The Baseball Encyclopedia

The Baseball Encyclopedia

EIGHTH EDITION · REVISED, UPDATED AND EXPANDED

The Complete and Official Record
of
Major League Baseball

Macmillan Publishing Company
New York

Collier Macmillan Publishers
London

EIGHTH EDITION

EDITORIAL AND RESEARCH STAFF:

Rick Wolff, *Editorial Director*   Warner Fusselle
Andrew Attaway   Paul Heacock
Jeanine Bucek   Robert Keefe
Carol-June Cassidy   Casey Kwang-Chong Lee
Fred Chase   Fred C. Richardson
Sean Devlin   Bill Rosen
Jackie Dickens   Ken Samelson

Special thanks to Richard Topp, Jack Carlson, Bob Tiemann,
Frank J. Williams, and the Society for American Baseball Research.

Copyright © 1969, 1974, 1976, 1979, 1982, 1985, 1986, 1987, 1988, 1990 by
Macmillan Publishing Company, a division of Macmillan, Inc.

Macmillan Publishing Company
866 Third Avenue, New York, NY 10022
Collier Macmillan Canada, Inc.

Library of Congress Cataloging-in-Publication Data
The Baseball encyclopedia : the complete and official record of major league base-
    ball.—8th ed., rev., updated, and expanded.
        p. cm.
    ISBN 0-02-579040-4
    1. Baseball—United States—Statistics.
GV877.B27 1990
796.357′0973′021—dc20   89-29902   CIP

Macmillan books are available at special discounts for bulk purchases for sales promotions, premiums,
fund-raising, or educational use. For details, contact:

Special Sales Director
Macmillan Publishing Company
866 Third Avenue
New York, NY 10022

Eighth Edition 1990

10 9 8 7 6 5 4 3 2 1

Portions of this book appeared in different form in *The Baseball Trade Register,*
copyright © 1984 by Joseph L. Reichler.

Printed in the United States of America

Contents

Preface

Part of the enduring beauty and charm of the game of baseball is that its history spans generation upon generation, a history of one generation handing down the tradition and legacy of the national pastime to the next generation.

And in a sense, the enduring beauty and charm of *The Baseball Encyclopedia* follows in that same path, because the *Encyclopedia* represents not just the work of a few dedicated baseball researchers and historians, but rather the passing along of a torch that keeps the flame of baseball lore and legend alive.

In keeping with that tradition, it is incumbent upon us, the editorial staff at Macmillan, to acknowledge the efforts of all baseball fans all over the world who breathe life into the *Encyclopedia* and keep its rich legacy growing. Whether it's used for a definitive purpose, such as to check on a player's batting average or a pitcher's shutouts, or merely for a leisurely stroll to find unusual nicknames, the *Encyclopedia* has been with us since 1969, and now, in its eighth edition, we feel we have added even more luster to the book by adding two more significant features—a listing of some of the best known stars of the old Negro leagues, and complete listings of all players' and pitchers' fielding statistics.

Both of these new additions have been carefully researched by the finest baseball historians, and we're most proud to make these new features part of our legacy. Of course, to accommodate these sections, in particular the fielding statistics, it was necessary to increase the *Encyclopedia* to its new trim size. We are the last ones to break with tradition, but after some long discussion, we decided that it was better to include the fielding statistics even though that meant enlarging the pages. The alternatives were either to leave the fielding statistics out, which nobody wanted to do, or else try and squeeze them into the *Encyclopedia*'s former trim size, which would make the book's print extremely difficult to read. As a compromise, then, the fielding statistics were included, and the book was made larger.

Keep in mind that nowhere else do these fielding statistics appear in any encyclopedic volume, and the same applies to the Negro league material. We of course welcome input from baseball fans everywhere to help us keep this data fresh and up-to-date.

The People Who Made the Encyclopedia Happen

As mentioned, the *Encyclopedia* represents the efforts of baseball fans everywhere, but there are certain individuals whose special efforts made the *Encyclopedia* come together.

Back in the late 1960s, two of baseball's finest historians were called upon to help put the *Encyclopedia* together. One was Lee Allen, the historian of the Baseball Hall of Fame in Cooperstown, New York, and the other was John Tattersall, an executive with a steamship firm in Philadelphia. Both men marveled at the idea of a complete reference work. Allen—long known as "the walking encyclopedia of baseball"—specialized in accumulating facts about the players. He had spent thirty years collecting the largest baseball demographic file in the country. A lot of that time had been spent visiting state record bureaus, speaking to ballplayers, corresponding with the descendants of ballplayers long dead, and even pursuing leads to graveyards to look at burial markers in search of birth and death dates.

Lee Allen suffered a fatal heart attack on May 20, 1969, and did not live to see the final product of his efforts, the culmination of a lifelong dream. Historian, columnist, reporter, and author, Lee was one of our foremost authorities on baseball.

Tattersall's forty-year plunge into nineteenth-century baseball history made him an expert on that period. The original material he gathered over the years was housed in a basement library that contained boxes of the sports sections of different newspapers from the early 1900s through the 1960s, a wide assortment of baseball publications, and a collection of scrapbooks from 1876 through 1900. There were box scores of every major league game played during that time, neatly preserved by year and league. By using these books, Tattersall was able to construct day-by-day playing records, which helped him to find or reconfirm past statistical achievements. The contribution of Allen and Tattersall and their invaluable collections really got the project off the ground.

Since the first edition of the *Encyclopedia* was published in 1969, there have been several "keepers of the flame." But in the most recent years, Joe Reichler, a former special assistant to the commissioner of baseball and a well-known baseball historian and author, came to head the editorial direction of the *Encyclopedia*. Joe's efforts to increase the growth and popularity of the *Encyclopedia* speak for themselves; the "bible of baseball" has indeed become an inseparable part of every baseball fan's library.

Joe Reichler passed away in 1988, and with his passing, the *Encyclopedia* lost a most valued friend. His contributions have been sorely missed, although Joe's legacy lives on in this and in future editions of the *Encyclopedia*.

The *Encyclopedia* lost another great admirer in 1989 with the death of Commissioner A. Bartlett Giamatti. With the commissioner's office giving its blessing to the *Encyclopedia* as the official record of Major League Baseball, Commissioner Giamatti spent several hours with the Macmillan editorial staff going over the proposed changes for this edition. Indeed, one of the last contributions the commissioner made was to appoint a special historical committee to oversee the accuracy of the *Encyclopedia*. Alas, only a few weeks after working directly with us, the commissioner was stricken. We'd like to think that Dr. Giamatti, like Joe Reichler, would have been proud to see this edition of the *Encyclopedia*.

A Special Word of Thanks

It's only appropriate to single out those individuals who physically made this edition of the *Encyclopedia* happen. Keep in mind that the research that goes into this mammoth book takes place on a yearly basis; this is a continuing project that demands ample quantities of time and enthusiasm.

First, on the Macmillan editorial side, Ken Samelson has devoted many of his waking hours in the last two years to improving the *Encyclopedia* and making it as perfect a record of baseball as the world has seen. Ken has been ably assisted in this joyous duty by Richard Topp, president of the Society for American Baseball Research (SABR), who has served as a most diligent consultant to Macmillan on this labor of love.

Other valuable editorial contributions in this edition include the efforts of Bill Rosen, Jeanine Bucek, John Holway, Dick Clark, and Jim Riley with the Negro league statistics; Bob Tiemann with the updating of the Home/Road Performance section; the Elias Sports Bureau (Seymour Siwoff and the Hirdt brothers, Steve, Peter, and Tom) with their yearly statistical updates; Dave Alworth, Marla Miller, and Maria Gomez of Major League Baseball; the Commissioner's Special Committee on the History of Baseball (David Voigt, George Kirsch, and Joseph Durso); Bill Deane of the Hall of Fame; and Warner Fusselle, one of the most knowledgeable men in baseball today.

On the production side, the terrific efforts of Casey Kwang-Chong Lee, Fred C. Richardson, Robert Keefe, Jackie Dickens, Robert Parker, John Ball, Janet Tingey, Andrew Attaway, David Frost, Carol-June Cassidy, Paul Heacock, and Joan Greenfield are all recognized and cherished. This book, which involves a tremendous amount of production and manufacturing skill, simply does not happen without these individuals.

Over the years, literally hundreds of people have made this book possible, and we gratefully acknowledge their efforts. To those individuals, please rest assured that we undertake our job quite seriously in our efforts to build upon your solid bedrock of baseball research.

And finally, here's a word of thanks to you, the baseball fan. Without your love and enthusiasm for the game of baseball, our national pastime, this book would never happen. We salute you all, with a tip of our cap.

—Rick Wolff
Editorial Director

PART ONE

Introduction

America's Game: A Brief History of Baseball

America's Game: A Brief History of Baseball

David Q. Voigt

Organized baseball emerged at a time when the American nation was transforming from an agrarian to an urban industrial society. By the 1840s games were being played in northeastern towns and cities where early forms of baseball supplied a necessary recreational outlet for young men and boys. As a field sport the game of baseball had no sire, and debunking scholars have relegated the fable of the game's purported 1839 invention by the young West Point cadet Abner Doubleday to the historical dustbin. Indeed, American baseball developed out of informal bat and ball games, such as rounders and town ball, and with some infusions from English cricket, a game that was formally organized in the eighteenth century.

In 1845 the evolving game of baseball reached a stable equilibrium when the New York Knickerbocker Club published a version of the game inspired by one of its members, Alexander J. Cartwright. Cartwright's version included the familiar diamond-shaped infield with bases set ninety feet apart, a forty-five-foot pitching distance, and nine-man teams playing under such rules as three outs to end a team's inning at bat and three strikes as one way to put a batter out. Once published, this version of the game caught on and eclipsed competing forms. But continuing modifications over the years pose a reminder that American baseball is a constantly evolving sport.

During the 1850s popular enthusiasm for baseball inspired a veritable mania in the northeastern sections of America. As organized clubs and players proliferated, the growing numbers of spectators prompted clubs to charge admission prices and to compete with each other for the services of good players. In 1858 the newly organized National Association of Base Ball Players (NABBP) attempted to impose its authority and its definition of amateurism on the various clubs. By 1860, sixty clubs were enrolled as members of the association. But if the association succeeded in standardizing playing rules and equipment, it failed to regulate championship play or to halt the growing trend of teams paying players for their services.

But ineffective leadership failed to stunt the game's sturdy growth. Nor did the Civil War; converts were won over to the game among soldiers of both armies who played and watched games at camp sites during the war years. And on the northern home front strong teams like the Brooklyn Excelsiors and Brooklyn Atlantics continued to attract enthusiastic fans, some of whom followed the Atlantics as the team posted undefeated seasons in 1864 and 1865.

As the war ended a second baseball mania swept the land. No longer a regional pastime, the game burst its bounds by 1867 as over 100 of the 300 member clubs of the association hailed from midwestern towns and cities. And fueling the latest boom were the writings of Henry Chadwick, who was already acclaimed as the "Father of the Game." A tireless reporter of games, Chadwick designed a box score, edited guidebooks, published a history of the game in 1867, and served on the association's playing rules committee. The doughty Chadwick continued to serve the game for forty years.

The 1870s

Although still lacking a formal league organization or set playing schedules, by the end of the 1860s baseball was widely touted as America's "national game." As fans flocked to playing fields of the organized clubs, whose membership rolls included gentlemanly patrons, many willingly paid to see exciting games played by teams who now employed deceptive underhand pitching and defensive and offensive teamwork. By 1869 the best players were being paid in various ways, a trend that the amateur leaders of the NABBP viewed with alarm. And when the Cincinnati Red Stockings that year opted to field an openly all-salaried team under player-manager Harry Wright, the Reds' undefeated record of that season (which continued until the early part of the 1870 campaign) boosted the cause of professional baseball supporters. Although the Reds returned no profits to their joint-stock company investors, their bold course of action inspired imitators and ignited the smoldering dispute between amateurs and professionals in NABBP councils to full flame by the end of the 1870 season.

In 1870 the hostilities between these factions so disrupted the association's annual meeting that the amateurs staged a walkout. But the professionals retaliated by forming their own league in March of 1871. That coup destroyed the amateur association and marked the beginnings of major league baseball in America. Thereafter the professional major leagues dominated organized baseball by effecting changes in rules and style of play.

As the first professional major league, the National Association of Professional Base Ball Players (NAPBBP) lasted five seasons and was controlled by the players, who enjoyed freedom of contract and a powerful voice in its councils. Although most member clubs were financed by profit-minded investors, player salaries came first. But with attendance averaging fewer than three thousand a game, most clubs lost money. Disenchanted investors blamed those losses on the players, whose excessive freedoms led to such chronic abuses as contract jumping, poor discipline, and shady dealings with gamblers.

The NAPBBP also suffered from serious organizational problems. Like its amateur predecessor, whose playing rules and organizational structure were carried on, the NAPBBP lacked a fixed playing schedule of games. Instead, each team was required to play each rival five times a season with playing dates arranged by correspondence. Each season's championship pennant went to the team with the most victories, but seldom did a team meet its full quota of games. And the league's easy entrance policy allowed any team to enter by paying a ten-dollar entry fee, a system that led to frequent dropouts by outclassed teams. Moreover, there were endless disputes over playing dates, ticket pricing, the division of gate receipts, and poor officiating by volunteer umpires. Worse still, the league lacked competitive balance, a perennial problem that would plague major league baseball until the 1980s. At this time four of the NAPBBP's five pennants were won by the Boston Red Stockings.

Nevertheless the NAPBBP popularized professional baseball in America. Large crowds often flocked to the wooden parks to watch contending teams like the Boston Reds, who hosted 70,000 home fans in 1875. By then Boston's budget was $35,000, and manager Harry Wright's innovations in equipment procurement, training of players, park administration, and even his profitless 1874 baseball junket to Britain, set standards for future promoters to emulate. At this time Wright was justly acclaimed as the "Father of Professional Baseball." And the short-lived NAPBBP, which Wright helped to found, furnished spectators with sprightly games and heroic players to worship. Expanded newspaper coverage and annual guides edited by Chadwick also stirred public interest in the professional game, which moved to a higher level of organization in 1876.

That year Chicago promoter William A. Hulbert staged a coup that replaced the player-controlled NAPBBP with a league dominated by club owners. Membership in the newly established National League of Professional Base Ball Clubs was limited to well-financed joint-stock company clubs from cities with populations of at least 75,000. The eight-team NL was organized along east-west lines, with each team holding monopoly rights to its territory. But the enfranchised clubs had to abide by Hulbert's moral code, which barred liquor sales, gamblers, and Sunday games. Until a fixed playing schedule was in place in 1877, teams in 1876 were ordered to play each rival ten times or face expulsion. Players were subjected to tight disciplinary codes and were bound to teams by rigid contracts. And Hulbert's chief lieutenant, Albert G. Spalding, was contracted to supply the league's official balls and to publish its guidebook.

But the NL's first four seasons sorely tested the resolve of its promoters. Attendance was low; in 1879 the champion Providence team drew only 42,000 spectators at home. Flagging profits forced austerity measures that kept player salaries below those of the 1875 Boston Reds. Moreover, at the close of the 1876 season the NL lost its two most lucrative sites when the Philadelphia and New York teams were expelled for failing to play their quota of games. And the following year the six-team NL suffered a major scandal when gamblers bribed four Louisville players to throw the pennant. For that outrage the players were barred from the NL for life and the Louisville club was replaced by Milwaukee. On yet another front in 1877, the NL faced stiff competition from the rival International Association, but when that league folded in 1879, NL control over organized baseball was secured. By then the NL was once again an eight-team circuit and its teams fielded the best players in the land. And to keep star players in their fold, NL owners in 1879 inserted reserve clauses in their playing contracts. At first players viewed reservation as a status symbol but when the practice was extended to all player contracts in 1883, players viewed the practice as an infringement on their freedom of contract. Thus the reserve clause became a perennial bone of contention between players and owners.

The 1880s

During the prosperous years of the 1880s the gathering storm of player unrest was lightly regarded by owners. Buoyed by national prosperity, NL attendance and profits improved during the early years and took wing during the latter years of the decade. And as the NL prospered, interlopers formed competing major leagues to cash in on the boom. In 1882 the American Association took the field with a seductive formula of twenty-five-cent admission prices, optional liquor sales, and Sunday games. That formula and raids on NL playing rosters made the AA's campaign a success. In response hard-pressed NL officials extended major league recognition to the AA provided that roster raids ceased and the circuit accepted the reserve clause system. This was done and under the National Agreement of 1883 the AA was recognized as a major league and the two majors extended their sway over the minor leagues. And in 1884 the two majors crushed a third rival, the Union Association, which sought to lure major league players by opposing the reserve clause.

Over the years 1885–89 professional baseball enjoyed a prosperous golden age under the dual major league system. But constant tensions marked the relations between the two leagues. On the playing field the rivalry was fought out in annual post-season championship encounters, which the NL dominated after 1886. But the AA more than held its own at the turnstiles, especially in St. Louis where promoter Chris Von der Ahe hosted large crowds with sideshows, liquor sales, Sunday games, and four consecutive pennants won by his Browns. However, in 1889 the AA's Brooklyn Bridegrooms set the nineteenth-century attendance record by hosting over 300,000 spectators at home. That year attendance at major league games peaked at over 2 million admissions and some clubs counted profits of $100,000 and more. By then both leagues had upped their playing schedules to 140 games.

During this brief golden age fans thronged to larger

wooden parks where they saw livelier games that resulted in part from a spate of rule changes. Some changes were short-lived, like the 1887 rule counting bases on balls as hits that produced twenty .400 hitters. But for that year such records were official and latter-day statisticians violated historical canons by revamping them. Meanwhile, by 1889 more permanent changes speeded the game's development, such as extending the pitching distance to 50 feet, permitting overhand pitching, adopting a single strike zone, and establishing the four ball and three strike rule. By then, too, a pair of weekly journals, *The Sporting News* and *Sporting Life,* with columns wholly devoted to baseball, sated the growing public appetite for baseball news, as did telegraphed reports of scores and electric board displays of games in progress posted at telegraph offices. Journalistic coverage included complete accounts of games, the deeds of star players like King Kelly, Cap Anson, Tip O'Neill, and Dan Brouthers, incidents of fans abusing the professional umpires, and unique events like promoter Spalding's world baseball tour of 1888–89 or Ernest Thayer's poem, "Casey at the Bat." But the big story of the decade recounted the sale of Mike "King" Kelly to the NL Boston club for the astonishing price of $10,000. The most celebrated player of this decade, Kelly's diamond exploits and colorful antics also made him an enduring folk hero.

As the game of the 1880s prospered, so to a much lesser degree did its players, whose salaries averaged $2,000 with superstars like Kelly earning $5,000 and more. But by decade's end only white players played in the majors; reflecting widening patterns of racial segregation in the nation, major and minor league clubs excluded black players, who took to playing in segregated leagues until 1946. But white major leaguers of the times chafed under such impositions as the reserve clause, uncompensated player sales by teams, harsh disciplinary rules, and a threatened salary ceiling. In 1885 disgruntled NL players joined the Brotherhood of Professional Base Ball Players founded by John M. Ward, a star player and a lawyer. Under Ward's leadership the brotherhood in 1887 sought recognition as a collective bargaining agency. And when the owners refused to budge on the reserve clause and salary ceiling issues, Ward persuaded the brotherhood, whose ranks included most NL and many AA players, to field a rival major league in 1890. With financial backers secured, the Players' National League of Baseball Clubs promised its men fair shares of power and profits with long-term contracts as their antidote to the hated reserve clause.

The 1890s

The bitter and costly Players' League War of 1890 ended major league baseball's brief golden age. With most of the star players in its fold, the PL opened play with eight well-stocked teams planted in seven NL cities. In head-to-head competition with the NL on most playing dates, the PL outdrew the NL and the hopelessly outclassed AA. Nevertheless, financial losses savaged all three leagues; however, Spalding headed a well-financed NL war committee that

forced the tremulous PL backers to sue for peace at the end of the season. The forsaken PL players were allowed to return to their former clubs without penalties, but within five years most ex-PL players no longer played in the major leagues.

Hard after this struggle, the NL and AA fought another baseball war in 1891 that was precipitated by disputes over the reassignments of PL players. When the AA pulled out of the National Agreement, a season-long struggle ended with the collapse of the AA. In the aftermath the NL annexed four AA teams and bought off the others at a cost of $130,000.

From 1892 to 1899 the single, twelve-team National League dominated major league baseball. In those years the owners styled themselves as magnates, pridefully comparing their monopoly "Big League" to the great economic trusts raised up by American captains of industry. But the big league failed to match the old dual major leagues in attendance and profits. For this failure such external factors as the nation's economic recession and the 1898 Spanish-American War were cited, but internally the league's competitive imbalance counted for more. In these years Boston, Baltimore, and Brooklyn teams outclassed all others, leaving scant cash and glory for the also-rans.

Efforts aimed at boosting attendance, such as staging post-season Temple Cup matches, increasing the playing schedule to 154 games, or attempting a split-season format in 1892, were failures. So were two abortive "syndicate" experiments, each involving single ownership of two major league clubs in 1899. That year another proposal aimed at pooling all players and receipts and redistributing the players among teams each new season. In rejecting this "baseball trust" scheme, the repentant owners voted instead to drop the four weakest teams and return to an eight-club format in 1900. This move saddled the owners with a hefty debt incurred by buying out the discarded teams; thus the big league that was born in debt in 1892, died in debt in 1900.

During this wayward era player salaries lagged well behind 1889 standards. With the collapse of the players' union the victorious owners imposed a salary cap, limiting salaries to a maximum of $2,400. Moreover, stricter disciplinary standards were laid on, including the unenforceable "brush rules" that threatened to banish players for such offenses as swearing and rowdy play. At this time rowdy tactics like brawling, umpire-baiting, bench-jockeying, and interfering with opposing players were widely used by aggressive teams like the Baltimore Orioles and Cleveland Spiders. Such tactics won games and excited fans and, when toned down, became a familiar part of the diamond drama. Likewise, bigger gloves and improved catcher's equipment made for better defensive play. And in this era two competing styles of offensive play, the "slugging" style and the "scientific" style, vied for acceptance. The slugging style was fostered by the 1893 rule which increased the pitching distance to its present length of sixty feet six inches and replaced the pitching box with a rubber slab atop a mound. Until pitchers adapted, sluggers feasted and set long-lasting batting and homer marks. But by the end of the decade the scientific style, with its emphasis on bunting, stealing, the hit and run, and sacrificing, became the dominant offensive style for the next twenty seasons.

In other ways the game continued to grow and evolve. Ballpark fans were tempted with concessionary items like hot dogs and soda pop. Opponents of Sunday games mounted a long and ultimately unsuccessful campaign to bar such games. In these years a rash of ballpark fires led to stricter safety codes that soon forced the replacement of wooden parks. And in this era professional baseball continued to expand in the minor leagues and among the flourishing black leagues. And prospects for continuing growth followed the spread of the game to Latin America and Japan.

From 1900 through World War I

As the twentieth century opened, major league baseball entered an era of expansion marked by unprecedented prosperity and stability. In 1900 the eight-team NL still reigned as the only major league, but that year Western League President Byron "Ban" Johnson mounted a challenge. Angered by NL draft policies, Johnson sought parity with the NL. That year he renamed his circuit the American League; his clubs occupied some of the abandoned NL sites and signed some surplus NL players. When the AL prospered, Johnson demanded major league recognition for his American League and launched a classic baseball war. In 1901 AL clubs occupied Philadelphia and Boston and enticed NL stars to jump to the new league. After two years of strife, NL owners, who faced a serious crisis of leadership, sued for peace. The National Agreement of 1903 recognized the AL as a major league and returned the major league game to the dual major league format of the 1880s. Under the 1903 agreement the NL and AL functioned as separate but equal major leagues; however, a three-member national commission was empowered to settle disputes and keep peace between the two leagues. The two league presidents and Cincinnati owner Garry Herrmann headed the National Commission, which successfully governed the game for seventeen years, during which time the two leagues respected each other's territories and playing rosters, agreed on playing rules and playing schedules, reclassified the minor leagues, and staged increasingly popular and profitable World Series matches.

The 1903 settlement ushered in a long period of stability for major league baseball. After the AL planted a team in New York City in 1903, both leagues retained the same teams for 50 years. During those years, except for the years of 1918–19, each league's teams played 154 games a season.

Rising attendance, averaging over 7 million fans a season from 1907–09, translated into profits that underscored the game's growing popularity. With no serious challenge from rival pro sports, baseball benefited from increasing coverage from big-city newspapers and from books, magazines, and films. Such coverage boosted public adulation of stars like Ty Cobb, Honus Wagner, Nap Lajoie, Walter Johnson, Christy Mathewson, and other heroes of the "deadball era," as the pitching-dominated, "scientific" style of play came to be

called. Trick deliveries like the spitball and various scuffed-ball tactics made for pitching dominance. Other innovations included improved offensive and defensive team tactics, equipment changes such as more efficient gloves, and rule changes such as restricting the size of pitching mounds and assigning two umpires to work each game. All contributed to the game's growing popularity. So did the game's enduring hymn, "Take Me Out to the Ball Game," written at this time, and the presence of American presidents at opening-day games and World Series matches. By 1910 owner optimism over the game's future prospects inspired a park building boom that replaced wooden parks with capacious concrete-and-steel edifices. The building boom climaxed with the construction of Yankee Stadium in 1923 and most of these privately financed parks served until a new building boom began in the 1950s.

However, chronic problems of competitive imbalance and unequal distribution of attendance and revenues persisted. In this era the Giants and Cubs captured the lion's share of attendance and championships in the NL as did the Boston, Detroit, and Philadelphia clubs of the AL. Moreover, player salaries rose slowly, averaging $2,500 by 1910 with a few superstars getting $12,000 and more marginal players getting less than $1,000. Widespread discontent over salaries and the reserve clause prompted players in 1900 and again in 1912 to organize for reforms, but both movements were quashed by the owners and the national commission.

For their part owners faced troubles of their own from the three major crises that affected the game over the years 1914–20. The troubles began with the Federal League War of 1914–15. A well-financed incursion by promoters of a rival major league, the invasion dropped annual attendance at NL and AL games below 5 million in those years. In 1915 the FL folded, but a dispute over the terms of the settlement prompted one Federal League club to sue major league baseball for monopoly practices. The case reached the Supreme Court in 1922 where it was ruled that the game was a sport and not subject to the laws of interstate commerce.

Soon after the FL war came the crisis of World War I. The total war effort drafted players for service and forced the majors to reduce playing schedules in 1918–19. Combined with a raging influenza epidemic, such restrictions reduced total attendance to 3 million in 1918.

Yet another crisis followed just as attendance rebounded to 6.5 million in the shortened playing season of 1919. That year the World Series was blighted by gamblers who bribed eight Chicago White Sox players to throw games to the victorious Cincinnati Reds. When news of the scandal broke in 1920, the furor it caused led to the suspension of the accused players and the fall of the national commission. In place of that ruling body, federal judge Kenesaw M. Landis was named sole commissioner of the game and empowered to act on his own volition to defend the integrity of the game. Although Landis banished the eight accused "Black Sox" players for life and later barred a few other players for consorting with gamblers, he failed to halt the long-established practice of betting on major league games. Such activity by players and managers is deeply rooted in baseball history. Among other incidents, Chicago manager Cap Anson bet on his team's games in the 1890s, contending teams often bribed rival teams to play harder against other contenders, and stars like Rube Waddell, Hal Chase, Ty Cobb, Tris Speaker, and Joe Wood were accused of betting or game fixing. Of those named, four (Anson, Waddell, Cobb, and Speaker) were later enshrined in the game's Hall of Fame.

Ironically the furor over the 1919 World Series fix failed to affect attendance, which rose to a record 9.1 million in 1920. Had the owners known of the coming boom, they likely would not have granted Commissioner Landis such sweeping powers. Certainly none of the commissioners who succeeded Landis, who died in 1944, were granted such powers.

The 1920s

Meanwhile big league baseball's stock soared during the 1920s. Externally, national prosperity enabled Americans to spend nearly $5 billion a year on recreational pursuits in 1929. Such monies fostered the growth of other sports where fans doted on the deeds of such heroes as Bobby Jones, Bill Tilden, Red Grange, Jack Dempsey, and Gene Tunney. Yet none of these champions matched the adulation heaped on baseball superstar Babe Ruth. In 1920 Ruth smote 54 homers, a record feat that drew a million fans to New York Yankees games and easily justified the record price Yankees owners spent to acquire the slugger from the Boston Red Sox.

Over the years 1920–31 Ruth won ten AL homer titles and he personified the new slugging style of play. Abetted in part by a ban on trick pitches and by the widespread use of lively cork-centered balls that were frequently replaced during games (and retained by souvenir-seeking fans when hit into the stands), the "big bang" became the perennially dominant offensive style. During the 1920s NL sluggers outhomered their AL counterparts, but hitters in both leagues set enduring records. Thus NL star Rogers Hornsby averaged .400 over a five-year period, while on four occasions AL star Harry Heilmann topped .390. The hitting frenzy peaked in 1930 when NL hitters averaged above .300.

That fans welcomed the batting assaults was evidenced at the turnstiles. During the 1920s annual attendance at major league games averaged about 9 million with a record 10.1 million admissions counted in 1930. Legalized Sunday games spurred attendance and radio broadcasts of World Series games won new fans, but most clubs refused to allow radio broadcasts of regular-season games. Moreover, expanding newspaper and magazine coverage supplied fans with plenteous information on teams and players. At this time baseball writers tended to use a highly romanticized, gee-whiz style of coverage that lionized players, especially Ruth, who became the most photographed and recognized American of the decade.

In retrospect the 1920s stand out as the game's second golden age. Annual revenues topped those of the 1900–20 era by 40 percent and player salaries averaged $7,000 by 1930. However, such figures were distorted by competitive imbalance. In this era the AL Yankees won six pennants and an inordinate share of attendance and revenues. In the NL the Giants won four consecutive pennants and outdrew all others at the gate. And the average player salary was dwarfed by Ruth's $80,000 salary of 1930.

Along with the new offensive style of play other innovations marked the game's continuing evolution. There was the bright promise of radio and films as new revenue sources, with the latter now serving as a useful training device. At St. Louis, Cardinal general manager Branch Rickey's farm system was revolutionizing the recruitment and training of young talent in the minors. Acquiring a network of minor league teams, Rickey stocked them with young players whose steady development enabled the poor-drawing Cardinals to win pennants and profit by the sales of surplus players. Yet another revolution of the decade occurred outside of organized baseball when promoter Rube Foster launched the Negro National League in 1920. Along with similar ventures by other promoters, the black majors enabled stars like pitchers Bullet Joe Rogan, Smokey Joe Williams, and Satchel Paige to display their formidable talents along with such hitting virtuosos as Pop Lloyd and Oscar Charleston. But such worthies continued to be shunned by white major and minor league teams; yet in time, when the walls of racial discrimination were finally razed, the wealth of black playing talent and their fans would revitalize major league baseball.

The 1930s

Reformists were battering at those walls in the 1930s, but their pleas made little headway during that depression-wracked decade. As the Great Depression idled millions of American workers, attendance at major league games hit a low point of 6.3 million in 1933. Recovering slowly thereafter, annual attendance still did not surpass the 1930 mark as late as 1940.

During the worst years of the depression, from 1932–34, most major league clubs lost money, especially the NL Braves and Phillies and the AL Athletics, Browns, and Senators. So did the players, whose salaries were sharply slashed; by 1933 salaries averaged $6,000, and in 1940 still lagged behind the 1929 peak of $7,500.

To weather the storm, poorer clubs like the Phillies and Athletics sold star players, but such medicine had the side effect of worsening attendance for the sellers. However, the talent-rich Cardinals compensated for poor attendance by selling surplus players from their vast farm system and retaining the best to stay in contention. But such financial disparities among clubs worsened the chronic problem of competitive imbalance. In this decade the AL Yankees won four world titles in as many tries, and in the NL the Giants, Cardinals, and Cubs dominated the campaigns.

To attract more fans promoters turned to night baseball, a rejected innovation of the 1880s but by now a proven success as demonstrated by the black majors and at the minor league level. In 1935 Cincinnati general manager Larry Mac-Phail successfully staged night games in the NL. By 1940 most major league clubs followed suit, setting a trend that within a few decades transformed the game into a mainly nocturnal spectacle. In like manner clubs increasingly sold radio broadcasting rights, fostering a trend that would later transform the game into an electronic media event. For now, owners welcomed the windfall, which amounted to 7.3 percent of major league revenues by 1939. At this time, too, owners wrung money from fans by expanded concession sales, especially beer sales that were revived after the failure of national prohibition, which halted such sales during the 1920s.

Scarcely touched by innovation was the game itself as teams of the 1930s continued to ply big-bang offensives in games now officiated by three-man umpire crews. As the game's towering hero Ruth faded from the scene, soon after his legendary feat of supposedly calling his homer shot in the 1932 World Series, new heroes emerged as worthy successors. Among them were pitcher Johnny Vander Meer (who hurled two consecutive no-hit games in 1938), Joe DiMaggio (who batted safely in 56 games in 1941), and Ted Williams (whose .406 batting mark of 1941 was the last .400 batting effort to this day).

In 1939 major league baseball's image as the national pastime was burnished by season-long celebrations of the game's mythical centennial birth date. At Cooperstown, New York, the purported site of the game's 1839 invention, the Baseball Hall of Fame was formally opened in June and the first five immortal players were enshrined. It attracted 25,000 visitors that year and now hosts more than 250,000 pilgrims annually.

World War II

Rebounding from the depression, major league baseball enjoyed profitable seasons in 1940–41 when the game was rocked by the crisis of World War II. As the nation mounted its total war effort against the Axis powers, some 500 major leaguers and 3,500 minor league players were called to the colors along with 11 million other Americans. The manpower drain affected major league attendance, which fell to 8.8 million in 1942 and to a nadir of 7.7 million the following year. The accompanying financial losses hit poorer clubs hard and one, the NL Phillies, went bankrupt in 1943, but soon fell into the hands of a wealthy backer.

Although given a "green light" to continue play by President Roosevelt, major league teams had to cope with shortages of players, equipment, and accommodations. For a time night games were curtailed, but were revived when government officials decided that such games provided useful recreation for war workers. But the biggest problem promoters faced was the scarcity of able players. To cope, clubs recruited draft rejects and some too old or too young to serve; some clubs turned to Latin America, where a virtually untapped pool of players existed. During the war years fifty Latin American players appeared in various lineups. However, another promising pool of talent, the black majors, remained off limits; owners rejected promoter Bill Veeck's

1943 bid to buy the bankrupt Phillies, which Veeck proposed to stock with black players. Thus major league clubs muddled through the war years by fielding teams of below-average playing skills. At this time, government-imposed wage freezes helped to hold player salaries to an average of $6,400 and widespread resentment among players made them receptive to postwar union movements.

Meanwhile major league owners won plaudits for supporting the war effort with bond sales, free admissions to servicemen, and donations of equipment and radio broadcasts of games to the armed forces. Moreover, most owners profited when attendance rebounded to 8.7 million in 1944 and then posted a record 10.8 million admissions in 1945. By then the war was over, but its aftermath unleashed pent-up demands for higher wages and racial equality in the land. In 1946 these and other tremors shook major league baseball as the game entered its postwar era.

The Postwar Era

Baseball's postwar era (1949–60) confronted owners and players with vexing problems caused by changing social conditions. Indeed, the era was barely underway when owners were forced to grapple with problems of racial integration and player unionism. Of the two, it was the former that immediately transformed the game as black activists, backed by federal and state antidiscrimination laws, demanded an end to segregation in organized baseball. Although most major league owners resisted integration, their position was crumbling. Until his death in 1944 Commissioner Landis opposed integration, but his successor, Commissioner A. B. Chandler, favored the cause. Thus while opponents feared to voice their opposition, Brooklyn Dodgers president Branch Rickey decided to force the issue. In 1945 Rickey signed black player Jackie Robinson to a Dodgers contract and assigned him to the club's Montreal farm team. After leading the International League in hitting in 1946, Robinson joined the NL Dodgers in 1947 and won Rookie of the Year honors. Robinson's successful debut and that of Larry Doby, who became the first AL black player that year, opened the doors to other black Americans and Latin Americans whose performances validated Rickey's bold experiment. In the NL, where most blacks played during this era, black stars won seven Most Valuable Player awards during the 1950s. However, the integration of organized baseball did not end racial discrimination practices. Nor were black promoters fairly compensated for the loss of players, which also led to the demise of the black majors in 1950.

Although the crisis caused by the game's integration was short-lived, that of player unionism confronted major league owners with an enduring and chronically festering problem. In 1946 cumulative grievances nursed by players, including many returning war veterans, led to the formation of the American Baseball Guild. Although the guild folded that year, the players won such concessions as a pension plan (funded by national radio and television revenues), a minimum salary, pay for spring training, and the right to negotiate further through elected player representatives. Among these gains, the pension plan was the most portentous and when owners sought to abolish the system in 1953, the players retaliated by forming the permanent Major League Players Association. That year the MLPA managed to confirm all previous concessions, including the continuation of the pension system. But the MLPA later languished as an ineffective company union until 1966, when under Marvin Miller's leadership it became a formidable labor organization.

Meanwhile on another front of the 1946 labor struggle, several players were blacklisted by Commissioner Chandler for violating reserve clauses in their contracts by joining an outlaw Mexican league. In opposing that sanction, player Danny Gardella filed suit and when his case reached a federal circuit court, tremulous owners settled out of court. However, Gardella's challenge prompted congressional investigations into major league baseball's monopoly practices. Although no punitive legislation resulted, the future of the reserve clause was clouded. Some owners blamed Chandler for precipitating the investigation and also faulted him for acting against their wishes by supporting racial integration and the players' pension movement. As a result Chandler was forced to resign in 1951. Thereafter, commissioners became figureheads for the owners, who wielded power. Until his death in 1979, Walter O'Malley of the Dodgers was a most important decision maker in owner councils.

Crises notwithstanding, major league baseball flourished during the postwar era. Stimulated by national prosperity, attendance topped 18 million in 1946 and peaked at 21.3 million in 1948. The increasing number of night games was a catalyst for this upsurge, with every club but the Chicago Cubs staging such games. At the same time Cleveland owner Bill Veeck demonstrated new ways of attracting crowds with his imaginative promotional schemes, including giveaways. In 1948 the AL champion Indians set a record by hosting over 2 million fans.

Unfortunately the boom of the late 1940s burst in the 1950s when annual attendance failed to reach 20 million. For this reversal, factors like population shifts away from major league cities, suburban growth, deteriorating parks in run-down neighborhoods, competition from rival sports, and the popularity of television were cited. Internally, competitive imbalance was a major factor; during the years 1947–60 the AL Yankees won eleven pennants and the NL Dodgers won seven.

By the 1950s financial losses forced the owners of the NL Braves and the AL Athletics and Browns to sell to new owners who were permitted to relocate these clubs to more promising sites. In 1953 the NL Braves became the first breakaway franchise in half a century by moving to Milwaukee. Over the next two years the AL Browns reincarnated as the Baltimore Orioles and the Athletics relocated to Kansas City. And in 1958 the NL Dodgers and Giants stunned their fans by moving to the flourishing West Coast cities of Los Angeles and San Francisco.

At the same time the popular television medium was transforming the game. Although TV broadcasts of games were blamed for flagging attendance, the medium pumped new revenues into team coffers. From $2.3 million in 1950, annual TV revenue rose to $12 million by 1960. However, much of this money was unevenly distributed because such revenues derived mainly from local TV contracts. But all clubs shared equally in increasing revenue from national TV networks, which vied with one another to purchase rights to televise World Series games, All-Star games, and selected seasonal games. Thus increasing TV revenues helped boost franchise values to figures that dwarfed the 1945 sale of the Yankees for $2.5 million. Yet few observers of this era envisioned a time when ever-increasing TV monies would also boost player salaries to undreamed-of heights.

At this time player salaries rose modestly, keeping pace with the dollar's continuing inflation. By the late 1950s, 75 percent of player salaries ranged from $10,000 to $25,000 with $100,000 checks going to five superstars (Joe DiMaggio, Ted Williams, Stan Musial, Mickey Mantle, and Willie Mays). However, salaries were being pushed upward by talent scarcity caused by declining numbers of minor leagues and by rival sports competing for top athletes. As a result teams of this era engaged in costly bidding wars that made high-priced "bonus babies" of promising rookies. Other replacements came from dwindling numbers of black professionals and to a greater extent from Latin American recruits. But the chronic shortage of talent was ending the longstanding practice of free-enterprise scouting and forcing owners to seek other solutions to the problem. At this time the flourishing Little League baseball movement introduced thousands of youngsters to the game, but fewer youth and adult leagues made it difficult to sustain the enthusiasm of youngsters for the game.

Meanwhile big league players continued to play the slugging game, with NL hitters averaging 1,100 homers a season during the 1950s. Whippier bats, protective helmets, and the strategy of platooning hitters bolstered offenses, but more efficient gloves boosted defenses, and varied deliveries, including the effective slider, enabled pitchers to better cope with the hitters. Moreover, teams now deployed better-trained relief pitchers to quell batting rallies. The increased use of specialized role performers also had teams using more coaches and improving their training techniques.

A new park-building boom began in this era as breakaway clubs occupied new, publicly financed ballparks. More commodious than the idiosyncratic parks that had served fans for half a century, the new parks were located closer to suburban population centers and were more accessible by automobiles. And a rule of 1959 ordained that all new parks constructed after that year must conform to minimum 325-foot distances from home plate to the right- and left-field fences.

The 1960s

The 1959 rule calling for standardized playing fields was linked with a larger plan calling for the major leagues to expand to twenty teams. When implemented by the AL in 1961 and by the NL in 1962, major league baseball embarked upon the first phase of its expansion era. Although inspired in part by professional football's profitable example, the precipitating cause of expansion was the threat from a rival major league, the Continental League, to field teams in baseball-hungry urban areas. In defusing that threat, major league owners voted to add two new teams to each league and to increase the playing schedule to 162 games.

For its part the NL occupied Houston and New York, while the AL took on Washington and Los Angeles clubs. The NL's choice of New York quelled protests arising from that city's loss of the Giants and Dodgers in 1958. Similarly the AL's reoccupation of Washington was prompted by theats of lawsuits arising over the 1961 move by the original Washington Senators to Minnesota. The first round of expansion cost each new club owner $2 million for his franchise plus additional spending for the purchase of players picked from a pool of surplus players made available by an expansion draft procedure. Thus arrayed, the AL played its first season under the ten-team format in 1961 with the NL following suit in 1962.

But the first expansion ventures of 1961–68 fell short of expectations. Three franchise relocations of these years, including the NL Milwaukee Braves' move to Atlanta and moves by the AL's Kansas City Athletics to Oakland and Los Angeles Angels to nearby Anaheim, indicated dissatisfaction with the format. The format also aggravated the competitive imbalance problem. Ten teams competing in each league made for too many losers, both on the field of play and at the turnstiles. The situation was worsened by dominant teams like the AL Yankees, winners of four consecutive pennants through 1964, and by the Dodgers and Cardinals winning all six races in the NL in 1963–68. As a result annual attendance was disappointing. The era's best attendance mark of 25 million bettered that of 1960 by little more than 5 million and by 1968 total attendance sagged to 23 million. Moreover, NL attendance of this era surpassed that of the AL by 15 million, an anomaly attributed to the NL's newer parks and better choices of expansion sites. In these years six of the eight new parks built housed NL clubs, including Houston's all-weather Astrodome with its artificial turf playing surface. Today ten major league teams play home games on artificial surfaces.

The NL also enjoyed batting superiority, but these were lackluster years for all hitters. Dominant pitching, backed by increasingly effective relief corps (whose stars now competed for annual Fireman of the Year honors) produced a hitting famine that by 1968 held hitters to a century-low .237 average. Although NL sluggers Willie Mays and Hank Aaron hit homers at a pace that threatened to topple Ruth's lifetime mark of 714 blows, most hitters were throttled by the dominant pitching of aces like Sandy Koufax, Bob Gibson, and Denny McLain. To restore a balance, rules makers in 1969 lowered pitching mounds and shortened strike zones.

Yet if players' bats were relatively silent, their demands for reforms were effectively voiced. Reflecting the social climate of this frenzied decade, which had protestors of all stripes clamoring for reforms, including demonstrating for an end to the Vietnam War and sometimes rioting in the streets, major league players battled for improved salaries, pension benefits, and working conditions. To revive their moribund union, players in 1966 chose the experienced labor organizer Marvin Miller to head the MLPA. In short order Miller united the players and invoked federal labor laws to force owners to bargain with the association. Such negotiations produced formal labor contracts (known as basic agreements) in 1967 and 1970 which boosted pension benefits and minimum salaries. By the end of the 1960s player salaries averaged $20,000 and those of twenty stars topped $100,000. Moreover, in 1966 Dodgers pitchers Sandy Koufax and Don Drysdale set a precedent by using a lawyer in their contract negotiations that season. Within a few years all players won the right to use agents in salary negotiations. Even umpires gained a measure of power when their organization, the Major League Umpires Association, won recognition as a bargaining agency.

Helping to strengthen the players' bargaining position at this time was the continuing problem of talent scarcity. As the number of minor leagues continued to shrink, alarmed owners adopted a player development plan to save these vital nurseries of talent. Under this 1962 plan each major league club was required to subsidize at least five minor league teams of various classes. As a further step the owners in 1965 established annual free agent (rookie) drafts of high school and college players. This equal sharing of annual crops of young players was accomplished by pooling the talent and allowing each team to choose in an order based on a team's finish in the previous year's standings. A dramatic departure from past practices, the rookie drafts ended free-enterprise scouting in the U.S., but not in foreign lands such as the productive Latin American countries.

At this time worried owners benefited from increasing television revenues, which helped meet expenses incurred by rising salaries and player development programs. By 1967 annual TV monies totaled $25 million with no signs of abating. Thus when major league owners embarked on a new expansion course in 1969, TV revenue played a vital part in the success of the venture.

The 1970s

By replacing the unwieldy ten-club format with a new expansion plan that would add two clubs to each league and subdivide each league into six-team Eastern and Western divisions, major league owners of 1969 hit upon a successful format that endures to this day. The new format retained the 162-game playing schedule, but added a postseason, best-of-five-games League Championship Series, which pitted each season's divisional winners in a test to determine the annual league champions. A proven success in professional football, which at this time rivaled big league baseball in popularity, divisional play in big league baseball also focused fan attention on divisional races where winning teams were rewarded with pennants.

In implementing the plan in 1969 the AL added the Kansas City Royals and Seattle Pilots, with the NL taking on the Montreal Expos (the first foreign franchise in major league history) and the San Diego Padres. A new AL franchise now cost $5.6 million with an NL franchise pegged at $10 million. Each owner also spent additional money to stock teams from player cullings made available in another expansion draft procedure.

Once underway the wisdom of this venture was demonstrated by rising attendance figures. From 30 million annual admissions in the early 1970s, annual attendance rose to 43 million by 1980. To be sure the early years were plagued with glitches, especially for the outclassed AL where shaky franchises, flagging attendance, and poor offensive performance continued. Thus after one season of play, the AL's Seattle owner was forced to sell his club to Milwaukee interests. The Milwaukee move provided a more stable franchise and also quashed a lawsuit against the NL for its earlier abandonment of that city. But by quitting Seattle and by allowing the unstable Washington Senators to move to Arlington, Texas, in 1972, the AL now faced similar suits. While the Washington protest was defused by the vague promise of a future franchise, the Seattle suit was headed off by the AL's unilateral expansion move of 1977. That year the AL added two new clubs, the Seattle Mariners and the Toronto Blue Jays, whose new owners paid $6 million each for their franchises. This unilateral expansion made the AL a fourteen-team circuit with seven teams arrayed in each division. The 162-game schedule was retained, but annual matchups between teams were necessarily skewed. Nevertheless, the bold move stabilized the AL, whose annual attendance thenceforth surpassed that of the NL.

By then another unilateral move by the AL was boosting its annual offensive figures above those of the NL. This was accomplished in 1973 by the adoption, over NL protests, of a designated hitter rule allowing a batter to hit in place of a pitcher. To this day the AL use of the DH rule remains controversial. But at this time the two leagues settled an argument over the use of designated hitters in World Series play by restricting its use to alternate years. (A recent modification of this rule limits its use to World Series games played in AL parks.) Although the NL still refuses to adopt the rule, nearly twenty years of using designated hitters attests to its popularity among offense-minded AL fans.

Meanwhile, if owners expected the new divisional format to solve the chronic problem of competitive imbalance, such hopes were misplaced. Over the years 1969–80 most divisional races were dominated by the same two teams. In the AL East the Orioles and Yankees won most of these as did the Athletics and Kansas City Royals in the West. And in the NL the Phillies and Pirates dominated in the East with the Reds and Dodgers ruling in the West.

At least the booming attendance of these years demonstrated that such imbalance posed no barrier to the game's dynamic growth. In this decade new park construction and the refurbishing of old parks like Yankee Stadium helped the AL match the NL's parks and gain parity in attendance. Moreover, attendance everywhere was boosted by the use of

promotional schemes such as free gift days, more varied concession items for sale, cavorting team mascots, sideshows, and enhanced season-ticket sales. Thus promoters now regarded a million admissions a year as a must, while the lordly Dodgers topped all others by drawing over 2 million fans a year.

At the same time surging TV revenues accounted for 30 percent of major league baseball's gross revenues of $500 million in 1980. Such revenues raised the value of franchises so that the Red Sox and Mets went for $16 million and $20 million respectively when sold to new buyers, while the Dodgers and Yankees were valued at an estimated $50 million each. Certainly TV played an important part in the rising values of clubs. By 1980 network contracts for World Series, League Championship Series, All-Star games, and other selected games provided each owner with $1.8 million a year; local TV revenues were also growing at a fast pace. However, TV interests altered the game by persuading owners to schedule mostly night games, including World Series contests. And because improving technology now afforded TV fans a better view of a game than ballpark fans, clubs responded by erecting large TV screens at parks. Thus, ball games increasingly became entertainment spectacles, a trend that some observers blamed for the increasing episodes of crowd violence that forced clubs in these years to beef up their security staffs.

Indeed, many episodes of crowd violence targeted players, who were now cast as highly paid celebrities. TV exposure made players more visible and more onstage. Clad in colorful uniforms, many players sported facial hair, most were more assertive, and some like Jim Bouton wrote controversial, best-selling books that probed deeply into the private lives of players.

For players such unprecedented freedom was accompanied by mind-boggling salaries; average player salaries soared from $25,000 in 1970 to $185,000 by 1980, with pitcher Nolan Ryan becoming the first million-dollar-a-year player. Although TV revenue provided the wherewithal for gains that boosted top payrolls from $1 million in 1970 to $9 million in 1980, it was the negotiating skills of MLPA director Marvin Miller that wrung the money from the owners. In this decade Miller negotiated three basic agreements that vastly benefited the players. The 1970 agreement won players the right to use agents in salary negotiations; the 1973 agreement, which followed after the players staged a thirteen-day strike in 1972, won players the right to seek binding arbitration in salary disputes. The passage of time soon demonstrated the significance of that concession. But its portent was overshadowed in 1975 by an arbitration panel's decision that pitchers Andy Messersmith and Dave McNally, each of whom played a full season without a contract, were free agents. When upheld by a federal court, it was apparent that this Seitz decision (named for arbitrator Peter Seitz) applied to all players and thus seemed to circumvent the reserve clause.

In 1976 the Seitz decision became the front of battle in negotiations over a new basic agreement. After staging an abortive lockout of spring training camps, the owners returned to the bargaining table where a compromise was reached. This latest agreement allowed six-year veterans to become free agents who could sell their services anew in annual re-entry drafts. And when some owners bid high salaries for the services of some free agents, these rates were soon matched by binding awards from arbitration panels acting under procedures established in 1973.

Still there was no gainsaying the claim that the fortune-favored stars of this era earned their inflation-eroded salaries. Among the record setters, slugger Hank Aaron broke Ruth's lifetime homer record of 714 in 1974; hitting dervish Pete Rose tied Willie Keeler's NL mark by hitting safely in 44 consecutive games in 1978 and continued his assault on Cobb's lifetime mark of 4,191 hits; base-stealer Lou Brock broke Cobb's lifetime mark of 892 steals in 1977; and pitcher Nolan Ryan broke Walter Johnson's lifetime record of 3,508 strikeouts in 1983.

The 1980s

Nevertheless the skyrocketing player salaries of this era incurred the wrath of owners, who determined to halt the trend. Thus the opening of the decade of the 1980s saw owners and players marshaling their forces for a renewed battle in a continuing power struggle.

When a cooling-off period failed to produce a new basic agreement, the 1981 season was gutted by a player strike that lasted from mid-June to the end of July. The strike was provoked by owner demands for a ceiling on salaries and for compensation "in kind" for players lost by clubs in annual re-entry drafts. In rejecting such givebacks, the players struck for fifty days and forced the cancellation of as many games. With both sides bloodied financially, a settlement was reached whereby the owners lost their demand for a salary cap, but won compensation for lost free agents by receiving either a minor league player or a major leaguer chosen from a pool of cullings from the rosters of all the clubs. In the wake of the great strike, a confusing split-season format was arranged in hopes of salvaging the playing season. However, the quixotic scheme failed to stimulate attendance, which fell to 26 million.

But fears of a continuing baseball recession were dispelled by three prosperous seasons that followed the 1981 debacle. Bucking the faltering national economy of those years, annual attendance averaged better than 40 million and average player salaries rose to $300,000 by 1984 with thirty stars joining the millionaire ranks.

Baseball was riding the same wave of prosperity when the expiring basic agreement renewed the struggle in 1985. Once again the owners demanded a salary cap and they also sought to limit the salary arbitration procedure which they blamed for the soaring salary trend. When no agreement was reached, the players struck in August, but the walkout lasted only two days. With neither side wanting a reprise of the 1981 attrition, a new agreement was reached in which the players agreed to extend the eligibility period for salary arbi-

tration to three years. For their part the owners dropped the salary cap demand and sweetened the pension fund so that a ten-year veteran of the major leagues could expect a pension of $91,000 a year.

Although the new basic agreement extended through the 1989 season, its peace was marred by such owner ploys as reducing playing rosters to twenty-four men and boycotting the free agent markets of 1985–86. The boycott prompted a grievance suit by the MLPA that resulted in a 1989 arbitrator's ruling that the owners were guilty of collusion and must pay $10.5 million in damages to the affected players. The two sides also locked horns over the issue of drug abuse. Reflecting the national epidemic of illegal drug use by Americans, many players were numbered among the estimated 20 million violators in the country. Early in the decade some players were caught and jailed, and in 1986 six admitted users testified under immunity at a Pittsburgh trial of an accused drug dealer. When these witnesses implicated other players as users, Commissioner Peter Ueberroth penalized those accused and sought to make all players submit to drug testing. But the MLPA successfully argued that drug testing be negotiated as part of a formal labor agreement.

At this time none of these divisive issues affected the game's continuing prosperity, which benefited both players and owners. By 1989 the average player salary rose to $500,000 with twenty players earning at least $2 million a year, headed by Dodgers pitcher Orel Hershiser's Olympian $2.7 million pact. At the same time attendance topped 50 million with revenues from ticket sales, now averaging $7 apiece but still the lowest price of any major sports ticket, augmented by expanding revenues from concession sales. This income flow and a continuing flood of TV revenues boosted baseball's 1988 gross revenues above $1 billion.

Indeed, lucrative network TV pacts provided each club with $7 million in 1989. And beginning with the 1990 season a new four-year, $1.45 billion contract doubled that owner windfall. With another $400 million coming from a shared four-year cable TV contract, and with local TV revenues continuing to rise, the game's marriage with TV seemed to be heaven blessed. Not surprisingly the values of franchises rose sharply; the Mets were sold for $100 million in 1986, and in 1989 the Seattle Mariners were sold for $77 million.

Moreover an unprecedented spate of competitive balance made for hotly contested division races throughout the 1980s. Over the years 1981–88, eleven different teams won divisional titles in the AL. And if domination by the Dodgers and Cardinals made the NL less balanced, still ten different teams won divisional races, including the Cubs, who had been pennantless since 1945.

Just as attractive to fans as the hotly contested races were the record homer barrages of these years. In the vintage year of 1987 sluggers set records in both leagues with the AL blasting 2,634 and the NL 1,824. However, such clubbing was deemed too much by alarmed rules makers, who aided shell-shocked pitchers by widening the strike zone. As a result homer production tailed off in 1988–89.

Among the splendid performers of this era, Pete Rose of

the Reds broke Cobb's total hit record in 1985. In 1982 Rickey Henderson of the Athletics set a new seasonal mark by stealing 130 bases. And among the pitching aces, forty-two-year-old Nolan Ryan, still firing ninety-mile-per-hour fastballs, recorded his 5,000th strikeout in 1989.

The Future of Baseball

As measured by the affluent 1980s, major league baseball's prospects for continuing prosperity never looked brighter. In 1989 sparkling performances like oldster Ryan's hurling and young slugger Kevin Mitchell's homerics dazzled fans. In Chicago, Cubs fans at last were treated to night baseball and were cheering on a winning team. And in Toronto, pennant-hopeful fans watched their team play in a new state-of-the-art stadium with a sliding roof that can be opened or closed depending on the quirks of Mother Nature.

Elsewhere the minor leagues were thriving and the player development plan was providing a dependable flow of young talent. At the grass roots level, youthful interest in baseball is sustained by organizations like the Little Leagues, a movement that celebrated its fiftieth anniversary in 1989. Amateur

baseball flourishes at the high school, American Legion, and college levels, with the College World Series established as an annual media event. Furthermore, amateur baseball will become a medal event at the 1992 Olympic Games, with teams from China and the Soviet Union joining other nations in the competition. And in Japan, where amateur and professional baseball rivals our own in popularity and prowess, investors have reached out to purchase interests in some American minor league clubs and are eyeing major league franchises.

The possibility of a competing major league in the 1990s could provide such investment opportunities, but this rumored venture would pose a threat to the established majors. To deflect such a threat another round of expansion by the two major leagues is under discussion. However, the most immediate threat to major league stability is the likelihood of a renewed struggle between owners and players over a new basic agreement.

Nonetheless the game has weathered such storms in the past and the voracious public appetite for the game has continued. So it does today and therein lies the best promise for the game's continuing success.

PART TWO

Special Achievements

Most Valuable Player Awards
Rookie of the Year Award
Cy Young Award
Gold Glove Award
Triple Crown Winners
Manager of the Year Award
Consecutive Games Played
No-Hit Games
Baseball Hall of Fame
The Commissioners of Baseball

Special Achievements

Most Valuable Player Award

From 1911 through 1914, an automobile was presented to the player adjudged to be the most outstanding in his respective league. Thus the short-lived Chalmers Award was born. This award lasted four years.

The practice of selecting the league's Most Valuable Player actually began in 1922 when a special committee named George Sisler of the St. Louis Browns as the American League's Most Valuable Player. It was not until two years later, 1924, that the National League decided to join and Dazzy Vance, Brooklyn's flame-throwing right-hander, was chosen his league's MVP. This selection by committee process prevailed until 1930 when, for some uncertain reason, it simply faded away and there were no selections that year. A portent of what was to come actually surfaced in 1929 when the American League Selection Committee failed to make a selection.

The responsibility of selecting the respective leagues' most valuable players was turned over to the Baseball Writers Association of America (BBWAA) in 1931, and this able body of baseball writers has continued ever since. The first selections made were Robert "Lefty" Grove of the Philadelphia Athletics in the American League and Frankie Frisch of the St. Louis Cardinals in the National League. The only player ever to be selected MVP in both leagues is Frank Robinson, who won the honor in the National League in 1961 with Cincinnati and in the American League in 1966 with Baltimore.

League Championship Series, World Series, and All-Star Game Most Valuable Players

The Most Valuable Player Award in the American League Championship Series is officially called the "Leland S. Mac-Phail, Jr. Award," and the trophy is a large pewter tray. It was first given in 1980. The National League Championship Series Most Valuable Player receives a sterling silver platter. That award was first presented in 1977.

The World Series Most Valuable Player Award was first awarded in 1955, and the recipient is selected by a media panel at the World Series. The All-Star Most Valuable Player Award was started in 1962.

Rookie of the Year Award

The Rookie of the Year Award did not come into being until 1947, and again it was the Baseball Writers Association that did the voting. The first two years saw a combined selection, with Jackie Robinson of the Brooklyn Dodgers named in 1947 and Alvin Dark of the Boston Braves in 1948. Separate league selections began in 1949 with Roy Sievers of the St. Louis Browns in the American League and Don Newcombe of the Brooklyn Dodgers in the National. The Dodgers, with eleven selections, and the Yankees, with seven, lead their respective leagues in boasting the most rookie winners.

Cy Young Award

The Cy Young Award, honoring the best pitcher in baseball, was the brainchild of Ford Frick. The former commissioner of baseball, disturbed to find that voters generally tended to pay more attention to players in the lineup every day, as opposed to pitchers who appeared every fourth or fifth day, concluded there should be a separate award for pitchers. Consequently, in 1956, he inaugurated the Cy Young Award and turned this project over to the BBWAA. Frick's choice of Cy Young was based on two important statistics—Young is baseball's biggest winner with 511 victories and is the only pitcher in history to win 200 or more games in both leagues.

Don Newcombe of the Brooklyn Dodgers was the first Cy Young Award winner. The year was 1956. The selection of a single pitcher as baseball's best lasted through 1966, when Los Angeles' Sandy Koufax won the honor for the third time in four years. In 1967, acceding to a petition from the BBWAA, Gen. William Eckert, successor to Ford Frick as baseball commissioner, decreed that hereafter each league would have its own Cy Young Award winner. Jim Lonborg of Boston and Mike McCormick of San Francisco were the first to share that honor. The year 1969 produced the only tie for top honors when Mike Cuellar of Baltimore and Denny McLain of Detroit were deadlocked for first place in the American League. In 1981, Fernando Valenzuela became the first rookie to win the award. In 1982, Steve Carlton became the first four-time Cy Young Award winner; Tom Seaver, Jim Palmer, and Sandy Koufax have won three each.

Gold Glove Award

Each year, the top defensive player at his position is selected by the individual league's managers and coaches. He is not necessarily the player with the highest fielding percentage at his position.

Triple Crown Winners

In 114 National League and 89 American League seasons, there have been only fourteen players, all but two since the turn of the century, who have led their respective leagues in the three major offensive departments—batting, home runs, and runs batted in. Only two players—Rogers Hornsby of the 1922 and 1925 St. Louis Cardinals and Ted Williams of the 1942 and 1947 Boston Red Sox—have accomplished it twice. Although the American League is twenty-five years younger than the National, it has had eight Triple Crown winners compared to six for its older rival. Two of the National League's six came before the twentieth century. Paul Hines of Providence won the batting, home run, and rbi titles in 1878, and Hugh Duffy of the Boston Nationals captured the coveted prize in 1894. Napoleon Lajoie of the 1901 Philadelphia Athletics, with a .422 batting average, 14 home runs, and 125 rbis, was the first American League Triple Crown winner.

Manager of the Year Award

The top manager for the American and National leagues respectively is selected at the end of each season by the Baseball Writers Association of America (BBWAA).

Consecutive Games Played

This listing consists of those "iron men" who played the most consecutive games without interruptions.

No-Hit Games

Including Joe Borden's gem on July 28, 1875, with the Philadelphia club in the National Association, 227 no-hit games of nine innings or more have been pitched in the major leagues. This total includes 2 in the Union Association, 5 in the Federal League, 15 in the American Association, 91 in the American League, and 113 in the National League. In three of these no-hitters, it took the combined efforts of two or more pitchers to do the trick.

Thirteen of the no-hitters were perfect games of nine or more innings. These include the twelve perfect innings of Harvey Haddix before the Pittsburgh left-hander permitted a hit to the Milwaukee Braves on May 26, 1959, but do not include the perfect game pitched by Don Larsen of the New York Yankees against the Brooklyn Dodgers in the 1956 World Series.

Three pitchers—Ted Breitenstein, Charlie Jones, and Bobo Holloman—pitched no-hitters in their first major league game. Four others—Cy Young, Tom Hughes, Jim Bunning, and Nolan Ryan—pitched no-hitters in both the National and American leagues. Bob Feller is the only pitcher to hurl a no-hitter on opening day. Nolan Ryan leads all pitchers with five no-hitters. Bob Forsch of St. Louis and Ken Forsch of Houston are the only brothers who have both pitched no-hitters. Several pitchers have hurled two or more no-hitters in a single season, but Johnny Vander Meer of the Cincinnati Reds is the only one to pitch his two no-hitters back to back. They came on June 11 and June 15, 1938.

Baseball Hall of Fame

Baseball's Hall of Fame was founded in 1936 when five of the game's immortals were enshrined. These Hall of Fame pioneers were Babe Ruth, Ty Cobb, Honus Wagner, Christy Mathewson, and Walter Johnson. The special committee appointed by Commissioner Kenesaw Mountain Landis followed up its original selections by electing Napoleon Lajoie, Tris Speaker, and Cy Young to the Hall of Fame the following year. The committee also honored five others for meritorious service as field managers and baseball executives. The National Baseball Hall of Fame was established in Cooperstown, N.Y., in 1939. Several years later, the voting was turned over to the Baseball Writers Association of America, which was obliged to follow specified guidelines. These included that a player needs ten years of major league experience to qualify and 75 percent of the votes to be elected. No player is eligible for election until he has been retired for a minimum of five years.

In addition to the BBWAA, a Special Veterans Committee of twelve was established to consider players in the nineteenth century. Its scope has since been expanded to include eligible players retired for a minimum of twenty-five years. A third body, a ten-man Special Committee on the Negro Leagues, was authorized in 1971 to consider players of the old Negro leagues. Through 1989 a total of 204 players, managers, umpires, and executives have been inducted into the Hall of Fame.

MOST VALUABLE PLAYERS

NATIONAL LEAGUE		AMERICAN LEAGUE	
		CHALMERS	
1911	Frank Schulte, Chicago (OF)	1911	Ty Cobb, Detroit (OF)
1912	Larry Doyle, New York (2B)	1912	Tris Speaker, Boston (OF)
1913	Jake Daubert, Brooklyn (1B)	1913	Walter Johnson, Washington (P)
1914	Johnny Evers, Boston (2B)	1914	Eddie Collins, Philadelphia (2B)
		LEAGUE	
1922	No Selection	1922	George Sisler, St. Louis (1B)
1923	No Selection	1923	Babe Ruth, New York (OF)
1924	Dazzy Vance, Brooklyn (P)	1924	Walter Johnson, Washington (P)
1925	Rogers Hornsby, St. Louis (2B)	1925	Roger Peckinpaugh, Washington (SS)
1926	Bob O'Farrell, St. Louis (C)	1926	George Burns, Cleveland (1B)
1927	Paul Waner, Pittsburgh (OF)	1927	Lou Gehrig, New York (1B)
1928	Jim Bottomley, St. Louis (1B)	1928	Mickey Cochrane, Philadelphia (C)
1929	Rogers Hornsby, Chicago (2B)	1929	No Selection
	BASEBALL WRITERS ASSOCIATION OF AMERICA		
1931	Frankie Frisch, St. Louis (2B)	1931	Lefty Grove, Philadelphia (P)
1932	Chuck Klein, Philadelphia (OF)	1932	Jimmie Foxx, Philadelphia (1B)
1933	Carl Hubbell, New York (P)	1933	Jimmie Foxx, Philadelphia (1B)
1934	Dizzy Dean, St. Louis (P)	1934	Mickey Cochrane, Detroit (C)
1935	Gabby Hartnett, Chicago (C)	1935	Hank Greenberg, Detroit (1B)
1936	Carl Hubbell, New York (P)	1936	Lou Gehrig, New York (1B)
1937	Joe Medwick, St. Louis (OF)	1937	Charlie Gehringer, Detroit (2B)
1938	Ernie Lombardi, Cincinnati (C)	1938	Jimmie Foxx, Boston (1B)
1939	Bucky Walters, Cincinnati (P)	1939	Joe DiMaggio, New York (OF)
1940	Frank McCormick, Cincinnati (1B)	1940	Hank Greenberg, Detroit (1B)
1941	Dolph Camilli, Brooklyn (1B)	1941	Joe DiMaggio, New York (OF)
1942	Mort Cooper, St. Louis (P)	1942	Joe Gordon, New York (2B)
1943	Stan Musial, St. Louis (OF)	1943	Spud Chandler, New York (P)
1944	Marty Marion, St. Louis (SS)	1944	Hal Newhouser, Detroit (P)
1945	Phil Cavarretta, Chicago (1B)	1945	Hal Newhouser, Detroit (P)
1946	Stan Musial, St. Louis (1B)	1946	Ted Williams, Boston (OF)
1947	Bob Elliott, Boston (3B)	1947	Joe DiMaggio, New York (OF)
1948	Stan Musial, St. Louis (OF)	1948	Lou Boudreau, Cleveland (SS)
1949	Jackie Robinson, Brooklyn (2B)	1949	Ted Williams, Boston (OF)
1950	Jim Konstanty, Philadelphia (P)	1950	Phil Rizzuto, New York (SS)
1951	Roy Campanella, Brooklyn (C)	1951	Yogi Berra, New York (C)
1952	Hank Sauer, Chicago (OF)	1952	Bobby Shantz, Philadelphia (P)
1953	Roy Campanella, Brooklyn (C)	1953	Al Rosen, Cleveland (3B)

NATIONAL LEAGUE		AMERICAN LEAGUE	
1954	Willie Mays, New York (OF)	1954	Yogi Berra, New York (C)
1955	Roy Campanella, Brooklyn (C)	1955	Yogi Berra, New York (C)
1956	Don Newcombe, Brooklyn (P)	1956	Mickey Mantle, New York (OF)
1957	Hank Aaron, Milwaukee (OF)	1957	Mickey Mantle, New York (OF)
1958	Ernie Banks, Chicago (SS)	1958	Jackie Jensen, Boston (OF)
1959	Ernie Banks, Chicago (SS)	1959	Nellie Fox, Chicago (2B)
1960	Dick Groat, Pittsburgh (SS)	1960	Roger Maris, New York (OF)
1961	Frank Robinson, Cincinnati (OF)	1961	Roger Maris, New York (OF)
1962	Maury Wills, Los Angeles (SS)	1962	Mickey Mantle, New York (OF)
1963	Sandy Koufax, Los Angeles (P)	1963	Elston Howard, New York (C)
1964	Ken Boyer, St. Louis (3B)	1964	Brooks Robinson, Baltimore (3B)
1965	Willie Mays, San Francisco (OF)	1965	Zoilo Versalles, Minnesota (SS)
1966	Roberto Clemente, Pittsburgh (OF)	1966	Frank Robinson, Baltimore (OF)
1967	Orlando Cepeda, St. Louis (1B)	1967	Carl Yastrzemski, Boston (OF)
1968	Bob Gibson, St. Louis (P)	1968	Denny McLain, Detroit (P)
1969	Willie McCovey, San Francisco (1B)	1969	Harmon Killebrew, Minnesota (3B)
1970	Johnny Bench, Cincinnati (C)	1970	Boog Powell, Baltimore (1B)
1971	Joe Torre, St. Louis (3B)	1971	Vida Blue, Oakland (P)
1972	Johnny Bench, Cincinnati (C)	1972	Richie Allen, Chicago (1B)
1973	Pete Rose, Cincinnati (OF)	1973	Reggie Jackson, Oakland (OF)
1974	Steve Garvey, Los Angeles (1B)	1974	Jeff Burroughs, Texas (OF)
1975	Joe Morgan, Cincinnati (2B)	1975	Fred Lynn, Boston (OF)
1976	Joe Morgan, Cincinnati (2B)	1976	Thurman Munson, New York (C)
1977	George Foster, Cincinnati (OF)	1977	Rod Carew, Minnesota (1B)
1978	Dave Parker, Pittsburgh (OF)	1978	Jim Rice, Boston (OF)
1979	Keith Hernandez, St. Louis (1B)	1979	Don Baylor, California (DH)
	Willie Stargell, Pittsburgh (1B)		
1980	Mike Schmidt, Philadelphia (3B)	1980	George Brett, Kansas City (3B)
1981	Mike Schmidt, Philadelphia (3B)	1981	Rollie Fingers, Milwaukee (P)
1982	Dale Murphy, Atlanta (OF)	1982	Robin Yount, Milwaukee (SS)
1983	Dale Murphy, Atlanta (OF)	1983	Cal Ripken, Baltimore (SS)
1984	Ryne Sandberg, Chicago (2B)	1984	Willie Hernandez, Detroit (P)
1985	Willie McGee, St. Louis (OF)	1985	Don Mattingly, New York (1B)
1986	Mike Schmidt, Philadelphia (3B)	1986	Roger Clemens, Boston (P)
1987	Andre Dawson, Chicago (OF)	1987	George Bell, Toronto (OF)
1988	Kirk Gibson, Los Angeles (OF)	1988	Jose Canseco, Oakland (OF)
1989	Kevin Mitchell, San Francisco (OF)	1989	Robin Yount, Milwaukee (OF)

LEAGUE CHAMPIONSHIP SERIES MOST VALUABLE PLAYERS

NATIONAL LEAGUE	YEAR	AMERICAN LEAGUE
Dusty Baker, Los Angeles	1977	—
Steve Garvey, Los Angeles	1978	—
Willie Stargell, Pittsburgh	1979	—
Manny Trillo, Philadelphia	1980	Frank White, Kansas City
Burt Hooton, Los Angeles	1981	Graig Nettles, New York
Darrell Porter, St. Louis	1982	Fred Lynn, California
Gary Matthews, Philadelphia	1983	Mike Boddicker, Baltimore
Steve Garvey, San Diego	1984	Kirk Gibson, Detroit
Ozzie Smith, St. Louis	1985	George Brett, Kansas City
Mike Scott, Houston	1986	Marty Barrett, Boston
Jeff Leonard, San Francisco	1987	Gary Gaetti, Minnesota
Orel Hershiser, Los Angeles	1988	Dennis Eckersley, Oakland
Will Clark, San Francisco	1989	Rickey Henderson, Oakland

WORLD SERIES MOST VALUABLE PLAYERS

1955	Johnny Podres, Brooklyn	1973	Reggie Jackson, Oakland
1956	Don Larsen, New York (AL)	1974	Rollie Fingers, Oakland
1957	Lew Burdette, Milwaukee	1975	Pete Rose, Cincinnati
1958	Bob Turley, New York (AL)	1976	Johnny Bench, Cincinnati
1959	Larry Sherry, Los Angeles	1977	Reggie Jackson, New York (AL)
1960	Bobby Richardson, New York (AL)	1978	Bucky Dent, New York (AL)
1961	Whitey Ford, New York (AL)	1979	Willie Stargell, Pittsburgh
1962	Ralph Terry, New York (AL)	1980	Mike Schmidt, Philadelphia
1963	Sandy Koufax, Los Angeles	1981	Ron Cey, Pedro Guerrero,
1964	Bob Gibson, St. Louis		Steve Yeager, Los Angeles
1965	Sandy Koufax, Los Angeles	1982	Darrell Porter, St. Louis
1966	Frank Robinson, Baltimore	1983	Rick Dempsey, Baltimore
1967	Bob Gibson, St. Louis	1984	Alan Trammell, Detroit
1968	Mickey Lolich, Detroit	1985	Bret Saberhagen, Kansas City
1969	Donn Clendenon, New York (NL)	1986	Ray Knight, New York (NL)
1970	Brooks Robinson, Baltimore	1987	Frank Viola, Minnesota
1971	Roberto Clemente, Pittsburgh	1988	Orel Hershiser, Los Angeles
1972	Gene Tenace, Oakland	1989	Dave Stewart, Oakland

ALL-STAR GAME MOST VALUABLE PLAYERS

ARCH WARD MEMORIAL AWARD

1962(1)	Maury Wills	Los Angeles	NL
1962(2)	Leon Wagner	Los Angeles	AL
1963	Willie Mays	San Francisco	NL
1964	Johnny Callison	Philadelphia	NL
1965	Juan Marichal	San Francisco	NL
1966	Brooks Robinson	Baltimore	AL
1967	Tony Perez	Cincinnati	NL
1968	Willie Mays	San Francisco	NL
1969	Willie McCovey	San Francisco	NL

COMMISSIONER'S TROPHY

1970	Carl Yastrzemski	Boston	AL	CF-1B
1971	Frank Robinson	Baltimore	AL	RF
1972	Joe Morgan	Cincinnati	NL	2B
1973	Bobby Bonds	San Francisco	NL	RF
1974	Steve Garvey	Los Angeles	NL	1B
1975	Bill Madlock	Chicago	NL	3B
	Jon Matlack	New York	NL	P
1976	George Foster	Cincinnati	NL	CF-RF
1977	Don Sutton	Los Angeles	NL	P
1978	Steve Garvey	Los Angeles	NL	1B
1979	Dave Parker	Pittsburgh	NL	RF
1980	Ken Griffey	Cincinnati	NL	OF
1981	Gary Carter	Montreal	NL	C
1982	Dave Concepcion	Cincinnati	NL	SS
1983	Fred Lynn	California	AL	OF
1984	Gary Carter	Montreal	NL	C

ARCH WARD MEMORIAL AWARD

1985	LaMarr Hoyt	San Diego	NL	P
1986	Roger Clemens	Boston	AL	P
1987	Tim Raines	Montreal	AL	OF
1988	Terry Steinbach	Oakland	AL	C
1989	Bo Jackson	Kansas City	AL	OF

ROOKIE OF THE YEAR
(one selection 1947–48)

NATIONAL LEAGUE		AMERICAN LEAGUE	
1947	Jackie Robinson, Brooklyn (1B)		—
1948	Alvin Dark, Boston (SS)		—
1949	Don Newcombe, Brooklyn (P)	1949	Roy Sievers, St. Louis (OF)
1950	Sam Jethroe, Boston (OF)	1950	Walt Dropo, Boston (1B)
1951	Willie Mays, New York (OF)	1951	Gil McDougald, New York (3B)
1952	Joe Black, Brooklyn (P)	1952	Harry Byrd, Philadelphia (P)
1953	Junior Gilliam, Brooklyn (2B)	1953	Harvey Kuenn, Detroit (SS)
1954	Wally Moon, St. Louis (OF)	1954	Bob Grim, New York (P)
1955	Bill Virdon, St. Louis (OF)	1955	Herb Score, Cleveland (P)
1956	Frank Robinson, Cincinnati (OF)	1956	Luis Aparicio, Chicago (SS)
1957	Jack Sanford, Philadelphia (P)	1957	Tony Kubek, New York (SS)
1958	Orlando Cepeda, San Francisco (1B)	1958	Albie Pearson, Washington (OF)
1959	Willie McCovey, San Francisco (1B)	1959	Bob Allison, Washington (OF)
1960	Frank Howard, Los Angeles (OF)	1960	Ron Hansen, Baltimore (SS)
1961	Billy Williams, Chicago (OF)	1961	Don Schwall, Boston (P)
1962	Ken Hubbs, Chicago (2B)	1962	Tom Tresh, New York (SS)
1963	Pete Rose, Cincinnati (2B)	1963	Gary Peters, Chicago (P)
1964	Richie Allen, Philadelphia (3B)	1964	Tony Oliva, Minnesota (OF)
1965	Jim Lefebvre, Los Angeles (2B)	1965	Curt Blefary, Baltimore (OF)
1966	Tommy Helms, Cincinnati (2B)	1966	Tommie Agee, Chicago (OF)
1967	Tom Seaver, New York (P)	1967	Rod Carew, Minnesota (2B)
1968	Johnny Bench, Cincinnati (C)	1968	Stan Bahnsen, New York (P)
1969	Ted Sizemore, Los Angeles (2B)	1969	Lou Piniella, Kansas City (OF)

NATIONAL LEAGUE		AMERICAN LEAGUE	
1970	Carl Morton, Montreal (P)	1970	Thurman Munson, New York (C)
1971	Earl Williams, Atlanta (C)	1971	Chris Chambliss, Cleveland (1B)
1972	Jon Matlack, New York (P)	1972	Carlton Fisk, Boston (C)
1973	Gary Matthews, San Francisco (OF)	1973	Al Bumbry, Baltimore (OF)
1974	Bake McBride, St. Louis (OF)	1974	Mike Hargrove, Texas (1B)
1975	John Montefusco, San Francisco (P)	1975	Fred Lynn, Boston (OF)
1976	Pat Zachry, Cincinnati (P)	1976	Mark Fidrych, Detroit (P)
	Butch Metzger, San Diego (P)		
1977	Andre Dawson, Montreal (OF)	1977	Eddie Murray, Baltimore (DH)
1978	Bob Horner, Atlanta (3B)	1978	Lou Whitaker, Detroit (2B)
1979	Rick Sutcliffe, Los Angeles (P)	1979	Alfredo Griffin, Toronto (SS)
			John Castino, Minnesota (3B)
1980	Steve Howe, Los Angeles (P)	1980	Joe Charboneau, Cleveland (OF)
1981	Fernando Valenzuela, Los Angeles (P)	1981	Dave Righetti, New York (P)
1982	Steve Sax, Los Angeles (2B)	1982	Cal Ripken, Baltimore (SS)
1983	Darryl Strawberry, New York (OF)	1983	Ron Kittle, Chicago (OF)
1984	Dwight Gooden, New York (P)	1984	Alvin Davis, Seattle (1B)
1985	Vince Coleman, St. Louis (OF)	1985	Ozzie Guillen, Chicago (SS)
1986	Todd Worrell, St. Louis (P)	1986	Jose Canseco, Oakland (OF)
1987	Benito Santiago, San Diego (C)	1987	Mark McGwire, Oakland (1B)
1988	Chris Sabo, Cincinnati (3B)	1988	Walt Weiss, Oakland (SS)
1989	Jerome Walton, Chicago (OF)	1989	Gregg Olson, Baltimore (P)

CY YOUNG AWARD WINNERS
(one selection 1956–66)

NATIONAL LEAGUE		AMERICAN LEAGUE		NATIONAL LEAGUE		AMERICAN LEAGUE	
1956	Don Newcombe, Brooklyn (RH)	1958	Bob Turley, New York (RH)	1976	Randy Jones, San Diego (LH)	1978	Ron Guidry, New York (LH)
1957	Warren Spahn, Milwaukee (LH)	1959	Early Wynn, Chicago (RH)	1977	Steve Carlton, Philadelphia (LH)	1979	Mike Flanagan, Baltimore (LH)
1960	Vernon Law, Pittsburgh (RH)	1961	Whitey Ford, New York (LH)	1978	Gaylord Perry, San Diego (RH)	1980	Steve Stone, Baltimore (RH)
1962	Don Drysdale, Los Angeles (RH)	1964	Dean Chance, Los Angeles (RH)	1979	Bruce Sutter, Chicago (RH)	1981	Rollie Fingers, Milwaukee (RH)
1963	Sandy Koufax, Los Angeles (LH)	1967	Jim Lonborg, Boston (RH)	1980	Steve Carlton, Philadelphia (LH)	1982	Pete Vuckovich, Milwaukee (RH)
1965	Sandy Koufax, Los Angeles (LH)	1968	Denny McLain, Detroit (RH)	1981	Fernando Valenzuela, Los Angeles (LH)	1983	LaMarr Hoyt, Chicago (RH)
1966	Sandy Koufax, Los Angeles (LH)	1969	Mike Cuellar, Baltimore (LH)	1982	Steve Carlton, Philadelphia (LH)	1984	Willie Hernandez, Detroit (LH)
1967	Mike McCormick, San Francisco (LH)		Denny McLain, Detroit (RH)	1983	John Denny, Philadelphia (RH)	1985	Bret Saberhagen, Kansas City (RH)
1968	Bob Gibson, St. Louis (RH)	1970	Jim Perry, Minnesota (RH)	1984	Rick Sutcliffe, Chicago (RH)	1986	Roger Clemens, Boston (RH)
1969	Tom Seaver, New York (RH)	1971	Vida Blue, Oakland (LH)	1985	Dwight Gooden, New York (RH)	1987	Roger Clemens, Boston (RH)
1970	Bob Gibson, St. Louis (RH)	1972	Gaylord Perry, Cleveland (RH)	1986	Mike Scott, Houston (RH)	1988	Frank Viola, Minnesota (LH)
1971	Ferguson Jenkins, Chicago (RH)	1973	Jim Palmer, Baltimore (RH)	1987	Steve Bedrosian, Philadelphia (RH)	1989	Bret Saberhagen, Kansas City (RH)
1972	Steve Carlton, Philadelphia (LH)	1974	Jim (Catfish) Hunter, Oakland (RH)	1988	Orel Hershiser, Los Angeles (RH)		
1973	Tom Seaver, New York (RH)	1975	Jim Palmer, Baltimore (RH)	1989	Mark Davis, San Diego (LH)		
1974	Mike Marshall, Los Angeles (RH)	1976	Jim Palmer, Baltimore (RH)				
1975	Tom Seaver, New York (RH)	1977	Sparky Lyle, New York (LH)				

GOLD GLOVE AWARD WINNERS

COMBINED SELECTION

1957	P	Bobby Shantz, New York (AL)
	C	Sherm Lollar, Chicago (AL)
	1B	Gil Hodges, Brooklyn
	2B	Nellie Fox, Chicago (AL)
	3B	Frank Malzone, Boston
	SS	Roy McMillan, Cincinnati
	LF	Minnie Minoso, Chicago (AL)
	CF	Willie Mays, New York (NL)
	RF	Al Kaline, Detroit

		AMERICAN LEAGUE		NATIONAL LEAGUE
1958	P	Bobby Shantz, New York	P	Harvey Haddix, Cincinnati
	C	Sherm Lollar, Chicago	C	Del Crandall, Milwaukee
	1B	Vic Power, Cleveland	1B	Gil Hodges, Los Angeles
	2B	Frank Bolling, Detroit	2B	Bill Mazeroski, Pittsburgh
	3B	Frank Malzone, Boston	3B	Ken Boyer, St. Louis
	SS	Luis Aparicio, Chicago	SS	Roy McMillan, Cincinnati
	LF	Norm Siebern, New York	LF	Frank Robinson, Cincinnati
	CF	Jimmy Piersall, Boston	CF	Willie Mays, San Francisco
	RF	Al Kaline, Detroit	RF	Hank Aaron, Milwaukee
1959	P	Bobby Shantz, New York	P	Harvey Haddix, Pittsburgh
	C	Sherm Lollar, Chicago	C	Del Crandall, Milwaukee
	1B	Vic Power, Cleveland	1B	Gil Hodges, Los Angeles
	2B	Nellie Fox, Chicago	2B	Charlie Neal, Los Angeles
	3B	Frank Malzone, Boston	3B	Ken Boyer, St. Louis
	SS	Luis Aparicio, Chicago	SS	Roy McMillan, Cincinnati
	LF	Minnie Minoso, Cleveland	LF	Jackie Brandt, St. Louis
	CF	Al Kaline, Detroit	CF	Willie Mays, San Francisco
	RF	Jackie Jensen, Boston	RF	Hank Aaron, Milwaukee
1960	P	Bobby Shantz, New York	P	Harvey Haddix, Pittsburgh
	C	Earl Battey, Washington	C	Del Crandall, Milwaukee
	1B	Vic Power, Cleveland	1B	Bill White, St. Louis
	2B	Nellie Fox, Chicago	2B	Bill Mazeroski, Pittsburgh
	3B	Brooks Robinson, Baltimore	3B	Ken Boyer, St. Louis
	SS	Luis Aparicio, Chicago	SS	Ernie Banks, Chicago
	LF	Minnie Minoso, Chicago	LF	Wally Moon, Los Angeles
	CF	Jim Landis, Chicago	CF	Willie Mays, San Francisco
	RF	Roger Maris, New York	RF	Hank Aaron, Milwaukee

		AMERICAN LEAGUE	NATIONAL LEAGUE
1961	P	Frank Lary, Detroit	Bobby Shantz, Pittsburgh
	C	Earl Battey, Chicago	John Roseboro, Los Angeles
	1B	Vic Power, Cleveland	Bill White, St. Louis
	2B	Bobby Richardson, New York	Bill Mazeroski, Pittsburgh
	3B	Brooks Robinson, Baltimore	Ken Boyer, St. Louis
	SS	Luis Aparicio, Chicago	Maury Wills, Los Angeles
	OF	Al Kaline, Detroit	Willie Mays, San Francisco
	OF	Jimmy Piersall, Cleveland	Roberto Clemente, Pittsburgh
	OF	Jim Landis, Chicago	Vada Pinson, Cincinnati
1962	P	Jim Kaat, Minnesota	Bobby Shantz, St. Louis
	C	Earl Battey, Minnesota	Del Crandall, Milwaukee
	1B	Vic Power, Minnesota	Bill White, St. Louis
	2B	Bobby Richardson, New York	Ken Hubbs, Chicago
	3B	Brooks Robinson, Baltimore	Jim Davenport, San Francisco
	SS	Luis Aparicio, Chicago	Maury Wills, Los Angeles
	OF	Jim Landis, Chicago	Willie Mays, San Francisco
	OF	Mickey Mantle, New York	Roberto Clemente, Pittsburgh
	OF	Al Kaline, Detroit	Bill Virdon, Pittsburgh
1963	P	Jim Kaat, Minnesota	Bobby Shantz, St. Louis
	C	Elston Howard, New York	Johnny Edwards, Cincinnati
	1B	Vic Power, Minnesota	Bill White, St. Louis
	2B	Bobby Richardson, New York	Bill Mazeroski, Pittsburgh
	3B	Brooks Robinson, Baltimore	Ken Boyer, St. Louis
	SS	Zoilo Versalles, Minnesota	Bobby Wine, Philadelphia
	OF	Al Kaline, Detroit	Willie Mays, San Francisco
	OF	Carl Yastrzemski, Boston	Roberto Clemente, Pittsburgh
	OF	Jim Landis, Chicago	Curt Flood, St. Louis
1964	P	Jim Kaat, Minnesota	Bobby Shantz, Philadelphia
	C	Elston Howard, New York	Johnny Edwards, Cincinnati
	1B	Vic Power, Los Angeles	Bill White, St. Louis
	2B	Bobby Richardson, New York	Bill Mazeroski, Pittsburgh
	3B	Brooks Robinson, Baltimore	Ron Santo, Chicago
	SS	Luis Aparicio, Baltimore	Ruben Amaro, Philadelphia
	OF	Al Kaline, Detroit	Willie Mays, San Francisco
	OF	Jim Landis, Chicago	Roberto Clemente, Pittsburgh
	OF	Vic Davalillo, Cleveland	Curt Flood, St. Louis

GOLD GLOVE AWARD WINNERS *cont.*

	AMERICAN LEAGUE	NATIONAL LEAGUE		AMERICAN LEAGUE	NATIONAL LEAGUE
1965	P Jim Kaat, Minnesota	P Bob Gibson, St. Louis	**1972**	P Jim Kaat, Minnesota	P Bob Gibson, St. Louis
	C Bill Freehan, Detroit	C Joe Torre, Atlanta		C Carlton Fisk, Boston	C Johnny Bench, Cincinnati
	1B Joe Pepitone, New York	1B Bill White, St. Louis		1B George Scott, Milwaukee	1B Wes Parker, Los Angeles
	2B Bobby Richardson, New York	2B Bill Mazeroski, Pittsburgh		2B Doug Griffin, Boston	2B Felix Millan, Atlanta
	3B Brooks Robinson, Baltimore	3B Ron Santo, Chicago		3B Brooks Robinson, Baltimore	3B Doug Rader, Houston
	SS Zoilo Versalles, Minnesota	SS Leo Cardenas, Cincinnati		SS Ed Brinkman, Detroit	SS Larry Bowa, Philadelphia
	OF Al Kaline, Detroit	OF Willie Mays, San Francisco		OF Paul Blair, Baltimore	OF Roberto Clemente, Pittsburgh
	OF Tom Tresh, New York	OF Roberto Clemente, Pittsburgh		OF Bobby Murcer, New York	OF Cesar Cedeno, Houston
	OF Carl Yastrzemski, Boston	OF Curt Flood, St. Louis		OF Ken Berry, California	OF Willie Davis, Los Angeles
1966	P Jim Kaat, Minnesota	P Bob Gibson, St. Louis	**1973**	P Jim Kaat, Chicago	P Bob Gibson, St. Louis
	C Bill Freehan, Detroit	C John Roseboro, Los Angeles		C Thurman Munson, New York	C Johnny Bench, Cincinnati
	1B Joe Pepitone, New York	1B Bill White, Philadelphia		1B George Scott, Milwaukee	1B Mike Jorgensen, Montreal
	2B Bobby Knoop, California	2B Bill Mazeroski, Pittsburgh		2B Bobby Grich, Baltimore	2B Joe Morgan, Cincinnati
	3B Brooks Robinson, Baltimore	3B Ron Santo, Chicago		3B Brooks Robinson, Baltimore	3B Doug Rader, Houston
	SS Luis Aparicio, Baltimore	SS Gene Alley, Pittsburgh		SS Mark Belanger, Baltimore	SS Roger Metzger, Houston
	OF Al Kaline, Detroit	OF Willie Mays, San Francisco		OF Paul Blair, Baltimore	OF Bobby Bonds, San Francisco
	OF Tommie Agee, Chicago	OF Curt Flood, St. Louis		OF Amos Otis, Kansas City	OF Cesar Cedeno, Houston
	OF Tony Oliva, Minnesota	OF Roberto Clemente, Pittsburgh		OF Mickey Stanley, Detroit	OF Willie Davis, Los Angeles
1967	P Jim Kaat, Minnesota	P Bob Gibson, St. Louis	**1974**	P Jim Kaat, Chicago	P Andy Messersmith, Los Angeles
	C Bill Freehan, Detroit	C Randy Hundley, Chicago		C Thurman Munson, New York	C Johnny Bench, Cincinnati
	1B George Scott, Boston	1B Wes Parker, Los Angeles		1B George Scott, Milwaukee	1B Steve Garvey, Los Angeles
	2B Bobby Knoop, California	2B Bill Mazeroski, Pittsburgh		2B Bobby Grich, Baltimore	2B Joe Morgan, Cincinnati
	3B Brooks Robinson, Baltimore	3B Ron Santo, Chicago		3B Brooks Robinson, Baltimore	3B Doug Rader, Houston
	SS Jim Fregosi, California	SS Gene Alley, Pittsburgh		SS Mark Belanger, Baltimore	SS Dave Concepcion, Cincinnati
	OF Carl Yastrzemski, Boston	OF Roberto Clemente, Pittsburgh		OF Paul Blair, Baltimore	OF Cesar Cedeno, Houston
	OF Paul Blair, Baltimore	OF Curt Flood, St. Louis		OF Amos Otis, Kansas City	OF Cesar Geronimo, Cincinnati
	OF Al Kaline, Detroit	OF Willie Mays, San Francisco		OF Joe Rudi, Oakland	OF Bobby Bonds, San Francisco
1968	P Jim Kaat, Minnesota	P Bob Gibson, St. Louis	**1975**	P Jim Kaat, Chicago	P Andy Messersmith, Los Angeles
	C Bill Freehan, Detroit	C Johnny Bench, Cincinnati		C Thurman Munson, New York	C Johnny Bench, Cincinnati
	1B George Scott, Boston	1B Wes Parker, Los Angeles		1B George Scott, Milwaukee	1B Steve Garvey, Los Angeles
	2B Bobby Knoop, California	2B Glenn Beckert, Chicago		2B Bobby Grich, Baltimore	2B Joe Morgan, Cincinnati
	3B Brooks Robinson, Baltimore	3B Ron Santo, Chicago		3B Brooks Robinson, Baltimore	3B Ken Reitz, St. Louis
	SS Luis Aparicio, Chicago	SS Dal Maxvill, St. Louis		SS Mark Belanger, Baltimore	SS Dave Concepcion, Cincinnati
	OF Mickey Stanley, Detroit	OF Willie Mays, San Francisco		OF Paul Blair, Baltimore	OF Cesar Cedeno, Houston
	OF Carl Yastrzemski, Boston	OF Roberto Clemente, Pittsburgh		OF Joe Rudi, Oakland	OF Cesar Geronimo, Cincinnati
	OF Reggie Smith, Boston	OF Curt Flood, St. Louis		OF Fred Lynn, Boston	OF Garry Maddox, Philadelphia
1969	P Jim Kaat, Minnesota	P Bob Gibson, St. Louis	**1976**	P Jim Palmer, Baltimore	P Jim Kaat, Philadelphia
	C Bill Freehan, Detroit	C Johnny Bench, Cincinnati		C Jim Sundberg, Texas	C Johnny Bench, Cincinnati
	1B Joe Pepitone, New York	1B Wes Parker, Los Angeles		1B George Scott, Milwaukee	1B Steve Garvey, Los Angeles
	2B Dave Johnson, Baltimore	2B Felix Millan, Atlanta		2B Bobby Grich, Baltimore	2B Joe Morgan, Cincinnati
	3B Brooks Robinson, Baltimore	3B Ken Boyer, Atlanta		3B Aurelio Rodriguez, Detroit	3B Mike Schmidt, Philadelphia
	SS Mark Belanger, Baltimore	SS Don Kessinger, Chicago		SS Mark Belanger, Baltimore	SS Dave Concepcion, Cincinnati
	OF Paul Blair, Baltimore	OF Roberto Clemente, Pittsburgh		OF Joe Rudi, Oakland	OF Cesar Cedeno, Houston
	OF Mickey Stanley, Detroit	OF Curt Flood, St. Louis		OF Dwight Evans, Boston	OF Cesar Geronimo, Cincinnati
	OF Carl Yastrzemski, Boston	OF Pete Rose, Cincinnati		OF Rick Manning, Cleveland	OF Garry Maddox, Philadelphia
1970	P Jim Kaat, Minnesota	P Bob Gibson, St. Louis	**1977**	P Jim Palmer, Baltimore	P Jim Kaat, Philadelphia
	C Ray Fosse, Cleveland	C Johnny Bench, Cincinnati		C Jim Sundberg, Texas	C Johnny Bench, Cincinnati
	1B Jim Spencer, California	1B Wes Parker, Los Angeles		1B Jim Spencer, Chicago	1B Steve Garvey, Los Angeles
	2B Dave Johnson, Baltimore	2B Tommy Helms, Cincinnati		2B Frank White, Kansas City	2B Joe Morgan, Cincinnati
	3B Brooks Robinson, Baltimore	3B Doug Rader, Houston		3B Graig Nettles, New York	3B Mike Schmidt, Philadelphia
	SS Luis Aparicio, Chicago	SS Don Kessinger, Chicago		SS Mark Belanger, Baltimore	SS Dave Concepcion, Cincinnati
	OF Mickey Stanley, Detroit	OF Roberto Clemente, Pittsburgh		OF Juan Beniquez, Texas	OF Cesar Geronimo, Cincinnati
	OF Paul Blair, Baltimore	OF Tommie Agee, New York		OF Carl Yastrzemski, Boston	OF Garry Maddox, Philadelphia
	OF Ken Berry, Chicago	OF Pete Rose, Cincinnati		OF Al Cowens, Kansas City	OF Dave Parker, Pittsburgh
1971	P Jim Kaat, Minnesota	P Bob Gibson, St. Louis	**1978**	P Jim Palmer, Baltimore	P Phil Niekro, Atlanta
	C Ray Fosse, Cleveland	C Johnny Bench, Cincinnati		C Jim Sundberg, Texas	C Bob Boone, Philadelphia
	1B George Scott, Boston	1B Wes Parker, Los Angeles		1B Chris Chambliss, New York	1B Keith Hernandez, St. Louis
	2B Dave Johnson, Baltimore	2B Tommy Helms, Cincinnati		2B Frank White, Kansas City	2B Davey Lopes, Los Angeles
	3B Brooks Robinson, Baltimore	3B Doug Rader, Houston		3B Graig Nettles, New York	3B Mike Schmidt, Philadelphia
	SS Mark Belanger, Baltimore	SS Bud Harrelson, New York		SS Mark Belanger, Baltimore	SS Larry Bowa, Philadelphia
	OF Paul Blair, Baltimore	OF Roberto Clemente, Pittsburgh		OF Fred Lynn, Boston	OF Garry Maddox, Philadelphia
	OF Amos Otis, Kansas City	OF Bobby Bonds, San Francisco		OF Dwight Evans, Boston	OF Dave Parker, Pittsburgh
	OF Carl Yastrzemski, Boston	OF Willie Davis, Los Angeles		OF Rick Miller, California	OF Ellis Valentine, Montreal

GOLD GLOVE AWARD WINNERS *cont.*

		AMERICAN LEAGUE	NATIONAL LEAGUE
1979	P	Jim Palmer, Baltimore	P Phil Niekro, Atlanta
	C	Jim Sundberg, Texas	C Bob Boone, Philadelphia
	1B	Cecil Cooper, Milwaukee	1B Keith Hernandez, St. Louis
	2B	Frank White, Kansas City	2B Manny Trillo, Philadelphia
	3B	Buddy Bell, Texas	3B Mike Schmidt, Philadelphia
	SS	Rick Burleson, Boston	SS Dave Concepcion, Cincinnati
	OF	Dwight Evans, Boston	OF Garry Maddox, Philadelphia
	OF	Sixto Lezcano, Milwaukee	OF Dave Parker, Pittsburgh
	OF	Fred Lynn, Boston	OF Dave Winfield, San Diego
1980	P	Mike Norris, Oakland	P Phil Niekro, Atlanta
	C	Jim Sundberg, Texas	C Gary Carter, Montreal
	1B	Cecil Cooper, Milwaukee	1B Keith Hernandez, St. Louis
	2B	Frank White, Kansas City	2B Doug Flynn, New York
	3B	Buddy Bell, Texas	3B Mike Schmidt, Philadelphia
	SS	Alan Trammell, Detroit	SS Ozzie Smith, San Diego
	OF	Fred Lynn, Boston	OF Andre Dawson, Montreal
	OF	Dwayne Murphy, Oakland	OF Garry Maddox, Philadelphia
	OF	Willie Wilson, Kansas City	OF Dave Winfield, San Diego
1981	P	Mike Norris, Oakland	P Steve Carlton, Philadelphia
	C	Jim Sundberg, Texas	C Gary Carter, Montreal
	1B	Mike Squires, Chicago	1B Keith Hernandez, St. Louis
	2B	Frank White, Kansas City	2B Manny Trillo, Philadelphia
	3B	Buddy Bell, Texas	3B Mike Schmidt, Philadelphia
	SS	Alan Trammell, Detroit	SS Ozzie Smith, San Diego
	OF	Dwayne Murphy, Oakland	OF Andre Dawson, Montreal
	OF	Dwight Evans, Boston	OF Garry Maddox, Philadelphia
	OF	Rickey Henderson, Oakland	OF Dusty Baker, Los Angeles
1982	P	Ron Guidry, New York	P Phil Niekro, Atlanta
	C	Bob Boone, California	C Gary Carter, Montreal
	1B	Eddie Murray, Baltimore	1B Keith Hernandez, St. Louis
	2B	Frank White, Kansas City	2B Manny Trillo, Philadelphia
	3B	Buddy Bell, Texas	3B Mike Schmidt, Philadelphia
	SS	Robin Yount, Milwaukee	SS Ozzie Smith, St. Louis
	OF	Dwight Evans, Boston	OF Andre Dawson, Montreal
	OF	Dave Winfield, New York	OF Dale Murphy, Atlanta
	OF	Dwayne Murphy, Oakland	OF Garry Maddox, Philadelphia
1983	P	Ron Guidry, New York	P Phil Niekro, Atlanta
	C	Lance Parrish, Detroit	C Tony Pena, Pittsburgh
	1B	Eddie Murray, Baltimore	1B Keith Hernandez, St. Louis/New York
	2B	Lou Whitaker, Detroit	2B Ryne Sandberg, Chicago
	3B	Buddy Bell, Texas	3B Mike Schmidt, Philadelphia
	SS	Alan Trammell, Detroit	SS Ozzie Smith, St. Louis
	OF	Dwight Evans, Boston	OF Andre Dawson, Montreal
	OF	Dave Winfield, New York	OF Dale Murphy, Atlanta
	OF	Dwayne Murphy, Oakland	OF Willie McGee, St. Louis
1984	P	Ron Guidry, New York	P Joaquin Andujar, St. Louis
	C	Lance Parrish, Detroit	C Tony Pena, Pittsburgh
	1B	Eddie Murray, Baltimore	1B Keith Hernandez, New York
	2B	Lou Whitaker, Detroit	2B Ryne Sandberg, Chicago
	3B	Buddy Bell, Texas	3B Mike Schmidt, Philadelphia
	SS	Alan Trammell, Detroit	SS Ozzie Smith, St. Louis
	OF	Dwight Evans, Boston	OF Dale Murphy, Atlanta
	OF	Dave Winfield, New York	OF Bob Dernier, Chicago
	OF	Dwayne Murphy, Oakland	OF Andre Dawson, Montreal

		AMERICAN LEAGUE	NATIONAL LEAGUE
1985	P	Ron Guidry, New York	P Rick Reuschel, Pittsburgh
	C	Lance Parrish, Detroit	C Tony Pena, Pittsburgh
	1B	Don Mattingly, New York	1B Keith Hernandez, New York
	2B	Lou Whitaker, Detroit	2B Ryne Sandberg, Chicago
	3B	George Brett, Kansas City	3B Tim Wallach, Montreal
	SS	Alfredo Griffin, Oakland	SS Ozzie Smith, St. Louis
	OF	Gary Pettis, California	OF Willie McGee, St. Louis
	OF	Dave Winfield, New York	OF Andre Dawson, Montreal
	OF	Dwight Evans, Boston	OF Dale Murphy, Atlanta
	OF	Dwayne Murphy, Oakland	
1986	P	Ron Guidry, New York	P Fernando Valenzuela, Los Angeles
	C	Bob Boone, California	C Jody Davis, Chicago
	1B	Don Mattingly, New York	1B Keith Hernandez, New York
	2B	Frank White, Kansas City	2B Ryne Sandberg, Chicago
	3B	Gary Gaetti, Minnesota	3B Mike Schmidt, Philadelphia
	SS	Tony Fernandez, Toronto	SS Ozzie Smith, St. Louis
	OF	Jesse Barfield, Toronto	OF Dale Murphy, Atlanta
	OF	Kirby Puckett, Minnesota	OF Willie McGee, St. Louis
	OF	Gary Pettis, California	OF Tony Gwynn, San Diego
1987	P	Mark Langston, Seattle	P Rick Reuschel, San Francisco
	C	Bob Boone, California	C Mike LaValliere, Pittsburgh
	1B	Don Mattingly, New York	1B Keith Hernandez, New York
	2B	Frank White, Kansas City	2B Ryne Sandberg, Chicago
	3B	Gary Gaetti, Minnesota	3B Terry Pendleton, St. Louis
	SS	Tony Fernandez, Toronto	SS Ozzie Smith, St. Louis
	OF	Jesse Barfield, Toronto	OF Eric Davis, Cincinnati
	OF	Kirby Puckett, Minnesota	OF Andre Dawson, Chicago
	OF	Dave Winfield, New York	OF Tony Gwynn, San Diego
1988	P	Mark Langston, Seattle	P Orel Hershiser, Los Angeles
	C	Bob Boone, California	C Benito Santiago, San Diego
	1B	Don Mattingly, New York	1B Keith Hernandez, New York
	2B	Harold Reynolds, Seattle	2B Ryne Sandberg, Chicago
	3B	Gary Gaetti, Minnesota	3B Tim Wallach, Montreal
	SS	Tony Fernandez, Toronto	SS Ozzie Smith, St. Louis
	OF	Devon White, California	OF Andre Dawson, Chicago
	OF	Gary Pettis, California	OF Eric Davis, Cincinnati
	OF	Kirby Puckett, Minnesota	OF Andy Van Slyke, Pittsburgh
1989	P	Bret Saberhagen, Kansas City	P Ron Darling, New York
	1B	Don Mattingly, New York	1B Andres Galarraga, Montreal
	2B	Harold Reynolds, Seattle	2B Ryne Sandberg, Chicago
	3B	Gary Gaetti, Minnesota	3B Terry Pendleton, St. Louis
	SS	Tony Fernandez, Toronto	SS Ozzie Smith, St. Louis
	OF	Devon White, California	OF Andy Van Slyke, Pittsburgh
	OF	Gary Pettis, Detroit	OF Eric Davis, Cincinnati
	OF	Kirby Puckett, Minnesota	OF Tony Gwynn, San Diego
	C	Bob Boone, Kansas City	C Benito Santiago, San Diego

SPECIAL ACHIEVEMENTS

TRIPLE CROWN WINNERS

NATIONAL LEAGUE

Paul Hines, Providence	1878
Hugh Duffy, Boston	1894
Heinie Zimmerman, Chicago	1912
Rogers Hornsby, St. Louis	1922
Rogers Hornsby, St. Louis	1925
Chuck Klein, Philadelphia	1933
Joe Medwick, St. Louis	1937

AMERICAN LEAGUE

Napoleon Lajoie, Philadelphia	1901
Ty Cobb, Detroit	1909
Jimmie Foxx, Philadelphia	1933
Lou Gehrig, New York	1934
Ted Williams, Boston	1942
Ted Williams, Boston	1947
Mickey Mantle, New York	1956
Frank Robinson, Baltimore	1966
Carl Yastrzemski, Boston	1967

MANAGER OF THE YEAR AWARD WINNERS

NATIONAL LEAGUE

1983	Tommy Lasorda, Los Angeles
1984	Jim Frey, Chicago
1985	Whitey Herzog, St. Louis
1986	Hal Lanier, Houston
1987	Buck Rodgers, Montreal
1988	Tommy Lasorda, Los Angeles
1989	Don Zimmer, Chicago

AMERICAN LEAGUE

1983	Tony LaRussa, Chicago
1984	Sparky Anderson, Detroit
1985	Bobby Cox, Toronto
1986	John McNamara, Boston
1987	Sparky Anderson, Detroit
1988	Tony LaRussa, Oakland
1989	Frank Robinson, Baltimore

CONSECUTIVE GAMES PLAYED
(500 or more games)

Lou Gehrig	2130	Pete Rose	745	Steve Brodie	574
Everett Scott	1307	Dale Murphy	740	Aaron Ward	565
Cal Ripken	1250*	Richie Ashburn	730	Candy LaChance	540
Steve Garvey	1207	Ernie Banks	717	Buck Freeman	535
Billy Williams	1117	Earl Averill	673	Fred Luderus	533
Joe Sewell	1103	Frank McCormick	652	Clyde Milan	512
Stan Musial	895	Sandy Alomar	648	Charlie Gehringer	511
Eddie Yost	829	Eddie Brown	618	Vada Pinson	508
Gus Suhr	822	Roy McMillan	598	Charlie Gehringer	504
Nellie Fox	798	George Pinckney	577	Omar Moreno	503

*Streak in progress at the end of the 1989 season.

NO-HIT GAMES
(9 innings or more)

NATIONAL LEAGUE

1876	July 15	George W. Bradley, St.L. vs Har. 2-0
1880	June 12	John Richmond, Wor. vs Cle. 1-0 (perfect game)
	June 17	John M. Ward, Pro. vs Buf. 5-0 (perfect game)
	Aug. 19	Larry Corcoran, Chi. vs Bos. 6-0
	Aug. 20	Jim Galvin, Buf. at Wor. 1-0
1882	Sep. 20	Larry Corcoran, Chi. vs Wor. 5-0
	Sep. 22	Tom Lovett, Bkn. vs N.Y. 4-0
1883	July 25	Charles Radbourn, Pro. at Cle. 8-0
	Sep. 13	Hugh Daily, Cle. at Phi. 1-0
1884	June 27	Larry Corcoran, Chi. vs Pro. 6-0
	Aug. 4	Jim Galvin, Buf. at Det. 18-0
1885	July 27	John Clarkson, Chi. vs Pro. 6-0
	Aug. 29	Charles Ferguson, Phi. vs Pro. 1-0
1891	July 31	Amos Rusie, N.Y. vs Bkn. 6-0
1892	Aug. 6	John Stivetts, Bos. vs Bkn. 11-0
	Aug. 22	Alex Sanders, Lou. vs Bal. 6-2
	Oct. 15	Charlie Jones, Cin. vs Pit. 7-1 (First Major League game)
1893	Aug. 16	Bill Hawke, Bal. vs Was. 5-0
1897	Sep. 18	Cy Young, Cle. vs Cin. 6-0
1898	Apr. 22	Ted Breitenstein, Cin. vs Pit. 11-0
	Apr. 22	Jim Hughes, Bal. vs Bos. 8-0
	July 8	Frank Donahue, Phi. vs Bos. 5-0
	Aug. 21	Walter Thornton, Chi. vs Bkn. 2-0
1899	May 25	Deacon Phillippe, Lou. vs N.Y. 7-0
	Aug. 7	Vic Willis, Bos. vs Was. 7-1
1900	July 12	Frank Hahn, Cin. vs Phi. 4-0
1901	July 15	Christy Mathewson, N.Y. at St.L. 5-0
1903	Sep. 18	Chick Fraser, Phi. at Chi. 10-0
1904	June 11	Bob Wicker, Chi. at N.Y. 1-0 (hit in 10th; won in 12th)
1905	June 13	Christy Mathewson, N.Y. at Chi. 1-0
1906	May 1	John Lush, Phi. at Bkn. 1-0
	July 20	Mal Eason, Bkn. at St.L. 2-0
	Aug. 1	Harry McIntyre, Bkn. vs Pit. 0-1 (hit in 11th; lost in 13th)
1907	May 8	Frank Pfeffer, Bos. vs Cin. 6-0
	Sep. 20	Nick Maddox, Pit. vs Bkn. 2-1

NATIONAL LEAGUE *cont.*

1908	July 4	George Wiltse, N.Y. vs Phi. 1-0 (10 innings)
	Sep. 5	Nap Rucker, Bkn. vs Bos. 6-0
1909	Apr. 15	Leon Ames, N.Y. vs Bkn. 0-3 (hit in 10th; lost in 13th)
1912	Sep. 6	Jeff Tesreau, N.Y. at Phi. 3-0
1914	Sep. 9	George Davis, Bos. vs Phi. 7-0
1915	Apr. 15	Rube Marquard, N.Y. vs Bkn. 2-0
	Aug. 31	Jimmy Lavender, Chi. at N.Y. 2-0
1916	June 16	Tom Hughes, Bos. vs Pit. 2-0
1917	May 2	Jim Vaughn, Chi. vs Cin. 0-1 (hit in 10th; lost in 10th)
	May 2	Fred Toney, Cin. at Chi. 1-0 (10 innings)
1919	May 11	Hod Eller, Cin. at St.L. 6-0
1922	May 7	Jesse Barnes, N.Y. vs Phi. 6-0
1924	July 17	Jesse Haines, St.L. vs Bos. 5-0
1925	Sep. 13	Dazzy Vance, Bkn. vs Phi. 10-1
1929	May 8	Carl Hubbell, N.Y. vs Pit 11-0
1934	Sep. 21	Paul Dean, St.L. vs Bkn. 3-0
1938	June 11	Johnny Vander Meer, Cin. vs Bos. 3-0
	June 15	Johnny Vander Meer, Cin. at Bkn. 6-0
1940	Apr. 30	Tex Carleton, Bkn. at Cin. 3-0
1941	Aug. 30	Lon Warneke, St.L. at Cin. 2-0
1944	Apr. 27	Jim Tobin, Bos. vs Bkn. 2-0
	May 15	Clyde Shoun, Cin. vs Bos. 1-0
1946	Apr. 23	Ed Head, Bkn. vs Bos. 5-0
1947	June 18	Ewell Blackwell, Cin. vs Bos. 6-0
1948	Sep. 9	Rex Barney, Bkn. at N.Y. 2-0
1950	Aug. 11	Vern Bickford, Bos. vs Bkn. 7-0
1951	May 6	Cliff Chambers, Pit. at Bos. 3-0
1952	June 19	Carl Erskine, Bkn. vs Chi. 5-0
1954	June 12	Jim Wilson, Mil. vs Phi. 2-0
1955	May 12	Sam Jones, Chi. vs Pit. 4-0
1956	May 12	Carl Erskine, Bkn. vs N.Y. 3-0
	Sep. 25	Sal Maglie, Bkn. vs Phi. 5-0
1959	May 26	Harvey Haddix, Pit. at Mil. 0-1 (hit in 13th; lost in 13th)

NO-HIT GAMES cont.
(9 innings or more)

NATIONAL LEAGUE cont.

1960	May 15	Don Cardwell, Chi. vs St.L. 4-0
	Aug. 18	Lew Burdette, Mil. vs Phi. 1-0
	Sep. 15	Warren Spahn, Mil. vs Phi. 4-0
1961	Apr. 28	Warren Spahn, Mil. vs S.F. 1-0
1962	June 30	Sandy Koufax, L.A. vs N.Y. 5-0
1963	May 11	Sandy Koufax, L.A. vs S.F. 8-0
	May 17	Don Nottebart, Hou. vs Phi. 4-1
	June 15	Juan Marichal, S.F. vs Hou. 1-0
1964	Apr. 23	Ken Johnson, Hou. vs Cin. 0-1
	June 4	Sandy Koufax, L.A. at Phi. 3-0
	June 21	Jim Bunning, Phi. at N.Y. 6-0 (perfect game)
1965	June 14	Jim Maloney, Cin. vs N.Y. 0-1 (hit in 10th; lost in 10th)
	Aug. 9	Jim Maloney, Cin. at Chi. 1-0 (10 innings)
	Sep. 9	Sandy Koufax, L.A. vs Chi. 1-0 (perfect game)
1967	June 18	Don Wilson, Hou. vs Atl. 2-0
1968	July 29	George Culver, Cin. at Phi. 6-1
	Sep. 17	Gaylord Perry, S.F. vs St.L. 1-0
	Sep. 18	Ray Washburn, St.L. at S.F. 2-0
1969	Apr. 17	Bill Stoneman, Mon. at Phi. 7-0
	Apr. 30	Jim Maloney, Cin. vs Hou. 1-0
	May 1	Don Wilson, Hou. at Cin. 4-0
	Aug. 19	Ken Holtzman, Chi. vs Atl. 3-0
	Sep. 20	Bob Moose, Pit. at N.Y. 4-0
1970	June 12	Dock Ellis, Pit. at S.D. 2-0
	July 20	Bill Singer, L.A. vs Phi. 5-0
1971	June 3	Ken Holtzman, Chi. at Cin. 1-0
	June 23	Rick Wise, Phi. at Cin. 4-0
	Aug. 14	Bob Gibson, St.L. at Pit. 11-0
1972	Apr. 16	Burt Hooton, Chi. vs Phi. 4-0
	Sep. 2	Milt Pappas, Chi. vs S.D. 8-0
	Oct. 2	Bill Stoneman, Mon. vs N.Y. 7-0
1973	Aug. 5	Phil Niekro, Atl. vs S.D. 9-0
1975	Aug. 24	Ed Halicki, S.F. vs N.Y. 6-0
1976	July 9	Larry Dierker, Hou. vs Mon. 6-0
	Aug. 9	John Candelaria, Pit. vs L.A. 2-0
	Sep. 29	John Montefusco, S.F. at Atl. 9-0
1978	Apr. 16	Bob Forsch, St.L. vs Phi. 5-0
	June 16	Tom Seaver, Cin. vs St.L. 4-0
1979	Apr. 7	Ken Forsch, Hou. vs Atl. 6-0
1980	June 27	Jerry Reuss, L.A. at S.F. 8-0
1981	May 10	Charlie Lea, Mon. vs S.F. 4-0
	Sep. 26	Nolan Ryan, Hou. vs L.A. 5-0
1983	Sep. 26	Bob Forsch, St.L. vs. Mon. 3-0
1986	Sep. 25	Mike Scott, Hou. vs. S.F. 2-0
1988	Sep. 16	Tom Browning, Cin. vs. L.A. 1-0 (perfect game)

AMERICAN LEAGUE

1901	May 9	Earl Moore, Cle. vs Chi. 2-4 (hit in 10th; lost in 10th)
1902	Sep. 20	Jimmy Callahan, Chi. vs Det. 3-0
1904	May 5	Cy Young, Bos. vs Phi. 3-0 (perfect game)
	Aug. 17	Jesse Tannehill, Bos. vs Chi. 6-0
1905	July 22	Weldon Henley, Phi. at St.L. 6-0
	Sep. 6	Frank Smith, Chi. at Det. 15-0
	Sep. 27	Bill Dinneen, Bos. vs Chi. 2-0
1908	June 30	Cy Young, Bos. at N.Y. 8-0
	Sep. 18	Bob Rhoades, Cle. vs Chi. 2-0
	Sep. 20	Frank Smith, Chi. vs Phi. 1-0
	Oct. 2	Addie Joss, Cle. vs Chi. 1-0 (perfect game)
1910	Apr. 20	Addie Joss, Cle. at Chi. 1-0
	May 12	Chief Bender, Phi. vs Cle. 4-0
	Aug. 30	Tom Hughes, N.Y. vs Cle. 0-5 (hit in 10th; lost in 11th)
1911	July 29	Joe Wood, Bos. vs St.L. 5-0
	Aug. 27	Ed Walsh, Chi. vs Bos. 5-0
1912	July 4	George Mullin, Det. vs St.L. 7-0
	Aug. 30	Earl Hamilton, St.L. at Det. 5-1
1914	May 14	Jim Scott, Chi. at Was. 0-1 (hit in 10th; lost in 10th)
	May 31	Joe Benz, Chi. vs Cle. 6-1

AMERICAN LEAGUE cont.

1916	June 21	George Foster, Bos. vs N.Y. 2-0
	Aug. 26	Joe Bush, Phi. vs Cle. 5-0
	Aug. 30	Hub Leonard, Bos. vs St.L. 4-0
1917	Apr. 14	Ed Cicotte, Chi. at St.L. 11-0
	Apr. 24	George Mogridge, N.Y. at Bos. 2-1
	May 5	Ernie Koob, St.L. vs Chi. 1-0
	May 6	Bob Groom, St.L. vs Chi. 3-0
	June 23	Ernie Shore, Bos. vs Was. 4-0 (perfect game)
1918	June 3	Hub Leonard, Bos. at Det. 5-0
1919	Sep. 10	Ray Caldwell, Bos. at N.Y. 3-0
1920	July 1	Walter Johnson, Was. at Bos. 1-0
1922	Apr. 30	Charlie Robertson, Chi. at Det. 2-0 (perfect game)
1923	Sep. 4	Sam Jones, N.Y. at Phi. 2-0
	Sep. 7	Howard Ehmke, Bos. at Phi. 4-0
1926	Aug. 21	Ted Lyons, Chi. at Bos. 6-0
1931	Apr. 29	Wes Ferrell, Cle. vs St.L. 9-0
	Aug. 8	Bob Burke, Was. vs Bos. 5-0
1934	Sep. 18	Bobo Newsom, St.L. vs Bos. 1-2 (hit in 10th; lost in 10th)
1935	Aug. 31	Vern Kennedy, Chi. vs St.L. 5-0
1937	June 1	Bill Dietrich, Chi. vs St.L. 8-0
1938	Aug. 27	Monte Pearson, N.Y. vs Cle. 13-0
1940	Apr. 16	Bob Feller, Cle. at Chi. 1-0 (opening day)
1945	Sep. 9	Dick Fowler, Phi. vs St.L. 1-0
1946	Apr. 30	Bob Feller, Cle. vs N.Y. 1-0
1947	July 10	Don Black, Cle. vs Phi. 3-0
	Sep. 3	Bill McCahan, Phi. vs Was. 3-0
1948	June 30	Bob Lemon, Cle. vs Det. 2-0
1951	July 1	Bob Feller, Cle. vs Det. 2-1
	July 12	Allie Reynolds, N.Y. at Cle. 1-0
	Sep. 28	Allie Reynolds, N.Y. vs Bos. 8-0
1952	May 15	Virgil Trucks, Det. vs Was. 1-0
	Aug. 25	Virgil Trucks, Det. at N.Y. 1-0
1953	May 6	Bobo Holloman, St.L. vs Phi. 6-0 (first major league start)
1956	July 14	Mel Parnell, Bos. vs Chi. 4-0
1957	Aug. 20	Bob Keegan, Chi. vs Was. 6-0
1958	July 20	Jim Bunning, Det. at Bos. 3-0
	Sep. 2	Hoyt Wilhelm, Bal. vs N.Y. 1-0
1962	May 5	Bo Belinsky, L.A. vs Bal. 2-0
	June 26	Earle Wilson, Bos. vs L.A. 2-0
	Aug. 1	Bill Monbouquette, Bos. at Chi. 1-0
	Aug. 26	Jack Kralick, Min. vs K.C. 1-0
1965	Sep. 16	Dave Morehead, Bos. vs Cle. 2-0
1966	June 10	Sonny Siebert, Cle. vs Was. 2-0
1967	Apr. 30	Steve Barber (8²⁄₃) and Stu Miller (¹⁄₃), Bal. vs Det. 1-2
	Aug. 25	Dean Chance, Min. at Cle. 2-1
	Sep. 10	Joel Horlen, Chi. vs Det. 6-0
1968	Apr. 27	Tom Phoebus, Bal. vs Bos. 6-0
	May 8	Jim Hunter, Oak. vs Min. 4-0 (perfect game)
1969	Aug. 13	Jim Palmer, Bal. vs Oak. 8-0
1970	July 3	Clyde Wright, Cal. vs Oak. 4-0
	Sep. 21	Vida Blue, Oak. vs Min. 6-0
1973	Apr. 27	Steve Busby, K.C. vs Det. 3-0
	May 15	Nolan Ryan, Cal. at K.C. 3-0
	July 15	Nolan Ryan, Cal. at Det. 6-0
	July 30	Jim Bibby, Tex. at Oak. 6-0
1974	June 19	Steve Busby, K.C. at Mil. 2-0
	July 19	Dick Bosman, Cle. vs Oak. 4-0
	Sep. 28	Nolan Ryan, Cal. vs Min. 4-0
1975	June 1	Nolan Ryan, Cal. vs Bal. 1-0
	Sep. 28	Blue (5), Abbott & Lindblad (1), Fingers (2), Oak. vs Cal. 5-0
1976	July 28	John Odom (5) and Francisco Barrios (4), Chi. at Oak. 2-1
1977	May 14	Jim Colborn, K.C. vs Tex. 6-0
	May 30	Dennis Eckersley, Cle. vs Cal. 1-0
	Sep. 22	Bert Blyleven, Tex. at Cal. 6-0
1981	May 15	Len Barker, Cle. vs Tor. 3-0 (perfect game)

NO-HIT GAMES *cont.*

AMERICAN LEAGUE *cont.*

1983	July 4	Dave Righetti, N.Y. vs Bos. 4-0
	Sep. 9	Mike Warren, Oak. vs Chi. 3-0
1984	Apr. 7	Jack Morris, Det. at Chi. 4-0
	Sep. 30	Mike Witt, Cal. at Tex. 1-0 (perfect game)
1986	Sep. 19	Joe Cowley, Chi. at Cal. 7-1
1987	Apr. 15	Juan Nieves, Mil. at Bal. 7-0

AMERICAN ASSOCIATION

1882		Tony Mullane, Lou. at Cin. 2-0
		Guy Hecker, Lou. at Pit. 3-1
1884		Al Atkisson, Phi. vs Pit. 10-1
		Ed Morris, Col. at Pit. 5-0
		Frank Mountain, Col. at Was. 12-0
		Sam Kimber, Bkn. vs Tol. 0-0 (11 innings, game called due to darkness)
1886		Al Atkisson, Phi. vs N.Y. 3-2
		Bill Terry, Bkn. vs St.L. 1-0
		Matt Kilroy, Bal. vs Tol. 6-0
1888	May 27	Bill Terry, Bkn. vs Lou. 4-0
	June 6	Henry Porter, K.C. at Bal. 4-0
	July 26	Ed Seward, Phi. vs Cin. 12-2
	July 31	Gus Weyhing, Phi. vs K.C. 4-0
1890	Sep. 15	Ledell Titcomb, Roc. vs Syr. 7-0
1891	Oct. 4	Ted Breitenstein, St.L. vs Lou. 8-0 (first major league start)

FEDERAL LEAGUE

1914	Sep. 19	Ed Lafitte, Bkn. vs K.C. 6-2
1915	Apr. 24	Frank Allen, Pit. vs St.L. 2-0
	May 15	Claude Hendrix, Chi. vs Pit. 10-0
	Aug. 16	Miles Main, K.C. vs Buf. 5-0
	Sep. 7	Art Davenport, St.L. vs Cin. 3-0

UNION ASSOCIATION

1884	Aug. 26	Dick Burns, Cin. at K.C. 3-1
	Sep. 28	Ed Cushman, Mil. vs Was. 5-0

NATIONAL ASSOCIATION

1875	July 28	Joe Borden, Phi. vs Chi. 4-0

BASEBALL HALL OF FAME

PLAYER	Position	Career Dates	Year Selected	PLAYER	Position	Career Dates	Year Selected	PLAYER	Position	Career Dates	Year Selected
Henry Aaron	OF	1954-1976	1982	Ray Dandridge*	3B		1987	Travis Jackson	SS	1922-1936	1982
Grover Alexander	P	1911-1930	1938	Dizzy Dean	P	1930-1947	1953	Hugh Jennings	SS	1891-1918	1945
Cap Anson	1B	1876-1897	1939	Ed Delahanty	OF	1888-1903	1945	Judy Johnson*	3B		1975
Luis Aparicio	SS	1956-1973	1984	Bill Dickey	C	1928-1946	1954	Walter Johnson	P	1907-1927	1936
Luke Appling	SS	1930-1950	1964	Martin DiHigo*	P		1977	Addie Joss	P	1902-1910	1978
Earl Averill	OF	1929-1941	1975	Joe DiMaggio	OF	1936-1951	1955	Al Kaline	OF	1953-1974	1980
J. Frank Baker	3B	1908-1922	1955	Bobby Doerr	2B	1937-1951	1986	Tim Keefe	P	1880-1893	1964
Dave Bancroft	SS	1915-1930	1971	Don Drysdale	P	1956-1969	1984	Willie Keeler	OF	1892-1910	1939
Ernie Banks	SS-1B	1953-1971	1977	Hugh Duffy	OF	1888-1906	1945	George Kell	3B	1943-1957	1983
Jake Beckley	1B	1888-1907	1971	Johnny Evers	2B	1902-1929	1939	Joe Kelley	OF	1891-1908	1971
James "Cool Papa" Bell*	OF		1974	Buck Ewing	C	1880-1897	1946	George Kelly	1B	1915-1932	1973
Johnny Bench	C	1967-1983	1989	Red Faber	P	1914-1933	1964	King Kelly	C	1878-1893	1945
Chief Bender	P	1903-1925	1953	Bob Feller	P	1936-1956	1962	Harmon Killebrew	1B-3B	1954-1975	1984
Yogi Berra	C	1946-1965	1972	Rick Ferrell	C	1929-1947	1984	Ralph Kiner	OF	1946-1955	1975
Jim Bottomley	1B	1922-1937	1974	Elmer Flick	OF	1898-1910	1963	Chuck Klein	OF	1928-1944	1980
Lou Boudreau	SS	1938-1952	1970	Whitey Ford	P	1950-1967	1974	Sandy Koufax	P	1955-1966	1972
Roger Bresnahan	C	1897-1915	1945	Jimmie Foxx	1B	1925-1945	1951	Nap Lajoie	2B	1896-1916	1937
Lou Brock	OF	1961-1979	1985	Frankie Frisch	2B	1919-1937	1947	Bob Lemon	P	1941-1958	1976
Dan Brouthers	1B	1879-1904	1945	Pud Galvin	P	1879-1892	1965	Buck Leonard*	1B		1972
Mordecai Brown	P	1903-1916	1949	Lou Gehrig	1B	1923-1939	1939	Fred Lindstrom	3B	1924-1936	1976
Jesse Burkett	OF	1890-1905	1946	Charlie Gehringer	2B	1924-1942	1949	John Henry Lloyd*	SS-1B		1977
Roy Campanella	C	1948-1957	1969	Bob Gibson	P	1959-1975	1981	Ernie Lombardi	C	1931-1947	1986
Max Carey	OF	1910-1929	1961	Josh Gibson*	C		1972	Ted Lyons	P	1923-1946	1955
Frank Chance	1B	1898-1914	1946	Lefty Gomez	P	1930-1943	1972	Mickey Mantle	OF	1951-1968	1974
Oscar Charleston*	OF		1976	Goose Goslin	OF	1921-1938	1968	Heinie Manush	OF	1923-1993	1964
Jack Chesbro	P	1899-1909	1946	Hank Greenberg	1B	1930-1947	1956	Rabbit Maranville	SS-2B	1912-1935	1954
Fred Clarke	OF	1894-1915	1945	Burleigh Grimes	P	1916-1934	1964	Juan Marichal	P	1960-1975	1983
John Clarkson	P	1882-1894	1963	Lefty Grove	P	1925-1941	1947	Rube Marquard	P	1908-1925	1971
Roberto Clemente	OF	1955-1972	1973	Chick Hafey	OF	1924-1937	1971	Eddie Mathews	3B	1952-1968	1978
Ty Cobb	OF	1905-1928	1936	Jesse Haines	P	1918-1937	1970	Christy Mathewson	P	1900-1916	1936
Mickey Cochrane	C	1925-1937	1947	Billy Hamilton	OF	1888-1901	1961	Willie Mays	OF	1951-1973	1979
Eddie Collins	2B	1906-1930	1939	Gabby Hartnett	C	1922-1941	1955	Tommy McCarthy	OF	1884-1896	1946
Jimmy Collins	3B	1895-1908	1945	Harry Heilmann	OF	1914-1932	1952	Willie McCovey	1B	1959-1980	1986
Earle Combs	OF	1924-1935	1970	Billy Herman	2B	1931-1947	1975	Joe McGinnity	P	1899-1908	1946
Roger Connor	1B	1880-1897	1976	Harry Hooper	OF	1909-1925	1971	Joe Medwick	OF	1932-1948	1968
Stan Coveleski	P	1912-1928	1969	Rogers Hornsby	2B	1915-1937	1942	Johnny Mize	1B	1936-1953	1981
Sam Crawford	OF	1899-1917	1957	Waite Hoyt	P	1918-1938	1969	Stan Musial	OF-1B	1941-1963	1969
Joe Cronin	SS	1926-1945	1956	Carl Hubbell	P	1928-1943	1947	Kid Nichols	P	1890-1906	1949
Candy Cummings	P	1872-1877	1939	Catfish Hunter	P	1965-1979	1987	Jim O'Rourke	OF	1876-1904	1945
Kiki Cuyler	OF	1921-1938	1968	Monte Irvin*	OF	1949-1956	1973	Mel Ott	OF	1926-1947	1951

BASEBALL HALL OF FAME *cont.*

PLAYER	Position	Career Dates	Year Selected	PLAYER	Position	Career Dates	Year Selected	PLAYER	Position	Career Dates	Year Selected
Satchel Paige*	P	1948-1965	1971	Warren Spahn	P	1942-1965	1973	Hack Wilson	OF	1923-1934	1979
Herb Pennock	P	1912-1934	1948	Al Spalding	P	1871-1878	1939	Early Wynn	P	1939-1963	1972
Eddie Plank	P	1901-1917	1946	Tris Speaker	OF	1907-1928	1937	Carl Yastrzemski	OF	1961-1983	1989
Hoss Radbourn	P	1880-1891	1939	Willie Stargell	OF-1B	1962-1982	1988	Cy Young	P	1890-1911	1937
Pee Wee Reese	SS	1940-1958	1984	Bill Terry	1B	1923-1936	1954	Ross Youngs	OF	1917-1926	1972
Sam Rice	OF	1915-1935	1963	Sam Thompson	OF	1885-1906	1974				
Eppa Rixey	P	1912-1933	1963	Joe Tinker	SS	1902-1916	1946	**MANAGERS**	**Year Selected**		
Robin Roberts	P	1948-1966	1976	Pie Traynor	3B	1920-1937	1948	Walt Alston	1983		
Brooks Robinson	3B	1955-1977	1983	Dazzy Vance	P	1915-1935	1955	Charles Comiskey	1939		
Frank Robinson	OF	1956-1976	1982	Arky Vaughan	SS	1932-1948	1985	Clark Griffith	1946		
Jackie Robinson	2B	1947-1956	1962	Rube Waddell	P	1897-1910	1946	Bucky Harris	1975		
Edd Roush	OF	1913-1931	1962	Honus Wagner	SS	1897-1917	1936	Miller Huggins	1964		
Red Ruffing	P	1924-1947	1967	Bobby Wallace	SS	1894-1918	1953	Al Lopez	1977		
Amos Rusie	P	1889-1901	1977	Ed Walsh	P	1904-1917	1946	Connie Mack	1937		
Babe Ruth	OF	1914-1935	1936	Lloyd Waner	OF	1927-1945	1967	Joe McCarthy	1957		
Ray Schalk	C	1912-1929	1955	Paul Waner	OF	1926-1945	1952	John McGraw	1937		
Red Schoendienst	2B	1945-1963	1989	Monte Ward	2B-P	1878-1894	1964	Bill McKechnie	1962		
Joe Sewell	SS	1920-1933	1977	Mickey Welch	P	1880-1892	1973	Wilbert Robinson	1945		
Al Simmons	OF	1924-1944	1953	Zach Wheat	OF	1909-1927	1959	Casey Stengel	1966		
George Sisler	1B	1915-1930	1939	Hoyt Wilhelm	P	1952-1972	1985	George Wright	1937		
Enos Slaughter	OF	1938-1959	1985	Billy Williams	OF	1959-1976	1987	Harry Wright	1953		
Duke Snider	OF	1947-1964	1980	Ted Williams	OF	1939-1960	1966				

Career Dates indicate first and last appearances in the majors.
*Elected on the basis of his career in the Negro leagues.

SELECTED FOR MERITORIOUS SERVICE

Al Barlick (Umpire)
Edward Barrow (Manager-Executive)
Morgan G. Bulkeley (Executive)
Alexander J. Cartwright (Executive)
Henry Chadwick (Writer-Statistician)
Happy Chandler (Commissioner-Executive)
John "Jocko" Conlan (Umpire)

Thomas Connolly (Umpire)
William G. Evans (Umpire-Executive)
Andrew "Rube" Foster (Player-Executive)
Ford C. Frick (Commissioner-Executive)
Warren Giles (Executive)
William Harridge (Executive)
Cal Hubbard (Umpire)

B. Bancroft Johnson (Executive)
William Klem (Umpire)
Kenesaw M. Landis (Commissioner)
Larry S. MacPhail (Executive)
W. Branch Rickey (Manager-Executive)
George M. Weiss (Executive)
Tom Yawkey (Executive)

THE COMMISSIONERS OF BASEBALL

Judge Kenesaw Mountain Landis	Elected November 12, 1920. Served until his death on November 25, 1944.
A. B. "Happy" Chandler	Elected April 24, 1945. Served until July 15, 1951.
Ford Frick	Elected September 20, 1951. Served until November 16, 1965.
General William Eckert	Elected November 17, 1965. Served until December 20, 1968.
Bowie Kuhn	Elected February 4, 1969. Served until September 30, 1984.
Peter V. Ueberroth	Elected March 3, 1984, took office October 1, 1984, and served through March 31, 1989.
A. Bartlett Giamatti	Elected September 8, 1988, took office April 1, 1989, and served until his death on September 1, 1989.
Francis T. Vincent, Jr.	Appointed Acting Commissioner September 2, 1989; elected Commissioner September 13, 1989.

PART THREE

All-Time Leaders

Individual Batting, Single Season
Individual Pitching, Single Season
Individual Fielding, Single Season
Individual Batting, Lifetime
Individual Pitching, Lifetime
Individual Fielding, Lifetime
World Series Lifetime Leaders

All-Time Leaders

The All-Time Leaders section provides information on individual all-time single season and lifetime leaders for all major leagues from 1876 through today. Included for all the various categories are leaders in batting, fielding, and pitching.

Much of the information has never been compiled, especially for the period 1876 through 1919. For certain other years some statistics are still missing or incomplete.

When teams in this section are listed by an abbreviation of the city in which the team played, the abbreviations are as follows:

ALT	Altoona	NWK	Newark
ATL	Atlanta	NY	New York
BAL	Baltimore	OAK	Oakland
BKN	Brooklyn	PHI	Philadelphia
BOS	Boston	PIT	Pittsburgh
BUF	Buffalo	PRO	Providence
CAL	California	RIC	Richmond
CHI	Chicago	ROC	Rochester
CIN	Cincinnati	SD	San Diego
CLE	Cleveland	SEA	Seattle
COL	Columbus	SF	San Francisco
DET	Detroit	STL	St. Louis
HAR	Hartford	STP	St. Paul
HOU	Houston	SYR	Syracuse
IND	Indianapolis	TEX	Texas
KC	Kansas City	TOL	Toledo
LA	Los Angeles	TOR	Toronto
LOU	Louisville	TRO	Troy
MIL	Milwaukee	WAS	Washington
MIN	Minnesota	WIL	Wilmington
MON	Montreal	WOR	Worcester

Individual All-Time Single Season Leaders

The top 20 men are shown in batting and base running, the top 15 in pitching and relief pitching. If required by ties, 1 additional player is shown. If ties would require more than 1 additional man to be shown, none of the last tied group is included. All the information is self-explanatory, with the possible exception of Home Run Percentage, which is the number of home runs per 100 times at bat.

Stolen Bases. As shown here, stolen bases start in 1898. Although stolen bases were first considered a statistical item in 1886, they were known as "bases advanced," which credited a stolen base to a man taking an extra base on another player's hit or out, until 1898.

Pitching Categories. Pitching information appears for two separate periods: 1876 through 1892; 1893 through today, except for relief pitching information, which is shown only from 1893. The reason for these separate categories is that the pitching rubber was not moved to its present distance of 60 feet 6 inches until 1893.

Estimated Earned Run Averages (applies to all parts of this section). Any time an earned run average appears in italics it indicates that not all the earned runs allowed by the pitcher are known, and the information had to be estimated. For example, it is known that a team allowed 560 runs in 112 games. Of these games, it is known that in 90 of them the team allowed 420 runs of which 315 or 75% were earned. The man pitched 207⅔ innings in 40 games and allowed 134 runs. In 35 of these games, it is known that he allowed 118 runs of which 83 were earned. By multiplying the team's known ratio of earned runs to total runs (75%) by the pitcher's 16 (134 minus 118) remaining runs allowed, a figure of 12 additional estimated earned runs is calculated. This means that the pitcher allowed an estimated total of 95 earned runs in 207⅔ innings for an estimated earned run average of 4.12. In all cases at least 50% of the runs allowed by the team were "known" as a basis for estimating earned run averages.

League Leader Qualifications. Throughout baseball there have been different rules used to determine the minimum appearances necessary to qualify for league leader in categories concerning averages (Batting Average, Earned Run Average, etc.). For the rules and the years they were in effect, see Appendix C.

Individual Lifetime Leaders

The ranking of the batting, base running, pitching, and fielding leaders is based on calculation to 5 decimal points, although no more than the first 3 decimal points are shown. Players with *identical* ranking (through 5 decimal points) are listed with the same rank number. The following minimum criteria were used to establish the lifetime leaders:

Batting

Batting average, all players .300, 4,000 times at bat

Slugging average, .500, 4,000 at bat

Total bases, 4,000

Games played, 2,000

At bats, 9,000

Hits, 2,000

Doubles, 400

Triples, 150

Home runs, 300

Home run percentage, top 35 players, 4,000 at bat

Extra base hits, 800

Runs batted in, 1,000

RBI per game, top 35 players, 4,000 at bat

Runs, 1,000

Runs per game, top 35 players, 4,000 at bat

Bases on balls, 1,000

Bases on balls average, top 35 players, 4,000 at bat

Stolen bases, 300

Pinch hits, 50

Pinch hit batting average, top 35 players, 150 pinch hit at bat

Fewest strikeouts per game, top 35 players, 4,000 at bat

Most strikeouts per game, top 35 players, 4,000 at bat

Strikeouts, 1,000

Pitching

Wins, 200 or more

Winning percentage, top 35 players, 300 games pitched

Earned run average, 2.50, 1,500 innings pitched

Games, 500

Completed games, 300

Innings pitched, 3,500

Strikeouts, 1,500

Strikeouts per nine innings, top 35 players, 1,500 innings

Shutouts, 30

Fewest hits per nine innings, top 35 players, 1,500 innings

Most bases on balls, top 35 players

Fewest bases on balls per nine innings, top 35 players, 1,500 innings

Most losses, top 35 players

Relief Pitching

Wins, 50

Winning percentage, top 35 players, 500 innings pitched

Saves, 75

Wins plus saves, 125

Games, 400

Fielding

The top 15 players in each category are shown for each position. A minimum 1,000 games played at the indicated position is required, except for pitchers, where 1,500 innings or more pitched is the criterion.

INDIVIDUAL BATTING (SINGLE SEASON)

BATTING AVERAGE

1. Hugh Duffy, 1894	.438
2. Tip O'Neill, 1887	.435
3. Willie Keeler, 1897	.432
4. Ross Barnes, 1876	.429
5. Rogers Hornsby, 1924	.424
6. Jesse Burkett, 1895	.423
7. Nap Lajoie, 1901	.422
8. George Sisler, 1922	.420
9. Ty Cobb, 1911	.420
10. Tuck Turner, 1894	.416
11. Fred Dunlap, 1884	.412
12. Ty Cobb, 1912	.410
13. Jesse Burkett, 1896	.410
14. Ed Delahanty, 1899	.408
15. Joe Jackson, 1911	.408
16. George Sisler, 1920	.407
17. Fred Clarke, 1897	.406
17. Ted Williams, 1941	.406
19. Harry Stovey, 1884	.404
20. Sam Thompson, 1894	.404

AT BATS

1. Willie Wilson, 1980	705
2. Juan Samuel, 1984	701
3. Dave Cash, 1975	699
4. Matty Alou, 1969	698
5. Woody Jensen, 1936	696
6. Omar Moreno, 1979	695
6. Maury Wills, 1962	695
8. Bobby Richardson, 1962	692
9. Kirby Puckett, 1985	691
10. Lou Brock, 1967	689
10. Sandy Alomar, 1971	689
12. Tony Fernandez, 1986	687
12. Dave Cash, 1974	687
14. Horace Clarke, 1970	686
15. Lloyd Waner, 1931	681
15. Joe Moore, 1935	681
17. Kirby Puckett, 1986	680
17. Pete Rose, 1973	680
17. Frank Taveras, 1979	680

TRIPLES

1. Owen Wilson, 1912	36
2. Heinie Reitz, 1894	31
2. Dave Orr, 1886	31
4. Perry Werden, 1893	29
5. Harry Davis, 1897	28
6. Sam Thompson, 1894	27
6. George Davis, 1893	27
6. Jimmy Williams, 1899	27
9. George Treadway, 1894	26
9. Long John Reilly, 1890	26
9. Joe Jackson, 1912	26
9. Sam Crawford, 1914	26
9. Kiki Cuyler, 1925	26
14. Harry Stovey, 1884	25
14. Roger Connor, 1894	25
14. Tommy Long, 1915	25
14. Larry Doyle, 1911	25
14. Sam Crawford, 1903	25
14. Buck Freeman, 1899	25
20. Ed McKean, 1893	24
20. Ty Cobb, 1911	24

EXTRA BASE HITS

1. Babe Ruth, 1921	119
2. Lou Gehrig, 1927	117
3. Chuck Klein, 1930	107
4. Hank Greenberg, 1937	103
4. Stan Musial, 1948	103
4. Chuck Klein, 1932	103
7. Rogers Hornsby, 1922	102
8. Lou Gehrig, 1930	100
8. Jimmie Foxx, 1932	100
10. Babe Ruth, 1920	99
10. Babe Ruth, 1923	99
10. Hank Greenberg, 1940	99
13. Hank Greenberg, 1935	98
14. Babe Ruth, 1927	97
14. Hack Wilson, 1930	97
14. Joe Medwick, 1937	97
17. Hank Greenberg, 1934	96
17. Joe DiMaggio, 1937	96
17. Hal Trosky, 1936	96
20. Lou Gehrig, 1934	95
20. Joe Medwick, 1936	95

SLUGGING AVERAGE

1. Babe Ruth, 1920	.847
2. Babe Ruth, 1921	.846
3. Babe Ruth, 1927	.772
4. Lou Gehrig, 1927	.765
5. Babe Ruth, 1923	.764
6. Rogers Hornsby, 1925	.756
7. Jimmie Foxx, 1932	.749
8. Babe Ruth, 1924	.739
9. Babe Ruth, 1926	.737
10. Ted Williams, 1941	.735
11. Babe Ruth, 1930	.732
12. Ted Williams, 1957	.731
13. Hack Wilson, 1930	.723
14. Rogers Hornsby, 1922	.722
15. Lou Gehrig, 1930	.721
16. Babe Ruth, 1928	.709
17. Al Simmons, 1930	.708
18. Lou Gehrig, 1934	.706
19. Mickey Mantle, 1956	.705
20. Jimmie Foxx, 1938	.704

HITS

1. George Sisler, 1920	257
2. Bill Terry, 1930	254
2. Lefty O'Doul, 1929	254
4. Al Simmons, 1925	253
5. Rogers Hornsby, 1922	250
5. Chuck Klein, 1930	250
7. Ty Cobb, 1911	248
8. George Sisler, 1922	246
9. Willie Keeler, 1897	243
10. Babe Herman, 1930	241
10. Heinie Manush, 1928	241
12. Wade Boggs, 1985	240
12. Jesse Burkett, 1896	240
14. Rod Carew, 1977	239
15. Don Mattingly, 1986	238
16. Harry Heilmann, 1921	237
16. Paul Waner, 1927	237
16. Joe Medwick, 1937	237
19. Hugh Duffy, 1894	236
19. Jack Tobin, 1921	236

HOME RUNS

1. Roger Maris, 1961	61
2. Babe Ruth, 1927	60
3. Babe Ruth, 1921	59
4. Hank Greenberg, 1938	58
4. Jimmie Foxx, 1932	58
6. Hack Wilson, 1930	56
7. Babe Ruth, 1920	54
7. Mickey Mantle, 1961	54
7. Babe Ruth, 1928	54
7. Ralph Kiner, 1949	54
11. Mickey Mantle, 1956	52
11. Willie Mays, 1965	52
11. George Foster, 1977	52
14. Ralph Kiner, 1947	51
14. Willie Mays, 1955	51
14. Johnny Mize, 1947	51
17. Jimmie Foxx, 1938	50

RUNS BATTED IN

1. Hack Wilson, 1930	190
2. Lou Gehrig, 1931	184
3. Hank Greenberg, 1937	183
4. Jimmie Foxx, 1938	175
4. Lou Gehrig, 1927	175
6. Lou Gehrig, 1930	174
7. Babe Ruth, 1921	171
8. Hank Greenberg, 1935	170
8. Chuck Klein, 1930	170
10. Jimmie Foxx, 1932	169
11. Joe DiMaggio, 1937	167
12. Sam Thompson, 1887	166
12. Sam Thompson, 1895	165
13. Al Simmons, 1930	165
13. Lou Gehrig, 1934	165
16. Babe Ruth, 1927	164
17. Babe Ruth, 1931	163
17. Jimmie Foxx, 1933	163
19. Hal Trosky, 1936	162

TOTAL BASES

1. Babe Ruth, 1921	457
2. Rogers Hornsby, 1922	450
3. Lou Gehrig, 1927	447
4. Chuck Klein, 1930	445
5. Jimmie Foxx, 1932	438
6. Stan Musial, 1948	429
7. Hack Wilson, 1930	423
8. Chuck Klein, 1932	420
9. Lou Gehrig, 1930	419
10. Joe DiMaggio, 1937	418
11. Babe Ruth, 1927	417
12. Babe Herman, 1930	416
13. Lou Gehrig, 1931	410
14. Lou Gehrig, 1934	409
14. Rogers Hornsby, 1929	409
16. Joe Medwick, 1937	406
16. Jim Rice, 1978	406
18. Chuck Klein, 1929	405
18. Hal Trosky, 1936	405
20. Jimmie Foxx, 1933	403
20. Lou Gehrig, 1936	403

DOUBLES

1. Earl Webb, 1931	67
2. George Burns, 1926	64
2. Joe Medwick, 1936	64
4. Hank Greenberg, 1934	63
5. Paul Waner, 1932	62
6. Charlie Gehringer, 1936	60
7. Tris Speaker, 1923	59
7. Chuck Klein, 1930	59
9. Billy Herman, 1936	57
9. Billy Herman, 1935	57
11. Ed Delahanty, 1899	56
11. Joe Medwick, 1937	56
11. George Kell, 1950	56
14. Gee Walker, 1936	55
15. Hal McRae, 1977	54
16. Don Mattingly, 1986	53
16. Tris Speaker, 1912	53
16. Al Simmons, 1926	53
16. Paul Waner, 1936	53
16. Stan Musial, 1953	53

HOME RUN PERCENTAGE

1. Babe Ruth, 1920	11.8
2. Babe Ruth, 1927	11.1
3. Babe Ruth, 1921	10.9
4. Mickey Mantle, 1961	10.5
5. Hank Greenberg, 1938	10.4
6. Roger Maris, 1961	10.3
7. Babe Ruth, 1928	10.1
8. Jimmie Foxx, 1932	9.9
9. Ralph Kiner, 1949	9.8
10. Mickey Mantle, 1956	9.8
11. Hack Wilson, 1930	9.6
12. Hank Aaron, 1971	9.5
12. Babe Ruth, 1926	9.5
14. Jim Gentile, 1961	9.5
15. Babe Ruth, 1930	9.5
16. Willie Stargell, 1971	9.4
17. Rudy York, 1937	9.3
18. Willie Mays, 1965	9.3
19. Babe Ruth, 1929	9.2
20. Willie McCovey, 1969	9.2

RUNS BATTED IN PER GAME

1. Sam Thompson, 1894	1.42
2. Sam Thompson, 1895	1.39
3. Sam Thompson, 1887	1.31
4. Hack Wilson, 1930	1.23
5. Al Simmons, 1930	1.20
6. Cap Anson, 1894	1.19
7. Hank Greenberg, 1937	1.19
8. Lou Gehrig, 1931	1.19
9. Cap Anson, 1886	1.18
10. Jimmie Foxx, 1938	1.17
11. Hugh Duffy, 1894	1.16
12. Dave Orr, 1890	1.16
13. Ed Delahanty, 1894	1.15
14. Babe Ruth, 1929	1.14
15. Lou Gehrig, 1930	1.13
16. Lou Gehrig, 1927	1.13
17. Babe Ruth, 1921	1.12
18. Babe Ruth, 1931	1.12
19. Hank Greenberg, 1935	1.12
20. Ed Delahanty, 1893	1.11

INDIVIDUAL BATTING (SINGLE SEASON), *cont.*

RUNS

1. Billy Hamilton, 1894 — 196
2. Babe Ruth, 1921 — 177
2. Tom Brown, 1891 — 177
4. Joe Kelley, 1894 — 167
4. Tip O'Neill, 1887 — 167
4. Lou Gehrig, 1936 — 167
7. Billy Hamilton, 1895 — 166
8. Willie Keeler, 1894 — 165
9. Babe Ruth, 1928 — 163
9. Lou Gehrig, 1931 — 163
9. Arlie Latham, 1887 — 163
12. Willie Keeler, 1895 — 162
13. Hugh Duffy, 1890 — 161
14. Fred Dunlap, 1884 — 160
14. Hugh Duffy, 1894 — 160
14. Jesse Burkett, 1896 — 160
17. Hughie Jennings, 1895 — 159
18. Babe Ruth, 1920 — 158
18. Babe Ruth, 1927 — 158
18. Bobby Lowe, 1894 — 158
18. Chuck Klein, 1930 — 158

RUNS PER GAME

1. Ross Barnes, 1876 — 1.91
2. Fred Dunlap, 1884 — 1.58
3. Billy Hamilton, 1894 — 1.50
4. George Gore, 1890 — 1.42
5. Billy Hamilton, 1895 — 1.35
6. Tip O'Neill, 1887 — 1.35
7. Billy Hamilton, 1893 — 1.34
8. Herman Long, 1894 — 1.32
9. King Kelly, 1886 — 1.31
10. Joe Kelley, 1894 — 1.29
11. Tom Brown, 1891 — 1.29
12. Ed Delahanty, 1894 — 1.29
13. Ed Delahanty, 1895 — 1.28
14. Hugh Duffy, 1894 — 1.28
15. Willie Keeler, 1894 — 1.28
16. George Gore, 1886 — 1.27
17. John McGraw, 1894 — 1.26
18. Dan Brouthers, 1887 — 1.24
19. Bill Dahlen, 1894 — 1.24
20. Willie Keeler, 1895 — 1.24

STOLEN BASES

1. Rickey Henderson, 1982 — 130
2. Lou Brock, 1974 — 118
3. Vince Coleman, 1985 — 110
4. Vince Coleman, 1987 — 109
5. Rickey Henderson, 1983 — 108
6. Vince Coleman, 1986 — 107
7. Maury Wills, 1962 — 104
8. Rickey Henderson, 1980 — 100
9. Ron LeFlore, 1980 — 97
10. Ty Cobb, 1915 — 96
10. Omar Moreno, 1980 — 96
12. Maury Wills, 1965 — 94
13. Rickey Henderson, 1988 — 93
14. Tim Raines, 1983 — 90
15. Clyde Milan, 1912 — 88
16. Rickey Henderson, 1986 — 87
17. Willie Wilson, 1979 — 83
17. Ty Cobb, 1911 — 83
19. Vince Coleman, 1988 — 81
19. Eddie Collins, 1910 — 81
19. Bob Bescher, 1911 — 81

BASES ON BALLS

1. Babe Ruth, 1923 — 170
2. Ted Williams, 1947 — 162
2. Ted Williams, 1949 — 162
4. Ted Williams, 1946 — 156
5. Eddie Yost, 1956 — 151
6. Eddie Joost, 1949 — 149
7. Babe Ruth, 1920 — 148
7. Jimmy Wynn, 1969 — 148
7. Eddie Stanky, 1945 — 148
10. Jimmy Sheckard, 1911 — 147
11. Mickey Mantle, 1957 — 146
12. Ted Williams, 1941 — 145
12. Ted Williams, 1942 — 145
12. Harmon Killebrew, 1969 — 145
15. Babe Ruth, 1926 — 144
15. Eddie Stanky, 1950 — 144
15. Babe Ruth, 1921 — 144
18. Ted Williams, 1951 — 143
19. Babe Ruth, 1924 — 142
20. Eddie Yost, 1950 — 141

PINCH HIT BATTING AVERAGE

1. Ed Kranepool, 1974 — .486
2. Smead Jolley, 1931 — .467
3. Frenchy Bordagaray, 1938 — .465
4. Gates Brown, 1968 — .462
5. Rick Miller, 1983 — .457
6. Jose Pagan, 1969 — .452
7. Elmer Valo, 1955 — .452
8. Randy Bush, 1986 — .433
8. Ted Easterly, 1912 — .433
8. Milt Thompson, 1985 — .433
11. Don Dillard, 1961 — .429
11. Joe Cronin, 1943 — .429
13. Candy Maldonado, 1986 — .425
14. Richie Ashburn, 1962 — .419
14. Bob Bowman, 1958 — .419
14. Dick Williams, 1962 — .419
17. Merritt Ranew, 1963 — .415
17. Kurt Bevacqua, 1983 — .412
18. Bob Hansen, 1974 — .412
20. Dave Philley, 1958 — .409

STRIKEOUTS

1. Bobby Bonds, 1970 — 189
2. Bobby Bonds, 1969 — 187
3. Rob Deer, 1987 — 186
4. Pete Incaviglia, 1986 — 185
5. Mike Schmidt, 1975 — 180
6. Rob Deer, 1986 — 179
7. Jose Canseco, 1986 — 175
7. Dave Nicholson, 1963 — 175
7. Gorman Thomas, 1979 — 175
10. Jim Presley, 1986 — 172
10. Bo Jackson, 1989 — 172
12. Reggie Jackson, 1968 — 171
13. Gorman Thomas, 1980 — 170
14. Pete Incaviglia, 1987 — 168
14. Juan Samuel, 1984 — 168
16. Cory Snyder, 1987 — 166
16. Steve Balboni, 1985 — 166
16. Gary Alexander, 1978 — 166
19. Donn Clendenon, 1968 — 163
20. Juan Samuel, 1987 — 162
20. Butch Hobson, 1977 — 162

PINCH HITS

1. Jose Morales, 1976 — 25
2. Dave Philley, 1961 — 24
2. Vic Davalillo, 1970 — 24
2. Rusty Staub, 1983 — 24
5. Wallace Johnson, 1988 — 22
5. Peanuts Lowrey, 1953 — 22
5. Sam Leslie, 1932 — 22
5. Red Schoendienst, 1962 — 22
9. Smoky Burgess, 1966 — 21
9. Merv Rettenmund, 1977 — 21
11. Thad Bosley, 1985 — 20
11. Chris Chambliss, 1986 — 20
11. Frenchy Bordagaray, 1938 — 20
11. Jerry Turner, 1978 — 20
11. Doc Miller, 1913 — 20
11. Ed Coleman, 1936 — 20
11. Joe Frazier, 1954 — 20
11. Smoky Burgess, 1965 — 20
11. Ken Boswell, 1976 — 20

INDIVIDUAL PITCHING (SINGLE SEASON)

WINS

1. Jack Chesbro, 1904 — 41
2. Ed Walsh, 1908 — 40
3. Christy Mathewson, 1908 — 37
4. Walter Johnson, 1913 — 36
4. Jouett Meekin, 1894 — 36
4. Amos Rusie, 1894 — 36
7. Joe McGinnity, 1904 — 35
7. Cy Young, 1895 — 35
9. Smoky Joe Wood, 1912 — 34
9. Frank Killen, 1893 — 34
11. Cy Young, 1901 — 33
11. Grover Alexander, 1916 — 33
11. Christy Mathewson, 1904 — 33
11. Kid Nichols, 1893 — 33

GAMES STARTED

1. Amos Rusie, 1893 — 52
2. Jack Chesbro, 1904 — 51
3. Frank Killen, 1896 — 50
3. Amos Rusie, 1894 — 50
3. Pink Hawley, 1895 — 50
3. Ted Breitenstein, 1894 — 50
3. Ted Breitenstein, 1895 — 50
8. Ed Walsh, 1908 — 49
8. Wilbur Wood, 1972 — 49
10. Joe McGinnity, 1903 — 48
10. Jouett Meekin, 1894 — 48
10. Frank Killen, 1893 — 48
10. Wilbur Wood, 1973 — 48
14. Cy Young, 1894 — 47
14. Jack Taylor, 1898 — 47
14. Amos Rusie, 1895 — 47

STRIKEOUTS PER 9 INNINGS

1. Nolan Ryan, 1987 — 11.48
2. Dwight Gooden, 1984 — 11.39
3. Nolan Ryan, 1989 — 11.32
4. Sam McDowell, 1965 — 10.71
5. Nolan Ryan, 1973 — 10.57
6. Sandy Koufax, 1962 — 10.55
7. Nolan Ryan, 1972 — 10.43
8. Sam McDowell, 1966 — 10.42
9. Nolan Ryan, 1976 — 10.36
10. Nolan Ryan, 1977 — 10.26
11. Sandy Koufax, 1965 — 10.24
12. Sandy Koufax, 1960 — 10.13
13. Mike Scott, 1986 — 10.00
14. Nolan Ryan, 1978 — 9.96
15. Roger Clemens, 1988 — 9.92

BASES ON BALLS

1. Amos Rusie, 1893 — 218
2. Cy Seymour, 1898 — 213
3. Bob Feller, 1938 — 208
4. Nolan Ryan, 1977 — 204
5. Nolan Ryan, 1974 — 202
6. Amos Rusie, 1894 — 200
7. Bob Feller, 1941 — 194
8. Bobo Newsom, 1938 — 192
9. Ted Breitenstein, 1894 — 191
10. Tony Mullane, 1893 — 189
11. Kid Gleason, 1893 — 187
12. Sam Jones, 1955 — 185
13. Nolan Ryan, 1976 — 183
14. Bob Turley, 1954 — 181
14. Willie McGill, 1893 — 181
14. Bob Harmon, 1911 — 181

WINNING PERCENTAGE

1. Roy Face, 1959 — .947
2. Johnny Allen, 1937 — .938
3. Ron Guidry, 1978 — .893
4. Freddie Fitzsimmons, 1940 — .889
5. Lefty Grove, 1931 — .886
6. Bob Stanley, 1978 — .882
7. Preacher Roe, 1951 — .880
8. Tom Seaver, 1981 — .875
9. Smoky Joe Wood, 1912 — .872
10. David Cone, 1988 — .870
11. Orel Hershiser, 1985 — .864
12. Wild Bill Donovan, 1907 — .862
12. Whitey Ford, 1961 — .862
14. Roger Clemens, 1986 — .857
14. Dwight Gooden, 1985 — .857

COMPLETE GAMES

1. Amos Rusie, 1893 — 50
2. Jack Chesbro, 1904 — 48
3. Ted Breitenstein, 1894 — 46
3. Ted Breitenstein, 1895 — 46
5. Vic Willis, 1902 — 45
5. Amos Rusie, 1894 — 45
7. Kid Nichols, 1893 — 44
7. Cy Young, 1894 — 44
7. Joe McGinnity, 1903 — 44
7. Pink Hawley, 1895 — 44
7. Frank Killen, 1896 — 44

SHUTOUTS

1. Grover Alexander, 1916 — 16
2. Bob Gibson, 1968 — 13
2. Jack Coombs, 1910 — 13
4. Grover Alexander, 1915 — 12
4. Christy Mathewson, 1908 — 12
6. Dean Chance, 1964 — 11
6. Walter Johnson, 1913 — 11
6. Sandy Koufax, 1963 — 11
6. Ed Walsh, 1908 — 11

BASES ON BALLS PER 9 INNINGS

1. Babe Adams, 1920 — .62
2. Christy Mathewson, 1913 — .62
3. Christy Mathewson, 1914 — .66
4. Cy Young, 1904 — .69
5. Red Lucas, 1933 — .74
6. Cy Young, 1906 — .78
7. Babe Adams, 1919 — .79
8. Babe Adams, 1922 — .79
9. Slim Sallee, 1919 — .79
10. Slim Sallee, 1918 — .82
11. Addie Joss, 1908 — .83
12. Cy Young, 1905 — .84
13. LaMarr Hoyt, 1985 — .86
14. Deacon Phillippe, 1902 — .86
15. Grover Alexander, 1923 — .89

EARNED RUN AVERAGE

1. Dutch Leonard, 1914 — 1.01
2. Three Finger Brown, 1906 — 1.04
3. Walter Johnson, 1913 — 1.09
4. Bob Gibson, 1968 — 1.12
5. Christy Mathewson, 1909 — 1.14
6. Jack Pfiester, 1907 — 1.15
7. Addie Joss, 1908 — 1.16
8. Carl Lundgren, 1907 — 1.17
9. Grover Alexander, 1915 — 1.22
10. Cy Young, 1908 — 1.26
11. Ed Walsh, 1910 — 1.27
12. Walter Johnson, 1918 — 1.27
13. Christy Mathewson, 1905 — 1.27
14. Jack Coombs, 1910 — 1.30
15. Three Finger Brown, 1909 — 1.31

INNINGS PITCHED

1. Amos Rusie, 1893 — 482
2. Ed Walsh, 1908 — 464
3. Jack Chesbro, 1904 — 455
4. Ted Breitenstein, 1894 — 447
5. Pink Hawley, 1895 — 444
6. Amos Rusie, 1894 — 444
7. Joe McGinnity, 1903 — 434
8. Frank Killen, 1896 — 432
9. Ted Breitenstein, 1895 — 430
10. Kid Nichols, 1893 — 425
11. Cy Young, 1893 — 423
12. Ed Walsh, 1907 — 422
13. Frank Killen, 1893 — 415
14. Cy Young, 1896 — 414
15. Vic Willis, 1902 — 410

HITS PER 9 INNINGS

1. Nolan Ryan, 1972 — 5.26
2. Luis Tiant, 1968 — 5.30
3. Ed Reulbach, 1906 — 5.33
4. Jim Hearn, 1950 — 5.64
5. Carl Lundgren, 1907 — 5.65
6. Dutch Leonard, 1914 — 5.70
7. Sid Fernandez, 1985 — 5.71
8. Tommy Byrne, 1949 — 5.74
9. Dave McNally, 1968 — 5.77
10. Sandy Koufax, 1965 — 5.79
11. Russ Ford, 1910 — 5.83
12. Al Downing, 1963 — 5.84
13. Herb Score, 1956 — 5.85
14. Bob Gibson, 1968 — 5.85
15. Sam McDowell, 1965 — 5.87

LOSSES

1. Red Donahue, 1897 — 33
2. Jim Hughey, 1899 — 30
2. Ted Breitenstein, 1895 — 30
4. Vic Willis, 1905 — 29
4. Bill Hart, 1896 — 29
4. Jack Taylor, 1898 — 29
7. Still Bill Hill, 1896 — 28
7. Duke Esper, 1893 — 28
9. Paul Derringer, 1933 — 27
9. Bill Hart, 1897 — 27
9. George Bell, 1910 — 27
9. Willie Sudhoff, 1898 — 27
9. Dummy Taylor, 1901 — 27
9. Pink Hawley, 1894 — 27

GAMES

1. Mike Marshall, 1974 — 106
2. Kent Tekulve, 1979 — 94
3. Mike Marshall, 1973 — 92
4. Kent Tekulve, 1978 — 91
5. Wayne Granger, 1969 — 90
5. Mike Marshall, 1979 — 90
5. Kent Tekulve, 1987 — 90
8. Mark Eichhorn, 1987 — 89
9. Wilbur Wood, 1968 — 88
10. Rob Murphy, 1987 — 87
11. Kent Tekulve, 1982 — 85
11. Mitch Williams, 1987 — 85
11. Frank Williams, 1987 — 85

STRIKEOUTS

1. Nolan Ryan, 1973 — 383
2. Sandy Koufax, 1965 — 382
3. Nolan Ryan, 1974 — 367
4. Rube Waddell, 1904 — 349
5. Bob Feller, 1946 — 348
6. Nolan Ryan, 1977 — 341
7. Nolan Ryan, 1972 — 329
8. Nolan Ryan, 1976 — 327
9. Sam McDowell, 1965 — 325
10. Sandy Koufax, 1966 — 317
11. J. R. Richard, 1979 — 313
11. Walter Johnson, 1910 — 313
13. Steve Carlton, 1972 — 310
14. Mickey Lolich, 1971 — 308
15. Mike Scott, 1986 — 306
15. Sandy Koufax, 1963 — 306

INDIVIDUAL PITCHING (RELIEF PITCHING)

WINS

1. Roy Face, 1959 — 18
2. Bill Campbell, 1976 — 17
2. John Hiller, 1974 — 17
4. Ron Perranoski, 1963 — 16
4. Jim Konstanty, 1950 — 16
4. Tom Johnson, 1977 — 16
4. Dick Radatz, 1964 — 16
8. Hoyt Wilhelm, 1952 — 15
8. Luis Arroyo, 1961 — 15
8. Dick Radatz, 1963 — 15
8. Eddie Fisher, 1965 — 15
8. Mace Brown, 1938 — 15
8. Dale Murray, 1975 — 15
8. Mike Marshall, 1974 — 15

WINNING PERCENTAGE

1. Dennis Lamp, 1985 — 1.000
1. Tom Hughes, 1915 — 1.000
1. Joe Pate, 1926 — 1.000
1. Frank DiPino, 1989 — 1.000
1. Lew Burdette, 1953 — 1.000
1. Sandy Consuegra, 1954 — 1.000
1. Nig Cuppy, 1894 — 1.000
1. Bob Grim, 1954 — 1.000
1. Grant Jackson, 1973 — 1.000
1. Emil Kush, 1946 — 1.000
1. George Mullin, 1914 — 1.000
1. Charlie Root, 1937 — 1.000
13. Roy Face, 1959 — .947
14. Phil Regan, 1966 — .933
15. Eddie Yuhas, 1952 — .917

SAVES

1. Dave Righetti, 1986 — 46
2. Bruce Sutter, 1984 — 45
2. Dan Quisenberry, 1983 — 45
2. Dennis Eckersley, 1988 — 45
5. Dan Quisenberry, 1984 — 44
5. Mark Davis, 1989 — 44
7. Jeff Reardon, 1988 — 42
8. Jeff Reardon, 1985 — 41
9. Steve Bedrosian, 1987 — 40
10. John Franco, 1988 — 39
11. John Hiller, 1973 — 38
11. Jeff Russell, 1989 — 38

WINS PLUS SAVES

1. Dave Righetti, 1986 — 54
2. Dan Quisenberry, 1984 — 50
2. Bruce Sutter, 1984 — 50
2. Dan Quisenberry, 1983 — 50
5. Dennis Eckersley, 1988 — 49
5. John Hiller, 1973 — 48
6. Mark Davis, 1989 — 48
8. Dick Radatz, 1964 — 45
8. Mike Marshall, 1973 — 45
8. Dan Quisenberry, 1980 — 45
8. Bruce Sutter, 1982 — 45
8. Bill Caudill, 1984 — 45
8. Todd Worrell, 1986 — 45
8. Dan Quisenberry, 1985 — 45
8. John Franco, 1988 — 45
8. Steve Bedrosian, 1987 — 45

GAMES

1. Mike Marshall, 1974 — 106
2. Kent Tekulve, 1979 — 94
3. Mike Marshall, 1973 — 92
4. Kent Tekulve, 1978 — 91
5. Wayne Granger, 1969 — 90
5. Kent Tekulve, 1987 — 90
7. Mark Eichhorn, 1987 — 89
7. Mike Marshall, 1979 — 89
9. Rob Murphy, 1987 — 87
10. Wilbur Wood, 1968 — 86
11. Frank Williams, 1987 — 85
11. Kent Tekulve, 1982 — 85

LOSSES

1. Gene Garber, 1979 — 16
2. Darold Knowles, 1970 — 14
2. Mike Marshall, 1975 — 14
2. Mike Marshall, 1979 — 14
2. John Hiller, 1974 — 14
6. Rollie Fingers, 1978 — 13
6. Skip Lockwood, 1978 — 13
6. Wilbur Wood, 1970 — 13

INDIVIDUAL PITCHING (PITCHING BEFORE 1893)

WINS

1. Old Hoss Radbourn, 1884 — 60
2. John Clarkson, 1885 — 53
3. Guy Hecker, 1884 — 52
4. John Clarkson, 1889 — 49
4. Old Hoss Radbourn, 1883 — 49
6. Al Spalding, 1876 — 47
6. Charlie Buffinton, 1884 — 47
6. Monte Ward, 1879 — 47
9. Matt Kilroy, 1887 — 46
9. Pud Galvin, 1884 — 46
9. Pud Galvin, 1883 — 46

GAMES

1. Will White, 1879 — 76
1. Guy Hecker, 1884 — 76
1. Pud Galvin, 1883 — 76
1. Old Hoss Radbourn, 1883 — 76
5. Old Hoss Radbourn, 1884 — 75
5. Bill Hutchinson, 1892 — 75
7. Jim McCormick, 1880 — 74
7. Lee Richmond, 1880 — 74
9. John Clarkson, 1889 — 73
10. Pud Galvin, 1884 — 72

STRIKEOUTS

1. Matt Kilroy, 1886 — 513
2. Toad Ramsey, 1886 — 499
3. One Arm Daily, 1884 — 483
4. Old Hoss Radbourn, 1884 — 441
5. Charlie Buffinton, 1884 — 417
6. Guy Hecker, 1884 — 385
7. Bill Sweeney, 1884 — 374
8. Pud Galvin, 1884 — 369
9. Mark Baldwin, 1889 — 368
10. Tim Keefe, 1883 — 361

HITS PER 9 INNINGS

1. Tim Keefe, 1880 — 6.09
2. Charlie Sweeney, 1884 — 6.23
3. Jim McCormick, 1884 — 6.47
4. Dupee Shaw, 1884 — 6.47
5. Jim Handiboe, 1886 — 6.47
6. Guy Hecker, 1882 — 6.49
7. Tim Keefe, 1888 — 6.55
8. Adonis Terry, 1888 — 6.69
9. Silver King, 1888 — 6.72
10. Tim Keefe, 1885 — 6.72

WINNING PERCENTAGE

1. Fred Goldsmith, 1880 — .875
1. Jim McCormick, 1884 — .875
3. Billy Taylor, 1884 — .862
4. Old Hoss Radbourn, 1884 — .833
5. Mickey Welch, 1885 — .800
5. Jocko Flynn, 1886 — .800
7. Bob Caruthers, 1889 — .784
8. Al Spalding, 1876 — .783
9. Jack Manning, 1876 — .783
10. Charlie Sweeney, 1884 — .774

COMPLETE GAMES

1. Will White, 1879 — 75
2. Old Hoss Radbourn, 1884 — 73
3. Guy Hecker, 1884 — 72
3. Jim McCormick, 1880 — 72
3. Pud Galvin, 1883 — 72
6. Pud Galvin, 1884 — 71
7. Tim Keefe, 1883 — 68
7. John Clarkson, 1885 — 68
7. John Clarkson, 1889 — 68
10. Bill Hutchinson, 1892 — 67

STRIKEOUTS PER 9 INNINGS

1. Dupee Shaw, 1884 — 8.81
2. One Arm Daily, 1884 — 8.68
3. Matt Kilroy, 1886 — 7.92
4. Charlie Gagus, 1884 — 7.92
5. John Clarkson, 1884 — 7.78
6. Toad Ramsey, 1886 — 7.63
7. Tony Mullane, 1890 — 7.51
8. Jim Whitney, 1884 — 7.23
9. Mike Dorgan, 1884 — 7.17
10. Walter Burke, 1884 — 7.13

BASES ON BALLS PER 9 INNINGS

1. George Zettlein, 1876 — .23
2. Cherokee Fisher, 1876 — .24
3. George Bradley, 1880 — .28
4. Tommy Bond, 1876 — .29
5. Tommy Bond, 1879 — .39
6. Bobby Mathews, 1876 — .42
7. Charlie Sweeney, 1884 — .43
8. Guy Hecker, 1882 — .43
9. Al Spalding, 1876 — .44
10. Pud Galvin, 1879 — .47

EARNED RUN AVERAGE

1. Tim Keefe, 1880 — .86
2. Denny Driscoll, 1882 — 1.21
3. George Bradley, 1876 — 1.23
4. Guy Hecker, 1882 — 1.30
5. George Bradley, 1880 — 1.38
6. Old Hoss Radbourn, 1884 — 1.38
7. Monte Ward, 1878 — 1.51
8. Harry McCormick, 1882 — 1.52
9. Will White, 1882 — 1.54
10. Jim McCormick, 1884 — 1.54

INNINGS PITCHED

1. Will White, 1879 — 680
2. Old Hoss Radbourn, 1884 — 679
3. Guy Hecker, 1884 — 671
4. Jim McCormick, 1880 — 658
5. Pud Galvin, 1883 — 656
6. Pud Galvin, 1884 — 636
7. Old Hoss Radbourn, 1883 — 632
8. Bill Hutchinson, 1892 — 627
9. John Clarkson, 1885 — 623
10. Jim Devlin, 1876 — 622

SHUTOUTS

1. George Bradley, 1876 — 16
2. Ed Morris, 1886 — 12
2. Tommy Bond, 1879 — 12
2. Pud Galvin, 1884 — 12
5. Dave Foutz, 1886 — 11
5. Old Hoss Radbourn, 1884 — 11
7. John Clarkson, 1885 — 10
8. Cy Young, 1892 — 9
8. George Derby, 1881 — 9
8. Tommy Bond, 1878 — 9
8. Monte Ward, 1880 — 9

LOSSES

1. John Coleman, 1883 — 48
2. Will White, 1880 — 42
3. Larry McKeon, 1884 — 41
4. George Bradley, 1879 — 40
4. Jim McCormick, 1879 — 40
6. George Cobb, 1892 — 37
6. Kid Carsey, 1891 — 37
6. Henry Porter, 1888 — 37
6. Pud Galvin, 1880 — 37
10. Stump Weidman, 1886 — 36

INDIVIDUAL FIELDING (SINGLE SEASON)

PUTOUTS

FIRST BASE

1. Jiggs Donahue, 1907 — 1846
2. George Kelly, 1920 — 1759
3. Phil Todt, 1926 — 1755
4. Wally Pipp, 1926 — 1710
5. Jiggs Donahue, 1906 — 1697
6. Candy LaChance, 1904 — 1691
7. Tom Jones, 1907 — 1687
8. Ernie Banks, 1965 — 1682
9. Wally Pipp, 1922 — 1667
10. Lou Gehrig, 1927 — 1662

SECOND BASE

1. Bid McPhee, 1886 — 529
2. Bobby Grich, 1974 — 484
3. Bucky Harris, 1922 — 479
4. Nellie Fox, 1956 — 478
5. Lou Bierbauer, 1889 — 472
6. Billy Herman, 1933 — 466
7. Cub Stricker, 1887 — 461
8. Buddy Myer, 1935 — 460
9. Bill Sweeney, 1912 — 459
9. Bill Wambsganss, 1924 — 459

THIRD BASE

1. Denny Lyons, 1887 — 255
2. Jimmy Collins, 1900 — 251
2. Jimmy Williams, 1899 — 251
4. Jimmy Collins, 1898 — 243
4. Willie Kamm, 1928 — 243
6. Willie Kamm, 1927 — 236
7. Frank Baker, 1913 — 233
8. Bill Coughlin, 1901 — 232
9. Ernie Courtney, 1905 — 229
10. Jimmy Austin, 1911 — 228

SHORTSTOP

1. Hughie Jennings, 1895 — 425
1. Donie Bush, 1914 — 425
3. Rabbit Maranville, 1914 — 407
4. Eddie Miller, 1940 — 405
4. Dave Bancroft, 1922 — 405
6. Monte Cross, 1898 — 404
7. Dave Bancroft, 1921 — 396
8. Mickey Doolan, 1906 — 395
9. Buck Weaver, 1913 — 392
10. Rabbit Maranville, 1915 — 391
10. Buck Herzog, 1915 — 391

OUTFIELD

1. Taylor Douthit, 1928 — 547
2. Richie Ashburn, 1951 — 538
3. Richie Ashburn, 1949 — 514
4. Chet Lemon, 1977 — 512
5. Dwayne Murphy, 1980 — 507
6. Richie Ashburn, 1956 — 503
6. Dom DiMaggio, 1948 — 503
8. Richie Ashburn, 1957 — 502
9. Richie Ashburn, 1953 — 496
10. Richie Ashburn, 1958 — 495

CATCHER

1. Johnny Edwards, 1969 — 1135
2. Johnny Edwards, 1963 — 1008
3. Randy Hundley, 1969 — 978
4. Tony Pena, 1983 — 976
5. Bill Freehan, 1968 — 971
6. Gary Carter, 1985 — 956
7. Gary Carter, 1982 — 954
8. Bill Freehan, 1967 — 950
9. Johnny Bench, 1968 — 942
10. Elston Howard, 1964 — 939

PITCHER

1. Dave Foutz, 1886 — 57
2. Tony Mullane, 1882 — 54
3. George Bradley, 1876 — 50
3. Guy Hecker, 1884 — 50
5. Mike Boddicker, 1984 — 49
6. Larry Corcoran, 1884 — 47
7. Ted Breitenstein, 1895 — 45
7. Al Spalding, 1876 — 45
9. Dave Foutz, 1887 — 44
9. Jim Devlin, 1876 — 44
9. Bill Hutchinson, 1890 — 44

ASSISTS

FIRST BASE

1. Bill Buckner, 1985 — 184
2. Sid Bream, 1986 — 166
3. Bill Buckner, 1983 — 161
4. Bill Buckner, 1982 — 159
5. Bill Buckner, 1986 — 157
6. Mickey Vernon, 1949 — 155
6. Eddie Murray, 1985 — 152
7. Fred Tenney, 1905 — 152
9. Ferris Fain, 1952 — 150

SECOND BASE

1. Frankie Frisch, 1927 — 641
2. Hughie Critz, 1926 — 588
3. Rogers Hornsby, 1927 — 582
4. Oscar Melillo, 1930 — 572
5. Ryne Sandberg, 1983 — 571
6. Rabbit Maranville, 1924 — 568
7. Frank Parkinson, 1922 — 562
8. Tony Cuccinello, 1936 — 559
9. Johnny Hodapp, 1930 — 557
10. Lou Bierbauer, 1892 — 555

THIRD BASE

1. Graig Nettles, 1971 — 412
2. Brooks Robinson, 1974 — 410
2. Graig Nettles, 1973 — 410
4. Harlond Clift, 1937 — 405
4. Brooks Robinson, 1967 — 405
6. Mike Schmidt, 1974 — 404
7. Doug DeCinces, 1982 — 399
8. Buddy Bell, 1982 — 396
8. Mike Schmidt, 1977 — 396
8. Clete Boyer, 1962 — 396

SHORTSTOP

1. Ozzie Smith, 1980 — 621
2. Glenn Wright, 1924 — 601
3. Dave Bancroft, 1920 — 598
4. Tommy Thevenow, 1926 — 597
5. Ivan DeJesus, 1977 — 595
6. Cal Ripken, 1984 — 583
7. Whitey Wietelmann, 1943 — 581
8. Dave Bancroft, 1922 — 579
9. Rabbit Maranville, 1914 — 574
10. Don Kessinger, 1968 — 573

OUTFIELD

1. Tom Dolan, 1883 — 62
2. Orator Shaffer, 1879 — 50
3. Hugh Nicol, 1884 — 48
4. Hardy Richardson, 1881 — 45
5. Pete Gillespie, 1887 — 44
5. Tommy McCarthy, 1888 — 44
5. Chuck Klein, 1930 — 44
8. Jimmy Bannon, 1894 — 43
8. Charlie Duffee, 1889 — 43
10. Jim Fogarty, 1889 — 42

CATCHER

1. Bill Rariden, 1915 — 238
2. Bill Rariden, 1914 — 215
3. Pat Moran, 1903 — 214
4. Art Wilson, 1914 — 212
4. Oscar Stanage, 1911 — 212
6. Gabby Street, 1909 — 210
7. Frank Snyder, 1915 — 204
8. George Gibson, 1910 — 203
9. Bill Bergen, 1909 — 202
9. Claude Berry, 1914 — 202

PITCHER

1. Ed Walsh, 1907 — 227
2. Will White, 1882 — 223
3. Ed Walsh, 1908 — 190
4. Harry Howell, 1905 — 178
5. Tony Mullane, 1882 — 177
6. John Clarkson, 1885 — 174
7. John Clarkson, 1889 — 172
8. Matt Kilroy, 1887 — 167
9. Jack Chesbro, 1904 — 166
10. George Mullin, 1904 — 163

FIELDING AVERAGE

FIRST BASE

1. Steve Garvey, 1984 — 1.000
2. Stuffy McInnis, 1921 — .999
3. Frank McCormick, 1946 — .999
4. Steve Garvey, 1981 — .999
4. Jim Spencer, 1973 — .999
6. Wes Parker, 1968 — .999
7. Eddie Murray, 1981 — .999
8. Jim Spencer, 1976 — .998
9. Jim Spencer, 1981 — .998
10. Joe Judge, 1930 — .998

SECOND BASE

1. Bobby Grich, 1985 — .997
2. Rob Wilfong, 1980 — .995
3. Bobby Grich, 1973 — .995
4. Frank White, 1988 — .994
5. Jose Oquendo, 1989 — .994
6. Jerry Adair, 1964 — .994
7. Ryne Sandberg, 1986 — .994
8. Tim Cullen, 1970 — .994
9. Manny Trillo, 1982 — .994
10. Johnny Ray, 1986 — .993

THIRD BASE

1. Don Money, 1974 — .989
2. Hank Majeski, 1947 — .988
3. Aurelio Rodriguez, 1978 — .987
4. Willie Kamm, 1933 — .984
5. George Kell, 1946 — .983
6. Heinie Groh, 1924 — .983
7. Carney Lansford, 1979 — .982
8. George Kell, 1950 — .982
9. Pinky Whitney, 1937 — .982
10. Buddy Bell, 1980 — .980

SHORTSTOP

1. Tony Fernandez, 1989 — .992
2. Larry Bowa, 1979 — .991
3. Ed Brinkman, 1972 — .990
4. Cal Ripken, 1989 — .990
5. Larry Bowa, 1972 — .987
6. Ozzie Smith, 1987 — .987
7. Larry Bowa, 1971 — .986
8. Larry Bowa, 1978 — .986
9. Frank Duffy, 1973 — .986
10. Roger Metzger, 1976 — .986

OUTFIELD

Many players tied with — 1.000

CATCHER

1. Buddy Rosar, 1946 — 1.000
1. Yogi Berra, 1958 — 1.000
1. Rick Cerone, 1988 — 1.000
1. Lou Berberet, 1957 — 1.000
1. Pete Daley, 1957 — 1.000
6. Joe Azcue, 1967 — .999
7. Wes Westrum, 1950 — .999
8. Thurman Munson, 1971 — .998
9. Rick Cerone, 1987 — .998
10. Gus Triandos, 1963 — .998

PITCHER

Many players tied with — 1.000

INDIVIDUAL FIELDING (SINGLE SEASON), cont.

TOTAL CHANCES			TOTAL CHANCES/GAME			DOUBLE PLAYS		
FIRST BASE			**FIRST BASE**			**FIRST BASE**		
1.	Jiggs Donahue, 1907	1998	1.	Joe Gerhardt, 1876	13.3	1.	Ferris Fain, 1949	194
2.	Phil Todt, 1926	1903	2.	Jiggs Donahue, 1907	12.7	2.	Ferris Fain, 1950	192
3.	George Kelly, 1920	1873	3.	Gene Paulette, 1917	12.7	3.	Donn Clendenon, 1966	182
4.	Jiggs Donahue, 1906	1837	4.	Frank Isbell, 1909	12.7	4.	Ron Jackson, 1979	175
5.	Tom Jones, 1907	1821	5.	Cap Anson, 1879	12.6	5.	Gil Hodges, 1951	171
6.	Wally Pipp, 1926	1817	6.	Oscar Walker, 1879	12.6	6.	Mickey Vernon, 1949	168
7.	Ernie Banks, 1965	1790	7.	Joe Start, 1878	12.5	7.	Ted Kluszewski, 1954	166
8.	Jiggs Donahue, 1905	1780	8.	Tim Murnane, 1878	12.5	7.	Rudy York, 1944	163
9.	Earl Sheely, 1921	1778	9.	Joe Start, 1879	12.5	9.	Rod Carew, 1977	161
10.	Fred Tenney, 1908	1769	10.	Jake Goodman, 1878	12.5	9.	Donn Clendenon, 1965	161
SECOND BASE			**SECOND BASE**			**SECOND BASE**		
1.	Frankie Frisch, 1927	1059	1.	Thorny Hawkes, 1879	8.4	1.	Bill Mazeroski, 1966	161
2.	Bid McPhee, 1886	1058	2.	Chick Fulmer, 1879	8.3	2.	Gerry Priddy, 1950	150
3.	Burgess Whitehead, 1936	1026	3.	Jack Burdock, 1878	8.3	3.	Bill Mazeroski, 1961	144
4.	Nap Lajoie, 1908	1025	4.	Ed Somerville, 1876	8.3	4.	Nellie Fox, 1957	141
5.	Billy Herman, 1933	1023	5.	Joe Gerhardt, 1877	8.1	4.	Dave Cash, 1974	141
6.	Oscar Melillo, 1931	1003	6.	Fred Pfeffer, 1884	8.1	6.	Buddy Myer, 1935	138
7.	Jimmy Dykes, 1921	1002	7.	Davy Force, 1881	8.1	6.	Bill Mazeroski, 1962	138
8.	Gerry Priddy, 1950	1001	8.	Jack Burdock, 1879	7.9	8.	Red Schoendienst, 1954	137
9.	Bucky Harris, 1922	992	9.	Joe Quest, 1878	7.8	8.	Jerry Coleman, 1950	137
10.	Fred Pfeffer, 1889	991	10.	Pop Smith, 1885	7.7	8.	Jackie Robinson, 1951	137
THIRD BASE			**THIRD BASE**			**THIRD BASE**		
1.	Jimmy Williams, 1899	671	1.	Al Nichols, 1876	5.8	1.	Graig Nettles, 1971	54
2.	Bill Shindle, 1892	660	2.	Bob Ferguson, 1877	5.6	2.	Harlond Clift, 1937	50
3.	Tommy Leach, 1904	643	3.	Arthur Irwin, 1882	5.4	3.	Johnny Pesky, 1949	48
4.	Harlond Clift, 1937	637	4.	Jumbo Davis, 1888	5.1	3.	Paul Molitor, 1982	48
5.	Bill Shindle, 1889	636	5.	John Shetzline, 1882	5.1	5.	Sammy Hale, 1927	46
6.	Jimmy Collins, 1899	629	6.	Cap Anson, 1876	5.0	5.	Clete Boyer, 1965	46
7.	Charlie Reilly, 1890	626	7.	Bill Shindle, 1892	4.9	5.	Gary Gaetti, 1983	46
8.	Arlie Latham, 1891	622	8.	Jack Gleason, 1882	4.9	8.	Frank Malzone, 1961	45
9.	Jimmy Collins, 1900	620	9.	Bill Bradley, 1900	4.9	8.	Eddie Yost, 1950	45
10.	Jimmy Collins, 1898	617	10.	George Bradley, 1880	4.8	8.	Darrell Evans, 1974	45
SHORTSTOP			**SHORTSTOP**			**SHORTSTOP**		
1.	Dave Bancroft, 1922	1046	1.	Herman Long, 1889	7.3	1.	Rick Burleson, 1980	147
1.	Rabbit Maranville, 1914	1046	2.	Hughie Jennings, 1895	7.2	2.	Roy Smalley, 1979	144
3.	Donie Bush, 1914	1027	3.	Dave Bancroft, 1918	7.1	3.	Bobby Wine, 1970	137
4.	Tommy Thevenow, 1926	1013	4.	Phil Tomney, 1889	7.1	4.	Lou Boudreau, 1944	134
5.	Dave Bancroft, 1920	1005	5.	George Davis, 1899	7.1	5.	Spike Owen, 1986	133
6.	Monte Cross, 1898	1003	6.	Hughie Jennings, 1896	7.1	6.	Rafael Ramirez, 1982	130
6.	Donie Bush, 1911	1003	7.	Hughie Jennings, 1897	7.0	7.	Roy McMillan, 1954	129
6.	Heinie Wagner, 1908	1003	8.	Bobby Wallace, 1901	7.0	8.	Gene Alley, 1966	128
9.	George McBride, 1908	992	9.	Monte Cross, 1897	7.0	8.	Hod Ford, 1928	128
10.	Monte Cross, 1899	989	10.	Bill Dahlen, 1895	6.9	8.	Vern Stephens, 1949	128
OUTFIELD			**OUTFIELD**			**OUTFIELD**		
1.	Taylor Douthit, 1928	566	1.	Fred Treacey, 1876	4.4	1.	Jack Tobin, 1919	15
2.	Richie Ashburn, 1951	560	2.	Tom Dolan, 1883	4.3	1.	Happy Felsch, 1919	15
3.	Richie Ashburn, 1949	538	3.	Redleg Snyder, 1876	3.8	3.	Jimmy Sheckard, 1899	14
4.	Chet Lemon, 1977	536	4.	Charley Jones, 1877	3.8	4.	Tom Brown, 1893	13
5.	Richie Ashburn, 1957	527	5.	Taylor Douthit, 1928	3.7			
6.	Dom DiMaggio, 1948	526	6.	Mike Mansell, 1879	3.6			
7.	Dwayne Murphy, 1980	525	7.	Richie Ashburn, 1951	3.6			
8.	Richie Ashburn, 1956	523	8.	Chet Lemon, 1977	3.5			
9.	Richie Ashburn, 1953	519	9.	Thurman Tucker, 1944	3.6			
10.	Lloyd Waner, 1931	515	10.	Kirby Puckett, 1984	3.5			
CATCHER			**CATCHER**			**CATCHER**		
1.	Johnny Edwards, 1969	1221	1.	Bill Holbert, 1883	10.6	1.	Steve O'Neill, 1916	36
2.	Johnny Edwards, 1963	1101	2.	Sam Trott, 1884	10.4	2.	Frankie Hayes, 1945	29
3.	Tony Pena, 1983	1075	3.	Bill Holbert, 1884	9.7	3.	Ray Schalk, 1916	25
4.	Gary Carter, 1982	1068	4.	Jocko Milligan, 1884	9.4	3.	Yogi Berra, 1951	25
5.	Randy Hundley, 1969	1065	4.	Mert Hackett, 1884	9.4	5.	Jack Lapp, 1915	23
6.	Johnny Bench, 1968	1053	6.	Barney Gilligan, 1884	9.3	5.	Tom Haller, 1968	23
7.	Bill Freehan, 1968	1050	7.	Mike Hines, 1883	9.3	5.	Muddy Ruel, 1924	23
8.	Tony Pena, 1985	1034	8.	George Baker, 1884	9.0	8.	Steve O'Neill, 1914	22
9.	Gary Carter, 1985	1031	9.	Jocko Milligan, 1885	8.8	8.	Bob O'Farrell, 1922	22
10.	Bill Freehan, 1967	1021	10.	Lew Brown, 1877	8.7	10.	Gabby Hartnett, 1927	21
						10.	Wes Westrum, 1950	21
PITCHER			**PITCHER**			**PITCHER**		
1.	Ed Walsh, 1907	266	1.	Guy Bush, 1933	6.5	1.	Lefty Gomez, 1938	15
2.	Will White, 1882	257	2.	Harry Howell, 1905	5.4	1.	Howie Fox, 1948	15
3.	Tony Mullane, 1882	241	3.	Harry Howell, 1904	5.1	1.	Bob Lemon, 1953	15
4.	Tim Keefe, 1883	238	4.	Harry Arundel, 1882	5.1	4.	Randy Jones, 1976	12
5.	Ed Walsh, 1908	237	5.	Will White, 1882	4.8	4.	Eddie Rommel, 1924	12
6.	John Clarkson, 1889	235	6.	Ed Walsh, 1907	4.8	4.	Curt Davis, 1934	12
7.	Matt Kilroy, 1887	224	7.	George Mullin, 1904	4.5			
8.	John Clarkson, 1885	220	8.	Tony Mullane, 1882	4.4			
9.	Harry Howell, 1905	206	9.	Red Donahue, 1902	4.4			
10.	Guy Hecker, 1884	205	10.	Nick Altrock, 1905	4.4			

INDIVIDUAL BATTING (LIFETIME)

BATTING AVERAGE

1. Ty Cobb	.367	
2. Rogers Hornsby	.358	
3. Joe Jackson	.356	
4. Wade Boggs	.352	
5. Ed Delahanty	.346	
6. Ted Williams	.344	
7. Tris Speaker	.344	
8. Billy Hamilton	.344	
9. Willie Keeler	.343	
10. Dan Brouthers	.342	
11. Babe Ruth	.342	
12. Harry Heilmann	.342	
13. Pete Browning	.341	
14. Bill Terry	.341	
15. George Sisler	.340	
16. Lou Gehrig	.340	
17. Jesse Burkett	.339	
18. Nap Lajoie	.338	
19. Riggs Stephenson	.336	
20. Al Simmons	.334	
21. Paul Waner	.333	
22. Eddie Collins	.333	
23. Tony Gwynn	.332	
24. Stan Musial	.331	
25. Sam Thompson	.331	
26. Heinie Manush	.330	
27. Cap Anson	.329	
28. Rod Carew	.328	
29. Honus Wagner	.327	
30. Tip O'Neill	.326	
31. Jimmie Foxx	.325	
32. Earle Combs	.325	
33. Joe DiMaggio	.325	
34. Babe Herman	.324	
35. Hugh Duffy	.324	
36. Joe Medwick	.324	
37. Don Mattingly	.323	
38. Edd Roush	.323	
39. Sam Rice	.322	
40. Ross Youngs	.322	
41. Kiki Cuyler	.321	
42. Charlie Gehringer	.320	
43. Chuck Klein	.320	
44. Pie Traynor	.320	
45. Mickey Cochrane	.320	
46. Ken Williams	.319	
47. Earl Averill	.318	
48. Arky Vaughan	.318	
49. Roberto Clemente	.317	
50. Chick Hafey	.317	
51. Joe Kelley	.317	
52. Zack Wheat	.317	
53. Roger Connor	.317	
54. Lloyd Waner	.316	
55. George Van Haltren	.316	
56. Frankie Frisch	.316	
57. Goose Goslin	.316	
58. Bibb Falk	.314	
59. Cecil Travis	.314	
60. Hank Greenberg	.313	
61. Elmer Flick	.313	
62. Jack Fournier	.313	
63. Bill Dickey	.313	
64. Hughie Jennings	.312	
65. Fred Clarke	.312	
66. Johnny Mize	.312	
67. Joe Sewell	.312	
68. Barney McCosky	.312	
69. Bing Miller	.312	
70. Freddie Lindstrom	.311	
71. Jackie Robinson	.311	
72. Baby Doll Jacobson	.311	
73. Rip Radcliff	.311	
74. Ginger Beaumont	.311	
75. Mike Tiernan	.311	
76. Denny Lyons	.310	
77. Irish Meusel	.310	
78. Luke Appling	.310	
79. George Brett	.310	
80. Elmer Smith	.310	
81. Bobby Veach	.310	
82. Jim O'Rourke	.310	
83. John Stone	.310	
84. Jim Bottomley	.310	
85. Sam Crawford	.309	
86. Bob Meusel	.309	
87. Jack Tobin	.309	
88. Spud Davis	.308	
89. Pedro Guerrero	.308	
90. Richie Ashburn	.308	
91. Jake Beckley	.308	
92. King Kelly	.308	
93. Stuffy McInnis	.308	
94. Joe Vosmik	.307	
95. Frank Baker	.307	
96. George Burns	.307	
97. Matty Alou	.307	
98. Hack Wilson	.307	
99. Jimmy Ryan	.307	
100. Johnny Pesky	.307	
101. George Kell	.306	
102. Dixie Walker	.306	
103. Chick Stahl	.306	
104. Cupid Childs	.306	
105. Ernie Lombardi	.306	
106. Ralph Garr	.306	
107. Hank Aaron	.305	
108. Bill Madlock	.305	
109. Billy Herman	.304	
110. Tony Oliva	.304	
111. Mel Ott	.304	
112. Curt Walker	.304	
113. Cy Seymour	.304	
114. Deacon White	.303	
115. Charlie Jamieson	.303	
116. Jake Daubert	.303	
117. Al Oliver	.303	
118. Henry Larkin	.303	
119. Buck Ewing	.303	
120. Steve Brodie	.303	
121. Pete Rose	.303	
122. Buddy Myer	.303	
123. Harvey Kuenn	.303	
124. Tim Raines	.303	
125. Hal Trosky	.302	
126. Ed McKean	.302	
127. George Grantham	.302	
128. Ben Chapman	.302	
129. Carl Reynolds	.302	
130. Tommy Holmes	.302	
131. Willie Mays	.302	
132. Joe Cronin	.301	
133. Stan Hack	.301	
134. George Gore	.301	
135. Paul Hines	.301	
136. Paul Molitor	.300	
137. Oyster Burns	.300	
138. Wally Berger	.300	
139. Ethan Allen	.300	
140. Enos Slaughter	.300	
141. Patsy Donovan	.300	
142. Earl Sheely	.300	
143. Billy Goodman	.300	

SLUGGING AVERAGE

1. Babe Ruth	.690
2. Ted Williams	.634
3. Lou Gehrig	.632
4. Jimmie Foxx	.609
5. Hank Greenberg	.605
6. Joe DiMaggio	.579
7. Rogers Hornsby	.577
8. Johnny Mize	.562
9. Stan Musial	.559
10. Willie Mays	.557
11. Mickey Mantle	.557
12. Hank Aaron	.555
13. Ralph Kiner	.548
14. Hack Wilson	.545
15. Chuck Klein	.543
16. Duke Snider	.540
17. Frank Robinson	.537
18. Al Simmons	.535
19. Dick Allen	.534
20. Earl Averill	.533
21. Mel Ott	.533
22. Babe Herman	.532
23. Ken Williams	.531
24. Willie Stargell	.529
25. Mike Schmidt	.527
26. Chick Hafey	.526
27. Hal Trosky	.522
28. Wally Berger	.522
29. Don Mattingly	.521
30. Harry Heilmann	.520
31. Dan Brouthers	.519
32. Joe Jackson	.518
33. Willie McCovey	.515
34. Ty Cobb	.513
35. Eddie Mathews	.509
36. Jeff Heath	.509
37. Harmon Killebrew	.509
38. Bob Johnson	.506
39. Bill Terry	.506
40. Sam Thompson	.505
41. Joe Medwick	.505
42. Pedro Guerrero	.504
43. Ed Delahanty	.504
44. Jim Rice	.502
45. George Brett	.501
46. Jim Bottomley	.500
47. Tris Speaker	.500
48. Goose Goslin	.500
49. Roy Campanella	.500
50. Ernie Banks	.500

TOTAL BASES

1. Hank Aaron	6856
2. Stan Musial	6134
3. Willie Mays	6066
4. Ty Cobb	5863
5. Babe Ruth	5793
6. Pete Rose	5752
7. Carl Yastrzemski	5539
8. Frank Robinson	5373
9. Tris Speaker	5104
10. Lou Gehrig	5059
11. Mel Ott	5041
12. Jimmie Foxx	4956
13. Ted Williams	4884
14. Honus Wagner	4868
15. Al Kaline	4852
16. Reggie Jackson	4834
17. Rogers Hornsby	4712
18. Ernie Banks	4706
19. Al Simmons	4685
20. Billy Williams	4599
21. Tony Perez	4532
22. Mickey Mantle	4511
23. Roberto Clemente	4492
24. Nap Lajoie	4473
25. Paul Waner	4471
26. Mike Schmidt	4404
27. Eddie Mathews	4349
28. Sam Crawford	4336
29. Goose Goslin	4325
30. Brooks Robinson	4270
31. Vada Pinson	4264
32. Eddie Collins	4263
33. Charlie Gehringer	4257
34. Lou Brock	4238
35. Willie McCovey	4219
36. Willie Stargell	4190
37. Rusty Staub	4185
38. Jake Beckley	4157
39. Harmon Killebrew	4143
40. Jim Rice	4129
41. Zack Wheat	4100
42. George Brett	4083
43. Al Oliver	4083
44. Cap Anson	4064
45. Harry Heilmann	4053
46. Dave Winfield	4052

GAMES

1. Pete Rose	3562
2. Carl Yastrzemski	3308
3. Hank Aaron	3298
4. Ty Cobb	3034
5. Stan Musial	3026
6. Willie Mays	2992
7. Rusty Staub	2951
8. Brooks Robinson	2896
9. Al Kaline	2834
10. Eddie Collins	2826
11. Reggie Jackson	2820
12. Frank Robinson	2808
13. Tris Speaker	2789
13. Honus Wagner	2789
15. Tony Perez	2777
16. Mel Ott	2734
17. Graig Nettles	2700
18. Darrell Evans	2687
19. Rabbit Maranville	2670
20. Joe Morgan	2649
21. Lou Brock	2616
22. Luis Aparicio	2599
23. Willie McCovey	2588
24. Paul Waner	2549
25. Ernie Banks	2528
26. Sam Crawford	2517
27. Babe Ruth	2503
28. Bill Buckner	2495
29. Billy Williams	2488
29. Dave Concepcion	2488
31. Nap Lajoie	2479
32. Max Carey	2476
33. Vada Pinson	2469
33. Rod Carew	2469
35. Ted Simmons	2456
36. Bill Dahlen	2443
37. Ron Fairly	2442
38. Harmon Killebrew	2435
39. Roberto Clemente	2433
40. Willie Davis	2429
41. Luke Appling	2422
42. Zack Wheat	2410
43. Mickey Vernon	2409
44. Buddy Bell	2405
45. Sam Rice	2404
45. Mike Schmidt	2404
47. Mickey Mantle	2401
48. Eddie Mathews	2388
49. Jake Beckley	2386
50. Bobby Wallace	2383
51. Dwight Evans	2382
52. Enos Slaughter	2380
53. George Davis	2376
54. Al Oliver	2368
55. Nellie Fox	2367
56. Willie Stargell	2360
57. Jose Cruz	2353
58. Steve Garvey	2332
59. Bert Campaneris	2328
60. Charlie Gehringer	2323
61. Jimmie Foxx	2317
62. Frankie Frisch	2311
63. Harry Hooper	2308
64. Ted Williams	2292
64. Don Baylor	2292
66. Robin Yount	2291
67. Goose Goslin	2287
68. Jimmy Dykes	2282
69. Cap Anson	2276
70. Lave Cross	2275
71. Dave Winfield	2269
72. Chris Speier	2260
73. Rogers Hornsby	2259
74. Larry Bowa	2247
75. Fred Clarke	2244
76. Ron Santo	2243
77. Frank White	2242
78. Doc Cramer	2239
79. Bob Boone	2224
80. Red Schoendienst	2216
81. Al Simmons	2215
82. Joe Torre	2209
83. Tommy Corcoran	2200
84. Tony Taylor	2195
85. Richie Ashburn	2189
86. Bill Russell	2181
87. Dave Parker	2177
88. Chris Chambliss	2173
89. Joe Judge	2171
90. Pee Wee Reese	2166
91. Lou Gehrig	2164
91. Charlie Grimm	2164
93. Bill Mazeroski	2163
94. Johnny Bench	2158
95. Tommy Leach	2155
95. Toby Harrah	2155
97. Harry Heilmann	2146
98. Duke Snider	2143
99. Carlton Fisk	2141
100. Bid McPhee	2137
100. George Brett	2137
102. Stuffy McInnis	2128
103. Orlando Cepeda	2124
103. Joe Cronin	2124
105. Willie Keeler	2122
106. Jimmy Sheckard	2121
107. Yogi Berra	2120
108. Eddie Yost	2109
109. Joe Kuhel	2104
110. Roy McMillan	2093
111. Norm Cash	2089
111. Jim Rice	2089
113. Sherry Magee	2085
114. Hal McRae	2084
115. Ed Konetchy	2083
116. Felipe Alou	2082
116. Ken Singleton	2082
118. Don Kessinger	2078
119. Ron Cey	2073
120. Gil Hodges	2071

INDIVIDUAL BATTING (LIFETIME), *cont.*

120. Lee May 2071
122. Jesse Burkett 2070
123. George Sisler 2055
124. George Hendrick 2048
125. Keith Hernandez 2045
126. Boog Powell 2042
127. Dusty Baker 2039
128. Ken Boyer 2034
128. George Scott 2034
130. Gary Matthews 2033

131. Phil Cavarretta 2030
132. Willie Horton 2028
133. Sal Bando 2019
134. Brian Downing 2018
135. Jose Cardenal 2017
135. Aurelio Rodriguez 2017
137. Dick Bartell 2016
137. Mark Belanger 2016
139. Jake Daubert 2014
140. Wally Moses 2012

140. Roger Peckinpaugh 2012
140. Jimmy Ryan 2012
143. Heinie Manush 2009
144. Gary Carter 2008
144. Bobby Grich 2008
146. Cesar Cedeno 2006
147. Cy Williams 2002
148. Ken Griffey 2000

AT BATS
1. Pete Rose 14053
2. Hank Aaron 12364
3. Carl Yastrzemski 11988
4. Ty Cobb 11429
5. Stan Musial 10972
6. Willie Mays 10881
7. Brooks Robinson 10654
8. Honus Wagner 10441
9. Lou Brock 10332
10. Luis Aparicio 10230

11. Tris Speaker 10208
12. Al Kaline 10116
13. Rabbit Maranville 10078
14. Frank Robinson 10006
15. Eddie Collins 9949
16. Reggie Jackson 9864
17. Tony Perez 9778
18. Rusty Staub 9720
19. Vada Pinson 9645
20. Nap Lajoie 9592

21. Sam Crawford 9580
22. Jake Beckley 9527
23. Paul Waner 9459
24. Mel Ott 9456
25. Roberto Clemente 9454
26. Ernie Banks 9421
27. Max Carey 9363
28. Bill Buckner 9354
29. Billy Williams 9350
30. Rod Carew 9315

31. Joe Morgan 9277
32. Sam Rice 9269
33. Nellie Fox 9232
34. Willie Davis 9174
35. Doc Cramer 9140
36. Frankie Frisch 9112
37. Cap Anson 9108
38. Zack Wheat 9106
39. Lave Cross 9064
40. George Davis 9050

41. Al Oliver 9049
42. Bill Dahlen 9039

HITS
1. Pete Rose 4256
2. Ty Cobb 4191
3. Hank Aaron 3771
4. Stan Musial 3630
5. Tris Speaker 3515
6. Carl Yastrzemski 3419
7. Honus Wagner 3418
8. Eddie Collins 3311
9. Willie Mays 3283
10. Nap Lajoie 3244

11. Paul Waner 3152
12. Rod Carew 3053
13. Lou Brock 3023
14. Al Kaline 3007
15. Cap Anson 3000
15. Roberto Clemente 3000
17. Sam Rice 2987
18. Sam Crawford 2964
19. Willie Keeler 2947
20. Frank Robinson 2943

21. Jake Beckley 2931
22. Rogers Hornsby 2930
23. Al Simmons 2927
24. Zack Wheat 2884
25. Frankie Frisch 2880
26. Mel Ott 2876
27. Babe Ruth 2873
28. Jesse Burkett 2853
29. Brooks Robinson 2848
30. Charlie Gehringer 2839

31. George Sisler 2812
32. Vada Pinson 2757
33. Luke Appling 2749
34. Al Oliver 2743
35. Goose Goslin 2735
36. Tony Perez 2732
37. Lou Gehrig 2721
38. Rusty Staub 2716
39. Billy Williams 2711
40. Bill Buckner 2707

41. Doc Cramer 2705
42. Luis Aparicio 2677
43. Fred Clarke 2675
44. George Davis 2667
45. Max Carey 2665
46. Nellie Fox 2663
47. Harry Heilmann 2660
48. Ted Williams 2654
49. Jimmie Foxx 2646
50. Lave Cross 2644

51. Rabbit Maranville 2605
52. Robin Yount 2602
53. Steve Garvey 2599
54. Ed Delahanty 2597
55. Reggie Jackson 2584
56. Ernie Banks 2583
57. Richie Ashburn 2574
58. Willie Davis 2561
59. George Van Haltren 2536
60. George Brett 2528

61. Heinie Manush 2524
62. Joe Morgan 2517
63. Buddy Bell 2514
64. Jimmy Ryan 2506
65. Mickey Vernon 2495
66. Ted Simmons 2472
67. Joe Medwick 2471
68. Roger Connor 2467
69. Harry Hooper 2466
70. Bill Dahlen 2460

71. Lloyd Waner 2459
72. Jim Rice 2452
73. Red Schoendienst 2449
74. Dave Winfield 2421

75. Pie Traynor 2416
75. Dave Parker 2416
77. Mickey Mantle 2415
78. Stuffy McInnis 2406
79. Enos Slaughter 2383
80. Edd Roush 2376

81. Joe Judge 2352
82. Orlando Cepeda 2351
83. Billy Herman 2345
84. Joe Torre 2342
85. Jake Daubert 2326
85. Dave Concepcion 2326
87. Eddie Mathews 2315
88. Jim Bottomley 2313
89. Jim O'Rourke 2304
90. Bobby Wallace 2303

91. Kiki Cuyler 2299
91. Charlie Grimm 2299
93. Dan Brouthers 2296
94. Joe Cronin 2285
95. Hugh Duffy 2283
96. Dwight Evans 2262
97. Bid McPhee 2260
98. Jimmy Dykes 2256
99. Ron Santo 2254
100. Jose Cruz 2251

100. Tommy Corcoran 2251
102. Bert Campaneris 2249
103. Patsy Donovan 2246
104. Mike Schmidt 2234
105. Willie Stargell 2232
106. Fred Tenney 2231
107. Joe Sewell 2226
108. Graig Nettles 2225
109. Darrell Evans 2223
110. Joe Kelley 2222

111. Joe DiMaggio 2214
112. Joe Kuhel 2212
113. Willie McCovey 2211
114. Bill Terry 2193
114. Stan Hack 2193
116. Cecil Cooper 2192
117. Larry Bowa 2191
118. Pee Wee Reese 2170
119. Sherry Magee 2169
120. Eddie Murray 2168

121. Dick Bartell 2165
122. Billy Hamilton 2163
123. Hal Chase 2158
124. Keith Hernandez 2156
125. Yogi Berra 2150
126. Ed Konetchy 2148
127. Tommy Leach 2146
128. Ken Boyer 2143
129. Wally Moses 2138
129. Dick Groat 2138

131. Don Baylor 2135
132. Maury Wills 2134
133. Herman Long 2132
134. Buddy Myer 2131
135. Tommy Davis 2121
136. Duke Snider 2116
137. Chris Chambliss 2109
138. Monte Ward 2105
139. Arky Vaughan 2103
140. Felipe Alou 2101

141. Clyde Milan 2100
142. Harvey Kuenn 2092
143. Hal McRae 2091
144. Alvin Dark 2089
145. Cesar Cedeno 2087
146. Harmon Killebrew 2086
147. Jimmy Sheckard 2085
148. Ed McKean 2083
149. Ken Griffey 2077

149. George Burns 2077
151. Chuck Klein 2076
152. Bobby Veach 2064
152. Dixie Walker 2064
154. Del Ennis 2063
154. Carlton Fisk 2063
156. Bob Elliott 2061
157. George Kell 2054
157. Dummy Hoy 2054
159. Bob Johnson 2051
160. Johnny Bench 2048

161. Bobby Doerr 2042
162. Jack Glasscock 2040
163. Andre Dawson 2037
164. Lee May 2031
165. Ken Singleton 2029
166. Earl Averill 2020
166. Reggie Smith 2020
166. Amos Otis 2020
169. George Burns 2018
170. Bill Mazeroski 2016

171. Johnny Mize 2011
171. Gary Matthews 2011
173. Bill Madlock 2008
174. Tony Taylor 2007
175. Dave Bancroft 2004

DOUBLES
1. Tris Speaker 792
2. Pete Rose 746
3. Stan Musial 725
4. Ty Cobb 724
5. Nap Lajoie 658
6. Carl Yastrzemski 646
7. Honus Wagner 643
8. Hank Aaron 624
9. Paul Waner 603
10. Charlie Gehringer 574

11. Harry Heilmann 542
12. Rogers Hornsby 541
13. Joe Medwick 540
14. Al Simmons 539
15. Lou Gehrig 535
16. Al Oliver 529
17. Cap Anson 528
17. Frank Robinson 528
19. Ted Williams 525
20. Willie Mays 523

21. Ed Delahanty 520
22. Joe Cronin 515
23. George Brett 514
24. Babe Ruth 506
25. Tony Perez 505
26. Goose Goslin 500
27. Rusty Staub 499
28. Bill Buckner 498
28. Al Kaline 498
30. Sam Rice 497

31. Heinie Manush 491
32. Mickey Vernon 490
33. Mel Ott 488
34. Billy Herman 486
34. Lou Brock 486
36. Vada Pinson 485
37. Hal McRae 484
38. Ted Simmons 483
39. Brooks Robinson 482
40. Robin Yount 481

41. Zack Wheat 476
41. Jake Beckley 476
43. Dave Parker 470
44. Frankie Frisch 466

45. Jim Bottomley 465
46. Reggie Jackson 463
47. Dan Brouthers 460
48. Jimmie Foxx 458
49. Sam Crawford 457
50. Dwight Evans 456

51. George Davis 455
52. Jimmy Dykes 453
53. Jimmy Ryan 451
54. Joe Morgan 449
55. Rod Carew 445
56. George Burns 444
57. Dick Bartell 442
58. Roger Connor 441
59. Steve Garvey 440
59. Luke Appling 440
59. Roberto Clemente 440
62. Eddie Collins 437
63. Joe Sewell 436
63. Cesar Cedeno 436
65. Wally Moses 435
66. Billy Williams 434
67. Joe Judge 433
68. Red Schoendienst 427
69. Sherry Magee 425
69. George Sisler 425
69. Buddy Bell 425
72. Keith Hernandez 424
73. Willie Stargell 423
74. Max Carey 419
75. Orlando Cepeda 417
76. Cecil Cooper 415
77. Jim O'Rourke 414
77. Bill Dahlen 414
79. Enos Slaughter 413
80. Joe Kuhel 412
80. Dave Winfield 412
82. Lave Cross 411
83. Mike Schmidt 408
84. Ben Chapman 407
84. Ernie Banks 407
86. Earl Averill 401
86. Marty McManus 401

TRIPLES
1. Sam Crawford 312
2. Ty Cobb 297
3. Honus Wagner 252
4. Jake Beckley 243
5. Roger Connor 233
6. Tris Speaker 223
7. Fred Clarke 220
8. Dan Brouthers 205
9. Joe Kelley 194
10. Paul Waner 190

11. Bid McPhee 188
12. Eddie Collins 187
13. Sam Rice 184
14. Ed Delahanty 183
14. Jesse Burkett 183
16. Edd Roush 182
17. Ed Konetchy 181
18. Buck Ewing 178
19. Harry Stovey 177
19. Rabbit Maranville 177
19. Stan Musial 177
22. Goose Goslin 173
23. Tommy Leach 172
23. Zack Wheat 172
25. Rogers Hornsby 169
26. Joe Jackson 168
27. Elmer Flick 166
27. Sherry Magee 166

INDIVIDUAL BATTING (LIFETIME), cont.

27. Roberto Clemente	166
30. Jake Daubert	165
30. George Sisler	165
32. Pie Traynor	164
33. Bill Dahlen	163
33. George Davis	163
35. Mike Tiernan	162
35. Lou Gehrig	162
35. George Van Haltren	162
39. Nap Lajoie	161
39. Sam Thompson	160
39. Heinie Manush	160
39. Harry Hooper	160
42. Joe Judge	159
42. Max Carey	159
44. Ed McKean	158
45. Kiki Cuyler	157
45. Jimmy Ryan	157
47. Tommy Corcoran	155
48. Earle Combs	154
49. Bobby Wallace	153
50. Jim Bottomley	151
50. Harry Heilmann	151
52. Willie Keeler	150

HOME RUNS

1. Hank Aaron	755
2. Babe Ruth	714
3. Willie Mays	660
4. Frank Robinson	586
5. Harmon Killebrew	573
6. Reggie Jackson	563
7. Mike Schmidt	548
8. Mickey Mantle	536
9. Jimmie Foxx	534
10. Ted Williams	521
10. Willie McCovey	521
12. Eddie Mathews	512
12. Ernie Banks	512
14. Mel Ott	511
15. Lou Gehrig	493
16. Willie Stargell	475
16. Stan Musial	475
18. Carl Yastrzemski	452
19. Dave Kingman	442
20. Billy Williams	426
21. Darrell Evans	414
22. Duke Snider	407
23. Al Kaline	399
24. Graig Nettles	390
25. Johnny Bench	389
26. Frank Howard	382
26. Jim Rice	382
28. Orlando Cepeda	379
28. Tony Perez	379
30. Norm Cash	377
31. Rocky Colavito	374
32. Gil Hodges	370
33. Ralph Kiner	369
34. Dwight Evans	366
35. Joe DiMaggio	361
36. Johnny Mize	359
37. Yogi Berra	358
38. Dave Winfield	357
39. Dale Murphy	354
39. Lee May	354
41. Eddie Murray	353
42. Dick Allen	351
43. George Foster	348
44. Ron Santo	342
45. Boog Powell	339
46. Don Baylor	338
47. Joe Adcock	336
47. Carlton Fisk	336
49. Bobby Bonds	332
50. Hank Greenberg	331
51. Willie Horton	325
52. Andre Dawson	319
53. Roy Sievers	318
54. Ron Cey	316
55. Reggie Smith	314
56. Greg Luzinski	307
56. Dave Parker	307
56. Al Simmons	307
59. Gary Carter	304
60. Rogers Hornsby	301
61. Chuck Klein	300
61. Fred Lynn	300

HOME RUN PERCENTAGE

1. Babe Ruth	8.5
2. Ralph Kiner	7.1
3. Harmon Killebrew	7.0
4. Ted Williams	6.8
5. Dave Kingman	6.6
6. Mickey Mantle	6.6
7. Jimmie Foxx	6.6
8. Mike Schmidt	6.6
9. Hank Greenberg	6.4
10. Willie McCovey	6.4
11. Lou Gehrig	6.2
12. Hank Aaron	6.1
13. Willie Mays	6.1
14. Hank Sauer	6.0
15. Eddie Mathews	6.0
16. Willie Stargell	6.0
17. Frank Howard	5.9
18. Frank Robinson	5.9
19. Roy Campanella	5.8
20. Rocky Colavito	5.8
21. Gus Zernial	5.7
22. Gorman Thomas	5.7
23. Reggie Jackson	5.7
24. Duke Snider	5.7
25. Norm Cash	5.6
26. Johnny Mize	5.6
27. Dick Allen	5.5
28. Ernie Banks	5.4
29. Mel Ott	5.4
30. Roger Maris	5.4
31. Joe DiMaggio	5.3
32. Gil Hodges	5.3
33. Dale Murphy	5.2
34. Wally Post	5.2
35. Hack Wilson	5.1

EXTRA BASE HITS

1. Hank Aaron	1477
2. Stan Musial	1377
3. Babe Ruth	1356
4. Willie Mays	1323
5. Lou Gehrig	1190
6. Frank Robinson	1186
7. Carl Yastrzemski	1157
8. Ty Cobb	1139
9. Tris Speaker	1132
10. Ted Williams	1117
10. Jimmie Foxx	1117
12. Reggie Jackson	1075
13. Mel Ott	1071
14. Pete Rose	1041
15. Mike Schmidt	1015
16. Rogers Hornsby	1011

RUNS BATTED IN

1. Hank Aaron	2297
2. Babe Ruth	2211
3. Lou Gehrig	1990
4. Ty Cobb	1961
5. Stan Musial	1951
6. Jimmie Foxx	1921
7. Willie Mays	1903
8. Mel Ott	1861
9. Carl Yastrzemski	1844
10. Ted Williams	1839
11. Al Simmons	1827
12. Frank Robinson	1812
13. Honus Wagner	1732
14. Cap Anson	1715
15. Reggie Jackson	1702
16. Tony Perez	1652
17. Ernie Banks	1636
18. Goose Goslin	1609
19. Nap Lajoie	1599
20. Mike Schmidt	1595
21. Rogers Hornsby	1584
21. Harmon Killebrew	1584
23. Al Kaline	1583
24. Jake Beckley	1575
25. Tris Speaker	1559
26. Willie McCovey	1555
27. Harry Heilmann	1551
28. Willie Stargell	1540
29. Joe DiMaggio	1537
30. Sam Crawford	1525
31. Mickey Mantle	1509
32. Billy Williams	1475
33. Rusty Staub	1466
34. Ed Delahanty	1464
35. Eddie Mathews	1453
36. Jim Rice	1451
37. Dave Winfield	1438
38. George Davis	1435
39. Yogi Berra	1430
40. Charlie Gehringer	1427
41. Joe Cronin	1424
42. Jim Bottomley	1422
43. Ted Simmons	1389
44. Joe Medwick	1383
45. Johnny Bench	1376
46. Orlando Cepeda	1365
47. Brooks Robinson	1357
48. Darrell Evans	1354
49. Lave Cross	1345
50. Dave Parker	1342
51. Johnny Mize	1337
52. Duke Snider	1333
53. Ron Santo	1331
54. Al Oliver	1326
55. Graig Nettles	1314
55. Pete Rose	1314
57. George Brett	1311
57. Mickey Vernon	1311
59. Paul Waner	1309
60. Steve Garvey	1308
61. Roberto Clemente	1305
62. Enos Slaughter	1304
63. Sam Thompson	1299
63. Hugh Duffy	1299
63. Eddie Collins	1299
66. Del Ennis	1284
67. Bob Johnson	1283
67. Dwight Evans	1283
69. Eddie Murray	1278
70. Hank Greenberg	1276
70. Don Baylor	1276
72. Gil Hodges	1274
73. Pie Traynor	1273
74. Zack Wheat	1261
75. Bobby Doerr	1247
76. Lee May	1244
76. Frankie Frisch	1244
78. George Foster	1239
79. Bill Dahlen	1233
80. Dave Kingman	1210
81. Bill Dickey	1209
82. Bill Buckner	1205
83. Chuck Klein	1202
84. Bob Elliott	1195
85. Joe Kelley	1193
86. Tony Lazzeri	1191
87. Boog Powell	1187
88. Joe Torre	1185
89. Sherry Magee	1182
90. Gabby Hartnett	1179
91. Vic Wertz	1178
92. George Sisler	1175
93. Vern Stephens	1174
94. Heinie Manush	1173
95. Vada Pinson	1170
96. Bobby Veach	1166
96. Carlton Fisk	1166
98. Earl Averill	1165
99. Willie Horton	1163
100. Rocky Colavito	1159
101. Rudy York	1152
102. Roy Sievers	1147
103. Gary Carter	1143
104. Ken Boyer	1141
105. Ron Cey	1139
106. Tommy Corcoran	1135
107. Joe Morgan	1133
108. Andre Dawson	1131
109. Greg Luzinski	1128
110. Cecil Cooper	1125
110. Roger Connor	1125
112. Robin Yount	1124
113. Joe Adcock	1122
114. Bobby Wallace	1121
115. Dick Allen	1119
115. Frank Howard	1119
117. Luke Appling	1116
118. George Hendrick	1111
119. Buddy Bell	1106
120. Norm Cash	1103
121. Hal McRae	1097
122. Jimmy Ryan	1093
123. Reggie Smith	1092
124. Dale Murphy	1088
124. Fred Lynn	1088
126. Bill Terry	1078
126. Charlie Grimm	1078
126. Sam Rice	1078
129. Jose Cruz	1077
130. Pinky Higgins	1075
131. Jimmy Dykes	1071
132. Ed McKean	1070
133. Bob Meusel	1067
134. Kiki Cuyler	1065
134. Ken Singleton	1065
136. Keith Hernandez	1063
137. Hack Wilson	1062
138. Stuffy McInnis	1060
139. Carl Furillo	1058
140. Dan Brouthers	1057
141. Willie Davis	1053
142. Herman Long	1052
142. Tommy Davis	1052
144. Joe Sewell	1051
144. George Scott	1051
146. Joe Kuhel	1049
147. Ron Fairly	1044
148. Bobby Murcer	1043
149. Sal Bando	1039
150. Joe Judge	1037
151. Ted Kluszewski	1028
152. Bobby Thomson	1026
153. Bobby Bonds	1024
154. Minnie Minoso	1023
154. Dixie Walker	1023
156. George Kelly	1020
157. Ralph Kiner	1015
157. Fred Clarke	1015
157. Rod Carew	1015
160. George Van Haltren	1014
161. Frank Baker	1013
161. Dusty Baker	1013
163. Hal Trosky	1012
164. Amos Otis	1007
165. Cy Williams	1005

RBI PER GAME

1. Sam Thompson	.92
2. Lou Gehrig	.92
3. Hank Greenberg	.92
4. Joe DiMaggio	.89
5. Babe Ruth	.88
6. Jimmie Foxx	.83
7. Al Simmons	.82
8. Ted Williams	.80
9. Ed Delahanty	.80
10. Hack Wilson	.79
11. Bob Meusel	.76

INDIVIDUAL BATTING (LIFETIME), *cont.*

12. Cap Anson .75
13. Hal Trosky .75
14. Hugh Duffy .75
15. Harry Heilmann .72
16. Rudy York .72
17. Jim Bottomley .71
18. Johnny Mize .71
19. Don Mattingly .71
20. Roy Campanella .70

21. Goose Goslin .70
22. Rogers Hornsby .70
23. Earl Averill .70
24. Joe Medwick .70
25. Hank Aaron .70
26. Jim Rice .69
27. Ralph Kiner .69
28. Bob Johnson .69
29. Chuck Klein .69
30. Tony Lazzeri .68

31. Vern Stephens .68
32. Mel Ott .68
33. Bill Dickey .68
34. Del Ennis .67
35. Yogi Berra .67

RUNS

1. Ty Cobb 2245
2. Babe Ruth 2174
3. Hank Aaron 2174
4. Pete Rose 2165
5. Willie Mays 2062
6. Stan Musial 1949
7. Lou Gehrig 1888
8. Tris Speaker 1881
9. Mel Ott 1859
10. Frank Robinson 1829

11. Eddie Collins 1818
12. Carl Yastrzemski 1816
13. Ted Williams 1798
14. Charlie Gehringer 1774
15. Jimmie Foxx 1751
16. Honus Wagner 1735
17. Willie Keeler 1727
18. Cap Anson 1719
19. Jesse Burkett 1718
20. Billy Hamilton 1692

21. Bid McPhee 1684
22. Mickey Mantle 1677
23. Joe Morgan 1650
24. Jimmy Ryan 1643
25. George Van Haltren 1639
26. Paul Waner 1626
27. Al Kaline 1622
28. Fred Clarke 1621
29. Roger Connor 1620
30. Lou Brock 1610

31. Ed Delahanty 1601
32. Jake Beckley 1600
33. Bill Dahlen 1590
34. Rogers Hornsby 1579
35. Hugh Duffy 1551
36. Reggie Jackson 1551
37. Max Carey 1545
38. George Davis 1544
39. Frankie Frisch 1532
40. Dan Brouthers 1523

41. Tom Brown 1521
42. Sam Rice 1515
43. Eddie Mathews 1509
44. Al Simmons 1507
45. Mike Schmidt 1506
46. Nap Lajoie 1503
47. Harry Stovey 1492

48. Goose Goslin 1483
49. Arlie Latham 1478
50. Herman Long 1459

51. Jim O'Rourke 1446
52. Harry Hooper 1429
53. Dummy Hoy 1426
54. Joe Kelley 1424
54. Rod Carew 1424
56. Roberto Clemente 1416
57. Billy Williams 1410
58. Monte Ward 1408
59. Mike Griffin 1406
60. Sam Crawford 1393

61. Joe DiMaggio 1390
62. Dwight Evans 1369
63. Vada Pinson 1366
64. King Kelly 1357
64. Doc Cramer 1357
66. Tommy Leach 1355
67. Darrell Evans 1344
68. Pee Wee Reese 1338
69. Robin Yount 1335
69. Luis Aparicio 1335

71. Lave Cross 1333
72. George Gore 1327
73. Richie Ashburn 1322
74. Luke Appling 1319
75. Patsy Donovan 1318
76. Dave Winfield 1314
77. Mike Tiernan 1313
78. Kiki Cuyler 1305
78. Ernie Banks 1305
80. George Brett 1300

81. Jimmy Sheckard 1296
82. Harry Heilmann 1291
83. Zack Wheat 1289
84. Heinie Manush 1287
85. George Sisler 1284
86. Harmon Killebrew 1283
87. Donie Bush 1280
88. Nellie Fox 1279
89. Fred Tenney 1275
90. Tony Perez 1272

91. Sam Thompson 1263
92. Duke Snider 1259
93. Bobby Bonds 1258
94. Rabbit Maranville 1255
95. Jim Rice 1249
96. Enos Slaughter 1247
97. Bob Johnson 1239
97. Stan Hack 1239
99. Joe Kuhel 1236
99. Don Baylor 1236

101. Joe Cronin 1233
102. Brooks Robinson 1232
103. Willie McCovey 1229
104. Ed McKean 1227
105. Earl Averill 1224
106. Red Schoendienst 1223
107. Willie Davis 1217
108. Eddie Yost 1215
109. Cupid Childs 1214
110. Lloyd Waner 1201

111. Joe Medwick 1198
112. Mickey Vernon 1196
113. Willie Stargell 1195
114. Graig Nettles 1193
115. Al Oliver 1189
115. Rusty Staub 1189
117. George Burns 1188
117. Tommy Corcoran 1188
119. Earle Combs 1186
120. Fielder Jones 1184
120. Joe Judge 1184

122. Pie Traynor 1183
123. Bert Campaneris 1181
124. Jim Bottomley 1177
125. Yogi Berra 1175
126. Buddy Myer 1174
127. Arky Vaughan 1173
128. Rickey Henderson 1171
129. Chuck Klein 1168
130. Jack Glasscock 1163

130. Billy Herman 1163
130. Jim Gilliam 1163
133. Carlton Fisk 1155
134. Dave Parker 1154
135. Lu Blue 1151
136. Buddy Bell 1150
137. Ben Chapman 1144
138. Steve Garvey 1143
139. Joe Sewell 1141
140. Ron Santo 1138

141. Minnie Minoso 1136
142. Bobby Lowe 1131
142. Orlando Cepeda 1131
144. Dick Bartell 1130
145. Buck Ewing 1129
146. Wally Moses 1124
147. Reggie Smith 1123
148. Hardy Richardson 1120
148. Bill Terry 1120
150. Johnny Mize 1118

151. Jake Daubert 1117
151. Keith Hernandez 1117
153. Toby Harrah 1115
154. Eddie Murray 1114
155. Sherry Magee 1112
156. Jimmy Dykes 1108
157. Jimmy Wynn 1105
157. Gil Hodges 1105
159. Ken Boyer 1104
160. Ken Griffey 1100

161. Dick Allen 1099
161. Edd Roush 1099
163. Willie Randolph 1098
164. Fred Pfeffer 1094
164. Bobby Doerr 1094
166. Amos Otis 1092
167. Johnny Bench 1091
168. Tommy Tucker 1084
168. Cesar Cedeno 1084
170. Paul Hines 1083

170. Gary Matthews 1083
172. Ted Simmons 1074
173. Bill Buckner 1073
174. Billy Nash 1072
175. Harlond Clift 1070
176. Tommy McCarthy 1069
177. Maury Wills 1067
178. Kip Selbach 1065
178. Dale Murphy 1065
180. Alvin Dark 1064

180. Bob Elliott 1064
182. Charlie Jamieson 1062
183. Bobby Wallace 1059
184. Andre Dawson 1058
185. Jimmy Collins 1055
186. Hank Greenberg 1051
187. Dave Bancroft 1048
188. Dom DiMaggio 1046
188. Norm Cash 1046
190. Fred Lynn 1045

191. Mickey Cochrane 1041
192. Dixie Walker 1037
193. Jose Cruz 1036
194. Bobby Grich 1033
195. John McGraw 1024
195. Cy Williams 1024

197. Davey Lopes 1023
198. Tom Daly 1022
199. Kid Gleason 1020
200. Cecil Cooper 1012

200. Brian Downing 1012
202. Willie Wilson 1011
203. Roy Thomas 1010
204. Marty McManus 1008
205. Frankie Crosetti 1006
205. Roger Peckinpaugh 1006
207. Tony Taylor 1005
208. Augie Galan 1004
208. Clyde Milan 1004
210. Vern Stephens 1001

RUNS PER 9 INNINGS

1. Billy Hamilton 1.06
2. George Gore 1.01
3. Harry Stovey 1.00
4. King Kelly .93
5. Mike Griffin .93
6. Dan Brouthers .91
7. Arlie Latham .91
8. Sam Thompson .90
9. Hugh Duffy .89
10. Mike Tiernan .89

11. Ed Delahanty .87
12. Lou Gehrig .87
13. Babe Ruth .87
14. Buck Ewing .86
15. Abner Dalrymple .85
16. Tom Brown .85
17. Hardy Richardson .84
18. Tommy McCarthy .84
19. Tip O'Neill .83
20. Denny Lyons .83

21. Jesse Burkett .83
22. Cupid Childs .83
23. Curt Welch .83
24. George Van Haltren .83
25. Jimmy Ryan .82
26. Earle Combs .82
27. Jim O'Rourke .82
28. Willie Keeler .81
29. Roger Connor .81
30. Pete Browning .81

31. Red Rolfe .80
32. Joe DiMaggio .80
33. Rickey Henderson .80
34. Dummy Hoy .79
35. Bid McPhee .79

BASES ON BALLS

1. Babe Ruth 2056
2. Ted Williams 2019
3. Joe Morgan 1865
4. Carl Yastrzemski 1845
5. Mickey Mantle 1734
6. Mel Ott 1708
7. Eddie Yost 1614
8. Darrell Evans 1605
9. Stan Musial 1599
10. Pete Rose 1566

11. Harmon Killebrew 1559
12. Lou Gehrig 1508
13. Mike Schmidt 1507
14. Eddie Collins 1503
15. Willie Mays 1463
16. Jimmie Foxx 1452
17. Eddie Mathews 1444
18. Frank Robinson 1420
19. Hank Aaron 1402

20. Tris Speaker 1381
21. Reggie Jackson 1375
22. Willie McCovey 1345
23. Luke Appling 1302
24. Al Kaline 1277
25. Dwight Evans 1270
26. Ken Singleton 1263
27. Rusty Staub 1255
28. Ty Cobb 1249
29. Jimmy Wynn 1224
30. Pee Wee Reese 1210

31. Richie Ashburn 1198
32. Billy Hamilton 1187
33. Charlie Gehringer 1185
34. Donie Bush 1158
35. Max Bishop 1153
35. Toby Harrah 1153
37. Harry Hooper 1136
38. Jimmy Sheckard 1135
39. Ron Santo 1108
40. Lu Blue 1092

40. Stan Hack 1092
42. Paul Waner 1091
43. Graig Nettles 1088
44. Bobby Grich 1087
45. Willie Randolph 1083
46. Bob Johnson 1073
47. Harlond Clift 1070
48. Bill Dahlen 1064
49. Joe Cronin 1059
50. Keith Hernandez 1056

51. Ron Fairly 1052
52. Billy Williams 1045
53. Norm Cash 1043
54. Roy Thomas 1042
55. Eddie Joost 1041
56. Max Carey 1040
57. Rogers Hornsby 1038
58. Jim Gilliam 1036
59. Sal Bando 1031
60. Jesse Burkett 1029

61. Brian Downing 1027
62. Enos Slaughter 1019
63. Rod Carew 1018
64. Ron Cey 1012
65. Ralph Kiner 1011
66. Jack Clark 1006
67. Dummy Hoy 1004
68. Miller Huggins 1002
68. Roger Connor 1002
70. Boog Powell 1001

BB AVERAGE

1. Ted Williams .208
2. Max Bishop .204
3. Babe Ruth .197
4. Eddie Stanky .188
5. Gene Tenace .183
6. Eddie Yost .180
7. Mickey Mantle .176
8. Joe Morgan .167
9. Earl Torgeson .165
10. Roy Thomas .164

11. Ralph Kiner .163
12. Harmon Killebrew .161
13. Billy Hamilton .159
14. Lou Gehrig .159
15. Elmer Valo .158
16. Harlond Clift .157
17. Eddie Joost .157
18. Lu Blue .156
19. Jimmy Wynn .155
20. Mel Ott .153

INDIVIDUAL BATTING (LIFETIME), *cont.*

21. Mike Schmidt .153
22. Rickey Henderson .153
23. Miller Huggins .153
24. Darrell Evans .152
25. Jimmie Foxx .151
26. Dolf Camilli .150
27. Cupid Childs .150
28. Ken Singleton .149
29. Elbie Fletcher .149
30. Jack Clark .148

31. Mike Hargrove .148
32. Topsy Hartsel .147
33. Dwayne Murphy .146
34. Jason Thompson .145
35. Eddie Mathews .145

STOLEN BASES
1. Lou Brock 938
2. Ty Cobb 892
3. Rickey Henderson 871
4. Eddie Collins 743
5. Max Carey 738
6. Honus Wagner 703
7. Joe Morgan 689
8. Bert Campaneris 649
9. Willie Wilson 588
10. Maury Wills 586

11. Tim Raines 585
12. Davey Lopes 557
13. Cesar Cedeno 550
14. Luis Aparicio 506
15. Clyde Milan 495
16. Omar Moreno 487
17. Vince Coleman 472
18. Bobby Bonds 461
19. Jimmy Sheckard 460
20. Ron LeFlore 455

21. Sherry Magee 441
22. Tris Speaker 433
23. Ozzie Smith 432
24. Bob Bescher 428
25. Frankie Frisch 419
26. Tommy Harper 408
27. Frank Chance 405
28. Donie Bush 403
29. Willie Davis 398
30. Billy North 395

31. Dave Collins 388
32. Freddie Patek 385
33. George Burns 383
34. Sam Mertes 377
35. George Sisler 375
35. Harry Hooper 375
37. Sam Crawford 366
38. Hal Chase 363
39. Tommy Leach 361
40. Nap Lajoie 355

41. Rod Carew 353
42. Sam Rice 351
43. Fred Clarke 350
44. George Case 349
45. Paul Molitor 344
46. Julio Cruz 343
47. Amos Otis 341
48. Willie Mays 338
49. Lonnie Smith 337
50. Joe Tinker 336

51. Elmer Flick 334
52. Steve Sax 333
53. Jose Cardenal 329
54. Kiki Cuyler 328
55. Miller Huggins 324
55. Johnny Evers 324

57. Red Murray 321
57. Dave Concepcion 321
59. Larry Bowa 318
60. Jose Cruz 317

61. Hans Lobert 316
62. Buck Herzog 312
63. Claudell Washington 309
64. Brett Butler 307
65. Vada Pinson 305
66. Frank Taveras 300

PINCH HITS
1. Manny Mota 150
2. Smoky Burgess 145
3. Greg Gross 143
4. Jose Morales 123
5. Jerry Lynch 116
6. Red Lucas 114
7. Steve Braun 113
8. Terry Crowley 108
9. Gates Brown 107
10. Mike Lum 103

11. Rusty Staub 100
12. Vic Davalillo 95
12. Larry Biittner 95
14. Jerry Hairston 94
14. Jim Dwyer 94
16. Dave Philley 93
16. Denny Walling 93
16. Joel Youngblood 93
19. Jay Johnstone 92
20. Ed Kranepool 90

20. Elmer Valo 90
20. Jesus Alou 82
22. Kurt Bevacqua 82
22. Tim McCarver 82
25. Dalton Jones 81
25. Tito Francona 81
27. Thad Bosley 79
27. Tom Hutton 79
27. Dave Collins 79
30. Enos Slaughter 77

31. Bob Fothergill 76
31. George Crowe 76
31. Harry Spilman 76
31. Lee Mazzilli 76
35. Wallace Johnson 74
36. Jerry Turner 73
37. Mike Jorgensen 72
38. Ed Kirkpatrick 71
38. Jimmy Stewart 71
40. Bob Skinner 69

40. Dane Iorg 69
42. Cliff Johnson 68
42. Champ Summers 68
42. Ron Fairly 68
45. Oscar Gamble 67
46. Merv Rettenmund 66
46. Bob Johnson 66
46. Willie McCovey 66
46. Ernie Lombardi 66
46. Ken Boswell 66

51. Gene Woodling 65
51. Lee Lacy 65
51. Jim Wohlford 65
54. Tommy Davis 63
54. Tony Taylor 63
54. Julio Becquer 63
54. Jim King 63
57. Peanuts Lowrey 62
58. Bob Bailey 62
58. Vic Wertz 62

58. Bob Hale 62
62. Ken Griffey 61
62. Mike Vail 61
64. Ty Cline 60
65. Ron Northey 59
65. Sam Leslie 59
65. Russ Nixon 59
65. Duke Snider 59
65. Johnny Grubb 59
65. Clarence Gaston 59

65. Gene Clines 59
72. Tom Paciorek 58
72. Bill Buckner 58
72. Red Ruffing 58
75. Ham Hyatt 57
75. Wes Covington 57
75. Lee Maye 57
78. Red Schoendienst 56
78. Jose Pagan 56
78. Fred Whitfield 56

78. Charlie Maxwell 56
78. Walker Cooper 56
78. Dave Bergman 56
84. Billy Sullivan 55
84. Jerry Mumphrey 55
84. Earl Torgeson 55
84. Bob Cerv 55
84. Richie Hebner 55
84. Len Gabrielson 55
84. John Lowenstein 55

84. Willie Stargell 55
84. Dusty Rhodes 55
84. Danny Heep 55
84. Phil Gagliano 55
95. Frenchy Bordagaray 54
95. Rick Miller 54
95. Debs Garms 54
95. Willie Smith 54
95. Del Unser 54
100. Johnny Mize 53

100. Ted Kluszewski 53
100. Lenny Green 53
100. Scot Thompson 53
104. Dom Dallessandro 52
104. Walt Williams 52
104. Irv Noren 52
104. Larry Stahl 52
108. Harvey Hendrick 51
108. Terry Puhl 51
108. Glenn Adams 51

108. Pat Kelly 51
108. Terry Whitfield 51
108. Dick Williams 51
108. Hal McRae 51
108. Max Venable 51
108. John Milner 51
117. Jose Cardenal 50
117. Tim Flannery 50

PH BATTING AVERAGE
1. Tommy Davis .320
2. Frenchy Bordagaray .312
3. Frankie Baumholtz .307
4. Red Schoendienst .303
5. Bob Fothergill .300
6. Dave Philley .299
7. Manny Mota .297
8. Ted Easterly .296
9. Rance Mulliniks .296
10. Harvey Hendrick .295

11. Larry Herndon .294
12. Manny Sanguillen .288
13. Thad Bosley .286

14. Smoky Burgess .286
15. Rick Miller .286
16. Ken Griffey .284
17. Johnny Mize .283
18. Terry Puhl .282
19. Bubba Morton .281
20. Steve Braun .281

21. Don Mueller .280
22. Rusty Staub .279
23. Mickey Vernon .279
24. Denny Walling .278
25. Wallace Johnson .278
26. Gene Woodling .278
27. Bobby Adams .277
28. Ed Kranepool .277
29. Jose Morales .276
30. Ron Northey .276

31. Glenn Adams .276
32. Candy Maldonado .276
33. Bill Stein .274
34. Merv Rettenmund .274
35. Sam Leslie .273

FEWEST STRIKEOUTS PER AT BAT
1. Joe Sewell .016
2. Willie Keeler .019
3. Lloyd Waner .022
4. Nellie Fox .023
5. Tommy Holmes .024
6. Lave Cross .028
7. Tris Speaker .028
8. Stuffy McInnis .028
9. Andy High .030
10. Sam Rice .030

11. Doggie Miller .030
12. Frankie Frisch .030
13. Jack Glasscock .031
14. Lou Bierbauer .032
15. Edd Roush .032
16. Charlie Comiskey .033
17. Frank McCormick .033
18. Don Mueller .033
19. Cap Anson .034
20. Billy Southworth .034

21. Jack Tobin .034
22. Rip Radcliff .035
23. Dan Brouthers .035
24. Ed McKean .036
25. Jack McCarthy .036
26. Pie Traynor .037
27. Patsy Donovan .038
28. Doc Cramer .038
29. Fielder Jones .038
30. Sam Thompson .038

31. Carson Bigbee .038
32. Cupid Childs .039
33. Eddie Collins .039
34. Steve Brodie .039
35. Hank Severeid .039

MOST STRIKEOUTS PER AT BAT
1. Gorman Thomas .286
2. Dave Kingman .272
3. Reggie Jackson .263
4. Bobby Bonds .249
5. Rick Monday .247
6. Dick Allen .246
7. Donn Clendenon .245
8. Willie Stargell .244
9. Woodie Held .235

10. Tony Armas .233
11. Greg Luzinski .230
12. Gene Tenace .227
13. Mike Schmidt .225
14. Frank Howard .225
15. Larry Hisle .224
16. Deron Johnson .222
17. Dale Murphy .222
18. Kirk Gibson .222
19. Dwayne Murphy .219
20. Jimmy Wynn .214

21. Mickey Mantle .211
22. Harmon Killebrew .209
23. Lee May .206
24. Bob Allison .205
25. Lance Parrish .205
26. Jeff Burroughs .205
27. Doug Rader .203
28. Wally Post .203
29. George Foster .202
30. Larry Parrish .200

31. Ron LeFlore .199
32. Lloyd Moseby .198
33. Jeffrey Leonard .198
34. Dick Green .196
35. Jack Clark .196

STRIKEOUTS
1. Reggie Jackson 2597
2. Willie Stargell 1936
3. Mike Schmidt 1883
4. Tony Perez 1867
5. Dave Kingman 1816
6. Bobby Bonds 1757
7. Lou Brock 1730
8. Mickey Mantle 1710
9. Harmon Killebrew 1699
10. Lee May 1570

10. Dwight Evans 1570
12. Dick Allen 1556
13. Willie McCovey 1550
14. Frank Robinson 1532
15. Willie Mays 1526
16. Rick Monday 1513
17. Dale Murphy 1497
18. Greg Luzinski 1495
19. Eddie Mathews 1487
20. Frank Howard 1460

21. Jimmy Wynn 1427
22. Jim Rice 1423
23. George Foster 1419
24. George Scott 1418
25. Darrell Evans 1410
26. Carl Yastrzemski 1393
27. Hank Aaron 1383
28. Larry Parrish 1359
29. Ron Santo 1343
30. Gorman Thomas 1339

31. Dave Parker 1337
32. Babe Ruth 1330
33. Deron Johnson 1318
34. Willie Horton 1313
35. Jimmie Foxx 1311
36. Bobby Grich 1278
37. Johnny Bench 1278
38. Ken Singleton 1246
39. Claudell Washington 1241
40. Duke Snider 1237

41. Ernie Banks 1236
42. Ron Cey 1235
43. Roberto Clemente 1230
44. Boog Powell 1226

INDIVIDUAL BATTING (LIFETIME), *cont.*

45.	Dave Winfield	1224
46.	Graig Nettles	1209
47.	Tony Armas	1201
48.	Vada Pinson	1196
49.	Dave Concepcion	1186
50.	Carlton Fisk	1178
51.	Orlando Cepeda	1169
52.	Lance Parrish	1148
53.	Pete Rose	1143
54.	Bert Campaneris	1142
55.	Donn Clendenon	1140
56.	Gil Hodges	1137
57.	Jeff Burroughs	1135
57.	Leo Cardenas	1135
59.	Andre Dawson	1134
60.	Jack Clark	1130
61.	Bob Bailey	1126
62.	Gary Matthews	1125
63.	Jim Fregosi	1097
64.	Joe Torre	1094
65.	Norm Cash	1091
66.	Tony Taylor	1083
67.	Tommy Harper	1080
68.	Fred Lynn	1073
69.	Don Baylor	1068
70.	Johnny Callison	1064
71.	Joe Adcock	1059
72.	Doug Rader	1055
73.	Billy Williams	1046
74.	Bob Allison	1033
75.	Jose Cruz	1031
76.	Reggie Smith	1030
77.	Rod Carew	1028
78.	Darrell Porter	1025
79.	Al Kaline	1020
80.	Ken Boyer	1017
81.	Lloyd Moseby	1015
81.	Joe Morgan	1015
83.	George Hendrick	1013
84.	Eddie Murray	1012
85.	Larry Doby	1011
86.	Amos Otis	1008
86.	Robin Yount	1008
88.	Frank White	1003
88.	Steve Garvey	1003

INDIVIDUAL PITCHING (LIFETIME)

WINS
1. Cy Young 511
2. Walter Johnson 416
3. Christy Mathewson 373
3. Grover Alexander 373
5. Warren Spahn 363
6. Kid Nichols 361
6. Pud Galvin 361
8. Tim Keefe 342
9. Steve Carlton 329
10. Eddie Plank 327
11. John Clarkson 326
12. Don Sutton 324
13. Phil Niekro 318
14. Gaylord Perry 314
15. Old Hoss Radbourn 311
15. Tom Seaver 311
17. Mickey Welch 308
18. Lefty Grove 300
18. Early Wynn 300
20. Nolan Ryan 289
21. Tommy John 288
22. Robin Roberts 286
23. Tony Mullane 285
24. Ferguson Jenkins 284
25. Jim Kaat 283
26. Red Ruffing 273
27. Bert Blyleven 271
28. Burleigh Grimes 270
29. Jim Palmer 268
30. Bob Feller 266
30. Eppa Rixey 266
32. Jim McCormick 265
33. Gus Weyhing 264
34. Ted Lyons 260
35. Red Faber 254
36. Carl Hubbell 253
37. Bob Gibson 251
38. Vic Willis 248
39. Joe McGinnity 247
39. Jack Quinn 247
41. Amos Rusie 246
42. Jack Powell 245
43. Juan Marichal 243
44. Clark Griffith 240
44. Herb Pennock 240
46. Three Finger Brown 239
47. Waite Hoyt 237
48. Whitey Ford 236
49. Charlie Buffinton 232
50. Will White 229
50. Luis Tiant 229
50. Sad Sam Jones 229
53. George Mullin 228
54. Catfish Hunter 224
54. Jim Bunning 224
56. Paul Derringer 223
56. Mel Harder 223
58. Hooks Dauss 222
58. Jerry Koosman 222
60. Joe Niekro 221
61. Jerry Reuss 220
62. Bob Caruthers 218
62. Earl Whitehill 218
64. Freddie Fitzsimmons 217
64. Mickey Lolich 217
66. Wilbur Cooper 216
67. Stan Coveleski 215
67. Jim Perry 215
69. Rick Reuschel 211
69. Billy Pierce 211
69. Bobo Newsom 211
72. Chief Bender 210
72. Jesse Haines 210
74. Vida Blue 209
74. Don Drysdale 209
74. Milt Pappas 209
77. Carl Mays 208
77. Eddie Cicotte 208
79. Silver King 207
79. Bob Lemon 207
79. Hal Newhouser 207
82. Jack Stivetts 204
83. Lew Burdette 203
84. Al Orth 202
85. Rube Marquard 201
85. Charlie Root 201
87. George Uhle 200

WINNING PERCENTAGE
1. Bob Caruthers .692
2. Dave Foutz .690
3. Whitey Ford .690
4. Lefty Grove .680
5. Vic Raschi .667
6. Christy Mathewson .665
7. Larry Corcoran .663
8. Sam Leever .658
9. Sal Maglie .657
10. Sandy Koufax .655
11. Johnny Allen .654
12. Ron Guidry .651
13. Lefty Gomez .649
14. Three Finger Brown .649
15. John Clarkson .648
16. Dizzy Dean .644
17. Grover Alexander .642
18. Deacon Phillippe .639
19. Jim Palmer .638
20. Kid Nichols .634
21. Ed Reulbach .633
22. Joe McGinnity .632
23. Juan Marichal .631
24. Mort Cooper .631
25. Allie Reynolds .630
26. Jesse Tannehill .629
27. Eddie Plank .629
28. Ray Kremer .627
29. Tommy Bond .627
30. Fred Goldsmith .626
31. Clark Griffith .625
32. Don Newcombe .623
33. Chief Bender .623
34. Nig Cuppy .623
35. Jeff Tesreau .623

EARNED RUN AVERAGE
1. Ed Walsh 1.82
2. Addie Joss 1.88
3. Three Finger Brown 2.06
4. Monte Ward 2.10
5. Christy Mathewson 2.13
6. Rube Waddell 2.16
7. Walter Johnson 2.17
8. Orval Overall 2.24
9. Tommy Bond 2.25
10. Will White 2.28
11. Ed Reulbach 2.28
12. Jim Scott 2.32
13. Eddie Plank 2.34
14. Larry Corcoran 2.36
15. Eddie Cicotte 2.37
16. George McQuillan 2.38
17. Ed Killian 2.38
18. Doc White 2.38
19. Nap Rucker 2.42
20. Jeff Tesreau 2.43
21. Jim McCormick 2.43
22. Terry Larkin 2.43
23. Chief Bender 2.46
24. Hooks Wiltse 2.47
25. Sam Leever 2.47
26. Lefty Leifield 2.47
27. Hippo Vaughn 2.49

GAMES
1. Hoyt Wilhelm 1070
2. Kent Tekulve 1050
3. Lindy McDaniel 987
4. Rollie Fingers 944
5. Gene Garber 931
6. Cy Young 906
7. Sparky Lyle 899
8. Jim Kaat 898
9. Don McMahon 874
10. Phil Niekro 864
11. Goose Gossage 853
12. Roy Face 848
13. Tug McGraw 824
14. Walter Johnson 801
15. Gaylord Perry 777
16. Don Sutton 774
17. Darold Knowles 765
18. Tommy John 760
19. Jack Quinn 755
20. Ron Reed 751
21. Warren Spahn 750
22. Tom Burgmeier 745
22. Gary Lavelle 745
24. Guillermo Hernandez 744
25. Steve Carlton 741
26. Ron Perranoski 737
27. Ron Kline 736
28. Clay Carroll 731
29. Mike Marshall 723
30. Charlie Hough 713
31. Johnny Klippstein 711
32. Nolan Ryan 710
33. Stu Miller 704
34. Joe Niekro 702
35. Bill Campbell 700
36. Greg Minton 699
37. Pud Galvin 697
38. Grover Alexander 696
39. Bob Miller 694
40. Grant Jackson 692
40. Eppa Rixey 692
42. Early Wynn 691
43. Eddie Fisher 690
44. Ted Abernathy 681
45. Robin Roberts 676
46. Waite Hoyt 674
47. Red Faber 669
48. Dan Quisenberry 669
49. Dave Giusti 668
50. Ferguson Jenkins 664
51. Bruce Sutter 661
52. Tom Seaver 656
53. Paul Lindblad 653
54. Wilbur Wood 651
55. Sad Sam Jones 647
55. Dave LaRoche 647
55. Jeff Reardon 647
58. Bert Blyleven 644
59. Dutch Leonard 640
59. Gerry Staley 640
61. Diego Segui 639
62. Bob Stanley 637
63. Christy Mathewson 634
64. Charlie Root 632
65. Jim Perry 630
66. Lew Burdette 626
67. Murry Dickson 625
67. Woodie Fryman 625
69. Red Ruffing 624
69. Jerry Reuss 624
71. Eddie Plank 622
72. Kid Nichols 620
72. Dick Tidrow 620
74. Burleigh Grimes 617
74. Herb Pennock 617
76. Lefty Grove 616
77. Terry Forster 614
78. Jerry Koosman 612
79. Bob Friend 602
79. Al Worthington 602
81. Elias Sosa 601
82. Tim Keefe 600
82. Bobo Newsom 600
84. Ted Lyons 594
85. Pedro Borbon 593
86. Jim Bunning 591
87. Dick Farrell 590
88. Moe Drabowsky 589
89. Mickey Lolich 586
89. Lee Smith 586
91. Billy Pierce 585
92. Jim Brewer 584
93. Mel Harder 582
93. Pedro Ramos 582
95. Paul Derringer 579
96. Jack Powell 577
97. Bob Locker 576
98. Stan Bahnsen 574
99. Luis Tiant 573
100. Mudcat Grant 571
101. Bob Feller 570
101. Larry French 570
103. Curt Simmons 569
104. Mickey Welch 564
105. Ray Sadecki 563
106. Doug Bair 562
107. Doyle Alexander 561
108. Larry Jackson 558
108. Jim Palmer 558
110. Jack Russell 557
110. Bob McClure 557
112. Tony Mullane 556
112. Dan Spillner 556
114. Jesse Haines 555
115. Firpo Marberry 551
115. Phil Regan 551
117. Dolf Luque 550
118. Tippy Martinez 546
119. John Hiller 545
119. Al Hrabosky 545
121. Rube Walberg 544
122. Tom Hume 543
123. Guy Bush 542
123. Syl Johnson 542
125. Claude Osteen 541
125. Earl Whitehill 541
125. Dennis Eckersley 541
128. Hooks Dauss 538
128. Gus Weyhing 538
128. Rick Reuschel 538
131. Bobby Shantz 537
132. Rube Marquard 536
133. Carl Hubbell 535
133. Rudy May 535
135. Randy Moffitt 534
136. Red Ames 533
136. Tom Zachary 533
138. John Clarkson 531
139. Camilo Pascual 529
140. Bob Gibson 528
140. Bump Hadley 528
140. Old Hoss Radbourn 528
143. Bill Henry 527
144. Joe Nuxhall 526
145. Dizzy Trout 521
145. Ken Forsch 521
147. Milt Pappas 520
147. Dennis Lamp 520
149. Gary Bell 519
149. Dick Drago 519
151. Don Drysdale 518
151. Dale Murray 518
153. Wilbur Cooper 517
153. Virgil Trucks 517
155. Frank Linzy 516
156. Bill Sherdel 514
156. Dave Smith 514
158. Freddie Fitzsimmons 513
158. Clem Labine 513
158. George Uhle 513
158. Vic Willis 513
162. Harry Gumbert 508
163. Frank Tanana 507
164. Rick Wise 506
165. Billy Hoeft 505
166. Turk Lown 504
167. Eddie Cicotte 502
168. Vida Blue 502
169. Chris Short 501
170. Catfish Hunter 500
170. Eddie Rommel 500

COMPLETE GAMES
1. Cy Young 750
2. Pud Galvin 639
3. Tim Keefe 557
4. Kid Nichols 532
5. Walter Johnson 531
6. Mickey Welch 525
7. Old Hoss Radbourn 489
8. John Clarkson 485
9. Tony Mullane 469
10. Jim McCormick 466
11. Gus Weyhing 448
12. Grover Alexander 438
13. Christy Mathewson 435
14. Jack Powell 422
15. Eddie Plank 412
16. Will White 394
17. Amos Rusie 392
18. Vic Willis 388
19. Warren Spahn 382
20. Jim Whitney 377
21. Adonis Terry 368
22. Ted Lyons 356
23. George Mullin 353
24. Charlie Buffinton 351
25. Chick Fraser 342
26. Clark Griffith 337
27. Red Ruffing 335
28. Silver King 329
29. Al Orth 324
30. Bill Hutchinson 321
31. Guy Hecker 314
31. Joe McGinnity 314
31. Burleigh Grimes 314
34. Red Donahue 312
35. Bill Dinneen 306
36. Robin Roberts 305
37. Gaylord Perry 303
38. Ted Breitenstein 300
38. Lefty Grove 300

INDIVIDUAL PITCHING (LIFETIME), cont.

INNINGS PITCHED

1. Cy Young	7356
2. Pud Galvin	5941
3. Walter Johnson	5923
4. Phil Niekro	5403
5. Gaylord Perry	5351
6. Don Sutton	5280
7. Warren Spahn	5244
8. Steve Carlton	5217
9. Grover Alexander	5189
10. Kid Nichols	5084
11. Tim Keefe	5061
12. Mickey Welch	4802
13. Nolan Ryan	4787
14. Tom Seaver	4783
15. Christy Mathewson	4782
16. Tommy John	4708
17. Bert Blyleven	4703
18. Robin Roberts	4689
19. Early Wynn	4564
20. Tony Mullane	4540
21. John Clarkson	4536
22. Old Hoss Radbourn	4535
23. Jim Kaat	4528
24. Eddie Plank	4505
25. Ferguson Jenkins	4500
26. Eppa Rixey	4495
27. Jack Powell	4388
28. Red Ruffing	4344
29. Gus Weyhing	4324
30. Jim McCormick	4276
31. Burleigh Grimes	4180
32. Ted Lyons	4161
33. Red Faber	4088
34. Vic Willis	3996
35. Jim Palmer	3948
36. Lefty Grove	3941
37. Jack Quinn	3935
38. Bob Gibson	3885
39. Sad Sam Jones	3883
40. Jerry Koosman	3839
41. Bob Feller	3827
42. Amos Rusie	3770
43. Waite Hoyt	3763
44. Jim Bunning	3760
45. Bobo Newsom	3759
46. George Mullin	3687
47. Jerry Reuss	3662
48. Paul Derringer	3645
49. Mickey Lolich	3639
50. Bob Friend	3611
51. Carl Hubbell	3589
52. Joe Niekro	3585
53. Earl Whitehill	3566
54. Herb Pennock	3558
55. Will White	3543
56. Adonis Terry	3523
57. Juan Marichal	3509

STRIKEOUTS

1. Nolan Ryan	5076
2. Steve Carlton	4136
3. Tom Seaver	3640
4. Don Sutton	3574
5. Bert Blyleven	3562
6. Gaylord Perry	3534
7. Walter Johnson	3508
8. Phil Niekro	3342
9. Ferguson Jenkins	3192
10. Bob Gibson	3117
11. Jim Bunning	2855
12. Mickey Lolich	2832
13. Cy Young	2796

14. Warren Spahn	2583
15. Bob Feller	2581
16. Jerry Koosman	2556
17. Tim Keefe	2527
18. Christy Mathewson	2502
19. Don Drysdale	2486
20. Jim Kaat	2461
21. Sam McDowell	2453
22. Luis Tiant	2416
23. Sandy Koufax	2396
24. Robin Roberts	2357
25. Frank Tanana	2345
26. Early Wynn	2334
27. Rube Waddell	2316
28. Juan Marichal	2303
29. Lefty Grove	2266
30. Eddie Plank	2246
31. Tommy John	2245
32. Jim Palmer	2212
33. Grover Alexander	2199
34. Vida Blue	2175
35. Camilo Pascual	2167
36. Bobo Newsom	2082
37. Dazzy Vance	2045
38. Catfish Hunter	2012
39. Billy Pierce	1999
40. Red Ruffing	1987
41. John Clarkson	1978
42. Rick Reuschel	1962
43. Whitey Ford	1956
44. Amos Rusie	1934
45. Jerry Reuss	1906
46. Kid Nichols	1877
47. Charlie Hough	1875
48. Dennis Eckersley	1865
49. Mickey Welch	1850
50. Old Hoss Radbourn	1830
51. Jack Morris	1819
52. Tony Mullane	1812
53. Pud Galvin	1799
54. Hal Newhouser	1796
55. Ron Guidry	1778
56. Rudy May	1760
57. Joe Niekro	1747
58. Ed Walsh	1736
59. Bob Friend	1734
60. Joe Coleman	1728
60. Milt Pappas	1728
62. Chief Bender	1711
63. Larry Jackson	1709
64. Jim McCormick	1704
65. Bob Veale	1703
66. Red Ames	1702
67. Charlie Buffinton	1700
68. Curt Simmons	1697
69. Carl Hubbell	1678
70. Floyd Bannister	1677
71. Tommy Bridges	1674
72. Gus Weyhing	1665
73. Vic Willis	1651
74. Rick Wise	1647
75. Fernando Valenzuela	1644
76. Al Downing	1639
77. Mike Cuellar	1632
78. Chris Short	1629
79. Andy Messersmith	1625
80. Steve Rogers	1621
80. Jack Powell	1621
82. Ray Sadecki	1614
83. Claude Osteen	1612
84. Hoyt Wilhelm	1610
85. Jim Maloney	1605
86. Ken Holtzman	1601
87. Rube Marquard	1593
88. Bob Welch	1587

88. Woodie Fryman	1587
90. Jim Perry	1576
91. Harvey Haddix	1575
92. Jim Whitney	1571
93. Adonis Terry	1555
94. Wild Bill Donovan	1552
95. Dean Chance	1534
95. Virgil Trucks	1534
97. John Candelaria	1532
98. Doyle Alexander	1528
99. Juan Pizarro	1522
100. Jon Matlack	1516
101. Toad Ramsey	1515
101. Bill Singer	1515
103. Sonny Siebert	1512
103. Dave McNally	1512
103. Burleigh Grimes	1512
106. Paul Derringer	1507

STRIKEOUTS PER 9 INNINGS

1. Nolan Ryan	9.54
2. Sandy Koufax	9.28
3. Sam McDowell	8.86
4. J. R. Richard	8.37
5. Bob Veale	7.96
6. Jim Maloney	7.81
7. Goose Gossage	7.59
8. Mario Soto	7.54
9. Sam Jones	7.54
10. Bob Gibson	7.22
11. Steve Carlton	7.14
12. Rube Waddell	7.04
13. Mickey Lolich	7.00
14. Fernando Valenzuela	6.90
15. Rollie Fingers	6.87
16. Tom Seaver	6.85
17. Jim Bunning	6.83
18. Bert Blyleven	6.82
19. Juan Pizarro	6.73
20. Bobby Bolin	6.71
21. Ray Culp	6.69
22. Ron Guidry	6.69
23. Stan Williams	6.66
24. Camilo Pascual	6.66
25. Bob Turley	6.65
26. Don Wilson	6.60
27. Tug McGraw	6.58
28. Denny Lemaster	6.57
29. Andy Messersmith	6.56
30. Mike Scott	6.52
31. Don Drysdale	6.52
32. Al Downing	6.50
33. Toad Ramsey	6.49
34. Floyd Bannister	6.49
35. Diego Segui	6.46

SHUTOUTS

1. Walter Johnson	110
2. Grover Alexander	90
3. Christy Mathewson	80
4. Cy Young	76
5. Eddie Plank	69
6. Warren Spahn	63
7. Tom Seaver	61
8. Bert Blyleven	60
9. Don Sutton	58
10. Nolan Ryan	57
10. Ed Walsh	57
10. Three Finger Brown	57
10. Pud Galvin	57
14. Bob Gibson	56

15. Steve Carlton	55
16. Jim Palmer	53
16. Gaylord Perry	53
18. Juan Marichal	52
19. Rube Waddell	50
19. Vic Willis	50
21. Don Drysdale	49
21. Luis Tiant	49
21. Ferguson Jenkins	49
21. Early Wynn	49
25. Red Ruffing	48
25. Kid Nichols	48
27. Babe Adams	47
27. Jack Powell	47
29. Tommy John	46
29. Addie Joss	46
29. Doc White	46
29. Bob Feller	46
33. Whitey Ford	45
33. Phil Niekro	45
33. Robin Roberts	45
36. Milt Pappas	43
37. Catfish Hunter	42
37. Bucky Walters	42
39. Mickey Lolich	41
39. Hippo Vaughn	41
39. Chief Bender	41
42. Sandy Koufax	40
42. Claude Osteen	40
42. Jim Bunning	40
42. Mel Stottlemyre	40
42. Larry French	40
42. Ed Reulbach	40
42. Mickey Welch	40
42. Tim Keefe	40
50. Sam Leever	39
50. Eppa Rixey	39
52. Jerry Reuss	38
52. Nap Rucker	38
52. Billy Pierce	38
52. Stan Coveleski	38
56. Steve Rogers	37
56. Vida Blue	37
56. Larry Jackson	37
56. John Clarkson	37
60. Camilo Pascual	36
60. Allie Reynolds	36
60. Bill Doak	36
60. Bob Friend	36
60. Curt Simmons	36
60. Mike Cuellar	36
60. Eddie Cicotte	36
60. Sad Sam Jones	36
60. Carl Hubbell	36
60. Wilbur Cooper	36
60. Tommy Bond	36
60. Will White	36
72. Virgil Trucks	35
72. Jack Coombs	35
72. Joe Bush	35
72. Herb Pennock	35
72. Jack Chesbro	35
72. Wild Bill Donovan	35
72. Lefty Grove	35
72. Burleigh Grimes	35
72. George Mullin	35
72. Old Hoss Radbourn	35
82. Earl Moore	34
82. Jesse Tannehill	34
84. Dean Chance	33
84. Dave McNally	33
84. Mort Cooper	33
84. Jerry Koosman	33
84. Lew Burdette	33
84. Lefty Tyler	33

84. Bob Shawkey	33
84. Tommy Bridges	33
84. Hal Newhouser	33
84. Charlie Buffinton	33
84. Jim McCormick	33
95. Jim Perry	32
95. Frank Tanana	32
95. Lefty Leifield	32
95. Dutch Leonard	32
95. Paul Derringer	32
95. Joe McGinnity	32
101. Ken Holtzman	31
101. Ken Raffensberger	31
101. Jim Kaat	31
101. Bob Lemon	31
101. Lon Warneke	31
101. Bobo Newsom	31
101. Al Orth	31
101. Tony Mullane	31
109. Jim Maloney	30
109. Bob Knepper	30
109. Jon Matlack	30
109. Johnny Vander Meer	30
109. Orval Overall	30
109. Rick Wise	30
109. Art Nehf	30
109. Dutch Leonard	30
109. Rube Marquard	30
109. Dazzy Vance	30
109. Red Faber	30
109. Amos Rusie	30

HITS PER 9 INNINGS

1. Nolan Ryan	6.57
2. Sandy Koufax	6.79
3. J. R. Richard	6.88
4. Andy Messersmith	6.94
5. Hoyt Wilhelm	7.02
6. Sam McDowell	7.03
7. Ed Walsh	7.12
8. Bob Turley	7.18
9. Orval Overall	7.22
10. Jeff Tesreau	7.24
11. Ed Reulbach	7.24
12. Mario Soto	7.26
13. Addie Joss	7.30
14. Goose Gossage	7.37
15. Jim Maloney	7.39
16. Tom Seaver	7.47
17. Rube Waddell	7.48
18. Walter Johnson	7.48
19. Bob Gibson	7.60
20. Don Wilson	7.61
21. Charlie Hough	7.63
22. Jim Palmer	7.63
23. Larry Cheney	7.68
24. Three Finger Brown	7.68
25. Sam Jones	7.68
26. Bob Feller	7.69
27. Johnny Vander Meer	7.69
28. Catfish Hunter	7.72
29. Al Downing	7.72
30. Stan Williams	7.79
30. Bobby Bolin	7.79
32. Rollie Fingers	7.80
33. Barney Pelty	7.80
34. Jim Scott	7.81
35. Dean Chance	7.81

INDIVIDUAL PITCHING (LIFETIME), cont.

BASES ON BALLS

1. Nolan Ryan — 2540
2. Steve Carlton — 1833
3. Phil Niekro — 1809
4. Early Wynn — 1775
5. Bob Feller — 1764
6. Bobo Newsom — 1732
7. Amos Rusie — 1704
8. Gus Weyhing — 1566
9. Red Ruffing — 1541
10. Bump Hadley — 1442

11. Warren Spahn — 1434
12. Earl Whitehill — 1431
13. Tony Mullane — 1409
14. Sad Sam Jones — 1396
15. Tom Seaver — 1390
16. Gaylord Perry — 1379
17. Mike Torrez — 1371
18. Walter Johnson — 1355
19. Don Sutton — 1343
20. Bob Gibson — 1336

21. Chick Fraser — 1332
22. Sam McDowell — 1312
23. Jim Palmer — 1311
24. Mark Baldwin — 1307
25. Adonis Terry — 1301
26. Mickey Welch — 1297
27. Burleigh Grimes — 1295
28. Kid Nichols — 1272
29. Bert Blyleven — 1268
30. Charlie Hough — 1263

30. Joe Bush — 1263
32. Joe Niekro — 1262
33. Allie Reynolds — 1261
34. Tommy John — 1259
35. Bob Lemon — 1251

BASES ON BALLS PER 9 INNINGS

1. Tommy Bond — .58
2. George Bradley — .67
3. Terry Larkin — .71
4. Monte Ward — .92
5. Fred Goldsmith — .96
6. Jim Whitney — 1.06
7. Bobby Mathews — 1.11
8. Pud Galvin — 1.13
9. Deacon Phillippe — 1.25
10. Will White — 1.26

11. Babe Adams — 1.29
12. Jack Lynch — 1.39
13. Addie Joss — 1.43
14. Cy Young — 1.49
15. Guy Hecker — 1.51
16. Lee Richmond — 1.53
17. Jesse Tannehill — 1.55
18. Jim McCormick — 1.58
19. Christy Mathewson — 1.58
20. Red Lucas — 1.61

21. Nick Altrock — 1.62
22. Grover Alexander — 1.65
23. Jumbo McGinnis — 1.65
24. Ernie Bonham — 1.67
25. Ed Morris — 1.67
26. Noodles Hahn — 1.70
27. Charlie Ferguson — 1.72
28. Fritz Peterson — 1.73
29. Robin Roberts — 1.73
30. Old Hoss Radbourn — 1.74

31. Dick Rudolph — 1.77
32. Al Orth — 1.77
33. Stump Weidman — 1.78
34. Pete Donohue — 1.80

35. Jesse Barnes — 1.80

LOSSES

1. Cy Young — 315
2. Pud Galvin — 308
3. Walter Johnson — 279
4. Phil Niekro — 274
5. Gaylord Perry — 265
6. Nolan Ryan — 263
7. Jack Powell — 256
7. Don Sutton — 256
9. Eppa Rixey — 251
10. Robin Roberts — 245

10. Warren Spahn — 245
12. Early Wynn — 244
12. Steve Carlton — 244
14. Jim Kaat — 237
15. Gus Weyhing — 235
16. Bert Blyleven — 231
16. Tommy John — 231
18. Ted Lyons — 230
18. Bob Friend — 230
20. Ferguson Jenkins — 226

21. Tim Keefe — 225
21. Red Ruffing — 225
23. Bobo Newsom — 222
24. Tony Mullane — 220
24. Sad Sam Jones — 217
25. Jack Quinn — 217
27. Chick Fraser — 213
27. Jim McCormick — 213
27. Red Faber — 213
30. Paul Derringer — 212

30. Burleigh Grimes — 212
32. Mickey Welch — 209
32. Jerry Koosman — 209
34. Kid Nichols — 208
34. Grover Alexander — 208

RELIEF WINS

1. Hoyt Wilhelm — 124
2. Lindy McDaniel — 119
3. Rollie Fingers — 107
4. Goose Gossage — 104
5. Sparky Lyle — 99
6. Roy Face — 96
7. Gene Garber — 94
7. Kent Tekulve — 94
9. Mike Marshall — 92
10. Don McMahon — 90

11. Tug McGraw — 89
12. Clay Carroll — 88
13. Bob Stanley — 85
14. Bill Campbell — 80
14. Gary Lavelle — 80
16. Stu Miller — 79
16. Ron Perranoski — 79
16. Tom Burgmeier — 79
19. Johnny Murphy — 73
20. John Hiller — 72

21. Dick Hall — 71
21. Mark Clear — 71
23. Guillermo Hernandez — 70
24. Pedro Borbon — 69
25. Bruce Sutter — 68
26. Al Hrabosky — 64
27. Clem Labine — 63
27. Darold Knowles — 63
29. Dick Farrell — 62
29. Frank Linzy — 62

29. Jim Brewer — 62
29. Grant Jackson — 62
29. Paul Lindblad — 62
29. Eddie Fisher — 62
29. Dave LaRoche — 62
36. Joe Heving — 60
37. Johnny Klippstein — 59
37. Elias Sosa — 59
39. Phil Regan — 58
39. Aurelio Lopez — 58

41. Bob Locker — 57
41. Ted Abernathy — 57
41. Jeff Reardon — 57
44. Mace Brown — 56
44. Gerry Staley — 56
44. Dan Quisenberry — 56
47. Dave Giusti — 55
47. Tippy Martinez — 55
47. Greg Minton — 55
50. Jack Quinn — 54

50. Ron Reed — 54
50. Ron Kline — 54
50. Al Worthington — 54
54. Firpo Marberry — 53
54. Jesse Orosco — 53
54. Dale Murray — 53
54. Doug Bair — 53
58. Sammy Stewart — 52
58. Dick Radatz — 52
58. Ed Roebuck — 52

61. Eddie Rommel — 51
61. Hugh Casey — 51
61. Jim Konstanty — 51
64. Jim Kern — 50
64. Dick Tidrow — 50
64. Lee Smith — 50

RELIEF WINNING PERCENTAGE

1. Hugh Casey — .708
2. Guy Bush — .683
3. Doug Bird — .677
4. Eddie Rommel — .662
5. Grant Jackson — .653
6. Danny Darwin — .652
7. Mace Brown — .651
8. Pedro Borbon — .651
9. Al Hrabosky — .646
10. Al Brazle — .641

11. Hooks Dauss — .635
12. Johnny Murphy — .635
13. Ed Roebuck — .634
14. Dick Hall — .634
15. Joe Heving — .632
16. Aurelio Lopez — .630
17. Clyde Shoun — .621
18. Charlie Root — .618
19. Tom Morgan — .615
20. Harry Gumbert — .611

21. Jack Quinn — .607
22. Tom Burgmeier — .598
23. Dave Giusti — .598
24. Sammy Stewart — .598
25. Mark Clear — .597
26. Johnny Klippstein — .596
27. Ellis Kinder — .595
28. Bob Locker — .594
29. Jim Konstanty — .593
30. Phil Regan — .592

31. Firpo Marberry — .589
32. Fred Gladding — .585
33. Moe Drabowsky — .584
33. Sid Monge — .584
35. Clem Labine — .583

35. John Franco — .583

SAVES

1. Rollie Fingers — 341
2. Goose Gossage — 307
3. Bruce Sutter — 300
4. Jeff Reardon — 266
5. Dan Quisenberry — 244
6. Sparky Lyle — 238
7. Lee Smith — 234
8. Hoyt Wilhelm — 227
9. Gene Garber — 218
10. Roy Face — 193

11. Dave Righetti — 188
11. Mike Marshall — 188
13. Kent Tekulve — 184
14. Tug McGraw — 180
15. Ron Perranoski — 179
16. Dave Smith — 176
17. Lindy McDaniel — 172
18. Steve Bedrosian — 161
19. Stu Miller — 154
20. Don McMahon — 153

21. Greg Minton — 150
22. John Franco — 148
22. Ted Abernathy — 148
24. Guillermo Hernandez — 147
25. Dave Giusti — 145
26. Clay Carroll — 143
26. Darold Knowles — 143
28. Gary Lavelle — 136
29. Jim Brewer — 132
29. Bob Stanley — 132

31. Ron Davis — 130
32. Terry Forster — 127
33. Todd Worrell — 126
33. Dave LaRoche — 126
33. Bill Campbell — 126
36. John Hiller — 125
37. Jack Aker — 123
38. Tom Henke — 122
38. Dick Radatz — 122
40. Jesse Orosco — 119

41. Jay Howell — 117
42. Tippy Martinez — 115
43. Frank Linzy — 111
44. Al Worthington — 110
45. Fred Gladding — 109
46. Wayne Granger — 108
46. Ron Kline — 108
48. Johnny Murphy — 107
49. Bill Caudill — 106
50. Roger McDowell — 103

50. John Wyatt — 103
50. Ron Reed — 103
53. Ellis Kinder — 102
53. Tom Burgmeier — 102
55. Firpo Marberry — 101
56. Dan Plesac — 100
57. Joe Hoerner — 99
58. Dennis Eckersley — 97
58. Al Hrabosky — 97
60. Clem Labine — 96

60. Randy Moffitt — 96
62. Tom Niedenfuer — 95
62. Bob Locker — 95
64. Aurelio Lopez — 93
65. Phil Regan — 92
66. Tom Hume — 92
67. Bobby Thigpen — 91
68. Bill Henry — 90
69. Donnie Moore — 89
70. Jim Kern — 88

71. Cecil Upshaw — 86
71. Ken Sanders — 86
73. Mark Davis — 85
74. Joe Sambito — 84
75. Claude Raymond — 83
75. Dick Farrell — 83
75. Mark Clear — 83
75. Elias Sosa — 83
79. Larry Sherry — 82
80. Doug Bair — 81

80. Eddie Fisher — 81
82. Eddie Watt — 80
82. Pedro Borbon — 80
84. Don Aase — 79
84. Grant Jackson — 79
86. Doug Jones — 78
86. Al Holland — 78
88. Joe Page — 76
88. Tim Burke — 76
88. Tim Stoddard — 76

91. Ed Farmer — 75
91. Neil Allen — 75

WINS PLUS SAVES

1. Rollie Fingers — 448
2. Goose Gossage — 411
3. Bruce Sutter — 368
4. Hoyt Wilhelm — 351
5. Sparky Lyle — 337
6. Jeff Reardon — 323
7. Gene Garber — 312
8. Dan Quisenberry — 300
9. Lindy McDaniel — 291
10. Roy Face — 289

11. Lee Smith — 284
12. Mike Marshall — 280
13. Kent Tekulve — 278
14. Tug McGraw — 269
15. Ron Perranoski — 258
16. Don McMahon — 243
17. Stu Miller — 233
18. Clay Carroll — 231
19. Dave Righetti — 228
20. Dave Smith — 223

21. Bob Stanley — 217
21. Guillermo Hernandez — 217
23. Gary Lavelle — 216
24. Steve Bedrosian — 206
24. Bill Campbell — 206
24. Darold Knowles — 206
27. Ted Abernathy — 205
27. Greg Minton — 205
29. Dave Giusti — 200
30. John Hiller — 197

31. Jim Brewer — 194
32. John Franco — 190
33. Dave LaRoche — 188
34. Tom Burgmeier — 181
35. Johnny Murphy — 180
36. Ron Davis — 177
37. Dick Radatz — 174
37. Terry Forster — 174
39. Frank Linzy — 173
40. Jesse Orosco — 172

41. Jack Aker — 170
41. Tippy Martinez — 170
43. Al Worthington — 164
44. Ron Kline — 162
45. Al Hrabosky — 161
46. Clem Labine — 159
47. Fred Gladding — 157
47. Ron Reed — 157
49. Todd Worrell — 154

INDIVIDUAL PITCHING (LIFETIME), *cont.*

49. Firpo Marberry	154	41. Dave Giusti	535
49. Mark Clear	154	42. Ron Kline	533
52. Bob Locker	152	42. Al Worthington	533
53. Aurelio Lopez	151	42. Randy Moffitt	533
54. Jay Howell	150	45. Dale Murray	517
54. Phil Regan	150	46. Ron Reed	515
56. Tom Henke	149	47. Frank Linzy	514
56. Pedro Borbon	149	48. Dave Smith	513
58. Ellis Kinder	146	49. John Hiller	502
59. Dick Farrell	145	50. Jack Aker	495
60. Wayne Granger	143		
		51. Joe Hoerner	493
60. Eddie Fisher	143	52. Jesse Orosco	492
62. John Wyatt	142	53. Tom Hume	488
62. Elias Sosa	142	54. Tim Stoddard	485
64. Grant Jackson	141	55. Bob McClure	484
65. Bill Caudill	140	56. Bill Henry	483
66. Roger McDowell	139	57. Dick Tidrow	482
66. Dick Hall	139	58. Ron Davis	481
66. Randy Moffitt	139	59. Mark Clear	476
69. Jim Kern	138	60. Clem Labine	475
69. Joe Hoerner	138		
		61. Ron Taylor	474
71. Doug Bair	134	62. Diego Segui	468
72. Tom Hume	133	62. Larry Andersen	468
73. Donnie Moore	132	64. Craig Lefferts	467
74. Tom Niedenfuer	131	65. Ed Roebuck	459
75. Larry Sherry	129	66. Jack Baldschun	457
76. Paul Lindblad	126	67. Dick Farrell	456
77. Jim Konstanty	125	67. Joe Sambito	456
77. Claude Raymond	125	69. Turk Lown	455
77. Johnny Klippstein	125	70. Gerry Staley	454
		71. Wayne Granger	451
		72. Aurelio Lopez	450
RELIEF GAMES		73. Fred Gladding	449
1. Kent Tekulve	1050	74. Phil Regan	446
2. Hoyt Wilhelm	1018	75. Claude Raymond	442
3. Gene Garber	922	76. Steve Bedrosian	438
4. Lindy McDaniel	913	77. Moe Drabowsky	435
5. Rollie Fingers	907	77. Don Elston	435
6. Sparky Lyle	899	79. Dan Spillner	433
7. Don McMahon	872	80. Tom Niedenfuer	432
8. Roy Face	821		
9. Goose Gossage	816	81. John Wyatt	426
10. Tug McGraw	785	81. Frank DiPino	426
		83. Dick Hall	421
11. Darold Knowles	757	83. Bill Caudill	421
12. Tom Burgmeier	742	85. Sid Monge	418
12. Gary Lavelle	742	86. Charlie Hough	416
14. Ron Perranoski	736	87. George Frazier	415
15. Guillermo Hernandez	733	88. Donnie Moore	412
16. Clay Carroll	703	89. Dave Tomlin	408
17. Mike Marshall	699	90. Ken Sanders	407
18. Greg Minton	692		
19. Bill Campbell	691	91. Steve Hamilton	404
20. Dan Quisenberry	669	92. Jim Kern	402
		93. Larry Sherry	400
21. Bruce Sutter	661		
22. Ted Abernathy	647		
22. Jeff Reardon	647		
24. Dave LaRoche	632		
25. Eddie Fisher	627		
26. Paul Lindblad	623		
27. Stu Miller	611		
28. Grant Jackson	609		
29. Elias Sosa	598		
30. Bob Miller	595		
31. Pedro Borbon	589		
32. Lee Smith	580		
33. Bob Locker	576		
34. Terry Forster	575		
35. Doug Bair	557		
36. Bob Stanley	552		
37. Jim Brewer	549		
37. Johnny Klippstein	549		
39. Tippy Martinez	544		
39. Al Hrabosky	544		

INDIVIDUAL FIELDING (LIFETIME)

GAMES

1B
1. Jake Beckley 2377
2. Mickey Vernon 2237
3. Lou Gehrig 2136
4. Charlie Grimm 2129
5. Joe Judge 2084
6. Ed Konetchy 2071
7. Steve Garvey 2061
8. Cap Anson 2058
9. Joe Kuhel 2057
10. Willie McCovey 2054
11. Jake Daubert 2001
12. Stuffy McInnis 1995
13. Chris Chambliss 1986
14. Keith Hernandez 1972
15. George Sisler 1970

2B
1. Eddie Collins 2650
2. Joe Morgan 2527
3. Nellie Fox 2295
4. Charlie Gehringer 2206
5. Bid McPhee 2125
6. Bill Mazeroski 2094
7. Frank White 2071
8. Nap Lajoie 2036
9. Bobby Doerr 1852
10. Willie Randolph 1842
11. Red Schoendienst 1834
12. Billy Herman 1829
13. Frankie Frisch 1775
14. Bobby Grich 1765
15. Johnny Evers 1736

3B
1. Brooks Robinson 2870
2. Graig Nettles 2412
3. Mike Schmidt 2212
4. Buddy Bell 2186
5. Eddie Mathews 2181
6. Ron Santo 2130
7. Eddie Yost 2008
8. Ron Cey 1989
9. Aurelio Rodriguez 1983
10. Sal Bando 1896
11. Pie Traynor 1864
12. Stan Hack 1836
13. Ken Boyer 1785
14. Pinky Higgins 1768
15. Lave Cross 1721

SS
1. Luis Aparicio 2581
2. Larry Bowa 2222
3. Luke Appling 2218
4. Dave Concepcion 2178
5. Rabbit Maranville 2154
6. Bill Dahlen 2132
7. Bert Campaneris 2097
8. Tommy Corcoran 2073
9. Roy McMillan 2028
10. Pee Wee Reese 2014
11. Roger Peckinpaugh 1983
12. Don Kessinger 1955
13. Mark Belanger 1942
14. Chris Speier 1900
15. Honus Wagner 1888

OF
1. Ty Cobb 2933
2. Willie Mays 2843
3. Hank Aaron 2760
4. Tris Speaker 2700
5. Lou Brock 2507
6. Al Kaline 2488
7. Max Carey 2422
8. Vada Pinson 2403
9. Roberto Clemente 2370
10. Zack Wheat 2350
11. Willie Davis 2323
12. Mel Ott 2313
13. Sam Crawford 2297
14. Paul Waner 2288
15. Harry Hooper 2282

C
1. Bob Boone 2185
2. Carlton Fisk 1928
3. Jim Sundberg 1927
4. Al Lopez 1918
5. Gary Carter 1823
6. Rick Ferrell 1806
7. Gabby Hartnett 1790
8. Ted Simmons 1772
9. Johnny Bench 1744
10. Ray Schalk 1726
11. Bill Dickey 1712
12. Yogi Berra 1696
13. Jim Hegan 1629
14. Deacon McGuire 1611
15. Bill Freehan 1581

P
1. Hoyt Wilhelm 1070
2. Kent Tekulve 1050
3. Lindy McDaniel 987
4. Rollie Fingers 944
5. Gene Garber 931
6. Cy Young 906
7. Sparky Lyle 899
8. Jim Kaat 898
9. Don McMahon 874
10. Phil Niekro 864
11. Goose Gossage 853
12. Roy Face 848
13. Tug McGraw 824
14. Walter Johnson 802
15. Gaylord Perry 777

FIELDING AVERAGE

1B
1. Steve Garvey .996
2. Wes Parker .996
3. Dan Driessen .995
4. Jim Spencer .995
5. Frank McCormick .995
6. Keith Hernandez .994
7. Vic Power .994
8. Carl Yastrzemski .994
9. Joe Adcock .994
10. Mike Jorgensen .994
11. Ernie Banks .994
12. John Mayberry .994
13. Lee May .994
14. Ed Kranepool .994
15. Eddie Murray .993

2B
1. Ryne Sandberg .989
2. Tommy Herr .989
3. Jim Gantner .985
4. Frank White .984
5. Bobby Grich .984
6. Jerry Lumpe .984
7. Cookie Rojas .984
8. Dave Cash .984
9. Nellie Fox .984
10. Tommy Helms .983
11. Lou Whitaker .983
12. Dick Green .983
13. Red Schoendienst .983
14. Bill Mazeroski .983
15. Glenn Hubbard .983

3B
1. Brooks Robinson .971
2. Ken Reitz .970
3. George Kell .969
4. Don Money .968
5. Don Wert .968
6. Willie Kamm .967
7. Heinie Groh .967
8. Ken Oberkfell .966
9. Gary Gaetti .966
10. Carney Lansford .965
11. Clete Boyer .965
12. Ken Keltner .965
13. Jim Davenport .964
14. Buddy Bell .964
15. Aurelio Rodriguez .964

SS
1. Larry Bowa .980
2. Ozzie Smith .978
3. Mark Belanger .977
4. Alan Trammell .976
5. Bucky Dent .976
6. Roger Metzger .976
7. Cal Ripken .975
8. Tim Foli .973
9. Dal Maxvill .973
10. Lou Boudreau .973
11. Eddie Miller .972
12. Luis Aparicio .972
13. Roy McMillan .972
14. Rick Burleson .971
15. Bobby Wine .971

OF
1. Terry Puhl .993
2. Pete Rose .991
3. Brett Butler .991
4. Amos Otis .991
5. Joe Rudi .991
6. Mickey Stanley .991
7. Jimmy Piersall .990
8. Jim Landis .989
9. Ken Berry .989
10. Tommy Holmes .989
11. Gene Woodling .989
12. Cesar Geronimo .988
13. Fred Lynn .988
14. Paul Blair .988
15. Tim Raines .988

C
1. Bill Freehan .993
2. Elston Howard .993
3. Jim Sundberg .993
4. Sherm Lollar .992
5. Tom Haller .992
6. Johnny Edwards .992
7. Jerry Grote .991
8. Ernie Whitt .991
9. Gary Carter .991
10. Lance Parrish .991
11. Johnny Bench .990
12. Randy Hundley .990
13. Rick Cerone .990
14. Earl Battey .990
15. Tim McCarver .990

P
1. Don Mossi .990
2. Gary Nolan .990
3. Rick Rhoden .989
4. Lon Warneke .988
5. Jim Wilson .988
6. Woodie Fryman .988
7. Larry Gura .986
8. Grover Alexander .985
9. General Crowder .984
10. Bill Monbouquette .984
11. Harry Brecheen .983
12. Rick Wise .982
13. Mike Flanagan .981
14. Red Lucas .981
15. Ron Guidry .981

PUTOUTS

1B
1. Jake Beckley 23709
2. Ed Konetchy 21361
3. Cap Anson 20761
4. Charlie Grimm 20711
5. Stuffy McInnis 20119
6. Mickey Vernon 19808
7. Jake Daubert 19634
8. Lou Gehrig 19510
9. Joe Kuhel 19386
10. Joe Judge 19277
11. Steve Garvey 18844
12. George Sisler 18814
13. Wally Pipp 18779
14. Jim Bottomley 18337
15. Hal Chase 18177

2B
1. Bid McPhee 6545
2. Eddie Collins 6526
3. Nellie Fox 6090
4. Joe Morgan 5742
5. Nap Lajoie 5407
6. Charlie Gehringer 5369
7. Bill Mazeroski 4974
8. Bobby Doerr 4928
9. Billy Herman 4780
10. Fred Pfeffer 4711
11. Red Schoendienst 4616
12. Frank White 4597
13. Frankie Frisch 4348
14. Willie Randolph 4275
15. Bobby Grich 4217

3B
1. Brooks Robinson 2697
2. Jimmy Collins 2372
3. Eddie Yost 2356
4. Lave Cross 2304
5. Pie Traynor 2291
6. Billy Nash 2219
7. Frank Baker 2154
8. Willie Kamm 2151
9. Eddie Mathews 2049
10. Willie Jones 2045
11. Jimmy Austin 2042
12. Arlie Latham 1975
13. Ron Santo 1955
14. Stan Hack 1944
15. Graig Nettles 1898

SS
1. Rabbit Maranville 5139
2. Bill Dahlen 4850
3. Dave Bancroft 4623
4. Honus Wagner 4576
5. Tommy Corcoran 4550
6. Luis Aparicio 4548
7. Luke Appling 4398
8. Herman Long 4219
9. Bobby Wallace 4142
10. Pee Wee Reese 4040
11. Donie Bush 4038
12. Monte Cross 3974
13. Roger Peckinpaugh 3919
14. Dick Bartell 3872
15. Joe Tinker 3758

OF
1. Willie Mays 7095
2. Tris Speaker 6791
3. Max Carey 6363
4. Ty Cobb 6361
5. Richie Ashburn 6089
6. Hank Aaron 5539
7. Willie Davis 5449
8. Doc Cramer 5412
9. Vada Pinson 5097
10. Al Kaline 5035
11. Zack Wheat 4996
12. Al Simmons 4988
13. Amos Otis 4936
14. Paul Waner 4881
15. Lloyd Waner 4860

C
1. Bob Boone 11017
2. Gary Carter 10626
3. Bill Freehan 9941
4. Carlton Fisk 9847
5. Jim Sundberg 9767
6. Johnny Roseboro 9291
7. Johnny Bench 9260
8. Johnny Edwards 8925
9. Ted Simmons 8906
10. Yogi Berra 8711
11. Tim McCarver 8206

INDIVIDUAL FIELDING (LIFETIME), *CONT.*

12.	Jerry Grote	8081
13.	Bill Dickey	7965
14.	Jim Hegan	7506
15.	Del Crandall	7352

P

1.	Guy Hecker	780
2.	Phil Niekro	386
3.	Ferguson Jenkins	363
4.	Gaylord Perry	349
5.	Don Sutton	334
6.	Tom Seaver	328
7.	Tony Mullane	327
8.	Rick Reuschel	326
9.	Pud Galvin	324
10.	Robin Roberts	316
11.	Chick Fraser	315
12.	Kid Nichols	311
13.	Jim Palmer	292
14.	Juan Marichal	291
14.	Bob Gibson	291

PUTOUTS/GAME

1B

1.	Tom Jones	10.5
2.	Candy LaChance	10.5
3.	George Stovall	10.4
4.	George Kelly	10.4
5.	Wally Pipp	10.3
6.	Ed Konetchy	10.3
7.	Bill Phillips	10.2
8.	Walter Holke	10.2
9.	Charlie Comiskey	10.1
10.	Long John Reilly	10.1
11.	George Burns	10.1
12.	Cap Anson	10.1
13.	Stuffy McInnis	10.1
14.	Bill Terry	10.1
15.	Hal Chase	10.0

2B

1.	Bid McPhee	3.1
2.	Fred Pfeffer	3.1
3.	Cub Stricker	3.0
4.	Gerry Priddy	2.7
5.	Lou Bierbauer	2.7
6.	Bucky Harris	2.7
7.	Bobby Doerr	2.7
8.	Cupid Childs	2.7
9.	Nap Lajoie	2.7
10.	Nellie Fox	2.7
11.	Eddie Stanky	2.6
12.	Billy Herman	2.6
13.	Oscar Melillo	2.6
14.	Buddy Myer	2.6
15.	Joe Quinn	2.5

3B

1.	Jerry Denny	1.6
2.	Denny Lyons	1.5
3.	Billy Nash	1.5
4.	Bill Shindle	1.4
5.	Jimmy Austin	1.4
6.	Jimmy Collins	1.4
7.	Frank Baker	1.4
8.	Hick Carpenter	1.4
9.	Lave Cross	1.3
10.	Hans Lobert	1.3
11.	Willie Kamm	1.3
12.	Harry Steinfeldt	1.3
13.	Bobby Byrne	1.3
14.	Willie Jones	1.3
15.	George Pinckney	1.3

SS

1.	Dave Bancroft	2.5
2.	Honus Wagner	2.4
3.	Rabbit Maranville	2.4
4.	Monte Cross	2.4
5.	Herman Long	2.4
6.	George Davis	2.3
7.	Dick Bartell	2.3
8.	Bill Dahlen	2.3
9.	Bobby Wallace	2.3
10.	Ivy Olson	2.3
11.	George McBride	2.2
12.	Mickey Doolan	2.2
13.	Tommy Corcoran	2.2
14.	Doc Lavan	2.2
15.	Travis Jackson	2.2

OF

1.	Taylor Douthit	3.0
2.	Richie Ashburn	2.9
3.	Mike Kreevich	2.8
4.	Dwayne Murphy	2.8
5.	Dom DiMaggio	2.8
6.	Sammy West	2.7
7.	Sam Chapman	2.7
8.	Fred Schulte	2.7
9.	Lloyd Waner	2.7
10.	Billy North	2.6
11.	Garry Maddox	2.6
12.	Rickey Henderson	2.6
13.	Vince DiMaggio	2.6
14.	Max Carey	2.6
15.	Joe DiMaggio	2.6

C

1.	Johnny Edwards	6.4
2.	Johnny Roseboro	6.3
3.	Bill Freehan	6.3
4.	Jerry Grote	6.0
5.	Mike Scioscia	5.9
6.	Tim McCarver	5.9
7.	Tom Haller	5.8
8.	Gary Carter	5.8
9.	Tony Pena	5.7
10.	Earl Battey	5.7
11.	Elston Howard	5.7
12.	Randy Hundley	5.6
13.	Clay Dalrymple	5.5
14.	Roy Campanella	5.5
15.	Alan Ashby	5.5

P

1.	Guy Hecker	2.3
2.	Mike Boddicker	.8
3.	Dave Foutz	.8
4.	Nick Altrock	.8
5.	Dan Petry	.8
6.	Chick Fraser	.7
7.	Jack Morris	.7
8.	Carl Morton	.7
9.	Mel Stottlemyre	.7
10.	Nixey Callahan	.7
11.	Dave Stieb	.6
12.	Ted Breitenstein	.6
13.	Juan Marichal	.6
14.	Rick Reuschel	.6
15.	Harry Howell	.6

ASSISTS

1B

1.	Keith Hernandez	1662
2.	George Sisler	1528
3.	Mickey Vernon	1448
4.	Eddie Murray	1380
5.	Fred Tenney	1363
6.	Chris Chambliss	1351
7.	Bill Buckner	1345
8.	Norm Cash	1317
9.	Jake Beckley	1315
10.	Joe Judge	1300
11.	Ed Konetchy	1292
12.	Gil Hodges	1281
13.	Stuffy McInnis	1238
14.	Jimmie Foxx	1222
14.	Willie McCovey	1222

2B

1.	Eddie Collins	7630
2.	Charlie Gehringer	7068
3.	Joe Morgan	6967
4.	Bid McPhee	6905
5.	Bill Mazeroski	6685
6.	Nellie Fox	6373
7.	Nap Lajoie	6259
8.	Frank White	6028
9.	Frankie Frisch	6026
10.	Bobby Doerr	5710
11.	Billy Herman	5681
12.	Willie Randolph	5450
13.	Bobby Grich	5381
14.	Red Schoendienst	5243
15.	Rogers Hornsby	5166

3B

1.	Brooks Robinson	6205
2.	Graig Nettles	5299
3.	Mike Schmidt	5045
4.	Buddy Bell	4925
5.	Ron Santo	4581
6.	Eddie Mathews	4323
7.	Aurelio Rodriguez	4150
8.	Ron Cey	4018
9.	Sal Bando	3720
10.	Lave Cross	3703
11.	Jimmy Collins	3702
12.	George Brett	3669
13.	Eddie Yost	3659
14.	Ken Boyer	3652
15.	Arlie Latham	3545

SS

1.	Luis Aparicio	8016
2.	Bill Dahlen	7500
3.	Rabbit Maranville	7354
4.	Luke Appling	7218
5.	Tommy Corcoran	7106
6.	Larry Bowa	6857
7.	Dave Concepcion	6594
8.	Dave Bancroft	6561
9.	Roger Peckinpaugh	6334
10.	Bobby Wallace	6303
11.	Don Kessinger	6212
12.	Roy McMillan	6191
13.	Ozzie Smith	6157
14.	Germany Smith	6154
15.	Herman Long	6130

OF

1.	Tris Speaker	448
2.	Ty Cobb	392
3.	Jimmy Ryan	375
4.	Tom Brown	348
4.	George Van Haltren	348
6.	Harry Hooper	344
7.	Max Carey	339
8.	Jimmy Sheckard	307
9.	Clyde Milan	294
10.	Orator Shaffer	289
11.	King Kelly	287
12.	Sam Thompson	283
13.	Sam Rice	278
14.	Dummy Hoy	273
15.	Jesse Burkett	270

C

1.	Deacon McGuire	1859
2.	Ray Schalk	1811
3.	Steve O'Neill	1698
4.	Red Dooin	1590
5.	Chief Zimmer	1580
6.	Johnny Kling	1552
7.	Ivy Wingo	1487
8.	Wilbert Robinson	1454
9.	Bill Bergen	1444
10.	Duke Farrell	1417
10.	Wally Schang	1417
12.	George Gibson	1386
13.	Oscar Stanage	1379
14.	Mal Kittridge	1363
15.	Lou Criger	1342

P

1.	Cy Young	2013
2.	Christy Mathewson	1503
3.	Grover Alexander	1419
4.	Pud Galvin	1390
5.	Walter Johnson	1348
6.	Burleigh Grimes	1252
7.	George Mullin	1244
8.	Jack Quinn	1240
9.	Ed Walsh	1210
10.	Eppa Rixey	1195
11.	John Clarkson	1143
12.	Carl Mays	1138
13.	Hooks Dauss	1128
14.	Vic Willis	1124
15.	Eddie Plank	1108
15.	Red Faber	1108

ASSISTS/GAME

1B

1.	Keith Hernandez	.8
2.	Ferris Fain	.8
3.	Vic Power	.8
4.	Bill Buckner	.8
5.	Pete O'Brien	.8
6.	George Sisler	.8
7.	Rudy York	.8
8.	Fred Tenney	.8
9.	Dick Stuart	.7
10.	Elbie Fletcher	.7
11.	Mike Hargrove	.7
12.	Eddie Murray	.7
13.	George McQuinn	.7
14.	Bill Terry	.7
15.	George Stovall	.7

2B

1.	Hughie Critz	3.5
2.	Frankie Frisch	3.4
3.	Oscar Melillo	3.4
4.	Lou Bierbauer	3.3
5.	Glenn Hubbard	3.3
6.	Fred Pfeffer	3.3
7.	Rogers Hornsby	3.3
8.	Ryne Sandberg	3.3
9.	Bid McPhee	3.2
10.	Tony Cuccinello	3.2
11.	Cupid Childs	3.2
12.	Charlie Gehringer	3.2
13.	Bill Mazeroski	3.2
14.	Bobby Lowe	3.2
15.	Max Bishop	3.1

3B

1.	Mike Schmidt	2.3
2.	Bill Shindle	2.3
3.	Arlie Latham	2.3
4.	Buddy Bell	2.3
5.	Clete Boyer	2.2
6.	Jimmy Collins	2.2
7.	Graig Nettles	2.2
8.	George Brett	2.2
9.	Darrell Evans	2.2
10.	Brooks Robinson	2.2
11.	Lave Cross	2.2
12.	Ron Santo	2.2
13.	Doug Rader	2.1
14.	Billy Nash	2.1
15.	Bill Bradley	2.1

SS

1.	Germany Smith	3.7
2.	Art Fletcher	3.6
3.	Bill Dahlen	3.5
4.	Dave Bancroft	3.5
5.	Bones Ely	3.5
6.	Travis Jackson	3.5
7.	Ozzie Smith	3.5
8.	George Davis	3.5
9.	Jack Glasscock	3.5
10.	Bobby Wallace	3.5
11.	Tommy Corcoran	3.4
12.	Herman Long	3.4
13.	Rabbit Maranville	3.4
14.	Freddy Parent	3.4
15.	Joe Tinker	3.4

OF

1.	Tommy McCarthy	.2
2.	Chicken Wolf	.2
3.	Pop Corkhill	.2
4.	Sam Thompson	.2

INDIVIDUAL FIELDING (LIFETIME), *CONT.*

5. Tom Brown	.2
6. Curt Welch	.2
7. Jimmy Ryan	.2
8. George Van Haltren	.2
9. George Gore	.2
10. Ed Delahanty	.2
11. Paul Hines	.2
12. Joe Hornung	.2
13. Ned Hanlon	.2
14. Tris Speaker	.2
15. Tilly Walker	.2

C
1. Duke Farrell	1.4
2. Red Dooin	1.3
3. Johnny Kling	1.3
4. Bill Killefer	1.3
5. Oscar Stanage	1.3
6. Chief Zimmer	1.3
7. Jack Warner	1.3
8. Ivy Wingo	1.2
9. Billy Sullivan	1.2
10. George Gibson	1.2
11. Deacon McGuire	1.2
12. Mal Kittridge	1.1
13. Steve O'Neill	1.1
14. Wilbert Robinson	1.1
15. Frank Snyder	1.1

P
1. Addie Joss	3.0
2. Harry Howell	2.8
3. Ed Walsh	2.8
4. Nick Altrock	2.8
5. Willie Sudhoff	2.7
6. Nixey Callahan	2.6
7. George Mullin	2.5
8. Ed Willett	2.5
9. Barney Pelty	2.5
10. Red Donahue	2.5
11. Bill Bernhard	2.4
12. Jack Taylor	2.4
13. Christy Mathewson	2.4
14. Bob Rhoads	2.3
15. Jesse Tannehill	2.3

CHANCES

1B
1. Jake Beckley	25505
2. Ed Konetchy	22877
3. Cap Anson	22299
4. Charlie Grimm	22087
5. Stuffy McInnis	21517
6. Mickey Vernon	21467
7. Jake Daubert	20943
8. Lou Gehrig	20790
9. Joe Kuhel	20722
10. Joe Judge	20719
11. George Sisler	20611
12. Wally Pipp	20099
13. Steve Garvey	19951
14. Hal Chase	19627
15. Fred Tenney	19610

2B
1. Eddie Collins	14591
2. Bid McPhee	14241
3. Joe Morgan	12953
4. Charlie Gehringer	12746
5. Nellie Fox	12672
6. Nap Lajoie	12117
7. Bill Mazeroski	11863
8. Bobby Doerr	10852
9. Billy Herman	10815
10. Frank White	10795
11. Fred Pfeffer	10672
12. Frankie Frisch	10654
13. Red Schoendienst	10029
14. Willie Randolph	9920
15. Bobby Grich	9754

3B
1. Brooks Robinson	9165
2. Graig Nettles	7492
3. Buddy Bell	6979
4. Mike Schmidt	6949
5. Ron Santo	6853
6. Eddie Mathews	6665
7. Jimmy Collins	6539
8. Lave Cross	6401
9. Arlie Latham	6342
10. Eddie Yost	6285
11. Pie Traynor	6140
12. Billy Nash	5952
13. Aurelio Rodriguez	5894
14. Ron Cey	5741
15. Stan Hack	5684

SS
1. Bill Dahlen	13325
2. Rabbit Maranville	13124
3. Luis Aparicio	12930
4. Tommy Corcoran	12612
5. Luke Appling	12259
6. Dave Bancroft	11844
7. Herman Long	11419
8. Honus Wagner	11292
9. Bobby Wallace	11130
10. Donie Bush	10846
11. Roger Peckinpaugh	10806
12. Dave Concepcion	10575
13. Larry Bowa	10382
14. Pee Wee Reese	10319
15. Joe Tinker	10241

OF
1. Tris Speaker	7461
2. Willie Mays	7431
3. Ty Cobb	7024
4. Max Carey	6937
5. Richie Ashburn	6377
6. Hank Aaron	5857
7. Willie Davis	5719
8. Doc Cramer	5702
9. Zack Wheat	5411
10. Vada Pinson	5370
11. Fred Clarke	5300
12. Al Kaline	5278
13. Paul Waner	5254
14. Al Simmons	5251
15. Sam Rice	5234

C
1. Bob Boone	12346
2. Gary Carter	11808
3. Carlton Fisk	10891
4. Jim Sundberg	10855
5. Bill Freehan	10734
6. Johnny Bench	10207
7. Johnny Roseboro	10073
8. Ted Simmons	9951
9. Johnny Edwards	9710
10. Yogi Berra	9619
11. Deacon McGuire	9291
12. Ray Schalk	9157
13. Bill Dickey	9047
14. Tim McCarver	8885
15. Jerry Grote	8794

P
1. Cy Young	2388
2. Pud Galvin	1875
3. Christy Mathewson	1836
4. Walter Johnson	1679
5. Grover Alexander	1633
6. George Mullin	1555
7. Burleigh Grimes	1548
8. Tim Keefe	1531
9. John Clarkson	1526
10. Ed Walsh	1499
11. Tony Mullane	1496
12. Vic Willis	1456
13. Jack Quinn	1451
14. Kid Nichols	1409

CHANCES/GAME

1B
1. Tom Jones	11.4
2. George Stovall	11.3
3. George Kelly	11.1
4. Wally Pipp	11.0
5. Ed Konetchy	11.0
6. Candy LaChance	11.0
7. George Burns	10.9
8. Bill Terry	10.9
9. Fred Tenney	10.9
10. Hal Chase	10.8
11. Cap Anson	10.8
12. Walter Holke	10.8
13. Bill Phillips	10.8
14. Charlie Comiskey	10.8
15. Stuffy McInnis	10.8

2B
1. Fred Pfeffer	6.9
2. Bid McPhee	6.7
3. Cub Stricker	6.6
4. Lou Bierbauer	6.5
5. Cupid Childs	6.3
6. Oscar Melillo	6.2
7. Hughie Critz	6.1
8. Bobby Lowe	6.0
9. Frankie Frisch	6.0
10. Bucky Harris	6.0
11. Nap Lajoie	6.0
12. Gerry Priddy	5.9
13. Billy Herman	5.9
14. Bobby Doerr	5.9
15. Hobe Ferris	5.8

3B
1. Jerry Denny	4.2
2. Bill Shindle	4.1
3. Billy Nash	4.1
4. Arlie Latham	4.0
5. Denny Lyons	4.0
6. Jimmy Collins	3.9
7. Hick Carpenter	3.8
8. Jimmy Austin	3.7
9. Lave Cross	3.7
10. Frank Baker	3.6
11. Bill Bradley	3.6
12. Harry Steinfeldt	3.6
13. George Pinckney	3.6
14. Doc Casey	3.5
15. Art Devlin	3.5

SS
1. Herman Long	6.4
2. Dave Bancroft	6.3
3. Bill Dahlen	6.3
4. George Davis	6.2
5. Bobby Wallace	6.1
6. Rabbit Maranville	6.1
7. Tommy Corcoran	6.1
8. Monte Cross	6.1
9. Bones Ely	6.1
10. Honus Wagner	6.0
11. Germany Smith	6.0
12. Travis Jackson	6.0
13. Art Fletcher	5.9
14. Joe Tinker	5.9
15. Dick Bartell	5.8

OF
1. Taylor Douthit	3.2
2. Richie Ashburn	3.0
3. Dom DiMaggio	3.0
4. Mike Kreevich	2.9
5. Dwayne Murphy	2.9
6. Sam Chapman	2.9
7. Sammy West	2.9
8. Max Carey	2.9
9. Fred Schulte	2.8
10. Lloyd Waner	2.8
11. Vince DiMaggio	2.8
12. Joe DiMaggio	2.8
13. Tris Speaker	2.8
14. Billy North	2.8
15. Terry Moore	2.7

C
1. Johnny Edwards	7.0
2. Johnny Roseboro	6.8
3. Bill Freehan	6.8
4. Mike Scioscia	6.6
5. Jerry Grote	6.5
6. Gary Carter	6.5
7. Tony Pena	6.4
8. Tim McCarver	6.4
9. Tom Haller	6.3
10. Bill Killefer	6.3
11. Earl Battey	6.2
12. Johnny Kling	6.2
13. Clay Dalrymple	6.2
14. Randy Hundley	6.2
15. Elston Howard	6.1

P
1. Guy Hecker	3.8
2. Nick Altrock	3.7
3. Addie Joss	3.6
4. Harry Howell	3.6
5. Ed Walsh	3.5
6. Nixey Callahan	3.5
7. Willie Sudhoff	3.3
8. George Mullin	3.2
9. Barney Pelty	3.2
10. Chick Fraser	3.1
11. Ed Willett	3.0
12. Red Donahue	2.9
13. Bill Bernhard	2.9
14. Jack Taylor	2.9
15. Doc White	2.9

DOUBLE PLAYS

1B
1. Mickey Vernon	2044
2. Joe Kuhel	1769
3. Charlie Grimm	1733
4. Chris Chambliss	1687
5. Keith Hernandez	1626
6. Gil Hodges	1614
7. Eddie Murray	1585
8. Lou Gehrig	1574
9. Jim Bottomley	1560
10. Jimmie Foxx	1528
10. Steve Garvey	1528
12. Joe Judge	1500
13. George Scott	1480
14. George Sisler	1467
15. Willie McCovey	1405

2B
1. Bill Mazeroski	1706
2. Nellie Fox	1619
3. Bobby Doerr	1507
4. Joe Morgan	1505
5. Charlie Gehringer	1444
6. Red Schoendienst	1363
7. Frank White	1330
8. Willie Randolph	1326
9. Bobby Grich	1302
10. Eddie Collins	1215
11. Bid McPhee	1186
12. Billy Herman	1183
13. Joe Gordon	1160
14. Lou Whitaker	1115
15. Frankie Frisch	1060

3B
1. Brooks Robinson	618
2. Graig Nettles	470
3. Mike Schmidt	450
4. Buddy Bell	430
5. Aurelio Rodriguez	408
6. Ron Santo	395
7. Eddie Mathews	369
8. Ken Boyer	355
9. Sal Bando	345
10. Eddie Yost	345
11. Doug DeCinces	331
12. Clete Boyer	315
12. Ron Cey	315

INDIVIDUAL FIELDING (LIFETIME), *CONT.*

	14. Harlond Clift	309
	15. Pie Traynor	308
SS	1. Luis Aparicio	1553
	2. Luke Appling	1424
	3. Roy McMillan	1304
	4. Dave Concepcion	1290
	5. Larry Bowa	1265
	6. Pee Wee Reese	1246
	7. Dick Groat	1237
	8. Phil Rizzuto	1217
	9. Bert Campaneris	1186
	10. Rabbit Maranville	1183
	11. Lou Boudreau	1180
	12. Don Kessinger	1170
	13. Joe Cronin	1165
	14. Ozzie Smith	1134
	15. Garry Templeton	1072
OF	1. Tris Speaker	139
	2. Ty Cobb	107
	3. Max Carey	86
	4. Tom Brown	85
	5. Jimmy Sheckard	81
	5. Harry Hooper	81
	7. Mike Griffin	75
	8. Dummy Hoy	72
	9. Jimmy Ryan	71
	10. Fielder Jones	70
	11. Patsy Donovan	69
	12. Sam Rice	67
	13. George Van Haltren	64
	14. Jesse Burkett	62
	15. Sam Thompson	61
C	1. Ray Schalk	221
	2. Steve O'Neill	175
	2. Yogi Berra	175
	4. Gabby Hartnett	173
	5. Bob Boone	154
	6. Jimmie Wilson	153
	7. Wally Schang	149
	8. Jim Sundberg	144
	9. Rollie Hemsley	143
	10. Deacon McGuire	142
	10. Gary Carter	142
	12. Ivy Wingo	141
	13. Rick Ferrell	139
	14. Luke Sewell	138
	15. Bill Dickey	137
	15. Al Lopez	137
P	1. Phil Niekro	83
	2. Warren Spahn	82
	3. Freddie Fitzsimmons	79
	4. Bob Lemon	78
	5. Bucky Walters	76
	6. Burleigh Grimes	74
	7. Walter Johnson	72
	8. Tommy John	69
	9. Jim Kaat	65
	10. Dizzy Trout	63
	11. Gaylord Perry	58
	12. Ted Lyons	57
	13. Carl Mays	56
	14. Don Drysdale	55
	14. Lew Burdette	55
	14. Eppa Rixey	55

WORLD SERIES BATTING LEADERS (LIFETIME)

BATTING AVERAGE
1. Pepper Martin .418
2. Lou Brock .391
3. Thurman Munson .373
4. George Brett .373
5. Hank Aaron .364
6. Frank Baker .363
7. Roberto Clemente .362
8. Lou Gehrig .361
9. Reggie Jackson .357
10. Carl Yastrzemski .352
11. Earle Combs .350
12. Stan Hack .348
13. Joe Jackson .345
14. Dave Henderson .345
15. Jimmie Foxx .344

TOTAL BASES
1. Mickey Mantle 123
2. Yogi Berra 117
3. Babe Ruth 96
4. Lou Gehrig 87
5. Joe DiMaggio 84
6. Duke Snider 79
7. Hank Bauer 75
8. Reggie Jackson 74
8. Frankie Frisch 74
10. Gil McDougald 72
11. Bill Skowron 69
12. Elston Howard 66
13. Goose Goslin 63
14. Pee Wee Reese 59
15. Lou Brock 57

HOME RUNS
1. Mickey Mantle 18
2. Babe Ruth 15
3. Yogi Berra 12
4. Duke Snider 11
5. Reggie Jackson 10
5. Lou Gehrig 10
7. Frank Robinson 8
7. Bill Skowron 8
7. Joe DiMaggio 8
10. Goose Goslin 7
10. Hank Bauer 7
10. Gil McDougald 7
13. Al Simmons 6
13. Reggie Smith 6
13. Roger Maris 6

BASES ON BALLS
1. Mickey Mantle 43
2. Babe Ruth 33
3. Yogi Berra 32
4. Phil Rizzuto 30
5. Lou Gehrig 26
6. Mickey Cochrane 25
7. Jim Gilliam 23
8. Jackie Robinson 21
9. Gil McDougald 20
10. Gene Woodling 19
10. Joe DiMaggio 19
12. Roger Maris 18
12. Pee Wee Reese 18
14. Gene Tenace 17
14. Ross Youngs 17
14. Gil Hodges 17

SLUGGING AVERAGE
1. Reggie Jackson .755
2. Babe Ruth .744
3. Lou Gehrig .731
4. Dave Henderson .672
5. Al Simmons .658
6. Lou Brock .655
7. Pepper Martin .636
8. Hank Greenberg .624
9. Charlie Keller .611
10. Jimmie Foxx .609
11. Hank Aaron .600
12. Duke Snider .594
13. Dwight Evans .580
14. Steve Yeager .579
15. Willie Stargell .574

HITS
1. Yogi Berra 71
2. Mickey Mantle 59
3. Frankie Frisch 58
4. Joe DiMaggio 54
5. Pee Wee Reese 46
5. Hank Bauer 46
7. Phil Rizzuto 45
7. Gil McDougald 45
9. Lou Gehrig 43
10. Eddie Collins 42
10. Babe Ruth 42
10. Elston Howard 42
13. Bobby Richardson 40
14. Bill Skowron 39
15. Duke Snider 38

HOME RUN PERCENTAGE
1. Babe Ruth 11.6
2. Reggie Jackson 10.2
3. Frank Robinson 8.7
4. Lou Gehrig 8.4
5. Duke Snider 8.3
6. Al Simmons 8.2
6. Reggie Smith 8.2
8. Mickey Mantle 7.8
9. Gene Tenace 7.0
9. Steve Yeager 7.0
11. Charlie Keller 6.9
12. Don Buford 6.9
12. Dave Henderson 6.9
14. Mel Ott 6.6
15. Jimmie Foxx 6.3

STOLEN BASES
1. Lou Brock 14
1. Eddie Collins 14
3. Frank Chance 10
3. Davey Lopes 10
3. Phil Rizzuto 10
6. Honus Wagner 9
6. Frankie Frisch 9
8. Johnny Evers 8
9. Pepper Martin 7
9. Joe Morgan 7
11. Jimmy Slagle 6
11. Vince Coleman 6
11. Bobby Tolan 6
11. Joe Tinker 6
11. Maury Wills 6
11. Jackie Robinson 6

GAMES
1. Yogi Berra 75
2. Mickey Mantle 65
3. Elston Howard 54
4. Hank Bauer 53
4. Gil McDougald 53
6. Phil Rizzuto 52
7. Joe DiMaggio 51
8. Frankie Frisch 50
9. Pee Wee Reese 44
10. Roger Maris 41
10. Babe Ruth 41
12. Carl Furillo 40
13. Jim Gilliam 39
13. Gil Hodges 39
13. Bill Skowron 39

DOUBLES
1. Frankie Frisch 10
1. Yogi Berra 10
3. Pete Fox 9
3. Jack Barry 9
3. Carl Furillo 9
6. Lonnie Smith 8
6. Lou Gehrig 8
6. Duke Snider 8

RUNS BATTED IN
1. Mickey Mantle 40
2. Yogi Berra 39
3. Lou Gehrig 35
4. Babe Ruth 33
5. Joe DiMaggio 30
6. Bill Skowron 29
7. Duke Snider 26
8. Reggie Jackson 24
8. Bill Dickey 24
8. Hank Bauer 24
8. Gil McDougald 24
12. Hank Greenberg 22
13. Gil Hodges 21

STRIKEOUTS
1. Mickey Mantle 54
2. Elston Howard 37
3. Duke Snider 33
4. Babe Ruth 30
5. Gil McDougald 29
6. Bill Skowron 26
7. Hank Bauer 25
8. Reggie Jackson 24
8. Bob Meusel 24
10. Frank Robinson 23
10. George Kelly 23
10. Tony Kubek 23
10. Joe DiMaggio 23
14. Jim Bottomley 22
14. Joe Collins 22
14. Gil Hodges 22

AT BATS
1. Yogi Berra 259
2. Mickey Mantle 230
3. Joe DiMaggio 199
4. Frankie Frisch 197
5. Gil McDougald 190
6. Hank Bauer 188
7. Phil Rizzuto 183
8. Elston Howard 171
9. Pee Wee Reese 169
10. Roger Maris 152
11. Jim Gilliam 147
12. Tony Kubek 146
13. Bill Dickey 145
14. Jackie Robinson 137
15. Duke Snider 133
15. Bill Skowron 133

TRIPLES
1. Tommy Leach 4
1. Billy Johnson 4
1. Tris Speaker 4
4. Buck Freeman 3
4. Freddy Parent 3
4. Chick Stahl 3
4. Bobby Brown 3
4. Dave Concepcion 3
4. Tim McCarver 3
4. Billy Martin 3
4. Lou Gehrig 3
4. Bob Meusel 3
4. Hank Bauer 3
4. Frankie Frisch 3

RUNS
1. Mickey Mantle 42
2. Yogi Berra 41
3. Babe Ruth 37
4. Lou Gehrig 30
5. Joe DiMaggio 27
6. Roger Maris 26
7. Elston Howard 25
8. Gil McDougald 23
9. Jackie Robinson 22
10. Gene Woodling 21
10. Reggie Jackson 21
10. Duke Snider 21
10. Phil Rizzuto 21
10. Hank Bauer 21
15. Eddie Collins 20
15. Pee Wee Reese 20

WORLD SERIES PITCHING LEADERS (LIFETIME)

WINS

1.	Whitey Ford	10
2.	Bob Gibson	7
2.	Red Ruffing	7
2.	Allie Reynolds	7
5.	Lefty Gomez	6
5.	Chief Bender	6
5.	Waite Hoyt	6
8.	Jack Coombs	5
8.	Three Finger Brown	5
8.	Herb Pennock	5
8.	Christy Mathewson	5
8.	Vic Raschi	5
8.	Catfish Hunter	5

GAMES STARTED

1.	Whitey Ford	22
2.	Waite Hoyt	11
2.	Christy Mathewson	11
4.	Chief Bender	10
4.	Red Ruffing	10
6.	Allie Reynolds	9
6.	Catfish Hunter	9
6.	Art Nehf	9
6.	Bob Gibson	9
10.	Bob Turley	8
10.	Rube Marquard	8
10.	Vic Raschi	8
10.	Jim Palmer	8
10.	George Earnshaw	8
10.	Don Sutton	8

STRIKEOUTS

1.	Whitey Ford	94
2.	Bob Gibson	92
3.	Allie Reynolds	62
4.	Sandy Koufax	61
4.	Red Ruffing	61
6.	Chief Bender	59
7.	George Earnshaw	56
8.	Waite Hoyt	49
9.	Christy Mathewson	48
10.	Bob Turley	46
11.	Jim Palmer	44
12.	Vic Raschi	43

BASES ON BALLS

1.	Whitey Ford	34
2.	Allie Reynolds	32
2.	Art Nehf	32
4.	Jim Palmer	31
5.	Bob Turley	29
6.	Paul Derringer	27
6.	Red Ruffing	27
8.	Don Gullett	26
8.	Burleigh Grimes	26
10.	Vic Raschi	25
11.	Carl Erskine	24
12.	Bill Hallahan	23
13.	Waite Hoyt	22
14.	Jack Coombs	21
14.	Chief Bender	21

WINNING PERCENTAGE

1.	Lefty Gomez	1.000
1.	Jack Coombs	1.000
1.	Herb Pennock	1.000
1.	Monte Pearson	1.000
1.	Babe Adams	1.000
1.	Mickey Lolich	1.000
1.	George Pipgras	1.000
1.	Babe Ruth	1.000
1.	Tom Zachary	1.000
1.	Jerry Koosman	1.000
1.	Jesse Barnes	1.000
1.	Ed Reulbach	1.000
1.	Luis Tiant	1.000
1.	Jack Billingham	1.000

COMPLETE GAMES

1.	Christy Mathewson	10
2.	Chief Bender	9
3.	Bob Gibson	8
4.	Red Ruffing	7
4.	Whitey Ford	7
6.	George Mullin	6
6.	Eddie Plank	6
6.	Art Nehf	6
6.	Waite Hoyt	6

MOST STRIKEOUTS PER 9 INNINGS

1.	Bob Gibson	10.22
2.	Sandy Koufax	9.63
3.	Steve Carlton	9.09
4.	Roger Craig	8.54
5.	Jesse Barnes	8.20
6.	Don Drysdale	8.17
7.	Tom Seaver	8.10
8.	George Earnshaw	8.04
9.	Danny Cox	7.71
9.	Bob Turley	7.71
11.	Ron Guidry	7.31
12.	Allie Reynolds	7.22
13.	Bill Dinneen	7.20
14.	Max Lanier	7.11
15.	Monte Pearson	7.07

FEWEST BASES ON BALLS PER 9 INNINGS

1.	Schoolboy Rowe	.39
2.	Deacon Phillippe	.72
3.	Christy Mathewson	.89
4.	Red Faber	1.00
5.	Lefty Grove	1.05
6.	Cy Young	1.06
6.	Scott McGregor	1.06
8.	Ralph Terry	1.17
9.	Carl Mays	1.26
10.	Herb Pennock	1.30
11.	Eddie Cicotte	1.41
12.	Lew Burdette	1.46
13.	Stan Coveleski	1.52
14.	Slim Sallee	1.57
15.	Dizzy Dean	1.57

EARNED RUN AVERAGE

1.	Jack Billingham	.36
2.	Harry Brecheen	.83
3.	Babe Ruth	.87
4.	Sherry Smith	.89
5.	Sandy Koufax	.95
6.	Hippo Vaughn	1.00
7.	Monte Pearson	1.01
8.	Christy Mathewson	1.15
9.	Babe Adams	1.29
10.	Eddie Plank	1.32
11.	Rollie Fingers	1.35
12.	Bill Hallahan	1.36

INNINGS PITCHED

1.	Whitey Ford	146
2.	Christy Mathewson	102
3.	Red Ruffing	86
4.	Chief Bender	85
5.	Waite Hoyt	84
6.	Bob Gibson	81
7.	Art Nehf	79
8.	Allie Reynolds	77
9.	Jim Palmer	65
10.	Catfish Hunter	63
11.	George Earnshaw	63
12.	Joe Bush	61
13.	Vic Raschi	60
14.	Rube Marquard	59
15.	George Mullin	58

SHUTOUTS

1.	Christy Mathewson	4
2.	Three Finger Brown	3
2.	Whitey Ford	3
4.	Bill Hallahan	2
4.	Lew Burdette	2
4.	Bill Dinneen	2
4.	Sandy Koufax	2
4.	Allie Reynolds	2
4.	Art Nehf	2
4.	Bob Gibson	2

LOSSES

1.	Whitey Ford	8
2.	Eddie Plank	5
2.	Schoolboy Rowe	5
2.	Joe Bush	5
2.	Rube Marquard	5
2.	Christy Mathewson	5

GAMES

1.	Whitey Ford	22
2.	Rollie Fingers	16
3.	Allie Reynolds	15
3.	Bob Turley	15
5.	Clay Carroll	14
6.	Clem Labine	13
7.	Waite Hoyt	12
7.	Catfish Hunter	12
7.	Art Nehf	12
10.	Paul Derringer	11
10.	Carl Erskine	11
10.	Rube Marquard	11
10.	Christy Mathewson	11
10.	Vic Raschi	11

SAVES

1.	Rollie Fingers	6
2.	Allie Reynolds	4
2.	Johnny Murphy	4
4.	Roy Face	3
4.	Herb Pennock	3
4.	Kent Tekulve	3
4.	Firpo Marberry	3
4.	Will McEnaney	3
4.	Todd Worrell	3
4.	Tug McGraw	3

FEWEST HITS PER 9 INNINGS

1.	Jesse Barnes	4.78
2.	Monte Pearson	4.79
3.	Jack Billingham	4.97
4.	Sherry Smith	5.04
5.	Jerry Koosman	5.47
6.	Babe Ruth	5.52
7.	George Earnshaw	5.60
8.	Ron Guidry	5.63
9.	Hippo Vaughn	5.67
10.	Sandy Koufax	5.68
11.	Art Nehf	5.70
12.	Eddie Plank	5.93
13.	Don Larsen	6.00
13.	Lefty Tyler	6.00
15.	Ernie Bonham	6.11

PART FOUR

The Teams and Their Players

Year-by-Year Order of Finish
The Lineups, Including Pitchers
Individual Batting, Pitching, and Fielding
The Managers
Team Statistics
League Leaders
Baseball Club Nicknames

The Teams and Their Players

The Teams and Their Players is a chronological listing of team standings, league leaders, basic team rosters, and player records for every major league from 1876 through today. This section, which serves as a cross-reference to the Player and Pitcher registers, makes it possible to find out such information as who played second base for the Brooklyn Dodgers in 1924, or who were the top pitchers for the Detroit Tigers in 1917. It also gives the yearly league leaders in many statistical categories and includes the names and records of the men who managed the teams. The information is presented on a year-by-year basis starting with the National League in 1876.

All information and abbreviations that may appear unfamiliar are explained in the sample format presented below. The National League team rosters of 1876 would normally appear first, but as an example to illustrate the information only the Chicago team is shown. They finished first in 1876, and all teams are presented in the order of final standing.

NATIONAL LEAGUE 1876

	POS	Player	AB	BA	HR	RBI	PO	A	E	DP	TC/G	FA	Pitcher	G	IP	W	L	SV	ERA
Chicago	1B	C. McVey	308	.347	1	53	485	10	21	21	9.4	.959	A. Spalding	61	529	46	12	0	1.75
	2B	R. Barnes	322	.429	1	59	167	199	36	22	6.1	.910							
W-52 L-14	SS	J. Peters	316	.351	1	47	95	193	21	16	4.7	.932							
	3B	C. Anson	309	.356	1	59	135	147	50	8	5.0	.849							
Al Spalding	RF	B. Addy	142	.282	0	16	46	6	13	0	2.0	.800							
	CF	P. Hines	305	.331	2	59	159	8	14	4	2.8	.923							
	LF	J. Glenn	276	.304	0	32	128	5	18	1	2.7	.881							
	C	D. White	303	.343	1	60	295	50	64	3	6.5	.844							
	P	A. Spalding	292	.312	0	44	45	92	7	7	2.4	.951							
	OF	O. Bielaski	139	.209	0	10	41	4	14	1	1.8	.763							

Roster Column Headings Information

POS   Fielding Position

AB   At Bats

BA   Batting Average

HR   Home Runs

RBI   Runs Batted In

PO   Putouts

A   Assists

E   Errors

DP   Double Plays

TC/G   Total Fielding Chances per Game

FA   Fielding Average

G   Games Pitched In

IP   Innings Pitched (rounded off to the nearest inning)

W   Wins

L   Losses

SV   Saves

ERA   Earned Run Average

Team Information Explanation

Directly beneath the city name is the team won and lost record and name of the man who managed the team. (Teams with more than one manager have the managers listed in the order of when they managed. The top listing would indicate the first manager.)

Multiple Team Players. If a man played for more than one team in the same year, the information shown is only his record for the indicated team.

Regulars. The men who appear first on the team roster are considered the regulars for that team at the positions indicated. There are several factors for determining regulars, of which "most games played at a position" and "most fielding chances at a position" are the two prime considerations. Fielding information applies only to the position indicated. For regular outfielders the fielding information is for all the outfield positions.

Substitutes. Appearing directly beneath the regulars are the substitutes for the team. Substitutes listed here must have a total of at least one at bat per scheduled game, or 20 or more runs batted in for the season. Substitutes are listed in order of most at bats, and can be someone who played most of the team's games as a regular, but not at one position. The rules for determining the listed positions of substitutes are as follows:

One Position Substitutes. If a man played at least 70% of his games in the field at one position, then he is listed only at that position, except for outfielders, where all three outfield positions are included under one category. Fielding information applies only to the position indicated.

Two Position Substitutes. If a man did not play at least 70% of his games in the field at one position, but did play more than 90% of his total games at two positions, then he is shown with a combination fielding position. For example, a player who has an "S2" shown in his position column played at least 90% of his games either at shortstop or at second base. These combinations are always indicated by the first letter or number of the position. Fielding information applies only to the two positions indicated. The position listed first is where the most games were played.

Utility Players. If a player has a "UT" shown in his position column, it means that he did not meet the above 70% or 90% requirement and is listed as a utility player. The fielding information is his total for all positions.

Pinch Hitters. Men who played less than 15 games in the field, but who had 20 runs batted in or more, are considered pinch hitters and are listed as "PH" and no fielding information is shown.

Total Fielding Chances per Game. This statistic is not shown for men who were two position substitutes or utility players, because total chances per game is only meaningful in reference to a specific fielding position.

Pitchers. A pitcher is included if he pitched 100 or more innings, or had ten decisions (a decision being a win, loss, or save). Pitchers are listed in order of innings pitched.

League Leader Qualifications (also applies to Yearly League Leaders Information). Throughout baseball, there have been different rules used to determine the minimum appearances necessary to qualify for league leader in categories concerning averages (Batting Average, Earned Run Average, etc.). For the rules and the years they were in effect, see Appendix C.

League Batting Leaders. Batting statistics that appear in boldfaced print indicate that the player led his league in a particular batting category. When there is a tie for league lead, the figures for all the men who tied are shown in boldface.

League Fielding Leaders. Fielding statistics that appear in boldfaced print indicate that the player led his league in a particular fielding category at his position. For the purpose of determining league leaders, all outfield positions are combined into one position. When there is a tie for league lead, the figures for all the men who tied are shown in boldface.

League Pitching Leaders. Pitching statistics that appear in boldfaced print indicate that the pitcher led his league in a particular pitching category. When there is a tie for league lead, the figures for all the men who tied are shown in boldface.

Traded League Leaders. An asterisk (*) next to a particular figure indicates that the player led the league that year in the particular statistical category, but since he played for more than one team, the figure does not necessarily represent his league leading total or average.

Unavailable Information. Any time a blank space is shown in a particular statistical column it indicates that the information was unavailable or incomplete. This, however, does not apply for *Total Chances per Game,* which is explained above.

Estimated Earned Run Averages (also applies to Yearly League Leaders Information). Any time an earned run average appears in italics it indicates that not all the earned runs allowed by the pitcher are known, and the information had to be estimated. For example, it is known that a pitcher's team allowed 560 runs in 112 games. Of these games, it is known that in 90 of them the team allowed 420 of which 315 or 75% were earned. The man is known to have pitched 207⅔ innings in 40 games and allowed 134 runs. In 35 of these games it is known that he allowed 118 runs of which 83 were earned. By multiplying the team's known ratio of earned runs to total runs (75%) by the pitcher's 16 (134 minus 118) remaining runs allowed, a figure of 12 additional estimated earned runs is calculated. This means that the pitcher allowed an estimated total of 95 earned runs in 207⅔ innings, for an estimated earned run average of 4.12. In all cases at least 50% of the runs allowed by the team were "known" as a basis for estimating earned run averages.

Yearly League Leaders Information

Appearing directly after the roster information are yearly league leaders. The categories generally include the top three and the top five players. However, there can be exceptions to the number of men included in the various categories if there are ties for a position. The exceptions if there are ties for any position other than first are explained below. The rule used for first place ties is that if more than six men tied for first (in a category that lists five), then the information in the categories shows only the number of players tied, along with the appropriate statistic. For categories of three, the most players that would be shown are four. The following is the list of categories included:

Batting and Base Running Leaders

Batting Average, Slugging Average. The top five players are shown. All ties are broken by carrying the average out to seven decimal places. If a tie still remains, then the players involved are considered tied but the man that had the most at bats is listed first. If required by ties, six players are shown. If ties would require more than six men to be shown, none of the last tied group are included.

Home Runs, Total Bases, Runs Batted In, Stolen Bases. The top five players are shown. If players are tied for a position, the man who had the fewest at bats is listed first. If required by ties, six players are shown. If ties would require more than six men to be shown, none of the last tied group are included.

Home Run Percentages (the number of home runs per 100 times at bat). The top three players are shown. All ties are broken by carrying the average out to seven decimal places. If a tie still remains, then the players involved are considered tied but the man that had the most at bats is listed first. If required by ties, four players are shown. However, if ties would require more than four men to be shown, none of the last tied group are included.

Runs Scored, Hits, Bases on Balls, Doubles, Triples. The top three players are shown. If players are tied for a position, the man who had the fewest at bats is listed first. If required by ties, four players are shown. If ties would require more than four men to be shown, none of the last tied group are included.

Pitching Leaders

Winning Percentage, Earned Run Average. The top five pitchers are shown. All ties are broken by carrying the average out to seven decimal places. If a tie still remains, then the pitchers involved are considered tied but the man that pitched the most innings is listed first. If required by ties, six pitchers are shown. If ties would require more than six men to be shown, none of the last tied group are included.

Wins, Strikeouts, Saves, Complete Games. The top five pitchers are shown. If pitchers are tied for a position in Wins or Strikeouts, the man that pitched the fewest innings is listed first. If pitchers are tied for a position in Saves, the man that pitched the fewest games in relief is listed first. If pitchers are tied for a position in Complete Games, the man that started the fewest games is listed first. If required by ties, six players are shown. If ties would require more than six men to be shown, none of the last tied group are included.

Fewest Hits per 9 Innings, Fewest Bases on Balls per 9 Innings, Most Strikeouts per 9 Innings. The top three pitchers are shown. All ties are broken by carrying the average out to seven decimal places. If a tie still remains, then the pitchers involved are considered tied but the man that pitched the most innings is listed first, except Most Strikeouts per 9 Innings. The man listed first in this category is the one who pitched the fewest innings. If required by ties, four pitchers are shown. If ties would require more than four men to be shown, none of the last tied group are included.

Games Pitched, Shutouts, Innings Pitched. The top three pitchers are shown. If pitchers are tied for a position in Games Pitched, the man who pitched the most innings is listed first. If pitchers are tied for a position in Shutouts, the man that started the fewest games is listed first. If pitchers are tied for a position in Innings Pitched, the man who pitched in the most games is listed first. If required by ties, four pitchers are shown. If ties would require more than four men to be shown, none of the last tied group are included.

League Column Headings Information

		W	L	PCT	GB	R	OR	2B	3B	HR	BA	SA	SB	E	DP	FA	CG	BB	SO	ShO	SV	ERA
East	Detroit	86	70	.551		558	514	179	32	122	.237	.356	17	96	137	.984	46	465	952	11	33	2.96
	Boston	85	70	.548	.5	640	620	229	34	124	.248	.376	66	130	141	.978	48	512	918	20	25	3.47
	Baltimore	80	74	.519	5	519	430	193	29	100	.229	.339	78	100	150	.983	62	395	788	20	21	2.53
	New York	79	76	.510	6.5	557	527	201	24	103	.249	.357	71	134	179	.978	35	419	625	19	39	3.05
	Cleveland	72	84	.462	14	472	519	187	18	91	.234	.330	49	116	157	.981	47	534	846	13	25	2.97
	Milwaukee	65	91	.417	21	493	595	167	22	88	.235	.328	64	139	145	.977	37	486	740	14	32	3.45
West	Oakland	93	62	.600		604	457	195	29	134	.240	.366	87	130	146	.979	42	418	862	23	43	2.58
	Chicago	87	67	.565	5.5	566	535	170	28	108	.238	.346	100	135	136	.977	36	431	936	14	42	3.12
	Minnesota	77	77	.500	15.5	537	535	182	31	93	.244	.344	53	159	133	.974	37	444	838	17	34	2.84
	Kansas City	76	78	.494	16.5	580	545	220	26	78	.255	.353	85	116	164	.981	44	405	801	16	28	3.24
	California	75	80	.484	18	454	533	171	26	78	.242	.330	57	114	135	.981	57	620	1000	18	16	3.06
	Texas	54	100	.351	38.5	461	628	166	17	56	.217	.290	126	166	147	.972	11	613	868	8	34	3.53
						6441	6438	2260	316	1175	.239	.343	853	1535	1770	.979	502	5742	10174	193	372	3.07

W   Wins
L   Losses
PCT   Winning Percentage
GB   Games Behind the League Leader
R   Runs Scored
OR   Opponents' Runs (Runs Scored Against)

Batting

2B   Doubles
3B   Triples
HR   Home Runs
BA   Batting Average
SA   Slugging Average
SB   Stolen Bases

Fielding

E   Errors
DP Double Plays
FA Fielding Average

Pitching

CG   Complete Games
BB   Bases on Balls
SO   Strikeouts
ShO Shutouts
SV   Saves
ERA Earned Run Average

League Leaders, Team Information. Statistics that appear in boldfaced print indicate that the team led the league that year in a particular statistical category. The leader for opponents' runs, pitcher's bases on balls, and errors are the teams that allowed or committed the fewest of these. When there is a tie for league lead the figures for all teams who tied are shown in boldface.

Unavailable Information. Any time a blank space is shown in a particular statistical column, it indicates that the information is unavailable or incomplete.

Team Estimated Earned Run Averages. Any time an earned run average appears in italics, it indicates that not all the earned runs allowed by the team are known, and the information had to be estimated. For example, it is known that a team allowed 560 runs in 112 games. Of these games, it is known that in 90 of them the team allowed 460 runs of which 345 or 75% were earned. By applying this percentage to the 100 remaining runs, it is estimated that 75 of these runs were earned. Thus, the earned runs allowed by the pitching staff is calculated as 420 (345 known plus 75 estimated). Since the pitchers worked a total of 1020 innings, the estimated team earned run average is 3.71. In all cases at least 50% of the runs allowed by the team were "known" as a basis for estimating earned run averages.

1981 Split Season.
The 1981 season was split into two halves as a result of the players' strike. The teams appear in order of their combined records for the two halves, and the managers' records as listed are also for the combined season. The standings for the two half-seasons appear below the combined standings and team statistics. The same applies to the 1892 National League season.

BASEBALL CLUB NICKNAMES
The following lists all the nicknames used by major league clubs,
including the years in which the nickname was applied.

UNION ASSOCIATION (1884)
Altoona Mountain Citys
Baltimore Monumentals
Boston Reds
Chicago Browns
Cincinnati Outlaw Reds
Kansas City Unions
Milwaukee Cream Citys
Philadelphia Keystones
Pittsburgh Stogies
St. Louis Maroons
St. Paul Saints
Washington Nationals
Wilmington Quicksteps

FEDERAL LEAGUE (1914–15)
Baltimore Terrapins
Brooklyn Tip-Tops
Buffalo Buffeds (1914)
Buffalo Blues (1915)
Chicago Chi-Feds (1914)
Chicago Whales (1915)
Indianapolis Hoosiers
Kansas City Packers
Newark Peppers
Pittsburgh Rebels
St. Louis Terriers

PLAYERS LEAGUE (1890)
Boston Reds
Brooklyn Wonders
Buffalo Bisons

Chicago Pirates
Cleveland Infants
New York Giants
Philadelphia Quakers
Pittsburgh Burghers

AMERICAN ASSOCIATION (1882–91)
Baltimore Orioles (1882–91)
Boston Reds (1891)
Brooklyn Trolley-Dodgers (1884–88)
Brooklyn Bridegrooms (1889)
Brooklyn Gladiators (1890)
Cincinnati Red Stockings (1882–89)
Cincinnati Kellys (1891)
Cleveland Blues (1887–88)
Columbus Buckeyes (1883–84)
Columbus Buckeyes (1889–91)
Indianapolis Hoosiers (1884)
Kansas City Cowboys (1888–89)
Louisville Eclipse (1882–84)
Louisville Colonels (1885–91)
Milwaukee Brewers (1891)
New York Metropolitans (1883–87)
Philadelphia Athletics (1882–91)
Pittsburgh Alleghenys (1882–86)
Richmond Virginians (1884)
Rochester Hop-Bitters (1890)
St. Louis Brown Stockings (1882)
St. Louis Browns (1883–91)
Syracuse Stars (1890)
Toledo Blue Stockings (1884)
Toledo Maumees (1890)

Washington Nationals (1884)
Washington Statesmen (1891)

NATIONAL ASSOCIATION (1871–75)
Baltimore Lord Baltimores (1872–74)
Baltimore Marylands (1873)
Boston Red Stockings (1871–75)
Brooklyn Atlantics (1872–75)
Brooklyn Eckfords (1872)
Chicago White Stockings (1871, 1874–75)
Cleveland Forest Citys (1871–72)
Elizabeth Resolutes (1873)
Ft. Wayne Kekiongas (1871)
Hartford Dark Blues (1874–75)
Keokuk Westerns (1875)
Middletown Mansfields (1872)
New Haven Elm Citys (1875)
New York Mutuals (1871–75)
Philadelphia Athletics (1871–75)
Philadelphia Centennials (1875)
Philadelphia Whites (1873–75)
Rockford Forest Citys (1871)
St. Louis Brown Stockings (1875)
St. Louis Red Stockings (1875)
Troy Haymakers (1871–72)
Washington Olympics (1871–72)
Washington Nationals (1872)
Washington Nationals (1875)

AMERICAN LEAGUE (1901—)
Baltimore Orioles (1901–02)
Baltimore Orioles (1954—)

BASEBALL CLUB NICKNAMES *cont.*

AMERICAN LEAGUE (1901—)

Boston Somersets (1901–02)
Boston Pilgrims (1903–06)
Boston Red Sox (1907—)
California Angels (1965—)
Chicago White Stockings (1901–03)
Chicago White Sox (1904—)
Cleveland Blues (1901–04)
Cleveland Naps (1905–14)
Cleveland Indians (1915—)
Detroit Tigers (1901—)
Kansas City Athletics (1955–67)
Kansas City Royals (1969—)
Los Angeles Angels (1961–64)
Milwaukee Brewers (1901)
Milwaukee Brewers (1970—)
Minnesota Twins (1961—)
New York Highlanders (1903–12)
New York Yankees (1913—)
Oakland Athletics (1968—)
Philadelphia Athletics (1901–54)
St. Louis Browns (1902–53)
Seattle Pilots (1969)
Seattle Mariners (1977—)
Texas Rangers (1972—)
Toronto Blue Jays (1977—)
Washington Nationals (1901–56)
Washington Senators (1957–71)

NATIONAL LEAGUE (1876—)

Atlanta Braves (1966—)
Baltimore Orioles (1892–99)
Boston Red Caps (1876–82)
Boston Beaneaters (1883–1906)
Boston Doves (1907–10)
Boston Rustlers (1911)
Boston Braves (1912–35, 1941–52)
Boston Bees (1936–40)
Brooklyn Bridegrooms (1890–98)
Brooklyn Superbas (1899–1910)
Brooklyn Dodgers (1911–13, 1932–57)
Brooklyn Robins (1914–31)
Buffalo Bisons (1879–85)
Chicago White Stockings (1876–89)
Chicago Colts (1890–97)
Chicago Orphans (1898–1901)
Chicago Cubs (1902—)
Cincinnati Red Stockings (1876–77)
Cincinnati Reds (1878–80)
Cincinnati Reds (1890–1952, 1959—)
Cincinnati Redlegs (1953–58)
Cleveland Blues (1879–84)
Cleveland Spiders (1889–99)
Detroit Wolverines (1881–88)
Hartford Dark Blues (1876–77)
Houston Colt .45's (1962–64)
Houston Astros (1965—)
Indianapolis Hoosiers (1878)
Indianapolis Hoosiers (1887–89)

Kansas City Cowboys (1886)
Los Angeles Dodgers (1958—)
Louisville Grays (1876–77)
Louisville Colonels (1892–99)
Milwaukee Cream Citys (1878)
Milwaukee Braves (1953–65)
Montreal Expos (1969—)
New York Mutuals (1876)
New York Gothams (1883–84)
New York Giants (1885–1957)
New York Mets (1962—)
Philadelphia Athletics (1876)
Philadelphia Quakers (1883–89)
Philadelphia Phillies (1890–1943, 1946—)
Philadelphia Blue Jays (1944–45)
Pittsburgh Alleghenys (1887–90)
Pittsburgh Pirates (1891—)
Providence Grays (1878–85)
St. Louis Brown Stockings (1876–77)
St. Louis Maroons (1885–86)
St. Louis Browns (1892–98)
St. Louis Perfectos (1899)
St. Louis Cardinals (1900—)
San Diego Padres (1969—)
San Francisco Giants (1958—)
Syracuse Stars (1879)
Troy Trojans (1879–82)
Washington Statesmen (1886–89)
Washington Senators (1892–99)
Worcester Ruby Legs (1880–82)

NATIONAL LEAGUE 1876

	POS	Player	AB	BA	HR	RBI	PO	A	E	DP	TC/G	FA	Pitcher	G	IP	W	L	SV	ERA
Chicago	1B	C. McVey	308	.347	1	53	485	10	21	21	9.4	.959	A. Spalding	61	529	**47**	13	0	1.75
	2B	R. Barnes	322	**.429**	1	59	167	199	36	22	6.1	**.910**							
W-52 L-14	SS	J. Peters	316	.351	1	47	95	193	21	16	4.7	**.932**							
	3B	C. Anson	309	.356	1	59	**135**	147	50	8	5.0	.849							
Al Spalding	RF	B. Addy	142	.282	0	16	46	6	13	0	2.0	.800							
	CF	P. Hines	305	.331	2	59	159	8	14	4	2.8	.923							
	LF	J. Glenn	276	.304	0	32	128	5	18	1	2.7	.881							
	C	D. White	303	.343	1	**60**	295	50	64	3	6.5	.844							
	P	A. Spalding	292	.312	0	44	45	92	7	7	2.4	.951							
	OF	O. Bielaski	139	.209	0	10	41	6	14	1	1.8	.763							
St. Louis	1B	D. Dehlman	245	.184	0	9	**750**	8	33	21	12.4	.958	G. Bradley	64	573	45	19	0	**1.23**
	2B	M. McGeary	276	.261	0	30	132	180	39	16	6.3	.889							
W-45 L-19	SS	D. Mack	180	.217	1	7	42	114	20	6	4.3	.886							
	3B	J. Battin	283	.300	0	46	115	145	40	8	4.8	**.867**							
Mase Graffen	RF	J. Blong	264	.235	0	30	64	13	9	2	1.4	.895							
W-39 L-17	CF	L. Pike	282	.323	1	50	82	13	11	5	1.7	.896							
	LF	N. Cuthbert	283	.247	0	25	95	7	19	2	1.9	.843							
George McManus	C	J. Clapp	298	.305	0	29	**333**	56	56	5	7.3	.874							
W-6 L-2	P	G. Bradley	265	.249	0	28	50	87	12	4	2.3	.919							
	SS	D. Pearce	102	.206	0	10	23	87	12	6	5.3	.902							
Hartford	1B	E. Mills	254	.260	0	23	644	7	42	13	11.0	.939	T. Bond	45	408	31	13	0	1.68
	2B	J. Burdock	309	.259	0	23	**211**	174	45	18	6.2	.895	C. Cummings	24	216	16	8	0	1.67
W-47 L-21	SS	T. Carey	289	.270	0	26	74	218	39	9	4.9	.882							
	3B	B. Ferguson	310	.265	0	32	124	133	54	5	4.5	.826							
Bob Ferguson	RF	D. Higham	312	.327	0	35	57	**16**	11	1	1.4	.869							
	CF	J. Remsen	324	.275	0	30	177	12	24	5	3.1	.887							
	LF	T. York	263	.259	1	39	153	8	18	1	2.7	.899							
	C	D. Allison	163	.264	0	15	201	43	33	2	6.9	**.881**							
	P	T. Bond	182	.275	0	21	25	93	15	0	**3.0**	.887							
	C	B. Harbidge	106	.217	0	6	97	30	32	0	6.6	.799							
	P	C. Cummings	105	.162	0	7	9	27	2	0	1.6	.947							
Boston	1B	T. Murnane	308	.282	0	34	689	5	**55**	**30**	11.5	.927	J. Borden	29	218	11	12	1	2.89
	2B	J. Morrill	278	.263	0	26	105	117	37	18	7.0	.857	J. Manning	34	197	18	5	5	2.14
W-39 L-31	SS	G. Wright	335	.299	1	34	89	251	43	16	5.6	.888	F. Bradley	22	173	9	10	1	2.49
	3B	H. Schafer	286	.252	0	35	122	146	63	8	4.7	.810							
Harry Wright	RF	J. Manning	288	.264	2	25	73	7	23	0	1.8	.777							
	CF	J. O'Rourke	312	.327	2	43	154	7	27	1	2.8	.856							
	LF	A. Leonard	303	.281	0	27	68	6	6	2	2.3	.925							
	C	L. Brown	195	.210	2	21	192	45	40	4	6.2	.856							
	OF	F. Whitney	139	.237	0	15	73	8	18	4	2.9	.818							
	PO	J. Borden	121	.207	0	7	20	34	29	0		.651							
	P	F. Bradley	82	.232	0	8	10	24	2	0	1.6	.944							
Louisville	1B	J. Gerhardt	292	.260	2	18	664	**13**	40	13	**13.3**	.944	J. Devlin	68	622	30	**35**	0	1.56
	2B	Somerville	256	.188	0	14	210	251	69	22	**8.3**	.870							
W-30 L-36	SS	C. Fulmer	267	.273	1	29	83	209	47	12	5.1	.861							
	3B	B. Hague	294	.265	0	22	67	89	51	5	3.1	.754							
Jack Chapman	RF	A. Allison	130	.208	0	10	34	11	12	1	2.5	.789							
	CF	S. Hastings	283	.258	0	21	98	11	16	4	1.9	.872							
	LF	J. Ryan	241	.253	1	18	131	1	17	1	2.3	.886							
	C	P. Snyder	224	.196	1	9	249	**86**	67	2	7.3	.833							
	P	J. Devlin	298	.315	0	28	44	**100**	9	4	2.3	.941							
New York	1B	J. Start	264	.277	0	21	547	10	21	11	10.3	**.964**	B. Mathews	56	516	21	34	0	2.86
	2B	B. Craver	246	.224	0	22	95	84	41	7	5.2	.814							
W-21 L-35	SS	J. Hallinan	240	.279	2	36	45	172	67	7	5.7	.764							
	3B	A. Nichols	212	.179	0	9	123	135	**73**	1	**5.8**	.779							
Bill Cammeyer	RF	E. Booth	228	.215	0	7	73	11	26	0	2.1	.764							
	CF	Holdsworth	241	.266	0	19	109	10	13	1	2.7	.902							
	LF	F. Treacey	256	.211	0	18	**202**	9	39	1	**4.4**	.844							
	C	N. Hicks	188	.234	0	15	222	47	**94**	3	**8.1**	.741							
	P	B. Mathews	218	.183	0	9	41	78	28	0	2.6	.810							
Philadelphia	1B	E. Sutton	236	.297	1	31	324	11	31	6	12.6	.915	L. Knight	34	282	10	22	0	2.62
	2B	W. Fisler	278	.288	1	30	45	65	22	7	6.3	.833	G. Zettlein	28	234	4	20	2	3.88
W-14 L-45	SS	D. Force	284	.232	0	17	108*	237	39	11	6.4*	.898							
	3B	L. Meyerle	256	.340	0	34	84	101	49	4	4.8	.791							
Al Wright	RF	W. Coon	220	.227	0	22	43	8	16	1	2.3	.761							
	CF	D. Eggler	174	.299	0	19	109	6	11	1	3.2	.913							
	LF	G. Hall	268	.366	5	45	150	7	39	3	3.3	.801							
	C	F. Malone	96	.229	0	6	78	30	31	0	7.0	.777							
	UT	L. Knight	240	.250	0	24	156	48	40	10		.836							
	P	G. Zettlein	128	.211	0	11	7	36	5	2	1.7	.896							
	20	B. Fouser	89	.135	0	2	45	55	21	3		.826							

NATIONAL LEAGUE 1876, cont.

	POS	Player	AB	BA	HR	RBI	PO	A	E	DP	TC/G	FA	Pitcher	G	IP	W	L	SV	ERA
	1B	C. Gould	258	.252	0	11	584	13	39	28	10.4	.939	D. Dean	30	263	4	26	0	3.73
	2B	C. Sweasy	225	.204	0	10	167	158	51	30	6.8	.864	C. Fisher	28	229	4	20	0	3.02
	SS	H. Kessler	248	.258	0	11	57	118	47	11	4.8	.788							
	3B	W. Foley	221	.226	0	9	67	101	41	4	4.5	.804							
	RF	D. Pierson	233	.236	0	13	46	9	9	2	2.1	.859							
	CF	C. Jones	276	.286	4	38	151	11	27	2	3.0	.857							
	LF	R. Snyder	205	.151	0	12	168	6	37	1	3.8	.825							
	C	A. Booth	272	.261	0	14	77	29	38	3	6.0	.736							
	P	D. Dean	138	.261	0	4	22	38	13	2	2.4	.822							
	PO	C. Fisher	129	.248	0	4	31	28	13	0		.819							
	UT	B. Clack	118	.161	0	5	105	33	26	1		.841							

Cincinnati

W-9 L-56

Charlie Gould

BATTING AND BASE RUNNING LEADERS

Batting Average
R. Barnes, CHI .429
G. Hall, PHI .366
C. Anson, CHI .356
J. Peters, CHI .351
C. McVey, CHI .347

Slugging Average
R. Barnes, CHI .590
G. Hall, PHI .545
L. Pike, STL .472
C. Anson, CHI .453
L. Meyerle, PHI .449

Home Runs
G. Hall, PHI 5
C. Jones, CIN 4

Total Bases
R. Barnes, CHI 190
G. Hall, PHI 146
C. Anson, CHI 140
P. Hines, CHI 134
L. Pike, STL 133
G. Wright, BOS 133

Runs Batted In
D. White, CHI 60
P. Hines, CHI 59
C. Anson, CHI 59
R. Barnes, CHI 59
C. McVey, CHI 53

Stolen Bases
(not available)

Hits
R. Barnes, CHI 138
J. Peters, CHI 111
C. Anson, CHI 110
C. McVey, CHI 107

Base on Balls
R. Barnes, CHI 20
J. O'Rourke, BOS 15
J. Burdock, HAR 13
J. Glenn, CHI 12

Home Run Percentage
G. Hall, PHI 1.9
C. Jones, CIN 1.4
L. Brown, BOS 1.0
J. Hallinan, NY 0.8

Runs Scored
R. Barnes, CHI 126
G. Wright, BOS 72
J. Peters, CHI 70
D. White, CHI 66

Doubles
P. Hines, CHI 21
D. Higham, HAR 21
R. Barnes, CHI 21
L. Pike, STL 19

Triples
R. Barnes, CHI 14
G. Hall, PHI 13
L. Pike, STL 10
L. Meyerle, PHI 8

PITCHING LEADERS

Winning Percentage
A. Spalding, CHI .783
J. Manning, BOS .783
T. Bond, HAR .705
G. Bradley, STL .703
C. Cummings, HAR .667

Earned Run Average
G. Bradley, STL 1.23
J. Devlin, LOU 1.56
C. Cummings, HAR 1.67
T. Bond, HAR 1.68
A. Spalding, CHI 1.75

Wins
A. Spalding, CHI 47
G. Bradley, STL 45
T. Bond, HAR 31
J. Devlin, LOU 30
B. Mathews, NY 21

Saves
J. Manning, BOS 5
C. McVey, CHI 2
G. Zettlein, PHI 2

Strikeouts
J. Devlin, LOU 122
G. Bradley, STL 103
T. Bond, HAR 88
A. Spalding, CHI 39
B. Mathews, NY 37

Complete Games
J. Devlin, LOU 66
G. Bradley, STL 63
B. Mathews, NY 55
A. Spalding, CHI 53
T. Bond, HAR 45

Fewest Hits/9 Innings
G. Bradley, STL 7.38
T. Bond, HAR 7.83
J. Devlin, LOU 8.19
C. Cummings, HAR 8.96

Shutouts
G. Bradley, STL 16
A. Spalding, CHI 8
T. Bond, HAR 6
C. Cummings, HAR 5

Fewest Walks/9 Innings
G. Zettlein, PHI 0.23
C. Fisher, CIN 0.24
T. Bond, HAR 0.29
B. Mathews, NY 0.42

Most Strikeouts/9 Inn.
T. Bond, HAR 1.94
J. Devlin, LOU 1.77
G. Bradley, STL 1.62
J. Borden, BOS 1.40

Innings
J. Devlin, LOU 622
G. Bradley, STL 573
A. Spalding, CHI 529
B. Mathews, NY 516

Games Pitched
J. Devlin, LOU 68
G. Bradley, STL 64
A. Spalding, CHI 61
B. Mathews, NY 56

	W	L	PCT	GB	R	OR	2B	3B	HR	BA	SA	SB	E	DP	FA	CG	BB	SO	ShO	SV	ERA
										Batting				Fielding			Pitching				
Chicago	52	14	.788		624	257	131	32	7	.337	.416	0	282	33	.899	58	29	51	8	4	1.76
St. Louis	45	19	.703	6	386	229	73	27	2	.259	.313	0	268	33	.902	63	39	103	16	0	1.22
Hartford	47	21	.691	6	429	261	96	22	2	.267	.322	0	337	27	.888	69	27	114	11	0	1.67
Boston	39	31	.557	15	471	450	96	24	9	.266	.328	0	442	42	.860	49	104	77	3	7	2.51
Louisville	30	36	.455	22	280	344	68	14	6	.249	.294	0	397	44	.875	67	38	125	5	0	1.69
New York	21	35	.375	26	260	412	39	15	2	.227	.261	0	473	18	.825	56	24	37	2	0	2.94
Philadelphia	14	45	.237	34.5	378	534	79	35	7	.271	.342	0	456	32	.839	53	41	22	1	2	3.22
Cincinnati	9	56	.138	42.5	238	579	51	12	4	.234	.271	0	469	45	.841	57	34	60		0	3.62
					3066	3066	633	181	39	.265	.321	0	3124	274	.866	472	336	589	46	13	2.31

NATIONAL LEAGUE 1877

	POS	Player	AB	BA	HR	RBI	PO	A	E	DP	TC/G	FA	Pitcher	G	IP	W	L	SV	ERA
	1B	D. White	266	.387	2	49	324	13	13	16	10.0	.963	T. Bond	58	521	40	17	0	2.11
	2B	G. Wright	290	.276	0	35	171	209	53	28	7.5	.878							
	SS	E. Sutton	253	.292	0	39	66	91	21	8	4.9	.882							
	3B	J. Morrill	242	.302	0	28	33	43	12	1	2.9	.864							
	RF	H. Schafer	141	.277	0	13	17	1	11	0	1.3	.621							
	CF	J. O'Rourke	265	.362	0	23	112	9	22	0	2.4	.846							
	LF	A. Leonard	272	.287	0	27	79	5	12	2	2.6	.875							
	C	L. Brown	221	.253	1	31	360	67	49	5	8.7	.897							
	P	T. Bond	259	.228	0	30	29	104	9	2	2.4	.937							
	OF	T. Murnane	140	.279	1	15	39	5	10	2	1.8	.815							

Boston

W-42 L-18

Harry Wright

NATIONAL LEAGUE 1877, *cont.*

	POS	Player	AB	BA	HR	RBI	PO	A	E	DP	TC/G	FA	Pitcher	G	IP	W	L	SV	ERA
Louisville	1B	J. Latham	278	.291	0	22	659	24	36	28	12.2	.950	J. Devlin	61	559	35	25	0	2.25
	2B	J. Gerhardt	250	.304	1	35	167	244	52	30	8.1	.888							
W-35 L-25	SS	B. Craver	238	.265	0	29	71	175	26	15	4.8	.904							
	3B	B. Hague	263	.266	1	24	78	78	29	4	3.1	.843							
Jack Chapman	RF	O. Shaffer	260	.285	3	34	121	21	28	1	2.8	.835							
	CF	B. Crowley	238	.282	1	23	109	20	23	2	2.6	.849							
	LF	G. Hall	269	.323	0	26	92	7	11	1	1.8	.900							
	C	P. Snyder	248	.258	2	28	292	102	39	8	7.1	.910							
	P	J. Devlin	268	.269	1	27	30	110	10	2	2.5	.933							
Hartford	1B	J. Start	271	.332	1	21	704	10	27	25	12.4	.964	T. Larkin	56	501	29	25	0	2.14
	2B	J. Burdock	277	.260	0	9	185	189	40	25	7.5	.903							
W-31 L-27	SS	T. Carey	274	.255	1	20	49	203	53	11	5.1	.826							
	3B	B. Ferguson	254	.255	0	35	109	155	50	6	5.6	.841							
Bob Ferguson	RF	J. Cassidy	251	.378	0	27	41	16	22	2	1.4	.722							
	CF	Holdsworth	260	.254	0	20	79	11	18	1	2.0	.833							
	LF	T. York	237	.283	1	37	130	5	21	1	2.8	.865							
	C	B. Harbidge	167	.222	0	8	143	27	23	2	6.0	.881							
	P	T. Larkin	228	.228	1	18	26	89	15	0	2.3	.885							
	C	D. Allison	115	.148	0	6	127	36	19	4	6.3	.896							
St. Louis	1B	D. Dehlman	119	.185	0	11	306	4	23	14	10.7	.931	T. Nichols	42	350	18	23	0	2.60
	2B	M. McGeary	258	.252	0	20	125	140	35	12	7.7	.883	J. Blong	25	187	10	9	0	2.74
W-28 L-32	SS	D. Force	225	.262	0	22	75	160	22	9	5.1	.914							
	3B	J. Battin	226	.199	1	22	58	77	29	6	5.1	.823							
George McManus	RF	J. Blong	218	.216	0	13	60	6	13	0	2.0	.835							
	CF	J. Remsen	123	.260	0	13	73	4	8	0	2.6	.906							
	LF	M. Dorgan	266	.308	0	23	70	5	16	3	1.8	.824							
	C	J. Clapp	255	.318	0	34	269	44	40	2	6.7	.887							
	10	A. Croft	220	.232	0	27	338	10	22	10		.941							
	P	T. Nichols	186	.167	0	9	14	62	4	1	1.9	.950							
Chicago	1B	A. Spalding	254	.256	0	35	472	21	21	23	11.4	.959	G. Bradley	50	394	18	23	0	3.31
	2B	R. Barnes	92	.272	0	5	49	70	23	5	6.5	.838	C. McVey	17	92	4	8	2	4.50
W-26 L-33	SS	J. Peters	265	.317	0	41	124	215	45	23	6.4	.883							
	3B	C. Anson	255	.337	0	32	74	77	20	9	4.3	.883							
Al Spalding	RF	P. Hines	261	.280	0	23	75	4	19	1	2.0	.806							
	CF	D. Eggler	136	.265	0	20	60	8	11	3	2.4	.861							
	LF	J. Glenn	202	.228	0	20	66	7	4	1	2.1	.948							
	C	C. McVey	266	.368	0	36	137	34	28	3	5.0	.859							
	P	G. Bradley	214	.243	0	12	25	71	5	1	2.0	.950							
	20	H. Smith	94	.202	0	3	47	32	18	2		.814							
	OF	J. Hallinan	89	.281	0	11	27	1	7	1	1.8	.800							
Cincinnati	1B	C. Gould	91	.275	0	13	229	9	20	13	10.8	.922	C. Cummings	19	156	5	14	0	4.34
	2B	J. Hallinan	73	.370	0	7	52	36	15	8	6.4	.854	B. Mathews	15	129	3	12	0	4.04
W-15 L-42	SS	J. Manning	252	.317	0	36	30	62	32	2	4.8	.742	B. Mitchell	12	100	6	5	0	3.51
	3B	W. Foley	216	.190	0	18	94	130	44	9	4.8	.836							
Lip Pike	RF	B. Addy	245	.278	0	31	74	17	22	5	2.0	.805							
W-3 L-11	CF	L. Pike	262	.298	4	23	79	10	22	1	2.9	.802							
	LF	C. Jones	232	.310	2	36	133*	14	28*	2	3.8*	.840							
Bob Addy	C	S. Hastings	71	.141	0	3	63	24	23	1	5.5	.791							
W-12 L-31	UT	A. Booth	157	.172	0	13	77	101	36	6		.832							
	S2	L. Meyerle	107	.327	0	15	54	86	24	5		.854							
	P	C. Cummings	70	.200	0	4	6	31	3	0	2.1	.925							

BATTING AND BASE RUNNING LEADERS

Batting Average
D. White, BOS .387
J. Cassidy, HAR .378
C. McVey, CHI .368
J. O'Rourke, BOS .362
C. Anson, CHI .337

Slugging Average
D. White, BOS .545
C. Jones, CHI, CIN .471
J. Cassidy, HAR .458
C. McVey, CHI .455
J. O'Rourke, BOS .445

Home Runs
L. Pike, CIN 4
O. Shaffer, LOU 3
C. Jones, CHI, CIN 2
P. Snyder, LOU 2
D. White, BOS 2

Total Bases
D. White, BOS 145
C. McVey, CHI 121
J. O'Rourke, BOS 118
G. Hall, LOU 118
J. Cassidy, HAR 115

Runs Batted In
D. White, BOS 49
J. Peters, CHI 41
E. Sutton, BOS 39
C. Jones, CHI, CIN 38
T. York, HAR 37

Stolen Bases
(not available)

PITCHING LEADERS

Winning Percentage
T. Bond, BOS .702
J. Devlin, LOU .583
T. Larkin, HAR .537
J. Blong, STL .526
G. Bradley, CHI .439
T. Nichols, STL .439

Earned Run Average
T. Bond, BOS 2.11
T. Larkin, HAR 2.14
J. Devlin, LOU 2.25
T. Nichols, STL 2.60
J. Blong, STL 2.74

Wins
T. Bond, BOS 40
J. Devlin, LOU 35
T. Larkin, HAR 29
G. Bradley, CHI 18
T. Nichols, STL 18

Saves
C. McVey, CHI 2
J. Manning, CIN 1
A. Spalding, CHI 1

Strikeouts
T. Bond, BOS 170
J. Devlin, LOU 141
T. Larkin, HAR 96
T. Nichols, STL 80
G. Bradley, CHI 59

Complete Games
J. Devlin, LOU 61
T. Bond, BOS 58
T. Larkin, HAR 55
T. Nichols, STL 35
G. Bradley, CHI 35

NATIONAL LEAGUE 1877, *cont.*

BATTING AND BASE RUNNING LEADERS

Hits
D. White, BOS	103
C. McVey, CHI	98
J. O'Rourke, BOS	96
J. Cassidy, BKN	95

Base on Balls
J. O'Rourke, BOS	20
C. Jones, CHI, CIN	15
A. Booth, CIN	12
G. Hall, LOU	12

Home Run Percentage
L. Pike, CIN	1.5
O. Shaffer, LOU	1.2
C. Jones, CHI, CIN	0.8
P. Snyder, LOU	0.8

Runs Scored
J. O'Rourke, BOS	68
C. McVey, CHI	58
G. Wright, BOS	58
J. Start, BKN	55

Doubles
C. Anson, CHI	19
T. York, HAR	16
J. Manning, CIN	16
G. Hall, LOU	15

Triples
D. White, BOS	11
C. Jones, CHI, CIN	10
L. Brown, BOS	8
G. Hall, LOU	8

PITCHING LEADERS

Fewest Hits/9 Innings
T. Bond, BOS	9.16
T. Larkin, HAR	9.16
T. Nichols, STL	9.67
J. Blong, STL	9.75

Shutouts
T. Bond, BOS	6
T. Larkin, HAR	4
J. Devlin, LOU	4
G. Bradley, CHI	2

Fewest Walks/9 Innings
T. Bond, BOS	0.62
J. Devlin, LOU	0.66
C. Cummings, CIN	0.75
G. Bradley, CHI	0.89

Most Strikeouts/9 Inn.
B. Mitchell, CIN	3.69
T. Bond, BOS	2.94
J. Blong, STL	2.45
J. Devlin, LOU	2.27

Innings
J. Devlin, LOU	559
T. Bond, BOS	521
T. Larkin, HAR	501
G. Bradley, CHI	394

Games Pitched
J. Devlin, LOU	61
T. Bond, BOS	58
T. Larkin, HAR	56
G. Bradley, CHI	50

	W	L	PCT	GB	R	OR	2B	3B	HR	BA	SA	SB	E	DP	FA	CG	BB	SO	ShO	SV	ERA
Boston	42	18	.700		419	263	91	37	4	.296	.370	0	290	36	.889	61	38	177	7	0	2.15
Louisville	35	25	.583	7	339	288	75	36	9	.280	.354	0	267	37	.904	61	41	141	4	0	2.25
Hartford	31	27	.534	10	341	311	63	31	4	.270	.328	0	313	32	.885	59	56	99	4	0	2.32
St. Louis	28	32	.467	14	284	318	51	36	1	.244	.302	0	281	29	.892	52	92	132	1	0	2.66
Chicago	26	33	.441	15.5	366	375	79	30		.278	.340	0	313	43	.883	45	58	92	3	3	3.37
Cincinnati	15	42	.263	25.5	291	485	72	34	6	.255	.329	0	394	33	.852	48	61	85	1	1	4.19
					2040	2040	431	204	24	.271	.338	0	1858	210	.884	326	346	726	20	4	2.81

NATIONAL LEAGUE 1878

	POS	Player	AB	BA	HR	RBI	PO	A	E	DP	TC/G	FA	Pitcher	G	IP	W	L	SV	ERA
Boston W-41 L-19 Harry Wright	1B	J. Morrill	233	.240	0	23	606	22	28	36	11.1	.957	T. Bond	59	533	40	19	0	2.06
	2B	J. Burdock	246	.260	0	25	245	212	41	34	8.3	.918							
	SS	G. Wright	267	.225	0	12	72	197	15	24	4.8	.947							
	3B	E. Sutton	239	.226	1	29	80	118	25	8	3.8	.888							
	RF	J. Manning	248	.254	0	23	61	9	23	1	1.6	.753							
	CF	J. O'Rourke	255	.278	1	29	102	15	19	4	2.4	.860							
	LF	A. Leonard	262	.260	0	16	65	8	21	1	1.6	.777							
	C	P. Snyder	226	.212	0	14	344	92	42	2	8.2	.912							
	P	T. Bond	236	.212	0	23	27	117	9	4	2.6	.941							
Cincinnati W-37 L-23 Cal McVey	1B	C. Sullivan	244	.258	0	20	680	23	18	33	11.8	.975	W. White	52	468	30	21	0	1.79
	2B	J. Gerhardt	259	.297	0	28	159	206	38	26	6.7	.906							
	SS	B. Geer	237	.219	0	20	58	177	36	15	4.5	.867							
	3B	C. McVey	271	.306	2	28	78	106	42	6	3.7	.814							
	RF	K. Kelly	237	.283	0	27	51	24	23	2	2.1	.765							
	CF	L. Pike	145	.324	0	11	38	4	9	1	1.6	.824							
	LF	C. Jones	261	.310	3	39	120	9	15	1	2.4	.896							
	C	D. White	258	.314	0	29	262	66	33	4	7.5	.909							
	P	W. White	197	.142	0	9	13	90	15	2	2.3	.873							
	OF	B. Dickerson	123	.309	0	9	56	1	8	0	2.2	.877							
Providence W-33 L-27 Tom York	1B	T. Murnane	188	.239	0	14	543	22	36	25	12.5	.940	M. Ward	37	334	22	13	0	1.51
	2B	C. Sweasy	212	.175	0	8	141	183	59	20	7.0	.846	T. Nichols	11	98	4	7	0	4.22
	SS	T. Carey	253	.237	0	24	56	207	38	8	4.9	.874							
	3B	B. Hague	250	.204	0	25	81	177	21	5	4.5	.925							
	RF	D. Higham	281	.320	1	29	76	27	24	4	2.0	.811							
	CF	P. Hines	257	.358	4	50	109	15	22	4	2.4	.849							
	LF	T. York	269	.309	1	26	89	14	15	3	1.9	.873							
	C	L. Brown	243	.305	1	43	232	84	43	11	8.0	.880							
	P	M. Ward	138	.196	1	15	23	74	15	4	3.0	.866							
	C	D. Allison	76	.289	0	7	96	27	12	1	7.1	.911							
Chicago W-30 L-30 Bob Ferguson	1B	J. Start	285	.351	1	27	719	13	33	28	12.5	.957	T. Larkin	56	506	29	26	0	2.24
	2B	McClellan	205	.224	0	29	87	139	35	15	6.2	.866							
	SS	B. Ferguson	259	.351	0	39	71	226	40	17	5.9	.881							
	3B	F. Hankinson	240	.267	1	27	94	138	33	9	4.6	.875							
	RF	J. Cassidy	256	.266	0	29	89	30	28	6	2.5	.810							
	CF	J. Remsen	224	.232	1	19	103	14	7	5	2.2	.944							
	LF	C. Anson	261	.341	0	40	60	6	14	0	1.7	.825							
	C	B. Harbidge	240	.296	0	37	257	66	45	1	7.4	.878							
	P	T. Larkin	226	.288	0	32	19	90	18	0	2.3	.858							
	O2	J. Hallinan	67	.284	0	2	26	14	12	1		.769							

NATIONAL LEAGUE 1878, cont.

	POS	Player	AB	BA	HR	RBI	PO	A	E	DP	TC/G	FA	Pitcher	G	IP	W	L	SV	ERA
Indianapolis	1B	A. Croft	222	.158	0	16	534	8	21	19	11.0	.963	T. Nolan	38	347	13	22	0	2.57
	2B	J. Quest	278	.205	0	13	228	196	60	27	7.8	.876	McCormick	14	117	5	8	0	1.69
W-24 L-36	SS	F. Warner	165	.248	0	10	41	124	17	9	4.4	.907	T. Healey	11	89	6	4	1	2.22
	3B	Williamson	250	.232	1	19	88	128	33	6	4.0	.867							
John Clapp	RF	O. Shaffer	266	.338	0	30	105	28	25	2	2.5	.842							
	CF	R. McKelvey	253	.225	2	36	119	18	25	2	2.6	.846							
	LF	J. Clapp	263	.304	0	29	60	5	8	0	1.7	.890							
	C	S. Flint	254	.224	0	18	285	102	39	7	7.2	.908							
	P	T. Nolan	152	.243	0	16	19	80	11	5	2.9	.900							
	SS	C. Nelson	84	.131	0	5	19	50	13	1	4.3	.841							
Milwaukee	1B	J. Goodman	252	.246	1	27	693	12	42	15	12.5	.944	S. Weaver	45	383	12	31	0	1.95
	2B	J. Peters	246	.309	0	22	97	136	42	14	8.0	.853	M. Golden	22	161	3	13	0	4.14
W-15 L-45	SS	B. Redmond	187	.230	0	21	31	97	35	5	4.2	.785							
	3B	W. Foley	229	.271	0	22	68	87	36	8	3.6	.812							
Jack Chapman	RF	B. Holbert	173	.185	0	12	35	19	12	1	2.2	.818							
	CF	M. Golden	214	.206	0	20	50	9	12	2	1.8	.831							
	LF	A. Dalrymple	271	.354	0	15	128	11	28	3	2.7	.832							
	C	C. Bennett	184	.245	1	12	176	31	42	4	7.1	.831							
	UT	G. Creamer	193	.212	0	15	82	117	37	7		.843							
	P	S. Weaver	170	.200	0	3	31	78	16	1	2.8	.872							

BATTING AND BASE RUNNING LEADERS

Batting Average
P. Hines, PRO .358
A. Dalrymple, MIL .354
B. Ferguson, CHI .351
J. Start, CHI .351
C. Anson, CHI .341

Slugging Average
P. Hines, PRO .486
T. York, PRO .465
O. Shaffer, IND .455
L. Brown, PRO .453
C. Jones, CIN .441

Home Runs
P. Hines, PRO 4
C. Jones, CIN 3
R. McKelvey, IND 2
C. McVey, CIN 2

Total Bases
P. Hines, PRO 125
T. York, PRO 125
J. Start, CHI 125
O. Shaffer, IND 121
D. Higham, PRO 117

Runs Batted In
P. Hines, PRO 50
L. Brown, PRO 43
C. Anson, CHI 40
B. Ferguson, CHI 39
C. Jones, CIN 39

Stolen Bases
(not available)

Hits
J. Start, CHI 100
A. Dalrymple, MIL 96
P. Hines, PRO 92
B. Ferguson, CHI 91

Base on Balls
J. Remsen, CHI 17
T. Larkin, CHI 17
C. Anson, CHI 13
J. Clapp, IND 13

Home Run Percentage
P. Hines, PRO 1.6
C. Jones, CIN 1.1
R. McKelvey, IND 0.8
C. McVey, CIN 0.7

Runs Scored
D. Higham, PRO 60
J. Start, CHI 58
T. York, PRO 56
C. Anson, CHI 55

Doubles
D. Higham, PRO 22
L. Brown, PRO 21
O. Shaffer, IND 19
T. York, PRO 19

Triples
T. York, PRO 10
J. O'Rourke, BOS 7
C. Jones, CIN 7
L. Brown, PRO 6

PITCHING LEADERS

Winning Percentage
T. Bond, BOS .678
M. Ward, PRO .629
W. White, CIN .588
T. Larkin, CHI .527
T. Nolan, IND .371

Earned Run Average
M. Ward, PRO 1.51
McCormick, IND 1.69
W. White, CIN 1.79
S. Weaver, MIL 1.95
T. Bond, BOS 2.06

Wins
T. Bond, BOS 40
W. White, CIN 30
T. Larkin, CHI 29
M. Ward, PRO 22
T. Nolan, IND 13

Saves
T. Healey, IND, PRO 1

Strikeouts
T. Bond, BOS 182
W. White, CIN 169
T. Larkin, CHI 163
T. Nolan, IND 125
M. Ward, PRO 116

Complete Games
T. Bond, BOS 57
T. Larkin, CHI 56
W. White, CIN 52
S. Weaver, MIL 39
M. Ward, PRO 37
T. Nolan, IND 37

Fewest Hits/9 Innings
M. Ward, PRO 8.30
S. Weaver, MIL 8.72
T. Larkin, CHI 9.09
W. White, CIN 9.17

Shutouts
T. Bond, BOS 9
M. Ward, PRO 6
W. White, CIN 5

Fewest Walks/9 Innings
S. Weaver, MIL 0.49
T. Larkin, CHI 0.55
T. Bond, BOS 0.56
W. White, CIN 0.87

Most Strikeouts/9 Inn.
W. White, CIN 3.25
T. Nolan, IND 3.24
M. Ward, PRO 3.13
T. Bond, BOS 3.08

Innings
T. Bond, BOS 533
T. Larkin, CHI 506
W. White, CIN 468
S. Weaver, MIL 383

Games Pitched
T. Bond, BOS 59
T. Larkin, CHI 56
W. White, CIN 52
S. Weaver, MIL 45

	W	L	PCT	GB	R	OR	2B	3B	HR	BA	SA	SB	E	DP	FA	CG	BB	SO	ShO	SV	ERA
							Batting						Fielding			Pitching					
Boston	41	19	.683		298	241	75	25	2	.241	.300	0	228	48	.914	58	38	184	9	0	2.32
Cincinnati	37	23	.617	4	333	281	67	22	5	.276	.331	0	269	37	.900	61	63	220	6	0	1.84
Providence	33	27	.550	8	353	337	107	30	8	.263	.346	0	311	42	.892	59	86	173	6	0	2.38
Chicago	30	30	.500	11	371	331	91	20	3	.290	.350	0	304	37	.891	61	35	175	1	0	2.37
Indianapolis	24	36	.400	17	293	328	76	15	3	.236	.286	0	290	37	.898	59	87	182	2	1	2.32
Milwaukee	15	45	.250	26	256	386	65	20	2	.250	.300	0	376	32	.866	54	55	147	1	0	2.60
					1904	1904	481	132	23	.259	.319	0	1778	233	.893	352	364	1081	25	1	2.30

NATIONAL LEAGUE 1879

	POS	Player	AB	BA	HR	RBI	PO	A	E	DP	TC/G	FA	Pitcher	G	IP	W	L	SV	ERA
Providence	1B	J. Start	317	.319	2	37	779	11	22	24	12.5	.973	M. Ward	70	587	47	17	1	2.15
	2B	M. McGeary	374	.275	0	35	218	255	62	21	7.3	.884	B. Mathews	27	189	12	8	1	2.29
W-59 L-25	SS	G. Wright	388	.276	1	42	96	319	34	17	5.3	.924							
	3B	B. Hague	209	.225	0	21	54	122	38	2	4.2	.822							
George Wright	RF	J. O'Rourke	362	.348	1	46	51	11	17	2	1.4	.785							
	CF	P. Hines	409	.357	2	52	146	24	26	3	2.3	.867							
	LF	T. York	342	.310	1	50	114	9	14	2	1.7	.898							
	C	L. Brown	229	.258	2	40	286	63	63*	5	8.6*	.847							
	P	M. Ward	364	.286	2	41	31	134	11	2	2.5	.938							
	PO	B. Mathews	173	.202	1	10	21	44	9	1		.878							
	C	E. Gross	132	.348	0	24	152	39	22	1	7.1	.897							

NATIONAL LEAGUE 1879, *cont.*

	POS	Player	AB	BA	HR	RBI	PO	A	E	DP	TC/G	FA	Pitcher	G	IP	W	L	SV	ERA
Boston	1B	E. Cogswell	236	.322	1	18	539	10	19	24	11.6	.967	T. Bond	64	555	43	19	0	**1.96**
	2B	J. Burdock	359	.240	0	36	**303**	300	59	43	7.9	.911	C. Foley	21	162	9	9	1	2.51
W-54 L-30	SS	E. Sutton	339	.248	0	34	53	167	29	15	4.9	.884							
	3B	J. Morrill	348	.282	0	49	70	96	23	2	3.7	**.878**							
Harry Wright	RF	S. Houck	356	.267	2	49	62	17	18	2	2.1	.814							
	CF	J. O'Rourke	317	.341	6	**62**	147	10	21	2	2.5	.882							
	LF	C. Jones	355	.315	9	**62**	162	20	13	1	2.3	**.933**							
	C	P. Snyder	329	.237	2	35	398	142	44	10	7.3	**.925**							
	P	T. Bond	257	.241	0	21	33	**144**	8	7	2.9	**.957**							
	OF	B. Hawes	155	.200	0	9	38	10	10	2	1.7	.828							
	PO	C. Foley	146	.315	0	17	13	28	12	0		.774							
Buffalo	1B	O. Walker	287	.275	1	35	**828**	**30**	49	**52**	12.6	.946	P. Galvin	66	593	37	27	0	2.28
	2B	C. Fulmer	306	.268	0	28	273	301	60	**46**	8.3	.905	McGunnigle	14	120	9	5	0	2.63
W-46 L-32	SS	D. Force	316	.209	0	8	74	264	26	**26**	4.7	**.929**							
	3B	Richardson	336	.283	0	37	83	153	44	13	3.6	.843							
John Clapp	RF	B. Crowley	261	.287	0	30	62	14	18	4	2.2	.809							
	CF	D. Eggler	317	.208	0	27	114	11	11	2	1.7	.919							
	LF	J. Hornung	319	.266	0	38	129	12	26	1	2.2	.844							
	C	J. Clapp	292	.264	1	36	286	60	36	4	6.1	.906							
	P	P. Galvin	265	.249	0	27	35	141	**26**	8	3.1	.871							
	OF	McGunnigle	171	.175	0	5	61	6	6	0	2.1	.918							
Chicago	1B	C. Anson	227	**.317**	0	34	620	8	16	26	**12.6**	**.975**	T. Larkin	58	513	31	23	0	2.44
	2B	J. Quest	334	.207	0	22	263	331	48	30	7.7	**.925**	F. Hankinson	26	231	15	10	0	2.50
W-46 L-33	SS	J. Peters	379	.245	1	31	94	271	**71**	14	5.3	.837							
	3B	Williamson	320	.294	1	36	84	**193**	41	13	4.5	.871							
Cap Anson	RF	O. Shaffer	316	.304	0	35	99	**50**	37	3	2.6	.801							
W-41 L-21	CF	G. Gore	266	.263	0	32	93	9	15	0	2.2	.872							
	LF	A. Dalrymple	333	.291	0	23	103	4	**40**	1	2.1	.728							
Silver Flint	C	S. Flint	324	.284	1	41	341	109	42	6	6.3	.915							
W-5 L-12	P	T. Larkin	228	.219	0	18	10	79	8	1	1.7	.918							
	UT	F. Hankinson	171	.181	0	8	42	87	14	1		.902							
	OF	J. Remsen	152	.217	0	8	52	4	9	1	2.1	.862							
Cincinnati	1B	C. McVey	354	.297	0	55	736	5	42	33	10.9	.946	W. White	**76**	**680**	43	31	0	1.99
	2B	J. Gerhardt	313	.198	1	39	191	192	39	23	7.7	.908							
W-43 L-37	SS	R. Barnes	323	.266	1	30	93	211	48	14	**5.8**	.864							
	3B	K. Kelly	345	.348	2	47	36	88	25	3	4.5	.832							
Deacon White	RF	W. Foley	218	.211	0	25	38	9	8	0	2.2	.855							
W-9 L-9	CF	P. Hotaling	369	.279	1	27	118	16	25	2	2.3	.843							
	LF	B. Dickerson	350	.291	2	57	144	9	38	1	2.4	.801							
Cal McVey	C	D. White	333	.330	1	52	307	92	44	3	7.5	.901							
W-34 L-28	P	W. White	294	.136	0	17	20	114	20	0	2.0	.870							
	UT	M. Burke	117	.222	0	8	36	62	32	3		.754							
Cleveland	1B	B. Phillips	365	.271	0	29	726	22	36	23	10.5	.954	McCormick	62	546	20	**40**	0	2.42
	2B	J. Glasscock	325	.209	0	29	201	208	36	18	6.7	.919	B. Mitchell	23	195	7	15	0	3.28
W-27 L-55	SS	T. Carey	335	.239	0	32	79	263	54	13	5.0	.864							
	3B	F. Warner	316	.244	0	22	78	109	39	5	4.2	.827							
Jim McCormick	RF	C. Eden	353	.272	3	34	101	21	29	3	1.9	.808							
	CF	G. Strief	264	.174	0	15	104	8	10	0	2.2	.918							
	LF	B. Riley	165	.145	0	9	79	12	16	1	2.5	.850							
	C	D. Kennedy	193	.290	1	18	277	50	40	2	8.0	.891							
	P	McCormick	282	.220	0	20	39	119	4	4	2.7	.946							
	CO	B. Gilligan	205	.171	0	11	179	47	36	0		.863							
	P	B. Mitchell	109	.147	0	6	11	24	14	2	2.1	.714							
Syracuse	1B	H. Carpenter	261	.203	0	20	298	10	17	12	9.6	.948	McCormick	54	457	18	33	0	2.99
	2B	J. Farrell	241	.303	1	22	162	186	52	16	7.4	.870	B. Purcell	22	180	4	15	0	3.76
W-22 L-48	SS	J. Macullar	246	.211	0	13	61	111	27	9	5.4	.864							
	3B	R. Woodhead	131	.160	0	2	52	51	27	4	3.8	.792							
Mike Dorgan	RF	B. Purcell	277	.260	0	24	64	4	20	0	1.9	.773							
W-17 L-26	CF	J. Richmond	254	.213	1	23	76	7	12	1	2.7	.874							
	LF	M. Mansell	242	.215	1	13	**204**	11	29	2	**3.6**	.881							
Bill Holbert	C	B. Holbert	229	.201	0	21	277	64	39	4	6.8	.897							
W-0 L-1	UT	M. Dorgan	270	.267	1	17	275	60	46	10		.879							
Jimmy Macullar	P	McCormick	230	.222	1	21	13	68	8	0	1.6	.910							
W-5 L-21																			

NATIONAL LEAGUE 1879, cont.

Troy

W-19 L-56

Horace Phillips
W-12 L-34

Bob Ferguson
W-7 L-22

POS	Player	AB	BA	HR	RBI	PO	A	E	DP	TC/G	FA	Pitcher	G	IP	W	L	SV	ERA
1B	D. Brouthers	168	.274	4	17	406	6	33	11	12.0	.926	G. Bradley	54	487	13	40	0	2.85
2B	T. Hawkes	250	.208	0	20	220	264	56	26	8.4	.896	H. Salisbury	10	89	4	6	0	2.22
SS	E. Caskin	304	.257	0	21	42	169	23	10	5.6	.902							
3B	H. Doscher	191	.220	0	18	49	96	35	7	3.8	.806							
RF	J. Evans	280	.232	0	17	153	30	24	4	2.9	.884							
CF	A. Hall	306	.258	0	14	126	18	27	3	2.6	.842							
LF	T. Mansell	177	.243	0	11	63	3	23	1	2.2	.742							
C	C. Reilley	236	.229	0	19	231	49	43	2	6.6	.867							
P	G. Bradley	251	.247	0	23	24	132	24	0	3.3	.867							
10	A. Clapp	146	.267	0	18	279	7	25	10		.920							
3B	B. Ferguson	123	.252	0	4	29	55	20	5	4.3	.808							
SS	C. Nelson	106	.264	0	10	37	89	25	8	6.3	.834							
OF	S. Taylor	97	.216	0	8	37	2	12	0	2.1	.765							

BATTING AND BASE RUNNING LEADERS

Batting Average
C. Anson, CHI — .396
P. Hines, PRO — .357
J. O'Rourke, PRO — .348
K. Kelly, CIN — .348
J. O'Rourke, BOS — .341

Slugging Average
J. O'Rourke, BOS — .521
C. Jones, BOS — .510
C. Anson, CHI — .493
K. Kelly, CIN — .493
P. Hines, PRO — .482

Home Runs
C. Jones, BOS — 9
J. O'Rourke, BOS — 6
D. Brouthers, TRO — 4
C. Eden, CLE — 3

Winning Percentage
M. Ward, PRO — .734
T. Bond, BOS — .694
B. Mathews, PRO — .667
F. Hankinson, CHI — .600
W. White, CIN — .581

Earned Run Average
T. Bond, BOS — 1.96
W. White, CIN — 1.99
M. Ward, PRO — 2.15
P. Galvin, BUF — 2.28
B. Mathews, PRO — 2.29

Wins
M. Ward, PRO — 47
T. Bond, BOS — 43
W. White, CIN — 43
P. Galvin, BUF — 37
T. Larkin, CHI — 31

Total Bases
P. Hines, PRO — 197
C. Jones, BOS — 181
K. Kelly, CIN — 170
J. O'Rourke, PRO — 166
J. O'Rourke, BOS — 165

Runs Batted In
J. O'Rourke, BOS — 62
C. Jones, BOS — 62
B. Dickerson, CIN — 57
C. McVey, CIN — 55
D. White, CIN — 52
P. Hines, PRO — 52

Stolen Bases
(not available)

Saves
M. Ward, PRO — 1
C. Foley, BOS — 1
B. Mathews, PRO — 1

Strikeouts
M. Ward, PRO — 239
W. White, CIN — 232
McCormick, CLE — 197
T. Bond, BOS — 155
T. Larkin, CHI — 142

Complete Games
W. White, CIN — 75
P. Galvin, BUF — 65
McCormick, CLE — 59
T. Bond, BOS — 59
M. Ward, PRO — 58

Hits
P. Hines, PRO — 146
J. O'Rourke, PRO — 126
K. Kelly, CIN — 120
C. Jones, BOS — 112

Base on Balls
C. Jones, BOS — 29
Williamson, CHI — 24
T. York, PRO — 19
R. Barnes, CIN — 16

Home Run Percentage
C. Jones, BOS — 2.5
J. O'Rourke, BOS — 1.9
C. Eden, CLE — 0.8
L. Brown, CHI, PRO — 0.8

Fewest Hits/9 Innings
McGunnigle, BUF — 8.47
M. Ward, PRO — 8.75
T. Bond, BOS — 8.80
P. Galvin, BUF — 8.88

Shutouts
T. Bond, BOS — 12
P. Galvin, BUF — 6
McCormick, SYR — 5
W. White, CIN — 4

Fewest Walks/9 Innings
T. Bond, BOS — 0.39
P. Galvin, BUF — 0.47
G. Bradley, TRO — 0.48
T. Larkin, CHI — 0.53

Runs Scored
C. Jones, BOS — 85
P. Hines, PRO — 81
G. Wright, PRO — 79
K. Kelly, CIN — 78

Doubles
C. Eden, CLE — 31
A. Dalrymple, CHI — 25
T. York, PRO — 25
P. Hines, PRO — 25

Triples
B. Dickerson, CIN — 14
Williamson, CHI — 13
K. Kelly, CIN — 12
J. O'Rourke, BOS — 11

Most Strikeouts/9 Inn.
McGunnigle, BUF — 4.65
B. Mathews, PRO — 4.29
B. Mitchell, CLE — 4.16
M. Ward, PRO — 3.66

Innings
W. White, CIN — 680
P. Galvin, BUF — 593
M. Ward, PRO — 587
T. Bond, BOS — 555

Games Pitched
W. White, CIN — 76
M. Ward, PRO — 70
P. Galvin, BUF — 66
T. Bond, BOS — 64

	W	L	PCT	GB	R	OR	2B	3B	HR	BA	SA	SB	E	DP	FA	CG	BB	SO	ShO	SV	ERA
Providence	59	25	.702		612	355	142	55	12	.296	.381	0	382	41	.902	73	62	329	2	2	2.18
Boston	54	30	.643	5	562	348	138	51	20	.274	.368	0	319	58	.913	79	46	230	12	1	2.19
Buffalo	46	32	.590	10	394	365	105	54	2	.252	.328	0	331	62	.906	78	47	198	8	0	2.34
Chicago	46	33	.582	10.5	485	411	167	32	3	.259	.336	0	381	52	.900	82	57	211	5	0	2.46
Cincinnati	43	37	.538	14	485	464	127	53	8	.264	.347	0	454	48	.877	79	81	246	4	0	2.29
Cleveland	27	55	.329	31	322	461	116	29	4	.223	.285	0	406	42	.889	79	116	287	3	0	2.65
Syracuse	22	48	.314	30	276	462	61	19	5	.227	.270	0	398	37	.872	64	52	132	5	0	3.19
Troy	19	56	.253	35.5	321	543	102	24	4	.237	.294	0	460	44	.875	75	47	210	3	0	2.80
					3409	3409	958	317	58	.255	.329	0	3131	384	.892	609	508	1843	42	3	2.50

NATIONAL LEAGUE 1880

Chicago

W-67 L-17

Cap Anson

POS	Player	AB	BA	HR	RBI	PO	A	E	DP	TC/G	FA	Pitcher	G	IP	W	L	SV	ERA
1B	C. Anson	356	.337	1	74	833	15	20	28	10.7	.977	L. Corcoran	63	536	43	14	2	1.95
2B	J. Quest	300	.237	0	27	223	270	58	26	6.9	.895	F. Goldsmith	26	210	21	3	1	1.75
SS	T. Burns	333	.309	0	43	62	186	39	9	3.6	.864							
3B	Williamson	311	.251	0	31	83	143	27	5	4.0	.893							
RF	K. Kelly	344	.291	1	60	49	32	23	1	1.6	.779							
CF	G. Gore	322	.360	2	47	124	18	21	4	2.2	.871							
LF	A. Dalrymple	382	.330	0	36	157	19	29	4	2.4	.859							
C	S. Flint	284	.162	0	17	388	117	37	4	8.1	.932							
P	L. Corcoran	286	.231	0	25	34	122	7	2	2.6	.957							
PO	F. Goldsmith	142	.261	0	15	21	53	8	0		.902							

NATIONAL LEAGUE 1880, *cont.*

	POS	Player	AB	BA	HR	RBI	PO	A	E	DP	TC/G	FA	Pitcher	G	IP	W	L	SV	ERA
Providence	1B	J. Start	345	.278	0	27	**954**	10	29	30	**12.1**	.971	M. Ward	70	595	40	23	1	1.74
	2B	J. Farrell	339	.271	3	36	207	274	61	26	6.8	.887	G. Bradley	28	196	12	9	1	1.38
W-52 L-32	SS	J. Peters	359	.228	0	24	111	268	42	26	4.9	**.900**							
	3B	G. Bradley	309	.227	0	23	71	**165**	40	8	**4.8**	.855							
Mike McGeary	RF	M. Dorgan	321	.246	0	31	96	25	20	4	1.8	.858							
W-8 L-7	CF	P. Hines	374	.307	3	35	148	17	13	**7**	2.4	.927							
	LF	T. York	203	.212	0	18	94	5	7	1	2.0	**.934**							
Monte Ward	C	E. Gross	347	.259	1	34	**429**	**126**	**86**	5	7.4	.866							
W-18 L-13	P	M. Ward	356	.228	0	27	43	133	3	1	2.6	.983							
	OF	S. Houck	184	.201	1	22	86	10	14	0	2.2	.873							
Mike Dorgan																			
W-26 L-12																			
Cleveland	1B	B. Phillips	334	.254	1	36	842	25	33	**37**	10.6	.963	McCormick	74	658	45	28	0	1.85
	2B	F. Dunlap	373	.276	4	30	252	**290**	53	44	7.0	.911							
W-47 L-37	SS	J. Glasscock	296	.243	0	27	107	252	44	21	5.2	.891							
	3B	F. Hankinson	263	.209	1	19	68	89	29	7	3.3	.844							
Jim McCormick	RF	O. Shaffer	338	.266	0	21	128	**35**	18	5	2.2	.901							
	CF	P. Hotaling	325	.240	4	41	115	14	15	4	1.8	.896							
	LF	N. Hanlon	280	.246	0	32	135	9	**35**	4	2.6	.804							
	C	D. Kennedy	250	.200	0	18	397	68	52	**9**	8.0	.899							
	P	McCormick	289	.246	0	26	36	135	22	3	2.6	.886							
	3B	M. McGeary	111	.252	0	3	37	49	11	4	3.3	.887							
	C	B. Gilligan	99	.172	1	13	124	33	5	4	7.0	.969							
Troy	1B	E. Cogswell	209	.301	0	13	475	15	20	18	10.9	.961	M. Welch	65	574	34	30	0	2.54
	2B	B. Ferguson	332	.262	0	22	294	255	58	38	7.4	.904	T. Keefe	12	105	6	6	0	**0.86**
W-41 L-42	SS	E. Caskin	333	.225	0	28	97	297	**51**	16	5.4	.885							
	3B	R. Connor	340	.332	3	47	116	159	**60**	10	4.0	.821							
Bob Ferguson	RF	J. Evans	180	.256	0	22	68	9	8	4	1.8	.906							
	CF	J. Cassidy	352	.253	0	29	128	18	20	1	2.0	.880							
	LF	P. Gillespie	346	.243	2	24	**185**	14	21	5	2.7	.905							
	C	B. Holbert	212	.189	0	8	261	107	36	6	7.0	.911							
	P	M. Welch	251	.287	0	27	35	86	21	4	2.2	.852							
	1B	B. Tobin	136	.162	0	8	297	8	16	25	9.7	.950							
	OF	B. Dickerson	119	.193	0	10	77	7	9	3	3.1	.903							
Worcester	1B	C. Sullivan	166	.259	0	0	447	12	8	19	10.9	**.983**	L. Richmond	74	591	32	32	3	2.15
	2B	G. Creamer	306	.199	0	27	238	274	68	34	6.8	.883	F. Corey	25	148	8	9	2	2.43
W-40 L-43	SS	A. Irwin	352	.259	1	35	95	**339**	**51**	**27**	5.9	.895							
	3B	A. Whitney	302	.222	1	36	83	162	40	6	3.8	.860							
Frank Bancroft	RF	L. Knight	201	.239	0	21	47	22	11	1	1.6	.863							
	CF	H. Stovey	355	.265	**6**	28	68	6	12	1	1.9	.860							
	LF	G. Wood	327	.245	0	28	123	10	17	0	1.9	.887							
	C	C. Bennett	193	.228	0	18	280	45	31	3	7.7	.913							
	P	L. Richmond	309	.227	0	34	13	97	**23**	1	1.8	.827							
	C	D. Bushong	146	.171	0	19	261	76	30	6	9.2	.918							
	OP	F. Corey	138	.174	0	6	25	19	13	2		.772							
	OF	B. Dickerson	133	.293	0	20	48	4	9	2	2.0	.852							
Boston	1B	J. Morrill	342	.237	2	44	434	**26**	16	26	10.3	.966	T. Bond	63	493	26	29	0	2.67
	2B	J. Burdock	356	.253	2	35	**328**	275	60	39	7.6	.923	C. Foley	36	238	14	14	0	3.89
W-40 L-44	SS	E. Sutton	288	.250	0	25	50	122	20	14	4.9	.896							
	3B	J. O'Rourke	363	.275	6	45	17	15	3	2	3.5	.914							
Harry Wright	RF	C. Foley	332	.292	2	31	35	6	8	1	1.4	.837							
	CF	J. O'Rourke	313	.275	3	36	156	19	26	0	2.5	.871							
	LF	C. Jones	280	.300	5	38	108	11	25	3	2.2	.826							
	C	P. Powers	126	.143	0	10	152	59	37	6	6.7	.851							
	PO	T. Bond	282	.220	0	24	60	152	16	8		.930							
	SS	J. Richmond	129	.248	0	9	30	73	19	14	3.9	.844							
	C	S. Trott	125	.208	0	9	170	56	27	0	7.0	.893							
Buffalo	1B	Esterbrook	253	.241	0	35	463	17	31	20	10.9	.939	P. Galvin	58	459	20	35	0	2.71
	2B	D. Force	290	.169	0	17	163	206	24	27	7.4	**.939**	S. Weidman	17	114	0	9	0	3.40
W-24 L-58	SS	M. Moynahan	100	.330	0	14	30	70	16	7	4.3	.862	T. Poorman	11	85	1	8	1	4.13
	3B	Richardson	343	.259	0	17	108	154	47	6	3.8	.848							
Sam Crane	RF	D. Stearns	104	.183	0	13	21	3	7	1	1.6	.774							
	CF	B. Crowley	354	.268	0	20	131	23	33	3	2.5	.824							
	LF	J. Hornung	342	.266	1	42	127	12	20	2	2.4	.874							
	C	J. Rowe	326	.252	0	36	231	56	33	3	5.3	.897							
	P	P. Galvin	241	.212	0	12	24	97	13	1	2.3	.903							
	10	O. Walker	126	.230	1	15	267	10	27	17		.911							

NATIONAL LEAGUE 1880, cont.

	POS	Player	AB	BA	HR	RBI	PO	A	E	DP	TC/G	FA	Pitcher	G	IP	W	L	SV	ERA
Cincinnati	1B	L. Reilly	272	.206	0	16	615	13	35	36	9.2	.947	W. White	62	517	18	42	0	2.14
	2B	P. Smith	334	.207	0	27	282	243	89	32	7.4	.855	B. Purcell	25	196	3	17	0	3.21
W-21 L-59	SS	L. Say	191	.199	0	15	54	164	44	11	5.5	.832							
	3B	H. Carpenter	300	.240	0	23	136	126	45	9	4.6	.853							
John Clapp	RF	J. Manning	190	.216	2	17	59	12	18	1	1.9	.798							
	CF	B. Purcell	325	.292	1	24	78	14	21	1	2.1	.814							
	LF	M. Mansell	187	.193	2	12	147	13	25	5	3.5	.865							
	C	J. Clapp	323	.282	1	20	420	121	62	5	8.3	.897							
	P	W. White	207	.169	0	14	17	68	10	2	1.5	.895							
	OF	D. White	141	.298	0	7	36	9	16	1	1.8	.738							
	S3	A. Leonard	133	.211	1	17	29	75	21	4		.832							
	UT	C. Reilley	103	.204	0	9	68	16	14	0		.857							
	OF	J. Sommer	88	.182	0	6	38	4	4	1	2.1	.913							

BATTING AND BASE RUNNING LEADERS

Batting Average
- G. Gore, CHI .360
- C. Anson, CHI .337
- R. Connor, TRO .332
- A. Dalrymple, CHI .330
- T. Burns, CHI .309

Slugging Average
- G. Gore, CHI .463
- R. Connor, TRO .459
- A. Dalrymple, CHI .458
- H. Stovey, WOR .454
- J. O'Rourke, BOS .441

Home Runs
- H. Stovey, WOR 6
- J. O'Rourke, BOS 6
- C. Jones, BOS 5
- F. Dunlap, CLE 4

Total Bases
- A. Dalrymple, CHI 175
- H. Stovey, WOR 161
- J. O'Rourke, BOS 160
- F. Dunlap, CLE 160
- R. Connor, TRO 156

Runs Batted In
(not available)

Stolen Bases
(not available)

Hits
- A. Dalrymple, CHI 126
- C. Anson, CHI 120
- G. Gore, CHI 116
- P. Hines, PRO 115

Base on Balls
- B. Ferguson, TRO 24
- G. Gore, CHI 21
- J. Clapp, CIN 21
- J. O'Rourke, BOS 21

Home Run Percentage
- C. Jones, BOS 1.8
- H. Stovey, WOR 1.7
- J. O'Rourke, BOS 1.7
- F. Dunlap, CLE 1.1

Runs Scored
- A. Dalrymple, CHI 91
- H. Stovey, WOR 76
- K. Kelly, CHI 72
- J. O'Rourke, BOS 71

Doubles
- F. Dunlap, CLE 27
- A. Dalrymple, CHI 25
- C. Anson, CHI 24
- G. Gore, CHI 23

Triples
- H. Stovey, WOR 14
- A. Dalrymple, CHI 12
- J. Hornung, BUF 11
- J. O'Rourke, BOS 11

PITCHING LEADERS

Winning Percentage
- F. Goldsmith, CHI .875
- L. Corcoran, CHI .754
- G. Bradley, PRO .636
- M. Ward, PRO .635
- McCormick, CLE .616

Earned Run Average
- T. Keefe, TRO 0.86
- G. Bradley, PRO 1.38
- M. Ward, PRO 1.74
- F. Goldsmith, CHI 1.75
- McCormick, CLE 1.85

Wins
- McCormick, CLE 45
- L. Corcoran, CHI 43
- M. Ward, PRO 40
- M. Welch, TRO 34
- L. Richmond, WOR 32

Saves
- L. Richmond, WOR 3
- L. Corcoran, CHI 2
- F. Corey, WOR 2

Strikeouts
- L. Corcoran, CHI 268
- McCormick, CLE 260
- L. Richmond, WOR 243
- M. Ward, PRO 230
- W. White, CIN 161

Complete Games
- McCormick, CLE 72
- M. Welch, TRO 64
- M. Ward, PRO 59
- W. White, CIN 58
- L. Corcoran, CHI 57
- L. Richmond, WOR 57

Fewest Hits/9 Innings
- T. Keefe, TRO 6.09
- L. Corcoran, CHI 6.78
- G. Bradley, PRO 7.26
- M. Ward, PRO 7.58

Shutouts
- M. Ward, PRO 9
- McCormick, CLE 7
- P. Galvin, BUF 5
- L. Corcoran, CHI 5

Fewest Walks/9 Innings
- G. Bradley, PRO 0.28
- P. Galvin, BUF 0.63
- M. Ward, PRO 0.68
- F. Goldsmith, CHI 0.77

Most Strikeouts/9 Inn.
- L. Corcoran, CHI 4.50
- F. Goldsmith, CHI 3.85
- L. Richmond, WOR 3.70
- T. Keefe, TRO 3.69

Innings
- McCormick, CLE 658
- M. Ward, PRO 595
- L. Richmond, WOR 591
- M. Welch, TRO 574

Games Pitched
- McCormick, CLE 74
- L. Richmond, WOR 74
- M. Ward, PRO 70
- M. Welch, TRO 65

	W	L	PCT	GB	R	OR	2B	3B	HR	BA	SA	SB	E	DP	FA	CG	BB	SO	ShO	SV	ERA
Chicago	67	17	.798		538	317	164	39	4	.279	.360	0	329	41	.911	80	129	367	9	3	1.93
Providence	52	32	.619	15	419	299	114	34	8	.248	.313	0	357	53	.910	75	51	286	12	2	1.64
Cleveland	47	37	.560	20	387	337	130	52	7	.242	.327	0	330	52	.910	83	98	289	7	1	1.90
Troy	41	42	.494	25.5	392	438	114	37	5	.251	.319	0	366	58	.900	81	113	173	4	0	2.74
Worcester	40	43	.482	26.5	412	370	129	52	8	.231	.316	0	355	49	.905	68	97	297	3	5	2.27
Boston	40	44	.476	27	416	456	134	41	20	.253	.343	0	367	54	.901	70	86	187	3	0	3.08
Buffalo	24	58	.293	42	331	502	104	37	3	.226	.289	0	408	55	.890	72	78	186	6	1	3.09
Cincinnati	21	59	.263	44	296	472	91	36	7	.224	.288	0	437	49	.877	79	88	208	3	0	2.44
					3191	3191	980	328	62	.245	.320	0	2949	411	.901	608	740	1993	51	12	2.37

NATIONAL LEAGUE 1881

	POS	Player	AB	BA	HR	RBI	PO	A	E	DP	TC/G	FA	Pitcher	G	IP	W	L	SV	ERA
Chicago	1B	C. Anson	343	.399	1	82	892	43	24	48	11.4	.975	L. Corcoran	45	397	31	14	0	2.31
	2B	J. Quest	293	.246	1	26	238	249	37	28	6.8	.929	F. Goldsmith	39	330	24	13	0	2.59
W-56 L-28	SS	T. Burns	342	.278	4	42	100	249	52	20	5.0	.870							
	3B	Williamson	343	.268	1	48	117	194	31	10	4.5	.909							
Cap Anson	RF	K. Kelly	353	.323	2	55	85	31	22	2	1.9	.841							
	CF	G. Gore	309	.298	1	44	146	21	24	3	2.7	.874							
	LF	A. Dalrymple	362	.323	1	37	143	14	31	1	2.3	.835							
	C	S. Flint	306	.310	1	34	319	92	27	6	5.5	.938							
	P	L. Corcoran	189	.222	0	9	29	63	11	0	2.3	.893							
	P	F. Goldsmith	158	.241	0	16	18	95	18	2	3.4	.863							
	OF	H. Nicol	108	.204	0	7	44	11	4	1	2.3	.932							

NATIONAL LEAGUE 1881, cont.

	POS	Player	AB	BA	HR	RBI	PO	A	E	DP	TC/G	FA	Pitcher	G	IP	W	L	SV	ERA
Providence	1B	J. Start	348	.328	0	29	837	17	33	50	11.2	.963	M. Ward	39	330	18	18	0	2.13
	2B	J. Farrell	345	.238	5	36	214	271	64	40	6.7	.883	O. Radbourn	41	325	25	11	0	2.43
W-47 L-37	SS	McClellan	259	.166	0	16	59	147	35	18	4.8	.855	B. Mathews	14	102	4	8	0	3.17
	3B	J. Denny	320	.241	1	24	144	181	62	12	4.6	.840							
Jack Farrell	RF	M. Ward	357	.244	0	53	64	14	9	0	2.2	.897							
W-24 L-27	CF	P. Hines	361	.285	2	31	178	14	22	2	2.7	.897							
	LF	T. York	316	.304	2	47	159	17	29	1	2.4	.859							
Tom York	C	E. Gross	182	.275	1	24	240	70	37	5	6.9	.893							
W-23 L-10	UT	O. Radbourn	270	.219	0	28	57	121	30	8		.856							
	C	B. Gilligan	183	.219	0	20	184	41	17	9	6.7	.930							
Buffalo	1B	D. Brouthers	270	.319	8	45	321	11	17	17	11.6	.951	P. Galvin	56	474	29	24	0	2.37
	2B	D. Force	278	.180	0	15	168	218	26	19	8.1	.937	J. Lynch	20	166	10	9	0	3.59
W-45 L-38	SS	J. Peters	229	.214	0	25	102	183	43	17	6.2	.869							
	3B	J. O'Rourke	348	.302	0	30	85	80	36	8	3.6	.821							
Jim O'Rourke	RF	C. Foley	375	.256	1	25	79	14	24	5	2.1	.795							
	CF	Richardson	344	.291	2	53	179	45	21	3	3.1	.914							
	LF	D. White	319	.310	0	53	19	8	11	0	2.2	.711							
	C	J. Rowe	246	.333	1	43	187	39	25	5	5.5	.900							
	P	P. Galvin	236	.212	0	21	36	123	19	7	3.2	.893							
	C	S. Sullivan	121	.190	0	15	108	31	24	1	5.3	.853							
	OF	B. Purcell	113	.292	0	17	32	4	15	0	2.0	.706							
Detroit	1B	M. Powell	219	.338	1	38	513	17	31	47	10.2	.945	G. Derby	56	495	29	26	0	2.20
	2B	J. Gerhardt	297	.242	0	36	259	242	51	62	7.0	.908	S. Weidman	13	115	8	5	0	1.80
W-41 L-43	SS	S. Houck	308	.279	1	36	88	241	50	40	5.1	.868							
	3B	A. Whitney	214	.182	0	9	73	141	38	10	4.3	.849							
Frank Bancroft	RF	L. Knight	340	.271	1	52	116	21	17	6	1.9	.890							
	CF	N. Hanlon	305	.279	2	28	141	15	18	4	2.4	.897							
	LF	G. Wood	337	.297	2	32	132	18	24	4	2.2	.862							
	C	C. Bennett	299	.301	7	64	418	85	20	6	7.5	.962							
	P	G. Derby	236	.186	0	12	25	97	9	4	2.3	.931							
	1B	L. Brown	108	.241	3	14	252	8	11	20	10.0	.959							
Troy	1B	R. Connor	367	.292	2	31	836	40	46	51	10.8	.950	T. Keefe	45	402	18	27	0	3.25
	2B	B. Ferguson	339	.283	1	35	263	254	55	47	6.7	.904	M. Welch	40	368	21	18	0	2.67
W-39 L-45	SS	E. Caskin	234	.226	0	21	85	205	30	18	5.1	.906							
	3B	F. Hankinson	321	.193	1	19	151	169	33	21	4.2	.907							
Bob Ferguson	RF	J. Evans	315	.241	0	28	145	31	14	5	2.3	.926							
	CF	J. Cassidy	370	.222	1	11	143	20	24	0	2.2	.872							
	LF	P. Gillespie	348	.276	0	41	180	16	14	5	2.5	.933							
	C	B. Ewing	272	.250	0	25	211	89	28	9	7.5	.915							
	C	B. Holbert	180	.272	0	14	201	69	24	10	6.8	.918							
	P	T. Keefe	152	.230	0	19	23	79	17	5	2.6	.857							
	P	M. Welch	148	.203	0	11	20	39	7	3	1.7	.894							
Boston	1B	J. Morrill	311	.289	1	39	743	37	25	32	10.9	.969	J. Whitney	66	552	31	33	0	2.48
	2B	J. Burdock	282	.238	1	24	202	207	40	35	6.2	.911	J. Fox	17	124	6	8	0	3.33
W-38 L-45	SS	R. Barnes	295	.271	0	17	91	214	52	17	5.7	.854							
	3B	E. Sutton	333	.291	0	31	114	157	38	10	3.8	.877							
Harry Wright	RF	F. Lewis	114	.219	0	9	35	6	8	1	1.8	.837							
	CF	B. Crowley	279	.254	0	31	130	17	20	5	2.3	.880							
	LF	J. Hornung	324	.241	2	25	198	19	12	5	2.8	.948							
	C	P. Snyder	219	.228	0	16	261	105	42	0	6.8	.897							
	P	J. Whitney	282	.255	0	32	19	99	28	3	2.2	.808							
	UT	P. Deasley	147	.238	0	8	159	48	21	6		.908							
	UT	J. Fox	118	.178	0	4	68	29	10	4		.907							
	OF	J. Richmond	98	.276	1	12	59	4	2	1	2.6	.969							
Cleveland	1B	B. Phillips	357	.272	1	44	806	24	29	51	10.1	.966	McCormick	59	526	26	30	0	2.45
	2B	F. Dunlap	351	.325	3	24	258	254	51	41	7.1	.909	T. Nolan	22	180	8	14	0	3.05
W-36 L-48	SS	J. Glasscock	335	.257	0	33	105	274	37	29	5.3	.911							
	3B	G. Bradley	241	.249	2	18	78	76	24	6	3.7	.865							
Mike McGeary	RF	O. Shaffer	343	.257	1	34	122	24	20	4	2.0	.880							
W-4 L-7	CF	J. Remsen	172	.174	0	13	117	7	18	1	3.0	.873							
	LF	M. Moynahan	135	.230	0	8	65	3	9	2	2.4	.883							
Jim McCormick	C	J. Clapp	261	.253	0	25	211	73	35	8	6.6	.890							
W-32 L-41	P	McCormick	309	.256	0	26	34	81	13	4	2.2	.898							
	UT	T. Nolan	168	.244	0	18	32	37	9	2		.885							
	C	D. Kennedy	150	.313	0	15	207	36	21	4	7.5	.920							
	OF	B. Taylor	103	.243	0	12	51	4	9	1	2.8	.859							

NATIONAL LEAGUE 1881, *cont.*

	POS	Player	AB	BA	HR	RBI	PO	A	E	DP	TC/G	FA	Pitcher	G	IP	W	L	SV	ERA
Worcester	1B	H. Stovey	341	.270	2	30	562	16	28	26	10.6	.954	L. Richmond	53	462	25	26	0	3.39
	2B	G. Creamer	309	.207	0	25	230	248	51	39	6.6	.904	F. Corey	23	189	6	15	0	3.72
W-32 L-50	SS	A. Irwin	206	.267	0	24	50	155	36	11	4.8	.851							
	3B	H. Carpenter	347	.216	2	31	141	172	56	14	4.4	.848							
Mike Dorgan	RF	M. Dorgan	220	.277	0	18	41	7	7	1	2.4	.873							
W-24 L-32	CF	P. Hotaling	317	.309	1	35	142	21	26	2	2.6	.862							
	LF	B. Dickerson	367	.316	1	31	153	28	22	6	2.5	.892							
Harry Stovey	C	D. Bushong	275	.233	0	21	368	124	44	10	7.1	.918							
W-8 L-18	P	L. Richmond	252	.250	0	28	18	100	8	3	2.4	.937							
	UT	F. Corey	203	.222	0	10	55	71	15	3		.894							
	SS	C. Nelson	103	.282	1	15	20	94	13	6	5.3	.898							

BATTING AND BASE RUNNING LEADERS

PITCHING LEADERS

Batting Average
C. Anson, CHI	.399
M. Powell, DET	.338
J. Rowe, BUF	.333
J. Start, PRO	.328
F. Dunlap, CLE	.325

Slugging Average
D. Brouthers, BUF	.541
C. Anson, CHI	.510
J. Rowe, BUF	.480
C. Bennett, DET	.478
F. Dunlap, CLE	.444

Home Runs
D. Brouthers, BUF	8
C. Bennett, DET	7
J. Farrell, PRO	5
T. Burns, CHI	4
L. Brown, DET, PRO	3
F. Dunlap, CLE	3

Winning Percentage
O. Radbourn, PRO	.694
L. Corcoran, CHI	.689
F. Goldsmith, CHI	.649
P. Galvin, BUF	.547
G. Derby, DET	.527

Earned Run Average
S. Weidman, DET	1.80
M. Ward, PRO	2.13
G. Derby, DET	2.20
L. Corcoran, CHI	2.31
P. Galvin, BUF	2.37

Wins
L. Corcoran, CHI	31
J. Whitney, BOS	31
P. Galvin, BUF	29
G. Derby, DET	29
McCormick, CLE	26

Total Bases
C. Anson, CHI	175
F. Dunlap, CLE	156
K. Kelly, CHI	153
A. Dalrymple, CHI	150
B. Dickerson, WOR	149

Runs Batted In
C. Anson, CHI	82
C. Bennett, DET	64
K. Kelly, CHI	55
D. White, BUF	53
Richardson, BUF	53
M. Ward, PRO	53

Stolen Bases
(not available)

Saves
B. Mathews, BOS, PRO	2
J. Morrill, BOS	1

Strikeouts
G. Derby, DET	212
McCormick, CLE	178
J. Whitney, BOS	162
L. Richmond, WOR	156
L. Corcoran, CHI	150

Complete Games
McCormick, CLE	57
J. Whitney, BOS	57
G. Derby, DET	55
L. Richmond, WOR	50
P. Galvin, BUF	48

Hits
C. Anson, CHI	137
A. Dalrymple, CHI	117
B. Dickerson, WOR	116
J. Start, PRO	114

Base on Balls
J. Clapp, CLE	35
T. York, PRO	29
B. Ferguson, TRO	29
J. Farrell, PRO	29

Home Run Percentage
D. Brouthers, BUF	3.0
C. Bennett, DET	2.3
J. Farrell, PRO	1.4
T. Burns, CHI	1.2

Fewest Hits/9 Innings
McCormick, CLE	8.28
S. Weidman, DET	8.45
O. Radbourn, PRO	8.55
L. Corcoran, CHI	8.62

Shutouts
G. Derby, DET	9
J. Whitney, BOS	6
F. Goldsmith, CHI	5
P. Galvin, BUF	5

Fewest Walks/9 Innings
P. Galvin, BUF	0.87
S. Weidman, DET	0.94
F. Goldsmith, CHI	1.20
L. Richmond, WOR	1.32

Runs Scored
G. Gore, CHI	86
K. Kelly, CHI	84
A. Dalrymple, CHI	72
J. O'Rourke, BUF	71

Doubles
K. Kelly, CHI	27
P. Hines, PRO	27
H. Stovey, WOR	25
F. Dunlap, CLE	25

Triples
J. Rowe, BUF	11
B. Phillips, CLE	10
D. Brouthers, BUF	9
G. Gore, CHI	9

Most Strikeouts/9 Inn.
G. Derby, DET	3.86
L. Corcoran, CHI	3.40
M. Ward, PRO	3.25
O. Radbourn, PRO	3.24

Innings
J. Whitney, BOS	552
McCormick, CLE	526
G. Derby, DET	495
P. Galvin, BUF	474

Games Pitched
J. Whitney, BOS	66
McCormick, CLE	59
G. Derby, DET	56
P. Galvin, BUF	56

	W	L	PCT	GB	R	OR	2B	3B	HR	BA	SA	SB	E	DP	FA	CG	BB	SO	ShO	SV	ERA
Chicago	56	28	.667		550	379	157	36	12	.295	.380	0	309	54	.916	81	122	228	9	0	2.43
Providence	47	37	.560	9	447	426	144	37	11	.253	.335	0	390	66	.896	76	138	264	7	0	2.40
Buffalo	45	38	.542	10.5	440	447	157	50	12	.264	.361	0	408	48	.891	72	89	185	5	0	2.84
Detroit	41	43	.488	15	439	429	131	53	17	.260	.357	0	338	80	.905	83	137	265	10	0	2.65
Troy	39	45	.464	17	399	429	124	31	5	.248	.314	0	311	70	.917	85	159	207	7	0	2.97
Boston	38	45	.458	17.5	349	410	121	27	5	.253	.317	0	325	54	.909	72	143	199	6	3	2.71
Cleveland	36	48	.429	20	392	414	120	39	7	.255	.326	0	348	68	.904	82	126	240	2	0	2.68
Worcester	32	50	.390	23	410	492	114	31	7	.253	.316	0	353	50	.903	80	120	196	5	0	3.54
					3426	3426	1068	304	76	.260	.338	0	2782	490	.905	631	1034	1784	51	3	2.77

NATIONAL LEAGUE 1882

	POS	Player	AB	BA	HR	RBI	PO	A	E	DP	TC/G	FA	Pitcher	G	IP	W	L	SV	ERA
Chicago	1B	C. Anson	348	.362	1	83	810	27	45	42	10.8	.949	F. Goldsmith	44	405	28	16	0	2.42
	2B	T. Burns	355	.248	0	48	129	127	25	21	6.5	.911	L. Corcoran	40	356	27	13	0	1.95
W-55 L-29	SS	K. Kelly	377	.305	1	55	66	117	43	9	5.4	.810							
	3B	Williamson	348	.282	3	60	108	210	43	16	4.3	.881							
Cap Anson	RF	H. Nicol	186	.199	1	16	59	27	11	1	2.1	.887							
	CF	G. Gore	367	.319	3	51	153	23	33	5	2.5	.842							
	LF	A. Dalrymple	397	.295	1	36	185	8	27	4	2.6	.877							
	C	S. Flint	331	.251	4	44	440	91	37	3	7.0	.935							
	P	F. Goldsmith	183	.230	0	19	7	0	1	0	.2	.875							
	P	L. Corcoran	169	.207	1	24	0	0	0	0		.000							
	2B	J. Quest	159	.201	0	15	113	127	33	18	6.7	.879							

NATIONAL LEAGUE 1882, *cont.*

	POS	Player	AB	BA	HR	RBI	PO	A	E	DP	TC/G	FA	Pitcher	G	IP	W	L	SV	ERA
Providence	1B	J. Start	356	.329	0		905	21	25	54	11.6	.974	O. Radbourn	55	474	33	19	0	2.09
	2B	J. Farrell	366	.254	2		212	283	71	41	6.7	.875	M. Ward	33	278	19	13	1	2.59
	SS	G. Wright	185	.162	0		46	133	26	16	4.5	.873							
W-52 L-32	3B	J. Denny	329	.246	2		136	206	55	7	4.7	.861							
	RF	M. Ward	355	.245	0		69	20	19	3	2.2	.824							
Harry Wright	CF	P. Hines	379	.309	4		151	16	27	4	2.4	.861							
	LF	T. York	321	.268	1		159	11	24	3	2.4	.876							
	C	B. Gilligan	201	.224	0		287	82	27	8	7.3	.932							
	PO	O. Radbourn	326	.239	1		71	97	16	4		.913							
	C	S. Nava	97	.206	0		112	31	22		6.1	.867							
Boston	1B	J. Morrill	349	.289	2	54	741	16	28	22	10.3	.964	J. Whitney	49	420	24	21	0	2.64
	2B	J. Burdock	319	.238	0	27	223	256	35	28	6.2	.932	B. Mathews	34	285	19	15	0	2.87
	SS	S. Wise	298	.221	4	34	84	197	49	13	4.6	.852							
W-45 L-39	3B	E. Sutton	319	.251	2	38	98	146	41	6	3.7	.856							
	RF	E. Rowen	327	.248	1	43	47	7	7	2	1.3	.885							
John Morrill	CF	P. Hotaling	378	.259	0	28	150	16	26	5	2.3	.865							
	LF	J. Hornung	388	.302	1	50	191	14	15	4	2.6	.932							
	C	P. Deasley	264	.265	0	29	357	54	18	0	7.7	.958							
	P	J. Whitney	251	.323	5	48	13	88	13	3	2.3	.886							
	P	B. Mathews	169	.225	0	13	5	34	6	1	1.3	.867							
Buffalo	1B	D. Brouthers	351	**.368**	6		882	19	24	35	11.0	.974	P. Galvin	52	445	28	23	0	3.17
	2B	Richardson	354	.271	2		**275**	280	63	28	7.4	.898	O. Daily	29	256	15	14	0	2.99
	SS	D. Force	278	.241	1		66	209	28	13	5.0	.908							
W-45 L-39	3B	D. White	337	.282	1		59	111	33	6	3.2	.837							
	RF	C. Foley	341	.305	3		118	22	28	7	2.0	.833							
Jim O'Rourke	CF	J. O'Rourke	370	.281	2		140	15	24	3	2.2	.866							
	LF	B. Purcell	380	.276	2		144	11	**34**	0	2.3	.820							
	C	J. Rowe	308	.266	1		246	41	15	5	6.6	.950							
	P	P. Galvin	206	.214	0		20	85	8	1	2.2	.929							
	P	O. Daily	110	.164	0		1	28	4	0	1.1	.879							
	C	T. Dolan	89	.157	0		70	26	6	1	5.7	.941							
Cleveland	1B	B. Phillips	335	.260	4	47	827	24	25	**55**	11.2	.971	McCormick	**68**	**596**	**36**	29	0	2.37
	2B	F. Dunlap	364	.280	0	28	268	**297**	63	**62**	7.5	.900	G. Bradley	18	147	6	10	0	3.73
	SS	J. Glasscock	358	.291	4	46	111	**311**	47	**40**	5.7	.900							
W-42 L-40	3B	M. Muldoon	341	.246	6	45	86	133	30	12	4.1	.880							
	RF	O. Shaffer	313	.214	3	28	111	17	31	2	1.9	.805							
Jim McCormick	CF	J. Richmond	140	.171	0	11	65	12	7	0	2.9	.917							
W-0 L-4	LF	Esterbrook	179	.246	0	19	102	15	14	6	2.9	.893							
	C	F. Briody	194	.258	0	13	251	89	37	6	7.1	.902							
Fred Dunlap	P	McCormick	262	.218	2	15	**43**	**100**	13	1	2.3	.917							
W-42 L-36	UT	G. Bradley	115	.183	0	6	82	47	13	8		.908							
	C	K. Kelly	104	.135	0	5	113	35	37	2	6.2	.800							
	3B	H. Doscher	104	.240	0	10	33	45	13	2	4.1	.857							
	OF	D. Rowe	97	.258	1	17	33	3	7	1	1.9	.837							
Detroit	1B	M. Powell	338	.240	1	29	680	14	44	27	9.2	.940	S. Weidman	46	411	25	20	0	2.63
	2B	D. Troy	152	.243	0	14	74	76	27	9	5.7	.847	G. Derby	40	362	17	20	0	3.26
	SS	M. McGeary	133	.143	0	2	56	112	13	5	5.5	.928							
W-42 L-41	3B	J. Farrell	283	.247	1	24	50	65	26	8	3.4	.816							
	RF	L. Knight	347	.207	0	24	112	25	21	2	1.9	.867							
Frank Bancroft	CF	N. Hanlon	347	.231	5	38	**194**	19	27	8	**2.9**	.888							
	LF	G. Wood	375	.269	**7**	29	161	14	23	**8**	2.4	.884							
	C	C. Bennett	342	.301	5	51	**446**	70	30	8	**8.4**	.945							
	P	S. Weidman	193	.218	0	20	35	71	11	2	2.5	.906							
	P	G. Derby	149	.195	0	8	19	69	4	1	2.3	**.957**							
	UT	S. Trott	129	.240	0	12	207	53	33	6		.887							
	3S	A. Whitney	115	.183	0	4	58	66	21	7		.855							
Troy	1B	J. Smith	149	.242	0	14	352	9	15	19	10.7	.960	T. Keefe	43	375	17	26	0	2.50
	2B	B. Ferguson	319	.257	0	33	247	221	44	38	6.5	.914	M. Welch	33	281	14	16	0	3.46
	SS	F. Pfeffer	330	.218	1	31	161	276	73	35	6.1	.857	J. Egan	12	100	4	6	0	4.14
W-35 L-48	3B	B. Ewing	328	.271	2	29	76	112	24	11	4.8	.887							
	RF	C. Roseman	331	.236	1	43	107	21	22	6	1.8	.853							
Bob Ferguson	CF	R. Connor	349	.330	4	42	52	2	11	0	2.7	.831							
	LF	P. Gillespie	298	.275	2	32	144	9	32	1	2.5	.827							
	C	B. Holbert	251	.183	0	23	247	124	45	**13**	7.2	.892							
	P	T. Keefe	189	.228	1	19	32	89	11	4	3.1	.917							
	P	M. Welch	151	.245	1	17	10	46	10	4	2.0	.848							
	OF	B. Harbidge	123	.187	0	13	43	3	9	1	2.4	.836							
	O3	J. Cassidy	121	.174	0	9	35	23	25	1		.699							
	OP	J. Egan	115	.200	0	10	23	13	20	3		.643							

NATIONAL LEAGUE 1882, cont.

	POS	Player	AB	BA	HR	RBI	PO	A	E	DP	TC/G	FA	Pitcher	G	IP	W	L	SV	ERA
Worcester	1B	H. Stovey	360	.289	5	26	469	13	22	25	11.7	.956	L. Richmond	48	411	14	**33**	0	3.74
	2B	G. Creamer	286	.227	1	29	241	283	54	50	7.1	.907	F. Corey	21	139	1	13	0	3.56
W-18 L-66	SS	F. Corey	255	.247	0	29	29	76	19	5	4.8	.847	F. Mountain	13	102	2	11	0	3.97
	3B	A. Irwin	333	.219	0	30	84	147	45	8	5.4	.837							
Freeman Brown	RF	J. Evans	334	.213	0	25	131	31	16	2	2.6	.910							
W-9 L-32	CF	J. Hayes	326	.270	4	54	93	13	18	2	2.1	.855							
	LF	J. Clinton	98	.163	0	3	43	4	17	1	2.5	.734							
Tommy Bond	C	D. Bushong	253	.158	1	15	308	101	47	8	6.6	.897							
W-2 L-4	P	L. Richmond	228	.281	2	28	15	97	14	2	2.6	.889							
	OF	T. O'Brien	89	.202	0	7	41	4	12	0	2.9	.789							
Jack Chapman	UT	F. Mountain	86	.233	2	6	29	23	7	3		.881							
W-7 L-30																			

BATTING AND BASE RUNNING LEADERS

Batting Average
- D. Brouthers, BUF .368
- C. Anson, CHI .362
- R. Connor, TRO .330
- J. Start, PRO .329
- J. Whitney, BOS .323

Slugging Average
- D. Brouthers, BUF .547
- R. Connor, TRO .530
- J. Whitney, BOS .510
- C. Anson, CHI .500
- P. Hines, PRO .467

Home Runs
- G. Wood, DET 7
- M. Muldoon, CLE 6
- D. Brouthers, BUF 6

Total Bases
- D. Brouthers, BUF 192
- R. Connor, TRO 185
- P. Hines, PRO 177
- C. Anson, CHI 174
- A. Dalrymple, CHI 167

Runs Batted In
(not available)

Stolen Bases
(not available)

Hits
- D. Brouthers, BUF 129
- C. Anson, CHI 126

Base on Balls
- G. Gore, CHI 29
- O. Shaffer, CLE 27
- Williamson, CHI 27
- N. Hanlon, DET 26

Home Run Percentage
- J. Whitney, BOS 2.0
- G. Wood, DET 1.9
- M. Muldoon, CLE 1.8
- D. Brouthers, BUF 1.7

Runs Scored
- G. Gore, CHI 99
- A. Dalrymple, CHI 96
- H. Stovey, WOR 90
- K. Kelly, CHI 81

Doubles
- K. Kelly, CHI 37
- C. Anson, CHI 29
- P. Hines, PRO 28
- Williamson, CHI 27

Triples
- R. Connor, TRO 18
- F. Corey, WOR 12
- G. Wood, DET 12

PITCHING LEADERS

Winning Percentage
- L. Corcoran, CHI .675
- F. Goldsmith, CHI .636
- O. Radbourn, PRO .620
- M. Ward, PRO .594
- B. Mathews, BOS .559

Earned Run Average
- L. Corcoran, CHI 1.95
- O. Radbourn, PRO 2.09
- McCormick, CLE 2.37
- F. Goldsmith, CHI 2.42
- T. Keefe, TRO 2.50

Wins
- McCormick, CLE 36
- O. Radbourn, PRO 31
- F. Goldsmith, CHI 28
- P. Galvin, BUF 28
- L. Corcoran, CHI 27

Saves
- M. Ward, PRO 1

Strikeouts
- O. Radbourn, PRO 201
- McCormick, CLE 200
- G. Derby, DET 182
- J. Whitney, BOS 180
- L. Corcoran, CHI 170

Complete Games
- McCormick, CLE 65
- O. Radbourn, PRO 51
- P. Galvin, BUF 48
- J. Whitney, BOS 46
- F. Goldsmith, CHI 44
- L. Richmond, WOR 44

Fewest Hits/9 Innings
- L. Corcoran, CHI 7.11
- O. Radbourn, PRO 8.15
- McCormick, CLE 8.31
- F. Goldsmith, CHI 8.38

Shutouts
- O. Radbourn, PRO 6
- M. Welch, TRO 5
- M. Ward, PRO 4
- F. Goldsmith, CHI 4

Fewest Walks/9 Innings
- B. Mathews, BOS 0.69
- P. Galvin, BUF 0.81
- F. Goldsmith, CHI 0.84
- S. Weidman, DET 0.85

Most Strikeouts/9 Inn.
- B. Mathews, BOS 4.83
- G. Derby, DET 4.52
- L. Corcoran, CHI 4.30
- O. Daily, BUF 4.08

Innings
- McCormick, CLE 596
- O. Radbourn, PRO 474
- P. Galvin, BUF 445
- J. Whitney, BOS 420

Games Pitched
- McCormick, CLE 68
- O. Radbourn, PRO 55
- P. Galvin, BUF 52
- J. Whitney, BOS 49

	W	L	PCT	GB	R	OR	2B	3B	HR	BA	SA	SB	E	DP	FA	CG	BB	SO	ShO	SV	ERA
Chicago	55	29	.655		**604**	353	**209**	54	15	**.277**	**.389**	0	376	54	.898	**83**	102	279	7	0	**2.22**
Providence	52	32	.619	3	463	356	121	54	10	.250	.333	0	371	67	.901	80	87	273	9	1	2.27
Boston	45	39	.536	10	472	414	114	50	15	.264	.347	0	**314**	37	**.910**	81	**77**	352	4	0	2.80
Buffalo	45	39	.536	10	500	461	146	47	18	.274	.368	0	315	42	.910	79	114	287	3	0	3.25
Cleveland	42	40	.512	12	402	411	139	40	20	.238	.331	0	358	**71**	.905	81	132	232	4	0	2.75
Detroit	42	41	.506	12.5	407	488	117	44	20	.230	.315	0	396	44	.893	82	129	**354**	7	0	2.98
Troy	35	48	.422	19.5	430	522	116	**59**	12	.244	.333	0	432	70	.887	81	168	189	6	0	3.08
Worcester	18	66	.214	37	379	652	109	57	16	.231	.322	0	468	66	.877	75	151	195		0	3.75
					3657	3657	1071	405	126	.251	.343	0	3030	451	.897	642	960	2161	40	1	2.89

AMERICAN ASSOCIATION 1882

	POS	Player	AB	BA	HR	RBI	PO	A	E	DP	TC/G	FA	Pitcher	G	IP	W	L	SV	ERA
Cincinnati	1B	D. Stearns	214	.257	0		305	5	23	16	9.5	.931	W. White	54	**480**	**40**	12	0	1.54
	2B	B. McPhee	311	.228	1		274	207	42	36	6.7	**.920**	McCormick	25	220	14	11	0	1.52
W-55 L-25	SS	C. Fulmer	324	.281	0		130	243	43	14	5.3	.897							
	3B	H. Carpenter	351	.342	1		**137**	167	60	7	4.6	**.835**							
Pop Snyder	RF	H. Wheeler	344	.250	1		94	11	25	1	2.0	.808							
	CF	J. Macullar	299	.234	0		141	13	13	2	2.1	.922							
	LF	J. Sommer	354	.288	1		**188**	9	16	2	2.7	**.925**							
	C	P. Snyder	309	.291	1		358	92	41	3	7.0	.916							
	P	W. White	207	.266	0		23	**223**	11	3	4.8	.957							
	1B	H. Luff	120	.233	0		266	7	23	12	11.0	.922							
	P	McCormick	93	.129	0		12	76	5	0	3.7	.946							

AMERICAN ASSOCIATION 1882, *cont.*

	POS	Player	AB	BA	HR	RBI	PO	A	E	DP	TC/G	FA	Pitcher	G	IP	W	L	SV	ERA
Philadelphia	1B	J. Latham	323	.285	0		792	12	23	28	11.2	**.972**	S. Weaver	42	371	26	15	0	2.74
	2B	C. Stricker	272	.217	0		239	251	52	29	7.5	.904	B. Sweeney	20	170	9	11	0	2.91
W-41 L-34	SS	L. Say	199	.226	1		69	192	40	7	6.1	.867							
	3B	F. Mann	121	.231	0		32	39	18	3	3.1	.798							
Juice Latham	RF	B. Blakiston	281	.228	0		52	13	11	0	2.0	.855							
	CF	J. Mansell	126	.238	0		49	4	14	0	2.2	.791							
	LF	J. Birchall	338	.263	0		134	14	24	0	2.3	.860							
	C	J. O'Brien	241	.303	3		205	66	22	1	6.5	**.925**							
	CO	J. Dorgan	181	.282	0		158	30	30	0		.862							
	P	S. Weaver	155	.232	0		16	127	9	1	3.6	.941							
	P	B. Sweeney	88	.159	0		9	51	6	0	3.3	.909							
	SS	J. Say	82	.207	0		31	76	14	10	5.5	.884							
Louisville	1B	G. Hecker	340	.276	3		689	**22**	31	43	11.2	.958	T. Mullane	**55**	460	30	24	0	1.88
	2B	P. Browning	288	**.378**	5		157	127	35	19	7.6	.890	G. Hecker	13	104	6	6	0	1.30
W-42 L-38	SS	D. Mack	264	.182	0		51	161	24	9	4.8	**.898**	J. Reccius	13	95	4	6	0	3.03
	3B	B. Schenck	231	.260	0		70	110	41	4	3.8	.814							
Denny Mack	RF	C. Wolf	318	.299	0		71	**21**	10	2	1.5	.902							
	CF	J. Reccius	266	.237	1		87	15	17	3	1.8	.857							
	LF	L. Maskrey	288	.226	0		136	11	16	1	2.1	.902							
	C	D. Sullivan	286	.273	0		294	95	54	3	8.2	.878							
	UT	T. Mullane	303	.257	0		187	191	24	10		.940							
	UT	J. Strike	110	.164	0		110	45	22	6		.876							
Pittsburgh	1B	C. Lane	214	.178	3		480	12	13	19	11.7	.974	H. Salisbury	38	335	20	18	0	2.63
	2B	G. Strief	297	.195	2		241	200	40	28	6.2	.917	D. Driscoll	23	201	13	9	0	1.21
W-39 L-39	SS	J. Peters	333	.288	0		90	280	49	21	5.4	.883	H. Arundel	14	120	4	10	0	4.65
	3B	J. Battin	133	.211	1		62	108	24	5	5.7	.876							
Al Pratt	RF	E. Swartwood	325	.329	5		99	9	29	2	1.9	.788							
	CF	J. Leary	257	.292	2		26	2	9	0	1.4	.757							
	LF	M. Mansell	347	.277	2		159	16	**36**	1	2.7	.829							
	C	B. Taylor	299	.281	4		116	40	25	0	6.7	.862							
	P	H. Salisbury	145	.152	0		10	96	11	1	3.1	.906							
	OF	C. Morton	103	.282	0		31	9	9	2	2.0	.816							
	C	R. Kemmler	99	.253	0		123	37	14	1	7.6	.920							
	C	J. Keenan	96	.219	1		142	21	17	3	8.2	.906							
	P	D. Driscoll	80	.138	1		4	50	7	1	2.7	.885							
St. Louis	1B	C. Comiskey	329	.243	1		**860**	14	30	25	**11.7**	.967	J. McGinnis	44	379	25	17	0	2.47
	2B	B. Smiley	240	.213	0		145	155	39	20	5.9	.885	J. Schappert	15	128	8	7	0	3.52
W-37 L-43	SS	B. Gleason	347	.288	1		131	**294**	85	**23**	6.5	.833							
	3B	J. Gleason	331	.254	2		107	**168**	83	11	4.9	.768							
Ned Cuthbert	RF	G. Seward	144	.215	0		40	12	15	1	1.9	.776							
	CF	O. Walker	318	.239	7		158	18	32	4	**2.8**	.846							
	LF	N. Cuthbert	233	.223	0		74	12	10	0	1.6	.896							
	C	S. Sullivan	188	.181	0		231	46	50	4	6.5	.847							
	P	J. McGinnis	203	.217	0		13	97	11	2	2.8	.909							
	UT	McCaffrey	153	.275	0		71	49	17	5		.876							
	UT	Fusselbach	136	.228	0		92	54	25	4		.854							
Baltimore	1B	Householder	307	.254	1		749	20	23	30	10.7	.971	D. Landis	42	341	11	27*	0	3.33
	2B	G. Pierce	151	.199	0		123	99	57*	17	7.3	.796	T. Nichols	16	118	1	12	0	5.02
W-19 L-54	SS	H. Myers	294	.180	0		66	257	70	15	5.8	.822	E. Geis	13	96	4	9	0	4.80
	3B	J. Shetzline	282	.220	0		91	121	53	9	**5.1**	.800							
Henry Myers	RF	T. Brown	181	.304	1		59	16	28	1	2.3	.728							
	CF	M. Cline	172	.221	0		78	16	20	1	2.9	.825							
	LF	C. Waitt	250	.156	0		142	11	22	2	2.4	.874							
	C	E. Whiting	308	.260	0		299	**108**	81	6	6.8	.834							
	P	D. Landis	175	.166	0		19	101	11*	2	3.1	.916							
	3O	H. Jacoby	121	.174	1		46	59	26	3		.802							
	PO	T. Nichols	95	.158	0		26	36	13	0		.827							

BATTING AND BASE RUNNING LEADERS

Batting Average
P. Browning, LOU .382
H. Carpenter, CIN .342
E. Swartwood, PIT .329
J. O'Brien, PHI .303
C. Wolf, LOU .299

Slugging Average
P. Browning, LOU .521
E. Swartwood, PIT .498
B. Taylor, PIT .455
M. Mansell, PIT .438
H. Carpenter, CIN .422

Home Runs
O. Walker, STL 7
P. Browning, LOU 5
E. Swartwood, PIT 5
B. Taylor, PIT 4

Total Bases
E. Swartwood, PIT 162
M. Mansell, PIT 152
P. Browning, LOU 150
H. Carpenter, CIN 148
B. Taylor, PIT 136

Runs Batted In
(not available)

Stolen Bases
(not available)

PITCHING LEADERS

Winning Percentage
W. White, CIN .769
S. Weaver, PHI .634
J. McGinnis, STL .581
McCormick, CIN .560
T. Mullane, LOU .556

Earned Run Average
D. Driscoll, PIT 1.21
G. Hecker, LOU 1.30
McCormick, CIN 1.52
W. White, CIN 1.54
T. Mullane, LOU 1.88

Wins
W. White, CIN 40
T. Mullane, LOU 30
S. Weaver, PHI 26
J. McGinnis, STL 25
H. Salisbury, PIT 20

Saves
Fusselbach, STL 1

Strikeouts
T. Mullane, LOU 170
H. Salisbury, PIT 135
J. McGinnis, STL 134
W. White, CIN 122
S. Weaver, PHI 104

Complete Games
W. White, CIN 52
T. Mullane, LOU 51
J. McGinnis, STL 42
S. Weaver, PHI 41
H. Salisbury, PIT 38

AMERICAN ASSOCIATION 1882, cont.

BATTING AND BASE RUNNING LEADERS

Hits
H. Carpenter, CIN	120
P. Browning, LOU	110
E. Swartwood, PIT	107
J. Sommer, CIN	102

Base on Balls
J. Gleason, STL	27
P. Browning, LOU	26
J. Sommer, CIN	24
J. Reccius, LOU	23

Home Run Percentage
O. Walker, STL	2.2
P. Browning, LOU	1.7
E. Swartwood, PIT	1.5
C. Lane, PIT	1.4

Fewest Hits/9 Innings
G. Hecker, LOU	6.49
McCormick, CIN	7.25
D. Driscoll, PIT	7.25
W. White, CIN	7.71

PITCHING LEADERS

Shutouts
W. White, CIN	8
T. Mullane, LOU	5
McCormick, CIN	3
J. McGinnis, STL	3

Fewest Walks/9 Innings
G. Hecker, LOU	0.43
D. Driscoll, PIT	0.54
S. Weaver, PHI	0.85
H. Salisbury, PIT	0.99

Runs Scored
E. Swartwood, PIT	86
J. Sommer, CIN	82
H. Carpenter, CIN	78
P. Browning, LOU	67

Doubles
P. Browning, LOU	19
E. Swartwood, PIT	18
M. Mansell, PIT	18
N. Cuthbert, STL	16

Triples
M. Mansell, PIT	16
B. Taylor, PIT	12
E. Swartwood, PIT	11
H. Wheeler, CIN	11

Most Strikeouts/9 Inn.
H. Salisbury, PIT	3.63
H. Arundel, PIT	3.52
T. Mullane, LOU	3.32
J. McGinnis, STL	3.18

Innings
W. White, CIN	480
T. Mullane, LOU	460
J. McGinnis, STL	379
S. Weaver, PHI	371

Games Pitched
T. Mullane, LOU	55
W. White, CIN	54
J. McGinnis, STL	44
D. Landis, BAL, PHI	44

	W	L	PCT	GB	R	OR	2B	3B	HR	BA	SA	SB	E	DP	FA	CG	BB	SO	ShO	SV	ERA
Cincinnati	55	25	.688		**489**	268	95	47	5	**.264**	.332	0	**332**	41	**.907**	77	125	165	**11**	0	**1.67**
Philadelphia	41	34	.547	11.5	406	389	89	21	4	.244	.297	0	361	36	.895	72	99	190	2	0	2.99
Louisville	42	38	.525	13	443	352	**110**	28	9	.259	.328	0	385	**57**	.893	73	112	240	6	0	2.08
Pittsburgh	39	39	.500	15	428	418	**110**	58	21	.251	**.351**	0	397	40	.889	**77**	**82**	**252**	2	0	2.87
St. Louis	37	43	.463	18	399	496	87	41	11	.231	.302	0	446	41	.875	75	103	225	3	1	2.95
Baltimore	19	54	.260	32.5	273	515	60	24	4	.207	.254	0	490	41	.859	64	108	113	1	0	3.87
					2438	2438	551	219	54	.244	.312	0	2411	256	.886	438	629	1185	25	1	2.72

NATIONAL LEAGUE 1883

	POS	Player	AB	BA	HR	RBI	PO	A	E	DP	TC/G	FA	Pitcher	G	IP	W	L	SV	ERA
Boston W-63 L-35 Jack Burdock W-30 L-24 John Morrill W-33 L-11	1B	J. Morrill	404	.319	6	68	794	20	22	33	10.3	**.974**	J. Whitney	62	514	37	21	2	2.24
	2B	J. Burdock	400	.330	5	88	224	290	44	39	5.8	.921	C. Buffinton	43	333	25	14	1	3.03
	SS	S. Wise	406	.271	4	58	134	274	88	21	5.2	.823							
	3B	E. Sutton	414	.324	3	73	120	152	42	14	3.4	.866							
	RF	P. Radford	258	.205	0	14	86	16	20	2	1.7	.836							
	CF	E. Smith	115	.217	0	16	54	3	6	3	2.1	.905							
	LF	J. Hornung	**446**	.278	8	66	175	15	13	3	2.1	**.936**							
	C	M. Hines	231	.225	0	16	**382**	103	62	5	9.3	.887							
	PO	J. Whitney	409	.281	5	57	67	100	25	2		.870							
	OP	C. Buffinton	341	.238	1	26	67	68	33	6		.804							
	C	M. Hackett	179	.235	2	24	254	57	31	2	7.8	.909							
Chicago W-59 L-39 Cap Anson	1B	C. Anson	413	.308	0		1031	**41**	40	59	11.3	.964	L. Corcoran	56	474	34	20	0	2.49
	2B	F. Pfeffer	371	.235	1		264	264	67	49	7.5	.887	F. Goldsmith	46	383	25	19	0	3.15
	SS	T. Burns	405	.294	2		121	260	56	25	5.5	.872							
	3B	Williamson	402	.276	2		111	**252**	87	**20**	4.6	.807							
	RF	K. Kelly	428	.255	3		101	38	32	5	2.1	.813							
	CF	G. Gore	392	.334	2		195	27	34	4	2.8	.867							
	LF	A. Dalrymple	363	.298	2		149	12	34	3	2.4	.826							
	C	S. Flint	332	.265	0		301	104	57	4	5.6	.877							
	P	L. Corcoran	263	.209	0		**37**	88	13	3	2.5	.906							
	P	F. Goldsmith	235	.221	1		23	86	17	3	2.7	.865							
Providence W-58 L-40 Harry Wright	1B	J. Start	370	.284	1		923	29	43	48	11.4	.957	O. Radbourn	**76**	632	**49**	25	1	2.05
	2B	J. Farrell	420	.305	3		258	**365**	51	**51**	7.1	**.924**	C. Sweeney	20	147	7	7	0	3.13
	SS	A. Irwin	406	.286	0		93	293	65	29	4.8	.856	L. Richmond	12	92	3	7	0	3.33
	3B	J. Denny	393	.275	8		**178**	188	52	13	4.3	**.876**							
	RF	J. Cassidy	366	.238	0		120	26	23	2	1.9	.864							
	CF	P. Hines	442	.299	4		169	21	20	2	2.4	.905							
	LF	C. Carroll	238	.265	1		109	11	13	4	2.3	.902							
	C	B. Gilligan	263	.198	0		379	**108**	54	10	7.3	.900							
	P	O. Radbourn	381	.283	3		33	**139**	15	3	2.5	.920							
	OF	L. Richmond	194	.284	1		47	3	20	0	1.7	.714							
	C	S. Nava	100	.240	0		98	41	32	4	6.3	.813							
Cleveland W-55 L-42 Frank Bancroft	1B	B. Phillips	382	.246	2		953	22	33	53	10.4	.967	O. Daily	45	379	23	19	1	2.42
	2B	F. Dunlap	396	.326	4		**304**	290	58	49	7.0	.911	McCormick	43	342	28	12	1	**1.84**
	SS	J. Glasscock	383	.287	0		134	313	38	28	5.2	**.922**	W. Sawyer	17	141	4	10	0	2.36
	3B	M. Muldoon	378	.228	0		122	170	62	9	3.6	.825							
	RF	J. Evans	332	.238	0		119	29	16	1	1.9	.902							
	CF	P. Hotaling	417	.259	0		181	23	**42**	5	2.5	.829							
	LF	T. York	381	.260	2		176	15	30	3	2.2	.864							
	C	D. Bushong	215	.172	0		370	88	46	5	8.0	.909							
	P	McCormick	157	.236	0		28	101	16	4	1.7	.889							
	C	F. Briody	145	.234	0		171	46	24	5	7.3	.900							
	P	O. Daily	142	.127	0		6	71	5	2	1.8	.939							

NATIONAL LEAGUE 1883, *cont.*

	POS	Player	AB	BA	HR	RBI	PO	A	E	DP	TC/G	FA	Pitcher	G	IP	W	L	SV	ERA
Buffalo	1B	D. Brouthers	425	**.374**	3		1040	35	44	40	11.5	.961	P. Galvin	76	656	46	29	0	2.72
	2B	Richardson	399	.311	1		289	344	68	33	7.6	.903	G. Derby	14	108	2	10	1	5.85
W-52 L-45	SS	D. Force	378	.217	0		79	240	42	22	4.6	.884							
	3B	D. White	391	.292	0		84	128	54	8	3.5	.797							
Jim O'Rourke	RF	O. Shaffer	401	.292	0		182	41	36	3	2.7	.861							
	CF	D. Eggler	153	.248	0		83	4	16	1	2.7	.845							
	LF	J. O'Rourke	436	.328	1		89	8	15	0	1.8	.866							
	C	J. Rowe	374	.278	1		234	50	32	3	6.4	.899							
	P	P. Galvin	322	.220	1		20	127	10	4	2.1	.936							
	OF	J. Lillie	201	.234	1		73	8	16	2	2.1	.835							
	OF	C. Foley	111	.270	0		44	2	6	0	2.3	.885							
New York	1B	R. Connor	409	.357	1		958	40	44	37	10.6	.958	M. Welch	54	426	25	23	0	2.73
	2B	D. Troy	316	.215	0		187	226	57	23	6.4	.879	M. Ward	33	277	16	13	0	2.70
W-46 L-50	SS	E. Caskin	383	.238	1		146	250	67	14	5.7	.855	T. O'Neill	19	148	5	12	0	4.07
	3B	F. Hankinson	337	.220	2		122	166	43	9	3.6	.870							
John Clapp	RF	M. Dorgan	261	.234	0		104	7	20	1	2.2	.847							
	CF	M. Ward	380	.255	7		118	28	24	2	3.0	.859							
	LF	P. Gillespie	411	.314	1		216	11	26	6	2.6	.897							
	C	B. Ewing	376	.303	**10**		270	96	31	8	6.3	.922							
	PO	M. Welch	320	.234	3		71	63	38	4		.779							
	CO	J. Humphries	107	.112	0		84	31	26	0		.816							
Detroit	1B	M. Powell	421	.273	1		995	32	**54**	**62**	10.7	.950	S. Weidman	52	402	20	24	2	3.53
	2B	S. Trott	295	.244	0		102	92	26	16	5.2	.882	D. Shaw	26	227	10	15	0	2.50
W-40 L-58	SS	S. Houck	416	.252	0		162	328	85	36	5.7	.852	D. Burns	17	128	2	12	0	4.51
	3B	J. Farrell	444	.243	1		111	248	66	13	4.2	.845	J. Jones	12	93	6	5	0	3.50
Jack Chapman	RF	T. Mansell	131	.221	0		35	12	15	1	1.8	.758							
	CF	N. Hanlon	413	.242	1		216	13	30	6	**2.9**	.884							
	LF	G. Wood	441	.302	5		**226**	15	34	3	2.8	.876							
	C	C. Bennett	371	.305	5		333	88	25	11	6.2	**.944**							
	PO	S. Weidman	313	.185	1		73	81	18	2		.895							
	PO	D. Shaw	141	.206	0		21	50	7	5		.910							
	OP	D. Burns	140	.186	0		22	32	14	2		.794							
	2B	J. Quest	137	.234	0		114	112	26	25	6.8	.897							
Philadelphia	1B	S. Farrar	377	.233	1		1038	31	39	45	11.2	.965	J. Coleman	65	538	12	**48**	0	4.87
	2B	B. Ferguson	329	.258	0		261	287	**88**	38	7.4	.862	A. Hagan	17	137	1	14	0	5.45
W-17 L-81	SS	McClellan	326	.230	1		152	254	72	25	**6.1**	.849							
	3B	F. Warner	141	.227	0		46	54	29	4	3.4	.775							
Bob Ferguson	RF	J. Manning	420	.267	0		155	37	33	5	2.3	.853							
W-4 L-13	CF	F. Lewis	160	.250	0		84	8	21	1	3.0	.814							
	LF	B. Purcell	425	.268	1		60	14	14	2	2.0	.841							
Blondie Purcell	C	E. Gross	231	.307	1		207	70	**74**		6.4	.789							
W-13 L-68	PO	J. Coleman	354	.234	0		91	132	31	6		.878							
	UT	B. Harbidge	280	.221	0		138	79	62	3		.778							
	UT	F. Ringo	221	.190	0		197	98	64	9		.822							

BATTING AND BASE RUNNING LEADERS

Batting Average
D. Brouthers, BUF	.374
R. Connor, NY	.357
G. Gore, CHI	.334
J. Burdock, BOS	.330
J. O'Rourke, BUF	.328

Slugging Average
D. Brouthers, BUF	.572
J. Morrill, BOS	.525
R. Connor, NY	.506
E. Sutton, BOS	.486
B. Ewing, NY	.481

Home Runs
B. Ewing, NY	10
J. Denny, PRO	8
J. Hornung, BOS	8
M. Ward, NY	7
J. Morrill, BOS	6

Total Bases
D. Brouthers, BUF	243
J. Morrill, BOS	212
R. Connor, NY	207
E. Sutton, BOS	201
J. Hornung, BOS	199

Runs Batted In
(not available)

Stolen Bases
(not available)

Hits
D. Brouthers, BUF	159
R. Connor, NY	146
J. O'Rourke, BUF	143
E. Sutton, BOS	134

Base on Balls
T. York, CLE	37
N. Hanlon, DET	34
M. Powell, DET	28
G. Gore, CHI	27

Home Run Percentage
B. Ewing, NY	2.7
J. Denny, PRO	2.0
M. Ward, NY	1.8
J. Hornung, BOS	1.8

Runs Scored
J. Hornung, BOS	107
G. Gore, CHI	105
J. O'Rourke, BUF	102
E. Sutton, BOS	101

Doubles
Williamson, CHI	49
D. Brouthers, BUF	41
T. Burns, CHI	37
C. Anson, CHI	36

Triples
D. Brouthers, BUF	17
J. Morrill, BOS	16
R. Connor, NY	15
E. Sutton, BOS	15

PITCHING LEADERS

Winning Percentage
McCormick, CLE	.675
O. Radbourn, PRO	.662
C. Buffinton, BOS	.649
J. Whitney, BOS	.638
L. Corcoran, CHI	.630

Earned Run Average
McCormick, CLE	1.84
O. Radbourn, PRO	2.05
J. Whitney, BOS	2.24
W. Sawyer, CLE	2.36
O. Daily, CLE	2.42

Wins
O. Radbourn, PRO	49
P. Galvin, BUF	46
J. Whitney, BOS	37
L. Corcoran, CHI	34
McCormick, CLE	27
M. Welch, NY	27

Saves
J. Whitney, BOS	2
S. Weidman, DET	2

Strikeouts
J. Whitney, BOS	345
O. Radbourn, PRO	315
P. Galvin, BUF	279
L. Corcoran, CHI	216
C. Buffinton, BOS	188

Complete Games
P. Galvin, BUF	72
O. Radbourn, PRO	66
J. Coleman, PHI	59
J. Whitney, BOS	54
L. Corcoran, CHI	51

Fewest Hits/9 Innings
W. Sawyer, CLE	7.60
O. Radbourn, PRO	8.01
McCormick, CLE	8.32
O. Daily, CLE	8.56

Shutouts
C. Buffinton, BOS	5
P. Galvin, BUF	5
O. Daily, CLE	4
M. Welch, NY	4

Fewest Walks/9 Innings
J. Whitney, BOS	0.61
P. Galvin, BUF	0.69
O. Radbourn, PRO	0.80
J. Coleman, PHI	0.80

Most Strikeouts/9 Inn.
J. Whitney, BOS	6.04
C. Buffinton, BOS	5.08
W. Sawyer, CLE	4.85
O. Radbourn, PRO	4.48

Innings
P. Galvin, BUF	656
O. Radbourn, PRO	632
J. Coleman, PHI	538
J. Whitney, BOS	514

Games Pitched
P. Galvin, BUF	76
O. Radbourn, PRO	76
J. Coleman, PHI	65
J. Whitney, BOS	62

NATIONAL LEAGUE 1883, cont.

	W	L	PCT	GB	R	OR	Batting 2B	3B	HR	BA	SA	SB	Fielding E	DP	FA	Pitching CG	BB	SO	ShO	SV	ERA
Boston	63	35	.643		669	456	209	86	34	.276	.408	0	409	58	.901	89	90	538	5	3	2.55
Chicago	59	39	.602	4	679	540	277	61	13	.273	.393	0	543	76	.879	91	123	299	5	1	2.78
Providence	58	40	.592	5	636	436	189	59	21	.272	.372	0	419	75	.903	88	111	376	4	1	2.37
Cleveland	55	42	.567	7.5	476	443	184	38	8	.246	.329	0	389	69	.909	92	217	402	5	2	2.22
Buffalo	52	45	.536	10.5	614	576	184	59	8	.284	.371	0	445	52	.896	90	101	362	5	2	3.32
New York	46	50	.479	16	530	577	138	69	25	.255	.355	0	468	52	.889	87	170	323	5	0	2.94
Detroit	40	58	.408	23	524	650	164	48	13	.250	.330	0	470	77	.893	89	184	324	4	2	3.56
Philadelphia	17	81	.173	46	437	887	181	47	4	.240	.320	0	639	62	.858	91	125	253	3	0	5.33
					4565	4565	1526	467	126	.262	.360	0	3782	521	.891	717	1121	2877	36	11	3.13

AMERICAN ASSOCIATION 1883

Team	POS	Player	AB	BA	HR	RBI	PO	A	E	DP	TC/G	FA	Pitcher	G	IP	W	L	SV	ERA
Philadelphia W-66 L-32 Lew Simmons	1B	H. Stovey	421	.302	14		984	22	37	31	11.2	.965	B. Mathews	44	381	30	13	0	2.46
	2B	C. Stricker	330	.273	1		253	223	93	23	6.5	.837	G. Bradley	26	214	16	7	0	3.15
	SS	M. Moynahan	400	.308	1		105	268	75	14	4.7	.833	F. Corey	18	148	10	7	0	3.40
	3B	G. Bradley	312	.234	1		46	106	43	6	4.4	.779							
	RF	L. Knight	429	.252	1		123	22	24	5	1.8	.858							
	CF	B. Blakiston	167	.246	0		51	5	10	0	1.8	.848							
	LF	J. Birchall	449	.241	1		168	22	45	0	2.4	.809							
	C	J. O'Brien	390	.290	0		301	58	51	3	7.1	.876							
	UT	F. Corey	298	.258	1		86	150	57	7		.805							
	C	E. Rowen	196	.219	0		266	52	54	2	8.5	.855							
	P	B. Mathews	167	.186	0		15	68	12	2	2.2	.874							
St. Louis W-65 L-33 Ted Sullivan W-53 L-26 Charlie Comiskey W-12 L-7	1B	C. Comiskey	401	.294	2		1085	20	43	49	12.0	.963	T. Mullane	53	461	35	15	1	2.19
	2B	G. Strief	302	.225	1		205	214	47	28	7.0	.899	J. McGinnis	45	383	28	16	0	2.33
	SS	B. Gleason	425	.287	2		120	257	56	22	4.4	.871							
	3B	A. Latham	406	.236	2		120	256	58	14	4.4	.866							
	RF	H. Nicol	368	.288	0		133	31	15	4	2.1	.916							
	CF	F. Lewis	209	.301	4		89	6	17	0	2.3	.848							
	LF	T. Dolan	295	.214	1		214	51	12	4	6.6	.957							
	C	P. Deasley	206	.257	0		301	59	27	6	6.9	.930							
	PO	T. Mullane	307	.225	0		58	104	25	5		.866							
	P	J. McGinnis	180	.200	0		14	80	21	3	2.6	.817							
	OF	T. Mansell	112	.402	0		32	1	9	0	1.5	.786							
Cincinnati W-61 L-37 Pop Snyder	1B	L. Reilly	437	.311	9		959	19	40	50	10.4	.961	W. White	65	577	43	22	0	2.09
	2B	B. McPhee	367	.245	2		314	277	46	48	6.6	.928	R. Deagle	18	148	10	8	0	2.31
	SS	C. Fulmer	361	.258	5		134	243	60	26	4.8	.863	McCormick	15	129	8	6	0	2.87
	3B	H. Carpenter	436	.296	3		133	181	47	6	3.8	.870							
	RF	P. Corkhill	375	.216	2		162	10	13	0	2.2	.930							
	CF	C. Jones	391	.294	11		172	12	26	1	2.3	.876							
	LF	J. Sommer	413	.278	3		171	11	31	1	2.3	.854							
	C	P. Snyder	250	.256	0		283	71	31	4	6.8	.919							
	P	W. White	240	.225	0		23	106	23	1	2.3	.849							
	CO	P. Powers	114	.246	0		74	20	12	0		.887							
	C	B. Traffley	105	.200	0		121	33	27	2	6.2	.851							
New York W-54 L-42 Jim Mutrie	1B	S. Brady	432	.271	0		824	29	35	31	11.0	.961	T. Keefe	68	619	41	27	0	2.41
	2B	S. Crane	349	.235	0		283	249	87	26	6.4	.859	J. Lynch	29	255	13	15	0	4.09
	SS	C. Nelson	417	.305	0		98	232	47	18	3.9	.875							
	3B	Esterbrook	407	.253	0		110	173	42	8	3.4	.871							
	RF	C. Roseman	398	.251	0		105	19	21	3	1.6	.855							
	CF	J. O'Rourke	315	.270	2		95	12	18	2	1.6	.856							
	LF	E. Kennedy	356	.219	2		112	10	16	0	1.5	.884							
	C	B. Holbert	299	.237	0		527	138	58	8	10.6	.920							
	P	T. Keefe	259	.220	0		31	148	59	3	3.5	.752							
	C	Reipschlager	145	.186	0		202	46	17	1	9.1	.936							
	P	J. Lynch	107	.187	0		18	46	20	0	2.9	.762							
Louisville W-52 L-45 Joe Gerhardt	1B	J. Latham	368	.250	0		625	21	30	40	10.1	.956	G. Hecker	55	451	28	25	0	3.33
	2B	J. Gerhardt	319	.263	0		278	263	56	42	7.7	.906	S. Weaver	46	419	24	20	0	3.70
	SS	J. Leary	165	.188	3		62	106	38	11	5.2	.816							
	3B	J. Gleason	355	.296	2		83	107	49	6	2.9	.795							
	RF	C. Wolf	389	.262	1		157	29	23	6	2.7	.890							
	CF	L. Maskrey	361	.202	1		193	19	20	1	2.4	.914							
	LF	P. Browning	358	.338	2		94	5	16	1	2.4	.861							
	C	E. Whiting	240	.292	2		244	62	40	5	6.9	.884							
	UT	G. Hecker	322	.273	1		144	100	24	7		.910							
	P	S. Weaver	203	.192	0		21	81	6	3	2.3	.944							
	C	D. Sullivan	147	.211	0		149	34	21	2	6.4	.897							
	UT	McLaughlin	146	.192	0		105	72	27	8		.868							

AMERICAN ASSOCIATION 1883, *cont.*

	POS	Player	AB	BA	HR	RBI	PO	A	E	DP	TC/G	FA	Pitcher	G	IP	W	L	SV	ERA
Columbus	1B	J. Field	295	.254	1		781	10	52	44	11.1	.938	F. Mountain	59	503	26	33	0	3.60
	2B	P. Smith	405	.262	4		250	247	62	38	7.7	.889	E. Dundon	20	167	3	16	0	4.48
W-32 L-65	SS	J. Richmond	385	.283	0		122	304	60	19	5.3	.877	J. Valentine	13	102	2	10	0	3.53
	3B	W. Kuehne	374	.227	1		61	133	39	11	3.4	.833							
Horace Phillips	RF	T. Brown	420	.274	5		151	22	42	3	2.2	.805							
	CF	F. Mann	394	.249	1		124	16	24	4	2.0	.854							
	LF	H. Wheeler	371	.226	1		131	15	35	2	2.2	.807							
	C	R. Kemmler	318	.208	0		388	97	71	10	6.8	.872							
	P	F. Mountain	276	.217	3		31	105	24	3	2.7	.850							
	C1	J. Straub	100	.130			182	22	21	8		.907							
Pittsburgh	1B	E. Swartwood	413	.356	3		632	23	45	28	11.7	.936	D. Driscoll	41	336	18	21	0	3.99
	2B	G. Creamer	369	.255	0		310	274	67	42	7.2	.897	B. Barr	26	203	6	18	1	4.38
W-31 L-67	SS	D. Mack	224	.196	0		29	106	25	7	4.2	.844	B. Taylor	19	127	4	7	0	5.39
	3B	J. Battin	388	.214	1		151	258	50	12	4.7	.891	J. Neagle	16	114	3	12	0	5.84
Al Pratt	RF	B. Dickerson	355	.248	0		106	28	34	2	2.2	.798							
W-12 L-20	CF	B. Taylor	369	.260	2		49	10	20	0	2.1	.747							
	LF	M. Mansell	412	.257	3		186	11	26	1	2.3	.883							
Ormond Butler	C	J. Hayes	351	.262	3		277	70	34	2	6.1	.911							
W-17 L-36	P	D. Driscoll	148	.182	0		14	99	14	2	3.1	.890							
	UT	B. Barr	142	.246	0		62	43	17	2		.861							
Joe Battin	UT	B. Morgan	114	.158	0		59	72	25	4		.840							
W-2 L-11	SS	McLaughlin	114	.219	1		19	78	24	4	4.8	.802							
	PO	J. Neagle	101	.188	0		23	22	10	0		.818							
Baltimore	1B	D. Stearns	382	.246	1		984	38	57	38	11.7	.947	H. Henderson	45	358	10	32	0	4.02
	2B	T. Manning	121	.215	0		105	106	20	8	6.6	.913	B. Emslie	24	201	9	13	0	3.17
W-28 L-68	SS	L. Say	324	.256	1		76	241	82	13	5.4	.794	J. Fox	20	165	6	13	0	4.03
	3B	McCormick	389	.262	0		138	196	84	10	4.5	.799							
Billy Barnie	RF	D. Rowe	256	.313	0		70	5	19	0	1.9	.798							
	CF	D. Eggler	202	.188	0		92	6	9	1	2.0	.916							
	LF	J. Clinton	399	.313	1		158	18	33	2	2.3	.842							
	C	K. Kelly	202	.228	0		169	35	50	3	6.7	.803							
	P	H. Henderson	191	.162	1		23	59	22	3	2.3	.788							
	OF	G. Gardner	161	.273	1		62	5	13	0	2.3	.838							
	2B	T. O'Brien	138	.268	0		77	93	36	8	7.1	.825							
	CO	P. Baker	121	.273	1		113	14	21	2		.858							
	C	R. Sweeney	101	.208	0		97	40	19	2	6.8	.878							

BATTING AND BASE RUNNING LEADERS

Batting Average
- E. Swartwood, PIT .356
- H. Stovey, PHI .352
- P. Browning, LOU .336
- J. Clinton, BAL .313
- D. Rowe, BAL .313

Slugging Average
- H. Stovey, PHI .565
- L. Reilly, CIN .485
- E. Swartwood, PIT .475
- C. Jones, CIN .473
- P. Browning, LOU .469

Home Runs
- H. Stovey, PHI 14
- C. Jones, CIN 11
- L. Reilly, CIN 9
- C. Fulmer, CIN 5
- T. Brown, COL 5

Total Bases
- H. Stovey, PHI 238
- L. Reilly, CIN 212
- E. Swartwood, PIT 196
- C. Jones, CIN 185
- P. Browning, LOU 169

Runs Batted In
(not available)

Stolen Bases
(not available)

Hits
- H. Stovey, PHI 148
- E. Swartwood, PIT 147
- L. Reilly, CIN 136
- C. Nelson, NY 127

Base on Balls
- D. Stearns, BAL 34
- C. Nelson, NY 31
- M. Moynahan, PHI 30
- J. Gleason, LOU, STL 29

Home Run Percentage
- H. Stovey, PHI 3.3
- C. Jones, CIN 2.8
- L. Reilly, CIN 2.1
- C. Fulmer, CIN 1.4

Runs Scored
- H. Stovey, PHI 110
- L. Reilly, CIN 103
- H. Carpenter, CIN 99
- L. Knight, PHI 98

Doubles
- H. Stovey, PHI 32
- E. Swartwood, PIT 24
- J. Hayes, PIT 23
- L. Knight, PHI 23

Triples
- P. Smith, COL 17
- W. Kuehne, COL 14
- L. Reilly, CIN 14
- F. Mann, COL 13

PITCHING LEADERS

Winning Percentage
- T. Mullane, STL .700
- B. Mathews, PHI .698
- G. Bradley, PHI .696
- W. White, CIN .662
- J. McGinnis, STL .636

Earned Run Average
- W. White, CIN 2.09
- T. Mullane, STL 2.19
- R. Deagle, CIN 2.31
- J. McGinnis, STL 2.33
- T. Keefe, NY 2.41

Wins
- W. White, CIN 43
- T. Keefe, NY 41
- T. Mullane, STL 35
- B. Mathews, PHI 30
- J. McGinnis, STL 28
- G. Hecker, LOU 28

Saves
- T. Mullane, STL 1
- B. Barr, PIT 1

Strikeouts
- T. Keefe, NY 361
- B. Mathews, PHI 203
- T. Mullane, STL 191
- F. Mountain, COL 159
- G. Hecker, LOU 153

Complete Games
- T. Keefe, NY 68
- W. White, CIN 64
- F. Mountain, COL 57
- G. Hecker, LOU 53
- T. Mullane, STL 49

Fewest Hits/9 Innings
- T. Keefe, NY 7.07
- T. Mullane, STL 7.27
- W. White, CIN 7.38
- J. McGinnis, STL 7.64

Shutouts
- J. McGinnis, STL 6
- W. White, CIN 6
- T. Keefe, NY 5
- S. Weaver, LOU 4

Fewest Walks/9 Innings
- B. Mathews, PHI 0.73
- S. Weaver, LOU 0.82
- J. Lynch, NY 0.88
- G. Bradley, PHI 0.92

Most Strikeouts/9 Inn.
- T. Keefe, NY 5.25
- B. Mathews, PHI 4.80
- J. Lynch, NY 4.20
- T. Mullane, STL 3.73

Innings
- T. Keefe, NY 619
- W. White, CIN 577
- F. Mountain, COL 503
- T. Mullane, STL 461

Games Pitched
- T. Keefe, NY 68
- W. White, CIN 65
- F. Mountain, COL 59
- G. Hecker, LOU 55

AMERICAN ASSOCIATION 1883, cont.

	W	L	PCT	GB	R	OR	Batting					SB	Fielding			Pitching					ERA
							2B	3B	HR	BA	SA		E	DP	FA	CG	BB	SO	ShO	SV	
Philadelphia	66	32	.673		**720**	547	**149**	50	20	.262	.345	0	584	40	.865	92	**95**	347	1	0	2.87
St. Louis	65	33	.663	1	549	409	118	46	7	.255	.321	0	388	62	**.909**	93	150	325	9	1	2.23
Cincinnati	61	37	.622	5	662	413	122	73	35	.262	.364	0	**383**	57	.905	96	168	213	8	0	2.26
New York	54	42	.563	11	498	**405**	111	58	6	.250	.319	0	439	45	.895	**97**	123	**480**	6	0	2.90
Louisville	52	45	.536	13.5	564	562	114	66	12	.251	.330	0	488	67	.884	96	110	269	7	0	3.50
Columbus	32	65	.330	33.5	476	659	101	**78**	16	.240	.326	0	540	**69**	.873	90	211	222	4	0	3.97
Pittsburgh	31	67	.316	35	525	728	120	58	13	.247	.323	0	506	55	.884	82	151	271	1	1	4.62
Baltimore	28	68	.292	37	471	742	125	49	5	.246	.314	0	624	44	.855	86	190	290	1	0	4.08
					4465	4465	960	478	114	.252	.331	0	3952	439	.884	732	1198	2417	37	2	3.30

NATIONAL LEAGUE 1884

	POS	Player	AB	BA	HR	RBI	PO	A	E	DP	TC/G	FA	Pitcher	G	IP	W	L	SV	ERA
Providence W-84 L-28 Frank Bancroft	1B	J. Start	381	.276	2		939	21	20	31	10.5	.980	O. Radbourn	75	679	60	12	1	1.38
	2B	J. Farrell	469	.217	1		249	351	51	36	6.0	.922	C. Sweeney	27	221	17	8	1	1.55
	SS	A. Irwin	404	.240	2		99	307	55	20	4.5	.881							
	3B	J. Denny	439	.248	6		144	168	45	5	3.6	.874							
	RF	P. Radford	355	.197	1		146	26	23	4	2.0	.882							
	CF	P. Hines	490	.302	3		202	20	26	5	2.3	.895							
	LF	C. Carroll	452	.261	3		206	11	23	1	2.1	.904							
	C	B. Gilligan	294	.245	1		**605**	94	54	7	9.3	.928							
	P	O. Radbourn	361	.230	1		21	119	17	1	2.1	.892							
	PO	C. Sweeney	168	.298	1		31	49	6	1		.930							
	C	S. Nava	116	.095	0		172	40	27	1	8.9	.887							
Boston W-73 L-38 John Morrill	1B	J. Morrill	438	.260	3		953	34	30	33	11.2	.971	C. Buffinton	67	587	48	16	0	2.15
	2B	J. Burdock	361	.269	6		183	278	39	23	5.7	.922	J. Whitney	41	336	23	14	0	2.09
	SS	S. Wise	426	.214	4		156	307	61	16	4.9	.884							
	3B	E. Sutton	468	.346	3		119	186	31	7	3.1	.908							
	RF	B. Crowley	407	.270	6		125	22	22	5	1.6	.870							
	CF	J. Manning	345	.241	2		115	15	18	2	2.0	.878							
	LF	J. Hornung	518	.268	7		182	14	18	1	1.9	.916							
	C	M. Hackett	268	.205	1		512	104	48	2	9.4	.928							
	P	C. Buffinton	352	.267	1		40	118	9	2	2.5	.946							
	UT	J. Whitney	270	.259	3		135	80	10	3		.956							
	C	M. Hines	132	.174	0		255	64	28	7	9.9	.919							
Buffalo W-64 L-47 Jim O'Rourke	1B	D. Brouthers	398	.327	14		958	30	37	38	11.0	.964	P. Galvin	72	636	46	22	0	1.99
	2B	Richardson	439	.301	6		191	243	50	18	6.8	.897	B. Serad	37	308	16	20	0	4.27
	SS	D. Force	403	.206	0		110	312	48	21	4.5	**.898**							
	3B	D. White	452	.325	5		113	198	60	11	3.5	.825							
	RF	J. Lillie	471	.223	3		190	**41**	**40**	7	2.4	.852							
	CF	D. Eggler	241	.195	0		104	14	15	1	2.1	.887							
	LF	J. O'Rourke	467	.347	5		112	6	14	2	1.5	.894							
	C	J. Rowe	400	.315	4		373	60	26	3	7.1	**.943**							
	CO	G. Myers	325	.182	2		320	61	78	5		.830							
	P	P. Galvin	274	.179	0		32	**154**	7	3	2.7	.964							
	2B	C. Collins	169	.178	0		108	137	23	15	6.4	.914							
	P	B. Serad	137	.175	0		4	57	14	1	2.0	.813							
Chicago W-62 L-50 Cap Anson	1B	C. Anson	475	.335	21		**1211**	40	**58**	**86**	11.7	.956	L. Corcoran	60	517	35	23	0	2.40
	2B	F. Pfeffer	467	.289	25		395	**422**	88	85	8.1	.903	F. Goldsmith	21	188	9	11	0	4.26
	SS	T. Burns	343	.245	7		99	254	68	21	5.3	.838	J. Clarkson	14	118	10	3	0	2.14
	3B	Williamson	417	.278	**27**		121	**250**	60	**25**	4.4	.861							
	RF	K. Kelly	452	**.354**	13		69	31	26	1	2.0	.794							
	CF	G. Gore	422	.318	5		185	25	32	5	2.3	.868							
	LF	A. Dalrymple	521	.309	22		176	18	26	5	2.0	.882							
	C	S. Flint	279	.204	9		354	110	61	9	7.2	.884							
	P	L. Corcoran	251	.243	1		**47**	132	**24**	5	3.4	.882							
	OF	B. Sunday	176	.222	4		45	8	27	1	1.9	.663							
New York W-62 L-50 Jim Price W-56 L-42 Monte Ward W-6 L-8	1B	A. McKinnon	470	.272	4		1097	31	53	57	10.2	.955	M. Welch	65	557	39	21	0	2.50
	2B	R. Connor	477	.317	4		230	205	71	30	7.6	.860	E. Begley	31	266	12	18	0	4.16
	SS	E. Caskin	351	.231	2		121	278	53	**28**	4.7	.883	M. Dorgan	14	113	8	6	0	3.50
	3B	F. Hankinson	389	.231	2		135	182	47	8	3.5	.871							
	RF	M. Dorgan	341	.276	1		101	13	20	3	2.1	.851							
	CF	M. Ward	482	.253	2		103	13	21	2	2.3	.847							
	LF	P. Gillespie	413	.264	2		159	8	20	1	1.9	.893							
	C	B. Ewing	382	.277	3		445	**127**	41	10	7.7	.933							
	OF	Richardson	277	.253	1		77	20	10	3	1.9	.907							
	P	M. Welch	249	.241	3		25	78	14	**6**	1.8	.880							
	P	E. Begley	121	.182	0		16	46	9	2	2.3	.873							

NATIONAL LEAGUE 1884, cont.

	POS	Player	AB	BA	HR	RBI	PO	A	E	DP	TC/G	FA	Pitcher	G	IP	W	L	SV	ERA
Philadelphia	1B	S. Farrar	428	.245	1		1142	**42**	42	41	11.0	.966	C. Ferguson	50	417	21	25	1	3.54
	2B	E. Andrews	420	.221	0		239	326	69	37	5.8	.891	B. Vinton	21	182	10	10	0	2.23
	SS	McClellan	450	.258	3		**165**	**313**	**83**	22	5.1	.852	J. Coleman	21	154	5	15	0	4.90
W-39 L-73	3B	J. Mulvey	401	.229	2		151	216	**73**	20	4.4	.834	J. McElroy	13	111	1	12	0	4.86
	RF	J. Manning	424	.271	5		140	26	30	**7**	1.9	.847							
Harry Wright	CF	J. Fogarty	378	.212	1		193	12	19	3	**2.9**	.915							
	LF	B. Purcell	428	.252	1		182	12	28	1	2.2	.874							
	C	J. Crowley	168	.244	0		198	49	50	2	6.2	.832							
	P	C. Ferguson	203	.246	0		23	72	12	4	2.1	.888							
	OP	J. Coleman	171	.246	0		61	44	13	2		.890							
Cleveland	1B	B. Phillips	464	.276	3	46	1107	30	48	59	10.7	.959	J. Harkins	46	391	12	**32**	0	3.68
	2B	G. Smith	291	.254	4	26	111	136	34	23	6.7	.879	McCormick	42	359	19	22	0	2.86
	SS	J. Glasscock	281	.249	1	22	118	267	46	16	**6.2**	.893	S. Moffett	24	198	3	19	0	3.87
W-35 L-77	3B	M. Muldoon	422	.239	2	38	126	204	66	15	3.6	.833							
	RF	J. Evans	313	.259	1	39	136	19	14	3	2.2	**.917**							
Charlie Hackett	CF	P. Hotaling	408	.243	3	37	174	23	35	5	2.3	.849							
	LF	W. Murphy	168	.226	1	9	60	7	26	0	2.2	.720							
	C	D. Bushong	203	.236	0	10	355	98	58	11	8.2	.886							
	OP	S. Moffett	256	.184	0	14	78	65	23	2		.861							
	P	J. Harkins	229	.205	0	20	15	81	17	3	2.5	.850							
	P	McCormick	190	.263	0	23	18	67	0	4	2.0	**1.000**							
	C	F. Briody	148	.169	1	12	243	74	27	5	8.2	.922							
	2S	G. Pinckney	144	.313	0	16	73	110	32	11		.851							
	OF	E. Burch	124	.210	0	7	52	10	7	1	2.2	.899							
Detroit	1B	M. Scott	438	.247	3		1120	26	38	37	10.8	.968	F. Meinke	35	289	8	22	0	3.18
	2B	B. Geiss	283	.177	2		190	217	65	27	6.5	.862	D. Shaw	28	228	9	18	0	3.04
	SS	F. Meinke	341	.164	6		57	146	39	16	4.7	.839	S. Weidman	26	213	4	21	0	3.72
W-28 L-84	3B	J. Farrell	461	.226	3		126	198	61	12	3.5	.842	C. Getzien	17	147	5	12	0	1.95
	RF	S. Weidman	300	.163	0		76	12	16	2	2.0	.846	F. Brill	12	103	2	10	0	5.50
Jack Chapman	CF	N. Hanlon	450	.264	5		**241**	30	39	5	2.7	.874							
	LF	G. Wood	473	.252	8		190	17	24	1	2.0	.896							
	C	C. Bennett	341	.264	3		454	97	50	9	7.5	.917							
	P	D. Shaw	136	.191	1		10	55	11	2	2.7	.855							
	UT	H. Jones	129	.209	0		52	90	17	1		.893							

BATTING AND BASE RUNNING LEADERS

Batting Average
K. Kelly, CHI .354
J. O'Rourke, BUF .347
E. Sutton, BOS .346
C. Anson, CHI .335
D. Brouthers, BUF .327

Slugging Average
D. Brouthers, BUF .568
Williamson, CHI .554
C. Anson, CHI .543
K. Kelly, CHI .524
F. Pfeffer, CHI .514

Home Runs
Williamson, CHI 27
F. Pfeffer, CHI 25
A. Dalrymple, CHI 22
C. Anson, CHI 21
D. Brouthers, BUF 14

Total Bases
A. Dalrymple, CHI 263
C. Anson, CHI 258
F. Pfeffer, CHI 240
K. Kelly, CHI 237
Williamson, CHI 231

Runs Batted In
(not available)

Stolen Bases
(not available)

Hits
J. O'Rourke, BUF 162
E. Sutton, BOS 162
A. Dalrymple, CHI 161
K. Kelly, CHI 160

Base on Balls
G. Gore, CHI 61
K. Kelly, CHI 46
P. Hines, PRO 44
Williamson, CHI 42

Home Run Percentage
Williamson, CHI 6.5
F. Pfeffer, CHI 5.4
C. Anson, CHI 4.4
A. Dalrymple, CHI 4.2

Runs Scored
K. Kelly, CHI 120
J. O'Rourke, BUF 119
J. Hornung, BOS 119
A. Dalrymple, CHI 111

Doubles
P. Hines, PRO 36
J. O'Rourke, BUF 33
C. Anson, CHI 30
J. Manning, PHI 29

Triples
B. Ewing, NY 20
D. Brouthers, BUF 16
J. Rowe, BUF 14
B. Phillips, CLE 12

PITCHING LEADERS

Winning Percentage
O. Radbourn, PRO .833
C. Buffinton, BOS .746
C. Sweeney, PRO .680
P. Galvin, BUF .676
M. Welch, NY .650

Earned Run Average
O. Radbourn, PRO 1.38
C. Sweeney, PRO 1.55
C. Getzien, DET 1.95
P. Galvin, BUF 1.99
J. Whitney, BOS 2.09

Wins
O. Radbourn, PRO 60
C. Buffinton, BOS 47
P. Galvin, BUF 46
M. Welch, NY 39
L. Corcoran, CHI 35

Saves
J. Morrill, BOS 2
O. Radbourn, PRO 1
C. Sweeney, PRO 1
C. Ferguson, PHI 1
J. O'Rourke, BUF 1

Strikeouts
O. Radbourn, PRO 441
C. Buffinton, BOS 417
P. Galvin, BUF 369
M. Welch, NY 345
L. Corcoran, CHI 272

Complete Games
O. Radbourn, PRO 73
P. Galvin, BUF 71
C. Buffinton, BOS 63
M. Welch, NY 62
L. Corcoran, CHI 57

Fewest Hits/9 Innings
C. Sweeney, PRO 6.23
O. Radbourn, PRO 7.00
J. Clarkson, CHI 7.17
C. Getzien, DET 7.21

Shutouts
P. Galvin, BUF 12
O. Radbourn, PRO 11
C. Buffinton, BOS 8
L. Corcoran, CHI 7

Fewest Walks/9 Innings
J. Whitney, BOS 0.72
P. Galvin, BUF 0.89
C. Buffinton, BOS 1.17
C. Sweeney, PRO 1.18

Most Strikeouts/9 Inn.
J. Clarkson, CHI 7.78
J. Whitney, BOS 7.23
M. Dorgan, NY 7.17
C. Getzien, DET 6.54

Innings
O. Radbourn, PRO 679
P. Galvin, BUF 636
C. Buffinton, BOS 587
M. Welch, NY 557

Games Pitched
O. Radbourn, PRO 75
P. Galvin, BUF 72
C. Buffinton, BOS 67
M. Welch, NY 65

NATIONAL LEAGUE 1884, cont.

	W	L	PCT	GB	R	OR	Batting					SB	Fielding			Pitching					ERA
							2B	3B	HR	BA	SA		E	DP	FA	CG	BB	SO	ShO	SV	
Providence	84	28	.750		665	**388**	153	43	21	.241	.315	0	398	50	.918	107	172	639	**16**	**2**	*1.59*
Boston	73	38	.658	10.5	684	468	**179**	60	36	.254	.351	0	**384**	46	**.922**	109	**135**	**742**	14	**2**	*2.47*
Buffalo	64	47	.577	19.5	700	626	163	**69**	39	.262	.361	0	462	71	.905	108	189	534	14	1	*2.95*
Chicago	62	50	.554	22	**834**	647	162	50	**142**	**.281**	**.446**	0	595	**107**	.886	106	231	472	9	0	*3.03*
New York	62	50	.554	22	693	623	148	67	24	.255	.341	0	514	69	.895	**111**	326	567	4	0	*3.12*
Philadelphia	39	73	.348	45	549	824	149	39	14	.234	.301	0	536	67	.888	106	254	411	3	1	*3.93*
Cleveland	35	77	.313	49	458	716	147	49	16	.237	.312	0	512	75	.897	107	269	482	7	0	*3.43*
Detroit	28	84	.250	56	445	736	114	47	31	.208	.284	0	549	60	.886	109	245	488	3	0	*3.38*
					5028	5028	1215	424	323	.247	.340	0	3950	545	.900	863	1821	4335	70	6	*2.98*

AMERICAN ASSOCIATION 1884

Team	POS	Player	AB	BA	HR	RBI	PO	A	E	DP	TC/G	FA	Pitcher	G	IP	W	L	SV	ERA
New York W-75 L-32 Jim Mutrie	1B	D. Orr	458	.354	9		1161	24	49	29	11.2	.960	T. Keefe	58	492	37	17	0	*2.29*
	2B	D. Troy	421	.264	2		224	314	74	25	5.7	.879	J. Lynch	54	487	37	15	0	*2.64*
	SS	C. Nelson	432	.255	1		113	292	56	16	4.2	.879							
	3B	Esterbrook	477	.314	1		126	208	43	11	3.4	.886							
	RF	S. Brady	485	.252	0		154	26	16	1	1.8	.918							
	CF	C. Roseman	436	.298	4		157	12	22	0	1.8	.885							
	LF	E. Kennedy	378	.190	1		138	13	14	4	1.7	.915							
	C	B. Holbert	255	.208	0		374	**142**	54	7	9.7	.905							
	C	Reipschlager	233	.240	0		369	109	39	3	10.1	.925							
	P	T. Keefe	213	.235	2		18	95	30	2	2.5	.790							
	P	J. Lynch	195	.154	0		24	80	**37**	3	2.6	.738							
Columbus W-69 L-39 Gus Schmelz	1B	J. Field	417	.233	4		1150	27	52	58	11.7	.958	E. Morris	52	430	34	13	0	*2.18*
	2B	P. Smith	445	.238	6		324	**394**	75	55	7.3	.905	F. Mountain	42	361	23	17	1	*2.45*
	SS	J. Richmond	398	.251	3		96	306	62	26	4.4	.866	E. Dundon	11	81	6	4	0	*3.78*
	3B	W. Kuehne	415	.236	5		117	218	46	13	3.5	.879							
	RF	T. Brown	451	.273	5		164	18	33	5	2.0	.847							
	CF	F. Mann	366	.276	7		120	12	22	2	1.6	.857							
	LF	J. Cahill	210	.219	0		62	8	13	0	1.5	.843							
	C	R. Kemmler	211	.199	0		268	77	36	3	6.6	.906							
	C	F. Carroll	252	.278	6		379	89	28	3	9.2	.944							
	P	F. Mountain	210	.238	4		14	88	9	0	2.6	.919							
	P	E. Morris	199	.186	0		19	88	23	3	2.5	.823							
Louisville W-68 L-40 Mike Walsh	1B	J. Latham	308	.169	0		788	32	33	48	11.2	.961	G. Hecker	**76**	**671**	**52**	20	0	*1.80*
	2B	J. Gerhardt	404	.220	0		334	389	64	64	7.5	.919	P. Reccius	18	129	6	7	0	*2.71*
	SS	McLaughlin	335	.200	1		121	330	55	**34**	5.4	.891	D. Driscoll	13	102	6	6	0	*3.44*
	3B	P. Browning	447	.336	3		79	66	35	4	3.5	.806	R. Deagle	12	87	4	6	0	*2.58*
	RF	C. Wolf	**486**	.300	3		173	26	26	4	2.2	.884							
	CF	M. Cline	396	.290	2		143	25	24	1	2.1	.875							
	LF	L. Maskrey	412	.250	0		138	17	18	2	1.7	.896							
	C	D. Sullivan	247	.239	0		340	61	30	2	6.8	.930							
	P	G. Hecker	316	.297	4		**50**	**145**	10	3	2.7	.951							
	UT	P. Reccius	263	.240	3		56	147	31	7		.868							
	C	E. Whiting	157	.223	0		199	54	31	6	7.1	.891							
St. Louis W-67 L-40 Jimmy Williams W-51 L-33 Charlie Comiskey W-16 L-7	1B	C. Comiskey	460	.239	2		**1193**	38	40	56	11.8	.969	J. McGinnis	40	354	24	16	0	*2.84*
	2B	J. Quest	310	.206	0		232	242	56	39	6.6	.894	D. Foutz	25	207	15	6	0	*2.18*
	SS	B. Gleason	472	.269	1		119	316	67	23	4.6	.867	D. Davis	25	198	10	12	0	*2.90*
	3B	A. Latham	474	.274	1		142	**302**	70	16	4.7	.864	T. O'Neill	17	141	11	4	0	*2.68*
	RF	H. Nicol	442	.260	0		144	**48**	28	3	**2.5**	.873							
	CF	F. Lewis	300	.323	0		118	15	23	1	2.1	.853							
	LF	T. O'Neill	297	.276	3		67	6	17	1	1.4	.811							
	C	P. Deasley	254	.205	0		428	120	48	3	7.9	.919							
	OF	G. Strief	184	.201	2		50	5	10	0	1.5	.846							
	P	J. McGinnis	146	.233	0		8	71	12	1	2.3	.868							
	C	T. Dolan	137	.263	0		188	45	34	2	7.9	.873							
	PO	D. Foutz	119	.227	0		26	45	6	6		.922							
Cincinnati W-68 L-41 Will White W-44 L-27 Pop Snyder W-24 L-14	1B	L. Reilly	448	.339	11		977	26	30	**60**	10.0	.971	W. White	52	456	34	18	0	*3.32*
	2B	B. McPhee	450	.278	5		**415**	365	64	**74**	7.5	.924	B. Mountjoy	33	289	19	12	0	*2.93*
	SS	J. Peoples	267	.169	0		54	140	40	19	5.0	.829	G. Shallix	23	200	11	10	0	*3.70*
	3B	H. Carpenter	474	.255	4		157	168	44	16	3.4	.881							
	RF	P. Corkhill	452	.274	4		169	29	14	5	2.3	**.934**							
	CF	T. Mansell	266	.248	0		88	3	30	0	1.9	.752							
	LF	C. Jones	472	.314	7		**207**	12	28	0	2.2	.887							
	C	P. Snyder	268	.257	0		341	135	40	5	7.9	.922							
	P	W. White	184	.190	1		8	72	18	2	1.9	.816							
	OF	B. West	131	.244	0		46	1	10	0	1.7	.825							
	C	P. Powers	130	.138	0		152	53	25	2	4.6	.891							
	SS	F. Fennelly	122	.352	2		25	84	25	12	4.8	.813							
	P	B. Mountjoy	119	.151	0		13	64	6	2	2.5	.928							
	SS	C. Fulmer	114	.175	0		22	66	24	7	3.9	.786							

AMERICAN ASSOCIATION 1884, cont.

	POS	Player	AB	BA	HR	RBI	PO	A	E	DP	TC/G	FA	Pitcher	G	IP	W	L	SV	ERA
Baltimore	1B	D. Stearns	396	.237	3		959	**48**	**54**	36	10.6	.949	B. Emslie	50	455	32	17	0	2.75
	2B	T. Manning	341	.205	2		228	277	52	28	6.1	.907	H. Henderson	52	439	27	23	0	2.62
W-63 L-43	SS	J. Macullar	358	.204	4		119	317	67	23	4.7	.867							
	3B	J. Sommer	479	.269	4		118	168	54	10	3.5	.841							
Billy Barnie	RF	G. Gardner	173	.214	2		62	12	12	0	2.2	.860							
	CF	J. Clinton	433	.273	3		133	17	35	5	1.8	.811							
	LF	T. York	314	.223	1		100	7	20	1	1.5	.843							
	C	S. Trott	284	.257	2		**491**	87	43	10	10.4	.931							
	C	B. Traffley	210	.176	0		321	57	30	6	8.7	.926							
	P	H. Henderson	203	.227	0		27	78	22	3	2.4	.827							
	P	B. Emslie	195	.190	0		27	83	22	0	2.6	.833							
	OF	D. Casey	149	.248	3		48	5	6	2	1.6	.898							
	O2	O. Burns	131	.298	6		49	34	13	2		.865							
Philadelphia	1B	H. Stovey	448	**.326**	10		1061	32	45	46	10.9	.960	B. Mathews	49	431	30	18	0	3.32
	2B	C. Stricker	399	.231	1		280	257	80	40	5.8	.870	B. Taylor	30	260	18	12	0	2.53
W-61 L-46	SS	S. Houck	472	.297	0		122	**379**	60	30	5.2	.893	A. Atkinson	22	184	11	11	0	4.20
	3B	F. Corey	439	.276	5		121	209	42	10	3.6	.887							
Charlie Mason	RF	L. Knight	484	.271	1		158	36	19	**6**	2.0	.911							
W-28 L-23	CF	H. Larkin	326	.276	3		106	7	19	0	1.6	.856							
	LF	J. Birchall	221	.258	0		81	7	17	1	2.0	.838							
Bill Sharsig	C	J. Milligan	268	.287	3		474	100	37	5	9.4	**.939**							
W-33 L-23	P	B. Mathews	184	.185	0		8	78	25	1	2.3	.775							
	C	J. O'Brien	138	.283	1		169	43	16	6	7.6	.930							
	OF	B. Blakiston	128	.258	0		48	7	6	1	2.2	.902							
	P	B. Taylor	111	.252	0		12	64	21	1	3.2	.784							
Toledo	1B	C. Lane	215	.228	1		474	20	27	17	11.3	.948	T. Mullane	68	576	37	26	0	2.48
	2B	S. Barkley	435	.306	1		318	358	51	46	7.1	.930	H. O'Day	39	309	7	28	1	3.97
W-46 L-58	SS	J. Miller	423	.239	1		125	320	70	26	4.9	.864							
	3B	E. Brown	153	.176	0		41	54	22	1	3.0	.812							
Charlie Morton	RF	T. Poorman	382	.233	0		129	29	29	5	2.0	.845							
	CF	C. Welch	425	.224	0		206	24	29	3	2.4	.888							
	LF	F. Olin	86	.256	1		22	6	4	0	1.2	.875							
	C	F. Walker	152	.263	0		220	70	37	4	8.0	.887							
	UT	T. Mullane	352	.276	3		139	161	41	10		.880							
	PO	H. O'Day	242	.211	0		38	90	17	2		.883							
	UT	J. Moffett	204	.201	0		421	42	33	23		.933							
	C	D. McGuire	151	.185	1		224	56	29	1	7.5	.906							
	3B	G. Meister	119	.193	0		27	40	15	3	2.4	.817							
	UT	C. Morton	111	.162	0		33	26	8	1		.881							
Brooklyn	1B	Householder	273	.242	3		426	18	19	17	11.6	.959	A. Terry	57	485	20	35	0	3.49
	2B	B. Greenwood	385	.216	3		230	300	59	40	6.4	.900	S. Kimber	40	352	17	20	0	3.91
W-40 L-64	SS	B. Geer	391	.210	0		176	360	81	34	5.8	.869	J. Conway	13	105	3	9	0	4.44
	3B	F. Warner	352	.222	1		94	147	52	13	3.5	.823							
George Taylor	RF	J. Cassidy	433	.252	2		124	25	26	5	1.8	.851							
	CF	J. Remsen	301	.223	3		152	7	15	2	1.9	.914							
	LF	O. Walker	382	.270	2		87	12	15	0	1.9	.868							
	C	J. Corcoran	185	.211	0		191	57	36	4	7.5	.873							
	P	A. Terry	240	.233	0		32	81	34	0	2.6	.769							
	OF	I. Benners	189	.201	1		64	1	13	0	1.6	.833							
	1B	J. Knowles	153	.235	1		304	17	16	18	11.6	.953							
	P	S. Kimber	138	.145	0		32	67	30	0	3.2	.767							
Richmond	1B	J. Powell	151	.245	0		380	18	24	15	10.3	.943	E. Dugan	20	166	5	14	0	4.49
	2B	T. Larkin	139	.201	0		94	129	23	14	6.2	.907	P. Meegan	17	140	5	9	0	4.37
W-12 L-30	SS	B. Schenck	151	.205	3		32	121	30	8	4.6	.836							
	3B	B. Nash	166	.199	1		77	87	34	8	4.4	.828							
Felix Moses	RF	M. Mansell	113	.301	0		24	5	9	1	1.3	.763							
	CF	D. Johnston	146	.281	2		86	10	15	3	3.0	.865							
	LF	E. Glenn	175	.246	1		85	5	18	2	2.5	.833							
	C	J. Hanna	67	.194	0		108	38	12	2	7.5	.924							
	CO	M. Quinton	94	.234	0		62	20	12	3		.872							
	P	E. Dugan	70	.114	0		13	23	13	0	2.5	.735							
	P	P. Meegan	59	.136	0		6	34	9	0	2.9	.816							
Pittsburgh	1B	J. Knowles	182	.231	0		499	15	21	20	11.6	.961	F. Sullivan	51	441	16	35	0	4.20
	2B	G. Creamer	339	.183	0		308	336	43	47	7.0	**.937**	J. Neagle	38	326	11	26	0	3.73
W-30 L-78	SS	B. White	291	.227	0		58	185	58	12	5.0	.807							
	3B	J. Battin	158	.177	0		53	95	13	4	3.7	.919							
Denny McKnight	RF	E. Swartwood	399	.288	0		109	22	32	2	2.1	.804							
W-4 L-8	CF	G. Taylor	152	.211	0		68	7	19	0	2.3	.798							
	LF	D. Miller	347	.225	0		74	13	22	1	2.2	.798							
Bob Ferguson	C	B. Colgan	161	.155	0		228	71	31	5	7.5	.906							
W-11 L-31	P	F. Sullivan	189	.153	0		24	90	24	2	2.7	.826							
	P	J. Neagle	148	.149	0		19	57	24	1	2.6	.760							
Joe Battin	30	J. McDonald	145	.159	0		43	38	19	2		.810							
W-6 L-7	SS	T. Forster	126	.222	0		45	103	17	8	5.9	.897							
	C	J. Hayes	124	.226	0		135	30	16	2	7.5	.912							
George Creamer	OF	C. Eden	122	.270	1		40	4	14	0	1.9	.759							
W-0 L-8	1B	J. Faatz	112	.241	0		283	6	11	16	10.3	.963							
Horace Phillips																			
W-9 L-4																			

AMERICAN ASSOCIATION 1884, *cont.*

	POS	Player	AB	BA	HR	RBI	PO	A	E	DP	TC/G	FA	Pitcher	G	IP	W	L	SV	ERA
Indianapolis	1B	J. Kerins	361	.216	6		887	41	27	20	11.0	**.972**	L. McKeon	61	512	18	41	0	3.50
	2B	E. Merrill	196	.179	0		144	162	34	15	6.2	.900	B. Barr	16	132	3	11	0	4.99
W-29 L-78	SS	M. Phillips	413	.269	0		108	335	71	16	5.3	.862	J. Aydelott	12	106	5	7	0	4.92
Jim Gifford	3B	P. Callahan	258	.260	2		66	94	37	5	3.2	.812							
W-25 L-59	RF	P. Weihe	256	.254	4		90	14	17	2	2.1	.860							
	CF	J. Morrison	182	.264	1		78	9	24	4	2.5	.784							
Bill Watkins	LF	J. Peltz	393	.219	3		155	16	38	1	2.0	.818							
W-4 L-19	C	J. Keenan	249	.293	3		399	71	39	5	8.6	.923							
	P	L. McKeon	247	.215	0		35	124	20	1	2.9	.888							
	OF	J. Dorgan	141	.298	0		37	9	12	1	2.0	.793							
	2B	C. Collins	138	.225	0		97	105	26	10	6.0	.886							
	UT	J. Donnelly	134	.254	0		33	62	21	2		.819							
	32	B. Watkins	127	.205	0		44	57	14	4		.878							
Washington	1B	W. Prince	166	.217	0		405	4	26	19	10.1	.940	B. Barr	32	281	9	23	0	3.45
	2B	T. Hawkes	151	.278	0		124	103	20	10	6.5	.919	J. Hamill	19	157	2	17	0	4.48
W-12 L-51	SS	F. Fennelly	257	.292	2		88	215	48	14	5.9	.863	E. Trumbull	10	84	1	9	0	4.71
	3B	B. Gladman	224	.156	1		62	90	39	5	3.6	.796							
Holly Hollingshead	RF	B. Morgan	162	.173	0		46	4	14	1	2.1	.781							
W-12 L-50	CF	H. Mullin	120	.142	0		47	6	8	0	1.8	.869							
	LF	T. Farley	52	.212	0		24	2	4	1	2.1	.867							
Bickerson	C	J. Humphries	193	.176	0		198	52	31	6	8.0	.890							
W-0 L-1	P	B. Barr	135	.148	2		13	57	24	1	2.9	.745							
	UT	E. Yewell	93	.247	0		40	55	17	7		.848							
	OP	E. Trumbull	86	.116	0		24	24	14	1		.774							
	20	F. Olin	83	.386	0		45	27	20	3		.783							
	C	J. Hanna	76	.066	0		94	31	18	1	7.9	.874							
	P	J. Hamill	71	.099	0		14	31	17	0	3.3	.726							

BATTING AND BASE RUNNING LEADERS

Batting Average
H. Stovey, PHI .404
D. Orr, NY .354
L. Reilly, CIN .339
P. Browning, LOU .330
F. Lewis, STL .323

Slugging Average
H. Stovey, PHI .648
L. Reilly, CIN .551
D. Orr, NY .539
F. Fennelly, CIN, WAS .480
C. Jones, CIN .470

Home Runs
H. Stovey, PHI 11
L. Reilly, CIN 11
D. Orr, NY 9
F. Mann, COL 7
C. Jones, CIN 7

Total Bases
H. Stovey, PHI 287
L. Reilly, CIN 247
D. Orr, NY 247
C. Jones, CIN 222
P. Browning, LOU 212

Runs Batted In
(not available)

Stolen Bases
(not available)

Hits
H. Stovey, PHI 179
D. Orr, NY 162
L. Reilly, CIN 152
C. Jones, CIN 148

Base on Balls
C. Nelson, NY 74
B. Geer, BKN 38
C. Jones, CIN 37
J. Macullar, BAL 35

Home Run Percentage
H. Stovey, PHI 2.5
L. Reilly, CIN 2.5
F. Carroll, COL 2.4
D. Orr, NY 2.0

Runs Scored
H. Stovey, PHI 126
C. Jones, CIN 117
A. Latham, STL 115
C. Nelson, NY 114

Doubles
S. Barkley, TOL 39
P. Browning, LOU 34
D. Orr, NY 32
Esterbrook, NY 29

Triples
H. Stovey, PHI 25
L. Reilly, CIN 19
F. Mann, COL 18
J. Peltz, IND 17

PITCHING LEADERS

Winning Percentage
J. Lynch, NY .725
E. Morris, COL .723
G. Hecker, LOU .722
D. Foutz, STL .714
T. Keefe, NY .685

Earned Run Average
G. Hecker, LOU 1.80
D. Foutz, STL 2.18
E. Morris, COL 2.18
T. Keefe, NY 2.29
F. Mountain, COL 2.45

Wins
G. Hecker, LOU 52
J. Lynch, NY 37
T. Keefe, NY 37
T. Mullane, TOL 35
E. Morris, COL 34
W. White, CIN 34

Saves
O. Burns, BAL 1
F. Mountain, COL 1
H. O'Day, TOL 1

Strikeouts
G. Hecker, LOU 385
H. Henderson, BAL 346
T. Mullane, TOL 334
T. Keefe, NY 323
L. McKeon, IND 308

Complete Games
G. Hecker, LOU 72
T. Mullane, TOL 65
L. McKeon, IND 59
T. Keefe, NY 57
A. Terry, BKN 55

Fewest Hits/9 Innings
E. Morris, COL 7.02
G. Hecker, LOU 7.06
T. Keefe, NY 7.10
F. Mountain, COL 7.21

Shutouts
T. Mullane, TOL 8
W. White, CIN 7
G. Hecker, LOU 6
J. McGinnis, STL 5

Fewest Walks/9 Innings
D. Driscoll, LOU 0.62
G. Hecker, LOU 0.75
J. Lynch, NY 0.78
E. Dugan, RIC 0.81

Most Strikeouts/9 Inn.
H. Henderson, BAL 7.09
D. Davis, STL 6.49
E. Morris, COL 6.33
B. Mathews, PHI 5.98

Innings
G. Hecker, LOU 671
T. Mullane, TOL 576
L. McKeon, IND 512
T. Keefe, NY 492

Games Pitched
G. Hecker, LOU 76
T. Mullane, TOL 68
L. McKeon, IND 61
T. Keefe, NY 58

	W	L	PCT	GB	R	OR	2B	3B	HR	BA	SA	SB	E	DP	FA	CG	BB	SO	ShO	SV	ERA
New York	75	32	.701		734	423	155	64	21	.262	.348	0	450	42	.905	111	119	611	9	0	2.46
Columbus	69	39	.639	6.5	585	459	107	96	40	.240	.351	0	433	74	.908	102	172	526	8	1	2.68
Louisville	68	40	.630	7.5	573	425	152	68	18	.254	.340	0	426	84	**.912**	101	97	470	6	0	**2.17**
St. Louis	67	40	.626	8	658	539	151	60	11	.249	.326	0	490	65	.900	99	172	477	8	0	2.67
Cincinnati	68	41	.624	8	754	512	109	98	34	.254	.353	0	430	82	.909	111	181	308	11	0	3.33
Baltimore	63	43	.594	11.5	636	515	133	84	30	.233	.335	0	459	61	.900	105	219	635	8	1	2.71
Philadelphia	61	46	.570	14	700	546	167	100	26	.267	.379	0	457	63	.901	105	127	530	5	0	3.40
Toledo	46	58	.442	27.5	463	571	153	48	8	.231	.305	0	469	67	.900	103	169	501	9	1	3.07
Brooklyn	40	64	.385	33.5	476	644	112	47	16	.225	.292	0	520	68	.889	105	163	378	6	0	3.79
Richmond	12	30	.286	30.5	194	294	40	33	7	.221	.308	0	239	27	.874	45	52	167	1	0	4.54
Pittsburgh	30	78	.278	45.5	406	725	105	50	2	.211	.268	0	524	71	.889	108	216	338	4	0	4.35
Indianapolis	29	78	.271	46	462	755	129	62	20	.234	.316	0	514	45	.889	107	199	479	2	0	4.21
Washington	12	51	.190	41	248	481	61	24	5	.200	.258	0	400	40	.858	62	110	235	3	0	4.00
					6889	6889	1574	834	238	.240	.325	0	5811	789	.897	1264	1996	5655	80	3	3.24

UNION ASSOCIATION 1884

Team	POS	Player	AB	BA	HR	RBI	PO	A	E	DP	TC/G	FA	Pitcher	G	IP	W	L	SV	ERA
St. Louis W-94 L-19 Ted Sullivan W-28 L-3 Fred Dunlap W-66 L-16	1B	J. Quinn	429	.270	0		1033	33	62	55	11.3	.945	C. Sweeney	33	271	24	7	0	1.83
	2B	F. Dunlap	449	.412	13		341	300	51	54	6.9	.926	B. Taylor	33	263	25	4	4	1.68
	SS	M. Whitehead	393	.211	1		85	269	87	19*	4.7	.803	H. Boyle	19	150	15	3	1	1.74
	3B	J. Gleason	395	.324	3		95	170	80	11	3.8	.768	P. Werden	16	141	12	1	0	1.97
	RF	O. Shaffer	467	.360	2		110	24	20	3	1.5	.870	C. Hodnett	14	121	12	2	0	2.01
	CF	D. Rowe	485	.293	3		146	15	9	5	1.8	.947							
	LF	B. Dickerson	211	.365	0		65	12	9	2	2.0	.895							
	C	G. Baker	317	.164	0		435	113	63	11	9.0	.897							
	UT	H. Boyle	262	.260	4		85	49	19	7		.876							
	UT	J. Brennan	231	.216	0		172	92	40	4		.868							
	P	B. Taylor	186	.366	3		17	51	10	2	2.4	.872							
	P	C. Sweeney	171	.316	1		23	76	6	4	3.2	.943							
Milwaukee W-8 L-4 Tom Loftus	1B	T. Griffin	41	.220	0		100	1	9	0	10.0	.918	H. Porter	6	51	3	3	0	3.00
	2B	A. Myers	46	.326	0		26	30	10	1	5.5	.848	E. Cushman	4	36	4	0	0	1.00
	SS	T. Sexton	47	.234	0		8	21	5	1	2.8	.853							
	3B	T. Morrissey	47	.170	0		7	15	9	1	2.6	.710							
	RF	E. Hogan	37	.081	0		16	9	6	1	2.8	.806							
	CF	L. Baldwin	27	.222	0		6	1	2	1	1.8	.778							
	LF	S. Behel	33	.242	0		4	1	0	0	.6	1.000							
	C	C. Broughton	39	.308	0		65	9	5	0	11.3	.937							
	PO	H. Porter	40	.275	0		2	10	0	0		1.000							
Cincinnati W-69 L-36 Dan O'Leary W-20 L-15 Sam Crane W-49 L-21	1B	M. Powell	185	.319	1		463	11	30	19	11.7	.940	G. Bradley	41	342	25	15	0	2.71
	2B	S. Crane	309	.233	1		224	217	73	27	6.4	.858	D. Burns	40	330	23	15	0	2.46
	SS	J. Jones	272	.261	2		54	140	32	9	5.5	.858	McCormick	26	210	21	3	0	1.54
	3B	C. Barber	204	.201	0		68	112	35	4	3.9	.837							
	RF	B. Hawes	349	.278	4		74	7	17	0	1.7	.827							
	CF	B. Harbidge	341	.279	2		101	24	13	2	1.7	.906							
	LF	L. Sylvester	333	.267	2		110	23	35	2	2.1	.792							
	C	K. Kelly	142	.282	1		210	60	42	3	8.4	.865							
	OP	D. Burns	350	.306	4		87	81	26	1		.866							
	UT	G. Bradley	226	.190	0		82	94	24	4		.880							
	SS	J. Glasscock	172	.419	3		45	107	19	4	4.8	.889							
	OF	D. O'Leary	132	.258	1		48	8	9	0	2.0	.862							
	1B	M. McQuery	132	.280	2		340	8	8	9	10.2	.978							
	3B	E. Cleveland	115	.322	1		48	54	19	0	4.2	.843							
Baltimore W-58 L-47 Bill Henderson	1B	C. Levis	373	.228	6		923	24	45	33	11.4*	.955	B. Sweeney	62	538	40	21	0	2.59
	2B	D. Phelan	402	.246	3		272	251	77	33	6.0	.872	T. Lee	15	122	5	8	0	3.39
	SS	L. Say	339	.239	2		103*	234*	87*	16*	5.4*	.795							
	3B	Y. Robinson	415	.267	2		98	163	53	10	4.4	.831							
	RF	B. Graham	167	.269	0		60	10	16	2	2.2	.814							
	CF	N. Cuthbert	168	.202	0		41	10	17	0	1.5	.750							
	LF	E. Seery	463	.311	2		157*	26*	38	3	2.1	.828							
	C	Fusselbach	303	.284	1		378	137	50	5	10.5	.912							
	P	B. Sweeney	296	.240	0		25	133	34	3	3.1	.823							
	CO	R. Sweeney	186	.226	0		218	60	35	1		.888							
	OF	H. Oberbeck	125	.184	0		33	10	6	1	1.8	.878							
Boston W-58 L-51 Tim Murnane	1B	T. Murnane	311	.235	0		588	7	31	8	9.9	.950	W. Burke	38	322	19	15	0	2.85
	2B	T. O'Brien	449	.263	4		257	267	90	23	6.2	.853	D. Shaw	39	316	21	15	0	1.77
	SS	W. Hackett	415	.243	1		126	294	71	12	4.8	.855	T. Bond	23	189	13	9	0	3.00
	3B	J. Irwin	432	.234	1		117	191	87	7	3.8	.780							
	RF	C. Crane	428	.285	12		74	21	20	3	2.0	.826							
	CF	M. Slattery	413	.208	0		140	26	41	3	2.2	.802							
	LF	F. Butler	255	.169	0		56	8	15	1	1.5	.810							
	C	L. Brown	325	.231	1		414	117	50	6	10.8	.914							
	OF	T. McCarthy	209	.215	0		39	11	13	1	1.3	.794							
	P	W. Burke	184	.223	0		13	45	11	2	1.8	.841							
	PO	T. Bond	162	.296	0		22	57	12	2		.868							
	P	D. Shaw	153	.242	0		18	59	17	1	2.4	.819							
Chicago W-34 L-39 Ed Hengle	1B	J. Schoeneck	289	.325	2		714	17	39	20	10.7	.949	O. Daily	46	397	22	23	0	2.43
	2B	M. Hengle	74	.203	0		40	39	15	2	4.9	.840							
	SS	S. Matthias	142	.275	0		30	101	25	5	4.3	.840							
	3B	W. Foley	71	.282	0		18	23	10	2	2.7	.804							
	RF	J. Ellick	314	.255	0		43	13	6	1	1.1	.903							
	CF	C. Briggs	182	.170	1		42	6	11	1	1.6	.814							
	LF	Householder	244	.234	1		24	0	3	0	1.2	.889							
	C	B. Krieg	240	.229	0		378	96	35	3	11.8	.931							
	P	O. Daily	160	.244	0		9	89	19	2	2.5	.838							
	UT	T. Suck	153	.144	0		146	68	35	2		.859							

UNION ASSOCIATION 1884, *cont.*

	POS	Player	AB	BA	HR	RBI	PO	A	E	DP	TC/G	FA	Pitcher	G	IP	W	L	SV	ERA
Washington	1B	P. Baker	371	.288	1		309	12	15	13	8.6	.955	B. Wise	50	364	23	18	0	3.04
	2B	T. Evers	427	.232	0		326	296	**94**	28	6.6	.869	A. Voss	27	186	5	14	0	3.57
W-47 L-65	SS	J. Halpin	168	.185	0		37	94	31	4	4.2	.809	C. Gagus	23	177	10	9	0	2.54
	3B	McCormick	157	.217	0		42*	42	22	5*	2.8	.792	A. Powell	18	134	6	12	0	3.43
Mike Scanlon	RF	B. Wise	339	.233	2		47	21	19	5	2.0	.782	M. Lockwood	11	68	1	9	0	7.32
	CF	A. Powell	191	.283	0		39	3	6	0	1.6	.875							
	LF	H. Moore	461	.336	1		134	16	33	4	1.7	.820							
	C	C. Fulmer	181	.276	0		213	41	17	4	8.0	.937							
	UT	A. Voss	245	.192	0		166	96	32	9		.891							
	CO	J. Gunson	166	.139	0		237	59	33	0		.900							
	PO	C. Gagus	154	.247	0		45	47	19	1		.829							
	SS	J. Deasley	134	.216	0		26	86	22	7	4.3	.836							
	1B	P. Joy	130	.215	0		331	7	12	14	9.7	.966							
	OF	F. Tenney	119	.235	0		34	5	6	2	1.7	.867							
	UT	E. McKenna	117	.188	0		124	46	35	5		.829							
Pittsburgh	1B	J. Schoeneck	77	.286	0		202	7	4	7	11.8	.981	K. Baldwin	38	322	19	15	0	2.85
	2B	G. Strief	53	.208	0		34	33	7	1	4.9	.905							
W-7 L-11	SS	J. Ellick	80	.163	0		13	43	5	3	3.4	.918							
	3B	J. Battin	69	.188	0		31	48	8	3	4.8	.908							
Joe Battin	RF	G. Gardner	64	.266	0		19	1	4	0	1.6	.833							
W-1 L-5	CF	H. Wheeler	73	.233	0		16	0	5	0	1.2	.762							
	LF	Householder	66	.258	0		17	3	6	2	1.5	.769							
Joe Ellick	C	T. Suck	35	.171	0		71	17	11	2	9.9	.889							
W-6 L-6																			
Philadelphia	1B	McGuinness	220	.236	0		550	12	24	19	12.2	.959	J. Bakely	39	345	14	25*	0	4.47
	2B	E. Peak	215	.195	0		145	137	60	14	7.3	.825	S. Weaver	17	136	5	12	0	5.76
	SS	H. Easterday	115	.243	0		35	98	19	6	5.4	.875							
W-21 L-46	3B	McCormick	295	.285	0		90*	116	48	8*	4.7	.811							
	RF	J. Flynn	209	.249	4		41	8	14	3	1.5	.778							
Fergy Malone	CF	B. Keinzil	299	.254	0		87	18	31	2	2.0	.772							
	LF	B. Hoover	275	.364	0		51	13	18	2	2.2	.780							
	C	T. Gillen	116	.155	0		152	61	25	1	8.8	.895							
	OC	J. Clements	177	.282	3		142	46	31	2		.858							
	P	J. Bakely	167	.132	0		14	69	23	3*	2.7	.783							
St. Paul	1B	S. Dunn	32	.250	0		64	5	2	2	7.9	.972	J. Brown	6	36	1	4	0	3.75
	2B	M. Hengle	33	.152	0		25	23	4	3	5.8	.923	L. Galvin	3	25	0	2	0	2.88
	SS	J. Werrick	27	.074	0		8	26	11	0	5.0	.756	B. O'Brien	2	10	1	0	0	1.80
W-2 L-6	3B	B. O'Brien	30	.233	0		7	14	4	0	3.1	.840							
	RF	S. Carroll	31	.097	0		9	5	3	1	2.1	.824							
Andrew Thompson	CF	B. Barnes	30	.200	0		8	0	3	1	1.4	.727							
	LF	J. Tilley	26	.154	0		14	1	1	0	1.8	.938							
	C	C. Ganzel	23	.217	0		36	7	2	0	7.5	.956							
	P	J. Brown	16	.313	0		0	12	5	0	2.8	.706							
	C	P. Dealey	15	.133	0		18	9	4	1	7.8	.871							
	P	L. Galvin	9	.222	0		1	1	1	0	1.0	.667							
Altoona	1B	F. Harris	95	.263	0		169	8	11	1	11.1	.941	J. Murphy	14	112	5	6	0	3.87
	2B	C. Dougherty	85	.259	0		47	41	15	2	6.4	.854	J. Brown	11	74	1	9	0	5.35
W-6 L-19	SS	G. Smith	108	.315	0		40	88	19	1	5.9	.871							
	3B	J. Koons	78	.231	0		39	45	13	1	4.6	.866							
Ed Curtis	RF	J. Brown	88	.250	1		14	2	10	0	1.9	.615							
	CF	J. Murphy	94	.149	0		11	4	4	2	1.9	.789							
	LF	F. Shaffer	74	.284	0		22	2	3	0	1.6	.889							
	C	J. Moore	80	.313	1		54	18	18	0	7.5	.800							
	C	P. Carroll	49	.265	0		40	6	4	0	6.3	.920							
	1B	J. Grady	36	.306	0		87	3	9	1	12.4	.909							
	OP	J. Leary	33	.091	0		10	7	7	0		.708							
Kansas City	1B	J. Sweeney	129	.264	0		304	14	14	15	10.7	.958	E. Hickman	17	137	4	13	0	4.52
	2B	C. Berry	118	.246	1		63	55	15	6	6.0	.887	B. Black	16	123	4	9	0	3.22
	SS	C. Cross	93	.215	0		15	92	21	3	5.3	.836	P. Veach	12	104	3	9	0	2.42
W-16 L-63	3B	P. Sullivan	114	.193	0		31	35	20	5	4.1	.767							
	RF	F. Shaffer	164	.171	0		51	12	19	0	2.0	.768							
Harry Wheeler	CF	F. Wyman	124	.218	0		41	11	18	3	2.8	.743							
W-0 L-4	LF	McLaughlin	162	.228	0		21	11	10	4	1.8	.762							
	C	K. Baldwin	191	.194	1		199	86	37	4	7.3	.885							
Matt Porter	UT	B. Black	146	.247	1		58	50	20	4		.844							
W-3 L-13	1B	J. Gorman	137	.277	0		264	4	13	7	11.7	.954							
	UT	McLaughlin	123	.228	1		55	50	30	4		.778							
Ted Sullivan																			
W-13 L-46																			

UNION ASSOCIATION 1884, *cont.*

	POS	Player	AB	BA	HR	RBI	PO	A	E	DP	TC/G	FA	Pitcher	G	IP	W	L	SV	ERA
Wilmington	1B	R. Snyder	52	.192	0		155	5	4	8	10.3	.976	J. Murphy	7	48	0	6	0	*3.00*
	2B	C. Bastian	60	.200	2		37	61	10	3	6.8	.907	T. Nolan	5	40	1	4	0	2.93
W-2 L-16	SS	H. Myers	24	.125	0		6	15	3	0	4.8	.875							
	3B	J. Say	59	.220	0		12	21	12	2	2.8	.733							
	RF	J. Munce	21	.190	0		4	2	3	0	1.3	.667							
Joe Simmons	CF	Fisher	29	.069	0		9	0	2	0	1.8	.818							
	LF	T. Lynch	58	.276	0		9	2	1	0	1.5	.917							
	C	T. Cusick	34	.147	0		42	19	9	2	11.7	.871							
	PO	T. Nolan	33	.273	0		5	11	1	0		.941							
	UT	J. Murphy	31	.065	0		4	11	9	2		.625							
	OS	J. Cullen	31	.194	0		9	8	9	0		.654							
	OC	McCloskey	30	.100	0		38	7	13	1		.776							
	OF	I. Benners	22	.045	0		8	1	3	1	2.0	.750							

BATTING AND BASE RUNNING LEADERS

Batting Average
F. Dunlap, STL .412
O. Shaffer, STL .360
H. Moore, WAS .336
J. Gleason, STL .324
E. Seery, BAL, KC .313

Slugging Average
F. Dunlap, STL .621
O. Shaffer, STL .501
D. Burns, CIN .457
C. Crane, BOS .451
J. Gleason, STL .433

Home Runs
F. Dunlap, STL 13
C. Crane, BOS 12
C. Levis, BAL, WAS 6

Total Bases
F. Dunlap, STL 279
O. Shaffer, STL 234
D. Rowe, STL 205
C. Crane, BOS 193
E. Seery, BAL, KC 192

Runs Batted In
(not available)

Stolen Bases
(not available)

Hits
F. Dunlap, STL 185
O. Shaffer, STL 168
H. Moore, WAS 155
E. Seery, BAL, KC 146

Base on Balls
Y. Robinson, BAL 37
O. Shaffer, STL 30
F. Dunlap, STL 29
B. Harbidge, CIN 25

Home Run Percentage
F. Dunlap, STL 2.9
C. Crane, BOS 2.8
C. Levis, BAL, WAS 1.6
B. Hawes, CIN 1.1

Runs Scored
F. Dunlap, STL 160
O. Shaffer, STL 130
E. Seery, BAL, KC 115
Y. Robinson, BAL 101

Doubles
O. Shaffer, STL 40
F. Dunlap, STL 39
D. Rowe, STL 32
T. O'Brien, BOS 31

Triples
D. Burns, CIN 12
D. Rowe, STL 11
O. Shaffer, STL 10

PITCHING LEADERS

Winning Percentage
McCormick, CIN .875
B. Taylor, STL .862
C. Sweeney, STL .774
B. Sweeney, BAL .656
G. Bradley, CIN .625

Earned Run Average
McCormick, CIN 1.54
B. Taylor, STL 1.68
H. Boyle, STL 1.74
D. Shaw, BOS 1.77
C. Sweeney, STL 1.83

Wins
B. Sweeney, BAL 40
O. Daily, CHI, PIT, WAS 28
B. Taylor, STL 25
G. Bradley, CIN 25
C. Sweeney, STL 24

Saves
B. Taylor, STL 4
H. Boyle, STL 1
L. Brown, BOS 1
F. Dunlap, STL 1
L. Sylvester, CIN 1

Strikeouts
O. Daily, CHI, PIT, WAS 483
B. Sweeney, BAL 374
D. Shaw, BOS 309
B. Wise, WAS 268
W. Burke, BOS 255

Complete Games
B. Sweeney, BAL 58
O. Daily, CHI, PIT, WAS 56
J. Bakely, KC, PHI, WIL 43
G. Bradley, CIN 36
D. Shaw, BOS 35

Fewest Hits/9 Innings
McCormick, CIN 6.47
D. Shaw, BOS 6.47
C. Sweeney, STL 6.87
H. Boyle, STL 7.08

Shutouts
McCormick, CIN 7
D. Shaw, BOS 5
B. Wise, WAS 4
O. Daily, CHI, PIT, WAS 4

Fewest Walks/9 Innings
C. Sweeney, STL 0.43
McCormick, CIN 0.60
H. Boyle, STL 0.60
G. Bradley, CIN 0.61

Most Strikeouts/9 Inn.
D. Shaw, BOS 8.81
O. Daily, CHI, PIT, WAS 8.68
C. Gagus, WAS 7.92
W. Burke, BOS 7.13

Innings
B. Sweeney, BAL 538
O. Daily, CHI, PIT, WAS 501
J. Bakely, KC, PHI, WIL 395
B. Wise, WAS 364

Games Pitched
B. Sweeney, BAL 62
O. Daily, CHI, PIT, WAS 58
B. Wise, WAS 50
J. Bakely, KC, PHI, WIL 46

	W	L	PCT	GB	R	OR	2B	3B	HR	BA	SA	SB	E	DP	FA	CG	BB	SO	ShO	SV	ERA
St. Louis	94	19	.832		**887**	429	**259**	41	30	**.292**	**.393**	0	554	**79**	.888	**104**	110	550	8	**6**	*1.95*
Milwaukee	8	4	.667	35.5	53	**34**	25			.223	.286	0	53	4	.892	12	**13**	139	3	0	2.25
Cincinnati	69	36	.657	21	703	466	118	**62**	27	.271	.357	0	532	45	.882	95	90	503	**11**	0	2.39
Baltimore	58	47	.552	32	662	627	150	26	17	.245	.310	0	616	53	.872	92	177	628	4	0	3.01
Boston	58	51	.532	34	636	558	168	32	19	.236	.309	0	633	39	.868	100	110	**753**	5	1	2.70
Chicago	34	39	.466	40	360	411	99	19	10	.234	.300	0	393	29	.875	68	111	560	4	0	2.74
Washington	47	65	.420	46.5	572	679	120	26	4	.237	.284	0	625	55	.869	94	168	684	5	0	3.43
Pittsburgh	7	11	.389	39.5	78	71	28	7		.218	.282	0	66	9	**.912**	18	26	119	1	0	2.64
Philadelphia	21	46	.313	50	414	545	108	35	7	.245	.324	0	501	36	.841	64	105	310	1	0	4.63
St. Paul	2	6	.250	39.5	24	57	13	1		.180	.235	0	**47**	6	.872	7	27	44	1	0	3.17
Altoona	6	19	.240	44	90	216	30	6	2	.248	.301	0	156	4	.862	20	52	93		0	4.67
Kansas City	16	63	.203	61	311	618	102	15	8	.199	.254	0	520	41	.861	70	127	334		0	4.05
Wilmington	2	16	.111	44.5	35	114	8	8	2	.175	.232	0	104	10	.860	15	18	113		0	3.04
					4825	4825	1228	278	126	.245	.316	0	4800	420	.872	759	1134	4830	43	8	3.04

NATIONAL LEAGUE 1885

	POS	Player	AB	BA	HR	RBI	PO	A	E	DP	TC/G	FA	Pitcher	G	IP	W	L	SV	ERA
Chicago	1B	C. Anson	464	.310	7	114	**1253**	39	57	62	**12.0**	.958	J. Clarkson	70	623	53	16	0	*1.85*
	2B	F. Pfeffer	469	.241	6	71	**325**	**391**	86	66	7.4	.893	McCormick	24	215	20	4	0	2.43
W-87 L-25	SS	T. Burns	445	.272	7	70	151	370	**96**	35	5.6	.844							
	3B	Williamson	407	.238	3	64	113	**258**	45	18	3.7	**.892**							
	RF	K. Kelly	438	.288	9	74	95	**29**	19	2	2.1	.867							
Cap Anson	CF	G. Gore	441	.313	5	51	204	17	29	2	2.3	.884							
	LF	A. Dalrymple	**492**	.274	11	58	180	16	27	2	2.0	.879							
	C	S. Flint	249	.209	1	19	**356**	100	36	2	7.2	**.927**							
	P	J. Clarkson	283	.216	4	31	26	**174**	20	8	3.1	.909							
	OF	B. Sunday	172	.256	2	20	46	6	11	2	1.4	.825							

NATIONAL LEAGUE 1885, *cont.*

	POS	Player	AB	BA	HR	RBI	PO	A	E	DP	TC/G	FA	Pitcher	G	IP	W	L	SV	ERA
New York W-85 L-27 Jim Mutrie	1B	R. Connor	455	.371	1		1178	42	31	66	11.4	.975	M. Welch	56	492	44	11	1	1.66
	2B	J. Gerhardt	399	.155	0		314	352	65	59	6.5	.911	T. Keefe	46	398	32	13	0	1.58
	SS	M. Ward	446	.226	0		167	350	55	36	5.2	.904							
	3B	Esterbrook	359	.256	0		111	159	35	14	3.6	.885							
	RF	M. Dorgan	347	.326	0		142	11	16	4	1.9	.905							
	CF	J. O'Rourke	477	.300	5		162	10	11	0	1.6	.940							
	LF	P. Gillespie	420	.293	0		133	12	9	2	1.5	.942							
	C	B. Ewing	342	.304	6		337	102	39	8	7.6	.918							
	C	P. Deasley	207	.256	0		281	80	25	4	7.1	.935							
	P	M. Welch	199	.206	2		16	70	14	0	1.8	.860							
	UT	Richardson	198	.263	0		52	58	5	1		.957							
	P	T. Keefe	166	.163	0		30	80	13	0	2.7	.894							
Philadelphia W-56 L-54 Harry Wright	1B	S. Farrar	420	.245	3	1	1153	41	31	50	11.0	.975	E. Daily	50	440	26	23	0	2.21
	2B	A. Myers	357	.204	1		201	287	64	31	5.9	.884	C. Ferguson	48	405	26	20	0	2.22
	SS	C. Bastian	389	.167	4		164	337	62	34	5.5	.890							
	3B	J. Mulvey	443	.269	6		144	201	62	12	3.8	.848							
	RF	J. Manning	445	.256	3		134	21	18	3	1.6	.896							
	CF	J. Fogarty	427	.232	0		227	26	16	5	3.1	.941							
	LF	E. Andrews	421	.266	0		175	11	16	1	2.0	.921							
	C	J. Clements	188	.191	1		181	47	28	2	6.2	.891							
	P	C. Ferguson	235	.306	1		27	87	9	3	2.6	.927							
	P	E. Daily	184	.207	1		11	87	12	2	2.2	.891							
	C	T. Cusick	141	.177	0		180	60	57	2	7.8	.808							
	C	C. Ganzel	125	.168	0		175	39	27	3	7.3	.888							
Providence W-53 L-57 Frank Bancroft	1B	J. Start	374	.275	0	41	1036	35	31	42	10.9	.972	O. Radbourn	49	446	28	21	0	2.20
	2B	J. Farrell	257	.206	1	19	158	194	39	16	5.8	.900	D. Shaw	49	400	23	26	0	2.57
	SS	A. Irwin	218	.179	0	14	70	209	40	17	5.5	.875							
	3B	J. Denny	318	.223	3	25	128	157	43	10	4.0	.869							
	RF	P. Radford	371	.243	0	32	141	26	29	7	2.2	.852							
	CF	P. Hines	411	.270	1	35	199	18	34	3	2.7	.865							
	LF	C. Carroll	426	.232	1	40	207	10	28	2	2.4	.886							
	C	B. Gilligan	252	.214	0	12	305	84	57	13	6.9	.872							
	UT	C. Bassett	285	.144	0	16	141	248	39	24		.909							
	P	O. Radbourn	249	.233	0	22	18	115	9	7	2.9	.937							
	C	C. Daily	223	.260	0	19	220	70	41	8	6.9	.876							
	P	D. Shaw	165	.133	0	9	11	76	8	2	1.9	.916							
Boston W-46 L-66 John Morrill	1B	J. Morrill	394	.226	4	44	952	32	31	53	11.0	.969	J. Whitney	51	441	18	32	0	2.98
	2B	J. Burdock	169	.142	0	7	99	134	21	16	5.6	.917	C. Buffinton	51	434	22	27	0	2.88
	SS	S. Wise	424	.283	4	66	135	270	67	29	6.0	.858	D. Davis	11	94	5	6	0	4.29
	3B	E. Sutton	457	.313	4	47	132	168	43	18	3.8	.875							
	RF	T. Poorman	227	.238	3	25	82	9	14	1	1.9	.867							
	CF	J. Manning	306	.206	2	27	164	21	21	3	2.5	.898							
	LF	T. McCarthy	148	.182	0	11	69	8	12	0	2.2	.865							
	C	T. Gunning	174	.184	0	15	252	68	45	4	7.6	.877							
	UT	C. Buffinton	338	.240	1	33	196	121	27	11		.922							
	PO	J. Whitney	290	.234	0	36	49	130	20	1		.899							
	OF	G. Whiteley	135	.185	1	7	42	8	14	2	2.0	.781							
	C	P. Dealey	130	.223	1	9	162	42	22	8	7.8	.903							
	2S	W. Hackett	125	.184	0	9	59	86	22	9		.868							
	C	M. Hackett	115	.183	0	4	194	53	27	6	8.1	.901							
	OF	D. Johnston	111	.234	1	23	40	8	9	2	2.2	.842							
Buffalo W-38 L-74 Pud Galvin W-7 L-17 Jack Chapman W-31 L-57	1B	D. Brouthers	407	.359	7	60	996	25	26	54	10.7	.975	P. Galvin	33	284	13	19	1	4.09
	2B	Richardson	426	.319	6	44	163	169	35	17	7.3	.905	B. Serad	30	241	7	21	0	4.10
	SS	J. Rowe	421	.290	2	51	71	186	51	26	4.7	.834	P. Conway	27	210	10	17	0	4.67
	3B	D. White	404	.292	0	57	118	198	40	12	3.6	.888	P. Wood	24	199	8	15	0	4.44
	RF	J. Lillie	430	.249	2	30	183	23	33	4	2.1	.862							
	CF	Richardson	426	.319	6	44	120	6	14	2	2.9	.900							
	LF	B. Crowley	344	.241	1	36	152	8	23	1	2.0	.874							
	C	G. Myers	326	.206	0	19	305	95	45	4	6.4	.899							
	2S	D. Force	253	.225	0	17	141	200	42	28		.890							
	P	P. Galvin	122	.189	1	10	17	83	13	3	3.4	.885							
Detroit W-41 L-67 Charlie Morton W-7 L-31 Bill Watkins W-34 L-36	1B	M. McQuery	278	.273	3	30	707	28	18	32	10.9	.976	S. Weidman	38	330	14	24	0	3.14
	2B	S. Crane	245	.192	2	20	179	197	38	21	6.1	.908	C. Getzien	37	330	12	25	0	3.03
	SS	M. Phillips	139	.209	0	17	35	120	21	6	5.3	.881	L. Baldwin	21	179	11	9	1	1.86
	3B	J. Donnelly	211	.232	1	22	73	102	31	3	3.7	.850	D. Casey	12	104	4	8	0	3.29
	RF	S. Thompson	254	.303	7	44	84	24	14	0	2.0	.885							
	CF	N. Hanlon	424	.302	1	29	220	19	38	2	2.6	.863							
	LF	G. Wood	362	.290	5	28	112	11	16	1	2.0	.885							
	C	C. Bennett	349	.269	5	60	347	87	38	10	7.6	.919							
	2B	J. Quest	200	.195	0	21	107	122	26	10	6.5	.898							
	OF	J. Dorgan	161	.286	0	24	55	5	10	2	1.8	.857							
	OP	S. Weidman	153	.157	1	14	5	2	7	1		.500							
	1B	M. Scott	148	.264	0	12	394	18	14	17	11.2	.967							
	P	C. Getzien	137	.212	0	16	17	66	8	0	2.5	.912							
	PO	L. Baldwin	124	.242	0	18	29	44	10	1		.880							
	C	D. McGuire	121	.190	0	9	249	52	26	2	10.5	.920							

AMERICAN ASSOCIATION 1885, *cont.*

	POS	Player	AB	BA	HR	RBI	PO	A	E	DP	TC/G	FA	Pitcher	G	IP	W	L	SV	ERA
Baltimore	1B	D. Stearns	253	.186	1		605	19	17	35	10.2	.973	H. Henderson	61	539	25	**35**	0	3.19
	2B	T. Manning	157	.204	0		118	132	22	19	6.6	.919	B. Emslie	13	107	3	10	0	4.28
W-41 L-68	SS	J. Macullar	320	.191	3		175	311	68	28	5.7	.877	O. Burns	15	106	7	4	3	3.58
	3B	M. Muldoon	410	.251	2		103	184	43	16	3.3	.870							
Billy Barnie	RF	E. Greer	211	.199	0		93	6	10	1	2.3	.908							
	CF	D. Casey	264	.288	3		100	10	24	0	2.1	.821							
	LF	J. Sommer	471	.251	1		230	14	21	2	2.5	.921							
	C	B. Traffley	254	.154	1		357	105	28	6	8.0	**.943**							
	UT	O. Burns	321	.231	5		121	83	27	12		.883							
	P	H. Henderson	229	.223	1		28	81	14	4	2.0	.886							
	2B	G. Gardner	170	.218	0		113	132	30	16	7.1	.891							
	1B	J. Field	144	.208	0		373	13*	15	15	10.6	.963							

BATTING AND BASE RUNNING LEADERS

Batting Average
P. Browning, LOU	.362
D. Orr, NY	.342
H. Stovey, PHI	.337
H. Larkin, PHI	.329
C. Jones, CIN	.322

Slugging Average
D. Orr, NY	.543
P. Browning, LOU	.530
H. Larkin, PHI	.525
H. Stovey, PHI	.519
C. Jones, CIN	.456

Home Runs
H. Stovey, PHI	13
F. Fennelly, CIN	10
P. Browning, LOU	9
H. Larkin, PHI	8
D. Orr, NY	6

Total Bases
P. Browning, LOU	255
H. Stovey, PHI	252
D. Orr, NY	241
H. Larkin, PHI	238
C. Jones, CIN	222

Runs Batted In
(not available)

Stolen Bases
(not available)

Hits
P. Browning, LOU	174
H. Stovey, PHI	164
C. Jones, CIN	157
D. Orr, NY	152

Base on Balls
C. Nelson, NY	61
J. Macullar, BAL	49
P. Hotaling, BKN	49
H. Stovey, PHI	39

Home Run Percentage
H. Stovey, PHI	2.7
F. Fennelly, CIN	2.2
P. Browning, LOU	1.9
H. Larkin, PHI	1.8

Runs Scored
H. Stovey, PHI	130
H. Larkin, PHI	114
C. Jones, CIN	108
C. Nelson, NY	98

Doubles
H. Larkin, PHI	37
P. Browning, LOU	34
D. Orr, NY	29
H. Stovey, PHI	27

Triples
D. Orr, NY	21
W. Kuehne, PIT	19
F. Fennelly, CIN	17
C. Wolf, LOU	17

PITCHING LEADERS

Winning Percentage
B. Caruthers, STL	.755
D. Foutz, STL	.702
B. Mathews, PHI	.638
E. Morris, PIT	.619
H. Porter, BKN	.611

Earned Run Average
B. Caruthers, STL	2.07
G. Hecker, LOU	2.18
E. Morris, PIT	2.35
B. Mathews, PHI	2.43
D. Foutz, STL	2.63

Wins
B. Caruthers, STL	40
E. Morris, PIT	39
D. Foutz, STL	33
H. Porter, BKN	33
B. Mathews, PHI	30
G. Hecker, LOU	30

Saves
O. Burns, BAL	3
P. Corkhill, CIN	1
P. Reccius, LOU	1
J. Sommer, BAL	1
A. Terry, BKN	1

Strikeouts
E. Morris, PIT	298
B. Mathews, PHI	286
H. Henderson, BAL	263
G. Hecker, LOU	209
H. Porter, BKN	197

Complete Games
E. Morris, PIT	63
H. Henderson, BAL	59
B. Caruthers, STL	53
H. Porter, BKN	53
G. Hecker, LOU	51

Fewest Hits/9 Innings
E. Morris, PIT	7.11
A. Mays, LOU	7.74
D. Foutz, STL	7.75
J. McGinnis, STL	7.88

Shutouts
B. Caruthers, STL	6
E. Morris, PIT	6
J. McGinnis, STL	3

Fewest Walks/9 Innings
J. Lynch, NY	1.00
G. Hecker, LOU	1.01
B. Caruthers, STL	1.06
B. Mathews, PHI	1.21

Most Strikeouts/9 Inn.
B. Mathews, PHI	6.09
E. Cushman, NY, PHI	5.50
E. Morris, PIT	4.62
H. Henderson, BAL	4.39

Innings
E. Morris, PIT	581
H. Henderson, BAL	539
B. Caruthers, STL	482
H. Porter, BKN	482

Games Pitched
E. Morris, PIT	63
H. Henderson, BAL	61
H. Porter, BKN	54
G. Hecker, LOU	54

	W	L	PCT	GB	R	OR	2B	3B	HR	BA	SA	SB	E	DP	FA	CG	BB	SO	ShO	SV	ERA
St. Louis	79	33	.705		677	**461**	132	57	14	.246	.319	0	**381**	64	**.920**	111	168	378	11	0	**2.43**
Cincinnati	63	49	.563	16	642	575	108	77	25	.258	.341	0	426	86	.910	102	250	330	7	1	3.27
Pittsburgh	56	55	.505	22.5	547	539	123	79	5	.240	.315	0	426	77	.912	104	201	454	7	0	2.92
Philadelphia	55	57	.491	24	**764**	691	169	77	29	**.265**	**.364**	0	483	79	.901	105	212	**506**	5	0	3.22
Brooklyn	53	59	.473	26	624	650	121	65	14	.245	.319	0	447	56	.908	110	211	436	3	1	3.45
Louisville	53	59	.473	26	564	598	126	**83**	19	.248	.336	0	466	75	.904	109	217	462	3	1	2.68
New York	44	64	.407	33	526	688	123	58	20	.247	.327	0	452	62	.901	103	204	408	2	0	4.15
Baltimore	41	68	.376	36.5	541	683	124	59	17	.219	.296	0	419	71	.909	104	222	395	2	4	3.89
					4885	4885	1026	555	143	.246	.328	0	3500	570	.908	848	1685	3369	40	7	3.24

NATIONAL LEAGUE 1886

	POS	Player	AB	BA	HR	RBI	PO	A	E	DP	TC/G	FA	Pitcher	G	IP	W	L	SV	ERA
Chicago	1B	C. Anson	504	.371	10	147	1188	**66**	**48**	69	10.4	.963	J. Clarkson	55	467	35	17	0	2.41
	2B	F. Pfeffer	474	.264	7	95	**343**	340	73	**66**	6.4	.903	McCormick	42	348	31	11	0	2.82
W-90 L-34	SS	Williamson	430	.216	6	58	161	355	78	36	4.9	.869	J. Flynn	32	257	24	6	1	2.24
	3B	T. Burns	445	.276	3	65	149	247	49	12	4.0	.890							
Cap Anson	RF	J. Ryan	327	.306	4	53	93	18	23	3	1.9	.828							
	CF	G. Gore	444	.304	6	63	184	20	29	4	2.0	.876							
	LF	A. Dalrymple	331	.233	3	26	126	15	7	1	1.8	**.953**							
	C	S. Flint	173	.202	1	13	300	93	**47**	2	8.1	.893							
	UT	K. Kelly	451	**.388**	4	79	387	141	59	11		.899							
	P	J. Clarkson	210	.233	3	23	19	**114**	19	3	2.8	.875							
	PO	J. Flynn	205	.200	4	19	34	59	9	2		.912							
	P	McCormick	174	.236	2	21	21	74	6	3	2.4	.941							

NATIONAL LEAGUE 1886, *cont.*

	POS	Player	AB	BA	HR	RBI	PO	A	E	DP	TC/G	FA	Pitcher	G	IP	W	L	SV	ERA
Detroit	1B	D. Brouthers	489	.370	11	72	1256	27	42	64	11.0	.968	L. Baldwin	56	487	**42**	13	0	*2.24*
	2B	F. Dunlap	196	.286	4	37	118	162*	25	22	6.0*	.918	C. Getzien	43	387	30	11	0	*3.03*
W-87 L-36	SS	J. Rowe	468	.303	6	87	86	310	54	26	4.1	.880	P. Conway	11	91	6	5	0	*3.36*
	3B	D. White	491	.289	1	76	131	245	68	18	3.6	.847							
Bill Watkins	RF	S. Thompson	503	.310	8	89	194	29	13	11	1.9	.945							
	CF	N. Hanlon	494	.235	4	60	205	18	17	4	1.9	.929							
	LF	Richardson	**538**	.351	11	61	131	21	17	1	2.1	.899							
	C	C. Bennett	235	.243	5	34	**425**	84	24	**13**	7.7	**.955**							
	C	C. Ganzel	213	.272	1	31	274	63	33	9	8.2	.911							
	P	L. Baldwin	204	.201	0	25	18	105	4	7	2.3	.969							
	2B	S. Crane	185	.141	1	12	104	111	23	19	6.3	.903							
	P	C. Getzien	165	.176	0	19	16	65	1	3	1.9	**.988**							
New York	1B	R. Connor	485	.355	7	71	1164	65	34	55	10.7	.973	T. Keefe	**64**	**540**	**42**	20	0	*2.53*
	2B	J. Gerhardt	426	.190	0	40	340	355	57	50	6.1	.924	M. Welch	59	500	33	22	0	*2.99*
W-75 L-44	SS	M. Ward	491	.273	2	81	91	369	69	36	4.3	.870							
	3B	Esterbrook	473	.264	3	43	148	219	43	9	3.3	**.895**							
Jim Mutrie	RF	M. Dorgan	442	.292	3	79	125	13	21	4	1.6	.888							
	CF	J. O'Rourke	440	.309	1	34	101	11	9	1	1.9	.926							
	LF	P. Gillespie	396	.273	0	58	121	6	14	0	1.5	.901							
	C	B. Ewing	275	.309	4	31	270	91	31	4	7.8	.921							
	OF	Richardson	237	.232	1	27	94	7	5	0	1.7	.953							
	P	M. Welch	213	.216	0	18	19	82	5	0	1.8	.953							
	P	T. Keefe	205	.171	1	20	29	107	15	3	2.4	.901							
	CO	P. Deasley	143	.266	0	17	167	42	21	4		.909							
Philadelphia	1B	S. Farrar	439	.248	5	50	1220	45	26	38	10.9	**.980**	C. Ferguson	48	396	30	9	2	*1.98*
	2B	C. Bastian	373	.217	2	38	157	286	26	19	5.4	**.945**	D. Casey	44	369	24	18	0	*2.41*
W-71 L-43	SS	A. Irwin	373	.233	0	34	137	322	56	21	5.2	.891	E. Daily	27	218	16	9	0	*3.06*
	3B	J. Mulvey	430	.267	2	53	99	191	40	2	3.1	.879							
Harry Wright	RF	J. Fogarty	280	.293	3	47	114	9	6	3	2.2	.953							
	CF	E. Andrews	437	.249	2	28	189	24	23	2	2.3	.903							
	LF	G. Wood	450	.273	4	50	148	13	17	2	1.8	.904							
	C	D. McGuire	167	.198	2	18	298	50	39	3	7.9	.899							
	OP	E. Daily	309	.227	4	50	98	70	27	3		.862							
	PO	C. Ferguson	261	.253	2	25	72	101	14	1		.925							
	C	J. Clements	185	.205	0	11	318	52	28	3	8.5	.930							
	P	D. Casey	151	.152	0	9	17	70	8	0	2.2	.916							
Boston	1B	S. Wise	387	.289	4	72	527	17	25	21	10.0	.956	O. Radbourn	58	509	27	31	0	*3.00*
	2B	J. Burdock	221	.217	0	25	145	165	33	22	5.8	.904	B. Stemmeyer	41	349	22	18	0	*3.02*
W-56 L-61	SS	J. Morrill	430	.247	7	69	92	156	29	13	5.0	.895	C. Buffinton	18	151	7	10	0	*4.59*
	3B	B. Nash	417	.281	1	45	137	177	50	9	4.0	.863							
John Morrill	RF	T. Poorman	371	.261	3	41	145	21	18	6	1.9	.902							
	CF	D. Johnston	413	.240	1	57	**243**	29	33	4	2.8	.892							
	LF	J. Hornung	424	.257	2	40	187	12	11	1	2.2	.948							
	C	C. Daily	180	.239	0	21	264	55	31	5	7.1	.911							
	UT	E. Sutton	499	.277	3	48	181	204	56	19		.873							
	P	O. Radbourn	253	.237	2	22	**39**	107	12	**8**	2.7	.924							
	1P	C. Buffinton	176	.290	1	30	181	35	11	8		.952							
	P	B. Stemmeyer	148	.277	0	20	6	61	17	0	2.0	.798							
St. Louis	1B	A. McKinnon	491	.301	8	72	1170	35	46	61	10.5	.963	E. Healy	42	354	17	23	0	*2.88*
	2B	F. Dunlap	285	.267	3	32	215	231*	33	42	6.7*	.931	J. Kirby	41	325	11	25	0	*3.30*
W-43 L-79	SS	J. Glasscock	486	.325	3	40	156	**392**	57	**43**	5.0	**.906**	H. Boyle	25	165	9	15	0	*2.24*
	3B	J. Denny	475	.257	9	62	**182**	**270**	53	**22**	4.3	.895	C. Sweeney	11	93	5	6	0	*4.16*
Gus Schmelz	RF	J. Cahill	463	.199	1	32	166	**34**	31	5	1.9	.866							
	CF	J. Quinn	271	.232	1	21	89	13	12	1	2.4	.895							
	LF	E. Seery	453	.238	2	48	176	20	26	2	1.8	.883							
	C	G. Myers	295	.190	0	27	368	80	35	8	6.7	.928							
	OF	J. McGeachy	226	.204	2	24	88	15	14	3	2.1	.880							
	P	E. Healy	145	.097	0	5	6	62	4	2	1.7	.944							
	C	F. Graves	138	.152	0	9	223	76	39	3	8.2	.885							
	P	J. Kirby	136	.110	0	5	14	61	9	2	2.0	.893							
Kansas City	1B	M. McQuery	449	.247	4	38	**1295**	50	43	61	**11.4**	.969	S. Weidman	51	428	12	**36**	0	*4.52*
	2B	A. Myers	473	.277	4	51	298	384	65	50	6.3	.913	J. Whitney	46	393	12	32	0	*4.49*
W-30 L-91	SS	C. Bassett	342	.260	2	32	120	277	51	25	**5.5**	.886	P. Conway	23	180	5	15	0	*5.75*
	3B	J. Donnelly	438	.201	2	38	153	245	**73**	13	4.2	.845							
Dave Rowe	RF	P. Radford	493	.229	0	20	125	29	19	5	1.9	.890							
	CF	D. Rowe	429	.240	3	57	154	11	29	2	2.2	.851							
	LF	J. Lillie	416	.175	0	22	199	30	30	3	2.3	.884							
	C	F. Briody	215	.237	0	29	258	95	31	4	7.1	.919							
	PO	J. Whitney	247	.239	2	23	38	116	15	6		.911							
	C	M. Hackett	230	.217	3	25	252	63	25	6	6.5	.926							
	OP	P. Conway	194	.242	1	18	56	39	18	3		.841							
	P	S. Weidman	179	.168	0	7	25	106	9	5	2.7	.936							

NATIONAL LEAGUE 1886, cont.

	POS	Player	AB	BA	HR	RBI	PO	A	E	DP	TC/G	FA	Pitcher	G	IP	W	L	SV	ERA
Washington	1B	P. Baker	325	.222	1	34	567	13	20	29	10.7	.967	D. Shaw	45	386	13	31	0	3.34
	2B	J. Knowles	443	.212	3	35	196	224	47	32	7.5	.899	B. Barr	22	191	3	18	0	4.30
W-28 L-92	SS	D. Force	242	.182	0	16	58	211	27	21	5.3	.909	T. Madigan	14	116	1	13	0	5.06
	3B	B. Gladman	152	.138	1	15	53	74	26	8	3.5	.830							
Mike Scanlon	RF	C. Crane	292	.171	0	20	107	16	19	4	2.1	.866							
W-13 L-67	CF	P. Hines	487	.312	9	56	167	19	21	1	2.3	.899							
	LF	C. Carroll	433	.229	2	22	153	22	28	4	1.8	.862							
John Gaffney	C	B. Gilligan	273	.190	0	17	358	101	37	7	7.0	.925							
W-15 L-25	SS	S. Houck	195	.215	0	14	58	159	36	9	5.0	.858							
	2B	J. Farrell	171	.240	2	18	99	131	22	12	5.4	.913							
	P	D. Shaw	148	.088	0	6	13	70	3	1	1.9	.965							

BATTING AND BASE RUNNING LEADERS

Batting Average
K. Kelly, CHI	.388
C. Anson, CHI	.371
D. Brouthers, DET	.370
R. Connor, NY	.355
Richardson, DET	.351

Slugging Average
D. Brouthers, DET	.581
C. Anson, CHI	.544
R. Connor, NY	.540
K. Kelly, CHI	.534
Richardson, DET	.504

Home Runs
D. Brouthers, DET	11
Richardson, DET	11
C. Anson, CHI	10
J. Denny, STL	9
P. Hines, WAS	9

Total Bases
D. Brouthers, DET	284
C. Anson, CHI	274
Richardson, DET	271
R. Connor, NY	262
K. Kelly, CHI	241

Runs Batted In
C. Anson, CHI	147
F. Pfeffer, CHI	95
S. Thompson, DET	89
J. Rowe, DET	87
M. Ward, NY	81

Stolen Bases
(not available)

Hits
Richardson, DET	189
C. Anson, CHI	187
D. Brouthers, DET	181
K. Kelly, CHI	175

Base on Balls
G. Gore, CHI	102
K. Kelly, CHI	83
Williamson, CHI	80
D. Brouthers, DET	66

Home Run Percentage
D. Brouthers, DET	2.2
Richardson, DET	2.0
C. Anson, CHI	2.0
J. Denny, STL	1.9

Runs Scored
K. Kelly, CHI	155
G. Gore, CHI	150
D. Brouthers, DET	139
Richardson, DET	125

Doubles
D. Brouthers, DET	40
C. Anson, CHI	35
K. Kelly, CHI	32
P. Hines, WAS	30

Triples
R. Connor, NY	20
G. Wood, PHI	15
D. Brouthers, DET	15
S. Thompson, DET	13

PITCHING LEADERS

Winning Percentage
J. Flynn, CHI	.800
C. Ferguson, PHI	.769
L. Baldwin, DET	.764
McCormick, CHI	.738
C. Getzien, DET	.732

Earned Run Average
C. Ferguson, PHI	1.98
L. Baldwin, DET	2.24
H. Boyle, STL	2.24
J. Flynn, CHI	2.24
J. Clarkson, CHI	2.41

Wins
L. Baldwin, DET	42
T. Keefe, NY	42
J. Clarkson, CHI	35
M. Welch, NY	33
McCormick, CHI	31

Saves
C. Ferguson, PHI	2
J. Flynn, CHI	1
J. Ryan, CHI	1
J. Devlin, NY	1
Williamson, CHI	1

Strikeouts
J. Clarkson, CHI	340
L. Baldwin, DET	323
T. Keefe, NY	291
M. Welch, NY	272
B. Stemmeyer, BOS	239

Complete Games
T. Keefe, NY	62
O. Radbourn, BOS	57
M. Welch, NY	56
L. Baldwin, DET	55
J. Clarkson, CHI	50

Fewest Hits/9 Innings
L. Baldwin, DET	6.86
C. Ferguson, PHI	7.21
J. Flynn, CHI	7.25
B. Stemmeyer, BOS	7.74

Shutouts
L. Baldwin, DET	7
D. Casey, PHI	4
C. Ferguson, PHI	4

Fewest Walks/9 Innings
J. Whitney, KC	1.26
C. Ferguson, PHI	1.57
J. Clarkson, CHI	1.66
T. Keefe, NY	1.67

Most Strikeouts/9 Inn.
B. Stemmeyer, BOS	6.17
J. Clarkson, CHI	6.04
L. Baldwin, DET	5.97
H. Boyle, STL	5.51

Innings
T. Keefe, NY	540
O. Radbourn, BOS	509
M. Welch, NY	500
L. Baldwin, DET	487

Games Pitched
T. Keefe, NY	64
M. Welch, NY	59
O. Radbourn, BOS	58
L. Baldwin, DET	56

	W	L	PCT	GB	R	OR	2B	3B	HR	BA	SA	SB	E	DP	FA	CG	BB	SO	ShO	SV	ERA
Chicago	90	34	.726		**900**	555	**198**	**87**	53	.279	**.401**	0	475	82	.912	116	262	**647**	7	**3**	2.54
Detroit	87	36	.707	2.5	829	538	176	80	**54**	**.280**	.391	0	373	82	**.928**	**122**	270	592	8	0	2.85
New York	75	44	.630	12.5	692	558	175	67	22	.269	.356	0	**359**	70	.927	119	278	582	3	1	2.85
Philadelphia	71	43	.623	14	621	**498**	145	66	26	.240	.327	0	393	46	.921	110	264	540	**9**	2	**2.45**
Boston	56	61	.479	30.5	657	661	151	59	24	.260	.341	0	457	63	.906	116	298	511	3	0	3.24
St. Louis	43	79	.352	46	547	712	183	46	30	.236	.321	0	452	92	**.914**	118	392	501	6	0	3.41
Kansas City	30	91	.248	58.5	494	872	177	48	19	.228	.306	0	482	79	.910	117	**246**	442	4	0	4.85
Washington	28	92	.233	60	445	791	135	51	23	.210	.285	0	458	69	.910	116	379	500	4	0	4.30
					5185	5185	1340	504	251	.251	.342	0	3449	583	.916	934	2389	4315	44	6	3.31

AMERICAN ASSOCIATION 1886

	POS	Player	AB	BA	HR	RBI	PO	A	E	DP	TC/G	FA	Pitcher	G	IP	W	L	SV	ERA
St. Louis	1B	C. Comiskey	578	.254	3		1156	49	31	67	10.1	.975	D. Foutz	59	504	**41**	16	1	**2.11**
	2B	Y. Robinson	481	.274	3		351	406	**95**	66	6.8	.888	B. Caruthers	44	387	30	14	0	2.32
W-93 L-46	SS	B. Gleason	524	.269	0		128	352	83	37	4.5	.853	N. Hudson	29	234	16	10	1	3.03
	3B	A. Latham	578	.301	1		138	284	**88**	22	3.8	.827	J. McGinnis	10	88	5	5	0	3.80
Charlie Comiskey	RF	H. Nicol	253	.206	0		86	11	6	0	1.8	.942							
	CF	C. Welch	563	.281	2		**297**	19	16	4	2.4	**.952**							
	LF	T. O'Neill	579	.328	3		279	14	23	4	2.3	.927							
	C	D. Bushong	386	.223	1		**647**	134	48	**14**	7.8	**.942**							
	UT	D. Foutz	414	.280	3		211	86	19	7		.940							
	PO	B. Caruthers	317	.334	4		67	75	18	5		.888							
	PO	N. Hudson	150	.233	0		31	36	6	1		.918							

AMERICAN ASSOCIATION 1886, *cont.*

	POS	Player	AB	BA	HR	RBI	PO	A	E	DP	TC/G	FA	Pitcher	G	IP	W	L	SV	ERA
Pittsburgh	1B	O. Schomberg	246	.272	1		702	6	25	34	10.2	.966	E. Morris	64	555	41	20	1	2.45
	2B	S. Barkley	478	.266	0		362	328	47	52	6.6	.936	P. Galvin	50	435	29	21	0	2.67
W-80 L-57	SS	P. Smith	483	.217	2		132	356	57	28	5.6	**.895**	J. Handiboe	14	114	7	7	0	3.32
	3B	A. Whitney	511	.239	1		120	209	34	17	3.8	**.906**							
Horace Phillips	RF	T. Brown	460	.285	1		185	30	42	**12**	2.2	.837							
	CF	F. Mann	440	.250	2		203	13	30	2	2.1	.878							
	LF	E. Glenn	277	.191	0		124	10	21	2	2.2	.865							
	C	F. Carroll	486	.288	5		435	87	45	8	**8.1**	.921							
	UT	W. Kuehne	481	.204	1		303	99	29	11		.933							
	C	D. Miller	317	.252	2		247	56	27	0	5.4	.918							
	P	E. Morris	227	.167	1		21	90	10	2	1.9	.917							
	P	P. Galvin	194	.253	0		22	101	8	3	2.6	.939							
Brooklyn	1B	B. Phillips	585	.274	0		1395	33	32	65	10.4	.978	H. Porter	48	424	27	19	0	3.42
	2B	McClellan	595	.255	1		423	435	88	64	6.7	.907	J. Harkins	34	292	15	16	0	3.60
W-76 L-61	SS	G. Smith	426	.246	2		142	381	85	30	5.8	.860	A. Terry	34	288	18	16	0	3.09
	3B	G. Pinckney	**597**	.261	0		**184**	234	69	17	3.5	.858	H. Henderson	14	124	10	4	0	2.90
Charlie Byrne	RF	E. Swartwood	471	.280	3		189	**32**	29	4	2.0	.884	S. Toole	13	104	6	6	0	4.41
	CF	J. McTamany	418	.254	2		215	27	29	5	2.4	.893							
	LF	E. Burch	456	.261	2		142	10	20	3	1.5	.884							
	C	J. Peoples	340	.218	3		379	145	**73**	6	7.9	.878							
	UT	A. Terry	299	.237	2		99	117	35	3		.861							
	UT	B. Clark	269	.216	0		246	106	64	11		.846							
	P	H. Porter	184	.179	0		17	70	15	0	2.1	.853							
	P	J. Harkins	142	.225	1		24	61	8	2	2.7	.914							
Louisville	1B	P. Cook	262	.206	0		420	13	25	21	10.7	.945	T. Ramsey	67	**589**	38	27	0	2.45
	2B	R. Mack	483	.244	1		350	446	88	60	6.5	.900	G. Hecker	52	421	26	23	0	2.87
W-66 L-70	SS	B. White	557	.257	1		**212**	430	95	48	5.5	.871							
	3B	J. Werrick	561	.250	3		162	257	72	9	3.6	.853							
Jim Hart	RF	C. Wolf	545	.272	3		197	28	16	5	2.0	.934							
	CF	P. Browning	467	.340	2		153	14	**44**	1	1.9	.791							
	LF	J. Strauss	297	.215	1		95	19	19	0	1.8	.857							
	C	J. Kerins	487	.269	4		487	**157**	46	12	10.6	.933							
	UT	G. Hecker	343	**.341**	4		260	102	35	16		.912							
	C1	A. Cross	283	.276	1		431	83	42	12		.924							
	P	T. Ramsey	241	.241	0		14	78	23	1	1.7	.800							
	OF	L. Sylvester	154	.227	0		54	9	6	3	1.5	.913							
Cincinnati	1B	L. Reilly	441	.265	4		1120	37	**40**	**80**	10.9	.967	T. Mullane	63	530	33	27	0	3.70
	2B	B. McPhee	560	.266	**7**		**529**	464	65	**90**	7.6	**.939**	G. Pechiney	40	330	15	21	0	4.14
W-65 L-73	SS	F. Fennelly	497	.249	6		169	**485**	**117**	54	5.8	.848	L. McKeon	19	156	8	8	0	5.08
	3B	H. Carpenter	458	.221	2		127	221	66	23	3.7	.841							
Ollie Caylor	RF	P. Corkhill	540	.265	4		156	25	16	6	1.8	.919							
	CF	F. Lewis	324	.318	4		126	11	18	1	2.0	.884							
	LF	C. Jones	500	.270	5		217	23	33	1	2.1	.879							
	C	K. Baldwin	315	.229	3		355	102	61	13	7.3	.882							
	PO	T. Mullane	324	.225	0		80	108	20	8		.904							
	C1	P. Snyder	220	.186	2		328	80	44	11		.903							
	UT	J. Keenan	148	.270	3		220	54	24	6		.919							
	P	G. Pechiney	144	.208	1		17	45	8	2	1.8	.886							
Philadelphia	1B	H. Stovey	489	.294	**7**		656	13	33	26	11.3	.953	A. Atkinson	45	397	25	17	0	3.95
	2B	L. Bierbauer	522	.226	2		380	429	80	54	6.7	.910	B. Mathews	24	198	13	9	0	3.96
W-63 L-72	SS	C. McGarr	267	.266	2		109	231	60	25	5.6	.850	B. Hart	22	186	9	13	0	3.19
	3B	J. Gleason	299	.187	1		85	150	60	19	3.8	.797	T. Kennedy	20	173	5	15	0	4.53
Lew Simmons	RF	J. Coleman	492	.246	2		183	27	33	6	2.1	.864	C. Miller	19	170	10	8	0	2.97
W-41 L-55	CF	E. Greer	264	.193	1		143	9	13	3	2.4	.921							
	LF	H. Larkin	565	.319	4		264	21	44	4	2.4	.866							
Bill Sharsig	C	W. Robinson	342	.202	1		265	109	45	12	6.9	.893							
W-22 L-17																			
	UT	J. O'Brien	423	.253	0		426	170	70	26		.895							
	C1	J. Milligan	301	.252	5		522	63	31	13		.950							
	SS	J. Quest	150	.207	0		56	138	35	15	5.6	.847							
	P	A. Atkinson	148	.122	0		21	59	7	1	1.9	.920							
New York	1B	D. Orr	571	.338	7		**1445**	34	28	62	11.1	**.981**	J. Lynch	51	433	20	30	0	3.95
	2B	T. Forster	251	.195	1		152	193	42	26	6.2	.891	A. Mays	41	350	11	28	0	3.39
W-53 L-82	SS	C. Nelson	413	.225	0		103	216	54	17	5.1	.855	E. Cushman	38	326	17	20	0	3.12
	3B	F. Hankinson	522	.241	2		181	**316**	72	**26**	**4.2**	.873							
Jim Gifford	RF	S. Brady	466	.240	0		169	25	38	1	1.9	.836							
W-5 L-12	CF	S. Behel	224	.205	0		84	7	15	0	1.8	.858							
	LF	C. Roseman	559	.227	5		203	18	27	6	1.9	.891							
Bob Ferguson	C	Reipschlager	232	.211	0		268	107	51	5	7.5	.880							
W-48 L-70																			
	SS	McLaughlin	250	.136	0		93	203	38	11	5.3	.886							
	2B	J. Meister	186	.237	2		130	121	26	18	6.2	.906							
	OC	J. Donahue	186	.199	0		141	37	22	1		.890							
	C	B. Holbert	171	.205	0		265	100	31	6	8.8	.922							
	P	J. Lynch	169	.160	0		9	65	11	0	1.7	.871							

AMERICAN ASSOCIATION 1886, *cont.*

	POS	Player	AB	BA	HR	RBI	PO	A	E	DP	TC/G	FA	Pitcher	G	IP	W	L	SV	ERA
Baltimore	1B	M. Scott	484	.190	2		1347	59	38	38	10.5	.974	M. Kilroy	68	583	29	34	0	3.37
	2B	M. Muldoon	381	.199	0		136	184	31	18	6.2	.912	J. McGinnis	26	209	11	13	0	3.48
W-48 L-83	SS	J. Macullar	268	.205	0		115	208	56	19	4.6	.852	H. Henderson	19	171	3	15	0	4.62
	3B	J. Davis	216	.194	1		82	114	35	6	3.9	.848							
Billy Barnie	RF	J. Manning	556	.223	1		165	16	23	3	1.5	.887							
	CF	B. Hoover	157	.217	0		70	3	14	0	2.2	.839							
	LF	J. Sommer	560	.209	1		186	12	22	4	2.3	.900							
	C	C. Fulmer	270	.244	1		465	113	35	5	9.0	.943							
	23	J. Farrell	301	.209	1		109	180	45	9		.865							
	SS	S. Houck	260	.192	0		73	152	40	4	4.8	.849							
	P	M. Kilroy	218	.174	0		32	116	28	1	2.6	.841							
	OF	P. O'Connell	166	.181	0		57	4	17	0	1.9	.782							

BATTING AND BASE RUNNING LEADERS

Batting Average
G. Hecker, LOU .342
P. Browning, LOU .340
D. Orr, NY .338
B. Caruthers, STL .334
T. O'Neill, STL .328

Slugging Average
D. Orr, NY .527
B. Caruthers, STL .527
H. Stovey, PHI .460
H. Larkin, PHI .450
P. Browning, LOU .448

Home Runs
H. Stovey, PHI 7
B. McPhee, CIN 7
D. Orr, NY 7
F. Fennelly, CIN 6

Total Bases
D. Orr, NY 301
T. O'Neill, STL 257
H. Larkin, PHI 254
H. Stovey, PHI 225
B. McPhee, CIN 221
C. Welch, STL 221

Runs Batted In
(not available)

Stolen Bases
(not available)

Hits
D. Orr, NY 193
T. O'Neill, STL 190
H. Larkin, PHI 180
A. Latham, STL 174

Base on Balls
E. Swartwood, BKN 70
G. Pinckney, BKN 70
R. Mack, LOU 68
J. Kerins, LOU 66

Home Run Percentage
H. Stovey, PHI 1.4
B. Caruthers, STL 1.3
B. McPhee, CIN 1.3
D. Orr, NY 1.2

Runs Scored
A. Latham, STL 152
B. McPhee, CIN 139
H. Larkin, PHI 133
McClellan, BKN 131

Doubles
H. Larkin, PHI 36
McClellan, BKN 33
S. Barkley, PIT 32
C. Welch, STL 31

Triples
D. Orr, NY 31
W. Kuehne, PIT 17
F. Fennelly, CIN 17
J. Coleman, PHI, PIT 17

PITCHING LEADERS

Winning Percentage
D. Foutz, STL .719
B. Caruthers, STL .682
E. Morris, PIT .672
N. Hudson, STL .615
A. Atkinson, PHI .595

Earned Run Average
D. Foutz, STL 2.11
B. Caruthers, STL 2.32
T. Ramsey, LOU 2.45
E. Morris, PIT 2.45
P. Galvin, PIT 2.67

Wins
D. Foutz, STL 41
E. Morris, PIT 41
T. Ramsey, LOU 38
T. Mullane, CIN 31
B. Caruthers, STL 30

Saves
D. Foutz, STL 1
N. Hudson, STL 1
B. Ely, LOU 1
E. Morris, PIT 1
J. Strauss, BKN, LOU 1

Strikeouts
M. Kilroy, BAL 513
T. Ramsey, LOU 499
E. Morris, PIT 326
D. Foutz, STL 283
T. Mullane, CIN 250

Complete Games
T. Ramsey, LOU 66
M. Kilroy, BAL 66
E. Morris, PIT 63
T. Mullane, CIN 55
D. Foutz, STL 55

Fewest Hits/9 Innings
J. Handiboe, PIT 6.47
T. Ramsey, LOU 6.83
M. Kilroy, BAL 7.35
E. Morris, PIT 7.37

Shutouts
E. Morris, PIT 12
D. Foutz, STL 11
A. Terry, BKN 5
M. Kilroy, BAL 5

Fewest Walks/9 Innings
P. Galvin, PIT 1.55
E. Morris, PIT 1.91
B. Caruthers, STL 2.00
J. McGinnis, BAL, STL 2.27

Most Strikeouts/9 Inn.
M. Kilroy, BAL 7.92
T. Ramsey, LOU 7.63
J. Handiboe, PIT 6.55
E. Morris, PIT 5.28

Innings
T. Ramsey, LOU 589
M. Kilroy, BAL 583
E. Morris, PIT 555
T. Mullane, CIN 530

Games Pitched
M. Kilroy, BAL 68
T. Ramsey, LOU 67
E. Morris, PIT 64
T. Mullane, CIN 63

	W	L	PCT	GB	R	OR	2B	3B	HR	BA	SA	SB	E	DP	FA	CG	BB	SO	ShO	SV	ERA
St. Louis	93	46	.669		944	592	206	85	20	.273	.360	0	494	96	.915	134	329	583	14	2	2.52
Pittsburgh	80	57	.584	12	810	647	187	96	15	.241	.329	0	487	90	.917	137	299	515	15	1	2.84
Brooklyn	76	61	.555	16	832	832	196	80	16	.250	.330	0	611	87	.900	138	464	540	6	0	3.41
Louisville	66	70	.485	25.5	833	805	182	88	20	.263	.348	0	593	89	.901	131	432	720	5	2	3.07
Cincinnati	65	73	.471	27.5	883	865	145	97	40	.249	.342	0	588	122	.904	129	481	495	3	0	4.18
Philadelphia	63	72	.467	28	772	942	192	89	21	.235	.321	0	637	99	.894	134	388	513	4	0	3.98
New York	53	82	.393	38	628	766	108	72	18	.224	.289	0	546	81	.907	134	386	559	5	0	3.50
Baltimore	48	83	.366	41	625	878	124	51	8	.204	.258	0	536	59	.908	134	403	805	5	0	4.08
					6327	6327	1340	651	158	.243	.323	0	4492	723	.906	1071	3182	4730	57	5	3.45

NATIONAL LEAGUE 1887

	POS	Player	AB	BA	HR	RBI	PO	A	E	DP	TC/G	FA	Pitcher	G	IP	W	L	SV	ERA
Detroit	1B	D. Brouthers	500	.338	12	101	1141	35	38	67	9.9	.969	C. Getzien	43	367	29	13	0	3.73
	2B	F. Dunlap	272	.265	5	45	212	225	24	44	7.1	.948	L. Baldwin	24	211	13	10	0	3.84
W-79 L-45	SS	J. Rowe	537	.318	6	96	119	378	51	36	4.4	.907	S. Weidman	21	183	13	7	0	5.36
	3B	D. White	449	.303	3	75	133	225	64	18	4.0	.848	P. Conway	17	146	8	9	0	2.90
Bill Watkins	RF	S. Thompson	545	.372	11	166	217	24	24	7	2.1	.909	L. Twitchell	15	112	11	1	1	4.33
	CF	N. Hanlon	471	.274	4	69	264	18	30	4	2.6	.904							
	LF	L. Twitchell	264	.333	0	51	84	4	13	1	1.9	.871							
	C	C. Ganzel	227	.260	0	20	275	71	33	5	7.4	.913							
	20	Richardson	543	.328	11	94	328	223	37	28		.937							
	C	C. Bennett	160	.244	3	20	197	57	13	9	5.9	.951							
	P	C. Getzien	156	.186	1	14	23	58	3	1	2.0	.964							
	C	F. Briody	128	.227	2	26	144	61	21	4	6.8	.907							

NATIONAL LEAGUE 1887, cont.

	POS	Player	AB	BA	HR	RBI	PO	A	E	DP	TC/G	FA	Pitcher	G	IP	W	L	SV	ERA
Philadelphia	1B	S. Farrar	443	.282	4	72	1149	46	28	55	10.5	.977	D. Casey	45	390	28	13	0	2.86
	2B	McLaughlin	205	.220	1	26	106	156	36	15	6.0	.879	C. Buffinton	40	332	21	17	0	3.66
W-75 L-48	SS	A. Irwin	374	.254	2	56	178	301	58	30	5.4	.892	C. Ferguson	37	297	22	10	1	3.00
	3B	J. Mulvey	474	.287	2	78	123	197	50	18	3.3	.865							
Harry Wright	RF	J. Fogarty	495	.261	8	50	273	39	27	9	2.8	.920							
	CF	E. Andrews	464	.325	4	67	203	18	24	1	2.5	.902							
	LF	G. Wood	491	.289	14	66	155	10	24	2	1.8	.873							
	C	J. Clements	246	.280	1	47	328	79	26	8	7.3	.940							
	UT	C. Buffinton	269	.268	1	46	124	93	23	8		.904							
	UT	C. Ferguson	264	.337	3	85	93	130	22	11		.910							
	2S	C. Bastian	221	.213	1	21	101	165	25	19		.914							
	P	D. Casey	164	.165	1	17	10	66	9	0	1.9	.894							
	C	D. McGuire	150	.307	2	23	214	52	35	6	7.3	.884							
Chicago	1B	C. Anson	472	.347	7	102	1232	**70**	36	75	11.0	.973	J. Clarkson	**60**	**523**	**38**	21	0	3.08
	2B	F. Pfeffer	479	.278	16	89	**393**	402	**72**	68	**7.0**	.917	M. Baldwin	40	334	18	17	1	3.40
W-71 L-50	SS	Williamson	439	.267	9	78	133	361	61	31	4.4	.890	Van Haltren	20	161	11	7	1	3.86
	3B	T. Burns	424	.264	3	60	168	246	61	**23**	4.4	.872							
Cap Anson	RF	B. Sunday	199	.291	3	32	78	4	25	2	2.1	.766							
	CF	J. Ryan	508	.285	11	74	164	33	33	7	1.9	.857							
	LF	M. Sullivan	472	.284	7	77	189	10	**36**	0	2.0	.847							
	C	T. Daly	256	.207	2	17	354	**148**	35	12	**8.4**	**.935**							
	P	J. Clarkson	215	.242	6	25	34	**125**	7	**5**	2.8	.958							
	C	S. Flint	187	.267	3	21	255	73	33	3	7.7	.909							
	OP	Van Haltren	172	.203	3	17	47	26	8	2		.901							
	OC	D. Darling	141	.319	3	20	132	45	23	3		.885							
	P	M. Baldwin	139	.187	4	17	7	45	6	0	1.5	.897							
	OF	B. Pettit	138	.261	2	12	34	8	5	0	1.5	.894							
New York	1B	R. Connor	471	.285	17	104	**1325**	44	10	67	10.9	**.993**	T. Keefe	56	479	35	19	0	3.10
	2B	Richardson	450	.278	3	62	257	384	50	46	6.4	.928	M. Welch	40	346	22	15	0	3.36
W-68 L-55	SS	M. Ward	**545**	.338	1	53	**226**	469	61	53	5.9	**.919**	B. George	13	108	3	9	0	5.25
	3B	B. Ewing	318	.305	6	44	76	101	28	6	4.0	.863							
Jim Mutrie	RF	M. Dorgan	283	.258	0	34	128	6	20	0	2.2	.870							
	CF	G. Gore	459	.290	1	49	221	20	30	7	2.4	.889							
	LF	M. Tiernan	407	.287	10	62	150	10	25	3	1.8	.865							
	C	W. Brown	170	.218	0	25	229	69	28	5	7.1	.914							
	UT	J. O'Rourke	397	.285	3	88	248	127	48	7		.887							
	OF	P. Gillespie	295	.264	3	37	91	44	6	1	1.9	**.957**							
	P	T. Keefe	191	.220	2	23	17	102	**15**	1	2.4	.888							
	P	M. Welch	148	.243	2	15	17	51	12	0	2.0	.850							
	C	P. Deasley	118	.314	0	23	86	31	18	0	5.6	.867							
Boston	1B	J. Morrill	504	.280	12	81	1231	50	21	**76**	10.3	.984	O. Radbourn	50	425	24	23	0	4.55
	2B	J. Burdock	237	.257	0	29	117	188	41	34	5.3	.882	K. Madden	37	321	21	14	0	3.79
W-61 L-60	SS	S. Wise	467	.334	9	92	152	233	58	22	6.2	.869	D. Conway	26	222	9	15	0	4.66
	3B	B. Nash	475	.295	7	94	**207**	242	59	19	4.3	.884	B. Stemmeyer	15	119	6	8	1	5.20
King Kelly	RF	K. Kelly	484	.322	8	63	78	11	15	2	1.7	.856							
W-49 L-43	CF	D. Johnston	507	.258	5	77	339	34	27	9	3.1	.933							
	LF	J. Hornung	437	.270	5	49	192	23	15	3	2.3	.935							
John Morrill	C	P. Tate	231	.260	0	27	209	109	26	6	6.5	.924							
W-12 L-17	UT	E. Sutton	326	.304	3	46	178	234	58	12		.877							
	P	O. Radbourn	175	.229	1	24	15	69	**15**	3	2.0	.848							
	OS	B. Wheelock	166	.253	2	15	68	69	19	5		.878							
	PO	D. Conway	145	.248	0	10	25	53	13	0		.857							
	P	K. Madden	132	.242	0	13	4	59	13	1	2.1	.829							
Pittsburgh	1B	S. Barkley	340	.224	1	35	552	15	12	24	10.9	.979	P. Galvin	49	441	28	21	0	3.29
	2B	P. Smith	456	.215	2	54	225	298	49	32	6.4	.914	McCormick	36	322	13	23	0	4.30
W-55 L-69	SS	W. Kuehne	402	.299	1	41	136	310	59	29	5.5	.883	E. Morris	38	318	14	22	0	4.31
	3B	A. Whitney	431	.260	0	51	166	237	33	13	3.7	**.924**							
Horace Phillips	RF	J. Coleman	475	.293	2	54	214	17	26	3	2.2	.899							
	CF	T. Brown	192	.245	0	6	130	10	21*	0	3.4	.870							
	LF	A. Dalrymple	358	.212	2	31	184	14	22	1	2.4	.900							
	C	D. Miller	342	.243	1	34	266	58	25	1	4.8	.928							
	UT	F. Carroll	421	.328	6	54	451	56	62	9		.891							
	1B	A. McKinnon	200	.340	1	30	483	25	12	27	10.8	.977							
	P	P. Galvin	193	.212	2	22	22	123	11	2	**3.2**	.929							
	OF	E. Beecher	169	.243	2	22	85	12	9	1	2.6	.915							
	UT	J. Fields	164	.268	0	17	141	29	18	2		.904							
	P	McCormick	136	.243	0	18	13	88	8	1	3.0	.927							
	P	E. Morris	126	.198	0	10	5	52	5	1	1.6	.919							

NATIONAL LEAGUE 1887, *cont.*

	POS	Player	AB	BA	HR	RBI	PO	A	E	DP	TC/G	FA	Pitcher	G	IP	W	L	SV	ERA
Washington	1B	B. O'Brien	453	.278	19	73	1159	26	32	53	11.7	.974	J. Whitney	47	405	24	21	0	3.22
	2B	A. Myers	362	.232	2	36	193	248	44	23	6.2	.909	H. O'Day	30	255	8	20	0	4.17
W-46 L-76	SS	J. Farrell	339	.221	0	41	91	156	35	14	5.9	.876	F. Gilmore	28	235	7	20	0	3.87
	3B	J. Donnelly	425	.200	1	46	136	275	63	21	4.1	.867	D. Shaw	21	181	7	13	0	6.45
John Gaffney	RF	E. Daily	311	.251	2	36	116	8	21	1	1.9	.855							
	CF	P. Hines	478	.308	10	72	180	14	25	5	2.0	.886							
	LF	C. Carroll	420	.248	4	37	146	19	18	6	1.8	.902							
	C	C. Mack	314	.201	0	20	391	119	53	15	7.4	.906							
	UT	P. Dealey	312	.272	1	18	171	105	34	9		.890							
	OF	G. Shoch	264	.239	1	18	115	15	15	3	2.3	.897							
	P	J. Whitney	201	.264	2	22	13	92	11	5	2.5	.905							
Indianapolis	1B	O. Schomberg	419	.308	5	83	1216	28	55	76	11.6	.958	E. Healy	41	341	12	29	0	5.17
	2B	C. Bassett	452	.230	1	47	273	444	53	62	6.5	.931	H. Boyle	38	328	13	24	0	3.65
W-37 L-89	SS	J. Glasscock	483	.294	0	40	211	493	73	58	6.4	.906	L. Shreve	14	122	5	9	0	4.72
	3B	J. Denny	510	.324	11	97	201	262	58	21	4.5	.889							
Watch Burnham	RF	J. Cahill	263	.205	0	26	84	11	20	1	2.1	.826							
W-6 L-22	CF	J. McGeachy	405	.269	1	56	231	22	30	3	2.9	.894							
	LF	E. Seery	465	.224	4	38	220	25	30	2	2.3	.891							
Fred Thomas	C	G. Myers	235	.217	1	20	176	58	18	8	5.0	.929							
W-11 L-18	C	T. Arundel	157	.197	0	13	153	64	34	5	6.0	.865							
	C	M. Hackett	147	.238	2	10	128	52	12	4	4.8	.938							
Horace Fogel	P	H. Boyle	141	.191	2	13	1	1	5	0	.2	.286							
W-20 L-49	OF	T. Brown	140	.179	2	9	58	7	15*	2	2.2	.813							
	P	E. Healy	138	.174	3	14	7	51	12	0	1.7	.829							

BATTING AND BASE RUNNING LEADERS

Batting Average
S. Thompson, DET	.372
C. Anson, CHI	.347
D. Brouthers, DET	.338
M. Ward, NY	.338
S. Wise, BOS	.334

Slugging Average
S. Thompson, DET	.571
D. Brouthers, DET	.562
R. Connor, NY	.541
S. Wise, BOS	.522
C. Anson, CHI	.517

Home Runs
B. O'Brien, WAS	19
R. Connor, NY	17
F. Pfeffer, CHI	16
G. Wood, PHI	14
D. Brouthers, DET	12
J. Morrill, BOS	12

Total Bases
S. Thompson, DET	311
D. Brouthers, DET	281
Richardson, DET	272
J. Denny, IND	256
R. Connor, NY	255

Runs Batted In
S. Thompson, DET	166
R. Connor, NY	104
C. Anson, CHI	102
D. Brouthers, DET	101
J. Denny, IND	97

Stolen Bases
M. Ward, NY	111
J. Fogarty, PHI	102
K. Kelly, BOS	84
N. Hanlon, DET	69
J. Glasscock, IND	62

Hits
S. Thompson, DET	203
M. Ward, NY	184
Richardson, DET	178
J. Rowe, DET	171

Base on Balls
J. Fogarty, PHI	82
R. Connor, NY	75
Williamson, CHI	73
E. Seery, IND	71

Home Run Percentage
B. O'Brien, WAS	4.2
R. Connor, NY	3.6
F. Pfeffer, CHI	3.3
G. Wood, PHI	2.9

Runs Scored
D. Brouthers, DET	153
J. Rowe, DET	135
Richardson, DET	131
K. Kelly, BOS	120

Doubles
D. Brouthers, DET	36
K. Kelly, BOS	34
J. Denny, IND	34
C. Anson, CHI	33

Triples
S. Thompson, DET	23
R. Connor, NY	22
D. Brouthers, DET	20
D. Johnston, BOS	20

PITCHING LEADERS

Winning Percentage
C. Getzien, DET	.690
C. Ferguson, PHI	.688
D. Casey, PHI	.683
T. Keefe, NY	.648
J. Clarkson, CHI	.644

Earned Run Average
D. Casey, PHI	2.86
P. Conway, DET	2.90
C. Ferguson, PHI	3.00
J. Clarkson, CHI	3.08
T. Keefe, NY	3.10

Wins
J. Clarkson, CHI	38
T. Keefe, NY	35
C. Getzien, DET	29
D. Casey, PHI	28
P. Galvin, PIT	28

Saves
8 tied with	1

Strikeouts
J. Clarkson, CHI	237
T. Keefe, NY	186
M. Baldwin, CHI	164
C. Buffinton, PHI	160
J. Whitney, WAS	146

Complete Games
J. Clarkson, CHI	56
T. Keefe, NY	54
O. Radbourn, BOS	48
P. Galvin, PIT	47
J. Whitney, WAS	46

Fewest Hits/9 Innings
P. Conway, DET	8.14
T. Keefe, NY	8.40
D. Casey, PHI	8.69
M. Welch, NY	8.82

Shutouts
D. Casey, PHI	4
K. Madden, BOS	3
E. Healy, IND	3
J. Whitney, WAS	3

Fewest Walks/9 Innings
J. Whitney, WAS	0.93
P. Galvin, PIT	1.37
C. Ferguson, PHI	1.42
J. Clarkson, CHI	1.58

Most Strikeouts/9 Inn.
M. Baldwin, CHI	4.42
F. Gilmore, WAS	4.37
C. Buffinton, PHI	4.33
Van Haltren, CHI	4.25

Innings
J. Clarkson, CHI	523
T. Keefe, NY	479
P. Galvin, PIT	441
O. Radbourn, BOS	425

Games Pitched
J. Clarkson, CHI	60
T. Keefe, NY	56
O. Radbourn, BOS	50
P. Galvin, PIT	49

	W	L	PCT	GB	R	OR	2B	3B	HR	BA	SA	SB	E	DP	FA	CG	BB	SO	ShO	SV	ERA
Detroit	79	45	.637		969	714	213	126	59	.299	.436	267	394	92	.925	122	344	337	3	1	3.95
Philadelphia	75	48	.610	3.5	901	702	213	89	47	.274	.389	355	471	76	.912	119	305	435	7	1	3.47
Chicago	71	50	.587	6.5	813	716	178	98	80	.271	.412	382	472	99	.914	117	338	510	4	3	3.46
New York	68	55	.553	10.5	816	723	167	93	48	.279	.389	415	431	83	.921	123	373	412	5	1	3.57
Boston	61	60	.504	16.5	831	792	185	94	54	.277	.395	373	522	94	.905	123	396	254	4	1	4.41
Pittsburgh	55	69	.444	24	621	750	183	78	20	.258	.349	221	425	70	.921	123	246	248	3	0	4.12
Washington	46	76	.377	32	601	818	149	63	47	.242	.336	334	483	77	.910	124	299	396	4	0	4.19
Indianapolis	37	89	.294	43	628	965	162	70	33	.247	.339	334	479	105	.912	118	431	245	4	1	5.25
					6180	6180	1450	711	388	.269	.381	2681	3677	696	.915	969	2732	2837	34	8	4.05

AMERICAN ASSOCIATION 1887

St. Louis
W-95 L-40

Charlie Comiskey

POS	Player	AB	BA	HR	RBI	PO	A	E	DP	TC/G	FA	Pitcher	G	IP	W	L	SV	ERA
1B	C. Comiskey	538	.335	4		1135	51	29	60	10.5	.976	S. King	46	390	34	11	1	3.78
2B	Y. Robinson	430	.305	1		320	355	76	52	6.4	.899	B. Caruthers	39	341	29	9	0	3.30
SS	B. Gleason	598	.288	0		169	411	83	27	4.9	.875	D. Foutz	40	339	25	12	0	3.87
3B	A. Latham	627	.316	2		155	288	62	17	3.8	.877							
RF	B. Caruthers	364	.357	8		91	11	11	1	2.1	.903							
CF	C. Welch	544	.278	3		336	29	23	7	3.2	.941							
LF	T. O'Neill	517	.435	14		247	8	30	2	2.3	.895							
C	J. Boyle	350	.189	2		339	114	56	7	5.9	.890							
UT	D. Foutz	423	.357	4		282	65	23	11		.938							
P	S. King	222	.207	0		16	69	6	0	2.0	.934							
C	D. Bushong	201	.254	0		201	93	23	3	6.1	.927							

Cincinnati
W-81 L-54

Gus Schmelz

POS	Player	AB	BA	HR	RBI	PO	A	E	DP	TC/G	FA	Pitcher	G	IP	W	L	SV	ERA
1B	L. Reilly	551	.309	10		1267	33	26	84	10.4	.980	E. Smith	52	447	34	18	0	2.94
2B	B. McPhee	540	.289	2		442	434	72	76	7.3	.924	T. Mullane	48	416	31	17	0	3.24
SS	F. Fennelly	526	.266	8		161	421	99	31	5.1	.855	B. Serad	22	187	10	11	1	4.08
3B	H. Carpenter	498	.249	1		144	242	70	17	3.6	.846							
RF	H. Nicol	475	.215	1		194	20	19	1	1.9	.918							
CF	P. Corkhill	541	.311	5		310	29	17	7	2.8	.952							
LF	W. Tebeau	318	.296	4		175	14	24	2	2.5	.887							
C	K. Baldwin	388	.253	1		381	165	79	9	6.5	.874							
P	T. Mullane	199	.221	3		29	72	6	5	2.2	.944							
P	E. Smith	186	.253	0		7	67	13	2	1.7	.851							
C	J. Keenan	174	.253	0		161	67	20	8	6.5	.919							
OF	C. Jones	153	.314	2		74	7	9	2*	2.2	.900							

Baltimore
W-77 L-58

Billy Barnie

POS	Player	AB	BA	HR	RBI	PO	A	E	DP	TC/G	FA	Pitcher	G	IP	W	L	SV	ERA
1B	T. Tucker	524	.275	6		1346	50	35	49	10.5	.976	M. Kilroy	69	589	46	19	0	3.07
2B	B. Greenwood	495	.263	0		357	360	56	33	6.6	.928	P. Smith	58	491	25	30	0	3.79
SS	O. Burns	551	.341	9		136	245	72	20	4.6	.841							
3B	J. Davis	485	.309	8		91	199	61	7	4.0	.826							
RF	B. Purcell	567	.250	4		203	18	18	5	1.7	.925							
CF	M. Griffin	532	.301	3		256	13	22	1	2.1	.924							
LF	J. Sommer	463	.266	0		191	20	22	4	2.1	.906							
C	S. Trott	300	.257	0		373	102	44	6	7.5	.915							
P	M. Kilroy	239	.247	0		37	167	20	2	3.2	.911							
P	P. Smith	205	.234	1		9	108	20	1	2.4	.854							
C	C. Fulmer	201	.269	0		201	73	28	5	6.3	.907							
UT	L. Daniels	165	.248	1		188	44	45	5		.838							

Louisville
W-76 L-60

Honest John Kelly

POS	Player	AB	BA	HR	RBI	PO	A	E	DP	TC/G	FA	Pitcher	G	IP	W	L	SV	ERA
1B	J. Kerins	476	.294	5		695	18	22	26	9.9	.970	T. Ramsey	65	561	37	27	0	3.43
2B	R. Mack	478	.308	1		366	395	73	48	6.5	.912	Chamberlain	36	309	18	16	0	3.79
SS	B. White	512	.252	2		204	431	91	45	5.5	.869	G. Hecker	33	285	18	12	1	4.16
3B	J. Werrick	533	.285	7		153	286	89	12	3.9	.831							
RF	C. Wolf	569	.281	1		207	27	15	5	1.9	.940							
CF	P. Browning	547	.402	4		281	21	46	7	2.6	.868							
LF	H. Collins	559	.290	1		192	19	27	1	2.2	.887							
C	P. Cook	223	.247	0		220	95	29	4	6.3	.916							
UT	G. Hecker	370	.319	4		429	82	29	27		.946							
P	T. Ramsey	225	.191	4		7	88	31	0	1.9	.754							
C	L. Cross	203	.266	0		251	66	31	7	7.9	.911							

Philadelphia
W-64 L-69

Charlie Mason

POS	Player	AB	BA	HR	RBI	PO	A	E	DP	TC/G	FA	Pitcher	G	IP	W	L	SV	ERA
1B	J. Milligan	377	.302	2		436	13	16	21	9.3	.966	E. Seward	55	471	25	25	0	4.13
2B	L. Bierbauer	530	.272	1		332	378	61	45	6.1	.921	G. Weyhing	55	466	26	28	0	4.27
SS	C. McGarr	536	.295	1		198	402	86	42	5.0	.875	A. Atkinson	15	125	6	8	0	5.92
3B	D. Lyons	570	.367	6		255	215	73	29	4.0	.866							
RF	T. Poorman	585	.265	4		237	18	25	6	2.1	.911							
CF	H. Stovey	497	.286	4		195	16	23	1	2.9	.902							
LF	H. Larkin	497	.310	3		183	14	23	0	2.4	.895							
C	W. Robinson	264	.227	1		281	137	46	9	6.9	.901							
P	E. Seward	266	.188	5		21	79	11	1	2.0	.901							
OF	F. Mann	229	.275	0		103	7	10	2	2.2	.917							
P	G. Weyhing	209	.201	0		18	88	24	5	2.4	.815							

Brooklyn
W-60 L-74

Charlie Byrne

POS	Player	AB	BA	HR	RBI	PO	A	E	DP	TC/G	FA	Pitcher	G	IP	W	L	SV	ERA
1B	B. Phillips	533	.266	2		1299	46	24	62	10.4	.982	H. Porter	40	340	15	24	0	4.21
2B	McClellan	548	.263	1		366	397	105	52	6.4	.879	A. Terry	40	318	16	16	3	4.02
SS	G. Smith	435	.294	4		157	387	70	23	6.1	.886	J. Harkins	24	199	10	14	0	6.02
3B	G. Pinckney	580	.267	3		196	290	60	26	4.0	.890	S. Toole	24	194	14	10	0	4.31
RF	E. Swartwood	363	.253	1		129	23	30	5	2.0	.835	H. Henderson	13	112	5	8	0	3.95
CF	J. McTamany	520	.258	1		281	32	28	8	2.5	.918							
LF	E. Greer	327	.254	1		155	8	14	1	2.3	.921							
C	J. Peoples	268	.254	1		226	106	59	3	6.9	.849							
OP	A. Terry	352	.293	3		124	86	23	1		.901							
OF	E. Burch	188	.293	2		90	8	11	1	2.2	.899							
C	B. Clark	177	.266	0		197	66	40	7	6.7	.868							
P	H. Porter	146	.199	1		8	66	12	1	2.2	.860							

AMERICAN ASSOCIATION 1887, cont.

	POS	Player	AB	BA	HR	RBI	PO	A	E	DP	TC/G	FA	Pitcher	G	IP	W	L	SV	ERA
New York	1B	D. Orr	345	.368	2		806	28	27	41	10.6	.969	A. Mays	52	441	17	**34**	0	4.73
	2B	J. Gerhardt	307	.221	0		288	271	65	48	7.4	.896	E. Cushman	26	220	10	14	0	5.97
W-44 L-89	SS	P. Radford	486	.265	4		121	229	70	28	5.5	.833	J. Lynch	21	187	7	14	0	5.10
	3B	F. Hankinson	512	.268	1		161	276	69	26	4.0	.864	J. Shaffer	13	112	2	11	0	6.19
Bob Ferguson	RF	C. Roseman	241	.228	0		99	6	16	2	2.1	.868	S. Weidman	12	97	4	8	0	4.64
W-6 L-24	CF	C. Jones	247	.255	3		114	18	12	6*	2.3	.917							
	LF	D. O'Brien	522	.301	5		244	20	25	4	2.4	.913							
Dave Orr	C	B. Holbert	255	.227	0		237	102	43	9	6.4	.887							
W-3 L-5	OS	C. Nelson	257	.245	0		120	111	27	18		.895							
	P	A. Mays	221	.204	2		21	144	24	4	**3.6**	.873							
Ollie Caylor	C	J. Donahue	220	.282	1		208	90	42	3	6.7	.876							
W-35 L-60	O2	J. Meister	158	.222	1		66	38	10	8		.912							
Cleveland	1B	J. Toy	423	.222	1		707	30	19	54	9.2	.975	B. Crowell	45	389	14	31	0	4.88
	2B	C. Stricker	534	.264	2		**461**	365	80	61	7.2	.912	M. Morrison	40	317	12	25	0	4.92
W-39 L-92	SS	E. McKean	539	.286	2		195	351	90	32	5.2	.847	O. Daily	16	140	4	12	0	3.67
	3B	P. Reccius	229	.205	0		85	137	31	18	4.1	.877	B. Gilks	13	108	7	5	0	3.08
Jimmy Williams	RF	F. Mann	259	.309	2		112	11	17	4	2.2	.879	G. Pechiney	10	86	1	9	0	7.12
	CF	P. Hotaling	505	.299	3		267	23	31	5	2.5	.903							
	LF	M. Allen	463	.276	4		222	22	29	6	2.4	.894							
	C	P. Snyder	282	.255	0		314	143	53	8	8.1	.896							
	C	Reipschlager	231	.212	0		196	105	43	9	7.2	.875							
	OF	S. Carroll	216	.199	0		79	7	16	1	1.9	.843							
	P	B. Crowell	156	.141	0		5	65	5	4	1.7	.933							
	P	M. Morrison	141	.191	0		14	109	11	4	3.4	.918							

BATTING AND BASE RUNNING LEADERS

Batting Average
- T. O'Neill, STL .435
- P. Browning, LOU .402
- D. Orr, NY .368
- D. Lyons, PHI .367
- B. Caruthers, STL .357

Slugging Average
- T. O'Neill, STL .691
- P. Browning, LOU .556
- B. Caruthers, STL .547
- O. Burns, BAL .525
- D. Lyons, PHI .523

Home Runs
- T. O'Neill, STL 14
- O. Burns, BAL 10
- L. Reilly, CIN 10
- B. Caruthers, STL 8
- J. Davis, BAL 8
- F. Fennelly, CIN 8

Winning Percentage
- B. Caruthers, STL .763
- S. King, STL .756
- M. Kilroy, BAL .697
- D. Foutz, STL .676
- E. Smith, CIN .647

PITCHING LEADERS

Earned Run Average
- E. Smith, CIN 2.94
- M. Kilroy, BAL 3.07
- B. Gilks, CLE 3.08
- T. Mullane, CIN 3.24
- B. Caruthers, STL 3.30

Wins
- M. Kilroy, BAL 46
- T. Ramsey, LOU 37
- S. King, STL 34
- E. Smith, CIN 33
- T. Mullane, CIN 31

Total Bases
- T. O'Neill, STL 357
- P. Browning, LOU 304
- D. Lyons, PHI 298
- O. Burns, BAL 289
- L. Reilly, CIN 263

(not available)

Stolen Bases
- H. Nicol, CIN 138
- A. Latham, STL 129
- C. Comiskey, STL 117
- P. Browning, LOU 103
- B. McPhee, CIN 95

Saves
- A. Terry, BKN 3

Strikeouts
- T. Ramsey, LOU 355
- M. Kilroy, BAL 217
- P. Smith, BAL 206
- G. Weyhing, PHI 193
- E. Smith, CIN 176

Complete Games
- M. Kilroy, BAL 66
- T. Ramsey, LOU 61
- P. Smith, BAL 54
- G. Weyhing, PHI 53
- E. Seward, PHI 52

Hits
- T. O'Neill, STL 225
- P. Browning, LOU 220
- D. Lyons, PHI 209
- A. Latham, STL 198

Base on Balls
- P. Radford, NY 106
- Y. Robinson, STL 92
- H. Nicol, CIN 86
- R. Mack, LOU 83

Home Run Percentage
- T. O'Neill, STL 2.7
- B. Caruthers, STL 2.2
- L. Reilly, CIN 1.8
- J. Davis, BAL 1.6

Fewest Hits/9 Innings
- E. Smith, CIN 8.05
- E. Seward, PHI 8.51
- S. Toole, BKN 8.63
- B. Gilks, CLE 8.67

Shutouts
- T. Mullane, CIN 6
- M. Kilroy, BAL 6
- E. Seward, PHI 3
- E. Smith, CIN 3

Fewest Walks/9 Innings
- G. Hecker, LOU 1.58
- B. Caruthers, STL 1.61
- J. Lynch, NY 1.73
- D. Foutz, STL 2.39

Runs Scored
- T. O'Neill, STL 167
- A. Latham, STL 163
- M. Griffin, BAL 142
- T. Poorman, PHI 140

Doubles
- T. O'Neill, STL 52
- D. Lyons, PHI 43
- P. Browning, LOU 36
- L. Reilly, CIN 35

Triples
- J. Kerins, LOU 19
- J. Davis, BAL 19
- T. O'Neill, STL 19
- B. McPhee, CIN 19

Most Strikeouts/9 Inn.
- T. Ramsey, LOU 5.70
- M. Morrison, CLE 4.49
- A. Terry, BKN 3.91
- P. Smith, BAL 3.77

Innings
- M. Kilroy, BAL 589
- T. Ramsey, LOU 561
- P. Smith, BAL 491
- E. Seward, PHI 471

Games Pitched
- M. Kilroy, BAL 69
- T. Ramsey, LOU 65
- P. Smith, BAL 58
- E. Seward, PHI 55

	W	L	PCT	GB	R	OR	Batting 2B	3B	HR	BA	SA	SB	Fielding E	DP	FA	Pitching CG	BB	SO	ShO	SV	ERA
St. Louis	95	40	.704		1131	761	**261**	78	**39**	**.307**	**.413**	581	485	86	.916	132	**323**	334	6	2	3.78
Cincinnati	81	54	.600	14	892	**745**	179	**102**	37	.268	.371	527	488	**106**	.915	129	396	330	**11**	1	3.59
Baltimore	77	58	.570	18	975	861	202	100	31	.277	.380	545	558	66	.906	132	418	470	8	0	3.87
Louisville	76	60	.559	19.5	956	854	195	98	26	.289	.384	466	576	83	.903	**133**	357	**544**	3	1	3.82
Philadelphia	64	69	.481	30	893	890	231	84	29	.277	.375	476	528	95	.907	131	433	417	5	1	4.59
Brooklyn	60	74	.448	34.5	904	918	200	82	25	.261	.350	409	565	88	.904	132	454	332	5	**3**	4.46
New York	44	89	.331	50	754	1093	193	66	20	.248	.328	305	643	102	.893	132	406	316	1	0	5.30
Cleveland	39	92	.298	54	729	1112	178	77	14	.252	.332	355	589	97	.897	127	533	332	2	1	4.99
					7234	7234	1639	687	221	.273	.367	3664	4432	723	.905	1048	3320	3075	39	9	4.29

NATIONAL LEAGUE 1888

	POS	Player	AB	BA	HR	RBI	PO	A	E	DP	TC/G	FA	Pitcher	G	IP	W	L	SV	ERA
New York	1B	R. Connor	481	.291	14	71	1337	43	26	57	10.6	.982	T. Keefe	51	434	**35**	12	0	**1.74**
	2B	Richardson	561	.226	8	61	321	423	46	43	5.9	**.942**	M. Welch	47	425	26	19	0	1.93
W-84 L-47	SS	M. Ward	510	.251	2	49	185	331	**86**	39	4.9	.857	C. Titcomb	23	197	14	8	0	2.24
	3B	A. Whitney	328	.220	1	28	90	184	35	11	3.4	.887	C. Crane	12	93	5	6	1	2.43
Jim Mutrie	RF	M. Tiernan	443	.293	9	52	174	16	8	2	1.8	.960							
	CF	M. Slattery	391	.246	1	35	187	16	18	3	2.1	.919							
	LF	J. O'Rourke	409	.274	4	50	130	13	6	1	1.7	**.960**							
	C	B. Ewing	415	.306	6	58	480	143	35	12	8.4	.947							
	OF	G. Gore	254	.220	2	17	88	4	18	0	1.7	.836							
	P	T. Keefe	181	.127	2	8	29	79	10	1	2.3	.915							
	P	M. Welch	169	.189	2	10	16	75	17	1	2.3	.843							
Chicago	1B	C. Anson	515	**.344**	12	84	1314	65	20	**85**	10.4	**.986**	G. Krock	39	340	25	14	0	2.44
	2B	F. Pfeffer	517	.250	8	57	**421**	**457**	65	**78**	7.0	.931	M. Baldwin	30	251	13	15	0	2.76
W-77 L-58	SS	Williamson	452	.250	8	73	120	**375**	65	**48**	4.2	.884	Van Haltren	30	246	13	13	1	3.52
	3B	T. Burns	483	.238	3	70	194	273	49	16	3.9	.905	J. Tener	12	102	7	5	0	2.74
Cap Anson	RF	H. Duffy	298	.282	7	41	103	19	12	5	2.0	.910							
	CF	J. Ryan	549	.332	**16**	64	217	**34**	35	5	2.2	.878							
	LF	M. Sullivan	314	.236	7	39	114	13	10	7	1.8	.927							
	C	T. Daly	219	.192	0	29	400	107	33	10	8.7	.939							
	OP	Van Haltren	318	.283	4	34	98	62	17	0		.904							
	CO	D. Farrell	241	.232	3	19	221	53	39	4		.875							
	OF	B. Pettit	169	.254	4	23	46	8	4	3	1.3	.931							
Philadelphia	1B	S. Farrar	508	.244	1	53	1345	53	30	57	10.9	.979	C. Buffinton	46	400	28	17	0	1.91
	2B	C. Bastian	275	.193	1	17	145	253	23	14	6.5	.945	D. Casey	33	286	14	18	0	3.15
W-69 L-61	SS	A. Irwin	448	.219	0	48	**204**	**374**	64	31	5.3	.900	B. Sanders	31	275	19	10	0	1.90
	3B	J. Mulvey	398	.216	1	39	87	174	32	9	2.9	.891	K. Gleason	24	200	7	16	0	2.84
Harry Wright	RF	J. Fogarty	454	.236	1	35	239	26	20	**9**	2.4	.930							
	CF	E. Andrews	528	.239	3	44	210	23	25	5	2.1	.903							
	LF	G. Wood	433	.229	6	15	175	15	20	3	2.0	.905							
	C	J. Clements	326	.245	1	32	**494**	104	47	6	7.6	.927							
	2B	E. Delahanty	290	.228	1	31	129	170	44	20	6.1	.872							
	PO	B. Sanders	236	.246	1	25	55	79	9	1		.937							
	P	C. Buffinton	160	.181	0	12	31	122	10	3	3.5	.939							
	UT	P. Schriver	134	.194	1	23	156	63	36	3		.859							
Boston	1B	J. Morrill	486	.198	4	39	**1398**	**72**	31	67	**11.3**	.979	J. Clarkson	54	**483**	33	20	0	2.76
	2B	J. Quinn	156	.301	4	29	97	115	20	11	6.1	.914	B. Sowders	36	317	19	15	0	2.07
W-70 L-64	SS	S. Wise	417	.240	4	40	179	271	57	34	**5.7**	.888	O. Radbourn	24	207	7	16	0	2.87
	3B	B. Nash	526	.283	4	75	139	250	37	**20**	4.1	**.913**	K. Madden	20	165	7	11	0	2.95
John Morrill	RF	T. Brown	420	.248	9	49	172	18	22	3	2.0	.896							
	CF	D. Johnston	**585**	.296	12	68	286	30	36	3	2.6	.898							
	LF	J. Hornung	431	.239	3	53	151	10	9	0	1.6	.947							
	C	K. Kelly	440	.318	9	71	367	146	**54**	8	7.5	.905							
	SS	I. Ray	206	.248	2	26	58	130	26	6	4.5	.879							
	P	J. Clarkson	205	.195	1	17	22	117	**19**	3	2.9	.880							
	C	P. Tate	148	.230	1	6	188	64	43	6	7.2	.854							
Detroit	1B	D. Brouthers	522	.307	9	66	1345	48	**42**	56	11.1	.971	C. Getzien	46	404	19	25	0	3.05
	2B	Richardson	266	.289	7	32	173	185	29	21	6.7	.925	P. Conway	45	391	30	14	0	2.26
W-68 L-63	SS	J. Rowe	451	.277	2	74	133	312	72	24	4.9	.861	H. Gruber	27	240	11	14	0	2.29
	3B	D. White	527	.298	4	71	146	244	65	19	3.6	.857	E. Beatin	12	107	5	7	0	2.86
Bill Watkins	RF	C. Campau	251	.203	1	18	101	10	8	3	1.7	.933							
W-49 L-44	CF	N. Hanlon	459	.266	5	39	230	7	21	3	2.4	.919							
	LF	L. Twitchell	524	.244	4	67	195	13	27	4	1.8	.885							
Bob Leadley	C	C. Bennett	258	.264	5	29	424	94	18	10	7.3	**.966**							
W-19 L-19	UT	C. Ganzel	386	.249	1	46	288	241	52	24		.910							
	OF	S. Thompson	238	.282	6	40	86	4	12	0	1.8	.882							
	UT	S. Sutcliffe	191	.257	0	23	172	127	39	13		.885							
	P	C. Getzien	167	.246	1	10	29	70	16	**5**	2.5	.861							
	P	P. Conway	167	.275	3	23	10	96	7	4	2.5	.938							
Pittsburgh	1B	J. Beckley	283	.343	0	27	744	19	16	38	11.0	.979	E. Morris	**55**	480	29	24	0	2.31
	2B	F. Dunlap	321	.262	1	36	240	279	33	44	6.7	.940	P. Galvin	50	437	23	25	0	2.63
W-66 L-68	SS	P. Smith	481	.206	4	52	91	247	37	18	5.0	.901	H. Staley	25	207	12	12	0	2.69
	3B	W. Kuehne	524	.235	3	62	96	168	26	10	3.9	.910							
Horace Phillips	RF	J. Coleman	438	.231	0	26	160	20	14	2	2.1	.928							
	CF	B. Sunday	505	.236	0	15	**297**	27	21	5	2.9	.939							
	LF	A. Dalrymple	227	.220	0	14	81	9	9	0	1.7	.909							
	C	D. Miller	404	.277	0	36	268	76	35	6	5.6	.908							
	CO	F. Carroll	366	.249	2	48	314	63	48	10		.887							
	10	A. Maul	259	.208	0	31	449	16	14	22		.971							
	P	E. Morris	189	.101	0	6	20	106	8	3	2.4	**.940**							
	P	P. Galvin	175	.143	1	3	23	113	10	2	2.9	.932							
	OC	J. Fields	169	.195	1	15	103	22	23	2		.845							

NATIONAL LEAGUE 1888, *cont.*

Indianapolis
W-50 L-85

Harry Spence

POS	Player	AB	BA	HR	RBI	PO	A	E	DP	TC/G	FA	Pitcher	G	IP	W	L	SV	ERA
1B	Esterbrook	246	.220	0	17	628	20	16	32	10.9	.976	H. Boyle	37	323	15	22	0	3.26
2B	C. Bassett	481	.241	2	60	250	423	57	44	5.7	.922	E. Healy	37	321	12	24	0	3.89
SS	J. Glasscock	442	.269	1	45	201	334	59	36	5.4	**.901**	L. Shreve	35	298	11	24	0	4.63
3B	J. Denny	524	.261	12	63	158	214	44	14	**4.3**	.894	B. Burdick	20	176	10	10	0	2.81
RF	J. McGeachy	452	.219	0	30	194	27	16	5	2.0	.932							
CF	P. Hines	513	.281	4	58	255	13	26	3	2.4	.912							
LF	E. Seery	500	.220	5	50	258	19	18	6	2.2	.939							
C	D. Buckley	260	.273	5	22	213	60	31	5	6.0	.898							
UT	G. Myers	248	.238	2	16	235	85	32	6		.909							
C	C. Daily	202	.218	0	14	215	69	34	6	7.6	.893							
1B	J. Schoeneck	169	.237	0	20	501	16	14	19	11.1	.974							

Washington
W-48 L-86

Walter Hewett
W-10 L-29

Ted Sullivan
W-38 L-57

POS	Player	AB	BA	HR	RBI	PO	A	E	DP	TC/G	FA	Pitcher	G	IP	W	L	SV	ERA
1B	B. O'Brien	528	.225	9	66	1272	38	33	55	10.2	.975	H. O'Day	46	403	16	**29**	0	3.10
2B	A. Myers	502	.207	2	46	271	399	60	37	5.5	.918	J. Whitney	39	325	18	21	0	3.05
SS	G. Shoch	317	.183	2	24	84	168	28	6	5.4	.900	W. Widner	13	115	5	7	0	2.82
3B	J. Donnelly	428	.201	0	24	126	230	51	15	3.5	.875	G. Keefe	13	114	6	7	0	2.84
RF	E. Daily	453	.225	8	39	179	19	19	4	2.2	.912	F. Gilmore	12	96	1	9	0	6.59
CF	D. Hoy	503	.274	2	29	296	26	37	7	2.6	.897							
LF	W. Wilmot	473	.224	4	43	260	19	**41**	4	2.7	.872							
C	C. Mack	300	.187	3	29	361	**152**	47	8	7.1	.916							
SS	S. Fuller	170	.182	0	12	67	140	38	14	5.2	.845							
P	H. O'Day	166	.139	0	6	19	64	7	1	2.0	.922							
P	J. Whitney	141	.170	1	17	15	67	11	2	2.4	.882							

BATTING AND BASE RUNNING LEADERS

Batting Average
C. Anson, CHI	.344
J. Ryan, CHI	.332
K. Kelly, BOS	.318
D. Brouthers, DET	.307
B. Ewing, NY	.306

Slugging Average
J. Ryan, CHI	.515
C. Anson, CHI	.499
R. Connor, NY	.480
K. Kelly, BOS	.480
D. Johnston, BOS	.472

Home Runs
J. Ryan, CHI	16
R. Connor, NY	14
C. Anson, CHI	12
J. Denny, IND	12
D. Johnston, BOS	12

Total Bases
J. Ryan, CHI	283
D. Johnston, BOS	276
C. Anson, CHI	257
D. Brouthers, DET	242
R. Connor, NY	231

Runs Batted In
C. Anson, CHI	84
B. Nash, BOS	75
J. Rowe, DET	74
Williamson, CHI	73

Stolen Bases
D. Hoy, WAS	82
E. Seery, IND	80
B. Sunday, PIT	71
F. Pfeffer, CHI	64
J. Ryan, CHI	60

Hits
J. Ryan, CHI	182
C. Anson, CHI	177
D. Johnston, BOS	173
D. Brouthers, DET	160

Base on Balls
R. Connor, NY	73
D. Hoy, WAS	69
D. Brouthers, DET	68
Williamson, CHI	65

Home Run Percentage
J. Ryan, CHI	2.9
R. Connor, NY	2.9
C. Anson, CHI	2.3
J. Denny, IND	2.3

Runs Scored
D. Brouthers, DET	118
J. Ryan, CHI	115
D. Johnston, BOS	102
C. Anson, CHI	101

Doubles
D. Brouthers, DET	33
J. Ryan, CHI	33
D. Johnston, BOS	31
J. Denny, IND	27

Triples
D. Johnston, BOS	18
R. Connor, NY	17
B. Ewing, NY	15
B. Nash, BOS	15

PITCHING LEADERS

Winning Percentage
T. Keefe, NY	.745
P. Conway, DET	.682
B. Sanders, PHI	.655
G. Krock, CHI	.632
J. Clarkson, BOS	.623

Earned Run Average
T. Keefe, NY	1.74
B. Sanders, PHI	1.90
C. Buffinton, PHI	1.91
M. Welch, NY	1.93
B. Sowders, BOS	2.07

Wins
T. Keefe, NY	35
J. Clarkson, BOS	33
P. Conway, DET	30
E. Morris, PIT	29
C. Buffinton, PHI	28

Saves
G. Wood, PHI	2

Strikeouts
T. Keefe, NY	333
J. Clarkson, BOS	223
C. Getzien, DET	202
C. Buffinton, PHI	199
H. O'Day, WAS	186

Complete Games
E. Morris, PIT	54
J. Clarkson, BOS	53
T. Keefe, NY	51
P. Galvin, PIT	49
M. Welch, NY	47

Fewest Hits/9 Innings
T. Keefe, NY	6.55
C. Titcomb, NY	6.81
G. Keefe, WAS	6.87
M. Welch, NY	6.94

Shutouts
T. Keefe, NY	8
P. Galvin, PIT	6
C. Buffinton, PHI	6

Fewest Walks/9 Innings
B. Sanders, PHI	1.08
P. Galvin, PIT	1.09
G. Krock, CHI	1.19
C. Getzien, DET	1.20

Most Strikeouts/9 Inn.
T. Keefe, NY	6.90
C. Titcomb, NY	5.89
M. Baldwin, CHI	5.63
Van Haltren, CHI	5.09

Innings
J. Clarkson, BOS	483
E. Morris, PIT	480
P. Galvin, PIT	437
T. Keefe, NY	434

Games Pitched
E. Morris, PIT	55
J. Clarkson, BOS	54
T. Keefe, NY	51
P. Galvin, PIT	50

	W	L	PCT	GB	R	OR	Batting 2B	3B	HR	BA	SA	SB	Fielding E	DP	FA	Pitching CG	BB	SO	ShO	SV	ERA
New York	84	47	.641		659	**479**	130	76	55	.242	.336	314	432	76	.924	**136**	308	**724**	19	1	**1.96**
Chicago	77	58	.570	9	**734**	659	147	**95**	**77**	.260	**.383**	287	417	112	.927	123	308	588	13	1	2.96
Philadelphia	69	61	.531	14.5	535	509	151	46	16	.225	.290	246	424	70	.923	125	196	519	9	**3**	2.38
Boston	70	64	.522	15.5	669	619	167	89	56	.245	.351	293	494	91	.917	134	269	484	7	0	2.61
Detroit	68	63	.519	16	721	629	177	71	52	.263	.361	193	463	83	.919	130	223	522	9	1	2.74
Pittsburgh	66	68	.493	19.5	534	580	150	49	14	.227	.289	287	416	88	**.927**	135	**183**	367	13	0	2.67
Indianapolis	50	85	.370	36	603	731	**180**	33	33	.238	.313	**350**	449	84	.921	132	308	388	6	0	3.81
Washington	48	86	.358	37.5	482	731	98	49	31	.208	.271	331	494	69	.912	133	298	406	6	0	3.54
					4937	4937	1200	508	334	.239	.325	2301	3589	673	.921	1048	2093	3998	82	6	2.83

AMERICAN ASSOCIATION 1888

	POS	Player	AB	BA	HR	RBI	PO	A	E	DP	TC/G	FA	Pitcher	G	IP	W	L	SV	ERA
St. Louis	1B	C. Comiskey	576	.273	6	83	1293	46	42	52	10.4	.970	S. King	66	586	45	21	0	1.64
	2B	Y. Robinson	455	.231	3	53	197	256	53	18	5.0	.895	N. Hudson	39	333	25	10	0	2.54
W-92 L-43	SS	B. White	275	.175	2	30	132*	205	41	10	5.1	.892	Chamberlain	14	112	11	2	0	1.61
	3B	A. Latham	570	.265	2	31	178	287	62	19	4.0	.882	J. Devlin	11	90	6	5	0	3.19
Charlie Comiskey	RF	T. McCarthy	511	.274	1	68	243	44	21	12	2.4	.932							
	CF	H. Lyons	499	.194	4	63	237	32	33	4	2.5	.891							
	LF	T. O'Neill	529	.335	5	98	231	8	16	1	2.0	.937							
	C	J. Boyle	257	.241	1	23	381	123	37	11	7.7	.932							
	C	J. Milligan	219	.251	5	37	317	85	25	11	7.4	.941							
	P	S. King	207	.208	1	14	32	119	12	4	2.5	.926							
	PO	N. Hudson	196	.255	2	28	72	55	9	4		.934							
	SO	E. Herr	172	.267	3	43	63	71	19	4		.876							
Brooklyn	1B	D. Orr	394	.305	1	59	976	44	22	41	10.5	.979	B. Caruthers	44	392	29	15	0	2.39
	2B	J. Burdock	246	.122	1	8	172	223	42	23	6.2	.904	M. Hughes	40	363	25	13	0	2.13
W-88 L-52	SS	G. Smith	402	.214	3	61	155	352	94	29	5.8	.844	A. Terry	23	195	13	8	0	2.03
	3B	G. Pinckney	575	.271	4	52	189	234	48	14	3.3	.898	D. Foutz	23	176	12	7	0	2.51
Bill McGunnigle	RF	D. Foutz	563	.277	3	99	115	13	15	3	1.8	.895	A. Mays	18	161	9	9	0	2.80
	CF	P. Radford	308	.218	2	29	180	22	12	2	2.4	.944							
	LF	D. O'Brien	532	.280	4	65	231	15	18	1	1.9	.932							
	C	D. Bushong	253	.209	0	16	347	105	42	8	7.2	.915							
	OP	B. Caruthers	335	.230	5	53	127	97	26	5		.896							
	2B	McClellan	278	.205	0	21	145	149	31	23	5.8	.905							
	SO	O. Burns	204	.284	2	25	72	98	31	6		.846							
	C	B. Clark	150	.240	1	20	197	61	36	6	8.2	.878							
Philadelphia	1B	H. Larkin	546	.269	7	101	1218	36	42	44	10.6	.968	E. Seward	57	519	35	19	0	2.01
	2B	L. Bierbauer	535	.267	0	80	342	399	68	39	6.7	.916	G. Weyhing	47	404	28	18	0	2.25
W-81 L-52	SS	B. Gleason	499	.224	0	61	112	370	80	32	4.6	.858	M. Mattimore	26	221	15	10	0	3.38
	3B	D. Lyons	456	.296	6	83	159	193	49	11	3.6	.878							
Bill Sharsig	RF	T. Poorman	383	.227	2	44	115	8	14	1	1.4	.898							
	CF	C. Welch	549	.282	1	61	272	23	15	6	2.3	.952							
	LF	H. Stovey	530	.287	9	65	204	12	13	4	1.9	.943							
	C	W. Robinson	254	.244	1	31	428	143	38	5	9.4	.938							
	P	E. Seward	225	.142	2	14	24	125	19	4	2.9	.887							
	P	G. Weyhing	184	.217	1	14	22	93	17	1	2.8	.871							
	C	G. Townsend	161	.155	0	12	225	76	31	2	7.9	.907							
	PO	M. Mattimore	142	.268	0	12	32	71	10	6		.912							
Cincinnati	1B	L. Reilly	527	.321	13	103	1264	42	31	73	11.4	.977	L. Viau	42	388	27	14	0	2.65
	2B	B. McPhee	458	.240	4	51	369	365	47	65	7.2	.940	T. Mullane	44	380	26	16	1	2.84
W-80 L-54	SS	F. Fennelly	448	.196	2	56	150	419*	94*	37*	5.9	.858	E. Smith	40	348	22	17	0	2.74
	3B	H. Carpenter	551	.267	3	67	142	286	66	15	3.6	.866							
Gus Schmelz	RF	H. Nicol	548	.239	1	35	188	17	9	4	1.7	.958							
	CF	P. Corkhill	490	.271	1	74	255*	17	12	5	2.4*	.958*							
	LF	W. Tebeau	411	.229	3	51	195	20	21	3	2.0	.911							
	C	J. Keenan	313	.233	1	40	356	114	29	7	7.2	.942							
	C	K. Baldwin	271	.218	1	25	350	107	41	6	7.7	.918							
	P	T. Mullane	175	.251	1	16	22	81	13	1	2.6	.888							
	P	L. Viau	149	.087	0	8	18	78	9	0	2.5	.914							
	S2	H. Kappel	143	.259	1	15	47	89	38	9		.782							
Baltimore	1B	T. Tucker	520	.287	6	61	1354	59	36	64	11.2	.975	Cunningham	51	453	22	29	0	3.39
	2B	B. Greenwood	409	.191	0	29	158	243	38	17	5.1	.913	M. Kilroy	40	321	17	21	0	4.04
W-57 L-80	SS	J. Farrell	398	.204	3	36	75	173	27	11	5.1	.902	P. Smith	35	292	14	19	0	3.61
	3B	B. Shindle	514	.208	1	53	218	340	47	26	4.5	.922							
Billy Barnie	RF	B. Purcell	406	.236	2	39	145	9	16	3	1.7	.906							
	CF	M. Griffin	542	.256	0	46	274	27	20	6	2.3	.938							
	LF	O. Burns	325	.298	4	42	97	3	17	1	2.1	.855							
	C	C. Fulmer	166	.187	0	10	237	42	30	5	6.9	.903							
	OS	J. Sommer	297	.219	0	35	107	105	29	13		.880							
	UT	J. O'Brien	196	.224	0	18	286	43	26	9		.927							
	P	Cunningham	177	.186	1	9	20	106	25	3	3.0	.834							
	OF	W. Goldsby	165	.236	0	14	53	3	6	0	1.4	.903							
	P	M. Kilroy	145	.179	0	19	17	60	6	2	2.1	.928							
	C	S. Trott	108	.278	0	22	156	32	19	4	7.7	.908							
Cleveland	1B	J. Faatz	470	.264	0	51	1171	39	13	50	10.2	.989	J. Bakely	61	533	25	33	0	2.97
	2B	C. Stricker	493	.233	1	33	387	361	57	58	6.6	.929	D. O'Brien	30	259	11	19	0	3.30
W-50 L-82	SS	E. McKean	548	.299	6	68	120	240	36	13	5.1	.909	B. Crowell	18	151	5	13	0	5.79
	3B	G. Alberts	364	.206	1	48	68	103	20	9	3.9	.895							
Jimmy Williams	RF	E. Hogan	269	.227	0	24	104	8	13	1	1.6	.896							
W-20 L-44	CF	P. Hotaling	403	.251	0	55	170	10	25	7	2.1	.878							
	LF	B. Gilks	484	.229	1	63	136	15	16	2	1.9	.904							
Tom Loftus	C	C. Zimmer	212	.241	0	22	311	111	40	6	7.8	.913							
W-30 L-38	OF	Goodfellow	269	.245	0	29	93	8	16	1	1.9	.863							
	C	P. Snyder	237	.215	0	14	308	130	48	11	8.4	.901							
	3B	J. McGlone	203	.182	1	22	70	93	44	5	4.3	.787							
	P	J. Bakely	194	.134	1	9	21	114	18	3	2.5	.882							

AMERICAN ASSOCIATION 1888, cont.

	POS	Player	AB	BA	HR	RBI	PO	A	E	DP	TC/G	FA	Pitcher	G	IP	W	L	SV	ERA
Louisville	1B	S. Smith	206	.238	1	31	568	22	18	15	10.5	.970	T. Ramsey	40	342	8	30	0	3.42
	2B	R. Mack	446	.217	3	34	307	344	67	35	6.4	.907	S. Stratton	33	270	10	17	0	3.64
W-48 L-87	SS	B. White	198	.278	1	30	52*	130	41	5	5.9	.816	G. Hecker	28	223	8	17	0	3.39
	3B	J. Werrick	413	.215	0	51	96	170	62	9	3.7	.811	Chamberlain	24	196	14	9	0	2.53
Honest John Kelly	RF	C. Wolf	538	.286	0	67	113	19	17	4	1.8	.886	J. Ewing	21	191	8	13	0	2.83
W-10 L-29	CF	P. Browning	383	.313	3	72	174	16	24	8	2.2	.888							
	LF	H. Collins	485	.307	2	50	175	20	24	6	2.7	.890							
Mordecai Davidson	C	P. Cook	185	.184	0	13	221	81	35	7	6.4	.896							
W-1 L-2	OC	J. Kerins	319	.235	2	41	308	65	47	5		.888							
	OP	S. Stratton	249	.257	1	29	66	70	17	1		.889							
John Kerins	UT	G. Hecker	211	.227	0	29	305	57	25	12		.935							
W-3 L-4	OC	F. Vaughn	189	.196	1	21	164	49	28	6		.884							
	C	L. Cross	181	.227	0	15	202	60	20	3	7.6	.929							
Mordecai Davidson	P	T. Ramsey	142	.120	0	9	8	57	18	1	2.1	.783							
W-34 L-52																			
Kansas City	1B	B. Phillips	509	.236	1	56	**1476**	55	32	66	12.1	.980	H. Porter	55	474	18	**37**	0	4.16
	2B	S. Barkley	482	.216	3	51	341	314	43	44	6.0	.938	T. Sullivan	24	215	8	16	0	3.40
W-43 L-89	SS	H. Easterday	401	.190	3	37	120	459	73	30	5.7	**.888**	B. Fagan	17	142	5	11	0	5.69
	3B	J. Davis	491	.267	3	61	155	334	**91**	27	5.1	.843	F. Hoffman	12	104	3	9	0	2.77
Dave Rowe	RF	M. Cline	293	.235	0	19	91	22	15	4	1.8	.883	S. Toole	12	92	5	6	0	6.68
W-14 L-36	CF	J. McTamany	516	.246	4	41	245	27	26	5	2.3	.913							
	LF	M. Allen	136	.213	0	10	72	9	6	1	2.5	.931							
Sam Barkley	C	J. Donahue	337	.234	1	28	282	106	42	9	6.4	.902							
W-21 L-36	OC	L. Daniels	218	.202	1	28	159	67	34	7		.869							
	P	H. Porter	195	.144	0	10	11	**133**	16	3	2.9	.900							
Bill Watkins	UT	F. Hankinson	155	.174	1	20	72	84	18	12		.897							
W-8 L-17																			

BATTING AND BASE RUNNING LEADERS

Batting Average
T. O'Neill, STL	.335
L. Reilly, CIN	.321
P. Browning, LOU	.313
H. Collins, BKN, LOU	.307
D. Orr, BKN	.305

Slugging Average
L. Reilly, CIN	.501
H. Stovey, PHI	.460
T. O'Neill, STL	.446
O. Burns, BAL, BKN	.441
P. Browning, LOU	.439

Home Runs
L. Reilly, CIN	13
H. Stovey, PHI	9
H. Larkin, PHI	7

Total Bases
L. Reilly, CIN	264
H. Stovey, PHI	244
T. O'Neill, STL	236
O. Burns, BAL, BKN	233
E. McKean, CLE	233

Runs Batted In
L. Reilly, CIN	103
L. Reilly, CIN	101
D. Foutz, BKN	99
T. O'Neill, STL	98
P. Corkhill, BKN, CIN	93

Stolen Bases
A. Latham, STL	109
H. Nicol, CIN	103
C. Welch, PHI	95
T. McCarthy, STL	93
H. Stovey, PHI	87

Hits
T. O'Neill, STL	177
L. Reilly, CIN	169
E. McKean, CLE	164
H. Collins, BKN, LOU	162

Base on Balls
Y. Robinson, STL	116
F. Fennelly, CIN, PHI	72
J. McTamany, KC	67
H. Nicol, CIN	67

Home Run Percentage
L. Reilly, CIN	2.5
H. Stovey, PHI	1.7
B. Caruthers, BKN	1.5
D. Lyons, PHI	1.3

Runs Scored
G. Pinckney, BKN	134
H. Collins, BKN, LOU	133
H. Stovey, PHI	127
C. Welch, PHI	125

Doubles
H. Collins, BKN, LOU	31
L. Reilly, CIN	28
C. Wolf, LOU	28
H. Larkin, PHI	28

Triples
H. Stovey, PHI	20
O. Burns, BAL, BKN	15
E. McKean, CLE	15
L. Reilly, CIN	14

PITCHING LEADERS

Winning Percentage
N. Hudson, STL	.714
Chamberlain, LOU, STL	.694
S. King, STL	.682
B. Caruthers, BKN	.659
L. Viau, CIN	.659

Earned Run Average
S. King, STL	1.64
E. Seward, PHI	2.01
A. Terry, BKN	2.03
M. Hughes, BKN	2.13
Chamberlain, LOU, STL	2.19

Wins
S. King, STL	45
E. Seward, PHI	35
B. Caruthers, BKN	29
G. Weyhing, PHI	28
L. Viau, CIN	27

Saves
T. Mullane, CIN	1
P. Corkhill, BKN, CIN	1
B. Gilks, CLE	1

Strikeouts
E. Seward, PHI	272
S. King, STL	258
T. Ramsey, LOU	228
J. Bakely, CLE	212
G. Weyhing, PHI	204

Complete Games
S. King, STL	64
J. Bakely, CLE	60
E. Seward, PHI	57
H. Porter, KC	53
Cunningham, BAL	50

Fewest Hits/9 Innings
A. Terry, BKN	6.69
S. King, STL	6.72
E. Seward, PHI	6.73
Chamberlain, LOU, STL	6.95

Shutouts
E. Seward, PHI	6
S. King, STL	6
N. Hudson, STL	5
E. Smith, CIN	5

Fewest Walks/9 Innings
S. King, STL	1.17
B. Caruthers, BKN	1.22
N. Hudson, STL	1.59
J. Ewing, LOU	1.60

Most Strikeouts/9 Inn.
A. Terry, BKN	6.37
T. Ramsey, LOU	5.99
Chamberlain, LOU, STL	5.14
P. Smith, BAL, PHI	4.90

Innings
S. King, STL	586
J. Bakely, CLE	533
E. Seward, PHI	519
H. Porter, KC	474

Games Pitched
S. King, STL	66
J. Bakely, CLE	61
E. Seward, PHI	57
H. Porter, KC	55

	W	L	PCT	GB	R	OR	Batting 2B	3B	HR	BA	SA	SB	Fielding E	DP	FA	Pitching CG	BB	SO	ShO	SV	ERA
St. Louis	92	43	.681		789	**501**	149	47	**36**	.250	.324	468	**430**	73	**.924**	132	**225**	517	12	0	**2.09**
Brooklyn	88	52	.629	6.5	758	584	172	70	25	.242	.321	334	507	88	.917	**138**	285	577	9	0	2.33
Philadelphia	81	52	.609	10	**827**	594	**183**	89	31	.250	**.344**	434	477	73	.918	133	324	596	**13**	0	2.41
Cincinnati	80	54	.597	11.5	745	628	132	82	32	.242	.323	**469**	458	100	.923	132	310	539	10	**2**	2.73
Baltimore	57	80	.416	36	653	779	162	70	18	.229	.306	326	461	88	.920	130	419	525	3	0	3.78
Cleveland	50	82	.379	40.5	651	839	128	59	12	.234	.295	353	490	87	.915	131	389	500	6	1	3.72
Louisville	48	87	.356	44	689	870	**183**	67	14	.241	.315	318	611	75	.900	128	281	**599**	6	0	3.25
Kansas City	43	89	.326	47.5	579	896	142	61	17	.218	.286	257	507	95	.914	128	401	381	4	0	4.29
					5691	5691	1251	545	185	.238	.315	2959	3941	679	.916	1057	2634	4234	63	3	3.06

NATIONAL LEAGUE 1889

	POS	Player	AB	BA	HR	RBI	PO	A	E	DP	TC/G	FA	Pitcher	G	IP	W	L	SV	ERA
New York W-83 L-43 Jim Mutrie	1B	R. Connor	496	.317	13	130	1265	32	30	68	10.1	.977	M. Welch	45	375	27	12	2	3.02
	2B	Richardson	497	.280	7	100	332	416	53	60	6.4	.934	T. Keefe	47	364	28	13	1	3.31
	SS	M. Ward	479	.299	1	67	229	319	68	38	5.7	.890	C. Crane	29	230	14	10	0	3.68
	3B	A. Whitney	473	.218	1	59	160	265	57	27	3.7	.882	H. O'Day	10	78	9	1	0	4.27
	RF	M. Tiernan	499	.335	11	73	179	19	23	2	1.8	.896							
	CF	G. Gore	488	.305	7	54	239	21	41	5	2.5	.864							
	LF	J. O'Rourke	502	.321	3	81	165	18	22	2	1.6	.893							
	C	B. Ewing	407	.327	4	87	524	149	45	10	7.4	.937							
	P	M. Welch	156	.192	0	12	13	59	4	2	1.7	.947							
	P	T. Keefe	149	.154	0	8	10	78	8	3	2.0	.917							
	C	W. Brown	139	.259	1	29	138	38	32	5	5.6	.846							
Boston W-83 L-45 Jim Hart	1B	D. Brouthers	485	**.373**	7	118	1243	58	35	**78**	10.6	.974	J. Clarkson	**73**	**620**	**49**	19	1	**2.73**
	2B	Richardson	536	.304	7	79	246	310	46	44	7.0	.924	O. Radbourn	33	277	20	11	0	3.67
	SS	J. Quinn	444	.261	2	69	67	167	38	19	4.3	.860	K. Madden	22	178	10	10	1	4.40
	3B	B. Nash	481	.274	3	76	205	274	50	25	4.1	.905							
	RF	K. Kelly	507	.294	9	78	155	24	32	4	1.9	.848							
	CF	D. Johnston	539	.228	5	67	267	22	26	6	2.4	.917							
	LF	T. Brown	362	.232	2	24	169	13	20	1	2.2	.901							
	C	C. Bennett	247	.231	4	28	419	74	23	9	6.3	**.955**							
	UT	C. Ganzel	275	.265	1	43	292	87	30	19		.927							
	P	J. Clarkson	262	.206	2	23	36	172	27	8	3.2	.885							
	SS	P. Smith	208	.260	0	32	121	170	36*	23	5.5	.890							
Chicago W-67 L-65 Cap Anson	1B	C. Anson	518	.311	7	117	**1409**	**79**	27	73	11.3	**.982**	Hutchinson	37	318	16	17	0	3.54
	2B	F. Pfeffer	531	.228	7	79	452	483	56	69	7.4	.943	J. Tener	35	287	15	15	0	3.64
	SS	Williamson	173	.237	1	30	48	130	33	7	4.5	.844	F. Dwyer	32	276	16	13	0	3.59
	3B	T. Burns	525	.242	4	66	**225**	**301**	72	**30**	4.4	.880	A. Gumbert	31	246	16	13	0	3.62
	RF	H. Duffy	**584**	.295	12	89	184	19	24	2	1.8	.894							
	CF	J. Ryan	576	.307	17	72	252	36	23	9	2.9	.926							
	LF	Van Haltren	543	.309	9	81	222	25	28	3	2.1	.898							
	C	D. Farrell	407	.248	11	75	344	119	46	3	6.7	.910							
	SS	C. Bastian	155	.135	0	10	63	153	19	9	5.2	.919							
	P	A. Gumbert	153	.288	7	29	17	44	6	1	2.2	.910							
	P	J. Tener	150	.273	1	19	22	69	7	1	2.8	.929							
Philadelphia W-63 L-64 Harry Wright	1B	S. Farrar	477	.268	3	58	1265	42	30	66	10.3	.978	C. Buffinton	47	380	28	16	0	3.24
	2B	A. Myers	305	.269	0	28	192	261	78*	33	7.1	.853	B. Sanders	44	350	19	18	1	3.55
	SS	B. Hallman	462	.253	2	60	237	337	67	39	**6.0**	.895	K. Gleason	29	205	9	15	0	5.58
	3B	J. Mulvey	544	.289	6	77	165	284	54	20	3.9	.893	D. Casey	20	153	6	10	0	3.77
	RF	S. Thompson	533	.296	**20**	111	173	19	21	7	1.7	.901							
	CF	J. Fogarty	499	.259	3	54	**302**	**42**	14	6	2.8	**.961**							
	LF	G. Wood	422	.251	5	53	164	9	16	1	2.1	.915							
	C	J. Clements	310	.284	4	35	380	77	42	7	6.4	.916							
	O2	E. Delahanty	246	.293	0	27	116	61	17	11		.912							
	C	P. Schriver	211	.265	1	19	233	76	27	4	7.0	.920							
	P	B. Sanders	169	.278	0	21	22	58	11	1	2.1	.879							
	P	C. Buffinton	154	.208	0	21	18	80	9	4	2.3	.916							
Pittsburgh W-61 L-71 Horace Phillips W-28 L-43 Fred Dunlap W-7 L-10 Ned Hanlon W-26 L-18	1B	J. Beckley	522	.301	9	97	1236	53	24	73	10.8	.982	H. Staley	49	420	21	**26**	1	3.51
	2B	F. Dunlap	451	.235	2	65	342	393	39	51	6.4	**.950**	P. Galvin	41	341	23	16	0	4.17
	SS	J. Rowe	317	.259	2	32	108	228	39	26	5.0	.896	E. Morris	21	170	6	13	0	4.13
	3B	W. Kuehne	390	.246	5	57	89	157	32	14	3.7	.885	B. Sowders	13	53	6	5	0	7.35
	RF	B. Sunday	321	.240	2	25	157	17	10	2	2.3	.946							
	CF	N. Hanlon	461	.239	2	37	277	18	26	2	2.8	.919							
	LF	A. Maul	257	.276	4	44	123	17	8	4	2.3	.946							
	C	D. Miller	422	.268	6	56	299	87	48	8	5.7	.889							
	CO	F. Carroll	318	.330	2	51	228	56	27	4		.913							
	OF	J. Fields	289	.311	2	43	97	7	17	2	2.0	.860							
	SS	P. Smith	258	.209	5	27	93	187	32*	21	5.4	.897							
	3B	D. White	225	.253	0	26	68	95	24	7	3.6	.872							
	P	H. Staley	186	.161	0	8	19	89	5	3	2.3	.956							
	P	P. Galvin	150	.187	0	16	20	72	11	6	2.5	.893							
Cleveland W-61 L-72 Tom Loftus	1B	J. Faatz	442	.231	2	38	1145	62	24	67	10.5	.981	D. O'Brien	41	347	22	17	0	4.15
	2B	C. Stricker	566	.251	1	47	434	429	63	65	6.9	.932	E. Beatin	36	318	20	15	0	3.57
	SS	E. McKean	500	.318	4	75	206	398	62	42	5.5	.907	J. Bakely	36	304	12	22	0	2.96
	3B	P. Tebeau	521	.282	8	76	185	287	54	26	3.9	.897	H. Gruber	25	205	7	16	1	3.64
	RF	P. Radford	487	.238	1	46	205	24	14	6	1.8	.942							
	CF	J. McAleer	447	.235	1	35	247	29	13	9	2.6	.955							
	LF	L. Twitchell	549	.275	4	95	220	10	21	0	1.9	.916							
	C	C. Zimmer	259	.259	1	21	315	131	33	10	5.9	.931							
	UT	B. Gilks	210	.238	0	18	172	54	9	9		.962							
	C	S. Sutcliffe	161	.248	1	21	179	70	30	3	7.5	.892							
	P	D. O'Brien	140	.250	0	18	25	70	7	3	2.5	.931							

NATIONAL LEAGUE 1889, cont.

	POS	Player	AB	BA	HR	RBI	PO	A	E	DP	TC/G	FA	Pitcher	G	IP	W	L	SV	ERA
Indianapolis	1B	P. Hines	486	.305	6	72	1090	57	**43**	66	10.9	.964	H. Boyle	46	379	21	23	0	3.92
	2B	C. Bassett	477	.245	4	68	322	451	52	67	6.5	.937	C. Getzien	45	349	18	22	1	4.54
W-59 L-75	SS	J. Glasscock	582	.352	7	85	**246**	478	67	60	6.0	.915	A. Rusie	33	225	12	10	0	5.32
	3B	J. Denny	578	.282	18	112	199	276	45	12	4.2	.913							
Frank Bancroft	RF	J. McGeachy	532	.267	2	63	189	36	20	8	1.9	.918							
W-25 L-43	CF	M. Sullivan	256	.285	4	35	133	9	14	4	2.4	.910							
	LF	E. Seery	526	.314	8	59	220	20	24	4	2.1	.909							
Jack Glasscock	C	D. Buckley	260	.258	8	41	182	53	33	2	4.9	.877							
W-34 L-32	C	C. Daily	219	.251	0	26	225	49	35	1	6.1	.887							
	OF	E. Andrews	173	.306	0	22	67	10	10	1	2.2	.885							
	P	H. Boyle	155	.245	1	17	17	51	3	0	1.5	.958							
	OC	G. Myers	149	.195	0	12	106	36	18	1		.888							
Washington	1B	J. Carney	273	.231	1	29	521	16	24	29	10.6	.957	A. Ferson	36	288	17	17	0	3.90
	2B	S. Wise	472	.250	4	62	170	225	36	26	6.0	.916	G. Haddock	33	276	11	19	0	4.20
W-41 L-83	SS	A. Irwin	313	.233	0	32	165	279	52	36	5.8	.895	G. Keefe	30	230	8	18	0	5.13
	3B	J. Irwin	228	.289	0	25	82	129	32	14	4.2	.868	H. O'Day	13	108	2	10	0	4.33
John Morrill	RF	E. Beecher	179	.296	0	30	61	7	11	1	2.0	.861	E. Healy	13	101	1	11	0	6.24
W-13 L-38	CF	D. Hoy	507	.274	0	39	255	29	35	4	2.5	.890							
	LF	W. Wilmot	432	.289	9	57	232	22	20	4	2.5	.927							
Arthur Irwin	C	T. Daly	250	.300	1	40	268	86	32	5	6.8	.917							
W-28 L-45	UT	C. Mack	386	.293	0	42	432	100	57	22		.903							
	3B	P. Sweeney	193	.228	1	23	67	83	37	6	4.0	.802							
	2B	A. Myers	176	.261	0	20	147	148	18*	26	6.8	.942							
	1B	J. Morrill	146	.185	2	16	369	18	8	15	9.9	.980							
	UT	S. Clark	145	.255	3	22	101	75	26	10		.871							

BATTING AND BASE RUNNING LEADERS

Batting Average
D. Brouthers, BOS .373
J. Glasscock, IND .352
C. Anson, CHI .342
M. Tiernan, NY .335
F. Carroll, PIT .330

Slugging Average
R. Connor, NY .528
J. Ryan, CHI .516
D. Brouthers, BOS .507
M. Tiernan, NY .501
S. Thompson, PHI .492

Home Runs
S. Thompson, PHI 20
J. Denny, IND 18
J. Ryan, CHI 17
R. Connor, NY 13
H. Duffy, CHI 12

Total Bases
J. Ryan, CHI 297
J. Glasscock, IND 272
R. Connor, NY 262
S. Thompson, PHI 262
H. Duffy, CHI 253

Runs Batted In
R. Connor, NY 130
D. Brouthers, BOS 118
C. Anson, CHI 117
J. Denny, IND 112
S. Thompson, PHI 111

Stolen Bases
J. Fogarty, PHI 99
K. Kelly, BOS 68
T. Brown, BOS 63
M. Ward, NY 62
J. Glasscock, IND 57

Hits
J. Glasscock, IND 205
J. Ryan, CHI 187
H. Duffy, CHI 182
Van Haltren, CHI 168

Base on Balls
M. Tiernan, NY 96
R. Connor, NY 93
P. Radford, CLE 91
C. Anson, CHI 86

Home Run Percentage
S. Thompson, PHI 3.8
J. Denny, IND 3.1
J. Ryan, CHI 3.0
D. Farrell, CHI 2.7

Runs Scored
M. Tiernan, NY 147
H. Duffy, CHI 144
J. Ryan, CHI 140
G. Gore, NY 132

Doubles
K. Kelly, BOS 41
J. Glasscock, IND 40
J. O'Rourke, NY 36
S. Thompson, PHI 36

Triples
W. Wilmot, WAS 19
R. Connor, NY 17
J. Fogarty, PHI 17
M. Tiernan, NY 14

PITCHING LEADERS

Winning Percentage
J. Clarkson, BOS .721
M. Welch, NY .692
T. Keefe, NY .683
O. Radbourn, BOS .645
C. Buffinton, PHI .614

Earned Run Average
J. Clarkson, BOS 2.73
J. Bakely, CLE 2.96
M. Welch, NY 3.02
C. Buffinton, PHI 3.24
T. Keefe, NY 3.31

Wins
J. Clarkson, BOS 49
T. Keefe, NY 28
M. Welch, NY 27
C. Buffinton, PHI 27
P. Galvin, PIT 23

Saves
B. Sowders, BOS, PIT 2
B. Bishop, CHI 2
M. Welch, NY 2

Strikeouts
J. Clarkson, BOS 284
T. Keefe, NY 209
H. Staley, PIT 159
C. Buffinton, PHI 153
C. Getzien, IND 139

Complete Games
J. Clarkson, BOS 68
H. Staley, PIT 46
D. O'Brien, CLE 39
M. Welch, NY 39

Fewest Hits/9 Innings
T. Keefe, NY 7.66
M. Welch, NY 8.16
J. Clarkson, BOS 8.55
C. Crane, NY 8.65

Shutouts
J. Clarkson, BOS 8
P. Galvin, PIT 4
Hutchinson, CHI 3
E. Beatin, CLE 3

Fewest Walks/9 Innings
P. Galvin, PIT 2.06
H. Boyle, IND 2.26
O. Radbourn, BOS 2.34
F. Dwyer, CHI 2.35

Most Strikeouts/9 Inn.
T. Keefe, NY 5.17
C. Crane, NY 5.09
A. Rusie, IND 4.36
E. Healy, CHI, WAS 4.35

Innings
J. Clarkson, BOS 620
H. Staley, PIT 420
C. Buffinton, PHI 380
H. Boyle, IND 379

Games Pitched
J. Clarkson, BOS 73
H. Staley, PIT 49
C. Buffinton, PHI 47
T. Keefe, NY 47

	W	L	PCT	GB	R	OR	2B	3B	HR	BA	SA	SB	E	DP	FA	CG	BB	SO	ShO	SV	ERA
										Batting				Fielding				Pitching			
New York	83	43	.659		**935**	708	207	**77**	53	**.282**	**.394**	292	437	90	.920	118	523	**542**	6	3	3.47
Boston	83	45	.648	1	826	**626**	196	53	43	.270	.363	331	413	105	.926	121	413	497	**10**	**4**	**3.36**
Chicago	67	65	.508	19	867	814	184	66	**79**	.263	.377	243	463	91	.923	123	408	434	4	2	3.73
Philadelphia	63	64	.496	20.5	742	748	215	52	44	.266	.362	269	466	92	.915	106	428	443	4	2	4.00
Pittsburgh	61	71	.462	25	726	801	209	65	42	.253	.351	231	385	94	.931	125	**374**	345	5	1	4.51
Cleveland	61	72	.459	25.5	656	720	131	59	25	.250	.319	237	**365**	**108**	**.936**	**132**	519	435	6	1	3.66
Indianapolis	59	75	.440	28	819	894	**228**	35	62	.278	.377	252	420	102	.926	109	420	408	3	2	4.85
Washington	41	83	.331	41	632	892	151	57	25	.251	.329	232	519	91	.904	113	527	388	1	0	4.68
					6203	6203	1521	464	373	.264	.359	2087	3468	773	.923	947	3612	3492	41	15	4.02

AMERICAN ASSOCIATION 1889

	POS	Player	AB	BA	HR	RBI	PO	A	E	DP	TC/G	FA	Pitcher	G	IP	W	L	SV	ERA
Brooklyn	1B	D. Foutz	553	.277	7	113	1371	33	30	65	10.7	.979	B. Caruthers	56	445	**40**	11	1	3.13
	2B	H. Collins	560	.266	2	73	385	410	61	56	6.2	.929	A. Terry	41	326	22	15	0	3.29
W-93 L-44	SS	G. Smith	446	.231	3	53	182	417	67	37	5.6	.899	T. Lovett	29	229	17	10	0	4.32
	3B	G. Pinckney	545	.246	4	82	183	278	53	19	3.7	**.897**	M. Hughes	20	153	9	8	0	4.35
Bill McGunnigle	RF	O. Burns	504	.304	5	100	139	23	14	5	1.6	.920							
	CF	P. Corkhill	537	.250	8	78	317	35	19	8	2.7	**.949**							
	LF	D. O'Brien	567	.300	5	80	255	14	28	5	2.2	.906							
	C	J. Visner	295	.258	8	68	198	72	40	7	5.8	.871							
	C	B. Clark	182	.275	0	22	275	86	54	4	7.8	.870							
	P	B. Caruthers	172	.250	2	31	29	95	4	4	2.3	.969							
	P	A. Terry	160	.300	2	26	24	86	4	2	2.8	.965							
St. Louis	1B	C. Comiskey	587	.286	3	102	1225	45	39	71	9.8	.970	S. King	56	458	33	17	1	3.14
	2B	Y. Robinson	452	.208	5	70	305	333	81	53	5.4	.887	Chamberlain	53	422	32	15	1	2.97
W-90 L-45	SS	S. Fuller	517	.226	0	51	240	459	67	46	5.5	**.913**	J. Stivetts	26	192	13	7	1	**2.25**
	3B	A. Latham	512	.246	4	49	197	249	59	22	4.4	.883							
Charlie Comiskey	RF	T. McCarthy	604	.291	2	63	229	38	32	11	2.1	.893							
	CF	C. Duffee	509	.244	15	86	296	**43**	23	7	**2.7**	.936							
	LF	T. O'Neill	534	.335	9	110	264	12	19	3	2.2	.936							
	C	J. Boyle	347	.245	4	42	378	108	27	11	6.4	.947							
	C	J. Milligan	273	.366	12	76	370	105	34	7	7.7	.933							
	P	S. King	189	.228	0	30	19	91	5	2	2.1	.957							
	P	Chamberlain	171	.199	2	31	15	67	7	0	1.7	.921							
Philadelphia	1B	H. Larkin	516	.318	3	74	1230	37	35	**88**	9.9	.973	G. Weyhing	54	449	30	21	0	2.95
	2B	L. Bierbauer	549	.304	7	105	**472**	406	55	80	**7.2**	.941	E. Seward	39	320	21	15	0	3.97
W-75 L-58	SS	F. Fennelly	513	.257	1	64	181	453	93	53	5.3	.872	S. McMahon	30	255	16	12	0	3.35
	3B	D. Lyons	510	.329	9	82	202	291	80	**29**	4.4	.860							
Bill Sharsig	RF	B. Purcell	507	.316	0	85	172	15	20	3	1.6	.903							
	CF	C. Welch	516	.271	0	39	282	29	26	10	2.7	.923							
	LF	H. Stovey	556	.308	**19**	119	287	38	37	9	2.6	.898							
	C	W. Robinson	264	.231	0	28	290	106	24	8	6.1	.943							
	C	L. Cross	199	.221	0	23	278	102	27	7	7.4	.934							
	P	G. Weyhing	191	.131	0	12	12	71	8	2	1.7	.912							
	P	E. Seward	143	.217	2	17	13	67	9	1	2.3	.899							
Cincinnati	1B	L. Reilly	427	.260	5	66	1143	30	19	76	10.9	**.984**	J. Duryea	53	401	32	19	1	2.56
	2B	B. McPhee	543	.269	5	57	429	**446**	50	**85**	6.9	**.946**	L. Viau	47	373	22	20	1	3.79
W-76 L-63	SS	O. Beard	558	.285	1	77	214	**537**	87	63	5.9	.896	T. Mullane	33	220	11	9	5	2.99
	3B	H. Carpenter	486	.261	0	63	143	207	69	18	3.5	.835	E. Smith	29	203	9	12	0	4.88
Gus Schmelz	RF	H. Nicol	474	.255	2	58	168	22	19	4	1.8	.918							
	CF	B. Holliday	563	.343	**19**	104	234	29	22	6	2.1	.923							
	LF	W. Tebeau	496	.252	7	70	241	18	33	3	2.2	.887							
	C	J. Keenan	300	.287	6	60	319	91	16	11	6.5	.962							
	C	K. Baldwin	223	.247	1	34	274	89	35	5	7.2	.912							
	UT	T. Mullane	196	.296	0	29	78	80	22	10		.878							
	OC	B. Earle	169	.266	4	31	157	31	34	5		.847							
	P	J. Duryea	162	.272	0	17	15	80	11	1	2.0	.896							
	P	L. Viau	147	.143	0	9	9	61	4	2	1.6	.946							
Baltimore	1B	T. Tucker	527	**.372**	5	99	1144	45	44	63	10.0	.964	M. Kilroy	59	481	29	25	0	2.85
	2B	R. Mack	519	.241	1	87	367	358	**83**	70	6.0	.897	F. Foreman	51	414	23	21	0	3.52
W-70 L-65	SS	J. Farrell	157	.210	1	26	65	131	24	13	5.2	.891	Cunningham	39	279	16	19	1	4.87
	3B	B. Shindle	567	.314	3	64	**225**	**323**	**88**	25	**4.6**	.862							
Billy Barnie	RF	J. Sommer	386	.220	1	36	172	24	15	7	2.0	.929							
	CF	M. Griffin	531	.279	4	48	246	17	26	5	2.7	.910							
	LF	J. Hornung	533	.229	1	78	250	32	27	10	2.3	.913							
	C	P. Tate	253	.182	1	27	306	75	25	3	6.5	.938							
	P	M. Kilroy	208	.274	1	26	25	139	**17**	4	3.1	.906							
	C	T. Quinn	194	.175	1	15	290	81	30	10	7.3	.925							
	P	F. Foreman	181	.144	1	11	9	72	14	1	1.9	.853							
	SS	W. Holland	143	.189	0	16	37	102	24	9	4.2	.853							
Columbus	1B	D. Orr	560	.327	4	87	1291	**61**	23	64	10.3	.983	M. Baldwin	63	514	27	**34**	1	3.61
	2B	B. Greenwood	414	.225	3	49	313	322	60	50	5.9	.914	W. Widner	41	294	12	20	1	5.20
W-60 L-78	SS	H. Easterday	324	.173	4	34	134	326	57	27	5.8	.890	H. Gastright	32	223	10	16	0	4.57
	3B	L. Marr	546	.306	1	75	111	151	44	13	4.6	.856	A. Mays	21	140	10	7	0	4.82
Al Buckenberger	RF	S. Johnson	459	.283	2	79	75	12	12	2	1.4	.879							
	CF	J. McTamany	529	.276	4	52	247	28	30	8	2.2	.902							
	LF	E. Daily	578	.256	3	70	212	27	**41**	4	2.1	.854							
	C	J. O'Connor	398	.269	4	60	**423**	128	26	7	6.9	**.955**							
	P	M. Baldwin	208	.188	2	25	**33**	91	13	1	2.2	.905							
	S3	H. Kappel	173	.272	3	21	69	128	40	7		.831							

AMERICAN ASSOCIATION 1889, *cont.*

	POS	Player	AB	BA	HR	RBI	PO	A	E	DP	TC/G	FA	Pitcher	G	IP	W	L	SV	ERA
Kansas City	1B	D. Stearns	560	.286	2	87	1398	56	49	75	11.1	.967	P. Swartzel	48	410	19	27	1	4.32
	2B	S. Barkley	176	.284	0	23	90	103	16	20	5.1	.923	J. Conway	41	335	19	19	0	3.25
W-55 L-82	SS	H. Long	574	.279	3	60	335	479	117	55	7.3	.874	J. Sowders	25	185	6	16	1	4.82
	3B	J. Davis	241	.266	0	30	93	140	57	14	4.7	.803	J. McCarty	15	120	8	6	0	3.91
Bill Watkins	RF	B. Hamilton	534	.301	3	77	202	20	37	6	1.9	.857	T. Sullivan	10	87	2	8	0	5.67
	CF	J. Burns	579	.304	5	97	323	11	32	4	2.7	.913							
	LF	J. Manning	506	.204	3	68	119	20	11	2	2.2	.927							
	C	C. Hoover	258	.248	1	25	266	105	34	8	6.1	.916							
	UT	J. Donahue	252	.234	0	32	187	100	46	7		.862							
	UT	J. Pickett	201	.224	0	12	77	44	23	4		.840							
	UT	B. Alvord	186	.231	0	18	66	140	43	17		.827							
	P	P. Swartzel	174	.144	0	20	19	145	11	6	3.6	.937							
	P	J. Conway	149	.208	0	12	10	85	7	2	2.5	.931							
Louisville	1B	G. Hecker	327	.284	1	36	7	32	3		.6	.929	R. Ehret	45	364	10	29	0	4.80
	2B	D. Shannon	498	.257	4	48	307	391	69	59	6.3	.910	J. Ewing	40	331	6	30	0	4.87
W-27 L-111	SS	P. Tomney	376	.213	4	38	229	454	114	57	7.1	.857	G. Hecker	17	151	5	11	0	5.59
	3B	H. Raymond	515	.239	0	47	206	261	60	23	4.1	.886	T. Ramsey	18	140	1	16	0	5.59
Dude Esterbrook	RF	C. Wolf	546	.291	3	57	159	16	10	2	2.1	.946	S. Stratton	19	134	3	13	1	3.23
W-2 L-8	CF	F. Weaver	499	.291	0	60	249	30	25	4	2.5	.918							
	LF	P. Browning	324	.256	2	32	152	12	22	4	2.2	.882							
Chicken Wolf	C	P. Cook	286	.227	0	15	293	138	35	6	6.3	.925							
W-14 L-51	UT	F. Vaughn	360	.239	3	45	441	121	51	18		.917							
	PO	R. Ehret	258	.252	1	31	36	101	22	3		.862							
Dan Shannon	UT	S. Stratton	229	.288	4	34	198	57	21	15		.924							
W-10 L-46																			
Jack Chapman																			
W-1 L-6																			

BATTING AND BASE RUNNING LEADERS

Batting Average
T. Tucker, BAL	.372
B. Holliday, CIN	.343
T. O'Neill, STL	.335
D. Lyons, PHI	.329
D. Orr, COL	.327

Slugging Average
H. Stovey, PHI	.527
B. Holliday, CIN	.519
T. Tucker, BAL	.484
T. O'Neill, STL	.478
D. Lyons, PHI	.469

Home Runs
H. Stovey, PHI	19
B. Holliday, CIN	19
C. Duffee, STL	15
J. Milligan, STL	12
D. Lyons, PHI	9
T. O'Neill, STL	9

Winning Percentage
B. Caruthers, BKN	.784
Chamberlain, STL	.681
S. King, STL	.660
J. Stivetts, STL	.650
T. Lovett, BKN	.630

Earned Run Average
J. Stivetts, STL	2.25
J. Duryea, CIN	2.56
M. Kilroy, BAL	2.85
G. Weyhing, PHI	2.95
Chamberlain, STL	2.97

Wins
B. Caruthers, BKN	40
S. King, STL	33
Chamberlain, STL	32
J. Duryea, CIN	32
G. Weyhing, PHI	30

Total Bases
H. Stovey, PHI	293
B. Holliday, CIN	292
T. Tucker, BAL	255
T. O'Neill, STL	255
D. Orr, COL	250

Runs Batted In
H. Stovey, PHI	119
D. Foutz, BKN	113
T. O'Neill, STL	110
L. Bierbauer, PHI	105
B. Holliday, CIN	104

Stolen Bases
B. Hamilton, KC	117
D. O'Brien, BKN	91
H. Long, KC	89
N. Nicol, CIN	80
A. Latham, STL	69

Saves
T. Mullane, CIN	5

Strikeouts
M. Baldwin, COL	368
M. Kilroy, BAL	217
G. Weyhing, PHI	213
Chamberlain, STL	202
S. King, STL	188

Complete Games
M. Kilroy, BAL	55
M. Baldwin, COL	54
G. Weyhing, PHI	50
S. King, STL	47
B. Caruthers, BKN	46

Hits
T. Tucker, BAL	196
B. Holliday, CIN	193
D. Orr, COL	183
T. O'Neill, STL	179

Base on Balls
Y. Robinson, STL	118
J. McTamany, COL	116
M. Griffin, BAL	91
B. Hamilton, KC	87

Home Run Percentage
H. Stovey, PHI	3.4
B. Holliday, CIN	3.4
C. Duffee, STL	2.9
J. Keenan, CIN	2.0

Fewest Hits/9 Innings
J. Stivetts, STL	7.18
G. Weyhing, PHI	7.66
A. Terry, BKN	7.87
F. Foreman, BAL	7.91

Shutouts
B. Caruthers, BKN	7
M. Baldwin, COL	6
F. Foreman, BAL	5
M. Kilroy, BAL	5

Fewest Walks/9 Innings
B. Caruthers, BKN	2.10
J. Conway, KC	2.42
S. King, STL	2.46
T. Lovett, BKN	2.55

Runs Scored
M. Griffin, BAL	152
H. Stovey, PHI	152
D. O'Brien, BKN	146
B. Hamilton, KC	144

Doubles
C. Welch, PHI	39
H. Stovey, PHI	37
D. Lyons, PHI	36
T. O'Neill, STL	33

Triples
L. Marr, COL	15
M. Griffin, BAL	14
H. Stovey, PHI	14
O. Beard, CIN	14

Most Strikeouts/9 Inn.
J. Stivetts, STL	6.71
M. Baldwin, COL	6.45
A. Terry, BKN	5.13
J. Sowders, KC	5.06

Innings
M. Baldwin, COL	514
M. Kilroy, BAL	481
S. King, STL	458
G. Weyhing, PHI	449

Games Pitched
M. Baldwin, COL	63
M. Kilroy, BAL	59
S. King, STL	56
B. Caruthers, BKN	56

PITCHING LEADERS

	W	L	PCT	GB	R	OR	2B	3B	HR	BA	SA	SB	E	DP	FA	CG	BB	SO	ShO	SV	ERA
Brooklyn	93	44	.679		995	706	188	79	48	.263	.365	389	421	92	.928	120	400	471	10	1	3.61
St. Louis	90	45	.667	2	957	680	211	64	58	.266	.370	336	438	100	.925	121	413	617	7	3	3.00
Philadelphia	75	58	.564	16	880	787	239	65	43	.275	.377	252	465	120	.921	130	509	479	9	1	3.53
Cincinnati	76	63	.547	18	897	769	197	96	52	.270	.382	462	440	121	.926	114	475	562	3	8	3.50
Baltimore	70	65	.519	22	791	795	155	68	20	.254	.328	311	536	104	.907	128	424	540	10	1	3.56
Columbus	60	78	.435	33.5	779	924	171	95	36	.259	.356	304	497	92	.916	114	551	610	9	4	4.39
Kansas City	55	82	.401	38	852	1031	162	77	17	.254	.328	472	611	109	.900	128	457	447		2	4.36
Louisville	27	111	.196	66.5	632	1091	170	75	22	.252	.330	203	584	117	.907	127	475	451	2	1	4.81
					6783	6783	1493	619	296	.262	.354	2729	3992	855	.916	982	3704	4177	50	21	3.84

NATIONAL LEAGUE 1890

	POS	Player	AB	BA	HR	RBI	PO	A	E	DP	TC/G	FA	Pitcher	G	IP	W	L	SV	ERA
Brooklyn	1B	D. Foutz	509	.303	5	98	1192	39	28	63	11.1	.978	T. Lovett	44	372	30	11	0	2.78
	2B	H. Collins	510	.278	3	69	298	420	42	56	5.9	.945	A. Terry	46	370	26	16	0	2.94
W-86 L-43	SS	G. Smith	481	.191	1	47	232	468	74	49	6.0	.904	B. Caruthers	37	300	23	11	0	3.09
	3B	G. Pinckney	485	.309	7	83	179	222	29	15	3.4	.933							
Bill McGunnigle	RF	O. Burns	472	.284	13	128	137	23	10	4	1.5	.941							
	CF	D. O'Brien	350	.314	2	63	176	14	8	2	2.3	.960							
	LF	P. Corkhill	204	.225	1	21	122	6	3	1	2.7	.977							
	C	T. Daly	292	.243	5	43	332	72	20	7	6.1	.953							
	OP	A. Terry	363	.278	4	59	123	79	19	6		.914							
	OP	B. Caruthers	238	.265	1	29	65	83	20	2		.881							
	P	T. Lovett	164	.201	1	20	10	79	10	3	2.3	.899							
	C	B. Clark	151	.219	0	15	164	40	40	5	5.8	.836							
Chicago	1B	C. Anson	504	.312	7	107	1345	**49**	31	61	10.6	.978	Hutchinson	**71**	**603**	**42**	25	2	2.70
	2B	B. Glenalvin	250	.268	4	26	128	194	25	20	5.3	.928	P. Luby	34	268	20	9	1	3.19
W-84 L-53	SS	J. Cooney	574	.272	4	52	237	452	47	50	5.5	**.936**	E. Stein	20	161	12	6	0	3.81
	3B	T. Burns	538	.277	6	86	188	290	54	25	3.8	.898	M. Sullivan	12	96	5	6	0	4.59
Cap Anson	RF	J. Andrews	202	.188	3	17	80	10	10	1	1.9	.900	R. Coughlin	11	95	4	6	0	4.26
	CF	W. Wilmot	571	.278	14	99	320	26	23	4	2.7	.938							
	LF	C. Carroll	582	.285	7	65	265	28	20	7	2.3	.936							
	C	M. Kittridge	333	.201	3	35	458	113	34	9	6.3	.944							
	O2	H. Earl	384	.247	6	51	144	145	42	11		.873							
	P	Hutchinson	261	.203	2	27	44	128	14	5	2.6	.925							
	C	T. Nagle	144	.271	1	11	161	25	12	0	6.0	.939							
	OF	E. Foster	105	.248	5	23	69	2	1	0	2.7	.986							
Philadelphia	1B	A. McCauley	418	.244	1	42	1053	26	30	68	9.9	.973	K. Gleason	60	506	38	17	2	2.63
	2B	A. Myers	487	.277	2	81	347	352	38	**62**	6.3	.948	T. Vickery	46	382	24	22	0	3.44
W-78 L-54	SS	B. Allen	456	.226	2	57	**337**	**500**	69	**68**	6.8	.924	P. Smith	24	204	8	12	0	4.28
	3B	E. Mayer	484	.242	1	70	173	224	55	22	3.9	.878							
Harry Wright	RF	S. Thompson	549	.313	4	102	170	29	13	5	1.6	.939							
W-14 L-8	CF	E. Burke	430	.263	4	50	202	23	24	4	2.6*	.904							
	LF	B. Hamilton	496	.325	2	49	232	23	**34**	4	2.3	.882							
Jack Clements	C	J. Clements	381	.315	7	74	**503**	92	35	12	**6.9**	.944							
W-13 L-6	P	K. Gleason	224	.210	0	17	24	95	8	4	2.1	.937							
	UT	P. Schriver	223	.274	0	35	272	63	33	12		.910							
Al Reach	P	T. Vickery	159	.208	0	11	17	71	**20**	3	2.3	.815							
W-4 L-7	UT	B. Grey	128	.242	0	21	69	42	18	4		.860							
Bob Allen																			
W-25 L-10																			
Harry Wright																			
W-22 L-23																			
Cincinnati	1B	L. Reilly	553	.300	6	86	**1392**	38	**33**	**77**	11.1	.977	B. Rhines	46	401	28	17	0	**1.95**
	2B	B. McPhee	528	.256	3	39	**404**	**431**	51	**62**	6.7	.942	J. Duryea	33	274	16	12	0	2.92
W-77 L-55	SS	O. Beard	492	.268	3	72	145	419	65	43	5.6	.897	T. Mullane	25	209	12	10	1	2.24
	3B	A. Latham	164	.250	0	15	54	103	27	10	4.5	.853	F. Foreman	25	198	13	10	0	3.95
Tom Loftus	RF	L. Marr	527	.300	2	73	68	12	6	3	1.3	.930	L. Viau	13	90	7	5	0	4.50
	CF	B. Holliday	518	.270	4	75	253	20	15	5	2.2	.948							
	LF	J. Knight	481	.312	4	67	224	11	19	0	2.0	.925							
	C	Harrington	236	.246	1	23	345	73	19	3	6.7	.957							
	UT	T. Mullane	286	.276	0	34	114	116	37	7		.861							
	C	J. Keenan	202	.139	3	19	244	63	16	5	6.5	.950							
	OF	H. Nicol	186	.210	0	19	62	8	6	3	1.7	.921							
	P	B. Rhines	154	.188	0	11	23	77	7	3	2.3	.935							
Boston	1B	T. Tucker	539	.295	1	62	1341	39	29	53	10.7	**.979**	K. Nichols	48	427	27	19	0	2.21
	2B	P. Smith	463	.229	1	53	234	401	57	41	5.2	.918	J. Clarkson	44	383	25	18	0	3.27
W-76 L-57	SS	H. Long	431	.251	8	52	230	352	66	40	6.4	.898	C. Getzien	40	350	23	17	0	3.19
	3B	C. McGarr	487	.236	1	51	151	228	27	13	3.5	**.933**							
Frank Selee	RF	S. Brodie	514	.296	0	67	225	19	12	6	1.9	.953							
	CF	P. Hines	273	.264	2	48	114	4	16	2	1.9	.881							
	LF	M. Sullivan	505	.285	6	61	241	13	13	1	2.2	.951							
	C	C. Bennett	281	.214	3	40	448	90	23	8	6.6	**.959**							
	UT	B. Lowe	207	.280	2	21	103	82	11	2		.944							
	UT	L. Hardie	185	.227	3	17	171	49	28	5		.887							
	P	K. Nichols	174	.247	0	23	14	85	13	1	2.3	.884							
	P	J. Clarkson	173	.249	2	26	21	72	14	3	2.4	.869							
	CO	C. Ganzel	163	.270	0	24	144	28	7	4		.961							
	P	C. Getzien	147	.231	2	25	14	63	19	2	2.4	.802							
	OF	P. Donovan	140	.257	0	9	45	4	6	1	1.7	.891							

NATIONAL LEAGUE 1890, cont.

	POS	Player	AB	BA	HR	RBI	PO	A	E	DP	TC/G	FA	Pitcher	G	IP	W	L	SV	ERA
New York	1B	L. Whistler	170	.288	2	29	490	10	9	28	11.3	.982	A. Rusie	67	549	29	34	1	2.56
	2B	C. Bassett	410	.239	0	54	201	332	27	43	5.6	**.952**	M. Welch	37	292	17	13	0	2.99
W-63 L-68	SS	J. Glasscock	512	**.336**	1	66	275	421	69	46	6.2	.910	J. Sharrott	25	184	11	10	0	2.89
	3B	J. Denny	437	.213	3	42	165	210	47	16	4.0	.889	J. Burkett	21	118	3	10	0	5.57
Jim Mutrie	RF	J. Burkett	401	.309	4	60	108	23	28	4	1.8	.824							
	CF	M. Tiernan	553	.304	13	59	210	13	26	5	1.9	.896							
	LF	J. Hornung	513	.238	0	65	110	12	9	3	1.7	.931							
	C	D. Buckley	266	.256	2	26	365	93	34	4	7.9	.931							
	UT	A. Clarke	395	.225	0	49	288	138	55	11		.886							
	P	A. Rusie	284	.278	0	28	25	**129**	20	5	2.6	.885							
	1B	Esterbrook	197	.289	0	29	430	13	7	24	10.0	.984							
	OF	J. Henry	144	.243	0	16	56	4	9	1	1.9	.870							
Cleveland	1B	P. Veach	238	.235	0	32	634	40	20	37	10.8	.971	E. Beatin	54	474	22	**31**	0	3.83
	2B	J. Ardner	323	.223	0	35	205	257	40	42	6.0	.920	J. Wadsworth	20	170	2	16	0	5.20
	SS	E. McKean	530	.296	7	61	266	433	**75**	46	5.8	.903	C. Young	17	148	9	6	0	3.47
W-44 L-88	3B	W. Smalley	502	.213	0	42	**221**	**327**	64	**27**	4.5	.895	E. Lincoln	15	118	3	11	0	4.42
	RF	V. Dailey	246	.289	0	32	103	13	19	2	2.1	.859	L. Viau	13	107	4	9	0	3.36
Gus Schmelz	CF	G. Davis	526	.264	6	73	282	**35**	18	9	2.5	.946							
W-21 L-55	LF	B. Gilks	544	.213	0	41	237	20	16	2	2.2	.941							
	C	C. Zimmer	444	.214	2	57	480	**188**	**45**	**14**	5.7	.937							
Bob Leadley	1B	J. Virtue	223	.305	2	25	633	21	12	33	10.7	.982							
W-23 L-33	P	E. Beatin	191	.141	1	21	30	101	8	**7**	2.6	.942							
	O1	T. Dowse	159	.208	0	9	140	10	8	10		.949							
	OF	B. West	151	.245	2	29	50	9	12	1	1.9	.831							
Pittsburgh	1B	G. Hecker	340	.226	0	38	610	31	25	26	9.7	.962	K. Baker	25	178	3	19	0	5.60
	2B	S. LaRoque	434	.242	1	40	227	244	38	32	6.5	.925	G. Hecker	14	120	2	9	0	5.11
	SS	E. Sales	189	.228	1	23	85	151	35	10	5.3	.871	D. Anderson	13	108	2	11	0	4.67
W-23 L-113	3B	D. Miller	549	.273	4	66	127	213	60	18	4.5	.850	B. Sowders	15	106	3	8	0	4.42
	RF	B. Sunday	358	.257	1	33	181	23	27	9*	2.7	.883	C. Schmit	11	83	1	9	0	5.83
Guy Hecker	CF	T. Berger	391	.266	0	40	72	11	8	1	2.2	.912	B. Phillips	10	82	1	9	0	7.57
	LF	J. Kelty	207	.237	1	27	100	6	12	1	2.0	.898	B. Gumbert	10	79	4	6	0	5.22
	C	H. Decker	354	.274	5	38	267	72	34	5	5.3	.909							
	UT	B. Wilson	304	.214	0	21	409	90	60	22		.893							
	3B	F. Roat	215	.223	2	17	64	102	30	9	4.5	.847							
	OF	F. Osborne	168	.238	1	14	64	8	15	0	2.5	.828							

BATTING AND BASE RUNNING LEADERS

Batting Average
J. Glasscock, NY	.336
B. Hamilton, PHI	.325
J. Clements, PHI	.315
D. O'Brien, BKN	.314
S. Thompson, PHI	.313

Slugging Average
M. Tiernan, NY	.495
J. Clements, PHI	.472
L. Reilly, CIN	.472
O. Burns, BKN	.468
J. Burkett, NY	.461

Home Runs
W. Wilmot, CHI	14
O. Burns, BKN	13
M. Tiernan, NY	13
H. Long, BOS	8

Total Bases
M. Tiernan, NY	274
L. Reilly, CIN	261
S. Thompson, PHI	243
W. Wilmot, CHI	240
J. Glasscock, NY	225

Runs Batted In
O. Burns, BKN	128
C. Anson, CHI	107
S. Thompson, PHI	102
W. Wilmot, CHI	99
D. Foutz, BKN	98

Stolen Bases
B. Hamilton, PHI	102
H. Collins, BKN	85
B. Sunday, PHI, PIT	84
W. Wilmot, CHI	76
M. Tiernan, NY	56

Hits
J. Glasscock, NY	172
S. Thompson, PHI	172
M. Tiernan, NY	168
L. Reilly, CIN	166

Base on Balls
C. Anson, CHI	113
B. Allen, PHI	87
E. McKean, CLE	87
H. Collins, BKN	85

Home Run Percentage
O. Burns, BKN	2.8
W. Wilmot, CHI	2.5
M. Tiernan, NY	2.4
H. Long, BOS	1.9

Runs Scored
H. Collins, BKN	148
C. Carroll, CHI	134
B. Hamilton, PHI	133
M. Tiernan, NY	132

Doubles
S. Thompson, PHI	41
H. Collins, BKN	32
J. Glasscock, NY	32
A. Myers, PHI	29

Triples
L. Reilly, CIN	26
B. McPhee, CIN	22
M. Tiernan, NY	21
O. Beard, CIN	15

PITCHING LEADERS

Winning Percentage
T. Lovett, BKN	.732
K. Gleason, PHI	.691
P. Luby, CHI	.690
B. Caruthers, BKN	.676
Hutchinson, CHI	.627

Earned Run Average
B. Rhines, CIN	1.95
K. Nichols, BOS	2.21
A. Rusie, NY	2.56
K. Gleason, PHI	2.63
Hutchinson, CHI	2.70

Wins
Hutchinson, CHI	42
K. Gleason, PHI	38
T. Lovett, BKN	30
A. Rusie, NY	29
B. Rhines, CIN	28

Saves
D. Foutz, BKN	2
K. Gleason, PHI	2
Hutchinson, CHI	2

Strikeouts
A. Rusie, NY	345
Hutchinson, CHI	289
K. Nichols, BOS	222
K. Gleason, PHI	222
A. Terry, BKN	185

Complete Games
Hutchinson, CHI	65
A. Rusie, NY	56
K. Gleason, PHI	54
E. Beatin, CLE	53
K. Nichols, BOS	47

Fewest Hits/9 Innings
A. Rusie, NY	7.15
Hutchinson, CHI	7.54
B. Rhines, CIN	7.56
P. Luby, CHI	7.60

Shutouts
K. Nichols, BOS	7
B. Rhines, CIN	6
K. Gleason, PHI	6
Hutchinson, CHI	5

Fewest Walks/9 Innings
C. Young, CLE	1.83
J. Duryea, CIN	1.97
C. Getzien, BOS	2.11
K. Nichols, BOS	2.36

Most Strikeouts/9 Inn.
T. Mullane, CIN	7.51
A. Rusie, NY	5.59
K. Nichols, BOS	4.68
A. Terry, BKN	4.50

Innings
Hutchinson, CHI	603
A. Rusie, NY	549
K. Gleason, PHI	506
E. Beatin, CLE	474

Games Pitched
Hutchinson, CHI	71
A. Rusie, NY	67
K. Gleason, PHI	60
E. Beatin, CLE	54

NATIONAL LEAGUE 1890, *cont.*

	W	L	PCT	GB	R	OR	2B	Batting 3B	HR	BA	SA	SB	E	Fielding DP	FA	CG	BB	Pitching SO	ShO	SV	ERA
Brooklyn	86	43	.667		**884**	620	184	75	43	.264	**.369**	**349**	320	92	**.940**	115	401	403	6	2	3.05
Chicago	84	53	.613	6	847	692	146	59	**68**	.260	.356	329	344	89	.940	126	481	504	6	**3**	3.24
Philadelphia	78	54	.591	9.5	823	707	**220**	78	23	**.269**	.364	334	398	**122**	.929	122	486	507	8	2	3.32
Cincinnati	77	55	.583	10.5	753	633	150	**120**	28	.259	.361	312	382	106	.932	124	407	488	9	1	3.05
Boston	76	57	.571	12	763	**593**	175	62	31	.258	.341	285	359	77	.934	**132**	**354**	506	**13**	1	**2.93**
New York	63	68	.481	24	713	698	208	89	25	.259	.354	289	449	104	.921	115	**607**	**612**	6	1	3.06
Cleveland	44	88	.333	43.5	630	832	132	59	21	.232	.299	152	405	108	.929	129	462	306	2	0	4.13
Pittsburgh	23	113	.169	66.5	597	1235	160	43	20	.230	.294	208	607	94	.896	119	573	381	3	0	*5.97*
					6010	6010	1375	585	259	.254	.342	2258	3264	792	.927	982	3771	3707	53	10	3.60

AMERICAN ASSOCIATION 1890

	POS	Player	AB	BA	HR	RBI	PO	A	E	DP	TC/G	FA	Pitcher	G	IP	W	L	SV	ERA
Louisville	1B	H. Taylor	553	.306	0		1301	51	25	54	**11.7**	.982	S. Stratton	50	431	34	14	0	**2.36**
	2B	T. Shinnick	493	.256	1		288	351	52	42	5.3	.925	R. Ehret	43	359	25	14	0	*2.53*
W-88 L-44	SS	P. Tomney	386	.277	1		180	406	64	31	6.0	.902	G. Meakim	28	192	12	7	1	*2.91*
	3B	H. Raymond	521	.259	2		182	241	61	18	4.1	.874	H. Goodall	18	109	8	5	4	*3.39*
Jack Chapman	RF	C. Wolf	543	**.363**	4		199	16	14	5	1.9	.939							
	CF	F. Weaver	557	.289	3		227	23	18	4	2.1	.933							
	LF	C. Hamburg	485	.272	3		229	16	14	3	1.9	.946							
	C	J. Ryan	337	.217	0		415	148	41	5	6.8	.932							
	P	S. Stratton	189	.323	0		18	111	3	2	2.6	**.977**							
	P	R. Ehret	146	.212	0		9	64	12	2	2.0	.859							
St. Louis	1B	Cartwright	300	.300	8		706	25	18	37	10.0	.976	J. Stivetts	54	419	29	20	0	*3.52*
	2B	B. Higgins	258	.252	0		168	204	19	34	5.8	.951	T. Ramsey	44	349	24	17	0	*3.69*
W-78 L-58	SS	S. Fuller	526	.278	1		222	389	91	**39**	5.4	.870	B. Hart	26	201	12	8	0	*3.67*
	3B	P. Sweeney	190	.179	0		40	28	16	3	4.0	.810	B. Whitrock	16	105	5	6	1	*3.51*
Tommy McCarthy	RF	T. McCarthy	548	.350	6		159	19	21	5	2.0	.894							
	CF	C. Duffee	378	.275	3		120	16	7	8	2.2	.951							
Chief Roseman	LF	C. Campau	314	.322	10		113	14	9	1	1.8	.934							
W-7 L-8	C	J. Munyan	342	.266	4		452	115	37	8	7.3	.939							
	OF	C. Roseman	302	.341	2		61	7	15	2	1.4	.819							
Count Campau	OF	T. Gettinger	227	.238	3		62	8	9	1	1.4	.886							
W-27 L-14	P	J. Stivetts	226	.288	7		24	86	13	3	2.3	.894							
	P	T. Ramsey	145	.228	0		12	31	16	2	1.3	.729							
Tommy McCarthy																			
Columbus	1B	M. Lehane	512	.211	0		**1430**	73	27	**80**	10.9	**.982**	H. Gastright	48	401	30	14	0	*2.94*
	2B	J. Crooks	485	.221	1		348	345	46	57	5.6	.938	F. Knauss	37	276	17	12	2	*2.81*
W-79 L-55	SS	H. Easterday	197	.157	0		82	202	39	20	5.6	.879	J. Easton	37	256	15	14	1	*3.52*
	3B	C. Reilly	530	.266	4		**205**	354	67	26	4.6	.893	Chamberlain	25	175	12	6	0	*2.21*
Al Buckenberger	RF	J. Sneed	484	.291	2		161	20	24	5	1.6	.883	W. Widner	13	96	4	8	0	*3.28*
W-39 L-41	CF	J. McTamany	466	.258	1		232	17	16	8	2.1	.940							
	LF	S. Johnson	538	.346	2		164	12	14	1	1.4	.926							
Gus Schmelz	C	J. O'Connor	457	.324	2		**539**	146	27	**13**	6.7	**.962**							
W-38 L-13	UT	J. Doyle	298	.268	2		231	153	54	14		.877							
	SS	B. Wheelock	190	.237	1		92	162	33	12	5.5	.885							
Pat Sullivan	P	H. Gastright	169	.213	0		12	55	5	2	1.5	.931							
W-2 L-1																			
Toledo	1B	P. Werden	498	.295	6		1178	59	**35**	57	10.3	.972	E. Healy	46	389	22	21	0	*2.89*
	2B	P. Nicholson	523	.268	4		294	385	52	45	5.5	.929	E. Cushman	40	316	17	21	1	*4.19*
W-68 L-64	SS	F. Scheibeck	485	.241	1		**282**	412	92	35	5.9	.883	F. Smith	35	286	19	13	0	*3.27*
	3B	B. Alvord	495	.273	2		203	252	67	13	4.5	.872	C. Sprague	19	123	9	5	0	*3.89*
Charlie Morton	RF	E. Swartwood	462	.327	3		224	23	20	2	2.1	.925							
	CF	W. Tebeau	381	.268	1		182	14	10	1	2.2	.951							
	LF	B. Van Dyke	502	.257	2		172	17	16	0	1.9	.922							
	C	H. Sage	275	.149	2		336	**153**	27	3	6.5	.948							
	OP	C. Sprague	199	.236	1		60	18	8	1		.907							
	P	E. Healy	156	.218	1		24	62	14	2	2.2	.860							
Rochester	1B	T. O'Brien	273	.190	0		675	20	21	40	10.5	.971	B. Barr	57	493	28	**24**	0	*3.25*
	2B	B. Greenwood	437	.222	2		331	343	**59**	59	6.0	.920	W. Calihan	37	296	18	15	0	*3.28*
W-63 L-63	SS	M. Phillips	257	.206	0		101	222	29	24	5.5	.918	C. Titcomb	20	169	10	9	0	*3.74*
	3B	J. Knowles	491	.281	5		162	303	63	19	4.3	.881	B. Miller	13	92	3	7	1	*4.29*
Pat Powers	RF	T. Scheffler	445	.245	3		196	**29**	22	6	2.1	.911	Fitzgerald	11	78	3	8	0	*4.04*
	CF	S. Griffin	407	.307	5		159	7	28	1	1.8	.856							
	LF	H. Lyons	584	.260	3		**264**	25	25	4	2.4	.920							
	C	D. McGuire	331	.299	4		389	99	32	9	**7.3**	.938							
	C	D. McKeough	218	.225	0		186	76	20	4	6.0	.929							
	P	B. Barr	201	.179	2		20	111	10	2	2.5	.929							
	UT	J. Grim	192	.266	2		151	99	27	15		.903							
	1B	J. Field	188	.202	4		486	12	18	24	10.1	.965							
	P	W. Calihan	159	.145	1		14	71	9	6	2.5	.904							

AMERICAN ASSOCIATION 1890, *cont.*

POS	Player	AB	BA	HR	RBI	PO	A	E	DP	TC/G	FA	Pitcher	G	IP	W	L	SV	ERA
Baltimore												L. German	17	132	5	11	0	4.84
1B	T. Power	125	.208	0		259	7	11	8	10.7	.960	S. McMahon	12	99	7	3	0	3.09
2B	R. Mack	95	.284	0		62	76	10	7	5.7	.932							
SS	I. Ray	139	.360	1		40	104	17	7	4.2	.894							
W-15 L-19	3B	P. Gilbert	100	.280	1		34	55	10	5	3.4	.899						
	RF	B. Johnson	95	.295	0		39	6	7	3	2.2	.865						
Billy Barnie	CF	D. Long	77	.156	0		26	5	2	0	1.6	.939						
	LF	J. Sommer	129	.256	0		69	5	9	3	2.2	.892						
	C	G. Townsend	67	.239	0		72	34	8	2	6.3	.930						
Syracuse	1B	M. McQuery	461	.308	2		1146	45	34	63	10.0	.972	D. Casey	45	361	19	22	0	4.14
	2B	C. Childs	493	.345	2		372	367	57	59	6.4	.928	J. Keefe	43	352	17	24	0	4.32
	SS	McLaughlin	329	.264	2		120	258	41	22	4.9	.902	M. Morrison	17	127	6	9	0	5.88
W-55 L-72	3B	T. O'Rourke	332	.283	1		117	168	44	9	3.8	.866	E. Mars	16	121	9	5	0	4.67
	RF	P. Friel	261	.249	3		77	7	8	2	1.5	.913						
George Frazer	CF	R. Wright	348	.305	0		170	15	19	7	2.3	.907						
W-31 L-40	LF	B. Ely	496	.262	0		179	14	18	1	2.7	.915						
	C	G. Briggs	316	.180	0		200	71	21	6	6.3	.928						
Wally Fessenden	P	D. Casey	160	.163	0		22	78	14	4	2.5	.877						
W-4 L-7	P	J. Keefe	157	.191	0		14	71	4	2	2.1	.955						
George Frazer	OF	H. Simon	156	.301	2		62	2	4	1	1.8	.941						
W-20 L-25	C	T. O'Rourke	153	.216	0		187	48	24	8	6.5	.907						
Philadelphia	1B	J. O'Brien	433	.261	4		1018	52	26	61	10.1	.976	S. McMahon	48*	410*	29*	18	1	3.34
	2B	T. Shaffer	261	.172	0		214	195	35	39	6.4	.921	E. Green	25	191	7	15	1	5.80
	SS	B. Conroy	404	.171	0		119	257	45	26	5.7	.893	E. Seward	21	154	6	12	0	4.73
W-54 L-78	3B	D. Lyons	339	.354	7		147	203	35	14	4.4	.909	D. Esper	18	144	8	9	0	4.89
	RF	O. Shaffer	390	.282	1		143	17	7	6	1.7	.958	C. Stecher	10	68	0	10	0	0.32
Bill Sharsig	CF	C. Welch	396	.268	2		225	23	22	8*	2.6*	.919						
	LF	B. Purcell	463	.276	2		170	17	10	3	1.8	.949						
	C	W. Robinson	329	.237	4		412	103	39	10*	6.8	.930						
	UT	J. Kappel	208	.240	1		75	92	31	8		.843						
	P	S. McMahon	175	.229	2		29*	112*	8	6*	3.1	.946						
Brooklyn	1B	B. O'Brien	388	.278	4		1015	35	29	66	11.2	.973	E. Daily	27	235	10	15	0	3.95
	2B	J. Gerhardt	369	.203	3		359	348	47	67	7.6	.938	McCullough	26	216	4	21	0	4.59
	SS	C. Nelson	223	.251	0		60	198	40	20	5.2	.866	M. Mattimore	19	178	6	13	0	4.44
W-26 L-72	3B	J. Davis	142	.303	2		49	87	25	9	4.2	.845	C. Murphy	12	95	3	9	0	5.78
	RF	E. Daily	394	.239	1		107	17	15	3	2.2	.892						
Jim Kennedy	CF	J. Peltz	384	.227	1		207	18	24	6	2.5	.904						
	LF	H. Simon	373	.257	0		176	17	10	4	2.3	.951						
	C	J. Toy	160	.181	0		148	86	36	4	6.1	.867						
	UT	F. Bowes	232	.220	0		164	67	35	8		.868						
	UT	H. Pitz	189	.138	0		156	88	43	6		.850						
	SS	F. Fennelly	178	.247	2		70	135	34	8	6.3	.858						

BATTING AND BASE RUNNING LEADERS

Batting Average
C. Wolf, LOU .363
D. Lyons, PHI .354
T. McCarthy, STL .350
S. Johnson, COL .346
C. Childs, SYR .345

Slugging Average
D. Lyons, PHI .531
C. Childs, SYR .481
C. Wolf, LOU .479
T. McCarthy, STL .467
S. Johnson, COL .461

Home Runs
C. Campau, STL 10
Cartwright, STL 8
J. Stivetts, STL 7
D. Lyons, PHI 7
P. Werden, TOL 6
T. McCarthy, STL 6

Total Bases
C. Wolf, LOU 260
T. McCarthy, STL 256
S. Johnson, COL 248
C. Childs, SYR 237
P. Werden, TOL 227

Runs Batted In
(not available)

Stolen Bases
T. McCarthy, STL 83
T. Scheffler, ROC 77
B. Van Dyke, TOL 73
C. Welch, BKN, BAL, PHI 72
E. Daily, BKN, BAL, LOU 62
T. Shinnick, LOU 62

Hits
C. Wolf, LOU 197
T. McCarthy, STL 192
S. Johnson, COL 186
C. Childs, SYR 170

Base on Balls
J. McTamany, COL 112
J. Crooks, COL 96
E. Swartwood, TOL 80
T. Scheffler, ROC 78

Home Run Percentage
D. Lyons, PHI 2.1
S. Griffin, ROC 1.2
D. McGuire, ROC 1.2
P. Werden, TOL 1.2

Runs Scored
J. McTamany, COL 140
T. McCarthy, STL 137
S. Fuller, STL 118
J. Sneed, COL, TOL 117

Doubles
C. Childs, SYR 33
D. Lyons, PHI 29
C. Wolf, LOU 29
S. Griffin, ROC 28

Triples
P. Werden, TOL 20
S. Johnson, COL 18
B. Alvord, TOL 16
J. Sneed, COL, TOL 15

PITCHING LEADERS

Winning Percentage
S. Stratton, LOU .708
H. Gastright, COL .682
Chamberlain, COL, STL .682
R. Ehret, LOU .641
McMahon, BAL, PHI .632
G. Meakim, LOU .632

Earned Run Average
S. Stratton, LOU 2.36
R. Ehret, LOU 2.53
F. Knauss, COL 2.81
Chamberlain, COL, STL 2.83
E. Healy, TOL 2.89

Wins
McMahon, BAL, PHI 36
S. Stratton, LOU 34
H. Gastright, COL 30
J. Stivetts, STL 29
B. Barr, ROC 28

Saves
H. Goodall, LOU 4
R. Ehret, LOU 2
F. Knauss, COL 2

Strikeouts
McMahon, BAL, PHI 291
J. Stivetts, STL 289
T. Ramsey, STL 257
E. Healy, TOL 225
B. Barr, ROC 209

Complete Games
McMahon, BAL, PHI 55
B. Barr, ROC 52
E. Healy, TOL 44
S. Stratton, LOU 44
H. Gastright, COL 41
J. Stivetts, STL 41

Fewest Hits/9 Innings
F. Knauss, COL 6.73
H. Gastright, COL 7.00
J. Easton, COL 7.50
Chamberlain, COL, STL 7.50

Shutouts
Chamberlain, COL, STL 6
R. Ehret, LOU 4
H. Gastright, COL 4
S. Stratton, LOU 4

Fewest Walks/9 Innings
S. Stratton, LOU 1.27
R. Ehret, LOU 1.98
T. Ramsey, STL 2.63
F. Smith, TOL 2.83

Most Strikeouts/9 Inn.
T. Ramsey, STL 6.63
J. Stivetts, STL 6.20
G. Meakim, LOU 5.77
Chamberlain, COL, STL 5.49

Innings
McMahon, BAL, PHI 509
B. Barr, ROC 493
S. Stratton, LOU 431
J. Stivetts, STL 419

Games Pitched
McMahon, BAL, PHI 60
B. Barr, ROC 57
J. Stivetts, STL 54
S. Stratton, LOU 50

AMERICAN ASSOCIATION 1890, cont.

	W	L	PCT	GB	R	OR	Batting 2B	3B	HR	BA	SA	SB	Fielding E	DP	FA	Pitching CG	BB	SO	ShO	SV	ERA
Louisville	88	44	.667		819	588	156	65	15	.279	.350	341	380	79	.933	114	293	587	13	7	2.58
St. Louis	78	58	.574	12	870	736	178	72	49	.273	.370	307	478	93	.916	118	447	733	4	1	3.67
Columbus	79	55	.590	10	831	617	159	78	15	.258	.334	353	401	101	.931	120	471	624	14	3	2.99
Toledo	68	64	.515	20	739	689	152	108	24	.252	.348	421	419	75	.925	122	429	533	4	2	3.56
Rochester	63	63	.500	22	709	711	131	64	31	.239	.316	310	416	95	.926	122	530	477	5	2	3.56
Baltimore	15	19	.441	24	182	192	34	16	2	.229	.289	101	109	21	.928	36	123	134	1	0	4.03
Syracuse	55	72	.433	30.5	698	831	151	59	14	.259	.329	292	391	90	.925	115	518	454	5	0	4.98
Philadelphia	54	78	.409	34	702	945	181	51	24	.235	.314	305	452	93	.918	119	514	461	3	2	5.22
Brooklyn	26	72	.265	45	492	733	116	46	14	.221	.293	182	403	92	.909	96	421	230		0	4.78
					6042	6042	1258	559	188	.253	.332	2612	3449	739	.923	962	3746	4233	49	17	3.87

PLAYERS' LEAGUE 1890

	POS	Player	AB	BA	HR	RBI	PO	A	E	DP	TC/G	FA	Pitcher	G	IP	W	L	SV	ERA
Boston W-81 L-48 King Kelly	1B	D. Brouthers	460	.330	1	97	1187	73	49	78	10.6	.963	O. Radbourn	41	343	27	12	0	3.31
	2B	J. Quinn	509	.301	7	82	431	395	51	70	6.7	.942	A. Gumbert	39	277	22	12	0	3.96
	SS	A. Irwin	354	.260	0	45	137	331	65	44	5.6	.878	B. Daley	34	235	18	7	2	3.60
	3B	B. Nash	488	.266	5	90	198	307	78	37	4.5	.866	M. Kilroy	30	218	10	15	0	4.26
	RF	H. Stovey	481	.297	11	83	186	24	18	3	1.7	.921							
	CF	T. Brown	543	.276	4	61	276	32	30	8	2.6	.911							
	LF	Richardson	555	.326	11	143	235	13	13	3	2.1	.950							
	C	M. Murphy	246	.228	2	32	257	59	34	8	5.2	.903							
	UT	K. Kelly	340	.326	4	66	274	145	55	12		.884							
	P	O. Radbourn	154	.253	0	16	16	99	8	4	3.0	.935							
	P	A. Gumbert	145	.241	3	20	15	83	13	0	2.8	.883							
Brooklyn W-76 L-56 Monte Ward	1B	D. Orr	464	.373	6	124	1009	42	30	67	10.1	.972	G. Weyhing	49	390	30	16	0	3.60
	2B	L. Bierbauer	589	.306	7	99	372	468	62	77	6.8	.931	J. Sowders	39	309	19	16	0	3.82
	SS	M. Ward	561	.337	4	60	303	450	105	59	6.7	.878	Van Haltren	28	223	15	10	2	4.28
	3B	B. Joyce	489	.252	1	78	176	284	107	22	4.3	.811	C. Murphy	20	139	4	10	2	4.79
	RF	J. McGeachy	443	.244	1	65	206	16	23	1	2.4	.906	G. Hemming	19	123	8	4	3	3.80
	CF	E. Andrews	395	.253	3	38	220	17	23	3	2.8	.912							
	LF	E. Seery	394	.223	1	50	216	21	28	3	2.5	.894							
	C	T. Kinslow	242	.264	4	46	298	72	37	7	6.4	.909							
	OP	Van Haltren	376	.335	5	54	138	84	21	6		.914							
	C1	P. Cook	218	.252	0	31	319	57	30	20		.926							
	C	C. Daily	168	.250	0	35	141	34	24	5	5.0	.879							
	P	G. Weyhing	165	.164	1	15	12	55	12	2	1.6	.848							
	P	J. Sowders	132	.189	1	20	7	75	7	1	2.3	.921							
New York W-74 L-57 Buck Ewing	1B	R. Connor	484	.349	13	103	1335	80	21	79	11.7	.985	C. Crane	43	330	16	19	0	4.63
	2B	D. Shannon	324	.216	3	44	162	262	43	35	6.1	.908	H. O'Day	43	329	22	13	3	4.21
	SS	Richardson	528	.256	4	80	153	263	46	33	6.8	.900	J. Ewing	35	267	18	12	2	4.24
	3B	A. Whitney	442	.219	0	45	129	172	47	11	4.0	.865	T. Keefe	30	229	17	11	0	3.38
	RF	J. O'Rourke	478	.360	9	115	175	25	15	3	1.9	.930							
	CF	G. Gore	399	.318	10	55	146	11	22	3	1.9	.877							
	LF	M. Slattery	411	.307	5	67	175	5	19	1	2.1	.905							
	C	B. Ewing	352	.338	8	72	372	107	26	7	6.2	.949							
	OF	D. Johnston	306	.242	1	43	164	18	21	3	2.7	.897							
	3S	G. Hatfield	287	.279	1	37	79	156	54	13		.813							
	UT	W. Brown	230	.278	4	43	241	49	26	5		.918							
	CO	F. Vaughn	166	.265	1	22	112	21	18	3		.881							
	P	H. O'Day	150	.227	1	23	11	71	7	0	2.1	.921							
	P	C. Crane	146	.315	0	16	17	71	16	0	2.4	.846							
Chicago W-75 L-62 Charlie Comiskey	1B	C. Comiskey	377	.244	0	59	882	41	33	52	10.9	.965	M. Baldwin	59	501	32	24	0	3.31
	2B	F. Pfeffer	499	.257	5	80	441	387	76	73	7.3	.916	S. King	56	461	32	22	0	2.69
	SS	C. Bastian	283	.191	0	29	85	202	39	24	5.1	.880	C. Bartson	25	188	8	10	1	4.26
	3B	Williamson	261	.195	1	26	53	91	34	6	3.4	.809	F. Dwyer	12	69	3	6	1	6.23
	RF	H. Duffy	596	.320	7	82	255	34	26	5	2.3	.917							
	CF	J. Ryan	486	.340	6	89	257	25	25	5	2.6	.919							
	LF	T. O'Neill	577	.302	3	75	231	8	19	1	1.9	.926							
	C	D. Farrell	451	.290	2	84	428	132	43	12	6.7	.929							
	UT	J. Boyle	369	.260	1	49	335	154	61	16		.889							
	UT	D. Darling	221	.258	2	39	296	72	37	24		.909							
	P	M. Baldwin	215	.209	1	25	26	146	15	2	3.2	.920							
	3B	A. Latham	214	.229	1	20	65	119	25	9	4.0	.880							
	P	S. King	185	.168	1	16	22	139	6	5	3.0	.964							

PLAYERS' LEAGUE 1890, *cont.*

	POS	Player	AB	BA	HR	RBI	PO	A	E	DP	TC/G	FA	Pitcher	G	IP	W	L	SV	ERA
Philadelphia	1B	S. Farrar	481	.254	1	69	1238	58	36	**79**	10.5	.973	B. Sanders	43	347	20	17	1	3.76
	2B	J. Pickett	407	.280	4	64	236	284	62	46	5.8	.893	P. Knell	35	287	22	11	0	3.83
W-68 L-63	SS	B. Shindle	584	.322	10	90	266	442	**119**	67	6.4	.856	C. Buffinton	36	283	19	14	1	3.81
	3B	J. Mulvey	519	.287	6	87	144	227	62	15	3.6	.857	B. Husted	18	129	5	12	0	4.88
Jim Fogarty	RF	J. Fogarty	347	.239	4	58	192	17	8	3	2.4	**.963**	Cunningham	14	109	3	9	0	5.22
W-7 L-9	CF	M. Griffin	489	.286	6	54	278	33	15	10	2.8	.954							
	LF	G. Wood	539	.289	9	102	254	**35**	34	9	2.4	.895							
Charlie Buffinton	C	J. Milligan	234	.295	3	57	260	66	39	13	6.2	.893							
W-61 L-54	UT	B. Hallman	356	.267	1	37	194	103	36	15		.892							
	C	L. Cross	245	.298	3	47	191	70	34	7	6.0	.885							
	P	B. Sanders	189	.312	0	30	17	93	9	5*	2.8	.924							
	P	C. Buffinton	150	.273	1	24	12	77	14	5	2.9	.864							
Pittsburgh	1B	J. Beckley	516	.324	10	120	1256	58	32	61	11.1	.976	H. Staley	46	388	21	25	0	3.23
	2B	Y. Robinson	306	.229	0	38	226	286	65	46	5.9	.887	A. Maul	30	247	16	12	0	3.79
W-60 L-68	SS	T. Corcoran	503	.233	1	61	210	431	84	36	5.9	.884	P. Galvin	26	217	12	13	0	4.35
	3B	W. Kuehne	528	.239	5	73	159	304	82	18	4.3	.850	E. Morris	18	144	8	7	0	4.86
Ned Hanlon	RF	J. Visner	521	.265	3	71	198	18	26	4	1.9	.893	J. Tener	14	117	3	11	0	7.31
	CF	N. Hanlon	472	.278	1	44	**291**	15	30	4	2.8	.911							
	LF	J. Fields	526	.283	9	86	153	21	24	3	2.5	.879							
	C	F. Carroll	416	.298	2	71	206	50	43	1	5.3	.856							
	C	T. Quinn	207	.213	1	15	203	58	33	3	5.3	.888							
	P	H. Staley	164	.207	1	25	11	86	6	**5**	2.2	.942							
	PO	A. Maul	162	.259	0	21	49	83	15	5		.898							
Cleveland	1B	H. Larkin	506	.332	5	112	1268	40	30	63	10.7	.978	H. Gruber	48	383	21	23	1	4.27
	2B	C. Stricker	544	.244	2	65	295	353	68	57	6.6	.905	J. Bakely	43	326	13	25	0	4.47
	SS	E. Delahanty	517	.298	3	64	143	244	79	33	6.1	.830	D. O'Brien	25	206	8	16	0	3.40
W-55 L-75	3B	P. Tebeau	450	.300	5	74	**204**	246	66	25	**4.7**	**.872**	W. McGill	24	184	11	9	0	4.12
	RF	P. Radford	466	.292	2	62	137	16	18	5	2.1	.895							
Henry Larkin	CF	J. McAleer	341	.267	1	42	249	15	17	4	**3.3**	.940							
W-34 L-45	LF	P. Browning	493	**.373**	5	93	248	18	32	4	2.5	.893							
	C	S. Sutcliffe	386	.329	2	60	264	115	**50**	9	5.1	.883							
Patsy Tebeau	OF	L. Twitchell	233	.223	2	36	61	8	15	1	1.5	.821							
W-21 L-30	C3	J. Brennan	233	.253	0	26	147	73	42	7		.840							
	P	H. Gruber	163	.221	0	9	8	109	14	3	2.7	.893							
	OF	J. Carney	89	.348	0	21	21	3	4	0	1.5	.857							
Buffalo	1B	D. White	439	.260	0	47	582	40	19	33	11.2	.970	G. Haddock	35	291	9	**26**	0	5.76
	2B	S. Wise	505	.293	6	102	328	375	73	58	6.5	.906	Cunningham	25	211	9	15	0	5.84
W-36 L-96	SS	J. Rowe	504	.250	2	76	228	381	67	56	5.4	**.901**	G. Keefe	25	196	6	16	0	6.52
	3B	J. Irwin	308	.234	1	34	79	139	29	13	3.9	.883	L. Twitchell	12	104	5	7	0	4.57
Jack Rowe	RF	J. Halligan	211	.251	3	33	73	11	18	1	2.4	.824	G. Stafford	12	98	3	9	0	5.14
W-28 L-58	CF	D. Hoy	493	.298	1	53	289	23	30	9	2.8	.912							
	LF	E. Beecher	536	.297	3	90	211	24	**55**	4	2.3	.810							
Jay Faatz	C	C. Mack	503	.266	0	53	**449**	140	48	**13**	5.7	.925							
W-9 L-24	UT	S. Clark	260	.265	1	25	168	63	19	14		.924							
	OP	L. Twitchell	172	.221	2	17	49	37	7	1		.925							
Jack Rowe	UT	J. Rainey	166	.235	1	20	72	42	17	8		.870							
W-5 L-14	P	G. Haddock	146	.247	0	24	20	86	8	2	3.3	.930							

BATTING AND BASE RUNNING LEADERS

Batting Average		Slugging Average		Home Runs	
P. Browning, CLE	.387	R. Connor, NY	.566	R. Connor, NY	13
D. Orr, BKN	.373	J. Beckley, PIT	.541	H. Stovey, BOS	11
R. Connor, NY	.372	D. Orr, BKN	.537	Richardson, BOS	11
M. Ward, BKN	.369	P. Browning, CLE	.531	G. Gore, NY	10
J. O'Rourke, NY	.360	J. O'Rourke, NY	.515	J. Beckley, PIT	10
				B. Shindle, PHI	10

Total Bases		Runs Batted In		Stolen Bases	
H. Duffy, CHI	283	Richardson, BOS	143	H. Stovey, BOS	97
B. Shindle, PHI	281	D. Orr, BKN	124	T. Brown, BOS	79
J. Beckley, PIT	279	J. Beckley, PIT	120	H. Duffy, CHI	79
R. Connor, NY	274	J. O'Rourke, NY	115	N. Hanlon, PIT	65
Richardson, BOS	268	H. Larkin, CLE	112	M. Ward, BKN	63

Hits		Base on Balls		Home Run Percentage	
M. Ward, BKN	207	B. Joyce, BKN	123	R. Connor, NY	2.7
H. Duffy, CHI	194	Y. Robinson, PIT	101	G. Gore, NY	2.5
P. Browning, CLE	191	D. Brouthers, BOS	99	H. Stovey, BOS	2.3
Richardson, BOS	181	D. Hoy, BUF	94	Richardson, BOS	2.0

PITCHING LEADERS

Winning Percentage		Earned Run Average		Wins	
O. Radbourn, BOS	.692	S. King, CHI	2.69	S. King, CHI	32
B. Daley, BOS	.692	H. Staley, PIT	3.23	M. Baldwin, CHI	32
A. Gumbert, BOS	.667	M. Baldwin, CHI	3.31	G. Weyhing, BKN	30
P. Knell, PHI	.667	O. Radbourn, BOS	3.31	O. Radbourn, BOS	27
G. Weyhing, BKN	.652	T. Keefe, NY	3.38	H. O'Day, NY	23

Saves		Strikeouts		Complete Games	
G. Hemming, BKN, CLE	3	M. Baldwin, CHI	211	M. Baldwin, CHI	54
H. O'Day, NY	3	S. King, CHI	185	S. King, CHI	48
B. Daley, BOS	2	G. Weyhing, BKN	177	H. Staley, PIT	44
J. Ewing, NY	2	J. Ewing, NY	145	H. Gruber, CLE	39
C. Murphy, BKN	2	H. Staley, PIT	145	G. Weyhing, BKN	38
Van Haltren, BKN	2				

Fewest Hits/9 Innings		Shutouts		Fewest Walks/9 Innings	
S. King, CHI	8.20	S. King, CHI	4	H. Staley, PIT	1.72
C. Crane, NY	8.80	H. Staley, PIT	3	B. Sanders, PHI	1.79
G. Hemming, BKN, CLE	8.87	G. Weyhing, BKN	3	P. Galvin, PIT	2.03
M. Baldwin, CHI	8.95			E. Morris, PIT	2.18

PLAYERS' LEAGUE 1890, cont.

BATTING AND BASE RUNNING LEADERS

Runs Scored		Doubles		Triples	
H. Duffy, CHI	161	P. Browning, CLE	40	J. Beckley, PIT	22
T. Brown, BOS	146	J. Beckley, PIT	38	J. Visner, PIT	22
H. Stovey, BOS	142	J. O'Rourke, NY	37	B. Shindle, PHI	21
M. Ward, BKN	134	D. Brouthers, BOS	36	J. Fields, PIT	20

PITCHING LEADERS

Most Strikeouts/9 Inn.		Innings		Games Pitched	
J. Ewing, NY	4.88	M. Baldwin, CHI	501	M. Baldwin, CHI	59
B. Daley, BOS	4.21	S. King, CHI	461	S. King, CHI	56
G. Weyhing, BKN	4.08	G. Weyhing, BKN	390	G. Weyhing, BKN	49
W. McGill, CLE	4.02	H. Staley, PIT	388	H. Gruber, CLE	48

	W	L	PCT	GB	R	OR	2B	3B	HR	BA	SA	SB	E	DP	FA	CG	BB	SO	ShO	SV	ERA
Boston	81	48	.628		992	767	223	77	51	.282	.397	412	460	109	.918	105	467	345	6	2	3.79
Brooklyn	76	56	.576	6.5	964	893	186	93	34	.277	.374	272	531	114	.909	111	570	377	4	7	3.95
New York	74	57	.565	8	1018	875	204	97	64	.284	.404	231	450	94	.921	111	569	449	3	6	4.17
Chicago	75	62	.547	10	886	770	200	96	30	.264	.361	276	492	107	.918	124	503	460	5	2	3.39
Philadelphia	68	63	.519	14	941	855	187	113	49	.278	.393	203	510	118	.910	118	495	361	4	2	4.05
Pittsburgh	60	68	.469	20.5	835	892	168	113	36	.260	.370	249	512	80	.907	121	334	318	7	0	4.22
Cleveland	55	75	.423	26.5	849	1027	213	94	27	.286	.386	180	533	103	.907	115	571	325	1	1	4.23
Buffalo	36	96	.273	46.5	793	1199	180	64	20	.260	.337	160	491	116	.914	125	673	351	2	0	6.11
					7278	7278	1561	747	311	.274	.378	1983	3979	841	.913	930	4182	2986	32	20	4.23

NATIONAL LEAGUE 1891

Boston
W-87 L-51 — Frank Selee

POS	Player	AB	BA	HR	RBI	PO	A	E	DP	TC/G	FA	Pitcher	G	IP	W	L	SV	ERA
1B	T. Tucker	548	.270	2	69	1313	55	34	66	10.0	.976	J. Clarkson	55	461	33	19	3	2.79
2B	J. Quinn	508	.240	3	63	275	364	42	44	5.5	.938	K. Nichols	52	426	30	17	3	2.39
SS	H. Long	577	.282	9	74	345	441	85	60	6.3	.902	H. Staley	31	252	20	8	0	2.50
3B	B. Nash	537	.276	5	95	213	264	53	20	3.8	.900							
RF	H. Stovey	544	.279	16	95	232	22	25	4	2.1	.910							
CF	S. Brodie	523	.260	2	78	268	25	15	9	2.3	.951							
LF	B. Lowe	497	.260	6	74	186	16	16	2	2.0	.927							
C	C. Bennett	256	.215	5	39	383	75	19	10	6.4	.960							
C	C. Ganzel	263	.259	1	29	288	59	16	3	6.2	.956							
P	J. Clarkson	187	.225	0	26	27	114	13	2	2.8	.916							
P	K. Nichols	183	.197	0	27	30	100	7	5	2.6	.949							

Chicago
W-82 L-53 — Cap Anson

POS	Player	AB	BA	HR	RBI	PO	A	E	DP	TC/G	FA	Pitcher	G	IP	W	L	SV	ERA
1B	C. Anson	540	.291	8	120	1407	79	29	86	11.1	.981	Hutchinson	66	561	44	19	1	2.81
2B	F. Pfeffer	498	.247	7	77	429	474	77	78	7.2	.921	A. Gumbert	32	256	17	11	0	3.58
SS	J. Cooney	465	.245	0	42	145	433	52	39	5.3	.917	P. Luby	30	206	8	11	1	4.76
3B	B. Dahlen	549	.260	9	76	120	211	42	13	4.4	.887	E. Stein	14	101	7	6	0	3.74
RF	C. Carroll	515	.256	7	80	168	15	17	5	1.5	.915	T. Vickery	14	80	5	5	0	4.07
CF	J. Ryan	505	.277	9	66	231	25	27	3	2.4	.905							
LF	W. Wilmot	498	.279	11	71	223	15	20	0	2.1	.922							
C	M. Kittridge	296	.209	2	27	384	87	30	5	6.3	.940							
P	Hutchinson	243	.185	2	25	22	103	13	0	2.1	.906							
3B	T. Burns	243	.226	1	17	92	107	24	11	4.2	.892							
P	P. Luby	98	.245	2	24	8	42	2	2	1.7	.962							
C	P. Schriver	90	.333	1	21	135	27	6	3	6.2	.964							

New York
W-71 L-61 — Jim Mutrie

POS	Player	AB	BA	HR	RBI	PO	A	E	DP	TC/G	FA	Pitcher	G	IP	W	L	SV	ERA
1B	R. Connor	479	.290	6	94	1362	56	25	77	11.2	.983	A. Rusie	61	500	33	20	1	2.55
2B	Richardson	516	.269	5	51	323	429	38	60	6.9	.952	J. Ewing	33	269	21	8	0	2.27
SS	J. Glasscock	369	.241	0	55	164	274	42	39	4.9	.913	M. Welch	22	160	6	9	1	4.28
3B	C. Bassett	524	.260	4	68	143	270	42	18	3.8	.908	J. Sharrott	10	69	4	5	1	2.60
RF	M. Tiernan	542	.306	17	73	138	16	17	4	1.3	.901							
CF	G. Gore	528	.284	2	48	234	16	25	3	2.1	.909							
LF	J. O'Rourke	555	.295	5	95	195	18	22	1	1.9	.906							
C	D. Buckley	253	.217	4	31	446	83	23	7	7.5	.958							
UT	L. Whistler	265	.245	4	38	143	128	49	11		.847							
P	A. Rusie	220	.245	0	15	10	106	14	4	2.1	.892							
C	A. Clarke	174	.190	0	21	189	50	22	6	6.2	.916							

Philadelphia
W-68 L-69 — Harry Wright

POS	Player	AB	BA	HR	RBI	PO	A	E	DP	TC/G	FA	Pitcher	G	IP	W	L	SV	ERA
1B	W. Brown	441	.243	0	50	997	48	12	60	10.9	.989	K. Gleason	53	418	24	22	1	3.51
2B	A. Myers	514	.230	2	69	354	438	53	67	6.3	.937	D. Esper	39	296	20	15	1	3.56
SS	B. Allen	438	.221	1	51	258	438	79	50	6.5	.896	J. Thornton	37	269	15	16	2	3.68
3B	B. Shindle	415	.210	0	38	153	248	58	24	4.6	.874	T. Keefe	11	78	3	6	1	3.91
RF	S. Thompson	554	.294	8	90	234	32	18	6	2.1	.937							
CF	E. Delahanty	543	.243	4	86	199	22	22	3	2.5	.909							
LF	B. Hamilton	527	.340	2	60	287	17	31	7	2.5	.907							
C	J. Clements	423	.310	4	75	415	108	41	10	5.3	.927							
UT	E. Mayer	268	.187	0	31	100	105	29	4		.876							
P	K. Gleason	214	.248	0	17	22	73	11	2	2.0	.896							

NATIONAL LEAGUE 1891, *cont.*

	POS	Player	AB	BA	HR	RBI	PO	A	E	DP	TC/G	FA	Pitcher	G	IP	W	L	SV	ERA
Cleveland	1B	J. Virtue	517	.261	2	72	**1465**	44	**44**	70	11.2	.972	C. Young	55	424	27	22	2	2.85
	2B	C. Childs	551	.281	2	83	371	455	**82**	54	6.4	.910	H. Gruber	44	349	17	22	0	4.13
W-65 L-74	SS	E. McKean	**603**	.282	6	69	248	463	**91**	42	5.7	.887	L. Viau	45	344	18	17	0	3.01
	3B	P. Tebeau	249	.261	1	41	102	150	33	13	4.7	.884							
Bob Leadley	RF	S. Johnson	327	.257	1	46	99	10	16	1	1.6	.872							
W-34 L-34	CF	G. Davis	570	.289	3	89	257	27	21	1	2.6	.931							
	LF	J. McAleer	565	.237	2	61	284	19	25	1	2.4	.924							
Patsy Tebeau	C	C. Zimmer	440	.255	3	69	476	181	45	7	6.1	.936							
W-34 L-40	UT	J. Doyle	250	.276	0	43	178	73	38	5		.869							
	P	C. Young	174	.167	1	18	10	89	9	0	2.0	.917							
	OF	J. Burkett	167	.269	0	13	53	5	7	1	1.5	.892							
	P	L. Viau	144	.160	0	6	12	79	**14**	2	2.3	.867							
	P	H. Gruber	141	.163	1	20	8	90	10	**5**	2.5	.907							
	3B	J. Denny	138	.225	0	21	39	60	13	1	3.9	.884							
Brooklyn	1B	D. Foutz	521	.257	2	73	1235	47	31	50	10.6	.976	T. Lovett	44	366	23	19	0	3.69
	2B	H. Collins	435	.276	3	31	180	222	40	19	6.1	.910	B. Caruthers	38	297	18	14	1	3.12
W-61 L-76	SS	M. Ward	441	.277	0	39	180	296	66	28	6.2	.878	G. Hemming	27	200	8	15	1	4.96
	3B	G. Pinckney	501	.273	2	71	146	261	43	10	3.5	.904	A. Terry	25	194	6	11	1	4.22
Monte Ward	RF	O. Burns	470	.285	4	83	173	16	16	5	1.8	.922	B. Inks	13	96	3	10	0	4.02
	CF	M. Griffin	521	.271	3	65	**353**	31	16	7	**3.0**	**.960**							
	LF	D. O'Brien	395	.253	5	57	203	11	11	4	2.2	.951							
	C	T. Kinslow	228	.237	0	33	252	54	26	6	5.4	.922							
	C	C. Daily	206	.320	0	30	230	65	24	2	5.8	.925							
	UT	T. Daly	200	.250	2	27	289	58	38	8		.901							
	PO	B. Caruthers	171	.281	2	23	29	68	10	2		.907							
	2B	J. O'Brien	167	.246	0	26	85	102	32	13	5.1	.854							
	P	T. Lovett	153	.163	0	17	23	59	6	2	2.0	.932							
Cincinnati	1B	L. Reilly	546	.242	4	64	1104	26	21	60	**11.5**	.982	T. Mullane	51	426	23	26	0	3.23
	2B	B. McPhee	562	.256	6	38	389	**492**	42	72	6.7	**.954**	B. Rhines	48	373	17	24	1	2.87
W-56 L-81	SS	G. Smith	512	.201	3	53	240	507	75	40	6.0	.909	O. Radbourn	26	218	11	13	0	4.25
	3B	A. Latham	533	.272	7	53	177	**370**	75	24	4.6	.879	C. Crane	15	117	4	8	0	4.09
Tom Loftus	RF	L. Marr	286	.259	0	32	75	6	16	2	1.3	.835	J. Duryea	10	77	1	9	0	5.38
	CF	B. Holliday	442	.319	9	84	186	13	13	3	1.9	.939							
	LF	P. Browning	216	.343	0	33	103	6	9	2	2.1	.924							
	C	Harrington	333	.228	2	41	388	106	**50**	6	5.9	.908							
	1C	J. Keenan	252	.202	4	33	587	51	30	22		.955							
	OF	J. Halligan	247	.312	3	44	89	6	16	1	1.8	.856							
	P	T. Mullane	209	.148	0	10	22	93	5	2	2.4	.958							
	OF	M. Slattery	158	.209	1	16	91	4	6	1	2.5	.941							
	P	B. Rhines	148	.122	0	5	8	95	7	3	2.3	.936							
Pittsburgh	1B	J. Beckley	554	.292	4	73	1250	**87**	24	63	10.2	.982	M. Baldwin	53	438	22	28	0	2.76
	2B	L. Bierbauer	500	.206	1	47	331	384	55	42	6.4	.929	S. King	48	384	14	**29**	1	3.11
W-55 L-80	SS	F. Shugart	320	.275	2	33	172	235	44	34	6.0	.902	P. Galvin	33	247	14	13	0	2.88
	3B	C. Reilly	415	.219	3	44	128	232	60	8	4.2	.857							
Ned Hanlon	RF	F. Carroll	353	.218	4	48	160	12	16	2	2.1	.915							
W-31 L-47	CF	N. Hanlon	455	.266	0	60	219	25	**33**	1	1.3	.881							
	LF	P. Browning	203	.291	4	28	115	8	13	0	2.7	.904							
Bill McGunnigle	C	C. Mack	280	.214	0	29	359	79	35	1	6.6	.926							
W-24 L-33	UT	D. Miller	548	.285	4	57	339	238	80	13		.878							
	P	M. Baldwin	177	.153	1	12	**37**	80	13	4	2.5	.900							
	OF	A. Maul	149	.188	0	14	58	7	9	2	1.9	.878							
	P	S. King	148	.169	0	9	19	67	10	**5**	2.0	.896							
	OF	P. Corkhill	145	.228	3	20	77	9	6	3	2.2	.935							
	OF	B. Lally	143	.224	1	17	45	2	9	0	1.4	.839							

BATTING AND BASE RUNNING LEADERS

Batting Average
B. Hamilton, PHI .340
B. Holliday, CIN .319
P. Browning, CIN, PIT .317
J. Clements, PHI .310
M. Tiernan, NY .306

Slugging Average
M. Tiernan, NY .500
H. Stovey, BOS .498
B. Holliday, CIN .473
J. Ryan, CHI .444
R. Connor, NY .443

Home Runs
M. Tiernan, NY 17
H. Stovey, BOS 16
W. Wilmot, CHI 11
H. Long, BOS 10

Total Bases
M. Tiernan, NY 271
H. Stovey, BOS 271
H. Long, BOS 241
G. Davis, CLE 235
J. Beckley, PIT 234

Runs Batted In
C. Anson, CHI 120
B. Nash, BOS 95
H. Stovey, BOS 95
J. O'Rourke, NY 95
R. Connor, NY 94

Stolen Bases
B. Hamilton, PHI 115
A. Latham, CIN 87
M. Griffin, BKN 65
H. Long, BOS 60
M. Ward, BKN 57
H. Stovey, BOS 57

PITCHING LEADERS

Winning Percentage
J. Ewing, NY .724
Hutchinson, CHI .694
H. Staley, BOS, PIT .649
K. Nichols, BOS .638
J. Clarkson, BOS .635

Earned Run Average
J. Ewing, NY 2.27
K. Nichols, BOS 2.39
A. Rusie, NY 2.55
H. Staley, BOS, PIT 2.58
M. Baldwin, PIT 2.76

Wins
Hutchinson, CHI 43
J. Clarkson, BOS 33
A. Rusie, NY 33
K. Nichols, BOS 30
C. Young, CLE 27

Saves
J. Clarkson, BOS 3
K. Nichols, BOS 3
C. Young, CLE 2
J. Thornton, PHI 2

Strikeouts
A. Rusie, NY 337
Hutchinson, CHI 261
K. Nichols, BOS 240
M. Baldwin, PIT 197
S. King, PIT 160

Complete Games
Hutchinson, CHI 56
A. Rusie, NY 52
M. Baldwin, PIT 48
J. Clarkson, BOS 47
K. Nichols, BOS 45

NATIONAL LEAGUE 1891, *cont.*

BATTING AND BASE RUNNING LEADERS

Hits
B. Hamilton, PHI	179
E. McKean, CLE	170
G. Davis, CLE	167
J. O'Rourke, NY	164

Base on Balls
B. Hamilton, PHI	102
C. Childs, CLE	97
R. Connor, NY	83
H. Long, BOS	80

Home Run Percentage
M. Tiernan, NY	3.1
H. Stovey, BOS	2.9
W. Wilmot, CHI	2.2
B. Holliday, CIN	2.0

Runs Scored
B. Hamilton, PHI	141
H. Long, BOS	129
C. Childs, CLE	120
A. Latham, CIN	119

Doubles
M. Griffin, BKN	36
G. Davis, CLE	35
H. Stovey, BOS	31
M. Tiernan, NY	30

Triples
H. Stovey, BOS	20
J. Beckley, PIT	20
B. McPhee, CIN	16
J. Ryan, CHI	15

PITCHING LEADERS

Fewest Hits/9 Innings
A. Rusie, NY	7.03
M. Baldwin, PIT	7.92
J. Ewing, NY	7.92
Hutchinson, CHI	8.15

Shutouts
A. Rusie, NY	6
J. Ewing, NY	5
K. Nichols, BOS	5
Hutchinson, CHI	4

Fewest Walks/9 Innings
K. Nichols, BOS	2.18
H. Staley, BOS, PIT	2.22
P. Galvin, PIT	2.26
O. Radbourn, CIN	2.56

Most Strikeouts/9 Inn.
A. Rusie, NY	6.06
K. Nichols, BOS	5.07
J. Ewing, NY	4.61
T. Keefe, NY, PHI	4.32

Innings
Hutchinson, CHI	561
A. Rusie, NY	500
J. Clarkson, BOS	461
M. Baldwin, PIT	438

Games Pitched
Hutchinson, CHI	66
A. Rusie, NY	61
J. Clarkson, BOS	55
C. Young, CLE	55

	W	L	PCT	GB	R	OR	2B	3B	HR	BA	SA	SB	E	DP	FA	CG	BB	SO	ShO	SV	ERA
							Batting						**Fielding**			**Pitching**					
Boston	87	51	.630		**847**	658	181	82	51	.255	.356	289	**358**	96	**.938**	126	364	525	9	**6**	**2.76**
Chicago	82	53	.607	3.5	832	730	159	88	**60**	.253	.359	238	397	**119**	.932	114	475	477	6	3	3.47
New York	71	61	.538	13	754	711	189	72	48	**.263**	**.362**	224	384	104	.933	117	593	**651**	11	3	2.99
Philadelphia	68	69	.496	18.5	756	773	180	51	21	.252	.322	232	443	108	.925	105	505	343	3	5	3.73
Cleveland	65	74	.468	22.5	835	888	183	87	23	.255	.339	242	485	86	.920	118	476	400	1	3	3.50
Brooklyn	61	76	.445	25.5	765	820	**200**	69	23	.260	.345	**337**	432	73	.924	121	459	407	8	3	3.86
Cincinnati	56	81	.409	30.5	646	790	148	**90**	40	.242	.335	244	409	101	.931	125	465	393	6	1	3.55
Pittsburgh	55	80	.407	30.5	679	744	148	71	28	.239	.317	205	475	76	.917	122	465	446	7	2	2.89
					6114	6114	1388	610	294	.252	.342	2011	3383	763	.928	948	3802	3642	51	26	3.34

AMERICAN ASSOCIATION 1891

	POS	Player	AB	BA	HR	RBI	PO	A	E	DP	TC/G	FA	Pitcher	G	IP	W	L	SV	ERA
Boston W-93 L-42 Arthur Irwin	1B	D. Brouthers	486	**.350**	5	108	1313	34	30	82	10.6	.978	G. Haddock	51	380	**34**	11	1	2.49
	2B	C. Stricker	514	.216	0	46	**405**	418	51	**78**	6.3	.942	C. Buffinton	48	364	29	9	1	2.55
	SS	P. Radford	456	.259	0	65	230	453	71	51	5.8	.906	D. O'Brien	40	269	18	13	2	3.65
	3B	D. Farrell	473	.302	12	110	87	160	22	8	4.1	.918	B. Daley	19	127	8	6	2	2.98
	RF	H. Duffy	536	.336	8	108	166	23	17	3	1.7	.917							
	CF	T. Brown	**589**	.321	5	71	228	23	35	7	2.1	.878							
	LF	Richardson	278	.255	7	51	101	5	5	2	1.9	.955							
	C	M. Murphy	402	.216	4	54	**532**	118	31	8	6.5	**.954**							
	3B	B. Joyce	243	.309	3	51	82	149	41	12	4.3	.849							
	P	G. Haddock	185	.243	3	23	21	116	12	2	2.9	.919							
	P	C. Buffinton	181	.188	1	16	10	117	9	3	2.8	.934							
	OF	J. McGeachy	178	.253	1	21	57	4	6	0	1.6	.910							
St. Louis W-86 L-52 Charlie Comiskey	1B	C. Comiskey	580	.262	3	93	**1433**	62	31	78	10.8	.980	J. Stivetts	64	440	33	22	1	2.86
	2B	B. Eagan	302	.215	4	43	177	278	35	29	5.9	.929	W. McGill	35	249	18	10	1	2.93
	SS	S. Fuller	586	.217	2	63	168	309	80	36	5.4	.856	C. Griffith	27	186	14	6	0	3.33
	3B	D. Lyons	451	.315	11	84	151	246	59	16	3.8	.871	J. Neale	15	110	8	4	1	4.24
	RF	T. McCarthy	578	.310	8	95	164	24	22	5	1.9	.895	G. Rettger	14	93	7	3	1	3.40
	CF	D. Hoy	567	.291	5	66	255	26	28	3	2.2	.909							
	LF	T. O'Neill	521	.321	10	95	197	5	14	0	1.7	.935							
	C	J. Boyle	439	.280	5	79	428	88	35	**11**	6.1	.936							
	P	J. Stivetts	302	.305	7	54	22	110	**15**	2	2.3	.898							
	UT	J. Munyan	182	.231	0	20	207	55	25	4		.913							
Milwaukee W-21 L-15 Charlie Cushman	1B	J. Carney	110	.300	3	23	324	20	5	16	11.3	.986	G. Davies	12	102	7	5	0	2.66
	2B	J. Canavan	142	.268	3	21	51	76	20	4	6.1	.864	F. Killen	11	96	7	4	0	1.68
	SS	G. Shoch	127	.315	1	16	51	85	10	4	5.8	.932	F. Dwyer	10	86	6	4	0	2.20
	3B	G. Alberts	41	.098	0	2	14	21	8	2	3.6	.814							
	RF	H. Earl	129	.248	1	17	43	2	1	1	1.5	.978							
	CF	E. Burke	144	.236	1	21	70	8	7	3	2.4	.918							
	LF	A. Dalrymple	135	.311	1	22	44	6	5	1	1.7	.909							
	C	F. Vaughn	99	.333	0	9	103	19	10	5	6.6	.924							
Baltimore W-72 L-63 Billy Barnie W-72 L-63 George Van Haltren W-4 L-2	1B	P. Werden	552	.290	6	104	1422	58	30	79	**10.9**	.980	S. McMahon	61	**503**	**34**	25	1	2.81
	2B	S. Wise	388	.247	1	48	225	299	66	30	6.0	.888	Cunningham	30	238	11	14	0	4.01
	SS	I. Ray	418	.278	0	58	71	103	28	9	5.1	.861	K. Madden	32	224	13	12	1	4.10
	3B	P. Gilbert	513	.230	3	72	201	324	84	34	4.4	.862	E. Healy	23	170	9	10	0	3.75
	RF	B. Johnson	480	.271	2	79	235	28	**37**	5	2.3	.877							
	CF	C. Welch	514	.268	3	55	258	25	16	4	**2.6**	.946							
	LF	Van Haltren	566	.318	9	83	143	21	22	7	2.3	.882							
	C	W. Robinson	334	.216	2	46	415	80	24	**11**	5.6	.954							
	P	S. McMahon	210	.205	1	15	14	141	11	4	2.7	.934							
	C	G. Townsend	204	.191	0	18	191	68	26	5	4.9	.909							

AMERICAN ASSOCIATION 1891, *cont.*

	POS	Player	AB	BA	HR	RBI	PO	A	E	DP	TC/G	FA	Pitcher	G	IP	W	L	SV	ERA
Philadelphia	1B	H. Larkin	526	.279	10	93	987	33	27	56	9.4	.974	G. Weyhing	52	450	31	20	0	3.18
	2B	B. Hallman	587	.283	6	69	327	399	55	53	5.5	.930	Chamberlain	49	406	22	23	0	4.22
W-73 L-66	SS	T. Corcoran	511	.254	7	71	**300**	434	72	5	**6.1**	.911	B. Sanders	19	145	11	5	0	3.79
	3B	J. Mulvey	453	.254	5	66	172	241	49	18	4.1	.894	W. Calihan	13	112	6	6	0	6.43
Bill Sharsig	RF	J. McGeachy	201	.229	2	13	82	10	8	0	2.0	.920							
W-6 L-11	CF	P. Corkhill	349	.209	0	31	182	14	9	3	2.5	.956							
	LF	G. Wood	528	.309	3	61	221	25	16	**10**	2.1	.939							
George Wood	C	J. Milligan	455	.303	11	106	470	101	37	9	**7.0**	.939							
W-67 L-55	UT	L. Cross	402	.301	5	52	297	103	28	12		.935							
	OF	J. McTamany	218	.225	3	21	118	10	14	1	2.4	.901							
	P	G. Weyhing	198	.111	0	11	27	73	8	2	2.1	.926							
	P	Chamberlain	176	.188	2	19	20	89	10	2	2.4	.916							
	OP	B. Sanders	156	.250	1	19	32	31	8	1		.887							
Columbus	1B	M. Lehane	511	.215	1	52	1362	**71**	28	**98**	10.7	**.981**	P. Knell	58	462	28	27	0	2.92
	2B	J. Crooks	519	.245	0	46	399	404	36	72	6.1	**.957**	H. Gastright	35	284	12	19	0	3.78
W-61 L-76	SS	B. Wheelock	498	.229	0	39	248	**474**	81	65	5.9	.899	J. Dolan	27	203	12	11	0	4.16
	3B	W. Kuehne	261	.215	2	22	85	146	30	15	3.8	.885	J. Easton	20	150	5	12	0	4.43
Gus Schmelz	RF	J. Sneed	366	.257	1	61	142	10	18	4	1.7	.894							
	CF	J. McTamany	304	.250	3	35	161	10	13	4	2.3	.929							
	LF	C. Duffee	552	.301	10	90	235	**33**	21	7	2.3	.927							
	C	J. Donahue	280	.218	0	35	343	108	28	**11**	6.4	.942							
	OC	J. O'Connor	229	.266	0	37	135	37	11	5		.940							
	OF	L. Twitchell	224	.277	2	35	67	4	9	0	1.4	.888							
	P	P. Knell	215	.158	0	19	**40**	119	10	1	2.9	.941							
	C	T. Dowse	201	.224	0	22	254	52	27	6	6.5	.919							
Cincinnati	1B	J. Carney	367	.278	3	43	984	45	28	42	10.7	.974	F. Dwyer	35	289	13	19	0	4.52
	2B	Y. Robinson	342	.178	1	37	222	287	78	33	6.1	.867	C. Crane	32	250	14	14	0	2.45
W-43 L-57	SS	J. Canavan	426	.228	7	46	217	304	85	31	6.0	.860	W. Mains	30	204	12	12	0	2.69
	3B	A. Whitney	347	.199	3	33	129	198	35	12	3.9	.903							
King Kelly	RF	E. Seery	372	.285	4	36	160	17	20	3	2.0	.898							
	CF	D. Johnston	376	.221	6	51	193	20	25	4	2.4	.895							
	LF	E. Andrews	356	.211	0	26	173	25	8	4	2.5	.961							
	C	K. Kelly	283	.297	1	53	217	102	34	11	5.3	.904							
	C	F. Vaughn	175	.257	1	14	170	58	19	6	5.6	.923							
	P	F. Dwyer	141	.284	0	18	15	74	6	1	2.7	.937							
Louisville	1B	H. Taylor	356	.295	2	37	927	45	21	56	10.8	.979	Fitzgerald	33	276	14	18	0	3.59
	2B	T. Shinnick	443	.221	1	54	226	332	52	45	5.1	.915	J. Meekin	29	228	10	16	0	4.30
W-55 L-84	SS	H. Jennings	360	.292	1	58	187	225	49	28	6.6	.894	R. Ehret	26	221	13	13	0	3.47
	3B	O. Beard	257	.241	0	24	84	149	32	16	4.3	.879	S. Stratton	20	172	6	13	0	4.08
Jack Chapman	RF	C. Wolf	537	.253	1	82	185	28	19	5	1.7	.918	J. Doran	15	126	5	10	0	5.43
	CF	F. Weaver	565	.283	1	55	**294**	**33**	15	7	2.6	**.956**	E. Daily	15	111	4	8	0	5.74
	LF	P. Donovan	439	.321	2	53	214	15	22	0	2.4	.912							
	C	J. Ryan	253	.225	2	25	223	83	23	10	5.9	.930							
	UT	T. Cahill	433	.256	3	47	389	242	69	32		.901							
	3B	W. Kuehne	159	.277	1	18	56	95	16	8	4.1	.904							
	C	P. Cook	153	.229	0	23	120	39	16	0	5.0	.909							
Washington	1B	M. McQuery	261	.241	2	37	701	30	17	39	11.0	.977	K. Carsey	54	415	14	**37**	0	4.99
	2B	T. Dowd	464	.259	1	44	230	287	67	38	5.5	.885	F. Foreman	43	345	18	21	1	3.73
W-43 L-92	SS	G. Hatfield	500	.256	1	48	211	334	82	40	6.0	.869	J. Bakely	13	104	2	10	0	5.35
	3B	B. Alvord	312	.234	0	30	147	210	57	10	5.1	.862							
Sam Trott	RF	L. Murphy	400	.265	1	35	164	10	25	3	2.0	.874							
W-4 L-7	CF	P. Hines	206	.282	0	31	81	8	15	4	2.2	.856							
	LF	E. Beecher	235	.243	2	28	109	13	26	4	2.6	.824							
Pop Snyder	C	D. McGuire	413	.303	3	66	442	**130**	**56**	8	6.4	.911							
W-23 L-46	1B	A. McCauley	206	.282	1	31	541	22	18	27	9.8	.969							
	OC	S. Sutcliffe	201	.353	2	33	115	36	15	4		.910							
Dan Shannon	P	K. Carsey	187	.150	0	15	22	120	12	5	2.9	.922							
W-15 L-34	P	F. Foreman	153	.222	4	19	13	66	4	4	1.9	.952							
Sandy Griffin																			
W-2 L-4																			

BATTING AND BASE RUNNING LEADERS

Batting Average		Slugging Average		Home Runs			Winning Percentage		Earned Run Average		Wins	
D. Brouthers, BOS	.350	D. Brouthers, BOS	.512	D. Farrell, BOS	12		C. Buffinton, BOS	.757	C. Crane, CIN, MIL	2.45	G. Haddock, BOS	34
H. Duffy, BOS	.336	J. Milligan, PHI	.505	D. Lyons, STL	11		G. Haddock, BOS	.756	G. Haddock, BOS	2.49	S. McMahon, BAL	34
T. Brown, BOS	.321	D. Farrell, BOS	.474	J. Milligan, PHI	11		C. Griffith, BOS, STL	.708	C. Buffinton, BOS	2.55	J. Stivetts, STL	33
T. O'Neill, STL	.321	T. Brown, BOS	.469				G. Weyhing, PHI	.608	G. Davies, CIN, MIL	2.65	G. Weyhing, PHI	31
Van Haltren, BAL	.318	L. Cross, PHI	.458				J. Stivetts, STL	.600	S. McMahon, BAL	2.81	C. Buffinton, BOS	28

PITCHING LEADERS

P. Knell, COL   28

AMERICAN ASSOCIATION 1891, *cont.*

BATTING AND BASE RUNNING LEADERS

Total Bases			Runs Batted In			Stolen Bases		
T. Brown, BOS	276		D. Farrell, BOS	110		T. Brown, BOS	106	
Van Haltren, BAL	251		D. Brouthers, BOS	108		H. Duffy, BOS	85	
D. Brouthers, BOS	249		H. Duffy, BOS	108		Van Haltren, BAL	75	
H. Duffy, BOS	240		J. Milligan, PHI	106		D. Hoy, STL	59	
T. McCarthy, STL	236		P. Werden, BAL	104		P. Radford, BOS	55	

Hits			Base on Balls			Home Run Percentage		
T. Brown, BOS	189		D. Hoy, STL	119		D. Farrell, BOS	2.5	
H. Duffy, BOS	180		J. Crooks, COL	103		D. Lyons, STL	2.4	
Van Haltren, BAL	180		J. McTamany, COL, PHI	101		J. Milligan, PHI	2.4	
T. McCarthy, STL	179		P. Radford, BOS	96		J. Stivetts, STL	2.3	

Runs Scored			Doubles			Triples		
T. Brown, BOS	177		J. Milligan, PHI	35		T. Brown, BOS	21	
Van Haltren, BAL	136		T. Brown, BOS	30		D. Brouthers, BOS	19	
D. Hoy, STL	136		T. O'Neill, STL	28		P. Werden, BAL	18	
H. Duffy, BOS	134		C. Duffee, COL	28		J. Canavan, CIN, MIL	18	

PITCHING LEADERS

Saves		Strikeouts		Complete Games	
C. Buffinton, BOS	3	J. Stivetts, STL	259	S. McMahon, BAL	53
B. Daley, BOS	2	P. Knell, COL	228	G. Weyhing, PHI	51
		G. Weyhing, PHI	219	P. Knell, COL	47
		S. McMahon, BAL	219	K. Carsey, WAS	46
		Chamberlain, PHI	204	Chamberlain, PHI	44

Fewest Hits/9 Innings		Shutouts		Fewest Walks/9 Innings	
P. Knell, COL	7.07	G. Haddock, BOS	5	S. Stratton, LOU	1.78
J. Stivetts, STL	7.30	P. Knell, COL	5	B. Sanders, PHI	2.30
C. Buffinton, BOS	7.50	S. McMahon, BAL	5	S. McMahon, BAL	2.67
C. Crane, CIN, MIL	7.78	Fitzgerald, LOU	3	R. Ehret, LOU	2.85

Most Strikeouts/9 Inn.		Innings		Games Pitched	
J. Meekin, LOU	5.68	S. McMahon, BAL	503	J. Stivetts, STL	64
G. Davies, CIN, MIL	5.38	P. Knell, COL	462	S. McMahon, BAL	61
J. Stivetts, STL	5.30	G. Weyhing, PHI	450	P. Knell, COL	58
W. McGill, CIN, MIL, STL	4.96	J. Stivetts, STL	440	K. Carsey, WAS	54

	W	L	PCT	GB	R	OR	2B	3B	HR	BA	SA	SB	E	DP	FA	CG	BB	SO	ShO	SV	ERA
Boston	93	42	.689		1028	675	163	100	51	.274	.380	447	392	115	.934	108	497	524	9	8	3.03
St. Louis	86	52	.623	8.5	976	753	169	51	58	.266	.355	283	468	91	.920	103	576	621	8	5	3.27
Milwaukee	21	15	.583	22.5	227	156	58	15	12	.261	.359	47	116	20	.922	35	120	137	3	0	2.50
Baltimore	72	63	.533	21	850	798	142	99	30	.255	.345	342	503	103	.915	118	472	408	6	2	3.43
Philadelphia	73	66	.525	22	817	794	182	55	45	.258	.376	149	389	109	.933	135	520	533	3	0	4.01
Columbus	61	76	.445	33	702	777	154	61	20	.237	.308	280	379	126	.935	118	588	502	6	0	3.75
Cincinnati	43	57	.430	32.5	549	643	105	58	24	.234	.320	164	389	68	.913	86	446	331	2	1	3.44
Louisville	55	84	.396	40	713	890	130	69	17	.258	.324	230	458	113	.922	128	464	485	9	1	4.27
Washington	43	92	.319	50	691	1067	147	84	19	.251	.330	219	589	95	.900	123	566	486	2	2	4.83
					6553	6553	1250	660	290	.255	.344	2161	3683	840	.922	954	4249	4027	48	19	3.72

NATIONAL LEAGUE 1892

	POS	Player	AB	BA	HR	RBI	PO	A	E	DP	TC/G	FA	Pitcher	G	IP	W	L	SV	ERA
Boston W-102 L-48 Frank Selee	1B	T. Tucker	542	.282	1	62	1484	51	45	96	10.6	.972	K. Nichols	53	454	35	16	0	2.83
	2B	J. Quinn	532	.218	1	59	356	426	40	75	5.7	.951	J. Stivetts	53	415	35	16	1	3.04
	SS	H. Long	646	.280	6	77	297	497	99	65	6.3	.889	H. Staley	37	300	22	10	0	3.03
	3B	B. Nash	526	.260	4	95	197	351	62	23	4.5	.898	J. Clarkson	16	146	8	6	0	2.35
	RF	T. McCarthy	603	.242	4	63	219	29	33	4	1.8	.883							
	CF	H. Duffy	612	.301	5	81	259	17	17	4	2.0	.942							
	LF	B. Lowe	475	.242	3	57	175	17	15	2	2.3	.928							
	C	K. Kelly	281	.189	2	41	319	98	40	11	6.3	.912							
	P	J. Stivetts	240	.296	3	36	17	96	12	5	2.4	.904							
	C	C. Ganzel	198	.268	0	25	202	50	18	1	5.3	.933							
	P	K. Nichols	197	.198	2	21	25	88	4	4	2.2	.966							
Cleveland W-93 L-56 Patsy Tebeau	1B	J. Virtue	557	.282	2	89	1500	61	26	61	10.8	.984	C. Young	53	453	36	12	0	**1.93**
	2B	C. Childs	558	.317	3	53	357	441	53	51	6.3	.938	N. Cuppy	47	376	28	13	1	2.51
	SS	E. McKean	531	.262	0	93	207	369	92	29	5.2	.862	J. Clarkson	29	243	17	10	1	2.55
	3B	G. Davis	597	.241	5	82	100	166	25	8	3.7	.914	G. Davies	26	216	10	16	0	2.59
	RF	J. O'Connor	572	.248	2	58	152	21	12	4	1.7	.935							
	CF	J. McAleer	571	.238	4	70	367	25	16		2.7	.961							
	LF	J. Burkett	608	.275	6	66	271	20	31	7	2.2	.904							
	C	C. Zimmer	413	.262	1	64	514	122	42	11	6.1	.938							
	3B	P. Tebeau	340	.244	2	49	99	156	25	17	3.8	.911							
	P	C. Young	196	.158	1	15	19	122	8	7	2.8	.946							
	P	N. Cuppy	168	.214	0	24	10	103	6	3	2.5	.950							
Brooklyn W-95 L-59 Monte Ward	1B	D. Brouthers	588	**.335**	5	124	1498	105	29	69	10.7	.982	G. Haddock	46	381	29	13	1	3.14
	2B	M. Ward	614	.265	2	47	377	472	74	48	6.2	.920	E. Stein	48	377	27	16	1	2.84
	SS	T. Corcoran	613	.237	1	74	291	495	64	49	5.6	.925	D. Foutz	27	203	13	8	1	3.41
	3B	B. Joyce	372	.245	6	45	141	146	49	8	3.8	.862	B. Hart	28	195	9	12	1	3.28
	RF	O. Burns	542	.315	4	96	162	16	12	4	1.5	.937	B. Kennedy	26	191	13	8	1	3.86
	CF	M. Griffin	452	.277	3	66	267	25	4	7	2.3	**.986**							
	LF	D. O'Brien	490	.243	1	56	222	16	11	3	2.0	.956							
	C	C. Daily	278	.234	0	28	342	85	26	9	6.7	.943							
	UT	T. Daly	446	.256	4	51	260	170	33	16		.929							
	C	T. Kinslow	246	.305	2	40	355	89	32	6	7.2	.933							
	OP	D. Foutz	220	.186	1	26	50	60	14	2		.887							
	P	G. Haddock	158	.177	0	11	21	80	11	5	2.4	.902							

NATIONAL LEAGUE 1892, cont.

	POS	Player	AB	BA	HR	RBI	PO	A	E	DP	TC/G	FA	Pitcher	G	IP	W	L	SV	ERA
Philadelphia	1B	R. Connor	564	.294	12	73	1483	59	23	99	10.1	.985	G. Weyhing	59	470	32	21	3	2.66
	2B	B. Hallman	586	.292	2	84	335	379	49	60	5.5	.936	K. Carsey	43	318	19	16	1	3.12
W-87 L-66	SS	B. Allen	563	.227	2	64	331	537	77	67	6.2	.919	T. Keefe	39	313	19	16	0	2.36
	3B	C. Reilly	331	.196	1	24	106	169	29	13	4.3	.905	D. Esper	21	160	11	6	1	3.42
Harry Wright	RF	S. Thompson	609	.305	9	104	223	28	17	7	1.8	.937	P. Knell	11	80	5	5	0	4.05
	CF	E. Delahanty	477	.306	6	91	261	25	17	6	2.5	.944							
	LF	B. Hamilton	554	.330	3	53	291	26	28	7	2.5	.919							
	C	J. Clements	402	.264	8	76	557	107	35	12	6.4	.950							
	UT	L. Cross	541	.275	4	69	327	236	35	17		.941							
	P	G. Weyhing	214	.136	0	13	20	63	20	2	1.7	.806							
Cincinnati	1B	C. Comiskey	551	.227	3	71	1469	73	25	103	11.1	.984	Chamberlain	52	406	19	23	0	3.39
	2B	B. McPhee	573	.274	4	60	451	471	51	86	6.8	.948	T. Mullane	37	295	21	13	1	2.59
W-82 L-68	SS	G. Smith	506	.239	8	63	239	561	70	55	6.3	.920	F. Dwyer	33	259	19	10	1	2.33
	3B	A. Latham	622	.238	0	44	167	329	66	26	4.0	.883	M. Sullivan	21	166	12	4	0	3.08
Charlie Comiskey	RF	B. Holliday	602	.292	13	81	271	20	21	6	2.1	.933	B. Rhines	12	84	4	7	0	5.06
	CF	P. Browning	307	.303	3	52	152	13	15	0	2.2	.917							
	LF	T. O'Neill	419	.251	2	52	188	13	17	3	2.0	.922							
	C	M. Murphy	234	.197	2	24	315	67	18	6	5.4	.955							
	UT	F. Vaughn	346	.254	2	50	394	80	33	22		.935							
	P	Chamberlain	160	.225	2	15	16	67	9	0	1.8	.902							
Pittsburgh	1B	J. Beckley	614	.236	10	96	1523	132	38	88	11.2	.978	M. Baldwin	56	440	26	27	0	3.47
	2B	L. Bierbauer	649	.236	8	65	385	555	79	66	6.5	.950	R. Ehret	39	316	16	20	0	2.65
W-80 L-73	SS	F. Shugart	554	.267	0	62	303	466	99	43	6.5	.886	A. Terry	30	240	17	7	1	2.51
	3B	D. Farrell	605	.215	8	77	180	286	64	20	4.0	.879	E. Smith	17	134	6	7	0	3.63
Al Buckenberger	RF	P. Donovan	388	.294	2	26	111	18	19	4	1.6	.872	P. Galvin	12	96	5	6	0	2.63
W-55 L-43	CF	J. Kelley	205	.239	0	28	101	13	10	4	2.2	.919							
	LF	E. Smith	511	.274	4	63	223	15	31	0	2.2	.885							
Tom Burns	C	C. Mack	346	.243	1	31	404	143	28	11	6.3	.951							
W-25 L-30	UT	D. Miller	623	.254	2	59	413	145	44	22		.927							
	OF	P. Corkhill	256	.184	0	25	148	13	8	4	2.5	.953							
	P	M. Baldwin	178	.101	1	13	37	86	18	2	2.5	.872							
Chicago	1B	C. Anson	559	.272	1	74	1491	67	44	62	11.0	.973	Hutchinson	75	627	37	36	0	2.74
	2B	J. Canavan	439	.166	0	32	282	349	53	40	6.1	.923	A. Gumbert	46	383	22	19	0	3.41
W-70 L-76	SS	B. Dahlen	581	.291	5	58	178	232	41	29	6.3	.909	P. Luby	31	247	10	16	1	3.13
	3B	J. Parrott	333	.201	2	48	115	164	34	7	4.0	.891							
Cap Anson	RF	S. Dungan	433	.284	0	53	183	8	20	2	1.9	.905							
	CF	J. Ryan	505	.293	10	65	241	26	23	5	2.4	.921							
	LF	W. Wilmot	380	.216	2	35	197	8	22	0	2.5	.903							
	C	P. Schriver	326	.224	1	34	367	102	36	5	6.2	.929							
	OF	G. Decker	291	.227	1	28	73	12	12	3	1.6	.876							
	P	Hutchinson	263	.217	1	22	21	156	13	4	2.5	.932							
	SS	J. Cooney	238	.172	0	20	101	211	30	15	5.3	.912							
	C	M. Kittridge	229	.179	0	10	359	87	26	5	6.8	.945							
	P	A. Gumbert	178	.236	1	8	10	97	9	1	2.5	.922							
	PO	P. Luby	163	.190	2	20	28	62	9	3		.909							
New York	1B	B. Ewing	393	.310	7	76	669	49	19	35	10.1	.974	A. Rusie	64	532	32	31	0	2.88
	2B	E. Burke	363	.259	6	41	149	181	55	19	6.5	.857	S. King	52	419	23	24	0	3.24
W-71 L-80	SS	S. Fuller	508	.226	1	48	294	434	92	44	5.8	.888	C. Crane	47	364	16	24	1	3.80
	3B	D. Lyons	389	.257	8	51	152	206	53	13	3.8	.871							
Pat Powers	RF	M. Tiernan	450	.287	5	66	155	15	19	2	1.6	.899							
	CF	H. Lyons	411	.238	0	53	186	16	20	1	2.3	.910							
	LF	J. O'Rourke	448	.304	0	56	146	11	15	1	1.5	.913							
	C	J. Boyle	436	.183	0	32	418	126	46	9	7.5	.922							
	UT	J. Doyle	366	.298	0	33	231	154	60	13		.865							
	P	A. Rusie	252	.210	1	26	27	132	21	5	2.8	.883							
	UT	Richardson	248	.214	2	34	218	136	24	16		.937							
	OF	G. Gore	193	.254	0	11	102	8	8	2	2.2	.932							
	P	S. King	167	.210	2	23	22	81	11	4	2.2	.904							
	P	C. Crane	163	.245	0	14	27	69	22	4	2.5	.814							
	1B	J. McMahon	147	.224	1	24	312	13	9	13	9.3	.973							
Louisville	1B	L. Whistler	285	.235	5	34	773	32	18	52	11.4*	.978	S. Stratton	42	352	21	19	0	2.92
	2B	F. Pfeffer	470	.257	2	76	313	377	50	72	6.4	.932	B. Sanders	31	268	12	19	0	3.22
W-63 L-89	SS	H. Jennings	594	.222	2	61	343	537	90	59	6.4	.907	F. Clausen	24	200	9	13	0	3.06
	3B	W. Kuehne	287	.167	0	36	104	160	38	16	4.0	.874	J. Meekin	19	156	7	10	0	4.03
Jack Chapman	RF	E. Seery	154	.201	0	15	65	10	3	1	1.9	.962	A. Jones	18	147	5	11	0	3.31
W-23 L-35	CF	T. Brown	660	.227	2	45	351	37	34	8	2.8	.919	L. Viau	16	131	4	11	0	3.99
	LF	F. Weaver	551	.254	0	57	185	18	22	3	1.8	.902							
Fred Pfeffer	C	J. Grim	370	.243	1	36	262	85	22	7	5.3	.940							
W-40 L-54	UT	H. Taylor	493	.260	0	34	498	74	29	29		.952							
	3B	C. Bassett	313	.214	2	34	76	179	41	13	4.1	.861							
	PO	S. Stratton	219	.256	0	23	35	91	14	4		.900							
	UT	B. Sanders	198	.273	3	18	172	61	12	7		.951							
	C	B. Merritt	168	.196	1	13	175	58	15	6	5.4	.940							

NATIONAL LEAGUE 1892, *cont.*

	POS	Player	AB	BA	HR	RBI	PO	A	E	DP	TC/G	FA	Pitcher	G	IP	W	L	SV	ERA
Washington	1B	H. Larkin	464	.280	8	96	1121	69	38	77	10.5	.969	F. Killen	60	460	29	26	0	3.31
	2B	T. Dowd	584	.243	1	50	208	264	58	33	5.4	.891	B. Abbey	27	196	5	18	1	3.45
W-58 L-93	SS	Richardson	551	.240	3	58	225	355	43	45	6.7	.931	P. Knell	22	170	9	13	0	3.65
	3B	Y. Robinson	218	.179	0	19	70	125	34	11	3.9	.852	J. Duryea	18	127	3	10	2	2.41
Billy Barnie	RF	P. Radford	510	.255	1	37	86	12	7	7	1.7	.933	J. Meekin	14	112	3	10	0	3.46
W-0 L-2	CF	D. Hoy	593	.280	3	75	275	16	38	3	2.2	.884							
	LF	C. Duffee	492	.248	6	51	230	34	25	8	2.3	.913							
Arthur Irwin	C	D. McGuire	315	.232	4	43	381	100	33	8	5.8	.936							
W-46 L-60	C1	J. Milligan	323	.276	5	43	522	99	24	22		.963							
	OF	L. Twitchell	192	.219	0	20	73	5	9	1	1.8	.897							
Danny Richardson	P	F. Killen	186	.199	4	23	20	121	22	2	2.7	.865							
W-12 L-31	OF	P. Donovan	163	.239	0	12	56	9	12	3	1.9	.844							
St. Louis	1B	P. Werden	598	.258	8	84	1467	102	28	81	10.7	.982	K. Gleason	47	400	16	24	0	3.33
	2B	J. Crooks	445	.213	7	38	286	300	44	43	6.2	.930	Breitenstein	39	282	14	20	0	4.69
W-56 L-94	SS	J. Glasscock	566	.267	3	72	280	472	69	46	5.9	.916	P. Hawley	20	166	6	14	0	3.19
	3B	G. Pinckney	290	.172	0	25	84	161	31	12	3.5	.888	C. Getzien	13	108	5	8	0	5.67
Jack Glasscock	RF	B. Caruthers	513	.277	3	69	159	14	21	2	1.6	.892	B. Caruthers	16	102	2	8	1	5.84
W-1 L-3	CF	S. Brodie	602	.252	4	60	296	21	19	4	2.5	.943	P. Galvin	12	92	5	7	0	3.23
	LF	C. Carroll	407	.273	4	49	181	19	22	1	2.2	.901	F. Dwyer	10	64	2	8	0	5.63
Cub Stricker	C	D. Buckley	410	.227	5	52	513	123	43	14	5.7	.937							
W-6 L-17	UT	K. Gleason	233	.215	3	25													
	OF	G. Moriarity	177	.175	3	19	96	9	23	0	2.7	.820							
Jack Crooks																			
W-27 L-33																			
George Gore																			
W-6 L-9																			
Bob Caruthers																			
W-16 L-32																			
Baltimore	1B	S. Sutcliffe	276	.279	1	27	678	24	31	39	11.1	.958	S. McMahon	48	397	20	25	0	3.24
	2B	C. Stricker	269	.264	3	37	212	224	39	31	6.3	.918	G. Cobb	53	394	10	37	0	4.86
W-48 L-105	SS	T. O'Rourke	239	.310	0	35	104	180	43	17	5.6	.869	T. Vickery	24	176	8	10	0	3.53
	3B	B. Shindle	619	.252	3	50	200	382	78	27	4.9	.882	C. Buffinton	13	97	3	8	0	4.92
George Van Haltren	RF	Van Haltren	556	.302	7	57	217	27	43*	5	2.2	.850							
W-1 L-14	CF	C. Welch	237	.236	1	22	129	4	14	1	2.3	.905							
	LF	H. Stovey	283	.272	4	55	109	6	11	2	2.0	.913							
John Waltz	C	W. Robinson	330	.267	2	57	332	86	36	8	5.2	.921							
W-2 L-6	C	J. Gunson	314	.213	0	32	281	92	32	3	6.0	.921							
	SS	G. Shoch	308	.276	1	50	96	197	43	17	5.9	.872							
Ned Hanlon	UT	J. McGraw	286	.269	1	26	165	144	28	16		.917							
W-45 L-85	1B	L. Whistler	209	.225	2	21	540	26	16	21	11.4*	.973							
	OF	P. Ward	186	.290	1	33	53	13	8	4	1.7	.892							
	UT	J. Halligan	178	.270	2	43	220	13	19	10		.925							
	P	S. McMahon	177	.141	0	18	7	94	12	2	2.4	.894							
	P	G. Cobb	172	.209	1	13	12	96	14	0	2.3	.885							

BATTING AND BASE RUNNING LEADERS

Batting Average
- D. Brouthers, BKN — .335
- B. Hamilton, PHI — .330
- C. Childs, CLE — .317
- O. Burns, BKN — .315
- B. Ewing, NY — .310

Slugging Average
- E. Delahanty, PHI — .495
- D. Brouthers, BKN — .480
- B. Ewing, NY — .466
- R. Connor, PHI — .463
- O. Burns, BKN — .454

Home Runs
- B. Holliday, CIN — 13
- R. Connor, PHI — 12
- J. Ryan, CHI — 10
- J. Beckley, PIT — 10
- S. Thompson, PHI — 9

Winning Percentage
- C. Young, CLE — .766
- G. Haddock, BKN — .690
- H. Staley, BOS — .688
- K. Nichols, BOS — .686
- J. Stivetts, BOS — .686

Earned Run Average
- C. Young, CLE — 1.93
- T. Keefe, PHI — 2.36
- J. Clarkson, BOS, CLE — 2.48
- N. Cuppy, CLE — 2.51
- A. Terry, BAL, PIT — 2.57

Wins
- Hutchinson, CHI — 37
- C. Young, CLE — 36
- K. Nichols, BOS — 35
- J. Stivetts, BOS — 35
- G. Weyhing, PHI — 32
- A. Rusie, NY — 32

Total Bases
- D. Brouthers, BKN — 282
- B. Holliday, CIN — 270
- S. Thompson, PHI — 263
- R. Connor, PHI — 261
- H. Duffy, BOS — 251

Runs Batted In
- D. Brouthers, BKN — 124
- S. Thompson, PHI — 104
- H. Larkin, WAS — 96
- O. Burns, BKN — 96
- J. Beckley, PIT — 96

Stolen Bases
- M. Ward, BKN — 88
- T. Brown, LOU — 78
- A. Latham, CIN — 66
- H. Duffy, BOS — 61
- B. Dahlen, CHI — 60
- D. Hoy, WAS — 60

Saves
- G. Weyhing, PHI — 3
- J. Duryea, CIN, WAS — 2

Strikeouts
- Hutchinson, CHI — 316
- A. Rusie, NY — 303
- G. Weyhing, PHI — 202
- E. Stein, BKN — 190
- K. Nichols, BOS — 187

Complete Games
- Hutchinson, CHI — 67
- A. Rusie, NY — 58
- K. Nichols, BOS — 50
- C. Young, CLE — 48

Hits
- D. Brouthers, BKN — 197
- S. Thompson, PHI — 186
- H. Long, BOS — 185
- B. Hamilton, PHI — 183

Base on Balls
- J. Crooks, STL — 136
- C. Childs, CLE — 117
- R. Connor, PHI — 116
- T. McCarthy, BOS — 93

Home Run Percentage
- B. Holliday, CIN — 2.2
- R. Connor, PHI — 2.1
- D. Lyons, NY — 2.1
- J. Clements, PHI — 2.0

Fewest Hits/9 Innings
- T. Mullane, CIN — 6.77
- A. Rusie, NY — 6.85
- A. Terry, BAL, PIT — 6.94
- C. Young, CLE — 7.21

Shutouts
- C. Young, CLE — 9
- E. Stein, BKN — 6
- G. Weyhing, PHI — 6
- J. Clarkson, BOS, CLE — 5

Fewest Walks/9 Innings
- S. Stratton, LOU — 1.79
- F. Dwyer, CIN, STL — 2.03
- B. Sanders, LOU — 2.08
- C. Young, CLE — 2.34

Runs Scored
- C. Childs, CLE — 136
- B. Hamilton, PHI — 132
- H. Duffy, BOS — 125
- R. Connor, PHI — 123

Doubles
- R. Connor, PHI — 37
- H. Long, BOS — 33
- E. Delahanty, PHI — 30
- D. Brouthers, BKN — 30

Triples
- E. Delahanty, PHI — 21
- J. Virtue, CLE — 20
- D. Brouthers, BKN — 20
- B. Dahlen, CHI — 19

Most Strikeouts/9 Inn.
- B. Kennedy, BKN — 5.09
- A. Rusie, NY — 4.87
- Hutchinson, CHI — 4.54
- E. Stein, BKN — 4.53

Innings
- Hutchinson, CHI — 627
- A. Rusie, NY — 532
- G. Weyhing, PHI — 470
- F. Killen, WAS — 460

Games Pitched
- Hutchinson, CHI — 75
- A. Rusie, NY — 64
- F. Killen, WAS — 60
- G. Weyhing, PHI — 59

PITCHING LEADERS

NATIONAL LEAGUE 1892, cont.

	W	L	PCT	GB	R	OR	Batting 2B	3B	HR	BA	SA	SB	Fielding E	DP	FA	Pitching CG	BB	SO	ShO	SV	ERA
Boston	102	48	.680		862	649	203	51	34	.250	.327	338	454	128	.929	143	460	509	**15**	1	2.86
Cleveland	93	56	.624	8.5	855	**613**	196	96	26	.254	.340	225	407	95	.935	140	**413**	472	11	2	**2.41**
Brooklyn	95	59	.617	9	**935**	733	183	105	30	**.262**	.350	**409**	398	98	**.940**	132	600	597	12	**5**	3.25
Philadelphia	87	66	.569	16.5	860	690	**225**	95	**50**	.262	**.367**	216	**393**	128	.939	131	492	502	10	**5**	2.93
Cincinnati	82	68	.547	20	766	731	155	75	44	.241	.322	270	402	**140**	.939	131	535	437	8	2	3.17
Pittsburgh	80	73	.523	23.5	802	796	143	108	38	.236	.322	222	483	113	.927	130	537	455	3	1	3.10
Chicago	70	76	.479	30	635	730	149	92	26	.235	.316	233	424	85	.932	133	424	518	6	1	3.16
New York	71	80	.470	31.5	811	826	173	85	38	.251	.337	301	565	97	.912	139	635	**641**	5	1	3.29
Louisville	63	89	.414	40	649	804	133	61	18	.226	.284	275	471	133	.928	**147**	447	430	9	0	3.34
Washington	58	93	.384	44.5	731	869	148	78	38	.239	.320	276	547	122	.916	129	556	479	5	3	3.46
St. Louis	56	94	.373	46	703	922	138	53	45	.226	.298	209	452	100	.929	139	543	478	4	1	4.20
Baltimore	48	105	.314	55.5	779	1020	160	**111**	30	.254	.343	227	584	100	.910	131	536	437	2	1	4.28
					9388	9388	2006	1010	417	.245	.327	3201	5580	1339	.928	1625	6178	5955	90	23	3.28

First Half

	W	L	PCT	GB
BOS*	52	22	.702	
BKN	51	26	.662	2.5
PHI	46	30	.662	7
CIN	44	31	.587	8.5
CLE	40	33	.548	11.5
PIT	37	39	.487	16
WAS	35	41	.461	18
CHI	31	39	.443	21
STL	31	42	.425	22.5
NY	31	43	.419	23
LOU	30	47	.390	25.5
BAL	20	55	.267	34.5

Second Half

	W	L	PCT	GB
CLE	53	23	.697	
BOS	50	26	.658	3
BKN	44	33	.571	9.5
PIT	43	34	.558	10.5
PHI	41	36	.532	12.5
NY	40	37	.532	13.5
CHI	39	37	.513	14
CIN	38	37	.513	14.5
LOU	33	42	.440	19.5
BAL	26	46	.361	25
STL	25	52	.325	28.5
WAS	23	52	.307	29.5

*Defeated Cleveland in playoff 5 games to 0 (1 tie).

NATIONAL LEAGUE 1893

POS	Player	AB	BA	HR	RBI	PO	A	E	DP	TC/G	FA	Pitcher	G	IP	W	L	SV	ERA
Boston W-86 L-43 Frank Selee																		
1B	T. Tucker	486	.284	7	91	1252	39	27	**89**	10.9	.980	K. Nichols	52	425	**34**	14	1	3.52
2B	B. Lowe	526	.298	13	89	308	409	49	58	6.3	.936	J. Stivetts	38	284	20	12	1	4.41
SS	H. Long	552	.288	6	58	271	469	98	67	6.8	.883	H. Staley	36	263	18	10	0	5.13
3B	B. Nash	485	.291	10	123	189	300	41	23	4.1	**.923**	H. Gastright	19	156	12	4	0	5.13
RF	C. Carroll	438	.224	2	54	226	18	22	5	2.2	.917							
CF	H. Duffy	560	.363	6	118	313	15	16	6	2.6	.953							
LF	T. McCarthy	462	.346	5	111	202	28	25	4	2.4	.902							
C	C. Bennett	191	.209	4	27	204	40	12	1	4.3	.953							
UT	C. Ganzel	281	.267	1	48	278	49	15	14		.956							
P	K. Nichols	177	.220	2	26	21	81	5	5	2.1	.953							
P	J. Stivetts	172	.297	3	25	13	50	3	2	1.8	.955							
C	B. Merritt	141	.348	3	26	129	25	9	6	4.4	.945							
P	H. Staley	113	.265	2	21	3	60	9	2	2.0	.875							
Pittsburgh W-81 L-48 Al Buckenberger																		
1B	J. Beckley	542	.303	5	106	1360	**95**	21	83	11.3	**.986**	F. Killen	55	415	**34**	14	0	3.64
2B	L. Bierbauer	528	.284	4	94	352	441	34	71	6.5	**.959**	R. Ehret	39	314	18	18	0	3.44
SS	J. Glasscock	293	.341	1	74	155	239	28	40	6.4	.934	A. Terry	26	170	12	8	0	4.45
3B	D. Lyons	490	.306	3	105	**214**	303	46	23	4.3	.918	A. Gumbert	22	163	12	7	0	5.15
RF	P. Donovan	499	.317	2	56	178	16	13	5	1.8	.937							
CF	Van Haltren	529	.338	3	79	227	24	38	3	2.6	.869							
LF	E. Smith	518	.346	7	103	271	20	25	7	2.5	.921							
C	D. Miller	154	.182	0	17	141	45	17	3	5.1	.916							
OF	J. Stenzel	224	.362	4	37	82	4	9	2	2.1	.905							
SS	F. Shugart	210	.262	1	32	98	178	37	15	6.1	.882							
P	F. Killen	171	.275	4	30	16	103	14	2	2.4	.895							
P	R. Ehret	136	.176	1	17	12	80	11	0	2.6	.893							
C	C. Mack	133	.286	0	15	128	47	11	5	5.0	.941							
Cleveland W-73 L-55 Patsy Tebeau																		
1B	J. Virtue	378	.265	1	60	777	47	21	48	11.6	.975	C. Young	53	423	34	16	1	3.36
2B	C. Childs	485	.326	3	65	348	424	62	56	6.8	.926	J. Clarkson	36	295	16	17	0	4.45
SS	E. McKean	545	.310	4	133	247	431	74	55	6.0	.902	N. Cuppy	31	244	17	10	0	4.47
3B	C. McGarr	249	.309	0	28	93	147	31	7	4.3	.886	C. Hastings	15	92	4	5	1	4.70
RF	B. Ewing	500	.344	6	122	201	14	17	3	2.1	.927							
CF	J. McAleer	350	.237	2	41	230	16	19	3	2.9	.908							
LF	J. Burkett	511	.348	6	82	239	19	**46**	5	2.4	.849							
C	C. Zimmer	227	.308	2	41	169	73	8	10	4.5	.968							
13	P. Tebeau	486	.329	2	102	652	177	41	35		.953							
CO	J. O'Connor	384	.286	3	75	252	70	19	2		.944							
P	C. Young	187	.235	1	27	27	112	8	1	2.8	.946							

NATIONAL LEAGUE 1893, *cont.*

Philadelphia

W-72 L-57

Harry Wright

POS	Player	AB	BA	HR	RBI	PO	A	E	DP	TC/G	FA	Pitcher	G	IP	W	L	SV	ERA
1B	J. Boyle	504	.286	4	81	1066	74	14	71	10.3	.988	G. Weyhing	42	345	23	16	0	4.74
2B	B. Hallman	596	.307	4	76	281	370	34	54	5.7	.950	K. Carsey	39	318	20	15	0	4.81
SS	B. Allen	471	.268	8	90	302	447	66	65	6.6	.919	T. Keefe	22	178	10	7	0	4.40
3B	C. Reilly	416	.245	4	56	164	235	47	21	4.3	.895	J. Taylor	25	170	10	9	1	4.24
RF	S. Thompson	600	.370	11	126	171	17	14	3	1.5	.931							
CF	B. Hamilton	355	.380	5	44	228	8	16	6	3.1	.937							
LF	E. Delahanty	595	.368	19	146	318	31	19	8	3.1	.948							
C	J. Clements	376	.285	17	80	329	75	25	5	4.7	.942							
UT	L. Cross	415	.299	4	78	291	182	27	27		.946							
OF	T. Turner	155	.323	1	13	79	5	6	2	2.5	.933							
OF	J. Sharrott	152	.250	1	22	51	5	12	0	2.1	.824							
P	G. Weyhing	147	.150	0	11	31	56	5	3	2.2	.946							
P	K. Carsey	145	.186	0	10	17	81	8	1	2.7	.925							

New York

W-68 L-64

Monte Ward

POS	Player	AB	BA	HR	RBI	PO	A	E	DP	TC/G	FA	Pitcher	G	IP	W	L	SV	ERA
1B	R. Connor	511	.305	11	105	1423	83	40	70	11.5	.974	A. Rusie	56	482	33	21	1	3.23
2B	M. Ward	588	.328	2	77	348	464	73	41	6.6	.918	M. Baldwin	45	331	16	20	2	4.10
SS	S. Fuller	474	.236	0	51	260	464	71	48	6.1	.911	L. German	20	152	8	8	0	4.14
3B	G. Davis	549	.355	11	119	181	305	64	27	4.1	.884							
RF	M. Tiernan	511	.309	15	102	178	12	15	2	1.6	.927							
CF	G. Stafford	281	.281	5	27	129	8	15	4	2.3	.901							
LF	E. Burke	537	.279	9	80	278	19	29	2	2.4	.911							
C	J. Doyle	318	.321	1	51	186	62	22	7	5.6	.919							
P	A. Rusie	212	.269	3	27	23	114	15	5	2.7	.901							
OF	H. Lyons	187	.273	0	21	113	9	11	3	2.8	.917							
C	J. Milligan	147	.231	1	25	188	67	18	5	6.5	.934							
P	M. Baldwin	134	.127	0	9	24	52	6	1	1.8	.927							
C	P. Wilson	114	.246	2	21	106	20	4	1	4.2	.969							

Brooklyn

W-65 L-63

Dave Foutz

POS	Player	AB	BA	HR	RBI	PO	A	E	DP	TC/G	FA	Pitcher	G	IP	W	L	SV	ERA
1B	D. Brouthers	282	.337	2	59	736	47	11	51	10.3	.986	B. Kennedy	46	383	25	20	1	3.72
2B	T. Daly	470	.289	8	70	207	265	44	22	6.3	.915	E. Stein	37	298	19	15	0	3.77
SS	T. Corcoran	459	.275	2	58	218	444	68	44	6.3	.907	G. Haddock	23	151	8	9	0	5.60
3B	G. Shoch	327	.263	2	54	48	66	9	5	3.3	.927	D. Daub	12	103	6	6	0	3.84
RF	O. Burns	415	.270	7	60	159	19	13	5	1.8	.932	G. Sharrott	13	95	4	6	1	5.87
CF	M. Griffin	362	.285	6	59	232	19	9	8	2.8	.965							
LF	D. Foutz	557	.246	7	67	157	10	16	1	2.4	.913							
C	T. Kinslow	312	.244	4	45	290	80	27	11	5.2	.932							
C	C. Daily	215	.265	1	32	215	46	18	2	5.5	.935							
2B	Richardson	206	.223	0	27	115	107	12	18	5.1	.949							
OF	H. Stovey	175	.251	1	29	115	3	13	0	2.7	.901							
P	B. Kennedy	157	.248	0	16	12	109	10	6	2.8	.924							

Cincinnati

W-65 L-63

Charlie Comiskey

POS	Player	AB	BA	HR	RBI	PO	A	E	DP	TC/G	FA	Pitcher	G	IP	W	L	SV	ERA
1B	C. Comiskey	259	.220	0	26	675	21	15	57	11.1	.979	F. Dwyer	37	287	18	15	2	4.13
2B	B. McPhee	491	.281	3	68	396	455	41	101	7.0	.954	Chamberlain	34	241	16	12	0	3.73
SS	G. Smith	500	.236	3	56	250	500	53	67	6.2	.934	M. Sullivan	27	184	8	11	1	5.05
3B	A. Latham	531	.282	2	49	172	281	55	23	4.0	.892	T. Parrott	22	154	10	7	0	4.09
RF	J. McCarthy	195	.282	0	22	87	7	12	0	2.3	.887	T. Mullane	15	122	6	6	1	4.41
CF	B. Holliday	500	.310	5	89	270	14	17	4	2.4	.944	S. King	17	105	5	6	1	4.89
LF	J. Canavan	461	.226	5	64	243	15	19	0	2.4	.931							
C	F. Vaughn	483	.280	1	108	270	77	11	10	4.5	.969							
C	M. Murphy	200	.235	1	19	162	45	15	6	4.0	.932							
1B	F. Motz	156	.256	2	25	426	38	9	27	11.0	.981							
OF	P. Ward	150	.280	0	10	54	8	13	4	1.9	.827							

Baltimore

W-60 L-70

Ned Hanlon

POS	Player	AB	BA	HR	RBI	PO	A	E	DP	TC/G	FA	Pitcher	G	IP	W	L	SV	ERA
1B	H. Taylor	360	.283	1	54	882	43	23	58	10.8	.976	S. McMahon	43	346	23	18	1	4.37
2B	H. Reitz	490	.286	1	76	315	421	48	62	6.0	.939	T. Mullane	34	245	12	16	1	4.45
SS	J. McGraw	480	.321	5	64	218	350	67	40	5.4	.894	B. Hawke	29	225	11	16	0	4.76
3B	B. Shindle	521	.261	1	75	176	308	63	24	4.4	.885	E. McNabb	21	142	8	7	0	4.12
RF	G. Treadway	458	.260	1	67	192	27	24	4	2.1	.901	K. Baker	15	92	3	8	0	8.44
CF	J. Kelley	502	.305	9	76	307	22	21	4	2.8	.940							
LF	J. Long	226	.212	2	25	109	8	14	1	2.4	.893							
C	W. Robinson	359	.334	3	57	349	70	26	8	4.8	.942							
C	B. Clarke	183	.175	1	24	135	45	18	3	5.2	.909							
P	S. McMahon	148	.243	0	22	16	75	18	2	2.5	.835							
OF	T. O'Rourke	135	.363	0	19	48	1	1	1	2.0	.980							

Chicago

W-56 L-71

Cap Anson

POS	Player	AB	BA	HR	RBI	PO	A	E	DP	TC/G	FA	Pitcher	G	IP	W	L	SV	ERA
1B	C. Anson	398	.314	0	91	997	44	20	59	10.5	.981	Hutchinson	44	348	16	24	0	4.75
2B	B. Lange	469	.281	8	88	151	181	42	21	6.6	.888	W. McGill	39	303	17	18	0	4.61
SS	B. Dahlen	485	.301	5	66	229	306	65	33	6.8	.892	H. Mauck	23	143	8	10	0	4.41
3B	J. Parrott	455	.244	1	65	145	251	42	21	4.4	.904							
RF	S. Dungan	465	.297	2	64	175	20	17	3	2.0	.920							
CF	J. Ryan	341	.299	3	30	122	16	18	2	2.7	.908							
LF	W. Wilmot	392	.301	3	61	198	16	31	1	2.6	.873							
C	M. Kittridge	255	.231	2	30	260	81	22	4	5.2	.939							
UT	G. Decker	328	.271	2	48	333	79	33	25		.926							
C	P. Schriver	229	.284	4	34	215	62	22	8	5.3	.926							
P	Hutchinson	162	.253	0	25	13	62	7	3	1.9	.915							
UT	L. Camp	156	.263	2	17	55	66	18	7		.871							

NATIONAL LEAGUE 1893, cont.

	POS	Player	AB	BA	HR	RBI	PO	A	E	DP	TC/G	FA	Pitcher	G	IP	W	L	SV	ERA
St. Louis	1B	P. Werden	500	.276	1	94	1194	81	**42**	75	10.6	.968	Breitenstein	48	383	19	20	1	**3.18**
	2B	J. Quinn	547	.230	0	71	354	366	44	63	5.7	.942	K. Gleason	48	380	21	25	1	4.61
W-57 L-75	SS	J. Glasscock	195	.287	1	26	85	159	25	19	5.6	.907	P. Hawley	31	227	5	17	1	4.60
	3B	J. Crooks	448	.237	1	48	210	286	50	19	**4.4**	.908	D. Clarkson	24	186	12	9	0	3.48
Bill Watkins	RF	T. Dowd	581	.282	1	54	225	27	15	9	2.0	.944							
	CF	S. Brodie	469	.318	2	79	273	21	15	7	2.9	.951							
	LF	C. Frank	164	.335	1	17	84	9	7	1	2.5	.930							
	C	H. Peitz	362	.254	1	45	296	86	21	7	5.4	.948							
	UT	F. Shugart	246	.280	0	28	107	101	34	11		.860							
	P	K. Gleason	199	.256	0	20	30	87	12	3	2.7	.907							
	SS	B. Ely	178	.253	0	16	98	139	25	16	6.0	.905							
	P	Breitenstein	160	.181	1	14	**42**	82	8	4	2.8	.939							
	C	J. Gunson	151	.272	0	15	130	36	13	4	5.1	.927							
	UT	D. Cooley	107	.346	0	21	46	12	4	2		.935							
Louisville	1B	W. Brown	461	.304	1	85	1082	51	13	76	10.3	.989*	G. Hemming	41	332	18	17	1	5.18
	2B	F. Pfeffer	508	.254	3	75	355	398	49	74	6.4	.939	S. Stratton	38	324	12	24	0	5.45
W-50 L-75	SS	T. O'Rourke	352	.281	0	53	118	176	46	26	5.7	.865	B. Rhodes	20	152	5	12	0	7.60
	3B	G. Pinckney	446	.235	1	62	126	279	34	26	3.7	.923	J. Menefee	15	129	8	7	0	4.24
Billy Barnie	RF	F. Weaver	439	.292	2	49	151	17	16	2	2.2	.913							
	CF	T. Brown	529	.240	5	54	**339**	39	29	**13**	3.3	.929							
	LF	P. Browning	220	.355	1	37	114	5	16	1	2.4	.881							
	C	J. Grim	415	.267	3	54	281	112	20	**15**	4.5	.952							
	PO	S. Stratton	221	.226	0	16	59	96	8	4		.951							
	OF	L. Twitchell	187	.310	1	31	91	6	14	0	2.5	.874							
	SS	J. Denny	175	.246	1	22	91	139	20	16	6.0	.920							
	P	G. Hemming	158	.203	0	19	19	80	7	2	2.6	.934							
Washington	1B	H. Larkin	319	.317	4	73	781	29	31	48	10.4	.963	D. Esper	42	334	12	**28**	0	4.71
	2B	S. Wise	521	.311	5	77	315	302	51	45	**7.3**	.924	A. Maul	37	297	12	21	0	5.30
W-40 L-89	SS	J. Sullivan	508	.266	2	64	233	396	**102**	34	5.7	.860	J. Meekin	31	245	10	15	0	4.96
	3B	J. Mulvey	226	.235	0	19	76	140	31	10	4.5	.874	J. Duryea	17	117	4	10	0	7.54
Jim O'Rourke	RF	P. Radford	464	.228	2	34	198	29	25	4	2.0	.901	Stocksdale	11	69	2	8	0	8.22
	CF	D. Hoy	564	.245	0	45	281	26	37	8	2.6	.892							
	LF	J. O'Rourke	547	.287	3	95	174	16	15	2	2.4	.927							
	C	D. Farrell	511	.280	4	75	304	**140**	**37**	5	**5.9**	.923							
	C	D. McGuire	237	.262	1	26	172	45	27	3	4.9	.889							
	UT	C. Stricker	218	.183	0	20	168	146	36	23		.897							
	P	D. Esper	143	.287	0	24	14	79	9	0	2.4	.912							
	P	A. Maul	134	.254	0	12	11	69	10	1	2.4	.889							
	P	J. Meekin	113	.257	3	20	12	53	7	3	2.3	.903							

BATTING AND BASE RUNNING LEADERS

Batting Average
B. Hamilton, PHI .380
S. Thompson, PHI .370
E. Delahanty, PHI .368
H. Duffy, BOS .363
G. Davis, NY .362

Slugging Average
E. Delahanty, PHI .583
G. Davis, NY .561
S. Thompson, PHI .530
E. Smith, PIT .525
B. Hamilton, PHI .524

Home Runs
E. Delahanty, PHI 19
J. Clements, PHI 17
M. Tiernan, NY 15
B. Lowe, BOS 13

Total Bases
E. Delahanty, PHI 347
S. Thompson, PHI 318
G. Davis, NY 308
E. Smith, PIT 272
E. McKean, CLE 258
H. Duffy, BOS 258

Runs Batted In
E. Delahanty, PHI 146
E. McKean, CLE 133
S. Thompson, PHI 126
B. Nash, BOS 123
B. Ewing, CLE 122

Stolen Bases
T. Brown, LOU 66
T. Dowd, STL 59
A. Latham, CIN 57
E. Burke, NY 54
H. Duffy, BOS 50

Hits
S. Thompson, PHI 222
E. Delahanty, PHI 219
H. Duffy, BOS 203
G. Davis, NY 195

Base on Balls
J. Crooks, STL 121
C. Childs, CLE 120
P. Radford, WAS 105
J. McGraw, BAL 101

Home Run Percentage
J. Clements, PHI 4.5
E. Delahanty, PHI 3.2
M. Tiernan, NY 2.9
B. Lowe, BOS 2.5

Runs Scored
H. Long, BOS 149
H. Duffy, BOS 147
C. Childs, CLE 145
J. Burkett, CLE 145

Doubles
S. Thompson, PHI 37
E. Delahanty, PHI 35
P. Tebeau, CLE 32
J. Beckley, PIT 32

Triples
P. Werden, STL 29
G. Davis, NY 27
E. McKean, CLE 24
E. Smith, PIT 23

PITCHING LEADERS

Winning Percentage
H. Gastright, BOS, PIT .750
F. Killen, PIT .733
K. Nichols, BOS .717
C. Young, CLE .667
H. Staley, BOS .643

Earned Run Average
Breitenstein, STL 3.18
A. Rusie, NY 3.23
C. Young, CLE 3.36
R. Ehret, PIT 3.44
D. Clarkson, STL 3.48

Wins
F. Killen, PIT 34
C. Young, CLE 34
K. Nichols, BOS 33
A. Rusie, NY 29
B. Kennedy, BKN 26

Saves
T. Mullane, BAL, CIN 2
M. Baldwin, NY, PIT 2
F. Dwyer, CIN 2
F. Donnelly, CHI 2

Strikeouts
A. Rusie, NY 208
B. Kennedy, BKN 107
Breitenstein, STL 102
C. Young, CLE 102
G. Weyhing, PHI 101

Complete Games
A. Rusie, NY 50
K. Nichols, BOS 44
C. Young, CLE 42
B. Kennedy, BKN 40

Fewest Hits/9 Innings
A. Rusie, NY 8.42
Breitenstein, STL 8.44
F. Killen, PIT 8.70
B. Kennedy, BKN 8.84

Shutouts
R. Ehret, PIT 4
A. Rusie, NY 4

Fewest Walks/9 Innings
C. Young, CLE 2.19
K. Nichols, BOS 2.50
N. Cuppy, CLE 2.77
H. Staley, BOS 2.77

Most Strikeouts/9 Inn.
A. Rusie, NY 3.88
J. Meekin, WAS 3.34
P. Hawley, STL 2.89
F. Clausen, CHI, LOU 2.89

Innings
A. Rusie, NY 482
K. Nichols, BOS 425
C. Young, CLE 423
F. Killen, PIT 415

Games Pitched
A. Rusie, NY 56
F. Killen, PIT 55
C. Young, CLE 53
K. Nichols, BOS 52

NATIONAL LEAGUE 1893, cont.

	W	L	PCT	GB	R	OR	Batting 2B	3B	HR	BA	SA	SB	Fielding E	DP	FA	Pitching CG	BB	SO	ShO	SV	ERA
Boston	86	43	.667		1008	795	178	50	64	.290	.391	243	353	118	.936	115	402	253	2	2	4.43
Pittsburgh	81	48	.628	5	970	766	176	127	37	.299	.411	210	347	112	.938	104	504	280	8	1	4.08
Cleveland	73	55	.570	12.5	976	839	222	98	31	.300	.408	252	395	92	.929	110	356	242	2	2	4.20
Philadelphia	72	57	.558	14	1011	841	246	90	79	.301	.430	202	318	121	.944	107	521	283	4	2	4.68
New York	68	64	.515	19.5	941	845	182	101	62	.293	.410	299	432	95	.927	111	581	395	6	4	4.29
Brooklyn	65	63	.508	20.5	775	845	173	83	45	.266	.371	213	385	88	.930	109	547	297	3	3	4.55
Cincinnati	65	63	.508	20.5	759	814	161	65	28	.259	.340	238	321	138	.943	97	549	258	4	5	4.59
Baltimore	60	70	.462	26.5	820	893	164	86	27	.275	.365	233	384	95	.929	104	534	275	1	2	4.97
Chicago	56	71	.441	29	829	874	186	93	32	.279	.379	255	421	92	.922	101	553	273	4	5	4.81
St. Louis	57	75	.432	30.5	745	829	152	98	10	.264	.341	250	398	110	.930	114	542	301	3	4	4.06
Louisville	50	75	.400	34	759	942	178	73	18	.260	.342	203	330	111	.937	114	479	190	4	1	5.90
Washington	40	89	.310	46	722	1032	180	83	24	.266	.354	154	497	96	.912	110	574	292	2	0	5.56
					10315	10315	2198	1047	457	.280	.379	2752	4581	1268	.931	1296	6142	3339	43	31	4.66

NATIONAL LEAGUE 1894

Baltimore
W-89 L-39
Ned Hanlon

POS	Player	AB	BA	HR	RBI	PO	A	E	DP	TC/G	FA	Pitcher	G	IP	W	L	SV	ERA
1B	D. Brouthers	525	.347	9	128	1184	65	31	83	10.4	.976	S. McMahon	35	276	25	8	0	4.21
2B	H. Reitz	446	.303	2	105	264	336	20	50	6.4	.968	B. Hawke	32	205	16	9	3	5.84
SS	H. Jennings	501	.335	4	109	307	499	63	69	6.8	.928	K. Gleason	21	172	15	5	0	4.45
3B	J. McGraw	512	.340	1	92	131	247	46	17	3.6	.892	B. Inks	22	133	9	4	1	5.55
RF	W. Keeler	590	.361	5	94	215	25	16	4	2.0	.938	T. Mullane	21	123	6	9	4	6.31
CF	S. Brodie	573	.366	3	113	310	14	17	4	2.6	.950	D. Esper	16	102	10	2	2	3.88
LF	J. Kelley	507	.393	6	111	276	16	15	3	2.4	.951							
C	W. Robinson	414	.353	1	98	370	84	27	8	4.4	.944							
P	S. McMahon	126	.286	0	25	17	62	5	2	2.4	.940							
2B	F. Bonner	118	.322	0	24	60	62	13	8	5.0	.904							

New York
W-88 L-44
Monte Ward

POS	Player	AB	BA	HR	RBI	PO	A	E	DP	TC/G	FA	Pitcher	G	IP	W	L	SV	ERA
1B	J. Doyle	425	.369	3	100	981	59	38	51	10.9	.965	A. Rusie	54	444	36	13	1	2.78
2B	M. Ward	540	.265	0	77	331	446	64	52	6.2	.924	J. Meekin	52	409	33	9	2	3.70
SS	S. Fuller	368	.283	2	46	205	291	65	39	6.3	.884	Westervelt	23	141	7	10	0	5.04
3B	G. Davis	492	.346	9	91	150	247	40	18	3.5	.908	L. German	23	134	9	8	1	5.78
RF	M. Tiernan	424	.276	5	77	169	9	15	1	1.7	.922							
CF	Van Haltren	519	.331	7	104	299	29	31	5	2.6	.914							
LF	E. Burke	566	.304	5	77	260	17	20	3	2.2	.933							
C	D. Farrell	401	.284	4	66	460	140	48	9	6.2	.926							
SO	Y. Murphy	280	.271	0	28	142	149	34	14		.895							
P	A. Rusie	186	.280	3	26	28	113	14	4	2.9	.910							
C1	P. Wilson	175	.331	1	32	246	28	31	9		.898							
P	J. Meekin	170	.282	5	29	15	60	4	3	1.5	.949							

Boston
W-83 L-49
Frank Selee

POS	Player	AB	BA	HR	RBI	PO	A	E	DP	TC/G	FA	Pitcher	G	IP	W	L	SV	ERA
1B	T. Tucker	500	.330	3	100	1108	68	18	82	9.7	.985	K. Nichols	50	407	32	13	0	4.75
2B	B. Lowe	613	.346	17	115	345	402	59	62	6.2	.927	J. Stivetts	45	338	25	14	0	4.90
SS	H. Long	475	.324	12	79	217	359	75	62	6.6	.885	H. Staley	27	209	13	10	0	6.81
3B	B. Nash	512	.289	8	87	204	267	34	24	3.8	.933	T. Lovett	15	104	8	6	0	5.97
RF	J. Bannon	494	.336	13	114	240	43	41	12	2.5	.873							
CF	H. Duffy	539	.438	18	145	315	27	27	5	3.0	.927							
LF	T. McCarthy	539	.349	13	126	291	28	34	10	2.8	.904							
C	C. Ganzel	266	.278	3	56	184	52	27	6	4.5	.897							
PO	J. Stivetts	244	.328	8	64	49	49	12	2		.891							
C	J. Ryan	201	.269	1	29	168	46	21	7	4.6	.911							
SS	Connaughton	171	.345	2	33	62	111	21	11	5.9	.892							
P	K. Nichols	170	.294	0	34	34	67	7	3	2.2	.935							
C	F. Tenney	86	.395	2	21	55	20	9	3	4.2	.893							
P	H. Staley	85	.235	2	25	5	28	6	0	1.4	.846							

Philadelphia
W-71 L-57
Arthur Irwin

POS	Player	AB	BA	HR	RBI	PO	A	E	DP	TC/G	FA	Pitcher	G	IP	W	L	SV	ERA
1B	J. Boyle	495	.301	4	88	950	61	18	76	9.0	.983	J. Taylor	41	298	23	13	1	4.08
2B	B. Hallman	505	.309	0	66	318	320	48	62	5.8	.930	K. Carsey	35	277	18	12	0	5.56
SS	J. Sullivan	304	.352	3	63	169	224	50	32	5.9	.887	G. Weyhing	38	266	16	14	1	5.81
3B	L. Cross	529	.386	7	125	177	234	36	24	4.5	.919	G. Harper	12	86	6	6	0	5.32
RF	S. Thompson	458	.404	4	141	159	12	4	2	1.7	.977							
CF	B. Hamilton	559	.399	4	87	361	15	14	4	3.0	.964							
LF	E. Delahanty	497	.400	4	131	212	23	19	4	2.9	.925							
C	J. Clements	159	.346	3	36	178	32	12	4	4.9	.946							
OF	T. Turner	339	.416	1	82	134	7	13	1	2.0	.916							
C	M. Grady	190	.363	0	40	101	29	18	7	3.4	.878							
C	D. Buckley	160	.294	1	26	157	39	7	2	4.8	.966							
SS	B. Allen	149	.255	0	19	87	129	20	15	5.9	.915							
P	J. Taylor	144	.333	0	22	13	68	12	3	2.3	.871							
3B	C. Reilly	135	.296	0	19	34	56	13	3	3.7	.874							

NATIONAL LEAGUE 1894, *cont.*

	POS	Player	AB	BA	HR	RBI	PO	A	E	DP	TC/G	FA	Pitcher	G	IP	W	L	SV	ERA
Brooklyn	1B	D. Foutz	293	.307	0	51	658	33	17	37	9.8	.976	B. Kennedy	48	361	24	20	2	4.92
	2B	T. Daly	492	.341	8	82	317	354	**68**	52	6.0	.908	E. Stein	45	359	27	14	1	4.54
W-70 L-61	SS	T. Corcoran	576	.300	5	92	280	439	76	45	6.2	.904	D. Daub	33	215	9	12	0	6.32
	3B	B. Shindle	476	.296	4	96	192	226	48	12	4.0	.897	H. Gastright	16	93	2	6	2	6.39
Dave Foutz	RF	O. Burns	513	.361	5	109	208	15	12	4	1.9	.949							
	CF	M. Griffin	405	.365	5	75	297	14	10	5	3.0	.969							
	LF	G. Treadway	479	.328	4	102	274	16	35	2	2.7	.892							
	C	T. Kinslow	223	.305	2	41	217	47	27	4	4.8	.907							
	1B	C. LaChance	257	.323	5	52	508	16	11	26	9.6	.979							
	UT	G. Shoch	239	.322	1	37	130	77	17	6		.924							
	C	C. Daily	234	.256	0	32	218	61	21	7	5.0	.930							
	P	B. Kennedy	161	.304	0	23	7	82	8	4	2.0	.918							
	P	E. Stein	146	.260	2	28	20	64	7	1	2.0	.923							
Cleveland	1B	P. Tebeau	523	.302	3	89	1077	46	26	66	10.0	.977	C. Young	52	409	26	21	1	3.94
	2B	C. Childs	479	.353	2	52	313	374	63	51	6.4	.916	N. Cuppy	43	316	24	15	0	4.56
W-68 L-61	SS	E. McKean	554	.357	8	128	269	411	71	43	5.8	.905	J. Clarkson	22	151	8	9	0	4.42
	3B	C. McGarr	523	.275	2	74	170	242	45	17	3.6	.902	M. Sullivan	13	91	6	5	0	6.35
Patsy Tebeau	RF	H. Blake	296	.264	1	51	120	16	10	4	2.0	.932							
	CF	J. McAleer	253	.289	2	40	175	9	9	3	3.0	.953							
	LF	J. Burkett	523	.358	8	94	242	17	24	5	2.3	.915							
	C	C. Zimmer	341	.284	4	65	289	100	15	**16**	4.5	**.963**							
	CO	J. O'Connor	330	.315	2	51	249	43	20	4		.936							
	OF	B. Ewing	211	.251	2	39	86	7	9	2	2.0	.912							
	P	C. Young	186	.215	2	26	16	108	7	4	2.5	.947							
	O1	W. Tebeau	150	.313	0	25	172	2	13	13		.930							
	P	N. Cuppy	135	.259	0	19	17	60	2	**5**	1.8	.975							
Pittsburgh	1B	J. Beckley	533	.343	8	120	**1227**	**84**	30	80	10.2	.978	R. Ehret	46	347	19	21	0	5.14
	2B	L. Bierbauer	525	.303	3	107	309	**453**	50	58	6.2	.938	A. Gumbert	37	269	15	14	0	6.02
W-65 L-65	SS	J. Glasscock	332	.280	1	63	189	295	35	46	6.1	**.933**	F. Killen	28	204	14	11	0	4.50
	3B	D. Lyons	254	.323	4	50	119	155	31	11	4.3	.898	Colcolough	22	149	8	5	0	7.08
Al Buckenberger	RF	P. Donovan	576	.302	4	76	267	22	21	5	2.3	.932	J. Menefee	13	112	5	8	0	5.40
W-53 L-55	CF	J. Stenzel	522	.354	13	121	311	23	27	6	2.8	.925							
	LF	E. Smith	489	.356	6	72	275	18	21	8	2.5	.933							
Connie Mack	C	C. Mack	228	.250	1	21	274	67	19	6	5.2	.947							
W-12 L-10	3B	F. Hartman	182	.319	2	20	65	97	23	6	3.8	.876							
	C	J. Sugden	139	.331	2	23	105	27	13	4	4.7	.910							
	P	R. Ehret	135	.170	0	11	12	61	12	2	1.8	.859							
	UT	F. Weaver	115	.348	0	24	73	47	15	6		.889							
Chicago	1B	C. Anson	347	.395	5	99	739	47	8	52	9.7	**.990**	Hutchinson	36	278	14	16	0	6.06
	2B	J. Parrott	532	.261	3	64	285	379	49	56	5.8	.931	C. Griffith	36	261	21	14	0	4.92
W-57 L-75	SS	B. Dahlen	508	.362	15	107	186	253	50	43	7.4	.898	W. McGill	27	208	7	19	0	5.84
	3B	C. Irwin	498	.289	8	95	89	123	46	15	3.9	.822	A. Terry	23	163	5	11	0	5.84
Cap Anson	RF	J. Ryan	481	.360	3	62	221	22	24	3	2.5	.910	S. Stratton	15	119	8	5	0	6.03
	CF	B. Lange	442	.328	6	90	267	25	29	10	2.9	.910							
	LF	W. Wilmot	597	.330	5	130	264	16	**41**	5	2.4	.872							
	C	P. Schriver	349	.275	3	47	290	91	32	12	4.7	.923							
	UT	G. Decker	384	.313	8	92	497	39	32	32		.944							
	C	M. Kittridge	168	.315	0	23	209	36	20	4	5.2	.925							
	P	C. Griffith	142	.232	0	15	20	45	4	1	1.9	.942							
	P	Hutchinson	136	.309	6	16	10	45	5	1	1.7	.917							
	PO	S. Stratton	96	.375	3	23	16	21	2	2		.949							
St. Louis	1B	R. Connor	380	.321	7	79	897	68	26	72*	10.0	.974	Breitenstein	**56**	447	27	25	0	4.79
	2B	J. Quinn	405	.286	4	61	341	339	34	**74**	6.7	.952	P. Hawley	53	393	19	**26**	0	4.90
W-56 L-76	SS	B. Ely	510	.306	12	89	273	442	**79**	51	6.3	.901	D. Clarkson	32	233	8	17	0	6.36
	3B	D. Miller	481	.339	8	86	68	96	33	6	3.8	.832							
George Miller	RF	T. Dowd	524	.271	4	62	199	14	16	4	2.0	.930							
	CF	F. Shugart	527	.292	7	72	276	26	29	2	2.7	.912							
	LF	C. Frank	319	.279	4	42	161	11	26	4	2.6	.869							
	C	H. Peitz	338	.263	3	49	146	51	13	3	5.4	.938							
	OF	D. Cooley	206	.296	1	21	74	1	15	1	2.3	.833							
	P	Breitenstein	182	.220	0	13	**42**	83	9	4	2.4	.933							
	P	P. Hawley	163	.264	2	23	29	77	12	2	2.2	.898							
Cincinnati	1B	C. Comiskey	220	.264	0	33	536	24	16	36	9.6	.972	F. Dwyer	45	348	19	22	1	5.07
	2B	B. McPhee	481	.320	5	88	**389**	446	49	72	**7.0**	.945	T. Parrott	41	309	17	19	1	5.60
W-55 L-75	SS	G. Smith	482	.263	3	76	233	**501**	72	**75**	6.3	.911	Chamberlain	23	178	10	9	0	5.77
	3B	A. Latham	524	.313	4	60	158	248	**66**	20	3.7	.860	C. Fisher	11	91	2	8	0	7.32
Charlie Comiskey	RF	J. Canavan	356	.272	13	70	188	9	21	6	2.3	.904							
	CF	D. Hoy	506	.312	5	70	314	29	40	3	3.0	.896							
	LF	B. Holliday	519	.383	13	119	243	22	25	5	2.4	.914							
	C	M. Murphy	255	.275	1	37	194	70	29	5	4.0	.901							
	UT	F. Vaughn	284	.310	7	64	362	64	26	19		.942							
	UT	T. Parrott	229	.323	4	40	143	87	22	10		.913							
	P	F. Dwyer	172	.267	2	28	31	62	5	2	2.2	.949							
	O1	J. McCarthy	167	.269	0	21	193	19	13	12		.942							
	C	B. Merritt	113	.327	1	21	55	26	4	0	3.5	.953							

NATIONAL LEAGUE 1894, *cont.*

Washington
W-45 L-87
Gus Schmelz

POS	Player	AB	BA	HR	RBI	PO	A	E	DP	TC/G	FA	Pitcher	G	IP	W	L	SV	ERA
1B	Cartwright	507	.294	12	106	1219	71	36	63	10.0	.973	W. Mercer	49	333	17	23	3	3.76
2B	P. Ward	347	.303	0	36	167	237	45	21	5.7	.900	A. Maul	28	202	11	15	0	5.98
SS	F. Scheibeck	196	.230	0	17	108	204	44	15	6.8	.876	D. Esper	19	122	5	10	0	7.50
3B	B. Joyce	355	.355	17	89	152	183	52	20	3.9	.866	M. Sullivan	20	118	2	10	1	6.58
RF	B. Hassamaer	494	.322	4	90	109	11	11	4	1.9	.916	Stocksdale	18	117	5	9	0	5.06
CF	C. Abbey	523	.314	7	101	344	26	37	6	3.2	.909	C. Petty	16	103	3	8	0	5.59
LF	K. Selbach	372	.306	7	71	153	8	15	2	2.2	.915							
C	D. McGuire	425	.306	6	78	288	114	36	8	4.2	.918							
UT	P. Radford	325	.240	0	49	219	247	73	23		.865							
OF	W. Tebeau	222	.225	0	28	118	8	21	1	2.4	.857							
P	W. Mercer	162	.284	2	29	14	68	5	1	1.8	.943							
C	D. Dugdale	134	.239	0	16	72	32	15	0	3.6	.874							
P	A. Maul	124	.242	2	20	8	49	8	0	2.3	.877							

Louisville
W-36 L-94
Billy Barnie

POS	Player	AB	BA	HR	RBI	PO	A	E	DP	TC/G	FA	Pitcher	G	IP	W	L	SV	ERA
1B	L. Lutenberg	250	.192	0	23	593	38	15	54	9.6	.977	G. Hemming	35	294	13	19	1	4.37
2B	F. Pfeffer	409	.308	5	59	255	284	36	58	6.4	.937	P. Knell	32	247	7	21	0	5.32
SS	Richardson	430	.253	1	40	232	360	54	59	6.0	.916	J. Menefee	28	212	8	17	0	4.29
3B	J. Denny	221	.276	0	32	85	124	30	12	4.0	.874	J. Wadsworth	22	173	4	18	0	7.60
RF	O. Smith	134	.299	3	20	63	5	9	0	2.0	.883							
CF	T. Brown	536	.254	9	57	331	21	34	8	3.0	.912							
LF	F. Clarke	310	.268	7	48	162	15	23	2	2.6	.885							
C	J. Grim	410	.298	7	70	262	100	27	9	5.1	.931							
UT	F. Weaver	244	.221	3	24	191	28	11	9		.952							
UT	T. O'Rourke	220	.277	0	27	316	41	22	36		.942							
OF	L. Twitchell	210	.267	2	32	103	15	12	4	2.5	.908							
3B	P. Flaherty	145	.297	0	15	42	70	19	7	3.4	.855							

BATTING AND BASE RUNNING LEADERS

Batting Average
H. Duffy, BOS .438
T. Turner, PHI .416
S. Thompson, PHI .404
E. Delahanty, PHI .400
B. Hamilton, PHI .399

Slugging Average
H. Duffy, BOS .679
S. Thompson, PHI .670
B. Joyce, WAS .648
J. Kelley, BAL .602
J. Stenzel, PIT .580

Home Runs
H. Duffy, BOS 18
B. Joyce, WAS 17
B. Lowe, BOS 17
B. Dahlen, CHI 15

Total Bases
H. Duffy, BOS 366
B. Lowe, BOS 319
S. Thompson, PHI 307
J. Kelley, BAL 305
W. Keeler, BAL 305

Runs Batted In
H. Duffy, BOS 145
S. Thompson, PHI 141
E. Delahanty, PHI 131
W. Wilmot, CHI 130
D. Brouthers, BAL 128
E. McKean, CLE 128

Stolen Bases
B. Hamilton, PHI 99
J. McGraw, BAL 78
W. Wilmot, CHI 74
T. Brown, LOU 66
B. Lange, CHI 65

Hits
H. Duffy, BOS 236
B. Hamilton, PHI 223
W. Keeler, BAL 219
B. Lowe, BOS 212

Base on Balls
B. Hamilton, PHI 126
C. Childs, CLE 107
J. Kelley, BAL 107
J. McGraw, BAL 91

Home Run Percentage
B. Joyce, WAS 4.8
J. Canavan, CIN 3.7
H. Duffy, BOS 3.3
B. Dahlen, CHI 3.0

Runs Scored
B. Hamilton, PHI 196
J. Kelley, BAL 167
W. Keeler, BAL 165
H. Duffy, BOS 160

Doubles
H. Duffy, BOS 50
J. Kelley, BAL 48
W. Wilmot, CHI 45
E. Delahanty, PHI 39

Triples
H. Reitz, BAL 31
S. Thompson, PHI 27
G. Treadway, BKN 26
R. Connor, NY, STL 25

PITCHING LEADERS

Winning Percentage
J. Meekin, NY .786
S. McMahon, BAL .758
A. Rusie, NY .735
K. Nichols, BOS .711
J. Stivetts, BOS .683

Earned Run Average
A. Rusie, NY 2.78
J. Meekin, NY 3.70
W. Mercer, WAS 3.76
C. Young, CLE 3.94
J. Taylor, PHI 4.08

Wins
J. Meekin, NY 36
A. Rusie, NY 36
K. Nichols, BOS 32
J. Stivetts, BOS 28
E. Stein, BKN 27
Breitenstein, STL 27

Saves
T. Mullane, BAL, CLE 4
B. Hawke, BAL 3
W. Mercer, WAS 3

Strikeouts
A. Rusie, NY 195
Breitenstein, STL 140
J. Meekin, NY 133
P. Hawley, STL 120
K. Nichols, BOS 113

Complete Games
Breitenstein, STL 46
A. Rusie, NY 45
C. Young, CLE 44
K. Nichols, BOS 40
J. Meekin, NY 40

Fewest Hits/9 Innings
A. Rusie, NY 8.64
J. Meekin, NY 8.89
E. Stein, BKN 9.93
Breitenstein, STL 10.00

Shutouts
N. Cuppy, CLE 3
K. Nichols, BOS 3
A. Rusie, NY 3
G. Weyhing, PHI 2

Fewest Walks/9 Innings
C. Young, CLE 2.33
J. Menefee, LOU, PIT 2.48
K. Gleason, BAL, STL 2.54
H. Staley, BOS 2.63

Most Strikeouts/9 Inn.
A. Rusie, NY 3.95
B. Hawke, BAL 2.99
J. Wadsworth, LOU 2.97
J. Meekin, NY 2.93

Innings
Breitenstein, STL 447
A. Rusie, NY 444
J. Meekin, NY 409
C. Young, CLE 409

Games Pitched
Breitenstein, STL 56
A. Rusie, NY 54
P. Hawley, STL 53
J. Meekin, NY 52

	W	L	PCT	GB	R	OR	2B	3B	HR	BA	SA	SB	E	DP	FA	CG	BB	SO	ShO	SV	ERA
Baltimore	89	39	.695		1171	820	271	150	33	.343	.483	324	293	105	.944	97	472	275	1	11	5.00
New York	88	44	.667	3	940	789	197	96	44	.301	.409	319	443	101	.924	111	539	395	5	5	3.83
Boston	83	49	.629	8	1222	1002	272	93	103	.331	.484	241	415	120	.925	108	411	262	3	1	5.41
Philadelphia	71	57	.555	18	1143	966	252	131	40	.349	.476	273	338	111	.935	102	469	262	3	4	5.63
Brooklyn	70	61	.534	20.5	1021	1007	228	130	42	.313	.440	282	390	85	.928	105	555	285	3	5	5.51
Cleveland	68	61	.527	21.5	932	896	241	90	37	.303	.414	220	344	107	.935	107	435	254	6	1	4.97
Pittsburgh	65	65	.500	25	955	972	222	123	49	.312	.443	256	354	106	.936	106	457	304	2	0	5.60
Chicago	57	75	.432	34	1041	1066	265	86	65	.314	.441	327	452	113	.918	117	557	281		0	5.68
St. Louis	56	76	.424	35	771	954	171	113	54	.286	.408	190	426	109	.923	114	500	319	2	0	5.29
Cincinnati	55	75	.423	35	910	1085	224	68	60	.294	.410	215	423	119	.925	110	491	219	4	3	5.99
Washington	45	87	.341	46	882	1122	218	118	59	.287	.425	249	499	81	.908	102	446	190	1	4	5.51
Louisville	36	94	.277	54	692	1001	173	88	42	.269	.375	217	428	130	.920	113	475	258	2	1	5.45
					11680	11680	2734	1286	628	.309	.435	3113	4805	1287	.927	1292	5807	3304	32	35	5.32

NATIONAL LEAGUE 1895

Baltimore — W-87 L-43 — Ned Hanlon

POS	Player	AB	BA	HR	RBI	PO	A	E	DP	TC/G	FA	Pitcher	G	IP	W	L	SV	ERA
1B	S. Carey	490	.261	1	75	1132	43	15	73	9.7	.987	B. Hoffer	41	314	31	6	0	3.21
2B	K. Gleason	421	.309	0	74	205	250	51	32	6.0	.899	G. Hemming	34	262	20	13	0	4.05
SS	H. Jennings	529	.386	4	125	425	457	56	71	7.2	.940	D. Esper	34	218	10	12	1	3.92
3B	J. McGraw	388	.369	2	48	100	239	47	19	4.1	.878	D. Clarkson	20	142	12	3	0	3.87
RF	W. Keeler	565	.391	4	78	244	21	10	5	2.1	.964	S. McMahon	15	122	10	4	0	2.94
CF	S. Brodie	528	.348	2	134	307	23	12	2	2.6	.965							
LF	J. Kelley	518	.365	10	134	260	20	16	5	2.3	.946							
C	W. Robinson	282	.262	0	48	243	78	7	6	4.4	.979							
2B	H. Reitz	245	.294	0	29	120	137	17	25	5.7	.938							
C	B. Clarke	241	.290	0	35	176	67	16	8	4.3	.938							

Cleveland — W-84 L-46 — Patsy Tebeau

POS	Player	AB	BA	HR	RBI	PO	A	E	DP	TC/G	FA	Pitcher	G	IP	W	L	SV	ERA
1B	P. Tebeau	264	.318	2	52	473	19	4	28	10.1	.992	C. Young	47	370	35	10	0	3.24
2B	C. Childs	462	.288	4	90	337	394	63	42	6.7	.921	N. Cuppy	47	353	26	14	2	3.54
SS	E. McKean	565	.342	8	119	246	424	67	42	5.6	.909	B. Wallace	30	229	12	14	1	4.09
3B	C. McGarr	419	.265	2	59	125	217	51	13	3.6	.870	P. Knell	20	117	7	5	0	5.40
RF	H. Blake	315	.276	3	45	119	13	15	3	1.8	.898							
CF	J. McAleer	528	.271	0	68	341	14	25	1	2.9	.934							
LF	J. Burkett	550	.409	5	83	273	17	38	4	2.5	.884							
C	C. Zimmer	315	.340	5	56	318	77	10	2	4.8	.975							
C1	J. O'Connor	340	.291	0	58	520	66	16	24		.973							
O1	W. Tebeau	337	.326	0	68	480	25	17	12		.967							
P	C. Young	140	.214	0	13	15	120	6	2	3.0	.957							
P	N. Cuppy	140	.286	0	25	30	90	7	2	2.6	.968							

Philadelphia — W-78 L-53 — Arthur Irwin

POS	Player	AB	BA	HR	RBI	PO	A	E	DP	TC/G	FA	Pitcher	G	IP	W	L	SV	ERA
1B	J. Boyle	565	.253	0	67	1245	61	36	69	10.1	.973	K. Carsey	44	342	24	16	1	4.92
2B	B. Hallman	539	.314	1	91	299	392	42	57	6.0	.943	J. Taylor	41	335	26	14	1	4.49
SS	J. Sullivan	373	.338	2	50	182	270	62	32	5.8	.879	W. McGill	20	146	10	8	0	5.55
3B	L. Cross	535	.271	2	101	191	308	32	23	4.2	.940	A. Orth	11	88	8	1	1	3.89
RF	S. Thompson	538	.392	18	165	186	31	13	2	1.9	.943							
CF	B. Hamilton	517	.389	7	74	313	11	31	5	2.6	.913							
LF	E. Delahanty	480	.404	11	106	237	16	15	4	2.6	.944							
C	J. Clements	322	.394	13	75	280	69	11	7	4.1	.969							
OF	T. Turner	210	.386	2	43	89	5	17	0	2.0	.847							
S3	C. Reilly	179	.268	0	25	70	123	23	14		.894							
P	J. Taylor	155	.290	3	35	19	89	5	3	2.8	.956							
P	K. Carsey	141	.291	0	20	9	77	12	2	2.2	.878							
C	M. Grady	123	.325	1	23	103	10	9	2	3.2	.926							

Chicago — W-72 L-58 — Cap Anson

POS	Player	AB	BA	HR	RBI	PO	A	E	DP	TC/G	FA	Pitcher	G	IP	W	L	SV	ERA
1B	C. Anson	474	.335	2	91	1176	60	19	82	10.3	.985	C. Griffith	42	353	26	14	0	3.93
2B	A. Stewart	365	.241	8	76	252	281	52	53	6.0	.911	A. Terry	38	311	21	14	0	4.80
SS	B. Dahlen	516	.254	7	62	281	527	86	70	6.9	.904	Hutchinson	38	291	13	21	0	4.73
3B	B. Everett	550	.358	3	88	174	263	75	12	3.9	.854							
RF	J. Ryan	438	.317	6	49	161	18	12	6	1.8	.937							
CF	B. Lange	478	.389	10	98	298	28	27	6	2.9	.924							
LF	W. Wilmot	466	.283	8	72	226	19	23	5	2.5	.914							
C	T. Donahue	219	.269	2	36	234	45	26	8	4.8	.915							
OF	G. Decker	297	.276	2	41	98	3	10	0	1.9	.910							
C	M. Kittridge	212	.226	3	29	197	48	6	4	4.3	.976							
P	C. Griffith	144	.319	1	27	27	81	9	2	2.8	.923							
P	A. Terry	137	.219	1	10	13	81	11	3	2.8	.895							

Brooklyn — W-71 L-60 — Dave Foutz

POS	Player	AB	BA	HR	RBI	PO	A	E	DP	TC/G	FA	Pitcher	G	IP	W	L	SV	ERA
1B	C. LaChance	536	.312	8	108	1286	53	23	68	10.9	.983	B. Kennedy	39	280	19	12	1	5.12
2B	T. Daly	455	.281	2	68	318	346	50	42	6.0	.930	E. Stein	32	255	15	13	1	4.72
SS	T. Corcoran	535	.265	2	69	293	488	64	49	6.7	.924	A. Gumbert	33	234	11	16	1	5.08
3B	B. Shindle	477	.279	3	69	142	257	46	16	3.8	.897	D. Daub	25	185	10	10	0	4.29
RF	G. Treadway	339	.257	7	54	117	7	16	4	1.6	.886	C. Lucid	21	137	10	7	0	5.52
CF	M. Griffin	519	.333	4	65	349	23	12	12	2.9	.969							
LF	J. Anderson	419	.286	9	87	205	11	29	4	2.4	.882							
C	J. Grim	329	.280	0	44	253	103	20	10	4.1	.947							
UT	G. Shoch	216	.259	0	29	98	63	14	6		.920							
C	C. Daily	142	.211	1	11	127	25	7	7	4.1	.956							
P	B. Kennedy	127	.307	0	21	5	66	5	1	1.9	.934							
OF	D. Foutz	115	.296	0	21	26	3	4	1	1.7	.879							

Boston — W-71 L-60 — Frank Selee

POS	Player	AB	BA	HR	RBI	PO	A	E	DP	TC/G	FA	Pitcher	G	IP	W	L	SV	ERA
1B	T. Tucker	462	.249	3	73	1159	82	28	78	10.2	.978	K. Nichols	47	394	26	16	3	3.29
2B	B. Lowe	412	.296	7	62	265	336	29	50	6.4	.954	J. Stivetts	38	291	17	17	0	4.64
SS	H. Long	535	.316	9	75	280	409	84	48	6.3	.891	C. Dolan	25	198	11	7	1	4.27
3B	B. Nash	508	.289	10	108	193	246	59	26	3.8	.882	J. Sullivan	21	179	11	9	0	4.82
RF	J. Bannon	489	.350	6	74	209	30	33	3	2.2	.879							
CF	H. Duffy	531	.352	9	100	322	20	20	7	2.8	.945							
LF	T. McCarthy	452	.290	2	73	199	16	28	2	2.2	.885							
C	C. Ganzel	277	.264	1	52	345	65	16	9	5.6	.962							
C	J. Ryan	189	.291	0	18	167	46	11	2	5.2	.951							
OC	F. Tenney	173	.272	1	21	109	24	7	2		.950							
P	J. Stivetts	158	.190	0	24	24	50	3	1	2.0	.961							
P	K. Nichols	157	.236	0	18	29	73	4	2	2.2	.962							

NATIONAL LEAGUE 1895, cont.

	POS	Player	AB	BA	HR	RBI	PO	A	E	DP	TC/G	FA	Pitcher	G	IP	W	L	SV	ERA
Pittsburgh	1B	J. Beckley	530	.328	5	110	1340	54	31	76	11.0	.978	P. Hawley	56	444	31	22	1	3.18
	2B	L. Bierbauer	466	.258	0	69	284	400	39	52	6.2	.946	B. Hart	36	262	14	17	1	4.75
W-71 L-61	SS	M. Cross	393	.257	3	54	254	327	77	42	6.1	.883	B. Foreman	19	140	8	6	2	3.22
	3B	B. Clingman	382	.259	0	45	137	256	50	16	4.2	.887	F. Killen	13	95	5	5	0	5.49
Connie Mack	RF	P. Donovan	519	.308	1	58	187	11	8	2	1.6	.961	J. Gardner	11	85	8	2	0	2.64
	CF	J. Stenzel	514	.374	7	97	257	23	27	6	2.4	.912							
	LF	E. Smith	480	.302	1	81	250	16	31	2	2.4	.896							
	C	B. Merritt	239	.285	0	27	245	58	21	7	5.1	.935							
	UT	F. Genins	252	.250	2	24	127	99	29	7		.886							
	P	P. Hawley	185	.308	5	42	16	110	13	2	2.5	.906							
	C	J. Sugden	155	.310	1	17	176	57	25	4	5.3	.903							
Cincinnati	1B	B. Ewing	434	.318	5	94	957	79	26	69	10.1	.976	F. Dwyer	37	280	18	15	0	4.24
	2B	B. McPhee	432	.299	1	75	355	366	34	57	6.6	.955	B. Rhines	38	268	19	10	0	4.81
W-66 L-64	SS	G. Smith	503	.300	4	74	251	457	59	58	6.0	.923	T. Parrott	41	263	11	18	3	5.47
	3B	A. Latham	460	.311	2	69	126	197	52	13	4.2	.861	F. Foreman	32	219	11	14	1	4.11
Buck Ewing	RF	D. Miller	529	.335	8	112	243	25	18	8	2.2	.937	B. Phillips	18	109	6	7	2	6.03
	CF	G. Hogriever	239	.272	2	34	174	10	13	3	3.0	.934							
	LF	D. Hoy	429	.277	3	55	235	14	33	6	2.6	.883							
	C	F. Vaughn	334	.305	0	48	262	78	24	10	4.7	.934							
	OF	E. Burke	228	.268	1	28	135	8	16	2	2.8	.899							
	UT	T. Parrott	201	.343	3	41	151	70	13	12		.944							
	UT	B. Grey	181	.304	1	29	89	108	24	13		.891							
	OF	B. Holliday	127	.299	0	20	60	3	4	1	2.1	.940							
	P	B. Rhines	113	.221	0	23	17	56	9	3	2.2	.890							
New York	1B	J. Doyle	319	.313	1	66	599	34	21	27	11.3	.968	A. Rusie	49	393	23	23	0	3.73
	2B	G. Stafford	463	.279	3	73	242	329	56	44	5.7	.911	D. Clarke	37	282	18	15	1	3.39
W-66 L-65	SS	S. Fuller	458	.225	0	32	270	499	73	59	6.7	.913	J. Meekin	29	226	16	11	0	5.30
	3B	G. Davis	430	.340	5	101	122	175	40	18	4.2	.881	L. German	25	178	7	11	0	5.96
George Davis	RF	M. Tiernan	476	.347	7	70	184	8	11	2	1.7	.946							
W-16 L-17	CF	Van Haltren	521	.340	8	103	252	26	26	3	2.3	.914							
	LF	E. Burke	167	.257	1	12	77	8	8	2	2.4	.914							
Jack Doyle	C	D. Farrell	312	.288	1	58	269	67	21	11	5.8	.941							
W-32 L-31	C	P. Wilson	238	.235	0	30	214	56	18	8	5.4	.938							
	UT	Y. Murphy	184	.201	0	16	82	39	18	4		.871							
Harvey Watkins	P	A. Rusie	179	.246	1	19	19	93	11	4	2.5	.911							
W-18 L-17	O1	T. Bannon	159	.270	0	8	198	18	19	16		.919							
	OF	O. Burns	114	.307	1	25	42	5	7	0	1.7	.870							
Washington	1B	Cartwright	472	.331	3	90	1102	95	19	69	10.0	.984	W. Mercer	43	311	13	23	2	4.46
	2B	J. Crooks	409	.279	6	57	327	364	32	43	6.2	.956	V. Anderson	29	205	9	16	0	5.89
W-43 L-85	SS	F. Scheibeck	167	.186	0	25	95	142	30	17	6.1	.888	Stocksdale	20	136	6	11	1	6.09
	3B	B. Joyce	474	.312	17	95	186	232	77	16	3.9	.844	A. Maul	16	136	10	5	0	2.45
Gus Schmelz	RF	B. Hassamaer	358	.279	1	60	104	4	4	1	1.5	.964	J. Malarkey	22	101	0	8	2	5.99
	CF	C. Abbey	511	.276	8	84	275	32	33	7	2.6	.903	J. Boyd	14	85	2	11	0	7.07
	LF	K. Selbach	516	.322	6	55	289	21	30	4	2.9	.912							
	C	D. McGuire	533	.336	10	97	408	179	40	11	4.8	.936							
	P	W. Mercer	196	.255	1	26	25	58	12	2	2.2	.874							
	UT	J. Boyd	157	.268	1	16	50	55	24	5		.814							
	OF	T. Brown	134	.239	2	16	59	1	6	0	1.9	.909							
St. Louis	1B	R. Connor	398	.329	8	77	953	62	14	60	10.0	.986	Breitenstein	54	430	18	30	1	4.44
	2B	J. Quinn	543	.311	2	74	359	390	43	63	5.9	.946	R. Ehret	37	232	6	19	0	6.02
W-39 L-92	SS	B. Ely	467	.259	1	46	247	407	53	52	6.0	.925	H. Staley	23	159	6	13	0	5.22
	3B	D. Miller	490	.292	5	74	54	72	26	5	3.3	.829	B. Kissinger	24	141	4	12	0	6.72
Al Buckenberger	RF	T. Dowd	505	.323	6	74	218	11	18	3	2.1	.927	J. McDougal	18	115	4	10	0	8.32
W-16 L-34	CF	T. Brown	350	.217	1	31	215	15	12	5	2.9	.950							
	LF	D. Cooley	563	.339	6	75	320	17	23	1	2.9	.936							
Chris Von Der Ahe	C	H. Peitz	334	.284	2	65	260	80	23	10	5.1	.937							
W-1 L-0	P	Breitenstein	218	.193	0	18	45	98	14	1	2.9	.911							
	OF	B. Sheehan	180	.317	1	18	56	7	4	1	1.6	.940							
Joe Quinn	3B	D. Lyons	129	.295	2	25	61	49	13	2	3.7	.894							
W-11 L-28																			
Lew Phelan																			
W-11 L-30																			
Louisville	1B	H. Spies	276	.268	2	35	439	22	9	30	10.0	.981	Cunningham	31	231	11	16	0	4.75
	2B	J. O'Brien	539	.256	1	50	304	396	46	56	6.0	.938	G. Weyhing	28	213	7	19	0	5.41
W-35 L-96	SS	F. Shugart	473	.264	4	70	178	258	63	39	5.7	.874	McDermott	33	207	4	19	0	5.99
	3B	J. Collins	373	.279	6	49	131	181	25	12	4.4	.926	B. Inks	28	205	7	20	0	6.40
John McCloskey	RF	T. Gettinger	260	.269	2	32	127	5	13	1	2.3	.910							
	CF	J. Wright	228	.276	1	30	127	4	5	1	2.3	.963							
	LF	F. Clarke	550	.347	4	82	344	20	49	4	3.1	.881							
	C	J. Warner	232	.267	1	20	195	47	18	4	4.1	.931							
	O3	W. Preston	197	.279	1	24	71	54	33	5		.791							
	UT	D. Holmes	161	.373	3	20	49	32	21	2		.794							
	C1	T. Welsh	153	.242	1	8	254	41	21	17		.934							

NATIONAL LEAGUE 1895, *cont.*

BATTING AND BASE RUNNING LEADERS

Batting Average
J. Burkett, CLE	.423
E. Delahanty, PHI	.399
J. Clements, PHI	.394
S. Thompson, PHI	.392
W. Keeler, BAL	.391

Slugging Average
S. Thompson, PHI	.654
J. Clements, PHI	.612
E. Delahanty, PHI	.611
B. Lange, CHI	.575
J. Kelley, BAL	.546

Home Runs
S. Thompson, PHI	18
B. Joyce, WAS	17
J. Clements, PHI	13
E. Delahanty, PHI	11

Total Bases
S. Thompson, PHI	352
J. Burkett, CLE	301
E. Delahanty, PHI	294
J. Kelley, BAL	283
E. McKean, CLE	283

Runs Batted In
S. Thompson, PHI	165
J. Kelley, BAL	134
S. Brodie, BAL	134
H. Jennings, BAL	125
E. McKean, CLE	119

Stolen Bases
B. Hamilton, PHI	95
B. Lange, CHI	67
J. McGraw, BAL	61
J. Kelley, BAL	54
J. Stenzel, PIT	53
H. Jennings, BAL	53

Hits
J. Burkett, CLE	235
S. Thompson, PHI	211
W. Keeler, BAL	211
H. Jennings, BAL	204

Base on Balls
B. Joyce, WAS	96
B. Hamilton, PHI	96
M. Griffin, BKN	93
E. Delahanty, PHI	86

Home Run Percentage
J. Clements, PHI	4.0
B. Joyce, WAS	3.6
S. Thompson, PHI	3.3
E. Delahanty, PHI	2.3

Runs Scored
B. Hamilton, PHI	166
W. Keeler, BAL	162
H. Jennings, BAL	159
J. Burkett, CLE	153

Doubles
E. Delahanty, PHI	49
S. Thompson, PHI	45
H. Jennings, BAL	41
J. Stenzel, PIT	38

Triples
K. Selbach, WAS	22
M. Tiernan, NY	21
S. Thompson, PHI	21
D. Cooley, STL	21

PITCHING LEADERS

Winning Percentage
B. Hoffer, BAL	.811
C. Young, CLE	.778
K. Nichols, BOS	.682
C. Griffith, CHI	.658
B. Rhines, CIN	.655

Earned Run Average
A. Maul, WAS	2.45
S. McMahon, BAL	2.94
P. Hawley, PIT	3.18
B. Hoffer, BAL	3.21
B. Foreman, PIT	3.22

Wins
C. Young, CLE	35
P. Hawley, PIT	32
B. Hoffer, BAL	30
K. Nichols, BOS	30

Saves
T. Parrott, CIN	3
E. Beam, PHI	3
K. Nichols, BOS	3

Strikeouts
A. Rusie, NY	201
K. Nichols, BOS	146
P. Hawley, PIT	142
Breitenstein, STL	127
C. Young, CLE	121

Complete Games
Breitenstein, STL	46
P. Hawley, PIT	44
K. Nichols, BOS	42
A. Rusie, NY	42
C. Griffith, CHI	39

Fewest Hits/9 Innings
S. McMahon, BAL	8.09
B. Foreman, PIT	8.44
B. Hoffer, BAL	8.48
A. Rusie, NY	8.79

Shutouts
5 tied with	4

Fewest Walks/9 Innings
C. Young, CLE	1.83
D. Clarke, NY	1.92
K. Nichols, BOS	2.04
H. Staley, STL	2.21

Most Strikeouts/9 Inn.
A. Rusie, NY	4.60
W. McGill, PHI	4.32
B. Foreman, PIT	3.48
J. Stivetts, BOS	3.43

Innings
P. Hawley, PIT	444
Breitenstein, STL	430
K. Nichols, BOS	394
C. Young, CLE	370

Games Pitched
P. Hawley, PIT	56
Breitenstein, STL	54
A. Rusie, NY	49
K. Nichols, BOS	48

	W	L	PCT	GB	R	OR	2B	3B	HR	BA	SA	SB	E	DP	FA	CG	BB	SO	ShO	SV	ERA
Baltimore	87	43	.669		1009	646	235	89	25	.324	.427	310	**288**	108	**.946**	104	430	244	**10**	4	**3.80**
Cleveland	84	46	.646	3	917	720	194	67	29	.305	.395	187	348	77	.936	108	**346**	326	6	3	3.90
Philadelphia	78	53	.595	9.5	**1068**	957	**272**	73	61	**.330**	**.450**	276	369	93	.933	106	485	330	2	**7**	5.47
Chicago	72	58	.554	15	866	854	171	85	55	.298	.405	260	401	**113**	.928	**119**	432	297	3	1	4.67
Brooklyn	71	60	.542	16.5	867	834	189	77	39	.282	.379	183	325	96	.941	103	395	216	5	6	4.94
Boston	71	60	.542	16.5	907	826	197	57	54	.290	.391	199	364	102	.934	115	363	370	4	4	4.27
Pittsburgh	71	61	.538	17	811	787	190	89	26	.290	.386	257	392	95	.930	106	500	382	4	6	4.05
Cincinnati	66	64	.508	21	903	854	235	**107**	33	.298	.415	**326**	377	112	.931	97	362	245	2	6	4.81
New York	66	65	.504	21.5	852	834	191	90	32	.288	.389	292	438	106	.922	115	415	**409**	6	1	4.51
Washington	43	85	.336	43	837	1048	207	101	55	.287	.412	237	447	96	.917	99	465	258		5	5.28
St. Louis	39	92	.298	48.5	747	1032	155	89	36	.281	.373	205	380	94	.930	105	439	280	1	1	5.76
Louisville	35	96	.267	52.5	698	1090	171	73	34	.279	.368	156	477	104	.913	104	469	245	3	1	5.90
					10482	10482	2407	997	479	.296	.399	2888	4606	1198	.930	1281	5101	3602	46	45	4.78

NATIONAL LEAGUE 1896

	POS	Player	AB	BA	HR	RBI	PO	A	E	DP	TC/G	FA	Pitcher	G	IP	W	L	SV	ERA
Baltimore W-90 L-39 Ned Hanlon	1B	J. Doyle	487	.339	1	101	1173	42	**32**	85	10.6	.974	B. Hoffer	35	309	25	7	0	3.38
	2B	H. Reitz	464	.287	4	106	256	335	30	54	5.3	.952	A. Pond	28	214	16	8	0	3.49
	SS	H. Jennings	521	.401	0	121	**377**	476	66	**70**	7.1	.928	G. Hemming	25	202	15	6	0	4.19
	3B	J. Donnelly	396	.328	0	71	140	217	47	15	3.8	.884	S. McMahon	22	176	11	9	0	3.48
	RF	W. Keeler	544	.386	4	82	227	20	8	6	2.0	.969	D. Esper	20	156	14	5	0	3.58
	CF	S. Brodie	516	.297	2	87	**320**	22	10	6	2.7	.972							
	LF	J. Kelley	519	.364	8	100	280	20	13	3	2.4	.958							
	C	W. Robinson	245	.347	2	38	260	48	17	5	4.9	.948							
	C	B. Clarke	300	.297	2	71	203	53	14	5	4.0	.948							
Cleveland W-80 L-48 Patsy Tebeau	1B	P. Tebeau	543	.269	2	94	**1340**	75	21	**88**	11.8	.985	C. Young	51	414	28	15	3	3.24
	2B	C. Childs	498	.355	1	106	**375**	**487**	53	**73**	6.9	.942	N. Cuppy	46	358	25	14	1	3.12
	SS	E. McKean	571	.338	7	112	214	400	57	57	5.0	.915	Z. Wilson	33	240	17	9	1	4.01
	3B	C. McGarr	455	.268	1	53	123	228	29	20	3.4	.924	B. Wallace	22	145	10	7	0	3.34
	RF	H. Blake	383	.240	1	43	184	17	12	5	2.1	.944							
	CF	J. McAleer	455	.288	1	54	278	18	13	5	2.7	.958							
	LF	J. Burkett	586	**.410**	6	72	269	18	23	4	2.3	.926							
	C	C. Zimmer	336	.277	3	46	338	81	12	9	4.7	**.972**							
	UT	J. O'Connor	256	.297	1	43	242	40	7	13		.976							
	P	C. Young	180	.289	3	28	8	**145**	12	3	3.2	.927							
	OP	B. Wallace	149	.235	1	17	42	35	5	4		.939							
	P	N. Cuppy	141	.270	1	20	14	106	4	3	2.7	.968							

NATIONAL LEAGUE 1896, *cont.*

	POS	Player	AB	BA	HR	RBI	PO	A	E	DP	TC/G	FA	Pitcher	G	IP	W	L	SV	ERA
Cincinnati	1B	B. Ewing	263	.278	1	38	669	49	15	41	10.6	.980	F. Dwyer	36	289	24	11	1	3.15
	2B	B. McPhee	433	.305	1	87	297	357	15	56	5.7	**.978**	R. Ehret	34	277	18	14	0	3.42
W-77 L-50	SS	G. Smith	456	.287	2	71	207	407	49	47	5.5	.926	F. Foreman	27	191	15	6	1	3.68
	3B	C. Irwin	476	.296	1	67	**200**	262	34	28	3.9	**.931**	C. Fisher	27	160	10	7	2	4.45
Buck Ewing	RF	D. Miller	504	.321	4	93	199	21	24	7	2.0	.902	B. Rhines	19	143	8	6	0	**2.45**
	CF	D. Hoy	443	.298	4	57	303	14	18	3	2.6	.946							
	LF	E. Burke	521	.340	1	52	290	13	21	3	2.7	.935							
	C	H. Peitz	211	.299	2	34	201	42	8	6	3.7	.968							
	C1	F. Vaughn	433	.293	2	66	740	82	21	41		.975							
	P	R. Ehret	102	.196	1	20	15	69	7	3	2.7	.923							
Boston	1B	T. Tucker	474	.304	2	72	1214	72	20	72	10.7	.985	K. Nichols	49	375	**30**	14	1	2.81
	2B	B. Lowe	305	.321	2	48	193	280	17	31	6.7	.965	J. Stivetts	42	329	21	14	0	4.10
W-74 L-57	SS	H. Long	501	.343	6	100	311	415	83	52	6.7	.897	J. Sullivan	31	225	11	12	1	4.03
	3B	J. Collins	304	.296	1	46	134	207	34	16	**4.7**	.909	F. Klobedanz	10	81	6	4	0	3.01
Frank Selee	RF	J. Bannon	343	.251	0	50	132	13	16	2	2.1	.901							
	CF	B. Hamilton	523	.365	3	52	276	8	20	2	2.3	.934							
	LF	H. Duffy	527	.300	5	112	250	15	12	2	2.2	.957							
	C	M. Bergen	245	.269	4	37	207	70	24	6	4.8	.920							
	OC	F. Tenney	348	.336	2	49	183	40	14	4		.941							
	P	J. Stivetts	221	.344	3	49	30	57	5	3	2.2	.946							
	3B	Harrington	198	.197	1	25	56	102	35	7	3.9	.819							
	C	C. Ganzel	179	.263	1	18	139	47	2	4	4.6	.989							
	2B	D. McGann	171	.322	2	30	88	111	21	10	5.1	.905							
	P	K. Nichols	147	.190	1	24	19	92	0	3	2.3	**1.000**							
Chicago	1B	C. Anson	402	.331	2	90	880	54	16	67	9.7	.983	C. Griffith	36	318	23	11	0	3.54
	2B	F. Pfeffer	360	.244	2	52	227	307	30	43	6.0	.947	D. Friend	36	291	18	14	0	4.74
W-71 L-57	SS	B. Dahlen	474	.352	9	74	310	456	71	66	6.7	.915	A. Terry	30	235	15	13	0	4.28
	3B	B. Everett	575	.320	2	46	148	180	44	10	3.8	.882	B. Briggs	26	194	12	8	1	4.31
Cap Anson	RF	J. Ryan	489	.313	3	86	207	21	22	4	2.0	.912							
	CF	B. Lange	469	.326	4	92	313	18	24	3	2.9	.932							
	LF	G. Decker	421	.280	5	61	131	10	11	0	2.1	.928							
	C	M. Kittridge	215	.223	1	19	251	56	12	12	5.0	.962							
	C	T. Donahue	188	.218	0	20	235	60	20	7	5.5	.937							
	3B	McCormick	168	.220	1	23	34	72	21	5	3.6	.835							
	P	C. Griffith	135	.267	1	16	20	79	9	3	3.0	.917							
	2B	H. Truby	109	.257	2	31	76	82	11	17	6.0	.935							
Pittsburgh	1B	J. Beckley	217	.253	3	32	558	31	11	42	10.7	.982	F. Killen	**52**	**432**	30	18	0	3.41
	2B	D. Padden	219	.242	2	24	176	149	24	14	5.7	.931	P. Hawley	49	378	22	21	0	3.57
W-66 L-63	SS	B. Ely	537	.285	3	77	258	432	62	52	5.9	.918	J. Hughey	25	155	6	8	0	4.99
	3B	D. Lyons	436	.307	4	71	165	201	44	15	3.5	.893	C. Hastings	17	104	5	10	1	5.88
Connie Mack	RF	P. Donovan	573	.319	3	59	224	24	12	8	2.0	.954							
	CF	J. Stenzel	479	.361	2	82	247	13	22	5	2.5	.922							
	LF	E. Smith	484	.362	6	94	302	14	18	6	2.7	.946							
	C	J. Sugden	301	.296	0	36	284	70	18	12	**5.3**	.952							
	C	B. Merritt	282	.291	1	42	242	75	20	5	5.4	.941							
	2B	L. Bierbauer	258	.287	0	39	140	206	12	32	6.1	.966							
	P	F. Killen	173	.231	2	25	15	115	10	1	2.7	.929							
	1B	H. Davis	168	.190	0	23	325	18	12	17	10.1	.966							
	P	P. Hawley	163	.239	1	21	12	108	10	2	2.7	.923							
New York	1B	W. Clark	247	.291	0	33	634	25	17	40	10.4	.975	D. Clarke	48	351	17	24	1	4.26
	2B	K. Gleason	541	.299	4	89	329	397	48	38	6.0	.938	J. Meekin	42	334	26	14	0	3.82
W-64 L-67	SS	Connaughton	315	.260	2	43	89	199	35	19	6.0	.892	M. Sullivan	25	185	10	13	0	4.66
	3B	G. Davis	494	.320	6	99	117	169	26	11	4.2	.917	E. Doheny	17	108	6	7	0	4.49
Arthur Irwin	RF	M. Tiernan	521	.369	7	89	213	15	7	4	1.8	.970							
W-36 L-53	CF	Van Haltren	562	.351	5	74	272	25	15	4	2.3	.952							
	LF	G. Stafford	230	.287	0	40	78	9	10	2	1.8	.897							
Bill Joyce	C	P. Wilson	253	.237	0	23	256	64	22	4	4.8	.936							
W-28 L-14	O1	H. Davis	233	.275	2	50	307	13	15	14		.955							
	UT	D. Farrell	191	.283	1	37	144	83	26	13		.897							
	1B	J. Beckley	182	.302	5	38	418	22	8	18	10.0	.982							
	3B	B. Joyce	165	.370	5*	43	71	103	23	4	4.0	.883							
	P	D. Clarke	147	.204	0	10	12	72	8	1	1.9	.913							
	P	J. Meekin	144	.299	2	16	17	62	8	2	2.1	.908							
Philadelphia	1B	D. Brouthers	218	.344	1	41	566	23	10	44	10.5	.983	J. Taylor	45	359	20	21	1	4.79
	2B	B. Hallman	469	.320	2	83	304	368	39	62	5.9	.945	A. Orth	25	196	15	10	0	4.41
W-62 L-68	SS	B. Hulen	339	.265	0	38	149	205	51	33	5.5	.874	K. Carsey	27	187	11	11	1	5.62
	3B	B. Nash	227	.247	3	30	87	148	23	12	4.0	.911	H. Keener	16	113	3	11	0	5.88
Billy Nash	RF	S. Thompson	517	.298	12	100	231	28	7	11	2.2	**.974**							
	CF	D. Cooley	287	.307	2	22	130	6	15	2	2.4	.901							
	LF	E. Delahanty	499	.397	13	**126**	262	18	14	4	**3.0**	.952							
	C	M. Grady	242	.318	1	44	167	60	14	12	4.0	.942							
	3S	L. Cross	406	.256	1	73	165	270	28	26		.940							
	OF	J. Sullivan	191	.251	2	24	99	3	4	0	2.4	.962							
	C	J. Clements	184	.359	5	45	149	51	7	3	3.9	.966							
	1B	N. Lajoie	175	.326	4	42	363	11	2	27	9.6	.995							
	P	J. Taylor	157	.185	0	18	19	107	11	3	3.0	.920							
	C	J. Boyle	145	.297	1	28	83	21	9	3	4.0	.920							
	OF	S. Mertes	143	.238	0	14	85	3	9	0	2.8	.907							

NATIONAL LEAGUE 1896, cont.

	POS	Player	AB	BA	HR	RBI	PO	A	E	DP	TC/G	FA	Pitcher	G	IP	W	L	SV	ERA
Brooklyn	1B	C. LaChance	348	.284	7	58	956	37	14	62	11.3	.986	B. Kennedy	42	306	17	20	1	4.42
	2B	T. Daly	224	.281	3	29	168	190	36	31	6.0	.909	H. Payne	34	242	14	16	0	3.39
W-58 L-73	SS	T. Corcoran	532	.289	3	73	323	477	64	69	6.5	.926	D. Daub	32	225	12	11	0	3.60
	3B	B. Shindle	516	.279	1	61	144	251	38	20	3.3	.912	B. Abbey	25	164	8	8	0	5.15
Dave Foutz	RF	F. Jones	395	.354	3	46	171	10	14	6	1.9	.928	G. Harper	16	86	4	8	0	5.55
	CF	M. Griffin	493	.308	4	51	316	8	13	1	2.8	.961							
	LF	T. McCarthy	377	.249	3	47	175	20	17	6	2.1	.920							
	C	J. Grim	281	.267	2	35	242	82	21	7	4.5	.939							
	O1	J. Anderson	430	.314	1	55	538	28	16	30		.973							
	2B	G. Shoch	250	.292	1	28	103	184	18	16	4.9	.941							
	C	B. Burrell	206	.301	0	23	176	42	17	3	3.9	.928							
Washington	1B	Cartwright	499	.277	1	62	1276	71	30	76	10.4	.978	W. Mercer	46	366	25	18	0	4.13
	2B	J. O'Brien	270	.267	4	33	166	228	20	33	5.7	.952	D. McJames	37	280	12	20	1	4.27
W-58 L-73	SS	DeMontreville	533	.343	8	77	305	479	97	53	6.6	.890	L. German	28	167	2	20	1	6.32
	3B	B. Joyce	310	.313	9*	51	50	108	20	6	3.7	.888	S. King	22	145	10	7	1	4.09
Gus Schmelz	RF	B. Lush	352	.247	4	45	142	19	21	4	2.0	.885							
	CF	T. Brown	435	.294	2	59	262	7	21	2	2.5	.928							
	LF	K. Selbach	487	.304	5	100	303	13	18	3	2.7	.946							
	C	D. McGuire	389	.321	2	70	**349**	87	**30**	**14**	4.8	.936							
	OF	C. Abbey	301	.262	1	49	105	10	16		1.7	.878							
	P	W. Mercer	156	.244	1	14	36	89	21	3	3.2	.856							
	3B	J. Rogers	154	.279	1	30	27	70	13	2	3.4	.882							
	C3	D. Farrell	130	.300	1	30	75	47	5	1		.961							
	2B	J. Crooks	84	.286	3	20	49	49	9	5	5.4	.916							
St. Louis	1B	R. Connor	483	.284	11	72	1217	**94**	16	48	10.5	**.988**	Breitenstein	44	340	18	26	0	4.48
	2B	T. Dowd	521	.265	5	46	182	220	35	22	5.6	.920	B. Hart	42	336	12	**29**	0	5.12
W-40 L-90	SS	M. Cross	427	.244	6	52	298	394	84	31	6.2	.892	R. Donahue	32	267	7	24	0	5.80
	3B	B. Myers	454	.256	0	37	162	242	**62**	16	3.9	.867	B. Kissinger	20	136	2	9	1	6.49
Harry Diddlebock	RF	T. Turner	203	.246	1	27	69	4	3	1	1.5	.961							
W-7 L-10	CF	T. Parrott	474	.291	7	70	276	16	15	7	2.8	.951							
	LF	K. Douglass	296	.264	1	28	105	13	14	3	1.8	.894							
Arlie Latham	C	McFarland	290	.241	3	36	276	**117**	16	6	5.1	.961							
W-0 L-3	OF	J. Sullivan	212	.292	2	21	81	4	4	1	2.0	.955							
	2B	J. Quinn	191	.209	1	17	92	167	12	7	5.6	.956							
Chris Von Der Ahe	C	M. Murphy	175	.257	0	11	178	48	18	5	5.1	.926							
W-0 L-2	OF	D. Cooley	166	.307	0	13	91	2	4	0	2.4	.959							
	P	Breitenstein	162	.259	0	12	34	89	7	4	3.0	.946							
Roger Connor	P	B. Hart	161	.186	0	15	29	106	8	3	3.4	.944							
W-8 L-37																			
Tommy Dowd																			
W-25 L-38																			
Louisville	1B	J. Rogers	290	.259	0	38	591	37	19	42	10.8	.971	C. Fraser	43	349	12	27	1	4.87
	2B	J. O'Brien	186	.339	2	24	125	147	24	19	6.0	.919	S. Hill	43	320	9	28	2	4.31
	SS	J. Dolan	165	.212	3	18	92	159	16	25	6.1	.940	Cunningham	27	189	7	14	1	5.09
W-38 L-93	3B	B. Clingman	423	.234	2	37	188	**281**	38	21	4.2	.925	A. Herman	14	94	4	6	0	5.63
	RF	T. McCreery	441	.351	7	65	177	20	18	4	1.9	.916							
John McCloskey	CF	O. Pickering	165	.303	1	22	97	12	12	4	2.7	.901							
W-2 L-17	LF	F. Clarke	517	.325	9	79	277	18	**30**	2	2.5	.908							
	C	C. Dexter	402	.279	3	37	179	63	26	9	4.9	.903							
Bill McGunnigle	UT	D. Miller	324	.275	1	33	202	130	31	14		.915							
W-36 L-76	1B	P. Cassidy	184	.212	0	12	348	17	10	14	9.9	.973							
	P	C. Fraser	146	.151	0	6	39	95	**25**	5	**3.7**	.843							
	OF	D. Holmes	141	.270	0	18	43	6	13	1	1.9	.790							

BATTING AND BASE RUNNING LEADERS

Batting Average		Slugging Average		Home Runs		Winning Percentage	
J. Burkett, CLE	.410	E. Delahanty, PHI	.631	B. Joyce, NY, WAS	14	B. Hoffer, BAL	.781
H. Jennings, BAL	.398	B. Dahlen, CHI	.561	E. Delahanty, PHI	13	F. Foreman, CIN	.714
E. Delahanty, PHI	.397	T. McCreery, LOU	.546	S. Thompson, PHI	12	G. Hemming, BAL	.714
W. Keeler, BAL	.392	J. Kelley, BAL	.543	R. Connor, STL	11	F. Dwyer, CIN	.686
M. Tiernan, NY	.369	J. Burkett, CLE	.541	B. Dahlen, CHI	9	A. Orth, PHI	.682
				F. Clarke, LOU	9		

PITCHING LEADERS

Earned Run Average		Wins	
B. Rhines, CIN	2.45	K. Nichols, BOS	30
K. Nichols, BOS	2.81	F. Killen, PIT	29
N. Cuppy, CLE	3.12	C. Young, CLE	28
F. Dwyer, CIN	3.15	J. Meekin, NY	26
C. Young, CLE	3.24		

Total Bases		Runs Batted In		Stolen Bases		Saves		Strikeouts		Complete Games	
J. Burkett, CLE	317	E. Delahanty, PHI	126	B. Hamilton, BOS	93	C. Young, CLE	3	P. Hawley, PIT	137	F. Killen, PIT	44
E. Delahanty, PHI	315	H. Jennings, BAL	121	J. Kelley, BAL	87	C. Fisher, CIN	2	C. Young, CLE	137	C. Young, CLE	42
J. Kelley, BAL	282	H. Duffy, BOS	112	B. Lange, CHI	84	S. Hill, LOU	2	F. Killen, PIT	134	W. Mercer, WAS	38
W. Keeler, BAL	274	E. McKean, CLE	112	D. Miller, CIN	76			Breitenstein, STL	114		
Van Haltren, NY	273	H. Reitz, BAL	106	J. Doyle, BAL	73			J. Meekin, NY	110		
		C. Childs, CLE	106								

NATIONAL LEAGUE 1896, cont.

BATTING AND BASE RUNNING LEADERS

Hits
J. Burkett, CLE	240
W. Keeler, BAL	214
H. Jennings, BAL	208
E. Delahanty, PHI	198

Base on Balls
B. Hamilton, BOS	110
B. Joyce, NY, WAS	101
C. Childs, CLE	100
J. Kelley, BAL	91

Home Run Percentage
B. Joyce, NY, WAS	2.9
E. Delahanty, PHI	2.6
S. Thompson, PHI	2.3
R. Connor, STL	2.3

Fewest Hits/9 Innings
B. Rhines, CIN	8.06
P. Hawley, PIT	9.10
M. Sullivan, NY	9.13
D. Friend, CHI	9.23

PITCHING LEADERS

Shutouts
C. Young, CLE	5
F. Killen, PIT	5

Fewest Walks/9 Innings
C. Young, CLE	1.35
D. Clarke, NY	1.54
F. Dwyer, CIN	1.87
N. Cuppy, CLE	1.89

Runs Scored
J. Burkett, CLE	160
B. Dahlen, CHI	153
W. Keeler, BAL	153
J. Kelley, BAL	148

Doubles
E. Delahanty, PHI	44
D. Miller, CIN	38
J. Kelley, BAL	31
B. Dahlen, CHI	30

Triples
T. McCreery, LOU	21
Van Haltren, NY	21
B. Dahlen, CHI	19
J. Kelley, BAL	19

Most Strikeouts/9 Inn.
B. Briggs, CHI	3.90
A. Pond, BAL	3.36
D. McJames, WAS	3.31
P. Hawley, PIT	3.26

Innings
F. Killen, PIT	432
C. Young, CLE	414
P. Hawley, PIT	378
K. Nichols, BOS	372

Games Pitched
F. Killen, PIT	52
C. Young, CLE	51
P. Hawiey, PIT	49
K. Nichols, BOS	49

	W	L	PCT	GB	R	OR	2B	3B	HR	BA	SA	SB	E	DP	FA	CG	BB	SO	ShO	SV	ERA
Baltimore	90	39	.698		**995**	662	207	**100**	23	**.328**	**.429**	**441**	296	114	.945	115	339	302	9	1	3.67
Cleveland	80	48	.625	9.5	840	650	207	72	28	.301	.391	175	288	117	.949	113	**280**	336	9	5	**3.46**
Cincinnati	77	50	.606	12	783	**620**	205	73	19	.294	.388	350	**252**	107	**.951**	105	310	219	**12**	4	3.67
Boston	74	57	.565	17	860	761	175	74	36	.300	.392	241	368	94	.934	110	397	277	6	3	3.78
Chicago	71	57	.555	18.5	815	799	182	97	34	.286	.390	332	366	115	.934	**118**	467	353	2	1	4.41
Pittsburgh	66	63	.512	24	787	741	169	94	27	.292	.385	217	317	103	.941	108	439	**362**	8	1	4.30
New York	64	67	.489	27	829	821	159	87	40	.297	.394	274	365	90	.933	104	403	312	1	2	4.54
Philadelphia	62	68	.477	28.5	890	891	**234**	84	**49**	.295	.413	191	313	112	.941	107	387	243	3	2	5.20
Brooklyn	58	73	.443	33	692	764	174	87	28	.284	.379	198	297	104	.945	97	400	259	3	1	4.25
Washington	58	73	.443	33	818	920	179	79	45	.286	.388	258	398	99	.927	106	435	292	2	3	4.61
St. Louis	40	90	.308	50.5	593	929	134	78	37	.257	.346	185	345	73	.936	115	456	279	1	1	5.33
Louisville	38	93	.290	53	653	997	142	80	37	.261	.351	195	475	110	.916	108	541	288	1	4	5.12
					9555	9555	2167	1005	403	.290	.387	3057	4080	1238	.938	1306	4854	3522	57	28	4.36

NATIONAL LEAGUE 1897

Boston
W-93 L-39

Frank Selee

POS	Player	AB	BA	HR	RBI	PO	A	E	DP	TC/G	FA	Pitcher	G	IP	W	L	SV	ERA
1B	F. Tenney	**566**	.318	1	85	1248	81	16	69	10.5	.988	K. Nichols	46	**368**	**31**	11	3	2.64
2B	B. Lowe	499	.309	5	106	270	404	34	33	5.8	.952	F. Klobedanz	38	309	26	7	0	4.60
SS	H. Long	450	.322	3	69	274	353	46	40	6.5	.905	T. Lewis	38	290	21	12	1	3.85
3B	J. Collins	529	.346	6	132	**214**	**303**	47	20	**4.2**	.917	J. Stivetts	18	129	11	4	0	3.41
RF	C. Stahl	469	.354	4	97	164	17	14	4	1.8	.928	J. Sullivan	13	89	4	5	2	3.94
CF	B. Hamilton	507	.343	3	61	296	10	12	0	2.5	.962							
LF	H. Duffy	550	.340	11	129	266	12	7	2	2.2	.975							
C	M. Bergen	327	.248	2	45	351	66	16	4	5.1	.963							
OP	J. Stivetts	199	.367	2	37	50	39	6	1		.937							
P	F. Klobedanz	148	.324	1	20	8	47	2	4	1.5	.965							
P	K. Nichols	147	.265	3	28	29	62	3	1	2.0	.968							
SS	B. Allen	119	.319	1	24	78	117	16	12	6.6	.924							

Baltimore
W-90 L-40

Ned Hanlon

POS	Player	AB	BA	HR	RBI	PO	A	E	DP	TC/G	FA	Pitcher	G	IP	W	L	SV	ERA
1B	J. Doyle	460	.354	1	87	1105	75	25	72	10.6	.979	J. Corbett	37	313	24	8	0	3.11
2B	H. Reitz	477	.289	2	84	280	**449**	29	**62**	5.9	.962	B. Hoffer	38	303	22	11	0	4.30
SS	H. Jennings	439	.355	2	79	335	425	55	54	**7.0**	.933	A. Pond	32	248	18	9	0	3.52
3B	J. McGraw	391	.325	0	48	112	182	38	16	3.2	.886	J. Nops	30	221	20	6	0	2.81
RF	W. Keeler	564	**.424**	1	74	217	12	7	2	1.8	.970							
CF	J. Stenzel	536	.353	5	116	264	12	20	2	2.3	.932							
LF	J. Kelley	505	.362	5	118	240	15	11	3	2.0	.959							
C	B. Clarke	241	.270	1	38	191	38	15	2	4.1	.939							
UT	J. Quinn	285	.260	1	45	142	176	16	22		.952							
C	W. Robinson	181	.315	0	23	184	36	8	2	4.8	.965							
P	J. Corbett	150	.247	0	22	21	76	16	1	3.1	.858							
10	T. O'Brien	147	.252	0	32	243	15	9	9		.966							
P	B. Hoffer	139	.237	1	16	22	64	4	4	2.4	.956							
C	F. Bowerman	130	.315	1	21	155	29	10	1	5.4	.948							

New York
W-83 L-48

Bill Joyce

POS	Player	AB	BA	HR	RBI	PO	A	E	DP	TC/G	FA	Pitcher	G	IP	W	L	SV	ERA
1B	W. Clark	431	.283	1	75	1038	64	18	69	10.5	.984	A. Rusie	38	322	28	10	0	**2.54**
2B	K. Gleason	540	.319	1	106	309	395	**53**	43	5.9	.930	J. Meekin	37	304	20	11	0	3.76
SS	G. Davis	519	.353	10	**134**	337	434	62	67	6.4	.926	C. Seymour	38	292	20	14	1	3.21
3B	B. Joyce	388	.304	3	64	165	199	**63**	17	4.0	.852	M. Sullivan	23	149	8	7	2	5.09
RF	M. Tiernan	528	.330	5	72	178	11	14	2	1.6	.931							
CF	Van Haltren	564	.330	3	64	267	31	20	4	2.5	.937							
LF	D. Holmes	306	.268	1	44	113	9	13	2	1.8	.904							
C	J. Warner	397	.275	2	51	**513**	127	32	17	6.1	.952							
OF	T. McCreery	177	.299	1	28	53	10	7*	1	1.6	.900							
UT	P. Wilson	154	.299	0	22	222	26	13	9		.950							
P	A. Rusie	144	.278	0	22	19	77	8	3	2.7	.923							
P	C. Seymour	137	.241	2	14	15	98	**20**	5	3.5	.850							
P	J. Meekin	137	.299	0	10	14	56	11	2	2.2	.864							

NATIONAL LEAGUE 1897, cont.

	POS	Player	AB	BA	HR	RBI	PO	A	E	DP	TC/G	FA	Pitcher	G	IP	W	L	SV	ERA
Cincinnati	1B	J. Beckley	365	.345	7	76	830	45	19	56	9.2	.979	Breitenstein	40	320	23	12	0	3.62
	2B	B. McPhee	282	.301	1	39	209	267	17	34	6.1	.966	B. Rhines	41	289	21	15	0	4.08
W-76 L-56	SS	C. Ritchey	337	.282	0	41	144	204	40	21	5.5	.897	F. Dwyer	37	247	18	13	0	3.78
	3B	C. Irwin	505	.289	0	74	186	236	27	19	3.4	.940	R. Ehret	34	184	8	10	2	4.78
Buck Ewing	RF	D. Miller	440	.316	4	70	203	18	17	2	2.0	.929	B. Dammann	16	95	6	4	0	4.74
	CF	D. Hoy	497	.292	2	42	359	10	26	5	3.1	.934							
	LF	E. Burke	387	.266	1	41	224	11	15	4	2.6	.940							
	C	H. Peitz	266	.293	1	44	260	67	7	8	4.7	.979							
	S2	T. Corcoran	445	.288	3	57	286	360	48	51		.931							
	1B	F. Vaughn	199	.291	0	30	342	17	5	19	10.4	.986							
	OF	B. Holliday	195	.313	2	20	76	2	5	4	2.0	.940							
	C	P. Schriver	178	.303	1	30	147	42	8	3	3.7	.959							
	P	Breitenstein	124	.266	0	23	16	65	3	3	2.1	.964							
Cleveland	1B	P. Tebeau	412	.267	0	59	912	44	6	47	10.5	.994	C. Young	46	335	21	19	0	3.79
	2B	C. Childs	444	.338	1	61	319	384	42	42	6.5	.944	Z. Wilson	34	264	16	11	0	4.16
W-69 L-62	SS	E. McKean	523	.273	2	78	226	385	53	36	5.3	.920	J. Powell	27	225	15	10	0	3.16
	3B	B. Wallace	516	.335	4	112	190	249	34	10	3.6	.928	N. Cuppy	19	139	10	6	0	3.18
Patsy Tebeau	RF	Sockalexis	278	.338	3	42	117	10	16	3	2.2	.888							
	CF	O. Pickering	182	.352	1	22	110	5	6	1	2.6	.950							
	LF	J. Burkett	517	.383	2	60	226	18	13	3	2.0	.949							
	C	C. Zimmer	294	.316	0	40	278	81	9	10	4.6	.976							
	UT	J. O'Connor	397	.290	2	69	477	23	16	10		.969							
	P	C. Young	153	.222	0	19	16	88	9	0	2.5	.920							
	C	L. Criger	138	.225	0	22	129	35	11	1	4.7	.937							
	UT	McAllister	137	.219	0	11	74	21	9	1		.913							
Brooklyn	1B	C. LaChance	520	.308	4	90	1289	64	30	76	11.0	.978	B. Kennedy	44	343	18	20	1	3.91
	2B	G. Shoch	284	.278	0	38	188	240	27	25	6.7	.941	H. Payne	40	280	14	16	0	4.63
W-61 L-71	SS	G. Smith	428	.201	0	29	201	399	61	36	5.9	.908	J. Dunn	25	217	14	9	0	4.57
	3B	B. Shindle	542	.284	3	105	185	241	45	13	5.3	.904	C. Fisher	20	149	9	7	1	4.23
Billy Barnie	RF	F. Jones	548	.314	0	49	233	22	16	8	2.0	.941	D. Daub	19	138	6	11	0	6.08
	CF	M. Griffin	534	.316	2	56	353	13	17	6	2.9	.956							
	LF	J. Anderson	492	.325	4	85	253	11	18	2	2.5	.936							
	C	J. Grim	290	.248	0	25	241	98	19	8	4.6	.947							
	2B	J. Canavan	240	.217	2	34	157	162	32	18	5.6	.909							
	CO	B. Smith	237	.300	1	39	138	51	19	8		.909							
	P	B. Kennedy	147	.272	1	18	14	87	4	4	2.4	.962							
Washington	1B	T. Tucker	352	.338	5	61	856	42	15	58	9.8	.984	W. Mercer	45	332	20	20	2	3.25
	2B	J. O'Brien	320	.244	3	45	223	260	30	43	6.0	.942	D. McJames	44	324	15	23	2	3.61
W-61 L-71	SS	DeMontreville	566	.341	3	93	254	352	78	47	6.6	.886	C. Swaim	27	194	10	11	0	4.41
	3B	C. Reilly	351	.276	2	60	149	224	39	17	4.1	.905	S. King	23	154	7	8	1	4.79
Gus Schmelz	RF	C. Abbey	300	.260	3	34	126	14	8	1	1.9	.946							
W-9 L-25	CF	T. Brown	469	.292	5	45	252	17	21	5	2.5	.928							
	LF	K. Selbach	486	.313	5	59	305	14	15	2	2.7	.955							
Tom Brown	C	D. McGuire	327	.343	4	53	290	88	21	6	5.5	.947							
W-52 L-46																			
	UT	Z. Wrigley	388	.284	3	64	175	209	50	18		.885							
	C	D. Farrell	261	.322	0	53	220	91	18	10	5.2	.945							
	OF	J. Gettman	143	.315	3	29	49	3	1	0	1.5	.981							
	P	W. Mercer	135	.319	0	19													
Pittsburgh	1B	H. Davis	429	.305	2	63	570	29	22	26	9.7	.965	F. Killen	42	337	17	23	0	4.46
	2B	D. Padden	517	.282	2	58	369	402	48	36	6.1	.941	P. Hawley	40	311	18	18	0	4.80
W-60 L-71	SS	B. Ely	516	.283	2	74	308	451	60	41	6.2	.927	J. Hughey	25	149	6	10	1	5.06
	3B	Hoffmeister	188	.309	3	36	48	70	31	7	3.1	.792	J. Tannehill	21	142	9	9	1	4.25
Patsy Donovan	RF	P. Donovan	479	.322	0	57	186	17	11	5	1.8	.949	C. Hastings	16	118	5	4	0	4.58
	CF	S. Brodie	370	.292	2	53	218	11	4	1	2.3	.983	J. Gardner	14	95	5	5	0	5.19
	LF	E. Smith	467	.310	6	54	245	19	28	1	2.4	.904							
	C	J. Sugden	288	.222	0	38	317	82	25	6	5.2	.941							
	C	B. Merritt	209	.263	1	26	202	43	14	6	4.9	.946							
	OP	J. Tannehill	184	.266	0	22	89	53	13	1		.916							
	3B	J. Donnelly	161	.193	0	14	51	87	12	1	3.4	.920							
Chicago	1B	C. Anson	424	.285	3	75	933	62	25	67	9.9	.975	C. Griffith	41	344	21	18	1	3.72
	2B	J. Connor	285	.291	3	38	176	293	32	40	6.6	.936	D. Friend	24	203	12	11	0	4.52
W-59 L-73	SS	B. Dahlen	276	.290	6	40	215	291	38	48	7.3	.930	N. Callahan	23	190	12	9	0	4.03
	3B	B. Everett	379	.314	5	39	119	147	42	9	3.7	.864	B. Briggs	22	187	4	17	0	5.26
Cap Anson	RF	J. Ryan	520	.300	5	85	211	28	14	7	1.9	.945	W. Thornton	16	130	6	7	0	4.70
	CF	B. Lange	479	.340	5	83	264	17	16	4	2.5	.946	R. Denzer	12	95	2	8	0	5.13
	LF	G. Decker	428	.290	5	63	112	12	10	1	1.8	.925							
	C	M. Kittridge	262	.202	1	30	324	75	20	6	5.3	.952							
	3S	McCormick	419	.267	2	55	171	268	59	26		.882							
	UT	N. Callahan	360	.292	3	47	147	201	42	25		.892							
	OF	W. Thornton	265	.321	0	55	74	8	23	0	1.8	.781							
	C	T. Donahue	188	.239	0	21	218	64	15	2	5.4	.949							
	P	C. Griffith	162	.235	0	21	23	85	6	3	2.8	.947							

NATIONAL LEAGUE 1897, cont.

	POS	Player	AB	BA	HR	RBI	PO	A	E	DP	TC/G	FA	Pitcher	G	IP	W	L	SV	ERA
Philadelphia	1B	N. Lajoie	545	.361	9	127	1079	37	18	45	10.5	.984	J. Taylor	40	317	16	20	2	4.23
	2B	L. Cross	344	.259	3	51	68	120	7	10	5.1	.964	A. Orth	36	282	14	19	0	4.62
W-55 L-77	SS	S. Gillen	270	.259	0	27	129	197	38	6	5.3	.896	J. Fifield	27	211	5	18	0	5.51
	3B	B. Nash	337	.258	0	39	114	146	23	10	3.6	.919	G. Wheeler	26	191	11	10	0	3.96
George Stallings	RF	T. Dowd	391	.292	0	43	116	9	11	3	1.9	.919							
	CF	D. Cooley	**566**	.329	4	40	322	16	14	6	2.7	.960							
	LF	E. Delahanty	530	.377	5	96	266	23	9	2	2.3	.970							
	C	J. Boyle	288	.253	2	36	215	4	4	3	4.5	.982							
	O2	P. Geier	316	.278	1	35	158	129	18	6		.941							
	C	J. Clements	185	.238	6	36	163	40	8	3	4.3	.962							
	SS	F. Shugart	163	.252	5	25	104	128	34	15	6.7	.872							
	P	A. Orth	152	.329	1	17	9	69	6	1	2.3	.929							
	P	J. Taylor	139	.252	1	17	12	89	16	2	2.9	.863							
Louisville	1B	P. Werden	506	.302	5	83	**1318**	**116**	23	70	**11.1**	.984	C. Fraser	35	286	15	19	0	4.09
	2B	J. Rogers	150	.147	2	22	86	120	15	12	5.7	.932	Cunningham	29	235	14	13	0	4.14
W-52 L-78	SS	G. Stafford	432	.278	7	53	197	353	70	33	6.0	.887	S. Hill	27	199	7	17	0	3.62
	3B	B. Clingman	395	.228	2	47	176	269	25	16	4.2	**.947**	B. Magee	22	155	4	12	0	5.39
Jim Rogers	RF	T. McCreery	338	.284	4	40	130	13	24*	2	1.9	.856							
W-17 L-24	CF	O. Pickering	246	.252	1	21	134	15	10	2	2.6	.937							
	LF	F. Clarke	518	.390	6	67	282	18	24	0	2.6	.926							
Fred Clarke	C	B. Wilson	381	.213	1	41	338	113	29	7	4.7	.940							
W-35 L-54	UT	C. Dexter	257	.280	2	46	132	68	27	8		.881							
	OF	H. Wagner	237	.338	2	39	101	17	12	5	2.5	.908							
	2B	A. Johnson	161	.242	0	23	68	92	22	8	5.5	.879							
	S2	J. Dolan	133	.211	0	7	84	113	26	14		.883							
St. Louis	1B	M. Grady	322	.280	7	55	797	48	23	54	10.5	.974	R. Donahue	**46**	348	11	**33**	1	6.13
	2B	B. Hallman	298	.221	0	26	189	244	28	35	6.0	.939	B. Hart	39	295	9	27	0	6.26
W-29 L-102	SS	M. Cross	462	.286	4	55	327	**513**	73	47	7.0	.920	K. Carsey	12	99	3	8	0	6.00
	3B	F. Hartman	516	.306	2	67	159	253	**63**	14	3.8	.867							
Tommy Dowd	RF	T. Turner	416	.291	2	41	146	10	9	3	1.6	.945							
W-6 L-22	CF	D. Harley	330	.291	3	55	186	19	23	3	2.6	.899							
	LF	B. Lally	355	.279	2	42	192	9	23	2	2.7	.897							
Hugh Nicol	C	K. Douglass	516	.329	6	50	171	64	13	4	4.1	.948							
W-8 L-32	20	J. Houseman	278	.245	0	21	168	131	24	10		.926							
	C	M. Murphy	207	.169	0	12	145	62	11	3	4.1	.950							
Bill Hallman	P	B. Hart	156	.250	2	14	21	76	8	4	2.7	.924							
W-13 L-36	P	R. Donahue	155	.213	1	14	24	97	3	1	2.7	.976							
Chris Von Der Ahe	OF	T. Dowd	145	.262	0	9	65	0	6	0	2.4	.915							
W-2 L-12																			

BATTING AND BASE RUNNING LEADERS

Batting Average
W. Keeler, BAL	.432
F. Clarke, LOU	.406
J. Kelley, BAL	.388
J. Burkett, CLE	.383
E. Delahanty, PHI	.377

Slugging Average
N. Lajoie, PHI	.578
W. Keeler, BAL	.553
F. Clarke, LOU	.550
E. Delahanty, PHI	.538
G. Davis, NY	.516

Home Runs
H. Duffy, BOS	11
N. Lajoie, PHI	10
G. Davis, NY	9
J. Beckley, CIN, NY	8
M. Grady, PHI, STL	7
G. Stafford, LOU, NY	7

Total Bases
N. Lajoie, PHI	315
W. Keeler, BAL	311
F. Clarke, LOU	289
E. Delahanty, PHI	285
G. Davis, NY	264

Runs Batted In
G. Davis, NY	134
J. Collins, BOS	132
H. Duffy, BOS	129
N. Lajoie, PHI	127
J. Kelley, BAL	118

Stolen Bases
B. Lange, CHI	73
B. Hamilton, BOS	70
J. Stenzel, BAL	69
G. Davis, NY	65
W. Keeler, BAL	64

Hits
W. Keeler, BAL	243
F. Clarke, LOU	213
E. Delahanty, PHI	200
J. Burkett, CLE	198

Base on Balls
B. Hamilton, BOS	105
J. McGraw, BAL	99
M. Griffin, BKN	81
K. Selbach, WAS	80

Home Run Percentage
M. Grady, PHI, STL	2.1
H. Duffy, BOS	2.0
G. Davis, NY	1.9
J. Beckley, CIN, NY	1.8

Runs Scored
B. Hamilton, BOS	152
W. Keeler, BAL	145
M. Griffin, BKN	136
F. Jones, BKN	134

Doubles
J. Stenzel, BAL	43
E. Delahanty, PHI	40
N. Lajoie, PHI	40
B. Wallace, CLE	33

Triples
H. Davis, PIT	28
N. Lajoie, PHI	23
B. Wallace, CLE	21
W. Keeler, BAL	19

PITCHING LEADERS

Winning Percentage
F. Klobedanz, BOS	.788
A. Rusie, NY	.784
J. Nops, BAL	.769
J. Corbett, BAL	.750
K. Nichols, BOS	.732

Earned Run Average
A. Rusie, NY	2.54
K. Nichols, BOS	2.64
J. Nops, BAL	2.81
J. Corbett, BAL	3.11
J. Powell, CLE	3.16

Wins
K. Nichols, BOS	30
A. Rusie, NY	29
F. Klobedanz, BOS	26
J. Corbett, BAL	24
Breitenstein, CIN	23

Saves
K. Nichols, BOS	3

Strikeouts
C. Seymour, NY	157
D. McJames, WAS	156
J. Corbett, BAL	149
K. Nichols, BOS	136
A. Rusie, NY	135

Complete Games
C. Griffith, CHI	38
F. Killen, PIT	38
R. Donahue, STL	38
K. Nichols, BOS	37
B. Kennedy, BKN	36

Fewest Hits/9 Innings
C. Seymour, NY	8.23
A. Rusie, NY	8.77
K. Nichols, BOS	8.85
S. Hill, LOU	9.45

Shutouts
D. McJames, WAS	3
W. Mercer, WAS	3

Fewest Walks/9 Innings
C. Young, CLE	1.32
J. Tannehill, PIT	1.52
K. Nichols, BOS	1.66
N. Cuppy, CLE	1.69

Most Strikeouts/9 Inn.
C. Seymour, NY	4.83
D. McJames, WAS	4.34
J. Corbett, BAL	4.28
W. Thornton, CHI	3.80

Innings
K. Nichols, BOS	368
R. Donahue, STL	348
C. Griffith, CHI	344
B. Kennedy, BKN	343

Games Pitched
K. Nichols, BOS	46
R. Donahue, STL	46
C. Young, CLE	46
W. Mercer, WAS	45

NATIONAL LEAGUE 1897, cont.

	W	L	PCT	GB	R	OR	2B	3B	HR	BA	SA	SB	E	DP	FA	CG	BB	SO	ShO	SV	ERA
							Batting						Fielding			Pitching					
Boston	93	39	.705		**1025**	**665**	230	83	**45**	.319	**.426**	233	272	80	**.951**	115	393	329	**8**	**7**	3.65
Baltimore	90	40	.692	2	964	674	**243**	66	20	**.325**	.414	**401**	277	110	.951	118	382	361	3	0	3.55
New York	83	48	.634	9.5	895	695	188	84	31	.299	.392	328	397	109	.930	118	486	**456**	8	3	**3.47**
Cincinnati	76	56	.576	17	763	705	219	69	22	.290	.383	194	273	100	.948	100	329	270	4	2	4.09
Cleveland	69	62	.527	23.5	773	680	192	88	16	.298	.389	181	**261**	74	.950	111	**289**	277	6	0	3.95
Brooklyn	61	71	.462	32	802	845	202	72	22	.279	.365	187	364	99	.936	114	410	256	4	2	4.60
Washington	61	71	.462	32	781	793	194	77	36	.297	.395	208	369	103	.933	103	400	348	7	5	4.01
Pittsburgh	60	71	.458	32.5	676	835	140	**108**	25	.276	.370	170	346	70	.936	112	318	342	2	2	4.67
Chicago	59	73	.447	34	832	894	189	97	38	.282	.386	264	393	**112**	.932	**131**	433	361	2	1	4.53
Philadelphia	55	77	.417	38	752	792	213	83	40	.293	.386	163	296	72	.944	115	364	253	4	2	4.60
Louisville	52	78	.400	40	669	859	160	70	40	.265	.358	195	395	85	.929	114	459	267	2	0	4.42
St. Louis	29	102	.221	63.5	588	1083	149	67	31	.275	.356	172	375	84	.933	109	453	207	1	1	6.21
					9520	9520	2319	964	366	.292	.386	2696	4018	1098	.939	1360	4716	3727	51	25	4.31

NATIONAL LEAGUE 1898

	POS	Player	AB	BA	HR	RBI	PO	A	E	DP	TC/G	FA	Pitcher	G	IP	W	L	SV	ERA
Boston W-102 L-47 Frank Selee	1B	F. Tenney	488	.328	0	62	1090	66	23	71	10.1	.980	K. Nichols	**50**	388	**31**	12	4	2.13
	2B	B. Lowe	559	.272	4	94	397	457	37	63	6.1	.958	T. Lewis	41	313	26	8	2	2.90
	SS	H. Long	589	.265	6	99	326	472	67	65	6.1	.923	V. Willis	41	311	25	13	0	2.84
	3B	J. Collins	597	.328	15	111	**243**	332	42	20	4.1	.932	F. Klobedanz	35	271	19	10	0	3.89
	RF	C. Stahl	467	.308	3	52	199	14	7	4	1.8	.968							
	CF	B. Hamilton	417	.369	3	90	189	8	21	2	2.0	.904							
	LF	H. Duffy	568	.298	8	108	332	18	16	2	2.4	.956							
	C	M. Bergen	446	.280	3	60	496	109	**24**	4	5.4	.962							
	UT	G. Yeager	221	.267	3	24	303	40	19	6		.948							
	P	K. Nichols	158	.241	2	23	21	78	4	1	2.1	.961							
Baltimore W-96 L-53 Ned Hanlon	1B	D. McGann	535	.301	5	106	1416	68	26	78	10.4	.983	D. McJames	45	374	27	15	0	2.36
	2B	DeMontreville	567	.328	0	86	303	386	41	35	5.9	.944	J. Hughes	38	301	23	12	0	3.20
	SS	H. Jennings	534	.328	1	87	289	368	50	41	6.1	.929	A. Maul	28	240	20	7	0	2.10
	3B	J. McGraw	515	.342	0	53	142	271	46	16	3.4	.900	J. Nops	33	235	16	9	0	3.56
	RF	W. Keeler	561	**.385**	1	44	210	14	9	2	1.8	.961	F. Kitson	17	119	8	6	0	3.24
	CF	J. Kelley	464	.321	2	110	235	18	8	4	2.1	.969							
	LF	D. Holmes	442	.285	1	64	247	13	18	4	2.5	.935							
	C	W. Robinson	289	.277	0	38	288	72	13	4	4.8	.965							
	C	B. Clarke	285	.242	0	27	289	69	14	6	5.3	.962							
	P	J. Hughes	164	.226	2	20	29	78	11	1	3.1	.907							
	OF	J. Stenzel	138	.254	0	22	57	6	5	1	1.9	.926							
Cincinnati W-92 L-60 Buck Ewing	1B	J. Beckley	459	.294	4	72	1167	53	21	76	10.5	.983	P. Hawley	43	331	27	11	0	3.37
	2B	B. McPhee	486	.249	1	60	299	396	32	74	5.6	.956	Breitenstein	39	316	20	14	0	3.42
	SS	T. Corcoran	619	.250	2	87	353	561	67	76	6.4	.932	S. Hill	33	262	13	14	0	3.98
	3B	C. Irwin	501	.240	3	55	223	305	34	20	**4.1**	.940	F. Dwyer	31	240	16	10	0	3.04
	RF	D. Miller	586	.299	3	90	292	23	24	4	2.2	.929	B. Dammann	35	225	16	10	2	3.61
	CF	A. McBride	486	.302	2	43	288	18	13	3	2.7	.959							
	LF	E. Smith	486	.342	1	66	280	15	16	5	2.5	.949							
	C	H. Peitz	330	.273	1	43	323	90	**24**	12	4.3	.945							
	UT	Steinfeldt	308	.295	0	43	202	158	41	17		.898							
	1C	F. Vaughn	275	.305	1	46	462	50	17	28		.968							
Chicago W-85 L-65 Tom Burns	1B	B. Everett	596	.319	0	69	1519	70	42	**123**	10.9	.974	C. Griffith	38	326	24	10	0	**1.88**
	2B	J. Connor	505	.226	0	76	330	437	44	75	5.9	.956	N. Callahan	31	274	20	10	0	2.46
	SS	B. Dahlen	521	.290	1	79	369	511	76	**77**	6.7	.921	W. Woods	27	215	9	13	0	3.14
	3B	McCormick	530	.247	2	78	152	322	**60**	31	3.9	.888	W. Thornton	28	215	13	10	0	3.34
	RF	S. Mertes	269	.297	1	47	97	13	15	6	2.1	.880	M. Kilroy	13	100	6	7	0	4.31
	CF	B. Lange	442	.319	6	69	269	19	9	4	2.7	.970	F. Isbell	13	81	4	7	0	3.56
	LF	J. Ryan	572	.323	4	79	267	20	27	2	2.2	.914							
	C	T. Donahue	396	.220	0	39	450	107	22	**16**	4.7	.962							
	OP	W. Thornton	210	.295	0	14	74	53	17	5		.882							
	OF	D. Green	188	.314	4	27	87	10	3	5	2.1	.970							
	P	N. Callahan	164	.262	0	22	27	63	5	3	3.1	.947							
	UT	F. Isbell	159	.233	0	8	54	43	19	5		.836							
	UT	W. Woods	154	.175	0	8	42	87	15	3		.896							
Cleveland W-81 L-68 Patsy Tebeau	1B	P. Tebeau	477	.258	1	63	956	43	16	43	11.2	.984	C. Young	46	378	25	13	0	2.53
	2B	C. Childs	413	.288	1	90	273	370	48	37	**6.3**	.931	J. Powell	42	342	23	15	0	3.00
	SS	E. McKean	604	.285	9	94	304	425	53	47	5.2	.932	Z. Wilson	33	255	13	18	0	3.60
	3B	B. Wallace	593	.270	3	99	201	329	36	19	4.0	.936	N. Cuppy	18	128	9	8	0	3.30
	RF	H. Blake	474	.245	0	58	234	25	13	3	2.0	.952							
	CF	J. McAleer	366	.238	0	48	239	10	9	4	2.5	.965							
	LF	J. Burkett	624	.341	0	42	268	17	19	3	2.0	.938							
	C	L. Criger	287	.279	1	32	322	105	19	9	5.4	.957							
	UT	J. O'Connor	478	.249	1	56	761	92	20	36		.977							
	P	C. Young	154	.253	2	13	12	122	4	2	3.0	.971							

NATIONAL LEAGUE 1898, *cont.*

	POS	Player	AB	BA	HR	RBI	PO	A	E	DP	TC/G	FA	Pitcher	G	IP	W	L	SV	ERA
Philadelphia	1B	K. Douglass	582	.258	2	48	1236	73	32	74	9.2	.976	W. Piatt	39	306	24	14	0	3.18
	2B	N. Lajoie	608	.324	6	**127**	442	406	46	59	6.1	.949	R. Donahue	35	284	17	17	0	3.55
W-78 L-71	SS	M. Cross	525	.257	1	50	404	506	93	65	6.7	.907	A. Orth	32	250	15	13	0	3.02
	3B	B. Lauder	361	.263	2	67	132	171	47	6	3.6	.866	J. Fifield	21	171	11	9	0	3.31
George Stallings	RF	E. Flick	453	.302	8	81	237	21	19	4	2.1	.931	G. Wheeler	15	112	6	8	0	4.17
W-19 L-27	CF	D. Cooley	629	.312	4	55	352	15	22	2	2.6	.943							
	LF	E. Delahanty	548	.334	4	92	302	20	12	5	2.3	.964							
Bill Shettsline	C	McFarland	429	.282	3	71	420	136	23	7	4.8	.960							
W-59 L-44																			
New York	1B	B. Joyce	508	.258	10	91	1252	**87**	47	73	10.7	.966	C. Seymour	45	357	25	19	0	3.18
	2B	K. Gleason	570	.221	0	62	366	**468**	55	57	6.2	.938	J. Meekin	38	320	16	18	0	3.77
W-77 L-73	SS	G. Davis	486	.307	2	86	349	421	55	61	**6.8**	.933	A. Rusie	37	300	20	11	1	3.03
	3B	F. Hartman	475	.272	2	88	146	280	57	16	3.9	.882	E. Doheny	28	213	7	19	0	3.68
Bill Joyce	RF	J. Doyle	297	.283	1	43	39	10	8	2	1.5	.860	C. Gettig	17	115	6	3	0	3.83
W-22 L-21	CF	Van Haltren	654	.312	2	68	299	22	29	5	2.2	.917							
	LF	M. Tiernan	415	.280	4	49	130	12	4	2	1.4	.973							
Cap Anson	C	J. Warner	373	.257	0	42	536	139	22	10	**6.4**	.968							
W-9 L-13	PO	C. Seymour	297	.276	4	23	71	119	25	9		.884							
Bill Joyce	UT	M. Grady	287	.296	3	49	321	74	34	7		.921							
W-46 L-39	UT	C. Gettig	196	.250	0	26	70	103	21	6		.892							
	OF	W. Wilmot	138	.239	2	22	35	4	5	0	1.3	.886							
Pittsburgh	1B	W. Clark	209	.306	1	31	601	27	10	29	11.2	.984	J. Tannehill	43	327	25	13	2	2.95
	2B	D. Padden	463	.257	2	43	301	407	40	46	5.8	.947	B. Rhines	31	258	12	16	0	3.52
W-72 L-76	SS	B. Ely	519	.212	2	44	311	527	51	58	6.0	**.943**	J. Gardner	25	185	10	13	0	3.21
	3B	B. Grey	528	.229	0	67	172	258	59	16	3.6	.879	F. Killen	23	178	10	11	0	3.75
Bill Watkins	RF	P. Donovan	610	.302	0	37	238	21	20	4	1.9	.928	C. Hastings	19	137	4	10	0	3.41
	CF	T. O'Brien	413	.259	1	45	144	15	13	4*	2.5	.924	B. Hart	16	125	5	9	1	4.82
	LF	J. McCarthy	537	.289	4	78	296	19	22	4	2.5	.935							
	C	P. Schriver	315	.229	0	32	302	95	18	6	4.5	.957							
	C	F. Bowerman	241	.274	0	29	204	76	16	8	5.0	.946							
	1B	H. Davis	222	.293	1	24	556	22	12	30	11.1	.980							
	OF	T. McCreery	190	.311	2	20	107	6	8	1	2.4	.934							
	OF	S. Brodie	156	.263	0	21	110	4	5	1	2.8	.958							
Louisville	1B	H. Wagner	588	.299	10	105	729	41	22	44	10.6	.972	Cunningham	44	362	28	15	0	3.16
	2B	H. Smith	121	.190	0	13	74	87	16	8	5.4	.910	B. Magee	38	295	16	15	0	4.05
W-70 L-81	SS	C. Ritchey	551	.254	5	51	194	228	37	32	5.7	.919	P. Dowling	36	286	13	20	0	4.16
	3B	B. Clingman	538	.257	0	50	119	191	29	12	4.3	.914	C. Fraser	26	203	7	17	0	5.32
Fred Clarke	RF	C. Dexter	421	.314	1	66	148	13	7	2	1.8	.958	R. Ehret	12	89	3	7	0	5.76
	CF	D. Hoy	582	.304	6	66	348	19	21	6	2.6	.946							
	LF	F. Clarke	599	.307	3	47	344	19	23	3	2.6	.940							
	C	M. Kittridge	287	.244	1	31	258	80	20	10	4.2	.944							
	20	G. Stafford	181	.298	1	25	91	82	17	9		.911							
Brooklyn	1B	C. LaChance	526	.247	5	65	807	20	10	53	11.3	.988	B. Kennedy	40	339	16	22	0	3.37
	2B	B. Hallman	509	.244	2	63	268	419	41	46	5.9	.944	J. Dunn	41	323	16	21	0	3.60
W-54 L-91	SS	G. Magoon	343	.224	1	39	199	357	45	38	6.5	.925	J. Yeager	36	291	12	22	0	3.65
	3B	B. Shindle	466	.225	1	41	154	278	42	23	4.0	.911	R. Miller	23	152	4	14	0	5.34
Billy Barnie	RF	F. Jones	596	.304	1	69	229	17	14	7	1.8	.946	K. McKenna	14	101	2	6	0	5.63
W-15 L-20	CF	M. Griffin	537	.300	2	40	314	20	9	7	2.6	**.974**							
	LF	J. Sheckard	408	.277	4	64	213	12	18	2	2.3	.926							
Mike Griffin	C	J. Ryan	301	.189	0	24	289	93	16	13	4.7	.960							
W-1 L-3	1B	T. Tucker	283	.279	1	34	797*	49	8	44	11.7*	.991							
	OC	B. Smith	199	.261	0	13	103	24	13	5		.907							
Charlie Ebbets	C	J. Grim	178	.281	0	11	155	56	11	6	4.3	.950							
W-38 L-68	P	J. Dunn	167	.246	0	19	22	70	6	2	2.4	.939							
Washington	1B	J. Doyle	177	.305	2	26	344	17	14	23	9.9	.963	G. Weyhing	45	361	15	26	0	4.51
	2B	H. Reitz	489	.303	2	47	323	401	31	56	5.7	**.959**	W. Mercer	33	234	12	18	0	4.81
W-51 L-101	SS	Z. Wrigley	400	.245	2	39	252	326	68	42	6.7	.895	B. Dinneen	29	218	9	16	0	4.00
	3B	J. Smith	234	.303	3	28	65	74	15	6	3.3	.903	F. Killen	17	128	6	9	0	3.58
Tom Brown	RF	J. Gettman	567	.277	5	47	234	18	20	4	2.2	.926	C. Swaim	16	101	3	11	1	4.26
W-12 L-26	CF	J. Anderson	430	.305	9	71	200	20	12	3	2.5	.948							
	LF	K. Selbach	515	.303	3	60	320	24	19	6	**2.8**	.948							
Jack Doyle	C	D. McGuire	489	.268	1	57	371	93	16	11	5.2	.967							
W-8 L-9	C1	D. Farrell	338	.314	1	53	434	96	27	22		.952							
	UT	W. Mercer	249	.321	2	25	91	116	29	8		.877							
Deacon McGuire	UT	B. Wagner	223	.224	1	31	82	102	37	8		.833							
W-21 L-47	OF	B. Freeman	107	.364	3	21	39	5	1	2	1.6	.978							
Arthur Irwin																			
W-10 L-19																			

NATIONAL LEAGUE 1898, cont.

		POS	Player	AB	BA	HR	RBI	PO	A	E	DP	TC/G	FA	Pitcher	G	IP	W	L	SV	ERA
St. Louis		1B	G. Decker	286	.259	1	45	772	17	16	31	10.7	.980*	J. Taylor	50	397	15	29	1	3.90
		2B	J. Crooks	225	.231	1	20	192	209	17	23	6.3	.959	W. Sudhoff	41	315	11	27	1	4.34
W-39 L-111		SS	G. Smith	157	.159	1	9	79	167	26	14	5.3	.904	J. Hughey	35	284	7	24	0	3.93
		3B	L. Cross	602	.317	3	79	215	351	33	20	4.0	.945	K. Carsey	20	124	2	12	0	6.33
Tim Hurst		RF	T. Dowd	586	.244	0	32	208	11	19	3	1.8	.920							
		CF	J. Stenzel	404	.282	1	33	257	8	16	2	2.6	.943							
		LF	D. Harley	549	.246	0	42	311	26	27	3	2.6	.926							
		C	J. Clements	335	.257	3	41	287	81	11	8	4.4	.971							
		2S	J. Quinn	375	.251	0	36	218	340	31	30		.947							
		C	J. Sugden	289	.253	0	34	181	88	18	8	4.8	.937							
		1B	T. Tucker	252	.238	0	20	755*	36	22	40	11.3*	.973							
		P	J. Taylor	157	.242	1	18	18	144	22	2	3.7	.880							

BATTING AND BASE RUNNING LEADERS

Batting Average		Slugging Average		Home Runs	
W. Keeler, BAL	.379	J. Anderson, BKN, WAS	.494	J. Collins, BOS	15
B. Hamilton, BOS	.369	J. Collins, BOS	.479	B. Joyce, NY	10
J. Burkett, CLE	.345	E. Flick, PHI	.457	H. Wagner, LOU	10
J. McGraw, BAL	.342	E. Delahanty, PHI	.454	J. Anderson, BKN, WAS	9
E. Smith, CIN	.342	B. Hamilton, BOS	.453	E. McKean, CLE	9

Total Bases		Runs Batted In		Stolen Bases	
J. Collins, BOS	286	N. Lajoie, PHI	127	B. Hamilton, BOS	59
N. Lajoie, PHI	275	J. Collins, BOS	111	E. Delahanty, PHI	58
Van Haltren, NY	270	J. Kelley, BAL	110	DeMontreville, BAL	49
J. Anderson, BKN, WAS	257	H. Duffy, BOS	108	C. Dexter, LOU	44
D. Cooley, PHI	256	D. McGann, BAL	106	J. McGraw, BAL	43

Hits		Base on Balls		Home Run Percentage	
J. Burkett, CLE	215	J. McGraw, BAL	112	J. Collins, BOS	2.5
W. Keeler, BAL	214	B. Joyce, NY	88	B. Joyce, NY	2.0
Van Haltren, NY	204	B. Hamilton, BOS	87	E. Flick, PHI	1.8
N. Lajoie, PHI	197	E. Flick, PHI	86	J. Anderson, BKN, WAS	1.7

Runs Scored		Doubles		Triples	
J. McGraw, BAL	143	N. Lajoie, PHI	40	J. Anderson, BKN, WAS	22
H. Jennings, BAL	135	E. Delahanty, PHI	36	D. Hoy, LOU	16
Van Haltren, NY	129	B. Dahlen, CHI	35	Van Haltren, NY	16
W. Keeler, BAL	126	J. Collins, BOS	35	H. Davis, LOU, PIT, WAS	15

PITCHING LEADERS

Winning Percentage		Earned Run Average		Wins	
A. Maul, BAL	.769	C. Griffith, CHI	1.88	K. Nichols, BOS	29
T. Lewis, BOS	.765	A. Maul, BAL	2.10	Cunningham, LOU	28
C. Griffith, CHI	.722	K. Nichols, BOS	2.13	P. Hawley, CIN	27
P. Hawley, CIN	.711	D. McJames, BAL	2.36	D. McJames, BAL	27
K. Nichols, BOS	.707	N. Callahan, CHI	2.46	T. Lewis, BOS	26
				C. Griffith, CHI	26

Saves		Strikeouts		Complete Games	
K. Nichols, BOS	3	C. Seymour, NY	244	J. Taylor, STL	42
B. Dammann, CIN	2	D. McJames, BAL	178	Cunningham, LOU	41
T. Lewis, BOS	2	V. Willis, BOS	160	C. Young, CLE	40
J. Tannehill, PIT	2	K. Nichols, BOS	138	D. McJames, BAL	40
P. Hickman, BOS	2	W. Piatt, PHI	121	K. Nichols, BOS	40

Fewest Hits/9 Innings		Shutouts		Fewest Walks/9 Innings	
K. Nichols, BOS	7.33	W. Piatt, PHI	6	C. Young, CLE	0.98
V. Willis, BOS	7.64	J. Powell, CLE	6	F. Dwyer, CIN	1.58
T. Lewis, BOS	7.67	J. Hughes, BAL	5	Cunningham, LOU	1.62
A. Maul, BAL	7.77	J. Tannehill, PIT	5	J. Tannehill, PIT	1.74

Most Strikeouts/9 Inn.		Innings		Games Pitched	
C. Seymour, NY	6.03	J. Taylor, STL	397	J. Taylor, STL	50
V. Willis, BOS	4.63	K. Nichols, BOS	388	K. Nichols, BOS	50
D. McJames, BAL	4.28	C. Young, CLE	378	C. Young, CLE	46
E. Doheny, NY	4.06	D. McJames, BAL	374	D. McJames, BAL	45

	W	L	PCT	GB	R	OR	2B	3B	HR	BA	SA	SB	E	DP	FA	CG	BB	SO	ShO	SV	ERA
Boston	102	47	.685		872	614	190	55	53	.290	.377	172	310	102	.950	127	470	432	9	7	2.98
Baltimore	96	53	.644	6	933	623	154	77	12	.302	.368	250	326	105	.947	138	400	422	12	0	2.90
Cincinnati	92	60	.605	11.5	831	740	207	101	19	.271	.359	165	325	128	.950	131	449	294	10	2	3.50
Chicago	85	65	.567	17.5	828	679	175	83	19	.274	.350	220	412	149	.936	137	364	323	13	0	2.83
Cleveland	81	68	.544	21	730	683	162	56	18	.263	.325	93	301	95	.952	142	309	339	9	0	3.20
Philadelphia	78	71	.523	24	823	784	238	81	33	.280	.377	182	379	102	.937	129	399	325	10	0	3.72
New York	77	73	.513	25.5	837	800	190	86	33	.266	.352	214	447	113	.932	141	587	558	9	1	3.44
Pittsburgh	72	76	.486	29.5	634	694	140	88	14	.258	.328	107	340	105	.946	131	346	330	10	3	3.41
Louisville	70	81	.464	33	728	833	150	71	32	.267	.342	235	382	114	.939	137	470	271	4	0	4.24
Brooklyn	54	91	.372	46	638	811	156	66	17	.256	.322	130	334	125	.947	134	476	294	1	0	4.01
Washington	51	101	.336	52.5	704	939	177	81	35	.271	.355	197	443	119	.939	129	450	371		1	4.52
St. Louis	39	111	.260	63.5	571	929	149	55	13	.247	.305	104	388	97	.939	133	372	288		2	4.53
					9129	9129	2088	900	298	.271	.347	2069	4387	1354	.942	1609	5092	4247	87	16	3.60

NATIONAL LEAGUE 1899

		POS	Player	AB	BA	HR	RBI	PO	A	E	DP	TC/G	FA	Pitcher	G	IP	W	L	SV	ERA
Brooklyn		1B	D. McGann	214	.243	2	32	645	31	10	49	11.2	.985*	J. Dunn	41	299	23	13	2	3.70
		2B	T. Daly	498	.313	5	88	377	453	63	69	6.3	.929	J. Hughes	35	292	28	6	0	2.68
W-101 L-47		SS	B. Dahlen	428	.283	4	76	256	377	40	48	6.1	.941	B. Kennedy	40	277	22	9	2	2.79
		3B	D. Casey	525	.269	1	43	162	258	51	20	3.5	.892	D. McJames	37	275	19	15	1	3.50
Ned Hanlon		RF	W. Keeler	570	.379	1	61	208	21	5	4	1.7	.979							
		CF	F. Jones	365	.285	2	38	199	11	12	2	2.3	.946							
		LF	J. Kelley	538	.325	6	93	307	26	8	7	2.4	.977							
		C	D. Farrell	254	.299	2	55	251	111	20	9	4.9	.948							
		O1	J. Anderson	439	.269	3	92	537	30	19	27		.968							
		1B	H. Jennings	216	.296	0	40	446	25	7	24	9.6	.985							
		C	D. McGuire	157	.318	0	23	144	58*	6	2	4.5	.971							

NATIONAL LEAGUE 1899, *cont.*

	POS	Player	AB	BA	HR	RBI	PO	A	E	DP	TC/G	FA	Pitcher	G	IP	W	L	SV	ERA
Boston	1B	F. Tenney	603	.347	1	67	1474	**99**	35	**107**	10.7	.978	K. Nichols	42	349	21	19	1	2.94
	2B	B. Lowe	559	.272	4	88	361	461	40	66	5.8	.954	V. Willis	41	343	27	8	2	2.50
W-95 L-57	SS	H. Long	578	.265	6	100	351	435	60	68	5.9	.929	T. Lewis	29	235	17	11	0	3.49
	3B	J. Collins	599	.277	5	92	217	**376**	36	23	4.2	.943	J. Meekin	13	108	7	6	0	2.83
Frank Selee	RF	C. Stahl	576	.351	8	53	253	26	9	6	1.9	.969	F. Killen	12	99	7	5	0	4.26
	CF	B. Hamilton	297	.310	1	33	166	11	9	2	2.3	.952	H. Bailey	12	87	6	4	0	3.95
	LF	H. Duffy	588	.279	5	102	344	9	11	1	2.5	.970							
	C	M. Bergen	260	.258	1	34	253	89	16	4	5.0	.955							
	C	B. Clarke	223	.224	2	32	213	69	18	4	5.0	.940							
	OF	G. Stafford	182	.302	3	40	86	0	4	0	2.2	.956							
	OF	C. Frisbee	152	.329	0	20	68	9	11	1	2.2	.875							
Philadelphia	1B	D. Cooley	406	.276	1	31	756	34	24	56	10.3	.971	W. Piatt	39	305	23	15	0	3.45
	2B	N. Lajoie	312	.378	6	70	224	231	22	39	7.1	.954	R. Donahue	35	279	21	8	0	3.39
W-94 L-58	SS	M. Cross	557	.257	3	65	**370**	**529**	90	55	6.4	.909	C. Fraser	35	271	21	12	0	3.36
	3B	B. Lauder	583	.268	3	90	210	307	62	22	3.8	.893	A. Orth	21	145	14	3	1	**2.49**
Bill Shettsline	RF	E. Flick	485	.342	2	98	234	24	19	7	2.2	.931	B. Bernhard	21	132	6	6	0	2.65
	CF	R. Thomas	547	.325	0	47	313	22	17	8	2.6	.952	J. Fifield	14	93	3	8	1	4.08
	LF	E. Delahanty	581	**.410**	9	137	284	26	10	4	2.2	.969							
	C	McFarland	324	.333	1	57	305	125	14	**14**	4.7	.968							
	UT	P. Chiles	338	.320	2	76	330	44	25	18		.937							
	C	K. Douglass	275	.255	0	27	179	76	8	7	4.0	.970							
	2B	J. Dolan	222	.257	1	30	113	190	28	10	5.4	.915							
Baltimore	1B	C. LaChance	472	.307	1	75	1272	40	21	72	10.7	.984	McGinnity	48	**380**	**28**	17	2	2.58
	2B	DeMontreville	240	.279	1	36	174	197	15	16	6.4	.961	F. Kitson	40	330	22	16	0	2.76
W-86 L-62	SS	B. Keister	523	.329	3	73	169	283	53	25	5.6	.895	J. Nops	33	259	17	11	0	4.03
	3B	J. McGraw	399	.391	1	33	142	270	24	14	3.7	.945	H. Howell	28	209	13	8	1	3.91
John McGraw	RF	J. Sheckard	536	.295	3	75	298	33	20	**14**	2.4	.943							
	CF	S. Brodie	531	.309	3	87	310	15	7	5	2.7	**.979**							
	LF	D. Holmes	553	.320	4	66	321	24	**27**	5	2.7	.927							
	C	W. Robinson	356	.284	0	47	286	83	20	2	3.7	.949							
	O3	D. Fultz	210	.295	0	18	94	41	16	1		.894							
	SS	G. Magoon	207	.256	0	31	143	215	30	19	6.3	.923							
	1C	P. Crisham	172	.291	0	20	282	23	8	7		.974							
	C	B. Smith	120	.383	0	25	109	26	7	3	3.9	.951							
St. Louis	1B	P. Tebeau	281	.246	1	26	648	22	14	33	10.5	.980	J. Powell	48	373	23	21	0	3.52
	2B	C. Childs	464	.265	1	48	323	355	48	45	5.8	.934	C. Young	44	369	26	16	1	2.58
W-84 L-67	SS	B. Wallace	577	.295	12	108	238	386	55	40	6.8	.919	W. Sudhoff	26	189	13	10	0	3.61
	3B	L. Cross	403	.303	4	64	157	277	18	25*	4.4	.960*	N. Cuppy	21	172	11	8	0	3.15
Patsy Tebeau	RF	E. Heidrick	591	.328	2	82	211	**34**	20	6	1.8	.925	C. Jones	12	85	6	5	0	3.59
	CF	H. Blake	292	.240	2	41	176	10	4	3	2.2	.979							
	LF	J. Burkett	558	.396	7	71	296	20	21	3	2.4	.938							
	C	L. Criger	258	.256	2	44	228	91	17	6	4.5	.949							
	C1	J. O'Connor	289	.253	0	43	427	76	18	20		.965							
	1C	Schreckengost	277	.278	2	37	516	49	23	35		.961							
	UT	E. McKean	277	.260	3	40	254	156	34	25		.923							
	OF	M. Donlin	266	.323	6	27	96	7	15	2	2.3	.873							
Cincinnati	1B	J. Beckley	513	.333	3	99	1291	72	19	74	10.3	.986	N. Hahn	38	309	23	8	0	2.68
	2B	B. McPhee	373	.279	1	65	245	312	26	41	5.5	.955	P. Hawley	34	250	14	17	1	4.24
W-83 L-67	SS	T. Corcoran	537	.277	0	81	281	416	52	52	6.1	.931	B. Phillips	33	228	17	9	1	3.32
	3B	C. Irwin	314	.232	1	52	108	142	25	5	3.5	.909	Breitenstein	26	211	13	9	0	3.59
Buck Ewing	RF	D. Miller	323	.251	0	37	148	18	13	4	2.2	.927	J. Taylor	24	168	9	10	2	4.12
	CF	E. Smith	339	.298	1	24	178	12	16	3	2.4	.922							
	LF	K. Selbach	521	.296	3	87	355	27	19	10	2.9	.953							
	C	H. Peitz	290	.272	1	43	**329**	89	10	12	4.7	.977							
	32	Steinfeldt	386	.244	0	43	175	239	41	17		.910							
	OF	A. McBride	251	.347	1	23	124	8	7	2	2.2	.950							
	C	B. Wood	194	.314	0	24	160	49	14	3	4.2	.937							
	S3	K. Elberfeld	138	.261	0	22	74	108	25	9		.879							
	OF	S. Crawford	127	.307	1	20	56	9	2	2	2.2	.970							
Pittsburgh	1B	W. Clark	298	.285	0	44	837	36	10	37	11.3	.989	S. Leever	**51**	379	21	23	3	3.18
	2B	J. O'Brien	279	.226	1	65	211	243	26	32	6.1	.946	J. Tannehill	41	333	24	14	1	2.57
W-76 L-73	SS	B. Ely	522	.278	3	72	274	472	58	45	6.1	.928	T. Sparks	28	170	8	6	0	3.86
	3B	J. Williams	617	.355	9	116	**251**	354	**66**	14	**4.4**	.902	B. Hoffer	23	164	8	10	0	3.63
Bill Watkins	RF	P. Donovan	531	.294	1	55	184	9	12	3	1.7	.941	J. Chesbro	19	149	6	9	0	4.11
W-7 L-15	CF	G. Beaumont	437	.352	3	38	235	20	21	6	2.7	.924							
	LF	J. McCarthy	560	.305	3	67	281	18	12	5	2.3	.961							
Patsy Donovan	C	F. Bowerman	424	.259	3	53	276	128	22	7	5.4	.948							
W-69 L-58																			
	OF	T. McCreery	455	.323	2	64	198	16	21	2	2.4	.911							
	C	P. Schriver	301	.282	1	49	275	94	16	6	4.9	.958							
	1B	P. Dillon	121	.256	0	20	301	17	4	16	10.7	.988							

NATIONAL LEAGUE 1899, cont.

Chicago — W-75 L-73 — Tom Burns

POS	Player	AB	BA	HR	RBI	PO	A	E	DP	TC/G	FA	Pitcher	G	IP	W	L	SV	ERA
1B	B. Everett	536	.310	1	74	1491	95	47	103	12.0	.971	J. Taylor	41	355	18	21	0	3.76
2B	McCormick	376	.258	2	52	200	344	34	47	5.8	.941	C. Griffith	38	320	22	14	0	2.79
SS	DeMontreville	310	.281	0	40	192	306	54	38	6.7	.902	N. Callahan	35	294	21	12	0	3.06
3B	H. Wolverton	389	.285	1	49	123	227	57	12	4.2	.860	N. Garvin	24	199	9	13	0	2.85
RF	D. Green	475	.295	6	56	175	22	11	11	1.8	.947	B. Phyle	10	84	1	8	1	4.20
CF	B. Lange	416	.325	1	58	224	22	6	11	2.7	.976							
LF	J. Ryan	525	.301	3	68	266	18	13	6	2.4	.956							
C	T. Donahue	278	.248	0	29	304	100	21	13	4.7	.951							
OF	S. Mertes	426	.298	9	81	197	20	18	4	2.2	.923							
23	J. Connor	234	.205	0	22	101	211	26	25		.923							
C	F. Chance	192	.286	1	22	166	64	12	6	4.2	.950							
SS	G. Magoon	189	.228	0	21	138	216	41	34	6.7	.896							

Louisville — W-75 L-77 — Fred Clarke

POS	Player	AB	BA	HR	RBI	PO	A	E	DP	TC/G	FA	Pitcher	G	IP	W	L	SV	ERA
1B	M. Kelley	282	.241	3	33	745	38	21	37	10.6	.974	Cunningham	39	324	17	17	0	3.84
2B	C. Ritchey	536	.300	4	71	352	414	51	54	6.0	.938	D. Phillippe	42	321	21	17	1	3.17
SS	B. Clingman	366	.262	2	44	195	381	53	43	5.8	.916	P. Dowling	34	290	13	17	0	3.11
3B	T. Leach	406	.288	5	57	135	200	34	13	4.6	.908	W. Woods	26	186	9	13	0	3.28
RF	C. Dexter	295	.258	1	33	131	16	9	2	2.2	.942	R. Waddell	10	79	7	2	1	3.08
CF	D. Hoy	633	.306	5	49	321	21	27	2	2.4	.927	B. Magee	12	71	3	7	0	5.20
LF	F. Clarke	602	.342	5	70	327	20	13	2	2.5	.964							
C	C. Zimmer	262	.298	2	29	184	77	4		4.3	.985*							
30	H. Wagner	571	.336	7	113	197	182	24	15		.940							
C	M. Powers	169	.207	0	22	118	27	9	5	4.1	.942							
P	Cunningham	154	.260	2	17	35	100	8	2	3.7	.944							

New York — W-60 L-90 — John Day W-29 L-35 — Fred Hoey W-31 L-55

POS	Player	AB	BA	HR	RBI	PO	A	E	DP	TC/G	FA	Pitcher	G	IP	W	L	SV	ERA
1B	J. Doyle	448	.299	3	76	1110	69	29	76	10.7	.976	B. Carrick	44	362	16	27	0	4.65
2B	K. Gleason	576	.264	0	59	403	465	50	60	6.3	.946	C. Seymour	32	268	14	18	0	3.56
SS	G. Davis	416	.337	1	57	311	412	42	57	7.1	.945	E. Doheny	35	265	14	17	0	4.51
3B	F. Hartman	174	.236	1	16	56	100	20	11	3.5	.886	J. Meekin	18	148	5	11	0	4.37
RF	P. Foster	301	.296	3	57	103	8	6	3	1.4	.949	C. Gettig	18	128	7	8	0	4.43
CF	Van Haltren	604	.301	2	58	284	31	23	8	2.2	.932							
LF	T. O'Brien	573	.297	6	77	243	21	19	7	2.2	.933							
C	J. Warner	293	.266	0	19	312	123	22	8	5.6	.952							
UT	P. Wilson	328	.268	0	42	416	140	49	34		.919							
C3	M. Grady	311	.334	2	54	147	137	26	9		.916							
P	C. Seymour	159	.327	2	27	16	88	20	1	3.9	.839							

Washington — W-54 L-98 — Arthur Irwin

POS	Player	AB	BA	HR	RBI	PO	A	E	DP	TC/G	FA	Pitcher	G	IP	W	L	SV	ERA
1B	D. McGann	280	.343	5	58	667	36	7	37	9.3	.990*	G. Weyhing	43	335	17	23	0	4.54
2B	F. Bonner	347	.274	2	44	192	264	29	34	5.7	.940	B. Dinneen	37	291	14	18	0	3.93
SS	D. Padden	451	.277	2	61	201	281	46	33	6.2	.913	D. McFarlan	32	212	8	18	0	4.76
3B	C. Atherton	242	.248	0	23	91	119	26	7	3.7	.890	W. Mercer	23	186	7	14	0	4.60
RF	B. Freeman	588	.318	25	122	220	14	14	3	1.6	.944							
CF	J. Slagle	599	.272	0	41	407	20	21	8	3.1	.953							
LF	J. O'Brien	468	.282	6	51	266	21	23	5	2.6	.926							
C	D. McGuire	199	.271	1	12	178	71*	7	3	4.6	.973							
UT	W. Mercer	375	.299	1	35	109	156	40	8		.869							
UT	S. Barry	247	.287	1	33	254	65	19	13		.944							
1B	P. Cassidy	178	.315	3	32	337	16	11	26	9.8	.970							

Cleveland — W-20 L-134 — Lave Cross W-8 L-30 — Joe Quinn W-12 L-104

POS	Player	AB	BA	HR	RBI	PO	A	E	DP	TC/G	FA	Pitcher	G	IP	W	L	SV	ERA
1B	T. Tucker	456	.241	0	40	1229	58	30	71	10.4	.977	J. Hughey	36	283	4	30	0	5.41
2B	J. Quinn	615	.286	0	72	350	440	31	61	5.6	.962	C. Knepper	27	220	4	22	0	5.78
SS	H. Lochhead	541	.238	1	43	319	490	81	54	6.1	.909	F. Bates	20	153	1	18	0	7.24
3B	S. Sullivan	473	.245	0	55	110	237	23	21	3.7	.938	C. Schmit	20	138	2	17	0	5.86
RF	McAllister	418	.237	1	31	106	10	7	4	1.6	.943	Colliflower	14	98	1	11	0	8.17
CF	T. Dowd	605	.278	2	35	341	10	17	2	2.5	.954	W. Sudhoff	11	86	3	8	0	6.98
LF	D. Harley	567	.250	1	50	299	27	27	7	2.5	.924							
C	J. Sugden	250	.276	0	14	196	108	21	11	4.9	.935							
OF	C. Hemphill	202	.277	2	23	61	6	11	1	1.4	.859							
3B	L. Cross	154	.286	1	20	66	81	7	7*	4.1	.955*							

BATTING AND BASE RUNNING LEADERS

Batting Average		Slugging Average		Home Runs		Total Bases		Runs Batted In		Stolen Bases	
E. Delahanty, PHI	.408	E. Delahanty, PHI	.585	B. Freeman, WAS	25	E. Delahanty, PHI	335	E. Delahanty, PHI	137	J. Sheckard, BAL	77
J. Burkett, STL	.402	B. Freeman, WAS	.563	B. Wallace, STL	12	B. Freeman, WAS	331	B. Freeman, WAS	122	J. McGraw, BAL	73
J. McGraw, BAL	.391	J. Williams, PIT	.532	S. Mertes, CHI	9	J. Williams, PIT	328	J. Williams, PIT	116	E. Heidrick, STL	55
W. Keeler, BKN	.377	H. Wagner, LOU	.530	E. Delahanty, PHI	9	H. Wagner, LOU	291	H. Wagner, LOU	113	D. Holmes, BAL	50
H. Wagner, LOU	.359	J. Burkett, STL	.504	J. Williams, PIT	9	J. Burkett, STL	286	B. Wallace, STL	108	F. Clarke, LOU	49

PITCHING LEADERS

Winning Percentage		Earned Run Average		Wins		Saves		Strikeouts		Complete Games	
J. Hughes, BKN	.824	A. Orth, PHI	2.49	J. Hughes, BKN	28	S. Leever, PIT	3	N. Hahn, CIN	145	C. Young, STL	40
N. Hahn, CIN	.767	V. Willis, BOS	2.50	McGinnity, BAL	28	McGinnity, BAL	2	C. Seymour, NY	142	B. Carrick, NY	40
B. Kennedy, BKN	.733	J. Tannehill, PIT	2.57	V. Willis, BOS	27	J. Dunn, BKN	2	S. Leever, PIT	121	J. Powell, STL	40
V. Willis, BOS	.730	McGinnity, BAL	2.58	C. Young, STL	26	B. Kennedy, BKN	2	V. Willis, BOS	120	J. Taylor, CHI	39
R. Donahue, PHI	.724	C. Young, STL	2.58	J. Tannehill, PIT	24	J. Taylor, CIN	2	E. Doheny, NY	115	McGinnity, BAL	38
						V. Willis, BOS	2				

NATIONAL LEAGUE 1899, *cont.*

BATTING AND BASE RUNNING LEADERS

Hits			Base on Balls			Home Run Percentage			Fewest Hits/9 Innings	
E. Delahanty, PHI	234		J. McGraw, BAL	124		B. Freeman, WAS	4.3		V. Willis, BOS	7.28
J. Burkett, STL	228		R. Thomas, PHI	115		S. Mertes, CHI	2.1		J. Hughes, BKN	7.71
J. Williams, PIT	219		C. Childs, STL	74		B. Wallace, STL	2.1		N. Hahn, CIN	8.16
W. Keeler, BKN	216		Van Haltren, NY	74		E. Delahanty, PHI	1.5		B. Bernhard, PHI	8.16

Runs Scored			Doubles			Triples			Most Strikeouts/9 Inn.	
J. McGraw, BAL	140		E. Delahanty, PHI	56		J. Williams, PIT	27		C. Seymour, NY	4.76
W. Keeler, BKN	140		H. Wagner, LOU	47		B. Freeman, WAS	25		N. Hahn, CIN	4.22
R. Thomas, PHI	137		D. Holmes, BAL	31		C. Stahl, BOS	18		E. Doheny, NY	3.90
E. Delahanty, PHI	135		H. Long, BOS	30		J. McCarthy, PIT	17		D. McJames, BKN	3.43

PITCHING LEADERS

Shutouts		Innings		Fewest Walks/9 Innings		Games Pitched	
V. Willis, BOS	5	McGinnity, BAL	380	C. Young, STL	1.07	S. Leever, PIT	51
		S. Leever, PIT	379	A. Orth, PHI	1.18	J. Powell, STL	48
		J. Powell, STL	373	N. Cuppy, STL	1.36	McGinnity, BAL	48
		B. Carrick, NY	362	J. Tannehill, PIT	1.47	C. Young, STL	44

	W	L	PCT	GB	R	OR	2B	3B	HR	BA	SA	SB	E	DP	FA	CG	BB	SO	ShO	SV	ERA
Brooklyn	101	47	.682		892	658	178	97	26	.291	.382	271	314	125	.948	121	463	331	9	9	3.25
Boston	95	57	.625	8	858	**645**	178	89	40	.287	.377	185	**303**	124	**.952**	138	432	385	13	4	3.26
Philadelphia	94	58	.618	9	**916**	743	**241**	84	30	**.301**	**.395**	212	379	110	.940	129	370	281	**15**	2	3.47
Baltimore	86	62	.581	15	827	691	204	71	17	.297	.376	**364**	308	96	.949	133	349	294	9	4	3.31
St. Louis	84	67	.556	18.5	819	739	172	89	46	.285	.377	210	397	117	.939	134	**321**	331	7	1	3.36
Cincinnati	83	67	.553	19	856	770	194	105	13	.275	.360	228	339	111	.947	130	370	360	8	5	3.70
Pittsburgh	76	73	.510	25.5	834	765	196	**121**	27	.289	.384	179	361	98	.945	117	437	334	9	4	3.60
Chicago	75	73	.507	26	812	763	173	82	27	.277	.359	247	428	**145**	.935	**147**	330	313	8	1	3.37
Louisville	75	77	.493	28	827	775	192	68	40	.280	.364	233	394	102	.939	134	323	287	5	2	3.45
New York	60	90	.400	42	734	863	161	65	23	.281	.352	234	433	140	.932	138	628	**397**	4	0	4.29
Washington	54	98	.355	49	743	983	162	87	**47**	.272	.363	176	403	99	.935	131	422	328	3	0	4.93
Cleveland	20	134	.130	84	529	1252	142	50	12	.253	.305	127	388	121	.937	138	527	215	1	0	6.37
					9647	9647	2193	1008	348	.282	.366	2666	4447	1388	.942	1590	4972	3856	90	32	3.85

NATIONAL LEAGUE 1900

	POS	Player	AB	BA	HR	RBI	PO	A	E	DP	TC/G	FA	Pitcher	G	IP	W	L	SV	ERA
Brooklyn W-82 L-54 Ned Hanlon	1B	H. Jennings	441	.272	1	69	1050	76	21	71	10.2	.982	McGinnity	**44**	**347**	**29**	9	0	2.90
	2B	T. Daly	343	.312	4	55	233	234	40	39	5.5	.921	B. Kennedy	42	292	20	13	0	3.91
	SS	B. Dahlen	483	.259	1	69	321	**517**	55	59	6.7	.938	F. Kitson	40	253	15	13	4	4.19
	3B	L. Cross	461	.293	4	67	162	282	27	10	4.0	.943*	H. Howell	21	110	6	5	0	3.75
	RF	W. Keeler	563	.362	4	68	227	22	16	4	1.9	.940							
	CF	F. Jones	552	.310	4	54	315	15	15	3	2.5	.957							
	LF	J. Kelley	454	.319	6	91	174	12	8	2	2.5	.959							
	C	D. Farrell	273	.275	0	39	252	88	20	8	4.9	.944							
	OF	J. Sheckard	273	.300	1	39	171	13	15	3	2.6	.925							
	C	D. McGuire	241	.286	0	34	218	77	15	7	4.5	.952							
	UT	DeMontreville	234	.244	0	28	159	176	25	19		.931							
	P	McGinnity	145	.193	0	16	15	75	12	4	2.3	.882							
Pittsburgh W-79 L-60 Fred Clarke	1B	D. Cooley	249	.201	0	22	683	20	8	39	10.8	.989	D. Phillippe	38	279	20	13	0	2.84
	2B	C. Ritchey	476	.292	1	67	303	357	33	51	5.6	.952	J. Tannehill	29	234	20	6	0	2.88
	SS	B. Ely	475	.244	0	51	242	503	52	62	6.1	.935	S. Leever	30	233	15	13	0	2.71
	3B	J. Williams	416	.264	5	68	153	254	51	21	4.4	.889	J. Chesbro	32	216	15	13	0	3.67
	RF	H. Wagner	527	**.381**	4	100	181	11	7	4	1.7	.965	R. Waddell	29	209	8	13	0	**2.37**
	CF	G. Beaumont	567	.279	4	50	274	10	17	3	2.2	.944							
	LF	F. Clarke	399	.276	3	32	263	8	16	2	2.8	.944							
	C	C. Zimmer	271	.295	0	35	**318**	100	17	8	5.6	.961							
	10	T. O'Brien	376	.290	3	61	718	27	31	37		.960							
	UT	T. Leach	160	.213	1	16	74	117	24	9		.888							
	C	J. O'Connor	147	.238	0	19	108	44	9	2	4.0	.944							
Philadelphia W-75 L-63 Bill Shettsline	1B	E. Delahanty	539	.323	2	109	1299	66	27	86	10.7	.981	A. Orth	33	262	12	13	1	3.78
	2B	N. Lajoie	451	.337	7	92	287	341	30	**69**	6.5	**.954**	R. Donahue	32	240	15	10	0	3.60
	SS	M. Cross	466	.202	3	62	**339**	459	62	68	6.6	.928	C. Fraser	29	223	16	10	0	3.14
	3B	H. Wolverton	383	.282	3	58	122	234	48	16	4.0	.881	B. Bernhard	32	219	15	10	2	4.77
	RF	E. Flick	545	.367	11	110	232	23	24	6	2.0	.914	W. Piatt	22	161	9	10	0	4.65
	CF	R. Thomas	531	.316	0	33	303	19	14	6	2.4	.958	J. Dunn	10	80	5	5	0	4.84
	LF	J. Slagle	574	.287	0	45	320	22	**29**	5	2.6	.922							
	C	McFarland	344	.305	0	38	278	**137**	16	9	4.6	**.963**							
	UT	J. Dolan	257	.198	1	27	136	198	26	17		.928							
	C	K. Douglass	160	.300	0	25	138	59	14	4	4.5	.934							
	P	A. Orth	129	.310	1	21	15	68	5	3	2.7	.943							
	12	P. Chiles	111	.216	1	23	165	42	6	14		.972							

NATIONAL LEAGUE 1900, *cont.*

	POS	Player	AB	BA	HR	RBI	PO	A	E	DP	TC/G	FA	Pitcher	G	IP	W	L	SV	ERA
Boston	1B	F. Tenney	437	.279	1	56	1021	82	21	50	10.1	.981	B. Dinneen	40	321	20	14	0	3.12
	2B	B. Lowe	474	.278	3	71	323	335	34	38	5.4	.951	V. Willis	32	236	10	17	0	4.19
W-66 L-72	SS	H. Long	486	.261	12	66	257	454	48	34	6.1	.937	K. Nichols	29	231	13	16	0	3.07
	3B	J. Collins	586	.304	6	95	251	329	40	21	4.4	.935	T. Lewis	30	209	13	12	0	4.13
Frank Selee	RF	B. Freeman	418	.301	6	65	130	3	7	1	1.5	.950	T. Pittinger	18	114	2	9	0	5.13
	CF	B. Hamilton	520	.333	1	47	326	14	19	6	2.6	.947	N. Cuppy	17	105	8	4	1	3.08
	LF	C. Stahl	553	.295	5	82	277	22	10	4	2.3	**.968**							
	C	B. Clarke	270	.315	1	30	246	104	27	8	5.6	.928							
	UT	S. Barry	254	.260	1	37	199	82	23	13		.924							
	C	B. Sullivan	238	.273	8	41	227	71	8	10	4.6	.974							
	OF	H. Duffy	181	.304	2	31	107	5	5	2	2.4	.957							
Chicago	1B	J. Ganzel	284	.275	4	32	817	34	17	40	11.1	.980	N. Callahan	32	285	13	16	0	3.82
	2B	C. Childs	531	.241	0	44	323	431	52	57	5.9	.935	C. Griffith	30	248	14	13	0	3.05
W-65 L-75	SS	McCormick	379	.219	3	48	161	307	48	32	6.1	.907	N. Garvin	30	246	10	18	0	2.41
	3B	B. Bradley	444	.282	5	49	164	291	61	11	4.9	.882	J. Taylor	28	222	10	17	1	2.55
Tom Loftus	RF	J. Ryan	415	.277	5	59	177	12	18	3	2.0	.913	J. Menefee	16	117	9	4	0	3.85
	CF	D. Green	389	.298	5	49	218	10	15	2	2.4	.938							
	LF	J. McCarthy	503	.294	0	48	233	20	15	4	2.2	.944							
	C	T. Donahue	216	.236	0	17	232	63	23	6	4.8	.928							
	O1	S. Mertes	481	.295	7	60	520	30	26	20		.955							
	SS	B. Clingman	159	.208	0	11	81	150	34	19	5.6	.872							
	C	F. Chance	149	.295	0	13	155	65	16	2	4.6	.932							
	CO	C. Dexter	125	.200	2	20	98	36	6	4		.957							
St. Louis	1B	D. McGann	444	.297	4	58	1212	58	13	41	10.6	**.990**	C. Young	41	321	19	19	0	3.00
	2B	B. Keister	497	.300	1	72	206	315	41	26	4.8	.927	C. Jones	39	293	13	19	0	3.54
W-65 L-75	SS	B. Wallace	485	.268	4	70	327	447	55	31	6.6	.934	J. Powell	38	288	17	17	0	4.44
	3B	J. McGraw	334	.344	2	33	106	213	32	7	3.5	.909	W. Sudhoff	16	127	6	8	0	2.76
Patsy Tebeau	RF	P. Donovan	503	.316	0	61	180	13	10	4	1.6	.951	J. Hughey	20	113	5	7	0	5.19
W-42 L-50	CF	E. Heidrick	339	.301	2	45	215	21	10	4	3.0	.959							
	LF	J. Burkett	559	.363	7	68	337	17	25	6	2.7	.934							
Louie Heilbroner	C	L. Criger	288	.271	2	38	282	105	19	8	5.4	.953							
W-23 L-25	O1	M. Donlin	276	.326	10	48	308	11	21	14		.938							
	C	W. Robinson	210	.248	0	28	189	72	7	3	5.0	.974							
	O3	P. Dillard	183	.230	0	12	74	47	14	2		.896							
Cincinnati	1B	J. Beckley	558	.341	2	94	**1389**	93	30	91	**10.8**	.980	E. Scott	43	323	17	21	1	3.82
	2B	J. Quinn	266	.274	0	25	154	169	17	24	4.6	.950	N. Hahn	38	303	16	19	0	3.29
W-62 L-77	SS	T. Corcoran	523	.245	1	54	262	436	60	56	6.1	.921	D. Newton	35	235	9	15	0	4.14
	3B	Steinfeldt	513	.248	2	66	107	175	24	11	4.6	.922	B. Phillips	29	208	9	11	0	4.28
Bob Allen	RF	A. McBride	436	.275	4	59	163	10	16	5	1.7	.915	Breitenstein	24	192	10	10	0	3.65
	CF	J. Barrett	545	.316	5	42	287	25	24	6	2.5	.929							
	LF	S. Crawford	389	.267	7	59	237	18	14	2	2.9	.948							
	C	H. Peitz	294	.255	2	34	310	125	19	13	5.7	.958							
	3B	C. Irwin	333	.273	1	44	74	128	15	11	3.6	.931							
	C	M. Kahoe	175	.189	1	9	207	79	11	5	5.8	.963							
	C3	B. Wood	139	.266	0	22	68	56	12	5		.912							
New York	1B	J. Doyle	505	.267	1	66	1269	**96**	41	92	10.6	.971	B. Carrick	45	342	19	21	0	3.53
	2B	K. Gleason	420	.248	1	29	321	326	48	51	6.3	.931	P. Hawley	41	329	18	18	0	3.53
W-60 L-78	SS	G. Davis	426	.319	3	61	279	450	43	**94**	6.8	**.944**	W. Mercer	32	242	13	17	0	3.86
	3B	P. Hickman	473	.313	9	91	183	276	86	19	4.5	.842	E. Doheny	20	134	4	14	0	5.45
Buck Ewing	RF	E. Smith	312	.260	2	34	91	10	5	2	1.3	.953							
W-21 L-41	CF	Van Haltren	571	.315	1	51	325	**28**	23	7	2.7	.939							
	LF	K. Selbach	523	.337	4	68	327	25	18	**8**	2.6	.951							
George Davis	C	F. Bowerman	270	.241	1	42	232	136	**28**	**15**	5.3	.929							
W-39 L-37	UT	M. Grady	251	.219	0	27	247	106	37	18		.905							
	UT	W. Mercer	248	.294	0	27	75	149	32	11		.875							

BATTING AND BASE RUNNING LEADERS

Batting Average		Slugging Average		Home Runs	
H. Wagner, PIT	.381	H. Wagner, PIT	.573	H. Long, BOS	12
E. Flick, PHI	.378	E. Flick, PHI	.545	E. Flick, PHI	11
W. Keeler, BKN	.368	N. Lajoie, PHI	.517	M. Donlin, STL	10
J. Burkett, STL	.363	J. Kelley, BKN	.485	P. Hickman, NY	9
N. Lajoie, PHI	.346	P. Hickman, NY	.482	B. Sullivan, BOS	8

Total Bases		Runs Batted In		Stolen Bases	
E. Flick, PHI	305	E. Flick, PHI	110	P. Donovan, STL	45
H. Wagner, PIT	302	E. Delahanty, PHI	109	Van Haltren, NY	45
J. Burkett, STL	262	H. Wagner, PIT	100	J. Barrett, CIN	44
W. Keeler, BKN	259	J. Collins, BOS	95	W. Keeler, BKN	41
J. Beckley, CIN	242	J. Beckley, CIN	94	S. Mertes, CHI	38
				H. Wagner, PIT	38

PITCHING LEADERS

Winning Percentage		Earned Run Average		Wins	
J. Tannehill, PIT	.769	R. Waddell, PIT	2.37	McGinnity, BKN	29
McGinnity, BKN	.763	N. Garvin, CHI	2.41	J. Tannehill, PIT	20
C. Fraser, PHI	.615	J. Taylor, CHI	2.55	B. Kennedy, BKN	20
B. Kennedy, BKN	.606	S. Leever, PIT	2.71	B. Dinneen, BOS	20
B. Bernhard, PHI	.600	W. Sudhoff, STL	2.76	C. Young, STL	20
R. Donahue, PHI	.600				

Saves		Strikeouts		Complete Games	
F. Kitson, BKN	4	R. Waddell, PIT	130	P. Hawley, NY	34
B. Bernhard, PHI	2	N. Hahn, CIN	127	B. Dinneen, BOS	33
		C. Young, STL	119		
		N. Garvin, CHI	107		
		B. Dinneen, BOS	107		

NATIONAL LEAGUE 1900, cont.

BATTING AND BASE RUNNING LEADERS

Hits		Base on Balls		Home Run Percentage	
W. Keeler, BKN	208	R. Thomas, PHI	115	H. Long, BOS	2.5
E. Flick, PHI	207	B. Hamilton, BOS	107	E. Flick, PHI	2.0
J. Burkett, STL	203	J. McGraw, STL	85	P. Hickman, NY	1.9
J. Beckley, CIN	190	B. Dahlen, BKN	73	S. Crawford, CIN	1.8

Runs Scored		Doubles		Triples	
R. Thomas, PHI	134	H. Wagner, PIT	45	H. Wagner, PIT	22
J. Slagle, PHI	115	E. Flick, PHI	33	J. Kelley, BKN	17
J. Barrett, CIN	114	N. Lajoie, PHI	32	P. Hickman, NY	17
Van Haltren, NY	114	E. Delahanty, PHI	32	E. Flick, PHI	16

PITCHING LEADERS

Fewest Hits/9 Innings		Shutouts		Fewest Walks/9 Innings	
R. Waddell, PIT	7.59	K. Nichols, BOS	4	C. Young, STL	1.01
N. Garvin, CHI	8.22	C. Griffith, CHI	4	D. Phillippe, PIT	1.35
K. Nichols, BOS	8.36	C. Young, STL	4	J. Tannehill, PIT	1.65
B. Dinneen, BOS	8.53	N. Hahn, CIN	4	E. Scott, CIN	1.84

Most Strikeouts/9 Inn.		Innings		Games Pitched	
R. Waddell, PIT	5.61	McGinnity, BKN	347	McGinnity, BKN	45
N. Garvin, CHI	3.91	B. Carrick, NY	342	B. Carrick, NY	45
N. Hahn, CIN	3.77	P. Hawley, NY	329	E. Scott, CIN	43
D. Newton, CIN	3.37	E. Scott, CIN	323	B. Kennedy, BKN	42

	W	L	PCT	GB	R	OR	2B	3B	HR	BA	SA	SB	E	DP	FA	CG	BB	SO	ShO	SV	ERA
							Batting						**Fielding**			**Pitching**					
Brooklyn	82	54	.603		**816**	722	199	81	26	**.293**	**.383**	**274**	303	102	.948	104	405	300	8	**4**	3.89
Pittsburgh	79	60	.568	4.5	733	**612**	185	**100**	25	.272	.368	174	322	106	.945	114	**295**	**415**	11	1	**3.06**
Philadelphia	75	63	.543	8	810	791	187	82	29	.290	.378	205	330	**125**	.945	116	402	284	7	3	4.12
Boston	66	72	.478	17	778	739	163	68	**48**	.283	.373	182	**273**	86	**.953**	116	463	340	8	2	3.72
Chicago	65	75	.464	19	635	751	**202**	51	33	.260	.342	189	418	98	.933	**137**	324	357	9	1	3.23
St. Louis	65	75	.464	19	743	747	141	81	36	.291	.375	243	331	73	.943	117	299	325	**12**	0	3.75
Cincinnati	62	77	.446	21.5	702	745	178	83	33	.266	.354	183	341	120	.945	118	404	399	9	1	3.83
New York	60	78	.435	23	713	823	177	61	23	.279	.357	236	439	124	.928	114	442	277	4	0	3.96
					5930	5930	1432	607	253	.279	.366	1686	2757	834	.942	936	3034	2697	68	12	3.69

NATIONAL LEAGUE 1901

	POS	Player	AB	BA	HR	RBI	PO	A	E	DP	TC/G	FA	Pitcher	G	IP	W	L	SV	ERA
Pittsburgh W-90 L-49 Fred Clarke	1B	Bransfield	566	.295	0	91	1374	52	28	72	10.5	.981	D. Phillippe	37	296	22	12	2	2.22
	2B	C. Ritchey	540	.296	1	74	340	**392**	**46**	53	5.6	.941	J. Chesbro	36	288	21	10	1	2.38
	SS	B. Ely	240	.208	0	28	112	215	30	23	5.6	.916	J. Tannehill	32	252	18	10	1	**2.18**
	3B	T. Leach	374	.305	1	44	122	196	34	9	3.8	.903	S. Leever	21	176	14	5	0	2.86
	RF	L. Davis	335	.313	2	33	140	18	4	7	1.9	.975							
	CF	G. Beaumont	558	.332	8	72	289	8	18	2	2.4	.943							
	LF	F. Clarke	527	.324	6	60	282	13	9	0	2.4	.970							
	C	C. Zimmer	236	.220	0	21	285	69	9	4	5.3	.975							
	UT	H. Wagner	556	.353	6	**126**	297	280	48	35		.923							
	C	J. O'Connor	202	.193	0	22	256	59	7	5	5.5	.978							
Philadelphia W-83 L-57 Bill Shettsline	1B	H. Jennings	302	.275	1	39	745	38	17	20	10.0	.979	R. Donahue	35	304	21	13	0	2.60
	2B	B. Hallman	445	.184	0	38	177	261	13	20	5.0	.971	A. Orth	35	282	20	12	0	2.27
	SS	M. Cross	483	.197	1	44	**343**	445	65	31	6.1	.924	B. Duggleby	34	276	19	12	0	2.87
	3B	H. Wolverton	379	.309	0	43	114	190	26	9	3.5	.921	D. White	31	237	14	13	0	3.19
	RF	E. Flick	542	.336	8	88	278	23	12	7	2.3	.962	J. Townsend	19	144	9	6	0	3.45
	CF	R. Thomas	479	.309	1	28	283	9	10	2	2.3	.967							
	LF	E. Delahanty	538	.357	8	108	179	9	10	2	2.4	.949							
	C	McFarland	295	.285	1	32	316	102	13	2	5.8	.970							
	UT	S. Barry	252	.246	1	22	122	123	31	8		.888							
	OF	J. Slagle	183	.202	1	20	108	12*	9	3	2.7	.930							
	C	K. Douglass	173	.324	0	23	201	29	5	2	5.7	.979							
	C	Jacklitsch	120	.250	0	24	126	39	5	3	5.7	.971							
Brooklyn W-79 L-57 Ned Hanlon	1B	J. Kelley	492	.309	4	65	984	82	27	63	9.5	.975	W. Donovan	**45**	351	**25**	15	1	2.77
	2B	T. Daly	520	.315	3	90	**370**	357	43	46	5.8	.944	F. Kitson	38	281	19	11	2	2.98
	SS	B. Dahlen	513	.261	4	82	301	450	57	49	6.3	.929	J. Hughes	31	251	17	12	0	3.27
	3B	C. Irwin	242	.215	0	20	88*	106	9	5	5.1	.956	D. Newton	13	105	6	5	0	2.83
	RF	W. Keeler	589	.355	2	43	181	17	3	4	1.6	**.985**	D. McJames	13	91	5	6	0	4.75
	CF	T. McCreery	335	.290	3	53	189	9	11	2	2.5	.947							
	LF	J. Sheckard	558	.353	11	104	287	15	18	5	2.6	.944							
	C	D. McGuire	301	.296	0	40	415	94	21	4	6.5	.960							
	C	D. Farrell	284	.296	1	31	285	90	8	8	6.5	.979							
	OF	C. Dolan	253	.261	0	29	108	9	4	2	1.9	.967							
	3B	F. Gatins	197	.228	1	21	56	58	10	5	2.7	.919							
St. Louis W-76 L-64 Patsy Donovan	1B	D. McGann	426	.289	6	56	1030	50	18	64	10.7	.984	J. Powell	**45**	338	19	19	3	3.54
	2B	D. Padden	488	.256	2	62	286	336	33	47	5.7	.950	J. Harper	39	309	23	13	0	3.62
	SS	B. Wallace	556	.322	2	91	326	**542**	66	67	7.0	.929	W. Sudhoff	38	276	17	11	2	3.52
	3B	O. Krueger	520	.275	2	79	171	**275**	60	11	3.6	.881	E. Murphy	23	165	10	9	0	4.20
	RF	P. Donovan	527	.292	1	73	215	19	5	8	1.9	.979							
	CF	E. Heidrick	502	.339	6	67	258	15	16	2	2.4	.945							
	LF	J. Burkett	**597**	**.382**	10	75	307	17	27	4	2.5	.923							
	C	J. Ryan	300	.197	0	31	292	84	7	7	5.9	.982							
	CO	A. Nichols	308	.244	1	33	256	60	13	9		.960							
	C1	P. Schriver	166	.271	1	23	273	61	10	13		.971							

NATIONAL LEAGUE 1901, cont.

	POS	Player	AB	BA	HR	RBI	PO	A	E	DP	TC/G	FA	Pitcher	G	IP	W	L	SV	ERA
Boston	1B	F. Tenney	457	.278	1	22	1059	86	28	58	10.4	.976	K. Nichols	38	321	19	16	0	3.22
	2B	DeMontreville	570	.304	5	72	272	344	30	35	5.4	.954	B. Dinneen	37	309	15	18	0	2.94
W-69 L-69	SS	H. Long	518	.228	3	68	304	468	44	55	5.9	.946	V. Willis	38	305	20	17	0	2.36
	3B	B. Lowe	491	.255	3	47	149	192	33	12	3.4	.912	T. Pittinger	34	281	13	16	0	3.01
Frank Selee	RF	J. Slagle	255	.271	0	7	89	11*	7	3	1.6	.935							
	CF	B. Hamilton	349	.292	3	38	232	7	14	4	2.6	.945							
	LF	D. Cooley	240	.258	0	27	127	5	8	1	2.6	.943							
	C	M. Kittridge	381	.252	2	40	581	136	12	7	6.5	.984							
	OF	F. Crolius	200	.240	1	13	65	3	12	1	1.6	.850							
	UT	P. Moran	180	.211	2	18	299	37	14	8		.960							
	OF	F. Murphy	176	.261	1	18	97	10	7	1	2.5	.939							
	P	K. Nichols	163	.282	4	28	27	69	4	1	2.6	.960							
	P	B. Dinneen	147	.211	1	6	14	72	7	2	2.5	.925							
Chicago	1B	J. Doyle	285	.232	0	39	698	60	21	32	10.4	.973	L. Hughes	37	308	11	21	0	3.24
	2B	C. Childs	237	.257	0	21	146	192	22	34	5.8	.939	J. Taylor	33	276	13	19	0	3.36
W-53 L-86	SS	McCormick	427	.234	1	32	202	405	59	47	5.9	.911	R. Waddell	29	244	13	15	0	2.81
	3B	F. Raymer	463	.233	0	43	79	143	30	5	3.1	.881	M. Eason	27	221	8	17	0	3.59
Tom Loftus	RF	F. Chance	241	.278	0	36	61	7	5	0	1.5	.932	J. Menefee	21	182	8	13	0	3.80
	CF	D. Green	537	.313	6	60	312	17	24	7	2.7	.932							
	LF	T. Hartsel	558	.335	7	54	273	16	15	3	2.2	.951							
	C	J. Kling	253	.277	0	21	319	75	20	7	6.0	.952							
	UT	C. Dexter	460	.267	1	66	618	125	27	32		.965							
	C	M. Kahoe	237	.224	1	21	368	74	12	8	7.2	.974							
	2B	P. Childs	213	.225	0	14	128	198	14	19	5.6	.959							
	OF	C. Dolan	171	.263	0	16	63	9	10	3	2.0	.878							
	OP	J. Menefee	152	.257	0	13	52	47	8	1		.925							
New York	1B	J. Ganzel	526	.215	2	66	1421	77	21	59	11.0	.986	D. Taylor	45	353	18	27	0	3.18
	2B	R. Nelson	130	.200	0	7	44	125	22	10	4.9	.885	C. Mathewson	40	336	20	17	0	2.41
W-52 L-85	SS	G. Davis	495	.309	7	65	296	396	45	42	6.5	.939	B. Phyle	24	169	7	10	1	4.27
	3B	S. Strang	493	.282	1	34	127	194	45	16	4.0	.877							
George Davis	RF	A. McBride	264	.280	2	29	84	8	5	3	1.5	.948							
	CF	Van Haltren	544	.342	1	47	263	23	18	5	2.3	.941							
	LF	K. Selbach	502	.289	1	56	215	11	14	2	1.9	.942							
	C	J. Warner	291	.241	0	20	361	107	16	11	5.8	.967							
	UT	P. Hickman	401	.282	4	62	154	154	35	10		.898							
	C	F. Bowerman	191	.199	0	14	256	67	17	6	7.4	.950							
Cincinnati	1B	J. Beckley	580	.307	3	79	1366	71	34	79	10.5	.977	N. Hahn	42	375	22	19	0	2.71
	2B	Steinfeldt	382	.249	6	47	138	142	18	23	6.0	.940	B. Phillips	37	281	14	20	0	4.64
W-52 L-87	SS	G. Magoon	460	.252	1	53	253	345	53	36	5.8	.919	D. Newton	20	168	4	14	0	4.12
	3B	C. Irwin	260	.238	0	25	87*	139	27	10	3.8	.893	A. Stimmel	20	153	4	14	0	4.11
Bid McPhee	RF	S. Crawford	515	.330	16	104	209	20	19	6	2.0	.923							
	CF	J. Dobbs	435	.274	2	27	189	11	11	4	2.1	.948							
	LF	D. Harley	535	.273	4	27	245	20	30	2	2.2	.898							
	C	B. Bergen	308	.179	1	17	406	117	16	8	6.2	.970							
	UT	H. Peitz	269	.305	1	24	321	127	9	14		.980							
	2B	B. Fox	159	.176	0	7	103	134	11	19	5.8	.956							
	OF	H. Bay	157	.210	1	3	78	3	4	3	2.1	.953							
	P	N. Hahn	141	.170	0	7	14	85	6	4	2.5	.943							

BATTING AND BASE RUNNING LEADERS

Batting Average
J. Burkett, STL	.382
E. Delahanty, PHI	.357
W. Keeler, BKN	.355
H. Wagner, PIT	.353
J. Sheckard, BKN	.353

Slugging Average
J. Sheckard, BKN	.536
E. Delahanty, PHI	.533
S. Crawford, CIN	.528
J. Burkett, STL	.524
E. Flick, PHI	.500

Home Runs
S. Crawford, CIN	16
J. Sheckard, BKN	11
J. Burkett, STL	10
E. Flick, PHI	8
E. Delahanty, PHI	8
G. Beaumont, PIT	8

Total Bases
J. Burkett, STL	313
J. Sheckard, BKN	299
E. Delahanty, PHI	287
H. Wagner, PIT	273
E. Flick, PHI	272
S. Crawford, CIN	272

Runs Batted In
H. Wagner, PIT	126
E. Delahanty, PHI	108
S. Crawford, CIN	104
J. Sheckard, BKN	104
B. Wallace, STL	91
Bransfield, PIT	91

Stolen Bases
H. Wagner, PIT	49
T. Hartsel, CHI	41
S. Strang, NY	40
D. Harley, CIN	37
G. Beaumont, PIT	36

Hits
J. Burkett, STL	228
W. Keeler, BKN	209
J. Sheckard, BKN	197
H. Wagner, PIT	194

Base on Balls
R. Thomas, PHI	100
T. Hartsel, CHI	74
L. Davis, BKN, PIT	66
E. Delahanty, PHI	65

Home Run Percentage
S. Crawford, CIN	3.1
J. Sheckard, BKN	2.0
J. Burkett, STL	1.7
Steinfeldt, CIN	1.6

PITCHING LEADERS

Winning Percentage
J. Chesbro, PIT	.677
J. Harper, STL	.657
D. Phillippe, PIT	.647
J. Tannehill, PIT	.643
R. Donahue, PHI	.629

Earned Run Average
J. Tannehill, PIT	2.18
D. Phillippe, PIT	2.22
A. Orth, PHI	2.27
V. Willis, BOS	2.36
J. Chesbro, PIT	2.38

Wins
W. Donovan, BKN	25
J. Harper, STL	23
D. Phillippe, PIT	22
N. Hahn, CIN	22

Saves
J. Powell, STL	3
F. Kitson, BKN	2
D. Phillippe, PIT	2
W. Sudhoff, STL	2

Strikeouts
N. Hahn, CIN	239
W. Donovan, BKN	226
L. Hughes, CHI	225
C. Mathewson, NY	221
R. Waddell, CHI, PIT	172

Complete Games
N. Hahn, CIN	41
D. Taylor, NY	37
W. Donovan, BKN	36
C. Mathewson, NY	36
R. Donahue, PHI	34

Fewest Hits/9 Innings
J. Townsend, PHI	7.39
C. Mathewson, NY	7.71
V. Willis, BOS	7.72
A. Orth, PHI	7.99

Shutouts
J. Chesbro, PIT	6
A. Orth, PHI	6
V. Willis, BOS	6
B. Duggleby, PHI	5

Fewest Walks/9 Innings
A. Orth, PHI	1.02
D. Phillippe, PIT	1.16
J. Tannehill, PIT	1.28
B. Duggleby, PHI	1.31

NATIONAL LEAGUE 1901, *cont.*

BATTING AND BASE RUNNING LEADERS

Runs Scored		Doubles		Triples	
J. Burkett, STL	139	E. Delahanty, PHI	39	J. Sheckard, BKN	19
W. Keeler, BKN	123	H. Wagner, PIT	39	E. Flick, PHI	17
G. Beaumont, PIT	120	J. Beckley, CIN	39	Bransfield, PIT	17
F. Clarke, PIT	118	T. Daly, BKN	38	J. Burkett, STL	17

PITCHING LEADERS

Most Strikeouts/9 Inn.		Innings		Games Pitched	
L. Hughes, CHI	6.57	N. Hahn, CIN	375	D. Taylor, NY	45
R. Waddell, CHI, PIT	6.16	D. Taylor, NY	353	W. Donovan, BKN	45
C. Mathewson, NY	5.92	W. Donovan, BKN	351	J. Powell, STL	45
W. Donovan, BKN	5.79	J. Powell, STL	338	N. Hahn, CIN	42

	W	L	PCT	GB	R	OR	2B	3B	HR	BA	SA	SB	E	DP	FA	CG	BB	SO	ShO	SV	ERA
										Batting				**Fielding**				**Pitching**			
Pittsburgh	90	49	.647		776	**534**	185	92	28	.286	.378	**203**	287	97	.950	119	**244**	505	15	4	**2.58**
Philadelphia	83	57	.593	7.5	668	543	194	58	24	.267	.347	199	262	65	**.954**	125	259	480	**16**	0	2.87
Brooklyn	79	57	.581	9.5	744	600	**206**	**97**	32	**.288**	**.390**	178	281	99	.950	111	435	583	7	3	3.14
St. Louis	76	64	.543	14.5	**792**	689	187	**97**	**39**	.285	.383	190	305	**108**	.949	118	332	445	5	**5**	3.68
Boston	69	69	.500	20.5	531	556	135	36	28	.250	.312	157	282	89	.952	128	349	558	11	0	2.90
Chicago	53	86	.381	37	578	699	153	61	18	.258	.326	**203**	336	87	.943	**131**	324	**586**	2	0	3.33
New York	52	85	.380	37	544	755	166	47	19	.255	.321	133	348	81	.941	118	377	542	11	1	3.87
Cincinnati	52	87	.374	38	561	818	179	70	38	.251	.339	137	355	102	.940	126	365	542	4	0	4.17
					5194	5194	1405	558	226	.268	.350	1400	2456	728	.947	976	2685	4241	71	13	3.32

AMERICAN LEAGUE 1901

	POS	Player	AB	BA	HR	RBI	PO	A	E	DP	TC/G	FA	Pitcher	G	IP	W	L	SV	ERA
Chicago	1B	F. Isbell	556	.257	3	70	**1387**	101	31	79	11.1	.980	R. Patterson	41	312	20	16	0	3.37
	2B	S. Mertes	545	.277	5	98	337	396	47	54	5.9	.940	C. Griffith	35	267	24	7	1	2.67
W-83 L-53	SS	F. Shugart	415	.251	2	47	223	338	73	32	5.9	.885	N. Callahan	27	215	15	8	0	2.42
	3B	F. Hartman	473	.309	3	89	151	263	49	15	3.9	.894	J. Katoll	27	208	11	10	0	2.81
Clark Griffith	RF	F. Jones	521	.311	2	65	216	20	16	5	1.9	.937	E. Harvey	16	92	3	6	1	3.62
	CF	D. Hoy	527	.294	2	60	278	16	13	6	2.3	.958							
	LF	McFarland	473	.275	4	59	283	14	17	3	2.4	.946							
	C	B. Sullivan	367	.245	4	56	396	104	17	13	5.3	**.967**							
	C	J. Sugden	153	.275	0	19	179	47	7	4	5.5	.970							
	SS	J. Burke	148	.264	0	21	56	94	23	10	5.6	.867							
Boston	1B	B. Freeman	490	.345	12	114	1278	55	**36**	71	10.7	.974	C. Young	43	371	**33**	10	0	**1.62**
	2B	H. Ferris	523	.250	2	63	359	450	61	**68**	6.3	.930	T. Lewis	39	316	16	17	1	3.53
W-79 L-57	SS	F. Parent	517	.306	4	59	260	446	63	52	5.6	.918	G. Winter	28	241	16	12	0	2.80
	3B	J. Collins	564	.332	6	94	203	**328**	50	24	**4.2**	.914	F. Mitchell	17	109	6	6	0	3.81
Jimmy Collins	RF	C. Hemphill	545	.261	3	62	188	22	17	4	1.7	.925	N. Cuppy	13	93	4	6	0	4.15
	CF	C. Stahl	515	.309	6	72	277	12	13	3	2.3	.957							
	LF	T. Dowd	594	.268	3	52	288	11	20	3	2.3	.937							
	C	Schreckengost	280	.304	0	38	273	102	**30**	8	5.6	.926							
	C	L. Criger	268	.231	0	24	300	109	14	11	6.2	.967							
	P	C. Young	153	.209	0	17	12	105	3	3	2.8	.975							
Detroit	1B	P. Dillon	281	.288	1	42	777	44	18	57	11.3	.979	R. Miller	38	332	23	13	1	2.95
	2B	K. Gleason	547	.274	3	75	334	**457**	64	67	6.3	.925	E. Siever	38	289	18	15	0	3.24
W-74 L-61	SS	K. Elberfeld	436	.310	3	76	**332**	411	76	**62**	6.8	.907	J. Cronin	30	220	13	15	0	3.89
	3B	D. Casey	540	.283	2	46	133	324	58	**25**	4.1	.887	J. Yeager	26	200	12	11	1	2.61
George Stallings	RF	D. Holmes	537	.294	4	62	217	18	24	5	2.0	.907							
	CF	J. Barrett	542	.293	4	65	300	**31**	21	7	**2.6**	.940							
	LF	D. Nance	461	.280	3	66	240	20	19	6	2.1	.932							
	C	F. Buelow	231	.225	2	29	213	84	10	4	4.4	.967							
	UT	McAllister	306	.301	3	57	381	66	42	19		.914							
	C	A. Shaw	171	.269	1	23	134	46	12	5	4.6	.938							
Philadelphia	1B	H. Davis	496	.306	8	76	1265	83	33	67	**11.8**	.976	C. Fraser	40	331	22	16	0	3.81
	2B	N. Lajoie	543	**.422**	14	125	395	381	32	60	6.8	**.960**	E. Plank	33	261	17	13	0	3.31
W-74 L-62	SS	J. Dolan	338	.216	1	38	88	223	42	30	5.8	.881	B. Bernhard	31	257	17	10	0	4.52
	3B	L. Cross	420	.331	2	73	140	236	33	7	4.1	.919	S. Wiltse	19	166	13	5	0	3.58
Connie Mack	RF	S. Seybold	457	.333	8	90	157	10	8	2	1.8	.954	W. Piatt	18	140	5	12	1	4.63
	CF	D. Fultz	561	.292	0	52	216	13	16	0	2.3	.935							
	LF	M. McIntyre	308	.276	0	46	155	8	14	0	2.2	.921							
	C	M. Powers	431	.251	1	47	**400**	137	27	6	5.1	.952							
	OF	J. Hayden	211	.265	0	17	63	11	14	0	1.8	.841							
	OF	P. Geier	211	.232	0	23	80	5	6	1	1.8	.934							
	SS	B. Ely	171	.216	0	16	85	156	23	19	5.9	.913							

AMERICAN LEAGUE 1901, *cont.*

	POS	Player	AB	BA	HR	RBI	PO	A	E	DP	TC/G	FA	Pitcher	G	IP	W	L	SV	ERA
Baltimore W-68 L-65 John McGraw	1B	B. Hart	206	.311	0	23	561	9	14	28	10.1	.976	McGinnity	48	**382**	26	20	1	3.56
	2B	J. Williams	501	.317	7	96	339	412	52	47	6.2	.935	H. Howell	37	295	14	21	0	3.67
	SS	B. Keister	442	.328	2	93	231	322	**97**	30	5.8	.851	F. Foreman	24	191	13	6	1	3.67
	3B	J. McGraw	232	.349	0	28	80	107	23	5	3.0	.890	J. Nops	27	177	11	10	1	4.08
	RF	C. Seymour	547	.303	1	77	271	23	17	4	2.3	.945							
	CF	S. Brodie	306	.310	2	41	178	4	7	0	2.3	.963							
	LF	M. Donlin	476	.347	5	67	179	12	17	2	2.8	.918							
	C	R. Bresnahan	295	.268	1	32	199	63	23	3	4.1	.919							
	OF	J. Jackson	364	.250	2	50	234	4	7	1	2.6	**.971**							
	UT	J. Dunn	362	.249	0	36	157	206	53	14		.873							
	C	W. Robinson	239	.301	0	26	235	61	16	4	4.7	.949							
	UT	H. Howell	188	.218	2	26	59	93	16	6		.905							
	P	McGinnity	148	.209	0	6	15	104	9	2	2.7	.930							
Washington W-61 L-73 Jimmy Manning	1B	M. Grady	347	.285	9	56	575	52	16	34	10.9	.975	B. Carrick	42	324	14	23	0	3.75
	2B	J. Farrell	555	.272	3	63	176	246	39	43	6.4	.915	W. Lee	36	262	16	16	0	4.40
	SS	B. Clingman	480	.242	2	55	290	**462**	55	56	5.9	**.932**	C. Patten	32	254	18	10	0	3.93
	3B	B. Coughlin	508	.278	6	68	**232**	275	43	16	4.0	.922	W. Mercer	24	180	9	13	1	4.56
	RF	S. Dungan	559	.320	1	73	145	15	9	4	1.6	.947	D. Gear	24	163	4	11	0	4.03
	CF	I. Waldron	332*	.322	0	22	140	7	7	0	2.0	.955							
	LF	P. Foster	392	.278	6	53	200	9	17	1	2.2	.925							
	C	B. Clarke	422	.280	3	54	358	122	24	11	4.7	.952							
	2B	J. Quinn	266	.252	3	36	158	177	16	17	5.3	.954							
	OP	D. Gear	199	.236	0	20	56	59	6	3		.950							
	UT	W. Mercer	140	.300	0	16	92	57	15	10		.909							
Cleveland W-55 L-82 Jimmy McAleer	1B	C. LaChance	548	.303	1	75	1342	58	30	73	10.8	.979	P. Dowling	33	256	11	22*	0	3.86
	2B	E. Beck	539	.289	6	79	310	404	56	44	5.8	2.90	E. Moore	31	251	16	14	0	2.90
	SS	F. Scheibeck	329	.213	0	38	176	268	51	26	5.4	.897	B. Hart	20	158	7	11	0	3.77
	3B	B. Bradley	516	.293	1	55	192	298	37	**25**	4.0	**.930**	E. Scott	17	125	7	6	1	4.40
	RF	J. O'Brien	375	.283	0	39	150	9	10	4	1.8	.941	J. Bracken	12	100	4	8	0	6.21
	CF	O. Pickering	547	.309	0	40	**315**	22	18	9	2.6	.949	B. Hoffer	16	99	3	8	3	4.55
	LF	J. McCarthy	343	.321	0	32	157	9	9	5	2.0	.949	H. McNeal	12	85	5	5	0	4.43
	C	B. Wood	346	.292	1	49	307	106	21	11	5.2	.952							
	OF	E. Harvey	170	.353	1	24	82	7	11	4	2.2	.890							
Milwaukee W-48 L-89 Hugh Duffy	1B	J. Anderson	576	.330	8	99	1310	66	25	**81**	11.2	**.982**	B. Reidy	37	301	16	20	0	4.21
	2B	B. Gilbert	492	.270	0	43	319	395	49	66	6.0	.936	N. Garvin	37	257	7	20	2	3.46
	SS	W. Conroy	503	.256	5	64	285	408	59	46	6.4	.922	B. Husting	34	217	10	15	1	4.27
	3B	J. Burke	233	.206	0	26	83	132	35	5	3.9	.860	T. Sparks	29	210	7	16	0	3.51
	RF	B. Hallman	549	.246	2	47	226	22	**26**	6	2.0	.905	P. Hawley	26	182	7	14	0	4.59
	CF	H. Duffy	286	.308	2	45	141	5	5	0	2.0	.967							
	LF	G. Hogriever	221	.235	0	16	134	3	15	1	2.8	.901							
	C	B. Maloney	290	.293	0	22	284	111	20	6	**5.8**	.952							
	UT	B. Friel	376	.266	4	35	142	183	46	16		.876							
	OF	I. Waldron	266*	.297	0	29	97	9	14	0	1.9	.883							

BATTING AND BASE RUNNING LEADERS

Batting Average
N. Lajoie, PHI	.422
B. Freeman, BOS	.345
M. Donlin, BAL	.341
S. Seybold, PHI	.333
J. Collins, BOS	.332

Slugging Average
N. Lajoie, PHI	.635
B. Freeman, BOS	.527
S. Seybold, PHI	.499
J. Williams, BAL	.495
J. Collins, BOS	.495

Home Runs
N. Lajoie, PHI	13
B. Freeman, BOS	12
M. Grady, WAS	9
S. Seybold, PHI	8
H. Davis, PHI	8
J. Anderson, MIL	8

Total Bases
N. Lajoie, PHI	342
J. Collins, BOS	279
J. Anderson, MIL	274
B. Freeman, BOS	258
J. Williams, BAL	248

Runs Batted In
N. Lajoie, PHI	125
B. Freeman, BOS	114
J. Anderson, MIL	99
S. Mertes, CHI	98
J. Williams, BAL	96

Stolen Bases
F. Isbell, CHI	52
S. Mertes, CHI	46
F. Jones, CHI	38
C. Seymour, BAL	38
O. Pickering, CLE	36
D. Fultz, PHI	36

Hits
N. Lajoie, PHI	229
J. Anderson, MIL	190
J. Collins, BOS	187
I. Waldron, MIL, WAS	186

Base on Balls
D. Hoy, CHI	86
F. Jones, CHI	84
J. Barrett, DET	76
McFarland, CHI	75

Home Run Percentage
M. Grady, WAS	2.6
B. Freeman, BOS	2.4
N. Lajoie, PHI	2.4
S. Seybold, PHI	1.8

Runs Scored
N. Lajoie, PHI	145
F. Jones, CHI	120
J. Williams, BAL	113
D. Hoy, CHI	112

Doubles
N. Lajoie, PHI	48
J. Anderson, MIL	46
J. Collins, BOS	42
J. Farrell, WAS	32

Triples
B. Keister, BAL	21
J. Williams, BAL	21
S. Mertes, CHI	17
C. Stahl, BOS	16

PITCHING LEADERS

Winning Percentage
C. Griffith, CHI	.774
C. Young, BOS	.767
N. Callahan, CHI	.652
C. Patten, WAS	.643
R. Miller, DET	.639

Earned Run Average
C. Young, BOS	1.62
N. Callahan, CHI	2.42
J. Yeager, DET	2.61
C. Griffith, CHI	2.67
G. Winter, BOS	2.80

Wins
C. Young, BOS	33
McGinnity, BAL	26
C. Griffith, CHI	24
R. Miller, DET	23
C. Fraser, PHI	22

Saves
B. Hoffer, CLE	3
McGinnity, BAL	3
N. Garvin, MIL	2

Strikeouts
C. Young, BOS	158
R. Patterson, CHI	127
P. Dowling, CLE, MIL	124
N. Garvin, MIL	122
C. Fraser, PHI	110

Complete Games
McGinnity, BAL	39
C. Young, BOS	38
R. Miller, DET	35
C. Fraser, PHI	35
B. Carrick, WAS	34

Fewest Hits/9 Innings
C. Young, BOS	7.85
N. Callahan, CHI	8.15
E. Moore, CLE	8.38
T. Lewis, BOS	8.51

Shutouts
C. Griffith, CHI	5
C. Young, BOS	5
E. Moore, CLE	4
C. Patten, WAS	4

Fewest Walks/9 Innings
C. Young, BOS	0.90
D. Gear, WAS	1.21
W. Lee, WAS	1.55
C. Griffith, CHI	1.69

Most Strikeouts/9 Inn.
N. Garvin, MIL	4.27
C. Patten, WAS	3.86
C. Young, BOS	3.83
R. Patterson, CHI	3.66

Innings
McGinnity, BAL	382
C. Young, BOS	371
R. Miller, DET	332
C. Fraser, PHI	331

Games Pitched
McGinnity, BAL	48
C. Young, BOS	43
P. Dowling, CLE, MIL	43
B. Carrick, WAS	42

AMERICAN LEAGUE 1901, *cont.*

	W	L	PCT	GB	R	OR	Batting 2B	3B	HR	BA	SA	SB	Fielding E	DP	FA	Pitching CG	BB	SO	ShO	SV	ERA
Chicago	83	53	.610		**819**	631	173	89	32	.276	.370	**280**	345	100	.941	110	312	394	**11**	2	**2.98**
Boston	79	57	.581	4	759	**608**	183	104	**37**	.279	.382	157	337	104	.943	123	294	**396**	7	1	3.04
Detroit	74	61	.548	8.5	741	694	180	80	29	.279	.370	205	410	**127**	.930	118	313	307	9	2	3.30
Philadelphia	74	62	.544	9	805	761	**239**	86	35	.288	.394	173	337	93	.942	**124**	374	350	6	1	4.00
Baltimore	68	65	.511	13.5	760	750	179	**111**	24	**.294**	**.397**	207	401	76	.926	115	344	271	4	3	3.73
Washington	61	73	.455	21	678	767	191	83	34	.269	.365	127	**323**	97	**.943**	118	**284**	308	8	1	4.09
Cleveland	55	82	.401	28.5	663	827	197	68	12	.271	.348	125	329	99	.942	122	464	334	7	4	4.12
Milwaukee	48	89	.350	35.5	641	828	192	66	26	.261	.345	176	393	106	.934	107	395	376	3	4	4.06
					5866	5866	1534	687	229	.277	.371	1450	2875	802	.938	937	2780	2736	55	18	3.66

NATIONAL LEAGUE 1902

Team	POS	Player	AB	BA	HR	RBI	PO	A	E	DP	TC/G	FA	Pitcher	G	IP	W	L	SV	ERA
Pittsburgh W-103 L-36 Fred Clarke	1B	Bransfield	417	.305	1	69	1064	41	18	40	11.1	.984	J. Chesbro	35	286	**28**	6	1	2.17
	2B	C. Ritchey	405	.277	2	55	275	341	22	48	5.6	**.966**	D. Phillippe	31	272	20	9	0	2.05
	SS	W. Conroy	365	.244	1	47	192	327	42	39	5.9	.925	J. Tannehill	26	231	20	6	0	1.95
	3B	T. Leach	514	.280	**6**	85	170	**316**	39	10	3.9	.926	S. Leever	28	222	16	7	2	2.39
	RF	L. Davis	232	.280	0	20	80	6	5	1	1.5	.945	E. Doheny	22	188	16	4	0	2.53
	CF	G. Beaumont	544	**.357**	0	67	260	15	7	8	2.2	.975							
	LF	F. Clarke	461	.321	2	53	215	13	10	2	2.1	.958							
	C	H. Smith	185	.189	0	12	265	49	7	3	6.5	.972							
	UT	H. Wagner	538	.329	3	**91**	532	176	32	33		.957							
	UT	J. Burke	203	.296	0	26	90	120	23	8		.901							
	C	J. O'Connor	170	.294	1	28	187	49	5	2	5.7	.979							
	PO	J. Tannehill	148	.291	1	17	25	57	4	3		.953							
	C	C. Zimmer	142	.268	0	17	202	48	8	8	6.3	.969							
Brooklyn W-75 L-63 Ned Hanlon	1B	T. McCreery	430	.244	4	57	1032	59	**23**	53	10.3	.979	W. Donovan	35	298	17	15	1	2.78
	2B	T. Flood	476	.218	3	50	297	374	**41**	33	5.4	.942	D. Newton	31	264	15	14	0	2.42
	SS	B. Dahlen	527	.264	2	74	278	440	66	34	5.7	.916	F. Kitson	31	260	19	12	0	2.84
	3B	C. Irwin	458	.273	2	43	173	244	33	21	3.5	.927	J. Hughes	31	254	15	11	0	2.87
	RF	W. Keeler	556	.338	0	38	208	14	5	4	1.7	**.978**	R. Evans	13	97	5	6*	0	2.68
	CF	C. Dolan	**592**	.280	1	54	283	10	20	2	2.5	.936							
	LF	J. Sheckard	486	.270	4	37	**284**	12	11	6	2.5	.964							
	C	H. Hearne	231	.281	0	28	298	67	13	7	5.8	.966							
	C1	D. Farrell	264	.242	0	24	469	90	12	8		.979							
	P	W. Donovan	161	.168	1	16	20	71	5	2	2.7	.948							
Boston W-73 L-64 Al Buckenberger	1B	F. Tenney	489	.315	2	30	1251	**105**	21	75	10.3	**.985**	V. Willis	51	410	27	**19**	3	2.20
	2B	DeMontreville	481	.268	0	53	271	294	36	24	5.4	.940	T. Pittinger	46	389	27	16	0	2.52
	SS	H. Long	429	.228	2	44	279	360	37	46	6.4	**.945**	M. Eason	27	206	9	11	0	2.75
	3B	Gremminger	522	.257	1	66	**222**	282	26	15	3.8	.951	J. Malarkey	21	170	8	10	1	2.59
	RF	P. Carney	522	.270	2	65	153	19	13	7	1.4	.930							
	CF	B. Lush	413	.223	2	19	251	24	14	5	1.5	.952							
	LF	D. Cooley	548	.296	0	58	250	7	13	2	2.1	.952							
	C	M. Kittridge	255	.235	2	30	363	99	9	5	6.5	.981							
	C	P. Moran	251	.239	1	24	332	95	8	5	6.1	**.982**							
	UT	C. Dexter	183	.257	1	18	111	113	19	12		.922							
	OF	E. Courtney	165	.218	0	17	71	5	2	0	2.0	.974							
	P	V. Willis	150	.153	0	7	**37**	105	4	**5**	2.9	.973							
	P	T. Pittinger	147	.136	0	10	20	83	6	2	2.4	.945							
Cincinnati W-70 L-70 Bid McPhee W-27 L-37 Frank Bancroft W-9 L-7 Joe Kelley W-34 L-26	1B	J. Beckley	532	.331	5	69	**1262**	64	**23**	**84**	10.5	.983	N. Hahn	36	312	22	12	0	1.76
	2B	H. Peitz	387	.315	1	60	124	126	22	23	5.7	.919	B. Phillips	33	263	16	15	0	2.50
	SS	T. Corcoran	537	.251	0	54	292	412	56	49	5.5	.926	H. Thielman	25	211	8	15	1	3.24
	3B	Steinfeldt	479	.278	1	49	190	315	49	29	4.3	.912	E. Poole	16	138	12	4	0	2.15
	RF	S. Crawford	555	.333	3	78	208	24	17	5	1.8	.932	B. Ewing	15	118	6	6	0	2.98
	CF	D. Hoy	279	.290	2	20	149	4	11	1	2.3	.933							
	LF	J. Dobbs	256	.297	1	16	146	11	6	2	2.6	.963							
	C	B. Bergen	322	.180	0	36	406	137	23	13	6.4	.959							
	OF	C. Seymour	235	.349	2	37	139	10	13	3	2.7	.920							
	2B	E. Beck	187	.305	1	20	70	92	11	11	5.4	.936							
	2B	G. Magoon	162	.272	0	23	83	144	17	16	6.0	.930							
	UT	J. Kelley	156	.321	1	12	78	59	6	9		.958							
	OF	M. Donlin	143	.294	0	9	59	5	9	1	2.3	.877							
Chicago W-68 L-69 Frank Selee	1B	F. Chance	236	.284	1	31	391	20	13	21	11.2	.969	J. Taylor	36	325	22	11	1	**1.33**
	2B	B. Lowe	472	.246	0	31	326	406	33	59	**6.5**	.957	P. Williams	31	254	12	16	0	2.51
	SS	J. Tinker	501	.273	2	54	243	**453**	72	47	6.2	.906	J. Menefee	22	197	12	10	0	2.42
	3B	G. Schaefer	291	.196	0	14	103	152	40	11	3.9	.864	C. Lundgren	18	160	9	9	0	1.97
	RF	D. Jones	243	.305	0	14	146	3	7	1	2.4	.955	B. Rhoads	16	118	4	8	1	3.20
	CF	J. Dobbs	235	.302	0	35	122	8	3	5	2.3	.977	J. St. Vrain	12	95	4	6	0	2.08
	LF	J. Slagle	454	.315	0	28	262	15	10	5	2.5	.965							
	C	J. Kling	434	.286	0	57	**471**	158	17	**16**	5.8	.974							
	UT	C. Dexter	266	.226	2	26	303	71	27	20		.933							
	UT	J. Menefee	216	.231	0	15	230	57	13	7		.957							
	OF	D. Miller	187	.246	0	13	97	9	5	0	2.2	.955							
	UT	J. Taylor	186	.237	0	17	42	133	9	5		.951							
	OF	B. Congalton	179	.223	1	24	71	6	1	1	1.7	.987							
	O1	A. Williams	160	.231	0	14	226	15	11	10		.956							

NATIONAL LEAGUE 1902, *cont.*

	POS	Player	AB	BA	HR	RBI	PO	A	E	DP	TC/G	FA	Pitcher	G	IP	W	L	SV	ERA
St. Louis	1B	K. Brashear	388	.276	1	40	751	36	16	49	12.0	.980	M. O'Neill	36	288	18	14	0	2.93
	2B	J. Farrell	565	.250	0	25	297	422	40	72	6.4	.947	S. Yerkes	39	273	11	20	0	3.66
W-56 L-78	SS	O. Krueger	467	.266	0	46	184	390	66	47	6.0	.897	E. Murphy	23	164	9	7	1	3.02
	3B	F. Hartman	416	.216	0	52	138	229	37	9	3.8	.908	B. Wicker	22	152	5	13	0	3.19
Patsy Donovan	RF	P. Donovan	502	.315	0	35	179	30	9	6	1.7	.959	C. Currie	15	118	6	5	0	2.75
	CF	H. Smoot	518	.311	3	48	284	14	22	5	2.5	.931							
	LF	G. Barclay	543	.300	3	53	247	16	28	3	2.1	.904							
	C	J. Ryan	267	.180	0	14	258	86	12	8	5.4	.966							
	1B	A. Nichols	251	.267	1	31	577	24	10	26	10.9	.984							
	C	J. O'Neill	192	.141	0	12	246	79	9	5	5.7	.973							
Philadelphia	1B	H. Jennings	289	.277	1	32	659	46	12	32	10.4	.983	D. White	36	306	16	20	1	2.53
	2B	P. Childs	403	.194	0	25	271	349	36	26	5.3	.945	B. Duggleby	33	259	11	17	0	3.38
W-56 L-81	SS	R. Hulswitt	497	.272	0	38	318	400	65	37	6.3	.917	H. Iburg	30	236	11	18	0	3.89
	3B	B. Hallman	254	.248	0	35	71	147	16	3	3.3	.932	C. Fraser	27	224	12	13	0	3.42
Bill Shettsline	RF	S. Barry	543	.287	3	57	185	15	13	3	1.6	.939							
	CF	R. Thomas	500	.286	0	24	277	23	8	3	2.2	.974							
	LF	G. Browne	281	.260	0	26	158	14	17*	2	2.7*	.910							
	C	R. Dooin	333	.231	0	35	433	117	29	10	6.9	.950							
	1C	K. Douglass	408	.233	0	37	792	63	18	28		.979							
	UT	H. Krug	198	.227	0	14	116	62	12	10		.937							
	PO	D. White	179	.263	1	15	35	84	12	0		.908							
New York	1B	D. McGann	227	.300	0	21	634	39	13	38	11.2	.981	C. Mathewson	34	277	14	17	0	2.11
	2B	H. Smith	511	.252	0	33	347	403	37	58	5.7	.953	D. Taylor	26	201	7	15	0	2.29
W-48 L-88	SS	J. Bean	176	.222	0	5	71	153	28	19	5.3	.889	R. Evans	23	176	8	13*	0	3.17
	3B	B. Lauder	482	.237	1	44	189	251	45	17	4.0	.907	McGinnity	19	153	8	8	0	2.06
Horace Fogel	RF	J. Dunn	342	.211	0	14	47	4	2	2	1.2	.962	T. Sparks	15	115	4	10	1	3.76
W-18 L-23	CF	S. Brodie	416	.281	3	42	219	22	12	7	2.3	.953	J. Cronin	13	114	5	6	0	2.45
	LF	J. Jones	249	.237	0	19	122	9	15	2	2.2	.897							
Heinie Smith	C	F. Bowerman	367	.253	0	26	428	143	26	10	6.1	.956							
W-5 L-27																			
	OF	G. Browne	216	.319	0	14	104	7	13*	1	2.3*	.895							
John McGraw	1B	J. Doyle	186	.301	1	19	490	34	5	28	10.8	.991							
W-25 L-38	UT	R. Bresnahan	178	.292	1	22	164	40	13	8		.940							

BATTING AND BASE RUNNING LEADERS

Batting Average		Slugging Average		Home Runs	
G. Beaumont, PIT	.357	H. Wagner, PIT	.467	T. Leach, PIT	6
W. Keeler, BKN	.338	S. Crawford, CIN	.461	J. Beckley, CIN	5
S. Crawford, CIN	.333	F. Clarke, PIT	.453	T. McCreery, BKN	4
J. Beckley, CIN	.331	T. Leach, PIT	.442	J. Sheckard, BKN	4
H. Wagner, PIT	.329	J. Beckley, CIN	.429		

Total Bases		Runs Batted In		Stolen Bases	
S. Crawford, CIN	256	H. Wagner, PIT	91	H. Wagner, PIT	42
H. Wagner, PIT	251	T. Leach, PIT	85	J. Slagle, CHI	40
J. Beckley, CIN	228	S. Crawford, CIN	78	P. Donovan, STL	34
T. Leach, PIT	227	B. Dahlen, BKN	74	G. Beaumont, PIT	33
G. Beaumont, PIT	226	Bransfield, PIT	69	H. Smith, NY	32
		J. Beckley, CIN	69		

Hits		Base on Balls		Home Run Percentage	
G. Beaumont, PIT	194	R. Thomas, PHI	107	T. Leach, PIT	1.2
W. Keeler, BKN	188	B. Lush, BOS	76	J. Beckley, CIN	0.9
S. Crawford, CIN	185	F. Tenney, BOS	73	T. McCreery, BKN	0.9
H. Wagner, PIT	176	J. Sheckard, BKN	57	J. Sheckard, BKN	0.8

Runs Scored		Doubles		Triples	
H. Wagner, PIT	105	H. Wagner, PIT	33	S. Crawford, CIN	23
F. Clarke, PIT	104	F. Clarke, PIT	27	T. Leach, PIT	22
G. Beaumont, PIT	100	D. Cooley, BOS	26	H. Wagner, PIT	16
T. Leach, PIT	97	B. Dahlen, BKN	25	F. Clarke, PIT	14

PITCHING LEADERS

Winning Percentage		Earned Run Average		Wins	
J. Chesbro, PIT	.824	J. Taylor, CHI	1.33	J. Chesbro, PIT	28
E. Doheny, PIT	.800	N. Hahn, CIN	1.76	T. Pittinger, BOS	27
J. Tannehill, PIT	.769	J. Tannehill, PIT	1.95	V. Willis, BOS	27
S. Leever, PIT	.696	C. Lundgren, CHI	1.97	J. Taylor, CHI	22
D. Phillippe, PIT	.690	D. Phillippe, PIT	2.05	N. Hahn, CIN	22

Saves		Strikeouts		Complete Games	
V. Willis, BOS	3	V. Willis, BOS	225	V. Willis, BOS	45
S. Leever, PIT	2	D. White, PHI	185	T. Pittinger, BOS	36
		T. Pittinger, BOS	174	N. Hahn, CIN	34
		W. Donovan, BKN	170	D. White, PHI	34
		C. Mathewson, NY	159	J. Taylor, CHI	33

Fewest Hits/9 Innings		Shutouts		Fewest Walks/9 Innings	
D. Newton, BKN	7.08	C. Mathewson, NY	8	D. Phillippe, PIT	0.86
McGinnity, NY	7.18	J. Chesbro, PIT	8	J. Tannehill, PIT	0.97
J. Taylor, CHI	7.51	J. Taylor, CHI	8	J. Menefee, CHI	1.19
W. Donovan, BKN	7.56	T. Pittinger, BOS	7	J. Taylor, CHI	1.19

Most Strikeouts/9 Inn.		Innings		Games Pitched	
D. White, PHI	5.44	V. Willis, BOS	410	V. Willis, BOS	51
C. Mathewson, NY	5.17	T. Pittinger, BOS	389	T. Pittinger, BOS	46
W. Donovan, BKN	5.14	J. Taylor, CHI	325	S. Yerkes, STL	39
V. Willis, BOS	4.94	N. Hahn, CIN	312	J. Taylor, CHI	36

NATIONAL LEAGUE 1902, *cont.*

	W	L	PCT	GB	R	OR	2B	3B	HR	BA	SA	SB	E	DP	FA	CG	BB	SO	ShO	SV	ERA
										Batting				**Fielding**				**Pitching**			
Pittsburgh	103	36	.741		**775**	440	**199**	**94**	**19**	**.287**	**.377**	**222**	247	87	.958	131	**250**	**564**	**21**	3	2.30
Brooklyn	75	63	.543	• 27.5	564	519	147	50	**19**	.257	.320	145	275	79	.952	131	363	536	15	1	2.69
Boston	73	64	.533	29	572	516	142	39	14	.250	.305	189	**240**	90	**.959**	124	372	523	14	**4**	2.61
Cincinnati	70	70	.500	33.5	633	566	188	77	18	.282	.363	131	322	**118**	.945	130	352	430	9	1	2.67
Chicago	68	69	.496	34	530	501	131	40	6	.251	.299	**222**	327	111	.946	**132**	279	437	18	2	**2.21**
St. Louis	56	78	.418	44.5	517	695	116	37	10	.258	.304	158	336	107	.944	112	338	400	7	2	3.47
Philadelphia	56	81	.409	46	484	649	113	42	5	.247	.293	108	305	81	.946	118	334	504	8	2	3.50
New York	48	88	.353	53.5	401	590	149	34	8	.238	.291	187	330	104	.943	118	332	501	11	1	2.82
					4476	4476	1185	413	99	.259	.320	1362	2382	777	.949	996	2620	3895	103	16	2.78

AMERICAN LEAGUE 1902

	POS	Player	AB	BA	HR	RBI	PO	A	E	DP	TC/G	FA	Pitcher	G	IP	W	L	SV	ERA
Philadelphia W-83 L-53 Connie Mack	1B	H. Davis	561	.307	6	92	1247	87	22	58	10.6	.984	E. Plank	36	300	20	15	0	3.30
	2B	D. Murphy	291	.313	1	48	167	197	14	22	5.0	.963	R. Waddell	33	276	24	7	0	2.05
	SS	M. Cross	497	.231	3	59	**373**	466	66	37	6.6	.927	B. Husting	32	204	14	5	0	3.79
	3B	L. Cross	559	.342	0	108	185	306	30	18	3.8	.942	S. Wiltse	19	138	8	8	1	5.15
	RF	S. Seybold	522	.316	**16**	97	246	11	10	3	2.0	.963	F. Mitchell	18	108	5	7	1	3.59
	CF	D. Fultz	506	.302	1	49	231	18	10	1	2.3	.961	H. Wilson	13	96	7	5	0	2.43
	LF	T. Hartsel	545	.283	5	58	238	18	12	2	2.0	.955							
	C	Schreckengost	284	.324	2	43	367*	108	20*	3	7.0*	.960							
	C	M. Powers	246	.264	2	39	229	110	18	5	5.3	.950							
	2B	L. Castro	143	.245	1	15	71	85	14	10	4.7	.918							
St. Louis W-78 L-58 Jimmy McAleer	1B	J. Anderson	524	.284	4	85	1361	47	22	78	11.3	.985	J. Powell	42	328	22	17	2	3.21
	2B	D. Padden	413	.264	1	40	288	363	22	64	5.8	.967	R. Donahue	35	316	22	11	0	2.76
	SS	B. Wallace	495	.287	1	63	299	474	42	64	6.2	.948	J. Harper	29	222	15	11	0	4.13
	3B	McCormick	504	.246	3	51	147	271	44	26	3.5	.905	W. Sudhoff	30	220	13	13	0	2.86
	RF	C. Hemphill	416	.317	6	58	164	15	9	6	1.9	.952							
	CF	E. Heidrick	447	.289	3	56	264	16	18	4	**2.7**	.940							
	LF	J. Burkett	549	.306	5	52	300	17	**26**	5	2.5	.924							
	C	J. Sugden	203	.246	0	15	192	67	12	**9**	4.4	.956							
	UT	B. Friel	267	.240	2	20	194	94	15	17		.950							
	C	M. Kahoe	197	.244	2	28	214	52	9	4	5.2	.967							
Boston W-77 L-60 Jimmy Collins	1B	C. LaChance	541	.279	6	56	**1544**	46	27	80	11.7	.983	C. Young	**45**	**385**	**32**	11	0	2.15
	2B	H. Ferris	499	.244	8	63	312	**461**	39	59	6.1	.952	B. Dinneen	42	371	21	21	0	2.93
	SS	F. Parent	**567**	.275	3	62	287	**496**	58	60	6.1	.931	G. Winter	20	168	11	9	0	2.99
	3B	J. Collins	429	.322	6	61	143	255	19	14	3.9	**.954**	T. Sparks	17	143	7	9	0	3.47
	RF	B. Freeman	564	.309	11	**121**	222	15	14	3	1.8	.944							
	CF	C. Stahl	508	.323	2	58	244	15	12	2	2.2	.956							
	LF	P. Dougherty	438	.342	0	34	170	8	20	1	1.9	.899							
	C	L. Criger	266	.256	0	28	330	117	16	6	5.8	.965							
	3O	H. Gleason	240	.225	2	25	91	67	11	7		.935							
	C	J. Warner	222	.234	0	12	252	81	7	8	5.3	.979							
	P	C. Young	148	.230	1	12	10	82	7	4	2.2	.929							
	P	B. Dinneen	141	.128	0	9	7	77	4	1	2.1	.955							
Chicago W-74 L-60 Clark Griffith	1B	F. Isbell	515	.252	4	59	1401	**93**	21	**97**	11.4	.986	N. Callahan	35	282	16	14	0	3.60
	2B	T. Daly	489	.225	1	54	312	370	31	**70**	5.2	.957	R. Patterson	34	268	19	14	0	3.06
	SS	G. Davis	485	.299	3	93	289	427	37	**72**	5.8	**.951**	W. Piatt	32	246	12	12	0	3.51
	3B	S. Strang	536	.295	3	46	170	**334**	62	21	4.1	.890	C. Griffith	28	213	15	9	0	4.19
	RF	D. Green	481	.312	0	62	217	11	14	4	1.9	.942	N. Garvin	23	175	10	10	0	2.21
	CF	F. Jones	532	.321	0	54	323	25	10	**11**	2.7	.972							
	LF	S. Mertes	497	.282	1	79	223	**26**	21	5	2.3	.922							
	C	B. Sullivan	263	.243	1	26	242	81	11	8	4.8	.967							
	C	McFarland	244	.230	1	25	282	71	12	7	5.3	.967							
	PO	N. Callahan	218	.234	0	13	54	107	9	7		.947							
Cleveland W-69 L-67 Bill Armour	1B	P. Hickman	426	.380	8	94	1079	47	40*	63	11.9*	.966	E. Moore	36	293	17	17	1	2.95
	2B	N. Lajoie	348	.368	7	64	270	283	15	49	6.6*	.974*	A. Joss	32	269	17	13	0	2.77
	SS	J. Gochnaur	459	.185	0	37	223	447	48	59	5.7	.933	B. Bernhard	27	217	17	5	1	2.20
	3B	B. Bradley	550	.340	11	77	**188**	324	43	21	4.1	.923	C. Wright	21	148	7	11	1	3.95
	RF	E. Flick	424	.297	2	61	156	13	13	2	1.7	.929							
	CF	H. Bay	455	.290	0	23	242	13	7	3	2.4	**.973**							
	LF	J. McCarthy	359	.284	0	41	178	6	11	0	2.1	.944							
	C	H. Bemis	317	.312	1	29	333	120	17	2	5.4	.964							
	OF	O. Pickering	293	.256	3	26	138	5	3	1	2.3	.979							
	C	B. Wood	258	.295	0	40	169	53	14	4	4.5	.941							

AMERICAN LEAGUE 1902, *cont.*

	POS	Player	AB	BA	HR	RBI	PO	A	E	DP	TC/G	FA	Pitcher	G	IP	W	L	SV	ERA
Washington	1B	S. Carey	452	.314	0	60	1190	69	14	54	10.6	.989	A. Orth	38	324	19	18	0	3.97
	2B	J. Doyle	312	.247	1	20	145	197	26	17	5.4	.929	C. Patten	36	300	17	16	1	4.05
W-61 L-75	SS	B. Ely	381	.262	1	62	238	350	49	31	6.1	.923	B. Carrick	31	258	11	17	0	4.86
	3B	B. Coughlin	469	.301	6	71	104	157	21	6	4.3	.926	J. Townsend	27	220	9	16	0	4.45
Tom Loftus	RF	W. Lee	391	.256	4	45	171	14	17	1	2.1	.916	W. Lee	13	98	5	7	0	5.05
	CF	J. Ryan	484	.320	6	44	280	16	16	0	2.6	.949							
	LF	E. Delahanty	473	**.376**	10	93	236	11	10	0	2.3	.961							
	C	B. Clarke	291	.268	7	42	288	97	11	8	4.6	**.972**							
	UT	B. Keister	483	.300	9	90	229	166	34	14		.921							
	3B	H. Wolverton	249	.249	1	23	86	139	24	8	4.2	.904							
	C	L. Drill	221	.262	1	29	175	51	19	2	4.6	.922							
	P	A. Orth	175	.217	2	10	25	95	10	3	3.4	.923							
Detroit	1B	P. Dillon	243	.206	0	22	709	52	19	45	11.8	.976	W. Mercer	35	282	15	18	1	3.04
	2B	K. Gleason	441	.247	1	38	**320**	349	**42**	66	6.0	.941	G. Mullin	35	260	13	16	0	3.67
W-52 L-83	SS	K. Elberfeld	488	.260	1	64	326	459	67	63	6.6	.921	E. Siever	25	188	8	11	1	**1.91**
	3B	D. Casey	520	.273	3	55	174	309	51	17	4.0	.904	R. Miller	20	149	6	12	1	3.69
Frank Dwyer	RF	D. Holmes	362	.257	2	33	155	16	9	5	2.0	.950	J. Yeager	19	140	6	12	0	4.82
	CF	J. Barrett	509	.303	4	44	326	22	14	6	2.7	.961							
	LF	D. Harley	491	.281	2	44	238	15	19	1	2.2	.930							
	C	D. McGuire	229	.227	2	23	210	65	14	6	4.1	.952							
	UT	McAllister	229	.210	1	32	301	67	14	19		.963							
	C	F. Buelow	224	.223	2	29	174	81	**20**	5	4.4	.927							
	1B	E. Beck	162	.296	2	22	343	26	11	24	10.6	.971							
	UT	J. Yeager	161	.242	1	23	59	94	9	3		.944							
Baltimore	1B	D. McGann	250	.316	0	42	658	41	9	52	10.4	.987	H. Howell	26	199	9	15	0	4.12
	2B	J. Williams	498	.313	8	83	248	332	34	46	5.9	.945	McGinnity	25	199	13	10	0	3.44
W-50 L-88	SS	B. Gilbert	445	.245	2	38	349	410	**78**	**72**	6.5	.907	S. Wiltse	19	164	7	11	0	5.10
	3B	R. Bresnahan	235	.272	4	34	33	55	12	4	3.3	.880	C. Shields	23	142	4	11	1	4.24
John McGraw	RF	C. Seymour	280	.268	3	41	121	9	6	2	1.9	.956	J. Katoll	15	123	5	10	0	4.02
W-26 L-31	CF	McFarland	242	.322	3	36	152	12	6	1	2.8	.965	I. Butler	16	116	1	10	0	5.34
	LF	K. Selbach	503	.320	3	60	286	17	19	3	2.5	.941	L. Hughes	13	108	7	6	0	3.90
Wilbert Robinson	C	W. Robinson	335	.293	1	57	262	75	18	4	4.1	.949							
W-24 L-57	UT	H. Howell	347	.268	2	42	152	208	26	10		.933							
	OF	H. Arndt	248	.254	2	28	106	10	17	1	2.1	.872							
	OF	J. Kelley	222	.311	1	34	101	7	3	2	2.3	.973							
	1B	T. Jones	159	.283	0	14	341	22	17	23	10.3	.955							
	UT	B. Smith	145	.234	0	21	135	34	7	5		.960							
	UT	S. Wiltse	132	.295	2	24	160	44	10	8		.953							

BATTING AND BASE RUNNING LEADERS

Batting Average
- E. Delahanty, WAS — .376
- N. Lajoie, CLE, PHI — .366
- P. Hickman, BOS, CLE — .363
- P. Dougherty, BOS — .342
- L. Cross, PHI — .342

Slugging Average
- E. Delahanty, WAS — .590
- N. Lajoie, CLE, PHI — .551
- P. Hickman, BOS, CLE — .541
- B. Bradley, CLE — .515
- S. Seybold, PHI — .506

Home Runs
- S. Seybold, PHI — 16
- P. Hickman, BOS, CLE — 11
- B. Bradley, CLE — 11
- B. Freeman, BOS — 11
- E. Delahanty, WAS — 10

Total Bases
- P. Hickman, BOS, CLE — 289
- B. Bradley, CLE — 283
- B. Freeman, BOS — 283
- E. Delahanty, WAS — 279
- S. Seybold, PHI — 264

Runs Batted In
- B. Freeman, BOS — 121
- P. Hickman, BOS, CLE — 110
- L. Cross, PHI — 108
- S. Seybold, PHI — 97
- E. Delahanty, WAS — 93
- G. Davis, CHI — 93

Stolen Bases
- T. Hartsel, PHI — 47
- S. Mertes, CHI — 46
- D. Fultz, PHI — 44
- B. Gilbert, BAL — 38
- F. Isbell, CHI — 38
- S. Strang, CHI — 38

Hits
- P. Hickman, BOS, CLE — 195
- L. Cross, PHI — 191
- B. Bradley, CLE — 187
- E. Delahanty, WAS — 178

Base on Balls
- T. Hartsel, PHI — 87
- S. Strang, CHI — 76
- J. Barrett, DET — 74
- J. Burkett, STL — 71

Home Run Percentage
- S. Seybold, PHI — 3.1
- B. Clarke, WAS — 2.4
- E. Delahanty, WAS — 2.1
- P. Hickman, BOS, CLE — 2.1

Runs Scored
- D. Fultz, PHI — 109
- T. Hartsel, PHI — 109
- S. Strang, CHI — 108
- B. Bradley, CLE — 104

Doubles
- E. Delahanty, WAS — 43
- H. Davis, PHI — 43
- B. Bradley, CLE — 39
- L. Cross, PHI — 39

Triples
- J. Williams, BAL — 21
- B. Freeman, BOS — 19
- E. Delahanty, WAS — 14
- H. Ferris, BOS — 14

PITCHING LEADERS

Winning Percentage
- B. Bernhard, CLE, PHI — .783
- R. Waddell, PHI — .774
- C. Young, BOS — .744
- R. Donahue, STL — .667
- C. Griffith, CHI — .625

Earned Run Average
- E. Siever, DET — 1.91
- R. Waddell, PHI — 2.05
- B. Bernhard, CLE, PHI — 2.15
- C. Young, BOS — 2.15
- N. Garvin, CHI — 2.21

Wins
- C. Young, BOS — 32
- R. Waddell, PHI — 24
- R. Donahue, STL — 22
- J. Powell, STL — 22
- B. Dinneen, BOS — 21

Saves
- J. Powell, STL — 3

Strikeouts
- R. Waddell, PHI — 210
- C. Young, BOS — 160
- J. Powell, STL — 137
- B. Dinneen, BOS — 136
- E. Plank, PHI — 107

Complete Games
- C. Young, BOS — 41
- B. Dinneen, BOS — 39
- A. Orth, WAS — 36
- J. Powell, STL — 36
- R. Donahue, STL — 33
- C. Patten, WAS — 33

Fewest Hits/9 Innings
- B. Bernhard, CLE, PHI — 7.01
- R. Waddell, PHI — 7.30
- A. Joss, CLE — 7.52
- E. Siever, DET — 7.93

Shutouts
- A. Joss, CLE — 5
- E. Siever, DET — 4
- W. Mercer, DET — 4
- E. Moore, CLE — 4

Fewest Walks/9 Innings
- A. Orth, WAS — 1.11
- C. Young, BOS — 1.24
- B. Bernhard, CLE, PHI — 1.47
- E. Siever, DET — 1.53

Most Strikeouts/9 Inn.
- R. Waddell, PHI — 6.84
- J. Powell, STL — 3.76
- C. Young, BOS — 3.74
- A. Joss, CLE — 3.54

Innings
- C. Young, BOS — 385
- B. Dinneen, BOS — 371
- J. Powell, STL — 328
- A. Orth, WAS — 324

Games Pitched
- C. Young, BOS — 45
- B. Dinneen, BOS — 42
- J. Powell, STL — 42
- A. Orth, WAS — 38

AMERICAN LEAGUE 1902, *cont.*

	W	L	PCT	GB	R	OR	Batting 2B	3B	HR	BA	SA	SB	Fielding E	DP	FA	Pitching CG	BB	SO	ShO	SV	ERA
Philadelphia	83	53	.610		**775**	636	235	67	38	.287	.389	201	270	75	.953	114	368	**455**	5	2	3.29
St. Louis	78	58	.574	5	619	607	208	61	29	.265	.353	137	274	122	.953	120	343	348	8	2	3.34
Boston	77	60	.562	6.5	664	**600**	195	46	42	.278	.383	132	263	101	.955	123	326	431	6	1	**3.02**
Chicago	74	60	.552	8	675	602	170	50	14	.268	.335	265	**257**	125	**.955**	116	331	346	11	0	3.41
Cleveland	69	67	.507	14	686	667	248	68	33	**.289**	.389	140	287	96	.950	116	411	361	**16**	**3**	3.28
Washington	61	75	.449	22	707	790	261	66	**48**	.283	**.396**	121	316	70	.945	**130**	312	300	2	1	4.36
Detroit	52	83	.385	30.5	566	657	141	55	22	.251	.320	130	332	111	.943	116	370	245	9	**3**	3.56
Baltimore	50	88	.362	34	715	848	202	**107**	33	.277	.385	189	357	109	.938	119	354	258	3	1	4.33
					5407	5407	1660	569	259	.275	.369	1315	2356	809	.949	954	2815	2744	60	13	3.57

NATIONAL LEAGUE 1903

	POS	Player	AB	BA	HR	RBI	PO	A	E	DP	TC/G	FA	Pitcher	G	IP	W	L	SV	ERA
Pittsburgh W-91 L-49 Fred Clarke	1B	Bransfield	505	.265	2	57	1347	88	28	**82**	11.5	.981	D. Phillippe	36	289	24	7	2	2.43
	2B	C. Ritchey	506	.287	0	59	281	**460**	30	45	5.6	**.961**	S. Leever	36	284	25	7	1	**2.06**
	SS	H. Wagner	512	**.355**	5	101	303	397	50	51	6.8	.933	E. Doheny	27	223	16	8	2	3.19
	3B	T. Leach	507	.298	7	87	178	292	65	16	**4.2**	.879	B. Kennedy	18	125	9	6	0	3.45
	RF	J. Sebring	506	.277	4	64	208	20	18	11	2.0	.927							
	CF	G. Beaumont	613	.341	7	68	258	15	15	2	2.0	.948							
	LF	F. Clarke	427	.351	5	70	168	10	7	3	1.8	.962							
	C	E. Phelps	273	.282	2	31	315	81	8	7	5.3	.980							
	UT	O. Krueger	256	.246	1	28	109	113	20	17		.917							
	C	H. Smith	212	.175	0	19	259	75	9	2	5.7	.974							
New York W-84 L-55 John McGraw	1B	D. McGann	482	.270	3	50	1188	64	15	58	9.8	**.988**	McGinnity	**55**	**434**	31	20	2	2.43
	2B	B. Gilbert	413	.252	1	40	314	366	47	42	5.7	.935	C. Mathewson	45	366	30	13	2	2.26
	SS	C. Babb	424	.248	0	46	238	343	56	35	5.6	.912	D. Taylor	33	245	13	13	0	4.23
	3B	B. Lauder	395	.281	0	53	140	194	34	10	3.4	.908	J. Cronin	20	116	6	4	1	3.81
	RF	G. Browne	591	.313	3	45	212	13	20	4	1.7	.918	R. Miller	15	85	2	5	3	4.13
	CF	R. Bresnahan	406	.350	4	55	150	14	6	6	2.0	.965							
	LF	S. Mertes	517	.280	7	104	265	24	8	5	2.2	**.973**							
	C	J. Warner	285	.284	0	34	450	123	8	9	**6.8**	**.986**							
	OF	Van Haltren	280	.257	0	28	136	3	6	1	1.9	.959							
	UT	J. Dunn	257	.241	0	37	101	173	26	24		.913							
	C	F. Bowerman	210	.276	1	31	316	66	9	9	7.1	.977							
	P	McGinnity	165	.206	0	11	31	94	**16**	3	2.6	.887							
	P	C. Mathewson	124	.226	1	20	18	93	3	0	2.5	.974							
Chicago W-82 L-56 Frank Selee	1B	F. Chance	441	.327	2	81	1204	68	**36**	49	10.8	.972	J. Taylor	37	312	21	14	1	2.45
	2B	J. Evers	464	.293	0	52	245	306	37	39	5.3	.937	J. Weimer	35	282	21	9	0	2.30
	SS	J. Tinker	460	.291	2	70	229	362	61	37	6.1	.906	B. Wicker	32	245	19	10	1	3.02
	3B	D. Casey	435	.290	1	40	143	190	31	5	3.3	.915	C. Lundgren	27	193	10	9	3	2.94
	RF	D. Harley	386	.231	0	33	162	18	15	2	1.9	.923	J. Menefee	20	147	8	8	0	3.00
	CF	D. Jones	497	.282	1	62	249	14	8	3	2.1	.970							
	LF	J. Slagle	543	.298	0	44	292	16	21	8	2.4	.936							
	C	J. Kling	491	.297	3	68	**565**	189	24	13	5.9	.969							
Cincinnati W-74 L-65 Joe Kelley	1B	J. Beckley	459	.327	2	81	1127	78	30	56	10.4	.976	N. Hahn	34	296	22	12	0	2.52
	2B	T. Daly	307	.293	1	38	151	221	25	22	5.0	.937	B. Ewing	29	247	14	13	1	2.77
	SS	T. Corcoran	459	.246	2	73	263	367	38	42	5.8	.943	J. Sutthoff	30	225	16	10	0	2.80
	3B	Steinfeldt	439	.312	6	83	159	212	25	11	3.8	.937	E. Poole	25	184	8	13	0	3.28
	RF	C. Dolan	385	.288	0	58	107	11	8	2	1.4	.937	J. Harper	17	135	6	8	0	4.33
	CF	C. Seymour	558	.342	7	72	**318**	14	**36**	2	**2.7**	.902	B. Phillips	16	118	8	6	0	3.35
	LF	M. Donlin	496	.351	7	67	209	15	25	4	2.1	.900							
	C	H. Peitz	358	.260	0	42	365	93	14	7	6.1	.970							
	UT	J. Kelley	383	.316	3	45	239	86	22	11		.937							
	C	B. Bergen	207	.227	0	19	251	85	7	3	5.9	.980							
Brooklyn W-70 L-66 Ned Hanlon	1B	J. Doyle	524	.313	0	91	**1418**	83	29	74	11.0	.981	O. Jones	38	324	20	16	0	2.94
	2B	T. Flood	309	.249	0	32	195	216	34	37	5.3	.924	H. Schmidt	40	301	21	13	2	3.83
	SS	B. Dahlen	474	.262	1	64	296	**477**	42	48	5.9	**.948**	N. Garvin	38	298	15	18	2	3.08
	3B	S. Strang	508	.272	0	38	147	245	37	13	3.5	.914	R. Evans	15	110	4	8	0	3.27
	RF	McCreedie	213	.324	0	20	68	6	6	3	1.4	.925	B. Reidy	15	104	7	6	0	3.46
	CF	J. Dobbs	414	.237	2	59	241	11	9	4	2.4	.966							
	LF	J. Sheckard	515	.332	**9**	75	314	**36**	18	7	2.6	.951							
	C	L. Ritter	259	.236	0	37	309	80	**25**	6	5.6	.940							
	2B	D. Jordan	267	.236	0	21	101	132	18	12	4.6	.928							
	C	Jacklitsch	176	.267	1	21	201	71	7	7	5.3	.975							
	OF	D. Gessler	154	.247	0	18	56	4	1	1	1.4	.984							
	OF	T. McCreery	141	.262	0	10	54	4	7	2	1.7	.892							

NATIONAL LEAGUE 1903, *cont.*

	POS	Player	AB	BA	HR	RBI	PO	A	E	DP	TC/G	FA	Pitcher	G	IP	W	L	SV	ERA
Boston W-58 L-80 Al Buckenberger	1B	F. Tenney	447	.313	3	41	1145	93	33	60	10.4	.974	T. Pittinger	44	352	19	23	0	3.48
	2B	Abbaticchio	489	.227	1	46	316	325	45	35	5.9	.934	V. Willis	33	278	12	18	0	2.98
	SS	H. Aubrey	325	.212	0	27	185	301	74	20	6.0	.868	J. Malarkey	32	253	11	16	0	3.09
	3B	Gremminger	511	.264	5	56	217	300	36	20	4.0	.935	W. Piatt	25	181	8	13	0	3.18
	RF	P. Carney	392	.240	1	49	112	10	6	4	1.4	.953							
	CF	C. Dexter	457	.223	3	34	177	13	12	6	1.9	.941							
	LF	D. Cooley	553	.289	1	70	246	11	13	4	2.1	.952							
	C	P. Moran	389	.262	7	54	400	214	24	17	6.0	.962							
	OF	J. Stanley	308	.250	1	47	117	21	15	2	2.0	.902							
	2S	F. Bonner	173	.220	1	10	104	116	15	19		.936							
Philadelphia W-49 L-86 Chief Zimmer	1B	K. Douglass	377	.255	1	36	902	51	15	41	10.0	.985	B. Duggleby	36	264	13	18	1	3.75
	2B	K. Gleason	412	.284	1	49	236	280	22	30	5.3	.959	C. Fraser	31	250	12	17	1	4.50
	SS	R. Hulswitt	519	.247	1	58	354	430	81	43	6.3	.906	T. Sparks	28	248	11	15	0	2.72
	3B	H. Wolverton	494	.308	0	53	182	247	27	8	3.7	.941	F. Mitchell	28	227	11	15	0	4.48
	RF	B. Keister	400	.320	3	63	133	22	10	1	1.7	.939	McFetridge	14	103	1	11	0	4.91
	CF	R. Thomas	477	.327	1	27	318	19	13	3	2.7	.963							
	LF	S. Barry	550	.276	1	60	211	14	7	2	2.2	.970							
	C	F. Roth	220	.273	0	22	235	82	22	9	5.7	.935							
	OF	J. Titus	280	.286	2	34	126	13	7	2	2.0	.952							
	UT	B. Hallman	198	.212	0	17	148	101	16	6		.940							
	C	R. Dooin	188	.218	0	14	186	82	17	1	5.6	.940							
St. Louis W-43 L-94 Patsy Donovan	1B	J. Hackett	351	.228	0	36	947	40	28	63	11.4	.972	McFarland	28	229	9	18	0	3.07
	2B	J. Farrell	519	.272	1	32	281	394	53	52	6.2	.927	T. Brown	26	201	9	13	0	2.60
	SS	D. Brain	464	.231	1	60	163	244	41	34	6.2	.908	C. Currie	22	148	4	12	1	4.01
	3B	J. Burke	431	.285	0	42	139	199	33	14	4.0	.911	B. Rhoads	17	129	5	8	0	4.60
	RF	P. Donovan	410	.327	0	39	142	16	8	5	1.6	.952	M. O'Neill	19	115	4	13	0	4.77
	CF	H. Smoot	500	.296	4	49	231	14	15	3	2.0	.942	E. Murphy	15	106	4	8	0	3.31
	LF	G. Barclay	419	.248	0	42	187	13	22	0	2.1	.901	J. Dunleavy	14	102	6	8	0	4.06
	C	J. O'Neill	246	.236	0	27	348	135	14	8	6.7	.972							
	C	J. Ryan	227	.238	1	10	168	65	7	4	5.1	.971							
	OF	J. Dunleavy	193	.249	0	10	58	11	2	5	1.9	.972							
	SS	O. Williams	187	.203	0	9	94	161	33	16	5.5	.885							

BATTING AND BASE RUNNING LEADERS

Batting Average
H. Wagner, PIT	.355
F. Clarke, PIT	.351
M. Donlin, CIN	.351
R. Bresnahan, NY	.350
C. Seymour, CIN	.342

Slugging Average
F. Clarke, PIT	.532
H. Wagner, PIT	.518
M. Donlin, CIN	.516
R. Bresnahan, NY	.493
Steinfeldt, CIN	.481

Home Runs
J. Sheckard, BKN	9

Total Bases
G. Beaumont, PIT	272
C. Seymour, CIN	267
H. Wagner, PIT	265
M. Donlin, CIN	256
J. Sheckard, BKN	245

Runs Batted In
S. Mertes, NY	104
H. Wagner, PIT	101
J. Doyle, BKN	91
T. Leach, PIT	87
Steinfeldt, CIN	83

Stolen Bases
F. Chance, CHI	67
J. Sheckard, BKN	67
S. Strang, BKN	46
H. Wagner, PIT	46
S. Mertes, NY	45

Hits
G. Beaumont, PIT	209
C. Seymour, CIN	191
G. Browne, NY	185
H. Wagner, PIT	182

Base on Balls
R. Thomas, PHI	107
B. Dahlen, BKN	82
J. Slagle, CHI	81
F. Chance, CHI	78

Home Run Percentage
P. Moran, BOS	1.8
J. Sheckard, BKN	1.7
M. Donlin, CIN	1.4
T. Leach, PIT	1.4

Runs Scored
G. Beaumont, PIT	137
M. Donlin, CIN	110
G. Browne, NY	105
J. Slagle, CHI	104

Doubles
F. Clarke, PIT	32
Steinfeldt, CIN	32
S. Mertes, NY	32
R. Bresnahan, NY	30

Triples
H. Wagner, PIT	19
M. Donlin, CIN	18
T. Leach, PIT	17
F. Clarke, PIT	15

PITCHING LEADERS

Winning Percentage
S. Leever, PIT	.781
D. Phillippe, PIT	.774
J. Weimer, CHI	.700
C. Mathewson, NY	.698
E. Doheny, PIT	.667

Earned Run Average
S. Leever, PIT	2.06
C. Mathewson, NY	2.26
J. Weimer, CHI	2.30
McGinnity, NY	2.43
D. Phillippe, PIT	2.43

Wins
McGinnity, NY	31
C. Mathewson, NY	30
S. Leever, PIT	25
D. Phillippe, PIT	24
N. Hahn, CIN	22

Saves
C. Lundgren, CHI	3
R. Miller, NY	3

Strikeouts
C. Mathewson, NY	267
McGinnity, NY	171
N. Garvin, BKN	154
T. Pittinger, BOS	140
J. Weimer, CHI	128

Complete Games
McGinnity, NY	44
C. Mathewson, NY	37
T. Pittinger, BOS	35
N. Hahn, CIN	34
J. Taylor, CHI	33

Fewest Hits/9 Innings
J. Weimer, CHI	7.69
C. Mathewson, NY	7.89
J. Taylor, CHI	7.98
S. Leever, PIT	8.07

Shutouts
S. Leever, PIT	7
N. Hahn, CIN	5
H. Schmidt, BKN	5
D. Phillippe, PIT	4

Fewest Walks/9 Innings
D. Phillippe, PIT	0.90
B. Reidy, BKN	1.21
N. Hahn, CIN	1.43
J. Taylor, CHI	1.64

Most Strikeouts/9 Inn.
C. Mathewson, NY	6.56
W. Piatt, BOS	4.97
N. Garvin, BKN	4.65
J. Weimer, CHI	4.09

Innings
McGinnity, NY	434
C. Mathewson, NY	366
T. Pittinger, BOS	352
O. Jones, BKN	324

Games Pitched
McGinnity, NY	55
C. Mathewson, NY	45
T. Pittinger, BOS	44
H. Schmidt, BKN	40

NATIONAL LEAGUE 1903, cont.

	W	L	PCT	GB	R	OR	Batting					SB	Fielding			Pitching					ERA
							2B	3B	HR	BA	SA		E	DP	FA	CG	BB	SO	ShO	SV	
Pittsburgh	91	49	.650		**793**	613	208	110	34	.287	**.393**	172	295	100	.951	117	384	454	16	5	2.91
New York	84	55	.604	6.5	729	**567**	181	49	20	.272	.344	264	287	87	**.951**	115	371	628	8	8	2.95
Chicago	82	56	.594	8	695	599	191	62	9	.275	.347	259	338	78	.942	117	**354**	451	6	6	**2.77**
Cincinnati	74	65	.532	16.5	765	656	**228**	92	28	.288	.390	144	312	84	.946	126	378	480	11	1	3.07
Brooklyn	70	66	.515	19	667	682	177	56	15	.265	.339	273	284	98	.951	118	377	438	11	4	3.44
Boston	58	80	.420	32	578	699	176	47	25	.245	.318	159	361	89	.937	125	460	516	5	0	3.34
Philadelphia	49	86	.363	39.5	617	738	186	62	12	.268	.341	120	300	76	.947	126	425	381	5	2	3.97
St. Louis	43	94	.314	46.5	505	795	138	65	8	.251	.313	171	354	**111**	.940	111	430	419	4	2	3.76
					5349	5349	1485	543	151	.269	.349	1562	2531	723	.946	955	3179	3767	66	28	3.27

AMERICAN LEAGUE 1903

	POS	Player	AB	BA	HR	RBI	PO	A	E	DP	TC/G	FA	Pitcher	G	IP	W	L	SV	ERA
Boston W-91 L-47 Jimmy Collins	1B	C. LaChance	522	.257	1	53	**1471**	57	25	68	11.0	.984	C. Young	40	342	**28**	9	2	2.08
	2B	H. Ferris	525	.251	9	66	313	434	39	50	5.7	.950	B. Dinneen	37	299	21	13	2	2.26
	SS	F. Parent	560	.304	4	80	296	456	57	36	5.8	.930	L. Hughes	33	245	20	7	0	2.57
	3B	J. Collins	540	.296	5	72	178	260	22	19	3.5	**.952**	N. Gibson	24	183	13	9	0	3.19
	RF	B. Freeman	567	.287	**13**	104	195	13	15	2	1.6	.933	G. Winter	24	178	9	8	0	3.08
	CF	C. Stahl	299	.274	2	44	135	11	6	2	2.1	.961							
	LF	P. Dougherty	**590**	.331	4	59	259	16	14	3	2.1	.952							
	C	L. Criger	317	.192	3	31	491	**156**	14	10	6.9	.979							
	OF	J. O'Brien	338	.210	3	38	128	9	6	2	2.0	.958							
Philadelphia W-75 L-60 Connie Mack	1B	H. Davis	420	.298	5	55	942	63	29	38	9.9	.972	E. Plank	**43**	336	23	16	0	2.38
	2B	D. Murphy	513	.273	1	60	241	349	32	34	4.7	.949	R. Waddell	39	324	21	16	0	2.44
	SS	M. Cross	470	.247	3	45	**305**	396	45	36	5.4	.940	C. Bender	36	270	17	15	0	3.07
	3B	L. Cross	559	.292	2	90	152	228	20	14	2.9	.950	W. Henley	29	186	12	9	0	3.91
	RF	S. Seybold	522	.299	8	84	177	9	7	4	1.6	.964							
	CF	O. Pickering	512	.281	1	36	272	17	9	5	2.2	.970							
	LF	T. Hartsel	373	.311	5	26	144	6	5	0	1.6	.968							
	C	Schreckengost	306	.255	3	30	**514**	106	16	4	**8.3**	.975							
	OF	D. Hoffman	248	.246	2	22	111	4	6	0	2.0	.950							
	C	M. Powers	247	.227	0	23	349	86	8	3	6.7	.982							
Cleveland W-77 L-63 Bill Armour	1B	P. Hickman	518	.330	12	97	1310	66	40	67	11.3	.972	A. Joss	32	293	18	13	0	2.15
	2B	N. Lajoie	488	**.355**	7	93	366	402	36	**61**	6.5	.955	E. Moore	29	239	19	9	1	**1.77**
	SS	J. Gochnaur	438	.185	0	48	236	414	98	45	5.6	.869	B. Bernhard	20	166	14	6	0	2.12
	3B	B. Bradley	543	.315	6	68	151	**299**	37	18	3.6	.924	R. Donahue	16	137	7	9	0	2.44
	RF	E. Flick	529	.299	2	51	219	15	11	3	1.8	.955	C. Wright	15	102	3	9	0	5.75
	CF	H. Bay	579	.292	1	35	293	13	16	3	2.3	.950							
	LF	J. McCarthy	415	.265	0	43	178	10	7	5	1.8	.964							
	C	H. Bemis	314	.261	1	41	315	82	5	6	5.4	**.988**							
	C	F. Abbott	255	.235	1	25	337	97	19	9	6.4	.958							
New York W-72 L-62 Clark Griffith	1B	J. Ganzel	476	.277	3	71	1385	94	18	68	**11.6**	**.988**	J. Chesbro	40	325	21	15	0	2.77
	2B	J. Williams	502	.267	3	82	266	**438**	32	59	5.6	.957	J. Tannehill	32	240	15	15	0	3.27
	SS	K. Elberfeld	349	.287	0	45	221	291	48	40	6.2*	.914	C. Griffith	25	213	14	11	0	2.70
	3B	W. Conroy	503	.272	1	45	164	243	36	11	**3.6**	.919	H. Howell	25	156	9	6	0	3.53
	RF	W. Keeler	515	.318	0	32	177	10	13	4	1.6	.935	B. Wolfe	20	148	6	9	0	2.97
	CF	McFarland	362	.243	5	45	207	9	14	2	2.2	.939							
	LF	L. Davis	372	.237	0	25	176	7	19	1	2.0	.906							
	C	M. Beville	258	.194	0	29	296	66	15	4	5.0	.960							
	OF	D. Fultz	295	.224	0	25	156	11	12	2	2.3	.933							
	C	J. O'Connor	212	.203	0	12	282	56	4	6	5.4	.988							
Detroit W-65 L-71 Ed Barrow	1B	C. Carr	548	.281	2	79	1276	**111**	25	60	10.5	.982	G. Mullin	41	321	19	15	2	2.25
	2B	H. Smith	336	.223	1	22	200	267	36	30	5.4	.928	W. Donovan	35	307	17	16	0	2.29
	SS	McAllister	265	.260	0	22	77	129	26	12	5.0	.888	F. Kitson	31	258	15	16	0	2.58
	3B	J. Yeager	402	.256	0	43	126	176	26	9	3.1	.921	R. Kisinger	16	119	7	9	0	2.96
	RF	S. Crawford	550	.335	4	89	225	16	10	3	1.8	.960							
	CF	J. Barrett	517	.315	2	31	303	**19**	15	7	2.5	.955							
	LF	B. Lush	423	.274	1	33	227	17	8	4	2.5	.968							
	C	D. McGuire	248	.250	0	21	330	73	17	9	6.1	.960							
	S2	H. Long	239	.222	0	23	161	198	32	18		.918							
	C	F. Buelow	192	.214	1	13	254	66	13	6	5.6	.961							
St. Louis W-65 L-74 Jimmy McAleer	1B	J. Anderson	550	.284	2	78	1416	91	22	**71**	11.5	.986	J. Powell	38	306	15	19	2	2.91
	2B	B. Friel	351	.228	0	25	108	171	26	15	4.8	.915	W. Sudhoff	38	294	21	15	0	2.27
	SS	B. Wallace	519	.245	1	54	282	**468**	42	53	6.0	.924	E. Siever	31	254	13	14	0	2.48
	3B	H. Hill	317	.243	0	25	110	165	23	10	3.5	.923	R. Donahue	16	131	8	7	0	2.75
	RF	C. Hemphill	383	.245	3	29	155	17	7	4	1.7	.961							
	CF	E. Heidrick	461	.280	1	42	252	17	13	5	2.4	.954							
	LF	J. Burkett	514	.296	3	40	230	10	15	4	1.9	.941							
	C	M. Kahoe	244	.189	0	23	333	64	12	8	5.8	.971							
	C	J. Sugden	241	.216	0	22	321	81	7	6	6.2	.983							
	32	McCormick	207	.217	1	16	79	131	10	14		.955							
	OF	J. Martin	173	.214	0	7	53	6	1	3	1.6	.983							

AMERICAN LEAGUE 1903, *cont.*

	POS	Player	AB	BA	HR	RBI	PO	A	E	DP	TC/G	FA	Pitcher	G	IP	W	L	SV	ERA
Chicago	1B	F. Isbell	546	.242	2	59	1180	87	20	57	11.0	.984	D. White	37	300	17	16	0	2.13
	2B	G. Magoon	334	.228	0	25	198	253	31	28	5.1	.936	R. Patterson	34	293	15	15	1	2.70
	SS	L. Tannehill	503	.225	2	50	291	457	76	**58**	6.0	.908	P. Flaherty	40	294	11	**25**	1	3.74
W-60 L-77	3B	N. Callahan	439	.292	2	56	113	203	**37**	5	3.5	.895	F. Owen	26	167	8	12	1	3.50
	RF	D. Green	499	.309	6	62	219	16	17	**8**	1.9	.933							
Nixey Callahan	CF	F. Jones	530	.287	0	45	**324**	11	5	3	2.5	**.985**							
	LF	D. Holmes	344	.279	0	18	151	14*	6	0	2.1	.965							
	C	J. Slattery	211	.218	0	20	215	44	7	0	4.8	.974							
	OF	B. Hallman	207	.208	0	18	114	7	6	0	2.2	.953							
	C	McFarland	201	.209	1	19	240	65	10	7	5.6	.968							
	2B	T. Daly	150	.207	0	19	96	103	11	12	4.9	.948							
Washington	1B	B. Clarke	465	.239	2	38	891	44	14	44	10.8	.985	C. Patten	36	300	11	22	1	3.60
	2B	McCormick	219	.215	1	24	130	205	14	27	5.5	.960*	A. Orth	36	280	10	22	2	4.34
	SS	C. Moran	373	.225	1	24	216	300	31	37	5.7	**.943**	H. Wilson	30	242	7	18	0	3.31
W-43 L-94	3B	B. Coughlin	470	.251	1	31	170	224	20	13	3.5	.952	W. Lee	22	167	8	12	0	3.08
	RF	W. Lee	231	.208	0	13	100	6	8	2	2.4	.930	J. Townsend	20	127	2	11	0	4.76
Tom Loftus	CF	J. Ryan	437	.245	7	46	288	7	9	1	2.7	.970	D. Dunkle	14	108	5	9	0	4.24
	LF	K. Selbach	536	.250	3	49	251	10	12	2	2.0	.956							
	C	M. Kittridge	192	.214	0	16	238	76	7	2	5.4	.978							
	UT	R. Robinson	373	.212	1	20	185	248	43	27		.910							
	1B	S. Carey	183	.202	0	23	435	23	11	18	10.0	.977							
	P	A. Orth	162	.302	0	11	17	86	9	0	3.1	.920							
	OF	E. Delahanty	156	.333	1	21	69	6	3	1	2.0	.962							
	C	L. Drill	154	.253	0	23	208	47	9	5	5.6	.966							

BATTING AND BASE RUNNING LEADERS

Batting Average
N. Lajoie, CLE   .355
S. Crawford, DET   .335
P. Dougherty, BOS   .331
P. Hickman, CLE   .330
W. Keeler, NY   .318

Slugging Average
N. Lajoie, CLE   .533
P. Hickman, CLE   .502
B. Freeman, BOS   .496
B. Bradley, CLE   .495
S. Crawford, DET   .489

Home Runs
B. Freeman, BOS   13
P. Hickman, CLE   12
H. Ferris, BOS   9
S. Seybold, PHI   8
J. Ryan, WAS   7
N. Lajoie, CLE   7

Winning Percentage
C. Young, BOS   .757
L. Hughes, BOS   .741
E. Moore, CLE   .679
B. Dinneen, BOS   .636
E. Plank, PHI   .590

Earned Run Average
E. Moore, CLE   1.77
C. Young, BOS   2.08
B. Bernhard, CLE   2.12
D. White, CHI   2.13
A. Joss, CLE   2.15

Wins
C. Young, BOS   28
E. Plank, PHI   23
B. Dinneen, BOS   21
W. Sudhoff, STL   21
J. Chesbro, NY   21
R. Waddell, PHI   21

Total Bases
B. Freeman, BOS   281
B. Bradley, CLE   269
S. Crawford, DET   269
N. Lajoie, CLE   260
P. Hickman, CLE   260

Runs Batted In
B. Freeman, BOS   104
P. Hickman, CLE   97
N. Lajoie, CLE   93
L. Cross, PHI   90
S. Crawford, DET   89

Stolen Bases
H. Bay, CLE   45
O. Pickering, PHI   40
D. Holmes, CHI, WAS   35
P. Dougherty, BOS   35
W. Conroy, NY   33

Saves
C. Young, BOS   2
A. Orth, WAS   2
J. Powell, STL   2
B. Dinneen, BOS   2
G. Mullin, DET   2

Strikeouts
R. Waddell, PHI   302
W. Donovan, DET   187
E. Plank, PHI   176
C. Young, BOS   176
G. Mullin, DET   170

Complete Games
W. Donovan, DET   34
C. Young, BOS   34
R. Waddell, PHI   34
J. Powell, STL   33
J. Chesbro, NY   33
E. Plank, PHI   33

Hits
P. Dougherty, BOS   195
S. Crawford, DET   184
N. Lajoie, CLE   173
H. Bay, CLE   169

Base on Balls
J. Barrett, DET   74
B. Lush, DET   70
O. Pickering, PHI   53
J. Burkett, STL   52

Home Run Percentage
P. Hickman, CLE   2.3
B. Freeman, BOS   2.3
H. Ferris, BOS   1.7
J. Ryan, WAS   1.6

Fewest Hits/9 Innings
E. Moore, CLE   7.13
W. Donovan, DET   7.24
A. Joss, CLE   7.35
R. Waddell, PHI   7.61

Shutouts
C. Young, BOS   7
B. Dinneen, BOS   6
G. Mullin, DET   6
L. Hughes, BOS   5

Fewest Walks/9 Innings
C. Young, BOS   0.97
B. Bernhard, CLE   1.14
R. Donahue, CLE, STL   1.14
J. Tannehill, NY   1.28

Runs Scored
P. Dougherty, BOS   108
B. Bradley, CLE   103
W. Keeler, NY   95
J. Barrett, DET   95

Doubles
S. Seybold, PHI   45
N. Lajoie, CLE   40
B. Freeman, BOS   39
B. Bradley, CLE   36

Triples
S. Crawford, DET   25
B. Bradley, CLE   22
B. Freeman, BOS   20
J. Collins, BOS   17

Most Strikeouts/9 Inn.
R. Waddell, PHI   8.39
W. Donovan, DET   5.48
E. Moore, CLE   5.35
J. Powell, STL   4.97

Innings
C. Young, BOS   342
E. Plank, PHI   336
J. Chesbro, NY   325
R. Waddell, PHI   324

Games Pitched
E. Plank, PHI   43
G. Mullin, DET   41
C. Young, BOS   40
J. Chesbro, NY   40

PITCHING LEADERS

	W	L	PCT	GB	R	OR	Batting						SB	Fielding			Pitching				
							2B	3B	HR	BA	SA			E	DP	FA	CG	BB	SO	ShO	SV	ERA
Boston	91	47	.659		708	504	222	113	48	**.272**	**.392**	141	239	86	**.959**	123	269	579	**20**	4	**2.57**
Philadelphia	75	60	.556	14.5	597	519	228	68	31	.264	.362	157	**217**	66	**.960**	112	315	**728**	10	1	2.97
Cleveland	77	63	.550	15	639	579	**230**	95	31	.270	.378	176	322	**99**	.946	**125**	271	521	**20**	1	2.66
New York	72	62	.537	17	579	573	193	62	19	.250	.331	160	264	82	.953	111	245	463	8	2	3.08
Detroit	65	71	.478	25	567	539	162	91	12	.268	.351	128	281	82	.950	123	336	554	15	2	2.75
St. Louis	65	74	.468	26.5	500	525	166	78	12	.242	.319	101	268	94	.953	124	**237**	511	12	4	2.77
Chicago	60	77	.438	30.5	516	613	176	49	14	.247	.314	**180**	297	86	.949	114	287	391	9	4	3.02
Washington	43	94	.314	47.5	437	691	172	72	18	.231	.311	131	260	86	.954	122	306	452	6	3	3.82
					4543	4543	1549	628	184	.256	.345	1174	2148	685	.953	954	2266	4199	100	21	2.95

NATIONAL LEAGUE 1904

New York
W-106 L-47
John McGraw

POS	Player	AB	BA	HR	RBI	PO	A	E	DP	TC/G	FA	Pitcher	G	IP	W	L	SV	ERA
1B	D. McGann	517	.286	6	71	1481	94	15	62	11.3	.991	McGinnity	51	408	35	8	5	1.61
2B	B. Gilbert	478	.253	1	54	305	466	44	48	5.6	.946	C. Mathewson	48	368	33	12	0	2.03
SS	B. Dahlen	523	.268	2	80	316	494	61	61	6.0	.930	D. Taylor	37	296	21	15	0	2.34
3B	A. Devlin	474	.281	1	66	126	285	42	10	3.5	.907	H. Wiltse	24	165	13	3	3	2.84
RF	G. Browne	596	.284	4	39	201	20	18	7	1.6	.925	R. Ames	16	115	4	6	3	2.27
CF	R. Bresnahan	402	.284	5	33	151	14	8	9	1.9	.954							
LF	S. Mertes	532	.276	4	78	244	17	12	1	1.9	.956							
C	J. Warner	287	.199	1	15	427	115	10	7	6.4	.982							
C	F. Bowerman	289	.232	2	27	413	96	12	11	6.6	.977							
OF	McCormick	203	.266	1	26	95	3	9	2	1.9	.916							
UT	J. Dunn	181	.309	1	19	61	89	15	7		.909							

Chicago
W-93 L-60
Frank Selee

POS	Player	AB	BA	HR	RBI	PO	A	E	DP	TC/G	FA	Pitcher	G	IP	W	L	SV	ERA
1B	F. Chance	451	.310	6	49	1205	106	13	48	10.8	.990	J. Weimer	37	307	20	14	0	1.91
2B	J. Evers	532	.265	0	47	381	518	54	53	6.3	.943	B. Briggs	34	277	19	11	2	2.05
SS	J. Tinker	488	.221	3	41	327	465	64	54	6.1	.925	C. Lundgren	31	242	17	10	1	2.60
3B	D. Casey	548	.268	1	43	157	241	39	11	3.3	.911	B. Wicker	30	229	17	8	1	2.67
RF	D. Jones	336	.244	3	39	128	8	10	0	1.5	.932	T. Brown	26	212	15	10	1	1.86
CF	J. McCarthy	432	.264	0	51	213	8	9	0	2.0	.961	F. Corridon	12	100	5	5	0	3.05
LF	J. Slagle	481	.260	1	31	194	15	18	7	1.9	.921							
C	J. Kling	452	.243	2	46	499	135	17	6	6.3	.974							
UT	S. Barry	263	.262	1	26	270	73	21	16		.942							
UT	O. Williams	185	.200	0	8	161	67	9	3		.962							
C	J. O'Neill	168	.214	1	19	256	62	6	5	6.6	.981							
PO	B. Wicker	155	.219	0	9	48	34	7	1		.921							

Cincinnati
W-88 L-65
Joe Kelley

POS	Player	AB	BA	HR	RBI	PO	A	E	DP	TC/G	FA	Pitcher	G	IP	W	L	SV	ERA
1B	J. Kelley	449	.281	0	63	1049	76	14	48	9.7	.988	N. Hahn	35	298	16	18	0	2.06
2B	M. Huggins	491	.263	2	30	337	448	46	32	5.9	.945	J. Harper	35	285	23	9	0	2.37
SS	T. Corcoran	578	.230	2	74	353	471	56	54	5.9	.936	W. Kellum	31	225	15	10	2	2.60
3B	Steinfeldt	349	.244	1	52	153	168	41	13	3.7	.887	T. Walker	24	217	15	8	0	2.24
RF	C. Dolan	465	.284	6	51	157	13	11	0	1.8	.939	B. Ewing	26	212	11	13	0	2.46
CF	C. Seymour	531	.313	5	58	308	20	17	4	2.7	.951	J. Sutthoff	12	90	5	6	0	2.30
LF	F. Odwell	468	.284	1	58	284	18	14	6	2.5	.956							
C	A. Schlei	291	.237	0	32	384	123	12	5	5.9	.977							
3B	O. Woodruff	306	.190	0	20	75	116	14	4	3.4	.932							
C	H. Peitz	272	.243	1	30	255	89	9	10	5.5	.975							
OF	M. Donlin	236	.356	1	38	87	8	14	1	2.1	.872							
OF	J. Sebring	222	.225	0	24	88	11*	0	3	1.8	1.000							

Pittsburgh
W-87 L-66
Fred Clarke

POS	Player	AB	BA	HR	RBI	PO	A	E	DP	TC/G	FA	Pitcher	G	IP	W	L	SV	ERA
1B	Bransfield	520	.223	0	60	1454	89	30	70	11.3	.981	S. Leever	34	253	18	11	0	2.17
2B	C. Ritchey	544	.263	0	51	330	482	36	48	5.4	.958	P. Flaherty	29	242	19	9	0	2.05
SS	H. Wagner	490	.349	4	75	274	367	49	46	5.7	.929	M. Lynch	27	223	15	11	0	2.71
3B	T. Leach	579	.257	2	56	212	371	60	18	4.4	.907	D. Phillippe	21	167	10	10	1	3.24
RF	J. Sebring	305	.269	0	32	146	16*	7	5	2.1	.959	C. Case	18	141	10	5	0	2.94
CF	G. Beaumont	615	.301	3	54	287	14	10	6	2.0	.968	R. Miller	19	134	7	8	0	3.35
LF	F. Clarke	278	.306	0	25	135	4	3	2	2.0	.979							
C	E. Phelps	302	.242	0	26	360	97	17	8	5.2	.964							
UT	O. Krueger	268	.194	1	26	115	117	23	10		.910							
OF	McCormick	238	.290	2	23	87	7	6	0	1.5	.940							

St. Louis
W-75 L-79
Kid Nichols

POS	Player	AB	BA	HR	RBI	PO	A	E	DP	TC/G	FA	Pitcher	G	IP	W	L	SV	ERA
1B	J. Beckley	551	.325	1	67	1526	64	20	65	11.3	.988	J. Taylor	41	352	21	19	1	2.22
2B	J. Farrell	509	.255	0	20	297	450	53	55	6.2	.934	K. Nichols	36	317	21	13	1	2.02
SS	D. Shay	340	.256	1	18	153	319	46	30	5.3	.911	McFarland	32	269	14	17	0	3.21
3B	J. Burke	406	.227	0	37	148	217	42	10	3.4	.897	M. O'Neill	25	220	10	14	0	2.09
RF	S. Shannon	500	.280	1	26	246	18	6	10	2.0	.978	J. Corbett	14	109	5	9	0	4.39
CF	H. Smoot	520	.281	3	66	270	17	10	6	2.2	.966							
LF	G. Barclay	375	.200	1	28	170	7	10	2	1.8	.947							
C	M. Grady	323	.313	5	43	323	77	19	7	5.4	.955							
UT	D. Brain	488	.266	7	72	259	308	45	26		.926							
OF	J. Dunleavy	172	.233	1	14	68	6	1	2	1.7	.987							

Brooklyn
W-56 L-97
Ned Hanlon

POS	Player	AB	BA	HR	RBI	PO	A	E	DP	TC/G	FA	Pitcher	G	IP	W	L	SV	ERA
1B	P. Dillon	511	.258	0	31	1304	99	25	56	10.7	.982	O. Jones	46	377	17	25	0	2.75
2B	D. Jordan	252	.179	0	19	142	176	14	17	4.7	.958	J. Cronin	40	307	12	23	0	2.70
SS	C. Babb	521	.265	0	53	370	459	65	44	5.9	.927	N. Garvin	23	182	5	15	0	1.68
3B	McCormick	347	.184	0	27	138	190	31	21	3.5	.914	E. Poole	25	178	8	13	1	3.39
RF	H. Lumley	577	.279	9	78	228	26	12	8	1.8	.955	D. Scanlan	13	104	7	6	0	2.16
CF	J. Dobbs	363	.248	0	30	200	6	14	0	2.4	.936							
LF	J. Sheckard	507	.239	1	46	291	16	14	5	2.3	.956							
C	B. Bergen	329	.182	0	12	414	151	24	10	6.3	.959							
OF	D. Gessler	341	.290	2	28	170	15	16	2	2.3	.920							
2B	S. Strang	271	.192	1	9	100	164	26	13	4.6	.910							
C	L. Ritter	214	.248	0	19	249	88	12	7	6.1	.966							

NATIONAL LEAGUE 1904, *cont.*

	POS	Player	AB	BA	HR	RBI	PO	A	E	DP	TC/G	FA	Pitcher	G	IP	W	L	SV	ERA
Boston	1B	F. Tenney	533	.270	1	37	1451	115	23	66	11.0	.986	V. Willis	43	350	18	25	0	2.85
	2B	F. Raymer	419	.210	1	27	272	351	27	38	5.7	.958	T. Pittinger	38	335	15	21	0	2.66
W-55 L-98	SS	Abbaticchio	579	.256	3	54	367	473	78	47	6.0	.915	K. Wilhelm	39	288	14	22	0	3.69
	3B	J. Delahanty	499	.285	3	60	158	223	48	12	3.8	.888	T. Fisher	31	214	6	15	0	4.25
Al Buckenberger	RF	R. Cannell	346	.234	0	18	135	5	16	1	1.7	.897	E. McNichol	17	122	2	12	0	4.28
	CF	P. Geier	580	.243	1	27	243	20	19	11	2.1	.933							
	LF	D. Cooley	467	.272	5	70	201	3	5	4	1.8	.976							
	C	T. Needham	269	.260	4	19	326	140	27	8	6.4	.945							
	C3	P. Moran	398	.226	4	34	373	197	36	16		.941							
	OF	P. Carney	279	.204	0	11	89	12	5	5	1.5	.953							
Philadelphia	1B	J. Doyle	236	.220	1	22	585	52	15	27	10.0	.977	C. Fraser	42	302	14	24	1	3.25
	2B	K. Gleason	587	.274	0	42	379	463	52	44	5.9	.942	B. Duggleby	32	224	12	13	1	3.78
W-52 L-100	SS	R. Hulswitt	406	.244	1	36	273	310	56	42	5.7	.912	T. Sparks	26	201	7	18	0	2.65
	3B	H. Wolverton	398	.266	0	49	143	191	27	15	3.5	.925	J. Sutthoff	19	164	6	13	0	3.68
Hugh Duffy	RF	S. Magee	364	.277	3	57	146	19	14	3	1.9	.922	McPherson	15	128	1	10	0	3.66
	CF	R. Thomas	496	.290	3	29	321	9	4	4	2.5	.974	F. Mitchell	13	109	4	7	0	3.40
	LF	J. Titus	504	.294	4	55	258	21	14	7	2.1	.952	F. Corridon	12	94	6	5	0	2.19
	C	R. Dooin	355	.242	6	36	411	149	37	12	6.2	.938							
	1O	J. Lush	369	.276	2	42	580	31	34	27		.947							
	C	F. Roth	229	.258	1	20	241	76	14	4	4.9	.958							
	S3	S. Donahue	200	.215	0	14	83	106	33	10		.851							
	UT	B. Hall	163	.160	0	17	149	80	31	13		.881							

BATTING AND BASE RUNNING LEADERS

Batting Average
- H. Wagner, PIT .349
- M. Donlin, CIN, NY .329
- J. Beckley, STL .325
- M. Grady, STL .313
- C. Seymour, CIN .313

Slugging Average
- H. Wagner, PIT .520
- M. Grady, STL .474
- M. Donlin, CIN, NY .457
- C. Seymour, CIN .439
- F. Chance, CHI .430

Home Runs
- H. Lumley, BKN 9
- D. Brain, STL 7
- R. Dooin, PHI 6
- F. Chance, CHI 6
- C. Dolan, CIN 6
- D. McGann, NY 6

Winning Percentage
- McGinnity, NY .814
- C. Mathewson, NY .733
- J. Harper, CIN .719
- B. Wicker, CHI .680
- P. Flaherty, PIT .679

Earned Run Average
- McGinnity, NY 1.61
- N. Garvin, BKN 1.68
- T. Brown, CHI 1.86
- J. Weimer, CHI 1.91
- K. Nichols, STL 2.02

Wins
- McGinnity, NY 35
- C. Mathewson, NY 33
- J. Harper, CIN 23
- K. Nichols, STL 21
- D. Taylor, NY 21
- J. Taylor, STL 21

Total Bases
- H. Wagner, PIT 255
- H. Lumley, BKN 247
- C. Seymour, CIN 233
- G. Beaumont, PIT 230
- J. Beckley, STL 222

Runs Batted In
- B. Dahlen, NY 80
- S. Mertes, NY 78
- H. Lumley, BKN 78
- H. Wagner, PIT 75
- T. Corcoran, CIN 74

Stolen Bases
- H. Wagner, PIT 53
- B. Dahlen, NY 47
- S. Mertes, NY 47
- F. Chance, CHI 42
- D. McGann, NY 42

Saves
- McGinnity, NY 5
- R. Ames, NY 3
- H. Wiltse, NY 3
- W. Kellum, CIN 2
- B. Briggs, CHI 2
- B. Milligan, NY 2

Strikeouts
- C. Mathewson, NY 212
- V. Willis, BOS 196
- J. Weimer, CHI 177
- T. Pittinger, BOS 146
- McGinnity, NY 144

Complete Games
- J. Taylor, STL 39
- V. Willis, BOS 39
- O. Jones, BKN 38
- McGinnity, NY 38
- K. Nichols, STL 35
- T. Pittinger, BOS 35

Hits
- G. Beaumont, PIT 185
- J. Beckley, STL 179
- H. Wagner, PIT 171
- G. Browne, NY 169

Base on Balls
- R. Thomas, PHI 102
- M. Huggins, CIN 88
- A. Devlin, NY 62
- H. Wagner, PIT 59

Home Run Percentage
- R. Dooin, PHI 1.7
- H. Lumley, BKN 1.6
- M. Grady, STL 1.5
- D. Brain, STL 1.4

Fewest Hits/9 Innings
- T. Brown, CHI 6.57
- J. Weimer, CHI 6.71
- McGinnity, NY 6.77
- N. Garvin, BKN 6.99

Shutouts
- McGinnity, NY 9
- J. Harper, CIN 6
- P. Flaherty, PIT 5
- D. Taylor, NY 5

Fewest Walks/9 Innings
- N. Hahn, CIN 1.06
- D. Phillippe, PIT 1.40
- K. Nichols, STL 1.42
- W. Kellum, CIN 1.84

Runs Scored
- G. Browne, NY 99
- H. Wagner, PIT 97
- G. Beaumont, PIT 97
- M. Huggins, CIN 96

Doubles
- H. Wagner, PIT 44
- S. Mertes, NY 28
- J. Delahanty, BOS 27
- B. Dahlen, NY 26

Triples
- H. Lumley, BKN 18
- H. Wagner, PIT 14
- J. Kelley, CIN 13
- J. Tinker, CHI 13

Most Strikeouts/9 Inn.
- R. Ames, NY 7.28
- H. Wiltse, NY 5.74
- J. Corbett, STL 5.63
- C. Mathewson, NY 5.19

Innings
- McGinnity, NY 408
- O. Jones, BKN 377
- C. Mathewson, NY 368
- J. Taylor, STL 352

Games Pitched
- McGinnity, NY 51
- C. Mathewson, NY 48
- O. Jones, BKN 46
- V. Willis, BOS 43

PITCHING LEADERS

	W	L	PCT	GB	R	OR	2B	3B	HR	BA	SA	SB	E	DP	FA	CG	BB	SO	ShO	SV	ERA
New York	106	47	.693		744	476	202	65	31	.262	.344	283	294	93	.956	127	349	707	21	14	2.17
Chicago	93	60	.608	13	599	517	157	62	22	.248	.315	227	298	89	.954	139	402	618	18	5	2.30
Cincinnati	88	65	.575	18	695	547	189	92	21	.255	.338	179	301	81	.954	142	343	502	12	2	2.35
Pittsburgh	87	66	.569	19	675	592	164	102	15	.258	.338	178	291	93	.955	133	379	455	15	1	2.89
St. Louis	75	79	.487	31.5	602	595	175	66	24	.253	.327	199	307	83	.952	146	319	529	7	2	2.64
Brooklyn	56	97	.366	50	497	614	159	53	15	.232	.295	205	343	87	.945	135	414	453	12	2	2.70
Boston	55	98	.359	51	491	749	153	50	24	.237	.300	143	348	91	.946	136	500	544	14	0	3.43
Philadelphia	52	100	.342	53.5	571	784	170	54	23	.248	.316	159	403	93	.937	131	425	469	10	2	3.39
					4874	4874	1369	544	175	.249	.322	1573	2585	710	.950	1089	3131	4277	109	28	2.73

AMERICAN LEAGUE 1904

Boston
W-95 L-59 — Jimmy Collins

POS	Player	AB	BA	HR	RBI	PO	A	E	DP	TC/G	FA	Pitcher	G	IP	W	L	SV	ERA
1B	C. LaChance	573	.227	1	47	**1691**	59	14	65	11.2	**.992**	C. Young	43	380	26	16	1	1.97
2B	H. Ferris	563	.213	3	63	**366**	460	33	42	5.5	.962	B. Dinneen	37	336	23	14	0	2.20
SS	F. Parent	591	.291	6	77	327	493	**63**	44	5.7	.929	J. Tannehill	33	282	21	11	0	2.04
3B	J. Collins	631	.266	3	67	191	320	30	15	3.5	.945	N. Gibson	33	273	17	14	0	2.21
RF	B. Freeman	597	.280	7	84	216	14	11	4	1.5	.954	G. Winter	20	136	8	4	0	2.32
CF	C. Stahl	587	.295	3	67	293	6	12	0	2.0	.961							
LF	K. Selbach	376	.258	0	30	190	8	8	2	2.1	.961							
C	L. Criger	299	.211	2	34	502	112	12	7	6.6	.981							
C	D. Farrell	198	.212	0	15	234	62	13	6	5.5	.958							
OF	P. Dougherty	195*	.272	0	4	95	4	8*	3	2.2	.925							

New York
W-92 L-59 — Clark Griffith

POS	Player	AB	BA	HR	RBI	PO	A	E	DP	TC/G	FA	Pitcher	G	IP	W	L	SV	ERA
1B	J. Ganzel	465	.260	6	48	1243	63	16	49	11.2	.988	J. Chesbro	**55**	**455**	41	12	0	1.82
2B	J. Williams	559	.263	2	74	315	**465**	40	52	5.6	.951	J. Powell	47	390	23	19	0	2.44
SS	K. Elberfeld	445	.263	2	46	237	432	48	44	5.9	.933	A. Orth	20	138	11	6	0	2.68
3B	W. Conroy	489	.243	1	52	137	231	22	8	3.5	.944	L. Hughes	19	136	7	11	0	3.70
RF	W. Keeler	543	.343	2	40	186	16	14	7	1.5	.935	C. Griffith	16	100	7	5	0	2.87
CF	D. Fultz	339	.274	2	32	194	8	5	2	2.3	.976							
LF	P. Dougherty	452*	.283	6	22	135	14	12*	1	1.5	.925							
C	D. McGuire	322	.208	0	20	530	120	20	11	6.9	.970							
OF	J. Anderson	558	.278	3	82	186	9	9	1	1.8	.956							
C	R. Kleinow	209	.206	0	16	276	66	12	5	5.7	.966							
P	J. Chesbro	174	.236	1	17	24	**166**	12	7	3.7	.941							

Chicago
W-89 L-65
Nixey Callahan W-23 L-18
Fielder Jones W-66 L-47

POS	Player	AB	BA	HR	RBI	PO	A	E	DP	TC/G	FA	Pitcher	G	IP	W	L	SV	ERA
1B	J. Donahue	367	.248	1	48	1067	85	25	49	**11.7**	.979	F. Owen	37	315	21	15	1	1.94
2B	G. Dundon	373	.228	0	36	186	282	13	25	4.7	**.973**	N. Altrock	38	307	19	14	1	2.96
SS	G. Davis	563	.252	1	69	**347**	**514**	58	62	6.0	.937	D. White	30	228	16	12	0	1.78
3B	L. Tannehill	547	.229	0	61	180	**369**	31	22	**3.8**	.947	F. Smith	26	202	16	9	0	2.09
RF	D. Green	536	.265	2	62	231	13	9	5	1.7	.964	R. Patterson	22	165	9	9	0	2.29
CF	F. Jones	564	.243	3	43	325	15	8	4	2.3	.977	E. Walsh	18	111	6	3	1	2.60
LF	N. Callahan	482	.261	0	54	158	9	4	0	1.6	.977							
C	B. Sullivan	371	.229	1	44	463	**130**	22	10	5.7	.964							
12	F. Isbell	314	.210	1	34	652	128	20	28		.975							
OF	D. Holmes	251	.311	1	19	111	8	3	3	1.9	.975							
C	McFarland	160	.275	0	20	195	39	6	2	4.9	.975							

Cleveland
W-86 L-65 — Bill Armour

POS	Player	AB	BA	HR	RBI	PO	A	E	DP	TC/G	FA	Pitcher	G	IP	W	L	SV	ERA
1B	P. Hickman	337	.288	4	45	391	22	14	17	10.7	.967	B. Bernhard	38	321	23	13	0	2.13
2B	N. Lajoie	554	**.381**	6	102	272	255	21	42	5.8	.962	R. Donahue	35	277	19	14	0	2.40
SS	T. Turner	404	.235	1	45	191	376	36	28	5.4	.940	E. Moore	26	228	12	11	0	2.25
3B	B. Bradley	607	.300	5	83	178	308	23	18	3.3	**.955**	A. Joss	25	192	14	10	0	**1.59**
RF	E. Flick	579	.306	6	56	234	19	12	5	1.8	.955	B. Rhoads	22	175	10	9	0	2.87
CF	H. Bay	506	.261	3	36	281	15	4	6	2.3	**.987**	O. Hess	21	151	8	7	0	1.67
LF	B. Lush	477	.258	1	50	269	11	12	4	2.1	.959							
C	H. Bemis	336	.226	0	25	393	86	21	8	6.3	.958							
1B	G. Stovall	182	.297	1	31	376	22	9	18	10.7	.978							

Philadelphia
W-81 L-70 — Connie Mack

POS	Player	AB	BA	HR	RBI	PO	A	E	DP	TC/G	FA	Pitcher	G	IP	W	L	SV	ERA
1B	H. Davis	404	.309	**10**	62	1011	57	19	33	10.7	.983	R. Waddell	46	383	25	19	0	1.62
2B	D. Murphy	557	.287	7	77	280	455	**46**	35	5.2	.941	E. Plank	43	357	26	16	0	2.14
SS	M. Cross	503	.189	1	38	276	424	47	26	4.9	.937	W. Henley	36	296	15	17	0	2.53
3B	L. Cross	607	.290	1	71	164	247	28	15	2.8	.936	C. Bender	29	204	10	11	0	2.87
RF	S. Seybold	510	.292	3	64	180	12	5	5	1.5	.975							
CF	O. Pickering	455	.226	0	30	217	13	15	2	2.0	.939							
LF	T. Hartsel	534	.253	2	25	216	15	10	2	1.6	.959							
C	Schreckengost	311	.186	1	21	**589**	76	14	5	**8.1**	.979							
OF	D. Hoffman	204	.299	3	17	83	5	6	1	1.8	.936							
C	M. Powers	184	.190	0	11	338	52	14	6	7.2	.965							

St. Louis
W-65 L-87 — Jimmy McAleer

POS	Player	AB	BA	HR	RBI	PO	A	E	DP	TC/G	FA	Pitcher	G	IP	W	L	SV	ERA
1B	T. Jones	625	.243	2	68	1443	92	19	51	11.6	.988	B. Pelty	39	301	15	18	0	2.84
2B	D. Padden	453	.238	0	36	288	373	28	31	5.2	.959	H. Howell	34	300	13	21	0	2.19
SS	B. Wallace	550	.273	2	69	303	482	44	37	6.0	**.947**	F. Glade	35	289	18	15	1	2.27
3B	C. Moran	272	.173	0	14	69	169	16	2	3.1	.937	W. Sudhoff	27	222	8	15	0	3.76
RF	C. Hemphill	438	.256	2	45	177	12	15	5	1.9	.926	E. Siever	29	217	10	15	0	2.65
CF	E. Heidrick	538	.273	1	36	291	22	12	6	**2.5**	.963							
LF	J. Burkett	576	.273	2	27	266	24	18	4	1.9	.942							
C	J. Sugden	347	.262	0	30	370	94	5	11	5.9	**.989**							
OF	P. Hynes	254	.236	0	15	72	1	8	0	1.3	.901							
C	M. Kahoe	236	.212	0	12	307	91	13	3	6.0	.968							
3B	H. Hill	219	.215	0	14	78	79	33*	3	3.4	.826							
UT	H. Gleason	155	.213	0	6	66	108	15	11		.921							

Detroit
W-62 L-90
Ed Barrow W-32 L-46
Bobby Lowe W-30 L-44

POS	Player	AB	BA	HR	RBI	PO	A	E	DP	TC/G	FA	Pitcher	G	IP	W	L	SV	ERA
1B	C. Carr	360	.214	0	40	901	99*	17	46	11.1	.983	G. Mullin	45	382	17	23	0	2.40
2B	B. Lowe	506	.208	0	40	328	402	27	44	5.4	.964	E. Killian	40	332	14	20	1	2.44
SS	C. O'Leary	456	.213	1	16	308	439	54	48	5.9	.933	W. Donovan	34	293	17	16	0	2.46
3B	Gremminger	309	.214	1	28	103	123	12	3	2.9	.950	F. Kitson	26	200	8	13	1	3.07
RF	S. Crawford	571	.250	2	73	230	18	7	**8**	1.7	.973	J. Stovall	22	147	3	13	0	4.42
CF	J. Barrett	624	.268	0	31	**339**	**29**	11	6	2.3	.971							
LF	M. McIntyre	578	.253	2	46	334	16	15	4	2.4	.959							
C	L. Drill	160	.244	0	13	195	51	13*	6*	5.3	.950							
UT	R. Robinson	320	.241	0	37	151	216	22	17		.943							
3B	B. Coughlin	206	.228	0	17	53	104	12	2	3.0	.929							
C	B. Wood	175	.246	1	17	232	69	8	5	6.6	.974							
C1	M. Beville	174	.207	0	13	354	41	16	11		.961							
1B	P. Hickman	144	.243	2	22	396	23	13	18	11.1	.970							

AMERICAN LEAGUE 1904, cont.

	POS	Player	AB	BA	HR	RBI	PO	A	E	DP	TC/G	FA	Pitcher	G	IP	W	L	SV	ERA
Washington	1B	J. Stahl	520	.262	3	50	1202	85	29	52	11.1	.978	C. Patten	45	358	14	23	3	3.07
	2B	McCormick	404	.218	0	39	204	355	37	39	5.3	.938	J. Townsend	36	291	5	26	0	3.58
W-38 L-113	SS	J. Cassidy	581	.241	1	33	249	301	37	38	5.9	.937	B. Jacobson	33	254	6	23	0	3.55
	3B	H. Hill	290	.197	0	17	86	126	25*	4	3.3	.895	B. Wolfe	17	127	6	9	0	3.27
Mal Kittridge	RF	P. Donovan	436	.229	0	19	217	15	9	4	2.0	.963	L. Hughes	16	124	2	13	1	3.47
W-1 L-16	CF	B. O'Neill	365	.244	1	16	141	9	18	1	1.8	.893	D. Dunkle	12	74	2	9	0	4.96
	LF	F. Huelsman	303	.248	2	30	138	7	6	2	1.8	.960							
Patsy Donovan	C	M. Kittridge	265	.242	0	24	346	99	8	4	5.7	.982							
W-37 L-97	C1	B. Clarke	275	.211	0	17	517	86	13	24		.979							
	3B	B. Coughlin	265	.275	0	17	95	121	14	7	3.6	.939							
	SS	C. Moran	243	.222	0	7	114	171	25	17	5.1	.919							
	OF	K. Selbach	178	.275	0	14	103	5	8	1	2.4	.931							

BATTING AND BASE RUNNING LEADERS

Batting Average
N. Lajoie, CLE .381
W. Keeler, NY .343
H. Davis, PHI .309
E. Flick, CLE .306
B. Bradley, CLE .300

Slugging Average
N. Lajoie, CLE .554
H. Davis, PHI .490
D. Murphy, PHI .440
P. Hickman, CLE, DET .437
C. Stahl, BOS .416

Home Runs
H. Davis, PHI 10
D. Murphy, PHI 7
B. Freeman, BOS 7

Total Bases
N. Lajoie, CLE 307
E. Flick, CLE 262
C. Stahl, BOS 247
B. Freeman, BOS 246
P. Dougherty, BOS, NY 245
D. Murphy, PHI 245

Runs Batted In
N. Lajoie, CLE 102
B. Freeman, BOS 84
B. Bradley, CLE 83
J. Anderson, NY 82
D. Murphy, PHI 77
F. Parent, BOS 77

Stolen Bases
E. Flick, CLE 42
H. Bay, CLE 38
E. Heidrick, STL 35
G. Davis, CHI 32
W. Conroy, NY 30

Hits
N. Lajoie, CLE 211
W. Keeler, NY 186
B. Bradley, CLE 182
P. Dougherty, BOS, NY 181

Base on Balls
J. Barrett, DET 79
J. Burkett, STL 78
T. Hartsel, PHI 75
B. Lush, CLE 72

Home Run Percentage
H. Davis, PHI 2.5
J. Ganzel, NY 1.3
D. Murphy, PHI 1.3
P. Hickman, CLE, DET 1.2

Runs Scored
P. Dougherty, BOS, NY 113
E. Flick, CLE 97
B. Bradley, CLE 94
N. Lajoie, CLE 92

Doubles
N. Lajoie, CLE 50
J. Collins, BOS 33

Triples
J. Cassidy, WAS 19
C. Stahl, BOS 19
B. Freeman, BOS 19
D. Murphy, PHI 17

PITCHING LEADERS

Winning Percentage
J. Chesbro, NY .774
J. Tannehill, BOS .656
F. Smith, CHI .640
B. Bernhard, CLE .639
B. Dinneen, BOS .622

Earned Run Average
A. Joss, CLE 1.59
R. Waddell, PHI 1.62
O. Hess, CLE 1.67
J. Chesbro, NY 1.82
F. Owen, CHI 1.94

Wins
J. Chesbro, NY 41
E. Plank, PHI 26
C. Young, BOS 26
R. Waddell, PHI 25

Saves
C. Patten, WAS 3

Strikeouts
R. Waddell, PHI 349
J. Chesbro, NY 239
C. Young, BOS 203
J. Powell, NY 202
E. Plank, PHI 201

Complete Games
J. Chesbro, NY 48
G. Mullin, DET 42
C. Young, BOS 40
R. Waddell, PHI 39
J. Powell, NY 38

Fewest Hits/9 Innings
J. Chesbro, NY 6.69
F. Owen, CHI 6.94
F. Smith, CHI 6.98
N. Gibson, BOS 7.12

Shutouts
C. Young, BOS 10
R. Waddell, PHI 8
D. White, CHI 7
E. Plank, PHI 7

Fewest Walks/9 Innings
C. Young, BOS 0.69
J. Tannehill, BOS 1.05
R. Patterson, CHI 1.31
A. Joss, CLE 1.40

Most Strikeouts/9 Inn.
R. Waddell, PHI 8.20
C. Bender, PHI 6.58
E. Moore, CLE 5.49
E. Plank, PHI 5.07

Innings
J. Chesbro, NY 455
J. Powell, NY 390
R. Waddell, PHI 383
G. Mullin, DET 382

Games Pitched
J. Chesbro, NY 55
J. Powell, NY 47
R. Waddell, PHI 46
G. Mullin, DET 45

	W	L	PCT	GB	R	OR	2B	3B	HR	BA	SA	SB	E	DP	FA	CG	BB	SO	ShO	SV	ERA
									Batting					Fielding				Pitching			
Boston	95	59	.617		608	**466**	194	**105**	26	.247	.340	101	242	83	.962	**148**	**233**	612	21	1	**2.12**
New York	92	59	.609	1.5	598	526	195	91	27	.259	.347	163	275	90	.958	123	311	684	15	1	2.57
Chicago	89	65	.578	6	600	482	193	68	14	.242	.316	**216**	**238**	95	**.964**	134	303	550	**26**	3	2.30
Cleveland	86	65	.570	7.5	647	482	**225**	90	27	**.264**	**.357**	189	255	86	.959	141	285	627	20	0	2.22
Philadelphia	81	70	.536	12.5	557	503	197	77	**31**	.249	.336	137	250	67	.959	137	366	887	**26**	0	2.35
St. Louis	65	87	.428	29	481	604	153	53	10	.239	.293	150	267	78	.960	135	333	577	13	1	2.83
Detroit	62	90	.408	32	505	627	154	70	11	.231	.293	112	273	92	.959	143	433	556	15	2	2.77
Washington	38	113	.252	55.5	437	743	171	57	10	.227	.288	150	314	**97**	.951	137	347	533	8	**4**	3.62
					4433	4433	1482	611	156	.245	.321	1218	2114	688	.959	1098	2611	5026	144	12	2.60

NATIONAL LEAGUE 1905

	POS	Player	AB	BA	HR	RBI	PO	A	E	DP	TC/G	FA	Pitcher	G	IP	W	L	SV	ERA
New York	1B	D. McGann	491	.299	5	75	1350	86	13	59	10.7	.991	C. Mathewson	43	339	**31**	8	2	**1.27**
	2B	B. Gilbert	376	.247	0	24	245	367	34	41	5.6	.947	McGinnity	46	320	21	15	3	2.87
W-105 L-48	SS	B. Dahlen	520	.242	7	81	313	501	45	58	5.8	.948	R. Ames	34	263	22	8	0	2.74
	3B	A. Devlin	525	.246	2	61	156	**299**	33	14	3.2	.932	D. Taylor	32	213	15	9	0	2.66
John McGraw	RF	G. Browne	536	.293	4	43	175	9	17	1	1.6	.915	H. Wiltse	32	197	15	6	3	2.47
	CF	M. Donlin	606	.356	7	80	250	17	19	4	1.9	.934							
	LF	S. Mertes	551	.279	5	108	230	10	10	3	1.7	.960							
	C	R. Bresnahan	331	.302	0	46	492	114	19	15	**7.2**	.970							
	C	F. Bowerman	297	.269	3	41	383	66	8	4	6.3	.982							
	UT	S. Strang	294	.259	3	29	123	144	25	11		.914							

NATIONAL LEAGUE 1905, *cont.*

	POS	Player	AB	BA	HR	RBI	PO	A	E	DP	TC/G	FA	Pitcher	G	IP	W	L	SV	ERA
Pittsburgh	1B	D. Howard	435	.292	2	63	912	48	22	57	10.9	.978	D. Phillippe	38	279	22	13	0	2.19
	2B	C. Ritchey	533	.255	0	52	279	478	31	**59**	5.2	**.961**	S. Leever	33	230	19	6	0	2.70
W-96 L-57	SS	H. Wagner	548	.363	6	101	353	517	60	64	**6.4**	.935	C. Case	31	217	12	10	1	2.57
	3B	D. Brain	307	.257	3	46	82	170	21	13	3.5	.923	M. Lynch	33	206	17	8	2	3.80
Fred Clarke	RF	O. Clymer	365	.296	0	23	136	7	2	5	1.6	.986	P. Flaherty	27	188	9	10	1	3.49
	CF	G. Beaumont	384	.328	3	40	200	12	6	5	2.2	.972	Robitaille	17	120	8	5	0	2.93
	LF	F. Clarke	525	.299	2	51	270	16	7	4	2.1	.976							
	C	H. Peitz	278	.223	0	27	337	105	16	14	5.3	.965							
	O3	T. Leach	499	.257	2	53	238	134	16	15		.959							
	1B	B. Clancy	227	.229	2	34	551	27	10	30	11.3	.983							
Chicago	1B	F. Chance	392	.316	2	70	1165	75	13	54	10.9	.990	E. Reulbach	34	292	18	13	1	1.42
	2B	J. Evers	340	.276	1	37	249	290	36	38	5.8	.937	J. Weimer	33	250	18	12	1	2.27
W-92 L-61	SS	J. Tinker	547	.247	2	66	345	527	56	**67**	6.2	.940	T. Brown	30	249	18	12	0	2.17
	3B	D. Casey	526	.232	1	56	160	252	22	7	3.1	**.949**	B. Wicker	22	178	13	7	0	2.02
Frank Selee	RF	B. Maloney	558	.260	2	56	251	18	13	4	1.9	.954	C. Lundgren	23	169	13	4	0	2.24
W-37 L-28	CF	J. Slagle	568	.269	0	37	306	**27**	13	6	2.2	.962	B. Briggs	20	168	8	8	0	2.14
	LF	W. Schulte	493	.274	1	47	189	14	4	0	1.7	.981	B. Pfeffer	15	101	4	5	0	2.50
Frank Chance	C	J. Kling	380	.218	1	52	**538**	136	24	12	6.6	.966							
W-55 L-33	2B	S. Hofman	287	.237	1	38	138	178	15	13	5.6	.955							
	C	J. O'Neill	172	.198	0	12	276	63	9	8	7.0	.974							
	OF	J. McCarthy	170	.276	0	14	63	9	1	4	2.0	.986							
Philadelphia	1B	Bransfield	580	.259	3	76	1398	92	23	**75**	10.0	.985	T. Pittinger	**46**	337	23	14	2	3.10
	2B	K. Gleason	608	.247	1	50	**365**	457	46	49	5.6	.947	B. Duggleby	38	289	18	17	0	2.46
W-83 L-69	SS	M. Doolan	492	.254	1	48	299	432	51	45	5.8	.935	T. Sparks	34	260	14	11	1	2.18
	3B	E. Courtney	601	.275	2	77	**229**	249	40	13	3.3	.923	F. Corridon	35	212	10	13	1	3.48
Hugh Duffy	RF	J. Titus	548	.308	2	89	255	24	11	4	2.0	.962	K. Nichols	17	139	10	6	0	2.27
	CF	R. Thomas	562	.317	0	31	**373**	27	7	6	**2.8**	.983							
	LF	S. Magee	603	.299	5	98	341	19	14	6	2.4	.963							
	C	R. Dooin	380	.250	0	36	505	152	24	9	6.4	.965							
Cincinnati	1B	S. Barry	494	.324	1	56	1216	61	23	7	10.6	.982	O. Overall	42	318	17	22	0	2.86
	2B	M. Huggins	564	.273	1	38	346	**525**	**51**	55	**6.2**	.945	B. Ewing	40	312	20	11	0	2.51
W-79 L-74	SS	T. Corcoran	605	.248	2	85	344	**531**	44	**67**	6.1	**.952**	C. Chech	39	268	14	15	0	2.89
	3B	Steinfeldt	384	.271	1	39	152	221	33	16	**3.9**	.919	J. Harper	26	179	10	13	0	3.87
Joe Kelley	RF	F. Odwell	468	.241	**9**	65	216	18	8	5	1.9	.967	T. Walker	23	145	9	7	0	3.23
	CF	C. Seymour	581	**.377**	8	**121**	347	25	21	**12**	2.6	.947							
	LF	J. Kelley	321	.277	1	37	137	11	4	0	1.8	.974							
	C	A. Schlei	314	.226	1	36	398	**153**	22	**16**	6.4	.962							
	UT	A. Bridwell	254	.252	0	17	104	118	17	15		.929							
	OF	J. Sebring	217	.286	2	28	63	6	9	2	1.4	.885							
	C	E. Phelps	156	.231	0	18	189	55	13	5	5.8	.949							
St. Louis	1B	J. Beckley	514	.286	1	57	1442	69	28	56	11.5	.982	J. Taylor	37	309	15	21	1	3.44
	2B	H. Arndt	415	.243	2	36	173	254	22	25	5.0	.951	McFarland	31	250	8	18	1	3.82
W-58 L-96	SS	G. McBride	281	.217	2	34	147	273	28	29	5.6	.930	J. Thielman	32	242	15	16	0	3.50
	3B	J. Burke	431	.225	0	30	174	238	34	13	3.7	.924	B. Brown	23	179	8	11	0	2.97
Kid Nichols	RF	J. Dunleavy	435	.241	1	25	177	25	8	7	1.8	.962	W. Egan	23	171	6	15	0	3.58
W-5 L-9	CF	H. Smoot	534	.311	4	58	295	18	8	6	2.3	.975							
	LF	S. Shannon	544	.268	0	41	299	7	5	3	2.2	**.984**							
Jimmy Burke	C	M. Grady	311	.286	4	41	288	79	17	7	5.4	.956							
W-34 L-56	S2	D. Shay	281	.238	0	28	172	230	35	22		.920							
	O2	J. Clarke	167	.257	0	18	74	49	12	3		.911							
Matt Robison	SS	D. Brain	158	.228	1	17	58	74	13	4	5.0	.910							
W-19 L-31																			
Boston	1B	F. Tenney	549	.288	0	28	**1556**	**152**	32	68	**11.8**	.982	I. Young	43	**378**	20	21	0	2.90
	2B	F. Raymer	498	.211	0	31	256	381	34	33	5.0	.949	V. Willis	41	342	11	**29**	0	3.21
W-51 L-103	SS	Abbaticchio	**610**	.279	3	41	**386**	468	75	53	6.1	.919	C. Fraser	39	334	14	21	0	3.29
	3B	H. Wolverton	463	.225	2	55	139	256	28	12	3.5	.934	K. Wilhelm	34	242	4	23	0	4.54
Fred Tenney	RF	C. Dolan	433	.275	3	48	175	19	11	2	1.8	.946							
	CF	R. Cannell	567	.247	0	36	315	14	**23**	6	2.3	.935							
	LF	J. Delahanty	461	.258	5	55	186	16	8	1	1.7	.962							
	C	P. Moran	267	.240	2	22	389	113	7	5	6.5	**.986**							
	C	T. Needham	271	.218	2	17	292	134	23	6	5.8	.949							
	32	Lauterborn	200	.185	0	9	82	127	27	3		.886							
	OF	B. Sharpe	170	.182	0	11	55	11	7	3	1.7	.904							
	P	C. Fraser	156	.224	0	10	36	80	9	1	3.2	.928							
Brooklyn	1B	D. Gessler	431	.290	3	46	1017	79	**33**	54	10.6	.971	H. McIntire	40	309	8	25	1	3.70
	2B	C. Malay	349	.252	1	31	138	216	26	17	5.1	.932	D. Scanlan	33	250	14	12	0	2.92
W-48 L-104	SS	P. Lewis	433	.254	1	33	253	371	66	43	5.8	.904	Stricklett	33	237	9	18	1	3.34
	3B	E. Batch	568	.252	5	49	203	246	**57**	**22**	3.5	.887	M. Eason	27	207	5	21	0	4.30
Ned Hanlon	RF	H. Lumley	505	.293	7	47	177	21	19	4	1.7	.912	O. Jones	29	174	8	15	1	4.66
	CF	J. Dobbs	460	.254	2	36	246	11	17	1	2.2	.938	F. Mitchell	12	96	3	7	0	4.78
	LF	J. Sheckard	480	.292	3	41	266	24	10	6	2.3	.967							
	C	L. Ritter	311	.219	1	28	397	106	**26**	4	6.3	.951							
	C	B. Bergen	247	.190	0	22	371	127	24	8	6.9	.954							
	S1	C. Babb	235	.187	0	17	388	132	24	32		.956							
	OF	B. Hall	203	.236	2	15	101	6	7	2	2.7	.939							
	2B	R. Owens	168	.214	1	20	102	132	18	19	5.9	.929							

NATIONAL LEAGUE 1905, *cont.*

BATTING AND BASE RUNNING LEADERS

Batting Average
C. Seymour, CIN	.377
H. Wagner, PIT	.363
M. Donlin, NY	.356
G. Beaumont, PIT	.328
R. Thomas, PHI	.317

Slugging Average
C. Seymour, CIN	.559
H. Wagner, PIT	.505
M. Donlin, NY	.495
J. Titus, PHI	.436
M. Grady, STL	.434

Home Runs
F. Odwell, CIN	9
C. Seymour, CIN	8
H. Lumley, BKN	7
B. Dahlen, NY	7
M. Donlin, NY	7

Total Bases
C. Seymour, CIN	325
M. Donlin, NY	300
H. Wagner, PIT	277
S. Magee, PHI	253
J. Titus, PHI	239

Runs Batted In
C. Seymour, CIN	121
S. Mertes, NY	108
H. Wagner, PIT	101
S. Magee, PHI	98
J. Titus, PHI	89

Stolen Bases
A. Devlin, NY	59
B. Maloney, CHI	59
H. Wagner, PIT	57
S. Mertes, NY	52
S. Magee, PHI	48

Hits
C. Seymour, CIN	219
M. Donlin, NY	216
H. Wagner, PIT	199
S. Barry, CHI, CIN	182

Base on Balls
M. Huggins, CIN	103
J. Slagle, CHI	97
R. Thomas, PHI	93
F. Chance, CHI	78

Home Run Percentage
F. Odwell, CIN	1.9
H. Lumley, BKN	1.4
C. Seymour, CIN	1.4
B. Dahlen, NY	1.3

Runs Scored
M. Donlin, NY	124
R. Thomas, PHI	118
M. Huggins, CIN	117
H. Wagner, PIT	114

Doubles
C. Seymour, CIN	40
J. Titus, PHI	36
H. Wagner, PIT	32
M. Donlin, NY	31

Triples
C. Seymour, CIN	21
S. Mertes, NY	17
S. Magee, PHI	17
H. Smoot, STL	16

PITCHING LEADERS

Winning Percentage
C. Mathewson, NY	.795
S. Leever, PIT	.760
R. Ames, NY	.733
H. Wiltse, NY	.714
M. Lynch, PIT	.680

Earned Run Average
C. Mathewson, NY	1.27
E. Reulbach, CHI	1.42
B. Wicker, CHI	2.02
B. Briggs, CHI	2.14
T. Brown, CHI	2.17

Wins
C. Mathewson, NY	31
T. Pittinger, PHI	23
R. Ames, NY	22
D. Phillippe, PIT	22
McGinnity, NY	21

Saves
C. Elliott, NY	6
H. Wiltse, NY	3
McGinnity, NY	3
M. Lynch, PIT	2
C. Mathewson, NY	2
T. Pittinger, PHI	2

Strikeouts
C. Mathewson, NY	206
R. Ames, NY	198
O. Overall, CIN	173
B. Ewing, CIN	164
I. Young, BOS	156

Complete Games
I. Young, BOS	41
V. Willis, BOS	36
C. Fraser, BOS	35
J. Taylor, STL	34
C. Mathewson, NY	33

Fewest Hits/9 Innings
E. Reulbach, CHI	6.41
C. Mathewson, NY	6.69
B. Wicker, CHI	7.03
C. Lundgren, CHI	7.03

Shutouts
C. Mathewson, NY	8
I. Young, BOS	7
B. Briggs, CHI	5
E. Reulbach, CHI	5

Fewest Walks/9 Innings
D. Phillippe, PIT	1.55
T. Brown, CHI	1.59
I. Young, BOS	1.69
C. Mathewson, NY	1.70

Most Strikeouts/9 Inn.
R. Ames, NY	6.78
H. Wiltse, NY	5.48
C. Mathewson, NY	5.47
O. Overall, CIN	4.90

Innings
I. Young, BOS	378
V. Willis, BOS	342
C. Mathewson, NY	339
T. Pittinger, PHI	337

Games Pitched
T. Pittinger, PHI	46
McGinnity, NY	46
I. Young, BOS	43
C. Mathewson, NY	43

	W	L	PCT	GB	R	OR	2B	3B	HR	BA	SA	SB	E	DP	FA	CG	BB	SO	ShO	SV	ERA
New York	105	48	.686		778	505	191	88	39	.273	.368	291	258	93	.960	118	364	760	18	14	2.39
Pittsburgh	96	57	.627	9	692	570	190	91	22	.266	.350	202	255	112	.961	113	389	512	12	4	2.86
Chicago	92	61	.601	13	667	442	157	82	12	.245	.314	267	248	99	.962	133	385	627	23	2	2.04
Philadelphia	83	69	.546	21.5	708	602	187	82	16	.260	.336	180	275	99	.957	119	411	516	12	5	2.81
Cincinnati	79	74	.516	26	735	698	160	101	27	.269	.354	181	310	122	.953	119	439	547	10	1	3.01
St. Louis	58	96	.377	47.5	535	734	140	85	20	.248	.321	162	274	83	.957	135	367	411	10	2	3.59
Boston	51	103	.331	54.5	468	731	148	52	17	.234	.293	132	325	89	.951	139	433	533	14	0	3.52
Brooklyn	48	104	.316	56.5	506	807	154	60	29	.246	.317	186	411	101	.936	125	476	556	7	3	3.76
					5089	5089	1327	641	182	.255	.332	1601	2356	798	.954	1001	3264	4462	106	31	2.99

AMERICAN LEAGUE 1905

	POS	Player	AB	BA	HR	RBI	PO	A	E	DP	TC/G	FA	Pitcher	G	IP	W	L	SV	ERA
Philadelphia W-92 L-56 Connie Mack	1B	H. Davis	602	.284	8	83	1621	91	24	43	11.7	.986	E. Plank	41	347	25	12	0	2.26
	2B	D. Murphy	533	.278	6	71	287	387	31	29	4.7	.956	R. Waddell	46	329	26	11	0	1.48
	SS	J. Knight	325	.203	3	29	143	188	39	9	4.6	.895	A. Coakley	35	255	20	7	0	1.84
	3B	L. Cross	583	.266	0	77	161	249	32	6	3.0	.928	C. Bender	35	229	16	10	0	2.83
	RF	S. Seybold	488	.270	6	59	213	13	4	5	1.7	.983	W. Henley	25	184	4	12	0	2.60
	CF	D. Hoffman	454	.262	1	35	214	12	14	4	2.0	.942							
	LF	T. Hartsel	533	.276	0	28	253	6	17	1	1.9	.938							
	C	Schreckengost	416	.272	0	45	790	114	15	11	8.2	.984							
	SS	M. Cross	248	.270	0	24	159	195	27	22	5.0	.929							
	OF	B. Lord	238	.239	0	13	94	9	4	3	1.8	.963							
Chicago W-92 L-60 Fielder Jones	1B	J. Donahue	533	.287	1	76	1645	114	21	77	11.9	.988	F. Owen	42	334	21	13	0	2.10
	2B	G. Dundon	364	.192	0	22	218	321	12	23	5.3	.978	N. Altrock	38	316	22	12	0	1.88
	SS	G. Davis	550	.278	1	55	330	501	46	56	5.6	.948	F. Smith	39	292	19	13	0	2.13
	3B	L. Tannehill	480	.200	0	39	168	358	39	17	4.0	.931	D. White	36	260	18	14	0	1.76
	RF	D. Green	379	.243	0	44	119	9	12	3	1.3	.914	E. Walsh	22	137	8	3	0	2.17
	CF	F. Jones	568	.245	2	38	337	21	11	5	2.4	.970							
	LF	D. Holmes	328	.201	0	22	150	11	11	1	1.9	.936							
	C	B. Sullivan	323	.201	2	26	389	104	13	8	5.4	.974							
	OF	N. Callahan	345	.272	1	43	120	10	6	0	1.5	.956							
	UT	F. Isbell	341	.296	2	45	219	136	13	18		.965							
	C	McFarland	250	.280	0	31	343	88	12	8	6.3	.973							

AMERICAN LEAGUE 1905, cont.

	POS	Player	AB	BA	HR	RBI	PO	A	E	DP	TC/G	FA	Pitcher	G	IP	W	L	SV	ERA
Detroit	1B	P. Lindsay	329	.267	0	31	761	57	18	40	9.5	.978	G. Mullin	44	348	21	21	0	2.51
	2B	G. Schaefer	554	.244	2	47	403	389	37	35	5.5	.955	E. Killian	39	313	23	14	0	2.27
W-79 L-74	SS	C. O'Leary	512	.213	1	33	358	411	55	40	5.6	.933	W. Donovan	34	281	18	15	0	2.60
	3B	B. Coughlin	489	.252	0	44	137	255	37	12	3.1	.914	F. Kitson	33	226	12	14	1	3.47
Bill Armour	RF	S. Crawford	575	.297	6	75	152	18	2	3	1.7	.988							
	CF	D. Cooley	377	.247	1	32	223	12	10	5	2.5	.959							
	LF	M. McIntyre	495	.263	0	30	286	18	10	6	2.4	.968							
	C	L. Drill	211	.261	0	24	345	73	13	10	6.2	.970							
	OF	P. Hickman	213	.221	2	20	72	7	5	3	1.8	.940							
	UT	B. Lowe	181	.193	0	9	93	54	4	1		.974							
Boston	1B	M. Grimshaw	285	.239	4	35	768	35	16	35	11.1	.980	C. Young	38	321	18	19	0	1.82
	2B	H. Ferris	523	.220	6	59	320	424	30	38	5.5	.961	J. Tannehill	37	272	22	9	0	2.48
W-78 L-74	SS	F. Parent	602	.234	0	33	294	461	66	48	5.4	.920	G. Winter	35	264	16	16	0	2.96
	3B	J. Collins	508	.276	4	65	164	268	36	12	3.6	.923	B. Dinneen	31	244	12	15	1	3.73
Jimmy Collins	RF	K. Selbach	418	.246	4	47	186	8	15	1	1.8	.928	N. Gibson	23	134	4	7	0	3.69
	CF	C. Stahl	500	.258	0	47	249	11	6	4	2.0	.977							
	LF	J. Burkett	573	.257	4	47	276	11	22	0	2.1	.929							
	C	L. Criger	313	.198	1	36	539	147	20	5	6.5	.972							
	10	B. Freeman	455	.240	3	49	647	25	19	20		.973							
Cleveland	1B	C. Carr	306	.235	1	31	940	50	9	33	11.5	.991	A. Joss	33	286	20	12	0	2.01
	2B	N. Lajoie	249	.329	2	41	148	177	3	25	5.6	.991	E. Moore	31	269	15	15	0	2.64
W-76 L-78	SS	T. Turner	582	.263	4	72	285	430	41	49	4.9	.946	B. Rhoads	28	235	16	9	0	2.83
	3B	B. Bradley	537	.268	0	51	187	312	29	17	3.6	.945	O. Hess	26	214	10	15	0	3.16
Nap Lajoie	RF	E. Flick	496	.306	4	64	177	18	13	3	1.6	.938	B. Bernhard	22	174	7	13	0	3.36
W-37 L-21	CF	H. Bay	550	.298	0	22	303	14	10	4	2.3	.969	R. Donahue	20	138	6	12	0	3.40
	LF	J. Jackson	421	.257	2	31	191	16	11	3	2.1	.950							
Bill Bradley	C	F. Buelow	236	.174	1	18	262	72	13	4	5.9	.963							
W-20 L-21	12	G. Stovall	419	.272	1	47	745	160	30	35		.968							
	C	H. Bemis	226	.292	0	28	256	52	9	4	5.5	.972							
Nap Lajoie	OP	O. Hess	175	.251	2	13	74	67	9	2		.940							
W-19 L-36	2B	N. Kahl	131	.221	0	21	60	94	9	3	5.3	.945							
New York	1B	H. Chase	465	.249	3	49	1171	61	31	63	10.4	.975	A. Orth	40	305	18	16	0	2.86
	2B	J. Williams	470	.228	6	60	335	332	25	51	5.4	.964	J. Chesbro	41	303	19	15	0	2.20
W-71 L-78	SS	K. Elberfeld	390	.262	0	53	244	317	57	35	5.7	.908	B. Hogg	39	205	9	13	1	3.20
	3B	J. Yeager	401	.267	0	42	103	173	23	6	3.3	.923	J. Powell	36	202	8	13	1	3.52
Clark Griffith	RF	W. Keeler	560	.302	4	38	194	17	7	1	1.6	.968	C. Griffith	25	103	9	6	1	1.67
	CF	D. Fultz	422	.232	0	42	252	14	9	2	2.3	.967	A. Puttmann	17	86	2	7	1	4.27
	LF	P. Dougherty	418	.263	3	29	173	11	21	2	1.9	.898							
	C	R. Kleinow	253	.221	1	24	361	82	10	4	5.5	.978							
	UT	W. Conroy	385	.273	2	25	287	142	24	14		.947							
	C	D. McGuire	228	.219	0	33	366	69	11	4	6.3	.975							
	OF	E. Hahn	160	.319	0	11	83	5	4	1	2.1	.957							
Washington	1B	J. Stahl	501	.244	5	66	1593	94	21	51	12.2	.988	C. Patten	42	310	14	21	0	3.14
	2B	P. Hickman	360	.311	2	46	170	281	38*	19	5.8	.922	L. Hughes	39	291	16	20	1	2.35
W-64 L-87	SS	J. Cassidy	576	.215	1	43	308	520	66	50	5.9	.926	J. Townsend	34	263	7	16	0	2.63
	3B	H. Hill	374	.209	1	24	130	206	34	10	3.6	.908	B. Wolfe	38	182	8	14	2	2.57
Jake Stahl	RF	J. Anderson	400	.290	1	38	161	7	7	1	2.0	.960	B. Jacobson	22	144	9	9	0	3.30
	CF	C. Jones	544	.208	2	41	240	24	11	6	1.9	.960							
	LF	F. Huelsman	421	.271	3	62	189	7	15	2	1.7	.929							
	C	M. Heydon	245	.192	1	26	368	125	23	7	6.7	.955							
	32	R. Nill	319	.182	3	31	138	188	28	15		.921							
	OF	P. Knoll	244	.213	0	29	101	8	8	1	1.7	.932							
	C	M. Kittridge	238	.164	0	14	323	113	10	8	5.9	.978							
	2B	J. Mullin	163	.190	0	13	83	97	14	8	5.0	.928							
St. Louis	1B	T. Jones	504	.242	0	48	1502	105	25	52	12.1	.985	H. Howell	38	323	15	22	0	1.98
	2B	Rockenfield	322	.217	0	16	210	255	37	19	5.3	.926	F. Glade	32	275	6	25	0	2.81
W-54 L-99	SS	B. Wallace	587	.271	1	59	385	506	62	40	6.1	.935	B. Pelty	31	259	14	14	0	2.75
	3B	H. Gleason	535	.217	1	57	118	271	38	8	3.0	.911	W. Sudhoff	32	244	10	19	0	2.99
Jimmy McAleer	RF	E. Frisk	429	.261	3	36	117	15	11	2	1.2	.923	J. Buchanan	22	141	5	10	2	3.50
	CF	B. Koehler	536	.237	2	47	227	24	8	11	2.0	.969							
	LF	G. Stone	632	.296	7	52	278	15	14	5	2.0	.954							
	C	J. Sugden	266	.173	0	23	407	112	9	6	7.4	.983							
	OF	I. Van Zandt	322	.233	1	20	69	7	11	0	1.2	.874							

BATTING AND BASE RUNNING LEADERS

Batting Average		Slugging Average		Home Runs		Winning Percentage		Earned Run Average		Wins	
E. Flick, CLE	.306	E. Flick, CLE	.466	H. Davis, PHI	8	A. Coakley, PHI	.741	R. Waddell, PHI	1.48	R. Waddell, PHI	26
W. Keeler, NY	.302	F. Isbell, CHI	.440	G. Stone, STL	7	J. Tannehill, BOS	.710	D. White, CHI	1.76	E. Killian, DET	25
H. Bay, CLE	.298	S. Crawford, DET	.433	S. Seybold, PHI	6	R. Waddell, PHI	.703	C. Young, BOS	1.82	E. Plank, PHI	23
S. Crawford, DET	.297	H. Davis, PHI	.422	H. Ferris, BOS	6	E. Plank, PHI	.676	A. Coakley, PHI	1.84	J. Tannehill, BOS	22
F. Isbell, CHI	.296	G. Stone, STL	.410	D. Murphy, PHI	6	N. Altrock, CHI	.647	N. Altrock, CHI	1.88	N. Altrock, CHI	22
				S. Crawford, DET	6						

PITCHING LEADERS

AMERICAN LEAGUE 1905, *cont.*

BATTING AND BASE RUNNING LEADERS

Total Bases
G. Stone, STL	259
H. Davis, PHI	254
S. Crawford, DET	249
P. Hickman, DET, WAS	232
E. Flick, CLE	229

Runs Batted In
H. Davis, PHI	83
L. Cross, PHI	77
J. Donahue, CHI	76
S. Crawford, DET	75
T. Turner, CLE	72

Stolen Bases
D. Hoffman, PHI	46
D. Fultz, NY	44
J. Stahl, WAS	41
T. Hartsel, PHI	36
H. Bay, CLE	36
H. Davis, PHI	36

Hits
G. Stone, STL	187
S. Crawford, DET	171
H. Davis, PHI	171
W. Keeler, NY	169

Base on Balls
T. Hartsel, PHI	121
F. Jones, CHI	73
K. Selbach, BOS	67
J. Burkett, BOS	67

Home Run Percentage
H. Davis, PHI	1.3
S. Seybold, PHI	1.2
H. Ferris, BOS	1.1
D. Murphy, PHI	1.1

Runs Scored
H. Davis, PHI	92
F. Jones, CHI	91
H. Bay, CLE	90
T. Hartsel, PHI	87

Doubles
H. Davis, PHI	47
S. Crawford, DET	40
S. Seybold, PHI	37
P. Hickman, DET, WAS	37

Triples
E. Flick, CLE	19
H. Ferris, BOS	16
T. Turner, CLE	14
J. Burkett, BOS	13

PITCHING LEADERS

Saves
R. Waddell, PHI	4
C. Griffith, NY	3
C. Bender, PHI	3
B. Wolfe, WAS	2
J. Buchanan, STL	2

Strikeouts
R. Waddell, PHI	287
E. Plank, PHI	210
C. Young, BOS	208
H. Howell, STL	198
F. Smith, CHI	171

Complete Games
E. Plank, PHI	36
H. Howell, STL	35
G. Mullin, DET	35
E. Killian, DET	33
C. Young, BOS	32
F. Owen, CHI	32

Fewest Hits/9 Innings
R. Waddell, PHI	6.33
F. Smith, CHI	6.63
C. Young, BOS	6.96
H. Howell, STL	7.02

Shutouts
E. Killian, DET	8
R. Waddell, PHI	7
J. Tannehill, BOS	6
A. Orth, NY	6

Fewest Walks/9 Innings
C. Young, BOS	0.84
A. Joss, CLE	1.45
F. Owen, CHI	1.51
R. Donahue, CLE	1.63

Most Strikeouts/9 Inn.
R. Waddell, PHI	7.86
C. Young, BOS	5.89
C. Bender, PHI	5.58
H. Howell, STL	5.52

Innings
G. Mullin, DET	348
E. Plank, PHI	347
F. Owen, CHI	334
R. Waddell, PHI	329

Games Pitched
R. Waddell, PHI	46
G. Mullin, DET	44
F. Owen, CHI	42
C. Patten, WAS	42

	W	L	PCT	GB	R	OR	2B	3B	HR	BA	SA	SB	E	DP	FA	CG	BB	SO	ShO	SV	ERA
								Batting						Fielding			Pitching				
Philadelphia	92	56	.622		623	492	256	51	24	.255	.339	189	264	64	.958	117	409	895	20	0	2.19
Chicago	92	60	.605	2	612	451	200	55	11	.237	.304	194	217	95	.968	131	329	613	17	0	1.99
Detroit	79	74	.516	15.5	512	602	190	54	14	.243	.312	129	265	80	.957	124	474	578	17	1	2.83
Boston	78	74	.513	16	579	564	165	69	29	.234	.311	131	294	75	.953	125	262	652	15	1	2.84
Cleveland	76	78	.494	19	567	587	211	72	6	.255	.335	188	229	84	.963	139	334	555	16	0	2.85
New York	71	78	.477	21.5	586	622	163	61	23	.248	.319	200	293	88	.952	88	396	642	19	4	2.93
Washington	64	87	.424	29.5	559	623	193	68	22	.223	.302	169	318	76	.951	118	385	539	11	3	2.87
St. Louis	54	99	.353	40.5	511	608	153	49	16	.232	.289	130	295	78	.955	133	389	633	11	2	2.74
					4549	4549	1531	479	157	.241	.314	1330	2175	640	.957	975	3008	5107	126	11	2.65

NATIONAL LEAGUE 1906

	POS	Player	AB	BA	HR	RBI	PO	A	E	DP	TC/G	FA	Pitcher	G	IP	W	L	SV	ERA
Chicago W-116 L-36 Frank Chance	1B	F. Chance	474	.319	3	71	1376	82	16	71	10.8	.989	T. Brown	36	277	26	6	3	1.04
	2B	J. Evers	533	.255	1	51	344	441	44	51	5.4	.947	J. Pfiester	31	242	20	8	0	1.56
	SS	J. Tinker	523	.233	1	64	288	472	45	55	5.5	.944	E. Reulbach	33	218	19	4	2	1.65
	3B	Steinfeldt	539	.327	3	83	160	253	20	13	2.9	.954	C. Lundgren	27	208	17	6	2	2.21
	RF	W. Schulte	563	.281	7	60	218	18	6	7	1.7	.975	J. Taylor	17	147	12	3	1	1.83
	CF	J. Slagle	498	.239	0	33	276	9	7	5	2.3	.976	O. Overall	18	144	12	3	1	1.88
	LF	J. Sheckard	549	.262	1	45	264	13	4	1	1.9	.986							
	C	J. Kling	343	.312	2	46	520	126	12	7	6.9	.982							
	C	P. Moran	226	.252	0	35	335	78	9	6	6.9	.979							
	UT	S. Hofman	195	.256	2	20	253	52	7	18		.978							
New York W-96 L-56 John McGraw	1B	D. McGann	451	.237	0	37	1391	83	8	61	11.1	.995	McGinnity	45	340	27	12	2	2.25
	2B	B. Gilbert	307	.231	1	27	223	324	35	32	5.9	.940	C. Mathewson	38	267	22	12	1	2.97
	SS	B. Dahlen	471	.240	1	49	287	454	49	36	5.5	.938	H. Wiltse	38	249	16	11	5	2.27
	3B	A. Devlin	498	.299	2	65	171	355	31	22	3.8	.944	D. Taylor	31	213	17	9	0	2.20
	RF	G. Browne	477	.264	0	38	153	17	12	3	1.5	.934	R. Ames	31	203	12	10	1	2.66
	CF	C. Seymour	269	.320	4	42	129	7	3	3	1.9	.978							
	LF	S. Shannon	287	.254	0	25	109	4	5	2	1.6	.958							
	C	R. Bresnahan	405	.281	0	43	407	125	14	6	6.7	.974							
	20	S. Strang	313	.319	4	49	176	175	21	13		.944							
	C	F. Bowerman	285	.228	1	42	300	80	6	8	5.8	.984							
	OF	S. Mertes	253	.237	1	33	119	10	4	0	1.9	.970							
Pittsburgh W-93 L-60 Fred Clarke	1B	J. Nealon	556	.255	3	83	1592	102	23	90	11.1	.987	V. Willis	41	322	22	13	1	1.73
	2B	C. Ritchey	484	.269	1	62	326	439	27	59	5.2	.966	S. Leever	36	260	22	7	0	2.32
	SS	H. Wagner	516	.339	2	71	334	473	51	57	6.3	.941	L. Leifield	37	256	18	13	1	1.87
	3B	T. Sheehan	315	.241	1	34	104	166	15	11	3.2	.947	D. Phillippe	33	219	15	10	0	2.47
	RF	B. Ganley	511	.258	0	31	207	16	8	5	1.7	.965	M. Lynch	18	119	6	5	0	2.42
	CF	G. Beaumont	310	.265	2	32	148	6	9	2	2.1	.945							
	LF	F. Clarke	417	.309	1	39	209	15	6	3	2.1	.974							
	C	G. Gibson	259	.178	0	20	336	97	13	10	5.5	.971							
	30	T. Leach	476	.286	1	39	204	141	20	4		.945							
	OF	D. Meier	273	.256	0	16	73	5	2	2	1.5	.975							
	C	H. Peitz	125	.240	0	20	186	45	5	2	6.2	.979							

NATIONAL LEAGUE 1906, cont.

Philadelphia
W-71 L-82

Hugh Duffy

POS	Player	AB	BA	HR	RBI	PO	A	E	DP	TC/G	FA	Pitcher	G	IP	W	L	SV	ERA
1B	Bransfield	524	.275	1	60	1318	88	29	57	10.3	.980	T. Sparks	42	317	19	16	3	2.16
2B	K. Gleason	494	.227	0	34	215	358	32	39	4.5	.947	J. Lush	37	281	18	15	0	2.37
SS	M. Doolan	535	.230	1	55	395	480	66	51	6.1	.930	B. Duggleby	42	280	13	19	2	2.25
3B	E. Courtney	398	.236	0	42	113	163	23	9	3.1	.923	L. Richie	33	206	9	11	0	2.41
RF	J. Titus	484	.267	1	57	236	23	7	7	1.9	.974	T. Pittinger	20	130	8	10	0	3.40
CF	R. Thomas	493	.254	0	16	340	12	5	5	2.5	.986							
LF	S. Magee	563	.282	6	67	316	18	6	2	2.2	.982							
C	R. Dooin	351	.245	0	32	475	111	32	9	5.8	.948							
PO	J. Lush	212	.264	0	15	59	92	12	3		.926							
32	P. Sentell	192	.229	1	14	70	105	19	4		.902							
C	J. Donovan	166	.199	0	15	222	52	13	4	5.5	.955							

Brooklyn
W-66 L-86

Patsy Donovan

POS	Player	AB	BA	HR	RBI	PO	A	E	DP	TC/G	FA	Pitcher	G	IP	W	L	SV	ERA
1B	T. Jordan	450	.262	12	78	1240	64	30	44	10.6	.978	Stricklett	41	292	14	18	5	2.72
2B	W. Alperman	441	.252	3	46	245	308	35	25	5.7	.940	D. Scanlan	38	288	18	13	1	3.19
SS	P. Lewis	452	.243	0	37	244	393	54	35	5.1	.922	H. McIntire	39	276	13	21	0	2.97
3B	D. Casey	571	.233	0	34	172	272	39	11	3.2	.919	M. Eason	34	227	10	17	0	3.25
RF	H. Lumley	484	.324	9	61	231	13	13	5	2.0	.949	J. Pastorius	29	212	10	14	0	3.61
CF	B. Maloney	566	.221	0	32	355	19	13	6	2.6	.966							
LF	J. McCarthy	322	.304	0	35	158	13	14	1	2.2	.924							
C	B. Bergen	353	.159	0	19	485	149	15	9	6.3	.977							
UT	J. Hummel	286	.199	1	21	310	156	18	25		.963							
C	L. Ritter	226	.208	0	15	211	61	6	4	5.2	.978							
OF	E. Batch	203	.256	0	11	101	5	4	0	2.2	.964							

Cincinnati
W-64 L-87

Ned Hanlon

POS	Player	AB	BA	HR	RBI	PO	A	E	DP	TC/G	FA	Pitcher	G	IP	W	L	SV	ERA
1B	S. Deal	231	.208	0	21	624	46	10	25	10.5	.985	J. Weimer	41	305	20	14	1	2.22
2B	M. Huggins	545	.292	0	26	341	458	44	62	5.8	.948	B. Ewing	33	288	13	14	0	2.38
SS	T. Corcoran	430	.207	1	33	263	379	40	51	5.8	.941	C. Fraser	31	236	10	20	0	2.67
3B	J. Delahanty	379	.280	1	39	136	170	33	4	3.2	.903	B. Wicker	20	150	6	14	0	2.70
RF	F. Jude	308	.208	1	31	95	14	4	1	1.4	.965	C. Hall	14	95	4	6	1	3.32
CF	C. Seymour	307	.257	4	38	202	10	7	3	2.8	.968							
LF	J. Kelley	465	.228	1	53	184	13	7	5	1.7	.966							
C	A. Schlei	388	.245	4	54	455	139	24	8	6.8	.961							
1O	S. Barry	279	.287	1	33	481	32	8	24		.985							
UT	H. Lobert	268	.310	0	19	118	178	20	8		.937							
OF	H. Smoot	220	.259	1	17	109	10	7	0	2.1	.944							
OF	F. Odwell	202	.223	0	21	94	10	4	0	1.9	.963							

St. Louis
W-52 L-98

John McCloskey

POS	Player	AB	BA	HR	RBI	PO	A	E	DP	TC/G	FA	Pitcher	G	IP	W	L	SV	ERA
1B	J. Beckley	320	.247	0	44	928	43	13	38	11.6	.987	B. Brown	32	238	8	16	0	2.64
2B	P. Bennett	595	.262	1	34	295	447	41	43	5.1	.948	E. Karger	25	192	5	16	1	2.72
SS	G. McBride	313	.169	0	13	194	310	30	33	5.9	.944	F. Beebe	20	161	9	9	0	3.02
3B	H. Arndt	256	.270	2	26	108	139	9	15	3.9	.965	J. Taylor	17	155	8	9	0	2.15
RF	A. Burch	335	.266	0	11	155	15	12	6	2.0	.934	C. Druhot	15	130	6	7	0	2.62
CF	H. Smoot	343	.248	0	31	174	8	9	4	2.2	.953	G. Thompson	17	103	2	11	0	4.28
LF	S. Shannon	302	.258	0	25	165	9	5	3	2.2	.972	W. Egan	16	86	2	9	0	4.59
C	M. Grady	280	.250	3	27	115	67	5	9	3.1	.973							
UT	Hoelskoetter	317	.224	0	14	109	173	19	10		.937							
O1	S. Barry	237	.249	0	12	261	16	11	9		.962							
OF	S. Mertes	191	.246	0	19	77	4	10	0	1.7	.890							
OF	J. Himes	155	.271	0	14	76	10	2	2	2.2	.977							

Boston
W-49 L-102

Fred Tenney

POS	Player	AB	BA	HR	RBI	PO	A	E	DP	TC/G	FA	Pitcher	G	IP	W	L	SV	ERA
1B	F. Tenney	544	.283	1	28	1456	118	28	78	11.2	.983	I. Young	43	358	16	25	0	2.91
2B	A. Strobel	317	.202	1	24	181	259	25	32	5.0	.946	V. Lindaman	39	307	12	23	0	2.43
SS	A. Bridwell	459	.227	0	22	322	390	54	43	6.4	.930	B. Pfeffer	35	302	13	22	0	2.95
3B	D. Brain	525	.250	5	45	208	321	48	26	4.2	.917	G. Dorner	34	257	8	25*	0	3.88
RF	C. Dolan	549	.248	0	39	207	26	18	4	1.7	.928							
CF	J. Bates	504	.252	6	54	238	12	11	4	1.9	.958							
LF	D. Howard	545	.261	1	54	118	14	13	3	1.7	.910							
C	T. Needham	285	.189	0	12	317	114	17	9	5.9	.962							
UT	S. Brown	231	.208	0	20	235	88	13	5		.961							
C	J. O'Neill	167	.180	0	4	259	72	10	6	7.1	.971							
P	B. Pfeffer	158	.196	1	11	13	91	4	0	3.1	.963							

BATTING AND BASE RUNNING LEADERS

Batting Average

H. Wagner, PIT	.339
Steinfeldt, CHI	.327
H. Lumley, BKN	.324
S. Strang, NY	.319
F. Chance, CHI	.319

Slugging Average

H. Wagner, PIT	.477
H. Wagner, PIT	.459
S. Strang, NY	.435
Steinfeldt, CHI	.430
F. Chance, CHI	.430

Home Runs

T. Jordan, BKN	12
H. Lumley, BKN	9
C. Seymour, CIN, NY	8
W. Schulte, CHI	7
J. Bates, BOS	6
S. Magee, PHI	6

Total Bases

H. Wagner, PIT	237
Steinfeldt, CHI	232
H. Lumley, BKN	231
S. Magee, PHI	229
W. Schulte, CHI	223

Runs Batted In

Steinfeldt, CHI	83
J. Nealon, PIT	83
C. Seymour, CIN, NY	80
T. Jordan, BKN	78
F. Chance, CHI	71
H. Wagner, PIT	71

Stolen Bases

F. Chance, CHI	57
S. Magee, PHI	55
A. Devlin, NY	54
H. Wagner, PIT	53
J. Evers, CHI	49

PITCHING LEADERS

Winning Percentage

E. Reulbach, CHI	.826
T. Brown, CHI	.813
S. Leever, PIT	.759
C. Lundgren, CHI	.739
J. Pfiester, CHI	.714

Earned Run Average

T. Brown, CHI	1.04
J. Pfiester, CHI	1.56
E. Reulbach, CHI	1.65
V. Willis, PIT	1.73
L. Leifield, PIT	1.87

Wins

McGinnity, NY	27
T. Brown, CHI	26
S. Leever, PIT	22
C. Mathewson, NY	22
V. Willis, PIT	22

Saves

G. Ferguson, NY	6
H. Wiltse, NY	5
Stricklett, BKN	5

Strikeouts

F. Beebe, CHI, STL	171
B. Pfeffer, BOS	158
R. Ames, NY	156
J. Pfiester, CHI	153
J. Lush, PHI	151
I. Young, BOS	151

Complete Games

I. Young, BOS	37
B. Pfeffer, BOS	33
J. Taylor, CHI, STL	32
V. Lindaman, BOS	32
V. Willis, PIT	32
McGinnity, NY	32

NATIONAL LEAGUE 1906, *cont.*

BATTING AND BASE RUNNING LEADERS

Hits			Base on Balls			Home Run Percentage			Fewest Hits/9 Innings	
Steinfeldt, CHI	176		R. Thomas, PHI	107		T. Jordan, BKN	2.7		E. Reulbach, CHI	5.33
H. Wagner, PIT	175		R. Bresnahan, NY	81		H. Lumley, BKN	1.9		T. Brown, CHI	6.43
C. Seymour, CIN, NY	165		J. Titus, PHI	78		C. Seymour, CIN, NY	1.4		J. Pfiester, CHI	6.44
M. Huggins, CIN	159		B. Dahlen, NY	76		S. Strang, NY	1.3		F. Beebe, CHI, STL	6.67

Runs Scored			Doubles			Triples			Most Strikeouts/9 Inn.	
F. Chance, CHI	103		H. Wagner, PIT	38		F. Clarke, PIT	13		R. Ames, NY	6.90
H. Wagner, PIT	103		S. Magee, PHI	36		W. Schulte, CHI	13		F. Beebe, CHI, STL	6.67
J. Sheckard, CHI	90		Bransfield, PHI	28		H. Lumley, BKN	12		J. Pfiester, CHI	5.70
J. Nealon, PIT	82		Steinfeldt, CHI	27		J. Nealon, PIT	12		O. Overall, CHI, CIN	5.05

PITCHING LEADERS

Shutouts			Fewest Walks/9 Innings	
T. Brown, CHI	10		D. Phillippe, PIT	1.07
L. Leifield, PIT	8		S. Leever, PIT	1.66
J. Weimer, CIN	7		T. Sparks, PHI	1.76
			B. Ewing, CIN	1.88

Innings			Games Pitched	
I. Young, BOS	358		McGinnity, NY	45
McGinnity, NY	340		I. Young, BOS	43
V. Willis, PIT	322		T. Sparks, PHI	42
T. Sparks, PHI	317		B. Duggleby, PHI	42

	W	L	PCT	GB	R	OR	Batting 2B	3B	HR	BA	SA	SB	Fielding E	DP	FA	Pitching CG	BB	SO	ShO	SV	ERA
Chicago	116	36	.763		705	381	181	71	20	.262	.339	283	194	100	.969	125	446	702	31	9	1.76
New York	96	56	.632	20	625	510	162	53	15	.255	.321	288	233	84	.963	105	394	639	19	16	2.49
Pittsburgh	93	60	.608	23.5	623	470	164	67	12	.261	.327	162	228	109	.964	116	309	532	27	2	2.21
Philadelphia	71	82	.464	45.5	528	564	197	47	12	.241	.307	180	271	83	.956	108	436	500	21	5	2.58
Brooklyn	66	86	.434	50	496	625	141	68	25	.236	.308	175	283	73	.955	119	453	476	22	9	3.13
Cincinnati	64	87	.424	51.5	533	582	140	71	16	.238	.304	170	262	97	.959	126	470	567	11	5	2.69
St. Louis	52	98	.347	63	470	607	137	69	10	.235	.296	110	272	92	.957	118	479	559	4	2	3.04
Boston	49	102	.325	66.5	408	649	136	43	16	.226	.281	93	337	102	.947	137	436	562	10	0	3.17
					4388	4388	1258	489	126	.244	.310	1461	2080	740	.959	954	3423	4537	145	48	2.63

AMERICAN LEAGUE 1906

	POS	Player	AB	BA	HR	RBI	PO	A	E	DP	TC/G	FA	Pitcher	G	IP	W	L	SV	ERA
Chicago W-93 L-58 Fielder Jones	1B	J. Donahue	556	.257	1	57	1697	118	22	62	11.9	.988	F. Owen	42	293	22	13	2	2.33
	2B	F. Isbell	549	.279	0	57	292	363	35	36	5.2	.949	N. Altrock	38	288	20	13	0	2.06
	SS	G. Davis	484	.277	0	80	263	475	42	44	6.0	.946	E. Walsh	41	278	17	13	1	1.88
	3B	L. Tannehill	378	.183	0	33	131	278	21	12	4.3	.951	D. White	28	219	18	6	0	1.52
	RF	B. O'Neill	330	.248	1	21	118	12	7	1	1.5	.949	R. Patterson	21	142	10	7	1	2.09
	CF	F. Jones	496	.230	2	34	312	23	4	5	2.4	.988	F. Smith	20	122	5	5	1	3.39
	LF	E. Hahn	484	.227	0	27	164	21	10	3	1.5	.949							
	C	B. Sullivan	387	.214	2	33	475	134	16	7	5.3	.974							
	OF	P. Dougherty	253	.233	1	27	118	10	2	1	1.8	.985							
	3B	G. Rohe	225	.258	0	25	66	122	15	6	3.6	.926							
New York W-90 L-61 Clark Griffith	1B	H. Chase	597	.323	0	76	1504	89	33	54	10.8	.980	A. Orth	45	339	27	17	0	2.34
	2B	J. Williams	501	.277	3	77	336	412	32	34	5.6	.959	J. Chesbro	49	325	24	16	1	2.96
	SS	K. Elberfeld	346	.306	2	31	200	317	42	18	5.7	.925	B. Hogg	28	206	14	13	0	2.93
	3B	F. LaPorte	454	.264	2	54	118	210	35	11	3.2	.904	W. Clarkson	32	151	9	4	0	2.32
	RF	W. Keeler	592	.304	2	33	213	16	3	3	1.5	.987	D. Newton	21	125	6	5	0	3.17
	CF	D. Hoffman	320	.256	0	23	176	7	12	1	2.0	.938							
	LF	F. Delahanty	307	.238	2	41	180	7	9	1	2.1	.954							
	C	R. Kleinow	268	.220	0	31	381	102	13	8	5.2	.974							
	OS	W. Conroy	567	.245	4	54	295	154	21	15		.955							
	3O	G. Moriarty	197	.234	0	23	78	79	15	3		.913							
Cleveland W-89 L-64 Nap Lajoie	1B	C. Rossman	396	.308	1	53	1145	45	19	47	11.5	.984	O. Hess	43	334	20	17	3	1.83
	2B	N. Lajoie	602	.355	0	91	354	415	21	76	6.1	.973	B. Rhoads	38	315	22	10	0	1.80
	SS	T. Turner	584	.291	2	62	287	570	36	61	6.1	.960	A. Joss	34	282	21	9	1	1.72
	3B	B. Bradley	302	.275	2	25	107	177	10	6	3.6	.966	B. Bernhard	31	255	16	15	0	2.54
	RF	B. Congalton	419	.320	1	50	174	6	8	0	1.6	.957	J. Townsend	17	93	3	7	0	2.91
	CF	E. Flick	624	.311	1	62	248	13	5	4	1.8	.981							
	LF	J. Jackson	374	.214	0	38	189	5	5	2	1.9	.975							
	C	H. Bemis	297	.276	2	30	340	73	16	7	5.3	.963							
	UT	G. Stovall	443	.273	0	37	666	153	21	53		.975							
	OF	H. Bay	280	.275	0	14	131	8	3	2	2.1	.979							
	C	N. Clarke	179	.358	1	21	211	58	9	4	5.1	.982							
	P	O. Hess	154	.201	0	11	25	86	6	4	2.7	.949							
Philadelphia W-78 L-67 Connie Mack	1B	H. Davis	551	.292	12	96	1352	91	37	66	10.2	.975	R. Waddell	43	273	15	17	0	2.21
	2B	D. Murphy	448	.301	2	60	239	308	26	38	4.8	.955	C. Bender	36	238	15	10	3	2.53
	SS	M. Cross	445	.200	1	40	305	411	47	48	5.7	.938	J. Dygert	35	214	11	13	0	2.70
	3B	J. Knight	253	.194	3	20	71	130	17	6	3.3	.922	E. Plank	26	212	19	6	0	2.25
	RF	S. Seybold	411	.316	5	59	150	10	13	3	1.5	.925	J. Coombs	23	173	10	10	0	2.50
	CF	B. Lord	434	.233	1	44	212	13	14	4	2.1	.941	A. Coakley	22	149	7	8	0	3.14
	LF	T. Hartsel	533	.255	1	30	238	15	8	5	1.8	.969							
	C	Schreckengost	338	.284	1	41	532	110	19	7	7.4	.971							
	OF	Armbruster	265	.238	2	24	124	9	4	1	1.9	.971							
	C	M. Powers	185	.157	0	7	297	79	10	2	6.8	.974							
	3B	R. Oldring	174	.241	0	19	53	87	16	5	3.2	.897							

AMERICAN LEAGUE 1906, cont.

St. Louis
W-76 L-73

Jimmy McAleer

POS	Player	AB	BA	HR	RBI	PO	A	E	DP	TC/G	FA	Pitcher	G	IP	W	L	SV	ERA
1B	T. Jones	539	.252	0	30	1476	116	25	55	11.3	.985	H. Howell	35	277	15	14	1	2.11
2B	P. O'Brien	524	.233	2	57	254	274	38	31	4.7	.933	F. Glade	35	267	15	14	1	2.36
SS	B. Wallace	476	.258	2	67	309	461	41	47	5.9	.949	B. Pelty	34	261	16	11	2	1.59
3B	R. Hartzell	404	.213	0	24	119	209	41	11	3.6	.889	J. Powell	28	244	13	14	1	1.77
RF	H. Niles	541	.229	2	31	140	34	6	5	1.7	.967	B. Jacobson	24	155	9	9	0	2.50
CF	C. Hemphill	585	.289	4	62	304	17	13	1	2.2	.961	E. Smith	19	155	8	11	0	3.72
LF	G. Stone	581	.358	6	71	295	10	10	3	2.0	.968							
C	T. Spencer	188	.176	0	17	226	60	20	3	5.7	.935							
C	B. Rickey	201	.284	3	24	233	58	14	2	5.6	.954							
OF	B. Koehler	186	.220	0	15	81	8	4	1	1.8	.957							
C	J. O'Connor	174	.190	0	11	248	64	3	2	5.8	.990							

Detroit
W-71 L-78

Bill Armour

POS	Player	AB	BA	HR	RBI	PO	A	E	DP	TC/G	FA	Pitcher	G	IP	W	L	SV	ERA
1B	P. Lindsay	499	.224	0	33	1122	66	28	55	10.0	.977	G. Mullin	40	330	21	18	0	2.78
2B	G. Schaefer	446	.238	2	44	348	328	37	42	6.3	.948	R. Donahue	28	241	13	14	0	2.73
SS	C. O'Leary	443	.219	2	34	326	398	58	37	6.2	.926	E. Siever	30	223	14	11	0	2.71
3B	B. Coughlin	498	.235	2	60	188	265	29	16	3.3	.940	W. Donovan	25	212	9	15	0	3.15
RF	S. Crawford	563	.295	2	72	171	19	3	2	1.7	.984	E. Killian	21	150	10	6	2	3.43
CF	T. Cobb	350	.320	1	41	208	14	9	4	2.4	.961	J. Eubank	24	135	4	10	2	3.53
LF	M. McIntyre	493	.260	1	39	254	25	5	8	2.1	.982							
C	B. Schmidt	216	.218	0	10	257	104	16	4	5.6	.958							
OF	D. Jones	323	.260	0	24	193	10	4	3	2.5	.981							
C	F. Payne	222	.270	0	20	177	49	8	3	5.0	.966							

Washington
W-55 L-95

Jake Stahl

POS	Player	AB	BA	HR	RBI	PO	A	E	DP	TC/G	FA	Pitcher	G	IP	W	L	SV	ERA
1B	J. Stahl	482	.222	0	51	1322	78	24	51	10.5	.983	Falkenberg	40	299	14	20	1	2.86
2B	H. Schlafly	426	.246	2	30	341	358	28	42	5.9	.961	C. Patten	38	283	19	16	0	2.17
SS	D. Altizer	433	.256	1	27	257	323	43	31	5.5	.931	C. Smith	33	235	9	16	0	2.91
3B	L. Cross	494	.263	1	46	157	242	20	9	3.2	.952	L. Hughes	30	204	7	17	0	3.62
RF	P. Hickman	451	.284	9	57	137	12	7	2	1.6	.955	F. Kitson	30	197	6	14	0	3.65
CF	C. Jones	497	.241	3	42	279	20	12	7	2.4	.961							
LF	J. Anderson	583	.271	3	70	286	19	15	2	2.1	.953							
C	H. Wakefield	211	.280	1	21	237	59	17	5	5.2	.954							
UT	R. Nill	315	.235	0	15	148	211	36	21		.909							
OF	J. Stanley	221	.163	0	9	78	7	6	0	1.4	.934							

Boston
W-49 L-105

Jimmy Collins
W-35 L-79

Chick Stahl
W-14 L-26

POS	Player	AB	BA	HR	RBI	PO	A	E	DP	TC/G	FA	Pitcher	G	IP	W	L	SV	ERA
1B	M. Grimshaw	428	.290	0	48	1165	64	16	39	11.3	.987	C. Young	39	288	13	21	2	3.19
2B	H. Ferris	495	.244	2	44	316	375	29	41	5.7	.960	J. Harris	30	235	2	21	2	3.52
SS	F. Parent	600	.235	1	49	312	472	56	45	5.9	.933	B. Dinneen	28	219	8	19	0	2.92
3B	R. Morgan	307	.215	1	21	126	139	41	8	3.5	.866	G. Winter	29	208	6	18	2	4.12
RF	J. Hayden	322	.280	1	13	136	7	4	1	1.7	.973	J. Tannehill	27	196	13	11	0	3.16
CF	C. Stahl	595	.286	4	51	344	24	15	9	2.5	.961	R. Glaze	19	123	4	6	0	3.59
LF	J. Hoey	361	.244	0	24	155	7	15	0	1.9	.915							
C	Armbruster	201	.144	0	6	262	99	17	6	5.7	.955							
O1	B. Freeman	392	.250	1	30	467	47	8	22		.985							
OF	K. Selbach	228	.211	0	23	109	6	4	2	2.1	.966							
UT	J. Godwin	193	.187	0	15	79	115	26	11		.882							

BATTING AND BASE RUNNING LEADERS

Batting Average
G. Stone, STL	.358	
N. Lajoie, CLE	.355	
H. Chase, NY	.323	
B. Congalton, CLE	.320	
S. Seybold, PHI	.316	

Slugging Average
G. Stone, STL	.501
N. Lajoie, CLE	.460
H. Davis, PHI	.459
E. Flick, CLE	.439
P. Hickman, WAS	.421

Home Runs
H. Davis, PHI	12
P. Hickman, WAS	9
G. Stone, STL	6
S. Seybold, PHI	5

Total Bases
G. Stone, STL	291
N. Lajoie, CLE	277
E. Flick, CLE	275
H. Davis, PHI	253
H. Chase, NY	236

Runs Batted In
H. Davis, PHI	96
N. Lajoie, CLE	91
G. Davis, CHI	80
J. Williams, NY	77
H. Chase, NY	76

Stolen Bases
J. Anderson, WAS	39
E. Flick, CLE	39
D. Altizer, WAS	37
F. Isbell, CHI	37
J. Donahue, CHI	36

Hits
N. Lajoie, CLE	214
G. Stone, STL	208
E. Flick, CLE	194
H. Chase, NY	193

Base on Balls
T. Hartsel, PHI	88
F. Jones, CHI	83
E. Hahn, CHI, NY	72
B. Wallace, STL	58

Home Run Percentage
H. Davis, PHI	2.2
P. Hickman, WAS	2.0
S. Seybold, PHI	1.2
G. Stone, STL	1.0

Runs Scored
E. Flick, CLE	98
T. Hartsel, PHI	96
W. Keeler, NY	96
H. Davis, PHI	94

Doubles
N. Lajoie, CLE	49
H. Davis, PHI	42
E. Flick, CLE	34
D. Murphy, PHI	28

Triples
E. Flick, CLE	22
G. Stone, STL	20
S. Crawford, DET	16
H. Ferris, BOS	13

PITCHING LEADERS

Winning Percentage
E. Plank, PHI	.760
D. White, CHI	.750
A. Joss, CLE	.700
B. Rhoads, CLE	.688
F. Owen, CHI	.629

Earned Run Average
D. White, CHI	1.52
B. Pelty, STL	1.59
A. Joss, CLE	1.72
J. Powell, STL	1.77
B. Rhoads, CLE	1.80

Wins
A. Orth, NY	27
J. Chesbro, NY	24
B. Rhoads, CLE	22
F. Owen, CHI	22
A. Joss, CLE	21
G. Mullin, DET	21

Saves
C. Bender, PHI	3
O. Hess, CLE	3

Strikeouts
R. Waddell, PHI	196
Falkenberg, WAS	178
E. Walsh, CHI	171
O. Hess, CLE	167
C. Bender, PHI	159

Complete Games
A. Orth, NY	36
G. Mullin, DET	35
O. Hess, CLE	33
B. Rhoads, CLE	31
H. Howell, STL	30
Falkenberg, WAS	30

Fewest Hits/9 Innings
B. Pelty, STL	6.53
D. White, CHI	6.57
E. Walsh, CHI	6.95
A. Joss, CLE	7.02

Shutouts
E. Walsh, CHI	10
A. Joss, CLE	9
R. Waddell, PHI	8

Fewest Walks/9 Innings
C. Young, BOS	0.78
R. Patterson, CHI	1.08
N. Altrock, CHI	1.31
A. Joss, CLE	1.37

Most Strikeouts/9 Inn.
R. Waddell, PHI	6.47
C. Bender, PHI	6.00
E. Walsh, CHI	5.53
Falkenberg, WAS	5.36

Innings
A. Orth, NY	339
O. Hess, CLE	334
G. Mullin, DET	330
J. Chesbro, NY	325

Games Pitched
J. Chesbro, NY	49
A. Orth, NY	45
O. Hess, CLE	44
F. Owen, CHI	42

AMERICAN LEAGUE 1906, cont.

	W	L	PCT	GB	R	OR	Batting 2B	3B	HR	BA	SA	SB	Fielding E	DP	FA	Pitching CG	BB	SO	ShO	SV	ERA
Chicago	93	58	.616		570	**460**	152	52	7	.230	.286	214	243	80	.963	117	**255**	543	**32**	5	2.13
New York	90	61	.596	3	644	543	166	**77**	17	.266	.339	192	272	69	.957	99	351	605	18	5	2.78
Cleveland	89	64	.582	5	**663**	482	**240**	73	11	**.279**	**.357**	203	**216**	**111**	**.967**	**133**	365	530	27	4	**2.09**
Philadelphia	78	67	.538	12	561	542	213	49	**32**	.247	.330	166	267	86	.956	107	425	**749**	19	4	2.60
St. Louis	76	73	.510	16	558	498	145	60	20	.247	.312	221	290	80	.954	**133**	314	558	17	5	2.23
Detroit	71	78	.477	21	518	599	154	66	10	.242	.306	206	260	86	.959	128	389	469	7	4	3.06
Washington	55	95	.367	37.5	518	664	144	65	26	.238	.309	**233**	279	78	.955	115	451	558	12	1	3.25
Boston	49	105	.318	45.5	462	706	160	75	13	.239	.306	99	335	84	.949	124	285	549	6	**6**	3.41
					4494	4494	1374	517	136	.249	.319	1534	2162	674	.958	956	2835	4561	138	34	2.69

NATIONAL LEAGUE 1907

	POS	Player	AB	BA	HR	RBI	PO	A	E	DP	TC/G	FA	Pitcher	G	IP	W	L	SV	ERA
Chicago W-107 L-45 Frank Chance	1B	F. Chance	382	.293	1	49	1129	80	10	64	11.2	**.992**	O. Overall	35	265	23	8	3	1.70
	2B	J. Evers	508	.250	2	51	346	**500**	32	58	5.8	.964	T. Brown	34	233	20	6	3	1.39
	SS	J. Tinker	402	.221	1	36	215	390	39	45	5.7	.939	C. Lundgren	28	207	18	7	0	1.17
	3B	Steinfeldt	542	.266	1	70	161	307	16	18	3.2	**.967**	J. Pfiester	30	195	15	9	0	**1.15**
	RF	W. Schulte	342	.287	2	32	130	11	4	1	1.6	.972	E. Reulbach	27	192	17	4	0	1.69
	CF	J. Slagle	489	.258	0	32	239	15	10	5	2.0	.962	C. Fraser	22	138	8	5	0	2.28
	LF	J. Sheckard	484	.267	1	36	223	13	6	2	1.7	.975	J. Taylor	18	123	6	5	0	3.29
	C	J. Kling	334	.284	1	43	499	109	8	11	6.3	**.987**							
	UT	S. Hofman	470	.268	1	36	433	144	31	36		.949							
	C	P. Moran	198	.227	1	19	258	72	9	9	5.7	.973							
Pittsburgh W-91 L-63 Fred Clarke	1B	J. Nealon	381	.257	0	47	998	68	24	35	10.5	.978	V. Willis	39	293	22	11	1	2.34
	2B	Abbaticchio	496	.262	2	82	320	380	33	37	5.0	.951	L. Leifield	40	286	20	16	0	2.33
	SS	H. Wagner	515	**.350**	6	82	314	428	49	32	5.7	.938	S. Leever	31	217	14	9	1	1.66
	3B	A. Storke	357	.258	1	39	75	123	16	10	3.2	.925	D. Phillippe	35	214	13	11	2	2.61
	RF	G. Anderson	413	.206	1	12	207	15	11	4	2.0	.953	H. Camnitz	31	180	13	8	1	2.15
	CF	T. Leach	547	.303	4	43	284	15	6	5	**2.7**	.980							
	LF	F. Clarke	501	.289	2	59	298	15	4	2	2.2	**.987**							
	C	G. Gibson	382	.220	3	35	499	125	18	12	5.9	.972							
	OF	B. Hallman	302	.222	0	15	134	9	5	1	1.8	.966							
	3B	T. Sheehan	226	.274	0	25	55	137	12	3	3.6	.941							
Philadelphia W-83 L-64 Billy Murray	1B	Bransfield	348	.233	0	38	862	53	21	46	10.2	.978	F. Corridon	37	274	18	14	1	2.46
	2B	O. Knabe	444	.255	1	34	293	336	26	53	5.4	.960	T. Sparks	33	265	22	8	1	2.00
	SS	M. Doolan	509	.204	1	47	**327**	463	60	**59**	5.9	.929	L. Moren	37	255	11	18	1	2.54
	3B	E. Courtney	440	.243	2	43	90	143	24	11	3.4	.907	B. Brown	21	130	9	6	0	2.42
	RF	J. Titus	523	.275	3	63	198	21	17	3	1.7	.928	L. Richie	25	117	6	6	0	1.77
	CF	R. Thomas	419	.243	1	23	274	15	6	4	2.4	.980	T. Pittinger	16	102	9	5	0	3.00
	LF	S. Magee	503	.328	4	**85**	297	13	7	7	2.3	.978							
	C	R. Dooin	313	.211	0	14	436	123	22	14	6.2	.959							
	3B	E. Grant	268	.243	0	19	106	145	23	6	3.7	.916							
	C	Jacklitsch	202	.213	0	17	270	97	6	**15**	6.4	.984							
	OF	F. Osborn	163	.276	0	9	60	2	0	0	1.7	1.000							
New York W-82 L-71 John McGraw	1B	D. McGann	262	.298	2	36	781	55	5	36	10.4	.994	C. Mathewson	41	316	**24**	13	2	1.99
	2B	L. Doyle	227	.260	0	16	128	158	26	7	4.5	.917	McGinnity	**47**	310	18	18	4	3.16
	SS	B. Dahlen	464	.207	0	34	292	426	45	39	5.3	.941	R. Ames	39	233	10	12	1	2.16
	3B	A. Devlin	491	.277	1	54	174	282	29	12	3.5	.940	H. Wiltse	33	190	13	12	1	2.18
	RF	G. Browne	458	.260	5	37	146	14	10	5	1.4	.941	D. Taylor	28	171	11	7	1	2.42
	CF	C. Seymour	473	.294	3	75	300	8	8	4	2.5	.975							
	LF	S. Shannon	585	.265	1	33	282	18	7	3	2.0	.977							
	C	R. Bresnahan	328	.253	4	38	483	94	8	11	6.2	.986							
	C1	F. Bowerman	311	.260	0	32	606	79	6	14		.991							
	OF	S. Strang	306	.252	4	30	112	13	7	5	1.9	.947							
	2B	T. Corcoran	226	.265	0	24	108	183	19	15	5.0	.939							
Brooklyn W-65 L-83 Patsy Donovan	1B	T. Jordan	485	.274	4	53	1417	78	**31**	71	10.7	.980	N. Rucker	37	275	15	13	0	2.06
	2B	W. Alperman	558	.233	2	39	298	378	33	41	**6.2**	.953	G. Bell	35	264	8	16	1	2.25
	SS	P. Lewis	475	.248	0	30	277	372	43	37	5.1	.938	Stricklett	29	230	12	14	0	2.27
	3B	D. Casey	527	.231	0	19	176	274	21	16	3.4	.955	J. Pastorius	28	222	16	12	0	2.35
	RF	H. Lumley	454	.267	9	66	171	15	8	7	1.6	.959	H. McIntire	28	200	7	15	0	2.39
	CF	B. Maloney	502	.229	0	32	**336**	18	12	5	2.0	.967	D. Scanlan	17	107	6	8	0	3.20
	LF	E. Batch	388	.247	0	31	178	14	13	4	2.0	.937							
	C	L. Ritter	271	.203	0	17	391	103	16	11	5.7	.969							
	UT	J. Hummel	342	.234	3	31	321	162	16	23		.968							

NATIONAL LEAGUE 1907, *cont.*

	POS	Player	AB	BA	HR	RBI	PO	A	E	DP	TC/G	FA	Pitcher	G	IP	W	L	SV	ERA
Cincinnati	1B	J. Ganzel	531	.254	2	64	1346	84	14	**89**	10.1	.990	B. Ewing	41	333	17	19	0	1.73
	2B	M. Huggins	561	.248	1	31	**353**	443	32	**73**	5.3	.961	A. Coakley	37	265	17	16	1	2.34
W-66 L-87	SS	H. Lobert	537	.246	1	41	299	382	43	53	5.1	.941	J. Weimer	29	209	11	14	0	2.41
	3B	M. Mowrey	448	.252	1	44	167	214	29	14	3.2	.929	R. Hitt	21	153	6	10	0	3.40
Ned Hanlon	RF	M. Mitchell	558	.292	3	47	265	**39**	12	9	2.2	.962	D. Mason	25	146	5	12	0	3.14
	CF	A. Kruger	317	.233	0	28	199	11	6	3	2.3	.972	F. Smith	18	85	2	7	1	2.85
	LF	F. Odwell	274	.270	0	24	186	9	5	2	2.4	.975							
	C	L. McLean	374	.289	0	54	365	110	12	12	5.5	.975							
	OF	L. Davis	266	.229	1	25	160	11	5	3	2.5	.972							
	UT	J. Kane	262	.248	3	19	120	80	19	2		.913							
	C	A. Schlei	246	.272	0	27	277	111	8	6	5.9	.980							
Boston	1B	F. Tenney	554	.273	0	26	**1587**	113	19	86	**11.5**	.989	G. Dorner	36	271	12	16	0	3.12
	2B	C. Ritchey	499	.255	0	26	340	460	24	55	5.7	**.971**	V. Lindaman	34	260	11	15	1	3.63
W-58 L-90	SS	A. Bridwell	509	.218	0	26	325	437	47	57	5.8	**.942**	I. Young	40	245	10	23	0	3.96
	3B	D. Brain	509	.279	10	56	191	323	47	**27**	**4.3**	.916	P. Flaherty	27	217	12	15	0	2.70
Fred Tenney	RF	J. Bates	447	.260	2	49	171	18	4	5	1.6	.979	B. Pfeffer	19	144	6	8	0	3.00
	CF	G. Beaumont	580	.322	4	62	296	30	13	**12**	2.3	.962	J. Boultes	24	140	5	9	0	2.71
	LF	N. Randall	258	.213	0	15	106	9	10	1	1.7	.920							
	C	T. Needham	260	.196	1	19	281	101	13	9	5.1	.967							
	C	S. Brown	208	.192	0	14	267	91	11	12	5.9	.970							
	UT	B. Sweeney	191	.262	0	18	86	106	24	9		.889							
	OF	D. Howard	187	.273	1	13	54	8	2	2	1.4	.969							
St. Louis	1B	E. Konetchy	330	.252	3	30	922	71	25	46	11.3	.975	S. McGlynn	45	352	14	**25**	1	2.91
	2B	P. Bennett	324	.222	0	21	175	208	25	26	4.9	.939	E. Karger	38	310	15	19	1	2.03
W-52 L-101	SS	E. Holly	544	.230	1	40	317	**474**	62	45	5.8	.927	F. Beebe	31	238	7	19	0	2.72
	3B	B. Byrne	558	.256	0	29	212	**348**	49	24	4.1	.920	A. Fromme	23	146	5	13	0	2.90
John McCloskey	RF	S. Barry	292	.247	0	19	94	11	4	0	1.3	.963	J. Lush	20	144	7	10	0	2.50
	CF	J. Burnett	206	.238	0	12	98	8	5	1	1.9	.955							
	LF	R. Murray	485	.262	7	46	232	25	18	4	2.1	.935							
	C	D. Marshall	268	.201	2	18	374	**142**	26	9	**6.5**	.952							
	UT	Hoelskoetter	396	.247	2	28	450	267	42	40		.945							
	C	P. Noonan	236	.225	1	16	369	98	24	12	7.0	.951							
	OF	J. Kelly	197	.188	0	6	85	7	3	4	1.8	.968							
	OF	T. O'Hara	173	.237	0	5	78	5	5	2	1.9	.943							
	OF	A. Burch	154	.227	0	5	85	10	8	4	2.1	.922							

BATTING AND BASE RUNNING LEADERS

Batting Average
H. Wagner, PIT	.350
S. Magee, PHI	.328
G. Beaumont, BOS	.322
T. Leach, PIT	.303
C. Seymour, NY	.294

Slugging Average
H. Wagner, PIT	.513
S. Magee, PHI	.455
H. Lumley, BKN	.425
G. Beaumont, BOS	.424
D. Brain, BOS	.420

Home Runs
D. Brain, BOS	10
H. Lumley, BKN	9
R. Murray, STL	7
H. Wagner, PIT	6
G. Browne, NY	5

Total Bases
H. Wagner, PIT	264
G. Beaumont, BOS	246
S. Magee, PHI	229
T. Leach, PIT	221
D. Brain, BOS	214

Runs Batted In
S. Magee, PHI	85
Abbaticchio, PIT	82
H. Wagner, PIT	82
C. Seymour, NY	75
Steinfeldt, CHI	70

Stolen Bases
H. Wagner, PIT	61
S. Magee, PHI	46
J. Evers, CHI	46
T. Leach, PIT	43
A. Devlin, NY	38

Hits
G. Beaumont, BOS	187
H. Wagner, PIT	180
T. Leach, PIT	166
S. Magee, PHI	165

Base on Balls
R. Thomas, PHI	83
M. Huggins, CIN	83
F. Tenney, BOS	82
S. Shannon, NY	82

Home Run Percentage
H. Lumley, BKN	2.0
D. Brain, BOS	2.0
R. Murray, STL	1.4
S. Strang, NY	1.3

Runs Scored
S. Shannon, NY	104
T. Leach, PIT	102
H. Wagner, PIT	98
F. Clarke, PIT	97

Doubles
H. Wagner, PIT	38
S. Magee, PHI	28
C. Seymour, NY	25
Steinfeldt, CHI	25

Triples
J. Ganzel, CIN	16
W. Alperman, BKN	16
H. Wagner, PIT	14
G. Beaumont, BOS	14

PITCHING LEADERS

Winning Percentage
E. Reulbach, CHI	.810
T. Brown, CHI	.769
O. Overall, CHI	.742
T. Sparks, PHI	.733
C. Lundgren, CHI	.720

Earned Run Average
J. Pfiester, CHI	1.15
C. Lundgren, CHI	1.17
T. Brown, CHI	1.39
S. Leever, PIT	1.66
E. Reulbach, CHI	1.69

Wins
C. Mathewson, NY	24
O. Overall, CHI	23
T. Sparks, PHI	22
V. Willis, PIT	22
T. Brown, CHI	20
L. Leifield, PIT	20

Saves
McGinnity, NY	4
T. Brown, CHI	3
O. Overall, CHI	3
D. Phillippe, PIT	2
C. Mathewson, NY	2

Strikeouts
C. Mathewson, NY	178
B. Ewing, CIN	147
R. Ames, NY	146
F. Beebe, STL	141
O. Overall, CHI	139

Complete Games
S. McGlynn, STL	33
B. Ewing, CIN	32
C. Mathewson, NY	31
E. Karger, STL	28
V. Willis, PIT	27

Fewest Hits/9 Innings
C. Lundgren, CHI	5.65
J. Pfiester, CHI	6.60
O. Overall, CHI	6.75
H. Camnitz, PIT	6.75

Shutouts
O. Overall, CHI	8
C. Mathewson, NY	8
C. Lundgren, CHI	7

Fewest Walks/9 Innings
D. Phillippe, PIT	1.51
C. Mathewson, NY	1.51
T. Brown, CHI	1.55
McGinnity, NY	1.68

Most Strikeouts/9 Inn.
R. Ames, NY	5.63
F. Beebe, STL	5.32
C. Mathewson, NY	5.09
D. Scanlan, BKN	4.96

Innings
S. McGlynn, STL	352
B. Ewing, CIN	333
C. Mathewson, NY	316
McGinnity, NY	310

Games Pitched
McGinnity, NY	47
S. McGlynn, STL	45
B. Ewing, CIN	41
C. Mathewson, NY	41

NATIONAL LEAGUE 1907, cont.

	W	L	PCT	GB	R	OR	Batting 2B	3B	HR	BA	SA	SB	Fielding E	DP	FA	Pitching CG	BB	SO	ShO	SV	ERA
Chicago	107	45	.704		572	**390**	**162**	48	13	.250	.311	235	**211**	110	**.967**	114	402	584	**30**	7	**1.73**
Pittsburgh	91	63	.591	17		**634**	133	78	19	**.254**	**.324**	**264**	256	75	.959	111	**368**	497	24	4	2.30
Philadelphia	83	64	.565	21.5	512	476	**162**	65	12	.236	.305	154	256	104	.957	110	422	499	21	3	2.43
New York	82	71	.536	25.5	574	510	160	48	**23**	.251	.317	205	232	75	.963	109	369	**655**	20	**11**	2.45
Brooklyn	65	83	.439	40	446	522	142	63	18	.232	.298	121	262	94	.959	125	463	479	20	1	2.38
Cincinnati	66	87	.431	41.5	526	519	126	**90**	15	.247	.318	158	227	118	.963	118	444	481	10	2	2.41
Boston	58	90	.392	47	502	652	142	61	22	.243	.309	120	249	**128**	.961	121	458	426	9	2	3.33
St. Louis	52	101	.340	55.5	419	606	121	51	19	.232	.288	125	349	105	.947	**126**	499	589	20	2	2.70
					4185	4185	1148	504	141	.243	.309	1382	2042	809	.959	934	3425	4210	154	32	2.46

AMERICAN LEAGUE 1907

	POS	Player	AB	BA	HR	RBI	PO	A	E	DP	TC/G	FA	Pitcher	G	IP	W	L	SV	ERA
Detroit W-92 L-58 Hughie Jennings	1B	C. Rossman	571	.277	0	69	1478	62	30	57	10.3	.981	G. Mullin	46	357	20	20	3	2.59
	2B	R. Downs	374	.219	1	42	149	207	27	10	4.8	.930	E. Killian	41	314	25	13	1	1.78
	SS	C. O'Leary	465	.241	0	34	**353**	448	44	35	6.1	.948	E. Siever	39	275	18	11	1	2.16
	3B	B. Coughlin	519	.243	0	46	163	236	30	9	3.2	.930	W. Donovan	32	271	25	4	1	2.19
	RF	T. Cobb	605	**.350**	5	116	238	30	11	**12**	1.9	.961							
	CF	S. Crawford	582	.323	4	81	311	22	12	2	2.4	.965							
	LF	D. Jones	491	.273	0	27	282	15	9	2	**2.4**	.971							
	C	B. Schmidt	349	.244	0	23	446	132	**34**	14	5.9	.944							
	UT	G. Schaefer	372	.258	1	32	239	286	23	23		.958							
	C	F. Payne	169	.166	0	14	205	55	5	4	5.8	.981							
	P	G. Mullin	157	.217	0	13	15	133	6	1	3.3	.961							
Philadelphia W-88 L-57 Connie Mack	1B	H. Davis	582	.266	**8**	87	1475	103	**38**	50	10.8	.976	E. Plank	43	344	24	16	0	2.20
	2B	D. Murphy	469	.271	2	57	271	386	24	28	5.6	.965	R. Waddell	44	285	19	13	0	2.15
	SS	S. Nicholls	460	.302	0	23	178	258	33	12	5.7	.934	J. Dygert	42	262	21	8	1	2.34
	3B	J. Collins	365	.274	0	35	97	185	30	11	3.1	.904	C. Bender	33	219	16	8	3	2.05
	RF	S. Seybold	564	.271	5	92	201	19	6	7	1.5	.973	J. Coombs	23	133	6	9	2	3.12
	CF	R. Oldring	441	.286	1	40	180	10	5	0	1.7	.974							
	LF	T. Hartsel	507	.280	3	29	191	11	7	2	1.5	.967							
	C	Schreckengost	356	.272	0	38	**640**	145	12	4	8.1	.985							
	SS	M. Cross	248	.206	0	18	169	226	19	17	5.6	.954							
	OF	B. Lord	170	.182	1	11	91	6	5	0	1.9	.951							
	C	M. Powers	159	.182	0	9	313	80	7	8	6.8	.983							
Chicago W-87 L-64 Fielder Jones	1B	J. Donahue	**609**	.259	1	68	**1846**	140	12	78	12.7	**.994**	E. Walsh	**56**	**422**	24	18	4	**1.60**
	2B	F. Isbell	486	.243	1	41	276	384	30	41	5.8	.957	F. Smith	41	310	23	10	0	2.47
	SS	G. Davis	466	.238	1	52	223	485	38	53	5.7	.949	D. White	46	291	**27**	13	1	2.26
	3B	G. Rohe	494	.213	2	51	58	161	25	14	3.2	.898	N. Altrock	30	214	7	13	2	2.57
	RF	E. Hahn	592	.255	0	45	182	24	2	6	1.3	**.990**	R. Patterson	19	96	4	6	0	2.63
	CF	F. Jones	559	.261	0	47	307	18	9	6	2.2	.973							
	LF	P. Dougherty	533	.270	1	59	209	19	13	4	1.6	.946							
	C	B. Sullivan	339	.174	0	36	477	117	10	12	5.6	.983							
	P	E. Walsh	154	.162	1	10	35	**227**	4	2	4.8	.985							
Cleveland W-85 L-67 Nap Lajoie	1B	G. Stovall	466	.236	1	36	1381	68	25	**90**	12.1	.983	A. Joss	42	339	**27**	11	2	1.83
	2B	N. Lajoie	509	.299	2	63	314	**461**	25	**86**	6.3	.969	G. Liebhardt	38	280	18	14	1	2.05
	SS	T. Turner	524	.242	0	46	258	477	39	67	5.3	.950	B. Rhoads	35	275	15	14	1	2.29
	3B	B. Bradley	498	.223	0	34	164	278	29	18	3.4	**.938**	J. Thielman	20	166	11	8	0	2.33
	RF	E. Flick	549	.302	3	58	219	22	11	7	1.7	.956	O. Hess	17	93	6	6	1	2.89
	CF	Birmingham	476	.235	1	33	273	**33**	17	8	2.4	.947	W. Clarkson	17	91	4	6	0	1.99
	LF	B. Hinchman	514	.228	1	50	231	18	11	3	1.7	.958							
	C	N. Clarke	390	.269	3	33	470	119	24	9	5.3	.961							
	C	H. Bemis	172	.250	0	19	180	42	10	3	4.5	.957							
New York W-70 L-78 Clark Griffith	1B	H. Chase	498	.287	2	68	1144	77	34	50	10.4	.973	A. Orth	36	249	14	**21**	0	2.61
	2B	J. Williams	504	.270	2	63	357	393	26	45	5.6	.966	J. Chesbro	30	206	10	10	0	2.53
	SS	K. Elberfeld	447	.271	0	51	295	400	52	31	6.3	.930	S. Doyle	29	194	11	11	1	2.65
	3B	G. Moriarty	437	.277	0	43	115	160	31	8	3.4	.899	B. Hogg	25	167	10	8	0	3.08
	RF	W. Keeler	423	.234	0	17	144	13	5	5	1.5	.969	D. Newton	19	133	7	10	0	3.18
	CF	D. Hoffman	517	.253	4	46	286	20	15	4	2.4	.953	B. Keefe	19	58	3	5	3	2.22
	LF	W. Conroy	530	.234	3	51	204	10	10	2	2.2	.955							
	C	R. Kleinow	269	.264	0	26	318	97	14	5	5.0	.967							
	3O	F. LaPorte	470	.270	0	48	149	125	30	4		.901							
	C	I. Thomas	208	.192	1	24	257	90	17	7	5.5	.953							

AMERICAN LEAGUE 1907, *cont.*

	POS	Player	AB	BA	HR	RBI	PO	A	E	DP	TC/G	FA	Pitcher	G	IP	W	L	SV	ERA
St. Louis	1B	T. Jones	549	.250	0	34	1687	103	31	69	11.7	.983	H. Howell	42	316	16	15	3	1.93
	2B	H. Niles	492	.289	2	35	280	352	**34**	41	5.7	.949	B. Pelty	36	273	12	21	1	2.57
W-69 L-83	SS	B. Wallace	538	.257	0	70	338	**517**	**54**	54	6.2	.941	J. Powell	32	256	13	16	1	2.68
	3B	J. Yeager	436	.239	1	44	108	194	20	12	3.5	.938	F. Glade	24	202	13	9	0	2.67
Jimmy McAleer	RF	O. Pickering	576	.276	0	60	210	14	12	5	1.6	.949	B. Dinneen	24	155	7	10	4	2.43
	CF	C. Hemphill	603	.259	0	38	**320**	12	15	2	2.3	.957							
	LF	G. Stone	596	.320	4	59	276	12	9	5	1.9	.970							
	C	T. Spencer	230	.265	0	24	250	80	15	6	5.5	.957							
	32	R. Hartzell	220	.236	0	13	85	114	14	6		.934							
	C	J. Stephens	173	.202	0	11	200	63	9	4	4.9	.967							
Boston	1B	B. Unglaub	544	.254	1	62	1504	84	22	71	11.6	.986	C. Young	43	343	21	15	1	1.99
	2B	H. Ferris	561	.241	4	60	**424**	459	30	43	6.1	.967	G. Winter	35	257	12	15	1	2.07
W-59 L-90	SS	H. Wagner	385	.213	2	21	283	387	50	31	**6.6**	.931	R. Glaze	32	182	8	13	0	2.32
	3B	J. Knight	364	.212	2	29	129*	211*	28*	15*	3.8*	.924	T. Pruiett	35	174	3	11	3	3.11
Cy Young	RF	B. Congalton	496	.286	2	47	169	18	6	4	1.5	.969	J. Tannehill	18	131	6	7	1	2.47
W-3 L-3	CF	D. Sullivan	551	.245	1	26	296	16	8	3	2.0	.975	C. Morgan	16	114	6	6	0	1.97
	LF	J. Barrett	390	.244	1	28	183	14	7	5	2.1	.966							
George Huff	C	L. Criger	226	.181	0	14	288	109	9	12	5.4	.978							
W-2 L-6	UT	F. Parent	409	.276	1	26	195	191	25	20		.939							
	C	A. Shaw	198	.192	0	7	294	106	12	10	5.6	.971							
Bob Unglaub	O1	M. Grimshaw	181	.204	0	33	163	8	5	10		.972							
W-9 L-20	3B	J. Collins	158	.291	0	10	46	72	17	2	3.3	.874							
Deacon McGuire W-45 L-61																			
Washington	1B	J. Anderson	333	.288	0	44	615	32	11	13	10.8	.983	C. Smith	36	259	10	20	0	2.61
	2B	J. Delahanty	404	.292	2	54	172	180	22	18	5.5	.941	C. Patten	36	237	12	16	0	3.56
W-49 L-102	SS	D. Altizer	540	.269	1	42	157	251	32	23	6.2	.927	Falkenberg	32	234	6	17	0	2.35
	3B	B. Shipke	189	.196	1	9	57	127	11	2	3.1	.944	L. Hughes	34	211	7	14	4	3.11
Joe Cantillon	RF	B. Ganley	605	.276	1	35	276	23	**19**	5	2.1	.940	W. Johnson	14	111	5	9	0	1.87
	CF	C. Jones	437	.265	0	37	226	6	8	2	2.2	.967	O. Graham	20	104	4	9	0	3.98
	LF	O. Clymer	206	.316	1	16	79	4	8	0	1.8	.912	H. Gehring	15	87	3	7	0	3.31
	C	J. Warner	207	.256	0	17	271	64	10	4	5.4	.971							
	20	R. Nill	215	.219	0	25	113	106	8	9		.965							
	1O	P. Hickman	193	.285	1	23	306	20	13	13		.962							
	OF	C. Milan	183	.279	0	9	80	12	7	1	2.1	.929							
	C	M. Heydon	164	.183	0	9	247	52	12	4	5.5	.961							
	3B	L. Cross	161	.199	0	10	38	98	3	2	3.4	.978							

BATTING AND BASE RUNNING LEADERS

Batting Average
T. Cobb, DET .350
S. Crawford, DET .323
G. Stone, STL .320
E. Flick, CLE .302
S. Nicholls, PHI .302

Slugging Average
T. Cobb, DET .473
S. Crawford, DET .460
E. Flick, CLE .412
G. Stone, STL .399
H. Davis, PHI .397

Home Runs
H. Davis, PHI 8
S. Seybold, PHI 5
T. Cobb, DET 5

Total Bases
T. Cobb, DET 286
S. Crawford, DET 268
G. Stone, STL 238
H. Davis, PHI 231
E. Flick, CLE 226

Runs Batted In
T. Cobb, DET 116
S. Seybold, PHI 92
H. Davis, PHI 87
S. Crawford, DET 81
B. Wallace, STL 70

Stolen Bases
T. Cobb, DET 49
W. Conroy, NY 41
E. Flick, CLE 41
B. Ganley, WAS 40
D. Altizer, WAS 38

Hits
T. Cobb, DET 212
G. Stone, STL 191
S. Crawford, DET 188
B. Ganley, WAS 167

Base on Balls
T. Hartsel, PHI 106
E. Hahn, CHI 84
F. Jones, CHI 67
E. Flick, CLE 64

Home Run Percentage
H. Davis, PHI 1.4
S. Seybold, PHI 0.9
T. Cobb, DET 0.8
D. Hoffman, NY 0.8

Runs Scored
S. Crawford, DET 102
D. Jones, DET 101
T. Cobb, DET 97
T. Hartsel, PHI 93

Doubles
H. Davis, PHI 36
S. Crawford, DET 34
N. Lajoie, CLE 30
J. Collins, BOS, PHI 30

Triples
E. Flick, CLE 18
S. Crawford, DET 17
T. Cobb, DET 15
B. Unglaub, BOS 13

PITCHING LEADERS

Winning Percentage
W. Donovan, DET .862
J. Dygert, PHI .724
A. Joss, CLE .711
C. Bender, PHI .708
D. White, CHI .675

Earned Run Average
E. Walsh, CHI 1.60
E. Killian, DET 1.78
A. Joss, CLE 1.83
W. Johnson, WAS 1.87
H. Howell, STL 1.93

Wins
A. Joss, CLE 27
D. White, CHI 27
W. Donovan, DET 25
E. Killian, DET 25
E. Plank, PHI 24
E. Walsh, CHI 24

Saves
L. Hughes, WAS 4
B. Dinneen, BOS, STL 4
E. Walsh, CHI 4

Strikeouts
R. Waddell, PHI 232
E. Walsh, CHI 206
E. Plank, PHI 183
J. Dygert, PHI 151
C. Young, BOS 147

Complete Games
E. Walsh, CHI 37
G. Mullin, DET 35
A. Joss, CLE 34
C. Young, BOS 33
E. Plank, PHI 33

Fewest Hits/9 Innings
J. Dygert, PHI 6.88
G. Winter, BOS 6.94
E. Walsh, CHI 7.27
H. Howell, STL 7.34

Shutouts
E. Plank, PHI 8
R. Waddell, PHI 7
D. White, CHI 7
C. Young, BOS 6

Fewest Walks/9 Innings
D. White, CHI 1.18
N. Altrock, CHI 1.31
C. Young, BOS 1.34
J. Tannehill, BOS 1.37

Most Strikeouts/9 Inn.
R. Waddell, PHI 7.33
W. Johnson, WAS 5.53
J. Dygert, PHI 5.19
J. Coombs, PHI 4.95

Innings
E. Walsh, CHI 422
G. Mullin, DET 357
E. Plank, PHI 344
C. Young, BOS 343

Games Pitched
E. Walsh, CHI 56
D. White, CHI 47
G. Mullin, DET 46
R. Waddell, PHI 44

AMERICAN LEAGUE 1907, *cont.*

	W	L	PCT	GB	R	OR	2B	3B	HR	BA	SA	SB	E	DP	FA	CG	BB	SO	ShO	SV	ERA
										Batting				**Fielding**				**Pitching**			
Detroit	92	58	.613		**694**	532	179	**76**	11	**.266**	**.336**	192	260	79	.959	120	380	512	15	7	2.33
Philadelphia	88	57	.607	1.5	582	511	220	45	22	.255	.330	138	263	67	.958	106	378	**789**	27	6	2.35
Chicago	87	64	.576	5.5	588	**474**	148	34	6	.237	.283	175	**233**	101	**.966**	112	305	604	17	**9**	**2.22**
Cleveland	85	67	.559	8	530	525	182	68	11	.241	.310	193	264	**137**	.960	127	362	513	20	5	2.26
New York	70	78	.473	21	605	665	150	67	14	.249	.314	206	334	79	.947	93	428	511	9	5	3.03
St. Louis	69	83	.454	24	542	555	154	63	9	.253	.312	144	266	97	.959	**129**	352	463	15	**9**	2.61
Boston	59	90	.396	32.5	464	558	155	48	18	.284	.292	124	274	103	.959	100	337	517	17	6	2.45
Washington	49	102	.325	43.5	506	691	137	57	12	.243	.300	**223**	311	69	.952	106	341	569	11	5	3.11
					4511	4511	1325	458	103	.247	.310	1395	2205	732	.958	893	2883	4478	131	52	2.54

NATIONAL LEAGUE 1908

	POS	Player	AB	BA	HR	RBI	PO	A	E	DP	TC/G	FA	Pitcher	G	IP	W	L	SV	ERA
Chicago W-99 L-55 Frank Chance	1B	F. Chance	452	.272	2	55	1291	86	15	56	11.0	.989	T. Brown	44	312	29	9	5	1.47
	2B	J. Evers	416	.300	0	37	237	361	25	39	5.1	.960	E. Reulbach	46	298	24	7	1	2.03
	SS	J. Tinker	548	.266	6	68	314	**570**	39	48	5.9	**.958**	J. Pfiester	33	252	12	10	0	2.00
	3B	Steinfeldt	539	.241	1	62	166	275	28	15	3.1	.940	O. Overall	37	225	15	11	2	1.92
	RF	W. Schulte	386	.236	1	43	148	11	1	3	1.6	**.994**	C. Fraser	26	163	11	9	2	2.27
	CF	J. Slagle	352	.222	0	26	199	6	5	2	2.1	.976	C. Lundgren	23	139	6	9	0	4.22
	LF	J. Sheckard	403	.231	2	22	201	13	10	3	1.9	.955							
	C	J. Kling	424	.276	4	59	596	149	16	11	**6.5**	.979							
	UT	S. Hofman	411	.243	2	42	532	97	23	16		.965							
	OF	D. Howard	315	.279	1	26	129	10	5	1	1.8	.965							
New York W-98 L-56 John McGraw	1B	F. Tenney	583	.256	2	49	**1634**	117	18	**68**	11.3	.990	C. Mathewson	**56**	**391**	**37**	11	5	**1.43**
	2B	L. Doyle	377	.308	0	33	180	291	33	28	4.9	.935	H. Wiltse	44	330	23	14	2	2.24
	SS	A. Bridwell	467	.285	0	46	277	486	55	39	5.6	.933	D. Crandall	32	215	12	12	0	2.93
	3B	A. Devlin	534	.253	2	45	**203**	**331**	30	19	3.6	**.947**	McGinnity	37	186	11	7	4	2.27
	RF	M. Donlin	593	.334	6	106	239	21	6	1	1.7	.977	D. Taylor	27	128	8	5	2	2.33
	CF	C. Seymour	587	.267	5	92	340	**29**	20	9	2.5	.949	R. Ames	18	114	7	4	0	1.81
	LF	S. Shannon	268	.224	1	21	114	8	3	3	1.7	.976							
	C	R. Bresnahan	449	.283	1	54	**657**	140	12	12	5.8	.985							
	OF	McCormick	252	.302	0	32	97	3	11	2	1.7	.901							
	2B	B. Herzog	160	.300	0	11	61	125	16	19	4.8	.921							
Pittsburgh W-98 L-56 Fred Clarke	1B	H. Swacina	176	.216	0	13	501	19	9	19	10.6	.983	V. Willis	41	305	23	11	0	2.07
	2B	Abbaticchio	500	.250	1	61	268	423	22	42	5.0	**.969**	N. Maddox	36	261	23	8	1	2.28
	SS	H. Wagner	568	**.354**	10	**109**	354	469	50	47	5.8	.943	H. Camnitz	38	237	16	9	1	1.56
	3B	T. Leach	583	.259	5	41	199	293	33	19	3.5	.937	L. Leifield	34	219	15	14	2	2.10
	RF	O. Wilson	529	.227	3	43	258	20	13	3	2.0	.955	S. Leever	38	193	15	7	2	2.10
	CF	R. Thomas	386	.256	1	24	269	7	7	4	2.8*	.975							
	LF	F. Clarke	551	.265	2	53	350	15	10	2	2.5	.973							
	C	G. Gibson	486	.228	2	45	607	136	21	10	5.5	.973							
	1B	A. Storke	202	.252	1	12	481	17	6	19	10.3	.988							
	1B	J. Kane	145	.241	0	22	378	24	14	19	10.4	.966							
Philadelphia W-83 L-71 Billy Murray	1B	Bransfield	527	.304	3	71	1472	89	22	67	11.1	.986	McQuillan	48	360	23	17	2	1.53
	2B	O. Knabe	555	.218	0	27	**344**	**470**	26	42	5.6	**.969**	T. Sparks	33	263	16	15	2	2.60
	SS	M. Doolan	445	.234	2	49	269	419	45	32	5.7	.939	F. Corridon	27	208	14	10	1	2.51
	3B	E. Grant	**598**	.244	0	32	197	271	**35**	**22**	3.8	.930	L. Richie	25	158	7	10	1	1.83
	RF	J. Titus	539	.286	2	48	215	22	9	3	1.7	.963	L. Moren	28	154	8	9	0	2.92
	CF	F. Osborn	555	.267	2	44	**359**	14	12	3	2.5	.969	B. Foxen	22	147	7	7	1	1.95
	LF	S. Magee	508	.283	2	57	279	15	9	5	2.1	.970							
	C	R. Dooin	435	.248	0	41	554	191	**26**	17	5.8	.966							
	UT	E. Courtney	160	.181	0	6	157	61	6	7		.973							
Cincinnati W-73 L-81 John Ganzel	1B	J. Ganzel	388	.250	1	53	1116	61	12	52	11.0	**.990**	B. Ewing	37	294	17	15	3	2.21
	2B	M. Huggins	498	.239	0	23	302	406	30	45	5.5	.959	B. Spade	35	249	17	12	1	2.74
	SS	R. Hulswitt	386	.228	1	28	242	368	42	37	5.5	.936	A. Coakley	32	242	8	18	2	1.86
	3B	H. Lobert	570	.293	4	63	121	181	26	11	3.3	.921	B. Campbell	35	221	12	13	1	2.60
	RF	M. Mitchell	406	.222	1	37	193	16	9	2	1.8	.959	J. Weimer	15	117	8	7	0	2.39
	CF	J. Kane	455	.213	3	6	292	15	6	2	2.5	.981	J. Dubuc	15	85	5	6	0	2.74
	LF	D. Paskert	395	.243	1	36	251	15	13	3	2.4	.953							
	C	A. Schlei	300	.220	1	22	355	96	18	10	5.3	.962							
	C	L. McLean	309	.217	1	28	280	82	14	9	5.4	.963							
	3B	M. Mowrey	227	.220	2	23	51	110	11	6	3.1	.936							

NATIONAL LEAGUE 1908, *cont.*

	POS	Player	AB	BA	HR	RBI	PO	A	E	DP	TC/G	FA	Pitcher	G	IP	W	L	SV	ERA
Boston	1B	D. McGann	475	.240	2	55	1229	93	16	66	11.1	.988	V. Lindaman	43	271	12	16	1	2.36
	2B	C. Ritchey	421	.273	2	36	325	368	24	**46**	6.0	.967	P. Flaherty	31	244	12	18	0	3.25
W-63 L-91	SS	B. Dahlen	524	.239	3	48	291	553	43	**58**	6.2	.952	G. Dorner	38	216	8	19	0	3.54
	3B	B. Sweeney	418	.244	0	40	174	277	34	14	**3.9**	.930	G. Ferguson	37	208	12	11	0	2.47
Joe Kelley	RF	G. Browne	536	.228	1	34	248	20	14	8	2.0	.950	I. Young	16	85	4	8	0	2.86
	CF	G. Beaumont	476	.267	2	52	259	17	10	3	2.4	.965							
	LF	J. Bates	445	.258	1	29	205	15	12	2	2.0	.948							
	C	F. Bowerman	254	.228	1	25	228	69	9	12	4.9	.971							
	UT	J. Hannifin	257	.206	2	22	152	179	19	15		.946							
	OF	J. Kelley	228	.259	2	17	71	5	5	1	2.1	.938							
	C	P. Graham	215	.274	0	22	242	75	15	6	5.4	.955							
	OF	B. Becker	171	.275	0	7	40	8	3	1	1.2	.941							
Brooklyn	1B	T. Jordan	515	.247	**12**	60	1462	55	**28**	52	10.6	.982	N. Rucker	42	333	17	19	0	2.08
	2B	H. Pattee	264	.216	0	9	158	246	15	15	5.7	.964	K. Wilhelm	42	332	16	22	0	1.87
W-53 L-101	SS	P. Lewis	415	.219	1	30	227	352	35	33	5.3	.943	H. McIntire	40	288	11	20	2	2.69
	3B	T. Sheehan	468	.214	0	29	174	280	34	13	3.4	.930	J. Pastorius	28	214	4	20	0	2.44
Patsy Donovan	RF	H. Lumley	440	.216	4	39	157	13	8	6	1.5	.955	G. Bell	29	155	4	15	1	3.59
	CF	B. Maloney	359	.195	3	17	238	11	14	4	2.6	.947							
	LF	A. Burch	456	.243	2	18	242	24	8	6	2.4	.971							
	C	B. Bergen	302	.175	0	15	470	137	7	9	6.2	**.989**							
	UT	J. Hummel	594	.241	4	41	367	182	18	25		.968							
	2B	W. Alperman	213	.197	1	15	74	110	13	8	4.7	.934							
St. Louis	1B	E. Konetchy	545	.248	5	50	1610	**122**	24	61	**11.4**	.986	B. Raymond	48	324	15	**25**	2	2.03
	2B	B. Gilbert	276	.214	0	10	222	254	24	23	5.6	.952	J. Lush	38	251	11	18	1	2.12
W-49 L-105	SS	P. O'Rourke	164	.195	0	16	80	171	41	10	5.5	.860	F. Beebe	29	174	5	13	0	2.63
	3B	B. Byrne	439	.191	0	14	183	248	**35**	14	3.8	.925	E. Karger	22	141	4	9	0	3.06
John McCloskey	RF	R. Murray	593	.282	7	62	274	22	**28**	4	2.1	.914	S. Sallee	25	129	3	8	0	3.15
	CF	A. Shaw	367	.264	1	19	179	23	15	7	2.4	.931	A. Fromme	20	116	5	13	0	2.72
	LF	J. Delahanty	499	.255	1	44	243	11	6	1	1.9	.977	Higginbotham	19	107	3	8	0	3.20
	C	B. Ludwig	187	.182	0	8	227	87	16	2	5.3	.952							
	UT	C. Charles	454	.205	1	17	215	322	49	25		.916							
	OF	S. Barry	268	.228	0	11	109	10	4	0	1.8	.967							
	C	Hoelskoetter	155	.232	0	6	182	56	13	6	6.1	.948							

BATTING AND BASE RUNNING LEADERS

Batting Average
H. Wagner, PIT — .354
M. Donlin, NY — .334
L. Doyle, NY — .308
Bransfield, PHI — .304
J. Evers, CHI — .300

Slugging Average
H. Wagner, PIT — .542
M. Donlin, NY — .452
S. Magee, PHI — .417
H. Lobert, CIN — .407
R. Murray, STL — .400

Home Runs
T. Jordan, BKN — 12
H. Wagner, PIT — 10
R. Murray, STL — 7
J. Tinker, CHI — 6
M. Donlin, NY — 6

Total Bases
H. Wagner, PIT — 308
M. Donlin, NY — 268
R. Murray, STL — 237
H. Lobert, CIN — 232
T. Leach, PIT — 222

Runs Batted In
H. Wagner, PIT — 109
M. Donlin, NY — 106
C. Seymour, NY — 92
Bransfield, PHI — 71
J. Tinker, CHI — 68

Stolen Bases
H. Wagner, PIT — 53
R. Murray, STL — 48
H. Lobert, CIN — 47
S. Magee, PHI — 40
J. Evers, CHI — 36

Hits
H. Wagner, PIT — 201
M. Donlin, NY — 198
H. Lobert, CIN — 167
R. Murray, STL — 167

Base on Balls
R. Bresnahan, NY — 83
F. Tenney, NY — 72
J. Evers, CHI — 66
F. Clarke, PIT — 65

Home Run Percentage
T. Jordan, BKN — 2.3
H. Wagner, PIT — 1.8
R. Murray, STL — 1.2
J. Tinker, CHI — 1.1

Runs Scored
F. Tenney, NY — 101
H. Wagner, PIT — 100
T. Leach, PIT — 93
J. Evers, CHI — 83

Doubles
H. Wagner, PIT — 39
S. Magee, PHI — 30
F. Chance, CHI — 27
O. Knabe, PHI — 26

Triples
H. Wagner, PIT — 19
H. Lobert, CIN — 18
S. Magee, PHI — 16
T. Leach, PIT — 16

PITCHING LEADERS

Winning Percentage
E. Reulbach, CHI — .774
C. Mathewson, NY — .771
T. Brown, CHI — .763
N. Maddox, PIT — .742
V. Willis, PIT — .676

Earned Run Average
C. Mathewson, NY — 1.43
T. Brown, CHI — 1.47
McQuillan, PHI — 1.53
H. Camnitz, PIT — 1.56
A. Coakley, CHI, CIN — 1.78

Wins
C. Mathewson, NY — 37
T. Brown, CHI — 29
E. Reulbach, CHI — 24

Saves
T. Brown, CHI — 5
C. Mathewson, NY — 5
McGinnity, NY — 4
B. Ewing, CIN — 3

Strikeouts
C. Mathewson, NY — 259
N. Rucker, BKN — 199
O. Overall, CHI — 167
B. Raymond, STL — 145
E. Reulbach, CHI — 133

Complete Games
C. Mathewson, NY — 34
K. Wilhelm, BKN — 33
McQuillan, PHI — 32
N. Rucker, BKN — 30
H. Wiltse, NY — 30

Fewest Hits/9 Innings
T. Brown, CHI — 6.17
B. Raymond, STL — 6.55
C. Mathewson, NY — 6.57
McQuillan, PHI — 6.58

Shutouts
C. Mathewson, NY — 12
T. Brown, CHI — 9
E. Reulbach, CHI — 7
H. Wiltse, NY — 7

Fewest Walks/9 Innings
C. Mathewson, NY — 0.97
T. Brown, CHI — 1.41
T. Sparks, PHI — 1.74
B. Ewing, CIN — 1.75

Most Strikeouts/9 Inn.
O. Overall, CHI — 6.68
C. Mathewson, NY — 5.97
N. Rucker, BKN — 5.37
H. Camnitz, PIT — 4.49

Innings
C. Mathewson, NY — 391
McQuillan, PHI — 360
N. Rucker, BKN — 333
K. Wilhelm, BKN — 332

Games Pitched
C. Mathewson, NY — 56
McQuillan, PHI — 48
B. Raymond, STL — 48
E. Reulbach, CHI — 46

NATIONAL LEAGUE 1908, *cont.*

	W	L	PCT	GB	R	OR	2B	3B	HR	BA	SA	SB	E	DP	FA	CG	BB	SO	ShO	SV	ERA
							|← Batting →|						|← Fielding →|		|← Pitching →|					
Chicago	99	55	.643		624	461	**197**	56	19	.249	.321	**212**	**206**	76	**.969**	108	437	**668**	**28**	10	2.14
New York	98	56	.636	1	**652**	456	182	43	20	.267	.333	181	250	79	.962	95	**288**	656	25	**15**	2.14
Pittsburgh	98	56	.636	1	585	469	162	**98**	25	.247	.332	186	226	74	.964	100	406	468	24	8	2.12
Philadelphia	83	71	.539	16	504	**445**	194	68	11	.244	.316	200	238	75	.963	116	379	476	22	6	**2.10**
Cincinnati	73	81	.474	26	489	544	129	77	14	.227	.294	196	255	72	.959	110	415	433	17	7	2.37
Boston	63	91	.409	36	537	622	137	43	17	.239	.293	134	252	**90**	.962	92	423	416	14	1	2.79
Brooklyn	53	101	.344	46	377	516	110	60	**28**	.213	.277	113	247	66	.961	**118**	444	535	20	3	2.47
St. Louis	49	105	.318	50	371	626	134	57	17	.223	.283	150	348	68	.946	97	430	528	13	4	2.64
					4139	4139	1245	502	151	.239	.306	1372	2022	600	.961	836	3222	4180	163	54	2.35

AMERICAN LEAGUE 1908

Team	POS	Player	AB	BA	HR	RBI	PO	A	E	DP	TC/G	FA	Pitcher	G	IP	W	L	SV	ERA
Detroit W-90 L-63 Hughie Jennings	1B	C. Rossman	524	.294	2	71	1429	102	29	70	11.3	.981	E. Summers	40	301	24	12	1	1.64
	2B	R. Downs	289	.221	1	35	180	265	36	24	5.9	.925	G. Mullin	39	291	17	13	0	3.10
	SS	G. Schaefer	584	.259	3	52	162	254	37	35	6.7	.918	W. Donovan	29	243	18	7	0	2.08
	3B	B. Coughlin	405	.215	0	23	129	214	21	12	3.1	.942	E. Willett	30	197	15	8	1	2.28
	RF	T. Cobb	581	**.324**	4	**108**	212	**23**	14	5	1.7	.944	E. Killian	27	181	12	9	1	2.99
	CF	S. Crawford	591	.311	**7**	80	252	9	8	2	2.0	.970							
	LF	M. McIntyre	569	.295	0	28	**329**	17	8	4	2.3	.977							
	C	B. Schmidt	419	.265	1	38	541	**184**	**37**	12	**6.3**	.951							
	SS	C. O'Leary	211	.251	0	17	130	179	27	15	5.3	.920							
Cleveland W-90 L-64 Nap Lajoie	1B	G. Stovall	534	.292	2	45	1509	87	16	**79**	12.2	**.990**	A. Joss	42	325	24	11	2	**1.16**
	2B	N. Lajoie	581	.289	2	74	**450**	**538**	**37**	**78**	**6.6**	.964	B. Rhoads	37	270	18	12	0	1.77
	SS	G. Perring	310	.216	0	19	74	159	18	15	5.2	.928	G. Liebhardt	39	262	15	16	0	2.20
	3B	B. Bradley	548	.243	1	46	142	209	23	13	3.2	.939	H. Berger	29	199	13	8	0	2.12
	RF	B. Hinchman	464	.231	6	59	106	13	3	1	1.6	.975	C. Chech	27	166	11	7	0	1.74
	CF	Birmingham	413	.213	2	38	250	20	12	6	2.3	.957							
	LF	J. Clarke	492	.242	1	21	220	13	9	1	1.8	.963							
	C	N. Clarke	290	.241	0	27	327	108	14	6	5.0	.969							
	C	H. Bemis	277	.224	0	33	326	74	15	5	5.5	.964							
	OS	T. Turner	201	.239	0	19	65	68	6	4		.957							
	O1	P. Hickman	197	.234	2	16	248	20	12	7		.957							
	OF	W. Good	154	.279	1	14	62	0	11	0	1.7	.849							
Chicago W-88 L-64 Fielder Jones	1B	J. Donahue	304	.204	0	22	968	57	6	30	12.4	.994	E. Walsh	**66**	**464**	**40**	15	6	1.42
	2B	G. Davis	419	.217	0	26	191	314	21	25	5.5	.960	F. Smith	41	298	16	17	1	2.03
	SS	F. Parent	391	.207	0	35	212	442	49	33	6.0	.930	D. White	41	296	18	13	0	2.55
	3B	L. Tannehill	482	.216	0	35	135	**341**	33	15	3.7	.935	F. Owen	25	140	6	7	0	3.41
	RF	E. Hahn	447	.251	0	21	160	4	6	2	1.4	.965	N. Altrock	23	136	5	7	2	2.71
	CF	F. Jones	529	.253	1	50	288	17	10	5	2.1	.968							
	LF	P. Dougherty	482	.278	0	45	173	7	10	1	1.4	.947							
	C	B. Sullivan	430	.191	0	29	553	156	11	11	5.3	**.985**							
	OF	J. Anderson	355	.262	0	47	96	9	4	7	1.2	.963							
	1B	F. Isbell	320	.247	1	49	824	46	9	30	13.5	.990							
	2B	J. Atz	206	.194	0	27	82	137	15	12	5.1	.936							
	P	E. Walsh	157	.172	1	10	**41**	**190**	6	**9**	**3.6**	.975							
St. Louis W-83 L-69 Jimmy McAleer	1B	T. Jones	549	.246	1	50	**1616**	90	24	**79**	11.2	.986	H. Howell	41	324	18	18	1	1.89
	2B	J. Williams	539	.236	4	53	352	445	31	50	5.6	.963	R. Waddell	43	286	19	14	3	1.89
	SS	B. Wallace	487	.253	1	60	286	510	41	45	6.1	**.951**	J. Powell	33	256	16	13	1	2.11
	3B	H. Ferris	555	.270	2	74	**222**	316	27	**27**	3.8	**.952**	B. Dinneen	27	167	14	7	0	2.10
	RF	R. Hartzell	422	.265	2	32	117	15	8	5	1.7	.943	B. Pelty	20	122	7	4	0	1.99
	CF	D. Hoffman	363	.251	1	25	185	19	8	**8**	2.1	.962	B. Graham	21	117	6	7	0	2.30
	LF	G. Stone	588	.281	5	31	274	11	16	3	2.0	.947	B. Bailey	22	107	3	5	0	3.04
	C	T. Spencer	286	.210	0	28	398	109	9	9	5.8	.983							
	OF	C. Jones	263	.232	0	17	116	13	5	2	1.9	.963							
	OF	Schweitzer	182	.291	1	14	86	14	5	3	1.9	.952							
Boston W-75 L-79 Deacon McGuire W-53 L-62 Fred Lake W-22 L-17	1B	J. Stahl	258	.248	0	23	830	45	12	34	11.2	.986	C. Young	36	299	21	11	2	1.26
	2B	McConnell	502	.279	2	43	237	349	**38**	32	5.0	.939	E. Cicotte	39	207	11	12	2	2.43
	SS	H. Wagner	526	.247	1	46	**373**	569	61	51	6.6	.939	C. Morgan	30	205	14	13	1	2.46
	3B	H. Lord	558	.260	2	37	181	271	**47**	13	3.5	.906	F. Burchell	31	180	10	8	0	2.96
	RF	D. Gessler	435	.308	3	63	162	8	9	4	1.4	.950	G. Winter	22	148	4	14	0	3.05
	CF	D. Sullivan	353	.241	0	25	193	18	4	4	2.2	.981*	E. Steele	16	118	5	7	0	1.83
	LF	J. Thoney	416	.255	2	30	208	12	12	4	2.3	.948	T. Pruiett	13	59	1	7	2	1.99
	C	L. Criger	237	.190	0	25	380	120	10	11	6.1	.980							
	OF	G. Cravath	277	.256	1	34	128	7	11	3	1.9	.925							
	1B	B. Unglaub	266	.263	1	25	744	50	16	22	11.3	.980							
	UT	F. LaPorte	156	.237	0	15	67	115	10	7		.948							

AMERICAN LEAGUE 1908, *cont.*

	POS	Player	AB	BA	HR	RBI	PO	A	E	DP	TC/G	FA	Pitcher	G	IP	W	L	SV	ERA
Philadelphia	1B	H. Davis	513	.248	5	62	1410	86	22	44	10.3	.986	R. Vickers	53	300	18	19	1	2.34
	2B	E. Collins	330	.273	1	40	111	127	14	5	5.4	.944	E. Plank	34	245	14	16	1	2.17
W-68 L-85	SS	S. Nicholls	550	.216	4	31	221	370	56	26	5.4	.913	J. Dygert	41	239	11	15	1	2.87
	3B	J. Collins	433	.217	0	30	117	216	26	14	3.1	.928	J. Coombs	26	153	7	5	0	2.00
Connie Mack	RF	D. Murphy	525	.265	4	66	145	11	6	4	1.9	.963	C. Bender	18	139	8	9	1	1.75
	CF	R. Oldring	434	.221	1	39	246	9	16	3	2.3	.941	B. Schlitzer	24	131	6	8	0	3.16
	LF	T. Hartsel	460	.243	4	29	211	6	9	2	1.8	.960							
	C	Schreckengost	207	.222	0	16	352	91	10	3	6.9	.978							
	OP	J. Coombs	220	.255	1	23	102	48	4	4		.974							
	C	M. Powers	172	.180	0	7	303	74	13	3	6.5	.967							
Washington	1B	J. Freeman	531	.252	1	45	1548	66	41	69	10.7	.975	L. Hughes	43	276	18	15	4	2.21
	2B	J. Delahanty	287	.317	1	30	181	232	16	25	5.4	.963	W. Johnson	36	257	14	14	1	1.64
W-67 L-85	SS	G. McBride	518	.232	0	34	372	568	52	58	6.4	.948	C. Smith	26	184	9	13	1	2.40
	3B	B. Shipke	341	.208	0	20	111	190	22	11	2.9	.932	B. Keeley	28	170	6	11	1	2.97
Joe Cantillon	RF	O. Clymer	368	.253	1	35	81	16	7	7	1.3	.933	B. Burns	23	165	6	11	0	1.69
	CF	C. Milan	485	.239	1	32	265	18	12	6	2.4	.959	E. Cates	19	115	4	8	0	2.51
	LF	B. Ganley	549	.239	1	36	280	13	11	1	2.0	.964							
	C	G. Street	394	.206	1	32	578	167	21	14	6.0	.973							
	OF	O. Pickering	373	.225	2	30	135	6	9	1	1.5	.940							
	32	B. Unglaub	276	.308	0	29	111	178	15	12		.951							
	23	D. Altizer	205	.224	0	18	87	145	13	13		.947							
New York	1B	H. Chase	405	.257	1	36	1020	54	22	35	11.4	.980	J. Chesbro	45	289	14	20	1	2.93
	2B	H. Niles	361	.249	4	24	166	220	30	15	4.9	.928	J. Lake	38	269	9	22	0	3.17
W-51 L-103	SS	N. Ball	446	.247	0	38	268	438	30	28	6.0	.898	R. Manning	41	245	13	16	1	2.94
	3B	W. Conroy	531	.237	1	39	179	249	28	12	3.8	.939	B. Hogg	24	152	4	16	0	3.01
Clark Griffith	RF	W. Keeler	323	.263	1	14	123	9	9	2	1.6	.936	A. Orth	21	139	2	13	0	3.42
W-24 L-32	CF	C. Hemphill	505	.297	0	44	285	13	20	2	2.2	.937	D. Newton	23	88	4	5	1	2.95
	LF	J. Stahl	274	.255	2	42	111	14	9	3	2.0	.933							
Kid Elberfeld	C	R. Kleinow	279	.168	1	13	281	116	14	5	4.6	.966							
W-27 L-71	UT	G. Moriarty	348	.236	0	27	609	117	24	30		.968							
	C	W. Blair	211	.190	1	13	225	58	12	4	4.9	.959							
	OF	I. McIlveen	169	.213	0	8	70	4	4	0	1.8	.949							

BATTING AND BASE RUNNING LEADERS

Batting Average
T. Cobb, DET	.324
S. Crawford, DET	.311
D. Gessler, BOS	.308
C. Hemphill, NY	.297
M. McIntyre, DET	.295

Slugging Average
T. Cobb, DET	.475
S. Crawford, DET	.457
D. Gessler, BOS	.423
C. Rossman, DET	.418
M. McIntyre, DET	.383

Home Runs
S. Crawford, DET	7
B. Hinchman, CLE	6
H. Niles, BOS, NY	5
H. Davis, PHI	5
G. Stone, STL	5

Total Bases
T. Cobb, DET	276
S. Crawford, DET	270
C. Rossman, DET	219
M. McIntyre, DET	218
N. Lajoie, CLE	218

Runs Batted In
T. Cobb, DET	108
S. Crawford, DET	80
H. Ferris, STL	74
N. Lajoie, CLE	74
C. Rossman, DET	71

Stolen Bases
P. Dougherty, CHI	47
C. Hemphill, NY	42
G. Schaefer, DET	40
T. Cobb, DET	39
J. Clarke, CLE	37

Hits
T. Cobb, DET	188
S. Crawford, DET	184
M. McIntyre, DET	168
N. Lajoie, CLE	168

Base on Balls
T. Hartsel, PHI	93
F. Jones, CHI	86
M. McIntyre, DET	83
J. Clarke, CLE	76

Home Run Percentage
B. Hinchman, CLE	1.3
H. Niles, BOS, NY	1.3
S. Crawford, DET	1.2
H. Davis, PHI	1.0

Runs Scored
M. McIntyre, DET	105
S. Crawford, DET	102
G. Schaefer, DET	96
F. Jones, CHI	92

Doubles
T. Cobb, DET	36
C. Rossman, DET	33
S. Crawford, DET	33
N. Lajoie, CLE	32

Triples
T. Cobb, DET	20
J. Stahl, BOS, NY	16
S. Crawford, DET	16
D. Gessler, BOS	14

PITCHING LEADERS

Winning Percentage
E. Walsh, CHI	.727
W. Donovan, DET	.720
A. Joss, CLE	.686
E. Summers, DET	.667
C. Young, BOS	.656

Earned Run Average
A. Joss, CLE	1.16
C. Young, BOS	1.26
E. Walsh, CHI	1.42
W. Johnson, WAS	1.64
E. Summers, DET	1.64

Wins
E. Walsh, CHI	40
A. Joss, CLE	24
E. Summers, DET	24
C. Young, BOS	21

Saves
E. Walsh, CHI	6
L. Hughes, WAS	4
J. Chesbro, NY	3
R. Waddell, STL	3

Strikeouts
E. Walsh, CHI	269
R. Waddell, STL	232
L. Hughes, WAS	165
J. Dygert, PHI	164
W. Johnson, WAS	160

Complete Games
E. Walsh, CHI	42
C. Young, BOS	30
A. Joss, CLE	29
H. Howell, STL	27
G. Mullin, DET	26

Fewest Hits/9 Innings
A. Joss, CLE	6.42
F. Smith, CHI	6.44
E. Walsh, CHI	6.65
W. Johnson, WAS	6.78

Shutouts
E. Walsh, CHI	11
A. Joss, CLE	9
W. Donovan, DET	6
W. Johnson, WAS	6

Fewest Walks/9 Innings
A. Joss, CLE	0.83
B. Burns, WAS	0.98
E. Walsh, CHI	1.09
C. Young, BOS	1.11

Most Strikeouts/9 Inn.
R. Waddell, STL	7.31
J. Dygert, PHI	6.18
W. Johnson, WAS	5.60
C. Bender, PHI	5.52

Innings
E. Walsh, CHI	464
A. Joss, CLE	325
H. Howell, STL	324
E. Summers, DET	301

Games Pitched
E. Walsh, CHI	66
R. Vickers, PHI	53
J. Chesbro, NY	45
R. Waddell, STL	43

AMERICAN LEAGUE 1908, *cont.*

	W	L	PCT	GB	R	OR	2B	3B	HR	BA	SA	SB	E	DP	FA	CG	BB	SO	ShO	SV	ERA
Detroit	90	63	.588		**647**	547	**199**	86	19	**.264**	**.347**	165	305	95	.953	**120**	318	553	15	5	2.40
Cleveland	90	64	.584	.5	568	**457**	188	58	18	.239	.309	169	257	95	.962	108	328	548	18	5	**2.02**
Chicago	88	64	.579	1.5	537	470	145	41	3	.224	.271	209	**232**	82	**.966**	107	284	623	**23**	10	2.22
St. Louis	83	69	.546	6.5	544	483	173	56	21	.245	.312	126	237	97	.964	107	387	607	16	5	2.15
Boston	75	79	.487	15.5	564	513	116	**88**	14	.246	.312	168	297	71	.955	102	366	624	12	7	2.27
Philadelphia	68	85	.444	22	486	562	183	49	**21**	.223	.291	116	272	68	.957	102	409	**740**	23	4	2.57
Washington	67	85	.441	22.5	479	539	131	74	8	.235	.295	170	275	89	.958	105	348	649	14	7	2.34
New York	51	103	.331	39.5	459	713	142	51	12	.236	.291	**230**	337	78	.947	91	457	584	11	3	3.16
					4284	4284	1277	503	116	.239	.304	1353	2212	675	.958	842	2897	4928	132	46	2.39

NATIONAL LEAGUE 1909

Team	POS	Player	AB	BA	HR	RBI	PO	A	E	DP	TC/G	FA	Pitcher	G	IP	W	L	SV	ERA
Pittsburgh W-110 L-42 Fred Clarke	1B	B. Abstein	512	.260	1	70	1412	65	27	70	11.1	.982	V. Willis	39	290	22	11	0	2.24
	2B	D. Miller	560	.279	3	87	260	**426**	34	50	4.8	.953	H. Camnitz	41	283	25	6	3	1.62
	SS	H. Wagner	495	**.339**	5	100	344	430	49	**58**	6.1	.940	N. Maddox	31	203	13	8	0	2.21
	3B	J. Barbeau	350	.220	0	25	99	139	29*	8	3.1	.891	L. Leifield	32	202	19	8	0	2.37
	RF	O. Wilson	569	.272	4	59	292	19	14	7	2.1	.957	D. Phillippe	22	132	8	3	0	2.32
	CF	T. Leach	587	.261	6	43	333	12	11	3	2.6	.969	B. Adams	25	130	12	3	2	1.11
	LF	F. Clarke	550	.287	3	68	**362**	17	5	2	2.5	**.987**	S. Leever	19	70	8	1	2	2.83
	C	G. Gibson	510	.265	2	52	**655**	192	15	9	5.7	**.983**							
	3B	B. Byrne	168	.256	0	7	50*	107*	2	3	3.5*	.987							
Chicago W-104 L-49 Frank Chance	1B	F. Chance	324	.272	0	46	901	40	6	43	10.3	**.994**	T. Brown	**50**	**343**	**27**	9	7	1.31
	2B	J. Evers	463	.263	1	24	262	354	38	49	5.2	.942	O. Overall	38	285	20	11	2	1.42
	SS	J. Tinker	516	.256	4	57	320	470	50	49	5.9	**.940**	E. Reulbach	35	263	19	10	0	1.78
	3B	Steinfeldt	528	.252	2	59	183	299	31	16	3.4	.940	J. Pfiester	29	197	17	6	0	2.43
	RF	W. Schulte	538	.264	4	60	169	14	6	1	1.4	.968	R. Kroh	17	120	9	4	0	1.65
	CF	S. Hofman	527	.285	2	58	347	16	13	5	2.5	.965							
	LF	J. Sheckard	525	.255	1	43	277	18	10	5	2.1	.967							
	C	J. Archer	261	.230	1	30	408	97	21	7	6.6	.960							
	C	P. Moran	246	.220	1	23	181	97	8	3	3.9	.972							
	1B	D. Howard	203	.197	1	24	593	32	13	29	11.2	.980							
	UT	H. Zimmerman	183	.273	0	21	100	93	19	12		.910							
New York W-92 L-61 John McGraw	1B	F. Tenney	375	.235	3	30	1046	72	16	53	**11.6**	.986	C. Mathewson	37	275	25	6	2	**1.14**
	2B	L. Doyle	570	.302	6	49	**292**	322	39	**51**	4.6	.940	B. Raymond	39	270	18	12	0	2.47
	SS	A. Bridwell	476	.294	0	55	268	439	45	55	5.2	.940	H. Wiltse	37	269	20	11	3	2.00
	3B	A. Devlin	491	.265	0	55	191	317	36	**21**	3.8	.934	R. Ames	34	240	15	10	1	2.70
	RF	R. Murray	570	.263	**7**	91	222	**30**	14	1	1.8	.947	R. Marquard	29	173	5	13	0	2.60
	CF	B. O'Hara	360	.236	1	30	202	19	5	4	2.0	.978	D. Crandall	30	122	6	4	4	2.88
	LF	McCormick	413	.291	3	27	144	13	13	6	1.6	.924							
	C	A. Schlei	279	.244	0	30	493	127	24	9	**7.2**	.963							
	OF	C. Seymour	280	.311	1	30	138	11	5	3	2.1	.968							
	1B	F. Merkle	236	.191	0	20	621	27	16	29	9.6	.976							
	C	C. Meyers	220	.277	1	30	376	71	17	4	7.3	.963							
Cincinnati W-77 L-76 Clark Griffith	1B	Hoblitzell	517	.308	4	67	1444	74	**28**	80	10.9	.982	A. Fromme	37	279	19	13	2	1.90
	2B	D. Egan	480	.275	2	53	271	376	34	45	**5.9**	.950	H. Gaspar	44	260	18	11	2	2.01
	SS	T. Downey	416	.231	1	32	260	363	**62**	35	5.8	.909	J. Rowan	38	226	11	12	0	2.79
	3B	H. Lobert	425	.212	4	52	182	204	33	16	3.4	.921	B. Ewing	31	218	11	12	2	2.43
	RF	M. Mitchell	523	.310	4	86	262	20	11	3	2.0	.962	B. Campbell	30	148	7	11	2	2.67
	CF	R. Oakes	415	.270	3	31	218	15	5	3	2.1	.979	B. Spade	14	98	5	5	0	2.85
	LF	B. Bescher	446	.240	1	34	247	14	13	4	2.3	.953	J. Dubuc	19	71	3	5	2	3.66
	C	L. McLean	324	.256	2	36	379	119	11	16	5.4	.978							
	OF	D. Paskert	322	.252	0	33	172	11	6	3	2.3	.968							
	23	M. Huggins	159	.214	0	6	95	125	16	14		.932							
Philadelphia W-74 L-79 Billy Murray	1B	Bransfield	527	.292	1	59	1377	89	16	71	10.7	**.989**	E. Moore	38	300	18	12	0	2.10
	2B	O. Knabe	402	.234	0	33	237	312	36	38	5.4	.938	L. Moren	39	254	16	15	1	2.66
	SS	M. Doolan	493	.219	1	35	**352**	**484**	54	**58**	6.1	.939	McQuillan	41	248	13	16	2	2.14
	3B	E. Grant	**631**	.269	1	37	184	310	22	18	3.4	.957	F. Corridon	27	171	11	7	0	2.11
	RF	J. Titus	540	.270	3	46	241	23	8	6	1.8	.971	T. Sparks	24	122	6	11	0	2.96
	CF	J. Bates	266	.293	1	15	130	12	6	3	2.0	.959	H. Coveleski	24	122	6	10	1	2.74
	LF	S. Magee	522	.270	2	66	283	11	9	0	2.1	.970	B. Foxen	18	83	3	7	0	3.35
	C	R. Dooin	468	.224	2	38	517	199	**40**	14	5.4	.947							
	OF	F. Osborn	189	.185	0	19	126	14	3	3	2.6	.979							
	2B	J. Ward	184	.266	0	23	58	77	8	12	3.0	.944							
	OF	P. Deininger	169	.260	0	16	83	5	1	0	2.0	.989							

NATIONAL LEAGUE 1909, *cont.*

	POS	Player	AB	BA	HR	RBI	PO	A	E	DP	TC/G	FA	Pitcher	G	IP	W	L	SV	ERA
Brooklyn	1B	T. Jordan	330	.273	3	36	937	29	17	36	10.3	.983	N. Rucker	38	309	13	19	1	2.24
	2B	W. Alperman	420	.248	1	41	266	297	**42**	32	5.6	.931	G. Bell	33	256	16	15	1	2.71
W-55 L-98	SS	T. McMillan	373	.212	0	24	190	310	47	32	5.2	.914	H. McIntire	32	228	7	17	0	3.63
	3B	E. Lennox	435	.262	2	44	167	210	16	18	3.2	**.959**	K. Wilhelm	22	163	3	13	0	3.26
Harry Lumley	RF	H. Lumley	172	.250	0	14	83	9	5	1	1.9	.948	D. Scanlan	19	141	8	7	0	2.93
	CF	A. Burch	601	.271	0	30	320	23	16	4	2.4	.955	G. Hunter	16	113	4	10	0	2.46
	LF	W. Clement	340	.256	0	17	179	14	7	4	2.3	.965	J. Pastorius	12	80	1	9	0	5.76
	C	B. Bergen	346	.139	1	15	436	**202**	18	**18**	5.9	.973							
	UT	J. Hummel	542	.280	4	52	728	207	35	38		.964							
	UT	P. McElveen	258	.198	3	25	147	107	14	11		.948							
	OF	J. Kustus	173	.145	1	11	92	6	5	1	2.1	.951							
St. Louis	1B	E. Konetchy	576	.286	4	80	**1584**	97	26	71	11.2	.985	F. Beebe	44	288	15	21	1	2.82
	2B	C. Charles	339	.236	0	29	162	186	31	28	5.3	.918	J. Lush	34	221	11	18	0	3.13
W-54 L-98	SS	R. Hulswitt	289	.280	0	29	147	200	26	16	5.7	.930	S. Sallee	32	219	10	11	0	2.42
	3B	B. Byrne	421	.214	1	33	164*	252*	35	11	4.3*	.922	B. Harmon	21	159	6	11	0	3.68
Roger Bresnahan	RF	S. Evans	498	.259	2	56	212	19	13	**10**	1.7	.947	L. Backman	21	128	3	11	0	4.14
	CF	A. Shaw	331	.248	2	34	189	14	13	1	2.3	.940	J. Raleigh	15	81	1	10	0	3.79
	LF	R. Ellis	575	.268	3	46	332	28	17	9	**2.6**	.955							
	C	E. Phelps	306	.248	0	22	330	87	20	11	5.3	.954							
	O2	J. Delahanty	411	.214	2	54	203	121	22	11		.936							
	C	R. Bresnahan	234	.244	0	23	211	78	12	3	5.1	.960							
	3B	J. Barbeau	175	.251	0	5	56	72	14*	7	3.1	.901							
	SS	A. Storke	174	.282	0	10	93	135	10	14	5.4	.958							
Boston	1B	F. Stem	245	.208	0	11	656	62	8	31	10.7	.989	A. Mattern	47	316	16	20	3	2.85
	2B	D. Shean	267	.247	1	29	164	209	17	34	5.4	.956	G. Ferguson	36	227	5	**23**	0	3.73
W-45 L-108	SS	J. Coffey	257	.187	0	20	133	213	40	18	5.3	.896	K. White	23	148	6	13	0	3.22
	3B	B. Sweeney	493	.243	1	36	156	243	**43**	14	3.9	.903	L. Richie	22	132	7	7	2	2.32
Frank Bowerman	RF	B. Becker	562	.246	6	24	222	26	**18**	8	1.8	.932	B. Brown	18	123	4	10	0	3.14
W-23 L-54	CF	G. Beaumont	407	.263	0	60	234	15	8	3	2.3	.969							
	LF	R. Thomas	281	.263	0	11	155	9	4	1	2.4	.976							
Harry Smith	C	P. Graham	267	.240	0	17	193	111	22	14	4.3	.933							
W-22 L-54	O1	F. Beck	334	.198	3	27	464	26	14	18		.972							
	OF	J. Bates	236	.288	1	23	123	15	8	0	2.4	.945							
	2B	C. Starr	216	.222	0	6	103	140	18	19	4.8	.931							
	1B	C. Autry	199	.196	0	13	605	38	4	27	10.6	.994							
	SS	B. Dahlen	197	.234	2	16	101	184	29	20	6.4	.908							

BATTING AND BASE RUNNING LEADERS

Batting Average
H. Wagner, PIT	.339
M. Mitchell, CIN	.310
Hoblitzell, CIN	.308
L. Doyle, NY	.301
A. Bridwell, NY	.294

Slugging Average
H. Wagner, PIT	.489
M. Mitchell, CIN	.430
L. Doyle, NY	.419
Hoblitzell, CIN	.418
McCormick, NY	.402

Home Runs
R. Murray, NY	7
B. Becker, BOS	6
L. Doyle, NY	6
T. Leach, PIT	6
H. Wagner, PIT	5

Total Bases
H. Wagner, PIT	242
L. Doyle, NY	238
E. Konetchy, STL	228
M. Mitchell, CIN	225
D. Miller, PIT	222

Runs Batted In
H. Wagner, PIT	100
R. Murray, NY	91
D. Miller, PIT	87
M. Mitchell, CIN	86
E. Konetchy, STL	80

Stolen Bases
B. Bescher, CIN	54
R. Murray, NY	48
D. Egan, CIN	39
S. Magee, PHI	38
A. Burch, BKN	38

Hits
L. Doyle, NY	172
E. Grant, PHI	170
H. Wagner, PIT	168
E. Konetchy, STL	165

Base on Balls
F. Clarke, PIT	80
B. Byrne, PIT, STL	78
J. Evers, CHI	73
J. Sheckard, CHI	72

Home Run Percentage
R. Murray, NY	1.2
B. Becker, BOS	1.1
L. Doyle, NY	1.1
T. Leach, PIT	1.0

Runs Scored
T. Leach, PIT	126
F. Clarke, PIT	97
H. Wagner, PIT	92
B. Byrne, PIT, STL	92

Doubles
H. Wagner, PIT	39
S. Magee, PHI	33
D. Miller, PIT	31
J. Sheckard, CHI	29

Triples
M. Mitchell, CIN	17
S. Magee, PHI	14
E. Konetchy, STL	14
D. Miller, PIT	13

PITCHING LEADERS

Winning Percentage
H. Camnitz, PIT	.806
C. Mathewson, NY	.806
T. Brown, CHI	.750
J. Pfiester, CHI	.739
L. Leifield, PIT	.704

Earned Run Average
C. Mathewson, NY	1.14
T. Brown, CHI	1.31
O. Overall, CHI	1.42
H. Camnitz, PIT	1.62
R. Kroh, CHI	1.65

Wins
T. Brown, CHI	27
H. Camnitz, PIT	25
C. Mathewson, NY	25
V. Willis, PIT	22
O. Overall, CHI	20
H. Wiltse, NY	20

Saves
T. Brown, CHI	7
D. Crandall, NY	4
H. Camnitz, PIT	3
A. Mattern, BOS	3
L. Richie, BOS, PHI	3
H. Wiltse, NY	3

Strikeouts
O. Overall, CHI	205
N. Rucker, BKN	201
E. Moore, PHI	173
T. Brown, CHI	172
R. Ames, NY	156

Complete Games
T. Brown, CHI	32
G. Bell, BKN	29
N. Rucker, BKN	28
C. Mathewson, NY	26

Fewest Hits/9 Innings
C. Mathewson, NY	6.28
A. Fromme, CIN	6.28
O. Overall, CHI	6.44
T. Brown, CHI	6.46

Shutouts
O. Overall, CHI	9
C. Mathewson, NY	8
T. Brown, CHI	8
G. Bell, BKN	6

Fewest Walks/9 Innings
C. Mathewson, NY	1.18
T. Brown, CHI	1.39
H. Wiltse, NY	1.70
N. Maddox, PIT	1.73

Most Strikeouts/9 Inn.
O. Overall, CHI	6.47
R. Ames, NY	5.85
N. Rucker, BKN	5.85
E. Moore, PHI	5.20

Innings
T. Brown, CHI	343
A. Mattern, BOS	316
N. Rucker, BKN	309
E. Moore, PHI	300

Games Pitched
T. Brown, CHI	50
A. Mattern, BOS	47
F. Beebe, STL	44
H. Gaspar, CIN	44

NATIONAL LEAGUE 1909, cont.

	W	L	PCT	GB	R	OR	2B	3B	HR	BA	SA	SB	E	DP	FA	CG	BB	SO	ShO	SV	ERA
							Batting						**Fielding**			**Pitching**					
Pittsburgh	110	42	.724		**699**	447	**218**	**92**	25	**.260**	**.353**	185	**227**	100	**.964**	94	**320**	490	20	9	2.07
Chicago	104	49	.680	6.5	635	390	203	60	20	.245	.322	187	244	95	.961	111	364	680	**32**	9	**1.75**
New York	92	61	.601	18.5	623	546	173	68	**26**	.255	.329	230	307	99	.954	105	397	**735**	16	**12**	2.27
Cincinnati	77	76	.503	33.5	606	599	159	72	22	.250	.323	**280**	308	**120**	.952	91	510	477	10	9	2.52
Philadelphia	74	79	.484	36.5	516	518	185	53	12	.244	.309	185	241	97	.961	89	470	610	17	6	2.44
Brooklyn	55	98	.359	55.5	444	627	176	59	16	.229	.296	141	282	86	.954	**126**	528	594	18	2	3.10
St. Louis	54	98	.355	56	583	731	148	56	15	.243	.303	161	322	90	.950	84	483	435	4	2	3.41
Boston	45	108	.294	65.5	435	683	124	43	15	.223	.274	135	340	101	.947	98	543	414	12	6	3.20
					4541	4541	1386	503	151	.244	.314	1504	2271	788	.955	798	3615	4435	129	55	2.59

AMERICAN LEAGUE 1909

Detroit
W-98 L-54

Hughie Jennings

POS	Player	AB	BA	HR	RBI	PO	A	E	DP	TC/G	FA	Pitcher	G	IP	W	L	SV	ERA
1B	C. Rossman	287	.261	0	39	913	36	18	30	12.9	.981	G. Mullin	40	304	**29**	8	1	2.22
2B	G. Schaefer	280	.250	0	22	180	273	16	26	5.5	.966	E. Willett	41	293	21	10	1	2.34
SS	D. Bush	532	.273	0	33	308	**567**	71	38	6.0	.925	E. Summers	35	282	19	9	1	2.24
3B	G. Moriarty	473	.273	1	39	117	253	24	11	3.7	**.939**	E. Killian	25	173	11	9	1	1.71
RF	T. Cobb	573	**.377**	**9**	**107**	222	24	14	7	1.7	.946	W. Donovan	21	140	8	7	2	2.31
CF	S. Crawford	589	.314	6	97	297	7	11	2	2.3	.965							
LF	M. McIntyre	476	.244	1	34	217	14	6	1	1.9	.975							
C	B. Schmidt	253	.209	1	28	315	107	**20**	7	5.5	.955							
3B	C. O'Leary	261	.203	0	13	59	118	15	4	3.6	.922							
C	O. Stanage	252	.262	0	21	324	80	15	12	5.4	.964							
OF	D. Jones	204	.279	0	10	103	4	2	1	1.9	.982							
2B	J. Delahanty	150	.253	0	20	88	127	13*	13	5.0	.943							

Philadelphia
W-95 L-58

Connie Mack

POS	Player	AB	BA	HR	RBI	PO	A	E	DP	TC/G	FA	Pitcher	G	IP	W	L	SV	ERA
1B	H. Davis	530	.268	4	75	1432	74	19	65	10.2	.988	E. Plank	34	275	19	10	0	1.70
2B	E. Collins	572	.346	3	56	**373**	**406**	27	**55**	5.3	.967	C. Bender	34	250	18	8	1	1.66
SS	J. Barry	409	.215	1	23	196	351	43	40	4.8	.927	C. Morgan	28	229	16	11	0	1.65
3B	F. Baker	541	.305	4	85	209	277	42	16	3.6	.920	H. Krause	32	213	18	8	1	**1.39**
RF	D. Murphy	541	.281	5	69	191	17	5	5	1.4	.977	J. Coombs	31	206	12	11	1	2.32
CF	R. Oldring	326	.230	1	28	174	7	7	1	2.1	.963	J. Dygert	32	137	9	5	0	2.42
LF	B. Ganley	274	.197	0	9	185	9	4	2	2.6	.980*							
C	I. Thomas	256	.223	0	31	479	112	9	5	7.1	**.985**							
OF	T. Hartsel	267	.270	0	18	140	0	5	0	2.0	.966							
OF	Heitmuller	210	.286	0	15	111	4	9	2	2.1	.927							
C	Livingston	175	.234	0	15	306	106	13	6	6.6	.969							

Boston
W-88 L-63

Fred Lake

POS	Player	AB	BA	HR	RBI	PO	A	E	DP	TC/G	FA	Pitcher	G	IP	W	L	SV	ERA
1B	J. Stahl	435	.294	6	60	1353	50	20	57	11.3	.986	F. Arellanes	45	231	16	12	8	2.18
2B	McConnell	453	.238	0	36	251	389	**31**	43	5.5	.954	E. Cicotte	27	160	13	5	2	1.97
SS	H. Wagner	430	.256	1	49	282	413	50	40	6.1	.933	S. Wood	24	159	11	7	0	2.21
3B	H. Lord	534	.311	0	31	180	268	34	10	3.6	.929	C. Chech	17	107	7	5	0	2.95
RF	D. Gessler	386	.298	0	46	135	18	11	1	1.5	.933	C. Hall	11	60	6	4	0	2.56
CF	T. Speaker	544	.309	7	77	**319**	35	10	**12**	2.6	.973							
LF	H. Niles	546	.245	1	38	197	20	11	3	1.9	.952							
C	B. Carrigan	280	.296	0	36	347	110	13	9	6.1	.972							
OF	H. Hooper	255	.282	0	12	124	14	7	3	2.0	.952							
C	P. Donahue	176	.239	2	25	249	71	6	3	5.6	.982							
2S	C. French	167	.251	0	13	86	140	24	14		.904							

Chicago
W-78 L-74

Billy Sullivan

POS	Player	AB	BA	HR	RBI	PO	A	E	DP	TC/G	FA	Pitcher	G	IP	W	L	SV	ERA
1B	F. Isbell	433	.224	0	33	1204	66	8	48	12.7	**.994**	F. Smith	51	**365**	25	17	1	1.80
2B	J. Atz	381	.236	0	22	202	311	25	40	4.6	.954	J. Scott	36	250	12	12	0	2.30
SS	F. Parent	472	.261	0	30	182	357	41	34	5.9	.929	E. Walsh	31	230	15	11	2	1.41
3B	L. Tannehill	531	.222	0	47	103	168	17	11	3.2	.941	D. White	24	178	11	9	0	1.72
RF	E. Hahn	287	.181	1	16	93	3	1	1	1.3	.990	B. Burns	22	174	7	13	0	1.96
CF	D. Altizer	382	.233	1	20	99	12	6	1	1.9	.949							
LF	P. Dougherty	491	.285	1	55	184	10	12	0	1.9	.942							
C	B. Sullivan	265	.162	0	16	452	119	10	6	6.0	.983							
32	B. Purtell	361	.258	0	40	162	248	24	24		.945							
OP	D. White	192	.234	0	7	71	54	8	1		.940							
C	F. Owens	174	.201	0	17	266	62	14	2	6.0	.959							
OF	W. Cole	165	.236	0	16	83	5	11	1	2.2	.889							
P	F. Smith	127	.173	0	20	**26**	**154**	4	3	3.6	.978							

New York
W-74 L-77

George Stallings

POS	Player	AB	BA	HR	RBI	PO	A	E	DP	TC/G	FA	Pitcher	G	IP	W	L	SV	ERA
1B	H. Chase	474	.283	4	63	1202	71	**28**	53	11.0	.978	J. Warhop	36	243	13	15	2	2.40
2B	F. LaPorte	309	.298	0	31	142	208	23	30	4.5	.938	J. Lake	31	215	14	11	1	1.88
SS	J. Knight	360	.236	0	40	141	204	38	19	4.9	.901	R. Manning	26	173	7	11	1	3.17
3B	J. Austin	437	.231	1	39	176	236	32	**19**	4.0	.928	L. Brockett	26	152	10	8	1	2.37
RF	W. Keeler	360	.264	1	32	111	9	4	2	1.3	.968	S. Doyle	17	126	8	6	0	2.58
CF	R. Demmitt	427	.246	4	30	185	22	**21**	7	2.1	.908	J. Quinn	23	119	9	5	1	1.97
LF	C. Engle	492	.278	3	71	299	17	18	5	2.5	.946	T. Hughes	24	119	7	8	1	2.65
C	R. Kleinow	206	.228	0	15	343	83	15	6	5.7	.966	P. Wilson	14	94	6	5	0	3.17
S3	K. Elberfeld	379	.237	0	26	196	269	26	30		.947							
OF	B. Cree	343	.262	2	27	121	9	7	2	1.8	.949							
OF	C. Hemphill	181	.243	0	10	75	6	2	1	1.8	.976							
C	J. Sweeney	176	.267	0	21	274	83	**20**	7	6.1	.947							

AMERICAN LEAGUE 1909, *cont.*

	POS	Player	AB	BA	HR	RBI	PO	A	E	DP	TC/G	FA	Pitcher	G	IP	W	L	SV	ERA
Cleveland	1B	G. Stovall	565	.246	2	49	**1478**	**109**	19	**80**	11.1	.988	C. Young	35	295	19	15	0	2.26
	2B	N. Lajoie	469	.324	1	47	193	370	28	**55**	4.9	.953	H. Berger	34	257	13	14	1	2.63
W-71 L-82	SS	N. Ball	324	.256	1	25	198	289	46	42	5.6	.914	A. Joss	33	243	14	13	0	1.71
	3B	B. Bradley	334	.186	0	22	89	157	11	16	3.0	.957	Falkenberg	24	165	10	9	0	2.40
Nap Lajoie	RF	W. Good	318	.214	0	17	110	12	6	2	1.6	.953	B. Rhoads	20	133	5	9	0	2.90
W-57 L-57	CF	Birmingham	343	.289	1	38	203	15	12	2	2.3	.948							
	LF	B. Hinchman	457	.258	2	53	233	0	20	1	1.9	.921							
Deacon McGuire	C	T. Easterly	287	.261	1	27	335	110	16	9	6.1	.965							
W-14 L-25	3B	G. Perring	283	.223	0	20	83	151	17	6	3.8	.932							
	OF	B. Lord	249	.269	1	25	110	13	1	4	1.8	.992							
	OF	E. Flick	235	.255	0	15	87	4	4	1	1.6	.958							
	S2	T. Turner	208	.250	0	16	112	176	11	21		.963							
	C	N. Clarke	164	.274	0	14	192	65	13	2	6.1	.952							
St. Louis	1B	T. Jones	337	.249	0	29	950	70	11	57	10.9	.989	J. Powell	34	239	12	16	3	2.11
	2B	J. Williams	374	.195	0	22	221	280	20	42	4.8	.962	R. Waddell	31	220	11	14	0	2.37
W-61 L-89	SS	B. Wallace	403	.238	1	35	193	279	27	34	5.7	.946	B. Pelty	27	199	11	11	0	2.30
	3B	H. Ferris	556	.216	3	58	157	242	27	15	3.7	.937	B. Bailey	32	199	9	10	0	2.44
Jimmy McAleer	RF	R. Hartzell	**595**	.271	0	32	120	21	9	5	1.8	.940	B. Graham	34	187	8	14	1	3.12
	CF	D. Hoffman	387	.269	2	26	230	10	8	6	2.3	.968	B. Dinneen	17	112	6	7	0	3.46
	LF	G. Stone	310	.287	1	15	147	8	12	4	2.1	.928							
	C	L. Criger	212	.170	0	9	387	98	7	16	6.7	.986							
	1O	A. Griggs	364	.280	0	43	504	38	14	22		.975							
	OF	J. McAleese	267	.213	0	12	120	11	13	2	1.8	.910							
	C	J. Stephens	223	.220	3	18	335	103	9	9	6.2	.980							
Washington	1B	J. Donahue	283	.237	0	28	766	36	13	28	10.1	.984	W. Johnson	40	297	13	25	1	2.21
	2B	J. Delahanty	302	.222	1	21	177	211	18*	26	4.8	.956	B. Groom	44	261	7	**26**	0	2.87
W-42 L-110	SS	G. McBride	504	.234	0	34	341	499	58	56	5.8	**.935**	D. Gray	36	218	5	19	0	3.59
	3B	W. Conroy	488	.244	1	20	136	239	25	14	3.3	.938	C. Smith	23	146	3	12	0	3.27
Joe Cantillon	RF	J. Lelivelt	318	.292	0	24	179	14	6	3	2.2	.970	L. Hughes	22	120	4	7	1	2.69
	CF	C. Milan	400	.200	1	15	222	19	7	3	2.1	.972							
	LF	G. Browne	393	.272	1	16	147	12	11	3	1.7	.935							
	C	G. Street	407	.211	0	29	**714**	**210**	18	**18**	6.9	.981							
	UT	B. Unglaub	480	.265	3	41	669	121	13	39		.984							

BATTING AND BASE RUNNING LEADERS

Batting Average
T. Cobb, DET	.377
E. Collins, PHI	.346
N. Lajoie, CLE	.324
S. Crawford, DET	.314
H. Lord, BOS	.311

Slugging Average
T. Cobb, DET	.517
S. Crawford, DET	.452
E. Collins, PHI	.449
F. Baker, PHI	.447
T. Speaker, BOS	.443

Home Runs
T. Cobb, DET	9
T. Speaker, BOS	7
J. Stahl, BOS	6
S. Crawford, DET	6
D. Murphy, PHI	5

Total Bases
T. Cobb, DET	296
S. Crawford, DET	266
E. Collins, PHI	257
F. Baker, PHI	242
T. Speaker, BOS	241

Runs Batted In
T. Cobb, DET	107
S. Crawford, DET	97
F. Baker, PHI	85
T. Speaker, BOS	77
H. Davis, PHI	75

Stolen Bases
T. Cobb, DET	76
E. Collins, PHI	67
D. Bush, DET	53
P. Dougherty, CHI	36
H. Lord, BOS	36

Hits
T. Cobb, DET	216
E. Collins, PHI	198
S. Crawford, DET	185
T. Speaker, BOS	168

Base on Balls
D. Bush, DET	88
E. Collins, PHI	62
R. Demmitt, NY	55
M. McIntyre, DET	54

Home Run Percentage
T. Cobb, DET	1.6
J. Stahl, BOS	1.4
T. Speaker, BOS	1.3
S. Crawford, DET	1.0

Runs Scored
T. Cobb, DET	116
D. Bush, DET	114
E. Collins, PHI	104
H. Lord, BOS	85

Doubles
S. Crawford, DET	35
N. Lajoie, CLE	33
T. Cobb, DET	33
E. Collins, PHI	30

Triples
F. Baker, PHI	19
D. Murphy, PHI	14
S. Crawford, DET	14
B. Hinchman, CLE	13

PITCHING LEADERS

Winning Percentage
G. Mullin, DET	.784
C. Bender, PHI	.692
H. Krause, PHI	.692
E. Summers, DET	.679
E. Willett, DET	.677

Earned Run Average
H. Krause, PHI	1.39
E. Walsh, CHI	1.41
C. Bender, PHI	1.66
E. Plank, PHI	1.70
A. Joss, CLE	1.71

Wins
G. Mullin, DET	29
F. Smith, CHI	25
E. Willett, DET	21

Saves
F. Arellanes, BOS	8
J. Warhop, NY	4
J. Powell, STL	3
T. Hughes, NY	3

Strikeouts
F. Smith, CHI	177
W. Johnson, WAS	164
H. Berger, CLE	162
C. Bender, PHI	161
R. Waddell, STL	141

Complete Games
F. Smith, CHI	37
C. Young, CLE	30
G. Mullin, DET	29
W. Johnson, WAS	27
C. Morgan, BOS, PHI	26

Fewest Hits/9 Innings
C. Morgan, BOS, PHI	6.26
H. Krause, PHI	6.38
E. Walsh, CHI	6.49
E. Cicotte, BOS	6.59

Shutouts
E. Walsh, CHI	8
H. Krause, PHI	7
F. Smith, CHI	7
J. Coombs, PHI	6

Fewest Walks/9 Innings
A. Joss, CLE	1.15
D. White, CHI	1.57
J. Powell, STL	1.58
C. Bender, PHI	1.62

Most Strikeouts/9 Inn.
H. Krause, PHI	5.87
C. Bender, PHI	5.80
R. Waddell, STL	5.76
H. Berger, CLE	5.67

Innings
F. Smith, CHI	365
G. Mullin, DET	304
W. Johnson, WAS	297
C. Young, CLE	295

Games Pitched
F. Smith, CHI	51
F. Arellanes, BOS	45
B. Groom, WAS	44
E. Willett, DET	41

AMERICAN LEAGUE 1909, cont.

	W	L	PCT	GB	R	OR	Batting 2B	3B	HR	BA	SA	SB	Fielding E	DP	FA	Pitching CG	BB	SO	ShO	SV	ERA
Detroit	98	54	.645		**666**	493	**209**	58	19	**.267**	.342	**280**	276	87	.959	**117**	359	528	17	12	2.26
Philadelphia	95	58	.621	3.5	605	**408**	186	**89**	20	.257	**.343**	205	**245**	92	.961	111	386	**728**	27	3	**1.92**
Boston	88	63	.583	9.5	597	550	151	69	20	.263	.333	215	292	95	.955	75	384	555	11	**15**	2.60
Chicago	78	74	.513	20	492	463	145	56	4	.221	.275	211	246	101	**.964**	112	**341**	671	26	4	2.04
New York	74	77	.490	23.5	590	587	143	61	16	.248	.311	187	329	94	.948	94	422	597	18	7	2.68
Cleveland	71	82	.464	27.5	493	532	173	81	10	.241	.313	174	275	**110**	.957	110	349	569	15	3	2.39
St. Louis	61	89	.407	36	441	575	116	45	11	.232	.280	136	267	107	.958	105	383	620	21	4	2.88
Washington	42	110	.276	56	380	656	148	41	9	.223	.275	136	280	100	.957	99	424	653	11	2	3.04
					4264	4264	1271	500	109	.244	.309	1544	2210	786	.957	823	3048	4921	146	50	2.47

NATIONAL LEAGUE 1910

Team	POS	Player	AB	BA	HR	RBI	PO	A	E	DP	TC/G	FA	Pitcher	G	IP	W	L	SV	ERA
Chicago W-104 L-50 Frank Chance	1B	F. Chance	295	.298	0	36	773	38	3	48	9.4	.996	T. Brown	46	295	25	13	7	1.86
	2B	J. Evers	433	.263	0	28	282	347	33	55	5.3	.950	K. Cole	33	240	20	4	0	1.80
	SS	J. Tinker	473	.288	3	69	277	411	42	54	5.6	.942	H. McIntire	28	176	13	9	0	3.07
	3B	Steinfeldt	448	.252	2	58	137	246	22	16	3.2	.946	E. Reulbach	24	173	12	8	0	3.12
	RF	W. Schulte	559	.301	10	68	221	18	8	5	1.6	.968	O. Overall	23	145	12	6	1	2.68
	CF	S. Hofman	477	.325	3	86	249	19	7	4	2.5	.975	L. Richie	30	130	11	4	3	2.70
	LF	J. Sheckard	507	.256	5	51	308	21	8	3	2.4	.976	J. Pfiester	14	100	6	3	0	1.79
	C	J. Kling	297	.269	2	32	407	118	11	10	6.2	.979							
	UT	H. Zimmerman	335	.284	3	38	164	181	33	28		.913							
	C1	J. Archer	313	.259	2	41	620	97	20	31		.973							
	OF	G. Beaumont	172	.267	2	22	107	5	5	0	2.1	.957							
New York W-91 L-63 John McGraw	1B	F. Merkle	506	.292	4	70	1390	84	**29**	87	10.4	.981	C. Mathewson	38	318	**27**	9	0	1.90
	2B	L. Doyle	575	.285	8	69	313	388	53	62	5.0	.930	H. Wiltse	36	235	14	12	1	2.72
	SS	A. Bridwell	492	.276	0	48	304	417	41	52	5.4	.946	L. Drucke	34	215	12	10	0	2.47
	3B	A. Devlin	493	.260	2	67	179	284	33	20	3.4	.933	D. Crandall	42	208	17	4	4	2.56
	RF	R. Murray	553	.277	4	87	246	**26**	15	3	1.9	.948	R. Ames	33	190	12	11	0	2.22
	CF	F. Snodgrass	396	.321	2	44	214	12	7	1	2.3	.970	B. Raymond	19	99	4	11	0	3.81
	LF	J. Devore	490	.304	2	27	191	18	16	3	1.7	.929							
	C	C. Meyers	365	.285	1	62	**638**	154	25	16	**7.0**	.969							
	OF	C. Seymour	287	.265	1	40	137	9	10	1	2.1	.936							
	OF	B. Becker	126	.286	3	24	63	7	2	0	1.6	.972							
Pittsburgh W-86 L-67 Fred Clarke	1B	J. Flynn	332	.274	6	52	869	49	22	54	10.1	.977	H. Camnitz	38	260	12	13	2	3.22
	2B	D. Miller	444	.227	1	48	263	318	33	45	5.2	.946	B. Adams	34	245	18	9	0	2.24
	SS	H. Wagner	556	.320	4	81	337	413	51	62	5.8	.936	L. Leifield	40	218	15	12	1	2.64
	3B	B. Byrne	602	.296	2	52	167	289	35	11	3.3	.929	K. White	30	153	10	9	2	3.46
	RF	O. Wilson	536	.276	4	50	255	23	8	5	2.0	.972	D. Phillippe	31	122	14	2	4	2.29
	CF	T. Leach	529	.270	4	52	352	14	13	4	2.9	.966	S. Leever	26	111	6	5	2	2.76
	LF	F. Clarke	429	.263	2	63	284	10	10	4	2.6	.967	B. Powell	12	75	4	6	0	2.40
	C	G. Gibson	482	.259	3	44	633	**203**	14	8	5.9	**.984**							
	OF	V. Campbell	282	.326	4	21	145	8	18	2	2.3	.895							
	UT	McKechnie	212	.217	0	12	146	166	12	20		.963							
	1B	H. Hyatt	175	.263	1	30	323	19	5	19	9.1	.986							
Philadelphia W-78 L-75 Red Dooin	1B	Bransfield	427	.239	3	52	1026	51	20	82	10.0	.982	E. Moore	46	283	22	15	0	2.58
	2B	O. Knabe	510	.261	1	44	383	381	37	72	5.9	.954	B. Ewing	34	255	16	14	0	3.00
	SS	M. Doolan	536	.263	2	57	283	**500**	43	**71**	5.6	.948	L. Moren	34	205	13	14	1	3.55
	3B	E. Grant	579	.268	1	67	**193**	256	31	22	3.2	.935	McQuillan	24	152	9	6	1	**1.60**
	RF	J. Titus	535	.241	3	35	226	22	6	4	1.8	.976	E. Stack	20	117	6	7	0	4.00
	CF	J. Bates	498	.305	3	61	308	24	16	8	2.7	.954	L. Schettler	27	107	2	6	1	3.20
	LF	S. Magee	519	**.331**	6	123	285	9	8	2	2.0	.974	B. Foxen	16	78	5	5	0	2.55
	C	R. Dooin	331	.242	0	30	472	131	**28**	14	6.9	.956							
	UT	J. Walsh	242	.248	3	31	122	101	23	11		.907							
	C	P. Moran	199	.236	0	11	278	83	4	5	6.5	.989							
Cincinnati W-75 L-79 Clark Griffith	1B	Hoblitzell	**611**	.278	4	70	1454	67	24	64	10.4	.984	H. Gaspar	48	275	15	17	5	2.59
	2B	D. Egan	474	.245	0	46	264	391	26	49	5.1	.961	G. Suggs	35	266	19	11	3	2.40
	SS	T. McMillan	248	.185	0	13	162	270	34	32	5.7	.927	J. Rowan	42	261	14	13	1	2.93
	3B	H. Lobert	314	.309	3	40	123	164	21	11	3.4	.932	F. Beebe	35	214	12	15	0	3.07
	RF	M. Mitchell	583	.286	5	88	257	19	12	4	1.9	.958	B. Burns	31	179	8	13	0	3.48
	CF	D. Paskert	506	.300	2	46	**355**	25	17	4	2.9	.957							
	LF	B. Bescher	589	.250	4	48	339	16	**20**	4	2.5	.947							
	C	L. McLean	423	.298	2	71	485	158	11	**18**	5.5	.983							
	S3	T. Downey	378	.270	2	32	201	281	60	26		.889							
	C	T. Clarke	151	.278	1	20	217	52	8	3	4.9	.971							

NATIONAL LEAGUE 1910, cont.

	POS	Player	AB	BA	HR	RBI	PO	A	E	DP	TC/G	FA	Pitcher	G	IP	W	L	SV	ERA
Brooklyn W-64 L-90 Bill Dahlen	1B	J. Daubert	552	.264	8	50	1418	72	16	81	10.5	.989	N. Rucker	41	320	17	18	0	2.58
	2B	J. Hummel	578	.244	5	74	344	424	28	67	5.2	.965	G. Bell	44	310	10	27	1	2.64
	SS	T. Smith	321	.181	1	16	254	318	36	57	6.0	.941	C. Barger	35	272	15	15	1	2.88
	3B	E. Lennox	367	.259	3	32	135	149	15	14	3.0	.950	D. Scanlan	34	217	9	11	2	2.61
	RF	J. Dalton	273	.227	1	21	129	12	5	3	2.0	.966	E. Knetzer	20	133	7	5	0	3.19
	CF	B. Davidson	509	.238	0	34	283	11	12	3	2.3	.961	K. Wilhelm	15	68	3	7	0	4.74
	LF	Z. Wheat	606	.284	2	55	354	21	15	6	2.5	.962							
	C	B. Bergen	249	.161	0	14	373	151	10	15	6.0	.981							
	OF	A. Burch	352	.236	1	20	124	11	6	6	2.0	.957							
	3B	P. McElveen	213	.225	1	26	72	78	9	12	2.9	.943							
	C	T. Erwin	202	.188	1	10	259	114	20	10	5.8	.949							
St. Louis W-63 L-90 Roger Bresnahan	1B	E. Konetchy	520	.302	3	78	1499	98	15	81	11.2	.991	B. Harmon	43	236	13	15	2	4.46
	2B	M. Huggins	547	.265	1	36	325	452	30	58	5.3	.963	J. Lush	36	225	14	13	1	3.20
	SS	A. Hauser	375	.205	2	36	212	345	41	31	5.1	.931	V. Willis	33	212	9	12	3	3.35
	3B	M. Mowrey	489	.282	2	70	171	301	37	30	3.6	.927	F. Corridon	30	156	6	14	2	3.81
	RF	S. Evans	506	.241	2	73	226	16	8	3	1.8	.968	L. Backman	26	116	6	7	1	3.03
	CF	R. Oakes	468	.252	0	43	266	12	18	3	2.3	.939	S. Sallee	18	115	7	8	2	2.97
	LF	R. Ellis	550	.258	4	54	268	25	18	4	2.2	.942							
	C	E. Phelps	270	.263	0	37	320	84	10	10	5.2	.976							
	C	R. Bresnahan	234	.278	0	27	295	100	16	11	5.3	.961							
Boston W-53 L-100 Fred Lake	1B	B. Sharpe	439	.239	0	29	1122	81	16	72	10.8	.987	A. Mattern	51	305	16	19	1	2.98
	2B	D. Shean	543	.239	3	36	408	493	44	92	6.4	.953	B. Brown	46	263	9	23	2	2.67
	SS	B. Sweeney	499	.267	5	46	232	300	57	52	5.4	.903	S. Frock	45	255	11	19	2	3.21
	3B	B. Herzog	380	.250	3	32	110	223	32	17	3.5	.915	C. Curtis	43	251	6	24	2	3.55
	RF	D. Miller	482	.286	3	55	203	9	11	3	1.7	.951	G. Ferguson	26	123	8	7	0	3.80
	CF	F. Beck	571	.275	10	64	293	19	12	6	2.4	.963							
	LF	B. Collins	584	.241	3	40	355	23	9	2	2.6	.977							
	C	P. Graham	291	.282	0	21	318	132	16	11	5.4	.966							
	SS	Abbaticchio	178	.247	0	10	73	149	22	19	5.3	.910							

BATTING AND BASE RUNNING LEADERS

Batting Average
S. Magee, PHI	.331
V. Campbell, PIT	.326
S. Hofman, CHI	.325
F. Snodgrass, NY	.321
H. Wagner, PIT	.320

Slugging Average
S. Magee, PHI	.507
S. Hofman, CHI	.461
W. Schulte, CHI	.460
F. Merkle, NY	.441
V. Campbell, PIT	.436

Home Runs
W. Schulte, CHI	10
F. Beck, BOS	10
J. Daubert, BKN	8
L. Doyle, NY	8
J. Flynn, PIT	6
S. Magee, PHI	6

Total Bases
S. Magee, PHI	263
W. Schulte, CHI	257
B. Byrne, PIT	251
Z. Wheat, BKN	244
H. Wagner, PIT	240

Runs Batted In
S. Magee, PHI	123
M. Mitchell, CIN	88
R. Murray, NY	87
S. Hofman, CHI	86
H. Wagner, PIT	81

Stolen Bases
B. Bescher, CIN	70
R. Murray, NY	57
D. Paskert, CIN	51
S. Magee, PHI	49
J. Devore, NY	43

Hits
H. Wagner, PIT	178
B. Byrne, PIT	178
S. Magee, PHI	172
Z. Wheat, BKN	172

Base on Balls
M. Huggins, STL	116
J. Evers, CHI	108
S. Magee, PHI	94
J. Titus, PHI	93

Home Run Percentage
J. Flynn, PIT	1.8
W. Schulte, CHI	1.8
F. Beck, BOS	1.8
J. Daubert, BKN	1.4

Runs Scored
S. Magee, PHI	110
M. Huggins, STL	101
B. Byrne, PIT	101
L. Doyle, NY	97

Doubles
B. Byrne, PIT	43
S. Magee, PHI	39
Z. Wheat, BKN	36
F. Merkle, NY	35

Triples
M. Mitchell, CIN	18
S. Magee, PHI	17
S. Hofman, CHI	16
E. Konetchy, STL	16

PITCHING LEADERS

Winning Percentage
K. Cole, CHI	.833
D. Crandall, NY	.810
C. Mathewson, NY	.750
B. Adams, PIT	.667
T. Brown, CHI	.658

Earned Run Average
McQuillan, PHI	1.60
K. Cole, CHI	1.80
T. Brown, CHI	1.86
C. Mathewson, NY	1.89
R. Ames, NY	2.22

Wins
C. Mathewson, NY	27
T. Brown, CHI	25
K. Cole, CHI	20
E. Moore, PHI	20

Saves
T. Brown, CHI	7
H. Gaspar, CIN	5
D. Crandall, NY	4
D. Phillippe, PIT	4

Strikeouts
E. Moore, PHI	185
C. Mathewson, NY	184
S. Frock, BOS, PIT	171
L. Drucke, NY	151
N. Rucker, BKN	147

Complete Games
T. Brown, CHI	27
C. Mathewson, NY	27
N. Rucker, BKN	27
C. Barger, BKN	25
G. Bell, BKN	25

Fewest Hits/9 Innings
McQuillan, PHI	6.44
K. Cole, CHI	6.53
O. Overall, CHI	6.59
D. Scanlan, BKN	7.25

Shutouts
T. Brown, CHI	7
E. Moore, PHI	6
A. Mattern, BOS	6
N. Rucker, BKN	6

Fewest Walks/9 Innings
G. Suggs, CIN	1.62
C. Mathewson, NY	1.70
D. Crandall, NY	1.86
T. Brown, CHI	1.95

Most Strikeouts/9 Inn.
L. Drucke, NY	6.31
S. Frock, BOS, PIT	5.98
E. Moore, PHI	5.88
O. Overall, CHI	5.72

Innings
N. Rucker, BKN	320
C. Mathewson, NY	318
G. Bell, BKN	310
A. Mattern, BOS	305

Games Pitched
A. Mattern, BOS	51
H. Gaspar, CIN	48
T. Brown, CHI	46
E. Moore, PHI	46

	W	L	PCT	GB	R	OR	Batting 2B	3B	HR	BA	SA	SB	Fielding E	DP	FA	Pitching CG	BB	SO	ShO	SV	ERA
Chicago	104	50	.675		712	499	219	84	34	.268	.366	173	230	110	.963	99	474	609	27	11	2.51
New York	91	63	.591	13	715	567	204	83	31	.275	.366	282	291	117	.955	96	397	717	9	8	2.68
Pittsburgh	86	67	.562	17.5	655	576	214	83	33	.266	.360	148	245	102	.961	73	392	479	13	11	2.83
Philadelphia	78	75	.510	25.5	674	639	223	71	26	.255	.338	199	258	132	.960	84	547	657	16	7	3.05
Cincinnati	75	79	.487	29	620	684	150	79	23	.259	.333	310	291	103	.955	86	528	497	16	9	3.08
Brooklyn	64	90	.416	40	497	623	166	73	25	.229	.305	151	235	125	.964	103	545	555	15	4	3.07
St. Louis	63	90	.412	40.5	639	718	167	70	15	.248	.319	179	261	105	.959	83	541	466	3	12	3.78
Boston	53	100	.346	50.5	495	701	173	49	31	.246	.317	152	305	137	.954	74	599	531	12	7	3.22
					5007	5007	1516	592	214	.256	.338	1594	2116	935	.959	698	4023	4511	111	69	3.02

AMERICAN LEAGUE 1910

Philadelphia
W-102 L-48
Connie Mack

POS	Player	AB	BA	HR	RBI	PO	A	E	DP	TC/G	FA	Pitcher	G	IP	W	L	SV	ERA
1B	H. Davis	492	.248	1	41	1353	64	20	**74**	10.3	.986	J. Coombs	**45**	353	**31**	9	1	1.30
2B	E. Collins	583	.322	3	81	**402**	**451**	25	67	5.7	.972	C. Morgan	36	291	18	12	0	1.55
SS	J. Barry	487	.259	3	60	279	406	**63**	54	5.2	.916	E. Plank	38	250	16	10	2	2.01
3B	F. Baker	561	.283	2	74	**207**	313	45	**35**	3.9	.920	C. Bender	30	250	23	5	0	1.58
RF	D. Murphy	560	.300	4	64	209	15	6	5	1.5	.974	H. Krause	16	112	6	6	0	2.88
CF	R. Oldring	546	.308	4	57	249	14	6	6	2.0	**.978**							
LF	T. Hartsel	285	.221	0	22	113	8	7	2	1.5	.945							
C	J. Lapp	192	.234	0	17	361	88	9	6	7.3	.980							
OF	B. Lord	288	.278	1	20	142	6	3	2	2.1	.980							
C	I. Thomas	180	.278	1	19	324	86	14	8	7.1	.967							

New York
W-88 L-63
George Stallings W-78 L-59
Hal Chase W-10 L-4

POS	Player	AB	BA	HR	RBI	PO	A	E	DP	TC/G	FA	Pitcher	G	IP	W	L	SV	ERA
1B	H. Chase	524	.290	3	73	1373	65	28	68	11.3	.981	R. Ford	36	300	26	6	1	1.65
2B	F. LaPorte	432	.264	2	67	127	220	15	21	4.6	.959	J. Warhop	37	254	14	14	2	2.87
SS	J. Knight	414	.312	3	45	169	247	32	39	5.7	.929	J. Quinn	35	237	18	12	0	2.36
3B	J. Austin	432	.218	2	36	204	284	30	10	3.9	.942	H. Vaughn	30	222	13	11	1	1.83
RF	H. Wolter	479	.267	4	42	192	11	13	3	1.7	.940	T. Hughes	23	152	7	9	1	3.50
CF	C. Hemphill	351	.239	0	21	159	10	5	2	1.9	.971							
LF	B. Cree	467	.287	4	73	202	11	10	3	1.7	.955							
C	J. Sweeney	215	.200	0	13	388	106	13	2	6.5	.974							
OF	B. Daniels	356	.253	1	17	170	9	8	2	2.2	.957							
2B	E. Gardner	271	.244	1	24	169	199	25	36	5.6	.936							
SS	R. Roach	220	.214	0	20	112	173	27	27	5.4	.913							
C	F. Mitchell	196	.230	0	18	262	69	11	2	5.0	.968							

Detroit
W-86 L-68
Hughie Jennings

POS	Player	AB	BA	HR	RBI	PO	A	E	DP	TC/G	FA	Pitcher	G	IP	W	L	SV	ERA
1B	T. Jones	432	.255	0	45	1405	67	23	50	11.1	.985	G. Mullin	38	289	21	12	0	2.87
2B	J. Delahanty	378	.294	2	45	246	267	33	36	5.2	.940	E. Summers	30	220	13	12	0	2.53
SS	D. Bush	496	.262	3	34	310	487	51	31	6.0	.940	W. Donovan	26	209	17	7	0	2.42
3B	G. Moriarty	490	.251	2	60	165	302	37	17	3.8	.927	E. Willett	37	147	16	11	0	3.60
RF	S. Crawford	588	.289	5	**120**	223	10	9	2	1.6	.963	S. Stroud	28	130	5	9	1	3.25
CF	T. Cobb	509	**.385**	8	91	305	18	14	4	2.5	.958	R. Works	18	86	3	6	1	3.57
LF	D. Jones	377	.265	0	24	181	13	9	2	2.0	.956							
C	O. Stanage	275	.207	2	25	344	148	25	6	6.2	.952							
OF	M. McIntyre	305	.236	0	25	147	12	9	2	2.2	.946							
2S	C. O'Leary	211	.242	0	9	116	153	16	12		.944							
C	B. Schmidt	197	.259	1	23	239	80	9	1	5.0	.973							

Boston
W-81 L-72
Patsy Donovan

POS	Player	AB	BA	HR	RBI	PO	A	E	DP	TC/G	FA	Pitcher	G	IP	W	L	SV	ERA
1B	J. Stahl	531	.271	**10**	77	**1488**	60	23	46	11.1	.985	E. Cicotte	36	250	15	11	0	2.74
2B	L. Gardner	413	.283	2	36	222	320	32	28	5.1	.944	R. Collins	35	245	13	11	1	1.62
SS	H. Wagner	491	.273	1	52	303	424	57	40	5.6	.927	S. Wood	35	198	12	13	0	1.68
3B	H. Lord	288	.250	1	32	90	138	18	10	3.5	.927	C. Hall	35	189	12	9	2	1.91
RF	H. Hooper	584	.267	2	27	241	**30**	**18**	7	1.9	.938	E. Karger	27	183	11	7	1	3.19
CF	T. Speaker	538	.340	7	65	**337**	20	16	7	2.7	.957	C. Smith	24	156	11	6	1	2.30
LF	D. Lewis	541	.283	8	68	261	28	17	9	2.1	.944	F. Arellanes	18	100	4	7	0	2.88
C	B. Carrigan	342	.249	3	53	**495**	134	25	12	5.9	.962							
UT	C. Engle	363	.264	2	38	129	223	29	17		.924							
3B	B. Purtell	168	.208	1	15	41	87*	13*	2	3.4	.908							

Cleveland
W-71 L-81
Deacon McGuire

POS	Player	AB	BA	HR	RBI	PO	A	E	DP	TC/G	FA	Pitcher	G	IP	W	L	SV	ERA
1B	G. Stovall	521	.261	0	52	1404	**91**	18	60	**11.5**	**.988**	Falkenberg	37	257	14	13	1	2.95
2B	N. Lajoie	**591**	.384	4	76	387	419	28	60	5.6	.966	W. Mitchell	35	184	12	8	0	2.60
SS	T. Turner	574	.230	0	33	194	320	14	42	5.6	**.973**	C. Young	21	163	7	10	0	2.53
3B	B. Bradley	214	.196	0	12	89	126	10	8	3.7	.956	E. Koestner	27	145	5	10	2	3.04
RF	J. Graney	454	.236	1	31	209	14	12	5	2.1	.949	S. Harkness	26	136	10	7	1	3.04
CF	Birmingham	364	.231	0	35	223	24	10	8	2.5	.961	F. Link	22	123	5	6	1	3.30
LF	A. Kruger	223	.170	0	14	116	10	6	3	2.1	.955	A. Joss	13	107	5	5	0	2.26
C	T. Easterly	363	.306	0	55	200	104	15	7	4.8	.953	G. Kahler	12	95	6	4	0	1.60
OF	H. Niles	240	.213	1	18	70	7	2	1	1.4	.975	H. Fanwell	17	92	2	9	0	3.62
OF	B. Lord	201	.219	0	17	77	14	4	4	1.7	.958							
C	H. Bemis	167	.216	1	16	186	63	10	4	5.6	.961							

Chicago
W-68 L-85
Hugh Duffy

POS	Player	AB	BA	HR	RBI	PO	A	E	DP	TC/G	FA	Pitcher	G	IP	W	L	SV	ERA
1B	C. Gandil	275	.193	2	21	854	57	10	34	12.4	.989	E. Walsh	**45**	**370**	18	**20**	5	**1.27**
2B	R. Zeider	498	.217	0	31	205	242	33	31	5.5	.931	D. White	33	246	15	13	1	2.56
SS	Blackburne	242	.174	0	10	173	265	43	29	6.5	.911	J. Scott	41	230	8	18	1	2.43
3B	B. Purtell	368	.234	1	36	117	233*	36*	16	3.8	.907	F. Olmstead	32	184	10	12	0	1.95
RF	S. Collins	315	.197	1	24	101	11	6	6	1.8	.949	I. Young	27	136	4	8	0	2.72
CF	P. Meloan	222	.243	0	23	76	16	5	1	1.5	.948	P. Lange	23	131	9	4	0	1.65
LF	P. Dougherty	443	.248	1	43	158	9	14	2	1.5	.923	F. Smith	19	129	4	9	0	2.03
C	F. Payne	257	.218	0	19	409	106	14	11	**6.8**	.974							
OF	F. Parent	258	.178	1	16	92	5	3	1	1.6	.970							
S1	L. Tannehill	230	.222	0	21	258	144	12	21		.971							
2O	C. French	170	.165	0	4	69	54	10	6		.925							
3B	H. Lord	165	.297	0	10	44	75	6	4	2.8	.952							

AMERICAN LEAGUE 1910, cont.

	POS	Player	AB	BA	HR	RBI	PO	A	E	DP	TC/G	FA	Pitcher	G	IP	W	L	SV	ERA
Washington	1B	B. Unglaub	431	.234	0	44	1230	79	20	51	10.7	.985	W. Johnson	45	373	25	17	1	1.35
	2B	R. Killefer	345	.229	0	24	173	231	26	27	4.9	.940	B. Groom	34	258	12	17	0	2.76
W-66 L-85	SS	G. McBride	514	.230	1	55	370	518	58	57	6.1	.939	D. Gray	34	229	8	19	0	2.63
	3B	K. Elberfeld	455	.251	2	42	139	223	22	15	3.4	.943	D. Walker	29	199	11	11	0	3.30
Jimmy McAleer	RF	D. Gessler	487	.259	2	50	161	23	9	3	1.3	.953	D. Reisling	30	191	10	10	1	2.54
	CF	C. Milan	531	.279	0	16	267	30	17	10	2.2	.946							
	LF	J. Lelivelt	347	.265	0	33	149	13	6	5	1.9	.964							
	C	G. Street	257	.202	1	16	417	151	13	8	6.8	.978							
	3O	W. Conroy	351	.254	1	27	151	91	10	6		.960							
	2O	G. Schaefer	229	.275	0	14	89	108	11	16		.947							
St. Louis	1B	P. Newnam	384	.216	2	26	1041	56	**32**	53	11.0	.972	J. Lake	35	261	11	17	2	2.20
	2B	F. Truesdale	415	.219	1	25	279	313	56	41	5.3	.914	B. Bailey	34	192	3	18	0	3.32
W-47 L-107	SS	B. Wallace	508	.258	0	37	258	344	33	37	**6.5**	.948	B. Pelty	27	165	5	11	0	3.48
	3B	R. Hartzell	542	.218	2	30	123	203	25	19	3.9	.929	F. Ray	21	141	4	10	0	3.58
Jack O'Connor	RF	Schweitzer	379	.230	2	37	149	15	11	3	1.6	.937	J. Powell	21	129	7	11	0	2.30
	CF	D. Hoffman	380	.237	0	27	202	14	9	5	2.1	.960							
	LF	G. Stone	562	.256	0	40	220	20	7	2	1.7	.972							
	C	J. Stephens	299	.241	0	23	418	**156**	17	**18**	6.2	.971							
	UT	A. Griggs	416	.236	2	30	322	120	32	29		.932							
	C	B. Killefer	193	.124	0	7	311	124	**29**	16	6.4	.938							

BATTING AND BASE RUNNING LEADERS

Batting Average		Slugging Average		Home Runs		Winning Percentage		Earned Run Average		Wins	
T. Cobb, DET	.385	T. Cobb, DET	.554	J. Stahl, BOS	10	C. Bender, PHI	.821	E. Walsh, CHI	1.27	J. Coombs, PHI	31
N. Lajoie, CLE	.384	N. Lajoie, CLE	.514	T. Cobb, DET	8	R. Ford, NY	.813	J. Coombs, PHI	1.30	R. Ford, NY	26
T. Speaker, BOS	.340	T. Speaker, BOS	.468	D. Lewis, BOS	8	J. Coombs, PHI	.775	W. Johnson, WAS	1.35	W. Johnson, WAS	25
E. Collins, PHI	.322	D. Murphy, PHI	.436	T. Speaker, BOS	7	W. Donovan, DET	.708	C. Morgan, PHI	1.55	C. Bender, PHI	23
J. Knight, NY	.312	R. Oldring, PHI	.430	S. Crawford, DET	5	G. Mullin, DET	.636	C. Bender, PHI	1.58	G. Mullin, DET	21

Total Bases		Runs Batted In		Stolen Bases		Saves		Strikeouts		Complete Games	
N. Lajoie, CLE	304	S. Crawford, DET	120	E. Collins, PHI	81	C. Hall, BOS	5	W. Johnson, WAS	313	W. Johnson, WAS	38
T. Cobb, DET	282	T. Cobb, DET	91	T. Cobb, DET	65	E. Walsh, CHI	5	E. Walsh, CHI	258	J. Coombs, PHI	35
T. Speaker, BOS	252	E. Collins, PHI	81	D. Bush, DET	49	F. Browning, DET	3	J. Coombs, PHI	224	E. Walsh, CHI	33
S. Crawford, DET	249	J. Stahl, BOS	77	R. Zeider, CHI	49			R. Ford, NY	209	R. Ford, NY	29
D. Murphy, PHI	244	N. Lajoie, CLE	76	C. Milan, WAS	44			C. Bender, PHI	155	G. Mullin, DET	27

Hits		Base on Balls		Home Run Percentage		Fewest Hits/9 Innings		Shutouts		Fewest Walks/9 Innings	
N. Lajoie, CLE	227	D. Bush, DET	78	J. Stahl, BOS	1.9	R. Ford, NY	5.83	J. Coombs, PHI	13	E. Walsh, CHI	1.49
T. Cobb, DET	196	C. Milan, WAS	71	T. Cobb, DET	1.6	E. Walsh, CHI	5.89	R. Ford, NY	8	C. Young, CLE	1.49
E. Collins, PHI	188	H. Wolter, NY	66	D. Lewis, BOS	1.5	J. Coombs, PHI	6.32	W. Johnson, WAS	8	R. Collins, BOS	1.51
T. Speaker, BOS	183	T. Cobb, DET	64	T. Speaker, BOS	1.3	W. Johnson, WAS	6.49	E. Walsh, CHI	7	C. Bender, PHI	1.69

Runs Scored		Doubles		Triples		Most Strikeouts/9 Inn.		Innings		Games Pitched	
T. Cobb, DET	106	N. Lajoie, CLE	51	S. Crawford, DET	19	W. Johnson, WAS	7.55	W. Johnson, WAS	373	W. Johnson, WAS	45
T. Speaker, BOS	92	T. Cobb, DET	36	B. Lord, CLE, PHI	18	S. Wood, BOS	6.60	E. Walsh, CHI	370	E. Walsh, CHI	45
N. Lajoie, CLE	92	D. Lewis, BOS	29	D. Murphy, PHI	18	E. Walsh, CHI	6.28	J. Coombs, PHI	353	J. Coombs, PHI	45
D. Bush, DET	90	D. Murphy, PHI	28	B. Cree, NY	16	R. Ford, NY	6.28	R. Ford, NY	300	J. Scott, CHI	41

PITCHING LEADERS

	W	L	PCT	GB	R	OR	2B	3B	HR	BA	SA	SB	E	DP	FA	CG	BB	SO	ShO	SV	ERA
Philadelphia	102	48	.680		673	**441**	**194**	**106**	19	**.266**	**.356**	207	**230**	117	**.965**	**123**	450	**789**	24	5	**1.79**
New York	88	63	.583	14.5	626	557	163	75	20	.248	.322	**288**	284	95	.956	110	**364**	654	14	**8**	2.59
Detroit	86	68	.558	18	**679**	582	192	73	26	.261	.344	249	288	79	.956	108	460	532	17	5	3.00
Boston	81	72	.529	22.5	638	564	175	87	**43**	.259	.351	194	309	80	.954	100	414	670	13	6	2.46
Cleveland	71	81	.467	32	548	657	185	63	9	.244	.308	189	247	112	.964	92	487	614	13	5	2.89
Chicago	68	85	.444	35.5	457	479	115	58	7	.211	.261	183	314	100	.954	103	381	785	23	7	2.01
Washington	66	85	.437	36.5	501	550	145	46	9	.236	.289	192	264	99	.959	119	374	675	19	3	2.46
St. Louis	47	107	.305	57	451	743	131	60	12	.220	.276	169	377	113	.944	100	532	557	9	3	3.09
					4573	4573	1300	568	145	.243	.314	1671	2313	795	.956	855	3462	5276	132	42	2.53

NATIONAL LEAGUE 1911

	POS	Player	AB	BA	HR	RBI	PO	A	E	DP	TC/G	FA	Pitcher	G	IP	W	L	SV	ERA
New York	1B	F. Merkle	541	.283	12	84	1375	**117**	**22**	73	10.2	.985	C. Mathewson	45	307	26	13	3	**1.99**
	2B	L. Doyle	526	.310	13	77	272	340	36	46	4.6	.944	R. Marquard	45	278	24	7	2	2.50
W-99 L-54	SS	A. Bridwell	263	.270	0	31	129	249	34	26	5.4	.917	R. Ames	34	205	11	10	1	2.68
	3B	A. Devlin	260	.273	0	25	75	144	13	3	2.9	.944	D. Crandall	41	199	15	5	5	2.63
John McGraw	RF	R. Murray	488	.291	3	78	196	12	10	1	1.7	.954	H. Wiltse	30	187	12	9	0	3.27
	CF	F. Snodgrass	534	.294	1	77	293	31	9	8	2.2	.973	B. Raymond	17	82	6	4	0	3.31
	LF	J. Devore	565	.280	3	50	241	29	19	5	1.9	.934							
	C	C. Meyers	391	.332	1	61	**729**	108	18	11	**6.7**	.979							
	UT	A. Fletcher	326	.319	1	37	153	285	32	27		.932							
	3B	B. Herzog	247	.267	1	26	88	138	18	7	3.8	.926							
	OF	B. Becker	172	.262	1	20	72	7	2	0	1.5	.975							
	P	D. Crandall	113	.239	2	21	9	59	3	2	1.7	.958							

NATIONAL LEAGUE 1911, *cont.*

	POS	Player	AB	BA	HR	RBI	PO	A	E	DP	TC/G	FA	Pitcher	G	IP	W	L	SV	ERA
Chicago	1B	V. Saier	259	.259	1	37	715	33	15	44	10.5	.980	T. Brown	53	270	21	11	13	2.80
	2B	H. Zimmerman	535	.307	9	85	256	304	32	42	5.5	.946	L. Richie	36	253	15	11	1	2.31
W-92 L-62	SS	J. Tinker	536	.278	4	69	333	486	55	56	6.1	.937	E. Reulbach	33	222	16	9	0	2.96
	3B	J. Doyle	472	.282	5	62	134	278	35	25	3.5	.922	K. Cole	32	221	18	7	0	3.13
Frank Chance	RF	W. Schulte	577	.300	21	121	246	19	8	8	1.8	.971	H. McIntire	25	149	11	7	0	4.11
	CF	S. Hofman	512	.252	2	70	230	11	8	5	2.3	.968							
	LF	J. Sheckard	539	.276	4	50	332	32	14	12	2.4	.963							
	C	J. Archer	387	.253	4	41	476	124	14	11	6.0	.977							
	2B	J. Evers	155	.226	0	7	66	90	4	17	4.8	.975							
	OF	W. Good	145	.269	2	21	74	3	6	1	2.1	.928							
Pittsburgh	1B	N. Hunter	209	.254	2	24	504	26	6	44	8.8	.989	L. Leifield	42	318	16	16	1	2.63
	2B	D. Miller	470	.268	6	78	273	357	38	65	5.2	.943	B. Adams	40	293	22	12	0	2.33
W-85 L-69	SS	H. Wagner	473	.334	9	89	221	312	39	55	5.7	.932	H. Camnitz	40	268	20	15	0	3.13
	3B	B. Byrne	598	.259	2	52	181	282	35	21	3.3	.930	E. Steele	31	166	9	9	2	2.60
Fred Clarke	RF	O. Wilson	544	.300	12	107	273	20	7	10	2.1	.977	C. Hendrix	22	119	4	6	1	2.73
	CF	M. Carey	427	.258	5	43	304	11	8	5	2.6	.975	J. Ferry	26	86	6	4	3	3.15
	LF	F. Clarke	392	.324	5	49	216	8	7	3	2.3	.970							
	C	G. Gibson	311	.209	0	19	452	117	12	16	5.9	.979							
	OF	T. Leach	386	.238	3	43	208	15	3	3	2.5	.987							
	UT	McKechnie	321	.227	2	37	598	109	21	49		.971							
	C	M. Simon	215	.228	0	22	320	75	13	6	6.0	.968							
	SS	A. McCarthy	150	.240	2	31	70	88	3	12	4.9	.981							
Philadelphia	1B	F. Luderus	551	.301	16	99	1373	77	22	85	10.1	.985	G. Alexander	48	367	28	13	3	2.57
	2B	O. Knabe	528	.237	1	42	310	412	38	54	5.4	.950	E. Moore	42	308	15	19	1	2.63
W-79 L-73	SS	M. Doolan	512	.238	1	49	295	474	53	68	5.7	.936	G. Chalmers	38	209	13	10	4	3.11
	3B	H. Lobert	541	.285	4	72	202	213	20	13	3.0	.954	B. Burns	21	121	6	10	0	3.42
Red Dooin	RF	J. Titus	236	.284	8	26	85	10	2	3	1.6	.979	E. Stack	13	78	5	5	0	3.59
	CF	D. Paskert	560	.273	4	47	361	20	8	6	2.5	.979							
	LF	S. Magee	445	.288	15	94	248	14	5	3	2.2	.981							
	C	R. Dooin	247	.328	1	16	436	97	18	5	7.4	.967							
	UT	J. Walsh	289	.270	1	31	148	79	12	14		.950							
	OF	F. Beck	210	.281	3	25	81	7	4	4	1.5	.957							
St. Louis	1B	E. Konetchy	571	.289	6	88	1652	71	16	85	11.0	.991	B. Harmon	51	348	23	16	4	3.13
	2B	M. Huggins	509	.261	1	24	281	439	29	62	5.5	.961	B. Steele	43	287	18	19	3	3.73
W-75 L-74	SS	A. Hauser	515	.241	3	46	223	400	56	51	5.1	.918	S. Sallee	36	245	15	9	2	2.76
	3B	M. Mowrey	471	.268	0	61	174	267	26	19	3.5	.944	R. Golden	30	149	4	9	0	5.02
Roger Bresnahan	RF	S. Evans	547	.294	5	71	258	17	8	5	1.9	.972	R. Geyer	29	149	9	6	0	3.27
	CF	R. Oakes	551	.263	2	47	364	26	16	8	2.7	.961							
	LF	R. Ellis	555	.250	3	66	297	21	21	3	2.3	.938							
	C	J. Bliss	258	.229	1	27	332	103	22	9	5.4	.952							
	C	R. Bresnahan	227	.278	3	41	323	100	13	9	5.7	.970							
	UT	W. Smith	194	.216	2	19	63	139	14	7		.935							
Cincinnati	1B	Hoblitzell	622	.289	11	97	1442	91	16	81	9.8	.990	G. Suggs	36	261	15	13	0	3.00
	2B	D. Egan	558	.249	1	56	341	480	44	67	5.7	.949	H. Gaspar	44	254	10	17	3	3.30
W-70 L-83	SS	T. Downey	360	.261	0	36	198	267	48	26	5.5	.906	B. Keefe	39	234	12	13	3	2.69
	3B	E. Grant	458	.223	1	53	158	208	18	21	3.1	.953	A. Fromme	38	208	10	11	0	3.46
Clark Griffith	RF	M. Mitchell	529	.291	2	84	280	23	9	8	2.2	.971	F. Smith	34	176	10	14	1	3.98
	CF	J. Bates	518	.292	1	61	352	21	13	4	2.6	.966							
	LF	B. Bescher	599	.275	4	45	267	21	14	2	2.0	.954							
	C	L. McLean	328	.287	0	34	414	138	18	16	5.8	.968							
	C	T. Clarke	203	.241	1	25	313	74	12	10	4.9	.970							
	SS	J. Esmond	198	.273	1	11	110	104	19	19	5.3	.918							
	OF	F. Beck	87	.184	2	20	25	2	0	0	1.7	1.000							
Brooklyn	1B	J. Daubert	573	.307	5	45	1485	88	18	91	10.7	.989	N. Rucker	48	316	22	18	4	2.71
	2B	J. Hummel	477	.270	5	58	296	352	19	58	5.3	.972	C. Barger	30	217	11	15	0	3.52
W-64 L-86	SS	B. Tooley	433	.206	1	49	226	340	46	42	5.4	.925	E. Knetzer	35	204	11	12	0	3.49
	3B	E. Zimmerman	417	.185	3	36	167	229	16	24	3.4	.961	B. Schardt	39	195	5	15	4	3.59
Bill Dahlen	RF	B. Coulson	521	.234	0	50	253	21	9	5	2.0	.968	D. Scanlan	22	114	3	10	1	3.64
	CF	B. Davidson	292	.233	1	26	168	4	8	1	2.4	.956	G. Bell	19	101	5	6	0	4.28
	LF	Z. Wheat	534	.287	5	76	287	12	14	0	2.3	.955							
	C	B. Bergen	227	.132	0	10	346	121	9	10	5.7	.981							
	C	T. Erwin	218	.271	7	34	273	98	11	6	5.2	.971							
	S2	D. Stark	193	.295	0	19	111	134	19	20		.971							
	OF	A. Burch	167	.228	0	7	98	6	3	3	2.5	.972							

NATIONAL LEAGUE 1911, *cont.*

Boston

W-44 L-107

Fred Tenney

POS	Player	AB	BA	HR	RBI	PO	A	E	DP	TC/G	FA	Pitcher	G	IP	W	L	SV	ERA
1B	F. Tenney	369	.263	1	36	901	64	15	47	10.5	.985	B. Brown	42	241	8	18	2	4.29
2B	B. Sweeney	523	.314	3	63	372	410	46	61	6.1	.944	A. Mattern	33	186	4	15	0	4.97
SS	B. Herzog	294	.310	5	41	149	248	28	31	5.7	.934	L. Tyler	28	165	7	10	0	5.06
3B	S. Ingerton	521	.250	5	61	92	119	13	6	3.9	.942	H. Perdue	24	137	6	10	1	4.98
RF	D. Miller	577	.333	7	91	243	26	11	4	1.9	.961	O. Weaver	27	121	3	12	0	6.47
CF	M. Donlin	222	.315	2	34	117	8	12	2	2.4	.912	B. Pfeffer	26	97	7	5	2	4.73
LF	A. Kaiser	197	.203	2	15	101	6	9	3	2.0	.922	C. Curtis	12	77	1	8	1	4.44
C	J. Kling	241	.224	2	24	302	106*	21*	6	6.0	.951							
C	B. Rariden	246	.228	0	21	291	110	20	12	6.5	.952							
SS	A. Bridwell	182	.291	0	10	78	149	12	19	4.7	.950							
3B	E. McDonald	175	.206	1	21	63	86	7	10	2.9	.955							
OF	W. Good	165	.267	0	15	108	13	7	1	3.0	.945							
UT	H. Spratt	154	.240	2	13	82	75	19	9		.892							
OF	G. Jackson	147	.347	0	25	74	4	6	1	2.2	.929							
OF	P. Flaherty	94	.287	2	20	26	2	2	0	1.6	.933							

BATTING AND BASE RUNNING LEADERS

Batting Average
H. Wagner, PIT .334
D. Miller, BOS .333
C. Meyers, NY .332
F. Clarke, PIT .324
A. Fletcher, NY .319

Slugging Average
W. Schulte, CHI .534
L. Doyle, NY .527
H. Wagner, PIT .507
F. Clarke, PIT .492
S. Magee, PHI .483

Home Runs
W. Schulte, CHI 21
F. Luderus, PHI 16
S. Magee, PHI 15
L. Doyle, NY 13
F. Merkle, NY 12
O. Wilson, PIT 12

Winning Percentage
R. Marquard, NY .781
D. Crandall, NY .750
K. Cole, CHI .720
G. Alexander, PHI .683
C. Mathewson, NY .667

Earned Run Average
C. Mathewson, NY 1.99
L. Richie, CHI 2.31
B. Adams, PIT 2.33
R. Marquard, NY 2.50
G. Alexander, PHI 2.57

Wins
G. Alexander, PHI 28
C. Mathewson, NY 26
R. Marquard, NY 24
B. Harmon, STL 23
N. Rucker, BKN 22

Total Bases
W. Schulte, CHI 308
L. Doyle, NY 277
F. Luderus, PHI 260
Hoblitzell, CIN 258
O. Wilson, PIT 257

Runs Batted In
W. Schulte, CHI 121
O. Wilson, PIT 107
F. Luderus, PHI 99
Hoblitzell, CIN 97
S. Magee, PHI 94

Stolen Bases
B. Bescher, CIN 81
J. Devore, NY 61
F. Snodgrass, NY 51
F. Merkle, NY 49
R. Murray, NY 48
B. Herzog, BOS, NY 48

Saves
T. Brown, CHI 13
D. Crandall, NY 5
N. Rucker, BKN 4
G. Chalmers, PHI 4
B. Harmon, STL 4

Strikeouts
R. Marquard, NY 237
G. Alexander, PHI 227
N. Rucker, BKN 190
E. Moore, STL 174
B. Harmon, STL 144

Complete Games
G. Alexander, PHI 31
C. Mathewson, NY 29
B. Harmon, STL 28
L. Leifield, PIT 26
B. Adams, PIT 24

Hits
D. Miller, BOS 192
Hoblitzell, CIN 180
J. Daubert, BKN 176
W. Schulte, CHI 173

Base on Balls
J. Sheckard, CHI 147
J. Bates, CIN 103
B. Bescher, CIN 102
M. Huggins, STL 96

Home Run Percentage
W. Schulte, CHI 3.6
S. Magee, PHI 3.4
F. Luderus, PHI 2.9
L. Doyle, NY 2.5

Fewest Hits/9 Innings
G. Alexander, PHI 6.99
R. Marquard, NY 7.16
N. Rucker, BKN 7.27
R. Ames, NY 7.46

Shutouts
B. Adams, PIT 7
G. Alexander, PHI 7
R. Marquard, NY 5
N. Rucker, BKN 5

Fewest Walks/9 Innings
C. Mathewson, NY 1.11
B. Adams, PIT 1.29
T. Brown, CHI 1.83
H. Wiltse, NY 1.87

Runs Scored
J. Sheckard, CHI 121
M. Huggins, STL 106
B. Bescher, CIN 106
W. Schulte, CHI 105

Doubles
E. Konetchy, STL 38
D. Miller, BOS 36
O. Wilson, PIT 34
B. Sweeney, BOS 33

Triples
L. Doyle, NY 25
M. Mitchell, CIN 22
W. Schulte, CHI 21
H. Zimmerman, CHI 17

Most Strikeouts/9 Inn.
R. Marquard, NY 7.68
G. Alexander, PHI 5.57
N. Rucker, BKN 5.42
R. Ames, NY 5.18

Innings
G. Alexander, PHI 367
B. Harmon, STL 348
L. Leifield, PIT 318
N. Rucker, BKN 316

Games Pitched
T. Brown, CHI 53
B. Harmon, STL 51
G. Alexander, PHI 48
N. Rucker, BKN 48

	W	L	PCT	GB	R	OR	2B	3B	HR	BA	SA	SB	E	DP	FA	CG	BB	SO	ShO	SV	ERA
New York	99	54	.647		756	542	225	105	41	.279	.391	347	255	86	.959	95	369	771	19	11	2.69
Chicago	92	62	.597	7.5	757	607	218	101	54	.260	.374	214	260	114	.960	85	525	582	12	16	2.90
Pittsburgh	85	69	.552	14.5	744	557	206	106	48	.262	.371	160	232	131	.963	91	375	605	14	10	2.84
Philadelphia	79	73	.520	19.5	658	669	214	56	60	.259	.359	153	231	113	.963	90	598	697	20	9	3.30
St. Louis	75	74	.503	22	671	745	199	85	27	.252	.340	175	261	106	.960	88	701	561	6	9	3.68
Cincinnati	70	83	.458	29	682	706	180	105	21	.261	.346	290	295	108	.955	77	476	557	4	10	3.26
Brooklyn	64	86	.427	33.5	539	659	151	71	28	.237	.311	184	243	112	.962	81	566	533	14	10	3.39
Boston	44	107	.291	54	699	1021	249	54	37	.267	.355	169	347	110	.947	73	672	486	5	6	5.08
					5506	5506	1642	683	316	.260	.356	1692	2124	880	.958	680	4282	4792	94	81	3.39

AMERICAN LEAGUE 1911

Philadelphia

W-101 L-50

Connie Mack

POS	Player	AB	BA	HR	RBI	PO	A	E	DP	TC/G	FA	Pitcher	G	IP	W	L	SV	ERA
1B	S. McInnis	468	.321	3	77	1048	55	17	55	11.5	.985	J. Coombs	47	337	28	12	2	3.53
2B	E. Collins	493	.365	3	73	348	349	24	49	5.5	.967	E. Plank	40	257	23	8	4	2.10
SS	J. Barry	442	.265	1	63	268	384	39	49	5.4	.944	C. Morgan	38	250	15	7	1	2.70
3B	F. Baker	592	.334	11	115	217	274	30	26	3.5	.942	C. Bender	31	216	17	5	3	2.16
RF	D. Murphy	508	.329	6	66	162	34	8	6	1.5	.961	H. Krause	27	169	11	8	2	3.04
CF	R. Oldring	495	.297	3	59	225	13	5	2	2.0	.979							
LF	B. Lord	574	.310	1	55	271	17	11	5	2.3	.963							
C	I. Thomas	297	.273	0	39	499	150	17	12	6.5	.974							
OF	A. Strunk	215	.256	1	21	127	11	3	4	2.3	.979							
1B	H. Davis	183	.197	1	22	427	36	11	21	8.9	.977							
C	J. Lapp	167	.353	1	26	270	47	9	8	5.7	.972							
P	J. Coombs	141	.319	2	23	24	71	9	3	2.2	.913							

AMERICAN LEAGUE 1911, *cont.*

	POS	Player	AB	BA	HR	RBI	PO	A	E	DP	TC/G	FA	Pitcher	G	IP	W	L	SV	ERA
Detroit	1B	J. Delahanty	542	.339	3	94	744	21	17	17	10.9	.978	G. Mullin	30	234	18	10	0	3.07
	2B	C. O'Leary	256	.266	0	25	169	201	13	19	5.7	.966	E. Willett	38	231	13	14	1	3.66
W-89 L-65	SS	D. Bush	561	.232	1	36	372	556	75	42	6.7	.925	E. Summers	30	179	11	11	0	3.66
	3B	G. Moriarty	478	.243	1	60	157	273	33	11	3.6	.929	E. Lafitte	29	172	11	8	1	3.92
Hughie Jennings	RF	S. Crawford	574	.378	7	115	181	16	5	3	1.4	.975	W. Donovan	20	168	10	9	0	3.31
	CF	T. Cobb	591	.420	8	144	376	24	18	10	2.9	.957	R. Works	30	167	11	5	1	3.87
	LF	D. Jones	341	.273	0	19	156	15	9	3	2.0	.950	J. Lively	18	114	7	5	0	4.59
	C	O. Stanage	503	.264	3	51	599	212	41	13	6.0	.952							
	OF	D. Drake	315	.279	1	36	141	4	9	1	1.9	.942							
	1B	D. Gainer	248	.302	2	25	671	38	18	36	10.5	.975							
Cleveland	1B	G. Stovall	458	.271	0	79	1073	87	17	56	10.0	.986	V. Gregg	34	244	23	7	0	1.81
	2B	N. Ball	412	.296	3	45	206	289	29	38	5.5	.945	G. Krapp	34	215	13	9	1	3.44
W-80 L-73	SS	I. Olson	545	.261	1	50	293	428	72	51	5.7	.909	W. Mitchell	30	177	7	14	0	3.76
	3B	T. Turner	417	.252	0	28	114	208	10	10	3.5	.970	F. Blanding	29	176	7	11	2	3.68
Deacon McGuire	RF	J. Jackson	571	.408	7	83	242	32	12	8	1.9	.958	G. Kahler	30	154	9	8	1	3.27
W-6 L-11	CF	Birmingham	447	.304	2	51	231	19	7	6	2.5	.973	Falkenberg	15	107	8	5	1	3.29
	LF	J. Graney	527	.269	1	45	258	22	22	5	2.1	.927							
George Stovall	C	G. Fisher	203	.261	0	12	298	96	18	11	7.1	.956							
W-74 L-62	12	N. Lajoie	315	.365	2	60	479	109	14	33		.977							
	OF	T. Easterly	287	.324	1	37	67	7	7	3	1.5	.914							
	C	S. Smith	154	.299	1	21	270	62	7	10	7.1	.979							
Chicago	1B	S. Collins	370	.262	4	48	878	67	19	46	9.9	.980	E. Walsh	56	369	27	18	4	2.22
	2B	McConnell	396	.280	1	34	189	280	13	31	4.4	.973	D. White	34	214	10	14	2	2.98
W-77 L-74	SS	L. Tannehill	516	.254	0	49	262	380	29	37	6.6	.957	J. Scott	39	202	14	11	0	2.63
	3B	H. Lord	561	.321	3	61	175	226	25	21	3.1	.941	F. Lange	29	162	8	8	3	3.23
Hugh Duffy	RF	M. McIntyre	569	.323	1	52	235	18	14	5	1.8	.948	F. Olmstead	25	118	6	6	2	4.21
	CF	P. Bodie	551	.289	4	97	256	24	9	9	2.3	.969	J. Baker	22	94	2	7	1	3.93
	LF	N. Callahan	466	.281	3	60	173	10	7	2	1.7	.963	I. Young	24	93	5	6	2	4.37
	C	B. Sullivan	256	.215	0	31	447	114	8	13	6.4	.986							
	UT	R. Zeider	217	.253	2	21	358	92	15	16		.968							
	OF	P. Dougherty	211	.289	0	32	78	6	6	1	1.6	.933							
	P	E. Walsh	155	.206	0	9	27	159	8	5	3.5	.959							
Boston	1B	C. Engle	514	.270	2	48	550	43	14	24	9.3	.977	S. Wood	44	277	23	17	3	2.02
	2B	H. Wagner	261	.257	1	38	106	104	12	11	5.6	.946	E. Cicotte	35	221	11	15	0	2.81
W-78 L-75	SS	S. Yerkes	502	.279	1	57	232	337	47	37	5.3	.924	R. Collins	31	204	11	12	1	2.39
	3B	L. Gardner	492	.285	4	44	92	161	10	3	3.7	.962	L. Pape	27	176	10	8	0	2.45
Patsy Donovan	RF	H. Hooper	524	.311	4	45	181	27	10	1	1.7	.954	C. Hall	32	147	8	7	4	3.73
	CF	T. Speaker	510	.327	8	80	297	26	15	5	2.4	.956	E. Karger	25	131	5	8	0	3.37
	LF	D. Lewis	469	.307	7	86	203	27	15	4	2.0	.939							
	C	B. Carrigan	232	.289	1	30	326	94	12	11	7.0	.972							
	1C	B. Williams	284	.239	0	31	727	73	20	28		.976							
	C	L. Nunamaker	183	.257	0	19	309	79	11	8	6.8	.972							
New York	1B	H. Chase	527	.315	3	62	1255	81	36	62	11.1	.974	R. Ford	37	281	22	11	0	2.27
	2B	E. Gardner	357	.263	0	39	181	290	20	44	4.9	.959	R. Caldwell	41	255	14	14	1	3.35
W-76 L-76	SS	J. Knight	470	.268	3	62	200	247	46	30	6.0	.907	J. Warhop	31	210	12	13	0	4.16
	3B	R. Hartzell	527	.296	3	91	158	221	26	18	3.3	.936	J. Quinn	40	175	8	10	2	3.76
Hal Chase	RF	H. Wolter	434	.304	4	39	178	18	10	8	1.8	.951	R. Fisher	29	172	10	11	0	3.25
	CF	B. Daniels	462	.286	2	31	256	15	17	6	2.4	.941	H. Vaughn	26	146	8	10	0	4.39
	LF	B. Cree	520	.348	4	88	245	19	10	2	2.0	.964							
	C	W. Blair	222	.194	0	26	379	101	15	12	5.9	.970							
	C	J. Sweeney	229	.231	0	18	394	94	18	8	6.1	.964							
	SS	O. Johnson	209	.234	3	36	78	126	21	17	4.8	.907							
	OF	C. Hemphill	201	.284	1	15	95	4	5	0	1.9	.952							
Washington	1B	G. Schaefer	440	.334	0	45	1038	71	23	57	10.5	.980	W. Johnson	40	323	25	13	1	1.89
	2B	Cunningham	331	.190	3	37	168	244	30	18	4.8	.932	B. Groom	37	255	13	17	2	3.82
W-64 L-90	SS	G. McBride	557	.235	0	59	353	546	56	60	6.2	.941	L. Hughes	34	223	11	17	0	3.47
	3B	W. Conroy	346	.231	2	28	87	177	20	11	3.3	.930	D. Walker	32	186	8	13	0	3.39
Jimmy McAleer	RF	D. Gessler	450	.282	4	78	130	19	9	2	1.3	.943	D. Gray	28	121	2	13	0	5.06
	CF	C. Milan	616	.315	3	35	347	33	17	2	2.6	.957							
	LF	T. Walker	356	.278	2	39	163	14	16	1	2.1	.917							
	C	G. Street	216	.222	0	14	362	102	13	10	6.7	.973							
	23	K. Elberfeld	404	.272	0	47	233	297	31	34		.945							
	C1	J. Henry	261	.203	0	21	549	123	21	15		.970							
	OF	J. Lelivelt	225	.320	0	22	82	11	6	1	2.0	.939							

AMERICAN LEAGUE 1911, *cont.*

	POS	Player	AB	BA	HR	RBI	PO	A	E	DP	TC/G	FA	Pitcher	G	IP	W	L	SV	ERA
St. Louis	1B	J. Black	186	.151	0	7	519	37	16	31	10.6	.972	J. Lake	30	215	10	15	0	3.30
	2B	F. LaPorte	507	.314	2	82	287	**398**	36	**59**	5.4	.950	J. Powell	31	208	8	**19**	1	3.29
W-45 L-107	SS	B. Wallace	410	.232	0	31	280	417	42	47	6.0	.943	B. Pelty	28	207	7	15	0	2.83
	3B	J. Austin	541	.261	2	45	228	337	42	27	4.1	.931	E. Hamilton	32	177	5	12	0	3.97
Bobby Wallace	RF	Schweitzer	237	.215	0	34	100	13	8	4	1.8	.934	R. Mitchell	28	134	4	8	0	3.84
	CF	B. Shotton	572	.255	0	36	356	21	20	2	2.9	.950	L. George	27	116	4	9	0	4.18
	LF	H. Hogan	443	.260	2	62	263	26	22*	3	2.7	.929	R. Nelson	16	81	3	9	0	5.22
	C	N. Clarke	256	.215	0	18	251	111	29	**15**	5.4	.926							
	C	J. Stephens	212	.231	0	17	223	94	17	7	5.1	.949							
	OF	P. Meloan	206	.262	3	14	69	6	8	1	1.5	.904							
	S2	E. Hallinan	169	.207	0	14	118	133	24	24		.913							

BATTING AND BASE RUNNING LEADERS

Batting Average
- T. Cobb, DET .420
- J. Jackson, CLE .408
- S. Crawford, DET .378
- E. Collins, PHI .365
- B. Cree, NY .348

Slugging Average
- T. Cobb, DET .621
- J. Jackson, CLE .590
- S. Crawford, DET .526
- B. Cree, NY .513
- F. Baker, PHI .505

Home Runs
- F. Baker, PHI 11
- T. Speaker, BOS 8
- T. Cobb, DET 8
- D. Lewis, BOS 7
- J. Jackson, CLE 7
- S. Crawford, DET 7

Total Bases
- T. Cobb, DET 367
- J. Jackson, CLE 337
- S. Crawford, DET 302
- F. Baker, PHI 299
- B. Cree, NY 267

Runs Batted In
- T. Cobb, DET 144
- S. Crawford, DET 115
- F. Baker, PHI 115
- P. Bodie, CHI 97
- J. Delahanty, DET 94

Stolen Bases
- T. Cobb, DET 83
- C. Milan, WAS 58
- B. Cree, NY 48
- N. Callahan, CHI 45
- H. Lord, CHI 43

Hits
- T. Cobb, DET 248
- J. Jackson, CLE 233
- S. Crawford, DET 217
- F. Baker, PHI 198

Base on Balls
- D. Bush, DET 98
- D. Gessler, WAS 74
- C. Milan, WAS 74
- H. Hooper, BOS 73

Home Run Percentage
- F. Baker, PHI 1.9
- T. Speaker, BOS 1.6
- D. Lewis, BOS 1.5
- T. Cobb, DET 1.4

Runs Scored
- T. Cobb, DET 147
- D. Bush, DET 126
- J. Jackson, CLE 126
- S. Crawford, DET 109

Doubles
- T. Cobb, DET 47
- J. Jackson, CLE 45
- F. Baker, PHI 40
- F. LaPorte, STL 37

Triples
- T. Cobb, DET 24
- B. Cree, NY 22
- J. Jackson, CLE 19
- H. Lord, CHI 18

PITCHING LEADERS

Winning Percentage
- C. Bender, PHI .773
- V. Gregg, CLE .767
- E. Plank, PHI .742
- J. Coombs, PHI .700
- C. Morgan, PHI .682

Earned Run Average
- V. Gregg, CLE 1.81
- W. Johnson, WAS 1.89
- S. Wood, BOS 2.02
- E. Plank, PHI 2.10
- C. Bender, PHI 2.16

Wins
- J. Coombs, PHI 28
- E. Walsh, CHI 27
- W. Johnson, WAS 25
- V. Gregg, CLE 23
- E. Plank, PHI 23

Saves
- E. Plank, PHI 5
- C. Hall, BOS 4
- E. Walsh, CHI 4
- S. Wood, BOS 3
- J. Quinn, NY 3
- C. Bender, PHI 3

Strikeouts
- E. Walsh, CHI 255
- S. Wood, BOS 231
- W. Johnson, WAS 207
- J. Coombs, PHI 185
- R. Ford, NY 158

Complete Games
- W. Johnson, WAS 36
- E. Walsh, CHI 33
- R. Ford, NY 26
- J. Coombs, PHI 26
- S. Wood, BOS 25
- G. Mullin, DET 25

Fewest Hits/9 Innings
- V. Gregg, CLE 6.34
- S. Wood, BOS 7.35
- G. Krapp, CLE 7.63
- C. Morgan, PHI 7.82

Shutouts
- E. Plank, PHI 6
- W. Johnson, WAS 6
- V. Gregg, CLE 5
- S. Wood, BOS 5

Fewest Walks/9 Innings
- D. White, CHI 1.47
- J. Lake, STL 1.67
- E. Walsh, CHI 1.76
- J. Warhop, NY 1.89

Most Strikeouts/9 Inn.
- S. Wood, BOS 7.51
- E. Walsh, CHI 6.23
- W. Johnson, WAS 5.76
- J. Scott, CHI 5.70

Innings
- E. Walsh, CHI 369
- J. Coombs, PHI 337
- W. Johnson, WAS 323
- R. Ford, NY 281

Games Pitched
- E. Walsh, CHI 56
- J. Coombs, PHI 47
- S. Wood, BOS 44
- R. Caldwell, NY 41

	W	L	PCT	GB	R	OR	2B	3B	HR	BA	SA	SB	E	DP	FA	CG	BB	SO	ShO	SV	ERA
										Batting				**Fielding**			**Pitching**				
Philadelphia	101	50	.669		**861**	601	235	93	**35**	**.296**	**.397**	226	**225**	100	**.965**	97	487	739	13	**13**	3.01
Detroit	89	65	.578	13.5	831	776	230	**96**	30	.292	.388	**276**	318	78	.951	**108**	460	538	8	3	3.73
Cleveland	80	73	.523	22	691	712	**238**	81	20	.282	.369	209	302	**108**	.954	93	550	673	6	6	3.37
Chicago	77	74	.510	24	719	624	179	92	20	.269	.350	201	252	98	.961	87	**384**	**752**	16	11	3.01
Boston	78	75	.510	24	680	643	203	66	**35**	.274	.362	190	323	93	.949	87	475	713	10	8	**2.73**
New York	76	76	.500	25.5	684	724	190	**96**	26	.272	.363	270	328	99	.949	91	406	667	5	3	3.54
Washington	64	90	.416	38.5	625	766	159	53	16	.258	.320	215	305	90	.945	106	410	628	13	3	3.52
St. Louis	45	107	.296	56.5	567	812	187	63	17	.239	.312	125	358	104	.945	92	463	383	8	1	3.83
					5658	5658	1621	640	199	.273	.358	1712	2411	770	.953	761	3635	5093	79	48	3.34

NATIONAL LEAGUE 1912

	POS	Player	AB	BA	HR	RBI	PO	A	E	DP	TC/G	FA	Pitcher	G	IP	W	L	SV	ERA
New York	1B	F. Merkle	479	.309	11	84	1229	72	**27**	77	10.3	.980	C. Mathewson	43	310	23	12	4	2.12
	2B	L. Doyle	558	.330	10	90	313	379	38	68	5.1	.948	R. Marquard	43	295	**26**	11	0	2.57
W-103 L-48	SS	A. Fletcher	419	.282	1	57	237	428	**52**	60	5.7	.927	J. Tesreau	36	243	17	7	1	**1.96**
	3B	B. Herzog	482	.263	2	47	**159**	**308**	29	21	3.5	.942	R. Ames	33	179	11	5	2	2.46
John McGraw	RF	R. Murray	549	.277	3	92	255	20	9	7	2.0	.968	D. Crandall	37	162	13	7	2	3.61
	CF	B. Becker	402	.264	6	58	230	20	11	4	2.2	.958	H. Wiltse	28	134	9	6	2	3.16
	LF	F. Snodgrass	535	.269	3	69	229	25	14	4	2.3	.948							
	C	C. Meyers	371	.358	6	54	576	111	19	10	5.8	.973							
	OF	J. Devore	327	.275	2	37	155	14	15	3	1.9	.918							
	UT	T. Shafer	163	.288	0	23	80	119	22	10		.900							

NATIONAL LEAGUE 1912, *cont.*

	POS	Player	AB	BA	HR	RBI	PO	A	E	DP	TC/G	FA	Pitcher	G	IP	W	L	SV	ERA
Chicago	1B	V. Saier	451	.288	2	61	1165	52	10	67	10.2	.992	L. Cheney	42	303	**26**	10	0	2.85
	2B	J. Evers	478	.341	1	63	319	439	32	71	5.5	.959	J. Lavender	42	252	16	13	3	3.04
W-91 L-59	SS	J. Tinker	550	.282	0	75	354	470	50	73	6.2	.943	L. Richie	39	238	16	8	0	2.95
	3B	H. Zimmerman	557	**.372**	14	103	142	242	35	16	3.5	.916	E. Reulbach	39	169	10	6	3	3.78
Frank Chance	RF	W. Schulte	553	.264	13	70	219	19	12	6	1.8	.952	C. Smith	21	94	7	4	1	4.21
	CF	T. Leach	265	.242	2	32	181	11	5	4	2.7*	.975*	T. Brown	15	89	5	6	0	2.64
	LF	J. Sheckard	523	.245	3	47	332	**26**	14	4	2.5	.962							
	C	J. Archer	385	.283	5	58	504	149	23	15	5.7	.966							
	OF	W. Miller	241	.307	0	22	109	6	7	2	1.9	.943							
Cincinnati	1B	Hoblitzell	558	.294	2	85	1326	87	21	73	9.8	.985	G. Suggs	42	303	19	16	3	2.94
	2B	D. Egan	507	.247	0	52	345	452	22	55	5.5	**.973**	R. Benton	50	302	18	21	2	3.10
W-75 L-78	SS	J. Esmond	231	.195	1	40	154	180	25	22	4.9	.930	A. Fromme	43	296	16	18	0	2.74
	3B	A. Phelan	461	.243	3	54	153	250	33	18	3.4	.924	B. Humphries	30	159	9	11	2	3.23
Hank O'Day	RF	M. Mitchell	552	.283	4	78	251	18	15	8	2.0	.947							
	CF	A. Marsans	416	.317	1	38	222	11	6	2	2.4	.975							
	LF	B. Bescher	548	.281	4	38	347	15	14	4	2.6	.963							
	C	L. McLean	333	.243	1	27	425	124	15	16	5.8	.973							
	SS	E. Grant	255	.239	2	20	102	171	15	20	5.1	.948							
	OF	J. Bates	239	.289	1	29	157	15	9	4	2.8	.950							
	C	T. Clarke	146	.281	0	22	239	58	5	7	4.8	.983							
Philadelphia	1B	F. Luderus	572	.257	10	69	**1421**	104	15	77	10.5	.990	G. Alexander	46	**310**	19	17	2	2.81
	2B	O. Knabe	426	.282	0	46	258	342	30	45	5.1	.952	T. Seaton	44	255	16	12	2	3.28
W-73 L-79	SS	M. Doolan	532	.258	1	62	289	**476**	40	49	5.5	.950	E. Moore	31	182	9	14	0	3.31
	3B	H. Lobert	257	.327	2	33	80	86	4	3	2.7	.976	A. Brennan	27	174	11	9	2	3.57
Red Dooin	RF	G. Cravath	436	.284	11	70	200	**26**	8	5	2.1	.966	E. Rixey	23	162	10	10	0	2.50
	CF	D. Paskert	540	.315	2	43	336	19	12	4	2.6	.967							
	LF	S. Magee	464	.306	6	72	251	8	10	2	2.2	.963							
	C	B. Killefer	268	.224	1	21	407	134	15	17	**6.5**	.973							
	C	R. Dooin	184	.234	0	22	254	69	14	2	5.8	.958							
	OF	D. Miller	177	.288	0	21	61	9	1	1	1.8	.986							
	3B	T. Downey	171	.292	1	23	57	76	16	3	3.2	.893							
	OF	J. Titus	157	.274	3	22	53	2	5	1	1.4	.917							
Pittsburgh	1B	D. Miller	567	.275	4	87	1385	85	23	**93**	10.2	.985	C. Hendrix	39	289	24	9	1	2.59
	2B	A. McCarthy	401	.277	1	41	237	320	22	52	5.5	.962	H. Camnitz	41	277	22	12	2	2.83
W-93 L-58	SS	H. Wagner	558	.324	7	102	341	462	32	**74**	5.8	.962	M. O'Toole	37	275	15	17	0	2.71
	3B	B. Byrne	528	.288	3	35	144	187	18	14	2.7	**.948**	H. Robinson	33	175	12	7	2	2.26
Fred Clarke	RF	M. Donlin	244	.316	2	35	102	8	2	1	1.8	.982	B. Adams	28	170	11	8	0	2.91
	CF	O. Wilson	583	.300	11	95	324	20	14	5	2.4	.961							
	LF	M. Carey	587	.302	5	66	**369**	19	13	**10**	2.7	.968							
	C	G. Gibson	300	.240	2	35	484	101	6	11	6.3	**.990**							
	2B	A. Butler	154	.273	1	17	71	99	7	12	4.1	.960							
	OF	H. Hyatt	97	.289	0	22	20	1	1	0	1.5	.955							
St. Louis	1B	E. Konetchy	538	.314	8	82	1392	90	13	77	10.5	.991	S. Sallee	48	294	16	17	6	2.60
	2B	M. Huggins	431	.304	0	29	272	337	37	50	5.7	.943	B. Harmon	43	268	18	18	0	3.93
W-63 L-90	SS	A. Hauser	479	.259	1	42	262	446	50	54	5.7	.934	B. Steele	40	194	9	13	1	4.69
	3B	M. Mowrey	408	.255	2	50	131	220	26	**22**	3.5	.931	R. Geyer	41	181	7	14	0	3.28
Roger Bresnahan	RF	S. Evans	491	.283	6	72	219	24	15	2	1.9	.942	J. Willis	31	130	4	9	2	4.44
	CF	R. Oakes	495	.281	3	58	324	15	19	5	2.6	.947							
	LF	L. Magee	458	.290	0	40	198	18	10	2	2.7	.956							
	C	I. Wingo	310	.265	2	44	360	148	**23**	11	5.8	.957							
	OF	R. Ellis	305	.269	4	33	173	10	14	5	2.6	.929							
	3S	W. Smith	219	.256	0	26	81	126	10	10		.954							
Brooklyn	1B	J. Daubert	559	.308	3	66	1373	76	10	68	10.2	**.993**	N. Rucker	45	298	18	21	4	2.21
	2B	G. Cutshaw	357	.280	0	28	192	290	21	31	5.6	.958	P. Ragan	36	208	7	18	1	3.63
W-58 L-95	SS	B. Tooley	265	.234	2	37	147	214	47	23	5.4	.885	E. Yingling	25	163	6	11	0	3.59
	3B	R. Smith	486	.286	4	57	156	251	27	16	3.5	.938	E. Stack	28	142	7	5	1	3.36
Bill Dahlen	RF	H. Northen	412	.282	2	46	178	11	10	3	2.0	.950	E. Knetzer	33	140	7	9	0	4.55
	CF	H. Moran	508	.276	1	40	273	24	12	5	2.4	.961	F. Allen	20	109	3	9	0	3.63
	LF	Z. Wheat	453	.305	8	65	285	13	10	2	2.5	.968	C. Barger	16	94	1	9	0	5.46
	C	O. Miller	316	.278	1	31	455	141	15	11	6.5	.975	M. Kent	20	93	5	5	0	4.84
	2O	J. Hummel	411	.282	5	54	175	161	11	17		.968	C. Curtis	19	80	4	7	0	3.94
	SS	B. Fisher	257	.233	0	26	121	200	29	23	4.7	.917							
	OF	J. Daley	199	.256	2	13	116	10	7	3	2.4	.947							
	C	E. Phelps	111	.288	0	23	130	35	4	4	5.3	.976							

NATIONAL LEAGUE 1912, *cont.*

	POS	Player	AB	BA	HR	RBI	PO	A	E	DP	TC/G	FA	Pitcher	G	IP	W	L	SV	ERA
Boston	1B	B. Houser	332	.286	8	52	759	37	11	48	9.7	.986	L. Tyler	42	256	12	22	0	4.18
	2B	B. Sweeney	593	.344	1	100	459	475	40	76	6.4	.959	O. Hess	33	254	12	17	0	3.76
W-52 L-101	SS	F. O'Rourke	196	.122	0	16	92	167	24	16	4.8	.915	H. Perdue	37	249	13	16	3	3.80
	3B	E. McDonald	459	.259	2	34	147	216	23	18	3.3	.940	W. Dickson	36	189	3	19	0	3.86
Johnny Kling	RF	J. Titus	345	.325	2	48	152	12	6	1	1.8	.965	E. Donnelly	37	184	5	10	0	4.35
	CF	V. Campbell	624	.296	3	48	340	20	24	6	2.7	.938	B. Brown	31	168	4	15	0	4.01
	LF	G. Jackson	397	.262	4	48	230	20	15	3	2.5	.943							
	C	J. Kling	252	.317	2	30	322	108	19	20	6.1	.958							
	UT	A. Devlin	436	.289	0	54	768	140	15	52		.984							
	O3	J. Kirke	359	.320	4	62	99	45	23	4		.862							
	C	B. Rariden	247	.223	1	14	297	103	15	6	5.7	.964							
	OF	D. Miller	201	.234	2	24	79	12	5	4	1.9	.948							

BATTING AND BASE RUNNING LEADERS

Batting Average
H. Zimmerman, CHI	.372
C. Meyers, NY	.358
B. Sweeney, BOS	.344
J. Evers, CHI	.341
L. Doyle, NY	.330

Slugging Average
H. Zimmerman, CHI	.571
O. Wilson, PIT	.513
H. Wagner, PIT	.496
C. Meyers, NY	.477
L. Doyle, NY	.471

Home Runs
H. Zimmerman, CHI	14
W. Schulte, CHI	13
G. Cravath, PHI	11
F. Merkle, NY	11
O. Wilson, PIT	11

Winning Percentage
C. Hendrix, PIT	.727
L. Cheney, CHI	.722
J. Tesreau, NY	.708
R. Marquard, NY	.703
L. Richie, CHI	.667

PITCHING LEADERS

Earned Run Average
J. Tesreau, NY	1.96
C. Mathewson, NY	2.12
N. Rucker, BKN	2.21
H. Robinson, PIT	2.26
E. Rixey, PHI	2.50

Wins
L. Cheney, CHI	26
R. Marquard, NY	26
C. Hendrix, PIT	24
C. Mathewson, NY	23
H. Camnitz, PIT	22

Total Bases
H. Zimmerman, CHI	318
O. Wilson, PIT	299
H. Wagner, PIT	277
B. Sweeney, BOS	264
L. Doyle, NY	263

Runs Batted In
H. Zimmerman, CHI	103
H. Wagner, PIT	102
B. Sweeney, BOS	100
O. Wilson, PIT	95
R. Murray, NY	92

Stolen Bases
B. Bescher, CIN	67
M. Carey, PIT	45
F. Snodgrass, NY	43
R. Murray, NY	38
F. Merkle, NY	37
B. Herzog, NY	37

Saves
S. Sallee, STL	6
N. Rucker, BKN	4
C. Mathewson, NY	4

Strikeouts
G. Alexander, PHI	195
C. Hendrix, PIT	176
R. Marquard, NY	175
R. Benton, CIN	162
N. Rucker, BKN	151

Complete Games
L. Cheney, CHI	28
C. Mathewson, NY	27
G. Alexander, PHI	26
C. Hendrix, PIT	25
G. Suggs, CIN	25

Hits
H. Zimmerman, CHI	207
B. Sweeney, BOS	204
V. Campbell, BOS	185
L. Doyle, NY	184

Base on Balls
J. Sheckard, CHI	122
D. Paskert, PHI	91
M. Huggins, STL	87
B. Bescher, CIN	83

Home Run Percentage
G. Cravath, PHI	2.5
H. Zimmerman, CHI	2.5
W. Schulte, CHI	2.4
F. Merkle, NY	2.3

Fewest Hits/9 Innings
J. Tesreau, NY	6.56
H. Robinson, PIT	7.51
M. O'Toole, PIT	7.75
L. Cheney, CHI	7.77

Shutouts
N. Rucker, BKN	6
M. O'Toole, PIT	6
G. Suggs, CIN	5
L. Richie, CHI	4

Fewest Walks/9 Innings
C. Mathewson, NY	0.99
H. Robinson, PIT	1.54
G. Suggs, CIN	1.66
B. Adams, PIT	1.85

Runs Scored
B. Bescher, CIN	120
M. Carey, PIT	114
D. Paskert, PHI	102
V. Campbell, BOS	102

Doubles
H. Zimmerman, CHI	41
D. Paskert, PHI	37
H. Wagner, PIT	35
L. Doyle, NY	33

Triples
O. Wilson, PIT	36
R. Murray, NY	20
H. Wagner, PIT	20
J. Daubert, BKN	16

Most Strikeouts/9 Inn.
G. Alexander, PHI	5.66
C. Hendrix, PIT	5.49
R. Marquard, NY	5.35
L. Tyler, BOS	5.06

Innings
G. Alexander, PHI	310
C. Mathewson, NY	310
L. Cheney, CHI	303
G. Suggs, CIN	303

Games Pitched
R. Benton, CIN	50
S. Sallee, STL	48
G. Alexander, PHI	46
N. Rucker, BKN	45

	W	L	PCT	GB	R	OR	2B	3B	HR	BA	SA	SB	E	DP	FA	CG	BB	SO	ShO	SV	ERA
New York	103	48	.682		823	571	231	89	47	.286	.395	319	280	123	.956	93	338	652	8	13	2.58
Chicago	91	59	.607	11.5	756	668	245	91	43	.277	.387	164	249	125	.960	80	493	554	14	8	3.42
Cincinnati	75	78	.490	29	656	722	183	89	21	.256	.339	248	247	102	.960	86	452	561	12	10	3.42
Philadelphia	73	79	.480	30.5	670	688	244	68	43	.267	.367	159	231	98	.963	81	515	616	10	8	3.25
Pittsburgh	93	58	.616	10	751	565	222	129	39	.284	.398	177	169	125	.972	94	497	664	18	6	2.85
St. Louis	63	90	.412	41	659	830	190	77	27	.259	.352	193	274	113	.957	62	560	487	6	11	3.85
Brooklyn	58	95	.379	46	651	754	220	73	32	.268	.358	179	255	96	.959	71	510	553	10	7	3.64
Boston	52	101	.340	52	693	861	227	68	35	.273	.360	137	295	129	.954	92	521	542	5	3	4.17
					5659	5659	1762	684	287	.272	.369	1576	2000	911	.960	659	3886	4629	83	66	3.40

AMERICAN LEAGUE 1912

	POS	Player	AB	BA	HR	RBI	PO	A	E	DP	TC/G	FA	Pitcher	G	IP	W	L	SV	ERA
Boston	1B	J. Stahl	326	.301	3	60	853	49	18	37	10.0	.980	S. Wood	43	344	34	5	1	1.91
	2B	S. Yerkes	523	.252	0	42	244	323	34	39	4.6	.943	B. O'Brien	37	276	20	13	0	2.58
W-105 L-47	SS	H. Wagner	504	.274	2	68	332	391	61	43	5.4	.922	H. Bedient	41	231	20	9	2	2.92
	3B	L. Gardner	517	.315	3	86	167	296	35	16	3.5	.930	R. Collins	27	199	13	8	0	2.53
Jake Stahl	RF	H. Hooper	590	.242	2	53	220	22	9	6	1.7	.964	C. Hall	34	191	15	8	2	3.02
	CF	T. Speaker	580	.383	10	98	372	35	18	9	2.8	.958							
	LF	D. Lewis	581	.284	6	109	301	23	18	4	2.2	.947							
	C	B. Carrigan	266	.263	0	24	413	102	16	7	6.1	.970							
	UT	C. Engle	171	.234	0	18	248	60	13	15		.960							

AMERICAN LEAGUE 1912, *cont.*

	POS	Player	AB	BA	HR	RBI	PO	A	E	DP	TC/G	FA	Pitcher	G	IP	W	L	SV	ERA
Washington	1B	C. Gandil	443	.305	2	81	1106	68	12	49	10.1	.990	W. Johnson	50	368	32	12	2	**1.39**
	2B	R. Morgan	273	.238	1	30	150	173	21	21	4.6	.939	B. Groom	43	316	24	13	1	2.62
W-91 L-61	SS	G. McBride	521	.226	1	52	349	498	53	55	5.9	.941	L. Hughes	31	196	13	10	0	2.94
	3B	E. Foster	618	.285	2	70	168	348	45	22	3.6	.920	J. Cashion	26	170	10	6	1	3.17
Clark Griffith	RF	D. Moeller	519	.276	6	46	227	25	15	5	2.0	.944							
	CF	C. Milan	601	.306	1	79	326	31	25	6	2.5	.935							
	LF	H. Shanks	399	.231	1	47	189	14	8	2	1.9	.962							
	C	J. Henry	191	.194	0	9	347	113	11	7	7.5	.977							
	C	E. Ainsmith	186	.226	0	22	415	85	22	5	9.0	.958							
	UT	G. Schaefer	166	.247	0	19	169	30	8	7		.961							
	C	B. Williams	157	.318	0	22	234	74	7	6	7.0	.978							
	P	W. Johnson	144	.264	2	20	15	93	4	4	2.2	.964							
Philadelphia	1B	S. McInnis	568	.327	3	101	**1533**	**100**	27	**88**	**10.8**	.984	J. Coombs	40	262	21	10	2	3.29
	2B	E. Collins	543	.348	0	64	**387**	**426**	38	63	5.6	.955	E. Plank	37	260	26	6	2	2.22
W-90 L-62	SS	J. Barry	483	.261	0	55	238	438	55	55	5.3	.925	B. Brown	34	199	13	11	1	3.66
	3B	F. Baker	577	.347	10	133	217	321	34	25	3.8	.941	B. Houck	30	181	8	8	0	2.94
Connie Mack	RF	B. Lord	378	.238	0	25	148	15	10	5	1.8	.942	C. Bender	27	171	13	8	2	2.74
	CF	R. Oldring	395	.301	1	24	214	8	6	1	2.4	.974	C. Morgan	16	94	3	8	0	3.75
	LF	A. Strunk	412	.289	3	63	278	16	3	3	2.5	**.990**							
	C	J. Lapp	281	.292	1	35	354	105	20	10	5.8	.958							
	OF	H. Maggert	242	.256	1	13	103	5	7	0	1.9	.939							
	OF	D. Murphy	130	.323	2	20	39	2	5	2	1.3	.891							
Chicago	1B	R. Zeider	420	.245	1	42	682	54	16	28	11.4	.979	E. Walsh	**62**	**393**	27	17	10	2.15
	2B	M. Rath	591	.272	1	19	353	386	27	46	5.4	**.963**	J. Benz	41	238	13	17	0	2.92
W-78 L-76	SS	B. Weaver	523	.224	1	43	342	425	71	53	5.7	.915	D. White	32	172	8	10	3	3.24
	3B	H. Lord	570	.267	5	54	127	172	35	11	3.2	.895	F. Lange	31	165	10	10	3	3.27
Nixey Callahan	RF	S. Collins	575	.292	2	81	177	11	6	0	1.8	.969	E. Cicotte	20	152	9	7	0	2.84
	CF	P. Bodie	472	.294	5	72	208	11	7	3	1.7	.969	R. Peters	28	109	5	6	0	4.14
	LF	N. Callahan	408	.272	1	52	166	3	11	0	1.7	.939	G. Mogridge	17	65	3	4	3	4.04
	C	W. Kuhn	178	.202	0	10	318	104	15	8	5.8	.966							
	OF	W. Mattick	285	.260	1	35	154	8	3	1	2.1	.982							
	C	B. Block	136	.257	0	26	222	65	6	4	6.4	.980							
Cleveland	1B	A. Griggs	273	.304	0	39	661	43	10	33	10.1	.986	V. Gregg	37	271	20	13	2	2.59
	2B	N. Lajoie	448	.368	0	90	241	249	21	49	5.3	.959	F. Blanding	39	262	18	14	1	2.92
W-75 L-78	SS	Peckinpaugh	236	.212	1	22	127	188	26	16	5.1	.924	G. Kahler	41	246	12	19	1	3.69
	3B	T. Turner	370	.308	0	33	129	199	17	21	3.3	**.951**	W. Mitchell	29	164	5	8	1	2.80
Harry Davis	RF	J. Jackson	572	.395	3	90	273	30	16	2	2.1	.950	B. Steen	26	143	9	8	0	3.77
W-54 L-71	CF	Birmingham	369	.255	0	45	198	18	11	8	2.4	.952	J. Baskette	29	116	8	4	1	3.18
	LF	B. Ryan	328	.271	1	31	167	11	7	2	2.1	.962							
Joe Birmingham	C	S. O'Neill	215	.228	0	14	316	108	17	9	6.6	.961							
W-21 L-7	UT	I. Olson	467	.253	0	33	230	318	44	18		.926							
	OF	J. Graney	264	.242	0	20	148	11	7	5	2.2	.958							
	C	T. Easterly	186	.296	1	21	226	69	13	11*	6.0	.958							
	1B	D. Johnston	164	.280	1	11	330	17	3	27	8.5	.991							
Detroit	1B	G. Moriarty	375	.248	0	54	800	27	11	19	11.8	.987	E. Willett	37	284	17	15	0	3.29
	2B	B. Louden	403	.241	1	36	200	288	25	25	6.0	.951	J. Dubuc	37	250	17	10	3	2.77
W-69 L-84	SS	D. Bush	511	.231	2	38	317	**547**	66	45	**6.5**	.929	G. Mullin	30	226	12	17	0	3.54
	3B	C. Deal	142	.225	0	11	48	113	10	3	4.2	.942	J. Lake	26	163	9	11	1	3.10
Hughie Jennings	RF	S. Crawford	581	.325	4	109	169	16	3	5	1.3	.984	R. Works	27	157	5	10	1	4.24
	CF	T. Cobb	553	**.410**	7	90	324	21	22	5	2.6	.940							
	LF	D. Jones	316	.294	0	24	141	13	6	4	2.0	.963							
	C	O. Stanage	394	.261	0	41	440	**168**	32	**14**	5.4	.950							
	UT	O. Vitt	273	.245	0	19	109	99	11	8		.950							
	20	J. Delahanty	266	.286	0	41	148	120	23	19		.921							
	1B	D. Gainer	179	.240	0	20	547	22	8	25	11.5	.986							
St. Louis	1B	G. Stovall	398	.254	0	45	845	68	16	64	9.9	.983	E. Hamilton	41	250	11	14	2	3.24
	2B	D. Pratt	570	.302	5	69	273	326	36	49	5.2	.943	J. Powell	32	235	9	16	0	3.10
W-53 L-101	SS	B. Wallace	323	.241	0	31	185	271	28	29	5.6	.942	Baumgardner	30	218	11	14	0	3.38
	3B	J. Austin	536	.252	2	44	**219**	292	50	22	3.8	.911	M. Allison	31	169	6	17	1	3.62
Bobby Wallace	RF	P. Compton	268	.280	2	30	139	9	12	1	2.2	.925	E. Brown	23	120	5	8	0	2.99
W-12 L-27	CF	B. Shotton	580	.290	2	40	**381**	20	25	7	2.8	.941							
	LF	H. Hogan	360	.214	1	36	229	14	7	6	2.5	.972							
George Stovall	C	J. Stephens	205	.249	0	22	262	110	18	10	5.9	.954							
W-41 L-74	20	F. LaPorte	266	.312	1	38	123	107	16	24		.935							
	OF	G. Williams	216	.292	2	32	94	12	8	3	1.8	.930							
	1B	J. Kutina	205	.205	1	18	489	24	8	28	10.2	.985							
	C	P. Krichell	161	.217	0	8	255	72	14	9	6.0	.959							

AMERICAN LEAGUE 1912, cont.

	POS	Player	AB	BA	HR	RBI	PO	A	E	DP	TC/G	FA	Pitcher	G	IP	W	L	SV	ERA
New York	1B	H. Chase	522	.274	4	58	1162	79	27	49	10.5	.979	R. Ford	36	292	13	21	0	3.55
	2B	H. Simmons	401	.239	0	41	162	207	21	23	4.4	.946	J. Warhop	39	258	10	19	3	2.86
W-50 L-102	SS	J. Martin	231	.225	0	17	123	201	36	18	5.6	.900	R. Caldwell	30	183	8	16	0	4.47
	3B	D. Paddock	156	.288	1	14	49	69	14	4	3.2	.894	McConnell	23	177	8	12	0	2.75
Harry Wolverton	RF	G. Zinn	401	.262	6	55	158	9	20	1	1.8	.893	J. Quinn	18	103	5	7	0	5.79
	CF	R. Hartzell	416	.272	1	38	101	9	7	2	2.1	.940	R. Fisher	17	90	2	8	0	5.88
	LF	B. Daniels	496	.274	2	41	277	13	17	1	2.3	.945	H. Vaughn	15	63	2	8	0	5.14
	C	J. Sweeney	351	.268	0	30	548	167	34	9	6.9	.955							
	UT	D. Sterrett	230	.265	1	32	259	22	5	4		.983							
	OF	B. Cree	190	.332	0	22	123	5	7	1	2.7	.948							
	2B	E. Gardner	160	.281	0	26	93	107	17	11	5.0	.922							
	OF	J. Lelivelt	149	.362	2	23	75	4	3	2	2.3	.963							

BATTING AND BASE RUNNING LEADERS

Batting Average		Slugging Average		Home Runs	
T. Cobb, DET	.410	T. Cobb, DET	.586	F. Baker, PHI	10
J. Jackson, CLE	.395	J. Jackson, CLE	.579	T. Speaker, BOS	10
T. Speaker, BOS	.383	T. Speaker, BOS	.567	T. Cobb, DET	7
N. Lajoie, CLE	.368	F. Baker, PHI	.541	G. Zinn, NY	6
E. Collins, PHI	.348	S. Crawford, DET	.470	D. Moeller, WAS	6
				D. Lewis, BOS	6

Total Bases		Runs Batted In		Stolen Bases	
J. Jackson, CLE	331	F. Baker, PHI	133	C. Milan, WAS	88
T. Speaker, BOS	329	S. Crawford, DET	109	E. Collins, PHI	63
T. Cobb, DET	324	D. Lewis, BOS	109	T. Cobb, DET	61
F. Baker, PHI	312	S. McInnis, PHI	101	T. Speaker, BOS	52
S. Crawford, DET	273	T. Speaker, BOS	98	R. Zeider, CHI	47

Hits		Base on Balls		Home Run Percentage	
T. Cobb, DET	227	D. Bush, DET	117	F. Baker, PHI	1.7
J. Jackson, CLE	226	E. Collins, PHI	101	T. Speaker, BOS	1.6
T. Speaker, BOS	222	M. Rath, CHI	95	G. Zinn, NY	1.5
F. Baker, PHI	200	B. Shotton, STL	86	T. Cobb, DET	1.3

Runs Scored		Doubles		Triples	
E. Collins, PHI	137	T. Speaker, BOS	53	J. Jackson, CLE	26
T. Speaker, BOS	136	J. Jackson, CLE	44	T. Cobb, DET	23
J. Jackson, CLE	121	F. Baker, PHI	40	F. Baker, PHI	21
T. Cobb, DET	119	D. Lewis, BOS	36	S. Crawford, DET	21

PITCHING LEADERS

Winning Percentage		Earned Run Average		Wins	
S. Wood, BOS	.872	W. Johnson, WAS	1.39	S. Wood, BOS	34
E. Plank, PHI	.813	S. Wood, BOS	1.91	W. Johnson, WAS	32
W. Johnson, WAS	.727	E. Walsh, CHI	2.15	E. Walsh, CHI	27
J. Coombs, PHI	.677	E. Plank, PHI	2.22	E. Plank, PHI	26
H. Bedient, BOS	.667	R. Collins, BOS	2.53	B. Groom, WAS	24

Saves		Strikeouts		Complete Games	
E. Walsh, CHI	10	W. Johnson, WAS	303	S. Wood, BOS	35
		S. Wood, BOS	258	W. Johnson, WAS	34
		E. Walsh, CHI	254	R. Ford, NY	32
		V. Gregg, CLE	184	E. Walsh, CHI	32
		B. Groom, WAS	179	E. Willett, DET	28
				B. Groom, WAS	28

Fewest Hits/9 Innings		Shutouts		Fewest Walks/9 Innings	
W. Johnson, WAS	6.33	S. Wood, BOS	10	C. Bender, PHI	1.74
S. Wood, BOS	6.99	W. Johnson, WAS	7	W. Johnson, WAS	1.86
B. Houck, PHI	7.37	E. Walsh, CHI	6	R. Collins, BOS	1.90
E. Walsh, CHI	7.60	R. Collins, BOS	4	J. Powell, STL	1.99

Most Strikeouts/9 Inn.		Innings		Games Pitched	
W. Johnson, WAS	7.24	E. Walsh, CHI	393	E. Walsh, CHI	62
S. Wood, BOS	6.75	W. Johnson, WAS	368	W. Johnson, WAS	50
V. Gregg, CLE	6.10	S. Wood, BOS	344	S. Wood, BOS	43
H. Vaughn, NY, WAS	5.94	B. Groom, WAS	316	B. Groom, WAS	43

	W	L	PCT	GB	R	OR	2B	3B	Batting HR	BA	SA	SB	Fielding E	DP	FA	Pitching CG	BB	SO	ShO	SV	ERA
Boston	105	47	.691		799	544	269	84	29	.277	.380	185	267	88	.957	108	385	712	18	6	2.76
Washington	91	61	.599	14	698	581	202	86	20	.256	.341	274	297	92	.954	98	525	828	11	6	2.69
Philadelphia	90	62	.592	15	779	658	204	108	22	.282	.377	258	263	115	.959	100	518	601	11	9	3.32
Chicago	78	76	.506	28	638	646	174	80	17	.255	.329	205	291	102	.956	85	426	697	14	16	3.06
Cleveland	75	78	.490	30.5	676	680	218	77	10	.273	.352	194	287	124	.956	94	523	622	7	7	3.30
Detroit	69	84	.451	36.5	720	777	189	86	19	.267	.349	270	338	91	.950	107	517	506	7	5	3.78
St. Louis	53	101	.344	53	552	764	166	71	19	.249	.320	176	341	127	.947	85	442	547	8	5	3.71
New York	50	102	.329	55	630	842	168	79	18	.259	.334	247	382	77	.940	105	436	637	4	3	4.13
					5492	5492	1590	671	154	.265	.348	1809	2466	816	.952	782	3772	5150	80	57	3.34

NATIONAL LEAGUE 1913

	POS	Player	AB	BA	HR	RBI	PO	A	E	DP	TC/G	FA	Pitcher	G	IP	W	L	SV	ERA
New York	1B	F. Merkle	563	.261	3	69	1463	76	22	86	10.2	.986	C. Mathewson	40	306	25	11	2	2.06
	2B	L. Doyle	482	.280	5	73	315	345	31	55	5.3	.955	R. Marquard	42	288	23	10	2	2.50
W-101 L-51	SS	A. Fletcher	538	.297	4	71	245	435	50	42	5.4	.932	J. Tesreau	41	282	22	13	0	2.17
	3B	B. Herzog	290	.286	3	31	95	139	13	18	2.9	.947	A. Demaree	31	200	13	4	2	2.21
John McGraw	RF	R. Murray	520	.267	2	59	279	24	11	3	2.1	.965	A. Fromme	26	112	11	6	0	4.01
	CF	F. Snodgrass	457	.291	3	49	312	19	11	1	2.6	.968	D. Crandall	35	98	4	4	6	2.86
	LF	G. Burns	605	.286	2	54	321	22	13	2	2.4	.963							
	C	C. Meyers	378	.312	3	47	579	143	25	12	6.4	.967							
	UT	T. Shafer	508	.287	5	52	220	254	43	26		.917							

NATIONAL LEAGUE 1913, *cont.*

	POS	Player	AB	BA	HR	RBI	PO	A	E	DP	TC/G	FA	Pitcher	G	IP	W	L	SV	ERA
Philadelphia	1B	F. Luderus	588	.262	18	86	1533	92	26	76	10.7	.984	T. Seaton	52	322	27	12	1	2.60
	2B	O. Knabe	571	.263	2	53	311	466	33	58	5.5	.959	G. Alexander	47	306	22	8	2	2.79
W-88 L-63	SS	M. Doolan	518	.218	1	43	338	482	51	63	5.9	.941	A. Brennan	40	207	14	12	1	2.39
	3B	H. Lobert	573	.300	7	55	181	225	11	13	2.9	.974	E. Mayer	39	171	9	9	1	3.11
Red Dooin	RF	G. Cravath	525	.341	19	128	208	20	10	1	1.7	.958	E. Rixey	35	156	9	5	2	3.12
	CF	D. Paskert	454	.262	4	29	330	19	10	8	3.0	.972	G. Chalmers	26	116	3	10	1	4.81
	LF	S. Magee	470	.306	11	70	236	7	8	2	2.0	.968							
	C	B. Killefer	360	.244	0	24	569	166	9	16	6.3	.988							
	OF	B. Becker	306	.324	9	44	172	6	3	1	2.4	.983							
Chicago	1B	V. Saier	518	.288	14	92	1469	71	26	79	10.6	.983	L. Cheney	54	305	21	14	11	2.57
	2B	J. Evers	444	.284	3	49	303	426	30	70	5.6	.960	J. Lavender	40	204	10	14	2	3.66
W-88 L-65	SS	A. Bridwell	405	.240	1	37	282	399	37	46	5.3	.948	B. Humphries	28	181	16	4	0	2.69
	3B	H. Zimmerman	447	.313	9	95	139	232	36	18	3.3	.912	G. Pearce	25	163	13	5	0	2.31
Johnny Evers	RF	W. Schulte	495	.279	9	72	180	13	9	2	1.6	.955	C. Smith	20	138	7	9	0	2.55
	CF	T. Leach	454	.289	6	32	270	15	3	5	2.4	.990							
	LF	M. Mitchell	278	.259	4	35	176	14	12*	0	2.5	.941							
	C	J. Archer	367	.267	2	44	454	138	19	6	5.9	.969							
	23	A. Phelan	259	.251	2	35	102	147	19	12		.929							
	OF	W. Miller	203	.236	1	16	136	9	3	5	2.3	.980							
	C	R. Bresnahan	161	.230	1	21	194	67	10	2	4.7	.963							
	OF	C. Williams	156	.224	4	32	77	4	2	0	1.9	.976							
Pittsburgh	1B	D. Miller	580	.272	7	90	1400	78	22	67	10.0	.985	B. Adams	43	314	21	10	0	2.15
	2B	J. Viox	492	.317	2	65	223	314	23	29	4.5	.959	C. Hendrix	42	241	14	15	3	2.84
W-78 L-71	SS	H. Wagner	413	.300	3	56	289	323	24	47	6.1	.962	H. Robinson	43	196	14	9	2	2.38
	3B	B. Byrne	448	.270	1	47	154	176	21	14	3.2	.940	H. Camnitz	36	192	6	17	2	3.74
Fred Clarke	RF	O. Wilson	580	.266	10	73	301	14	10	3	2.1	.969	M. O'Toole	26	145	6	8	1	3.30
	CF	M. Mitchell	199	.271	1	16	150	9	9*	0	3.1	.946	McQuillan	25	142	8	6	1	3.43
	LF	M. Carey	620	.277	5	49	363	28	16	6	2.6	.961							
	C	M. Simon	255	.247	1	17	393	151	14	6	6.1	.975							
	2S	A. Butler	214	.280	0	20	126	144	25	14		.915							
	OF	F. Kommers	155	.232	0	22	94	1	2	0	2.4	.979							
Boston	1B	H. Myers	524	.273	2	50	1344	85	19	57	10.7	.987	L. Tyler	39	290	16	17	2	2.79
	2B	B. Sweeney	502	.257	0	47	301	391	45	42	5.4	.939	D. Rudolph	33	249	14	13	0	2.92
W-69 L-82	SS	Maranville	571	.247	2	48	317	475	43	49	5.8	.949	O. Hess	29	218	7	17	0	3.83
	3B	A. Devlin	210	.229	0	12	83	134	6	4	3.2	.973	H. Perdue	38	212	16	13	1	3.26
George Stallings	RF	J. Titus	269	.297	5	38	94	8	9	1	1.5	.919	B. James	24	136	6	10	2	2.79
	CF	L. Mann	407	.253	3	51	250	14	11	2	2.3	.960	W. Dickson	19	128	6	7	0	3.23
	LF	J. Connolly	427	.281	5	57	214	16	11	2	1.9	.954							
	C	B. Rariden	246	.236	3	30	377	111	12	6	5.7	.976							
	UT	F. Smith	285	.228	0	27	104	150	27	11		.904							
	OF	B. Lord	235	.251	6	26	81	4	8	0	1.5	.914							
	C	B. Whaling	211	.242	0	25	328	84	4	4	5.4	.990							
Brooklyn	1B	J. Daubert	508	.350	2	52	1279	80	13	91	9.9	.991	P. Ragan	44	265	15	18	0	3.77
	2B	G. Cutshaw	592	.267	7	80	402	448	38	79	6.0	.957	N. Rucker	41	260	14	15	3	2.87
W-65 L-84	SS	B. Fisher	474	.262	4	54	263	364	52	60	5.2	.923	F. Allen	34	175	4	18	2	2.83
	3B	R. Smith	540	.296	6	76	175	295	34	13	3.3	.933	C. Curtis	30	152	8	9	1	3.26
Bill Dahlen	RF	H. Moran	515	.266	0	26	231	15	13	7	2.0	.950	E. Yingling	26	147	8	8	0	2.58
	CF	C. Stengel	438	.272	7	43	270	16	12	1	2.5	.960	E. Reulbach	15	110	7	6	0	2.05
	LF	Z. Wheat	535	.301	7	71	338	13	8	7	2.8	.978							
	C	O. Miller	320	.272	0	26	448	148	18	13	6.0	.971							
	UT	J. Hummel	198	.242	2	24	126	66	8	24		.960							
	C	B. Fischer	165	.267	1	12	193	65	7	2	5.2	.974							
Cincinnati	1B	Hoblitzell	502	.285	3	68	1373	60	17	76	10.8	.988	C. Johnson	44	269	14	16	0	3.01
	2B	H. Groh	397	.282	3	48	249	358	23	43	5.6	.963	G. Suggs	36	199	8	15	2	4.03
W-64 L-89	SS	J. Tinker	382	.317	1	57	223	320	18	34	5.6	.968	G. Packard	39	191	7	11	0	2.97
	3B	J. Dodge	323	.241	4	45	96	170	27	10	3.2	.908	J. Ames	31	187	11	13	2	2.88
Joe Tinker	RF	J. Bates	407	.278	6	51	192	19	12	6	2.0	.946	T. Brown	39	173	11	12	6	2.91
	CF	A. Marsans	435	.297	0	38	170	12	7	2	2.0	.963	R. Benton	23	144	11	7	0	3.49
	LF	B. Bescher	511	.258	1	37	283	22	10	2	2.3	.968							
	C	T. Clarke	330	.264	1	38	378	131	11	5	5.2	.979							
	OF	J. Devore	217	.267	3	14	106	9	10	3	2.2	.920							
	C	J. Kling	209	.273	0	23	259	94	9	3	5.7	.975							
	2S	D. Egan	195	.282	0	22	115	150	12	20		.957							
	SS	Berghammer	188	.218	1	13	97	143	24	16	5.0	.909							
	3B	R. Almeida	130	.262	3	21	42	71	10	6	3.3	.919							

NATIONAL LEAGUE 1913, *cont.*

	POS	Player	AB	BA	HR	RBI	PO	A	E	DP	TC/G	FA	Pitcher	G	IP	W	L	SV	ERA
St. Louis	1B	E. Konetchy	502	.273	7	68	1432	91	7	71	11.0	.995	S. Sallee	49	273	18	15	5	2.70
	2B	M. Huggins	381	.286	0	27	266	339	14	44	5.5	.977	B. Harmon	42	273	8	21	1	3.92
W-51 L-99	SS	C. O'Leary	404	.218	0	31	193	297	25	22	5.0	.951	D. Griner	34	225	10	22	0	5.08
	3B	M. Mowrey	449	.258	0	33	143	284	21	23	3.4	.953	P. Perritt	36	175	6	14	0	5.25
Miller Huggins	RF	S. Evans	245	.249	1	31	111	5	2	0	1.6	.983	B. Doak	15	93	2	8	1	3.10
	CF	R. Oakes	537	.291	0	49	321	16	11	2	2.4	.968							
	LF	L. Magee	529	.265	2	31	250	21	5	5	2.6	.982							
	C	I. Wingo	305	.256	2	35	346	132	28	12	5.2	.945							
	UT	P. Whitted	402	.221	0	38	225	207	27	27		.941							
	OF	T. Cather	183	.213	0	12	67	8	7	0	1.4	.915							

BATTING AND BASE RUNNING LEADERS

Batting Average
J. Daubert, BKN .350
G. Cravath, PHI .341
J. Viox, PIT .317
J. Tinker, CIN .317
B. Becker, CIN, PHI .316

Slugging Average
G. Cravath, PHI .568
B. Becker, CIN, PHI .502
H. Zimmerman, CHI .490
S. Magee, PHI .479
V. Saier, CHI .477

Home Runs
G. Cravath, PHI 19
F. Luderus, PHI 18
V. Saier, CHI 14
S. Magee, PHI 11
O. Wilson, PIT 10

Total Bases
G. Cravath, PHI 298
F. Luderus, PHI 254
V. Saier, CHI 247
H. Lobert, PHI 243
D. Miller, PIT 243

Runs Batted In
G. Cravath, PHI 128
H. Zimmerman, CHI 95
V. Saier, CHI 92
D. Miller, PIT 90
F. Luderus, PHI 86

Stolen Bases
M. Carey, PIT 61
H. Myers, BOS 57
H. Lobert, PHI 41
G. Burns, NY 40
G. Cutshaw, BKN 39

Hits
G. Cravath, PHI 179
J. Daubert, BKN 178
G. Burns, NY 173
H. Lobert, PHI 172

Base on Balls
B. Bescher, CIN 94
M. Huggins, STL 91
T. Leach, CHI 77
A. Bridwell, CHI 74

Home Run Percentage
G. Cravath, PHI 3.6
F. Luderus, PHI 3.1
V. Saier, CHI 2.7
S. Magee, PHI 2.3

Runs Scored
T. Leach, CHI 99
M. Carey, PIT 99
H. Lobert, PHI 98
V. Saier, CHI 93

Doubles
R. Smith, BKN 40
G. Burns, NY 37
S. Magee, PHI 36
G. Cravath, PHI 34

Triples
V. Saier, CHI 21
D. Miller, PIT 20
E. Konetchy, STL 17
G. Cravath, PHI 14

PITCHING LEADERS

Winning Percentage
B. Humphries, CHI .800
G. Alexander, PHI .733
R. Marquard, NY .697
C. Mathewson, NY .694
T. Seaton, PHI .692

Earned Run Average
C. Mathewson, NY 2.06
B. Adams, PIT 2.15
J. Tesreau, NY 2.17
A. Demaree, NY 2.21
G. Pearce, CHI 2.31

Wins
T. Seaton, PHI 27
C. Mathewson, NY 25
R. Marquard, NY 23
G. Alexander, PHI 22
J. Tesreau, NY 22

Saves
L. Cheney, CHI 11
T. Brown, CIN 6
D. Crandall, NY, STL 6
S. Sallee, STL 5

Strikeouts
T. Seaton, PHI 168
J. Tesreau, NY 167
G. Alexander, PHI 159
R. Marquard, NY 151
B. Adams, PIT 144

Complete Games
L. Tyler, BOS 28
C. Mathewson, NY 25
L. Cheney, CHI 25
B. Adams, PIT 24
G. Alexander, PHI 23

Fewest Hits/9 Innings
J. Tesreau, NY 7.09
T. Seaton, PHI 7.32
F. Allen, BKN 7.42
G. Pearce, CHI 7.55

Shutouts
G. Alexander, PHI 9
T. Seaton, PHI 6

Fewest Walks/9 Innings
C. Mathewson, NY 0.62
B. Humphries, CHI 1.19
B. Adams, PIT 1.41
R. Marquard, NY 1.53

Most Strikeouts/9 Inn.
J. Tesreau, NY 5.33
C. Hendrix, PIT 5.15
B. James, BOS 4.84
R. Marquard, NY 4.72

Innings
T. Seaton, PHI 322
B. Adams, PIT 314
G. Alexander, PHI 306
C. Mathewson, NY 306

Games Pitched
L. Cheney, CHI 54
T. Seaton, PHI 52
S. Sallee, STL 49
G. Alexander, PHI 47

	W	L	PCT	GB	R	OR	2B	3B	HR	BA	SA	SB	E	DP	FA	CG	BB	SO	ShO	SV	ERA
New York	101	51	.664		684	515	226	70	31	.273	.361	296	254	107	.961	82	315	651	12	16	2.43
Philadelphia	88	63	.583	12.5	693	636	257	78	73	.265	.382	156	214	112	.968	77	512	667	20	11	3.15
Chicago	88	65	.575	13.5	720	625	194	96	59	.257	.369	181	259	112	.959	89	478	556	12	14	3.13
Pittsburgh	78	71	.523	21.5	673	585	210	86	35	.263	.356	181	226	94	.964	74	434	590	9	7	2.90
Boston	69	82	.457	31.5	641	690	191	60	32	.256	.335	177	273	82	.957	105	419	597	12	3	3.19
Brooklyn	65	84	.436	34.5	595	613	193	86	34	.270	.363	188	243	125	.961	70	439	548	9	6	3.13
Cincinnati	64	89	.418	37.5	607	717	170	96	27	.261	.347	226	251	104	.961	71	456	522	10	10	3.46
St. Louis	51	99	.340	49	523	755	152	72	14	.247	.315	171	219	113	.965	73	476	464	6	10	4.24
					5136	5136	1593	644	310	.262	.354	1576	1939	843	.962	641	3529	4595	90	77	3.20

AMERICAN LEAGUE 1913

	POS	Player	AB	BA	HR	RBI	PO	A	E	DP	TC/G	FA	Pitcher	G	IP	W	L	SV	ERA
Philadelphia	1B	S. McInnis	543	.326	4	90	1504	80	12	85	10.8	.992	E. Plank	41	243	18	10	4	2.60
	2B	E. Collins	534	.345	3	73	314	449	28	54	5.3	.965	C. Bender	48	237	21	10	13	2.21
W-96 L-57	SS	J. Barry	455	.275	3	85	248	403	32	60	5.1	.953	B. Brown	43	235	17	11	1	2.94
	3B	F. Baker	565	.336	12	126	233	280	44	19	3.7	.921	J. Bush	39	200	14	6	3	3.82
Connie Mack	RF	E. Murphy	508	.295	1	30	166	14	11	2	1.4	.942	B. Houck	41	176	14	6	0	4.14
	CF	J. Walsh	303	.254	0	27	184	11	8	4	2.3	.961	B. Shawkey	18	111	6	5	0	2.34
	LF	R. Oldring	538	.283	5	71	236	9	8	3	1.9	.968							
	C	J. Lapp	238	.227	1	20	313	110	14	3	5.7	.968							
	OF	A. Strunk	292	.305	0	46	168	9	7	3	2.3	.962							
	C	W. Schang	207	.266	3	30	317	97	14	9	6.0	.967							

AMERICAN LEAGUE 1913, *cont.*

	POS	Player	AB	BA	HR	RBI	PO	A	E	DP	TC/G	FA	Pitcher	G	IP	W	L	SV	ERA
Washington	1B	C. Gandil	550	.318	1	72	1436	**103**	15	**89**	10.7	.990	W. Johnson	47	**346**	**36**	7	2	**1.09**
	2B	R. Morgan	481	.272	0	57	254	359	32	61	4.8	.950	B. Groom	37	264	16	16	0	3.23
W-90 L-64	SS	G. McBride	499	.214	1	52	316	490	34	62	5.6	**.960**	J. Boehling	38	235	17	7	4	2.14
	3B	E. Foster	409	.247	1	41	112	217	36	20	3.5	.901	J. Engel	36	165	8	9	0	3.06
Clark Griffith	RF	D. Moeller	589	.236	5	42	249	27	22	4	1.9	.926	L. Hughes	36	130	4	12	6	4.30
	CF	C. Milan	579	.301	3	54	296	20	23	7	2.2	.932							
	LF	H. Shanks	390	.254	1	37	207	13	5	3	2.1	.978							
	C	J. Henry	273	.223	1	26	476	127	11	9	6.4	**.982**							
	UT	F. LaPorte	242	.252	0	18	83	114	9	13		.956							
	C	E. Ainsmith	229	.214	2	20	418	82	17	10	6.5	.967							
Cleveland	1B	D. Johnston	530	.255	2	39	1319	76	15	76	10.6	.989	V. Gregg	44	286	20	13	3	2.24
	2B	N. Lajoie	465	.335	1	68	279	363	20	59	5.3	**.970**	Falkenberg	39	276	23	10	0	2.22
W-86 L-66	SS	R. Chapman	508	.258	3	39	299	408	48	59	5.5	.936	W. Mitchell	34	217	14	8	0	1.74
	3B	I. Olson	370	.249	0	32	97	145	12	7	3.5	.953	F. Blanding	41	215	15	10	0	2.55
Joe Birmingham	RF	J. Jackson	528	.373	7	71	211	28	18	5	1.7	.930	B. Steen	22	128	4	5	2	2.45
	CF	N. Leibold	286	.259	0	12	142	12	9	1	2.3	.945	G. Kahler	24	118	5	9	0	3.14
	LF	J. Graney	517	.267	3	68	275	16	9	5	2.0	.970	N. Cullop	23	98	3	7	0	4.42
	C	F. Carisch	222	.216	0	26	391	114	15	10	**6.6**	.971							
	UT	T. Turner	388	.247	0	44	188	279	18	35		.963							
	OF	B. Ryan	243	.296	0	32	138	7	2	2		.986							
	C	S. O'Neill	234	.295	0	29	353	119	13	9	6.2	.973							
Boston	1B	C. Engle	498	.289	2	50	1239	57	17	55	9.9	.987	D. Leonard	42	259	14	16	1	2.39
	2B	S. Yerkes	487	.267	1	48	220	341	25	31	4.5	.957	H. Bedient	43	259	15	14	5	2.78
W-79 L-71	SS	H. Wagner	365	.227	2	34	274	311	39	36	5.9	.938	R. Collins	30	247	19	8	0	2.63
	3B	L. Gardner	473	.281	4	63	126	220	21	13	2.8	.943	S. Wood	23	146	11	5	2	2.29
Jake Stahl	RF	H. Hooper	586	.288	4	40	248	25	9	7	1.9	.968	E. Moseley	24	121	9	5	0	3.13
W-39 L-41	CF	T. Speaker	520	.365	3	81	**374**	**30**	**25**	7	3.1	.942	C. Hall	35	105	4	4	3	3.43
	LF	D. Lewis	551	.298	0	90	262	29	12	3	2.1	.960	B. O'Brien	15	90	4	9	0	3.69
Bill Carrigan	C	B. Carrigan	256	.242	0	28	383	127	11	8	6.4	.979							
W-40 L-30	UT	H. Janvrin	276	.207	3	25	172	177	26	17		.931							
Chicago	1B	H. Chase	384	.286	2	39	1009	71	27*	53	10.9	.976	R. Russell	**51**	316	22	16	4	1.91
	2B	M. Rath	295	.200	0	12	159	251	16	32	5.0	.962	J. Scott	48	312	20	**20**	1	1.90
W-78 L-74	SS	B. Weaver	533	.272	4	52	**392**	**520**	70	**73**	6.5	.929	E. Cicotte	41	268	18	12	1	1.58
	3B	H. Lord	547	.263	1	42	142	221	30	13	2.6	.924	J. Benz	33	151	7	10	1	2.74
Nixey Callahan	RF	S. Collins	535	.239	1	47	244	19	14	3	1.9	.949	D. White	19	103	2	4	0	3.50
	CF	P. Bodie	406	.264	8	48	226	14	8	1	2.1	.968	E. Walsh	16	98	8	3	1	2.58
	LF	W. Mattick	207	.188	0	11	116	14	3	2	2.1	.977							
	C	R. Schalk	401	.244	1	38	599	154	15	**18**	6.1	.980							
	2B	J. Berger	223	.215	2	20	111	214	14	18	4.9	.959							
	OF	L. Chappell	208	.231	0	15	114	5	6	1	2.1	.952							
	10	J. Fournier	172	.233	1	23	306	23	5	10		.985							
Detroit	1B	D. Gainer	363	.267	2	25	1118	50	14	55	**11.6**	.988	E. Willett	34	242	13	14	0	3.09
	2B	O. Vitt	359	.240	2	33	151	234	16	24	5.1	.960	J. Dubuc	36	243	15	14	2	2.89
W-66 L-87	SS	D. Bush	593	.251	1	40	331	510	56	61	5.9	.938	H. Dauss	33	225	13	12	1	2.68
	3B	G. Moriarty	347	.239	0	30	122	183	20	9	3.5	.938	M. Hall	30	165	10	12	1	3.27
Hughie Jennings	RF	S. Crawford	**610**	.316	9	83	201	14	8	5	1.6	.964	J. Lake	28	137	8	7	1	3.28
	CF	T. Cobb	428	**.390**	4	67	262	22	16	8	2.5	.947							
	LF	B. Veach	494	.269	0	64	250	16	24	3	2.1	.917							
	C	O. Stanage	241	.224	0	21	277	106	16	6	5.2	.960							
	UT	B. Louden	191	.241	0	23	76	146	17	11		.929							
	2B	P. Baumann	191	.298	1	22	97	136	14	15	5.0	.943							
	C	R. McKee	187	.283	1	20	237	84	17	5	5.5	.950							
	OF	H. High	183	.230	0	16	104	8	2	0	2.3	.982							
New York	1B	J. Knight	250	.236	0	24	494	45	11	26	11.0	.980	R. Fisher	43	246	12	16	1	3.18
	2B	R. Hartzell	490	.259	0	38	203	234	27	29	5.7	.942	R. Ford	33	237	12	18	2	2.66
W-57 L-94	SS	Peckinpaugh	340	.268	1	32	184	303	36	30	5.6	.931	A. Schulz	38	193	7	13	0	3.73
	3B	E. Midkiff	284	.197	0	14	102	185	13	12	3.9	.957	McConnell	35	180	4	15	3	3.20
Frank Chance	RF	B. Daniels	320	.216	0	22	128	15	5	3	1.7	.966	R. Caldwell	27	164	9	8	0	2.41
	CF	H. Wolter	425	.254	2	43	228	15	14	1	2.1	.946	R. Keating	28	151	6	12	0	3.21
	LF	B. Cree	534	.272	1	63	239	17	3	5	1.8	**.988**	J. Warhop	15	62	4	6	0	3.75
	C	J. Sweeney	351	.265	2	40	511	**180**	26	9	6.4	.964							
	3B	F. Maisel	187	.257	0	12	70	83	8	3	3.2	.950							
	UT	R. Zeider	159	.233	0	12	138	102	17	13		.934							
St. Louis	1B	G. Stovall	303	.287	1	24	751	65	10	38	10.9	.988	Baumgardner	38	253	10	19	1	3.13
	2B	D. Pratt	592	.296	2	87	**364**	425	41	56	**5.7**	.951	C. Weilman	39	252	10	**20**	0	3.40
W-57 L-96	SS	M. Balenti	211	.180	0	11	107	169	23	25	5.3	.923	R. Mitchell	33	245	13	16	1	3.01
	3B	J. Austin	489	.266	2	42	216	**288**	30	21	3.8	**.944**	E. Hamilton	31	217	13	12	1	2.57
George Stovall	RF	G. Williams	538	.273	5	53	225	26	13	7	1.8	.951	W. Leverenz	30	203	6	17	1	2.58
W-50 L-84	CF	B. Shotton	549	.297	1	28	357	29	20	**11**	2.8	.951							
	LF	J. Johnston	380	.224	2	27	222	23	9	3	2.4	.965							
Jimmy Austin	C	S. Agnew	307	.208	2	24	383	170	**28**	17	5.6	.952							
W-2 L-6	1B	B. Brief	258	.217	1	26	622	34	9	41	10.7	.986							
	SS	B. Wallace	147	.211	0	21	67	96	12	8	4.6	.931							
Branch Rickey																			
W-5 L-6																			

AMERICAN LEAGUE 1913, *cont.*

BATTING AND BASE RUNNING LEADERS

Batting Average
T. Cobb, DET	.390
J. Jackson, CLE	.373
T. Speaker, BOS	.365
E. Collins, PHI	.345
F. Baker, PHI	.336

Slugging Average
J. Jackson, CLE	.551
T. Cobb, DET	.535
T. Speaker, BOS	.535
F. Baker, PHI	.492
S. Crawford, DET	.489

Home Runs
F. Baker, PHI	12
S. Crawford, DET	9
P. Bodie, CHI	8
J. Jackson, CLE	7

Winning Percentage
W. Johnson, WAS	.837
R. Collins, BOS	.714
J. Boehling, WAS	.708
Falkenberg, CLE	.697
C. Bender, PHI	.677

Earned Run Average
W. Johnson, WAS	1.09
E. Cicotte, CHI	1.58
W. Mitchell, CLE	1.74
J. Scott, CHI	1.90
R. Russell, CHI	1.91

Wins
W. Johnson, WAS	36
Falkenberg, CLE	23
R. Russell, CHI	22
C. Bender, PHI	21

Total Bases
S. Crawford, DET	298
J. Jackson, CLE	291
T. Speaker, BOS	278
F. Baker, PHI	278
E. Collins, PHI	242

Runs Batted In
F. Baker, PHI	126
S. McInnis, PHI	90
D. Lewis, BOS	90
D. Pratt, STL	87
J. Barry, PHI	85

Stolen Bases
C. Milan, WAS	75
D. Moeller, WAS	62
E. Collins, PHI	55
T. Cobb, DET	51
T. Speaker, BOS	46

Saves
C. Bender, PHI	12
L. Hughes, WAS	6

Strikeouts
W. Johnson, WAS	243
Falkenberg, CLE	166
V. Gregg, CLE	166
J. Scott, CHI	158
B. Groom, WAS	156

Complete Games
W. Johnson, WAS	29
R. Russell, CHI	26
J. Scott, CHI	25
Baumgardner, STL	23
V. Gregg, CLE	23
Falkenberg, CLE	23

Hits
J. Jackson, CLE	197
S. Crawford, DET	193
F. Baker, PHI	190
T. Speaker, BOS	189

Base on Balls
B. Shotton, STL	99
E. Collins, PHI	85
H. Wolter, NY	80
J. Jackson, CLE	80

Home Run Percentage
F. Baker, PHI	2.1
P. Bodie, CHI	2.0
S. Crawford, DET	1.5
J. Jackson, CLE	1.3

Fewest Hits/9 Innings
W. Johnson, WAS	5.98
W. Mitchell, CLE	6.35
W. Leverenz, STL	7.06
R. Russell, CHI	7.09

Shutouts
W. Johnson, WAS	11
R. Russell, CHI	8
E. Plank, PHI	7
Falkenberg, CLE	6

Fewest Walks/9 Innings
W. Johnson, WAS	0.99
R. Collins, BOS	1.35
R. Mitchell, STL	1.72
E. Plank, PHI	2.11

Runs Scored
E. Collins, PHI	125
F. Baker, PHI	116
J. Jackson, CLE	109
E. Murphy, PHI	105

Doubles
J. Jackson, CLE	39
T. Speaker, BOS	35
F. Baker, PHI	34
S. Crawford, DET	32

Triples
S. Crawford, DET	23
T. Speaker, BOS	22
J. Jackson, CLE	17
T. Cobb, DET	16

Most Strikeouts/9 Inn.
S. Wood, BOS	7.60
W. Johnson, WAS	6.32
W. Mitchell, CLE	5.85
E. Plank, PHI	5.60

Innings
W. Johnson, WAS	346
R. Russell, CHI	316
J. Scott, CHI	312
V. Gregg, CLE	286

Games Pitched
R. Russell, CHI	51
J. Scott, CHI	48
C. Bender, PHI	48
W. Johnson, WAS	47

	W	L	PCT	GB	R	OR	2B	3B	HR	BA	SA	SB	E	DP	FA	CG	BB	SO	ShO	SV	ERA
Philadelphia	96	57	.627		**794**	592	**223**	80	**33**	**.280**	**.376**	221	**212**	108	**.966**	69	532	630	17	**22**	3.19
Washington	90	64	.584	6.5	596	561	156	80	20	.252	.327	**287**	261	122	.960	78	465	**757**	**23**	20	2.72
Cleveland	86	66	.566	9.5	633	536	205	74	16	.268	.348	191	242	124	.962	95	502	689	18	5	2.52
Boston	79	71	.527	15.5	631	610	221	**101**	17	.269	.364	189	237	84	.961	87	442	710	11	11	2.93
Chicago	78	74	.513	17.5	488	**498**	157	66	23	.236	.310	156	255	104	.960	84	**438**	602	17	8	**2.33**
Detroit	66	87	.431	30	624	716	180	**101**	24	.265	.355	219	300	105	.954	90	504	468	4	7	3.41
New York	57	94	.377	38	529	668	154	45	9	.237	.293	203	293	94	.954	75	455	530	8	7	3.27
St. Louis	57	96	.373	39	528	642	179	73	18	.237	.312	209	301	**125**	.954	**104**	454	476	14	5	3.06
					4823	4823	1475	620	160	.256	.336	1675	2101	866	.959	682	3792	4862	112	85	2.93

NATIONAL LEAGUE 1914

	POS	Player	AB	BA	HR	RBI	PO	A	E	DP	TC/G	FA	Pitcher	G	IP	W	L	SV	ERA
Boston	1B	B. Schmidt	537	.285	1	71	1485	88	16	**109**	10.8	.990	D. Rudolph	42	336	**27**	10	0	2.35
	2B	J. Evers	491	.279	1	40	301	397	17	73	5.1	**.976**	B. James	46	332	26	7	2	1.90
W-94 L-59	SS	Maranville	586	.246	4	78	**407**	**574**	65	92	6.7	.938	L. Tyler	38	271	16	14	2	2.69
	3B	C. Deal	257	.210	0	23	86	133	12	8	3.1	.948	D. Crutcher	33	159	5	6	3	3.46
George Stallings	RF	L. Gilbert	224	.268	5	25	79	14	2	2	1.6	.979	O. Hess	14	89	5	6	1	3.03
	CF	L. Mann	389	.247	4	40	273	24	15	8	2.5	.952							
	LF	J. Connolly	399	.306	9	65	168	19	5	1	1.6	.974							
	C	H. Gowdy	366	.243	3	46	475	151	21	11	5.6	.968							
	UT	P. Whitted	218	.261	2	31	161	61	12	9		.949							
	3B	R. Smith	207	.314	3	37	84*	139*	15	12*	4.0*	.937							
	C	B. Whaling	172	.209	0	12	272	91	7	7	6.3	.981							
	OF	H. Moran	154	.266	0	4	59	4	4	0	1.6	.940							
	OF	T. Cather	145	.297	0	27	57	4	3	1	1.3	.953							
New York	1B	F. Merkle	512	.258	7	63	1463	88	16	80	10.7	.990	J. Tesreau	42	322	26	10	1	2.37
	2B	L. Doyle	539	.260	5	63	307	379	29	61	4.9	.959	C. Mathewson	41	312	24	13	2	3.00
W-84 L-70	SS	A. Fletcher	514	.286	2	79	299	446	63	0	6.0	.922	R. Marquard	39	268	12	22	2	3.06
	3B	M. Stock	365	.263	3	41	95	261	23	17	3.4	.939	A. Demaree	38	224	10	17	0	3.09
John McGraw	RF	F. Snodgrass	392	.263	0	44	200	11	5	4	2.3	.977	A. Fromme	38	138	9	5	2	3.20
	CF	B. Bescher	512	.270	6	35	298	14	13	7	2.6	.960							
	LF	G. Burns	561	.303	3	60	326	19	18	5	2.4	.950							
	C	C. Meyers	381	.286	1	55	**487**	150	20	**16**	5.2	.970							
	UT	E. Grant	282	.277	0	29	97	191	23	16		.926							
	OF	D. Robertson	256	.266	2	32	101	13	6	2	1.7	.950							
	C	L. McLean	154	.260	0	14	211	42	7	8	3.5	.973							
	OF	R. Murray	139	.223	0	23	56	2	0	0	1.2	1.000							

NATIONAL LEAGUE 1914, *cont.*

	POS	Player	AB	BA	HR	RBI	PO	A	E	DP	TC/G	FA	Pitcher	G	IP	W	L	SV	ERA
St. Louis W-81 L-72 Miller Huggins	1B	D. Miller	573	.290	4	88	1019	57	8	46	11.1	.993	P. Perritt	41	286	16	13	2	2.36
	2B	M. Huggins	509	.263	1	24	328	428	28	58	5.3	.964	S. Sallee	46	282	18	17	6	2.10
	SS	A. Butler	274	.201	1	24	155	228	30	24	4.9	.927	B. Doak	36	256	20	6	0	**1.72**
	3B	Z. Beck	457	.232	3	45	141	264	28	24	3.5	.935	D. Griner	37	179	9	13	2	2.51
	RF	O. Wilson	580	.259	9	73	312	34	6	11	2.3	**.983**	H. Perdue	22	153	8	8	1	2.82
	CF	L. Magee	529	.284	2	40	210	14	7	4	2.3	.970	H. Robinson	26	126	6	8	0	3.00
	LF	C. Dolan	421	.240	4	32	182	10	9	2	2.1	.955							
	C	F. Snyder	326	.230	1	25	419	130	12	12	5.7	**.979**							
	OF	W. Cruise	256	.227	4	28	158	6	4	1	2.1	.976							
	C	I. Wingo	237	.300	4	26	276	93	16	7	5.5	.958							
Chicago W-78 L-76 Hank O'Day	1B	V. Saier	537	.240	18	72	1521	59	22	62	10.5	.986	L. Cheney	**50**	311	20	18	5	2.54
	2B	B. Sweeney	463	.218	1	38	301	426	35	40	5.7	.954	H. Vaughn	· 42	294	21	13	1	2.05
	SS	R. Corriden	318	.230	3	29	174	212	46	29	4.5	.894	J. Lavender	37	214	11	11	0	3.07
	3B	H. Zimmerman	564	.296	4	87	141	197	**39**	13	3.2	.897	B. Humphries	34	171	10	11	0	2.68
	RF	W. Good	580	.272	2	43	242	25	**20**	10	1.9	.930	G. Pearce	30	141	8	12	1	3.51
	CF	T. Leach	577	.263	7	46	321	16	11	5	2.5	.968	Z. Zabel	29	128	4	4	1	2.18
	LF	W. Schulte	465	.241	5	61	217	9	11	2	1.8	.954							
	C	R. Bresnahan	248	.278	0	24	365	113	11	6	5.8	.978							
	C	J. Archer	248	.258	2	19	367	105	13	8	6.4	.973							
Brooklyn W-75 L-79 Wilbert Robinson	1B	J. Daubert	474	**.329**	6	45	1097	48	8	68	9.2	.993	J. Pfeffer	43	315	23	12	4	1.97
	2B	G. Cutshaw	583	.257	2	78	**455**	**444**	38	**74**	6.1	.959	E. Reulbach	44	256	11	18	3	2.64
	SS	D. Egan	337	.226	1	21	150	232	36	16	5.0	.914	P. Ragan	38	208	10	15	3	2.98
	3B	R. Smith	330	.245	4	48	136*	193*	22	16*	3.9*	.937	R. Aitchison	26	172	12	7	0	2.66
	RF	C. Stengel	412	.316	4	60	173	15	7	3	1.6	.964	F. Allen	36	171	8	14	0	3.10
	CF	J. Dalton	442	.319	1	45	240	7	9	2	2.2	.965	N. Rucker	16	104	7	6	0	3.39
	LF	Z. Wheat	533	.319	9	89	**331**	21	14	5	2.5	.962							
	C	L. McCarty	284	.254	1	30	398	117	16	9	6.3	.970							
	SS	O. O'Mara	247	.263	1	7	110	183	26	17	5.1	.918							
	OF	H. Myers	227	.286	0	17	102	4	4	0	1.8	.964							
	3B	G. Getz	210	.248	0	20	69	134	11	12	3.9	.949							
	10	J. Hummel	208	.264	0	20	338	21	6	13		.984							
	C	O. Miller	169	.231	0	9	236	66	11	5	6.3	.965							
Philadelphia W-74 L-80 Red Dooin	1B	F. Luderus	443	.248	12	55	1102	76	**30**	49	10.0	.975	G. Alexander	46	**355**	**27**	15	1	2.38
	2B	B. Byrne	467	.272	0	26	187	312	35	19	5.3	.934	E. Mayer	48	321	21	19	2	2.58
	SS	J. Martin	292	.253	0	21	185	251	33	24	5.7	.930	B. Tincup	28	155	7	10	1	2.61
	3B	H. Lobert	505	.275	1	52	188	174	22	10	2.9	**.943**	R. Marshall	27	134	6	7	1	3.75
	RF	G. Cravath	499	.299	**19**	100	205	**34**	18	7	1.8	.930	J. Oeschger	32	124	4	8	1	3.77
	CF	D. Paskert	451	.264	3	44	303	19	14	4	**2.6**	.958	E. Rixey	24	103	2	11	1	4.37
	LF	B. Becker	514	.325	9	66	270	17	16	3	2.4	.947							
	C	B. Killefer	299	.234	0	27	464	**154**	14	11	**7.0**	.978							
	UT	S. Magee	544	.314	15	**103**	549	187	37	20		.952							
	2B	H. Irelan	165	.236	1	16	98	142	24	12	6.0	.909							
Pittsburgh W-69 L-85 Fred Clarke	1B	E. Konetchy	563	.249	4	51	**1576**	**93**	8	70	10.9	**.995**	B. Adams	40	283	13	16	1	2.51
	2B	J. Viox	506	.265	1	57	250	400	42	43	5.0	.939	W. Cooper	40	267	16	15	0	2.13
	SS	H. Wagner	552	.252	1	50	322	424	39	45	5.9	**.950**	McQuillan	45	259	13	17	4	2.98
	3B	M. Mowrey	284	.254	1	25	83	156	10	8	3.2	.960	B. Harmon	37	245	13	17	3	2.53
	RF	M. Mitchell	273	.234	2	23	174	11	3	6	2.5	.984	J. Conzelman	33	101	5	6	1	2.94
	CF	J. Kelly	508	.222	1	48	319	15	19	3	2.6	.946							
	LF	M. Carey	**593**	.243	1	31	318	23	12	3	2.3	.966							
	C	G. Gibson	274	.285	0	30	358	126	13	8	4.9	.974							
	OF	Z. Collins	182	.242	0	15	92	8	4	2	2.1	.962							
	UT	A. McCarthy	173	.150	1	14	63	136	11	10		.948							
Cincinnati W-60 L-94 Buck Herzog	1B	Hoblitzell	248	.210	0	29	802	31	10	43	11.2	.988	R. Ames	47	297	15	**23**	6	2.64
	2B	H. Groh	455	.288	2	32	252	394	**44**	56	5.1	.936	R. Benton	41	271	17	18	2	2.96
	SS	B. Herzog	498	.281	1	40	324	474	52	58	6.2	.939	P. Douglas	45	239	11	18	1	2.56
	3B	B. Niehoff	484	.242	4	49	154	272	35	15	3.4	.924	E. Yingling	34	198	8	13	0	3.45
	RF	H. Moran	395	.235	1	35	175	11	9	4	1.8	.954	P. Schneider	29	144	5	13	1	2.81
	CF	B. Daniels	269	.219	0	19	144	7	4	2	2.2	.974							
	LF	G. Twombly	240	.233	0	19	111	11	4	2	1.9	.968							
	C	T. Clarke	313	.262	2	25	448	132	16	12	5.5	.973							
	OF	D. Miller	192	.255	0	33	79	2	3	1	1.8	.976							
	C	M. Gonzalez	176	.233	0	10	252	101	17	5	4.5	.954							
	OF	J. Bates	163	.245	2	15	91	4	9	1	1.8	.913							
	OF	A. Marsans	124	.298	0	22	72	4	7	1	2.3	.916							

BATTING AND BASE RUNNING LEADERS

Batting Average		Slugging Average		Home Runs	
J. Daubert, BKN	.329	S. Magee, PHI	.509	G. Cravath, PHI	19
B. Becker, PHI	.325	G. Cravath, PHI	.499	V. Saier, CHI	18
J. Dalton, BKN	.319	J. Connolly, BOS	.494	S. Magee, PHI	15
Z. Wheat, BKN	.319	Z. Wheat, BKN	.452	F. Luderus, PHI	12
C. Stengel, BKN	.316	B. Becker, PHI	.446		

PITCHING LEADERS

Winning Percentage		Earned Run Average		Wins	
B. James, BOS	.788	B. Doak, STL	1.72	D. Rudolph, BOS	27
B. Doak, STL	.769	B. James, BOS	1.90	G. Alexander, PHI	27
D. Rudolph, BOS	.730	J. Pfeffer, BKN	1.97	B. James, BOS	26
J. Tesreau, NY	.722	H. Vaughn, CHI	2.05	J. Tesreau, NY	26
J. Pfeffer, BKN	.657	S. Sallee, STL	2.10	C. Mathewson, NY	24

NATIONAL LEAGUE 1914, cont.

BATTING AND BASE RUNNING LEADERS

Total Bases			Runs Batted In			Stolen Bases		
S. Magee, PHI	277		S. Magee, PHI	103		G. Burns, NY	62	
G. Cravath, PHI	249		G. Cravath, PHI	100		B. Herzog, CIN	46	
Z. Wheat, BKN	241		Z. Wheat, BKN	89		C. Dolan, STL	42	
H. Zimmerman, CHI	239		D. Miller, STL	88		M. Carey, PIT	38	
G. Burns, NY	234		H. Zimmerman, CHI	87		B. Bescher, NY	36	
						L. Magee, STL	36	

Hits			Base on Balls			Home Run Percentage		
S. Magee, PHI	171		M. Huggins, STL	105		G. Cravath, PHI	3.8	
Z. Wheat, BKN	170		V. Saier, CHI	94		V. Saier, CHI	3.4	
G. Burns, NY	170		G. Burns, NY	89		S. Magee, PHI	2.8	
B. Becker, PHI	167		J. Evers, BOS	87		F. Luderus, PHI	2.7	

Runs Scored			Doubles			Triples		
G. Burns, NY	100		S. Magee, PHI	39		M. Carey, PIT	17	
S. Magee, PHI	96		H. Zimmerman, CHI	36		H. Zimmerman, CHI	12	
J. Daubert, BKN	89		G. Burns, NY	35		O. Wilson, STL	12	
V. Saier, CHI	87		J. Connolly, BOS	28		G. Cutshaw, BKN	12	

PITCHING LEADERS

Saves			Strikeouts			Complete Games		
S. Sallee, STL	6		G. Alexander, PHI	214		G. Alexander, PHI	32	
R. Ames, CIN	6		J. Tesreau, NY	189		D. Rudolph, BOS	31	
L. Cheney, CHI	5		H. Vaughn, CHI	165		B. James, BOS	30	
McQuillan, PIT	4		L. Cheney, CHI	157		C. Mathewson, NY	29	
J. Pfeffer, BKN	4		B. James, BOS	156		J. Pfeffer, BKN	27	

Fewest Hits/9 Innings			Shutouts			Fewest Walks/9 Innings		
J. Tesreau, NY	6.65		J. Tesreau, NY	8		C. Mathewson, NY	0.66	
B. Doak, STL	6.79		B. Doak, STL	7		B. Adams, PIT	1.24	
L. Cheney, CHI	6.91		D. Rudolph, BOS	6		R. Marquard, NY	1.58	
P. Douglas, CIN	6.99		G. Alexander, PHI	6		D. Rudolph, BOS	1.63	

Most Strikeouts/9 Inn.			Innings			Games Pitched		
G. Alexander, PHI	5.43		G. Alexander, PHI	355		L. Cheney, CHI	50	
J. Tesreau, NY	5.28		D. Rudolph, BOS	336		E. Mayer, PHI	48	
H. Vaughn, CHI	5.06		B. James, BOS	332		R. Ames, CIN	47	
L. Tyler, BOS	4.64		J. Tesreau, NY	322		G. Alexander, PHI	46	

	W	L	PCT	GB	R	OR	2B	3B	HR	BA	SA	SB	E	DP	FA	CG	BB	SO	ShO	SV	ERA
										Batting				Fielding			Pitching				
Boston	94	59	.614		657	548	213	60	35	.251	.335	139	246	**143**	.963	**104**	477	606	19	5	2.74
New York	84	70	.545	10.5	**672**	576	**222**	59	30	.265	.348	**239**	254	119	.961	88	**367**	563	**20**	9	2.94
St. Louis	81	72	.529	13	558	**540**	203	65	33	.248	.333	204	239	109	.964	83	422	531	16	11	**2.38**
Chicago	78	76	.506	16.5	615	638	199	74	42	.243	.337	164	310	87	.951	70	528	**651**	14	9	2.71
Brooklyn	75	79	.487	19.5	622	618	172	**90**	31	**.269**	.355	173	248	112	.961	80	466	605	11	10	2.82
Philadelphia	74	80	.481	20.5	651	687	211	52	**62**	.263	**.361**	145	324	81	.950	85	452	650	14	6	3.06
Pittsburgh	69	85	.448	25.5	503	**540**	148	79	18	.233	.303	147	**223**	96	**.966**	86	392	488	10	9	2.70
Cincinnati	60	94	.390	34.5	530	651	142	64	16	.236	.299	224	314	113	.952	74	489	607	15	**14**	2.94
					4798	4798	1510	543	267	.251	.334	1435	2158	860	.958	670	3593	4701	119	73	2.78

AMERICAN LEAGUE 1914

		POS	Player	AB	BA	HR	RBI	PO	A	E	DP	TC/G	FA	Pitcher	G	IP	W	L	SV	ERA
Philadelphia		1B	S. McInnis	576	.314	1	95	1423	85	7	**89**	10.2	**.995**	B. Shawkey	38	237	16	8	2	2.73
		2B	E. Collins	526	.344	2	85	354	387	23	55	5.0	.970	J. Bush	38	206	16	12	3	3.06
W-99 L-53		SS	J. Barry	467	.242	0	42	244	447	39	61	5.2	.947	J. Wyckoff	32	185	11	7	2	3.02
		3B	F. Baker	570	.319	9	97	221	292	24	20	3.6	.955	E. Plank	34	185	15	7	3	2.87
Connie Mack		RF	E. Murphy	573	.272	3	43	194	15	13	4	1.5	.941	C. Bender	28	179	17	3	2	2.26
		CF	A. Strunk	404	.275	2	45	280	14	4	3	2.5	**.987**	H. Pennock	28	152	11	4	3	2.79
		LF	R. Oldring	466	.277	3	49	215	7	8	5	2.0	.965	R. Bressler	29	148	10	4	2	1.77
		C	W. Schang	307	.287	3	45	498	154	**30**	11	6.8	.956							
		OF	J. Walsh	216	.236	3	36	107	7	4	3	2.1	.966							
		C	J. Lapp	199	.231	0	19	330	88	10	4	6.4	.977							
Boston		1B	Hoblitzell	229	.319	0	33	627	30	14	22	9.9	.979	R. Collins	39	272	20	13	0	2.51
		2B	S. Yerkes	293	.218	1	23	177	241	12	38	4.7	.972	D. Leonard	36	223	19	5	3	**1.01**
W-91 L-62		SS	E. Scott	539	.239	2	37	324	408	39	50	5.4	.949	R. Foster	32	213	14	8	0	1.65
		3B	L. Gardner	553	.259	3	68	187	312	31	18	3.5	.942	H. Bedient	42	177	8	12	2	3.60
Bill Carrigan		RF	H. Hooper	530	.258	1	41	231	23	7	5	1.9	.973	E. Shore	20	148	10	4	1	1.89
		CF	T. Speaker	571	.338	4	90	**423**	29	15	**12**	3.0	.968	S. Wood	18	113	9	3	1	2.62
		LF	D. Lewis	510	.278	2	79	254	22	14	2	2.0	.952	A. Johnson	16	99	4	9	0	3.08
		C	B. Carrigan	178	.253	1	22	350	84	7	8	5.7	**.984**							
		UT	H. Janvrin	492	.238	1	51	669	237	43	50		.955							
		C	H. Cady	159	.258	0	8	217	80	9	1	5.3	.971							
Washington		1B	C. Gandil	526	.259	3	75	1284	**143**	13	84	9.9	.991	W. Johnson	**51**	**372**	**28**	18	1	1.72
		2B	R. Morgan	491	.257	1	49	290	379	37	**58**	4.8	.948	D. Ayers	49	265	12	15	4	2.54
W-81 L-73		SS	G. McBride	503	.203	0	24	367	460	36	**72**	5.5	**.958**	J. Shaw	48	257	15	17	4	2.70
		3B	E. Foster	616	.282	2	50	200	247	34	**25**	3.1	.929	J. Boehling	27	196	12	8	1	3.03
Clark Griffith		RF	D. Moeller	571	.250	1	45	208	19	17	4	1.6	.930	J. Bentley	30	125	5	7	2	2.37
		CF	C. Milan	437	.295	1	39	230	10	13	0	2.2	.949	J. Engel	35	124	7	5	3	2.97
		LF	H. Shanks	500	.224	4	64	276	14	13	3	2.2	.954							
		C	J. Henry	261	.169	0	20	513	124	13	9	**7.1**	.980							
		OF	M. Mitchell	193	.285	1	20	99	11	5	0	2.2	.957							
		C	B. Williams	169	.278	1	22	181	54	6	0	5.5	.975							

AMERICAN LEAGUE 1914, *cont.*

	POS	Player	AB	BA	HR	RBI	PO	A	E	DP	TC/G	FA	Pitcher	G	IP	W	L	SV	ERA
Detroit W-80 L-73 Hughie Jennings	1B	G. Burns	478	.291	5	57	1576	79	30	72	12.3	.982	H. Coveleski	44	303	22	12	2	2.49
	2B	M. Kavanagh	439	.248	4	35	228	333	43	30	5.3	.929	H. Dauss	45	302	18	15	4	2.86
	SS	D. Bush	596	.252	0	32	425	544	58	64	6.5	.944	J. Dubuc	36	224	13	14	1	3.46
	3B	G. Moriarty	465	.254	1	40	125	312	20	16	3.6	.956	P. Cavet	31	151	7	7	2	2.44
	RF	S. Crawford	582	.314	8	104	193	18	5	4	1.4	.977	A. Main	32	138	6	6	3	2.67
	CF	T. Cobb	345	.368	2	57	177	8	10	0	2.0	.949	M. Hall	25	90	4	6	0	2.69
	LF	B. Veach	531	.275	1	72	282	22	11	6	2.2	.965							
	C	O. Stanage	400	.193	0	25	532	190	30	11	6.2	.960							
	23	O. Vitt	195	.251	0	8	63	154	9	13		.960							
	OF	H. High	184	.266	0	17	92	2	4	1	1.8	.959							
	UT	H. Heilmann	182	.225	2	22	209	31	11	11		.956							
St. Louis W-71 L-82 Branch Rickey	1B	J. Leary	533	.265	0	45	1256	75	17	64	10.4	.987	E. Hamilton	44	302	17	18	2	2.50
	2B	D. Pratt	584	.283	5	65	358	423	46	48	5.4	.944	C. Weilman	44	299	18	13	1	2.08
	SS	D. Lavan	239	.264	1	21	178	193	34	17	5.5	.916	B. James	44	284	15	14	1	2.85
	3B	J. Austin	466	.238	0	30	183	249	30	18	3.6	.935	Baumgardner	45	184	14	13	3	2.79
	RF	G. Williams	499	.253	4	47	200	24	16	2	1.7	.933	W. Leverenz	27	111	1	12	0	3.80
	CF	B. Shotton	579	.269	0	38	359	15	24	4	2.6	.940	R. Mitchell	28	103	4	5	4	4.35
	LF	T. Walker	517	.298	6	78	311	30	10	5	2.4	.972							
	C	S. Agnew	311	.212	0	16	451	163	25	10	5.7	.961							
	SS	B. Wares	215	.209	0	23	128	196	35	23	5.3	.903							
	31	I. Howard	209	.244	0	20	252	63	9	5		.972							
Chicago W-70 L-84 Nixey Callahan	1B	J. Fournier	379	.311	6	44	1025	78	25	30	11.6	.978	J. Benz	48	283	14	19	2	2.26
	2B	Blackburne	474	.222	1	35	239	433	26	28	4.9	.963	E. Cicotte	45	269	11	16	3	2.04
	SS	B. Weaver	541	.246	2	28	367	389	59	50	6.1	.928	J. Scott	43	253	14	18	1	2.84
	3B	J. Breton	231	.212	0	24	84	159	24	6	3.4	.910	R. Faber	40	181	10	9	4	2.68
	RF	S. Collins	598	.274	3	65	268	21	19	5	2.0	.938	R. Russell	38	167	8	12	1	2.90
	CF	P. Bodie	327	.229	3	29	175	14	8	2	2.1	.959	M. Wolfgang	24	119	9	5	0	1.89
	LF	R. Demmitt	515	.258	2	46	217	24	12	3	1.8	.953							
	C	R. Schalk	392	.270	0	36	613	183	21	20	6.6	.974							
	1B	H. Chase	206	.267	0	20	632	43	13	27	11.9	.981							
	3B	S. Alcock	156	.173	0	7	57	95	16	10	3.5	.905							
New York W-70 L-84 Frank Chance W-60 L-74 Roger Peckinpaugh W-10 L-10	1B	C. Mullen	323	.260	0	44	898	62	6	54	10.4	.994	J. Warhop	37	217	8	15	0	2.37
	2B	L. Boone	370	.222	0	21	238	294	22	32	6.2	.960	R. Caldwell	31	213	17	9	1	1.94
	SS	Peckinpaugh	570	.223	3	51	356	500	39	45	5.7	.956	R. Keating	34	210	7	11	1	2.96
	3B	F. Maisel	548	.239	2	47	206	245	35	17	3.3	.928	R. Fisher	29	209	10	12	1	2.28
	RF	D. Cook	470	.283	1	40	171	15	10	2	1.6	.949	M. McHale	31	191	7	16	1	2.97
	CF	B. Cree	275	.309	0	40	190	10	5	4	2.7	.976	K. Cole	33	142	11	9	0	3.30
	LF	R. Hartzell	481	.233	1	32	241	15	7	2	2.1	.973	B. Brown	20	122	5	5	1	3.24
	C	J. Sweeney	258	.213	1	22	369	120	10	7	6.4	.980							
	C	L. Nunamaker	257	.265	2	29	304	126	13	12	6.3	.971							
	2B	F. Truesdale	217	.212	0	13	121	185	17	19	4.8	.947							
	OF	T. Daley	191	.251	0	9	26	12	6	2	.8	.864							
	1B	H. Williams	178	.163	1	17	577	25	15	19	10.6	.976							
	OF	B. Holden	165	.182	0	12	98	3	2	0	2.3	.981							
Cleveland W-51 L-102 Joe Birmingham	1B	D. Johnston	340	.244	0	23	847	36	12	43	10.1	.987	W. Mitchell	39	257	12	17	1	3.19
	2B	N. Lajoie	419	.258	0	50	187	215	17	45	5.2	.959	B. Steen	30	201	9	14	0	2.60
	SS	R. Chapman	375	.275	2	42	161	187	33	24	5.3	.913	R. Hagerman	37	198	9	15	1	3.09
	3B	T. Turner	428	.245	1	33	138	229	14	23	3.7	.963	G. Morton	25	128	1	13	1	3.02
	RF	J. Jackson	453	.338	3	53	195	13	7	4	1.8	.967	F. Blanding	29	116	3	9	1	3.96
	CF	N. Leibold	402	.264	0	32	221	22	18	4	2.4	.931	A. Collamore	27	105	3	7	0	3.25
	LF	J. Graney	460	.265	1	39	274	15	20	0	2.4	.935	V. Gregg	17	97	9	3	0	3.07
	C	S. O'Neill	269	.253	0	20	393	134	24	22	6.8	.956							
	UT	I. Olson	310	.242	1	20	197	197	17	20		.959							
	OF	J. Kirke	242	.273	1	25	73	3	2	1	1.9	.974							
	O1	R. Wood	220	.236	1	15	209	16	7	13		.970							

BATTING AND BASE RUNNING LEADERS

Batting Average
T. Cobb, DET .368
E. Collins, PHI .344
T. Speaker, BOS .338
J. Jackson, CLE .338
F. Baker, PHI .319

Slugging Average
T. Cobb, DET .513
T. Speaker, BOS .503
S. Crawford, DET .483
J. Jackson, CLE .464
E. Collins, PHI .452

Home Runs
F. Baker, PHI 9
S. Crawford, DET 8
J. Fournier, CHI 6
T. Walker, STL 6
G. Burns, DET 5
D. Pratt, STL 5

Total Bases
T. Speaker, BOS 287
S. Crawford, DET 281
F. Baker, PHI 252
D. Pratt, STL 240
E. Collins, PHI 238

Runs Batted In
S. Crawford, DET 104
F. Baker, PHI 97
S. McInnis, PHI 95
T. Speaker, BOS 90
E. Collins, PHI 85

Stolen Bases
F. Maisel, NY 74
E. Collins, PHI 58
T. Speaker, BOS 42
B. Shotton, STL 40
C. Milan, WAS 38
Peckinpaugh, NY 38

PITCHING LEADERS

Winning Percentage
C. Bender, PHI .850
D. Leonard, BOS .783
E. Plank, PHI .682
B. Shawkey, PHI .667
R. Caldwell, NY .654

Earned Run Average
D. Leonard, BOS 1.01
R. Foster, BOS 1.65
W. Johnson, WAS 1.72
E. Shore, BOS 1.89
R. Caldwell, NY 1.94

Wins
W. Johnson, WAS 28
H. Coveleski, DET 22
R. Collins, BOS 20
D. Leonard, BOS 19

Saves
D. Leonard, BOS 4
J. Shaw, WAS 4
H. Dauss, DET 4
R. Faber, CHI 4
R. Mitchell, STL 4
J. Bentley, WAS 4

Strikeouts
W. Johnson, WAS 225
W. Mitchell, CLE 179
D. Leonard, BOS 174
J. Shaw, WAS 164
H. Dauss, DET 150

Complete Games
W. Johnson, WAS 33
H. Coveleski, DET 23
R. Caldwell, NY 22
H. Dauss, DET 22

AMERICAN LEAGUE 1914, *cont.*

BATTING AND BASE RUNNING LEADERS

Hits
T. Speaker, BOS	193
S. Crawford, DET	183
F. Baker, PHI	182
E. Collins, PHI	181

Runs Scored
E. Collins, PHI	122
E. Murphy, PHI	101
T. Speaker, BOS	100
D. Bush, DET	97

Base on Balls
D. Bush, DET	112
E. Collins, PHI	97
E. Murphy, PHI	87
T. Speaker, BOS	77

Doubles
T. Speaker, BOS	46
D. Lewis, BOS	37
D. Pratt, STL	34
S. Collins, CHI	34

Home Run Percentage
J. Fournier, CHI	1.6
F. Baker, PHI	1.6
S. Crawford, DET	1.4
T. Walker, STL	1.2

Triples
S. Crawford, DET	26
L. Gardner, BOS	19
T. Speaker, BOS	18
T. Walker, STL	16

Fewest Hits/9 Innings
D. Leonard, BOS	5.70
R. Caldwell, NY	6.46
E. Shore, BOS	6.77
R. Foster, BOS	6.86

Most Strikeouts/9 Inn.
D. Leonard, BOS	7.03
W. Mitchell, CLE	6.27
J. Shaw, WAS	5.74
W. Johnson, WAS	5.45

PITCHING LEADERS

Shutouts
W. Johnson, WAS	9
C. Bender, PHI	7
D. Leonard, BOS	7
R. Collins, BOS	6

Innings
W. Johnson, WAS	372
H. Coveleski, DET	303
E. Hamilton, STL	302
H. Dauss, DET	302

Fewest Walks/9 Innings
M. McHale, NY	1.55
W. Johnson, WAS	1.79
J. Warhop, NY	1.83
R. Collins, BOS	1.85

Games Pitched
W. Johnson, WAS	51
D. Ayers, WAS	49
J. Benz, CHI	48
J. Shaw, WAS	48

	W	L	PCT	GB	R	OR	2B	3B	HR	BA	SA	SB	E	DP	FA	CG	BB	SO	ShO	SV	ERA
Philadelphia	99	53	.651		**749**	529	165	80	**29**	**.272**	**.352**	231	**213**	116	**.966**	89	521	720	24	17	2.78
Boston	91	62	.595	8.5	588	**511**	**226**	**85**	18	.250	.338	177	242	99	.963	88	397	605	24	8	**2.35**
Washington	81	73	.526	19	572	519	176	81	18	.244	.320	220	254	116	.961	75	520	**784**	**25**	**20**	2.54
Detroit	80	73	.523	19.5	615	618	195	84	25	.258	.344	211	286	101	.958	81	498	567	14	12	2.86
St. Louis	71	82	.464	28.5	523	614	185	75	17	.243	.319	233	317	114	.952	81	540	553	15	11	2.85
Chicago	70	84	.455	30	487	560	161	71	19	.239	.311	167	299	90	.955	74	460	617	11	11	2.48
New York	70	84	.455	30	538	550	149	52	12	.229	.287	**251**	238	93	.963	**98**	**390**	563	9	5	2.81
Cleveland	51	102	.333	48.5	538	709	178	70	10	.245	.312	167	300	**119**	.953	69	666	688	10	3	3.21
	4610	4610					1435	598	148	.248	.323	1657	2149	848	.959	655	3933	5140	138	87	2.73

FEDERAL LEAGUE 1914

Indianapolis
W-88 L-65
Bill Phillips

POS	Player	AB	BA	HR	RBI	PO	A	E	DP	TC/G	FA	Pitcher	G	IP	W	L	SV	ERA
1B	C. Carr	441	.293	3	69	1088	59	11	67	10.1	**.991**	Falkenberg	**49**	377	25	16	3	2.22
2B	F. LaPorte	505	.311	4	**107**	300	373	31	61	5.3	.956	E. Moseley	43	317	19	18	1	3.47
SS	J. Esmond	542	.295	2	49	317	448	67	54	5.5	.919	Kaiserling	37	275	17	10	0	3.11
3B	McKechnie	570	.304	2	38	195	**327**	34	**28**	**3.7**	.939	G. Mullin	36	203	14	10	2	2.70
RF	B. Kauff	571	**.370**	8	95	310	31	17	5	2.3	.953	H. Billiard	32	126	8	7	1	3.72
CF	V. Campbell	544	.318	7	44	218	18	19	6	1.9	.925							
LF	A. Scheer	363	.306	3	45	150	13	13	2	1.7	.926							
C	B. Rariden	396	.235	0	47	**714**	**215**	18	14	7.3	.981							
OF	A. Kaiser	187	.230	1	16	98	3	9	0	2.2	.918							
OF	E. Roush	166	.325	1	30	85	5	1	1	2.1	.989							
P	G. Mullin	77	.312	0	21	9	45	5	1	1.6	.915							

Chicago
W-87 L-67
Joe Tinker

POS	Player	AB	BA	HR	RBI	PO	A	E	DP	TC/G	FA	Pitcher	G	IP	W	L	SV	ERA
1B	F. Beck	555	.279	11	77	1614	55	**31**	**86**	10.8	.982	C. Hendrix	**49**	362	**29**	11	5	1.69
2B	J. Farrell	524	.235	0	35	354	**457**	39	54	5.5	.954	M. Fiske	38	198	12	9	0	3.14
SS	J. Tinker	438	.256	2	46	271	408	38	48	**5.7**	.947	E. Lange	36	190	12	10	2	2.23
3B	R. Zeider	452	.274	1	36	151	217	25	27	3.4	.936	D. Watson	26	172	9	11	0	2.04
RF	A. Wickland	536	.276	6	68	252	23	11	3	1.8	.962	Prendergast	30	136	5	9	0	2.38
CF	D. Zwilling	592	.313	**15**	95	**340**	15	14	3	2.4	.962	T. McGuire	24	131	5	7	0	3.70
LF	M. Flack	502	.247	2	39	232	18	7	2	1.9	.973	A. Johnson	16	120	9	5	0	**1.58**
C	A. Wilson	440	.291	10	64	674	212	**24**	19	6.9	.974							
3B	H. Fritz	174	.213	0	13	34	59	9	7	2.2	.912							

Baltimore
W-84 L-70
Otto Knabe

POS	Player	AB	BA	HR	RBI	PO	A	E	DP	TC/G	FA	Pitcher	G	IP	W	L	SV	ERA
1B	H. Swacina	**617**	.280	0	90	**1616**	**104**	26	74	11.1	.985	J. Quinn	46	343	26	14	1	2.60
2B	O. Knabe	469	.226	2	42	287	389	31	49	4.9	.956	G. Suggs	46	319	24	14	3	2.90
SS	M. Doolan	486	.245	1	53	305	**476**	42	**55**	5.7	**.949**	K. Wilhelm	47	244	12	17	4	4.03
3B	J. Walsh	428	.308	10	65	125	217	25	18	3.2	.932	F. Smith	39	175	10	8	2	2.99
RF	B. Meyer	500	.304	5	40	172	14	17	6	1.5	.916	B. Bailey	19	129	7	9	0	3.08
CF	V. Duncan	557	.287	2	53	255	20	26	**8**	2.0	.914	S. Conley	35	125	4	6	0	2.52
LF	H. Simmons	352	.270	1	38	91	10	12	2	1.5	.894							
C	Jacklitsch	337	.276	2	48	580	167	9	13	6.4	**.988**							
OF	G. Zinn	225	.280	3	25	82	5	6	1	1.6	.935							
OF	J. Bates	190	.305	1	29	108	7	6	0	2.1	.950							
3B	Kirkpatrick	174	.253	2	16	28	40	5	1	2.0	.932							
C	H. Russell	168	.232	0	13	193	44	11	2	5.3	.956							

Buffalo
W-80 L-71
Harry Schlafly

POS	Player	AB	BA	HR	RBI	PO	A	E	DP	TC/G	FA	Pitcher	G	IP	W	L	SV	ERA
1B	J. Agler	463	.272	0	20	734	49	12	44	10.5	.985	F. Anderson	37	260	13	16	0	3.08
2B	T. Downey	541	.218	2	42	265	388	26	49	5.3	**.962**	G. Krapp	36	253	14	14	0	2.49
SS	B. Louden	431	.313	6	63	299	285	43	34	5.5	.931	R. Ford	35	247	20	6	6	1.82
3B	F. Smith	473	.220	2	45	170	229	30	14	3.4	.930	E. Moore	36	195	10	14	2	4.30
RF	T. McDonald	250	.296	3	32	94	7	5	2	1.7	.953	A. Schulz	27	171	10	11	1	3.37
CF	C. Hanford	597	.291	13	90	331	24	10	5	2.4	.973	H. Moran	34	154	11	8	1	4.27
LF	F. Delahanty	274	.201	2	27	116	8	3	1	1.6	.976*							
C	W. Blair	378	.243	0	33	604	194	13	17	6.3	.984							
1B	H. Chase	291	.347	3	48	690	38	15	33	10.2	.980							
OF	E. Booe	241	.224	0	14	86	8	4	2	1.7	.959							
OF	D. Young	174	.276	4	22	49	2	3	2	1.3	.944							

197

FEDERAL LEAGUE 1914, cont.

Brooklyn
W-77 L-77
Bill Bradley

POS	Player	AB	BA	HR	RBI	PO	A	E	DP	TC/G	FA	Pitcher	G	IP	W	L	SV	ERA
1B	H. Myers	305	.220	1	29	784	44	9	47	9.5	.989	T. Seaton	44	303	25	13	2	3.03
2B	S. Hofman	515	.287	5	83	232	289	27	39	5.1	.951	E. Lafitte	42	291	16	16	2	2.63
SS	E. Gagnier	337	.187	0	25	219	244	33	37	5.6	.933	H. Finneran	27	175	12	11	1	3.18
3B	T. Wisterzil	534	.257	0	66	207	294	23	24	3.5	.956	R. Sommers	23	82	4	7	0	4.06
RF	S. Evans	514	.348	12	96	163	13	11	2	1.7	.941	Bluejacket	17	67	4	5	1	3.76
CF	A. Shaw	376	.324	5	49	198	14	10	4	2.2	.955							
LF	G. Anderson	364	.316	3	24	176	15	11	2	2.2	.946							
C	G. Land	335	.275	0	29	490	147	20	11	6.8	.970							
OF	C. Cooper	399	.241	2	25	188	12	16	4	2.1	.926							
SS	A. Halt	261	.234	3	25	164	184	43	30	5.5	.890							
2B	J. Delahanty	214	.290	0	15	104	117	10	15	4.2	.957							
C	F. Owens	184	.277	2	20	228	67	10	10	5.3	.967							
OF	D. Murphy	161	.304	4	32	65	8	1	2	1.6	.986							

Kansas City
W-67 L-84
George Stovall

POS	Player	AB	BA	HR	RBI	PO	A	E	DP	TC/G	FA	Pitcher	G	IP	W	L	SV	ERA
1B	G. Stovall	450	.284	7	75	1201	70	14	82	11.1	.989	G. Packard	42	302	21	13	4	2.89
2B	D. Kenworthy	545	.317	15	91	437	407	43	79	6.1	.952	N. Cullop	44	296	14	17	1	2.34
SS	P. Goodwin	374	.235	1	32	85	208	30	21	4.8	.907	D. Stone	39	187	7	14	0	4.34
3B	G. Perring	496	.278	2	69	100	223	23	20	3.4	.934	B. Harris	31	154	7	8	1	4.09
RF	E. Gilmore	530	.287	1	32	196	24	6	7	1.7	.973	P. Henning	28	138	6	12	1	4.83
CF	A. Kruger	441	.259	4	47	249	14	10	1	2.3	.963	D. Adams	36	136	3	9	3	3.51
LF	Chadbourne	581	.277	1	37	238	34	10	6	1.9	.965	C. Johnson	20	134	9	10	0	3.16
C	T. Easterly	436	.335	1	67	570	173	24	16	6.0	.969							
OF	C. Coles	194	.253	1	25	52	4	7	0	1.6	.889							
SS	J. Rawlings	193	.212	0	15	121	222	23	25	6.0	.937							
UT	C. Daringer	160	.263	0	16	70	142	19	16		.918							

Pittsburgh
W-64 L-86
Doc Gessler
W-3 L-8
Rebel Oakes
W-61 L-78

POS	Player	AB	BA	HR	RBI	PO	A	E	DP	TC/G	FA	Pitcher	G	IP	W	L	SV	ERA
1B	H. Bradley	427	.307	0	61	1132	60	12	52	10.2	.990	E. Knetzer	37	272	19	11	1	2.88
2B	J. Lewis	394	.234	1	48	304	332	34	33	5.8	.949	H. Camnitz	36	262	14	18	1	3.23
SS	E. Holly	350	.246	0	26	238	263	31	30	5.7	.942	W. Dickson	40	257	9	21	1	3.16
3B	E. Lennox	430	.312	11	84	136	193	16	12	2.8	.954	C. Barger	33	228	10	16	1	4.34
RF	J. Savage	479	.284	1	26	141	15	6	3	1.7	.963	M. Walker	35	169	3	16	0	4.31
CF	R. Oakes	571	.312	7	75	313	23	14	2	2.4	.960	G. LaClaire	22	103	5	2	0	4.07
LF	D. Jones	352	.273	2	24	216	11	7	1	2.5	.970							
C	C. Berry	411	.238	2	36	550	202	23	18	6.4	.970							
O2	T. McDonald	223	.318	3	29	77	83	13	10		.925							
UT	C. Rheam	214	.210	0	20	431	55	16	16		.968							
OF	F. Delahanty	159	.239	1	7	57	5	1	0	1.8	.984*							
SS	S. Yerkes	142	.338	1	25	89	139	6	13	6.0	.974							

St. Louis
W-62 L-89
Three Finger Brown
W-50 L-63
Fielder Jones
W-12 L-26

POS	Player	AB	BA	HR	RBI	PO	A	E	DP	TC/G	FA	Pitcher	G	IP	W	L	SV	ERA
1B	H. Miller	490	.222	0	46	1256	65	14	48	10.3	.990	B. Groom	42	281	13	20	1	3.24
2B	D. Crandall	278	.309	2	46	98	152	20	10	4.3	.926	D. Davenport	33	216	8	13	4	3.46
SS	A. Bridwell	381	.236	1	33	217	291	30	36	5.2	.944	H. Keupper	42	213	8	20	0	4.27
3B	A. Boucher	516	.231	2	49	193	263	42	18	3.4	.916	D. Crandall	27	196	13	9	0	3.54
RF	J. Tobin	529	.270	7	35	185	31	11	3	1.7	.952	E. Willett	27	175	4	16	0	4.22
CF	D. Drake	514	.251	3	42	207	16	10	2	2.0	.957	T. Brown	26	175	12	6	0	3.30
LF	W. Miller	402	.294	4	50	248	15	13	3	2.5	.953							
C	M. Simon	276	.207	0	21	433	132	9	9	7.4	.984							
2S	J. Misse	306	.196	0	22	229	279	43	29		.922							
OF	F. Kommers	244	.307	3	41	107	11	12	1	1.9	.908							
UT	G. Hartley	212	.288	1	25	249	79	11	12		.968							
OF	L. Kirby	195	.246	2	18	100	7	3	2	2.2	.973							
C	H. Chapman	181	.210	0	14	247	77	9	8	6.5	.973							

BATTING AND BASE RUNNING LEADERS

Batting Average
B. Kauff, IND .370
S. Evans, BKN .348
T. Easterly, KC .335
A. Shaw, BKN .324
V. Campbell, IND .318

Slugging Average
S. Evans, BKN .556
B. Kauff, IND .534
D. Kenworthy, KC .525
E. Lennox, PIT .493
D. Zwilling, CHI .480

Home Runs
D. Kenworthy, KC 15
D. Zwilling, CHI 15
C. Hanford, BUF 13
S. Evans, BKN 12
E. Lennox, PIT 11
F. Beck, CHI 11

Total Bases
B. Kauff, IND 305
S. Evans, BKN 286
D. Kenworthy, KC 286
D. Zwilling, CHI 284
C. Hanford, BUF 267

Runs Batted In
F. LaPorte, IND 107
S. Evans, BKN 96
B. Kauff, IND 95
D. Zwilling, CHI 95
D. Kenworthy, KC 91

Stolen Bases
B. Kauff, IND 75
McKechnie, IND 47
H. Myers, BKN 43
Chadbourne, KC 42

Hits
B. Kauff, IND 211
D. Zwilling, CHI 185
S. Evans, BKN 179
R. Oakes, PIT 178

Base on Balls
A. Wickland, CHI 81
J. Agler, BUF 77
B. Kauff, IND 72
A. Bridwell, STL 71

Home Run Percentage
D. Kenworthy, KC 2.8
E. Lennox, PIT 2.6
D. Zwilling, CHI 2.5
J. Walsh, BAL 2.3

PITCHING LEADERS

Winning Percentage
R. Ford, BUF .769
C. Hendrix, CHI .725
G. Suggs, BAL .676
T. Seaton, BKN .658
Kaiserling, IND .654

Earned Run Average
A. Johnson, CHI 1.58
C. Hendrix, CHI 1.69
R. Ford, BUF 1.82
D. Watson, CHI, STL 2.01
Falkenberg, IND 2.22

Wins
C. Hendrix, CHI 29
J. Quinn, BAL 26
G. Suggs, BAL 25
T. Seaton, BKN 25
Falkenberg, IND 25

Saves
R. Ford, BUF 6
C. Hendrix, CHI 5
K. Wilhelm, BAL 4
G. Packard, KC 4
D. Davenport, STL 4

Strikeouts
Falkenberg, IND 236
E. Moseley, IND 205
C. Hendrix, CHI 189
T. Seaton, BKN 172
B. Groom, STL 167

Complete Games
C. Hendrix, CHI 34
Falkenberg, IND 33
E. Moseley, IND 29
J. Quinn, BAL 27
T. Seaton, BKN 26
G. Suggs, BAL 26

Fewest Hits/9 Innings
C. Hendrix, CHI 6.51
A. Johnson, CHI 6.60
R. Ford, BUF 6.91
G. Krapp, BUF 7.05

Shutouts
Falkenberg, IND 9
T. Seaton, BKN 7
C. Hendrix, CHI 6
G. Suggs, BAL 6

Fewest Walks/9 Innings
R. Ford, BUF 1.49
G. Suggs, BAL 1.61
J. Quinn, BAL 1.71
C. Hendrix, CHI 1.91

FEDERAL LEAGUE 1914, *cont.*

BATTING AND BASE RUNNING LEADERS

Runs Scored		Doubles		Triples			Most Strikeouts/9 Inn.		PITCHING LEADERS Innings		Games Pitched	
B. Kauff, IND	120	B. Kauff, IND	44	S. Evans, BKN	15		B. Bailey, BAL	9.16	Falkenberg, IND	377	Falkenberg, IND	49
McKechnie, IND	107	S. Evans, BKN	41	J. Esmond, IND	15		D. Davenport, STL	5.93	C. Hendrix, CHI	362	C. Hendrix, CHI	49
V. Duncan, BAL	99	D. Kenworthy, KC	40	D. Kenworthy, KC	14		E. Moseley, IND	5.83	J. Quinn, BAL	343	K. Wilhelm, BAL	47
S. Evans, BKN	93	D. Zwilling, CHI	38	T. McDonald, BUF, PIT	13		Falkenberg, IND	5.63	G. Suggs, BAL	319	J. Quinn, BAL	46

	W	L	PCT	GB	R	OR	2B	3B	HR	BA	SA	SB	E	DP	FA	CG	BB	SO	ShO	SV	ERA
Indianapolis	88	65	.575		762	622	230	90	33	.285	.383	273	289	113	.956	104	476	664	15	8	3.06
Chicago	87	67	.565	1.5	621	517	227	50	51	.258	.352	171	249	113	.962	93	393	650	17	8	2.44
Baltimore	84	70	.545	4.5	645	628	222	67	32	.268	.357	152	263	105	.960	88	392	732	15	10	3.13
Buffalo	80	71	.530	7	620	602	177	74	38	.250	.336	228	242	109	.962	89	505	662	15	13	3.16
Brooklyn	77	77	.500	11.5	662	677	225	85	42	.269	.368	220	283	120	.956	91	559	636	11	7	3.33
Kansas City	67	84	.444	20	644	683	226	77	39	.267	.364	171	279	135	.957	82	445	600	10	10	3.41
Pittsburgh	64	86	.427	22.5	605	698	180	90	34	.262	.352	153	253	92	.960	97	444	510	9	4	3.56
St. Louis	62	89	.411	25	565	697	193	65	26	.247	.326	113	273	94	.957	97	409	661	9	6	3.59
					5124	5124	1680	598	295	.263	.355	1481	2131	881	.959	741	3623	5115	101	66	3.20

NATIONAL LEAGUE 1915

	POS	Player	AB	BA	HR	RBI	PO	A	E	DP	TC/G	FA	Pitcher	G	IP	W	L	SV	ERA
Philadelphia W-90 L-62 Pat Moran	1B	F. Luderus	499	.315	7	62	1409	99	11	76	10.8	.993	G. Alexander	49	376	31	10	3	1.22
	2B	B. Niehoff	529	.238	2	49	307	411	41	55	5.1	.946	E. Mayer	43	275	21	15	2	2.36
	SS	D. Bancroft	563	.254	7	30	336	492	64	60	5.8	.928	A. Demaree	32	210	14	11	1	3.05
	3B	B. Byrne	387	.209	0	21	98	183	9	9	2.8	.969	E. Rixey	29	177	11	12	1	2.39
	RF	G. Cravath	522	.285	24	115	233	28	15	2	1.8	.946	G. Chalmers	26	170	8	9	1	2.48
	CF	D. Paskert	328	.244	3	39	181	10	6	2	1.9	.970							
	LF	B. Becker	338	.246	11	35	177	5	11	0	2.0	.943							
	C	B. Killefer	320	.238	0	24	539	126	19	6	6.5	.972							
	OF	P. Whitted	448	.281	1	43	266	7	6	2	2.6	.978							
	3B	M. Stock	227	.260	1	15	62	106	5	7	3.1	.971							
	C	E. Burns	174	.241	0	16	241	61	6	6	4.6	.981							
Boston W-83 L-69 George Stallings	1B	B. Schmidt	458	.251	2	60	1221	60	17	80	10.2	.987	D. Rudolph	44	341	22	19	1	2.37
	2B	J. Evers	278	.263	1	22	170	209	16	33	4.8	.959	T. Hughes	50	280	16	14	5	2.12
	SS	Maranville	509	.244	2	43	391	473	26	63	6.3	.941	P. Ragan	33	227	15	12	0	2.46
	3B	R. Smith	549	.264	2	65	170	292	26	26	3.1	.947	L. Tyler	32	205	10	9	0	2.86
	RF	H. Moran	419	.200	0	21	168	17	7	3	1.6	.964							
	CF	S. Magee	571	.280	2	87	346	16	7	4	2.8	.981							
	LF	J. Connolly	305	.298	0	23	158	10	5	2	1.9	.971							
	C	H. Gowdy	316	.247	2	30	460	148	16	11	5.3	.974							
	2B	Fitzpatrick	303	.221	0	24	135	160	10	23	4.3	.967							
	UT	D. Egan	220	.259	0	21	179	92	16	20		.944							
	C	B. Whaling	190	.221	0	13	292	68	5	2	5.1	.986							
Brooklyn W-80 L-72 Wilbert Robinson	1B	J. Daubert	544	.301	2	47	1441	102	11	73	10.4	.993	J. Pfeffer	40	292	19	14	3	2.10
	2B	G. Cutshaw	566	.246	0	62	397	473	26	53	5.8	.971	W. Dell	40	215	11	10	1	2.34
	SS	O. O'Mara	577	.244	0	31	319	431	78	44	5.6	.906	J. Coombs	29	196	15	10	0	2.58
	3B	G. Getz	477	.258	2	46	140	290	22	14	3.5	.951	S. Smith	29	174	14	8	2	2.59
	RF	C. Stengel	459	.237	3	50	220	13	10	2	1.9	.959	E. Appleton	34	138	4	10	0	3.32
	CF	H. Myers	605	.248	2	46	352	23	14	5	2.6	.964	N. Rucker	19	123	9	4	1	2.42
	LF	Z. Wheat	528	.258	5	66	345	18	18	4	2.6	.953	P. Douglas	20	117	5	5	0	2.62
	C	O. Miller	254	.224	0	25	363	91	9	8	5.5	.981							
	C	L. McCarty	276	.239	0	19	310	101	13	5	5.0	.969							
Chicago W-73 L-80 Roger Bresnahan	1B	V. Saier	497	.264	11	64	1348	65	21	71	10.3	.985	H. Vaughn	41	270	20	12	1	2.87
	2B	H. Zimmerman	520	.265	3	62	211	267	29	30	5.1	.943	J. Lavender	41	220	10	16	3	2.58
	SS	B. Fisher	568	.287	5	53	277	434	51	35	5.2	.933	G. Pearce	36	176	13	9	0	3.32
	3B	A. Phelan	448	.219	3	35	136	203	22	14	3.3	.939	B. Humphries	31	172	8	13	2	2.31
	RF	W. Good	498	.253	2	27	192	13	14	4	1.8	.936	Z. Zabel	36	163	7	10	0	3.20
	CF	C. Williams	518	.257	13	64	347	14	12	2	2.5	.968	L. Cheney	25	131	8	9	0	3.56
	LF	W. Schulte	550	.249	12	69	280	24	12	3	2.1	.962	Standridge	29	112	4	1	0	3.61
	C	J. Archer	309	.243	1	27	447	126	13	11	6.7	.978	K. Adams	26	107	1	9	0	4.71
	C	R. Bresnahan	221	.204	1	19	345	95	8	9	6.6	.982							

NATIONAL LEAGUE 1915, cont.

	POS	Player	AB	BA	HR	RBI	PO	A	E	DP	TC/G	FA	Pitcher	G	IP	W	L	SV	ERA
Pittsburgh W-73 L-81 Fred Clarke	1B	D. Johnston	543	.265	5	64	1453	48	13	65	10.3	.991	B. Harmon	37	270	16	17	1	2.50
	2B	J. Viox	503	.256	2	45	239	362	29	35	4.7	.954	A. Mamaux	38	252	21	8	0	2.04
	SS	H. Wagner	566	.274	6	78	298	395	38	53	5.6	.948	B. Adams	40	245	14	14	2	2.87
	3B	D. Baird	512	.219	1	53	142	226	24	13	3.0	.939	W. Cooper	38	186	5	16	4	3.30
	RF	B. Hinchman	577	.307	5	77	261	17	9	5	1.8	.969	Kantlehner	29	163	5	12	2	2.26
	CF	Z. Collins	354	.294	1	23	217	11	14	3	2.4	.942	McQuillan	30	149	8	10	1	2.84
	LF	M. Carey	564	.254	3	27	307	21	6	5	2.4	.982							
	C	G. Gibson	351	.251	1	30	551	134	25	14	5.9	.965							
St. Louis W-72 L-81 Miller Huggins	1B	D. Miller	553	.264	2	72	1000	50	10	54	12.8	.991	B. Doak	38	276	16	18	1	2.64
	2B	M. Huggins	353	.241	2	24	194	315	23	44	5.0	.957	S. Sallee	46	275	13	17	3	2.84
	SS	A. Butler	469	.254	1	31	235	351	53	43	4.9	.917	L. Meadows	39	244	13	11	0	2.99
	3B	B. Betzel	367	.251	0	27	105	221	22	10	3.3	.937	D. Griner	37	150	5	11	3	2.81
	RF	T. Long	507	.294	2	61	236	18	20	1	2.0	.927	H. Robinson	32	143	7	8	0	2.45
	CF	O. Wilson	348	.276	3	39	234	20	4	3	2.4	.984	H. Perdue	31	115	6	12	1	4.21
	LF	B. Bescher	486	.263	4	34	257	12	8	1	2.1	.971	R. Ames	15	113	9	3	1	2.46
	C	F. Snyder	473	.298	2	55	592	204	14	9	5.6	.983							
	OF	C. Dolan	322	.280	2	38	179	4	14	0	2.0	.929							
	1B	H. Hyatt	295	.268	2	46	616	21	6	31	7.9	.991							
	3B	Z. Beck	223	.233	0	15	59	127	13	10	3.3	.935							
Cincinnati W-71 L-83 Buck Herzog	1B	F. Mollwitz	525	.259	1	51	1545	79	7	107	10.7	.996	G. Dale	49	297	18	17	3	2.46
	2B	B. Rodgers	213	.239	0	12	96	170	15	30	5.0	.947	P. Schneider	48	276	13	19	2	2.48
	SS	B. Herzog	579	.264	1	42	391	513	53	90	6.3	.945	F. Toney	36	223	15	6	1	1.58
	3B	H. Groh	587	.290	3	50	153	280	14	34	3.4	.969	R. Benton	35	176	9	13	4	3.32
	RF	T. Griffith	583	.307	4	85	225	11	12	1	1.8	.952	K. Lear	40	168	6	10	0	3.01
	CF	R. Killefer	555	.272	1	41	334	17	9	5	2.4	.975	L. McKenry	21	110	5	5	0	2.94
	LF	K. Williams	219	.242	0	16	117	11	7	4	2.2	.948							
	C	I. Wingo	339	.221	3	29	413	124	19	15	5.7	.966							
	OF	T. Leach	335	.224	0	17	200	9	9	2	2.3	.959							
	C	T. Clarke	226	.288	0	21	294	71	7	7	5.2	.981							
	UT	I. Olson	207	.232	0	14	170	166	19	20		.946							
	2B	J. Wagner	197	.178	0	13	99	122	9	28	5.0	.961							
New York W-69 L-83 John McGraw	1B	F. Merkle	505	.299	4	62	1123	53	13	62	10.7	.989	J. Tesreau	43	306	19	16	3	2.29
	2B	L. Doyle	591	.320	4	70	313	396	40	66	5.0	.947	P. Perritt	35	220	12	18	0	2.66
	SS	A. Fletcher	562	.254	3	74	302	544	58	76	6.1	.936	C. Mathewson	27	186	8	14	0	3.58
	3B	H. Lobert	386	.251	0	38	109	192	16	9	3.0	.950	S. Stroud	32	184	11	9	1	2.79
	RF	D. Robertson	544	.294	3	58	225	13	11	4	1.8	.956	R. Marquard	27	169	9	8	2	3.73
	CF	F. Snodgrass	252	.194	0	20	160	12	12	2	1.8	.935	R. Schauer	32	105	2	8	0	3.50
	LF	G. Burns	622	.272	3	51	278	13	12	4	2.0	.960	R. Benton	10	61	4	5	1	2.82
	C	C. Meyers	289	.232	1	26	464	90	8	15	5.1	.986							
	UT	F. Brainerd	249	.201	1	21	443	94	18	37		.968							
	3B	E. Grant	192	.208	0	10	39	57	3	3	1.8	.970							

BATTING AND BASE RUNNING LEADERS

Batting Average
L. Doyle, NY .320
F. Luderus, PHI .315
T. Griffith, CIN .307
B. Hinchman, PIT .307
J. Daubert, BKN .301

Slugging Average
G. Cravath, PHI .510
F. Luderus, PHI .457
T. Long, STL .446
V. Saier, CHI .445
L. Doyle, NY .442

Home Runs
G. Cravath, PHI 24
C. Williams, CHI 13
W. Schulte, CHI 12
B. Becker, PHI 11
V. Saier, CHI 11

Total Bases
G. Cravath, PHI 266
L. Doyle, NY 261
T. Griffith, CIN 254
B. Hinchman, PIT 253
H. Wagner, PIT 239

Runs Batted In
G. Cravath, PHI 115
S. Magee, BOS 87
T. Griffith, CIN 85
H. Wagner, PIT 78
B. Hinchman, PIT 77

Stolen Bases
M. Carey, PIT 36
B. Herzog, CIN 35
V. Saier, CHI 29
D. Baird, PIT 29
G. Cutshaw, BKN 28

Hits
L. Doyle, NY 189
T. Griffith, CIN 179
B. Hinchman, PIT 177
H. Groh, CIN 170

Base on Balls
G. Cravath, PHI 86
D. Bancroft, PHI 77
J. Viox, PIT 75
M. Huggins, STL 74

Home Run Percentage
G. Cravath, PHI 4.6
B. Becker, PHI 3.3
C. Williams, CHI 2.5
V. Saier, CHI 2.2

Runs Scored
G. Cravath, PHI 89
L. Doyle, NY 86
D. Bancroft, PHI 85
G. Burns, NY 83

Doubles
L. Doyle, NY 40
F. Luderus, PHI 36
V. Saier, CHI 35
R. Smith, BOS 34

Triples
T. Long, STL 25
H. Wagner, PIT 17
T. Griffith, CIN 16
B. Hinchman, PIT 14

PITCHING LEADERS

Winning Percentage
G. Alexander, PHI .756
A. Mamaux, PIT .724
F. Toney, CIN .714
H. Vaughn, CHI .625
J. Coombs, BKN .600

Earned Run Average
G. Alexander, PHI 1.22
F. Toney, CIN 1.58
A. Mamaux, PIT 2.04
J. Pfeffer, BKN 2.10
T. Hughes, BOS 2.12

Wins
G. Alexander, PHI 31
D. Rudolph, BOS 22
A. Mamaux, PIT 21
E. Mayer, PHI 21
H. Vaughn, CHI 20

Saves
T. Hughes, BOS 5
R. Benton, CIN, NY 5
W. Cooper, PIT 4

Strikeouts
G. Alexander, PHI 241
J. Tesreau, NY 176
T. Hughes, BOS 171
A. Mamaux, PIT 152
H. Vaughn, CHI 148

Complete Games
G. Alexander, PHI 36
D. Rudolph, BOS 30
J. Pfeffer, BKN 26
B. Harmon, PIT 25
J. Tesreau, NY 24

Fewest Hits/9 Innings
G. Alexander, PHI 6.05
F. Toney, CIN 6.47
A. Mamaux, PIT 6.51
T. Hughes, BOS 6.68

Shutouts
G. Alexander, PHI 12
A. Mamaux, PIT 8
J. Tesreau, NY 8
F. Toney, CIN 6

Fewest Walks/9 Innings
C. Mathewson, NY 0.97
B. Humphries, CHI 1.21
B. Adams, PIT 1.25
G. Alexander, PHI 1.53

Most Strikeouts/9 Inn.
G. Alexander, PHI 5.76
T. Hughes, BOS 5.49
A. Mamaux, PIT 5.44
J. Tesreau, NY 5.18

Innings
G. Alexander, PHI 376
D. Rudolph, BOS 341
J. Tesreau, NY 306
G. Dale, CIN 297

Games Pitched
T. Hughes, BOS 50
G. Alexander, PHI 49
G. Dale, CIN 49
P. Schneider, CIN 48

NATIONAL LEAGUE 1915, cont.

	W	L	PCT	GB	R	OR	Batting 2B	3B	HR	BA	SA	SB	Fielding E	DP	FA	Pitching CG	BB	SO	ShO	SV	ERA
Philadelphia	90	62	.592		589	**463**	202	39	**58**	.247	.340	121	216	99	.966	**98**	342	652	**20**	8	**2.17**
Boston	83	69	.546	7	582	545	**231**	57	17	.240	.319	121	**213**	115	**.966**	95	366	630	15	9	2.57
Brooklyn	80	72	.526	10	536	560	165	75	14	.248	.317	131	238	96	.963	87	473	499	16	7	2.66
Chicago	73	80	.477	17.5	570	620	212	66	53	.244	**.342**	166	268	94	.958	71	480	**657**	18	6	3.11
Pittsburgh	73	81	.474	18	557	520	197	91	24	.246	.334	**182**	214	100	.966	91	384	544	18	10	2.60
St. Louis	72	81	.471	18.5	**590**	601	159	**92**	20	**.254**	.333	162	235	109	.964	79	402	538	13	9	2.89
Cincinnati	71	83	.461	20	516	585	194	84	15	.253	.331	156	222	**148**	.966	80	497	572	19	**12**	2.84
New York	69	83	.454	21	582	628	195	68	24	.251	.329	155	256	119	.960	78	**325**	637	15	8	3.11
					4522	4522	1555	572	225	.248	.331	1194	1862	880	.964	679	3269	4729	134	69	2.75

AMERICAN LEAGUE 1915

	POS	Player	AB	BA	HR	RBI	PO	A	E	DP	TC/G	FA	Pitcher	G	IP	W	L	SV	ERA
Boston W-101 L-50 Bill Carrigan	1B	Hoblitzell	399	.283	2	61	1095	63	15	51	10.0	.987	R. Foster	37	255	19	8	1	2.11
	2B	H. Wagner	267	.240	0	29	161	195	28	18	4.9	.927	E. Shore	38	247	19	8	0	1.64
	SS	E. Scott	359	.201	0	28	198	298	20	31	5.2	.961	B. Ruth	32	218	18	8	0	2.44
	3B	L. Gardner	430	.258	1	55	134	227	26	16	3.0	.933	D. Leonard	35	183	15	7	0	2.36
	RF	H. Hooper	566	.235	2	51	255	23	8	7	1.9	.972	S. Wood	25	157	15	5	1	**1.49**
	CF	T. Speaker	547	.322	0	69	**378**	21	10	**8**	2.7	.976	C. Mays	38	132	6	5	7	2.60
	LF	D. Lewis	557	.291	2	76	263	15	14	3	1.9	.952	R. Collins	25	105	4	7	2	4.30
	C	P. Thomas	203	.236	0	21	325	81	13	7	5.1	.969							
	S3	H. Janvrin	316	.269	0	37	122	191	31	16		.910							
	2B	J. Barry	248	.262	0	26	143	216	14	19	4.8	.962							
	C	H. Cady	205	.278	0	17	313	79	8	12	5.2	.980							
	1B	D. Gainer	200	.295	1	29	457	33	6	22	8.9	.988							
	P	B. Ruth	92	.315	4	21	17	63	2	3	2.6	.976							
Detroit W-100 L-54 Hughie Jennings	1B	G. Burns	392	.253	5	50	1155	57	17	65	**11.8**	.986	H. Coveleski	**50**	313	22	13	4	2.45
	2B	R. Young	378	.243	0	31	233	371	**32**	44	5.3	.950	H. Dauss	46	310	24	13	2	2.50
	SS	D. Bush	561	.228	1	44	340	**504**	57	61	5.8	.937	J. Dubuc	39	258	17	12	2	3.21
	3B	O. Vitt	560	.250	1	48	191	324	19	19	**3.5**	**.964**	B. Boland	45	203	13	7	2	3.11
	RF	S. Crawford	612	.299	4	112	219	8	6	1	1.9	.974	B. Steen	20	79	5	1	4	2.72
	CF	T. Cobb	563	**.369**	3	99	328	22	18	7	2.4	.951	B. James	11	67	7	3	0	2.42
	LF	B. Veach	569	.313	3	112	297	19	8	4	2.1	.975							
	C	O. Stanage	300	.223	1	31	395	111	19	0	5.3	.964							
	12	M. Kavanagh	332	.295	4	49	559	119	19	23		.973							
Chicago W-93 L-61 Pants Rowland	1B	J. Fournier	422	.322	5	77	674	41	10	31	11.2	.986	R. Faber	50	300	24	14	2	2.55
	2B	E. Collins	521	.332	4	77	344	**487**	22	54	5.5	**.974**	J. Scott	48	296	24	11	2	2.03
	SS	B. Weaver	563	.268	3	49	281	470	49	54	5.4	.939	J. Benz	39	238	15	11	0	2.11
	3B	Blackburne	283	.216	0	25	88	134	12	13	2.8	.949	R. Russell	41	229	11	10	2	2.59
	RF	E. Murphy	273	.315	0	26	113	7	6	0	1.8	.952	E. Cicotte	39	223	13	12	3	3.02
	CF	H. Felsch	427	.248	3	53	247	9	11	1	2.3	.959							
	LF	S. Collins	576	.257	2	85	197	13	8	2	2.1	.963							
	C	R. Schalk	413	.266	1	54	655	159	13	8	6.2	**.984**							
	30	B. Roth	240	.250	3*	35	79	48	18	1		.876							
	OF	J. Jackson	162	.265	2	36	84	6	5	1	2.1	.947							
	1B	B. Brief	154	.214	2	17	458	23	7	21	10.6	.986							
Washington W-85 L-68 Clark Griffith	1B	C. Gandil	485	.291	2	64	1237	77	**19**	65	9.9	.986	W. Johnson	47	337	**27**	13	4	1.55
	2B	R. Morgan	193	.233	0	21	102	175	10	23	5.0	.965	B. Gallia	43	260	17	11	1	2.29
	SS	G. McBride	476	.204	1	30	326	422	25	47	5.3	**.968**	J. Boehling	40	229	14	13	0	3.22
	3B	E. Foster	**618**	.275	0	52	92	147	21	14	3.3	.919	D. Ayers	40	211	14	9	3	2.21
	RF	D. Moeller	438	.226	2	23	167	13	9	6	1.6	.952	J. Shaw	25	133	6	11	1	2.50
	CF	C. Milan	573	.288	2	66	352	13	21	3	2.6	.946	H. Harper	19	86	4	4	2	1.77
	LF	H. Shanks	492	.250	0	47	151	13	3	1	2.1	.982							
	C	J. Henry	277	.220	1	22	478	122	17	4	6.6	.972							
	C	B. Williams	197	.244	0	31	213	51	9	4	6.8	.967							
	OF	M. Acosta	163	.209	0	18	75	4	3	2	1.5	.963							
New York W-69 L-83 Wild Bill Donovan	1B	W. Pipp	479	.246	4	60	**1396**	**85**	12	**85**	11.1	**.992**	R. Caldwell	36	305	19	16	0	2.89
	2B	L. Boone	431	.204	5	43	249	392	23	59	**5.8**	.965	R. Fisher	30	248	18	11	0	2.11
	SS	Peckinpaugh	540	.220	5	44	291	468	47	60	5.7	.942	J. Warhop	21	143	7	9	0	3.96
	3B	F. Maisel	530	.281	4	40	184	223	26	20	3.2	.940	B. Shawkey	16	86	4	7	0	3.26
	RF	D. Cook	476	.271	2	33	188	20	9	4	1.7	.959	M. McHale	13	78	3	7	0	4.25
	CF	H. High	427	.258	1	43	254	10	5	1	2.3	.981							
	LF	R. Hartzell	387	.251	3	60	200	10	8	2	2.0	.963							
	C	L. Nunamaker	249	.225	0	17	324	99	16	9	5.7	.964							
	23	P. Baumann	219	.292	2	28	129	140	6	20		.978							
	OF	B. Cree	196	.214	0	15	97	6	6	1	2.1	.945							
	P	R. Caldwell	144	.243	4	20	12	72	1	5	2.4	**.988**							

AMERICAN LEAGUE 1915, cont.

	POS	Player	AB	BA	HR	RBI	PO	A	E	DP	TC/G	FA	Pitcher	G	IP	W	L	SV	ERA
St. Louis	1B	J. Leary	227	.242	0	15	433	32	7	41	8.9	.985	C. Weilman	47	296	18	19	4	2.34
	2B	D. Pratt	602	.291	3	78	417	441	31	82	5.6	.965	Lowdermilk	38	222	9	17	0	3.12
W-63 L-91	SS	D. Lavan	514	.218	1	48	313	475	75	81	5.5	.913	E. Hamilton	35	204	9	17	0	2.87
	3B	J. Austin	477	.266	1	30	188	264	41	32	3.5	.917	B. James	34	170	7	10	1	3.59
Branch Rickey	RF	D. Walsh	150	.220	0	6	66	11	4	0	1.8	.951	E. Koob	28	134	4	5	1	2.36
	CF	T. Walker	510	.269	5	49	333	27	23	5	2.8	.940							
	LF	B. Shotton	559	.283	1	30	295	15	23	4	2.2	.931							
	C	S. Agnew	295	.203	0	19	398	153	39	16	5.8	.934							
	UT	I. Howard	324	.278	1	43	488	90	12	33		.980							
	UT	G. Sisler	274	.285	3	29	413	38	7	21		.985							
	C	H. Severeid	203	.222	1	22	247	66	11	2	5.1	.966							
Cleveland	1B	J. Kirke	339	.310	2	40	886	52	13	37	10.9	.986	G. Morton	34	240	16	15	1	2.14
	2B	Wambsganss	375	.195	0	21	138	237	25	24	5.1	.938	W. Mitchell	36	236	11	14	1	2.82
W-57 L-95	SS	R. Chapman	570	.270	3	67	378	469	50	38	5.8	.944	R. Hagerman	29	151	6	14	0	3.52
	3B	W. Barbare	246	.191	0	11	99	141	10	12	3.7	.960	S. Jones	48	146	4	9	4	3.65
Joe Birmingham	RF	E. Smith	476	.248	3	67	202	15	18	4	1.9	.923	R. Walker	25	131	4	9	1	3.98
W-12 L-16	CF	N. Leibold	207	.256	0	4	147	10	5	0	3.1	.969	F. Coumbe	30	114	4	7	2	3.47
	LF	J. Graney	404	.260	1	56	227	17	7	1	2.2	.972							
Lee Fohl	C	S. O'Neill	386	.236	2	34	556	175	24	17	6.6	.968							
W-45 L-79	O1	J. Jackson	299	.331	3	45	352	21	10	12		.974							
	2B	T. Turner	262	.252	0	14	82	136	8	11	4.4	.965							
	OF	Southworth	177	.220	0	8	90	7	6	3	2.3	.942							
	OF	B. Roth	144	.299	4*	20	60	5	9	1	1.9	.878							
Philadelphia	1B	S. McInnis	456	.314	0	49	1123	83	13	63	10.2	.989	J. Wyckoff	43	276	10	22	0	3.52
	2B	N. Lajoie	490	.280	1	61	251	332	23	61	5.5	.962	R. Bressler	32	178	4	17	0	5.20
W-43 L-109	SS	L. Kopf	386	.225	1	33	152	205	31	24	5.2	.920	J. Bush	25	146	5	15	0	4.14
	3B	W. Schang	359	.248	1	44	64	81	18	9	3.8	.890	T. Sheehan	15	102	4	9	0	4.15
Connie Mack	RF	J. Walsh	417	.206	1	20	231	15	6	1	2.3	.976	B. Shawkey	17	100	6	6	0	4.05
	CF	A. Strunk	485	.297	1	45	225	24	5	4	2.3	.980	T. Knowlson	18	101	4	6	0	3.49
	LF	R. Oldring	408	.248	6	42	212	9	4	3	2.3	.982	H. Pennock	11	44	3	6	1	5.32
	C	J. Lapp	312	.272	2	31	376	115	17	23	5.7	.967							
	OF	E. Murphy	260	.231	0	17	55	7	7	0	1.2	.899							
	2B	L. Malone	201	.204	1	17	117	109	20	9	5.7	.919							
	SS	J. Barry	194	.222	0	15	106	150	13	21	5.0	.952							
	C	W. McAvoy	184	.190	0	6	235	130	25	8	6.1	.936							

BATTING AND BASE RUNNING LEADERS

Batting Average
T. Cobb, DET	.369
E. Collins, CHI	.332
J. Fournier, CHI	.322
T. Speaker, BOS	.322
S. McInnis, PHI	.314

Slugging Average
J. Fournier, CHI	.491
T. Cobb, DET	.487
M. Kavanagh, DET	.452
J. Jackson, CHI, CLE	.445
B. Roth, CHI, CLE	.438

Home Runs
B. Roth, CHI, CLE	7
R. Oldring, PHI	6

Total Bases
T. Cobb, DET	274
S. Crawford, DET	264
B. Veach, DET	247
D. Pratt, STL	237
E. Collins, CHI	227

Runs Batted In
B. Veach, DET	112
S. Crawford, DET	112
T. Cobb, DET	99
S. Collins, CHI	85
J. Jackson, CHI, CLE	81

Stolen Bases
T. Cobb, DET	96
F. Maisel, NY	51
E. Collins, CHI	46
B. Shotton, STL	43
C. Milan, WAS	40

Hits
T. Cobb, DET	208
S. Crawford, DET	183
B. Veach, DET	178
T. Speaker, BOS	176

Base on Balls
E. Collins, CHI	119
B. Shotton, STL	118
D. Bush, DET	118
T. Cobb, DET	118

Home Run Percentage
B. Roth, CHI, CLE	1.8
R. Oldring, PHI	1.5
G. Burns, DET	1.3
M. Kavanagh, DET	1.2

Runs Scored
T. Cobb, DET	144
E. Collins, CHI	118
O. Vitt, DET	116
T. Speaker, BOS	108

Doubles
B. Veach, DET	40
D. Lewis, BOS	31
T. Cobb, DET	31
D. Pratt, STL	31

Triples
S. Crawford, DET	19
J. Fournier, CHI	18
B. Roth, CHI, CLE	17
R. Chapman, CLE	17

PITCHING LEADERS

Winning Percentage
S. Wood, BOS	.750
R. Foster, BOS	.704
E. Shore, BOS	.692
E. Shore, BOS	.692
J. Scott, CHI	.686

Earned Run Average
S. Wood, BOS	1.49
W. Johnson, WAS	1.55
E. Shore, BOS	1.64
J. Scott, CHI	2.03
R. Fisher, NY	2.11

Wins
W. Johnson, WAS	28
J. Scott, CHI	24
H. Dauss, DET	24
R. Faber, CHI	24
H. Coveleski, DET	22

Saves
C. Mays, BOS	5

Strikeouts
W. Johnson, WAS	203
R. Faber, CHI	182
J. Wyckoff, PHI	157
H. Coveleski, DET	150
W. Mitchell, CLE	149

Complete Games
W. Johnson, WAS	35
R. Caldwell, NY	31
H. Dauss, DET	27
J. Scott, CHI	23

Fewest Hits/9 Innings
D. Leonard, BOS	6.38
B. Ruth, BOS	6.86
S. Wood, BOS	6.86
W. Johnson, WAS	6.90

Shutouts
J. Scott, CHI	7
W. Johnson, WAS	7
G. Morton, CLE	6
J. Dubuc, DET	5

Fewest Walks/9 Innings
W. Johnson, WAS	1.50
J. Benz, CHI	1.62
R. Russell, CHI	1.84
E. Cicotte, CHI	1.93

Most Strikeouts/9 Inn.
D. Leonard, BOS	5.69
W. Mitchell, CLE	5.68
R. Faber, CHI	5.47
W. Johnson, WAS	5.43

Innings
W. Johnson, WAS	337
H. Coveleski, DET	313
H. Dauss, DET	310
R. Caldwell, NY	305

Games Pitched
H. Coveleski, DET	50
R. Faber, CHI	50
J. Scott, CHI	48
S. Jones, CLE	48

AMERICAN LEAGUE 1915, cont.

	W	L	PCT	GB	R	OR	Batting 2B	3B	HR	BA	SA	SB	Fielding E	DP	FA	Pitching CG	BB	SO	ShO	SV	ERA
Boston	101	50	.669		668	499	202	76	14	.260	.339	118	226	95	.964	82	446	634	19	15	2.39
Detroit	100	54	.649	2.5	778	597	207	94	23	.268	.358	241	258	107	.961	86	489	550	9	19	2.86
Chicago	93	61	.604	9.5	717	509	163	102	25	.258	.348	233	222	95	.965	92	350	635	17	9	2.43
Washington	85	68	.556	17	569	491	152	79	12	.244	.312	186	230	101	.964	87	455	715	21	13	2.31
New York	69	83	.454	32.5	584	588	167	50	31	.233	.305	198	217	118	.966	101	517	559	12	2	3.09
St. Louis	63	91	.409	39.5	521	679	166	65	19	.246	.315	202	335	144	.949	76	612	566	6	7	3.07
Cleveland	57	95	.375	44.5	539	670	169	79	20	.241	.317	138	280	82	.957	62	518	610	11	10	3.13
Philadelphia	43	109	.283	58.5	545	888	183	72	16	.237	.311	127	338	118	.947	78	827	588	6	2	4.33
					4921	4921	1409	617	160	.248	.326	1443	2106	860	.959	664	4214	4857	101	77	2.94

FEDERAL LEAGUE 1915

Chicago
W-86 L-66
Joe Tinker

POS	Player	AB	BA	HR	RBI	PO	A	E	DP	TC/G	FA	Pitcher	G	IP	W	L	SV	ERA
1B	F. Beck	373	.223	5	38	1073	42	9	57	9.6	.992	McConnell	44	303	25	10	1	2.20
2B	R. Zeider	494	.227	0	34	208	240	28	39	5.7	.941	C. Hendrix	40	285	16	15	4	3.00
SS	J. Smith	318	.217	4	30	187	246	46*	28	5.2	.904	Prendergast	42	254	14	12	0	2.48
3B	H. Fritz	236	.250	3	26	79	106	7	8	2.7	.964	T. Brown	35	236	17	8	3	2.09
RF	M. Flack	523	.314	3	45	226	24	8	5	1.9	.969	D. Black	25	121	6	7	0	2.45
CF	D. Zwilling	548	.286	13	94	356	20	8	6	2.6	.979	A. Brennan	19	106	3	9	0	3.74
LF	L. Mann	470	.306	4	58	269	17	9	3	2.3	.969							
C	A. Wilson	269	.305	7	31	391	96	10	6	5.7	.980							
C	B. Fischer	292	.329	4	50	324	100	12	9	5.5	.972							
2B	J. Farrell	222	.216	0	14	138	182	20	26	4.9	.941							
OF	C. Hanford	179	.240	0	22	66	2	2	0	1.6	.971							
3B	T. Wisterzil	164	.244	0	14	65	109	6	6	3.8	.967							

St. Louis
W-87 L-67
Fielder Jones

POS	Player	AB	BA	HR	RBI	PO	A	E	DP	TC/G	FA	Pitcher	G	IP	W	L	SV	ERA
1B	B. Borton	549	.286	3	83	1571	58	12	91	10.3	.993	D. Davenport	55	393	22	18	1	2.20
2B	B. Vaughn	521	.280	0	32	249	357	30	43	5.0	.953	D. Crandall	51	274	21	15	0	2.59
SS	E. Johnson	512	.240	7	67	348	477	51	64	5.8	.942	E. Plank	42	268	21	11	3	2.08
3B	C. Deal	223	.323	1	27	76	136	11	9	3.4	.951	B. Groom	37	209	11	11	1	3.27
RF	J. Tobin	625	.294	6	51	279	21	11	3	2.0	.965	D. Watson	33	136	9	9	0	3.98
CF	D. Drake	343	.265	1	41	180	10	5	2	2.0	.974							
LF	W. Miller	536	.306	1	63	299	16	12	3	2.1	.963							
C	G. Hartley	394	.274	1	50	565	151	21	11	6.5	.972							
3B	A. Kores	201	.234	1	22	80	161	10	12	4.2	.960							
C	H. Chapman	186	.199	1	29	293	79	4	6	7.1	.989							
OF	L. Kirby	178	.213	0	16	87	8	3	2	1.9	.969							
2B	A. Bridwell	175	.229	0	9	60	98	8	9	4.0	.952							

Pittsburgh
W-86 L-67
Rebel Oakes

POS	Player	AB	BA	HR	RBI	PO	A	E	DP	TC/G	FA	Pitcher	G	IP	W	L	SV	ERA
1B	E. Konetchy	576	.314	10	93	1536	81	10	83	10.7	.994	F. Allen	41	283	23	12	0	2.51
2B	S. Yerkes	434	.288	1	49	242	322	19	38	5.1	.967	E. Knetzer	41	279	18	15	3	2.58
SS	Berghammer	469	.243	0	33	286	359	39	55	5.2	.943	C. Rogge	37	254	17	12	0	2.55
3B	M. Mowrey	521	.280	1	49	174	268	19	15	3.1	.959	B. Hearn	29	176	6	11	0	3.38
RF	B. Kelly	524	.294	4	50	292	27	16	5	2.3	.952	C. Barger	34	153	10	7	5	2.29
CF	R. Oakes	580	.278	0	82	348	12	10	2	2.4	.973	W. Dickson	27	97	6	5	0	4.19
LF	A. Wickland	389	.301	1	30	234	11	8	0	2.3	.968							
C	C. Berry	292	.192	1	26	384	144	11	8	5.4	.980							
UT	J. Lewis	231	.264	0	26	150	152	11	20		.965							
C	P. O'Connor	219	.228	0	16	275	112	5	4	5.9	.987							

Kansas City
W-81 L-72
George Stovall

POS	Player	AB	BA	HR	RBI	PO	A	E	DP	TC/G	FA	Pitcher	G	IP	W	L	SV	ERA
1B	G. Stovall	480	.231	0	44	1417	87	20	61	11.8	.987	N. Cullop	44	302	22	11	2	2.44
2B	D. Kenworthy	396	.298	3	52	230	283	35	35	5.1	.936	G. Packard	42	282	20	11	2	2.68
SS	J. Rawlings	399	.216	2	24	209	366	46	36	5.2	.926	C. Johnson	46	281	18	17	1	2.75
3B	G. Perring	553	.259	6	67	135	226	16	14	3.7	.958	A. Main	35	230	13	14	3	2.54
RF	E. Gilmore	411	.285	1	47	215	17	5	4	2.0	.979	P. Henning	40	207	8	16	2	3.17
CF	Chadbourne	587	.227	1	35	308	24	7	7	2.2	.979							
LF	A. Shaw	448	.281	6	67	184	11	12	0	1.7	.942							
C	T. Easterly	309	.272	3	32	398	132	17	11	6.2	.969							
OF	A. Kruger	240	.238	2	26	116	8	2	2	1.9	.984							
S2	P. Goodwin	229	.236	0	16	106	180	24	17		.923							
C	D. Brown	227	.242	1	26	270	104	15	4	6.0	.961							
3B	B. Bradley	203	.187	0	9	55	95	8	4	2.6	.949							

Newark
W-80 L-72
Bill Phillips
W-26 L-27
Bill McKechnie
W-54 L-45

POS	Player	AB	BA	HR	RBI	PO	A	E	DP	TC/G	FA	Pitcher	G	IP	W	L	SV	ERA
1B	E. Huhn	415	.227	1	41	1001	53	16	68	10.6	.985	E. Reulbach	33	270	20	10	1	2.23
2B	F. LaPorte	550	.253	2	56	330	431	32	69	5.4	.960	E. Moseley	38	268	16	16	0	1.91
SS	J. Esmond	569	.258	5	62	353	482	54	67	5.7	.939	Kaiserling	41	261	13	14	2	2.24
3B	McKechnie	451	.251	1	41	184	226	19	17	3.7	.956	H. Moran	34	206	13	10	0	2.54
RF	V. Campbell	525	.310	1	44	200	15	12	3	1.8	.947	Falkenberg	25	172	9	11	1	3.24
CF	E. Roush	551	.298	3	60	331	20	10	3	2.5	.972	T. Seaton	12	75	3	6	1	2.28
LF	A. Scheer	546	.267	2	60	287	16	9	5	2.0	.971							
C	B. Rariden	444	.270	4	40	709	238	21	18	6.8	.978							
UT	G. Schaefer	154	.214	0	8	146	31	7	12		.962							

FEDERAL LEAGUE 1915, *cont.*

	POS	Player	AB	BA	HR	RBI	PO	A	E	DP	TC/G	FA	Pitcher	G	IP	W	L	SV	ERA
Buffalo	1B	H. Chase	567	.291	17	89	1460	83	26	84	11.0	.983	A. Schulz	42	310	21	14	0	3.08
	2B	B. Louden	469	.281	4	48	191	262	10	36	5.3	.978	H. Bedient	53	269	15	18	10	3.17
W-74 L-78	SS	R. Roach	346	.269	2	31	212	297	22	38	5.8	.959	F. Anderson	36	240	19	13	0	2.51
	3B	H. Lord	359	.270	1	21	85	158	14	13	2.8	.946	G. Krapp	38	231	9	19	0	3.51
Harry Schlafly	RF	T. McDonald	251	.271	6	39	93	4	8	1	1.6	.924	R. Ford	21	127	5	9	0	4.52
W-13 L-28	CF	C. Engle	501	.261	3	71	211	8	7	2	2.3	.969							
	LF	B. Meyer	333	.231	1	29	134	9	8	1	1.7	.947							
Walter Blair	C	W. Blair	290	.224	2	20	404	150	11	15	5.8	.981							
W-1 L-1	OF	J. Dalton	437	.293	2	46	218	11	8	4	2.0	.966							
	OF	S. Hofman	346	.234	0	27	132	16	6	5	1.9	.961							
Harry Lord	23	T. Downey	282	.199	1	19	165	193	22	25		.942							
W-60 L-49	C	N. Allen	215	.205	0	17	347	110	21	8	6.0	.956							
Brooklyn	1B	H. Myers	341	.287	1	36	961	56	10	52	9.6	.990	H. Finneran	37	215	12	13	0	2.80
	2B	L. Magee	452	.323	4	49	271	321	40	46	5.5	.937	D. Marion	35	208	10	9	0	3.20
W-70 L-82	SS	F. Smith	385	.247	5	58	203	281	42	24	5.6	.920	T. Seaton	32	189	12	11	3	4.56
	3B	A. Halt	524	.250	3	64	174	224	30	23	3.9	.930	Bluejacket	24	163	9	11	0	3.15
Lee Magee	RF	G. Anderson	511	.264	2	39	200	16	10	5	1.7	.956	B. Upham	33	121	7	8	4	3.05
W-53 L-64	CF	B. Kauff	483	.342	12	83	317	32	15	7	2.7	.959	E. Lafitte	17	118	6	9	0	3.98
	LF	C. Cooper	527	.294	2	63	274	26	13	3	2.6	.958	F. Wilson	18	102	1	7	0	3.78
John Ganzel	C	G. Land	290	.259	0	22	314	114	18	13	5.5	.960	H. Wiltse	18	59	3	5	5	2.28
W-17 L-18	OF	S. Evans	216	.296	3	30	89	8	4	2	1.7	.960							
	3B	T. Wisterzil	106	.311	0	21	45	67	6	7	3.8	.949							
Baltimore	1B	H. Swacina	301	.246	1	38	735	57	11	50	10.7	.986	J. Quinn	44	274	9	22	1	3.45
	2B	O. Knabe	320	.253	1	25	203	264	12	52	5.1	.975	G. Suggs	35	233	13	17	1	4.14
W-47 L-107	SS	M. Doolan	404	.186	2	21	303	400	40	67*	6.2*	.946	B. Bailey	36	190	5	19	0	4.63
	3B	J. Walsh	401	.302	9	60	131	190	22	15	3.2	.936	C. Bender	26	178	4	16	1	3.99
Otto Knabe	RF	S. Evans	340	.315	1	37	111	12	10	4	1.5	.925	A. Johnson	23	151	7	11	1	3.35
	CF	V. Duncan	531	.267	2	43	257	19	10	6	2.3	.965	G. LaClaire	18	84	2	8	0	2.46
	LF	G. Zinn	312	.269	5	43	139	11	8	4	1.8	.949							
	C	F. Owens	334	.251	3	28	462	146	15	19	6.3	.976							
	OF	McCandless	406	.214	5	34	209	16	13	8	2.3	.945							
	1B	J. Agler	214	.215	0	14	573	44	12	42	10.8	.981							
	UT	Kirkpatrick	171	.240	0	19	101	108	20	11		.913							

BATTING AND BASE RUNNING LEADERS

Batting Average
B. Kauff, BKN .342
B. Fischer, CHI .329
L. Magee, BKN .323
E. Konetchy, PIT .314
M. Flack, CHI .314

Slugging Average
B. Kauff, BKN .509
E. Konetchy, PIT .483
H. Chase, BUF .471
B. Fischer, CHI .449
D. Zwilling, CHI .442

Home Runs
H. Chase, BUF 17
D. Zwilling, CHI 13
B. Kauff, BKN 12
E. Konetchy, PIT 10
J. Walsh, BAL, STL 9

Total Bases
E. Konetchy, PIT 278
H. Chase, BUF 267
J. Tobin, STL 254
B. Kauff, BKN 246
D. Zwilling, CHI 242

Runs Batted In
D. Zwilling, CHI 94
E. Konetchy, PIT 93
H. Chase, BUF 89
B. Kauff, BKN 83
B. Borton, STL 83

Stolen Bases
B. Kauff, BKN 55
M. Mowrey, PIT 40
B. Kelly, PIT 38
M. Flack, CHI 37
L. Magee, BKN 34

Hits
J. Tobin, STL 184
E. Konetchy, PIT 181
S. Evans, BAL, BKN 171
B. Kauff, BKN 165

Base on Balls
B. Borton, STL 92
B. Kauff, BKN 85
Berghammer, PIT 83
W. Miller, STL 79

Home Run Percentage
H. Chase, BUF 3.0
A. Wilson, CHI 2.6
B. Kauff, BKN 2.5
D. Zwilling, CHI 2.4

Runs Scored
B. Borton, STL 97
Berghammer, PIT 96
S. Evans, BAL, BKN 94
B. Kauff, BKN 92

Doubles
S. Evans, BAL, BKN 34
D. Zwilling, CHI 32
H. Chase, BUF 31
E. Konetchy, PIT 31

Triples
L. Mann, CHI 19
E. Konetchy, PIT 18
B. Kelly, PIT 17
E. Gilmore, KC 15

PITCHING LEADERS

Winning Percentage
McConnell, CHI .714
T. Brown, CHI .680
N. Cullop, KC .667
E. Reulbach, NWK .667
F. Allen, PIT .657

Earned Run Average
E. Moseley, NWK 1.91
E. Plank, STL 2.08
T. Brown, CHI 2.09
McConnell, CHI 2.20
D. Davenport, STL 2.20

Wins
McConnell, CHI 25
F. Allen, PIT 23
N. Cullop, KC 22
D. Davenport, STL 22

Saves
H. Bedient, BUF 10
C. Barger, PIT 5
H. Wiltse, BKN 5
B. Upham, BKN 4
C. Hendrix, CHI 4
T. Seaton, BKN, NWK 4

Strikeouts
D. Davenport, STL 229
A. Schulz, BUF 160
McConnell, CHI 151
E. Plank, STL 147
F. Anderson, BUF 142
E. Moseley, NWK 142

Complete Games
D. Davenport, STL 30
C. Hendrix, CHI 26
A. Schulz, BUF 25
F. Allen, PIT 24

Fewest Hits/9 Innings
D. Davenport, STL 6.88
A. Main, KC 7.08
E. Plank, STL 7.11
T. Brown, CHI 7.20

Shutouts
D. Davenport, STL 10
E. Plank, STL 6
F. Allen, PIT 6

Fewest Walks/9 Innings
E. Plank, STL 1.81
C. Bender, BAL 1.87
N. Cullop, KC 1.99
J. Quinn, BAL 2.07

Most Strikeouts/9 Inn.
F. Anderson, BUF 5.32
D. Davenport, STL 5.25
E. Plank, STL 4.93
B. Bailey, BAL, CHI 4.91

Innings
D. Davenport, STL 393
D. Crandall, STL 313
A. Schulz, BUF 310
McConnell, CHI 303

Games Pitched
D. Davenport, STL 55
H. Bedient, BUF 53
D. Crandall, STL 51
C. Johnson, KC 46

FEDERAL LEAGUE 1915, *cont.*

	W	L	PCT	GB	R	OR	Batting 2B	3B	HR	BA	SA	SB	Fielding E	DP	FA	Pitching CG	BB	SO	ShO	SV	ERA
Chicago	86	66	.566		640	538	185	77	**50**	.257	.352	161	233	102	.964	97	402	576	21	9	2.64
St. Louis	87	67	.565		634	527	199	81	23	.261	.345	195	212	111	.967	94	396	**698**	24	7	2.73
Pittsburgh	86	67	.562	.5	592	**524**	180	80	20	.262	.341	224	**182**	98	**.971**	88	441	517	16	11	2.79
Kansas City	81	72	.529	5.5	547	551	200	66	27	.244	.328	144	246	96	.962	95	**390**	526	16	10	2.82
Newark	80	72	.526	6	585	562	**210**	80	17	.252	.334	184	239	124	.963	**100**	453	581	16	5	**2.60**
Buffalo	74	78	.487	12	574	634	193	68	40	.249	.338	184	232	112	.964	79	553	594	14	11	3.38
Brooklyn	70	82	.461	16	**647**	673	205	75	36	**.268**	**.360**	249	290	103	.955	78	536	467	10	**13**	3.37
Baltimore	47	107	.305	40	550	760	196	53	36	.244	.325	128	273	140	.957	85	466	570	5	4	3.96
					4769	4769	1568	580	249	.255	.340	1469	1907	886	.963	716	3637	4529	122	70	3.03

NATIONAL LEAGUE 1916

	POS	Player	AB	BA	HR	RBI	PO	A	E	DP	TC/G	FA	Pitcher	G	IP	W	L	SV	ERA
Brooklyn W-94 L-60 Wilbert Robinson	1B	J. Daubert	478	.316	3	33	1195	66	9	56	10.1	.993	J. Pfeffer	41	329	25	11	1	1.92
	2B	G. Cutshaw	581	.260	2	63	361	467	36	51	5.6	.958	L. Cheney	41	253	18	12	0	1.92
	SS	I. Olson	351	.254	1	38	234	303	47	28	5.7	.920	S. Smith	36	219	14	10	1	2.34
	3B	M. Mowrey	495	.244	0	60	154	291	16	17	3.2	.965	R. Marquard	36	205	13	6	5	1.58
	RF	J. Johnston	425	.252	1	26	224	16	9	3	2.3	.964	J. Coombs	27	159	13	8	0	2.66
	CF	H. Myers	412	.262	3	36	242	11	8	5	2.5	.969	W. Dell	32	155	8	9	1	2.26
	LF	Z. Wheat	568	.312	9	73	333	14	9	0	2.4	.975							
	C	C. Meyers	239	.247	0	21	389	95	8	9	6.6	.984							
	OF	C. Stengel	462	.279	8	53	206	14	8	4	1.9	.965							
	C	O. Miller	216	.255	1	17	311	85	13	6	5.9	.968							
	SS	O. O'Mara	193	.202	0	15	117	148	30	13	5.8	.898							
Philadelphia W-91 L-62 Pat Moran	1B	F. Luderus	508	.281	5	53	1499	71	**28**	83	10.9	.982	G. Alexander	48	**389**	33	12	3	**1.55**
	2B	B. Niehoff	548	.243	4	61	285	437	**49**	**65**	5.3	.936	E. Rixey	38	287	22	10	0	1.85
	SS	D. Bancroft	477	.212	3	33	326	510	**60**	64	**6.3**	.933	A. Demaree	39	285	19	14	1	2.62
	3B	M. Stock	509	.281	1	43	128	213	16	22	3.1	.955	E. Mayer	28	140	7	7	0	3.15
	RF	G. Cravath	448	.283	11	70	182	17	7	2	1.6	.966	C. Bender	27	123	7	7	3	3.74
	CF	D. Paskert	555	.279	8	46	332	14	6	4	2.4	.983	McQuillan	21	62	1	7	2	2.76
	LF	P. Whitted	526	.281	6	68	285	13	11	3	2.3	.964							
	C	B. Killefer	286	.217	3	27	443	89	8	15	5.9	**.985**							
	C	E. Burns	219	.233	0	14	283	87	7	5	5.0	.981							
Boston W-89 L-63 George Stallings	1B	E. Konetchy	566	.260	3	70	**1626**	96	18	**96**	11.0	.990	D. Rudolph	41	312	19	12	3	2.16
	2B	J. Evers	241	.216	0	15	98	175	14	29	4.0	.951	L. Tyler	34	249	17	10	1	2.02
	SS	Maranville	604	.235	4	38	386	515	50	79	6.1	**.947**	P. Ragan	28	182	9	9	0	2.08
	3B	R. Smith	509	.259	3	60	166	299	36	15	3.3	.928	J. Barnes	33	163	6	14	1	2.37
	RF	J. Wilhoit	383	.230	2	38	177	12	4	3	1.8	.979	T. Hughes	40	161	16	3	5	2.35
	CF	F. Snodgrass	382	.249	1	32	274	19	5	5	2.7	.983	A. Nehf	22	121	7	5	0	2.01
	LF	S. Magee	419	.241	3	54	220	6	5	0	1.9	.979	F. Allen	19	113	8	2	1	2.07
	C	H. Gowdy	349	.252	1	34	533	158	14	**19**	6.1	.980	E. Reulbach	21	109	7	6	0	2.47
	OF	Z. Collins	268	.209	1	18	114	10	7	3	1.7	.947							
	2B	D. Egan	238	.223	0	16	81	125	11	11	4.1	.949							
	2O	Fitzpatrick	216	.213	1	18	114	96	9	14		.959							
	P	L. Tyler	93	.204	3	20	9	72	3	3	2.5	.964							
New York W-86 L-66 John McGraw	1B	F. Merkle	401	.237	7	44	1183	58	20	61	11.3	.984	J. Tesreau	40	268	18	14	1	2.92
	2B	L. Doyle	441	.268	2	47	270	352	26	53	5.7	.960	P. Perritt	40	251	18	11	2	2.62
	SS	A. Fletcher	500	.286	3	66	253	497	48	56	6.0	.940	R. Benton	38	239	16	8	2	2.87
	3B	McKechnie	260	.246	0	17	70	134	13	8	3.1	.940	F. Anderson	38	188	9	13	0	3.40
	RF	D. Robertson	587	.307	**12**	69	248	17	11	5	1.9	.960	F. Schupp	30	140	9	3	1	0.90
	CF	B. Kauff	552	.264	9	74	329	22	14	6	2.4	.962	S. Sallee	15	112	9	4	0	1.37
	LF	G. Burns	**623**	.279	5	41	289	19	12	3	2.1	.963							
	C	B. Rariden	351	.222	1	29	**576**	144	21	10	**6.2**	.972							
	UT	B. Herzog	280	.261	0	25	140	238	17	28		.957							
Chicago W-67 L-86 Joe Tinker	1B	V. Saier	498	.253	7	50	1622	74	27	78	**11.7**	.984	H. Vaughn	44	294	17	15	1	2.20
	2B	O. Knabe	145	.276	0	7	72	128	13	17	5.1	.939	C. Hendrix	36	218	8	16	2	2.68
	SS	C. Wortman	234	.201	2	16	124	191	32	24	5.0	.908	J. Lavender	36	188	10	14	2	2.82
	3B	H. Zimmerman	398	.291	6	64*	88	198	21	11	4.1*	.932	McConnell	28	171	4	12	0	2.57
	RF	M. Flack	465	.258	3	20	193	22	2	4	1.6	**.991**	G. Packard	37	155	10	6	5	2.78
	CF	C. Williams	405	.279	**12**	66	260	7	3	0	2.3	.989	Prendergast	35	152	6	11	2	2.31
	LF	L. Mann	415	.272	2	29	200	9	6	1	1.9	.972	T. Seaton	31	121	6	6	1	3.27
	C	J. Archer	205	.220	1	30	236	84	7	5	5.0	.979							
	UT	R. Zeider	345	.235	1	22	140	199	21	19	5.0	.942							
	OF	W. Schulte	230	.296	5	27	108	8	6	0	1.9	.951							
	SS	E. Mulligan	189	.153	0	9	116	200	40	27	6.1	.888							
	C	B. Fischer	179	.196	1	14	246	73	9	3	5.9	.973							
	OF	J. Kelly	169	.254	2	15	98	4	5	0	2.3	.953							

NATIONAL LEAGUE 1916, *cont.*

Pittsburgh
W-65 L-89
Nixey Callahan

POS	Player	AB	BA	HR	RBI	PO	A	E	DP	TC/G	FA	Pitcher	G	IP	W	L	SV	ERA
1B	D. Johnston	404	.213	0	39	1042	47	14	44	10.0	.987	A. Mamaux	45	310	21	15	2	2.53
2B	J. Farmer	166	.271	0	14	53	77	10	6	4.5	.929	W. Cooper	42	246	12	11	2	1.87
SS	H. Wagner	432	.287	1	39	226	261	30	32	5.6	.942	F. Miller	30	173	7	10	1	2.29
3B	D. Baird	430	.216	1	28	90	145	17	12	3.2	.933	B. Harmon	31	173	8	11	0	2.81
RF	B. Hinchman	555	.315	4	76	222	8	9	2	1.9	.962	Kantlehner	34	165	5	15	2	3.16
CF	M. Carey	599	.264	7	42	419	32	8	10	3.0	.983	E. Jacobs	34	153	6	10	0	2.94
LF	D. Costello	159	.239	0	8	82	0	2	0	2.0	.976	B. Adams	16	72	2	9	0	5.72
C	W. Schmidt	184	.190	2	15	232	88	8	6	5.8	.976							
UT	J. Schultz	204	.260	0	22	75	86	22	3		.880							
OF	W. Schulte	177	.254	0	14	89	2	3	0	2.0	.968							
3B	H. Warner	168	.238	2	14	60	56	13	5	3.1	.899							
2O	C. Bigbee	164	.250	0	3	81	54	9	7		.938							

Cincinnati
W-60 L-93
Buck Herzog
W-34 L-49
Ivy Wingo
W-1 L-1
Christy Mathewson
W-25 L-43

POS	Player	AB	BA	HR	RBI	PO	A	E	DP	TC/G	FA	Pitcher	G	IP	W	L	SV	ERA
1B	H. Chase	542	.339	4	82	932	37	14	66	10.0	.986	F. Toney	41	300	14	17	1	2.28
2B	B. Louden	439	.219	1	32	238	345	19	48	5.6	.968	P. Schneider	44	274	10	19	1	2.69
SS	B. Herzog	281	.267	1	24	162	203	27	30	6.0	.931	A. Schulz	44	215	8	19	2	3.14
3B	H. Groh	553	.269	2	28	123	252	17	32	3.6	.957	C. Mitchell	29	195	11	10	1	3.14
RF	T. Griffith	595	.266	2	61	238	28	9	5	1.8	.967	E. Knetzer	36	171	5	12	1	2.89
CF	E. Roush	272	.287	0	15	192	7	6	1	3.0	.971	E. Moseley	31	150	7	10	1	3.89
LF	G. Neale	530	.262	0	20	307	20	9	6	2.5	.973							
C	I. Wingo	347	.245	2	40	463	170	28	15	6.2	.958							
OF	R. Killefer	234	.244	1	18	138	6	5	2	2.2	.966							
1B	F. Mollwitz	183	.224	0	16	482	23	10	29	9.5	.981							
C	T. Clarke	177	.237	0	17	187	58	7	3	5.0	.965							

St. Louis
W-60 L-93
Miller Huggins

POS	Player	AB	BA	HR	RBI	PO	A	E	DP	TC/G	FA	Pitcher	G	IP	W	L	SV	ERA
1B	D. Miller	505	.238	1	46	948	43	7	60	10.7	.993	L. Meadows	51	289	12	23	2	2.58
2B	B. Betzel	510	.233	1	37	275	366	27	64	5.9	.960	R. Ames	45	228	11	16	7	2.64
SS	R. Corhan	295	.210	0	18	153	278	39	35	5.6	.917	B. Doak	29	192	12	8	0	2.63
3B	R. Hornsby	495	.313	6	65	82	174	20	7	3.3	.928	B. Steele	29	148	5	15	0	3.41
RF	T. Long	403	.293	1	33	143	13	9	2	1.6	.945	H. Jasper	21	107	5	6	1	3.28
CF	J. Smith	357	.244	6	34	212	12	12	4	2.0	.949	S. Williams	36	105	6	7	1	4.20
LF	B. Bescher	561	.235	6	43	284	18	15	2	2.1	.953	M. Watson	18	103	4	6	0	3.06
C	M. Gonzalez	331	.239	0	29	367	136	10	8	5.5	.981	S. Sallee	16	70	5	5	1	3.47
C1	F. Snyder	406	.259	0	39	731	138	19	35		.979							
OF	O. Wilson	355	.239	3	32	181	11	9	3	1.8	.955							
3B	Z. Beck	184	.223	0	10	45	86	13	7	2.8	.910							

BATTING AND BASE RUNNING LEADERS

Batting Average
H. Chase, CIN	.339
J. Daubert, BKN	.316
B. Hinchman, PIT	.315
R. Hornsby, STL	.313
Z. Wheat, BKN	.312

Slugging Average
Z. Wheat, BKN	.461
H. Chase, CIN	.459
C. Williams, CHI	.459
R. Hornsby, STL	.444
G. Cravath, PHI	.440

Home Runs
C. Williams, CHI	12
D. Robertson, NY	12
G. Cravath, PHI	11
B. Kauff, NY	9
Z. Wheat, BKN	9

Total Bases
Z. Wheat, BKN	262
D. Robertson, NY	250
H. Chase, CIN	249
B. Hinchman, PIT	237
G. Burns, NY	229

Runs Batted In
H. Zimmerman, CHI, NY	83
H. Chase, CIN	82
B. Hinchman, PIT	76
B. Kauff, NY	74
Z. Wheat, BKN	73

Stolen Bases
M. Carey, PIT	63
B. Kauff, NY	40
B. Bescher, STL	39
G. Burns, NY	37
B. Herzog, CIN, NY	34

Hits
H. Chase, CIN	184
D. Robertson, NY	180
Z. Wheat, BKN	177
B. Hinchman, PIT	175

Base on Balls
H. Groh, CIN	84
V. Saier, CHI	79
D. Bancroft, PHI	74
B. Kauff, NY	68

Home Run Percentage
C. Williams, CHI	3.0
G. Cravath, PHI	2.5
D. Robertson, NY	2.0
C. Stengel, BKN	1.7

Runs Scored
G. Burns, NY	105
M. Carey, PIT	90
D. Robertson, NY	88
H. Groh, CIN	85

Doubles
B. Niehoff, PHI	42
Z. Wheat, BKN	32
D. Paskert, PHI	30

Triples
B. Hinchman, PIT	16
E. Roush, CIN, NY	15
R. Hornsby, STL	15
B. Kauff, NY	15

PITCHING LEADERS

Winning Percentage
T. Hughes, BOS	.842
G. Alexander, PHI	.733
J. Pfeffer, BKN	.694
E. Rixey, PHI	.688
R. Benton, NY	.667

Earned Run Average
G. Alexander, PHI	1.55
R. Marquard, BKN	1.58
E. Rixey, PHI	1.85
W. Cooper, PIT	1.87
J. Pfeffer, BKN	1.92

Wins
G. Alexander, PHI	33
J. Pfeffer, BKN	25
E. Rixey, PHI	22
A. Mamaux, PIT	21
D. Rudolph, BOS	19
A. Demaree, PHI	19

Saves
R. Ames, STL	7
T. Hughes, BOS	5
G. Packard, CHI	5
R. Marquard, BKN	5

Strikeouts
G. Alexander, PHI	167
L. Cheney, BKN	166
A. Mamaux, PIT	163
F. Toney, CIN	146
H. Vaughn, CHI	144

Complete Games
G. Alexander, PHI	38
J. Pfeffer, BKN	30
D. Rudolph, BOS	27
A. Mamaux, PIT	26
A. Demaree, PHI	25

Fewest Hits/9 Innings
L. Cheney, BKN	6.33
W. Cooper, PIT	6.91
F. Miller, PIT	7.02
P. Ragan, BOS	7.07

Shutouts
G. Alexander, PHI	16
L. Tyler, BOS	6
J. Pfeffer, BKN	6

Fewest Walks/9 Innings
D. Rudolph, BOS	1.10
G. Alexander, PHI	1.16
A. Demaree, PHI	1.52
S. Sallee, NY, STL	1.63

Most Strikeouts/9 Inn.
L. Cheney, BKN	5.91
C. Hendrix, CHI	4.83
A. Mamaux, PIT	4.73
R. Marquard, BKN	4.70

Innings
G. Alexander, PHI	389
J. Pfeffer, BKN	329
D. Rudolph, BOS	312
A. Mamaux, PIT	310

Games Pitched
L. Meadows, STL	51
G. Alexander, PHI	48
A. Mamaux, PIT	45
R. Ames, STL	45

NATIONAL LEAGUE 1916, cont.

	W	L	PCT	GB	R	OR	2B	3B	Batting HR	BA	SA	SB	Fielding E	DP	FA	Pitching CG	BB	SO	ShO	SV	ERA
Brooklyn	94	60	.610		585	471	195	80	28	.261	.345	187	224	90	.965	96	372	634	22	9	2.12
Philadelphia	91	62	.595	2.5	581	489	223	53	42	.250	.341	149	234	119	.963	97	295	601	26	9	2.36
Boston	89	63	.586	4	542	453	166	73	22	.233	.307	141	212	124	.967	97	325	644	21	11	2.19
New York	86	66	.566	7	597	504	188	74	42	.253	.343	206	217	108	.966	88	310	638	22	11	2.60
Chicago	67	86	.438	26.5	520	541	194	56	46	.239	.325	133	286	104	.957	72	365	616	17	13	2.65
Pittsburgh	65	89	.422	29	484	586	147	91	20	.240	.316	173	260	97	.959	88	443	596	10	7	2.76
Cincinnati	60	93	.392	33.5	505	617	187	88	14	.254	.331	157	228	126	.965	86	458	569	7	6	3.10
St. Louis	60	93	.392	33.5	476	629	155	74	25	.243	.318	182	278	124	.957	58	445	529	11	14	3.14
					4290	4290	1455	589	239	.247	.328	1328	1939	892	.963	682	3013	4827	136	80	2.61

AMERICAN LEAGUE 1916

Boston
W-91 L-63
Bill Carrigan

POS	Player	AB	BA	HR	RBI	PO	A	E	DP	TC/G	FA	Pitcher	G	IP	W	L	SV	ERA
1B	Hoblitzell	417	.259	0	50	1225	67	15	64	10.4	.989	B. Ruth	44	324	23	12	1	1.75
2B	J. Barry	330	.203	0	20	200	282	13	30	5.3	.974	D. Leonard	48	274	18	12	6	2.36
SS	E. Scott	366	.232	0	27	217	339	19	36	4.8	.967	C. Mays	44	245	18	13	3	2.39
3B	L. Gardner	493	.308	2	62	149	278	21	24	3.0	.953	E. Shore	38	226	16	10	1	2.63
RF	H. Hooper	575	.271	1	37	266	19	10	5	2.0	.966	R. Foster	33	182	14	7	2	3.06
CF	T. Walker	467	.266	3	46	290	12	13	4	2.5	.959							
LF	D. Lewis	563	.268	1	56	306	16	10	4	2.2	.970							
C	P. Thomas	216	.264	1	21	321	86	8	7	4.6	.981							
S2	H. Janvrin	310	.223	0	26	166	225	27	37		.935							
C	H. Cady	162	.191	0	13	188	49	8	4	3.9	.967							

Chicago
W-89 L-65
Pants Rowland

POS	Player	AB	BA	HR	RBI	PO	A	E	DP	TC/G	FA	Pitcher	G	IP	W	L	SV	ERA
1B	J. Fournier	313	.240	3	44	855	49	20	47	10.9	.978	R. Russell	56	264	18	11	3	2.42
2B	E. Collins	545	.308	0	52	346	415	19	75	5.0	.976	L. Williams	43	224	13	7	1	2.89
SS	Z. Terry	269	.190	0	17	148	243	27	36	4.5	.935	R. Faber	35	205	17	9	1	2.02
3B	B. Weaver	582	.227	3	38	124	193	20	22	4.0	.941	E. Cicotte	44	187	15	7	5	1.78
RF	S. Collins	527	.243	0	42	238	20	11	6	2.0	.959	J. Scott	32	165	7	14	3	2.72
CF	H. Felsch	546	.300	7	70	340	19	7	5	2.6	.981	J. Benz	28	142	9	5	0	2.03
LF	J. Jackson	592	.341	3	78	290	17	8	5	2.0	.975	M. Wolfgang	27	127	4	6	1	1.98
C	R. Schalk	410	.232	0	41	653	166	10	25	6.7	.988	D. Danforth	28	94	6	5	2	3.27
1B	J. Ness	258	.267	1	34	655	31	15	45	10.2	.979							
3B	F. McMullin	187	.257	0	10	74	115	10	11	3.2	.950							

Detroit
W-87 L-67
Hughie Jennings

POS	Player	AB	BA	HR	RBI	PO	A	E	DP	TC/G	FA	Pitcher	G	IP	W	L	SV	ERA
1B	G. Burns	479	.286	4	73	1355	54	22	71	11.5	.985	H. Coveleski	44	324	21	11	2	1.97
2B	R. Young	528	.263	1	45	352	417	27	55	5.5	.966	H. Dauss	39	239	19	12	4	3.21
SS	D. Bush	550	.225	0	34	278	435	34	41	5.2	.954	J. Dubuc	36	170	10	10	1	2.96
3B	O. Vitt	597	.226	0	42	208	385	22	32	4.1	.964	B. James	30	152	8	12	1	3.68
RF	H. Heilmann	451	.282	2	76	110	10	6	0	1.6	.952	Cunningham	35	150	7	10	2	2.75
CF	T. Cobb	542	.371	5	68	325	18	17	9	2.5	.953	B. Boland	46	130	10	3	3	3.94
LF	B. Veach	566	.306	3	91	342	14	12	4	2.5	.967	W. Mitchell	23	128	7	5	0	3.31
C	O. Stanage	291	.237	0	30	387	108	15	11	5.4	.971							
OF	S. Crawford	322	.286	0	42	85	6	2	2	1.2	.978							

New York
W-80 L-74
Wild Bill Donovan

POS	Player	AB	BA	HR	RBI	PO	A	E	DP	TC/G	FA	Pitcher	G	IP	W	L	SV	ERA
1B	W. Pipp	545	.262	12	93	1513	99	13	89	11.0	.992	B. Shawkey	53	277	24	14	8	2.21
2B	J. Gedeon	435	.211	0	27	235	341	27	55	4.9	.955	G. Mogridge	30	195	6	12	0	2.31
SS	Peckinpaugh	552	.255	4	58	285	468	43	50	5.5	.946	R. Fisher	31	179	11	8	2	3.17
3B	F. Baker	360	.269	10	52	133	210	22	16	3.8	.940	A. Russell	34	171	6	10	6	3.20
RF	F. Gilhooley	223	.278	1	10	93	9	3	3	1.8	.971	N. Cullop	28	167	13	6	1	2.05
CF	L. Magee	510	.257	3	45	301	17	8	3	2.5	.975	R. Caldwell	21	166	5	12	0	2.99
LF	H. High	377	.263	1	28	216	14	12	2	2.2	.950	R. Keating	14	91	5	6	0	3.07
C	L. Nunamaker	260	.296	0	28	353	102	8	13	5.9	.983							
UT	P. Baumann	237	.287	1	25	93	64	8	8		.952							
C	R. Walters	203	.266	0	23	346	102	12	13	7.1	.974							
OF	R. Oldring	158	.234	1	12	66	1	3	3	1.6	.957							
O3	F. Maisel	158	.228	0	7	60	26	4	4		.956							

St. Louis
W-79 L-75
Fielder Jones

POS	Player	AB	BA	HR	RBI	PO	A	E	DP	TC/G	FA	Pitcher	G	IP	W	L	SV	ERA
1B	G. Sisler	580	.305	4	76	1507	83	24	85	11.6	.985	D. Davenport	59	291	12	11	2	2.85
2B	D. Pratt	596	.267	5	103	438	491	33	74	6.1	.966	C. Weilman	46	276	17	18	2	2.15
SS	D. Lavan	343	.236	0	19	217	386	32	52	6.0	.950	E. Plank	37	236	16	15	3	2.33
3B	J. Austin	411	.207	1	28	128	274	26	21	3.5	.939	B. Groom	41	217	13	9	4	2.57
RF	W. Miller	485	.266	1	50	215	12	14	0	1.8	.942	E. Koob	33	167	11	8	2	2.54
CF	A. Marsans	528	.254	1	60	351	25	9	7	2.6	.977	E. Hamilton	22	91	5	7	0	3.05
LF	B. Shotton	618	.282	1	36	357	25	20	6	2.6	.950							
C	H. Severeid	293	.273	0	34	313	99	10	6	4.7	.976							
SS	E. Johnson	236	.229	0	19	115	192	21	19	5.5	.936							
C	G. Hartley	222	.225	0	12	263	98	12	10	5.0	.968							

AMERICAN LEAGUE 1916, *cont.*

Cleveland
W-77 L-77
Lee Fohl

POS	Player	AB	BA	HR	RBI	PO	A	E	DP	TC/G	FA	Pitcher	G	IP	W	L	SV	ERA
1B	C. Gandil	533	.259	0	72	1557	105	9	84	11.5	.995	J. Bagby	48	279	16	16	5	2.55
2B	I. Howard	246	.187	0	23	108	219	10	17	5.2	.970	S. Coveleski	45	232	15	13	3	3.41
SS	Wambsganss	475	.246	0	45	208	325	43	38	5.4	.925	G. Morton	27	150	12	8	0	2.89
3B	T. Turner	428	.262	0	38	87	173	10	10	3.5	.963	E. Klepfer	31	143	6	6	2	2.52
RF	B. Roth	409	.286	4	72	166	20	9	6	1.7	.954	F. Coumbe	29	120	7	5	0	2.02
CF	T. Speaker	546	.386	2	83	359	25	10	10	2.6	.975	A. Gould	30	107	5	7	1	2.53
LF	J. Graney	589	.241	5	54	309	22	14	5	2.2	.959	F. Beebe	20	101	5	3	2	2.41
C	S. O'Neill	378	.235	0	29	540	154	21	36	5.6	.971							
UT	R. Chapman	346	.231	0	27	207	310	32	35		.942							
OF	E. Smith	213	.277	3	40	77	7	3	3	1.5	.966							

Washington
W-76 L-77
Clark Griffith

POS	Player	AB	BA	HR	RBI	PO	A	E	DP	TC/G	FA	Pitcher	G	IP	W	L	SV	ERA
1B	J. Judge	336	.220	0	31	935	69	14	53	9.9	.986	W. Johnson	48	371	25	20	1	1.89
2B	R. Morgan	315	.267	1	29	133	222	16	34	4.5	.957	B. Gallia	49	284	17	12	2	2.76
SS	G. McBride	466	.227	1	36	282	438	32	53	5.4	.957	H. Harper	36	250	14	10	2	2.45
3B	E. Foster	606	.252	1	44	104	143	19	14	3.2	.929	D. Ayers	43	157	5	9	2	3.78
RF	D. Moeller	240	.246	1	23	94	11	4	3	1.7	.963	J. Boehling	27	140	9	11	0	3.09
CF	C. Milan	565	.273	1	45	372	27	16	8	2.8	.961	J. Shaw	26	106	3	8	1	2.62
LF	H. Shanks	471	.253	1	48	203	19	3	4	2.6	.987							
C	J. Henry	305	.249	0	46	538	124	13	17	5.8	.981							
1C	B. Williams	202	.267	0	20	388	30	6	21		.986							
OF	S. Rice	197	.299	1	17	83	5	4	1	2.0	.957							
OF	E. Smith	168	.214	2	27	75	5	1	1	1.8	.988							
3B	J. Leonard	168	.274	0	14	53	65	6	6	3.0	.952							
OF	H. Rondeau	162	.222	1	28	110	4	5	0	2.5	.958							

Philadelphia
W-36 L-117
Connie Mack

POS	Player	AB	BA	HR	RBI	PO	A	E	DP	TC/G	FA	Pitcher	G	IP	W	L	SV	ERA
1B	S. McInnis	512	.295	1	60	1404	96	12	87	10.8	.992	E. Myers	44	315	14	23	1	3.66
2B	N. Lajoie	426	.246	2	35	254	325	16	61	5.7	.973	J. Bush	40	287	15	24	0	2.57
SS	W. Witt	563	.245	2	36	299	423	78	59	5.6	.903	J. Nabors	40	213	1	20	1	3.47
3B	C. Pick	398	.241	0	20	143	230	42	25	3.8	.899	T. Sheehan	38	188	1	16	0	3.69
RF	J. Walsh	390	.233	1	27	172	13	12	4	1.7	.939	J. Johnson	12	84	2	8	0	3.74
CF	A. Strunk	544	.316	3	49	291	20	7	5	2.2	.978							
LF	R. Oldring	146	.247	0	14	64	6	8	2	2.0	.897							
C	B. Meyer	138	.232	1	12	217	79	12	5	6.4	.961							
OC	W. Schang	338	.266	7	38	266	77	19	6		.948							
3O	L. McElwee	155	.265	0	10	52	61	13	7		.897							

BATTING AND BASE RUNNING LEADERS

Batting Average
T. Speaker, CLE	.386
T. Cobb, DET	.371
J. Jackson, CHI	.341
A. Strunk, PHI	.316
L. Gardner, BOS	.308

Slugging Average
T. Speaker, CLE	.502
J. Jackson, CHI	.495
T. Cobb, DET	.493
B. Veach, DET	.433
F. Baker, NY	.428

Home Runs
W. Pipp, NY	12
F. Baker, NY	10
W. Schang, PHI	7
H. Felsch, CHI	7

Total Bases
J. Jackson, CHI	293
T. Speaker, CLE	274
T. Cobb, DET	267
B. Veach, DET	245
H. Felsch, CHI	233
D. Pratt, STL	233

Runs Batted In
D. Pratt, STL	103
W. Pipp, NY	93
B. Veach, DET	91
T. Speaker, CLE	83
J. Jackson, CHI	78

Stolen Bases
T. Cobb, DET	68
A. Marsans, STL	46
B. Shotton, STL	41
E. Collins, CHI	40
T. Speaker, CLE	35

Hits
T. Speaker, CLE	211
J. Jackson, CHI	202
T. Cobb, DET	201
G. Sisler, STL	177

Base on Balls
B. Shotton, STL	111
J. Graney, CLE	102
E. Collins, CHI	86
T. Speaker, CLE	82

Home Run Percentage
F. Baker, NY	2.8
W. Pipp, NY	2.2
W. Schang, PHI	2.1
E. Smith, CLE, WAS	1.3

Runs Scored
T. Cobb, DET	113
J. Graney, CLE	106
T. Speaker, CLE	102
B. Shotton, STL	97

Doubles
T. Speaker, CLE	41
J. Graney, CLE	41
J. Jackson, CHI	40
D. Pratt, STL	35

Triples
J. Jackson, CHI	21
E. Collins, CHI	17
W. Witt, PHI	15
B. Veach, DET	15

PITCHING LEADERS

Winning Percentage
E. Cicotte, CHI	.682
B. Ruth, BOS	.657
H. Coveleski, DET	.656
R. Faber, CHI	.654
B. Shawkey, NY	.632

Earned Run Average
B. Ruth, BOS	1.75
E. Cicotte, CHI	1.78
W. Johnson, WAS	1.89
H. Coveleski, DET	1.97
R. Faber, CHI	2.02

Wins
W. Johnson, WAS	25
B. Shawkey, NY	24
B. Ruth, BOS	23
H. Coveleski, DET	21
H. Dauss, DET	19
C. Mays, BOS	19

Saves
B. Shawkey, NY	8
A. Russell, NY	6
J. Bagby, CLE	5
E. Cicotte, CHI	5
D. Leonard, BOS	5

Strikeouts
W. Johnson, WAS	228
E. Myers, PHI	182
B. Ruth, BOS	170
J. Bush, PHI	157
H. Harper, WAS	149

Complete Games
W. Johnson, WAS	36
E. Myers, PHI	31
J. Bush, PHI	25
B. Ruth, BOS	23
H. Coveleski, DET	22

Fewest Hits/9 Innings
B. Ruth, BOS	6.40
B. Shawkey, NY	6.64
E. Cicotte, CHI	6.64
J. Bush, PHI	6.97

Shutouts
B. Ruth, BOS	9
J. Bush, PHI	8
D. Leonard, BOS	6
R. Russell, CHI	5

Fewest Walks/9 Innings
R. Russell, CHI	1.43
H. Coveleski, DET	1.75
E. Shore, BOS	1.95
J. Bagby, CLE	2.16

Most Strikeouts/9 Inn.
L. Williams, CHI	5.54
W. Johnson, WAS	5.53
H. Harper, WAS	5.37
E. Myers, PHI	5.20

Innings
W. Johnson, WAS	371
H. Coveleski, DET	324
B. Ruth, BOS	324
E. Myers, PHI	315

Games Pitched
D. Davenport, STL	59
R. Russell, CHI	56
B. Shawkey, NY	53
B. Gallia, WAS	49

AMERICAN LEAGUE 1916, *cont.*

	W	L	PCT	GB	R	OR	2B	3B	HR	BA	SA	SB	E	DP	FA	CG	BB	SO	ShO	SV	ERA
Boston	91	63	.591		550	**480**	196	56	14	.248	.318	129	**183**	108	**.972**	76	463	584	**24**	16	2.48
Chicago	89	65	.578	2	601	497	194	**100**	17	.251	.339	197	203	**134**	.968	73	**405**	644	20	15	**2.36**
Detroit	87	67	.565	4	**670**	595	202	96	17	**.264**	**.350**	190	211	110	.968	81	578	531	8	13	2.97
New York	80	74	.519	11	577	561	194	59	**35**	.246	.326	179	219	119	.967	84	476	616	12	**17**	2.77
St. Louis	79	75	.513	12	588	545	181	50	14	.245	.307	**234**	248	120	.963	74	478	505	9	13	2.58
Cleveland	77	77	.500	14	630	602	**233**	66	16	.250	.331	160	232	130	.965	65	467	537	9	16	2.89
Washington	76	77	.497	14.5	536	543	170	60	12	.242	.306	185	231	119	.964	84	490	**706**	11	7	2.66
Philadelphia	36	117	.235	54.5	447	776	169	65	19	.242	.313	151	314	126	.951	94	715	575	11	3	3.84
					4599	4599	1539	552	144	.248	.324	1425	1841	966	.965	631	4072	4698	104	100	2.81

NATIONAL LEAGUE 1917

	POS	Player	AB	BA	HR	RBI	PO	A	E	DP	TC/G	FA	Pitcher	G	IP	W	L	SV	ERA
New York	1B	W. Holke	527	.277	2	55	**1635**	70	19	104	11.3	.989	F. Schupp	36	272	21	7	0	1.95
	2B	B. Herzog	417	.235	2	31	251	327	32	60	5.4	.948	S. Sallee	34	216	18	7	4	2.17
W-98 L-56	SS	A. Fletcher	557	.260	4	56	276	**565**	39	71	5.8	**.956**	P. Perritt	35	215	17	7	1	1.88
	3B	H. Zimmerman	585	.297	5	**102**	148	349	28	22	3.3	.947	R. Benton	35	215	15	9	3	2.72
John McGraw	RF	D. Robertson	532	.259	**12**	54	266	12	17	1	2.1	.942	J. Tesreau	33	184	13	8	3	3.09
	CF	B. Kauff	559	.308	5	68	357	12	9	4	2.5	.976	F. Anderson	38	162	8	8	3	1.44
	LF	G. Burns	597	.302	5	45	325	16	9	4	2.3	.974							
	C	B. Rariden	266	.271	0	25	354	74	13	7	4.4	.971							
	C	L. McCarty	162	.247	2	19	235	43	6	0	5.3	.979							
Philadelphia	1B	F. Luderus	522	.261	5	72	1597	**91**	16	91	11.1	.991	G. Alexander	45	**388**	**30**	13	0	**1.86**
	2B	B. Niehoff	361	.255	2	42	203	326	31	37	5.8	.945	E. Rixey	39	281	16	21	1	2.27
W-87 L-65	SS	D. Bancroft	478	.243	4	43	274	439	49	56	6.4	.936	J. Oeschger	42	262	16	14	0	2.75
	3B	M. Stock	564	.264	3	53	132	255	24	16	3.1	.942	E. Mayer	28	160	11	6	0	2.76
Pat Moran	RF	G. Cravath	503	.280	**12**	83	209	17	13	3	1.7	.946	J. Lavender	28	129	5	8	1	3.55
	CF	D. Paskert	546	.251	4	43	286	19	5	4	2.2	**.984**	C. Bender	20	113	8	2	2	1.67
	LF	P. Whitted	553	.280	3	70	275	19	7	0	2.1	.977							
	C	B. Killefer	409	.274	0	31	**617**	138	12	**14**	6.4	**.984**							
	2B	J. Evers	183	.224	1	12	83	145	4	15	4.7	.983							
St. Louis	1B	G. Paulette	332	.265	0	34	1130	45	8	82	12.7	.993	B. Doak	44	281	16	20	2	3.10
	2B	D. Miller	544	.248	2	45	219	308	22	56	6.0	.960	L. Meadows	43	265	15	9	2	3.09
W-82 L-70	SS	R. Hornsby	523	.327	8	66	268	527	52	82	5.9	.939	R. Ames	43	209	15	10	3	2.71
	3B	D. Baird	364	.253	0	24	110	259	23	24	3.8*	.941	M. Watson	41	161	10	13	0	3.51
Miller Huggins	RF	T. Long	530	.232	3	41	173	9	16	2	1.4	.919	G. Packard	34	153	9	6	2	2.47
	CF	J. Smith	462	.297	3	34	233	12	10	6	2.0	.961	O. Horstmann	35	138	9	4	1	3.45
	LF	W. Cruise	529	.295	5	59	285	15	11	6	2.0	.965	M. Goodwin	14	85	6	4	0	2.21
	C	F. Snyder	313	.236	1	33	341	134	12	10	5.2	.975							
	2B	B. Betzel	328	.216	1	17	159	217	15	40	5.2	.962							
	C	M. Gonzalez	290	.262	1	28	241	97	8	8	5.1	.977							
	3B	F. Smith	165	.182	1	17	62	110	9	5	3.5	.950							
Cincinnati	1B	H. Chase	**602**	.277	4	86	1499	80	**28**	100	10.6	.983	P. Schneider	46	342	20	19	0	1.98
	2B	D. Shean	442	.210	2	35	**332**	**412**	30	**69**	5.9	.961	F. Toney	43	340	24	16	1	2.20
W-78 L-76	SS	L. Kopf	573	.255	2	26	276	470	**68**	59	5.6	.916	M. Regan	32	216	11	10	0	2.71
	3B	H. Groh	599	.304	1	53	**178**	331	18	28	3.4	**.966**	C. Mitchell	32	159	9	15	1	3.22
Christy Mathewson	RF	T. Griffith	363	.270	1	45	165	19	5	3	1.9	.974	H. Eller	37	152	10	5	1	2.36
	CF	E. Roush	522	**.341**	4	67	335	15	14	0	2.4	.962	J. Ring	24	88	3	7	2	4.40
	LF	G. Neale	385	.294	3	33	216	13	5	1	2.0	.979							
	C	I. Wingo	399	.266	2	39	459	**151**	21	12	5.3	.967							
	OF	J. Thorpe	251	.247	4	36	143	7	6	2	2.3	.962							
	OF	S. Magee	137	.321	0	23	83	7	1	1	2.2	.989							
Chicago	1B	F. Merkle	549	.266	3	57	1415	66	26	84	10.8	.983	H. Vaughn	41	296	23	13	0	2.01
	2B	L. Doyle	476	.254	6	61	300	348	**33**	54	5.3	.952	P. Douglas	**51**	293	14	20	1	2.55
W-74 L-80	SS	C. Wortman	190	.174	0	9	85	162	22	26	4.1	.918	C. Hendrix	40	215	10	12	1	2.60
	3B	C. Deal	449	.254	0	47	151	254	18	**31**	3.3	.957	A. Demaree	24	141	5	9	1	2.55
Fred Mitchell	RF	M. Flack	447	.248	0	21	199	14	12	3	1.9	.947	P. Carter	23	113	5	8	2	3.26
	CF	C. Williams	468	.241	5	42	340	23	15	4	2.8	.960	V. Aldridge	30	107	6	6	2	3.12
	LF	L. Mann	444	.273	1	44	203	20	11	2	2.0	.953	Prendergast	35	99	3	6	1	3.35
	C	A. Wilson	211	.213	2	25	361	92	15	5	6.2	.968	T. Seaton	16	75	5	4	1	2.53
	UT	R. Zeider	354	.243	0	27	151	226	28	35		.931							
	OF	H. Wolter	353	.249	0	28	131	14	9	5	1.6	.942							
	C	R. Elliott	223	.251	0	28	307	93	13	9	5.7	.969							
	SS	P. Kilduff	202	.277	0	15	91	128	19	19	4.7	.920							

NATIONAL LEAGUE 1917, cont.

	POS	Player	AB	BA	HR	RBI	PO	A	E	DP	TC/G	FA	Pitcher	G	IP	W	L	SV	ERA
Boston W-72 L-81 George Stallings	1B	E. Konetchy	474	.272	2	54	1351	70	8	65	11.1	**.994**	J. Barnes	50	295	13	**21**	1	2.68
	2B	J. Rawlings	371	.256	2	31	177	290	11	40	5.0	**.977**	D. Rudolph	32	243	13	13	0	3.41
	SS	Maranville	561	.260	3	43	**341**	474	46	67	6.1	.947	L. Tyler	32	239	14	12	1	2.52
	3B	R. Smith	505	.295	2	62	141	264	**33**	27	3.0	.925	A. Nehf	38	233	17	8	0	2.16
	RF	W. Rehg	341	.270	1	31	122	9	6	2	1.6	.956	P. Ragan	30	148	6	9	1	2.93
	CF	R. Powell	357	.272	4	30	231	14	6	2	2.9	.976	F. Allen	29	112	3	11	0	3.94
	LF	J. Kelly	445	.222	3	36	284	16	**17**	8	2.7	.946							
	C	W. Tragesser	297	.222	0	25	433	105	16	11	5.7	.971							
	OF	S. Magee	246	.256	1	29	137	7	7	3	2.3	.954							
	OF	J. Wilhoit	186	.274	1	10	70	7	6	1	1.6	.928							
	UT	Fitzpatrick	178	.253	0	17	71	67	15	5		.902							
	C	H. Gowdy	154	.214	0	14	204	75	9	3	5.9	.969							
Brooklyn W-70 L-81 Wilbert Robinson	1B	J. Daubert	468	.261	2	30	1188	82	12	59	10.3	.991	J. Pfeffer	30	266	11	15	0	2.23
	2B	G. Cutshaw	487	.259	4	49	319	377	27	43	5.4	.963	L. Cadore	37	264	13	13	3	2.45
	SS	I. Olson	580	.269	2	38	283	431	45	53	5.7	.941	R. Marquard	37	233	19	12	0	2.55
	3B	M. Mowrey	271	.214	0	25	73	164	12	13	3.1	.952	S. Smith	38	211	12	12	3	3.32
	RF	C. Stengel	549	.257	6	73	256	**30**	9	**9**	2.0	.969	L. Cheney	35	210	8	12	2	2.35
	CF	J. Hickman	370	.219	6	36	222	22	15	6	2.6	.942	J. Coombs	31	141	7	11	0	3.96
	LF	Z. Wheat	362	.312	1	41	216	12	5	5	2.1	.979							
	C	O. Miller	274	.230	1	17	412	95	11	8	5.7	.979							
	UT	H. Myers	471	.268	1	41	410	102	19	15		.964							
	OF	J. Johnston	330	.270	0	25	150	8	7	1	1.8	.958							
	3B	F. O'Rourke	198	.237	0	15	72	134	10	6	3.7	.954							
Pittsburgh W-51 L-103 Nixey Callahan W-20 L-40 Honus Wagner W-1 L-4 Hugo Bezdek W-30 L-59	1B	H. Wagner	230	.265	0	24	433	22	7	27	9.8	.985	W. Cooper	40	298	17	11	1	2.36
	2B	J. Pitler	382	.233	0	23	283	277	20	46	5.5	.966	E. Jacobs	38	227	6	19	2	2.81
	SS	C. Ward	423	.236	0	43	206	312	50	45	5.1	.912	F. Miller	38	224	10	19	1	3.13
	3B	T. Boeckel	219	.265	0	23	71	116	13	9	3.2	.935	B. Grimes	37	194	3	16	0	3.53
	RF	L. King	381	.249	1	35	198	16	7	6	2.2	.968	B. Steele	27	180	5	11	1	2.76
	CF	M. Carey	588	.296	1	51	**440**	28	10	8	3.1	.979	H. Carlson	34	161	7	11	1	2.90
	LF	C. Bigbee	469	.239	0	21	235	9	10	2	2.4	.961	A. Mamaux	16	86	2	11	0	5.25
	C	B. Fischer	245	.286	3	25	272	77	14	8	5.3	.961							
	OF	B. Hinchman	244	.189	2	29	99	5	6	0	2.3	.945							
	C	W. Schmidt	183	.246	0	17	229	84	7	9	5.2	.978							

BATTING AND BASE RUNNING LEADERS

Batting Average
E. Roush, CIN	.341
R. Hornsby, STL	.327
Z. Wheat, BKN	.312
B. Kauff, NY	.308
H. Groh, CIN	.304

Slugging Average
R. Hornsby, STL	.484
G. Cravath, PHI	.473
E. Roush, CIN	.454
Z. Wheat, BKN	.423
G. Burns, NY	.412

Home Runs
G. Cravath, PHI	12
D. Robertson, NY	12
R. Hornsby, STL	8
J. Hickman, BKN	6
L. Doyle, CHI	6
C. Stengel, BKN	6

Total Bases
R. Hornsby, STL	253
G. Burns, NY	246
H. Groh, CIN	246
G. Cravath, PHI	238
E. Roush, CIN	237
H. Chase, CIN	237

Runs Batted In
H. Zimmerman, NY	102
H. Chase, CIN	86
G. Cravath, PHI	83
C. Stengel, BKN	73
F. Luderus, PHI	72

Stolen Bases
M. Carey, PIT	46
G. Burns, NY	40
B. Kauff, NY	30
Maranville, BOS	27
D. Baird, PIT, STL	26

Hits
H. Groh, CIN	182
G. Burns, NY	180
E. Roush, CIN	178
H. Zimmerman, NY	174

Base on Balls
G. Burns, NY	75
H. Groh, CIN	71
G. Cravath, PHI	70
F. Luderus, PHI	65

Home Run Percentage
G. Cravath, PHI	2.4
D. Robertson, NY	2.3
J. Hickman, BKN	1.6
R. Hornsby, STL	1.5

Runs Scored
G. Burns, NY	103
H. Groh, CIN	91
B. Kauff, NY	89
R. Hornsby, STL	86

Doubles
H. Groh, CIN	39
R. Smith, BOS	31
F. Merkle, BKN, CHI	31
G. Cravath, PHI	29

Triples
R. Hornsby, STL	17
G. Cravath, PHI	16
H. Chase, CIN	15
E. Roush, CIN	14

PITCHING LEADERS

Winning Percentage
F. Schupp, NY	.750
S. Sallee, NY	.720
P. Perritt, NY	.708
G. Alexander, PHI	.698
A. Nehf, BOS	.680

Earned Run Average
G. Alexander, PHI	1.86
P. Perritt, NY	1.88
F. Schupp, NY	1.95
P. Schneider, CIN	1.98
H. Vaughn, CHI	2.01

Wins
G. Alexander, PHI	30
F. Toney, CIN	24
H. Vaughn, CHI	23
F. Schupp, NY	21
P. Schneider, CIN	20

Saves
S. Sallee, NY	4
R. Ames, STL	3
F. Anderson, NY	3
S. Smith, BKN	3
R. Benton, NY	3
L. Cadore, BKN	3

Strikeouts
G. Alexander, PHI	201
H. Vaughn, CHI	195
P. Douglas, CHI	151
F. Schupp, NY	147
P. Schneider, CIN	142

Complete Games
G. Alexander, PHI	35
F. Toney, CIN	31
J. Barnes, BOS	27
H. Vaughn, CHI	27
F. Schupp, NY	25
P. Schneider, CIN	25

Fewest Hits/9 Innings
F. Schupp, NY	6.68
A. Nehf, BOS	7.60
J. Pfeffer, BKN	7.61
L. Tyler, BOS	7.64

Shutouts
G. Alexander, PHI	8
W. Cooper, PIT	7
F. Toney, CIN	7
F. Schupp, NY	6

Fewest Walks/9 Innings
G. Alexander, PHI	1.35
S. Sallee, NY	1.42
A. Nehf, BOS	1.50
J. Barnes, BOS	1.53

Most Strikeouts/9 Inn.
H. Vaughn, CHI	5.94
F. Schupp, NY	4.86
G. Alexander, PHI	4.67
P. Douglas, CHI	4.63

Innings
G. Alexander, PHI	388
P. Schneider, CIN	342
F. Toney, CIN	340
W. Cooper, PIT	298

Games Pitched
P. Douglas, CHI	51
J. Barnes, BOS	50
P. Schneider, CIN	46
G. Alexander, PHI	45

NATIONAL LEAGUE 1917, *cont.*

	W	L	PCT	GB	R	OR	Batting 2B	3B	HR	BA	SA	SB	Fielding E	DP	FA	Pitching CG	BB	SO	ShO	SV	ERA
New York	98	56	.636		**635**	457	170	71	**39**	.261	.343	**162**	**208**	122	**.968**	92	**327**	551	18	**14**	2.27
Philadelphia	87	65	.572	10	578	500	**225**	60	38	.248	.339	109	212	112	.967	103	**327**	617	**22**	4	2.46
St. Louis	82	70	.539	15	531	567	159	93	26	.250	.333	159	221	**153**	.967	66	421	502	16	10	3.03
Cincinnati	78	76	.506	20	601	611	196	**100**	26	**.264**	**.354**	153	247	120	.962	95	404	492	12	6	2.66
Chicago	74	80	.481	24	552	567	194	67	17	.239	.313	127	267	121	.959	79	374	**654**	15	9	2.62
Boston	72	81	.471	25.5	536	552	169	75	22	.246	.320	155	224	122	.966	**105**	371	593	21	3	2.77
Brooklyn	70	81	.464	26.5	511	559	159	78	25	.247	.322	130	245	102	.962	99	405	582	7	9	2.78
Pittsburgh	51	103	.331	47	464	595	160	61	9	.238	.298	150	251	119	.961	84	432	509	17	6	3.01
					4408	4408	1432	605	202	.249	.328	1145	1875	971	.964	723	3061	4500	128	61	2.70

AMERICAN LEAGUE 1917

Chicago
W-100 L-54

Pants Rowland

POS	Player	AB	BA	HR	RBI	PO	A	E	DP	TC/G	FA	Pitcher	G	IP	W	L	SV	ERA
1B	C. Gandil	553	.273	0	57	1405	77	8	84	10.0	**.995**	E. Cicotte	49	**347**	**28**	12	4	**1.53**
2B	E. Collins	564	.289	0	67	353	388	24	68	4.9	.969	R. Faber	41	248	16	13	3	1.92
SS	S. Risberg	474	.203	1	45	291	352	61	57	4.8	.913	L. Williams	45	230	17	8	1	2.97
3B	B. Weaver	447	.284	3	32	154	218	20	18	3.7	.949	R. Russell	35	189	15	5	3	1.95
RF	N. Leibold	428	.236	0	29	204	18	9	3	1.9	.961	D. Danforth	50	173	11	6	9	2.65
CF	H. Felsch	575	.308	6	102	**440**	24	7	5	3.1	.985	J. Scott	24	125	6	7	1	1.87
LF	J. Jackson	538	.301	5	75	341	18	6	4	2.5	.984	J. Benz	19	95	7	3	0	2.47
C	R. Schalk	424	.226	3	51	**624**	148	15	13	5.7	.981							
OF	S. Collins	252	.234	1	14	125	6	1	4	1.8	.992							
3B	F. McMullin	194	.237	0	12	61	90	11	4	3.1	.932							

Boston
W-90 L-62

Jack Barry

POS	Player	AB	BA	HR	RBI	PO	A	E	DP	TC/G	FA	Pitcher	G	IP	W	L	SV	ERA
1B	Hoblitzell	420	.257	1	47	1274	52	14	58	11.4	.990	B. Ruth	41	326	24	13	2	2.01
2B	J. Barry	388	.214	2	30	196	339	14	40	4.7	**.974**	D. Leonard	37	294	16	17	1	2.17
SS	E. Scott	528	.241	0	50	315	483	39	64	5.3	.953	C. Mays	35	289	22	9	0	1.74
3B	L. Gardner	501	.265	1	61	148	315	31	18	3.4	.937	E. Shore	29	227	13	10	1	2.22
RF	H. Hooper	559	.256	3	45	245	20	8	3	1.8	.971	R. Foster	17	125	8	7	0	2.53
CF	T. Walker	337	.246	2	37	225	20	7	7	2.6	.972	H. Pennock	24	101	5	5	1	3.31
LF	D. Lewis	553	.302	1	65	324	20	10	6	2.4	.972							
C	S. Agnew	260	.208	0	16	297	88	14	5	4.7	.965							
C	P. Thomas	202	.238	0	24	296	69	5	8	4.8	**.986**							
OF	J. Walsh	185	.265	0	12	103	8	2	0	2.4	.982							
1B	D. Gainer	172	.308	2	16	490	27	6	29	10.5	.989							
OF	C. Shorten	168	.179	0	16	82	2	2	0	2.0	.977							

Cleveland
W-88 L-66

Lee Fohl

POS	Player	AB	BA	HR	RBI	PO	A	E	DP	TC/G	FA	Pitcher	G	IP	W	L	SV	ERA
1B	J. Harris	369	.304	0	65	1019	86	17	58	**11.8**	.985	J. Bagby	49	321	23	13	7	1.96
2B	Wambsganss	499	.255	0	43	316	442	33	**70**	5.8	.952	S. Coveleski	45	298	19	14	4	1.81
SS	R. Chapman	563	.302	3	36	**360**	**528**	59	71	6.1	.938	E. Klepfer	41	213	14	4	1	2.37
3B	J. Evans	385	.190	2	33	138	279	27	20	3.5	.939	G. Morton	35	161	10	10	2	2.74
RF	B. Roth	495	.285	1	72	228	18	11	6	1.9	.957	F. Coumbe	34	134	8	6	5	2.14
CF	T. Speaker	523	.352	2	60	365	23	8	5	2.8	.980	O. Lambeth	26	97	7	6	2	3.14
LF	J. Graney	535	.228	3	35	288	14	13	6	2.2	.959							
C	S. O'Neill	370	.184	0	34	446	145	12	**19**	4.7	.980							
1B	L. Guisto	200	.185	0	29	611	33	7	45	11.0	.989							
32	T. Turner	180	.206	0	15	86	119	4	7		.981							
OF	E. Smith	161	.261	3	22	64	5	1	2	1.8	.986							

Detroit
W-78 L-75

Hughie Jennings

POS	Player	AB	BA	HR	RBI	PO	A	E	DP	TC/G	FA	Pitcher	G	IP	W	L	SV	ERA
1B	G. Burns	407	.226	1	40	1127	57	12	44	11.5	.990	H. Dauss	37	271	17	14	2	2.43
2B	R. Young	503	.231	1	35	300	**449**	33	46	5.5	.958	B. Boland	43	238	16	11	6	2.68
SS	D. Bush	581	.281	0	24	281	423	51	41	5.1	.932	H. Ehmke	35	206	10	15	2	2.97
3B	O. Vitt	512	.254	0	47	164	260	27	18	3.2	.940	B. James	34	198	13	10	1	2.09
RF	H. Heilmann	556	.281	5	86	200	17	9	4	1.8	.960	W. Mitchell	30	185	12	8	0	2.19
CF	T. Cobb	588	**.383**	7	102	373	27	11	9	2.7	.973	Cunningham	44	139	2	7	4	2.91
LF	B. Veach	571	.319	8	103	356	17	**17**	5	2.5	.956	H. Coveleski	16	69	4	6	0	2.61
C	O. Stanage	297	.205	0	30	385	88	11	13	5.1	.977							
C	T. Spencer	192	.240	0	30	250	57	7	10	5.1	.978							

Washington
W-74 L-79

Clark Griffith

POS	Player	AB	BA	HR	RBI	PO	A	E	DP	TC/G	FA	Pitcher	G	IP	W	L	SV	ERA
1B	J. Judge	393	.285	2	30	906	60	12	59	9.8	.988	W. Johnson	47	328	23	16	3	2.30
2B	R. Morgan	338	.266	1	33	206	243	18	45	4.9	.961	J. Shaw	47	266	15	14	1	3.21
SS	H. Shanks	430	.202	0	28	205	255	35	44	5.5	.929	B. Gallia	42	208	9	13	1	2.99
3B	E. Foster	554	.235	0	43	95	178	19	15	3.4	.935	D. Ayers	40	208	11	10	1	2.17
RF	S. Rice	586	.302	0	69	265	26	12	5	2.0	.960	G. Dumont	37	205	5	14	2	2.55
CF	C. Milan	579	.294	0	48	339	18	14	3	2.4	.962	H. Harper	31	179	11	12	0	3.01
LF	M. Menosky	322	.258	1	34	208	15	4	3	2.4	.982							
C	E. Ainsmith	350	.191	0	42	580	154	22	15	**6.4**	.971							
3B	J. Leonard	297	.192	0	23	78	119	16	15	3.2	.925							
1B	P. Gharrity	176	.284	0	18	371	29	8	19	8.9	.980							
C	J. Henry	163	.190	0	18	274	54	4	6	5.6	.988							

AMERICAN LEAGUE 1917, cont.

	POS	Player	AB	BA	HR	RBI	PO	A	E	DP	TC/G	FA	Pitcher	G	IP	W	L	SV	ERA
New York	1B	W. Pipp	587	.244	9	70	1609	109	17	97	11.2	.990	B. Shawkey	32	236	13	15	0	2.44
	2B	F. Maisel	404	.198	0	20	219	280	17	37	5.2	.967	R. Caldwell	32	236	13	16	0	2.86
W-71 L-82	SS	Peckinpaugh	543	.260	0	41	292	467	54	84	5.5	.934	G. Mogridge	29	196	9	11	0	2.98
	3B	F. Baker	553	.282	6	71	202	317	28	21	3.7	.949	N. Cullop	30	146	5	9	1	3.32
Wild Bill Donovan	RF	E. Miller	379	.251	3	35	204	16	9	2	2.0	.961	U. Shocker	26	145	8	5	1	2.61
	CF	T. Hendryx	393	.249	5	44	215	17	11	1	2.3	.955	R. Fisher	23	144	8	9	0	2.19
	LF	H. High	365	.236	1	19	188	16	3	3	2.1	.986	S. Love	33	130	6	5	1	2.35
	C	L. Nunamaker	310	.261	0	33	372	113	12	12	5.5	.976	A. Russell	25	104	7	8	2	2.24
	OF	L. Magee	173	.220	0	8	84	6	6	1	1.9	.938							
	C	R. Walters	171	.263	0	14	263	73	11	6	6.1	.968							
	OF	F. Gilhooley	165	.242	0	8	78	5	6	1	1.9	.933							
St. Louis	1B	G. Sisler	539	.353	2	52	1384	101	22	97	11.3	.985	D. Davenport	47	281	17	17	2	3.08
	2B	D. Pratt	450	.247	1	53	324	353	29	64	5.9	.959	A. Sothoron	48	277	14	19	4	2.83
W-57 L-97	SS	D. Lavan	355	.239	0	30	229	338	47	67	5.6	.923	B. Groom	38	233	8	19	3	2.94
	3B	J. Austin	455	.240	0	19	159	248	23	22	3.6	.947	E. Koob	39	134	6	14	1	3.91
Fielder Jones	RF	B. Jacobson	529	.248	4	55	292	18	8	6	2.4	.975	E. Plank	20	131	5	6	1	1.79
	CF	A. Marsans	257	.230	0	20	155	3	6	1	2.4	.963	T. Rogers	24	109	3	6	0	3.89
	LF	B. Shotton	398	.224	1	20	182	10	16	6	1.9	.923	E. Hamilton	27	83	0	9	1	3.14
	C	H. Severeid	501	.265	1	57	529	156	24	10	5.1	.966							
	OF	T. Sloan	313	.230	2	25	120	10	5	4	1.8	.963							
	OF	E. Smith	199	.281	0	10	114	12	3	5	2.5	.977							
	UT	E. Johnson	199	.246	2	20	122	197	25	19		.927							
Philadelphia	1B	S. McInnis	567	.303	0	44	1658	95	12	81	11.8	.993	J. Bush	37	233	11	17	2	2.47
	2B	R. Grover	482	.224	0	34	279	425	29	51	5.3	.960	R. Schauer	33	215	7	16	1	3.14
W-55 L-98	SS	W. Witt	452	.252	0	28	190	354	38	41	5.2	.935	E. Myers	38	202	9	16	3	4.42
	3B	R. Bates	485	.237	2	66	168	267	31	17	3.8	.933	J. Johnson	34	191	9	12	0	2.78
Connie Mack	RF	C. Jamieson	347	.265	0	27	121	12	9	4	1.7	.937	W. Noyes	27	171	10	10	1	2.95
	CF	A. Strunk	540	.281	1	45	346	13	5	5	2.5	.986	S. Seibold	33	160	4	16	1	3.94
	LF	P. Bodie	557	.291	7	74	258	32	11	7	2.1	.963							
	C	W. Schang	316	.285	3	36	260	102	17	11	4.8	.955							
	C	B. Meyer	162	.235	0	9	235	66	12	2	5.7	.962							

BATTING AND BASE RUNNING LEADERS

Batting Average
T. Cobb, DET	.383
G. Sisler, STL	.353
T. Speaker, CLE	.352
B. Veach, DET	.319
H. Felsch, CHI	.308

Slugging Average
T. Cobb, DET	.571
T. Speaker, CLE	.486
B. Veach, DET	.457
G. Sisler, STL	.453
J. Jackson, CHI	.429

Home Runs
W. Pipp, NY	9
B. Veach, DET	8
P. Bodie, PHI	7
T. Cobb, DET	7
F. Baker, NY	6
H. Felsch, CHI	6

Total Bases
T. Cobb, DET	336
B. Veach, DET	261
T. Speaker, CLE	254
G. Sisler, STL	244
P. Bodie, PHI	233

Runs Batted In
B. Veach, DET	103
H. Felsch, CHI	102
T. Cobb, DET	102
H. Heilmann, DET	86
J. Jackson, CHI	75

Stolen Bases
T. Cobb, DET	55
E. Collins, CHI	53
R. Chapman, CLE	52
B. Roth, CLE	51
G. Sisler, STL	37

Hits
T. Cobb, DET	225
G. Sisler, STL	190
T. Speaker, CLE	184
B. Veach, DET	182

Base on Balls
J. Graney, CLE	94
E. Collins, CHI	89
H. Hooper, BOS	80
D. Bush, DET	80

Home Run Percentage
W. Pipp, NY	1.5
B. Veach, DET	1.4
T. Hendryx, NY	1.3
P. Bodie, PHI	1.3

Runs Scored
D. Bush, DET	112
T. Cobb, DET	107
R. Chapman, CLE	98
J. Jackson, CHI	91

Doubles
T. Cobb, DET	44
T. Speaker, CLE	42
B. Veach, DET	31
B. Roth, CLE	30

Triples
T. Cobb, DET	23
J. Jackson, CHI	17
J. Judge, WAS	15

PITCHING LEADERS

Winning Percentage
R. Russell, CHI	.750
D. Danforth, CHI	.714
C. Mays, BOS	.710
E. Cicotte, CHI	.700
L. Williams, CHI	.680

Earned Run Average
E. Cicotte, CHI	1.53
C. Mays, BOS	1.74
S. Coveleski, CLE	1.81
R. Faber, CHI	1.92
R. Russell, CHI	1.95

Wins
E. Cicotte, CHI	28
B. Ruth, BOS	24
J. Bagby, CLE	23
W. Johnson, WAS	23
C. Mays, BOS	22

Saves
D. Danforth, CHI	9
J. Bagby, CLE	7
B. Boland, DET	6

Strikeouts
W. Johnson, WAS	188
E. Cicotte, CHI	150
D. Leonard, BOS	144
S. Coveleski, CLE	133
B. Ruth, BOS	128

Complete Games
B. Ruth, BOS	35
W. Johnson, WAS	30
E. Cicotte, CHI	29
C. Mays, BOS	27
D. Leonard, BOS	26
J. Bagby, CLE	26

Fewest Hits/9 Innings
S. Coveleski, CLE	6.09
E. Cicotte, CHI	6.39
B. Ruth, BOS	6.73
W. Johnson, WAS	7.11

Shutouts
S. Coveleski, CLE	9
W. Johnson, WAS	8
J. Bagby, CLE	8
E. Cicotte, CHI	7

Fewest Walks/9 Innings
R. Russell, CHI	1.52
G. Mogridge, NY	1.79
E. Cicotte, CHI	1.82
W. Johnson, WAS	1.84

Most Strikeouts/9 Inn.
W. Johnson, WAS	5.16
H. Harper, WAS	4.97
J. Bush, PHI	4.67
D. Leonard, BOS	4.40

Innings
E. Cicotte, CHI	347
W. Johnson, WAS	328
B. Ruth, BOS	326
J. Bagby, CLE	321

Games Pitched
D. Danforth, CHI	50
E. Cicotte, CHI	49
J. Bagby, CLE	49
A. Sothoron, STL	48

AMERICAN LEAGUE 1917, *cont.*

	W	L	PCT	GB	R	OR	2B	3B	HR	BA	SA	SB	E	DP	FA	CG	BB	SO	ShO	SV	ERA
								Batting						Fielding				Pitching			
Chicago	100	54	.649		**656**	464	152	**80**	19	.253	.326	**219**	204	117	.967	78	**413**	517	**22**	21	**2.16**
Boston	90	62	.592	9	555	**454**	198	64	14	.246	.319	105	**183**	116	**.972**	**115**	**413**	509	15	7	2.20
Cleveland	88	66	.571	12	584	543	**218**	63	14	.245	.322	210	242	136	.964	73	438	451	20	**22**	2.52
Detroit	78	75	.510	21.5	639	577	204	76	26	**.259**	**.344**	163	234	95	.964	78	504	516	20	15	2.56
Washington	74	79	.484	25.5	543	566	173	70	4	.241	.304	166	251	127	.961	84	536	**637**	21	10	2.77
New York	71	82	.464	28.5	524	558	172	52	**27**	.239	.308	136	225	129	.965	87	427	571	10	6	2.66
St. Louis	57	97	.370	43	510	687	183	63	15	.245	.315	157	281	**139**	.957	65	537	429	12	12	3.20
Philadelphia	55	98	.359	44.5	529	691	177	62	17	.254	.322	112	251	106	.961	80	562	516	8	8	3.27
					4540	4540	1477	530	136	.248	.320	1268	1871	965	.964	660	3830	4146	128	101	2.66

NATIONAL LEAGUE 1918

	POS	Player	AB	BA	HR	RBI	PO	A	E	DP	TC/G	FA	Pitcher	G	IP	W	L	SV	ERA
Chicago W-84 L-45 Fred Mitchell	1B	F. Merkle	482	.297	3	65	**1388**	82	15	69	11.5	.990	H. Vaughn	35	**290**	**22**	10	0	**1.74**
	2B	R. Zeider	251	.223	0	26	142	207	16	22	4.6	.956	L. Tyler	33	269	19	9	1	2.00
	SS	C. Hollocher	**509**	.316	2	38	278	418	53	39	5.7	.929	C. Hendrix	32	233	19	7	0	2.78
	3B	C. Deal	414	.239	2	34	144	247	24	21	3.5	.942	P. Douglas	25	157	9	9	2	2.13
	RF	M. Flack	478	.257	4	41	199	20	5	5	1.9	.978							
	CF	D. Paskert	461	.286	3	59	283	12	6	1	2.5	.980							
	LF	L. Mann	489	.288	2	55	229	15	10	3	2.0	.961							
	C	B. Killefer	331	.233	0	22	**487**	110	11	12	**5.8**	**.982**							
New York W-71 L-53 John McGraw	1B	W. Holke	326	.252	1	27	938	68	10	50	11.5	.990	P. Perritt	35	233	18	13	0	2.74
	2B	L. Doyle	257	.261	3	36	121	221	11	24	4.8	.969	R. Causey	29	158	11	6	2	2.79
	SS	A. Fletcher	468	.263	0	47	268	484	32	54	6.3	.959	A. Demaree	26	142	8	6	1	2.47
	3B	H. Zimmerman	463	.272	1	56	128	209	16	8	3.5	.955	S. Sallee	18	132	8	8	2	2.25
	RF	R. Youngs	474	.302	1	25	197	22	12	3	1.9	.948							
	CF	B. Kauff	270	.315	2	39	147	11	8	4	2.5	.952							
	LF	G. Burns	465	.290	4	51	292	10	11	1	2.6	.965							
	C	L. McCarty	257	.268	0	24	288	67	9	3	4.9	.975							
	C	B. Rariden	183	.224	0	17	195	45	4	3	3.9	.984							
Cincinnati W-68 L-60 Christy Mathewson W-61 L-57 Heinie Groh W-7 L-3	1B	H. Chase	259	.301	2	38	607	38	13	59	9.8	.980	P. Schneider	33	218	10	15	0	3.51
	2B	L. Magee	459	.290	0	28	275	361	**29**	**73**	5.8	.956	H. Eller	37	218	16	12	1	2.36
	SS	Blackburne	435	.228	1	45	319	413	48	**69**	6.2	.938	J. Ring	21	142	9	5	0	2.85
	3B	H. Groh	493	.320	1	37	**180**	253	14	**37**	5.6	**.969**	F. Toney	21	137	6	10	2	2.90
	RF	T. Griffith	427	.265	2	48	201	18	7	3	1.9	.969	B. Bressler	17	128	8	5	2	2.46
	CF	E. Roush	435	.333	5	62	320	13	14	2	3.1	.960	M. Regan	22	80	5	5	2	3.26
	LF	G. Neale	371	.270	1	32	249	11	5	2	2.6	**.981**							
	C	I. Wingo	323	.254	0	31	315	111	**12**	13	4.7	.973							
	10	S. Magee	400	.298	2	**76**	685	41	14	40		**.981**							
Pittsburgh W-65 L-60 Hugo Bezdek	1B	F. Mollwitz	432	.269	0	45	1252	73	13	67	11.2	.990	W. Cooper	38	273	19	14	3	2.11
	2B	G. Cutshaw	463	.285	5	68	**323**	**366**	26	60	5.7	**.964**	F. Miller	23	170	11	8	0	2.38
	SS	B. Caton	303	.234	0	17	136	276	32	35	5.6	.928	R. Sanders	28	156	7	9	1	2.60
	3B	McKechnie	435	.255	2	43	162	261	15	26	3.5	.966	E. Mayer	15	123	9	3	0	2.26
	RF	Southworth	246	.341	2	43	137	12	3	4	2.4	.980	R. Comstock	15	81	5	6	1	3.00
	CF	M. Carey	468	.274	3	48	**359**	**25**	**17**	9	**3.2**	.958							
	LF	C. Bigbee	310	.255	1	19	168	13	8	1	2.1	.958							
	C	W. Schmidt	323	.238	0	27	373	**153**	10	**19**	5.2	.981							
Brooklyn W-57 L-69 Wilbert Robinson	1B	J. Daubert	396	.308	2	47	1069	63	10	43	10.9	.991	B. Grimes	**41**	270	19	9	1	2.14
	2B	M. Doolan	308	.179	0	18	230	283	17	37	5.8	.968	R. Marquard	34	239	9	**18**	0	2.64
	SS	I. Olson	506	.239	1	17	265	388	58	42	5.6	.918	L. Cheney	32	201	11	13	1	3.00
	3B	O. O'Mara	450	.213	1	24	126	262	20	15	3.4	.951	J. Coombs	27	189	8	14	0	3.81
	RF	J. Johnston	484	.281	0	27	178	19	9	4	2.1	.956							
	CF	H. Myers	407	.256	4	40	294	17	8	7	3.0	.975							
	LF	Z. Wheat	409	**.335**	0	51	219	11	5	2	2.2	.979							
	C	O. Miller	228	.193	0	8	276	77	10	6	5.9	.972							
	OF	J. Hickman	167	.234	1	16	76	9	8	1	2.0	.914							
	C	M. Wheat	157	.217	1	3	151	50	7	1	5.5	.966							
Philadelphia W-55 L-68 Pat Moran	1B	F. Luderus	468	.288	5	67	1307	**98**	17	**74**	11.4	.988	Prendergast	33	252	13	14	1	2.89
	2B	McGaffigan	192	.203	1	8	100	155	14	19	5.1	.948	B. Hogg	29	228	13	12	1	2.53
	SS	D. Bancroft	499	.265	0	26	**371**	457	64	57	**7.1**	.928	J. Oeschger	30	184	6	**18**	3	3.03
	3B	M. Stock	481	.274	1	42	132	273	23	16	3.5	.946	E. Jacobs	18	123	9	5	1	2.41
	RF	G. Cravath	426	.232	**8**	54	184	19	15	3	1.8	.931	M. Watson	23	113	5	7	0	3.43
	CF	C. Williams	351	.276	6	39	229	10	8	4	2.7	.968	E. Mayer	13	104	7	4	0	3.12
	LF	I. Meusel	473	.279	4	62	296	14	9	2	2.7	.972							
	C	B. Adams	227	.176	0	12	261	69	8	8	4.4	.976							
	C	E. Burns	184	.207	0	9	184	77	5	3	3.9	.981							
	2B	H. Pearce	164	.244	0	18	97	157	15	18	5.8	.944							

NATIONAL LEAGUE 1918, *cont.*

	POS	Player	AB	BA	HR	RBI	PO	A	E	DP	TC/G	FA	Pitcher	G	IP	W	L	SV	ERA
Boston	1B	E. Konetchy	437	.236	2	56	1226	61	11	69	11.6	**.992**	A. Nehf	32	284	15	15	0	2.69
	2B	B. Herzog	473	.228	0	26	240	322	23	43	**5.9**	.961	P. Ragan	30	206	8	17	0	3.23
W-53 L-71	SS	J. Rawlings	410	.207	0	21	137	256	18	27	5.8	.956	D. Rudolph	21	154	9	10	0	2.57
	3B	R. Smith	429	.298	2	65	123	**291**	**35**	16	3.8	.922	B. Hearn	17	126	5	6	0	2.49
George Stallings	RF	A. Wickland	332	.262	4	32	183	11	5	2	2.1	.975	D. Fillingim	14	113	7	6	0	2.23
	CF	R. Powell	188	.213	0	20	121	8	7	2	2.6	.949							
	LF	R. Massey	203	.291	0	18	75	4	3	2	1.8	.963							
	C	A. Wilson	280	.246	0	19	292	96	9	7	4.7	.977							
	OF	J. Kelly	155	.232	0	15	93	4	7	0	2.3	.933							
St. Louis	1B	G. Paulette	461	.273	0	52	1093	59	**20**	64	**12.1**	.983	B. Doak	31	211	9	15	1	2.43
	2B	B. Fisher	246	.317	2	20	147	232	8	34	6.1	.979	R. Ames	27	207	9	14	1	2.31
W-51 L-78	SS	R. Hornsby	416	.281	5	60	208	434	46	55	6.3	.933	B. Sherdel	35	182	6	12	0	2.71
	3B	D. Baird	316	.247	2	25	99	219	11	12	4.1	.967	G. Packard	30	182	12	12	2	3.50
Jack Hendricks	RF	W. Cruise	240	.271	6	39	103	4	4	0	1.7	.964	L. Meadows	30	165	8	14	1	3.59
	CF	C. Heathcote	348	.259	4	32	222	6	16	0	2.8	.934	J. May	29	153	5	6	0	3.83
	LF	A. McHenry	272	.261	1	29	145	14	8	3	2.1	.952							
	C	M. Gonzalez	349	.252	3	20	362	124	11	17	5.0	.978							
	UT	B. Betzel	230	.222	0	13	100	103	17	10		.923							
	OF	J. Smith	166	.211	0	4	87	9	6	6	2.4	.941							

BATTING AND BASE RUNNING LEADERS

Batting Average
Z. Wheat, BKN	.335
E. Roush, CIN	.333
H. Groh, CIN	.320
C. Hollocher, CHI	.316
J. Daubert, BKN	.308

Slugging Average
E. Roush, CIN	.455
J. Daubert, BKN	.429
R. Hornsby, STL	.416
S. Magee, CIN	.415
A. Wickland, BOS	.398

Home Runs
G. Cravath, PHI	8
W. Cruise, STL	6
C. Williams, PHI	6

Total Bases
C. Hollocher, CHI	202
E. Roush, CIN	198
H. Groh, CIN	195
L. Mann, CHI	188
F. Merkle, CHI	187

Runs Batted In
S. Magee, CIN	76
G. Cutshaw, PIT	68
F. Luderus, PHI	67
R. Smith, BOS	65
F. Merkle, CHI	65

Stolen Bases
M. Carey, PIT	58
G. Burns, NY	40
C. Hollocher, CHI	26
D. Baird, STL	25
G. Cutshaw, PIT	25

Hits
C. Hollocher, CHI	161
H. Groh, CIN	158
E. Roush, CIN	145
R. Youngs, NY	143

Base on Balls
M. Carey, PIT	62
M. Flack, CHI	56
G. Cravath, PHI	54
H. Groh, CIN	54

Home Run Percentage
G. Cravath, PHI	1.9
C. Williams, PHI	1.7
A. Wickland, BOS	1.2
R. Hornsby, STL	1.2

Runs Scored
H. Groh, CIN	88
G. Burns, NY	80
M. Flack, CHI	74
C. Hollocher, CHI	72

Doubles
H. Groh, CIN	28
G. Cravath, PHI	27
L. Mann, CHI	27
I. Meusel, PHI	25

Triples
J. Daubert, BKN	15
A. Wickland, BOS	13
S. Magee, CIN	13
L. Magee, CIN	13

PITCHING LEADERS

Winning Percentage
C. Hendrix, CHI	.731
E. Mayer, PHI, PIT	.696
H. Vaughn, CHI	.688
B. Grimes, BKN	.679
L. Tyler, CHI	.679

Earned Run Average
H. Vaughn, CHI	1.74
L. Tyler, CHI	2.00
W. Cooper, PIT	2.11
P. Douglas, CHI	2.13
B. Grimes, BKN	2.14

Wins
H. Vaughn, CHI	22
C. Hendrix, CHI	19
B. Grimes, BKN	19
L. Tyler, CHI	19
W. Cooper, PIT	19

Saves
W. Cooper, PIT	3
F. Anderson, NY	3
J. Oeschger, PHI	3
F. Toney, CIN, NY	3

Strikeouts
H. Vaughn, CHI	148
W. Cooper, PIT	117
B. Grimes, BKN	113
L. Tyler, CHI	102
A. Nehf, BOS	96

Complete Games
A. Nehf, BOS	28
H. Vaughn, CHI	27
W. Cooper, PIT	26
L. Tyler, CHI	22
C. Hendrix, CHI	21

Fewest Hits/9 Innings
H. Vaughn, CHI	6.70
B. Grimes, BKN	7.01
W. Cooper, PIT	7.21
L. Tyler, CHI	7.28

Shutouts
L. Tyler, CHI	8
H. Vaughn, CHI	8
B. Grimes, BKN	7
P. Perritt, NY	6

Fewest Walks/9 Innings
S. Sallee, NY	0.82
P. Perritt, NY	1.47
F. Toney, CIN, NY	1.54
G. Packard, STL	1.63

Most Strikeouts/9 Inn.
H. Vaughn, CHI	4.59
W. Cooper, PIT	3.85
B. Grimes, BKN	3.77
L. Cheney, BKN	3.72

Innings
H. Vaughn, CHI	290
A. Nehf, BOS	284
W. Cooper, PIT	273
B. Grimes, BKN	270

Games Pitched
B. Grimes, BKN	40
W. Cooper, PIT	38
H. Eller, CIN	37
H. Vaughn, CHI	35

	W	L	PCT	GB	R	OR	2B	3B	HR	BA	SA	SB	E	DP	FA	CG	BB	SO	ShO	SV	ERA
								Batting					Fielding				Pitching				
Chicago	84	45	.651		**538**	393	164	53	21	.265	.342	159	188	91	.966	92	296	**472**	25	6	**2.18**
New York	71	53	.573	10.5	480	415	150	53	13	.260	.330	130	**152**	78	**.970**	74	**228**	330	18	11	2.64
Cincinnati	68	60	.531	15.5	530	496	165	84	15	**.278**	**.366**	128	192	127	.964	84	381	321	14	6	3.00
Pittsburgh	65	60	.520	17	466	412	107	72	15	.248	.321	**200**	179	108	.966	85	299	367	12	7	2.48
Brooklyn	57	69	.452	25.5	360	463	121	62	10	.250	.315	113	193	74	.963	85	320	395	17	2	2.81
Philadelphia	55	68	.447	26	430	507	158	28	25	.244	.313	97	211	91	.961	78	369	312	10	6	3.15
Boston	53	71	.427	28.5	424	469	107	59	13	.244	.307	83	184	89	.965	**96**	277	340	13	0	2.90
St. Louis	51	78	.395	33	454	527	147	64	**27**	.244	.325	119	220	116	.962	72	352	361	5	3	2.96
					3682	3682	1119	475	139	.254	.328	1029	1519	774	.965	666	2522	2898	112	43	2.76

AMERICAN LEAGUE 1918

	POS	Player	AB	BA	HR	RBI	PO	A	E	DP	TC/G	FA	Pitcher	G	IP	W	L	SV	ERA
Boston	1B	S. McInnis	423	.272	0	56	1066	71	9	45	**12.2**	**.992**	C. Mays	35	293	21	13	0	2.21
	2B	D. Shean	425	.264	0	34	241	341	20	38	5.2	.967	J. Bush	36	273	15	15	2	2.11
W-75 L-51	SS	E. Scott	443	.221	0	43	270	419	17	38	5.6	.976	S. Jones	24	184	16	5	0	2.25
	3B	F. Thomas	144	.257	1	11	54	97	5	4	3.8	.968	B. Ruth	20	166	13	7	0	2.22
Ed Barrow	RF	H. Hooper	474	.289	1	44	221	16	9	**8**	2.0	.963	D. Leonard	16	126	8	6	0	2.72
	CF	A. Strunk	413	.257	0	35	230	13	3	4	2.2	**.988**							
	LF	B. Ruth	317	.300	**11**	66	121	8	7	3	2.3	.949							
	C	S. Agnew	199	.166	0	9	254	104	13	10	5.2	.965							
	C	W. Schang	225	.244	0	20	188	49	9	4	4.3	.963							
	OF	G. Whiteman	214	.266	1	28	95	5	7	1	1.6	.935							

AMERICAN LEAGUE 1918, cont.

	POS	Player	AB	BA	HR	RBI	PO	A	E	DP	TC/G	FA	Pitcher	G	IP	W	L	SV	ERA
Cleveland	1B	D. Johnston	273	.227	0	25	738	40	9	25	10.8	.989	S. Coveleski	38	311	22	13	1	1.82
	2B	Wambsganss	315	.295	0	40	204	251	23	35	5.5	.952	J. Bagby	45	271	17	16	6	2.69
W-73 L-54	SS	R. Chapman	446	.267	1	32	321	398	49	42	6.0	.936	G. Morton	30	215	14	8	0	2.64
	3B	J. Evans	243	.263	1	22	91	155	18	17	3.6	.932	F. Coumbe	30	150	13	7	3	3.00
Lee Fohl	RF	B. Roth	375	.283	1	59	175	16	13	3	1.9	.936	J. Enzmann	30	137	5	7	2	2.37
	CF	T. Speaker	471	.318	0	61	352	15	10	6	3.0	.973							
	LF	S. Wood	422	.296	5	66	193	10	8	4	2.2	.962							
	C	S. O'Neill	359	.242	1	35	409	154	10	10	5.1	.983							
	32	T. Turner	233	.249	0	23	77	170	5	6		.980							
	OF	J. Graney	177	.237	0	9	77	2	2	0	1.8	.975							
Washington	1B	J. Judge	502	.261	1	46	1304	92	21	71	10.9	.985	W. Johnson	39	325	23	13	3	1.27
	2B	R. Morgan	300	.233	0	30	172	251	18	29	5.5	.959	H. Harper	35	244	11	10	1	2.18
W-72 L-56	SS	D. Lavan	464	.278	0	45	275	354	57	43	5.9	.917	J. Shaw	41	241	16	12	1	2.42
	3B	E. Foster	519	.283	0	29	156	281	30	31	3.7	.936	D. Ayers	40	220	10	12	3	2.83
Clark Griffith	RF	W. Schulte	267	.288	0	44	145	10	5	4	2.1	.969							
	CF	C. Milan	503	.290	0	56	299	17	9	3	2.6	.972							
	LF	B. Shotton	505	.261	0	21	277	15	18	6	2.5	.942							
	C	E. Ainsmith	292	.212	0	20	413	131	14	13	6.3	.975							
	O2	H. Shanks	436	.257	1	56	279	143	21	21		.953							
New York	1B	W. Pipp	349	.304	2	44	918	61	12	75	10.9	.988	G. Mogridge	45	230	16	13	7	2.27
	2B	D. Pratt	477	.275	2	55	340	386	23	82	5.9	.969	S. Love	38	229	13	12	1	3.07
W-60 L-63	SS	Peckinpaugh	446	.231	0	43	260	439	28	75	6.0	.961	R. Caldwell	24	177	9	8	1	3.06
	3B	F. Baker	504	.306	6	68	175	282	13	30	3.7	.972	A. Russell	27	141	7	11	4	3.26
Miller Huggins	RF	F. Gilhooley	427	.276	1	23	206	15	9	8	2.1	.961	H. Finneran	23	114	3	6	0	3.78
	CF	E. Miller	202	.243	1	22	149	13	9	0	2.8	.947	Thormahlen	16	113	7	3	0	2.48
	LF	P. Bodie	324	.256	3	46	181	17	6	3	2.3	.971							
	C	T. Hannah	250	.220	2	21	343	111	12	16	5.3	.974							
	C	R. Walters	191	.199	0	12	199	47	12	6	5.2	.953							
St. Louis	1B	G. Sisler	452	.341	2	41	1244	95	13	64	11.9	.990	A. Sothoron	29	209	12	12	0	1.94
	2B	J. Gedeon	441	.213	1	41	309	409	17	45	6.0	.977	D. Davenport	31	180	10	11	1	3.25
W-58 L-64	SS	J. Austin	367	.264	0	20	117	158	18	13	5.1	.939	T. Rogers	29	154	8	10	2	3.27
	3B	F. Maisel	284	.232	0	16	108	154	14	10	3.5	.949	B. Gallia	19	124	8	6	0	3.48
Fielder Jones	RF	R. Demmitt	405	.281	1	61	206	25	12	8	2.1	.951	R. Wright	18	111	8	2	0	2.51
W-22 L-24	CF	J. Tobin	480	.277	0	36	244	20	8	8	2.2	.971	U. Shocker	14	95	6	5	2	1.81
	LF	E. Smith	286	.269	0	32	164	14	9	4	2.3	.952							
Jimmy Austin	C	L. Nunamaker	274	.259	0	22	315	108	9	10	5.3	.979							
W-7 L-9	OF	T. Hendryx	219	.279	0	33	108	4	2	2	1.8	.982							
	SS	W. Gerber	171	.240	0	10	109	174	24	20	5.5	.922							
Jimmy Burke																			
W-29 L-31																			
Chicago	1B	C. Gandil	439	.271	0	55	1123	64	10	70	10.5	.992	E. Cicotte	38	266	12	19	2	2.64
	2B	E. Collins	330	.276	2	30	231	285	14	53	5.5	.974	Shellenback	28	183	9	12	2	2.66
W-57 L-67	SS	B. Weaver	420	.300	0	29	191	319	32	50	5.5	.941	J. Benz	29	154	8	8	0	2.51
	3B	F. McMullin	235	.277	1	23	74	151	14	9	3.5	.941	D. Danforth	39	159	6	15	2	3.43
Pants Rowland	RF	H. Felsch	206	.252	1	20	149	7	7	5	3.1	.957	R. Russell	19	125	7	5	0	2.60
	CF	S. Collins	365	.274	1	56	230	20	7	1	2.8	.973	L. Williams	15	106	6	4	1	2.73
	LF	N. Leibold	440	.250	1	31	259	16	6	5	2.5	.979							
	C	R. Schalk	333	.219	0	22	422	114	12	15	5.2	.978							
	OF	E. Murphy	286	.297	0	23	111	3	5	1	1.9	.958							
	UT	S. Risberg	273	.256	1	27	168	160	21	27		.940							
	OF	J. Jackson	65	.354	1	20	36	1	0		2.2	1.000							
Detroit	1B	H. Heilmann	286	.276	5	44	367	18	5	11	10.5	.987	H. Dauss	33	250	12	16	3	2.99
	2B	R. Young	298	.188	0	21	190	271	30	28	5.4	.939	B. Boland	29	204	14	10	0	2.65
W-55 L-71	SS	D. Bush	500	.234	0	22	280	364	48	29	5.4	.931	R. Kallio	30	181	8	14	0	3.62
	3B	O. Vitt	267	.240	0	17	106	137	12	15	3.9	.953	Cunningham	27	140	6	7	1	3.15
Hughie Jennings	RF	G. Harper	227	.242	0	16	125	5	6	2	2.1	.956	B. James	19	122	6	11	0	3.76
	CF	T. Cobb	421	.382	3	64	225	12	6	1	2.6	.975	E. Erickson	12	94	4	5	1	2.48
	LF	B. Veach	499	.279	3	78	277	14	7	3	2.3	.977							
	C	A. Yelle	144	.174	0	7	172	81	14	5	5.1	.948							
	3B	B. Jones	287	.275	0	21	81	83	11	6	2.8	.937							
	C	O. Stanage	186	.253	1	14	188	54	5	9	5.3	.980							
	OF	F. Walker	167	.198	1	20	102	5	9	1	2.6	.922							
	C	T. Spencer	155	.219	0	8	153	46	7		4.3	.966							
Philadelphia	1B	G. Burns	505	.352	6	70	1384	104	26	109	11.8	.983	S. Perry	44	332	21	19	1	1.98
	2B	J. Dykes	186	.188	0	13	139	189	21	33	6.2	.940	V. Gregg	30	199	8	14	2	3.12
W-52 L-76	SS	J. Dugan	406	.195	3	34	211	281	37	46	6.2	.930	W. Adams	32	169	5	12	0	4.42
	3B	L. Gardner	463	.285	1	52	158	291	17	33	3.7	.964	M. Watson	21	142	7	10	0	3.37
Connie Mack	RF	C. Jamieson	416	.202	0	11	182	15	6	4	2.0	.970	E. Myers	18	95	4	8	1	4.63
	CF	T. Walker	414	.295	11	48	242	25	13	4	2.6	.954	B. Geary	16	87	2	5	4	2.69
	LF	M. Kopp	363	.234	0	18	221	20	7	6	2.6	.972							
	C	W. McAvoy	271	.244	0	32	235	123	15	15	5.0	.960							
	S2	R. Shannon	225	.240	0	16	155	223	39	40		.906							
	C	C. Perkins	218	.188	1	14	201	103	3	11	5.1	.990							
	OF	M. Acosta	169	.302	0	14	77	7	5	2	2.0	.944							

AMERICAN LEAGUE 1918, *cont.*

BATTING AND BASE RUNNING LEADERS

Batting Average		Slugging Average		Home Runs		Winning Percentage	
T. Cobb, DET	.382	B. Ruth, BOS	.555	B. Ruth, BOS	11	S. Jones, BOS	.762
G. Burns, PHI	.352	T. Cobb, DET	.515	T. Walker, PHI	11	W. Johnson, WAS	.639
G. Sisler, STL	.341	G. Burns, PHI	.467	F. Baker, NY	6	S. Coveleski, CLE	.629
T. Speaker, CLE	.318	G. Sisler, STL	.440	G. Burns, PHI	6	C. Mays, BOS	.618
F. Baker, NY	.306	T. Speaker, CLE	.435	H. Heilmann, DET	5	J. Shaw, WAS	.571
				S. Wood, CLE	5		

Total Bases		Runs Batted In		Stolen Bases		Saves	
G. Burns, PHI	236	B. Veach, DET	78	G. Sisler, STL	45	G. Mogridge, NY	7
T. Cobb, DET	217	G. Burns, PHI	70	B. Roth, CLE	35	J. Bagby, CLE	6
F. Baker, NY	206	F. Baker, NY	68	T. Cobb, DET	34		
T. Speaker, CLE	205	B. Ruth, BOS	66	R. Chapman, CLE	30		
G. Sisler, STL	199	S. Wood, CLE	66	T. Speaker, CLE	27		

Hits		Base on Balls		Home Run Percentage		Fewest Hits/9 Innings	
G. Burns, PHI	178	R. Chapman, CLE	84	B. Ruth, BOS	3.5	A. Sothoron, STL	6.55
T. Cobb, DET	161	D. Bush, DET	79	T. Walker, PHI	2.7	W. Johnson, WAS	6.67
G. Sisler, STL	154	H. Hooper, BOS	75	F. Baker, NY	1.2	H. Harper, WAS	6.71
F. Baker, NY	154	E. Collins, CHI	73	G. Burns, PHI	1.2	B. Ruth, BOS	6.76

Runs Scored		Doubles		Triples		Most Strikeouts/9 Inn.	
R. Chapman, CLE	84	T. Speaker, CLE	33	T. Cobb, DET	14	G. Morton, CLE	5.16
T. Cobb, DET	83	B. Ruth, BOS	26	H. Hooper, BOS	13	J. Shaw, WAS	4.81
H. Hooper, BOS	81	H. Hooper, BOS	26	B. Veach, DET	13	W. Johnson, WAS	4.49
D. Bush, DET	74	F. Baker, NY	24	B. Roth, CLE	12	J. Bush, BOS	4.13

PITCHING LEADERS

Earned Run Average		Wins	
W. Johnson, WAS	1.27	W. Johnson, WAS	23
S. Coveleski, CLE	1.82	S. Coveleski, CLE	22
A. Sothoron, STL	1.94	C. Mays, BOS	21
S. Perry, PHI	1.98	S. Perry, PHI	21
J. Bush, BOS	2.11	J. Bagby, CLE	17

Strikeouts		Complete Games	
W. Johnson, WAS	162	C. Mays, BOS	30
J. Shaw, WAS	129	S. Perry, PHI	30
J. Bush, BOS	125	W. Johnson, WAS	29
G. Morton, CLE	123	J. Bush, BOS	26
C. Mays, BOS	114	S. Coveleski, CLE	25

Shutouts		Fewest Walks/9 Innings	
W. Johnson, WAS	8	E. Cicotte, CHI	1.35
C. Mays, BOS	8	J. Benz, CHI	1.64
J. Bush, BOS	7	G. Mogridge, NY	1.68
S. Jones, BOS	5	W. Johnson, WAS	1.94

Innings		Games Pitched	
S. Perry, PHI	332	J. Bagby, CLE	45
W. Johnson, WAS	325	G. Mogridge, NY	45
S. Coveleski, CLE	311	S. Perry, PHI	44
C. Mays, BOS	293	J. Shaw, WAS	41

	W	L	PCT	GB	R	OR	2B	3B	HR	BA	SA	SB	E	DP	FA	CG	BB	SO	ShO	SV	ERA
Boston	75	51	.595		474	380	159	54	15	.249	.327	110	149	89	.971	105	380	392	26	2	2.31
Cleveland	73	54	.575	2.5	504	447	176	67	9	.260	.341	165	207	82	.962	78	343	364	5	13	2.63
Washington	72	56	.563	4	461	412	156	48	5	.256	.316	137	226	95	.960	75	395	505	19	8	2.14
New York	60	63	.488	13.5	493	475	160	45	20	.257	.330	88	161	137	.970	59	463	369	8	13	3.03
St. Louis	58	64	.475	15	426	448	152	40	5	.259	.320	138	190	86	.963	67	402	346	8	8	2.75
Chicago	57	67	.460	17	457	446	136	54	9	.256	.321	116	169	98	.967	76	300	349	9	8	2.69
Detroit	55	71	.437	20	476	557	141	56	13	.249	.318	123	211	77	.960	74	437	374	8	7	3.40
Philadelphia	52	76	.406	24	412	538	124	44	22	.243	.308	83	228	136	.959	80	479	279	13	8	3.22
					3703	3703	1204	408	98	.254	.323	960	1541	800	.964	614	3199	2978	96	67	2.77

NATIONAL LEAGUE 1919

	POS	Player	AB	BA	HR	RBI	PO	A	E	DP	TC/G	FA	Pitcher	G	IP	W	L	SV	ERA
Cincinnati W-96 L-44 Pat Moran	1B	J. Daubert	537	.276	2	44	1437	80	17	75	11.0	.989	H. Eller	38	248	20	9	2	2.39
	2B	M. Rath	537	.264	1	29	345	452	21	59	5.9	.974	D. Ruether	33	243	19	6	0	1.82
	SS	L. Kopf	503	.270	0	58	273	407	41	39	5.3	.943	S. Sallee	29	228	21	7	0	2.06
	3B	H. Groh	448	.310	5	63	171	226	12	22	3.4	.971	J. Ring	32	183	10	9	3	2.26
	RF	G. Neale	500	.242	1	54	285	16	13	4	2.3	.959	R. Fisher	26	174	14	5	1	2.17
	CF	E. Roush	504	.321	4	71	335	22	4	5	2.7	.989	D. Luque	30	106	9	3	3	2.63
	LF	R. Bressler	165	.206	2	17	105	4	4	1	2.4	.965							
	C	I. Wingo	245	.273	0	27	266	106	12	6	5.1	.969							
	C	B. Rariden	218	.216	1	24	283	67	6	5	5.1	.983							
	OF	S. Magee	163	.215	0	21	98	2	1	0	2.1	.990							
New York W-87 L-53 John McGraw	1B	H. Chase	408	.284	5	45	1205	65	21	62	12.1	.984	J. Barnes	38	296	25	9	1	2.40
	2B	L. Doyle	381	.289	7	52	214	311	24	48	5.5	.956	R. Benton	35	209	17	11	2	2.63
	SS	A. Fletcher	488	.277	3	54	265	521	47	49	6.6	.944	F. Toney	24	181	13	6	1	1.84
	3B	H. Zimmerman	444	.255	4	58	122	268	25	15	3.4	.940	J. Dubuc	36	132	6	4	3	2.66
	RF	R. Youngs	489	.311	2	43	235	23	16	7	2.1	.942	R. Causey	19	105	9	3	0	3.69
	CF	B. Kauff	491	.277	10	67	306	18	17	3	2.5	.950	A. Nehf	13	102	9	2	0	1.50
	LF	G. Burns	534	.303	2	46	290	15	3	4	2.2	.990							
	C	L. McCarty	210	.281	2	21	203	56	8	1	4.5	.970							
	23	F. Frisch	190	.226	2	24	100	130	6	7		.975							
	C	M. Gonzalez	158	.190	0	8	179	49	9	3	4.6	.962							

NATIONAL LEAGUE 1919, *cont.*

Team	POS	Player	AB	BA	HR	RBI	PO	A	E	DP	TC/G	FA	Pitcher	G	IP	W	L	SV	ERA
Chicago W-75 L-65 Fred Mitchell	1B	F. Merkle	498	.267	3	62	1494	56	23	66	11.9	.985	H. Vaughn	38	307	21	14	1	1.79
	2B	C. Pick	269	.242	0	18	135	253	22*	31	5.8	.946	G. Alexander	30	235	16	11	1	1.72
	SS	C. Hollocher	430	.270	3	26	219	418	40	49	5.9	.941	C. Hendrix	33	206	10	14	0	2.62
	3B	C. Deal	405	.289	2	52	157	233	11	14	3.5	.973	S. Martin	35	164	8	8	2	2.47
	RF	M. Flack	469	.294	6	35	194	18	3	1	1.9	.986	P. Douglas	25	162	10	6	0	2.00
	CF	D. Paskert	270	.196	2	29	146	12	5	1	2.0	.969	P. Carter	28	85	5	4	1	2.65
	LF	L. Mann	299	.227	1	22	155	10	3	2	2.2	.982							
	C	B. Killefer	315	.286	0	22	478	124	8	7	6.1	.987							
	UT	L. Magee	267	.292	1	17	130	88	13	5		.944							
	OF	T. Barber	230	.313	0	21	123	7	7	1	2.0	.949							
	2B	B. Herzog	193	.275	0	17	81	151	3	14	4.5	.987							
Pittsburgh W-71 L-68 Hugo Bezdek	1B	F. Mollwitz	168	.173	0	12	478	19	3	21	9.6	.994	W. Cooper	35	287	19	13	1	2.67
	2B	G. Cutshaw	512	.242	3	51	344	392	15	56	5.4	.980	B. Adams	34	263	17	10	1	1.98
	SS	Z. Terry	472	.227	0	27	207	395	25	41	4.9	.960	F. Miller	32	202	13	12	0	3.03
	3B	W. Barbare	293	.273	1	34	109	136	10	11	3.2	.961	E. Hamilton	28	160	8	11	1	3.31
	RF	C. Stengel	321	.293	4	43	195	7	9	3	2.4	.957	H. Carlson	22	141	8	10	0	2.23
	CF	C. Bigbee	478	.276	2	27	343	21	11	5	3.0	.971							
	LF	Southworth	453	.280	4	61	253	17	9	5	2.3	.968							
	C	W. Schmidt	267	.251	0	29	315	110	8	8	5.1	.982							
	OF	M. Carey	244	.307	0	9	173	5	10	1	3.0	.947							
	1B	V. Saier	166	.223	2	17	493	17	8	18	10.2	.985							
	1B	P. Whitted	131	.389	0	21	311	27	4	21	10.4	.988							
Brooklyn W-69 L-71 Wilbert Robinson	1B	E. Konetchy	486	.298	1	47	1288	89	9	62	10.5	.994	J. Pfeffer	30	267	17	13	0	2.66
	2B	J. Johnston	405	.281	1	23	157	294	19	31	5.4	.960	L. Cadore	35	251	14	12	0	2.37
	SS	I. Olson	590	.278	1	38	349	445	44	57	6.0	.947	A. Mamaux	30	199	10	12	0	2.66
	3B	L. Malone	162	.204	0	11	52	75	9	4	2.9	.934	B. Grimes	25	181	10	11	0	3.47
	RF	T. Griffith	484	.281	6	57	210	20	11	3	1.9	.954	S. Smith	30	173	7	12	1	2.24
	CF	H. Myers	512	.307	5	73	358	13	8	5	2.9	.979	C. Mitchell	23	109	7	5	0	3.06
	LF	Z. Wheat	536	.297	5	62	297	9	9	2	2.3	.971							
	C	E. Krueger	226	.248	5	36	305	88	15	2	6.2	.963							
	2B	L. Magee	181	.238	0	7	74	124	13	10	5.9	.938							
	C	O. Miller	164	.226	0	5	223	58	10	5	5.7	.966							
Boston W-57 L-82 George Stallings	1B	W. Holke	518	.292	0	48	1474	95	11	86	11.6	.993	D. Rudolph	37	274	13	18	2	2.17
	2B	B. Herzog	275	.280	1	25	130	191	16	23	4.8	.953	D. Fillingim	32	186	6	13	2	3.38
	SS	Maranville	480	.267	5	43	361	488	53	74	6.9	.941	A. Nehf	22	169	8	9	0	3.09
	3B	T. Boeckel	365	.249	1	26	98	188	12	11	3.2	.960	R. Keating	22	136	7	11	0	2.98
	RF	R. Powell	470	.236	2	33	213	21	12	7	2.0	.951	A. Demaree	25	128	6	6	3	3.80
	CF	J. Riggert	240	.283	4	17	165	6	9	2	3.0	.950	J. Scott	19	104	6	6	1	3.13
	LF	W. Cruise	241	.216	1	21	124	7	3	1	2.0	.978							
	C	H. Gowdy	219	.279	1	22	230	105	8	11	4.6	.977							
	2B	J. Rawlings	275	.255	1	16	105	169	11	20	4.9	.961							
	O3	R. Smith	241	.245	1	25	128	64	9	5		.955							
	C	A. Wilson	191	.257	0	16	213	82	7	4	4.7	.977							
	OF	J. Thorpe	156	.327	1	25	73	2	6	0	2.1	.926							
	OF	L. Mann	145	.283	3	20	82	9	7	1	2.5	.929							
St. Louis W-54 L-83 Branch Rickey	1B	D. Miller	346	.231	1	24	687	40	14	34	10.9	.981	B. Doak	31	203	13	14	0	3.11
	2B	M. Stock	492	.307	0	52	168	254	15	32	5.7	.966	M. Goodwin	33	179	11	9	0	2.51
	SS	D. Lavan	356	.242	1	25	207	352	43	49	6.1	.929	O. Tuero	45	155	5	7	4	3.20
	3B	R. Hornsby	512	.318	8	71	73	151	16	11	3.3	.933	B. Sherdel	36	137	5	9	1	3.47
	RF	J. Smith	408	.223	0	15	197	19	9	6	2.0	.960	J. May	28	126	3	12	0	3.22
	CF	C. Heathcote	401	.279	1	29	225	10	8	3	2.4	.967	L. Meadows	22	92	4	10*	0	3.03
	LF	A. McHenry	371	.286	1	47	183	20	3	3	2.0	.985	E. Jacobs	17	85	3	6	1	2.53
	C	V. Clemons	239	.264	2	22	289	89	7	8	5.1	.982							
	OF	B. Shotton	270	.285	1	20	104	10	9	2	1.8	.927							
	OF	J. Schultz	229	.253	2	21	75	6	0	1	1.7	1.000							
	C	F. Snyder	154	.182	0	14	149	80	4	4	4.9	.983							
Philadelphia W-47 L-90 Jack Coombs W-18 L-44 Gavvy Cravath W-29 L-46	1B	F. Luderus	509	.293	5	54	1385	108	22	82	11.0	.985	G. Smith	31	185	5	11	0	3.22
	2B	G. Paulette	243	.259	1	31	141	173	14	28	6.2	.957	E. Rixey	23	154	6	12	0	3.97
	SS	D. Bancroft	335	.272	0	25	242	306	28	43	6.5	.951	B. Hogg	22	150	5	12	0	4.43
	3B	Blackburne	291	.199	2	19	85	167	18	11	3.8*	.933	L. Meadows	18	149	8	10*	0	2.47
	RF	L. Callahan	235	.230	1	9	102	13	6	1	2.1	.950	G. Packard	21	134	6	8	1	4.15
	CF	C. Williams	435	.278	9	39	278	13	9	2	2.8	.970	E. Jacobs	17	129	6	10	0	3.85
	LF	I. Meusel	521	.305	5	59	256	14	9	4	2.2	.968	F. Woodward	17	101	6	9	0	4.74
	C	B. Adams	232	.233	1	17	249	90	12	15	4.8	.966							
	O2	P. Whitted	289	.249	3	32	169	74	9	8		.964							
	2S	H. Pearce	244	.180	0	9	129	198	17	30		.951							
	3B	D. Baird	242	.252	2	30	100	147	13	17	3.9	.950							
	OF	G. Cravath	214	.341	12	45	89	7	9	2	1.9	.914							
	S2	E. Sicking	185	.216	0	15	117	157	15	37		.948							

NATIONAL LEAGUE 1919, *cont.*

BATTING AND BASE RUNNING LEADERS

Batting Average
E. Roush, CIN	.321
R. Hornsby, STL	.318
R. Youngs, NY	.311
H. Groh, CIN	.310
M. Stock, STL	.307

Slugging Average
H. Myers, BKN	.436
L. Doyle, NY	.433
H. Groh, CIN	.431
E. Roush, CIN	.431
R. Hornsby, STL	.430

Home Runs
G. Cravath, PHI	12
B. Kauff, NY	10
C. Williams, PHI	9
R. Hornsby, STL	8
L. Doyle, NY	7

Winning Percentage
D. Ruether, CIN	.760
S. Sallee, CIN	.750
J. Barnes, NY	.735
H. Eller, CIN	.690
B. Adams, PIT	.630

PITCHING LEADERS

Earned Run Average
G. Alexander, CHI	1.72
H. Vaughn, CHI	1.79
D. Ruether, CIN	1.82
F. Toney, NY	1.84
B. Adams, PIT	1.98

Wins
J. Barnes, NY	25
S. Sallee, CIN	21
H. Vaughn, CHI	21
H. Eller, CIN	20
D. Ruether, CIN	19
W. Cooper, PIT	19

Total Bases
H. Myers, BKN	223
R. Hornsby, STL	220
Z. Wheat, BKN	219
E. Roush, CIN	217
G. Burns, NY	216

Runs Batted In
H. Myers, BKN	73
E. Roush, CIN	71
R. Hornsby, STL	71
B. Kauff, NY	67
H. Groh, CIN	63

Stolen Bases
G. Burns, NY	40
G. Cutshaw, PIT	36
C. Bigbee, PIT	31
J. Smith, STL	30
B. Herzog, BOS, CHI	28
G. Neale, CIN	28

Saves
O. Tuero, STL	4
J. Dubuc, NY	3
D. Luque, CIN	3
A. Demaree, BOS	3
J. Ring, CIN	3
J. Winters, NY	3

Strikeouts
H. Vaughn, CHI	141
H. Eller, CIN	137
G. Alexander, CHI	116
L. Meadows, PHI, STL	116
W. Cooper, PIT	106

Complete Games
W. Cooper, PIT	27
J. Pfeffer, BKN	26
H. Vaughn, CHI	25
D. Rudolph, BOS	24
B. Adams, PIT	23
J. Barnes, NY	23

Hits
I. Olson, BKN	164
R. Hornsby, STL	163
E. Roush, CIN	162
G. Burns, NY	162

Base on Balls
G. Burns, NY	82
M. Rath, CIN	64
H. Groh, CIN	56
F. Luderus, PHI	54

Home Run Percentage
C. Williams, PHI	2.1
B. Kauff, NY	2.0
L. Doyle, NY	1.8
R. Hornsby, STL	1.6

Fewest Hits/9 Innings
G. Alexander, CHI	6.89
W. Cooper, PIT	7.19
D. Ruether, CIN	7.23
R. Fisher, CIN	7.28

Shutouts
G. Alexander, CHI	9
B. Adams, PIT	7
H. Eller, CIN	7
R. Fisher, CIN	5

Fewest Walks/9 Innings
B. Adams, PIT	0.79
S. Sallee, CIN	0.79
J. Barnes, NY	1.07
L. Cadore, BKN	1.40

Runs Scored
G. Burns, NY	86
H. Groh, CIN	79
J. Daubert, CIN	79
M. Rath, CIN	77

Doubles
R. Youngs, NY	31
F. Luderus, PHI	30
G. Burns, NY	30
B. Kauff, NY	27

Triples
Southworth, PIT	14
H. Myers, BKN	14
E. Roush, CIN	13

Most Strikeouts/9 Inn.
H. Eller, CIN	4.97
G. Alexander, CHI	4.63
L. Meadows, PHI, STL	4.33
H. Vaughn, CHI	4.14

Innings
H. Vaughn, CHI	307
J. Barnes, NY	296
W. Cooper, PIT	287
D. Rudolph, BOS	274

Games Pitched
O. Tuero, STL	45
L. Meadows, PHI, STL	40
H. Vaughn, CHI	38
J. Barnes, NY	38

	W	L	PCT	GB	R	OR	2B	3B	HR	BA	SA	SB	E	DP	FA	CG	BB	SO	ShO	SV	ERA
Cincinnati	96	44	.686		577	401	135	83	20	.263	.342	143	152	98	.974	89	298	407	23	9	2.23
New York	87	53	.621	9	605	470	204	64	40	.269	.366	157	216	96	.964	72	305	340	11	13	2.70
Chicago	75	65	.536	21	454	407	166	58	21	.256	.332	150	186	87	.969	80	294	495	21	5	2.21
Pittsburgh	71	68	.511	24.5	472	466	130	82	17	.249	.325	196	166	89	.970	92	263	214	16	4	2.88
Brooklyn	69	71	.493	27	525	513	167	66	25	.263	.340	112	218	84	.972	98	292	476	12	1	2.73
Boston	57	82	.410	38.5	465	563	142	62	24	.253	.324	145	204	111	.966	79	337	374	5	9	3.17
St. Louis	54	83	.394	40.5	463	552	163	52	18	.256	.326	148	217	112	.963	55	415	414	6	8	3.23
Philadelphia	47	90	.343	47.5	510	699	208	50	42	.251	.342	114	219	112	.963	93	408	397	6	2	4.17
					4071	4071	1315	517	207	.258	.337	1165	1578	789	.968	658	2612	3294	100	51	2.91

AMERICAN LEAGUE 1919

	POS	Player	AB	BA	HR	RBI	PO	A	E	DP	TC/G	FA	Pitcher	G	IP	W	L	SV	ERA
Chicago W-88 L-52 Kid Gleason	1B	C. Gandil	441	.290	1	60	1116	60	3	71	10.3	.997	E. Cicotte	40	307	29	7	1	1.82
	2B	E. Collins	518	.319	4	80	347	401	20	66	5.5	.974	L. Williams	41	297	23	11	1	2.64
	SS	S. Risberg	414	.256	2	38	175	278	32	39	5.0	.934	D. Kerr	39	212	13	7	0	2.88
	3B	B. Weaver	571	.296	3	75	113	200	12	14	3.4	.963	R. Faber	25	162	11	9	0	3.83
	RF	N. Leibold	434	.302	0	26	218	26	19	4	2.2	.928	Lowdermilk	20	97	5	5	0	2.79
	CF	H. Felsch	502	.275	7	86	360	32	13	15	3.0	.968							
	LF	J. Jackson	516	.351	7	96	252	15	9	4	2.0	.967							
	C	R. Schalk	394	.282	0	34	551	130	13	14	5.4	.981							
	OF	S. Collins	179	.279	1	16	82	7	4	5	2.0	.957							
	3B	F. McMullin	170	.294	0	19	45	90	10	10	3.2	.931							
Cleveland W-84 L-55 Lee Fohl W-44 L-34 Tris Speaker W-40 L-21	1B	D. Johnston	331	.305	1	33	957	57	16	57	10.5	.984	S. Coveleski	43	296	24	12	4	2.52
	2B	Wambsganss	526	.278	2	60	342	436	30	60	5.8	.963	J. Bagby	35	241	17	11	3	2.80
	SS	R. Chapman	433	.300	3	53	255	347	36	44	5.5	.944	G. Morton	26	147	9	9	0	2.81
	3B	L. Gardner	524	.300	2	79	143	291	25	23	3.3	.946	E. Myers	23	135	8	7	1	3.74
	RF	E. Smith	395	.278	9	54	167	12	8	8	1.7	.957	G. Uhle	26	127	10	5	0	2.91
	CF	T. Speaker	494	.296	2	63	375	25	7	6	3.0	.983							
	LF	J. Graney	461	.234	1	30	281	13	12	2	2.4	.961							
	C	S. O'Neill	398	.289	2	47	472	125	14	13	5.0	.977							
	OF	S. Wood	192	.255	1	27	90	6	7	1	1.6	.932							
	1B	J. Harris	184	.375	1	46	451	38	6	22	10.8	.988							

AMERICAN LEAGUE 1919, *cont.*

New York
W-80 L-59
Miller Huggins

POS	Player	AB	BA	HR	RBI	PO	A	E	DP	TC/G	FA	Pitcher	G	IP	W	L	SV	ERA
1B	W. Pipp	523	.275	7	50	1488	94	15	77	11.6	.991	J. Quinn	38	264	15	14	0	2.63
2B	D. Pratt	527	.292	4	56	315	491	26	64	5.9	.969	B. Shawkey	41	261	20	11	4	2.72
SS	Peckinpaugh	453	.305	7	33	271	434	43	57	6.2	.943	Thormahlen	30	189	12	10	1	2.62
3B	F. Baker	567	.293	10	83	176	286	22	28	3.4	.955	G. Mogridge	35	187	10	7	0	2.50
RF	S. Vick	407	.248	2	27	166	11	9	2	1.9	.952	C. Mays	13	120	9	3	0	1.65
CF	P. Bodie	475	.278	6	59	293	19	13	6	2.4	.960	E. Shore	20	95	5	8	0	4.17
LF	D. Lewis	559	.272	7	89	254	13	4	4	1.9	.985	A. Russell	23	91	5	5	1	3.47
C	M. Ruel	233	.240	0	31	340	90	11	6	5.4	.975							
OS	C. Fewster	244	.283	1	15	118	80	17	8		.921							
C	T. Hannah	227	.238	1	21	298	66	6	12	5.1	.984							

Detroit
W-80 L-60
Hughie Jennings

POS	Player	AB	BA	HR	RBI	PO	A	E	DP	TC/G	FA	Pitcher	G	IP	W	L	SV	ERA
1B	H. Heilmann	537	.320	8	95	1402	78	31	61	10.8	.979	H. Dauss	34	256	21	9	0	3.55
2B	R. Young	456	.211	1	25	300	389	22	38	5.9	.969	H. Ehmke	33	249	17	10	0	3.18
SS	D. Bush	509	.244	0	26	290	376	40	38	5.5	.943	B. Boland	35	243	14	16	1	3.04
3B	B. Jones	439	.260	1	57	134	219	21	14	2.9	.944	D. Leonard	29	217	14	13	0	2.77
RF	I. Flagstead	287	.331	5	41	140	15	8	4	2.0	.951	S. Love	22	90	6	4	1	3.01
CF	T. Cobb	497	.384	1	70	272	19	8	3	2.4	.973							
LF	B. Veach	538	.355	3	101	338	14	12	3	2.6	.967							
C	E. Ainsmith	364	.272	3	32	456	107	22	7	5.5	.962							
OF	C. Shorten	270	.315	0	22	143	2	4	2	2.0	.973							

St. Louis
W-67 L-72
Jimmy Burke

POS	Player	AB	BA	HR	RBI	PO	A	E	DP	TC/G	FA	Pitcher	G	IP	W	L	SV	ERA
1B	G. Sisler	511	.352	10	83	1249	120	13	62	10.5	.991	A. Sothoron	40	270	20	13	3	2.20
2B	J. Gedeon	437	.254	0	27	290	345	16	44	5.5	.975	B. Gallia	34	222	11	14	2	3.60
SS	W. Gerber	462	.227	1	37	287	422	45	42	5.4	.940	U. Shocker	30	211	13	11	0	2.69
3B	J. Austin	396	.237	1	21	161	207	24	15	4.0	.939	C. Weilman	20	148	10	6	0	2.07
RF	E. Smith	252	.250	1	36	155	13	5	4	2.5	.971	D. Davenport	24	123	3	11	0	3.94
CF	B. Jacobson	455	.323	4	51	270	9	15	2	2.8	.949	L. Leifield	19	92	6	4	0	2.93
LF	J. Tobin	486	.327	6	57	247	16	13	15	2.2	.953							
C	H. Severeid	351	.248	0	36	401	106	9	12	5.0	.983							
OF	K. Williams	227	.300	6	35	168	10	12	3	3.0	.937							
OF	R. Demmitt	202	.238	1	19	60	6	10	0	1.6	.868							
32	H. Bronkie	196	.255	0	14	75	113	11	13		.945							

Boston
W-66 L-71
Ed Barrow

POS	Player	AB	BA	HR	RBI	PO	A	E	DP	TC/G	FA	Pitcher	G	IP	W	L	SV	ERA
1B	S. McInnis	440	.305	1	58	1236	82	7	84	11.2	.995	S. Jones	35	245	12	20	1	3.75
2B	R. Shannon	290	.259	0	17	171	228	11	40	5.2	.973	H. Pennock	32	219	16	8	0	2.71
SS	E. Scott	507	.278	0	38	276	423	17	63	5.2	.976	C. Mays	21	145	5	11	2	2.48
3B	O. Vitt	469	.243	0	40	129	254	13	24	3.0	.967	B. Ruth	17	133	9	5	1	2.97
RF	H. Hooper	491	.267	3	49	262	19	6	2	2.2	.979	A. Russell	21	120	10	4	4	2.54
CF	B. Roth	227	.256	0	23	125	7	8	1	2.2	.943	W. Hoyt	13	105	4	6	0	3.25
LF	B. Ruth	432	.322	29	114	230	16	2	6	2.2	.992	R. Caldwell	18	86	7	4	0	3.75
C	W. Schang	330	.306	0	55	359	131	14	15	4.9	.972							
OF	A. Strunk	184	.272	0	17	118	4	4	0	2.6	.968							

Washington
W-56 L-84
Clark Griffith

POS	Player	AB	BA	HR	RBI	PO	A	E	DP	TC/G	FA	Pitcher	G	IP	W	L	SV	ERA
1B	J. Judge	521	.288	2	31	1177	78	15	66	9.5	.988	J. Shaw	45	307	16	17	4	2.73
2B	H. Janvrin	208	.178	1	13	108	120	18	14	4.4	.927	W. Johnson	39	290	20	14	2	1.49
SS	H. Shanks	491	.248	1	54	238	260	42	2	5.7	.922	H. Harper	35	208	6	21	0	3.72
3B	E. Foster	478	.264	0	26	120	267	22	16	3.2	.946	E. Erickson	20	132	6	11	0	3.95
RF	S. Rice	557	.321	3	71	285	18	12	3	2.2	.962							
CF	C. Milan	321	.287	0	37	195	9	10	2	2.5	.953							
LF	M. Menosky	342	.287	6	39	222	7	5	1	2.3	.979							
C	V. Picinich	212	.274	3	22	303	92	9	5	5.9	.978							
CO	P. Gharrity	347	.271	2	43	329	72	15	7		.964							
OF	B. Murphy	252	.262	0	28	177	8	8	2	2.6	.959							
23	J. Leonard	198	.258	2	20	81	98	8	14		.957							

Philadelphia
W-36 L-104
Connie Mack

POS	Player	AB	BA	HR	RBI	PO	A	E	DP	TC/G	FA	Pitcher	G	IP	W	L	SV	ERA
1B	G. Burns	470	.296	8	57	918	71	20	44	11.7	.980	R. Naylor	31	205	5	18	0	3.34
2B	R. Shannon	155	.271	0	14	66	116	10	10	5.2	.980	W. Kinney	43	203	9	15	2	3.64
SS	J. Dugan	387	.271	1	30	228	307	42	39	5.9	.927	J. Johnson	34	202	9	15	0	3.61
3B	F. Thomas	453	.212	2	23	168	242	24	14	3.5	.945	S. Perry	25	184	4	17	1	3.58
RF	M. Kopp	235	.226	1	12	127	7	11	0	2.2	.924	T. Rogers	23	140	4	12	0	4.31
CF	T. Walker	456	.292	10	64	253	13	19	4	2.5	.933							
LF	W. Witt	460	.267	0	33	134	3	4	0	2.4	.972							
C	C. Perkins	305	.252	2	29	340	134	14	15	5.6	.971							
OF	B. Roth	195	.323	5	29	78	1	2	2	1.7	.975							
OF	A. Strunk	194	.211	0	13	98	7	2	0	2.1	.981							
1B	D. Burrus	194	.258	0	8	337	21	5	15	9.6	.986							
C	W. McAvoy	170	.141	0	11	182	73	7	6	4.6	.973							

BATTING AND BASE RUNNING LEADERS

Batting Average		Slugging Average		Home Runs	
T. Cobb, DET	.384	B. Ruth, BOS	.657	B. Ruth, BOS	29
B. Veach, DET	.355	G. Sisler, STL	.530	T. Walker, PHI	10
G. Sisler, STL	.352	B. Veach, DET	.519	G. Sisler, STL	10
J. Jackson, CHI	.351	T. Cobb, DET	.515	F. Baker, NY	10
I. Flagstead, DET	.331	J. Jackson, CHI	.506	E. Smith, CLE	9

PITCHING LEADERS

Winning Percentage		Earned Run Average		Wins	
E. Cicotte, CHI	.806	W. Johnson, WAS	1.49	E. Cicotte, CHI	29
H. Dauss, DET	.700	E. Cicotte, CHI	1.82	S. Coveleski, CLE	24
L. Williams, CHI	.676	C. Weilman, STL	2.07	L. Williams, CHI	23
S. Coveleski, CLE	.667	C. Mays, BOS, NY	2.11	H. Dauss, DET	21
H. Pennock, BOS	.667	A. Sothoron, STL	2.20		

AMERICAN LEAGUE 1919, *cont.*

BATTING AND BASE RUNNING LEADERS

Total Bases
B. Ruth, BOS	284
B. Veach, DET	279
G. Sisler, STL	271
J. Jackson, CHI	261
T. Cobb, DET	256
H. Heilmann, DET	256

Hits
T. Cobb, DET	191
B. Veach, DET	191
J. Jackson, CHI	181
G. Sisler, STL	180

Runs Scored
B. Ruth, BOS	103
G. Sisler, STL	96
T. Cobb, DET	92
Peckinpaugh, NY	89

Runs Batted In
B. Ruth, BOS	114
B. Veach, DET	101
J. Jackson, CHI	96
H. Heilmann, DET	95
D. Lewis, NY	89

Base on Balls
J. Graney, CLE	105
B. Ruth, BOS	101
J. Judge, WAS	81
H. Hooper, BOS	79

Doubles
B. Veach, DET	45
T. Speaker, CLE	38
T. Cobb, DET	36
S. O'Neill, CLE	35

Stolen Bases
E. Collins, CHI	33
T. Cobb, DET	28
G. Sisler, STL	28
S. Rice, WAS	26
H. Hooper, BOS	23
J. Judge, WAS	23

Home Run Percentage
B. Ruth, BOS	6.7
E. Smith, CLE	2.3
T. Walker, PHI	2.2
G. Sisler, STL	2.0

Triples
B. Veach, DET	17
G. Sisler, STL	15
H. Heilmann, DET	15
J. Jackson, CHI	14

Saves
A. Russell, BOS, NY	5
B. Shawkey, NY	4
S. Coveleski, CLE	4
J. Shaw, WAS	4
A. Sothoron, STL	3
J. Bagby, CLE	3

Fewest Hits/9 Innings
W. Johnson, WAS	7.28
Thormahlen, NY	7.39
B. Shawkey, NY	7.51
E. Cicotte, CHI	7.51

Most Strikeouts/9 Inn.
A. Russell, BOS, NY	4.82
W. Johnson, WAS	4.56
W. Kinney, PHI	4.31
D. Leonard, DET	4.22

PITCHING LEADERS

Strikeouts
W. Johnson, WAS	147
J. Shaw, WAS	128
L. Williams, CHI	125
B. Shawkey, NY	122
S. Coveleski, CLE	118

Shutouts
W. Johnson, WAS	7
U. Shocker, STL	5
H. Pennock, BOS	5
S. Jones, BOS	5

Innings
J. Shaw, WAS	307
E. Cicotte, CHI	307
L. Williams, CHI	297
S. Coveleski, CLE	296

Complete Games
E. Cicotte, CHI	30
W. Johnson, WAS	27
L. Williams, CHI	27
S. Coveleski, CLE	24
C. Mays, BOS, NY	23
J. Shaw, WAS	23

Fewest Walks/9 Innings
E. Cicotte, CHI	1.44
W. Johnson, WAS	1.58
J. Bagby, CLE	1.64
L. Williams, CHI	1.76

Games Pitched
J. Shaw, WAS	45
A. Russell, BOS, NY	44
S. Coveleski, CLE	43
W. Kinney, PHI	43

	W	L	PCT	GB	R	OR	2B	3B	HR	BA	SA	SB	E	DP	FA	CG	BB	SO	ShO	SV	ERA
Chicago	88	52	.629		**667**	534	218	70	25	**.287**	.380	**150**	176	116	.969	88	**342**	468	14	3	3.04
Cleveland	84	55	.604	3.5	636	537	**254**	71	25	.278	.381	113	201	102	.965	80	362	432	10	**10**	2.92
New York	80	59	.576	7.5	578	**506**	193	49	**45**	.267	.356	101	192	108	.968	85	433	500	14	6	**2.78**
Detroit	80	60	.571	8	618	578	222	**84**	23	.283	**.381**	121	205	81	.964	85	431	428	10	4	3.30
St. Louis	67	72	.482	20.5	533	540	187	73	31	.264	.355	74	216	98	.963	77	421	415	14	5	3.13
Boston	66	71	.482	20.5	564	552	181	49	33	.261	.344	108	**141**	**118**	**.975**	**89**	420	380	**15**	8	3.30
Washington	56	84	.400	32	533	570	177	63	24	.260	.339	142	227	86	.960	69	451	**536**	12	8	3.01
Philadelphia	36	104	.257	52	457	742	175	71	35	.244	.334	103	259	96	.956	72	503	417	1	3	4.26
					4586	4586	1607	530	241	.268	.359	912	1617	805	.965	645	3363	3576	90	47	3.21

NATIONAL LEAGUE 1920

		POS	Player	AB	BA	HR	RBI	PO	A	E	DP	TC/G	FA	Pitcher	G	IP	W	L	SV	ERA
Brooklyn		1B	E. Konetchy	497	.308	5	63	1332	79	14	70	11.0	.990	B. Grimes	40	304	23	11	2	2.22
		2B	P. Kilduff	478	.272	0	58	316	454	26	69	5.9	.967	L. Cadore	35	254	15	14	0	2.62
W-93 L-61		SS	I. Olson	637	.254	1	46	275	404	40	48	5.8	.935	J. Pfeffer	30	215	16	9	0	3.01
		3B	J. Johnston	635	.291	1	52	159	282	31	21	3.2	.934	A. Mamaux	41	191	12	8	4	2.69
Wilbert Robinson		RF	T. Griffith	334	.260	2	30	132	7	4	1	1.6	.972	R. Marquard	28	190	10	7	0	3.23
		CF	H. Myers	582	.304	4	80	386	17	9	5	2.7	.978	S. Smith	33	136	11	9	3	1.85
		LF	Z. Wheat	583	.328	9	73	287	10	9	5	2.1	.971							
		C	O. Miller	301	.289	0	33	**418**	65	7	8	**5.5**	**.986**							
		OF	B. Neis	249	.253	2	22	145	11	7	4	2.0	.957							
New York		1B	G. Kelly	590	.266	11	**94**	**1759**	103	11	**115**	**12.1**	.994	J. Barnes	43	293	20	15	0	2.64
		2B	L. Doyle	471	.285	4	50	278	389	23	61	5.2	.967	A. Nehf	40	281	21	12	0	3.08
W-86 L-68		SS	D. Bancroft	442	.299	0	31	256*	445*	40	67*	6.9*	.946*	F. Toney	42	278	21	11	1	2.65
		3B	F. Frisch	440	.280	4	77	104	251	12	23	3.3	.967	P. Douglas	46	226	14	10	2	2.71
John McGraw		RF	R. Youngs	581	.351	6	78	288	**26**	**22**	7	2.2	.935	R. Benton	33	193	9	16	2	3.03
		CF	L. King	261	.276	7	42	167	8	9	1	2.2	.951							
		LF	G. Burns	631	.287	6	46	336	11	9	5	2.3	.983							
		C	F. Snyder	264	.250	3	27	269	92	8	6	4.4	.978							
		C	E. Smith	262	.294	1	30	252	73	8	12	4.1	.976							
		SS	A. Fletcher	171	.257	0	24	79	154	22	16	6.2	.914							
		OF	B. Kauff	157	.274	3	26	111	10	5	2	2.5	.960							
Cincinnati		1B	J. Daubert	553	.304	4	48	1358	63	15	90	10.3	.990	J. Ring	42	293	17	16	1	3.23
		2B	M. Rath	506	.267	2	28	310	399	17	60	5.8	**.977**	D. Ruether	37	266	16	12	3	2.47
W-82 L-71		SS	L. Kopf	458	.245	0	59	249	363	47	0	5.4	.929	H. Eller	35	210	13	12	0	2.95
		3B	H. Groh	550	.298	0	49	179	252	14	**30**	3.1	.969	D. Luque	37	208	13	9	1	2.51
Pat Moran		RF	G. Neale	530	.255	3	46	347	19	5	**7**	2.5	.987	R. Fisher	33	201	10	11	1	2.73
		CF	E. Roush	579	.339	4	90	**410**	18	11	6	**3.2**	.975	S. Sallee	21	116	5	6	2	3.34
		LF	P. Duncan	576	.295	2	83	334	15	13	4	2.4	.964							
		C	I. Wingo	364	.264	2	38	368	115	21	14	4.7	.958							

NATIONAL LEAGUE 1920, *cont.*

	POS	Player	AB	BA	HR	RBI	PO	A	E	DP	TC/G	FA	Pitcher	G	IP	W	L	SV	ERA
Pittsburgh	1B	C. Grimm	533	.227	2	54	1496	95	8	95	10.8	.995	W. Cooper	44	327	24	15	2	2.39
	2B	G. Cutshaw	488	.252	0	47	336	423	25	62	6.1	.968	B. Adams	35	263	17	13	2	2.16
W-79 L-75	SS	B. Caton	352	.236	0	27	191	296	37	40	5.5	.929	H. Carlson	39	247	14	13	3	3.36
	3B	P. Whitted	494	.261	1	74	166	229	16	16	3.3	.961	E. Hamilton	39	231	10	13	3	3.24
George Gibson	RF	Southworth	546	.284	2	53	337	12	3	3	2.5	.991	E. Ponder	33	196	11	15	0	2.62
	CF	M. Carey	485	.289	1	35	345	10	12	0	2.8	.967							
	LF	C. Bigbee	550	.280	4	32	289	16	9	4	2.4	.971							
	C	W. Schmidt	310	.277	0	20	323	109	13	10	4.8	.971							
	OF	F. Nicholson	247	.360	4	30	125	9	6	2	2.4	.957							
	S2	W. Barbare	186	.274	0	12	75	151	13	20		.946							
	C	B. Haeffner	175	.194	0	14	192	48	7	1	4.8	.972							
Chicago	1B	F. Merkle	330	.285	3	38	906	54	15	52	11.5	.985	G. Alexander	46	363	**27**	14	5	**1.91**
	2B	Z. Terry	496	.280	0	52	138	222	9	30	5.9	.976	H. Vaughn	40	301	19	16	0	2.54
W-75 L-79	SS	C. Hollocher	301	.319	0	22	196	280	23	34	6.2	.954	C. Hendrix	27	204	9	12	0	3.58
	3B	C. Deal	450	.240	3	39	129	268	11	22	3.2	**.973**	L. Tyler	27	193	11	12	0	3.31
Fred Mitchell	RF	M. Flack	520	.302	4	49	216	16	8	2	1.8	.967	S. Martin	35	136	4	15	2	4.83
	CF	D. Paskert	487	.279	5	71	306	23	15	3	2.5	.956	P. Carter	31	106	3	6	2	4.67
	LF	D. Robertson	500	.300	10	75	230	10	8	1	1.9	.968							
	C	B. O'Farrell	270	.248	3	19	317	100	19	6	5.1	.956							
	1B	T. Barber	340	.265	0	50	739	30	9	40	11.3	.988							
	23	B. Herzog	305	.193	0	19	153	241	29	32		.931							
	C	B. Killefer	191	.220	0	16	304	80	9	6	6.4	.977							
	OF	B. Twombly	183	.235	2	14	91	6	3	0	2.2	.970							
St. Louis	1B	J. Fournier	530	.306	3	61	1373	88	**25**	100	10.8	.983	J. Haines	**47**	302	13	20	2	2.98
	2B	R. Hornsby	589	**.370**	9	94	343	**524**	34	76	6.0	.962	B. Doak	39	270	20	12	1	2.53
W-75 L-79	SS	D. Lavan	516	.289	1	63	327	489	50	77	6.3	.942	F. Schupp	38	251	16	13	0	3.52
	3B	M. Stock	**639**	.319	0	76	158	**300**	30	23	3.1	.939	B. Sherdel	43	170	11	10	6	3.28
Branch Rickey	RF	J. Schultz	320	.263	0	32	147	7	9	3	2.0	.945	M. Goodwin	32	116	3	8	1	4.95
	CF	C. Heathcote	489	.284	3	56	296	**26**	12	3	2.6	.964	E. Jacobs	23	78	4	8	1	5.21
	LF	A. McHenry	504	.282	10	65	297	21	16	1	2.5	.952							
	C	V. Clemons	338	.281	1	36	408	111	12	11	5.2	.977							
	OF	J. Smith	313	.332	1	28	144	12	6	1	2.0	.963							
	UT	H. Janvrin	270	.274	1	28	307	93	13	33		.969							
	C	Dillhoefer	224	.263	0	13	291	72	18	6	5.2	.953							
	OF	B. Shotton	180	.228	1	12	85	9	4	2	1.9	.959							
Boston	1B	W. Holke	551	.294	3	64	1528	81	14	97	11.3	.991	J. Oeschger	38	299	15	13	0	3.46
	2B	C. Pick	383	.274	2	28	219	333	28	45	6.2	.952	J. Scott	44	291	10	21	1	3.53
W-62 L-90	SS	Maranville	493	.266	1	43	354	462	45	62	6.5	.948	D. Fillingim	37	272	12	21	0	3.11
	3B	T. Boeckel	582	.268	3	62	**219**	266	33	**30**	3.4	.936	McQuillan	38	226	11	15	5	3.55
George Stallings	RF	W. Cruise	288	.278	1	21	122	10	7	3	1.7	.950	D. Rudolph	18	89	4	8	0	4.04
	CF	R. Powell	609	.225	6	29	370	25	18	5	2.8	.956							
	LF	L. Mann	424	.276	3	32	228	13	5	1	2.2	.980							
	C	M. O'Neil	304	.283	0	18	304	**153**	18	10	4.5	.962							
	2B	H. Ford	257	.241	1	30	122	219	10	21	5.9	.972							
	OF	J. Sullivan	250	.296	1	28	115	10	3	2	1.9	.977							
	OF	E. Eayrs	244	.328	1	24	108	6	6	2	1.9	.950							
	C	H. Gowdy	214	.243	0	18	231	104	7	12	4.6	.980							
Philadelphia	1B	G. Paulette	562	.288	1	36	1428	99	18	94	11.1	.988	E. Rixey	41	284	11	**22**	2	3.48
	2B	J. Rawlings	384	.234	3	30	221	321	17	53	5.8	.970	G. Smith	43	251	13	18	2	3.45
W-62 L-91	SS	A. Fletcher	379	.296	4	38	223	368	26	47	6.1	.958	L. Meadows	35	247	16	14	0	2.84
	3B	R. Miller	338	.219	0	28	89	179	17	15	3.1	.940	R. Causey	35	181	7	14	3	4.32
Gavvy Cravath	RF	C. Stengel	445	.292	9	50	212	16	11	1	2.0	.954	B. Hubbell	24	150	9	9	2	3.84
	CF	C. Williams	590	.325	**15**	72	388	22	12	4	2.9	.972	B. Gallia	18	72	2	6	2	4.50
	LF	I. Meusel	518	.309	14	69	260	16	21	6	2.3	.929							
	C	M. Wheat	230	.226	3	20	262	105	15	8	5.2	.961							
	UT	D. Miller	343	.254	1	27	254	234	27	48		.948							
	OF	LeBourveau	261	.257	3	12	133	16	8	1	2.2	.949							
	3B	Wrightstone	206	.262	3	17	75	109	13	7	3.5	.934							
	C	W. Tragesser	176	.210	6	26	157	46	12	4	4.1	.944							
	SS	D. Bancroft	171	.298	0	5	106*	153*	5	28*	6.3*	.981*							

BATTING AND BASE RUNNING LEADERS

Batting Average		Slugging Average		Home Runs		Winning Percentage	
R. Hornsby, STL	.370	R. Hornsby, STL	.559	C. Williams, PHI	15	B. Grimes, BKN	.676
R. Youngs, NY	.351	C. Williams, PHI	.497	I. Meusel, PHI	14	G. Alexander, CHI	.659
E. Roush, CIN	.339	R. Youngs, NY	.477	G. Kelly, NY	11	F. Toney, NY	.656
Z. Wheat, BKN	.328	I. Meusel, PHI	.473	D. Robertson, CHI	10	J. Pfeffer, BKN	.640
C. Williams, PHI	.325	Z. Wheat, BKN	.463	A. McHenry, STL	10	A. Nehf, NY	.636

PITCHING LEADERS

Earned Run Average		Wins	
G. Alexander, CHI	1.91	G. Alexander, CHI	27
B. Adams, PIT	2.16	W. Cooper, PIT	24
B. Grimes, BKN	2.22	B. Grimes, BKN	23
W. Cooper, PIT	2.39	F. Toney, NY	21
D. Ruether, CIN	2.47	A. Nehf, NY	21

NATIONAL LEAGUE 1920, *cont.*

BATTING AND BASE RUNNING LEADERS

Total Bases
R. Hornsby, STL	329
C. Williams, PHI	293
R. Youngs, NY	277
Z. Wheat, BKN	270
H. Myers, BKN	269

Runs Batted In
R. Hornsby, STL	94
G. Kelly, NY	94
E. Roush, CIN	90
P. Duncan, CIN	83
H. Myers, BKN	80

Stolen Bases
M. Carey, PIT	52
E. Roush, CIN	36
F. Frisch, NY	34
C. Bigbee, PIT	31
G. Neale, CIN	29

Saves
B. Sherdel, STL	6
G. Alexander, CHI	5
McQuillan, BOS	5
A. Mamaux, BKN	4
B. Hubbell, NY, PHI	4

Hits
R. Hornsby, STL	218
R. Youngs, NY	204
M. Stock, STL	204
E. Roush, CIN	196

Base on Balls
G. Burns, NY	76
R. Youngs, NY	75
D. Paskert, CHI	64
H. Groh, CIN	60

Home Run Percentage
I. Meusel, PHI	2.7
C. Williams, PHI	2.5
C. Stengel, PHI	2.0
D. Robertson, CHI	2.0

Fewest Hits/9 Innings
D. Luque, CIN	7.28
D. Ruether, CIN	7.96
B. Grimes, BKN	8.03
B. Adams, PIT	8.21

Runs Scored
G. Burns, NY	115
D. Bancroft, NY, PHI	102
J. Daubert, CIN	97
R. Hornsby, STL	96

Doubles
R. Hornsby, STL	44
H. Myers, BKN	36
C. Williams, PHI	36
D. Bancroft, NY, PHI	36

Triples
H. Myers, BKN	22
R. Hornsby, STL	20
E. Roush, CIN	16
Maranville, BOS	15

Most Strikeouts/9 Inn.
G. Alexander, CHI	4.29
F. Schupp, STL	4.27
R. Marquard, BKN	4.22
H. Vaughn, CHI	3.92

PITCHING LEADERS

Strikeouts
G. Alexander, CHI	173
H. Vaughn, CHI	131
B. Grimes, BKN	131
J. Haines, STL	120
F. Schupp, STL	119

Shutouts
B. Adams, PIT	8
G. Alexander, CHI	7

Innings
G. Alexander, CHI	363
W. Cooper, PIT	327
B. Grimes, BKN	304
J. Haines, STL	302

Complete Games
G. Alexander, CHI	33
W. Cooper, PIT	28
B. Grimes, BKN	25
E. Rixey, PHI	25
H. Vaughn, CHI	24

Fewest Walks/9 Innings
B. Adams, PIT	0.62
W. Cooper, PIT	1.43
A. Nehf, NY	1.44
R. Benton, NY	1.44

Games Pitched
J. Haines, STL	47
G. Alexander, CHI	46
P. Douglas, NY	46
W. Cooper, PIT	44

	W	L	PCT	GB	R	OR	2B	3B	HR	BA	SA	SB	E	DP	FA	CG	BB	SO	ShO	SV	ERA
Brooklyn	93	61	.604		660	**528**	205	**99**	28	.277	.367	70	226	118	.966	89	327	**553**	17	10	**2.62**
New York	86	68	.558	7	**682**	543	210	76	46	.269	.363	131	210	**137**	.969	86	297	380	**18**	9	2.80
Cincinnati	82	71	.536	10.5	639	569	169	76	18	.277	.349	158	200	125	.968	90	393	435	12	9	2.84
Pittsburgh	79	75	.513	14	530	552	162	90	16	.257	.332	**181**	**186**	119	**.971**	92	**280**	444	17	10	2.89
Chicago	75	79	.487	18	619	635	223	67	34	.264	.354	115	225	112	.965	**95**	382	508	13	9	3.27
St. Louis	75	79	.487	18	675	682	**238**	96	32	**.289**	**.385**	126	256	136	.961	72	479	529	9	**12**	3.43
Boston	62	90	.408	30	523	670	168	86	23	.260	.339	88	239	125	.964	93	415	368	13	6	3.54
Philadelphia	62	91	.405	30.5	565	714	229	54	**64**	.263	.364	100	232	135	.964	77	444	419	8	11	3.63
					4893	4893	1604	644	261	.270	.357	969	1774	1007	.966	694	3017	3636	107	76	3.13

AMERICAN LEAGUE 1920

	POS	Player	AB	BA	HR	RBI	PO	A	E	DP	TC/G	FA	Pitcher	G	IP	W	L	SV	ERA
Cleveland W-98 L-56 Tris Speaker	1B	D. Johnston	535	.292	2	71	1427	91	12	83	10.4	.992	J. Bagby	**48**	**340**	**31**	12	0	2.89
	2B	Wambsganss	565	.244	1	55	414	489	38	75	6.2	.960	S. Coveleski	41	315	24	14	2	2.49
	SS	R. Chapman	435	.303	3	49	243	371	26	43	**5.8**	.959	R. Caldwell	34	238	20	10	0	3.86
	3B	L. Gardner	597	.310	3	118	156	362	13	**32**	3.4	**.976**	G. Morton	29	137	8	6	1	4.47
	RF	E. Smith	456	.316	12	103	217	8	7	1	1.8	.970	G. Uhle	27	85	4	5	1	5.21
	CF	T. Speaker	552	.388	8	107	363	24	9	8	2.7	.977							
	LF	C. Jamieson	370	.319	1	40	185	14	7	0	2.1	.966							
	C	S. O'Neill	489	.321	3	55	576	128	17	1	4.9	.976							
	OF	J. Evans	172	.349	0	23	79	6	3	0	2.0	.966							
	OF	S. Wood	137	.270	1	30	71	6	1	0	1.4	.987							
Chicago W-96 L-58 Kid Gleason	1B	S. Collins	495	.303	1	63	1146	63	15	69	10.5	.988	R. Faber	40	319	23	13	1	2.99
	2B	E. Collins	601	.369	3	75	**449**	471	23	76	6.2	**.976**	E. Cicotte	37	303	21	10	2	3.26
	SS	S. Risberg	458	.266	2	65	238	400	45	59	5.5	.934	L. Williams	39	299	22	14	0	3.91
	3B	B. Weaver	630	.333	2	75	153	276	**31**	15	3.7	.933	D. Kerr	45	254	21	9	5	3.37
	RF	N. Leibold	413	.220	1	28	190	18	5	5	2.0	.977	R. Wilkinson	34	145	7	9	2	4.03
	CF	H. Felsch	556	.338	14	115	385	25	8	**10**	2.9	.981							
	LF	J. Jackson	570	.382	12	121	314	14	12	2	2.3	.965							
	C	R. Schalk	485	.270	1	61	**581**	138	10	**19**	4.8	**.986**							
	OF	A. Strunk	183	.230	1	14	96	3	2		2.1	.980*							
New York W-95 L-59 Miller Huggins	1B	W. Pipp	610	.280	11	76	**1649**	100	15	**101**	**11.5**	.991	C. Mays	45	312	26	11	2	3.06
	2B	D. Pratt	574	.314	4	97	354	**515**	26	**77**	5.8	.971	B. Shawkey	38	268	20	13	2	**2.45**
	SS	Peckinpaugh	534	.270	8	54	263	441	28	56	5.3	.962	J. Quinn	41	253	18	10	3	3.20
	3B	A. Ward	496	.256	11	54	132	303	16	23	**4.0**	.965	R. Collins	36	187	14	8	1	3.17
	RF	B. Ruth	458	.376	**54**	**137**	259	21	19	3	2.2	.936	Thormahlen	29	143	9	6	1	4.14
	CF	P. Bodie	471	.295	7	79	264	12	9	2	2.2	.968	G. Mogridge	26	125	5	9	1	4.31
	LF	D. Lewis	365	.271	4	61	182	14	8	1	2.1	.961							
	C	M. Ruel	261	.268	1	15	317	62	6	2	4.8	.984							
	O3	B. Meusel	460	.328	11	83	150	85	20	6		.922							
	C	T. Hannah	259	.247	2	25	308	64	15	1	5.0	.961							

AMERICAN LEAGUE 1920, *cont.*

St. Louis
W-76 L-77

Jimmy Burke

POS	Player	AB	BA	HR	RBI	PO	A	E	DP	TC/G	FA	Pitcher	G	IP	W	L	SV	ERA
1B	G. Sisler	631	.407	19	122	1477	140	16	87	10.6	.990	D. Davis	38	269	18	12	0	3.17
2B	J. Gedeon	606	.292	0	61	365	421	29	75	5.3	.964	U. Shocker	38	246	20	10	5	2.71
SS	W. Gerber	584	.279	2	60	288	513	52	65	5.5	.939	A. Sothoron	36	218	8	15	2	4.70
3B	J. Austin	280	.271	1	32	108	171	17	14	3.9	.943	C. Weilman	30	183	9	13	2	4.47
RF	J. Tobin	593	.341	4	62	293	18	13	1	2.2	.960	B. Burwell	33	113	6	4	4	3.65
CF	B. Jacobson	609	.355	9	122	394	18	9	5	2.7	.979	E. Vangilder	24	105	3	8	0	5.50
LF	K. Williams	521	.307	10	72	331	17	14	6	2.6	.961	B. Bayne	18	100	5	6	0	3.70
C	H. Severeid	422	.277	2	49	480	111	10	11	5.1	.983							
3B	E. Smith	353	.306	3	55	73	146	20	2	3.4	.916							
C	J. Billings	155	.277	0	11	138	36	6	4	4.5	.967							

Boston
W-72 L-81

Ed Barrow

POS	Player	AB	BA	HR	RBI	PO	A	E	DP	TC/G	FA	Pitcher	G	IP	W	L	SV	ERA
1B	S. McInnis	559	.297	2	71	1586	91	7	101	11.4	.996	S. Jones	37	274	13	16	0	3.94
2B	M. McNally	312	.256	0	23	168	233	30	38	5.7	.930	J. Bush	35	244	15	15	1	4.25
SS	E. Scott	569	.269	4	61	330	496	23	64	5.5	.973	H. Pennock	37	242	16	13	2	3.68
3B	E. Foster	386	.259	0	41	99	233	15	20	3.9	.957	H. Harper	27	163	5	14	0	3.04
RF	M. Menosky	532	.297	3	64	281	17	12	2	2.2	.961	W. Hoyt	22	121	6	6	1	4.38
CF	T. Hendryx	363	.328	4	73	208	6	8	1	2.3	.964	A. Russell	16	108	5	6	1	3.01
LF	H. Hooper	536	.312	7	53	263	22	11	2	2.1	.963	E. Myers	12	97	9	1	0	2.13
C	R. Walters	258	.198	0	28	351	94	9	15	5.3	.980	B. Karr	26	92	3	8	1	4.81
CO	W. Schang	387	.305	4	51	377	83	18	8		.962							
3B	O. Vitt	296	.220	1	28	61	148	3	5	3.3	.986							
2B	C. Brady	180	.228	0	12	111	193	8	21	5.9	.974							

Washington
W-68 L-84

Clark Griffith

POS	Player	AB	BA	HR	RBI	PO	A	E	DP	TC/G	FA	Pitcher	G	IP	W	L	SV	ERA
1B	J. Judge	493	.333	5	51	1194	62	10	67	10.2	.992	T. Zachary	44	263	15	16	2	3.77
2B	B. Harris	506	.300	1	68	345	401	33	59	5.8	.958	E. Erickson	39	239	12	16	1	3.84
SS	J. O'Neill	294	.289	1	40	130	251	23	22	5.1	.943	J. Shaw	38	236	11	18	1	4.27
3B	F. Ellerbe	336	.292	0	36	101	167	19	8	3.8	.934	H. Courtney	37	188	8	11	0	4.74
RF	B. Roth	468	.291	9	92	184	15	10	0	1.6	.952	W. Johnson	21	144	8	10	3	3.13
CF	S. Rice	624	.338	3	80	454	24	20	5	3.3	.960	A. Schacht	22	99	6	4	1	4.44
LF	C. Milan	506	.322	3	41	291	15	9	1	2.6	.971	J. Acosta	17	83	5	4	1	4.03
C	P. Gharrity	428	.245	3	44	409	148	20	13	4.8	.965							
UT	H. Shanks	444	.268	4	37	294	154	17	12		.963							
UT	R. Shannon	222	.288	0	30	89	148	18	14		.929							

Detroit
W-61 L-93

Hughie Jennings

POS	Player	AB	BA	HR	RBI	PO	A	E	DP	TC/G	FA	Pitcher	G	IP	W	L	SV	ERA
1B	H. Heilmann	543	.309	9	89	1207	80	19	52	10.7	.985	H. Dauss	38	270	13	21	0	3.56
2B	R. Young	594	.291	0	33	405	436	27	46	5.8	.969	H. Ehmke	38	268	15	18	3	3.29
SS	D. Bush	506	.263	1	33	258	421	45	39	5.2	.938	R. Oldham	39	215	8	13	1	3.85
3B	B. Pinelli	284	.229	0	21	110	183	14	20	4.1	.954	D. Ayers	46	209	7	14	1	3.88
RF	C. Shorten	364	.288	1	40	168	14	2	3	1.9	.989	D. Leonard	28	191	10	17	0	4.33
CF	T. Cobb	428	.334	2	63	246	8	9	2	2.3	.966							
LF	B. Veach	612	.307	11	113	357	26	13	4	2.6	.967							
C	O. Stanage	238	.231	0	17	248	75	14	4	4.3	.958							
OF	I. Flagstead	311	.235	3	35	164	13	6	4	2.2	.967							
3B	B. Jones	265	.249	1	18	80	146	14	7	3.6	.942							
C	E. Ainsmith	186	.231	1	19	219	55	13	4	4.7	.955							
1B	B. Ellison	155	.219	0	21	363	26	1	13	10.3	.997							

Philadelphia
W-48 L-106

Connie Mack

POS	Player	AB	BA	HR	RBI	PO	A	E	DP	TC/G	FA	Pitcher	G	IP	W	L	SV	ERA
1B	I. Griffin	467	.238	0	20	1252	96	13	77	10.8	.990	S. Perry	42	264	11	25	1	3.62
2B	J. Dykes	546	.256	8	35	305	373	32	38	6.6	.955	R. Naylor	42	251	10	23	0	3.47
SS	C. Galloway	298	.201	0	18	184	252	34	22	5.6	.928	S. Harriss	31	192	9	14	0	4.08
3B	F. Thomas	255	.231	1	11	78	140	9	9	3.7	.960	E. Rommel	33	174	7	7	1	2.85
RF	W. Witt	218	.321	1	25	68	2	3	0	1.5	.959	R. Moore	24	133	1	13	0	4.68
CF	F. Welch	360	.258	4	40	194	14	14	4	2.3	.937	D. Keefe	31	130	6	7	0	2.97
LF	T. Walker	585	.268	17	82	318	26	22	5	2.5	.940							
C	C. Perkins	493	.260	5	52	524	179	15	15	4.9	.979							
UT	J. Dugan	491	.322	3	60	225	328	35	48		.940							
OF	A. Strunk	202	.297	0	20	97	2	1	0	1.9	.990*							
OC	G. Myatt	196	.250	0	18	83	22	10	3		.913							

BATTING AND BASE RUNNING LEADERS

Batting Average

G. Sisler, STL	.407
T. Speaker, CLE	.388
J. Jackson, CHI	.382
B. Ruth, NY	.376
E. Collins, CHI	.369

Slugging Average

B. Ruth, NY	.847
G. Sisler, STL	.632
J. Jackson, CHI	.589
T. Speaker, CLE	.562
H. Felsch, CHI	.540

Home Runs

B. Ruth, NY	54
G. Sisler, STL	19
T. Walker, PHI	17
H. Felsch, CHI	14
E. Smith, CLE	12
J. Jackson, CHI	12

Total Bases

G. Sisler, STL	399
B. Ruth, NY	388
J. Jackson, CHI	336
T. Speaker, CLE	310
B. Jacobson, STL	305

Runs Batted In

B. Ruth, NY	137
B. Jacobson, STL	122
G. Sisler, STL	122
J. Jackson, CHI	121
L. Gardner, CLE	118

Stolen Bases

S. Rice, WAS	63
G. Sisler, STL	42
B. Roth, WAS	24
M. Menosky, BOS	23
J. Tobin, STL	21

PITCHING LEADERS

Winning Percentage

J. Bagby, CLE	.721
C. Mays, NY	.703
D. Kerr, CHI	.700
E. Cicotte, CHI	.677
R. Caldwell, CLE	.667
U. Shocker, STL	.667

Earned Run Average

B. Shawkey, NY	2.45
S. Coveleski, CLE	2.49
U. Shocker, STL	2.71
J. Bagby, CLE	2.89
R. Faber, CHI	2.99

Wins

J. Bagby, CLE	31
C. Mays, NY	26
S. Coveleski, CLE	24
R. Faber, CHI	23
L. Williams, CHI	22

Saves

D. Kerr, CHI	5
U. Shocker, STL	5
B. Burwell, STL	4
W. Johnson, WAS	3
J. Quinn, NY	3
H. Ehmke, DET	3

Strikeouts

S. Coveleski, CLE	133
L. Williams, CHI	128
B. Shawkey, NY	126
R. Faber, CHI	108
U. Shocker, STL	107

Complete Games

J. Bagby, CLE	30
E. Cicotte, CHI	28
R. Faber, CHI	28
S. Coveleski, CLE	26
C. Mays, NY	26
L. Williams, CHI	26

AMERICAN LEAGUE 1920, cont.

BATTING AND BASE RUNNING LEADERS

Hits		Base on Balls		Home Run Percentage	
G. Sisler, STL	257	B. Ruth, NY	148	B. Ruth, NY	11.8
E. Collins, CHI	222	T. Speaker, CLE	97	G. Sisler, STL	3.0
J. Jackson, CHI	218	H. Hooper, BOS	88	T. Walker, PHI	2.9
B. Jacobson, STL	216	R. Young, DET	85	E. Smith, CLE	2.6

Runs Scored		Doubles		Triples	
B. Ruth, NY	158	T. Speaker, CLE	50	J. Jackson, CHI	20
T. Speaker, CLE	137	G. Sisler, STL	49	G. Sisler, STL	18
G. Sisler, STL	137	J. Jackson, CHI	42	H. Hooper, BOS	17
E. Collins, CHI	113	B. Meusel, NY	40	J. Judge, WAS	15

PITCHING LEADERS

Fewest Hits/9 Innings		Shutouts		Fewest Walks/9 Innings	
S. Coveleski, CLE	8.11	C. Mays, NY	6	W. Johnson, WAS	1.69
U. Shocker, STL	8.21	U. Shocker, STL	5	J. Quinn, NY	1.71
R. Collins, NY	8.22	B. Shawkey, NY	5	S. Coveleski, CLE	1.86
B. Shawkey, NY	8.27	W. Johnson, WAS	4	J. Bagby, CLE	2.09

Most Strikeouts/9 Inn.		Innings		Games Pitched	
W. Johnson, WAS	4.89	J. Bagby, CLE	340	J. Bagby, CLE	48
B. Shawkey, NY	4.24	R. Faber, CHI	319	D. Ayers, DET	46
H. Harper, BOS	3.93	S. Coveleski, CLE	315	C. Mays, NY	45
U. Shocker, STL	3.92	C. Mays, NY	312	D. Kerr, CHI	45

	W	L	PCT	GB	R	OR	2B	3B	HR	BA	SA	SB	E	DP	FA	CG	BB	SO	ShO	SV	ERA
Cleveland	98	56	.636		857	642	301	95	35	.303	.417	73	185	124	.971	93	401	466	10	7	3.41
Chicago	96	58	.623	2	794	665	263	97	35	.295	.402	108	198	142	.968	112	405	440	9	10	3.59
New York	95	59	.617	3	838	629	268	71	115	.280	.426	64	193	129	.970	88	420	480	16	11	3.31
St. Louis	76	77	.497	21.5	797	766	278	84	50	.308	.419	121	232	119	.963	84	578	444	9	14	4.03
Boston	72	81	.471	25.5	650	698	216	71	22	.269	.351	98	183	131	.972	91	461	481	11	6	3.82
Washington	68	84	.447	29	723	802	232	81	36	.290	.386	161	232	95	.963	80	520	418	10	10	4.17
Detroit	61	93	.396	37	652	833	228	72	30	.270	.358	75	229	95	.965	76	561	483	9	7	4.04
Philadelphia	48	106	.312	50	558	834	218	49	44	.252	.337	51	267	126	.959	81	461	423	5	2	3.93
					5869	5869	2004	620	369	.283	.387	751	1719	961	.966	705	3807	3635	79	67	3.79

NATIONAL LEAGUE 1921

New York
W-94 L-59

John McGraw

POS	Player	AB	BA	HR	RBI	PO	A	E	DP	TC/G	FA	Pitcher	G	IP	W	L	SV	ERA
1B	G. Kelly	587	.308	23	122	1552	115	17	132	11.3	.990	A. Nehf	41	261	20	10	1	3.63
2B	J. Rawlings	307	.267	1	30	204*	280*	15*	61*	5.8	.970	J. Barnes	42	259	15	9	6	3.10
SS	D. Bancroft	606	.318	6	67	396	546	39	105	6.4	.960	F. Toney	42	249	18	11	3	3.61
3B	F. Frisch	618	.341	8	100	79	200	19	16	3.2	.936	P. Douglas	40	222	15	10	2	4.22
RF	R. Youngs	504	.327	3	102	122	11	3	3	1.0	.978	R. Ryan	36	147	7	10	3	3.73
CF	G. Burns	605	.299	4	61	360	16	11	2	2.6	.972	S. Sallee	37	96	6	4	2	3.64
LF	I. Meusel	243	.329	2	36	122	10	4	0	2.2	.971							
C	F. Snyder	309	.320	8	45	299	98	6	7	4.0	.985							
C	E. Smith	229	.336	10	51	195	56	9	4	3.3	.965							
OF	C. Walker	192	.286	3	35	247	16	6	5	4.6	.978							
3B	G. Rapp	181	.215	0	15	55	135	12	12	3.6*	.941							

Pittsburgh
W-90 L-63

George Gibson

POS	Player	AB	BA	HR	RBI	PO	A	E	DP	TC/G	FA	Pitcher	G	IP	W	L	SV	ERA
1B	C. Grimm	562	.274	7	71	1517	67	9	93	10.6	.994	W. Cooper	38	327	22	14	0	3.25
2B	G. Cutshaw	350	.340	0	53	196	253	23	36	5.6	.951	W. Glazner	36	234	14	5	1	2.77
SS	Maranville	612	.294	1	70	325	529	34	72	5.8	.962	E. Hamilton	35	225	13	15	0	3.36
3B	C. Barnhart	449	.258	3	62	101	204	14	19	2.7	.956	B. Adams	25	160	14	5	0	2.64
RF	P. Whitted	403	.283	7	63	247	9	3	6	2.5	.988	J. Morrison	21	144	9	7	0	2.88
CF	M. Carey	521	.309	7	56	431	16	20	6	3.4	.957	J. Zinn	32	127	7	6	4	3.68
LF	C. Bigbee	632	.323	3	42	351	27	9	6	2.7	.977	H. Carlson	31	110	4	8	4	4.27
C	W. Schmidt	393	.282	0	38	438	120	8	15	5.1	.986							
23	C. Tierney	442	.299	3	52	191	237	18	37		.960							
OF	D. Robertson	230	.322	6	48	117	2	5	0	2.1	.960							

St. Louis
W-87 L-66

Branch Rickey

POS	Player	AB	BA	HR	RBI	PO	A	E	DP	TC/G	FA	Pitcher	G	IP	W	L	SV	ERA
1B	J. Fournier	574	.343	16	86	1416	73	19	91	10.1	.987	J. Haines	37	244	18	12	0	3.50
2B	R. Hornsby	592	.397	21	126	305	477	25	59	5.7	.969	B. Pertica	38	208	14	10	2	3.37
SS	D. Lavan	560	.259	2	82	382	540	49	88	6.5	.950	B. Doak	32	209	15	6	1	2.59
3B	M. Stock	587	.307	3	84	148	243	25	21	2.8	.940	R. Walker	38	171	11	12	3	4.22
RF	J. Smith	411	.328	7	33	179	11	9	3	1.9	.955	B. Sherdel	38	144	9	8	1	3.18
CF	L. Mann	256	.328	7	30	174	11	6	2	2.4	.969	J. Pfeffer	18	99	9	3	0	4.29
LF	A. McHenry	574	.350	17	102	371	13	14	3	2.6	.965	L. North	40	86	4	4	7	3.54
C	V. Clemons	341	.320	2	48	357	101	7	12	4.3	.985							
OF	J. Schultz	275	.309	6	45	120	7	3	4	1.9	.977							
OF	H. Mueller	176	.352	1	34	117	5	3	1	2.3	.976							
C	Dillhoefer	162	.241	0	15	170	52	11	0	3.4	.953							
OF	C. Heathcote	156	.244	0	9	83	5	7	0	1.9	.926							

Boston
W-79 L-74

Fred Mitchell

POS	Player	AB	BA	HR	RBI	PO	A	E	DP	TC/G	FA	Pitcher	G	IP	W	L	SV	ERA
1B	W. Holke	579	.261	3	63	1471	86	4	100	10.4	.997	J. Oeschger	46	299	20	14	0	3.52
2B	H. Ford	555	.279	2	61	297	417	20	48	6.2	.973	M. Watson	44	259	14	13	0	3.85
SS	W. Barbare	550	.302	0	49	294	393	31	58	5.9	.957	McQuillan	45	250	13	17	5	4.00
3B	T. Boeckel	592	.313	10	84	184	276	33	19	3.2	.933	D. Fillingim	44	240	15	10	1	3.45
RF	Southworth	569	.308	7	79	288	25	8	6	2.3	.975	J. Scott	47	234	15	13	3	3.70
CF	R. Powell	624	.306	12	74	377	21	19	3	2.8	.954							
LF	W. Cruise	344	.346	8	55	232	2	9	3	2.4	.963							
C	M. O'Neil	277	.249	2	29	276	117	13	8	4.3	.968							
OF	F. Nicholson	245	.327	5	41	112	4	2	0	2.0	.983							
C	H. Gowdy	164	.299	2	17	162	50	4	3	4.1	.981							

NATIONAL LEAGUE 1921, *cont.*

	POS	Player	AB	BA	HR	RBI	PO	A	E	DP	TC/G	FA	Pitcher	G	IP	W	L	SV	ERA
Brooklyn	1B	R. Schmandt	350	.306	1	43	941	52	11	74	10.9	.989	B. Grimes	37	302	**22**	13	0	2.83
	2B	P. Kilduff	372	.288	3	45	243	379	24	57	6.2	.963	D. Ruether	36	211	10	13	2	4.26
W-77 L-75	SS	I. Olson	652	.267	3	35	343	465	49	77	6.4	.943	L. Cadore	35	212	13	14	0	4.17
	3B	J. Johnston	624	.325	5	56	162	312	33	34	3.4	.935	C. Mitchell	37	190	11	9	2	2.89
Wilbert Robinson	RF	T. Griffith	455	.312	12	71	215	27	7	5	2.0	.972	S. Smith	35	175	7	11	4	3.90
	CF	H. Myers	549	.288	4	68	278	25	10	5	2.5	.968	J. Miljus	28	94	6	3	1	4.23
	LF	Z. Wheat	568	.320	14	85	283	18	11	3	2.1	.965							
	C	O. Miller	286	.234	1	27	338	107	13	10	5.0	.972							
	OF	B. Neis	230	.257	4	34	126	13	8	1	1.9	.946							
	1B	E. Konetchy	197	.269	3	23	564	28	8*	41	11.1*	.987							
	C	E. Krueger	163	.264	3	20	179	39	7	4	4.3	.969							
Cincinnati	1B	J. Daubert	516	.306	2	64	1290	78	10	98	10.1	.993	D. Luque	41	304	17	19	3	3.38
	2B	S. Bohne	613	.285	3	44	256	327	16	56	5.9	**.973**	E. Rixey	40	301	19	18	1	2.78
W-70 L-83	SS	L. Kopf	367	.218	1	25	195	304	28	39	5.7	.947	R. Marquard	39	266	17	14	0	3.39
	3B	H. Groh	357	.331	0	48	97	188	15	27	3.1	.950	P. Donohue	21	118	7	6	1	3.35
Pat Moran	RF	R. Bressler	323	.307	1	54	155	6	8	2	2.0	.953	L. Brenton	17	60	1	8	1	4.05
	CF	E. Roush	418	.352	4	71	286	9	6	0	2.8	.980							
	LF	P. Duncan	532	.308	2	60	349	19	11	2	2.6	.971							
	C	I. Wingo	295	.268	3	38	318	101	18	11	4.8	.959							
	UT	L. Fonseca	297	.276	1	41	307	155	14	30		.971							
	C	B. Hargrave	263	.289	1	38	270	50	9	2	4.5	.973							
	OF	G. Neale	241	.241	0	12	128	7	5	2	2.3	.964							
	SS	S. Crane	215	.233	0	16	129	173	15	32	5.0	.953							
Chicago	1B	R. Grimes	530	.321	6	79	1544	68	12	93	11.0	.993	G. Alexander	31	252	15	13	1	3.39
	2B	Z. Terry	488	.275	2	45	272	413	20	57	5.7	.972	S. Martin	37	217	11	15	1	4.35
W-64 L-89	SS	C. Hollocher	558	.289	3	37	282	491	30	72	5.9	**.963**	B. Freeman	38	177	9	10	3	4.11
	3B	C. Deal	422	.289	3	66	122	239	10	19	3.3	**.973**	V. Cheeves	37	163	11	12	0	4.64
Johnny Evers	RF	M. Flack	572	.301	6	37	244	19	3	2	2.0	**.989**	L. York	40	139	5	9	1	4.73
W-41 L-55	CF	G. Maisel	393	.310	0	43	259	12	6	2	2.6	.978	H. Vaughn	17	109	3	11	0	6.01
	LF	T. Barber	452	.314	1	54	234	23	8	4	2.2	.970							
Bill Killefer	C	B. O'Farrell	260	.250	4	32	269	87	12	8	4.1	.967							
W-23 L-34	UT	J. Kelleher	301	.309	4	47	192	194	15	31		.963							
	OF	J. Sullivan	240	.329	4	41	122	3	5	0	2.0	.962							
	OF	B. Twombly	175	.377	1	18	81	11	3	0	2.1	.968							
	C	T. Daly	143	.238	0	22	171	48	6	10	4.8	.973							
Philadelphia	1B	E. Konetchy	268	.321	8	59	771	55	12*	38	11.8*	.986	J. Ring	34	246	10	19	1	4.24
	2B	J. Smith	247	.231	4	22	125	239	11	19	5.7	.971	G. Smith	39	221	4	**20**	1	4.76
W-51 L-103	SS	F. Parkinson	391	.253	5	32	233	404	47	55	6.5	.931	B. Hubbell	36	220	9	16	2	4.33
	3B	Wrightstone	372	.296	9	51	58	108	14	6	3.3	.922	L. Meadows	28	194	11	16	0	4.31
Wild Bill Donovan	RF	LeBourveau	281	.295	6	35	126	7	13	2	1.9	.911	J. Winters	18	114	5	10	0	3.63
W-25 L-62	CF	C. Williams	562	.320	18	75	382	29	9	5	2.9	.979	H. Betts	32	101	3	7	4	4.47
	LF	I. Meusel	343	.353	12	51	153	18	13	4	2.2	.929							
Kaiser Wilhelm	C	F. Bruggy	277	.310	5	28	231	73	15	14	3.7	.953							
W-26 L-41	3I	D. Miller	320	.297	0	23	433	96	18	35		.967							
	1O	C. Lee	286	.308	4	29	542	22	10	35		.983							
	2B	J. Rawlings	254	.291	1	16	138*	215*	17*	32*	6.2	.954							
	OF	L. King	216	.269	4	32	115	8	12	0	2.4	.911							
	SS	R. Miller	204	.304	3	26	91	132	22	20	5.3	.910							
	3B	G. Rapp	202	.277	1	10	62	90	8	7	3.2*	.950							
	C	J. Peters	155	.290	3	23	116	24	10	0	3.4	.933							

BATTING AND BASE RUNNING LEADERS

Batting Average
R. Hornsby, STL .397
E. Roush, CIN .352
A. McHenry, STL .350
W. Cruise, BOS .346
J. Fournier, STL .343

Slugging Average
R. Hornsby, STL .639
A. McHenry, STL .531
G. Kelly, NY .528
I. Meusel, NY, PHI .515
J. Fournier, STL .505

Home Runs
G. Kelly, NY 23
R. Hornsby, STL 21
C. Williams, PHI 18
A. McHenry, STL 17
J. Fournier, STL 16

Winning Percentage
B. Doak, STL .714
A. Nehf, NY .667
B. Grimes, BKN .629
B. Barnes, NY .625
F. Toney, NY .621

PITCHING LEADERS

Earned Run Average
B. Doak, STL 2.59
B. Adams, PIT 2.64
W. Glazner, PIT 2.77
E. Rixey, CIN 2.78
B. Grimes, BKN 2.83

Wins
B. Grimes, BKN 22
W. Cooper, PIT 22
A. Nehf, NY 20
J. Oeschger, BOS 20
E. Rixey, CIN 19

Total Bases
R. Hornsby, STL 378
G. Kelly, NY 310
A. McHenry, STL 305
I. Meusel, NY, PHI 302
F. Frisch, NY 300

Runs Batted In
R. Hornsby, STL 126
G. Kelly, NY 122
R. Youngs, NY 102
A. McHenry, STL 102
F. Frisch, NY 100

Stolen Bases
F. Frisch, NY 49
M. Carey, PIT 37
J. Johnston, BKN 28
S. Bohne, CIN 26
Maranville, PIT 25

Saves
L. North, STL 7
J. Barnes, NY 6
McQuillan, BOS 5

Strikeouts
B. Grimes, BKN 136
W. Cooper, PIT 134
D. Luque, CIN 102
McQuillan, BOS 94

Complete Games
B. Grimes, BKN 30
W. Cooper, PIT 29
D. Luque, CIN 25
G. Alexander, CHI 21
J. Ring, PHI 21
E. Rixey, CIN 21

Hits
R. Hornsby, STL 235
F. Frisch, NY 211
C. Bigbee, PIT 204
J. Johnston, BKN 203

Base on Balls
G. Burns, NY 80
R. Youngs, NY 71
M. Carey, PIT 70
R. Grimes, CHI 70

Home Run Percentage
G. Kelly, NY 3.9
R. Hornsby, STL 3.5
C. Williams, PHI 3.2
A. McHenry, STL 3.0

Fewest Hits/9 Innings
J. Morrison, PIT 8.19
W. Glazner, PIT 8.23
B. Adams, PIT 8.72
J. Oeschger, BOS 9.12

Shutouts
7 tied with 3

Fewest Walks/9 Innings
B. Adams, PIT 1.01
G. Alexander, CHI 1.18
J. Barnes, NY 1.53
B. Hubbell, PHI 1.55

NATIONAL LEAGUE 1921, *cont.*

BATTING AND BASE RUNNING LEADERS

Runs Scored		Doubles		Triples	
R. Hornsby, STL	131	R. Hornsby, STL	44	R. Hornsby, STL	18
D. Bancroft, NY	121	G. Kelly, NY	42	R. Powell, BOS	18
F. Frisch, NY	121	J. Johnston, BKN	41	C. Grimm, PIT	17
R. Powell, BOS	114	R. Grimes, CHI	38	F. Frisch, NY	17

PITCHING LEADERS

Most Strikeouts/9 Inn.		Innings		Games Pitched	
B. Grimes, BKN	4.05	W. Cooper, PIT	327	J. Scott, BOS	47
W. Cooper, PIT	3.69	D. Luque, CIN	304	J. Oeschger, BOS	46
B. Doak, STL	3.58	B. Grimes, BKN	302	McQuillan, BOS	45
S. Martin, CHI	3.56	E. Rixey, CIN	301	M. Watson, BOS	44

	W	L	PCT	GB	R	OR	Batting 2B	3B	HR	BA	SA	SB	Fielding E	DP	FA	Pitching CG	BB	SO	ShO	SV	ERA
New York	94	59	.614		840	637	237	93	75	.298	.421	**137**	187	**155**	.971	71	295	357	9	**18**	3.55
Pittsburgh	90	63	.588	4	692	**595**	231	**104**	37	.285	.387	134	172	129	.973	**88**	322	**500**	10	10	**3.17**
St. Louis	87	66	.569	7	809	681	**260**	88	83	**.308**	**.437**	94	219	130	.965	71	399	464	10	16	3.62
Boston	79	74	.516	15	721	697	209	100	61	.290	.400	94	199	122	.969	74	420	382	**11**	12	3.90
Brooklyn	77	75	.507	16.5	667	681	209	85	59	.280	.386	91	232	142	.964	82	361	471	8	12	3.70
Cincinnati	70	83	.458	24	618	649	221	94	20	.278	.370	117	193	139	.969	83	305	408	7	9	3.46
Chicago	64	89	.418	30	668	773	234	56	37	.292	.378	70	**166**	129	**.974**	73	409	441	7	7	4.39
Philadelphia	51	103	.331	43.5	617	919	238	50	**88**	.284	.397	66	295	127	.955	82	371	333	5	8	4.48
					5632	5632	1839	670	460	.289	.397	803	1663	1073	.967	624	2882	3356	67	92	3.78

AMERICAN LEAGUE 1921

New York
W-98 L-55

Miller Huggins

POS	Player	AB	BA	HR	RBI	PO	A	E	DP	TC/G	FA	Pitcher	G	IP	W	L	SV	ERA
1B	W. Pipp	588	.296	8	97	1624	89	16	116	11.3	.991	C. Mays	**49**	337	**27**	9	7	3.05
2B	A. Ward	556	.306	5	75	262	409	26	35	5.7	.963	W. Hoyt	43	282	19	13	3	3.09
SS	Peckinpaugh	577	.288	8	71	318	443	42	75	5.4	.948	B. Shawkey	38	245	18	12	2	4.08
3B	F. Baker	330	.294	9	71	84	173	11	16	3.2	.959	R. Collins	28	137	11	5	0	5.44
RF	B. Meusel	598	.318	24	135	253	**28**	20	8	2.0	.934	J. Quinn	33	129	8	7	0	3.48
CF	E. Miller	242	.298	4	36	134	10	8	2	2.7	.947							
LF	B. Ruth	540	.378	59	171	348	17	13	6	2.5	.966							
C	W. Schang	424	.316	6	55	500	101	19	13	4.7	.969							
3B	M. McNally	215	.260	1	24	54	131	5	5	4.0	.974							
OF	C. Fewster	207	.280	1	19	71	5	2	1	1.8	.974							
P	C. Mays	143	.343	2	22	8	104	2	4	2.3	.982							

Cleveland
W-94 L-60

Tris Speaker

POS	Player	AB	BA	HR	RBI	PO	A	E	DP	TC/G	FA	Pitcher	G	IP	W	L	SV	ERA
1B	D. Johnston	384	.297	2	44	960	62	12	72	8.9	.988	S. Coveleski	43	316	23	13	2	3.36
2B	Wambsganss	410	.285	2	46	268	255	20	51	5.3	.963	G. Uhle	41	238	16	13	2	4.01
SS	J. Sewell	572	.318	4	91	319	480	47	75	5.5	.944	D. Mails	34	194	14	8	2	3.94
3B	L. Gardner	586	.319	3	115	179	**335**	27	23	3.6	.950	J. Bagby	40	192	14	12	4	4.70
RF	E. Smith	431	.290	16	84	183	16	6	1	1.6	.971	R. Caldwell	37	147	6	6	4	4.90
CF	T. Speaker	506	.362	3	74	345	15	6	2	2.9	**.984**	A. Sothoron	22	145	12	4	0	3.24
LF	C. Jamieson	536	.310	1	45	277	17	8	3	2.2	.974	G. Morton	30	108	8	3	0	2.76
C	S. O'Neill	335	.322	1	50	393	92	9	8	4.7	.982							
1B	G. Burns	244	.361	0	48	534	41	6	40	8.0	.990							
2B	Stephenson	206	.330	2	34	122	153	17	30	5.4	.942							
OF	S. Wood	194	.366	4	60	105	3	3	1	1.7	.973							
OF	J. Evans	153	.333	0	21	90	8	7	2	2.2	.933							
C	L. Nunamaker	131	.359	0	24	166	31	6	3	4.4	.970							

St. Louis
W-81 L-73

Lee Fohl

POS	Player	AB	BA	HR	RBI	PO	A	E	DP	TC/G	FA	Pitcher	G	IP	W	L	SV	ERA
1B	G. Sisler	582	.371	11	104	1267	108	10	86	10.0	.993	U. Shocker	47	327	**27**	12	4	3.55
2B	M. McManus	412	.260	3	64	212	269	24	44	5.3	.952	D. Davis	40	265	16	16	0	4.44
SS	W. Gerber	436	.278	2	48	269	331	36	60	5.6	.943	E. Vangilder	31	180	11	12	0	3.94
3B	F. Ellerbe	430	.288	0	48	158	226	19	9	3.8	.953	R. Kolp	37	167	8	7	0	4.97
RF	J. Tobin	**671**	.352	8	59	277	**28**	14	5	2.1	.956	B. Bayne	47	164	11	5	3	4.72
CF	B. Jacobson	599	.352	5	69	375	7	7	1	2.8	.982	E. Palmero	24	90	4	7	0	5.00
LF	K. Williams	547	.347	24	117	331	24	**26**	3	2.6	.932							
C	H. Severeid	472	.324	2	78	481	117	17	11	4.9	.972							
S2	D. Lee	180	.167	0	11	138	151	19	30		.938							

Washington
W-80 L-73

George McBride

POS	Player	AB	BA	HR	RBI	PO	A	E	DP	TC/G	FA	Pitcher	G	IP	W	L	SV	ERA
1B	J. Judge	622	.301	7	72	1417	89	6	109	9.9	.996	G. Mogridge	38	288	18	14	0	3.00
2B	B. Harris	584	.289	0	54	407	481	38	**91**	6.0	.959	W. Johnson	35	264	17	14	1	3.51
SS	F. O'Rourke	444	.234	3	54	272	378	**55**	52	5.8	.922	T. Zachary	39	250	18	16	1	3.96
3B	H. Shanks	562	.302	7	69	**218**	330	23	35	3.7	**.960**	E. Erickson	32	179	8	10	0	3.62
RF	C. Milan	406	.288	1	40	196	19	16	2	2.4	.931	H. Courtney	30	133	6	9	1	5.63
CF	S. Rice	561	.330	4	79	380	18	15	3	**2.9**	.964	J. Acosta	33	116	5	4	3	4.36
LF	B. Miller	420	.288	9	71	247	13	15	4	2.5	.945	A. Schacht	29	83	6	6	1	4.90
C	P. Gharrity	387	.310	7	55	408	110	12	14	4.6	.977							
OF	F. Brower	203	.261	1	35	88	10	9	3	2.3	.916							
OF	E. Smith	180	.217	2	12	84	10	5	2	2.3	.949							

AMERICAN LEAGUE 1921, *cont.*

	POS	Player	AB	BA	HR	RBI	PO	A	E	DP	TC/G	FA	Pitcher	G	IP	W	L	SV	ERA
Boston	1B	S. McInnis	584	.307	0	74	1549	102	1	109	10.9	**.999**	S. Jones	40	299	23	16	1	3.22
	2B	D. Pratt	521	.324	5	100	283	408	28	90	5.4	.961	J. Bush	37	254	16	9	1	3.50
W-75 L-79	SS	E. Scott	576	.262	1	60	**380**	**528**	26	94	6.1	.972	H. Pennock	32	223	12	14	0	4.04
	3B	E. Foster	412	.284	0	30	74	189	16	18	3.0	.943	A. Russell	39	173	7	11	3	4.11
Hugh Duffy	RF	S. Collins	542	.286	4	65	264	22	10	8	2.1	.966	E. Myers	30	172	8	12	0	4.87
	CF	N. Leibold	467	.306	0	30	283	15	16	9	2.7	.949	B. Karr	26	118	8	7	0	3.67
	LF	M. Menosky	477	.300	3	43	278	12	9	3	2.2	.970							
	C	M. Ruel	358	.277	1	43	375	86	11	7	4.3	.977							
	3B	O. Vitt	232	.190	0	12	63	138	8	14	2.9	.962							
	C	R. Walters	169	.201	0	13	232	53	3	11	5.3	.990							
	OF	T. Hendryx	137	.241	0	21	66	2	3	0	1.7	.958							
Detroit	1B	L. Blue	585	.308	5	75	1478	85	16	75	10.4	.990	D. Leonard	36	245	11	13	1	3.75
	2B	R. Young	401	.299	0	29	285	270	31	44	5.5	.947	H. Dauss	32	233	10	15	1	4.33
W-71 L-82	SS	D. Bush	402	.281	0	27	172	260	23	35	5.6	.949	R. Oldham	40	229	11	14	1	4.24
	3B	B. Jones	554	.303	1	72	194	324	**27**	12	3.9	.950	H. Ehmke	30	196	13	14	0	4.54
	RF	H. Heilmann	602	**.394**	19	139	233	10	10	1	1.8	.960	C. Holling	35	136	3	7	4	4.30
Ty Cobb	CF	T. Cobb	507	.389	12	101	301	27	10	2	2.8	.970	J. Middleton	38	122	6	11	7	5.03
	LF	B. Veach	612	.338	16	128	**384**	21	11	4	2.8	.974	B. Cole	20	110	7	4	1	4.27
	C	J. Bassler	388	.307	0	56	433	113	14	7	4.9	.975							
	SS	I. Flagstead	259	.305	0	31	111	139	27	8	5.0	.903							
	OF	C. Shorten	217	.272	0	23	101	3	2	2	2.0	.981							
	UT	J. Sargent	178	.253	2	22	112	134	21	21		.921							
Chicago	1B	E. Sheely	563	.304	11	95	**1637**	119	22	121	11.5	.988	R. Faber	43	331	25	15	1	**2.48**
	2B	E. Collins	526	.337	2	58	376	458	28	84	6.3	**.968**	D. Kerr	44	309	19	17	1	4.72
W-62 L-92	SS	E. Johnson	613	.295	1	51	291	494	44	80	5.9	.947	R. Wilkinson	36	198	4	20	3	5.13
	3B	E. Mulligan	609	.251	1	45	162	307	22	28	3.2	.955	S. Hodge	36	143	6	8	2	6.56
Kid Gleason	RF	H. Hooper	419	.327	8	58	182	12	5	3	1.8	.975	D. McWeeny	27	98	3	6	2	6.08
	CF	A. Strunk	401	.332	3	69	214	10	7	2	1.1	.970	D. Mulrenan	12	56	2	8	0	7.23
	LF	B. Falk	585	.285	5	82	288	9	13	5	2.1	.958							
	C	R. Schalk	416	.252	0	47	453	129	9	**19**	4.7	**.985**							
	OF	J. Mostil	326	.301	3	42	215	12	13	1	2.6	.946							
	UT	McClellan	196	.179	1	14	112	141	8	23		.969							
Philadelphia	1B	J. Walker	423	.258	2	45	1008	49	12	71	10.8	.989	E. Rommel	46	285	16	**23**	3	3.94
	2B	J. Dykes	613	.274	17	77	**434**	**522**	46	88	6.5	.954	S. Harriss	39	228	11	16	2	4.27
W-53 L-100	SS	C. Galloway	465	.265	3	47	205	305	43	52	5.0	.922	R. Moore	29	192	10	10	0	4.51
	3B	J. Dugan	461	.295	10	58	118	208	16	19	2.9	.953	B. Hasty	35	179	5	16	0	4.87
Connie Mack	RF	W. Witt	629	.315	4	45	288	15	13	3	2.1	.959	D. Keefe	44	173	2	9	1	4.68
	CF	F. Welch	403	.285	7	45	251	16	16	1	2.7	.943	R. Naylor	32	169	3	13	0	4.84
	LF	T. Walker	556	.304	23	101	337	24	17	3	2.7	.955	S. Perry	12	70	3	6	1	4.11
	C	C. Perkins	538	.288	12	73	**540**	**137**	**20**	16	**4.9**	.971							
	1B	F. Brazill	177	.271	0	19	340	22	6	28	10.2	.984							
	SS	E. McCann	157	.223	0	15	55	93	8	12	4.9	.949							

BATTING AND BASE RUNNING LEADERS

Batting Average
H. Heilmann, DET	.394
T. Cobb, DET	.389
B. Ruth, NY	.378
G. Sisler, STL	.371
T. Speaker, CLE	.362

Slugging Average
B. Ruth, NY	.846
H. Heilmann, DET	.606
T. Cobb, DET	.596
K. Williams, STL	.561
B. Meusel, NY	.559

Home Runs
B. Ruth, NY	59
K. Williams, STL	24
B. Meusel, NY	24
T. Walker, PHI	23
H. Heilmann, DET	19

Total Bases
B. Ruth, NY	457
H. Heilmann, DET	365
B. Meusel, NY	334
J. Tobin, STL	327
B. Veach, DET	324

Runs Batted In
B. Ruth, NY	171
H. Heilmann, DET	139
B. Meusel, NY	135
B. Veach, DET	128
K. Williams, STL	117

Stolen Bases
G. Sisler, STL	35
B. Harris, WAS	29
S. Rice, WAS	25
T. Cobb, DET	22
E. Johnson, CHI	22

Hits
H. Heilmann, DET	237
J. Tobin, STL	236
G. Sisler, STL	216
B. Jacobson, STL	211

Base on Balls
B. Ruth, NY	144
L. Blue, DET	103
Peckinpaugh, NY	84
J. Sewell, CLE	80

Home Run Percentage
B. Ruth, NY	10.9
K. Williams, STL	4.4
T. Walker, PHI	4.1
B. Meusel, NY	4.0

Runs Scored
B. Ruth, NY	177
J. Tobin, STL	132
Peckinpaugh, NY	128
G. Sisler, STL	125

Doubles
T. Speaker, CLE	52
B. Ruth, NY	44
H. Heilmann, DET	43
B. Veach, DET	43

Triples
H. Shanks, WAS	19
G. Sisler, STL	18
J. Tobin, STL	18
T. Cobb, DET	16

PITCHING LEADERS

Winning Percentage
C. Mays, NY	.750
U. Shocker, STL	.692
J. Bush, STL	.640
S. Coveleski, CLE	.639
R. Faber, CHI	.625

Earned Run Average
R. Faber, CHI	2.48
G. Mogridge, WAS	3.00
C. Mays, NY	3.05
W. Hoyt, NY	3.09
S. Jones, BOS	3.22

Wins
C. Mays, NY	27
U. Shocker, STL	27
C. Mays, NY	25
S. Coveleski, CLE	23
S. Jones, BOS	23

Saves
J. Middleton, DET	7
C. Mays, NY	7
J. Bagby, CLE	4
R. Caldwell, CLE	4
U. Shocker, STL	4
C. Holling, DET	4

Strikeouts
W. Johnson, WAS	143
U. Shocker, STL	132
B. Shawkey, NY	126
R. Faber, CHI	124
D. Leonard, DET	120

Complete Games
R. Faber, CHI	32
U. Shocker, STL	31
C. Mays, NY	30
S. Coveleski, CLE	29

Fewest Hits/9 Innings
R. Faber, CHI	7.97
J. Bush, BOS	8.63
C. Mays, NY	8.88
B. Shawkey, NY	9.00

Shutouts
S. Jones, BOS	5
G. Mogridge, WAS	4
R. Faber, CHI	4
U. Shocker, STL	4

Fewest Walks/9 Innings
C. Mays, NY	2.03
G. Mogridge, WAS	2.06
J. Bagby, CLE	2.07
T. Zachary, WAS	2.12

Most Strikeouts/9 Inn.
W. Johnson, WAS	4.87
B. Shawkey, NY	4.63
D. Leonard, DET	4.41
D. Mails, CLE	4.03

Innings
C. Mays, NY	337
R. Faber, CHI	331
U. Shocker, STL	327
S. Coveleski, CLE	316

Games Pitched
C. Mays, NY	49
U. Shocker, STL	47
B. Bayne, STL	47
E. Rommel, PHI	46

AMERICAN LEAGUE 1921, *cont.*

	W	L	PCT	GB	R	OR	2B	3B	HR	BA	SA	SB	E	DP	FA	CG	BB	SO	ShO	SV	ERA
										Batting				Fielding				Pitching			
New York	98	55	.641		**948**	708	285	87	**134**	.300	**.464**	89	222	138	.965	**92**	470	**481**	7	15	**3.79**
Cleveland	94	60	.610	4.5	925	712	**355**	90	42	.308	.430	58	204	124	.967	81	**430**	475	11	14	3.90
St. Louis	81	73	.526	17.5	835	845	246	**106**	66	.304	.425	92	224	127	.964	79	557	478	9	9	4.62
Washington	80	73	.523	18	704	738	240	96	42	.277	.383	**111**	235	153	.963	80	442	452	8	10	3.97
Boston	75	79	.487	23.5	668	**696**	248	69	17	.277	.361	83	**157**	151	**.975**	88	452	446	9	5	3.98
Detroit	71	82	.464	27	883	852	268	100	58	**.316**	.433	95	232	107	.963	73	495	452	4	**17**	4.40
Chicago	62	92	.403	36.5	683	858	242	82	35	.283	.379	97	200	**155**	.969	86	549	392	7	9	4.94
Philadelphia	53	100	.346	45	657	894	256	64	83	.274	.390	68	274	144	.958	75	548	431	1	7	4.60
					6303	6303	2140	694	477	.292	.408	693	1748	1099	.965	654	3943	3607	56	86	4.28

NATIONAL LEAGUE 1922

	POS	Player	AB	BA	HR	RBI	PO	A	E	DP	TC/G	FA	Pitcher	G	IP	W	L	SV	ERA
New York W-93 L-61 John McGraw	1B	G. Kelly	592	.328	17	107	1642	**103**	13	123	**11.6**	.993	A. Nehf	37	268	19	13	1	3.29
	2B	F. Frisch	514	.327	5	51	176	288	12	40	5.6	.975	J. Barnes	37	213	13	8	0	3.51
	SS	D. Bancroft	651	.321	4	60	**405**	579	62	93	6.7	.941	R. Ryan	46	192	17	12	3	**3.01**
	3B	H. Groh	426	.265	3	51	100	207	11	25	2.9	**.965**	P. Douglas	24	158	11	4	0	2.63
	RF	R. Youngs	559	.331	7	86	280	**28**	19	6	2.2	.942	C. Jonnard	33	96	6	1	5	3.84
	CF	C. Stengel	250	.368	7	48	179	7	6	2	2.5	.969	McQuillan	15	94	6	5	1	3.82
	LF	I. Meusel	617	.331	16	132	279	15	6	1	1.9	.980	F. Toney	13	86	5	6	0	4.17
	C	F. Snyder	318	.343	5	51	272	74	7	10	3.6	.980	J. Scott	17	80	8	2	2	4.41
	2B	J. Rawlings	308	.282	1	30	166	252	7	44	5.5	.984							
	C	E. Smith	234	.278	9	39	214	56	6	3	3.7	.978							
	OF	Cunningham	229	.328	2	33	155	7	2	3	2.3	.988							
Cincinnati W-86 L-68 Pat Moran	1B	J. Daubert	610	.336	12	66	**1652**	79	11	**127**	11.2	**.994**	E. Rixey	40	**313**	**25**	13	0	3.53
	2B	S. Bohne	383	.274	3	51	183	320	22	50	6.2	.958	J. Couch	43	264	16	9	1	3.89
	SS	I. Caveney	394	.239	3	54	256	404	41	74	6.0	.934	D. Luque	39	261	13	23	0	3.31
	3B	B. Pinelli	547	.305	1	72	**204**	350	32	19	3.8	.945	P. Donohue	33	242	18	9	1	3.12
	RF	G. Harper	430	.340	2	68	220	15	11	2	2.3	.955	C. Keck	27	131	7	6	1	3.37
	CF	G. Burns	631	.285	1	53	386	20	10	3	2.7	.976							
	LF	P. Duncan	607	.328	8	94	316	19	10	4	2.3	.971							
	C	B. Hargrave	320	.316	7	57	261	60	6	5	3.8	.982							
	2B	L. Fonseca	291	.361	4	45	197	251	14	40	6.5	.970							
	C	I. Wingo	260	.285	3	45	211	81	11	6	3.9	.964							
	OF	E. Roush	165	.352	1	24	96	8	1	0	2.4	.990							
Pittsburgh W-85 L-69 George Gibson W-32 L-33 Bill McKechnie W-53 L-36	1B	C. Grimm	593	.292	0	76	1478	68	10	104	10.1	.994	W. Cooper	41	295	23	14	0	3.18
	2B	C. Tierney	441	.345	7	86	179	302	18	52	4.8	.964	J. Morrison	45	286	17	11	1	3.43
	SS	Maranville	**672**	.295	0	63	359	453	33	81	6.1	.961	W. Glazner	34	193	11	12	1	4.38
	3B	P. Traynor	571	.282	4	81	147	216	21	19	3.1	.945	B. Adams	27	171	8	11	0	3.57
	RF	R. Russell	220	.368	12	75	115	5	4	2	2.1	.968	E. Hamilton	33	160	11	7	2	3.99
	CF	M. Carey	629	.329	10	70	**449**	22	15	4	3.1	.969	H. Carlson	39	145	9	12	2	5.70
	LF	C. Bigbee	614	.350	5	99	345	27	17	5	2.6	.956							
	C	J. Gooch	353	.329	1	42	382	102	15	10	**4.8**	.970							
	3O	C. Barnhart	209	.330	1	38	76	34	8	4		.932							
	C	W. Schmidt	152	.329	0	22	159	22	1		4.6	.995							
	OF	R. Rohwer	129	.295	3	22	56	5	4	1	2.2	.938							
St. Louis W-85 L-69 Branch Rickey	1B	J. Fournier	404	.295	10	61	902	60	18	63	9.0	.982	J. Pfeffer	44	261	19	12	2	3.58
	2B	R. Hornsby	623	**.401**	**42**	**152**	398	473	30	**81**	5.9	**.967**	B. Sherdel	47	241	17	13	2	3.88
	SS	S. Toporcer	352	.324	3	36	168	246	27	31	4.8	.939	J. Haines	29	183	11	9	0	3.84
	3B	M. Stock	581	.305	5	79	172	245	22	22	2.9	.950	B. Doak	37	180	11	13	2	5.54
	RF	M. Flack	267	.292	2	21	116	5	4	3	1.9	.968	L. North	53	150	10	3	4	4.45
	CF	J. Smith	510	.310	8	46	282	11	15	3	2.3	.951	B. Pertica	34	117	8	8	0	5.91
	LF	J. Schultz	344	.314	2	64	195	7	5	1	2.3	.976	C. Barfoot	42	118	4	5	2	4.21
	C	E. Ainsmith	379	.293	13	59	428	99	**20**	14	4.7	.963							
	SS	D. Lavan	264	.227	0	27	169	246	28	40	5.4	.937							
	OF	A. McHenry	238	.303	5	43	132	13	10	3	2.5	.935							
	C	V. Clemons	160	.256	0	15	172	50	1	2	3.5	.996							
	OF	H. Mueller	159	.270	3	26	83	6	5	2	2.1	.947							
	1B	J. Bottomley	151	.325	5	35	346	12	5	20	10.7	.986							
	OF	L. Mann	147	.347	2	20	87	3	2	1	1.6	.978							
	OF	R. Blades	130	.300	3	21	61	6	5	0	2.5	.931							
	1B	D. Gainer	97	.268	2	23	175	9	4	6	7.2	.979							
Chicago W-80 L-74 Bill Killefer	1B	R. Grimes	509	.354	14	99	1378	68	**19**	106	10.6	.987	V. Aldridge	36	258	16	15	0	3.52
	2B	Z. Terry	496	.286	0	67	298	442	28	75	6.1	.964	G. Alexander	33	246	16	13	1	3.63
	SS	C. Hollocher	592	.340	3	69	332	502	30	89	5.7	**.965**	T. Osborne	41	184	9	5	3	4.50
	3B	M. Krug	450	.276	4	65	129	184	21	19	3.2	.937	V. Cheeves	39	183	12	11	2	4.09
	RF	B. Friberg	296	.311	0	23	126	13	4	5	1.9	.972	P. Jones	44	164	8	9	1	4.72
	CF	J. Statz	462	.297	1	34	309	16	14	4	3.1	.959	T. Kaufmann	37	153	7	13	3	4.06
	LF	H. Miller	466	.352	12	78	219	15	10	3	2.1	.959	G. Stueland	35	111	9	4	0	5.92
	C	B. O'Farrell	392	.324	4	60	446	143	14	**22**	4.8	.977							
	OF	C. Heathcote	243	.280	1	34	131	5	2	1	2.3	.986							
	OF	T. Barber	226	.310	0	29	78	4	4	2	1.8	.953							
	3B	J. Kelleher	193	.259	0	20	44	93	10	9	3.2	.932							
	OF	M. Callaghan	175	.257	0	20	85	2	5	0	1.7	.946							

NATIONAL LEAGUE 1922, *cont.*

	POS	Player	AB	BA	HR	RBI	PO	A	E	DP	TC/G	FA	Pitcher	G	IP	W	L	SV	ERA
Brooklyn	1B	R. Schmandt	396	.268	2	44	1017	65	12	83	9.9	.989	D. Ruether	35	267	21	12	0	3.53
	2B	I. Olson	551	.272	1	47	193	283	20	43	5.8	.960	B. Grimes	36	259	17	14	1	4.76
W-76 L-78	SS	J. Johnston	567	.319	4	49	102	189	16	33	6.1	.948	D. Vance	36	246	18	12	0	3.70
	3B	A. High	579	.283	6	65	131	257	17	23	3.1	.958	L. Cadore	29	190	8	15	0	4.35
Wilbert Robinson	RF	T. Griffith	329	.316	4	49	167	13	9	4	2.3	.952	S. Smith	28	109	4	8	2	4.56
	CF	H. Myers	618	.317	6	89	399	16	11	2	2.8	.974	H. Shriver	25	108	4	6	0	2.99
	LF	Z. Wheat	600	.335	16	112	317	14	3	1	2.2	**.991**							
	C	H. DeBerry	259	.301	3	35	309	64	11	5	4.7	.971							
	OF	B. Griffith	325	.308	2	35	148	7	3	3	2.1	.981							
	C	O. Miller	180	.261	1	23	216	56	9	3	4.9	.968							
	1B	C. Mitchell	155	.290	3	28	365	27	3	32	9.4	.992							
	P	D. Ruether	125	.208	2	20	9	56	0	**6**	1.9	1.000							
Philadelphia	1B	R. Leslie	513	.271	6	50	1517	63	16	110	11.5	.990	J. Ring	40	249	12	18	1	4.58
	2B	F. Parkinson	545	.275	15	70	323	**562**	**34**	78	**6.6**	.963	L. Meadows	33	237	12	18	0	4.03
W-57 L-96	SS	A. Fletcher	396	.280	7	53	202	379	38	63	5.8	.939	G. Smith	42	194	5	14	0	4.78
	3B	G. Rapp	502	.253	0	38	117	249	20	20	3.3	.948	B. Hubbell	35	189	7	15	1	5.00
Kaiser Wilhelm	RF	C. Walker	581	.337	12	89	295	24	15	**8**	2.3	.955	L. Weinert	34	167	8	11	1	3.40
	CF	C. Williams	584	.308	26	92	376	19	11	2	2.7	.973	J. Winters	34	138	6	6	2	5.33
	LF	C. Lee	422	.322	17	77	167	10	6	2	2.1	.967	J. Singleton	22	93	1	10	0	5.90
	C	B. Henline	430	.316	14	64	400	113	9	13	4.4	**.983**							
	3S	Wrightstone	331	.305	5	33	109	227	11	25		.968							
	OF	LeBourveau	167	.269	2	20	77	4	7	1	2.1	.920							
	OF	J. Mokan	151	.252	3	27	62	5	7	1	2.4	.905							
	C	J. Peters	143	.245	4	24	118	24	7	3	3.8	.953							
Boston	1B	W. Holke	395	.291	0	46	1017	44	8	65	10.2	.993	M. Watson	41	201	8	14	1	4.70
	2B	L. Kopf	466	.266	1	37	175	243	25	35	5.7	.944	F. Miller	31	200	11	13	1	3.51
W-53 L-100	SS	H. Ford	515	.272	2	60	267	387	32	57	6.0	.953	R. Marquard	39	198	11	15	1	5.09
	3B	T. Boeckel	402	.289	6	47	128	168	15	13	2.9	.952	J. Oeschger	46	196	6	21	1	5.06
Fred Mitchell	RF	W. Cruise	352	.278	4	46	212	9	12	3	2.3	.948	McQuillan	28	136	5	10	0	4.24
	CF	R. Powell	550	.296	6	37	377	18	8	2	3.0	.980	D. Fillingim	25	117	5	9	2	4.54
	LF	A. Nixon	318	.264	2	22	189	6	5	0	2.5	.975							
	C	M. O'Neil	251	.223	0	26	239	70	7	3	4.0	.978							
	UT	W. Barbare	373	.231	0	40	241	238	14	44		.972							
	OF	F. Nicholson	222	.252	2	29	125	5	12	0	2.3	.915							
	C	H. Gowdy	221	.317	1	27	204	63	8	6	3.8	.971							
	C1	F. Gibson	164	.299	3	20	245	28	5	14		.982							
	OF	Southworth	158	.323	4	18	100	7	5	0	2.7	.955							

BATTING AND BASE RUNNING LEADERS

Batting Average		Slugging Average		Home Runs		Winning Percentage		Earned Run Average		Wins	
R. Hornsby, STL	.401	R. Hornsby, STL	.722	R. Hornsby, STL	42	P. Donohue, CIN	.667	R. Ryan, NY	3.01	E. Rixey, CIN	25
R. Grimes, CHI	.354	R. Grimes, CHI	.572	C. Williams, PHI	26	E. Rixey, CIN	.658	P. Donohue, CIN	3.12	W. Cooper, PIT	23
H. Miller, CHI	.352	C. Lee, PHI	.540	C. Lee, PHI	17	J. Couch, CIN	.640	W. Cooper, PIT	3.18	D. Ruether, BKN	21
C. Bigbee, PIT	.350	C. Tierney, PIT	.515	G. Kelly, NY	17	D. Ruether, BKN	.636	A. Nehf, NY	3.29	J. Pfeffer, STL	19
C. Tierney, PIT	.345	C. Williams, PHI	.514	Z. Wheat, BKN	16	W. Cooper, PIT	.622	D. Luque, CIN	3.31	A. Nehf, NY	19
				I. Meusel, NY	16						

Total Bases		Runs Batted In		Stolen Bases		Saves		Strikeouts		Complete Games	
R. Hornsby, STL	450	R. Hornsby, STL	152	M. Carey, PIT	51	C. Jonnard, NY	5	D. Vance, BKN	134	W. Cooper, PIT	27
I. Meusel, NY	314	I. Meusel, NY	132	F. Frisch, NY	31	L. North, STL	4	W. Cooper, PIT	129	D. Ruether, BKN	26
Z. Wheat, BKN	302	Z. Wheat, BKN	112	G. Burns, CIN	30	R. Ryan, NY	3	J. Ring, PHI	116	E. Rixey, CIN	26
C. Williams, PHI	300	G. Kelly, NY	107	C. Bigbee, PIT	24	T. Osborne, CHI	3	J. Morrison, PIT	104		
J. Daubert, CIN	300	R. Grimes, CHI	99	Maranville, PIT	24	T. Kaufmann, CHI	3	B. Grimes, BKN	99		
		C. Bigbee, PIT	99			A. Mamaux, BKN	3				

Hits		Base on Balls		Home Run Percentage		Fewest Hits/9 Innings		Shutouts		Fewest Walks/9 Innings	
R. Hornsby, STL	250	M. Carey, PIT	80	R. Hornsby, STL	6.7	R. Ryan, NY	9.11	D. Vance, BKN	5	B. Adams, PIT	0.79
C. Bigbee, PIT	215	B. O'Farrell, CHI	79	C. Williams, PHI	4.5	D. Luque, CIN	9.17	J. Morrison, PIT	5	G. Alexander, CHI	1.25
D. Bancroft, NY	209	D. Bancroft, NY	79	C. Lee, PHI	4.0	D. Vance, BKN	9.49	B. Adams, PIT	4	E. Rixey, CIN	1.29
M. Carey, PIT	207	G. Burns, CIN	78	E. Ainsmith, STL	3.4	P. Donohue, CIN	9.56	W. Cooper, PIT	4	P. Donohue, CIN	1.60

Runs Scored		Doubles		Triples		Most Strikeouts/9 Inn.		Innings		Games Pitched	
R. Hornsby, STL	141	R. Hornsby, STL	46	J. Daubert, CIN	22	D. Vance, BKN	4.91	E. Rixey, CIN	313	L. North, STL	53
M. Carey, PIT	140	R. Grimes, CHI	45	I. Meusel, NY	17	J. Ring, PHI	4.19	W. Cooper, PIT	295	B. Sherdel, STL	47
J. Smith, STL	117	P. Duncan, CIN	44	C. Bigbee, PIT	15	W. Cooper, PIT	3.94	J. Morrison, PIT	286	J. Oeschger, BOS	46
D. Bancroft, NY	117	D. Bancroft, NY	41	Maranville, PIT	15	W. Glazner, PIT	3.59	A. Nehf, NY	268	R. Ryan, NY	46

PITCHING LEADERS

NATIONAL LEAGUE 1922, *cont.*

	W	L	PCT	GB	R	OR	Batting					SB	Fielding			Pitching					
							2B	3B	HR	BA	SA		E	DP	FA	CG	BB	SO	ShO	SV	ERA
New York	93	61	.604		852	658	253	90	80	.305	.428	116	194	145	.970	73	393	388	7	15	3.45
Cincinnati	86	68	.558	7	766	677	226	99	45	.296	.401	130	205	147	.968	88	326	357	8	3	3.53
Pittsburgh	85	69	.552	8	865	736	239	110	52	.308	.419	145	187	126	.970	88	358	490	15	7	3.98
St. Louis	85	69	.552	8	863	819	280	88	107	.301	.444	73	239	122	.961	60	447	465	8	12	4.44
Chicago	80	74	.519	13	771	808	248	71	42	.293	.390	97	204	154	.968	74	475	402	8	12	4.34
Brooklyn	76	78	.494	17	743	754	235	76	56	.290	.392	79	208	139	.967	82	490	499	12	8	4.05
Philadelphia	57	96	.373	35.5	738	920	268	55	116	.282	.415	48	225	152	.965	73	460	394	6	5	4.64
Boston	53	100	.346	39.5	596	822	162	73	32	.263	.341	67	215	121	.965	62	489	360	7	6	4.37
					6194	6194	1911	662	530	.292	.404	755	1677	1106	.967	600	3438	3355	71	68	4.10

AMERICAN LEAGUE 1922

	POS	Player	AB	BA	HR	RBI	PO	A	E	DP	TC/G	FA	Pitcher	G	IP	W	L	SV	ERA
New York	1B	W. Pipp	577	.329	9	90	1667	88	13	106	11.6	.993	B. Shawkey	39	300	20	12	1	2.91
	2B	A. Ward	558	.267	7	68	358	489	23	73	5.7	.974	W. Hoyt	37	265	19	12	0	3.43
W-94 L-60	SS	E. Scott	557	.269	3	45	302	538	31	74	5.7	.964	S. Jones	45	260	13	13	8	3.67
	3B	J. Dugan	252	.286	3	25	59	117	6	10	3.0	.967	J. Bush	39	255	26	7	3	3.31
Miller Huggins	RF	B. Meusel	473	.319	16	84	202	24	12	0	2.0	.950	C. Mays	34	240	13	14	2	3.60
	CF	W. Witt	528	.297	4	40	312	9	8	1	2.4	.976							
	LF	B. Ruth	406	.315	35	99	225	14	9	3	2.3	.964							
	C	W. Schang	408	.319	1	53	456	102	14	12	4.6	.976							
	3B	F. Baker	234	.278	7	36	68	108	7	7	3.1	.962							
	OF	E. Miller	172	.267	3	18	101	7	2	0	2.2	.982							
St. Louis	1B	G. Sisler	586	.420	8	105	1293	125	17	116	10.2	.988	U. Shocker	48	348	24	17	3	2.97
	2B	M. McManus	606	.312	11	109	398	467	32	103	5.9	.964	E. Vangilder	43	245	19	13	4	3.42
W-93 L-61	SS	W. Gerber	604	.267	1	51	322	470	47	93	5.5	.944	D. Davis	25	174	11	6	0	4.08
	3B	F. Ellerbe	342	.246	1	33	137	224	17	20	4.2	.955	R. Kolp	32	170	14	4	0	3.93
Lee Fohl	RF	J. Tobin	625	.331	13	66	221	15	15	5	1.7	.940	R. Wright	31	154	9	7	5	2.92
	CF	B. Jacobson	555	.317	9	102	367	9	12	3	2.8	.969	H. Pruett	39	120	7	7	7	2.33
	LF	K. Williams	585	.332	39	155	372	16	12	4	2.6	.970	B. Bayne	26	93	4	5	2	4.56
	C	H. Severeid	517	.321	3	78	552	123	11	10	5.1	.984							
	C	P. Collins	127	.307	8	23	129	19	3	4	5.6	.980							
Detroit	1B	L. Blue	584	.300	6	45	1506	75	15	107	11.1	.991	H. Ehmke	45	280	17	17	1	4.22
	2B	G. Cutshaw	499	.267	2	61	334	390	21	69	5.6	.972	H. Pillette	40	275	19	12	1	2.85
W-79 L-75	SS	T. Rigney	536	.300	2	63	262	493	50	74	5.2	.938	H. Dauss	39	219	13	13	4	4.20
	3B	B. Jones	455	.257	3	44	161	267	17	22	3.7	.962	R. Oldham	43	212	10	13	3	4.67
Ty Cobb	RF	H. Heilmann	455	.356	21	92	175	6	10	2	1.7	.953	O. Olsen	37	137	7	6	3	4.53
	CF	T. Cobb	526	.401	4	99	330	14	7	3	2.6	.980	S. Johnson	29	97	7	3	1	3.71
	LF	B. Veach	618	.327	9	126	375	16	7	3	2.6	.982							
	C	J. Bassler	372	.323	0	41	421	113	11	12	4.6	.980							
	3B	F. Haney	213	.352	0	25	43	105	10	11	3.8	.937							
	2B	D. Clark	185	.292	3	26	72	99	10	16	4.8	.945							
	OF	Fothergill	152	.322	0	29	50	2	3	1	1.4	.945							
Cleveland	1B	S. McInnis	537	.305	1	78	1376	73	5	96	10.4	.997	G. Uhle	50	287	22	16	3	4.07
	2B	Wambsganss	538	.262	0	47	297	376	27	72	5.6	.961	S. Coveleski	35	277	17	14	2	3.32
W-78 L-76	SS	J. Sewell	558	.299	2	83	295	462	49	72	5.8	.939	G. Morton	38	203	14	9	0	4.00
	3B	L. Gardner	470	.285	2	68	133	259	20	24	3.2	.951	D. Mails	26	104	4	7	0	5.28
Tris Speaker	RF	S. Wood	505	.297	8	92	247	18	11	5	2.0	.960	J. Bagby	25	98	4	5	1	6.32
	CF	T. Speaker	426	.378	11	71	285	13	5	6	2.8	.983	J. Edwards	25	88	3	8	0	4.70
	LF	C. Jamieson	567	.323	3	57	289	18	7	5	2.2	.978	J. Lindsey	29	84	4	5	1	6.02
	C	S. O'Neill	392	.311	2	65	450	116	15	9	4.5	.974	D. Boone	11	75	4	6	0	4.06
	32	Stephenson	233	.339	2	32	75	135	12	11		.946							
	OF	J. Evans	145	.269	0	22	92	1	3	0	2.0	.969							
Chicago	1B	E. Sheely	526	.317	6	80	1512	103	12	101	10.9	.993	R. Faber	43	353	21	17	2	2.80
	2B	E. Collins	598	.324	1	69	406	451	21	73	5.7	.976	C. Robertson	37	272	14	15	0	3.64
W-77 L-77	SS	E. Johnson	603	.254	0	56	259	468	37	74	5.4	.952	D. Leverett	33	225	13	10	2	3.32
	3B	E. Mulligan	372	.234	0	31	94	200	11	14	3.5	.964	S. Hodge	35	139	7	6	1	4.14
Kid Gleason	RF	H. Hooper	602	.304	11	80	288	19	12	7	2.1	.962	Blankenship	24	128	8	10	1	3.81
	CF	J. Mostil	458	.303	7	70	333	9	12	2	2.7	.966	H. Courtney	18	88	5	6	0	4.93
	LF	B. Falk	483	.298	12	79	253	10	10	2	2.1	.963							
	C	R. Schalk	442	.281	4	60	591	150	8	16	5.3	.989							
	OF	A. Strunk	311	.289	0	33	170	9	2	2	2.4	.989							
	3B	McClellan	301	.226	2	28	77	158	7	15	3.4	.971							

AMERICAN LEAGUE 1922, *cont.*

	POS	Player	AB	BA	HR	RBI	PO	A	E	DP	TC/G	FA	Pitcher	G	IP	W	L	SV	ERA
Washington	1B	J. Judge	591	.294	10	81	1413	101	6	**131**	10.3	.996	W. Johnson	41	280	15	16	4	2.99
	2B	B. Harris	602	.269	2	40	479	483	30	116	**6.4**	.970	G. Mogridge	34	252	18	13	0	3.58
W-69 L-85	SS	Peckinpaugh	520	.254	2	48	265	524	41	93	5.6	.951	R. Francis	39	225	7	18	2	4.28
	3B	B. LaMotte	214	.252	1	23	90	138	11	10	3.9	.954	T. Zachary	32	185	15	10	1	3.12
Clyde Milan	RF	F. Brower	471	.293	9	71	208	9	5	1	1.8	.977	E. Erickson	30	142	4	12	2	4.96
	CF	S. Rice	**633**	.295	6	69	385	23	**21**	3	2.8	.951	Brillheart	31	120	4	6	1	3.61
	LF	G. Goslin	358	.324	3	53	197	8	15	1	2.4	.932	T. Phillips	17	70	3	7	0	4.89
	C	P. Gharrity	273	.256	5	45	282	85	7	9	4.3	.981							
	30	H. Shanks	272	.283	1	32	125	112	16	16		.937							
	C	V. Picinich	210	.229	0	19	273	55	8	4	4.4	.976							
	OF	E. Smith	205	.259	1	23	88	12	9	3	2.2	.917							
Philadelphia	1B	J. Hauser	368	.323	9	43	936	55	14	61	10.7	.986	E. Rommel	**51**	294	**27**	13	2	3.28
	2B	R. Young	470	.223	1	35	302	350	27	53	5.7	.960	S. Harriss	47	230	9	20	3	5.02
W-65 L-89	SS	C. Galloway	571	.324	6	69	321	493	41	76	5.5	.952	B. Hasty	28	193	9	14	4	4.25
	3B	J. Dykes	501	.275	12	68	186	295	28	21	3.6	.945	R. Naylor	35	171	10	15	0	4.73
Connie Mack	RF	F. Welch	375	.259	11	49	191	12	11	2	2.1	.949	F. Heimach	37	172	7	11	1	5.03
	CF	B. Miller	535	.336	21	90	314	19	8	3	2.5	.977							
	LF	T. Walker	565	.283	37	99	309	19	15	4	2.3	.981							
	C	C. Perkins	505	.267	6	69	432	130	9	10	4.0	.984							
	OF	F. McGowan	300	.230	1	20	210	13	8	2	2.8	.965							
	1B	D. Johnston	260	.250	1	29	641	31	7	34	10.4	.990							
Boston	1B	G. Burns	558	.306	12	73	1412	94	**20**	103	10.9	.987	J. Quinn	40	256	13	15	0	3.48
	2B	D. Pratt	607	.301	6	86	362	484	30	80	5.7	.966	R. Collins	32	211	14	11	0	3.76
W-61 L-93	SS	J. Mitchell	203	.251	1	8	98	184	11	31	5.1	.962	H. Pennock	32	202	10	17	1	4.32
	3B	J. Dugan	341	.287	3	38	72	143	13	13	3.6	.943	A. Ferguson	39	198	9	16	2	4.31
Hugh Duffy	RF	S. Collins	472	.271	1	52	245	6	13	1	2.3	.951	B. Karr	41	183	5	12	2	4.47
	CF	J. Harris	408	.316	6	54	186	15	10	2	2.5	.953	A. Russell	34	126	6	7	2	5.01
	LF	M. Menosky	406	.283	1	32	240	14	6	3	2.5	.977	B. Piercy	29	121	3	9	0	4.67
	C	M. Ruel	361	.255	0	28	359	96	10	**17**	4.2	.978							
	OF	N. Leibold	271	.258	1	18	190	10	7	3	2.9	.966							
	OF	E. Smith	231	.286	6	32	117	7	7	3	2.2	.947							
	SS	F. O'Rourke	216	.264	1	17	86	134	22	17	5.0	.909							
	3S	P. Pittenger	186	.258	0	7	88	148	22	19		.915							

BATTING AND BASE RUNNING LEADERS

Batting Average		Slugging Average		Home Runs	
G. Sisler, STL	.420	B. Ruth, NY	.672	K. Williams, STL	39
T. Cobb, DET	.401	K. Williams, STL	.627	T. Walker, PHI	37
T. Speaker, CLE	.378	T. Speaker, CLE	.606	B. Ruth, NY	35
H. Heilmann, DET	.356	H. Heilmann, DET	.598	H. Heilmann, DET	21
B. Miller, PHI	.336	G. Sisler, STL	.594	B. Miller, PHI	21

Total Bases		Runs Batted In		Stolen Bases	
K. Williams, STL	367	K. Williams, STL	155	G. Sisler, STL	51
G. Sisler, STL	348	B. Veach, DET	126	K. Williams, STL	37
T. Walker, PHI	310	M. McManus, STL	109	B. Harris, WAS	25
T. Cobb, DET	297	G. Sisler, STL	105	E. Johnson, CHI	21
B. Miller, PHI	296	B. Jacobson, STL	102	E. Collins, CHI	20
J. Tobin, STL	296			S. Rice, WAS	20

Hits		Base on Balls		Home Run Percentage	
G. Sisler, STL	246	W. Witt, NY	89	B. Ruth, NY	8.6
T. Cobb, DET	211	B. Ruth, NY	84	K. Williams, STL	6.7
J. Tobin, STL	207	L. Blue, DET	82	T. Walker, PHI	6.5
B. Veach, DET	202	T. Speaker, CLE	77	H. Heilmann, DET	4.6

Runs Scored		Doubles		Triples	
G. Sisler, STL	134	T. Speaker, CLE	48	G. Sisler, STL	18
L. Blue, DET	131	D. Pratt, BOS	44	T. Cobb, DET	16
K. Williams, STL	128	T. Cobb, DET	42	B. Jacobson, STL	16
J. Tobin, STL	122	G. Sisler, STL	42	J. Judge, WAS	15

PITCHING LEADERS

Winning Percentage		Earned Run Average		Wins	
J. Bush, NY	.788	R. Faber, CHI	2.80	E. Rommel, PHI	27
E. Rommel, PHI	.675	H. Pillette, DET	2.85	J. Bush, NY	26
B. Shawkey, NY	.625	B. Shawkey, NY	2.91	U. Shocker, STL	24
W. Hoyt, NY	.613	U. Shocker, STL	2.97	G. Uhle, CLE	22
H. Pillette, DET	.613	W. Johnson, WAS	2.99	R. Faber, CHI	21

Saves		Strikeouts		Complete Games	
S. Jones, NY	8	U. Shocker, STL	149	R. Faber, CHI	31
H. Pruett, STL	7	R. Faber, CHI	148	U. Shocker, STL	29
R. Wright, STL	5	B. Shawkey, NY	130	W. Johnson, WAS	23
H. Dauss, DET	4	H. Ehmke, DET	108	G. Uhle, CLE	23
E. Vangilder, STL	4	W. Johnson, WAS	105	E. Rommel, PHI	22
W. Johnson, WAS	4				

Fewest Hits/9 Innings		Shutouts		Fewest Walks/9 Innings	
U. Shocker, STL	6.85	G. Uhle, CLE	5	U. Shocker, STL	1.53
J. Bush, NY	8.46	D. Leverett, CHI	4	E. Vangilder, STL	1.76
R. Faber, CHI	8.52	W. Johnson, WAS	4	C. Mays, NY	1.87
B. Shawkey, NY	8.59	J. Quinn, BOS	4	B. Hasty, PHI	1.92

Most Strikeouts/9 Inn.		Innings		Games Pitched	
G. Morton, CLE	4.53	R. Faber, CHI	353	E. Rommel, PHI	51
S. Harriss, PHI	4.00	U. Shocker, STL	348	G. Uhle, CLE	50
B. Shawkey, NY	3.90	B. Shawkey, NY	300	U. Shocker, STL	48
U. Shocker, STL	3.85	E. Rommel, PHI	294	S. Harriss, PHI	47

AMERICAN LEAGUE 1922, cont.

	W	L	PCT	GB	R	OR	2B	3B	HR	BA	SA	SB	E	DP	FA	CG	BB	SO	ShO	SV	ERA
									Batting					Fielding				Pitching			
New York	94	60	.610		758	**618**	220	75	95	.287	.412	62	157	122	.975	**98**	423	458	7	14	3.39
St. Louis	93	61	.604	1	**867**	643	291	**94**	98	**.313**	**.455**	132	201	158	.968	79	**421**	534	8	**22**	**3.38**
Detroit	79	75	.513	15	828	791	250	87	54	.305	.414	- 78	191	135	.970	67	473	461	7	15	4.27
Cleveland	78	76	.506	16	768	817	**320**	73	32	.292	.398	89	202	140	.968	76	464	489	**14**	7	4.60
Chicago	77	77	.500	17	691	691	243	62	45	.278	.373	106	**155**	132	**.975**	86	529	484	13	8	3.93
Washington	69	85	.448	25	650	706	229	76	45	.268	.367	94	196	**161**	.969	84	500	422	11	10	3.81
Philadelphia	65	89	.422	29	705	830	229	63	111	.269	.400	60	215	119	.966	73	469	373	4	6	4.59
Boston	61	93	.396	33	598	769	250	55	45	.260	.352	60	224	139	.965	71	503	359	10	6	4.30
					5865	5865	2032	585	525	.284	.397	681	1541	1106	.969	634	3782	3580	74	88	4.03

NATIONAL LEAGUE 1923

	POS	Player	AB	BA	HR	RBI	PO	A	E	DP	TC/G	FA	Pitcher	G	IP	W	L	SV	ERA
New York W-95 L-58 John McGraw	1B	G. Kelly	560	.307	16	103	**1568**	60	12	111	**11.3**	.993	McQuillan	38	230	15	14	0	3.41
	2B	F. Frisch	641	.348	12	111	307	451	21	79	5.8	**.973**	J. Scott	40	220	16	7	1	3.89
	SS	D. Bancroft	444	.304	1	31	246	381	43	53	7.0	.936	A. Nehf	34	196	13	10	2	4.50
	3B	H. Groh	465	.290	4	48	117	233	9	18	3.0	**.975**	J. Bentley	31	183	13	8	3	4.48
	RF	R. Youngs	596	.336	3	87	282	22	13	7	2.1	.959	R. Ryan	45	173	16	5	4	3.49
	CF	J. O'Connell	252	.250	6	39	145	2	3	1	2.3	.980	M. Watson	17	108	8	5	0	3.43
	LF	I. Meusel	595	.297	19	125	268	10	15	2	2.0	.949	C. Jonnard	45	96	4	3	5	3.28
	C	F. Snyder	402	.256	5	63	**428**	90	5	12	4.7	**.990**							
	S3	T. Jackson	327	.275	4	37	103	257	23	29		.940							
	OF	C. Stengel	218	.339	5	43	115	4	2	1	2.1	.983							
	OF	Cunningham	203	.271	5	27	123	8	1	2	1.9	.992							
Cincinnati W-91 L-63 Pat Moran	1B	J. Daubert	500	.292	2	54	1224	77	9	95	10.8	.993	D. Luque	41	322	**27**	8	2	**1.93**
	2B	S. Bohne	539	.252	3	47	243	333	15	46	6.2	.975	E. Rixey	42	309	20	15	1	2.80
	SS	I. Caveney	488	.277	4	63	313	477	**49**	86	6.1	.942	P. Donohue	42	274	21	15	3	3.38
	3B	B. Pinelli	423	.277	0	51	131	250	25	17	**3.5**	.938	R. Benton	33	219	14	10	1	3.66
	RF	G. Burns	614	.274	3	45	327	11	14	3	2.3	.960	C. Keck	35	87	3	6	2	3.72
	CF	E. Roush	527	.351	6	88	337	14	11	3	2.6	.970							
	LF	P. Duncan	566	.327	7	83	291	11	2	2	2.1	**.993**							
	C	B. Hargrave	378	.333	10	78	404	90	6	12	4.6	.988							
	2B	L. Fonseca	237	.278	3	28	123	169	13	27	6.8	.957							
	C	I. Wingo	171	.263	1	24	172	44	7	2	3.9	.969							
Pittsburgh W-87 L-67 Bill McKechnie	1B	C. Grimm	563	.345	7	99	1453	81	8	130	10.1	**.995**	J. Morrison	42	302	25	13	2	3.49
	2B	J. Rawlings	461	.284	1	45	294	388	30	68	6.0	.958	W. Cooper	39	295	17	**19**	0	3.57
	SS	Maranville	581	.277	1	41	**332**	**505**	30	**94**	6.1	**.965**	L. Meadows	31	227	16	10	0	3.01
	3B	P. Traynor	616	.338	12	101	**191**	**310**	26	30	3.4	.951	B. Adams	26	159	13	7	1	4.42
	RF	C. Barnhart	327	.324	9	72	179	14	3	1	2.1	.985	E. Hamilton	28	141	7	9	1	3.77
	CF	M. Carey	610	.308	6	63	**450**	**28**	19	4	**3.2**	.962							
	LF	C. Bigbee	499	.299	0	54	283	12	3	3	2.4	.990							
	C	W. Schmidt	335	.248	0	37	279	88	7	10	3.9	.981							
	OF	R. Russell	291	.289	9	58	156	4	5	0	2.2	.970							
	C	J. Gooch	202	.277	1	20	217	56	7	7	4.2	.975							
	2B	C. Tierney	120	.292	2	23	65	94	10	22*	5.8	.941							
	OF	W. Mueller	111	.306	0	20	62	2	4	0	2.6	.941							
Chicago W-83 L-71 Bill Killefer	1B	R. Grimes	216	.329	2	36	629	30	6	46	10.7	.991	G. Alexander	39	305	22	12	2	3.19
	2B	G. Grantham	570	.281	8	70	**374**	**518**	**55**	90	**6.3**	.942	V. Aldridge	30	217	16	9	0	3.48
	SS	S. Adams	311	.289	4	35	153	248	28	45	5.4	.935	T. Kaufmann	33	206	14	10	3	3.10
	3B	B. Friberg	547	.318	12	88	168	294	22	33	3.3	.955	T. Osborne	37	180	8	15	1	4.56
	RF	C. Heathcote	393	.249	1	27	231	14	5	1	2.2	.980	V. Keen	35	177	12	8	1	3.00
	CF	J. Statz	**655**	.319	10	70	438	26	12	**7**	3.1	.975	F. Fussell	28	76	3	5	3	5.54
	LF	H. Miller	485	.301	20	88	256	17	6	4	2.2	.978							
	C	B. O'Farrell	452	.319	12	84	418	**118**	13	11	4.4	.976							
	SS	C. Hollocher	260	.342	1	28	124	212	13	35	5.4	.963							
	C1	G. Hartnett	231	.268	8	39	413	39	5	25		.989							
	UT	J. Kelleher	193	.306	6	21	228	84	22	21		.934							
	1B	A. Elliott	168	.250	2	29	450	19	4	36	9.1	.992							
St. Louis W-79 L-74 Branch Rickey	1B	J. Bottomley	523	.371	8	94	1264	43	18	95	10.2	.986	J. Haines	37	266	20	13	0	3.11
	2B	R. Hornsby	424	**.384**	17	83	192	283	19	47	5.1	.962	B. Sherdel	39	225	15	13	2	4.32
	SS	H. Freigau	358	.263	1	35	193	290	37	42	6.0	.929	F. Toney	29	197	11	12	0	3.84
	3B	M. Stock	603	.289	2	96	165	261	20	24	3.0	.955	B. Doak	30	185	8	13	0	3.26
	RF	M. Flack	505	.291	3	28	242	8	13	4	2.2	.951	J. Pfeffer	26	152	8	9	0	4.02
	CF	H. Myers	330	.300	2	48	239	15	6	0	3.0	.977	J. Stuart	37	150	9	5	3	4.27
	LF	J. Smith	407	.310	5	41	247	11	7	3	2.5	.974	C. Barfoot	33	101	3	3	1	3.73
	C	E. Ainsmith	263	.213	3	34	235	57	6	3	3.7	.980							
	OF	R. Blades	317	.246	5	44	194	11	7	1	2.6	.967							
	2S	S. Toporcer	303	.254	3	35	192	239	24	57		.947							
	OF	H. Mueller	265	.343	5	41	197	9	8	3	2.9	.963							
	C	H. McCurdy	185	.265	0	15	157	30	6	4	3.3	.969							

NATIONAL LEAGUE 1923, cont.

	POS	Player	AB	BA	HR	RBI	PO	A	E	DP	TC/G	FA	Pitcher	G	IP	W	L	SV	ERA
Brooklyn	1B	J. Fournier	515	.351	22	102	1281	82	21	90	10.4	.985	B. Grimes	39	327	21	18	0	3.58
	2B	J. Johnston	625	.325	4	60	221	291	28	25	6.4	.948	D. Vance	37	280	18	15	0	3.50
W-76 L-78	SS	A. High	426	.270	3	37	94	122	15	23	5.1	.935	D. Ruether	34	275	15	14	0	4.22
	3B	B. McCarren	216	.245	3	27	72	106	14	11	2.9	.927	L. Dickerman	35	166	8	12	0	3.59
Wilbert Robinson	RF	T. Griffith	481	.293	8	66	215	14	18	4	1.9	.927	A. Decatur	36	105	3	3	3	2.67
	CF	B. Neis	445	.274	5	37	268	20	18	3	2.8	.941	D. Henry	17	94	4	6	0	3.91
	LF	G. Bailey	411	.265	1	42	245	10	11	0	2.7	.959	G. Smith	25	91	3	6	1	3.66
	C	Z. Taylor	337	.288	0	46	354	118	16	6	5.8	.967							
	OF	Z. Wheat	349	.375	8	65	135	4	14	1	1.8	.908							
	2B	I. Olson	292	.260	1	35	161	244	11	36	5.8	.974							
	OF	B. Griffith	248	.294	2	37	111	1	6	0	1.9	.949							
	C	H. DeBerry	235	.285	1	48	273	65	10	8	5.8	.971							
Boston	1B	S. McInnis	607	.315	2	95	1500	89	14	136	10.4	.991	R. Marquard	38	239	11	14	0	3.73
	2B	H. Ford	380	.271	2	50	213	300	16	61	5.6	.970	J. Genewich	43	227	13	14	1	3.72
W-54 L-100	SS	B. Smith	375	.251	0	40	234	360	35	69	6.2	.944	J. Barnes	31	195	10	14	2	2.76
	3B	T. Boeckel	568	.298	7	79	169	265	28	27	3.1	.939	J. Oeschger	44	166	5	15	2	5.68
Fred Mitchell	RF	Southworth	611	.319	6	78	326	22	21	6	2.4	.943	T. McNamara	32	139	3	13	0	4.91
	CF	R. Powell	338	.302	4	38	214	8	14	0	2.8	.941	L. Benton	35	128	5	9	0	4.99
	LF	G. Felix	506	.273	6	44	276	11	15	2	2.5	.950	D. Fillingim	35	100	1	9	0	5.20
	C	M. O'Neil	306	.212	0	20	298	104	11	5	4.3	.973							
	OF	A. Nixon	321	.274	0	19	214	14	3	4	2.9	.987							
	C	E. Smith	191	.288	3	19	141	51	5	7	5.8	.975							
Philadelphia	1B	W. Holke	.562	.311	7	70	1425	69	13	136	10.3	.991	J. Ring	39	313	18	16	0	3.76
	2B	C. Tierney	480	.317	2	65	249	416	17	82*	6.0	.975	W. Glazner	28	161	7	14	1	4.69
W-50 L-104	SS	H. Sand	470	.228	4	32	277	411	49	91	6.1	.934	L. Weinert	38	156	4	17	1	5.42
	3B	Wrightstone	392	.273	7	57	73	121	12	12	2.9	.942	C. Mitchell	29	139	9	10	0	4.72
Art Fletcher	RF	C. Walker	527	.281	5	66	284	19	17	5	2.3	.947	R. Head	35	132	2	9	0	6.66
	CF	C. Williams	535	.293	41	114	350	9	7	3	2.7	.981	P. Behan	31	131	3	12	2	5.50
	LF	J. Mokan	400	.313	10	48	235	16	8	0	2.5	.969							
	C	B. Henline	330	.324	7	46	288	71	8	8	3.8	.978							
	OF	C. Lee	355	.321	11	47	136	4	6	3	1.8	.959							
	C	J. Wilson	252	.262	1	25	235	50	12	10	4.3	.960							
	UT	F. Parkinson	219	.242	3	28	118	175	18	36		.942							
	3B	G. Rapp	179	.263	1	10	58	84	8	9	3.3	.947							

BATTING AND BASE RUNNING LEADERS

Batting Average
R. Hornsby, STL	.384
J. Bottomley, STL	.371
J. Fournier, BKN	.351
E. Roush, CIN	.351
F. Frisch, NY	.348

Slugging Average
R. Hornsby, STL	.627
J. Fournier, BKN	.588
C. Williams, PHI	.576
C. Barnhart, PIT	.563
J. Bottomley, STL	.535

Home Runs
C. Williams, PHI	41
J. Fournier, BKN	22
H. Miller, CHI	20
I. Meusel, NY	19
R. Hornsby, STL	17

Total Bases
F. Frisch, NY	311
C. Williams, PHI	308
J. Fournier, BKN	303
P. Traynor, PIT	301
J. Statz, CHI	288

Runs Batted In
I. Meusel, NY	125
C. Williams, PHI	114
F. Frisch, NY	111
G. Kelly, NY	103
J. Fournier, BKN	102

Stolen Bases
M. Carey, PIT	51
G. Grantham, CHI	43
C. Heathcote, CHI	32
J. Smith, STL	32
F. Frisch, NY	29
J. Statz, CHI	29

Hits
F. Frisch, NY	223
J. Statz, CHI	209
P. Traynor, PIT	208
J. Johnston, BKN	203

Base on Balls
G. Burns, CIN	101
H. Sand, PHI	82
R. Youngs, NY	73
M. Carey, PIT	73

Home Run Percentage
C. Williams, PHI	7.7
J. Fournier, BKN	4.3
H. Miller, CHI	4.1
R. Hornsby, STL	4.0

Runs Scored
R. Youngs, NY	121
M. Carey, PIT	120
F. Frisch, NY	116
J. Johnston, BKN	111

Doubles
E. Roush, CIN	41
G. Grantham, CHI	36
C. Tierney, PHI, PIT	36
J. Bottomley, STL	34

Triples
M. Carey, PIT	19
P. Traynor, PIT	19
E. Roush, CIN	18
Southworth, BOS	16

PITCHING LEADERS

Winning Percentage
D. Luque, CIN	.771
R. Ryan, NY	.762
J. Scott, NY	.696
J. Morrison, PIT	.658
G. Alexander, CHI	.647

Earned Run Average
D. Luque, CIN	1.93
E. Rixey, CIN	2.80
V. Keen, CHI	3.00
T. Kaufmann, CHI	3.10
J. Haines, STL	3.11

Wins
D. Luque, CIN	27
J. Morrison, PIT	25
G. Alexander, CHI	22
P. Donohue, CIN	21
B. Grimes, BKN	21

Saves
C. Jonnard, NY	5
R. Ryan, NY	4

Strikeouts
D. Vance, BKN	197
D. Luque, CIN	151
B. Grimes, BKN	119
J. Morrison, PIT	114
J. Ring, PHI	112

Complete Games
B. Grimes, BKN	33
D. Luque, CIN	28
J. Morrison, PIT	27
G. Alexander, CHI	26
W. Cooper, PIT	26

Fewest Hits/9 Innings
D. Luque, CIN	7.80
D. Vance, BKN	8.44
J. Morrison, PIT	8.56
V. Keen, CHI	8.59

Shutouts
D. Luque, CIN	6
J. Barnes, BOS, NY	5
McQuillan, NY	5

Fewest Walks/9 Innings
G. Alexander, CHI	0.89
B. Adams, PIT	1.42
J. Genewich, BOS	1.82
E. Rixey, CIN	1.89

Most Strikeouts/9 Inn.
D. Vance, BKN	6.32
D. Luque, CIN	4.22
J. Bentley, NY	3.93
J. Morrison, PIT	3.40

Innings
B. Grimes, BKN	327
D. Luque, CIN	322
J. Ring, PHI	313
E. Rixey, CIN	309

Games Pitched
R. Ryan, NY	45
C. Jonnard, NY	45
J. Oeschger, BOS	44
J. Barnes, BOS, NY	43

NATIONAL LEAGUE 1923, *cont.*

	W	L	PCT	GB	R	OR	2B	3B	HR	BA	SA	SB	E	DP	FA	CG	BB	SO	ShO	SV	ERA
								Batting						Fielding			Pitching				
New York	95	58	.621		854	679	248	76	85	.295	.415	106	176	141	.972	62	424	453	10	18	3.90
Cincinnati	91	63	.591	4.5	708	629	237	95	45	.285	.392	96	202	144	.969	88	359	450	11	9	3.21
Pittsburgh	87	67	.565	8.5	786	696	224	111	49	.295	.404	154	179	157	.971	92	402	414	5	9	3.87
Chicago	83	71	.539	12.5	756	704	243	52	90	.288	.406	181	208	144	.967	80	435	408	8	11	3.82
St. Louis	79	74	.516	16	746	732	274	76	63	.286	.398	89	232	141	.963	77	456	398	9	7	3.87
Brooklyn	76	78	.494	19.5	753	741	214	81	62	.273	.353	71	293	137	.955	94	477	549	8	5	3.73
Boston	54	100	.351	41.5	636	798	213	58	32	.273	.353	57	230	157	.964	55	394	351	13	7	4.22
Philadelphia	50	104	.325	45.5	748	1008	259	39	112	.278	.401	70	217	172	.966	68	549	385	3	8	5.30
					5987	5987	1912	588	538	.286	.395	824	1737	1193	.966	616	3496	3408	67	74	3.99

AMERICAN LEAGUE 1923

	POS	Player	AB	BA	HR	RBI	PO	A	E	DP	TC/G	FA	Pitcher	G	IP	W	L	SV	ERA
New York W-98 L-54 Miller Huggins	1B	W. Pipp	569	.304	6	108	1461	81	12	97	10.8	.992	J. Bush	37	276	19	15	0	3.43
	2B	A. Ward	567	.284	10	82	387	493	18	86	5.9	.980	B. Shawkey	36	259	16	11	1	3.51
	SS	E. Scott	533	.246	6	60	245	414	27	65	4.5	.961	S. Jones	39	243	21	8	4	3.63
	3B	J. Dugan	644	.283	7	67	155	300	12	28	3.2	.974	W. Hoyt	37	239	17	9	1	3.02
	RF	B. Ruth	522	.393	41	131	378	20	11	2	2.8	.973	H. Pennock	35	224	19	6	3	3.33
	CF	W. Witt	596	.314	6	56	357	14	8	4	2.6	.979							
	LF	B. Meusel	460	.313	9	91	206	17	11	2	1.9	.953							
	C	W. Schang	272	.276	2	29	292	60	11	6	4.5	.970							
	C	F. Hofmann	238	.290	3	26	292	34	7	7	4.8	.979							
	OF	E. Smith	183	.306	7	35	86	5	5	2	2.0	.948							
Detroit W-83 L-71 Ty Cobb	1B	L. Blue	504	.284	1	46	1347	93	12	74	11.3	.992	H. Dauss	50	316	21	13	3	3.62
	2B	F. Haney	503	.282	4	67	162	178	16	29	5.2	.955	H. Pillette	47	250	14	19	1	3.85
	SS	T. Rigney	470	.315	1	74	209	383	35	46	4.9	.944	K. Holloway	42	194	11	10	1	4.45
	3B	B. Jones	372	.250	1	40	109	224	16	17	3.2	.954	S. Johnson	37	176	12	7	0	3.98
	RF	H. Heilmann	524	.403	18	115	272	13	12	2	2.3	.960	B. Cole	52	163	13	5	5	4.14
	CF	T. Cobb	556	.340	6	88	362	14	12	2	2.8	.969	R. Collins	17	92	3	7	0	4.87
	LF	H. Manush	308	.334	4	54	158	6	8	0	2.2	.953	R. Francis	33	79	5	8	1	4.42
	C	J. Bassler	383	.298	0	49	447	133	7	8	4.6	.988							
	UT	D. Pratt	297	.310	0	40	281	179	18	32		.962							
	OF	B. Veach	293	.321	2	39	127	6	8	0	1.7	.943							
	OF	Fothergill	241	.315	1	49	121	4	3	0	1.9	.977							
Cleveland W-82 L-71 Tris Speaker	1B	F. Brower	397	.285	16	66	1047	66	13	87	10.1	.988	G. Uhle	54	358	26	16	5	3.77
	2B	Wambsganss	345	.290	1	59	252	275	20	46	6.2	.963	S. Coveleski	33	228	13	14	2	2.76
	SS	J. Sewell	553	.353	3	109	286	497	59	82	5.6	.930	J. Edwards	38	179	10	10	1	3.71
	3B	R. Lutzke	511	.256	3	65	186	358	35	23	4.0	.940	J. Shaute	33	172	10	8	0	3.51
	RF	H. Summa	525	.328	3	69	216	15	11	5	1.8	.955	G. Morton	33	129	6	6	1	4.24
	CF	T. Speaker	574	.380	17	130	369	26	13	7	2.7	.968	S. Smith	30	124	9	6	1	4.27
	LF	C. Jamieson	644	.345	2	51	360	18	10	1	2.6	.974	D. Boone	27	70	4	6	0	6.01
	C	S. O'Neill	330	.248	0	50	354	68	14	3	3.9	.968							
	2B	Stephenson	301	.319	5	65	205	214	13	49	6.5	.970							
	C	G. Myatt	220	.286	3	40	188	37	16	3	3.5	.934							
	P	G. Uhle	144	.361	0	22	18	89	2	9	2.0	.982							
	OF	J. Connolly	109	.303	3	25	42	2	2	0	1.2	.957							
Washington W-75 L-78 Donie Bush	1B	J. Judge	405	.314	2	63	1070	88	8	113	10.4	.993	W. Johnson	42	261	17	12	4	3.48
	2B	B. Harris	532	.282	2	70	418	449	35	120	6.3	.961	G. Mogridge	33	211	13	13	1	3.11
	SS	Peckinpaugh	568	.264	2	62	311	510	45	105	5.6	.948	T. Zachary	35	204	10	16	0	4.49
	3B	O. Bluege	379	.245	2	42	126	247	25	30	3.7	.937	A. Russell	52	181	10	8	9	3.03
	RF	S. Rice	595	.316	3	75	307	21	10	8	2.3	.970	P. Zahniser	33	177	9	10	0	3.86
	CF	N. Leibold	315	.305	1	22	186	13	4	2	2.4	.980	C. Warmoth	21	105	7	4	0	4.29
	LF	G. Goslin	600	.300	9	99	310	26	15	5	2.4	.957	Hollingsworth	17	73	3	7	0	4.09
	C	M. Ruel	449	.316	0	54	528	146	14	14	5.2	.980							
	OF	J. Evans	372	.263	0	38	159	5	3	2	2.3	.982							
	C1	P. Gharrity	251	.207	3	33	417	47	8	27		.983							
St. Louis W-74 L-78 Lee Fohl W-52 L-49 Jimmy Austin W-22 L-29	1B	Schliebner	444	.275	4	52	1141	79	13	102	9.7	.989	E. Vangilder	41	282	16	17	1	3.06
	2B	M. McManus	582	.309	15	94	386	373	32	86	5.9	.960	U. Shocker	43	277	20	12	5	3.41
	SS	W. Gerber	605	.281	1	62	334	461	42	86	5.4	.950	D. Danforth	38	226	16	14	1	3.94
	3B	G. Robertson	251	.247	0	17	86	117	14	6	2.9	.935	R. Kolp	34	171	5	12	1	3.89
	RF	J. Tobin	637	.317	13	73	269	14	9	3	1.9	.969	D. Davis	19	109	4	6	0	3.62
	CF	B. Jacobson	592	.309	8	81	409	10	11	4	2.9	.974	H. Pruett	32	104	4	7	2	4.31
	LF	K. Williams	555	.357	29	91	333	23	12	5	2.5	.967	R. Wright	20	83	7	4	0	6.42
	C	H. Severeid	432	.308	3	51	513	88	4	9	5.2	.993							
	3B	H. Ezzell	279	.244	0	14	88	159	10	13	3.5	.961							
	C	P. Collins	181	.177	3	30	161	31	4	4	4.2	.980							

AMERICAN LEAGUE 1923, cont.

POS	Player	AB	BA	HR	RBI	PO	A	E	DP	TC/G	FA	Pitcher	G	IP	W	L	SV	ERA
1B	J. Hauser	537	.307	16	94	1475	86	15	109	10.8	.990	E. Rommel	56	298	18	19	5	3.27
2B	J. Dykes	416	.252	4	43	245	315	21	55	5.7	.964	B. Hasty	44	243	13	15	1	4.44
SS	C. Galloway	504	.278	2	62	285	408	41	73	5.5	.944	S. Harriss	46	209	10	16	6	4.00
3B	S. Hale	434	.288	3	51	85	222	28	17	3.1	.916	F. Heimach	40	208	6	12	0	4.32
RF	F. Welch	421	.297	4	55	253	13	9	4	2.4	.967	R. Naylor	26	143	12	7	0	3.46
CF	W. Matthews	485	.274	1	25	316	3	18	0	2.7	.947	R. Walberg	26	115	4	8	0	5.32
LF	B. Miller	458	.299	12	64	262	10	6	0	2.3	.978							
C	C. Perkins	500	.270	2	65	475	102	17	12	4.3	.971							
OF	F. McGowan	287	.254	1	19	154	12	5	1	2.2	.971							
2B	H. Scheer	210	.238	2	21	147	156	9	30	5.1	.971							
3B	H. Riconda	175	.263	0	12	45	114	15	9	3.7	.914							

Philadelphia W-69 L-83 Connie Mack

POS	Player	AB	BA	HR	RBI	PO	A	E	DP	TC/G	FA	Pitcher	G	IP	W	L	SV	ERA
1B	E. Sheely	570	.296	4	88	1563	96	14	113	10.7	.992	C. Robertson	38	255	13	18	0	3.81
2B	E. Collins	505	.360	5	67	347	430	20	77	5.6	.975	R. Faber	32	232	14	11	0	3.41
SS	McClellan	550	.235	1	41	217	394	27	63	4.6	.958	M. Cvengros	41	215	12	13	3	4.39
3B	W. Kamm	544	.292	6	87	173	352	22	29	3.7	.960	Blankenship	44	209	9	14	0	4.27
RF	H. Hooper	576	.288	10	65	272	15	12	3	2.1	.960	D. Leverett	38	193	10	13	3	4.06
CF	J. Mostil	546	.291	3	64	422	21	12	5	3.2	.974	S. Thurston	44	192	7	8	4	3.05
LF	B. Falk	274	.307	5	38	148	6	8	3	2.0	.951							
C	R. Schalk	382	.228	1	44	481	93	10	20	4.8	.983							
OF	R. Elsh	209	.249	0	24	127	7	6	1	2.5	.957							
OF	B. Barrett	162	.272	2	23	89	5	6	1	2.5	.940							

Chicago W-69 L-85 Kid Gleason

POS	Player	AB	BA	HR	RBI	PO	A	E	DP	TC/G	FA	Pitcher	G	IP	W	L	SV	ERA
1B	G. Burns	551	.328	7	82	1485	92	16	103	10.9	.990	H. Ehmke	43	317	20	17	3	3.78
2B	C. Fewster	284	.236	0	15	103	140	16	21	5.4	.938	J. Quinn	42	243	13	17	7	3.89
SS	J. Mitchell	347	.225	0	19	184	264	18	40	5.4	.961	A. Ferguson	34	198	9	13	0	4.04
3B	H. Shanks	464	.254	3	57	89	169	17	16	3.2	.938	B. Piercy	30	187	8	17	0	3.41
RF	I. Flagstead	382	.312	8	53	218	33*	10	8*	2.6	.962	G. Murray	39	178	7	11	0	4.91
CF	D. Reichle	361	.258	1	39	190	10	5	2	2.2	.976	C. Fullerton	37	143	2	15	1	5.09
LF	J. Harris	483	.335	13	76	289	13	10	2	2.4	.968							
C	V. Picinich	268	.276	2	31	247	89	15	7	4.3	.957							
UT	N. McMillan	459	.253	0	42	261	327	35	48		.944							
OF	S. Collins	342	.231	0	18	164	17	9	2	2.1	.953							
C	A. DeVormer	209	.258	0	18	181	48	5	3	4.3	.979							
OF	M. Menosky	188	.229	0	25	103	12	10	1	2.6	.920							
2B	P. Pittenger	177	.215	0	15	77	86	7	12	4.0	.959							

Boston W-61 L-91 Frank Chance

BATTING AND BASE RUNNING LEADERS

Batting Average
H. Heilmann, DET	.403
B. Ruth, NY	.393
T. Speaker, CLE	.380
E. Collins, CHI	.360
K. Williams, STL	.357

Slugging Average
B. Ruth, NY	.764
H. Heilmann, DET	.632
K. Williams, STL	.623
T. Speaker, CLE	.610
J. Harris, BOS	.520

Home Runs
B. Ruth, NY	41
K. Williams, STL	29
H. Heilmann, DET	18
T. Speaker, CLE	17
F. Brower, CLE	16
J. Hauser, PHI	16

Total Bases
B. Ruth, NY	399
T. Speaker, CLE	350
K. Williams, STL	346
H. Heilmann, DET	331
J. Tobin, STL	303

Runs Batted In
B. Ruth, NY	130
T. Speaker, CLE	130
H. Heilmann, DET	115
J. Sewell, CLE	109
W. Pipp, NY	108

Stolen Bases
E. Collins, CHI	47
J. Mostil, CHI	41
B. Harris, WAS	23
S. Rice, WAS	20
C. Jamieson, CLE	19

Hits
C. Jamieson, CLE	222
T. Speaker, CLE	218
H. Heilmann, DET	211
B. Ruth, NY	205

Base on Balls
B. Ruth, NY	170
J. Sewell, CLE	98
L. Blue, DET	96
T. Speaker, CLE	93

Home Run Percentage
B. Ruth, NY	7.9
K. Williams, STL	5.2
F. Brower, CLE	4.0
H. Heilmann, DET	3.4

Runs Scored
B. Ruth, NY	151
T. Speaker, CLE	133
C. Jamieson, CLE	130
H. Heilmann, DET	121

Doubles
T. Speaker, CLE	59
G. Burns, BOS	47
B. Ruth, NY	45
H. Heilmann, DET	44

Triples
S. Rice, WAS	18
G. Goslin, WAS	18
J. Mostil, CHI	15
J. Tobin, STL	15

PITCHING LEADERS

Winning Percentage
H. Pennock, NY	.760
S. Jones, NY	.724
W. Hoyt, NY	.654
U. Shocker, STL	.625
G. Uhle, CLE	.619

Earned Run Average
S. Coveleski, CLE	2.76
W. Hoyt, NY	3.02
E. Vangilder, STL	3.06
G. Mogridge, WAS	3.11
E. Rommel, PHI	3.27

Wins
G. Uhle, CLE	26
S. Jones, NY	21
H. Dauss, DET	21
U. Shocker, STL	20
H. Ehmke, BOS	20

Saves
A. Russell, WAS	9
J. Quinn, BOS	7
S. Harriss, PHI	6

Strikeouts
W. Johnson, WAS	130
B. Shawkey, NY	125
J. Bush, NY	125
H. Ehmke, BOS	121
U. Shocker, STL	109
G. Uhle, CLE	109

Complete Games
G. Uhle, CLE	29
H. Ehmke, BOS	28
U. Shocker, STL	24
J. Bush, NY	23
H. Dauss, DET	22

Fewest Hits/9 Innings
B. Shawkey, NY	8.07
W. Hoyt, NY	8.56
J. Bush, NY	8.59
D. Danforth, STL	8.79

Shutouts
S. Coveleski, CLE	5
W. Johnson, WAS	4
E. Vangilder, STL	4
H. Dauss, DET	4

Fewest Walks/9 Innings
U. Shocker, STL	1.59
S. Coveleski, CLE	1.66
J. Quinn, BOS	1.96
H. Dauss, DET	2.22

Most Strikeouts/9 Inn.
W. Johnson, WAS	4.47
B. Shawkey, NY	4.35
J. Bush, NY	4.08
D. Danforth, STL	3.82

Innings
G. Uhle, CLE	358
H. Ehmke, BOS	317
H. Dauss, DET	316
E. Rommel, PHI	298

Games Pitched
E. Rommel, PHI	56
G. Uhle, CLE	54
A. Russell, WAS	52
B. Cole, DET	52

AMERICAN LEAGUE 1923, cont.

	W	L	PCT	GB	R	OR	2B	3B	Batting HR	BA	SA	SB	E	Fielding DP	FA	CG	BB	Pitching SO	ShO	SV	ERA
New York	98	54	.645		823	622	231	79	105	.291	.422	69	144	131	.977	102	491	506	9	10	3.66
Detroit	83	71	.539	16	831	741	270	69	41	.300	.401	87	200	103	.968	61	459	447	9	12	4.09
Cleveland	82	71	.536	16.5	888	746	301	75	59	.301	.420	79	226	143	.964	76	466	407	10	11	3.91
Washington	75	78	.490	23.5	720	747	224	93	26	.274	.367	102	216	182	.966	70	559	474	8	16	3.99
St. Louis	74	78	.487	24	688	720	248	62	82	.281	.398	64	177	145	.971	83	528	488	10	10	3.93
Philadelphia	69	83	.454	29	661	761	229	65	52	.271	.370	72	221	127	.965	65	550	400	6	12	4.08
Chicago	69	85	.448	30	692	741	254	57	42	.279	.373	191	184	138	.971	74	534	467	5	11	4.03
Boston	61	91	.401	37	584	809	253	54	34	.261	.351	77	232	126	.963	78	520	412	3	11	4.20
					5887	5887	2010	554	441	.282	.388	741	1600	1095	.968	609	4107	3601	60	93	3.99

NATIONAL LEAGUE 1924

	POS	Player	AB	BA	HR	RBI	PO	A	E	DP	TC/G	FA	Pitcher	G	IP	W	L	SV	ERA
New York W-93 L-60 John McGraw W-16 L-13 Hughie Jennings W-32 L-12 John McGraw W-45 L-35	1B	G. Kelly	571	.324	21	136	1309	60	10	105	11.0	.993	V. Barnes	35	229	16	10	3	3.06
	2B	F. Frisch	603	.328	7	69	391	537	27	100	6.7	.972	J. Bentley	28	188	16	5	1	3.78
	SS	T. Jackson	596	.302	11	76	332	534	58	101	6.1	.937	McQuillan	27	184	14	8	3	2.69
	3B	H. Groh	559	.281	2	46	121	286	7	13	2.9	.983	A. Nehf	30	172	14	4	2	3.62
	RF	R. Youngs	526	.356	10	74	236	17	12	3	2.0	.955	W. Dean	26	126	6	12	0	5.01
	CF	H. Wilson	383	.295	10	57	230	8	8	2	2.4	.967	R. Ryan	37	125	8	6	5	4.26
	LF	I. Meusel	549	.310	6	102	287	4	10	0	2.2	.967	M. Watson	22	100	7	4	0	3.79
	C	F. Snyder	354	.302	5	53	308	79	5	8	3.6	.987	C. Jonnard	34	90	4	5	5	2.41
	OF	Southworth	281	.256	3	36	167	5	12	2	2.5	.935							
	C	H. Gowdy	191	.325	4	37	223	51	5	8	3.6	.982							
	1B	B. Terry	163	.239	5	24	325	14	4	30	8.2	.988							
Brooklyn W-92 L-62 Wilbert Robinson	1B	J. Fournier	563	.334	27	116	1388	99	22	102	9.9	.985	B. Grimes	38	311	22	13	1	3.82
	2B	A. High	582	.328	6	61	295	437	27	52	5.7	.964	D. Vance	35	309	28	6	0	2.16
	SS	J. Mitchell	243	.263	1	16	131	216	18	30	5.7	.951	D. Ruether	30	167	8	13	3	3.94
	3B	M. Stock	561	.242	2	52	139	200	25	14	2.6	.931	B. Doak	21	149	11	5	0	3.07
	RF	T. Griffith	482	.251	3	67	210	9	8	3	1.6	.965	A. Decatur	31	128	10	9	1	4.07
	CF	E. Brown	455	.308	5	78	311	3	8	0	2.8	.975	T. Osborne	21	104	6	5	0	5.09
	LF	Z. Wheat	566	.375	14	97	288	13	11	4	2.2	.965							
	C	Z. Taylor	345	.290	1	39	388	96	6	13	5.3	.988							
	SS	J. Johnston	315	.298	2	29	136	203	22	32	5.7	.939							
	C	H. DeBerry	218	.243	3	26	394	57	3	8	7.2	.993							
	OF	B. Neis	211	.303	4	26	114	5	8	1	2.0	.937							
Pittsburgh W-90 L-63 Bill McKechnie	1B	C. Grimm	542	.288	2	63	1596	72	8	139	11.1	.995	W. Cooper	38	269	20	14	1	3.28
	2B	Maranville	594	.266	2	71	365	568	26	109	6.3	.973	R. Kremer	41	259	18	10	1	3.19
	SS	G. Wright	616	.287	7	111	310	601	52	102	6.3	.946	J. Morrison	41	238	11	16	2	3.75
	3B	P. Traynor	545	.294	5	82	179	268	15	31	3.0	.968	L. Meadows	36	229	13	12	0	3.26
	RF	C. Barnhart	344	.276	3	51	186	8	6	3	2.3	.970	E. Yde	33	194	16	3	0	2.83
	CF	M. Carey	599	.297	7	55	428	16	16	3	3.1	.965							
	LF	K. Cuyler	466	.354	9	85	246	19	16	4	2.5	.943							
	C	J. Gooch	224	.290	0	25	198	47	3	12	3.6	.988							
	OF	C. Bigbee	282	.262	0	15	155	9	10	2	2.3	.943							
	O3	E. Moore	209	.359	2	13	92	30	1	2		.992							
	C	W. Schmidt	177	.243	1	20	166	51	3	6	3.9	.986							
	C	E. Smith	111	.369	4	21	127	23	4	3	4.4	.974							
Cincinnati W-83 L-70 Jack Hendricks	1B	J. Daubert	405	.281	1	31	1128	74	12	84	11.9	.990	E. Rixey	35	238	15	14	1	2.76
	2B	H. Critz	413	.322	3	35	229	357	27	58	6.4	.956	C. Mays	37	226	20	9	0	3.15
	SS	I. Caveney	337	.273	4	32	200	310	42	59	6.1	.924	P. Donohue	35	222	16	9	0	3.60
	3B	B. Pinelli	510	.306	0	70	182	318	23	21	3.7	.956	D. Luque	31	219	10	15	1	3.16
	RF	C. Walker	397	.300	4	46	213	14	5	4	2.1	.978	T. Sheehan	39	167	9	11	1	3.24
	CF	E. Roush	483	.348	3	72	270	10	12	4	2.5	.959	R. Benton	32	163	7	9	1	2.77
	LF	P. Duncan	319	.270	2	37	124	3	10	0	1.7	.927	J. May	38	99	3	3	6	3.00
	C	B. Hargrave	312	.301	3	33	322	80	7	7	4.5	.983							
	1O	R. Bressler	383	.347	4	49	561	35	9	36		.985							
	UT	S. Bohne	349	.255	4	46	194	294	23	40		.955							
	OF	G. Burns	336	.256	2	33	168	13	7	4	2.1	.963							
	C	I. Wingo	192	.286	1	23	215	50	3	7	4.1	.989							
Chicago W-81 L-72 Bill Killefer	1B	H. Cotter	310	.261	4	33	873	59	10	72	10.5	.989	V. Aldridge	32	244	15	12	0	3.50
	2B	G. Grantham	469	.316	12	60	273	426	44	78	6.3	.941	V. Keen	40	235	15	14	3	3.80
	SS	S. Adams	418	.280	1	27	169	277	28	62	5.4	.941	T. Kaufmann	34	208	16	11	0	4.02
	3B	B. Friberg	495	.279	5	82	163	268	21	21	3.2	.954	E. Jacobs	38	190	11	12	1	3.74
	RF	C. Heathcote	392	.309	0	30	228	7	5	3	2.2	.979	G. Alexander	21	169	12	5	0	3.03
	CF	J. Statz	549	.277	9	49	373	22	16	5	3.1	.961	S. Blake	29	106	6	6	1	4.57
	LF	D. Grigsby	411	.299	3	48	244	16	7	4	2.2	.974	R. Wheeler	29	101	3	6	0	3.91
	C	G. Hartnett	354	.299	16	67	369	97	18	12	4.6	.963							
	SS	C. Hollocher	286	.245	2	21	156	248	13	42	5.9	.969							
	C	B. O'Farrell	183	.240	3	28	204	40	4	5	4.4	.984							
	1B	R. Grimes	177	.299	5	34	530	12	10	40	11.0	.982							
	OF	O. Vogel	172	.267	1	24	101	7	5	2	2.1	.956							
	OF	B. Weis	133	.278	0	23	81	8	2	2	2.5	.978							
	UT	B. Barrett	133	.241	5	21	123	80	13	20		.940							
	OF	H. Miller	131	.336	4	25	54	1	3	0	1.8	.948							

NATIONAL LEAGUE 1924, cont.

	POS	Player	AB	BA	HR	RBI	PO	A	E	DP	TC/G	FA	Pitcher	G	IP	W	L	SV	ERA
St. Louis	1B	J. Bottomley	528	.316	14	111	1297	48	24	110	10.3	.982	J. Haines	35	223	8	19	0	4.41
	2B	R. Hornsby	536	.424	25	94	301	517	30	102	5.9	.965	A. Sothoron	29	197	10	16	0	3.57
W-65 L-89	SS	J. Cooney	383	.295	1	57	242	322	18	68	5.9	.969	B. Sherdel	35	169	8	9	1	3.42
	3B	H. Freigau	376	.269	2	39	127	171	13	24	3.2	.958	J. Stuart	28	159	9	11	0	4.75
Branch Rickey	RF	J. Smith	459	.283	2	33	251	18	9	8	2.4	.968	E. Dyer	29	137	8	11	0	4.61
	CF	W. Holm	293	.294	0	23	162	9	2	1	2.7	.988	L. Dickerman	18	120	7	4	0	2.41
	LF	R. Blades	456	.311	11	68	256	6	12	1	2.5	.956	H. Bell	28	113	3	8	1	4.92
	C	M. Gonzalez	402	.296	3	53	413	96	7	15	4.3	.986							
	O1	H. Mueller	296	.264	2	37	335	15	9	17		.975							
	OF	M. Flack	209	.263	2	21	90	9	3	0	2.0	.971							
	3S	S. Toporcer	198	.313	1	24	54	103	7	8		.957							
	OF	T. Douthit	173	.277	0	13	118	5	3	2	2.5	.976							
	OF	C. Hafey	91	.253	2	22	48	3	4	1	2.3	.927							
Philadelphia	1B	W. Holke	563	.300	6	64	1516	90	12	134	10.9	.993	J. Ring	32	215	10	12	0	3.97
	2B	H. Ford	530	.272	3	53	337	543	27	96	6.3	.970	H. Carlson	38	204	8	17	2	4.86
W-55 L-96	SS	H. Sand	539	.245	6	40	333	460	34	95	6.0	.959	B. Hubbell	36	179	10	9	2	4.83
	3B	Wrightstone	388	.307	7	58	114	154	16	19	2.9	.944	C. Mitchell	30	165	6	13	1	5.62
Art Fletcher	RF	G. Harper	411	.294	16	55	219	13	2	4	2.1	.991*	W. Glazner	35	157	7	16	0	5.92
	CF	C. Williams	558	.328	24	93	368	13	15	0	2.7	.962	H. Betts	37	144	7	10	2	4.30
	LF	J. Mokan	366	.260	7	44	195	9	3	1	2.2	.986	J. Couch	37	137	4	8	3	4.73
	C	B. Henline	289	.284	5	35	248	76	9	12	4.0	.973							
	OF	J. Schultz	284	.282	5	29	137	7	6	0	2.0	.960							
	C	J. Wilson	280	.279	6	39	240	93	11	14	4.2	.968							
	UT	F. Parkinson	156	.212	1	19	63	127	7	23		.964							
Boston	1B	S. McInnis	581	.291	1	59	1435	95	10	129	10.5	.994	J. Barnes	37	268	15	20	0	3.23
	2B	C. Tierney	505	.259	6	58	235	399	24	83	5.7	.964	J. Genewich	34	200	10	19	1	5.21
W-53 L-100	SS	B. Smith	347	.228	2	38	180	273	20	54	5.9	.958	J. Cooney	34	181	8	9	2	3.18
	3B	E. Padgett	502	.255	1	46	95	194	10	23	2.6	.967	T. McNamara	35	179	8	12	0	5.18
Dave Bancroft	RF	C. Stengel	461	.280	5	39	211	12	5	4	1.8	.978	J. Yeargin	32	141	1	11	0	5.09
W-27 L-38	CF	F. Wilson	215	.237	1	15	140	5	4	1	2.7	.973	L. Benton	30	128	5	7	1	4.15
	LF	Cunningham	437	.272	1	40	243	16	8	3	2.4	.970	D. Stryker	20	73	3	8	0	6.01
Dick Rudolph	C	M. O'Neil	362	.246	0	22	362	108	7	8	4.5	.985							
W-11 L-27	SS	D. Bancroft	319	.279	2	21	186	259	18	57	5.9	.961							
	C	F. Gibson	229	.310	1	30	159	52	6	4	4.7	.972							
Dave Bancroft	OF	G. Felix	204	.211	1	10	147	6	8	1	3.2	.950							
W-15 L-35	OF	R. Powell	188	.261	1	15	117	9	7	3	2.9	.947							

BATTING AND BASE RUNNING LEADERS

Batting Average
R. Hornsby, STL .424
Z. Wheat, BKN .375
R. Youngs, NY .356
K. Cuyler, PIT .354
E. Roush, CIN .348

Slugging Average
R. Hornsby, STL .696
C. Williams, PHI .552
Z. Wheat, BKN .549
K. Cuyler, PIT .539
G. Kelly, NY .531

Home Runs
J. Fournier, BKN 27
R. Hornsby, STL 25
C. Williams, PHI 24
G. Kelly, NY 21
G. Hartnett, CHI 16
G. Harper, CIN, PHI 16

Total Bases
R. Hornsby, STL 373
Z. Wheat, BKN 311
C. Williams, PHI 308
G. Kelly, NY 303
J. Fournier, BKN 302

Runs Batted In
G. Kelly, NY 136
J. Fournier, BKN 116
J. Bottomley, STL 111
G. Wright, PIT 111
I. Meusel, NY 102

Stolen Bases
M. Carey, PIT 49
K. Cuyler, PIT 32
C. Heathcote, CHI 26
J. Smith, STL 24
P. Traynor, PIT 24

Hits
R. Hornsby, STL 227
Z. Wheat, BKN 212
F. Frisch, NY 198
A. High, BKN 191

Base on Balls
R. Hornsby, STL 89
J. Fournier, BKN 83
R. Youngs, NY 77
C. Williams, PHI 67

Home Run Percentage
R. Hornsby, STL 4.7
G. Hartnett, CHI 4.5
C. Williams, PHI 4.3
G. Kelly, NY 3.7

Runs Scored
R. Hornsby, STL 121
F. Frisch, NY 121
M. Carey, PIT 113
R. Youngs, NY 112

Doubles
R. Hornsby, STL 43
Z. Wheat, BKN 41
G. Kelly, NY 37
R. Youngs, NY 33

Triples
E. Roush, CIN 21
Maranville, PIT 20
G. Wright, PIT 18
K. Cuyler, PIT 16

PITCHING LEADERS

Winning Percentage
E. Yde, PIT .842
D. Vance, BKN .824
J. Bentley, NY .762
C. Mays, CIN .690
R. Kremer, PIT .643

Earned Run Average
D. Vance, BKN 2.16
McQuillan, NY 2.69
E. Rixey, CIN 2.76
E. Yde, PIT 2.83
G. Alexander, CHI 3.03

Wins
D. Vance, BKN 28
B. Grimes, BKN 22
C. Mays, CIN 20
W. Cooper, PIT 20
R. Kremer, PIT 18

Saves
J. May, CIN 6
R. Ryan, NY 5
C. Jonnard, NY 5

Strikeouts
D. Vance, BKN 262
B. Grimes, BKN 135
D. Luque, CIN 86
J. Morrison, PIT 85
T. Kaufmann, CHI 79

Complete Games
D. Vance, BKN 30
B. Grimes, BKN 30
W. Cooper, PIT 25
J. Barnes, BOS 21
V. Aldridge, CHI 20

Fewest Hits/9 Innings
D. Vance, BKN 6.94
E. Yde, PIT 7.93
J. Morrison, PIT 8.07
E. Rixey, CIN 8.27

Shutouts
5 tied with 4

Fewest Walks/9 Innings
G. Alexander, CHI 1.33
W. Cooper, PIT 1.34
C. Mays, CIN 1.43
P. Donohue, CIN 1.46

Most Strikeouts/9 Inn.
D. Vance, BKN 7.64
B. Grimes, BKN 3.91
A. Nehf, NY 3.77
D. Luque, CIN 3.53

Innings
B. Grimes, BKN 311
D. Vance, BKN 309
W. Cooper, PIT 269
J. Barnes, BOS 268

Games Pitched
R. Kremer, PIT 41
J. Morrison, PIT 41
V. Keen, CHI 40
T. Sheehan, CIN 39

NATIONAL LEAGUE 1924, cont.

	W	L	PCT	GB	R	OR	Batting 2B	3B	HR	BA	SA	SB	Fielding E	DP	FA	Pitching CG	BB	SO	ShO	SV	ERA
New York	93	60	.608		**857**	641	269	81	**95**	**.300**	**.432**	82	186	160	.971	71	392	406	4	21	3.62
Brooklyn	92	62	.597	1.5	717	675	227	54	72	.287	.391	34	196	121	.968	**98**	403	**640**	10	5	3.64
Pittsburgh	90	63	.588	3	724	588	222	**122**	43	.287	.399	**181**	183	161	.971	85	323	364	**15**	5	3.27
Cincinnati	83	70	.542	10	649	**579**	236	111	36	.290	.397	103	217	142	.966	77	**293**	451	14	9	**3.12**
Chicago	81	72	.529	12	698	699	207	59	66	.276	.378	137	218	153	.966	85	438	416	4	6	3.83
St. Louis	65	89	.422	28.5	740	750	**270**	87	67	.290	.411	86	191	162	.969	79	486	393	7	6	4.15
Philadelphia	55	96	.364	37	676	849	256	56	94	.275	.397	57	175	168	.972	59	469	349	7	10	4.87
Boston	53	100	.346	40	520	800	194	52	25	.256	.327	74	**168**	154	**.973**	66	402	364	10	4	4.46
					5581	5581	1881	622	498	.283	.392	754	1534	1221	.970	620	3206	3383	71	66	3.87

AMERICAN LEAGUE 1924

	POS	Player	AB	BA	HR	RBI	PO	A	E	DP	TC/G	FA	Pitcher	G	IP	W	L	SV	ERA
Washington W-92 L-62 Bucky Harris	1B	J. Judge	516	.324	3	79	1276	86	8	108	9.8	.994	W. Johnson	38	278	**23**	7	0	**2.72**
	2B	B. Harris	544	.268	1	58	393	386	26	**100**	5.6	.968	G. Mogridge	30	213	16	11	0	3.76
	SS	Peckinpaugh	523	.272	2	73	278	487	29	81	5.3	.963	T. Zachary	33	203	15	9	2	2.75
	3B	O. Bluege	402	.281	2	49	88	195	16	11	2.9	.946	F. Marberry	50	195	11	12	15	3.09
	RF	S. Rice	**646**	.334	1	76	331	18	12	4	2.3	.967	J. Martina	24	125	6	8	0	4.67
	CF	N. Leibold	246	.293	0	20	148	7	1	0	2.2	.994	C. Ogden	16	108	9	5	0	2.59
	LF	G. Goslin	579	.344	12	**129**	369	12	16	4	2.6	.960	P. Zahniser	24	92	5	7	0	4.40
	C	M. Ruel	501	.283	0	57	**612**	112	15	**23**	5.0	.980	A. Russell	37	82	5	1	8	4.37
	OF	E. McNeely	179	.330	0	15	105	3	3	1	2.6	.973							
	OF	W. Matthews	169	.302	0	13	121	7	2	2	3.0	.985							
	3B	D. Prothro	159	.333	0	24	40	68	10	6	2.6	.915							
New York W-89 L-63 Miller Huggins	1B	W. Pipp	589	.295	9	113	1447	106	9	106	10.2	**.994**	H. Pennock	40	286	21	9	3	2.83
	2B	A. Ward	400	.253	8	66	303	385	27	60	5.9	.973	J. Bush	39	252	17	16	1	3.57
	SS	E. Scott	548	.250	4	64	322	455	27	80	5.3	.966	W. Hoyt	46	247	18	13	4	3.79
	3B	J. Dugan	610	.302	3	56	177	250	17	22	3.0	.962	B. Shawkey	38	208	16	11	0	4.12
	RF	B. Ruth	529	**.378**	46	121	340	18	14	4	2.4	.962	S. Jones	36	179	9	6	3	3.63
	CF	W. Witt	600	.297	1	36	362	11	9	1	2.7	.976							
	LF	B. Meusel	579	.325	12	120	252	17	14	4	2.0	.951							
	C	W. Schang	356	.292	5	52	423	89	15	9	4.8	.972							
	C	F. Hofmann	166	.175	1	11	179	45	2	2	4.2	.991							
Detroit W-86 L-68 Ty Cobb	1B	L. Blue	395	.311	2	50	1099	85	17	72	11.1	.986	E. Whitehill	35	233	17	9	0	3.86
	2B	D. Pratt	429	.303	1	77	133	192	18	38	5.4	.948	R. Collins	34	216	14	7	0	3.21
	SS	T. Rigney	499	.289	4	93	273	463	25	72	5.2	**.967**	L. Stoner	36	216	11	11	0	4.72
	3B	B. Jones	393	.272	0	47	108	196	14	12	3.0	.956	K. Holloway	49	181	14	6	3	4.07
	RF	H. Heilmann	570	.346	10	113	263	**31**	9	6	2.1	.970	H. Dauss	40	131	12	11	6	4.59
	CF	T. Cobb	625	.338	4	74	417	12	6	**8**	2.6	**.986**	B. Cole	28	109	3	9	2	4.69
	LF	H. Manush	422	.289	9	68	224	4	5	1	2.2	.979	S. Johnson	29	104	5	4	3	4.93
	C	J. Bassler	379	.346	1	68	402	103	11	11	4.2	.979	E. Wells	29	102	6	8	4	4.06
	3B	F. Haney	256	.309	1	30	48	146	14	9	3.5	.933							
	2B	L. Burke	241	.253	0	17	125	167	13	30	5.3	.957							
	2B	F. O'Rourke	181	.276	0	19	115	140	8	27	6.6	.970							
	OF	Fothergill	166	.301	0	15	89	2	3	1	2.1	.968							
	C	L. Woodall	165	.309	0	24	174	41	3	5	3.5	.986							
	OF	A. Wingo	150	.287	1	26	59	3	5	2	1.6	.925							
St. Louis W-74 L-78 George Sisler	1B	G. Sisler	636	.305	9	74	1319	111	**23**	114	9.6	.984	U. Shocker	39	239	16	13	1	4.17
	2B	M. McManus	442	.333	5	80	324	365	20	67	6.0	.972	D. Danforth	41	220	15	12	4	4.51
	SS	W. Gerber	496	.272	0	55	317	422	**42**	77	5.3	.946	E. Wingard	36	218	13	12	1	3.51
	3B	G. Robertson	439	.319	4	52	112	203	14	22	3.0	.957	D. Davis	29	160	11	13	0	4.10
	RF	J. Tobin	569	.299	2	48	248	19	12	5	2.1	.957	E. Vangilder	43	145	5	10	1	5.76
	CF	B. Jacobson	579	.318	19	97	**484**	7	7	4	3.3	.986	R. Kolp	25	97	5	7	0	5.68
	LF	K. Williams	398	.324	18	84	257	13	9	2	2.6	.968							
	C	H. Severeid	432	.308	4	48	436	104	6	12	4.2	**.989**							
	OF	J. Evans	209	.254	0	18	118	3	4	1	2.6	.968							
	UT	N. McMillan	201	.279	0	27	132	122	11	19		.958							
Philadelphia W-71 L-81 Connie Mack	1B	J. Hauser	562	.288	27	115	**1513**	94	12	**131**	11.1	.993	E. Rommel	43	278	18	15	1	3.95
	2B	M. Bishop	294	.255	2	21	189	273	15	50	6.0	.969	F. Heimach	40	198	14	12	0	4.73
	SS	C. Galloway	464	.276	2	48	285	389	34	71	5.5	.952	Baumgartner	36	181	13	6	4	2.88
	3B	H. Riconda	281	.253	1	21	95	147	19	14	3.6	.927	D. Burns	37	154	6	8	1	5.08
	RF	B. Miller	398	.342	6	62	172	11	5	4	2.0	.973	S. Gray	34	152	8	7	2	3.98
	CF	A. Simmons	594	.308	8	102	390	17	10	4	2.7	.976	R. Meeker	30	146	5	12	0	4.68
	LF	B. Lamar	367	.330	7	48	184	13	6	4	2.3	.970	S. Harriss	36	123	6	10	2	4.68
	C	C. Perkins	392	.242	0	32	415	102	9	9	4.1	.983							
	2B	J. Dykes	410	.312	3	50	213	253	19	46	6.2	.961							
	OF	F. Welch	293	.290	5	31	120	15	2	2	1.9	.985							
	3B	S. Hale	261	.318	2	17	39	108	8	10	2.8	.948							
	OF	P. Strand	167	.228	0	13	80	3	1	0	1.9	.988							

AMERICAN LEAGUE 1924, *cont.*

POS	Player	AB	BA	HR	RBI	PO	A	E	DP	TC/G	FA	Pitcher	G	IP	W	L	SV	ERA
Cleveland W-67 L-86 Tris Speaker																		
1B	G. Burns	462	.310	4	66	1227	110	18	85	10.7	.987	J. Shaute	46	283	20	17	2	3.75
2B	C. Fewster	322	.267	0	36	194	229	17	36	4.7	.961	S. Smith	39	248	12	14	1	3.02
SS	J. Sewell	594	.316	4	104	**349**	**514**	36	76	**5.9**	.960	S. Coveleski	37	240	15	16	0	4.04
3B	R. Lutzke	341	.243	0	42	154	238	**22**	25	**4.0**	.947	G. Uhle	28	196	9	15	1	4.77
RF	H. Summa	390	.290	2	38	167	10	11	2	2.0	.941							
CF	T. Speaker	486	.344	9	65	323	20	13	3	2.8	.963							
LF	C. Jamieson	594	.359	3	53	330	11	9	6	2.5	.974							
C	G. Myatt	342	.342	8	73	248	63	7	7	3.3	.978							
OF	P. McNulty	291	.268	0	26	137	9	6	2	2.0	.961							
2B	Stephenson	240	.371	4	44	114	179	12	20	5.3	.961							
C	L. Sewell	165	.291	0	17	171	42	9	5	4.0	.959							
1B	F. Brower	107	.280	3	20	187	17	2	11	7.9	.990							
Boston W-67 L-87 Lee Fohl																		
1B	J. Harris	491	.301	3	77	1266	101	10	100	10.8	.993	H. Ehmke	45	**315**	19	17	4	3.46
2B	Wambsganss	636	.274	0	49	**459**	**490**	37	98	6.4	.962	A. Ferguson	40	235	14	17	2	3.79
SS	D. Lee	288	.253	0	29	198	246	30	43	5.3	.937	J. Quinn	43	228	12	13	7	3.20
3B	D. Clark	325	.277	2	54	88	173	15	8	3.0	.946	C. Fullerton	33	152	7	12	2	4.32
RF	I. Boone	486	.333	13	96	189	17	5	3	1.7	.976	B. Piercy	22	115	5	7	0	6.20
CF	I. Flagstead	560	.305	5	43	370	9	10	2	2.7	.974	G. Murray	28	80	2	9	0	6.72
LF	B. Veach	519	.295	5	99	268	15	13	2	2.3	.956							
C	S. O'Neill	307	.238	0	38	342	75	13	2	4.7	.970							
3B	H. Ezzell	273	.275	0	32	59	127	2	6	3.0	.989							
OF	S. Collins	240	.292	0	28	85	4	4	0	1.7	.957							
UT	H. Shanks	193	.259	0	25	118	129	9	23		.965							
C	V. Picinich	158	.266	1	24	155	36	10	2	3.9	.950							
Chicago W-66 L-87 Johnny Evers W-10 L-11 Ed Walsh W-1 L-2 Eddie Collins W-14 L-13 Johnny Evers W-41 L-61																		
1B	E. Sheely	535	.320	3	103	1423	79	14	97	10.4	.991	S. Thurston	38	291	20	14	1	3.80
2B	E. Collins	556	.349	6	86	396	446	20	83	5.7	**.977**	T. Lyons	41	216	12	11	3	4.87
SS	B. Barrett	406	.271	2	56	167	199	39	36	5.3	.904	R. Faber	21	161	9	11	0	3.85
3B	W. Kamm	528	.254	6	93	190	312	15	31	3.6	**.971**	S. Connally	44	160	7	13	6	4.05
RF	H. Hooper	476	.328	10	62	251	22	4	**8**	2.3	.986	Blankenship	25	125	7	6	1	5.17
CF	J. Mostil	385	.325	4	49	281	13	8	2	3.0	.974	M. Cvengros	26	106	3	12	0	5.88
LF	B. Falk	526	.352	6	99	292	26	10	4	2.4	.970	C. Robertson	17	97	4	10	0	4.99
C	B. Crouse	305	.259	1	44	298	97	**23**	9	4.6	.945							
OF	Archdeacon	288	.319	0	25	173	8	8	2	2.5	.958							

BATTING AND BASE RUNNING LEADERS

Batting Average		Slugging Average		Home Runs	
B. Ruth, NY	.378	B. Ruth, NY	.739	B. Ruth, NY	46
C. Jamieson, CLE	.359	H. Heilmann, DET	.533	J. Hauser, PHI	27
B. Falk, CHI	.352	K. Williams, STL	.533	B. Jacobson, STL	19
E. Collins, CHI	.349	B. Jacobson, STL	.528	K. Williams, STL	18
J. Bassler, DET	.346	G. Myatt, CLE	.518	I. Boone, BOS	13

Total Bases		Runs Batted In		Stolen Bases	
B. Ruth, NY	391	G. Goslin, WAS	129	E. Collins, CHI	42
B. Jacobson, STL	306	B. Ruth, NY	121	B. Meusel, NY	26
H. Heilmann, DET	304	B. Meusel, NY	120	S. Rice, WAS	24
G. Goslin, WAS	299	J. Hauser, PHI	115	T. Cobb, DET	23
J. Hauser, PHI	290	H. Heilmann, DET	113	C. Jamieson, CLE	21
		W. Pipp, NY	113		

Hits		Base on Balls		Home Run Percentage	
S. Rice, WAS	216	B. Ruth, NY	142	B. Ruth, NY	8.7
C. Jamieson, CLE	213	T. Rigney, DET	102	J. Hauser, PHI	4.8
T. Cobb, DET	211	E. Sheely, CHI	95	K. Williams, STL	4.5
B. Ruth, NY	200	E. Collins, CHI	89	B. Jacobson, STL	3.3

Runs Scored		Doubles		Triples	
B. Ruth, NY	143	H. Heilmann, DET	45	W. Pipp, NY	19
T. Cobb, DET	115	J. Sewell, CLE	45	G. Goslin, WAS	17
E. Collins, CHI	108	B. Jacobson, STL	41	H. Heilmann, DET	16
H. Hooper, CHI	107	Wambsganss, BOS	41	S. Rice, WAS	14

PITCHING LEADERS

Winning Percentage		Earned Run Average		Wins	
W. Johnson, WAS	.767	W. Johnson, WAS	2.72	W. Johnson, WAS	23
H. Pennock, NY	.700	T. Zachary, WAS	2.75	H. Pennock, NY	21
E. Whitehill, DET	.654	H. Pennock, NY	2.83	S. Thurston, CHI	20
T. Zachary, WAS	.625	Baumgartner, PHI	2.88	J. Shaute, CLE	20
G. Mogridge, WAS	.593	S. Smith, CLE	3.02	H. Ehmke, BOS	19
B. Shawkey, NY	.593				

Saves		Strikeouts		Complete Games	
F. Marberry, WAS	15	W. Johnson, WAS	158	S. Thurston, CHI	28
A. Russell, WAS	8	H. Ehmke, BOS	119	H. Ehmke, BOS	26
J. Quinn, BOS	7	B. Shawkey, NY	114	H. Pennock, NY	25
H. Dauss, DET	6	H. Pennock, NY	101	E. Rommel, PHI	21
S. Connally, CHI	6	U. Shocker, STL	84	J. Shaute, CLE	21

Fewest Hits/9 Innings		Shutouts		Fewest Walks/9 Innings	
W. Johnson, WAS	7.55	W. Johnson, WAS	6	S. Smith, CLE	1.53
R. Collins, DET	8.29	D. Davis, STL	5	U. Shocker, STL	1.84
T. Zachary, WAS	8.79	U. Shocker, STL	4	S. Thurston, CHI	1.86
E. Wingard, STL	8.88	H. Pennock, NY	4	H. Pennock, NY	2.01

Most Strikeouts/9 Inn.		Innings		Games Pitched	
W. Johnson, WAS	5.12	H. Ehmke, BOS	315	F. Marberry, WAS	50
B. Shawkey, NY	4.94	S. Thurston, CHI	291	K. Holloway, DET	49
H. Ehmke, BOS	3.40	H. Pennock, NY	286	J. Shaute, CLE	46
H. Pennock, NY	3.17	J. Shaute, CLE	283	W. Hoyt, NY	46

AMERICAN LEAGUE 1924, cont.

	W	L	PCT	GB	R	OR	Batting 2B	3B	HR	BA	SA	SB	Fielding E	DP	FA	Pitching CG	BB	SO	ShO	SV	ERA
Washington	92	62	.597		755	613	255	88	22	.294	.387	115	171	149	.972	74	505	469	12	25	3.35
New York	89	63	.586	2	798	667	248	86	98	.289	.426	69	156	131	.974	76	522	487	13	13	3.86
Detroit	86	68	.558	6	849	796	315	76	35	.298	.404	100	187	142	.971	60	466	441	5	20	4.19
St. Louis	74	78	.487	17	764	797	265	62	67	.294	.408	85	183	141	.969	68	512	382	11	7	4.55
Philadelphia	71	81	.467	20	685	778	251	59	63	.281	.389	79	180	157	.971	68	597	371	7	10	4.39
Cleveland	67	86	.438	24.5	755	814	306	59	41	.296	.399	84	205	130	.967	87	503	315	7	7	4.40
Boston	67	87	.435	25	725	801	300	61	30	.277	.374	79	210	124	.967	73	519	414	8	16	4.36
Chicago	66	87	.431	25.5	793	858	254	58	41	.288	.382	138	229	136	.963	76	512	360	1	11	4.75
					6124	6124	2194	549	397	.290	.396	749	1521	1110	.969	580	4136	3239	64	109	4.23

NATIONAL LEAGUE 1925

Team	POS	Player	AB	BA	HR	RBI	PO	A	E	DP	TC/G	FA	Pitcher	G	IP	W	L	SV	ERA
Pittsburgh W-95 L-58 Bill McKechnie	1B	G. Grantham	359	.326	8	52	925	44	11	96	9.6	.989	L. Meadows	35	255	19	10	1	3.67
	2B	E. Moore	547	.298	6	77	307	401	36	82	6.1	.952	R. Kremer	40	215	17	8	2	3.69
	SS	G. Wright	614	.308	18	121	338	530	56	109	6.0	.939	V. Aldridge	30	213	15	7	0	3.63
	3B	P. Traynor	591	.320	6	106	226	303	24	41	3.7	.957	J. Morrison	44	211	17	14	4	3.88
	RF	K. Cuyler	617	.357	17	102	362	21	13	4	2.6	.967	E. Yde	33	207	17	9	0	4.13
	CF	M. Carey	542	.343	5	44	363	20	20	2	3.1	.950	B. Adams	33	101	6	5	3	5.42
	LF	C. Barnhart	539	.325	4	114	295	11	12	2	2.3	.962							
	C	E. Smith	329	.313	8	64	317	77	13	15	4.2	.968							
	C	J. Gooch	215	.298	0	30	172	39	7	8	2.9	.968							
	1B	S. McInnis	155	.368	0	24	377	24	3	40	8.8	.993							
New York W-86 L-66 John McGraw	1B	B. Terry	489	.319	11	70	1270	77	14	83	10.8	.990	J. Scott	36	240	14	15	3	3.15
	2B	G. Kelly	586	.309	20	99	273	394	13	68	6.3	.981	V. Barnes	32	222	15	11	2	3.53
	SS	T. Jackson	411	.285	9	59	277	366	40	64	6.2	.941	Greenfield	29	172	12	8	0	3.88
	3B	F. Lindstrom	356	.287	4	33	123	147	12	9	2.9	.957	J. Bentley	28	157	11	9	1	5.04
	RF	R. Youngs	500	.264	6	53	214	24	12	2	2.0	.952	A. Nehf	29	155	11	9	1	3.77
	CF	Southworth	473	.292	6	44	289	7	11	1	2.6	.964	W. Dean	33	151	10	7	1	4.64
	LF	I. Meusel	516	.328	21	111	244	16	11	2	2.2	.959							
	C	F. Snyder	325	.240	11	51	336	71	6	7	4.3	.985							
	UT	F. Frisch	502	.331	11	48	215	393	37	45		.943							
	OF	H. Wilson	180	.239	6	30	75	3	2	2	1.6	.975							
Cincinnati W-80 L-73 Jack Hendricks	1B	W. Holke	232	.280	1	20	642	35	2	60	10.4	.997	P. Donohue	42	301	21	14	2	3.08
	2B	H. Critz	541	.277	2	51	340	542	27	96	6.3	.970	D. Luque	36	291	16	18	0	2.63
	SS	I. Caveney	358	.249	2	47	209	349	35	72	5.3	.941	E. Rixey	39	287	21	11	1	2.88
	3B	B. Pinelli	492	.283	2	49	113	265	22	21	3.7	.945	R. Benton	33	147	9	10	1	4.05
	RF	C. Walker	509	.318	6	71	332	12	6	4	2.5	.983	J. May	36	137	8	9	2	3.87
	CF	E. Roush	540	.339	8	83	343	15	8	3	2.7	.978	C. Mays	12	52	3	5	2	3.31
	LF	B. Zitzmann	301	.252	0	21	135	5	6	0	1.6	.959							
	C	B. Hargrave	273	.300	2	33	283	42	7	1	4.0	.979							
	10	R. Bressler	319	.348	4	61	602	23	12	46		.981							
	OF	E. Smith	284	.271	8	46	139	8	5	5	1.9	.967							
	3B	C. Dressen	215	.274	3	19	40	95	7	8	3.0	.951							
	SS	S. Bohne	214	.257	2	24	84	138	16	24	4.9	.933							
St. Louis W-77 L-76 Branch Rickey W-13 L-25 Rogers Hornsby W-64 L-51	1B	J. Bottomley	619	.367	21	128	1466	74	21	133	10.2	.987	J. Haines	29	207	13	14	0	4.57
	2B	R. Hornsby	504	.403	39	143	287	416	34	95	5.4	.954	B. Sherdel	32	200	15	6	1	3.11
	SS	S. Toporcer	268	.284	2	26	141	215	15	40	5.6	.960	F. Rhem	30	170	8	13	1	4.92
	3B	L. Bell	586	.285	11	88	151	284	36	39	3.1	.924	A. Sothoron	28	156	10	10	0	4.05
	RF	C. Hafey	358	.302	5	57	180	9	9	2	2.3	.955	A. Reinhart	20	145	11	5	0	3.05
	CF	H. Mueller	243	.313	1	26	165	6	8	3	2.5	.955	D. Mails	21	131	7	7	0	4.60
	LF	R. Blades	462	.342	12	57	266	13	6	4	2.5	.979	L. Dickerman	29	131	4	11	1	5.58
	C	B. O'Farrell	317	.278	3	32	324	67	10	5	4.4	.975	E. Dyer	27	82	4	3	3	4.15
	OF	R. Shinners	251	.295	7	36	161	2	3	1	2.5	.982							
	OF	J. Smith	243	.251	4	31	152	7	7	2	2.6	.958							
	OF	M. Flack	241	.249	0	28	103	8	1	1	1.9	.991							
	S2	J. Cooney	187	.273	0	18	97	137	6	31		.975							
	SS	T. Thevenow	175	.269	0	17	98	169	14	18	5.6	.950							
Boston W-70 L-83 Dave Bancroft	1B	D. Burrus	588	.340	5	87	1416	85	15	110	10.0	.990	J. Cooney	31	246	14	14	0	3.48
	2B	D. Gautreau	279	.262	0	23	171	231	10	39	6.1	.976	J. Barnes	32	216	11	16	0	4.53
	SS	D. Bancroft	479	.319	2	49	300	459	44	81	6.4	.945	L. Benton	31	183	14	7	1	3.09
	3B	B. Marriott	370	.268	1	40	96	187	22	13	3.4	.928	J. Genewich	34	169	12	10	0	3.99
	RF	J. Welsh	484	.312	7	63	237	27	11	7	2.4	.960	K. Graham	34	157	7	12	1	4.41
	CF	G. Felix	459	.307	2	66	328	15	10	3	3.1	.972	R. Ryan	37	123	2	8	2	6.31
	LF	B. Neis	355	.285	5	45	282	8	9	1	3.4	.970	R. Marquard	26	72	2	8	0	5.75
	C	F. Gibson	316	.278	2	50	271	60	11	7	3.9	.968							
	OF	D. Harris	340	.265	5	36	217	12	9	3	2.6	.962							
	2S	E. Padgett	256	.305	0	29	118	152	11	29		.961							
	C	M. O'Neil	222	.257	2	30	208	31	7	3	3.6	.972							
	3B	A. High	219	.288	4	28	47	93	3	7	2.4	.979							
	OF	L. Mann	184	.342	2	20	116	7	1	1	2.2	.992							
	UT	B. Smith	174	.282	0	23	78	145	17	20		.929							

NATIONAL LEAGUE 1925, cont.

	POS	Player	AB	BA	HR	RBI	PO	A	E	DP	TC/G	FA	Pitcher	G	IP	W	L	SV	ERA
Brooklyn	1B	J. Fournier	545	.350	22	130	1317	82	15	105	9.8	.989	D. Vance	31	265	**22**	9	0	3.53
	2B	M. Stock	615	.328	1	62	305	477	18	74	5.7	.978	B. Grimes	33	247	12	19	0	5.04
W-68 L-85	SS	J. Mitchell	336	.250	0	18	184	266	25	49	5.3	.947	R. Ehrhardt	36	208	10	14	1	5.03
	3B	J. Johnston	431	.297	2	43	76	110	24	10	2.6	.886	T. Osborne	41	175	8	15	1	4.94
Wilbert Robinson	RF	D. Cox	434	.329	7	64	197	14	7	4	2.0	.968	J. Petty	28	153	9	9	0	4.88
	CF	E. Brown	618	.306	5	99	449	7	13	3	3.1	.972	B. Hubbell	33	87	3	6	1	5.30
	LF	Z. Wheat	616	.359	14	103	320	7	13	2	2.3	.962							
	C	Z. Taylor	352	.310	3	44	294	102	17	12	4.3	.959							
	3B	C. Tierney	265	.257	2	39	54	102	6	6	2.7	.963							
	SS	H. Ford	216	.273	1	15	126	185	11	33	4.9	.966							
	C	H. DeBerry	193	.259	2	24	309	50	7	4	6.7	.981							
Philadelphia	1B	C. Hawks	320	.322	5	45	775	45	12	64	9.2	.986	J. Ring	38	270	14	16	0	4.37
	2B	B. Friberg	304	.270	5	22	181	257	16	37	5.9	.965	H. Carlson	35	234	13	14	0	4.23
W-68 L-85	SS	H. Sand	496	.278	3	55	352	420	60	91	5.8	.928	C. Mitchell	32	199	10	17	1	5.28
	3B	C. Huber	436	.284	5	54	107	199	17	16	2.7	.947	A. Decatur	25	128	4	13	2	5.27
Art Fletcher	RF	C. Williams	314	.331	13	60	173	12	2	3	1.9	.989	J. Knight	33	105	7	6	3	6.84
	CF	G. Harper	495	.349	18	97	319	16	10	5	2.7	.971	H. Betts	35	97	4	5	1	5.55
	LF	G. Burns	349	.292	1	22	189	9	2	2	2.3	.990	J. Couch	34	94	5	6	2	5.44
	C	J. Wilson	335	.328	3	54	275	50	6	9	3.7	.982							
	21	L. Fonseca	467	.319	7	60	648	245	20	68		.978							
	OF	F. Leach	292	.312	5	28	178	2	9	1	2.9	.952							
	UT	Wrightstone	286	.346	14	61	152	62	16	11		.930							
	C	B. Henline	263	.304	8	48	209	53	12	9	4.0	.956							
	OF	J. Mokan	209	.330	6	42	120	1	2	0	1.8	.984							
Chicago	1B	C. Grimm	519	.306	10	76	1317	73	15	125	10.1	.989	G. Alexander	32	236	15	11	0	3.39
	2B	S. Adams	**627**	.287	2	48	**354**	551	16	90	6.4	**.983**	S. Blake	36	231	10	18	2	4.86
W-68 L-86	SS	Maranville	266	.233	0	23	162	261	20	51	6.0	.955	W. Cooper	32	212	12	14	0	4.28
	3B	H. Freigau	476	.307	8	71	98	185	27	20	3.2	.913	T. Kaufmann	31	196	13	13	2	4.50
Bill Killefer	RF	C. Heathcote	380	.263	5	39	241	21	8	**8**	2.7	.970	G. Bush	42	182	6	13	0	4.30
W-33 L-42	CF	M. Brooks	349	.281	13	72	249	9	6	2	3.0	.977	P. Jones	28	124	6	6	0	4.65
	LF	A. Jahn	226	.301	0	37	124	5	2	3	2.3	.985							
Rabbit Maranville	C	G. Hartnett	398	.289	24	67	**409**	114	23	15	5.0	.958							
W-23 L-30	OF	T. Griffith	235	.285	7	27	109	9	8	1	2.1	.937							
	C	M. Gonzalez	197	.264	3	18	155	31	2	7	3.8	.989							
George Gibson	OF	B. Weis	180	.267	2	25	78	3	3	0	1.8	.964							
W-12 L-14	S3	P. Pittenger	173	.312	0	15	71	127	11	13		.947							
	OF	D. Grigsby	137	.255	0	20	81	4	3	2	2.3	.966							

BATTING AND BASE RUNNING LEADERS

Batting Average
R. Hornsby, STL .403
J. Bottomley, STL .367
Z. Wheat, BKN .359
K. Cuyler, PIT .357
J. Fournier, BKN .350

Slugging Average
R. Hornsby, STL .756
K. Cuyler, PIT .593
J. Bottomley, STL .578
J. Fournier, BKN .569
G. Harper, PHI .558

Home Runs
R. Hornsby, STL 39
G. Hartnett, CHI 24
J. Fournier, BKN 22
I. Meusel, NY 21
J. Bottomley, STL 21

Winning Percentage
B. Sherdel, STL .714
D. Vance, BKN .710
V. Aldridge, PIT .682
R. Kremer, PIT .680
E. Rixey, CIN .656

Earned Run Average
D. Luque, CIN 2.63
E. Rixey, CIN 2.88
A. Reinhart, STL 3.05
P. Donohue, CIN 3.08
L. Benton, BOS 3.09

Wins
D. Vance, BKN 22
E. Rixey, CIN 21
P. Donohue, CIN 21
L. Meadows, PIT 19

Total Bases
R. Hornsby, STL 381
K. Cuyler, PIT 366
J. Bottomley, STL 358
Z. Wheat, BKN 333
J. Fournier, BKN 310

Runs Batted In
R. Hornsby, STL 143
J. Fournier, BKN 130
J. Bottomley, STL 128
G. Wright, PIT 121
C. Barnhart, PIT 114

Stolen Bases
M. Carey, PIT 46
K. Cuyler, PIT 41
S. Adams, CHI 26
E. Roush, CIN 22
F. Frisch, NY 21

Saves
J. Morrison, PIT 4
G. Bush, CHI 4

Strikeouts
D. Vance, BKN 221
D. Luque, CIN 140
S. Blake, CHI 93
J. Ring, PHI 93
V. Aldridge, PIT 88

Complete Games
P. Donohue, CIN 27
D. Vance, BKN 26
D. Luque, CIN 22
E. Rixey, CIN 22
J. Ring, PHI 21

Hits
J. Bottomley, STL 227
Z. Wheat, BKN 221
K. Cuyler, PIT 220
R. Hornsby, STL 203

Base on Balls
J. Fournier, BKN 86
R. Hornsby, STL 83
E. Moore, PIT 73
R. Youngs, NY 66

Home Run Percentage
R. Hornsby, STL 7.7
G. Hartnett, CHI 6.0
C. Williams, PHI 4.1
I. Meusel, NY 4.1

Fewest Hits/9 Innings
D. Luque, CIN 8.13
L. Benton, BOS 8.35
D. Vance, BKN 8.38
V. Aldridge, PIT 9.20

Shutouts
D. Vance, BKN 4
H. Carlson, PHI 4
D. Luque, CIN 4
P. Donohue, CIN 3

Fewest Walks/9 Innings
G. Alexander, CHI 1.11
P. Donohue, CIN 1.47
E. Rixey, CIN 1.47
J. Cooney, BOS 1.83

Runs Scored
K. Cuyler, PIT 144
R. Hornsby, STL 133
Z. Wheat, BKN 125
P. Traynor, PIT 114

Doubles
J. Bottomley, STL 44
K. Cuyler, PIT 43
Z. Wheat, BKN 42
R. Hornsby, STL 41

Triples
K. Cuyler, PIT 26
C. Walker, CIN 16
E. Roush, CIN 16
J. Fournier, BKN 16

Most Strikeouts/9 Inn.
D. Vance, BKN 7.50
D. Luque, CIN 4.33
V. Aldridge, PIT 3.71
S. Blake, CHI 3.62

Innings
P. Donohue, CIN 301
D. Luque, CIN 291
E. Rixey, CIN 287
J. Ring, PHI 270

Games Pitched
J. Morrison, PIT 44
P. Donohue, CIN 42
G. Bush, CHI 42
T. Osborne, BKN 41

PITCHING LEADERS

NATIONAL LEAGUE 1925, cont.

	W	L	PCT	GB	R	OR	2B	3B	HR	BA	SA	SB	E	DP	FA	CG	BB	SO	ShO	SV	ERA
										Batting				**Fielding**			**Pitching**				
Pittsburgh	95	58	.621		912	715	316	105	77	.307	.448	159	224	171	.964	77	387	386	2	13	3.87
New York	86	66	.566	8.5	736	702	239	61	114	.283	.415	79	199	129	.968	80	408	446	6	8	3.94
Cincinnati	80	73	.523	15	690	643	221	90	44	.285	.387	108	203	161	.968	92	324	437	11	12	3.38
St. Louis	77	76	.503	18	828	764	292	80	109	.299	.445	70	204	156	.966	82	470	428	8	7	4.36
Boston	70	83	.458	25	708	802	260	70	41	.292	.390	77	221	145	.964	77	458	351	5	4	4.39
Brooklyn	68	85	.444	27	786	866	250	80	64	.296	.406	37	210	130	.966	82	477	518	4	4	4.77
Philadelphia	68	85	.444	27	812	930	288	58	100	.295	.425	48	211	147	.966	69	444	371	8	9	5.02
Chicago	68	86	.442	27.5	723	773	254	70	85	.275	.396	94	198	161	.969	75	485	435	5	10	4.41
					6195	6195	2120	614	634	.292	.414	672	1670	1200	.966	634	3453	3372	49	67	4.27

AMERICAN LEAGUE 1925

	POS	Player	AB	BA	HR	RBI	PO	A	E	DP	TC/G	FA	Pitcher	G	IP	W	L	SV	ERA
Washington	1B	J. Judge	376	.314	8	66	901	71	7	92	9.0	.993	S. Coveleski	32	241	20	5	0	2.84
	2B	B. Harris	551	.287	1	66	402	429	26	107	6.0	.970	W. Johnson	30	229	20	7	0	3.07
W-96 L-55	SS	Peckinpaugh	422	.294	4	64	215	345	28	71	4.7	.952	D. Ruether	30	223	18	7	0	3.87
	3B	O. Bluege	522	.287	4	79	158	285	22	29	3.2	.953	T. Zachary	38	218	12	15	2	3.85
Bucky Harris	RF	S. Rice	649	.350	1	87	339	20	12	7	2.4	.968	F. Marberry	55	93	8	6	15	3.47
	CF	E. McNeely	385	.286	3	37	259	13	7	3	2.5	.975							
	LF	G. Goslin	601	.334	18	113	385	24	12	1	2.8	.971							
	C	M. Ruel	393	.310	0	54	491	103	11	18	4.8	.982							
	1O	J. Harris	300	.323	12	59	461	41	6	40		.988							
	P	W. Johnson	97	.433	2	20	5	37	0	2	1.4	1.000							
Philadelphia	1B	J. Poole	480	.298	5	67	1166	65	23	102	10.2	.982	E. Rommel	52	261	21	10	3	3.69
	2B	M. Bishop	368	.280	4	27	233	352	26	53	5.9	.957	S. Harriss	46	252	19	12	1	3.50
W-88 L-64	SS	C. Galloway	481	.241	3	71	296	431	35	89	5.1	.954	L. Grove	45	197	10	12	1	4.75
	3B	S. Hale	391	.345	8	63	98	173	24	19	3.1	.919	S. Gray	32	196	16	8	3	3.40
Connie Mack	RF	B. Miller	474	.319	10	81	158	7	5	1	1.5	.971	R. Walberg	53	192	8	14	7	3.99
	CF	A. Simmons	658	.384	24	129	447	8	16	2	3.1	.966	Baumgartner	37	113	6	3	3	3.57
	LF	B. Lamar	568	.356	3	77	283	18	15	4	2.4	.953							
	C	M. Cochrane	420	.331	6	55	419	79	8	9	3.8	.984							
	32	J. Dykes	465	.323	5	55	225	302	21	45		.962							
	OF	F. Welch	202	.277	4	41	85	6	3	3	1.6	.968							
St. Louis	1B	G. Sisler	649	.345	12	105	1330	131	26	120	9.9	.983	M. Gaston	42	239	15	14	1	4.41
	2B	M. McManus	587	.288	13	90	430	479	31	93	6.1	.967	J. Bush	33	214	14	14	0	4.97
W-82 L-71	SS	B. LaMotte	356	.272	2	51	220	270	39	57	5.7	.926	E. Vangilder	52	193	14	8	6	4.70
	3B	G. Robertson	582	.271	14	76	201	287	32	41	3.4	.938	D. Davis	35	180	12	7	1	4.59
George Sisler	RF	H. Rice	354	.359	11	47	175	13	3	1	2.2	.984	J. Giard	30	161	10	5	0	5.04
	CF	B. Jacobson	540	.341	15	76	383	18	13	9	3.0	.969	D. Danforth	38	159	7	9	2	4.36
	LF	K. Williams	411	.331	25	105	242	11	12	4	2.6	.955	E. Wingard	32	153	9	10	0	5.06
	C	L. Dixon	205	.224	1	19	233	70	6	8	4.1	.981							
	OF	H. Bennett	298	.279	2	37	140	12	14	1	2.3	.916							
	SS	W. Gerber	246	.272	0	19	144	206	19	39	5.2	.949							
	C	P. Hargrave	225	.284	8	43	211	44	5	4	4.2	.981							
	OF	J. Tobin	193	.301	2	27	61	1	0	0	1.6	1.000							
	OF	J. Evans	159	.314	0	20	96	3	0	2	2.1	1.000							
	C	H. Severeid	109	.367	1	21	114	24	1	3	4.5	.993							
Detroit	1B	L. Blue	532	.306	3	94	1480	101	19	115	10.8	.988	E. Whitehill	35	239	11	11	2	4.66
	2B	F. O'Rourke	482	.293	5	57	309	382	21	67	6.0	.971	H. Dauss	35	228	16	11	1	3.16
W-81 L-73	SS	J. Tavener	453	.245	0	47	229	398	24	73	4.9	.963	K. Holloway	38	158	13	4	2	4.62
	3B	F. Haney	398	.279	0	40	115	207	16	22	3.2	.953	L. Stoner	34	152	10	9	1	4.26
Ty Cobb	RF	H. Heilmann	573	.393	13	133	278	9	9	1	2.0	.970	R. Collins	26	140	6	11	0	4.56
	CF	T. Cobb	415	.378	12	102	267	9	15	1	2.0	.948	E. Wells	35	134	6	9	2	6.23
	LF	A. Wingo	440	.370	5	68	282	16	9	6	2.5	.971	D. Leonard	18	126	11	4	0	4.51
	C	J. Bassler	344	.279	0	52	375	87	8	14	4.0	.983	J. Doyle	45	118	4	7	8	5.93
	OF	H. Manush	277	.303	5	47	153	7	3	0	2.2	.982							
	OF	Fothergill	204	.353	2	38	120	6	3	2	2.2	.977							
	2B	L. Burke	180	.289	0	24	100	130	9	27	4.6	.962							
	C	L. Woodall	171	.205	0	13	165	38	7	4	2.8	.967							
Chicago	1B	E. Sheely	600	.315	9	111	1565	95	20	136	11.0	.988	T. Lyons	43	263	21	11	3	3.26
	2B	E. Collins	425	.346	3	80	290	346	20	74	5.7	.970	R. Faber	34	238	12	11	0	3.78
W-79 L-75	SS	I. Davis	562	.240	0	61	313	472	53	97	5.8	.937	Blankenship	40	222	17	8	1	3.16
	3B	W. Kamm	509	.279	6	83	182	310	22	32	3.4	.957	S. Thurston	36	175	10	14	1	6.17
Eddie Collins	RF	H. Hooper	442	.265	6	55	231	16	6	4	2.0	.976	C. Robertson	24	137	8	12	0	5.26
	CF	J. Mostil	605	.299	2	50	446	11	7	5	3.0	.985	M. Cvengros	22	105	3	9	0	4.30
	LF	B. Falk	602	.301	4	99	306	18	14	4	2.2	.959	S. Connally	40	105	6	7	8	4.64
	C	R. Schalk	343	.274	0	52	368	99	8	15	3.8	.983							
	UT	B. Barrett	245	.363	3	40	132	131	19	24		.933							
	C	B. Crouse	131	.351	2	25	104	36	7	5	3.1	.952							

AMERICAN LEAGUE 1925, cont.

	POS	Player	AB	BA	HR	RBI	PO	A	E	DP	TC/G	FA	Pitcher	G	IP	W	L	SV	ERA
Cleveland	1B	G. Burns	488	.336	6	79	1195	82	14	94	10.2	.989	S. Smith	31	237	11	14	1	4.86
	2B	C. Fewster	294	.248	1	38	222	237	30	41	5.7	.939	G. Uhle	29	211	13	11	0	4.10
W-70 L-84	SS	J. Sewell	608	.336	1	98	314	529	29	80	5.7	.967	B. Karr	32	198	11	12	0	4.78
	3B	R. Lutzke	238	.218	1	16	61	129	13	9	2.9	.936	J. Miller	32	190	10	13	2	3.31
Tris Speaker	RF	P. McNulty	373	.314	6	43	206	16	8	2	2.1	.965	G. Buckeye	30	153	13	8	0	3.65
	CF	T. Speaker	429	.389	12	87	311	16	11	9	3.1	.967	J. Shaute	26	131	4	12	4	5.43
	LF	C. Jamieson	557	.296	4	42	324	16	16	4	2.6	.955							
	C	G. Myatt	358	.271	11	54	273	53	9	2	3.4	.973							
	32	F. Spurgeon	376	.287	0	32	155	250	21	30		.951							
	OF	C. Lee	230	.322	4	42	129	7	7	2	2.0	.951							
	OF	H. Summa	224	.330	2	25	83	2	3	0	1.6	.966							
	C	L. Sewell	220	.232	0	18	216	54	8	13	4.2	.971							
New York	1B	L. Gehrig	437	.295	20	68	1126	53	13	72	10.5	.989	H. Pennock	47	277	16	17	2	2.96
	2B	A. Ward	439	.246	4	38	246	317	20	57	5.2	.966	S. Jones	43	247	15	21	2	4.63
W-69 L-85	SS	P. Wanninger	403	.236	1	22	214	296	30	59	4.9	.944	U. Shocker	41	244	12	12	3	3.65
	3B	J. Dugan	404	.292	0	31	118	202	10	19	3.4	.970	W. Hoyt	46	243	11	14	6	4.00
Miller Huggins	RF	B. Ruth	359	.290	25	66	207	15	6	3	2.3	.974	B. Shawkey	33	186	6	14	0	4.11
	CF	E. Combs	593	.342	3	61	401	12	9	2	2.8	.979							
	LF	B. Meusel	624	.290	33	138	249	9	4	6	2.0	.985							
	C	B. Bengough	283	.258	0	23	325	83	3	12	4.4	.993							
	OF	B. Paschal	247	.360	12	56	117	6	6	0	2.0	.953							
	1B	W. Pipp	178	.230	3	24	399	38	4	40	9.4	.991							
	2S	E. Johnson	170	.282	5	17	87	107	9	21		.956							
	C	W. Schang	167	.240	2	24	172	55	6	8	4.0	.974							
	32	H. Shanks	155	.258	1	18	64	87	6	13		.962							
Boston	1B	P. Todt	544	.278	11	75	1408	100	13	126	10.9	.991	H. Ehmke	34	261	9	20	1	3.73
	2B	Wambsganss	360	.231	1	41	254	326	26	60	5.9	.957	T. Wingfield	41	254	12	19	2	3.96
W-47 L-105	SS	D. Lee	255	.224	0	19	188	260	37	64	5.8	.924	R. Ruffing	37	217	9	18	1	5.01
	3B	D. Prothro	415	.313	0	51	115	211	19	16	3.2	.945	P. Zahniser	37	177	5	12	1	5.15
Lee Fohl	RF	I. Boone	476	.330	9	68	198	9	13	1	1.9	.941	J. Quinn	19	105	7	8	0	4.37
	CF	I. Flagstead	572	.280	6	61	429	24	11	6	3.2	.976	B. Ross	33	94	3	8	0	6.20
	LF	R. Carlyle	276	.326	7	49	122	5	13	0	2.1	.907							
	C	V. Picinich	251	.255	1	25	222	53	9	3	3.8	.968							
	OF	T. Vache	252	.313	3	48	87	2	9	0	1.8	.908							
	OF	D. Williams	218	.229	0	13	117	4	6	1	2.4	.953							
	3B	H. Ezzell	186	.285	0	15	53	89	13	5	3.3	.916							
	2B	B. Rogell	169	.195	0	17	98	145	17	29	5.3	.935							
	SS	B. Connolly	107	.262	0	21	60	72	7	13	4.1	.950							

BATTING AND BASE RUNNING LEADERS

Batting Average
H. Heilmann, DET	.393
T. Speaker, CLE	.389
A. Simmons, PHI	.384
T. Cobb, DET	.378
A. Wingo, DET	.370

Slugging Average
K. Williams, STL	.613
T. Cobb, DET	.598
A. Simmons, PHI	.596
A. Simmons, PHI	.578
H. Heilmann, DET	.569

Home Runs
B. Meusel, NY	33
B. Ruth, NY	25
K. Williams, STL	25
A. Simmons, PHI	24
L. Gehrig, NY	20

Total Bases
A. Simmons, PHI	392
B. Meusel, NY	338
G. Goslin, WAS	329
H. Heilmann, DET	326
G. Sisler, STL	311

Runs Batted In
B. Meusel, NY	138
H. Heilmann, DET	133
A. Simmons, PHI	129
G. Goslin, WAS	113
E. Sheely, CHI	111

Stolen Bases
J. Mostil, CHI	43
G. Goslin, WAS	26
S. Rice, WAS	26
E. Collins, CHI	19
L. Blue, DET	19
I. Davis, CHI	19

Hits
A. Simmons, PHI	253
S. Rice, WAS	227
H. Heilmann, DET	225
G. Sisler, STL	224

Base on Balls
W. Kamm, CHI	90
J. Mostil, CHI	90
M. Bishop, PHI	87
E. Collins, CHI	87

Home Run Percentage
K. Williams, STL	6.1
B. Meusel, NY	5.3
L. Gehrig, NY	4.6
J. Harris, BOS, WAS	4.1

Runs Scored
J. Mostil, CHI	135
A. Simmons, PHI	122
E. Combs, NY	117
G. Goslin, WAS	116

Doubles
M. McManus, STL	44
E. Sheely, CHI	43
A. Simmons, PHI	43
G. Burns, CLE	41

Triples
G. Goslin, WAS	20
J. Mostil, CHI	16
G. Sisler, STL	15
P. Todt, BOS	13

PITCHING LEADERS

Winning Percentage
S. Coveleski, WAS	.800
W. Johnson, WAS	.741
D. Ruether, WAS	.720
Blankenship, CHI	.680
E. Rommel, PHI	.677

Earned Run Average
S. Coveleski, WAS	2.84
H. Pennock, NY	2.96
W. Johnson, WAS	3.07
H. Dauss, DET	3.16
Blankenship, CHI	3.16

Wins
E. Rommel, PHI	21
T. Lyons, CHI	21
S. Coveleski, WAS	20
W. Johnson, WAS	20
S. Harriss, PHI	19

Saves
F. Marberry, WAS	15
S. Connally, CHI	8
J. Doyle, DET	8
R. Walberg, PHI	7
E. Vangilder, STL	6
W. Hoyt, NY	6

Strikeouts
L. Grove, PHI	116
W. Johnson, WAS	108
S. Harriss, PHI	95
H. Ehmke, BOS	95
S. Jones, NY	92

Complete Games
S. Smith, CLE	22
H. Ehmke, BOS	22
H. Pennock, NY	21
T. Lyons, CHI	19
T. Wingfield, BOS	18

Fewest Hits/9 Innings
W. Johnson, WAS	8.29
S. Coveleski, WAS	8.59
H. Pennock, NY	8.68
Blankenship, CHI	8.84

Shutouts
T. Lyons, CHI	5
J. Giard, STL	4
S. Gray, PHI	4

Fewest Walks/9 Innings
S. Smith, CLE	1.82
J. Quinn, BOS, PHI	1.85
U. Shocker, NY	2.14
R. Faber, CHI	2.23

Most Strikeouts/9 Inn.
W. Johnson, WAS	4.24
S. Gray, PHI	3.68
S. Harriss, PHI	3.39
S. Jones, NY	3.36

Innings
H. Pennock, NY	277
T. Lyons, CHI	263
E. Rommel, PHI	261
H. Ehmke, BOS	261

Games Pitched
F. Marberry, WAS	55
R. Walberg, PHI	53
E. Rommel, PHI	52
E. Vangilder, STL	52

AMERICAN LEAGUE 1925, *cont.*

	W	L	PCT	GB	R	OR	2B	3B	HR	BA	SA	SB	E	DP	FA	CG	BB	SO	ShO	SV	ERA
								Batting						**Fielding**			**Pitching**				
Washington	96	55	.636		829	**669**	251	71	56	.303	.411	**134**	170	**166**	.972	69	543	464	9	21	**3.67**
Philadelphia	88	64	.579	8.5	830	714	298	79	76	**.307**	.434	67	211	148	.966	61	544	**495**	8	18	3.89
St. Louis	82	71	.536	15	897	909	304	68	110	.298	**.439**	85	226	164	.964	67	675	419	7	10	4.85
Detroit	81	73	.526	16.5	**903**	829	277	**84**	50	.302	.413	97	173	143	.972	66	556	419	2	18	4.61
Chicago	79	75	.513	18.5	811	771	299	59	38	.284	.385	129	200	162	.968	71	**489**	374	**12**	13	4.34
Cleveland	70	84	.455	27.5	782	810	285	58	52	.297	.399	90	210	146	.967	**93**	493	345	6	9	4.49
New York	69	85	.448	28.5	706	774	247	74	110	.275	.410	67	**160**	150	**.974**	80	505	492	8	13	4.33
Boston	47	105	.309	49.5	639	921	257	64	41	.266	.364	42	271	150	.957	68	510	310	6	6	4.97
					6397	6397	2218	557	533	.292	.407	711	1621	1229	.968	575	4315	3318	58	108	4.39

NATIONAL LEAGUE 1926

	POS	Player	AB	BA	HR	RBI	PO	A	E	DP	TC/G	FA	Pitcher	G	IP	W	L	SV	ERA
St. Louis W-89 L-65 Rogers Hornsby	1B	J. Bottomley	603	.299	19	**120**	1607	54	19	118	10.9	.989	F. Rhem	34	258	**20**	7	0	3.21
	2B	R. Hornsby	527	.317	11	93	245	433	27	73	5.3	.962	B. Sherdel	34	235	16	12	0	3.49
	SS	T. Thevenow	563	.256	2	63	371	**597**	45	98	**6.5**	.956	J. Haines	33	183	13	4	1	3.25
	3B	L. Bell	581	.325	17	100	165	254	22	25	2.8	.950	V. Keen	26	152	10	9	0	4.56
	RF	Southworth	391	.317	11	69	228	5	7	0	2.4	.971	G. Alexander	23	148	9	7	2	2.91
	CF	T. Douthit	530	.308	3	52	**440**	14	20	2	3.4	.958	A. Reinhart	27	143	10	5	0	4.22
	LF	R. Blades	416	.305	8	43	229	10	5	1	2.3	.980	H. Bell	27	85	6	6	2	3.18
	C	B. O'Farrell	492	.293	7	68	**466**	117	10	12	4.1	.983							
	OF	C. Hafey	225	.271	4	38	106	6	3	1	2.1	.974							
	OF	H. Mueller	191	.267	3	28	106	7	6	3	2.3	.950							
	OF	W. Holm	144	.285	0	21	75	1	3	1	2.0	.962							
Cincinnati W-87 L-67 Jack Hendricks	1B	W. Pipp	574	.291	6	99	**1710**	92	15	**140**	11.7	.992	P. Donohue	47	286	**20**	14	2	3.37
	2B	H. Critz	607	.270	3	79	357	**588**	18	**107**	6.2	**.981**	C. Mays	39	281	19	12	1	3.14
	SS	F. Emmer	224	.196	0	18	141	242	34	40	5.3	.918	E. Rixey	37	233	14	8	0	3.40
	3B	C. Dressen	474	.266	4	48	108	**284**	14	19	3.3	.966	D. Luque	34	234	13	16	0	3.43
	RF	C. Walker	571	.306	6	78	325	21	14	8	2.4	.961	J. May	45	168	13	9	3	3.22
	CF	E. Roush	563	.323	7	79	304	12	15	2	2.3	.955	R. Lucas	39	154	8	5	2	3.68
	LF	Christensen	329	.350	0	41	170	6	4	2	1.9	.978							
	C	B. Hargrave	326	**.353**	6	62	276	50	4	7	3.5	**.988**							
	OF	R. Bressler	297	.357	1	51	155	4	5	1	2.1	.970							
	C	V. Picinich	240	.263	2	31	240	52	10	6	3.5	.967							
	3S	B. Pinelli	207	.222	0	24	52	141	11	9		.946							
	SS	H. Ford	197	.279	0	18	152	190	13	57	6.2	.963							
Pittsburgh W-84 L-69 Bill McKechnie	1B	G. Grantham	449	.318	8	70	1203	66	13	106	9.7	.990	R. Kremer	37	231	**20**	6	5	**2.61**
	2B	H. Rhyne	366	.251	2	39	167	220	13	46	6.1	.968	L. Meadows	36	227	**20**	9	0	3.97
	SS	G. Wright	458	.308	8	77	242	382	49	82	5.8	.927	V. Aldridge	30	190	10	13	4	4.07
	3B	P. Traynor	574	.317	3	92	**182**	279	**23**	**39**	3.3	.952	E. Yde	37	187	8	7	0	3.65
	RF	P. Waner	536	.336	8	79	307	21	8	3	2.4	.976	D. Songer	35	126	7	8	2	3.13
	CF	M. Carey	324	.222	0	28	225	8	14	3	3.0	.943	J. Morrison	26	122	6	8	3	3.38
	LF	K. Cuyler	614	.321	8	92	405	19	14	4	2.8	.968	J. Bush	19	111	6	6	3	3.01
	C	E. Smith	292	.346	2	46	307	63	14	10	3.9	.964							
	C	J. Gooch	218	.271	1	42	202	38	5	6	3.1	.980							
	OF	C. Barnhart	203	.192	0	10	101	5	1	1	1.8	.991							
	2B	J. Rawlings	181	.232	0	20	126	164	9	25	5.1	.970							
Chicago W-82 L-72 Joe McCarthy	1B	C. Grimm	524	.277	8	82	1416	68	18	139	10.2	.988	C. Root	42	271	18	**17**	2	2.82
	2B	S. Adams	**624**	.309	0	39	324	485	29	93	6.2	.965	S. Blake	39	198	11	12	1	3.60
	SS	J. Cooney	513	.251	1	47	344	492	24	**107**	6.1	**.972**	T. Kaufmann	26	170	9	7	2	3.02
	3B	H. Freigau	508	.270	3	51	133	242	13	22	2.9	**.966**	P. Jones	30	160	12	7	2	3.09
	RF	C. Heathcote	510	.276	10	53	306	22	5	8	2.5	**.985**	G. Bush	35	157	13	9	2	2.86
	CF	H. Wilson	529	.321	**21**	109	348	11	10	5	2.6	.973	B. Osborn	31	136	6	5	1	3.63
	LF	Stephenson	281	.338	3	44	126	7	7	0	1.9	.950	B. Piercy	19	90	6	5	0	4.48
	C	G. Hartnett	284	.275	8	41	307	86	9	6	4.6	.978							
	C	M. Gonzalez	253	.249	1	23	306	53	4	5	4.7	.989							
	OF	P. Scott	189	.286	3	34	114	7	4	2	2.1	.968							
	OF	J. Kelly	176	.335	0	32	58	3	3	0	1.6	.953							
New York W-74 L-77 John McGraw	1B	G. Kelly	499	.303	13	80	1196	79	9	89	11.3	**.993**	J. Scott	**50**	226	13	15	5	4.34
	2B	F. Frisch	545	.314	5	44	261	471	19	69	5.9	.975	Greenfield	39	223	13	12	1	3.96
	SS	T. Jackson	385	.327	8	51	256	351	24	71	5.8	.962	Fitzsimmons	37	219	14	10	0	2.88
	3B	F. Lindstrom	543	.302	9	76	151	251	16	23	3.0	.962	V. Barnes	31	185	8	13	2	2.87
	RF	R. Youngs	372	.306	4	43	170	18	5	5	2.1	.974	J. Ring	39	183	11	10	2	4.57
	CF	T. Tyson	335	.293	3	35	232	9	5	5	2.7	.980	McQuillan	33	167	11	10	0	3.72
	LF	I. Meusel	449	.292	6	65	197	10	9	1	1.9	.958	C. Davies	38	89	2	4	6	3.94
	C	P. Florence	188	.229	2	14	212	41	**17**	7	3.6	.937							
	OF	H. Mueller	305	.249	4	29	194	13	11	2	2.7	.950							
	1B	B. Terry	225	.289	5	43	391	31	9	36	11.3	.979							
	SS	D. Farrell	171	.287	2	23	106	124	12	22	4.6	.950							
	OF	Southworth	116	.328	5	30	62	2	2	1	2.4	.970							

NATIONAL LEAGUE 1926, cont.

POS	Player	AB	BA	HR	RBI	PO	A	E	DP	TC/G	FA	Pitcher	G	IP	W	L	SV	ERA
Brooklyn																		
W-71 L-82																		
Wilbert Robinson																		
1B	B. Herman	496	.319	11	81	918	60	14	55	9.8	.986	J. Petty	38	276	17	17	1	2.84
2B	C. Fewster	337	.243	2	24	225	297	26	38	5.3	.953	B. Grimes	30	225	12	13	0	3.71
SS	J. Butler	501	.269	1	68	243	317	30	43	5.8	.949	D. McWeeny	42	216	11	13	1	3.04
3B	B. Marriott	360	.267	3	42	80	173	20	6	2.6	.927	B. McGraw	33	174	9	13	1	4.59
RF	D. Cox	398	.296	1	45	201	12	8	2	1.9	.964	D. Vance	24	169	9	10	1	3.89
CF	G. Felix	432	.280	3	53	270	11	13	2	2.4	.956	J. Barnes	31	158	10	11	1	5.24
LF	Z. Wheat	411	.290	5	35	202	9	10	3	2.2	.955	R. Ehrhardt	44	97	2	5	4	3.90
C	M. O'Neil	201	.209	0	20	247	53	11	5	4.2	.965							
OF	M. Jacobson	288	.247	0	23	191	5	5	2	2.3	.975							
1B	J. Fournier	243	.284	11	48	548	28	8	19	9.1	.986							
SS	Maranville	234	.235	0	24	138	192	18	28	5.8	.948							
C	Hargreaves	208	.250	2	23	224	65	4	6	4.2	.986							
Boston																		
W-66 L-86																		
Dave Bancroft																		
1B	D. Burrus	486	.270	3	61	1153	**103**	12	97	9.8	.991	L. Benton	43	232	14	14	1	3.85
2B	D. Gautreau	266	.267	0	8	170	205	23	42	5.4	.942	J. Genewich	37	216	8	16	2	3.88
SS	D. Bancroft	453	.311	1	44	317	398	33	75	6.1	.956	B. Smith	33	193	10	13	1	3.91
3B	A. High	476	.296	2	66	99	155	10	15	3.3	.962	J. Wertz	32	189	11	9	0	3.28
RF	J. Welsh	490	.278	3	57	283	**23**	11	**8**	2.5	.965	G. Mogridge	39	142	6	10	3	4.50
CF	J. Smith	322	.311	2	25	206	8	6	0	2.7	.973	B. Hearn	34	117	4	9	2	4.22
LF	E. Brown	612	.328	2	84	401	10	15	2	2.8	.965	H. Goldsmith	19	101	5	7	0	4.37
C	Z. Taylor	432	.255	0	42	394	**123**	8	**17**	4.3	.985							
3S	E. Taylor	272	.268	0	33	117	174	13	28		.957							
OF	F. Wilson	236	.237	0	23	121	6	9	1	2.4	.934							
2B	E. Moore	184	.266	0	15	90	123	6	27	5.8	.973							
OF	L. Mann	129	.302	1	20	79	5	3	0	1.9	.966							
Philadelphia																		
W-58 L-93																		
Art Fletcher																		
1B	J. Bentley	240	.258	2	27	516	28	4	41	9.8	.993	H. Carlson	35	267	17	12	0	3.23
2B	B. Friberg	478	.268	1	51	**381**	512	22	89	6.4	.976	C. Mitchell	28	179	9	14	1	4.58
SS	H. Sand	567	.272	4	37	358	495	**55**	88	6.1	.939	Willoughby	47	168	8	12	1	5.95
3B	C. Huber	376	.245	1	34	110	214	15	22	2.9	.956	W. Dean	33	164	8	16	0	6.10
RF	C. Williams	336	.345	18	53	143	14	6	3	1.8	.963	D. Ulrich	45	148	8	13	1	4.08
CF	F. Leach	492	.329	11	71	313	15	7	2	2.7	.979	J. Knight	35	143	3	12	2	6.62
LF	J. Mokan	456	.303	6	62	221	16	8	4	2.0	.967							
C	J. Wilson	279	.305	4	32	228	78	16	5	4.1	.950							
UT	Wrightstone	368	.307	7	57	549	125	19	64		.973							
OF	A. Nixon	311	.293	4	41	206	7	5	3	2.5	.977							
C	B. Henline	283	.283	2	30	217	46	8	9	3.5	.970							
OF	G. Harper	194	.314	7	38	111	2	7	1	2.2	.942							

BATTING AND BASE RUNNING LEADERS   PITCHING LEADERS

Batting Average
B. Hargrave, CIN	.353
Christensen, CIN	.350
E. Smith, PIT	.346
C. Williams, PHI	.345
P. Waner, PIT	.336

Slugging Average
C. Williams, PHI	.568
H. Wilson, CHI	.539
P. Waner, PIT	.528
B. Hargrave, CIN	.525
L. Bell, STL	.518

Home Runs
H. Wilson, CHI	21
J. Bottomley, STL	19
C. Williams, PHI	18
L. Bell, STL	17
Southworth, NY, STL	16

Winning Percentage
R. Kremer, PIT	.769
F. Rhem, STL	.741
L. Meadows, PIT	.690
C. Mays, CIN	.613
P. Donohue, CIN	.588

Earned Run Average
R. Kremer, PIT	2.61
C. Root, CHI	2.82
J. Petty, BKN	2.84
Fitzsimmons, NY	2.88
T. Kaufmann, CHI	3.02

Wins
R. Kremer, PIT	20
F. Rhem, STL	20
L. Meadows, PIT	20
P. Donohue, CIN	20
C. Mays, CIN	19

Total Bases
J. Bottomley, STL	305
L. Bell, STL	301
H. Wilson, CHI	285
P. Waner, PIT	283
K. Cuyler, PIT	282

Runs Batted In
J. Bottomley, STL	120
H. Wilson, CHI	109
L. Bell, STL	100
Southworth, NY, STL	99
W. Pipp, CIN	99

Stolen Bases
K. Cuyler, PIT	35
S. Adams, CHI	27
T. Douthit, STL	23
F. Frisch, NY	23
R. Youngs, NY	21

Saves
C. Davies, NY	6
J. Scott, NY	5
R. Kremer, PIT	5
R. Ehrhardt, BKN	4

Strikeouts
D. Vance, BKN	140
C. Root, CHI	127
J. May, CIN	103
L. Benton, BOS	103
J. Petty, BKN	101

Complete Games
C. Mays, CIN	24
J. Petty, BKN	23
C. Root, CHI	21
H. Carlson, PHI	20
F. Rhem, STL	20

Hits
E. Brown, BOS	201
K. Cuyler, PIT	197
S. Adams, CHI	193
L. Bell, STL	189

Base on Balls
H. Wilson, CHI	69
P. Waner, PIT	66
H. Sand, PHI	66
D. Bancroft, BOS	64

Home Run Percentage
C. Williams, PHI	5.4
H. Wilson, CHI	4.0
Southworth, NY, STL	3.2
J. Bottomley, STL	3.2

Fewest Hits/9 Innings
J. Petty, BKN	8.03
F. Rhem, STL	8.41
P. Jones, CHI	8.48
G. Alexander, CHI, STL	8.58

Shutouts
P. Donohue, CIN	5
B. Smith, BOS	4
S. Blake, CHI	4

Fewest Walks/9 Innings
P. Donohue, CIN	1.23
G. Alexander, CHI, STL	1.39
H. Carlson, PHI	1.58
C. Mays, CIN	1.70

Runs Scored
K. Cuyler, PIT	113
P. Waner, PIT	101
Southworth, NY, STL	99
H. Sand, PHI	99

Doubles
J. Bottomley, STL	40
E. Roush, CIN	37
H. Wilson, CHI	36
B. Herman, BKN	35

Triples
P. Waner, PIT	22
C. Walker, CIN	20
P. Traynor, PIT	17
G. Wright, PIT	15

Most Strikeouts/9 Inn.
D. Vance, BKN	7.46
P. Jones, CHI	4.49
S. Blake, CHI	4.33
C. Root, CHI	4.21

Innings
P. Donohue, CIN	286
C. Mays, CIN	281
J. Petty, BKN	276
C. Root, CHI	271

Games Pitched
J. Scott, NY	50
P. Donohue, CIN	47
Willoughby, PHI	47
J. May, CIN	45

NATIONAL LEAGUE 1926, cont.

	W	L	PCT	GB	R	OR	Batting					SB	Fielding			Pitching					ERA
							2B	3B	HR	BA	SA		E	DP	FA	CG	BB	SO	ShO	SV	
St. Louis	89	65	.578		817	678	259	82	90	.286	.415	83	198	141	.969	90	397	365	10	6	3.67
Cincinnati	87	67	.565	2	747	651	242	120	35	.290	.400	51	183	160	.972	88	324	424	14	8	3.42
Pittsburgh	84	69	.549	4.5	769	689	243	106	44	.285	.396	91	220	161	.965	83	455	387	12	18	3.67
Chicago	82	72	.532	7	682	602	291	49	66	.278	.390	85	162	174	.974	77	486	508	13	14	3.26
New York	74	77	.490	13.5	663	668	214	58	73	.278	.384	94	186	150	.970	61	427	419	4	15	3.77
Brooklyn	71	82	.464	17.5	623	705	246	62	40	.263	.358	76	229	95	.963	83	472	517	5	9	3.82
Boston	66	86	.434	22	624	719	209	62	16	.277	.350	81	208	150	.967	60	455	408	9	9	4.03
Philadelphia	58	93	.384	29.5	687	900	244	50	75	.281	.390	47	224	153	.964	68	454	331	5	5	5.19
					5612	5612	1948	589	439	.280	.386	608	1610	1184	.968	610	3470	3359	72	84	3.84

AMERICAN LEAGUE 1926

Team	POS	Player	AB	BA	HR	RBI	PO	A	E	DP	TC/G	FA	Pitcher	G	IP	W	L	SV	ERA
New York W-91 L-63 Miller Huggins	1B	L. Gehrig	572	.313	16	107	1566	73	15	87	10.7	.991	H. Pennock	40	266	23	11	2	3.62
	2B	T. Lazzeri	589	.275	18	114	298	461	31	72	5.3	.961	U. Shocker	41	258	19	11	2	3.38
	SS	M. Koenig	617	.271	5	62	281	422	52	66	5.4	.931	W. Hoyt	40	218	16	12	4	3.85
	3B	J. Dugan	434	.288	1	64	122	221	16	10	2.9	.955	S. Jones	39	161	9	8	5	4.98
	RF	B. Ruth	495	.372	47	145	308	11	7	5	2.2	.979	M. Thomas	33	140	6	6	0	4.23
	CF	E. Combs	606	.299	8	56	375	8	12	2	2.7	.970	B. Shawkey	29	104	8	7	3	3.62
	LF	B. Meusel	413	.315	12	81	211	4	9	1	2.1	.960							
	C	P. Collins	290	.286	7	35	394	76	14	14	4.8	.971							
	OF	B. Paschal	258	.287	7	33	134	10	10	0	2.1	.935							
	3B	M. Gazella	168	.232	0	21	37	78	11	5	2.8	.913							
Cleveland W-88 L-66 Tris Speaker	1B	G. Burns	603	.358	4	114	1499	99	19	122	10.7	.988	G. Uhle	39	318	27	11	1	2.83
	2B	F. Spurgeon	614	.295	0	49	341	479	32	93	5.7	.962	D. Levsen	33	237	16	13	0	3.41
	SS	J. Sewell	578	.324	4	85	326	463	37	86	5.4	.955	J. Shaute	34	207	14	10	1	3.53
	3B	R. Lutzke	475	.261	0	59	160	302	19	27	3.4	.960	S. Smith	27	188	11	10	0	3.73
	RF	H. Summa	581	.308	4	76	328	18	9	5	2.3	.975	G. Buckeye	32	166	6	9	0	3.10
	CF	T. Speaker	540	.304	7	86	394	20	8	7	2.8	.981	B. Karr	30	113	5	6	1	5.00
	LF	C. Jamieson	555	.299	2	45	293	15	13	5	2.2	.960	J. Miller	18	83	7	4	1	3.27
	C	L. Sewell	433	.238	0	46	437	91	9	3	4.3	.983							
Philadelphia W-83 L-67 Connie Mack	1B	J. Poole	361	.294	8	63	887	55	8	71	9.4	.992	L. Grove	45	258	13	13	6	2.51
	2B	M. Bishop	400	.265	0	33	235	365	8	55	5.1	.987	E. Rommel	37	219	11	11	0	3.08
	SS	C. Galloway	408	.240	0	49	274	315	41	49	4.7	.935	J. Quinn	31	164	10	11	1	3.41
	3B	S. Hale	327	.281	4	43	82	152	13	16	3.2	.947	R. Walberg	40	151	12	10	2	2.80
	RF	W. French	397	.305	1	36	186	12	6	7	2.1	.971	S. Gray	38	151	11	12	0	3.64
	CF	A. Simmons	581	.343	19	109	333	11	9	5	2.4	.975	H. Ehmke	20	147	12	4	0	2.81
	LF	B. Lamar	419	.284	5	50	199	10	10	2	2.1	.954	J. Pate	47	113	9	0	6	2.71
	C	M. Cochrane	370	.273	8	47	502	90	15	5	5.3	.975							
	32	J. Dykes	429	.287	1	44	197	322	20	42		.963							
	1B	J. Hauser	229	.192	8	36	630	35	3	39	10.3	.996							
	OF	F. Welch	174	.282	4	23	75	4	2	1	1.7	.975							
Washington W-81 L-69 Bucky Harris	1B	J. Judge	453	.291	7	92	1145	95	8	90	9.8	.994	W. Johnson	33	262	15	16	0	3.61
	2B	B. Harris	537	.283	1	63	356	427	30	74	5.8	.963	S. Coveleski	36	245	14	11	1	3.12
	SS	B. Myer	434	.304	1	62	215	297	40	47	4.7	.928	D. Ruether	23	169	12	6	0	4.84
	3B	O. Bluege	487	.271	3	65	139	256	20	13	3.1	.952	F. Marberry	64	138	12	7	22	3.00
	RF	S. Rice	641	.337	3	76	342	25	15	5	2.5	.961	G. Crowder	19	100	7	4	1	3.96
	CF	E. McNeely	442	.303	0	48	274	9	9	3	2.4	.969							
	LF	G. Goslin	567	.354	17	108	373	25	15	8	2.8	.964							
	C	M. Ruel	368	.299	1	53	452	81	6	13	4.6	.989							
	10	J. Harris	257	.307	5	55	354	20	3	20		.992							
Chicago W-81 L-72 Eddie Collins	1B	E. Sheely	525	.299	6	89	1380	84	8	87	10.2	.995	T. Lyons	39	284	18	16	2	3.01
	2B	E. Collins	375	.344	1	62	228	307	15	53	5.4	.973	T. Thomas	44	249	15	12	2	3.80
	SS	Hunnefield	470	.274	3	48	185	259	32	44	4.9	.933	Blankenship	29	209	13	10	1	3.61
	3B	W. Kamm	480	.294	0	62	177	323	11	16	3.6	.978	R. Faber	27	185	15	9	0	3.56
	RF	B. Barrett	368	.307	6	61	179	8	6	2	1.9	.969	J. Edwards	32	142	6	9	1	4.18
	CF	J. Mostil	600	.328	4	42	440	15	15	4	3.2	.968	S. Thurston	31	134	6	8	3	5.02
	LF	B. Falk	566	.345	8	108	338	16	3	4	2.3	.992	S. Connally	31	108	6	5	3	3.16
	C	R. Schalk	226	.265	0	32	251	45	7	6	3.8	.977							
	OF	S. Harris	222	.252	2	27	106	6	6	2	1.9	.949							
	2B	R. Morehart	192	.318	0	21	71	136	11	13	4.5	.950							
Detroit W-79 L-75 Ty Cobb	1B	L. Blue	429	.287	1	52	1153	56	17	95	11.2	.986	E. Whitehill	36	252	16	13	0	3.99
	2B	C. Gehringer	459	.277	1	62	255	323	16	56	5.3	.973	S. Gibson	35	196	12	9	2	3.48
	SS	J. Tavener	532	.265	1	58	300	470	39	92	5.2	.952	E. Wells	36	178	12	10	0	4.15
	3B	J. Warner	311	.251	0	34	105	175	13	9	3.1	.956	L. Stoner	32	160	7	10	0	5.47
	RF	H. Heilmann	502	.367	9	103	228	18	7	4	1.9	.975	K. Holloway	36	139	4	6	2	5.12
	CF	H. Manush	498	.378	14	86	283	7	10	3	2.5	.967	H. Dauss	35	124	12	6	9	4.20
	LF	Fothergill	387	.367	3	73	245	3	10	0	2.5	.961	R. Collins	30	122	8	8	1	2.73
	C	C. Manion	176	.199	0	14	227	48	8	2	3.8	.972	A. Johns	35	113	6	4	1	5.35
	32	F. O'Rourke	363	.242	1	41	181	256	23	42		.950							
	OF	A. Wingo	298	.282	1	45	155	13	14	2	2.5	.923							
	1B	J. Neun	242	.298	0	15	433	22	3	34	9.3	.993							
	OF	T. Cobb	233	.339	4	62	109	4	6	2	2.2	.950							
	C	J. Bassler	174	.305	0	22	223	61	0	6	4.5	1.000							

AMERICAN LEAGUE 1926, *cont.*

	POS	Player	AB	BA	HR	RBI	PO	A	E	DP	TC/G	FA	Pitcher	G	IP	W	L	SV	ERA
St. Louis	1B	G. Sisler	613	.290	7	71	1467	87	21	**141**	10.6	.987	T. Zachary	34	247	14	15	0	3.60
	2B	O. Melillo	385	.255	1	30	225	297	19	65	6.1	.965	M. Gaston	32	214	10	**18**	0	4.33
W-62 L-92	SS	W. Gerber	411	.270	0	42	261	358	37	**92**	5.1	.944	E. Vangilder	42	181	9	11	1	5.17
	3B	M. McManus	549	.284	9	68	119	197	14	17	3.9	.958	E. Wingard	39	169	5	8	3	3.57
George Sisler	RF	B. Miller	353	.331	4	50	219	12	15*	2	2.6	.939	W. Ballou	43	154	11	10	2	4.79
	CF	H. Rice	578	.313	9	59	300	22	10	4	2.5	.970	J. Giard	22	90	3	10	0	7.00
	LF	K. Williams	347	.280	17	74	189	12	11	2	2.3	.948	D. Davis	27	83	3	8	1	4.66
	C	W. Schang	285	.330	8	50	224	75	10	7	3.8	.968							
	3B	G. Robertson	247	.251	1	19	58	112	14	9	3.3	.924							
	C	P. Hargrave	235	.281	7	37	165	50	5	7	3.7	.977							
	OF	H. Bennett	225	.267	1	26	106	9	6	3	2.4	.950							
	OF	C. Durst	219	.237	3	16	143	5	3	0	2.6	.980							
	OF	B. Jacobson	182	.286	2	21	105	2	4	0	2.2	.964							
Boston	1B	P. Todt	599	.255	7	69	1755	126	22	114	12.4	.988	H. Wiltse	37	196	8	15	0	4.22
	2B	B. Regan	403	.263	4	34	264	392	24	66	6.4	.965	T. Wingfield	43	191	11	16	3	4.44
W-46 L-107	SS	T. Rigney	525	.270	4	53	286	**492**	25	80	**5.5**	**.969**	P. Zahniser	30	172	6	**18**	0	4.97
	3B	F. Haney	462	.221	0	52	149	322	21	30	3.6	.957	R. Ruffing	37	166	6	15	2	4.39
Lee Fohl	RF	B. Jacobson	394	.305	6	69	193	7	4	1	2.1	.980	T. Welzer	40	141	4	3	0	4.79
	CF	I. Flagstead	415	.299	3	31	264	14	5	4	2.9	.982	S. Harriss	21	113	6	10	0	4.46
	LF	S. Rosenthal	285	.267	4	34	100	0	4	0	1.6	.962	F. Heimach	20	102	2	9	0	5.65
	C	A. Gaston	301	.223	0	21	284	69	7	5	3.7	.981	H. Ehmke	14	97	3	10	0	5.46
	2B	M. Herrera	237	.257	0	19	112	168	11	23	6.1	.962							
	OF	J. Tobin	209	.273	1	14	79	7	3	1	1.7	.966							
	OF	W. Shaner	191	.283	0	21	106	3	4	2	2.4	.965							
	OF	F. Bratschi	167	.275	0	19	55	1	3	0	1.6	.949							
	OF	R. Carlyle	164	.287	2	16	62	4	7	0	2.0	.904							

BATTING AND BASE RUNNING LEADERS

Batting Average
- H. Manush, DET — .378
- B. Ruth, NY — .372
- Fothergill, DET — .367
- H. Heilmann, DET — .367
- G. Burns, CLE — .358

Slugging Average
- B. Ruth, NY — .737
- A. Simmons, PHI — .566
- H. Manush, DET — .564
- L. Gehrig, NY — .549
- G. Goslin, WAS — .543

Home Runs
- B. Ruth, NY — 47
- A. Simmons, PHI — 19
- T. Lazzeri, NY — 18
- K. Williams, STL — 17
- G. Goslin, WAS — 17

Winning Percentage
- G. Uhle, CLE — .711
- H. Pennock, NY — .676
- R. Faber, CHI — .652
- U. Shocker, NY — .633
- W. Hoyt, NY — .571

Earned Run Average
- L. Grove, PHI — 2.51
- G. Uhle, CLE — 2.83
- T. Lyons, CHI — 3.01
- E. Rommel, PHI — 3.08
- S. Coveleski, WAS — 3.12

Wins
- G. Uhle, CLE — 27
- H. Pennock, NY — 23
- U. Shocker, NY — 19
- T. Lyons, CHI — 18

Total Bases
- B. Ruth, NY — 365
- A. Simmons, PHI — 329
- L. Gehrig, NY — 314
- G. Goslin, WAS — 308
- G. Burns, CLE — 298

Runs Batted In
- B. Ruth, NY — 145
- T. Lazzeri, NY — 114
- G. Burns, CLE — 114
- A. Simmons, PHI — 109
- B. Falk, CHI — 108
- G. Goslin, WAS — 108

Stolen Bases
- J. Mostil, CHI — 35
- S. Rice, WAS — 25
- Hunnefield, CHI — 24
- E. McNeely, WAS — 18
- J. Sewell, CLE — 17

Saves
- F. Marberry, WAS — 22
- H. Dauss, DET — 9
- J. Pate, PHI — 6
- L. Grove, PHI — 6
- S. Jones, NY — 5

Strikeouts
- L. Grove, PHI — 194
- G. Uhle, CLE — 159
- T. Thomas, CHI — 127
- W. Johnson, WAS — 125
- E. Whitehill, DET — 109

Complete Games
- G. Uhle, CLE — 32
- T. Lyons, CHI — 24
- W. Johnson, WAS — 22
- L. Grove, PHI — 20
- H. Pennock, NY — 19
- U. Shocker, NY — 19

Hits
- G. Burns, CLE — 216
- S. Rice, WAS — 216
- G. Goslin, WAS — 201
- A. Simmons, PHI — 199

Base on Balls
- B. Ruth, NY — 144
- M. Bishop, PHI — 116
- T. Rigney, BOS — 108
- L. Gehrig, NY — 105

Home Run Percentage
- B. Ruth, NY — 9.5
- K. Williams, STL — 4.9
- A. Simmons, PHI — 3.3
- T. Lazzeri, NY — 3.1

Fewest Hits/9 Innings
- L. Grove, PHI — 7.92
- T. Thomas, CHI — 8.13
- G. Uhle, CLE — 8.48
- T. Lyons, CHI — 8.50

Shutouts
- E. Wells, DET — 4

Fewest Walks/9 Innings
- H. Pennock, NY — 1.45
- S. Smith, CLE — 1.48
- E. Rommel, PHI — 2.22
- U. Shocker, NY — 2.47

Runs Scored
- B. Ruth, NY — 139
- L. Gehrig, NY — 135
- J. Mostil, CHI — 120
- E. Combs, NY — 113

Doubles
- G. Burns, CLE — 64
- A. Simmons, PHI — 53
- T. Speaker, CLE — 52
- B. Jacobson, BOS, STL — 51

Triples
- L. Gehrig, NY — 20
- C. Gehringer, DET — 17
- G. Goslin, WAS — 15
- J. Mostil, CHI — 15

Most Strikeouts/9 Inn.
- L. Grove, PHI — 6.77
- T. Thomas, CHI — 4.59
- G. Uhle, CLE — 4.50
- W. Johnson, WAS — 4.30

Innings
- G. Uhle, CLE — 318
- T. Lyons, CHI — 284
- H. Pennock, NY — 266
- W. Johnson, WAS — 262

Games Pitched
- F. Marberry, WAS — 64
- J. Pate, PHI — 47
- L. Grove, PHI — 45
- T. Thomas, CHI — 44

PITCHING LEADERS

	W	L	PCT	GB	R	OR	2B	3B	HR	BA	SA	SB	E	DP	FA	CG	BB	SO	ShO	SV	ERA
New York	91	63	.591		**847**	713	262	75	**121**	.289	**.437**	79	210	117	.966	64	478	486	4	20	3.86
Cleveland	88	66	.571	3	738	612	**333**	49	27	.289	.386	88	173	153	.972	**96**	**450**	381	11	4	3.40
Philadelphia	83	67	.553	6	677	**570**	259	65	61	.269	.383	56	171	131	.972	62	451	**571**	10	16	**3.00**
Washington	81	69	.540	8	802	761	244	**97**	43	**.292**	.401	**122**	184	129	.969	65	566	418	5	**26**	4.34
Chicago	81	72	.529	9.5	730	665	314	60	32	.289	.390	121	**165**	122	**.973**	85	506	458	11	12	3.74
Detroit	79	75	.513	12	793	830	281	90	36	.291	.398	88	193	151	.969	57	555	469	10	18	4.41
St. Louis	62	92	.403	29	682	845	253	78	72	.276	.394	62	235	**167**	.963	64	654	337	5	9	4.66
Boston	46	107	.301	44.5	562	835	249	54	32	.256	.343	48	193	143	.970	53	546	336	6	5	4.72
					5831	5831	2195	568	424	.281	.392	664	1524	1113	.969	546	4206	3456	62	110	4.02

NATIONAL LEAGUE 1927

	POS	Player	AB	BA	HR	RBI	PO	A	E	DP	TC/G	FA	Pitcher	G	IP	W	L	SV	ERA
Pittsburgh	1B	J. Harris	411	.326	5	73	1056	78	11	84	9.9	.990	L. Meadows	40	299	19	10	0	3.40
	2B	G. Grantham	531	.305	8	66	279	363	32	65	5.4	.953	C. Hill	43	278	22	11	3	3.24
W-94 L-60	SS	G. Wright	570	.281	9	105	296	430	45	82	5.4	.942	V. Aldridge	35	239	15	10	1	4.25
	3B	P. Traynor	573	.342	5	106	212	265	19	23	3.5	.962	R. Kremer	35	226	19	8	2	2.47
Donie Bush	RF	P. Waner	623	**.380**	9	131	326	20	7	4	2.5	.980	J. Dawson	20	81	3	7	0	4.46
	CF	L. Waner	629	.355	2	27	396	9	10	0	2.8	.976	J. Miljus	19	76	8	3	0	1.90
	LF	C. Barnhart	360	.319	3	54	222	5	5	2	2.5	.978							
	C	J. Gooch	291	.258	2	48	285	57	9	7	3.9	.974							
	OF	K. Cuyler	285	.309	3	31	195	6	4	0	2.8	.980							
	C	E. Smith	189	.270	5	25	187	32	3	2	3.6	.986							
	2B	H. Rhyne	168	.274	0	17	105	101	8	19	4.8	.963							
St. Louis	1B	J. Bottomley	574	.303	19	124	**1656**	70	20	**149**	11.5	.989	J. Haines	38	301	24	10	1	2.72
	2B	F. Frisch	617	.337	10	78	396	**641**	22	104	6.9	.979	G. Alexander	37	268	21	10	3	2.52
W-92 L-61	SS	H. Schuble	218	.257	4	28	120	192	29	36	5.2	.915	B. Sherdel	39	232	17	12	6	3.53
	3B	L. Bell	390	.259	9	65	85	142	24	13	2.5	.904	F. Rhem	27	169	10	12	0	4.41
Bob O'Farrell	RF	W. Holm	419	.286	3	66	201	3	7	0	2.2	.967							
	CF	T. Douthit	488	.262	5	50	396	8	15	4	**3.4**	.964							
	LF	C. Hafey	346	.329	18	63	179	19	4	7	2.1	.980							
	C	F. Snyder	194	.258	1	30	174	37	4	5	3.5	.981							
	OF	Southworth	306	.301	2	39	153	6	5	2	2.0	.970							
	3S	S. Toporcer	290	.248	0	19	86	157	12	21		.953							
	SS	T. Thevenow	191	.194	0	4	111	199	18	38	5.6	.945							
	OF	R. Blades	180	.317	2	29	64	0	6	0	1.4	.914							
	C	B. O'Farrell	178	.264	0	18	141	45	4	5	3.6	.979							
	C	J. Schulte	156	.288	9	32	172	45	10	6	3.8	.956							
New York	1B	B. Terry	580	.326	20	121	1621	**105**	12	135	**11.6**	.993	B. Grimes	39	260	19	8	2	3.54
	2B	R. Hornsby	568	.361	26	125	299	582	25	98	5.8	.972	Fitzsimmons	42	245	17	10	3	3.72
W-92 L-62	SS	T. Jackson	469	.318	14	98	287	**444**	37	85	6.2	.952	V. Barnes	35	229	14	11	2	3.98
	3B	F. Lindstrom	562	.306	7	58	93	178	9	12	3.2	.968	L. Benton	29	173	13	5	2	3.95
John McGraw	RF	G. Harper	483	.331	16	87	299	13	8	5	2.3	.975	D. Henry	45	164	11	6	4	4.23
W-70 L-52	CF	E. Roush	570	.304	7	58	327	19	9	4	2.6	.975	B. Clarkson	26	87	3	9	2	4.36
	LF	H. Mueller	190	.289	3	19	100	1	6	0	1.9	.944							
Rogers Hornsby	C	Z. Taylor	258	.233	4	21	267	51	9	8	4.0	.972							
W-22 L-10	3B	A. Reese	355	.265	4	21	50	126	17	14	3.0	.912							
	OF	M. Ott	163	.282	1	19	52	2	1	1	1.7	.982							
	OF	T. Tyson	159	.264	1	17	73	5	6	1	2.0	.929							
	SS	D. Farrell	142	.387	3	34	77	116	17	19	5.8	.919							
	C	A. DeVormer	141	.248	2	21	115	27	7	0	2.8	.953							
Chicago	1B	C. Grimm	543	.311	2	74	1437	99	15	117	10.6	.990	C. Root	**48**	**309**	**26**	15	2	3.76
	2B	C. Beck	391	.258	2	44	238	358	19	62	6.2	.969	S. Blake	32	224	13	14	0	3.29
W-85 L-68	SS	W. English	334	.290	1	28	177	281	29	47	5.8	.940	G. Bush	36	193	10	10	2	3.03
	3B	S. Adams	647	.292	0	49	45	107	6	12	3.0	.962	H. Carlson	27	184	12	8	0	3.17
Joe McCarthy	RF	E. Webb	332	.301	14	52	171	14	8	5	2.2	.959	Brillheart	32	129	4	2	0	4.13
	CF	H. Wilson	551	.318	**30**	129	**400**	13	14	3	2.9	.967	P. Jones	30	113	7	8	0	4.07
	LF	Stephenson	579	.344	7	82	297	18	8	5	2.2	.975	B. Osborn	24	108	5	5	0	4.18
	C	G. Hartnett	449	.294	10	80	**479**	99	16	21	4.8	.973							
	OF	C. Heathcote	228	.294	2	25	136	13	2	7	2.6	.987							
	3B	E. Pick	181	.171	2	15	60	71	13	9	2.9	.910							
	OF	P. Scott	156	.314	0	21	70	3	1	1	2.1	.986							
Cincinnati	1B	W. Pipp	443	.260	2	41	1145	66	5	86	10.7	**.996**	R. Lucas	37	240	18	11	2	3.38
	2B	H. Critz	396	.278	4	49	239	388	20	69	5.7	.969	J. May	44	236	15	12	1	3.51
W-75 L-78	SS	H. Ford	409	.274	1	46	218	323	27	75	5.5	.952	D. Luque	29	231	13	12	0	3.20
	3B	C. Dressen	548	.292	2	55	131	**315**	15	20	3.2	**.967**	E. Rixey	34	220	12	10	1	3.48
Jack Hendricks	RF	C. Walker	527	.292	6	80	316	15	**15**	8	2.5	.957	P. Donohue	33	191	6	16	1	4.11
	CF	E. Allen	359	.295	2	20	250	6	3	3	2.6	.988	C. Mays	14	82	3	7	0	3.51
	LF	R. Bressler	467	.291	3	77	261	15	8	5	2.4	.972	A. Nehf	21	45	3	5	1	5.56
	C	B. Hargrave	305	.308	0	35	261	57	4	10	3.5	**.988**							
	OF	B. Zitzmann	232	.284	0	24	135	2	6	0	2.4	.958							
	1B	G. Kelly	222	.270	5	21	456	32	4	46	10.0	.992							
	OF	Christensen	185	.254	0	16	106	6	5	3	2.3	.957							
	C	V. Picinich	173	.254	0	21	218	31	5	8	4.2	.980							
	P	R. Lucas	150	.313	0	28	7	51	1	2	1.6	.983							
Brooklyn	1B	B. Herman	412	.272	14	73	968	68	**21**	64	10.1	.980	D. Vance	34	273	16	15	1	2.70
	2B	J. Partridge	572	.260	7	40	330	454	**52**	63	6.0	.938	J. Petty	42	272	13	18	1	2.98
W-65 L-88	SS	J. Butler	521	.238	2	57	214	251	20	49	5.4	.959	J. Elliott	30	188	6	13	3	3.30
	3B	B. Barrett	355	.259	5	38	76	167	21	12	2.8	.920	D. McWeeny	34	164	4	8	1	3.56
Wilbert Robinson	RF	M. Carey	538	.266	1	54	331	19	11	6	2.6	.970	B. Doak	27	145	11	8	0	3.48
	CF	J. Statz	507	.274	1	21	371	14	4	5	3.2	.990	R. Ehrhardt	46	96	3	7	3	3.57
	LF	G. Felix	445	.265	0	57	221	13	13	1	2.1	.947	J. Barnes	18	79	2	10	0	5.72
	C	H. DeBerry	201	.234	1	21	339	59	5	8	6.0	.988	W. Clark	27	74	7	2	2	2.32
	O1	H. Hendrick	458	.310	0	24	556	37	10	37		.983							
	SS	J. Flowers	231	.234	2	20	137	184	19	29	5.2	.944							
	C	B. Henline	177	.266	1	18	216	50	15	6	4.7	.947							

NATIONAL LEAGUE 1927, cont.

POS	Player	AB	BA	HR	RBI	PO	A	E	DP	TC/G	FA	Pitcher	G	IP	W	L	SV	ERA
Boston												B. Smith	41	261	10	18	3	3.76
1B	J. Fournier	374	.283	10	53	901	63	11	63	9.6	.989	Greenfield	27	190	11	14	0	3.84
2B	D. Gautreau	236	.246	0	20	136	196	12	22	6.0	.965	J. Genewich	40	181	11	8	1	3.83
SS	D. Bancroft	375	.243	1	31	275	329	39	66	6.2	.939	J. Wertz	42	164	4	10	1	4.55
3B	A. High	384	.302	4	46	93	122	20	9	2.6	.915	C. Robertson	28	154	7	17	0	4.72
RF	L. Richbourg	450	.309	2	34	233	10	12	0	2.3	.953	F. Edwards	29	92	2	8	0	4.99
CF	J. Welsh	497	.288	9	54	377	24	13	6	3.2	.969	G. Mogridge	20	49	6	4	5	3.70
LF	E. Brown	558	.306	2	75	335	10	7	1	2.3	.980							
C	S. Hogan	229	.288	3	32	215	54	4	3	4.5	.985							
W-60 L-94																		
Dave Bancroft																		
UT	D. Farrell	424	.292	1	58	252	335	37	47		.941							
UT	E. Moore	411	.302	1	32	200	223	16	36		.964							
1B	D. Burrus	220	.318	0	32	505	44	16	51	9.3	.972							
OF	J. Smith	183	.317	1	24	106	7	6	1	2.5	.950							
C	F. Gibson	167	.222	0	19	130	35	6	3	3.6	.965							

POS	Player	AB	BA	HR	RBI	PO	A	E	DP	TC/G	FA	Pitcher	G	IP	W	L	SV	ERA
Philadelphia												J. Scott	**48**	233	9	**21**	1	5.09
1B	Wrightstone	533	.306	6	75	1268	90	15	114	10.1	.989	A. Ferguson	31	227	8	16	0	4.84
2B	F. Thompson	597	.303	1	70	424	485	35	97	6.2	.963	D. Ulrich	32	193	8	11	1	3.17
SS	H. Sand	535	.299	1	49	201	247	24	36	5.5	.949	H. Pruett	31	186	7	17	1	6.05
3B	B. Friberg	335	.233	1	28	124	226	15	**23**	3.5	.959	L. Sweetland	21	104	2	10	0	6.16
RF	C. Williams	492	.274	**30**	98	241	22	8	8	2.1	.970	Willoughby	35	98	3	7	2	6.54
CF	F. Leach	536	.306	12	83	385	**26**	8	**10**	3.0	.981	H. Carlson	11	64	4	5	1	5.23
LF	D. Spalding	442	.296	0	25	250	7	2	1	2.3	**.992**							
C	J. Wilson	443	.275	2	45	377	82	12	12	3.8	.975							
W-51 L-103																		
Stuffy McInnis																		
SS	J. Cooney	259	.270	0	15	155	238	8	51	5.4	.980*							
OF	J. Mokan	213	.286	0	33	97	5	4	0	1.7	.962							
OF	A. Nixon	154	.312	0	18	121	3	4	0	2.9	.969							

BATTING AND BASE RUNNING LEADERS

Batting Average
P. Waner, PIT	.380
R. Hornsby, NY	.361
L. Waner, PIT	.355
Stephenson, CHI	.344
P. Traynor, PIT	.342

Slugging Average
C. Hafey, STL	.590
R. Hornsby, NY	.586
H. Wilson, CHI	.579
P. Waner, PIT	.543
B. Terry, NY	.529

Home Runs
C. Williams, PHI	30
H. Wilson, CHI	30
R. Hornsby, NY	26
B. Terry, NY	20
J. Bottomley, STL	19

Total Bases
P. Waner, PIT	338
R. Hornsby, NY	333
H. Wilson, CHI	319
B. Terry, NY	307
J. Bottomley, STL	292

Runs Batted In
P. Waner, PIT	131
H. Wilson, CHI	129
R. Hornsby, NY	125
J. Bottomley, STL	124
B. Terry, NY	121

Stolen Bases
F. Frisch, STL	48
M. Carey, BKN	32
H. Hendrick, BKN	29
S. Adams, CHI	26
L. Richbourg, BOS	24

Hits
P. Waner, PIT	237
L. Waner, PIT	223
F. Frisch, STL	208
R. Hornsby, NY	205

Base on Balls
R. Hornsby, NY	86
G. Harper, NY	84
G. Grantham, PIT	74
J. Bottomley, STL	74

Home Run Percentage
C. Williams, PHI	6.1
H. Wilson, CHI	5.4
C. Hafey, STL	5.2
R. Hornsby, NY	4.6

Runs Scored
R. Hornsby, NY	133
L. Waner, PIT	133
H. Wilson, CHI	119
P. Waner, PIT	113

Doubles
Stephenson, CHI	46
P. Waner, PIT	40
C. Dressen, CIN	36
F. Lindstrom, NY	36

Triples
P. Waner, PIT	17
J. Bottomley, STL	15
F. Thompson, PHI	14
B. Terry, NY	13

Winning Percentage
L. Benton, BOS, NY	.708
J. Haines, STL	.706
B. Grimes, NY	.704
R. Kremer, PIT	.704
G. Alexander, STL	.677

Saves
B. Sherdel, STL	6
G. Mogridge, BOS	5
A. Nehf, CHI, CIN	5
D. Henry, NY	4

Fewest Hits/9 Innings
D. Vance, BKN	7.97
R. Kremer, PIT	8.16
J. Haines, STL	8.17
C. Hill, PIT	8.43

Most Strikeouts/9 Inn.
D. Vance, BKN	6.06
J. Elliott, BKN	4.73
J. May, CIN	4.62
H. Pruett, PHI	4.35

PITCHING LEADERS

Earned Run Average
R. Kremer, PIT	2.47
G. Alexander, STL	2.52
D. Vance, BKN	2.70
J. Haines, STL	2.72
J. Petty, BKN	2.98

Strikeouts
D. Vance, BKN	184
C. Root, CHI	145
J. May, CIN	121
B. Grimes, NY	102
J. Petty, BKN	101

Shutouts
J. Haines, STL	6
R. Lucas, CIN	4
C. Root, CHI	4
R. Kremer, PIT	3

Innings
C. Root, CHI	309
J. Haines, STL	301
L. Meadows, PIT	299
C. Hill, PIT	278

Wins
C. Root, CHI	26
J. Haines, STL	24
C. Hill, PIT	22
G. Alexander, STL	21

Complete Games
D. Vance, BKN	25
J. Haines, STL	25
L. Meadows, PIT	25
G. Alexander, STL	22
C. Hill, PIT	22

Fewest Walks/9 Innings
G. Alexander, STL	1.28
R. Lucas, CIN	1.46
P. Donohue, CIN	1.51
H. Carlson, CHI, PHI	1.63

Games Pitched
C. Root, CHI	48
J. Scott, PHI	48
R. Ehrhardt, BKN	46
D. Henry, NY	45

	W	L	PCT	GB	R	OR	2B	3B	HR	BA	SA	SB	E	DP	FA	CG	BB	SO	ShO	SV	ERA
								Batting						Fielding				Pitching			
Pittsburgh	94	60	.610		**817**	659	258	78	54	**.305**	.412	65	187	130	.969	**90**	418	435	10	10	3.66
St. Louis	92	61	.601	1.5	754	665	264	**79**	84	.278	.408	**110**	213	**170**	.966	89	363	394	**14**	11	3.57
New York	92	62	.597	2	**817**	720	251	62	**109**	.297	**.427**	73	195	160	.969	65	453	442	7	**16**	3.97
Chicago	85	68	.556	8.5	750	661	**266**	63	74	.284	.400	65	181	152	.971	75	514	465	11	5	3.65
Cincinnati	75	78	.490	18.5	643	653	222	77	29	.278	.367	62	**165**	160	**.973**	87	316	407	12	12	3.54
Brooklyn	65	88	.425	28.5	541	**619**	195	74	39	.253	.342	106	229	117	.963	74	418	**574**	7	10	**3.36**
Boston	60	94	.390	34	651	771	216	61	37	.279	.363	100	231	130	.963	52	468	402	3	11	4.22
Philadelphia	51	103	.331	43	678	903	216	46	57	.280	.370	68	169	152	.972	81	462	377	5	6	5.35
					5651	5651	1888	540	483	.282	.386	649	1570	1171	.969	613	3412	3496	69	81	3.91

AMERICAN LEAGUE 1927

	POS	Player	AB	BA	HR	RBI	PO	A	E	DP	TC/G	FA	Pitcher	G	IP	W	L	SV	ERA
New York	1B	L. Gehrig	584	.373	47	175	1662	88	15	108	11.4	.992	W. Hoyt	36	256	**22**	7	1	**2.63**
	2B	T. Lazzeri	570	.309	18	102	213	398	18	60	5.6	.971	W. Moore	50	213	19	7	13	2.28
W-110 L-44	SS	M. Koenig	526	.285	3	62	262	423	**47**	76	**6.0**	.936	H. Pennock	34	210	19	8	2	3.00
	3B	J. Dugan	387	.269	2	43	93	196	19	15	2.8	.938	U. Shocker	31	200	18	6	0	2.84
Miller Huggins	RF	B. Ruth	540	.356	**60**	164	328	14	13	4	2.4	.963	D. Ruether	27	184	13	6	0	3.38
	CF	E. Combs	648	.356	6	64	411	6	14	0	2.8	.968	G. Pipgras	29	166	10	3	0	4.11
	LF	B. Meusel	516	.337	8	103	249	15	14	1	2.1	.950	M. Thomas	21	89	7	4	0	4.87
	C	P. Collins	251	.275	7	36	267	56	8	1	3.7	.976							
	2B	R. Morehart	195	.256	1	20	101	175	16	27	5.5	.945							
	C	J. Grabowski	195	.277	0	25	197	47	4	3	3.6	.984							
	OF	C. Durst	129	.248	0	25	47	1	1	0	1.4	.980							
Philadelphia	1B	J. Dykes	417	.324	3	60	816	49	10	59	10.7	.989	L. Grove	51	262	20	13	9	3.19
	2B	M. Bishop	372	.277	0	22	211	342	19	48	5.4	.967	R. Walberg	46	249	16	12	4	3.97
W-91 L-63	SS	J. Boley	370	.311	1	52	182	318	26	49	4.6	.951	J. Quinn	34	207	15	10	1	3.17
	3B	S. Hale	501	.313	5	81	152	247	16	**46**	3.2	.961	H. Ehmke	30	190	12	10	0	4.22
Connie Mack	RF	T. Cobb	490	.357	5	93	243	9	8	2	2.1	.969	E. Rommel	30	147	11	3	1	4.36
	CF	A. Simmons	406	.392	15	108	247	10	4	2	2.5	.985	S. Gray	37	141	9	6	3	4.60
	LF	W. French	326	.304	0	41	190	6	9	2	2.2	.956							
	C	M. Cochrane	432	.338	12	80	559	85	9	11	**5.3**	.986							
	OF	B. Lamar	324	.299	4	47	148	9	8	1	2.1	.952							
	OF	Z. Wheat	247	.324	1	38	105	8	2	1	1.9	.983							
	2B	E. Collins	225	.338	1	15	124	150	10	31	5.1	.965							
	SS	C. Galloway	181	.265	0	22	115	150	15	20	4.6	.946							
	1B	J. Foxx	130	.323	3	20	258	15	7	10	8.8	.975							
Washington	1B	J. Judge	522	.308	2	71	1309	71	6	79	10.2	**.996**	H. Lisenbee	39	242	18	9	0	3.57
	2B	B. Harris	475	.267	1	55	316	413	21	68	5.9	.972	S. Thurston	29	205	13	13	0	4.47
W-85 L-69	SS	B. Reeves	380	.255	1	39	194	296	41	36	5.5	.923	B. Hadley	30	199	14	6	0	2.85
	3B	O. Bluege	503	.274	1	66	185	**337**	21	20	3.7	.961	F. Marberry	56	155	10	7	9	4.64
Bucky Harris	RF	S. Rice	603	.297	2	65	258	12	7	2	2.0	.975	G. Braxton	58	155	10	9	13	2.95
	CF	T. Speaker	523	.327	2	73	278	12	10	5	2.5	.967	T. Zachary	15	110	4	7	0	3.67
	LF	G. Goslin	581	.334	13	120	356	8	17	3	2.6	.955	W. Johnson	18	108	5	6	0	5.10
	C	M. Ruel	428	.308	1	52	495	100	7	8	4.7	**.988**	B. Burke	36	100	3	2	0	3.96
	OF	E. McNeely	185	.276	0	16	81	3	2	1	1.8	.977	G. Crowder	15	67	4	7	0	4.54
	C	B. Tate	131	.313	1	24	148	24	4	4	4.5	.977							
Detroit	1B	L. Blue	365	.260	1	42	1019	68	18	99	10.6	.984	E. Whitehill	41	236	16	14	3	3.36
	2B	C. Gehringer	508	.317	4	61	304	**438**	27	**84**	**6.4**	.965	L. Stoner	38	215	10	13	5	3.98
W-82 L-71	SS	J. Tavener	419	.274	5	59	246	356	33	79	5.6	.948	S. Gibson	33	190	11	12	0	3.69
	3B	J. Warner	559	.267	1	45	156	277	**24**	34	3.3	.947	K. Holloway	36	183	11	12	6	4.07
George Moriarty	RF	H. Heilmann	505	**.398**	14	120	218	11	8	5	1.8	.966	R. Collins	30	173	13	7	0	4.69
	CF	H. Manush	593	.298	6	80	361	9	11	3	2.5	.971	O. Carroll	31	172	10	6	0	3.98
	LF	Fothergill	527	.359	9	114	315	3	13	1	2.4	.961							
	C	L. Woodall	246	.280	0	39	265	72	1	6	3.9	.997							
	UT	M. McManus	369	.268	9	69	245	263	17	54		.968							
	1B	J. Neun	204	.324	0	27	548	30	12	45	11.1	.980							
	C	J. Bassler	200	.285	0	24	206	56	7	8	4.0	.974							
	OF	A. Wingo	137	.234	0	20	43	6	6	2	1.6	.891							
Chicago	1B	B. Clancy	464	.300	3	53	1184	81	11	76	10.4	.991	T. Thomas	40	**308**	19	16	1	2.98
	2B	A. Ward	463	.270	5	56	275	437	27	66	5.4	.963	T. Lyons	39	**308**	**22**	14	2	2.84
W-70 L-83	SS	Hunnefield	365	.285	2	36	150	210	26	38	4.9	.933	Blankenship	37	237	12	17	0	5.06
	3B	W. Kamm	540	.270	0	59	**236**	279	15	21	3.6	**.972**	S. Connally	43	198	10	15	5	4.08
Ray Schalk	RF	B. Barrett	556	.286	4	83	289	22	12	6	2.2	.963	R. Faber	18	111	4	7	0	4.55
	CF	A. Metzler	543	.319	3	61	397	16	15	6	**3.2**	.965							
	LF	B. Falk	535	.327	9	83	372	22	9	**9**	2.8	.978							
	C	H. McCurdy	262	.286	1	27	261	55	9	8	4.0	.972							
	C	B. Crouse	222	.239	0	20	202	79	8	10	3.6	.972							
	SS	Peckinpaugh	217	.295	0	23	101	170	10	30	4.7	.964							
Cleveland	1B	G. Burns	549	.319	3	78	1362	102	15	111	10.6	.990	W. Hudlin	43	265	18	12	0	4.01
	2B	L. Fonseca	428	.311	2	40	229	304	15	51	5.7	.973	J. Shaute	45	230	9	16	2	4.22
W-66 L-87	SS	J. Sewell	569	.316	1	92	**361**	**480**	33	80	5.7	**.962**	G. Buckeye	35	205	10	17	1	3.96
	3B	R. Lutzke	311	.251	0	41	120	199	21	24	3.5	.938	J. Miller	34	185	10	8	3	3.21
Jack McCallister	RF	H. Summa	574	.286	4	74	242	12	12	3	1.8	.955	G. Uhle	25	153	8	9	1	4.34
	CF	F. Eichrodt	267	.221	0	25	170	13	4	6	2.3	.979	D. Levsen	25	80	3	7	0	5.49
	LF	C. Jamieson	489	.309	0	36	300	13	10	2	2.5	.969	G. Grant	25	75	4	6	1	4.46
	C	L. Sewell	470	.294	0	53	402	**119**	**20**	**14**	4.3	.963							
	3B	J. Hodapp	240	.304	5	40	69	132	14	15	3.2	.935							
	2B	F. Spurgeon	179	.251	1	19	124	150	18	28	5.6	.938							

AMERICAN LEAGUE 1927, *cont.*

	POS	Player	AB	BA	HR	RBI	PO	A	E	DP	TC/G	FA	Pitcher	G	IP	W	L	SV	ERA
St. Louis	1B	G. Sisler	614	.327	5	97	1374	131	24	138	10.3	.984	M. Gaston	37	254	13	17	1	5.00
	2B	O. Melillo	356	.225	0	26	229	293	36	72	5.5	.935	E. Vangilder	44	203	10	12	1	4.79
W-59 L-94	SS	W. Gerber	438	.224	0	45	290	427	41	91	5.4	.946	S. Jones	30	190	8	14	0	4.32
	3B	F. O'Rourke	538	.268	1	39	183	244	20	27	3.7	.955	E. Wingard	38	156	2	13	0	6.56
Dan Howley	RF	H. Rice	520	.287	7	68	277	26	20	7	2.5	.938	L. Stewart	27	156	8	11	1	4.28
	CF	B. Miller	492	.325	5	75	309	9	10	3	2.6	.970	E. Nevers	27	95	3	8	2	4.94
	LF	K. Williams	421	.323	17	74	260	15	10	4	2.5	.965	W. Ballou	21	90	5	6	0	4.78
	C	W. Schang	263	.319	5	42	213	73	7	10	3.9	.976	T. Zachary	13	78	4	6	0	4.37
	23	S. Adams	259	.266	0	29	159	190	21	35		.943	G. Crowder	21	74	3	5	3	5.01
	OF	H. Bennett	256	.266	3	30	118	5	7	1	2.4	.946							
	C	S. O'Neill	191	.230	1	22	180	57	4	8	4.0	.983							
	OF	F. Schulte	189	.317	3	34	117	3	11	0	2.7	.916							
Boston	1B	P. Todt	516	.236	6	52	1401	112	13	121	11.0	.991	H. Wiltse	36	219	10	18	1	5.10
	2B	B. Regan	468	.274	2	66	283	397	28	76	5.9	.960	S. Harriss	44	218	14	21	1	4.18
W-51 L-103	SS	B. Myer	469	.288	2	47	239	311	35	64	5.8	.940	T. Welzer	37	182	6	11	1	4.46
	3B	B. Rogell	207	.266	2	28	49	123	6	8	3.4	.966	MacFayden	34	160	5	8	2	4.27
Bill Carrigan	RF	J. Tobin	374	.310	2	40	152	10	9	4	1.8	.947	R. Ruffing	26	158	5	13	2	4.66
	CF	I. Flagstead	466	.285	4	69	326	19	5	4	2.7	.986	J. Russell	34	147	4	9	0	4.10
	LF	W. Shaner	406	.273	3	49	220	13	11	1	2.3	.955	D. Lundgren	30	136	5	12	0	6.27
	C	G. Hartley	244	.275	1	31	214	51	9	5	3.2	.967							
	UT	J. Rothrock	428	.259	1	36	323	284	26	63		.959							
	OF	C. Carlyle	278	.234	1	28	127	10	5	0	1.7	.965							
	C	F. Hofmann	217	.272	0	24	241	59	18	4	3.9	.943							
	3B	R. Rollings	184	.266	0	9	39	66	7	2	2.5	.938							
	OF	B. Jacobson	155	.245	0	24	90	4	2	0	2.5	.979							

BATTING AND BASE RUNNING LEADERS

Batting Average
H. Heilmann, DET	.398
A. Simmons, PHI	.392
L. Gehrig, NY	.373
Fothergill, DET	.359
T. Cobb, PHI	.357

Slugging Average
B. Ruth, NY	.772
L. Gehrig, NY	.765
A. Simmons, PHI	.645
H. Heilmann, DET	.616
K. Williams, STL	.527

Home Runs
B. Ruth, NY	60
L. Gehrig, NY	47
T. Lazzeri, NY	18
K. Williams, STL	17
A. Simmons, PHI	15

Total Bases
L. Gehrig, NY	447
B. Ruth, NY	417
E. Combs, NY	331
H. Heilmann, DET	311
G. Goslin, WAS	300

Runs Batted In
L. Gehrig, NY	175
B. Ruth, NY	164
H. Heilmann, DET	120
G. Goslin, WAS	120
Fothergill, DET	114

Stolen Bases
G. Sisler, STL	27
B. Meusel, NY	24
J. Neun, DET	22
T. Cobb, PHI	22
T. Lazzeri, NY	22

Hits
E. Combs, NY	231
L. Gehrig, NY	218
H. Heilmann, DET	201
G. Sisler, STL	201

Base on Balls
B. Ruth, NY	138
L. Gehrig, NY	109
M. Bishop, PHI	105
H. Heilmann, DET	72

Home Run Percentage
B. Ruth, NY	11.1
L. Gehrig, NY	8.0
K. Williams, STL	4.0
A. Simmons, PHI	3.7

Runs Scored
B. Ruth, NY	158
L. Gehrig, NY	149
E. Combs, NY	137
C. Gehringer, DET	110

Doubles
L. Gehrig, NY	52
G. Burns, CLE	51
H. Heilmann, DET	50
J. Sewell, CLE	48

Triples
E. Combs, NY	23
L. Gehrig, NY	18
H. Manush, DET	18
G. Goslin, WAS	15

PITCHING LEADERS

Winning Percentage
W. Hoyt, NY	.759
U. Shocker, NY	.750
W. Moore, NY	.731
H. Pennock, NY	.704
H. Lisenbee, WAS	.667

Earned Run Average
W. Hoyt, NY	2.63
U. Shocker, NY	2.84
T. Lyons, CHI	2.84
B. Hadley, WAS	2.85
T. Thomas, CHI	2.98

Wins
W. Hoyt, NY	22
T. Lyons, CHI	22
L. Grove, PHI	20
W. Moore, NY	19
H. Pennock, NY	19
T. Thomas, CHI	19

Saves
W. Moore, NY	13
G. Braxton, WAS	13
F. Marberry, WAS	9
L. Grove, PHI	9
K. Holloway, DET	6
J. Pate, PHI	6

Strikeouts
L. Grove, PHI	174
R. Walberg, PHI	136
T. Thomas, CHI	107
H. Lisenbee, WAS	105
G. Braxton, WAS	95
E. Whitehill, DET	95

Complete Games
T. Lyons, CHI	30
T. Thomas, CHI	24
W. Hoyt, NY	23
M. Gaston, STL	21
H. Pennock, NY	18
W. Hudlin, CLE	18

Fewest Hits/9 Innings
T. Thomas, CHI	7.93
B. Hadley, WAS	8.02
H. Lisenbee, WAS	8.22
W. Hoyt, NY	8.50

Shutouts
H. Lisenbee, WAS	4

Fewest Walks/9 Innings
J. Quinn, PHI	1.61
U. Shocker, NY	1.85
W. Hoyt, NY	1.90
T. Lyons, CHI	1.96

Most Strikeouts/9 Inn.
L. Grove, PHI	5.97
R. Walberg, PHI	4.91
R. Ruffing, BOS	4.38
G. Uhle, CLE	4.05

Innings
T. Thomas, CHI	308
T. Lyons, CHI	308
W. Hudlin, CLE	265
L. Grove, PHI	262

Games Pitched
G. Braxton, WAS	58
F. Marberry, WAS	56
L. Grove, PHI	51
W. Moore, NY	50

	W	L	PCT	GB	R	OR	2B	3B	HR	BA	SA	SB	E	DP	FA	CG	BB	SO	ShO	SV	ERA
New York	110	44	.714		975	599	291	103	158	.307	.489	90	195	123	.969	82	409	431	11	20	3.20
Philadelphia	91	63	.591	19	841	726	281	70	56	.303	.414	98	190	124	.970	66	442	553	8	24	3.95
Washington	85	69	.552	25	782	730	268	87	29	.287	.386	133	195	125	.969	62	491	497	10	23	3.95
Detroit	82	71	.536	27.5	845	805	282	100	51	.289	.409	141	206	173	.968	75	577	421	5	17	4.12
Chicago	70	83	.458	39.5	662	708	285	61	36	.278	.378	90	178	131	.971	85	440	365	10	8	3.91
Cleveland	66	87	.431	43.5	668	766	321	52	26	.283	.379	63	201	146	.968	72	508	366	5	8	4.27
St. Louis	59	94	.386	50.5	724	904	262	59	55	.276	.380	91	248	166	.960	80	604	385	4	8	4.95
Boston	51	103	.331	59	597	856	271	78	28	.259	.357	82	228	162	.964	63	558	381	6	7	4.68
					6094	6094	2261	610	439	.285	.399	788	1641	1150	.967	585	4029	3399	59	115	4.12

NATIONAL LEAGUE 1928

	POS	Player	AB	BA	HR	RBI	PO	A	E	DP	TC/G	FA	Pitcher	G	IP	W	L	SV	ERA
St. Louis W-95 L-59 Bill McKechnie	1B	J. Bottomley	576	.325	31	136	1454	52	20	113	10.3	.987	B. Sherdel	38	249	21	10	5	2.86
	2B	F. Frisch	547	.300	10	86	383	474	21	80	6.3	.976	G. Alexander	34	244	16	9	2	3.36
	SS	Maranville	366	.240	1	34	236	362	19	57	5.5	.969	J. Haines	33	240	20	8	0	3.18
	3B	W. Holm	386	.277	3	47	100	145	22	9	3.2	.918	F. Rhem	28	170	11	8	3	4.14
	RF	G. Harper	272	.305	17	58	156	13	2	2	2.0	.988	C. Mitchell	19	150	8	9	0	3.30
	CF	T. Douthit	648	.295	3	43	547	10	9	4	3.7	.984	S. Johnson	34	120	8	4	3	3.90
	LF	C. Hafey	520	.337	27	111	287	13	11	3	2.3	.965	A. Reinhart	23	75	4	6	2	2.87
	C	J. Wilson	411	.258	2	50	394*	82*	8	13*	4.0	.983							
	3B	A. High	368	.285	6	37	56	117	12	10	2.5	.935							
	OF	W. Roettger	261	.341	6	44	152	2	3	1	2.4	.981							
	SS	T. Thevenow	171	.205	0	13	100	158	19	29	4.3	.931							
New York W-93 L-61 John McGraw	1B	B. Terry	568	.326	17	101	1584	78	12	148	11.2	.993	L. Benton	42	310	25	9	4	2.73
	2B	A. Cohen	504	.274	9	59	304	434	24	90	6.0	.969	Fitzsimmons	40	261	20	9	1	3.68
	SS	T. Jackson	537	.270	14	77	354	547	45	112	6.3	.952	J. Genewich	26	158	11	4	3	3.18
	3B	F. Lindstrom	646	.358	14	107	145	340	21	34	3.3	.958	C. Hubbell	20	124	10	6	1	2.83
	RF	M. Ott	435	.322	18	77	214	14	7	4	2.0	.970	V. Aldridge	22	119	4	7	2	4.83
	CF	J. Welsh	476	.307	9	54	310	8	6	3	2.8	.981	J. Faulkner	38	117	9	8	2	3.53
	LF	L. O'Doul	354	.319	8	46	149	4	6	0	1.7	.962	D. Henry	17	64	3	6	1	3.80
	C	S. Hogan	411	.333	10	71	389	57	10	11	3.7	.978							
	UT	A. Reese	406	.308	6	44	232	136	16	21		.958							
	OF	L. Mann	193	.264	2	25	97	3	5	1	1.5	.952							
	OF	E. Roush	163	.252	2	13	100	7	5	0	2.9	.955							
	C	B. O'Farrell	133	.195	2	20	138	27	2	1	2.7	.988							
Chicago W-91 L-63 Joe McCarthy	1B	C. Grimm	547	.294	5	62	1458	70	10	147	10.5	.993	P. Malone	42	251	18	13	2	2.84
	2B	F. Maguire	574	.279	1	41	410	524	23	126	6.9	.976	S. Blake	34	241	17	11	1	2.47
	SS	W. English	475	.299	2	34	245	382	36	85	5.8	.946	C. Root	40	237	14	18	2	3.57
	3B	C. Beck	483	.257	3	52	74	156	10	24	2.8	.958	G. Bush	42	204	15	6	2	3.83
	RF	K. Cuyler	499	.285	17	79	257	18	5	3	2.2	.982	A. Nehf	31	177	13	7	0	2.65
	CF	H. Wilson	520	.313	31	120	321	11	14	2	2.4	.960	P. Jones	39	154	10	6	3	4.03
	LF	Stephenson	512	.324	8	90	268	10	5	1	2.1	.982							
	C	G. Hartnett	388	.302	14	57	455	103	6	14	4.8	.989							
	3B	J. Butler	174	.270	0	16	51	120	9	9	3.1	.950							
	C	M. Gonzalez	158	.272	1	21	198	35	4	8	5.3	.983							
	OF	E. Webb	140	.250	3	23	65	4	1	0	2.3	.986							
Pittsburgh W-85 L-67 Donie Bush	1B	G. Grantham	440	.323	10	85	1117	71	17	83	10.1	.986	B. Grimes	48	331	25	14	3	2.99
	2B	S. Adams	539	.276	0	38	265	343	18	54	5.9	.971	C. Hill	36	237	16	10	2	3.53
	SS	G. Wright	407	.310	8	66	194	301	39	59	5.3	.927	R. Kremer	34	219	15	13	0	4.64
	3B	P. Traynor	569	.337	3	124	175	296	27	15	3.5	.946	F. Fussell	28	160	8	9	1	3.61
	RF	P. Waner	602	.370	6	86	299	14	8	0	2.5	.975	J. Dawson	31	129	7	7	3	3.29
	CF	L. Waner	659	.335	5	61	418	15	9	4	2.9	.980	E. Brame	24	96	7	4	0	5.08
	LF	F. Brickell	202	.322	3	41	107	6	5	1	2.4	.958	J. Miljus	21	70	5	7	1	5.30
	C	Hargreaves	260	.285	1	32	230	47	11*	7	3.7	.962							
	2S	D. Bartell	233	.305	1	36	158	199	16	40		.957							
	OF	C. Barnhart	196	.296	4	30	96	3	3	0	2.1	.971							
	OF	P. Scott	177	.311	5	33	90	5	2	5	2.3	.979							
	OF	A. Comorosky	176	.295	2	34	118	2	4	1	2.5	.968							
Cincinnati W-78 L-74 Jack Hendricks	1B	G. Kelly	402	.296	3	58	894	69	9	99	9.8	.991	E. Rixey	43	291	19	18	2	3.43
	2B	H. Critz	641	.296	5	52	333	497	25	124	5.6	.971	D. Luque	33	234	11	10	1	3.57
	SS	H. Ford	506	.241	0	54	355	508	25	128	6.0	.972	R. Kolp	44	209	13	10	3	3.19
	3B	C. Dressen	498	.291	1	59	122	283	27	27	3.2	.938	R. Lucas	27	167	13	9	1	3.39
	RF	C. Walker	427	.279	6	73	289	9	14	3	2.6	.955	P. Donohue	23	150	7	11	0	4.74
	CF	E. Allen	485	.305	1	62	348	12	7	4	2.8	.981							
	LF	B. Zitzmann	266	.297	3	33	155	4	7	2	2.1	.958							
	C	V. Picinich	324	.302	7	35	279	65	6	6	3.8	.983							
	1B	W. Pipp	272	.283	2	26	673	40	8	69	10.0	.989							
	OF	M. Callaghan	238	.290	0	24	140	5	3	2	2.1	.980							
	OF	P. Purdy	223	.309	0	25	137	3	5	1	2.4	.966							
	C	B. Hargrave	190	.295	0	23	181	37	2	2	3.9	.991							
Brooklyn W-77 L-76 Wilbert Robinson	1B	Bissonette	587	.320	25	106	1482	77	20	95	10.2	.987	D. Vance	38	280	22	10	2	**2.09**
	2B	J. Flowers	339	.274	2	44	260	270	16	46	5.8	.971	D. McWeeny	42	244	14	14	1	3.17
	SS	D. Bancroft	515	.247	0	51	350	484	46	66	5.9	.948	J. Petty	40	234	15	15	1	4.04
	3B	H. Hendrick	425	.318	11	59	74	200	26	19	3.3	.913	W. Clark	40	195	12	9	3	2.68
	RF	B. Herman	486	.340	12	91	225	12	16	2	2.0	.937	J. Elliott	41	192	9	14	1	3.89
	CF	M. Carey	296	.247	2	19	202	8	3	1	2.2	.986	B. Doak	28	99	3	8	3	3.26
	LF	R. Bressler	501	.295	4	70	254	7	4	0	1.9	**.985**							
	C	H. DeBerry	258	.252	0	23	377	56	10	5	5.5	.977							
	UT	H. Riconda	281	.224	3	35	181	222	20	25		.953							
	OF	T. Tyson	210	.271	1	21	130	6	5	3	2.6	.965							
	OF	J. Statz	171	.234	0	16	107	3	4	2	1.5	.965							

NATIONAL LEAGUE 1928, *cont.*

	POS	Player	AB	BA	HR	RBI	PO	A	E	DP	TC/G	FA	Pitcher	G	IP	W	L	SV	ERA
Boston	1B	G. Sisler	491	.340	4	68	1188	86	15	100	10.9	.988	B. Smith	38	244	13	17	2	3.87
	2B	R. Hornsby	486	.387	21	94	295	450	21	85	5.5	.973	E. Brandt	38	225	9	21	0	5.07
W-50 L-103	SS	D. Farrell	483	.215	3	43	289	418	51	73	5.7	.933	A. Delaney	39	192	9	17	2	3.79
	3B	L. Bell	591	.277	10	91	177	314	27	37	3.4	.948	Greenfield	32	144	3	11	0	5.32
Jack Slattery	RF	L. Richbourg	612	.337	2	52	367	8	11	1	2.6	.972	J. Cooney	24	90	3	7	1	4.32
W-11 L-20	CF	J. Smith	254	.280	1	32	165	4	2	0	2.6	.988	J. Genewich	13	81	3	7	0	4.13
	LF	E. Brown	523	.268	2	59	302	6	13	3	2.5	.960							
Rogers Hornsby	C	Z. Taylor	399	.251	2	30	367	83	7	8	3.7	.985							
W-39 L-83	OF	E. Moore	215	.237	2	18	131	7	6	3	2.7	.958							
Philadelphia	1B	D. Hurst	396	.285	19	64	964	68	12	92	10.0	.989	R. Benge	40	202	8	18	1	4.55
	2B	F. Thompson	634	.287	3	50	409	509	32	109	6.3	.966	J. Ring	35	173	4	17	1	6.40
W-43 L-109	SS	H. Sand	426	.211	0	38	290	410	36	94	5.4	.951	L. Sweetland	37	135	3	15	2	6.58
	3B	P. Whitney	585	.301	10	103	171	293	22	27	3.3	.955	B. McGraw	39	132	7	8	1	4.64
Burt Shotton	RF	C. Klein	253	.360	11	34	128	7	3	0	2.2	.978	A. Ferguson	34	132	5	10	2	5.67
	CF	D. Sothern	579	.285	5	38	358	19	14	7	2.9	.964	Willoughby	35	131	6	5	1	5.30
	LF	F. Leach	588	.304	13	96	296	11	7	5	2.6	.978	A. Walsh	38	122	4	9	2	6.18
	C	W. Lerian	239	.272	2	25	239	61	7	12	4.1	.977	R. Miller	33	108	0	12	1	5.42
	OF	C. Williams	238	.256	12	37	118	9	0	0	1.8	1.000							
	C	S. Davis	163	.282	3	18	149	46	4	7	4.1	.980							

BATTING AND BASE RUNNING LEADERS

PITCHING LEADERS

Batting Average
R. Hornsby, BOS	.387
P. Waner, PIT	.370
F. Lindstrom, NY	.358
G. Sisler, BOS	.340
B. Herman, BKN	.340

Slugging Average
R. Hornsby, BOS	.632
J. Bottomley, STL	.628
C. Hafey, STL	.604
H. Wilson, CHI	.588
P. Waner, PIT	.547

Home Runs
H. Wilson, CHI	31
J. Bottomley, STL	31
C. Hafey, STL	27
Bissonette, BKN	25
R. Hornsby, BOS	21

Winning Percentage
L. Benton, NY	.735
J. Haines, STL	.714
G. Bush, CHI	.714
Fitzsimmons, NY	.690
D. Vance, BKN	.688

Earned Run Average
D. Vance, BKN	2.09
S. Blake, CHI	2.47
A. Nehf, CHI	2.65
W. Clark, BKN	2.68
L. Benton, NY	2.73

Wins
L. Benton, NY	25
B. Grimes, PIT	25
D. Vance, BKN	22
B. Sherdel, STL	21
J. Haines, STL	20
Fitzsimmons, NY	20

Total Bases
J. Bottomley, STL	362
F. Lindstrom, NY	330
P. Waner, PIT	329
Bissonette, BKN	319
C. Hafey, STL	314

Runs Batted In
J. Bottomley, STL	136
P. Traynor, PIT	124
H. Wilson, CHI	120
C. Hafey, STL	111
F. Lindstrom, NY	107

Stolen Bases
K. Cuyler, CHI	37
F. Frisch, STL	29
C. Walker, CIN	19
F. Thompson, PHI	19
M. Carey, BKN	18
H. Critz, CIN	18

Saves
B. Sherdel, STL	5
H. Haid, STL	5
H. Carlson, CHI	4
L. Benton, NY	4

Strikeouts
D. Vance, BKN	200
P. Malone, CHI	155
C. Root, CHI	122
L. Benton, NY	90

Complete Games
L. Benton, NY	28
B. Grimes, PIT	28
D. Vance, BKN	24
B. Sherdel, STL	20
J. Haines, STL	20

Hits
F. Lindstrom, NY	231
P. Waner, PIT	223
L. Waner, PIT	221
L. Richbourg, BOS	206

Base on Balls
R. Hornsby, BOS	107
T. Douthit, STL	84
R. Bressler, BKN	80
H. Wilson, CHI	77

Home Run Percentage
H. Wilson, CHI	6.0
G. Harper, NY, STL	5.8
J. Bottomley, STL	5.4
C. Hafey, STL	5.2

Fewest Hits/9 Innings
D. Vance, BKN	7.26
S. Blake, CHI	7.82
P. Malone, CHI	7.83
D. McWeeny, BKN	8.04

Shutouts
5 tied with	4

Fewest Walks/9 Innings
G. Alexander, STL	1.37
B. Sherdel, STL	2.03
L. Benton, NY	2.06
E. Rixey, CIN	2.07

Runs Scored
P. Waner, PIT	142
J. Bottomley, STL	123
L. Waner, PIT	121
T. Douthit, STL	111

Doubles
P. Waner, PIT	50
C. Hafey, STL	46
R. Hornsby, BOS	42
J. Bottomley, STL	42

Triples
J. Bottomley, STL	20
P. Waner, PIT	19
L. Waner, PIT	14
R. Bressler, BKN	13

Most Strikeouts/9 Inn.
D. Vance, BKN	6.42
P. Malone, CHI	5.57
C. Root, CHI	4.63
W. Clark, BKN	3.93

Innings
B. Grimes, PIT	331
L. Benton, NY	310
E. Rixey, CIN	291
D. Vance, BKN	280

Games Pitched
B. Grimes, PIT	48
R. Kolp, CIN	44
E. Rixey, CIN	43

	W	L	PCT	GB	R	OR	2B	3B	HR	BA	SA	SB	E	DP	FA	CG	BB	SO	ShO	SV	ERA
St. Louis	95	59	.617		807	636	292	70	113	.281	.425	82	160	134	.974	83	399	422	4	21	3.38
New York	93	61	.604	2	807	653	276	59	118	.293	.430	62	178	175	.972	79	405	399	7	16	3.67
Chicago	91	63	.591	4	714	615	251	64	92	.278	.402	83	156	176	.975	75	508	531	12	14	3.40
Pittsburgh	85	67	.559	9	837	704	246	100	52	.309	.421	64	201	123	.967	82	446	385	8	11	3.95
Cincinnati	78	74	.513	16	648	686	229	67	32	.280	.368	83	162	194	.974	68	410	355	11	11	3.94
Brooklyn	77	76	.503	17.5	665	640	229	70	66	.266	.374	81	217	113	.965	75	468	551	16	15	3.25
Boston	50	103	.327	44.5	631	878	241	41	52	.275	.367	60	193	141	.969	54	524	343	1	6	4.83
Philadelphia	43	109	.283	51	660	957	257	47	85	.267	.382	53	181	171	.971	42	671	403	4	11	5.52
					5769	5769	2021	518	610	.281	.397	568	1448	1227	.971	558	3831	3389	63	105	3.98

AMERICAN LEAGUE 1928

	POS	Player	AB	BA	HR	RBI	PO	A	E	DP	TC/G	FA	Pitcher	G	IP	W	L	SV	ERA
New York	1B	L. Gehrig	562	.374	27	**142**	**1488**	79	18	112	10.3	.989	G. Pipgras	46	**301**	**24**	13	3	3.38
	2B	T. Lazzeri	404	.332	10	82	236	331	26	56	5.1	.956	W. Hoyt	42	273	23	7	8	3.36
W-101 L-53	SS	M. Koenig	533	.319	4	63	260	328	49	69	5.1	.923	H. Pennock	28	211	17	6	3	2.56
	3B	J. Dugan	312	.276	6	34	87	129	11	13	2.5	.952	H. Johnson	31	199	14	9	0	4.30
Miller Huggins	RF	B. Ruth	536	.323	54	142	304	9	8	0	2.1	.975	A. Shealy	23	96	8	6	2	5.06
	CF	E. Combs	626	.310	7	56	**424**	11	9	7	3.0	.980	W. Moore	35	60	4	4	2	4.18
	LF	B. Meusel	518	.297	11	113	259	16	7	6	2.2	.975							
	C	J. Grabowski	202	.238	1	21	265	32	4	8	4.0	.987							
	2S	L. Durocher	296	.270	0	31	158	274	18	42		.960							
	3B	G. Robertson	251	.291	1	36	75	112	15	5	2.9	.926							
	C	B. Bengough	161	.267	0	9	206	37	2	7	4.2	.992							
Philadelphia	1B	J. Hauser	300	.260	16	59	811	41	12	51	9.8	.986	L. Grove	39	262	**24**	8	4	2.58
	2B	M. Bishop	472	.316	6	50	284	371	15	62	5.4	**.978**	R. Walberg	38	236	17	12	1	3.55
W-98 L-55	SS	J. Boley	425	.264	0	49	244	320	30	51	4.5	.949	J. Quinn	31	211	18	7	1	2.90
	3B	S. Hale	314	.309	4	58	86	189	20	17	3.7	.932	E. Rommel	43	174	13	5	4	3.06
Connie Mack	RF	T. Cobb	353	.323	1	40	154	7	6	0	2.0	.964	G. Earnshaw	26	158	7	7	1	3.81
	CF	B. Miller	510	.329	8	85	298	8	10	2	2.4	.968	H. Ehmke	23	139	9	8	0	3.62
	LF	A. Simmons	464	.351	15	107	231	10	3	2	2.1	.988	O. Orwoll	27	106	6	5	2	4.58
	C	M. Cochrane	468	.293	10	57	**645**	71	25	8	**5.7**	.966							
	UT	J. Foxx	400	.328	13	79	412	154	17	32		.971							
	OF	M. Haas	332	.280	6	39	175	9	5	1	2.3	.974							
	UT	J. Dykes	242	.277	5	30	166	164	9	21		.973							
	OF	T. Speaker	191	.267	3	29	111	8	3	1	2.4	.975							
	1P	O. Orwoll	170	.306	0	22	328	41	7	32		.981							
St. Louis	1B	L. Blue	549	.281	14	80	1472	**107**	17	**121**	10.4	.989	S. Gray	35	263	20	12	3	3.19
	2B	O. Brannan	483	.244	10	66	272	434	26	74	5.4	.964	G. Crowder	41	244	21	5	2	3.69
W-82 L-72	SS	R. Kress	560	.273	9	81	318	400	55	99	5.2	.929	J. Ogden	38	243	15	16	0	4.15
	3B	F. O'Rourke	391	.263	1	62	149	160	15	13	3.4	.954	Blaeholder	38	214	10	15	3	4.37
Dan Howley	RF	E. McNeely	496	.236	0	44	229	19	4	2	2.1	.984	L. Stewart	29	143	7	9	3	4.67
	CF	F. Schulte	556	.286	7	85	419	21	12	6	3.2	.973	D. Coffman	29	86	4	5	1	6.09
	LF	H. Manush	638	.378	13	108	355	6	3	2	2.4	.992							
	C	W. Schang	245	.286	3	39	263	46	5	5	3.8	.984							
	C	C. Manion	243	.226	2	31	302	49	7	10	5.0	.980							
	OF	F. McGowan	168	.363	2	18	99	3	4	1	2.3	.962							
	3B	Bettencourt	159	.283	4	24	38	68	6	4	2.7	.946							
Washington	1B	J. Judge	542	.306	3	93	1412	92	6	118	10.1	.996	B. Hadley	33	232	12	13	0	3.54
	2B	B. Harris	358	.204	0	28	251	326	18	61	6.2	.970	S. Jones	30	225	17	7	0	2.84
W-75 L-79	SS	B. Reeves	353	.303	3	42	159	190	35	32	5.8	.909	G. Braxton	38	218	13	11	6	**2.51**
	3B	O. Bluege	518	.297	2	75	150	**330**	20	34	**3.5**	.960	F. Marberry	48	161	13	13	3	3.85
Bucky Harris	RF	S. Rice	616	.328	2	55	240	11	7	5	1.8	.973	M. Gaston	28	149	6	12	0	5.51
	CF	R. Barnes	417	.302	6	51	255	16	6	2	2.7	.978	L. Brown	27	107	4	4	1	4.04
	LF	G. Goslin	456	**.379**	17	102	266	14	11	4	2.3	.962	T. Zachary	20	103	6	9	0	5.44
	C	M. Ruel	350	.257	0	55	397	73	5	5	4.7	**.989**							
	OF	S. West	378	.302	3	40	210	13	1	0	1.9	**.996**							
	SS	J. Cronin	227	.242	0	25	133	190	16	42	5.4	.953							
	2B	J. Hayes	210	.257	0	22	101	123	6	26	5.6	.974							
	C	E. Kenna	118	.297	1	20	104	26	8	3	4.1	.942							
Chicago	1B	B. Clancy	487	.271	2	37	1175	93	12	104	10.0	.991	T. Thomas	36	283	17	16	2	3.08
	2B	Hunnefield	333	.294	2	24	160	239	14	47	5.0	.966	T. Lyons	39	240	15	14	6	3.98
W-72 L-82	SS	B. Cissell	443	.260	1	60	255	360	41	77	5.3	.938	G. Adkins	36	225	10	16	1	3.73
	3B	W. Kamm	552	.308	1	84	**243**	278	12	33	3.4	**.977**	R. Faber	27	201	13	9	0	3.75
Ray Schalk	RF	A. Metzler	464	.304	0	55	288	11	10	3	2.3	.968	Blankenship	27	158	9	11	0	4.61
W-32 L-42	CF	J. Mostil	503	.270	0	51	394	18	10	3	**3.2**	.976	E. Walsh	14	78	4	7	0	4.96
	LF	B. Falk	286	.290	1	37	164	9	5	0	2.3	.972							
Lena Blackburne	C	B. Crouse	218	.252	2	20	196	61	11	3	3.5	.959							
W-40 L-40	OF	C. Reynolds	291	.323	2	36	135	6	3	2	1.9	.979							
	2S	B. Redfern	261	.234	0	35	166	223	24	39		.942							
	O2	B. Barrett	235	.277	3	26	122	62	5	7		.974							
	C	M. Berg	224	.246	0	29	256	52	3	8	4.3	.990							
Detroit	1B	B. Sweeney	309	.252	0	19	675	55	5	51	9.8	.993	O. Carroll	34	231	16	12	2	3.27
	2B	C. Gehringer	603	.320	6	74	377	**507**	35	101	6.0	.962	E. Whitehill	31	196	11	16	0	4.31
W-68 L-86	SS	J. Tavener	473	.260	5	52	302	405	42	81	5.7	.944	V. Sorrell	29	171	8	11	0	4.79
	3B	M. McManus	500	.288	8	73	114	183	14	12	3.4	.955	E. Vangilder	38	156	11	10	5	3.91
George Moriarty	RF	H. Heilmann	558	.328	14	107	215	17	7	2	1.9	.971	L. Stoner	36	126	5	8	4	4.35
	CF	H. Rice	510	.302	6	81	346	9	14	0	2.9	.962	K. Holloway	30	120	4	8	2	4.34
	LF	Fothergill	347	.317	3	63	179	6	8	0	2.1	.959	S. Gibson	20	120	5	8	0	5.42
	C	P. Hargrave	321	.274	10	63	301	35	8	5	3.9	.977	H. Billings	21	111	5	10	0	5.12
	OF	A. Wingo	242	.285	2	30	144	5	5	1	2.2	.968	G. Smith	39	106	1	1	3	4.42
	3B	J. Warner	206	.214	0	13	62	107	10	6	3.4	.944							
	C	L. Woodall	186	.210	0	13	218	44	2	3	4.3	.992							
	OF	J. Stone	113	.354	2	21	49	2	2	0	2.0	.962							

AMERICAN LEAGUE 1928, *cont.*

	POS	Player	AB	BA	HR	RBI	PO	A	E	DP	TC/G	FA	Pitcher	G	IP	W	L	SV	ERA
Cleveland	1B	L. Fonseca	263	.327	3	36	541	41	0	65	10.4	1.000	J. Shaute	36	254	13	17	2	4.04
	2B	C. Lind	650	.294	1	54	390	505	37	116	6.1	.960	W. Hudlin	42	220	14	14	7	4.04
W-62 L-92	SS	J. Sewell	588	.323	4	70	297	438	28	103	5.6	.963	G. Uhle	31	214	12	17	1	4.07
	3B	J. Hodapp	449	.323	2	73	103	220	19	20	3.4	.944	J. Miller	25	158	8	9	0	4.44
Roger Peckinpaugh	RF	H. Summa	504	.284	3	57	223	12	7	5	1.8	.971	G. Grant	28	155	10	8	0	5.04
	CF	S. Langford	427	.276	4	50	239	5	7	2	2.3	.972	B. Bayne	37	109	2	5	3	5.13
	LF	C. Jamieson	433	.307	1	37	282	22	5	1	2.8	.984							
	C	L. Sewell	411	.270	3	52	430	117	16	13	4.8	.972							
	UT	E. Morgan	265	.313	4	54	387	69	18	41		.962							
	1B	G. Burns	209	.249	5	30	470	38	8	44	9.7	.984							
Boston	1B	P. Todt	539	.252	12	73	1486	94	5	96	11.0	.997	R. Ruffing	42	289	10	25	2	3.89
	2B	B. Regan	511	.264	7	75	294	467	29	87	5.8	.963	E. Morris	47	258	19	15	5	3.53
W-57 L-96	SS	W. Gerber	300	.213	0	28	201	328	25	50	5.4	.955	J. Russell	32	201	11	14	0	3.84
	3B	B. Myer	536	.313	1	44	137	306	14	35	3.2	.969	MacFayden	33	195	9	15	0	4.75
Bill Carrigan	RF	D. Taitt	482	.299	3	61	251	19	7	8	2.0	.975	S. Harriss	27	128	8	11	1	4.63
	CF	I. Flagstead	510	.290	1	39	346	18	10	4	2.8	.973							
	LF	K. Williams	462	.303	8	67	253	10	8	0	2.1	.970							
	C	F. Hofmann	199	.226	0	16	223	44	5	7	3.8	.982							
	UT	J. Rothrock	344	.267	3	22	242	61	12	14		.962							
	S2	B. Rogell	296	.233	0	29	150	232	23	34		.943							
	C	C. Berry	177	.260	1	19	153	34	8	2	3.1	.959							
	C	J. Heving	158	.259	0	11	153	25	6	2	3.0	.967							

BATTING AND BASE RUNNING LEADERS

Batting Average		Slugging Average		Home Runs		Winning Percentage		Earned Run Average		Wins	
G. Goslin, WAS	.379	B. Ruth, NY	.709	B. Ruth, NY	54	G. Crowder, STL	.808	G. Braxton, WAS	2.51	L. Grove, PHI	24
H. Manush, STL	.378	L. Gehrig, NY	.648	L. Gehrig, NY	27	W. Hoyt, NY	.767	H. Pennock, NY	2.56	G. Pipgras, NY	24
L. Gehrig, NY	.374	G. Goslin, WAS	.614	G. Goslin, WAS	17	L. Grove, PHI	.750	L. Grove, PHI	2.58	W. Hoyt, NY	23
A. Simmons, PHI	.351	H. Manush, STL	.575	J. Hauser, PHI	16	H. Pennock, NY	.739	S. Jones, WAS	2.84	G. Crowder, STL	21
T. Lazzeri, NY	.332	A. Simmons, PHI	.558	A. Simmons, PHI	15	J. Quinn, PHI	.720	J. Quinn, PHI	2.90	S. Gray, STL	20

Total Bases		Runs Batted In		Stolen Bases		Saves		Strikeouts		Complete Games	
B. Ruth, NY	380	B. Ruth, NY	142	B. Myer, BOS	30	W. Hoyt, NY	8	L. Grove, PHI	183	R. Ruffing, BOS	25
H. Manush, STL	367	L. Gehrig, NY	142	J. Mostil, CHI	23	W. Hudlin, CLE	7	G. Pipgras, NY	139	L. Grove, PHI	24
L. Gehrig, NY	364	B. Meusel, NY	113	H. Rice, DET	20	T. Lyons, CHI	6	T. Thomas, CHI	129	T. Thomas, CHI	24
E. Combs, NY	290	H. Manush, STL	108	B. Cissell, CHI	18	G. Braxton, WAS	6	R. Ruffing, BOS	118	G. Pipgras, NY	22
H. Heilmann, DET	283	A. Simmons, PHI	107	O. Bluege, WAS	18	E. Vangilder, DET	5	G. Earnshaw, PHI	117		
		H. Heilmann, DET	107			E. Morris, BOS	5				

Hits		Base on Balls		Home Run Percentage		Fewest Hits/9 Innings		Shutouts		Fewest Walks/9 Innings	
H. Manush, STL	241	B. Ruth, NY	135	B. Ruth, NY	10.1	G. Braxton, WAS	7.30	H. Pennock, NY	5	J. Quinn, PHI	1.45
L. Gehrig, NY	210	L. Blue, STL	105	L. Gehrig, NY	4.8	L. Grove, PHI	7.84	S. Jones, WAS	4	H. Pennock, NY	1.71
S. Rice, WAS	202	M. Bishop, PHI	97	G. Goslin, WAS	3.7	S. Jones, WAS	8.37	J. Quinn, PHI	4	G. Braxton, WAS	1.81
E. Combs, NY	194	L. Gehrig, NY	95	J. Foxx, PHI	3.3	H. Johnson, NY	8.50	L. Grove, PHI	4	J. Russell, BOS	1.83

Runs Scored		Doubles		Triples		Most Strikeouts/9 Inn.		Innings		Games Pitched	
B. Ruth, NY	163	L. Gehrig, NY	47	E. Combs, NY	21	L. Grove, PHI	6.29	G. Pipgras, NY	301	F. Marberry, WAS	48
L. Gehrig, NY	139	H. Manush, STL	47	H. Manush, STL	20	H. Johnson, NY	4.97	R. Ruffing, BOS	289	E. Morris, BOS	47
E. Combs, NY	118	B. Meusel, NY	45	C. Gehringer, DET	16	R. Walberg, PHI	4.28	T. Thomas, CHI	283	G. Pipgras, NY	46
L. Blue, STL	116	F. Schulte, STL	44	R. Barnes, WAS	15	E. Whitehill, DET	4.26	W. Hoyt, NY	273	E. Rommel, PHI	43

	W	L	PCT	GB	R	OR	2B	3B	HR	BA	SA	SB	E	DP	FA	CG	BB	SO	ShO	SV	ERA
New York	101	53	.656		894	685	269	79	133	.296	.450	51	194	136	.968	83	452	487	13	21	3.74
Philadelphia	98	55	.641	2.5	829	615	323	75	89	.295	.436	59	181	124	.970	81	424	607	15	16	3.36
St. Louis	82	72	.532	19	772	742	276	76	63	.274	.393	76	189	146	.969	80	454	456	6	15	4.17
Washington	75	79	.487	26	718	705	277	93	40	.284	.393	110	178	146	.972	77	466	462	15	10	3.88
Chicago	72	82	.468	29	656	725	231	77	24	.270	.358	139	186	140	.970	88	501	418	6	11	3.98
Detroit	68	86	.442	33	744	804	265	97	62	.279	.401	113	218	140	.965	65	567	451	5	16	4.32
Cleveland	62	92	.403	39	674	830	299	61	34	.285	.382	50	221	187	.965	71	511	416	4	15	4.47
Boston	57	96	.373	43.5	589	770	260	62	38	.264	.361	99	178	139	.971	70	452	407	5	9	4.39
					5876	5876	2200	620	483	.281	.397	697	1545	1167	.969	615	3827	3704	69	113	4.04

NATIONAL LEAGUE 1929

	POS	Player	AB	BA	HR	RBI	PO	A	E	DP	TC/G	FA	Pitcher	G	IP	W	L	SV	ERA
Chicago W-98 L-54 Joe McCarthy	1B	C. Grimm	463	.298	10	91	1228	74	10	114	10.9	.992	C. Root	43	272	19	6	5	3.47
	2B	R. Hornsby	602	.380	39	149	286	547	23	106	5.5	.973	G. Bush	50	271	18	7	8	3.66
	SS	W. English	608	.276	1	52	332	497	39	107	6.0	.955	P. Malone	40	267	22	10	2	3.57
	3B	N. McMillan	495	.271	5	55	131	226	21	21	3.2	.944	S. Blake	35	218	14	13	1	4.29
	RF	K. Cuyler	509	.360	15	102	288	15	8	6	2.4	.974	A. Nehf	32	121	8	5	1	5.59
	CF	H. Wilson	574	.345	39	159	380	14	12	4	2.7	.970	H. Carlson	31	112	11	5	2	5.16
	LF	Stephenson	495	.362	17	110	245	9	4	4	2.0	.984	M. Cvengros	32	64	5	4	2	4.64
	C	Z. Taylor	215	.274	1	31	247	36	6	4	4.5*	.979							
	OF	C. Heathcote	224	.313	2	31	131	4	2	2	2.6	.985							
	3B	C. Beck	190	.211	0	9	18	70	2	5	2.7	.978							
	C	M. Gonzalez	167	.240	0	18	212	34	2	7	4.1	.992							
Pittsburgh W-88 L-65 Donie Bush W-67 L-51 Jewel Ens W-21 L-14	1B	E. Sheely	485	.293	6	88	1292	83	5	102	9.9	.996	B. Grimes	33	233	17	7	2	3.13
	2B	G. Grantham	349	.307	12	90	205	239	15	54	6.0	.967	E. Brame	37	230	16	11	0	4.55
	SS	D. Bartell	610	.302	2	57	179	246	21	21	4.6	.953	R. Kremer	34	222	18	10	0	4.26
	3B	P. Traynor	540	.356	4	108	148	238	20	23	3.1	.951	J. Petty	36	184	11	10	0	3.71
	RF	P. Waner	596	.336	15	100	328	15	5	5	2.4	.986	S. Swetonic	41	144	8	10	5	4.82
	CF	L. Waner	662	.353	5	74	450	22	6	6	3.2	.987	L. French	30	123	7	5	1	4.90
	LF	A. Comorosky	473	.321	6	97	256	6	10	3	2.2	.963	H. Meine	22	108	7	6	1	4.50
	C	Hargreaves	328	.268	1	44	308	56	7	7	3.6	.981							
	C	R. Hemsley	235	.289	0	37	240	48	14	7	3.8	.954							
	UT	S. Adams	196	.260	0	11	75	130	17	14		.923							
	SS	S. Clarke	178	.264	2	21	73	132	18	19	5.4	.919							
	P	E. Brame	116	.310	4	25	7	36	3	0	1.2	.935							
New York W-84 L-67 John McGraw	1B	B. Terry	607	.372	14	117	1575	111	11	146	11.4	.994	C. Hubbell	39	268	18	11	1	3.69
	2B	A. Cohen	347	.294	5	47	227	315	20	52	6.0	.964	L. Benton	39	237	11	17	3	4.14
	SS	T. Jackson	551	.294	21	94	329	552	28	110	6.1	.969	Fitzsimmons	37	222	15	11	1	4.10
	3B	F. Lindstrom	549	.319	15	91	134	258	14	24	3.2	.966	B. Walker	29	178	14	7	0	3.09
	RF	M. Ott	545	.328	42	152	335	26	6	12	2.5	.973	C. Mays	37	123	7	2	4	4.32
	CF	E. Roush	450	.324	8	52	248	18	5	5	2.5	.982	D. Henry	27	101	5	6	1	3.82
	LF	F. Leach	411	.290	8	47	149	2	4	0	1.6	.974	J. Scott	30	92	7	6	1	3.53
	C	S. Hogan	317	.300	5	45	286	47	7	5	3.7	.979	J. Genewich	21	85	3	7	1	6.78
	OF	C. Fullis	274	.288	7	29	151	3	6	0	2.1	.963							
	C	B. O'Farrell	248	.306	4	42	254	22	6	2	3.4	.979							
	2B	A. Reese	209	.263	0	21	104	163	11	24	6.3	.960							
	32	D. Farrell	178	.213	0	16	87	114	13	18		.939							
	PH	P. Crawford	57	.298	3	24													
St. Louis W-78 L-74 Billy Southworth W-43 L-45 Gabby Street W-1 L-0 Bill McKechnie W-34 L-29	1B	J. Bottomley	560	.314	29	137	1347	75	13	122	9.9	.991	B. Sherdel	33	196	10	15	0	5.93
	2B	F. Frisch	527	.334	5	74	295	374	21	66	5.7	.970	S. Johnson	42	182	13	7	3	3.60
	SS	C. Gelbert	512	.262	3	65	338	499	46	95	6.0	.948	J. Haines	28	180	13	10	0	5.71
	3B	A. High	603	.295	10	63	91	204	10	17	2.5	.967	C. Mitchell	25	173	8	11	0	4.27
	RF	E. Orsatti	346	.332	3	39	176	12	5	5	2.5	.974	H. Haid	38	155	9	9	4	4.07
	CF	T. Douthit	613	.336	9	62	442	8	12	1	3.1	.974	Frankhouse	30	133	7	2	1	4.12
	LF	C. Hafey	517	.338	29	125	278	8	10	1	2.3	.966	G. Alexander	22	132	9	8	0	3.89
	C	J. Wilson	394	.325	4	71	410	80	14	16	4.2	.972							
	OF	W. Roettger	269	.253	3	42	137	4	1	0	2.1	.993							
	OF	W. Holm	176	.233	0	14	115	4	7	2	2.9	.944							
	C	E. Smith	145	.345	1	22	131	21	6	1	3.2	.962							
Philadelphia W-71 L-82 Burt Shotton	1B	D. Hurst	589	.304	31	125	1509	112	24	125	10.7	.985	Willoughby	49	243	15	14	4	4.99
	2B	F. Thompson	623	.324	4	53	395	512	33	103	6.4	.965	L. Sweetland	43	204	13	11	2	5.11
	SS	T. Thevenow	317	.227	0	35	188	296	24	56	5.6	.953	R. Benge	38	199	11	15	4	6.29
	3B	P. Whitney	612	.327	8	115	168	333	17	29	3.4	.967	P. Collins	43	153	9	7	5	5.75
	RF	C. Klein	616	.356	43	145	321	18	12	3	2.4	.966	H. Elliott	40	114	3	7	2	6.06
	CF	D. Sothern	294	.306	5	27	193	9	7	2	2.9	.967	B. McGraw	41	86	5	5	4	5.73
	LF	L. O'Doul	638	.398	32	122	320	14	10	5	2.2	.971	L. Koupal	15	87	5	5	2	4.78
	C	W. Lerian	273	.223	7	25	271	69	5	13	3.3	.986	H. Smythe	19	69	4	6	1	5.24
	SO	B. Friberg	455	.301	7	55	234	195	28	33		.939							
	C	S. Davis	263	.342	7	48	198	47	10	7	2.6	.961							
	OF	H. Peel	156	.269	0	19	94	2	1	1	2.5	.990							
	PH	C. Williams	65	.292	5	21													
Brooklyn W-70 L-83 Wilbert Robinson	1B	Bissonette	431	.281	12	75	1093	47	15	70	10.2	.987	W. Clark	41	279	16	19	1	3.74
	2B	E. Moore	402	.296	0	48	135	228	17	31	5.1	.955	D. Vance	31	231	14	13	0	3.89
	SS	D. Bancroft	358	.277	1	44	224	309	25	45	5.5	.955	R. Moss	39	182	11	6	0	5.04
	3B	W. Gilbert	569	.304	3	58	137	271	19	16	3.0	.956	C. Dudley	35	157	6	14	0	5.69
	RF	B. Herman	569	.381	21	113	244	10	16	2	1.9	.941	D. McWeeny	36	146	4	10	1	6.10
	CF	J. Frederick	628	.328	24	75	410	13	11	1	3.0	.975	J. Morrison	39	137	13	7	8	4.48
	LF	R. Bressler	456	.318	9	77	263	7	13	0	2.3	.954							
	C	V. Picinich	273	.260	4	31	311	62	8	8	4.5	.979							
	UT	H. Hendrick	384	.354	14	82	467	62	16	29		.971							
	C	H. DeBerry	210	.262	1	25	304	36	3	3	5.0	.991							
	2B	B. Rhiel	205	.278	4	25	94	137	5	16	5.0	.979							

NATIONAL LEAGUE 1929, *cont.*

	POS	Player	AB	BA	HR	RBI	PO	A	E	DP	TC/G	FA	Pitcher	G	IP	W	L	SV	ERA
Cincinnati	1B	G. Kelly	577	.293	5	103	1537	103	11	127	11.2	.993	R. Lucas	32	270	19	12	0	3.60
	2B	H. Critz	425	.247	1	50	210	395	16	72	5.9	**.974**	E. Rixey	35	201	10	13	1	4.16
W-66 L-88	SS	H. Ford	529	.276	3	50	239	368	30	86	5.9	.953	J. May	41	199	10	14	3	4.61
	3B	C. Dressen	401	.244	1	36	77	157	17	9	2.6	.932	P. Donohue	32	178	10	13	0	5.42
Jack Hendricks	RF	C. Walker	492	.313	7	83	298	11	10	2	2.3	.969	D. Luque	32	176	5	16	0	4.50
	CF	E. Allen	538	.292	6	64	393	12	5	2	3.0	**.988**	R. Kolp	30	145	8	10	0	4.03
	LF	E. Swanson	574	.300	4	43	317	9	10	2	2.4	.970							
	C	J. Gooch	287	.300	0	34	251	61	8	7	3.7	.975							
	C	C. Sukeforth	237	.354	1	33	171	40	4	4	2.8	.981							
	SS	P. Pittenger	210	.295	0	27	107	153	12	37	5.4	.956							
	3B	J. Stripp	187	.214	3	20	49	120	7	4	3.2	.960							
	OF	P. Purdy	181	.271	1	16	84	3	2	0	2.1	.978							
Boston	1B	G. Sisler	629	.326	1	79	1398	111	**28**	131	10.0	.982	B. Smith	34	231	11	17	3	4.68
	2B	F. Maguire	496	.252	0	41	334	437	23	94	5.8	.971	S. Seibold	33	206	12	17	1	4.73
W-56 L-98	SS	Maranville	560	.284	0	55	319	536	35	104	6.1	.961	P. Jones	35	188	7	15	0	4.64
	3B	L. Bell	483	.298	9	72	107	198	15	15	2.5	.953	E. Brandt	26	168	8	13	0	5.53
Judge Fuchs	RF	L. Richbourg	557	.305	3	56	323	14	10	2	2.6	.971	B. Cantwell	27	157	4	13	2	4.47
	CF	E. Clark	279	.315	1	30	216	7	5	3	3.1	.978	D. Leverett	24	98	3	7	1	6.36
	LF	G. Harper	457	.291	10	68	266	7	8	2	2.2	.972	Cunningham	17	92	4	6	1	4.52
	C	A. Spohrer	342	.272	2	48	314	57	**18**	5	3.6	.954							
	OF	J. Welsh	186	.290	2	16	177	6	4	1	3.7	.979							

BATTING AND BASE RUNNING LEADERS

Batting Average
L. O'Doul, PHI .398
B. Herman, BKN .381
R. Hornsby, CHI .380
B. Terry, NY .372
Stephenson, CHI .362

Slugging Average
R. Hornsby, CHI .679
C. Klein, PHI .657
M. Ott, NY .635
C. Hafey, STL .632
L. O'Doul, PHI .622

Home Runs
C. Klein, PHI 43
M. Ott, NY 42
H. Wilson, CHI 39
R. Hornsby, CHI 39
L. O'Doul, PHI 32

Total Bases
R. Hornsby, CHI 409
C. Klein, PHI 405
L. O'Doul, PHI 397
H. Wilson, CHI 355
B. Herman, BKN 348

Runs Batted In
H. Wilson, CHI 159
M. Ott, NY 151
R. Hornsby, CHI 149
C. Klein, PHI 145
J. Bottomley, STL 137

Stolen Bases
K. Cuyler, CHI 43
E. Swanson, CIN 33
F. Frisch, STL 24
E. Allen, CIN 21
B. Herman, BKN 21

Hits
L. O'Doul, PHI 254
L. Waner, PIT 234
R. Hornsby, CHI 229
B. Terry, NY 226

Base on Balls
M. Ott, NY 113
G. Grantham, PIT 93
P. Waner, PIT 89
R. Hornsby, CHI 87

Home Run Percentage
M. Ott, NY 7.7
C. Klein, PHI 7.0
H. Wilson, CHI 6.8
R. Hornsby, CHI 6.6

Runs Scored
R. Hornsby, CHI 156
L. O'Doul, PHI 152
M. Ott, NY 138
H. Wilson, CHI 135

Doubles
J. Frederick, BKN 52
C. Hafey, STL 47
R. Hornsby, CHI 47
G. Kelly, CIN 45

Triples
L. Waner, PIT 20
C. Walker, CIN 15
P. Waner, PIT 15
P. Whitney, PHI 14

PITCHING LEADERS

Winning Percentage
C. Root, CHI .760
G. Bush, CHI .720
B. Grimes, PIT .708
P. Malone, CHI .688
R. Kremer, PIT .643

Earned Run Average
B. Walker, NY 3.09
B. Grimes, PIT 3.13
C. Root, CHI 3.47
P. Malone, CHI 3.57
R. Lucas, CIN 3.60

Wins
P. Malone, CHI 22
C. Root, CHI 19
R. Lucas, CIN 19
G. Bush, CHI 18
R. Kremer, PIT 18
C. Hubbell, NY 18

Saves
J. Morrison, BKN 8
G. Bush, CHI 8
L. Koupal, BKN, PHI 6
P. Collins, PHI 5
S. Swetonic, PIT 5
C. Root, CHI 5

Strikeouts
P. Malone, CHI 166
W. Clark, BKN 140
D. Vance, BKN 126
C. Root, CHI 124
C. Hubbell, NY 106

Complete Games
R. Lucas, CIN 28

Fewest Hits/9 Innings
R. Lucas, CIN 8.90
C. Hubbell, NY 9.17
R. Kremer, PIT 9.18
S. Johnson, STL 9.18

Shutouts
P. Malone, CHI 5
Fitzsimmons, NY 4
C. Root, CHI 4
S. Johnson, STL 3

Fewest Walks/9 Innings
D. Vance, BKN 1.83
R. Lucas, CIN 1.93
J. Petty, PIT 2.05
C. Hubbell, NY 2.25

Most Strikeouts/9 Inn.
P. Malone, CHI 5.60
D. Vance, BKN 4.90
W. Clark, BKN 4.52
J. May, CIN 4.16

Innings
W. Clark, BKN 279
C. Root, CHI 272
G. Bush, CHI 271
R. Lucas, CIN 270

Games Pitched
G. Bush, CHI 50
Willoughby, PHI 49
C. Root, CHI 43
L. Sweetland, PHI 43

	W	L	PCT	GB	R	OR	2B	3B	HR	BA	SA	SB	E	DP	FA	CG	BB	SO	ShO	SV	ERA
										Batting				**Fielding**			**Pitching**				
Chicago	98	54	.645		**982**	758	**310**	45	140	.303	.452	103	**154**	**169**	**.975**	79	537	548	**14**	21	4.16
Pittsburgh	88	65	.575	10.5	904	780	285	**116**	60	.303	.430	94	181	136	.970	79	439	409	5	13	4.36
New York	84	67	.556	13.5	897	**709**	251	47	136	.296	.436	85	158	163	.975	68	**387**	431	9	13	**3.97**
St. Louis	78	74	.513	20	831	806	**310**	84	100	.293	.438	72	174	149	.971	**83**	474	453	6	8	4.66
Philadelphia	71	82	.464	27.5	897	1032	305	51	**153**	**.309**	**.467**	59	191	153	.969	45	616	369	5	**24**	6.13
Brooklyn	70	83	.458	28.5	755	888	282	69	99	.291	.427	80	192	113	.968	59	549	**549**	7	16	4.92
Cincinnati	66	88	.429	33	686	760	258	79	34	.281	.379	**134**	162	148	.974	75	413	347	5	8	4.41
Boston	56	98	.364	43	657	876	252	78	32	.280	.375	65	204	146	.967	78	530	366	4	12	5.12
					6609	6609	2253	569	754	.294	.426	692	1416	1177	.971	566	3945	3472	55	115	4.71

AMERICAN LEAGUE 1929

	POS	Player	AB	BA	HR	RBI	PO	A	E	DP	TC/G	FA	Pitcher	G	IP	W	L	SV	ERA
Philadelphia	1B	J. Foxx	517	.354	33	117	1226	74	6	98	9.2	.995	L. Grove	42	275	20	6	4	**2.81**
	2B	M. Bishop	475	.232	3	36	301	371	21	58	5.4	.970	R. Walberg	40	268	18	11	4	3.60
W-104 L-46	SS	J. Boley	303	.251	2	47	161	229	15	50	4.6	.963	G. Earnshaw	44	255	**24**	8	1	3.29
	3B	S. Hale	379	.277	1	40	90	171	12	13	2.8	.956	J. Quinn	35	161	11	9	2	3.97
Connie Mack	RF	B. Miller	556	.335	8	93	311	10	10	4	2.3	.970	B. Shores	39	153	11	6	7	3.60
	CF	M. Haas	578	.313	16	82	373	10	7	2	2.8	.982	E. Rommel	32	114	12	2	4	2.85
	LF	A. Simmons	581	.365	34	**157**	349	19	4	2	2.6	.989							
	C	M. Cochrane	514	.331	7	95	**659**	77	13	9	5.5	**.983**							
	UT	J. Dykes	401	.327	13	79	203	273	33	41		.935							
New York	1B	L. Gehrig	553	.300	35	126	1458	82	9	134	10.1	.994	G. Pipgras	39	225	18	12	0	4.23
	2B	T. Lazzeri	545	.354	18	106	368	467	**27**	**101**	5.9	.969	W. Hoyt	30	202	10	9	1	4.24
W-88 L-66	SS	L. Durocher	341	.246	0	32	197	299	22	59	5.6	.958	E. Wells	31	193	13	9	0	4.33
	3B	G. Robertson	309	.298	0	35	80	116	7	6	2.6	.966	R. Sherid	33	160	6	6	1	3.49
Miller Huggins	RF	B. Ruth	499	.345	**46**	154	240	5	4	2	1.9	.984	H. Pennock	27	158	9	11	2	4.90
W-82 L-61	CF	E. Combs	586	.345	3	65	358	10	13	5	2.7	.966	F. Heimach	35	135	11	6	4	4.01
	LF	B. Meusel	391	.261	10	57	206	9	7	2	2.3	.968	T. Zachary	26	120	12	0	2	2.48
Art Fletcher	C	B. Dickey	447	.324	10	65	476	**95**	12	**13**	4.6	.979	W. Moore	41	62	6	4	8	4.06
W-6 L-5	S3	M. Koenig	373	.292	3	41	137	216	32	34		.917							
	3B	L. Lary	236	.309	5	26	38	95	8	10	2.6	.943							
	OF	C. Durst	202	.257	4	31	151	5	2	1	2.2	.987							
	OF	S. Byrd	170	.312	5	28	108	6	6	2	2.2	.950							
Cleveland	1B	L. Fonseca	566	**.369**	6	103	1486	**107**	8	**141**	10.9	.995	W. Hudlin	40	280	17	15	1	3.34
	2B	J. Hodapp	294	.327	4	51	162	271	10	32	6.2	.977	W. Ferrell	43	243	21	10	5	3.60
	SS	J. Tavener	250	.212	2	27	158	275	25	59	5.1	.945	J. Miller	29	206	14	12	0	3.58
W-81 L-71	3B	J. Sewell	578	.315	7	73	163	**336**	13	28	3.4	.975	J. Shaute	26	162	8	8	0	4.28
	RF	B. Falk	430	.309	13	94	219	15	14	4	2.0	.944	J. Miljus	34	128	8	8	2	5.19
Roger Peckinpaugh	CF	E. Averill	602	.331	18	97	**388**	14	14	3	2.7	.966	K. Holloway	25	119	6	5	0	3.03
	LF	C. Jamieson	364	.291	0	26	192	8	4	1	2.2	.980	J. Zinn	18	105	4	6	2	5.04
	C	L. Sewell	406	.236	1	39	433	81	**18**	11	4.3	.966							
	OF	E. Morgan	318	.318	3	37	100	8	11	1	1.5	.908							
	SS	R. Gardner	256	.262	1	24	175	240	21	50	5.3	.952							
	2B	C. Lind	224	.241	0	13	190	209	18	60	6.5	.957							
	O2	D. Porter	192	.328	1	24	95	63	8	8		.952							
St. Louis	1B	L. Blue	573	.293	6	61	**1491**	88	10	127	10.5	.994	S. Gray	43	**305**	18	15	1	3.72
	2B	O. Melillo	494	.296	5	67	342	**519**	24	98	6.3	.975	G. Crowder	40	267	17	15	4	3.92
W-79 L-73	SS	R. Kress	557	.305	9	107	312	441	43	**94**	5.5	.946	Blaeholder	42	222	14	15	2	4.18
	3B	F. O'Rourke	585	.251	2	62	171	242	25	**30**	2.9	.943	R. Collins	26	155	11	6	1	4.00
Dan Howley	RF	F. McGowan	441	.254	2	51	257	16	7	5	2.4	.975	L. Stewart	23	149	9	6	0	3.25
	CF	F. Schulte	446	.307	3	71	361	12	4	2	**3.3**	.989	J. Ogden	34	131	4	8	0	4.93
	LF	H. Manush	574	.355	6	81	293	11	4	3	2.2	.987	C. Kimsey	24	64	3	6	1	5.04
	C	W. Schang	249	.237	5	36	268	56	4	6	3.9	.988							
	OF	E. McNeely	230	.243	1	18	96	4	2	0	1.6	.980							
	C	R. Ferrell	144	.229	0	20	140	35	7	3	4.0	.962							
Washington	1B	J. Judge	543	.315	6	71	1323	88	6	116	10.0	**.996**	F. Marberry	**49**	250	19	12	11	3.06
	2B	B. Myer	563	.300	3	82	205	271	21	51	5.6	.958	B. Hadley	37	194	6	16	0	5.65
W-71 L-81	SS	J. Cronin	494	.281	8	61	285	**459**	62	92	5.6	.923	G. Braxton	37	182	12	10	4	4.85
	3B	J. Hayes	424	.276	2	57	56	132	11	15	3.2	.945	L. Brown	40	168	8	7	0	4.18
Walter Johnson	RF	S. Rice	616	.323	1	62	272	20	9	5	2.0	.970	S. Jones	24	154	9	9	0	3.92
	CF	S. West	510	.267	3	75	376	**25**	9	**8**	2.9	.978	B. Burke	37	141	6	8	0	4.79
	LF	G. Goslin	553	.288	18	91	299	7	10	1	2.2	.968	M. Thomas	22	125	7	8	2	3.52
	C	B. Tate	265	.294	0	30	291	49	10	10	4.7	.971	A. Liska	24	94	3	9	0	4.77
	UT	O. Bluege	220	.295	5	31	74	145	6	24		.973							
	C	M. Ruel	188	.245	0	20	247	52	3	6	4.8	.990							
Detroit	1B	D. Alexander	626	.343	25	137	1443	90	**18**	129	10.0	.988	G. Uhle	32	249	15	11	0	4.08
	2B	C. Gehringer	634	.339	13	106	**404**	501	23	93	6.0	**.975**	E. Whitehill	38	245	14	15	1	4.62
	SS	H. Schuble	258	.233	2	28	141	216	46	43	4.7	.886	V. Sorrell	36	226	14	15	1	5.18
W-70 L-84	3B	M. McManus	599	.280	18	90	206	289	14	29	3.4	.972	O. Carroll	34	202	9	17	1	4.63
	RF	H. Heilmann	453	.344	15	120	193	8	7	3	1.8	.966	E. Yde	29	87	7	3	0	5.30
Bucky Harris	CF	H. Rice	536	.304	6	69	345	16	15	6	3.0	.960	L. Stoner	24	53	3	3	4	5.26
	LF	R. Johnson	**640**	.314	10	69	377	**25**	**31**	5	3.0	.928							
	C	E. Phillips	221	.235	2	21	255	34	10	4	4.7	.967							
	OF	Fothergill	277	.354	6	62	116	2	4	1	2.1	.967							
	C	P. Hargrave	185	.330	3	26	175	38	6	7	4.6	.973							
	C	M. Shea	162	.290	3	24	157	32	7	4	3.9	.964							

AMERICAN LEAGUE 1929, *cont.*

	POS	Player	AB	BA	HR	RBI	PO	A	E	DP	TC/G	FA	Pitcher	G	IP	W	L	SV	ERA
Chicago	1B	A. Shires	353	.312	3	41	815	58	8	78	10.0	.991	T. Thomas	36	260	14	18	1	3.19
	2B	J. Kerr	419	.258	1	39	307	459	23	84	6.5	.971	T. Lyons	37	259	14	20	2	4.10
W-59 L-93	SS	B. Cissell	618	.280	5	62	357	459	55	90	5.7	.937	R. Faber	31	234	13	13	0	3.88
	3B	W. Kamm	523	.268	3	63	221	270	11	27	3.5	.978	H. McKain	34	158	6	9	1	3.65
Lena Blackburne	RF	C. Reynolds	517	.317	11	67	268	13	15	5	2.3	.949	G. Adkins	31	138	2	11	0	5.33
	CF	D. Hoffman	337	.258	3	37	237	4	4	2	2.8	.984	E. Walsh	24	129	6	11	0	5.65
	LF	A. Metzler	568	.275	2	49	316	16	14	3	2.5	.960							
	C	M. Berg	351	.288	0	47	290	86	7	12	3.6	.982							
	1B	B. Clancy	290	.283	3	45	647	49	6	47	9.5	.991							
	OF	C. Watwood	278	.302	2	18	188	7	12	2	2.7	.942							
Boston	1B	P. Todt	534	.262	4	64	1467	102	14	128	10.3	.991	R. Ruffing	35	244	9	22	1	4.86
	2B	B. Regan	371	.288	1	54	193	282	19	66	5.4	.962	M. Gaston	39	244	12	19	2	3.73
W-58 L-96	SS	H. Rhyne	346	.251	0	38	220	297	36	71	4.9	.935	J. Russell	35	226	6	18	0	3.94
	3B	B. Reeves	460	.248	2	28	152	242	38	27	3.3	.912	MacFayden	32	221	10	18	0	3.62
Bill Carrigan	RF	B. Barrett	370	.270	3	35	204	16	6	4	2.1	.973	E. Morris	33	208	14	14	1	4.45
	CF	J. Rothrock	473	.300	6	59	342	12	11	3	2.9	.970	B. Bayne	27	84	5	5	0	6.72
	LF	R. Scarritt	540	.294	1	71	302	16	19	6	2.3	.944							
	C	C. Berry	207	.242	1	21	236	51	5	8	4.1	.983							
	UT	B. Narleski	260	.277	0	25	146	200	15	41		.958							
	OF	E. Bigelow	211	.284	1	26	63	5	4	1	1.2	.944							
	C	J. Heving	188	.319	0	23	207	40	3	4	4.5	.988							
	OF	K. Williams	139	.345	3	21	75	3	3	2	2.3	.963							

BATTING AND BASE RUNNING LEADERS

Batting Average
L. Fonseca, CLE .369
A. Simmons, PHI .365
H. Manush, STL .355
T. Lazzeri, NY .354
J. Foxx, PHI .354

Slugging Average
B. Ruth, NY .697
A. Simmons, PHI .642
J. Foxx, PHI .625
L. Gehrig, NY .582
D. Alexander, DET .580

Home Runs
B. Ruth, NY 46
L. Gehrig, NY 35
A. Simmons, PHI 34
J. Foxx, PHI 33
D. Alexander, DET 25

Total Bases
A. Simmons, PHI 373
D. Alexander, DET 363
B. Ruth, NY 348
C. Gehringer, DET 337
J. Foxx, PHI 323

Runs Batted In
A. Simmons, PHI 157
B. Ruth, NY 154
D. Alexander, DET 137
L. Gehrig, NY 126
H. Heilmann, DET 120

Stolen Bases
C. Gehringer, DET 28
B. Cissell, CHI 26
B. Miller, PHI 24
J. Rothrock, BOS 23
R. Johnson, DET 20

Hits
D. Alexander, DET 215
C. Gehringer, DET 215
A. Simmons, PHI 212
L. Fonseca, CLE 209

Base on Balls
M. Bishop, PHI 128
L. Blue, STL 126
L. Gehrig, NY 122
J. Foxx, PHI 103

Home Run Percentage
B. Ruth, NY 9.2
J. Foxx, PHI 6.4
L. Gehrig, NY 6.3
A. Simmons, PHI 5.9

Runs Scored
C. Gehringer, DET 131
R. Johnson, DET 128
L. Gehrig, NY 127
J. Foxx, PHI 123

Doubles
H. Manush, STL 45
C. Gehringer, DET 45
R. Johnson, DET 45
L. Fonseca, CLE 44

Triples
C. Gehringer, DET 19
R. Scarritt, BOS 17
B. Miller, PHI 16
L. Fonseca, CLE 15

PITCHING LEADERS

Winning Percentage
L. Grove, PHI .769
G. Earnshaw, PHI .750
W. Ferrell, CLE .677
R. Walberg, PHI .621
F. Marberry, WAS .613

Earned Run Average
L. Grove, PHI 2.81
F. Marberry, WAS 3.06
T. Thomas, CHI 3.19
G. Earnshaw, PHI 3.29
W. Hudlin, CLE 3.34

Wins
G. Earnshaw, PHI 24
W. Ferrell, CLE 21
L. Grove, PHI 20
F. Marberry, WAS 19

Saves
F. Marberry, WAS 11
W. Moore, NY 8
B. Shores, PHI 7
W. Ferrell, CLE 5

Strikeouts
L. Grove, PHI 170
G. Earnshaw, PHI 149
G. Pipgras, NY 125
F. Marberry, WAS 121
R. Ruffing, BOS 109
S. Gray, STL 109

Complete Games
T. Thomas, CHI 24
G. Uhle, DET 23
S. Gray, STL 23
W. Hudlin, CLE 22
T. Lyons, CHI 21
L. Grove, PHI 21

Fewest Hits/9 Innings
G. Earnshaw, PHI 8.23
E. Wells, NY 8.33
F. Marberry, WAS 8.38
R. Walberg, PHI 8.61

Shutouts
Blaeholder, STL 4
MacFayden, BOS 4
G. Crowder, STL 4
S. Gray, STL 4

Fewest Walks/9 Innings
J. Russell, BOS 1.59
T. Thomas, CHI 2.08
G. Uhle, DET 2.10
W. Hudlin, CLE 2.34

Most Strikeouts/9 Inn.
L. Grove, PHI 5.56
G. Earnshaw, PHI 5.27
G. Pipgras, NY 4.99
F. Marberry, WAS 4.35

Innings
S. Gray, STL 305
W. Hudlin, CLE 280
L. Grove, PHI 275
R. Walberg, PHI 268

Games Pitched
F. Marberry, WAS 49
G. Earnshaw, PHI 44
S. Gray, STL 43
W. Ferrell, CLE 43

	W	L	PCT	GB	R	OR	2B	3B	HR	BA	SA	SB	E	DP	FA	CG	BB	SO	ShO	SV	ERA
										Batting				**Fielding**			**Pitching**				
Philadelphia	104	46	.693		901	615	288	76	122	.296	.451	61	146	117	.975	72	487	573	8	24	3.44
New York	88	66	.571	18	899	775	262	74	142	.295	.450	51	178	152	.971	64	485	484	12	18	4.17
Cleveland	81	71	.533	24	717	736	294	79	62	.294	.417	75	198	162	.968	80	488	389	8	10	4.05
St. Louis	79	73	.520	26	733	713	276	63	46	.276	.380	72	156	148	.975	83	462	415	15	10	4.08
Washington	71	81	.467	34	730	776	244	66	48	.276	.375	86	195	156	.968	61	496	494	3	17	4.34
Detroit	70	84	.455	36	926	928	339	97	110	.299	.453	95	242	156	.961	82	646	467	5	9	4.96
Chicago	59	93	.388	46	627	792	240	74	37	.268	.363	106	188	153	.970	78	505	328	5	7	4.41
Boston	58	96	.377	48	605	803	285	69	28	.267	.365	85	218	159	.965	84	496	416	9	5	4.43
					6138	6138	2228	598	595	.284	.407	631	1521	1196	.969	604	4065	3566	65	100	4.24

NATIONAL LEAGUE 1930

	POS	Player	AB	BA	HR	RBI	PO	A	E	DP	TC/G	FA	Pitcher	G	IP	W	L	SV	ERA
St. Louis	1B	J. Bottomley	487	.304	15	97	1164	41	12	127	9.8	.990	B. Hallahan	35	237	15	9	2	4.66
	2B	F. Frisch	540	.346	10	114	307	473	25	93	6.5	.969	S. Johnson	32	188	12	10	2	4.65
W-92 L-62	SS	C. Gelbert	513	.304	3	72	322	472	44	104	6.0	.947	J. Haines	29	182	13	8	1	4.30
	3B	S. Adams	570	.314	0	55	66	159	8	18	2.2	.966	B. Grimes	22	152	13	6	0	3.01
Gabby Street	RF	G. Watkins	391	.373	17	87	163	10	8	4	2.0	.956	F. Rhem	26	140	12	8	0	4.45
	CF	T. Douthit	664	.303	7	93	425	8	16	3	2.9	.964	H. Bell	39	115	4	3	8	3.90
	LF	C. Hafey	446	.336	26	107	189	11	5	0	1.8	.976	A. Grabowski	33	106	6	4	1	4.84
	C	J. Wilson	362	.318	1	58	456	67	7	11	5.0	.987	J. Lindsey	39	106	7	5	5	4.43
	OF	S. Fisher	254	.374	8	61	122	6	5	0	2.0	.962							
	C	G. Mancuso	227	.366	7	59	277	33	10	5	5.2	.969							
	3B	A. High	215	.279	2	29	34	68	1	5	2.1	.990							
	OF	R. Blades	101	.396	4	25	66	1	3	0	2.2	.957							
Chicago	1B	C. Grimm	429	.289	6	66	1040	68	6	103	9.9	.995	P. Malone	45	272	20	9	4	3.94
	2B	F. Blair	578	.273	6	59	257	429	30	83	6.2	.958	G. Bush	46	225	15	10	3	6.20
W-90 L-64	SS	C. Beck	244	.213	6	34	97	165	13	36	4.8	.953	C. Root	37	220	16	14	3	4.33
	3B	W. English	638	.335	14	59	83	135	6	19	2.7	.973	S. Blake	34	187	10	14	0	4.82
Joe McCarthy	RF	K. Cuyler	642	.355	13	134	377	21	8	7	2.6	.980	B. Teachout	40	153	11	4	0	4.06
W-86 L-64	CF	H. Wilson	585	.356	56	190	357	9	19	2	2.5	.951	B. Osborn	35	127	10	6	1	4.97
	LF	Stephenson	341	.367	5	68	132	5	6	1	1.8	.958							
Rogers Hornsby	C	G. Hartnett	508	.339	37	122	646	68	8	11	5.3	.989							
W-4 L-0	3B	L. Bell	248	.278	5	47	63	102	9	14	2.5	.948							
	OF	D. Taylor	219	.283	2	37	97	3	3	0	2.0	.971							
	1B	G. Kelly	166	.331	3	19	414	32	1	31	11.5	.998							
New York	1B	B. Terry	633	.401	23	129	1538	128	17	128	10.9	.990	B. Walker	39	245	17	15	1	3.93
	2B	H. Critz	558	.265	4	50	346*	413*	22	88*	6.3	.972*	C. Hubbell	37	242	17	12	2	3.76
W-87 L-67	SS	T. Jackson	431	.339	13	82	218	441	30	72	6.0	.956	Fitzsimmons	41	224	19	7	4	4.25
	3B	F. Lindstrom	609	.379	22	106	132	291	21	24	3.0	.953	H. Pruett	45	136	5	4	3	4.78
John McGraw	RF	M. Ott	521	.349	25	119	320	23	11	6	2.4	.969	C. Mitchell	24	129	10	3	0	3.98
	CF	W. Roettger	420	.283	5	51	233	9	2	1	2.1	.992	J. Heving	41	90	7	5	6	5.22
	LF	F. Leach	544	.327	13	71	208	11	5	4	1.8	.978	P. Donohue	18	87	7	6	1	6.13
	C	S. Hogan	389	.339	13	75	386	46	8	5	4.6	.982	J. Genewich	18	61	2	5	3	5.61
	C	B. O'Farrell	249	.301	4	54	259	34	8	0	4.4	.973							
	OF	E. Allen	238	.307	7	31	122	6	2	0	2.1	.985							
	S2	D. Marshall	223	.309	0	21	106	175	12	28		.959							
	OF	A. Reese	172	.273	4	25	66	1	5	0	2.2	.957							
Brooklyn	1B	Bissonette	572	.336	16	113	1427	72	20	142	10.4	.987	D. Vance	35	259	17	15	0	2.61
	2B	M. Finn	273	.278	3	30	182	235	23	63	5.4	.948	W. Clark	44	200	13	13	6	4.19
W-86 L-68	SS	G. Wright	532	.321	22	126	297	462	28	97	5.9	.964	D. Luque	31	199	14	8	2	4.30
	3B	W. Gilbert	623	.294	6	67	130	312	26	27	3.1	.944	J. Elliott	35	198	10	7	1	3.95
Wilbert Robinson	RF	B. Herman	614	.393	35	130	260	10	6	1	1.8	.978	R. Phelps	36	180	14	7	0	4.11
	CF	J. Frederick	616	.334	17	76	394	12	4	3	2.9	.990	R. Moss	36	118	9	6	1	5.10
	LF	R. Bressler	335	.299	3	52	200	5	1	1	2.3	.995	S. Thurston	24	106	6	4	1	3.40
	C	A. Lopez	421	.309	6	57	465	66	9	9	4.3	.983							
	2B	J. Flowers	253	.320	2	50	153	200	19	42	5.7	.949							
	UT	E. Moore	196	.281	1	20	117	115	10	23		.959							
	OF	H. Hendrick	167	.257	5	28	68	4	4	2	1.8	.947							
Pittsburgh	1B	G. Suhr	542	.286	17	107	1445	79	13	142	10.2	.992	R. Kremer	39	276	20	12	0	5.02
	2B	G. Grantham	552	.324	18	99	324	488	36	84	6.0	.957	L. French	42	275	17	18	1	4.36
W-80 L-74	SS	D. Bartell	475	.320	4	75	304	458	48	111	6.4	.941	E. Brame	32	236	17	8	1	4.70
	3B	P. Traynor	497	.366	9	119	130	268	25	18	3.3	.941	G. Spencer	41	157	8	9	4	5.40
Jewel Ens	RF	P. Waner	589	.368	8	77	344	9	15	4	2.6	.959	H. Meine	20	117	6	8	1	6.14
	CF	L. Waner	260	.362	1	36	165	6	3	1	2.7	.983	S. Swetonic	23	97	6	6	5	4.47
	LF	A. Comorosky	597	.313	12	119	337	12	11	2	2.4	.969							
	C	R. Hemsley	324	.253	2	45	325	50	8	11	3.9	.979							
	OF	F. Brickell	219	.297	1	14	134	3	7	1	2.4	.951							
	UT	C. Engle	216	.264	0	15	113	161	15	18		.948							
	C	A. Bool	216	.259	7	46	190	42	8	4	3.7	.967							
	OF	I. Flagstead	156	.250	2	21	70	4	3	1	1.9	.961							
	P	E. Brame	116	.353	3	22	1	39	2	0	1.3	.952							
Boston	1B	G. Sisler	431	.309	3	67	915	81	13	103	9.4	.987	S. Seibold	36	251	15	16	2	4.12
	2B	F. Maguire	516	.267	0	52	387	476	28	104	6.1	.969	B. Smith	38	220	10	14	5	4.26
W-70 L-84	SS	Maranville	558	.281	2	43	343	445	29	98	5.9	.965	B. Cantwell	31	173	9	15	4	4.88
	3B	B. Chatham	404	.267	5	56	89	152	21	26	2.8	.920	T. Zachary	24	151	11	5	0	4.58
Bill McKechnie	RF	L. Richbourg	529	.304	5	54	294	9	9	4	2.4	.971	E. Brandt	41	147	4	11	1	5.01
	CF	J. Welsh	422	.275	3	36	329	8	7	2	3.1	.980	B. Sherdel	21	119	6	5	1	4.75
	LF	W. Berger	555	.310	38	119	307	10	11	3	2.3	.966	Frankhouse	27	111	7	6	0	5.61
	C	A. Spohrer	356	.317	2	37	322	36	16	4	3.5	.957	Cunningham	36	107	5	6	0	5.48
	OF	E. Clark	233	.296	3	28	165	3	4	0	2.7	.977							
	1B	J. Neun	212	.325	2	23	431	31	4	46	8.5	.991							
	OF	R. Moore	191	.288	2	34	70	3	1	0	2.2	.986							
	C	B. Cronin	178	.253	0	17	203	31	4	5	3.7	.983							

NATIONAL LEAGUE 1930, *cont.*

	POS	Player	AB	BA	HR	RBI	PO	A	E	DP	TC/G	FA	Pitcher	G	IP	W	L	SV	ERA
Cincinnati	1B	J. Stripp	464	.306	3	64	722	38	3	76	10.2	.996	B. Frey	44	245	11	18	1	4.70
	2B	H. Ford	424	.231	1	34	152	217	6	45	5.7	.984	R. Lucas	33	211	14	16	1	5.38
W-59 L-95	SS	L. Durocher	354	.243	3	32	216	350	24	77	5.7	.959	L. Benton	35	178	7	12	1	5.12
	3B	Cuccinello	443	.312	10	78	85	181	23	15	2.7	.920	R. Kolp	37	168	7	12	3	4.22
Dan Howley	RF	H. Heilmann	459	.333	19	91	279	16	14	5	2.9	.955	E. Rixey	32	164	9	13	0	5.10
	CF	B. Meusel	443	.289	10	62	223	8	9	3	2.1	.963	J. May	26	112	3	11	0	5.77
	LF	C. Walker	472	.307	8	51	241	5	9	2	2.1	.965	A. Campbell	23	58	2	4	4	5.43
	C	C. Sukeforth	296	.284	1	19	234	46	7	8	3.5	.976							
	OF	E. Swanson	301	.309	2	22	178	5	7	1	2.7	.963							
	C	J. Gooch	276	.243	2	30	233	42	13	4	3.6	.955							
	OF	M. Callaghan	225	.276	0	16	142	3	2	1	2.7	.986							
	2B	P. Crawford	224	.290	3	26	94	153	8	23	4.7	.969							
	1B	G. Kelly	188	.287	5	35	503	35	4	44	10.8	.993							
Philadelphia	1B	D. Hurst	391	.327	17	78	845	59	15	92	9.6	.984	P. Collins	47	239	16	11	3	4.78
	2B	F. Thompson	478	.282	4	46	287	386	32	95	6.3	.955	R. Benge	38	226	11	15	1	5.70
W-52 L-102	SS	T. Thevenow	573	.286	0	78	344	554	56	113	6.1	.941	L. Sweetland	34	167	7	15	0	7.71
	3B	P. Whitney	606	.342	8	117	186	313	16	29	3.5	.965	Willoughby	41	153	4	17	1	7.59
Burt Shotton	RF	C. Klein	648	.386	40	170	362	44	17	10	2.7	.960	H. Collard	30	127	6	12	0	6.80
	CF	D. Sothern	347	.280	5	36	217	15	8	3	2.9	.967	H. Elliott	48	117	6	11	0	7.67
	LF	L. O'Doul	528	.383	22	97	262	3	13	1	2.1	.953							
	C	S. Davis	329	.313	14	65	307	50	5	5	3.8	.986							
	UT	B. Friberg	331	.341	4	42	185	175	21	29		.945							
	1B	M. Sherlock	299	.324	0	8	623	51	7	57	9.7	.990							
	OF	F. Brickell	240	.246	0	17	151	6	6	0	3.1	.963							
	C	T. Rensa	172	.285	3	31	131	20	11	5	3.3	.932							
	C	H. McCurdy	148	.331	1	25	97	16	4	1	2.9	.966							

BATTING AND BASE RUNNING LEADERS

Batting Average
B. Terry, NY — .401
B. Herman, BKN — .393
C. Klein, PHI — .386
L. O'Doul, PHI — .383
F. Lindstrom, NY — .379

Slugging Average
H. Wilson, CHI — .723
C. Klein, PHI — .687
B. Herman, BKN — .678
C. Hafey, STL — .652
G. Hartnett, CHI — .630

Home Runs
H. Wilson, CHI — 56
C. Klein, PHI — 40
W. Berger, BOS — 38
G. Hartnett, CHI — 37
B. Herman, BKN — 35

Total Bases
C. Klein, PHI — 445
H. Wilson, CHI — 423
B. Herman, BKN — 416
B. Terry, NY — 392
K. Cuyler, CHI — 351

Runs Batted In
H. Wilson, CHI — 190
C. Klein, PHI — 170
K. Cuyler, CHI — 134
B. Herman, BKN — 130
B. Terry, NY — 129

Stolen Bases
K. Cuyler, CHI — 37
P. Waner, PIT — 18
B. Herman, BKN — 18
J. Stripp, CIN — 15
F. Frisch, STL — 15
F. Lindstrom, NY — 15

Hits
B. Terry, NY — 254
C. Klein, PHI — 250
B. Herman, BKN — 241
F. Lindstrom, NY — 231

Base on Balls
H. Wilson, CHI — 105
M. Ott, NY — 103
W. English, CHI — 100
G. Grantham, PIT — 81

Home Run Percentage
H. Wilson, CHI — 9.6
G. Hartnett, CHI — 7.3
W. Berger, BOS — 6.8
C. Klein, PHI — 6.2

Runs Scored
C. Klein, PHI — 158
K. Cuyler, CHI — 155
W. English, CHI — 152
H. Wilson, CHI — 146

Doubles
C. Klein, PHI — 59
K. Cuyler, CHI — 50
B. Herman, BKN — 48
A. Comorosky, PIT — 47

Triples
A. Comorosky, PIT — 23
P. Waner, PIT — 18
W. English, CHI — 17
K. Cuyler, CHI — 17

PITCHING LEADERS

Winning Percentage
Fitzsimmons, NY — .731
P. Malone, CHI — .690
E. Brame, PIT — .680
R. Kremer, PIT — .625
B. Hallahan, STL — .625

Earned Run Average
D. Vance, BKN — 2.61
C. Hubbell, NY — 3.76
B. Walker, NY — 3.93
P. Malone, CHI — 3.94
B. Grimes, BOS, STL — 4.07

Wins
P. Malone, CHI — 20
R. Kremer, PIT — 20
Fitzsimmons, NY — 19

Saves
H. Bell, STL — 8
J. Heving, NY — 6
W. Clark, BKN — 6
J. Lindsey, STL — 5
S. Swetonic, PIT — 5
B. Smith, BOS — 5

Strikeouts
B. Hallahan, STL — 177
D. Vance, BKN — 173
P. Malone, CHI — 142
C. Root, CHI — 124
C. Hubbell, NY — 117

Complete Games
E. Brame, PIT — 22
P. Malone, CHI — 22
L. French, PIT — 21
D. Vance, BKN — 20
S. Seibold, BOS — 20

Fewest Hits/9 Innings
D. Vance, BKN — 8.39
B. Hallahan, STL — 8.84
Fitzsimmons, NY — 9.23
B. Walker, NY — 9.46

Shutouts
C. Root, CHI — 4
D. Vance, BKN — 4
C. Hubbell, NY — 3
L. French, PIT — 3

Fewest Walks/9 Innings
R. Lucas, CIN — 1.88
D. Vance, BKN — 1.91
R. Kremer, PIT — 2.05
E. Brame, PIT — 2.14

Most Strikeouts/9 Inn.
B. Hallahan, STL — 6.71
D. Vance, BKN — 6.02
C. Root, CHI — 5.07
P. Malone, CHI — 4.70

Innings
R. Kremer, PIT — 276
L. French, PIT — 275
P. Malone, CHI — 272
D. Vance, BKN — 259

Games Pitched
H. Elliott, PHI — 48
P. Collins, PHI — 47
G. Bush, CHI — 46
P. Malone, CHI — 45

	W	L	PCT	GB	R	OR	2B	3B	HR	BA	SA	SB	E	DP	FA	CG	BB	SO	ShO	SV	ERA
St. Louis	92	62	.597		1004	784	373	89	104	.314	.471	72	183	176	.970	63	477	641	5	21	4.40
Chicago	90	64	.584	2	998	870	305	72	171	.309	.481	70	170	167	.973	67	528	601	6	12	4.80
New York	87	67	.565	5	959	814	264	83	143	.319	.473	59	164	164	.974	64	439	522	6	19	4.59
Brooklyn	86	68	.558	6	871	738	303	73	122	.304	.454	53	174	167	.972	74	526	526	13	15	4.03
Pittsburgh	80	74	.519	12	891	928	285	119	86	.303	.449	76	216	164	.965	80	438	393	7	13	5.24
Boston	70	84	.455	22	693	835	246	78	66	.281	.393	69	178	167	.971	71	475	424	6	11	4.91
Cincinnati	59	95	.383	33	665	857	265	67	74	.281	.400	48	161	164	.973	61	394	361	6	11	5.08
Philadelphia	52	102	.338	40	944	1199	345	44	126	.315	.458	34	239	169	.962	54	543	384	3	7	6.71
					7025	7025	2386	625	892	.303	.448	481	1485	1338	.970	534	3688	3852	52	109	4.97

AMERICAN LEAGUE 1930

	POS	Player	AB	BA	HR	RBI	PO	A	E	DP	TC/G	FA	Pitcher	G	IP	W	L	SV	ERA
Philadelphia	1B	J. Foxx	562	.335	37	156	**1362**	79	14	101	9.5	.990	G. Earnshaw	49	296	22	13	2	4.44
	2B	M. Bishop	441	.252	10	38	267	418	17	61	5.5	.976	L. Grove	**50**	291	**28**	5	9	**2.54**
W-102 L-52	SS	J. Boley	420	.276	4	55	221	296	16	62	4.4	**.970**	R. Walberg	38	205	13	12	1	4.69
	3B	J. Dykes	435	.301	6	73	124	191	13	18	2.7	.960	B. Shores	31	159	12	4	0	4.19
Connie Mack	RF	B. Miller	585	.303	9	100	309	10	8	3	2.1	.976	R. Mahaffey	33	153	9	5	0	5.01
	CF	M. Haas	532	.299	2	68	360	11	9	**5**	2.9	.976	E. Rommel	35	130	9	4	3	4.28
	LF	A. Simmons	554	**.381**	36	165	275	10	3	1	2.1	**.990**	J. Quinn	35	90	9	7	6	4.42
	C	M. Cochrane	487	.357	10	85	**654**	69	5	11	5.6	**.993**							
	S3	E. McNair	237	.266	0	34	93	104	17	12		.921							
	2S	D. Williams	191	.262	3	22	108	149	12	23		.955							
Washington	1B	J. Judge	442	.326	10	80	1050	67	2	95	9.6	**.998**	B. Hadley	42	260	15	11	2	3.73
	2B	B. Myer	541	.303	2	61	330	405	27	89	5.7	.965	G. Crowder	27	202	15	9	1	3.60
W-94 L-60	SS	J. Cronin	587	.346	13	126	**336**	**509**	35	95	5.7	.960	L. Brown	38	197	16	12	0	4.25
	3B	O. Bluege	476	.290	3	69	138	**258**	15	20	3.1	.964	F. Marberry	33	185	15	5	1	4.09
Walter Johnson	RF	S. Rice	593	.349	1	73	297	13	12	4	2.2	.963	S. Jones	25	183	15	7	0	4.07
	CF	S. West	411	.328	6	67	310	8	9	1	2.8	.972	A. Liska	32	151	9	7	1	3.29
	LF	H. Manush	356	.362	7	65	159	5	2	0	1.9	.988	B. Burke	24	74	3	4	3	3.63
	C	R. Spencer	321	.255	0	36	395	44	5	3	4.8	.989	G. Braxton	15	27	3	2	5	3.29
	OF	D. Harris	205	.317	4	44	106	8	2	3	2.0	.983							
	C	M. Ruel	198	.253	0	26	243	32	4	5	4.7	.986							
	OF	G. Goslin	188	.271	7	38	72	5	5	1	1.7	.937							
	UT	J. Hayes	166	.283	1	20	149	110	5	33		.981							
New York	1B	L. Gehrig	581	.379	41	**174**	1298	**89**	15	109	9.2	.989	G. Pipgras	44	221	15	15	4	4.11
	2B	T. Lazzeri	571	.303	9	121	184	245	13	39	5.7	.971	R. Ruffing	34	198	15	5	1	4.14
W-86 L-68	SS	L. Lary	464	.289	3	52	224	324	35	58	5.2	.940	R. Sherid	37	184	12	13	4	5.23
	3B	B. Chapman	513	.316	10	81	100	149	**24**	11	3.0	.912	H. Johnson	44	175	14	11	2	4.67
Bob Shawkey	RF	B. Ruth	518	.359	**49**	153	266	10	10	0	2.1	.965	H. Pennock	25	156	11	7	0	4.32
	CF	H. Rice	346	.298	7	74	244	7	8	2	3.0	.969	E. Wells	27	151	12	3	0	5.20
	LF	E. Combs	532	.344	7	82	275	5	9	1	2.1	.969							
	C	B. Dickey	366	.339	5	65	418	51	**11**	5	4.8	.977							
	OF	S. Byrd	218	.284	2	31	119	2	1	0	1.4	.992							
	OF	D. Cooke	216	.255	6	29	133	2	3	1	1.9	.978							
	2B	J. Reese	188	.346	3	18	86	99	5	26	4.0	.974							
	P	R. Ruffing	99	.374	4	21	3	27	2	0	.9	.938							
Cleveland	1B	E. Morgan	584	.349	26	136	1275	80	18	116	9.2	.987	W. Ferrell	43	297	25	13	3	3.31
	2B	J. Hodapp	635	.354	9	121	**403**	557	30	103	6.4	.970	W. Hudlin	37	217	13	16	1	4.57
W-81 L-73	SS	J. Goldman	306	.242	1	44	203	246	26	54	5.1	.945	C. Brown	35	214	11	12	1	4.97
	3B	J. Sewell	353	.289	0	48	83	184	14	16	2.9	.950	M. Harder	36	175	11	10	2	4.21
Roger Peckinpaugh	RF	D. Porter	480	.350	4	57	189	12	8	4	1.8	.962	P. Appleton	39	119	8	7	1	4.02
	CF	E. Averill	534	.339	19	119	345	11	**19**	5	2.8	.949							
	LF	C. Jamieson	366	.301	1	52	162	7	8	0	1.9	.955							
	C	L. Sewell	292	.257	1	43	283	49	9	5	4.5	.974							
	OF	B. Seeds	277	.285	3	32	156	6	8	0	2.4	.953							
	C	G. Myatt	265	.294	2	37	214	43	6	8	3.7	.977							
	OF	B. Falk	191	.325	4	36	84	4	3	3	2.2	.967							
	SS	E. Montague	179	.263	1	16	84	104	17	19	4.5	.917							
	3S	J. Burnett	170	.312	0	20	44	105	11	14		.931							
Detroit	1B	D. Alexander	602	.326	20	135	1338	71	**22**	132	9.3	.985	G. Uhle	33	239	12	12	3	3.65
	2B	C. Gehringer	610	.330	16	98	399	501	19	97	6.0	**.979**	V. Sorrell	35	233	16	11	1	3.86
W-75 L-79	SS	M. Koenig	267	.240	1	16	115	181	25	40	4.6	.922	E. Whitehill	34	221	17	13	1	4.24
	3B	M. McManus	484	.320	9	89	**152**	241	14	**23**	3.1	.966	C. Hogsett	33	146	9	8	1	5.42
Bucky Harris	RF	R. Johnson	462	.275	2	35	218	15	16	4	2.1	.936	W. Hoyt	26	136	9	8	4	4.78
	CF	L. Funk	527	.275	4	65	354	8	13	4	2.9	.965	C. Sullivan	40	94	1	5	5	6.53
	LF	J. Stone	422	.313	3	56	222	5	8	1	2.2	.966	W. Wyatt	21	86	4	5	2	3.57
	C	R. Hayworth	227	.278	0	22	277	27	7	4	4.1	.977							
	S3	B. Akers	233	.279	9	40	119	184	20	43		.938							
	OF	H. Rice	128	.305	2	24	66	2	4	0	2.1	.944							
	P	G. Uhle	117	.308	2	21	10	29	1	2	1.2	.975							
St. Louis	1B	L. Blue	425	.235	4	42	1110	68	16	91	**10.8**	.987	L. Stewart	35	271	20	12	0	3.45
	2B	O. Melillo	574	.256	5	59	384	**572**	21	**107**	6.6	.979	D. Coffman	38	196	8	18	1	5.14
W-64 L-90	SS	R. Kress	614	.313	16	112	271	349	**41**	83	5.4	.938	Blaeholder	37	191	11	13	4	4.61
	3B	F. O'Rourke	400	.268	1	41	116	150	14	16	3.3	.950	R. Collins	35	172	9	7	2	4.35
Bill Killefer	RF	T. Gullic	308	.250	4	44	136	12	5	3	1.9	.967	S. Gray	27	168	4	15	0	6.28
	CF	F. Schulte	392	.278	5	62	250	5	9	2	2.7	.966	C. Kimsey	42	113	6	10	1	6.35
	LF	G. Goslin	396	.326	30	100	237	13	7	0	2.5	.973	R. Stiles	20	102	3	6	0	5.89
	C	R. Ferrell	314	.268	1	41	336	66	7	5	4.0	.983	G. Crowder	13	77	3	7	1	4.66
	O1	E. McNeely	235	.272	0	20	302	18	8	30		.976							
	OF	R. Badgro	234	.239	1	27	112	8	6	3	2.1	.952							
	OF	A. Metzler	209	.258	1	23	114	2	6	0	2.2	.951							
	OF	H. Manush	198	.328	2	29	96	5	1	0	2.1	.990							
	3B	S. Hale	190	.274	2	25	46	80	7	5	2.8	.947							

AMERICAN LEAGUE 1930, cont.

	POS	Player	AB	BA	HR	RBI	PO	A	E	DP	TC/G	FA	Pitcher	G	IP	W	L	SV	ERA
Chicago W-62 L-92 Donie Bush	1B	B. Clancy	234	.244	3	27	583	24	3	38	9.7	.995	T. Lyons	42	298	22	15	1	3.78
	2B	B. Cissell	562	.270	2	48	251	336	32	60	5.8	.948	P. Caraway	38	193	10	10	1	3.86
	SS	G. Mulleavy	289	.263	0	28	137	219	32	41	5.3	.918	T. Thomas	34	169	5	13	0	5.22
	3B	W. Kamm	331	.269	3	47	142	209	23	17	3.6	.939	R. Faber	29	169	8	13	1	4.21
	RF	S. Jolley	616	.313	16	114	249	17	14	4	1.9	.950	D. Henry	35	155	2	17	0	4.88
	CF	R. Barnes	266	.248	1	31	179	6	12	3	2.7	.939	E. Walsh	37	104	1	4	0	5.38
	LF	C. Reynolds	563	.359	22	100	336	11	9	1	2.7	.975	G. Braxton	19	91	4	10	1	6.45
	C	B. Tate	230	.317	0	27	219	40	5	5	3.8	.981	H. McKain	32	89	6	4	5	5.56
	1O	C. Watwood	427	.302	2	51	707	46	11	59		.986							
	2B	J. Kerr	266	.289	3	27	130	166	6	33	5.9	.980							
	OF	Fothergill	135	.296	0	24	49	2	7	0	1.9	.879							
Boston W-52 L-102 Heinie Wagner	1B	P. Todt	383	.269	11	62	1001	65	8	84	10.3	.993	M. Gaston	38	273	13	20	2	3.92
	2B	B. Regan	507	.266	3	53	308	439	29	92	6.1	.963	MacFayden	36	269	11	14	2	4.21
	SS	H. Rhyne	296	.203	0	23	188	284	28	63	4.7	.944	H. Lisenbee	37	237	10	17	0	4.40
	3B	O. Miller	370	.286	0	48	78	160	13	13	3.0	.948	J. Russell	35	230	9	20	0	5.45
	RF	E. Webb	449	.323	16	66	200	8	9	4	1.9	.959	E. Durham	33	140	4	15	1	4.69
	CF	T. Oliver	646	.293	0	46	477	9	9	3	3.2	.982	E. Morris	18	65	4	9	0	4.13
	LF	R. Scarritt	447	.289	2	48	256	5	9	0	2.5	.967							
	C	C. Berry	256	.289	6	35	279	56	4	4	4.0	.988							
	OF	C. Durst	302	.245	1	24	145	4	5	1	2.1	.968							
	3B	B. Reeves	272	.217	2	18	63	125	22	21	3.4	.895							
	1B	B. Sweeney	243	.309	4	30	541	30	2	49	10.2	.997							
	C	J. Heving	220	.277	0	17	195	37	3	7	3.3	.987							
	SS	R. Warstler	162	.185	1	13	100	149	14	30	4.9	.947							

BATTING AND BASE RUNNING LEADERS

Batting Average
A. Simmons, PHI	.381
L. Gehrig, NY	.379
B. Ruth, NY	.359
C. Reynolds, CHI	.359
M. Cochrane, PHI	.357

Slugging Average
B. Ruth, NY	.732
L. Gehrig, NY	.721
A. Simmons, PHI	.708
J. Foxx, PHI	.637
G. Goslin, STL, WAS	.601
E. Morgan, CLE	.601

Home Runs
B. Ruth, NY	49
L. Gehrig, NY	41
J. Foxx, PHI	37
G. Goslin, STL, WAS	37
A. Simmons, PHI	36

Total Bases
L. Gehrig, NY	419
A. Simmons, PHI	392
B. Ruth, NY	379
J. Foxx, PHI	358
G. Goslin, STL, WAS	351
E. Morgan, CLE	351

Runs Batted In
L. Gehrig, NY	174
A. Simmons, PHI	165
J. Foxx, PHI	156
B. Ruth, NY	153
G. Goslin, STL, WAS	138

Stolen Bases
M. McManus, DET	23
C. Gehringer, DET	19
R. Johnson, DET	17
G. Goslin, STL, WAS	17
J. Cronin, WAS	17

Hits
J. Hodapp, CLE	225
L. Gehrig, NY	220
A. Simmons, PHI	211
S. Rice, WAS	207

Base on Balls
B. Ruth, NY	136
M. Bishop, PHI	128
L. Gehrig, NY	101
J. Foxx, PHI	93

Home Run Percentage
B. Ruth, NY	9.5
L. Gehrig, NY	7.1
J. Foxx, PHI	6.6
A. Simmons, PHI	6.5

Runs Scored
A. Simmons, PHI	152
B. Ruth, NY	150
C. Gehringer, DET	144
L. Gehrig, NY	143

Doubles
J. Hodapp, CLE	51
H. Manush, STL, WAS	49
E. Morgan, CLE	47
C. Gehringer, DET	47

Triples
E. Combs, NY	22
C. Reynolds, CHI	18
L. Gehrig, NY	17
A. Simmons, PHI	16

PITCHING LEADERS

Winning Percentage
L. Grove, PHI	.848
F. Marberry, WAS	.750
S. Jones, WAS	.682
W. Ferrell, CLE	.658
R. Ruffing, BOS, NY	.652

Earned Run Average
L. Grove, PHI	2.54
W. Ferrell, CLE	3.31
L. Stewart, STL	3.45
G. Uhle, DET	3.65
B. Hadley, WAS	3.73

Wins
L. Grove, PHI	28
W. Ferrell, CLE	25
G. Earnshaw, PHI	22
T. Lyons, CHI	22
L. Stewart, STL	20

Saves
L. Grove, PHI	9
J. Quinn, PHI	6
G. Braxton, CHI, WAS	6
C. Sullivan, DET	5
H. McKain, CHI	5

Strikeouts
L. Grove, PHI	209
G. Earnshaw, PHI	193
B. Hadley, WAS	162
W. Ferrell, CLE	143
R. Ruffing, BOS, NY	131

Complete Games
T. Lyons, CHI	29
G. Crowder, STL, WAS	25
W. Ferrell, CLE	25
L. Stewart, STL	23
L. Grove, PHI	22

Fewest Hits/9 Innings
B. Hadley, WAS	8.37
L. Grove, PHI	8.44
G. Crowder, STL, WAS	8.88
M. Gaston, BOS	8.97

Shutouts
| G. Pipgras, NY | 3 |
| G. Earnshaw, PHI | 3 |

Fewest Walks/9 Innings
H. Pennock, NY	1.15
T. Lyons, CHI	1.72
L. Grove, PHI	1.86
J. Russell, BOS	2.08

Most Strikeouts/9 Inn.
L. Grove, PHI	6.46
G. Earnshaw, PHI	5.87
B. Hadley, WAS	5.60
R. Ruffing, BOS, NY	5.32

Innings
T. Lyons, CHI	298
W. Ferrell, CLE	297
G. Earnshaw, PHI	296
L. Grove, PHI	291

Games Pitched
L. Grove, PHI	50
G. Earnshaw, PHI	49
G. Pipgras, NY	44
H. Johnson, NY	44

	W	L	PCT	GB	R	OR	2B	3B	HR	BA	SA	SB	E	DP	FA	CG	BB	SO	ShO	SV	ERA
Philadelphia	102	52	.662		951	751	319	74	125	.294	.452	48	**145**	121	**.975**	72	488	**672**	8	21	4.28
Washington	94	60	.610	8	892	**689**	300	98	57	.302	.426	**101**	159	150	.974	**78**	504	524	4	14	3.96
New York	86	68	.558	16	1062	898	298	110	152	**.309**	**.488**	91	207	132	.965	65	524	572	6	15	4.88
Cleveland	81	73	.526	21	890	915	**358**	59	72	.304	.431	51	237	156	.962	69	528	441	4	14	4.88
Detroit	75	79	.487	27	783	833	298	90	82	.284	.421	98	192	156	.967	68	570	574	3	17	4.70
St. Louis	64	90	.416	38	751	886	289	67	75	.268	.391	93	188	152	.970	68	449	470	5	10	5.07
Chicago	62	92	.403	40	729	884	255	90	63	.276	.391	74	235	136	.962	67	**407**	471	2	10	4.71
Boston	52	102	.338	50	612	814	257	67	47	.264	.364	42	196	**161**	.968	**78**	488	356	4	5	4.70
					6670	6670	2374	655	673	.288	.421	598	1559	1164	.968	565	3958	4080	36	106	4.65

NATIONAL LEAGUE 1931

	POS	Player	AB	BA	HR	RBI	PO	A	E	DP	TC/G	FA	Pitcher	G	IP	W	L	SV	ERA
St. Louis	1B	J. Bottomley	382	.348	9	75	897	43	12	95	10.2	.987	B. Hallahan	37	249	**19**	9	4	3.29
	2B	F. Frisch	518	.311	4	82	290	424	19	93	5.7	.974	B. Grimes	29	212	17	9	0	3.65
W-101 L-53	SS	C. Gelbert	447	.289	1	62	281	435	31	91	5.7	.959	P. Derringer	35	212	18	8	2	3.36
	3B	S. Adams	608	.293	1	40	118	223	13	**29**	2.6	**.963**	F. Rhem	33	207	11	10	1	3.56
Gabby Street	RF	G. Watkins	503	.288	13	51	263	12	12	4	2.2	.958	S. Johnson	32	186	11	9	2	3.00
	CF	P. Martin	413	.300	7	75	282	10	10	2	2.7	.967	J. Haines	19	122	12	3	0	3.02
	LF	C. Hafey	450	**.349**	16	95	226	4	4	1	2.0	.983	J. Lindsey	35	75	6	4	7	2.77
	C	J. Wilson	383	.274	0	51	498	75	9	15	**5.3**	.985							
	1B	R. Collins	279	.301	4	59	563	42	3	54	8.9	.995							
	C	G. Mancuso	187	.262	1	23	239	40	8	6	5.1	.972							
	OF	E. Orsatti	158	.291	0	19	83	0	1	0	1.9	.988							
	OF	T. Douthit	133	.331	1	21	105	0	3	0	3.0	.972							
New York	1B	B. Terry	611	.349	9	112	1411	**105**	16	108	10.0	.990	Fitzsimmons	35	254	18	11	0	3.05
	2B	Hunnefield	196	.270	1	17	112	140	13	27	4.7	.951	C. Hubbell	36	247	14	12	3	2.66
W-87 L-65	SS	T. Jackson	555	.310	5	71	303	**496**	25	79	5.7	**.970**	B. Walker	37	239	17	9	3	**2.26**
	3B	J. Vergez	565	.278	13	81	146	268	30	23	2.9	.932	C. Mitchell	27	190	13	11	4	4.07
John McGraw	RF	F. Lindstrom	303	.300	5	36	150	4	4	1	2.2	.975	J. Berly	27	111	7	8	0	3.88
	CF	M. Ott	497	.292	29	115	332	20	7	4	2.6	.981	J. Heving	22	42	1	6	3	4.89
	LF	F. Leach	515	.309	6	61	239	6	6	1	2.0	.976							
	C	S. Hogan	396	.301	12	65	469	54	2	10	4.6	**.996**							
	OF	C. Fullis	302	.328	3	28	154	5	2	4	2.4	.988							
	OF	E. Allen	298	.329	5	43	151	2	4	1	2.0	.975							
	2B	H. Critz	238	.290	4	17	139	164	5	27	5.7	.984							
	2B	D. Marshall	194	.201	0	10	102	135	11	26	5.3	.956							
	C	B. O'Farrell	174	.224	1	19	223	27	5	1	3.2	.980							
Chicago	1B	C. Grimm	531	.331	4	66	1357	79	10	107	10.0	**.993**	C. Root	39	251	17	14	2	3.48
	2B	R. Hornsby	357	.331	16	90	107	205	16	24	4.8	.951	B. Smith	36	240	15	12	2	3.22
W-84 L-70	SS	W. English	634	.319	2	53	**322**	441	28	75	5.7	.965	P. Malone	36	228	16	9	0	3.90
	3B	L. Bell	252	.282	4	32	66	118	11	18	2.8	.944	G. Bush	39	180	16	8	2	4.49
Rogers Hornsby	RF	K. Cuyler	613	.330	9	88	347	11	11	4	2.4	.970	L. Sweetland	26	130	8	7	0	5.04
	CF	H. Wilson	395	.261	13	61	210	9	5	1	2.2	.978	J. May	31	79	5	5	2	3.87
	LF	Stephenson	263	.319	1	52	134	1	2	1	1.7	.985							
	C	G. Hartnett	380	.282	8	70	444	68	10	**16**	5.0	.981							
	32	B. Jurges	293	.201	0	23	108	198	11	32		.965							
	OF	D. Taylor	270	.300	5	41	170	3	2	0	2.6	.989							
	21	F. Blair	240	.258	2	29	245	120	12	28		.968							
	OF	V. Barton	239	.238	13	50	133	2	5	0	2.3	.964							
	C	R. Hemsley	204	.309	3	31	236	40	7	5	4.3	.975							
Brooklyn	1B	Bissonette	587	.290	12	87	**1460**	66	16	136	10.1	.990	W. Clark	34	233	14	10	1	3.20
	2B	M. Finn	413	.274	0	45	260	331	15	65	5.4	.975	D. Vance	30	219	11	13	0	3.38
W-79 L-73	SS	G. Slade	272	.239	1	29	173	274	25	54	5.8	.947	R. Phelps	28	149	7	9	0	5.00
	3B	W. Gilbert	552	.266	0	46	125	**295**	23	14	3.1	.948	S. Thurston	24	143	9	9	0	3.97
Wilbert Robinson	RF	B. Herman	610	.313	18	97	287	24	13	7	2.2	.960	F. Heimach	31	135	9	7	1	3.46
	CF	J. Frederick	611	.270	17	71	398	10	**15**	2	2.9	.965	J. Shaute	25	129	11	8	0	4.83
	LF	L. O'Doul	512	.336	7	75	285	4	14	0	2.3	.954	D. Luque	19	103	7	6	0	4.56
	C	A. Lopez	360	.269	0	40	390	69	11	6	4.5	.977	J. Quinn	39	64	5	4	15	2.66
	SS	G. Wright	268	.284	9	32	151	255	25	52	5.7	.942							
	C	E. Lombardi	182	.297	4	23	218	23	4	5	4.9	.984							
	2B	F. Thompson	181	.265	1	21	89	120	12	36	3.5	.946							
	OF	R. Bressler	153	.281	0	26	54	1	1	0	1.6	.982							
Pittsburgh	1B	G. Suhr	270	.211	4	32	684	39	5	72	9.6	.993	H. Meine	36	**284**	**19**	13	0	2.98
	2B	G. Grantham	465	.305	10	46	114	142	23	34	5.5	.918	L. French	39	276	15	13	1	3.26
W-75 L-79	SS	T. Thevenow	404	.213	0	38	245	432	25	92	5.9	.964	R. Kremer	30	230	11	15	0	3.33
	3B	P. Traynor	615	.298	2	103	**172**	284	**37**	21	**3.2**	.925	G. Spencer	38	187	11	12	3	3.42
Jewel Ens	RF	P. Waner	559	.322	6	70	342	**28**	9	**8**	2.7	.976	E. Brame	26	180	9	13	0	4.21
	CF	L. Waner	681	.314	4	57	**484**	20	11	5	**3.4**	.979							
	LF	A. Comorosky	350	.243	1	48	214	4	5	2	2.5	.978							
	C	E. Phillips	353	.232	7	44	293	49	5	12	3.4	.986							
	OF	W. Jensen	267	.243	3	17	182	2	5	1	2.8	.974							
	2B	T. Piet	167	.299	0	24	103	133	3	17	5.4	.987							
	2B	H. Grossklos	161	.280	0	20	92	115	4	35	5.4	.981							
	C	E. Grace	150	.280	1	20	128	23	4	5	3.4	.974							
Philadelphia	1B	D. Hurst	489	.305	11	91	1206	104	**18**	117	9.8	.986	J. Elliott	**52**	249	**19**	14	5	4.27
	2B	L. Mallon	375	.309	1	45	231	290	24	57	5.6	.956	R. Benge	38	247	14	18	2	3.17
W-66 L-88	SS	D. Bartell	554	.289	0	34	315	432	**41**	**96**	5.9	.948	P. Collins	42	240	12	16	4	3.86
	3B	P. Whitney	501	.287	9	74	131	217	19	1	2.9	.948	C. Dudley	30	179	8	14	0	3.52
Burt Shotton	RF	B. Arlett	418	.313	18	72	196	14	10	6	2.3	.955	F. Watt	38	123	5	5	2	4.84
	CF	F. Brickell	514	.253	1	31	341	8	8	2	2.9	.978	S. Bolen	28	99	3	12	0	6.39
	LF	C. Klein	594	.337	31	121	292	10	9	2	2.1	.971	S. Blake	14	71	4	5	1	5.58
	C	S. Davis	393	.326	4	51	420	**78**	3	10	4.4	.994							
	23	B. Friberg	353	.261	1	26	180	252	20	43		.956							
	C	H. McCurdy	150	.287	1	25	157	27	6	1	4.2	.968							

NATIONAL LEAGUE 1931, cont.

	POS	Player	AB	BA	HR	RBI	PO	A	E	DP	TC/G	FA	Pitcher	G	IP	W	L	SV	ERA
Boston W-64 L-90 Bill McKechnie	1B	E. Sheely	538	.273	1	77	1374	70	12	108	10.2	.992	E. Brandt	33	250	18	11	2	2.92
	2B	F. Maguire	492	.228	0	26	372	478	21	94	5.9	.976	T. Zachary	33	229	11	15	2	3.10
	SS	Maranville	562	.260	0	33	271	432	38	93	5.4	.949	S. Seibold	33	206	10	18	0	4.67
	3B	B. Urbanski	303	.238	0	17	76	145	9	15	3.4	.961	B. Cantwell	33	156	7	9	2	3.63
	RF	Schulmerich	327	.309	2	43	190	6	7	0	2.3	.966	B. Sherdel	27	138	6	10	0	4.25
	CF	W. Berger	617	.323	19	84	457	16	11	5	3.1	.977	Cunningham	33	137	3	12	1	4.48
	LF	Worthington	491	.291	4	44	242	8	3	1	2.0	.988	Frankhouse	26	127	8	8	1	4.03
	C	A. Spohrer	350	.240	0	27	392	54	8	5	4.1	.982							
	OF	L. Richbourg	286	.287	2	29	154	3	3	2	2.3	.981							
	O3	R. Moore	192	.260	3	34	71	39	6	3		.948							
	3B	B. Dreesen	180	.222	1	10	28	83	11	1	2.6	.910							
Cincinnati W-58 L-96 Dan Howley	1B	H. Hendrick	530	.315	1	75	1348	67	18*	147*	10.5*	.987	S. Johnson	42	262	11	19	0	3.77
	2B	Cuccinello	575	.315	2	93	376	499	28	128	5.9	.969	R. Lucas	29	238	14	13	0	3.59
	SS	L. Durocher	361	.227	1	29	212	344	20	86	4.8	.965	L. Benton	38	204	10	15	2	3.35
	3B	J. Stripp	426	.324	3	42	101	191	13	22	3.2	.957	B. Frey	34	134	8	12	2	4.92
	RF	E. Crabtree	443	.269	4	37	240	19	7	6	2.6	.974	E. Rixey	22	127	4	7	0	3.91
	CF	T. Douthit	374	.262	0	24	286	6	5	3	3.1	.983	R. Kolp	30	107	4	9	1	4.96
	LF	E. Roush	376	.271	1	41	197	5	4	1	2.3	.981	O. Carroll	29	107	3	9	0	5.53
	C	C. Sukeforth	351	.256	0	25	300	59	13	9	3.5	.965	J. Ogden	22	89	4	8	1	2.93
	OF	N. Cullop	334	.263	8	48	177	5	6	3	2.3	.968							
	OF	C. Heathcote	252	.258	0	28	164	13	2	4	3.0	.989							
	OF	W. Roettger	185	.351	1	20	95	3	1	1	2.3	.990							
	SS	H. Ford	175	.229	0	13	107	162	13	41	3.9	.954							
	C	Asbjornson	118	.305	0	22	82	24	2	2	3.5	.981							

BATTING AND BASE RUNNING LEADERS

Batting Average
C. Hafey, STL .349
B. Terry, NY .349
J. Bottomley, STL .348
C. Klein, PHI .337
L. O'Doul, BKN .336

Slugging Average
C. Klein, PHI .584
R. Hornsby, CHI .574
C. Hafey, STL .569
M. Ott, NY .545
B. Arlett, PHI .538

Home Runs
C. Klein, PHI 31
M. Ott, NY 29
W. Berger, BOS 19
B. Arlett, PHI 18
B. Herman, BKN 18

Total Bases
C. Klein, PHI 347
B. Terry, NY 323
B. Herman, BKN 320
W. Berger, BOS 316
K. Cuyler, CHI 290

Runs Batted In
C. Klein, PHI 121
M. Ott, NY 115
B. Terry, NY 112
P. Traynor, PIT 103
B. Herman, BKN 97

Stolen Bases
F. Frisch, STL 28
B. Herman, BKN 17
P. Martin, STL 16
S. Adams, STL 16
G. Watkins, STL 15

Hits
L. Waner, PIT 214
B. Terry, NY 213
K. Cuyler, CHI 202
W. English, CHI 202

Base on Balls
M. Ott, NY 80
P. Waner, PIT 73
K. Cuyler, CHI 72
G. Grantham, PIT 71

Home Run Percentage
M. Ott, NY 5.8
C. Klein, PHI 5.2
R. Hornsby, CHI 4.5
B. Arlett, PHI 4.3

Runs Scored
C. Klein, PHI 121
B. Terry, NY 121
W. English, CHI 117
K. Cuyler, CHI 110

Doubles
S. Adams, STL 46
W. Berger, BOS 44
D. Bartell, PHI 43
B. Herman, BKN 43

Triples
B. Terry, NY 20
B. Herman, BKN 16
P. Traynor, PIT 15
Bissonette, BKN 14

PITCHING LEADERS

Winning Percentage
P. Derringer, STL .692
B. Hallahan, STL .679
G. Bush, CHI .667
B. Grimes, STL .654
B. Walker, NY .654

Earned Run Average
B. Walker, NY 2.26
C. Hubbell, NY 2.66
E. Brandt, BOS 2.92
H. Meine, PIT 2.98
S. Johnson, STL 3.00

Wins
B. Hallahan, STL 19
H. Meine, PIT 19
J. Elliott, PHI 19
P. Derringer, STL 18
E. Brandt, BOS 18
Fitzsimmons, NY 18

Saves
J. Quinn, BKN 15
J. Lindsey, STL 7
J. Elliott, PHI 5
B. Hallahan, STL 4
P. Collins, PHI 4

Strikeouts
B. Hallahan, STL 159
C. Hubbell, NY 156
D. Vance, BKN 150
P. Derringer, STL 134
C. Root, CHI 131

Complete Games
R. Lucas, CIN 24
E. Brandt, BOS 23
H. Meine, PIT 22
C. Hubbell, NY 21
L. French, PIT 20

Fewest Hits/9 Innings
C. Hubbell, NY 7.76
B. Walker, NY 7.97
E. Brandt, BOS 8.21
Fitzsimmons, NY 8.59

Shutouts
B. Walker, NY 6
P. Derringer, STL 4
C. Hubbell, NY 4
Fitzsimmons, NY 4

Fewest Walks/9 Innings
S. Johnson, STL 1.40
R. Lucas, CIN 1.47
W. Clark, BKN 2.01
T. Zachary, BOS 2.08

Most Strikeouts/9 Inn.
D. Vance, BKN 6.17
B. Hallahan, STL 5.75
P. Derringer, STL 5.70
C. Hubbell, NY 5.68

Innings
H. Meine, PIT 284
L. French, PIT 276
S. Johnson, CIN 262
Fitzsimmons, NY 254

Games Pitched
J. Elliott, PHI 52
S. Johnson, CIN 42
P. Collins, PHI 42

	W	L	PCT	GB	R	OR	2B	3B	HR	BA	SA	SB	E	DP	FA	CG	BB	SO	ShO	SV	ERA
St. Louis	101	53	.656		815	614	353	74	60	.286	.411	114	160	169	.974	80	449	626	17	20	3.45
New York	87	65	.572	13	768	599	251	64	101	.289	.416	83	159	126	.974	90	421	571	17	12	3.30
Chicago	84	70	.545	17	828	710	340	67	83	.289	.422	49	169	141	.973	80	524	541	8	8	3.97
Brooklyn	79	73	.520	21	681	673	240	77	71	.276	.390	45	187	154	.969	64	351	546	9	18	3.84
Pittsburgh	75	79	.487	26	636	691	243	70	41	.266	.360	59	194	167	.968	89	442	345	9	5	3.66
Philadelphia	66	88	.429	35	684	828	299	52	81	.279	.400	42	210	149	.966	60	511	499	4	16	4.58
Boston	64	90	.416	37	533	680	221	59	34	.258	.341	46	170	141	.973	78	406	419	12	9	3.90
Cincinnati	58	96	.377	43	592	742	241	70	21	.269	.352	24	165	194	.973	70	399	317	4	6	4.22
					5537	5537	2188	533	492	.277	.387	462	1414	1241	.971	611	3503	3864	80	94	3.86

AMERICAN LEAGUE 1931

	POS	Player	AB	BA	HR	RBI	PO	A	E	DP	TC/G	FA	Pitcher	G	IP	W	L	SV	ERA
Philadelphia	1B	J. Foxx	515	.291	30	120	964	49	7	89	9.1	.993	R. Walberg	44	291	20	12	3	3.74
	2B	M. Bishop	497	.294	5	37	314	414	12	84	5.7	.984	L. Grove	41	289	31	4	5	2.06
W-107 L-45	SS	D. Williams	294	.269	6	40	152	214	27	59	5.5	.931	G. Earnshaw	43	282	21	7	6	3.67
	3B	J. Dykes	355	.273	3	46	105	153	7	19	3.0	.974	R. Mahaffey	30	162	15	4	2	4.21
Connie Mack	RF	B. Miller	534	.281	8	77	305	7	4	1	2.3	.987	E. Rommel	25	118	7	5	0	2.97
	CF	M. Haas	440	.323	8	56	272	6	3	4	2.8	.989	W. Hoyt	16	111	10	5	0	4.22
	LF	A. Simmons	513	**.390**	22	128	287	10	4	0	2.4	.987							
	C	M. Cochrane	459	.349	17	89	560	63	9	9	5.4	.986							
	UT	E. McNair	280	.271	5	33	97	155	19	36		.930							
	SS	J. Boley	224	.228	0	20	102	149	12	31	4.2	.954							
	OF	D. Cramer	223	.260	2	20	133	5	3	1	2.6	.979							
	1B	P. Todt	197	.244	5	44	403	13	2	36	8.0	.995							
	OF	J. Moore	143	.224	2	21	70	3	2	2	2.1	.973							
New York	1B	L. Gehrig	619	.341	**46**	**184**	1352	58	13	120	9.2	.991	L. Gomez	40	243	21	9	3	2.63
	2B	T. Lazzeri	484	.267	8	83	216	288	22	52	5.8	.958	R. Ruffing	37	237	16	14	2	4.41
W-94 L-59	SS	L. Lary	610	.280	10	107	321	484	46	85	5.5	.946	H. Johnson	40	196	13	8	4	4.72
	3B	J. Sewell	484	.302	6	64	131	227	18	14	3.1	.952	H. Pennock	25	189	11	6	0	4.28
Joe McCarthy	RF	B. Ruth	534	.373	46	163	237	5	7	2	1.8	.972	G. Pipgras	36	138	7	6	3	3.79
	CF	E. Combs	563	.318	5	58	335	5	9	2	2.7	.974	E. Wells	27	117	9	5	2	4.32
	LF	B. Chapman	600	.315	17	122	300	14	12	1	2.4	.963	R. Sherid	17	74	5	5	2	5.69
	C	B. Dickey	477	.327	6	78	**670**	78	3	6	6.0	**.996**							
	OF	S. Byrd	248	.270	3	32	148	3	4	1	1.8	.974							
	2B	J. Reese	245	.241	3	26	173	168	10	44	5.8	.972							
Washington	1B	J. Kuhel	524	.269	8	85	1255	57	12	119	9.5	.991	L. Brown	42	259	15	14	0	3.20
	2B	B. Myer	591	.293	4	56	333	398	12	87	5.4	**.984**	G. Crowder	44	234	18	11	2	3.88
W-92 L-62	SS	J. Cronin	611	.306	12	126	**323**	488	43	**94**	5.5	.950	F. Marberry	45	219	16	4	7	3.45
	3B	O. Bluege	570	.272	8	98	151	**286**	18	24	3.0	**.960**	C. Fischer	46	191	13	9	3	4.38
Walter Johnson	RF	S. Rice	413	.310	0	42	221	7	7	2	2.2	.970	B. Hadley	55	180	11	10	8	3.06
	CF	S. West	526	.333	3	91	402	13	4	3	**3.3**	.990	S. Jones	25	148	9	10	1	4.32
	LF	H. Manush	616	.307	6	70	245	5	6	1	1.8	.977	B. Burke	30	129	8	3	2	4.27
	C	R. Spencer	483	.275	1	60	642	69	11	9	5.0	.985							
	OF	D. Harris	231	.312	5	50	111	4	6	1	2.0	.950							
	OF	H. Rice	162	.265	0	15	89	3	3	0	2.3	.968							
Cleveland	1B	E. Morgan	462	.351	11	86	1114	72	**19**	102	10.3	.984	W. Ferrell	40	276	22	12	3	3.75
	2B	J. Hodapp	468	.295	2	56	274	413	22	73	5.9	.969	W. Hudlin	44	254	15	14	4	4.60
W-78 L-76	SS	E. Montague	193	.285	1	26	127	202	27	30	5.6	.924	C. Brown	39	233	11	15	0	4.71
	3B	W. Kamm	410	.295	0	66	129*	208	19	29*	3.1*	.947	M. Harder	40	194	13	14	1	4.36
Roger Peckinpaugh	RF	D. Porter	414	.312	1	38	184	7	6	0	1.8	.970	S. Connally	17	86	5	5	1	4.20
	CF	E. Averill	**627**	.333	32	143	398	9	10	3	2.7	.976							
	LF	J. Vosmik	591	.320	7	117	315	12	10	2	2.3	.970							
	C	L. Sewell	375	.275	1	53	384	61	9	5	4.3	.980							
	UT	J. Burnett	427	.300	1	52	194	296	34	52		.935							
	C	G. Myatt	195	.246	1	29	176	34	2	2	3.7	.991							
	OF	B. Falk	161	.304	2	28	55	1	3	0	1.8	.949							
	P	W. Ferrell	116	.319	9	30	19	**74**	3	3	2.4	.969							
St. Louis	1B	J. Burns	570	.260	4	70	1346	**125**	11	**131**	10.4	.993	L. Stewart	36	258	14	17	0	4.40
	2B	O. Melillo	617	.306	2	75	**428**	**543**	32	118	6.6	.968	S. Gray	43	258	11	**24**	2	5.09
W-63 L-91	SS	J. Levey	498	.209	5	38	269	398	58	92	5.2	.920	Blaeholder	35	226	11	15	0	4.53
	3B	R. Kress	605	.311	16	114	92	141	16	12	3.0	.936	D. Coffman	32	169	9	13	1	3.88
Bill Killefer	RF	T. Jenkins	230	.265	3	25	93	6	5	1	1.952	.952	R. Collins	17	107	5	5	0	3.79
	CF	F. Schulte	553	.304	9	65	361	13	11	4	2.9	.971	W. Hebert	23	103	6	7	0	5.07
	LF	G. Goslin	591	.328	24	105	319	14	14	1	2.3	.960	C. Kimsey	42	94	4	6	7	4.39
	C	R. Ferrell	386	.306	3	57	412	**86**	**14**	11	4.7	.973							
	3B	L. Storti	273	.220	3	26	78	134	17	20	3.4	.926							
	OF	Bettencourt	206	.257	3	26	99	6	4	1	1.9	.963							
Boston	1B	B. Sweeney	498	.295	1	58	1283	92	9	89	**11.2**	**.993**	J. Russell	36	232	10	18	0	5.16
	2B	R. Warstler	181	.243	0	10	74	135	15	20	5.3	.933	MacFayden	35	231	16	12	0	4.02
W-62 L-90	SS	H. Rhyne	565	.273	0	51	295	**502**	31	74	5.6	.963	W. Moore	53	185	11	13	10	3.88
	3B	O. Miller	389	.272	0	43	75	147	11	12	3.1	.953	E. Durham	38	165	8	10	0	4.25
Shano Collins	RF	E. Webb	589	.333	14	103	270	21	**16**	5	2.0	.948	H. Lisenbee	41	165	5	12	0	5.19
	CF	T. Oliver	586	.276	0	70	**433**	15	3	4	3.0	**.993**	E. Morris	37	131	5	7	0	4.75
	LF	J. Rothrock	475	.278	4	42	153	9	3	1	2.1	.982	M. Gaston	23	119	2	13	0	4.46
	C	C. Berry	357	.283	6	49	312	78	6	8	3.9	.985	B. Kline	28	98	5	5	0	4.41
	3B	U. Pickering	341	.252	9	52	90	143	8	8	3.3	.967							
	OF	A. Van Camp	324	.275	0	33	107	3	3	0	1.9	.973							

AMERICAN LEAGUE 1931, cont.

	POS	Player	AB	BA	HR	RBI	PO	A	E	DP	TC/G	FA	Pitcher	G	IP	W	L	SV	ERA
Detroit	1B	D. Alexander	517	.325	3	87	1197	53	16	91	10.0	.987	E. Whitehill	34	272	13	16	0	4.06
	2B	C. Gehringer	383	.311	4	53	224	236	10	54	6.0	.979	V. Sorrell	35	247	13	14	1	4.12
W-61 L-93	SS	B. Rogell	185	.303	2	24	91	182	12	26	5.9	.958	G. Uhle	29	193	11	12	2	3.50
	3B	M. McManus	362	.271	3	53	92	172	14	18	3.5	.950	T. Bridges	35	173	8	16	0	4.99
Bucky Harris	RF	R. Johnson	621	.279	8	55	332	25	15	8	2.5	.960	A. Herring	35	165	7	13	1	4.31
	CF	H. Walker	252	.286	0	16	170	4	7	1	2.7	.961	C. Hogsett	22	112	3	9	2	5.93
	LF	J. Stone	584	.327	10	76	319	11	14	6	2.3	.959	W. Hoyt	16	92	3	8	0	5.87
	C	R. Hayworth	273	.256	0	25	334	61	11	5	4.6	.973							
	UT	M. Owen	377	.223	3	39	308	220	24	46		.957							
	2S	M. Koenig	364	.253	1	39	191	236	28	41		.938							
	OF	G. Walker	189	.296	1	28	99	2	5	1	2.4	.953							
	OF	F. Doljack	187	.278	4	20	140	8	12	1	3.0	.925							
Chicago	1B	L. Blue	589	.304	1	62	1452	81	16	105	10.0	.990	V. Frasier	46	254	13	15	4	4.46
	2B	J. Kerr	444	.268	2	50	297	366	22	78	5.9	.968	T. Thomas	42	242	10	14	2	4.80
W-56 L-97	SS	B. Cissell	409	.220	1	46	168	233	24	47	5.1	.944	P. Caraway	51	220	10	24	2	6.22
	3B	B. Sullivan	363	.275	2	33	96	152	24	9	3.3	.912	R. Faber	44	184	10	14	1	3.82
Donie Bush	RF	C. Reynolds	462	.290	6	77	233	10	13	3	2.3	.949	H. McKain	27	112	6	9	0	5.71
	CF	C. Watwood	367	.283	1	47	259	13	16	2	2.8	.944	T. Lyons	22	101	4	6	0	4.01
	LF	L. Fonseca	465	.299	2	71	183	4	5	1	2.0	.974							
	C	B. Tate	273	.267	0	22	310	69	5	11	4.5	.987							
	OF	Fothergill	312	.282	3	56	169	2	5	0	2.4	.972							
	SS	L. Appling	297	.232	1	28	147	232	42	37	5.5	.900							
	C	F. Grube	265	.219	1	24	248	50	7	3	3.8	.977							
	3B	I. Jeffries	223	.224	2	16	69	100	7	4	2.9	.949							
	OF	M. Simons	189	.275	0	12	112	3	6	0	2.1	.950							
	OF	S. Jolley	110	.300	3	28	29	1	5	1	1.5	.857							

BATTING AND BASE RUNNING LEADERS

Batting Average
- A. Simmons, PHI — .390
- B. Ruth, NY — .373
- E. Morgan, CLE — .351
- M. Cochrane, PHI — .349
- L. Gehrig, NY — .341

Slugging Average
- B. Ruth, NY — .700
- L. Gehrig, NY — .662
- A. Simmons, PHI — .641
- E. Averill, CLE — .576
- J. Foxx, PHI — .567

Home Runs
- B. Ruth, NY — 46
- L. Gehrig, NY — 46
- E. Averill, CLE — 32
- J. Foxx, PHI — 30
- G. Goslin, STL — 24

Winning Percentage
- L. Grove, PHI — .886
- F. Marberry, WAS — .800
- R. Mahaffey, PHI — .789
- G. Earnshaw, PHI — .750
- L. Gomez, NY — .700

Earned Run Average
- L. Grove, PHI — 2.06
- L. Gomez, NY — 2.63
- L. Brown, WAS — 3.20
- F. Marberry, WAS — 3.45
- G. Uhle, DET — 3.50

Wins
- L. Grove, PHI — 31
- W. Ferrell, CLE — 22
- G. Earnshaw, PHI — 21
- L. Gomez, NY — 21
- R. Walberg, PHI — 20

Total Bases
- L. Gehrig, NY — 410
- B. Ruth, NY — 374
- E. Averill, CLE — 361
- A. Simmons, PHI — 329
- G. Goslin, STL — 328

Runs Batted In
- L. Gehrig, NY — 184
- B. Ruth, NY — 163
- E. Averill, CLE — 143
- A. Simmons, PHI — 128
- J. Cronin, WAS — 126

Stolen Bases
- B. Chapman, NY — 61
- R. Johnson, DET — 33
- J. Burns, STL — 19
- B. Cissell, CHI — 18
- T. Lazzeri, NY — 18

Saves
- W. Moore, BOS — 10
- B. Hadley, WAS — 8
- C. Kimsey, STL — 7
- F. Marberry, WAS — 7
- G. Earnshaw, PHI — 6

Strikeouts
- L. Grove, PHI — 175
- G. Earnshaw, PHI — 152
- L. Gomez, NY — 150
- R. Ruffing, NY — 132
- B. Hadley, WAS — 124

Complete Games
- L. Grove, PHI — 27
- W. Ferrell, CLE — 27
- G. Earnshaw, PHI — 23
- E. Whitehill, DET — 22
- L. Stewart, STL — 20

Hits
- L. Gehrig, NY — 211
- E. Averill, CLE — 209
- A. Simmons, PHI — 200
- B. Ruth, NY — 199

Base on Balls
- B. Ruth, NY — 128
- L. Blue, CHI — 127
- L. Gehrig, NY — 117
- M. Bishop, PHI — 112

Home Run Percentage
- B. Ruth, NY — 8.6
- L. Gehrig, NY — 7.4
- J. Foxx, PHI — 5.8
- E. Averill, CLE — 5.1

Fewest Hits/9 Innings
- L. Gomez, NY — 7.63
- L. Grove, PHI — 7.76
- G. Earnshaw, PHI — 8.15
- D. Coffman, STL — 8.45

Shutouts
- L. Grove, PHI — 4
- G. Earnshaw, PHI — 3

Fewest Walks/9 Innings
- H. Pennock, NY — 1.43
- S. Gray, STL — 1.88
- L. Grove, PHI — 1.93
- C. Brown, CLE — 2.12

Runs Scored
- L. Gehrig, NY — 163
- B. Ruth, NY — 149
- E. Averill, CLE — 140
- E. Combs, NY — 120

Doubles
- E. Webb, BOS — 67
- D. Alexander, DET — 47
- R. Kress, STL — 46
- J. Cronin, WAS — 44

Triples
- R. Johnson, DET — 19
- L. Blue, CHI — 15
- L. Gehrig, NY — 15
- C. Reynolds, CHI — 14

Most Strikeouts/9 Inn.
- L. Gomez, NY — 5.56
- T. Bridges, DET — 5.46
- L. Grove, PHI — 5.46
- R. Ruffing, NY — 5.01

Innings
- R. Walberg, PHI — 291
- L. Grove, PHI — 289
- G. Earnshaw, PHI — 282
- W. Ferrell, CLE — 276

Games Pitched
- B. Hadley, WAS — 55
- W. Moore, BOS — 53
- P. Caraway, CHI — 51
- V. Frasier, CHI — 46

PITCHING LEADERS

	W	L	PCT	GB	R	OR	2B	3B	HR	BA	SA	SB	E	DP	FA	CG	BB	SO	ShO	SV	ERA
Philadelphia	107	45	.704		858	626	311	64	118	.287	.435	27	141	151	.976	97	457	574	12	16	3.47
New York	94	59	.614	13.5	1067	760	277	78	155	.297	.457	138	169	131	.972	78	543	686	4	17	4.20
Washington	92	62	.597	16	843	691	308	93	49	.285	.400	72	142	148	.976	60	498	582	6	24	3.76
Cleveland	78	76	.506	30	885	833	321	69	71	.296	.419	63	232	143	.963	76	561	470	6	9	4.63
St. Louis	63	91	.409	45	722	870	287	62	76	.271	.390	73	232	160	.963	65	448	436	4	10	4.76
Boston	62	90	.408	45	625	800	289	34	37	.262	.349	43	188	127	.970	61	473	365	5	10	4.60
Detroit	61	93	.396	47	651	836	292	69	43	.268	.371	117	220	139	.964	93	597	511	5	6	4.56
Chicago	56	97	.366	51.5	704	939	238	69	27	.260	.343	94	245	131	.961	54	588	420	6	10	5.05
					6355	6355	2323	538	576	.278	.396	627	1569	1130	.968	584	4165	4044	48	102	4.38

NATIONAL LEAGUE 1932

	POS	Player	AB	BA	HR	RBI	PO	A	E	DP	TC/G	FA	Pitcher	G	IP	W	L	SV	ERA
Chicago	1B	C. Grimm	570	.307	7	80	1429	123	11	127	10.5	.993	L. Warneke	35	277	22	6	0	2.37
	2B	B. Herman	656	.314	1	51	401	527	38	102	6.3	.961	G. Bush	40	239	19	11	0	3.21
W-90 L-64	SS	B. Jurges	396	.253	2	52	223	394	23	69	6.2	.964	P. Malone	37	237	15	17	0	3.38
	3B	W. English	522	.272	3	47	96	173	12	13	3.0	.957	C. Root	39	216	15	10	3	3.58
Rogers Hornsby	RF	K. Cuyler	446	.291	10	77	239	7	8	1	2.3	.969	B. Grimes	30	141	6	11	1	4.78
W-53 L-46	CF	J. Moore	443	.305	13	64	272	12	5	2	2.7	.983	B. Smith	34	119	4	3	2	4.61
	LF	Stephenson	583	.324	4	85	298	7	5	2	2.1	.984							
Charlie Grimm	C	G. Hartnett	406	.271	12	52	484	75	10	8	4.9	.982							
W-37 L-18	3B	S. Hack	178	.236	2	19	36	90	12	5	2.7	.913							
	C	R. Hemsley	151	.238	4	20	173	17	5	3	4.1	.974							
	OF	L. Richbourg	148	.257	1	21	70	2	1	1	2.2	.986							
Pittsburgh	1B	G. Suhr	581	.263	5	81	1388	84	18	111	9.7	.988	L. French	47	274	18	16	4	3.02
	2B	T. Piet	574	.282	7	85	378	454	26	80	5.6	.970	B. Swift	39	214	14	10	4	3.61
W-86 L-68	SS	A. Vaughan	497	.318	4	61	247	403	46	74	5.4	.934	H. Meine	28	172	12	9	1	3.86
	3B	P. Traynor	513	.329	2	68	173	222	27	14	3.3	.936	B. Harris	37	168	10	9	2	3.64
George Gibson	RF	P. Waner	630	.341	7	82	367	13	10	3	2.5	.974	S. Swetonic	24	163	11	6	0	2.82
	CF	L. Waner	565	.333	3	38	426	9	6	0	3.4	.986	G. Spencer	39	138	4	8	1	4.97
	LF	A. Comorosky	370	.286	4	46	255	4	5	2	2.9	.981	L. Chagnon	30	128	9	6	0	3.94
	C	E. Grace	390	.274	7	55	364	48	1	10	3.6	.998							
	OF	D. Barbee	327	.257	5	55	190	5	5	2	2.6	.975							
	S3	T. Thevenow	194	.237	0	26	82	126	14	24		.937							
Brooklyn	1B	G. Kelly	202	.243	4	22	575	36	10	48	10.0	.984	W. Clark	40	273	20	12	0	3.49
	2B	Cuccinello	597	.281	12	77	385	525	25	113	6.1	.973	V. Mungo	39	223	13	11	2	4.43
W-81 L-73	SS	G. Wright	446	.274	10	60	231	386	40	83	5.4	.939	D. Vance	27	176	12	11	1	4.20
	3B	J. Stripp	534	.303	6	64	92	201	14	22	3.3	.954	F. Heimach	36	168	9	4	0	3.97
Max Carey	RF	H. Wilson	481	.297	23	123	220	14	11	4	2.0	.955	S. Thurston	28	153	12	8	0	4.06
	CF	D. Taylor	395	.324	11	48	271	8	3	1	2.9	.989	J. Shaute	34	117	7	7	4	4.62
	LF	L. O'Doul	595	.368	21	90	317	4	7	0	2.2	.979	J. Quinn	42	87	3	7	8	3.30
	C	A. Lopez	404	.275	1	43	456	82	13	10	4.4	.976							
	OF	J. Frederick	384	.299	16	56	201	6	5	2	2.4	.976							
	SS	G. Slade	250	.240	1	23	101	148	15	30	4.8	.943							
	1B	B. Clancy	196	.306	0	16	524	40	2	55	10.7	.996							
	3B	M. Finn	189	.238	0	14	34	92	9	7	2.7	.933							
Philadelphia	1B	D. Hurst	579	.339	24	143	1341	94	10	105	9.6	.993	E. Holley	34	228	11	14	0	3.95
	2B	L. Mallon	347	.259	5	31	199	228	20	42	5.5	.955	R. Benge	41	222	13	12	6	4.05
W-78 L-76	SS	D. Bartell	614	.308	1	53	359	529	34	83	6.0	.963	S. Hansen	39	191	10	10	2	3.72
	3B	P. Whitney	624	.298	13	124	177	276	19	31	3.1	.960	P. Collins	43	184	14	12	3	5.27
Burt Shotton	RF	C. Klein	650	.348	38	137	331	29	15	3	2.4	.960	F. Rhem	26	169	11	7	1	3.74
	CF	K. Davis	576	.309	5	57	411	15	11	6	3.3	.975	J. Elliott	39	166	11	10	0	5.42
	LF	H. Lee	595	.303	18	85	380	11	14	3	2.7	.965							
	C	S. Davis	402	.336	14	70	408	54	6	15	3.9	.987							
	2B	B. Friberg	154	.240	0	14	107	137	11	22	4.6	.957							
Boston	1B	A. Shires	298	.238	5	30	715	48	9	61	9.4	.988	E. Brandt	35	254	16	16	1	3.97
	2B	Maranville	571	.235	0	37	402	473	22	91	6.0	.975	H. Betts	31	222	13	11	1	2.80
W-77 L-77	SS	B. Urbanski	563	.272	8	46	316	461	44	91	6.0	.946	B. Brown	35	213	14	7	1	3.30
	3B	F. Knothe	344	.238	1	36	81	168	14	7	3.0	.947	T. Zachary	32	212	12	11	0	3.10
Bill McKechnie	RF	Schulmerich	404	.260	11	57	232	11	8	5	2.5	.968	B. Cantwell	37	146	13	11	5	2.96
	CF	W. Berger	602	.307	17	73	396	10	3	3	3.3	.993	S. Seibold	28	137	3	10	0	4.68
	LF	Worthington	435	.303	8	61	216	8	3	2	2.2	.987	Frankhouse	37	109	4	6	0	3.56
	C	A. Spohrer	335	.269	0	33	374	62	4	2	4.4	.991							
	UT	R. Moore	351	.293	3	43	258	67	5	34		.985							
	OF	F. Leach	223	.247	1	29	126	2	3	0	2.6	.977							
	C	P. Hargrave	217	.263	4	33	206	39	8	4	3.5	.968							
	1B	B. Jordan	212	.321	2	29	514	31	5	48	11.2	.991							
	OF	D. Holland	156	.295	1	18	94	3	1	0	2.5	.990							
New York	1B	B. Terry	643	.350	28	117	1493	137	14	125	10.7	.991	C. Hubbell	40	284	18	11	2	2.50
	2B	H. Critz	659	.276	2	50	392	471	23	94	5.9	.974	Fitzsimmons	35	238	11	11	0	4.43
W-72 L-82	SS	D. Marshall	226	.248	0	28	119	199	27	37	5.5	.922	B. Walker	31	163	8	12	2	4.14
	3B	J. Vergez	376	.261	9	43	94	208	21	22	2.9	.935	J. Mooney	29	125	6	10	0	5.05
John McGraw	RF	M. Ott	566	.318	38	123	347	11	6	5	2.4	.984	H. Bell	35	120	8	4	2	3.68
W-17 L-23	CF	F. Lindstrom	595	.271	15	92	315	18	6	2	2.6	.982	D. Luque	38	110	6	7	5	4.01
	LF	J. Moore	361	.305	2	27	160	6	3	10	2.0	.982	Schumacher	27	101	5	6	0	3.55
Bill Terry	C	S. Hogan	502	.287	8	77	522	71	10	11	4.4	.983	W. Hoyt	18	97	5	7	0	3.42
W-55 L-59	OF	C. Fullis	235	.298	1	21	97	1	1	0	1.8	.990	S. Gibson	41	82	4	8	3	4.85
	3S	G. English	204	.225	2	19	77	133	14	18		.938							
	SS	T. Jackson	195	.256	4	38	106	166	22	31	5.7	.925							

NATIONAL LEAGUE 1932, *cont.*

	POS	Player	AB	BA	HR	RBI	PO	A	E	DP	TC/G	FA	Pitcher	G	IP	W	L	SV	ERA
St. Louis	1B	R. Collins	549	.279	21	91	701	46	1	72	9.2	.999	D. Dean	46	286	18	15	2	3.30
	2B	J. Reese	309	.265	2	26	209	220	9	48	5.7	.979	P. Derringer	39	233	11	14	0	4.05
W-72 L-82	SS	C. Gelbert	455	.268	1	45	246	389	37	69	5.5	.945	T. Carleton	44	196	10	13	0	4.08
	3B	J. Flowers	247	.255	2	18	59	91	3	10	2.8	.980	B. Hallahan	25	176	12	7	1	3.11
Gabby Street	RF	G. Watkins	458	.312	9	63	267	11	15	1	2.4	.949	S. Johnson	32	165	5	14	2	4.92
	CF	P. Martin	323	.238	4	34	151	10	4	3	2.4	.976	A. Stout	36	74	4	5	1	4.40
	LF	E. Orsatti	375	.336	2	44	197	3	5	0	2.1	.976							
	C	G. Mancuso	310	.284	5	43	454	53	12	7	6.3	.977							
	23	F. Frisch	486	.292	3	60	252	309	14	58		.976							
	1B	J. Bottomley	311	.296	11	48	662	41	10	67	9.6	.986							
	C	J. Wilson	274	.248	2	28	326	55	7	9	5.2	.982							
	OF	R. Blades	201	.229	3	29	117	2	3	0	2.0	.975							
Cincinnati	1B	H. Hendrick	398	.302	4	40	922	60	14	72	10.6	.986	R. Lucas	31	269	13	17	0	2.94
	2B	G. Grantham	493	.292	6	39	258	347	26	45	5.5	.959	S. Johnson	42	245	13	15	2	3.27
W-60 L-94	SS	L. Durocher	457	.217	1	33	283	429	30	76	5.2	.960	O. Carroll	32	210	10	19	1	4.50
	3B	W. Gilbert	420	.214	1	40	90	198	22	16	2.8	.929	L. Benton	35	180	6	13	2	4.31
Dan Howley	RF	B. Herman	577	.326	16	87	392	18	13	6	2.9	.969	R. Kolp	32	160	6	10	1	3.89
	CF	E. Crabtree	402	.274	2	35	288	9	3	3	3.2	.990	B. Frey	28	131	4	10	0	4.32
	LF	W. Roettger	347	.277	3	43	214	3	2	2	2.3	.991	E. Rixey	25	112	5	5	0	2.66
	C	E. Lombardi	413	.303	11	68	288	76	14	6	3.5	.963							
	OF	T. Douthit	333	.243	0	25	251	6	4	2	3.0	.985							
	UT	J. Morrissey	269	.242	0	13	144	240	8	38		.980							
	OF	C. Hafey	253	.344	2	36	131	5	5	0	1.7	.965							
	3B	A. High	191	.188	0	12	34	62	5	2	2.2	.950							

BATTING AND BASE RUNNING LEADERS

Batting Average
L. O'Doul, BKN	.368
B. Terry, NY	.350
C. Klein, PHI	.348
P. Waner, PIT	.341
D. Hurst, PHI	.339

Slugging Average
C. Klein, PHI	.646
M. Ott, NY	.601
B. Terry, NY	.580
L. O'Doul, BKN	.555
D. Hurst, PHI	.547

Home Runs
M. Ott, NY	38
C. Klein, PHI	38
B. Terry, NY	28
D. Hurst, PHI	24
H. Wilson, BKN	23

Winning Percentage
L. Warneke, CHI	.786
G. Bush, CHI	.633
W. Clark, BKN	.625
F. Rhem, PHI, STL	.625
C. Hubbell, NY	.621

PITCHING LEADERS

Earned Run Average
L. Warneke, CHI	2.37
C. Hubbell, NY	2.50
H. Betts, BOS	2.80
S. Swetonic, PIT	2.82
R. Lucas, CIN	2.94

Wins
L. Warneke, CHI	22
W. Clark, BKN	20
G. Bush, CHI	19
C. Hubbell, NY	18
D. Dean, STL	18
L. French, PIT	18

Total Bases
C. Klein, PHI	420
B. Terry, NY	373
M. Ott, NY	340
L. O'Doul, BKN	330
P. Waner, PIT	318

Runs Batted In
D. Hurst, PHI	143
C. Klein, PHI	137
P. Whitney, PHI	124
H. Wilson, BKN	123
M. Ott, NY	123

Stolen Bases
C. Klein, PHI	20
T. Piet, PIT	19
G. Watkins, STL	18
F. Frisch, STL	18
K. Davis, PHI	16

Saves
J. Quinn, BKN	8
R. Benge, PHI	6
B. Cantwell, BOS	5
D. Luque, NY	5

Strikeouts
D. Dean, STL	191
C. Hubbell, NY	137
P. Malone, CHI	120
T. Carleton, STL	113
B. Brown, BOS	110

Complete Games
R. Lucas, CIN	28
L. Warneke, CHI	25
C. Hubbell, NY	22
L. French, PIT	20
E. Brandt, BOS	19
W. Clark, BKN	19

Hits
C. Klein, PHI	226
B. Terry, NY	225
L. O'Doul, BKN	219
P. Waner, PIT	215

Base on Balls
M. Ott, NY	100
D. Hurst, PHI	65
D. Bartell, PHI	64
G. Suhr, PIT	63

Home Run Percentage
M. Ott, NY	6.7
C. Klein, PHI	5.8
H. Wilson, BKN	4.8
B. Terry, NY	4.4

Fewest Hits/9 Innings
S. Swetonic, PIT	7.41
L. Warneke, CHI	8.03
C. Hubbell, NY	8.24
P. Malone, CHI	8.43

Shutouts
S. Swetonic, PIT	4
L. Warneke, CHI	4
D. Dean, STL	4
T. Carleton, STL	3

Fewest Walks/9 Innings
B. Swift, PIT	1.09
R. Lucas, CIN	1.17
C. Hubbell, NY	1.27
H. Betts, BOS	1.42

Runs Scored
C. Klein, PHI	152
B. Terry, NY	124
L. O'Doul, BKN	120
M. Ott, NY	119

Doubles
P. Waner, PIT	62
C. Klein, PHI	50
Stephenson, CHI	49
D. Bartell, PHI	48

Triples
B. Herman, CIN	19
G. Suhr, PIT	16
C. Klein, PHI	15
L. Waner, PIT	11

Most Strikeouts/9 Inn.
D. Dean, STL	6.01
B. Hallahan, STL	5.51
P. Malone, CHI	4.56
C. Hubbell, NY	4.34

Innings
D. Dean, STL	286
C. Hubbell, NY	284
L. Warneke, CHI	277
L. French, PIT	274

Games Pitched
L. French, PIT	47
D. Dean, STL	46
T. Carleton, STL	44
P. Collins, PHI	43

	W	L	PCT	GB	R	OR	2B	3B	HR	BA	SA	SB	E	DP	FA	CG	BB	SO	ShO	SV	ERA
Chicago	90	64	.584		720	633	296	60	69	.278	.392	48	173	146	.973	79	409	527	9	7	3.44
Pittsburgh	86	68	.558	4	701	711	274	90	47	.285	.394	71	185	124	.969	72	338	377	12	12	3.75
Brooklyn	81	73	.526	9	752	747	296	59	109	.283	.419	61	183	146	.971	61	403	499	7	16	4.28
Philadelphia	78	76	.506	12	844	796	330	67	122	.292	.442	71	194	133	.968	59	450	459	4	17	4.47
Boston	77	77	.500	13	649	655	262	53	63	.265	.366	36	152	145	.976	72	420	440	8	8	3.53
New York	72	82	.468	18	755	706	263	54	116	.276	.406	31	191	143	.969	57	387	506	3	10	3.83
St. Louis	72	82	.468	18	684	717	307	51	76	.269	.385	92	175	155	.971	70	455	681	13	9	3.97
Cincinnati	60	94	.390	30	575	715	265	68	47	.263	.362	35	178	129	.971	83	276	359	6	6	3.79
					5680	5680	2293	502	649	.276	.396	445	1431	1144	.971	553	3138	3848	62	91	3.88

AMERICAN LEAGUE 1932

	POS	Player	AB	BA	HR	RBI	PO	A	E	DP	TC/G	FA	Pitcher	G	IP	W	L	SV	ERA
New York	1B	L. Gehrig	596	.349	34	151	1293	75	18	101	8.9	.987	L. Gomez	37	265	24	7	1	4.21
	2B	T. Lazzeri	510	.300	15	113	362	405	17	70	5.9	.978	R. Ruffing	35	259	18	7	2	3.09
W-107 L-47	SS	F. Crosetti	398	.241	5	57	155	216	25	49	4.8	.937	G. Pipgras	32	219	16	9	0	4.19
	3B	J. Sewell	503	.272	11	68	122	221	9	15	2.9	.974	J. Allen	33	192	17	4	4	3.70
Joe McCarthy	RF	B. Ruth	457	.341	41	137	209	10	9	1	1.8	.961	H. Pennock	22	147	9	5	0	4.60
	CF	E. Combs	591	.321	9	65	343	6	12	3	2.6	.967	MacFayden	17	121	7	5	1	3.93
	LF	B. Chapman	581	.299	10	107	303	13	17	2	2.2	.949							
	C	B. Dickey	423	.310	15	84	639	53	9	6	6.5	.987							
	SS	L. Lary	280	.232	3	39	152	218	23	39	4.9	.941							
	OF	S. Byrd	209	.297	8	30	129	4	5	1	1.5	.964							
Philadelphia	1B	J. Foxx	585	.364	**58**	**169**	1328	79	9	115	10.0	**.994**	L. Grove	44	292	25	10	7	**2.84**
	2B	M. Bishop	409	.254	5	37	232	340	20	68	5.5	**.988**	R. Walberg	41	272	17	10	1	4.73
W-94 L-60	SS	E. McNair	554	.285	18	95	242	391	31	89	5.0	.953	G. Earnshaw	36	245	19	13	0	4.77
	3B	J. Dykes	558	.265	7	90	142	251	8	20	2.8	**.980**	R. Mahaffey	37	223	13	13	0	5.09
Connie Mack	RF	D. Cramer	384	.336	3	46	233	7	6	2	2.9	.976	T. Freitas	23	150	12	5	0	3.83
	CF	M. Haas	558	.305	6	65	372	6	5	2	2.8	.987							
	LF	A. Simmons	**670**	.322	35	151	290	9	6	4	2.0	.980							
	C	M. Cochrane	518	.293	23	112	652	94	5	15	5.5	**.993**							
	OF	B. Miller	305	.295	8	58	180	3	4	0	2.2	.979							
	2B	D. Williams	215	.251	4	24	122	175	15	30	5.9	.952							
Washington	1B	J. Kuhel	347	.291	4	52	761	45	5	64	9.5	.994	G. Crowder	50	**327**	**26**	13	1	3.33
	2B	B. Myer	577	.279	5	52	352	426	20	97	5.7	.975	M. Weaver	43	234	22	10	2	4.08
W-93 L-61	SS	J. Cronin	557	.318	6	116	306	448	32	95	5.6	**.959**	L. Brown	46	203	15	12	5	4.44
	3B	O. Bluege	507	.258	5	64	158	295	14	**28**	3.1	.970	F. Marberry	**54**	198	8	4	**13**	4.01
Walter Johnson	RF	C. Reynolds	406	.305	9	63	229	3	4	0	2.5	.983	T. Thomas	18	117	8	7	0	3.54
	CF	S. West	554	.287	6	83	**450**	15	10	**7**	3.3	.979							
	LF	H. Manush	625	.342	14	116	318	6	4	3	2.2	.988							
	C	R. Spencer	317	.246	1	41	313	44	8	9	3.7	.978							
	1B	J. Judge	291	.258	3	29	668	46	2	71	9.2	.997							
	OF	S. Rice	288	.323	1	34	132	7	4	2	2.1	.972							
	C	M. Berg	195	.236	1	26	229	35	0	9	3.5	1.000							
	OF	D. Harris	156	.327	6	29	66	3	5	0	2.2	.932							
Cleveland	1B	E. Morgan	532	.293	4	68	**1430**	74	**23**	100	10.8	.985	W. Ferrell	38	288	23	13	1	3.66
	2B	B. Cissell	541	.320	6	93	329	475	30*	82	6.5*	.964	C. Brown	37	263	15	12	1	4.08
W-87 L-65	SS	J. Burnett	512	.297	4	53	184	304	28	52	5.0	.946	M. Harder	39	255	15	13	0	3.75
	3B	W. Kamm	524	.286	3	83	164	299	16	20	3.2	.967	W. Hudlin	33	182	12	8	2	4.71
Roger Peckinpaugh	RF	D. Porter	621	.308	4	62	269	2	5	0	1.9	.982	Hildebrand	27	129	8	6	0	3.69
	CF	E. Averill	631	.314	32	124	412	12	16	3	2.9	.964	J. Russell	18	113	5	7	1	4.70
	LF	J. Vosmik	621	.312	10	97	432	12	5	4	2.9	**.989**	S. Connally	35	112	8	6	3	4.33
	C	L. Sewell	300	.253	2	52	306	50	8	8	4.3	.978							
	C	G. Myatt	252	.246	8	46	211	32	3	3	3.8	.988							
	SS	E. Montague	192	.245	0	24	91	129	27	22	4.3	.891							
Detroit	1B	H. Davis	590	.269	4	74	1327	75	16	123	10.1	.989	E. Whitehill	33	244	16	12	0	4.54
	2B	C. Gehringer	618	.298	19	107	**396**	495	**30**	**110**	6.1	.967	V. Sorrell	32	234	14	14	0	4.03
W-76 L-75	SS	B. Rogell	554	.271	9	61	275	433	42	88	5.4	.944	W. Wyatt	43	206	9	13	1	5.03
	3B	H. Schuble	340	.271	5	52	70	152	14	10	3.1	.941	T. Bridges	34	201	14	12	1	3.36
Bucky Harris	RF	E. Webb	338	.287	3	51	163	8	8	0	2.1	.955	C. Hogsett	47	178	11	9	7	3.54
	CF	G. Walker	480	.323	8	78	309	9	17	1	2.9	.949	G. Uhle	33	147	6	6	5	4.48
	LF	J. Stone	582	.297	17	108	334	11	14	2	2.5	.961							
	C	R. Hayworth	338	.293	2	44	399	59	4	4	4.4	.991							
	UT	B. Rhiel	250	.280	3	38	150	65	5	21		.977							
	OF	J. White	208	.260	2	21	96	6	4	0	2.3	.962							
	OF	R. Johnson	195	.251	3	22	102	3	8	2	2.4	.929							
	3B	Richardson	155	.219	0	12	51	92	2	8	2.2	.986							
St. Louis	1B	J. Burns	617	.305	11	70	1399	**101**	12	**130**	10.1	.992	L. Stewart	41	260	14	19	1	4.61
	2B	O. Melillo	612	.242	3	66	393	**526**	18	**110**	6.1	.981	Blaeholder	42	258	14	14	0	4.70
W-63 L-91	SS	J. Levey	568	.280	4	63	284	439	**47**	83	5.1	.939	B. Hadley	40	230	13	20*	1	5.53
	3B	A. Scharein	303	.304	0	42	100	172	10	23	3.7	.965	S. Gray	52	207	8	12	4	4.53
Bill Killefer	RF	B. Campbell	593	.285	14	85	297	12	20*	4	2.4	.939	W. Hebert	35	108	1	12	1	6.48
	CF	F. Schulte	565	.294	9	73	331	9	5	1	2.7	.986	C. Fischer	24	97	3	7	0	5.57
	LF	G. Goslin	572	.299	17	104	330	**16**	8	5	2.4	.951							
	C	R. Ferrell	438	.315	2	65	486	78	8	9	4.8	.986							
	3B	L. Storti	193	.259	3	26	50	81	6	8	2.7	.956							
Chicago	1B	L. Blue	373	.249	0	43	1014	88	16	106	10.6	.986	T. Lyons	33	231	10	15	2	3.28
	2B	J. Hayes	475	.257	2	54	241	346	20	78	6.3	.967	S. Jones	30	200	10	15	0	4.22
W-49 L-102	SS	L. Appling	489	.274	3	63	195	287	37	66	6.1	.929	M. Gaston	28	167	7	17	1	4.00
	3B	C. Selph	396	.283	0	51	83	120	20	14	3.1	.910	V. Frasier	29	146	3	13	0	6.23
Lew Fonseca	RF	B. Seeds	434	.290	2	45	234	7	9	1	2.2	.964	P. Gregory	33	118	5	3	0	4.51
	CF	L. Funk	440	.259	2	40	318	15	7	4	2.8	.979	R. Faber	42	106	2	11	6	3.74
	LF	Fothergill	346	.295	7	50	136	4	7	0	1.7	.952							
	C	F. Grube	277	.282	0	31	303	55	16	5	4.1	.957							
	UT	R. Kress	515	.285	9	57	281	201	32	41		.938							
	1B	B. Sullivan	307	.316	1	45	485	35	5	42	10.1	.990							
	C	C. Berry	226	.305	4	31	212	52	5	5	3.8	.981							
	OF	J. Hodapp	176	.227	3	20	58	0	2	0	1.9	.967							

AMERICAN LEAGUE 1932, *cont.*

	POS	Player	AB	BA	HR	RBI	PO	A	E	DP	TC/G	FA	Pitcher	G	IP	W	L	SV	ERA
Boston	1B	D. Alexander	376	.372*	8	56	1051	67	9	93	11.2*	.992	B. Weiland	43	196	6	16	1	4.51
	2B	M. Olson	403	.248	0	25	266	324	28	68	5.8	.955	E. Durham	34	175	6	13	0	3.80
W-43 L-111	SS	R. Warstler	388	.211	0	34	254	373	41	84	6.2	.939	B. Kline	47	172	11	13	2	5.28
	3B	U. Pickering	457	.260	2	40	110	222	21	22	2.8	.941	I. Andrews	25	142	8	6	0	3.81
Shano Collins	RF	R. Johnson	348	.299	11	47	167	6	13	0	2.2	.930	W. Moore	37	84	4	10	4	5.23
W-11 L-44	CF	T. Oliver	455	.264	0	37	328	12	6	4	3.0	.983	MacFayden	12	78	1	10	0	5.10
	LF	S. Jolley	531	.309	18	99	234	12	15	3	2.1	.943	J. Welch	20	72	4	6	0	5.23
Marty McManus	C	B. Tate	273	.245	2	26	244	50	8	7	4.0	.974							
W-32 L-67	23	M. McManus	302	.235	5	24	147	227	17	28		.957							
	OF	C. Watwood	266	.248	0	30	101	3	6	0	2.4	.945							
	C	E. Connolly	222	.225	0	21	233	55	13	0	4.0	.957							
	SS	H. Rhyne	207	.227	0	14	92	161	9	31	4.8	.966							
	OF	E. Webb	192	.281	5	27	74	7	3	2	1.7	.964							
	OF	G. Stumpf	169	.201	1	18	78	2	4	0	1.6	.952							

BATTING AND BASE RUNNING LEADERS

Batting Average
D. Alexander, BOS, DET	.367
J. Foxx, PHI	.364
L. Gehrig, NY	.349
H. Manush, WAS	.342
B. Ruth, NY	.341

Slugging Average
J. Foxx, PHI	.749
B. Ruth, NY	.661
L. Gehrig, NY	.621
E. Averill, CLE	.569
A. Simmons, PHI	.548

Home Runs
J. Foxx, PHI	58
B. Ruth, NY	41
A. Simmons, PHI	35
L. Gehrig, NY	34
E. Averill, CLE	32

Winning Percentage
J. Allen, NY	.810
L. Gomez, NY	.774
R. Ruffing, NY	.720
L. Grove, PHI	.714
M. Weaver, WAS	.688

PITCHING LEADERS

Earned Run Average
L. Grove, PHI	2.84
R. Ruffing, NY	3.09
T. Lyons, CHI	3.28
G. Crowder, WAS	3.33
T. Bridges, DET	3.36

Wins
G. Crowder, WAS	26
L. Grove, PHI	25
L. Gomez, NY	24
W. Ferrell, CLE	23
M. Weaver, WAS	22

Total Bases
J. Foxx, PHI	438
L. Gehrig, NY	370
A. Simmons, PHI	367
E. Averill, CLE	359
H. Manush, WAS	325

Runs Batted In
J. Foxx, PHI	169
L. Gehrig, NY	151
A. Simmons, PHI	151
B. Ruth, NY	137
E. Averill, CLE	124

Stolen Bases
B. Chapman, NY	38
G. Walker, DET	30
R. Johnson, BOS, DET	20
B. Cissell, CHI, CLE	18

Saves
F. Marberry, WAS	13
W. Moore, BOS, NY	8
C. Hogsett, DET	7
L. Grove, PHI	7
R. Faber, CHI	6

Strikeouts
R. Ruffing, NY	190
L. Grove, PHI	188
L. Gomez, NY	176
B. Hadley, CHI, STL	145
G. Pipgras, NY	111

Complete Games
L. Grove, PHI	27
W. Ferrell, CLE	26
R. Ruffing, NY	22

Hits
A. Simmons, PHI	216
H. Manush, WAS	214
J. Foxx, PHI	213
L. Gehrig, NY	208

Base on Balls
B. Ruth, NY	130
J. Foxx, PHI	116
M. Bishop, PHI	110
L. Gehrig, NY	108

Home Run Percentage
J. Foxx, PHI	9.9
B. Ruth, NY	9.0
L. Gehrig, NY	5.7
A. Simmons, PHI	5.2

Fewest Hits/9 Innings
J. Allen, NY	7.59
R. Ruffing, NY	7.61
T. Bridges, DET	7.79
L. Grove, PHI	8.30

Shutouts
| T. Bridges, DET | 4 |
| L. Grove, PHI | 4 |

Fewest Walks/9 Innings
C. Brown, CLE	1.71
G. Crowder, WAS	2.12
M. Harder, CLE	2.40
L. Grove, PHI	2.44

Runs Scored
J. Foxx, PHI	151
A. Simmons, PHI	144
E. Combs, NY	143
L. Gehrig, NY	138

Doubles
E. McNair, PHI	47
C. Gehringer, DET	44
J. Cronin, WAS	43
R. Kress, CHI, STL	42

Triples
J. Cronin, WAS	18
T. Lazzeri, NY	16
B. Myer, WAS	16
B. Chapman, NY	15

Most Strikeouts/9 Inn.
R. Ruffing, NY	6.60
L. Gomez, NY	5.97
L. Grove, PHI	5.80
B. Hadley, CHI, STL	5.26

Innings
G. Crowder, WAS	327
L. Grove, PHI	292
W. Ferrell, CLE	288
R. Walberg, PHI	272

Games Pitched
F. Marberry, WAS	54
S. Gray, STL	52
G. Crowder, WAS	50
C. Hogsett, DET	47

	W	L	PCT	GB	R	OR	2B	3B	HR	BA	SA	SB	E	DP	FA	CG	BB	SO	ShO	SV	ERA
										Batting				**Fielding**			**Pitching**				
New York	107	47	.695		1002	724	279	82	160	.286	.454	77	188	124	.969	95	561	770	11	15	3.98
Philadelphia	94	60	.610	13	981	752	303	51	173	.290	.457	38	124	142	.979	95	511	595	10	10	4.45
Washington	93	61	.604	14	840	716	303	100	61	.284	.408	70	125	157	.979	66	526	437	10	22	4.16
Cleveland	87	65	.572	19	845	747	310	74	78	.285	.413	52	191	129	.969	94	446	439	6	8	4.12
Detroit	76	75	.503	29.5	799	787	291	80	80	.273	.401	103	187	154	.969	67	592	521	9	17	4.30
St. Louis	63	91	.409	44	736	898	274	69	67	.276	.388	69	188	156	.969	63	574	496	8	11	5.01
Chicago	49	102	.325	56.5	667	897	274	56	36	.267	.360	89	264	170	.958	50	580	379	2	12	4.82
Boston	43	111	.279	64	566	915	253	57	53	.251	.351	46	233	165	.963	42	612	365	2	7	5.02
					6436	6436	2287	569	708	.277	.404	544	1500	1197	.969	572	4402	4002	58	102	4.48

NATIONAL LEAGUE 1933

	POS	Player	AB	BA	HR	RBI	PO	A	E	DP	TC/G	FA	Pitcher	G	IP	W	L	SV	ERA
New York	1B	B. Terry	475	.322	6	58	1246	76	11	103	11.4	.992	C. Hubbell	45	309	23	12	5	1.66
	2B	H. Critz	558	.246	2	33	316	541	16	87	6.6	.982	Schumacher	35	259	19	12	1	2.16
W-91 L-61	SS	B. Ryan	525	.238	3	48	296	494	42	95	5.7	.950	Fitzsimmons	36	252	16	11	0	2.90
	3B	J. Vergez	458	.271	16	72	101	222	25	17	2.8	.928	R. Parmelee	32	218	13	8	0	3.17
Bill Terry	RF	M. Ott	580	.283	23	103	283	12	5	5	2.0	.983	H. Bell	38	105	6	5	5	2.05
	CF	K. Davis	434	.258	7	37	248	7	3	3	2.2	.988	D. Luque	35	80	8	2	4	2.69
	LF	J. Moore	524	.292	0	42	266	19	10	6	2.2	.966							
	C	G. Mancuso	481	.264	6	56	580	83	19	15	4.8	.972							
	OF	L. O'Doul	229	.306	9	35	109	4	3	0	1.8	.974							
	1B	S. Leslie	137	.321	3	27	371	21	4	28	11.3	.990							

NATIONAL LEAGUE 1933, *cont.*

	POS	Player	AB	BA	HR	RBI	PO	A	E	DP	TC/G	FA	Pitcher	G	IP	W	L	SV	ERA
Pittsburgh	1B	G. Suhr	566	.267	10	75	1451	90	14	**151**	10.1	.991	L. French	47	291	18	13	1	2.72
	2B	T. Piet	362	.323	1	42	241	305	26	61	5.9	.955	B. Swift	37	218	14	10	0	3.13
W-87 L-67	SS	A. Vaughan	573	.314	9	97	310	487	**46**	95	5.5	.945	H. Meine	32	207	15	8	0	3.65
	3B	P. Traynor	624	.304	1	82	176	**300**	27	16	**3.3**	.946	S. Swetonic	31	165	12	12	0	3.50
George Gibson	RF	P. Waner	618	.309	7	70	346	16	7	2	2.4	.981	H. Smith	28	145	8	7	1	2.86
	CF	F. Lindstrom	538	.310	5	55	388	7	5	2	**3.1**	.988	W. Hoyt	36	117	5	7	4	2.92
	LF	L. Waner	500	.276	0	26	267	9	5	2	2.5	.982	L. Chagnon	39	100	6	4	1	3.69
	C	E. Grace	291	.289	3	44	305	37	7	7	4.0	.980	B. Harris	31	59	4	4	5	3.22
	2B	T. Thevenow	253	.312	0	34	137	172	8	31	5.2	.975							
	OF	W. Jensen	196	.296	0	15	95	1	2	0	2.5	.980							
	OF	A. Comorosky	162	.284	1	15	66	1	0	0	2.2	1.000							
Chicago	1B	C. Grimm	384	.247	3	37	979	84	4	94	10.3	**.996**	L. Warneke	36	287	18	13	1	2.00
	2B	B. Herman	619	.279	0	44	**466**	512	45	**114**	6.7	.956	G. Bush	41	259	20	12	2	2.75
W-86 L-68	SS	B. Jurges	487	.269	5	50	298	476	34	95	5.7	.958	C. Root	35	242	15	10	0	2.60
	3B	W. English	398	.261	3	41	80	173	7	9	2.5	**.973**	P. Malone	31	186	10	14	0	3.91
Charlie Grimm	RF	B. Herman	508	.289	16	93	252	12	12	1	2.1	.957	B. Tinning	32	175	13	6	1	3.18
	CF	F. Demaree	515	.272	6	51	321	12	12	1	2.6	.965	L. Nelson	24	76	5	5	1	3.21
	LF	Stephenson	346	.329	4	51	187	5	3	2	2.1	.985	B. Grimes	17	70	3	6	3	3.49
	C	G. Hartnett	490	.276	16	88	550	77	7	**17**	4.5	.989							
	OF	K. Cuyler	262	.317	5	35	130	2	3	0	2.0	.978							
	3S	M. Koenig	218	.284	3	25	65	132	14	24		.934							
	1B	H. Hendrick	189	.291	4	23	328	23	6	31	9.4	.983							
Boston	1B	B. Jordan	588	.286	4	46	**1513**	88	14	117	10.8	.991	E. Brandt	41	288	18	14	4	2.60
	2B	Maranville	478	.218	0	38	362	384	22	82	5.4	.971	B. Cantwell	40	255	20	10	2	2.62
W-83 L-71	SS	B. Urbanski	566	.251	0	35	299	473	38	91	5.7	.953	Frankhouse	43	245	16	15	3	3.16
	3B	P. Whitney	382	.246	8	47	77	187	8	23*	3.2	.971	H. Betts	35	242	11	11	4	2.79
Bill McKechnie	RF	R. Moore	497	.302	8	70	275	11	6	1	2.4	.979	T. Zachary	26	125	7	9	2	3.53
	CF	W. Berger	528	.313	27	106	382	6	9	4	2.9	.977							
	LF	H. Lee	312	.221	1	28	207	6	5	2	2.5	.977							
	C	S. Hogan	328	.253	3	30	280	56	1	11	3.5	**.997**							
	OF	J. Mowry	249	.221	0	20	155	2	1	0	2.5	.994							
	C	A. Spohrer	184	.250	1	28	150	26	5	4	2.8	.972							
	3B	F. Knothe	158	.228	1	6	34	56	2	6	2.8	.978							
	3B	D. Gyselman	155	.239	0	12	45	93	11	4	3.5	.926							
St. Louis	1B	R. Collins	493	.310	10	68	1054	79	7	82	9.3	.994	D. Dean	**48**	293	20	18	4	3.04
	2B	F. Frisch	585	.303	4	66	371	378	14	71	5.8	.982	T. Carleton	44	277	17	11	3	3.38
W-82 L-71	SS	L. Durocher	395	.258	2	41	238	358	24	64	5.0	.961*	B. Hallahan	36	244	16	13	0	3.50
	3B	P. Martin	599	.316	8	57	139	273	25	14	3.0	.943	B. Walker	29	158	9	10	0	3.42
Gabby Street	RF	G. Watkins	525	.278	5	62	295	9	15	3	2.4	.953	J. Haines	32	115	9	6	1	2.50
W-46 L-45	CF	E. Orsatti	436	.298	0	38	274	5	4	1	2.8	.986	D. Vance	28	99	6	2	3	3.55
	LF	J. Medwick	595	.306	18	98	318	17	7	2	2.3	.980							
Frankie Frisch	C	J. Wilson	369	.255	1	45	498	58	10	13	**5.3**	.982							
W-36 L-26	OF	E. Allen	261	.241	0	36	179	8	3	1	2.8	.984							
	UT	P. Crawford	224	.268	0	21	287	62	6	25		.983							
	C	B. O'Farrell	163	.239	2	20	211	19	7	1	4.7	.970							
	2B	R. Hornsby	83	.325	2	21	24	35	2	7	3.6	.967							
Brooklyn	1B	S. Leslie	364	.286	5	46	855	49	17	44	9.7	.982	B. Beck	43	257	12	20	1	3.54
	2B	Cuccinello	485	.252	9	65	311	334	15	64	5.5	.977	V. Mungo	41	248	16	15	0	2.72
W-65 L-88	SS	G. Wright	192	.255	1	37	95	124	15	29	4.6	.936	R. Benge	37	229	10	17	1	3.42
	3B	J. Stripp	537	.277	1	51	170	264	15	17	3.2	.967	O. Carroll	33	226	13	15	0	3.78
Max Carey	RF	J. Frederick	556	.308	7	64	289	8	9	1	2.2	.971	S. Thurston	32	131	6	8	3	4.52
	CF	D. Taylor	358	.285	9	40	247	4	6	1	2.8	.977	J. Shaute	41	108	3	4	2	3.49
	LF	H. Wilson	360	.267	9	54	181	3	7	0	2.1	.963							
	C	A. Lopez	372	.301	3	41	449	**84**	5	14	4.3	.991							
	OF	B. Boyle	338	.299	0	35	195	2	5	0	2.2	.975							
	SS	J. Jordan	211	.256	0	17	104	182	6	25	5.8	.969							
	UT	J. Flowers	210	.233	2	22	130	158	11	21		.963							
	OF	J. Hutcheson	184	.234	6	21	84	8	1	2	2.1	.989							
	OF	L. O'Doul	159	.252	5	21	88	1	5	0	2.3	.947							
Philadelphia	1B	D. Hurst	550	.267	8	76	1355	**114**	**23**	132	10.5	.985	E. Holley	30	207	13	15	0	3.53
	2B	J. Warner	340	.224	0	22	177	224	11	45	5.8	.973	S. Hansen	32	168	6	14	1	4.44
W-60 L-92	SS	D. Bartell	587	.271	1	37	**381**	493	46	**100**	6.0	.951	C. Moore	36	161	8	9	1	3.74
	3B	J. McLeod	232	.194	0	15	60	120	17	8	2.9	.914	J. Elliott	35	162	6	10	2	3.84
Burt Shotton	RF	C. Klein	606	**.368**	28	120	339	**21**	5	5	2.4	.986	P. Collins	42	151	8	13	6	4.11
	CF	C. Fullis	**647**	.309	1	45	410	15	10	3	2.9	.977	F. Rhem	28	126	5	14	2	6.57
	LF	Schulmerich	365	.334	8	59	210	6	5	0	2.3	.977							
	C	S. Davis	495	.349	9	65	395	69	8	9	3.6	.983							
	2B	M. Finn	169	.237	0	13	107	164	10	34	5.5	.964							
	OF	H. Lee	167	.287	0	12	97	5	2	0	2.3	.981							

NATIONAL LEAGUE 1933, *cont.*

Cincinnati
W-58 L-94

Donie Bush

POS	Player	AB	BA	HR	RBI	PO	A	E	DP	TC/G	FA	Pitcher	G	IP	W	L	SV	ERA
1B	J. Bottomley	549	.250	13	83	1511	72	15	112	11.0	.991	P. Derringer	33	231	7	25*	1	3.23
2B	J. Morrissey	534	.230	0	26	187	295	18	46	5.7	.964	R. Lucas	29	220	10	16	0	3.40
SS	O. Bluege	291	.213	0	18	162	256	28	48	4.7	.937	S. Johnson	34	211	7	18	1	3.49
3B	S. Adams	538	.262	1	22	121	272	15	15	3.1	.963	L. Benton	34	153	10	11	2	3.71
RF	H. Rice	510	.261	0	54	315	14	3	3	2.4	.991	R. Kolp	30	150	6	9	3	3.53
CF	C. Hafey	568	.303	7	62	364	16	5	5	2.7	.987	B. Frey	37	132	6	4	0	3.82
LF	J. Moore	514	.263	1	44	329	12	9	4	2.7	.974							
C	E. Lombardi	350	.283	4	47	223	52	8	3	3.0	.972							
2B	G. Grantham	260	.204	4	28	160	189	19	33	5.1	.948							
OF	W. Roettger	209	.239	1	17	124	4	3	2	2.4	.977							

BATTING AND BASE RUNNING LEADERS

Batting Average
C. Klein, PHI .368
S. Davis, PHI .349
T. Piet, PIT .323
B. Terry, NY .322
Schulmerich, BOS, PHI .318

Slugging Average
C. Klein, PHI .602
W. Berger, BOS .566
B. Herman, CHI .502
J. Medwick, STL .497
A. Vaughan, PIT .478

Home Runs
C. Klein, PHI 28
W. Berger, BOS 27
M. Ott, NY 23
J. Medwick, STL 18

Total Bases
C. Klein, PHI 365
W. Berger, BOS 299
J. Medwick, STL 296
P. Waner, PIT 282
A. Vaughan, PIT 274

Runs Batted In
C. Klein, PHI 120
W. Berger, BOS 106
M. Ott, NY 103
J. Medwick, STL 98
A. Vaughan, PIT 97

Stolen Bases
P. Martin, STL 26
F. Frisch, STL 18
C. Fullis, PHI 18
C. Klein, PHI 15
E. Orsatti, STL 14

Hits
C. Klein, PHI 223
C. Fullis, PHI 200
P. Waner, PIT 191
P. Traynor, PIT 190

Base on Balls
M. Ott, NY 75
G. Suhr, PIT 72
P. Martin, STL 67
A. Vaughan, PIT 64

Home Run Percentage
W. Berger, BOS 5.1
C. Klein, PHI 4.6
M. Ott, NY 4.0
L. O'Doul, BKN, NY 3.6

Runs Scored
P. Martin, STL 122
C. Klein, PHI 101
P. Waner, PIT 101
M. Ott, NY 98

Doubles
C. Klein, PHI 44
J. Medwick, STL 40
F. Lindstrom, PIT 39
P. Waner, PIT 38

Triples
A. Vaughan, PIT 19
P. Waner, PIT 16
B. Herman, CHI 12
P. Martin, STL 12

PITCHING LEADERS

Winning Percentage
B. Cantwell, BOS .667
C. Hubbell, NY .657
H. Meine, PIT .652
G. Bush, CHI .625
Schumacher, NY .613

Earned Run Average
C. Hubbell, NY 1.66
L. Warneke, CHI 2.00
Schumacher, NY 2.16
E. Brandt, BOS 2.60
C. Root, CHI 2.60

Wins
C. Hubbell, NY 23
B. Cantwell, BOS 20
G. Bush, CHI 20
D. Dean, STL 20
Schumacher, NY 19

Saves
P. Collins, PHI 6
H. Bell, NY 5
B. Harris, PIT 5
C. Hubbell, NY 5

Strikeouts
D. Dean, STL 199
C. Hubbell, NY 156
T. Carleton, STL 147
L. Warneke, CHI 133
R. Parmelee, NY 132

Complete Games
D. Dean, STL 26
L. Warneke, CHI 26
E. Brandt, BOS 23
C. Hubbell, NY 22

Fewest Hits/9 Innings
Schumacher, NY 6.92
C. Hubbell, NY 7.46
R. Parmelee, NY 7.87
E. Brandt, BOS 8.01

Shutouts
C. Hubbell, NY 10
Schumacher, NY 7
L. French, PIT 5

Fewest Walks/9 Innings
R. Lucas, CIN 0.74
C. Hubbell, NY 1.37
B. Swift, PIT 1.48
L. French, PIT 1.70

Most Strikeouts/9 Inn.
D. Dean, STL 6.11
R. Parmelee, NY 5.44
T. Carleton, STL 4.78
C. Hubbell, NY 4.55

Innings
C. Hubbell, NY 309
D. Dean, STL 293
L. French, PIT 291
E. Brandt, BOS 288

Games Pitched
D. Dean, STL 48
L. French, PIT 47
C. Hubbell, NY 45
A. Liska, PHI 45

	W	L	PCT	GB	R	OR	2B	3B	HR	BA	SA	SB	E	DP	FA	CG	BB	SO	ShO	SV	ERA
New York	91	61	.599		636	515	204	41	82	.263	.361	31	178	156	.973	75	400	555	22	15	2.71
Pittsburgh	87	67	.565	5	667	619	249	84	39	.285	.383	34	166	133	.972	70	313	401	16	12	3.27
Chicago	86	68	.558	6	646	536	256	51	72	.271	.380	52	168	163	.973	95	413	488	16	9	2.93
Boston	83	71	.539	9	552	531	217	56	54	.252	.345	25	138	148	.978	85	355	383	14	16	2.96
St. Louis	82	71	.536	9.5	687	609	256	61	57	.276	.378	99	162	119	.973	73	452	635	10	16	3.37
Brooklyn	65	88	.425	26.5	617	695	224	51	62	.263	.359	82	177	120	.971	71	374	415	9	10	3.73
Philadelphia	60	92	.395	31	607	760	240	41	60	.274	.369	55	183	156	.970	52	410	341	10	13	4.34
Cincinnati	58	94	.382	33	496	643	208	37	34	.246	.320	30	177	139	.971	74	257	310	13	8	3.42
					4908	4908	1854	422	460	.266	.362	408	1349	1134	.973	595	2974	3528	110	99	3.34

AMERICAN LEAGUE 1933

Washington
W-99 L-53

Joe Cronin

POS	Player	AB	BA	HR	RBI	PO	A	E	DP	TC/G	FA	Pitcher	G	IP	W	L	SV	ERA
1B	J. Kuhel	602	.322	11	107	1498	61	7	126	10.2	.996	G. Crowder	52	299	24	15	4	3.97
2B	B. Myer	530	.302	4	61	356	417	17	92	6.1	.978	E. Whitehill	39	270	22	8	1	3.33
SS	J. Cronin	602	.309	5	118	297	528	34	95	5.7	.960	L. Stewart	34	231	15	6	0	3.82
3B	O. Bluege	501	.261	6	71	116	247	13	25	2.7	.965	M. Weaver	23	152	10	5	0	3.25
RF	G. Goslin	549	.297	10	64	261	17	10	7	2.3	.965	T. Thomas	35	135	7	7	3	4.80
CF	F. Schulte	550	.295	5	87	433	10	9	4	3.2	.980	J. Russell	50	124	12	6	13	2.69
LF	H. Manush	658	.336	5	95	325	10	6	1	2.3	.982	B. McAfee	27	53	3	2	5	6.62
C	L. Sewell	474	.264	2	61	516	61	6	12	4.1	.990							
OF	D. Harris	177	.260	5	38	79	1	3	0	1.8	.964							
UT	B. Boken	133	.278	3	26	72	91	7	13		.959							

AMERICAN LEAGUE 1933, *cont.*

	POS	Player	AB	BA	HR	RBI	PO	A	E	DP	TC/G	FA	Pitcher	G	IP	W	L	SV	ERA
New York W-91 L-59 Joe McCarthy	1B	L. Gehrig	593	.334	32	139	1290	64	9	102	9.0	.993	R. Ruffing	35	235	9	14	3	3.91
	2B	T. Lazzeri	523	.294	18	104	338	407	**25**	71	5.6	.968	L. Gomez	35	235	16	10	2	3.18
	SS	F. Crosetti	451	.253	9	60	245	384	43	58	5.1	.936	J. Allen	25	185	15	7	1	4.39
	3B	J. Sewell	524	.273	2	54	123	224	13	27	2.7	.964	R. Van Atta	26	157	12	4	1	4.18
	RF	B. Ruth	459	.301	34	103	215	9	7	4	1.8	.970	J. Brown	21	74	7	5	0	5.23
	CF	E. Combs	419	.298	5	60	227	3	6	1	2.3	.975	H. Pennock	23	65	7	4	4	5.54
	LF	B. Chapman	565	.312	9	98	288	**24**	8	4	2.2	.975	W. Moore	35	62	5	6	8	5.52
	C	B. Dickey	478	.318	14	97	721	82	6	15	**6.4**	.993							
	OF	D. Walker	328	.274	15	51	194	7	8	1	2.7	.962							
Philadelphia W-79 L-72 Connie Mack	1B	J. Foxx	573	**.356**	48	163	1402	**93**	15	98	10.1	.990	L. Grove	45	275	**24**	8	6	3.20
	2B	M. Bishop	391	.294	4	42	254	359	16	52	5.6	.975	S. Cain	38	218	13	12	1	4.25
	SS	D. Williams	408	.289	11	73	199	243	38	34	5.7	.921	R. Walberg	40	201	9	13	4	4.88
	3B	P. Higgins	567	.314	14	99	159	270	**24**	23	3.0	.947	R. Mahaffey	33	179	13	10	5	5.17
	RF	E. Coleman	388	.281	6	68	178	5	10	2	2.2	.948	G. Earnshaw	21	118	5	10	0	5.97
	CF	D. Cramer	661	.295	8	75	387	13	12	2	2.7	.971							
	LF	B. Johnson	535	.290	21	93	298	16	16	3	2.3	.952							
	C	M. Cochrane	429	.322	15	60	476	67	6	8	4.3	.989							
	S2	E. McNair	310	.261	7	48	169	216	17	39		.958							
	OF	L. Finney	240	.267	3	32	136	6	8	1	2.4	.947							
Cleveland W-75 L-76 Roger Peckinpaugh W-26 L-25 Bibb Falk W-1 L-0 Walter Johnson W-48 L-51	1B	H. Boss	438	.269	1	53	1062	71	7	89	10.4	.994	M. Harder	43	253	15	17	4	2.95
	2B	O. Hale	351	.276	10	64	213	259	23	45	6.8	.954	Hildebrand	36	220	16	11	0	3.76
	SS	Knickerbocker	279	.226	2	32	151	233	25	37	5.1	.939	W. Ferrell	28	201	11	12	0	4.21
	3B	W. Kamm	447	.282	1	47	153	221	6	16	2.9	**.984**	C. Brown	33	185	11	12	1	3.41
	RF	D. Porter	499	.267	0	41	236	9	1	3	2.0	**.996**	W. Hudlin	34	147	5	13	1	3.97
	CF	E. Averill	599	.301	11	92	390	8	12	3	2.3	.971	M. Pearson	19	135	10	5	0	**2.33**
	LF	J. Vosmik	438	.263	4	56	242	15	4	3	2.3	.985	S. Connally	41	103	5	3	1	4.89
	C	R. Spencer	227	.203	0	23	258	42	3	4	4.2	.990							
	2S	B. Cissell	409	.230	6	33	238	351	28	47		.955							
	UT	J. Burnett	261	.272	1	29	124	198	23	31		.933							
	C	F. Pytlak	248	.310	2	33	246	57	0	11	4.4	1.000							
	OF	M. Galatzer	160	.238	1	17	74	4	2	0	2.0	.975							
	PO	W. Ferrell	140	.271	7	26	43	49	0	5		1.000							
Detroit W-75 L-79 Bucky Harris W-73 L-79 Del Baker W-2 L-0	1B	H. Greenberg	449	.301	12	87	1133	63	14	111	10.3	.988	F. Marberry	37	238	16	11	2	3.29
	2B	C. Gehringer	628	.325	12	105	358	**542**	17	**111**	5.9	.981	T. Bridges	33	233	14	12	2	3.09
	SS	B. Rogell	587	.295	0	57	**326**	526	51	**116**	5.4	.944	V. Sorrell	36	233	11	15	1	3.79
	3B	M. Owen	550	.262	2	65	143	226	22	19	2.9	.944	C. Fischer	35	183	11	15	3	3.55
	RF	J. Stone	574	.280	11	80	280	11	9	1	2.1	.970	S. Rowe	19	123	7	4	0	3.58
	CF	P. Fox	535	.288	7	57	313	5	7	0	2.6	.978	C. Hogsett	45	116	6	10	9	4.50
	LF	G. Walker	483	.280	9	64	234	10	15	3	2.3	.942	V. Frasier	20	104	5	5	0	6.64
	C	R. Hayworth	425	.245	1	45	546	79	4	14	4.7	.994							
	OF	J. White	234	.252	2	34	122	4	3	1	2.4	.977							
	1B	H. Davis	173	.214	0	14	433	13	10	33	10.4	.978							
	OF	F. Doljack	147	.286	0	22	74	6	5	3	2.3	.941							
Chicago W-67 L-83 Lew Fonseca	1B	R. Kress	467	.248	10	78	1169	60	**28**	83	**11.3**	.978	T. Lyons	36	228	10	**21**	1	4.38
	2B	J. Hayes	535	.258	2	47	344	497	16	89	6.2	.981	S. Jones	27	177	10	12	0	3.36
	SS	L. Appling	612	.322	6	85	314	**534**	55	107	6.0	.939	M. Gaston	30	167	8	12	0	4.85
	3B	J. Dykes	554	.260	1	68	132	**296**	21	22	3.0	.953	E. Durham	24	139	10	6	0	4.48
	RF	E. Swanson	539	.306	1	63	281	7	8	0	2.1	.973	J. Heving	40	118	7	5	6	2.67
	CF	M. Haas	585	.287	1	51	347	9	6	2	2.5	.983	J. Miller	26	106	5	6	0	5.62
	LF	A. Simmons	605	.331	14	119	372	15	4	1	2.7	.990	P. Gregory	23	104	4	11	0	4.95
	C	F. Grube	256	.230	0	23	266	44	5	5	3.8	.984	R. Faber	36	86	3	4	5	3.44
	C	C. Berry	271	.255	2	28	260	39	4	1	3.7	.987							
Boston W-63 L-86 Marty McManus	1B	D. Alexander	313	.281	5	40	728	47	6	51	9.9	.992	G. Rhodes	34	232	12	15	0	4.03
	2B	J. Hodapp	413	.312	3	54	273	334	**25**	65	6.3	.960	B. Weiland	39	216	8	14	3	3.87
	SS	R. Warstler	322	.217	1	17	150	275	22	40	5.1	.951	L. Brown	33	163	8	11	1	4.02
	3B	M. McManus	366	.284	3	36	79	123	9	9	2.8	.957	H. Johnson	25	155	8	6	1	4.06
	RF	R. Johnson	483	.313	10	95	280	14	**25**	3	2.6	.922	I. Andrews	34	140	7	13	1	4.95
	CF	D. Cooke	454	.291	5	54	257	6	12	5	2.3	.956	J. Welch	47	129	4	9	3	4.60
	LF	S. Jolley	411	.282	9	65	178	12	9	3	2.0	.955	G. Pipgras	22	128	9	8	1	4.07
	C	R. Ferrell	421	.297	3	72	500	76*	6*	9	5.0	.990	B. Kline	46	127	7	8	4	4.54
	S3	B. Werber	425	.259	3	39	167	257	39	43		.916							
	OF	T. Oliver	244	.258	0	23	187	9	3	3	2.3	.985							
	1O	B. Seeds	230	.243	0	23	422	22	8	33		.982							
	3B	B. Walters	195	.256	4	28	42	84	8	11	3.1	.940							
	1B	J. Judge	108	.296	0	22	259	12	0	21	9.7	1.000							

AMERICAN LEAGUE 1933, *cont.*

St. Louis

W-55 L-96

Bill Killefer
W-34 L-57

Allen Sothoron
W-2 L-6

Rogers Hornsby
W-19 L-33

POS	Player	AB	BA	HR	RBI	PO	A	E	DP	TC/G	FA	Pitcher	G	IP	W	L	SV	ERA
1B	J. Burns	556	.288	7	71	1336	81	12	129	10.0	.992	B. Hadley	45	317	15	20	3	3.92
2B	O. Melillo	496	.292	3	79	362	451	7	110	6.3	.991	Blaeholder	38	256	15	19	0	4.72
SS	J. Levey	529	.195	2	36	298	428	42	73	5.6	.945	E. Wells	36	204	6	14	1	4.20
3B	A. Scharein	471	.204	0	26	113	208	17	31	3.6	.950	R. Stiles	31	115	3	7	1	5.01
RF	B. Campbell	567	.277	16	106	250	18	14	4	2.0	.950	S. Gray	38	112	7	4	4	4.10
CF	S. West	517	.300	11	48	329	14	4	3	2.7	.988	W. Hebert	33	88	4	6	0	5.30
LF	C. Reynolds	475	.286	8	71	269	8	10	3	2.3	.965	D. Coffman	21	81	3	7	1	5.89
C	M. Shea	279	.262	1	27	328	60	2	15*	4.6	.995*							
UT	T. Gullic	304	.243	5	35	229	74	5	8		.984							
32	L. Storti	210	.195	3	21	105	113	8	26		.965							
OF	D. Garms	189	.317	4	24	91	5	4	1	2.1	.960							

BATTING AND BASE RUNNING LEADERS

Batting Average		Slugging Average		Home Runs	
J. Foxx, PHI	.356	J. Foxx, PHI	.703	J. Foxx, PHI	48
H. Manush, WAS	.336	L. Gehrig, NY	.605	B. Ruth, NY	34
L. Gehrig, NY	.334	B. Ruth, NY	.582	L. Gehrig, NY	32
A. Simmons, CHI	.331	M. Cochrane, PHI	.515	B. Johnson, PHI	21
C. Gehringer, DET	.325	B. Johnson, PHI	.505	T. Lazzeri, NY	18

Total Bases		Runs Batted In		Stolen Bases	
J. Foxx, PHI	403	J. Foxx, PHI	163	B. Chapman, NY	27
L. Gehrig, NY	359	L. Gehrig, NY	139	G. Walker, DET	26
H. Manush, WAS	302	A. Simmons, CHI	119	E. Swanson, CHI	19
C. Gehringer, DET	294	J. Cronin, WAS	118	J. Kuhel, WAS	17
A. Simmons, CHI	291	J. Kuhel, WAS	107	B. Werber, BOS, NY	15
				T. Lazzeri, NY	15

Hits		Base on Balls		Home Run Percentage	
H. Manush, WAS	221	B. Ruth, NY	114	J. Foxx, PHI	8.4
J. Foxx, PHI	204	M. Bishop, PHI	106	B. Ruth, NY	7.4
C. Gehringer, DET	204	M. Cochrane, PHI	106	L. Gehrig, NY	5.4
A. Simmons, CHI	200	J. Foxx, PHI	96	B. Johnson, PHI	3.9

Runs Scored		Doubles		Triples	
L. Gehrig, NY	138	J. Cronin, WAS	45	H. Manush, WAS	17
J. Foxx, PHI	125	B. Johnson, PHI	44	E. Combs, NY	16
H. Manush, WAS	115	J. Burns, STL	43	E. Averill, CLE	16
B. Chapman, NY	112	B. Rogell, DET	42	B. Myer, WAS	15

PITCHING LEADERS

Winning Percentage		Earned Run Average		Wins	
L. Grove, PHI	.750	M. Pearson, CLE	2.33	L. Grove, PHI	24
E. Whitehill, WAS	.733	M. Harder, CLE	2.95	G. Crowder, WAS	24
L. Stewart, WAS	.714	T. Bridges, DET	3.09	E. Whitehill, WAS	22
J. Allen, NY	.682	L. Gomez, NY	3.18	L. Gomez, NY	16
G. Crowder, WAS	.615	L. Grove, PHI	3.20	Hildebrand, CLE	16
L. Gomez, NY	.615			F. Marberry, DET	16

Saves		Strikeouts		Complete Games	
J. Russell, WAS	13	L. Gomez, NY	163	L. Grove, PHI	21
C. Hogsett, DET	9	B. Hadley, STL	149	B. Hadley, STL	19
W. Moore, NY	8	R. Ruffing, NY	122	E. Whitehill, WAS	19
L. Grove, PHI	6	T. Bridges, DET	120	R. Ruffing, NY	18
J. Heving, CHI	6	J. Allen, NY	119	T. Bridges, DET	17
				G. Crowder, WAS	17

Fewest Hits/9 Innings		Shutouts		Fewest Walks/9 Innings	
M. Pearson, CLE	7.38	Hildebrand, CLE	6	C. Brown, CLE	1.65
T. Bridges, DET	7.42	L. Gomez, NY	4	F. Marberry, DET	2.30
B. Weiland, BOS	8.20	Blaeholder, STL	3	L. Stewart, WAS	2.34
J. Allen, NY	8.33			M. Harder, CLE	2.38

Most Strikeouts/9 Inn.		Innings		Games Pitched	
L. Gomez, NY	6.25	B. Hadley, STL	317	G. Crowder, WAS	52
J. Allen, NY	5.80	G. Crowder, WAS	299	J. Russell, WAS	50
R. Ruffing, NY	4.67	L. Grove, PHI	275	J. Welch, BOS	47
T. Bridges, DET	4.64	E. Whitehill, WAS	270	B. Kline, BOS	46

	W	L	PCT	GB	R	OR	2B	3B	HR	BA	SA	SB	E	DP	FA	CG	BB	SO	ShO	SV	ERA
Washington	99	53	.651		850	665	281	86	60	.287	.402	65	131	149	.979	68	452	447	5	26	3.82
New York	91	59	.607	7	927	768	241	75	144	.283	.440	74	165	122	.972	70	612	711	8	22	4.36
Philadelphia	79	72	.523	19.5	875	853	297	56	140	.285	.441	33	203	121	.966	69	644	423	6	14	4.81
Cleveland	75	76	.497	23.5	654	669	218	77	50	.261	.360	36	156	127	.974	74	465	437	12	7	3.71
Detroit	75	76	.487	23.5	722	733	283	78	57	.269	.380	68	178	167	.971	69	561	575	6	17	3.96
Chicago	67	83	.447	31	683	814	231	53	43	.272	.360	43	186	143	.970	53	519	423	8	13	4.45
Boston	63	86	.423	34.5	700	758	294	56	50	.271	.377	62	204	133	.966	60	591	473	4	14	4.35
St. Louis	55	96	.364	43.5	669	820	244	64	64	.253	.360	70	149	162	.976	55	531	426	7	10	4.82
					6080	6080	2089	545	608	.273	.390	451	1372	1124	.972	518	4375	3915	56	123	4.28

NATIONAL LEAGUE 1934

St. Louis

W-95 L-58

Frankie Frisch

POS	Player	AB	BA	HR	RBI	PO	A	E	DP	TC/G	FA	Pitcher	G	IP	W	L	SV	ERA
1B	R. Collins	600	.333	35	128	1289	110	13	115	9.2	.991	D. Dean	50	312	30	7	7	2.66
2B	F. Frisch	550	.305	3	75	294	351	15	74	5.7	.977	T. Carleton	40	241	16	11	2	4.26
SS	L. Durocher	500	.260	3	70	320	407	33	86	5.2	.957	P. Dean	39	233	19	11	3	3.43
3B	P. Martin	454	.289	5	49	85	195	19	7	2.8	.936	B. Hallahan	32	163	8	12	0	4.26
RF	J. Rothrock	647	.284	11	72	343	10	9	4	2.4	.975	B. Walker	24	153	12	4	0	3.12
CF	E. Orsatti	337	.300	0	31	207	5	3	0	2.4	.986							
LF	J. Medwick	620	.319	18	106	322	10	14	1	2.3	.960							
C	S. Davis	347	.300	9	65	459	42	6	7	5.4	.988							
UT	B. Whitehead	332	.277	1	24	158	220	16	38		.959							
C	B. DeLancey	253	.316	13	40	363	35	8	5	5.3	.980							
OF	C. Fullis	199	.261	0	26	124	2	4	1	2.3	.969							

NATIONAL LEAGUE 1934, cont.

	POS	Player	AB	BA	HR	RBI	PO	A	E	DP	TC/G	FA	Pitcher	G	IP	W	L	SV	ERA
New York W-93 L-60 Bill Terry	1B	B. Terry	602	.354	8	83	1592	105	10	131	11.2	.994	C. Hubbell	49	313	21	12	8	2.30
	2B	H. Critz	571	.242	6	40	353	510	19	90	6.4	.978	Schumacher	41	297	23	10	0	3.18
	SS	T. Jackson	523	.268	16	101	283	458	43	60	6.0	.945	Fitzsimmons	38	263	18	14	1	3.04
	3B	J. Vergez	320	.200	7	27	86	195	17	11	2.9	.943	R. Parmelee	22	153	10	6	0	3.42
	RF	M. Ott	582	.326	35	135	286	12	8	1	2.0	.974	J. Bowman	30	107	5	4	3	3.61
	CF	G. Watkins	296	.247	6	33	165	3	10	1	2.2	.944	A. Smith	30	67	3	5	5	4.32
	LF	J. Moore	580	.331	15	61	242	8	12	1	2.0	.954	H. Bell	22	54	4	6	6	3.67
	C	G. Mancuso	383	.245	7	46	448	67	12	7	4.3	.977	D. Luque	26	42	4	3	7	3.83
	UT	B. Ryan	385	.242	2	41	159	283	26	33		.944							
	OF	H. Leiber	187	.241	2	25	99	3	3	1	2.1	.971							
	OF	L. O'Doul	177	.316	9	46	60	1	2	0	1.7	.968							
Chicago W-86 L-65 Charlie Grimm	1B	C. Grimm	267	.296	5	47	683	43	4	39	9.9	.995	L. Warneke	43	291	22	10	3	3.21
	2B	B. Herman	456	.303	3	42	278	385	17	64	6.1	.975	B. Lee	35	214	13	14	1	3.40
	SS	B. Jurges	358	.246	8	33	205	334	19	63	5.7	.966	G. Bush	40	209	18	10	2	3.83
	3B	S. Hack	402	.289	1	21	102	198	16	10	2.9	.949	P. Malone	34	191	14	7	0	3.53
	RF	B. Herman	467	.304	14	84	192	7	6	2	1.8	.971	J. Weaver	27	159	11	9	0	3.91
	CF	K. Cuyler	559	.338	6	69	319	15	10	1	2.4	.971	B. Tinning	39	129	4	6	3	3.34
	LF	C. Klein	435	.301	20	80	222	6	9	2	2.2	.962	C. Root	34	118	4	7	0	4.28
	C	G. Hartnett	438	.299	22	90	605	86	3	11	5.4	.996							
	S3	W. English	421	.278	3	31	72	126	8	27		.961							
	OF	T. Stainback	359	.306	2	46	185	4	9	1	2.1	.955							
	2B	A. Galan	192	.260	5	22	90	106	8	16	4.7	.961							
Boston W-78 L-73 Bill McKechnie	1B	B. Jordan	489	.311	2	58	1165	66	14	85	10.6	.989	E. Brandt	40	255	16	14	5	3.53
	2B	M. McManus	435	.276	8	47	156	247	15	39	5.7	.964	Frankhouse	37	234	17	9	1	3.20
	SS	B. Urbanski	605	.293	7	53	298	457	31	84	5.4	.961	H. Betts	40	213	17	10	3	4.06
	3B	P. Whitney	563	.259	12	79	105	227	11	11	3.1	.968	F. Rhem	25	153	8	8	0	3.60
	RF	T. Thompson	343	.265	0	37	205	12	8	3	2.7	.964	B. Cantwell	27	143	5	11	5	4.33
	CF	W. Berger	615	.298	34	121	385	9	9	2	2.7	.978	B. Smith	39	122	6	9	5	4.66
	LF	H. Lee	521	.292	8	79	317	5	5	1	2.6	.985							
	C	A. Spohrer	265	.223	0	17	296	45	8	5	3.6	.977							
	O1	R. Moore	422	.284	7	64	496	23	12	24		.977							
	C	S. Hogan	279	.262	4	34	291	53	5	8	3.9	.986							
	2B	L. Mallon	166	.295	0	18	92	145	8	17	5.8	.967							
Pittsburgh W-74 L-76 George Gibson W-27 L-24 Pie Traynor W-47 L-52	1B	G. Suhr	573	.283	13	103	1326	75	9	108	9.3	.994	L. French	49	264	12	18	1	3.58
	2B	C. Lavagetto	304	.220	3	46	214	234	18	39	5.6	.961	B. Swift	37	213	11	13	0	3.98
	SS	A. Vaughan	558	.333	12	94	329	480	41	77	5.7	.952	R. Birkofer	41	204	11	12	1	4.10
	3B	P. Traynor	444	.309	1	61	116	176	14	16	2.8	.954	W. Hoyt	48	191	15	6	5	2.93
	RF	P. Waner	599	.362	14	90	323	15	5	1	2.4	.985	R. Lucas	29	173	10	9	0	4.38
	CF	L. Waner	611	.283	1	48	405	8	9	1	3.0	.979	H. Meine	26	106	7	6	0	4.32
	LF	F. Lindstrom	383	.290	4	49	181	8	2	1	2.1	.990							
	C	E. Grace	289	.270	4	24	304	26	6	4	4.0	.982							
	23	T. Thevenow	446	.271	0	54	214	280	19	37		.963							
	OF	W. Jensen	283	.290	0	27	143	1	1	0	2.2	.993							
	C	T. Padden	237	.321	0	22	297	20	7	3	4.3	.978							
Brooklyn W-71 L-81 Casey Stengel	1B	S. Leslie	546	.332	9	102	1262	93	9	104	9.9	.993	V. Mungo	45	315	18	16	3	3.37
	2B	Cuccinello	528	.261	14	94	246	347	16	54	6.0	.974	B. Benge	36	227	14	12	0	4.32
	SS	L. Frey	490	.284	8	57	232	375	35	81	5.9	.945	D. Leonard	44	184	14	11	5	3.28
	3B	J. Stripp	384	.315	1	40	93	147	15	20	2.7	.941	J. Babich	25	135	7	11	1	4.20
	RF	B. Boyle	472	.305	7	48	275	20	9	1	2.5	.970	T. Zachary	22	102	5	6	2	4.43
	CF	L. Koenecke	460	.320	14	73	310	6	2	0	2.6	.994	L. Munns	33	99	3	7	0	4.71
	LF	D. Taylor	405	.299	7	57	188	8	5	1	1.9	.975							
	C	A. Lopez	439	.273	7	54	542	62	11	4	4.5	.982							
	S2	J. Jordan	369	.266	0	43	157	246	19	40		.955							
	OF	J. Frederick	307	.296	4	35	121	11	6	3	1.8	.957							
	OF	H. Wilson	172	.262	6	27	71	3	2	3*	1.8	.974							
Philadelphia W-56 L-93 Jimmie Wilson	1B	D. Camilli	378	.265	12	68	882	55	14*	102	9.3	.985	C. Davis	51	274	19	17	5	2.95
	2B	L. Chiozza	484	.304	0	44	215	257	31	37	5.9	.938	P. Collins	45	254	13	18	1	4.18
	SS	D. Bartell	604	.310	0	37	350	483	40	93	6.0	.954	S. Hansen	50	151	6	12	3	5.42
	3B	B. Walters	300	.260	4	38	74	136	11	12	2.8	.950	S. Johnson	42	134	5	9	3	3.50
	RF	J. Moore	458	.343	11	93	244	18	5	2	2.3	.981	C. Moore	35	127	4	9	0	6.47
	CF	K. Davis	393	.293	3	48	304	13	3	3	3.2*	.991	E. Moore	20	122	5	7	1	4.05
	LF	E. Allen	581	.330	10	85	337	19	8	3	2.5	.978							
	C	A. Todd	302	.318	4	41	291	32	8	7	4.0	.976							
	C	J. Wilson	277	.292	3	35	265	42	4	7	4.0	.987							
	2B	I. Jeffries	175	.246	4	19	122	157	11	42	5.6	.962							
	32	M. Haslin	166	.265	1	11	61	89	8	9		.949							
	1B	D. Hurst	130	.262	2	21	317	17	2	30	8.4	.994							

NATIONAL LEAGUE 1934, *cont.*

	POS	Player	AB	BA	HR	RBI	PO	A	E	DP	TC/G	FA	Pitcher	G	IP	W	L	SV	ERA
Cincinnati	1B	J. Bottomley	556	.284	11	78	1303	77	15	106	10.0	.989	P. Derringer	47	261	15	21	4	3.59
	2B	T. Piet	421	.259	1	38	126	149	15	27	5.9	.948	B. Frey	39	245	11	16	2	3.52
W-52 L-99	SS	G. Slade	555	.285	4	52	200	315	26	60	5.6	.952	S. Johnson	46	216	7	22	3	5.22
	3B	M. Koenig	633	.272	1	67	57	130	14	1	3.1	.930	T. Freitas	30	153	6	12	1	4.01
Bob O'Farrell	RF	A. Comorosky	446	.258	0	40	285	5	9	1	2.5	.970	A. Stout	41	141	6	8	1	4.86
W-30 L-60	CF	C. Hafey	535	.293	18	67	380	7	13	1	2.9	.968							
	LF	H. Pool	358	.327	2	50	196	8	10	1	2.3	.953							
Burt Shotton	C	E. Lombardi	417	.305	9	62	383	61	5	8	4.0	.989							
W-1 L-0	32	S. Adams	278	.252	0	14	92	156	8	21		.969							
	OF	Schulmerich	209	.263	5	19	121	4	3	1	2.2	.976							
Chuck Dressen																			
W-21 L-39																			

BATTING AND BASE RUNNING LEADERS

Batting Average
P. Waner, PIT	.362
B. Terry, NY	.354
K. Cuyler, CHI	.338
R. Collins, STL	.333
A. Vaughan, PIT	.333

Slugging Average
R. Collins, STL	.615
M. Ott, NY	.591
W. Berger, BOS	.546
P. Waner, PIT	.539
J. Medwick, STL	.529

Home Runs
M. Ott, NY	35
R. Collins, STL	35
W. Berger, BOS	34
G. Hartnett, CHI	22
C. Klein, CHI	20

Total Bases
R. Collins, STL	369
M. Ott, NY	344
W. Berger, BOS	336
J. Medwick, STL	328
P. Waner, PIT	323

Runs Batted In
M. Ott, NY	135
R. Collins, STL	128
W. Berger, BOS	121
J. Medwick, STL	106
G. Suhr, PIT	103

Stolen Bases
P. Martin, STL	23
K. Cuyler, CHI	15
D. Bartell, PHI	13
D. Taylor, BKN	12

Hits
P. Waner, PIT	217
B. Terry, NY	213
R. Collins, STL	200
J. Medwick, STL	198

Base on Balls
A. Vaughan, PIT	94
M. Ott, NY	85
L. Koenecke, BKN	70
S. Leslie, BKN	69

Home Run Percentage
M. Ott, NY	6.0
R. Collins, STL	5.8
W. Berger, BOS	5.5
G. Hartnett, CHI	5.0

Runs Scored
P. Waner, PIT	122
M. Ott, NY	119
R. Collins, STL	116
A. Vaughan, PIT	115

Doubles
K. Cuyler, CHI	42
E. Allen, PHI	42
A. Vaughan, PIT	41
R. Collins, STL	40

Triples
J. Medwick, STL	18
P. Waner, PIT	16
G. Suhr, PIT	13
R. Collins, STL	12

PITCHING LEADERS

Winning Percentage
D. Dean, STL	.811
W. Hoyt, PIT	.714
Schumacher, NY	.697
L. Warneke, CHI	.688
Frankhouse, BOS	.654

Earned Run Average
C. Hubbell, NY	2.30
D. Dean, STL	2.66
C. Davis, PHI	2.95
Fitzsimmons, NY	3.04
B. Walker, STL	3.12

Wins
D. Dean, STL	30
Schumacher, NY	23
L. Warneke, CHI	22
C. Hubbell, NY	21
P. Dean, STL	19
C. Davis, PHI	19

Saves
C. Hubbell, NY	8
D. Dean, STL	7
D. Luque, NY	7
H. Bell, NY	6

Strikeouts
D. Dean, STL	195
V. Mungo, BKN	184
P. Dean, STL	150
L. Warneke, CHI	143
P. Derringer, CIN	122

Complete Games
D. Dean, STL	24
C. Hubbell, NY	23
L. Warneke, CHI	23
V. Mungo, BKN	22
E. Brandt, BOS	20

Fewest Hits/9 Innings
C. Hubbell, NY	8.22
D. Dean, STL	8.32
L. Warneke, CHI	8.43
V. Mungo, BKN	8.56

Shutouts
D. Dean, STL	7
C. Hubbell, NY	5
C. Hubbell, NY	5
B. Lee, CHI	4

Fewest Walks/9 Innings
C. Hubbell, NY	1.06
B. Frey, CIN	1.54
D. Leonard, BKN	1.67
Fitzsimmons, NY	1.74

Most Strikeouts/9 Inn.
P. Dean, STL	5.79
D. Dean, STL	5.63
V. Mungo, BKN	5.25
B. Walker, STL	4.47

Innings
V. Mungo, BKN	315
C. Hubbell, NY	313
D. Dean, STL	312
Schumacher, NY	297

Games Pitched
C. Davis, PHI	51
D. Dean, STL	50
S. Hansen, PHI	50
C. Hubbell, NY	49

	W	L	PCT	GB	R	OR	2B	3B	HR	BA	SA	SB	E	DP	FA	CG	BB	SO	ShO	SV	ERA
St. Louis	95	58	.621		**799**	656	**294**	75	104	**.288**	**.425**	**69**	166	**141**	.972	**78**	411	**689**	15	16	3.69
New York	93	60	.608	2	760	583	240	41	**126**	.275	.405	19	179	**141**	.972	66	351	499	12	**30**	**3.19**
Chicago	86	65	.570	8	705	639	263	44	101	.279	.402	59	**137**	135	**.977**	73	417	633	11	9	3.76
Boston	78	73	.517	16	683	714	233	44	83	.272	.378	30	169	120	.972	62	405	462	11	20	4.11
Pittsburgh	74	76	.493	19.5	735	713	281	**77**	52	.287	.398	44	145	118	.975	61	354	487	8	8	4.20
Brooklyn	71	81	.467	23.5	748	795	284	52	79	.281	.396	55	180	**141**	.970	66	476	520	6	12	4.48
Philadelphia	56	93	.376	37	675	794	286	35	56	.284	.384	52	197	140	.966	52	437	416	8	15	4.76
Cincinnati	52	99	.344	42	590	801	227	65	55	.266	.364	34	181	136	.970	51	389	438	3	19	4.37
					5695	5695	2108	433	656	.279	.394	362	1354	1072	.972	509	3240	4144	74	129	4.06

AMERICAN LEAGUE 1934

	POS	Player	AB	BA	HR	RBI	PO	A	E	DP	TC/G	FA	Pitcher	G	IP	W	L	SV	ERA
Detroit	1B	H. Greenberg	593	.339	26	139	1454	84	16	124	10.2	.990	T. Bridges	36	275	22	11	1	3.67
	2B	C. Gehringer	601	.356	11	127	355	**516**	17	100	5.8	.981	S. Rowe	45	266	24	8	1	3.45
W-101 L-53	SS	B. Rogell	592	.296	3	100	259	**518**	31	99	5.2	.962	E. Auker	43	205	15	7	1	3.42
	3B	M. Owen	565	.317	8	96	202	253	21	33	3.1	.956	F. Marberry	38	156	15	5	3	4.57
Mickey Cochrane	RF	P. Fox	516	.285	2	45	245	13	7	**4**	2.2	.974	V. Sorrell	28	130	6	9	2	4.79
	CF	J. White	384	.313	0	44	225	9	10	2	2.4	.959	C. Fischer	20	95	6	4	1	4.37
	LF	G. Goslin	614	.305	13	100	290	15	15	2	2.1	.953							
	C	M. Cochrane	437	.320	2	76	517	69	7	7	4.8	.988							
	OF	G. Walker	347	.300	6	39	191	5	11	2	2.6	.947							
	C	R. Hayworth	167	.293	0	27	226	23	4	3	4.7	.984							
	P	S. Rowe	109	.303	2	22	9	46	0	3	1.2	**1.000**							

AMERICAN LEAGUE 1934, cont.

	POS	Player	AB	BA	HR	RBI	PO	A	E	DP	TC/G	FA	Pitcher	G	IP	W	L	SV	ERA
New York	1B	L. Gehrig	579	**.363**	49	165	1284	80	8	126	9.0	.994	L. Gomez	38	**282**	**26**	5	1	**2.33**
	2B	T. Lazzeri	438	.267	14	67	218	265	12	52	5.4	.976	R. Ruffing	36	256	19	11	0	3.93
W-94 L-60	SS	F. Crosetti	554	.265	11	67	242	356	35	77	5.3	.945	J. Murphy	40	208	14	10	4	3.12
	3B	Saltzgaver	350	.271	6	36	71	130	10	10	2.5	.953	J. Broaca	26	177	12	9	0	4.16
Joe McCarthy	RF	B. Ruth	365	.288	22	84	197	3	8	0	1.9	.962	J. DeShong	31	134	6	7	3	4.11
	CF	B. Chapman	588	.308	5	86	368	12	13	2	2.6	.967							
	LF	S. Byrd	191	.246	3	23	156	2	2	1	1.5	**.988**							
	C	B. Dickey	395	.322	12	72	527	49	8	13	**5.6**	.986							
	S3	R. Rolfe	279	.287	0	18	121	159	19	31		.936							
	OF	M. Hoag	251	.267	3	34	142	7	4	2	1.8	.974							
	OF	E. Combs	251	.319	2	25	145	1	1	0	2.4	.993							
	2B	D. Heffner	241	.261	0	25	158	179	10	46	5.1	.971							
	C	A. Jorgens	183	.208	0	20	288	20	5	1	5.6	.984							
	OF	G. Selkirk	176	.313	5	38	90	3	1	1	2.0	.989							
Cleveland	1B	H. Trosky	625	.330	35	142	**1487**	86	**22**	145	10.4	.986	M. Harder	44	255	20	12	4	2.61
	2B	O. Hale	563	.302	13	101	408	480	41	107	6.8	.956	M. Pearson	39	255	18	13	2	4.52
W-85 L-69	SS	Knickerbocker	593	.317	4	67	262	451	28	106	5.1	.962	Hildebrand	33	198	11	9	1	4.50
	3B	W. Kamm	386	.269	0	42	109	248	8	24	3.1	**.978**	W. Hudlin	36	195	15	10	4	4.75
Walter Johnson	RF	S. Rice	335	.293	1	33	129	2	5	0	1.7	.963	L. Brown	38	117	5	10	6	3.85
	CF	E. Averill	598	.313	31	113	**410**	12	13	3	**2.8**	.970							
	LF	J. Vosmik	405	.341	6	78	199	7	5	2	2.0	.976							
	C	F. Pytlak	289	.260	0	35	325	38	4	4	4.2	.989							
	3B	J. Burnett	208	.293	3	30	43	59	2	6	2.5	.981							
	OF	M. Galatzer	196	.270	0	15	91	7	2	0	2.0	.980							
	OF	B. Seeds	186	.247	0	18	83	2	2	0	1.8	.977							
Boston	1B	E. Morgan	528	.267	3	79	1283	56	16	111	9.9	.988	G. Rhodes	44	219	12	12	2	4.56
	2B	B. Cissell	416	.267	4	44	280	281	24	62	6.1	.959	J. Welch	41	206	13	15	0	4.49
W-76 L-76	SS	L. Lary	419	.241	2	54	260	396	24	66	5.3	.965*	Ostermueller	33	199	10	13	3	3.49
	3B	B. Werber	623	.321	11	67	136	**323**	29	25	3.8	.941	W. Ferrell	26	181	14	5	1	3.63
Bucky Harris	RF	M. Solters	365	.299	7	58	197	11	15	1	2.5	.933	H. Johnson	31	124	6	8	1	5.36
	CF	C. Reynolds	413	.303	4	86	244	6	6	3	2.6	.977	L. Grove	22	109	8	8	0	6.50
	LF	R. Johnson	569	.320	7	119	260	12	15	1	2.1	.948	R. Walberg	30	105	6	7	1	4.04
	C	R. Ferrell	437	.297	1	48	**531**	72	6	7	4.8	**.990**							
	OF	D. Porter	265	.302	0	56	109	1	7	1	1.6	.940							
	2B	M. Bishop	253	.261	1	22	147	155	3	37	5.4	.990							
	OF	D. Cooke	168	.244	1	26	79	1	2	0	1.9	.976							
Philadelphia	1B	J. Foxx	539	.334	44	130	1378	85	10	133	**10.5**	.993	J. Marcum	37	232	14	11	0	4.50
	2B	R. Warstler	419	.236	1	36	228	392	20	87	6.0	.969	S. Cain	36	231	9	17	0	4.41
W-68 L-82	SS	E. McNair	599	.280	17	82	305	489	41	109	5.5	.951	B. Dietrich	39	208	11	12	3	4.68
	3B	P. Higgins	543	.330	16	90	147	247	37	34	3.0	.914	Cascarella	42	194	12	15	1	4.68
Connie Mack	RF	E. Coleman	329	.280	14	60	140	8	3	2	1.8	.980	A. Benton	32	155	7	9	1	4.88
	CF	D. Cramer	**649**	.311	6	46	385	12	6	0	2.7	.985	R. Mahaffey	37	129	6	7	2	5.37
	LF	B. Johnson	547	.307	34	92	304	**17**	11	3	2.4	.967							
	C	C. Berry	269	.268	0	34	339	48	5	9	4.0	.987							
	OF	L. Finney	272	.279	1	28	112	3	7	1	2.3	.943							
	C	F. Hayes	248	.226	6	30	279	36	15	4	3.7	.955							
	2B	D. Williams	205	.273	2	17	110	171	13	31	5.5	.956							
	OF	B. Miller	177	.243	1	22	72	2	0	1	1.6	1.000							
St. Louis	1B	J. Burns	612	.257	13	73	1365	81	12	132	9.5	.992	B. Newsom	47	262	16	**20**	5	4.01
	2B	O. Melillo	552	.241	2	55	**412**	462	17	**110**	6.3	**.981**	Blaeholder	39	234	14	18	3	4.22
W-67 L-85	SS	A. Strange	430	.233	1	45	260	392	31	84	5.5	.955	B. Hadley	39	213	10	16	1	4.35
	3B	H. Clift	572	.260	14	56	150	245	30	28	3.0	.929	D. Coffman	40	173	9	10	3	4.53
Rogers Hornsby	RF	B. Campbell	481	.279	9	74	230	14	**17**	3	2.1	.935	I. Andrews	43	139	4	11	3	4.66
	CF	S. West	482	.326	9	55	303	14	9	3	2.7	.972	J. Knott	45	138	10	3	4	4.96
	LF	R. Pepper	564	.298	7	101	299	15	12	**4**	2.4	.963							
	C	R. Hemsley	431	.309	2	52	487	**92**	16	**15**	5.2	.973							
	UT	O. Bejma	262	.271	2	29	129	145	11	27		.961							
	OF	D. Garms	232	.293	0	31	111	2	7	0	2.1	.942							
	C	F. Grube	170	.288	0	11	186	21	8	4	3.9	.963							
Washington	1B	J. Kuhel	263	.289	3	25	618	23	4	62	10.2	.994	E. Whitehill	32	235	14	11	0	4.52
	2B	B. Myer	524	.305	3	57	367	420	20	101	6.0	.975	M. Weaver	31	205	11	15	0	4.79
W-66 L-86	SS	J. Cronin	504	.284	7	101	246	486	38	86	**6.1**	.951	B. Burke	37	168	8	8	0	3.21
	3B	C. Travis	392	.319	1	53	88	210	20	23	3.2	.937	J. Russell	**54**	158	5	10	7	4.17
Joe Cronin	RF	J. Stone	419	.315	7	67	245	13	9	3	2.4	.966	L. Stewart	24	152	7	11	0	4.03
	CF	F. Schulte	524	.298	3	73	351	5	5	0	2.7	.986	T. Thomas	33	133	8	9	1	5.47
	LF	H. Manush	556	.349	11	89	293	5	6	2	2.3	.980	A. McColl	42	112	3	4	1	3.86
	C	E. Phillips	169	.195	2	16	162	21	3	4	3.5	.984	G. Crowder	29	101	4	10	3	6.79
	UT	O. Bluege	285	.246	0	11	114	202	10	28		.969							
	OF	D. Harris	235	.251	2	37	103	7	3	1	1.8	.973							
	1B	P. Susko	224	.286	2	25	608	40	8	58	11.3	.988							
	C	L. Sewell	207	.237	2	21	143	23	1	6	3.3	.994							
	UT	R. Kress	171	.228	4	24	327	32	3	21		.994							

AMERICAN LEAGUE 1934, *cont.*

	POS	Player	AB	BA	HR	RBI	PO	A	E	DP	TC/G	FA	Pitcher	G	IP	W	L	SV	ERA
Chicago	1B	Z. Bonura	510	.302	27	110	1239	77	5	94	10.4	.996	G. Earnshaw	33	227	14	11	0	4.52
	2B	J. Hayes	226	.257	1	31	147	188	7	35	5.6	.980	T. Lyons	30	205	11	13	1	4.87
W-53 L-99	SS	L. Appling	452	.303	2	61	243	341	34	55	5.6	.945	M. Gaston	29	194	6	19	0	5.85
	3B	J. Dykes	456	.268	7	82	74	160	14	9	3.4	.944	S. Jones	27	183	8	12	0	5.11
Lew Fonseca	RF	E. Swanson	426	.298	0	34	193	4	4	1	1.9	.980	L. Tietje	34	176	5	14	0	4.81
W-4 L-11	CF	M. Haas	351	.268	2	22	204	5	2	1	2.4	.991	P. Gallivan	35	127	4	7	1	5.61
	LF	A. Simmons	558	.344	18	104	286	14	4	3	2.2	.987	J. Heving	33	88	1	7	4	7.26
Jimmy Dykes	C	E. Madjeski	281	.221	5	32	348	49	11	11	5.2	.973	W. Wyatt	23	68	4	11	2	7.18
W-49 L-88	2B	B. Boken	297	.236	3	40	121	165	22	28	5.4	.929							
	OF	J. Conlan	225	.249	0	16	122	5	6	1	2.5	.955							
	3B	M. Hopkins	210	.214	2	28	63	136	9	4	3.3	.957							
	C	M. Shea	176	.159	0	5	240	35	8	4	4.7	.972							
	OF	F. Uhalt	165	.242	0	16	85	2	6	1	2.3	.935							

BATTING AND BASE RUNNING LEADERS

Batting Average
L. Gehrig, NY	.363
C. Gehringer, DET	.356
H. Manush, WAS	.349
A. Simmons, CHI	.344
J. Vosmik, CLE	.341

Slugging Average
L. Gehrig, NY	.706
J. Foxx, PHI	.653
H. Greenberg, DET	.600
H. Trosky, CLE	.598
E. Averill, CLE	.569

Home Runs
L. Gehrig, NY	49
J. Foxx, PHI	44
H. Trosky, CLE	35
B. Johnson, PHI	34
E. Averill, CLE	31

Winning Percentage
L. Gomez, NY	.839
S. Rowe, DET	.750
F. Marberry, DET	.750
E. Auker, DET	.682
T. Bridges, DET	.667

Earned Run Average
L. Gomez, NY	2.33
M. Harder, CLE	2.61
J. Murphy, NY	3.12
E. Auker, DET	3.42
S. Rowe, DET	3.45

Wins
L. Gomez, NY	26
S. Rowe, DET	24
T. Bridges, DET	22
M. Harder, CLE	20
R. Ruffing, NY	19

Total Bases
L. Gehrig, NY	409
H. Trosky, CLE	374
H. Greenberg, DET	356
J. Foxx, PHI	352
E. Averill, CLE	340

Runs Batted In
L. Gehrig, NY	165
H. Trosky, CLE	142
H. Greenberg, DET	139
J. Foxx, PHI	130
C. Gehringer, DET	127

Stolen Bases
B. Werber, BOS	40
J. White, DET	28
B. Chapman, NY	26
P. Fox, DET	25
G. Walker, DET	20

Saves
J. Russell, WAS	7
L. Brown, CLE	6
B. Newsom, STL	5

Strikeouts
L. Gomez, NY	158
T. Bridges, DET	151
R. Ruffing, NY	149
S. Rowe, DET	149
M. Pearson, CLE	140

Complete Games
L. Gomez, NY	25
T. Bridges, DET	23
T. Lyons, CHI	21
S. Rowe, DET	20
R. Ruffing, NY	19
M. Pearson, CLE	19

Hits
C. Gehringer, DET	214
L. Gehrig, NY	210
H. Trosky, CLE	206
D. Cramer, PHI	202

Base on Balls
J. Foxx, PHI	111
L. Gehrig, NY	109
B. Ruth, NY	103
B. Myer, WAS	102

Home Run Percentage
L. Gehrig, NY	8.5
J. Foxx, PHI	8.2
B. Johnson, PHI	6.2
B. Ruth, NY	6.0

Fewest Hits/9 Innings
L. Gomez, NY	7.13
R. Ruffing, NY	8.15
T. Bridges, DET	8.15
J. Murphy, NY	8.36

Shutouts
M. Harder, CLE	6
L. Gomez, NY	6
R. Ruffing, NY	5
B. Dietrich, PHI	4

Fewest Walks/9 Innings
W. Ferrell, BOS	2.44
E. Auker, DET	2.46
Blaeholder, STL	2.61
S. Rowe, DET	2.74

Runs Scored
C. Gehringer, DET	134
B. Werber, BOS	129
L. Gehrig, NY	128
E. Averill, CLE	128

Doubles
H. Greenberg, DET	63
C. Gehringer, DET	50
E. Averill, CLE	48
H. Trosky, CLE	45

Triples
B. Chapman, NY	13
H. Manush, WAS	11

Most Strikeouts/9 Inn.
R. Ruffing, NY	5.23
L. Gomez, NY	5.05
S. Rowe, DET	5.04
M. Pearson, CLE	4.95

Innings
L. Gomez, NY	282
T. Bridges, DET	275
S. Rowe, DET	266
B. Newsom, STL	262

Games Pitched
J. Russell, WAS	54
B. Newsom, STL	47
S. Rowe, DET	45
J. Knott, STL	45

	W	L	PCT	GB	R	OR	2B	3B	HR	BA	SA	SB	E	DP	FA	CG	BB	SO	ShO	SV	ERA
Detroit	101	53	.656		**958**	708	**349**	53	74	**.300**	.424	**124**	159	150	.974	74	**488**	640	10	14	4.06
New York	94	60	.610	7	842	**669**	226	61	135	.278	.419	71	**157**	151	.973	**83**	542	**656**	**13**	10	**3.76**
Cleveland	85	69	.552	16	814	763	340	46	100	.287	.423	52	172	164	.972	72	582	554	8	19	4.28
Boston	76	76	.500	24	820	775	287	**70**	51	.274	.383	116	188	141	.969	68	543	538	8	8	4.32
Philadelphia	68	82	.453	31	764	838	236	50	**144**	.280	**.425**	57	196	166	.967	68	693	480	8	8	5.01
St. Louis	67	85	.441	33	674	800	252	59	62	.268	.373	42	187	160	.969	50	632	499	6	**20**	4.49
Washington	66	86	.434	34	729	806	278	**70**	51	.278	.382	49	162	**167**	**.974**	61	503	412	3	12	4.68
Chicago	53	99	.349	47	704	946	237	40	71	.263	.363	36	207	126	.966	72	628	506	4	8	5.41
					6305	6305	2205	449	688	.279	.399	547	1428	1225	.970	548	4611	4285	60	100	4.50

NATIONAL LEAGUE 1935

	POS	Player	AB	BA	HR	RBI	PO	A	E	DP	TC/G	FA	Pitcher	G	IP	W	L	SV	ERA
Chicago	1B	Cavarretta	589	.275	8	82	1347	98	**20**	129	10.1	.986	L. Warneke	42	262	20	13	4	3.06
	2B	B. Herman	666	.341	7	83	416	**520**	35	109	6.3	.964	B. Lee	39	252	20	6	1	2.96
W-100 L-54	SS	B. Jurges	519	.241	1	59	348	484	31	99	5.9	.964	L. French	42	246	17	10	2	2.96
	3B	S. Hack	427	.311	4	64	87	237	20	21	3.1	.942	C. Root	38	201	15	8	2	3.08
Charlie Grimm	RF	C. Klein	434	.293	21	73	215	11	10	7	2.1	.958	T. Carleton	31	171	11	8	1	3.89
	CF	F. Demaree	385	.325	2	66	204	13	6	3	2.3	.973	R. Henshaw	31	143	13	5	1	3.28
	LF	A. Galan	646	.314	12	79	351	12	8	4	2.4	.978							
	C	G. Hartnett	413	.344	13	91	477	77	9	11	5.1	**.984**							
	O3	F. Lindstrom	342	.275	3	62	167	40	7	7		.967							
	C	K. O'Dea	202	.257	6	38	213	27	9	3	4.0	.964							
	OF	K. Cuyler	157	.268	4	18	98	5	2	1	2.5	.981							

NATIONAL LEAGUE 1935, *cont.*

St. Louis
W-96 L-58
Frankie Frisch

POS	Player	AB	BA	HR	RBI	PO	A	E	DP	TC/G	FA	Pitcher	G	IP	W	L	SV	ERA
1B	R. Collins	578	.313	23	122	1269	95	18	107	9.2	.987	D. Dean	50	325	28	12	5	3.04
2B	F. Frisch	354	.294	1	55	193	252	8	48	5.1	.982	P. Dean	46	270	19	12	5	3.37
SS	L. Durocher	513	.265	8	78	313	420	28	81	5.4	.963	B. Walker	37	193	13	8	1	3.82
3B	P. Martin	539	.299	9	54	113	171	30	17	2.8	.904	B. Hallahan	40	181	15	8	1	3.42
RF	J. Rothrock	502	.273	3	56	283	5	6	1	2.3	.980	E. Heusser	33	123	5	5	2	2.92
CF	T. Moore	456	.287	6	53	354	11	6	3	3.2	.984	J. Haines	30	115	6	5	2	3.59
LF	J. Medwick	634	.353	23	126	352	8	13	0	2.4	.965	P. Collins	26	83	7	6	2	4.57
C	B. DeLancey	301	.279	6	41	372	29	12	6	5.0	.971							
2B	B. Whitehead	338	.263	0	33	172	218	8	43	5.0	.980							
C	S. Davis	315	.317	1	60	335	34	3	2	4.6	.992							
OF	E. Orsatti	221	.240	1	24	115	3	3	2	2.0	.975							
3S	C. Gelbert	168	.292	2	21	62	95	5	16		.969							
P	D. Dean	128	.234	2	21	13	42	2	0	1.1	.965							

New York
W-91 L-62
Bill Terry

POS	Player	AB	BA	HR	RBI	PO	A	E	DP	TC/G	FA	Pitcher	G	IP	W	L	SV	ERA
1B	B. Terry	596	.341	6	64	1379	99	6	105	10.4	.996	C. Hubbell	42	303	23	12	0	3.27
2B	M. Koenig	396	.283	3	37	123	206	11	20	5.3	.968	Schumacher	33	262	19	9	0	2.89
SS	D. Bartell	539	.262	14	53	339	424	37	71	5.8	.954	R. Parmelee	34	226	14	10	0	4.22
3B	T. Jackson	511	.301	9	80	139	220	20	13	3.0	.947	S. Castleman	29	174	15	6	0	4.09
RF	M. Ott	593	.322	31	114	285	17	3	7	2.2	.990	A. Smith	40	124	10	8	5	3.41
CF	H. Leiber	613	.331	22	107	357	5	13	2	2.4	.965	Fitzsimmons	18	94	4	8	0	4.02
LF	J. Moore	681	.295	15	71	342	11	10	2	2.3	.972	A. Stout	40	88	1	4	5	4.91
C	G. Mancuso	447	.298	5	56	484	71	16	4	4.5	.972							
2B	H. Critz	219	.187	2	14	140	175	11	31	5.5	.966							
2B	Cuccinello	165	.248	4	20	113	140	13	26	5.5	.951							
C	H. Danning	152	.243	2	20	153	22	4	6	4.1	.978							
P	Schumacher	107	.196	2	21	14	89	0	4	3.1	1.000							

Pittsburgh
W-86 L-67
Pie Traynor

POS	Player	AB	BA	HR	RBI	PO	A	E	DP	TC/G	FA	Pitcher	G	IP	W	L	SV	ERA
1B	G. Suhr	529	.272	10	81	1315	73	15	83	9.4	.989	C. Blanton	35	254	18	13	1	2.58
2B	P. Young	494	.265	7	82	282	315	30	47	5.9	.952	G. Bush	41	204	11	11	2	4.32
SS	A. Vaughan	499	.385	19	99	249	422	35	55	5.2	.950	B. Swift	39	204	15	8	1	2.70
3B	T. Thevenow	408	.238	0	47	94	161	13	11	3.3	.951	J. Weaver	33	176	14	8	0	3.42
RF	P. Waner	549	.321	11	78	283	13	5	2	2.2	.983	W. Hoyt	39	164	7	11	6	3.40
CF	L. Waner	537	.309	0	46	350	5	4	1	3.0	.989	R. Birkofer	37	150	9	7	1	4.07
LF	W. Jensen	627	.324	8	62	290	6	7	1	2.1	.977	R. Lucas	20	126	8	6	0	3.44
C	T. Padden	302	.272	1	30	425	64	17	2	5.4	.966							
2B	C. Lavagetto	231	.290	0	19	92	120	11	10	5.3	.951							
C	E. Grace	224	.263	3	29	269	35	3	9	4.4	.990							
3B	P. Traynor	204	.279	1	36	59	84	18	2	3.3	.888							
OF	B. Hafey	184	.228	6	16	125	5	4	3	2.9	.970							

Brooklyn
W-70 L-83
Casey Stengel

POS	Player	AB	BA	HR	RBI	PO	A	E	DP	TC/G	FA	Pitcher	G	IP	W	L	SV	ERA
1B	S. Leslie	520	.308	5	93	1233	81	14	106	9.6	.989	V. Mungo	37	214	16	10	2	3.65
2B	Cuccinello	360	.292	8	53	158	186	8	48	5.5	.977	W. Clark	33	207	13	8	0	3.30
SS	L. Frey	515	.262	11	77	264	388	44	72	5.5	.937	G. Earnshaw	25	166	8	12	0	4.12
3B	J. Stripp	373	.306	3	43	63	162	9	17	2.7	.962	T. Zachary	25	158	7	12	4	3.59
RF	B. Boyle	475	.272	4	44	244	18	10	5	2.2	.963	J. Babich	37	143	7	14	6	6.66
CF	Bordagaray	422	.282	1	39	227	14	5	2	2.3	.980	D. Leonard	43	138	2	9	8	3.92
LF	D. Taylor	352	.290	7	59	193	4	6	0	2.1	.970	R. Benge	23	125	9	9	1	4.48
C	A. Lopez	379	.251	3	39	472	65	11	8	4.3	.980							
UT	J. Bucher	473	.302	7	58	194	188	18	29		.955							
OF	L. Koenecke	325	.283	4	27	222	3	8	0	2.6	.966							
2S	J. Jordan	295	.278	0	30	174	273	12	39		.974							
C	B. Phelps	121	.364	5	22	118	16	6	4	4.1	.957							

Cincinnati
W-68 L-85
Chuck Dressen

POS	Player	AB	BA	HR	RBI	PO	A	E	DP	TC/G	FA	Pitcher	G	IP	W	L	SV	ERA
1B	J. Bottomley	399	.258	1	49	934	53	8	74	10.3	.992	P. Derringer	45	277	22	13	2	3.51
2B	A. Kampouris	499	.246	7	62	367	411	35	88	5.8	.957	Hollingsworth	38	173	6	13	0	3.89
SS	B. Myers	445	.267	5	36	230	335	37	77	5.4	.939	G. Schott	33	159	8	11	3	3.91
3B	L. Riggs	532	.278	5	46	132	269	31	21	3.2	.928	T. Freitas	31	144	5	10	2	4.57
RF	I. Goodman	592	.269	12	72	322	17	14	4	2.4	.960	S. Johnson	30	130	5	11	0	6.23
CF	S. Byrd	416	.262	9	52	284	10	9	1	2.6	.970	B. Frey	38	114	6	10	0	6.85
LF	B. Herman	349	.335	10	58	156	5	4	0	2.2	.976	D. Brennan	38	114	5	5	5	3.15
C	E. Lombardi	332	.343	12	64	298	49	6	4	4.3	.983	L. Herrmann	29	108	3	5	0	3.58
13	B. Sullivan	241	.266	2	36	368	61	4	40		.991							
OF	K. Cuyler	223	.251	2	22	123	5	2	2	2.3	.985							
C	G. Campbell	218	.257	3	30	238	36	4	1	4.2	.986							
UT	G. Slade	196	.281	1	14	91	115	11	20		.949							

Philadelphia
W-64 L-89
Jimmie Wilson

POS	Player	AB	BA	HR	RBI	PO	A	E	DP	TC/G	FA	Pitcher	G	IP	W	L	SV	ERA
1B	D. Camilli	602	.261	25	83	1442	96	20	118	10.0	.987	C. Davis	44	231	16	14	2	3.66
2B	L. Chiozza	472	.284	3	47	296	405	39	54	6.2	.947	O. Jorgens	53	188	10	15	2	4.83
SS	M. Haslin	407	.265	3	52	212	249	34	52	5.7	.931	S. Johnson	37	175	10	8	6	3.56
3B	J. Vergez	546	.249	9	63	188	222	20	25	2.9	.953	J. Bivin	47	162	2	9	1	5.79
RF	J. Moore	600	.323	19	93	233	18	7	6	1.7	.973	B. Walters	24	151	9	9	0	4.17
CF	E. Allen	645	.307	8	63	412	26	9	6	2.9	.980	J. Bowman	33	148	7	10	1	4.25
LF	G. Watkins	600	.270	17	76	325	18	15	4	2.4	.958							
C	A. Todd	328	.290	3	42	292	37	11	5	3.9	.968							
C	J. Wilson	290	.279	1	37	329	44	7	9	4.9	.982							
S2	C. Gomez	222	.230	0	16	150	216	19	36		.951							

NATIONAL LEAGUE 1935, cont.

Boston

W-38 L-115

Bill McKechnie

POS	Player	AB	BA	HR	RBI	PO	A	E	DP	TC/G	FA	Pitcher	G	IP	W	L	SV	ERA
1B	B. Jordan	470	.279	5	35	857	66	16	59	9.9	.983	Frankhouse	40	231	11	15	0	4.76
2B	L. Mallon	412	.274	2	25	166	219	10	31	5.4	.975	B. Cantwell	39	211	4	25	0	4.61
SS	B. Urbanski	514	.230	4	30	258	356	40	52	5.1	.939	B. Smith	46	203	8	18	5	3.94
3B	P. Whitney	458	.273	4	60	83	144	10	8	3.2	.958	E. Brandt	29	175	5	19	0	5.00
RF	R. Moore	407	.275	4	42	161	10	9	3	2.3	.950	H. Betts	44	160	2	9	0	5.47
CF	W. Berger	589	.295	34	130	458	8	17	1	3.2	.965	MacFayden	28	152	5	13	0	5.10
LF	H. Lee	422	.303	0	39	273	7	11	0	2.6	.962							
C	A. Spohrer	260	.242	1	16	230	45	12	4	3.2	.958							
OF	T. Thompson	297	.273	4	30	184	9	7	3	2.4	.965							
UT	J. Coscarart	284	.236	1	29	115	177	14	20		.954							
C	S. Hogan	163	.301	2	25	175	25	2	2	3.6	.990							

BATTING AND BASE RUNNING LEADERS

Batting Average
A. Vaughan, PIT .385
J. Medwick, STL .353
G. Hartnett, CHI .344
E. Lombardi, CIN .343
B. Herman, CHI .341

Slugging Average
A. Vaughan, PIT .607
J. Medwick, STL .576
M. Ott, NY .555
W. Berger, BOS .548
G. Hartnett, CHI .545

Home Runs
W. Berger, BOS 34
M. Ott, NY 31
D. Camilli, PHI 25
R. Collins, STL 23
J. Medwick, STL 23

Winning Percentage
B. Lee, CHI .769
S. Castleman, NY .714
D. Dean, STL .700
Schumacher, NY .679
C. Hubbell, NY .657

PITCHING LEADERS

Earned Run Average
C. Blanton, PIT 2.58
B. Swift, PIT 2.70
Schumacher, NY 2.89
L. French, CHI 2.96
B. Lee, CHI 2.96

Wins
D. Dean, STL 28
C. Hubbell, NY 23
P. Derringer, CIN 22
B. Lee, CHI 20
L. Warneke, CHI 20

Total Bases
J. Medwick, STL 365
M. Ott, NY 329
W. Berger, BOS 323
B. Herman, CHI 317
H. Leiber, NY 314

Runs Batted In
W. Berger, BOS 130
J. Medwick, STL 126
R. Collins, STL 122
M. Ott, NY 114
H. Leiber, NY 107

Stolen Bases
A. Galan, CHI 22
P. Martin, STL 20
Bordagaray, BKN 18
S. Hack, CHI 14
I. Goodman, CIN 14

Saves
D. Leonard, BKN 8
W. Hoyt, PIT 6
S. Johnson, PHI 6

Strikeouts
D. Dean, STL 182
C. Hubbell, NY 150
V. Mungo, BKN 143
P. Dean, STL 143
C. Blanton, PIT 142

Complete Games
D. Dean, STL 29
C. Hubbell, NY 24
C. Blanton, PIT 23
L. Warneke, CHI 20
P. Derringer, CIN 20

Hits
B. Herman, CHI 227
J. Medwick, STL 224
B. Terry, NY 203
H. Leiber, NY 203

Base on Balls
A. Vaughan, PIT 97
A. Galan, CHI 87
M. Ott, NY 82
G. Suhr, PIT 70

Home Run Percentage
W. Berger, BOS 5.8
M. Ott, NY 5.2
C. Klein, CHI 4.8
D. Camilli, PHI 4.2

Fewest Hits/9 Innings
C. Blanton, PIT 7.79
Schumacher, NY 8.08
R. Parmelee, NY 8.52
B. Swift, PIT 8.53

Shutouts
5 tied with 4

Fewest Walks/9 Innings
W. Clark, BKN 1.22
C. Hubbell, NY 1.46
P. Derringer, CIN 1.59
L. French, CHI 1.61

Runs Scored
A. Galan, CHI 133
J. Medwick, STL 132
P. Martin, STL 121
M. Ott, NY 113

Doubles
B. Herman, CHI 57
J. Medwick, STL 46
E. Allen, PHI 46
P. Martin, STL 41

Triples
I. Goodman, CIN 18
L. Waner, PIT 14
J. Medwick, STL 13

Most Strikeouts/9 Inn.
V. Mungo, BKN 6.00
D. Dean, STL 5.05
C. Blanton, PIT 5.02
P. Dean, STL 4.77

Innings
D. Dean, STL 324
C. Hubbell, NY 303
P. Derringer, CIN 277
P. Dean, STL 270

Games Pitched
O. Jorgens, PHI 53
D. Dean, STL 50
J. Bivin, PHI 47
P. Dean, STL 46

	W	L	PCT	GB	R	OR	2B	3B	HR	BA	SA	SB	E	DP	FA	CG	BB	SO	ShO	SV	ERA
Chicago	100	54	.649		847	597	303	62	88	.288	.414	66	186	163	.970	81	400	589	12	14	3.26
St. Louis	96	58	.623	4	829	625	286	59	86	.284	.405	71	164	133	.972	73	382	594	9	18	3.54
New York	91	62	.595	8.5	770	675	248	56	123	.286	.416	32	174	129	.972	76	411	524	10	11	3.78
Pittsburgh	86	67	.562	13.5	743	647	255	90	66	.285	.402	30	190	94	.968	76	312	549	15	11	3.42
Brooklyn	70	83	.458	29.5	711	767	235	62	59	.277	.376	60	188	146	.969	62	436	480	11	20	4.22
Cincinnati	68	85	.444	31.5	646	772	244	68	73	.265	.378	72	204	139	.966	59	438	500	9	12	4.30
Philadelphia	64	89	.418	35.5	685	871	249	32	92	.269	.378	52	228	145	.963	53	505	475	8	15	4.76
Boston	38	115	.248	61.5	575	852	233	33	75	.263	.362	20	197	101	.967	54	404	355	6	5	4.93
					5806	5806	2053	462	662	.277	.391	403	1531	1050	.968	534	3288	4066	80	106	4.02

AMERICAN LEAGUE 1935

Detroit

W-93 L-58

Mickey Cochrane

POS	Player	AB	BA	HR	RBI	PO	A	E	DP	TC/G	FA	Pitcher	G	IP	W	L	SV	ERA
1B	H. Greenberg	619	.328	36	170	1437	99	13	142	10.2	.992	S. Rowe	42	276	19	13	3	3.69
2B	C. Gehringer	610	.330	19	108	349	489	13	99	5.7	.985	T. Bridges	36	274	21	10	1	3.51
SS	B. Rogell	560	.275	6	71	280	512	24	104	5.4	.971	G. Crowder	33	241	16	10	0	4.26
3B	M. Owen	483	.263	2	71	148	215	16	19	2.9	.958	E. Auker	36	195	18	7	0	3.83
RF	P. Fox	517	.321	15	73	244	9	3	1	2.0	.988	J. Sullivan	25	126	6	6	0	3.51
CF	J. White	412	.240	2	32	247	7	10	1	2.7	.962	C. Hogsett	40	97	6	6	5	3.54
LF	G. Goslin	590	.292	9	109	326	6	12	2	2.4	.965							
C	M. Cochrane	411	.319	5	47	504	50	6	6	5.1	.989							
OF	G. Walker	362	.301	7	53	204	2	10	1	2.5	.954							
C	R. Hayworth	175	.309	0	22	211	35	1	4	5.1	.996							
P	S. Rowe	109	.312	3	28	11	42	1	1	1.3	.981							

AMERICAN LEAGUE 1935, cont.

	POS	Player	AB	BA	HR	RBI	PO	A	E	DP	TC/G	FA	Pitcher	G	IP	W	L	SV	ERA
New York	1B	L. Gehrig	535	.329	30	119	1337	82	15	96	9.6	.990	L. Gomez	34	246	12	15	1	3.18
	2B	T. Lazzeri	477	.273	13	83	285	329	19	72	5.4	.970	R. Ruffing	30	222	16	11	0	3.12
	SS	F. Crosetti	305	.256	8	50	153	261	16	42	4.9	.963	J. Broaca	29	201	15	7	0	3.58
W-89 L-60	3B	R. Rolfe	639	.300	5	67	166	239	15	16	3.1	**.964**	J. Allen	23	167	13	6	0	3.61
	RF	G. Selkirk	491	.312	11	94	269	9	7	1	2.2	.975	V. Tamulis	30	161	10	5	1	4.09
Joe McCarthy	CF	B. Chapman	553	.289	8	74	372	25	15	7	3.0	.964	J. Murphy	40	117	10	5	5	4.08
	LF	J. Hill	392	.293	4	33	203	9	11	1	2.4	.951	J. Brown	20	87	6	5	0	3.61
	C	B. Dickey	448	.279	14	81	536	62	3	7	**5.1**	**.995**	P. Malone	29	56	3	5	3	5.43
	OF	E. Combs	298	.282	3	35	143	2	1	0	2.1	.993							
Cleveland	1B	H. Trosky	632	.271	26	113	**1567**	88	11	129	10.9	.993	M. Harder	42	287	22	11	2	3.29
	2B	B. Berger	461	.258	5	43	309	419	27	91	6.3	.964	W. Hudlin	36	232	15	11	5	3.69
	SS	Knickerbocker	540	.298	0	55	247	453	32	82	5.7	.956	M. Pearson	30	182	8	13	0	4.90
W-82 L-71	3B	O. Hale	589	.304	16	101	160	**312**	**31**	17	3.4	.938	T. Lee	32	181	7	10	1	4.04
	RF	B. Campbell	308	.325	7	54	129	2	1	1	1.8	.992	Hildebrand	34	171	9	8	5	3.94
Walter Johnson	CF	E. Averill	563	.288	19	79	371	6	7	2	2.8	.982	L. Brown	42	122	8	7	4	3.61
W-46 L-48	LF	J. Vosmik	620	.348	10	110	347	5	5	3	2.4	.986	L. Stewart	24	91	6	6	2	5.44
	C	E. Phillips	220	.273	1	41	233	18	5	3	3.7	.980							
Steve O'Neill	2S	R. Hughes	266	.293	0	14	151	215	13	44		.966							
W-36 L-23	OF	M. Galatzer	259	.301	0	19	134	7	10	0	1.9	.934							
	OF	A. Wright	160	.238	2	18	56	4	1	0	1.3	.984							
Boston	1B	B. Dahlgren	525	.263	9	63	1433	69	**18**	109	10.2	.988	W. Ferrell	41	**322**	**25**	14	0	3.52
	2B	O. Melillo	399	.261	1	39	286	372	18	85	6.4*	.973	L. Grove	35	273	20	12	1	**2.70**
	SS	J. Cronin	556	.295	9	95	264	431	37	86	5.3	.949	G. Rhodes	34	146	2	10	2	5.41
W-78 L-75	3B	B. Werber	462	.255	14	61	**174**	264	27	20	3.8	.942	J. Welch	31	143	10	9	4	4.47
	RF	D. Cooke	294	.306	3	34	172	4	5	1	2.2	.972	R. Walberg	44	143	5	9	3	3.91
Joe Cronin	CF	M. Almada	607	.290	3	59	337	22	12	3	2.5	.968	Ostermueller	22	138	7	8	1	3.92
	LF	R. Johnson	553	.315	4	66	267	21	17	1	2.1	.944							
	C	R. Ferrell	458	.301	3	61	520	79	**13**	**12**	4.7	.979							
	UT	D. Williams	251	.251	3	25	122	154	12	21	·	.958							
	OF	C. Reynolds	244	.270	6	35	146	7	4	0	2.5	.975							
	P	W. Ferrell	150	.347	7	32	9	76	2	1	2.1	.977							
	OF	B. Miller	138	.304	3	26	48	2	2	0	1.8	.962							
Chicago	1B	Z. Bonura	550	.295	21	92	1421	83	9	109	**11.0**	.994	J. Whitehead	28	222	13	13	0	3.72
	2B	J. Hayes	329	.267	4	45	202	275	17	48	5.8	.966	V. Kennedy	31	212	11	11	1	3.91
	SS	L. Appling	525	.307	1	71	**335**	**556**	**39**	93	6.1	.958	T. Lyons	23	191	15	8	0	3.02
W-74 L-78	3B	J. Dykes	403	.288	4	61	100	166	13	12	2.8	.953	J. Tietje	30	170	9	15	0	4.30
	RF	M. Haas	327	.291	2	40	183	4	2	1	2.3	.989	S. Jones	21	140	8	7	0	4.05
Jimmy Dykes	CF	A. Simmons	525	.267	16	79	349	5	7	1	2.9	.981	R. Phelps	27	125	4	8	1	4.82
	LF	R. Radcliff	623	.286	10	68	231	8	8	1	1.7	.968	C. Fischer	24	89	5	5	0	6.19
	C	L. Sewell	421	.285	2	67	399	83	6	10	4.4	.988	W. Wyatt	30	52	4	3	5	6.75
	OF	Washington	339	.283	8	47	137	10	4	2	1.9	.974							
	2B	T. Piet	292	.298	3	27	129	216	9	32	6.0	.975							
Washington	1B	J. Kuhel	633	.261	2	74	1425	87	14	**150**	10.1	.991	E. Whitehill	34	279	14	13	0	4.29
	2B	B. Myer	616	**.349**	5	100	**460**	473	20	**138**	6.3	.979	B. Hadley	35	230	10	15	0	4.92
	SS	O. Bluege	320	.263	0	34	117	177	10	32	5.2	.967	B. Newsom	28	198	11	12*	2	4.45
W-67 L-86	3B	C. Travis	534	.318	0	61	136	254	15	**29**	3.6	.963	E. Linke	40	178	11	7	3	5.01
	RF	J. Stone	454	.315	1	78	224	12	11	4	2.2	.955	J. Russell	43	126	4	9	3	5.71
Bucky Harris	CF	J. Powell	551	.312	6	98	361	10	9	4	2.8	.976	L. Pettit	41	109	8	5	3	4.95
	LF	H. Manush	479	.273	4	56	251	8	4	5	2.4	.985							
	C	C. Bolton	375	.304	2	55	356	52	12	8	4.0	.971							
	SS	R. Kress	252	.298	2	42	118	204	12	53	6.3	.964							
	OF	F. Schulte	224	.268	2	23	96	2	2	0	1.8	.980							
	OF	D. Miles	216	.264	0	29	92	5	3	1	2.2	.970							
	C	S. Holbrook	135	.259	0	25	145	12	8	0	3.5	.952							
St. Louis	1B	J. Burns	549	.286	5	67	1239	57	11	115	9.3	.992	I. Andrews	50	213	13	7	1	3.54
	2B	T. Carey	296	.291	0	42	189	253	18	52	6.1	.961	J. Knott	48	188	11	8	7	4.60
	SS	L. Lary	371	.288	2	35	258	306	22	66	6.3	.962	J. Walkup	55	181	6	9	0	6.25
W-65 L-87	3B	H. Clift	475	.295	11	69	130	240	26	12	3.1	.934	R. Van Atta	53*	170	9	16	3	5.34
	RF	E. Coleman	397	.287	17	71	173	11	5	1	1.9	.974	S. Cain	31	168	9	8	0	5.26
Rogers Hornsby	CF	S. West	527	.300	10	70	**449**	7	5	2	**3.4**	**.989**	F. Thomas	49	147	7	15	1	4.78
	LF	M. Solters	552	.330	18	104	328	18	4	1	2.8	.989	D. Coffman	41	144	5	11	2	6.14
	C	R. Hemsley	504	.290	0	48	510	**105**	**13**	10	4.5	.979							
	OF	R. Pepper	261	.253	4	37	103	5	2	1	1.9	.982							
	O1	B. Bell	220	.250	3	17	187	8	9	11		.956							
	UT	J. Burnett	206	.223	0	26	71	136	13	18		.941							
	2B	O. Bejma	198	.192	2	26	105	153	13	32	5.8	.952							

AMERICAN LEAGUE 1935, cont.

Philadelphia
W-58 L-91

Connie Mack

POS	Player	AB	BA	HR	RBI	PO	A	E	DP	TC/G	FA	Pitcher	G	IP	W	L	SV	ERA
1B	J. Foxx	535	.346	**36**	115	1109	77	3	107	9.8	**.997**	J. Marcum	39	243	17	12	3	4.08
2B	R. Warstler	496	.250	3	59	308	482	**34**	94	6.1	.959	B. Dietrich	43	185	7	13	5	5.39
SS	E. McNair	526	.270	4	57	232	346	27	78	5.0	.955	Blaeholder	23	149	6	10	0	3.99
3B	P. Higgins	524	.296	23	94	162	214	21	15	3.0	.947	W. Wilshere	27	142	9	9	1	4.05
RF	W. Moses	345	.325	5	35	157	7	10	1	2.2	.943	R. Mahaffey	27	136	8	4	0	3.90
CF	D. Cramer	644	.332	3	70	429	6	11	1	3.0	.975							
LF	B. Johnson	582	.299	28	109	337	13	**20**	4	2.5	.946							
C	P. Richards	257	.245	4	29	293	40	8	5	4.3	.977							
OF	L. Finney	410	.273	0	31	145	5	9	1	2.1	.943							
C	C. Berry	190	.253	3	29	189	37	3	7	4.1	.987							

BATTING AND BASE RUNNING LEADERS

Batting Average
B. Myer, WAS	.349
J. Vosmik, CLE	.348
J. Foxx, PHI	.346
D. Cramer, PHI	.332
C. Gehringer, DET	.330

Slugging Average
J. Foxx, PHI	.636
H. Greenberg, DET	.628
L. Gehrig, NY	.583
J. Vosmik, CLE	.537
P. Fox, DET	.513

Home Runs
J. Foxx, PHI	36
H. Greenberg, DET	36
L. Gehrig, NY	30
B. Johnson, PHI	28
H. Trosky, CLE	26

Total Bases
H. Greenberg, DET	389
J. Foxx, PHI	340
J. Vosmik, CLE	333
M. Solters, BOS, STL	314
L. Gehrig, NY	312

Runs Batted In
H. Greenberg, DET	170
L. Gehrig, NY	119
J. Foxx, PHI	115
H. Trosky, CLE	113
M. Solters, BOS, STL	112

Stolen Bases
B. Werber, BOS	29
L. Lary, STL, WAS	28
M. Almada, BOS	20
J. White, DET	19
B. Chapman, NY	17

Hits
J. Vosmik, CLE	216
B. Myer, WAS	215
D. Cramer, PHI	214
H. Greenberg, DET	203

Base on Balls
L. Gehrig, NY	132
L. Appling, CHI	122
J. Foxx, PHI	114
M. Cochrane, DET	96

Home Run Percentage
J. Foxx, PHI	6.7
H. Greenberg, DET	5.8
L. Gehrig, NY	5.6
B. Johnson, PHI	4.8

Runs Scored
L. Gehrig, NY	125
C. Gehringer, DET	123
H. Greenberg, DET	121
J. Foxx, PHI	118

Doubles
J. Vosmik, CLE	47
H. Greenberg, DET	46
M. Solters, BOS, STL	45
P. Fox, DET	38

Triples
J. Vosmik, CLE	20
J. Stone, WAS	18
H. Greenberg, DET	16
J. Cronin, BOS	14

PITCHING LEADERS

Winning Percentage
E. Auker, DET	.720
J. Broaca, NY	.682
T. Bridges, DET	.677
M. Harder, CLE	.667
T. Lyons, CHI	.652

Earned Run Average
L. Grove, BOS	2.70
T. Lyons, CHI	3.02
R. Ruffing, NY	3.12
L. Gomez, NY	3.18
M. Harder, CLE	3.29

Wins
W. Ferrell, BOS	25
M. Harder, CLE	22
T. Bridges, DET	21
L. Grove, BOS	20
S. Rowe, DET	19

Saves
J. Knott, STL	7
C. Hogsett, DET	5
J. Murphy, NY	5
W. Wyatt, CHI	5
Hildebrand, CLE	5
W. Hudlin, CLE	5

Strikeouts
T. Bridges, DET	163
S. Rowe, DET	140
L. Gomez, NY	138
L. Grove, BOS	121
J. Allen, NY	113

Complete Games
W. Ferrell, BOS	31
L. Grove, BOS	23
T. Bridges, DET	23
S. Rowe, DET	21

Fewest Hits/9 Innings
J. Allen, NY	8.03
R. Ruffing, NY	8.15
L. Gomez, NY	8.16
J. Whitehead, CHI	8.46

Shutouts
S. Rowe, DET	6
T. Bridges, DET	4
M. Harder, CLE	4

Fewest Walks/9 Innings
M. Harder, CLE	1.66
L. Grove, BOS	2.14
S. Rowe, DET	2.22
I. Andrews, STL	2.24

Most Strikeouts/9 Inn.
J. Allen, NY	6.09
T. Bridges, DET	5.35
L. Gomez, NY	5.05
S. Rowe, DET	4.57

Innings
W. Ferrell, BOS	322
M. Harder, CLE	287
E. Whitehill, WAS	279
S. Rowe, DET	276

Games Pitched
R. Van Atta, NY, STL	58
J. Walkup, STL	55
I. Andrews, STL	50
F. Thomas, STL	49

	W	L	PCT	GB	R	OR	2B	3B	HR	BA	SA	SB	E	DP	FA	CG	BB	SO	ShO	SV	ERA
Detroit	93	58	.616		**919**	665	301	83	106	**.290**	**.435**	70	**128**	154	**.978**	87	522	584	**16**	11	3.82
New York	89	60	.597	3	818	**632**	255	70	104	.280	.416	68	151	114	.974	76	516	**594**	12	13	**3.60**
Cleveland	82	71	.536	12	776	739	**324**	77	93	.284	.421	63	177	147	.972	67	**457**	498	11	**21**	4.15
Boston	78	75	.510	16	718	732	281	63	69	.276	.392	**89**	194	136	.969	82	520	470	6	11	4.05
Chicago	74	78	.487	19.5	738	750	262	42	74	.275	.382	46	146	133	.976	80	574	436	8	8	4.38
Washington	67	86	.438	27	823	903	255	**95**	32	.285	.381	54	171	**186**	.972	67	613	456	5	12	5.25
St. Louis	65	87	.428	28.5	718	930	291	51	73	.284	.384	45	187	138	.970	42	640	435	4	15	5.26
Philadelphia	58	91	.389	34	710	869	243	44	**112**	.279	.406	42	190	150	.968	58	**704**	469	7	10	5.12
					6220	6220	2212	525	663	.280	.402	477	1344	1158	.972	559	4546	3942	69	101	4.45

NATIONAL LEAGUE 1936

New York
W-92 L-62

Bill Terry

POS	Player	AB	BA	HR	RBI	PO	A	E	DP	TC/G	FA	Pitcher	G	IP	W	L	SV	ERA
1B	S. Leslie	417	.295	6	54	1030	68	10	81	11.2	.991	C. Hubbell	42	304	**26**	6	3	**2.31**
2B	B. Whitehead	632	.278	4	47	442	552	**32**	107	6.7	.969	Schumacher	35	214	11	13		3.49
SS	D. Bartell	510	.298	8	42	317	**559**	40	**106**	6.4	.956	A. Smith	43	209	14	13	2	3.78
3B	T. Jackson	465	.230	7	53	99	196	15	8	2.7	.952	F. Gabler	43	162	9	8	6	3.12
RF	M. Ott	534	.328	**33**	135	250	20	4	3	1.9	.985	Fitzsimmons	28	141	10	7		3.32
CF	H. Leiber	337	.279	9	67	165	9	7	3	2.1	.961	H. Gumbert	39	141	11	3	0	3.90
LF	J. Moore	649	.316	9	63	291	25	6	3	2.2	.981	S. Castleman	29	112	4	7	1	5.64
C	G. Mancuso	519	.301	9	63	524	104	15	15	4.7	.977	D. Coffman	42	102	7	5	7	3.90
OF	J. Ripple	311	.305	7	47	190	5	4	**10**	2.6	.980							
1B	B. Terry	229	.310	2	39	525	41	2	55	10.1	.996							

NATIONAL LEAGUE 1936, *cont.*

	POS	Player	AB	BA	HR	RBI	PO	A	E	DP	TC/G	FA	Pitcher	G	IP	W	L	SV	ERA
Chicago	1B	Cavarretta	458	.273	9	56	980	71	14	93	9.3	.987	B. Lee	43	259	18	11	1	3.31
	2B	B. Herman	632	.334	5	93	457	492	24	110	6.4	**.975**	L. French	43	252	18	9	3	3.39
W-87 L-67	SS	B. Jurges	429	.280	1	42	249	379	26	80	5.6	.960	L. Warneke	40	241	16	13	1	3.44
	3B	S. Hack	561	.298	6	78	121	202	17	13	2.4	.950	T. Carleton	35	197	14	10	1	3.65
Charlie Grimm	RF	F. Demaree	605	.350	16	96	285	16	10	1	2.0	.968	C. Davis	24	153	11	9	1	3.00
	CF	A. Galan	575	.264	8	81	381	9	5	3	2.7	.987	R. Henshaw	39	129	6	5	1	3.97
	LF	E. Allen	373	.295	3	39	191	2	4	2	2.2	.980	C. Root	33	74	3	6	1	4.15
	C	G. Hartnett	424	.307	7	64	504	75	5	8	**5.1**	**.991**							
	C	K. O'Dea	189	.307	2	38	211	27	5	1	4.4	.979							
	SS	W. English	182	.247	0	20	75	127	5	27	4.9	.976							
	OF	J. Gill	174	.253	7	28	72	3	5	1	2.0	.938							
St. Louis	1B	J. Mize	414	.329	19	93	897	66	6	63	10.0	.994	D. Dean	51	315	24	13	11	3.17
	2B	S. Martin	332	.298	6	41	169	242	22	50	5.2	.949	R. Parmelee	37	221	11	11	2	4.56
W-87 L-67	SS	L. Durocher	510	.286	1	58	300	392	21	80	5.2	**.971**	J. Winford	39	192	11	10	3	3.80
	3B	C. Gelbert	280	.229	3	27	60	104	6	11	2.8	.965	E. Heusser	42	104	7	3	3	5.43
Frankie Frisch	RF	P. Martin	572	.309	11	76	226	13	6	5	1.9	.976	J. Haines	25	99	7	5	1	3.90
	CF	T. Moore	590	.264	5	47	418	14	10	7	3.3	.977	P. Dean	17	92	5	5	1	4.60
	LF	J. Medwick	636	.351	18	138	367	16	6	4	2.5	.985	B. Walker	21	80	5	6	1	5.87
	C	S. Davis	363	.273	4	59	390	59	7	7	4.4	.985							
	2B	F. Frisch	303	.274	1	26	124	176	11	27	5.1	.965							
	1B	R. Collins	277	.292	13	48	475	37	5	48	8.5	.990							
	C	Ogrodowski	237	.228	1	20	314	32	4	6	4.1	.989							
	32	A. Garibaldi	232	.276	1	20	97	119	11	7		.952							
Pittsburgh	1B	G. Suhr	583	.312	11	118	1432	93	10	100	9.8	**.993**	B. Swift	45	262	16	16	2	4.01
	2B	P. Young	475	.248	6	77	318	361	24	39	5.7	.966	C. Blanton	44	236	13	15	3	3.51
W-84 L-70	SS	A. Vaughan	568	.335	9	78	327	477	47	86	5.5	.945	J. Weaver	38	226	14	8	0	4.31
	3B	B. Brubaker	554	.289	6	102	134	209	22	8	2.5	.940	R. Lucas	27	176	15	4	0	3.18
Pie Traynor	RF	P. Waner	585	.373	5	94	323	15	14	7	2.4	.960	M. Brown	47	165	10	11	3	3.87
	CF	L. Waner	414	.321	1	31	245	2	4	2	2.7	.984	W. Hoyt	22	117	7	5	1	2.70
	LF	W. Jensen	**696**	.283	10	58	338	6	9	1	2.3	.975	R. Birkofer	34	109	7	5	0	4.69
	C	T. Padden	281	.249	1	31	342	62	10	6	4.8	.976							
	C	A. Todd	267	.273	2	28	332	39	9	2	5.4	.976							
	OF	F. Schulte	238	.261	1	17	129	1	3	1	2.4	.977							
	2B	C. Lavagetto	197	.244	2	26	85	110	10	24	5.5	.951							
Cincinnati	1B	L. Scarsella	485	.313	3	65	1109	84	13	90	**10.5**	.989	P. Derringer	51	282	19	19	5	4.02
	2B	A. Kampouris	355	.239	5	46	270	376	21	71	5.6	.969	Hollingsworth	29	184	9	10	0	4.16
W-74 L-80	SS	B. Myers	323	.269	6	27	225	304	35	73	5.8	.938	G. Schott	31	180	11	11	1	3.80
	3B	L. Riggs	538	.257	6	57	122	267	14	19	2.9	.968	B. Hallahan	23	135	5	9	0	4.33
Chuck Dressen	RF	I. Goodman	489	.284	17	71	274	6	8	2	2.4	.972	B. Frey	31	131	10	8	0	4.25
	CF	K. Cuyler	567	.326	7	74	322	9	9	3	2.4	.974	P. Davis	26	126	8	8	5	3.58
	LF	B. Herman	380	.279	13	71	175	3	6	0	2.0	.967	L. Stine	40	122	3	8	2	5.03
	C	E. Lombardi	387	.333	12	68	330	54	15	10	3.8	.962	D. Brennan	41	94	5	2	9	4.39
	UT	T. Thevenow	321	.234	0	36	178	248	23	49	2.3	.949							
	OF	H. Walker	258	.275	4	23	158	4	5	2	2.3	.970							
	C	G. Campbell	235	.268	1	40	257	49	5	9	4.4	.984							
	O2	C. Chapman	219	.247	1	22	85	49	4	6		.971							
Boston	1B	B. Jordan	555	.323	3	66	1307	96	10	**137**	10.4	.993	MacFayden	37	267	17	13	0	2.87
	2B	Cuccinello	565	.308	7	86	383	**559**	28	**128**	6.5	.971	T. Chaplin	40	231	10	15	2	4.12
W-71 L-83	SS	B. Urbanski	494	.261	0	26	188	211	27	56	5.3	.937	J. Lanning	28	153	7	11	0	3.65
	3B	J. Coscarart	367	.245	2	44	91	168	18	16	2.9	.935	B. Reis	35	139	6	5	0	4.48
Bill McKechnie	RF	G. Moore	637	.290	13	67	314	32	8	0	2.3	.977	B. Smith	35	136	6	7	8	3.77
	CF	W. Berger	534	.288	25	91	384	10	14	1	3.1	.966	B. Cantwell	34	133	9	9	2	3.04
	LF	H. Lee	565	.253	3	64	319	5	9	1	2.2	.973	R. Benge	21	115	7	9	0	5.79
	C	A. Lopez	426	.242	8	50	447	**107**	14	9	4.5	.975							
	SS	R. Warstler	304	.211	0	17	157	278	24	59	6.2	.948							
	O1	T. Thompson	266	.286	4	36	359	20	5	19		.987							
Brooklyn	1B	B. Hassett	635	.310	3	82	1401	**121**	**26**	89	9.9	.983	V. Mungo	45	312	18	19	3	3.35
	2B	J. Jordan	398	.234	2	28	209	247	14	41	4.8	.970	Frankhouse	41	234	13	10	2	3.65
W-67 L-87	SS	L. Frey	524	.279	4	60	238	331	51	52	5.3	.918	E. Brandt	38	234	11	13	2	3.50
	3B	J. Stripp	439	.317	1	60	132	174	10	13	3.0	**.968**	M. Butcher	38	148	6	6	2	3.96
Casey Stengel	RF	Bordagaray	372	.315	4	31	207	8	2	0	2.4	.991	W. Clark	33	120	7	11	2	4.43
	CF	J. Cooney	507	.282	0	30	336	11	2	3	2.7	**.994**	G. Jeffcoat	40	96	5	6	3	4.52
	LF	G. Watkins	364	.255	4	43	183	5	6	1	2.0	.969	G. Earnshaw	19	93	4	9	1	5.32
	C	R. Berres	267	.240	1	13	436	59	6	7	4.8	.988	T. Baker	35	88	1	8	2	4.72
	UT	J. Bucher	370	.251	2	41	145	138	19	15		.937							
	C	B. Phelps	319	.367	5	57	334	49	9	6	4.0	.977							
	OF	E. Wilson	173	.347	3	25	72	3	6	0	1.7	.926							

NATIONAL LEAGUE 1936, cont.

	POS	Player	AB	BA	HR	RBI	PO	A	E	DP	TC/G	FA	Pitcher	G	IP	W	L	SV	ERA
Philadelphia	1B	D. Camilli	530	.315	28	102	**1446**	79	18	122	10.3	.988	B. Walters	40	258	11	**21**	0	4.26
	2B	C. Gomez	332	.232	0	28	137	229	20	33	5.4	.948	C. Passeau	49	217	11	15	3	3.48
W-54 L-100	SS	L. Norris	581	.265	11	76	317	345	45	70	5.8	.936	J. Bowman	40	204	9	20	1	5.04
	3B	P. Whitney	411	.294	6	59	106	212	15	15	3.0*	.955	O. Jorgens	39	167	8	8	0	4.79
Jimmie Wilson	RF	C. Klein	492	.309	20	87	213	13	17*	2	2.1	.930	S. Johnson	39	111	5	7	7	4.30
	CF	L. Chiozza	572	.297	1	48	235	7	7	10	2.8	.972							
	LF	J. Moore	472	.328	16	68	214	5	12	1	2.1	.948							
	C	E. Grace	221	.249	4	32	217	29	6	3	3.9	.976							
	OF	E. Sulik	404	.287	6	36	227	6	7	1	2.3	.971							
	C	J. Wilson	230	.278	1	27	187	31	9	5	3.6	.960							
	C	B. Atwood	192	.302	2	29	184	27	6	3	4.1	.972							

BATTING AND BASE RUNNING LEADERS

Batting Average
P. Waner, PIT .373
B. Phelps, BKN .367
J. Medwick, STL .351
F. Demaree, CHI .350
A. Vaughan, PIT .335

Slugging Average
M. Ott, NY .588
D. Camilli, PHI .577
J. Mize, STL .577
J. Medwick, STL .577
P. Waner, PIT .520

Home Runs
M. Ott, NY 33
D. Camilli, PHI 28
W. Berger, BOS 25
C. Klein, CHI, PHI 25
J. Mize, STL 19

Total Bases
J. Medwick, STL 367
M. Ott, NY 314
C. Klein, CHI, PHI 308
D. Camilli, PHI 306
P. Waner, PIT 304

Runs Batted In
J. Medwick, STL 138
M. Ott, NY 135
G. Suhr, PIT 118
C. Klein, CHI, PHI 104
D. Camilli, PHI 102
B. Brubaker, PIT 102

Stolen Bases
P. Martin, STL 23
S. Martin, STL 17
S. Hack, CHI 17
L. Chiozza, PHI 17

Hits
J. Medwick, STL 223
P. Waner, PIT 218
F. Demaree, CHI 212
B. Herman, CHI 211

Base on Balls
A. Vaughan, PIT 118
D. Camilli, PHI 116
M. Ott, NY 111
G. Suhr, PIT 95

Home Run Percentage
M. Ott, NY 6.2
D. Camilli, PHI 5.3
R. Collins, STL 4.7
W. Berger, BOS 4.7

Runs Scored
A. Vaughan, PIT 122
P. Martin, STL 121
M. Ott, NY 120
J. Medwick, STL 115

Doubles
J. Medwick, STL 64
B. Herman, CHI 57
P. Waner, PIT 53
T. Moore, STL 39

Triples
I. Goodman, CIN 14
D. Camilli, PHI 13
J. Medwick, STL 13
L. Riggs, CIN 12

PITCHING LEADERS

Winning Percentage
C. Hubbell, NY .813
R. Lucas, PIT .789
L. French, CHI .667
D. Dean, STL .649
B. Lee, CHI .621

Earned Run Average
C. Hubbell, NY 2.31
MacFayden, BOS 2.87
D. Dean, STL 3.17
R. Lucas, PIT 3.18
B. Lee, CHI 3.31

Wins
C. Hubbell, NY 26
D. Dean, STL 24
P. Derringer, CIN 19
L. French, CHI 18
B. Lee, CHI 18
V. Mungo, BKN 18

Saves
D. Dean, STL 11
D. Brennan, CIN 9
B. Smith, BOS 8
D. Coffman, NY 7
S. Johnson, PHI 7

Strikeouts
V. Mungo, BKN 238
D. Dean, STL 195
C. Blanton, PIT 127
C. Hubbell, NY 123
P. Derringer, CIN 121

Complete Games
D. Dean, STL 28
C. Hubbell, NY 25
V. Mungo, BKN 22
MacFayden, BOS 21
B. Lee, CHI 20

Fewest Hits/9 Innings
C. Hubbell, NY 7.85
V. Mungo, BKN 7.94
B. Lee, CHI 8.28
D. Dean, STL 8.86

Shutouts
7 tied with 4

Fewest Walks/9 Innings
R. Lucas, PIT 1.33
P. Derringer, CIN 1.34
D. Dean, STL 1.51
C. Hubbell, NY 1.69

Most Strikeouts/9 Inn.
V. Mungo, BKN 6.87
D. Dean, STL 5.57
C. Blanton, PIT 4.85
J. Weaver, PIT 4.31

Innings
D. Dean, STL 315
V. Mungo, BKN 312
C. Hubbell, NY 304
P. Derringer, CIN 282

Games Pitched
D. Dean, STL 51
P. Derringer, CIN 51
C. Passeau, PHI 49
M. Brown, PIT 47

	W	L	PCT	GB	R	OR	2B	3B	HR	BA	SA	SB	E	DP	FA	CG	BB	SO	ShO	SV	ERA
New York	92	62	.597		742	621	237	48	97	.281	.395	31	168	164	.974	58	401	500	12	22	**3.46**
Chicago	87	67	.565	5	755	603	275	36	76	.286	.392	68	**146**	156	**.976**	**77**	434	597	**18**	10	3.53
St. Louis	87	67	.565	5	795	794	**332**	60	88	.281	**.410**	69	156	156	.974	65	477	561	5	**24**	4.48
Pittsburgh	84	70	.545	8	**804**	718	283	**80**	60	**.286**	.397	37	199	113	.967	67	379	559	5	12	3.89
Cincinnati	74	80	.481	18	722	760	224	73	82	.274	.388	68	191	150	.969	50	418	459	6	23	4.22
Boston	71	83	.461	21	631	715	207	44	68	.265	.356	23	189	**175**	.971	60	451	421	7	13	3.94
Brooklyn	67	87	.435	25	662	752	263	43	33	.272	.353	55	208	107	.966	59	528	**654**	7	18	3.98
Philadelphia	54	100	.351	38	726	874	250	46	**103**	.281	.401	50	252	144	.959	51	515	454	7	14	4.64
					5837	5837	2071	430	607	.278	.386	401	1509	1143	.969	487	3603	4205	67	136	4.02

AMERICAN LEAGUE 1936

	POS	Player	AB	BA	HR	RBI	PO	A	E	DP	TC/G	FA	Pitcher	G	IP	W	L	SV	ERA
New York	1B	L. Gehrig	579	.354	**49**	152	1377	82	9	128	9.5	.994	R. Ruffing	33	271	20	12	0	3.85
	2B	T. Lazzeri	537	.287	14	109	346	414	**25**	88	5.3	.968	M. Pearson	33	223	19	7	1	3.71
W-102 L-51	SS	F. Crosetti	632	.288	15	78	320	463	**43**	95	5.5	.968	J. Broaca	37	206	12	7	3	4.24
	3B	R. Rolfe	568	.319	10	70	162	265	19	20	3.4	**.957**	L. Gomez	31	189	13	7	0	4.39
Joe McCarthy	RF	G. Selkirk	493	.308	18	107	290	10	8	3	2.3	.974	B. Hadley	31	174	14	4	1	4.35
	CF	J. Powell	324	.306	7	48	196	6	5	2	2.5	.976	P. Malone	35	135	12	4	9	3.81
	LF	J. DiMaggio	637	.323	29	125	339	**22**	8	2	2.7	.978	J. Murphy	27	88	9	3	5	3.38
	C	B. Dickey	423	.362	22	107	499	61	14	10	**5.4**	.976							
	OF	M. Hoag	156	.301	3	34	82	2	4	1	2.3	.955							
	OF	B. Chapman	139	.266	1	21	106	3	4	0	3.1	.965							
	C	J. Glenn	129	.271	1	20	167	24	6	2	4.5	.970							
	P	R. Ruffing	127	.291	5	22	13	56	1	6	2.1	.986							
	P	M. Pearson	91	.253	1	20	12	39	1	3	1.6	.981							

AMERICAN LEAGUE 1936, cont.

	POS	Player	AB	BA	HR	RBI	PO	A	E	DP	TC/G	FA	Pitcher	G	IP	W	L	SV	ERA
Detroit	1B	J. Burns	558	.283	4	63	1280	73	8	126	9.9	.994	T. Bridges	39	295	**23**	11	0	3.60
	2B	C. Gehringer	641	.354	15	116	397	**524**	25	116	6.1	**.974**	S. Rowe	41	245	19	10	3	4.51
W-83 L-71	SS	B. Rogell	585	.274	6	68	286	462	27	98	5.3	.965	E. Auker	35	215	13	16	0	4.89
	3B	M. Owen	583	.295	9	105	**190**	281	24	**28**	3.2	.952	V. Sorrell	30	131	6	7	3	5.28
Mickey Cochrane	RF	G. Walker	550	.353	12	93	280	14	16	5	2.5	.948	R. Lawson	41	128	8	6	3	5.48
	CF	A. Simmons	568	.327	13	112	352	8	5	1	2.6	**.986**							
	LF	G. Goslin	572	.315	24	125	266	11	13	1	2.0	.955							
	C	R. Hayworth	250	.240	1	30	305	28	4	5	4.2	.988							
	OF	P. Fox	220	.305	4	26	118	3	4	0	2.3	.968							
Chicago	1B	Z. Bonura	587	.330	12	138	**1500**	**107**	7	**150**	11.1	**.996**	V. Kennedy	35	274	21	9	0	4.63
	2B	J. Hayes	417	.312	5	84	216	334	12	70	6.3	.979	J. Whitehead	34	231	13	13	1	4.64
W-81 L-70	SS	L. Appling	526	**.388**	6	128	320	471	41	119	6.1	.951	S. Cain	30	195	14	10	0	4.75
	3B	J. Dykes	435	.267	7	60	108	240	18	14	2.9	.951	T. Lyons	26	182	10	13	0	5.14
Jimmy Dykes	RF	M. Haas	408	.284	0	46	176	7	2	2	1.9	.989	M. Stratton	16	95	5	7	0	5.21
	CF	M. Kreevich	550	.307	5	69	300	17	12	5	2.5	.964	C. Brown	38	83	6	2	5	4.99
	LF	R. Radcliff	618	.335	8	82	213	6	15	2	1.8	.936	R. Phelps	15	69	4	6	0	6.03
	C	L. Sewell	451	.251	5	73	461	**87**	9	12	4.4	.984							
	23	T. Piet	352	.273	7	42	167	317	18	49		.964							
	OF	L. Rosenthal	317	.281	3	46	243	7	6	3	3.2	.977							
Washington	1B	J. Kuhel	588	.321	16	118	1452	73	10	138	10.3	.993	B. Newsom	43	286	17	15	2	4.32
	2B	O. Bluege	319	.288	1	55	128	158	2	35	5.5	.993	J. DeShong	34	224	18	10	2	4.63
W-82 L-71	SS	C. Travis	517	.317	2	92	135	213	23	53	5.2	.938	E. Whitehill	28	212	14	11	0	4.87
	3B	B. Lewis	601	.291	6	67	152	297	**32**	24	3.5	.933	P. Appleton	38	202	14	9	3	3.53
Bucky Harris	RF	C. Reynolds	293	.276	4	41	142	8	5	0	2.2	.968	Cascarella	22	139	9	8	1	4.07
	CF	B. Chapman	401	.332	4	60	271	10	12	4	3.0	.959	M. Weaver	26	91	6	4	1	4.35
	LF	J. Stone	437	.341	15	90	249	12	9	5	2.4	.967							
	C	C. Bolton	289	.291	2	51	287	44	7	4	4.1	.979							
	S2	R. Kress	391	.284	8	51	229	312	29	73		.949							
	OF	J. Hill	233	.305	0	34	83	5	3	1	1.5	.967							
	C	W. Millies	215	.312	0	25	205	40	8	3	3.5	.968							
	OF	J. Powell	214	.290	1	30	115	2	6	1	2.3	.951							
	2B	B. Myer	156	.269	0	15	120	143	4	31	6.2	.985							
	OF	F. Sington	94	.319	1	28	52	1	3	0	2.2	.946							
Cleveland	1B	H. Trosky	629	.343	42	162	1367	85	**22**	126	9.8	.985	J. Allen	36	243	20	10	1	3.44
	2B	R. Hughes	638	.295	0	63	421	466	**25**	98	6.0	.973	M. Harder	36	225	15	15	1	5.17
W-80 L-74	SS	Knickerbocker	618	.294	8	73	313	486	40	97	5.4	.952	Hildebrand	36	175	10	11	4	4.90
	3B	O. Hale	620	.316	14	87	169	**323**	28	26	**3.5**	.946	D. Galehouse	36	148	8	7	1	4.85
Steve O'Neill	RF	R. Weatherly	349	.335	8	53	164	15	5	2	2.2	.973	L. Brown	24	140	8	10	1	4.17
	CF	E. Averill	614	.378	28	126	369	11	12	2	2.6	.969	Blaeholder	35	134	8	4	0	5.09
	LF	J. Vosmik	506	.287	7	94	258	11	6	1	2.0	.978	T. Lee	43	127	3	5	3	4.89
	C	B. Sullivan	319	.351	2	48	324	40	12	8	5.2	.968							
	C	F. Pytlak	224	.321	0	31	224	35	1	6	4.5	.996							
	OF	B. Campbell	172	.372	6	30	68	4	3	2	1.6	.960							
Boston	1B	J. Foxx	585	.338	41	143	1226	76	12	108	9.5	.991	W. Ferrell	39	**301**	20	15	0	4.19
	2B	O. Melillo	327	.226	0	32	239	242	10	59	5.3	.980	L. Grove	35	253	17	12	2	**2.81**
W-74 L-80	SS	E. McNair	494	.285	4	74	171	230	14	47	4.9	.966	Ostermueller	43	181	10	16	2	4.87
	3B	B. Werber	535	.275	10	67	112	161	19	16	2.9	.935	J. Marcum	31	174	8	13	1	4.81
Joe Cronin	RF	M. Almada	320	.253	1	21	144	9	2	2	1.9	.987	J. Wilson	43	136	6	8	3	4.42
	CF	D. Cramer	643	.292	0	41	**443**	20	12	6	3.1	.975	R. Walberg	24	100	5	4	0	4.40
	LF	D. Cooke	341	.273	6	47	207	3	6	2	2.4	.972							
	C	R. Ferrell	410	.312	8	55	**556**	55	8	5	5.1	**.987**							
	OF	H. Manush	313	.291	0	45	110	3	4	1	1.6	.966							
	UT	J. Kroner	298	.292	4	62	146	211	18	36		.952							
	SS	J. Cronin	295	.281	2	43	115	191	23	34	5.5	.930							
	P	W. Ferrell	135	.267	5	24	9	42	2	2	1.4	.962							
St. Louis	1B	J. Bottomley	544	.298	12	95	1250	47	10	103	9.3	.992	C. Hogsett	39	215	13	15	1	5.52
	2B	T. Carey	488	.273	1	57	308	434	**25**	82	6.0	.967	J. Knott	47	193	9	17	6	7.29
W-57 L-95	SS	L. Lary	620	.289	2	52	**339**	**495**	38	88	5.6	.956	I. Andrews	36	191	7	12	1	4.84
	3B	H. Clift	576	.302	20	73	158	310	24	27	3.2	.951	E. Caldwell	41	189	7	16	2	6.00
Rogers Hornsby	RF	B. Bell	616	.344	11	123	291	11	8	**6**	2.2	.974	T. Thomas	36	180	11	9	0	5.26
	CF	S. West	533	.278	7	70	442	10	8	2	3.1	.983	R. Van Atta	52	123	4	7	2	6.60
	LF	M. Solters	628	.291	17	134	356	16	**17**	5	2.6	.956							
	C	R. Hemsley	377	.263	2	39	340	68	13	**16**	3.7	.969							
	C	T. Giuliani	198	.217	0	13	226	29	9	7	4.0	.966							
	OF	E. Coleman	137	.292	2	34	31	0	2	0	1.8	.939							
	OF	R. Pepper	124	.282	2	23	31	1	2	0	1.9	.941							

AMERICAN LEAGUE 1936, cont.

	POS	Player	AB	BA	HR	RBI	PO	A	E	DP	TC/G	FA	Pitcher	G	IP	W	L	SV	ERA
Philadelphia	1B	L. Finney	**653**	.302	1	41	782	34	8	70	10.6	.990	H. Kelley	35	235	15	12	3	3.86
	2B	R. Warstler	236	.250	1	24	139	265	11	45	6.3	.973	G. Rhodes	35	216	9	**20**	1	5.74
W-53 L-100	SS	S. Newsome	471	.225	0	46	273	417	31	87	5.9	.957	B. Ross	30	201	9	14	0	5.83
	3B	P. Higgins	550	.289	12	80	151	266	26	24	3.1	.941	H. Fink	34	189	8	16	3	5.39
Connie Mack	RF	Puccinelli	457	.278	11	78	245	11	14	1	2.3	.948	B. Dietrich	21	72	4	6	3	6.53
	CF	W. Moses	585	.345	7	66	396	12	11	3	2.9	.974							
	LF	B. Johnson	566	.292	25	121	289	13	12	3	2.4	.962							
	C	F. Hayes	505	.271	10	67	489	69	**16**	8	4.0	.972							
	1B	C. Dean	342	.287	1	48	680	37	8	62	9.4	.989							
	2B	A. Niemiec	203	.197	1	20	134	180	9	32	6.2	.972							

BATTING AND BASE RUNNING LEADERS

Batting Average		Slugging Average		Home Runs		Winning Percentage			PITCHING LEADERS Earned Run Average		Wins	
L. Appling, CHI	.388	L. Gehrig, NY	.696	L. Gehrig, NY	49	M. Pearson, NY	.731		L. Grove, BOS	2.81	T. Bridges, DET	23
E. Averill, CLE	.378	H. Trosky, CLE	.644	H. Trosky, CLE	42	V. Kennedy, CHI	.700		J. Allen, CLE	3.44	V. Kennedy, CHI	21
B. Dickey, NY	.362	J. Foxx, BOS	.631	J. Foxx, BOS	41	T. Bridges, DET	.676		P. Appleton, WAS	3.53	J. Allen, CLE	20
C. Gehringer, DET	.354	E. Averill, CLE	.627	J. DiMaggio, NY	29	J. Allen, CLE	.667		T. Bridges, DET	3.60	R. Ruffing, NY	20
L. Gehrig, NY	.354	B. Dickey, NY	.617	E. Averill, CLE	28	S. Rowe, DET	.655		M. Pearson, NY	3.71	W. Ferrell, BOS	20

Total Bases		Runs Batted In		Stolen Bases		Saves		Strikeouts		Complete Games	
H. Trosky, CLE	405	H. Trosky, CLE	162	L. Lary, STL	37	P. Malone, NY	9	T. Bridges, DET	175	W. Ferrell, BOS	28
L. Gehrig, NY	403	L. Gehrig, NY	152	J. Powell, NY, WAS	26	J. Knott, STL	6	J. Allen, CLE	165	T. Bridges, DET	26
E. Averill, CLE	385	J. Foxx, BOS	143	B. Werber, BOS	23	C. Brown, CHI	5	B. Newsom, WAS	156	R. Ruffing, NY	25
J. Foxx, BOS	369	Z. Bonura, CHI	138	B. Chapman, NY, WAS	20	J. Murphy, NY	5	L. Grove, BOS	130	B. Newsom, WAS	24
J. DiMaggio, NY	367	M. Solters, STL	134	R. Hughes, CLE	20	Hildebrand, CLE	4	M. Pearson, NY	118	L. Grove, BOS	22

Hits		Base on Balls		Home Run Percentage		Fewest Hits/9 Innings		Shutouts		Fewest Walks/9 Innings	
E. Averill, CLE	232	L. Gehrig, NY	130	L. Gehrig, NY	8.5	M. Pearson, NY	7.71	L. Grove, BOS	6	T. Lyons, CHI	2.23
C. Gehringer, DET	227	L. Lary, STL	117	J. Foxx, BOS	7.0	L. Grove, BOS	8.42	T. Bridges, DET	5	L. Grove, BOS	2.31
H. Trosky, CLE	216	H. Clift, STL	115	H. Trosky, CLE	6.7	J. Allen, CLE	8.67	J. Allen, CLE	4	S. Rowe, DET	2.35
B. Bell, STL	212	J. Foxx, BOS	105	B. Dickey, NY	5.2	L. Gomez, NY	8.78	S. Rowe, DET	4	I. Andrews, STL	2.35

Runs Scored		Doubles		Triples		Most Strikeouts/9 Inn.		Innings		Games Pitched	
L. Gehrig, NY	167	C. Gehringer, DET	60	R. Rolfe, NY	15	J. Allen, CLE	6.11	W. Ferrell, BOS	301	R. Van Atta, STL	52
H. Clift, STL	145	G. Walker, DET	55	E. Averill, CLE	15	T. Bridges, DET	5.35	T. Bridges, DET	295	J. Knott, STL	47
C. Gehringer, DET	144	B. Chapman, NY, WAS	50	J. DiMaggio, NY	15	L. Gomez, NY	5.01	B. Newsom, WAS	286	B. Newsom, WAS	43
F. Crosetti, NY	137	O. Hale, CLE	50	B. Johnson, PHI	14	B. Newsom, WAS	4.91	V. Kennedy, CHI	274	Ostermueller, BOS	43

	W	L	PCT	GB	R	OR	2B	3B	HR	BA	SA	SB	E	DP	FA	CG	BB	SO	ShO	SV	ERA
New York	102	51	.667		**1065**	731	315	83	**182**	.300	**.483**	76	163	148	.973	77	663	**624**	6	**21**	**4.17**
Detroit	83	71	.539	19.5	921	871	326	55	94	.300	.431	72	**153**	159	**.975**	76	562	526	**13**	13	5.00
Chicago	81	70	.536	20	920	873	282	56	60	.292	.397	66	168	**174**	.973	**80**	578	414	5	8	5.06
Washington	82	71	.536	20	889	799	293	**84**	62	.295	.414	**103**	182	163	.970	78	588	462	8	14	4.58
Cleveland	80	74	.519	22.5	921	862	**357**	82	123	**.304**	.461	66	178	154	.971	**80**	**607**	619	6	12	4.83
Boston	74	80	.481	28.5	775	764	288	62	86	.276	.400	54	165	139	.972	78	**552**	584	11	9	4.39
St. Louis	57	95	.375	44.5	804	1064	299	66	79	.279	.403	62	188	143	.969	54	609	399	3	13	6.24
Philadelphia	53	100	.346	49	714	1045	240	60	72	.269	.376	59	209	152	.965	68	696	405	3	12	6.08
					7009	7009	2400	548	758	.289	.421	558	1406	1232	.971	591	4855	4033	55	102	5.04

NATIONAL LEAGUE 1937

	POS	Player	AB	BA	HR	RBI	PO	A	E	DP	TC/G	FA	Pitcher	G	IP	W	L	SV	ERA
New York	1B	J. McCarthy	420	.279	10	65	1123	82	16	89	11.1	.987	C. Hubbell	39	262	**22**	8	4	3.20
	2B	B. Whitehead	574	.286	5	52	**394**	514	24	**106**	6.1	**.974**	C. Melton	46	248	20	7	1	2.61
W-95 L-57	SS	D. Bartell	516	.306	14	62	281	476	33	96	6.2	.958	Schumacher	38	218	13	12	1	3.60
	3B	L. Chiozza	439	.232	4	29	90	171	17	9	3.0	.939	H. Gumbert	34	200	10	11	1	3.68
Bill Terry	RF	M. Ott	545	.294	**31**	95	156	13	0	1	1.9	**1.000**	S. Castleman	23	160	11	6	0	3.31
	CF	J. Ripple	426	.317	5	66	193	6	4	1	1.8	.980	D. Coffman	42	80	8	3	3	3.04
	LF	J. Moore	580	.310	6	57	226	12	6	0	1.7	.975							
	C	H. Danning	292	.288	8	51	332	57	7	7	4.6	.982							
	C	G. Mancuso	287	.279	4	39	410	69	9	4	6.0	.982							
	OF	W. Berger	199	.291	12	43	107	4	4	0	2.2	.965							
	1B	S. Leslie	191	.309	3	30	444	38	5	45	11.1	.990							
	OF	H. Leiber	184	.293	4	32	78	1	1	0	1.7	.988							

NATIONAL LEAGUE 1937, *cont.*

	POS	Player	AB	BA	HR	RBI	PO	A	E	DP	TC/G	FA	Pitcher	G	IP	W	L	SV	ERA
Chicago	1B	R. Collins	456	.274	16	71	1068	80	11	94	10.4	.991	B. Lee	42	272	14	15	3	3.54
	2B	B. Herman	564	.335	8	65	384	468	41	97	6.5	.954	L. French	42	208	16	10	0	3.98
	SS	B. Jurges	450	.298	1	65	258	370	16	74	5.0	.975	T. Carleton	32	208	16	8	2	3.15
W-93 L-61	3B	S. Hack	582	.297	2	63	151	247	13	25	2.7	.968	C. Root	43	179	13	5	5	3.38
	RF	F. Demaree	615	.324	17	115	283	17	6	6	2.0	.980	R. Parmelee	33	146	7	8	0	5.13
Charlie Grimm	CF	J. Marty	290	.290	5	44	196	4	5	0	2.4	.976	C. Bryant	38	135	9	3	3	4.26
	LF	A. Galan	611	.252	18	78	328	9	7	3	2.5	.980	C. Davis	28	124	10	5	1	4.08
	C	G. Hartnett	356	.354	12	82	436	65	2	7	5.0	.996	C. Shoun	37	93	7	7	0	5.61
	O1	Cavarretta	329	.286	5	56	454	40	10	28		.980							
	C	K. O'Dea	219	.301	4	32	234	29	4	4	4.2	.985							
	UT	L. Frey	198	.278	1	22	90	101	10	18		.950							
	OF	T. Stainback	160	.231	0	14	99	4	2	1	2.1	.981							
Pittsburgh	1B	G. Suhr	575	.278	5	97	1452	91	11	108	10.3	.993	C. Blanton	36	243	14	12	0	3.30
	2B	L. Handley	480	.250	3	37	296	375	35	67	5.6	.950	R. Bauers	34	188	13	6	1	2.88
	SS	A. Vaughan	469	.322	5	72	231	335	26	58	5.5	.956	E. Brandt	33	176	11	10	2	3.11
W-86 L-68	3B	B. Brubaker	413	.254	6	48	98	216	16	16	2.9	.952	B. Swift	36	164	9	10	3	3.95
	RF	P. Waner	619	.354	2	74	271	16	9	3	2.0	.970	J. Bowman	30	128	8	8	1	4.57
Pie Traynor	CF	L. Waner	537	.330	1	45	312	8	4	0	2.6	.988	R. Lucas	20	126	8	10	0	4.27
	LF	W. Jensen	509	.279	5	45	256	5	10	1	2.3	.963	J. Weaver	32	110	8	5	0	3.20
	C	A. Todd	514	.307	8	86	603	89	20	15	5.6	.972	M. Brown	50	108	7	2	7	4.18
	UT	P. Young	408	.260	9	54	195	328	24	52		.956	J. Tobin	20	87	6	3	1	3.00
	OF	J. Dickshot	264	.254	3	33	109	5	6	2	1.9	.950							
St. Louis	1B	J. Mize	560	.364	25	113	1308	67	17	104	9.7	.988	B. Weiland	41	264	15	14	0	3.54
	2B	J. Brown	525	.276	2	53	235	360	22	57	5.5	.964	L. Warneke	36	239	18	11	0	4.53
	SS	L. Durocher	477	.203	1	47	279	381	28	72	5.1	.959	D. Dean	27	197	13	10	1	2.69
W-81 L-73	3B	Gutteridge	447	.271	7	61	133	176	7	18	3.0	.978	S. Johnson	38	192	12	12	1	3.32
	RF	D. Padgett	446	.314	10	74	225	9	11	5	2.2	.955	M. Ryba	38	135	9	6	0	4.13
Frankie Frisch	CF	T. Moore	461	.267	5	43	307	9	4	2	3.0	.988	R. Harrell	35	97	3	7	1	5.87
	LF	J. Medwick	633	.374	31	154	329	9	4	1	2.2	.988							
	C	Ogrodowski	279	.233	3	31	387	50	7	2	5.1	.984							
	OF	P. Martin	339	.304	5	38	204	12	6	3	2.7	.973							
	3O	Bordagaray	300	.293	1	37	105	72	9	2		.952							
	C	M. Owen	234	.231	0	20	287	49	9	6	4.4	.974							
	2B	S. Martin	223	.260	1	17	93	134	13	27	5.0	.946							
Boston	1B	E. Fletcher	539	.247	1	38	1587	108	12	117	11.5	.993	L. Fette	35	259	20	10	0	2.88
	2B	Cuccinello	575	.271	11	80	330	524	29	92	5.8	.967	J. Turner	33	257	20	11	1	2.38
	SS	R. Warstler	555	.223	3	36	298	493	49	85	5.6	.942	MacFayden	32	246	14	14	0	2.93
W-79 L-73	3B	G. English	269	.290	2	37	61	121	8	9	2.7	.958	G. Bush	32	181	8	15	1	3.54
	RF	G. Moore	561	.283	16	70	340	21	8	1	2.5	.978	J. Lanning	32	117	5	7	3	3.93
Bill McKechnie	CF	V. DiMaggio	493	.256	13	69	351	21	7	2	2.9	.982	Hutchinson	31	92	4	6	0	3.73
	LF	D. Garms	478	.259	2	37	168	1	4	0	2.1	.977	F. Gabler	19	76	4	7	2	5.09
	C	A. Lopez	334	.204	3	38	342	83	7	5	4.2	.984							
	OF	R. Johnson	260	.277	3	22	131	5	5	0	2.2	.965							
	C	R. Mueller	187	.251	2	26	169	44	1	6	3.8	.995							
	3B	E. Mayo	172	.227	1	18	57	73	6	2	2.7	.956							
	OF	W. Berger	113	.274	5	22	51	1	0	0	1.9	1.000							
Brooklyn	1B	B. Hassett	556	.304	1	53	1125	116	20	96	9.6	.984	M. Butcher	39	192	11	15	0	4.27
	2B	C. Lavagetto	503	.282	8	70	229	294	28	56	5.5	.949	L. Hamlin	39	186	11	13	1	3.59
	SS	W. English	378	.238	1	42	220	303	24	51	4.7	.956	Frankhouse	33	179	10	13	0	4.27
W-62 L-91	3B	J. Stripp	300	.243	1	26	75	91	5	4	2.6	.971	W. Hoyt	27	167	7	7	3	3.23
	RF	H. Manush	466	.333	4	73	187	7	6	1	1.6	.970	V. Mungo	25	161	9	11	2	2.91
Burleigh Grimes	CF	J. Cooney	430	.293	0	37	279	9	7	2	2.7	.976	R. Henshaw	42	156	5	12	2	5.07
	LF	T. Winsett	350	.237	5	42	209	6	9	1	2.2	.960	Fitzsimmons	13	91	4	8	0	4.27
	C	B. Phelps	409	.313	7	58	465	76	16	10	5.0	.971							
	23	J. Bucher	380	.253	4	37	165	192	23	35		.939							
	OF	G. Brack	372	.274	5	38	208	10	7	0	2.2	.969							
Philadelphia	1B	D. Camilli	475	.339	27	80	1256	99	8	104	10.4	.994	C. Passeau	50	292	14	18	2	4.34
	2B	D. Young	360	.194	0	24	200	333	28	63	5.2	.950	B. Walters	37	246	14	15	0	4.75
	SS	G. Scharein	511	.241	0	57	335	456	44	98	5.7	.947	W. LaMaster	50	220	15	19	4	5.31
W-61 L-92	3B	P. Whitney	487	.341	8	79	136	238	7	17	2.9	.982	H. Mulcahy	56	216	8	18	3	5.13
	RF	C. Klein	406	.325	15	57	175	11	10	3	1.9	.949	O. Jorgens	52	141	3	4	3	4.41
Jimmie Wilson	CF	H. Martin	579	.283	8	49	353	9	8	1	2.7	.978	S. Johnson	32	138	4	10	3	5.02
	LF	M. Arnovich	410	.290	10	60	237	10	7	5	2.4	.972							
	C	B. Atwood	279	.244	2	32	290	48	11	5	4.4	.968							
	UT	L. Norris	381	.257	9	36	212	264	22	43		.956							
	OF	E. Browne	332	.292	6	52	92	7	2	1	1.9	.980							
	OF	J. Moore	307	.319	9	59	124	9	8	1	2.0	.943							
	C	E. Grace	223	.211	6	29	275	30	3	10	4.8	.990							

NATIONAL LEAGUE 1937, cont.

Cincinnati

W-56 L-98

Chuck Dressen
W-51 L-78

Bobby Wallace
W-5 L-20

POS	Player	AB	BA	HR	RBI	PO	A	E	DP	TC/G	FA	Pitcher	G	IP	W	L	SV	ERA
1B	B. Jordan	316	.282	1	28	669	46	8	55	9.5	.989	L. Grissom	50	224	12	17	6	3.26
2B	A. Kampouris	458	.249	17	71	367	439	33	87	5.7	.961	P. Derringer	43	223	10	14	1	4.04
SS	B. Myers	335	.251	7	43	190	360	30	67	4.8	.948	P. Davis	42	218	11	13	3	3.59
3B	L. Riggs	384	.242	6	45	112	223	21	16	3.6	.941	Hollingsworth	43	202	9	15	5	3.91
RF	I. Goodman	549	.273	12	55	291	13	8	0	2.2	.974	G. Schott	37	154	4	13	1	2.97
CF	C. Hafey	257	.261	9	41	128	5	4	0	2.1	.971	B. Hallahan	21	63	3	9	0	6.14
LF	K. Cuyler	406	.271	0	32	174	8	5	1	1.8	.973							
C	E. Lombardi	368	.334	9	59	333	58	11	3	4.5	.973							
1B	L. Scarsella	329	.246	3	34	589	37	10	55	9.8	.984							
OF	H. Walker	221	.249	1	19	135	5	1	3	2.4	.993							
C	S. Davis	209	.268	3	33	300	40	7	3	5.9	.980							
OF	P. Weintraub	177	.271	3	20	78	3	2	1	1.8	.976							
3B	J. Outlaw	165	.273	0	11	41	87	12	4	3.4	.914							

BATTING AND BASE RUNNING LEADERS

Batting Average
J. Medwick, STL	.374
J. Mize, STL	.364
G. Hartnett, CHI	.354
P. Waner, PIT	.354
P. Whitney, PHI	.341

Slugging Average
J. Medwick, STL	.641
J. Mize, STL	.595
D. Camilli, PHI	.587
G. Hartnett, CHI	.548
M. Ott, NY	.523

Home Runs
M. Ott, NY	31
J. Medwick, STL	31
D. Camilli, PHI	27
J. Mize, STL	25
A. Galan, CHI	18

Winning Percentage
C. Hubbell, NY	.733
C. Melton, NY	.690
L. Fette, BOS	.667
T. Carleton, CHI	.667
J. Turner, BOS	.645

Earned Run Average
J. Turner, BOS	2.38
C. Melton, NY	2.61
J. Dean, STL	2.69
R. Bauers, PIT	2.88
L. Fette, BOS	2.88

Wins
C. Hubbell, NY	22
C. Melton, NY	20
L. Fette, BOS	20
J. Turner, BOS	20
L. Warneke, STL	18

Total Bases
J. Medwick, STL	406
J. Mize, STL	333
F. Demaree, CHI	298
M. Ott, NY	285
D. Camilli, PHI	279

Runs Batted In
J. Medwick, STL	154
F. Demaree, CHI	115
J. Mize, STL	113
G. Suhr, PIT	97
M. Ott, NY	95

Stolen Bases
A. Galan, CHI	23
S. Hack, CHI	16
T. Moore, STL	13
C. Lavagetto, BKN	13
G. Scharein, PHI	13
B. Hassett, BKN	13

Saves
M. Brown, PIT	7
C. Melton, NY	7
L. Grissom, CIN	6
C. Root, CHI	5
Hollingsworth, CIN	5

Strikeouts
C. Hubbell, NY	159
L. Grissom, CIN	149
C. Blanton, PIT	143
C. Melton, NY	142
W. LaMaster, PHI	135
C. Passeau, PHI	135

Complete Games
J. Turner, BOS	24
L. Fette, BOS	23
B. Weiland, STL	21

Hits
J. Medwick, STL	237
P. Waner, PIT	219
J. Mize, STL	204
F. Demaree, CHI	199

Base on Balls
M. Ott, NY	102
D. Camilli, PHI	90
S. Hack, CHI	83
G. Suhr, PIT	83

Home Run Percentage
M. Ott, NY	5.7
D. Camilli, PHI	5.7
J. Medwick, STL	4.9
J. Mize, STL	4.5

Fewest Hits/9 Innings
V. Mungo, BKN	7.60
L. Grissom, CIN	7.77
C. Melton, NY	7.84
T. Carleton, CHI	7.91

Shutouts
L. Grissom, CIN	5
J. Turner, BOS	5
L. Fette, BOS	5

Fewest Walks/9 Innings
D. Dean, STL	1.51
W. Hoyt, BKN, PIT	1.66
J. Turner, BOS	1.82
S. Castleman, NY	1.85

Runs Scored
J. Medwick, STL	111
B. Herman, CHI	106
S. Hack, CHI	106
A. Galan, CHI	104

Doubles
J. Medwick, STL	56
J. Mize, STL	40
D. Bartell, NY	38
B. Phelps, BKN	37

Triples
A. Vaughan, PIT	17
G. Suhr, PIT	14
L. Handley, PIT	12
I. Goodman, CIN	12

Most Strikeouts/9 Inn.
V. Mungo, BKN	6.82
L. Grissom, CIN	6.00
R. Bauers, PIT	5.66
W. LaMaster, PHI	5.51

Innings
C. Passeau, PHI	292
B. Lee, CHI	272
B. Weiland, STL	264
C. Hubbell, NY	262

Games Pitched
H. Mulcahy, PHI	56
O. Jorgens, PHI	52
C. Passeau, PHI	50
L. Grissom, CIN	50

	W	L	PCT	GB	R	OR	| 2B	3B	Batting HR	BA	SA	SB	| E	Fielding DP	FA	| CG	BB	Pitching SO	ShO	SV	| ERA
New York	95	57	.625		732	602	251	41	111	.278	.403	45	159	143	.974	67	404	653	11	17	3.43
Chicago	93	61	.604	3	811	682	253	74	96	.287	.416	71	151	141	.975	73	502	596	11	13	3.97
Pittsburgh	86	68	.558	10	704	646	223	86	47	.285	.384	32	181	135	.970	67	428	643	12	17	3.56
St. Louis	81	73	.526	15	789	733	264	67	94	.282	.406	78	164	127	.973	81	448	573	10	4	3.95
Boston	79	73	.520	16	579	556	200	41	63	.247	.339	45	157	128	.975	85	372	387	16	10	3.22
Brooklyn	62	91	.405	33.5	616	772	258	53	37	.265	.354	69	217	127	.964	63	476	592	5	8	4.13
Philadelphia	61	92	.399	34.5	724	869	258	37	103	.273	.391	66	184	157	.970	59	501	529	6	15	5.06
Cincinnati	56	98	.364	40	612	707	215	59	73	.254	.360	53	208	139	.966	64	533	581	10	18	3.94
					5567	5567	1922	458	624	.272	.382	459	1421	1097	.971	559	3664	4554	81	102	3.91

AMERICAN LEAGUE 1937

New York

W-102 L-52

Joe McCarthy

POS	Player	AB	BA	HR	RBI	PO	A	E	DP	TC/G	FA	Pitcher	G	IP	W	L	SV	ERA
1B	L. Gehrig	569	.351	37	159	1370	74	16	113	9.3	.989	L. Gomez	34	278	21	11	0	2.33
2B	T. Lazzeri	446	.244	14	70	251	382	22	64	5.2	.966	R. Ruffing	31	256	20	7	0	2.98
SS	F. Crosetti	611	.234	11	49	313	467	43	86	5.6	.948	B. Hadley	29	178	11	8	0	5.30
3B	R. Rolfe	648	.276	4	62	195	309	20	27	3.4	.962	M. Pearson	22	145	9	3	1	3.17
RF	M. Hoag	362	.301	3	46	181	8	9	2	2.0	.955	J. Murphy	39	110	13	4	10	4.17
CF	J. DiMaggio	621	.346	46	167	413	21	17	4	3.0	.962	P. Malone	28	92	4	4	6	5.48
LF	J. Powell	365	.263	4	45	201	5	4	2	2.2	.981	K. Wicker	16	88	7	3	0	4.40
C	B. Dickey	530	.332	29	133	692	80	7	11	5.7	.991	S. Chandler	12	82	7	4	0	2.84
OF	G. Selkirk	256	.328	18	68	140	9	2	1	2.2	.987	F. Makosky	26	58	5	2	3	4.97
OF	T. Henrich	206	.320	8	42	90	6	3	1	1.7	.970							
2S	D. Heffner	201	.249	0	21	123	126	6	30		.976							

AMERICAN LEAGUE 1937, cont.

Detroit — W-89 L-65 — Mickey Cochrane W-16 L-13 — Del Baker W-34 L-20 — Mickey Cochrane W-39 L-32

POS	Player	AB	BA	HR	RBI	PO	A	E	DP	TC/G	FA	Pitcher	G	IP	W	L	SV	ERA
1B	H. Greenberg	594	.337	40	183	1477	102	13	133	10.3	.992	E. Auker	39	253	17	9	1	3.88
2B	C. Gehringer	564	.371	14	96	331	485	12	102	5.8	.986	T. Bridges	34	245	15	12	0	4.07
SS	B. Rogell	536	.276	8	64	323	451	26	103	5.5	.968	R. Lawson	37	217	18	7	1	5.26
3B	M. Owen	396	.288	1	45	108	219	10	17	3.2	.970	J. Wade	33	165	7	10	0	5.39
RF	P. Fox	628	.331	12	82	321	6	8	0	2.3	.976	Poffenberger	29	137	10	5	3	4.65
CF	J. White	305	.246	0	21	216	4	6	0	2.8	.973	G. Gill	31	128	11	4	1	4.51
LF	G. Walker	635	.335	18	113	316	9	15	2	2.3	.956	S. Coffman	28	101	7	5	0	4.37
C	R. York	375	.307	35	103	190	27	9	6	4.2	.960	J. Russell	25	40	2	5	4	7.59
OF	C. Laabs	242	.240	8	37	133	2	4	0	2.2	.971							
OF	G. Goslin	181	.238	4	35	81	2	4	1	2.2	.954							
C	B. Tebbetts	162	.191	2	16	155	25	7	1	3.9	.963							

Chicago — W-86 L-68 — Jimmy Dykes

POS	Player	AB	BA	HR	RBI	PO	A	E	DP	TC/G	FA	Pitcher	G	IP	W	L	SV	ERA
1B	Z. Bonura	447	.345	19	100	1114	63	13	123	10.3	.989	V. Kennedy	32	221	14	13	0	5.09
2B	J. Hayes	573	.229	2	79	353	490	14	115	6.0	.984	T. Lee	30	205	12	10	0	3.52
SS	L. Appling	574	.317	4	77	280	541	49	111	5.6	.944	T. Lyons	22	169	12	7	0	4.15
3B	T. Piet	332	.235	4	38	83	163	16	12	3.0	.939	J. Whitehead	26	166	11	8	0	4.07
RF	D. Walker	593	.302	9	95	270	10	14	1	1.9	.952	M. Stratton	22	165	15	5	0	2.40
CF	M. Kreevich	583	.302	12	73	401	13	5	4	3.0	.988	B. Dietrich	29	143	8	10	1	4.90
LF	R. Radcliff	584	.325	4	79	273	9	10	5	2.1	.966	C. Brown	53	100	7	7	18	3.42
C	L. Sewell	412	.269	1	61	502	72	9	11	4.9	.985							
13	J. Dykes	85	.306	1	23	152	27	1	15		.994							

Cleveland — W-83 L-71 — Steve O'Neill

POS	Player	AB	BA	HR	RBI	PO	A	E	DP	TC/G	FA	Pitcher	G	IP	W	L	SV	ERA
1B	H. Trosky	601	.298	32	128	1403	76	10	131	9.8	.993	M. Harder	38	234	15	12	2	4.28
2B	J. Kroner	283	.237	2	26	155	189	11	45	5.5	.969	D. Galehouse	36	201	9	14	3	4.57
SS	L. Lary	644	.290	8	77	325	489	31	95	5.4	.963	W. Hudlin	35	176	12	11	2	4.10
3B	O. Hale	561	.267	6	82	96	199	11	24	3.4	.964	J. Allen	24	173	15	1	0	2.55
RF	B. Campbell	448	.301	4	61	204	14	5	5	1.8	.978	B. Feller	26	149	9	7	1	3.39
CF	E. Averill	609	.299	21	92	362	11	9	3	2.4	.976	E. Whitehill	33	147	8	8	2	6.49
LF	M. Solters	589	.323	20	109	283	19	15	3	2.1	.953	J. Heving	40	73	8	4	5	4.83
C	F. Pytlak	397	.315	1	44	559	80	9	13	5.6	.986							
32	R. Hughes	346	.277	1	40	157	233	13	32		.968							
C	B. Sullivan	168	.286	3	22	146	20	9	1	4.6	.949							

Boston — W-80 L-72 — Joe Cronin

POS	Player	AB	BA	HR	RBI	PO	A	E	DP	TC/G	FA	Pitcher	G	IP	W	L	SV	ERA
1B	J. Foxx	569	.285	36	127	1287	106	8	122	9.3	.994	L. Grove	32	262	17	9	0	3.02
2B	E. McNair	455	.292	12	76	242	316	18	67	5.4	.969	W. Wilson	51	221	16	10	7	3.70
SS	J. Cronin	570	.307	18	110	300	414	31	89	5.0	.958	B. Newsom	30	208	13	10	0	4.38
3B	P. Higgins	570	.302	9	106	161	258	29	29	2.9	.935	J. Marcum	37	184	13	11	3	4.85
RF	B. Chapman	423	.307	7	57	262	9	4	4	2.5	.985	A. McKain	36	137	8	8	2	4.66
CF	D. Cramer	560	.305	0	51	365	12	12	4	2.9	.969	R. Walberg	32	105	5	7	1	5.59
LF	B. Mills	505	.295	7	58	239	8	14	0	2.2	.946	Ostermueller	25	87	3	7	1	4.98
C	G. Desautels	305	.243	0	27	491	44	4	4	5.7	.993							
OF	F. Gaffke	184	.288	6	34	80	3	3	0	1.7	.965							
C	M. Berg	141	.255	0	20	208	24	5	2	5.0	.979							

Washington — W-73 L-80 — Bucky Harris

POS	Player	AB	BA	HR	RBI	PO	A	E	DP	TC/G	FA	Pitcher	G	IP	W	L	SV	ERA
1B	J. Kuhel	547	.283	6	61	1242	85	9	141	9.8	.993	J. DeShong	37	264	14	15	1	4.90
2B	B. Myer	430	.293	1	65	308	338	23	99	5.6	.966	W. Ferrell	25	208*	11	13	0	3.94
SS	C. Travis	526	.344	3	66	229	396	23	99	5.0	.965	M. Weaver	30	189	12	9	0	4.20
3B	B. Lewis	668	.314	10	79	146	293	29	32	3.0	.938	P. Appleton	35	168	8	15	2	4.39
RF	J. Stone	542	.330	6	88	300	15	5	3	2.3	.984	E. Linke	36	129	6	1	3	5.60
CF	M. Almada	433	.309	4	33	308	16	12	3	3.4	.964	C. Fischer	17	72	4	5	2	4.38
LF	A. Simmons	419	.279	8	84	240	7	4	5	2.5	.984	S. Cohen	33	55	2	4	4	3.11
C	R. Ferrell	279	.229	1	32	341	42	5	5	4.6	.987							
OF	F. Sington	228	.237	3	36	120	4	5	0	2.0	.961							
C	W. Millies	179	.223	0	28	199	33	7	7	4.3	.971							

Philadelphia — W-54 L-97 — Connie Mack W-39 L-80 — Earle Mack W-15 L-17

POS	Player	AB	BA	HR	RBI	PO	A	E	DP	TC/G	FA	Pitcher	G	IP	W	L	SV	ERA
1B	C. Dean	309	.262	2	31	705	38	7	55	9.6	.991	G. Caster	34	232	12	19	0	4.43
2B	R. Peters	339	.260	3	43	138	170	11	34	4.6	.966	H. Kelley	41	205	13	21	0	5.36
SS	S. Newsome	438	.253	1	30	256	408	32	76	5.7	.954	E. Smith	38	197	4	17	5	3.94
3B	B. Werber	493	.292	7	70	132	260	17	25	3.3	.958	B. Thomas	35	170	8	15	0	4.99
RF	W. Moses	649	.320	25	86	323	16	15	4	2.3	.958	B. Ross	28	147	5	10	0	4.89
CF	J. Hill	242	.293	1	37	163	4	8	0	2.6	.954	L. Nelson	30	116	4	9	2	5.90
LF	B. Johnson	477	.306	25	108	313	14	8	3	2.5	.976							
C	E. Brucker	317	.259	6	37	323	48	11	13	4.2	.971							
10	L. Finney	379	.251	1	20	519	30	12	39		.979							
OF	J. Rothrock	232	.267	0	21	130	2	1	0	2.3	.992							
C	F. Hayes	188	.261	10	38	208	23	7	4	4.3	.971							
2B	W. Ambler	162	.216	0	11	107	149	12	34	4.8	.955							
P	L. Nelson	113	.354	4	29	3	14	0	0	.6	1.000							

AMERICAN LEAGUE 1937, cont.

	POS	Player	AB	BA	HR	RBI	PO	A	E	DP	TC/G	FA	Pitcher	G	IP	W	L	SV	ERA
St. Louis	1B	H. Davis	450	.276	3	35	1065	54	10	108	10.1	.991	Hildebrand	30	201	8	17	1	5.14
	2B	T. Carey	487	.275	1	40	202	253	8	58	5.3	.983	J. Knott	38	191	8	18	2	4.89
W-46 L-108	SS	Knickerbocker	491	.261	4	61	205	368	25	59	5.2	.958	C. Hogsett	37	177	6	19	2	6.29
	3B	H. Clift	571	.306	29	118	198	405	34	50	4.1	.947	J. Walkup	27	150	9	12	0	7.36
Rogers Hornsby	RF	B. Bell	642	.340	14	117	222	22	4	6	1.9	.984	J. Bonetti	28	143	4	11	1	5.84
W-25 L-52	CF	S. West	457	.328	7	58	298	17	4	6	3.0	.987	B. Trotter	34	122	2	9	1	5.81
	LF	J. Vosmik	594	.325	4	93	333	12	10	4	2.5	.972	L. Koupal	26	106	4	9	0	6.56
Jim Bottomley	C	R. Hemsley	334	.222	3	28	332	70	13	13	4.4	.969							
W-21 L-56																			
	OF	E. Allen	320	.316	0	31	186	8	4	1	2.5	.980							
	C	B. Huffman	176	.273	1	24	140	20	5	4	3.9	.970							

BATTING AND BASE RUNNING LEADERS

Batting Average		Slugging Average		Home Runs		Winning Percentage	
C. Gehringer, DET	.371	J. DiMaggio, NY	.673	J. DiMaggio, NY	46	J. Allen, CLE	.938
L. Gehrig, NY	.351	H. Greenberg, DET	.668	H. Greenberg, DET	40	M. Stratton, CHI	.750
J. DiMaggio, NY	.346	R. York, DET	.651	L. Gehrig, NY	37	R. Ruffing, NY	.741
Z. Bonura, CHI	.345	L. Gehrig, NY	.643	J. Foxx, BOS	36	R. Lawson, DET	.720
C. Travis, WAS	.344	Z. Bonura, CHI	.573	R. York, DET	35	L. Gomez, NY	.656

Total Bases		Runs Batted In		Stolen Bases		Saves	
J. DiMaggio, NY	418	H. Greenberg, DET	183	B. Werber, PHI	35	C. Brown, CHI	18
H. Greenberg, DET	397	J. DiMaggio, NY	167	B. Chapman, BOS, WAS	35	J. Murphy, NY	10
L. Gehrig, NY	366	L. Gehrig, NY	159	G. Walker, DET	23	J. Wilson, BOS	7
W. Moses, PHI	357	B. Dickey, NY	133	J. Hill, PHI, WAS	18	P. Malone, NY	6
H. Trosky, CLE	329	H. Trosky, CLE	128	L. Appling, CHI	18	J. Heving, CLE	5
				L. Lary, CLE	18	E. Smith, PHI	5

Hits		Base on Balls		Home Run Percentage		Fewest Hits/9 Innings	
B. Bell, STL	218	L. Gehrig, NY	127	R. York, DET	9.3	L. Gomez, NY	7.53
J. DiMaggio, NY	215	H. Greenberg, DET	102	J. DiMaggio, NY	7.4	M. Stratton, CHI	7.76
G. Walker, DET	213	J. Foxx, BOS	99	H. Greenberg, DET	6.7	E. Smith, PHI	8.15
B. Lewis, WAS	210	B. Johnson, PHI	98	L. Gehrig, NY	6.5	J. Allen, CLE	8.17

Runs Scored		Doubles		Triples		Most Strikeouts/9 Inn.	
J. DiMaggio, NY	151	B. Bell, STL	51	M. Kreevich, CHI	16	L. Gomez, NY	6.27
R. Rolfe, NY	143	H. Greenberg, DET	49	D. Walker, CHI	16	J. Wilson, BOS	5.57
L. Gehrig, NY	138	W. Moses, PHI	48	J. Stone, WAS	15	B. Newsom, BOS, WAS	5.43
H. Greenberg, DET	137	J. Vosmik, STL	47	J. DiMaggio, NY	15	L. Grove, BOS	5.26

PITCHING LEADERS

Earned Run Average		Wins	
L. Gomez, NY	2.33	L. Gomez, NY	21
M. Stratton, CHI	2.40	R. Ruffing, NY	20
J. Allen, CLE	2.55	R. Lawson, DET	18
R. Ruffing, NY	2.98	E. Auker, DET	17
L. Grove, BOS	3.02	L. Grove, BOS	17

Strikeouts		Complete Games	
L. Gomez, NY	194	W. Ferrell, BOS, WAS	26
B. Newsom, BOS, WAS	166	L. Gomez, NY	25
L. Grove, BOS	153	R. Ruffing, NY	22
B. Feller, CLE	150	L. Grove, BOS	21
T. Bridges, DET	138	J. DeShong, WAS	20

Shutouts		Fewest Walks/9 Innings	
L. Gomez, NY	6	M. Stratton, CHI	2.02
M. Stratton, CHI	5	W. Hudlin, CLE	2.05
P. Appleton, WAS	4	R. Ruffing, NY	2.39
J. Whitehead, CHI	4	T. Lyons, CHI	2.39

Innings		Games Pitched	
W. Ferrell, BOS, WAS	281	C. Brown, CHI	53
L. Gomez, NY	278	J. Wilson, BOS	51
B. Newsom, BOS, WAS	275	B. Newsom, BOS, WAS	41
J. DeShong, WAS	264	H. Kelley, PHI	41

	W	L	PCT	GB	R	OR	2B	3B	HR	BA	SA	SB	E	DP	FA	CG	BB	SO	ShO	SV	ERA
New York	102	52	.662		**979**	671	282	73	**174**	.283	**.456**	60	170	134	.972	**82**	506	652	15	21	**3.65**
Detroit	89	65	.578	13	935	841	309	62	150	**.292**	.452	89	**147**	149	**.976**	70	635	485	6	11	4.87
Chicago	86	68	.558	16	780	730	280	76	67	.280	.400	70	174	173	.971	70	532	533	15	21	4.17
Cleveland	83	71	.539	19	817	768	304	76	103	.280	.423	76	159	153	.974	64	563	630	4	15	4.39
Boston	80	72	.526	21	821	775	269	64	100	.281	.411	79	177	139	.970	74	597	**682**	6	14	4.48
Washington	73	80	.477	28.5	757	841	245	**84**	47	.279	.379	61	170	**181**	.972	75	676	535	5	14	4.58
Philadelphia	54	97	.358	46.5	699	854	278	60	94	.267	.397	**95**	198	150	.967	65	613	469	6	9	4.85
St. Louis	46	108	.299	56	715	1023	**327**	44	71	.285	.399	30	173	166	.972	55	653	468	2	8	6.00
					6503	6503	2294	539	806	.281	.415	560	1368	1245	.972	555	4775	4454	59	113	4.62

NATIONAL LEAGUE 1938

	POS	Player	AB	BA	HR	RBI	PO	A	E	DP	TC/G	FA	Pitcher	G	IP	W	L	SV	ERA
Chicago	1B	R. Collins	490	.267	13	61	1264	111	6	118	10.2	**.996**	B. Lee	44	291	**22**	9	2	**2.66**
	2B	B. Herman	624	.277	1	56	**404**	517	18	111	6.2	**.981**	C. Bryant	44	270	19	11	2	3.10
W-89 L-63	SS	B. Jurges	465	.245	1	47	277	417	34	82	5.4	.953	L. French	43	201	10	19	0	3.80
	3B	S. Hack	609	.320	4	67	178	300	23	26	3.3	.954	T. Carleton	33	168	10	9	0	5.42
Charlie Grimm	RF	F. Demaree	476	.273	8	62	199	12	6	1	1.7	.972	C. Root	44	161	8	7	8	2.86
W-45 L-36	CF	C. Reynolds	497	.302	3	67	328	10	6	4	2.8	.983	J. Russell	42	102	6	1	3	3.34
	LF	A. Galan	395	.286	6	69	211	10	3	3	2.2	.987	V. Page	13	68	5	4	1	3.84
Gabby Hartnett	C	G. Hartnett	299	.274	10	59	358	40	2	8	4.8	.995							
W-44 L-27																			
	O1	Cavarretta	268	.239	1	28	277	21	4	14		.987							
	C	K. O'Dea	247	.263	3	33	294	32	10	3	4.7	.970							
	OF	J. Marty	235	.243	7	35	143	6	2	1	2.2	.987							
	UT	T. Lazzeri	120	.267	5	23	49	75	7	12		.947							

NATIONAL LEAGUE 1938, *cont.*

	POS	Player	AB	BA	HR	RBI	PO	A	E	DP	TC/G	FA	Pitcher	G	IP	W	L	SV	ERA
Pittsburgh	1B	G. Suhr	530	.294	3	64	**1512**	81	12	**150**	11.1	.993	R. Bauers	40	243	13	14	3	3.07
	2B	P. Young	562	.278	4	79	370	**554**	26	**120**	6.4	.973	J. Tobin	40	241	14	12	0	3.47
W-86 L-64	SS	A. Vaughan	541	.322	7	68	306	**507**	33	107	5.8	.961	C. Blanton	29	173	11	7	0	3.70
	3B	L. Handley	570	.268	6	51	119	**304**	23	**26**	3.3	.948	B. Klinger	28	159	12	5	1	2.99
Pie Traynor	RF	P. Waner	625	.280	6	69	284	11	7	0	2.1	.977	B. Swift	36	150	7	5	4	3.24
	CF	L. Waner	619	.313	5	57	341	15	5	5	2.5	.986	M. Brown	**51**	133	15	9	5	3.80
	LF	J. Rizzo	555	.301	23	111	284	5	15	1	2.2	.951							
	C	A. Todd	491	.265	7	75	**574**	89	10	7	**5.1**	**.985**							
New York	1B	J. McCarthy	470	.272	8	59	1315	77	10	111	**11.2**	.993	C. Melton	36	243	14	14	0	3.89
	2B	A. Kampouris	268	.246	5	37	198	255	13	52	5.9	.972	H. Gumbert	38	236	15	13	0	4.01
W-83 L-67	SS	D. Bartell	481	.262	9	49	288	447	37	85	6.1	.952	Schumacher	28	185	13	8	0	3.50
	3B	M. Ott	527	.311	**36**	116	98	238	15	14	3.1	.957	C. Hubbell	24	179	13	10	1	3.07
Bill Terry	RF	J. Ripple	501	.261	10	60	236	13	6	2	1.9	.976	B. Lohrman	31	152	9	6	0	3.32
	CF	H. Leiber	360	.269	12	65	181	6	5	3	2.2	.974	D. Coffman	**51**	111	8	4	12	3.48
	LF	J. Moore	506	.302	11	56	214	8	5	1	2.0	.978	J. Brown	43	90	5	3	5	1.80
	C	H. Danning	448	.306	9	60	449	50	8	7	4.4	.984							
	OF	B. Seeds	296	.291	9	52	147	6	2	1	2.0	.987							
	2O	L. Chiozza	179	.235	3	17	80	111	11	9		.946							
	S3	G. Myatt	170	.306	3	10	77	128	17	24		.923							
	C	G. Mancuso	158	.348	2	15	184	24	5	5	4.8	.977							
	1B	S. Leslie	154	.253	1	16	304	15	4	21	10.1	.988							
Cincinnati	1B	McCormick	**640**	.327	5	106	1441	95	7	127	10.2	.995	P. Derringer	41	**307**	21	14	3	2.93
	2B	L. Frey	501	.265	4	36	278	390	25	80	5.7	.964	Vander Meer	32	225	15	10	0	3.12
W-82 L-68	SS	B. Myers	442	.253	12	47	255	380	41	74	5.5	.939	B. Walters	27	168	11	6	1	3.69
	3B	L. Riggs	531	.252	2	55	146	280	24	18	3.2	.947	P. Davis	29	168	7	12	1	3.97
Bill McKechnie	RF	I. Goodman	568	.292	30	92	306	10	4	1	2.3	.988	J. Weaver	30	129	6	4	3	3.13
	CF	H. Craft	612	.270	15	83	**436**	15	8	3	**3.0**	.983	W. Moore	19	90	6	4	0	3.49
	LF	W. Berger	407	.307	16	56	192	7	7	2	2.1	.966	G. Schott	31	83	5	5	2	4.45
	C	E. Lombardi	489	**.342**	19	95	512	73	9	8	4.8	.985	Cascarella	33	61	4	7	4	4.57
	OF	D. Cooke	233	.275	2	33	126	4	5	1	2.6	.963							
Boston	1B	E. Fletcher	529	.272	6	48	1424	**126**	15	108	10.7	.990	J. Turner	35	268	14	18	0	3.46
	2B	Cuccinello	555	.265	9	76	323	458	21	84	5.5	.974	L. Fette	33	240	11	13	1	3.15
W-77 L-75	SS	R. Warstler	467	.231	0	40	285	428	**48**	76	5.6	.937	MacFayden	29	220	14	9	0	2.95
	3B	J. Stripp	229	.275	1	19	61	111	6	12	3.1	.966*	Hutchinson	36	151	9	8	4	2.74
Casey Stengel	RF	J. Cooney	432	.271	0	17	209	6	4	2	2.0	.982	M. Shoffner	26	140	8	7	1	3.54
	CF	V. DiMaggio	540	.228	14	61	415	**19**	12	**10**	3.0	.973	J. Lanning	32	138	8	7	0	3.72
	LF	M. West	418	.234	10	63	205	6	3	2	2.0	.986	D. Errickson	34	123	9	7	6	3.15
	C	R. Mueller	274	.237	4	35	239	47	2	4	3.8	.993							
	O3	D. Garms	428	.315	0	47	174	104	11	8		.962							
	C	A. Lopez	236	.267	1	14	240	42	3	4	4.0	.989							
	OF	G. Moore	180	.272	3	19	97	4	2	0	2.2	.981							
	3B	G. English	165	.248	2	21	33	75	5	3	2.6	.956							
St. Louis	1B	J. Mize	531	.337	27	102	1297	93	**15**	117	10.0	.989	B. Weiland	35	228	16	11	1	3.59
	2B	S. Martin	417	.278	1	27	225	301	18	59	5.5	.967	B. McGee	47	216	7	12	5	3.21
W-71 L-80	SS	L. Myers	227	.242	1	19	110	195	18	36	4.7	.944	L. Warneke	31	197	13	8	0	3.97
	3B	Gutteridge	552	.255	9	64	94	148	14	17	3.5	.945	C. Davis	40	173	12	8	3	3.63
Frankie Frisch	RF	E. Slaughter	395	.276	8	58	189	7	6	0	2.2	.970	R. Henshaw	27	130	5	11	0	4.02
W-63 L-72	CF	T. Moore	312	.272	4	21	219	5	3	1	3.0	.987	M. Macon	38	129	4	11	2	4.11
	LF	J. Medwick	590	.322	21	**122**	330	12	9	6	2.4	.974	C. Shoun	40	117	6	6	1	4.14
Mike Gonzalez	C	M. Owen	397	.267	4	36	463	67	11	8	4.7	.980							
W-8 L-8	OF	D. Padgett	388	.271	8	65	140	14	6	3	2.3	.963							
	UT	J. Brown	382	.301	0	38	195	264	21	55		.956							
	OF	P. Martin	269	.294	2	38	138	1	2	1	2.3	.986							
	3B	J. Stripp	199	.286	0	18	53	76	3	9	2.6	.977*							
	OF	Bordagaray	156	.282	0	21	67	3	3	0	2.5	.959							
Brooklyn	1B	D. Camilli	509	.251	24	100	1356	95	8	129	10.1	.995	L. Hamlin	44	237	12	15	6	3.68
	2B	J. Hudson	498	.261	2	37	304	395	**27**	79	5.5	.963	Fitzsimmons	27	203	11	8	0	3.02
W-69 L-80	SS	L. Durocher	479	.219	1	56	287	399	24	90	5.0	**.966**	T. Pressnell	43	192	11	14	3	3.56
	3B	C. Lavagetto	487	.273	6	79	136	229	**28**	**26**	3.0	.929	V. Tamulis	38	160	12	6	2	3.83
Burleigh Grimes	RF	G. Rosen	473	.281	4	51	263	**19**	5	4	2.5	**.989**	B. Posedel	33	140	8	9	1	5.66
	CF	E. Koy	521	.299	11	76	306	7	5	4	2.4	.984	V. Mungo	24	133	4	11	0	3.92
	LF	B. Hassett	335	.293	0	40	154	0	9	0	2.3	.945	M. Butcher	24	73	5	4	2	6.56
	C	B. Phelps	208	.308	5	46	218	25	5	5	4.5	.980							
	OF	K. Cuyler	253	.273	2	23	125	9	1	1	2.0	.993							
	OF	T. Stainback	104	.327	0	20	52	1	1	0	2.3	.981							

NATIONAL LEAGUE 1938, cont.

	POS	Player	AB	BA	HR	RBI	PO	A	E	DP	TC/G	FA	Pitcher	G	IP	W	L	SV	ERA
Philadelphia	1B	P. Weintraub	351	.311	4	45	913	75	12	70	10.2	.988	H. Mulcahy	46	267	10	**20**	1	4.61
	2B	E. Mueller	444	.250	4	34	229	266	17	44	4.6	.967	C. Passeau	44	239	11	18	1	4.52
W-45 L-105	SS	D. Young	340	.229	0	31	156	263	30	44	5.2	.933	Hollingsworth	24	174	5	16	0	3.82
Jimmie Wilson	3B	P. Whitney	300	.277	3	38	68	131	14	8	2.8	.934	P. Sivess	39	116	3	6	3	5.51
W-45 L-103	RF	C. Klein	458	.247	8	61	229	8	10	1	2.1	.960	M. Butcher	12	98	4	8	0	2.93
	CF	H. Martin	466	.298	3	39	298	7	11	2	2.7	.965	B. Walters	12	83	4	8	0	5.23
Hans Lobert	LF	M. Arnovich	502	.275	4	72	327	18	6	0	2.6	.983	W. LaMaster	18	64	4	7	0	7.77
W-0 L-2	C	B. Atwood	281	.196	3	28	350	53	13	12	4.4	.969							
	S2	G. Scharein	390	.238	1	29	246	327	37	57		.939							
	3B	B. Jordan	310	.300	0	18	42	103	4	13	2.6	.973							
	OF	G. Brack	282	.287	4	28	156	5	6	2	2.5	.964							
	C	S. Davis	215	.247	2	23	217	27	5	5	4.0	.980							

BATTING AND BASE RUNNING LEADERS

Batting Average		Slugging Average		Home Runs	
E. Lombardi, CIN	.342	J. Mize, STL	.614	M. Ott, NY	36
J. Mize, STL	.337	M. Ott, NY	.583	I. Goodman, CIN	30
McCormick, CIN	.327	J. Medwick, STL	.536	J. Mize, STL	27
J. Medwick, STL	.322	I. Goodman, CIN	.533	D. Camilli, BKN	24
A. Vaughan, PIT	.322	E. Lombardi, CIN	.524	J. Rizzo, PIT	23

Total Bases		Runs Batted In		Stolen Bases	
J. Mize, STL	326	J. Medwick, STL	122	S. Hack, CHI	16
J. Medwick, STL	316	M. Ott, NY	116	C. Lavagetto, BKN	15
M. Ott, NY	307	J. Rizzo, PIT	111	E. Koy, BKN	15
I. Goodman, CIN	303	McCormick, CIN	106	A. Vaughan, PIT	14
J. Rizzo, PIT	285	J. Mize, STL	102	Gutteridge, STL	14

Hits		Base on Balls		Home Run Percentage	
McCormick, CIN	209	D. Camilli, BKN	119	M. Ott, NY	6.8
S. Hack, CHI	195	M. Ott, NY	118	I. Goodman, CIN	5.3
L. Waner, PIT	194	A. Vaughan, PIT	104	J. Mize, STL	5.1
J. Medwick, STL	190	S. Hack, CHI	94	D. Camilli, BKN	4.7

Runs Scored		Doubles		Triples	
M. Ott, NY	116	J. Medwick, STL	47	J. Mize, STL	16
S. Hack, CHI	109	McCormick, CIN	40	Gutteridge, STL	15
D. Camilli, BKN	106	H. Martin, PHI	36	G. Suhr, PIT	14
I. Goodman, CIN	103	P. Young, PIT	36	E. Koy, BKN	13

PITCHING LEADERS

Winning Percentage		Earned Run Average		Wins	
B. Lee, CHI	.710	B. Lee, CHI	2.66	B. Lee, CHI	22
C. Bryant, CHI	.633	P. Derringer, CIN	2.93	P. Derringer, CIN	21
M. Brown, PIT	.625	MacFayden, BOS	2.95	C. Bryant, CHI	19
P. Derringer, CIN	.600	B. Klinger, PIT	2.99	B. Weiland, STL	16
Vander Meer, CIN	.600	Fitzsimmons, BKN	3.02		

Saves		Strikeouts		Complete Games	
D. Coffman, NY	12	C. Bryant, CHI	135	P. Derringer, CIN	26
C. Root, CHI	8	P. Derringer, CIN	132	J. Turner, BOS	22
D. Errickson, BOS	6	Vander Meer, CIN	125	B. Walters, CIN, PHI	20
L. Hamlin, BKN	6	B. Lee, CHI	121	MacFayden, BOS	19
		B. Weiland, STL	117	B. Lee, CHI	19
		R. Bauers, PIT	117		

Fewest Hits/9 Innings		Shutouts		Fewest Walks/9 Innings	
Vander Meer, CIN	7.07	B. Lee, CHI	9	P. Derringer, CIN	1.44
R. Bauers, PIT	7.67	MacFayden, BOS	5	C. Hubbell, NY	1.66
C. Bryant, CHI	7.82	L. Warneke, STL	4	J. Turner, BOS	1.81
B. Klinger, PIT	8.59	Schumacher, NY	4	Fitzsimmons, BKN	1.91

Most Strikeouts/9 Inn.		Innings		Games Pitched	
C. Hubbell, NY	5.23	P. Derringer, CIN	307	M. Brown, PIT	51
Vander Meer, CIN	4.99	B. Lee, CHI	291	D. Coffman, NY	51
B. Weiland, STL	4.61	C. Bryant, CHI	270	B. McGee, STL	47
C. Bryant, CHI	4.49	J. Turner, BOS	268	H. Mulcahy, PHI	46

	W	L	PCT	GB	R	OR	2B	3B	HR	BA	SA	SB	E	DP	FA	CG	BB	SO	ShO	SV	ERA
Chicago	89	63	.586		713	598	242	70	65	.269	.377	49	**135**	151	**.978**	67	454	**583**	16	18	3.37
Pittsburgh	86	64	.573	2	707	630	265	66	65	.279	.388	47	163	**168**	.974	57	432	557	8	15	3.46
New York	83	67	.553	5	705	637	210	36	125	.271	.396	31	168	147	.973	59	**389**	497	8	18	3.62
Cincinnati	82	68	.547	6	723	634	251	57	110	.277	.406	19	172	133	.971	72	463	542	11	16	3.62
Boston	77	75	.507	12	561	618	199	39	54	.250	.333	49	173	136	.972	**83**	465	413	15	12	3.40
St. Louis	71	80	.470	17.5	725	721	288	74	91	.279	.407	55	199	145	.967	58	474	534	10	16	3.84
Brooklyn	69	80	.463	18.5	704	710	225	**79**	61	.257	.367	**66**	157	148	.973	56	446	469	12	14	4.07
Philadelphia	45	105	.300	43	550	840	233	29	40	.254	.333	38	201	135	.966	68	582	492	3	6	4.93
					5388	5388	1913	450	611	.267	.376	354	1368	1163	.972	520	3705	4087	83	115	3.78

AMERICAN LEAGUE 1938

	POS	Player	AB	BA	HR	RBI	PO	A	E	DP	TC/G	FA	Pitcher	G	IP	W	L	SV	ERA
New York	1B	L. Gehrig	576	.295	29	114	1483	100	14	**157**	10.2	.991	R. Ruffing	31	247	**21**	7	0	3.31
	2B	J. Gordon	458	.255	25	97	290	450	**31**	98	6.1	.960	L. Gomez	32	239	18	12	0	3.35
W-99 L-53	SS	F. Crosetti	631	.263	9	55	**352**	**506**	47	120	5.8	.948	M. Pearson	28	202	16	7	0	3.97
	3B	R. Rolfe	631	.311	10	80	151	294	19	26	3.1	.959	S. Chandler	23	172	14	5	0	4.03
Joe McCarthy	RF	T. Henrich	471	.270	22	91	239	14	4	1	2.0	.984	B. Hadley	29	167	9	8	1	3.60
	CF	J. DiMaggio	599	.324	32	140	366	20	15	4	2.8	.963	S. Sundra	25	94	6	4	0	4.80
	LF	G. Selkirk	335	.254	10	62	176	7	5	3	2.0	.973	J. Murphy	32	91	8	2	11	4.24
	C	B. Dickey	454	.313	27	115	518	94	8	7	4.0	.987							
	OF	M. Hoag	267	.277	0	48	132	5	5	3	2.0	.965							
	OF	J. Powell	164	.256	2	20	86	1	2	0	2.1	.978							
	2B	Knickerbocker	128	.250	1	21	78	86	3	23	4.9	.982							
	C	J. Glenn	123	.260	0	25	134	15	4	3	3.8	.974							

AMERICAN LEAGUE 1938, *cont.*

	POS	Player	AB	BA	HR	RBI	PO	A	E	DP	TC/G	FA	Pitcher	G	IP	W	L	SV	ERA
Boston	1B	J. Foxx	565	.349	50	175	1282	116	19	153	9.5	.987	J. Bagby	43	199	15	11	2	4.21
	2B	B. Doerr	509	.289	5	80	372	420	26	118	5.6	.968	J. Wilson	37	195	15	15	1	4.30
W-88 L-61	SS	J. Cronin	530	.325	17	94	304	449	36	110	5.6	.954	Ostermueller	31	177	13	5	2	4.58
	3B	P. Higgins	524	.303	5	106	140	272	39	28	3.3	.914	L. Grove	24	164	14	4	1	**3.08**
Joe Cronin	RF	B. Chapman	480	.340	6	80	267	15	10	5	2.3	.966	E. Dickman	32	104	5	5	0	5.28
	CF	D. Cramer	658	.301	0	71	417	15	6	3	3.0	.986	A. McKain	37	100	5	4	6	4.52
	LF	J. Vosmik	621	.324	9	86	302	14	7	4	2.2	.978	J. Marcum	15	92	5	6	0	4.09
	C	G. Desautels	333	.291	2	48	423	52	7	7	4.5	.985	J. Heving	16	82	8	1	2	3.73
	C	J. Peacock	195	.303	1	39	177	12	3	2	4.4	.984	B. Harris	13	80	5	5	1	4.03
	OF	Nonnenkamp	180	.283	0	18	85	5	3	1	2.4	.968							
Cleveland	1B	H. Trosky	554	.334	19	110	1232	102	10	124	9.1	.993	B. Feller	39	278	17	11	1	4.08
	2B	O. Hale	496	.278	8	69	304	343	25	72	5.3	.963	M. Harder	38	240	17	10	4	3.83
W-86 L-66	SS	L. Lary	568	.268	3	51	296	399	26	88	5.1	.964	J. Allen	30	200	14	8	0	4.19
	3B	K. Keltner	576	.276	26	113	141	271	19	19	2.9	.956	E. Whitehill	26	160	9	8	0	5.56
Ossie Vitt	RF	B. Campbell	511	.290	12	72	220	13	8	3	2.0	.967	W. Hudlin	29	127	8	8	1	4.89
	CF	E. Averill	482	.330	14	93	331	14	9	2	2.7	.975	D. Galehouse	36	114	7	8	3	4.34
	LF	J. Heath	502	.343	21	112	254	5	7	2	2.2	.974	J. Humphries	45	103	9	8	6	5.23
	C	F. Pytlak	364	.308	1	43	475	56	7	11	5.4	.987							
	OF	R. Weatherly	210	.262	2	18	110	7	3	3	2.2	.975							
	C	R. Hemsley	203	.296	2	28	358	38	8	5	7.0	.980							
	OF	M. Solters	199	.201	2	22	91	4	3	3	2.1	.969							
Detroit	1B	H. Greenberg	556	.315	58	146	1484	120	14	146	10.4	.991	V. Kennedy	33	190	12	9	2	5.06
	2B	C. Gehringer	568	.306	20	107	393	455	21	115	5.7	.976	G. Gill	24	164	12	9	0	4.12
W-84 L-70	SS	B. Rogell	501	.259	3	55	291	431	31	101	5.6	.959	E. Auker	27	161	11	10	0	5.27
	3B	D. Ross	265	.260	1	30	90	157	14	15	3.5	.946	T. Bridges	25	151	13	9	1	4.59
Mickey Cochrane	RF	P. Fox	634	.293	7	96	301	13	2	2	2.1	**.994**	R. Lawson	27	127	8	9	1	5.46
W-47 L-51	CF	C. Morgan	306	.284	0	27	192	6	4	2	2.7	.980	Poffenberger	25	125	6	7	1	4.82
	LF	D. Walker	454	.308	6	43	224	8	5	1	2.1	.979	H. Eisenstat	32	125	9	6	4	3.73
Del Baker	C	R. York	463	.298	33	127	406	70	5	10	4.1	.990	S. Coffman	39	96	4	4	2	6.02
W-37 L-19	3B	M. Christman	318	.248	1	44	86	146	4	14	3.4	.983							
	OF	C. Laabs	211	.237	7	37	128	4	4	1	2.6	.971							
	OF	J. White	206	.262	0	15	141	4	5	0	2.7	.967							
	C	B. Tebbetts	143	.294	1	25	108	20	2	4	2.5	.985							
Washington	1B	Z. Bonura	540	.289	22	114	1209	93	9	132	10.2	**.993**	D. Leonard	33	223	12	15	0	3.43
	2B	B. Myer	437	.336	6	71	308	355	12	91	5.6	**.982**	P. Appleton	43	164	7	9	5	4.60
W-75 L-76	SS	C. Travis	567	.335	5	67	304	457	40	113	5.6	.950	K. Chase	32	150	9	10	1	5.58
	3B	B. Lewis	656	.296	12	91	161	329	47	32	3.6	.912	W. Ferrell	23	149	13	8	0	5.92
Bucky Harris	RF	G. Case	433	.305	2	40	207	7	8	2	2.2	.964	H. Kelley	38	148	9	8	1	4.49
	CF	S. West	344	.302	5	47	221	4	4	3	2.7	.983	M. Weaver	31	139	7	6	0	5.24
	LF	A. Simmons	470	.302	21	95	232	4	4	1	2.1	.983	J. DeShong	31	131	5	8	0	6.58
	C	R. Ferrell	411	.292	1	58	512	69	11	15	4.5	.981	Krakauskas	29	121	7	5	0	3.12
	OF	T. Wright	263	.350	2	36	107	3	2	3	1.9	.982	C. Hogsett	31	91	5	6	3	6.03
	OF	J. Stone	213	.244	3	28	107	5	3	0	2.2	.974							
	OF	M. Almada	197	.244	1	15	147	7	5	1	3.4	.969							
	2B	O. Bluege	184	.261	0	21	85	110	2	26	5.2	.990							
Chicago	1B	J. Kuhel	412	.267	8	51	1136	59	14	97	**10.9**	.988	T. Lee	33	245	13	12	1	3.49
	2B	J. Hayes	238	.328	1	20	146	183	8	51	5.5	.976	T. Lyons	23	195	9	11	0	3.70
W-65 L-83	SS	L. Appling	294	.303	0	44	149	258	20	37	5.5	.953	M. Stratton	26	186	15	9	2	4.01
	3B	M. Owen	577	.281	6	55	136	305	24	29	3.3	.948	J. Whitehead	32	183	10	11	4	4.76
Jimmy Dykes	RF	Steinbacher	399	.331	4	61	202	7	8	2	2.1	.963	J. Rigney	38	167	9	9	1	3.56
	CF	M. Kreevich	489	.297	6	73	379	7	10	2	3.1	.975	J. Knott	20	131	5	10	0	4.05
	LF	G. Walker	442	.305	16	87	197	9	9	4	2.0	.958							
	C	L. Sewell	211	.213	0	27	205	55	4	7	4.1	.985							
	OF	R. Radcliff	503	.330	5	81	230	5	5	0	2.4	.979							
	S2	B. Berger	470	.217	3	36	230	341	36	78		.941							
	C	T. Rensa	165	.248	3	19	185	36	4	4	3.9	.982							
St. Louis	1B	G. McQuinn	602	.324	12	82	1207	90	10	134	8.8	.992	B. Newsom	44	**330**	20	16	1	5.08
	2B	D. Heffner	473	.245	2	69	365	363	22	103	5.3	.971	L. Mills	30	210	10	12	0	5.31
W-55 L-97	SS	R. Kress	566	.302	7	79	321	388	26	100	4.9	.965	Hildebrand	23	163	8	10	1	5.69
	3B	H. Clift	534	.290	34	118	176	306	19	31	3.4	**.962**	R. Van Atta	25	104	4	7	0	6.06
Gabby Street	RF	B. Bell	526	.262	13	84	266	12	6	3	2.2	.979	J. Walkup	18	94	1	12	0	6.80
	CF	M. Almada	436	.342	3	37	247	9	9	1	2.6	.966	F. Johnson	17	69	3	7	3	5.61
	LF	B. Mills	466	.285	3	46	235	9	9	2	2.2	.964							
	C	B. Sullivan	375	.277	7	49	441	65	5	10	5.2	**.990**							
	OF	M. Mazzera	204	.279	6	29	74	7	2	1	1.8	.976							
	C	T. Heath	194	.227	2	22	315	42	5	5	5.6	.986							
	OF	S. West	165	.309	1	27	101	0	3	0	2.5	.971							

AMERICAN LEAGUE 1938, cont.

	POS	Player	AB	BA	HR	RBI	PO	A	E	DP	TC/G	FA	Pitcher	G	IP	W	L	SV	ERA
Philadelphia	1B	L. Finney	454	.275	10	48	574	24	6	35	9.4	.990	G. Caster	42	280	16	**20**	1	4.37
	2B	D. Lodigiani	325	.280	6	44	193	233	21	45	5.6	.953	B. Thomas	42	212	9	14	0	4.92
W-53 L-99	SS	W. Ambler	393	.234	0	38	209	310	32	54	4.8	.942	L. Nelson	32	191	10	11	2	5.65
	3B	B. Werber	499	.259	11	69	168	266	30	21	3.5	.935	B. Ross	29	184	9	16	0	5.32
Connie Mack	RF	W. Moses	589	.307	8	49	304	11	11	3	2.3	.966	E. Smith	43	131	3	10	4	5.92
	CF	B. Johnson	563	.313	30	113	400	21	16	3	2.9	.963	N. Potter	35	111	2	12	5	6.47
	LF	S. Chapman	406	.259	17	63	229	8	12	0	2.2	.952							
	C	F. Hayes	316	.291	11	55	319	38	9	2	4.1	.975							
	2B	S. Sperry	253	.273	0	27	121	185	13	26	5.3	.959							
	1B	D. Siebert	194	.284	0	28	403	41	0	35	9.7	1.000							
	C	E. Brucker	171	.374	3	35	188	20	3	1	4.8	.986							

BATTING AND BASE RUNNING LEADERS

Batting Average
- J. Foxx, BOS .349
- J. Heath, CLE .343
- B. Chapman, BOS .340
- B. Myer, WAS .336
- C. Travis, WAS .335

Slugging Average
- J. Foxx, BOS .704
- H. Greenberg, DET .683
- J. Heath, CLE .602
- J. DiMaggio, NY .581
- R. York, DET .579

Home Runs
- H. Greenberg, DET 58
- J. Foxx, BOS 50
- H. Clift, STL 34
- R. York, DET 33
- J. DiMaggio, NY 32

Total Bases
- J. Foxx, BOS 398
- H. Greenberg, DET 380
- J. DiMaggio, NY 348
- B. Johnson, PHI 311
- J. Heath, CLE 302

Runs Batted In
- J. Foxx, BOS 175
- H. Greenberg, DET 146
- J. DiMaggio, NY 140
- R. York, DET 127
- H. Clift, STL 118

Stolen Bases
- F. Crosetti, NY 27
- L. Lary, CLE 23
- B. Werber, PHI 19
- B. Lewis, WAS 17
- P. Fox, DET 16

Hits
- J. Vosmik, BOS 201
- D. Cramer, BOS 198
- J. Foxx, BOS 197
- M. Almada, STL, WAS 197

Base on Balls
- H. Greenberg, DET 119
- J. Foxx, BOS 119
- H. Clift, STL 118
- C. Gehringer, DET 112

Home Run Percentage
- H. Greenberg, DET 10.4
- J. Foxx, BOS 8.8
- R. York, DET 7.1
- H. Clift, STL 6.4

Runs Scored
- H. Greenberg, DET 144
- J. Foxx, BOS 139
- C. Gehringer, DET 133
- R. Rolfe, NY 132

Doubles
- J. Cronin, BOS 51
- G. McQuinn, STL 42
- B. Chapman, BOS 40
- H. Trosky, CLE 40

Triples
- J. Heath, CLE 18
- E. Averill, CLE 15
- J. DiMaggio, NY 13
- L. Finney, PHI 12

PITCHING LEADERS

Winning Percentage
- R. Ruffing, NY .750
- M. Pearson, NY .696
- M. Harder, CLE .630
- M. Stratton, CHI .625
- B. Feller, CLE .607

Earned Run Average
- L. Grove, BOS 3.08
- R. Ruffing, NY 3.31
- L. Gomez, NY 3.35
- D. Leonard, WAS 3.43
- T. Lee, CHI 3.49

Wins
- R. Ruffing, NY 21
- B. Newsom, STL 20
- L. Gomez, NY 18
- M. Harder, CLE 17
- B. Feller, CLE 17

Saves
- J. Murphy, NY 11
- J. Humphries, CLE 6
- A. McKain, BOS 6
- P. Appleton, WAS 5
- N. Potter, PHI 5

Strikeouts
- B. Feller, CLE 240
- B. Newsom, STL 226
- L. Mills, STL 134
- L. Gomez, NY 129
- R. Ruffing, NY 127

Complete Games
- B. Newsom, STL 31
- R. Ruffing, NY 22
- L. Gomez, NY 20
- B. Feller, CLE 20
- G. Caster, PHI 20

Fewest Hits/9 Innings
- B. Feller, CLE 7.29
- J. Allen, CLE 8.51
- M. Pearson, NY 8.82
- D. Leonard, WAS 8.91

Shutouts
- R. Ruffing, NY 4
- L. Gomez, NY 4
- J. Wilson, BOS 3
- D. Leonard, WAS 3

Fewest Walks/9 Innings
- D. Leonard, WAS 2.14
- M. Harder, CLE 2.32
- T. Lyons, CHI 2.40
- S. Chandler, NY 2.46

Most Strikeouts/9 Inn.
- B. Feller, CLE 7.78
- B. Newsom, STL 6.17
- T. Bridges, DET 6.02
- L. Mills, STL 5.73

Innings
- B. Newsom, STL 330
- G. Caster, PHI 280
- B. Feller, CLE 278
- R. Ruffing, NY 247

Games Pitched
- J. Humphries, CLE 45
- B. Newsom, STL 44
- J. Bagby, BOS 43
- P. Appleton, WAS 43

	W	L	PCT	GB	R	OR	2B	3B	HR	BA	SA	SB	E	DP	FA	CG	BB	SO	ShO	SV	ERA
New York	99	53	.651		**966**	710	283	63	**174**	.274	**.446**	91	169	169	.973	**91**	566	567	**10**	13	**3.91**
Boston	88	61	.591	9.5	902	751	298	56	98	**.299**	.434	55	190	172	.968	67	**528**	484	**10**	15	4.46
Cleveland	86	66	.566	13	847	782	**300**	**89**	113	.281	.434	83	151	174	.974	68	681	**717**	5	17	4.60
Detroit	84	70	.545	16	862	795	219	52	137	.272	.411	76	147	172	**.976**	75	608	435	2	11	4.79
Washington	75	76	.497	23.5	814	873	278	72	85	.293	.416	65	180	**179**	.970	59	655	515	6	11	4.94
Chicago	65	83	.439	32	709	752	239	55	67	.277	.383	56	196	163	.967	83	550	432	5	9	4.36
St. Louis	55	97	.362	44	755	962	273	36	92	.281	.397	51	**145**	163	.975	71	737	632	3	7	5.80
Philadelphia	53	99	.349	46	726	956	243	62	98	.270	.396	65	206	119	.965	56	599	473	4	12	5.48
					6581	6581	2133	485	864	.281	.415	542	1384	1274	.971	570	4924	4255	45	95	4.79

NATIONAL LEAGUE 1939

	POS	Player	AB	BA	HR	RBI	PO	A	E	DP	TC/G	FA	Pitcher	G	IP	W	L	SV	ERA
Cincinnati	1B	McCormick	630	.332	18	**128**	1518	100	7	**153**	10.4	.996	B. Walters	39	**319**	**27**	11	0	**2.29**
	2B	L. Frey	484	.291	11	55	324	412	18	83	6.1	.976	P. Derringer	38	301	25	7	0	2.93
W-97 L-57	SS	B. Myers	509	.281	9	56	309	512	**42**	110	5.7	.951	W. Moore	42	188	13	12	3	3.45
	3B	B. Werber	599	.289	5	57	165	**308**	34	32	3.4	.933	L. Grissom	33	154	9	7	0	4.10
Bill McKechnie	RF	I. Goodman	470	.323	7	84	246	16	5	4	2.2	.981	J. Thompson	42	152	13	5	2	2.54
	CF	H. Craft	502	.257	13	67	300	13	6	4	2.4	.981	Vander Meer	30	129	5	9	0	4.67
	LF	W. Berger	329	.258	14	44	158	6	5	0	1.8	.970							
	C	E. Lombardi	450	.287	20	85	536	63	**10**	7	5.1	.984							
	OF	L. Gamble	221	.267	0	14	87	5	1	0	1.7	.989							
	C	Hershberger	174	.345	0	32	204	21	3	2	3.8	.987							
	OF	Bongiovanni	159	.258	0	16	89	1	1	1	2.3	.989							

NATIONAL LEAGUE 1939, cont.

	POS	Player	AB	BA	HR	RBI	PO	A	E	DP	TC/G	FA	Pitcher	G	IP	W	L	SV	ERA
St. Louis	1B	J. Mize	564	.349	28	108	1348	90	19	123	9.6	.987	C. Davis	49	248	22	16	7	3.63
	2B	S. Martin	425	.268	3	30	242	304	13	62	5.2	.977	M. Cooper	45	211	12	6	4	3.25
	SS	J. Brown	645	.298	3	51	208	349	25	67	5.6	.957	B. Bowman	51	169	13	5	9	2.60
W-92 L-61	3B	Gutteridge	524	.269	7	54	136	203	24	24	2.5	.934	L. Warneke	34	162	13	7	2	3.78
	RF	E. Slaughter	604	.320	12	86	348	18	12	5	2.5	.968	B. McGee	43	156	12	5	0	3.81
Ray Blades	CF	T. Moore	417	.295	17	77	291	16	2	1	2.6	.994	B. Weiland	32	146	10	12	1	3.57
	LF	J. Medwick	606	.332	14	117	313	10	8	1	2.2	.976	C. Shoun	53	103	3	1	9	3.76
	C	M. Owen	344	.259	3	35	452	52	9	7	4.1	.982							
	O3	P. Martin	281	.306	3	37	128	34	7	2		.959							
	C	D. Padgett	233	.399	5	53	249	18	6	5	4.5	.978							
Brooklyn	1B	D. Camilli	565	.290	26	104	1515	129	17	138	10.6	.990	L. Hamlin	40	270	20	13	0	3.64
	2B	P. Coscarart	419	.277	4	43	256	338	25	69	5.8	.960	H. Casey	40	227	15	10	1	2.93
	SS	L. Durocher	390	.277	1	34	228	322	25	73	5.1	.957	V. Tamulis	39	159	9	8	4	4.37
W-84 L-69	3B	C. Lavagetto	587	.300	10	87	163	278	24	28	3.1	.948	T. Pressnell	31	157	9	7	2	4.02
	RF	A. Parks	239	.272	1	19	125	2	3	0	2.0	.977	Fitzsimmons	27	151	7	9	3	3.87
Leo Durocher	CF	G. Moore	306	.225	3	39	140	8	6	3	1.8	.961	W. Wyatt	16	109	8	3	0	2.31
	LF	E. Koy	425	.278	8	67	252	4	10	1	2.3	.962	Hutchinson	41	106	5	2	1	4.34
	C	B. Phelps	323	.285	6	42	361	40	8	6	4.4	.980	R. Evans	24	64	1	8	1	5.18
	S2	J. Hudson	343	.254	2	32	175	259	18	56		.960							
	C	A. Todd	245	.278	5	32	284	35	5	5	4.4	.985							
	OF	D. Walker	225	.280	2	38	144	5	5	3	2.6	.968							
	OF	T. Stainback	201	.269	3	19	121	0	8	0	2.3	.938							
	OF	G. Rosen	183	.251	1	12	106	0	0	0	2.3	1.000							
	OF	J. Ripple	106	.330	0	28	55	0	0	0	2.0	1.000							
Chicago	1B	R. Russell	542	.273	9	79	1383	83	18	109	10.4	.988	B. Lee	37	282	19	15	0	3.44
	2B	B. Herman	623	.307	7	70	377	485	29	95	5.7	.967	C. Passeau	34	221	13	9	3	3.05
	SS	D. Bartell	336	.238	3	34	241	307	33	62	5.8	.943	L. French	36	194	15	8	1	3.29
W-84 L-70	3B	S. Hack	641	.298	8	56	177	278	21	15	3.1	.956	C. Root	35	167	8	8	4	4.03
	RF	J. Gleeson	332	.223	4	45	175	5	8	1	2.1	.957	V. Page	27	139	7	7	1	3.88
Gabby Hartnett	CF	H. Leiber	365	.310	24	88	249	5	6	0	2.7	.977	D. Dean	19	96	6	4	0	3.36
	LF	A. Galan	549	.304	6	71	290	6	9	0	2.1	.970	E. Whitehill	24	89	4	7	1	5.14
	C	G. Hartnett	306	.278	12	59	336	47	3	8	4.5	.992	J. Russell	39	69	4	3	3	3.67
	OF	C. Reynolds	281	.246	4	44	168	5	5	1	2.5	.972							
	C	G. Mancuso	251	.231	2	17	333	36	7	6	4.9	.981							
	OF	B. Nicholson	220	.295	5	38	123	5	6	0	2.3	.955							
	SS	B. Mattick	178	.287	0	23	102	179	22	28	6.3	.927							
New York	1B	Z. Bonura	455	.321	11	85	1205	90	11	110	10.7	.992	H. Gumbert	36	244	18	11	0	4.32
	2B	B. Whitehead	335	.239	2	24	232	320	17	60	6.3	.970	C. Melton	41	207	12	15	5	3.56
	SS	B. Jurges	543	.285	6	63	295	482	28	95	5.9	.965	B. Lohrman	38	186	12	13	1	4.07
W-77 L-74	3B	T. Hafey	256	.242	6	26	61	130	8	10	2.8	.960	Schumacher	29	182	13	10	0	4.81
	RF	M. Ott	396	.308	27	80	175	6	5	2	1.9	.973	C. Hubbell	29	154	11	9	2	2.75
Bill Terry	CF	F. Demaree	560	.304	11	79	329	11	5	2	2.3	.986	M. Salvo	32	136	4	10	1	4.63
	LF	J. Moore	562	.269	10	47	260	13	4	2	2.0	.986	J. Brown	31	56	4	0	7	4.15
	C	H. Danning	520	.313	16	74	550	80	6	13	4.8	.991							
	2B	A. Kampouris	201	.249	5	29	146	179	9	34	5.4	.973							
	OF	B. Seeds	173	.266	5	26	77	2	2	0	1.6	.975							
Pittsburgh	1B	E. Fletcher	370	.303	12	71	1010	56	8	97	10.6*	.993	B. Klinger	37	225	14	17	0	4.36
	2B	P. Young	293	.276	3	29	202	270	16	61	5.8	.967	M. Brown	47	200	9	13	7	3.37
	SS	A. Vaughan	595	.306	6	62	330	531	34	103	5.9	.962	J. Bowman	37	185	10	14	1	4.48
W-68 L-85	3B	L. Handley	376	.285	1	42	83	180	18	14	2.8	.936	R. Sewell	52	176	10	9	2	4.08
	RF	P. Waner	461	.328	3	45	206	12	5	4	2.1	.978	J. Tobin	25	145	9	9	0	4.52
Pie Traynor	CF	L. Waner	379	.285	0	24	225	9	2	1	2.6	.992	B. Swift	36	130	5	7	4	3.89
	LF	J. Rizzo	330	.261	6	55	186	2	5	0	2.2	.974							
	C	R. Mueller	180	.233	2	18	203	32	7	5	3.0	.971							
	23	B. Brubaker	345	.232	7	43	183	286	26	47		.947							
	OF	C. Klein	270	.300	11	47	133	4	7	0	2.2	.951							
	OF	F. Bell	262	.286	2	34	152	6	4	0	2.4	.975							
	C	R. Berres	231	.229	0	16	269	36	2	4	3.8	.993							
	1B	G. Suhr	204	.289	1	31	521	23	4	42	10.5	.993							
Boston	1B	B. Hassett	590	.308	2	60	1143	112	19	127	10.0	.985	B. Posedel	33	221	15	13	0	3.92
	2B	Cuccinello	310	.306	2	40	208	246	14	66	5.9	.970	MacFayden	33	192	8	14	2	3.90
	SS	E. Miller	296	.267	4	31	183	275	14	76	6.1	.970	J. Turner	25	158	4	11	0	4.28
W-63 L-88	3B	H. Majeski	367	.272	7	54	111	196	18	19	3.3	.945	L. Fette	27	146	10	10	0	2.96
	RF	D. Garms	513	.298	2	37	183	6	7	2	1.9	.964	M. Shoffner	25	132	4	6	1	3.13
Casey Stengel	CF	J. Cooney	368	.274	2	27	236	10	2	2	2.1	.992	J. Lanning	37	129	5	6	4	3.42
	LF	M. West	449	.285	19	82	287	8	8	2	2.4	.974	D. Errickson	28	128	6	9	1	4.00
	C	A. Lopez	412	.252	8	49	424	72	7	11	3.9	.986	J. Sullivan	31	114	6	9	2	3.64
	UT	R. Warstler	342	.243	0	24	194	301	20	75		.961							
	OF	A. Simmons	330	.282	7	43	158	7	3	2	2.0	.982							
	UT	S. Sisti	215	.228	1	11	136	152	8	8		.973							

NATIONAL LEAGUE 1939, cont.

	POS	Player	AB	BA	HR	RBI	PO	A	E	DP	TC/G	FA	Pitcher	G	IP	W	L	SV	ERA
Philadelphia	1B	G. Suhr	198	.318	3	24	520	37	3	50	9.3	.995	H. Mulcahy	38	226	9	16	4	4.99
	2B	R. Hughes	237	.228	1	16	183	184	6	30	5.7	.984	K. Higbe	34	187	10	14	2	4.85
W-45 L-106	SS	G. Scharein	399	.238	1	33	258	331	26	69	5.3	.958	B. Beck	34	183	7	14	3	4.73
	3B	P. May	464	.287	2	62	153	263	19	28	3.3	**.956**	I. Pearson	26	125	2	13	0	5.76
Doc Prothro	RF	J. Marty	299	.254	9	44	176	9	5	3	2.4	.974	S. Johnson	22	111	8	8	2	3.81
	CF	H. Martin	393	.282	1	22	276	5	7	1	3.0	.976	M. Butcher	19	104	2	13*	0	5.61
	LF	M. Arnovich	491	.324	5	67	335	10	6	0	**2.7**	.983	R. Harrell	22	95	3	7	0	5.42
	C	S. Davis	202	.307	0	23	260	40	0	1	3.5	1.000	Hollingsworth	15	60	1	9	0	5.85
	UT	E. Mueller	341	.279	9	43	163	166	11	38		.968							
	OF	G. Brack	270	.289	6	41	89	4	4	1	2.0	.959							
	OF	L. Scott	232	.280	1	26	109	7	5	1	2.2	.959							
	SS	D. Young	217	.263	3	20	70	104	10	16	3.3	.946							
	1B	J. Bolling	211	.289	3	13	392	38	8	35	9.1	.982							
	C	W. Millies	205	.234	0	12	229	37	**10**	3	3.3	.964							

BATTING AND BASE RUNNING LEADERS

Batting Average
J. Mize, STL — .349
McCormick, CIN — .332
J. Medwick, STL — .332
P. Waner, PIT — .328
M. Arnovich, PHI — .324

Slugging Average
J. Mize, STL — .626
M. Ott, NY — .581
H. Leiber, CHI — .556
D. Camilli, BKN — .524
I. Goodman, CIN — .515

Home Runs
J. Mize, STL — 28
M. Ott, NY — 27
D. Camilli, BKN — 26
H. Leiber, CHI — 24
E. Lombardi, CIN — 20

Total Bases
J. Mize, STL — 353
McCormick, CIN — 312
J. Medwick, STL — 307
D. Camilli, BKN — 296
E. Slaughter, STL — 291

Runs Batted In
McCormick, CIN — 128
J. Medwick, STL — 117
J. Mize, STL — 108
D. Camilli, BKN — 104
H. Leiber, CHI — 88

Stolen Bases
L. Handley, PIT — 17
S. Hack, CHI — 17
B. Werber, CIN — 15
C. Lavagetto, BKN — 14
B. Hassett, BOS — 13

Hits
McCormick, CIN — 209
J. Medwick, STL — 201
J. Mize, STL — 197
E. Slaughter, STL — 193

Base on Balls
D. Camilli, BKN — 110
M. Ott, NY — 100
J. Mize, STL — 92
B. Werber, CIN — 91

Home Run Percentage
M. Ott, NY — 6.8
H. Leiber, CHI — 6.6
J. Mize, STL — 5.0
D. Camilli, BKN — 4.6

Runs Scored
B. Werber, CIN — 115
S. Hack, CHI — 112
B. Herman, CHI — 111
D. Camilli, BKN — 105

Doubles
E. Slaughter, STL — 52
J. Medwick, STL — 48
J. Mize, STL — 44
McCormick, CIN — 41

Triples
B. Herman, CHI — 18
I. Goodman, CIN — 16
J. Mize, STL — 14
D. Camilli, BKN — 12

PITCHING LEADERS

Winning Percentage
P. Derringer, CIN — .781
B. Walters, CIN — .711
L. French, CHI — .652
H. Gumbert, NY — .621
L. Hamlin, BKN — .606

Earned Run Average
B. Walters, CIN — 2.29
C. Hubbell, NY — 2.75
H. Casey, BKN — 2.93
P. Derringer, CIN — 2.93
L. Fette, BOS — 2.96

Wins
B. Walters, CIN — 27
P. Derringer, CIN — 25
C. Davis, STL — 22
L. Hamlin, BKN — 20
B. Lee, CHI — 19

Saves
B. Bowman, STL — 9
C. Shoun, STL — 9
J. Brown, NY — 7
C. Davis, STL — 7
M. Brown, PIT — 7

Strikeouts
C. Passeau, CHI, PHI — 137
B. Walters, CIN — 137
M. Cooper, STL — 130
P. Derringer, CIN — 128
B. Lee, CHI — 105

Complete Games
B. Walters, CIN — 31
P. Derringer, CIN — 28
B. Lee, CHI — 20
L. Hamlin, BKN — 19
B. Posedel, BOS — 18

Fewest Hits/9 Innings
B. Walters, CIN — 7.05
L. Fette, BOS — 7.58
L. Hamlin, BKN — 8.51
C. Hubbell, NY — 8.77

Shutouts
L. Fette, BOS — 6
B. Posedel, BOS — 5
P. Derringer, CIN — 5
B. McGee, STL — 4

Fewest Walks/9 Innings
P. Derringer, CIN — 1.05
C. Hubbell, NY — 1.40
C. Davis, STL — 1.74
L. Hamlin, BKN — 1.80

Most Strikeouts/9 Inn.
L. French, CHI — 4.55
C. Passeau, CHI, PHI — 4.49
K. Higbe, CHI, PHI — 4.07
B. Walters, CIN — 3.87

Innings
B. Walters, CIN — 319
P. Derringer, CIN — 301
B. Lee, CHI — 282
C. Passeau, CHI, PHI — 274

Games Pitched
C. Shoun, STL — 53
R. Sewell, PIT — 52
B. Bowman, STL — 51
C. Davis, STL — 49

	W	L	PCT	GB	R	OR	2B	3B	HR	BA	SA	SB	E	DP	FA	CG	BB	SO	ShO	SV	ERA
Cincinnati	97	57	.630		767	**595**	269	60	98	.278	.405	46	162	170	.974	**86**	499	**637**	13	9	**3.27**
St. Louis	92	61	.601	4.5	779	633	**332**	62	98	**.294**	**.432**	44	177	140	.971	45	498	603	**18**	**32**	3.59
Brooklyn	84	69	.549	12.5	708	645	265	57	78	.265	.380	59	176	157	.972	69	**399**	528	9	13	3.64
Chicago	84	70	.545	13	724	678	263	62	91	.266	.391	**61**	186	126	.970	72	430	584	8	13	3.80
New York	77	74	.510	18.5	703	685	211	38	**116**	.272	.396	26	**153**	152	**.975**	55	478	505	6	20	4.07
Pittsburgh	68	85	.444	28.5	666	721	261	60	63	.276	.384	44	168	153	.972	53	423	524	10	15	4.15
Boston	63	88	.417	32.5	572	659	199	39	56	.264	.348	41	181	**178**	.971	68	513	430	11	15	3.71
Philadelphia	45	106	.298	50.5	553	856	232	40	49	.261	.351	47	171	133	.970	67	579	447	3	12	5.17
					5472	5472	2032	418	649	.272	.386	368	1374	1209	.972	515	3819	4258	78	129	3.92

AMERICAN LEAGUE 1939

	POS	Player	AB	BA	HR	RBI	PO	A	E	DP	TC/G	FA	Pitcher	G	IP	W	L	SV	ERA
New York	1B	B. Dahlgren	531	.235	15	89	1303	68	13	**140**	9.6	.991	R. Ruffing	28	233	21	7	0	2.93
	2B	J. Gordon	567	.284	28	111	**370**	461	28	116	5.7	.967	L. Gomez	26	198	12	8	0	3.41
W-106 L-45	SS	F. Crosetti	656	.233	10	56	323	460	26	118	5.3	**.968**	B. Hadley	26	154	12	6	2	2.98
	3B	R. Rolfe	648	.329	14	80	151	282	19	22	3.0	.958	A. Donald	24	153	13	3	1	3.71
Joe McCarthy	RF	C. Keller	398	.334	11	83	213	5	7	1	2.1	.969	M. Pearson	22	146	12	5	0	4.49
	CF	J. DiMaggio	462	**.381**	30	126	328	13	6	2	3.0	.986	Hildebrand	21	127	10	4	2	3.06
	LF	G. Selkirk	418	.306	21	101	254	4	3	1	2.1	**.989**	S. Sundra	24	121	11	1	0	2.76
	C	B. Dickey	480	.302	24	105	**571**	57	7	8	5.0	.989	M. Russo	21	116	8	3	2	2.41
	OF	T. Henrich	347	.277	9	57	205	7	2	1	2.4	.991	J. Murphy	38	61	3	6	19	4.40
	P	R. Ruffing	114	.307	1	20	8	32	2	2	1.5	.952							

AMERICAN LEAGUE 1939, cont.

	POS	Player	AB	BA	HR	RBI	PO	A	E	DP	TC/G	FA	Pitcher	G	IP	W	L	SV	ERA
Boston	1B	J. Foxx	467	.360	35	105	1101	91	10	104	9.8	.992	L. Grove	23	191	15	4	0	**2.54**
	2B	B. Doerr	525	.318	12	73	336	431	19	95	6.2	.976	J. Wilson	36	177	11	11	2	4.67
W-89 L-62	SS	J. Cronin	520	.308	19	107	306	437	32	93	5.5	.959	Ostermueller	34	159	11	7	4	4.24
	3B	J. Tabor	577	.289	14	95	144	338	40	32	3.5	.923	E. Auker	31	151	9	10	0	5.36
Joe Cronin	RF	T. Williams	565	.327	31	145	318	11	19	3	2.3	.945	D. Galehouse	30	147	9	10	0	4.54
	CF	D. Cramer	589	.311	0	56	356	12	6	0	2.8	.984	E. Dickman	48	114	8	3	5	4.43
	LF	J. Vosmik	554	.276	7	84	296	9	8	0	2.2	.974	J. Heving	46	107	11	3	7	3.70
	C	J. Peacock	274	.277	0	36	314	33	10	6	4.3	.972	J. Bagby	21	80	5	5	0	7.09
	1O	L. Finney	249	.325	1	46	328	12	6	28		.983							
	C	G. Desautels	226	.243	0	21	310	48	2	5	4.9	.994							
	2B	T. Carey	161	.242	0	20	75	87	0	19	4.6	1.000							
Cleveland	1B	H. Trosky	448	.335	25	104	1004	97	9	97	9.4	.992	B. Feller	39	**297**	**24**	9	1	2.85
	2B	O. Hale	253	.312	4	48	141	146	10	31	4.1	.966	A. Milnar	37	209	14	12	3	3.79
W-87 L-67	SS	S. Webb	269	.264	2	26	165	203	27	40	4.9	.932	M. Harder	29	208	15	9	1	3.50
	3B	K. Keltner	587	.325	13	97	**187**	297	13	**40**	3.2	**.974**	J. Allen	28	175	9	7	0	4.58
Ossie Vitt	RF	B. Campbell	450	.287	8	72	200	12	13	3	2.0	.942	W. Hudlin	27	143	9	10	3	4.91
	CF	B. Chapman	545	.290	6	82	356	12	11	0	2.6	.971	H. Eisenstat	26	104	6	7	2	3.30
	LF	J. Heath	431	.292	14	69	263	7	10	2	2.6	.964							
	C	R. Hemsley	395	.263	2	36	499	58	9	7	5.3	.984							
	UT	O. Grimes	364	.269	4	56	501	192	22	75		.969							
	OF	R. Weatherly	323	.310	1	32	146	3	6	1	2.0	.961							
	SS	L. Boudreau	225	.258	0	19	103	184	11	31	4.9	.953							
	C	F. Pytlak	183	.268	0	14	227	24	0	5	4.9	1.000							
Chicago	1B	J. Kuhel	546	.300	15	56	1256	72	11	113	**9.8**	.992	T. Lee	33	235	15	11	3	4.21
	2B	O. Bejma	307	.251	8	44	170	199	7	36	4.6	.981	J. Rigney	35	219	15	8	0	3.70
W-85 L-69	SS	L. Appling	516	.314	0	56	289	**461**	39	78	5.3	.951	E. Smith	29	177	9	11	0	3.67
	3B	E. McNair	479	.324	7	82	90	194	19	23	2.9	.937	T. Lyons	21	173	14	6	0	2.76
Jimmy Dykes	RF	L. Rosenthal	324	.265	10	51	193	5	2	1	2.2	.990	J. Knott	25	150	11	6	0	4.15
	CF	M. Kreevich	541	.323	5	77	419	18	11	4	3.2	.975	B. Dietrich	25	128	7	8	0	5.22
	LF	G. Walker	598	.291	13	111	365	11	13	3	2.6	.967	C. Brown	**61**	118	11	10	18	3.88
	C	M. Tresh	352	.259	0	38	480	59	8	7	4.6	.985							
	OF	R. Radcliff	397	.264	2	53	130	1	4	0	1.7	.970							
	2B	J. Hayes	269	.249	0	23	172	201	10	51	5.6	.974							
	3B	M. Owen	194	.237	0	15	63	99	8	11	3.1	.953							
Detroit	1B	H. Greenberg	500	.312	33	112	1205	75	9	108	9.5	**.993**	B. Newsom	35	246	17	10	2	3.37
	2B	C. Gehringer	406	.325	16	86	245	312	13	67	5.3	**.977**	T. Bridges	29	198	17	7	2	3.50
W-81 L-73	SS	F. Croucher	324	.269	5	40	139	256	28	47	4.5	.934	S. Rowe	28	164	10	12	0	4.99
	3B	P. Higgins	489	.276	8	76	140	241	36	22	3.2	.914	D. Trout	33	162	9	10	2	3.61
Del Baker	RF	P. Fox	519	.295	7	66	275	12	9	3	2.3	.970	A. Benton	37	150	6	8	4	4.56
	CF	B. McCosky	611	.311	4	58	**428**	7	6	2	3.0	.986	A. McKain	32	130	5	6	4	3.68
	LF	E. Averill	309	.262	10	58	157	3	4	0	2.1	.976							
	C	B. Tebbetts	341	.261	4	53	449	**64**	16	10	5.3	.970							
	C	R. York	329	.307	20	68	283	38	5	5	4.9	.985							
	2S	B. McCoy	192	.302	1	33	108	150	11	25		.959							
	OF	Cullenbine	179	.240	6	23	81	2	9	1	2.0	.902							
	S3	B. Rogell	174	.230	2	23	76	130	15	24		.932							
	S2	R. Kress	157	.242	1	22	77	116	11	28		.946							
	OF	D. Walker	154	.305	4	19	93	4	3	1	2.7	.970							
	OF	B. Bell	134	.239	0	24	73	4	0	1	2.1	1.000							
Washington	1B	M. Vernon	276	.257	1	30	690	40	11	75	9.9	.985	D. Leonard	34	269	20	8	0	3.54
	2B	Bloodworth	318	.289	4	40	226	219	13	66	6.3	.972	K. Chase	32	232	10	19	0	3.80
W-65 L-87	SS	C. Travis	476	.292	5	63	194	359	24	74	4.9	.958	Krakauskas	39	217	11	17	1	4.60
	3B	B. Lewis	536	.319	10	75	122	326	32	31	3.6	.933	J. Haynes	27	173	8	12	0	5.36
Bucky Harris	RF	G. Case	530	.302	2	35	332	7	16	2	2.9	.955	Carrasquel	40	159	5	9	2	4.69
	CF	S. West	390	.282	3	52	232	7	2	3	2.7	.992	P. Appleton	40	103	5	10	6	4.56
	LF	T. Wright	499	.309	4	93	236	10	13	4	2.1	.950							
	C	R. Ferrell	274	.281	0	31	327	46	9	9	4.6	.976							
	OF	B. Estalella	280	.275	8	41	157	3	6	1	2.2	.964							
	2B	B. Myer	258	.302	1	32	175	188	12	48	5.8	.968							
	OF	J. Welaj	201	.274	1	33	113	2	3	1	2.1	.975							
	S3	C. Gelbert	188	.255	3	29	60	122	7	20		.963							
	C	T. Giuliani	172	.250	0	18	201	28	5	3	4.7	.979							
Philadelphia	1B	D. Siebert	402	.294	6	47	874	74	9	73	9.7	.991	L. Nelson	35	198	10	13	1	4.78
	2B	Gantenbein	348	.290	4	36	165	179	19	26	4.8	.948	N. Potter	41	196	8	12	2	6.60
W-55 L-97	SS	S. Newsome	248	.222	0	17	176	221	21	44	4.5	.950	B. Ross	29	174	6	14	0	6.00
	3B	D. Lodigiani	393	.260	6	44	103	181	17	8	3.4	.944	B. Beckmann	27	155	7	11	0	5.39
Connie Mack	RF	W. Moses	437	.307	3	33	209	10	8	2	2.2	.965	G. Caster	28	136	9	9	0	4.90
W-25 L-37	CF	S. Chapman	498	.269	15	64	350	11	17	2	**3.2**	.955	C. Pippen	25	119	4	11	1	5.99
	LF	B. Johnson	544	.338	23	114	369	15	13	3	2.6	.967	C. Dean	54	117	5	8	7	5.25
Earle Mack	C	F. Hayes	431	.283	20	83	380	60	10	**12**	3.9	.978	B. Joyce	30	108	3	5	0	6.69
W-30 L-60	23	B. Nagel	341	.252	12	39	134	218	21	32		.944							
	OF	D. Miles	320	.300	1	37	146	4	5	1	2.0	.968							
	SS	W. Ambler	227	.211	0	24	126	184	15	31	4.2	.954							
	C	E. Brucker	172	.291	3	31	150	18	0	5	3.6	1.000							
	1B	N. Etten	155	.252	3	29	376	19	4	29	9.7	.990							

AMERICAN LEAGUE 1939, *cont.*

	POS	Player	AB	BA	HR	RBI	PO	A	E	DP	TC/G	FA	Pitcher	G	IP	W	L	SV	ERA
	1B	G. McQuinn	617	.316	20	94	1377	116	11	122	9.8	.993	J. Kramer	40	212	9	16	0	5.83
	2B	J. Berardino	468	.256	5	58	315	339	29	67	6.0	.958	V. Kennedy	33	192	9	17*	0	5.73
	SS	D. Heffner	375	.267	1	35	138	218	21	33	5.2	.944	B. Trotter	41	157	6	13	0	5.34
	3B	H. Clift	526	.270	15	84	184	324	25	34	3.6	.953	R. Lawson	36	151	3	7	0	5.32
	RF	M. Hoag	482	.295	10	75	218	13	7	2	2.0	.971	L. Mills	34	144	4	11	2	6.55
	CF	C. Laabs	317	.300	10	62	199	7	6	0	2.7	.972	B. Harris	28	126	3	12	0	5.71
	LF	J. Gallagher	266	.282	9	40	143	8	9	1	2.4	.944	G. Gill	27	95	1	12	0	7.11
	C	J. Glenn	286	.273	4	29	280	48	11	4	4.1	.968							
St. Louis																			
W-43 L-111	OF	B. Sullivan	332	.289	5	50	139	7	7	3	2.6	.954							
	SS	M. Christman	222	.216	0	20	151	209	15	45	5.9	.960							
Fred Haney	OF	J. Grace	207	.304	3	22	83	9	3	0	1.8	.968							
	OF	M. Mazzera	111	.297	3	22	56	1	1	0	2.3	.983							

BATTING AND BASE RUNNING LEADERS

Batting Average		Slugging Average		Home Runs		Winning Percentage		Earned Run Average		Wins	
J. DiMaggio, NY	.381	J. Foxx, BOS	.694	J. Foxx, BOS	35	L. Grove, BOS	.789	L. Grove, BOS	2.54	B. Feller, CLE	24
J. Foxx, BOS	.360	J. DiMaggio, NY	.671	H. Greenberg, DET	33	R. Ruffing, NY	.750	T. Lyons, CHI	2.76	R. Ruffing, NY	21
B. Johnson, PHI	.338	H. Greenberg, DET	.622	T. Williams, BOS	31	B. Feller, CLE	.727	B. Feller, CLE	2.85	D. Leonard, WAS	20
H. Trosky, CLE	.335	T. Williams, BOS	.609	J. DiMaggio, NY	30	D. Leonard, WAS	.714	R. Ruffing, NY	2.93	B. Newsom, DET, STL	20
C. Keller, NY	.334	H. Trosky, CLE	.589	J. Gordon, NY	28	T. Bridges, DET	.708	L. Gomez, NY	3.41	T. Bridges, DET	17

Total Bases		Runs Batted In		Stolen Bases		Saves		Strikeouts		Complete Games	
T. Williams, BOS	344	T. Williams, BOS	145	G. Case, WAS	51	J. Murphy, NY	19	B. Feller, CLE	246	B. Feller, CLE	24
J. Foxx, BOS	324	J. DiMaggio, NY	126	P. Fox, DET	23	C. Brown, CHI	18	B. Newsom, DET, STL	192	B. Newsom, DET, STL	24
R. Rolfe, NY	321	B. Johnson, PHI	114	M. Kreevich, CHI	23	J. Heving, BOS	7	T. Bridges, DET	129	R. Ruffing, NY	22
G. McQuinn, STL	318	H. Greenberg, DET	112	B. McCosky, DET	20	C. Dean, PHI	7	J. Rigney, CHI	119	D. Leonard, WAS	21
H. Greenberg, DET	311	J. Gordon, NY	111	B. Chapman, CLE	18	P. Appleton, WAS	6	K. Chase, WAS	118	L. Grove, BOS	17
		G. Walker, CHI	111	J. Kuhel, CHI	18						

Hits		Base on Balls		Home Run Percentage		Fewest Hits/9 Innings		Shutouts		Fewest Walks/9 Innings	
R. Rolfe, NY	213	H. Clift, STL	111	J. Foxx, BOS	7.5	B. Feller, CLE	6.89	R. Ruffing, NY	5	T. Lyons, CHI	1.36
G. McQuinn, STL	195	T. Williams, BOS	107	H. Greenberg, DET	6.6	L. Gomez, NY	7.86	B. Feller, CLE	4	D. Leonard, WAS	1.97
K. Keltner, CLE	191	L. Appling, CHI	105	J. DiMaggio, NY	6.5	R. Ruffing, NY	8.14			T. Lee, CHI	2.68
B. McCosky, DET	190	G. Selkirk, NY	103	R. York, DET	6.1	K. Chase, WAS	8.34			L. Grove, BOS	2.73

Runs Scored		Doubles		Triples		Most Strikeouts/9 Inn.		Innings		Games Pitched	
R. Rolfe, NY	139	R. Rolfe, NY	46	B. Lewis, WAS	16	B. Feller, CLE	7.46	B. Feller, CLE	297	C. Brown, CHI	61
T. Williams, BOS	131	T. Williams, BOS	44	B. McCosky, DET	14	B. Newsom, DET, STL	5.92	B. Newsom, DET, STL	292	C. Dean, PHI	54
J. Foxx, BOS	130	H. Greenberg, DET	42	B. Campbell, CLE	13	T. Bridges, DET	5.86	D. Leonard, WAS	269	E. Dickman, BOS	48
B. McCosky, DET	120	G. McQuinn, STL	37	G. McQuinn, STL	13	J. Rigney, CHI	4.90	T. Lee, CHI	235	J. Heving, BOS	46

PITCHING LEADERS

	W	L	PCT	GB	R	OR	2B	3B	Batting HR	BA	SA	SB	Fielding E	DP	FA	Pitching CG	BB	SO	ShO	SV	ERA
New York	106	45	.702		967	556	259	55	166	.287	.451	72	126	159	.978	87	567	565	12	26	3.31
Boston	89	62	.589	17	890	795	287	57	124	.291	.436	42	180	147	.970	52	543	539	4	20	4.56
Cleveland	87	67	.565	20.5	797	700	291	79	85	.280	.413	72	180	148	.970	69	602	614	9	13	4.08
Chicago	85	69	.552	22.5	755	737	220	56	64	.275	.374	113	167	140	.972	62	454	535	5	21	4.31
Detroit	81	73	.526	26.5	849	762	277	67	124	.279	.426	88	198	147	.967	64	574	633	6	16	4.29
Washington	65	87	.428	41.5	702	797	249	79	44	.278	.379	94	205	167	.966	72	602	521	4	10	4.60
Philadelphia	55	97	.362	51.5	711	1022	282	55	98	.271	.400	60	210	131	.964	50	579	397	5	12	5.79
St. Louis	43	111	.279	64.5	733	1035	242	50	91	.268	.381	48	199	144	.968	56	739	516	3	3	6.01
					6404	6404	2107	498	796	.279	.407	589	1465	1183	.969	512	4660	4320	48	121	4.62

NATIONAL LEAGUE 1940

	POS	Player	AB	BA	HR	RBI	PO	A	E	DP	TC/G	FA	Pitcher	G	IP	W	L	SV	ERA
	1B	McCormick	618	.309	19	127	1587	98	8	146	10.9	.995	B. Walters	36	305	22	10	0	2.48
	2B	L. Frey	563	.266	8	54	366	512	21	111	6.0	.977	P. Derringer	37	297	20	12	0	3.06
	SS	B. Myers	282	.202	5	30	155	269	17	62	5.0	.961	J. Thompson	33	225	16	9	0	3.32
	3B	B. Werber	584	.277	12	48	139	287	17	24	3.1	.962	J. Turner	24	187	14	7	0	2.89
	RF	I. Goodman	519	.258	12	63	252	6	8	0	2.0	.970	W. Moore	25	117	8	8	1	3.63
Cincinnati	CF	H. Craft	422	.244	6	48	284	7	1	2	2.7	.997	J. Beggs	37	77	12	3	7	2.00
W-100 L-53	LF	McCormick	417	.300	1	30	266	9	4	2	2.6	.986							
	C	E. Lombardi	376	.319	14	44	397	46	5	5	4.4	.989							
Bill McKechnie	SS	E. Joost	278	.216	1	24	145	240	16	48	5.1	.960							
	OF	M. Arnovich	211	.284	0	21	129	5	0	0	2.2	1.000							
	C	Hershberger	123	.309	0	26	121	11	2	0	3.6	.985							
	OF	J. Ripple	101	.307	4	20	45	0	0	0	1.5	1.000							

NATIONAL LEAGUE 1940, cont.

	POS	Player	AB	BA	HR	RBI	PO	A	E	DP	TC/G	FA	Pitcher	G	IP	W	L	SV	ERA
Brooklyn	1B	D. Camilli	512	.287	23	96	1299	79	11	85	9.9	.992	W. Wyatt	37	239	15	14	0	3.46
	2B	P. Coscarart	506	.237	9	58	326	379	31	58	5.3	.958	L. Hamlin	33	182	9	8	0	3.06
W-88 L-65	SS	P. Reese	312	.272	5	28	190	238	18	41	5.4	.960	V. Tamulis	41	154	8	5	3	3.09
	3B	C. Lavagetto	448	.257	4	43	137	191	24	12	3.0	.932	H. Casey	44	154	11	8	2	3.62
Leo Durocher	RF	J. Vosmik	404	.282	1	42	193	9	5	1	2.1	.976	T. Carleton	34	149	6	6	2	3.81
	CF	D. Walker	556	.308	6	66	360	6	10	3	2.8	.973	C. Davis	22	137	8	7	2	3.81
	LF	J. Medwick	423	.300	14	66	240	7	5	0	2.4	.980	Fitzsimmons	20	134	16	2	1	2.81
	C	B. Phelps	370	.295	13	61	428	35	11	3	4.8	.977	T. Pressnell	24	68	6	5	2	3.69
	OF	J. Wasdell	230	.278	3	37	70	1	4	0	1.8	.947							
	3O	P. Reiser	225	.293	3	20	59	58	5	7		.959							
	S2	J. Hudson	179	.218	0	19	94	145	15	20		.941							
	SS	L. Durocher	160	.231	1	14	102	131	10	22	4.6	.959							
St. Louis	1B	J. Mize	579	.314	43	137	1376	80	14	105	9.6	.990	L. Warneke	33	232	16	10	0	3.14
	2B	J. Orengo	415	.287	7	56	204	216	21	45	5.7	.952	M. Cooper	38	231	11	12	3	3.63
W-84 L-69	SS	M. Marion	435	.278	3	46	245	366	33	76	5.2	.949	B. McGee	38	218	16	10	0	3.80
	3B	S. Martin	369	.238	4	32	52	89	4	2	2.0	.972	C. Shoun	54	197	13	11	5	3.92
Ray Blades	RF	E. Slaughter	516	.306	17	73	267	8	3	5	2.1	.989	B. Bowman	28	114	7	5	0	4.33
W-14 L-24	CF	T. Moore	537	.304	17	64	383	11	5	4	3.0	.987	M. Lanier	35	105	9	6	3	3.34
	LF	E. Koy	348	.310	8	52	192	2	6	0	2.2	.970							
Mike Gonzalez	C	M. Owen	307	.264	0	27	378	56	9	8	3.9	.980							
W-1 L-5	UT	J. Brown	454	.280	0	30	198	243	22	42		.952							
	C	D. Padgett	240	.242	6	41	243	34	11	5	4.0	.962							
Billy Southworth	OF	P. Martin	228	.316	3	39	103	8	3	0	1.8	.974							
W-69 L-40	OF	J. Medwick	158	.304	3	20	81	1	1	0	2.2	.988							
Pittsburgh	1B	E. Fletcher	510	.273	16	104	1512	104	11	128	11.1	.993	R. Sewell	33	190	16	5	1	2.80
	2B	F. Gustine	524	.281	1	55	288	402	43	92	5.6	.941	J. Bowman	32	188	9	10	2	4.46
W-78 L-76	SS	A. Vaughan	594	.300	7	95	308	542	52	94	5.8	.942	M. Brown	48	173	10	9	7	3.49
	3B	L. Handley	302	.281	1	19	84	139	18	12	3.0	.925	Heintzelman	39	165	8	8	3	4.47
Frankie Frisch	RF	B. Elliott	551	.292	5	64	302	12	7	0	2.2	.978	B. Klinger	39	142	8	13	5	5.39
	CF	V. DiMaggio	356	.289	19	54	220	13	5	3	2.2	.979	M. Butcher	35	136	8	9	2	6.01
	LF	Van Robays	572	.273	11	116	276	10	11	3	2.1	.963	J. Lanning	38	116	8	4	4	4.05
	C	S. Davis	285	.326	5	39	288	61	12	11	4.1	.967	D. Lanahan	40	108	6	8	2	4.25
	3B	D. Garms	358	.355	5	57	65	123	7	15	3.0	.964	MacFayden	35	91	5	4	2	3.55
	OF	P. Waner	238	.290	1	32	62	3	1	0	1.5	.985							
	C	A. Lopez	174	.259	1	24	224	29	2	7	4.3	.992*							
	OF	L. Waner	166	.259	0	3	90	3	1	1	2.2	.989							
	2B	P. Young	136	.250	2	20	51	79	13	9	4.3	.909							
Chicago	1B	Cavarretta	193	.280	2	22	524	30	5	57	10.8	.991	C. Passeau	46	281	20	13	5	2.50
	2B	B. Herman	558	.292	5	57	366	448	22	94	6.2	.974	L. French	40	246	14	14	2	3.29
W-75 L-79	SS	B. Mattick	441	.218	0	33	233	431	38	76	5.6	.946	B. Lee	37	211	9	17	0	5.03
	3B	S. Hack	603	.317	8	40	175	302	23	27	3.4	.954	V. Olsen	34	173	13	9	0	2.97
Gabby Hartnett	RF	B. Nicholson	491	.297	25	98	235	10	13	2	2.1	.950	Raffensberger	43	115	7	9	3	3.38
	CF	H. Leiber	440	.302	17	86	187	8	3	0	1.9	.985	J. Mooty	20	114	6	6	1	2.92
	LF	J. Gleeson	485	.313	5	61	273	14	5	3	2.4	.983	C. Root	36	113	2	4	1	3.82
	C	A. Todd	381	.255	6	42	418	59	8	11	4.7	.984							
	OF	Dallessandro	287	.268	1	36	156	1	5	0	2.2	.969							
	1B	R. Russell	215	.247	5	33	518	18	10	22	10.7	.982							
	OF	A. Galan	209	.230	3	22	114	6	2	2	2.3	.984							
	1B	Z. Bonura	182	.264	4	20	408	40	4	34	10.3	.991							
	S2	R. Warstler	159	.226	1	18	90	141	14	20		.943							
New York	1B	B. Young	556	.286	17	101	1505	86	13	112	10.9	.992	H. Gumbert	35	237	12	14	2	3.76
	2B	Cuccinello	307	.208	5	36	106	130	3	17	5.1	.987	Schumacher	34	227	13	13	1	3.25
W-72 L-80	SS	M. Witek	433	.256	3	31	192	307	22	46	5.9	.958	C. Hubbell	31	214	11	12	0	3.65
	3B	B. Whitehead	568	.282	4	36	68	130	11	5	2.8	.947	B. Lohrman	31	195	10	15	1	3.78
Bill Terry	RF	M. Ott	536	.289	19	79	210	9	4	2	2.0	.982	C. Melton	37	167	10	11	2	4.91
	CF	F. Demaree	460	.302	7	61	233	6	5	5	2.1	.980	J. Brown	41	55	2	4	7	3.42
	LF	J. Moore	543	.276	6	46	259	9	5	1	2.1	.982	R. Lynn	33	42	4	3	3	3.83
	C	H. Danning	524	.300	13	91	634	91	15	13	5.6	.980							
	OF	J. Rucker	277	.296	4	23	121	3	6	0	2.3	.954							
	SS	B. Jurges	214	.252	2	36	123	196	11	36	5.2	.967							
	OF	B. Seeds	155	.290	4	16	64	3	1	0	1.7	.985							
Boston	1B	B. Hassett	458	.234	0	27	877	91	21	102	10.1	.979	D. Errickson	34	236	12	13	4	3.16
	2B	B. Rowell	486	.305	3	58	251	360	30	81	5.6	.953	B. Posedel	35	233	12	17	1	4.13
W-65 L-87	SS	E. Miller	569	.276	14	79	405	487	28	122	6.1	.970	J. Sullivan	36	177	10	14	1	3.55
	3B	S. Sisti	459	.251	6	34	117	192	21	21	3.2	.936	M. Salvo	21	161	10	9	0	3.08
Casey Stengel	RF	M. West	524	.261	7	72	220	16	6	1	2.4	.975	Strincevich	32	129	4	8	1	5.53
	CF	J. Cooney	365	.318	0	21	238	5	2	0	2.5	.992	J. Tobin	15	96	7	3	0	3.83
	LF	C. Ross	569	.281	17	89	347	12	14	2	2.5	.962							
	C	R. Berres	229	.192	0	14	254	56	6	6	3.7	.981							
	OF	G. Moore	363	.292	5	39	198	11	3	3	2.3	.986							

NATIONAL LEAGUE 1940, cont.

	POS	Player	AB	BA	HR	RBI	PO	A	E	DP	TC/G	FA	Pitcher	G	IP	W	L	SV	ERA
Philadelphia	1B	A. Mahan	544	.244	2	39	1380	102	12	120	10.3	.992	K. Higbe	41	283	14	19	1	3.72
	2B	H. Schulte	436	.236	1	21	282	317	12	70	5.1	**.980**	H. Mulcahy	36	280	13	**22**	0	3.60
W-50 L-103	SS	B. Bragan	474	.222	7	44	268	443	49	83	5.8	.936	I. Pearson	29	145	3	14	1	5.45
	3B	P. May	501	.293	1	48	139	297	21	12	**3.4**	.954	S. Johnson	37	138	5	14	1	4.88
Doc Prothro	RF	C. Klein	354	.218	7	37	180	4	3	2	1.6	.984	B. Beck	29	129	4	9	0	4.31
	CF	J. Marty	455	.270	13	50	296	7	8	0	2.6	.974	L. Smoll	33	109	2	8	0	5.37
	LF	J. Rizzo	367	.292	20	53	207	6	7	2	2.4	.968							
	C	B. Warren	289	.246	12	34	326	63	10	9	4.1	.975							
	UT	E. Mueller	263	.247	3	28	146	96	5	13		.980							
	C	B. Atwood	203	.192	0	22	238	43	3	3	4.1	.989							
	OF	M. Mazzera	156	.237	0	13	62	5	1	2	1.6	.985							

BATTING AND BASE RUNNING LEADERS

Batting Average
D. Garms, PIT	.355
E. Lombardi, CIN	.319
J. Cooney, BOS	.318
S. Hack, CHI	.317
J. Mize, STL	.314

Slugging Average
J. Mize, STL	.636
B. Nicholson, CHI	.534
D. Camilli, BKN	.529
V. DiMaggio, CIN, PIT	.519
E. Slaughter, STL	.504

Home Runs
J. Mize, STL	43
B. Nicholson, CHI	25
J. Rizzo, CIN, PHI, PIT	24
D. Camilli, BKN	23

Total Bases
J. Mize, STL	368
McCormick, CIN	298
J. Medwick, BKN, STL	280
D. Camilli, BKN	271
A. Vaughan, PIT	269

Runs Batted In
J. Mize, STL	137
McCormick, CIN	127
Van Robays, PIT	116
E. Fletcher, PIT	104
B. Young, NY	101

Stolen Bases
L. Frey, CIN	22
S. Hack, CHI	21
T. Moore, STL	18
B. Werber, CIN	16
P. Reese, BKN	15

Hits
S. Hack, CHI	191
McCormick, CIN	191
J. Mize, STL	182
A. Vaughan, PIT	178

Base on Balls
E. Fletcher, PIT	119
M. Ott, NY	100
D. Camilli, BKN	89
A. Vaughan, PIT	88

Home Run Percentage
J. Mize, STL	7.4
V. DiMaggio, CIN, PIT	5.3
B. Nicholson, CHI	5.1
J. Rizzo, CIN, PHI, PIT	4.8

Runs Scored
A. Vaughan, PIT	113
J. Mize, STL	111
B. Werber, CIN	105
L. Frey, CIN	102

Doubles
McCormick, CIN	44
A. Vaughan, PIT	40
J. Gleeson, CHI	39
S. Hack, CHI	38

Triples
A. Vaughan, PIT	15
C. Ross, BOS	14
D. Camilli, BKN	13
E. Slaughter, STL	13

PITCHING LEADERS

Winning Percentage
Fitzsimmons, BKN	.889
R. Sewell, PIT	.762
B. Walters, CIN	.688
J. Thompson, CIN	.640
P. Derringer, CIN	.625

Earned Run Average
B. Walters, CIN	2.48
C. Passeau, CHI	2.50
R. Sewell, PIT	2.80
Fitzsimmons, BKN	2.81
J. Turner, CIN	2.89

Wins
B. Walters, CIN	22
P. Derringer, CIN	20
C. Passeau, CHI	20

Saves
J. Beggs, CIN	7
M. Brown, PIT	7
J. Brown, NY	7
C. Passeau, CHI	5
C. Shoun, STL	5

Strikeouts
K. Higbe, PHI	137
W. Wyatt, BKN	124
C. Passeau, CHI	124
Schumacher, NY	123
P. Derringer, CIN	115
B. Walters, CIN	115

Complete Games
B. Walters, CIN	29
P. Derringer, CIN	26
H. Mulcahy, PHI	21
C. Passeau, CHI	20
K. Higbe, PHI	20

Fewest Hits/9 Innings
B. Walters, CIN	7.11
K. Higbe, PHI	7.70
J. Thompson, CIN	7.87
R. Sewell, PIT	8.02

Shutouts
M. Salvo, BOS	5
B. Lohrman, NY	5
W. Wyatt, BKN	5
Fitzsimmons, BKN	4

Fewest Walks/9 Innings
P. Derringer, CIN	1.46
J. Turner, CIN	1.54
Fitzsimmons, BKN	1.67
L. Warneke, STL	1.82

Most Strikeouts/9 Inn.
Schumacher, NY	4.88
W. Wyatt, BKN	4.66
K. Higbe, PHI	4.36
J. Thompson, CIN	4.11

Innings
B. Walters, CIN	305
P. Derringer, CIN	297
K. Higbe, PHI	283
C. Passeau, CHI	281

Games Pitched
C. Shoun, STL	54
M. Brown, PIT	48
C. Passeau, CHI	46
H. Casey, BKN	44

	W	L	PCT	GB	R	OR	2B	3B	HR	BA	SA	SB	E	DP	FA	CG	BB	SO	ShO	SV	ERA
										Batting				Fielding				Pitching			
Cincinnati	100	53	.654		707	**528**	264	38	89	.266	.379	72	**117**	158	**.981**	91	445	557	10	11	**3.05**
Brooklyn	88	65	.575	12	697	621	256	**70**	93	.260	.383	56	183	110	.970	65	**393**	**634**	17	14	3.50
St. Louis	84	69	.549	16	747	699	266	61	**119**	.275	**.411**	97	174	134	.971	71	488	550	10	14	3.83
Pittsburgh	78	76	.506	22.5	**809**	783	**276**	68	76	**.276**	.394	69	217	160	.966	49	492	491	8	**24**	4.36
Chicago	75	79	.487	25.5	681	636	272	48	86	.267	.384	63	199	143	.968	69	430	564	12	14	3.54
New York	72	80	.474	27.5	663	659	201	46	91	.267	.374	45	139	132	.977	57	473	606	11	18	3.79
Boston	65	87	.428	34.5	623	745	219	50	59	.256	.349	48	184	**169**	.970	76	573	435	9	12	4.36
Philadelphia	50	103	.327	50	494	750	180	35	75	.238	.331	25	181	136	.970	66	475	485	5	8	4.40
					5421	5421	1934	416	688	.264	.376	475	1394	1142	.972	544	3769	4322	82	115	3.85

AMERICAN LEAGUE 1940

	POS	Player	AB	BA	HR	RBI	PO	A	E	DP	TC/G	FA	Pitcher	G	IP	W	L	SV	ERA
Detroit	1B	R. York	588	.316	33	134	1390	107	15	101	9.8	.990	B. Newsom	36	264	21	5	0	2.83
	2B	C. Gehringer	515	.313	10	81	276	374	19	72	4.8	.972	T. Bridges	29	198	12	9	0	3.37
	SS	D. Bartell	528	.233	7	53	295	394	34	74	5.2	.953	S. Rowe	27	169	16	3	0	3.46
W-90 L-64	3B	P. Higgins	480	.271	13	76	133	239	29	16	3.1	.928	J. Gorsica	29	160	7	7	0	4.33
	RF	P. Fox	350	.289	5	48	169	6	6	0	2.1	.967	H. Newhouser	28	133	9	9	0	4.86
Del Baker	CF	B. McCosky	589	.340	4	57	349	7	6	2	2.6	.983	D. Trout	33	101	3	7	2	4.47
	LF	H. Greenberg	573	.340	41	150	298	14	15	1	2.2	.954	A. Benton	42	79	6	10	17	4.42
	C	B. Tebbetts	379	.296	4	46	572	89	17	10	6.3	.975	Hutchinson	17	76	3	7	0	5.68
	OF	B. Campbell	297	.283	8	44	133	6	6	0	2.0	.959							
	C	B. Sullivan	220	.309	3	41	292	29	8	4	5.8	.976							
	OF	E. Averill	118	.280	2	20	23	2	1	0	1.2	.962							

AMERICAN LEAGUE 1940, *cont.*

	POS	Player	AB	BA	HR	RBI	PO	A	E	DP	TC/G	FA	Pitcher	G	IP	W	L	SV	ERA
Cleveland W-89 L-65 Ossie Vitt	1B	H. Trosky	522	.295	25	93	1207	70	11	129	9.3	.991	B. Feller	43	320	27	11	4	2.61
	2B	R. Mack	530	.283	12	69	323	417	27	109	5.3	.965	A. Milnar	37	242	18	10	3	3.27
	SS	L. Boudreau	627	.295	9	101	277	454	24	116	4.9	.968	M. Harder	31	186	12	11	0	4.06
	3B	K. Keltner	543	.254	15	77	170	277	22	27	3.2	.953	A. Smith	31	183	15	7	2	3.44
	RF	B. Bell	444	.279	4	58	193	5	6	1	2.1	.971	J. Allen	32	139	9	8	5	3.44
	CF	R. Weatherly	578	.303	12	59	370	10	12	3	2.9	.969	J. Dobson	40	100	3	7	3	4.95
	LF	B. Chapman	548	.286	4	50	307	10	12	3	2.4	.964							
	C	R. Hemsley	416	.267	4	42	591	65	4	8	5.6	.994							
	OF	J. Heath	356	.219	14	50	197	6	6	1	2.3	.971							
New York W-88 L-66 Joe McCarthy	1B	B. Dahlgren	568	.264	12	73	1488	75	15	143	10.2	.990	R. Ruffing	30	226	15	12	0	3.38
	2B	J. Gordon	616	.281	30	103	374	505	23	116	5.8	.975	M. Russo	30	189	14	8	1	3.28
	SS	F. Crosetti	546	.194	4	31	246	396	31	73	4.6	.954	S. Chandler	27	172	8	7	0	4.60
	3B	R. Rolfe	588	.250	10	53	161	288	24	24	3.4	.949	M. Breuer	27	164	8	9	0	4.55
	RF	C. Keller	500	.286	21	93	317	5	11	2	2.4	.967	A. Donald	24	119	8	3	0	3.03
	CF	J. DiMaggio	508	.352	31	133	359	5	8	2	2.9	.978	M. Pearson	16	110	7	5	0	3.69
	LF	G. Selkirk	379	.269	19	71	220	9	9	6	2.1	.962	S. Sundra	27	99	4	6	2	5.53
	C	B. Dickey	372	.247	9	54	425	55	3	9	4.7	.994	E. Bonham	12	99	9	3	0	1.90
	OF	T. Henrich	293	.307	10	53	147	10	5	2	2.1	.969	B. Hadley	25	80	3	5	2	5.74
	C	B. Rosar	228	.298	4	37	258	30	5	8	4.7	.983	J. Murphy	35	63	8	4	9	3.69
Boston W-82 L-72 Joe Cronin	1B	J. Foxx	515	.297	36	119	844	79	9	87	9.8	.990	J. Bagby	36	183	10	16	2	4.73
	2B	B. Doerr	595	.291	22	105	401	480	21	118	6.0	.977	J. Wilson	41	158	12	6	5	5.08
	SS	J. Cronin	548	.285	24	111	252	443	38	89	5.0	.948	L. Grove	22	153	7	6	0	3.99
	3B	J. Tabor	459	.285	21	81	143	267	33	25	3.7	.926	Ostermueller	31	144	5	9	0	4.95
	RF	D. DiMaggio	418	.301	8	46	239	16	6	5	2.8	.977	H. Hash	34	120	7	7	3	4.95
	CF	D. Cramer	661	.303	1	51	333	11	11	2	2.4	.969	D. Galehouse	25	120	6	6	0	5.18
	LF	T. Williams	561	.344	23	113	302	13	13	2	2.3	.960	J. Heving	39	119	12	7	3	4.01
	C	G. Desautels	222	.225	0	17	325	27	3	8	5.1	.992	E. Dickman	35	100	8	6	3	6.03
	O1	L. Finney	534	.320	5	73	652	33	7	41		.990							
Chicago W-82 L-72 Jimmy Dykes	1B	J. Kuhel	603	.280	27	94	1395	91	18	112	9.7	.988	J. Rigney	39	281	14	18	3	3.11
	2B	S. Webb	334	.237	1	29	143	229	12	44	5.2	.969	T. Lee	28	228	12	13	0	3.47
	SS	L. Appling	566	.348	0	79	307	436	37	83	5.2	.953	E. Smith	32	207	14	9	0	3.21
	3B	B. Kennedy	606	.252	3	52	178	322	33	25	3.5	.938	T. Lyons	22	186	12	8	0	3.24
	RF	T. Wright	581	.337	5	88	278	11	11	2	2.1	.963	J. Knott	25	158	11	9	0	4.56
	CF	M. Kreevich	582	.265	8	55	428	12	8	3	3.1	.982	B. Dietrich	23	150	10	6	0	4.03
	LF	M. Solters	428	.308	12	80	266	6	8	2	2.6	.971	C. Brown	37	66	4	6	10	3.68
	C	M. Tresh	480	.281	1	64	619	69	12	7	5.2	.983							
	OF	L. Rosenthal	276	.301	6	42	208	4	5	0	2.4	.977							
	2B	E. McNair	251	.227	7	31	128	170	13	27	4.8	.958							
St. Louis W-67 L-87 Fred Haney	1B	G. McQuinn	594	.279	16	84	1436	124	13	157	10.5	.992	E. Auker	38	264	16	11	0	3.96
	2B	D. Heffner	487	.236	3	53	311	426	17	102	6.0	.977	V. Kennedy	34	222	12	17	0	5.59
	SS	J. Berardino	523	.258	16	85	250	336	38	83	5.6	.939	B. Harris	35	194	11	15	1	4.93
	3B	H. Clift	523	.273	20	87	161	329	21	32	3.5	.959	J. Niggeling	28	154	7	11	0	4.45
	RF	C. Laabs	218	.271	10	40	124	3	4	1	2.1	.969	B. Trotter	36	98	7	6	2	3.77
	CF	W. Judnich	519	.303	24	89	356	7	4	4	2.8	.989	R. Lawson	30	72	5	3	4	5.13
	LF	R. Radcliff	584	.342	7	81	282	8	8	2	2.1	.973	J. Kramer	16	65	3	7	0	6.26
	C	B. Swift	398	.244	0	39	389	55	9	8	3.5	.980							
	OF	Cullenbine	257	.230	7	31	114	5	3	2	2.1	.975							
	OF	J. Grace	229	.258	5	25	86	6	4	0	1.9	.958							
	OF	M. Hoag	191	.262	3	26	64	4	2	0	1.5	.971							
	SS	A. Strange	167	.186	0	16	65	112	7	24	5.3	.962							
Washington W-64 L-90 Bucky Harris	1B	Z. Bonura	311	.273	3	45	712	42	14	70	9.7	.982	D. Leonard	35	289	14	19	0	3.49
	2B	Bloodworth	469	.245	11	70	260	274	12	74	5.7	.978	K. Chase	35	262	15	17	0	3.23
	SS	J. Pofahl	406	.234	2	36	191	302	25	69	4.6	.952	S. Hudson	38	252	17	16	1	4.57
	3B	C. Travis	528	.322	2	76	116	265	27	30	3.6	.934	W. Masterson	31	130	3	13	2	4.90
	RF	B. Lewis	600	.317	6	63	206	11	9	1	2.0	.960	Krakauskas	32	109	1	6	2	6.44
	CF	G. Case	656	.293	5	56	384	10	12	0	2.6	.970	Monteagudo	27	101	2	6	2	6.08
	LF	G. Walker	595	.294	13	96	285	10	10	2	2.2	.967							
	C	R. Ferrell	326	.273	0	28	427	67	10	5	5.1	.980							
	OF	J. Welaj	215	.256	3	21	132	1	3	0	2.6	.978							
	2B	B. Myer	210	.290	0	29	119	176	10	34	5.6	.967							
	C	J. Early	206	.257	5	14	276	41	10	5	5.8	.969							
Philadelphia W-54 L-100 Connie Mack	1B	D. Siebert	595	.286	5	77	1322	119	22	112	9.5	.985	J. Babich	31	229	14	13	0	3.73
	2B	B. McCoy	490	.257	7	62	261	392	34	82	5.3	.951	N. Potter	31	201	9	14	0	4.44
	SS	A. Brancato	298	.191	1	23	136	180	17	35	4.2	.949	G. Caster	36	178	4	19	2	6.56
	3B	A. Rubeling	376	.245	4	38	96	184	20	13	3.1	.933	C. Dean	30	159	6	13	1	6.61
	RF	W. Moses	537	.309	9	50	295	10	8	1	2.4	.974	B. Ross	24	156	5	10	1	4.38
	CF	S. Chapman	508	.276	23	75	348	13	14	2	2.9	.963	B. Beckmann	34	127	8	4	1	4.17
	LF	B. Johnson	512	.268	31	103	310	15	13	4	2.5	.962	E. Heusser	41	110	6	13	5	4.99
	C	F. Hayes	465	.308	16	70	515	63	17	9	4.4	.971	P. Vaughn	18	99	2	9	2	5.35
	OF	D. Miles	236	.301	1	23	117	3	7	0	2.5	.945							
	SS	B. Lillard	206	.238	1	21	112	157	23	28	4.2	.921							
	3B	Gantenbein	197	.239	4	23	31	75	8	11	2.5	.930							

AMERICAN LEAGUE 1940, *cont.*

BATTING AND BASE RUNNING LEADERS

Batting Average
J. DiMaggio, NY	.352
L. Appling, CHI	.348
T. Williams, BOS	.344
R. Radcliff, STL	.342
H. Greenberg, DET	.340

Slugging Average
H. Greenberg, DET	.670
J. DiMaggio, NY	.626
T. Williams, BOS	.594
R. York, DET	.583
J. Foxx, BOS	.581

Home Runs
H. Greenberg, DET	41
J. Foxx, BOS	36
R. York, DET	33
J. DiMaggio, NY	31
B. Johnson, PHI	31

Winning Percentage
S. Rowe, DET	.842
B. Newsom, DET	.808
B. Feller, CLE	.711
A. Smith, CLE	.682
A. Milnar, CLE	.643

Earned Run Average
E. Bonham, NY	1.90
B. Feller, CLE	2.61
B. Newsom, DET	2.83
J. Rigney, CHI	3.11
E. Smith, CHI	3.21

Wins
B. Feller, CLE	27
B. Newsom, DET	21
A. Milnar, CLE	18
S. Hudson, WAS	17
S. Rowe, DET	16
E. Auker, STL	16

Total Bases
H. Greenberg, DET	384
R. York, DET	343
T. Williams, BOS	333
J. DiMaggio, NY	318
J. Gordon, NY	315

Runs Batted In
H. Greenberg, DET	150
R. York, DET	134
J. DiMaggio, NY	133
J. Foxx, BOS	119
T. Williams, BOS	113

Stolen Bases
G. Case, WAS	35
G. Walker, WAS	21
J. Gordon, NY	18
M. Kreevich, CHI	15
B. Lewis, WAS	15

Saves
A. Benton, DET	17
C. Brown, CHI	10
J. Murphy, NY	9

Strikeouts
B. Feller, CLE	261
B. Newsom, DET	164
J. Rigney, CHI	141
T. Bridges, DET	133
K. Chase, WAS	129

Complete Games
B. Feller, CLE	31
T. Lee, CHI	24
D. Leonard, WAS	23

Hits
R. Radcliff, STL	200
B. McCosky, DET	200
D. Cramer, BOS	200
L. Appling, CHI	197

Base on Balls
C. Keller, NY	106
H. Clift, STL	104
J. Foxx, BOS	101
C. Gehringer, DET	101

Home Run Percentage
H. Greenberg, DET	7.2
J. Foxx, BOS	7.0
J. DiMaggio, NY	6.1
B. Johnson, PHI	6.1

Fewest Hits/9 Innings
B. Feller, CLE	6.88
E. Bonham, NY	7.52
J. Rigney, CHI	7.70
E. Smith, CHI	7.77

Shutouts
T. Lyons, CHI	4
A. Milnar, CLE	4
B. Feller, CLE	4

Fewest Walks/9 Innings
E. Bonham, NY	1.18
T. Lyons, CHI	1.79
T. Lee, CHI	2.21
S. Rowe, DET	2.29

Runs Scored
T. Williams, BOS	134
H. Greenberg, DET	129
B. McCosky, DET	123
J. Gordon, NY	112

Doubles
H. Greenberg, DET	50
R. York, DET	46
L. Boudreau, CLE	46
T. Williams, BOS	43

Triples
B. McCosky, DET	19
C. Keller, NY	15
L. Finney, BOS	15
T. Williams, BOS	14

Most Strikeouts/9 Inn.
B. Feller, CLE	7.33
T. Bridges, DET	6.06
B. Newsom, DET	5.59
E. Smith, CHI	5.17

Innings
B. Feller, CLE	320
D. Leonard, WAS	289
J. Rigney, CHI	281
B. Newsom, DET	264

Games Pitched
B. Feller, CLE	43
A. Benton, DET	42
J. Wilson, BOS	41
E. Heusser, PHI	41

	W	L	PCT	GB	R	OR	2B	3B	HR	BA	SA	SB	E	DP	FA	CG	BB	SO	ShO	SV	ERA
Detroit	90	64	.584		**888**	717	**312**	65	134	**.286**	.442	66	194	116	.968	59	570	**752**	10	**23**	4.01
Cleveland	89	65	.578	1	710	**637**	287	61	101	.265	.398	53	**149**	164	**.975**	72	512	686	**13**	22	**3.63**
New York	88	66	.571	2	817	671	243	66	**155**	.259	.418	59	152	158	.975	76	511	559	10	14	3.89
Boston	82	72	.532	8	872	825	301	**80**	145	.286	**.449**	55	173	156	.972	51	625	613	4	16	4.89
Chicago	82	72	.532	8	735	672	238	63	73	.278	.387	52	185	125	.969	**83**	480	574	10	18	3.74
St. Louis	67	87	.435	23	757	882	278	58	118	.263	.401	51	158	**179**	.974	64	646	439	4	9	5.12
Washington	64	90	.416	26	665	811	266	67	52	.271	.374	**94**	194	166	.968	74	618	618	6	7	4.59
Philadelphia	54	100	.351	36	703	932	242	53	105	.262	.387	48	238	131	.960	72	534	488	4	12	5.22
					6147	6147	2167	513	883	.271	.407	478	1443	1195	.970	551	4496	4729	61	121	4.38

NATIONAL LEAGUE 1941

	POS	Player	AB	BA	HR	RBI	PO	A	E	DP	TC/G	FA	Pitcher	G	IP	W	L	SV	ERA
Brooklyn	1B	D. Camilli	529	.285	**34**	120	1379	98	16	107	10.1	.989	K. Higbe	**48**	298	**22**	9	3	3.14
	2B	B. Herman	536	.291	3	41	297	354	20	64	5.0	.970	W. Wyatt	38	288	**22**	10	1	2.34
W-100 L-54	SS	P. Reese	595	.229	2	46	346	473	47	76	**5.7**	.946	H. Casey	45	162	14	11	7	3.89
	3B	C. Lavagetto	441	.277	1	78	117	215	22	17	3.0	.938	C. Davis	28	154	13	7	2	2.97
Leo Durocher	RF	D. Walker	531	.311	9	71	309	19	8	8	2.3	.976	L. Hamlin	30	136	8	8	1	4.24
	CF	P. Reiser	536	**.343**	14	76	356	14	7	0	**2.8**	.981							
	LF	J. Medwick	538	.318	18	88	270	11	5	2	2.2	.983							
	C	M. Owen	386	.231	1	44	**530**	64	3	7	4.7	.995							
	OF	J. Wasdell	265	.298	4	48	84	2	4	0	1.7	.956							
	3B	L. Riggs	197	.305	5	36	48	75	9	4	3.1	.932							
	P	W. Wyatt	109	.239	3	22	11	47	2	5	1.6	.967							
St. Louis	1B	J. Mize	473	.317	16	100	1157	82	8	104	10.2	.994	L. Warneke	37	246	17	9	0	3.15
	2B	C. Crespi	560	.279	4	46	**382**	421	32	**94**	5.8	.962	E. White	32	210	17	7	2	2.40
W-97 L-56	SS	M. Marion	547	.252	3	58	299	**489**	38	85	5.3	.954	M. Cooper	29	187	13	9	0	3.91
	3B	J. Brown	549	.306	3	56	135	276	15	22	3.5	.952	M. Lanier	35	153	10	8	3	2.82
Billy Southworth	RF	E. Slaughter	425	.311	13	76	173	5	10	1	1.7	.947	H. Gumbert	33	144	11	5	1	2.74
	CF	T. Moore	493	.294	6	68	293	14	5	3	2.6	.984	H. Krist	37	114	10	0	2	4.03
	LF	J. Hopp	445	.303	4	50	213	4	4	1	2.4	.982	Hutchinson	29	47	1	5	5	3.86
	C	G. Mancuso	328	.229	2	37	482	58	6	6	5.2	.989							
	OF	D. Padgett	324	.247	5	44	115	1	5	0	2.0	.959							
	C	W. Cooper	200	.245	1	20	247	39	10	11	4.7	.966							
	OF	C. Triplett	185	.286	3	21	78	4	3	0	1.8	.965							
	OF	E. Crabtree	167	.341	5	28	71	2	0	0	1.5	1.000							

NATIONAL LEAGUE 1941, *cont.*

	POS	Player	AB	BA	HR	RBI	PO	A	E	DP	TC/G	FA	Pitcher	G	IP	W	L	SV	ERA
Cincinnati	1B	McCormick	603	.269	17	97	**1464**	92	8	**130**	10.2	**.995**	B. Walters	37	**302**	19	15	2	2.83
	2B	L. Frey	543	.254	6	59	340	432	24	93	5.5	**.970**	P. Derringer	29	228	12	14	1	3.31
W-88 L-66	SS	E. Joost	537	.253	4	40	310	415	45	85	5.2	.942	Vander Meer	33	226	16	13	0	2.82
	3B	B. Werber	418	.239	4	46	120	256	16	30	3.7	.959	E. Riddle	33	217	19	4	1	**2.24**
Bill McKechnie	RF	J. Gleeson	301	.233	3	34	153	1	3	0	1.9	.981	J. Turner	23	113	6	4	0	3.11
	CF	H. Craft	413	.249	10	59	280	6	5	1	2.5	.983	J. Thompson	27	109	6	6	1	4.87
	LF	McCormick	369	.287	4	31	240	9	6	2	2.5	.976	J. Beggs	37	57	4	3	5	3.79
	C	E. Lombardi	398	.264	10	60	496	70	10	9	5.0	.983							
	OF	E. Koy	204	.250	2	27	92	3	1	1	2.0	.990							
	C	D. West	172	.215	1	17	209	21	7	3	3.7	.970							
	3B	C. Aleno	169	.243	1	18	41	77	3	6	3.0	.975							
	OF	L. Waner	164	.256	0	6	68	3	1	1	1.6	.986							
Pittsburgh	1B	E. Fletcher	521	.288	11	74	1444	118	14	113	**10.4**	.991	R. Sewell	39	249	14	**17**	2	3.72
	2B	F. Gustine	463	.270	1	46	269	317	28	45	5.9	.954	M. Butcher	33	236	17	12	0	3.05
W-81 L-73	SS	A. Vaughan	374	.316	6	38	172	289	20	42	5.0	.958	Heintzelman	35	196	11	11	0	3.44
	3B	L. Handley	459	.288	0	33	125	247	21	19	3.4	.947	J. Lanning	34	176	11	11	1	3.13
Frankie Frisch	RF	B. Elliott	527	.273	3	76	281	9	9	2	2.2	.970	B. Klinger	35	117	9	4	4	3.93
	CF	V. DiMaggio	528	.267	21	100	391	11	10	3	2.7	.976	D. Dietz	33	100	7	2	1	2.33
	LF	Van Robays	457	.282	4	78	292	9	8	3	2.6	.974							
	C	A. Lopez	317	.265	5	43	345	54	8	5	3.6	.980							
	2B	S. Martin	233	.305	0	19	127	154	8	26	5.5	.972							
	SS	A. Anderson	223	.215	1	10	97	161	19	29	4.8	.931							
	3O	D. Garms	220	.264	3	42	73	44	9	1		.929							
	OF	B. Stewart	172	.267	0	10	71	5	3	2	1.9	.962							
New York	1B	B. Young	574	.265	25	104	1395	87	21	124	10.0	.986	Schumacher	30	206	12	10	1	3.36
	2B	B. Whitehead	403	.228	1	23	288	285	18	60	5.7	.970	C. Melton	42	194	8	11	1	3.01
W-74 L-79	SS	B. Jurges	471	.293	5	61	230	432	30	82	5.2	.957	C. Hubbell	26	164	11	9	1	3.57
	3B	D. Bartell	373	.303	5	35	91	169	11	16	3.2	.959	B. Lohrman	33	159	9	10	3	4.02
Bill Terry	RF	M. Ott	525	.286	27	90	256	**19**	9	3	2.0	.968	B. Carpenter	29	132	11	6	2	3.83
	CF	J. Rucker	**622**	.288	1	42	344	13	12	5	2.6	.967	B. McGee	22	106	2	9	0	4.91
	LF	J. Moore	428	.273	7	40	237	5	7	0	2.1	.972	B. Bowman	29	80	6	7	1	5.71
	C	H. Danning	459	.244	7	56	**530**	77	4	8	5.3	.993	J. Brown	31	57	1	5	8	3.32
	3B	J. Orengo	252	.214	4	25	74	132	9	12	3.6	.958							
	OF	M. Arnovich	207	.280	2	22	103	5	2	0	1.8	.982							
	C	G. Hartnett	150	.300	5	26	138	15	1	1	4.5	.994							
Chicago	1B	B. Dahlgren	359	.281	16	59	957	38	9	84	10.2	.991	C. Passeau	34	231	14	14	0	3.35
	2B	L. Stringer	512	.246	5	53	356	**455**	34	84	**6.2**	.960	V. Olsen	37	186	10	8	1	3.15
W-70 L-84	SS	B. Sturgeon	433	.245	0	25	215	366	27	68	4.8	.956	B. Lee	28	167	8	14	1	3.76
	3B	S. Hack	586	.317	7	45	138	295	21	22	3.0	.954	J. Mooty	33	153	8	9	4	3.35
Jimmie Wilson	RF	B. Nicholson	532	.254	26	98	293	10	9	2	2.2	.971	P. Erickson	32	141	5	7	1	3.70
	CF	Cavarretta	346	.286	6	40	128	3	1	2	2.0	.992	L. French	26	138	5	14	0	4.63
	LF	Dallessandro	486	.272	6	85	292	4	4	0	2.3	.987	C. Root	19	107	8	7	0	5.40
	C	McCullough	418	.227	9	53	481	64	10	6	4.7	.982							
	OF	L. Novikoff	203	.241	5	24	92	3	0	0	1.8	1.000							
	O1	H. Leiber	162	.216	7	25	192	8	5	13		.976							
	C	B. Scheffing	132	.242	1	20	126	17	5	1	4.4	.966							
Boston	1B	B. Hassett	405	.296	1	33	895	78	9	92	9.9	.991	J. Tobin	33	238	12	12	0	3.10
	2B	B. Rowell	483	.267	7	60	265	312	**40**	81	5.5	.935	M. Salvo	35	195	7	16	0	4.06
W-62 L-92	SS	E. Miller	585	.239	6	68	336	485	29	**112**	5.5	**.966**	A. Johnson	43	183	7	15	1	3.53
	3B	S. Sisti	541	.259	1	45	162	287	**41**	28	3.6	.916	D. Errickson	38	166	6	12	1	4.78
Casey Stengel	RF	G. Moore	397	.272	5	43	229	13	8	2	2.3	.968	A. Javery	34	161	10	11	1	4.31
	CF	J. Cooney	442	.319	0	29	274	9	1	3	2.6	**.996**	T. Earley	33	139	6	8	3	2.53
	LF	M. West	484	.277	12	68	302	13	6	5	2.4	.981	F. LaManna	35	73	5	4	1	5.33
	C	R. Berres	279	.201	1	19	356	64	2	3	3.5	**.995**							
	OF	P. Waner	294	.279	2	46	129	7	5	3	1.8	.965							
	C	P. Masi	180	.222	3	18	194	31	5	3	2.8	.978							
	2B	S. Roberge	167	.216	0	15	95	132	5	31	5.0	.978							
	1B	B. Dahlgren	166	.235	7	30	379	28	3	45	10.5	.993							
Philadelphia	1B	N. Etten	540	.311	14	79	1286	89	**23**	124	9.3	.984	J. Podgajny	34	181	9	12	0	4.62
	2B	D. Murtaugh	347	.219	0	11	233	247	11	49	5.8	.978	T. Hughes	34	170	9	14	0	4.45
W-43 L-111	SS	B. Bragan	557	.251	4	69	322	437	45	86	5.2	.944	S. Johnson	39	163	5	12	2	4.52
	3B	P. May	490	.267	0	39	**194**	324	15	**31**	**3.8**	**.972**	C. Blanton	28	164	6	13	0	4.51
Doc Prothro	RF	S. Benjamin	480	.235	3	27	185	11	4	3	1.8	.980	I. Pearson	46	136	4	14	6	3.57
	CF	J. Marty	477	.268	8	39	286	7	11	0	2.3	.964	L. Grissom	29	131	2	13	0	3.97
	LF	D. Litwhiler	590	.305	18	66	**393**	12	**15**	3	2.8	.964	F. Hoerst	37	106	3	10	1	5.20
	C	B. Warren	345	.214	9	35	412	**84**	**14**	**16**	4.6	.973	B. Beck	34	95	1	9	0	4.63
	OF	J. Rizzo	235	.217	4	24	114	8	4	2	2.0	.968							
	UT	E. Mueller	233	.227	1	22	114	107	6	21		.974							
	C	Livingston	207	.203	1	18	263	34	8	5	4.3	.974							
	2S	H. Marnie	158	.241	0	11	129	103	2	24		.991							

NATIONAL LEAGUE 1941, *cont.*

BATTING AND BASE RUNNING LEADERS

Batting Average		Slugging Average		Home Runs		Winning Percentage		Earned Run Average		Wins	
P. Reiser, BKN	.343	P. Reiser, BKN	.558	D. Camilli, BKN	34	E. Riddle, CIN	.826	E. Riddle, CIN	2.24	K. Higbe, BKN	22
J. Cooney, BOS	.319	D. Camilli, BKN	.556	M. Ott, NY	27	K. Higbe, BKN	.710	W. Wyatt, BKN	2.34	W. Wyatt, BKN	22
J. Medwick, BKN	.318	J. Mize, STL	.535	B. Nicholson, CHI	26	E. White, STL	.708	E. White, STL	2.40	E. Riddle, CIN	19
S. Hack, CHI	.317	J. Medwick, BKN	.517	B. Young, NY	25	W. Wyatt, BKN	.688	Vander Meer, CIN	2.82	B. Walters, CIN	19
J. Mize, STL	.317	E. Slaughter, STL	.496	B. Dahlgren, BOS, CHI	23	L. Warneke, STL	.654	B. Walters, CIN	2.83		

Total Bases		Runs Batted In		Stolen Bases		Saves		Strikeouts		Complete Games	
P. Reiser, BKN	299	D. Camilli, BKN	120	D. Murtaugh, PHI	18	J. Brown, NY	8	Vander Meer, CIN	202	B. Walters, CIN	27
D. Camilli, BKN	294	B. Young, NY	104	S. Benjamin, PHI	17	H. Casey, BKN	7	W. Wyatt, BKN	176	W. Wyatt, BKN	23
J. Medwick, BKN	278	J. Mize, STL	100	L. Handley, PIT	16	B. Crouch, PHI, STL	7	B. Walters, CIN	129	J. Tobin, BOS	20
D. Litwhiler, PHI	275	V. DiMaggio, PIT	100	L. Frey, CIN	16	I. Pearson, PHI	6	K. Higbe, BKN	121	C. Passeau, CHI	20
B. Young, NY	265	B. Nicholson, CHI	98	J. Hopp, STL	15	J. Beggs, CIN	5	M. Cooper, STL	118	M. Butcher, PIT	19
						Hutchinson, STL	5			K. Higbe, BKN	19

Hits		Base on Balls		Home Run Percentage		Fewest Hits/9 Innings		Shutouts		Fewest Walks/9 Innings	
S. Hack, CHI	186	E. Fletcher, PIT	118	D. Camilli, BKN	6.4	Vander Meer, CIN	6.84	W. Wyatt, BKN	7	C. Davis, BKN	1.57
P. Reiser, BKN	184	D. Camilli, BKN	104	M. Ott, NY	5.1	W. Wyatt, BKN	6.96	Vander Meer, CIN	6	C. Passeau, CHI	2.03
D. Litwhiler, PHI	180	M. Ott, NY	100	B. Nicholson, CHI	4.9	E. White, STL	7.24	C. Davis, BKN	5	P. Derringer, CIN	2.13
J. Rucker, NY	179	S. Hack, CHI	99	B. Dahlgren, BOS, CHI	4.4	K. Higbe, BKN	7.37	B. Walters, CIN	5	J. Tobin, BOS	2.27

Runs Scored		Doubles		Triples		Most Strikeouts/9 Inn.		Innings		Games Pitched	
P. Reiser, BKN	117	J. Mize, STL	39	P. Reiser, BKN	17	Vander Meer, CIN	8.03	B. Walters, CIN	302	K. Higbe, BKN	48
S. Hack, CHI	111	P. Reiser, BKN	39	E. Fletcher, PIT	13	M. Cooper, STL	5.69	K. Higbe, BKN	298	I. Pearson, PHI	46
J. Medwick, BKN	100	J. Rucker, NY	38	J. Hopp, STL	11	W. Wyatt, BKN	5.49	W. Wyatt, BKN	288	H. Casey, BKN	45
E. Fletcher, PIT	95	Dallessandro, CHI	36	B. Elliott, PIT	10	E. White, STL	5.01	R. Sewell, PIT	249	J. Hutchings, BOS, CIN	44

PITCHING LEADERS

	W	L	PCT	GB	R	OR	Batting 2B	3B	HR	BA	SA	SB	Fielding E	DP	FA	Pitching CG	BB	SO	ShO	SV	ERA
Brooklyn	100	54	.649		800	581	286	69	101	.272	.405	36	162	125	.974	66	495	603	17	22	3.14
St. Louis	97	56	.634	2.5	734	589	254	56	70	.272	.377	47	172	146	.973	64	502	659	15	20	3.19
Cincinnati	88	66	.571	12	616	564	213	33	64	.247	.337	68	152	147	.975	89	510	627	19	10	3.17
Pittsburgh	81	73	.526	19	690	643	233	65	56	.268	.368	59	196	130	.968	71	492	410	8	12	3.48
New York	74	79	.484	25.5	667	706	248	35	95	.260	.371	36	160	144	.974	55	539	566	12	18	3.94
Chicago	70	84	.455	30	666	670	239	25	99	.253	.365	39	180	139	.970	74	449	548	8	9	3.72
Boston	62	92	.403	38	592	720	231	38	48	.251	.334	61	191	174	.969	62	554	446	10	9	3.95
Philadelphia	43	111	.279	57	501	793	188	38	64	.244	.331	65	187	147	.969	35	606	552	4	9	4.50
					5266	5266	1892	359	597	.258	.361	411	1400	1152	.972	516	4147	4411	93	109	3.63

AMERICAN LEAGUE 1941

New York
W-101 L-53
Joe McCarthy

POS	Player	AB	BA	HR	RBI	PO	A	E	DP	TC/G	FA	Pitcher	G	IP	W	L	SV	ERA
1B	J. Sturm	524	.239	3	36	1099	85	12	117	9.6	.990	M. Russo	28	210	14	10	1	3.09
2B	J. Gordon	588	.276	24	87	332	397	32	109	5.8	.958	R. Ruffing	23	186	15	6	0	3.54
SS	P. Rizzuto	515	.307	3	46	252	399	29	109	5.3	.957	S. Chandler	28	164	10	4	4	3.19
3B	R. Rolfe	561	.264	8	42	140	263	23	28	3.2	.946	A. Donald	22	159	9	5	0	3.57
RF	T. Henrich	538	.277	31	85	280	13	6	4	2.2	.980	L. Gomez	23	156	15	5	0	3.74
CF	J. DiMaggio	541	.357	30	125	385	16	9	5	2.9	.978	M. Breuer	26	141	9	7	2	4.09
LF	C. Keller	507	.298	33	122	328	7	7	2	2.5	.980	E. Bonham	23	127	9	6	2	2.98
C	B. Dickey	348	.284	7	71	422	45	3	11	4.5	.994	J. Murphy	35	77	8	3	15	1.98
C	B. Rosar	209	.287	1	36	246	24	1	6	4.5	.996							
UT	G. Priddy	174	.213	1	26	167	119	8	46		.973							
OF	G. Selkirk	164	.220	6	25	84	4	3	2	1.9	.967							
SS	F. Crosetti	148	.223	1	22	80	89	10	20	5.6	.944							
P	R. Ruffing	89	.303	2	22	7	21	0	3	1.2	1.000							

Boston
W-84 L-70
Joe Cronin

POS	Player	AB	BA	HR	RBI	PO	A	E	DP	TC/G	FA	Pitcher	G	IP	W	L	SV	ERA
1B	J. Foxx	487	.300	19	105	1155	112	10	105	10.3	.992	D. Newsome	36	214	19	10	0	4.13
2B	B. Doerr	500	.282	16	93	290	389	20	85	5.3	.971	M. Harris	35	194	8	14	1	3.25
SS	J. Cronin	518	.311	16	95	225	324	24	64	4.8	.958	C. Wagner	29	187	12	8	0	3.07
3B	J. Tabor	498	.279	16	101	123	277	30	24	3.4	.930	L. Grove	21	134	7	7	0	4.37
RF	L. Finney	497	.288	4	53	181	7	11	2	2.2	.945	J. Dobson	27	134	12	5	0	4.49
CF	D. DiMaggio	584	.283	8	58	386	16	15	2	2.9	.964	M. Ryba	40	121	7	3	6	4.46
LF	T. Williams	456	.406	37	120	262	11	11	2	2.1	.961	J. Wilson	27	116	4	13	1	5.03
C	F. Pytlak	336	.271	2	39	416	41	4	7	5.1	.991							
OF	P. Fox	268	.302	0	31	123	5	3	2	2.1	.977							
C	J. Peacock	261	.284	0	27	298	33	4	7	4.8	.988							
SS	S. Newsome	227	.225	2	17	95	133	10	28	3.4	.958							
OF	S. Spence	203	.232	2	28	97	6	0	2	2.0	1.000							

AMERICAN LEAGUE 1941, *cont.*

	POS	Player	AB	BA	HR	RBI	PO	A	E	DP	TC/G	FA	Pitcher	G	IP	W	L	SV	ERA
Chicago W-77 L-77 Jimmy Dykes	1B	J. Kuhel	600	.250	12	63	**1444**	108	10	113	10.3	.994	T. Lee	35	300	22	11	1	**2.37**
	2B	Knickerbocker	343	.245	7	29	204	221	13	58	5.0	.970	E. Smith	34	263	13	17	1	3.18
	SS	L. Appling	592	.314	1	57	294	**473**	42	95	5.3	.948	J. Rigney	30	237	13	13	0	3.84
	3B	D. Lodigiani	322	.239	4	40	120	187	12	22	3.7	.962	T. Lyons	22	187	12	10	0	3.70
	RF	T. Wright	513	.322	10	97	279	8	8	3	2.2	.973	B. Dietrich	19	109	5	8	0	5.35
	CF	M. Kreevich	436	.232	0	37	302	7	2	2	2.8	**.994**	B. Ross	20	108	3	8	0	3.16
	LF	M. Hoag	380	.255	1	44	215	6	10	1	2.3	.957	J. Hallett	22	75	5	5	0	6.03
	C	M. Tresh	390	.251	0	33	**488**	81	11	12	5.0	.981							
	2B	D. Kolloway	280	.271	3	24	118	181	14	23	5.0	.955							
	3B	B. Kennedy	257	.206	1	29	88	153	17	12	3.6	.934							
	OF	M. Solters	251	.259	4	43	135	7	5	1	2.3	.966							
	OF	B. Chapman	190	.226	2	19	122	4	5	1	2.6	.992							
Cleveland W-75 L-79 Roger Peckinpaugh	1B	H. Trosky	310	.294	11	51	727	54	9	77	9.3	.989	B. Feller	**44**	**343**	**25**	13	2	3.15
	2B	R. Mack	501	.228	9	44	363	386	23	**109**	5.3	.970	A. Milnar	35	229	12	19	0	4.36
	SS	L. Boudreau	579	.257	10	56	**296**	444	26	97	5.2	**.966**	A. Smith	29	207	12	13	0	3.83
	3B	K. Keltner	581	.269	23	84	181	**346**	16	36	3.6	**.971**	J. Bagby	33	201	9	15	2	4.04
	RF	J. Heath	585	.340	24	123	259	20	**15**	1	1.9	.949	C. Brown	41	74	5	3	3	3.27
	CF	R. Weatherly	363	.289	3	37	208	1	7	1	2.5	.968	J. Heving	27	71	5	2	5	2.29
	LF	G. Walker	445	.283	6	48	257	9	5	0	2.6	.982	M. Harder	15	69	5	4	1	5.24
	C	R. Hemsley	288	.240	2	24	401	42	9	8	4.7	.980							
	OF	S. Campbell	328	.250	3	35	202	6	4	0	2.7	.981							
	1B	O. Grimes	244	.238	4	24	544	31	3	53	9.3	.995							
	C	G. Desautels	189	.201	1	17	300	32	1	5	5.0	.997							
Detroit W-75 L-79 Del Baker	1B	R. York	590	.259	27	111	1393	110	**21**	111	9.8	.986	B. Newsom	43	250	12	**20**	2	4.60
	2B	C. Gehringer	436	.220	3	46	279	324	11	59	5.3	**.982**	H. Newhouser	33	173	9	11	0	4.79
	SS	F. Croucher	489	.254	2	39	270	361	44	85	5.0	.935	J. Gorsica	33	171	9	11	2	4.47
	3B	P. Higgins	540	.298	11	73	153	304	26	14	3.3	.946	A. Benton	38	158	15	6	7	2.97
	RF	B. Campbell	512	.275	15	93	241	5	6	1	1.9	.976	D. Trout	37	152	9	9	2	3.74
	CF	B. McCosky	494	.324	3	55	328	6	5	2	2.8	.985	T. Bridges	25	148	9	12	0	3.41
	LF	R. Radcliff	379	.317	3	39	155	6	5	1	1.9	.970	S. Rowe	27	139	8	6	1	3.14
	C	B. Tebbetts	359	.284	2	47	461	**83**	13	11	**5.7**	.977							
	C	B. Sullivan	234	.282	3	29	339	33	9	7	6.0	.976							
	OF	P. Mullin	220	.345	5	23	117	2	7	0	2.5	.944							
	OF	T. Stainback	200	.245	2	10	107	3	6	0	1.5	.948							
St. Louis W-70 L-84 Fred Haney W-15 L-29 Luke Sewell W-55 L-55	1B	G. McQuinn	495	.297	18	80	1138	109	6	109	10.0	**.995**	E. Auker	34	216	14	15	0	5.50
	2B	D. Heffner	399	.233	0	17	224	307	14	52	5.2	.974	B. Muncrief	36	214	13	9	1	3.65
	SS	J. Berardino	469	.271	5	89	261	305	27	81	4.8	.954	D. Galehouse	30	190	9	10	3	3.64
	3B	H. Clift	584	.255	17	84	**195**	316	22	27	3.5	.959	B. Harris	34	187	12	14	1	5.21
	RF	C. Laabs	392	.278	15	59	217	6	4	2	2.6	.982	J. Niggeling	24	168	7	9	0	3.80
	CF	W. Judnich	546	.284	14	83	383	11	8	3	2.9	.980	G. Caster	32	104	3	7	3	5.00
	LF	Cullenbine	501	.317	9	98	258	12	10	3	2.3	.964							
	C	R. Ferrell	321	.252	2	23	340	51	2	11	4.0	.995							
	OF	J. Grace	362	.309	6	60	164	13	3	1	2.0	.983							
	2B	J. Lucadello	351	.279	2	31	147	185	13	36	4.9	.962							
	C	B. Swift	170	.259	0	21	180	22	3	3	3.5	.985							
Washington W-70 L-84 Bucky Harris	1B	M. Vernon	531	.299	9	93	1186	80	10	**122**	9.7	.992	D. Leonard	34	256	18	13	0	3.45
	2B	Bloodworth	506	.245	7	66	**380**	436	24	107	**6.4**	.971	S. Hudson	33	250	13	14	0	3.46
	SS	C. Travis	608	.359	7	101	279	388	25	99	5.1	.964	K. Chase	33	206	6	18	0	5.08
	3B	G. Archie	379	.269	3	48	71	150	15	12	3.2	.936	S. Sundra	28	168	9	13	0	5.29
	RF	B. Lewis	569	.297	9	72	229	16	7	3	1.9	.972	R. Anderson	32	112	4	6	0	4.18
	CF	D. Cramer	**660**	.273	2	66	369	9	6	1	2.5	.984	B. Zuber	36	96	6	4	2	5.42
	LF	G. Case	649	.271	2	53	362	**21**	10	3	2.6	.975	Carrasquel	35	97	6	2	2	3.44
	C	J. Early	355	.287	10	54	385	52	**16**	13	4.5	.965	W. Masterson	34	78	4	3	3	5.97
	C	A. Evans	159	.277	1	19	195	24	7	6	4.4	.969							
Philadelphia W-64 L-90 Connie Mack	1B	D. Siebert	467	.334	5	79	1102	106	12	95	9.9	.990	Marchildon	30	204	10	15	0	3.57
	2B	B. McCoy	517	.271	8	61	285	423	27	87	5.4	.963	J. Knott	27	194	13	11	0	4.40
	SS	A. Brancato	530	.234	2	49	263	395	**61**	80	5.2	.915	L. McCrabb	26	157	9	13	2	5.49
	3B	P. Suder	531	.245	4	52	175	271	20	25	3.4	.957	L. Harris	33	132	4	4	2	4.78
	RF	W. Moses	438	.301	4	35	263	12	7	5	2.6	.975	B. Beckmann	22	130	5	9	1	4.57
	CF	S. Chapman	552	.322	25	106	416	21	15	5	3.2	.967	T. Ferrick	36	119	8	10	3	3.77
	LF	B. Johnson	552	.275	22	107	287	17	3	0	2.5	.990	B. Hadley	25	102	4	6	3	5.01
	C	F. Hayes	439	.280	12	63	403	65	8	11	3.9	.983							
	OF	E. Collins	219	.242	0	12	119	3	4	1	2.5	.968							
	OF	D. Miles	170	.312	0	15	79	2	0	1	2.3	1.000							

BATTING AND BASE RUNNING LEADERS

Batting Average		Slugging Average		Home Runs	
T. Williams, BOS	.406	T. Williams, BOS	.735	T. Williams, BOS	37
C. Travis, WAS	.359	J. DiMaggio, NY	.643	C. Keller, NY	33
J. DiMaggio, NY	.357	J. Heath, CLE	.586	T. Henrich, NY	31
J. Heath, CLE	.340	C. Keller, NY	.580	J. DiMaggio, NY	30
D. Siebert, PHI	.334	S. Chapman, PHI	.543	R. York, DET	27

PITCHING LEADERS

Winning Percentage		Earned Run Average		Wins	
L. Gomez, NY	.750	T. Lee, CHI	2.37	B. Feller, CLE	25
A. Benton, DET	.714	C. Wagner, BOS	3.07	T. Lee, CHI	22
R. Ruffing, NY	.714	M. Russo, NY	3.09	D. Newsome, BOS	19
T. Lee, CHI	.667	B. Feller, CLE	3.15	D. Leonard, WAS	18
B. Feller, CLE	.658	E. Smith, CHI	3.18		

AMERICAN LEAGUE 1941, *cont.*

BATTING AND BASE RUNNING LEADERS

Total Bases
J. DiMaggio, NY	348
J. Heath, CLE	343
T. Williams, BOS	335
C. Travis, WAS	316
S. Chapman, PHI	300

Runs Batted In
J. DiMaggio, NY	125
J. Heath, CLE	123
C. Keller, NY	122
T. Williams, BOS	120
R. York, DET	111

Stolen Bases
G. Case, WAS	33
J. Kuhel, CHI	20
J. Heath, CLE	18
M. Kreevich, CHI	17
J. Tabor, BOS	17

PITCHING LEADERS

Saves
J. Murphy, NY	15
A. Benton, DET	7
T. Ferrick, PHI	7
M. Ryba, BOS	6
C. Brown, CLE	5
J. Heving, CLE	5

Strikeouts
B. Feller, CLE	260
B. Newsom, DET	175
T. Lee, CHI	130
J. Rigney, CHI	119
M. Harris, BOS	111
E. Smith, CHI	111

Complete Games
T. Lee, CHI	30
B. Feller, CLE	28
E. Smith, CHI	21
T. Lyons, CHI	19
D. Leonard, WAS	19

Hits
C. Travis, WAS	218
J. Heath, CLE	199
J. DiMaggio, NY	193
L. Appling, CHI	186

Base on Balls
T. Williams, BOS	145
Cullenbine, STL	121
H. Clift, STL	113
C. Keller, NY	102

Home Run Percentage
T. Williams, BOS	8.1
C. Keller, NY	6.5
T. Henrich, NY	5.8
J. DiMaggio, NY	5.5

Fewest Hits/9 Innings
B. Feller, CLE	7.45
T. Lee, CHI	7.73
T. Bridges, DET	7.80
A. Donald, NY	7.98

Shutouts
B. Feller, CLE	6
J. Humphries, CHI	4
S. Chandler, NY	4
D. Leonard, WAS	4

Fewest Walks/9 Innings
T. Lyons, CHI	1.78
D. Leonard, WAS	1.90
B. Muncrief, STL	2.23
R. Ruffing, NY	2.62

Runs Scored
T. Williams, BOS	135
J. DiMaggio, NY	122
D. DiMaggio, BOS	117
H. Clift, STL	108

Doubles
L. Boudreau, CLE	45
J. DiMaggio, NY	43
W. Judnich, STL	40
J. Kuhel, CHI	39

Triples
J. Heath, CLE	20
C. Travis, WAS	19
K. Keltner, CLE	13

Most Strikeouts/9 Inn.
B. Feller, CLE	6.82
B. Newsom, DET	6.29
T. Bridges, DET	5.49
M. Harris, BOS	5.15

Innings
B. Feller, CLE	343
T. Lee, CHI	300
E. Smith, CHI	263
D. Leonard, WAS	256

Games Pitched
B. Feller, CLE	44
B. Newsom, DET	43
C. Brown, CLE	41
M. Ryba, BOS	40

	W	L	PCT	GB	R	OR	2B	3B	HR	BA	SA	SB	E	DP	FA	CG	BB	SO	ShO	SV	ERA
New York	101	53	.656	—	830	631	243	60	151	.269	.419	51	165	196	.973	75	598	589	13	26	3.53
Boston	84	70	.545	17	865	750	304	55	124	.283	.430	67	172	139	.972	70	611	574	8	11	4.19
Chicago	77	77	.500	24	638	649	245	47	47	.255	.343	91	180	145	.971	106	521	564	14	4	3.52
Cleveland	75	79	.487	26	677	668	249	84	103	.256	.393	63	142	158	.976	68	660	617	10	19	3.90
Detroit	75	79	.487	26	686	743	247	55	81	.263	.375	43	186	129	.969	52	645	697	8	16	4.18
St. Louis	70	84	.455	31	765	823	281	58	91	.266	.390	50	151	156	.975	65	549	454	7	10	4.72
Washington	70	84	.455	31	728	798	257	80	52	.272	.376	79	187	169	.969	69	603	544	8	7	4.35
Philadelphia	64	90	.416	37	713	840	240	69	85	.268	.387	27	200	150	.967	64	557	386	3	18	4.83
					5902	5902	2066	508	734	.266	.389	471	1383	1242	.972	569	4744	4425	71	111	4.15

NATIONAL LEAGUE 1942

	POS	Player	AB	BA	HR	RBI	PO	A	E	DP	TC/G	FA	Pitcher	G	IP	W	L	SV	ERA
St. Louis W-106 L-48 Billy Southworth	1B	J. Hopp	314	.258	3	37	746	44	14	68	9.1	.983	M. Cooper	37	279	22	7	0	1.78
	2B	C. Crespi	292	.243	0	35	219	190	14	42	5.1	.967	J. Beazley	43	215	21	6	3	2.13
	SS	M. Marion	485	.276	0	54	296	448	31	87	5.3	.960	H. Gumbert	38	163	9	5	5	3.26
	3B	W. Kurowski	366	.254	9	42	124	194	19	19	3.2	.944	M. Lanier	34	160	13	8	2	2.98
	RF	E. Slaughter	591	.318	13	98	287	15	4	2	2.0	.987	E. White	26	128	7	5	2	2.52
	CF	T. Moore	489	.288	6	49	271	9	4	0	2.3	.986	M. Dickson	36	121	6	3	2	2.91
	LF	S. Musial	467	.315	10	72	296	6	5	0	2.3	.984	H. Krist	34	118	13	3	1	2.51
	C	W. Cooper	438	.281	7	65	519	62	17	5	5.2	.972	H. Pollet	27	109	7	5	0	2.88
	23	J. Brown	606	.256	1	71	296	326	24	65		.963	L. Warneke	12	82	6	4	0	3.29
	1B	R. Sanders	282	.252	5	39	626	35	6	54	8.7	.991							
	C	K. O'Dea	192	.234	2	32	247	37	6	6	5.9	.979							
	OF	H. Walker	191	.314	0	16	115	6	4	0	2.2	.968							
	OF	C. Triplett	154	.273	1	23	82	2	3	0	1.9	.966							
Brooklyn W-104 L-50 Leo Durocher	1B	D. Camilli	524	.252	26	109	1334	85	12	123	9.5	.992	K. Higbe	38	222	16	11	0	3.25
	2B	B. Herman	571	.256	2	65	383	402	22	97	5.3	.973	W. Wyatt	31	217	19	7	0	2.73
	SS	P. Reese	564	.255	3	53	337	482	35	99	5.7	.959	C. Davis	32	206	15	6	2	2.36
	3B	A. Vaughan	495	.277	2	49	118	208	14	18	2.9	.959	L. French	38	148	15	4	0	1.83
	RF	D. Walker	393	.290	6	54	207	8	3	2	2.0	.986	E. Head	36	137	10	6	4	3.56
	CF	P. Reiser	480	.310	10	64	277	9	9	2	2.4	.969	J. Allen	27	118	10	6	3	3.20
	LF	J. Medwick	553	.300	4	96	287	5	3	1	2.1	.990	H. Casey	50	112	6	3	13	2.25
	C	M. Owen	421	.259	0	44	595	66	9	12	5.0	.987							
	OF	J. Rizzo	217	.230	4	27	124	6	3	1	1.9	.977							
	OF	A. Galan	209	.263	0	22	101	2	1	0	1.9	.990							
	3B	L. Riggs	180	.278	3	22	36	65	6	7	2.3	.944							
New York W-85 L-67 Mel Ott	1B	J. Mize	541	.305	26	110	1393	74	8	98	10.7	.995	Schumacher	29	216	12	13	0	3.04
	2B	M. Witek	553	.260	5	48	371	441	18	72	5.6	.978	B. Carpenter	28	186	11	10	0	3.15
	SS	B. Jurges	464	.256	2	30	251	401	15	67	5.4	.978	B. Lohrman	26	158	13	4	0	2.56
	3B	B. Werber	370	.205	1	13	79	227	24	14	3.5	.927	C. Hubbell	24	157	11	8	0	3.95
	RF	M. Ott	549	.295	30	93	269	15	3	3	1.9	.990	C. Melton	23	144	9	5	1	2.63
	CF	W. Marshall	401	.257	11	59	222	13	6	4	2.3	.975	H. Feldman	31	114	7	1	0	3.16
	LF	B. Barna	331	.257	6	58	169	4	3	0	2.0	.983	B. McGee	31	104	6	3	1	2.93
	C	H. Danning	408	.279	1	34	459	55	11	7	4.5	.979	A. Adams	61	88	7	4	11	1.84
	3S	D. Bartell	316	.244	5	24	135	191	14	27	.	.959							
	OF	B. Young	287	.279	11	59	101	4	3	2	2.0	.972							
	OF	B. Maynard	190	.247	4	32	103	6	2	2	1.9	.982							
	OF	H. Leiber	147	.218	4	23	93	2	1	1	2.3	.990							

NATIONAL LEAGUE 1942, *cont.*

	POS	Player	AB	BA	HR	RBI	PO	A	E	DP	TC/G	FA	Pitcher	G	IP	W	L	SV	ERA
Cincinnati	1B	McCormick	564	.277	13	89	**1403**	101	10	**132**	10.5	.993	R. Starr	37	277	15	13	0	2.67
	2B	L. Frey	523	.266	2	39	340	424	18	95	5.6	.977	B. Walters	34	254	15	14	0	2.66
W-76 L-76	SS	E. Joost	562	.224	6	41	248	380	45	79	5.2	.933	Vander Meer	33	244	18	12	0	2.43
	3B	B. Haas	585	.239	6	54	160	273	35	**33**	3.2	.925	P. Derringer	29	209	10	11	0	3.06
Bill McKechnie	RF	M. Marshall	530	.255	7	43	245	3	6	2	2.0	.976	E. Riddle	29	158	7	11	0	3.69
	CF	G. Walker	422	.230	5	50	277	7	8	2	2.7	.973	J. Thompson	29	102	4	7	0	3.36
	LF	E. Tipton	207	.222	4	18	126	3	3	0	2.3	.977	J. Beggs	38	89	6	5	8	2.13
	C	R. Lamanno	371	.264	12	43	421	59	11	7	4.7	.978							
	OF	I. Goodman	226	.243	0	15	101	7	1	2	1.9	.991							
Pittsburgh	1B	E. Fletcher	506	.289	7	57	1379	**118**	12	104	10.5	.992	R. Sewell	40	248	17	15	2	3.41
	2B	F. Gustine	388	.229	2	35	227	312	26	53	5.2	.954	B. Klinger	37	153	8	11	1	3.24
W-66 L-81	SS	P. Coscarart	487	.228	3	29	203	315	26	50	5.0	.952	M. Butcher	24	151	5	8	1	2.93
	3B	B. Elliott	560	.296	9	89	**173**	**285**	**36**	22	3.5	.927	D. Dietz	40	134	6	9	3	3.95
Frankie Frisch	RF	J. Barrett	332	.247	0	26	202	11	6	4	2.3	.973	Heintzelman	27	130	8	11	0	4.57
	CF	V. DiMaggio	496	.238	15	75	**383**	**20**	9	**5**	**3.0**	.978	J. Lanning	34	119	6	8	1	3.32
	LF	J. Wasdell	409	.259	3	38	191	8	9	1	2.1	.957	L. Hamlin	23	112	4	4	0	3.94
	C	A. Lopez	289	.256	1	26	327	53	2	14	3.9	**.995**	H. Gornicki	25	112	5	6	2	2.57
	OF	Van Robays	328	.232	1	46	199	6	3	3	2.5	.986	L. Wilkie	35	107	6	7	1	4.19
	C	B. Phelps	257	.284	9	41	244	40	12	5	4.1	.959							
	UT	B. Stewart	183	.219	0	20	87	23	3	0		.973							
	SS	A. Anderson	166	.271	0	7	77	103	11	17	4.0	.942							
Chicago	1B	Cavarretta	482	.270	3	54	567	44	5	48	10.1	.992	C. Passeau	35	278	19	14	0	2.68
	2B	L. Stringer	406	.236	9	41	268	343	29	59	5.7	.955	B. Lee	32	220	13	13	0	3.85
W-68 L-86	SS	L. Merullo	515	.256	2	37	299	438	42	80	5.4	.946	H. Bithorn	38	171	9	14	5	3.68
	3B	S. Hack	553	.300	6	39	154	261	15	21	3.1	**.965**	V. Olsen	32	140	6	9	1	4.49
Jimmie Wilson	RF	B. Nicholson	588	.294	21	78	327	18	5	2	2.3	.986	B. Fleming	33	134	5	6	2	3.01
	CF	Dallessandro	264	.261	4	43	134	6	2	1	2.2	.986	L. Warneke	15	99	5	7	2	2.27
	LF	L. Novikoff	483	.300	7	64	232	11	9	2	2.1	.964	J. Schmitz	23	87	3	7	2	3.43
	C	McCullough	337	.282	5	31	386	61	9	10	4.7	.980							
	UT	R. Russell	302	.242	8	41	392	90	14	40		.972							
	1B	J. Foxx	205	.205	3	19	489	24	9	32	10.0	.983							
	OF	C. Gilbert	179	.184	0	7	99	6	2	2	2.3	.981							
	2S	B. Sturgeon	162	.247	0	7	112	163	4	33		.986							
Boston	1B	M. West	452	.254	16	56	807	47	8	66	10.1	.991	J. Tobin	37	**288**	12	**21**	0	3.97
	2B	S. Sisti	407	.211	4	35	304	351	20	66	5.4	.970	A. Javery	42	261	12	16	0	3.03
W-59 L-89	SS	E. Miller	534	.243	6	47	285	450	13	78	5.2	**.983**	L. Tost	35	148	10	10	0	3.53
	3B	N. Fernandez	577	.255	6	55	123	206	31	16	3.7	.914	M. Salvo	25	131	7	8	0	3.03
Casey Stengel	RF	P. Waner	333	.258	1	39	150	6	5	3	1.7	.969	T. Earley	27	113	6	11	1	4.71
	CF	T. Holmes	558	.278	4	41	373	16	4	4	2.8	.990	J. Sain	40	97	4	7	6	3.90
	LF	C. Ross	220	.195	5	19	123	2	1	0	2.2	.992							
	C	E. Lombardi	309	**.330**	11	46	251	41	6	3	3.5	.980							
	C	C. Kluttz	210	.267	1	31	200	29	5	5	4.1	.979							
	1B	B. Gremp	207	.217	3	19	504	33	5	45	8.7	.991							
	OF	J. Cooney	198	.207	0	7	59	2	1	0	1.1	.984							
	OF	F. Demaree	187	.225	3	24	114	4	0	1	2.4	1.000							
	23	S. Roberge	172	.215	1	12	87	127	6	19		.973							
Philadelphia	1B	N. Etten	459	.264	8	41	1152	83	**19**	99	9.3	.985	T. Hughes	40	253	12	18	1	3.06
	2B	A. Glossop	454	.225	4	40	322	351	27	79	**5.9**	.961	R. Melton	42	209	9	20	4	3.70
W-42 L-109	SS	B. Bragan	335	.218	2	15	161	238	26	49	5.4	.939	S. Johnson	39	195	8	19	0	3.69
	3B	P. May	345	.238	0	18	109	227	13	23	3.3	.963	J. Podgajny	43	187	6	14	0	3.91
Hans Lobert	RF	R. Northey	402	.251	5	31	206	12	**11**	2	2.1	.952	F. Hoerst	33	151	4	16	1	5.20
	CF	L. Waner	287	.261	0	10	170	6	6	0	2.4	.967							
	LF	D. Litwhiler	591	.271	9	56	308	9	0	0	2.1	**1.000**							
	C	B. Warren	225	.209	7	20	264	50	9	4	4.1	.972							
	UT	D. Murtaugh	506	.241	0	27	302	377	43	61		.940							
	OF	E. Koy	258	.244	4	26	149	4	3	1	2.0	.981							
	C	Livingston	239	.205	2	22	275	36	4	8	4.0	.987							
	OF	S. Benjamin	210	.224	2	8	75	7	2	1	1.9	.976							
	OP	E. Naylor	168	.196	0	14	66	11	1	0		.987							

BATTING AND BASE RUNNING LEADERS

Batting Average		Slugging Average		Home Runs		Winning Percentage	
E. Lombardi, BOS	.330	J. Mize, NY	.521	M. Ott, NY	30	L. French, BKN	.789
E. Slaughter, STL	.318	M. Ott, NY	.497	D. Camilli, BKN	26	J. Beazley, STL	.778
S. Musial, STL	.315	E. Slaughter, STL	.494	J. Mize, NY	26	M. Cooper, STL	.759
P. Reiser, BKN	.310	S. Musial, STL	.490	B. Nicholson, CHI	21	W. Wyatt, BKN	.731
J. Mize, NY	.305	E. Lombardi, BOS	.482	M. West, BOS	16	C. Davis, BKN	.714

PITCHING LEADERS

Earned Run Average		Wins	
M. Cooper, STL	1.78	M. Cooper, STL	22
J. Beazley, STL	2.13	J. Beazley, STL	21
C. Davis, BKN	2.36	W. Wyatt, BKN	19
Vander Meer, CIN	2.43	C. Passeau, CHI	19
B. Lohrman, NY, STL	2.48	Vander Meer, CIN	18

NATIONAL LEAGUE 1942, *cont.*

BATTING AND BASE RUNNING LEADERS

Total Bases			Runs Batted In			Stolen Bases		
E. Slaughter, STL	292		J. Mize, NY	110		P. Reiser, BKN	20	
J. Mize, NY	282		D. Camilli, BKN	109		P. Reese, BKN	15	
B. Nicholson, CHI	280		E. Slaughter, STL	98		N. Fernandez, BOS	15	
M. Ott, NY	273		J. Medwick, BKN	96		J. Hopp, STL	14	
D. Camilli, BKN	247		M. Ott, NY	93		L. Merullo, CHI	14	

Hits			Base on Balls			Home Run Percentage		
E. Slaughter, STL	188		M. Ott, NY	109		M. Ott, NY	5.5	
B. Nicholson, CHI	173		E. Fletcher, PIT	105		D. Camilli, BKN	5.0	
S. Hack, CHI	166		D. Camilli, BKN	97		J. Mize, NY	4.8	
J. Medwick, BKN	166		S. Hack, CHI	94		B. Young, NY	3.8	

Runs Scored			Doubles			Triples		
M. Ott, NY	118		M. Marion, STL	38		E. Slaughter, STL	17	
E. Slaughter, STL	100		J. Medwick, BKN	37		B. Nicholson, CHI	11	
J. Mize, NY	97		S. Hack, CHI	36		S. Musial, STL	10	
S. Hack, CHI	91		B. Herman, BKN	34		D. Litwhiler, PHI	9	

PITCHING LEADERS

Saves			Strikeouts			Complete Games		
H. Casey, BKN	13		Vander Meer, CIN	186		J. Tobin, BOS	28	
A. Adams, NY	11		M. Cooper, STL	152		C. Passeau, CHI	24	
J. Beggs, CIN	8		K. Higbe, BKN	115		M. Cooper, STL	22	
J. Sain, BOS	6		B. Walters, CIN	109		B. Walters, CIN	21	
H. Gumbert, STL	5		R. Melton, PHI	107		Vander Meer, CIN	21	

Fewest Hits/9 Innings			Shutouts			Fewest Walks/9 Innings		
M. Cooper, STL	6.69		M. Cooper, STL	10		L. Warneke, CHI, STL	1.79	
Vander Meer, CIN	6.93		C. Davis, BKN	5		B. Lohrman, NY, STL	1.85	
K. Higbe, BKN	7.31		R. Sewell, PIT	5		C. Hubbell, NY	1.94	
R. Starr, CIN	7.42		A. Javery, BOS	5		C. Melton, NY	2.07	

Most Strikeouts/9 Inn.			Innings			Games Pitched		
Vander Meer, CIN	6.86		J. Tobin, BOS	288		A. Adams, NY	61	
M. Cooper, STL	4.91		M. Cooper, STL	279		H. Casey, BKN	50	
K. Higbe, BKN	4.67		C. Passeau, CHI	278		J. Beazley, STL	43	
R. Melton, PHI	4.60		R. Starr, CIN	277		J. Podgajny, PHI	43	

	W	L	PCT	GB	R	OR	2B	3B	HR	BA	SA	SB	E	DP	FA	CG	BB	SO	ShO	SV	ERA
St. Louis	106	48	.688		755	482	282	69	60	.268	.379	71	169	137	.972	70	473	651	18	15	2.55
Brooklyn	104	50	.675	2	742	510	263	34	62	.265	.362	79	138	150	.977	67	493	612	16	24	2.84
New York	85	67	.559	20	675	600	162	35	109	.254	.361	39	138	128	.977	70	493	497	12	13	3.31
Cincinnati	76	76	.500	29	527	545	198	39	66	.231	.321	42	177	158	.971	80	526	616	12	8	2.82
Pittsburgh	66	81	.449	36.5	585	631	173	49	54	.245	.330	41	184	129	.969	64	435	426	13	11	3.58
Chicago	68	86	.442	38	591	665	224	41	75	.254	.353	61	170	169	.973	71	525	507	10	14	3.60
Boston	59	89	.399	44	515	645	210	19	68	.240	.329	49	142	138	.976	68	518	414	9	8	3.76
Philadelphia	42	109	.278	62.5	394	706	168	37	44	.232	.306	37	194	147	.968	51	605	472	2	6	4.12
					4784	4784	1680	323	538	.249	.343	419	1312	1156	.973	541	4068	4195	92	99	3.31

AMERICAN LEAGUE 1942

	POS	Player	AB	BA	HR	RBI	PO	A	E	DP	TC/G	FA	Pitcher	G	IP	W	L	SV	ERA
New York	1B	B. Hassett	538	.284	5	48	1128	118	11	130	9.5	.991	E. Bonham	28	226	21	5	0	2.27
	2B	J. Gordon	538	.322	18	103	354	442	28	121	5.6	.966	S. Chandler	24	201	16	5	0	2.38
W-103 L-51	SS	P. Rizzuto	553	.284	4	68	324	445	30	114	5.5	.962	R. Ruffing	24	194	14	7	0	3.21
	3B	F. Crosetti	285	.242	4	23	70	105	9	14	3.0	.951	H. Borowy	25	178	15	4	1	2.52
Joe McCarthy	RF	T. Henrich	483	.267	13	67	219	10	3	5	1.9	.987	M. Breuer	27	164	8	9	1	3.07
	CF	J. DiMaggio	610	.305	21	114	409	10	8	3	2.8	.981	A. Donald	20	148	11	3	0	3.11
	LF	C. Keller	544	.292	26	108	321	10	5	1	2.2	.985	L. Gomez	13	80	6	4	0	4.28
	C	B. Dickey	268	.295	2	37	322	44	9	7	4.7	.976	J. Murphy	31	58	4	10	11	3.41
	3B	R. Rolfe	265	.219	8	25	57	132	8	16	3.3	.959							
	C	B. Rosar	209	.230	2	34	249	26	1	7	4.8	.996							
	UT	G. Priddy	189	.280	2	28	146	114	9	26		.967							
Boston	1B	T. Lupien	463	.281	3	70	1091	68	9	99	9.7	.992	T. Hughson	38	281	22	6	4	2.59
	2B	B. Doerr	545	.290	15	102	376	453	21	105	6.0	.975	C. Wagner	29	205	14	11	0	3.29
W-93 L-59	SS	J. Pesky	620	.331	2	51	320	465	37	94	5.6	.955	J. Dobson	30	183	11	9	0	3.30
	3B	J. Tabor	508	.252	12	75	168	236	33	24	3.2	.924	D. Newsome	24	158	8	10	0	5.01
Joe Cronin	RF	L. Finney	397	.285	3	61	199	8	5	2	2.2	.976	O. Judd	31	150	8	10	2	3.89
	CF	D. DiMaggio	622	.286	14	48	439	19	6	7	3.1	.987	B. Butland	23	111	7	1	1	2.51
	LF	T. Williams	522	.356	36	137	313	15	4	4	2.2	.988	Y. Terry	20	85	6	5	1	3.92
	C	B. Conroy	250	.200	4	20	324	40	11	6	4.5	.971	M. Brown	34	60	9	3	6	3.43
	C	J. Peacock	286	.266	0	25	280	44	4	8	4.0	.988							
	OF	P. Fox	256	.262	3	42	111	2	4	0	1.6	.966							
	31	J. Cronin	79	.304	4	24	46	26	6	7		.923							
St. Louis	1B	G. McQuinn	554	.262	12	78	1384	105	13	116	10.4	.991	E. Auker	35	249	14	13	0	4.08
	2B	Gutteridge	616	.255	1	50	377	454	23	94	5.9	.973	J. Niggeling	28	206	15	11	0	2.66
W-82 L-69	SS	V. Stephens	575	.294	14	92	290	415	42	82	5.2	.944	D. Galehouse	32	191	12	12	1	3.62
	3B	H. Clift	541	.274	7	55	160	287	28	28	3.4	.941	Hollingsworth	33	161	10	6	4	2.96
Luke Sewell	RF	C. Laabs	520	.275	27	99	276	13	9	3	2.1	.970	B. Muncrief	24	134	6	8	0	3.89
	CF	W. Judnich	457	.313	17	82	330	4	3	0	2.8	.991	S. Sundra	20	111	8	3	0	3.82
	LF	McQuillen	339	.283	3	47	156	2	5	0	2.1	.969	G. Caster	39	80	8	2	5	2.81
	C	R. Ferrell	273	.223	0	26	356	57	6	7	4.4	.986							
	OF	M. Chartak	237	.249	9	43	142	10	4	3	2.4	.974							
	C	F. Hayes	159	.252	2	17	175	25	6	2	4.0	.971							
	OF	T. Criscola	158	.297	1	13													

AMERICAN LEAGUE 1942, cont.

	POS	Player	AB	BA	HR	RBI	PO	A	E	DP	TC/G	FA	Pitcher	G	IP	W	L	SV	ERA
Cleveland	1B	L. Fleming	548	.292	14	82	**1503**	90	12	152	10.3	**.993**	J. Bagby	38	271	17	9	1	2.96
	2B	R. Mack	481	.225	2	45	340	434	25	105	5.6	.969	M. Harder	29	199	13	14	0	3.44
W-75 L-79	SS	L. Boudreau	506	.283	2	58	281	426	26	107	5.0	.965	C. Dean	27	173	8	11	1	3.81
	3B	K. Keltner	624	.287	6	78	166	**353**	30	**38**	**3.6**	**.945**	A. Smith	30	168	10	15	0	3.96
Lou Boudreau	RF	O. Hockett	601	.250	7	48	284	12	6	3	2.1	.980	A. Milnar	28	157	6	8	0	4.13
	CF	R. Weatherly	473	.258	5	39	324	7	3	4	2.9	.991	V. Kennedy	28	108	4	8	1	4.08
	LF	J. Heath	568	.278	10	76	326	12	7	3	2.4	.980	J. Heving	27	46	5	3	3	4.86
	C	O. Denning	214	.210	1	19	213	36	2	6	3.2	.992							
	OF	B. Mills	195	.277	1	26	142	4	4	2	2.8	.973							
	C	J. Hegan	170	.194	0	11	227	32	6	7	4.0	.977							
	C	G. Desautels	162	.247	0	9	180	16	5	3	3.3	.975							
Detroit	1B	R. York	577	.260	21	90	1413	**146**	19	117	10.4	.988	A. Benton	35	227	7	13	2	2.90
	2B	Bloodworth	533	.242	13	57	334	431	22	66	5.9	.972	D. Trout	35	223	12	18	0	3.43
W-73 L-81	SS	B. Hitchcock	280	.211	0	29	157	199	21	39	4.7	.944	H. White	34	217	12	12	1	2.91
	3B	P. Higgins	499	.267	11	79	134	243	30	24	3.0	.926	H. Newhouser	38	184	8	14	5	2.45
Del Baker	RF	B. Harris	398	.271	9	45	164	5	10	2	1.7	.944	T. Bridges	23	174	9	7	1	2.74
	CF	D. Cramer	630	.263	0	43	352	15	7	6	2.5	.981	V. Trucks	28	168	14	8	0	2.74
	LF	B. McCosky	600	.293	7	50	351	7	7	2	2.4	.981							
	C	B. Tebbetts	308	.247	1	27	**446**	69	**12**	10	**5.4**	.977							
	O3	D. Ross	226	.274	3	30	94	30	7	4		.947							
	C	D. Parsons	188	.197	2	11	274	44	6	6	5.2	.981							
	SS	M. Franklin	154	.260	2	16	67	79	5	14	4.7	.967							
	OF	R. Radcliff	144	.250	1	20	43	1	1	1	1.9	.978							
Chicago	1B	J. Kuhel	413	.249	4	52	1085	70	11	94	10.4	.991	J. Humphries	28	228	12	12	0	2.68
	2B	D. Kolloway	601	.273	3	60	308	345	23	80	5.8	.966	E. Smith	29	215	7	**20**	1	3.98
W-66 L-82	SS	L. Appling	543	.262	3	53	269	418	38	77	5.1	.948	T. Lyons	20	180	14	6	0	**2.10**
	3B	B. Kennedy	412	.231	0	48	99	207	14	17	3.3	.956	B. Dietrich	26	160	6	11	0	4.89
Jimmy Dykes	RF	W. Moses	577	.270	7	49	323	14	7	3	2.4	.980	B. Ross	22	113	5	7	1	5.00
	CF	M. Hoag	412	.240	2	37	266	12	8	4	2.6	.972	J. Haynes	**40**	103	8	5	6	2.62
	LF	T. Wright	300	.333	0	47	176	6	6	1	2.3	.968	J. Wade	15	51	5	5	0	4.10
	C	M. Tresh	233	.232	0	15	258	37	7	2	4.2	.977	O. Grove	12	66	4	6	0	5.16
	C	T. Turner	182	.242	3	21	199	35	7	4	4.5	.971							
	3B	D. Lodigiani	168	.280	0	15	40	96	8	4	3.3	.944							
	OF	S. West	151	.232	0	25	112	1	2	1	2.6	.983							
Washington	1B	M. Vernon	621	.271	9	86	1360	95	**26**	109	9.8	.982	S. Hudson	35	239	10	17	2	4.36
	2B	E. Clary	240	.275	0	16	162	181	11	37	5.1	.969	B. Newsom	30	214	11	17	0	4.93
W-62 L-89	SS	J. Sullivan	357	.235	0	42	217	235	31	51	5.3	.936	E. Wynn	30	190	10	16	0	5.12
	3B	B. Estalella	429	.277	8	65	89	134	14	4	3.0	.941	Carrasquel	35	152	7	7	4	3.43
Bucky Harris	RF	B. Campbell	378	.278	5	63	188	4	9	1	2.3	.955	W. Masterson	25	143	5	9	2	3.34
	CF	S. Spence	629	.323	4	79	395	7	11	0	2.8	.973	B. Zuber	37	127	9	9	1	3.84
	LF	G. Case	513	.320	5	43	270	4	**14**	1	2.4	.951							
	C	J. Early	353	.204	3	46	392	**71**	9	**11**	4.8	.981							
	UT	J. Pofahl	283	.208	0	28	166	204	18	45		.954							
	UT	B. Repass	259	.239	2	23	142	178	12	21		.964							
	O3	Cullenbine	241	.286	2	35	125	69	11	5		.946							
	C	A. Evans	223	.229	0	10	254	42	**12**	5	4.6	.961							
Philadelphia	1B	D. Siebert	612	.260	2	74	1345	104	16	109	9.6	.989	Marchildon	38	244	17	14	1	4.20
	2B	Knickerbocker	289	.253	1	19	178	220	15	45	5.1	.964	R. Wolff	32	214	12	15	3	3.32
W-55 L-99	SS	P. Suder	476	.256	4	54	141	193	16	31	5.1	.954	L. Harris	26	166	11	15	0	3.74
	3B	B. Blair	484	.279	5	66	143	234	28	21	3.2	.931	Christopher	30	165	4	13	1	3.82
Connie Mack	RF	E. Valo	459	.251	2	40	264	5	10	0	2.3	.964	D. Fowler	31	140	6	11	1	4.95
	CF	M. Kreevich	444	.255	1	30	314	4	6	0	3.0	.981	H. Besse	30	133	2	9	1	6.50
	LF	B. Johnson	550	.291	13	80	318	18	13	1	2.3	.963	J. Knott	20	95	2	10	0	5.57
	C	H. Wagner	288	.236	1	30	371	47	6	7	4.5	**.986**							
	OF	D. Miles	346	.272	0	22	177	6	3	0	2.3	.984							
	2S	C. Davis	272	.224	2	26	175	210	19	30		.953							
	C	B. Swift	192	.229	0	15	253	39	9	5	5.0	.970							

BATTING AND BASE RUNNING LEADERS

Batting Average		Slugging Average		Home Runs	
T. Williams, BOS	.356	T. Williams, BOS	.648	T. Williams, BOS	36
J. Pesky, BOS	.331	C. Keller, NY	.513	C. Laabs, STL	27
S. Spence, WAS	.323	W. Judnich, STL	.499	C. Keller, NY	26
J. Gordon, NY	.322	J. DiMaggio, NY	.498	R. York, DET	21
G. Case, WAS	.320	C. Laabs, STL	.498	J. DiMaggio, NY	21

Total Bases		Runs Batted In		Stolen Bases	
T. Williams, BOS	338	T. Williams, BOS	137	G. Case, WAS	44
J. DiMaggio, NY	304	J. DiMaggio, NY	114	M. Vernon, WAS	25
C. Keller, NY	279	C. Keller, NY	108	J. Kuhel, CHI	22
D. DiMaggio, BOS	272	J. Gordon, NY	103	P. Rizzuto, NY	22
S. Spence, WAS	272	B. Doerr, BOS	102	M. Hoag, CHI	17
				L. Appling, CHI	17

PITCHING LEADERS

Winning Percentage		Earned Run Average		Wins	
E. Bonham, NY	.808	T. Lyons, CHI	2.10	T. Hughson, BOS	22
H. Borowy, NY	.789	E. Bonham, NY	2.27	E. Bonham, NY	21
T. Hughson, BOS	.786	S. Chandler, NY	2.38	J. Bagby, CLE	17
S. Chandler, NY	.762	H. Newhouser, DET	2.45	Marchildon, PHI	17
J. Bagby, CLE	.654	H. Borowy, NY	2.52	S. Chandler, NY	16

Saves		Strikeouts		Complete Games	
J. Murphy, NY	11	B. Newsom, WAS	113	E. Bonham, NY	22
M. Brown, BOS	6	T. Hughson, BOS	113	T. Hughson, BOS	22
J. Haynes, CHI	6	A. Benton, DET	110	T. Lyons, CHI	20
G. Caster, STL	5	Marchildon, PHI	110	S. Hudson, WAS	19
H. Newhouser, DET	5	J. Niggeling, STL	107	E. Smith, CHI	18
				Marchildon, PHI	18

AMERICAN LEAGUE 1942, *cont.*

BATTING AND BASE RUNNING LEADERS

Hits			Base on Balls			Home Run Percentage			Fewest Hits/9 Innings	
J. Pesky, BOS	205		T. Williams, BOS	145		T. Williams, BOS	6.9		H. Newhouser, DET	6.71
S. Spence, WAS	203		C. Keller, NY	114		C. Laabs, STL	5.2		J. Niggeling, STL	7.55
T. Williams, BOS	186		H. Clift, STL	106		C. Keller, NY	4.8		J. Dobson, BOS	7.64
J. DiMaggio, NY	186		L. Fleming, CLE	106		W. Judnich, STL	3.7		S. Chandler, NY	7.89

Runs Scored			Doubles			Triples			Most Strikeouts/9 Inn.	
T. Williams, BOS	141		D. Kolloway, CHI	40		S. Spence, WAS	15		H. Newhouser, DET	5.05
J. DiMaggio, NY	123		H. Clift, STL	39		J. Heath, CLE	13		T. Bridges, DET	5.02
D. DiMaggio, BOS	110		J. Heath, CLE	37		J. DiMaggio, NY	13		B. Newsom, WAS	4.76
H. Clift, STL	108		D. DiMaggio, BOS	36		McQuillen, STL	12		J. Niggeling, STL	4.67

PITCHING LEADERS

Shutouts		Fewest Walks/9 Innings	
E. Bonham, NY	6	E. Bonham, NY	0.96
		T. Lyons, CHI	1.30
		R. Ruffing, NY	1.91
		J. Bagby, CLE	2.13

Innings		Games Pitched	
T. Hughson, BOS	281	J. Haynes, CHI	40
J. Bagby, CLE	271	G. Caster, STL	39
E. Auker, STL	249	T. Hughson, BOS	38
Marchildon, PHI	244	J. Bagby, CLE	38

	W	L	PCT	GB	R	OR	2B	3B	HR	BA	SA	SB	E	DP	FA	CG	BB	SO	ShO	SV	ERA
New York	103	51	.669		**801**	507	223	57	**108**	.269	.394	69	142	190	.976	88	431	558	18	17	**2.91**
Boston	93	59	.612	9	761	594	**244**	55	103	**.276**	**.403**	68	157	156	.974	84	553	500	11	17	3.44
St. Louis	82	69	.543	19.5	730	637	239	**62**	98	.259	.385	37	167	143	.972	68	505	488	12	13	3.59
Cleveland	75	79	.487	28	590	659	223	58	50	.253	.345	46	163	175	.974	61	560	448	12	11	3.59
Detroit	73	81	.474	30	589	587	217	37	76	.246	.344	39	194	142	.969	65	598	**671**	12	14	3.13
Chicago	66	82	.446	34	538	609	214	36	25	.246	.318	**114**	173	144	.970	86	473	432	8	8	3.58
Washington	62	89	.411	39.5	653	817	224	49	40	.245	.341	98	222	133	.962	68	558	496	12	11	4.58
Philadelphia	55	99	.357	48	549	801	213	46	33	.249	.325	44	188	124	.969	67	639	546	5	9	4.48
					5211	5211	1797	400	533	.257	.357	538	1406	1207	.971	587	4317	4139	90	100	3.66

NATIONAL LEAGUE 1943

	POS	Player	AB	BA	HR	RBI	PO	A	E	DP	TC/G	FA	Pitcher	G	IP	W	L	SV	ERA
St. Louis W-105 L-49 Billy Southworth	1B	R. Sanders	478	.280	11	73	1302	71	7	**142**	9.8	.995	M. Cooper	37	274	**21**	8	3	2.30
	2B	L. Klein	627	.287	7	62	301	356	18	99	5.4	.973	M. Lanier	32	213	15	7	3	1.90
	SS	M. Marion	418	.280	1	52	232	424	20	93	5.3	.970	H. Krist	34	164	11	5	3	2.90
	3B	W. Kurowski	522	.287	13	70	166	255	21	29	3.2	.952	H. Brecheen	29	135	9	6	4	2.26
	RF	S. Musial	617	**.357**	13	81	376	15	7	4	2.6	.982	H. Gumbert	21	133	10	5	0	2.84
	CF	H. Walker	564	.294	2	53	321	14	12	4	2.4	.965	H. Pollet	16	118	8	4	0	**1.75**
	LF	D. Litwhiler	258	.279	7	31	139	7	0	1	2.1	**1.000***	M. Dickson	31	116	8	2	0	3.58
	C	W. Cooper	449	.318	9	81	504	49	14	5	5.1	.975	G. Munger	32	93	9	5	2	3.95
	O3	D. Garms	249	.257	0	22	111	25	9	5		.938	A. Brazle	13	88	8	2	0	1.53
	O1	J. Hopp	241	.224	2	25	286	17	12	23		.962	E. White	14	79	5	5	0	3.78
	C	K. O'Dea	203	.281	3	25	237	32	3	6	4.9	.989							
Cincinnati W-87 L-67 Bill McKechnie	1B	McCormick	472	.303	8	59	1156	85	6	116	10.4	.995	Vander Meer	36	289	15	16	0	2.87
	2B	L. Frey	586	.263	2	43	399	461	13	**112**	6.1	**.985**	E. Riddle	36	260	**21**	11	3	2.63
	SS	E. Miller	576	.224	2	71	335	543	19	**123**	5.8	.979	B. Walters	34	246	15	15	0	3.54
	3B	S. Mesner	504	.272	0	52	132	274	24	29	3.3	.944	R. Starr	36	217	11	10	1	3.64
	RF	M. Marshall	508	.236	4	39	240	12	5	4	2.0	.981	C. Shoun	45	147	14	5	7	3.06
	CF	G. Walker	429	.245	3	54	231	8	5	3	2.3	.980	J. Beggs	39	115	7	6	6	2.34
	LF	E. Tipton	493	.288	9	49	298	8	5	2	2.2	.984							
	C	R. Mueller	427	.260	8	52	**579**	100	8	**17**	4.9	.988							
	UT	B. Haas	332	.262	4	44	432	97	9	52		.983							
	OF	E. Crabtree	254	.276	2	26	135	4	9	2	2.3	.939							
Brooklyn W-81 L-72 Leo Durocher	1B	D. Camilli	353	.246	6	43	853	60	7	78	9.7	.992	K. Higbe	35	185	13	10	0	3.70
	2B	B. Herman	585	.330	2	100	291	322	18	69	5.4	.971	W. Wyatt	26	181	14	5	0	2.49
	SS	A. Vaughan	610	.305	5	66	175	291	17	55	4.9	.965	E. Head	47	170	9	10	6	3.66
	3B	Bordagaray	268	.302	0	19	28	26	7	0	2.4	.885	C. Davis	31	164	10	13	3	3.78
	RF	D. Walker	540	.302	5	71	262	20	9	2	2.1	.969	B. Newsom	22	125	9	4	1	3.02
	CF	A. Galan	495	.287	9	67	347	12	7	1	3.0	.981	R. Melton	30	119	5	8	0	3.92
	LF	L. Olmo	238	.303	4	37	128	6	6	0	2.5	.957	L. Webber	54	116	2	2	10	3.81
	C	M. Owen	365	.260	0	54	414	47	6	11	4.7	.987	M. Macon	25	77	7	5	0	5.96
	OF	P. Waner	225	.311	1	26	116	4	5	1	2.2	.960							
	C	B. Bragan	220	.264	2	24	253	34	8	6	5.2	.973							
	UT	A. Glossop	217	.171	3	21	102	161	24	24		.916							
	1B	H. Schultz	182	.269	1	34	386	33	6	27	9.4	.986							
	OF	J. Medwick	173	.272	0	25	65	2	2	0	1.6	.971							
Pittsburgh W-80 L-74 Frankie Frisch	1B	E. Fletcher	544	.283	9	70	**1541**	108	6	141	10.7	**.996**	R. Sewell	35	265	**21**	9	3	2.54
	2B	P. Coscarart	491	.242	0	48	186	263	18	54	5.5	.961	B. Klinger	33	195	11	8	0	2.72
	SS	F. Gustine	414	.290	0	43	135	230	24	41	5.7	.938	M. Butcher	33	194	10	8	1	2.60
	3B	B. Elliott	581	.315	7	101	149	**294**	24	34	3.1	.949	W. Hebert	34	184	10	11	0	2.98
	RF	J. Barrett	290	.231	1	32	165	6	2	0	1.7	.988	H. Gornicki	42	147	9	13	4	3.98
	CF	V. DiMaggio	580	.248	15	88	**457**	16	7	3	3.1	.985	X. Rescigno	37	133	6	9	2	3.05
	LF	J. Russell	533	.259	4	44	285	16	3	3	2.3	.990							
	C	A. Lopez	372	.263	1	39	378	66	4	9	3.9	**.991**							
	OF	Van Robays	236	.288	1	35	120	5	8	1	2.2	.940							
	OF	T. O'Brien	232	.310	2	26	76	4	3	0	1.7	.964							
	C	B. Baker	172	.273	1	26	157	29	4	3	3.4	.979							
	2B	A. Rubeling	168	.262	0	9	87	138	6	27	5.3	.974							
	SS	H. Geary	166	.151	1	13	92	127	10	25	5.0	.956							

NATIONAL LEAGUE 1943, *cont.*

	POS	Player	AB	BA	HR	RBI	PO	A	E	DP	TC/G	FA	Pitcher	G	IP	W	L	SV	ERA
Chicago	1B	Cavarretta	530	.291	8	73	1290	67	18	103	10.3	.987	C. Passeau	35	257	15	12	1	2.91
	2B	E. Stanky	510	.245	0	47	362	416	27	78	6.1	.966	H. Bithorn	39	250	18	12	2	2.60
W-74 L-79	SS	L. Merullo	453	.254	1	25	218	396	39	68	5.2	.940	P. Derringer	32	174	10	14	3	3.57
	3B	S. Hack	533	.289	3	35	149	264	17	11	3.2	.960	H. Wyse	38	156	9	7	2	2.94
Jimmie Wilson	RF	B. Nicholson	608	.309	**29**	**128**	340	16	8	2	2.4	.978	Hanyzewski	33	130	8	7	0	2.56
	CF	P. Lowrey	480	.292	1	63	315	13	6	4	3.0	.982	B. Lee	13	78	3	7	0	3.56
	LF	I. Goodman	225	.320	3	45	120	2	4	1	2.1	.968							
	C	McCullough	266	.237	2	23	271	25	7	2	3.7	.977							
	OF	L. Novikoff	233	.279	0	28	96	2	2	1	1.6	.980							
	OF	Dallessandro	176	.222	1	31	87	2	3	0	2.0	.967							
Boston	1B	J. McCarthy	313	.304	2	33	839	53	4	51	11.5	.996	A. Javery	41	**303**	17	16	0	3.21
	2B	C. Ryan	457	.212	1	24	224	306	21	41	5.5	.962	N. Andrews	36	284	14	**20**	0	2.57
W-68 L-85	SS	Wietelmann	534	.215	0	39	307	**581**	**40**	91	**6.1**	.957	R. Barrett	38	255	12	18	0	3.18
	3B	E. Joost	421	.185	2	20	104	171	16	15	4.3	.945	J. Tobin	33	250	14	14	0	2.66
Bob Coleman	RF	C. Workman	615	.249	10	67	310	**22**	4	7	2.3	.988	M. Salvo	20	93	5	6	0	3.28
W-21 L-25	CF	T. Holmes	**629**	.270	5	41	408	18	3	3	2.8	.993							
	LF	B. Nieman	335	.251	7	46	195	12	8	1	2.3	.963							
Casey Stengel	C	P. Masi	238	.273	2	28	192	40	2	1	3.2	.991							
W-47 L-60	OF	C. Ross	285	.218	7	32	165	8	4	1	2.3	.977							
	1B	K. Farrell	280	.268	0	21	740	50	3	61	11.5	.996							
	C	C. Kluttz	207	.246	0	20	176	43	6	5	4.1	.973							
Philadelphia	1B	J. Wasdell	522	.261	4	67	749	56	10	62	9.9	.988	Gerheauser	38	215	10	19	0	3.60
	2B	D. Murtaugh	451	.273	1	35	321	345	18	76	6.1	.974	S. Rowe	27	199	14	8	1	2.94
	SS	G. Stewart	336	.211	2	24	128	232	20	41	4.9	.947	T. Kraus	34	200	9	15	2	3.16
W-64 L-90	3B	P. May	415	.282	1	48	142	280	16	20	**3.3**	**.963**	D. Barrett	23	169	10	9	1	2.39
	RF	R. Northey	586	.278	16	68	292	19	7	6	2.2	.978	S. Johnson	21	113	8	3	2	3.27
Bucky Harris	CF	B. Adams	418	.256	4	38	298	6	5	8*	2.9	.984	C. Fuchs	17	78	2	7	1	4.29
W-38 L-52	LF	C. Triplett	360	.272	14	52	184	11	6	0	2.2	.970							
	C	Livingston	265	.249	3	28	268	49	4	5	3.8	.988*							
Freddie Fitzsimmons	UT	B. Dahlgren	508	.287	5	56	800	151	24	81		.975							
W-26 L-38	2B	R. Hamrick	160	.200	0	9	67	78	6	9	4.9	.960							
	SS	C. Brewster	159	.220	0	12	73	110	20	18	4.4	.901							
New York	1B	J. Orengo	266	.218	6	29	730	61	6	49	9.7	.992	C. Melton	34	186	9	13	0	3.19
	2B	M. Witek	622	.314	6	55	**401**	**505**	31	90	6.1	.967	J. Wittig	40	164	5	15	4	4.23
	SS	B. Jurges	481	.229	4	29	209	303	24	44	5.4	.955	V. Mungo	45	154	3	7	2	3.91
W-55 L-98	3B	D. Bartell	337	.270	5	28	62	131	4	9	3.6	.980	A. Adams	**70**	140	11	7	9	2.82
	RF	M. Ott	380	.234	18	47	219	12	6	1	2.1	.975	R. Fischer	22	131	5	10	1	4.61
Mel Ott	CF	J. Rucker	505	.273	2	46	300	9	10	3	2.7	.969	K. Chase	21	129	4	12	0	4.11
	LF	J. Medwick	324	.281	5	45	130	9	5	2	1.9	.965	H. Feldman	31	105	4	5	0	4.30
	C	G. Mancuso	252	.198	2	20	336	40	10	1	5.0	.974	B. Lohrman	17	80	5	6	1	5.15
	UT	S. Gordon	474	.251	9	63	551	148	17	59		.976							
	OF	B. Maynard	393	.206	9	32	157	10	2	0	2.3	.988							
	C	E. Lombardi	295	.305	10	51	296	36	10	8	4.7	.971							

BATTING AND BASE RUNNING LEADERS

Batting Average
S. Musial, STL .357
B. Herman, BKN .330
W. Cooper, STL .318
B. Elliott, PIT .315
M. Witek, NY .314

Slugging Average
S. Musial, STL .562
B. Nicholson, CHI .531
W. Cooper, STL .463
B. Elliott, PIT .444
C. Triplett, PHI, STL .439

Home Runs
B. Nicholson, CHI 29
M. Ott, NY 18
R. Northey, PHI 16
C. Triplett, PHI, STL 15
V. DiMaggio, PIT 15

Total Bases
S. Musial, STL 347
B. Nicholson, CHI 323
B. Elliott, PIT 258
L. Klein, STL 257
R. Northey, PHI 252
A. Vaughan, BKN 252

Runs Batted In
B. Nicholson, CHI 128
B. Elliott, PIT 101
B. Herman, BKN 100
V. DiMaggio, PIT 88
W. Cooper, STL 81
S. Musial, STL 81

Stolen Bases
A. Vaughan, BKN 20
P. Lowrey, CHI 13
F. Gustine, PIT 12
J. Russell, PIT 12
C. Workman, BOS 12

Hits
S. Musial, STL 220
M. Witek, NY 195
B. Herman, BKN 193
B. Nicholson, CHI 188

Base on Balls
A. Galan, BKN 103
M. Ott, NY 95
E. Fletcher, PIT 95
E. Stanky, CHI 92

Home Run Percentage
B. Nicholson, CHI 4.8
M. Ott, NY 4.7
C. Triplett, PHI, STL 3.9
E. Lombardi, NY 3.4

Runs Scored
A. Vaughan, BKN 112
S. Musial, STL 108
B. Nicholson, CHI 95
Cavarretta, CHI 93

Doubles
S. Musial, STL 48
V. DiMaggio, PIT 41
B. Herman, BKN 41
A. Vaughan, BKN 39

Triples
S. Musial, STL 20
L. Klein, STL 14
P. Lowrey, CHI 12
B. Elliott, PIT 12

PITCHING LEADERS

Winning Percentage
M. Cooper, STL .724
R. Sewell, PIT .700
M. Lanier, STL .682
E. Riddle, CIN .656
H. Bithorn, CHI .600

Earned Run Average
H. Pollet, STL 1.75
M. Lanier, STL 1.90
M. Cooper, STL 2.30
W. Wyatt, BKN 2.49
R. Sewell, PIT 2.54

Wins
M. Cooper, STL 21
R. Sewell, PIT 21
E. Riddle, CIN 21
H. Bithorn, CHI 18
A. Javery, BOS 17

Saves
L. Webber, BKN 10
A. Adams, NY 9
C. Shoun, CIN 7
J. Beggs, CIN 6
E. Head, BKN 6

Strikeouts
Vander Meer, CIN 174
M. Cooper, STL 141
A. Javery, BOS 134
M. Lanier, STL 123
K. Higbe, BKN 108

Complete Games
R. Sewell, PIT 25
J. Tobin, BOS 24
M. Cooper, STL 24
N. Andrews, BOS 23
B. Walters, CIN 21
Vander Meer, CIN 21

Fewest Hits/9 Innings
H. Pollet, STL 6.31
W. Wyatt, BKN 6.92
Vander Meer, CIN 7.10
M. Cooper, STL 7.49

Shutouts
H. Bithorn, CHI 7
M. Cooper, STL 6
H. Pollet, STL 5
E. Riddle, CIN 5

Fewest Walks/9 Innings
S. Rowe, PHI 1.31
P. Derringer, CHI 2.02
W. Wyatt, BKN 2.14
W. Hebert, PIT 2.20

Most Strikeouts/9 Inn.
Vander Meer, CIN 5.42
M. Lanier, STL 5.19
H. Pollet, STL 4.64
M. Cooper, STL 4.63

Innings
A. Javery, BOS 303
Vander Meer, CIN 289
N. Andrews, BOS 284
M. Cooper, STL 274

Games Pitched
A. Adams, NY 70
L. Webber, BKN 54
E. Head, BKN 47
V. Mungo, NY 45

NATIONAL LEAGUE 1943, *cont.*

	W	L	PCT	GB	R	OR	2B	3B	HR	BA	SA	SB	E	DP	FA	CG	BB	SO	ShO	SV	ERA
							Batting						Fielding			Pitching					
St. Louis	105	49	.682		679	**475**	259	72	70	**.279**	**.391**	40	151	183	.976	**94**	477	**639**	**21**	15	**2.57**
Cincinnati	87	67	.565	18	608	543	229	47	43	.256	.340	49	**125**	**193**	**.980**	78	581	498	18	17	3.13
Brooklyn	81	72	.529	23.5	**716**	674	**263**	35	39	.272	.357	58	168	137	.972	50	637	588	12	**22**	3.88
Pittsburgh	80	74	.519	25	669	605	240	**73**	42	.262	.357	**64**	170	159	.973	74	421	396	11	12	3.06
Chicago	74	79	.484	30.5	632	600	207	56	52	.261	.351	53	168	138	.973	67	**394**	513	12	14	3.24
Boston	68	85	.444	36.5	465	612	202	36	39	.233	.309	56	176	139	.972	87	440	409	13	4	3.25
Philadelphia	64	90	.416	41	571	676	186	36	66	.249	.335	29	189	143	.969	66	456	431	11	14	3.79
New York	55	98	.359	49.5	558	713	153	33	**81**	.247	.335	35	166	140	.973	35	626	588	6	19	4.08
					4898	4898	1739	388	432	.258	.347	384	1313	1232	.974	551	4032	4062	104	117	3.37

AMERICAN LEAGUE 1943

POS	Player	AB	BA	HR	RBI	PO	A	E	DP	TC/G	FA	Pitcher	G	IP	W	L	SV	ERA
New York																		
W-98 L-56																		
Joe McCarthy																		
1B	N. Etten	583	.271	14	107	1410	79	**17**	148	9.8	.989	S. Chandler	30	253	**20**	4	0	**1.64**
2B	J. Gordon	543	.249	17	69	407	**490**	**29**	114	6.1	.969	E. Bonham	28	226	15	8	1	2.27
SS	F. Crosetti	348	.233	2	20	194	260	26	58	5.3	.946	B. Wensloff	29	223	13	11	1	2.54
3B	B. Johnson	592	.280	5	94	**183**	**326**	18	**32**	3.4	.966	H. Borowy	29	217	14	9	0	2.82
RF	B. Metheny	360	.261	9	36	156	1	6	0	1.8	.963	A. Donald	22	119	6	4	0	4.60
CF	J. Lindell	441	.245	4	51	269	11	10	1	2.4	.966	B. Zuber	20	118	8	4	1	3.89
LF	C. Keller	512	.271	31	86	338	8	2	0	2.5	.994	M. Russo	24	102	5	10	3	3.72
C	B. Dickey	242	.351	4	33	322	37	2	5	5.1	.994	J. Murphy	37	68	12	4	8	2.51
OF	R. Weatherly	280	.264	7	28	174	2	3	0	2.6	.983							
SS	Stirnweiss	274	.219	1	25	110	192	20	50	4.7	.938							
OF	T. Stainback	231	.260	0	10	141	3	1	2	2.4	.993							
C	K. Sears	187	.278	2	22	233	31	7	5	5.4	.974							
C	R. Hemsley	180	.239	2	24	234	31	5	3	5.2	.981							
Washington																		
W-84 L-69																		
Ossie Bluege																		
1B	M. Vernon	553	.268	7	70	1351	75	14	125	10.1	.990	E. Wynn	37	257	18	12	0	2.91
2B	G. Priddy	560	.271	4	62	364	411	23	105	6.0	.971	D. Leonard	31	220	11	13	1	3.28
SS	J. Sullivan	456	.208	1	55	276	445	41	89	5.7	.946	M. Candini	28	166	11	7	1	2.49
3B	E. Clary	254	.256	0	19	86	119	12	6	3.2	.945	M. Haefner	36	165	11	5	6	2.29
RF	G. Case	613	.294	1	52	318	8	5	2	2.4	.985	Carrasquel	39	144	11	7	5	3.68
CF	S. Spence	570	.267	12	88	396	12	7	1	2.8	.983	J. Mertz	33	117	5	7	3	4.63
LF	B. Johnson	438	.265	7	63	212	11	1	1	2.5	.996	Scarborough	24	86	4	4	2	2.83
C	J. Early	423	.258	5	60	443	83	**11**	10	4.4	.980	E. Pyle	18	73	4	8	1	4.09
OF	G. Moore	254	.268	2	39	125	5	2	0	2.3	.985							
C	T. Giuliani	133	.226	0	20	154	24	7	1	3.8	.962							
OF	J. Powell	132	.265	0	20	83	4	2	0	2.7	.978							
Cleveland																		
W-82 L-71																		
Lou Boudreau																		
1B	M. Rocco	405	.240	5	46	1012	61	5	111	10.0	**.995**	J. Bagby	36	**273**	17	14	1	3.10
2B	R. Mack	545	.220	7	62	381	444	28	123	5.6	.967	A. Smith	29	208	17	7	1	2.55
SS	L. Boudreau	539	.286	3	67	**328**	488	25	**122**	5.5	.970	A. Reynolds	34	199	11	12	3	2.99
3B	K. Keltner	427	.260	4	39	113	228	11	24	3.3	.969	V. Kennedy	28	147	10	7	0	2.45
RF	Cullenbine	488	.289	8	56	245	14	5	**6**	2.2	.981	M. Harder	19	135	8	7	0	3.06
CF	O. Hockett	601	.276	2	51	347	13	**15**	3	2.7	.960	J. Salveson	23	86	5	3	3	3.35
LF	J. Heath	424	.274	18	79	264	4	9	1	2.5	.968	C. Dean	17	76	5	5	0	4.50
C	B. Rosar	382	.283	1	41	480	**91**	10	11	5.1	.983	J. Heving	30	72	1	1	9	2.75
OF	H. Edwards	297	.276	3	28	173	4	3	0	2.4	.983	M. Naymick	29	63	4	4	2	2.30
UT	R. Peters	215	.219	1	19	66	98	11	17	5.1	.937							
C	G. Desautels	185	.205	0	19	251	28	5	4	4.3	.982							
Chicago																		
W-82 L-72																		
Jimmy Dykes																		
1B	J. Kuhel	531	.213	5	46	1471	106	8	143	10.4	.995	O. Grove	32	216	15	9	2	2.75
2B	D. Kolloway	348	.216	1	33	246	240	16	71	5.9	.968	J. Humphries	28	188	11	11	0	3.30
SS	L. Appling	585	**.328**	3	80	300	**500**	36	115	5.4	.957	E. Smith	25	188	11	11	0	3.69
3B	R. Hodgin	407	.314	1	50	34	120	9	7	2.9	.945	B. Dietrich	26	187	12	10	0	2.80
RF	W. Moses	599	.245	3	48	370	12	8	2	2.6	.979	B. Ross	21	149	11	7	0	3.19
CF	T. Tucker	528	.235	3	39	**399**	14	5	1	**3.2**	.988	T. Lee	19	127	5	9	0	4.18
LF	G. Curtright	488	.291	3	48	301	7	9	1	2.5	.972	J. Haynes	35	109	7	2	3	2.96
C	M. Tresh	279	.215	0	20	321	62	7	4	4.6	.982	Maltzberger	37	99	7	4	14	2.46
2B	S. Webb	213	.235	0	22	118	169	14	35	5.6	.953	J. Wade	21	84	3	7	0	3.01
3B	J. Grant	197	.259	4	22	43	115	19	11	3.5	.893							
C	T. Turner	154	.240	2	11	186	34	5	5	4.6	.978							
Detroit																		
W-78 L-76																		
Steve O'Neill																		
1B	R. York	571	.271	**34**	**118**	1349	**149**	15	105	9.8	.990	D. Trout	44	247	**20**	12	6	2.48
2B	Bloodworth	474	.241	6	52	349	393	21	74	5.9	.972	V. Trucks	33	203	16	10	2	2.84
SS	J. Hoover	575	.243	4	38	301	393	**41**	84	5.1	.944	H. Newhouser	37	196	8	17	1	3.04
3B	P. Higgins	523	.277	10	84	156	253	**26**	22	3.2	.940	T. Bridges	25	192	12	7	0	2.39
RF	B. Harris	354	.254	6	32	192	6	8	2	2.1	.961	H. White	32	178	7	12	2	3.39
CF	D. Cramer	606	.300	1	43	346	9	4	3	2.6	.989	S. Overmire	29	147	7	6	1	3.18
LF	D. Wakefield	**633**	.316	7	79	314	11	14	1	2.2	.959	J. Gorsica	35	96	4	5	5	3.36
C	P. Richards	313	.220	5	33	**537**	86	9	**12**	6.3	**.986**							
UT	D. Ross	247	.267	0	18	106	65	9	10		.950							
23	J. Wood	164	.323	1	17	70	64	12	6		.918							

AMERICAN LEAGUE 1943, *cont.*

	POS	Player	AB	BA	HR	RBI	PO	A	E	DP	TC/G	FA	Pitcher	G	IP	W	L	SV	ERA
St. Louis W-72 L-80 Luke Sewell	1B	G. McQuinn	449	.243	12	74	1072	86	9	88	9.6	.992	D. Galehouse	31	224	11	11	1	2.77
	2B	Gutteridge	538	.273	1	36	328	331	29	64	5.2	.958	S. Sundra	32	208	15	11	0	3.25
	SS	V. Stephens	512	.289	22	91	220	339	34	51	4.8	.943	B. Muncrief	35	205	13	12	1	2.81
	3B	H. Clift	379	.232	3	25	126	252	20	20	3.8*	.950	N. Potter	33	168	10	5	1	2.78
	RF	M. Chartak	344	.256	10	37	160	4	5	2	2.2	.970	Hollingsworth	35	154	6	13	3	4.21
	CF	M. Byrnes	429	.280	4	50	289	13	1	3	2.7	.997	J. Niggeling	20	150	6	8	0	3.17
	LF	C. Laabs	580	.250	17	85	346	16	9	4	2.5	.976	G. Caster	35	76	6	8	8	2.12
	C	F. Hayes	250	.188	5	30	301	40	6	8	4.6	.983							
	UT	M. Christman	336	.271	2	35	279	172	3	41		.993							
	OF	A. Zarilla	228	.254	2	17	123	5	5	2	2.2	.962							
	C	R. Ferrell	209	.239	0	20	327	52	5	7	5.5	.987							
	OF	M. Kreevich	161	.255	0	10	146	5	1	1	3.0	.993							
Boston W-68 L-84 Joe Cronin	1B	T. Lupien	608	.255	4	47	**1487**	118	12	**149**	10.6	.993	T. Hughson	35	266	12	15	2	2.64
	2B	B. Doerr	604	.270	16	75	415	490	9	132	5.9	**.990**	J. Dobson	25	164	7	11	0	3.12
	SS	S. Newsome	449	.265	1	22	222	310	21	69	5.6	.962	Y. Terry	30	164	7	9	1	3.52
	3B	J. Tabor	537	.242	13	85	135	261	**26**	**32**	3.2	.938	O. Judd	23	155	11	6	2	2.90
	RF	P. Fox	489	.288	2	44	261	10	11	2	2.3	.961	D. Newsome	25	154	8	13	0	4.49
	CF	C. Metkovich	321	.246	5	27	183	7	9	3	2.6	.955	M. Ryba	40	144	7	5	3	3.26
	LF	L. Culberson	312	.272	3	34	211	10	5	2	2.9	.978	P. Woods	23	101	5	6	1	4.92
	C	R. Partee	299	.281	0	31	349	57	7	11	4.5	.983	M. Brown	**49**	93	6	6	9	2.12
	SS	E. Lake	216	.199	3	16	128	195	13	43	5.3	.961							
	OF	J. Lazor	208	.226	0	13	135	7	3	0	2.3	.979							
	PH	J. Cronin	77	.312	5	29													
Philadelphia W-49 L-105 Connie Mack	1B	D. Siebert	558	.251	4	72	1332	111	15	117	10.1	.990	J. Flores	31	231	12	14	0	3.11
	2B	P. Suder	475	.221	3	41	231	269	15	58	5.4	.971	R. Wolff	41	221	10	15	6	3.54
	SS	I. Hall	544	.256	0	54	298	435	40	91	5.2	.948	L. Harris	32	216	7	**21**	1	4.20
	3B	E. Mayo	471	.219	0	28	176	223	10	18	3.3	**.976**	D. Black	33	208	6	16	1	4.20
	RF	J. Welaj	281	.242	0	15	187	3	8	0	2.8	.960	O. Arntzen	32	164	4	13	0	4.22
	CF	J. White	500	.248	1	30	335	8	12	2	2.7	.966	Christopher	24	133	5	8	2	3.45
	LF	B. Estalella	367	.259	11	63	225	5	6	1	2.4	.975	E. Fagan	18	37	2	6	3	6.27
	C	H. Wagner	289	.239	1	26	340	56	8	3	4.1	.980							
	OF	E. Valo	249	.221	3	18	134	4	2	0	2.2	.986							
	C	B. Swift	224	.192	1	11	278	53	8	9	4.4	.976							
	2B	D. Heffner	178	.208	0	8	98	127	5	27	4.9	.978							
	OF	J. Tyack	155	.258	0	23	82	4	2	0	2.3	.977							

BATTING AND BASE RUNNING LEADERS

Batting Average
L. Appling, CHI	.328
D. Wakefield, DET	.316
R. Hodgin, CHI	.314
D. Cramer, DET	.300
G. Case, WAS	.294

Slugging Average
R. York, DET	.527
C. Keller, NY	.525
V. Stephens, STL	.482
J. Heath, CLE	.481
D. Wakefield, DET	.434

Home Runs
R. York, DET	34
C. Keller, NY	31
V. Stephens, STL	22
J. Heath, CLE	18
J. Gordon, NY	17
C. Laabs, STL	17

Total Bases
R. York, DET	301
D. Wakefield, DET	275
C. Keller, NY	269
B. Doerr, BOS	249
V. Stephens, STL	247

Runs Batted In
R. York, DET	118
N. Etten, NY	107
B. Johnson, NY	94
V. Stephens, STL	91
S. Spence, WAS	88

Stolen Bases
G. Case, WAS	61
W. Moses, CHI	56
T. Tucker, CHI	29
L. Appling, CHI	27
M. Vernon, WAS	24

Hits
D. Wakefield, DET	200
L. Appling, CHI	192
D. Cramer, DET	182
G. Case, WAS	180

Base on Balls
C. Keller, NY	106
J. Gordon, NY	98
Cullenbine, CLE	96
L. Boudreau, CLE	90

Home Run Percentage
C. Keller, NY	6.1
R. York, DET	6.0
V. Stephens, STL	4.3
J. Heath, CLE	4.2

Runs Scored
G. Case, WAS	102
C. Keller, NY	97
D. Wakefield, DET	91
R. York, DET	90

Doubles
D. Wakefield, DET	38
G. Case, WAS	36
Gutteridge, STL	35
N. Etten, NY	35

Triples
J. Lindell, NY	12
W. Moses, CHI	12
C. Keller, NY	11
R. York, DET	11

PITCHING LEADERS

Winning Percentage
S. Chandler, NY	.833
A. Smith, CLE	.708
E. Bonham, NY	.652
D. Trout, DET	.625
O. Grove, CHI	.625

Earned Run Average
S. Chandler, NY	1.64
E. Bonham, NY	2.27
T. Bridges, DET	2.39
D. Trout, DET	2.48
B. Wensloff, NY	2.54

Wins
S. Chandler, NY	20
D. Trout, DET	20
E. Wynn, WAS	18
A. Smith, CLE	17
J. Bagby, CLE	17

Saves
Maltzberger, CHI	14
M. Brown, BOS	9
J. Heving, CLE	9
J. Murphy, NY	8
G. Caster, STL	8

Strikeouts
A. Reynolds, CLE	151
H. Newhouser, DET	144
S. Chandler, NY	134
T. Bridges, DET	124
V. Trucks, DET	118

Complete Games
S. Chandler, NY	20
T. Hughson, BOS	20
O. Grove, CHI	18
B. Wensloff, NY	18
D. Trout, DET	18

Fewest Hits/9 Innings
A. Reynolds, CLE	6.34
J. Niggeling, STL, WAS	6.66
S. Chandler, NY	7.01
B. Wensloff, NY	7.21

Shutouts
S. Chandler, NY	5
D. Trout, DET	5
E. Bonham, NY	4
T. Hughson, BOS	4

Fewest Walks/9 Innings
D. Leonard, WAS	1.88
S. Chandler, NY	1.92
E. Bonham, NY	2.07
B. Muncrief, STL	2.11

Most Strikeouts/9 Inn.
A. Reynolds, CLE	6.84
H. Newhouser, DET	6.62
T. Bridges, DET	5.82
V. Trucks, DET	5.24

Innings
J. Bagby, CLE	273
T. Hughson, BOS	266
E. Wynn, WAS	257
S. Chandler, NY	253

Games Pitched
M. Brown, BOS	49
D. Trout, DET	44
R. Wolff, PHI	41
M. Ryba, BOS	40

AMERICAN LEAGUE 1943, cont.

	W	L	PCT	GB	R	OR	Batting 2B	3B	HR	BA	SA	SB	Fielding E	DP	FA	Pitching CG	BB	SO	ShO	SV	ERA
New York	98	56	.636		**669**	542	218	**59**	100	.256	**.376**	46	160	166	.974	**83**	489	653	14	13	**2.93**
Washington	84	69	.549	13.5	666	595	245	50	47	.254	.347	142	179	145	.971	61	540	495	16	**21**	3.18
Cleveland	82	71	.536	15.5	600	577	**246**	45	55	.255	.350	47	157	**183**	.975	64	606	585	14	20	3.15
Chicago	82	72	.532	16	573	594	193	46	33	.247	.320	**173**	166	167	.973	70	501	476	12	19	3.20
Detroit	78	76	.506	20	632	560	200	47	77	**.261**	.359	40	177	130	.971	67	549	**706**	**18**	20	3.00
St. Louis	72	80	.474	25	596	604	229	36	78	.245	.349	37	**152**	127	.975	64	**488**	572	10	14	3.41
Boston	68	84	.447	29	563	607	223	42	57	.244	.332	86	153	179	**.976**	62	615	513	13	16	3.45
Philadelphia	49	105	.318	49	497	717	174	44	26	.232	.297	55	162	148	.973	73	536	503	5	13	4.05
					4796	4796	1728	369	473	.249	.341	626	1306	1245	.973	544	4324	4503	102	136	3.30

NATIONAL LEAGUE 1944

St. Louis
W-105 L-49
Billy Southworth

POS	Player	AB	BA	HR	RBI	PO	A	E	DP	TC/G	FA	Pitcher	G	IP	W	L	SV	ERA
1B	R. Sanders	601	.295	12	102	1370	64	8	**142**	9.5	**.994**	M. Cooper	34	252	22	7	1	2.46
2B	E. Verban	498	.257	0	43	319	380	23	**105**	4.9	.968	M. Lanier	33	224	17	12	0	2.65
SS	M. Marion	506	.267	6	63	268	461	21	90	5.2	.972	T. Wilks	36	207	17	4	0	2.65
3B	W. Kurowski	555	.270	20	87	**188**	281	17	20	3.3	**.965**	H. Brecheen	30	189	16	5	0	2.85
RF	S. Musial	568	.347	12	94	353	16	5	2	2.6	.987	G. Munger	21	121	11	3	2	1.34
CF	J. Hopp	527	.336	11	72	316	2	1	1	2.4	**.997**	A. Jurisich	30	130	7	9	1	3.39
LF	D. Litwhiler	492	.264	15	82	294	6	8	1	2.3	.974	F. Schmidt	37	114	7	3	5	3.15
C	W. Cooper	397	.317	13	72	442	40	10	7	**5.1**	.980							
C	K. O'Dea	265	.249	6	37	326	34	2	4	5.2	.994							
OF	A. Bergamo	192	.286	2	19	83	0	1	0	1.7	.988							

Pittsburgh
W-90 L-63
Frankie Frisch

POS	Player	AB	BA	HR	RBI	PO	A	E	DP	TC/G	FA	Pitcher	G	IP	W	L	SV	ERA
1B	B. Dahlgren	599	.289	12	101	1440	128	**20**	105	10.1	.987	R. Sewell	38	286	21	12	2	3.18
2B	P. Coscarart	554	.264	4	42	371	389	26	71	5.8	.967	Ostermueller	28	205	11	7	1	2.73
SS	F. Gustine	405	.230	2	42	183	330	34	52	4.7	.938	M. Butcher	35	199	13	11	2	3.12
3B	B. Elliott	538	.297	10	108	169	**285**	**27**	22	3.4	.944	Strincevich	40	190	14	7	2	3.08
RF	J. Barrett	568	.269	7	83	373	12	11	4	2.7	.972	P. Roe	39	185	13	11	1	3.11
CF	V. DiMaggio	342	.240	9	50	234	8	4	2	2.4	.984	X. Rescigno	48	124	10	8	5	4.35
LF	J. Russell	580	.312	8	66	345	20	5	**7**	2.5	.986	Cuccurullo	32	106	2	1	4	4.06
C	A. Lopez	331	.230	1	34	372	52	7	6	3.7	**.984**	R. Starr	27	90	6	5	3	5.02
OF	F. Colman	226	.270	6	53	102	4	4	0	2.1	.964							
UT	A. Rubeling	184	.245	4	30	70	56	2	7		.984							
SS	F. Zak	160	.300	0	11	93	162	14	24	4.0	.948							
OF	T. O'Brien	156	.250	3	20	50	5	2	1	1.2	.965							

Cincinnati
W-89 L-65
Bill McKechnie

POS	Player	AB	BA	HR	RBI	PO	A	E	DP	TC/G	FA	Pitcher	G	IP	W	L	SV	ERA
1B	McCormick	581	.305	20	102	**1508**	135	13	130	**10.8**	.992	B. Walters	34	285	**23**	8	1	2.40
2B	W. Williams	653	.240	1	35	377	**542**	27	97	6.1	**.971**	C. Shoun	38	203	13	10	2	3.02
SS	E. Miller	536	.209	4	55	357	544	27	**100**	6.0	.971	E. Heusser	30	193	13	11	1	**2.38**
3B	S. Mesner	414	.242	1	47	120	246	19	21	3.2	.951	De La Cruz	34	191	9	9	1	3.25
RF	G. Walker	478	.278	5	62	293	3	10	0	2.6	.967	H. Gumbert	24	155	10	8	2	3.30
CF	D. Clay	356	.250	0	17	272	4	2	0	2.8	.993	A. Carter	33	148	11	7	3	2.61
LF	E. Tipton	479	.301	3	36	329	8	6	1	2.5	.983	J. Konstanty	20	113	6	4	0	2.80
C	R. Mueller	555	.286	10	73	471	**65**	9	5	3.5	.983							
OF	M. Marshall	229	.245	4	23	131	6	5	3	2.4	.965							
OF	T. Criscola	157	.229	0	14	80	4	2	0	2.5	.977							

Chicago
W-75 L-79
Jimmie Wilson
W-1 L-9
Roy Johnson
W-0 L-1
Charlie Grimm
W-74 L-69

POS	Player	AB	BA	HR	RBI	PO	A	E	DP	TC/G	FA	Pitcher	G	IP	W	L	SV	ERA
1B	Cavarretta	614	.321	5	82	1337	77	11	121	10.3	.992	H. Wyse	41	257	16	15	1	3.15
2B	D. Johnson	608	.278	2	71	**385**	462	**47**	85	5.8	.947	C. Passeau	34	227	15	9	3	2.89
SS	L. Merullo	193	.212	1	16	115	167	19	26	5.4	.937	P. Derringer	42	180	7	13	3	4.15
3B	S. Hack	383	.282	3	32	96	164	17	3	3.7	.939	B. Fleming	39	158	9	10	3	3.13
RF	B. Nicholson	582	.287	33	122	305	18	7	4	2.1	.979	B. Chipman	26	129	9	9	2	3.49
CF	A. Pafko	469	.269	6	62	333	24	6	4	3.0	.983	Vandenburg	35	126	7	4	2	3.63
LF	Dallessandro	381	.304	8	74	212	9	4	2	2.1	.982	P. Erickson	33	124	5	9	1	3.55
C	D. Williams	262	.240	0	27	317	50	7	7	4.9	.981	R. Lynn	22	84	5	4	1	4.06
3S	R. Hughes	478	.287	1	28	220	303	20	54		.963							
SS	B. Schuster	154	.221	1	14	57	100	9	18	4.4	.946							

New York
W-67 L-87
Mel Ott

POS	Player	AB	BA	HR	RBI	PO	A	E	DP	TC/G	FA	Pitcher	G	IP	W	L	SV	ERA
1B	P. Weintraub	361	.316	13	77	928	72	8	72	10.2	.992	B. Voiselle	43	**313**	21	16	0	3.02
2B	G. Hausmann	466	.266	1	30	301	350	27	66	5.6	.960	H. Feldman	40	205	11	13	2	4.16
SS	B. Kerr	548	.266	9	63	328	507	**40**	81	5.9	.954	E. Pyle	31	164	7	10	0	4.34
3B	H. Luby	323	.254	2	35	83	134	13	14	3.5	.943	A. Adams	65	138	8	11	13	4.27
RF	M. Ott	399	.288	26	82	199	6	3	0	2.0	.986	R. Fischer	38	129	6	14	2	5.18
CF	J. Rucker	587	.244	6	39	310	14	5	0	2.4	.985	J. Allen	18	84	4	7	0	4.07
LF	J. Medwick	490	.337	7	85	290	8	2	2	2.5	.993							
C	E. Lombardi	373	.255	10	58	350	47	**13**	11	4.1	.968							
13	N. Reyes	374	.289	8	53	580	120	12	49		.983							
3B	B. Jurges	246	.211	1	23	48	124	7	7	2.9	.961							
C	G. Mancuso	195	.251	1	25	249	37	7	4	4.1	.976							
OF	R. Treadway	170	.300	0	5	87	3	4	0	2.5	.957							

NATIONAL LEAGUE 1944, *cont.*

	POS	Player	AB	BA	HR	RBI	PO	A	E	DP	TC/G	FA	Pitcher	G	IP	W	L	SV	ERA
Boston	1B	B. Etchison	308	.214	8	33	757	48	6	64	9.5	.993	J. Tobin	43	299	18	19	3	3.01
	2B	C. Ryan	332	.295	4	25	210	272	13	57	6.2	.974	N. Andrews	37	257	16	15	2	3.22
W-65 L-89	SS	Wietelmann	417	.240	2	32	215	287	24	60	5.1	.954	A. Javery	40	254	10	19	3	3.54
	3B	D. Phillips	489	.258	1	53	84	177	19	22	3.1	.932	R. Barrett	42	230	9	16	2	4.06
Bob Coleman	RF	C. Workman	418	.208	11	53	161	16	3	3	1.7	.983	Hutchinson	40	120	9	7	1	4.21
	CF	T. Holmes	631	.309	13	73	426	14	4	7	2.9	.991							
	LF	B. Nieman	468	.265	16	65	261	13	7	2	2.2	.975							
	C	P. Masi	251	.275	3	23	180	34	5	3	3.5	.977							
	1B	M. Macon	366	.273	3	36	625	49	16	62	9.6	.977							
	C	C. Kluttz	229	.279	2	19	199	40	5	5	4.2	.980							
	OF	A. Wright	195	.256	7	35	88	2	3	1	2.0	.968							
	C	S. Hofferth	180	.200	1	26	158	32	3	3	3.9	.984							
	OF	C. Ross	154	.227	5	26	75	8	0	2	2.2	1.000							
Brooklyn	1B	H. Schultz	526	.255	11	83	1091	85	14	90	8.8	.988	H. Gregg	39	198	9	16	2	5.46
	2B	E. Stanky	261	.276	0	16	132	138	11	28	4.8	.961	C. Davis	31	194	10	11	4	3.34
W-63 L-91	SS	B. Bragan	266	.267	0	17	77	109	9	16	3.8	.954	R. Melton	37	187	9	13	0	3.46
	3B	Bordagaray	501	.281	6	51	107	150	15	14	2.8	.945	L. Webber	48	140	7	8	3	4.94
Leo Durocher	RF	D. Walker	535	.357	13	91	260	17	11	4	2.1	.962	C. McLish	23	84	3	10	0	7.82
	CF	G. Rosen	264	.261	0	23	199	12	2	0	3.3	.991							
	LF	A. Galan	547	.318	12	93	323	10	4	3	2.3	.988							
	C	M. Owen	461	.273	1	42	506	57	12	8	4.6	.979							
	UT	L. Olmo	520	.258	9	85	316	138	27	18		.944							
	1B	J. Bolling	131	.351	1	25	206	20	2	7	8.4	.991							
Philadelphia	1B	T. Lupien	597	.283	5	52	1453	103	13	114	10.4	.992	Raffensberger	37	259	13	20	0	3.06
	2B	M. Mullen	464	.267	0	31	291	316	23	52	5.5	.963	C. Schanz	40	241	13	16	3	3.32
W-61 L-92	SS	R. Hamrick	292	.205	1	23	160	293	25	55	6.5	.948	D. Barrett	37	221	12	18	0	3.86
	3B	G. Stewart	377	.220	0	29	77	181	10	12	3.2	.963	B. Lee	31	208	10	11	1	3.15
Freddie Fitzsimmons	RF	R. Northey	570	.288	22	104	286	24	6	7	2.1	.981	Gerheauser	30	183	8	16	0	4.58
	CF	B. Adams	584	.283	17	64	449	14	10	1	3.1	.979							
	LF	J. Wasdell	451	.277	3	40	243	6	5	0	2.1	.980							
	C	B. Finley	281	.249	1	21	289	34	11	7	4.5	.967							
	UT	C. Letchas	396	.237	0	33	219	300	16	54		.970							
	C	J. Peacock	253	.225	0	21	274	38	3	4	4.3	.990							
	3B	T. Cieslak	220	.245	2	11	35	72	15	1	2.5	.877							
	OF	C. Triplett	184	.234	1	25	90	3	1	1	2.1	.989							

BATTING AND BASE RUNNING LEADERS

Batting Average
D. Walker, BKN .357
S. Musial, STL .347
J. Medwick, NY .337
J. Hopp, STL .336
Cavarretta, CHI .321

Slugging Average
S. Musial, STL .549
B. Nicholson, CHI .545
M. Ott, NY .544
D. Walker, BKN .529
P. Weintraub, NY .524

Home Runs
B. Nicholson, CHI 33
M. Ott, NY 26
R. Northey, PHI 22
W. Kurowski, STL 20
McCormick, CIN 20

Total Bases
B. Nicholson, CHI 317
S. Musial, STL 312
T. Holmes, BOS 288
D. Walker, BKN 283
R. Northey, PHI 283

Runs Batted In
B. Nicholson, CHI 122
B. Elliott, PIT 108
R. Northey, PHI 104
McCormick, CIN 102
R. Sanders, STL 102

Stolen Bases
J. Barrett, PIT 28
T. Lupien, PHI 18
R. Hughes, CHI 16
J. Hopp, STL 15
B. Kerr, NY 14

Hits
S. Musial, STL 197
Cavarretta, CHI 197
T. Holmes, BOS 195
D. Walker, BKN 191

Base on Balls
A. Galan, BKN 101
B. Nicholson, CHI 93
M. Ott, NY 90
S. Musial, STL 90

Home Run Percentage
M. Ott, NY 6.5
B. Nicholson, CHI 5.7
R. Northey, PHI 3.9
W. Kurowski, STL 3.6

Runs Scored
B. Nicholson, CHI 116
S. Musial, STL 112
J. Russell, PIT 109
J. Hopp, STL 106

Doubles
S. Musial, STL 51
A. Galan, BKN 43
T. Holmes, BOS 42
D. Walker, BKN 37

Triples
J. Barrett, PIT 19
B. Elliott, PIT 16
Cavarretta, CHI 15
S. Musial, STL 14

PITCHING LEADERS

Winning Percentage
T. Wilks, STL .810
H. Brecheen, STL .762
M. Cooper, STL .759
B. Walters, CIN .742
R. Sewell, PIT .636

Earned Run Average
E. Heusser, CIN 2.38
B. Walters, CIN 2.40
M. Cooper, STL 2.46
M. Lanier, STL 2.65
T. Wilks, STL 2.65

Wins
B. Walters, CIN 23
M. Cooper, STL 22
R. Sewell, PIT 21
B. Voiselle, NY 21
J. Tobin, BOS 18

Saves
A. Adams, NY 13
X. Rescigno, PIT 5
F. Schmidt, STL 5
Cuccurullo, PIT 4
C. Davis, BKN 4

Strikeouts
B. Voiselle, NY 161
M. Lanier, STL 141
A. Javery, BOS 137
Raffensberger, PHI 136
Ostermueller, BKN, PIT 97
M. Cooper, STL 97

Complete Games
J. Tobin, BOS 28
B. Walters, CIN 27
B. Voiselle, NY 25
R. Sewell, PIT 24
M. Cooper, STL 22

Fewest Hits/9 Innings
B. Walters, CIN 7.36
T. Wilks, STL 7.51
M. Lanier, STL 7.70
E. Heusser, CIN 7.71

Shutouts
M. Cooper, STL 7
B. Walters, CIN 6
M. Butcher, PIT 5
M. Lanier, STL 5

Fewest Walks/9 Innings
Raffensberger, PHI 1.57
Strincevich, PIT 1.75
C. Davis, BKN 1.81
C. Shoun, CIN 1.87

Most Strikeouts/9 Inn.
M. Lanier, STL 5.66
A. Javery, BOS 4.85
Raffensberger, PHI 4.73
B. Voiselle, NY 4.63

Innings
B. Voiselle, NY 313
J. Tobin, BOS 299
R. Sewell, PIT 286
B. Walters, CIN 285

Games Pitched
A. Adams, NY 65
L. Webber, BKN 48
X. Rescigno, PIT 48
B. Voiselle, NY 43

NATIONAL LEAGUE 1944, cont.

	W	L	PCT	GB	R	OR	2B	3B	Batting HR	BA	SA	SB	Fielding E	DP	FA	CG	Pitching BB	SO	ShO	SV	ERA
St. Louis	105	49	.682		772	490	274	59	100	.275	.402	37	112	162	.982	89	468	637	26	12	2.67
Pittsburgh	90	63	.588	14.5	744	662	248	80	70	.265	.379	87	191	122	.970	77	435	452	10	19	3.44
Cincinnati	89	65	.578	16	573	537	229	31	51	.254	.338	51	137	153	.978	93	384	359	17	12	2.97
Chicago	75	79	.487	30	702	669	236	46	71	.261	.360	53	186	151	.970	70	452	535	11	13	3.59
New York	67	87	.435	38	682	773	191	47	93	.263	.370	38	179	128	.971	47	587	499	4	21	4.29
Boston	65	89	.422	40	593	674	250	39	79	.246	.353	37	182	160	.971	70	527	454	13	12	3.67
Brooklyn	63	91	.409	42	690	832	255	51	56	.269	.366	43	197	112	.966	50	660	487	4	13	4.68
Philadelphia	61	92	.399	43.5	539	658	199	42	55	.251	.336	32	177	138	.972	66	459	496	11	6	3.64
					5295	5295	1882	395	575	.261	.363	378	1361	1126	.972	562	3972	3919	96	108	3.61

AMERICAN LEAGUE 1944

	POS	Player	AB	BA	HR	RBI	PO	A	E	DP	TC/G	FA	Pitcher	G	IP	W	L	SV	ERA
St. Louis	1B	G. McQuinn	516	.250	11	72	1332	72	9	116	9.7	.994	J. Kramer	33	257	17	13	0	2.49
	2B	Gutteridge	603	.245	3	36	368	407	35	95	5.5	.957	N. Potter	32	232	19	7	0	2.83
W-89 L-65	SS	V. Stephens	559	.293	20	109	239	480	35	71	5.3	.954	B. Muncrief	33	219	13	8	1	3.08
	3B	M. Christman	547	.271	6	83	172	316	14	34	3.3	.972	S. Jakucki	35	198	13	9	3	3.55
Luke Sewell	RF	G. Moore	390	.238	6	58	208	5	7	2	2.2	.968	D. Galehouse	24	153	9	10	0	3.12
	CF	M. Byrnes	407	.295	4	45	282	7	7	1	2.4	.976	Hollingsworth	26	93	5	7	1	4.47
	LF	M. Kreevich	402	.301	5	44	282	4	4	0	2.9	.986	G. Caster	42	81	6	6	12	2.44
	C	F. Mancuso	244	.205	1	24	311	35	17	9	4.2	.953							
	OF	A. Zarilla	288	.299	6	45	167	4	4	1	2.2	.977							
	C	R. Hayworth	269	.223	1	25	336	39	13	4	4.5	.966							
	OF	C. Laabs	201	.234	5	23	108	3	0	2	2.0	1.000							
Detroit	1B	R. York	583	.276	18	98	1453	107	17	163	10.4	.989	D. Trout	49	352	27	14	0	2.12
	2B	E. Mayo	607	.249	5	63	384	458	19	120	6.0	.978	H. Newhouser	47	312	29	9	2	2.22
W-88 L-66	SS	J. Hoover	441	.236	0	29	256	405	48	102	6.0	.932	R. Gentry	37	204	12	14	0	4.24
	3B	P. Higgins	543	.297	7	76	146	311	22	21	3.3	.954	S. Overmire	32	200	11	11	1	3.07
Steve O'Neill	RF	J. Outlaw	535	.273	3	57	254	14	10	2	2.0	.964	J. Gorsica	34	162	6	14	4	4.11
	CF	D. Cramer	578	.292	2	42	337	13	7	2	2.5	.980							
	LF	D. Wakefield	276	.355	12	53	155	3	6	1	2.1	.963							
	C	P. Richards	300	.237	3	37	413	60	10	13	5.4	.979							
	OF	C. Hostetler	265	.298	0	20	129	5	2	1	2.1	.985							
	C	B. Swift	247	.255	1	19	288	48	6	4	4.5	.982							
	OF	D. Ross	167	.210	2	15	67	2	3	1	1.9	.958							
	UT	J. Orengo	154	.201	0	10	124	124	20	24	2.4	.925							
	P	D. Trout	133	.271	5	24	21	94	4	8	2.4	.966							
New York	1B	N. Etten	573	.293	22	91	1382	106	16	144	9.8	.989	H. Borowy	35	253	17	12	2	2.64
	2B	Stirnweiss	643	.319	8	43	433	481	17	113	6.0	.982	M. Dubiel	30	232	13	13	0	3.38
W-83 L-71	SS	Milosevich	312	.247	0	32	176	281	22	68	5.3	.954	E. Bonham	26	214	12	9	0	2.99
	3B	O. Grimes	387	.279	5	46	105	189	17	14	3.2	.945	A. Donald	30	159	13	10	0	3.34
Joe McCarthy	RF	B. Metheny	518	.239	14	67	232	8	11	2	1.9	.956	B. Zuber	22	107	5	7	0	4.21
	CF	J. Lindell	594	.300	18	103	468	9	7	3	3.2	.986	J. Page	19	103	5	7	0	4.56
	LF	H. Martin	328	.302	9	47	177	8	7	4	2.4	.964	J. Turner	35	42	4	4	7	3.46
	C	M. Garbark	299	.261	1	33	372	47	5	9	5.0	.988							
	C	R. Hemsley	284	.268	2	36	298	41	6	7	4.5	.983							
	3B	D. Savage	239	.264	4	24	66	109	10	11	3.1	.946							
	SS	F. Crosetti	197	.239	5	30	115	150	11	33	5.0	.960							
	OF	E. Levy	153	.242	4	29	75	2	3	0	2.2	.963							
Boston	1B	L. Finney	251	.287	0	32	521	23	7	53	9.3	.987	T. Hughson	28	203	18	5	5	2.26
	2B	B. Doerr	468	.325	15	81	341	363	17	96	5.8	.976	P. Woods	38	171	4	8	0	3.27
W-77 L-77	SS	S. Newsome	472	.242	0	41	249	421	26	79	5.5	.963	J. Bowman	26	168	12	8	0	4.81
	3B	J. Tabor	438	.285	13	72	125	258	20	14	3.5	.950	E. O'Neill	28	152	6	11	0	4.63
Joe Cronin	RF	P. Fox	496	.315	1	64	228	7	3	1	2.0	.987	M. Ryba	42	138	12	7	2	3.33
	CF	C. Metkovich	549	.277	9	59	242	8	10	2	3.2	.962	C. Hausmann	32	137	4	7	2	3.42
	LF	B. Johnson	525	.324	17	106	270	23	7	3	2.1	.977	Y. Terry	27	133	6	10	0	4.21
	C	R. Partee	280	.243	2	41	326	40	4	5	4.4	.989	F. Barrett	38	90	8	7	8	3.69
	OF	L. Culberson	282	.238	2	21	182	6	4	2	2.7	.979							
	32	J. Bucher	277	.274	4	31	99	138	11	25		.956							
	C	H. Wagner	223	.332	1	38	299	29	10	4	5.3	.970							
	OF	T. McBride	216	.245	0	24	113	8	1	1	2.1	.992							
	1B	J. Cronin	191	.241	5	28	428	27	9	39	9.5	.981							
Cleveland	1B	M. Rocco	653	.266	13	70	1467	138	11	158	10.4	.993	S. Gromek	35	204	10	9	1	2.56
	2B	R. Mack	284	.232	0	29	226	243	24	73	5.9	.951	M. Harder	30	196	12	10	0	3.71
W-72 L-82	SS	L. Boudreau	584	.327	3	67	339	516	19	134	5.9	.978	A. Smith	28	182	7	13	0	3.42
	3B	K. Keltner	573	.295	13	91	168	369	18	37	3.7	.968	E. Klieman	47	178	11	13	5	3.38
Lou Boudreau	RF	Cullenbine	571	.284	16	80	275	15	10	6	2.0	.967	A. Reynolds	28	158	11	8	1	3.30
	CF	O. Hockett	457	.289	1	50	275	6	5	1	2.6	.983	J. Heving	63	119	8	3	10	1.96
	LF	P. Seerey	342	.234	15	39	196	8	3	1	2.4	.986	R. Poat	36	81	4	8	1	5.13
	C	B. Rosar	331	.263	0	30	409	59	5	13	4.8	.989							
	2B	R. Peters	282	.223	1	24	151	181	8	45	5.4	.976							
	OF	M. Hoag	277	.285	1	27	171	9	10*	3	2.9	.947							
	OF	P. O'Dea	173	.318	0	13	72	2	4	1	1.9	.949							
	OF	J. Heath	151	.331	5	33	76	4	4	2	2.3	.952							

AMERICAN LEAGUE 1944, *cont.*

	POS	Player	AB	BA	HR	RBI	PO	A	E	DP	TC/G	FA	Pitcher	G	IP	W	L	SV	ERA
Philadelphia	1B	B. McGhee	287	.289	1	19	701	46	8	51	10.1	.989	B. Newsom	37	265	13	15	1	2.82
	2B	I. Hall	559	.268	0	45	248	286	11	40	5.6	.980	Christopher	35	215	14	14	1	2.97
W-72 L-82	SS	E. Busch	484	.271	0	40	204	330	34	50	5.1	.940	L. Hamlin	29	190	6	12	0	3.74
	3B	G. Kell	514	.268	0	44	167	289	20	25	3.4	.958	J. Flores	27	186	9	11	0	3.39
Connie Mack	RF	J. White	267	.221	1	21	162	5	9	2	2.4	.949	D. Black	29	177	10	12	0	4.06
	CF	B. Estalella	506	.298	7	60	318	12	4	4	2.6	.988	L. Harris	23	174	10	9	0	3.30
	LF	F. Garrison	449	.269	4	37	289	6	4	0	2.5	.987	J. Berry	53	111	10	8	12	1.94
	C	F. Hayes	581	.248	13	78	**636**	**89**	13	10	4.8	.982							
	1O	D. Siebert	468	.306	6	52	759	53	10	60		.988							
	OF	H. Epps	229	.262	0	13	141	4	4	1	2.5	.973							
Chicago	1B	H. Trosky	497	.241	10	70	1310	57	9	122	**10.6**	.993	B. Dietrich	36	246	16	**17**	0	3.62
	2B	R. Schalk	587	.220	1	44	360	391	28	109	5.5	.964	O. Grove	34	235	14	15	0	3.72
W-71 L-83	SS	S. Webb	513	.211	0	30	202	461	39	81	5.2	.944	E. Lopat	27	210	11	10	0	3.26
	3B	R. Hodgin	465	.295	1	51	77	215	18	22	3.8	.942	J. Humphries	30	169	8	10	1	3.67
Jimmy Dykes	RF	W. Moses	535	.280	3	34	267	7	7	2	2.1	.975	J. Haynes	33	154	5	6	2	2.57
	CF	T. Tucker	446	.287	2	46	414	12	4	2	.991		T. Lee	15	113	3	9	0	3.02
	LF	E. Carnett	457	.276	1	60	199	7	11	0	2.5	.949	Maltzberger	46	91	10	5	12	2.96
	C	M. Tresh	312	.260	0	25	370	47	8	5	4.6	.981							
	OF	G. Curtright	198	.253	2	23	101	8	6	3	2.3	.948							
	3B	G. Clarke	169	.260	0	27	36	107	6	6	3.4	.941							
	OF	J. Dickshot	162	.253	3	15	72	3	2	1	1.9	.974							
Washington	1B	J. Kuhel	518	.278	4	51	1251	83	**17**	119	9.8	.987	D. Leonard	32	229	14	14	0	3.06
	2B	G. Myatt	538	.284	0	40	341	299	29	81	5.5	.957	M. Haefner	31	228	12	15	1	3.04
W-64 L-90	SS	J. Sullivan	471	.251	0	30	276	426	**50**	89	5.4	.934	E. Wynn	33	208	8	**17**	2	3.38
	3B	G. Torres	524	.267	0	58	120	297	21	25	3.6	.952	J. Niggeling	24	206	10	8	0	2.32
Ossie Bluege	RF	J. Powell	367	.240	1	37	196	5	4	0	2.3	.980	R. Wolff	33	155	4	15	2	4.99
	CF	S. Spence	592	.316	18	100	434	**29**	5	**9**	3.1	.989	Carrasquel	43	134	8	7	3	3.43
	LF	G. Case	465	.249	2	32	288	7	9	2	2.7	.970	M. Candini	28	103	6	7	1	4.11
	C	R. Ferrell	339	.277	0	25	403	71	9	8	5.0	.981							
	OF	R. Ortiz	316	.253	5	35	165	2	9	1	2.2	.949							
	C	M. Guerra	210	.281	1	29	211	32	10	8	4.4	.960							
	2B	F. Vaughn	109	.257	1	21	61	70	8	16	5.3	.942							

BATTING AND BASE RUNNING LEADERS

Batting Average
L. Boudreau, CLE	.327
B. Doerr, BOS	.325
B. Johnson, BOS	.324
Stirnweiss, NY	.319
S. Spence, WAS	.316

Slugging Average
B. Doerr, BOS	.528
B. Johnson, BOS	.528
J. Lindell, NY	.500
S. Spence, WAS	.486
N. Etten, NY	.466
K. Keltner, CLE	.466

Home Runs
N. Etten, NY	22
V. Stephens, STL	20
R. York, DET	18
S. Spence, WAS	18
J. Lindell, NY	18

Total Bases
J. Lindell, NY	297
Stirnweiss, NY	296
S. Spence, WAS	288
B. Johnson, BOS	277
N. Etten, NY	267
K. Keltner, CLE	267

Runs Batted In
V. Stephens, STL	109
B. Johnson, BOS	106
J. Lindell, NY	103
S. Spence, WAS	100
R. York, DET	98

Stolen Bases
Stirnweiss, NY	55
G. Case, WAS	49
G. Myatt, WAS	26
W. Moses, CHI	21
Gutteridge, STL	20

Hits
Stirnweiss, NY	205
L. Boudreau, CLE	191
S. Spence, WAS	187
J. Lindell, NY	178

Base on Balls
N. Etten, NY	97
B. Johnson, BOS	95
Cullenbine, CLE	87
G. McQuinn, STL	85

Home Run Percentage
P. Seerey, CLE	4.4
N. Etten, NY	3.8
V. Stephens, STL	3.6
B. Johnson, BOS	3.2

Runs Scored
Stirnweiss, NY	125
B. Johnson, BOS	106
Cullenbine, CLE	98
B. Doerr, BOS	95

Doubles
L. Boudreau, CLE	45
K. Keltner, CLE	41
B. Johnson, BOS	40
P. Fox, BOS	38

Triples
J. Lindell, NY	16
Stirnweiss, NY	16
Gutteridge, STL	11
B. Doerr, BOS	10

PITCHING LEADERS

Winning Percentage
T. Hughson, BOS	.783
H. Newhouser, DET	.763
N. Potter, STL	.731
D. Trout, DET	.659
H. Borowy, NY	.586

Earned Run Average
D. Trout, DET	2.12
H. Newhouser, DET	2.22
T. Hughson, BOS	2.26
J. Niggeling, WAS	2.32
J. Kramer, STL	2.49

Wins
H. Newhouser, DET	29
D. Trout, DET	27
N. Potter, STL	19
T. Hughson, BOS	18
H. Borowy, NY	17
J. Kramer, STL	17

Saves
J. Berry, PHI	12
Maltzberger, CHI	12
G. Caster, STL	12
J. Heving, CLE	10
F. Barrett, BOS	8

Strikeouts
H. Newhouser, DET	187
D. Trout, DET	144
B. Newsom, PHI	142
J. Kramer, STL	124
J. Niggeling, WAS	121

Complete Games
D. Trout, DET	33
H. Newhouser, DET	25
T. Hughson, BOS	19
E. Wynn, WAS	19
M. Dubiel, NY	19
H. Borowy, NY	19

Fewest Hits/9 Innings
S. Gromek, CLE	7.07
J. Niggeling, WAS	7.16
H. Newhouser, DET	7.61
T. Hughson, BOS	7.61

Shutouts
D. Trout, DET	7
H. Newhouser, DET	6
S. Jakucki, STL	4
R. Gentry, DET	4

Fewest Walks/9 Innings
L. Harris, PHI	1.34
D. Leonard, WAS	1.45
E. Bonham, NY	1.73
T. Hughson, BOS	1.81

Most Strikeouts/9 Inn.
H. Newhouser, DET	5.39
J. Niggeling, WAS	5.29
S. Gromek, CLE	5.08
T. Hughson, BOS	4.96

Innings
D. Trout, DET	352
H. Newhouser, DET	312
B. Newsom, PHI	265
J. Kramer, STL	257

Games Pitched
J. Heving, CLE	63
J. Berry, PHI	53
D. Trout, DET	49
H. Newhouser, DET	47

AMERICAN LEAGUE 1944, *cont.*

	W	L	PCT	GB	R	OR	Batting 2B	3B	HR	BA	SA	SB	Fielding E	DP	FA	Pitching CG	BB	SO	ShO	SV	ERA
St. Louis	89	65	.578	1	684	587	223	45	72	.252	.352	44	171	142	.972	71	469	**581**	16	17	3.17
Detroit	88	66	.571	1	658	581	220	44	60	.263	.354	61	190	184	.970	**87**	452	568	**20**	8	**3.09**
New York	83	71	.539	6	674	617	216	**74**	**96**	.264	**.387**	91	**156**	170	**.974**	78	532	529	9	13	3.39
Boston	77	77	.500	12	**739**	676	**277**	56	69	**.270**	.380	60	171	154	.972	58	592	524	5	17	3.82
Cleveland	72	82	.468	17	643	677	270	50	70	.266	.372	48	165	**192**	.974	48	621	524	7	**18**	3.65
Philadelphia	72	82	.468	17	525	594	169	47	36	.257	.327	42	176	127	.971	72	**390**	534	9	14	3.26
Chicago	71	83	.461	18	543	662	210	55	23	.247	.320	66	183	154	.970	64	420	481	5	17	3.58
Washington	64	90	.416	25	592	664	186	42	33	.261	.330	**127**	218	156	.964	83	475	503	12	11	3.49
					5058	5058	1771	413	459	.260	.353	539	1430	1279	.971	561	3951	4244	83	115	3.43

NATIONAL LEAGUE 1945

Chicago
W-98 L-56
Charlie Grimm

POS	Player	AB	BA	HR	RBI	PO	A	E	DP	TC/G	FA	Pitcher	G	IP	W	L	SV	ERA
1B	Cavarretta	498	**.355**	6	97	1149	77	9	83	10.3	.993	H. Wyse	38	278	22	10	0	2.68
2B	D. Johnson	557	.302	2	58	309	440	19	74	5.6	.975	C. Passeau	34	227	17	9	1	2.46
SS	L. Merullo	394	.239	2	37	209	336	30	49	4.9	.948	P. Derringer	35	214	16	11	4	3.45
3B	S. Hack	597	.323	2	43	**195**	312	13	27	**3.6**	**.975**	R. Prim	34	165	13	8	2	2.40
RF	B. Nicholson	559	.243	13	88	300	12	3	4	2.1	.990	H. Borowy	15	122	11	2	1	**2.13**
CF	A. Pafko	534	.298	12	110	371	11	2	0	2.7	**.995**	P. Erickson	28	108	7	4	3	3.32
LF	P. Lowrey	523	.283	7	89	280	17	4	1	2.2	.987	Vandenburg	30	95	6	3	2	3.49
C	Livingston	224	.254	2	23	263	27	3	2	4.3	.990							
UT	R. Hughes	222	.261	0	8	120	157	13	28		.955							
C	P. Gillespie	163	.288	3	25	161	20	2	1	4.1	.989							
1B	H. Becker	133	.286	2	27	222	12	0	21	8.4	1.000							

St. Louis
W-95 L-59
Billy Southworth

POS	Player	AB	BA	HR	RBI	PO	A	E	DP	TC/G	FA	Pitcher	G	IP	W	L	SV	ERA
1B	R. Sanders	537	.276	8	78	1259	90	**19**	113	9.6	.986	R. Barrett	36	247*	21*	9	0	2.74
2B	E. Verban	597	.278	0	72	398	406	18	95	5.3	**.978**	K. Burkhart	42	217	19	8	2	2.90
SS	M. Marion	430	.277	1	59	237	372	21	70	5.2	.967	B. Donnelly	31	166	8	10	2	3.52
3B	W. Kurowski	511	.323	21	102	172	235	15	28	3.2	.964	H. Brecheen	24	157	14	4	2	2.52
RF	J. Hopp	446	.289	3	44	244	5	5	2	2.4	.980	G. Dockins	31	126	8	6	0	3.21
CF	B. Adams	578	.292	20	101	382	9	9	3	2.9	.978	T. Wilks	18	98	4	7	0	2.93
LF	Schoendienst	565	.278	1	47	286	10	5	1	2.6	.983	J. Creel	26	87	5	4	2	4.14
C	K. O'Dea	307	.254	4	43	321	50	2	**14**	4.1	**.995**							
OF	A. Bergamo	304	.316	3	44	146	9	5	3	2.1	.969							
C	D. Rice	253	.261	1	28	284	39	2	6	4.2	.994							

Brooklyn
W-87 L-67
Leo Durocher

POS	Player	AB	BA	HR	RBI	PO	A	E	DP	TC/G	FA	Pitcher	G	IP	W	L	SV	ERA
1B	A. Galan	576	.307	9	92	558	34	7	53	9.1	.988	H. Gregg	42	254	18	13	2	3.47
2B	E. Stanky	555	.258	1	39	**429**	441	**34**	101	5.9	.962	V. Lombardi	38	204	10	11	4	3.31
SS	E. Basinski	336	.262	0	33	166	262	34	59	4.6	.926	C. Davis	24	150	10	10	0	3.25
3B	Bordagaray	273	.256	2	49	54	93	19	7	2.9	.886	A. Herring	22	124	7	4	2	3.48
RF	D. Walker	607	.300	8	**124**	346	18	3	4	2.4	.992	T. Seats	31	122	10	7	0	4.36
CF	G. Rosen	606	.325	12	75	392	7	3	1	2.9	.993	C. King	42	112	5	5	3	4.09
LF	L. Olmo	556	.313	10	110	225	8	7	2	2.3	.971	R. Branca	16	110	5	6	1	3.04
C	M. Sandlock	195	.282	2	17	196	20	2	3	4.6	.991	C. Buker	42	87	7	2	5	3.30
1B	E. Stevens	201	.274	4	29	478	38	7	40	9.5	.987	L. Webber	17	75	7	3	0	3.58
SS	T. Brown	196	.245	2	19	93	164	23	27	5.1	.918							
3B	B. Hart	161	.230	3	27	54	62	11	8	3.3	.913							

Pittsburgh
W-82 L-72
Frankie Frisch

POS	Player	AB	BA	HR	RBI	PO	A	E	DP	TC/G	FA	Pitcher	G	IP	W	L	SV	ERA
1B	B. Dahlgren	531	.250	5	75	1373	93	6	**115**	10.4	**.996**	P. Roe	33	235	14	13	1	2.87
2B	P. Coscarart	392	.242	8	38	257	361	14	74	5.2	.978	Strincevich	36	228	16	10	2	3.31
SS	F. Gustine	478	.280	2	66	177	291	**35**	52	4.8	.930	R. Sewell	33	188	11	9	1	4.07
3B	B. Elliott	541	.290	8	108	94	178	21	18	3.6	.928	M. Butcher	28	169	10	8	0	3.03
RF	J. Barrett	507	.256	15	67	318	8	8	0	2.5	.976	Gerheauser	32	140	5	10	1	3.91
CF	Gionfriddo	409	.284	2	42	235	6	9	2	2.4	.964	K. Gables	29	139	11	7	1	4.15
LF	J. Russell	510	.284	12	77	313	9	9	1	2.4	.973	X. Rescigno	44	79	3	5	9	5.72
C	A. Lopez	243	.218	0	18	326	38	3	7	4.0	.992							
3B	L. Handley	312	.298	1	32	85	183	15	13	3.6	.947							
C	B. Salkeld	267	.311	15	52	279	40	9	8	3.8	.973							
SS	V. Barnhart	201	.269	0	19	104	166	21	31	4.9	.928							
OF	T. O'Brien	161	.335	0	18	72	2	3	0	1.7	.961							
1O	F. Colman	153	.209	4	30	143	14	1	10		.994							

New York
W-78 L-74
Mel Ott

POS	Player	AB	BA	HR	RBI	PO	A	E	DP	TC/G	FA	Pitcher	G	IP	W	L	SV	ERA
1B	P. Weintraub	283	.272	10	42	774	60	6	49	10.9	.993	B. Voiselle	41	232	14	14	0	4.49
2B	G. Hausmann	623	.279	2	45	376	**489**	29	65	5.8	.968	H. Feldman	35	218	12	13	1	3.27
SS	B. Kerr	546	.249	4	40	**333**	**515**	32	**81**	5.9	.964	V. Mungo	26	183	14	7	0	3.20
3B	N. Reyes	431	.288	5	44	111	232	14	12	3.1	.961	J. Brewer	28	160	8	6	0	3.83
RF	M. Ott	451	.308	21	79	217	11	4	1	2.0	.983	A. Adams	65	113	11	9	15	3.42
CF	J. Rucker	429	.273	7	51	256	6	6	2	2.7	.978	S. Emmerich	31	100	4	4	0	4.86
LF	D. Gardella	430	.272	18	71	182	6	9	1	2.1	.954	A. Hansen	23	93	4	3	3	4.66
C	E. Lombardi	368	.307	19	70	**425**	49	8	8	**5.0**	.983	R. Fischer	31	77	3	8	1	5.63
OF	R. Treadway	224	.241	4	23	107	3	7	0	2.0	.940							
C	C. Kluttz	222	.279	4	21	195	32	5	5	4.1	.978							
3B	B. Jurges	176	.324	3	24	40	94	9	3	3.3	.937							

NATIONAL LEAGUE 1945, *cont.*

	POS	Player	AB	BA	HR	RBI	PO	A	E	DP	TC/G	FA	Pitcher	G	IP	W	L	SV	ERA
Boston	1B	V. Shupe	283	.269	0	15	650	53	8	81	9.2	.989	J. Tobin	27	197	9	14	0	3.84
	2B	Wietelmann	428	.271	4	33	222	232	13	58	5.4	.972	B. Logan	34	187	7	11	1	3.18
W-67 L-85	SS	D. Culler	527	.262	2	30	252	386	31	71	5.3	.954	J. Hutchings	57	185	7	6	3	3.75
	3B	C. Workman	514	.274	25	87	97	205	30	18	3.1	.910	N. Andrews	21	138	7	12	0	4.58
Bob Coleman	RF	T. Holmes	636	.352	28	117	334	13	6	4	2.3	.983	E. Wright	15	111	8	3	0	2.51
W-42 L-51	CF	Gillenwater	517	.288	7	72	451	24	10	5	3.5	.979	B. Lee	16	106	6	3	0	2.79
	LF	B. Nieman	247	.247	14	56	132	4	10	1	2.6	.932	M. Cooper	20	78	7	4	1	3.35
Del Bissonette	C	P. Masi	371	.272	7	46	335	52	8	7	4.2	.980	Hendrickson	37	73	4	8	5	4.91
W-25 L-34	1B	J. Mack	260	.231	0	44	635	48	6	48	10.6	.991							
	OF	J. Medwick	218	.284	0	26	78	7	0	2	2.2	1.000							
	C	S. Hofferth	170	.235	3	15	168	31	4	7	4.5	.980							
Cincinnati	1B	McCormick	580	.276	10	81	**1469**	**118**	9	104	**10.6**	.994	E. Heusser	31	223	11	16	1	3.71
	2B	W. Williams	482	.237	0	27	295	393	22	61	5.3	.969	J. Bowman	25	186	11	13	0	3.59
W-61 L-93	SS	E. Miller	421	.238	13	49	245	382	16	61	5.6	**.975**	B. Walters	22	168	10	10	0	2.68
	3B	S. Mesner	540	.254	1	52	170	**326**	15	**35**	3.5	.971	H. Fox	45	164	8	13	0	4.93
Bill McKechnie	RF	A. Libke	449	.283	4	53	223	13	9	6	2.3	.963	V. Kennedy	24	158	5	12	1	4.00
	CF	D. Clay	**656**	.280	1	50	446	10	5	3	3.0	.989							
	LF	E. Tipton	331	.242	5	34	192	2	6	1	2.4	.970							
	C	A. Lakeman	258	.256	8	31	226	31	10	4	3.6	.963							
	OF	G. Walker	316	.253	2	21	123	4	5	1	2.0	.962							
	C	A. Unser	204	.265	3	21	207	30	11	5	4.1	.956							
	2S	K. Wahl	194	.201	0	10	135	170	15	22		.953							
	OF	D. Sipek	156	.244	0	13	68	2	2	0	2.3	.972							
	OF	H. Sauer	116	.293	5	20	69	0	2	0	2.5	.972							
Philadelphia	1B	J. Wasdell	500	.300	7	60	597	43	7	51	10.3	.989	D. Barrett	36	191	7	**20**	1	5.43
	2B	F. Daniels	230	.200	0	10	171	215	18	41	5.4	.955	A. Karl	**67**	181	9	8	15	2.99
W-46 L-108	SS	B. Mott	289	.221	0	22	134	189	19	41	5.4	.944	C. Schanz	35	145	4	15	5	4.35
	3B	J. Antonelli	504	.256	1	28	129	201	14	24	3.2	.959	C. Sproull	34	130	4	10	1	5.94
Freddie Fitzsimmons	RF	V. Dinges	397	.287	1	36	132	10	2	5	2.2	.986	D. Mauney	20	123	6	10	1	3.08
W-18 L-51	CF	V. DiMaggio	452	.257	19	84	337	16	2	4	2.9	.994	O. Judd	23	83	5	4	2	3.81
	LF	C. Triplett	363	.240	7	46	202	3	**12**	1	2.4	.945	T. Kraus	19	82	4	9	0	5.40
Ben Chapman	C	A. Seminick	188	.239	6	26	198	30	5	3	3.3	.979							
W-28 L-57	UT	G. Crawford	302	.295	2	24	152	148	17	18		.946							
	UT	J. Foxx	224	.268	7	38	304	54	8	19		.978							
	OF	Monteagudo	193	.301	0	11	61	6	6	2	2.1	.918							
	C	G. Mancuso	176	.199	0	16	215	34	3	4	3.6	.988							
	OF	J. Powell	173	.231	1	14	67	5	1	2	1.7	.986							
	SS	W. Flager	168	.250	2	15	98	145	14	25	5.4	.946							

BATTING AND BASE RUNNING LEADERS

Batting Average
Cavarretta, CHI	.355
T. Holmes, BOS	.352
G. Rosen, BKN	.325
S. Hack, CHI	.323
W. Kurowski, STL	.323

Slugging Average
T. Holmes, BOS	.577
W. Kurowski, STL	.511
Cavarretta, CHI	.500
M. Ott, NY	.499
L. Olmo, BKN	.462

Home Runs
T. Holmes, BOS	28
C. Workman, BOS	25
B. Adams, PHI, STL	22
M. Ott, NY	21
W. Kurowski, STL	21

Total Bases
T. Holmes, BOS	367
G. Rosen, BKN	279
B. Adams, PHI, STL	279
D. Walker, BKN	266
W. Kurowski, STL	261

Runs Batted In
D. Walker, BKN	124
T. Holmes, BOS	117
A. Pafko, CHI	110
L. Olmo, BKN	110
B. Adams, PHI, STL	109

Stolen Bases
Schoendienst, STL	26
J. Barrett, PIT	25
D. Clay, CIN	19
J. Russell, PIT	15
L. Olmo, BKN	15
T. Holmes, BOS	15

Hits
T. Holmes, BOS	224
G. Rosen, BKN	197
S. Hack, CHI	193
D. Clay, CIN	184

Base on Balls
E. Stanky, BKN	148
A. Galan, BKN	114
S. Hack, CHI	99
B. Nicholson, CHI	92

Home Run Percentage
C. Workman, BOS	4.9
M. Ott, NY	4.7
T. Holmes, BOS	4.4
V. DiMaggio, PHI	4.2

Runs Scored
E. Stanky, BKN	128
G. Rosen, BKN	126
T. Holmes, BOS	125
A. Galan, BKN	114

Doubles
T. Holmes, BOS	47
D. Walker, BKN	42
B. Elliott, PIT	36
A. Galan, BKN	36

Triples
L. Olmo, BKN	13
A. Pafko, CHI	12
J. Rucker, NY	11
G. Rosen, BKN	11

PITCHING LEADERS

Winning Percentage
K. Burkhart, STL	.704
H. Wyse, CHI	.688
R. Barrett, BOS, STL	.657
C. Passeau, CHI	.654
Strincevich, PIT	.615

Earned Run Average
H. Borowy, CHI	2.13
C. Passeau, CHI	2.46
H. Brecheen, STL	2.52
B. Walters, CIN	2.68
H. Wyse, CHI	2.68

Wins
R. Barrett, BOS, STL	23
H. Wyse, CHI	22
K. Burkhart, STL	19
H. Gregg, BKN	18
C. Passeau, CHI	17

Saves
A. Adams, NY	15
A. Karl, PHI	15
X. Rescigno, PIT	9
Hendrickson, BOS	5
C. Buker, BKN	5
C. Schanz, PHI	5

Strikeouts
P. Roe, PIT	148
H. Gregg, BKN	139
B. Voiselle, NY	115
V. Mungo, NY	101
J. Hutchings, BOS	99

Complete Games
R. Barrett, BOS, STL	24
H. Wyse, CHI	23
C. Passeau, CHI	19
Strincevich, PIT	18
E. Heusser, CIN	18

Fewest Hits/9 Innings
H. Borowy, CHI	7.72
H. Brecheen, STL	7.78
H. Gregg, BKN	7.82
C. Passeau, CHI	8.13

Shutouts
C. Passeau, CHI	5
K. Burkhart, STL	4
B. Donnelly, STL	4
E. Heusser, CIN	4

Fewest Walks/9 Innings
C. Davis, BKN	1.26
R. Barrett, BOS, STL	1.71
P. Roe, PIT	1.76
H. Wyse, CHI	1.78

Most Strikeouts/9 Inn.
P. Roe, PIT	5.67
H. Gregg, BKN	4.92
B. Voiselle, NY	4.45
C. Passeau, CHI	3.89

Innings
R. Barrett, BOS, STL	285
H. Wyse, CHI	278
H. Gregg, BKN	254
P. Roe, PIT	235

Games Pitched
A. Karl, PHI	67
A. Adams, NY	65
J. Hutchings, BOS	57
R. Barrett, BOS, STL	45

NATIONAL LEAGUE 1945, *cont.*

	W	L	PCT	GB	R	OR	Batting 2B	3B	HR	BA	SA	SB	Fielding E	DP	FA	Pitching CG	BB	SO	ShO	SV	ERA
Chicago	98	56	.636		735	**532**	229	52	57	**.277**	.372	69	**121**	124	**.980**	**86**	385	541	15	14	**2.98**
St. Louis	95	59	.617	3	756	583	256	44	64	.273	.371	55	137	150	.977	77	497	510	**18**	9	3.24
Brooklyn	87	67	.565	11	**795**	724	257	**71**	57	.271	.376	75	230	144	.962	61	586	**557**	7	18	3.70
Pittsburgh	82	72	.532	16	753	686	**259**	56	72	.267	.377	81	178	141	.971	73	455	518	8	16	3.76
New York	78	74	.513	19	668	700	175	35	**114**	.269	**.379**	38	166	112	.973	53	529	530	13	21	4.06
Boston	67	85	.441	30	721	728	229	25	101	.267	.374	**82**	193	**160**	.969	57	557	404	7	13	4.04
Cincinnati	61	93	.396	37	536	694	221	26	56	.249	.333	71	146	138	.976	77	534	372	11	6	4.00
Philadelphia	46	108	.299	52	548	865	197	27	56	.246	.326	54	234	150	.962	31	608	433	4	**26**	4.64
					5512	5512	1823	336	577	.265	.364	525	1405	1119	.971	515	4151	3865	83	123	3.80

AMERICAN LEAGUE 1945

Detroit
W-88 L-65
Steve O'Neill

POS	Player	AB	BA	HR	RBI	PO	A	E	DP	TC/G	FA	Pitcher	G	IP	W	L	SV	ERA
1B	R. York	595	.264	18	87	**1464**	113	19	142	10.3	.988	H. Newhouser	40	**313**	**25**	9	2	**1.81**
2B	E. Mayo	501	.285	10	54	326	393	15	91	5.9	**.980**	D. Trout	41	246	18	15	2	3.14
SS	S. Webb	407	.199	0	21	215	343	25	71	5.6	.957	A. Benton	31	192	13	8	3	2.02
3B	B. Maier	486	.263	1	34	142	226	25	19	3.2	.936	S. Overmire	31	162	9	9	4	3.88
RF	Cullenbine	523	.277	18	93	321	23*	7	3	2.4	.980	L. Mueller	26	135	6	8	1	3.68
CF	D. Cramer	541	.275	6	58	314	7	3	4	2.3	**.991**	J. Tobin	14	58	4	5	1	3.55
LF	J. Outlaw	446	.271	0	34	192	13	7	**6**	2.0	.967							
C	B. Swift	279	.233	0	24	358	60	5	12	4.5	.988							
OF	H. Greenberg	270	.311	13	60	129	3	0	0	1.8	1.000							
C	P. Richards	234	.256	3	32	361	44	2	7	4.9	.995							
SS	J. Hoover	222	.257	1	17	126	163	17	35	4.5	.944							

Washington
W-87 L-67
Ossie Bluege

POS	Player	AB	BA	HR	RBI	PO	A	E	DP	TC/G	FA	Pitcher	G	IP	W	L	SV	ERA
1B	J. Kuhel	533	.285	2	75	1323	94	16	101	10.2	.989	R. Wolff	33	250	20	10	2	2.12
2B	G. Myatt	490	.296	1	39	228	231	13	48	5.6	.972	M. Haefner	37	238	16	14	3	3.47
SS	G. Torres	562	.237	0	48	**272**	437	35	65	5.1	.953	M. Pieretti	44	233	14	13	2	3.32
3B	H. Clift	375	.211	8	53	111	214	23	18	3.1	.934	D. Leonard	31	216	17	7	1	2.13
RF	B. Lewis	258	.333	2	37	151	8	3	3	2.3	.981	J. Niggeling	26	177	7	12	0	3.16
CF	G. Binks	550	.278	6	81	321	13	8	4	2.7	.977	Carrasquel	35	123	7	5	1	2.71
LF	G. Case	504	.294	1	31	316	17	7	3	2.8	.979							
C	R. Ferrell	286	.266	1	38	331	64	4	3	4.8	.990							
2B	F. Vaughn	268	.235	1	25	177	189	21	35	5.1	.946							
OF	M. Kreevich	158	.278	1	23	98	2	3	0	2.6*	.971							

St. Louis
W-81 L-70
Luke Sewell

POS	Player	AB	BA	HR	RBI	PO	A	E	DP	TC/G	FA	Pitcher	G	IP	W	L	SV	ERA
1B	G. McQuinn	483	.277	7	61	1143	105	11	87	9.3	.991	N. Potter	32	255	15	11	0	2.47
2B	Gutteridge	543	.238	2	49	334	334	21	66	5.4	.970	J. Kramer	29	193	10	15	2	3.36
SS	V. Stephens	571	.289	**24**	89	256	439	28	69	5.0	.961	S. Jakucki	30	192	12	10	2	3.51
3B	M. Christman	289	.277	4	34	79	137	6	12	2.9	.973	T. Shirley	32	184	8	12	0	3.63
RF	G. Moore	354	.260	5	50	184	10	6	0	2.0	.970	Hollingsworth	26	173	12	9	1	2.70
CF	M. Kreevich	295	.237	2	21	230	4	2	0	3.0*	.992	B. Muncrief	27	146	13	4	1	2.72
LF	M. Byrnes	442	.249	8	59	319	12	4	0	2.7	.988							
C	F. Mancuso	365	.268	1	38	467	55	6	10	4.6	.989							
UT	L. Schulte	430	.247	0	36	167	245	23	24		.947							
OF	P. Gray	234	.218	0	13	162	3	7	1	2.8	.959							
O1	L. Finney	213	.277	2	22	233	18	2	14		.992							
OF	B. Martin	185	.200	2	16	116	7	1	2	2.6	.992							
C	R. Hayworth	160	.194	0	17	216	23	2	5	4.4	.992							

New York
W-81 L-71
Joe McCarthy

POS	Player	AB	BA	HR	RBI	PO	A	E	DP	TC/G	FA	Pitcher	G	IP	W	L	SV	ERA
1B	N. Etten	565	.285	18	**111**	1401	94	17	**149**	9.9	.989	B. Bevens	29	184	13	9	0	3.67
2B	Stirnweiss	632	**.309**	10	64	432	492	29	119	6.3	.970	E. Bonham	23	181	8	11	0	3.29
SS	F. Crosetti	441	.238	4	48	264	380	37	86	5.4	.946	A. Gettel	27	155	9	8	3	3.90
3B	O. Grimes	480	.265	4	45	162	296	**31**	35	3.5	.937	M. Dubiel	26	151	10	9	0	4.64
RF	B. Metheny	509	.248	8	53	227	12	4	2	1.9	.984	H. Borowy	18	132	10	5	0	3.13
CF	T. Stainback	327	.257	5	32	233	10	8	**6**	3.0	.968	B. Zuber	21	127	5	11	0	3.19
LF	H. Martin	408	.267	7	53	233	8	4	1	2.4	.984	J. Page	20	102	6	3	0	2.82
C	M. Garbark	176	.216	1	26	202	41	7	10	4.2	.972	R. Ruffing	11	87	7	3	0	2.89
OF	R. Derry	253	.225	13	45	170	4	4	2	2.6	.978	J. Turner	30	54	3	4	10	3.64
OF	C. Keller	163	.301	10	34	110	4	0	2	2.6	1.000							
C	A. Robinson	160	.281	8	24	186	16	0	3	4.5	1.000							
OF	J. Lindell	159	.283	1	20	108	2	2	0	2.7	.982							

Cleveland
W-73 L-72
Lou Boudreau

POS	Player	AB	BA	HR	RBI	PO	A	E	DP	TC/G	FA	Pitcher	G	IP	W	L	SV	ERA
1B	M. Rocco	565	.264	10	56	1203	115	10	112	9.4	**.992**	S. Gromek	33	251	19	9	1	2.55
2B	D. Meyer	524	.292	7	48	317	313	14	66	5.0	.978	A. Reynolds	44	247	18	12	4	3.20
SS	L. Boudreau	346	.306	3	48	217	289	9	73	5.3	.983	J. Bagby	25	159	8	11	1	3.73
3B	D. Ross	363	.262	2	43	119	175	13	14	2.9	.958	A. Smith	21	134	5	12	1	3.84
RF	P. Seerey	414	.237	14	56	227	7	6	3	2.1	.975	E. Klieman	38	126	5	8	4	3.85
CF	Mackiewicz	359	.273	2	37	288	11	4	4	2.7	.987	P. Center	31	86	6	3	1	3.99
LF	J. Heath	370	.305	15	61	214	3	6	1	2.2	.973	M. Harder	11	76	3	7	0	3.67
C	F. Hayes	385	.236	6	43	508*	63	7	23*	4.9*	.988*							
UT	A. Cihocki	283	.212	0	24	154	208	15	42		.960							
OF	P. O'Dea	221	.235	1	21	118	4	1	2	2.3	.992							
OF	L. Fleming	140	.329	3	22	59	2	4	2	2.0	.938							

AMERICAN LEAGUE 1945, cont.

	POS	Player	AB	BA	HR	RBI	PO	A	E	DP	TC/G	FA	Pitcher	G	IP	W	L	SV	ERA
Chicago	1B	K. Farrell	396	.258	0	34	913	74	11	76	10.3	.989	T. Lee	29	228	15	12	0	2.44
	2B	R. Schalk	513	.248	1	65	380	389	18	90	5.9	.977	O. Grove	33	217	14	12	1	3.44
W-71 L-78	SS	C. Michaels	445	.245	2	54	259	426	47	74	5.8	.936	E. Lopat	26	199	10	13	1	4.11
	3B	Cuccinello	402	.308	2	49	73	221	20	22	2.8	.936	J. Humphries	22	153	6	14	1	4.24
Jimmy Dykes	RF	W. Moses	569	.295	2	50	329	12	8	1	2.5	.977	B. Dietrich	18	122	7	10	0	4.19
	CF	O. Hockett	417	.293	2	55	273	7	5	3	2.7	.982	E. Caldwell	27	105	6	7	4	3.59
	LF	J. Dickshot	486	.302	4	58	253	13	8	3	2.2	.971	J. Haynes	14	104	5	5	1	3.55
	C	M. Tresh	458	.249	0	47	575	102	11	7	4.6	.984							
	OF	G. Curtright	324	.281	4	32	196	8	3	0	2.5	.986							
	1B	B. Nagel	220	.209	3	27	503	34	9	42	9.6	.984							
	3B	F. Baker	208	.250	0	19	36	99	4	6	2.4	.971							
Boston	1B	C. Metkovich	539	.260	5	62	935	76	15	96	10.6	.985	B. Ferriss	35	265	21	10	2	2.96
	2B	S. Newsome	438	.290	1	48	206	231	17	54	5.5	.963	J. Wilson	23	144	6	8	0	3.30
W-71 L-83	SS	E. Lake	473	.279	11	51	265	459	40	112	5.9	.948	E. O'Neill	24	142	8	11	0	5.15
	3B	J. Tobin	278	.252	0	21	82	151	12	17	3.4	.951	C. Hausmann	31	125	5	7	2	5.04
Joe Cronin	RF	J. Lazor	335	.310	5	45	141	6	6	0	1.9	.961	M. Ryba	34	123	7	6	2	2.49
	CF	L. Culberson	331	.275	6	45	219	14	8	6	2.6	.967	P. Woods	24	107	4	7	2	4.19
	LF	B. Johnson	529	.280	12	74	296	15	8	4	2.3	.975	R. Heflin	20	102	4	10	0	4.06
	C	B. Garbark	199	.261	0	17	249	31	2	9	4.2	.993	F. Barrett	37	86	4	3	3	2.62
	OF	T. McBride	344	.305	1	47	180	10	3	4	2.4	.984	V. Johnson	26	85	6	4	2	4.01
	2B	B. Steiner	304	.257	3	20	202	213	14	63	5.6	.967							
	OF	P. Fox	208	.245	0	20	84	5	1	1	1.6	.989							
	3B	T. LaForest	204	.250	2	16	45	97	5	11	3.3	.966							
	1B	D. Camilli	198	.212	2	19	505	44	5	62	10.3	.991							
Philadelphia	1B	D. Siebert	573	.267	7	51	1427	135	14	129	10.7	.991	B. Newsom	36	257	8	20	0	3.29
	2B	I. Hall	616	.261	0	50	422	498	21	108	6.2	.978	Christopher	33	227	13	13	2	3.17
W-52 L-98	SS	E. Busch	416	.250	0	35	209	370	29	67	5.2	.952	J. Flores	29	191	7	10	1	3.43
	3B	G. Kell	567	.272	4	56	186	345	20	32	3.7	.964	L. Knerr	27	130	5	11	0	4.22
Connie Mack	RF	H. Peck	449	.276	5	39	190	9	12	3	1.9	.943	J. Berry	52	130	8	7	5	2.35
	CF	B. Estalella	451	.299	8	52	314	10	4	3	2.6	.988	D. Black	26	125	5	11	0	5.17
	LF	C. Metro	200	.210	3	15	100	5	3	0	1.9	.972	C. Gassaway	24	118	4	7	0	3.74
	C	B. Rosar	300	.210	1	25	338	54	5	6	4.7	.987	S. Gerkin	21	102	0	12	0	3.62
	OF	B. McGhee	250	.252	0	19	84	2	1	0	1.8	.989							
	OF	M. Smith	203	.212	0	11	120	4	3	0	2.0	.976							
	SS	B. Wilkins	154	.260	0	4	74	118	16	23	5.2	.923							

BATTING AND BASE RUNNING LEADERS

Batting Average
Stirnweiss, NY	.309
Cuccinello, CHI	.308
J. Dickshot, CHI	.302
B. Estalella, PHI	.299
G. Myatt, WAS	.296

Slugging Average
Stirnweiss, NY	.476
V. Stephens, STL	.473
Cullenbine, CLE, DET	.444
N. Etten, NY	.437
B. Estalella, PHI	.435

Home Runs
V. Stephens, STL	24
Cullenbine, CLE, DET	18
N. Etten, NY	18
R. York, DET	18
J. Heath, CLE	15

Total Bases
Stirnweiss, NY	301
V. Stephens, STL	270
N. Etten, NY	247
R. York, DET	246
W. Moses, CHI	239

Runs Batted In
N. Etten, NY	111
Cullenbine, CLE, DET	93
V. Stephens, STL	89
R. York, DET	87
G. Binks, WAS	81

Stolen Bases
Stirnweiss, NY	33
G. Myatt, WAS	30
G. Case, WAS	30
C. Metkovich, BOS	19
J. Dickshot, CHI	18

Hits
Stirnweiss, NY	195
W. Moses, CHI	168
V. Stephens, STL	165
N. Etten, NY	161

Base on Balls
Cullenbine, CLE, DET	112
E. Lake, BOS	106
O. Grimes, NY	97
N. Etten, NY	90

Home Run Percentage
V. Stephens, STL	4.2
P. Seerey, CLE	3.4
Cullenbine, CLE, DET	3.4
N. Etten, NY	3.2

Runs Scored
Stirnweiss, NY	107
V. Stephens, STL	90
Cullenbine, CLE, DET	83
E. Lake, BOS	81

Doubles
W. Moses, CHI	35
G. Binks, WAS	32
Stirnweiss, NY	32
G. McQuinn, STL	31

Triples
Stirnweiss, NY	22
W. Moses, CHI	15
J. Kuhel, WAS	13
J. Dickshot, CHI	10

PITCHING LEADERS

Winning Percentage
H. Newhouser, DET	.735
D. Leonard, WAS	.708
S. Gromek, CLE	.679
B. Ferriss, BOS	.677
R. Wolff, WAS	.667

Earned Run Average
H. Newhouser, DET	1.81
A. Benton, DET	2.02
R. Wolff, WAS	2.12
D. Leonard, WAS	2.13
T. Lee, CHI	2.44

Wins
H. Newhouser, DET	25
B. Ferriss, BOS	21
R. Wolff, WAS	20
S. Gromek, CLE	19
A. Reynolds, CLE	18
D. Trout, DET	18

Saves
J. Turner, NY	10
J. Berry, PHI	5

Strikeouts
H. Newhouser, DET	212
N. Potter, STL	129
B. Newsom, PHI	127
A. Reynolds, CLE	112
T. Lee, CHI	108
R. Wolff, WAS	108

Complete Games
H. Newhouser, DET	29
B. Ferriss, BOS	26
R. Wolff, WAS	21
S. Gromek, CLE	21
N. Potter, STL	21

Fewest Hits/9 Innings
H. Newhouser, DET	6.86
R. Wolff, WAS	7.20
N. Potter, STL	7.47
B. Muncrief, STL	8.16

Shutouts
H. Newhouser, DET	8
A. Benton, DET	5
B. Ferriss, BOS	5

Fewest Walks/9 Innings
E. Bonham, NY	1.10
D. Leonard, WAS	1.46
R. Wolff, WAS	1.91
S. Gromek, CLE	2.37

Most Strikeouts/9 Inn.
H. Newhouser, DET	6.09
J. Kramer, STL	4.62
N. Potter, STL	4.55
B. Newsom, PHI	4.44

Innings
H. Newhouser, DET	313
B. Ferriss, BOS	265
B. Newsom, PHI	257
N. Potter, STL	255

Games Pitched
J. Berry, PHI	52
A. Reynolds, CLE	44
M. Pieretti, WAS	44
D. Trout, DET	41

AMERICAN LEAGUE 1945, cont.

	W	L	PCT	GB	R	OR	Batting 2B	3B	HR	BA	SA	SB	Fielding E	DP	FA	Pitching CG	BB	SO	ShO	SV	ERA
Detroit	88	65	.575		633	565	**227**	47	77	.256	.361	60	158	173	.975	78	538	**588**	19	16	2.99
Washington	87	67	.565	1.5	622	562	197	**63**	27	.258	.334	**110**	183	124	.970	82	**440**	550	19	11	**2.92**
St. Louis	81	70	.536	6	597	548	215	37	63	.249	.341	25	143	123	.976	**91**	506	570	10	8	3.14
New York	81	71	.533	6.5	**676**	606	189	61	**93**	.259	**.373**	64	175	170	.971	78	485	474	9	14	3.45
Cleveland	73	72	.503	11	557	**548**	216	48	65	.255	.359	19	**126**	149	**.977**	76	501	497	14	12	3.31
Chicago	71	78	.477	15	596	633	204	55	22	**.262**	.337	78	180	139	.970	84	448	486	13	13	3.69
Boston	71	83	.461	17.5	599	674	225	44	50	.260	.346	72	169	198	.973	71	656	490	15	13	3.80
Philadelphia	52	98	.347	34.5	494	638	201	37	33	.245	.316	25	168	160	.973	65	571	531	11	8	3.62
					4774	4774	1674	392	430	.255	.346	453	1302	1236	.973	625	4145	4186	110	95	3.36

NATIONAL LEAGUE 1946

	POS	Player	AB	BA	HR	RBI	PO	A	E	DP	TC/G	FA	Pitcher	G	IP	W	L	SV	ERA
St. Louis W-98 L-58 Eddie Dyer	1B	S. Musial	**624**	**.365**	16	103	1056	65	13	119	9.9	.989	H. Pollet	40	**266**	**21**	10	5	**2.10**
	2B	Schoendienst	606	.281	0	34	340	354	11	87	5.5	**.984**	H. Brecheen	36	231	15	15	3	2.49
	SS	M. Marion	498	.233	3	46	**290**	359	17	**105**	5.5	.973	M. Dickson	47	184	15	6	1	2.88
	3B	W. Kurowski	519	.301	14	89	175	249	15	17	3.2	.966	A. Brazle	37	153	11	10	0	3.29
	RF	E. Slaughter	609	.300	18	**130**	284	23	6	6	2.0	.981	J. Beazley	19	103	7	5	0	4.46
	CF	H. Walker	346	.237	3	27	215	11	6	2	1.7	.974	K. Burkhart	25	100	6	3	2	2.88
	LF	E. Dusak	275	.240	9	42	139	12	1	1	2.0	.993							
	C	J. Garagiola	211	.237	3	22	260	25	3	6	4.1	.990							
	OF	T. Moore	278	.263	3	28	158	5	3	0	2.5	.982							
	1O	D. Sisler	235	.260	3	42	334	31	6	31		.984							
	OF	B. Adams	173	.185	5	22	95	1	1	1	1.7	.990							
Brooklyn W-96 L-60 Leo Durocher	1B	E. Stevens	310	.242	10	60	716	48	11	59	7.8	.986	J. Hatten	42	222	14	11	2	2.84
	2B	E. Stanky	483	.273	0	36	**356**	359	17	**88**	5.2	.977	K. Higbe	42	211	17	8	1	3.03
	SS	P. Reese	542	.284	5	60	285	463	26	104	5.1	.966	V. Lombardi	41	193	13	10	3	2.89
	3B	C. Lavagetto	242	.236	3	27	70	108	14	11	2.9	.927	H. Behrman	47	151	11	5	4	2.93
	RF	D. Walker	576	.319	9	116	237	15	8	3	1.7	.969	H. Gregg	26	117	6	4	2	2.99
	CF	C. Furillo	335	.284	3	35	292	9	5	4	2.7	.984	R. Melton	24	100	6	3	1	1.99
	LF	P. Reiser	423	.277	11	73	205	14	5	2	2.3	.978	H. Casey	46	100	11	5	5	1.99
	C	B. Edwards	292	.267	1	25	431	53	9	9	**5.4**	.982	A. Herring	35	86	7	2	5	3.35
	UT	A. Galan	274	.310	3	38	211	44	16	3		.941							
	OF	D. Whitman	265	.260	2	31	178	5	0	0	2.2	1.000							
	1B	H. Schultz	249	.253	3	27	576	58	7	65	7.4	.989							
	C	F. Anderson	199	.256	2	14	258	35	11	5	4.3	.964							
	32	B. Herman	184	.288	0	28	73	91	5	13		.970							
Chicago W-82 L-71 Charlie Grimm	1B	E. Waitkus	441	.304	4	55	992	81	4	76	10.2	.996	J. Schmitz	41	224	11	11	2	2.61
	2B	D. Johnson	314	.242	1	19	192	228	8	34	5.2	.981	H. Wyse	40	201	14	12	1	2.68
	SS	B. Jurges	221	.222	0	17	119	204	8	26	4.5	.976	H. Borowy	32	201	12	10	0	3.76
	3B	S. Hack	323	.285	0	26	102	168	9	6	3.1	.968	P. Erickson	32	137	9	7	0	2.43
	RF	Cavarretta	510	.294	8	78	196	7	7	2	2.4	.967	C. Passeau	21	129	9	8	0	3.13
	CF	P. Lowrey	540	.257	4	54	308	15	7	3	2.6	.979	E. Kush	40	130	9	2	3	3.05
	LF	M. Rickert	392	.263	7	47	200	5	6	1	2.0	.972	B. Chipman	34	109	6	5	2	3.13
	C	McCullough	307	.287	4	34	390	40	4	4	4.9	.991	H. Bithorn	26	87	6	5	1	3.84
	OF	B. Nicholson	296	.220	8	41	179	4	5	1	2.4	.973							
	SS	B. Sturgeon	294	.296	1	21	109	158	19	31	4.0	.934							
	OF	A. Pafko	234	.282	3	39	165	13	4	4	2.8	.978							
	2B	L. Stringer	209	.244	3	19	135	150	13	17	4.8	.956							
	C	Livingston	176	.256	2	20	239	25	5	3	4.8	.981							
	3B	J. Ostrowski	160	.213	3	12	33	80	8	5	2.4	.934							
Boston W-81 L-72 Billy Southworth	1B	R. Sanders	259	.243	6	35	659	61	9	57	9.5	.988	J. Sain	37	265	20	14	2	2.21
	2B	C. Ryan	502	.241	1	48	285	317	20	53	5.2	.968	M. Cooper	28	199	13	11	1	3.12
	SS	D. Culler	482	.255	0	33	279	380	36	68	5.3	.948	E. Wright	36	176	12	9	0	3.52
	3B	N. Fernandez	372	.255	2	42	83	150	15	10	3.1	.940	B. Lee	25	140	10	9	0	4.18
	RF	T. Holmes	568	.310	6	79	294	17	4	**7**	2.2	.987	S. Johnson	28	127	6	5	1	2.76
	CF	Gillenwater	224	.228	1	14	180	6	4	2	2.4	.979	W. Spahn	24	126	8	5	1	2.94
	LF	B. Rowell	293	.280	3	11	168	8	4	2	2.1	.978							
	C	P. Masi	397	.267	3	62	**470**	56	10	5	4.3	.981							
	1O	J. Hopp	445	.333	3	48	670	45	11	45		.985							
	UT	B. Herman	252	.306	3	22	279	116	11	48		.973							
	OF	D. Litwhiler	247	.291	4	38	128	2	2	0	2.0	.985							
	3B	S. Roberge	169	.231	2	20	63	80	4	11	3.1	.973							
	OF	McCormick	164	.262	1	16	109	1	3	0	2.4	.973							
	C	D. Padgett	98	.255	2	21	65	12	5	1	3.2	.939							

NATIONAL LEAGUE 1946, *cont.*

	POS	Player	AB	BA	HR	RBI	PO	A	E	DP	TC/G	FA	Pitcher	G	IP	W	L	SV	ERA
Philadelphia	1B	McCormick	504	.284	11	66	1185	98	1	92	9.6	.999	Raffensberger	39	196	8	15	6	3.63
	2B	E. Verban	473	.275	0	34	353	381*	28*	83	5.5	.963	O. Judd	30	173	11	12	2	3.53
W-69 L-85	SS	S. Newsome	375	.232	1	23	179	310	23	53	4.8	.955	S. Rowe	17	136	11	4	0	2.12
	3B	J. Tabor	463	.268	10	50	156	221	18	17	3.2	.954	C. Schanz	32	116	6	6	4	5.80
Ben Chapman	RF	R. Northey	438	.249	16	62	194	7	6	3	1.9	.971	T. Hughes	29	111	6	9	1	4.38
	CF	J. Wyrostek	545	.281	6	45	388	18	8	4	2.9	.981	D. Mauney	24	90	6	4	2	2.70
	LF	D. Ennis	540	.313	17	73	332	16	9	4	2.6	.975	A. Karl	39	65	3	7	5	4.96
	C	A. Seminick	406	.264	12	52	461	61	14	12	4.5	.974							
	UT	R. Hughes	276	.236	0	22	123	144	11	27		.960							
	OF	C. Gilbert	260	.242	1	17	154	9	0	4	2.4	1.000							
Cincinnati	1B	B. Haas	535	.264	3	50	1346	91	9	140	11.0	.994	Vander Meer	29	204	10	12	0	3.17
	2B	B. Adams	311	.244	4	24	190	251	15	67	6.2	.967	E. Blackwell	33	194	9	13	0	2.45
W-67 L-87	SS	E. Miller	299	.194	6	36	184	297	15	79	5.6	.970	J. Beggs	28	190	12	10	1	2.32
	3B	G. Hatton	436	.271	14	69	108	194	19	14	2.8	.941	E. Heusser	29	168	7	14	0	3.22
Bill McKechnie	RF	A. Libke	431	.253	5	42	191	14	6	4	1.8	.972	B. Walters	22	151	10	7	0	2.56
	CF	D. Clay	435	.228	2	22	312	10	4	3	2.7	.988	J. Hetki	32	126	6	6	1	2.99
	LF	E. Lukon	312	.250	12	34	190	5	3	1	2.4	.985	H. Gumbert	36	119	6	8	4	3.24
	C	R. Mueller	378	.254	8	48	405	65	3	12	4.7	.994							
	20	L. Frey	333	.246	3	24	210	176	15	33		.963							
	23	B. Zientara	280	.289	0	16	114	219	11	38		.968							
	SS	C. Corbitt	274	.248	1	16	126	229	20	45	4.9	.947							
	C	R. Lamanno	239	.243	1	30	222	37	7	6	4.4	.974							
	OF	M. West	202	.213	5	18	112	6	6	3	2.1	.952							
Pittsburgh	1B	E. Fletcher	532	.256	4	66	1356	106	8	97	10.0	.995	Ostermueller	27	193	13	10	0	2.84
	2B	F. Gustine	495	.259	8	52	290	328	21	61	5.7	.967	Strincevich	32	176	10	15	1	3.58
W-63 L-91	SS	B. Cox	411	.290	2	36	235	323	39	59	5.2	.935	Heintzelman	32	158	8	12	1	3.77
	3B	L. Handley	416	.238	1	28	107	237	15	13	3.5	.958	R. Sewell	25	149	8	12	0	3.68
Frankie Frisch	RF	B. Elliott	486	.263	5	68	188	8	1	5	2.1	.995	E. Bahr	27	137	8	6	0	2.63
W-62 L-89	CF	J. Russell	516	.277	8	50	308	7	11	1	2.4	.966	J. Hallett	35	115	5	7	0	3.29
	LF	R. Kiner	502	.247	23	81	339	6	11	0	2.5	.969	K. Gables	32	101	2	4	1	5.27
Spud Davis	C	A. Lopez	150	.307	1	12	173	30	3	4	3.7	.985	J. Lanning	27	91	4	5	1	3.07
W-1 L-2	UT	J. Brown	241	.241	0	12	127	168	16	28		.949	P. Roe	21	70	3	8	2	5.14
	C	B. Salkeld	160	.294	3	19	176	31	6	3	4.2	.972							
New York	1B	J. Mize	377	.337	22	70	928	83	11	80	10.1	.989	D. Koslo	40	265	14	19	1	3.63
	2B	B. Blattner	420	.255	11	49	285	315	15	62	5.4	.976	M. Kennedy	38	187	9	10	1	3.42
W-61 L-93	SS	B. Kerr	497	.249	6	40	240	400	12	66	5.2	.982	B. Voiselle	36	178	9	15	0	3.74
	3B	B. Rigney	360	.236	3	31	77	143	8	8	3.0	.965	K. Trinkle	48	151	7	14	2	3.87
Mel Ott	RF	G. Rosen	310	.281	5	30	200	3	5	0	2.5	.976	J. Thompson	39	63	4	6	4	1.29
	CF	W. Marshall	510	.282	13	48	253	14	6	2	2.2	.978							
	LF	S. Gordon	450	.293	5	45	197	8	1	0	2.0	.995							
	C	W. Cooper	280	.268	8	46	277	38	9	3	4.4	.972							
	10	B. Young	291	.278	7	33	492	24	7	25		.987							
	23	M. Witek	284	.264	4	29	138	150	20	23		.935							
	OF	J. Graham	270	.219	14	47	105	7	6	0	1.9	.949							
	C	E. Lombardi	238	.290	12	39	272	36	7	7	5.0	.978							
	OF	J. Rucker	197	.264	1	13	91	1	5	0	1.8	.948							

BATTING AND BASE RUNNING LEADERS

Batting Average
S. Musial, STL .365
J. Hopp, BOS .333
D. Walker, BKN .319
D. Ennis, PHI .313
T. Holmes, BOS .310

Slugging Average
S. Musial, STL .587
D. Ennis, PHI .485
E. Slaughter, STL .465
W. Kurowski, STL .462
D. Walker, BKN .448

Home Runs
R. Kiner, PIT 23
J. Mize, NY 22
E. Slaughter, STL 18
D. Ennis, PHI 17
R. Northey, PHI 16
S. Musial, STL 16

Total Bases
S. Musial, STL 366
E. Slaughter, STL 283
D. Ennis, PHI 262
D. Walker, BKN 258
T. Holmes, BOS 241

Runs Batted In
E. Slaughter, STL 130
D. Walker, BKN 116
S. Musial, STL 103
W. Kurowski, STL 89
R. Kiner, PIT 81

Stolen Bases
P. Reiser, BKN 34
B. Haas, CIN 22
J. Hopp, BOS 21
B. Adams, CIN 16
D. Walker, BKN 14

Hits
S. Musial, STL 228
D. Walker, BKN 184
E. Slaughter, STL 183
T. Holmes, BOS 176

Base on Balls
E. Stanky, BKN 137
E. Fletcher, PIT 111
Cavarretta, CHI 88
P. Reese, BKN 87

Home Run Percentage
R. Kiner, PIT 4.6
R. Northey, PHI 3.7
G. Hatton, CIN 3.2
D. Ennis, PHI 3.1

PITCHING LEADERS

Winning Percentage
M. Dickson, STL .714
K. Higbe, BKN .680
H. Pollet, STL .677
J. Sain, BOS .588
H. Brecheen, STL .500

Earned Run Average
H. Pollet, STL 2.10
J. Sain, BOS 2.21
J. Beggs, CIN 2.32
E. Blackwell, CIN 2.45
H. Brecheen, STL 2.49

Wins
H. Pollet, STL 21
J. Sain, BOS 20
K. Higbe, BKN 17
M. Dickson, STL 15
H. Brecheen, STL 15

Saves
Raffensberger, PHI 6
H. Casey, BKN 5
A. Herring, BKN 5
A. Karl, PHI 5
H. Pollet, STL 5

Strikeouts
J. Schmitz, CHI 135
K. Higbe, BKN 134
J. Sain, BOS 129
D. Koslo, NY 121
H. Brecheen, STL 117

Complete Games
J. Sain, BOS 24
H. Pollet, STL 22
D. Koslo, NY 17
Ostermueller, PIT 16
M. Cooper, BOS 15

Fewest Hits/9 Innings
M. Kennedy, NY 7.38
J. Schmitz, CHI 7.38
E. Blackwell, CIN 7.41
K. Higbe, BKN 7.60

Shutouts
E. Blackwell, CIN 6
Vander Meer, CIN 5
H. Brecheen, STL 5
M. Cooper, BOS 4

Fewest Walks/9 Innings
M. Cooper, BOS 1.76
Raffensberger, PHI 1.79
J. Beggs, CIN 1.85
Strincevich, PIT 2.25

NATIONAL LEAGUE 1946, cont.

BATTING AND BASE RUNNING LEADERS

Runs Scored		Doubles		Triples	
S. Musial, STL	124	S. Musial, STL	50	S. Musial, STL	20
E. Slaughter, STL	100	T. Holmes, BOS	35	Cavarretta, CHI	10
E. Stanky, BKN	98	W. Kurowski, STL	32	P. Reese, BKN	10
Schoendienst, STL	94	B. Herman, BKN, BOS	31	D. Walker, BKN	9

PITCHING LEADERS

Most Strikeouts/9 Inn.		Innings		Games Pitched	
K. Higbe, BKN	5.72	H. Pollet, STL	266	K. Trinkle, NY	48
J. Schmitz, CHI	5.42	D. Koslo, NY	265	M. Dickson, STL	47
E. Blackwell, CIN	4.63	J. Sain, BOS	265	H. Behrman, BKN	47
H. Brecheen, STL	4.55	H. Brecheen, STL	231	H. Casey, BKN	46

	W	L	PCT	GB	R	OR	2B	3B	HR	BA	SA	SB	E	DP	FA	CG	BB	SO	ShO	SV	ERA
St. Louis	98	58	.628		712	545	265	56	81	.265	.381	58	124	167	.980	75	493	607	18	15	3.01
Brooklyn	96	60	.615	2	701	570	233	66	55	.260	.361	100	174	154	.972	52	671	647	14	28	3.05
Chicago	82	71	.536	14.5	626	581	223	50	56	.254	.346	43	146	119	.976	59	527	609	14	11	3.24
Boston	81	72	.529	15.5	630	592	238	48	44	.264	.353	60	169	129	.972	74	478	531	10	12	3.37
Philadelphia	69	85	.448	28	560	705	209	40	80	.258	.359	41	148	144	.975	55	542	490	11	23	3.99
Cincinnati	67	87	.435	30	523	570	206	33	65	.239	.327	82	155	192	.975	69	467	506	11	11	3.07
Pittsburgh	63	91	.409	34	552	668	202	52	60	.250	.344	48	184	127	.970	61	541	458	10	6	3.72
New York	61	93	.396	36	612	685	176	37	121	.255	.374	46	159	121	.973	48	660	581	8	13	3.92
					4916	4916	1752	382	562	.256	.355	478	1259	1153	.974	493	4379	4429	101	119	3.42

* Defeated Brooklyn in a playoff 2 games to 0.

AMERICAN LEAGUE 1946

	POS	Player	AB	BA	HR	RBI	PO	A	E	DP	TC/G	FA	Pitcher	G	IP	W	L	SV	ERA
Boston	1B	R. York	579	.276	17	119	1327	116	8	154	9.4	.994	T. Hughson	39	278	20	11	3	2.75
	2B	B. Doerr	583	.271	18	116	420	483	13	129	6.1	.986	B. Ferriss	40	274	25	6	3	3.25
W-104 L-50	SS	J. Pesky	621	.335	2	55	296	479	25	96	5.2	.969	M. Harris	34	223	17	9	0	3.64
	3B	R. Russell	274	.208	6	35	59	137	12	24	3.0	.942	J. Dobson	32	167	13	7	0	3.24
Joe Cronin	RF	C. Metkovich	281	.246	4	25	125	3	7	0	1.7	.948	J. Bagby	21	107	7	6	0	3.71
	CF	D. DiMaggio	534	.316	7	73	390	9	6	2	2.9	.985	E. Johnson	29	80	5	4	3	3.71
	LF	T. Williams	514	.342	38	123	325	7	10	2	2.3	.971	B. Klinger	28	57	3	2	9	2.37
	C	H. Wagner	370	.230	6	52	553	39	10	3	5.2	.983							
	3B	P. Higgins	200	.275	2	28	52	109	9	14	2.9	.947							
	OF	L. Culberson	179	.313	3	18	87	1	3	0	1.9	.967							
	OF	W. Moses	175	.206	2	17	92	3	2	1	2.2	.979							
Detroit	1B	H. Greenberg	523	.277	44	127	1272	93	15	110	9.9	.989	H. Newhouser	37	292	26	9	1	1.94
	2B	Bloodworth	249	.245	5	36	157	184	9	46	4.9	.974	D. Trout	38	276	17	13	3	2.34
W-92 L-62	SS	E. Lake	587	.254	8	31	232	391	35	85	5.4	.947	V. Trucks	32	237	14	9	0	3.23
	3B	G. Kell	434	.327	4	41	105*	210*	5	22*	3.0*	.984*	Hutchinson	28	207	14	11	2	3.09
Steve O'Neill	RF	Cullenbine	328	.335	15	56	125	12	5	1	1.8	.965	A. Benton	28	141	11	7	1	3.65
	CF	H. Evers	304	.266	4	33	196	2	5	0	2.7	.975	S. Overmire	24	97	5	7	1	4.62
	LF	D. Wakefield	396	.268	12	59	210	6	8	1	2.2	.964							
	C	B. Tebbetts	280	.243	1	34	486	53	10	4	6.3	.982							
	O3	J. Outlaw	299	.261	2	31	101	64	7	4		.959							
	OF	P. Mullin	276	.246	3	35	121	8	7	1	1.8	.949							
	OF	D. Cramer	204	.294	1	26	89	2	0	0	1.8	1.000							
	2B	E. Mayo	202	.252	0	22	96	125	8	28	4.7	.965							
	2B	S. Webb	169	.219	0	17	97	143	7	28	4.9	.972							
New York	1B	N. Etten	323	.232	9	49	717	55	7	80	9.3	.991	S. Chandler	34	257	20	8	2	2.10
	2B	J. Gordon	376	.210	11	47	281	346	17	87	6.0	.974	B. Bevens	31	250	16	13	0	2.23
W-87 L-67	SS	P. Rizzuto	471	.257	2	38	267	378	26	97	5.4	.961	J. Page	31	136	9	8	3	3.57
	3B	Stirnweiss	487	.251	0	37	66	152	2	18	2.8	.991	R. Gumpert	33	133	11	3	1	2.31
Joe McCarthy	RF	T. Henrich	565	.251	19	83	224	10	2	5	2.1	.992	E. Bonham	18	105	5	8	3	3.70
W-22 L-13	CF	J. DiMaggio	503	.290	25	95	314	15	6	3	2.6	.982	A. Gettel	26	103	6	7	0	2.97
	LF	C. Keller	538	.275	30	101	324	4	7	0	2.2	.979	J. Murphy	27	45	4	2	7	3.40
Bill Dickey	C	A. Robinson	330	.297	16	64	410	50	8	5	4.9	.983							
W-57 L-48	OF	J. Lindell	332	.259	10	40	159	8	3	3	2.3	.982							
	3B	B. Johnson	296	.260	4	35	71	163	11	15	3.3	.955							
Johnny Neun																			
W-8 L-6																			
Washington	1B	M. Vernon	587	.353	8	85	1320	101	15	133	9.8	.990	M. Haefner	33	228	14	11	1	2.85
	2B	G. Priddy	511	.254	6	58	378	428	32	105	6.1	.962	B. Newsom	24	178	11	8	1	2.78
W-76 L-78	SS	C. Travis	465	.252	1	56	133	196	14	45	4.6	.959	D. Leonard	26	162	10	10	0	3.56
	3B	B. Hitchcock	354	.212	0	25	53	87	12	7	3.3	.921	Scarborough	32	156	7	11	1	4.05
Ossie Bluege	RF	B. Lewis	582	.292	7	45	304	16	10	5	2.3	.970	S. Hudson	31	142	8	11	0	3.60
	CF	S. Spence	578	.292	16	87	412	15	8	3	2.9	.982	R. Wolff	21	122	5	8	0	2.58
	LF	J. Grace	321	.302	2	31	185	4	8	2	2.7	.959	E. Wynn	17	107	8	5	0	3.11
	C	A. Evans	272	.254	2	30	336	30	13	5	4.7	.966	W. Masterson	29	91	5	6	1	6.01
	UT	S. Robertson	230	.200	6	19	88	132	19	22		.921							
	C	J. Early	189	.201	4	18	246	45	12	7	4.7	.960							
	UT	G. Torres	185	.254	0	13	82	137	11	20		.952							
	OF	J. Heath	166	.283	4	27	92	3	3		2.1	.969							

AMERICAN LEAGUE 1946, *cont.*

	POS	Player	AB	BA	HR	RBI	PO	A	E	DP	TC/G	FA	Pitcher	G	IP	W	L	SV	ERA
Chicago	1B	H. Trosky	299	.254	2	31	729	33	7	63	9.6	.991	E. Lopat	29	231	13	13	0	2.73
	2B	D. Kolloway	482	.280	3	53	235	281	15	74	5.9	.972	O. Grove	33	205	8	13	0	3.02
W-74 L-80	SS	L. Appling	582	.309	1	55	252	505	39	99	5.3	.951	J. Haynes	32	177	7	9	2	3.76
	3B	D. Lodigiani	155	.245	0	13	41	88	9	4	3.1	.935	E. Smith	24	145	8	11	1	2.85
Jimmy Dykes	RF	T. Wright	422	.275	7	52	217	5	2	0	2.1	.991	F. Papish	31	138	7	5	0	2.74
W-10 L-20	CF	T. Tucker	438	.288	1	36	276	11	3	1	2.6	.990	E. Caldwell	39	91	13	4	8	2.08
	LF	B. Kennedy	411	.258	5	34	157	10	6	1	2.3	.965	J. Rigney	15	83	5	5	0	4.03
Ted Lyons	C	M. Tresh	217	.217	0	21	330	48	2	13	4.8	.995	R. Hamner	25	71	2	7	1	4.42
W-64 L-60																			
	2B	C. Michaels	291	.258	1	22	185	195	17	51	6.0	.957							
	OF	R. Hodgin	258	.252	0	25	114	3	2	0	1.8	.983							
	OF	W. Platt	247	.251	3	32	130	4	4	1	2.3	.971							
	1B	J. Kuhel	238	.273	4	20	596	38	4	65	10.3	.994							
	C	F. Hayes	179	.212	2	16	199	32	5	4	4.7*	.979							
	OF	W. Moses	168	.274	4	16	84	2	0	0	2.4	1.000							
Cleveland	1B	L. Fleming	306	.278	8	42	607	62	11	60	8.5	.984	B. Feller	48	371	26	15	4	2.18
	2B	D. Meyer	207	.232	0	16	110	150	6	26	4.2	.977	R. Embree	28	200	8	12	0	3.47
	SS	L. Boudreau	515	.293	6	62	315	405	22	94	5.3	.970	A. Reynolds	31	183	11	15	0	3.88
W-68 L-86	3B	K. Keltner	398	.241	13	45	112	195	11	18	2.8	.965	S. Gromek	29	154	5	15	4	4.33
	RF	H. Edwards	458	.301	10	54	226	13	8	1	2.0	.968	B. Lemon	32	94	4	5	1	2.49
Lou Boudreau	CF	P. Seerey	404	.225	26	62	248	4	5	1	2.2	.981	J. Berry	21	37	3	6	1	3.38
	LF	G. Case	484	.225	1	22	226	5	4	0	2.0	.983							
	C	J. Hegan	271	.236	0	17	486	47	5	11	6.2	.991							
	OF	Mackiewicz	258	.260	0	16	172	2	3	1	2.5	.983							
	2B	J. Conway	258	.225	0	18	125	131	12	27	5.4	.955							
	2B	R. Mack	171	.205	1	9	118	142	8	37	4.4	.970							
	C	F. Hayes	156	.256	3	18	302	16	6	2	6.5*	.981							
St. Louis	1B	C. Stevens	432	.248	3	27	1020	86	6	98	9.3	.995	J. Kramer	31	195	13	11	0	3.19
	2B	J. Berardino	582	.265	5	68	374	414	23	96	5.7	.972	D. Galehouse	30	180	8	12	0	3.65
	SS	V. Stephens	450	.307	14	64	224	343	30	71	5.3	.950	S. Zoldak	35	170	9	11	2	3.43
W-66 L-88	3B	M. Christman	458	.258	1	41	61	171	6	21	3.1	.975	N. Potter	23	145	8	9	0	3.72
	RF	A. Zarilla	371	.259	4	43	236	13	7	6	2.4	.973	T. Shirley	27	140	6	12	0	4.96
Luke Sewell	CF	W. Judnich	511	.262	15	72	409	6	2	2	3.0	.995	B. Muncrief	29	115	3	12	0	4.99
W-53 L-71	LF	J. Heath	316	.275	12	57	147	5	6	1	1.9	.962	S. Ferens	34	88	2	9	0	4.50
	C	F. Mancuso	262	.240	3	23	298	31	9	3	4.0	.973	T. Ferrick	25	32	4	1	5	2.78
Zack Taylor	OF	C. Laabs	264	.261	16	52	151	5	2	2	2.2	.987							
W-13 L-17	3B	B. Dillinger	225	.280	0	11	56	98	13	11	3.1	.922							
	32	J. Lucadello	210	.248	1	15	84	102	7	14		.964							
	C	H. Helf	182	.192	6	21	251	51	11	7	4.5	.965							
	OF	McQuillen	166	.241	1	12	77	8	2	0	1.8	.977							
	OF	J. Grace	161	.230	1	13	82	6	3	1	2.1	.967							
Philadelphia	1B	G. McQuinn	484	.225	3	35	1098	99	15	107	9.0	.988	Marchildon	36	227	13	16	1	3.49
	2B	G. Handley	251	.251	0	21	159	146	17	32	4.7	.947	D. Fowler	32	206	9	16	0	3.28
	SS	P. Suder	455	.281	2	25	151	204	15	39	5.5	.959	B. Savage	40	164	3	15	2	4.06
W-49 L-105	3B	H. Majeski	264	.250	1	25	78	159	8	22	3.4	.967	J. Flores	29	155	9	7	1	2.32
	RF	E. Valo	348	.307	1	31	182	7	5	0	2.2	.974	L. Knerr	30	148	3	16	0	5.40
Connie Mack	CF	B. McCosky	308	.354	1	34	207	2	4	0	2.5	.981	L. Harris	34	125	3	14	0	5.24
	LF	S. Chapman	545	.261	20	67	369	13	12	4	2.7	.970	Christopher	30	119	5	7	0	4.30
	C	B. Rosar	424	.283	2	47	532	73	0	9	5.2	1.000							
	OF	T. Stainback	291	.244	0	20	153	5	6	1	2.5	.963							
	SS	J. Wallaesa	194	.196	5	11	111	130	22	31	4.5	.916							
	2B	O. Grimes	191	.262	1	20	98	105	9	30	4.9	.958							
	2B	I. Hall	185	.249	0	19	105	113	6	20	5.6	.973							
	OF	R. Derry	184	.207	0	14	127	3	2	2	2.6	.985							

BATTING AND BASE RUNNING LEADERS

Batting Average		Slugging Average		Home Runs		Winning Percentage		Earned Run Average		Wins	
M. Vernon, WAS	.353	T. Williams, BOS	.667	H. Greenberg, DET	44	B. Ferriss, BOS	.806	H. Newhouser, DET	1.94	H. Newhouser, DET	26
T. Williams, BOS	.342	H. Greenberg, DET	.604	T. Williams, BOS	38	H. Newhouser, DET	.743	S. Chandler, NY	2.10	B. Feller, CLE	26
J. Pesky, BOS	.335	C. Keller, NY	.533	C. Keller, NY	30	S. Chandler, NY	.714	B. Feller, CLE	2.18	B. Ferriss, BOS	25
G. Kell, DET, PHI	.322	J. DiMaggio, NY	.511	P. Seerey, CLE	26	M. Harris, BOS	.654	B. Bevens, NY	2.23	S. Chandler, NY	20
D. DiMaggio, BOS	.316	H. Edwards, CLE	.509	J. DiMaggio, NY	25	T. Hughson, BOS	.645	D. Trout, DET	2.34	T. Hughson, BOS	20

PITCHING LEADERS

Total Bases		Runs Batted In		Stolen Bases		Saves		Strikeouts		Complete Games	
T. Williams, BOS	343	H. Greenberg, DET	127	G. Case, CLE	28	B. Klinger, BOS	9	B. Feller, CLE	348	B. Feller, CLE	36
H. Greenberg, DET	316	T. Williams, BOS	123	Stirnweiss, NY	18	E. Caldwell, CHI	8	H. Newhouser, DET	275	H. Newhouser, DET	29
M. Vernon, WAS	298	R. York, BOS	119	E. Lake, DET	15	J. Murphy, NY	7	T. Hughson, BOS	172	B. Ferriss, BOS	26
C. Keller, NY	287	B. Doerr, BOS	116	P. Rizzuto, NY	14	T. Ferrick, CLE, STL	6	V. Trucks, DET	161	D. Trout, DET	23
S. Spence, WAS	287	C. Keller, NY	101	D. Kolloway, CHI	14			D. Trout, DET	151	T. Hughson, BOS	21
				M. Vernon, WAS	14						

AMERICAN LEAGUE 1946, *cont.*

BATTING AND BASE RUNNING LEADERS

Hits

J. Pesky, BOS	208
M. Vernon, WAS	207
L. Appling, CHI	180
T. Williams, BOS	176

Base on Balls

T. Williams, BOS	156
C. Keller, NY	113
E. Lake, DET	103
Cullenbine, DET	88

Home Run Percentage

H. Greenberg, DET	8.4
T. Williams, BOS	7.4
P. Seerey, CLE	6.4
C. Keller, NY	5.6

Fewest Hits/9 Innings

H. Newhouser, DET	6.62
B. Feller, CLE	6.71
S. Chandler, NY	6.99
B. Bevens, NY	7.68

PITCHING LEADERS

Shutouts

B. Feller, CLE	10
S. Chandler, NY	6
H. Newhouser, DET	6
B. Ferriss, BOS	6

Fewest Walks/9 Innings

T. Hughson, BOS	1.65
E. Lopat, CHI	1.87
B. Ferriss, BOS	2.33
D. Galehouse, STL	2.60

Runs Scored

T. Williams, BOS	142
J. Pesky, BOS	115
E. Lake, DET	105
C. Keller, NY	98

Doubles

M. Vernon, WAS	51
S. Spence, WAS	50
J. Pesky, BOS	43
T. Williams, BOS	37

Triples

H. Edwards, CLE	16
B. Lewis, WAS	13
G. Kell, DET, PHI	10
C. Keller, NY	10

Most Strikeouts/9 Inn.

H. Newhouser, DET	8.47
B. Feller, CLE	8.43
V. Trucks, DET	6.12
Hutchinson, DET	6.00

Innings

B. Feller, CLE	371
H. Newhouser, DET	292
T. Hughson, BOS	278
D. Trout, DET	276

Games Pitched

B. Feller, CLE	48
B. Ferriss, BOS	40
B. Savage, PHI	40
T. Hughson, BOS	39

	W	L	PCT	GB	R	OR	2B	3B	HR	BA	SA	SB	E	DP	FA	CG	BB	SO	ShO	SV	ERA
Boston	104	50	.675		**792**	594	**268**	50	109	**.271**	**.402**	45	**139**	165	**.977**	79	501	667	15	**20**	3.38
Detroit	92	62	.597	12	704	567	212	41	108	.258	.374	65	155	138	.974	**94**	**497**	**896**	**18**	15	3.22
New York	87	67	.565	17	684	547	208	50	**136**	.248	.387	48	150	**174**	.975	68	552	653	17	17	3.13
Washington	76	78	.494	28	608	706	260	**63**	60	.260	.366	51	211	162	.966	71	547	537	8	10	3.74
Chicago	74	80	.481	30	562	595	206	44	37	.257	.333	**78**	175	170	.972	62	508	550	9	16	**3.10**
Cleveland	68	86	.442	36	537	637	233	56	79	.245	.356	57	147	147	.975	63	649	789	16	13	3.62
St. Louis	66	88	.429	38	621	711	220	46	84	.251	.356	23	159	157	.974	63	573	574	13	12	3.95
Philadelphia	49	105	.318	55	529	680	220	51	40	.253	.338	39	167	141	.971	61	577	562	10	5	3.90
					5037	5037	1827	401	653	.256	.364	406	1303	1254	.973	561	4404	5228	106	108	3.50

NATIONAL LEAGUE 1947

	POS	Player	AB	BA	HR	RBI	PO	A	E	DP	TC/G	FA	Pitcher	G	IP	W	L	SV	ERA
Brooklyn	1B	J. Robinson	590	.297	12	48	1323	92	16	**144**	9.5	.989	R. Branca	43	280	21	12	1	2.67
	2B	E. Stanky	559	.252	3	53	402	406	12	123	5.6	**.985**	J. Hatten	42	225	17	8	0	3.63
W-94 L-60	SS	P. Reese	476	.284	12	73	266	441	25	99	5.2	.966	V. Lombardi	33	175	12	11	3	2.99
	3B	S. Jorgensen	441	.274	5	67	116	235	19	26	2.9	.949	H. Taylor	33	162	10	5	1	3.11
Clyde Sukeforth	RF	D. Walker	529	.306	9	94	261	9	10	0	1.9	.964	H. Gregg	37	104	4	5	1	5.87
W-2 L-0	CF	C. Furillo	437	.295	8	88	287	9	9	3	2.5	.977	H. Behrman	40	92	5	3	8	5.48
	LF	P. Reiser	388	.309	5	46	240	3	3	0	2.3	.988	C. King	29	88	6	5	0	2.77
Burt Shotton	C	B. Edwards	471	.295	9	80	592	58	11	11	5.2	.983	H. Casey	46	77	10	4	18	3.99
W-92 L-60	OF	G. Hermanski	189	.275	7	39	105	5	2	0	1.7	.982							
	O3	A. Vaughan	126	.325	2	25	56	20	0	3		1.000							
St. Louis	1B	S. Musial	587	.312	19	95	1360	77	8	138	9.7	.994	M. Dickson	47	232	13	16	3	3.07
	2B	Schoendienst	**659**	.253	3	48	357	404	19	109	5.5	.976	G. Munger	40	224	16	5	3	3.37
W-89 L-65	SS	M. Marion	540	.272	4	74	**329**	452	15	**104**	5.3	**.981**	H. Brecheen	29	223	16	11	1	3.30
	3B	W. Kurowski	513	.310	27	104	140	250	19	17	2.9	.954	H. Pollet	37	176	9	11	2	4.34
Eddie Dyer	RF	E. Dusak	328	.284	6	28	178	13	6	2	2.2	.970	A. Brazle	44	168	14	8	4	2.84
	CF	T. Moore	460	.283	7	45	292	6	6	2	2.5	.983	J. Hearn	37	162	12	7	1	3.22
	LF	E. Slaughter	551	.294	10	86	306	15	6	5	2.3	.982	K. Burkhart	34	95	3	6	1	5.21
	C	D. Rice	261	.218	12	44	380	33	8	7	4.5	.981							
	OF	R. Northey	311	.293	15	63	122	8	7	1	1.5	.949							
	C	J. Garagiola	183	.257	5	25	281	23	4	2	4.2	.987							
	OF	J. Medwick	150	.307	4	28	56	3	0	2	1.4	1.000							
Boston	1B	E. Torgeson	399	.281	16	78	1033	76	**18**	83	9.6	.984	W. Spahn	40	**290**	21	10	3	**2.33**
	2B	C. Ryan	544	.265	5	69	393	432	**23**	88	5.7	.973	J. Sain	38	266	21	12	1	3.52
	SS	D. Culler	214	.248	0	19	106	212	11	31	4.4	.967	R. Barrett	36	211	11	12	1	3.55
W-86 L-68	3B	B. Elliott	555	.317	22	113	129	302	20	25	3.0	.956	B. Voiselle	22	131	8	7	0	4.32
	RF	T. Holmes	618	.309	9	53	336	12	4	4	2.4	.989	S. Johnson	36	113	6	8	2	4.23
Billy Southworth	CF	J. Hopp	430	.288	2	32	296	2	6	0	2.4	.980							
	LF	B. Rowell	384	.276	5	40	202	4	12	0	2.2	.945							
	C	P. Masi	411	.304	9	50	411	58	5	1	3.9	**.989**							
	OF	McCormick	284	.285	3	36	155	4	3	0	2.1	.981							
	OF	D. Litwhiler	226	.261	7	31	119	2	3	0	1.9	.976							
	1B	McCormick	212	.354	2	43	428	26	2	31	9.5	.996							
	SS	N. Fernandez	209	.206	2	21	89	146	17	22	4.1	.933							
New York	1B	J. Mize	586	.302	51	138	1380	117	6	120	9.8	**.996**	L. Jansen	42	248	21	5	1	3.16
	2B	B. Rigney	531	.267	17	59	184	229	11	41	5.9	.974	D. Koslo	39	217	15	10	0	4.39
	SS	B. Kerr	547	.287	7	49	270	**460**	17	77	5.4	.977	M. Kennedy	34	148	9	12	0	4.85
W-81 L-73	3B	L. Lohrke	329	.240	11	35	118	187	20	20	2.9	.938	C. Hartung	23	138	9	7	0	4.57
	RF	W. Marshall	587	.291	36	107	334	19	10	6	2.3	.972	K. Trinkle	62	94	8	4	10	3.75
Mel Ott	CF	B. Thomson	545	.283	29	85	330	12	7	2	2.7	.980	H. Iott	20	71	3	8	0	5.93
	LF	S. Gordon	437	.272	13	57	254	12	8	0	2.2	.971							
	C	W. Cooper	515	.305	35	122	560	51	**13**	8	4.7	.979							
	OF	L. Gearhart	179	.246	6	17	94	4	4	1	2.3	.961							
	2B	M. Witek	160	.219	3	17	102	125	4	27	5.8	.983							
	C	E. Lombardi	110	.282	4	21	86	11	2	2	4.1	.980							

NATIONAL LEAGUE 1947, cont.

	POS	Player	AB	BA	HR	RBI	PO	A	E	DP	TC/G	FA	Pitcher	G	IP	W	L	SV	ERA
Cincinnati	1B	B. Young	364	.283	14	79	730	56	8	66	8.5	.990	E. Blackwell	33	273	22	8	0	2.47
	2B	B. Zientara	418	.258	2	24	243	247	12	53	5.0	.976	Vander Meer	30	186	9	14	0	4.40
W-73 L-81	SS	E. Miller	545	.268	19	87	295	445	21	88	5.0	.972	K. Peterson	37	152	6	13	2	4.25
	3B	G. Hatton	524	.281	16	77	143	248	26	18	3.1	.938	B. Lively	38	123	4	7	0	4.68
Johnny Neun	RF	F. Baumholtz	643	.283	5	45	282	18	7	2	2.0	.977	B. Walters	20	122	8	8	0	5.75
	CF	B. Haas	482	.286	3	67	170	2	8	0	2.6	.956	E. Erautt	36	119	4	9	0	5.07
	LF	A. Galan	392	.314	6	61	246	2	3	0	2.1	.988	Raffensberger	19	107	6	5	1	4.13
	C	R. Lamanno	413	.257	5	50	556	62	9	6	5.8	.986	H. Gumbert	46	90	10	10	10	3.89
	2B	B. Adams	217	.272	4	20	172	177	12	46	5.2	.967							
	OF	E. Lukon	200	.205	11	33	103	4	0	2	1.9	1.000							
	C	R. Mueller	192	.250	6	33	221	28	4	2	4.6	.984							
	OF	T. Tatum	176	.273	1	16	117	6	0	3	2.5	1.000							
	OF	C. Vollmer	155	.219	1	13	125	2	2	0	2.0	.984							
Chicago	1B	E. Waitkus	514	.292	2	35	1161	101	8	109	10.1	.994	J. Schmitz	38	207	13	18	4	3.22
	2B	D. Johnson	402	.259	3	26	255	291	17	65	5.2	.970	D. Lade	34	187	11	10	0	3.94
W-69 L-85	SS	L. Merullo	373	.241	0	29	219	322	29	77	5.3	.949	H. Borowy	40	183	8	12	2	4.38
	3B	P. Lowrey	448	.281	5	37	83	194	16	21	3.2	.945	P. Erickson	40	174	7	12	1	4.34
Charlie Grimm	RF	B. Nicholson	487	.244	26	75	281	7	3	1	2.1	.990	H. Wyse	37	142	6	9	1	4.31
	CF	A. Pafko	513	.302	13	66	327	9	5	3	2.7	.985	B. Chipman	32	135	7	6	0	3.68
	LF	Cavarretta	459	.314	2	63	203	11	5	3	2.7	.977	E. Kush	47	91	8	3	5	3.36
	C	B. Scheffing	363	.264	5	50	379	52	7	4	4.5	.984	C. Passeau	19	63	2	6		6.25
	3B	S. Hack	240	.271	0	12	64	136	8	11	3.2	.962							
	C	McCullough	234	.252	3	30	280	35	5	3	5.0	.984							
	S2	B. Sturgeon	232	.254	0	21	135	192	6	42		.982							
	OF	C. Aberson	140	.279	4	20	62	7	6	1	1.9	.920							
Philadelphia	1B	H. Schultz	403	.223	6	35	986	67	7	92	9.3	.993	D. Leonard	32	235	17	12	0	2.68
	2B	E. Verban	540	.285	0	42	450	453	17	111	5.9	.982	S. Rowe	31	196	14	10	1	4.32
W-62 L-92	SS	S. Newsome	310	.229	2	22	131	247	12	60	4.6	.969	O. Judd	32	147	4	15	0	4.60
	3B	L. Handley	277	.253	0	42	87	144	6	8	2.9	.975	Heintzelman	24	136	7	10	1	4.04
Ben Chapman	RF	J. Wyrostek	454	.273	5	51	261	11	8	2	2.2	.971	T. Hughes	29	127	4	11	1	3.47
	CF	H. Walker	488	.371*	1	41	350	15	13*	2	3.0	.966	B. Donnelly	38	121	4	6	5	2.98
	LF	D. Ennis	541	.275	12	81	320	12	7	2	2.5	.979	A. Jurisich	34	118	1	7	3	4.94
	C	A. Seminick	337	.252	13	50	438	53	11	6	4.7	.978	C. Schanz	34	102	2	4	2	4.16
	3B	J. Tabor	251	.235	4	31	68	96	15	8	2.7	.916	F. Schmidt	29	77	5	8	0	4.70
	SS	R. LaPointe	211	.308	1	15	82	158	11	25	4.6	.956							
	1C	A. Lakeman	182	.159	6	19	286	18	4	16		.987							
	OF	B. Adams	182	.247	2	15	78	5	4	2	1.7	.954							
	C	D. Padgett	158	.316	0	24	111	16	5	1	3.4	.962							
Pittsburgh	1B	H. Greenberg	402	.249	25	74	983	79	9	85	9.0	.992	K. Higbe	46	225	11	17	5	3.72
	2B	Bloodworth	316	.250	7	48	222	206	9	56	5.0	.979	Ostermueller	26	183	12	10	0	3.84
W-62 L-92	SS	B. Cox	529	.274	15	54	220	388	20	63	4.9	.968	E. Bonham	33	150	11	8	3	3.85
	3B	F. Gustine	616	.297	9	67	198	330	31	35	3.6	.945	P. Roe	38	144	4	15	2	5.25
Billy Herman	RF	W. Westlake	407	.273	17	69	239	8	3	0	2.3	.988	R. Sewell	24	121	6	4	0	3.57
W-61 L-92	CF	J. Russell	478	.253	8	51	343	6	7	3	3.0	.980	J. Bagby	37	116	5	4	0	4.67
	LF	R. Kiner	565	.313	51	127	390	8	7	1	2.7	.983	M. Queen	14	74	3	7	0	4.01
Bill Burwell	C	D. Howell	214	.276	4	25	272	30	8	4	4.2	.974							
W-1 L-0	OF	C. Rikard	324	.287	4	32	177	2	4	0	2.3	.978							
	C	C. Kluttz	232	.302	6	42	247	55	4	7	4.4	.987							
	2B	E. Basinski	161	.199	4	17	116	130	7	34	4.5	.972							
	1B	E. Fletcher	157	.242	1	20	324	25	5	28	7.1	.986							

BATTING AND BASE RUNNING LEADERS

Batting Average		Slugging Average		Home Runs		Winning Percentage		Earned Run Average		Wins	
H. Walker, PHI, STL	.363	R. Kiner, PIT	.639	R. Kiner, PIT	51	L. Jansen, NY	.808	W. Spahn, BOS	2.33	E. Blackwell, CIN	22
B. Elliott, BOS	.317	J. Mize, NY	.614	J. Mize, NY	51	G. Munger, STL	.762	E. Blackwell, CIN	2.47	L. Jansen, NY	21
Cavarretta, CHI	.314	W. Cooper, NY	.586	W. Marshall, NY	36	E. Blackwell, CIN	.733	R. Branca, BKN	2.67	W. Spahn, BOS	21
R. Kiner, PIT	.313	W. Kurowski, STL	.544	W. Cooper, NY	35	J. Hatten, BKN	.680	D. Leonard, PHI	2.68	R. Branca, BKN	21
S. Musial, STL	.312	W. Marshall, NY	.528	B. Thomson, NY	29	W. Spahn, BOS	.677	M. Dickson, STL	3.07	J. Sain, BOS	21

Total Bases		Runs Batted In		Stolen Bases		Saves		Strikeouts		Complete Games	
R. Kiner, PIT	361	J. Mize, NY	138	J. Robinson, BKN	29	H. Casey, BKN	18	E. Blackwell, CIN	193	E. Blackwell, CIN	23
J. Mize, NY	360	R. Kiner, PIT	127	P. Reiser, BKN	14	H. Gumbert, CIN	10	R. Branca, BKN	148	J. Sain, BOS	22
W. Marshall, NY	310	W. Cooper, NY	122	J. Hopp, BOS	13	K. Trinkle, NY	10	J. Sain, BOS	132	W. Spahn, BOS	22
W. Cooper, NY	302	B. Elliott, BOS	113	H. Walker, PHI, STL	13	H. Behrman, BKN, PIT	8	G. Munger, STL	123	L. Jansen, NY	20
S. Musial, STL	296	W. Marshall, NY	107	E. Torgeson, BOS	11			W. Spahn, BOS	123	D. Leonard, PHI	19

Hits		Base on Balls		Home Run Percentage		Fewest Hits/9 Innings		Shutouts		Fewest Walks/9 Innings	
T. Holmes, BOS	191	H. Greenberg, PIT	104	R. Kiner, PIT	9.0	H. Taylor, BKN	7.22	W. Spahn, BOS	7	L. Jansen, NY	2.07
H. Walker, PHI, STL	186	P. Reese, BKN	104	J. Mize, NY	8.7	E. Blackwell, CIN	7.48	G. Munger, STL	6	S. Rowe, PHI	2.07
S. Musial, STL	183	E. Stanky, BKN	103	W. Cooper, NY	6.8	W. Spahn, BOS	7.61	E. Blackwell, CIN	6	D. Leonard, PHI	2.18
F. Gustine, PIT	183	R. Kiner, PIT	98	H. Greenberg, PIT	6.2	R. Branca, BKN	8.07	M. Dickson, STL	4	Raffensberger, CIN, PHI	2.26

NATIONAL LEAGUE 1947, *cont.*

BATTING AND BASE RUNNING LEADERS

Runs Scored		Doubles		Triples		Most Strikeouts/9 Inn.	
J. Mize, NY	137	E. Miller, CIN	38	H. Walker, PHI, STL	16	E. Blackwell, CIN	6.36
J. Robinson, BKN	125	B. Elliott, BOS	35	E. Slaughter, STL	13	G. Munger, STL	4.93
R. Kiner, PIT	118	C. Ryan, BOS	33	S. Musial, STL	13	R. Branca, BKN	4.76
S. Musial, STL	113	T. Holmes, BOS	33	F. Baumholtz, CIN	9	J. Sain, BOS	4.47

PITCHING LEADERS

Innings		Games Pitched	
W. Spahn, BOS	290	K. Trinkle, NY	62
R. Branca, BKN	280	K. Higbe, BKN, PIT	50
E. Blackwell, CIN	273	H. Behrman, BKN, PIT	50
J. Sain, BOS	266	M. Dickson, STL	47

	W	L	PCT	GB	R	OR	2B	3B	HR	BA	SA	SB	E	DP	FA	CG	BB	SO	ShO	SV	ERA
									Batting					**Fielding**				**Pitching**			
Brooklyn	94	60	.610		774	668	241	50	83	.272	.384	**88**	129	164	.978	47	626	592	**14**	34	3.82
St. Louis	89	65	.578	5	780	634	235	**65**	115	.270	.401	28	**128**	169	**.979**	65	495	**642**	13	20	**3.53**
Boston	86	68	.558	8	701	622	**265**	42	85	**.275**	.390	58	153	124	.974	**74**	**453**	486	**14**	13	3.62
New York	81	73	.526	13	830	761	220	48	221	.271	.454	29	155	136	.974	58	590	553	6	14	4.44
Cincinnati	73	81	.474	21	681	755	242	43	95	.259	.375	46	138	134	.977	54	589	633	13	13	4.41
Chicago	69	85	.448	25	567	722	231	48	75	.259	.361	22	150	159	.975	46	618	571	8	15	4.10
Philadelphia	62	92	.403	32	589	687	210	52	60	.258	.352	60	152	140	.974	70	501	514	8	14	3.96
Pittsburgh	62	92	.403	32	744	817	216	44	156	.261	.406	30	149	131	.975	44	592	501	9	13	4.68
					5666	5666	1860	392	886	.265	.390	361	1154	1157	.976	458	4464	4492	85	136	4.07

AMERICAN LEAGUE 1947

	POS	Player	AB	BA	HR	RBI	PO	A	E	DP	TC/G	FA	Pitcher	G	IP	W	L	SV	ERA
New York W-97 L-57 Bucky Harris	1B	G. McQuinn	517	.304	13	80	1198	93	8	120	9.1	.994	A. Reynolds	34	242	19	8	2	3.20
	2B	Stirnweiss	571	.256	5	41	337	402	13	107	5.1	.983	S. Shea	27	179	14	5	1	3.07
	SS	P. Rizzuto	549	.273	2	60	340	450	25	111	5.4	.969	B. Bevens	28	165	7	13	0	3.82
	3B	B. Johnson	494	.285	10	95	136	204	17	12	2.7	.952	J. Page	56	141	14	8	17	2.48
	RF	T. Henrich	550	.287	16	98	278	13	5	2	2.2	.983	S. Chandler	17	128	9	5	0	**2.46**
	CF	J. DiMaggio	534	.315	20	97	316	2	1	0	2.1	**.997**	B. Newsom	17	116	7	5	0	2.80
	LF	J. Lindell	476	.275	11	67	308	6	7	1	2.7	.978	V. Raschi	15	105	7	2	0	3.87
	C	A. Robinson	252	.270	5	36	346	38	1	3	5.2	.997	K. Drews	30	92	6	6	1	4.91
	CO	Y. Berra	293	.280	11	54	307	18	9	5		.973							
	OF	C. Keller	151	.238	13	36	85	2	3	0	2.1	.967							
Detroit W-85 L-69 Steve O'Neill	1B	Cullenbine	464	.224	24	78	1184	139	15	111	9.7	.989	H. Newhouser	40	285	17	**17**	2	2.87
	2B	E. Mayo	535	.279	6	48	326	365	12	80	5.0	.983	Hutchinson	33	220	18	10	2	3.03
	SS	E. Lake	602	.211	12	46	268	450	43	94	4.8	.943	D. Trout	32	186	10	11	2	3.48
	3B	G. Kell	588	.320	5	93	167	333	20	25	3.4	.962	V. Trucks	36	181	10	12	2	4.53
	RF	P. Mullin	398	.256	15	62	229	10	3	2	2.3	.988	S. Overmire	28	141	11	5	0	3.77
	CF	H. Evers	460	.296	10	67	354	10	8	2	2.3	.978	A. Benton	36	133	6	7	7	4.40
	LF	D. Wakefield	368	.283	8	51	197	10	11	2	2.2	.950	A. Houtteman	23	111	7	2	0	3.42
	C	B. Swift	279	.251	1	21	401	45	5	6	4.6	.989	H. White	35	85	4	5	2	3.61
	OF	V. Wertz	333	.288	6	44	160	6	6	0	2.1	.965							
	C	H. Wagner	191	.288	5	33	275	25	3	3	4.3	.990							
	OF	D. Cramer	157	.268	2	30	79	3	3	0	2.4	.965							
Boston W-83 L-71 Joe Cronin	1B	J. Jones	404	.235	16	76	1018*	73	10	11	10.1*	.991	J. Dobson	33	229	18	8	1	2.95
	2B	B. Doerr	561	.258	17	95	376	466	16	118	5.9	.981	B. Ferriss	33	218	12	11	0	4.04
	SS	J. Pesky	638	.324	0	39	251	391	16	90	4.9	.976	T. Hughson	29	189	12	11	0	3.33
	3B	S. Dente	168	.232	0	11	40	83	8	11	2.8	.939	D. Galehouse	21	149	11	7	0	3.32
	RF	S. Mele	453	.302	12	73	233	10	2	1	2.1	.992	E. Johnson	45	142	12	11	8	2.97
	CF	D. DiMaggio	513	.283	8	71	413	19	10	4	3.3	.977	H. Dorish	41	136	7	8	2	4.70
	LF	T. Williams	528	**.343**	32	114	347	10	9	2	2.3	.975							
	C	B. Tebbetts	291	.299	1	28	332	50	10*	6	4.4	.974							
	OF	W. Moses	255	.275	2	27	109	2	3	0	2.0	.974							
	3S	Pellagrini	231	.203	4	19	73	142	14	17		.939							
	1B	R. York	184	.212	6	27	395	36	2	45*	9.0	.995*							
	C	R. Partee	169	.231	0	16	207	26	6	4	4.4	.975							
Cleveland W-80 L-74 Lou Boudreau	1B	E. Robinson	318	.245	14	52	800	55	5	79	9.9	.994	B. Feller	42	**299**	**20**	11	3	2.68
	2B	J. Gordon	562	.272	29	93	341	466	18	110	5.3	.978	D. Black	30	191	10	12	0	3.92
	SS	L. Boudreau	538	.307	4	67	305	475	14	120	5.4	**.982**	B. Lemon	37	167	11	5	3	3.44
	3B	K. Keltner	541	.257	11	76	156	266	12	29	2.9	.972	R. Embree	27	163	8	10	0	3.15
	RF	H. Edwards	393	.260	15	59	199	3	2	0	2.0	.990	A. Gettel	31	149	11	10	0	3.20
	CF	C. Metkovich	473	.254	5	40	349	2	4	2	2.0	.989	B. Stephens	31	92	5	10	1	4.01
	LF	D. Mitchell	493	.316	1	34	252	8	6	1	2.3	.977	E. Klieman	58	92	5	4	17	3.03
	C	J. Hegan	378	.249	4	42	**566**	54	7	14	**4.7**	.989	S. Gromek	29	84	3	5	4	3.74
	OF	H. Peck	392	.293	8	44	166	5	3	3	1.8	.983	M. Harder	15	80	6	4	0	4.50
	1B	L. Fleming	281	.242	4	43	662	63	8	78	9.5	.989							
	OF	P. Seerey	216	.171	11	29	105	7	5	1	1.7	.957							

AMERICAN LEAGUE 1947, *cont.*

	POS	Player	AB	BA	HR	RBI	PO	A	E	DP	TC/G	FA	Pitcher	G	IP	W	L	SV	ERA
Philadelphia	1B	F. Fain	461	.291	7	71	1141	101	**19**	118	9.6	.985	Marchildon	35	277	19	9	0	3.22
	2B	P. Suder	528	.241	5	60	304	413	10	94	5.2	**.986**	D. Fowler	36	227	12	11	0	2.81
W-78 L-76	SS	E. Joost	540	.206	13	64	**370**	452	38	100	**5.7**	.956	B. McCahan	29	165	10	5	0	3.32
	3B	H. Majeski	479	.280	8	72	160	263	6	28	3.2	**.988**	J. Coleman	32	160	6	12	1	4.32
Connie Mack	RF	E. Valo	370	.300	5	36	205	9	6	0	2.1	.973	J. Flores	28	151	4	13	0	3.39
	CF	S. Chapman	551	.252	14	83	**428**	16	6	2	3.1	.987	B. Savage	44	146	8	10	2	3.76
	LF	B. McCosky	546	.328	1	52	346	8	6	2	2.6	.983	C. Scheib	21	116	4	6	0	5.04
	C	B. Rosar	359	.259	1	33	406	**70**	2	12	4.7	**.996**	Christopher	44	81	10	7	12	2.90
	OF	G. Binks	333	.258	2	34	157	8	6	1	2.3	.965							
	C	M. Guerra	209	.215	0	18	203	36	9	5	4.0	.964							
Chicago	1B	R. York	400	.243	15	64	932	71	5	104*	9.9	.995*	E. Lopat	31	253	16	13	0	2.81
	2B	D. Kolloway	485	.278	2	35	274	306	**23**	76	6.1	.962	F. Papish	38	199	12	12	3	3.26
W-70 L-84	SS	L. Appling	503	.306	8	49	232	422	35	86	5.3	.949	J. Haynes	29	182	14	6	0	2.42
	3B	F. Baker	371	.264	0	22	84	253	7	28	3.4	.980	O. Grove	25	136	6	8	0	4.44
Ted Lyons	RF	B. Kennedy	428	.262	6	48	204	8	7	3	2.1	.968	B. Gillespie	25	118	5	8	0	4.73
	CF	D. Philley	551	.258	2	45	355	9	5	2	2.8	.986	E. Harrist	33	94	3	8	5	3.56
	LF	T. Wright	401	.324	4	47	198	6	6	1	2.1	.971	T. Lee	21	87	3	7	1	4.47
	C	M. Tresh	274	.241	0	20	313	38	9	10	4.0	.975	P. Gebrian	27	66	2	3	5	4.23
	23	C. Michaels	355	.273	3	34	208	264	15	61		.969	Maltzberger	33	64	1	4	5	3.39
	OF	T. Tucker	254	.236	1	17	171	5	4	2	2.8	.978	E. Caldwell	40	54	1	4	8	3.64
	C	G. Dickey	211	.223	1	27	285	35	5	5	4.1	.985							
	SO	J. Wallaesa	205	.195	7	32	129	95	5	22		.978							
	OF	R. Hodgin	180	.294	1	24	99	2	1	0	2.5	.990							
	1B	J. Jones	171	.240	3	20	444*	31	6	49	11.2*	.988							
Washington	1B	M. Vernon	600	.265	7	85	1299	105	**19**	123	9.2	.987	W. Masterson	35	253	12	16	1	3.13
	2B	G. Priddy	505	.214	3	49	**382**	405	16	89	5.5	.980	E. Wynn	33	247	17	15	0	3.64
W-64 L-90	SS	M. Christman	374	.222	1	31	203	291	11	75	4.8	.978	M. Haefner	31	193	10	14	1	3.64
	3B	E. Yost	428	.238	0	14	125	198	14	11	3.0	.958	Scarborough	33	161	6	13	0	3.41
Ossie Bluege	RF	B. Lewis	506	.261	6	48	259	11	9	2	2.1	.968	S. Hudson	20	106	6	9	0	5.60
	CF	S. Spence	506	.279	16	73	408	12	7	3	3.0	.984	B. Newsom	14	84	4	6	0	4.09
	LF	J. Grace	234	.248	3	17	162	4	4	0	2.5	.976	T. Ferrick	31	60	1	7	9	3.15
	C	A. Evans	319	.241	2	23	389	48	5	**14**	4.7	.989							
	OF	S. Robertson	266	.233	1	23	126	5	7	1	2.5	.949							
	3B	C. Travis	204	.216	1	10	28	68	7	6	2.6	.932							
	OF	T. McBride	166	.271	0	15	103	2	3	0	2.1	.972							
St. Louis	1B	W. Judnich	500	.258	18	64	1067	76	13	118	9.0	.989	J. Kramer	33	199	11	16	1	4.97
	2B	J. Berardino	306	.261	1	24	242	221	11	61	5.5	.977	E. Kinder	34	194	8	15	1	4.49
W-59 L-95	SS	V. Stephens	562	.279	15	83	283	**494**	24	113	5.4	.970	F. Sanford	34	187	7	16	4	3.71
	3B	B. Dillinger	571	.294	3	37	**169**	265	19	21	3.3	.958	B. Muncrief	31	176	8	14	0	4.90
Muddy Ruel	RF	A. Zarilla	380	.224	3	38	209	6	3	0	2.0	.986	S. Zoldak	35	171	9	10	1	3.47
	CF	P. Lehner	483	.248	7	48	344	1	7	0	2.8	.980	C. Fannin	26	146	6	8	1	3.58
	LF	J. Heath	491	.251	27	85	297	7	4	4	2.2	.987	N. Potter	32	123	4	10	2	4.04
	C	L. Moss	274	.157	6	24	362	43	7	6	4.3	.983							
	OF	R. Coleman	343	.259	2	30	174	7	3	4	2.0	.984							
	UT	B. Hitchcock	275	.222	1	28	209	190	14	45		.966							
	C	J. Early	214	.224	3	19	301	43	4	5	4.1	.989							

BATTING AND BASE RUNNING LEADERS

Batting Average		Slugging Average		Home Runs		Winning Percentage	
T. Williams, BOS	.343	T. Williams, BOS	.634	T. Williams, BOS	32	A. Reynolds, NY	.704
B. McCosky, PHI	.328	J. DiMaggio, NY	.522	J. Gordon, CLE	29	J. Dobson, BOS	.692
J. Pesky, BOS	.324	J. Gordon, CLE	.496	J. Heath, STL	27	Marchildon, PHI	.679
T. Wright, CHI	.324	T. Henrich, NY	.485	Cullenbine, DET	24	B. Feller, CLE	.645
G. Kell, DET	.320	J. Heath, STL	.485	R. York, BOS, CHI	21	Hutchinson, DET	.643

Total Bases		Runs Batted In		Stolen Bases		Saves	
T. Williams, BOS	335	T. Williams, BOS	114	B. Dillinger, STL	34	J. Page, NY	17
J. DiMaggio, NY	279	T. Henrich, NY	98	D. Philley, CHI	21	E. Klieman, CLE	17
J. Gordon, CLE	279	J. DiMaggio, NY	97	M. Vernon, WAS	12	Christopher, PHI	12
T. Henrich, NY	267	J. Jones, BOS, CHI	96	J. Pesky, BOS	12	T. Ferrick, WAS	9
J. Pesky, BOS	250	B. Johnson, NY	95			E. Johnson, BOS	8
		B. Doerr, BOS	95			E. Caldwell, CHI	8

Hits		Base on Balls		Home Run Percentage		Fewest Hits/9 Innings	
J. Pesky, BOS	207	T. Williams, BOS	162	T. Williams, BOS	6.1	S. Shea, NY	6.40
G. Kell, DET	188	Cullenbine, DET	137	J. Heath, STL	5.5	B. Feller, CLE	6.92
T. Williams, BOS	181	E. Lake, DET	120	Cullenbine, DET	5.2	S. Chandler, NY	7.03
B. McCosky, PHI	179	E. Joost, PHI	114	J. Gordon, CLE	5.2	Marchildon, PHI	7.42

PITCHING LEADERS

Earned Run Average		Wins	
S. Chandler, NY	2.46	B. Feller, CLE	20
B. Feller, CLE	2.68	A. Reynolds, NY	19
D. Fowler, PHI	2.81	Marchildon, PHI	19
E. Lopat, CHI	2.81	J. Dobson, BOS	18
H. Newhouser, DET	2.87	Hutchinson, DET	18

Strikeouts		Complete Games	
B. Feller, CLE	196	H. Newhouser, DET	24
H. Newhouser, DET	176	E. Lopat, CHI	22
W. Masterson, WAS	135	E. Wynn, WAS	22
A. Reynolds, NY	129	Marchildon, PHI	21
Marchildon, PHI	128	B. Feller, CLE	20

Shutouts		Fewest Walks/9 Innings	
B. Feller, CLE	5	D. Galehouse, BOS, STL	2.48
M. Haefner, WAS	4	Hutchinson, DET	2.50
A. Reynolds, NY	4	E. Lopat, CHI	2.60
W. Masterson, WAS	4	J. Dobson, BOS	2.87

AMERICAN LEAGUE 1947, *cont.*

BATTING AND BASE RUNNING LEADERS

Runs Scored		Doubles		Triples		Most Strikeouts/9 Inn.	
T. Williams, BOS	125	L. Boudreau, CLE	45	T. Henrich, NY	13	B. Feller, CLE	5.90
T. Henrich, NY	109	T. Williams, BOS	40	M. Vernon, WAS	12	T. Hughson, BOS	5.66
J. Pesky, BOS	106	T. Henrich, NY	35	D. Philley, CHI	11	H. Newhouser, DET	5.56
Stirnweiss, NY	102	J. DiMaggio, NY	31	D. Mitchell, CLE	10	E. Kinder, STL	5.09

PITCHING LEADERS

Innings		Games Pitched	
B. Feller, CLE	299	E. Klieman, CLE	58
H. Newhouser, DET	285	J. Page, NY	56
Marchildon, PHI	277	E. Johnson, BOS	45
W. Masterson, WAS	253	B. Savage, PHI	44

	W	L	PCT	GB	R	OR	2B	3B	HR	BA	SA	SB	E	DP	FA	CG	BB	SO	ShO	SV	ERA
							Batting						Fielding			Pitching					
New York	97	57	.630		794	568	230	72	115	.271	.407	27	109	151	.981	73	628	691	14	21	3.39
Detroit	85	69	.552	12	714	642	234	42	103	.258	.377	52	155	142	.975	77	531	648	15	18	3.57
Boston	83	71	.539	14	720	669	206	54	103	.265	.382	41	137	172	.977	64	575	586	13	19	3.81
Cleveland	80	74	.519	17	687	588	234	51	112	.259	.385	29	104	178	.983	55	628	590	13	29	3.44
Philadelphia	78	76	.506	19	633	614	218	52	61	.252	.349	37	143	161	.976	70	597	493	12	15	3.51
Chicago	70	84	.455	27	553	661	211	41	53	.256	.342	91	155	180	.975	47	603	522	11	27	3.64
Washington	64	90	.416	33	496	675	186	48	42	.241	.321	53	143	161	.976	67	579	551	15	12	3.97
St. Louis	59	95	.383	38	564	744	189	52	90	.241	.350	69	134	169	.977	50	604	552	7	13	4.33
					5161	5161	1708	412	679	.256	.364	399	1080	1304	.977	503	4745	4633	100	154	3.71

NATIONAL LEAGUE 1948

	POS	Player	AB	BA	HR	RBI	PO	A	E	DP	TC/G	FA	Pitcher	G	IP	W	L	SV	ERA
Boston W-91 L-62 Billy Southworth	1B	E. Torgeson	438	.253	10	67	1069	81	8	85	9.0	.993	J. Sain	42	315	24	15	1	2.60
	2B	E. Stanky	247	.320	2	29	168	202	7	45	5.7	.981	W. Spahn	36	257	15	12	1	3.71
	SS	A. Dark	543	.322	3	48	253	393	25	66	5.0	.963	B. Voiselle	37	216	13	13	2	3.63
	3B	B. Elliott	540	.283	23	100	146	298	26	18	3.1	.945	V. Bickford	33	146	11	5	1	3.27
	RF	T. Holmes	585	.325	6	61	283	8	5	4	2.2	.983	R. Barrett	34	128	7	8	0	3.65
	CF	McCormick	343	.303	1	39	187	7	5	3	2.0	.975	B. Hogue	40	86	8	2	2	3.23
	LF	J. Heath	364	.319	20	76	223	6	2	2	2.2	.991	C. Shoun	36	74	5	1	4	4.01
	C	P. Masi	376	.253	5	44	458	39	6	5	4.6	.988							
	OF	J. Russell	322	.264	9	54	246	3	2	0	3.0	.992							
	OF	C. Conatser	224	.277	3	23	146	3	4	1	2.0	.974							
	2S	S. Sisti	221	.244	0	21	140	173	14	32		.957							
	C	B. Salkeld	198	.242	8	28	254	32	3	5	4.9	.990							
	1B	McCormick	180	.250	4	34	343	33	5	30	7.6	.987							
St. Louis W-85 L-69 Eddie Dyer	1B	N. Jones	481	.254	10	81	1148	63	17	98	9.6	.986	M. Dickson	42	252	12	16	1	4.14
	2B	Schoendienst	408	.272	4	36	230	269	10	57	5.3	.980	H. Brecheen	33	233	20	7	1	2.24
	SS	M. Marion	567	.252	4	43	263	445	19	80	5.1	.974	H. Pollet	36	186	13	8	0	4.54
	3B	D. Lang	323	.269	4	31	81	188	10	13	2.9	.964	G. Munger	39	166	10	11	0	4.50
	RF	E. Slaughter	549	.321	11	90	330	9	10	1	2.4	.971	A. Brazle	42	156	10	6	1	3.80
	CF	T. Moore	207	.232	4	18	131	2	1	0	1.9	.993	T. Wilks	57	131	6	6	13	2.62
	LF	S. Musial	611	.376	39	131	347	10	7	3	2.3	.981	J. Hearn	34	90	8	6	1	4.22
	C	D. Rice	290	.197	4	34	447	46	2	5	5.0	.996							
	UT	E. Dusak	311	.209	6	19	191	80	5	14		.982							
	OF	R. Northey	246	.321	13	64	85	2	1	0	1.3	.989							
	2S	R. LaPointe	222	.225	0	15	142	158	12	36		.962							
	3B	W. Kurowski	220	.214	2	33	55	100	10	7	2.5	.939							
Brooklyn W-84 L-70 Leo Durocher W-35 L-37 Ray Blades W-1 L-0 Burt Shotton W-48 L-33	1B	G. Hodges	481	.249	11	70	830	60	13	85	9.4	.986	R. Barney	44	247	15	13	0	3.10
	2B	J. Robinson	574	.296	12	85	308	315	13	80	5.5	.980	R. Branca	36	216	14	9	1	3.51
	SS	P. Reese	566	.274	9	75	335	453	31	93	5.5	.962	J. Hatten	42	209	13	10	0	3.58
	3B	B. Cox	237	.249	3	15	51	107	7	7	2.4	.958	P. Roe	34	178	12	8	2	2.63
	RF	G. Hermanski	400	.290	15	60	225	13	7	1	2.1	.971	E. Palica	41	125	6	6	4	4.45
	CF	C. Furillo	364	.297	4	44	274	13	5	2	2.8	.983	H. Behrman	34	91	5	4	7	4.05
	LF	M. Rackley	281	.327	0	15	143	7	8	1	2.1	.949	W. Ramsdell	27	50	4	4	4	5.19
	C	Campanella	279	.258	9	45	413	45	9	12	6.0	.981							
	UT	B. Edwards	286	.276	8	54	264	43	12	2		.962							
	23	E. Miksis	221	.213	2	16	122	143	9	19		.967							
	OF	D. Whitman	165	.291	0	29	93	3	1	0	2.0	.990							
	OF	G. Shuba	161	.267	4	32	87	1	6	1	1.7	.936							
	OF	D. Snider	160	.244	5	21	87	5	1	0	2.0	.989							
	1B	P. Ward	146	.260	1	21	268	20	3	21	7.7	.990							
	3B	T. Brown	145	.241	2	20	43	60	7	7	2.6	.936							
	OF	A. Vaughan	123	.244	3	22	47	4	0	0	2.0	1.000							
Pittsburgh W-83 L-71 Billy Meyer	1B	E. Stevens	429	.254	10	69	1021	83	4	94	9.5	.996	B. Chesnes	25	194	14	6	0	3.57
	2B	D. Murtaugh	514	.290	1	71	375	412	17	95	5.5	.979	E. Riddle	28	191	12	10	1	3.49
	SS	S. Rojek	641	.290	4	51	262	475	29	91	4.9	.962	V. Lombardi	38	163	10	9	4	3.70
	3B	F. Gustine	449	.267	9	42	119	256	21	23	3.3	.947	K. Higbe	56	158	8	7	10	3.36
	RF	D. Walker	408	.316	2	54	168	4	4	0	1.6	.977	E. Bonham	22	136	6	10	0	4.31
	CF	W. Westlake	428	.285	17	65	274	8	7	2	2.3	.976	Ostermueller	23	134	8	11	0	4.42
	LF	R. Kiner	555	.265	40	123	382	6	10	1	2.6	.975	R. Sewell	21	122	13	3	0	3.48
	C	Fitz Gerald	262	.267	1	35	338	36	15	4	4.1	.961	E. Singleton	38	92	4	6	2	4.97
	OF	J. Hopp	392	.278	1	31	192	3	0	1	2.4	1.000							
	C	C. Kluttz	271	.221	4	20	298	54	8	8	4.0	.978							
	3B	E. Bockman	176	.239	4	23	50	100	6	9	3.1	.962							
	10	M. West	146	.178	8	21	209	20	2	14		.991							

NATIONAL LEAGUE 1948, cont.

	POS	Player	AB	BA	HR	RBI	PO	A	E	DP	TC/G	FA	Pitcher	G	IP	W	L	SV	ERA
New York	1B	J. Mize	560	.289	40	125	1359	111	13	114	9.8	.991	L. Jansen	42	277	18	12	2	3.61
	2B	B. Rigney	424	.264	10	43	258	275	18	48	5.2	.967	S. Jones	55	201	16	8	5	3.35
W-78 L-76	SS	B. Kerr	496	.240	0	46	269	456	25	72	5.2	.967	R. Poat	39	158	11	10	0	4.34
	3B	S. Gordon	521	.299	30	107	126	220	19	19	3.2	.948	C. Hartung	36	153	8	8	1	4.75
Mel Ott	RF	W. Marshall	537	.272	14	86	266	16	5	2	2.0	.983	D. Koslo	35	149	8	10	3	3.87
W-37 L-38	CF	W. Lockman	584	.286	18	59	388	6	5	0	2.8	.987	M. Kennedy	25	114	3	9	0	4.01
Leo Durocher	LF	B. Thomson	471	.248	16	63	313	10	10	2	2.7	.970	A. Hansen	36	100	5	3	1	2.97
W-41 L-38	C	W. Cooper	290	.266	16	54	307	21	7	3	4.2	.979	K. Trinkle	53	71	4	5	7	3.18
	32	L. Lohrke	280	.250	5	31	125	170	22	21		.931							
Philadelphia	1B	D. Sisler	446	.274	11	56	986	73	18	88	9.0	.983	D. Leonard	34	226	11	18	0	2.51
	2B	G. Hamner	446	.260	3	48	210	224	15	46	5.2	.967	C. Simmons	31	170	7	12	0	4.87
	SS	E. Miller	468	.246	14	61	229	341	20	63	4.8	.966	M. Dubiel	37	150	9	10	4	3.89
W-66 L-88	3B	P. Caballero	351	.245	0	19	105	147	10	14	3.3	.962	S. Rowe	30	148	10	10	2	4.07
	RF	D. Ennis	589	.290	30	95	297	15	14	4	2.2	.957	R. Roberts	20	147	7	9	0	3.19
Ben Chapman	CF	R. Ashburn	463	.333	2	40	344	14	7	2	3.1	.981	B. Donnelly	26	132	5	7	2	3.69
W-37 L-42	LF	J. Blatnik	415	.260	6	45	220	9	13	1	2.3	.946	Heintzelman	27	130	6	11	2	4.29
	C	A. Seminick	391	.225	13	44	541	74	22	8	5.1	.965							
Dusty Cooke	31	B. Haas	333	.282	4	34	366	107	24	26		.952							
W-6 L-6	OF	H. Walker	332	.292	2	23	198	6	4	1	2.6	.981							
Eddie Sawyer	UT	B. Rowell	196	.240	1	22	76	42	12	7		.908							
W-23 L-40	2B	E. Verban	169	.231	0	11	104	126	6	25	4.4	.975							
Cincinnati	1B	Kluszewski	379	.274	12	57	833	65	9	60	9.3	.990	Vander Meer	33	232	17	14	0	3.41
	2B	B. Adams	262	.298	1	21	160	143	11	33	4.9	.965	Raffensberger	40	180	11	12	0	3.84
	SS	V. Stallcup	539	.228	3	65	264	433	32	84	4.9	.956	H. Fox	34	171	6	9	1	4.53
W-64 L-89	3B	G. Hatton	458	.240	9	44	141	243	28	21	3.3	.932	H. Wehmeier	33	147	11	8	0	5.86
	RF	F. Baumholtz	415	.296	4	30	216	11	3	2	2.1	.987	E. Blackwell	22	139	7	9	1	4.54
Johnny Neun	CF	J. Wyrostek	512	.273	17	76	331	8	8	1	2.7	.977	K. Peterson	43	137	2	15	1	4.60
W-44 L-56	LF	H. Sauer	530	.260	35	97	270	14	8	6	2.2	.973	H. Gumbert	61	106	10	8	17	3.47
	C	R. Lamanno	385	.242	0	27	537	49	13	11	4.8	.978							
Bucky Walters																			
W-20 L-33	OF	D. Litwhiler	338	.275	14	44	165	3	2	2	2.0	.988							
	UT	C. Corbitt	258	.256	0	18	138	160	7	24		.977							
	2B	B. Zientara	187	.187	0	7	143	140	3	32	4.8	.990							
Chicago	1B	E. Waitkus	562	.295	7	44	1064	92	9	77	10.0	.992	J. Schmitz	34	242	18	13	1	2.64
	2B	H. Schenz	337	.261	1	14	184	190	10	45	4.9	.974	R. Meyer	29	165	10	10	0	3.66
	SS	R. Smalley	361	.216	4	36	189	351	34	70	4.6	.941	D. McCall	30	151	4	13	0	4.82
W-64 L-90	3B	A. Pafko	548	.312	26	101	125	314	29	29	3.4	.938	B. Rush	36	133	5	11	0	3.92
	RF	B. Nicholson	494	.261	19	67	244	7	5	1	1.9	.980	H. Borowy	39	127	5	10	1	4.89
Charlie Grimm	CF	H. Jeffcoat	473	.279	4	42	307	12	8	3	2.7	.976	R. Hamner	27	111	5	9	0	4.69
	LF	P. Lowrey	435	.294	2	54	225	9	4	2	2.3	.983	C. Chambers	29	104	2	9	0	4.43
	C	B. Scheffing	293	.300	5	45	332	36	4	5	4.8	.989	D. Lade	19	87	5	6	0	4.02
	1O	Cavarretta	334	.278	3	40	446	32	3	46		.994	J. Dobernic	54	86	7	2	1	3.15
	2B	E. Verban	248	.294	1	16	134	164	11	47	5.5	.964							
	OF	C. Maddern	214	.252	4	27	98	6	2	0	1.9	.981							
	C	McCullough	172	.209	1	7	225	25	7	5	5.0	.973							
	C	R. Walker	171	.275	5	26	178	22	4	3	4.6	.980							

BATTING AND BASE RUNNING LEADERS

Batting Average
- S. Musial, STL — .376
- R. Ashburn, PHI — .333
- T. Holmes, BOS — .325
- A. Dark, BOS — .322
- E. Slaughter, STL — .321

Slugging Average
- S. Musial, STL — .702
- J. Mize, NY — .564
- S. Gordon, NY — .537
- R. Kiner, PIT — .533
- D. Ennis, PHI — .525

Home Runs
- R. Kiner, PIT — 40
- J. Mize, NY — 40
- S. Musial, STL — 39
- H. Sauer, CIN — 35
- S. Gordon, NY — 30
- D. Ennis, PHI — 30

Total Bases
- S. Musial, STL — 429
- J. Mize, NY — 316
- D. Ennis, PHI — 309
- R. Kiner, PIT — 296
- A. Pafko, CHI — 283

Runs Batted In
- S. Musial, STL — 131
- J. Mize, NY — 125
- R. Kiner, PIT — 123
- S. Gordon, NY — 107
- A. Pafko, CHI — 101

Stolen Bases
- R. Ashburn, PHI — 32
- P. Reese, BKN — 25
- S. Rojek, PIT — 24
- J. Robinson, BKN — 22
- E. Torgeson, BOS — 19

Hits
- S. Musial, STL — 230
- T. Holmes, BOS — 190
- S. Rojek, PIT — 186
- E. Slaughter, STL — 176

Base on Balls
- B. Elliott, BOS — 131
- R. Kiner, PIT — 112
- J. Mize, NY — 94
- E. Torgeson, BOS — 81

Home Run Percentage
- R. Kiner, PIT — 7.2
- J. Mize, NY — 7.1
- H. Sauer, CIN — 6.6
- S. Musial, STL — 6.4

PITCHING LEADERS

Winning Percentage
- H. Brecheen, STL — .741
- S. Jones, NY — .667
- J. Sain, BOS — .615
- L. Jansen, NY — .600
- J. Schmitz, CHI — .581

Earned Run Average
- H. Brecheen, STL — 2.24
- D. Leonard, PHI — 2.51
- J. Sain, BOS — 2.60
- J. Schmitz, CHI — 2.64
- R. Barney, BKN — 3.10

Wins
- J. Sain, BOS — 24
- H. Brecheen, STL — 20
- L. Jansen, NY — 18
- J. Schmitz, CHI — 18
- Vander Meer, CIN — 17

Saves
- H. Gumbert, CIN — 17
- T. Wilks, STL — 13
- K. Higbe, PIT — 10
- K. Trinkle, NY — 7
- H. Behrman, BKN — 7

Strikeouts
- H. Brecheen, STL — 149
- R. Barney, BKN — 138
- J. Sain, BOS — 137
- L. Jansen, NY — 126
- R. Branca, BKN — 122

Complete Games
- J. Sain, BOS — 28
- H. Brecheen, STL — 21
- J. Schmitz, CHI — 18
- D. Leonard, PHI — 16
- W. Spahn, BOS — 16

Fewest Hits/9 Innings
- J. Schmitz, CHI — 6.92
- R. Barney, BKN — 7.04
- H. Brecheen, STL — 7.44
- V. Bickford, BOS — 7.71

Shutouts
- H. Brecheen, STL — 7
- Raffensberger, CIN — 4
- R. Barney, BKN — 4
- L. Jansen, NY — 4

Fewest Walks/9 Innings
- L. Jansen, NY — 1.75
- H. Brecheen, STL — 1.89
- D. Leonard, PHI — 2.15
- J. Sain, BOS — 2.37

NATIONAL LEAGUE 1948, cont.

BATTING AND BASE RUNNING LEADERS

Runs Scored		Doubles		Triples		Most Strikeouts/9 Inn.	
S. Musial, STL	135	S. Musial, STL	46	S. Musial, STL	18	H. Brecheen, STL	5.75
W. Lockman, NY	117	D. Ennis, PHI	40	J. Hopp, PIT	12	R. Branca, BKN	5.09
J. Mize, NY	110	A. Dark, BOS	39	E. Slaughter, STL	11	R. Barney, BKN	5.04
J. Robinson, BKN	108	J. Robinson, BKN	38	E. Waitkus, CHI	10	Vander Meer, CIN	4.66

PITCHING LEADERS

Innings		Games Pitched	
J. Sain, BOS	315	H. Gumbert, CIN	61
L. Jansen, NY	277	T. Wilks, STL	57
W. Spahn, BOS	257	K. Higbe, PIT	56
M. Dickson, STL	252	S. Jones, NY	55

	W	L	PCT	GB	R	OR	2B	3B	HR	BA	SA	SB	E	DP	FA	CG	BB	SO	ShO	SV	ERA
Boston	91	62	.595		739	584	272	49	95	.275	.399	43	143	132	.976	70	430	579	10	17	3.38
St. Louis	85	69	.552	6.5	742	646	238	58	105	.263	.389	24	119	138	.980	60	476	635	13	18	3.91
Brooklyn	84	70	.545	7.5	744	667	256	54	91	.261	.381	114	161	151	.973	52	633	670	9	22	3.75
Pittsburgh	83	71	.539	8.5	706	699	191	54	108	.263	.380	68	137	150	.973	65	564	519	5	19	4.15
New York	78	76	.506	13.5	780	704	210	49	164	.256	.408	51	156	134	.974	54	551	527	15	21	3.93
Philadelphia	66	88	.429	25.5	591	729	227	39	91	.259	.368	68	210	126	.964	61	561	552	6	15	4.08
Cincinnati	64	89	.418	27	588	752	221	37	104	.247	.365	42	158	135	.973	40	572	599	9	20	4.47
Chicago	64	90	.416	27.5	597	706	225	44	87	.262	.369	39	172	152	.972	51	609	636	7	10	4.00
					5487	5487	1840	384	845	.261	.383	449	1256	1118	.974	453	4396	4717	74	142	3.95

AMERICAN LEAGUE 1948

	POS	Player	AB	BA	HR	RBI	PO	A	E	DP	TC/G	FA	Pitcher	G	IP	W	L	SV	ERA
Cleveland	1B	E. Robinson	493	.254	16	83	1213	79	7	123	9.9	.995	B. Lemon	43	294	20	14	2	2.82
	2B	J. Gordon	550	.280	32	124	330	436	23	97	5.5	.971	B. Feller	44	280	19	15	3	3.56
W-97 L-58	SS	L. Boudreau	560	.355	18	106	297	483	20	119	5.3	.975	G. Bearden	37	230	20	7	1	2.43
	3B	K. Keltner	558	.297	31	119	123	312	14	27	2.9	.969	S. Gromek	38	130	9	3	2	2.84
Lou Boudreau	RF	L. Doby	439	.301	14	66	287	12	14	3	2.7	.955	S. Zoldak	23	106	9	6	0	2.81
	CF	T. Tucker	242	.260	1	19	172	5	0	2	2.7	1.000	Christopher	45	59	3	2	17	2.90
	LF	D. Mitchell	608	.336	4	56	307	12	3	3	2.3	.991							
	C	J. Hegan	472	.248	14	61	637	76	7	17	5.1	.990							
	OF	A. Clark	271	.310	9	38	108	4	2	1	1.8	.982							
	OF	W. Judnich	218	.257	2	29	93	4	3	0	2.0	.970							
	OF	H. Edwards	160	.269	3	18	76	1	1	0	1.9	.987							
	P	B. Lemon	119	.286	5	21	23	86	4	8	2.6	.965							
Boston	1B	B. Goodman	445	.310	1	66	1101	69	8	118	10.1	.993	J. Dobson	38	245	16	10	2	3.56
	2B	B. Doerr	527	.285	27	111	366	430	6	119	5.8	.993	M. Parnell	35	212	15	8	0	3.14
W-96 L-59	SS	V. Stephens	635	.269	29	137	269	540	24	113	5.4	.971	J. Kramer	29	205	18	5	0	4.35
	3B	J. Pesky	565	.281	3	55	121	303	22	35	3.2	.951	E. Kinder	28	178	10	7	0	3.74
Joe McCarthy	RF	S. Spence	391	.235	12	61	206	4	5	1	2.3	.977	D. Galehouse	27	137	8	8	0	4.00
	CF	D. DiMaggio	648	.285	9	87	503	13	10	4	3.4	.981	B. Ferriss	31	115	7	3	3	5.23
	LF	T. Williams	509	.369	25	127	289	9	5	2	2.3	.983	M. Harris	20	114	7	10	0	5.30
	C	B. Tebbetts	446	.280	5	68	470	56	10	8	4.3	.981	E. Johnson	35	91	10	4	5	4.53
	OF	W. Moses	189	.259	2	29	101	2	2	1	2.3	.981							
	OF	S. Mele	180	.233	2	25	99	2	3	0	1.9	.971							
	32	B. Hitchcock	124	.298	1	20	54	82	4	15		.971							
	C	M. Batts	118	.314	1	24	118	18	2	3	3.4	.986							
New York	1B	G. McQuinn	302	.248	11	41	693	48	5	79	8.3	.993	A. Reynolds	39	236	16	7	3	3.77
	2B	Stirnweiss	515	.252	3	32	346	364	5	103	5.1	.993	E. Lopat	33	227	17	11	0	3.65
W-94 L-60	SS	P. Rizzuto	464	.252	6	50	259	348	17	85	4.9	.973	V. Raschi	36	223	19	8	1	3.84
	3B	B. Johnson	446	.294	12	64	147	213	20	25	3.2	.947	S. Shea	28	156	9	10	1	3.41
Bucky Harris	RF	T. Henrich	588	.308	25	100	216	8	5	4	2.2	.978	T. Byrne	31	134	8	5	2	3.30
	CF	J. DiMaggio	594	.320	39	155	441	8	13	1	3.0	.972	J. Page	55	108	7	8	16	4.26
	LF	J. Lindell	309	.317	13	55	165	7	1	1	2.2	.994							
	C	G. Niarhos	228	.268	0	19	376	33	4	7	5.0	.990							
	CO	Y. Berra	469	.305	14	98	390	40	9	7		.979							
	UT	B. Brown	363	.300	3	48	130	173	18	33		.944							
	OF	C. Keller	247	.267	6	44	126	1	3	0	2.0	.977							
Philadelphia	1B	F. Fain	520	.281	7	88	1284	120	16	148	9.8	.989	Marchildon	33	226	9	15	0	4.53
	2B	P. Suder	519	.241	7	60	342	461	10	114	5.5	.988	J. Coleman	33	216	14	13	0	4.09
W-84 L-70	SS	E. Joost	509	.250	16	55	325	409	20	115	5.6	.973	D. Fowler	29	205	15	8	2	3.78
	3B	H. Majeski	590	.310	12	120	163	268	11	19	3.1	.975	C. Scheib	32	199	14	8	0	3.94
Connie Mack	RF	E. Valo	383	.305	3	46	231	4	4	1	2.2	.983	L. Brissie	39	194	14	10	5	4.13
	CF	S. Chapman	445	.258	13	70	368	8	7	2	3.2	.982	C. Harris	45	94	5	2	5	4.13
	LF	B. McCosky	515	.326	0	46	277	9	3	1	2.2	.990	B. McCahan	17	87	4	7	0	5.71
	C	B. Rosar	302	.255	4	41	335	39	1	10	4.2	.997	B. Savage	33	75	5	1	5	6.21
	OF	D. White	253	.245	1	28	108	3	5	1	2.1	.957							
	OF	R. Coleman	210	.243	0	21	126	7	3	3	2.6	.978							
	C	M. Guerra	142	.211	1	23	163	20	5	1	4.0	.973							
	P	C. Scheib	104	.298	2	21	14	36	1	5	1.6	.980							

AMERICAN LEAGUE 1948, cont.

	POS	Player	AB	BA	HR	RBI	PO	A	E	DP	TC/G	FA	Pitcher	G	IP	W	L	SV	ERA
Detroit	1B	G. Vico	521	.267	8	58	1169	85	15	112	8.9	.988	H. Newhouser	39	272	21	12	1	3.01
	2B	E. Mayo	370	.249	2	42	202	223	11	48	5.1	.975	Hutchinson	33	221	13	11	0	4.32
W-78 L-76	SS	J. Lipon	458	.290	5	52	211	346	17	63	4.9	.970	V. Trucks	43	212	14	13	2	3.78
	3B	G. Kell	368	.304	2	44	108	146	8	15	2.8	.969	D. Trout	32	184	10	14	2	3.43
Steve O'Neill	RF	P. Mullin	496	.288	23	80	274	7	8	0	2.2	.972	A. Houtteman	43	164	2	16	10	4.66
	CF	H. Evers	538	.314	10	103	392	8	11	0	3.0	.973	S. Overmire	37	66	3	4		5.97
	LF	V. Wertz	391	.248	7	67	196	11	10	3	2.2	.954							
	C	B. Swift	292	.223	4	33	476	55	5	13	4.8	.991							
	OF	D. Wakefield	322	.276	11	53	198	3	11	1	2.5	.948							
	S2	N. Berry	256	.266	0	16	138	199	17	46		.952							
	3B	J. Outlaw	198	.283	0	25	39	87	11	8	2.9	.920							
	2B	E. Lake	198	.263	2	18	110	132	7	31	5.5	.972							
St. Louis	1B	C. Stevens	287	.261	1	26	737	56	7	89	9.4	.991	F. Sanford	42	227	12	21	2	4.64
	2B	G. Priddy	560	.296	8	79	407	471	29	132	6.2	.968	C. Fannin	34	214	10	14	1	4.17
W-59 L-94	SS	Pellagrini	290	.238	2	27	194	292	18	85	5.1	.964	N. Garver	38	198	7	11	5	3.41
	3B	B. Dillinger	644	.321	2	44	187	242	20	30	2.9	.955	B. Kennedy	26	132	7	8	0	4.70
Zack Taylor	RF	A. Zarilla	529	.329	12	74	322	5	13	0	2.5	.962	B. Stephens	43	123	3	6	3	6.02
	CF	P. Lehner	333	.276	2	46	223	4	6	2	2.6	.974	F. Biscan	47	99	6	7	2	6.11
	LF	W. Platt	454	.271	7	82	230	5	13	2	2.2	.948	J. Ostrowski	26	78	4	6	3	5.97
	C	L. Moss	335	.257	14	46	357	52	5	8	4.0	.988							
	SS	S. Dente	267	.270	0	22	138	207	14	46	4.7	.958							
	OF	D. Kokos	258	.298	4	40	126	8	5	2	2.0	.964							
	1B	H. Arft	248	.238	5	38	598	43	3	81	9.3	.995							
	C	R. Partee	231	.203	0	17	297	22	6	7	4.3	.982							
	OF	D. Lund	161	.248	3	25	72	3	0	0	1.7	1.000							
Washington	1B	M. Vernon	558	.242	3	48	1297	113	15	128	9.5	.989	E. Wynn	33	198	8	19	0	5.82
	2B	A. Kozar	577	.250	1	58	348	444	22	89	5.5	.967	W. Masterson	33	188	8	15	2	3.83
W-56 L-97	SS	M. Christman	409	.259	1	40	207	259	15	59	4.7	.969	Scarborough	31	185	15	8	1	2.82
	3B	E. Yost	555	.249	2	50	189	240	15	21	3.1	.966	S. Hudson	39	182	4	16	1	5.88
Joe Kuhel	RF	B. Stewart	401	.279	7	69	265	5	7	1	2.4	.975	M. Haefner	28	148	5	13	0	4.02
	CF	Gillenwater	221	.244	3	21	186	4	5	0	2.9	.974	D. Thompson	46	131	6	10	4	3.84
	LF	G. Coan	513	.232	7	60	341	11	11	3	2.8	.970	T. Ferrick	37	74	2	5	10	4.15
	C	J. Early	246	.220	1	28	268	51	3	7	3.5	.991							
	OF	E. Wooten	258	.256	1	23	178	9	4	2	2.6	.979							
	C	A. Evans	228	.259	2	28	245	38	5	6	3.4	.983							
	OF	T. McBride	206	.257	1	29	108	7	2	3	2.1	.983							
	OF	S. Robertson	187	.246	2	22	105	3	7	0	2.3	.939							
	SS	J. Sullivan	173	.208	0	12	94	138	12	33	4.3	.951							
Chicago	1B	T. Lupien	617	.246	6	54	1436	92	11	155	10.0	.993	B. Wight	34	223	9	20	1	4.80
	2B	D. Kolloway	417	.273	6	38	241	276	18	62	6.4	.966	J. Haynes	27	150	9	10	0	3.97
W-51 L-101	SS	C. Michaels	484	.248	5	56	164	285	20	65	5.5	.957	A. Gettel	22	148	8	10	1	4.01
	3B	L. Appling	497	.314	0	47	84	163	15	13	3.6	.943	M. Pieretti	21	120	8	10	1	4.95
Ted Lyons	RF	T. Wright	455	.279	4	61	227	9	3	3	2.1	.987	H. Judson	40	107	4	5	8	4.78
	CF	D. Philley	488	.287	5	42	381	22	9	6	3.2	.978	F. Papish	32	95	2	8	4	5.00
	LF	P. Seerey	340	.229	18	64	198	9	4	5	2.3	.981	O. Grove	32	88	2	10	1	6.16
	C	A. Robinson	326	.252	8	39	303	50	4	4	3.9	.989	G. Moulder	33	86	3	6	2	6.41
	3B	F. Baker	335	.215	0	18	78	170	10	17	3.6	.961							
	OF	R. Hodgin	331	.266	1	34	184	9	6	0	2.5	.970							
	C	R. Weigel	163	.233	0	26	108	19	4	4	3.4	.969							

BATTING AND BASE RUNNING LEADERS

Batting Average
- T. Williams, BOS — .369
- L. Boudreau, CLE — .355
- D. Mitchell, CLE — .336
- A. Zarilla, STL — .329
- B. McCosky, PHI — .326

Slugging Average
- T. Williams, BOS — .615
- J. DiMaggio, NY — .598
- T. Henrich, NY — .554
- L. Boudreau, CLE — .534
- K. Keltner, CLE — .522

Home Runs
- J. DiMaggio, NY — 39
- J. Gordon, CLE — 32
- K. Keltner, CLE — 31
- V. Stephens, BOS — 29
- B. Doerr, BOS — 27

Total Bases
- J. DiMaggio, NY — 355
- T. Henrich, NY — 326
- T. Williams, BOS — 313
- L. Boudreau, CLE — 299
- V. Stephens, BOS — 299

Runs Batted In
- J. DiMaggio, NY — 155
- V. Stephens, BOS — 137
- T. Williams, BOS — 127
- J. Gordon, CLE — 124
- H. Majeski, PHI — 120

Stolen Bases
- B. Dillinger, STL — 28
- G. Coan, WAS — 23
- M. Vernon, WAS — 15
- D. Mitchell, CLE — 13

Hits
- B. Dillinger, STL — 207
- D. Mitchell, CLE — 204
- L. Boudreau, CLE — 199
- J. DiMaggio, NY — 190

Base on Balls
- T. Williams, BOS — 126
- E. Joost, PHI — 119
- F. Fain, PHI — 113
- D. DiMaggio, BOS — 101

Home Run Percentage
- J. DiMaggio, NY — 6.6
- J. Gordon, CLE — 5.8
- K. Keltner, CLE — 5.6
- B. Doerr, BOS — 5.1

PITCHING LEADERS

Winning Percentage
- J. Kramer, BOS — .783
- G. Bearden, CLE — .741
- V. Raschi, NY — .704
- A. Reynolds, NY — .696

Earned Run Average
- G. Bearden, CLE — 2.43
- B. Lemon, CLE — 2.82
- H. Newhouser, DET — 3.01
- M. Parnell, BOS — 3.14
- D. Trout, DET — 3.43

Wins
- H. Newhouser, DET — 21
- G. Bearden, CLE — 20
- B. Lemon, CLE — 20
- V. Raschi, NY — 19
- B. Feller, CLE — 19

Saves
- Christopher, CLE — 17
- J. Page, NY — 16
- T. Ferrick, WAS — 10
- A. Houtteman, DET — 10
- H. Judson, CHI — 8

Strikeouts
- B. Feller, CLE — 164
- B. Lemon, CLE — 147
- H. Newhouser, DET — 143
- L. Brissie, PHI — 127
- V. Raschi, NY — 124

Complete Games
- B. Lemon, CLE — 20
- H. Newhouser, DET — 19
- V. Raschi, NY — 18
- B. Feller, CLE — 18

Fewest Hits/9 Innings
- B. Lemon, CLE — 7.08
- G. Bearden, CLE — 7.33
- B. Feller, CLE — 8.19
- H. Newhouser, DET — 8.23

Shutouts
- B. Lemon, CLE — 10
- G. Bearden, CLE — 6
- V. Raschi, NY — 6
- J. Dobson, BOS — 5

Fewest Walks/9 Innings
- Hutchinson, DET — 1.95
- E. Lopat, NY — 2.62
- J. Kramer, BOS — 2.81
- V. Raschi, NY — 2.99

AMERICAN LEAGUE 1948, *cont.*

BATTING AND BASE RUNNING LEADERS

Runs Scored		Doubles		Triples			Most Strikeouts/9 Inn.	
T. Henrich, NY	138	T. Williams, BOS	44	T. Henrich, NY	14		L. Brissie, PHI	5.89
D. DiMaggio, BOS	127	T. Henrich, NY	42	B. Stewart, NY, WAS	13		B. Feller, CLE	5.27
T. Williams, BOS	124	H. Majeski, PHI	41	P. Mullin, DET	11		V. Raschi, NY	5.01
J. Pesky, BOS	124	G. Priddy, STL	40	E. Yost, WAS	11		H. Newhouser, DET	4.73

PITCHING LEADERS

Innings		Games Pitched	
B. Lemon, CLE	294	J. Page, NY	55
B. Feller, CLE	280	A. Widmar, STL	49
H. Newhouser, DET	272	F. Biscan, STL	47
J. Dobson, BOS	245	D. Thompson, WAS	46

	W	L	PCT	GB	R	OR	2B	3B	HR	BA	SA	SB	E	DP	FA	CG	BB	SO	ShO	SV	ERA
Cleveland *	97	58	.626		840	568	242	54	155	.282	.431	54	114	183	.982	66	628	595	26	30	3.22
Boston	96	59	.619	1	907	720	277	40	121	.274	.409	38	116	174	.981	70	592	513	11	13	4.20
New York	94	60	.610	2.5	857	633	251	75	139	.278	.432	24	120	161	.979	62	641	654	16	24	3.75
Philadelphia	84	70	.545	12.5	729	735	231	47	68	.260	.362	39	113	180	.981	74	638	486	7	18	4.43
Detroit	78	76	.506	18.5	700	726	219	58	78	.267	.375	22	155	143	.974	60	589	678	5	22	4.15
St. Louis	59	94	.386	37	671	849	251	62	63	.271	.378	63	168	190	.972	35	737	531	4	20	5.01
Washington	56	97	.366	40	578	796	203	75	31	.244	.331	76	154	144	.974	42	734	446	4	22	4.65
Chicago	51	101	.336	44.5	559	814	172	39	55	.251	.331	46	160	176	.974	35	673	403	2	23	4.89
					5841	5841	1846	450	710	.266	.382	362	1100	1351	.977	444	5232	4306	75	172	4.28

* Defeated Boston in a 1 game playoff.

NATIONAL LEAGUE 1949

	POS	Player	AB	BA	HR	RBI	PO	A	E	DP	TC/G	FA	Pitcher	G	IP	W	L	SV	ERA
Brooklyn W-97 L-57 Burt Shotton	1B	G. Hodges	596	.285	23	115	1336	80	7	142	9.1	.995	D. Newcombe	38	244	17	8	1	3.17
	2B	J. Robinson	593	.342	16	124	395	421	16	119	5.3	.981	P. Roe	30	213	15	6	1	2.79
	SS	P. Reese	617	.279	16	73	316	454	18	93	5.1	.977	J. Hatten	37	187	12	8	2	4.18
	3B	B. Cox	390	.233	8	40	104	213	12	28	3.3	.964	R. Branca	34	187	13	5	1	4.39
	RF	C. Furillo	549	.322	18	106	286	13	11	2	2.2	.965	J. Banta	48	152	10	6	3	3.37
	CF	D. Snider	552	.292	23	92	355	12	6	2	2.6	.984	R. Barney	38	141	9	8	1	4.41
	LF	G. Hermanski	224	.299	8	42	140	7	3	1	1.9	.980	E. Palica	49	97	8	9	6	3.62
	C	Campanella	436	.287	22	82	684	55	11	5	5.9	.985							
	C	B. Edwards	148	.209	8	25	184	13	2	0	4.9	.990							
St. Louis W-96 L-58 Eddie Dyer	1B	N. Jones	380	.300	8	62	876	40	15	85	9.5	.984	H. Pollet	39	231	20	9	1	2.77
	2B	Schoendienst	640	.297	3	54	399	424	11	105	6.0	.987	H. Brecheen	32	215	14	11	1	3.35
	SS	M. Marion	515	.272	5	70	242	441	17	74	5.2	.976	A. Brazle	39	206	14	8	0	3.18
	3B	E. Kazak	326	.304	6	42	64	175	19	20	3.2	.926	G. Munger	35	188	15	8	2	3.87
	RF	S. Musial	612	.338	36	123	326	10	3	5	2.2	.991	G. Staley	45	171	10	10	6	2.73
	CF	C. Diering	369	.263	3	38	300	7	4	1	2.5	.987	T. Wilks	59	118	10	3	9	3.73
	LF	E. Slaughter	568	.336	13	96	330	10	6	1	2.3	.983							
	C	D. Rice	284	.236	4	29	355	29	3	4	4.2	.992							
	OF	R. Northey	265	.260	7	50	93	4	2	2	1.4	.980							
	3B	T. Glaviano	258	.267	6	36	67	181	19	15	3.7	.929							
	1B	R. Nelson	244	.221	4	32	564	24	0	48	8.4	1.000							
	C	J. Garagiola	241	.261	3	26	332	35	6	1	4.7	.984							
Philadelphia W-81 L-73 Eddie Sawyer	1B	D. Sisler	412	.289	7	50	815	40	11	93	9.0	.987	Heintzelman	33	250	17	10	0	3.02
	2B	E. Miller	266	.207	6	29	240	189	6	54	5.3	.986	R. Roberts	43	227	15	15	4	3.69
	SS	G. Hamner	662	.263	6	53	280	506	32	101	5.3	.961	R. Meyer	37	213	17	8	1	3.08
	3B	W. Jones	532	.244	19	77	181	308	27	19	3.6	.948	H. Borowy	28	193	12	12	0	4.19
	RF	B. Nicholson	299	.234	11	40	185	10	1	1	2.2	.995	C. Simmons	38	131	4	10	1	4.59
	CF	R. Ashburn	662	.284	1	37	514	13	11	3	3.5	.980	J. Konstanty	53	97	9	5	7	3.25
	LF	D. Ennis	610	.302	25	110	359	16	13	1	2.5	.966	S. Rowe	23	65	3	7	0	4.82
	C	A. Seminick	334	.243	24	68	411	54	12	6	4.9	.975							
	OF	S. Hollmig	251	.255	2	26	108	5	5	1	1.8	.958							
	C	S. Lopata	240	.271	8	27	236	19	7	2	4.5	.973							
	1B	E. Waitkus	209	.306	1	28	452	36	3	55	9.1	.994							
	2B	M. Goliat	189	.212	3	19	140	143	9	31	5.8	.969							
	3B	B. Blattner	97	.247	5	21	11	11	1	2	.4	.957							
Boston W-75 L-79 Billy Southworth W-55 L-54 Johnny Cooney W-20 L-25	1B	E. Fletcher	413	.262	11	51	965	71	9	96	8.6	.991	W. Spahn	38	302	21	14	0	3.07
	2B	E. Stanky	506	.285	1	42	357	354	15	92	5.4	.979	J. Sain	37	243	10	17	0	4.81
	SS	A. Dark	529	.276	3	53	232	387	25	76	5.2	.961	V. Bickford	37	231	16	11	0	4.25
	3B	B. Elliott	482	.280	17	76	141	300	17	27	3.5	.963	B. Voiselle	30	169	7	8	1	4.04
	RF	T. Holmes	380	.266	8	59	210	10	3	4	2.2	.987	N. Potter	41	97	6	11	7	4.19
	CF	J. Russell	415	.231	8	54	269	3	7	3	2.3	.975	J. Antonelli	22	96	3	7	0	3.56
	LF	M. Rickert	277	.292	6	49	149	9	3	2	2.1	.981	B. Hall	31	74	6	4	0	4.36
	C	B. Salkeld	161	.255	5	25	230	21	5	3	4.1	.980							
	UT	S. Sisti	268	.257	5	22	156	80	7	11		.971							
	C	D. Crandall	228	.263	4	34	287	39	6	5	5.3	.982							
	OF	P. Reiser	221	.271	8	40	139	5	3	2	2.3	.980							
	OF	E. Sauer	214	.266	3	31	134	3	4	1	2.0	.972							
	UT	C. Ryan	208	.250	6	20	118	131	8	24		.969							
	OF	J. Heath	111	.306	9	23	56	2	1	1	1.9	.983							

NATIONAL LEAGUE 1949, *cont.*

	POS	Player	AB	BA	HR	RBI	PO	A	E	DP	TC/G	FA	Pitcher	G	IP	W	L	SV	ERA
New York	1B	J. Mize	388	.263	18	62	906	65	6	77	9.7	.994	L. Jansen	37	260	15	16	0	3.85
	2B	H. Thompson	275	.280	9	34	197	175	15	44	5.6	.961	M. Kennedy	38	223	12	14	1	3.43
W-73 L-81	SS	B. Kerr	220	.209	0	19	125	224	15	33	4.1	.959	D. Koslo	38	212	11	14	4	**2.50**
	3B	S. Gordon	489	.284	26	90	112	206	14	18	2.7	.958	S. Jones	42	207	15	12	0	3.34
Leo Durocher	RF	W. Marshall	499	.307	12	70	292	13	8	3	2.3	.974	C. Hartung	33	155	9	11	0	5.00
	CF	B. Thomson	641	.309	27	109	488	10	9	4	3.3	.982							
	LF	W. Lockman	617	.301	11	65	353	10	10	1	2.5	.973							
	C	W. Westrum	169	.243	7	28	224	18	5	4	4.0	.980							
	UT	B. Rigney	389	.278	6	47	185	317	32	46		.940							
	UT	L. Lohrke	180	.267	5	22	86	143	9	13		.962							
	C	R. Mueller	170	.224	5	23	197	21	4	2	4.0	.982							
	C	W. Cooper	147	.211	4	21	148	18*	3	2	4.2	.982							
Pittsburgh	1B	J. Hopp	371	.318	5	39	642	44	7	69	9.0	.990	M. Dickson	44	224	12	14	0	3.29
	2B	M. Basgall	308	.218	2	26	224	224	13	58	4.7	.972	B. Werle	35	221	12	13	0	4.24
W-71 L-83	SS	S. Rojek	557	.244	0	31	240	461	25	92	5.0	.966	C. Chambers	34	177	13	7	0	3.96
	3B	Castiglione	448	.268	6	43	100	213	14	26	3.3	.959	B. Chesnes	27	145	7	13	1	5.88
Billy Meyer	RF	W. Westlake	525	.282	23	104	319	12	6	4	2.4	.982	V. Lombardi	34	134	5	5	1	4.57
	CF	D. Restelli	232	.250	12	40	167	4	7	2	2.9	.961	E. Bonham	18	89	7	4	0	4.25
	LF	R. Kiner	549	.310	54	127	311	12	7	3	2.2	.979	E. Riddle	16	74	1	8	1	5.33
	C	McCullough	241	.237	4	21	363	39	6	8*	4.5	.985	H. Casey	33	39	4	1	5	4.66
	2B	D. Murtaugh	236	.203	2	24	202	182	10	58	5.3	.975							
	1B	E. Stevens	221	.262	4	32	533	58	3	65	10.2	.995							
	3B	E. Bockman	220	.223	6	19	59	127	8	14	2.9	.959							
	OF	T. Saffell	205	.322	2	25	122	2	1	1	2.4	.992							
	OF	D. Walker	181	.282	1	18	58	2	1	0	1.6	.984							
	C	Fitz Gerald	160	.263	2	18	163	22	5	5	3.4	.974							
Cincinnati	1B	Kluszewski	531	.309	8	68	1140	65	14	109	9.1	.989	Raffensberger	41	284	18	17	0	3.39
	2B	Bloodworth	452	.261	9	59	229	234	9	56	5.1	.981	H. Fox	38	215	6	**19**	0	3.98
W-62 L-92	SS	V. Stallcup	575	.254	3	45	256	437	27	87	5.1	.963	H. Wehmeier	33	213	11	12	0	4.68
	3B	G. Hatton	537	.263	11	69	143	290	11	**29**	3.3	**.975**	Vander Meer	28	160	5	10	0	4.90
Bucky Walters	RF	J. Wyrostek	474	.249	9	46	293	10	9	1	2.4	.971	E. Erautt	39	113	4	11	1	3.36
W-61 L-90	CF	L. Merriman	287	.230	4	26	214	7	7	1	2.7	.969	B. Lively	31	103	4	6	1	3.92
	LF	P. Lowrey	309	.275	2	25	202	7	1	2	2.7	.995	E. Blackwell	30	77	5	5	1	4.23
Luke Sewell	C	W. Cooper	307	.280	16	62	316	43*	8	3	4.8	.978							
W-1 L-2	OF	H. Walker	314	.318	1	23	177	7	7	1	2.5	.963							
	OF	D. Litwhiler	292	.291	11	48	143	6	2	1	1.8	.987							
	2B	B. Adams	277	.253	0	25	162	138	5	29	4.8	.984							
	C	D. Howell	172	.244	2	18	191	35	3	2	4.1	.987							
Chicago	1B	H. Reich	386	.280	4	34	759	**83**	9	57	10.0	.989	J. Schmitz	36	207	11	13	3	4.35
	2B	E. Verban	343	.289	0	22	218	249	**17**	60	5.5	.965	B. Rush	35	201	10	18	4	4.07
W-61 L-93	SS	R. Smalley	477	.245	8	35	265	438	**39**	91	**5.6**	.947	D. Leonard	33	180	7	16	0	4.15
	3B	F. Gustine	261	.226	4	27	52	110	12	13	3.2	.931	M. Dubiel	32	148	6	9	4	4.14
Charlie Grimm	RF	H. Jeffcoat	363	.245	2	26	250	12	10	2	2.7	.963	D. Lade	36	130	4	5	1	5.00
W-19 L-31	CF	A. Pafko	519	.281	18	69	217	8	3	2	2.3	.987	W. Hacker	30	126	5	8	0	4.23
	LF	H. Sauer	357	.291	27	83	199	10*	4	2	2.2	.981	B. Chipman	38	113	7	8	1	3.97
Frankie Frisch	C	M. Owen	198	.273	2	18	219	35	8	5	4.4	.969	B. Muncrief	34	75	5	6	2	4.56
W-42 L-62	1B	Cavarretta	360	.294	8	49	673	63	5	58	10.6	.993							
	3S	Ramazzotti	190	.179	0	6	48	112	3	15		.982							
	OF	H. Edwards	176	.290	7	21	80	4	1	2	1.7	.988							
	C	R. Walker	172	.244	3	22	166	23	7	2	4.6	.964							
	OF	F. Baumholtz	164	.226	1	15	67	3	1	3	1.7	.986							
	OF	H. Walker	159	.264	1	14	69	3	4	0	1.9	.947							

BATTING AND BASE RUNNING LEADERS

Batting Average
J. Robinson, BKN	.342
S. Musial, STL	.338
E. Slaughter, STL	.336
C. Furillo, BKN	.322
R. Kiner, PIT	.310

Slugging Average
R. Kiner, PIT	.658
S. Musial, STL	.624
J. Robinson, BKN	.528
D. Ennis, PHI	.525
B. Thomson, NY	.518

Home Runs
R. Kiner, PIT	54
S. Musial, STL	36
H. Sauer, CHI, CIN	31
B. Thomson, NY	27
S. Gordon, NY	26

Winning Percentage
P. Roe, BKN	.714
H. Pollet, STL	.690
R. Meyer, PHI	.680
D. Newcombe, BKN	.680
G. Munger, STL	.652

PITCHING LEADERS

Earned Run Average
D. Koslo, NY	2.50
H. Pollet, STL	2.77
P. Roe, BKN	2.79
Heintzelman, PHI	3.02
W. Spahn, BOS	3.07

Wins
W. Spahn, BOS	21
H. Pollet, STL	20
Raffensberger, CIN	18
R. Meyer, PHI	17
D. Newcombe, BKN	17
Heintzelman, PHI	17

Total Bases
S. Musial, STL	382
R. Kiner, PIT	361
B. Thomson, NY	332
D. Ennis, PHI	320
J. Robinson, BKN	313

Runs Batted In
R. Kiner, PIT	127
J. Robinson, BKN	124
S. Musial, STL	123
G. Hodges, BKN	115
D. Ennis, PHI	110

Stolen Bases
J. Robinson, BKN	37
P. Reese, BKN	26
G. Hermanski, BKN	12
H. Jeffcoat, CHI	12
D. Snider, BKN	12
W. Lockman, NY	12

Saves
T. Wilks, STL	9
J. Konstanty, PHI	7
N. Potter, BOS	7
G. Staley, STL	6
E. Palica, BKN	6

Strikeouts
W. Spahn, BOS	151
D. Newcombe, BKN	149
L. Jansen, NY	113
R. Branca, BKN	109
P. Roe, BKN	109

Complete Games
W. Spahn, BOS	25
Raffensberger, CIN	20
D. Newcombe, BKN	19
H. Pollet, STL	17
L. Jansen, NY	17

NATIONAL LEAGUE 1949, *cont.*

BATTING AND BASE RUNNING LEADERS

Hits
S. Musial, STL	207
J. Robinson, BKN	203
B. Thomson, NY	198
E. Slaughter, STL	191

Base on Balls
R. Kiner, PIT	117
P. Reese, BKN	116
E. Stanky, BOS	113
S. Musial, STL	107

Home Run Percentage
R. Kiner, PIT	9.8
H. Sauer, CHI, CIN	6.1
S. Musial, STL	5.9
S. Gordon, NY	5.3

Runs Scored
P. Reese, BKN	132
S. Musial, STL	128
J. Robinson, BKN	122
R. Kiner, PIT	116

Doubles
S. Musial, STL	41
D. Ennis, PHI	39
G. Hatton, CIN	38
J. Robinson, BKN	38

Triples
E. Slaughter, STL	13
S. Musial, STL	13
J. Robinson, BKN	12
D. Ennis, PHI	11

PITCHING LEADERS

Fewest Hits/9 Innings
D. Koslo, NY	8.19
D. Newcombe, BKN	8.21
M. Kennedy, NY	8.38
R. Meyer, PHI	8.41

Shutouts
H. Pollet, STL	5
D. Newcombe, BKN	5
Heintzelman, PHI	5
Raffensberger, CIN	5

Fewest Walks/9 Innings
D. Koslo, NY	1.83
P. Roe, BKN	1.86
B. Werle, PIT	2.08
L. Jansen, NY	2.15

Most Strikeouts/9 Inn.
D. Newcombe, BKN	5.49
C. Chambers, PIT	4.72
P. Roe, BKN	4.61
W. Spahn, BOS	4.49

Innings
W. Spahn, BOS	302
Raffensberger, CIN	284
L. Jansen, NY	260
Heintzelman, PHI	250

Games Pitched
T. Wilks, STL	59
J. Konstanty, PHI	53
E. Palica, BKN	49
J. Banta, BKN	48

	W	L	PCT	GB	R	OR	2B	3B	HR	BA	SA	SB	E	DP	FA	CG	BB	SO	ShO	SV	ERA
Brooklyn	97	57	.630		879	651	236	47	152	.274	.419	117	122	162	.980	62	582	743	15	17	3.80
St. Louis	96	58	.623	1	766	616	281	54	102	.277	.404	17	146	149	.976	64	506	606	13	19	3.45
Philadelphia	81	73	.526	16	662	668	232	55	122	.254	.388	27	156	141	.974	58	502	495	12	15	3.89
Boston	75	79	.487	22	706	719	246	33	103	.258	.374	28	148	144	.976	68	520	591	12	11	3.99
New York	73	81	.474	24	736	693	203	52	147	.261	.401	43	161	134	.973	68	544	516	10	9	3.82
Pittsburgh	71	83	.461	26	681	760	191	41	126	.259	.384	48	132	173	.978	53	535	556	9	15	4.57
Cincinnati	62	92	.403	35	627	770	264	35	86	.260	.368	31	138	150	.977	55	640	538	10	6	4.33
Chicago	61	93	.396	36	593	773	212	53	97	.256	.373	53	186	160	.970	44	564	532	8	17	4.50
					5650	5650	1865	370	935	.262	.389	364	1189	1213	.975	472	4393	4577	89	109	4.04

AMERICAN LEAGUE 1949

New York
W-97 L-57
Casey Stengel

POS	Player	AB	BA	HR	RBI	PO	A	E	DP	TC/G	FA	Pitcher	G	IP	W	L	SV	ERA
1B	T. Henrich	411	.287	24	85	445	28	2	64	9.1	.996	V. Raschi	38	275	21	10	0	3.34
2B	J. Coleman	447	.275	2	42	298	315	12	102	5.1	.981	E. Lopat	31	215	15	10	1	3.26
SS	P. Rizzuto	614	.275	5	64	329	440	23	118	5.2	.971	A. Reynolds	35	214	17	6	1	4.00
3B	B. Brown	343	.283	6	61	84	158	13	17	3.0	.949	T. Byrne	32	196	15	7	0	3.72
RF	H. Bauer	301	.272	10	45	156	11	4	3	1.8	.977	J. Page	60	135	13	8	27	2.59
CF	C. Mapes	304	.247	7	38	228	14	6	4	2.3	.976	F. Sanford	29	95	7	3	0	3.87
LF	G. Woodling	296	.270	5	44	163	5	3	1	1.7	.982							
C	Y. Berra	415	.277	20	91	544	60	7	18	5.6	.989							
3B	B. Johnson	329	.249	8	56	77	136	11	16	2.8	.951							
OF	J. DiMaggio	272	.346	14	67	195	1	3	0	2.6	.985							
OF	J. Lindell	211	.242	6	27	114	4	2	1	1.8	.983							
1B	D. Kryhoski	177	.294	1	27	363	31	7	39	7.9	.983							
2B	Stirnweiss	157	.261	0	11	121	106	6	34	4.6	.974							

Boston
W-96 L-58
Joe McCarthy

POS	Player	AB	BA	HR	RBI	PO	A	E	DP	TC/G	FA	Pitcher	G	IP	W	L	SV	ERA
1B	B. Goodman	443	.298	0	56	1069	79	9	148	9.9	.992	M. Parnell	39	295	25	7	2	2.77
2B	B. Doerr	541	.309	18	109	395	439	17	134	6.1	.980	E. Kinder	43	252	23	6	4	3.36
SS	V. Stephens	610	.290	39	159	257	508	27	128	5.1	.966	J. Dobson	33	213	14	12	2	3.85
3B	J. Pesky	604	.306	2	69	184	333	16	48	3.6	.970	C. Stobbs	26	152	11	6	0	4.03
RF	A. Zarilla	474	.281	9	71	241	6	4	4	2.1	.984	J. Kramer	21	112	6	8	1	5.16
CF	D. DiMaggio	605	.307	8	60	420	13	10	1	3.1	.977	W. Masterson	18	55	3	4	4	4.25
LF	T. Williams	566	.343	43	159	337	12	6	3	2.3	.983							
C	B. Tebbetts	404	.270	5	48	481	51	11	13	4.6	.980							
C	M. Batts	157	.242	3	31	193	23	5	2	4.4	.977							

Cleveland
W-89 L-65
Lou Boudreau

POS	Player	AB	BA	HR	RBI	PO	A	E	DP	TC/G	FA	Pitcher	G	IP	W	L	SV	ERA
1B	M. Vernon	584	.291	18	83	1438	155	14	168	10.5	.991	B. Lemon	37	280	22	10	1	2.99
2B	J. Gordon	541	.251	20	84	297	430	15	123	5.1	.980	B. Feller	36	211	15	14	0	3.75
SS	L. Boudreau	475	.284	4	60	176	272	8	78	5.2	.982	M. Garcia	41	176	14	5	2	2.36
3B	K. Keltner	246	.232	8	30	51	145	4	11	2.9	.980	E. Wynn	26	165	11	7	0	4.15
RF	B. Kennedy	424	.276	9	57	190	12	2	4	2.1	.990	A. Benton	40	136	9	6	10	2.12
CF	L. Doby	547	.280	24	85	355	7	9	2	2.5	.976	G. Bearden	32	127	8	8	0	5.10
LF	D. Mitchell	640	.317	3	56	337	10	2	2	2.3	.994	S. Gromek	27	92	4	6	0	3.33
C	J. Hegan	468	.224	8	55	651	73	7	16	4.8	.990	S. Paige	31	83	4	7	5	3.04
SS	R. Boone	258	.252	4	26	162	210	21	58	5.2	.947							
OF	T. Tucker	197	.244	0	14	119	2	2	0	2.4	.984							

Detroit
W-87 L-67
Red Rolfe

POS	Player	AB	BA	HR	RBI	PO	A	E	DP	TC/G	FA	Pitcher	G	IP	W	L	SV	ERA
1B	P. Campbell	255	.278	3	30	461	38	7	67	6.8	.986	H. Newhouser	38	292	18	11	1	3.36
2B	N. Berry	329	.237	0	18	225	234	14	56	5.0	.970	V. Trucks	41	275	19	11	4	2.81
SS	J. Lipon	439	.251	3	59	240	364	22	92	5.2	.965	A. Houtteman	34	204	15	10	0	3.71
3B	G. Kell	522	.343	3	59	154	271	11	23	3.3	.975	T. Gray	34	195	10	10	1	3.51
RF	V. Wertz	608	.304	20	133	302	14	6	4	2.1	.981	Hutchinson	33	189	15	7	1	2.96
CF	J. Groth	348	.293	11	73	247	8	9	3	2.7	.966	D. Trout	33	59	3	6	3	4.40
LF	H. Evers	432	.303	7	72	319	12	2	2	2.7	.994							
C	A. Robinson	331	.269	13	56	458	44	7	9	4.7	.986							
21	D. Kolloway	483	.294	2	47	607	184	18	93		.978							
OF	P. Mullin	310	.268	12	59	169	4	2	0	2.2	.989							
UT	E. Lake	240	.196	1	15	113	167	10	37		.966							
C	B. Swift	189	.238	2	18	232	26	3	6	3.8	.989							

AMERICAN LEAGUE 1949, cont.

	POS	Player	AB	BA	HR	RBI	PO	A	E	DP	TC/G	FA	Pitcher	G	IP	W	L	SV	ERA
Philadelphia	1B	F. Fain	525	.263	3	78	1275	122	22	194	9.5	.984	A. Kellner	38	245	20	12	1	3.75
	2B	P. Suder	445	.267	10	75	203	259	12	85	5.3	.975	J. Coleman	33	240	13	14	1	3.86
W-81 L-73	SS	E. Joost	525	.263	23	81	352	442	25	126	5.7	.969	L. Brissie	34	229	16	11	3	4.28
	3B	H. Majeski	448	.277	9	67	117	219	15	37	3.1	.957	D. Fowler	31	214	15	11	1	3.75
Connie Mack	RF	W. Moses	308	.276	1	25	169	7	3	3	1.9	.983	C. Scheib	38	183	9	12	0	5.12
	CF	S. Chapman	589	.278	24	108	450	11	10	3	3.1	.979	B. Shantz	33	127	6	8	2	3.40
	LF	E. Valo	547	.283	5	85	395	8	8	0	2.7	.981							
	C	M. Guerra	298	.265	3	31	328	48	7	3	4.0	.982							
	2B	N. Fox	247	.255	0	21	191	196	7	68	5.1	.982							
	OF	D. White	169	.213	0	10	89	4	1	0	2.0	.989							
	OF	T. Wright	149	.235	2	25	60	5	2	0	1.9	.970							
Chicago	1B	C. Kress	353	.278	1	44	907	66	6	103	10.3	.994	B. Wight	35	245	15	13	1	3.31
	2B	C. Michaels	561	.308	6	83	392	484	22	135	5.8	.976	R. Gumpert	34	234	13	16	1	3.81
W-63 L-91	SS	L. Appling	492	.301	5	58	253	450	26	95	5.2	.964	B. Pierce	32	172	7	15	0	3.88
	3B	F. Baker	388	.260	1	40	106	269	9	31	3.1	.977	B. Kuzava	29	157	10	6	0	4.02
Jack Onslow	RF	D. Philley	598	.286	0	44	282	16	7	3	2.1	.977	M. Pieretti	39	116	4	6	1	5.51
	CF	C. Metkovich	338	.237	5	45	212	1	7	0	2.5	.968	H. Judson	26	108	1	14	1	4.58
	LF	H. Adams	208	.293	0	16	112	4	3	1	2.5	.975	M. Surkont	44	96	3	5	4	4.78
	C	D. Wheeler	192	.240	1	22	210	36	6	4	4.3	.976	M. Haefner	14	80	4	6	1	4.37
	O1	S. Souchock	252	.234	7	37	346	21	6	30		.984							
	OF	G. Zernial	198	.318	5	38	73	4	0	0	1.7	1.000							
	C	J. Tipton	191	.204	3	19	203	32	2	4	4.5	.992							
	C	E. Malone	170	.271	1	16	186	22	2	2	4.1	.990							
	OF	J. Ostrowski	158	.266	5	31	81	3	5	0	2.2	.944							
St. Louis	1B	J. Graham	500	.238	24	79	1118	87	19	120	9.0	.984	N. Garver	41	224	12	17	3	3.98
	2B	G. Priddy	544	.290	11	63	407	415	27	96	5.9	.968	B. Kennedy	48	154	4	11	1	4.69
W-53 L-101	SS	Pellagrini	235	.238	2	15	164	227	16	52	5.4	.961	C. Fannin	30	143	8	14	1	6.17
	3B	B. Dillinger	544	.324	1	51	166	209	25	22	3.0	.938	A. Papai	42	142	4	11	2	5.06
Zack Taylor	RF	D. Kokos	501	.261	23	77	290	16	6	5	2.3	.981	J. Ostrowski	40	141	8	8	2	4.79
	CF	S. Spence	314	.245	13	45	205	10	1	2	2.5	.995	K. Drews	31	140	4	12	0	6.64
	LF	R. Sievers	471	.306	16	91	314	14	9	1	2.7	.973	R. Embree	35	127	3	13	1	5.37
	C	S. Lollar	284	.261	8	49	279	39	4	3	3.5	.988	T. Ferrick	50	104	6	4	6	3.88
	OF	P. Lehner	297	.229	3	37	153	1	2	0	2.8	.987							
	C	L. Moss	278	.291	10	39	283	41	10	9	4.0	.970							
	OF	W. Platt	244	.258	3	29	135	3	2	0	2.4	.986							
	SS	J. Sullivan	243	.226	0	18	117	144	16	35	3.9	.942							
Washington	1B	E. Robinson	527	.294	18	78	1299	100	18	133	9.9	.987	S. Hudson	40	209	8	17	1	4.22
	2B	A. Kozar	350	.269	4	31	232	235	11	57	4.7	.977	Scarborough	34	200	13	11	0	4.60
W-50 L-104	SS	S. Dente	590	.273	1	53	314	462	35	106	5.3	.957	P. Calvert	34	161	6	17	1	5.43
	3B	E. Yost	435	.253	9	45	158	232	19	23	3.4	.954	M. Harris	23	129	2	12	0	5.16
Joe Kuhel	RF	B. Stewart	388	.284	8	43	207	8	4	3	2.1	.982	L. Hittle	36	109	5	7	0	4.21
	CF	C. Vollmer	443	.253	14	59	324	3	6	1	2.9	.982	J. Haynes	37	96	2	9	2	6.26
	LF	G. Coan	358	.218	3	29	225	8	6	3	2.5	.975	D. Weik	27	95	3	12	1	5.38
	C	A. Evans	321	.271	2	42	322	47	3	2	3.5	.992	M. Haefner	19	92	5	5	0	4.42
	UT	S. Robertson	374	.251	11	42	185	253	25	43		.946							
	OF	S. Mele	264	.242	3	25	108	5	4	3	1.9	.966							
	OF	B. Lewis	257	.245	3	28	136	4	3	1	2.1	.979							

BATTING AND BASE RUNNING LEADERS

Batting Average
G. Kell, DET .343
T. Williams, BOS .343
B. Dillinger, STL .324
D. Mitchell, CLE .317
B. Doerr, BOS .309

Slugging Average
T. Williams, BOS .650
V. Stephens, BOS .539
T. Henrich, NY .526
B. Doerr, BOS .497
Y. Berra, NY .480

Home Runs
T. Williams, BOS 43
V. Stephens, BOS 39
T. Henrich, NY 24
J. Graham, STL 24
L. Doby, CLE 24
S. Chapman, PHI 24

Winning Percentage
E. Kinder, BOS .793
M. Parnell, BOS .781
A. Reynolds, NY .739
B. Lemon, CLE .688
T. Byrne, NY .682
Hutchinson, DET .682

PITCHING LEADERS

Earned Run Average
M. Parnell, BOS 2.77
V. Trucks, DET 2.81
B. Lemon, CLE 2.99
E. Lopat, NY 3.26
B. Wight, CHI 3.31

Wins
M. Parnell, BOS 25
E. Kinder, BOS 23
B. Lemon, CLE 22
V. Raschi, NY 21
A. Kellner, PHI 20

Total Bases
T. Williams, BOS 368
V. Stephens, BOS 329
V. Wertz, DET 283
D. Mitchell, CLE 274
B. Doerr, BOS 269

Runs Batted In
T. Williams, BOS 159
V. Stephens, BOS 159
V. Wertz, DET 133
B. Doerr, BOS 109
S. Chapman, PHI 108

Stolen Bases
B. Dillinger, STL 20
P. Rizzuto, NY 18
E. Valo, PHI 14
D. Philley, CHI 13

Saves
J. Page, NY 27
A. Benton, CLE 10
T. Ferrick, STL 6
S. Paige, CLE 5

Strikeouts
V. Trucks, DET 153
H. Newhouser, DET 144
E. Kinder, BOS 138
B. Lemon, CLE 138
T. Byrne, NY 129

Complete Games
M. Parnell, BOS 27
B. Lemon, CLE 22
H. Newhouser, DET 22
V. Raschi, NY 21
A. Kellner, PHI 19
E. Kinder, BOS 19

Hits
D. Mitchell, CLE 203
T. Williams, BOS 194
D. DiMaggio, BOS 186
J. Pesky, BOS 185

Base on Balls
T. Williams, BOS 162
E. Joost, PHI 149
F. Fain, PHI 136
L. Appling, CHI 121

Home Run Percentage
T. Williams, BOS 7.6
V. Stephens, BOS 6.4
T. Henrich, NY 5.8
Y. Berra, NY 4.8

Fewest Hits/9 Innings
T. Byrne, NY 5.74
B. Lemon, CLE 6.79
V. Trucks, DET 6.84
M. Parnell, BOS 7.86

Shutouts
E. Kinder, BOS 6
V. Trucks, DET 6
M. Garcia, CLE 5

Fewest Walks/9 Innings
A. Houtteman, DET 2.61
E. Lopat, NY 2.88
R. Gumpert, CHI 3.19
H. Newhouser, DET 3.42

AMERICAN LEAGUE 1949, cont.

BATTING AND BASE RUNNING LEADERS

Runs Scored		Doubles		Triples		Most Strikeouts/9 Inn.	
T. Williams, BOS	150	T. Williams, BOS	39	D. Mitchell, CLE	23	T. Byrne, NY	5.92
E. Joost, PHI	128	G. Kell, DET	38	B. Dillinger, STL	13	V. Trucks, DET	5.01
D. DiMaggio, BOS	126	D. DiMaggio, BOS	34	E. Valo, PHI	12	E. Kinder, BOS	4.93
V. Stephens, BOS	113	A. Zarilla, BOS, STL	33	G. Kell, DET	9	L. Brissie, PHI	4.63

PITCHING LEADERS

Innings		Games Pitched	
M. Parnell, BOS	295	J. Page, NY	60
H. Newhouser, DET	292	D. Welteroth, WAS	52
B. Lemon, CLE	280	T. Ferrick, STL	50
V. Trucks, DET	275	B. Kennedy, STL	48

	W	L	PCT	GB	R	OR	2B	3B	HR	BA	SA	SB	E	DP	FA	CG	BB	SO	ShO	SV	ERA
New York	97	57	.630	1	829	637	215	60	115	.269	.400	58	138	195	.977	59	812	671	12	36	3.69
Boston	96	58	.623	1	896	667	272	36	131	.282	.420	43	120	207	.980	84	661	598	16	16	3.97
Cleveland	89	65	.578	8	675	574	194	58	112	.260	.384	44	103	192	.983	65	611	594	10	19	3.36
Detroit	87	67	.565	10	751	655	215	51	88	.267	.378	39	131	174	.978	70	628	631	19	12	3.77
Philadelphia	81	73	.526	16	726	725	214	49	82	.260	.369	36	140	217	.976	85	758	490	9	11	4.23
Chicago	63	91	.409	34	648	737	207	66	43	.257	.347	62	141	180	.977	57	693	502	10	17	4.30
St. Louis	53	101	.344	44	667	913	213	30	117	.254	.377	38	166	154	.971	43	685	432	3	16	5.21
Washington	50	104	.325	47	584	868	207	41	81	.254	.356	46	161	168	.973	44	779	451	9	9	5.10
					5776	5776	1737	391	769	.263	.379	366	1100	1487	.977	507	5627	4369	88	136	4.20

NATIONAL LEAGUE 1950

	POS	Player	AB	BA	HR	RBI	PO	A	E	DP	TC/G	FA	Pitcher	G	IP	W	L	SV	ERA
Philadelphia	1B	E. Waitkus	641	.284	2	44	1387	99	10	142	9.7	.993	R. Roberts	40	304	20	11	1	3.02
	2B	M. Goliat	483	.234	13	64	345	393	21	89	5.5	.972	C. Simmons	31	215	17	8	1	3.40
W-91 L-63	SS	G. Hamner	637	.270	11	82	293	513	48	100	5.4	.944	B. Miller	35	174	11	6	1	3.57
	3B	W. Jones	610	.267	25	88	190	323	25	30	3.4	.954	R. Meyer	32	160	9	11	1	5.30
Eddie Sawyer	RF	D. Ennis	595	.311	31	126	279	10	9	3	2.0	.970	J. Konstanty	74	152	16	7	22	2.66
	CF	R. Ashburn	594	.303	2	41	405	8	5	2	2.8	.988	B. Church	31	142	8	6	1	2.73
	LF	D. Sisler	523	.296	13	83	293	9	4	0	2.2	.987	Heintzelman	23	125	3	9	0	4.09
	C	A. Seminick	393	.288	24	68	551	54	15	9	5.0	.976							
Brooklyn	1B	G. Hodges	561	.283	32	113	1273	100	8	159	9.0	.994	D. Newcombe	40	267	19	11	3	3.70
	2B	J. Robinson	518	.328	14	81	359	390	11	133	5.3	.986	P. Roe	36	251	19	11	1	3.30
W-89 L-65	SS	P. Reese	531	.260	11	52	282	398	26	94	5.3	.963	E. Palica	43	201	13	8	1	3.58
	3B	B. Cox	451	.257	8	44	102	233	15	35	3.3	.957	R. Branca	43	142	7	9	7	4.69
Burt Shotton	RF	C. Furillo	620	.305	18	106	246	18	8	2	1.8	.971	D. Bankhead	41	129	9	4	3	5.50
	CF	D. Snider	620	.321	31	107	378	15	7	1	2.6	.983	C. Erskine	22	103	7	6	1	4.72
	LF	G. Hermanski	289	.298	7	34	172	5	2	0	2.3	.989	B. Podbielan	20	73	5	4	1	5.33
	C	Campanella	437	.281	31	89	683	54	11	14	6.1	.985	J. Banta	16	41	4	4	2	4.35
	OF	J. Russell	214	.229	10	32	131	3	1	0	2.5	.993							
	3B	B. Morgan	199	.226	7	21	33	121	5	15	3.1	.969							
	OF	T. Brown	86	.291	8	20	31	2	3	0	2.3	.917							
New York	1B	T. Gilbert	322	.220	4	32	784	65	10	80	7.7	.988	L. Jansen	40	275	19	13	3	3.01
	2B	E. Stanky	527	.300	8	51	407	418	26	128	5.6	.976	S. Maglie	47	206	18	4	1	2.71
W-86 L-68	SS	A. Dark	587	.279	16	67	288	465	30	101	5.1	.962	S. Jones	40	199	13	16	4	4.61
	3B	H. Thompson	512	.289	20	91	136	303	26	43	3.4	.944	D. Koslo	40	187	13	15	3	3.91
Leo Durocher	RF	D. Mueller	525	.291	7	84	205	7	3	2	1.7	.986	J. Hearn	16	125	11	3	0	1.94*
	CF	B. Thomson	563	.252	25	85	394	15	9	5	2.8	.978	M. Kennedy	36	114	5	4	2	4.72
	LF	W. Lockman	532	.295	6	52	305	11	7	3	2.5	.978	J. Kramer	35	87	3	6	1	3.53
	C	W. Westrum	437	.236	23	71	608	71	1	21	4.9	.999							
	10	M. Irvin	374	.299	15	66	568	50	12	62		.981							
Boston	1B	E. Torgeson	576	.290	23	87	1365	110	21	126	9.6	.986	V. Bickford	40	312	19	14	0	3.47
	2B	Hartsfield	419	.277	7	24	236	247	26	53	5.3	.949	W. Spahn	41	293	21	17	1	3.16
W-83 L-71	SS	B. Kerr	507	.227	2	46	310	471	28	97	5.2	.965	J. Sain	37	278	20	13	0	3.94
	3B	B. Elliott	531	.305	24	107	141	256	20	26	3.0	.952	B. Chipman	27	124	7	7	1	4.43
Billy Southworth	RF	T. Holmes	322	.298	9	51	151	6	0	0	1.8	1.000	B. Hogue	36	63	3	5	7	5.03
	CF	S. Jethroe	582	.273	18	58	355	17	12	6	2.7	.969							
	LF	S. Gordon	481	.304	27	103	278	8	3	1	2.3	.990							
	C	W. Cooper	337	.329	14	60	386	47	12	9	5.1	.973							
	OF	W. Marshall	298	.235	5	40	150	11	7	2	2.0	.958							
	C	D. Crandall	255	.220	4	37	311	41	12	7	4.9	.967							
	OF	L. Olmo	154	.227	5	22	74	1	2	0	1.4	.974							
St. Louis	1B	R. Nelson	235	.247	1	20	596	51	5	66	9.3	.992	H. Pollet	37	232	14	13	2	3.29
	2B	Schoendienst	642	.276	7	63	393	403	12	124	5.7	.985	M. Lanier	27	181	11	9	0	3.13
W-78 L-75	SS	M. Marion	372	.247	4	40	180	313	11	73	5.0	.978	G. Staley	42	170	13	13	4	4.99
	3B	T. Glaviano	410	.285	11	44	103	255	25	16	3.6	.935	A. Brazle	46	165	11	9	6	4.10
Eddie Dyer	RF	E. Slaughter	556	.290	10	101	260	9	6	1	1.9	.978	H. Brecheen	27	163	8	11	1	3.80
	CF	C. Diering	204	.250	3	18	178	8	2	2	2.3	.989	G. Munger	32	155	7	8	3	3.90
	LF	B. Howerton	313	.281	10	59	183	2	6	0	2.0	.969	C. Boyer	36	120	7	7	1	3.52
	C	D. Rice	414	.244	9	54	572	63	10	12	5.0	.984							
	O1	S. Musial	555	.346	28	109	760	39	8	67		.990							
	3B	E. Kazak	207	.256	5	23	36	95	9	7	2.9	.936							
	SS	E. Miller	172	.227	3	22	72	173	5	29	4.9	.980							
	C	J. Garagiola	88	.318	2	20	99	8	0	2	3.6	1.000							

NATIONAL LEAGUE 1950, *cont.*

	POS	Player	AB	BA	HR	RBI	PO	A	E	DP	TC/G	FA	Pitcher	G	IP	W	L	SV	ERA
Cincinnati	1B	Kluszewski	538	.307	25	111	1123	61	15	101	9.2	.987	E. Blackwell	40	261	17	15	4	2.97
	2B	C. Ryan	367	.259	3	43	304	283	16	13	5.9*	.973	Raffensberger	38	239	14	19	0	4.26
W-66 L-87	SS	V. Stallcup	483	.251	8	54	253	389	18	79	4.9	.973	H. Wehmeier	41	230	10	18	4	5.67
	3B	G. Hatton	438	.260	11	54	145	230	18	19	3.1	.954	H. Fox	34	187	11	8	1	4.33
Luke Sewell	RF	J. Wyrostek	509	.285	8	76	238	8	5	0	1.9	.980	W. Ramsdell	27	157	7	12	0	3.72
	CF	L. Merriman	298	.258	2	31	181	4	2	1	2.2	.989	F. Smith	38	91	2	7	3	3.87
	LF	B. Usher	321	.259	6	35	190	7	3	1	2.1	.985							
	C	D. Howell	224	.223	2	22	338	26	5	4	4.6	.986							
	OF	J. Adcock	372	.293	8	55	177	6	6	3	2.5	.968							
	23	B. Adams	348	.282	3	25	170	200	14	34		.964							
	OF	P. Lowrey	264	.227	1	11	153	4	2	1	2.2	.987							
	C	J. Pramesa	228	.307	5	30	328	37	7	2	5.1	.981							
Chicago	1B	P. Ward	285	.253	6	33	734	73	4	78	10.7	.995	B. Rush	39	255	13	**20**	1	3.71
	2B	Terwilliger	480	.242	10	32	314	380	24	80	5.7	.967	J. Schmitz	39	193	10	16	0	4.99
W-64 L-89	SS	R. Smalley	557	.230	21	85	**332**	**541**	**51**	**115**	6.0	.945	P. Minner	39	190	8	13	4	4.11
	3B	B. Serena	435	.239	17	61	122	274	23	24	3.4	.945	F. Hiller	38	153	12	5	1	3.53
Frankie Frisch	RF	B. Borkowski	256	.273	4	29	150	3	4	1	2.4	.975	M. Dubiel	39	143	6	10	2	4.16
	CF	A. Pafko	514	.304	36	92	342	12	8	1	2.5	.978	D. Lade	34	118	5	6	2	4.74
	LF	H. Sauer	540	.274	32	103	236	12	9	1	2.1	.965	Klippstein	33	105	2	9	1	5.25
	C	M. Owen	259	.243	2	21	318	39	8	8	4.2	.978	D. Leonard	35	74	5	1	6	3.77
	1B	Cavarretta	256	.273	10	31	606	47	9	55	9.9	.986							
	C	R. Walker	213	.230	6	16	240	34	7	6	4.5	.975							
	OF	C. Mauro	185	.227	1	10	86	2	5	0	1.9	.946							
	OF	H. Jeffcoat	179	.235	2	18	83	6	3	0	1.7	.967							
	OF	R. Northey	114	.281	4	20	38	3	1	2	1.6	.976							
	OF	H. Edwards	110	.364	2	21	38	2	1	0	1.4	.976							
Pittsburgh	1B	J. Hopp	318	.340	8	47	534	32	6	61	8.2	.990	C. Chambers	37	249	12	15	0	4.30
	2B	D. Murtaugh	367	.294	2	37	273	292	14	84	5.4	.976	M. Dickson	51	225	10	15	3	3.80
W-57 L-96	SS	S. Rojek	230	.257	0	17	102	160	9	39	4.0	.967	B. Werle	48	215	8	16	8	4.60
	3B	B. Dillinger	222	.288	1	9	60	116	8	13	3.6	.957	MacDonald	32	153	8	10	1	4.29
Billy Meyer	RF	G. Bell	422	.282	8	53	203	10	5	3	2.1	.977	V. Law	27	128	7	9	0	4.92
	CF	W. Westlake	477	.285	24	95	329	4	3	3	2.7	**.991**	M. Queen	33	120	5	14	0	5.98
	LF	R. Kiner	547	.272	**47**	118	287	13	11	2	2.1	.965							
	C	McCullough	279	.254	6	34	362	45	6	3	4.1	.985							
	SS	D. O'Connell	315	.292	8	32	147	228	9	47	5.9	.977							
	UT	Castiglione	263	.255	3	22	116	125	10	23		.960							
	1B	J. Phillips	208	.293	5	34	450	39	7	46	9.2	.986							
	3B	N. Fernandez	198	.258	6	27	48	101	12	6	3.1	.925							
	OF	T. Saffell	182	.203	2	6	128	5	1	0	3.1	.993							
	OF	T. Beard	177	.232	4	12	112	4	2	0	2.4	.983							
	C	R. Mueller	156	.269	6	24	204	30	1	3	3.7	.996							

BATTING AND BASE RUNNING LEADERS

Batting Average
S. Musial, STL .346
J. Robinson, BKN .328
D. Snider, BKN .321
D. Ennis, PHI .311
Kluszewski, CIN .307

Slugging Average
S. Musial, STL .596
A. Pafko, CHI .591
R. Kiner, PIT .590
S. Gordon, BOS .557
D. Snider, BKN .553

Home Runs
R. Kiner, PIT 47
A. Pafko, CHI 36
H. Sauer, CHI 32
G. Hodges, BKN 32

Total Bases
D. Snider, BKN 343
S. Musial, STL 331
D. Ennis, PHI 328
R. Kiner, PIT 323
A. Pafko, CHI 304

Runs Batted In
D. Ennis, PHI 126
R. Kiner, PIT 118
G. Hodges, BKN 113
Kluszewski, CIN 111
S. Musial, STL 109

Stolen Bases
S. Jethroe, BOS 35
P. Reese, BKN 17
D. Snider, BKN 16
E. Torgeson, BOS 15
R. Ashburn, PHI 14

Hits
D. Snider, BKN 199
S. Musial, STL 192
C. Furillo, BKN 189
D. Ennis, PHI 185

Base on Balls
E. Stanky, NY 144
R. Kiner, PIT 122
E. Torgeson, BOS 119
W. Westrum, NY 92

Home Run Percentage
R. Kiner, PIT 8.6
Campanella, BKN 7.1
A. Pafko, CHI 7.0
H. Sauer, CHI 5.9

Runs Scored
E. Torgeson, BOS 120
E. Stanky, NY 115
R. Kiner, PIT 112
D. Snider, BKN 109

Doubles
Schoendienst, STL 43
S. Musial, STL 41
J. Robinson, BKN 39
Kluszewski, CIN 37

Triples
R. Ashburn, PHI 14
G. Bell, PIT 11
D. Snider, BKN 10
R. Smalley, CHI 9

PITCHING LEADERS

Winning Percentage
S. Maglie, NY .818
J. Konstanty, PHI .696
C. Simmons, PHI .680
R. Roberts, PHI .645
D. Newcombe, BKN .633
P. Roe, BKN .633

Earned Run Average
J. Hearn, NY, STL 2.49
S. Maglie, NY 2.71
E. Blackwell, CIN 2.97
L. Jansen, NY 3.01
R. Roberts, PHI 3.02

Wins
W. Spahn, BOS 21
R. Roberts, PHI 20
J. Sain, BOS 20

Saves
J. Konstanty, PHI 22
B. Werle, PIT 8
B. Hogue, BOS 7
B. Branca, BKN 7
A. Brazle, STL 6
D. Leonard, CHI 6

Strikeouts
W. Spahn, BOS 191
E. Blackwell, CIN 188
L. Jansen, NY 161
C. Simmons, PHI 146
R. Roberts, PHI 146

Complete Games
V. Bickford, BOS 27
J. Sain, BOS 25
W. Spahn, BOS 25
L. Jansen, NY 21
R. Roberts, PHI 21

Fewest Hits/9 Innings
J. Hearn, NY, STL 5.64
E. Blackwell, CIN 7.00
S. Maglie, NY 7.38
C. Simmons, PHI 7.46

Shutouts
J. Hearn, NY, STL 5
S. Maglie, NY 5
L. Jansen, NY 5
R. Roberts, PHI 5

Fewest Walks/9 Innings
Raffensberger, CIN 1.51
L. Jansen, NY 1.80
J. Sain, BOS 2.26
R. Roberts, PHI 2.28

Most Strikeouts/9 Inn.
E. Blackwell, CIN 6.48
C. Simmons, PHI 6.12
W. Spahn, BOS 5.87
E. Palica, BKN 5.86

Innings
V. Bickford, BOS 312
R. Roberts, PHI 304
W. Spahn, BOS 293
J. Sain, BOS 278

Games Pitched
J. Konstanty, PHI 74
M. Dickson, PIT 51
B. Werle, PIT 48
S. Maglie, NY 47

NATIONAL LEAGUE 1950, *cont.*

	W	L	PCT	GB	R	OR	2B	3B	HR	BA	SA	SB	E	DP	FA	CG	BB	SO	ShO	SV	ERA
							Batting						**Fielding**			**Pitching**					
Philadelphia	91	63	.591		722	**624**	225	55	125	.265	.396	33	151	155	.975	57	530	620	13	**27**	**3.50**
Brooklyn	89	65	.578	2	**847**	724	247	46	**194**	**.272**	**.444**	**77**	127	**183**	**.979**	62	591	**772**	10	21	4.28
New York	86	68	.558	5	735	643	204	50	133	.258	.392	42	137	181	.977	70	536	596	**19**	15	3.71
Boston	83	71	.539	8	785	736	246	36	148	.263	.405	71	182	146	.970	**88**	554	615	7	10	4.14
St. Louis	78	75	.510	12.5	693	670	255	50	102	.259	.386	23	130	172	.978	57	535	603	10	14	3.97
Cincinnati	66	87	.431	24.5	654	734	**257**	27	99	.260	.376	37	140	132	.976	67	582	686	7	13	4.32
Chicago	64	89	.418	26.5	643	772	224	47	161	.248	.401	46	201	169	.968	55	593	559	9	19	4.28
Pittsburgh	57	96	.373	33.5	681	857	227	**59**	138	.264	.406	43	136	165	.977	42	616	556	6	16	4.96
					5760	5760	1885	370	1100	.261	.401	372	1204	1303	.975	498	4537	5007	81	135	4.14

AMERICAN LEAGUE 1950

Team	POS	Player	AB	BA	HR	RBI	PO	A	E	DP	TC/G	FA	Pitcher	G	IP	W	L	SV	ERA
New York W-98 L-56 Casey Stengel	1B	J. Collins	205	.234	8	28	480	36	7	62	5.3	.987	V. Raschi	33	257	21	8	1	4.00
	2B	J. Coleman	522	.287	6	69	384	384	18	137	5.2	.977	A. Reynolds	35	241	16	12	2	3.74
	SS	P. Rizzuto	617	.324	7	66	**301**	452	14	123	4.9	**.982**	E. Lopat	35	236	18	8	1	3.47
	3B	B. Johnson	327	.260	6	40	82	169	11	20	2.6	.958	T. Byrne	31	203	15	9	0	4.74
	RF	H. Bauer	415	.320	13	70	228	8	3	3	2.2	.987	F. Sanford	26	113	5	4	0	4.55
	CF	J. DiMaggio	525	.301	32	122	363	9	9	1	2.8	.976	W. Ford	20	112	9	1	1	2.81
	LF	G. Woodling	449	.283	6	60	263	16	2	3	2.4	.993	T. Ferrick	30	57	8	4	9	3.65
	C	Y. Berra	597	.322	28	124	**777**	64	13	16	5.8	.985	J. Page	37	55	3	7	13	5.04
	OF	C. Mapes	356	.247	12	61	183	8	10	4	2.0	.950							
	3B	B. Brown	277	.267	4	37	63	140	9	13	2.6	.958							
	1B	J. Mize	274	.277	25	72	490	31	2	73	7.3	.996							
	1B	T. Henrich	151	.272	6	34	224	7	3	23	6.9	.987							
Detroit W-95 L-59 Red Rolfe	1B	D. Kolloway	467	.289	6	62	1087	85	13	133	**10.0**	.989	A. Houtteman	41	275	19	12	4	3.54
	2B	G. Priddy	618	.277	13	75	440	**542**	19	**150**	6.4	.981	Hutchinson	39	232	17	8	0	3.96
	SS	J. Lipon	601	.293	2	63	273	**483**	33	126	5.4	.958	H. Newhouser	35	214	15	13	3	4.34
	3B	G. Kell	**641**	.340	8	101	186	315	9	30	3.2	**.982**	D. Trout	34	185	13	5	4	3.75
	RF	V. Wertz	559	.308	27	123	286	5	10	3	2.1	.967	T. Gray	27	149	10	7	1	4.40
	CF	J. Groth	566	.306	12	85	374	9	6	0	2.5	.985	H. White	42	111	9	6	1	4.54
	LF	H. Evers	526	.323	21	103	325	15	1	3	2.5	**.997**							
	C	A. Robinson	283	.226	9	37	355	43	3	4	3.9	.993							
	1B	D. Kryhoski	169	.219	4	19	409	27	4	44	9.4	.991							
	OF	P. Mullin	142	.218	6	23	62	4	0	1	2.1	1.000							
	P	Hutchinson	95	.326	0	20	17	50	4	6	1.8	.944							
Boston W-94 L-60 Joe McCarthy W-31 L-28 Steve O'Neill W-63 L-32	1B	W. Dropo	559	.322	34	144	1142	77	15	147	9.2	.988	M. Parnell	40	249	18	10	3	3.61
	2B	B. Doerr	586	.294	27	120	**443**	431	11	130	5.9	**.988**	E. Kinder	48	207	14	12	9	4.26
	SS	V. Stephens	628	.295	30	144	258	431	13	115	4.8	.981	J. Dobson	39	207	15	10	4	4.18
	3B	J. Pesky	490	.312	1	49	160	257	11	29	3.7	.974	C. Stobbs	32	169	12	7	1	5.10
	RF	A. Zarilla	471	.325	9	74	230	12	6	1	1.9	.976	McDermott	38	130	7	3	5	5.19
	CF	D. DiMaggio	588	.328	7	70	390	15	7	2	2.9	.983	W. Masterson	33	129	8	6	1	5.64
	LF	T. Williams	334	.317	28	97	165	7	8	0	2.1	.956	W. Nixon	22	101	8	6	2	6.04
	C	B. Tebbetts	268	.310	8	45	285	44	4	5	4.5	.988							
	UT	B. Goodman	424	**.354**	4	68	344	89	9	28		.980							
	C	I. Batts	238	.273	4	34	306	29	2	3	4.6	.994							
	OF	C. Vollmer	169	.284	7	37	80	3	4	0	2.2	.954							
	OF	T. Wright	107	.318	0	20	40	1	2	1	1.8	.953							
Cleveland W-92 L-62 Lou Boudreau	1B	L. Easter	540	.280	28	107	1100	82	11	114	9.3	.991	B. Lemon	44	**288**	**23**	11	3	3.84
	2B	J. Gordon	368	.236	19	57	224	283	16	69	5.0	.969	B. Feller	35	247	16	11	0	3.43
	SS	R. Boone	365	.301	7	58	178	267	26	64	4.6	.945	E. Wynn	32	214	18	8	0	**3.20**
	3B	A. Rosen	554	.287	**37**	116	151	**322**	15	24	3.2	.969	M. Garcia	33	184	11	11	0	3.86
	RF	B. Kennedy	540	.291	9	54	294	13	4	3	2.2	.987	S. Gromek	31	113	10	7	0	3.65
	CF	L. Doby	503	.326	25	102	367	2	5	1	2.7	.987	S. Zoldak	33	64	4	2	4	3.96
	LF	D. Mitchell	506	.308	3	49	236	3	7	1	1.9	.972	A. Benton	36	63	2	4	4	3.57
	C	J. Hegan	415	.219	14	58	656	**64**	5	14	5.6	.993	J. Flores	28	53	3	3	4	3.74
	SS	L. Boudreau	260	.269	1	29	118	170	4	44	4.8	.986							
	2B	B. Avila	201	.299	1	21	153	135	5	46	4.7	.983							
	OF	A. Clark	163	.215	6	21	75	2	5	0	1.9	.987							
	P	B. Lemon	136	.272	6	26	22	66	4	6	2.1	.957							
Washington W-67 L-87 Bucky Harris	1B	M. Vernon	327	.306	9	65	743	61	8	93	9.6	.990*	S. Hudson	30	238	14	14	0	4.09
	2B	C. Michaels	388	.250	4	47	298	323	16*	91	6.1	.975	B. Kuzava	22	155	8	7	0	3.95
	SS	S. Dente	603	.239	2	54	225	406	32	88	5.2	.952	C. Marrero	27	152	6	10	1	4.50
	3B	E. Yost	573	.295	11	58	**205**	307	**30**	45	3.5	.945	S. Consuegra	21	125	7	8	2	4.40
	RF	B. Stewart	378	.267	4	35	202	10	2	3	2.1	.991	J. Haynes	27	102	7	5	0	5.84
	CF	I. Noren	542	.295	14	98	357	**20**	6	5	3.2	.984	M. Harris	**53**	98	5	9	15	4.78
	LF	G. Coan	366	.303	7	50	220	4	7	1	2.4	.970							
	C	A. Evans	289	.235	2	30	289	23	4	8	3.6	.987							
	OF	S. Mele	435	.274	12	86	192	8	2	0	2.0	.990							
	C	M. Grasso	195	.287	1	22	238	38	**17**	6	4.2	.942							
	OF	J. Ostrowski	141	.227	4	23	105	3	6	1	2.5	.947							

AMERICAN LEAGUE 1950, *cont.*

	POS	Player	AB	BA	HR	RBI	PO	A	E	DP	TC/G	FA	Pitcher	G	IP	W	L	SV	ERA
Chicago	1B	E. Robinson	424	.314	20	73	982*	60	14	105	8.9	.987	B. Pierce	33	219	12	16	1	3.98
	2B	N. Fox	457	.247	0	30	340	344	18	100	5.8	.974	B. Wight	30	206	10	16	0	3.58
W-60 L-94	SS	Carrasquel	524	.282	4	46	234	458	28	113	5.1	.961	B. Cain	34	172	9	12	2	3.93
	3B	H. Majeski	414	.309	6	46	115	246	11	31	3.3	.970	R. Gumpert	40	155	5	12	0	4.75
Jack Onslow	RF	M. Rickert	278	.237	4	27	150	3	5	1	2.0	.968	Scarborough	27	149	10	13	1	5.30
W-8 L-22	CF	D. Philley	619	.242	14	80	367	19	8	8	2.6	.980	H. Judson	46	112	2	3	0	3.94
	LF	G. Zernial	543	.280	29	93	306	9	10	2	2.4	.969	K. Holcombe	24	96	3	10	1	4.59
Red Corriden	C	P. Masi	377	.279	7	55	440	52	2	9	4.3	**.996**	L. Aloma	42	88	7	2	4	3.80
W-52 L-72																			
	3B	F. Baker	186	.317	0	11	50	102	2	7	2.9	.987							
	1B	Goldsberry	127	.268	1	25	235	29	3	37	6.7	.989							
St. Louis	1B	D. Lenhardt	480	.273	22	81	618	39	8	77	7.7	.988	N. Garver	37	260	13	18	0	3.39
	2B	O. Friend	372	.237	8	50	244	302	22	62	6.1	.961	A. Widmar	36	195	7	15	4	4.76
W-58 L-96	SS	T. Upton	389	.237	2	30	198	328	30	65	4.8	.946	S. Overmire	31	161	9	12	0	4.19
	3B	B. Sommers	137	.255	0	14	25	52	7	5	2.3	.917	D. Starr	32	124	7	5	2	5.02
Zack Taylor	RF	K. Wood	369	.225	13	62	162	16	9	2	2.0	.952	H. Dorish	29	109	4	9	0	6.44
	CF	R. Coleman	384	.271	8	55	253	7	4	1	2.7	.985	C. Fannin	25	102	5	9	1	6.53
	LF	D. Kokos	490	.261	18	67	342	8	**11**	2	2.8	.970	D. Johnson	25	96	5	6	1	6.09
	C	S. Lollar	396	.280	13	65	367	48	8	9	3.9	.981	D. Pillette	24	74	3	5	2	7.09
	OF	R. Sievers	370	.238	10	57	222	12	4	3	3.1	.983							
	23	Stirnweiss	326	.218	1	24	191	206	12	51		.971							
	1B	H. Arft	280	.268	1	32	701	51	4	59	9.0	.995							
	C	L. Moss	222	.266	8	34	204	20	10	4	3.9	.957							
	OF	J. Delsing	209	.263	0	15	150	4	1	3	2.9	.994							
	SS	B. DeMars	178	.247	0	13	113	123	17	32	4.7	.933							
Philadelphia	1B	F. Fain	522	.282	10	83	1286	**124**	19	**192**	9.5	.987	L. Brissie	46	246	7	19	8	4.02
	2B	B. Hitchcock	399	.273	1	54	297	319	21	105	6.0	.967	A. Kellner	36	225	8	**20**	2	5.47
W-52 L-102	SS	E. Joost	476	.233	18	58	241	389	29	117	5.0	.956	B. Shantz	36	215	8	14	0	4.61
	3B	B. Dillinger	356	.309	3	41	92	173	12	18	3.3	.957	H. Wyse	41	171	9	14	0	5.85
Connie Mack	RF	E. Valo	446	.280	10	46	264	9	5	3	2.4	.982	B. Hooper	45	170	15	10	5	5.02
	CF	S. Chapman	553	.251	23	95	**428**	11	10	4	**3.2**	.978	C. Scheib	43	106	3	10	3	7.22
	LF	P. Lehner	427	.309	9	52	247	10	5	1	2.6	.981							
	C	M. Guerra	252	.282	2	26	253	33	3	8	3.7	.990							
	3B	K. Wahl	280	.257	2	27	70	141	12	11	3.7	.946							
	OF	W. Moses	265	.264	2	21	147	7	2	2	2.5	.987							
	UT	P. Suder	248	.246	8	35	167	181	9	55		.975							
	C	J. Tipton	184	.266	6	20	201	24	3	3	3.9	.987							
	OF	B. McCosky	179	.240	0	11	73	1	1	1	1.8	.987							

BATTING AND BASE RUNNING LEADERS

Batting Average		Slugging Average		Home Runs	
B. Goodman, BOS	.354	J. DiMaggio, NY	.585	A. Rosen, CLE	37
G. Kell, DET	.340	W. Dropo, BOS	.583	W. Dropo, BOS	34
D. DiMaggio, BOS	.328	H. Evers, DET	.551	J. DiMaggio, NY	32
L. Doby, CLE	.326	L. Doby, CLE	.545	V. Stephens, BOS	30
A. Zarilla, BOS	.325	A. Rosen, CLE	.543	G. Zernial, CHI	29

Total Bases		Runs Batted In		Stolen Bases	
W. Dropo, BOS	326	W. Dropo, BOS	144	D. DiMaggio, BOS	15
V. Stephens, BOS	321	V. Stephens, BOS	144	E. Valo, PHI	12
Y. Berra, NY	318	Y. Berra, NY	124	P. Rizzuto, NY	12
G. Kell, DET	310	V. Wertz, DET	123	G. Coan, WAS	10
J. DiMaggio, NY	307	J. DiMaggio, NY	122	J. Lipon, DET	9

Hits		Base on Balls		Home Run Percentage	
G. Kell, DET	218	E. Yost, WAS	141	A. Rosen, CLE	6.7
P. Rizzuto, NY	200	F. Fain, PHI	132	J. DiMaggio, NY	6.1
D. DiMaggio, BOS	193	J. Pesky, BOS	104	W. Dropo, BOS	6.1
Y. Berra, NY	192	E. Joost, PHI	101	G. Zernial, CHI	5.3

Runs Scored		Doubles		Triples	
D. DiMaggio, BOS	131	G. Kell, DET	56	H. Evers, DET	11
P. Rizzuto, NY	125	V. Wertz, DET	37	B. Doerr, BOS	11
V. Stephens, BOS	125	P. Rizzuto, NY	36	D. DiMaggio, BOS	11
Y. Berra, NY	116	H. Evers, DET	35		

PITCHING LEADERS

Winning Percentage		Earned Run Average		Wins	
V. Raschi, NY	.724	E. Wynn, CLE	3.20	B. Lemon, CLE	23
E. Lopat, NY	.692	N. Garver, STL	3.39	V. Raschi, NY	21
E. Wynn, CLE	.692	B. Feller, CLE	3.43	A. Houtteman, DET	19
Hutchinson, DET	.680	E. Lopat, NY	3.47	E. Lopat, NY	18
B. Lemon, CLE	.676	A. Houtteman, DET	3.54	E. Wynn, CLE	18
				M. Parnell, BOS	18

Saves		Strikeouts		Complete Games	
M. Harris, WAS	15	B. Lemon, CLE	170	N. Garver, STL	22
J. Page, NY	13	A. Reynolds, NY	160	B. Lemon, CLE	22
T. Ferrick, NY, STL	11	V. Raschi, NY	155	M. Parnell, BOS	21
E. Kinder, BOS	9	E. Wynn, CLE	143	A. Houtteman, DET	21
L. Brissie, PHI	8	B. Feller, CLE	119	S. Hudson, WAS	17
				V. Raschi, NY	17

Fewest Hits/9 Innings		Shutouts		Fewest Walks/9 Innings	
E. Wynn, CLE	6.99	A. Houtteman, DET	4	Hutchinson, DET	1.86
B. Pierce, CHI	7.76	B. Wight, CHI	3	E. Lopat, NY	2.48
B. Cain, CHI	8.02	Scarborough, CHI, WAS	3	D. Trout, DET	3.12
A. Reynolds, NY	8.04	E. Lopat, NY	3	A. Houtteman, DET	3.24

Most Strikeouts/9 Inn.		Innings		Games Pitched	
E. Wynn, CLE	6.02	B. Lemon, CLE	288	M. Harris, WAS	53
A. Reynolds, NY	5.98	A. Houtteman, DET	275	E. Kinder, BOS	48
V. Raschi, NY	5.44	N. Garver, STL	260	L. Brissie, PHI	46
B. Lemon, CLE	5.31	V. Raschi, NY	257	H. Judson, CHI	46

AMERICAN LEAGUE 1950, cont.

	W	L	PCT	GB	R	OR	Batting 2B	3B	HR	BA	SA	SB	Fielding E	DP	FA	Pitching CG	BB	SO	ShO	SV	ERA
New York	98	56	.636		914	691	234	70	159	.282	.441	41	119	188	.980	66	708	712	12	31	4.15
Detroit	95	59	.617	3	837	713	285	50	114	.282	.417	23	120	194	.981	72	553	576	9	20	4.12
Boston	94	60	.610	4	1027	804	287	61	161	.302	.464	32	111	181	.981	66	748	630	6	28	4.88
Cleveland	92	62	.597	6	806	654	222	46	164	.269	.422	40	129	160	.978	69	647	674	11	16	3.74
Washington	67	87	.435	31	690	813	190	53	76	.260	.360	42	167	181	.972	59	648	486	7	18	4.66
Chicago	60	94	.390	38	625	749	172	47	93	.260	.364	19	140	181	.977	62	734	566	7	9	4.41
St. Louis	58	96	.377	40	684	916	235	43	106	.246	.370	39	196	155	.967	56	651	448	7	14	5.20
Philadelphia	52	102	.338	46	670	913	204	53	100	.261	.378	42	155	208	.974	50	729	466	3	18	5.49
					6253	6253	1829	423	973	.271	.402	278	1137	1448	.976	500	5418	4558	62	154	4.58

NATIONAL LEAGUE 1951

New York — W-98 L-59 — Leo Durocher

POS	Player	AB	BA	HR	RBI	PO	A	E	DP	TC/G	FA	Pitcher	G	IP	W	L	SV	ERA
1B	W. Lockman	614	.282	12	73	1045	89	16	113	9.7	.986	S. Maglie	42	298	23	6	4	2.93
2B	E. Stanky	515	.247	14	43	356	412	18	117	5.6	.977	L. Jansen	39	278	23	11	0	3.04
SS	A. Dark	646	.303	14	69	295	465	45	114	5.2	.944	J. Hearn	34	211	17	9	0	3.62
3B	H. Thompson	264	.235	8	33	64	120	15	16	2.8	.925	D. Koslo	39	150	10	9	3	3.31
RF	D. Mueller	469	.277	16	69	233	5	4	1	2.1	.983	G. Spencer	57	132	10	4	3	3.75
CF	W. Mays	464	.274	20	68	353	12	9	2	3.1	.976	S. Jones	41	120	6	11	4	4.26
LF	M. Irvin	558	.312	24	121	237	10	1	1	2.2	.996							
C	W. Westrum	361	.219	20	70	554	62	8	9	5.1	.987							
O3	B. Thomson	518	.293	32	101	258	139	20	14		.952							
C	R. Noble	141	.234	5	26	144	8	4	3	3.8	.974							

Brooklyn — W-97 L-60 — Chuck Dressen

POS	Player	AB	BA	HR	RBI	PO	A	E	DP	TC/G	FA	Pitcher	G	IP	W	L	SV	ERA
1B	G. Hodges	582	.268	40	103	1365	126	12	171	9.5	.992	D. Newcombe	40	272	20	9	0	3.28
2B	J. Robinson	548	.338	19	88	390	435	7	137	5.4	.992	P. Roe	34	258	22	3	0	3.04
SS	P. Reese	616	.286	10	84	292	422	35	106	4.9	.953	R. Branca	42	204	13	12	3	3.26
3B	B. Cox	455	.279	9	51	140	264	14	26	3.0	.967	C. Erskine	46	190	16	12	4	4.46
RF	C. Furillo	667	.295	16	91	330	24	5	6	2.3	.986	C. King	48	121	14	7	6	4.15
CF	D. Snider	606	.277	29	101	382	12	5	1	2.7	.987							
LF	A. Pafko	277	.249	18	58	144	8	1	0	2.0	.993							
C	Campanella	505	.325	33	108	722	72	11	12	5.8	.986							

St. Louis — W-81 L-73 — Marty Marion

POS	Player	AB	BA	HR	RBI	PO	A	E	DP	TC/G	FA	Pitcher	G	IP	W	L	SV	ERA
1B	N. Jones	300	.263	3	41	698	48	7	7	10.6	.991	G. Staley	42	227	19	13	3	3.81
2B	Schoendienst	553	.289	6	54	339	386	7	113	5.9	.990	T. Poholsky	38	195	7	13	1	4.43
SS	S. Hemus	420	.281	2	32	181	344	19	72	5.2	.965	M. Lanier	31	160	11	9	1	3.26
3B	B. Johnson	442	.262	14	64	99	316	10	32	3.4	.976	A. Brazle	56	154	6	5	7	3.09
RF	E. Slaughter	409	.281	4	64	198	10	1	3	2.5	.995	H. Brecheen	24	139	8	4	2	3.25
CF	P. Lowrey	370	.303	5	40	220	6	4	3	2.7	.983	C. Chambers	21	129	11	6	0	3.83
LF	S. Musial	578	.355	32	108	216	13	6	4	2.6	.974	G. Munger	23	95	4	6	2	5.32
C	D. Rice	374	.251	9	47	447	66	8	12	4.3	.985	J. Presko	15	89	7	4	2	3.45
OF	W. Westlake	267	.255	6	39	154	7	3	1	2.4	.982							
OF	H. Rice	236	.254	4	38	116	6	6	0	2.0	.953							
SS	S. Rojek	186	.274	0	14	95	131	6	36	4.5	.974							

Boston — W-76 L-78 — Billy Southworth W-28 L-31 — Tommy Holmes W-48 L-47

POS	Player	AB	BA	HR	RBI	PO	A	E	DP	TC/G	FA	Pitcher	G	IP	W	L	SV	ERA
1B	E. Torgeson	581	.263	24	92	1330	107	17	137	9.4	.988	W. Spahn	39	311	22	14	0	2.98
2B	Hartsfield	450	.271	6	31	336	293	20	87	5.7	.969	M. Surkont	37	237	12	16	1	3.99
SS	B. Kerr	172	.186	1	18	110	173	9	34	4.6	.969	V. Bickford	25	165	11	9	0	3.12
3B	B. Elliott	480	.285	15	70	138	242	24	31	3.2	.941	J. Sain	26	160	5	13	1	3.94
RF	W. Marshall	469	.281	11	62	220	11	0	3	1.8	1.000	C. Nichols	33	156	11	8	2	2.88
CF	S. Jethroe	572	.280	18	65	356	18	10	5	2.7	.974	J. Wilson	20	110	7	7	1	5.40
LF	S. Gordon	550	.287	29	109	249	4	4	1	2.1	.984	B. Chipman	33	52	4	4	4	4.85
C	W. Cooper	342	.313	18	59	367	57	8	9	4.8	.981							
2S	S. Sisti	362	.279	2	38	220	227	18	47		.961							
C	St. Claire	220	.282	1	25	267	29	7	5	4.9	.977							
OF	B. Addis	199	.276	1	24	107	1	2	1	2.4	.982							
SS	J. Logan	169	.219	0	16	98	155	11	31	4.6	.958							

Philadelphia — W-73 L-81 — Eddie Sawyer

POS	Player	AB	BA	HR	RBI	PO	A	E	DP	TC/G	FA	Pitcher	G	IP	W	L	SV	ERA
1B	E. Waitkus	610	.257	1	46	1214	94	10	121	9.2	.992	R. Roberts	44	315	21	15	2	3.03
2B	P. Caballero	161	.186	1	11	133	124	4	37	4.6	.985	B. Church	38	247	15	11	1	3.53
SS	G. Hamner	589	.255	9	72	255	458	31	93	5.0	.958	R. Meyer	28	168	8	9	0	3.48
3B	W. Jones	564	.285	22	81	190	286	17	33	3.4	.966	J. Thompson	29	119	4	8	1	3.85
RF	D. Ennis	532	.267	15	73	268	14	9	3	2.0	.969	Heintzelman	35	118	6	12	2	4.18
CF	R. Ashburn	643	.344	4	63	538	15	7	6	3.6	.988	J. Konstanty	58	116	4	11	9	4.05
LF	D. Sisler	428	.287	8	52	233	8	8	3	2.2	.968	K. Johnson	20	106	5	8	4	4.57
C	A. Seminick	291	.227	11	37	378	47	9	6	4.8	.979							
C	D. Wilber	245	.278	8	34	326	26	8	5	4.9	.978							
2B	Pellagrini	197	.234	5	30	80	110	2	19	3.6	.990							
UT	T. Brown	196	.219	10	32	174	36	8	14		.963							
OF	B. Nicholson	170	.241	8	30	75	1	1	0	1.9	.987							

NATIONAL LEAGUE 1951, cont.

Cincinnati
W-68 L-86
Luke Sewell

POS	Player	AB	BA	HR	RBI	PO	A	E	DP	TC/G	FA	Pitcher	G	IP	W	L	SV	ERA
1B	Kluszewski	607	.259	13	77	1381	88	5	115	9.6	.997	Raffensberger	42	249	16	17	5	3.44
2B	C. Ryan	473	.237	16	53	332	344	21	73	5.8	.970	E. Blackwell	38	232	16	15	2	3.45
SS	V. Stallcup	428	.241	8	49	190	333	17	61	4.6	.969	H. Fox	40	228	9	14	2	3.83
3B	G. Hatton	331	.254	4	37	103	178	8	24	3.3	.972	W. Ramsdell	31	196	9	17	0	4.04
RF	J. Wyrostek	537	.311	2	61	255	8	8	2	1.9	.970	H. Wehmeier	39	185	7	10	2	3.70
CF	L. Merriman	359	.242	5	36	309	5	1	2	3.1	.997	H. Perkowski	35	102	3	6	1	2.82
LF	J. Adcock	395	.243	10	47	221	8	4	2	2.2	.983	F. Smith	50	76	5	5	11	3.20
C	D. Howell	207	.251	2	18	275	24	4	5	4.2	.987							
32	B. Adams	403	.266	5	24	184	215	18	33		.957							
OF	B. Usher	303	.208	5	25	218	9	6	4	2.4	.974							
C	J. Pramesa	227	.229	6	22	241	27	9	4	4.4	.968							
SS	R. McMillan	199	.211	1	8	78	132	8	23	4.0	.963							
OF	H. Edwards	127	.315	3	20	64	0	1	0	1.9	.985							

Pittsburgh
W-64 L-90
Billy Meyer

POS	Player	AB	BA	HR	RBI	PO	A	E	DP	TC/G	FA	Pitcher	G	IP	W	L	SV	ERA
1B	J. Phillips	156	.237	0	12	322	21	3	37	6.5	.991	M. Dickson	45	289	20	16	2	4.02
2B	D. Murtaugh	151	.199	1	11	110	113	7	35	3.5	.970	M. Queen	39	168	7	9	0	4.44
SS	Strickland	454	.216	9	47	222	386	37	89	5.2	.943	B. Werle	59	150	8	6	0	5.65
3B	Castiglione	482	.261	7	42	103	228	15	25	3.5	.957	B. Friend	34	150	6	10	0	4.27
RF	G. Bell	600	.278	16	89	267	18	4	4	2.0	.986	H. Pollet	21	129	6	10	0	5.04
CF	C. Metkovich	423	.293	3	40	171	4	1	0	2.6	.994	V. Law	28	114	6	9	2	4.50
LF	R. Kiner	531	.309	42	109	195	7	7	1	2.2	.967	T. Wilks	48*	83	3	5	12	2.83
C	McCullough	259	.297	8	39	364	52	5	10	4.9	.988							
OF	B. Howerton	219	.274	11	37	93	3	5	1	1.9	.950							
C	J. Garagiola	212	.255	9	35	255	30	4	4	4.7	.986							
1B	R. Nelson	195	.267	1	4	275	24	3	32	9.4	.990							
3B	W. Westlake	181	.282	16	45	32	87	12	12	3.9	.908							

Chicago
W-62 L-92
Frankie Frisch
W-35 L-45
Phil Cavarretta
W-27 L-47

POS	Player	AB	BA	HR	RBI	PO	A	E	DP	TC/G	FA	Pitcher	G	IP	W	L	SV	ERA
1B	C. Connors	201	.239	2	18	452	33	8	41	8.6	.984	B. Rush	37	211	11	12	2	3.83
2B	E. Miksis	421	.266	4	35	279	317	19	71	6.0*	.969	P. Minner	33	202	6	17	1	3.79
SS	R. Smalley	238	.231	8	31	117	190	15	42	4.4	.953	C. McLish	30	146	4	10	0	4.45
3B	R. Jackson	557	.275	16	76	198	323	24	32	3.8	.956	F. Hiller	24	141	6	12	1	4.84
RF	H. Jeffcoat	278	.273	4	27	166	11	2	5	2.1	.989	T. Lown	31	127	4	9	0	5.46
CF	F. Baumholtz	560	.284	2	50	307	6	8	2	2.5	.975	Klippstein	35	124	6	6	2	4.29
LF	H. Sauer	525	.263	30	89	286	19	6	2	2.4	.981	B. Kelly	35	124	7	4	0	4.66
C	S. Burgess	219	.251	2	20	210	35	5	6	3.9	.980	D. Leonard	41	82	10	6	3	2.64
OF	G. Hermanski	231	.281	3	20	134	9	5	1	2.0	.966							
1B	Cavarretta	206	.311	6	28	444	42	3	51	9.2	.994							
2B	Terwilliger	192	.214	0	10	136	142	9	37	5.9	.969							
OF	A. Pafko	178	.264	12	35	119	6	1	3	2.6	.992							
1B	D. Fondy	170	.271	3	20	387	27	10	40	9.6	.976							
SS	J. Cusick	164	.177	2	16	78	147	11	25	4.2	.953							
SS	Ramazzotti	158	.247	1	15	73	137	11	32	4.3	.950							

BATTING AND BASE RUNNING LEADERS

Batting Average
S. Musial, STL	.355
R. Ashburn, PHI	.344
J. Robinson, BKN	.338
Campanella, BKN	.325
M. Irvin, NY	.312

Slugging Average
R. Kiner, PIT	.627
S. Musial, STL	.614
Campanella, BKN	.590
B. Thomson, NY	.562
G. Hodges, BKN	.527

Home Runs
R. Kiner, PIT	42
G. Hodges, BKN	40
Campanella, BKN	33
B. Thomson, NY	32
S. Musial, STL	32

Total Bases
S. Musial, STL	355
R. Kiner, PIT	333
G. Hodges, BKN	307
Campanella, BKN	298
D. Snider, BKN	293
A. Dark, NY	293

Runs Batted In
M. Irvin, NY	121
R. Kiner, PIT	109
S. Gordon, BOS	109
Campanella, BKN	108
S. Musial, STL	108

Stolen Bases
S. Jethroe, BOS	35
R. Ashburn, PHI	29
J. Robinson, BKN	25
E. Torgeson, BOS	20
P. Reese, BKN	20

Hits
R. Ashburn, PHI	221
S. Musial, STL	205
C. Furillo, BKN	197
A. Dark, NY	196

Base on Balls
R. Kiner, PIT	137
E. Stanky, NY	127
W. Westrum, NY	104
E. Torgeson, BOS	102

Home Run Percentage
R. Kiner, PIT	7.9
G. Hodges, BKN	6.9
A. Pafko, BKN, CHI	6.6
Campanella, BKN	6.5

Runs Scored
R. Kiner, PIT	124
S. Musial, STL	124
G. Hodges, BKN	118
A. Dark, NY	114

Doubles
A. Dark, NY	41
Kluszewski, CIN	35
Campanella, BKN	33
J. Robinson, BKN	33

Triples
S. Musial, STL	12
G. Bell, PIT	12
M. Irvin, NY	11
F. Baumholtz, CHI	10

PITCHING LEADERS

Winning Percentage
P. Roe, BKN	.880
S. Maglie, NY	.793
D. Newcombe, BKN	.690
L. Jansen, NY	.676
J. Hearn, NY	.654

Earned Run Average
C. Nichols, BOS	2.88
S. Maglie, NY	2.93
W. Spahn, BOS	2.98
R. Roberts, PHI	3.03
P. Roe, BKN	3.04

Wins
S. Maglie, NY	23
L. Jansen, NY	23
P. Roe, BKN	22
W. Spahn, BOS	22
R. Roberts, PHI	21

Saves
T. Wilks, PIT, STL	13
F. Smith, CIN	11
J. Konstanty, PHI	9
A. Brazle, STL	7

Strikeouts
D. Newcombe, BKN	164
W. Spahn, BOS	164
S. Maglie, NY	146
L. Jansen, NY	145
B. Rush, CHI	129

Complete Games
W. Spahn, BOS	26
S. Maglie, NY	22
R. Roberts, PHI	22
P. Roe, BKN	19
M. Dickson, PIT	19

Fewest Hits/9 Innings
S. Maglie, NY	7.67
D. Newcombe, BKN	7.78
E. Blackwell, CIN	7.90
R. Branca, BKN	7.94

Shutouts
R. Roberts, PHI	6
Raffensberger, CIN	5
H. Fox, CIN	4
G. Staley, STL	4

Fewest Walks/9 Innings
Raffensberger, CIN	1.38
L. Jansen, NY	1.81
R. Roberts, PHI	1.83
P. Roe, BKN	2.24

Most Strikeouts/9 Inn.
M. Queen, PIT	6.58
B. Rush, CHI	5.49
D. Newcombe, BKN	5.43
R. Branca, BKN	5.21

Innings
R. Roberts, PHI	315
W. Spahn, BOS	311
S. Maglie, NY	298
M. Dickson, PIT	289

Games Pitched
T. Wilks, PIT, STL	65
B. Werle, PIT	59
J. Konstanty, PHI	58
G. Spencer, NY	57

NATIONAL LEAGUE 1951, *cont.*

	W	L	PCT	GB	R	OR	Batting 2B	3B	HR	BA	SA	SB	Fielding E	DP	FA	Pitching CG	BB	SO	ShO	SV	ERA
New York *	98	59	.624		781	641	201	53	179	.260	.418	55	171	175	.972	64	482	625	9	18	3.48
Brooklyn	97	60	.618	1	855	672	249	37	184	.275	.434	89	129	192	.979	64	549	693	10	13	3.88
St. Louis	81	73	.526	15.5	683	671	230	57	95	.264	.382	30	125	187	.980	58	558	546	9	23	3.95
Boston	76	78	.494	20.5	723	662	234	37	130	.262	.394	78	145	157	.976	73	595	604	10	12	3.75
Philadelphia	73	81	.474	23.5	648	644	199	47	108	.260	.375	64	138	146	.977	57	496	570	19	15	3.81
Cincinnati	68	86	.442	28.5	559	667	215	33	88	.248	.351	44	140	141	.977	55	490	584	14	23	3.70
Pittsburgh	64	90	.416	32.5	689	845	218	56	137	.258	.397	26	170	178	.972	40	627	582	9	22	4.78
Chicago	62	92	.403	34.5	614	750	200	47	103	.250	.364	63	181	161	.971	48	572	544	10	10	4.34
					5552	5552	1746	367	1024	.260	.390	449	1199	1337	.975	459	4369	4748	90	136	3.96

* Defeated Brooklyn in a playoff 2 games to 1.

AMERICAN LEAGUE 1951

New York
W-98 L-56
Casey Stengel

POS	Player	AB	BA	HR	RBI	PO	A	E	DP	TC/G	FA	Pitcher	G	IP	W	L	SV	ERA
1B	J. Collins	262	.286	9	48	556	56	8	65	5.4	.987	V. Raschi	35	258	21	10	0	3.27
2B	J. Coleman	362	.249	3	43	245	268	17	84	5.2	.968	E. Lopat	31	235	21	9	0	2.91
SS	P. Rizzuto	540	.274	2	43	317	407	24	113	5.2	.968	A. Reynolds	40	221	17	8	7	3.05
3B	B. Brown	313	.268	6	51	80	151	11	14	2.7	.955	T. Morgan	27	125	9	3	2	3.68
RF	H. Bauer	348	.296	10	54	188	7	2	1	1.8	.990	S. Shea	25	96	5	5	0	4.33
CF	J. DiMaggio	415	.263	12	71	288	11	3	3	2.7	.990	J. Ostrowski	34	95	6	4	5	3.49
LF	G. Woodling	420	.281	15	71	265	5	2	0	2.3	.993	B. Kuzava	23	82	8	4	5	2.40
C	Y. Berra	547	.294	27	88	693	82	13	25	5.6	.984							
32	McDougald	402	.306	14	63	174	249	14	46		.968							
OF	M. Mantle	341	.267	13	65	135	4	6	1	1.7	.959							
1B	J. Mize	332	.259	10	49	632	44	4	86	7.3	.994							
OF	J. Jensen	168	.298	8	25	106	6	3	1	2.4	.974							

Cleveland
W-93 L-61
Al Lopez

POS	Player	AB	BA	HR	RBI	PO	A	E	DP	TC/G	FA	Pitcher	G	IP	W	L	SV	ERA
1B	L. Easter	486	.270	27	103	1043	68	14	108	9.0	.988	E. Wynn	37	274	20	13	1	3.02
2B	B. Avila	542	.304	10	58	349	417	14	87	5.7	.982	B. Lemon	42	263	17	14	2	3.52
SS	R. Boone	544	.233	12	51	311	425	33	108	5.1	.957	M. Garcia	47	254	20	13	6	3.15
3B	A. Rosen	573	.265	24	102	157	277	19	20	2.9	.958	B. Feller	33	250	22	8	0	3.50
RF	B. Kennedy	321	.246	7	29	174	9	6	2	1.8	.968	L. Brissie	54	112	4	3	9	3.20
CF	L. Doby	447	.295	20	69	321	12	8	3	2.6	.977	S. Gromek	27	107	7	4	1	2.77
LF	D. Mitchell	510	.290	11	62	253	3	2	0	2.1	.992							
C	J. Hegan	416	.238	6	43	597	66	6	8	5.2	.991							
O1	H. Simpson	332	.229	7	24	458	20	8	29		.984							
OF	S. Chapman	246	.228	6	36	132	2	2	1	1.6	.985							

Boston
W-87 L-67
Steve O'Neill

POS	Player	AB	BA	HR	RBI	PO	A	E	DP	TC/G	FA	Pitcher	G	IP	W	L	SV	ERA
1B	W. Dropo	360	.239	11	57	878	63	12	91	10.2	.987	M. Parnell	36	221	18	11	2	3.26
2B	B. Doerr	402	.289	13	73	303	311	12	99	5.9	.981	Scarborough	37	184	12	9	0	5.09
SS	J. Pesky	480	.313	3	41	204	340	22	74	5.3	.961	McDermott	34	172	8	8	3	3.35
3B	V. Stephens	377	.300	17	78	105	207	7	19	3.6	.978	C. Stobbs	34	170	10	9	0	4.76
RF	C. Vollmer	386	.251	22	85	206	5	3	0	2.0	.986	E. Kinder	63	127	11	2	14	2.55
CF	D. DiMaggio	639	.296	12	72	376	15	11	1	2.8	.973	W. Nixon	33	125	7	4	1	4.90
LF	T. Williams	531	.318	30	126	315	12	4	6	2.3	.988	B. Wight	34	118	7	7	0	5.10
C	L. Moss	202	.198	3	26	284	28	5	4	4.6	.984	L. Kiely	17	113	7	7	0	3.34
UT	B. Goodman	546	.297	0	50	742	170	14	96		.985	H. Taylor	31	81	4	9	2	5.75
SS	L. Boudreau	273	.267	5	47	80	153	12	45	4.7	.951							
C	B. Rosar	170	.229	1	13	235	20	1	6	4.6	.996							
3B	F. Hatfield	163	.172	2	14	40	124	7	15	3.5	.959							

Chicago
W-81 L-73
Paul Richards

POS	Player	AB	BA	HR	RBI	PO	A	E	DP	TC/G	FA	Pitcher	G	IP	W	L	SV	ERA
1B	E. Robinson	564	.282	29	117	1296	91	17	143	9.6	.988	B. Pierce	37	240	15	14	2	3.03
2B	N. Fox	604	.313	4	55	413	449	17	112	6.0	.981	S. Rogovin	22	193	11	7	0	2.48*
SS	Carrasquel	538	.264	2	58	306	477	20	107	5.5	.975	K. Holcombe	28	159	11	12	0	3.78
3B	B. Dillinger	299	.301	0	20	70	116	14	10	2.9	.930	J. Dobson	28	147	7	6	3	3.62
RF	A. Zarilla	382	.257	10	60	164	7	3	2	1.5	.983	R. Gumpert	33	142	9	8	2	4.32
CF	J. Busby	477	.283	5	68	360	16	7	4	2.8	.982	L. Kretlow	26	137	6	9	0	4.20
LF	M. Minoso	516	.324	10	74	145	4	6	0	1.9	.961	H. Judson	27	122	5	6	1	3.77
C	P. Masi	225	.271	4	28	299	24	7	7	4.2	.979	H. Dorish	32	97	5	6	0	3.54
OF	B. Stewart	217	.276	6	40	111	4	2	0	1.9	.983							
OF	D. Lenhardt	199	.266	10	45	116	2	2	0	2.3	.983							
OF	R. Coleman	181	.276	3	21	141	3	3	1	2.9	.980							
C	G. Niarhos	168	.256	1	10	240	31	4	5	4.7	.985							

Detroit
W-73 L-81
Red Rolfe

POS	Player	AB	BA	HR	RBI	PO	A	E	DP	TC/G	FA	Pitcher	G	IP	W	L	SV	ERA
1B	D. Kryhoski	421	.287	12	57	964	81	9	95	9.4	.991	T. Gray	34	197	7	14	1	4.06
2B	G. Priddy	584	.260	8	57	437	463	18	118	6.0	.980	D. Trout	42	192	9	14	5	4.04
SS	J. Lipon	487	.265	0	38	244	364	33	80	5.1	.949	Hutchinson	31	188	10	10	2	3.68
3B	G. Kell	598	.319	2	59	175	310	20	34	3.4	.960	V. Trucks	37	154	13	8	1	4.33
RF	V. Wertz	501	.285	27	94	254	7	3	1	2.0	.989	B. Cain	35	149	11	10	2	4.70
CF	J. Groth	428	.299	3	49	266	12	2	3	2.5	.993	M. Stuart	29	124	4	6	1	3.77
LF	H. Evers	393	.224	11	46	234	9	6	1	2.3	.976	G. Bearden	37	106	3	4	0	4.33
C	J. Ginsberg	304	.260	8	37	388	56	10	7	4.8	.978	H. Newhouser	15	96	6	6	0	3.92
OF	P. Mullin	295	.281	12	51	151	4	10	1	2.0	.939	H. White	38	76	3	4	4	4.74
1B	D. Kolloway	212	.255	1	17	452	49	4	53	8.6	.992							
OF	S. Souchock	188	.245	11	28	92	3	6	1	1.7	.941							
UT	N. Berry	157	.229	0	9	78	127	12	22		.945							
PH	C. Keller	62	.258	3	21													

AMERICAN LEAGUE 1951, *cont.*

Philadelphia
W-70 L-84

Jimmy Dykes

POS	Player	AB	BA	HR	RBI	PO	A	E	DP	TC/G	FA	Pitcher	G	IP	W	L	SV	ERA
1B	F. Fain	425	.344	6	57	931	113	11	124	9.8	.990	A. Kellner	33	210	11	14	2	4.46
2B	P. Suder	440	.245	1	42	274	313	8	93	5.8	.987	B. Shantz	32	205	18	10	0	3.94
SS	E. Joost	553	.289	19	78	325	422	20	115	5.5	.974	B. Hooper	38	189	12	10	5	4.38
3B	H. Majeski	323	.285	5	42	82	217	8	17	3.5	.974	C. Scheib	46	143	1	12	10	4.47
RF	E. Valo	444	.302	7	55	247	5	5	0	2.2	.981	M. Martin	35	138	11	4	0	3.78
CF	D. Philley	468	.263	7	59	299	15	7	4	2.7	.978	S. Zoldak	26	128	6	10	0	3.16
LF	G. Zernial	552	.274	33*	125*	321	17*	9	3	2.5	.974	D. Fowler	22	125	5	11	0	5.62
C	J. Tipton	213	.239	3	20	230	52	9	12	4.0	.969	J. Kucab	30	75	4	3	4	4.22
32	B. Hitchcock	222	.306	1	36	92	150	14	30		.945							
1B	L. Limmer	214	.159	5	30	450	40	6	54	8.6	.988							
C	J. Astroth	187	.246	2	19	228	18	2	2	4.4	.992							
OF	A. Clark	161	.248	4	22	60	2	1	1	2.0	.984							

Washington
W-62 L-92

Bucky Harris

POS	Player	AB	BA	HR	RBI	PO	A	E	DP	TC/G	FA	Pitcher	G	IP	W	L	SV	ERA
1B	M. Vernon	546	.293	9	87	1157	87	8	121	9.1	.994	C. Marrero	25	187	11	9	0	3.90
2B	C. Michaels	485	.258	4	45	258	391	24	86	5.3	.964	S. Consuegra	40	146	7	8	3	4.01
SS	P. Runnels	273	.278	0	25	159	176	18	41	4.8	.949	D. Johnson	21	144	7	11	0	3.95
3B	E. Yost	568	.283	12	65	203	234	21	22	3.0	.954	S. Hudson	23	139	5	12	0	5.13
RF	S. Mele	558	.274	5	94	263	8	2	1	2.2	.993	Porterfield	19	133	9	8	0	3.24
CF	I. Noren	509	.279	8	86	420	15	10	1	3.5	.978	J. Moreno	31	133	5	11	2	4.88
LF	G. Coan	538	.303	9	62	374	17	14	2	3.1	.965	M. Harris	41	87	6	8	4	3.81
C	M. Guerra	214	.201	1	20	192	25	5	0	3.4	.977	A. Sima	18	77	3	7	0	4.79
SS	S. Dente	273	.238	0	29	128	173	12	43	4.8	.962							
OF	McCormick	243	.288	1	23	134	7	5	0	2.4	.966							
S2	G. Verble	177	.203	0	15	101	123	5	28		.978							
C	M. Grasso	175	.206	1	14	182	26	7	6	4.4	.967							
C	C. Kluttz	159	.308	1	22	162	15	6	2	4.2	.967							

St. Louis
W-52 L-102

Zack Taylor

POS	Player	AB	BA	HR	RBI	PO	A	E	DP	TC/G	FA	Pitcher	G	IP	W	L	SV	ERA
1B	H. Arft	345	.261	7	42	820	86	10	100	9.4	.989	N. Garver	33	246	20	12	0	3.73
2B	B. Young	611	.260	1	31	361	462	17	118	5.7	.980	D. Pillette	35	191	6	14	0	4.99
SS	B. Jennings	195	.179	0	13	141	165	15	39	5.0	.953	T. Byrne	19	123	4	10	0	3.82
3B	F. Marsh	445	.243	4	43	137	225	28	31	3.3	.928	A. Widmar	26	108	4	9	0	6.52
RF	K. Wood	333	.237	15	44	179	7	8	0	1.9	.959	J. McDonald	16	84	4	7	1	4.07
CF	J. Delsing	449	.249	8	45	340	15	6	5	2.9	.983	L. Sleater	20	81	1	9	1	5.11
LF	R. Coleman	341	.282	5	55	185	9	5	1	2.3	.975	S. Paige	23	62	3	4	5	4.79
C	S. Lollar	310	.252	8	44	361	48	2	4	4.8	.995							
C	M. Batts	248	.302	5	31	259	30	12*	4	4.7	.960							
OF	C. Mapes	201	.274	7	30	111	4	2	1	2.2	.983							
SS	J. Bero	160	.213	5	17	91	137	11	30	4.3	.954							

BATTING AND BASE RUNNING LEADERS

Batting Average
F. Fain, PHI	.344
M. Minoso, CHI, CLE	.326
G. Kell, DET	.319
T. Williams, BOS	.318
N. Fox, CHI	.313

Slugging Average
T. Williams, BOS	.556
L. Doby, CLE	.512
G. Zernial, CHI, PHI	.511
V. Wertz, DET	.511
M. Minoso, CHI, CLE	.500

Home Runs
G. Zernial, CHI, PHI	33
T. Williams, BOS	30
E. Robinson, CHI	29
L. Easter, CLE	27
V. Wertz, DET	27
Y. Berra, NY	27

Total Bases
T. Williams, BOS	295
G. Zernial, CHI, PHI	292
E. Robinson, CHI	279
Y. Berra, NY	269
D. DiMaggio, BOS	267

Runs Batted In
G. Zernial, CHI, PHI	129
E. Robinson, CHI	126
E. Robinson, CHI	117
L. Easter, CLE	103
A. Rosen, CLE	102

Stolen Bases
M. Minoso, CHI, CLE	31
J. Busby, CHI	26
P. Rizzuto, NY	18
McDougald, NY	14
Carrasquel, CHI	14
B. Avila, CLE	14

Hits
G. Kell, DET	191
N. Fox, CHI	189
D. DiMaggio, BOS	189
M. Minoso, CHI, CLE	173

Base on Balls
T. Williams, BOS	143
E. Yost, WAS	126
E. Joost, PHI	106
L. Doby, CLE	101

Home Run Percentage
G. Zernial, CHI, PHI	5.8
T. Williams, BOS	5.6
L. Easter, CLE	5.6
V. Wertz, DET	5.4

Runs Scored
D. DiMaggio, BOS	113
M. Minoso, CHI, CLE	112
T. Williams, BOS	109
E. Yost, WAS	109

Doubles
S. Mele, WAS	36
E. Yost, WAS	36
G. Kell, DET	36
M. Minoso, CHI, CLE	34

Triples
M. Minoso, CHI, CLE	14
R. Coleman, CHI, STL	12
N. Fox, CHI	12
B. Young, STL	9

PITCHING LEADERS

Winning Percentage
B. Feller, CLE	.733
E. Lopat, NY	.700
A. Reynolds, NY	.680
V. Raschi, NY	.677
B. Shantz, PHI	.643

Earned Run Average
S. Rogovin, CHI, DET	2.78
E. Lopat, NY	2.91
E. Wynn, CLE	3.02
B. Pierce, CHI	3.03
A. Reynolds, NY	3.05

Wins
B. Feller, CLE	22
E. Lopat, NY	21
V. Raschi, NY	21
N. Garver, STL	20
M. Garcia, CLE	20
E. Wynn, CLE	20

Saves
E. Kinder, BOS	14
C. Scheib, PHI	10
L. Brissie, CLE, PHI	9
A. Reynolds, NY	7
M. Garcia, CLE	6

Strikeouts
V. Raschi, NY	164
E. Wynn, CLE	133
B. Lemon, CLE	132
T. Gray, DET	131
McDermott, BOS	127

Complete Games
N. Garver, STL	24
E. Wynn, CLE	21
E. Lopat, NY	20
B. Pierce, CHI	18
S. Rogovin, CHI, DET	17
B. Lemon, CLE	17

Fewest Hits/9 Innings
A. Reynolds, NY	6.96
McDermott, BOS	7.38
E. Wynn, CLE	7.45
S. Rogovin, CHI, DET	7.85

Shutouts
A. Reynolds, NY	7
E. Lopat, NY	5
B. Shantz, PHI	4
B. Feller, CLE	4

Fewest Walks/9 Innings
Hutchinson, DET	1.29
E. Lopat, NY	2.72
B. Pierce, CHI	2.73
B. Hooper, PHI	2.90

Most Strikeouts/9 Inn.
McDermott, BOS	6.65
T. Gray, DET	5.97
V. Raschi, NY	5.71
A. Reynolds, NY	5.13

Innings
E. Wynn, CLE	274
B. Lemon, CLE	263
V. Raschi, NY	258
M. Garcia, CLE	254

Games Pitched
E. Kinder, BOS	63
L. Brissie, CLE, PHI	56
M. Garcia, CLE	47
C. Scheib, PHI	46

AMERICAN LEAGUE 1951, cont.

	W	L	PCT	GB	R	OR	2B	3B	HR	BA	SA	SB	E	DP	FA	CG	BB	SO	ShO	SV	ERA
										Batting				Fielding				Pitching			
New York	98	56	.636		798	621	208	48	140	.269	.408	78	144	190	.975	66	562	664	24	22	3.56
Cleveland	93	61	.604	5	696	594	208	35	140	.256	.389	52	134	151	.978	76	577	642	10	19	3.38
Boston	87	67	.565	11	804	725	233	32	127	.266	.392	20	141	184	.977	46	599	658	7	24	4.14
Chicago	81	73	.526	17	714	644	229	64	86	.270	.385	99	151	176	.975	74	549	572	11	14	3.50
Detroit	73	81	.474	25	685	741	231	35	104	.265	.380	37	163	166	.973	51	602	597	8	17	4.29
Philadelphia	70	84	.455	28	736	745	262	43	102	.262	.386	48	136	204	.978	52	569	437	7	22	4.47
Washington	62	92	.403	36	672	764	242	45	54	.263	.355	45	160	148	.973	58	630	475	6	13	4.49
St. Louis	52	102	.338	46	611	882	223	47	86	.247	.357	35	172	179	.971	56	801	550	5	9	5.17
					5716	5716	1836	349	839	.262	.381	414	1201	1398	.975	479	4889	4595	78	140	4.12

NATIONAL LEAGUE 1952

	POS	Player	AB	BA	HR	RBI	PO	A	E	DP	TC/G	FA	Pitcher	G	IP	W	L	SV	ERA
Brooklyn	1B	G. Hodges	508	.254	32	102	1322	116	11	152	9.5	.992	C. Erskine	33	207	14	6	2	2.70
	2B	J. Robinson	510	.308	19	75	353	400	20	113	5.3	.974	B. Loes	39	187	13	8	1	2.69
W-96 L-57	SS	P. Reese	559	.272	6	58	282	376	21	89	4.7	.969	B. Wade	37	180	11	9	3	3.60
	3B	B. Cox	455	.259	6	34	100	157	8	26	2.7	.970	P. Roe	27	159	11	2	0	3.12
Chuck Dressen	RF	C. Furillo	425	.247	8	59	225	12	3	2	1.8	.988	J. Black	56	142	15	4	15	2.15
	CF	D. Snider	534	.303	21	92	341	13	3	3	2.5	.992	C. Van Cuyk	23	98	5	6	1	5.16
	LF	A. Pafko	551	.287	19	85	229	18	3	2	1.8	.988	Rutherford	22	97	7	7	2	4.25
	C	Campanella	468	.269	22	97	662	55	4	7	5.9	.994	C. Labine	25	77	8	4	0	5.14
	OF	G. Shuba	256	.305	9	40	116	2	1	0	1.8	.992							
	3B	B. Morgan	191	.236	7	16	45	107	5	10	2.6	.968							
New York	1B	W. Lockman	606	.290	13	58	1435	111	13	155	10.1	.992	J. Hearn	37	224	14	7	1	3.78
	2B	D. Williams	540	.254	13	55	279	375	18	102	4.9	.973	S. Maglie	35	216	18	8	1	2.92
W-92 L-62	SS	A. Dark	589	.301	14	73	324	423	27	116	5.2	.965	L. Jansen	34	167	11	11	2	4.09
	3B	B. Thomson	608	.270	24	108	82	184	17	13	3.1	.940	D. Koslo	41	166	10	7	5	3.19
Leo Durocher	RF	D. Mueller	456	.281	12	49	221	8	3	4	1.9	.987	H. Wilhelm	71	159	15	3	11	2.43
	CF	H. Thompson	423	.260	17	67	182	5	4	1	2.7	.979	M. Lanier	37	137	7	12	5	3.94
	LF	B. Elliott	272	.228	10	35	83	6	2	0	1.4	.978	G. Spencer	35	60	3	5	3	5.55
	C	W. Westrum	322	.220	14	43	481	64	12	11	5.0	.978							
	OF	D. Rhodes	176	.250	10	36	97	3	9	0	1.9	.917							
	OF	W. Mays	127	.236	4	23	109	6	1	2	3.4	.991							
	OF	M. Irvin	126	.310	4	21	44	3	0	1	1.5	1.000							
St. Louis	1B	D. Sisler	418	.261	13	60	1022	84	17*	116	9.9	.985	G. Staley	35	240	17	14	0	3.27
	2B	Schoendienst	620	.303	7	67	399	424	19	108	5.9	.977	V. Mizell	30	190	10	8	0	3.65
W-88 L-66	SS	S. Hemus	570	.268	15	52	253	452	29	104	5.0	.960	J. Presko	28	147	7	10	0	4.05
	3B	B. Johnson	282	.252	2	34	56	177	12	10	2.8	.951	C. Boyer	23	110	6	6	0	4.24
Eddie Stanky	RF	E. Slaughter	510	.300	11	101	250	11	3	3	1.9	.989	A. Brazle	46	109	12	5	16	2.72
	CF	S. Musial	578	.336	21	91	298	6	4	2	2.3	.987	H. Brecheen	25	100	7	5	2	3.32
	LF	P. Lowrey	374	.286	1	48	174	3	4	1	1.7	.978	E. Yuhas	54	99	12	2	6	2.72
	C	D. Rice	495	.259	11	65	677	81	6	8	5.2	.992							
	OF	H. Rice	295	.288	7	45	132	5	4	0	1.7	.972							
	3B	T. Glaviano	162	.241	3	19	46	95	10	5	2.9	.934							
Philadelphia	1B	E. Waitkus	499	.289	2	49	1281	95	12	119	9.7	.991	R. Roberts	39	330	28	7	2	2.59
	2B	C. Ryan	577	.241	12	49	348	462	23	95	5.4	.972	R. Meyer	37	232	13	14	1	3.14
W-87 L-67	SS	G. Hamner	596	.275	17	87	267	470	38	102	5.1	.951	K. Drews	33	229	14	15	0	2.72
	3B	W. Jones	541	.250	18	72	216	281	16	31	3.5	.969	C. Simmons	28	201	14	8	0	2.82
Eddie Sawyer	RF	J. Wyrostek	321	.274	1	37	202	10	6	1	2.5	.972	J. Konstanty	42	80	5	3	6	3.94
W-28 L-35	CF	R. Ashburn	613	.282	1	42	428	23	9	5	3.0	.980	A. Hansen	43	77	5	6	4	3.26
	LF	D. Ennis	592	.289	20	107	277	11	9	1	2.0	.970							
Steve O'Neill	C	S. Burgess	371	.296	6	56	439	47	11	6	4.8	.978							
W-59 L-32	C	S. Lopata	179	.274	4	27	274	21	4	6	5.4	.987							
	OF	M. Clark	155	.335	1	15	81	5	0	1	2.3	1.000							
Chicago	1B	D. Fondy	554	.300	10	67	1257	103	14	92	9.6	.990	B. Rush	34	250	17	13	0	2.70
	2B	E. Miksis	383	.232	2	19	126	140	14	22	5.2	.950	Klippstein	41	203	9	14	3	4.44
W-77 L-77	SS	R. Smalley	261	.222	5	30	139	200	17	33	4.3	.952	W. Hacker	33	185	15	9	1	2.58
	3B	R. Jackson	379	.232	9	34	91	203	13	13	3.0	.958	P. Minner	28	181	14	9	0	3.74
Phil Cavarretta	RF	F. Baumholtz	409	.325	4	35	248	10	7	3	2.6	.974	T. Lown	33	157	4	11	0	4.37
	CF	H. Jeffcoat	297	.219	4	30	218	16	1	2	2.5	.996	B. Kelly	31	125	4	9	0	3.59
	LF	H. Sauer	567	.270	37	121	327	17	6	3	2.3	.983	D. Leonard	45	67	2	2	11	2.16
	C	T. Atwell	362	.290	2	31	451	50	12	2	5.1	.977							
	32	B. Serena	390	.274	15	61	198	234	8	30		.982							
	OF	B. Addis	292	.295	1	20	160	8	2	2	2.2	.988							
	OF	G. Hermanski	275	.255	4	34	146	7	3	3	2.1	.981							
	SS	T. Brown	200	.320	3	24	58	85	14	17	4.0	.911							
	2B	Ramazzotti	183	.284	1	12	90	143	5	28	4.8	.979							

NATIONAL LEAGUE 1952, cont.

Cincinnati
W-69 L-85
Luke Sewell W-39 L-59
Earle Brucker W-3 L-2
Rogers Hornsby W-27 L-24

POS	Player	AB	BA	HR	RBI	PO	A	E	DP	TC/G	FA	Pitcher	G	IP	W	L	SV	ERA
1B	Kluszewski	497	.320	16	86	1121	66	8	116	9.0	.993	Raffensberger	38	247	17	13	1	2.81
2B	G. Hatton	433	.212	9	57	316	289	6	68	5.1	.990	H. Perkowski	33	194	12	10	0	3.80
SS	R. McMillan	540	.244	7	57	297	495	24	101	5.3	.971	H. Wehmeier	33	190	9	11	0	5.15
3B	B. Adams	637	.283	6	48	176	328	20	28	3.4	.962	B. Church	29	153	5	9	0	4.34
RF	W. Marshall	397	.267	8	46	188	13	3	2*	1.9	.985	F. Hiller	28	124	5	8	1	4.63
CF	B. Borkowski	377	.252	4	24	219	5	2	1	2.2	.991	F. Smith	53	122	12	11	7	3.75
LF	J. Adcock	378	.278	13	52	189	5	3	1	2.3	.985	E. Blackwell	23	102	3	12	0	5.38
C	A. Seminick	336	.256	14	50	416	47	13	7	4.8	.973	B. Podbielan	24	87	4	5	1	2.80
OF	H. Edwards	184	.283	6	28	80	2	1	0	1.6	.988							
OF	W. Westlake	183	.202	3	14	127	5	1	0	2.4	.992							
OF	C. Abrams	158	.278	2	13	87	1	0	1	2.0	1.000							
OF	Greengrass	68	.309	5	24	55	0	2	0	3.4	.965							

Boston
W-64 L-89
Tommy Holmes W-13 L-22
Charlie Grimm W-51 L-67

POS	Player	AB	BA	HR	RBI	PO	A	E	DP	TC/G	FA	Pitcher	G	IP	W	L	SV	ERA
1B	E. Torgeson	382	.230	5	34	931	73	11	86	9.7	.989	W. Spahn	40	290	14	19	3	2.98
2B	J. Dittmer	326	.193	7	41	228	267	9	60	5.6	.982	J. Wilson	33	234	12	14	0	4.23
SS	J. Logan	456	.283	4	42	247	385	18	81	5.6	.972	M. Surkont	31	215	12	13	0	3.77
3B	E. Mathews	528	.242	25	58	160	259	19	21	3.1	.957	V. Bickford	26	161	7	12	0	3.74
RF	B. Thorpe	292	.260	3	26	132	9	4	3	2.0	.972	L. Burdette	45	137	6	11	7	3.61
CF	S. Jethroe	608	.232	13	58	413	10	13	3	2.9	.970	E. Johnson	29	92	6	3	1	4.11
LF	S. Gordon	522	.289	25	75	263	9	1	0	1.9	.996							
C	W. Cooper	349	.235	10	55	417	55	8	8	5.4	.983							
UT	S. Sisti	245	.212	4	24	142	129	16	22		.944							
OF	J. Daniels	219	.187	2	14	119	6	3	2	1.5	.977							
1B	G. Crowe	217	.258	4	20	476	42	8	40	9.6	.985							
C	P. Burris	168	.220	2	21	208	16	0	3	4.5	1.000							

Pittsburgh
W-42 L-112
Billy Meyer

POS	Player	AB	BA	HR	RBI	PO	A	E	DP	TC/G	FA	Pitcher	G	IP	W	L	SV	ERA
1B	T. Bartirome	355	.220	0	16	909	72	11	91	8.4	.989	M. Dickson	43	278	14	21	2	3.57
2B	J. Merson	398	.246	5	38	190	214	9	59	5.1	.978	H. Pollet	31	214	7	16	0	4.12
SS	D. Groat	384	.284	1	29	229	272	25	61	5.6	.952	B. Friend	35	185	7	17	0	4.18
3B	Castiglione	214	.266	4	18	67	129	10	7	3.6	.951	W. Main	48	153	2	12	2	4.46
RF	G. Bell	468	.250	16	59	202	8	6	2	1.8	.972	T. Wilks	44	72	5	5	4	3.61
CF	B. Del Greco	341	.217	1	20	246	11	6	3	2.8	.977							
LF	R. Kiner	516	.244	37	87	250	9	8	0	1.8	.970							
C	J. Garagiola	344	.273	8	54	418	63	11	9	4.7	.978							
1O	C. Metkovich	373	.271	7	41	602	34	7	59		.989							
UT	C. Koshorek	322	.261	0	15	149	232	18	47		.955							
2S	Strickland	232	.177	5	22	142	217	19	54		.950							
C	McCullough	172	.233	1	15	227	38	5	4	4.4	.981							

BATTING AND BASE RUNNING LEADERS

Batting Average
S. Musial, STL	.336
F. Baumholtz, CHI	.325
Kluszewski, CIN	.320
J. Robinson, BKN	.308
D. Snider, BKN	.303

Slugging Average
S. Musial, STL	.538
H. Sauer, CHI	.531
Kluszewski, CIN	.509
R. Kiner, PIT	.500
G. Hodges, BKN	.500

Home Runs
R. Kiner, PIT	37
H. Sauer, CHI	37
G. Hodges, BKN	32
S. Gordon, BOS	25
E. Mathews, BOS	25

Total Bases
S. Musial, STL	311
H. Sauer, CHI	301
B. Thomson, NY	293
D. Ennis, PHI	281
D. Snider, BKN	264

Runs Batted In
H. Sauer, CHI	121
B. Thomson, NY	108
D. Ennis, PHI	107
G. Hodges, BKN	102
E. Slaughter, STL	101

Stolen Bases
P. Reese, BKN	30
S. Jethroe, BOS	28
J. Robinson, BKN	24
R. Ashburn, PHI	16
B. Fondy, CHI	13
C. Ryan, PHI	13

Hits
S. Musial, STL	194
Schoendienst, STL	188
B. Adams, CIN	180
A. Dark, NY	177

Base on Balls
R. Kiner, PIT	110
G. Hodges, BKN	107
J. Robinson, BKN	106
S. Hemus, STL	96

Home Run Percentage
R. Kiner, PIT	7.2
H. Sauer, CHI	6.5
G. Hodges, BKN	6.3
S. Gordon, BOS	4.8

Runs Scored
S. Hemus, STL	105
S. Musial, STL	105
J. Robinson, BKN	104
W. Lockman, NY	99

Doubles
S. Musial, STL	42
Schoendienst, STL	40
R. McMillan, CIN	32
H. Sauer, CHI	31

Triples
B. Thomson, NY	14
E. Slaughter, STL	12
Kluszewski, CIN	11
D. Ennis, PHI	10

PITCHING LEADERS

Winning Percentage
H. Wilhelm, NY	.833
R. Roberts, PHI	.800
J. Black, BKN	.789
S. Maglie, NY	.692
W. Hacker, CHI	.625

Earned Run Average
H. Wilhelm, NY	2.43
W. Hacker, CHI	2.58
R. Roberts, PHI	2.59
B. Loes, BKN	2.69
B. Rush, CHI	2.70

Wins
R. Roberts, PHI	28
S. Maglie, NY	18
Raffensberger, CIN	17
B. Rush, CHI	17
G. Staley, STL	17

Saves
A. Brazle, STL	16
J. Black, BKN	15
H. Wilhelm, NY	11
D. Leonard, CHI	11
F. Smith, CIN	7
L. Burdette, BOS	7

Strikeouts
W. Spahn, BOS	183
B. Rush, CHI	157
R. Roberts, PHI	148
V. Mizell, STL	146
C. Simmons, PHI	141

Complete Games
R. Roberts, PHI	30
M. Dickson, PIT	21
W. Spahn, BOS	19
Raffensberger, CIN	18
B. Rush, CHI	17

Fewest Hits/9 Innings
W. Hacker, CHI	7.01
H. Wilhelm, NY	7.17
C. Erskine, BKN	7.27
B. Rush, CHI	7.37

Shutouts
C. Simmons, PHI	6
Raffensberger, CIN	6
W. Hacker, CHI	5
K. Drews, PHI	5

Fewest Walks/9 Innings
R. Roberts, PHI	1.23
W. Hacker, CHI	1.51
Raffensberger, CIN	1.64
G. Staley, STL	1.95

Most Strikeouts/9 Inn.
V. Mizell, STL	6.92
C. Simmons, PHI	6.30
H. Wilhelm, NY	6.10
B. Wade, BKN	5.90

Innings
R. Roberts, PHI	330
W. Spahn, BOS	290
M. Dickson, PIT	278
B. Rush, CHI	250

Games Pitched
H. Wilhelm, NY	71
J. Black, BKN	56
E. Yuhas, STL	54
F. Smith, CIN	53

NATIONAL LEAGUE 1952, cont.

	W	L	PCT	GB	R	OR	2B	3B	HR	BA	SA	SB	E	DP	FA	CG	BB	SO	ShO	SV	ERA
										Batting				Fielding				Pitching			
Brooklyn	96	57	.627		**775**	603	199	32	**153**	.262	.399	**90**	106	169	**.982**	45	544	**773**	11	24	3.53
New York	92	62	.597	4.5	722	639	186	**56**	151	.256	**.399**	30	158	**175**	.974	49	538	655	11	**31**	3.59
St. Louis	88	66	.571	8.5	677	630	**247**	54	97	**.267**	.366	33	141	159	.977	49	501	712	11	27	3.66
Philadelphia	87	67	.565	9.5	657	**552**	237	45	93	.260	.376	60	150	145	.975	**80**	373	609	**16**	16	**3.07**
Chicago	77	77	.500	19.5	628	631	223	45	107	.264	.383	50	146	123	.976	59	534	661	15	15	3.58
Cincinnati	69	85	.448	27.5	615	659	212	45	104	.249	.366	32	107	145	.982	56	517	579	11	12	4.01
Boston	64	89	.418	32	569	651	187	31	110	.233	.343	58	154	143	.975	63	525	687	11	13	3.78
Pittsburgh	42	112	.273	54.5	515	793	181	30	92	.231	.331	43	182	167	.970	43	615	564	4	8	4.65
					5158	5158	1672	338	907	.253	.374	396	1144	1226	.976	444	4147	5240	90	146	3.73

AMERICAN LEAGUE 1952

	POS	Player	AB	BA	HR	RBI	PO	A	E	DP	TC/G	FA	Pitcher	G	IP	W	L	SV	ERA
New York W-95 L-59 Casey Stengel	1B	J. Collins	428	.280	18	59	1047	73	11	123	9.5	.990	A. Reynolds	35	244	20	8	6	**2.06**
	2B	B. Martin	363	.267	3	33	244	323	9	92	5.4	.984	V. Raschi	31	223	16	6	0	2.78
	SS	P. Rizzuto	578	.254	2	43	308	458	19	116	5.2	.976	E. Lopat	20	149	10	5	0	2.53
	3B	McDougald	555	.263	11	78	124	273	13	38	3.5	.968	J. Sain	35	148	11	6	7	3.46
	RF	H. Bauer	553	.293	17	74	233	16	4	2	1.8	.984	B. Kuzava	28	133	8	8	3	3.45
	CF	M. Mantle	549	.311	23	87	347	15	14	5	2.7	.968	T. Morgan	16	94	5	4	2	3.07
	LF	G. Woodling	408	.309	12	63	241	12	1	4	2.2	**.996**	B. Miller	21	88	4	6	0	3.48
	C	Y. Berra	534	.273	30	98	**700**	73	6	10	5.6	.992	B. Hogue	27	47	3	5	4	5.32
	OF	I. Noren	272	.235	5	21	95	3	0	1	1.6	1.000							
	1B	J. Mize	137	.263	4	29	218	18	3	32	8.9	.987							
Cleveland W-93 L-61 Al Lopez	1B	L. Easter	437	.263	31	97	940	90	18	87	8.9	.983	B. Lemon	42	310	22	11	4	2.50
	2B	B. Avila	597	.300	7	45	355	431	**28**	81	5.5	.966	M. Garcia	46	292	22	11	4	2.37
	SS	R. Boone	316	.263	7	45	177	251	27	55	4.7	.941	E. Wynn	42	286	23	12	3	2.90
	3B	A. Rosen	567	.302	28	**105**	159	256	18	25	2.9	.958	B. Feller	30	192	9	13	0	4.74
	RF	H. Simpson	545	.266	10	65	226	11	3	4	1.9	.988	S. Gromek	29	123	7	7	1	3.67
	CF	L. Doby	519	.276	32	104	398	11	6	3	3.1	.986							
	LF	D. Mitchell	511	.323	5	58	258	2	2	0	2.0	.992							
	C	J. Hegan	333	.225	4	41	498	53	7	7	5.2	.987							
	OF	J. Fridley	175	.251	4	16	87	3	2	0	1.7	.978							
	C	J. Tipton	105	.248	6	22	118	18	4	1	4.0	.971							
Chicago W-81 L-73 Paul Richards	1B	E. Robinson	594	.296	22	104	**1329**	89	14	145	9.2	.990	B. Pierce	33	255	15	12	1	2.57
	2B	N. Fox	648	.296	0	39	406	433	13	111	5.6	**.985**	S. Rogovin	33	232	14	9	1	3.85
	SS	Carrasquel	359	.248	1	42	176	248	16	50	4.4	.964	J. Dobson	29	201	14	10	1	2.51
	3B	H. Rodriguez	407	.265	1	40	145	232	16	26	3.5	.959	M. Grissom	28	166	12	10	0	3.74
	RF	S. Mele	423	.248	14	59	157	8	0	1	1.5	1.000	C. Stobbs	38	135	7	12	1	3.13
	CF	R. Coleman	195	.215	2	14	130	5	3	0	1.9	.978	H. Dorish	39	91	8	4	11	2.47
	LF	M. Minoso	569	.281	13	61	322	11	7	3	2.4	.979	L. Aloma	25	40	3	1	6	4.28
	C	S. Lollar	375	.240	13	50	590	53	7	4	5.4	.989							
	OF	B. Stewart	225	.267	5	30	108	1	2	0	1.9	.982							
	OF	J. Rivera	201	.249	3	18	157	2	2	1	3.0	.988							
	OF	T. Wright	132	.258	1	21	60	2	2	0	1.9	.969							
Philadelphia W-79 L-75 Jimmy Dykes	1B	F. Fain	538	**.327**	2	59	1245	**150**	**22**	124	**9.8**	.984	B. Shantz	33	280	**24**	7	0	2.48
	2B	S. Kell	213	.221	0	14	143	169	12	35	4.8	.963	A. Kellner	34	231	12	14	0	4.36
	SS	E. Joost	540	.244	20	75	278	431	**28**	81	5.0	.962	H. Byrd	37	228	15	15	2	3.31
	3B	B. Hitchcock	407	.246	1	56	105	222	20	26	3.3	.942	C. Scheib	30	158	11	7	2	4.39
	RF	E. Valo	388	.281	5	47	223	7	9	1	2.0	.962	B. Hooper	43	144	8	15	6	5.18
	CF	D. Philley	586	.263	7	71	442	13	4	3	3.1	.991							
	LF	G. Zernial	549	.262	29	100	302	6	9	0	2.2	.972							
	C	J. Astroth	337	.249	1	36	436	36	4	9	4.7	.992							
	UT	P. Suder	228	.241	1	20	136	179	8	40		.975							
	2B	C. Michaels	200	.250	1	18	151	133	2	30	5.2	.993							
	OF	A. Clark	186	.274	7	29	78	2	1	0	1.7	.988							
	3B	H. Majeski	117	.256	2	20	33	87	3	3	3.6	.976							
Washington W-78 L-76 Bucky Harris	1B	M. Vernon	569	.251	10	80	1291	115	10	139	9.3	**.993**	Porterfield	31	231	13	14	0	2.72
	2B	F. Baker	263	.262	0	33	151	176	2	36	4.8	.994	C. Marrero	22	184	11	8	0	2.88
	SS	P. Runnels	555	.285	1	64	314	406	25	97	5.1	.966	S. Shea	22	169	11	7	0	2.93
	3B	E. Yost	587	.233	12	49	**212**	249	18	26	3.1	.962	W. Masterson	24	161	9	8	2	3.70
	RF	J. Jensen	570	.286	10	80	283	17*	7	1	2.1	.977	J. Moreno	26	147	9	9	0	3.97
	CF	J. Busby	512	.244	2	47	430*	4	3	0	3.4*	.993	R. Gumpert	20	104	4	9	0	4.24
	LF	G. Coan	332	.205	5	20	185	4	3	1	2.2	.984	S. Consuegra	30	74	6	0	5	3.05
	C	M. Grasso	361	.216	0	27	485	64	**17**	4	5.0	.970							
	OF	K. Wood	210	.238	6	32	161	6	8	1	3.1	.954							
	2B	M. Hoderlein	208	.269	0	17	138	168	7	43	5.4	.978							

AMERICAN LEAGUE 1952, cont.

	POS	Player	AB	BA	HR	RBI	PO	A	E	DP	TC/G	FA	Pitcher	G	IP	W	L	SV	ERA
Boston	1B	D. Gernert	367	.243	19	67	877	67	12	104	9.7	.987	M. Parnell	33	214	12	12	2	3.62
	2B	B. Goodman	513	.306	4	56	284	340	16	95	6.2	.975	McDermott	30	162	10	9	0	3.72
W-76 L-78	SS	J. Lipon	234	.205	0	18	118	218	6	53	5.0	.982*	S. Hudson	21	134	7	9	0	3.62
	3B	G. Kell	276	.319	6	40	75	138	9	14	3.0	.959	D. Trout	26	134	9	8	1	3.64
Lou Boudreau	RF	Throneberry	310	.258	5	23	141	9	7	5	1.8	.955	D. Brodowski	20	115	5	5	0	4.40
	CF	D. DiMaggio	486	.294	6	33	303	12	8	4	2.6	.975	W. Nixon	23	104	5	4	0	4.86
	LF	H. Evers	401	.262	14	59	219	8	6	3	2.2	.974	E. Kinder	23	98	5	6	4	2.58
	C	S. White	381	.281	10	49	464	59	9	7	4.8	.983	I. Delock	39	95	4	9	5	4.26
	S3	V. Stephens	295	.254	7	44	110	227	16	48		.955	Scarborough	28	77	1	5	4	4.81
	23	T. Lepcio	274	.263	5	26	164	212	14	46		.964	A. Benton	24	38	4	3	6	2.39
	OF	C. Vollmer	250	.264	11	50	143	3	0	1	2.1	1.000							
	SO	J. Piersall	161	.267	1	16	79	78	9	13		.946							
	C	D. Wilber	135	.267	3	23	160	22	1	5	4.7	.995							
	1B	W. Dropo	132	.265	6	27	319	21	2	31	9.8	.994							
	OF	D. Lenhardt	105	.295	7	24	52	0	1	0	2.0	.981							
St. Louis	1B	D. Kryhoski	342	.243	11	42	680	49	8	80	8.6	.989	D. Pillette	30	205	10	13	0	3.59
	2B	B. Young	575	.247	4	56	380	407	13	127	5.4	.984	T. Byrne	29	162	7	14	0	4.68
W-64 L-90	SS	DeMaestri	186	.226	1	18	105	156	17	29	3.6	.939	B. Cain	29	170	12	10	2	4.13
	3B	J. Dyck	402	.269	15	64	79	152	9	14	3.2	.963	G. Bearden	34	151	7	8	0	4.30
Rogers Hornsby	RF	B. Nieman	478	.289	18	74	230	10	6	5	2.0	.976	N. Garver	21	149	7	10	0	3.69
W-22 L-29	CF	J. Rivera	336	.256	4	30	273	7	7	1	3.3	.976	S. Paige	46	138	12	10	10	3.07
	LF	J. Delsing	298	.255	1	34	206	4	3	2	2.5	.986	E. Harrist	36	117	2	8	5	4.01
Marty Marion	C	C. Courtney	413	.286	5	50	487	60	2	7	4.9	.996							
W-42 L-61	S3	F. Marsh	247	.279	2	27	87	162	17	39		.936							
	1B	Goldsberry	227	.229	3	17	524	40	10	56	8.0	.983							
	SS	M. Marion	186	.247	2	19	105	138	5	41	3.9	.980							
	3B	C. Michaels	166	.265	3	25	43	88	12	12	3.4	.916							
Detroit	1B	W. Dropo	459	.279	23	70	1005	78	12	104	9.5	.989	T. Gray	35	224	12	17	0	4.14
	2B	G. Priddy	279	.283	4	20	211	209	14	48	5.8	.968	A. Houtteman	35	221	8	20	1	4.36
	SS	N. Berry	189	.228	0	13	90	158	9	26	3.9	.965	V. Trucks	35	197	5	19	1	3.97
W-50 L-104	3B	F. Hatfield	441	.236	2	25	114	253*	9	32	3.5	.968*	H. Newhouser	25	154	9	9	0	3.74
	RF	V. Wertz	285	.246	17	51	134	8	2	3	1.8	.986	B. Wight	23	144	5	9	0	3.88
Red Rolfe	CF	J. Groth	524	.284	4	51	329	14	5	3	2.5	.986	B. Hoeft	34	125	2	7	4	4.32
W-23 L-49	LF	P. Mullin	255	.251	7	35	131	6	3	2	2.2	.979	H. White	41	63	1	8	5	3.69
	C	J. Ginsberg	307	.221	6	36	442	41	8	7	4.9	.984							
Fred Hutchinson	OF	S. Souchock	265	.249	13	45	103	4	4	2	2.0	.964							
W-27 L-55	2B	A. Federoff	231	.242	0	14	136	184	8	42	4.7	.976							
	OF	C. Mapes	193	.197	9	23	86	3	3	1	1.5	.967							
	S2	J. Pesky	177	.254	1	9	105	137	11	37		.957							
	1B	D. Kolloway	173	.243	2	21	252	28	6	15	8.9	.979							
	C	M. Batts	173	.237	3	13	262	36	5	4	5.5	.983							

BATTING AND BASE RUNNING LEADERS

Batting Average
F. Fain, PHI .327
D. Mitchell, CLE .323
M. Mantle, NY .311
G. Kell, BOS, DET .311
G. Woodling, NY .309

Slugging Average
L. Doby, CLE .541
M. Mantle, NY .530
A. Rosen, CLE .524
L. Easter, CLE .513
V. Wertz, DET, STL .506

Home Runs
L. Doby, CLE 32
L. Easter, CLE 31
Y. Berra, NY 30
G. Zernial, PHI 29
W. Dropo, BOS, DET 29

Total Bases
A. Rosen, CLE 297
M. Mantle, NY 291
W. Dropo, BOS, DET 282
L. Doby, CLE 281
E. Robinson, CHI 277

Runs Batted In
A. Rosen, CLE 105
L. Doby, CLE 104
E. Robinson, CHI 104
G. Zernial, PHI 100
Y. Berra, NY 98

Stolen Bases
M. Minoso, CHI 22
J. Rivera, CHI, STL 21
J. Jensen, NY, WAS 18
P. Rizzuto, NY 17
Throneberry, BOS 16

Hits
N. Fox, CHI 192
B. Avila, CLE 179
F. Fain, PHI 176
E. Robinson, CHI 176

Base on Balls
E. Yost, WAS 129
E. Joost, PHI 122
F. Fain, PHI 105
E. Valo, PHI 101

Home Run Percentage
L. Easter, CLE 7.1
L. Doby, CLE 6.2
Y. Berra, NY 5.6
V. Wertz, DET, STL 5.5

Runs Scored
L. Doby, CLE 104
B. Avila, CLE 102
A. Rosen, CLE 101
Y. Berra, NY 97

Doubles
F. Fain, PHI 43
M. Mantle, NY 37
M. Vernon, WAS 33
E. Robinson, CHI 33

Triples
B. Avila, CLE 11
H. Simpson, CLE 10
P. Rizzuto, NY 10
N. Fox, CHI 10

PITCHING LEADERS

Winning Percentage
B. Shantz, PHI .774
V. Raschi, NY .727
A. Reynolds, NY .714
M. Garcia, CLE .667
B. Lemon, CLE .667

Earned Run Average
A. Reynolds, NY 2.06
M. Garcia, CLE 2.37
B. Shantz, PHI 2.48
B. Lemon, CLE 2.50
J. Dobson, CHI 2.51

Wins
B. Shantz, PHI 24
E. Wynn, CLE 23
M. Garcia, CLE 22
B. Lemon, CLE 22
A. Reynolds, NY 20

Saves
H. Dorish, CHI 11
S. Paige, STL 10
J. Sain, NY 7

Strikeouts
A. Reynolds, NY 160
E. Wynn, CLE 153
B. Shantz, PHI 152
B. Pierce, CHI 144
M. Garcia, CLE 143

Complete Games
B. Lemon, CLE 28
B. Shantz, PHI 27
A. Reynolds, NY 24
E. Wynn, CLE 19
M. Garcia, CLE 19

Fewest Hits/9 Innings
B. Lemon, CLE 6.86
V. Raschi, NY 7.02
A. Reynolds, NY 7.15
J. Dobson, CHI 7.36

Shutouts
A. Reynolds, NY 6
M. Garcia, CLE 6
B. Shantz, PHI 5
B. Lemon, CLE 5

Fewest Walks/9 Innings
B. Shantz, PHI 2.03
D. Pillette, STL 2.41
C. Marrero, WAS 2.59
A. Houtteman, DET 2.65

Most Strikeouts/9 Inn.
McDermott, BOS 6.50
A. Reynolds, NY 5.89
V. Trucks, DET 5.89
T. Gray, DET 5.54

Innings
B. Lemon, CLE 310
M. Garcia, CLE 292
E. Wynn, CLE 286
B. Shantz, PHI 280

Games Pitched
B. Kennedy, CHI 47
M. Garcia, CLE 46
S. Paige, STL 46
B. Hooper, PHI 43

AMERICAN LEAGUE 1952, cont.

	W	L	PCT	GB	R	OR	2B	3B	HR	BA	SA	SB	E	DP	FA	CG	BB	SO	ShO	SV	ERA
								Batting						Fielding			Pitching				
New York	95	59	.617		727	**557**	221	**56**	129	**.267**	.403	52	127	**199**	.979	72	581	666	**17**	27	**3.14**
Cleveland	93	61	.604	2	**763**	606	211	49	**148**	.262	**.404**	46	155	141	.975	**80**	556	671	16	18	3.32
Chicago	81	73	.526	14	610	568	199	38	80	.252	.348	**61**	**123**	158	**.980**	53	578	**774**	13	**28**	3.25
Philadelphia	79	75	.513	16	664	723	212	35	89	.253	.359	52	140	148	.977	73	**526**	562	11	16	4.15
Washington	78	76	.506	17	598	608	225	44	50	.239	.326	48	132	152	.978	75	577	574	10	15	3.37
Boston	76	78	.494	19	668	658	**233**	34	113	.255	.377	59	145	181	.976	53	623	624	7	24	3.80
St. Louis	64	90	.416	31	604	733	225	46	82	.250	.356	30	155	176	.974	48	598	581	6	18	4.12
Detroit	50	104	.325	45	557	738	190	37	103	.243	.352	27	152	145	.975	51	591	702	10	14	4.25
					5191	5191	1716	339	794	.253	.365	375	1129	1300	.977	505	4630	5154	90	160	3.67

NATIONAL LEAGUE 1953

Brooklyn
W-105 L-49
Chuck Dressen

POS	Player	AB	BA	HR	RBI	PO	A	E	DP	TC/G	FA	Pitcher	G	IP	W	L	SV	ERA
1B	G. Hodges	520	.302	31	122	1025	99	8	105	8.9	.993	C. Erskine	39	247	20	6	3	3.54
2B	J. Gilliam	605	.278	6	63	332	426	19	102	5.2	.976	R. Meyer	34	191	15	5	0	4.56
SS	P. Reese	524	.271	13	61	265	380	23	83	4.9	.966	B. Loes	32	163	14	8	0	4.54
3B	B. Cox	327	.291	10	44	86	142	6	20	2.6	.974	P. Roe	25	157	11	3	0	4.36
RF	C. Furillo	479	.344	21	92	232	11	3	3	1.9	.988	B. Milliken	37	118	8	4	2	3.37
CF	D. Snider	590	.336	42	126	370	7	5	3	2.5	.987	J. Podres	33	115	9	4	0	4.23
LF	J. Robinson	484	.329	12	95	145	9	3	0	2.1	.981	C. Labine	37	110	11	6	7	2.77
C	Campanella	519	.312	41	**142**	807	57	10	9	6.2	.989	B. Wade	32	90	7	5	3	3.79
3S	B. Morgan	196	.260	7	33	71	105	10	19		.946	J. Hughes	48	86	4	3	9	3.47
OF	G. Shuba	169	.254	5	23	59	1	1	1	1.4	.984	J. Black	34	73	6	3	5	5.33
1B	W. Belardi	163	.239	11	34	283	23	5	34	8.2	.984							

Milwaukee
W-92 L-62
Charlie Grimm

POS	Player	AB	BA	HR	RBI	PO	A	E	DP	TC/G	FA	Pitcher	G	IP	W	L	SV	ERA
1B	J. Adcock	590	.285	18	80	1389	96	13	146	9.5	.991	W. Spahn	35	266	**23**	7	3	**2.10**
2B	J. Dittmer	504	.266	9	63	290	343	**23**	95	4.8	.965	L. Burdette	46	175	15	5	8	3.24
SS	J. Logan	611	.273	11	73	**295**	481	20	104	5.3	**.975**	J. Antonelli	31	175	12	12	1	3.18
3B	E. Mathews	579	.302	**47**	135	154	311	30	33	3.2	.939	M. Surkont	28	170	11	5	0	4.18
RF	A. Pafko	516	.297	17	72	241	5	6	1	1.8	.976	B. Buhl	30	154	13	8	0	2.97
CF	B. Bruton	613	.250	1	41	397	15	9	**5**	2.8	.979	D. Liddle	31	129	7	6	2	3.08
LF	S. Gordon	464	.274	19	75	245	10	6	2	1.9	.977	J. Wilson	20	114	4	9	0	4.34
C	D. Crandall	382	.272	15	51	566	**62**	9	**13**	5.9	.986							
OF	J. Pendleton	251	.299	7	27	141	7	6	1	1.5	.961							

Philadelphia
W-83 L-71
Steve O'Neill

POS	Player	AB	BA	HR	RBI	PO	A	E	DP	TC/G	FA	Pitcher	G	IP	W	L	SV	ERA
1B	E. Torgeson	379	.274	11	64	916	65	13	83	9.5	.987	R. Roberts	44	**347**	**23**	16	2	2.75
2B	G. Hamner	609	.276	21	92	194	290	15	65	5.4	.970	C. Simmons	32	238	16	13	0	3.21
SS	T. Kazanski	360	.217	2	27	185	239	23	53	4.7	.949	K. Drews	47	185	9	10	3	4.52
3B	W. Jones	481	.225	19	70	**176**	253	11	36	3.0	**.975**	J. Konstanty	48	171	14	10	5	4.43
RF	J. Wyrostek	409	.271	6	47	192	11	8	2	1.9	.962	B. Miller	35	157	8	9	2	4.00
CF	R. Ashburn	622	.330	2	57	**496**	18	5	4	3.3	.990	S. Ridzik	42	124	9	6	0	3.77
LF	D. Ennis	578	.285	29	125	284	14	6	4	2.0	.980							
C	S. Burgess	312	.292	4	36	395	23	3	8	4.4	**.993**							
1B	E. Waitkus	247	.291	1	16	480	37	6	65	8.9	.989							
2B	C. Ryan	247	.296	5	26	134	166	13	39	4.8	.958							
C	S. Lopata	234	.239	8	31	344	27	5	2	4.7	.987							
OF	M. Clark	198	.298	0	19	104	2	1	0	2.1	.991							

St. Louis
W-83 L-71
Eddie Stanky

POS	Player	AB	BA	HR	RBI	PO	A	E	DP	TC/G	FA	Pitcher	G	IP	W	L	SV	ERA
1B	S. Bilko	570	.251	21	84	**1446**	124	15	145	10.3	.991	H. Haddix	36	253	20	9	1	3.06
2B	Schoendienst	564	.342	15	79	**365**	430	14	109	5.8	.983	G. Staley	40	230	18	9	4	3.99
SS	S. Hemus	585	.279	14	61	257	476	**27**	90	5.1	.964	V. Mizell	33	224	13	11	0	3.49
3B	R. Jablonski	604	.268	21	112	94	278	27	27	2.5	.932	J. Presko	34	162	6	13	1	5.01
RF	E. Slaughter	492	.291	6	89	235	2	1	0	1.7	**.996**	S. Miller	40	138	7	8	4	5.56
CF	R. Repulski	567	.275	15	66	361	7	5	1	2.4	.987	A. Brazle	60	92	6	7	18	4.21
LF	S. Musial	593	.337	30	113	294	9	5	1	2.0	.984	H. White	49	85	6	5	7	2.98
C	D. Rice	419	.236	6	37	627	60	8	6	5.1	.988							
OF	P. Lowrey	182	.269	5	27	42	1	0	0	1.1	1.000							

New York
W-70 L-84
Leo Durocher

POS	Player	AB	BA	HR	RBI	PO	A	E	DP	TC/G	FA	Pitcher	G	IP	W	L	SV	ERA
1B	W. Lockman	607	.295	9	61	1042	100	13	96	9.6	.989	R. Gomez	29	204	13	11	0	3.40
2B	D. Williams	340	.297	3	34	191	254	8	54	4.8	.982	J. Hearn	36	197	9	12	0	4.53
SS	A. Dark	647	.300	23	88	219	343	19	79	5.3	.967	L. Jansen	36	185	11	16	1	4.14
3B	H. Thompson	388	.302	24	74	90	194	13	18	2.9	.956	H. Wilhelm	68	145	7	8	15	3.04
RF	D. Mueller	480	.333	6	60	203	7	6	0	1.8	.972	S. Maglie	27	145	8	9	0	4.15
CF	B. Thomson	608	.288	26	106	391	16	7	0	2.7	.983	D. Koslo	37	112	6	12	2	4.76
LF	M. Irvin	444	.329	21	97	244	10	7	4	2.3	.973	A. Corwin	48	107	6	4	2	4.98
C	W. Westrum	290	.224	12	30	441	53	9	9	4.7	.982	Worthington	20	102	4	8	0	3.44
UT	D. Spencer	408	.208	20	56	179	269	32	52		.933							
32	B. Hofman	169	.266	12	34	55	83	7	18		.952							
OF	D. Rhodes	163	.233	11	30	76	6	3	4	1.8	.965							
1B	T. Gilbert	160	.169	3	16	381	26	2	34	9.3	.995							

NATIONAL LEAGUE 1953, *cont.*

	POS	Player	AB	BA	HR	RBI	PO	A	E	DP	TC/G	FA	Pitcher	G	IP	W	L	SV	ERA
Cincinnati	1B	Kluszewski	570	.316	40	108	1285	58	7	**149**	9.2	**.995**	H. Perkowski	33	193	12	11	2	4.52
	2B	R. Bridges	432	.227	1	21	329	320	16	94	**5.8**	.976	B. Podbielan	36	186	6	16	1	4.73
W-68 L-86	SS	R. McMillan	557	.233	5	43	288	**519**	23	**114**	5.4	.972	Raffensberger	26	174	7	14	0	3.93
	3B	B. Adams	607	.275	8	49	159	**324**	25	**39**	3.4	.951	J. Nuxhall	30	142	9	11	2	4.32
Rogers Hornsby	RF	W. Marshall	357	.266	17	62	187	11	1	1	2.1	.995	F. Baczewski	24	138	11	4	1	3.45
W-64 L-82	CF	G. Bell	610	.300	30	105	447	16	**11**	5	3.1	.977	J. Collum	30	125	7	11	3	3.75
	LF	Greengrass	606	.285	20	100	341	11	6	0	2.3	.983	F. Smith	50	84	8	1	2	5.49
Buster Mills	C	A. Seminick	387	.235	19	64	436	44	9	2	4.4	.982	C. King	35	76	3	6	2	5.21
W-4 L-4	OF	B. Borkowski	249	.269	7	29	104	3	2	0	1.6	.982							
	2B	G. Hatton	159	.233	7	22	56	49	1	15	3.0	.991							
	C	H. Landrith	154	.240	3	16	179	13	3	4	4.1	.985							
Chicago	1B	D. Fondy	595	.309	18	78	1274	115	**18**	105	9.4	.987	W. Hacker	39	222	12	**19**	2	4.38
	2B	E. Miksis	577	.251	8	39	210	262	**23**	65	5.4	.954	P. Minner	31	201	12	15	1	4.21
W-65 L-89	SS	R. Smalley	253	.249	6	25	153	191	25	39	4.8	.932	Klippstein	48	168	10	11	6	4.83
	3B	R. Jackson	498	.285	19	66	141	265	22	24	3.2	.949	B. Rush	29	167	9	14	0	4.54
Phil Cavarretta	RF	H. Sauer	395	.263	19	60	221	5	7	1	2.2	.970	T. Lown	49	148	8	7	3	5.16
	CF	F. Baumholtz	520	.306	3	25	290	6	6	0	2.3	.980	H. Pollet	25	111	5	6	1	4.12
	LF	R. Kiner	414	.283	28	87	211	6	8	2	1.9	.964	B. Church	27	104	4	5	1	5.00
	C	McCullough	229	.258	6	23	273	31	4	7	4.2	.987	D. Leonard	45	63	2	3	8	4.60
	23	B. Serena	275	.251	10	52	135	160	7	31		.977							
	C	J. Garagiola	228	.272	1	21	296	34	4	2	4.9	.988							
	OF	H. Jeffcoat	183	.235	4	22	175	6	5	2	1.9	.973							
Pittsburgh	1B	P. Ward	281	.210	8	27	693	64	7	65	9.8	.991	M. Dickson	45	201	10	**19**	4	4.53
	2B	J. O'Brien	279	.247	2	22	172	210	7	48	5.1	.982	P. LaPalme	35	176	8	16	2	4.59
W-50 L-104	SS	E. O'Brien	261	.238	0	14	122	207	23	39	4.3	.935	J. Lindell	27	176	5	16	0	4.71
	3B	D. O'Connell	588	.294	7	55	119	221	15	16	3.4	.958	B. Friend	32	171	8	11	0	4.90
Fred Haney	RF	C. Abrams	448	.286	15	43	205	13	6	3	2.0	.973	B. Hall	37	152	3	12	1	5.39
	CF	C. Bernier	310	.213	3	31	220	8	7	1	2.7	.970	R. Face	41	119	6	8	0	6.58
	LF	F. Thomas	455	.255	30	102	306	17	8	1	2.8	.976	J. Hetki	54	118	3	6	3	3.95
	C	M. Sandlock	186	.231	0	12	290	49	3	4	5.3	.991							
	1B	P. Smith	389	.283	4	44	622	52	10	53	9.2	.985							
	OF	H. Rice	286	.311	4	42	167	14	5	2	2.7	.973							
	SS	D. Cole	235	.272	0	23	139	192	12	40	4.5	.965							
	23	Pellagrini	174	.253	4	19	75	95	6	13		.966							
	3B	Castiglione	159	.208	4	21	44	88	3	6	3.1	.978							
	OF	R. Kiner	148	.270	7	29	71	5	0	1	1.9	1.000							

BATTING AND BASE RUNNING LEADERS

Batting Average
C. Furillo, BKN	.344
Schoendienst, STL	.342
S. Musial, STL	.337
D. Snider, BKN	.336
D. Mueller, NY	.333

Slugging Average
D. Snider, BKN	.627
E. Mathews, MIL	.627
Campanella, BKN	.611
S. Musial, STL	.609
C. Furillo, BKN	.580

Home Runs
E. Mathews, MIL	47
D. Snider, BKN	42
Campanella, BKN	41
Kluszewski, CIN	40
R. Kiner, CHI, PIT	35

Total Bases
D. Snider, BKN	370
E. Mathews, MIL	363
S. Musial, STL	361
Kluszewski, CIN	325
G. Bell, CIN	320

Runs Batted In
Campanella, BKN	142
E. Mathews, MIL	135
D. Snider, BKN	126
D. Ennis, PHI	125
G. Hodges, BKN	122

Stolen Bases
B. Bruton, MIL	26
P. Reese, BKN	22
J. Gilliam, BKN	21
J. Robinson, BKN	17
D. Snider, BKN	16

Hits
R. Ashburn, PHI	205
S. Musial, STL	200
D. Snider, BKN	198
A. Dark, NY	194

Base on Balls
S. Musial, STL	105
R. Kiner, CHI, PIT	100
J. Gilliam, BKN	100
E. Mathews, MIL	99

Home Run Percentage
E. Mathews, MIL	8.1
Campanella, BKN	7.9
D. Snider, BKN	7.1
Kluszewski, CIN	7.0

Runs Scored
D. Snider, BKN	132
S. Musial, STL	127
A. Dark, NY	126
J. Gilliam, BKN	125

Doubles
S. Musial, STL	53
A. Dark, NY	41
C. Furillo, BKN	38
D. Snider, BKN	38

Triples
J. Gilliam, BKN	17
B. Bruton, MIL	14
S. Hemus, STL	11
D. Fondy, CHI	11

PITCHING LEADERS

Winning Percentage
C. Erskine, BKN	.769
W. Spahn, MIL	.767
L. Burdette, MIL	.750
R. Meyer, BKN	.750
H. Haddix, STL	.690

Earned Run Average
W. Spahn, MIL	2.10
R. Roberts, PHI	2.75
B. Buhl, MIL	2.97
H. Haddix, STL	3.06
J. Antonelli, MIL	3.18

Wins
W. Spahn, MIL	23
R. Roberts, PHI	23
C. Erskine, BKN	20
H. Haddix, STL	20
G. Staley, STL	18

Saves
A. Brazle, STL	18
H. Wilhelm, NY	15
J. Hughes, BKN	9
L. Burdette, MIL	8
D. Leonard, CHI	8

Strikeouts
R. Roberts, PHI	198
C. Erskine, BKN	187
V. Mizell, STL	173
H. Haddix, STL	163
W. Spahn, MIL	148

Complete Games
R. Roberts, PHI	33
W. Spahn, MIL	24
C. Simmons, PHI	19
H. Haddix, STL	19
C. Erskine, BKN	16

Fewest Hits/9 Innings
W. Spahn, MIL	7.15
R. Gomez, NY	7.32
V. Mizell, STL	7.74
B. Buhl, MIL	7.76

Shutouts
H. Haddix, STL	6
W. Spahn, MIL	5
R. Roberts, PHI	5
C. Simmons, PHI	4

Fewest Walks/9 Innings
R. Roberts, PHI	1.58
Raffensberger, CIN	1.71
P. Minner, CHI	1.79
G. Staley, STL	2.11

Most Strikeouts/9 Inn.
V. Mizell, STL	6.94
C. Erskine, BKN	6.82
J. Antonelli, MIL	6.72
Klippstein, CHI	6.07

Innings
R. Roberts, PHI	347
W. Spahn, MIL	266
H. Haddix, STL	253
C. Erskine, BKN	247

Games Pitched
H. Wilhelm, NY	68
A. Brazle, STL	60
J. Hetki, PIT	54
F. Smith, CIN	50

NATIONAL LEAGUE 1953, *cont.*

	W	L	PCT	GB	R	OR	Batting					SB	Fielding			Pitching					ERA
							2B	3B	HR	BA	SA		E	DP	FA	CG	BB	SO	ShO	SV	
Brooklyn	105	49	.682		**955**	689	274	59	**208**	**.285**	**.474**	**90**	**118**	161	**.980**	51	509	**819**	11	29	4.10
Milwaukee	92	62	.597	13	738	**589**	227	52	156	.266	.415	46	143	169	.976	72	539	738	**14**	15	**3.30**
Philadelphia	83	71	.539	22	716	666	228	**62**	115	.265	.396	42	147	161	.975	**76**	**410**	637	13	15	3.80
St. Louis	83	71	.539	22	768	713	**281**	56	140	.273	.424	18	138	161	.977	51	533	732	11	**36**	4.23
New York	70	84	.455	35	768	747	195	45	176	.271	.422	31	151	151	.975	46	610	647	10	20	4.25
Cincinnati	68	86	.442	37	714	788	190	34	166	.261	.403	25	129	**176**	.978	47	488	506	7	15	4.64
Chicago	65	89	.422	40	633	835	204	57	137	.260	.399	49	193	141	.967	38	554	623	3	22	4.79
Pittsburgh	50	104	.325	55	622	887	178	49	99	.247	.356	41	163	139	.973	49	577	607	4	10	5.22
					5914	5914	1777	414	1197	.266	.411	342	1182	1259	.975	430	4220	5309	73	162	4.29

AMERICAN LEAGUE 1953

	POS	Player	AB	BA	HR	RBI	PO	A	E	DP	TC/G	FA	Pitcher	G	IP	W	L	SV	ERA
New York W-99 L-52 Casey Stengel	1B	J. Collins	387	.269	17	44	826	65	10	100	8.0	.989	W. Ford	32	207	18	6	0	3.00
	2B	B. Martin	587	.257	15	75	376	390	12	121	5.3	.985	J. Sain	40	189	14	7	9	3.00
	SS	P. Rizzuto	413	.271	2	54	214	409	24	100	4.9	.963	V. Raschi	28	181	13	6	1	3.33
	3B	McDougald	541	.285	10	83	147	299	**22**	36	3.4	.953	E. Lopat	25	178	16	4	0	**2.42**
	RF	H. Bauer	437	.304	10	57	230	13	2	3	1.9	.992	A. Reynolds	41	145	13	7	13	3.41
	CF	M. Mantle	461	.295	21	92	322	10	6	2	2.8	.982	J. McDonald	27	130	9	7	0	3.82
	LF	G. Woodling	395	.306	10	58	240	6	1	2	2.1	**.996**	B. Kuzava	33	92	6	5	4	3.31
	C	Y. Berra	503	.296	27	108	566	64	9	9	4.8	.986	T. Gorman	40	77	4	5	6	3.39
	OF	I. Noren	345	.267	6	46	208	11	2	1	2.3	.991							
	1B	D. Bollweg	155	.297	6	24	323	15	6	37	8.0	.983							
	1B	J. Mize	104	.250	4	27	113	7	0	19	8.0	1.000							
Cleveland W-92 L-62 Al Lopez	1B	B. Glynn	411	.243	3	30	1036	81	8	133	8.3	.993	B. Lemon	41	**287**	21	15	1	3.36
	2B	B. Avila	559	.286	8	55	346	**445**	11	114	5.7	.986	M. Garcia	38	272	18	9	0	3.25
	SS	Strickland	419	.284	5	47	238	400	17	**103**	5.4	.974	E. Wynn	36	252	17	12	0	3.93
	3B	A. Rosen	599	.336	**43**	**145**	174	338	19	38	3.4	.964	B. Feller	25	176	10	7	0	3.59
	RF	W. Westlake	218	.330	9	46	128	3	5	2	1.9	.963	D. Hoskins	26	113	9	3	1	3.99
	CF	L. Doby	513	.263	29	102	354	10	6	3	2.5	.984	A. Houtteman	22	109	7	7	3	3.80
	LF	D. Mitchell	500	.300	13	60	224	2	7	1	1.9	.970	B. Hooper	43	69	5	4	7	4.02
	C	J. Hegan	299	.217	9	37	399	42	**11**	3	4.3	.976							
	OF	H. Simpson	242	.227	7	22	118	4	4	0	1.8	.968							
	1B	L. Easter	211	.303	7	31	442	30	9	54	8.6	.981							
	OF	B. Kennedy	161	.236	3	22	91	2	0	0	1.0	1.000							
	SS	R. Boone	112	.241	4	21	64	94	8	24	5.4	.952							
Chicago W-89 L-65 Paul Richards	1B	F. Fain	446	.256	6	52	1108	106	13	98	9.7	.989	B. Pierce	40	271	18	12	3	2.72
	2B	N. Fox	624	.285	3	72	**451**	426	15	101	**5.8**	.983	V. Trucks	24	176	15	6	1	2.86
	SS	Carrasquel	552	.279	2	47	278	462	18	87	5.1	.976	M. Fornieles	39	153	8	7	3	3.59
	3B	B. Elliott	208	.260	4	32	54	104	6	9	2.8	.963	H. Dorish	55	146	10	6	18	3.40
	RF	S. Mele	481	.274	12	82	213	14	1	1	1.7	.996	S. Rogovin	22	131	7	12	1	5.22
	CF	J. Rivera	567	.259	11	78	385	15	10	5	2.6	.976	S. Consuegra	29	124	7	5	2	2.54
	LF	M. Minoso	556	.313	15	104	279	15	10	3	2.1	.967	J. Dobson	23	101	5	5	1	3.67
	C	S. Lollar	334	.287	8	54	470	51	3	2	4.9	**.994**	B. Keegan	22	99	7	5	1	2.74
	10	B. Boyd	165	.297	3	23	301	16	1	25		.997							
	C	R. Wilson	164	.250	0	10	282	24	6	1	5.0	.981							
	OF	T. Wright	132	.250	2	25	44	1	1	0	1.4	.978							
Boston W-84 L-69 Lou Boudreau	1B	D. Gernert	494	.253	21	71	1223	84	**19**	139	**9.8**	.986	M. Parnell	38	241	21	8	0	3.06
	2B	B. Goodman	514	.313	2	41	267	306	15	88	5.3	.974	McDermott	32	206	18	10	0	3.01
	SS	M. Bolling	323	.263	5	28	174	321	23	71	4.8	.956	H. Brown	30	166	11	6	0	4.65
	3B	G. Kell	460	.307	12	73	114	231	10	23	2.9	**.972**	S. Hudson	30	156	6	9	2	3.52
	RF	J. Piersall	585	.272	3	52	352	15	5	**7**	2.5	.987	W. Nixon	23	117	4	8	0	3.93
	CF	T. Umphlett	495	.283	3	59	382	12	7	1	2.9	.983	E. Kinder	**69**	107	10	6	27	1.85
	LF	H. Evers	300	.240	11	31	161	3	2	0	1.8	.988	B. Henry	21	86	5	5	1	3.26
	C	S. White	476	.273	13	64	**588**	68	9	9	5.1	.986							
	OF	G. Stephens	221	.204	3	18	113	2	4	0	1.7	.966							
	32	F. Baker	172	.273	0	24	67	93	4	18		.976							
	UT	T. Lepcio	161	.236	4	11	96	155	6	37		.977							
	C	D. Wilber	112	.241	7	29	90	7	2	0	3.5	.980							
	OF	T. Williams	91	.407	13	34	31	1	1	1	1.3	.970							
Washington W-76 L-76 Bucky Harris	1B	M. Vernon	608	**.337**	15	115	**1376**	94	12	**158**	**9.8**	.992	Porterfield	34	255	**22**	10	0	3.35
	2B	Terwilliger	464	.252	4	46	333	395	13	108	5.6	.982	W. Masterson	29	166	10	12	0	3.63
	SS	P. Runnels	486	.257	2	50	195	324	23	87	4.5	.958	S. Shea	23	165	12	7	0	3.94
	3B	E. Yost	577	.272	9	45	**190**	300	18	31	3.3	.965	C. Stobbs	27	153	11	8	0	3.29
	RF	J. Jensen	552	.266	10	84	274	9	5	0	2.0	.983	C. Marrero	22	146	8	7	2	3.03
	CF	J. Busby	586	.312	6	82	**482**	15	6	4	**3.4**	.988	S. Dixon	43	120	5	8	3	3.75
	LF	C. Vollmer	408	.260	11	74	227	8	5	1	2.3	.979	J. Schmitz	24	108	2	7	4	3.68
	C	Fitz Gerald	288	.250	3	39	319	33	4	3	4.2	.989							
	C	M. Grasso	196	.209	2	22	219	24	4	4	4.2	.984							
	OF	G. Coan	168	.196	2	17	105	2	0	1	2.3	1.000							

AMERICAN LEAGUE 1953, *cont.*

	POS	Player	AB	BA	HR	RBI	PO	A	E	DP	TC/G	FA	Pitcher	G	IP	W	L	SV	ERA
Detroit	1B	W. Dropo	606	.248	13	96	1260	**127**	14	121	9.3	.990	N. Garver	30	198	11	11	1	4.45
	2B	J. Pesky	308	.292	2	24	166	183	3	49	4.8	.991	B. Hoeft	29	198	9	14	2	4.83
W-60 L-94	SS	H. Kuenn	679	.308	2	48	308	441	21	78	5.0	.973	T. Gray	30	176	10	15	0	4.60
	3B	R. Boone	385	.312	22	93	111	211	14	32	3.5	.958	S. Gromek	19	126	6	8	1	4.51
Fred Hutchinson	RF	D. Lund	421	.257	9	47	275	12	6	0	2.4	.980	D. Marlowe	42	120	6	7	0	5.26
	CF	J. Delsing	479	.288	11	62	354	7	3	2	2.7	.992	R. Branca	17	102	4	7	1	4.15
	LF	B. Nieman	508	.281	15	69	271	10	6	1	2.1	.979	R. Herbert	43	88	4	6	6	5.24
	C	M. Batts	374	.278	6	42	463	44	7	7	5.0	.986							
	32	F. Hatfield	311	.254	3	19	120	208	9	34		.973							
	OF	S. Souchock	278	.302	11	46	144	7	6	3	2.0	.962							
	2B	G. Priddy	196	.235	1	24	111	106	5	28	4.9	.977							
	C	J. Bucha	158	.222	1	14	218	22	4	4	4.4	.984							
Philadelphia	1B	E. Robinson	615	.247	22	102	1366	71	17	135	9.4	.988	H. Byrd	40	237	11	**20**	0	5.51
	2B	C. Michaels	411	.251	12	42	304	302	**19**	81	5.7	.970	M. Fricano	39	211	9	12	0	3.88
W-59 L-95	SS	DeMaestri	420	.255	6	35	191	297	18	53	4.7	.964	A. Kellner	25	202	11	12	0	3.93
	3B	L. Babe	343	.224	0	20	114	192	16	24	3.5	.950	C. Bishop	39	161	3	14	2	5.66
Jimmy Dykes	RF	D. Philley	620	.303	9	59	296	18	6	0	2.0	.981	M. Martin	58	156	10	12	7	4.43
	CF	E. McGhee	358	.263	1	29	319	4	6	0	3.3	.982	B. Shantz	16	106	5	9	0	4.09
	LF	G. Zernial	556	.284	42	108	300	17	9	2	2.3	.972	C. Scheib	28	96	3	7	2	4.88
	C	J. Astroth	260	.296	3	24	341	47	5	**13**	5.0	.987							
	32	P. Suder	454	.286	4	35	178	279	10	42		.979							
	C	R. Murray	268	.284	6	41	330	45	4	8	4.9	.989							
	SS	E. Joost	177	.249	6	15	102	147	11	33	5.1	.958							
	OF	C. Mauro	165	.267	0	17	119	5	4	0	2.6	.969							
St. Louis	1B	D. Kryhoski	338	.278	16	50	685	66	6	7	8.6	.992	D. Larsen	38	193	7	12	2	4.16
	2B	B. Young	537	.255	4	25	397	363	18	120	5.3	.977	D. Pillette	31	167	7	13	0	4.48
W-54 L-100	SS	B. Hunter	567	.219	1	37	284	**512**	**25**	99	5.4	.970	Littlefield	36	152	7	12	0	5.08
	3B	J. Dyck	334	.213	9	27	62	101	13	12	3.5	.926	S. Paige	57	117	3	9	11	3.53
Marty Marion	RF	V. Wertz	440	.268	19	70	243	15	7	4	2.2	.974	H. Brecheen	26	117	5	13	1	3.07
	CF	J. Groth	557	.253	10	57	425	18	4	5	3.2	.991	M. Stuart	60	114	8	2	7	3.94
	LF	D. Kokos	299	.241	13	38	152	5	6	1	2.0	.963	B. Cain	32	100	4	10	1	6.23
	C	C. Courtney	355	.251	4	19	436	47	10	7	4.8	.980	V. Trucks	16	88	5	4	2	3.07
	OF	D. Lenhardt	303	.317	10	35	148	8	5	1	2.1	.969	B. Holloman	22	65	3	7	0	5.23
	1B	R. Sievers	285	.270	8	35	604	31	5	64	8.4	.992							
	C	L. Moss	239	.276	2	28	296	21	7	4	4.6	.978							
	3B	V. Stephens	165	.321	4	17	54	91	7	9	3.3	.954							
	3B	B. Elliott	160	.250	5	29	51	93	7	12	3.4	.954							

BATTING AND BASE RUNNING LEADERS

Batting Average
M. Vernon, WAS	.337
A. Rosen, CLE	.336
B. Goodman, BOS	.313
M. Minoso, CHI	.313
J. Busby, WAS	.312

Slugging Average
A. Rosen, CLE	.613
G. Zernial, PHI	.559
Y. Berra, NY	.523
R. Boone, CLE, DET	.519
M. Vernon, WAS	.518

Home Runs
A. Rosen, CLE	43
G. Zernial, PHI	42
L. Doby, CLE	29
Y. Berra, NY	27
R. Boone, CLE, DET	26

Total Bases
A. Rosen, CLE	367
M. Vernon, WAS	315
G. Zernial, PHI	311
Y. Berra, NY	263
D. Philley, PHI	263

Runs Batted In
A. Rosen, CLE	145
M. Vernon, WAS	115
R. Boone, CLE, DET	114
Y. Berra, NY	108
G. Zernial, PHI	108

Stolen Bases
M. Minoso, CHI	25
J. Rivera, CHI	22
J. Jensen, WAS	18
J. Busby, WAS	13
D. Philley, PHI	13

Hits
H. Kuenn, DET	209
M. Vernon, WAS	205
A. Rosen, CLE	201
D. Philley, PHI	188

Base on Balls
E. Yost, WAS	123
F. Fain, CHI	108
L. Doby, CLE	96
D. Gernert, BOS	88

Home Run Percentage
G. Zernial, PHI	7.6
A. Rosen, CLE	7.2
L. Doby, CLE	5.7
Y. Berra, NY	5.4

Runs Scored
A. Rosen, CLE	115
E. Yost, WAS	107
M. Mantle, NY	105
M. Minoso, CHI	104

Doubles
M. Vernon, WAS	43
G. Kell, BOS	41
S. White, BOS	34
B. Goodman, BOS	33

Triples
J. Rivera, CHI	16
M. Vernon, WAS	11
J. Piersall, BOS	9
D. Philley, PHI	9

PITCHING LEADERS

Winning Percentage
E. Lopat, NY	.800
W. Ford, NY	.750
M. Parnell, BOS	.724
Porterfield, WAS	.688
V. Trucks, CHI, STL	.667
M. Garcia, CLE	.667

Saves
E. Kinder, BOS	27
H. Dorish, CHI	18
A. Reynolds, NY	13
S. Paige, STL	11
J. Sain, NY	9

Fewest Hits/9 Innings
B. Pierce, CHI	7.16
McDermott, BOS	7.37
V. Raschi, NY	7.46
W. Masterson, WAS	7.85

Most Strikeouts/9 Inn.
B. Pierce, CHI	6.17
T. Gray, DET	5.88
W. Masterson, WAS	5.14
M. Parnell, BOS	5.08

Earned Run Average
E. Lopat, NY	2.42
B. Pierce, CHI	2.72
V. Trucks, CHI, STL	2.93
W. Ford, NY	3.00
J. Sain, NY	3.00

Strikeouts
B. Pierce, CHI	186
V. Trucks, CHI, STL	149
E. Wynn, CLE	138
M. Parnell, BOS	136
M. Garcia, CLE	134

Shutouts
Porterfield, WAS	9
B. Pierce, CHI	7
V. Trucks, CHI, STL	5
M. Parnell, BOS	5

Innings
B. Lemon, CLE	287
M. Garcia, CLE	272
B. Pierce, CHI	271
V. Trucks, CHI, STL	264

Wins
Porterfield, WAS	22
M. Parnell, BOS	21
B. Lemon, CLE	21
V. Trucks, CHI, STL	20

Complete Games
Porterfield, WAS	24
B. Lemon, CLE	23
M. Garcia, CLE	21
B. Pierce, CHI	19
V. Trucks, CHI, STL	17

Fewest Walks/9 Innings
E. Lopat, NY	1.61
J. Sain, NY	2.14
A. Kellner, PHI	2.28
Porterfield, WAS	2.58

Games Pitched
E. Kinder, BOS	69
M. Stuart, STL	60
M. Martin, PHI	58
S. Paige, STL	57

AMERICAN LEAGUE 1953, *cont.*

	W	L	PCT	GB	R	OR	2B	3B	HR	BA	SA	SB	E	DP	FA	CG	BB	SO	ShO	SV	ERA
							Batting						Fielding			Pitching					
New York	99	52	.656		801	547	226	52	139	.273	.417	34	126	182	.979	50	500	604	16	39	3.20
Cleveland	92	62	.597	8.5	770	627	201	29	160	.270	.410	33	127	197	.979	81	519	586	11	15	3.64
Chicago	89	65	.578	11.5	716	592	226	53	74	.258	.364	73	125	144	.980	57	583	714	16	33	3.41
Boston	84	69	.549	16	656	632	255	37	101	.264	.384	33	148	173	.975	41	584	642	14	37	3.59
Washington	76	76	.500	23.5	687	614	230	53	69	.263	.368	65	120	173	.979	76	478	515	16	10	3.66
Detroit	60	94	.390	40.5	695	923	259	44	108	.266	.387	30	135	149	.978	50	585	645	2	16	5.25
Philadelphia	59	95	.383	41.5	632	799	205	38	116	.256	.372	41	137	161	.977	51	594	566	6	11	4.67
St. Louis	54	100	.351	46.5	555	778	214	25	112	.249	.363	17	152	165	.974	28	626	639	7	24	4.48
					5512	5512	1816	331	879	.262	.383	326	1070	1344	.978	434	4469	4911	88	185	4.00

NATIONAL LEAGUE 1954

New York
W-97 L-57
Leo Durocher

POS	Player	AB	BA	HR	RBI	PO	A	E	DP	TC/G	FA	Pitcher	G	IP	W	L	SV	ERA
1B	W. Lockman	570	.251	16	60	1261	88	18	122	9.4	.987	J. Antonelli	39	259	21	7	2	2.30
2B	D. Williams	544	.222	9	46	353	396	14	112	5.4	.982	R. Gomez	37	222	17	9	0	2.88
SS	A. Dark	644	.293	20	70	289	487	36	105	5.3	.956	S. Maglie	34	218	14	6	2	3.26
3B	H. Thompson	448	.263	26	86	125	267	23	27	3.2	.945	J. Hearn	29	130	8	8	1	4.15
RF	D. Mueller	619	.342	4	71	263	14	6	5	1.8	.979	D. Liddle	28	127	9	4	0	3.06
CF	W. Mays	565	.345	41	110	448	13	7	9	3.1	.985	M. Grissom	56	122	10	7	19	2.35
LF	M. Irvin	432	.262	19	64	274	7	7	0	2.3	.976	H. Wilhelm	57	111	12	4	7	2.10
C	W. Westrum	246	.187	8	27	419	45	7	8	4.8	.985							
C	R. Katt	200	.255	9	33	265	23	8	4	3.6	.973							
OF	D. Rhodes	164	.341	15	50	62	1	1	0	1.7	.984							
UT	B. Hofman	125	.224	8	30	192	32	4	25		.982							

Brooklyn
W-92 L-62
Walter Alston

POS	Player	AB	BA	HR	RBI	PO	A	E	DP	TC/G	FA	Pitcher	G	IP	W	L	SV	ERA
1B	G. Hodges	579	.304	42	130	1381	132	7	129	9.9	.995	C. Erskine	38	260	18	15	1	4.15
2B	J. Gilliam	607	.282	13	52	340	388	17	99	5.2	.977	R. Meyer	36	180	11	6	0	3.99
SS	P. Reese	554	.309	10	69	270	426	25	74	5.2	.965	J. Podres	29	152	11	7	0	4.27
3B	D. Hoak	261	.245	7	26	71	139	11	12	2.9	.950	B. Loes	28	148	13	5	0	4.14
RF	C. Furillo	547	.294	19	96	306	10	9	3	2.2	.972	D. Newcombe	29	144	9	8	0	4.55
CF	D. Snider	584	.341	40	130	360	8	7	1	2.5	.981	C. Labine	47	108	7	6	5	4.15
LF	S. Amoros	263	.274	9	34	149	6	2	1	2.2	.987	J. Hughes	60	87	8	4	24	3.22
C	Campanella	397	.207	19	51	600	58	7	7	6.0	.989							
O3	J. Robinson	386	.311	15	59	153	99	7	6		.973							
3B	B. Cox	226	.235	2	17	57	90	6	7	2.6	.961							
C	R. Walker	155	.181	5	23	259	19	1	4	5.9	.996							

Milwaukee
W-89 L-65
Charlie Grimm

POS	Player	AB	BA	HR	RBI	PO	A	E	DP	TC/G	FA	Pitcher	G	IP	W	L	SV	ERA
1B	J. Adcock	500	.308	23	87	1229	67	6	125	9.8	.995	W. Spahn	39	283	21	12	3	3.14
2B	D. O'Connell	541	.279	2	37	244	314	12	83	5.5	.979	L. Burdette	38	238	15	14	0	2.76
SS	J. Logan	560	.275	8	66	324	489	26	104	5.4	.969	G. Conley	28	194	14	9	0	2.96
3B	E. Mathews	476	.290	40	103	112	254	13	28	3.0	.966	J. Wilson	27	128	8	2	0	3.52
RF	A. Pafko	510	.286	14	69	245	9	8	3	1.9	.969	N. Nichols	35	122	9	11	1	4.41
CF	B. Bruton	567	.284	4	30	350	14	7	3	2.6	.981	D. Jolly	47	111	11	6	10	2.43
LF	H. Aaron	468	.280	13	69	223	5	7	0	2.0	.970	B. Buhl	31	110	2	7	3	4.00
C	D. Crandall	463	.242	21	64	665	79	8	11	5.5	.989							
2B	J. Dittmer	192	.245	6	20	119	141	6	31	4.8	.977							
OF	J. Pendleton	173	.220	1	16	90	5	5	0	2.0	.950							

Philadelphia
W-75 L-79
Steve O'Neill
W-40 L-37
Terry Moore
W-35 L-42

POS	Player	AB	BA	HR	RBI	PO	A	E	DP	TC/G	FA	Pitcher	G	IP	W	L	SV	ERA
1B	E. Torgeson	490	.271	5	54	1146	74	12	103	9.3	.990	R. Roberts	45	337	23	15	4	2.97
2B	G. Hamner	596	.299	13	89	361	412	17	97	5.2	.978	C. Simmons	34	253	14	15	1	2.81
SS	B. Morgan	455	.262	14	50	237	361	29	71	4.9	.954	M. Dickson	40	226	10	20	3	3.78
3B	W. Jones	535	.271	12	56	184	277	15	23	3.4	.968	B. Miller	30	150	7	9	0	4.56
RF	M. Clark	233	.240	1	24	114	9	5	2	2.0	.961	H. Wehmeier	25	147	10	8	0	3.85
CF	R. Ashburn	559	.313	1	41	483	12	8	2	3.3	.984							
LF	D. Ennis	556	.261	25	119	303	9	14	1	2.3	.957							
C	S. Burgess	345	.368	4	46	356	30	10	4	4.4	.975							
OF	D. Schell	272	.283	7	33	143	4	4	0	2.2	.974							
OF	J. Wyrostek	259	.239	3	28	90	5	1	1	1.7	.990							
C	S. Lopata	259	.290	14	42	336	26	4	1	4.9	.989							

Cincinnati
W-74 L-80
Birdie Tebbetts

POS	Player	AB	BA	HR	RBI	PO	A	E	DP	TC/G	FA	Pitcher	G	IP	W	L	SV	ERA
1B	Kluszewski	573	.326	49	141	1237	101	5	166	9.0	.996	A. Fowler	40	228	12	10	0	3.83
2B	J. Temple	505	.307	0	44	428	374	22	117	5.7	.973	C. Valentine	36	194	12	11	1	4.45
SS	R. McMillan	588	.250	4	42	341	464	34	129	5.4	.959	J. Nuxhall	35	167	12	5	0	3.89
3B	B. Adams	390	.269	3	23	127	186	16	24	3.5	.951	B. Podbielan	27	131	7	10	0	5.36
RF	W. Post	451	.255	18	83	231	13	11	2	2.2	.957	F. Baczewski	29	130	6	6	0	5.26
CF	G. Bell	619	.299	17	101	406	12	6	2	2.8	.986	H. Perkowski	28	96	2	8	0	6.11
LF	Greengrass	542	.280	27	95	298	9	10	0	2.3	.968	H. Judson	37	93	5	7	3	3.95
C	A. Seminick	247	.235	7	30	327	44	4	11	4.6	.989	F. Smith	50	81	5	8	20	2.67
3B	C. Harmon	286	.238	2	25	70	129	8	19	3.1	.961	J. Collum	36	79	7	3	0	3.74
C	E. Bailey	183	.197	9	20	194	20	6	2	3.6	.973							
OF	B. Borkowski	162	.265	1	19	69	3	0	0	2.0	1.000							

NATIONAL LEAGUE 1954, cont.

	POS	Player	AB	BA	HR	RBI	PO	A	E	DP	TC/G	FA	Pitcher	G	IP	W	L	SV	ERA
St. Louis	1B	Cunningham	310	.284	11	50	814	68	10	96	10.5	.989	H. Haddix	43	260	18	13	4	3.57
	2B	Schoendienst	610	.315	5	79	394	477	18	137	6.2	.980	V. Raschi	30	179	8	9	0	4.73
W-72 L-82	SS	A. Grammas	401	.264	2	29	252	432	24	100	5.0	.966	B. Lawrence	35	159	15	6	.1	3.74
	3B	R. Jablonski	611	.296	12	104	122	298	34	25	3.0	.925	G. Staley	48	156	7	13	2	5.26
Eddie Stanky	RF	S. Musial	591	.330	35	126	271	13	3	4	1.9	.990	T. Poholsky	25	106	5	7	0	3.06
	CF	W. Moon	635	.304	12	76	387	11	9	2	2.8	.978	A. Brazle	58	84	5	4	8	4.16
	LF	R. Repulski	619	.283	19	79	302	4	8	0	2.1	.975	J. Presko	37	72	4	9	0	6.91
	C	B. Sarni	380	.300	9	70	486	41	2	12	4.5	.996							
	1B	T. Alston	244	.246	4	34	552	72	7	57	9.7	.989							
	UT	S. Hemus	214	.304	2	27	85	151	10	29		.959							
Chicago	1B	D. Fondy	568	.285	9	49	1228	119	9	129	9.8	.993	B. Rush	33	236	13	15	0	3.77
	2B	G. Baker	541	.275	13	61	355	385	25	102	5.7	.967	P. Minner	32	218	11	11	1	3.96
W-64 L-90	SS	E. Banks	593	.275	19	79	312	475	34	105	5.3	.959	W. Hacker	39	159	6	13	2	4.25
	3B	R. Jackson	484	.273	19	67	118	266	18	21	3.2	.955	Klippstein	36	148	4	11	1	5.29
Stan Hack	RF	H. Sauer	520	.288	41	103	282	8	11	2	2.1	.963	H. Pollet	20	128	8	10	3	3.58
	CF	D. Talbot	403	.241	1	19	245	10	4	1	2.4	.985	J. Davis	46	128	11	7	4	3.52
	LF	R. Kiner	557	.285	22	73	298	6	9	1	2.1	.971	H. Jeffcoat	43	104	5	6	7	5.19
	C	J. Garagiola	153	.281	5	21	191	23	4	0	4.0	.982	D. Cole	18	84	3	8	0	5.36
	OF	F. Baumholtz	303	.297	4	28	168	2	2	0	2.4	.988							
	C	W. Cooper	158	.310	7	32	190	31	5	4	4.7	.978							
Pittsburgh	1B	B. Skinner	470	.249	8	46	1026	84	16	87	9.5	.986	M. Surkont	33	208	9	18	0	4.41
	2B	C. Roberts	496	.232	1	36	357	394	24	82	5.9	.969	B. Friend	35	170	7	12	2	5.07
W-53 L-101	SS	G. Allie	418	.199	3	30	192	260	23	59	5.0	.952	V. Law	39	162	9	13	3	5.51
	3B	D. Cole	486	.270	1	40	48	112	10	7	3.1	.941	Littlefield	23	155	10	11	0	3.60
Fred Haney	RF	S. Gordon	363	.306	12	49	121	9	3	1	1.8	.977	B. Purkey	36	131	3	8	0	5.07
	CF	F. Thomas	577	.298	23	94	418	14	5	2	2.9	.989	J. Thies	33	130	3	9	0	3.87
	LF	J. Lynch	284	.239	8	36	127	10	5	2	1.7	.965	P. LaPalme	33	121	4	10	0	5.52
	C	T. Atwell	287	.289	3	26	360	39	4	4	4.6	.990	G. O'Donnell	21	87	3	9	1	4.53
	UT	P. Ward	360	.269	1	48	419	69	15	34		.970	J. Hetki	58	83	4	4	9	4.99
	OF	D. Hall	310	.239	2	27	235	5	11	1	2.5	.956							
	C	J. Shepard	227	.304	3	22	257	46	7	4	4.6	.977							

BATTING AND BASE RUNNING LEADERS

Batting Average
W. Mays, NY	.345
D. Mueller, NY	.342
D. Snider, BKN	.341
S. Musial, STL	.330
Kluszewski, CIN	.326

Slugging Average
W. Mays, NY	.667
D. Snider, BKN	.647
Kluszewski, CIN	.642
S. Musial, STL	.607
E. Mathews, MIL	.603

Home Runs
Kluszewski, CIN	49
G. Hodges, BKN	42
H. Sauer, CHI	41
W. Mays, NY	41
E. Mathews, MIL	40
D. Snider, BKN	40

Total Bases
D. Snider, BKN	378
W. Mays, NY	377
Kluszewski, CIN	368
S. Musial, STL	359
G. Hodges, BKN	335

Runs Batted In
Kluszewski, CIN	141
G. Hodges, BKN	130
D. Snider, BKN	130
S. Musial, STL	126
D. Ennis, PHI	119

Stolen Bases
B. Bruton, MIL	34
J. Temple, CIN	21
D. Fondy, CHI	20
W. Moon, STL	18
R. Ashburn, PHI	11

Hits
D. Mueller, NY	212
D. Snider, BKN	199
W. Mays, NY	195
S. Musial, STL	195

Base on Balls
R. Ashburn, PHI	125
E. Mathews, MIL	113
S. Musial, STL	103
H. Thompson, NY	90

Home Run Percentage
Kluszewski, CIN	8.6
E. Mathews, MIL	8.4
H. Sauer, CHI	7.9
W. Mays, NY	7.3

Runs Scored
D. Snider, BKN	120
S. Musial, STL	120
W. Mays, NY	119
R. Ashburn, PHI	111

Doubles
S. Musial, STL	41
D. Snider, BKN	39
G. Hamner, PHI	39
R. Repulski, STL	39

Triples
W. Mays, NY	13
G. Hamner, PHI	11
D. Snider, BKN	10
B. Skinner, PIT	9

PITCHING LEADERS

Winning Percentage
J. Antonelli, NY	.750
B. Lawrence, STL	.714
R. Gomez, NY	.654
W. Spahn, MIL	.636
R. Roberts, PHI	.605

Earned Run Average
J. Antonelli, NY	2.30
L. Burdette, MIL	2.76
C. Simmons, PHI	2.81
R. Gomez, NY	2.88
G. Conley, MIL	2.96

Wins
R. Roberts, PHI	23
J. Antonelli, NY	21
W. Spahn, MIL	21
H. Haddix, STL	18
C. Erskine, BKN	18

Saves
J. Hughes, BKN	24
F. Smith, CIN	20
M. Grissom, NY	19
D. Jolly, MIL	10
J. Hetki, PIT	9

Strikeouts
R. Roberts, PHI	185
H. Haddix, STL	184
C. Erskine, BKN	166
J. Antonelli, NY	152
W. Spahn, MIL	136

Complete Games
R. Roberts, PHI	29
W. Spahn, MIL	23
C. Simmons, PHI	21
J. Antonelli, NY	18
L. Burdette, MIL	13
H. Haddix, STL	13

Fewest Hits/9 Innings
J. Antonelli, NY	7.27
R. Roberts, PHI	7.73
G. Conley, MIL	7.92
B. Lawrence, STL	8.00

Shutouts
J. Antonelli, NY	6
J. Wilson, MIL	4
M. Dickson, PHI	4
L. Burdette, MIL	4

Fewest Walks/9 Innings
R. Roberts, PHI	1.50
P. Minner, CHI	2.06
W. Hacker, CHI	2.10
L. Burdette, MIL	2.34

Most Strikeouts/9 Inn.
H. Haddix, STL	6.38
C. Erskine, BKN	5.74
Littlefield, PIT	5.34
J. Antonelli, NY	5.29

Innings
R. Roberts, PHI	337
W. Spahn, MIL	283
C. Erskine, BKN	260
H. Haddix, STL	260

Games Pitched
J. Hughes, BKN	60
A. Brazle, STL	58
J. Hetki, PIT	58
H. Wilhelm, NY	57

NATIONAL LEAGUE 1954, *cont.*

	W	L	PCT	GB	R	OR	Batting 2B	3B	HR	BA	SA	SB	Fielding E	DP	FA	Pitching CG	BB	SO	ShO	SV	ERA
New York	97	57	.630		732	**550**	194	42	**186**	.264	.424	30	154	172	.975	45	613	692	**19**	33	**3.09**
Brooklyn	92	62	.597	5	778	740	246	56	**186**	.270	**.444**	46	129	138	.978	39	533	**762**	8	**36**	4.31
Milwaukee	89	65	.578	8	670	556	217	41	139	.265	.401	54	**116**	171	**.981**	63	553	698	13	21	3.19
Philadelphia	75	79	.487	22	659	614	243	**58**	102	.267	.395	30	145	133	.975	**78**	**450**	570	14	12	3.59
Cincinnati	74	80	.481	23	729	763	221	46	147	.262	.406	47	137	**194**	.977	34	547	537	8	27	4.50
St. Louis	72	82	.468	25	**799**	790	**285**	**58**	119	**.281**	.421	**63**	146	178	.976	40	535	680	11	18	4.50
Chicago	64	90	.416	33	700	766	229	45	159	.263	.412	46	154	164	.974	41	619	622	6	19	4.51
Pittsburgh	53	101	.344	44	557	845	181	57	76	.248	.350	21	173	136	.971	37	564	525	4	15	4.92
					5624	5624	1816	403	1114	.265	.407	337	1154	1286	.976	377	4414	5086	83	181	4.07

AMERICAN LEAGUE 1954

	POS	Player	AB	BA	HR	RBI	PO	A	E	DP	TC/G	FA	Pitcher	G	IP	W	L	SV	ERA
Cleveland W-111 L-43 Al Lopez	1B	B. Glynn	171	.251	5	18	424	35	6	38	4.8	.987	E. Wynn	40	**271**	**23**	11	2	2.73
	2B	B. Avila	555	**.341**	15	67	356	**406**	**19**	100	**5.5**	.976	B. Lemon	36	258	**23**	7	0	2.72
	SS	Strickland	361	.213	6	37	193	321	21	61	4.8	.961	M. Garcia	45	259	19	8	5	**2.64**
	3B	A. Rosen	466	.300	24	102	110	149	11	14	3.1	.959	A. Houtteman	32	188	15	7	0	3.35
	RF	D. Philley	452	.226	12	60	237	6	4	0	1.9	.984	B. Feller	19	140	13	3	0	3.09
	CF	L. Doby	577	.272	**32**	**126**	411	14	2	6	2.8	.995	D. Mossi	40	93	6	1	7	1.94
	LF	A. Smith	481	.281	11	50	241	8	4	1	2.3	.984	R. Narleski	42	89	3	3	13	2.22
	C	J. Hegan	423	.234	11	40	661	49	4	9	5.2	**.994**	H. Newhouser	26	47	7	2	7	2.51
	1B	V. Wertz	295	.275	14	48	557	52	7	57	7.4	.989							
	OF	W. Westlake	240	.263	11	42	131	1	5	0	2.0	.964							
	3B	R. Regalado	180	.250	2	24	62	84	5	7	3.0	.967							
	SS	S. Dente	169	.266	1	19	66	133	6	33	3.4	.971							
New York W-103 L-51 Casey Stengel	1B	J. Collins	343	.271	12	46	759	60	7	105	7.1	.992	W. Ford	34	211	16	8	1	2.82
	2B	McDougald	394	.259	12	48	224	233	5	84	5.0	.989	B. Grim	37	199	20	6	0	3.26
	SS	P. Rizzuto	307	.195	2	15	184	294	16	84	3.9	.968	E. Lopat	26	170	12	4	0	3.55
	3B	A. Carey	411	.302	8	65	154	283	15	32	**3.8**	.967	A. Reynolds	36	157	13	4	7	3.32
	RF	H. Bauer	377	.294	12	54	179	6	2	1	1.7	.989	T. Morgan	32	143	11	5	1	3.34
	CF	M. Mantle	543	.300	27	102	327	**20**	9	5	2.5	.975	H. Byrd	25	132	9	7	0	2.99
	LF	I. Noren	426	.319	12	66	242	9	5	2	2.2	.980	J. Sain	45	77	6	6	22	3.16
	C	Y. Berra	584	.307	22	125	**717**	63	8	**14**	5.3	.990							
	OF	G. Woodling	304	.250	3	40	164	5	3	1	1.9	.983							
	2B	J. Coleman	300	.217	3	21	183	198	9	62	4.9	.977							
	1B	B. Skowron	215	.340	7	41	395	28	6	48	7.0	.986							
	1B	E. Robinson	142	.261	3	27	227	19	5	21	8.7	.980							
Chicago W-94 L-60 Paul Richards W-91 L-54 Marty Marion W-3 L-6	1B	F. Fain	235	.302	5	51	565	31	8	54	9.4	.987	V. Trucks	40	265	19	12	3	2.79
	2B	N. Fox	631	.319	2	47	**400**	392	9	**103**	5.1	**.989**	B. Keegan	31	210	16	9	3	3.09
	SS	Carrasquel	620	.255	12	62	280	492	20	**102**	5.1	.975	B. Pierce	36	189	9	10	3	3.48
	3B	C. Michaels	282	.262	7	44	95	180	12	10	3.2	.958	J. Harshman	35	177	14	8	1	2.95
	RF	J. Rivera	490	.286	13	61	255	5	**11**	0	1.9	.959	S. Consuegra	39	154	16	3	3	2.69
	CF	J. Groth	422	.275	7	60	314	7	4	3	2.6	.988	D. Johnson	46	144	8	7	7	3.13
	LF	M. Minoso	568	.320	19	116	340	14	8	3	2.5	.978	H. Dorish	37	109	6	4	6	2.72
	C	S. Lollar	316	.244	7	34	395	38	3	8	4.7	.993	M. Martin	35	70	5	4	5	2.06
	13	G. Kell	233	.283	5	48	272	56	4	31		.988							
	1B	Cavarretta	158	.316	3	24	261	17	2	29	6.4	.993							
	C	M. Batts	158	.228	3	19	225	19	2	3	5.9	.992							
Boston W-69 L-85 Lou Boudreau	1B	H. Agganis	434	.251	11	57	1064	**89**	12	101	9.8	.990	F. Sullivan	36	206	15	12	1	3.14
	2B	T. Lepcio	398	.256	8	45	233	230	14	58	6.0	.971	W. Nixon	31	200	11	12	0	4.06
	SS	M. Bolling	370	.249	6	36	186	370	**32**	73	**5.5**	.946	T. Brewer	33	163	10	9	0	4.65
	3B	G. Hatton	302	.281	5	33	77	204	10	20	3.1	.966*	L. Kiely	28	131	5	8	0	3.50
	RF	J. Piersall	474	.285	8	38	249	10	4	2	2.1	.985	H. Brown	40	118	1	8	0	4.12
	CF	J. Jensen	580	.276	25	117	331	12	5	0	2.3	.986	E. Kinder	48	107	8	8	15	3.62
	LF	T. Williams	386	.345	29	89	213	5	4	0	1.9	.982	B. Henry	24	96	3	7	0	4.52
	C	S. White	493	.282	14	75	677	**80**	16	11	**5.8**	.979	M. Parnell	19	92	3	7	0	3.70
	UT	B. Goodman	489	.303	1	36	393	248	14	90		.979	S. Hudson	33	71	3	4	5	4.42
	UT	B. Consolo	242	.227	1	11	113	184	15	30		.952							
	OF	K. Olson	227	.260	1	20	122	10	6	1	1.8	.957							
	1O	S. Mele	132	.318	7	23	188	9	2	18		.990							
Detroit W-68 L-86 Fred Hutchinson	1B	W. Dropo	320	.281	4	44	681	54	3	60	7.8	.996	S. Gromek	36	253	18	16	1	2.74
	2B	F. Bolling	368	.236	6	38	248	232	13	54	4.4	.974	N. Garver	35	246	14	11	1	2.81
	SS	H. Kuenn	**656**	.306	5	48	**294**	**496**	28	85	5.3	.966	G. Zuverink	35	203	9	13	4	3.59
	3B	R. Boone	543	.295	20	85	170	332	19	22	3.5	.964	B. Hoeft	34	175	7	15	1	4.58
	RF	A. Kaline	504	.276	4	43	283	16	9	0	2.0	.971	A. Aber	32	125	5	11	3	3.97
	CF	B. Tuttle	530	.266	7	58	364	18	6	3	2.7	.985	D. Marlowe	38	84	5	4	2	4.18
	LF	J. Delsing	371	.248	6	38	221	5	1	0	2.1	**.996**							
	C	F. House	352	.250	9	38	434	56	4	7	4.6	.992							
	OF	B. Nieman	251	.263	8	35	119	2	2	0	2.0	.984							
	1B	W. Belardi	250	.232	11	24	636	51	8	54	8.8	.988							
	2B	F. Hatfield	218	.294	2	25	114	126	7	29	4.6	.972							
	C	R. Wilson	170	.282	2	22	245	25	1	7	5.1	.996							

AMERICAN LEAGUE 1954, cont.

Washington
W-66 L-88
Bucky Harris

POS	Player	AB	BA	HR	RBI	PO	A	E	DP	TC/G	FA	Pitcher	G	IP	W	L	SV	ERA
1B	M. Vernon	597	.290	20	97	1365	76	11	144	9.8	.992	Porterfield	32	244	13	15	0	3.32
2B	Terwilliger	337	.208	3	24	213	243	13	72	5.2	.972	McDermott	30	196	7	15	1	3.44
SS	P. Runnels	488	.268	3	56	174	313	24	69	4.8	.953	J. Schmitz	29	185	11	8	1	2.91
3B	E. Yost	539	.256	11	47	170	347	17	29	3.4	.968	C. Stobbs	31	182	11	11	0	4.10
RF	T. Umphlett	342	.219	1	33	169	13	2	4	1.8	.989	D. Stone	31	179	12	10	0	3.22
CF	J. Busby	628	.298	7	80	491	6	6	1	3.2	.988	C. Pascual	48	119	4	7	3	4.22
LF	R. Sievers	514	.232	24	102	296	10	9	1	2.4	.971	S. Shea	23	71	2	9	0	6.18
C	Fitz Gerald	360	.289	4	40	396	38	12	5	4.2	.973							
OF	T. Wright	171	.246	1	17	84	0	0	0	2.0	1.000							
2B	J. Pesky	158	.253	0	9	92	91	4	22	5.1	.979							
C	J. Tipton	157	.223	1	10	220	30	2	6	4.8	.992							
SS	J. Snyder	154	.234	0	17	81	145	5	31	4.8	.978							

Baltimore
W-54 L-100
Jimmy Dykes

POS	Player	AB	BA	HR	RBI	PO	A	E	DP	TC/G	FA	Pitcher	G	IP	W	L	SV	ERA
1B	E. Waitkus	311	.283	2	33	618	48	0	72	8.5	1.000	B. Turley	35	247	14	15	0	3.46
2B	B. Young	432	.245	4	24	299	310	15	76	4.9	.976	J. Coleman	33	221	13	17	0	3.50
SS	B. Hunter	411	.243	2	27	249	333	32	76	5.0	.948	D. Larsen	29	202	3	21	0	4.37
3B	V. Stephens	365	.285	8	46	102	186	10	19	3.1	.966	D. Pillette	25	179	10	14	0	3.12
RF	C. Abrams	423	.293	6	25	248	6	6	1	2.3	.977	L. Kretlow	32	167	6	11	0	4.37
CF	C. Diering	418	.258	2	29	330	17	6	6	3.0	.983	B. Chakales	38	89	3	7	3	3.73
LF	J. Fridley	240	.246	4	36	132	1	2	0	2.0	.985							
C	C. Courtney	397	.270	4	37	539	53	6	8	5.4	.990							
3B	B. Kennedy	323	.251	6	45	81	131	14	10	3.2	.938							
1B	D. Kryhoski	300	.260	1	34	591	52	5	52	9.4	.992							
OF	G. Coan	265	.279	2	20	148	1	5	0	2.3	.968							
OF	S. Mele	230	.239	5	32	97	5	4	1	1.7	.962							
SS	Brideweser	204	.265	0	12	67	103	10	22	3.8	.944							

Philadelphia
W-51 L-103
Eddie Joost

POS	Player	AB	BA	HR	RBI	PO	A	E	DP	TC/G	FA	Pitcher	G	IP	W	L	SV	ERA
1B	L. Limmer	316	.231	14	32	597	56	8	63	8.4	.988	Portocarrero	34	248	9	18	0	4.06
2B	S. Jacobs	508	.258	0	26	347	300	17	98	5.1	.974	A. Kellner	27	174	6	17	0	5.39
SS	DeMaestri	539	.230	8	40	285	406	25	90	5.0	.965	M. Fricano	37	152	5	11	0	5.16
3B	J. Finigan	487	.302	7	51	151	305	25	34	3.5	.948	B. Trice	19	119	7	8	0	5.60
RF	B. Renna	422	.232	13	53	226	13	7	5	2.1	.972	S. Dixon	38*	107	5	7	4	4.86
CF	B. Wilson	323	.238	15	33	270	7	3	4	1.8	.989	J. Gray	18	105	3	12	0	6.51
LF	V. Power	462	.255	8	38	256	13	4	3	2.7	.985	C. Bishop	20	96	4	6	1	4.41
C	J. Astroth	226	.221	1	23	300	39	4	5	4.8	.988	M. Burtschy	46	95	5	4	4	3.80
OF	G. Zernial	336	.250	14	62	180	4	9	1	2.1	.953							
1B	D. Bollweg	268	.224	5	24	530	51	13	55	8.4	.978							
OF	E. Valo	224	.214	1	33	135	3	5	1	2.3	.965							
23	P. Suder	205	.200	0	16	97	134	8	25	3.8	.967							
C	B. Shantz	164	.256	1	17	170	28	5	1	4.0	.975							

BATTING AND BASE RUNNING LEADERS

Batting Average
B. Avila, CLE	.341
M. Minoso, CHI	.320
I. Noren, NY	.319
N. Fox, CHI	.319
Y. Berra, NY	.307

Slugging Average
T. Williams, BOS	.635
M. Minoso, CHI	.535
M. Mantle, NY	.525
A. Rosen, CLE	.506
M. Vernon, WAS	.492

Home Runs
L. Doby, CLE	32
T. Williams, BOS	29
M. Mantle, NY	27
J. Jensen, BOS	25
A. Rosen, CLE	24
R. Sievers, WAS	24

Total Bases
M. Minoso, CHI	304
M. Vernon, WAS	294
M. Mantle, NY	285
Y. Berra, NY	285
L. Doby, CLE	279

Runs Batted In
L. Doby, CLE	126
Y. Berra, NY	125
J. Jensen, BOS	117
M. Minoso, CHI	116

Stolen Bases
J. Jensen, BOS	22
J. Rivera, CHI	18
M. Minoso, CHI	18
S. Jacobs, PHI	17
J. Busby, WAS	17

Hits
N. Fox, CHI	201
H. Kuenn, DET	201
B. Avila, CLE	189
J. Busby, WAS	187

Base on Balls
T. Williams, BOS	136
E. Yost, WAS	131
M. Mantle, NY	102
A. Smith, CLE	88

Home Run Percentage
L. Doby, CLE	5.5
A. Rosen, CLE	5.2
M. Mantle, NY	5.0
R. Sievers, WAS	4.7

Runs Scored
M. Mantle, NY	129
M. Minoso, CHI	119
B. Avila, CLE	112
N. Fox, CHI	111

Doubles
M. Vernon, WAS	33
A. Smith, CLE	29
M. Minoso, CHI	29
Y. Berra, NY	28

Triples
M. Minoso, CHI	18
P. Runnels, WAS	15
M. Vernon, WAS	14
M. Mantle, NY	12

PITCHING LEADERS

Winning Percentage
S. Consuegra, CHI	.842
B. Grim, NY	.769
B. Lemon, CLE	.767
M. Garcia, CLE	.704
A. Houtteman, CLE	.682

Earned Run Average
M. Garcia, CLE	2.64
S. Consuegra, CHI	2.69
B. Lemon, CLE	2.72
E. Wynn, CLE	2.73
S. Gromek, DET	2.74

Wins
B. Lemon, CLE	23
E. Wynn, CLE	23
B. Grim, NY	20
M. Garcia, CLE	19
V. Trucks, CHI	19

Saves
J. Sain, NY	22
E. Kinder, BOS	15
R. Narleski, CLE	13

Strikeouts
B. Turley, BAL	185
E. Wynn, CLE	155
V. Trucks, CHI	152
B. Pierce, CHI	148
J. Harshman, CHI	134

Complete Games
Porterfield, WAS	21
B. Lemon, CLE	21
E. Wynn, CLE	20
S. Gromek, DET	17

Fewest Hits/9 Innings
B. Turley, BAL	6.48
W. Ford, NY	7.26
E. Wynn, CLE	7.48
J. Coleman, BAL	7.48

Shutouts
V. Trucks, CHI	5
M. Garcia, CLE	5

Fewest Walks/9 Innings
E. Lopat, NY	1.75
S. Gromek, DET	2.03
S. Consuegra, CHI	2.05
N. Garver, DET	2.27

Most Strikeouts/9 Inn.
B. Pierce, CHI	7.06
J. Harshman, CHI	6.81
B. Turley, BAL	6.73
B. Hoeft, DET	5.86

Innings
E. Wynn, CLE	271
V. Trucks, CHI	265
M. Garcia, CLE	259
B. Lemon, CLE	258

Games Pitched
S. Dixon, PHI, WAS	54
M. Martin, CHI, PHI	48
C. Pascual, WAS	48
E. Kinder, BOS	48

AMERICAN LEAGUE 1954, *cont.*

	W	L	PCT	GB	R	OR	2B	3B	HR	BA	SA	SB	E	DP	FA	CG	BB	SO	ShO	SV	ERA
									Batting					Fielding				Pitching			
Cleveland	111	43	.721		746	**504**	188	39	**156**	.262	.403	30	128	148	.979	**77**	486	678	12	36	**2.78**
New York	103	51	.669	8	805	563	215	59	133	.268	.408	34	126	198	.979	51	552	655	15	37	3.26
Chicago	94	60	.610	17	711	521	203	47	94	.267	.379	98	108	149	.982	60	517	701	21	33	3.05
Boston	69	85	.448	42	700	728	244	41	123	.266	.395	51	176	163	.972	41	612	707	9	22	4.01
Detroit	68	86	.442	43	584	664	215	41	90	.258	.367	48	129	131	.978	58	506	603	13	13	3.81
Washington	66	88	.429	45	632	680	188	69	81	.246	.355	37	137	172	.977	69	573	562	10	7	3.84
Baltimore	54	100	.351	57	483	668	195	49	52	.251	.338	30	147	152	.975	58	688	668	6	8	3.88
Philadelphia	51	103	.331	60	542	875	191	41	94	.236	.342	30	169	163	.972	49	685	555	3	13	5.18
					5203	5203	1639	386	823	.257	.373	358	1120	1276	.977	463	4619	5129	89	169	3.72

NATIONAL LEAGUE 1955

	POS	Player	AB	BA	HR	RBI	PO	A	E	DP	TC/G	FA	Pitcher	G	IP	W	L	SV	ERA
Brooklyn	1B	G. Hodges	546	.289	27	102	1274	105	12	126	10.0	.991	D. Newcombe	34	234	20	5	0	3.20
	2B	J. Gilliam	538	.249	7	40	213	269	16	64	5.0	.968	C. Erskine	31	195	11	8	1	3.79
W-98 L-55	SS	P. Reese	553	.282	10	61	239	404	23	86	4.7	.965	J. Podres	27	159	9	10	0	3.95
	3B	J. Robinson	317	.256	8	36	74	180	9	18	3.1	.966	C. Labine	60	144	13	5	11	3.24
Walter Alston	RF	C. Furillo	523	.314	26	95	249	10	5	4	1.9	.981	B. Loes	22	128	10	4	0	3.59
	CF	D. Snider	538	.309	42	**136**	348	9	4	0	2.5	.989	K. Spooner	29	99	8	6	2	3.65
	LF	S. Amoros	388	.247	10	51	201	10	6	1	2.0	.972	R. Craig	21	91	5	3	0	2.78
	C	Campanella	446	.318	32	107	**672**	54	6	8	**6.0**	.992	E. Roebuck	47	84	5	6	12	4.71
	2S	D. Zimmer	280	.239	15	50	182	199	12	63		.969	D. Bessent	24	63	8	1	3	2.70
	3B	D. Hoak	279	.240	5	19	82	183	11	15	3.5	.960							
	P	D. Newcombe	117	.359	7	23	15	24	4	5	1.3	.907							
Milwaukee	1B	G. Crowe	303	.281	15	55	677	61	8	62	9.4	.989	W. Spahn	39	246	17	14	1	3.26
	2B	D. O'Connell	453	.225	6	40	309	357	13	76	6.0	.981	L. Burdette	42	230	13	8	0	4.03
W-85 L-69	SS	J. Logan	595	.297	13	83	268	**511**	30	100	5.3	.963	B. Buhl	38	202	13	11	1	3.21
	3B	E. Mathews	499	.289	41	101	140	**280**	21	23	**3.2**	.952	G. Conley	22	158	11	7	0	4.16
Charlie Grimm	RF	H. Aaron	602	.314	27	106	254	9	9	2	2.2	.967	N. Nichols	34	144	9	8	1	4.00
	CF	B. Bruton	636	.275	9	47	412	17	14	6	3.0	.968	R. Crone	33	140	10	9	0	3.46
	LF	B. Thomson	343	.257	12	56	182	5	6	0	2.1	.969	E. Johnson	40	92	5	7	4	3.42
	C	D. Crandall	440	.236	26	62	611	67	10	8	5.3	.985							
	1B	J. Adcock	288	.264	15	45	725	44	8	68	10.0	.990							
	OF	A. Pafko	252	.266	5	34	96	1	2	0	1.7	.980							
	OF	C. Tanner	243	.247	6	27	101	4	2	0	1.7	.981							
New York	1B	G. Harris	263	.232	12	36	617	50	12	65	9.1	.982	J. Antonelli	38	235	14	16	1	3.33
	2B	Terwilliger	257	.257	1	18	212	240	7	70	5.9	.985	J. Hearn	39	227	14	16	0	3.73
W-80 L-74	SS	A. Dark	475	.282	9	45	213	324	21	70	4.9	.962	R. Gomez	33	185	9	10	1	4.56
	3B	H. Thompson	432	.245	17	63	104	262	22	23	3.1	.943	S. Maglie	23	130	9	5	0	3.75
Leo Durocher	RF	D. Mueller	605	.306	8	83	239	5	6	1	1.7	.976	D. Liddle	33	106	10	4	1	4.23
	CF	W. Mays	580	.319	51	127	407	**23**	8	**8**	2.9	.982	H. Wilhelm	59	103	4	1	0	3.93
	LF	W. Lockman	576	.273	15	49	167	4	3	1	2.1	.983	W. McCall	42	95	6	5	3	3.69
	C	R. Katt	326	.215	7	28	482	45	7	7	4.4	.987	R. Monzant	28	95	4	8	0	3.99
	2B	D. Williams	247	.251	4	15	139	162	10	39	4.4	.968	M. Grissom	55	89	5	4	8	2.92
	UT	B. Hofman	207	.266	10	28	259	59	1	30		.997							
	OF	D. Rhodes	187	.305	6	32	68	2	1	0	1.6	.986							
	SS	B. Gardner	187	.203	3	17	65	122	12	28	5.2	.940							
	3O	S. Gordon	144	.243	7	25	57	61	0	6		1.000							
Philadelphia	1B	M. Blaylock	259	.208	3	24	528	44	5	35	7.5	.991	R. Roberts	41	**305**	**23**	14	3	3.28
	2B	B. Morgan	483	.232	10	49	192	204	8	46	4.6	.980	M. Dickson	36	216	12	11	0	3.50
W-77 L-77	SS	R. Smalley	260	.196	7	39	136	205	9	32	4.0	.974	H. Wehmeier	31	194	10	12	0	4.41
	3B	W. Jones	516	.258	16	81	**202**	235	18	22	3.1	**.960**	C. Simmons	25	130	8	8	0	4.92
Mayo Smith	RF	Greengrass	323	.272	12	37	159	10	2	0	2.1	.988	J. Meyer	50	110	6	11	16	3.43
	CF	R. Ashburn	533	**.338**	3	42	387	10	7	3	2.9	.983	B. Miller	40	90	8	4	1	2.41
	LF	D. Ennis	564	.296	29	120	298	9	4	2	2.1	.987							
	C	A. Seminick	289	.246	11	34	435	45	3	6	5.5	.994*							
	2B	G. Hamner	405	.257	5	43	152	183	14	39	4.3	.960							
	C	S. Lopata	303	.271	22	58	332	37	2	9	5.6	.995							
	OF	G. Gorbous	224	.237	4	23	113	10	2	2	2.2	.984							
Cincinnati	1B	Kluszewski	612	.314	47	113	**1388**	86	8	**153**	9.7	.995	J. Nuxhall	50	257	17	12	3	3.47
	2B	J. Temple	588	.281	0	50	408	410	24	119	5.7	.971	A. Fowler	46	208	11	10	2	3.90
W-75 L-79	SS	R. McMillan	470	.268	1	37	290	495	25	111	5.4	.969	Klippstein	39	138	9	10	0	3.39
	3B	R. Bridges	168	.286	1	18	48	88	5	7	2.4	.965	J. Collum	32	134	9	8	1	3.63
Birdie Tebbetts	RF	W. Post	601	.309	40	109	298	13	7	2	2.1	.978	G. Staley	30	120	5	8	0	4.66
	CF	G. Bell	610	.308	27	104	364	4	5	0	2.4	.987	R. Minarcin	41	116	5	9	1	4.90
	LF	S. Palys	222	.230	7	30	116	3	1	0	2.2	.992	J. Black	32	102	5	2	3	4.22
	C	S. Burgess	421	.306	20	77	457	35	7	6	4.7	.986	H. Freeman	52	92	7	4	11	2.16
	O3	R. Jablonski	221	.240	9	28	69	46	11	3		.913							
	3O	C. Harmon	198	.253	5	28	114	50	6	4		.965							
	OF	B. Thurman	152	.217	7	22	54	2	3	0	1.6	.949							
	3B	B. Adams	150	.273	2	20	35	88	4	11	3.0	.969							

NATIONAL LEAGUE 1955, cont.

	POS	Player	AB	BA	HR	RBI	PO	A	E	DP	TC/G	FA	Pitcher	G	IP	W	L	SV	ERA
Chicago	1B	D. Fondy	574	.265	17	65	1304	107	13	135	9.7	.991	S. Jones	36	242	14	20	0	4.10
	2B	G. Baker	609	.268	11	52	432	444	30	114	5.9	.967	B. Rush	33	234	13	11	0	3.50
W-72 L-81	SS	E. Banks	596	.295	44	117	290	482	22	102	5.2	.972	W. Hacker	35	213	11	15	3	4.27
	3B	R. Jackson	499	.265	21	70	125	247	20	26	2.9	.949	P. Minner	22	158	9	9	0	3.48
Stan Hack	RF	J. King	301	.256	11	45	184	10	2	2	2.1	.990	J. Davis	42	134	7	11	3	4.44
	CF	E. Miksis	481	.235	9	41	267	6	3	1	2.5	.989	H. Jeffcoat	50	101	8	6	6	2.95
	LF	H. Sauer	261	.211	12	28	122	4	2	1	1.9	.984	H. Pollet	24	61	4	3	5	5.61
	C	H. Chiti	338	.231	11	41	495	69	9	10	5.1	.984							
	OF	F. Baumholtz	280	.289	1	27	131	3	1	1	2.1	.993							
	OF	B. Speake	261	.218	12	43	90	4	4	1	1.8	.959							
	OF	J. Bolger	160	.206	0	7	125	1	6	0	2.6	.955							
St. Louis	1B	S. Musial	562	.319	33	108	925	92	8	93	9.3	.992	H. Haddix	37	208	12	16	1	4.46
	2B	Schoendienst	553	.268	11	51	296	381	10	96	4.8	.985	L. Jackson	37	177	9	14	2	4.31
W-68 L-86	SS	A. Grammas	366	.240	3	15	235	340	19	76	4.7	.968	L. Arroyo	35	159	11	8	0	4.19
	3B	K. Boyer	530	.264	18	62	124	253	19	24	2.8	.952	T. Poholsky	30	151	9	11	0	3.81
Eddie Stanky	RF	W. Moon	593	.295	19	76	188	5	5	1	2.0	.975	W. Schmidt	20	130	7	6	0	2.78
W-17 L-19	CF	B. Virdon	534	.281	17	68	339	7	12	1	2.5	.966	B. Lawrence	46	96	3	8	1	6.56
	LF	R. Repulski	512	.270	23	73	260	5	7	1	1.9	.974	P. LaPalme	56	92	4	3	3	2.75
Harry Walker	C	B. Sarni	325	.255	3	34	482	39	7	8	5.3	.987							
W-51 L-67	32	S. Hemus	206	.243	5	21	56	90	5	10		.967							
	C	N. Burbrink	170	.276	0	15	261	24	6	4	5.3	.979							
Pittsburgh	1B	D. Long	419	.291	16	79	968	97	13	114	9.1	.988	V. Law	43	201	10	10	1	3.81
	2B	J. O'Brien	278	.299	1	25	185	220	13	53	5.4	.969	B. Friend	44	200	14	9	2	2.83
W-60 L-94	SS	D. Groat	521	.267	4	51	330	450	32	107	5.4	.961	M. Surkont	35	166	7	14	2	5.57
	3B	G. Freese	455	.253	14	44	55	127	11	16	3.0	.943	R. Kline	36	137	6	13	2	4.15
Fred Haney	RF	R. Clemente	474	.255	5	47	253	18	6	5	2.3	.978	Littlefield	35	130	5	12	0	5.12
	CF	E. O'Brien	236	.233	0	8	132	8	1	1	2.5	.993	R. Face	42	126	5	7	5	3.58
	LF	F. Thomas	510	.245	25	72	307	8	5	3	2.3	.984	L. Donoso	25	95	4	6	1	5.31
	C	J. Shepard	264	.239	2	23	288	34	6	6	4.3	.982	D. Hall	15	94	6	6	1	3.91
	OF	J. Lynch	282	.284	5	28	104	11	6	3	1.7	.950	B. Purkey	14	68	2	7	1	5.32
	UT	D. Cole	239	.226	0	21	103	158	10	25		.963							
	C	T. Atwell	207	.213	1	18	334	24	3	3	5.4	.992							
	1B	P. Ward	179	.212	5	25	384	35	1	41	8.8	.998							
	3B	G. Freese	179	.257	3	21	50	82	9	3	2.8	.936							
	OF	R. Mejias	167	.216	3	21	67	8	6	2	1.9	.926							

BATTING AND BASE RUNNING LEADERS

Batting Average
R. Ashburn, PHI .338
W. Mays, NY .319
S. Musial, STL .319
Campanella, BKN .318
H. Aaron, MIL .314

Slugging Average
W. Mays, NY .659
D. Snider, BKN .628
E. Mathews, MIL .601
E. Banks, CHI .596
Kluszewski, CIN .585

Home Runs
W. Mays, NY 51
Kluszewski, CIN 47
E. Banks, CHI 44
D. Snider, BKN 42
E. Mathews, MIL 41

Total Bases
W. Mays, NY 382
Kluszewski, CIN 358
E. Banks, CHI 355
W. Post, CIN 345
D. Snider, BKN 338

Runs Batted In
D. Snider, BKN 136
W. Mays, NY 127
D. Ennis, PHI 120
E. Banks, CHI 117
Kluszewski, CIN 113

Stolen Bases
B. Bruton, MIL 25
W. Mays, NY 24
K. Boyer, STL 22
J. Temple, CIN 19
J. Gilliam, BKN 15

Hits
Kluszewski, CIN 192
H. Aaron, MIL 189
G. Bell, CIN 188
W. Post, CIN 186

Base on Balls
E. Mathews, MIL 109
R. Ashburn, PHI 105
D. Snider, BKN 104
H. Thompson, NY 84

Home Run Percentage
W. Mays, NY 8.8
E. Mathews, MIL 8.2
D. Snider, BKN 7.8
Kluszewski, CIN 7.7

Runs Scored
D. Snider, BKN 126
W. Mays, NY 123
W. Post, CIN 116
Kluszewski, CIN 116

Doubles
J. Logan, MIL 37
H. Aaron, MIL 37
D. Snider, BKN 34
W. Post, CIN 33

Triples
D. Long, PIT 13
W. Mays, NY 13
B. Bruton, MIL 12
R. Clemente, PIT 11

PITCHING LEADERS

Winning Percentage
D. Newcombe, BKN .800
R. Roberts, PHI .622
J. Nuxhall, CIN .586
W. Spahn, MIL .548

Earned Run Average
B. Friend, PIT 2.83
D. Newcombe, BKN 3.20
B. Buhl, MIL 3.21
W. Spahn, MIL 3.26
R. Roberts, PHI 3.28

Wins
R. Roberts, PHI 23
D. Newcombe, BKN 20
J. Nuxhall, CIN 17
W. Spahn, MIL 17

Saves
J. Meyer, PHI 16
E. Roebuck, BKN 12
C. Labine, BKN 11
H. Freeman, CIN 11
M. Grissom, NY 8

Strikeouts
S. Jones, CHI 198
R. Roberts, PHI 160
H. Haddix, STL 150
D. Newcombe, BKN 143
J. Antonelli, NY 143

Complete Games
R. Roberts, PHI 26
D. Newcombe, BKN 17
W. Spahn, MIL 16
J. Nuxhall, CIN 14
B. Rush, CHI 14
J. Antonelli, NY 14

Fewest Hits/9 Innings
S. Jones, CHI 6.52
B. Buhl, MIL 7.50
B. Rush, CHI 7.85
J. Antonelli, NY 7.88

Shutouts
J. Nuxhall, CIN 5
M. Dickson, PHI 4
S. Jones, CHI 4
A. Fowler, CIN 3

Fewest Walks/9 Innings
D. Newcombe, BKN 1.46
R. Roberts, PHI 1.56
W. Hacker, CHI 1.82
B. Friend, PIT 2.34

Most Strikeouts/9 Inn.
S. Jones, CHI 7.37
H. Haddix, STL 6.49
J. Podres, BKN 6.44
G. Conley, MIL 6.09

Innings
R. Roberts, PHI 305
J. Nuxhall, CIN 257
W. Spahn, MIL 246
S. Jones, CHI 242

Games Pitched
C. Labine, BKN 60
H. Wilhelm, NY 59
P. LaPalme, STL 56
M. Grissom, NY 55

NATIONAL LEAGUE 1955, cont.

	W	L	PCT	GB	R	OR	2B	3B	HR	BA	SA	SB	E	DP	FA	CG	BB	SO	ShO	SV	ERA
							Batting						**Fielding**			**Pitching**					
Brooklyn	98	55	.641	—	**857**	650	**230**	44	**201**	**.271**	**.448**	**79**	133	156	.978	46	483	773	11	**37**	3.68
Milwaukee	85	69	.552	13.5	743	668	219	55	182	.261	.427	42	152	155	.975	**61**	591	654	5	12	3.85
New York	80	74	.519	18.5	702	673	173	34	169	.260	.402	38	142	165	.976	52	560	721	6	14	3.77
Philadelphia	77	77	.500	21.5	675	666	214	50	132	.255	.395	44	**110**	117	**.981**	58	477	657	11	21	3.93
Cincinnati	75	79	.487	23.5	761	684	216	28	181	.270	.425	51	139	169	.977	38	443	576	**12**	22	3.95
Chicago	72	81	.471	26	626	713	187	55	164	.247	.398	37	147	147	.975	47	601	686	10	23	4.17
St. Louis	68	86	.442	30.5	654	757	228	36	143	.261	.400	64	146	152	.975	42	549	730	10	15	4.56
Pittsburgh	60	94	.390	38.5	560	767	210	**60**	91	.244	.361	22	166	**175**	.972	41	536	622	5	16	4.39
					5578	5578	1677	362	1263	.259	.407	377	1135	1236	.976	385	4240	5419	70	160	4.04

AMERICAN LEAGUE 1955

New York
W-96 L-58
Casey Stengel

POS	Player	AB	BA	HR	RBI	PO	A	E	DP	TC/G	FA	Pitcher	G	IP	W	L	SV	ERA
1B	B. Skowron	288	.319	12	61	517	37	6	63	7.6	.989	W. Ford	39	254	**18**	7	2	2.63
2B	McDougald	533	.285	13	53	352	348	11	**119**	5.6	**.985**	B. Turley	36	247	17	13	1	3.06
SS	B. Hunter	255	.227	3	20	115	249	16	60	3.9	.958	T. Byrne	27	160	16	5	2	3.15
3B	A. Carey	510	.257	7	47	**154**	**301**	22	37	3.5	.954	J. Kucks	29	127	8	7	0	3.41
RF	H. Bauer	492	.278	20	53	248	13	5	3	2.0	.981	D. Larsen	19	97	9	2	2	3.06
CF	M. Mantle	517	.306	**37**	99	372	11	2	2	2.7	.995	B. Grim	26	92	7	5	4	4.19
LF	I. Noren	371	.253	8	59	238	9	5	0	2.0	.980	E. Lopat	16	87	4	8	0	3.74
C	Y. Berra	541	.272	27	108	**721**	54	13	10	5.4	.984	J. Konstanty	45	74	7	2	11	2.32
OF	E. Howard	279	.290	10	43	124	10	3	3	1.8	.978	T. Morgan	40	72	7	3	10	3.25
1B	J. Collins	278	.234	13	45	395	42	1	63	6.0	.998							
1B	E. Robinson	173	.208	16	42	390	20	2	35	9.0	.995							
OF	B. Cerv	85	.341	3	22	25	1	0	0	1.3	1.000							

Cleveland
W-93 L-61
Al Lopez

POS	Player	AB	BA	HR	RBI	PO	A	E	DP	TC/G	FA	Pitcher	G	IP	W	L	SV	ERA
1B	V. Wertz	257	.253	14	55	449	33	8	49	7.8	.984	E. Wynn	32	230	17	11	0	2.82
2B	B. Avila	537	.272	13	61	348	342	13	108	5.0	.982	H. Score	33	227	16	10	0	2.85
SS	Strickland	388	.209	2	34	221	360	14	84	4.6	.976	B. Lemon	35	211	**18**	10	2	3.88
3B	A. Rosen	492	.244	21	81	119	195	12	17	3.1	.963	M. Garcia	38	211	11	13	4	4.02
RF	A. Smith	607	.306	22	77	206	5	5	1	1.8	.977	A. Houtteman	35	124	10	6	0	3.98
CF	L. Doby	491	.291	26	75	313	6	2	1	2.5	.994	R. Narleski	60	112	9	1	19	3.71
LF	R. Kiner	321	.243	18	54	141	2	2	0	1.7	.986	D. Mossi	57	82	4	3	9	2.42
C	J. Hegan	304	.220	9	40	583	34	2	12	5.6	.997							
OF	G. Woodling	259	.278	5	35	129	4	1	0	1.9	.993*							
OF	D. Pope	104	.298	6	22	62	0	3	0	2.1	.954							

Chicago
W-91 L-63
Marty Marion

POS	Player	AB	BA	HR	RBI	PO	A	E	DP	TC/G	FA	Pitcher	G	IP	W	L	SV	ERA
1B	W. Dropo	453	.280	19	79	1101	62	6	104	8.4	.995	B. Pierce	33	206	15	10	1	**1.97**
2B	N. Fox	636	.311	6	59	**399**	**483**	24	110	**5.9**	.974	D. Donovan	29	187	15	9	0	3.32
SS	Carrasquel	523	.256	11	52	222	424	18	81	4.6	.973	J. Harshman	32	179	11	7	0	3.36
3B	G. Kell	429	.312	8	81	83	165	6	8	2.4	**.976**	V. Trucks	32	175	13	8	0	3.96
RF	J. Rivera	454	.264	10	52	288	22	6	7	2.2	.981	S. Consuegra	44	126	6	5	7	2.64
CF	J. Busby	337	.243	1	27	243	6	4	3	2.6	.984	C. Johnson	17	99	7	4	0	3.45
LF	M. Minoso	517	.288	10	70	287	19	9	3	2.3	.971	H. Byrd	25	91	4	6	1	4.65
C	S. Lollar	426	.261	16	61	664	62	4	12	5.4	.995	M. Fornieles	26	86	6	3	2	3.86
OF	B. Nieman	272	.283	11	53	118	4	3	2	1.6	.976	D. Howell	35	74	8	3	9	2.93
3B	B. Kennedy	214	.304	9	43	32	73	7	10	2.0	.938							

Boston
W-84 L-70
Pinky Higgins

POS	Player	AB	BA	HR	RBI	PO	A	E	DP	TC/G	FA	Pitcher	G	IP	W	L	SV	ERA
1B	N. Zauchin	477	.239	27	93	1137	84	6	106	9.7	.995	F. Sullivan	35	**260**	**18**	13	0	2.91
2B	B. Goodman	599	.294	0	52	348	373	23	93	5.2	.969	W. Nixon	31	208	12	10	0	4.07
SS	B. Klaus	541	.283	7	60	207	391	28	55	5.0	.955	T. Brewer	31	193	11	10	0	4.20
3B	G. Hatton	380	.245	4	49	97	225	8	22	3.0	.976	G. Susce	29	144	9	7	1	3.06
RF	J. Jensen	574	.275	26	**116**	281	11	7	3	2.0	.977	I. Delock	29	144	9	7	3	3.76
CF	J. Piersall	515	.283	13	62	425	7	3	2	3.0	.993	L. Kiely	33	90	3	3	6	2.80
LF	T. Williams	320	.356	28	83	170	5	2	0	1.9	.989	T. Hurd	43	81	8	6	5	3.01
C	S. White	544	.261	11	64	671	71	12	8	5.3	.984	E. Kinder	43	67	5	5	18	2.84
OF	G. Stephens	157	.293	3	18	82	7	5	1	1.3	.947							
OF	Throneberry	144	.257	6	27	69	3	3	0	2.2	.960							

Detroit
W-79 L-75
Bucky Harris

POS	Player	AB	BA	HR	RBI	PO	A	E	DP	TC/G	FA	Pitcher	G	IP	W	L	SV	ERA
1B	E. Torgeson	300	.283	9	50	695	53	6	79	9.1	.992	F. Lary	36	235	14	15	1	3.10
2B	F. Hatfield	413	.232	8	33	216	251	12	74	5.2	.975	N. Garver	33	231	12	16	0	3.98
SS	H. Kuenn	620	.306	8	62	253	378	29	83	4.7	.956	B. Hoeft	32	220	16	7	0	2.99
3B	R. Boone	500	.284	20	**116**	135	252	19	33	3.2	.953	S. Gromek	28	181	13	10	0	3.98
RF	A. Kaline	588	**.340**	27	102	306	14	7	4	2.2	.979	D. Maas	18	87	5	6	0	4.88
CF	B. Tuttle	603	.279	14	78	**442**	12	7	2	3.0	.985	B. Birrer	36	80	4	3	3	4.15
LF	J. Delsing	356	.239	10	60	178	3	1	1	1.8	.995	A. Aber	39	80	6	3	3	3.38
C	F. House	328	.259	15	53	423	35	6	5	5.0	.987							
C	R. Wilson	241	.220	2	17	292	25	5	5	4.5	.984							
2B	H. Malmberg	208	.216	0	19	155	181	5	42	5.2	.985							
OF	B. Phillips	184	.234	3	23	128	2	1	0	2.0	.992							
1B	F. Fain	140	.264	2	23	370	29	5	42	9.2	.988							
1B	J. Phillips	117	.316	1	20	236	13	2	16	7.2	.992							

AMERICAN LEAGUE 1955, *cont.*

	POS	Player	AB	BA	HR	RBI	PO	A	E	DP	TC/G	FA	Pitcher	G	IP	W	L	SV	ERA
Kansas City	1B	V. Power	596	.319	19	76	**1281**	130	10	140	9.9	.993	A. Ditmar	35	175	12	12	1	5.03
	2B	J. Finigan	545	.255	9	68	236	228	12	72	5.3	.975	A. Kellner	30	163	11	8	0	4.20
W-63 L-91	SS	DeMaestri	457	.249	6	37	206	358	21	78	4.8	.964	B. Shantz	23	125	5	10	0	4.54
	3B	H. Lopez	483	.290	15	68	104	233	**23**	26	3.9	.936	Ceccarelli	31	124	4	7	0	5.31
Lou Boudreau	RF	E. Slaughter	267	.322	5	34	126	5	2	2	1.7	.985	Portocarrero	24	111	5	9	0	4.77
	CF	H. Simpson	396	.301	5	52	262	5	6	2	2.7	.978	T. Gorman	57	109	7	6	18	3.55
	LF	G. Zernial	413	.254	30	84	231	9	9	4	2.4	.964	V. Raschi	20	101	4	6	0	5.42
	C	J. Astroth	274	.252	5	23	420	50	5	9	4.8	.989	C. Boyer	30	98	5	5	0	6.22
	OF	E. Valo	283	.364	3	37	147	5	2	2	2.1	.987							
	OF	B. Wilson	273	.223	15	38	186	4	6	0	2.4	.969							
	OF	B. Renna	249	.213	7	28	118	5	1	2	1.6	.992							
	C	B. Shantz	217	.258	1	12	261	27	3	8	3.7	.990							
Baltimore	1B	G. Triandos	481	.277	12	65	839	69	10	92	8.9	.989	J. Wilson	34	235	12	**18**	0	3.44
	2B	F. Marsh	303	.218	2	19	197	158	6	51	4.8	.983	E. Palica	33	170	5	11	2	4.14
W-57 L-97	SS	W. Miranda	487	.255	1	38	**300**	481	34	101	5.3	.958	R. Moore	46	152	10	10	6	3.92
	3B	W. Causey	175	.194	1	9	25	79	10	10	2.1	.912	B. Wight	19	117	6	8	2	2.45
Paul Richards	RF	C. Abrams	309	.243	6	32	191	7	3	1	2.1	.985	G. Zuverink	28	86	4	3	4	2.19
	CF	C. Diering	371	.256	3	31	242	6	6	2	2.4	.976	H. Dorish	35	66	3	3	6	3.15
	LF	D. Philley	311	.299	6	41	154	6	5	2	2.0	.970							
	C	H. Smith	424	.271	4	52	497	58	8	4	4.5	.986							
	OF	D. Pope	222	.248	1	30	152	3	0	1	2.1	1.000							
	OF	J. Dyck	197	.279	2	22	86	4	1	1	2.0	.989							
	32	B. Cox	194	.211	3	14	53	95	3	9		.980							
	2B	B. Young	186	.199	1	8	121	146	4	42	4.7	.985							
	OF	H. Evers	185	.238	6	30	106	1	1	0	2.0	.991							
	1B	B. Hale	182	.357	0	29	300	33	7	25	7.8	.974							
Washington	1B	M. Vernon	538	.301	14	85	1258	69	8	137	9.3	.994	D. Stone	43	180	6	13	1	4.15
	2B	P. Runnels	503	.284	2	49	349	338	17	107	5.3	.976	Porterfield	30	178	10	17	0	4.45
W-53 L-101	SS	Valdivielso	294	.221	2	28	160	317	22	69	5.3	.956	J. Schmitz	32	165	7	10	1	3.71
	3B	E. Yost	375	.243	7	48	100	217	19	22	3.1	.943	McDermott	31	156	10	10	1	3.75
Chuck Dressen	RF	C. Paula	351	.299	6	45	154	5	**10**	3	2.0	.941	C. Stobbs	41	140	4	14	3	5.00
	CF	T. Umphlett	323	.217	2	19	237	8	3	1	2.4	.988	P. Ramos	45	130	5	11	3	3.88
	LF	R. Sievers	509	.271	25	106	247	5	3	6		.988	C. Pascual	43	129	2	12	3	6.14
	C	Fitz Gerald	236	.237	4	19	304	30	6	5	4.7	.982	T. Abernathy	40	119	5	9	0	5.96
	OF	E. Oravetz	263	.270	0	25	117	1	4	0	2.1	.967							
	C	C. Courtney	238	.298	2	30	252	27	5	4	4.2	.982							
	OF	J. Busby	191	.230	6	14	132	1	1	0	2.9	.993							
	OF	J. Groth	183	.219	2	17	121	2	2	1	2.6	.984							

BATTING AND BASE RUNNING LEADERS

Batting Average
A. Kaline, DET .340
V. Power, KC .319
G. Kell, CHI .312
N. Fox, CHI .311
H. Kuenn, DET .306

Slugging Average
M. Mantle, NY .611
A. Kaline, DET .546
G. Zernial, KC .508
L. Doby, CLE .505
V. Power, KC .505

Home Runs
M. Mantle, NY 37
G. Zernial, KC 30
T. Williams, BOS 28
N. Zauchin, BOS 27
Y. Berra, NY 27
A. Kaline, DET 27

Total Bases
A. Kaline, DET 321
M. Mantle, NY 316
V. Power, KC 301
A. Smith, CLE 287
J. Jensen, BOS 275

Runs Batted In
R. Boone, DET 116
J. Jensen, BOS 116
Y. Berra, NY 108
R. Sievers, WAS 106
A. Kaline, DET 102

Stolen Bases
J. Rivera, CHI 25
M. Minoso, CHI 19
J. Jensen, BOS 16
J. Busby, CHI, WAS 12
A. Smith, CLE 11

Hits
A. Kaline, DET 200
N. Fox, CHI 198
V. Power, KC 190
H. Kuenn, DET 190

Base on Balls
M. Mantle, NY 113
B. Goodman, BOS 99
E. Yost, WAS 95
F. Fain, CLE, DET 94

Home Run Percentage
G. Zernial, KC 7.3
M. Mantle, NY 7.2
N. Zauchin, BOS 5.7
L. Doby, CLE 5.3

Runs Scored
A. Smith, CLE 123
M. Mantle, NY 121
A. Kaline, DET 121
B. Tuttle, DET 102

Doubles
H. Kuenn, DET 38
V. Power, KC 34
B. Goodman, BOS 31
S. White, BOS 30

Triples
A. Carey, NY 11
M. Mantle, NY 11
V. Power, KC 10

PITCHING LEADERS

Winning Percentage
T. Byrne, NY .762
W. Ford, NY .720
B. Hoeft, DET .696
B. Lemon, CLE .643
D. Donovan, CHI .625

Earned Run Average
B. Pierce, CHI 1.97
W. Ford, NY 2.63
E. Wynn, CLE 2.82
H. Score, CLE 2.85
F. Sullivan, BOS 2.91

Wins
W. Ford, NY 18
B. Lemon, CLE 18
F. Sullivan, BOS 18
E. Wynn, CLE 17
B. Turley, NY 17

Saves
R. Narleski, CLE 19
T. Gorman, KC 18
E. Kinder, BOS 18
J. Konstanty, NY 11
T. Morgan, NY 10

Strikeouts
H. Score, CLE 245
B. Turley, NY 210
B. Pierce, CHI 157
W. Ford, NY 137
B. Hoeft, DET 133

Complete Games
W. Ford, NY 18
B. Hoeft, DET 17

Fewest Hits/9 Innings
B. Turley, NY 6.13
H. Score, CLE 6.26
W. Ford, NY 6.67
B. Pierce, CHI 7.09

Shutouts
B. Hoeft, DET 7
B. Pierce, CHI 6
E. Wynn, CLE 6
B. Turley, NY 6

Fewest Walks/9 Innings
S. Gromek, DET 1.84
D. Donovan, CHI 2.31
M. Garcia, CLE 2.39
N. Garver, DET 2.61

Most Strikeouts/9 Inn.
H. Score, CLE 9.70
B. Turley, NY 7.66
B. Pierce, CHI 6.87
J. Harshman, CHI 5.82

Innings
F. Sullivan, BOS 260
W. Ford, NY 254
B. Turley, NY 247
J. Wilson, BAL 235

Games Pitched
R. Narleski, CLE 60
T. Gorman, KC 57
D. Mossi, CLE 57
H. Dorish, BAL, CHI 48

AMERICAN LEAGUE 1955, cont.

	W	L	PCT	GB	R	OR	Batting 2B	3B	HR	BA	SA	SB	Fielding E	DP	FA	Pitching CG	BB	SO	ShO	SV	ERA
New York	96	58	.623		762	569	179	55	175	.260	.418	55	128	180	.978	52	689	731	18	33	3.23
Cleveland	93	61	.604	3	698	601	195	31	148	.257	.394	28	108	152	.981	45	558	877	13	36	3.39
Chicago	91	63	.591	5	725	557	204	36	116	.268	.388	69	111	147	.981	55	499	720	17	23	3.37
Boston	84	70	.545	12	755	652	241	39	137	.264	.402	43	136	140	.977	44	582	674	9	34	3.72
Detroit	79	75	.513	17	775	658	211	38	130	.266	.394	41	139	159	.976	66	517	629	15	12	3.79
Kansas City	63	91	.409	33	638	911	189	46	121	.261	.382	22	146	174	.976	29	707	572	7	23	5.35
Baltimore	57	97	.370	39	540	754	177	39	54	.240	.320	34	167	159	.972	35	625	595	9	22	4.21
Washington	53	101	.344	43	598	789	178	54	80	.248	.351	25	154	170	.974	37	637	607	9	16	4.62
					5491	5491	1574	338	961	.258	.381	317	1089	1281	.977	363	4814	5405	97	199	3.96

NATIONAL LEAGUE 1956

Team	POS	Player	AB	BA	HR	RBI	PO	A	E	DP	TC/G	FA	Pitcher	G	IP	W	L	SV	ERA
Brooklyn W-93 L-61 Walter Alston	1B	G. Hodges	550	.265	32	87	1190	103	10	105	9.4	.992	D. Newcombe	38	268	27	7	0	3.06
	2B	J. Gilliam	594	.300	6	43	233	326	11	64	5.6	.981	R. Craig	35	199	12	11	1	3.71
	SS	P. Reese	572	.257	9	46	263	367	23	79	4.8	.965	S. Maglie	28	191	13	5	0	2.87
	3B	R. Jackson	307	.274	8	53	84	184	2	19	3.4	.993	C. Erskine	31	186	13	11	0	4.25
	RF	C. Furillo	523	.289	21	83	230	10	4	2	1.7	.984	C. Labine	62	116	10	6	19	3.35
	CF	D. Snider	542	.292	43	101	358	11	6	1	2.5	.984	D. Drysdale	25	99	5	5	0	2.64
	LF	S. Amoros	292	.260	16	58	123	3	6	0	1.5	.955	E. Roebuck	43	89	5	4	1	3.93
	C	Campanella	388	.219	20	73	659	49	11	3	5.9	.985	D. Bessent	38	79	4	3	9	2.50
	UT	J. Robinson	357	.275	10	43	169	230	9	37		.978							
	C	R. Walker	146	.212	3	20	184	20	3	4	4.8	.986							
Milwaukee W-92 L-62 Charlie Grimm W-24 L-22 Fred Haney W-68 L-40	1B	J. Adcock	454	.291	38	103	1086	75	6	109	9.0	.995	W. Spahn	39	281	20	11	3	2.78
	2B	D. O'Connell	498	.239	2	42	295	381	10	98	5.0	.985	L. Burdette	39	256	19	10	1	2.70
	SS	J. Logan	545	.281	15	46	266	467	24	94	5.1	.968	B. Buhl	38	217	18	8	0	3.32
	3B	E. Mathews	552	.272	37	95	133	287	25	22	3.0	.944	R. Crone	35	170	11	10	2	3.87
	RF	H. Aaron	609	.328	26	92	316	17	13	4	2.3	.962	G. Conley	31	158	8	9	3	3.13
	CF	B. Bruton	525	.272	8	56	391	10	13	1	2.9	.969	T. Phillips	23	88	5	3	2	2.26
	LF	B. Thomson	451	.235	20	74	257	7	7	0	2.0	.974	E. Johnson	36	51	4	3	6	3.71
	C	D. Crandall	311	.238	16	48	448	44	2	9	4.5	.996	D. Jolly	29	46	2	3	7	3.74
	C	D. Rice	188	.213	3	17	271	21	5	2	4.6	.983							
	1B	F. Torre	159	.258	0	16	390	42	3	34	4.9	.993							
Cincinnati W-91 L-63 Birdie Tebbetts	1B	Kluszewski	517	.302	35	102	1166	89	13	110	9.7	.990	B. Lawrence	49	219	19	10	0	3.99
	2B	J. Temple	632	.285	2	41	389	432	16	89	5.4	.981	Klippstein	37	211	12	11	1	4.09
	SS	R. McMillan	479	.263	3	62	319	511	21	105	5.7	.975	J. Nuxhall	44	201	13	11	3	3.72
	3B	R. Jablonski	407	.256	15	66	117	172	9	11	2.3	.970	A. Fowler	45	178	11	11	1	4.05
	RF	W. Post	539	.249	36	83	292	16	10	1	2.3	.969	H. Jeffcoat	38	171	8	2	2	3.84
	CF	G. Bell	603	.292	29	84	330	12	5	4	2.3	.986	H. Freeman	64	109	14	5	18	3.40
	LF	F. Robinson	572	.290	38	83	323	5	8	1	2.2	.976							
	C	E. Bailey	383	.300	28	75	511	52	9	10	5.4	.984							
	C	S. Burgess	229	.275	12	39	257	18	0	2	5.0	1.000							
	1B	G. Crowe	144	.250	10	23	225	25	3	15	7.9	.988							
	OF	B. Thurman	139	.295	8	22	39	2	2	1	1.5	.953							
St. Louis W-76 L-78 Fred Hutchinson	1B	S. Musial	594	.310	27	109	870	90	7	96	9.4	.993	V. Mizell	33	209	14	14	0	3.62
	2B	Blasingame	587	.261	0	27	280	303	8	89	6.0	.986	T. Poholsky	33	203	9	14	0	3.59
	SS	A. Dark	413	.286	4	37	178	292	20	66	4.9	.959	M. Dickson	28	196	13	8	0	3.07
	3B	K. Boyer	595	.306	26	98	130	309	18	37	3.1	.961	H. Wehmeier	34	171	12	9	1	3.69
	RF	W. Moon	540	.298	16	68	159	8	2	2	1.7	.988	W. Schmidt	33	148	6	8	1	3.84
	CF	B. Del Greco	270	.215	5	18	217	3	3	0	2.0	.987	L. McDaniel	39	116	7	6	0	3.40
	LF	R. Repulski	376	.277	11	55	187	3	5	0	2.3	.974	L. Jackson	51	85	2	2	9	4.11
	C	H. Smith	227	.282	5	23	300	34	6	3	5.2	.982	J. Collum	38	60	6	2	7	4.20
	OF	W. Lockman	193	.249	0	10	103	2	5	0	1.9	.955							
	C	R. Katt	158	.259	6	20	231	16	4	0	5.3	.984							
	OF	H. Sauer	151	.298	5	24	55	2	0	1	1.5	1.000							
	C	B. Sarni	148	.291	5	22	219	25*	2	1*	6.0	.992							
	UT	B. Morgan	113	.195	3	20	42	56	6	6		.942							
Philadelphia W-71 L-83 Mayo Smith	1B	M. Blaylock	460	.254	10	50	949	72	8	86	8.3	.992	R. Roberts	43	297	19	18	3	4.45
	2B	T. Kazanski	379	.211	4	34	246	261	11	68	4.5	.979	H. Haddix	31	207	12	8	2	3.48
	SS	G. Hamner	401	.224	4	42	177	302	32	69	4.6	.937	C. Simmons	33	198	15	10	0	3.36
	3B	W. Jones	520	.277	17	78	202	264	13	23	3.2	.973	B. Miller	49	122	3	6	5	3.24
	RF	E. Valo	291	.289	5	37	167	4	6	0	2.0	.966	S. Rogovin	22	107	7	6	0	4.98
	CF	R. Ashburn	628	.303	3	50	503	11	9	3	3.4	.983	S. Miller	24	107	5	8	0	4.47
	LF	D. Ennis	630	.260	26	95	269	8	11	0	1.9	.962	J. Meyer	41	96	7	11	2	4.41
	C	S. Lopata	535	.267	32	95	573	24	11	10	6.0	.982							
	OF	Greengrass	215	.205	5	25	104	3	1	1	1.7	.991							
	2B	S. Hemus	187	.289	5	24	94	93	5	18	3.9	.974							
	SS	R. Smalley	168	.226	0	16	81	142	12	32	3.9	.949							
	C	A. Seminick	161	.199	7	23	266	23	7	2	5.5	.976							

NATIONAL LEAGUE 1956, *cont.*

	POS	Player	AB	BA	HR	RBI	PO	A	E	DP	TC/G	FA	Pitcher	G	IP	W	L	SV	ERA
New York W-67 L-87 Bill Rigney	1B	B. White	508	.256	22	59	**1256**	111	15	106	10.0	.989	J. Antonelli	41	258	20	13	1	2.86
	2B	Schoendienst	334	.296	2	14	199	215	3	52	4.9	.993*	R. Gomez	40	196	7	17	0	4.58
	SS	D. Spencer	489	.221	14	42	113	169	6	33	4.4	.979	Worthington	28	166	7	14	0	3.97
	3B	F. Castleman	385	.226	14	45	90	213	17	10	3.0	.947	J. Hearn	30	129	5	11	1	3.97
	RF	D. Mueller	453	.269	5	41	180	4	2	2	1.6	.989	Littlefield	31	97	4	4	2	4.08
	CF	W. Mays	578	.296	36	84	415	14	9	6	2.9	.979	J. Margoneri	23	92	6	6	0	3.93
	LF	J. Brandt	351	.299	11	47	165	8	2	0	1.8	.989*	H. Wilhelm	64	89	4	9	8	3.83
	C	B. Sarni	238	.231	5	23	367	36*	3	9*	5.4	.993	W. McCall	46	77	3	4	7	3.61
	OF	D. Rhodes	244	.217	8	33	85	6	4	1	1.4	.958							
	SS	A. Dark	206	.252	2	17	89	132	9	27	4.8	.961							
	3B	H. Thompson	183	.235	8	29	25	94	12	7	3.0	.908							
	OF	W. Lockman	169	.272	1	10	69	3	3	1	1.9	.960							
	SS	E. Bressoud	163	.227	0	9	67	125	10	26	4.2	.950							
Pittsburgh W-66 L-88 Bobby Bragan	1B	D. Long	517	.263	27	91	1201	99	**24**	92	9.6	.982	B. Friend	49	**314**	17	17	3	3.46
	2B	B. Mazeroski	255	.243	3	14	163	242	8	56	5.1	.981	R. Kline	44	264	14	**18**	2	3.38
	SS	D. Groat	520	.273	0	37	287	420	**34**	74	5.3	.954	V. Law	39	196	8	16	2	4.32
	3B	F. Thomas	588	.282	25	80	118	176	18	21	2.8	.942	R. Face	**68**	135	12	13	6	3.52
	RF	R. Clemente	543	.311	7	60	274	17	**13**	2	2.2	.957	G. Munger	35	107	3	4	2	4.04
	CF	B. Virdon	509	.334	8	37	334	10	4	2	2.7	.989	N. King	38	60	4	1	5	3.15
	LF	L. Walls	474	.274	11	54	284	10	10	1	2.3	.967							
	C	J. Shepard	256	.242	7	30	356	36	4	4	4.6	.990							
	O1	B. Skinner	233	.202	5	29	216	8	2	21		.991							
	C	H. Foiles	222	.212	7	25	291	30	4	8	4.5	.988							
	32	G. Freese	207	.208	3	14	69	115	4	9		.979							
Chicago W-60 L-94 Stan Hack	1B	D. Fondy	543	.269	9	46	1048	94	17	101	8.7	.985	B. Rush	32	240	13	10	0	3.19
	2B	G. Baker	546	.258	12	57	362	426	**25**	99	5.8	.969	S. Jones	33	189	9	14	0	3.91
	SS	E. Banks	538	.297	28	85	279	357	25	92	4.8	.962	W. Hacker	34	168	3	13	0	4.66
	3B	D. Hoak	424	.215	5	37	122	158	15	16	2.7	.949	D. Kaiser	27	150	4	9	0	3.59
	RF	W. Moryn	529	.285	23	67	268	18	5	2	1.8	.983	J. Davis	46	120	5	7	2	3.66
	CF	P. Whisenant	314	.239	11	46	242	6	2	0	2.7	.992	T. Lown	61	111	9	8	13	3.58
	LF	M. Irvin	339	.271	15	50	216	6	2	0	2.3	.991	Valentinetti	42	95	6	4	1	3.78
	C	H. Landrith	312	.221	4	32	483	55	**14**	9	5.6	.975	J. Brosnan	30	95	5	9	1	3.79
	UT	E. Miksis	356	.239	9	27	144	151	7	14		.977							
	OF	J. King	317	.249	15	54	187	10	2	2	2.4	.990							
	OF	S. Drake	215	.256	2	15	142	3	1	1	2.8	.993							
	C	H. Chiti	203	.212	4	18	327	35	7	2	5.5	.981							

BATTING AND BASE RUNNING LEADERS

Batting Average
H. Aaron, MIL .328
B. Virdon, PIT, STL .319
R. Clemente, PIT .311
S. Musial, STL .310
K. Boyer, STL .306

Slugging Average
D. Snider, BKN .598
J. Adcock, MIL .597
H. Aaron, MIL .558
F. Robinson, CIN .558
W. Mays, NY .557

Home Runs
D. Snider, BKN 43
J. Adcock, MIL 38
F. Robinson, CIN 38
E. Mathews, MIL 37
W. Post, CIN 36
W. Mays, NY 36

Winning Percentage
D. Newcombe, BKN .794
B. Buhl, MIL .692
L. Burdette, MIL .655
B. Lawrence, CIN .655
W. Spahn, MIL .645

PITCHING LEADERS

Earned Run Average
L. Burdette, MIL 2.70
W. Spahn, MIL 2.78
J. Antonelli, NY 2.86
S. Maglie, BKN 2.87
D. Newcombe, BKN 3.06

Wins
D. Newcombe, BKN 27
W. Spahn, MIL 20
J. Antonelli, NY 20
L. Burdette, MIL 19
B. Lawrence, CIN 19
R. Roberts, PHI 19

Total Bases
H. Aaron, MIL 340
D. Snider, BKN 324
W. Mays, NY 322
F. Robinson, CIN 319
S. Musial, STL 310

Runs Batted In
S. Musial, STL 109
J. Adcock, MIL 103
Kluszewski, CIN 102
D. Snider, BKN 101
K. Boyer, STL 98

Stolen Bases
W. Mays, NY 40
J. Gilliam, BKN 21
B. White, NY 15
J. Temple, CIN 14
P. Reese, BKN 13

Saves
C. Labine, BKN 19
H. Freeman, CIN 18
T. Lown, CHI 13
D. Bessent, BKN 9
L. Jackson, STL 9

Strikeouts
S. Jones, CHI 176
H. Haddix, PHI, STL 170
B. Friend, PIT 166
R. Roberts, PHI 157
V. Mizell, STL 153

Complete Games
R. Roberts, PHI 22
W. Spahn, MIL 20
B. Friend, PIT 19
D. Newcombe, BKN 18
L. Burdette, MIL 16

Hits
H. Aaron, MIL 200
R. Ashburn, PHI 190
B. Virdon, PIT, STL 185
S. Musial, STL 184

Base on Balls
D. Snider, BKN 99
J. Gilliam, BKN 95
W. Jones, PHI 92
E. Mathews, MIL 91

Home Run Percentage
J. Adcock, MIL 8.4
D. Snider, BKN 7.9
Kluszewski, CIN 6.8
E. Mathews, MIL 6.7

Fewest Hits/9 Innings
S. Maglie, BKN 7.26
D. Newcombe, BKN 7.35
S. Jones, CHI 7.39
V. Mizell, STL 7.42

Shutouts
L. Burdette, MIL 6
J. Antonelli, NY 6
D. Newcombe, BKN 5
B. Friend, PIT 4

Fewest Walks/9 Innings
R. Roberts, PHI 1.21
D. Newcombe, BKN 1.54
W. Spahn, MIL 1.66
A. Fowler, CIN 1.77

Runs Scored
F. Robinson, CIN 122
D. Snider, BKN 112
H. Aaron, MIL 106
E. Mathews, MIL 103

Doubles
H. Aaron, MIL 34
S. Lopata, PHI 33
D. Snider, BKN 33
S. Musial, STL 33

Triples
B. Bruton, MIL 15
H. Aaron, MIL 14
L. Walls, PIT 11
W. Moon, STL 11

Most Strikeouts/9 Inn.
S. Jones, CHI 8.40
H. Haddix, PHI, STL 6.64
V. Mizell, STL 6.60
J. Nuxhall, CIN 5.38

Innings
B. Friend, PIT 314
R. Roberts, PHI 297
W. Spahn, MIL 281
D. Newcombe, BKN 268

Games Pitched
R. Face, PIT 68
H. Freeman, CIN 64
H. Wilhelm, NY 64
C. Labine, BKN 62

NATIONAL LEAGUE 1956, *cont.*

	W	L	PCT	GB	R	OR	Batting 2B	3B	HR	BA	SA	SB	Fielding E	DP	FA	Pitching CG	BB	SO	ShO	SV	ERA
Brooklyn	93	61	.604		720	601	212	36	179	.258	.419	65	**111**	149	**.981**	46	441	**772**	12	30	3.57
Milwaukee	92	62	.597	1	709	**569**	212	54	177	.259	.423	29	130	159	.979	**64**	467	639	12	27	**3.11**
Cincinnati	91	63	.591	2	**775**	658	201	32	**221**	.266	**.441**	45	113	147	.981	47	458	653	4	29	3.85
St. Louis	76	78	.494	17	678	698	**234**	49	124	**.268**	.399	41	134	**172**	.978	41	546	709	12	30	3.97
Philadelphia	71	83	.461	22	668	738	207	49	121	.252	.381	45	144	140	.975	57	**437**	750	4	15	4.20
New York	67	87	.435	26	540	650	192	45	145	.244	.382	**67**	144	143	.976	31	551	765	9	28	3.78
Pittsburgh	66	88	.429	27	588	653	199	**57**	110	.257	.380	24	162	140	.973	37	469	662	8	24	3.74
Chicago	60	94	.390	33	597	708	202	50	142	.244	.382	55	144	141	.976	37	613	744	6	17	3.96
					5275	5275	1659	372	1219	.256	.401	371	1082	1191	.977	360	3982	5694	67	200	3.77

AMERICAN LEAGUE 1956

POS	Player	AB	BA	HR	RBI	PO	A	E	DP	TC/G	FA	Pitcher	G	IP	W	L	SV	ERA
New York W-97 L-57 Casey Stengel																		
1B	B. Skowron	464	.308	23	90	968	**80**	7	**138**	8.8	.993	W. Ford	31	226	19	6	1	**2.47**
2B	B. Martin	458	.264	9	49	241	260	10	84	4.9	.980	J. Kucks	34	224	18	9	0	3.85
SS	McDougald	438	.311	13	56	177	273	14	77	5.0	.970	D. Larsen	38	180	11	5	1	3.26
3B	A. Carey	422	.237	7	50	114	265	21	26	3.1	.948	Sturdivant	32	158	16	8	5	3.30
RF	H. Bauer	539	.241	26	84	242	10	8	2	1.8	.969	B. Turley	27	132	8	4	1	5.05
CF	M. Mantle	533	**.353**	52	130	370	10	4	3	2.7	.990	T. Byrne	37	110	7	3	6	3.36
LF	E. Howard	290	.262	5	34	97	2	1	0	1.5	.990	R. Coleman	29	88	3	5	2	3.67
C	Y. Berra	521	.298	30	105	**732**	55	11	15	5.9	.986	B. Grim	26	75	6	1	5	2.77
O1	J. Collins	262	.225	7	43	346	32	1	37		.997	T. Morgan	41	71	6	7	11	4.16
UT	J. Coleman	183	.257	0	18	138	152	9	46		.970							
OF	N. Siebern	162	.204	4	21	100	1	3	0	2.0	.971							
OF	B. Cerv	115	.304	3	25	59	4	1	2	1.5	.984							
Cleveland W-88 L-66 Al Lopez																		
1B	V. Wertz	481	.264	32	106	**971**	77	9	99	7.9	.991	E. Wynn	38	278	20	9	2	2.72
2B	B. Avila	513	.224	10	54	322	351	16	83	5.1	.977	B. Lemon	39	255	20	14	3	3.03
SS	Carrasquel	474	.243	7	48	240	352	20	70	4.3	.967	H. Score	35	249	20	9	0	2.53
3B	A. Rosen	416	.267	15	61	89	219	18	20	2.8	.945	M. Garcia	35	198	11	12	0	3.78
RF	R. Colavito	322	.276	21	65	177	6	6	0	1.9	.968	D. Mossi	48	88	6	5	11	3.59
CF	J. Busby	494	.235	12	50	344	3	4	0	2.6	.989							
LF	A. Smith	526	.274	16	71	248	6	5	1	2.1	.981							
C	J. Hegan	315	.222	6	34	648	28	10	5	5.8	.985							
OF	G. Woodling	317	.262	8	38	154	3	3	0	1.9	.981							
UT	Strickland	171	.211	3	17	118	145	9	34		.981							
1B	P. Ward	150	.253	6	21	226	21	3	20	4.2	.988							
OF	S. Mele	114	.254	4	20	29	2	1	0	1.6	.969							
Chicago W-85 L-69 Marty Marion																		
1B	W. Dropo	361	.266	8	52	855	50	6	95	7.8	**.993**	B. Pierce	35	276	20	9	1	3.32
2B	N. Fox	**649**	.296	4	52	**478**	**396**	12	124	5.8	.986	D. Donovan	34	235	12	10	0	3.64
SS	L. Aparicio	533	.266	3	56	**250**	**474**	35	91	5.0	.954	J. Harshman	34	227	15	11	0	3.10
3B	F. Hatfield	321	.262	7	33	83	189	11	21	2.8	.961	J. Wilson	28	160	9	12	0	4.06
RF	J. Rivera	491	.255	12	66	271	9	7	4	2.1	.976	B. Keegan	20	105	5	7	0	3.93
CF	L. Doby	504	.268	24	102	371	4	5	2	2.8	.987	G. Staley	26	102	8	3	0	2.92
LF	M. Minoso	545	.316	21	88	284	10	8	1	2.0	.974	D. Howell	34	64	5	6	4	4.62
C	S. Lollar	450	.293	11	75	679	40	5	6	5.5	**.993**							
1O	D. Philley	279	.265	4	47	349	19	7	31		.981							
3B	S. Esposito	184	.228	3	25	41	109	6	17	2.6	.962							
C	L. Moss	127	.244	10	22	149	10	1	1	3.3	.994							
PH	R. Northey	48	.354	3	23													
Boston W-84 L-70 Pinky Higgins																		
1B	M. Vernon	403	.310	15	84	930	58	**11**	96	**9.3**	.989	T. Brewer	32	244	19	9	0	3.50
2B	B. Goodman	399	.293	2	38	215	266	**17**	69	5.2	.966	F. Sullivan	34	242	14	7	0	3.42
SS	D. Buddin	377	.239	5	37	213	370	29	**98**	5.4	.953	W. Nixon	23	145	9	8	0	4.21
3B	B. Klaus	520	.271	7	59	120	242	21	18	3.6	.945	D. Sisler	39	142	9	8	3	4.62
RF	J. Jensen	578	.315	20	97	291	13	12	2	2.1	.962	M. Parnell	21	131	7	6	0	3.77
CF	J. Piersall	601	.293	14	87	**455**	10	4	1	3.0	.991	I. Delock	48	128	13	7	4	4.21
LF	T. Williams	400	.345	24	82	174	7	5	2	1.7	.973	Porterfield	25	126	3	12	5	5.14
C	S. White	392	.245	5	44	547	**60**	11	13	5.4	.984	T. Hurd	40	76	3	4	5	5.33
O1	D. Gernert	306	.291	16	68	367	41	4	38		.990							
2B	T. Lepcio	284	.261	15	51	143	166	11	47	5.6	.966							
C	P. Daley	187	.267	5	29	228	14	2	1	4.3	.992							
Detroit W-82 L-72 Bucky Harris																		
1B	E. Torgeson	318	.264	12	42	623	32	5	62	8.0	.992	F. Lary	41	**294**	**21**	13	1	3.15
2B	F. Bolling	366	.281	7	45	223	260	11	72	4.8	.978	P. Foytack	43	256	15	13	1	3.59
SS	H. Kuenn	591	.332	12	88	219	388	20	86	4.4	**.968**	B. Hoeft	38	248	20	14	0	4.06
3B	R. Boone	481	.308	25	81	151	243	17	23	3.2	.959	S. Gromek	40	141	8	6	4	4.28
RF	A. Kaline	617	.314	27	128	343	**18**	6	4	3.2	.984	V. Trucks	22	120	6	5	1	3.83
CF	B. Tuttle	546	.253	9	65	348	13	9	2	2.7	.976	A. Aber	42	63	4	4	7	3.43
LF	C. Maxwell	500	.326	28	87	281	12	4	1	2.2	.987							
C	F. House	321	.240	10	44	450	33	7	8	5.6	.986							
C	R. Wilson	228	.289	7	38	393	34	4	7	5.5	.991							
1B	J. Phillips	224	.295	1	20	422	32	9	49	8.3	.981							
O3	B. Kennedy	177	.232	4	22	87	40	12	3		.914							
S2	Brideweser	156	.218	0	10	111	134	5	32		.980							
1B	W. Belardi	154	.279	6	15	240	17	3	21	8.4	.988							

AMERICAN LEAGUE 1956, cont.

	POS	Player	AB	BA	HR	RBI	PO	A	E	DP	TC/G	FA	Pitcher	G	IP	W	L	SV	ERA
Baltimore	1B	B. Boyd	225	.311	2	11	469	24	5	46	8.3	.990	R. Moore	32	185	12	7	0	4.18
	2B	B. Gardner	515	.231	11	50	274	331	16	76	4.7	.974	C. Johnson	26	184	9	10	0	3.43
W-69 L-85	SS	W. Miranda	461	.217	2	34	229	436	26	91	4.7	.962	B. Wight	35	175	9	12	0	4.02
	3B	G. Kell	345	.261	8	37	97	165	7	19	2.8	.974*	H. Brown	35	152	9	7	2	4.04
Paul Richards	RF	T. Francona	445	.258	9	57	240	10	6	1	2.1	.977	E. Palica	29	116	4	11	0	4.49
	CF	D. Williams	353	.286	11	37	205	2	2	0	2.6	.990	M. Fornieles	30	111	4	7	1	3.97
	LF	B. Nieman	388	.322	12	64	243	4	5	1	2.2	.980	D. Ferrarese	36	102	4	10	2	5.03
	C	G. Triandos	452	.279	21	88	417	50	5	12	5.3	.989	G. Zuverink	**62**	97	7	6	16	4.16
	C	H. Smith	229	.262	3	18	313	33	2	11	4.9	.994	B. Loes	21	57	2	7	3	4.76
	1B	B. Hale	207	.237	1	24	366	29	10	33	7.9	.975							
	OF	J. Pyburn	156	.173	2	11	114	5	3	3	1.6	.975							
Washington	1B	R. Sievers	550	.253	29	95	638	51	7	75	9.2	.990	C. Stobbs	37	240	15	15	1	3.60
	2B	P. Runnels	578	.310	8	76	179	177	10	56	4.3	.973	C. Pascual	39	189	6	18	2	5.87
W-59 L-95	SS	Valdivielso	246	.236	4	29	144	266	23	58	4.8	.947	P. Ramos	37	152	12	10	0	5.27
	3B	E. Yost	515	.231	11	53	164	303	18	31	3.6	.963	D. Stone	41	132	5	7	3	6.27
Chuck Dressen	RF	J. Lemon	538	.271	27	96	301	11	**12**	6	2.3	.963	B. Wiesler	37	123	3	12	0	6.44
	CF	K. Olson	313	.246	4	22	192	4	2	0	2.0	.990	B. Stewart	33	105	5	7	2	5.57
	LF	W. Herzog	421	.245	4	35	240	9	5	0	2.5	.980	B. Chakales	43	96	4	4	4	4.03
	C	C. Courtney	283	.300	5	44	290	35	7	7	4.4	.979	G. Grob	37	79	4	5	1	7.83
	2B	H. Plews	256	.270	1	25	137	166	**17**	38	4.8	.947	B. Byerly	25	52	2	4	4	2.96
	C	L. Berberet	207	.261	4	27	266	28	1	6	5.0	.997							
Kansas City	1B	V. Power	530	.309	14	63	671	62	5	73	9.7	.993	A. Ditmar	44	254	12	**22**	1	4.42
	2B	J. Finigan	250	.216	2	21	114	105	7	35	4.3	.969	T. Gorman	52	171	9	10	3	3.83
W-52 L-102	SS	DeMaestri	434	.233	6	39	210	407	23	95	4.8	.964	J. Crimian	54	129	4	8	3	5.51
	3B	H. Lopez	561	.273	18	69	152	254	**26**	23	3.6	.940	W. Burnette	18	121	6	8	0	2.89
Lou Boudreau	RF	H. Simpson	543	.293	21	105	188	3	7	2	1.8	.965	L. Kretlow	25	119	4	9	0	5.31
	CF	J. Groth	244	.258	5	37	140	8	0	3	1.8	1.000	T. Herriage	31	103	1	13	0	6.64
	LF	L. Skizas	297	.316	11	39	148	9	4	0	2.2	.975	B. Shantz	45	101	2	7	9	4.35
	C	T. Thompson	268	.272	1	27	328	38	7	7	5.5	.981	A. Kellner	20	92	7	4	0	4.32
	OF	G. Zernial	272	.224	16	44	111	9	2	1	1.8	.984							
	OF	A. Pilarcik	239	.251	4	22	154	9	4	1	2.5	.976							
	OF	E. Slaughter	223	.278	2	23	105	1	2	0	1.9	.981							
	C	J. Ginsberg	195	.246	1	12	238	28	3	3	4.7	.989							
	1B	E. Robinson	172	.198	2	12	360	19	9	43	8.3	.977							
	C	H. Smith	142	.275	2	24	183	22	3	3	5.8	.986							

BATTING AND BASE RUNNING LEADERS

Batting Average
M. Mantle, NY	.353
T. Williams, BOS	.345
H. Kuenn, DET	.332
C. Maxwell, DET	.326
B. Nieman, BAL, CHI	.320

Slugging Average
M. Mantle, NY	.705
T. Williams, BOS	.605
C. Maxwell, DET	.534
Y. Berra, NY	.534
A. Kaline, DET	.530

Home Runs
M. Mantle, NY	52
V. Wertz, CLE	32
Y. Berra, NY	30
R. Sievers, WAS	29
C. Maxwell, DET	28

Total Bases
M. Mantle, NY	376
A. Kaline, DET	327
J. Jensen, BOS	287
M. Minoso, CHI	286
Y. Berra, NY	278
H. Kuenn, DET	278

Runs Batted In
M. Mantle, NY	130
A. Kaline, DET	128
V. Wertz, CLE	106
Y. Berra, NY	105
H. Simpson, KC	105

Stolen Bases
L. Aparicio, CHI	21
J. Rivera, CHI	20
B. Avila, CLE	17
M. Minoso, CHI	12
T. Francona, BAL	11
J. Jensen, BOS	11

Hits
H. Kuenn, DET	196
A. Kaline, DET	194
N. Fox, CHI	192
M. Mantle, NY	188

Base on Balls
E. Yost, WAS	151
M. Mantle, NY	112
T. Williams, BOS	102
L. Doby, CHI	102

Home Run Percentage
M. Mantle, NY	9.8
V. Wertz, CLE	6.7
T. Williams, BOS	6.0
Y. Berra, NY	5.8

Runs Scored
M. Mantle, NY	132
N. Fox, CHI	109
M. Minoso, CHI	106

Doubles
J. Piersall, BOS	40
H. Kuenn, DET	32
A. Kaline, DET	32

Triples
J. Lemon, WAS	11
H. Simpson, KC	11
M. Minoso, CHI	11
J. Jensen, BOS	11

PITCHING LEADERS

Winning Percentage
W. Ford, NY	.760
B. Pierce, CHI	.690
H. Score, CLE	.690
E. Wynn, CLE	.690
T. Brewer, BOS	.679

Earned Run Average
W. Ford, NY	2.47
H. Score, CLE	2.53
E. Wynn, CLE	2.72
B. Lemon, CLE	3.03
J. Harshman, CHI	3.10

Wins
F. Lary, DET	21
B. Pierce, CHI	20
H. Score, CLE	20
E. Wynn, CLE	20
B. Hoeft, DET	20
B. Lemon, CLE	20

Saves
G. Zuverink, BAL	16
T. Morgan, NY	11
D. Mossi, CLE	11
I. Delock, BOS	9
B. Shantz, KC	9

Strikeouts
H. Score, CLE	263
B. Pierce, CHI	192
P. Foytack, DET	184
B. Hoeft, DET	172
F. Lary, DET	165

Complete Games
B. Pierce, CHI	21
B. Lemon, CLE	21
F. Lary, DET	20
W. Ford, NY	18
B. Hoeft, DET	18
E. Wynn, CLE	18

Fewest Hits/9 Innings
H. Score, CLE	5.85
D. Larsen, NY	6.66
J. Harshman, CHI	7.27
T. Brewer, BOS	7.37

Shutouts
H. Score, CLE	5
M. Garcia, CLE	4
J. Harshman, CHI	4
T. Brewer, BOS	4

Fewest Walks/9 Innings
C. Stobbs, WAS	2.03
D. Donovan, CHI	2.26
J. Kucks, NY	2.89
E. Wynn, CLE	2.95

Most Strikeouts/9 Inn.
H. Score, CLE	9.49
C. Pascual, WAS	7.73
P. Foytack, DET	6.47
B. Pierce, CHI	6.25

Innings
F. Lary, DET	294
E. Wynn, CLE	278
B. Pierce, CHI	276
P. Foytack, DET	256

Games Pitched
G. Zuverink, BAL	62
J. Crimian, KC	54
T. Gorman, KC	52
I. Delock, BOS	48

AMERICAN LEAGUE 1956, *cont.*

	W	L	PCT	GB	R	OR	2B	3B	HR	BA	SA	SB	E	DP	FA	CG	BB	SO	ShO	SV	ERA
New York	97	57	.630		**857**	631	193	55	**190**	.270	**.434**	51	136	**214**	.977	50	652	732	9	**35**	3.63
Cleveland	88	66	.571	9	712	**581**	199	23	153	.244	.381	40	129	130	.978	**67**	564	**845**	**17**	24	**3.32**
Chicago	85	69	.552	12	776	634	218	43	128	.267	.397	**70**	**122**	160	**.979**	65	**524**	722	11	13	3.73
Boston	84	70	.545	13	780	751	**261**	45	139	.275	.419	28	169	168	.972	50	668	712	8	20	4.17
Detroit	82	72	.532	15	789	699	209	50	150	**.279**	.420	43	140	151	.976	62	655	788	10	15	4.06
Baltimore	69	85	.448	28	571	705	198	34	91	.244	.350	39	137	142	.977	38	547	715	10	24	4.20
Washington	59	95	.383	38	652	924	198	**62**	112	.250	.377	37	171	173	.972	36	730	663	1	18	5.33
Kansas City	52	102	.338	45	619	831	204	41	112	.252	.370	40	166	187	.973	30	679	636	3	18	4.86
					5756	5756	1680	353	1075	.260	.394	348	1170	1325	.975	398	5019	5813	69	167	4.16

NATIONAL LEAGUE 1957

Milwaukee
W-95 L-59 — Fred Haney

POS	Player	AB	BA	HR	RBI	PO	A	E	DP	TC/G	FA	Pitcher	G	IP	W	L	SV	ERA
1B	F. Torre	364	.272	5	40	859	71	4	89	8.0	**.996**	W. Spahn	39	271	**21**	11	3	2.69
2B	Schoendienst	394	.310	6	32	238	282	7	72	5.7	.987	L. Burdette	37	257	17	9	0	3.72
SS	J. Logan	494	.273	10	49	263	**440**	29	94	**5.7**	.960	B. Buhl	34	217	18	7	0	2.74
3B	E. Mathews	572	.292	32	94	131	**299**	16	27	3.0	.964	G. Conley	35	148	9	9	1	3.16
RF	H. Aaron	615	.322	**44**	**132**	346	9	6	0	2.4	.983	Trowbridge	32	126	7	5	1	3.64
CF	B. Bruton	306	.278	5	30	206	5	4	2	2.7	.981	J. Pizarro	24	99	5	6	0	4.62
LF	W. Covington	328	.284	21	65	150	9	3	1	1.8	.981	E. Johnson	30	65	7	3	4	3.88
C	D. Crandall	383	.253	15	46	414	**59**	6	11	4.7	.987	D. McMahon	32	47	2	3	9	1.54
OF	A. Pafko	220	.277	8	27	108	1	2	1	1.6	.982							
1B	J. Adcock	209	.287	12	38	477	30	2	60	9.1	.996							
2B	D. O'Connell	183	.235	1	8	128	145	5	43	5.8	.982							
UT	F. Mantilla	182	.236	4	21	87	136	12	28		.949							
OF	B. Thomson	148	.236	4	23	78	2	1	0	2.1	.988							
C	D. Rice	144	.229	9	20	235	14	2	3	5.2	.992							
OF	B. Hazle	134	.403	7	27	57	1	6	0	1.6	.906							

St. Louis
W-87 L-67 — Fred Hutchinson

POS	Player	AB	BA	HR	RBI	PO	A	E	DP	TC/G	FA	Pitcher	G	IP	W	L	SV	ERA
1B	S. Musial	502	**.351**	29	102	1167	99	10	131	**9.8**	.992	L. Jackson	41	210	15	9	1	3.47
2B	Blasingame	650	.271	8	58	372	**512**	14	128	5.8	.984	L. McDaniel	30	191	15	9	0	3.49
SS	A. Dark	583	.290	4	64	**276**	419	25	105	5.2	.965	S. Jones	28	183	12	9	0	3.60
3B	E. Kasko	479	.273	1	35	100	224	13	21	2.8	.961	H. Wehmeier	36	165	10	7	0	4.31
RF	D. Ennis	490	.286	24	105	180	3	11	0	1.5	.943	V. Mizell	33	149	8	10	0	3.74
CF	K. Boyer	544	.265	19	62	275	2	1	1	2.6	**.996**	W. Schmidt	40	117	10	3	0	4.78
LF	W. Moon	516	.295	24	73	245	8	9	1	2.0	.966	V. McDaniel	17	87	7	5	0	3.22
C	H. Smith	333	.279	2	37	468	42	5	8	5.3	.990	L. Merritt	44	65	1	2	7	3.31
1O	Cunningham	261	.318	9	52	360	18	3	17		.992	H. Wilhelm	40	55	1	4	11	4.25
C	H. Landrith	214	.243	3	26	339	29	5	3	5.6	.987	B. Muffett	23	44	3	2	8	2.25
OF	B. Smith	185	.211	3	18	138	6	4	4	1.9	.973							

Brooklyn
W-84 L-70 — Walter Alston

POS	Player	AB	BA	HR	RBI	PO	A	E	DP	TC/G	FA	Pitcher	G	IP	W	L	SV	ERA
1B	G. Hodges	579	.299	27	98	**1317**	115	14	115	9.6	.990	D. Drysdale	34	221	17	9	0	2.69
2B	J. Gilliam	617	.250	2	37	**407**	390	11	90	5.5	.986	D. Newcombe	28	199	11	12	0	3.49
SS	C. Neal	448	.270	12	62	151	298	24	60	4.7	.949	J. Podres	31	196	12	9	3	**2.66**
3B	P. Reese	330	.224	1	29	51	166	13	5	3.1	.943	D. McDevitt	22	119	7	4	0	3.25
RF	C. Furillo	395	.306	12	66	153	7	2	1	1.5	.988	R. Craig	32	111	6	9	0	4.61
CF	D. Snider	508	.274	40	92	304	6	3	1	2.3	.990	C. Labine	58	104	5	7	17	3.44
LF	G. Cimoli	532	.293	10	57	265	11	6	2	2.0	.979	S. Koufax	34	104	5	4	0	3.88
C	Campanella	330	.242	13	62	618	51	5	5	**6.7**	.993	S. Maglie	19	101	6	6	1	2.93
3S	D. Zimmer	269	.219	6	19	99	170	13	20		.954	E. Roebuck	44	96	8	2	8	2.71
OF	S. Amoros	238	.277	7	26	122	2	2	0	1.9	.984							
C	R. Walker	166	.181	2	23	230	20	2	3	5.0	.992							
OF	E. Valo	161	.273	4	26	57	0	0		1.6	1.000							

Cincinnati
W-80 L-74 — Birdie Tebbetts

POS	Player	AB	BA	HR	RBI	PO	A	E	DP	TC/G	FA	Pitcher	G	IP	W	L	SV	ERA
1B	G. Crowe	494	.271	31	92	932	86	11	86	8.6	.989	B. Lawrence	49	250	16	13	4	3.52
2B	J. Temple	557	.284	0	37	391	372	20	81	5.4	.974	H. Jeffcoat	37	207	12	13	0	4.52
SS	R. McMillan	448	.272	1	55	253	418	16	86	4.5	**.977**	J. Nuxhall	39	174	10	10	1	4.75
3B	D. Hoak	529	.293	19	89	**193**	269	14	29	3.2	**.971**	D. Gross	43	148	7	9	1	4.31
RF	W. Post	467	.244	20	74	252	12	4	4	2.2	.985	Klippstein	46	146	8	11	3	5.05
CF	G. Bell	510	.292	13	61	311	7	4	4	2.7	.988	T. Acker	49	109	10	5	4	4.97
LF	F. Robinson	611	.322	29	75	336	11	4	3	2.6	.989	H. Freeman	52	84	7	2	8	4.52
C	E. Bailey	391	.261	20	48	542	41	5	5	5.1	.991	R. Sanchez	38	62	3	2	5	4.76
C	S. Burgess	205	.283	14	39	223	15	3	0	5.4	.988							
OF	B. Thurman	190	.247	16	40	75	3	1	1	1.8	.987							
1B	Kluszewski	127	.268	6	21	161	15	2	11	7.7	.989							

Philadelphia
W-77 L-77 — Mayo Smith

POS	Player	AB	BA	HR	RBI	PO	A	E	DP	TC/G	FA	Pitcher	G	IP	W	L	SV	ERA
1B	E. Bouchee	574	.293	17	76	1182	**125**	16	93	8.6	.988	R. Roberts	39	250	10	**22**	2	4.07
2B	G. Hamner	502	.227	10	62	260	282	**21**	54	4.5	.963	J. Sanford	33	237	19	8	0	3.08
SS	C. Fernandez	500	.262	5	51	241	377	26	69	4.3	.960	C. Simmons	32	212	12	11	0	3.44
3B	W. Jones	440	.218	9	47	140	197	12	18	2.8	.966	H. Haddix	27	171	10	13	0	4.06
RF	R. Repulski	516	.260	20	68	264	6	9	2	2.1	.968	D. Cardwell	30	128	4	8	1	4.91
CF	R. Ashburn	626	.297	0	33	**502**	18	7	7	3.4	.987	D. Farrell	52	83	10	2	10	2.38
LF	H. Anderson	400	.268	17	61	213	5	3	1	2.0	.986	B. Miller	32	60	2	5	6	2.69
C	S. Lopata	388	.237	18	67	634	36	8	9	6.3	.988							
OF	B. Bowman	237	.266	6	23	123	8	10	2	1.7	.929							
32	T. Kazanski	185	.265	3	11	63	95	5	21		.969							
C	J. Lonnett	160	.169	5	15	305	16	1	3	5.0	.997							

NATIONAL LEAGUE 1957, *cont.*

	POS	Player	AB	BA	HR	RBI	PO	A	E	DP	TC/G	FA	Pitcher	G	IP	W	L	SV	ERA
New York	1B	W. Lockman	456	.248	7	30	981	71	10	94	10.4	.991	R. Gomez	38	238	15	13	0	3.78
	2B	D. O'Connell	364	.266	7	28	156	194	7	50	5.3	.980	J. Antonelli	40	212	12	18	0	3.77
W-69 L-85	SS	D. Spencer	534	.249	11	50	213	342	29	95	5.3	.950	C. Barclay	37	183	9	9	0	3.44
	3B	R. Jablonski	305	.289	9	57	44	130	11	15	2.6	.941	Worthington	55	158	8	11	4	4.22
Bill Rigney	RF	D. Mueller	450	.258	6	37	174	13	2	4	1.6	.989	S. Miller	38	124	7	9	1	3.63
	CF	W. Mays	585	.333	35	97	422	14	9	5	3.0	.980	R. Crone	25	121	4	8	1	4.33
	LF	H. Sauer	378	.259	26	76	125	4	1	0	1.3	.992	M. Grissom	55	83	4	4	14	2.61
	C	V. Thomas	241	.249	6	31	396	31	4	8	4.9	.991							
	2B	Schoendienst	254	.307	9	33	141	166	5	41	5.5	.984							
	3B	O. Virgil	226	.235	4	24	27	111	11	10	2.4	.926							
	1B	G. Harris	225	.240	9	31	502	37	8	53	9.0	.985							
	OF	B. Thomson	215	.242	8	38	124	2	1	0	1.8	.992							
	OF	D. Rhodes	190	.205	4	19	63	0	0	0	1.4	1.000							
	C	R. Katt	165	.230	2	17	238	25	5	4	3.9	.981							
Chicago	1B	D. Long	397	.305	21	62	908	72	5	81	9.5	.995	M. Drabowsky	36	240	13	15	0	3.53
	2B	B. Morgan	425	.207	5	27	220	343	14	58	5.0	.976	D. Drott	38	229	15	11	0	3.58
W-62 L-92	SS	E. Banks	594	.285	43	102	168	261	11	59	4.4	.975	B. Rush	31	205	6	16	0	4.38
	3B	B. Adams	187	.251	1	10	43	68	6	5	2.5	.949	D. Elston	39	144	6	7	8	3.56
Bob Scheffing	RF	W. Moryn	568	.289	19	88	276	13	12	3	2.0	.960	D. Hillman	32	103	6	11	1	4.35
	CF	C. Tanner	318	.286	7	42	156	5	2	2	2.0	.988	J. Brosnan	41	99	5	5	0	3.38
	LF	L. Walls	366	.240	6	33	174	6	3	0	1.9	.984	T. Lown	67	93	5	7	12	3.77
	C	C. Neeman	415	.258	10	39	703	56	8	13	6.5	.990							
	O1	B. Speake	418	.232	16	50	480	41	7	21		.987							
	OF	J. Bolger	273	.275	5	29	152	4	2	1	2.5	.987							
	UT	J. Kindall	181	.160	6	12	73	109	15	10		.924							
Pittsburgh	1B	D. Fondy	323	.313	2	35	698	54	14	63	10.5	.982	B. Friend	40	277	14	18	0	3.38
	2B	B. Mazeroski	526	.283	8	54	308	443	17	96	5.3	.978	R. Kline	40	205	9	16	0	4.04
W-62 L-92	SS	D. Groat	501	.315	7	54	226	380	20	74	5.1	.968	B. Purkey	48	180	11	14	2	3.86
	3B	G. Freese	346	.283	6	31	62	132	16	16	2.8	.924	V. Law	31	173	10	8	1	2.87
Bobby Bragan	RF	R. Clemente	451	.253	4	30	272	9	6	1	2.6	.979	L. Arroyo	54	131	3	11	1	4.68
W-36 L-67	CF	B. Virdon	561	.251	8	50	403	13	6	2	3.0	.986	R. Face	59	94	4	6	10	3.07
	LF	B. Skinner	387	.305	13	45	172	9	7	2	2.0	.963							
Danny Murtaugh	C	H. Foiles	281	.270	9	36	436	32	9	2	4.4	.981							
W-26 L-25	UT	F. Thomas	594	.290	23	89	729	119	25	60		.971							
	UT	G. Baker	365	.266	2	36	129	219	20	35		.946							

BATTING AND BASE RUNNING LEADERS

Batting Average
S. Musial, STL	.351
W. Mays, NY	.333
F. Robinson, CIN	.322
H. Aaron, MIL	.322
D. Groat, PIT	.315

Slugging Average
W. Mays, NY	.626
S. Musial, STL	.612
H. Aaron, MIL	.600
D. Snider, BKN	.587
E. Banks, CHI	.579

Home Runs
H. Aaron, MIL	44
E. Banks, CHI	43
D. Snider, BKN	40
W. Mays, NY	35
E. Mathews, MIL	32

Hits
Schoendienst, MIL, NY	200
H. Aaron, MIL	198
F. Robinson, CIN	197
W. Mays, NY	195

Base on Balls
J. Temple, CIN	94
R. Ashburn, PHI	94
E. Mathews, MIL	90
E. Bouchee, PHI	84

Home Run Percentage
D. Snider, BKN	7.9
E. Banks, CHI	7.2
H. Aaron, MIL	7.2
G. Crowe, CIN	6.3

Runs Scored
H. Aaron, MIL	118
E. Banks, CHI	113
W. Mays, NY	112
E. Mathews, MIL	109

Doubles
D. Hoak, CIN	39
S. Musial, STL	38
E. Bouchee, PHI	35
E. Banks, CHI	34

Triples
W. Mays, NY	20
B. Virdon, PIT	11
B. Bruton, MIL	9
E. Mathews, MIL	9

Total Bases
H. Aaron, MIL	369
W. Mays, NY	366
E. Banks, CHI	344
F. Robinson, CIN	323
E. Mathews, MIL	309

Runs Batted In
H. Aaron, MIL	132
D. Ennis, STL	105
S. Musial, STL	102
E. Banks, CHI	102
G. Hodges, BKN	98

Stolen Bases
W. Mays, NY	38
J. Gilliam, BKN	26
Blasingame, STL	21
J. Temple, CIN	19
C. Fernandez, PHI	18

PITCHING LEADERS

Winning Percentage
B. Buhl, MIL	.720
J. Sanford, PHI	.704
W. Spahn, MIL	.656
L. Burdette, MIL	.654
D. Drysdale, BKN	.654

Saves
C. Labine, BKN	17
M. Grissom, NY	14
T. Lown, CHI	12
H. Wilhelm, STL	11
D. Farrell, PHI	10
R. Face, PIT	10

Fewest Hits/9 Innings
J. Sanford, PHI	7.38
J. Podres, BKN	7.71
D. Drott, CHI	7.86
B. Buhl, MIL	7.93

Most Strikeouts/9 Inn.
S. Jones, STL	7.59
H. Haddix, PHI	7.17
J. Sanford, PHI	7.15
D. Drott, CHI	6.68

Earned Run Average
J. Podres, BKN	2.66
D. Drysdale, BKN	2.69
W. Spahn, MIL	2.69
B. Buhl, MIL	2.74
V. Law, PIT	2.87

Strikeouts
J. Sanford, PHI	188
D. Drott, CHI	170
M. Drabowsky, CHI	170
S. Jones, STL	154
D. Drysdale, BKN	148

Shutouts
J. Podres, BKN	6
D. Newcombe, BKN	4
D. Drysdale, BKN	4
W. Spahn, MIL	4

Innings
B. Friend, PIT	277
W. Spahn, MIL	271
L. Burdette, MIL	257
B. Lawrence, CIN	250

Wins
W. Spahn, MIL	21
J. Sanford, PHI	19
B. Buhl, MIL	18
L. Burdette, MIL	17
D. Drysdale, BKN	17

Complete Games
W. Spahn, MIL	18
B. Friend, PIT	17
R. Gomez, NY	16
J. Sanford, PHI	15

Fewest Walks/9 Innings
D. Newcombe, BKN	1.49
R. Roberts, PHI	1.55
V. Law, PIT	1.67
B. Purkey, PIT	1.90

Games Pitched
T. Lown, CHI	67
R. Face, PIT	59
C. Labine, BKN	58
Worthington, NY	55

NATIONAL LEAGUE 1957, *cont.*

	W	L	PCT	GB	R	OR	2B	3B	HR	BA	SA	SB	E	DP	FA	CG	BB	SO	ShO	SV	ERA
									Batting					**Fielding**				**Pitching**			
Milwaukee	95	59	.617		**772**	613	221	62	**199**	.269	**.442**	35	120	173	.981	**60**	570	693	9	24	3.47
St. Louis	87	67	.565	8	737	666	235	43	132	**.274**	.405	58	131	168	.979	46	506	778	11	**29**	3.78
Brooklyn	84	70	.545	11	690	591	188	38	147	.253	.387	60	127	136	.979	44	456	**891**	18	**29**	**3.35**
Cincinnati	80	74	.519	15	747	781	**251**	33	187	.269	.432	51	**107**	139	**.982**	40	429	707	5	**29**	4.62
Philadelphia	77	77	.500	18	623	656	213	44	117	.250	.375	57	136	117	.976	54	**412**	858	9	23	3.80
New York	69	85	.448	26	643	701	171	54	157	.252	.393	**64**	161	**180**	.974	35	471	701	9	20	4.01
Chicago	62	92	.403	33	628	722	223	31	147	.244	.380	28	149	140	.975	30	601	859	5	26	4.13
Pittsburgh	62	92	.403	33	586	696	231	60	92	.268	.384	46	170	143	.972	47	421	663	9	15	3.88
					5426	5426	1733	365	1178	.260	.400	399	1101	1196	.977	356	3866	6150	75	195	3.88

AMERICAN LEAGUE 1957

	POS	Player	AB	BA	HR	RBI	PO	A	E	DP	TC/G	FA	Pitcher	G	IP	W	L	SV	ERA
New York W-98 L-56 Casey Stengel	1B	B. Skowron	457	.304	17	88	1026	86	9	116	**9.7**	.992	Sturdivant	28	202	16	6	0	2.54
	2B	Richardson	305	.256	0	19	206	223	9	60	4.7	.979	J. Kucks	37	179	8	10	2	3.56
	SS	McDougald	539	.289	13	62	247	391	16	104	5.4	.976	B. Turley	32	176	13	6	3	2.71
	3B	A. Carey	247	.255	6	33	66	147	5	9	2.7	.977	B. Shantz	30	173	11	5	5	**2.45**
	RF	H. Bauer	479	.259	18	65	200	7	3	1	1.6	.986	D. Larsen	27	140	10	4	0	3.74
	CF	M. Mantle	474	.365	34	94	324	6	7	1	2.4	.979	W. Ford	24	129	11	5	0	2.57
	LF	E. Slaughter	209	.254	5	34	97	2	0	1	1.5	1.000	A. Ditmar	46	127	8	3	6	3.25
	C	Y. Berra	482	.251	24	82	**704**	61	4	12	**6.4**	.995	T. Byrne	30	85	4	6	2	4.36
	UT	T. Kubek	431	.297	3	39	189	183	20	33		.949	B. Grim	46	72	12	8	19	2.63
	OC	E. Howard	356	.253	8	44	246	16	6	4		.978							
	O1	H. Simpson	224	.250	7	39	198	13	3	19		.986							
	23	J. Coleman	157	.268	2	12	89	115	7	33		.967							
Chicago W-90 L-64 Al Lopez	1B	E. Torgeson	251	.295	7	46	612	29	1	72	9.2	.998	B. Pierce	37	257	**20**	12	2	3.26
	2B	N. Fox	619	.317	6	61	**453**	453	13	**141**	5.9	.986	D. Donovan	28	221	16	6	0	2.77
	SS	L. Aparicio	575	.257	3	41	246	449	20	85	5.0	.972	J. Wilson	30	202	15	8	0	3.48
	3B	B. Phillips	393	.270	7	42	91	227	14	17	3.4	.958	J. Harshman	30	151	8	8	1	4.10
	RF	J. Landis	274	.212	2	16	192	8	3	4	2.3	.985	B. Keegan	30	143	10	8	2	3.53
	CF	L. Doby	416	.288	14	79	255	3	4	0	2.4	.985	B. Fischer	33	124	7	8	1	3.48
	LF	M. Minoso	568	.310	12	103	293	9	5	2	2.0	.984	G. Staley	47	105	5	1	5	2.06
	C	S. Lollar	351	.256	11	70	454	45	1	5	5.2	.998	D. Howell	37	68	6	5	6	3.29
	OF	J. Rivera	402	.256	14	52	141	6	4	0	1.8	.974	P. LaPalme	35	40	1	4	7	3.35
	1B	W. Dropo	223	.256	13	49	483	39	7	49	7.7	.987							
	3S	S. Esposito	176	.205	2	15	80	165	9	22		.965							
Boston W-82 L-72 Pinky Higgins	1B	D. Gernert	316	.237	14	58	681	50	8	82	10.4	.989	F. Sullivan	31	241	14	11	0	2.73
	2B	T. Lepcio	232	.241	9	37	136	194	8	58	5.0	.976	T. Brewer	32	238	16	13	0	3.85
	SS	B. Klaus	477	.252	10	42	204	417	25	93	5.5	.961	W. Nixon	29	191	12	13	0	3.68
	3B	F. Malzone	634	.292	15	103	151	370	25	**31**	3.6	.954	M. Fornieles	25	125	8	7	2	3.52
	RF	J. Jensen	544	.281	23	103	251	16	11	4	1.9	.960	D. Sisler	22	122	7	8	1	4.71
	CF	J. Piersall	609	.261	19	63	**397**	12	4	0	2.7	.990	Porterfield	28	102	4	4	1	4.05
	LF	T. Williams	420	**.388**	38	87	215	2	1	0	1.7	.995	I. Delock	49	94	9	8	11	3.83
	C	S. White	340	.215	3	31	489	49	8	13	4.9	.985	G. Susce	29	88	7	3	1	4.28
	1B	M. Vernon	270	.241	7	38	662	51	6	47	10.3	.992							
	2B	G. Mauch	222	.270	2	28	127	153	11	41	5.0	.962							
	SS	B. Consolo	196	.270	4	19	61	149	15	30	5.4	.933							
	C	P. Daley	191	.225	3	25	289	20	0	5	4.0	**1.000**							
	OF	G. Stephens	173	.266	3	26	70	4	1	2	.8	.987							
Detroit W-78 L-76 Jack Tighe	1B	R. Boone	462	.273	12	65	972	45	10	103	8.8	.990	J. Bunning	45	**267**	**20**	8	1	2.69
	2B	F. Bolling	576	.259	15	40	394	401	**16**	112	5.6	.980	F. Lary	40	238	11	16	3	3.98
	SS	H. Kuenn	624	.277	9	44	225	354	27	86	4.5	.955	D. Maas	45	219	10	14	1	3.28
	3B	R. Bertoia	295	.275	4	28	76	125	10	8	2.5	.953	P. Foytack	38	212	14	11	1	3.14
	RF	A. Kaline	577	.295	23	90	319	13	5	2	2.3	.985	B. Hoeft	34	207	9	11	1	3.48
	CF	B. Tuttle	451	.251	5	47	331	5	6	1	2.7	.982	H. Byrd	37	59	4	3	5	3.36
	LF	C. Maxwell	492	.276	24	82	317	6	1	1	2.4	**.997**							
	C	F. House	348	.259	7	36	535	54	2	5	6.1	.997							
	C	R. Wilson	178	.242	3	13	277	29	0	5	5.2	1.000							
	3B	J. Finigan	174	.270	0	17	58	108	8	9	2.9	.954							
	1O	D. Philley	173	.283	2	16	219	25	2	19		.992							
Baltimore W-76 L-76 Paul Richards	1B	B. Boyd	485	.318	4	34	**1073**	70	10	107	8.7	.991	C. Johnson	35	242	14	11	0	3.20
	2B	B. Gardner	**644**	.262	6	55	393	424	11	96	5.6	**.987**	R. Moore	34	227	11	13	0	3.72
	SS	W. Miranda	314	.194	0	20	166	324	17	59	4.4	.966	B. Loes	31	155	12	7	4	3.24
	3B	G. Kell	310	.297	9	44	66	122	4	15	2.4	.979	H. Brown	25	150	7	8	1	3.90
	RF	A. Pilarcik	407	.278	9	49	234	15	1	2	2.0	.996	B. O'Dell	35	140	4	10	4	2.69
	CF	J. Busby	288	.250	3	19	233	8	4	1	2.9	.984	B. Wight	27	121	6	6	0	3.64
	LF	B. Nieman	445	.276	13	70	237	6	5	1	2.1	.980	G. Zuverink	**56**	113	10	6	9	2.48
	C	G. Triandos	418	.254	19	72	580	**64**	5	**13**	5.4	.992	K. Lehman	30	68	8	3	6	2.78
	OF	T. Francona	279	.233	7	38	119	0	1	0	1.6	.992							
	UT	B. Goodman	263	.308	3	33	134	110	4	20		.957							
	C	J. Ginsberg	175	.274	1	18	252	20	4	6	4.2	.986							
	UT	D. Williams	167	.234	1	17	150	41	2	15		.990							
	OF	J. Durham	157	.185	4	17	70	1	0	0	1.2	1.000							

AMERICAN LEAGUE 1957, *cont.*

	POS	Player	AB	BA	HR	RBI	PO	A	E	DP	TC/G	FA	Pitcher	G	IP	W	L	SV	ERA
Cleveland	1B	V. Wertz	515	.282	28	105	1025	83	14	122	8.1	.988	E. Wynn	40	263	14	17	1	4.31
	2B	B. Avila	463	.268	5	48	280	254	9	72	5.1	.983	M. Garcia	38	211	12	8	0	3.75
W-76 L-77	SS	Carrasquel	392	.276	8	57	212	357	24	75	4.9	.960	D. Mossi	36	159	11	10	2	4.13
	3B	A. Smith	507	.247	11	49	95	156	24	16	3.3	.913	R. Narleski	46	154	11	5	16	3.09
Kerby Farrell	RF	R. Colavito	461	.252	25	84	268	12	11	2	2.2	.962	C. McLish	42	144	9	7	1	2.74
	CF	R. Maris	358	.235	14	51	266	10	7	2	2.5	.975	B. Lemon	21	117	6	11	0	4.60
	LF	G. Woodling	430	.321	19	78	225	10	2	0	2.1	.992	B. Daley	34	87	2	8	2	4.43
	C	J. Hegan	148	.216	4	15	287	14	0	4	5.2	1.000							
	UT	L. Raines	244	.262	2	16	84	109	13	15		.937							
	O3	D. Williams	205	.283	6	17	94	31	6	5		.954							
	UT	Strickland	201	.234	1	19	146	164	6	38		.981							
	C	R. Nixon	185	.281	2	18	268	31	5	5	5.3	.984							
	C	D. Brown	114	.263	4	22	190	18	3	4	6.4	.986							
Kansas City	1B	V. Power	467	.259	14	42	968	99	2	95	9.5	.998	N. Garver	24	145	6	13	0	3.84
	2B	B. Hunter	319	.191	8	29	111	152	7	40	4.2	.974	T. Morgan	46	144	9	7	7	4.64
W-59 L-94	SS	DeMaestri	461	.245	9	33	248	387	13	87	4.8	.980	A. Kellner	28	133	6	5	0	4.27
	3B	H. Lopez	391	.294	11	35	117	227	23	20	3.3	.937	R. Terry	21	131	4	11	0	3.38
Lou Boudreau	RF	B. Cerv	345	.272	11	44	157	6	6	1	1.9	.964	J. Urban	31	129	7	4	0	3.34
W-36 L-67	CF	W. Held	326	.239	20	50	266	12	1	2	3.0	.996	T. Gorman	38	125	5	9	3	3.83
	LF	G. Zernial	437	.236	27	69	213	4	11	1	2.0	.952	V. Trucks	48	116	9	7	7	3.03
Harry Craft	C	H. Smith	360	.303	13	41	463	55	9	8	5.1	.983	Portocarrero	33	115	4	9	0	3.92
W-23 L-27	OF	L. Skizas	376	.245	18	44	119	5	3	2	1.7	.976	W. Burnette	38	113	7	12	1	4.30
	23	B. Martin	265	.257	9	27	150	135	5	32		.983							
	C	T. Thompson	230	.204	7	19	272	29	2	7	4.9	.993							
	10	H. Simpson	179	.296	6	24	272	24	2	21		.993							
	1B	I. Noren	160	.213	2	16	191	12	2	24	8.2	.990							
	2B	M. Graff	155	.181	0	10	110	127	3	36	4.5	.988							
Washington	1B	P. Runnels	473	.230	2	35	616	44	3	59	9.2	.995	P. Ramos	43	231	12	16	0	4.79
	2B	H. Plews	329	.271	1	26	199	175	8	42	4.8	.979	C. Stobbs	42	212	8	20	1	5.36
W-55 L-99	SS	R. Bridges	391	.228	3	47	226	382	18	77	5.8	.971	C. Pascual	29	176	8	17	0	4.10
	3B	E. Yost	414	.251	9	38	109	207	16	18	3.1	.952	R. Kemmerer	39	172	7	11	0	4.96
Chuck Dressen	RF	J. Lemon	518	.284	17	64	227	4	7	2	1.8	.971	T. Clevenger	52	140	7	6	8	4.12
W-4 L-16	CF	B. Usher	295	.261	5	27	228	7	5	2	2.5	.979	D. Hyde	52	109	4	3	1	4.12
	LF	R. Sievers	572	.301	42	114	254	4	4	2	2.0	.985	B. Byerly	47	95	6	6	6	3.13
Cookie Lavagetto	C	L. Berberet	264	.261	7	36	349	48	0	8	5.2	1.000	T. Abernathy	26	85	2	10	0	6.78
W-51 L-83	2S	M. Bolling	277	.227	4	19	168	232	11	53		.973							
	10	A. Schult	247	.263	4	35	366	15	6	35		.984							
	C	C. Courtney	232	.267	6	27	288	35	2	6	5.5	.994							
	OF	Throneberry	195	.185	2	12	116	2	2	0	2.1	.983							
	1B	J. Becquer	186	.226	2	22	300	19	0	29	7.4	1.000							

BATTING AND BASE RUNNING LEADERS

Batting Average
T. Williams, BOS	.388
M. Mantle, NY	.365
G. Woodling, CLE	.321
B. Boyd, BAL	.318
N. Fox, CHI	.317

Slugging Average
T. Williams, BOS	.731
M. Mantle, NY	.665
R. Sievers, WAS	.579
G. Woodling, CLE	.521
V. Wertz, CLE	.485

Home Runs
R. Sievers, WAS	42
T. Williams, BOS	38
M. Mantle, NY	34
V. Wertz, CLE	28
G. Zernial, KC	27

Total Bases
R. Sievers, WAS	331
M. Mantle, NY	315
T. Williams, BOS	307
A. Kaline, DET	276
F. Malzone, BOS	271

Runs Batted In
R. Sievers, WAS	114
V. Wertz, CLE	105
J. Jensen, BOS	103
M. Minoso, CHI	103
F. Malzone, BOS	103

Stolen Bases
L. Aparicio, CHI	28
J. Rivera, CHI	18
M. Minoso, CHI	18
M. Mantle, NY	16

Hits
N. Fox, CHI	196
F. Malzone, BOS	185
M. Minoso, CHI	176
M. Mantle, NY	173

Base on Balls
M. Mantle, NY	146
T. Williams, BOS	119
A. Smith, CLE	79
M. Minoso, CHI	79

Home Run Percentage
T. Williams, BOS	9.0
R. Sievers, WAS	7.3
M. Mantle, NY	7.2
V. Wertz, CLE	5.4

Runs Scored
M. Mantle, NY	121
N. Fox, CHI	110
J. Piersall, BOS	103
R. Sievers, WAS	99

Doubles
M. Minoso, CHI	36
B. Gardner, BAL	36
F. Malzone, BOS	31
H. Kuenn, DET	30

Triples
H. Simpson, KC, NY	9
H. Bauer, NY	9
McDougald, NY	9
B. Boyd, BAL	8

PITCHING LEADERS

Winning Percentage
D. Donovan, CHI	.727
Sturdivant, NY	.727
J. Bunning, DET	.714
J. Wilson, CHI	.652
B. Pierce, CHI	.625

Earned Run Average
B. Shantz, NY	2.45
Sturdivant, NY	2.54
J. Bunning, DET	2.69
B. Turley, NY	2.71
F. Sullivan, BOS	2.73

Wins
J. Bunning, DET	20
B. Pierce, CHI	20
D. Donovan, CHI	16
Sturdivant, NY	16
T. Brewer, BOS	16

Saves
B. Grim, NY	19
R. Narleski, CLE	16
I. Delock, BOS	11
G. Zuverink, BAL	9
T. Clevenger, WAS	8

Strikeouts
E. Wynn, CLE	184
J. Bunning, DET	182
C. Johnson, BAL	177
B. Pierce, CHI	171
B. Turley, NY	152

Complete Games
D. Donovan, CHI	16
B. Pierce, CHI	16
T. Brewer, BOS	15
J. Bunning, DET	14
C. Johnson, BAL	14
F. Sullivan, BOS	14

Fewest Hits/9 Innings
B. Turley, NY	6.12
J. Bunning, DET	7.20
P. Foytack, DET	7.43
Sturdivant, NY	7.59

Shutouts
J. Wilson, CHI	5
B. Turley, NY	4
B. Pierce, CHI	4
B. Loes, BAL	3

Fewest Walks/9 Innings
F. Sullivan, BOS	1.79
D. Donovan, CHI	1.84
B. Shantz, NY	2.08
B. Loes, BAL	2.14

Most Strikeouts/9 Inn.
B. Turley, NY	7.76
C. Johnson, BAL	6.58
E. Wynn, CLE	6.30
J. Bunning, DET	6.13

Innings
J. Bunning, DET	267
E. Wynn, CLE	263
B. Pierce, CHI	257
C. Johnson, BAL	242

Games Pitched
G. Zuverink, BAL	56
T. Clevenger, WAS	52
D. Hyde, WAS	52
I. Delock, BOS	49

AMERICAN LEAGUE 1957, *cont.*

	W	L	PCT	GB	R	OR	2B	3B	HR	BA	SA	SB	E	DP	FA	CG	BB	SO	ShO	SV	ERA
										Batting				Fielding				Pitching			
New York	98	56	.636	—	**723**	534	200	**54**	145	**.268**	**.409**	49	123	**183**	.980	41	580	**810**	13	**42**	**3.00**
Chicago	90	64	.584	8	707	566	208	41	106	.260	.375	**109**	107	169	**.982**	59	470	665	**16**	27	3.35
Boston	82	72	.532	16	721	668	**231**	32	153	.262	.405	29	149	179	.976	55	498	692	9	23	3.88
Detroit	78	76	.506	20	614	614	224	37	116	.257	.378	36	121	151	.980	52	505	756	9	21	3.56
Baltimore	76	76	.500	21	597	588	191	39	87	.252	.353	57	112	159	.981	44	493	767	13	25	3.46
Cleveland	76	77	.497	21.5	682	722	199	26	140	.252	.382	40	153	154	.974	46	618	807	7	23	4.05
Kansas City	59	94	.386	38.5	563	710	195	40	**166**	.244	.394	35	125	162	.979	26	565	626	6	19	4.19
Washington	55	99	.357	43	603	808	215	38	111	.244	.363	13	128	159	.979	31	580	691	5	16	4.85
					5210	5210	1663	307	1024	.255	.382	368	1018	1316	.979	354	4309	5814	78	196	3.79

NATIONAL LEAGUE 1958

	POS	Player	AB	BA	HR	RBI	PO	A	E	DP	TC/G	FA	Pitcher	G	IP	W	L	SV	ERA
Milwaukee W-92 L-62 Fred Haney	1B	F. Torre	372	.309	6	55	960	80	6	85	8.6	**.994**	W. Spahn	38	**290**	**22**	11	1	3.07
	2B	Schoendienst	427	.262	1	24	233	301	7	77	5.2	**.987**	L. Burdette	40	275	20	10	0	2.91
	SS	J. Logan	530	.226	11	53	273	481	32	99	5.5	.959	B. Rush	28	147	10	6	0	3.42
	3B	E. Mathews	546	.251	31	77	116	351	22	24	3.3	.955	C. Willey	23	140	9	7	0	2.70
	RF	H. Aaron	601	.326	30	95	305	12	5	0	2.1	.984	J. Pizarro	16	97	6	4	1	2.70
	CF	B. Bruton	325	.280	3	28	203	6	5	0	2.2	.977	J. Jay	18	97	7	5	0	2.14
	LF	W. Covington	294	.330	24	74	118	3	6	2	1.5	.953	D. McMahon	38	59	7	2	8	3.68
	C	D. Crandall	427	.272	18	63	**659**	64	7	6	5.9	**.990**							
	1B	J. Adcock	320	.275	19	54	525	36	6	55	8.0	.989							
	O2	F. Mantilla	226	.221	7	19	114	49	4	12		.976							
	OF	A. Pafko	164	.238	3	23	107	2	0	0	1.2	1.000							
Pittsburgh W-84 L-70 Danny Murtaugh	1B	Kluszewski	301	.292	4	37	591	36	4	62	8.8	.994	B. Friend	38	274	**22**	14	0	3.68
	2B	B. Mazeroski	567	.275	19	68	344	496	17	118	**5.6**	.980	R. Kline	32	237	13	16	0	3.53
	SS	D. Groat	584	.300	3	66	**307**	461	20	**127**	5.3	.975	V. Law	35	202	14	12	3	3.96
	3B	F. Thomas	562	.281	35	109	122	240	**29**	21	2.8	.926	C. Raydon	31	134	8	4	1	3.62
	RF	R. Clemente	519	.289	6	50	312	**22**	6	3	2.5	.982	G. Witt	18	106	9	2	0	1.61
	CF	B. Virdon	604	.267	9	46	401	11	3	0	2.9	.993	Porterfield	37	88	4	6	5	3.29
	LF	B. Skinner	529	.321	13	70	232	19	6	2	1.8	.977	R. Face	57	84	5	2	20	2.89
	C	H. Foiles	264	.205	8	30	456	41	5	5	4.9	.990	D. Gross	40	75	5	7	7	3.98
	1B	D. Stuart	254	.268	16	48	529	49	**16**	69	9.3	.973							
	OF	R. Mejias	157	.268	5	19	104	3	3	0	1.9	.973							
San Francisco W-80 L-74 Bill Rigney	1B	O. Cepeda	603	.312	25	96	**1322**	97	16	131	**9.8**	.989	J. Antonelli	41	242	16	13	3	3.28
	2B	D. O'Connell	306	.232	3	23	222	278	7	70	4.9	.986	R. Gomez	42	208	10	12	1	4.38
	SS	D. Spencer	539	.256	17	74	238	438	**32**	95	5.3	.955	S. Miller	41	182	6	9	0	**2.47**
	3B	J. Davenport	434	.256	12	41	92	221	13	19	2.5	.960	McCormick	42	178	11	8	1	4.59
	RF	W. Kirkland	418	.258	14	56	187	12	8	**4**	1.8	.961	Worthington	54	151	11	7	6	3.63
	CF	W. Mays	600	.347	29	96	429	17	9	2	3.0	.980	R. Monzant	43	151	8	11	1	4.72
	LF	F. Alou	182	.253	4	16	126	2	2	1	1.9	.985	M. Grissom	51	65	7	5	10	3.99
	C	B. Schmidt	393	.244	14	54	616	54	**12**	10	5.5	.982							
	OF	H. Sauer	236	.250	12	46	93	3	5	1	1.5	.950							
	3B	R. Jablonski	230	.230	12	46	49	91	8	2	2.6	.946							
	OF	L. Wagner	221	.317	13	35	89	5	5	0	1.7	.949							
Cincinnati W-76 L-78 Birdie Tebbetts W-52 L-61 Jimmy Dykes W-24 L-17	1B	G. Crowe	345	.275	7	61	713	53	6	65	8.3	.992	B. Purkey	37	250	17	11	0	3.60
	2B	J. Temple	542	.306	3	47	**395**	353	16	90	5.4	.979	H. Haddix	29	184	8	7	0	3.52
	SS	R. McMillan	393	.229	1	25	278	394	14	81	4.7	**.980**	B. Lawrence	46	181	8	13	5	4.13
	3B	D. Hoak	417	.261	6	50	132	244	14	29	3.5	.964	J. Nuxhall	36	176	12	11	0	3.79
	RF	J. Lynch	420	.312	16	68	154	5	5	2	1.6	.970	D. Newcombe	20	133	7	7	1	3.85
	CF	G. Bell	385	.252	10	46	235	7	1	2	2.3	**.996**	T. Acker	38	125	4	3	1	4.55
	LF	F. Robinson	554	.269	31	83	310	12	3	1	2.4	.991	A. Kellner	18	82	7	3	0	2.30
	C	E. Bailey	360	.250	11	59	438	44	6	6	4.9	.988	H. Jeffcoat	49	75	6	8	9	3.72
	C	S. Burgess	251	.283	6	31	297	21	4	2	5.6	.988							
	UT	A. Grammas	216	.218	0	12	126	174	6	32		.980							
	OF	P. Whisenant	203	.236	11	40	122	3	0	1	1.9	1.000							
	OF	B. Thurman	178	.230	4	20	80	2	2	1	2.0	.976							
	1B	W. Dropo	162	.290	7	31	300	27	0	31	7.6	1.000							
Chicago W-72 L-82 Bob Scheffing	1B	D. Long	480	.271	20	75	1173	84	10	130	9.2	.992	T. Phillips	39	170	7	10	1	4.76
	2B	T. Taylor	497	.235	6	27	311	374	23	103	5.2	.968	G. Hobbie	55	168	10	6	2	3.74
	SS	E. Banks	**617**	.313	**47**	**129**	292	468	**32**	100	5.1	.960	D. Drott	39	167	7	11	0	5.43
	3B	A. Dark	464	.295	3	43	107	225	18	24	3.2	.949	D. Hillman	31	126	4	8	1	3.15
	RF	L. Walls	513	.304	24	72	241	10	2	1	1.9	.992	M. Drabowsky	22	126	9	11	0	4.51
	CF	B. Thomson	547	.283	21	82	353	13	4	3	2.5	.989	D. Elston	69	97	9	8	10	2.88
	LF	W. Moryn	512	.264	26	77	265	4	6	1	2.0	.978	J. Briggs	20	96	5	5	0	4.52
	C	S. Taylor	301	.259	6	36	460	23	6	4	5.6	.988	B. Henry	44	81	5	4	6	2.88
	32	J. Goryl	219	.242	4	14	91	153	16	26		.938							
	C	C. Neeman	201	.259	12	29	340	25	3	6	5.2	.992							

NATIONAL LEAGUE 1958, *cont.*

	POS	Player	AB	BA	HR	RBI	PO	A	E	DP	TC/G	FA	Pitcher	G	IP	W	L	SV	ERA
St. Louis	1B	S. Musial	472	.337	17	62	1019	100	13	127	9.1	.989	S. Jones	35	250	14	13	0	2.88
	2B	Blasingame	547	.274	2	36	312	380	26	97	5.2	.964	L. Jackson	49	198	13	13	8	3.68
W-72 L-82	SS	E. Kasko	259	.220	2	22	111	186	12	47	4.0	.961	V. Mizell	30	190	10	14	0	3.42
	3B	K. Boyer	570	.307	23	90	156	350	20	41	3.7	.962	J. Brosnan	33	115	8	4	7	3.44
Fred Hutchinson	RF	W. Moon	290	.238	7	38	122	5	2	0	1.6	.984	B. Mabe	31	112	3	9	0	4.51
W-69 L-75	CF	C. Flood	422	.261	10	41	346	18	8	3	3.1	.978	L. McDaniel	26	109	5	7	0	5.80
	LF	D. Ennis	329	.261	3	47	122	11	1	2	1.6	.993	B. Muffett	35	84	4	6	5	4.93
Stan Hack	C	H. Smith	220	.227	1	24	346	22	4	4	5.2	.989							
W-3 L-7	OC	G. Green	442	.281	13	55	428	35	9	5		.981							
	1O	Cunningham	337	.312	12	57	418	26	3	21		.993							
	S2	G. Freese	191	.257	6	16	77	77	12	14		.928							
	OF	I. Noren	178	.264	4	22	75	1	2	0	1.0	.974							
Los Angeles	1B	G. Hodges	475	.259	22	64	907	69	8	134	8.1	.992	D. Drysdale	44	212	12	13	0	4.17
	2B	C. Neal	473	.254	22	65	334	343	17	121	5.3	.976	J. Podres	39	210	13	15	1	3.72
W-71 L-83	SS	D. Zimmer	455	.262	17	60	265	372	23	100	5.8	.965	S. Koufax	40	159	11	11	1	4.48
	3B	D. Gray	197	.249	9	30	56	139	15	18	3.8	.929	S. Williams	27	119	9	7	0	4.01
Walter Alston	RF	C. Furillo	411	.290	18	83	187	5	5	0	1.7	.975	C. Labine	52	104	6	6	14	4.15
	CF	D. Snider	327	.312	15	58	151	4	2	0	1.7	.987	F. Kipp	40	102	6	6	0	5.01
	LF	G. Cimoli	325	.246	9	27	180	10	5	2	1.9	.974	Klippstein	45	90	3	5	9	3.80
	C	J. Roseboro	384	.271	14	43	594	36	8	5	6.1	.987							
	UT	J. Gilliam	555	.261	2	43	245	176	12	37		.972							
	O1	N. Larker	253	.277	4	29	239	17	5	18		.981							
Philadelphia	1B	E. Bouchee	334	.257	9	39	690	58	5	59	8.5	.993	R. Roberts	35	270	17	14	0	3.24
	2B	S. Hemus	334	.284	8	36	188	220	13	52	5.0	.969	R. Semproch	36	204	13	11	0	3.92
W-69 L-85	SS	C. Fernandez	522	.230	6	51	296	415	18	88	4.9	.975	J. Sanford	38	186	10	13	0	4.44
	3B	W. Jones	398	.271	14	60	137	186	11	13	3.0	.967	C. Simmons	29	168	7	14	1	4.38
Mayo Smith	RF	W. Post	379	.282	12	62	185	12	10	0	2.3	.952	D. Cardwell	16	108	3	6	0	4.51
W-39 L-45	CF	R. Ashburn	615	.350	2	33	495	8	8	2	3.4	.984	D. Farrell	54	94	8	9	11	3.35
	LF	H. Anderson	515	.301	23	97	155	4	4	1	1.9	.975	J. Meyer	37	90	3	6	2	3.59
Eddie Sawyer	C	S. Lopata	258	.248	9	33	418	28	6	6	5.7	.987							
W-30 L-40	UT	T. Kazanski	289	.228	3	35	140	175	8	41		.975							
	OF	R. Repulski	238	.244	13	40	90	3	5	0	1.8	.949							
	O1	D. Philley	207	.309	3	31	183	12	1	12		.995							
	OF	B. Bowman	184	.288	8	24	82	1	1	0	1.5	.988							
	C	C. Sawatski	183	.230	5	12	271	17	4	2	5.5	.986							

BATTING AND BASE RUNNING LEADERS

Batting Average
R. Ashburn, PHI	.350
W. Mays, SF	.347
S. Musial, STL	.337
H. Aaron, MIL	.326
B. Skinner, PIT	.321

Slugging Average
E. Banks, CHI	.614
W. Mays, SF	.583
H. Aaron, MIL	.546
F. Thomas, PIT	.528
S. Musial, STL	.528

Home Runs
E. Banks, CHI	47
F. Thomas, PIT	35
E. Mathews, MIL	31
F. Robinson, CIN	31
H. Aaron, MIL	30

Total Bases
E. Banks, CHI	379
W. Mays, SF	350
H. Aaron, MIL	328
O. Cepeda, SF	309
F. Thomas, PIT	297

Runs Batted In
E. Banks, CHI	129
F. Thomas, PIT	109
H. Anderson, PHI	97
W. Mays, SF	96
O. Cepeda, SF	96

Stolen Bases
W. Mays, SF	31
R. Ashburn, PHI	30
T. Taylor, CHI	21
Blasingame, STL	20
J. Gilliam, LA	18

Hits
R. Ashburn, PHI	215
W. Mays, SF	208
H. Aaron, MIL	196
E. Banks, CHI	193

Base on Balls
R. Ashburn, PHI	97
J. Temple, CIN	91
E. Mathews, MIL	85
Cunningham, STL	82

Home Run Percentage
E. Banks, CHI	7.6
F. Thomas, PIT	6.2
E. Mathews, MIL	5.7
F. Robinson, CIN	5.6

Runs Scored
W. Mays, SF	121
E. Banks, CHI	119
H. Aaron, MIL	109
K. Boyer, STL	101

Doubles
O. Cepeda, SF	38
D. Groat, PIT	36
S. Musial, STL	35
H. Anderson, PHI	34

Triples
R. Ashburn, PHI	13
W. Mays, SF	11
B. Virdon, PIT	11
E. Banks, CHI	11

PITCHING LEADERS

Winning Percentage
W. Spahn, MIL	.667
L. Burdette, MIL	.667
B. Friend, PIT	.611
B. Purkey, CIN	.607
J. Antonelli, SF	.552

Earned Run Average
S. Miller, SF	2.47
S. Jones, STL	2.88
L. Burdette, MIL	2.91
W. Spahn, MIL	3.07
R. Roberts, PHI	3.24

Wins
W. Spahn, MIL	22
B. Friend, PIT	22
L. Burdette, MIL	20
B. Purkey, CIN	17
R. Roberts, PHI	17

Saves
R. Face, PIT	20
C. Labine, LA	14
D. Farrell, PHI	11
D. Elston, CHI	10
M. Grissom, SF	10
Klippstein, CIN, LA	10

Strikeouts
S. Jones, STL	225
W. Spahn, MIL	150
J. Podres, LA	143
J. Antonelli, SF	143
B. Friend, PIT	135

Complete Games
W. Spahn, MIL	23
R. Roberts, PHI	21
L. Burdette, MIL	19
B. Purkey, CIN	17
B. Friend, PIT	16

Fewest Hits/9 Innings
S. Jones, STL	7.34
S. Koufax, LA	7.49
S. Miller, SF	7.91
W. Spahn, MIL	7.98

Shutouts
C. Willey, MIL	4
J. Jay, MIL	3
G. Witt, PIT	3
B. Purkey, CIN	3

Fewest Walks/9 Innings
L. Burdette, MIL	1.63
R. Roberts, PHI	1.70
V. Law, PIT	1.73
B. Purkey, CIN	1.76

Most Strikeouts/9 Inn.
S. Jones, STL	8.10
S. Koufax, LA	7.43
D. Drott, CHI	6.83
J. Podres, LA	6.12

Innings
W. Spahn, MIL	290
L. Burdette, MIL	275
B. Friend, PIT	274
R. Roberts, PHI	270

Games Pitched
D. Elston, CHI	69
Klippstein, CIN, LA	57
R. Face, PIT	57
G. Hobbie, CHI	55

NATIONAL LEAGUE 1958, *cont.*

	W	L	PCT	GB	R	OR	2B	3B	HR	BA	SA	SB	E	DP	FA	CG	BB	SO	ShO	SV	ERA
									Batting					**Fielding**			**Pitching**				
Milwaukee	92	62	.597		675	**541**	221	21	167	**.266**	.412	26	120	152	.980	**72**	426	773	**16**	17	3.21
Pittsburgh	84	70	.545	8	662	607	229	**68**	134	.264	.410	30	133	173	.978	43	470	679	10	**41**	3.56
San Francisco	80	74	.519	12	**727**	698	**250**	42	170	.263	.422	64	152	156	.975	38	512	775	7	25	3.98
Cincinnati	76	78	.494	16	695	621	242	40	123	.258	.389	61	**100**	148	**.983**	50	**419**	705	7	20	3.73
Chicago	72	82	.468	20	709	725	207	49	**182**	.265	.425	39	150	161	.975	27	619	805	5	24	4.22
St. Louis	72	82	.468	20	619	704	216	39	111	.261	.380	44	153	163	.974	45	567	822	6	25	4.12
Los Angeles	71	83	.461	21	668	761	166	50	172	.251	.402	**73**	146	**198**	.975	30	606	**855**	7	31	4.47
Philadelphia	69	85	.448	23	664	762	238	56	124	.266	.400	51	129	136	.978	51	446	778	6	15	4.32
					5419	5419	1769	365	1183	.262	.405	388	1083	1287	.977	356	4065	6192	64	198	3.95

AMERICAN LEAGUE 1958

Team	POS	Player	AB	BA	HR	RBI	PO	A	E	DP	TC/G	FA	Pitcher	G	IP	W	L	SV	ERA
New York W-92 L-62 Casey Stengel	1B	B. Skowron	465	.273	14	73	1040	71	8	112	9.5	.993	B. Turley	33	245	**21**	7	1	2.97
	2B	McDougald	503	.250	14	65	265	298	13	97	5.0	.977	W. Ford	30	219	14	7	1	**2.01**
	SS	T. Kubek	559	.265	2	48	242	453	28	98	5.4	.961	A. Ditmar	38	140	9	8	4	3.42
	3B	A. Carey	315	.286	12	45	99	195	12	22	3.1	.961	B. Shantz	33	126	7	6	0	3.36
	RF	H. Bauer	452	.268	12	50	186	7	4	0	1.6	.980	J. Kucks	34	126	8	8	4	3.93
	CF	M. Mantle	519	.304	**42**	97	331	5	8	2	2.3	.977	D. Larsen	19	114	9	6	0	3.07
	LF	N. Siebern	460	.300	14	55	259	8	5	2	2.0	.982	D. Maas	22	101	7	3	0	3.82
	C	Y. Berra	433	.266	22	90	509	41	0	8	6.5	**1.000**	R. Duren	44	76	6	4	20	2.02
	CO	E. Howard	376	.314	11	66	409	27	2	8		.995							
	3B	J. Lumpe	232	.254	3	32	57	126	11	13	3.0	.943							
	2B	Richardson	182	.247	0	14	104	110	6	35	4.3	.973							
Chicago W-82 L-72 Al Lopez	1B	E. Torgeson	188	.266	10	30	470	30	11	54	7.0	.978	D. Donovan	34	248	15	14	0	3.01
	2B	N. Fox	623	.300	0	49	**444**	399	13	**117**	5.5	.985	B. Pierce	35	245	17	11	2	2.68
	SS	L. Aparicio	557	.266	2	40	**289**	463	21	90	5.3	.973	E. Wynn	40	240	14	16	2	4.13
	3B	B. Goodman	425	.299	0	40	67	204	14	16	2.6	.951	J. Wilson	28	156	9	9	1	4.10
	RF	J. Rivera	276	.225	9	35	153	7	1	3	1.6	.994	R. Moore	32	137	9	7	2	3.82
	CF	J. Landis	523	.277	15	64	331	9	5	1	2.4	.986	G. Staley	50	85	4	5	8	3.16
	LF	A. Smith	480	.252	12	58	249	9	8	2	1.9	.970	T. Lown	27	41	3	3	8	3.98
	C	S. Lollar	421	.273	20	84	597	63	9	8	5.8	.987							
	3O	B. Phillips	260	.273	5	30	122	87	8	13		.963							
	1B	R. Boone	246	.244	7	41	511	34	8	45	8.8	.986							
	C	E. Battey	168	.226	8	26	220	27	3	6	5.1	.988							
	OF	D. Mueller	166	.253	0	16	57	3	2	1	1.4	.968							
	1B	R. Jackson	146	.233	7	21	289	16	1	29	8.1	.997							
Boston W-79 L-75 Pinky Higgins	1B	D. Gernert	431	.237	20	69	**1101**	**93**	11	**118**	10.6	.991	T. Brewer	33	227	12	12	0	3.72
	2B	P. Runnels	568	.322	8	59	267	320	9	88	5.6	.985	F. Sullivan	32	199	13	9	3	3.57
	SS	D. Buddin	497	.237	12	43	269	445	**31**	102	5.5	.958	I. Delock	31	160	14	8	2	3.38
	3B	F. Malzone	**627**	.295	15	87	139	**378**	**27**	36	3.5	.950	D. Sisler	30	149	8	9	0	4.94
	RF	J. Jensen	548	.286	35	**122**	293	14	6	3	2.0	.981	M. Wall	52	114	8	9	10	3.62
	CF	J. Piersall	417	.237	8	48	314	8	5	2	2.6	.985	M. Fornieles	37	111	4	6	1	4.96
	LF	T. Williams	411	**.328**	26	85	154	3	7	0	1.4	.957	L. Kiely	47	81	5	2	12	3.00
	C	S. White	328	.259	6	35	450	38	6	8	4.8	.988							
	OF	G. Stephens	270	.219	9	25	149	5	4	2	1.4	.975							
	C	L. Berberet	167	.210	2	18	234	18	4	2	5.2	.984							
Cleveland W-77 L-76 Bobby Bragan W-31 L-36 Joe Gordon W-46 L-40	1B	M. Vernon	355	.293	8	55	774	50	11	90	8.7	.987	C. McLish	39	226	16	8	1	2.99
	2B	B. Avila	375	.253	5	30	175	177	5	62	4.4	.986	M. Grant	44	204	10	11	4	3.84
	SS	B. Hunter	190	.195	0	9	124	165	16	46	4.1	.948	R. Narleski	44	183	13	10	1	4.07
	3B	B. Harrell	229	.218	7	19	21	50	1	7	1.6	.986	G. Bell	33	182	12	10	1	3.31
	RF	R. Colavito	489	.303	41	113	243	14	5	6	2.0	.981	D. Mossi	43	102	7	8	3	3.90
	CF	L. Doby	247	.283	13	45	141	5	0	0	2.1	1.000	H. Wilhelm	30	90	2	7	5	2.49
	LF	M. Minoso	556	.302	24	80	301	13	8	1	2.2	.975	Woodeshick	14	72	6	6	0	3.64
	C	R. Nixon	376	.301	9	46	499	31	5	4	5.3	.991							
	UT	V. Power	385	.317	12	53	365	172	8	68		.985							
	2S	B. Moran	257	.226	1	18	174	210	15	56		.962							
	OF	G. Geiger	195	.231	1	6	133	3	2	1	2.6	.986							
	OF	R. Maris	182	.225	9	27	109	6	4*	1	2.5	.966							
	C	D. Brown	173	.237	7	20	278	23	4	6	4.9	.987							
	S3	Carrasquel	156	.256	2	21	54	84	8	17		.945							
	31	P. Ward	148	.338	4	21	162	40	2	12		.990							
Detroit W-77 L-77 Jack Tighe W-21 L-28 Bill Norman W-56 L-49	1B	G. Harris	451	.273	20	83	942	79	**15**	90	8.5	.986	F. Lary	39	**260**	16	15	1	2.90
	2B	F. Bolling	610	.269	14	75	342	**445**	12	109	5.2	**.985**	P. Foytack	39	230	15	13	1	3.44
	SS	B. Martin	498	.255	7	42	159	229	17	58	4.6	.958	J. Bunning	35	220	14	12	0	3.52
	3B	R. Bertoia	240	.233	6	27	70	139	11	13	3.2	.950	B. Hoeft	36	143	10	9	3	4.15
	RF	A. Kaline	543	.313	16	85	316	23	2	4	2.4	.994	H. Moford	25	110	4	9	1	3.61
	CF	H. Kuenn	561	.319	8	54	**358**	9	6	1	2.7	.984	H. Aguirre	44	70	3	4	5	3.75
	LF	C. Maxwell	397	.272	13	65	201	4	3	0	1.8	.986							
	C	R. Wilson	298	.299	3	29	565	34	5	6	6.0	.992							
	SS	C. Veal	207	.256	0	16	95	160	5	30	4.5	.981							
	3B	O. Virgil	193	.244	3	19	55	101	3	7	3.2	.981							
	OF	G. Zernial	124	.323	5	23	30	1	2	0	1.4	.939							
	1B	R. Boone	114	.237	6	20	236	15	3	26	7.9	.988							

AMERICAN LEAGUE 1958, cont.

	POS	Player	AB	BA	HR	RBI	PO	A	E	DP	TC/G	FA	Pitcher	G	IP	W	L	SV	ERA
Baltimore	1B	B. Boyd	401	.309	7	36	757	53	5	85	8.2	.994	J. Harshman	34	236	12	15	4	2.89
	2B	B. Gardner	560	.225	3	33	349	350	11	113	4.7	.985	B. O'Dell	41	221	14	11	8	2.97
W-74 L-79	SS	W. Miranda	214	.201	1	8	137	216	14	53	3.6	.962	Portocarrero	32	205	15	11	2	3.25
	3B	B. Robinson	463	.238	3	32	151	275	21	30	3.2	.953	M. Pappas	31	135	10	10	0	4.06
Paul Richards	RF	A. Pilarcik	379	.243	1	24	213	5	3	0	1.9	.986	C. Johnson	26	118	6	9	1	3.88
	CF	J. Busby	215	.237	3	19	196	1	1	0	1.9	.995	B. Loes	32	114	3	9	5	3.63
	LF	G. Woodling	413	.276	15	65	181	7	5	1	1.7	.974	H. Brown	19	97	7	5	1	3.07
	C	G. Triandos	474	.245	30	79	698	61	10	11	5.8	.987	G. Zuverink	45	69	2	2	7	3.39
	UT	D. Williams	409	.276	4	32	359	61	8	27		.981							
	OF	B. Nieman	366	.325	16	60	145	3	6	0	1.9	.961							
	SS	F. Castleman	200	.170	3	14	102	165	10	37	3.0	.964							
	1B	J. Marshall	191	.215	5	19	382	19	0	37	7.7	1.000							
Kansas City	1B	V. Power	205	.302	4	27	439	48	4	54	9.6	.992	R. Terry	40	217	11	13	2	4.24
	2B	H. Lopez	564	.261	17	73	251	282	14	78	5.7	.974	N. Garver	31	201	12	11	1	4.03
W-73 L-81	SS	DeMaestri	442	.219	6	38	226	417	13	95	4.8	.980	R. Herbert	42	175	8	8	3	3.50
	3B	H. Smith	315	.273	5	46	44	87	7	9	3.2	.949	J. Urban	30	132	8	11	1	5.93
Harry Craft	RF	R. Maris	401	.247	19	53	194	9	5*	3	2.1	.976	B. Grim	26	114	7	6	0	3.56
	CF	B. Tuttle	511	.231	11	51	311	12	4	2	2.3	.988	M. Dickson	27	99	9	5	1	3.27
	LF	B. Cerv	515	.305	38	104	311	13	5	3	2.4	.985	T. Gorman	50	90	4	4	8	3.51
	C	H. Chiti	295	.268	9	44	425	41	6	9	5.7	.987	D. Tomanek	36	72	5	5	5	3.61
	13	P. Ward	268	.254	6	24	358	76	12	34		.973	D. Maas	10	55	4	5	1	3.90
	2B	M. Baxes	231	.212	0	8	134	151	9	40	4.8	.969							
	OF	B. Martyn	226	.261	2	23	112	4	4	2	1.9	.967							
	1B	H. Simpson	212	.264	7	27	384	18	4	44	9.4	.990							
	C	F. House	202	.252	4	24	236	22	2	4	4.7	.992							
	3S	Carrasquel	160	.213	2	13	53	97	4	16		.974							
Washington	1B	N. Zauchin	303	.228	15	37	749	56	4	74	8.9	.995	P. Ramos	43	259	14	18	3	4.23
	2B	Aspromonte	253	.225	5	27	139	184	12	49	4.7	.964	R. Kemmerer	40	224	6	15	0	4.61
W-61 L-93	SS	R. Bridges	377	.263	5	28	191	331	13	73	4.8	.976	C. Pascual	31	177	8	12	0	3.15
	3B	E. Yost	406	.224	8	37	109	186	11	20	2.7	.964	H. Griggs	32	137	3	11	0	5.52
Cookie Lavagetto	RF	J. Lemon	501	.246	26	75	255	8	6	2	2.0	.978	T. Clevenger	55	124	9	9	6	4.35
	CF	A. Pearson	530	.275	3	33	338	6	7	1	2.5	.980	D. Hyde	53	103	10	3	18	1.75
	LF	R. Sievers	550	.295	39	108	216	5	2	0	1.9	.991	Valentinetti	23	96	4	6	0	5.08
	C	C. Courtney	450	.251	8	62	682	64	7	17	5.9	.991							
	23	H. Plews	380	.258	2	29	156	208	16	45		.958							
	OF	N. Chrisley	233	.215	5	26	117	6	1	2	1.8	.992							
	SS	O. Alvarez	196	.209	0	5	113	158	9	33	4.4	.968							
	1B	J. Becquer	164	.238	0	12	319	34	2	26	8.5	.994							

BATTING AND BASE RUNNING LEADERS

Batting Average
T. Williams, BOS	.328
P. Runnels, BOS	.322
H. Kuenn, DET	.319
A. Kaline, DET	.313
V. Power, CLE, KC	.312

Slugging Average
R. Colavito, CLE	.620
B. Cerv, KC	.592
M. Mantle, NY	.592
T. Williams, BOS	.584
R. Sievers, WAS	.544

Home Runs
M. Mantle, NY	42
R. Colavito, CLE	41
R. Sievers, WAS	39
B. Cerv, KC	38
J. Jensen, BOS	35

Total Bases
M. Mantle, NY	307
B. Cerv, KC	305
R. Colavito, CLE	303
R. Sievers, WAS	299
J. Jensen, BOS	293

Runs Batted In
J. Jensen, BOS	122
R. Colavito, CLE	113
R. Sievers, WAS	108
B. Cerv, KC	104
M. Mantle, NY	97

Stolen Bases
L. Aparicio, CHI	29
J. Rivera, CHI	21
J. Landis, CHI	19
M. Mantle, NY	18
M. Minoso, CLE	14

Hits
N. Fox, CHI	187
F. Malzone, BOS	185
V. Power, CLE, KC	184
P. Runnels, BOS	183

Base on Balls
M. Mantle, NY	129
J. Jensen, BOS	99
T. Williams, BOS	98
P. Runnels, BOS	87

Home Run Percentage
R. Colavito, CLE	8.4
M. Mantle, NY	8.1
B. Cerv, KC	7.4
R. Sievers, WAS	7.1

Runs Scored
M. Mantle, NY	127
P. Runnels, BOS	103
V. Power, CLE, KC	98
M. Minoso, CLE	94

Doubles
H. Kuenn, DET	39
V. Power, CLE, KC	37
A. Kaline, DET	34
P. Runnels, BOS	32

Triples
V. Power, CLE, KC	10
J. Lemon, WAS	9
B. Tuttle, KC	9
L. Aparicio, CHI	9

PITCHING LEADERS

Winning Percentage
B. Turley, NY	.750
C. McLish, CLE	.667
B. Pierce, CHI	.607
Portocarrero, BAL	.577
P. Foytack, DET	.536

Earned Run Average
W. Ford, NY	2.01
B. Pierce, CHI	2.68
J. Harshman, BAL	2.89
F. Lary, DET	2.90
B. O'Dell, BAL	2.97

Wins
B. Turley, NY	21
B. Pierce, CHI	17
C. McLish, CLE	16
F. Lary, DET	16

Saves
R. Duren, NY	20
D. Hyde, WAS	18
L. Kiely, BOS	12
M. Wall, BOS	10

Strikeouts
E. Wynn, CHI	179
J. Bunning, DET	177
B. Turley, NY	168
J. Harshman, BAL	161
C. Pascual, WAS	146

Complete Games
B. Turley, NY	19
B. Pierce, CHI	19
F. Lary, DET	19
J. Harshman, BAL	17
P. Foytack, DET	16
D. Donovan, CHI	16

Fewest Hits/9 Innings
B. Turley, NY	6.53
G. Bell, CLE	6.97
W. Ford, NY	7.14
B. Pierce, CHI	7.49

Shutouts
W. Ford, NY	7
B. Turley, NY	6
D. Donovan, CHI	4
E. Wynn, CHI	4

Fewest Walks/9 Innings
D. Donovan, CHI	1.92
B. O'Dell, BAL	2.07
F. Sullivan, BOS	2.21
F. Lary, DET	2.35

Most Strikeouts/9 Inn.
C. Pascual, WAS	7.41
J. Bunning, DET	7.25
E. Wynn, CHI	6.72
B. Turley, NY	6.16

Innings
F. Lary, DET	260
P. Ramos, WAS	259
D. Donovan, CHI	248
B. Turley, NY	245

Games Pitched
T. Clevenger, WAS	55
D. Tomanek, CLE, KC	54
D. Hyde, WAS	53
M. Wall, BOS	52

AMERICAN LEAGUE 1958, *cont.*

	W	L	PCT	GB	R	OR	Batting 2B	3B	HR	BA	SA	SB	Fielding E	DP	FA	Pitching CG	BB	SO	ShO	SV	ERA
New York	92	62	.597		**759**	577	212	39	**164**	**.268**	**.416**	48	128	**182**	.978	53	557	796	**21**	**33**	**3.22**
Chicago	82	72	.532	10	634	615	191	42	101	.257	.367	**101**	114	160	.981	55	515	751	15	25	3.61
Boston	79	75	.513	13	697	691	**229**	30	155	.256	.400	29	145	172	.976	44	521	695	5	28	3.92
Cleveland	77	76	.503	14.5	694	635	210	31	161	.258	.403	50	152	171	.974	51	604	766	2	20	3.73
Detroit	77	77	.500	15	659	606	**229**	41	109	.266	.389	48	**106**	140	**.982**	59	437	**797**	8	19	3.59
Baltimore	74	79	.484	17.5	521	**575**	195	19	108	.241	.350	33	114	159	.980	55	**403**	749	15	28	3.40
Kansas City	73	81	.474	19	642	713	196	**50**	138	.247	.381	22	125	166	.979	42	467	720	9	25	4.15
Washington	61	93	.396	31	553	747	161	38	121	.240	.357	22	118	163	.980	28	558	762	6	28	4.53
					5159	5159	1623	290	1057	.254	.383	353	1002	1313	.979	387	4062	6036	81	206	3.77

NATIONAL LEAGUE 1959

Team	POS	Player	AB	BA	HR	RBI	PO	A	E	DP	TC/G	FA	Pitcher	G	IP	W	L	SV	ERA
Los Angeles W-88 L-68 Walter Alston	1B	G. Hodges	413	.276	25	80	891	66	8	77	8.5	.992	D. Drysdale	44	271	17	13	2	3.46
	2B	C. Neal	616	.287	19	83	**386**	413	9	**110**	5.4	.989	J. Podres	34	195	14	9	0	4.11
	SS	D. Zimmer	249	.165	4	28	115	226	10	43	4.0	.972	S. Koufax	35	153	8	6	2	4.05
	3B	J. Gilliam	553	.282	3	34	121	245	16	18	2.9	.958	R. Craig	29	153	11	5	0	2.06
	RF	D. Snider	370	.308	23	88	157	2	4	1	1.5	.975	D. McDevitt	39	145	10	8	4	3.97
	CF	D. Demeter	371	.256	18	70	223	5	4	1	1.9	.983	S. Williams	35	125	5	5	0	3.97
	LF	W. Moon	543	.302	19	74	224	13	4	2	1.7	.983	L. Sherry	23	94	7	2	3	2.19
	C	J. Roseboro	397	.232	10	38	**848**	54	8	10	**7.8**	.991	C. Labine	56	85	5	10	9	3.93
	1O	N. Larker	311	.289	8	49	491	48	5	53		.991							
	OF	R. Fairly	244	.238	4	23	97	8	4	1	1.2	.963							
	SS	M. Wills	242	.260	0	7	121	220	12	39	4.3	.966							
Milwaukee W-86 L-70 Fred Haney	1B	J. Adcock	404	.292	25	76	761	80	2	67	9.5	.998	W. Spahn	40	**292**	**21**	15	0	2.96
	2B	F. Mantilla	251	.215	3	19	97	126	7	26	3.8	.970	L. Burdette	41	290	**21**	15	1	4.07
	SS	J. Logan	470	.291	13	50	260	431	18	78	5.1	.975	B. Buhl	31	198	15	9	0	2.86
	3B	E. Mathews	594	.306	**46**	114	144	305	18	21	3.2	.961	J. Jay	34	136	6	11	0	4.09
	RF	H. Aaron	629	**.355**	39	123	261	12	5	3	1.8	.982	J. Pizarro	29	134	6	2	0	3.77
	CF	B. Bruton	478	.289	6	41	309	6	3	2	2.4	.991	C. Willey	26	117	5	9	0	4.15
	LF	W. Covington	373	.279	7	45	148	6	6	2	1.7	.963	B. Rush	31	101	5	6	0	2.40
	C	D. Crandall	518	.257	21	72	783	**71**	5	15	5.9	**.994**	D. McMahon	60	81	5	3	15	2.57
	1B	F. Torre	263	.228	1	33	622	46	4	43	7.7	.994							
	2B	B. Avila	172	.238	3	19	103	131	8	21	4.7	.967							
San Francisco W-83 L-71 Bill Rigney	1B	O. Cepeda	605	.317	27	105	929	70	16	74	8.3	.984	J. Antonelli	40	282	19	10	1	3.10
	2B	D. Spencer	555	.265	12	62	350	413	24	82	5.2	.970	S. Jones	50	271	**21**	15	4	**2.83**
	SS	E. Bressoud	315	.251	9	26	151	267	11	37	4.7	.974	McCormick	47	226	12	16	3	3.99
	3B	J. Davenport	469	.258	6	38	91	221	7	15	2.6	**.978**	J. Sanford	36	222	15	12	1	3.16
	RF	W. Kirkland	463	.272	22	68	212	8	7	0	1.9	.969	S. Miller	59	168	8	7	8	2.84
	CF	W. Mays	575	.313	34	104	353	6	6	2	2.5	.984							
	LF	J. Brandt	429	.270	12	57	176	10	3	2	1.6	.984							
	C	H. Landrith	283	.251	3	29	576	45	5	5	5.7	.992							
	OF	F. Alou	247	.275	10	33	111	2	3	0	1.7	.974							
	SS	A. Rodgers	228	.250	6	24	110	197	22	35	5.0	.933							
	1B	W. McCovey	192	.354	13	38	424	29	5	29	9.0	.989							
	C	B. Schmidt	181	.243	5	20	307	30	0	1	4.8	1.000							
	OF	L. Wagner	129	.225	5	22	48	0	3	0	1.8	.941							
Pittsburgh W-78 L-76 Danny Murtaugh	1B	D. Stuart	397	.297	27	78	831	81	**22**	87	8.9	.976	V. Law	34	266	18	9	1	2.98
	2B	B. Mazeroski	493	.241	7	59	303	373	13	100	5.2	.981	B. Friend	35	235	8	**19**	0	4.03
	SS	D. Groat	593	.275	5	51	**301**	473	**29**	97	5.5	.964	H. Haddix	31	224	12	12	0	3.13
	3B	D. Hoak	564	.294	8	65	169	**322**	20	31	3.3	.961	R. Kline	33	186	11	13	0	4.26
	RF	R. Clemente	432	.296	4	50	229	10	**13**	1	2.4	.948	B. Daniels	34	101	7	9	1	5.45
	CF	B. Virdon	519	.254	8	41	404	16	9	5	3.0	.979	R. Face	57	93	18	1	10	2.70
	LF	B. Skinner	547	.280	13	61	285	9	11	1	2.1	.964							
	C	S. Burgess	377	.297	11	59	441	39	8	4	4.8	.984							
	OF	R. Mejias	276	.236	7	28	155	8	5	2	2.0	.970							
	1B	R. Nelson	175	.291	6	32	337	18	2	45	6.4	.994							
	C	D. Kravitz	162	.253	3	21	198	19	3	3	4.9	.986							
Chicago W-74 L-80 Bob Scheffing	1B	D. Long	296	.236	14	37	731	49	12	63	9.3	.985	B. Anderson	37	235	12	13	0	4.13
	2B	T. Taylor	624	.280	8	38	352	**456**	25	105	**5.6**	.970	G. Hobbie	46	234	16	13	0	3.69
	SS	E. Banks	589	.304	**45**	**143**	271	**519**	12	95	5.2	**.985**	D. Hillman	39	191	8	11	0	3.53
	3B	A. Dark	477	.264	6	45	111	255	20	20	2.9	.948	M. Drabowsky	31	142	5	10	0	4.13
	RF	L. Walls	354	.257	8	33	203	1	7	0	1.8	.967	B. Henry	65	134	9	8	12	2.68
	CF	G. Altman	420	.245	12	47	278	7	3	2	2.4	.990	Ceccarelli	18	102	5	5	0	4.76
	LF	B. Thomson	374	.259	11	52	223	9	3	4	2.0	.987	J. Buzhardt	31	101	4	5	0	4.97
	C	S. Taylor	353	.269	13	43	497	37	**10**	1	5.0	.982	D. Elston	65	98	10	8	13	3.32
	OF	W. Moryn	381	.234	14	48	175	9	2	1	1.8	.989							
	1B	J. Marshall	294	.252	11	40	558	51	2	52	8.5	.997							
	UT	E. Averill	186	.237	10	34	197	49	13	4		.950							
	OF	I. Noren	156	.321	4	19	81	4	0	1	2.1	1.000							

NATIONAL LEAGUE 1959, cont.

	POS	Player	AB	BA	HR	RBI	PO	A	E	DP	TC/G	FA	Pitcher	G	IP	W	L	SV	ERA
Cincinnati	1B	F. Robinson	540	.311	36	125	998	75	17	111	8.7	.984	D. Newcombe	30	222	13	8	1	3.16
	2B	J. Temple	598	.311	8	67	322	390	19	96	4.9	.974	B. Purkey	38	218	13	18	1	4.25
W-74 L-80	SS	E. Kasko	329	.283	2	31	182	271	11	61	5.5	.976	O. Pena	46	136	5	9	5	4.76
	3B	W. Jones	233	.249	7	31	92	105	7	9	3.0	.966	J. Nuxhall	28	132	9	9	1	4.24
Mayo Smith	RF	G. Bell	580	.293	19	115	269	15	1	1	2.0	.996	J. O'Toole	28	129	5	8	0	5.15
W-35 L-45	CF	V. Pinson	648	.316	20	84	423	11	7	4	2.9	.984	B. Lawrence	43	128	7	12	10	4.77
	LF	J. Lynch	379	.269	17	58	180	5	4	3	1.9	.979	J. Brosnan	26	83	8	3	2	3.35
Fred Hutchinson	C	E. Bailey	379	.264	12	40	549	64	6	6	5.3	.990	J. Hook	17	79	5	5	0	5.13
W-39 L-35																			
	UT	F. Thomas	374	.225	12	47	206	126	19	19		.946							
	SS	R. McMillan	246	.264	9	24	163	205	10	50	5.2	.974							
	C	D. Dotterer	161	.267	2	17	230	20	2	3	4.9	.992							
	P	D. Newcombe	105	.305	3	21	14	31	1	4	1.5	.978							
St. Louis	1B	S. Musial	341	.255	14	44	623	63	7	72	7.7	.990	L. Jackson	40	256	14	13	0	3.30
	2B	Blasingame	615	.289	1	24	362	439	17	104	5.5	.979	V. Mizell	31	201	13	10	0	4.20
W-71 L-83	SS	A. Grammas	368	.269	3	30	216	373	22	80	4.7	.964	E. Broglio	35	181	7	12	0	4.72
	3B	K. Boyer	563	.309	28	94	134	300	20	32	3.2	.956	L. McDaniel	62	132	14	12	15	3.82
Solly Hemus	RF	Cunningham	458	.345	7	60	201	5	6	1	1.8	.972	G. Blaylock	26	100	4	5	0	5.13
	CF	G. Cimoli	519	.279	8	72	267	12	6	2	2.0	.979	M. Bridges	27	76	6	3	1	4.26
	LF	B. White	517	.302	12	72	175	2	7	1	2.0	.962							
	C	H. Smith	452	.270	13	50	758	60	9	13	5.9	.989							
	OF	C. Flood	208	.255	7	26	147	1	5	1	1.4	.967							
	OF	G. Oliver	172	.244	6	28	62	1	3	0	1.6	.955							
	PH	G. Crowe	103	.301	8	29													
Philadelphia	1B	E. Bouchee	499	.285	15	74	1127	95	17	96	9.2	.986	R. Roberts	35	257	15	17	0	4.27
	2B	S. Anderson	477	.218	0	34	343	403	12	70	5.0	.984	J. Owens	31	221	12	12	1	3.21
W-64 L-90	SS	J. Koppe	422	.261	7	28	218	347	27	67	5.2	.954	G. Conley	25	180	12	7	1	3.00
	3B	G. Freese	400	.268	23	70	83	156	22	15	2.4	.916	D. Cardwell	25	153	9	10	0	4.06
Eddie Sawyer	RF	W. Post	468	.254	22	94	226	12	2	3	2.0	.992	R. Semproch	30	112	3	10	5	5.40
	CF	R. Ashburn	564	.266	1	20	359	4	11	1	2.5	.971	R. Gomez	20	72	3	8	1	6.10
	LF	H. Anderson	508	.240	14	63	283	17	6	4	2.2	.980	D. Farrell	38	57	1	6	6	4.74
	C	C. Sawatski	198	.293	9	43	306	23	7	4	4.9	.979							
	O1	D. Philley	254	.291	7	37	238	15	4	18		.984							
	3B	W. Jones	160	.269	7	24	40	76	3	5	2.6	.975							

BATTING AND BASE RUNNING LEADERS

Batting Average
H. Aaron, MIL	.355
Cunningham, STL	.345
O. Cepeda, SF	.317
V. Pinson, CIN	.316
W. Mays, SF	.313

Slugging Average
H. Aaron, MIL	.636
E. Banks, CHI	.596
E. Mathews, MIL	.593
F. Robinson, CIN	.583
W. Mays, SF	.583

Home Runs
E. Mathews, MIL	46
E. Banks, CHI	45
H. Aaron, MIL	39
F. Robinson, CIN	36
W. Mays, SF	34

Total Bases
H. Aaron, MIL	400
E. Mathews, MIL	352
E. Banks, CHI	351
W. Mays, SF	335
V. Pinson, CIN	330

Runs Batted In
E. Banks, CHI	143
F. Robinson, CIN	125
H. Aaron, MIL	123
G. Bell, CIN	115
E. Mathews, MIL	114

Stolen Bases
W. Mays, SF	27
J. Gilliam, LA	23
O. Cepeda, SF	23
T. Taylor, CHI	23
V. Pinson, CIN	21

Hits
H. Aaron, MIL	223
V. Pinson, CIN	205
O. Cepeda, SF	192
J. Temple, CIN	186

Base on Balls
J. Gilliam, LA	96
Cunningham, STL	88
W. Moon, LA	81
E. Mathews, MIL	80

Home Run Percentage
E. Mathews, MIL	7.7
E. Banks, CHI	7.6
F. Robinson, CIN	6.7
H. Aaron, MIL	6.2

Runs Scored
V. Pinson, CIN	131
W. Mays, SF	125
E. Mathews, MIL	118
H. Aaron, MIL	116

Doubles
V. Pinson, CIN	47
H. Aaron, MIL	46
W. Mays, SF	43
G. Cimoli, STL	40

Triples
W. Moon, LA	11
C. Neal, LA	11
A. Dark, CHI	9
B. White, STL	9

PITCHING LEADERS

Winning Percentage
R. Face, PIT	.947
V. Law, PIT	.667
J. Antonelli, SF	.655
B. Buhl, MIL	.625

Earned Run Average
S. Jones, SF	2.83
S. Miller, SF	2.84
B. Buhl, MIL	2.86
W. Spahn, MIL	2.96
V. Law, PIT	2.98

Wins
L. Burdette, MIL	21
S. Jones, SF	21
W. Spahn, MIL	21
J. Antonelli, SF	19
R. Face, PIT	18
V. Law, PIT	18

Saves
L. McDaniel, STL	15
D. McMahon, MIL	15
D. Elston, CHI	13
B. Henry, CHI	12
R. Face, PIT	10
B. Lawrence, CIN	10

Strikeouts
D. Drysdale, LA	242
S. Jones, SF	209
S. Koufax, LA	173
J. Antonelli, SF	165
McCormick, SF	151

Complete Games
W. Spahn, MIL	21
V. Law, PIT	20
L. Burdette, MIL	20
R. Roberts, PHI	19
D. Newcombe, CIN	17
J. Antonelli, SF	17

Fewest Hits/9 Innings
H. Haddix, PIT	7.58
S. Jones, SF	7.71
G. Hobbie, CHI	7.85
D. Drysdale, LA	7.88

Shutouts
7 tied with	4

Fewest Walks/9 Innings
D. Newcombe, CIN	1.09
L. Burdette, MIL	1.18
R. Roberts, PHI	1.22
B. Purkey, CIN	1.78

Most Strikeouts/9 Inn.
D. Drysdale, LA	8.05
S. Jones, SF	6.95
J. Podres, LA	6.69
E. Broglio, STL	6.60

Innings
W. Spahn, MIL	292
L. Burdette, MIL	290
J. Antonelli, SF	282
S. Jones, SF	271

Games Pitched
B. Henry, CHI	65
D. Elston, CHI	65
L. McDaniel, STL	62
D. McMahon, MIL	60

NATIONAL LEAGUE 1959, cont.

	W	L	PCT	GB	R	OR	2B	3B	Batting HR	BA	SA	SB	E	Fielding DP	FA	CG	Pitching BB	SO	ShO	SV	ERA
Los Angeles *	88	68	.564		705	670	196	46	148	.257	.396	**84**	114	154	**.981**	43	614	**1077**	14	**26**	3.79
Milwaukee	86	70	.551	2	724	623	216	36	**177**	.265	.417	41	127	138	.979	**69**	429	775	**18**	18	3.51
San Francisco	83	71	.539	4	705	**613**	239	35	167	.261	.414	81	152	118	.974	52	500	873	12	23	**3.47**
Pittsburgh	78	76	.506	9	651	680	230	42	112	.263	.384	32	154	**165**	.975	48	**418**	730	7	17	3.90
Chicago	74	80	.481	13	673	688	209	44	163	.249	.398	32	140	142	.977	30	519	765	11	25	4.01
Cincinnati	74	80	.481	13	**764**	738	258	34	161	**.274**	**.427**	65	126	157	.978	44	456	690	7	**26**	4.31
St. Louis	71	83	.461	16	641	725	244	**49**	118	.269	.400	65	146	158	.975	36	564	846	8	25	4.34
Philadelphia	64	90	.416	23	599	725	196	38	113	.242	.362	39	154	132	.973	54	474	769	8	15	4.27
					5462	5462	1788	324	1159	.260	.400	439	1113	1164	.977	376	3974	6525	85	175	3.95

* Defeated Milwaukee in a playoff 2 games to 0.

AMERICAN LEAGUE 1959

	POS	Player	AB	BA	HR	RBI	PO	A	E	DP	TC/G	FA	Pitcher	G	IP	W	L	SV	ERA
Chicago	1B	E. Torgeson	277	.220	9	45	717	37	13	58	7.4	.983	E. Wynn	37	**256**	**22**	10	0	3.17
	2B	N. Fox	**624**	.306	2	70	**364**	**453**	10	93	5.3	**.988**	B. Shaw	47	231	18	6	3	2.69
W-94 L-60	SS	L. Aparicio	612	.257	6	51	282	**460**	23	87	5.0	**.970**	B. Pierce	34	224	14	15	0	3.62
	3B	B. Phillips	379	.264	5	40	90	202	15	13	3.1	.951	D. Donovan	31	180	9	10	0	3.66
Al Lopez	RF	J. McAnany	210	.276	0	27	106	6	4	4	1.7	.966	B. Latman	37	156	8	5	0	3.75
	CF	J. Landis	515	.272	5	60	**420**	10	3	2	2.9	.993	G. Staley	**67**	116	8	5	14	2.24
	LF	A. Smith	472	.237	17	55	303	8	6	2	2.5	.981	T. Lown	60	93	9	2	15	2.89
	C	S. Lollar	505	.265	22	84	623	51	5	**14**	5.6	.993							
	3B	B. Goodman	268	.250	1	28	57	135	10	10	2.7	.950							
	OF	J. Rivera	177	.220	4	19	75	5	2	3	1.2	.976							
	C	J. Romano	126	.294	5	25	169	16	4	5	5.0	.979							
Cleveland	1B	V. Power	595	.289	10	60	**1039**	110	6	98	9.5	**.995**	C. McLish	35	235	19	8	1	3.63
	2B	B. Martin	242	.260	9	24	147	149	1	37	4.4	.997	G. Bell	44	234	16	11	5	4.04
W-89 L-65	SS	W. Held	525	.251	29	71	177	277	18	43	4.6	.962	M. Grant	38	165	10	7	0	4.14
	3B	Strickland	441	.238	3	48	69	131	6	11	2.6	.971	H. Score	30	161	9	11	0	4.71
Joe Gordon	RF	R. Colavito	588	.257	**42**	111	319	7	5	1	2.1	.985	J. Perry	44	153	12	10	4	2.65
	CF	J. Piersall	317	.246	4	30	216	3	4	2	2.5	.982	M. Garcia	29	72	3	6	1	4.00
	LF	M. Minoso	570	.302	21	92	314	14	5	1	2.3	.985							
	C	R. Nixon	258	.240	1	29	374	31	6	8	5.6	.985							
	O1	T. Francona	399	.363	20	79	432	21	5	21		.989							
	23	J. Baxes	247	.239	15	34	123	148	15	31		.948							
New York	1B	B. Skowron	282	.298	15	59	626	43	6	68	9.4	.991	W. Ford	35	204	16	10	1	3.04
	2B	Richardson	469	.301	2	33	256	292	17	85	5.2	.970	A. Ditmar	38	202	13	9	1	2.90
W-79 L-75	SS	T. Kubek	512	.279	6	51	121	217	11	42	5.2	.968	B. Turley	33	154	8	11	0	4.32
	3B	H. Lopez	406	.283	16	69	66	147	17	15	3.0	.926	D. Maas	38	138	14	8	4	4.43
Casey Stengel	RF	H. Bauer	341	.238	9	39	139	2	4	0	1.3	.972	R. Terry	24	127	3	7	0	3.39
	CF	M. Mantle	541	.285	31	75	366	7	2	3	2.6	**.995**	D. Larsen	25	125	6	7	0	4.33
	LF	N. Siebern	380	.271	11	53	175	1	2	0	1.9	.989	J. Coates	37	100	6	1	3	2.87
	C	Y. Berra	472	.284	19	69	**698**	61	2	9	6.6	**.997**	B. Shantz	33	95	7	3	3	2.38
	UT	E. Howard	443	.273	18	73	712	49	10	41		.987	R. Duren	41	77	3	6	14	1.88
	UT	McDougald	434	.251	4	34	190	345	10	70		.982							
	1B	Throneberry	192	.240	8	22	337	27	4	40	6.8	.989							
	OF	E. Slaughter	99	.172	6	21	27	0	1	0	1.1	.964							
Detroit	1B	G. Harris	349	.221	9	39	728	57	6	59	8.5	.992	J. Bunning	40	250	17	13	1	3.89
	2B	F. Bolling	459	.266	13	55	281	340	8	81	5.0	.987	P. Foytack	39	240	14	14	1	4.64
W-76 L-78	SS	R. Bridges	381	.268	3	35	179	293	24	66	4.5	.952	D. Mossi	34	228	17	9	0	3.36
	3B	E. Yost	521	.278	21	61	168	259	17	21	3.0	**.962**	F. Lary	32	223	17	10	0	3.55
Bill Norman	RF	H. Kuenn	561	**.353**	9	71	247	6	3	0	1.9	.988	R. Narleski	42	104	4	12	5	5.78
W-2 L-15	CF	A. Kaline	511	.327	27	94	364	4	4	0	2.7	.989	T. Morgan	46	93	1	4	9	3.98
	LF	C. Maxwell	518	.251	31	95	285	6	4	1	2.2	.986	D. Sisler	32	52	1	3	7	4.01
Jimmy Dykes	C	L. Berberet	338	.216	13	44	511	39	6	4	5.9	.989							
W-74 L-63	C	R. Wilson	228	.263	4	35	374	55	5	8	6.3	.988							
	UT	T. Lepcio	215	.279	7	24	96	143	11	30		.956							
	1B	B. Osborne	209	.191	3	21	377	27	7	36	7.3	.983							
	1B	G. Zernial	132	.227	7	26	197	10	6	20	6.7	.972							
Boston	1B	D. Gernert	298	.262	11	42	552	49	3	54	8.1	**.995**	T. Brewer	36	215	10	12	2	3.76
	2B	P. Runnels	560	.314	6	57	273	272	10	82	5.5	.982	J. Casale	31	180	13	8	0	4.31
W-75 L-79	SS	D. Buddin	485	.241	10	53	235	412	**35**	89	4.5	.949	F. Sullivan	30	178	9	11	1	3.95
	3B	F. Malzone	604	.280	19	92	134	**357**	24	40	3.3	.953	Monbouquette	34	152	7	7	0	4.15
Pinky Higgins	RF	J. Jensen	535	.277	28	**112**	311	12	6	4	2.3	.982	I. Delock	28	134	11	6	0	2.95
W-31 L-42	CF	G. Geiger	335	.245	11	48	173	5	2	1	1.9	.989	F. Baumann	26	96	6	4	1	4.05
	LF	T. Williams	272	.254	10	43	94	4	3	0	1.3	.970	M. Fornieles	46	82	5	3	11	3.07
Rudy York	C	S. White	377	.284	1	42	557	56	6	8	5.2	.990	L. Kiely	41	56	3	3	7	4.20
W-0 L-1	OF	G. Stephens	270	.278	3	39	141	11	3	0	1.8	.981							
	OF	M. Keough	251	.243	7	27	147	5	1	1	2.2	.993							
Bill Jurges	1B	V. Wertz	247	.275	7	49	440	38	4	44	7.5	.992							
W-44 L-36	2B	P. Green	172	.233	1	10	109	132	7	38	5.5	.972							
	C	P. Daley	169	.225	1	11	245	28	1	5	4.7	.996							

AMERICAN LEAGUE 1959, cont.

	POS	Player	AB	BA	HR	RBI	PO	A	E	DP	TC/G	FA	Pitcher	G	IP	W	L	SV	ERA
Baltimore	1B	B. Boyd	415	.265	3	41	927	46	15	88	9.1	.985	H. Wilhelm	32	226	15	11	0	**2.19**
	2B	B. Gardner	401	.217	6	27	333	392	18	104	5.3	.976	M. Pappas	33	209	15	9	3	3.27
W-74 L-80	SS	Carrasquel	346	.223	4	28	124	237	11	63	4.2	.970	B. O'Dell	38	199	10	12	1	2.93
	3B	B. Robinson	313	.284	4	24	92	187	13	25	3.4	.955	J. Walker	30	182	11	10	4	2.92
Paul Richards	RF	G. Woodling	440	.300	14	77	210	2	4	0	1.7	.981	H. Brown	31	164	11	9	3	3.79
	CF	W. Tasby	505	.250	13	48	320	13	11	4	2.5	.968	B. Loes	37	64	4	7	14	4.06
	LF	B. Nieman	360	.292	21	60	171	6	5	0	1.9	.973							
	C	G. Triandos	393	.216	25	73	597	63	13	5	5.4	.981							
	S3	B. Klaus	321	.249	3	25	120	231	13	28		.964							
	OF	A. Pilarcik	273	.282	3	16	133	3	3	1	1.3	.978							
	C	J. Ginsberg	166	.181	1	14	241	29	2	4	4.4	.993							
	1B	W. Dropo	151	.278	6	21	386	18	4	42	7.6	.990							
Kansas City	1B	K. Hadley	288	.253	10	39	656	42	8	66	7.4	.989	B. Daley	39	216	16	13	1	3.16
	2B	Terwilliger	180	.267	2	18	144	166	9	42	5.1	.972	N. Garver	32	201	10	13	1	3.71
W-66 L-88	SS	DeMaestri	352	.244	6	34	167	320	22	63	4.4	.957	R. Herbert	37	184	11	11	1	4.85
	3B	D. Williams	488	.266	16	75	83	164	11	10	3.2	.957	J. Kucks	33	151	8	11	1	3.87
Harry Craft	RF	R. Maris	433	.273	16	72	231	7	6	4	2.1	.975	B. Grim	40	125	6	10	4	4.09
	CF	B. Tuttle	463	.300	7	43	294	17	5	3	2.6	.984	R. Coleman	29	81	2	10	2	4.56
	LF	B. Cerv	463	.285	20	87	231	8	5	2	2.1	.980	Sturdivant	36	72	2	6	5	4.65
	C	F. House	347	.236	1	30	447	43	9	7	5.3	.982							
	2S	J. Lumpe	403	.243	3	28	218	306	12	80		.978							
	3B	H. Smith	292	.288	5	31	85	119	10	10	2.8	.953							
	OF	R. Snyder	243	.313	3	21	127	9	2	2	2.2	.986							
	C	H. Chiti	162	.272	5	25	228	25	3	5	5.4	.988							
	2B	H. Lopez	135	.281	6	24	81	71	11	15	4.9	.933							
Washington	1B	R. Sievers	385	.242	21	49	846	72	10	72	10.0	.989	C. Pascual	32	239	17	10	0	2.64
	2B	R. Bertoia	308	.237	8	29	139	198	10	40	4.9	.971	P. Ramos	37	234	13	19	0	4.16
W-63 L-91	SS	B. Consolo	202	.213	0	10	111	229	17	44	4.8	.952	R. Kemmerer	37	206	8	17	0	4.50
	3B	H. Killebrew	546	.242	42	105	129	325	30	18	3.2	.938	B. Fischer	34	187	9	11	0	4.28
Cookie Lavagetto	RF	Throneberry	327	.251	10	42	136	7	7	2	1.7	.953	T. Clevenger	50	117	8	5	8	3.91
	CF	B. Allison	570	.261	30	85	333	8	9	1	2.3	.974	H. Griggs	37	98	2	8	2	5.25
	LF	J. Lemon	531	.279	33	100	281	4	9	0	2.1	.969	C. Stobbs	41	91	1	8	7	2.98
	C	H. Naragon	195	.241	0	11	262	13	2	0	5.1	.993	D. Hyde	37	54	2	5	4	4.97
	SS	R. Samford	237	.224	5	22	92	177	15	33	4.4	.947							
	2B	Aspromonte	225	.244	2	14	101	137	10	25	4.8	.960							
	1B	J. Becquer	220	.268	1	26	454	32	5	38	9.3	.990							
	OF	L. Green	190	.242	2	15	89	4	2	0	1.6	.979							
	C	C. Courtney	189	.233	2	18	213	11	3	2	4.3	.987							

BATTING AND BASE RUNNING LEADERS

Batting Average
H. Kuenn, DET	.353
A. Kaline, DET	.327
P. Runnels, BOS	.314
N. Fox, CHI	.306
M. Minoso, CLE	.302

Slugging Average
A. Kaline, DET	.530
H. Killebrew, WAS	.516
M. Mantle, NY	.514
R. Colavito, CLE	.512
J. Lemon, WAS	.510

Home Runs
H. Killebrew, WAS	42
R. Colavito, CLE	42
J. Lemon, WAS	33
C. Maxwell, DET	31
M. Mantle, NY	31

Winning Percentage
B. Shaw, CHI	.750
C. McLish, CLE	.704
E. Wynn, CHI	.688
D. Mossi, DET	.654
F. Lary, DET	.630
C. Pascual, WAS	.630

PITCHING LEADERS

Earned Run Average
H. Wilhelm, BAL	2.19
C. Pascual, WAS	2.64
B. Shaw, CHI	2.69
A. Ditmar, NY	2.90
J. Walker, BAL	2.92

Wins
E. Wynn, CHI	22
C. McLish, CLE	19
B. Shaw, CHI	18

Total Bases
R. Colavito, CLE	301
H. Killebrew, WAS	282
H. Kuenn, DET	281
M. Mantle, NY	278
B. Allison, WAS	275

Runs Batted In
J. Jensen, BOS	112
R. Colavito, CLE	111
H. Killebrew, WAS	105
J. Lemon, WAS	100
C. Maxwell, DET	95

Stolen Bases
L. Aparicio, CHI	56
M. Mantle, NY	21
J. Landis, CHI	20
J. Jensen, BOS	20
B. Allison, WAS	13

Saves
T. Lown, CHI	15
G. Staley, CHI	14
B. Loes, BAL	14
R. Duren, NY	14
M. Fornieles, BOS	11

Strikeouts
J. Bunning, DET	201
C. Pascual, WAS	185
E. Wynn, CHI	179
H. Score, CLE	147
H. Wilhelm, BAL	139

Complete Games
C. Pascual, WAS	17
M. Pappas, BAL	15
D. Mossi, DET	15
J. Bunning, DET	14
E. Wynn, CHI	14

Hits
H. Kuenn, DET	198
N. Fox, CHI	191
P. Runnels, BOS	176
M. Minoso, CLE	172

Base on Balls
E. Yost, DET	135
P. Runnels, BOS	95
M. Mantle, NY	94
D. Buddin, BOS	92

Home Run Percentage
H. Killebrew, WAS	7.7
R. Colavito, CLE	7.1
J. Lemon, WAS	6.2
C. Maxwell, DET	6.0

Fewest Hits/9 Innings
H. Score, CLE	6.89
A. Ditmar, NY	6.95
H. Wilhelm, BAL	7.09
E. Wynn, CHI	7.11

Shutouts
C. Pascual, WAS	6
E. Wynn, CHI	5
M. Pappas, BAL	4

Fewest Walks/9 Innings
H. Brown, BAL	1.76
F. Lary, DET	1.86
N. Garver, KC	1.88
D. Mossi, DET	1.93

Runs Scored
E. Yost, DET	115
M. Mantle, NY	104
V. Power, CLE	102
J. Jensen, BOS	101

Doubles
H. Kuenn, DET	42
F. Malzone, BOS	34
N. Fox, CHI	34
D. Williams, KC	33

Triples
B. Allison, WAS	9
McDougald, NY	8
R. Maris, KC	7
T. Kubek, NY	7

Most Strikeouts/9 Inn.
H. Score, CLE	8.23
J. Bunning, DET	7.25
C. Pascual, WAS	6.98
B. Turley, NY	6.47

Innings
E. Wynn, CHI	256
J. Bunning, DET	250
P. Foytack, DET	240
C. Pascual, WAS	239

Games Pitched
G. Staley, CHI	67
T. Lown, CHI	60
T. Clevenger, WAS	50
B. Shaw, CHI	47

AMERICAN LEAGUE 1959, cont.

	W	L	PCT	GB	R	OR	Batting					SB	Fielding			Pitching					ERA
							2B	3B	HR	BA	SA		E	DP	FA	CG	BB	SO	ShO	SV	
Chicago	94	60	.610		669	**588**	220	**46**	97	.250	.364	**113**	130	141	**.979**	44	525	761	13	**36**	**3.29**
Cleveland	89	65	.578	5	**745**	646	216	25	**167**	**.263**	**.408**	33	126	138	.978	**58**	635	799	7	23	3.75
New York	79	75	.513	15	687	647	224	40	153	.260	.402	45	131	160	.978	38	594	**836**	15	28	3.60
Detroit	76	78	.494	18	713	732	196	30	160	.258	.400	34	**124**	131	.978	53	**432**	829	9	24	4.20
Boston	75	79	.487	19	726	696	**248**	28	125	.256	.385	68	131	**167**	.978	38	589	724	9	25	4.17
Baltimore	74	80	.481	20	551	621	182	23	109	.238	.345	36	147	163	.976	45	476	735	**15**	30	3.56
Kansas City	66	88	.429	28	681	760	231	43	117	.263	.390	34	159	156	.973	44	492	703	8	21	4.35
Washington	63	91	.409	31	619	701	173	32	163	.237	.379	51	162	140	.973	46	467	694	10	21	4.01
					5391	5391	1690	267	1091	.253	.384	414	1110	1196	.977	366	4210	6081	86	208	3.86

NATIONAL LEAGUE 1960

	POS	Player	AB	BA	HR	RBI	PO	A	E	DP	TC/G	FA	Pitcher	G	IP	W	L	SV	ERA
Pittsburgh W-95 L-59 Danny Murtaugh	1B	D. Stuart	438	.260	23	83	920	77	14	90	9.4	.986	B. Friend	38	276	18	12	1	3.00
	2B	B. Mazeroski	538	.273	11	64	**413**	449	10	**127**	5.8	**.989**	V. Law	35	272	20	9	0	3.08
	SS	D. Groat	573	**.325**	2	50	237	443	24	92	5.2	.966	H. Haddix	29	172	11	10	1	3.97
	3B	D. Hoak	553	.282	16	79	132	**324**	25	34	3.1	.948	V. Mizell	23	156	13	5	0	3.12
	RF	R. Clemente	570	.314	16	94	246	19	8	2	1.9	.971	R. Face	68	115	10	8	24	2.90
	CF	B. Virdon	409	.264	8	40	272	10	5	0	2.6	.983	F. Green	45	70	8	4	3	3.21
	LF	B. Skinner	571	.273	15	86	250	13	5	2	1.9	.981							
	C	S. Burgess	337	.294	7	39	485	38	3	7	5.9	**.994**							
	OF	G. Cimoli	307	.267	0	28	181	5	7	1	2.1	.964							
	C	H. Smith	258	.295	11	45	356	30	6	5	5.5	.985							
	1B	R. Nelson	200	.300	7	35	463	37	2	48	6.9	.996							
Milwaukee W-88 L-66 Chuck Dressen	1B	J. Adcock	514	.298	25	91	**1229**	104	9	105	**9.9**	.993	L. Burdette	45	276	19	13	4	3.36
	2B	C. Cottier	229	.227	3	19	180	214	13	40	4.4	.968	W. Spahn	40	268	**21**	10	2	3.50
	SS	J. Logan	482	.245	7	42	235	417	30	77	5.0	.956	B. Buhl	36	239	16	9	0	3.09
	3B	E. Mathews	548	.277	39	124	**141**	280	22	23	2.9	.950	C. Willey	28	145	6	7	0	4.35
	RF	H. Aaron	590	.292	40	**126**	320	13	6	6	2.2	.982	J. Jay	32	133	9	8	1	3.24
	CF	B. Bruton	629	.286	12	54	351	10	5	3	2.5	.986	J. Pizarro	21	115	6	7	0	4.55
	LF	W. Covington	281	.249	10	35	106	2	4	1	1.6	.964	D. McMahon	48	64	3	6	10	5.94
	C	D. Crandall	537	.294	19	77	**764**	70	10	9	6.0	.988	R. Piche	37	48	3	5	9	3.56
	2B	Schoendienst	226	.257	1	19	120	148	10	34	4.5	.964							
St. Louis W-86 L-68 Solly Hemus	1B	B. White	554	.283	16	79	994	65	11	**109**	8.7	.990	L. Jackson	43	**282**	18	13	0	3.48
	2B	J. Javier	451	.237	4	21	272	338	**24**	71	5.3	.962	E. Broglio	52	226	**21**	9	0	2.74
	SS	D. Spencer	507	.258	16	58	215	323	31	66	4.1	.946	R. Sadecki	26	157	9	9	0	3.78
	3B	K. Boyer	552	.304	32	97	140	300	19	**37**	3.1	.959	C. Simmons	23	152	7	4	0	2.66
	RF	Cunningham	492	.280	6	39	184	6	**10**	1	1.7	.950	R. Kline	34	118	4	9	1	6.04
	CF	C. Flood	396	.237	8	38	290	7	2	0	2.2	**.993**	L. McDaniel	65	116	12	4	26	2.09
	LF	S. Musial	331	.275	17	63	97	2	1	0	1.7	.990							
	C	H. Smith	337	.228	2	28	664	61	7	9	5.9	.990							
	OF	W. Moryn	200	.245	11	35	100	4	1	0	1.7	.990							
	UT	A. Grammas	196	.245	4	17	102	171	9	33		.968							
	OF	B. Nieman	188	.287	4	31	63	0	4	0	1.2	.940							
	C	C. Sawatski	179	.229	6	27	279	25	2	5	4.6	.993							
Los Angeles W-82 L-72 Walter Alston	1B	N. Larker	440	.323	5	78	914	80	7	81	8.4	.993	D. Drysdale	41	269	15	14	2	2.84
	2B	C. Neal	477	.256	8	40	250	291	13	78	4.1	.977	J. Podres	34	228	14	12	0	3.08
	SS	M. Wills	516	.295	0	27	260	431	**40**	78	5.0	.945	S. Williams	38	207	14	10	1	3.00
	3B	J. Gilliam	557	.248	5	40	101	262	15	21	2.9	.960	S. Koufax	37	175	8	13	1	3.91
	RF	F. Howard	448	.268	23	77	177	8	3	1	1.6	.984	L. Sherry	57	142	14	10	7	3.79
	CF	T. Davis	352	.276	11	44	151	7	4	2	1.9	.975	E. Roebuck	58	117	8	3	8	2.78
	LF	W. Moon	469	.299	13	69	194	15	3	3	1.7	.986	R. Craig	21	116	8	3	0	3.27
	C	J. Roseboro	287	.213	8	42	640	48	5	10	8.0	.993							
	OF	D. Snider	235	.243	14	36	108	3	4	1	1.5	.965							
	1B	G. Hodges	197	.198	8	30	403	33	2	40	4.8	.995							
	OF	D. Demeter	168	.274	9	29	92	2	1	1	1.5	.989							
San Francisco W-79 L-75 Bill Rigney W-33 L-25 Tom Sheehan W-46 L-50	1B	W. McCovey	260	.238	13	51	557	39	9	42	8.5	.985	McCormick	40	253	15	12	3	**2.70**
	2B	Blasingame	523	.235	2	31	318	329	14	66	5.0	.979	S. Jones	39	234	18	14	0	3.19
	SS	E. Bressoud	386	.225	9	43	191	339	22	53	4.8	.960	J. Sanford	37	219	12	14	0	3.82
	3B	J. Davenport	363	.251	6	38	77	171	10	12	2.5	**.961**	B. O'Dell	43	203	8	13	0	3.17
	RF	W. Kirkland	515	.252	21	65	252	16	6	5	1.9	.978	J. Antonelli	41	112	6	7	11	3.77
	CF	W. Mays	595	.319	29	103	392	12	8	2	2.9	.981	S. Miller	47	102	7	6	2	3.90
	LF	O. Cepeda	569	.297	24	96	163	10	3	3	1.9	.983	B. Loes	37	46	3	2	5	4.93
	C	B. Schmidt	344	.267	8	37	631	31	**13**	6	6.3	.981							
	32	Amalfitano	328	.277	1	27	99	184	14	24		.953							
	OF	F. Alou	322	.264	8	44	156	5	7	0	1.8	.958							
	UT	A. Rodgers	217	.244	2	22	112	129	12	26		.953							
	C	H. Landrith	190	.242	1	20	346	23	13	5	5.5	.966							

NATIONAL LEAGUE 1960, *cont.*

	POS	Player	AB	BA	HR	RBI	PO	A	E	DP	TC/G	FA	Pitcher	G	IP	W	L	SV	ERA
Cincinnati	1B	F. Robinson	464	.297	31	83	663	54	5	60	9.3	.993	B. Purkey	41	253	17	11	0	3.60
	2B	B. Martin	317	.246	3	16	228	207	11	52	4.6	.975	J. Hook	36	222	11	18	0	4.50
W-67 L-87	SS	R. McMillan	399	.236	10	42	171	315	18	68	4.3	.964	J. O'Toole	34	196	12	12	1	3.80
	3B	E. Kasko	479	.292	6	51	98	186	10	20	3.4	.966	C. McLish	37	151	4	14	0	4.16
Fred Hutchinson	RF	G. Bell	515	.262	12	62	239	13	3	1	1.9	.988	J. Nuxhall	38	112	1	8	0	4.42
	CF	V. Pinson	**652**	.287	20	61	**401**	11	8	1	2.7	.981	J. Brosnan	57	99	7	2	12	2.36
	LF	W. Post	249	.281	17	38	125	8	2	0	2.0	.985	D. Newcombe	16	83	4	6	0	4.57
	C	E. Bailey	441	.261	13	67	621	52	7	8	5.3	.990	B. Henry	51	68	1	5	17	3.19
	1B	G. Coleman	251	.271	6	32	559	63	1	69	9.4	.998							
	OF	J. Lynch	159	.289	6	27	41	1	4	1	1.4	.913							
	3B	W. Jones	149	.268	3	27	43	59	4	5	2.3	.962							
Chicago	1B	E. Bouchee	299	.237	5	44	709	56	7	56	9.7	.991	G. Hobbie	46	259	16	**20**	1	3.97
	2B	J. Kindall	246	.240	2	23	147	218	13	44	4.6	.966	B. Anderson	38	204	9	11	1	4.11
W-60 L-94	SS	E. Banks	597	.271	41	117	283	488	18	94	5.1	**.977**	D. Cardwell	31	177	8	14	0	4.37
	3B	R. Santo	347	.251	9	44	78	144	13	6	2.5	.945	D. Ellsworth	31	177	7	13	0	3.72
Charlie Grimm	RF	B. Will	475	.255	6	53	224	10	2	2	2.0	.992	D. Elston	60	127	8	9	11	3.40
W-6 L-11	CF	R. Ashburn	547	.291	0	40	317	11	8	2	2.3	.976	S. Morehead	45	123	2	9	4	3.94
	LF	G. Altman	334	.266	13	51	144	2	1	0	1.9	.993							
Lou Boudreau	C	M. Thacker	90	.156	0	6	170	23	4	2	3.9	.980							
W-54 L-83	UT	F. Thomas	479	.238	21	64	528	92	17	40		.973							
	23	D. Zimmer	368	.258	6	35	208	266	16	30		.967							
Philadelphia	1B	P. Herrera	512	.281	17	71	1017	**109**	14	88	8.5	.988	R. Roberts	35	237	12	16	1	4.02
	2B	T. Taylor	505	.287	4	35	283	356	21	67	5.4	.968	J. Buzhardt	30	200	5	16	0	3.86
W-59 L-95	SS	R. Amaro	264	.231	0	16	153	230	14	47	4.3	.965	G. Conley	29	183	8	14	0	3.68
	3B	A. Dark	198	.242	3	14	57	84	7	7	2.8	.953	J. Owens	31	150	4	14	0	5.04
Eddie Sawyer	RF	K. Walters	426	.239	8	37	220	17	3	4	2.0	.988	D. Green	23	109	3	6	0	4.06
W-0 L-1	CF	B. Del Greco	300	.237	10	26	247	10	8	1	3.0	.970	C. Short	42	107	6	9	3	3.94
	LF	J. Callison	288	.260	9	30	176	7	2	4	2.2	.989	D. Farrell	59	103	10	6	11	2.70
Andy Cohen	C	J. Coker	252	.214	6	34	394	43	8	5	5.9	.982	A. Mahaffey	14	93	7	3	0	2.31
W-1 L-0	OF	T. Curry	245	.261	6	34	96	2	8	0	1.7	.925							
	OF	T. Gonzalez	241	.299	6	33	146	6	3	0	2.3	.981							
Gene Mauch	OF	B. Smith	217	.286	4	27	125	4	0	1	1.8	1.000							
W-58 L-94	UT	L. Walls	181	.199	3	19	75	49	6	8		.954							
	SS	J. Koppe	170	.171	1	13	107	133	11	23	4.6	.956							
	C	C. Neeman	160	.181	4	13	252	31	6	2	5.6	.979							
	C	C. Dalrymple	158	.272	4	21	172	25	7	3	4.3	.966							

BATTING AND BASE RUNNING LEADERS

Batting Average
- D. Groat, PIT — .325
- W. Mays, SF — .319
- R. Clemente, PIT — .314
- K. Boyer, STL — .304
- W. Moon, LA — .299

Slugging Average
- F. Robinson, CIN — .595
- H. Aaron, MIL — .566
- K. Boyer, STL — .562
- W. Mays, SF — .555
- E. Banks, CHI — .554

Home Runs
- E. Banks, CHI — 41
- H. Aaron, MIL — 40
- E. Mathews, MIL — 39
- K. Boyer, STL — 32
- F. Robinson, CIN — 31

Total Bases
- H. Aaron, MIL — 334
- E. Banks, CHI — 331
- W. Mays, SF — 330
- K. Boyer, STL — 310
- V. Pinson, CIN — 308

Runs Batted In
- H. Aaron, MIL — 126
- E. Mathews, MIL — 124
- E. Banks, CHI — 117
- W. Mays, SF — 103
- K. Boyer, STL — 97

Stolen Bases
- M. Wills, LA — 50
- V. Pinson, CIN — 32
- T. Taylor, CHI, PHI — 26
- W. Mays, SF — 25
- B. Bruton, MIL — 22

Hits
- W. Mays, SF — 190
- V. Pinson, CIN — 187
- D. Groat, PIT — 186
- B. Bruton, MIL — 180

Base on Balls
- R. Ashburn, CHI — 116
- E. Mathews, MIL — 111
- J. Gilliam, LA — 96
- F. Robinson, CIN — 82

Home Run Percentage
- E. Mathews, MIL — 7.1
- E. Banks, CHI — 6.9
- H. Aaron, MIL — 6.8
- F. Robinson, CIN — 6.7

Runs Scored
- B. Bruton, MIL — 112
- E. Mathews, MIL — 108
- W. Mays, SF — 107
- V. Pinson, CIN — 107

Doubles
- V. Pinson, CIN — 37
- O. Cepeda, SF — 36
- F. Robinson, CIN — 33
- B. Skinner, PIT — 33

Triples
- B. Bruton, MIL — 13
- W. Mays, SF — 12
- V. Pinson, CIN — 12
- H. Aaron, MIL — 11

PITCHING LEADERS

Winning Percentage
- E. Broglio, STL — .700
- V. Law, PIT — .690
- W. Spahn, MIL — .677
- B. Buhl, MIL — .640
- B. Purkey, CIN — .607

Earned Run Average
- McCormick, SF — 2.70
- E. Broglio, STL — 2.74
- D. Drysdale, LA — 2.84
- S. Williams, LA — 3.00
- B. Friend, PIT — 3.00

Wins
- E. Broglio, STL — 21
- W. Spahn, MIL — 21
- V. Law, PIT — 20
- L. Burdette, MIL — 19

Saves
- L. McDaniel, STL — 26
- R. Face, PIT — 24
- B. Henry, CIN — 17
- J. Brosnan, CIN — 12

Strikeouts
- D. Drysdale, LA — 246
- S. Koufax, LA — 197
- S. Jones, SF — 190
- E. Broglio, STL — 188
- B. Friend, PIT — 183

Complete Games
- L. Burdette, MIL — 18
- W. Spahn, MIL — 18
- V. Law, PIT — 18
- G. Hobbie, CHI — 16
- B. Friend, PIT — 16

Fewest Hits/9 Innings
- E. Broglio, STL — 6.84
- S. Koufax, LA — 6.84
- S. Williams, LA — 7.03
- D. Drysdale, LA — 7.16

Shutouts
- J. Sanford, SF — 6
- D. Drysdale, LA — 5

Fewest Walks/9 Innings
- L. Burdette, MIL — 1.14
- R. Roberts, PHI — 1.29
- V. Law, PIT — 1.33
- B. Friend, PIT — 1.47

Most Strikeouts/9 Inn.
- S. Koufax, LA — 10.13
- D. Drysdale, LA — 8.23
- S. Williams, LA — 7.60
- E. Broglio, STL — 7.48

Innings
- L. Jackson, STL — 282
- L. Burdette, MIL — 276
- B. Friend, PIT — 276
- V. Law, PIT — 272

Games Pitched
- R. Face, PIT — 68
- L. McDaniel, STL — 65
- D. Elston, CHI — 60
- D. Farrell, PHI — 59

NATIONAL LEAGUE 1960, cont.

	W	L	PCT	GB	R	OR	Batting 2B	3B	HR	BA	SA	SB	Fielding E	DP	FA	Pitching CG	BB	SO	ShO	SV	ERA
Pittsburgh	95	59	.617		734	593	236	56	120	.276	.407	34	128	163	.979	47	386	811	11	33	3.49
Milwaukee	88	66	.571	7	724	658	198	48	170	.265	.417	69	141	137	.976	55	518	807	13	28	3.76
St. Louis	86	68	.558	9	639	616	213	48	138	.254	.393	48	141	152	.976	37	511	906	11	30	3.64
Los Angeles	82	72	.532	13	662	593	216	38	126	.255	.383	95	125	142	.979	46	564	1122	13	20	3.40
San Francisco	79	75	.513	16	671	631	220	62	130	.255	.393	86	166	117	.972	55	512	897	16	26	3.44
Cincinnati	67	87	.435	28	640	692	230	40	140	.250	.388	73	125	155	.979	33	442	740	8	35	4.00
Chicago	60	94	.390	35	634	776	213	48	119	.243	.369	51	143	133	.977	36	565	805	6	25	4.35
Philadelphia	59	95	.383	36	546	691	196	44	99	.239	.351	45	155	129	.974	45	439	736	6	16	4.01
					5250	5250	1722	384	1042	.255	.388	501	1124	1128	.977	354	3937	6824	84	213	3.76

AMERICAN LEAGUE 1960

POS	Player	AB	BA	HR	RBI	PO	A	E	DP	TC/G	FA	Pitcher	G	IP	W	L	SV	ERA
New York W-97 L-57 — Casey Stengel																		
1B	B. Skowron	538	.309	26	91	1202	115	12	130	9.4	.991	A. Ditmar	34	200	15	9	0	3.06
2B	Richardson	460	.252	1	26	312	337	18	103	4.7	.973	W. Ford	33	193	12	9	0	3.08
SS	T. Kubek	568	.273	14	62	228	443	22	84	5.1	.968	B. Turley	34	173	9	3	5	3.27
3B	C. Boyer	393	.242	14	46	102	219	11	24	3.4	.967	R. Terry	35	167	10	8	1	3.40
RF	R. Maris	499	.283	39	112	263	6	4	1		.985	J. Coates	35	149	13	3	1	4.28
CF	M. Mantle	527	.275	40	94	326	9	3	1	2.3	.991	E. Grba	24	81	6	4	1	3.68
LF	H. Lopez	408	.284	9	42	199	8	5	2	2.0	.976	D. Maas	35	70	5	1	4	4.09
C	E. Howard	323	.245	6	39	410	40	6	9	5.0	.987	B. Shantz	42	68	5	4	11	2.79
CO	Y. Berra	359	.276	15	62	312	24	5	6		.985	R. Duren	42	49	3	4	9	4.96
32	McDougald	337	.258	8	34	127	236	13	31		.965	L. Arroyo	29	41	5	1	7	2.88
OF	B. Cerv	216	.250	8	28	101	6	2	0	2.1	.982							
Baltimore W-89 L-65 — Paul Richards																		
1B	J. Gentile	384	.292	21	98	885	52	7	98	7.6	.993	C. Estrada	36	209	18	11	2	3.58
2B	M. Breeding	551	.267	3	43	359	422	18	116	5.3	.977	M. Pappas	30	206	15	11	0	3.37
SS	R. Hansen	530	.255	22	86	325	456	29	110	5.3	.964	J. Fisher	40	198	12	11	2	3.41
3B	B. Robinson	595	.294	14	88	171	328	12	34	3.4	.977	S. Barber	36	182	10	7	2	3.22
RF	G. Stephens	193	.238	5	11	124	5	1	0	1.7	.992	H. Brown	30	159	12	5	0	3.06
CF	J. Brandt	511	.254	15	65	284	10	5	2	2.1	.983	H. Wilhelm	41	147	11	8	7	3.31
LF	G. Woodling	435	.283	11	62	202	7	1	0	1.7	.995	J. Walker	29	118	3	4	5	3.74
C	G. Triandos	364	.269	12	54	516	45	6	5	5.4	.989							
OF	A. Pilarcik	194	.247	4	17	75	4	0	0	1.1	1.000							
1B	W. Dropo	179	.268	4	21	397	27	3	50	6.4	.993							
OF	J. Busby	159	.258	0	12	133	2	2	1	1.9	.985							
C	C. Courtney	154	.227	1	12	246	23	7	2	4.8	.975							
Chicago W-87 L-67 — Al Lopez																		
1B	R. Sievers	444	.295	28	93	1079	63	8	117	10.1	.993	E. Wynn	36	237	13	12	1	3.49
2B	N. Fox	605	.289	2	59	412	447	13	126	5.9	.985	B. Pierce	32	196	14	7	0	3.62
SS	L. Aparicio	600	.277	2	61	305	551	18	117	5.7	.979	B. Shaw	36	193	13	13	0	4.06
3B	G. Freese	455	.273	17	79	88	263	20	29	3.0	.946	F. Baumann	44	185	13	6	3	2.67
RF	A. Smith	536	.315	12	72	252	5	9	2	1.9	.966	R. Kemmerer	36	121	6	3	2	2.98
CF	J. Landis	494	.253	10	49	372	10	6	3	2.6	.985	G. Staley	64	115	13	8	10	2.42
LF	M. Minoso	591	.311	20	105	282	14	6	3	2.0	.980	H. Score	23	114	5	10	0	3.72
C	S. Lollar	421	.252	7	46	555	54	3	12	5.0	.995	D. Donovan	33	79	6	1	5	5.38
1B	Kluszewski	181	.293	5	39	325	19	1	38	8.8	.997	T. Lown	45	67	2	5	5	3.88
Cleveland W-76 L-78 — Joe Gordon W-49 L-46; Jo-Jo White W-1 L-0; Jimmy Dykes W-26 L-32																		
1B	V. Power	580	.288	10	84	1177	145	5	145	9.0	.996	J. Perry	41	261	18	10	1	3.62
2B	Aspromonte	459	.290	10	48	192	215	10	63	5.2	.976	M. Grant	33	160	9	8	0	4.40
SS	W. Held	376	.258	21	67	208	345	19	87	5.2	.967	G. Bell	28	155	9	10	1	4.13
3B	B. Phillips	304	.207	4	33	87	135	11	18	2.7	.953	B. Latman	31	147	7	7	0	4.03
RF	H. Kuenn	474	.308	9	54	222	7	8	3	2.0	.966	D. Stigman	41	134	5	11	9	4.51
CF	J. Piersall	486	.282	18	66	355	5	3	0	2.7	.992	L. Locke	32	123	3	5	2	3.37
LF	T. Francona	544	.292	17	79	278	4	3	2	2.1	.989	Klippstein	49	74	5	5	14	2.91
C	J. Romano	316	.272	16	52	470	30	6	6	5.1	.988							
2B	J. Temple	381	.268	2	19	169	164	9	55	4.4	.974							
SS	de la Hoz	160	.256	6	23	58	94	8	13	4.2	.950							
Washington W-73 L-81 — Cookie Lavagetto																		
1B	J. Becquer	298	.252	4	35	611	38	7	59	8.5	.989	P. Ramos	43	274	11	18	2	3.45
2B	B. Gardner	592	.257	9	56	355	407	21	101	5.4	.973	D. Lee	44	165	8	7	3	3.44
SS	Valdivielso	268	.213	2	19	178	294	23	68	4.3	.954	C. Pascual	26	152	12	8	2	3.03
3B	R. Bertoia	460	.265	4	45	94	227	13	19	3.0	.961	J. Kralick	35	151	8	6	1	3.04
RF	B. Allison	501	.251	15	69	290	10	11	3	2.2	.965	T. Clevenger	53	129	5	11	7	4.20
CF	L. Green	330	.294	5	33	219	4	2	0	2.3	.991	C. Stobbs	40	119	12	7	2	3.32
LF	J. Lemon	528	.269	38	100	251	11	11	1	1.9	.960	Woodeshick	41	115	4	5	4	4.70
C	E. Battey	466	.270	15	60	749	65	15	10	6.1	.982	R. Moore	37	66	3	2	13	2.88
13	H. Killebrew	442	.276	31	80	629	135	17	76		.978							
OF	D. Dobbek	248	.218	10	30	141	5	4	1	1.9	.973							
SS	B. Consolo	174	.207	3	15	83	158	16	36	3.1	.938							
OF	Throneberry	157	.248	1	23	52	2	3	0	1.7	.947							

AMERICAN LEAGUE 1960, *cont.*

	POS	Player	AB	BA	HR	RBI	PO	A	E	DP	TC/G	FA	Pitcher	G	IP	W	L	SV	ERA
Detroit	1B	N. Cash	353	.286	18	63	739	59	7	68	8.1	.991	F. Lary	38	**274**	15	15	1	3.51
	2B	F. Bolling	536	.254	9	59	375	377	17	93	5.6	.978	J. Bunning	36	252	11	14	0	2.79
W-71 L-83	SS	C. Fernandez	435	.241	4	35	226	381	34	67	4.9	.947	D. Mossi	23	158	9	8	0	3.47
	3B	E. Yost	497	.260	14	47	155	208	26	18	2.7	.933	B. Bruce	34	130	4	7	0	3.74
Jimmy Dykes	RF	R. Colavito	555	.249	35	87	271	11	7	5	2.0	.976	P. Burnside	31	114	7	7	2	4.28
W-44 L-52	CF	A. Kaline	551	.278	15	68	367	5	5	1	2.7	.987	P. Foytack	28	97	2	11	2	6.14
	LF	C. Maxwell	482	.237	24	81	254	5	1	0	2.2	**.996**	H. Aguirre	37	95	5	3	10	2.85
Billy Hitchcock	C	L. Berberet	232	.194	5	23	396	36	3	4	5.4	.993	D. Sisler	41	80	7	5	6	2.48
W-1 L-0																			
	1B	S. Bilko	222	.207	9	25	501	36	5	47	8.7	.991							
Joe Gordon	OF	N. Chrisley	220	.255	5	24	101	2	5	0	2.2	.981							
W-26 L-31																			
Boston	1B	V. Wertz	443	.282	19	103	841	78	12	89	8.0	.987	Monbouquette	35	215	14	11	0	3.64
	2B	P. Runnels	528	**.320**	2	35	274	360	9	99	5.0	**.986**	T. Brewer	34	187	10	15	1	4.82
	SS	D. Buddin	428	.245	6	36	230	356	30	79	5.0	.951	F. Sullivan	40	154	6	16	1	5.10
W-65 L-89	3B	F. Malzone	595	.271	14	79	159	318	26	36	3.3	.948	I. Delock	24	129	9	10	0	4.73
	RF	L. Clinton	298	.228	6	37	165	4	6	2	2.0	.966	B. Muffett	23	125	6	4	0	3.24
Bill Jurges	CF	W. Tasby	385	.281	7	37	232	6	5	1	2.4	.979	M. Fornieles	**70**	109	10	5	14	2.64
W-15 L-27	LF	T. Williams	310	.316	29	72	131	6	1	1	1.6	.993	Sturdivant	40	101	3	3	1	4.97
	C	R. Nixon	272	.298	5	33	354	26	5	3	5.2	.987	J. Casale	29	96	2	9	0	6.17
Del Baker	2S	P. Green	260	.242	3	21	151	169	11	33		.967							
W-2 L-5	OF	G. Geiger	245	.302	9	33	121	9	0	1	2.0	1.000							
	OF	R. Repulski	136	.243	3	20	56	0	0	0	1.7	1.000							
Pinky Higgins	OF	B. Thomson	114	.263	5	20	65	1	2	1	2.5	.971							
W-48 L-57																			
Kansas City	1B	Throneberry	236	.250	11	41	508	40	5	56	7.8	.991	R. Herbert	37	253	14	15	1	3.28
	2B	J. Lumpe	574	.272	8	53	355	364	13	99	5.6	.982	B. Daley	37	231	16	16	0	4.56
	SS	K. Hamlin	428	.224	2	24	195	341	25	61	4.0	.955	D. Hall	29	182	8	13	0	4.05
W-58 L-96	3B	A. Carey	343	.233	12	53	95	180	7	26	3.1	.975	N. Garver	28	122	4	9	0	3.83
	RF	R. Snyder	304	.260	4	26	135	4	2	2	1.5	.986	K. Johnson	42	120	5	10	3	4.26
Bob Elliott	CF	B. Tuttle	559	.256	8	40	**381**	16	5	3	**2.7**	.988	J. Kucks	31	114	4	10	0	6.00
	LF	N. Siebern	520	.279	19	69	151	4	2	0	2.1	.987	D. Larsen	22	84	1	10	0	5.38
	C	P. Daley	228	.263	5	25	263	33	3	3	4.9	.990							
	UT	D. Williams	420	.288	12	65	376	131	11	28		.979							
	OF	H. Bauer	255	.275	3	31	85	4	2	1	1.4	.978							
	OF	W. Herzog	252	.266	8	38	128	4	2	1	1.9	.985							
	C	H. Chiti	190	.221	5	28	263	24	5	1	5.6	.983							
	C	D. Kravitz	175	.234	4	14	216	16	7	3	5.1	.971							

BATTING AND BASE RUNNING LEADERS

Batting Average
P. Runnels, BOS	.320
A. Smith, CHI	.315
M. Minoso, CHI	.311
B. Skowron, NY	.309
H. Kuenn, CLE	.308

Slugging Average
R. Maris, NY	.581
M. Mantle, NY	.558
H. Killebrew, WAS	.534
R. Sievers, CHI	.534
B. Skowron, NY	.528

Home Runs
M. Mantle, NY	40
R. Maris, NY	39
J. Lemon, WAS	38
R. Colavito, DET	35
H. Killebrew, WAS	31

Total Bases
M. Mantle, NY	294
R. Maris, NY	290
B. Skowron, NY	284
M. Minoso, CHI	284
J. Lemon, WAS	268

Runs Batted In
R. Maris, NY	112
M. Minoso, CHI	105
V. Wertz, BOS	103
J. Lemon, WAS	100
J. Gentile, BAL	98

Stolen Bases
L. Aparicio, CHI	51
J. Landis, CHI	23
L. Green, WAS	21
A. Kaline, DET	19
J. Piersall, CLE	18

Hits
M. Minoso, CHI	184
B. Robinson, BAL	175
N. Fox, CHI	175
P. Runnels, BOS	169

Base on Balls
E. Yost, DET	125
M. Mantle, NY	111
B. Allison, WAS	92
G. Woodling, BAL	84

Home Run Percentage
R. Maris, NY	7.8
M. Mantle, NY	7.6
J. Lemon, WAS	7.2
H. Killebrew, WAS	7.0

Runs Scored
M. Mantle, NY	119
R. Maris, NY	98
J. Landis, CHI	89
M. Minoso, CHI	89

Doubles
T. Francona, CLE	36
B. Skowron, NY	34
G. Freese, CHI	32
M. Minoso, CHI	32

Triples
N. Fox, CHI	10
B. Robinson, BAL	9

PITCHING LEADERS

Winning Percentage
J. Perry, CLE	.643
A. Ditmar, NY	.625
C. Estrada, BAL	.621
M. Pappas, BAL	.577

Earned Run Average
F. Baumann, CHI	2.67
J. Bunning, DET	2.79
H. Brown, BAL	3.06
A. Ditmar, NY	3.06
W. Ford, NY	3.08

Wins
J. Perry, CLE	18
C. Estrada, BAL	18
B. Daley, KC	16
A. Ditmar, NY	15
M. Pappas, BAL	15
F. Lary, DET	15

Saves
M. Fornieles, BOS	14
Klippstein, CLE	14
R. Moore, CHI, WAS	13
B. Shantz, NY	11
G. Staley, CHI	10
H. Aguirre, DET	10

Strikeouts
J. Bunning, DET	201
P. Ramos, WAS	160
E. Wynn, CHI	158
F. Lary, DET	149
C. Estrada, BAL	144

Complete Games
F. Lary, DET	15
R. Herbert, KC	14
P. Ramos, WAS	14
B. Daley, KC	13
E. Wynn, CHI	13

Fewest Hits/9 Innings
C. Estrada, BAL	6.99
B. Turley, NY	7.17
S. Barber, BAL	7.33
J. Bunning, DET	7.75

Shutouts
W. Ford, NY	4
E. Wynn, CHI	4
J. Perry, CLE	4

Fewest Walks/9 Innings
H. Brown, BAL	1.25
D. Mossi, DET	1.82
D. Hall, KC	1.88
F. Lary, DET	2.03

Most Strikeouts/9 Inn.
J. Bunning, DET	7.18
G. Bell, CLE	6.34
C. Estrada, BAL	6.21
E. Wynn, CHI	5.99

Innings
F. Lary, DET	274
P. Ramos, WAS	274
J. Perry, CLE	261
R. Herbert, KC	253

Games Pitched
M. Fornieles, BOS	70
G. Staley, CHI	64
T. Clevenger, WAS	53
R. Moore, CHI, WAS	51

AMERICAN LEAGUE 1960, *cont.*

	W	L	PCT	GB	R	OR	2B	3B	HR	BA	SA	SB	E	DP	FA	CG	BB	SO	ShO	SV	ERA
								Batting						Fielding			Pitching				
New York	97	57	.630		**746**	627	215	40	**193**	.260	**.426**	37	129	162	.979	38	609	712	**16**	42	3.52
Baltimore	89	65	.578	8	682	**606**	206	33	123	.253	.377	37	**108**	172	.982	48	552	785	11	22	3.52
Chicago	87	67	.565	10	741	617	242	38	112	**.270**	.396	122	109	175	**.982**	42	533	695	11	26	3.60
Cleveland	76	78	.494	21	667	693	218	20	127	.267	.388	58	128	165	.978	32	636	771	10	30	3.95
Washington	73	81	.474	24	672	696	205	**43**	147	.244	.384	52	165	159	.973	34	538	775	10	35	3.77
Detroit	71	83	.461	26	633	644	188	34	150	.239	.375	66	138	138	.977	40	**474**	**824**	7	25	3.64
Boston	65	89	.422	32	658	775	234	32	124	.261	.389	34	141	156	.976	34	580	767	6	23	4.62
Kansas City	58	96	.377	39	615	756	212	34	110	.249	.366	16	127	149	.979	44	525	664	4	14	4.38
					5414	5414	1720	274	1086	.255	.388	422	1045	1276	.978	312	4447	5993	75	217	3.87

NATIONAL LEAGUE 1961

	POS	Player	AB	BA	HR	RBI	PO	A	E	DP	TC/G	FA	Pitcher	G	IP	W	L	SV	ERA
Cincinnati	1B	G. Coleman	520	.287	26	87	1162	121	11	93	8.6	.991	J. O'Toole	39	253	19	9	2	3.10
	2B	Blasingame	450	.222	1	21	277	304	17	53	5.2	.972	J. Jay	34	247	**21**	10	0	3.53
W-93 L-61	SS	E. Kasko	469	.271	2	27	201	286	18	59	4.5	.964	B. Purkey	36	246	16	12	1	3.73
	3B	G. Freese	575	.277	26	87	123	254	20	23	2.6	.950	K. Hunt	29	136	9	10	0	3.96
Fred Hutchinson	RF	F. Robinson	545	.323	37	124	284	15	3	3	2.0	.990	J. Maloney	27	95	6	7	2	4.37
	CF	V. Pinson	607	.343	16	87	**391**	19	10	4	**2.7**	.976	J. Brosnan	53	80	10	4	16	3.04
	LF	W. Post	282	.294	20	57	133	7	6	3	1.8	.959	B. Henry	47	53	2	1	16	2.19
	C	J. Zimmerman	204	.206	0	10	374	22	10	8	5.3	.975							
	OF	G. Bell	235	.255	3	33	112	1	1	0	1.5	.991							
	SS	L. Cardenas	198	.308	5	24	83	133	6	21	3.5	.973							
	OF	J. Lynch	181	.315	13	50	53	2	3	0	1.3	.948							
Los Angeles	1B	G. Hodges	215	.242	8	31	454	37	1	44	4.9	.998	S. Koufax	42	256	18	13	1	3.52
	2B	C. Neal	341	.235	10	48	211	246	11	63	4.5	.976	D. Drysdale	40	244	13	10	0	3.69
W-89 L-65	SS	M. Wills	**613**	.282	1	31	253	428	29	104	4.8	.959	S. Williams	41	235	15	12	0	3.90
	3B	J. Gilliam	439	.244	4	32	48	104	7	9	2.1	.956	J. Podres	32	183	18	5	0	3.74
Walter Alston	RF	T. Davis	460	.278	15	58	143	3	4	2	1.7	.973	R. Craig	40	113	5	6	2	6.15
	CF	W. Davis	339	.254	12	45	224	4	4	1	2.0	.983	L. Sherry	53	95	4	4	15	3.90
	LF	W. Moon	463	.328	17	88	186	5	6	1	1.5	.970	Perranoski	53	92	7	5	6	2.65
	C	J. Roseboro	394	.251	18	59	877	56	13	16	7.6	.986	D. Farrell	50	89	6	6	10	5.06
	1B	N. Larker	282	.270	5	38	589	52	3	68	7.5	.995							
	OF	F. Howard	267	.296	15	45	79	6	6	0	1.4	.934							
	OF	R. Fairly	245	.322	10	48	85	7	1	1	1.3	.989							
	OF	D. Snider	233	.296	16	56	113	6	3	3	1.8	.975							
	3B	D. Spencer	189	.243	8	27	42	92	5	14	2.4	.964							
	C	N. Sherry	121	.256	5	21	253	16	2	3	6.0	.993							
San Francisco	1B	W. McCovey	328	.271	18	50	669	55	11	55	8.8	.985	McCormick	40	250	13	16	0	3.20
	2B	Amalfitano	384	.255	2	23	201	223	13	48	4.6	.970	J. Sanford	38	217	13	9	0	4.22
W-85 L-69	SS	J. Pagan	434	.253	5	46	227	334	21	55	4.4	.964	J. Marichal	29	185	13	10	0	3.89
	3B	J. Davenport	436	.278	12	65	119	235	13	25	2.8	**.965**	B. O'Dell	46	130	7	5	2	3.59
Alvin Dark	RF	F. Alou	415	.289	18	52	196	10	2	1	1.7	.990	S. Jones	37	128	8	8	1	4.49
	CF	W. Mays	572	.308	40	123	385	7	8	3	2.6	.980	S. Miller	63	122	14	5	17	2.66
	LF	H. Kuenn	471	.265	5	46	157	9	2	0	1.8	.988	B. Loes	26	115	6	5	0	4.24
	C	E. Bailey	340	.238	13	51	629	40	10	4	6.6	.985	D. LeMay	27	83	5	5	3	3.56
	10	O. Cepeda	585	.311	**46**	**142**	774	51	5	50		.994							
	2B	C. Hiller	240	.238	2	12	133	158	8	34	4.5	.973							
	OF	M. Alou	200	.310	6	24	85	2	2	0	1.5	.978							
Milwaukee	1B	J. Adcock	562	.285	35	108	**1471**	102	11	133	**10.7**	.993	L. Burdette	40	**272**	18	11	0	4.00
	2B	F. Bolling	585	.262	15	56	326	489	19	112	5.6	**.988**	W. Spahn	38	263	**21**	13	0	**3.02**
W-83 L-71	SS	R. McMillan	505	.220	7	48	**257**	**496**	19	110	5.0	.975	B. Buhl	32	188	9	10	0	4.11
	3B	E. Mathews	572	.306	32	91	168	281	18	30	3.1	.961	C. Willey	35	160	6	12	0	3.83
Chuck Dressen	RF	L. Maye	373	.271	14	41	169	6	5	0	1.9	.972	D. Nottebart	38	126	6	7	3	4.06
W-71 L-58	CF	H. Aaron	603	.327	34	120	377	13	7	3	2.6	.982	B. Hendley	19	97	5	7	0	3.90
	LF	F. Thomas	423	.284	25	67	202	4	10	0	2.0	.954	D. McMahon	53	92	6	4	8	2.84
Birdie Tebbetts	C	J. Torre	406	.278	10	42	494	50	10	4	4.9	.982							
W-12 L-13																			
St. Louis	1B	B. White	591	.286	20	90	1373	104	17	125	9.9	.989	R. Sadecki	31	223	14	10	0	3.72
	2B	J. Javier	445	.279	2	41	239	332	20	82	5.2	.966	L. Jackson	33	211	14	11	0	3.75
W-80 L-74	SS	A. Grammas	170	.212	0	21	81	136	9	29	3.5	.960	B. Gibson	35	211	13	12	1	3.24
	3B	K. Boyer	589	.329	24	95	117	346	24	23	3.2	.951	C. Simmons	30	196	9	10	0	3.13
Solly Hemus	RF	C. James	349	.255	4	44	151	3	6	1	1.8	.963	E. Broglio	29	175	9	12	0	4.12
W-33 L-41	CF	C. Flood	335	.322	2	21	241	13	4	4	2.2	.984	L. McDaniel	55	94	10	6	9	4.87
	LF	S. Musial	372	.288	15	70	149	9	1	0	1.5	**.994**							
Johnny Keane	C	J. Schaffer	153	.255	1	16	244	23	1	6	3.9	.996							
W-47 L-33	OF	Cunningham	322	.286	7	40	131	2	5	1	1.6	.964							
	SS	B. Lillis	230	.217	0	21	73	134	16	19	4.0	.928							
	OF	D. Taussig	188	.287	2	25	123	6	1	2	1.5	.992							
	C	C. Sawatski	174	.299	10	33	218	19	1	3	4.0	.996							
	SS	D. Spencer	130	.254	4	21	66	109	8	26	4.9	.956							

NATIONAL LEAGUE 1961, *cont.*

	POS	Player	AB	BA	HR	RBI	PO	A	E	DP	TC/G	FA	Pitcher	G	IP	W	L	SV	ERA
Pittsburgh	1B	D. Stuart	532	.301	35	117	1152	99	21	141	9.6	.983	B. Friend	41	236	14	19	1	3.85
	2B	B. Mazeroski	558	.265	13	59	410	505	23	144	6.2	.975	J. Gibbon	30	195	13	10	0	3.32
W-75 L-79	SS	D. Groat	596	.275	6	55	235	473	32	117	5.1	.957	H. Haddix	29	156	10	6	0	4.10
	3B	D. Hoak	503	.298	12	61	137	267	20	29	3.0	.953	E. Francis	23	103	2	8	0	4.21
Danny Murtaugh	RF	R. Clemente	572	.351	23	89	256	27	9	5	2.0	.969	V. Mizell	25	100	7	10	0	5.04
	CF	B. Virdon	599	.260	9	58	384	6	6	4	2.7	.985	C. Labine	56	93	4	1	8	3.69
	LF	B. Skinner	381	.268	3	42	175	5	5	1	1.9	.973	R. Face	62	92	6	12	17	3.82
	C	S. Burgess	323	.303	12	52	426	27	4	4	5.0	.991	B. Shantz	43	89	6	3	2	3.32
	C	H. Smith	193	.223	3	26	290	18	3	1	4.8	.990							
	OF	Christopher	186	.263	0	14	86	2	2	1	1.6	.978							
Chicago	1B	E. Bouchee	319	.248	12	38	852	76	16	97	8.8	.983	D. Cardwell	39	259	15	14	0	3.82
	2B	D. Zimmer	477	.252	13	40	282	323	17	99	5.4	.973	G. Hobbie	36	199	7	13	2	4.26
W-64 L-90	SS	E. Banks	511	.278	29	80	173	358	19	68	5.3	.965	D. Ellsworth	37	187	10	11	0	3.86
	3B	R. Santo	578	.284	23	83	157	307	31	41	3.2	.937	J. Curtis	31	180	10	13	0	4.89
	RF	G. Altman	518	.303	27	96	258	11	6	2	2.1	.978	B. Anderson	57	152	7	10	8	4.26
	CF	A. Heist	321	.255	7	37	211	9	5	0	2.3	.978	D. Elston	58	93	6	7	8	5.59
	LF	B. Williams	529	.278	25	86	220	9	11	3	1.8	.954	B. Schultz	41	67	7	6	7	2.70
	C	D. Bertell	267	.273	2	33	396	49	8	10	5.0	.982							
	2S	J. Kindall	310	.242	9	44	206	233	26	61		.944							
	OF	R. Ashburn	307	.257	0	19	131	4	3	0	1.8	.978							
	C	S. Taylor	235	.238	8	23	319	25	4	5	4.6	.989							
	1S	A. Rodgers	214	.266	6	23	404	83	9	44		.982							
Philadelphia	1B	P. Herrera	400	.258	13	51	1003	96	8	104	9.6	.993	A. Mahaffey	36	219	11	19	0	4.10
	2B	T. Taylor	400	.250	2	26	231	270	10	74	5.6	.980	J. Buzhardt	41	202	6	18	0	4.49
W-47 L-107	SS	R. Amaro	381	.257	1	32	243	379	19	91	4.9	.970	F. Sullivan	49	159	3	16	6	4.29
	3B	C. Smith	411	.248	9	47	75	194	22	19	3.1	.924	D. Ferrarese	42	139	5	12	1	3.76
Gene Mauch	RF	D. Demeter	382	.257	20	68	173	9	1	2	2.3	.995	D. Green	42	128	2	4	1	4.85
	CF	T. Gonzalez	426	.277	12	58	246	7	4	4	2.2	.984	C. Short	39	127	6	12	1	5.94
	LF	J. Callison	455	.266	9	47	227	10	8	2	2.0	.967	R. Roberts	26	117	1	10	0	5.85
	C	C. Dalrymple	378	.220	5	42	551	86	14	10	5.3	.978	J. Owens	20	107	5	10	0	4.47
	UT	B. Malkmus	342	.231	7	31	210	299	12	67		.977	J. Baldschun	65	100	5	3	3	3.88
	UT	L. Walls	261	.280	8	30	247	59	8	33		.975							
	OF	K. Walters	180	.228	2	14	73	4	2	0	1.4	.975							
	OF	B. Smith	174	.253	2	18	91	8	3	1	2.2	.971							
	OF	W. Covington	165	.303	7	26	53	4	3	1	1.3	.950							

Chicago coaching records:

Vedie Himsl W-5 L-6
Harry Craft W-4 L-8
Vedie Himsl W-5 L-12
El Tappe W-2 L-0
Harry Craft W-3 L-1
Vedie Himsl W-0 L-3
El Tappe W-35 L-43
Lou Klein W-5 L-6
El Tappe W-5 L-11

BATTING AND BASE RUNNING LEADERS

Batting Average
R. Clemente, PIT .351
V. Pinson, CIN .343
K. Boyer, STL .329
W. Moon, LA .328
H. Aaron, MIL .327

Slugging Average
F. Robinson, CIN .611
O. Cepeda, SF .609
H. Aaron, MIL .594
W. Mays, SF .584
D. Stuart, PIT .581

Home Runs
O. Cepeda, SF 46
W. Mays, SF 40
F. Robinson, CIN 37
D. Stuart, PIT 35
J. Adcock, MIL 35

Total Bases
H. Aaron, MIL 358
O. Cepeda, SF 356
W. Mays, SF 334
F. Robinson, CIN 333
R. Clemente, PIT 320

Runs Batted In
O. Cepeda, SF 142
F. Robinson, CIN 124
W. Mays, SF 123
H. Aaron, MIL 120
D. Stuart, PIT 117

Stolen Bases
M. Wills, LA 35
V. Pinson, CIN 23
F. Robinson, CIN 22
H. Aaron, MIL 21
W. Mays, SF 18

Hits
V. Pinson, CIN 208
R. Clemente, PIT 201
H. Aaron, MIL 197
K. Boyer, STL 194

Base on Balls
E. Mathews, MIL 93
W. Moon, LA 89
W. Mays, SF 81
J. Gilliam, LA 79

Home Run Percentage
O. Cepeda, SF 7.9
W. Mays, SF 7.0
F. Robinson, CIN 6.8
D. Stuart, PIT 6.6

Runs Scored
W. Mays, SF 129
F. Robinson, CIN 117
H. Aaron, MIL 115
K. Boyer, STL 109

Doubles
H. Aaron, MIL 39
V. Pinson, CIN 34
F. Robinson, CIN 32
W. Mays, SF 32

Triples
G. Altman, CHI 12
J. Callison, PHI 11
K. Boyer, STL 11
B. White, STL 11

PITCHING LEADERS

Winning Percentage
J. Podres, LA .783
J. O'Toole, CIN .679
J. Jay, CIN .677
L. Burdette, MIL .621
W. Spahn, MIL .618

Earned Run Average
W. Spahn, MIL 3.02
J. O'Toole, CIN 3.10
C. Simmons, STL 3.13
McCormick, SF 3.20
B. Gibson, STL 3.24

Wins
J. Jay, CIN 21
W. Spahn, MIL 21
J. O'Toole, CIN 19
J. Podres, LA 18
L. Burdette, MIL 18
S. Koufax, LA 18

Saves
S. Miller, SF 17
R. Face, PIT 17
J. Brosnan, CIN 16
B. Henry, CIN 16
L. Sherry, LA 15

Strikeouts
S. Koufax, LA 269
S. Williams, LA 205
D. Drysdale, LA 182
J. O'Toole, CIN 178
B. Gibson, STL 166

Complete Games
W. Spahn, MIL 21
S. Koufax, LA 15
J. Jay, CIN 14
L. Burdette, MIL 14

Fewest Hits/9 Innings
S. Koufax, LA 7.46
J. Jay, CIN 7.90
B. Gibson, STL 7.92
R. Sadecki, STL 7.92

Shutouts
J. Jay, CIN 4
W. Spahn, MIL 4

Fewest Walks/9 Innings
L. Burdette, MIL 1.09
B. Friend, PIT 1.72
B. Purkey, CIN 1.86
W. Spahn, MIL 2.19

Most Strikeouts/9 Inn.
S. Koufax, LA 9.47
S. Williams, LA 7.84
B. Gibson, STL 7.07
D. Drysdale, LA 6.71

Innings
L. Burdette, MIL 272
W. Spahn, MIL 263
D. Cardwell, CHI 259
S. Koufax, LA 256

Games Pitched
J. Baldschun, PHI 65
S. Miller, SF 63
R. Face, PIT 62
D. Elston, CHI 58

NATIONAL LEAGUE 1961, *cont.*

	W	L	PCT	GB	R	OR	Batting 2B	3B	HR	BA	SA	SB	Fielding E	DP	FA	Pitching CG	BB	SO	ShO	SV	ERA
Cincinnati	93	61	.604		710	653	247	35	158	.270	.421	70	134	124	.977	46	500	829	12	40	3.78
Los Angeles	89	65	.578	4	735	697	193	40	157	.262	.405	86	144	162	.975	40	544	1105	10	35	4.04
San Francisco	85	69	.552	8	773	655	219	32	183	.264	.423	79	133	126	.977	39	502	924	9	30	3.77
Milwaukee	83	71	.539	10	712	656	199	34	188	.258	.415	70	111	152	.982	57	493	652	8	16	3.89
St. Louis	80	74	.519	13	703	668	236	51	103	.271	.393	46	166	165	.972	49	570	823	10	24	3.74
Pittsburgh	75	79	.487	18	694	675	232	57	128	.273	.410	26	150	187	.975	34	400	759	9	29	3.92
Chicago	64	90	.416	29	689	800	238	51	176	.255	.418	35	183	175	.970	34	465	755	6	25	4.48
Philadelphia	47	107	.305	46	584	796	185	50	103	.243	.357	56	146	179	.976	29	521	775	9	13	4.61
					5600	5600	1749	350	1196	.262	.405	468	1167	1270	.976	328	3995	6622	73	212	4.03

AMERICAN LEAGUE 1961

Team	POS	Player	AB	BA	HR	RBI	PO	A	E	DP	TC/G	FA	Pitcher	G	IP	W	L	SV	ERA
New York W-109 L-53 Ralph Houk	1B	B. Skowron	561	.267	28	89	1228	102	10	146	9.0	.993	W. Ford	39	283	25	4	0	3.21
	2B	Richardson	662	.261	3	49	413	376	18	136	5.0	.978	B. Stafford	36	195	14	9	2	2.68
	SS	T. Kubek	617	.276	8	46	261	449	30	107	5.1	.959	R. Terry	31	188	16	3	0	3.15
	3B	C. Boyer	504	.224	11	55	151	353	17	36	3.7	.967	R. Sheldon	35	163	11	5	0	3.60
	RF	R. Maris	590	.269	61	142	266	9	9	1	1.8	.968	J. Coates	43	141	11	5	5	3.44
	CF	M. Mantle	514	.317	54	128	351	6	6	0	2.4	.983	B. Daley	23	130	8	9	0	3.96
	LF	Y. Berra	395	.271	22	61	161	7	2	2	2.0	.988	L. Arroyo	65	119	15	5	29	2.19
	C	E. Howard	446	.348	21	77	635	43	5	4	6.2	.993							
	OF	H. Lopez	243	.222	3	22	123	7	3	0	1.8	.977							
	C	J. Blanchard	243	.305	21	54	268	18	3	2	6.0	.990							
	OF	B. Cerv	118	.271	6	20	55	2	1	0	1.9	.983							
Detroit W-101 L-61 Bob Scheffing	1B	N. Cash	535	.361	41	132	1231	127	11	121	8.7	.992	F. Lary	36	275	23	9	0	3.24
	2B	J. Wood	663	.258	11	69	380	396	25	83	4.9	.969	J. Bunning	38	268	17	11	1	3.19
	SS	C. Fernandez	435	.248	3	40	207	312	23	59	4.5	.958	D. Mossi	35	240	15	7	1	2.96
	3B	S. Boros	396	.270	5	62	115	192	15	15	2.8	.953	P. Foytack	32	170	11	10	0	3.93
	RF	A. Kaline	586	.324	19	82	378	9	4	3	2.7	.990	P. Regan	32	120	10	7	2	5.25
	CF	B. Bruton	596	.257	17	63	410	4	5	2	2.7	.988	T. Fox	39	57	5	2	12	1.41
	LF	R. Colavito	583	.290	45	140	329	16	9	4	2.2	.975	H. Aguirre	45	55	4	4	8	3.25
	C	D. Brown	308	.266	16	45	460	38	5	7	5.5	.990							
	SS	McAuliffe	285	.256	6	33	79	115	14	29	3.8	.933							
	C	M. Roarke	229	.223	2	22	383	22	5	5	4.8	.988							
Baltimore W-95 L-67 Paul Richards W-78 L-57 Lum Harris W-17 L-10	1B	J. Gentile	486	.302	46	141	1209	100	14	129	9.2	.989	S. Barber	37	248	18	12	1	3.33
	2B	J. Adair	386	.264	9	37	233	237	6	57	4.4	.987	C. Estrada	33	212	15	9	0	3.69
	SS	R. Hansen	533	.248	12	51	256	437	30	110	4.9	.959	J. Fisher	36	196	10	13	1	3.90
	3B	B. Robinson	668	.287	7	61	151	331	14	34	3.0	.972	M. Pappas	26	178	13	9	1	3.04
	RF	W. Herzog	323	.291	5	35	143	2	0	0	1.5	1.000	H. Brown	27	167	10	6	1	3.19
	CF	J. Brandt	516	.297	16	72	293	6	8	2	2.3	.974	B. Hoeft	35	138	7	4	3	2.02
	LF	R. Snyder	312	.292	1	13	168	3	6	0	1.6	.966	D. Hall	29	122	7	5	4	3.09
	C	G. Triandos	397	.244	17	63	642	55	8	9	6.2	.989	H. Wilhelm	51	110	9	7	18	2.30
	OF	D. Williams	310	.206	8	24	86	4	3	1	1.2	.968							
	2B	M. Breeding	244	.209	1	16	179	179	11	53	4.6	.970							
	OF	E. Robinson	222	.266	8	30	136	6	4	3	1.8	.973							
	OF	D. Philley	144	.250	1	23	21	0	0	0	.8	1.000							
Chicago W-86 L-76 Al Lopez	1B	R. Sievers	492	.295	27	92	1096	94	8	93	9.1	.993	J. Pizarro	39	195	14	7	2	3.05
	2B	N. Fox	606	.251	2	51	413	407	15	97	5.3	.982	F. Baumann	53	188	10	13	3	5.61
	SS	L. Aparicio	625	.272	6	45	264	487	30	86	5.0	.962	B. Pierce	39	180	10	9	3	3.80
	3B	A. Smith	532	.278	28	93	58	161	12	12	2.9	.948	C. McLish	31	162	10	13	0	4.38
	RF	F. Robinson	432	.310	11	59	218	7	2	0	2.1	.991	R. Herbert	21	138	9	6	0	4.05
	CF	J. Landis	534	.283	22	85	389	9	5	3	2.9	.988	E. Wynn	17	110	8	2	0	3.51
	LF	M. Minoso	540	.280	14	82	273	10	13	2	2.0	.956	T. Lown	59	101	7	5	11	2.76
	C	S. Lollar	337	.282	7	41	464	48	1	6	4.8	.998	D. Larsen	25	74	7	2	2	4.12
	13	J. Martin	274	.230	5	32	353	118	10	38		.979	W. Hacker	42	57	3	3	8	3.77
	C	C. Carreon	229	.271	4	27	395	25	2	6	5.9	.995							
Cleveland W-78 L-83 Jimmy Dykes W-77 L-83 Mel Harder W-1 L-0	1B	V. Power	563	.268	5	63	1154	142	8	101	9.2	.994	M. Grant	35	245	15	9	0	3.86
	2B	J. Temple	518	.276	3	30	239	317	18	79	4.4	.969	G. Bell	34	228	12	16	0	4.10
	SS	W. Held	509	.267	23	78	258	393	27	90	4.7	.960	J. Perry	35	224	10	17	0	4.71
	3B	B. Phillips	546	.264	18	72	188	246	19	23	3.2	.958	B. Latman	45	177	13	5	5	4.02
	RF	W. Kirkland	525	.259	27	95	290	12	8	5	2.2	.974	W. Hawkins	30	133	7	9	1	4.06
	CF	J. Piersall	484	.322	6	40	328	9	3	3	2.8	.991	L. Locke	37	95	4	4	2	4.53
	LF	T. Francona	592	.301	16	85	289	5	4	1	2.2	.987	F. Funk	56	92	11	11	11	3.31
	C	J. Romano	509	.299	21	80	752	58	9	8	5.8	.989							
	UT	de la Hoz	173	.260	3	23	77	116	9	10		.955							
	OF	C. Essegian	166	.289	12	35	85	5	3	1	1.9	.968							

AMERICAN LEAGUE 1961, *cont.*

	POS	Player	AB	BA	HR	RBI	PO	A	E	DP	TC/G	FA	Pitcher	G	IP	W	L	SV	ERA
Boston	1B	P. Runnels	360	.317	3	38	701	50	4	92	6.7	**.995**	Monbouquette	32	236	14	14	0	3.39
	2B	C. Schilling	646	.259	5	62	397	449	8	121	5.4	**.991**	G. Conley	33	200	11	14	1	4.91
W-76 L-86	SS	D. Buddin	339	.263	6	42	204	294	23	70	4.8	.956	D. Schwall	25	179	15	7	0	3.22
	3B	F. Malzone	590	.266	14	87	136	304	**23**	**45**	3.1	.950	I. Delock	28	156	6	9	0	4.90
Pinky Higgins	RF	J. Jensen	498	.263	13	66	274	14	4	2	2.2	.986	T. Stallard	43	133	2	7	2	4.88
	CF	G. Geiger	499	.232	18	64	324	12	4	1	2.5	.988	M. Fornieles	57	119	9	8	15	4.68
	LF	Yastrzemski	583	.266	11	80	248	12	10	1	1.8	.963	B. Muffett	38	113	3	11	2	5.67
	C	Pagliaroni	376	.242	16	58	586	39	**10**	5	5.9	.984	A. Earley	33	50	2	4	7	3.99
	1B	V. Wertz	317	.262	11	60	664	67	7	65	8.6	.991							
	OF	C. Hardy	281	.263	3	36	142	7	6	3	2.0	.961							
	C	R. Nixon	242	.289	1	19	330	24	9	2	5.5	.975							
	SS	P. Green	219	.260	6	27	84	166	16	35	4.7	.940							
Minnesota	1B	H. Killebrew	541	.288	46	122	972	67	14	91	8.8	.987	P. Ramos	42	264	11	**20**	2	3.95
	2B	B. Martin	374	.246	6	36	217	224	17	61	4.4	.963	C. Pascual	35	252	15	16	0	3.46
W-70 L-90	SS	Z. Versalles	510	.280	7	53	229	371	30	74	4.9	.952	J. Kralick	33	242	13	11	0	3.61
	3B	B. Tuttle	370	.246	5	38	66	165	14	15	2.9	.943	J. Kaat	36	201	9	17	0	3.90
Cookie Lavagetto	RF	B. Allison	556	.245	29	105	300	14	8	3	2.1	.975	D. Lee	37	115	3	6	3	3.52
W-19 L-30	CF	L. Green	600	.285	9	50	356	3	8	0	2.4	.978	R. Moore	46	56	4	4	14	3.67
	LF	J. Lemon	423	.258	14	52	182	7	12	0	1.7	.940							
Sam Mele	C	E. Battey	460	.302	17	55	**812**	60	6	9	6.7	.993							
W-2 L-5																			
Cookie Lavagetto																			
W-4 L-6																			
Sam Mele																			
W-45 L-49																			
Los Angeles	1B	S. Bilko	294	.279	20	59	577	61	7	56	7.5	.989	K. McBride	38	242	12	15	1	3.65
	2B	Aspromonte	238	.223	2	14	156	196	11	55	5.9	.970	E. Grba	40	212	11	13	2	4.25
W-70 L-91	SS	J. Koppe	338	.251	5	40	127	250	21	51	4.5	.947	T. Bowsfield	41	157	11	8	0	3.73
	3B	E. Yost	213	.202	3	15	57	103	6	4	2.5	.964	R. Moeller	33	113	4	8	0	5.83
Bill Rigney	RF	A. Pearson	427	.288	7	41	233	7	11	2	2.2	.956	R. Kline	26	105	3	6	1	4.90
	CF	K. Hunt	479	.255	25	84	261	6	**14**	1	2.1	.950	J. Donohue	38	100	4	6	5	4.31
	LF	L. Wagner	453	.280	28	79	187	12	6	2	1.8	.971	R. Duren	40	99	6	12	2	5.18
	C	E. Averill	323	.266	21	59	542	38	5	6	6.6	.991	T. Morgan	59	92	8	2	10	2.36
	OF	L. Thomas	450	.284	24	70	159	9	6	1	2.0	.966	A. Fowler	53	89	5	8	11	3.64
	O3	G. Thomas	282	.280	13	59	96	63	13	5		.924							
	1B	Kluszewski	263	.243	15	39	520	28	6	51	8.4	.989							
	2S	R. Bridges	229	.240	2	15	145	196	6	35		.983							
	3B	G. Leek	199	.226	5	20	54	127	8	11	3.9	.958							
	2B	B. Moran	173	.260	2	22	108	116	8	31	4.5	.966							
	C	E. Sadowski	164	.232	4	12	295	17	4	4	5.6	.987							
Kansas City	1B	N. Siebern	560	.296	18	98	907	76	11	88	9.1	.989	J. Archer	39	205	9	15	5	3.20
	2B	J. Lumpe	569	.293	3	54	403	426	18	105	**5.8**	.979	N. Bass	40	171	11	11	0	4.69
W-61 L-100	SS	D. Howser	611	.280	3	45	**299**	427	**38**	85	4.9	.950	J. Walker	36	168	8	14	2	4.82
	3B	W. Causey	312	.276	8	49	102	193	14	20	3.5	.955	B. Shaw	26	150	9	10	0	4.31
Joe Gordon	RF	D. Johnson	283	.216	8	42	104	6	6	0	2.5	.948	J. Nuxhall	37	128	5	8	1	5.34
W-26 L-33	CF	B. Del Greco	239	.230	5	21	168	8	3	2	2.5	.983	E. Rakow	45	125	2	8	1	4.76
	LF	L. Posada	344	.253	7	53	205	8	6	0	2.1	.973	B. Kunkel	58	89	3	4	4	5.18
Hank Bauer	C	H. Sullivan	331	.242	6	40	387	32	7	7	4.8	.984	B. Daley	16	64	4	8	1	4.95
W-35 L-67																			
	C	J. Pignatano	243	.243	4	22	379	35	9	7	5.1	.979							
	OF	G. Stephens	183	.208	4	26	114	6	4	4*	2.3	.968							
	OF	J. Hankins	173	.185	3	6	97	1	3	0	1.6	.970							
	1B	Throneberry	130	.238	6	24	241	25	2	31	8.9	.996							
Washington	1B	D. Long	377	.249	17	49	827	62	**15**	87	9.5	.983	J. McClain	33	212	8	18	1	3.86
	2B	C. Cottier	337	.234	2	34	233	316	10	73	5.6	.982	B. Daniels	32	212	12	11	0	3.44
W-61 L-100	SS	C. Veal	218	.202	0	8	130	172	8	43	4.9	.974	D. Donovan	23	169	10	10	0	**2.40**
	3B	D. O'Connell	493	.260	1	37	75	173	16	14	3.6	.939	M. Kutyna	50	143	6	8	3	3.97
Mickey Vernon	RF	M. Keough	390	.249	9	34	213	7	5	2	2.3	.978	E. Hobaugh	26	126	7	9	0	4.42
	CF	W. Tasby	494	.251	17	63	332	5	5	0	2.5	.985	P. Burnside	33	113	4	9	2	4.53
	LF	C. Hinton	339	.260	6	34	175	6	7	4	2.0	.963	J. Gabler	29	93	3	8	4	4.86
	C	G. Green	364	.280	18	62	326	22	5	3	4.5	.986	D. Sisler	45	60	2	8	11	4.18
	OF	G. Woodling	342	.313	10	57	154	8	2	0	1.8	.988							
	OF	J. King	263	.270	11	46	138	7	3	2	1.6	.980							
	3B	B. Klaus	251	.227	7	30	40	107	6	3	3.0	.961							
	SS	B. Johnson	224	.295	6	28	110	172	13	31	5.2	.956							
	C	P. Daley	203	.192	2	17	285	34	4	6	4.5	.988							
	3B	H. Bright	183	.240	4	21	47	95	11	14	3.8	.928							
	1B	B. Zipfel	170	.200	4	18	429	25	8	40	10.5	.983							

BATTING AND BASE RUNNING LEADERS

Batting Average		Slugging Average		Home Runs		Winning Percentage	
N. Cash, DET	.361	M. Mantle, NY	.687	R. Maris, NY	61	W. Ford, NY	.862
A. Kaline, DET	.324	N. Cash, DET	.662	M. Mantle, NY	54	R. Terry, NY	.842
J. Piersall, CLE	.322	J. Gentile, BAL	.646	J. Gentile, BAL	46	L. Arroyo, NY	.750
M. Mantle, NY	.317	R. Maris, NY	.620	H. Killebrew, MIN	46	F. Lary, DET	.719
J. Gentile, BAL	.302	H. Killebrew, MIN	.606	R. Colavito, DET	45	D. Mossi, DET	.682
						D. Schwall, BOS	.682

PITCHING LEADERS

Earned Run Average		Wins	
D. Donovan, WAS	2.40	W. Ford, NY	25
B. Stafford, NY	2.68	F. Lary, DET	23
D. Mossi, DET	2.96	S. Barber, BAL	18
M. Pappas, BAL	3.04	J. Bunning, DET	17
J. Pizarro, CHI	3.05	R. Terry, NY	16

AMERICAN LEAGUE 1961, *cont.*

BATTING AND BASE RUNNING LEADERS

Total Bases			Runs Batted In			Stolen Bases	
R. Maris, NY		366	R. Maris, NY		142	L. Aparicio, CHI	53
N. Cash, DET		354	J. Gentile, BAL		141	D. Howser, KC	37
M. Mantle, NY		353	R. Colavito, DET		140	J. Wood, DET	30
R. Colavito, DET		338	N. Cash, DET		132	C. Hinton, WAS	22
H. Killebrew, MIN		328	M. Mantle, NY		128	B. Bruton, DET	22

Hits			Base on Balls			Home Run Percentage	
N. Cash, DET		193	M. Mantle, NY		126	M. Mantle, NY	10.5
B. Robinson, BAL		192	N. Cash, DET		124	R. Maris, NY	10.3
A. Kaline, DET		190	R. Colavito, DET		113	J. Gentile, BAL	9.5
T. Francona, CLE		178	H. Killebrew, MIN		107	H. Killebrew, MIN	8.5

Runs Scored			Doubles			Triples	
M. Mantle, NY		132	A. Kaline, DET		41	J. Wood, DET	14
R. Maris, NY		132	T. Kubek, NY		38	M. Keough, WAS	9
R. Colavito, DET		129	B. Robinson, BAL		38	J. Lumpe, KC	9
N. Cash, DET		119	N. Siebern, KC		36	J. Landis, CHI	8

PITCHING LEADERS

Saves			Strikeouts			Complete Games	
L. Arroyo, NY		29	C. Pascual, MIN		221	F. Lary, DET	22
H. Wilhelm, BAL		18	W. Ford, NY		209	C. Pascual, MIN	15
M. Fornieles, BOS		15	J. Bunning, DET		194	S. Barber, BAL	14
R. Moore, MIN		14	J. Pizarro, CHI		188		
T. Fox, DET		12	K. McBride, LA		180		

Fewest Hits/9 Innings		Shutouts			Fewest Walks/9 Innings	
C. Estrada, BAL	6.75	C. Pascual, MIN		8	D. Mossi, DET	1.76
M. Pappas, BAL	6.79	S. Barber, BAL		8	H. Brown, BAL	1.78
S. Barber, BAL	7.03	M. Pappas, BAL		4	D. Donovan, WAS	1.87
C. Pascual, MIN	7.31	F. Lary, DET		4	R. Terry, NY	2.01

Most Strikeouts/9 Inn.		Innings			Games Pitched	
J. Pizarro, CHI	8.69	W. Ford, NY		283	L. Arroyo, NY	65
C. Pascual, MIN	7.88	F. Lary, DET		275	T. Lown, CHI	59
C. Estrada, BAL	6.79	J. Bunning, DET		268	T. Morgan, LA	59
K. McBride, LA	6.70	P. Ramos, MIN		264	B. Kunkel, KC	58

	W	L	PCT	GB	R	OR	2B	3B	HR	BA	SA	SB	E	DP	FA	CG	BB	SO	ShO	SV	ERA
New York	109	53	.673		827	612	194	40	240	.263	.442	28	124	180	.980	47	542	866	14	39	3.46
Detroit	101	61	.623	8	841	671	215	53	180	.266	.421	98	146	147	.976	62	469	836	12	30	3.55
Baltimore	95	67	.586	14	691	588	227	36	149	.254	.390	39	128	173	.980	54	617	926	21	33	3.22
Chicago	86	76	.531	23	765	726	216	46	138	.265	.395	100	128	138	.980	39	498	814	3	33	4.06
Cleveland	78	83	.484	30.5	737	752	257	39	150	.266	.406	34	139	142	.977	35	599	801	12	23	4.15
Boston	76	86	.469	33	729	792	251	37	112	.254	.374	56	144	170	.977	35	679	831	6	30	4.29
Minnesota	70	90	.438	38	707	778	215	40	167	.250	.397	47	174	150	.971	49	570	914	14	23	4.28
Los Angeles	70	91	.435	38.5	744	784	218	22	189	.245	.398	37	192	154	.969	25	713	973	5	34	4.31
Kansas City	61	100	.379	47.5	683	863	216	47	90	.247	.354	58	175	160	.972	32	629	703	5	23	4.74
Washington	61	100	.379	47.5	618	776	217	44	119	.244	.367	81	156	171	.975	39	586	666	8	21	4.23
					7342	7342	2226	404	1534	.256	.395	578	1506	1585	.976	417	5902	8330	100	289	4.02

NATIONAL LEAGUE 1962

	POS	Player	AB	BA	HR	RBI	PO	A	E	DP	TC/G	FA	Pitcher	G	IP	W	L	SV	ERA
San Francisco	1B	O. Cepeda	625	.306	35	114	1353	88	13	125	9.1	.991	B. O'Dell	43	281	19	14	0	3.53
	2B	C. Hiller	602	.276	3	48	367	417	29	105	5.0	.964	J. Sanford	39	265	24	7	0	3.43
W-103 L-62	SS	J. Pagan	580	.259	7	57	286	461	21	84	4.7	.973	J. Marichal	37	263	18	11	1	3.36
	3B	J. Davenport	485	.297	14	58	125	256	19	28	2.8	.953	B. Pierce	30	162	16	6	1	3.49
Alvin Dark	RF	F. Alou	561	.316	25	98	262	7	8	3	1.8	.971	S. Miller	59	107	5	8	19	4.12
	CF	W. Mays	621	.304	49	141	429	6	4	1	2.7	.991	McCormick	28	99	5	5	0	5.38
	LF	H. Kuenn	487	.304	10	68	160	3	5	1	1.6	.970	B. Bolin	41	92	7	3	5	3.62
	C	T. Haller	272	.261	18	55	472	38	4	6	5.6	.992	D. Larsen	49	86	5	4	11	4.38
	C	E. Bailey	254	.232	17	45	419	25	6	3	6.0	.987							
	OF	W. McCovey	229	.293	20	54	81	2	2	1	1.5	.976							
	OF	M. Alou	195	.292	3	14	80	3	2	0	1.5	.976							
Los Angeles	1B	R. Fairly	460	.278	14	71	968	43	11	76	8.5	.989	D. Drysdale	43	314	25	9	1	2.83
	2B	L. Burright	249	.205	4	30	176	206	15	35	3.6	.962	J. Podres	40	255	15	13	0	3.81
W-102 L-63	SS	M. Wills	695	.299	6	48	295	493	36	86	5.0	.956	S. Williams	40	186	14	12	1	4.46
	3B	J. Gilliam	588	.270	4	43	51	126	11	12	2.1	.941	S. Koufax	28	184	14	7	1	2.54
Walter Alston	RF	F. Howard	493	.296	31	119	187	19	6	4	1.6	.972	E. Roebuck	64	119	10	2	9	3.09
	CF	W. Davis	600	.285	21	85	379	13	15	0	2.6	.963	Perranoski	70	107	6	6	20	2.85
	LF	T. Davis	665	.346	27	153	240	9	10	0	1.8	.961	L. Sherry	58	90	7	3	11	3.20
	C	J. Roseboro	389	.249	7	55	842	57	14	10	7.1	.985	J. Moeller	19	86	6	5	1	5.25
	O1	W. Moon	244	.242	4	31	300	20	7	29		.979							
	OF	D. Snider	158	.278	5	30	56	3	2	0	1.6	.967							
	C	D. Camilli	88	.284	4	22	162	8	3	1	4.4	.983							
Cincinnati	1B	G. Coleman	476	.277	28	86	1021	83	12	100	8.7	.989	B. Purkey	37	288	23	5	0	2.81
	2B	Blasingame	494	.281	2	35	334	352	17	66	5.1	.976	J. Jay	39	273	21	14	0	3.76
W-98 L-64	SS	L. Cardenas	589	.294	10	60	273	443	21	84	4.9	.972	J. O'Toole	36	252	16	13	0	3.50
	3B	E. Kasko	533	.278	4	41	101	204	19	18	2.8	.941	J. Maloney	22	115	9	7	1	3.51
Fred Hutchinson	RF	F. Robinson	609	.342	39	136	315	10	2	2	2.0	.994	Klippstein	40	109	7	6	4	4.47
	CF	V. Pinson	619	.292	23	100	344	13	4	1	2.4	.989	J. Brosnan	48	65	4	4	13	3.34
	LF	W. Post	285	.263	17	62	110	5	8	0	1.4	.935	B. Henry	40	37	4	2	11	4.58
	C	J. Edwards	452	.254	8	50	807	92	12	11	7.0	.987							
	OF	J. Lynch	288	.281	12	57	89	7	3	1	1.4	.970							
	OF	M. Keough	230	.278	7	27	88	2	3	1	1.3	.968							
	3B	D. Zimmer	192	.250	2	16	45	66	6	6	2.7	.949							
	C	H. Foiles	131	.275	7	25	249	14	5	1	6.5	.981							

NATIONAL LEAGUE 1962, *cont.*

Pittsburgh
W-93 L-68

Danny Murtaugh

POS	Player	AB	BA	HR	RBI	PO	A	E	DP	TC/G	FA	Pitcher	G	IP	W	L	SV	ERA
1B	D. Stuart	394	.228	16	64	868	78	17	98	9.5	.982	B. Friend	39	262	18	14	1	3.06
2B	B. Mazeroski	572	.271	14	81	**425**	**509**	14	**138**	6.0	.985	A. McBean	33	190	15	10	0	3.70
SS	D. Groat	678	.294	2	61	**314**	**521**	38	126	5.4	.956	E. Francis	36	176	9	8	0	3.07
3B	D. Hoak	411	.241	5	48	93	220	10	19	2.8	**.969**	H. Haddix	28	141	9	6	0	4.20
RF	R. Clemente	538	.312	10	74	269	19	8	1	2.1	.973	V. Law	23	139	10	7	0	3.94
CF	B. Virdon	663	.247	6	47	360	11	9	0	2.4	.976	Sturdivant	49	125	9	5	2	3.73
LF	B. Skinner	510	.302	20	75	210	6	9	0	1.6	.960	R. Face	63	91	8	7	28	1.88
C	S. Burgess	360	.328	13	61	550	45	7	5	6.0	.988	D. Olivo	62	84	5	1	7	2.77
1B	D. Clendenon	222	.302	7	28	382	24	4	44	7.9	.990							

Milwaukee
W-86 L-76

Birdie Tebbetts

POS	Player	AB	BA	HR	RBI	PO	A	E	DP	TC/G	FA	Pitcher	G	IP	W	L	SV	ERA
1B	J. Adcock	391	.248	29	78	907	57	3	72	8.6	**.997**	W. Spahn	34	269	18	14	0	3.04
2B	F. Bolling	406	.271	9	43	252	298	6	70	4.7	**.989**	B. Shaw	38	225	15	9	2	3.07
SS	R. McMillan	468	.246	12	41	243	424	19	85	5.1	.972	B. Hendley	35	200	11	13	1	3.60
3B	E. Mathews	536	.265	29	90	141	283	16	22	3.1	.964	L. Burdette	37	144	10	9	2	4.89
RF	M. Jones	333	.255	10	36	142	3	4	0	1.6	.973	T. Cloninger	24	111	8	3	0	4.30
CF	H. Aaron	592	.323	45	128	340	11	7	1	2.3	.980	C. Raymond	26	43	5	5	10	2.74
LF	L. Maye	349	.244	10	41	209	2	5	1	2.3	.977							
C	D. Crandall	350	.297	8	45	460	54	3	7	5.7	**.994**							
1B	T. Aaron	334	.231	8	38	507	45	6	55	5.1	.989							
C	J. Torre	220	.282	5	26	325	39	5	4	5.9	.986							
OF	G. Bell	214	.285	5	24	75	3	1	0	1.4	.987							
S2	A. Samuel	209	.206	3	20	81	155	10	29		.959							

St. Louis
W-84 L-78

Johnny Keane

POS	Player	AB	BA	HR	RBI	PO	A	E	DP	TC/G	FA	Pitcher	G	IP	W	L	SV	ERA
1B	B. White	614	.324	20	102	1221	94	9	114	9.1	.993	L. Jackson	36	252	16	11	0	3.75
2B	J. Javier	598	.263	7	39	344	414	18	96	5.1	.977	B. Gibson	32	234	15	13	1	2.85
SS	J. Gotay	369	.255	2	27	179	339	24	65	4.5	.956	E. Broglio	34	222	12	9	0	3.00
3B	K. Boyer	611	.291	24	98	158	318	22	**34**	3.1	.956	R. Washburn	34	176	12	9	0	4.10
RF	C. James	388	.276	8	59	156	7	2	1	1.4	.988	C. Simmons	31	154	10	10	0	3.51
CF	C. Flood	635	.296	12	70	387	12	4	5	2.7	.990	L. McDaniel	55	107	3	10	14	4.12
LF	S. Musial	433	.330	19	82	164	6	4	1	1.5	.977	R. Sadecki	22	102	6	8	1	5.54
C	G. Oliver	345	.258	14	45	494	46	5	7	5.6	.991	B. Shantz	28	58	5	3	4	2.18
C	C. Sawatski	222	.252	13	42	354	24	1	4	5.4	.997							
SS	D. Maxvill	189	.222	1	18	111	169	11	41	3.8	.962							
1B	F. Whitfield	158	.266	8	34	282	25	4	32	8.2	.987							

Philadelphia
W-81 L-80

Gene Mauch

POS	Player	AB	BA	HR	RBI	PO	A	E	DP	TC/G	FA	Pitcher	G	IP	W	L	SV	ERA
1B	R. Sievers	477	.262	21	80	975	93	10	102	8.3	.991	A. Mahaffey	41	274	19	14	0	3.94
2B	T. Taylor	625	.259	7	43	372	385	22	101	5.2	.972	J. Hamilton	41	182	9	12	2	5.09
SS	B. Wine	311	.244	4	25	140	237	8	51	4.3	.979	D. Bennett	31	175	9	9	3	3.81
3B	D. Demeter	550	.307	29	107	91	177	18	18	2.7	.937	C. McLish	32	155	11	5	1	4.25
RF	J. Callison	603	.300	23	83	327	**24**	7	7	2.4	.988	C. Short	47	142	11	9	3	3.42
CF	T. Gonzalez	437	.302	20	63	268	8	0	2	2.4	**1.000**	D. Green	37	129	6	6	1	3.83
LF	T. Savage	335	.266	7	39	185	4	5	1	1.8	.974	J. Baldschun	67	113	12	7	13	2.96
C	C. Dalrymple	370	.276	11	54	635	61	9	**11**	5.9	.987							
OF	W. Covington	304	.283	9	44	98	3	6	2	1.2	.944							
UT	B. Klaus	248	.206	4	20	93	142	9	21		.963							
SS	R. Amaro	226	.243	0	19	143	224	12	50	4.9	.968							
1B	F. Torre	168	.310	0	20	347	37	8	40	5.2	.980							

Houston
W-64 L-96

Harry Craft

POS	Player	AB	BA	HR	RBI	PO	A	E	DP	TC/G	FA	Pitcher	G	IP	W	L	SV	ERA
1B	N. Larker	506	.263	9	63	1148	103	11	103	9.3	.991	D. Farrell	43	242	10	20	4	3.02
2B	Amalfitano	380	.237	1	27	230	268	17	72	4.7	.988	K. Johnson	33	197	7	16	0	3.84
SS	B. Lillis	457	.249	1	40	169	290	13	54	4.8	.972	B. Bruce	32	175	10	9	0	4.06
3B	Aspromonte	534	.266	11	59	150	233	13	21	2.8	.967	J. Golden	37	153	7	11	1	4.07
RF	R. Mejias	566	.286	24	76	217	10	13	2	1.7	.946	Woodeshick	31	149	5	16	0	4.39
CF	C. Warwick	477	.260	16	60	262	12	4	1	2.2	.986	D. McMahon	51	77	5	5	8	1.53
LF	A. Spangler	418	.285	5	35	183	7	8	2	1.6	.960	R. Kemmerer	36	68	5	3	3	4.10
C	H. Smith	345	.235	12	35	570	65	9	9	7.0	.986							
OF	J. Pendleton	321	.246	8	36	126	4	5	0	1.5	.963							
C	M. Ranew	218	.234	4	24	357	35	8	1	6.9	.980							

Chicago
W-59 L-103

El Tappe
W-4 L-16

Lou Klein
W-12 L-18

Charlie Metro
W-43 L-69

POS	Player	AB	BA	HR	RBI	PO	A	E	DP	TC/G	FA	Pitcher	G	IP	W	L	SV	ERA
1B	E. Banks	610	.269	37	104	**1458**	**106**	11	**134**	10.6	.993	B. Buhl	34	212	12	13	0	3.69
2B	K. Hubbs	661	.260	5	49	363	489	15	103	5.5	.983	D. Ellsworth	37	209	9	20	1	5.09
SS	A. Rodgers	461	.278	5	44	239	433	28	91	5.3	.960	D. Cardwell	41	196	7	16	4	4.92
3B	R. Santo	604	.227	17	83	161	332	23	33	3.3	.955	C. Koonce	35	191	10	10	3	3.97
RF	G. Altman	534	.318	22	74	234	8	7	3	1.9	.972	G. Hobbie	42	162	5	14	0	5.22
CF	L. Brock	434	.263	9	35	243	7	9	2	2.4	.965	B. Anderson	57	108	2	7	4	5.02
LF	B. Williams	618	.298	22	91	273	18	10	4	1.9	.967	B. Schultz	51	78	5	5	5	3.82
C	D. Bertell	215	.302	2	18	306	36	5	0	4.6	.986	D. Elston	57	66	4	8	8	2.44
OF	D. Landrum	238	.282	1	15	122	3	4	3	2.2	.969							

NATIONAL LEAGUE 1962, *cont.*

	POS	Player	AB	BA	HR	RBI	PO	A	E	DP	TC/G	FA	Pitcher	G	IP	W	L	SV	ERA
New York	1B	Throneberry	357	.244	16	49	785	77	17	87	9.1	.981	R. Craig	42	233	10	24	3	4.51
	2B	C. Neal	508	.260	11	58	187	240	13	54	5.2	.970	A. Jackson	36	231	8	20	0	4.40
W-40 L-120	SS	E. Chacon	368	.236	2	27	204	332	22	64	5.1	.961	J. Hook	37	214	8	19	0	4.84
	3B	F. Mantilla	466	.275	11	59	76	179	14	22	2.8	.948	B. Miller	33	144	1	12	1	4.89
Casey Stengel	RF	R. Ashburn	389	.306	7	28	187	9	5	1	2.1	.975	C. Anderson	50	131	3	17	4	5.35
	CF	J. Hickman	392	.245	13	46	265	7	8	0	2.3	.971	B. Moorhead	38	105	0	2	0	4.53
	LF	F. Thomas	571	.266	34	94	216	14	9	0	1.9	.962	MacKenzie	42	80	5	4	1	4.95
	C	Cannizzaro	133	.241	0	9	218	34	7	3	4.6	.973							
	UT	R. Kanehl	351	.248	4	27	235	230	32	57		.936							
	OF	Christopher	271	.244	6	32	133	5	4	4	1.5	.972							
	OF	G. Woodling	190	.274	5	24	68	0	1	0	1.4	.986							
	C	S. Taylor	158	.222	3	20	202	25	2	3	4.6	.991							

BATTING AND BASE RUNNING LEADERS

Batting Average
- T. Davis, LA .346
- F. Robinson, CIN .342
- S. Musial, STL .330
- B. White, STL .324
- H. Aaron, MIL .323

Slugging Average
- F. Robinson, CIN .624
- H. Aaron, MIL .618
- W. Mays, SF .615
- F. Howard, LA .560
- T. Davis, LA .535

Home Runs
- W. Mays, SF 49
- H. Aaron, MIL 45
- F. Robinson, CIN 39
- E. Banks, CHI 37
- O. Cepeda, SF 35

Total Bases
- W. Mays, SF 382
- F. Robinson, CIN 380
- H. Aaron, MIL 366
- T. Davis, LA 356
- O. Cepeda, SF 324

Runs Batted In
- T. Davis, LA 153
- W. Mays, SF 141
- F. Robinson, CIN 136
- H. Aaron, MIL 128
- F. Howard, LA 119

Stolen Bases
- M. Wills, LA 104
- W. Davis, LA 32
- J. Javier, STL 26
- V. Pinson, CIN 26
- T. Taylor, PHI 20

Hits
- T. Davis, LA 230
- F. Robinson, CIN 208
- M. Wills, LA 208
- B. White, STL 199

Base on Balls
- E. Mathews, MIL 101
- J. Gilliam, LA 93
- R. Ashburn, NY 81
- W. Mays, SF 78

Home Run Percentage
- W. Mays, SF 7.9
- H. Aaron, MIL 7.6
- F. Robinson, CIN 6.4
- F. Howard, LA 6.3

Runs Scored
- F. Robinson, CIN 134
- W. Mays, SF 130
- M. Wills, LA 130
- H. Aaron, MIL 127

Doubles
- F. Robinson, CIN 51
- W. Mays, SF 36
- D. Groat, PIT 34
- L. Cardenas, CIN 31

Triples
- W. Davis, LA 10
- J. Callison, PHI 10
- B. Virdon, PIT 10
- M. Wills, LA 10

PITCHING LEADERS

Winning Percentage
- B. Purkey, CIN .821
- J. Sanford, SF .774
- D. Drysdale, LA .735
- B. Pierce, SF .727
- B. Shaw, MIL .625

Earned Run Average
- S. Koufax, LA 2.54
- B. Shaw, MIL 2.80
- B. Purkey, CIN 2.81
- D. Drysdale, LA 2.83
- B. Gibson, STL 2.85

Wins
- D. Drysdale, LA 25
- J. Sanford, SF 24
- B. Purkey, CIN 23
- J. Jay, CIN 21
- A. Mahaffey, PHI 19
- B. O'Dell, SF 19

Saves
- R. Face, PIT 28
- Perranoski, LA 20
- S. Miller, SF 19
- L. McDaniel, STL 14
- J. Baldschun, PHI 13
- J. Brosnan, CIN 13

Strikeouts
- D. Drysdale, LA 232
- S. Koufax, LA 216
- B. Gibson, STL 208
- D. Farrell, HOU 203
- B. O'Dell, SF 195

Complete Games
- W. Spahn, MIL 22
- A. Mahaffey, PHI 20
- B. O'Dell, SF 20
- D. Drysdale, LA 19
- J. Marichal, SF 18
- B. Purkey, CIN 18

Fewest Hits/9 Innings
- S. Koufax, LA 6.54
- B. Gibson, STL 6.70
- D. Bennett, PHI 7.42
- D. Drysdale, LA 7.79

Shutouts
- B. Gibson, STL 5
- B. Friend, PIT 5
- C. Simmons, STL 4
- E. Broglio, STL 4

Fewest Walks/9 Innings
- B. Shaw, MIL 1.76
- B. Friend, PIT 1.82
- W. Spahn, MIL 1.84
- B. Pierce, SF 1.94

Most Strikeouts/9 Inn.
- S. Koufax, LA 10.55
- K. Johnson, HOU 8.13
- B. Gibson, STL 8.01
- D. Bennett, PHI 7.68

Innings
- D. Drysdale, LA 314
- B. Purkey, CIN 288
- B. O'Dell, SF 281
- A. Mahaffey, PHI 274

Games Pitched
- Perranoski, LA 70
- J. Baldschun, PHI 67
- E. Roebuck, LA 64
- R. Face, PIT 63

	W	L	PCT	GB	R	OR	2B	3B	HR	BA	SA	SB	E	DP	FA	CG	BB	SO	ShO	SV	ERA
San Francisco*	103	62	.624		878	690	235	32	204	.278	.441	73	142	153	.977	62	503	886	10	39	3.79
Los Angeles	102	63	.618	1	842	697	192	65	140	.268	.400	198	193	144	.970	44	588	1104	8	46	3.62
Cincinnati	98	64	.605	3.5	802	685	252	40	167	.270	.417	66	145	144	.977	51	567	964	13	35	3.75
Pittsburgh	93	68	.578	8	706	626	240	65	108	.268	.394	50	152	177	.976	40	466	897	13	41	3.37
Milwaukee	86	76	.531	15.5	730	665	204	38	181	.252	.403	57	124	154	.980	59	407	802	10	24	3.68
St. Louis	84	78	.519	17.5	774	664	221	31	137	.271	.394	86	132	170	.979	53	517	914	17	25	3.55
Philadelphia	81	80	.503	20	705	759	199	39	142	.260	.390	79	138	167	.977	43	574	863	7	24	4.28
Houston	64	96	.400	36.5	592	717	170	47	105	.246	.351	42	173	149	.973	34	471	1047	9	19	3.83
Chicago	59	103	.364	42.5	632	827	196	56	126	.253	.377	78	146	171	.977	29	601	783	4	26	4.54
New York	40	120	.250	60.5	617	948	166	40	139	.240	.361	59	210	167	.967	43	571	772	4	10	5.04
					7278	7278	2075	453	1449	.261	.393	788	1555	1596	.975	458	5265	9032	95	289	3.94

* Defeated Los Angeles in a playoff 2 games to 1.

AMERICAN LEAGUE 1962

	POS	Player	AB	BA	HR	RBI	PO	A	E	DP	TC/G	FA	Pitcher	G	IP	W	L	SV	ERA
New York	1B	B. Skowron	478	.270	23	80	1054	77	10	101	8.5	.991	R. Terry	43	299	23	12	2	3.19
	2B	Richardson	692	.302	8	59	378	452	15	116	5.2	.982	W. Ford	38	258	17	8	0	2.90
W-96 L-66	SS	T. Tresh	622	.286	20	93	201	312	16	51	4.8	.970	B. Stafford	35	213	14	9	0	3.67
	3B	C. Boyer	566	.272	18	68	187	396	22	41	3.9	.964	J. Bouton	36	133	7	7	2	3.99
Ralph Houk	RF	R. Maris	590	.256	33	100	316	4	3	0	2.1	.991	R. Sheldon	34	118	7	8	1	5.49
	CF	M. Mantle	377	.321	30	89	214	4	5	1	1.9	.978	J. Coates	50	118	7	6	6	4.44
	LF	H. Lopez	335	.275	6	48	176	3	3	0	2.2	.984	B. Daley	43	105	7	5	4	3.59
	C	E. Howard	494	.279	21	91	713	44	4	12	5.9	.995	M. Bridges	52	72	8	4	18	3.14
	OF	J. Blanchard	246	.232	13	39	76	2	1	0	1.7	.987	L. Arroyo	27	34	1	3	7	4.81
	CO	Y. Berra	232	.224	10	35	238	17	6	6		.977							
	SS	T. Kubek	169	.314	4	17	71	117	9	27	5.6	.954							

AMERICAN LEAGUE 1962, *cont.*

	POS	Player	AB	BA	HR	RBI	PO	A	E	DP	TC/G	FA	Pitcher	G	IP	W	L	SV	ERA
Minnesota	1B	V. Power	611	.290	16	63	1193	**134**	10	**133**	9.4	.993	J. Kaat	39	269	18	14	1	3.14
	2B	B. Allen	573	.269	12	64	357	394	13	109	4.8	.983	C. Pascual	34	258	20	11	0	3.32
W-91 L-71	SS	Z. Versalles	568	.241	17	67	**335**	**501**	26	**127**	**5.4**	.970	J. Kralick	39	243	12	11	0	3.86
	3B	R. Rollins	624	.298	16	96	137	324	**28**	33	3.1	.943	D. Stigman	40	143	12	5	3	3.66
Sam Mele	RF	B. Allison	519	.266	29	102	287	10	7	1	2.1	.977	Bonikowski	30	100	5	7	2	3.88
	CF	L. Green	619	.271	14	63	361	8	2	2	2.4	.995	L. Stange	44	95	4	3	3	4.45
	LF	H. Killebrew	552	.243	**48**	**126**	227	5	8	0	1.6	.967	R. Moore	49	65	8	3	9	4.73
	C	E. Battey	522	.280	11	57	**872**	82	9	9	**6.6**	.991	B. Pleis	21	45	2	5	3	4.40
	1B	D. Mincher	121	.240	9	29	211	13	5	17	9.2	.978	F. Sullivan	21	33	4	1	5	3.24
Los Angeles	1B	L. Thomas	583	.290	26	104	735	42	14	66	8.8	.982	D. Chance	50	207	14	10	8	2.96
	2B	B. Moran	659	.282	17	74	**422**	477	13	103	**5.7**	.986	B. Belinsky	33	187	10	11	1	3.56
W-86 L-76	SS	J. Koppe	375	.227	4	40	197	356	25	63	4.9	.957	E. Grba	40	176	8	9	1	4.54
	3B	F. Torres	451	.259	11	74	110	250	24	20	3.1	.938	D. Lee	27	153	8	8	2	3.11
Bill Rigney	RF	G. Thomas	181	.238	4	12	107	4	5	1	2.3	.957	K. McBride	24	149	11	5	0	3.50
	CF	A. Pearson	614	.261	5	42	366	8	4	0	2.4	.989	T. Bowsfield	34	139	9	8	1	4.40
	LF	L. Wagner	612	.268	37	107	269	7	8	1	1.8	.972	A. Fowler	48	77	4	3	5	2.81
	C	B. Rodgers	565	.258	6	61	826	73	**10**	**14**	6.1	.989	R. Duren	42	71	2	9	8	4.42
	OF	E. Averill	187	.219	4	22	70	2	0	0	1.5	1.000	J. Spring	57	65	4	2	6	4.02
	SS	J. Fregosi	175	.291	3	23	96	150	15	35	5.0	.943	T. Morgan	48	59	5	2	9	2.91
	1B	S. Bilko	164	.287	8	38	371	28	2	36	8.0	.995	D. Osinski	33	54	6	4	4	2.82
Detroit	1B	N. Cash	507	.243	39	89	1081	116	10	94	8.3	.992	J. Bunning	41	258	19	10	6	3.59
	2B	J. Wood	367	.226	8	30	185	197	**20**	33	4.5	.950	H. Aguirre	42	216	16	8	3	**2.21**
W-85 L-76	SS	C. Fernandez	503	.249	20	59	235	336	24	53	4.3	.960	D. Mossi	35	180	11	13	1	4.19
	3B	S. Boros	356	.228	16	47	105	151	19	15	2.6	.931	P. Regan	35	171	11	9	0	4.04
Bob Scheffing	RF	A. Kaline	398	.304	29	94	225	8	4	1	2.4	.983	P. Foytack	29	144	10	7	0	4.39
	CF	B. Bruton	561	.278	16	74	**394**	5	7	2	2.8	.983	R. Kline	36	77	3	6	2	4.31
	LF	R. Colavito	601	.273	37	112	359	10	3	1	2.3	.992	R. Nischwitz	48	65	4	5	4	3.90
	C	D. Brown	431	.241	12	40	742	42	5	8	6.0	.994	T. Fox	44	58	3	1	16	1.71
	UT	McAuliffe	471	.263	12	63	260	257	30	45		.945							
	OF	B. Morton	195	.262	4	17	110	4	1	1	1.9	.991							
Chicago	1B	Cunningham	526	.295	8	70	1282	90	8	118	9.7	**.994**	R. Herbert	35	237	20	9	0	3.27
	2B	N. Fox	621	.267	2	54	376	428	8	93	5.3	**.990**	J. Pizarro	36	203	12	14	1	3.81
W-85 L-77	SS	L. Aparicio	581	.241	7	40	280	452	20	102	4.9	**.973**	E. Fisher	57	183	9	5	5	3.10
	3B	A. Smith	511	.292	16	82	76	185	18	8	2.7	.935	E. Wynn	27	168	7	15	0	4.46
Al Lopez	RF	Hershberger	427	.262	4	46	236	7	4	0	1.8	.984	J. Buzhardt	28	152	8	12	0	4.19
	CF	J. Landis	534	.228	15	61	360	2	2	1	2.5	.995	F. Baumann	40	120	7	6	4	3.38
	LF	F. Robinson	600	.312	11	109	278	13	8	2	1.9	.973	J. Horlen	20	109	7	6	0	4.89
	C	C. Carreon	313	.256	4	37	519	30	3	5	5.9	.995	D. Zanni	44	86	6	5	5	3.75
	C	S. Lollar	220	.268	2	26	298	23	3	0	4.9	.991	T. Lown	42	56	4	2	6	3.04
	OF	C. Maxwell	206	.296	9	43	100	2	1	1	1.8	.990							
	32	B. Sadowski	130	.231	6	24	33	62	2	9		.979							
Cleveland	1B	T. Francona	621	.272	14	70	1402	127	**22**	5	**9.8**	.986	D. Donovan	34	251	20	10	0	3.59
	2B	J. Kindall	530	.232	13	55	358	**494**	19	114	5.7	.956	P. Ramos	37	201	10	12	1	3.71
W-80 L-82	SS	W. Held	466	.249	19	58	221	371	27	101	4.7	.956	J. Perry	35	194	12	12	0	4.14
	3B	B. Phillips	562	.258	10	54	175	243	10	16	3.0	.977	B. Latman	45	179	8	13	5	4.17
Mel McGaha	RF	W. Kirkland	419	.200	21	72	233	11	7	0	2.0	.972	M. Grant	26	150	7	10	0	4.27
	CF	T. Cline	375	.248	2	28	238	3	2	1	2.0	.992	G. Bell	57	108	10	9	12	4.26
	LF	C. Essegian	336	.274	21	50	154	1	1	0	1.7	.994	S. McDowell	25	88	3	7	1	6.06
	C	J. Romano	459	.261	25	81	657	63	7	6	5.6	.990							
	OF	A. Luplow	318	.277	14	45	162	4	7	0	2.0	.960							
	OF	W. Tasby	199	.241	4	17	105	1	0	0	1.6	1.000							
	OF	D. Dillard	174	.230	5	14	54	1	2	0	1.1	.965							
	OF	G. Green	143	.280	11	28	51	2	2	1	1.7	.964							
Baltimore	1B	J. Gentile	545	.251	33	87	1214	121	16	121	9.0	.988	C. Estrada	34	223	9	**17**	0	3.83
	2B	M. Breeding	240	.246	2	18	146	196	8	47	4.8	.977	M. Pappas	35	205	12	10	0	4.03
W-77 L-85	SS	J. Adair	538	.284	11	48	216	285	16	72	4.6	.969	R. Roberts	27	191	10	9	0	2.78
	3B	B. Robinson	634	.303	23	86	163	339	11	32	3.2	**.979**	J. Fisher	32	152	7	9	1	5.09
Billy Hitchcock	RF	R. Snyder	416	.305	9	40	218	8	6	2	1.9	.974	S. Barber	28	140	9	6	0	3.46
	CF	J. Brandt	505	.255	19	75	310	9	8	2	2.4	.976	D. Hall	43	118	6	6	6	2.28
	LF	B. Powell	400	.243	15	53	184	1	6	0	1.7	.969	B. Hoeft	57	114	4	8	7	4.59
	C	G. Triandos	207	.159	6	23	355	28	6	2	6.2	.985	H. Wilhelm	52	93	7	10	15	1.94
	2B	J. Temple	270	.263	1	17	141	169	6	41	4.5	.981	H. Brown	22	86	6	4	1	4.10
	OF	W. Herzog	263	.266	1	35	132	4	3	0	2.0	.978							
	C	C. Lau	197	.294	6	37	269	15	1	1	5.1	.996							
	SS	R. Hansen	196	.173	3	17	114	159	10	37	4.4	.965							
	O1	D. Williams	178	.247	1	18	180	13	0	13		1.000							
	OF	D. Nicholson	173	.173	9	15	111	4	2	0	1.5	.983							
	C	H. Landrith	167	.222	4	17	289	34	6	5	5.5	.982							

AMERICAN LEAGUE 1962, cont.

Boston
W-76 L-84

Pinky Higgins

POS	Player	AB	BA	HR	RBI	PO	A	E	DP	TC/G	FA	Pitcher	G	IP	W	L	SV	ERA
1B	P. Runnels	562	.326	10	60	1309	104	10	125	9.4	.993	G. Conley	34	242	15	14	1	3.95
2B	C. Schilling	413	.230	7	35	267	331	9	85	5.1	.985	Monbouquette	35	235	15	13	0	3.33
SS	E. Bressoud	599	.277	14	68	291	482	28	107	5.2	.965	E. Wilson	31	191	12	8	0	3.90
3B	F. Malzone	619	.283	21	95	154	313	16	32	3.1	.967	D. Schwall	33	182	9	15	0	4.94
RF	L. Clinton	398	.294	18	75	185	6	4	1	1.9	.979	D. Radatz	62	125	9	6	24	2.24
CF	G. Geiger	466	.249	16	54	287	8	4	1	2.3	.987	G. Cisco	23	83	4	7	0	6.72
LF	Yastrzemski	646	.296	19	94	329	15	11	3	2.2	.969	M. Fornieles	42	82	3	6	5	5.36
C	Pagliaroni	260	.258	11	37	411	33	6	4	6.2	.987	A. Earley	38	68	4	5	5	5.80
OF	C. Hardy	362	.215	8	36	205	7	2	1	2.0	.991							
C	B. Tillman	249	.229	14	38	389	19	7	1	6.3	.983							
2B	B. Gardner	199	.271	0	12	67	91	6	21	4.3	.963							

Kansas City
W-72 L-90

Hank Bauer

POS	Player	AB	BA	HR	RBI	PO	A	E	DP	TC/G	FA	Pitcher	G	IP	W	L	SV	ERA
1B	N. Siebern	600	.308	25	117	1405	127	10	122	9.5	.994	E. Rakow	42	235	14	17	1	4.25
2B	J. Lumpe	641	.301	10	83	343	435	11	97	5.1	.986	D. Pfister	41	196	4	14	1	4.54
SS	D. Howser	286	.238	6	34	138	191	13	37	4.8	.962	J. Walker	31	143	8	9	0	5.90
3B	E. Charles	535	.288	17	74	145	285	16	27	3.2	.964	B. Fischer	34	128	4	12	2	3.95
RF	G. Cimoli	550	.275	10	71	231	8	8	2	1.7	.968	J. Wyatt	59	125	10	7	11	4.46
CF	B. Del Greco	338	.254	9	38	245	9	4	0	2.1	.984	D. Segui	37	117	8	5	6	3.86
LF	M. Jimenez	479	.301	11	69	185	7	3	0	1.6	.985	Wickersham	30	110	11	4	1	4.17
C	H. Sullivan	274	.248	4	29	447	31	10	2	5.2	.980	O. Pena	13	90	6	4	0	3.01
OF	J. Tartabull	310	.277	0	22	185	6	5	0	2.3	.974	G. Jones	21	33	3	2	6	6.34
UT	W. Causey	305	.252	4	38	143	200	14	25		.961							
C	J. Azcue	223	.229	2	25	363	42	6	5	5.9	.985							
OF	G. Alusik	209	.273	11	35	87	3	3	0	1.9	.968							

Washington
W-60 L-101

Mickey Vernon

POS	Player	AB	BA	HR	RBI	PO	A	E	DP	TC/G	FA	Pitcher	G	IP	W	L	SV	ERA
1B	H. Bright	392	.273	17	67	800	70	10	83	8.9	.989	D. Stenhouse	34	197	11	12	0	3.65
2B	C. Cottier	443	.242	6	40	368	354	14	100	5.5	.981	D. Rudolph	37	176	8	10	0	3.62
SS	K. Hamlin	292	.253	3	22	126	210	13	47	4.0	.963	T. Cheney	37	173	7	9	1	3.17
3B	B. Johnson	466	.288	12	43	79	142	13	12	3.3	.944	B. Daniels	44	161	7	16	2	4.85
RF	J. King	333	.243	11	35	178	9	4	4	1.9	.979	C. Osteen	28	150	8	13	1	3.65
CF	J. Piersall	471	.244	4	31	308	5	1	0	2.4	.997	P. Burnside	40	150	5	11	2	4.45
LF	C. Hinton	542	.310	17	75	233	7	3	1	1.8	.988	S. Hamilton	41	107	3	8	2	3.77
C	K. Retzer	340	.285	8	37	488	44	8	5	5.5	.985	M. Kutyna	54	78	5	6	0	4.04
C	B. Schmidt	256	.242	10	31	342	40	1	3	4.4	.997	J. Hannan	42	68	2	4	4	3.31
32	D. O'Connell	236	.263	2	18	70	141	10	21		.955							
3B	J. Schaive	225	.253	6	29	42	105	5	7	3.1	.967							
OF	D. Lock	225	.253	12	37	144	2	4	0	2.2	.973							
1B	D. Long	191	.241	4	24	459	32	2	67	9.7	.996							
1O	B. Zipfel	184	.239	6	21	228	17	8	13		.968							
OF	J. Hicks	174	.224	6	14	74	1	3	1	1.9	.962							

BATTING AND BASE RUNNING LEADERS

Batting Average
P. Runnels, BOS	.326
F. Robinson, CHI	.312
C. Hinton, WAS	.310
N. Siebern, KC	.308
B. Robinson, BAL	.303

Slugging Average
H. Killebrew, MIN	.545
R. Colavito, DET	.514
N. Cash, DET	.513
B. Allison, MIN	.511
L. Wagner, LA	.500

Home Runs
H. Killebrew, MIN	48
N. Cash, DET	39
R. Colavito, DET	37
L. Wagner, LA	37
J. Gentile, BAL	33
R. Maris, NY	33

Total Bases
R. Colavito, DET	309
B. Robinson, BAL	308
L. Wagner, LA	306
Yastrzemski, BOS	303
H. Killebrew, MIN	301

Runs Batted In
H. Killebrew, MIN	126
N. Siebern, KC	117
R. Colavito, DET	112
F. Robinson, CHI	109
L. Wagner, LA	107

Stolen Bases
L. Aparicio, CHI	31
C. Hinton, WAS	28
J. Wood, DET	24
E. Charles, KC	20

Hits
Richardson, NY	209
J. Lumpe, KC	193
B. Robinson, BAL	192
Yastrzemski, BOS	191

Base on Balls
M. Mantle, NY	122
N. Siebern, KC	110
H. Killebrew, MIN	106
N. Cash, DET	104

Home Run Percentage
H. Killebrew, MIN	8.7
N. Cash, DET	7.7
R. Colavito, DET	6.2
J. Gentile, BAL	6.1

Runs Scored
A. Pearson, LA	115
N. Siebern, KC	114
B. Allison, MIN	102
Yastrzemski, BOS	99

Doubles
F. Robinson, CHI	45
Yastrzemski, BOS	43
E. Bressoud, BOS	40
Richardson, NY	38

Triples
G. Cimoli, KC	15
L. Clinton, BOS	10
F. Robinson, CHI	10
J. Lumpe, KC	10

PITCHING LEADERS

Winning Percentage
R. Herbert, CHI	.690
W. Ford, NY	.680
D. Donovan, CLE	.667
H. Aguirre, DET	.667
R. Terry, NY	.657

Earned Run Average
H. Aguirre, DET	2.21
R. Roberts, BAL	2.78
W. Ford, NY	2.90
D. Chance, LA	2.96
E. Fisher, CHI	3.10

Wins
R. Terry, NY	23
R. Herbert, CHI	20
D. Donovan, CLE	20
C. Pascual, MIN	20
J. Bunning, DET	19

Saves
D. Radatz, BOS	24
M. Bridges, NY	18
T. Fox, DET	16
H. Wilhelm, BAL	15
G. Bell, CLE	12

Strikeouts
C. Pascual, MIN	206
J. Bunning, DET	184
R. Terry, NY	176
J. Pizarro, CHI	173
J. Kaat, MIN	173

Complete Games
C. Pascual, MIN	18
D. Donovan, CLE	16
J. Kaat, MIN	16
R. Terry, NY	14
J. Bunning, DET	12
R. Herbert, CHI	12

Fewest Hits/9 Innings
H. Aguirre, DET	6.75
T. Cheney, WAS	6.96
B. Belinsky, LA	7.16
E. Wilson, BOS	7.67

Shutouts
C. Pascual, MIN	5
D. Donovan, CLE	5
J. Kaat, MIN	5
K. McBride, LA	4

Fewest Walks/9 Innings
D. Donovan, CLE	1.69
R. Terry, NY	1.72
D. Mossi, DET	1.80
R. Roberts, BAL	1.93

Most Strikeouts/9 Inn.
J. Pizarro, CHI	7.66
T. Cheney, WAS	7.63
C. Pascual, MIN	7.20
B. Belinsky, LA	6.97

Innings
R. Terry, NY	299
J. Kaat, MIN	269
J. Bunning, DET	258
W. Ford, NY	258

Games Pitched
D. Radatz, BOS	62
J. Wyatt, KC	59
E. Fisher, CHI	57
B. Hoeft, BAL	57

AMERICAN LEAGUE 1962, cont.

	W	L	PCT	GB	R	OR	2B	3B	HR	BA	SA	SB	E	DP	FA	CG	BB	SO	ShO	SV	ERA
								Batting						Fielding			Pitching				
New York	96	66	.593		**817**	680	240	29	199	**.267**	**.426**	42	131	151	.979	33	499	838	10	42	3.70
Minnesota	91	71	.562	5	798	713	215	39	185	.260	.412	33	129	**173**	.979	**53**	493	**948**	11	27	3.89
Los Angeles	86	76	.531	10	718	706	232	35	137	.250	.380	46	175	153	.972	23	616	858	8	35	3.70
Detroit	85	76	.528	10.5	758	692	191	36	**209**	.248	.411	69	156	114	.974	46	503	873	8	35	3.81
Chicago	85	77	.525	11	707	**658**	250	56	92	.257	.372	76	**110**	153	**.982**	50	537	821	13	28	3.73
Cleveland	80	82	.494	16	682	745	202	22	180	.245	.388	35	139	168	.977	45	594	780	12	31	4.14
Baltimore	77	85	.475	19	652	680	225	34	156	.248	.387	45	122	152	.980	32	549	898	8	33	**3.69**
Boston	76	84	.475	19	707	756	**257**	53	146	.258	.403	39	131	152	.979	34	632	923	10	40	4.22
Kansas City	72	90	.444	24	745	837	220	58	116	.263	.386	76	132	131	.979	32	655	825	4	33	4.79
Washington	60	101	.373	35.5	599	716	206	38	132	.250	.373	**99**	139	160	.978	38	593	771	11	13	4.04
					7183	7183	2238	400	1552	.255	.394	560	1364	1507	.978	386	5671	8535	102	329	3.97

NATIONAL LEAGUE 1963

Team	POS	Player	AB	BA	HR	RBI	PO	A	E	DP	TC/G	FA	Pitcher	G	IP	W	L	SV	ERA
Los Angeles W-99 L-63 Walter Alston	1B	R. Fairly	490	.271	12	77	884	45	5	74	7.8	**.995**	D. Drysdale	42	315	19	17	0	2.63
	2B	J. Gilliam	525	.282	6	49	242	277	8	61	4.4	.985	S. Koufax	40	311	**25**	5	0	**1.88**
	SS	M. Wills	527	.302	0	34	171	322	21	47	4.7	.959	J. Podres	37	198	14	12	1	3.54
	3B	K. McMullen	233	.236	5	28	47	133	13	8	2.7	.933	B. Miller	42	187	10	8	1	2.89
	RF	F. Howard	417	.273	28	64	190	4	8	0	1.8	.960	Perranoski	**69**	129	16	3	21	1.67
	CF	W. Davis	515	.245	9	60	337	16	8	3	2.4	.978	L. Sherry	36	80	2	6	3	3.73
	LF	T. Davis	556	**.326**	16	88	181	7	6	3	1.5	.969							
	C	J. Roseboro	470	.236	9	49	908	66	8	6	7.3	.992							
	OF	W. Moon	343	.262	8	48	125	2	5	0	1.4	.962							
	1B	B. Skowron	237	.203	4	19	518	34	5	44	8.4	.991							
	SS	D. Tracewski	217	.226	1	10	92	196	13	32	3.7	.957							
	2B	N. Oliver	163	.239	1	9	109	112	9	26	4.0	.961							
St. Louis W-93 L-69 Johnny Keane	1B	B. White	658	.304	27	109	1389	105	13	126	9.3	.991	B. Gibson	36	255	18	9	0	3.39
	2B	J. Javier	609	.263	9	46	**377**	415	25	93	5.1	.969	E. Broglio	39	250	18	8	0	2.99
	SS	D. Groat	631	.319	6	73	257	448	26	91	4.6	.964	C. Simmons	32	233	15	9	0	2.48
	3B	K. Boyer	617	.285	24	111	129	293	**34**	23	2.9	.925	R. Sadecki	36	193	10	10	1	4.10
	RF	G. Altman	464	.274	9	47	220	8	5	1	1.9	.979	R. Taylor	54	133	9	7	11	2.84
	CF	C. Flood	**662**	.302	5	63	401	12	5	2	**2.6**	.988	L. Burdette	21	98	3	8	2	3.75
	LF	C. James	347	.268	10	45	169	4	1	1	1.7	.994	B. Shantz	55	79	6	4	11	2.61
	C	T. McCarver	405	.289	4	51	722	55	5	7	6.2	.994	E. Bauta	38	53	3	4	3	3.93
	OF	S. Musial	337	.255	12	58	121	1	4	0	1.3	.968							
	P	B. Gibson	87	.207	3	20	27	28	5	0	1.7	.917							
San Francisco W-88 L-74 Alvin Dark	1B	O. Cepeda	579	.316	34	97	1262	83	**21**	91	9.1	.985	J. Marichal	41	**321**	**25**	8	0	2.41
	2B	C. Hiller	417	.223	6	33	224	277	19	48	4.8	.963	J. Sanford	42	284	16	13	0	3.51
	SS	J. Pagan	483	.234	6	39	262	375	20	69	4.6	.970	B. O'Dell	36	222	14	10	1	3.16
	3B	J. Davenport	460	.252	4	36	122	183	12	9	2.5	.962	B. Bolin	47	137	10	6	7	3.28
	RF	F. Alou	565	.281	20	82	279	9	4	2	1.9	.986	J. Fisher	36	116	6	10	1	4.58
	CF	W. Mays	596	.314	38	103	397	7	8	1	2.6	.981	B. Pierce	38	99	3	11	8	4.27
	LF	W. McCovey	564	.280	44	102	220	7	**14**	0	1.8	.942	D. Larsen	46	62	7	7	3	3.05
	C	E. Bailey	308	.263	21	68	560	44	8	3	7.0	.987							
	O3	H. Kuenn	417	.290	6	31	115	60	13	3		.931							
	C	T. Haller	298	.255	14	44	499	38	3	7	6.4	.994							
Philadelphia W-87 L-75 Gene Mauch	1B	R. Sievers	450	.240	19	82	981	77	12	93	8.5	.989	C. McLish	32	210	13	11	0	3.26
	2B	T. Taylor	640	.281	5	49	319	396	10	86	4.9	**.986**	R. Culp	34	203	14	11	0	2.97
	SS	B. Wine	418	.215	6	44	220	359	17	73	4.5	.971	C. Short	38	198	9	12	0	2.95
	3B	D. Hoak	377	.231	6	24	88	205	13	13	2.9	.958	A. Mahaffey	26	149	7	10	0	3.99
	RF	J. Callison	626	.284	26	78	298	**26**	2	4	2.1	.994	D. Green	40	120	7	5	2	3.23
	CF	T. Gonzalez	555	.306	4	66	263	11	4	2	1.8	.986	D. Bennett	23	119	9	5	1	2.64
	LF	W. Covington	353	.303	17	64	114	4	8	0	1.2	.937	J. Baldschun	65	114	11	7	16	2.30
	C	C. Dalrymple	452	.252	10	40	881	**90**	19	**16**	7.0	.981	Klippstein	49	112	5	6	8	1.93
	UT	D. Demeter	515	.258	22	83	375	86	14	15		.971	R. Duren	33	87	6	2	2	3.30
	S3	R. Amaro	217	.217	2	19	105	169	13	28		.955							
Cincinnati W-86 L-76 Fred Hutchinson	1B	G. Coleman	365	.247	14	59	752	65	11	66	7.7	.987	J. Maloney	33	250	23	7	0	2.77
	2B	P. Rose	623	.273	6	41	360	366	22	78	4.8	.971	J. O'Toole	33	234	17	14	0	2.88
	SS	L. Cardenas	565	.235	7	48	270	420	20	84	4.5	**.972**	J. Nuxhall	35	217	15	8	2	2.61
	3B	G. Freese	217	.244	6	26	44	103	11	8	2.5	.930	J. Tsitouris	30	191	12	8	0	3.16
	RF	T. Harper	408	.260	10	37	224	7	4	1	2.0	.983	J. Jay	30	170	7	18	1	4.29
	CF	V. Pinson	652	.313	22	106	357	9	8	0	2.3	.979	B. Purkey	21	137	6	10	0	3.55
	LF	F. Robinson	482	.259	21	91	237	13	4	1	1.8	.984	Worthington	50	81	4	4	10	2.99
	C	J. Edwards	495	.259	11	67	**1008**	87	6	**16**	7.4	**.995**	B. Henry	47	52	1	3	14	4.15
	3B	E. Kasko	199	.241	3	10	41	75	5	5	2.5	.959							
	OF	B. Skinner	194	.253	3	17	74	3	0	1	1.5	1.000							
	1B	D. Pavletich	183	.208	5	18	317	16	3	20	5.9	.991							
	1O	M. Keough	172	.227	6	21	250	24	2	25		.993							
	3B	D. Spencer	155	.239	1	23	45	92	3	9	2.9	.979							

NATIONAL LEAGUE 1963, *cont.*

	POS	Player	AB	BA	HR	RBI	PO	A	E	DP	TC/G	FA	Pitcher	G	IP	W	L	SV	ERA
Milwaukee	1B	G. Oliver	296	.250	11	47	440	19	7	39	8.5	.985	W. Spahn	33	260	23	7	0	2.60
	2B	F. Bolling	542	.244	5	43	326	379	14	107	5.1	.981	D. Lemaster	46	237	11	14	1	3.04
W-84 L-78	SS	R. McMillan	320	.250	4	29	143	283	9	60	4.6	.979	B. Hendley	41	169	9	9	3	3.93
	3B	E. Mathews	547	.263	23	84	113	276	13	23	3.3	.968	B. Shaw	48	159	7	11	13	2.66
Bobby Bragan	RF	H. Aaron	631	.319	44	130	267	10	6	1	1.8	.979	T. Cloninger	41	145	9	11	1	3.78
	CF	M. Jones	228	.219	3	22	135	1	3	0	1.7	.978	B. Sadowski	19	117	5	7	0	2.62
	LF	L. Maye	442	.271	11	34	231	4	4	1	2.2	.983	L. Burdette	15	84	6	5	0	3.63
	C	J. Torre	501	.293	14	71	584	46	4	9	6.0	.994	C. Raymond	45	53	4	6	5	5.40
	UT	D. Menke	518	.234	11	50	234	398	24	67		.963							
	C	D. Crandall	259	.201	3	28	413	38	4	2	6.1	.991							
	OF	T. Cline	174	.236	0	10	116	5	1	3	2.0	.992							
Chicago	1B	E. Banks	432	.227	18	64	1178	78	9	97	10.1	.993	D. Ellsworth	37	291	22	10	0	2.11
	2B	K. Hubbs	566	.235	8	47	338	493	22	96	5.6	.974	L. Jackson	37	275	14	18	0	2.55
W-82 L-80	SS	A. Rodgers	516	.229	5	33	271	454	35	100	5.1	.954	B. Buhl	37	226	11	14	0	3.38
	3B	R. Santo	630	.297	25	99	136	374	26	25	3.3	.951	G. Hobbie	36	165	7	10	0	3.92
Bob Kennedy	RF	L. Brock	547	.258	9	37	269	17	8	7	2.1	.973	P. Toth	27	131	5	9	0	3.10
	CF	E. Burton	322	.230	12	41	151	6	4	1	1.8	.975	L. McDaniel	57	88	13	7	22	2.86
	LF	B. Williams	612	.286	25	95	298	13	4	2	2.0	.987							
	C	D. Bertell	322	.233	2	14	549	84	8	15	6.5	.988							
	OF	D. Landrum	227	.242	1	10	100	3	3	0	1.9	.972							
Pittsburgh	1B	D. Clendenon	563	.275	15	57	1450	118	15	154	10.5	.991	B. Friend	39	269	17	16	0	2.34
	2B	B. Mazeroski	534	.245	8	52	340	506	14	131	6.2	.984	D. Cardwell	33	214	13	15	0	3.07
W-74 L-88	SS	D. Schofield	541	.246	3	32	232	366	21	95	5.3	.966	D. Schwall	33	168	6	12	0	3.33
	3B	B. Bailey	570	.228	12	45	113	332	32	38	3.1	.933	J. Gibbon	37	147	5	12	1	3.30
Danny Murtaugh	RF	R. Clemente	600	.320	17	76	239	11	11	2	1.7	.958	A. McBean	55	122	13	3	11	2.57
	CF	B. Virdon	554	.269	8	53	323	6	4	2	2.3	.988	T. Sisk	57	108	1	3	1	2.92
	LF	W. Stargell	304	.243	11	47	78	3	4	0	1.3	.953	E. Francis	33	97	4	6	0	4.53
	C	Pagliaroni	252	.230	11	26	435	56	6	4	5.8	.988	B. Veale	34	78	5	2	3	1.04
	C	S. Burgess	264	.280	6	37	364	40	4	4	5.7	.990	R. Face	56	70	3	9	16	3.23
	OF	J. Lynch	237	.266	10	36	70	2	3	0	1.2	.960							
	SS	J. Logan	181	.232	0	9	74	122	17	28	4.8	.920							
Houston	1B	R. Staub	513	.224	6	45	881	58	10	52	8.7	.989	K. Johnson	37	224	11	17	1	2.65
	2B	E. Fazio	228	.184	2	5	132	145	8	18	3.4	.972	D. Farrell	34	202	14	13	1	3.02
W-66 L-96	SS	B. Lillis	469	.198	1	19	223	336	25	52	4.7	.957	D. Nottebart	31	193	11	8	0	3.17
	3B	Aspromonte	468	.214	8	49	134	213	23	4	2.8	.938	B. Bruce	30	170	5	9	0	3.59
Harry Craft	RF	C. Warwick	528	.254	7	47	240	7	3	2	1.8	.988	H. Brown	26	141	5	11	0	3.31
	CF	H. Goss	411	.209	9	44	276	7	2	2	2.3	.993	Woodeshick	55	114	11	9	10	1.97
	LF	A. Spangler	430	.281	4	27	215	5	3	1	2.0	.987	D. Drott	27	98	2	12	0	4.98
	C	J. Bateman	404	.210	10	59	690	81	23	7	6.9	.971	D. McMahon	49	80	1	5	5	4.05
	12	P. Runnels	388	.253	2	23	590	104	6	49		.991							
	23	J. Temple	322	.264	1	17	146	188	16	19		.954							
	OS	J. Wynn	250	.244	4	27	121	33	8	3		.951							
New York	1B	T. Harkness	375	.211	10	41	898	112	14	73	9.7	.986	R. Craig	46	236	5	22	2	3.78
	2B	R. Hunt	533	.272	10	42	350	416	26	85	5.6	.967	A. Jackson	37	227	13	17	1	3.96
W-51 L-111	SS	A. Moran	331	.193	1	23	189	332	27	57	4.7	.951	C. Willey	30	183	9	14	0	3.10
	3B	C. Neal	253	.225	3	18	61	135	8	10	3.1	.961	G. Cisco	51	156	7	15	0	4.34
Casey Stengel	RF	D. Snider	354	.243	14	45	139	5	2	0	1.4	.986	T. Stallard	39	155	6	17	1	4.71
	CF	J. Hickman	494	.229	17	51	149	6	6	2	2.0	.963	J. Hook	41	153	4	14	1	5.48
	LF	F. Thomas	420	.260	15	60	158	8	2	1	1.8	.988	L. Bearnarth	58	126	3	8	4	3.42
	C	C. Coleman	247	.178	3	9	418	54	15	9	5.4	.969							
	OF	E. Kranepool	273	.209	2	14	78	5	4	1	1.6	.954							
	UT	R. Kanehl	191	.241	1	9	128	35	12	7		.931							
	OF	J. Hicks	159	.226	5	22	83	1	3	0	2.1	.966							

BATTING AND BASE RUNNING LEADERS

Batting Average		Slugging Average		Home Runs		Winning Percentage	
T. Davis, LA	.326	H. Aaron, MIL	.586	W. McCovey, SF	44	Perranoski, LA	.842
R. Clemente, PIT	.320	W. Mays, SF	.582	H. Aaron, MIL	44	S. Koufax, LA	.833
H. Aaron, MIL	.319	W. McCovey, SF	.566	W. Mays, SF	38	J. Maloney, CIN	.767
D. Groat, STL	.319	O. Cepeda, SF	.563	O. Cepeda, SF	34	W. Spahn, MIL	.767
O. Cepeda, SF	.316	V. Pinson, CIN	.514	F. Howard, LA	28	J. Marichal, SF	.758

Total Bases		Runs Batted In		Stolen Bases		Saves	
H. Aaron, MIL	370	H. Aaron, MIL	130	M. Wills, LA	40	L. McDaniel, CHI	22
W. Mays, SF	347	K. Boyer, STL	111	H. Aaron, MIL	31	Perranoski, LA	21
V. Pinson, CIN	335	B. White, STL	109	V. Pinson, CIN	27	J. Baldschun, PHI	16
O. Cepeda, SF	326	V. Pinson, CIN	106	F. Robinson, CIN	26	R. Face, PIT	16
B. White, STL	323	W. Mays, SF	103	W. Davis, LA	25	B. Henry, CIN	14

PITCHING LEADERS

Earned Run Average		Wins	
S. Koufax, LA	1.88	S. Koufax, LA	25
D. Ellsworth, CHI	2.11	J. Marichal, SF	25
B. Friend, PIT	2.34	J. Maloney, CIN	23
J. Marichal, SF	2.41	W. Spahn, MIL	23
C. Simmons, STL	2.48	D. Ellsworth, CHI	22

Strikeouts		Complete Games	
S. Koufax, LA	306	W. Spahn, MIL	22
J. Maloney, CIN	265	S. Koufax, LA	20
D. Drysdale, LA	251	D. Ellsworth, CHI	19
J. Marichal, SF	248	J. Marichal, SF	18
B. Gibson, STL	204	D. Drysdale, LA	17

NATIONAL LEAGUE 1963, *cont.*

BATTING AND BASE RUNNING LEADERS

Hits		Base on Balls		Home Run Percentage		Fewest Hits/9 Innings	
V. Pinson, CIN	204	E. Mathews, MIL	124	W. McCovey, SF	7.8	S. Koufax, LA	6.19
H. Aaron, MIL	201	F. Robinson, CIN	81	H. Aaron, MIL	7.0	R. Culp, PHI	6.55
D. Groat, STL	201	H. Aaron, MIL	78	W. Mays, SF	6.4	J. Maloney, CIN	6.58
B. White, STL	200	K. Boyer, STL	70	O. Cepeda, SF	5.9	D. Ellsworth, CHI	6.90

Runs Scored		Doubles		Triples		Most Strikeouts/9 Inn.	
H. Aaron, MIL	121	D. Groat, STL	43	V. Pinson, CIN	14	J. Maloney, CIN	9.53
W. Mays, SF	115	V. Pinson, CIN	37	T. Gonzalez, PHI	12	S. Koufax, LA	8.86
C. Flood, STL	112	T. Gonzalez, PHI	36	L. Brock, CHI	11	R. Culp, PHI	7.79
B. White, STL	106	B. Williams, CHI	36	J. Callison, PHI	11	C. Short, PHI	7.27

PITCHING LEADERS

Shutouts		Fewest Walks/9 Innings	
S. Koufax, LA	11	B. Friend, PIT	1.47
W. Spahn, MIL	7	D. Farrell, HOU	1.56
C. Simmons, STL	6	J. Nuxhall, CIN	1.61
J. Maloney, CIN	6	D. Drysdale, LA	1.63

Innings		Games Pitched	
J. Marichal, SF	321	Perranoski, LA	69
D. Drysdale, LA	315	J. Baldschun, PHI	65
S. Koufax, LA	311	L. Bearnarth, NY	58
D. Ellsworth, CHI	291	T. Sisk, PIT	57

	W	L	PCT	GB	R	OR	Batting 2B	3B	HR	BA	SA	SB	Fielding E	DP	FA	Pitching CG	BB	SO	ShO	SV	ERA
Los Angeles	99	63	.611		640	550	178	34	110	.251	.357	124	159	129	.975	51	402	1095	24	29	2.85
St. Louis	93	69	.574	6	747	628	231	66	128	.271	.403	77	147	136	.976	49	463	978	17	32	3.32
San Francisco	88	74	.543	11	725	641	206	35	197	.258	.414	55	156	113	.975	46	464	954	9	30	3.35
Philadelphia	87	75	.537	12	642	578	228	54	126	.252	.381	56	142	147	.978	45	553	1052	12	31	3.09
Cincinnati	86	76	.531	13	648	594	225	44	122	.246	.371	92	135	127	.978	55	400	1048	22	36	3.29
Milwaukee	84	78	.519	15	677	603	204	39	139	.244	.370	75	129	161	.980	56	489	924	18	25	3.26
Chicago	82	80	.506	17	570	578	205	44	127	.238	.363	68	155	172	.976	45	400	851	15	28	3.08
Pittsburgh	74	88	.457	25	567	595	181	49	108	.250	.359	57	182	195	.972	34	457	900	16	33	3.10
Houston	66	96	.407	33	464	640	170	39	62	.220	.301	39	162	100	.974	36	378	937	16	20	3.44
New York	51	111	.315	48	501	774	156	35	96	.219	.315	41	210	151	.967	42	529	806	5	12	4.12
					6181	6181	1984	439	1215	.245	.364	684	1577	1431	.975	459	4560	9545	154	276	3.29

AMERICAN LEAGUE 1963

	POS	Player	AB	BA	HR	RBI	PO	A	E	DP	TC/G	FA	Pitcher	G	IP	W	L	SV	ERA
New York W-104 L-57 Ralph Houk	1B	J. Pepitone	580	.271	27	89	1140	103	6	111	8.7	.995	W. Ford	38	269	24	7	1	2.74
	2B	Richardson	630	.265	3	48	335	424	12	105	5.1	.984	R. Terry	40	268	17	15	1	3.22
	SS	T. Kubek	557	.257	7	44	227	403	13	80	4.9	.980	J. Bouton	40	249	21	7	1	2.53
	3B	C. Boyer	557	.251	12	54	165	309	23	32	3.5	.954	A. Downing	24	176	13	5	2	2.56
	RF	R. Maris	312	.269	23	53	162	6	2	1	2.0	.988	S. Williams	29	146	9	8	0	3.20
	CF	T. Tresh	520	.269	25	71	305	6	6	1	2.2	.981	B. Stafford	28	90	4	8	3	6.02
	LF	H. Lopez	433	.249	14	52	187	11	9	2	1.7	.957	H. Reniff	48	89	4	3	18	2.62
	C	E. Howard	487	.287	28	85	786	51	5	8	6.4	.994	S. Hamilton	34	62	5	1	5	2.60
	OF	J. Blanchard	218	.225	16	45	76	2	1	0	1.2	.987							
	UT	P. Linz	186	.269	2	12	69	103	4	17		.977							
	OF	M. Mantle	172	.314	15	35	99	2	1	0	2.0	.990							
	1B	H. Bright	157	.236	7	23	263	8	4	32	7.9	.985							
	C	Y. Berra	147	.293	8	28	244	13	3	5	7.4	.988							
Chicago W-94 L-68 Al Lopez	1B	T. McCraw	280	.254	6	33	673	47	5	65	7.5	.993	G. Peters	41	243	19	8	1	**2.33**
	2B	N. Fox	539	.260	2	44	305	342	8	71	4.9	**.988**	R. Herbert	33	225	13	10	0	3.24
	SS	R. Hansen	482	.226	13	67	247	**483**	13	95	5.2	.983	J. Pizarro	32	215	16	8	1	2.39
	3B	P. Ward	600	.295	22	84	156	302	**38**	27	3.2	.923	H. Wilhelm	55	136	5	8	21	2.64
	RF	F. Robinson	527	.283	13	71	245	8	4	4	1.9	.984	J. Buzhardt	19	126	9	4	0	2.42
	CF	J. Landis	396	.225	13	45	264	6	2	0	1.9	**.993**	J. Horlen	33	124	11	7	0	3.27
	LF	D. Nicholson	449	.229	22	70	213	10	7	1	1.9	.970	E. Fisher	33	121	9	8	0	3.95
	C	J. Martin	259	.205	5	28	468	48	9	9	5.4	.983	J. Brosnan	45	73	3	8	14	2.84
	OF	Hershberger	476	.279	3	45	230	13	6	3	2.1	.976							
	C	C. Carreon	270	.274	2	35	429	36	6	7	5.1	.987							
	2S	A. Weis	210	.271	0	18	123	168	10	41		.967							
	1B	Cunningham	210	.286	1	31	535	24	6	39	9.7	.989							
Minnesota W-91 L-70 Sam Mele	1B	V. Power	541	.270	10	52	896	76	8	86	7.9	.992	C. Pascual	31	248	21	9	0	2.46
	2B	B. Allen	421	.240	9	43	236	256	12	65	3.9	.976	D. Stigman	33	241	15	15	0	3.25
	SS	Z. Versalles	621	.261	10	54	301	448	30	87	4.9	.961	J. Kaat	31	178	10	10	1	4.19
	3B	R. Rollins	531	.307	16	61	121	225	26	22	2.8	.930	J. Perry	35	168	9	9	1	3.74
	RF	B. Allison	527	.271	35	91	326	11	10	4	2.4	.971	L. Stange	32	165	12	5	0	2.62
	CF	J. Hall	497	.260	33	80	306	13	6	5	2.3	.982	B. Dailey	66	126	6	3	21	1.99
	LF	H. Killebrew	515	.258	**45**	96	219	7	3	0	1.7	.987	Roggenburk	36	50	2	4	4	2.16
	C	E. Battey	508	.285	26	84	**861**	**66**	6	11	6.4	.994							
	OF	L. Green	280	.239	4	27	165	1	2	0	1.4	.988							
	1B	D. Mincher	225	.258	17	42	446	27	8	34	8.0	.983							
	UT	J. Goryl	150	.287	9	24	75	92	7	18		.960							

AMERICAN LEAGUE 1963, *cont.*

	POS	Player	AB	BA	HR	RBI	PO	A	E	DP	TC/G	FA	Pitcher	G	IP	W	L	SV	ERA
Baltimore	1B	J. Gentile	496	.248	24	72	1185	110	6	**122**	9.1	**.995**	S. Barber	39	259	20	13	0	2.75
	2B	J. Adair	382	.228	6	30	242	268	8	67	5.0	.985	R. Roberts	35	251	14	13	0	3.33
W-86 L-76	SS	L. Aparicio	601	.250	5	45	275	403	12	76	4.8	.983	M. Pappas	34	217	16	9	0	3.03
	3B	B. Robinson	589	.251	11	67	153	**330**	12	**43**	3.1	.976	McCormick	25	136	6	8	0	4.30
Billy Hitchcock	RF	R. Snyder	429	.256	7	36	238	5	3	1	1.9	.988	D. McNally	29	126	7	8	1	4.58
	CF	J. Brandt	451	.248	15	61	272	9	4	1	2.1	.986	S. Miller	71	112	5	8	27	2.24
	LF	B. Powell	491	.265	25	82	181	6	6	1	1.6	.969	D. Hall	47	112	5	5	12	2.98
	C	J. Orsino	379	.272	19	56	636	37	7	8	6.2	.990							
	OF	A. Smith	368	.272	10	39	160	6	5	0	1.8	.971							
	2B	B. Johnson	254	.295	8	32	97	131	3	34	4.6	.987							
	C	D. Brown	171	.246	2	13	317	23	5	7	5.9	.986							
	UT	B. Saverine	167	.234	1	12	99	89	2	19		.989							
	OF	J. Gaines	126	.286	6	20	52	0	3	0	1.4	.945							
Cleveland	1B	F. Whitfield	346	.251	21	54	690	51	10	64	8.2	.987	M. Grant	38	229	13	14	1	3.69
	2B	W. Held	416	.248	17	61	188	251	8	50	4.7	.982	D. Donovan	30	206	11	13	0	4.24
W-79 L-83	SS	J. Kindall	234	.205	5	20	63	97	7	15	3.6	.958	J. Kralick	28	197	13	9	0	2.92
	3B	M. Alvis	602	.274	22	67	170	285	28	32	3.1	.942	P. Ramos	36	185	9	8	0	3.12
Birdie Tebbetts	RF	W. Kirkland	427	.230	15	47	234	11	4	2	2.2	.984	B. Latman	38	149	7	12	2	4.94
	CF	V. Davalillo	370	.292	7	36	247	10	3	0	2.9	.988	G. Bell	58	119	8	5	5	2.95
	LF	T. Francona	500	.228	10	41	215	2	3	0	1.8	.986	J. Walker	39	88	6	6	1	4.91
	C	J. Azcue	320	.284	14	46	564	42	5	13*	6.7	.992	T. Abernathy	43	59	7	2	12	2.88
	OF	A. Luplow	295	.234	7	27	157	7	1	1	1.9	.994							
	1B	J. Adcock	283	.251	13	49	608	36	3	46	8.3	.995							
	C	J. Romano	255	.216	10	34	408	28	3	5	6.2	.993							
	S2	L. Brown	247	.255	5	18	113	176	14	25		.954							
	SS	D. Howser	162	.247	1	10	80	90	9	15	4.1	.950							
	2B	de la Hoz	150	.267	5	25	63	89	6	20	4.6	.962							
Detroit	1B	N. Cash	493	.270	26	79	1161	99	7	93	8.9	.994	J. Bunning	39	248	12	13	1	3.88
	2B	J. Wood	351	.271	11	27	188	202	17	47	5.0	.958	H. Aguirre	38	226	14	15	0	3.67
W-79 L-83	SS	McAuliffe	568	.262	13	61	220	356	22	68	4.5	.963	P. Regan	38	189	15	9	1	3.86
	3B	B. Phillips	464	.246	6	45	116	226	14	26	3.0	.961	M. Lolich	33	144	5	9	0	3.55
Bob Scheffing	RF	A. Kaline	551	.312	27	101	257	5	2	0	1.9	.992	D. Mossi	24	123	7	7	2	3.74
W-24 L-36	CF	B. Bruton	524	.256	8	48	339	6	3	3	2.5	.991	F. Lary	16	107	4	9	0	3.27
	LF	R. Colavito	597	.271	22	91	319	10	4	0	2.1	.988	B. Faul	28	97	5	6	1	4.64
Chuck Dressen	C	G. Triandos	327	.239	14	41	535	29	1	4	6.3	**.998**	T. Fox	46	80	8	6	11	3.59
W-55 L-47	C	B. Freehan	300	.243	9	36	407	22	2	5	5.9	.995							
	UT	D. Wert	251	.259	7	25	85	173	10	20		.963							
	2B	G. Smith	171	.216	0	17	120	157	5	28	5.4	.982							
Boston	1B	D. Stuart	612	.261	42	**118**	**1207**	**134**	**29**	100	8.8	.979	Monbouquette	37	267	20	10	0	3.81
	2B	C. Schilling	576	.234	8	33	276	369	10	74	4.6	.985	E. Wilson	37	211	11	16	0	3.76
W-76 L-85	SS	E. Bressoud	497	.260	20	60	260	351	24	76	4.6	.962	D. Morehead	29	175	10	13	0	3.81
	3B	F. Malzone	580	.291	15	71	151	283	16	18	3.0	.964	J. Lamabe	65	151	7	4	6	3.15
Johnny Pesky	RF	L. Clinton	560	.232	22	77	319	7	6	0	2.3	.982	D. Radatz	66	132	15	6	25	1.97
	CF	G. Geiger	399	.263	16	44	234	11	4	1	2.6	.984	B. Heffner	20	125	4	9	0	4.26
	LF	Yastrzemski	570	**.321**	14	68	283	18	6	3	2.0	.980	A. Earley	53	116	3	7	1	4.75
	C	B. Tillman	307	.225	8	32	621	26	5	5	**6.9**	.992							
	OF	R. Mejias	357	.227	11	39	177	6	5	1	2.2	.973							
	C	R. Nixon	287	.268	5	30	483	22	4	1	6.7	.992							
	UT	F. Mantilla	178	.315	6	15	83	74	4	19		.975							
Kansas City	1B	N. Siebern	556	.272	16	83	1193	102	12	95	**10.0**	.991	Wickersham	38	238	12	15	1	4.09
	2B	J. Lumpe	595	.271	5	59	341	452	10	92	5.2	.988	O. Pena	35	217	12	**20**	0	3.69
W-73 L-89	SS	W. Causey	554	.280	8	44	266	402	15	81	5.1	.978	E. Rakow	34	174	9	10	0	3.92
	3B	E. Charles	603	.267	15	79	153	310	25	19	3.1	.949	M. Drabowsky	26	174	7	13	0	3.05
Ed Lopat	RF	G. Cimoli	529	.263	4	48	256	14	4	3	2.0	.985	D. Segui	38	167	9	6	0	3.77
	CF	B. Del Greco	306	.212	8	29	207	5	4	0	2.0	.981	T. Bowsfield	41	111	5	7	3	4.45
	LF	J. Tartabull	242	.240	1	19	135	3	2	1	2.0	.986	B. Fischer	45	96	9	6	3	3.57
	C	D. Edwards	240	.250	6	35	341	30	5	4	6.0	.987	J. Wyatt	63	92	6	4	21	3.13
	OF	C. Essegian	231	.225	5	27	95	2	1	0	1.8	.990							
	1O	K. Harrelson	226	.230	6	23	326	17	7	24		.980							
	OF	G. Alusik	221	.267	9	37	98	5	0	1	1.6	1.000							
	C	C. Lau	187	.294	3	26	258	15	5	2	5.6	.982							
Los Angeles	1B	L. Thomas	528	.220	9	55	961	84	4	88	10.1	.996	K. McBride	36	251	13	12	0	3.26
	2B	B. Moran	597	.275	7	65	352	455	22	98	5.5	.973	D. Chance	45	248	13	18	3	3.19
W-70 L-91	SS	J. Fregosi	592	.287	9	50	271	446	27	90	4.9	.964	D. Osinski	47	159	8	8	3	3.28
	3B	F. Torres	463	.261	4	51	101	237	22	29	3.0	.939	D. Lee	40	154	8	11	1	3.68
Bill Rigney	RF	B. Perry	166	.253	3	14	86	1	5	0	1.7	.946	J. Navarro	57	90	4	5	12	2.89
	CF	A. Pearson	578	.304	6	47	340	10	6	5	2.4	.983	A. Fowler	57	89	5	3	10	2.42
	LF	L. Wagner	550	.291	26	90	254	7	**11**	1	1.9	.960	B. Belinsky	13	77	2	9	0	5.75
	C	B. Rodgers	300	.233	4	23	416	48	**10**	5	5.6	.979	P. Foytack	25	70	5	5	0	3.71
	1B	C. Dees	202	.307	4	27	474	32	7	41	9.2	.986							
	C	E. Sadowski	174	.172	4	15	340	38	1	7	5.6	.997							
	OF	G. Thomas	167	.210	4	15	63	1	4	0	1.7	.941							
	OF	B. Sadowski	144	.250	1	22	41	0	0	0	1.6	1.000							

AMERICAN LEAGUE 1963, *cont.*

	POS	Player	AB	BA	HR	RBI	PO	A	E	DP	TC/G	FA	Pitcher	G	IP	W	L	SV	ERA
Washington	1B	B. Osborne	358	.212	12	44	713	55	9	68	9.6	.988	C. Osteen	40	212	9	14	0	3.35
	2B	C. Cottier	337	.205	5	21	200	221	16	49	5.1	.963	D. Rudolph	37	174	7	19	1	4.55
W-56 L-106	SS	E. Brinkman	514	.228	7	45	241	462	37	97	5.2	.950	B. Daniels	35	169	5	10	1	4.38
	3B	D. Zimmer	298	.248	13	44	88	173	18	17	3.6	.935	T. Cheney	23	136	8	9	0	2.71
Mickey Vernon	RF	J. King	459	.231	24	62	213	13	3	2	1.9	.987	J. Duckworth	37	121	4	12	0	6.04
W-14 L-26	CF	D. Lock	531	.252	27	82	377	14	8	6	2.7	.980	R. Kline	62	94	3	8	17	2.79
	LF	C. Hinton	566	.269	15	55	274	8	3	1	2.3	.989	S. Ridzik	20	90	5	6	1	4.82
Eddie Yost	C	K. Retzer	265	.242	5	31	320	35	7	5	4.5	.981	D. Stenhouse	16	87	3	9	0	4.55
W-0 L-1	1B	D. Phillips	321	.237	10	32	655	59	4	73	10.6	.994							
	OF	M. Minoso	315	.229	4	30	103	4	5	0	1.5	.955							
Gil Hodges	2B	Blasingame	254	.256	2	12	162	177	3	52	5.3	.991							
W-42 L-79	C	D. Leppert	211	.237	6	24	281	20	5	4	5.1	.984							
	32	M. Breeding	197	.274	1	14	76	110	11	15		.944							

BATTING AND BASE RUNNING LEADERS

Batting Average		Slugging Average		Home Runs		Winning Percentage		Earned Run Average		Wins	
Yastrzemski, BOS	.321	H. Killebrew, MIN	.555	H. Killebrew, MIN	45	W. Ford, NY	.774	G. Peters, CHI	2.33	W. Ford, NY	24
A. Kaline, DET	.312	B. Allison, MIN	.533	D. Stuart, BOS	42	J. Bouton, NY	.750	J. Pizarro, CHI	2.39	J. Bouton, NY	21
R. Rollins, MIN	.307	E. Howard, NY	.528	B. Allison, MIN	35	D. Radatz, BOS	.714	C. Pascual, MIN	2.46	C. Pascual, MIN	21
A. Pearson, LA	.304	D. Stuart, BOS	.521	J. Hall, MIN	33	G. Peters, CHI	.704	J. Bouton, NY	2.53	Monbouquette, BOS	20
P. Ward, CHI	.295	J. Hall, MIN	.521	E. Howard, NY	28	C. Pascual, MIN	.700	A. Downing, NY	2.56	S. Barber, BAL	20

Total Bases		Runs Batted In		Stolen Bases		Saves		Strikeouts		Complete Games	
D. Stuart, BOS	319	D. Stuart, BOS	118	L. Aparicio, BAL	40	S. Miller, BAL	27	C. Pascual, MIN	202	C. Pascual, MIN	18
P. Ward, CHI	289	A. Kaline, DET	101	C. Hinton, WAS	25	D. Radatz, BOS	25	J. Bunning, DET	196	R. Terry, NY	18
H. Killebrew, MIN	286	H. Killebrew, MIN	96	J. Wood, DET	18	B. Dailey, MIN	21	D. Stigman, MIN	193	D. Stigman, MIN	15
A. Kaline, DET	283	B. Allison, MIN	91	R. Snyder, BAL	18	J. Wyatt, KC	21	G. Peters, CHI	189	H. Aguirre, DET	14
B. Allison, MIN	281	R. Colavito, DET	91	A. Pearson, LA	17	H. Wilhelm, CHI	21	W. Ford, NY	189	R. Herbert, CHI	14

Hits		Base on Balls		Home Run Percentage		Fewest Hits/9 Innings		Shutouts		Fewest Walks/9 Innings	
Yastrzemski, BOS	183	Yastrzemski, BOS	95	H. Killebrew, MIN	8.7	A. Downing, NY	5.84	R. Herbert, CHI	7	D. Donovan, CLE	1.22
P. Ward, CHI	177	A. Pearson, LA	92	D. Stuart, BOS	6.9	J. Bouton, NY	6.89	J. Bouton, NY	6	R. Terry, NY	1.31
A. Pearson, LA	176	B. Allison, MIN	90	B. Allison, MIN	6.6	M. Drabowsky, KC	6.97			R. Herbert, CHI	1.40
A. Kaline, DET	172	N. Cash, DET	89	J. Hall, MIN	6.6	D. Morehead, BOS	7.06			Monbouquette, BOS	1.42

Runs Scored		Doubles		Triples		Most Strikeouts/9 Inn.		Innings		Games Pitched	
B. Allison, MIN	99	Yastrzemski, BOS	40	Z. Versalles, MIN	13	A. Downing, NY	8.76	W. Ford, NY	269	S. Miller, BAL	71
A. Pearson, LA	92	P. Ward, CHI	34	C. Hinton, WAS	12	P. Ramos, CLE	8.24	R. Terry, NY	268	D. Radatz, BOS	66
T. Tresh, NY	91	F. Torres, LA	32	J. Fregosi, LA	12	C. Pascual, MIN	7.32	Monbouquette, BOS	267	B. Dailey, MIN	66
Yastrzemski, BOS	91	W. Causey, KC	32	G. Cimoli, KC	11	D. Stigman, MIN	7.21	S. Barber, BAL	259	J. Lamabe, BOS	65

PITCHING LEADERS

									Batting						Fielding				Pitching				
	W	L	PCT	GB	R	OR	2B	3B	HR	BA	SA	SB	E	DP	FA	CG	BB	SO	ShO	SV	ERA
New York	104	57	.646		714	547	197	35	188	.252	.403	42	110	162	.982	**59**	476	965	17	31	3.07
Chicago	94	68	.580	10.5	683	**544**	208	34	114	.250	.365	64	131	163	.979	49	**440**	932	19	39	**2.97**
Minnesota	91	70	.565	13	**767**	602	223	35	**225**	**.255**	**.430**	32	144	140	.976	58	459	941	12	30	3.28
Baltimore	86	76	.531	18.5	644	621	207	32	146	.249	.380	**97**	**99**	157	**.984**	35	507	913	8	**43**	3.45
Cleveland	79	83	.488	25.5	635	702	214	29	169	.239	.365	59	143	129	.977	40	478	**1018**	11	25	3.79
Detroit	79	83	.488	25.5	700	703	195	36	148	.252	.382	73	113	124	.981	42	533	930	6	28	3.90
Boston	76	85	.472	28	666	704	**247**	34	171	.252	.400	27	135	119	.978	29	539	1009	6	32	3.97
Kansas City	73	89	.451	31.5	615	704	225	38	95	.247	.353	47	127	131	.980	35	540	887	9	29	3.92
Los Angeles	70	91	.435	34	597	660	208	38	95	.250	.354	43	163	155	.974	30	578	889	9	31	3.52
Washington	56	106	.346	48.5	578	812	190	35	138	.227	.351	68	182	**165**	.971	29	537	744	8	25	4.42
					6599	6599	2114	352	1489	.247	.380	552	1347	1445	.978	406	5031	9228	105	313	3.63

NATIONAL LEAGUE 1964

	POS	Player	AB	BA	HR	RBI	PO	A	E	DP	TC/G	FA	Pitcher	G	IP	W	L	SV	ERA
St. Louis	1B	B. White	631	.303	21	102	1513	101	6	**125**	10.1	**.996**	B. Gibson	40	287	19	12	1	3.01
	2B	J. Javier	535	.241	12	65	**360**	401	**27**	97	5.1	.966	C. Simmons	34	244	18	9	0	3.43
W-93 L-69	SS	D. Groat	636	.292	1	70	249	**499**	**40**	91	4.9	.949	R. Sadecki	37	220	20	11	1	3.68
	3B	K. Boyer	628	.295	24	119	131	337	24	30	3.0	.951	R. Craig	39	166	7	9	5	3.25
Johnny Keane	RF	M. Shannon	253	.261	9	43	110	7	2	2	1.4	.983	R. Taylor	63	101	8	4	7	4.62
	CF	C. Flood	679	.311	5	46	391	10	5	2	2.5	.988	M. Cuellar	32	72	5	5	4	4.50
	LF	L. Brock	419	.348	12	44	180	7	10*	0	1.9	.949	B. Schultz	30	49	1	3	14	1.64
	C	T. McCarver	465	.288	9	52	762	43	**11**	9	6.0	.987							
	OF	C. James	233	.223	5	17	76	3	3	0	1.4	.963							

NATIONAL LEAGUE 1964, *cont.*

	POS	Player	AB	BA	HR	RBI	PO	A	E	DP	TC/G	FA	Pitcher	G	IP	W	L	SV	ERA
Cincinnati	1B	D. Johnson	477	.273	21	79	940	81	10	82	7.9	.990	J. O'Toole	30	220	17	7	0	2.66
	2B	P. Rose	516	.269	4	34	263	301	12	63	4.5	.979	J. Maloney	31	216	15	10	0	2.71
W-92 L-70	SS	L. Cardenas	597	.251	9	69	336	436	32	87	4.9	.960	B. Purkey	34	196	11	9	1	3.04
	3B	S. Boros	370	.257	2	31	95	204	12	18	2.7	.961	J. Jay	34	183	11	11	2	3.39
Fred Hutchinson	RF	F. Robinson	568	.306	29	96	279	7	4	3	1.9	.986	J. Tsitouris	37	175	9	13	2	3.80
W-54 L-45	CF	V. Pinson	625	.266	23	84	299	14	9	1	2.1	.972	J. Nuxhall	32	155	9	8	2	4.07
	LF	T. Harper	317	.243	4	22	149	4	1	2	1.7	.994	S. Ellis	52	122	10	3	14	2.57
Dick Sisler	C	J. Edwards	423	.281	7	55	890	73	8	17	8.1	.992	B. McCool	40	89	6	5	7	2.42
W-3 L-3	32	C. Ruiz	311	.244	9	16	95	149	11	28		.957	B. Henry	37	52	2	2	6	0.87
	OF	M. Keough	276	.257	9	28	105	4	1	1	1.4	.991							
Fred Hutchinson	1B	G. Coleman	198	.242	5	27	352	35	4	28	8.0	.990							
W-6 L-4																			
Dick Sisler																			
W-29 L-18																			
Philadelphia	1B	Herrnstein	303	.234	6	25	488	22	5	33	7.6	.990	J. Bunning	41	284	19	8	2	2.63
	2B	T. Taylor	570	.251	4	46	325	358	16	94	4.7	.977	C. Short	42	221	17	9	2	2.20
W-92 L-70	SS	B. Wine	283	.212	4	34	153	257	15	55	3.9	.965	D. Bennett	41	208	12	14	1	3.68
	3B	D. Allen	632	.318	29	91	154	325	41	30	3.2	.921	A. Mahaffey	34	157	12	9	0	4.52
Gene Mauch	RF	J. Callison	654	.274	31	104	319	19	4	3	2.1	.988	R. Culp	30	135	8	7	0	4.13
	CF	T. Gonzalez	421	.278	4	40	243	5	1	2	2.1	.996	J. Baldschun	71	118	6	9	21	3.12
	LF	W. Covington	339	.280	13	58	99	4	3	0	1.0	.972	E. Roebuck	60	77	5	3	12	2.21
	C	C. Dalrymple	382	.238	6	46	737	61	7	11	6.5	.991							
	UT	C. Rojas	340	.291	2	31	164	76	7	11		.972							
	S1	R. Amaro	299	.264	4	34	295	200	10	55		.980							
	C	G. Triandos	188	.250	8	33	371	24	6	4	6.3	.985							
	1B	F. Thomas	143	.294	7	26	297	28	8	37	8.5	.976							
San Francisco	1B	O. Cepeda	529	.304	31	97	1211	80	18	89	9.4	.986	J. Marichal	33	269	21	8	0	2.48
	2B	H. Lanier	383	.274	2	28	224	294	11	48	5.4	.979	G. Perry	44	206	12	11	5	2.75
W-90 L-72	SS	J. Pagan	367	.223	1	28	204	302	22	52	4.0	.958	B. Bolin	38	175	6	9	1	3.25
	3B	J. Hart	566	.286	31	81	139	277	28	24	3.0	.937	B. Hendley	30	163	10	11	0	3.64
Alvin Dark	RF	J. Alou	376	.274	3	28	172	8	5	2	1.7	.973	R. Herbel	40	161	9	9	1	3.07
	CF	W. Mays	578	.296	47	111	370	10	6	4	2.5	.984	J. Sanford	18	106	5	7	1	3.30
	LF	W. McCovey	364	.220	18	54	96	5	7	1	1.3	.935	B. Shaw	61	93	7	6	11	3.76
	C	T. Haller	388	.253	16	48	739	50	9	12	7.1	.989	B. O'Dell	36	85	8	7	2	5.40
	OF	H. Kuenn	351	.262	4	22	97	2	5	0	1.2	.952							
	UT	J. Davenport	297	.236	2	26	138	237	11	29		.972							
	OF	M. Alou	250	.264	1	14	120	2	3	1	1.6	.976							
	2B	C. Hiller	205	.180	1	17	111	143	6	29	4.3	.977							
	C	D. Crandall	195	.231	3	11	402	30	3	7	6.7	.993							
	OF	D. Snider	167	.210	4	17	44	2	1	0	1.1	.979							
Milwaukee	1B	G. Oliver	279	.276	13	49	622	34	12	50	8.8	.982	T. Cloninger	38	243	19	14	2	3.56
	2B	F. Bolling	352	.199	5	34	212	255	7	68	4.1	.985	D. Lemaster	39	221	17	11	1	4.15
W-88 L-74	SS	D. Menke	505	.283	20	65	253	422	25	76	5.0	.964	W. Spahn	38	174	6	13	4	5.29
	3B	E. Mathews	502	.233	23	74	130	247	15	19	3.1	.962	H. Fischer	37	168	11	10	2	4.01
Bobby Bragan	RF	H. Aaron	570	.328	24	95	270	13	5	5	2.1	.983	B. Sadowski	51	167	9	10	5	4.10
	CF	L. Maye	588	.304	10	74	264	7	11	1	2.1	.961	Blasingame	28	117	9	5	2	4.24
	LF	R. Carty	455	.330	22	88	176	5	4	1	1.5	.978	Tiefenauer	46	73	4	6	13	3.21
	C	J. Torre	601	.321	20	109	518	46	3	4	5.9	.995							
	OF	F. Alou	415	.253	9	51	191	2	5	0	2.2	.975							
	C	E. Bailey	271	.262	5	34	416	28	8	3	5.7	.982							
	UT	de la Hoz	189	.291	4	12	65	109	10	17		.946							
Los Angeles	1B	R. Fairly	454	.256	10	74	1081	82	15	89	8.4	.987	D. Drysdale	40	321	18	16	0	2.18
	2B	N. Oliver	321	.243	0	21	194	247	15	44	4.7	.967	S. Koufax	29	223	19	5	1	1.74
W-80 L-82	SS	M. Wills	630	.275	2	34	273	422	27	77	4.8	.963	P. Ortega	34	157	7	9	0	4.00
	3B	J. Gilliam	334	.228	2	27	54	121	12	7	2.2	.936	J. Moeller	27	145	7	13	0	4.21
Walter Alston	RF	F. Howard	433	.226	24	69	183	2	4	0	1.5	.979	B. Miller	74	138	7	7	9	2.62
	CF	W. Davis	613	.294	12	77	400	16	7	2	2.7	.983	Perranoski	72	125	5	7	14	3.09
	LF	T. Davis	592	.275	14	86	264	9	5	1	1.9	.982	L. Miller	16	80	4	8	0	4.18
	C	J. Roseboro	414	.287	3	45	809	64	6	8	6.9	.993							
	UT	D. Tracewski	304	.247	1	26	152	218	15	35		.961							
	3O	D. Griffith	238	.290	4	23	57	56	23	3		.831							
	O1	W. Parker	214	.257	3	10	326	26	6	18		.983							
Pittsburgh	1B	D. Clendenon	457	.282	12	64	1153	75	14	116	10.4	.989	B. Veale	40	280	18	12	0	2.74
	2B	B. Mazeroski	601	.268	10	64	346	543	23	122	5.6	.975	B. Friend	35	240	13	18	0	3.33
W-80 L-82	SS	D. Schofield	398	.246	3	36	184	349	28	78	5.1	.950	V. Law	35	192	12	13	0	3.61
	3B	B. Bailey	530	.281	11	88	81	218	18	19	3.0	.943	J. Gibbon	28	147	10	7	0	3.68
Danny Murtaugh	RF	R. Clemente	622	.339	12	87	289	13	10	2	2.0	.968	S. Blass	24	105	5	8	0	4.04
	CF	B. Virdon	473	.243	3	27	243	5	6	1	1.9	.976	A. McBean	58	90	8	3	22	1.91
	LF	M. Mota	271	.277	5	32	120	4	5	1	1.4	.961	R. Face	55	80	3	3	4	5.20
	C	Pagliaroni	302	.295	10	36	584	42	5	5	6.6	.992							
	O1	W. Stargell	421	.273	21	78	565	24	10	50		.983							
	OF	J. Lynch	297	.273	16	66	59	0	1	0	.8	.983							
	3B	G. Freese	289	.225	9	40	48	112	14	12	2.4	.920							
	SS	G. Alley	209	.211	6	13	100	211	11	43	5.3	.966							
	C	S. Burgess	171	.246	2	17	237	18	2	3	5.8	.992							

NATIONAL LEAGUE 1964, *cont.*

	POS	Player	AB	BA	HR	RBI	PO	A	E	DP	TC/G	FA	Pitcher	G	IP	W	L	SV	ERA
Chicago	1B	E. Banks	591	.264	23	95	**1565**	**132**	10	122	**10.9**	.994	L. Jackson	40	298	**24**	11	0	3.14
	2B	Amalfitano	324	.241	4	27	201	254	17	47	5.5	.964	D. Ellsworth	37	257	14	18	0	3.75
W-76 L-86	SS	A. Rodgers	448	.239	12	46	232	428	24	68	5.4	.965	B. Buhl	36	228	15	14	0	3.83
	3B	R. Santo	592	.313	30	114	156	367	20	**31**	3.4	.963	L. Burdette	28	131	9	9	0	4.88
Bob Kennedy	RF	Gabrielson	272	.246	5	23	116	5	2	0	1.8	.984	E. Broglio	18	100	4	7	1	4.04
	CF	B. Cowan	497	.241	19	50	297	2	10	0	2.3	.968	L. McDaniel	63	95	1	7	15	3.88
	LF	B. Williams	645	.312	33	98	233	14	13	0	1.6	.950							
	C	D. Bertell	353	.238	4	35	531	52	11	3	5.4	.981							
	2S	J. Stewart	415	.253	3	33	214	307	12	64		.977							
	OF	L. Brock	215	.251	2	14	86	8	4*	1	1.9	.959							
Houston	1B	W. Bond	543	.254	20	85	685	40	8	46	9.6	.989	K. Johnson	35	218	11	16	0	3.63
	2B	N. Fox	442	.265	0	28	231	317	13	51	4.9	.977	B. Bruce	35	202	15	9	0	2.76
W-66 L-96	SS	E. Kasko	448	.243	0	22	228	388	14	72	4.9	**.978**	D. Farrell	32	198	11	10	0	3.27
	3B	Aspromonte	553	.280	12	69	133	261	11	10	2.6	**.973**	D. Nottebart	28	157	6	11	0	3.90
Harry Craft	RF	J. Gaines	307	.254	7	34	130	4	6	1	1.7	.957	H. Brown	27	132	3	15	1	3.95
W-61 L-88	CF	M. White	280	.271	0	27	127	4	3	1	1.9	.978	J. Owens	48	118	8	7	6	3.28
	LF	A. Spangler	449	.245	4	38	185	3	7	1	1.5	.964	D. Larsen	30	103	4	8	1	2.26
Lum Harris	C	J. Grote	298	.181	3	24	522	52	9	5	5.9	.985	C. Raymond	38	80	5	5	0	2.82
W-5 L-8	UT	B. Lillis	332	.268	0	17	169	236	12	40		.976	Woodeshick	61	78	2	9	23	2.76
	10	R. Staub	292	.216	8	35	512	30	9	34		.984							
	C	J. Bateman	221	.190	5	19	400	43	6	4	6.2	.987							
	OF	J. Wynn	219	.224	5	18	129	8	6	3	2.2	.958							
New York	1B	E. Kranepool	420	.257	10	45	975	80	10	78	10.2	.991	J. Fisher	40	228	10	17	0	4.23
	2B	R. Hunt	475	.303	6	42	244	317	12	73	5.3	.979	T. Stallard	36	226	10	**20**	0	3.79
W-53 L-109	SS	R. McMillan	379	.211	1	25	217	353	14	64	5.3	.976	A. Jackson	40	213	11	16	1	4.26
	3B	C. Smith	443	.239	20	58	89	166	23	9	3.3	.917	G. Cisco	36	192	6	19	0	3.62
Casey Stengel	RF	Christopher	543	.300	16	76	251	10	7	2	1.8	.974	B. Wakefield	62	120	3	5	2	3.61
	CF	J. Hickman	409	.257	11	57	237	8	6	1	2.2	.976	L. Bearnarth	44	78	5	5	3	4.15
	LF	G. Altman	422	.230	9	47	202	12	7	3	2.0	.968	W. Hunter	41	49	3	3	5	4.41
	C	J. Gonder	341	.270	7	35	397	70	10	7	4.9	.979							
	UT	R. Kanehl	254	.232	1	11	161	125	6	26		.979							
	C	H. Taylor	225	.240	4	23	182	28	4	5	4.8	.981							
	OF	L. Elliot	224	.228	9	22	130	2	2	1	2.1	.985							
	32	B. Klaus	209	.244	2	11	81	128	6	14		.972							
	O1	F. Thomas	197	.254	3	19	200	16	1	12		.995							
	C	Cannizzaro	164	.311	0	10	225	28	3	6	4.8	.988							

BATTING AND BASE RUNNING LEADERS

Batting Average
R. Clemente, PIT	.339
H. Aaron, MIL	.328
J. Torre, MIL	.321
D. Allen, PHI	.318
L. Brock, CHI, STL	.315

Slugging Average
W. Mays, SF	.607
R. Santo, CHI	.564
D. Allen, PHI	.557
F. Robinson, CIN	.548
O. Cepeda, SF	.539

Home Runs
W. Mays, SF	47
B. Williams, CHI	33
O. Cepeda, SF	31
J. Hart, SF	31
J. Callison, PHI	31

Winning Percentage
S. Koufax, LA	.792
J. Marichal, SF	.724
J. O'Toole, CIN	.708
J. Bunning, PHI	.704
L. Jackson, CHI	.686

PITCHING LEADERS

Earned Run Average
S. Koufax, LA	1.74
D. Drysdale, LA	2.18
C. Short, PHI	2.20
J. Marichal, SF	2.48
J. Bunning, PHI	2.63

Wins
L. Jackson, CHI	24
J. Marichal, SF	21
R. Sadecki, STL	20

Total Bases
D. Allen, PHI	352
W. Mays, SF	351
B. Williams, CHI	343
R. Santo, CHI	334
J. Callison, PHI	322

Runs Batted In
K. Boyer, STL	119
R. Santo, CHI	114
W. Mays, SF	111
J. Torre, MIL	109
J. Callison, PHI	104

Stolen Bases
M. Wills, LA	53
L. Brock, CHI, STL	43
W. Davis, LA	42
T. Harper, CIN	24
F. Robinson, CIN	23

Saves
Woodeshick, HOU	23
A. McBean, PIT	22
J. Baldschun, PHI	21
L. McDaniel, CHI	15

Strikeouts
B. Veale, PIT	250
B. Gibson, STL	245
D. Drysdale, LA	237
S. Koufax, LA	223
J. Bunning, PHI	219

Complete Games
J. Marichal, SF	22
D. Drysdale, LA	21
L. Jackson, CHI	19
B. Gibson, STL	17
D. Ellsworth, CHI	16

Hits
R. Clemente, PIT	211
C. Flood, STL	211
D. Allen, PHI	201
B. Williams, CHI	201

Base on Balls
R. Santo, CHI	86
E. Mathews, MIL	85
W. Mays, SF	82
F. Robinson, CIN	79

Home Run Percentage
W. Mays, SF	8.1
O. Cepeda, SF	5.9
J. Hart, SF	5.5
B. Williams, CHI	5.1

Fewest Hits/9 Innings
S. Koufax, LA	6.22
D. Drysdale, LA	6.78
C. Short, PHI	7.10
B. Veale, PIT	7.14

Shutouts
S. Koufax, LA	7
H. Fischer, MIL	5
V. Law, PIT	5
J. Bunning, PHI	5

Fewest Walks/9 Innings
J. Bunning, PHI	1.46
B. Bruce, HOU	1.47
V. Law, PIT	1.50
J. Marichal, SF	1.74

Runs Scored
D. Allen, PHI	125
W. Mays, SF	121
L. Brock, CHI, STL	111
F. Robinson, CIN	103

Doubles
L. Maye, MIL	44
R. Clemente, PIT	40
B. Williams, CHI	39
F. Robinson, CIN	38

Triples
R. Santo, CHI	13
D. Allen, PHI	13
V. Pinson, CIN	11
L. Brock, CHI, STL	11

Most Strikeouts/9 Inn.
S. Koufax, LA	9.00
J. Maloney, CIN	8.92
B. Veale, PIT	8.05
B. Gibson, STL	7.67

Innings
D. Drysdale, LA	321
L. Jackson, CHI	298
B. Gibson, STL	287
J. Bunning, PHI	284

Games Pitched
B. Miller, LA	74
Perranoski, LA	72
J. Baldschun, PHI	71
R. Taylor, STL	63

NATIONAL LEAGUE 1964, *cont.*

	W	L	PCT	GB	R	OR	2B	3B	HR	BA	SA	SB	E	DP	FA	CG	BB	SO	ShO	SV	ERA
							Batting						**Fielding**			**Pitching**					
St. Louis	93	69	.574		715	652	240	53	109	.272	.392	73	172	147	.973	47	410	877	10	38	3.43
Cincinnati	92	70	.568	1	660	**566**	220	38	130	.249	.372	90	**130**	137	**.979**	54	436	**1122**	14	35	3.07
Philadelphia	92	70	.568	1	693	632	241	51	130	.258	.391	30	157	150	.975	37	440	1009	17	**41**	3.36
San Francisco	90	72	.556	3	656	587	185	38	**165**	.246	.382	64	159	136	.975	48	480	1023	17	30	3.19
Milwaukee	88	74	.543	5	**803**	744	**274**	32	159	**.272**	**.418**	53	143	139	.977	45	452	906	14	39	4.12
Los Angeles	80	82	.494	13	614	572	180	39	79	.250	.340	**141**	170	126	.973	47	458	1062	**19**	27	**2.95**
Pittsburgh	80	82	.494	13	663	636	225	**54**	121	.264	.389	39	177	**179**	.972	42	476	951	14	29	3.52
Chicago	76	86	.469	17	649	724	239	50	145	.251	.390	70	162	147	.975	**58**	423	737	11	19	4.08
Houston	66	96	.407	27	495	628	162	41	70	.229	.315	40	149	124	.976	30	**353**	852	9	31	3.41
New York	53	109	.327	40	569	776	195	31	103	.246	.348	36	167	154	.974	40	466	717	10	15	4.25
					6517	6517	2161	427	1211	.254	.374	636	1586	1439	.975	448	4394	9256	135	304	3.54

AMERICAN LEAGUE 1964

	POS	Player	AB	BA	HR	RBI	PO	A	E	DP	TC/G	FA	Pitcher	G	IP	W	L	SV	ERA
New York W-99 L-63 Yogi Berra	1B	J. Pepitone	613	.251	28	100	**1333**	121	18	**128**	9.5	.988	J. Bouton	38	271	18	13	0	3.02
	2B	Richardson	**679**	.267	4	50	**400**	410	15	108	5.3	.982	W. Ford	39	245	17	6	1	2.13
	SS	T. Kubek	415	.229	8	31	186	307	11	52	5.1	.978	A. Downing	37	244	13	8	2	3.47
	3B	C. Boyer	510	.218	8	52	118	278	13	28	**3.3**	.968	R. Terry	27	115	7	11	4	4.54
	RF	R. Maris	513	.281	26	71	250	6	1	0	1.9	.996	R. Sheldon	19	102	5	2	1	3.61
	CF	M. Mantle	465	.303	35	111	217	3	5	1	1.7	.978	Stottlemyre	13	96	9	3	0	2.06
	LF	T. Tresh	533	.246	16	73	259	7	1	0	1.8	**.996**	P. Mikkelsen	50	86	7	4	12	3.56
	C	E. Howard	550	.313	15	84	**939**	67	2	9	6.9	**.998**	H. Reniff	41	69	6	4	9	3.12
	S3	P. Linz	368	.250	5	25	121	275	20	42		.952	S. Hamilton	30	60	7	2	3	3.28
	OF	H. Lopez	285	.260	10	34	130	2	4	1	1.3	.971							
	CO	J. Blanchard	161	.255	7	28	139	8	2	1		.987							
Chicago W-98 L-64 Al Lopez	1B	T. McCraw	368	.261	6	36	601	37	5	57	7.7	.992	G. Peters	37	274	**20**	8	0	2.50
	2B	A. Weis	328	.247	2	23	199	255	16	64	4.1	.966	J. Pizarro	33	239	19	9	0	2.56
	SS	R. Hansen	575	.261	20	68	**292**	514	21	105	5.2	.975	J. Horlen	32	211	13	9	0	1.88
	3B	P. Ward	539	.282	23	94	126	309	19	24	3.3	.958	J. Buzhardt	31	160	10	8	0	2.98
	RF	Hershberger	452	.230	2	31	231	10	4	2	1.8	.984	H. Wilhelm	73	131	12	9	27	1.99
	CF	J. Landis	298	.208	1	18	183	7	1	0	1.9	.995	E. Fisher	59	125	6	3	9	3.02
	LF	F. Robinson	525	.301	11	59	225	5	3	0	1.7	.987	R. Herbert	20	112	6	7	0	3.47
	C	J. Martin	294	.197	4	22	530	43	8	6	4.8	.986	D. Mossi	34	40	3	1	4	2.93
	2B	D. Buford	442	.262	4	30	196	198	13	60	4.4	.968							
	OF	D. Nicholson	294	.204	13	39	136	4	4	0	1.6	.972							
	1B	B. Skowron	273	.293	4	38	621	40	1	53	9.5*	.998							
	C	McNertney	186	.215	3	23	360	30	5	5	5.7	.987							
Baltimore W-97 L-65 Hank Bauer	1B	N. Sieburn	478	.245	12	56	1171	101	6	121	8.6	.995	M. Pappas	37	252	16	7	0	2.97
	2B	J. Adair	569	.248	9	47	395	422	5	107	5.4	**.994**	W. Bunker	29	214	19	5	0	2.69
	SS	L. Aparicio	578	.266	10	37	260	437	15	98	4.9	**.979**	R. Roberts	31	204	13	7	0	2.91
	3B	B. Robinson	612	.317	28	**118**	153	327	14	40	3.0	.972	D. McNally	30	159	9	11	0	3.67
	RF	S. Bowens	501	.263	22	71	249	8	5	1	1.9	.981	S. Barber	36	157	9	13	1	3.84
	CF	J. Brandt	523	.243	13	47	345	14	7	2	**2.7**	.981	S. Miller	66	97	7	7	23	3.06
	LF	B. Powell	424	.290	39	99	178	13	5	1	1.6	.974	H. Haddix	49	90	5	5	10	2.31
	C	D. Brown	230	.257	8	32	380	29	5	4	4.9	.988	D. Hall	45	88	9	1	7	1.85
	C	J. Orsino	248	.222	8	23	384	31	10	3	6.4	.976							
	UT	B. Johnson	210	.248	3	29	164	77	5	27		.980							
	OF	W. Kirkland	150	.200	3	22	86	7	1	3	1.6	.989							
Detroit W-85 L-77 Chuck Dressen	1B	N. Cash	479	.257	23	83	1105	92	4	97	8.8	**.997**	Wickersham	40	254	19	12	1	3.44
	2B	J. Lumpe	624	.256	6	46	339	394	13	95	4.7	.983	M. Lolich	44	232	18	9	2	3.26
	SS	McAuliffe	557	.241	24	66	262	467	**32**	84	4.8	.958	H. Aguirre	32	162	5	10	1	3.79
	3B	D. Wert	525	.257	9	55	126	283	15	30	3.0	.965	E. Rakow	42	152	8	9	3	3.72
	RF	A. Kaline	525	.293	17	68	278	6	3	2	2.1	.990	P. Regan	32	147	5	10	1	5.03
	CF	G. Thomas	308	.286	12	44	164	4	2	1	1.9	.988	D. McLain	19	100	4	5	0	4.05
	LF	G. Brown	426	.272	15	54	205	4	4	0	2.0	.981	J. Sparma	21	84	5	6	0	3.00
	C	B. Freehan	520	.300	18	80	923	61	7	7	7.0	.993	F. Gladding	42	67	7	4	7	3.07
	OF	D. Demeter	441	.256	22	80	164	3	0	1	1.9	**1.000**	L. Sherry	38	66	7	5	11	3.66
	OF	B. Bruton	296	.277	5	33	143	7	2	3	1.9	.987	T. Fox	32	61	4	3	5	3.39
Los Angeles W-82 L-80 Bill Rigney	1B	J. Adcock	366	.268	21	64	959	54	7	94	9.7	.993	D. Chance	46	**278**	20	9	4	**1.65**
	2B	B. Knoop	486	.216	7	38	357	**522**	20	123	5.6	.978	F. Newman	32	190	13	10	0	2.75
	SS	J. Fregosi	505	.277	18	72	225	421	23	89	4.9	.966	B. Latman	40	138	6	10	2	3.85
	3B	F. Torres	277	.231	12	28	73	122	6	10	2.8	.970	B. Lee	64	137	5	5	19	1.51
	RF	L. Clinton	306	.248	9	38	123	12	2	3	1.6	.985	B. Belinsky	23	135	9	8	0	2.86
	CF	A. Pearson	265	.223	2	16	132	1	3	1	2.1	.978	K. McBride	29	116	4	13	1	5.26
	LF	W. Smith	359	.301	11	51	128	2	3	1	1.5	.977	D. Lee	33	89	5	4	2	2.72
	C	B. Rodgers	514	.243	4	54	884	**87**	13	14	6.7	.987	B. Duliba	58	73	6	4	9	3.59
	UT	T. Satriano	255	.200	1	17	383	72	8	32		.983							
	OF	J. Piersall	255	.314	2	13	115	2	0	2	1.6	**1.000**							
	13	V. Power	221	.249	3	13	302	79	3	26		.992							
	OF	B. Perry	221	.276	3	16	115	2	3	0	1.9	.975							
	OF	Kirkpatrick	219	.242	2	27	90	3	3	0	1.5	.969							
	3B	B. Moran	198	.268	0	11	47	86	10	5	3.0	.930							
	OF	L. Thomas	172	.273	2	24	71	4	4	1	1.7	.949							

AMERICAN LEAGUE 1964, cont.

	POS	Player	AB	BA	HR	RBI	PO	A	E	DP	TC/G	FA	Pitcher	G	IP	W	L	SV	ERA
Cleveland	1B	B. Chance	390	.279	14	75	567	24	7	47	7.4	.988	J. Kralick	30	191	12	7	0	3.21
	2B	L. Brown	335	.230	12	40	185	270	9	56	4.5	.981	S. McDowell	31	173	11	6	1	2.70
	SS	D. Howser	637	.256	3	52	291	463	20	100	4.8	.974	D. Donovan	30	158	7	9	1	4.55
W-79 L-83	3B	M. Alvis	381	.252	18	53	83	191	13	18	2.7	.955	S. Siebert	41	156	7	9	3	3.23
George Strickland	RF	T. Francona	270	.248	8	24	65	2	1	0	1.0	.985	P. Ramos	36	133	7	10	0	5.14
W-33 L-39	CF	V. Davalillo	577	.270	6	51	346	11	5	5	2.5	.986	L. Tiant	19	127	10	4	1	2.83
	LF	L. Wagner	641	.253	31	100	254	5	11	0	1.7	.959	G. Bell	56	106	8	6	4	4.33
Birdie Tebbetts	C	J. Romano	352	.241	19	47	714	38	7	3	7.9	.991	D. McMahon	70	101	6	4	16	2.41
W-46 L-44	UT	W. Held	364	.236	18	49	183	182	14	40		.963	T. John	25	94	2	9	0	3.91
	1B	F. Whitfield	293	.270	10	29	596	36	5	63	8.1	.992	L. Stange	23	92	4	8	0	4.12
	UT	C. Salmon	283	.307	4	25	191	67	2	14		.992	T. Abernathy	53	73	2	6	11	4.33
	C	J. Azcue	271	.273	4	34	510	36	4	2	7.2	.993							
Minnesota	1B	B. Allison	492	.287	32	86	715	55	11	63	8.4	.986	C. Pascual	36	267	15	12	0	3.30
	2B	B. Allen	243	.214	6	20	161	173	7	40	4.8	.979	J. Kaat	36	243	17	11	1	3.22
	SS	Z. Versalles	659	.259	20	64	271	427	31	89	4.6	.957	D. Stigman	32	190	6	15	0	4.03
W-79 L-83	3B	R. Rollins	596	.270	12	68	134	297	24	17	3.1	.947	M. Grant	26	166	11	9	1	2.82
	RF	T. Oliva	672	.323	32	94	313	5	6	0	2.0	.981	J. Arrigo	41	105	7	4	1	3.84
Sam Mele	CF	J. Hall	510	.282	25	75	323	13	5	0	2.5	.985	J. Roland	30	94	2	6	3	4.10
	LF	H. Killebrew	577	.270	49	111	232	1	7	0	1.5	.971	Worthington	41	72	5	6	14	1.37
	C	E. Battey	405	.272	12	52	813	52	9	4	7.0	.990	J. Perry	42	65	6	3	2	3.44
	1B	D. Mincher	287	.237	23	56	549	43	5	50	7.9	.992							
Boston	1B	D. Stuart	603	.279	33	114	1159	104	24	105	8.3	.981	Monbouquette	36	234	13	14	1	4.04
	2B	D. Jones	374	.230	6	39	181	193	16	41	4.6	.959	E. Wilson	33	202	11	12	0	4.49
	SS	E. Bressoud	566	.293	15	55	248	411	19	78	4.3	.972	J. Lamabe	39	177	9	13	1	5.89
W-72 L-90	3B	F. Malzone	537	.264	13	56	141	259	17	24	2.9	.957	D. Morehead	32	167	8	15	0	4.97
	RF	L. Thomas	401	.257	13	42	176	6	1	1	1.7	.995	B. Heffner	55	159	7	9	4	4.08
Johnny Pesky	CF	Yastrzemski	567	.289	15	67	372	19	11	3	2.7	.973	D. Radatz	79	157	16	9	29	2.29
W-70 L-90	LF	Conigliaro	404	.290	24	52	176	7	5	0	1.8	.973	E. Connolly	27	81	4	11	0	4.91
	C	B. Tillman	425	.278	17	61	897	49	11	5	7.3	.989							
Billy Herman	UT	F. Mantilla	425	.289	30	64	173	146	5	29		.985							
W-2 L-0	2B	C. Schilling	163	.196	0	7	89	101	5	20	4.6	.974							
	C	R. Nixon	163	.233	1	20	273	11	3	3	6.4	.990							
Washington	1B	B. Skowron	262	.271	13	41	591	40	4	41	9.6*	.994	C. Osteen	37	257	15	13	0	3.33
	2B	Blasingame	506	.267	1	34	259	336	14	70	4.5	.977	B. Narum	38	199	9	15	0	4.30
	SS	E. Brinkman	447	.224	8	34	234	364	19	75	4.9	.969	B. Daniels	33	163	8	10	0	3.70
W-62 L-100	3B	J. Kennedy	482	.230	7	35	97	190	16	14	2.9	.947	A. Koch	32	114	3	10	0	4.89
	RF	J. King	415	.241	18	56	240	10	7	0	2.1	.973	S. Ridzik	49	112	5	5	2	2.89
Gil Hodges	CF	D. Lock	512	.248	28	80	354	19	5	3	2.5	.973	J. Hannan	49	106	4	7	3	4.16
	LF	C. Hinton	514	.274	11	53	258	7	4	3	2.1	.985	D. Stenhouse	26	88	2	7	1	4.81
	C	M. Brumley	426	.244	2	35	628	44	6	4	5.1	.991	R. Kline	61	81	10	7	14	2.32
	3B	D. Zimmer	341	.246	12	38	68	143	10	6	2.5	.955	J. Duckworth	30	56	1	6	3	4.34
	1B	D. Phillips	234	.231	2	13	473	39	3	50	8.4	.990							
	OF	F. Valentine	212	.226	4	20	86	2	2	1	1.6	.978							
Kansas City	1B	J. Gentile	439	.251	28	71	1018	84	13	92	8.7	.988	O. Pena	40	219	12	14	0	4.43
	2B	D. Green	435	.264	11	37	262	361	6	69	5.2	.990	D. Segui	40	217	8	17	0	4.56
	SS	W. Causey	604	.281	8	49	266	352	21	75	4.9	.967	O'Donoghue	39	174	10	14	0	4.92
W-57 L-105	3B	E. Charles	557	.241	16	63	138	259	19	25	2.8	.954	M. Drabowsky	53	168	5	13	1	5.29
	RF	R. Colavito	588	.274	34	102	275	10	8	1	1.8	.973	J. Wyatt	81	128	9	8	20	3.59
Ed Lopat	CF	N. Mathews	573	.239	14	60	384	5	13	2	2.6	.968	T. Bowsfield	50	119	4	7	0	4.10
W-17 L-35	LF	M. Jimenez	204	.225	12	38	59	3	4	1	1.3	.939	W. Stock	50	93	6	3	1	1.94
	C	D. Edwards	294	.224	5	28	469	31	7	5	6.4	.986							
Mel McGaha	SO	Campaneris	269	.257	4	22	97	96	5	14		.975							
W-40 L-70	C	B. Bryan	220	.241	13	36	317	22	3	5	5.3	.991							
	OF	G. Alusik	204	.240	3	19	61	1	1	1	1.4	.984							

BATTING AND BASE RUNNING LEADERS

Batting Average		Slugging Average		Home Runs	
T. Oliva, MIN	.323	B. Powell, BAL	.606	H. Killebrew, MIN	49
B. Robinson, BAL	.317	M. Mantle, NY	.591	B. Powell, BAL	39
E. Howard, NY	.313	T. Oliva, MIN	.557	M. Mantle, NY	35
M. Mantle, NY	.303	B. Allison, MIN	.553	R. Colavito, KC	34
F. Robinson, CHI	.301	H. Killebrew, MIN	.548	D. Stuart, BOS	33

Total Bases		Runs Batted In		Stolen Bases	
T. Oliva, MIN	374	B. Robinson, BAL	118	L. Aparicio, BAL	57
B. Robinson, BAL	319	D. Stuart, BOS	114	A. Weis, CHI	22
H. Killebrew, MIN	316	M. Mantle, NY	111	V. Davalillo, CLE	21
R. Colavito, KC	298	H. Killebrew, MIN	111	D. Howser, CLE	20
D. Stuart, BOS	296	R. Colavito, KC	102	C. Hinton, WAS	17

PITCHING LEADERS

Winning Percentage		Earned Run Average		Wins	
W. Bunker, BAL	.792	D. Chance, LA	1.65	G. Peters, CHI	20
W. Ford, NY	.739	J. Horlen, CHI	1.88	D. Chance, LA	20
G. Peters, CHI	.714	W. Ford, NY	2.13	W. Bunker, BAL	19
M. Pappas, BAL	.696	G. Peters, CHI	2.50	J. Pizarro, CHI	19
D. Chance, LA	.690	J. Pizarro, CHI	2.56	Wickersham, DET	19

Saves		Strikeouts		Complete Games	
D. Radatz, BOS	29	A. Downing, NY	217	D. Chance, LA	15
H. Wilhelm, CHI	27	C. Pascual, MIN	213	C. Pascual, MIN	14
S. Miller, BAL	23	D. Chance, LA	207	J. Kaat, MIN	13
J. Wyatt, KC	20	G. Peters, CHI	205	C. Osteen, WAS	13
B. Lee, LA	19	M. Lolich, DET	192	M. Pappas, BAL	13

AMERICAN LEAGUE 1964, *cont.*

BATTING AND BASE RUNNING LEADERS

Hits
T. Oliva, MIN	217
B. Robinson, BAL	194
Richardson, NY	181
E. Howard, NY	172

Base on Balls
N. Siebern, BAL	106
M. Mantle, NY	99
H. Killebrew, MIN	93
B. Allison, MIN	92

Home Run Percentage
H. Killebrew, MIN	8.5
M. Mantle, NY	7.5
B. Allison, MIN	6.5
J. Gentile, KC	6.4

Runs Scored
T. Oliva, MIN	109
D. Howser, CLE	101
H. Killebrew, MIN	95
L. Wagner, CLE	94

Doubles
T. Oliva, MIN	43
E. Bressoud, BOS	41
B. Robinson, BAL	35
Z. Versalles, MIN	33

Triples
R. Rollins, MIN	10
Z. Versalles, MIN	10
J. Fregosi, LA	9
Yastrzemski, BOS	9

PITCHING LEADERS

Fewest Hits/9 Innings
J. Horlen, CHI	6.07
D. Chance, LA	6.27
W. Bunker, BAL	6.77
G. Peters, CHI	7.14

Most Strikeouts/9 Inn.
S. McDowell, CLE	9.19
A. Downing, NY	8.00
O. Pena, KC	7.55
D. Stigman, MIN	7.53

Shutouts
D. Chance, LA	11
W. Ford, NY	8
M. Pappas, BAL	7
M. Lolich, DET	6

Innings
D. Chance, LA	278
G. Peters, CHI	274
J. Bouton, NY	271
C. Pascual, MIN	267

Fewest Walks/9 Innings
Monbouquette, BOS	1.54
M. Pappas, BAL	1.72
F. Newman, LA	1.85
J. Bouton, NY	1.99

Games Pitched
J. Wyatt, KC	81
D. Radatz, BOS	79
H. Wilhelm, CHI	73
D. McMahon, CLE	70

	W	L	PCT	GB	R	OR	2B	3B	HR	BA	SA	SB	E	DP	FA	CG	BB	SO	ShO	SV	ERA
New York	99	63	.611		730	577	208	35	162	.253	.387	54	109	158	.983	46	504	989	18	45	3.15
Chicago	98	64	.605	1	642	501	184	40	106	.247	.353	75	122	164	.981	44	401	955	20	45	2.72
Baltimore	97	65	.599	2	679	567	229	20	162	.248	.383	78	95	159	.985	44	456	939	17	41	3.16
Detroit	85	77	.525	14	699	678	199	57	157	.253	.395	60	111	137	.982	35	536	993	11	35	3.84
Los Angeles	82	80	.506	17	544	551	186	27	102	.242	.344	49	138	168	.978	30	530	965	28	41	2.91
Cleveland	79	83	.488	20	689	693	208	22	164	.247	.380	79	118	149	.981	37	565	1162	16	37	3.75
Minnesota	79	83	.488	20	737	678	227	46	221	.252	.427	46	145	131	.977	47	545	1099	4	29	3.57
Boston	72	90	.444	27	688	793	253	29	186	.258	.416	18	138	123	.977	21	571	1094	9	38	4.50
Washington	62	100	.383	37	578	733	199	28	125	.231	.348	47	127	145	.979	27	505	794	5	26	3.98
Kansas City	57	105	.352	42	621	836	216	29	166	.239	.379	34	158	152	.974	18	614	966	6	27	4.71
					6607	6607	2109	333	1551	.247	.382	540	1261	1486	.980	349	5227	9956	134	364	3.63

NATIONAL LEAGUE 1965

	POS	Player	AB	BA	HR	RBI	PO	A	E	DP	TC/G	FA	Pitcher	G	IP	W	L	SV	ERA
Los Angeles W-97 L-65 Walter Alston	1B	W. Parker	542	.238	8	51	1434	95	5	112	10.0	.997	S. Koufax	43	336	26	8	2	2.04
	2B	J. Lefebvre	544	.250	12	69	349	429	24	91	5.1	.970	D. Drysdale	44	308	23	12	1	2.77
	SS	M. Wills	650	.286	0	33	267	535	25	89	5.3	.970	C. Osteen	40	287	15	15	0	2.79
	3B	J. Gilliam	372	.280	4	39	55	135	8	13	2.5	.960	J. Podres	27	134	7	6	1	3.43
	RF	R. Fairly	555	.274	9	70	262	7	5	1	1.9	.982	Perranoski	59	105	6	6	17	2.24
	CF	W. Davis	558	.238	10	57	318	6	11	1	2.4	.967	B. Miller	61	103	6	7	9	2.97
	LF	L. Johnson	468	.259	12	58	199	3	3	2	1.6	.985	H. Reed	38	78	7	5	1	3.12
	C	J. Roseboro	437	.233	8	57	824	55	5	7	6.7	.994							
	3B	D. Tracewski	186	.215	1	20	30	103	7	6	2.6	.950							
San Francisco W-95 L-67 Herman Franks	1B	W. McCovey	540	.276	39	92	1310	87	13	93	9.0	.991	J. Marichal	39	295	22	13	1	2.13
	2B	H. Lanier	522	.226	0	39	294	445	18	75	4.8	.976	B. Shaw	42	235	16	9	2	2.64
	SS	D. Schofield	379	.203	2	19	145	274	7	52	4.6	.984*	G. Perry	47	196	8	12	1	4.19
	3B	J. Hart	591	.299	23	96	134	231	32	16	2.8	.919	R. Herbel	47	171	12	9	1	3.85
	RF	J. Alou	543	.298	9	52	238	7	5	0	1.8	.980	B. Bolin	45	163	14	6	2	2.76
	CF	W. Mays	558	.317	52	112	337	13	6	4	2.4	.983	J. Sanford	23	91	4	5	2	3.96
	LF	M. Alou	324	.231	2	18	139	6	2	1	1.4	.986	F. Linzy	57	82	9	3	21	1.43
	C	T. Haller	422	.251	16	49	864	50	12	9	7.0	.987	M. Murakami	45	74	4	1	8	3.75
	UT	J. Davenport	271	.251	4	31	97	147	14	21		.946							
	OF	Gabrielson	269	.301	4	26	112	3	3	1	1.5	.975							
Pittsburgh W-90 L-72 Harry Walker	1B	D. Clendenon	612	.301	14	96	1572	119	28	161	10.9	.984	B. Veale	39	266	17	12	0	2.84
	2B	B. Mazeroski	494	.271	6	54	290	439	9	113	5.8	.988	D. Cardwell	37	240	13	10	0	3.18
	SS	G. Alley	500	.252	5	47	163	376	18	79	5.1	.968	B. Friend	34	222	8	12	0	3.24
	3B	B. Bailey	626	.256	11	49	96	243	22	25	2.5	.939	V. Law	29	217	17	9	0	2.15
	RF	R. Clemente	589	.329	10	65	288	16	10	1	2.2	.970	A. McBean	62	114	6	6	18	2.29
	CF	B. Virdon	481	.279	4	24	260	3	8	1	2.1	.970	T. Sisk	38	111	7	3	0	3.40
	LF	W. Stargell	533	.272	27	107	208	12	8	3	1.7	.965	J. Gibbon	31	106	4	9	1	4.51
	C	Pagliaroni	403	.268	17	56	669	42	4	14	5.5	.994	D. Schwall	43	77	9	6	1	2.92
	OF	M. Mota	294	.279	4	29	127	5	2	1	1.4	.985							
	UT	A. Rodgers	178	.287	2	25	88	110	8	27		.961							
Cincinnati W-89 L-73 Dick Sisler	1B	T. Perez	281	.260	12	47	525	40	6	55	6.1	.989	S. Ellis	44	264	22	10	2	3.79
	2B	P. Rose	670	.312	11	81	382	403	20	93	5.0	.975	J. Maloney	33	255	20	9	0	2.54
	SS	L. Cardenas	557	.287	11	57	292	440	19	92	4.8	.975	J. Jay	37	156	9	8	1	4.22
	3B	D. Johnson	616	.287	32	130	132	266	22	26	2.6	.948	J. Nuxhall	32	149	11	4	2	3.45
	RF	F. Robinson	582	.296	33	113	282	5	3	1	1.9	.990	J. Tsitouris	31	131	6	9	1	4.95
	CF	V. Pinson	669	.305	22	94	354	9	3	1	2.3	.992	J. O'Toole	29	128	3	10	1	5.92
	LF	T. Harper	646	.257	18	64	277	6	5	0	1.8	.983	B. McCool	62	105	9	10	21	4.27
	C	J. Edwards	371	.267	17	51	761	61	8	9	7.5	.990							
	1B	G. Coleman	325	.302	14	57	621	48	6	52	7.6	.991							
	C	D. Pavletich	191	.319	8	32	335	16	5	5	6.6	.986							

NATIONAL LEAGUE 1965, *cont.*

POS	Player	AB	BA	HR	RBI	PO	A	E	DP	TC/G	FA	Pitcher	G	IP	W	L	SV	ERA
Milwaukee												T. Cloninger	40	279	24	11	1	3.29
1B	F. Alou	555	.297	23	78	476	37	3	39	7.5	.994	Blasingame	38	225	16	10	1	3.77
2B	F. Bolling	535	.264	7	50	310	393	17	90	4.9	.976	K. Johnson	29	180	13	8	2	3.21
SS	W. Woodward	265	.208	0	11	146	243	9	61	3.7	.977	D. Lemaster	32	146	7	13	0	4.43
3B	E. Mathews	546	.251	32	95	113	301	19	19	2.8	.956	B. Sadowski	34	123	5	9	3	4.32
RF	H. Aaron	570	.318	32	89	298	9	4	2	2.1	.987	H. Fischer	31	123	8	9	0	3.89
CF	M. Jones	504	.262	31	75	239	2	5	2	1.8	.980	B. O'Dell	62	111	10	6	18	2.18
LF	F. Alou	555	.297	23	78	148	2	3	0	1.7	.980	P. Niekro	41	75	2	3	6	2.89
C	J. Torre	523	.291	27	80	589	43	6	4	6.4	.991							
C1	G. Oliver	392	.270	21	58	750	71	17	37		.980							
OF	R. Carty	271	.310	10	35	112	3	5	1	1.6	.958							
OF	T. Cline	220	.191	0	10	119	5	4	1	1.5	.969							
SS	D. Menke	181	.243	4	18	65	140	7	22	3.9	.967							
UT	de la Hoz	176	.256	2	11	61	99	8	20		.952							
Philadelphia												C. Short	47	297	18	11	2	2.82
1B	D. Stuart	538	.234	28	95	1119	98	17	100	8.6	.986	J. Bunning	39	291	19	9	0	2.60
2B	T. Taylor	323	.229	3	27	169	220	17	51	4.7	.958	R. Culp	33	204	14	10	0	3.22
SS	B. Wine	394	.228	5	33	221	387	21	84	4.7	.967	R. Herbert	25	131	5	8	1	3.86
3B	D. Allen	619	.302	20	85	129	305	26	**29**	2.9	.943	B. Belinsky	30	110	4	9	1	4.84
RF	J. Callison	619	.262	32	101	313	21	6	2	2.1	.982	G. Wagner	59	105	7	7	7	3.00
CF	T. Gonzalez	370	.295	13	41	167	3	3	1	1.7	.983	J. Baldschun	65	99	5	8	6	3.82
LF	A. Johnson	262	.294	8	28	109	3	4	0	1.4	.966	E. Roebuck	44	50	5	3	3	3.40
C	C. Dalrymple	301	.213	4	23	657	70	5	10	7.2	.993							
20	C. Rojas	521	.303	3	42	264	236	7	57		.986							
OF	W. Covington	235	.247	15	45	88	2	3	0	1.5	.968							
OF	J. Briggs	229	.236	4	23	110	2	2	0	1.7	.982							
S1	R. Amaro	184	.212	0	15	172	126	10	32		.968							
C	P. Corrales	174	.224	2	15	358	24	7	2	6.3	.982							
St. Louis												B. Gibson	38	299	20	12	1	3.07
1B	B. White	543	.289	24	73	1308	109	11	114	9.9	.992	C. Simmons	34	203	9	15	0	4.08
2B	J. Javier	229	.227	2	23	128	179	8	40	4.6	.975	T. Stallard	40	194	11	8	0	3.38
SS	D. Groat	587	.254	0	52	242	450	27	86	4.9	.962	R. Sadecki	36	173	6	15	1	5.21
3B	K. Boyer	535	.260	13	75	113	250	12	18	2.6	**.968**	B. Purkey	32	124	10	9	2	5.79
RF	M. Shannon	244	.221	3	25	170	5	1	1	1.7	.994	R. Washburn	28	119	9	11	3	3.62
CF	C. Flood	617	.310	11	83	349	7	5	3	2.4	.986	N. Briles	37	82	3	3	4	3.50
LF	L. Brock	631	.288	16	69	272	11	**12**	1	1.9	.959	Woodeshick	51	60	3	2	15	1.81
C	T. McCarver	409	.276	11	48	687	43	4	4	6.6	**.995**	D. Dennis	41	55	2	3	6	2.29
UT	P. Gagliano	363	.240	8	53	201	169	16	34		.959							
OF	T. Francona	174	.259	5	19	35	0	1	0	1.1	.972							
2S	J. Buchek	166	.247	3	21	92	154	5	38		.980							
OF	B. Skinner	152	.309	5	26	43	0	1	0	1.4	.935							
Chicago												L. Jackson	39	257	14	21	0	3.85
1B	E. Banks	612	.265	28	106	**1682**	93	15	143	**11.0**	.992	D. Ellsworth	36	222	14	15	1	3.81
2B	G. Beckert	614	.239	3	30	326	**494**	23	101	5.5	.973	B. Buhl	32	184	13	11	0	4.39
SS	D. Kessinger	309	.201	0	14	176	338	**28**	69	5.2	.948	C. Koonce	38	173	7	9	5	3.69
3B	R. Santo	608	.285	33	101	155	373	24	27	**3.4**	.957	T. Abernathy	**84**	136	4	6	31	2.57
RF	B. Williams	645	.315	34	108	296	10	10	2	1.9	.968	L. McDaniel	71	129	5	6	2	2.59
CF	D. Landrum	425	.226	6	34	241	3	3	0	2.1	.988	B. Faul	17	97	6	6	0	3.54
LF	D. Clemens	340	.221	4	26	145	7	3	0	1.5	.981							
C	V. Roznovsky	172	.221	3	15	270	30	5	6	4.8	.984							
OS	J. Stewart	282	.223	0	19	117	58	4	11		.956							
OF	G. Altman	196	.235	4	23	66	0	4	0	1.6	.943							
SS	R. Pena	170	.218	2	12	74	151	17	29	4.8	.930							
C	C. Krug	169	.201	5	24	273	27	6	5	5.3	.980							
C	E. Bailey	150	.253	5	23	237	23	5	3	4.9	.981							
Houston												B. Bruce	35	230	9	18	0	3.72
1B	W. Bond	407	.263	7	47	650	49	12	52	9.6	.983	D. Farrell	33	208	11	11	1	3.50
2B	J. Morgan	601	.271	14	40	348	492	**27**	82	5.5	.969	D. Nottebart	29	158	4	15	0	4.67
SS	B. Lillis	408	.221	0	20	188	273	15	49	4.6	.968	L. Dierker	26	147	7	8	0	3.50
3B	Aspromonte	578	.263	5	52	123	281	16	25	2.9	.962	D. Giusti	38	131	8	7	3	4.32
RF	R. Staub	410	.256	14	63	202	12	11	1	2.0	.951	C. Raymond	33	96	7	4	5	2.90
CF	J. Wynn	564	.275	22	73	**382**	13	9	1	**2.6**	.978	J. Owens	50	71	6	5	8	3.28
LF	L. Maye	415	.251	3	36	177	6	9	1	1.9	.953	R. Taylor	32	58	1	5	4	6.40
C	R. Brand	391	.235	2	37	585	54	8	8	6.3	.988	Woodeshick	27	32	3	4	3	3.06
OF	J. Gaines	229	.227	6	31	83	1	8	0	1.4	.913							
1B	J. Gentile	227	.242	7	31	544	43	4	41	8.7	.993							
SS	E. Kasko	215	.247	1	10	96	152	6	27	4.3	.976							
New York												J. Fisher	43	254	8	**24**	1	3.94
1B	E. Kranepool	525	.253	10	53	1375	93	12	116	10.1	.992	A. Jackson	37	205	8	20	1	4.34
2B	C. Hiller	286	.238	5	21	145	182	14	39	4.3	.959	W. Spahn	20	126	4	12	0	4.36
SS	R. McMillan	528	.242	1	42	248	477	27	80	4.9	.964	G. Cisco	35	112	4	8	0	4.49
3B	C. Smith	499	.244	16	62	119	281	18	27	3.2	.957	T. McGraw	37	98	2	7	1	3.32
RF	J. Lewis	477	.245	15	45	257	14	7	3	2.0	.975	T. Parsons	35	91	1	10	4	4.67
CF	J. Hickman	369	.236	15	40	136	3	5	0	1.6	.965	G. Kroll	32	87	6	6	1	4.45
LF	R. Swoboda	399	.228	19	50	188	9	11	2	1.9	.947							
C	Cannizzaro	251	.183	0	7	435	69	**12**	8	4.6	.977							
OF	Christopher	437	.249	5	40	180	3	2	0	1.7	.989							
UT	B. Klaus	288	.191	2	12	179	254	11	54		.975							
2B	R. Hunt	196	.240	1	10	106	128	5	17	5.2	.979							

Milwaukee W-86 L-76 — Bobby Bragan

Philadelphia W-85 L-76 — Gene Mauch

St. Louis W-80 L-81 — Red Schoendienst

Chicago W-72 L-90 — Bob Kennedy W-24 L-32; Lou Klein W-48 L-58

Houston W-65 L-97 — Lum Harris

New York W-50 L-112 — Casey Stengel W-31 L-64; Wes Westrum W-19 L-48

NATIONAL LEAGUE 1965, *cont.*

BATTING AND BASE RUNNING LEADERS

Batting Average		Slugging Average		Home Runs		Winning Percentage		Earned Run Average		Wins	
R. Clemente, PIT	.329	W. Mays, SF	.645	W. Mays, SF	52	S. Koufax, LA	.765	S. Koufax, LA	2.04	S. Koufax, LA	26
H. Aaron, MIL	.318	H. Aaron, MIL	.560	W. McCovey, SF	39	J. Maloney, CIN	.690	J. Marichal, SF	2.13	T. Cloninger, MIL	24
W. Mays, SF	.317	B. Williams, CHI	.552	B. Williams, CHI	34	S. Ellis, CIN	.688	V. Law, PIT	2.15	D. Drysdale, LA	23
B. Williams, CHI	.315	F. Robinson, CIN	.540	F. Robinson, CIN	33	T. Cloninger, MIL	.686	J. Maloney, CIN	2.54	S. Ellis, CIN	22
P. Rose, CIN	.312	W. McCovey, SF	.539	R. Santo, CHI	33	J. Bunning, PHI	.679	J. Bunning, PHI	2.60	J. Marichal, SF	22

Total Bases		Runs Batted In		Stolen Bases		Saves		Strikeouts		Complete Games	
W. Mays, SF	360	D. Johnson, CIN	130	M. Wills, LA	94	T. Abernathy, CHI	31	S. Koufax, LA	382	S. Koufax, LA	27
B. Williams, CHI	356	F. Robinson, CIN	113	L. Brock, STL	63	F. Linzy, SF	21	B. Veale, PIT	276	J. Marichal, SF	24
V. Pinson, CIN	324	W. Mays, SF	112	J. Wynn, HOU	43	B. McCool, CIN	21	B. Gibson, STL	270	B. Gibson, STL	20
H. Aaron, MIL	319	B. Williams, CHI	108	T. Harper, CIN	35	B. O'Dell, MIL	18	J. Bunning, PHI	268	D. Drysdale, LA	20
D. Johnson, CIN	317	W. Stargell, PIT	107	W. Davis, LA	25	Woodeshick, HOU, STL	18	J. Maloney, CIN	244	T. Cloninger, MIL	16
						A. McBean, PIT	18				

Hits		Base on Balls		Home Run Percentage		Fewest Hits/9 Innings		Shutouts		Fewest Walks/9 Innings	
P. Rose, CIN	209	J. Morgan, HOU	97	W. Mays, SF	9.3	S. Koufax, LA	5.79	J. Marichal, SF	10	J. Marichal, SF	1.40
V. Pinson, CIN	204	W. McCovey, SF	88	W. McCovey, SF	7.2	J. Maloney, CIN	6.66	S. Koufax, LA	8	V. Law, PIT	1.45
B. Williams, CHI	203	R. Santo, CHI	88	M. Jones, MIL	6.2	J. Marichal, SF	6.83	B. Veale, PIT	7	B. Bruce, HOU	1.49
R. Clemente, PIT	194	J. Wynn, HOU	84	E. Mathews, MIL	5.9	B. Bolin, SF	6.90	J. Bunning, PHI	7	D. Farrell, HOU	1.51

Runs Scored		Doubles		Triples		Most Strikeouts/9 Inn.		Innings		Games Pitched	
T. Harper, CIN	126	H. Aaron, MIL	40	J. Callison, PHI	16	S. Koufax, LA	10.24	S. Koufax, LA	336	T. Abernathy, CHI	84
W. Mays, SF	118	B. Williams, CHI	39	R. Clemente, PIT	14	B. Veale, PIT	9.34	D. Drysdale, LA	308	Woodeshick, HOU, STL	78
P. Rose, CIN	117	L. Brock, STL	35	D. Clendenon, PIT	14	J. Maloney, CIN	8.60	B. Gibson, STL	299	L. McDaniel, CHI	71
B. Williams, CHI	115	P. Rose, CIN	35	D. Allen, PHI	14	J. Bunning, PHI	8.29	C. Short, PHI	297	J. Baldschun, PHI	65

PITCHING LEADERS (headers shown above within the leader groups)

	W	L	PCT	GB	R	OR	2B	3B	HR	BA	SA	SB	E	DP	FA	CG	BB	SO	ShO	SV	ERA
Los Angeles	97	65	.599		608	521	193	32	78	.245	.335	172	134	135	.979	58	425	1079	23	34	2.81
San Francisco	95	67	.586	2	682	593	169	43	159	.252	.385	47	148	124	.976	42	408	1060	17	42	3.20
Pittsburgh	90	72	.556	7	675	580	217	57	111	.265	.382	51	152	189	.977	49	469	882	17	27	3.01
Cincinnati	89	73	.549	8	825	704	268	61	183	.273	.439	82	117	142	.981	43	587	1113	9	34	3.88
Milwaukee	86	76	.531	11	708	633	243	28	196	.256	.416	64	140	145	.978	43	541	966	4	38	3.52
Philadelphia	85	76	.528	11.5	654	667	205	53	144	.250	.384	64	157	153	.975	50	466	1071	18	21	3.53
St. Louis	80	81	.497	16.5	707	674	234	46	109	.254	.371	100	130	152	.979	40	467	916	11	35	3.77
Chicago	72	90	.444	25	635	723	202	33	134	.238	.358	65	171	166	.974	33	481	855	9	35	3.78
Houston	65	97	.401	32	569	711	188	42	97	.237	.340	90	166	130	.974	29	388	931	7	26	3.84
New York	50	112	.309	47	495	752	203	27	107	.221	.327	28	171	153	.974	29	449	776	11	14	4.06
					6558	6558	2122	422	1318	.249	.374	745	1486	1489	.977	416	4730	9649	126	306	3.54

AMERICAN LEAGUE 1965

	POS	Player	AB	BA	HR	RBI	PO	A	E	DP	TC/G	FA	Pitcher	G	IP	W	L	SV	ERA
Minnesota W-102 L-60 Sam Mele	1B	D. Mincher	346	.251	22	65	818	45	7	64	8.8	.992	M. Grant	41	270	21	7	0	3.30
	2B	J. Kindall	342	.196	6	36	242	252	19	62	4.9	.963	J. Kaat	45	264	18	11	2	2.83
	SS	Z. Versalles	666	.273	19	77	248	487	39	105	4.8	.950	J. Perry	36	168	12	7	0	2.63
	3B	R. Rollins	469	.249	5	32	112	229	15	21	3.2	.958	C. Pascual	27	156	9	3	0	3.35
	RF	T. Oliva	576	.321	16	98	284	10	11	3	2.1	.964	D. Boswell	27	106	6	5	0	3.40
	CF	J. Hall	522	.285	20	86	282	7	7	2	2.1	.976	Worthington	62	80	10	7	21	2.13
	LF	B. Allison	438	.233	23	78	231	11	7	4	2.0	.972	J. Merritt	16	77	5	4	2	3.17
	C	E. Battey	394	.297	6	60	652	56	10	10	5.6	.986	Klippstein	56	76	9	3	5	2.24
	13	H. Killebrew	401	.269	25	75	743	113	12	67		.986	D. Stigman	33	70	4	2	4	4.37
	OF	Valdespino	245	.261	1	22	94	4	1	1	1.7	.990	B. Pleis	41	51	4	4	4	2.98
	OF	J. Nossek	170	.218	2	16	64	1	2	1	1.4	.970							
Chicago W-95 L-67 Al Lopez	1B	B. Skowron	559	.274	18	78	1297	74	8	116	9.5	.994	J. Horlen	34	219	13	13	0	2.88
	2B	D. Buford	586	.283	10	47	326	357	13	93	5.0	.981	J. Buzhardt	32	189	13	8	1	3.01
	SS	R. Hansen	587	.235	11	66	287	527	26	97	5.2	.969	T. John	39	184	14	7	3	3.09
	3B	P. Ward	507	.247	10	57	97	319	21	22	3.3	.952	G. Peters	33	176	10	12	0	3.62
	RF	F. Robinson	577	.265	14	66	254	6	4	0	1.7	.985	E. Fisher	82	165	15	7	24	2.40
	CF	K. Berry	472	.218	12	44	331	6	7	1	2.2	.980	B. Howard	30	148	9	8	0	3.47
	LF	D. Cater	514	.270	14	55	174	6	4	2	1.4	.978	H. Wilhelm	66	144	7	7	20	1.81
	C	J. Romano	356	.242	18	48	569	61	5	10	5.7	.992							
	10	T. McCraw	273	.238	5	21	336	24	4	18		.989							
	C	J. Martin	230	.261	2	21	348	41	7	4	3.5	.982							
	PH	S. Burgess	77	.286	2	24													

AMERICAN LEAGUE 1965, *cont.*

Baltimore — W-94 L-68 — Hank Bauer

POS	Player	AB	BA	HR	RBI	PO	A	E	DP	TC/G	FA	Pitcher	G	IP	W	L	SV	ERA
1B	B. Powell	472	.248	17	72	538	52	5	50	7.6	.992	M. Pappas	34	221	13	9	0	2.60
2B	J. Adair	582	.259	7	66	395	446	12	99	5.4	.986	S. Barber	37	221	15	10	0	2.69
SS	L. Aparicio	564	.225	8	40	238	439	20	87	4.9	.971	D. McNally	35	199	11	6	0	2.85
3B	B. Robinson	559	.297	18	80	144	296	15	36	3.2	.967	W. Bunker	34	189	10	8	2	3.38
RF	R. Snyder	345	.270	1	29	188	4	0	0	1.8	1.000	S. Miller	67	119	14	7	24	1.89
CF	P. Blair	364	.234	5	25	241	5	2	0	1.8	.992	R. Roberts	20	115	5	7	0	3.38
LF	C. Blefary	462	.260	22	70	227	10	5	3	1.8	.979	J. Miller	16	93	6	4	0	3.18
C	D. Brown	255	.231	5	30	466	40	9	6	5.6	.983	D. Hall	48	94	11	8	12	3.07
1B	N. Siebern	297	.256	8	32	631	48	6	64	9.0	.991	J. Palmer	27	92	5	4	1	3.72
UT	B. Johnson	273	.242	5	27	310	106	9	29		.979							
OF	J. Brandt	243	.243	8	24	143	6	6	0	1.8	.961							
C	J. Orsino	232	.233	9	28	342	25	5	3	6.0	.987							
OF	S. Bowens	203	.163	7	20	108	3	2	1	1.7	.982							

Detroit — W-89 L-73 — Bob Swift W-24 L-18 — Chuck Dressen W-65 L-55

POS	Player	AB	BA	HR	RBI	PO	A	E	DP	TC/G	FA	Pitcher	G	IP	W	L	SV	ERA
1B	N. Cash	467	.266	30	82	1091	97	9	96	8.6	.992	M. Lolich	43	244	15	9	3	3.44
2B	J. Lumpe	502	.257	4	39	281	308	9	69	4.3	.985	D. McLain	33	220	16	6	1	2.61
SS	McAuliffe	404	.260	15	54	190	286	22	58	4.4	.956	H. Aguirre	32	208	14	10	0	3.59
3B	D. Wert	609	.261	12	54	163	331	12	33	3.1	.976	Wickersham	34	195	9	14	0	3.78
RF	A. Kaline	399	.281	18	72	193	2	3	2	1.8	.985	J. Sparma	30	167	13	8	0	3.18
CF	D. Demeter	389	.278	16	58	158	1	2	1	2.0	.988	L. Sherry	39	78	3	6	5	3.10
LF	W. Horton	512	.273	29	104	249	7	3	1	1.8	.988	T. Fox	42	78	6	4	10	2.78
C	B. Freehan	431	.234	10	43	865	57	4	4	7.2	.996	F. Gladding	46	70	6	2	5	2.83
OF	G. Brown	227	.256	10	43	108	1	3	0	2.0	.973	O. Pena	30	57	4	6	4	2.51
OF	J. Northrup	219	.205	2	16	82	0	2	0	1.6	.976							
SS	R. Oyler	194	.186	5	13	79	156	11	17	4.3	.955							
OF	G. Thomas	169	.213	3	10	87	4	5	0	1.6	.948							

Cleveland — W-87 L-75 — Birdie Tebbetts

POS	Player	AB	BA	HR	RBI	PO	A	E	DP	TC/G	FA	Pitcher	G	IP	W	L	SV	ERA
1B	F. Whitfield	468	.293	26	90	932	80	7	79	8.4	.993	S. McDowell	42	273	17	11	4	2.18
2B	P. Gonzalez	400	.253	5	39	265	287	11	59	5.0	.980	L. Tiant	41	196	11	11	1	3.53
SS	L. Brown	438	.253	8	40	167	262	10	55	4.6	.977	S. Siebert	39	189	16	8	1	2.43
3B	M. Alvis	604	.247	21	61	169	264	19	17	2.9	.958	R. Terry	30	166	11	6	0	3.69
RF	R. Colavito	592	.287	26	108	265	9	0	1	1.7	1.000	L. Stange	41	132	8	4	0	3.34
CF	V. Davalillo	505	.301	5	40	320	5	4	0	2.5	.988	G. Bell	60	104	6	5	17	3.04
LF	L. Wagner	517	.294	28	79	175	3	8	0	1.4	.957	J. Kralick	30	86	5	11	0	4.92
C	J. Azcue	335	.230	2	35	714	53	5	2	7.1	.994	D. McMahon	58	85	3	3	11	3.28
UT	C. Hinton	431	.255	18	54	408	71	13	30		.974							
SS	D. Howser	307	.235	1	6	119	173	7	33	4.1	.977							

New York — W-77 L-85 — Johnny Keane

POS	Player	AB	BA	HR	RBI	PO	A	E	DP	TC/G	FA	Pitcher	G	IP	W	L	SV	ERA
1B	J. Pepitone	531	.247	18	62	1036	71	3	104	9.7	.997	Stottlemyre	37	291	20	9	0	2.63
2B	Richardson	664	.247	6	47	372	403	15	121	5.0	.981	W. Ford	37	244	16	13	1	3.24
SS	T. Kubek	339	.218	5	35	134	237	14	53	4.1	.964	A. Downing	35	212	12	14	0	3.40
3B	C. Boyer	514	.251	18	58	134	354	16	46	3.4	.968	J. Bouton	30	151	4	15	0	4.82
RF	H. Lopez	283	.261	7	39	94	3	6	0	1.4	.942	B. Stafford	22	111	3	8	0	3.56
CF	T. Tresh	602	.279	26	74	283	11	9	1	2.0	.970	P. Ramos	65	92	5	5	19	2.92
LF	M. Mantle	361	.255	19	46	165	3	6	0	1.6	.966	H. Reniff	51	85	3	4	3	3.80
C	E. Howard	391	.233	9	45	614	43	6	6	7.0	.991	P. Mikkelsen	41	82	4	9	1	3.28
SS	P. Linz	285	.207	2	16	126	205	16	29	4.9	.954							
OF	R. Repoz	218	.220	12	28	133	1	1	0	2.0	.993							
1B	R. Barker	205	.254	7	31	398	45	4	41	7.3	.991							
OF	R. Maris	155	.239	8	27	66	1	2	0	1.6	.971							

California — W-75 L-87 — Bill Rigney

POS	Player	AB	BA	HR	RBI	PO	A	E	DP	TC/G	FA	Pitcher	G	IP	W	L	SV	ERA
1B	J. Adcock	349	.241	14	47	789	45	3	68	8.6	.996	F. Newman	36	261	14	16	0	2.93
2B	B. Knoop	465	.269	7	43	331	402	22	89	5.3	.971	D. Chance	36	226	15	10	0	3.15
SS	J. Fregosi	602	.277	15	64	312	481	26	93	5.1	.968	M. Lopez	35	215	14	13	1	2.93
3B	P. Schaal	483	.224	9	45	101	321	13	20	2.8	.970	G. Brunet	41	197	9	11	2	2.56
RF	A. Pearson	360	.278	4	21	166	5	2	1	1.7	.988	B. Lee	69	131	9	7	23	1.92
CF	J. Cardenal	512	.250	11	57	286	12	11	2	2.4	.964	R. May	30	124	4	9	0	3.92
LF	W. Smith	459	.261	14	57	187	10	4	1	1.6	.980							
C	B. Rodgers	411	.209	1	32	682	52	7	7	5.8	.991							
OF	L. Clinton	222	.243	1	8	107	6	2	1	1.6	.983							
1B	V. Power	197	.259	1	20	419	41	2	35	4.3	.996							

Washington — W-70 L-92 — Gil Hodges

POS	Player	AB	BA	HR	RBI	PO	A	E	DP	TC/G	FA	Pitcher	G	IP	W	L	SV	ERA
1B	D. Nen	246	.260	6	31	519	61	4	48	9.0	.993	P. Richert	34	194	15	12	0	2.60
2B	Blasingame	403	.223	1	18	235	248	8	68	4.5	.984	P. Ortega	35	180	12	15	0	5.11
SS	E. Brinkman	444	.185	5	35	292	369	25	76	4.6	.964	B. Narum	46	174	4	12	0	4.46
3B	K. McMullen	555	.263	18	54	155	299	22	29	3.4	.954	McCormick	44	158	8	8	1	3.36
RF	W. Held	332	.247	16	54	175	5	7	2	1.8	.963	B. Daniels	33	116	5	13	1	4.72
CF	D. Lock	418	.215	16	39	278	6	9	3	2.2	.969	S. Ridzik	63	110	6	4	8	4.02
LF	F. Howard	516	.289	21	84	204	5	4	0	1.5	.981	H. Koplitz	33	107	4	7	1	4.05
C	M. Brumley	216	.208	3	15	376	25	4	2	6.1	.990	R. Kline	74	99	7	6	29	2.63
2S	K. Hamlin	362	.273	4	22	185	210	12	45		.971							
OF	W. Kirkland	312	.231	14	54	151	3	2	0	1.7	.987							
OF	J. King	258	.213	14	49	127	7	1	1	1.5	.993							
UT	D. Zimmer	226	.199	2	17	181	81	12	7		.956							
1B	Cunningham	201	.229	3	20	393	24	6	44	7.2	.986							
1B	B. Chance	199	.256	4	14	391	25	5	39	8.8	.988							
C	D. Camilli	193	.192	3	18	319	23	7	2	5.9	.980							

AMERICAN LEAGUE 1965, *cont.*

	POS	Player	AB	BA	HR	RBI	PO	A	E	DP	TC/G	FA	Pitcher	G	IP	W	L	SV	ERA
Boston	1B	L. Thomas	521	.271	22	75	1035	97	18	86	9.1	.984	E. Wilson	36	231	13	14	0	3.98
	2B	F. Mantilla	534	.275	18	92	251	286	13	64	4.5	.976	Monbouquette	35	229	10	18	0	3.70
W-62 L-100	SS	Petrocelli	323	.232	13	33	151	278	19	45	4.8	.958	D. Morehead	34	193	10	18	0	4.06
	3B	F. Malzone	364	.239	3	34	79	170	8	19	2.7	.969	J. Lonborg	32	185	9	17	0	4.47
Billy Herman	RF	Conigliaro	521	.269	32	82	277	11	7	1	2.2	.976	D. Bennett	34	142	5	7	0	4.38
	CF	L. Green	373	.276	7	24	198	2	4	1	2.1	.980	D. Radatz	63	124	9	11	22	3.91
	LF	Yastrzemski	494	.312	20	72	222	11	3	2	1.8	.987							
	C	B. Tillman	368	.215	6	35	676	45	9	6	6.9	.988							
	3B	D. Jones	367	.270	5	37	63	163	17	14	3.0	.930							
	OF	J. Gosger	324	.256	9	35	195	4	5	2	2.5	.975							
	SS	E. Bressoud	296	.226	8	25	147	195	13	45	4.1	.963							
	2B	C. Schilling	171	.240	3	9	90	116	5	22	5.1	.976							
	1B	T. Horton	163	.294	7	23	311	24	7	30	7.8	.980							
Kansas City	1B	K. Harrelson	483	.238	23	66	1044	70	9	93	9.0	.992	F. Talbot	39	198	10	12	0	4.14
	2B	D. Green	474	.232	15	55	252	341	12	73	4.8	.976	R. Sheldon	32	187	10	8	0	3.95
W-59 L-103	SS	Campaneris	578	.270	6	42	187	269	30	50	4.5	.938	O'Donoghue	34	178	9	18	0	3.95
	3B	E. Charles	480	.269	8	56	150	251	12	28	3.2	.971	D. Segui	40	163	5	15	0	4.64
Mel McGaha	RF	Hershberger	494	.231	5	48	238	14	3	7	1.8	.985	C. Hunter	32	133	8	8	0	4.26
W-5 L-21	CF	J. Landis	364	.239	3	36	258	0	4	0	2.4	.985	J. Wyatt	65	89	2	6	18	3.25
	LF	T. Reynolds	270	.237	1	22	154	8	3	2	2.0	.982	D. Mossi	51	55	5	8	7	3.74
Haywood Sullivan	C	B. Bryan	325	.252	14	51	527	44	9	6	6.1	.982	J. Aker	34	51	4	3	3	3.16
W-54 L-82	UT	W. Causey	513	.261	3	34	221	313	15	60		.973							
	OF	J. Tartabull	218	.312	1	19	133	5	2	0	2.6	.986							
	C	R. Lachemann	216	.227	9	29	361	27	8	3	5.3	.980							
	OF	N. Mathews	184	.212	2	15	103	1	2	0	1.9	.981							
	1B	J. Gentile	118	.246	10	22	239	17	5	24	7.5	.981							

BATTING AND BASE RUNNING LEADERS

Batting Average

T. Oliva, MIN	.321
Yastrzemski, BOS	.312
V. Davalillo, CLE	.301
B. Robinson, BAL	.297
L. Wagner, CLE	.294

Slugging Average

Yastrzemski, BOS	.536
Conigliaro, BOS	.512
N. Cash, DET	.512
L. Wagner, CLE	.495
T. Oliva, MIN	.491

Home Runs

Conigliaro, BOS	32
N. Cash, DET	30
W. Horton, DET	29
L. Wagner, CLE	28

PITCHING LEADERS

Winning Percentage

M. Grant, MIN	.750
D. McLain, DET	.727
Stottlemyre, NY	.690
E. Fisher, CHI	.682
S. Siebert, CLE	.667

Earned Run Average

S. McDowell, CLE	2.18
E. Fisher, CHI	2.40
S. Siebert, CLE	2.43
G. Brunet, CAL	2.56
P. Richert, WAS	2.60

Wins

M. Grant, MIN	21
Stottlemyre, NY	20
J. Kaat, MIN	18
S. McDowell, CLE	17

Total Bases

Z. Versalles, MIN	308
T. Tresh, NY	287
T. Oliva, MIN	283
R. Colavito, CLE	277
Conigliaro, BOS	267

Runs Batted In

R. Colavito, CLE	108
W. Horton, DET	104
T. Oliva, MIN	98
F. Mantilla, BOS	92
F. Whitfield, CLE	90

Stolen Bases

Campaneris, KC	51
J. Cardenal, CAL	37
Z. Versalles, MIN	27
V. Davalillo, CLE	26
L. Aparicio, BAL	26

Saves

R. Kline, WAS	29
E. Fisher, CHI	24
S. Miller, BAL	24
B. Lee, CAL	23
D. Radatz, BOS	22

Strikeouts

S. McDowell, CLE	325
M. Lolich, DET	226
D. McLain, DET	192
S. Siebert, CLE	191
A. Downing, NY	179

Complete Games

Stottlemyre, NY	18
S. McDowell, CLE	14
M. Grant, MIN	14
D. McLain, DET	13

Hits

T. Oliva, MIN	185
Z. Versalles, MIN	182
R. Colavito, CLE	170
T. Tresh, NY	168

Base on Balls

R. Colavito, CLE	93
C. Blefary, BAL	88
F. Mantilla, BOS	79
N. Cash, DET	77

Home Run Percentage

N. Cash, DET	6.4
Conigliaro, BOS	6.1
W. Horton, DET	5.7
L. Wagner, CLE	5.4

Fewest Hits/9 Innings

S. McDowell, CLE	5.87
E. Fisher, CHI	6.42
S. Siebert, CLE	6.63
P. Richert, WAS	6.77

Shutouts

M. Grant, MIN	6
D. McLain, DET	4
D. Chance, CAL	4
J. Horlen, CHI	4

Fewest Walks/9 Innings

R. Terry, CLE	1.25
Monbouquette, BOS	1.57
J. Horlen, CHI	1.60
W. Ford, NY	1.84

Runs Scored

Z. Versalles, MIN	126
T. Oliva, MIN	107
T. Tresh, NY	94
D. Buford, CHI	93

Doubles

Yastrzemski, BOS	45
Z. Versalles, MIN	45
T. Oliva, MIN	40
T. Tresh, NY	29

Triples

Campaneris, KC	12
Z. Versalles, MIN	12
L. Aparicio, BAL	10
W. Smith, CAL	9

Most Strikeouts/9 Inn.

S. McDowell, CLE	10.71
S. Siebert, CLE	9.11
M. Lolich, DET	8.35
D. McLain, DET	7.84

Innings

Stottlemyre, NY	291
S. McDowell, CLE	273
M. Grant, MIN	270
J. Kaat, MIN	264

Games Pitched

E. Fisher, CHI	82
R. Kline, WAS	74
B. Lee, CAL	69
J. Dickson, KC	68

	W	L	PCT	GB	R	OR	2B	3B	Batting HR	BA	SA	SB	Fielding E	DP	FA	Pitching CG	BB	SO	ShO	SV	ERA
Minnesota	102	60	.630		774	600	257	42	150	.254	.399	92	172	158	.973	32	503	934	12	45	3.14
Chicago	95	67	.586	7	647	555	200	38	125	.246	.364	50	127	156	.980	21	460	946	14	53	2.99
Baltimore	94	68	.580	8	641	578	227	38	125	.238	.363	67	126	152	.980	32	510	939	15	41	2.98
Detroit	89	73	.549	13	680	602	190	27	162	.238	.374	57	116	126	.981	45	509	1069	14	31	3.35
Cleveland	87	75	.537	15	663	613	198	21	156	.250	.379	109	114	127	.981	41	500	1156	13	41	3.30
New York	77	85	.475	25	611	604	196	31	149	.235	.364	35	137	166	.978	41	511	1001	11	31	3.28
California	75	87	.463	27	527	569	200	36	92	.239	.341	107	123	149	.981	39	563	847	14	33	3.17
Washington	70	92	.432	32	591	721	179	33	136	.228	.350	30	143	149	.976	21	633	867	8	40	3.93
Boston	62	100	.383	40	669	791	244	40	165	.251	.400	47	162	129	.974	33	543	993	9	25	4.24
Kansas City	59	103	.364	43	585	755	186	59	110	.240	.358	110	139	142	.977	18	574	882	7	32	4.24
					6388	6388	2077	365	1370	.242	.369	704	1359	1453	.978	323	5306	9634	117	372	3.46

NATIONAL LEAGUE 1966

Los Angeles — W-95 L-67 — Walter Alston

POS	Player	AB	BA	HR	RBI	PO	A	E	DP	TC/G	FA	Pitcher	G	IP	W	L	SV	ERA
1B	W. Parker	475	.253	12	51	1118	70	9	74	8.6	.992	S. Koufax	41	323	27	9	0	1.73
2B	J. Lefebvre	544	.274	24	74	246	332	12	59	5.0	.980	D. Drysdale	40	274	13	16	0	3.42
SS	M. Wills	594	.273	1	39	227	453	23	79	5.1	.967	C. Osteen	39	240	17	14	0	2.85
3B	J. Kennedy	274	.201	3	24	39	127	6	10	2.0	.965	D. Sutton	37	226	12	12	0	2.99
RF	R. Fairly	351	.288	14	61	110	2	3	0	1.2	.974	P. Regan	65	117	14	1	21	1.62
CF	W. Davis	624	.284	11	61	347	9	11	0	2.4	.970	B. Miller	46	84	4	2	5	2.77
LF	L. Johnson	526	.272	17	73	249	8	4	2	1.8	.985	Perranoski	55	82	6	7	7	3.18
C	J. Roseboro	445	.276	9	53	904	65	7	11	7.1	.993							
OF	T. Davis	313	.313	3	27	98	5	3	1	1.3	.972							
3B	J. Gilliam	235	.217	1	16	40	103	7	8	2.1	.953							
OF	A. Ferrara	115	.270	5	23	43	0	2	0	1.4	.956							

San Francisco — W-93 L-68 — Herman Franks

POS	Player	AB	BA	HR	RBI	PO	A	E	DP	TC/G	FA	Pitcher	G	IP	W	L	SV	ERA
1B	W. McCovey	502	.295	36	96	1287	81	22	91	9.6	.984	J. Marichal	37	307	25	6	0	2.23
2B	H. Lanier	459	.231	3	37	254	313	5	66	5.1	.991	G. Perry	36	256	21	8	0	2.99
SS	T. Fuentes	541	.261	9	40	145	233	17	44	5.2	.957	B. Bolin	36	224	11	10	1	2.89
3B	J. Hart	578	.285	33	93	100	282	24	24	2.9	.941	R. Herbel	32	130	4	5	1	4.16
RF	O. Brown	348	.233	7	33	163	12	4	1	1.6	.978	L. McDaniel	64	122	10	5	6	2.66
CF	W. Mays	552	.288	37	103	370	8	7	2	2.6	.982	R. Sadecki	26	105	3	7	0	5.40
LF	J. Alou	370	.259	1	20	141	4	5	1	1.5	.967	F. Linzy	51	100	7	11	16	2.96
C	T. Haller	471	.240	27	67	797	57	8	5	6.3	.991	B. Priddy	38	91	6	3	1	3.96
UT	J. Davenport	305	.249	9	30	107	201	14	27		.957	J. Gibbon	37	81	4	6	1	3.67
OF	Gabrielson	240	.217	4	16	72	1	4	0	1.1	.948							
OF	C. Peterson	190	.237	2	19	62	2	0	1	1.3	1.000							

Pittsburgh — W-92 L-70 — Harry Walker

POS	Player	AB	BA	HR	RBI	PO	A	E	DP	TC/G	FA	Pitcher	G	IP	W	L	SV	ERA
1B	D. Clendenon	571	.299	28	98	1452	96	24	182	10.3	.985	B. Veale	38	268	16	12	0	3.02
2B	B. Mazeroski	621	.262	16	82	411	538	8	161	5.9	.992	W. Fryman	36	182	12	9	1	3.81
SS	G. Alley	579	.299	7	43	235	472	15	128	5.0	.979	V. Law	31	178	12	8	0	4.05
3B	B. Bailey	380	.279	13	46	57	201	12	20	2.8	.956	S. Blass	34	156	11	7	0	3.87
RF	R. Clemente	638	.317	29	119	318	17	12	3	2.3	.965	T. Sisk	34	150	10	5	1	4.14
CF	M. Alou	535	.342	2	27	264	11	8	3	2.1	.972	P. Mikkelsen	71	126	9	8	14	3.07
LF	W. Stargell	485	.315	33	102	180	9	11	0	1.6	.945	D. Cardwell	32	102	6	6	1	4.60
C	Pagliaroni	374	.235	11	49	613	37	2	6	5.5	.997	A. McBean	47	87	4	3	3	3.22
3B	J. Pagan	368	.264	4	54	57	166	12	18	2.8	.949	R. Face	54	70	6	6	18	2.70
OF	M. Mota	322	.332	5	46	150	3	1	0	1.6	.994							

Philadelphia — W-87 L-75 — Gene Mauch

POS	Player	AB	BA	HR	RBI	PO	A	E	DP	TC/G	FA	Pitcher	G	IP	W	L	SV	ERA
1B	B. White	577	.276	22	103	1422	109	9	118	9.7	.994	J. Bunning	43	314	19	14	1	2.41
2B	C. Rojas	626	.268	6	55	218	288	9	68	4.9	.983	C. Short	42	272	20	10	0	3.54
SS	D. Groat	584	.260	2	53	260	454	19	79	5.3	.974	L. Jackson	35	247	15	13	0	2.99
3B	D. Allen	524	.317	40	110	81	180	9	15	3.0	.967	B. Buhl	32	132	6	8	1	4.77
RF	J. Callison	612	.276	11	55	275	12	3	2	1.9	.990	R. Culp	34	111	7	4	1	5.04
CF	J. Briggs	255	.282	10	23	126	3	3	0	1.9	.977	D. Knowles	69	100	6	5	13	3.05
LF	T. Gonzalez	384	.286	6	40	206	7	3	1	1.6	.986	R. Wise	22	99	5	6	0	3.71
C	C. Dalrymple	331	.245	4	39	615	48	5	5	6.1	.993							
23	T. Taylor	434	.242	5	40	187	281	9	45		.981							
C	B. Uecker	207	.208	7	30	368	33	6	7	5.4	.985							
OF	J. Brandt	164	.250	1	15	78	3	1	0	1.2	.988							

Atlanta — W-85 L-77 — Bobby Bragan W-52 L-59 — Billy Hitchcock W-33 L-18

POS	Player	AB	BA	HR	RBI	PO	A	E	DP	TC/G	FA	Pitcher	G	IP	W	L	SV	ERA
1B	F. Alou	666	.327	31	74	769	53	10	63	9.2	.988	T. Cloninger	39	258	14	11	1	4.12
2B	W. Woodward	455	.264	0	43	154	208	10	46	4.7	.973	K. Johnson	32	216	14	8	0	3.30
SS	D. Menke	454	.251	15	60	165	282	21	50	4.4	.955	D. Lemaster	27	171	11	8	0	3.74
3B	E. Mathews	452	.250	16	53	114	237	20	31	2.9	.946	C. Carroll	73	144	8	7	11	2.37
RF	H. Aaron	603	.279	44	127	315	12	4	5	2.1	.988	D. Kelley	20	81	7	5	0	3.22
CF	M. Jones	417	.264	23	66	251	1	5	0	2.3	.981	Blasingame	16	68	3	7	0	5.32
LF	R. Carty	521	.326	15	76	226	8	7	0	1.9	.971	C. Olivo	47	66	5	4	7	4.23
C	J. Torre	546	.315	36	101	607	67	11	9	6.0	.984	T. Abernathy	38	65	4	3	4	3.86
2B	F. Bolling	227	.211	1	18	134	150	5	35	4.3	.983	B. O'Dell	24	41	2	3	6	2.40
C	G. Oliver	191	.194	8	24	286	22	3	3	6.5	.990							
P	T. Cloninger	111	.234	5	23	14	43	8	1	1.7	.877							

St. Louis — W-83 L-79 — Red Schoendienst

POS	Player	AB	BA	HR	RBI	PO	A	E	DP	TC/G	FA	Pitcher	G	IP	W	L	SV	ERA
1B	O. Cepeda	452	.303	17	58	1109	62	13	111	9.9	.989	B. Gibson	35	280	21	12	0	2.44
2B	J. Javier	460	.228	7	31	306	364	13	89	4.7	.981	A. Jackson	36	233	13	15	0	2.51
SS	D. Maxvill	394	.244	0	24	219	428	22	88	5.2	.967	R. Washburn	27	170	11	9	0	3.76
3B	C. Smith	391	.266	10	43	84	213	11	26	2.9	.964	N. Briles	49	154	4	15	6	3.21
RF	M. Shannon	459	.288	16	64	247	10	4	4	2.1	.985	L. Jaster	26	152	11	5	0	3.26
CF	C. Flood	626	.267	10	78	391	5	0	1	2.5	1.000	J. Hoerner	57	76	5	1	13	1.54
LF	L. Brock	643	.285	15	46	269	9	19	1	1.9	.936							
C	T. McCarver	543	.274	12	68	841	62	7	7	6.1	.992							
2S	J. Buchek	284	.236	4	25	148	220	18	52		.953							
3B	P. Gagliano	213	.254	2	15	30	77	2	7	2.7	.982							

NATIONAL LEAGUE 1966, cont.

	POS	Player	AB	BA	HR	RBI	PO	A	E	DP	TC/G	FA	Pitcher	G	IP	W	L	SV	ERA
Cincinnati W-76 L-84 Don Heffner W-37 L-46 Dave Bristol W-39 L-38	1B	T. Perez	257	.265	4	39	530	23	6	46	7.5	.989	J. Maloney	32	225	16	8	0	2.80
	2B	P. Rose	654	.313	16	70	385	344	14	79	5.3	.981	S. Ellis	41	221	12	19	0	5.29
	SS	L. Cardenas	568	.255	20	81	279	446	15	87	4.6	.980	M. Pappas	33	210	12	11	0	4.29
	3B	T. Helms	542	.284	9	49	110	208	13	16	2.9	.961	J. O'Toole	25	142	5	7	0	3.55
	RF	T. Harper	553	.278	5	31	257	5	1	2	1.8	.996	J. Nuxhall	35	130	6	8	0	4.50
	CF	V. Pinson	618	.288	16	76	344	9	13	4	2.4	.964	D. Nottebart	59	111	5	4	11	3.07
	LF	D. Johnson	505	.257	24	81	141	4	3	1	1.4	.980	B. McCool	57	105	8	8	18	2.48
	C	J. Edwards	282	.191	6	39	617	40	5	3	6.8	.992	T. Davidson	54	85	5	4	4	3.90
	C	D. Pavletich	235	.294	12	38	323	30	9	2	6.6	.975							
	OF	A. Shamsky	234	.231	21	47	104	3	3	1	1.5	.973							
	1B	G. Coleman	227	.251	5	37	399	29	6	33	6.7	.986							
Houston W-72 L-90 Grady Hatton	1B	C. Harrison	434	.256	9	52	974	78	8	68	9.3	.992	M. Cuellar	38	227	12	10	2	2.22
	2B	J. Morgan	425	.285	5	42	256	316	21	61	5.1	.965	D. Giusti	34	210	15	14	0	4.20
	SS	S. Jackson	596	.292	3	25	270	449	37	73	5.0	.951	L. Dierker	29	187	10	8	0	3.18
	3B	Aspromonte	560	.252	8	52	149	261	16	18	2.9	.962	D. Farrell	32	153	6	10	2	4.60
	RF	R. Staub	554	.280	13	81	289	13	12	2	2.1	.962	B. Bruce	25	130	3	13	0	5.34
	CF	J. Wynn	418	.256	18	62	259	6	6	4	2.6	.978	B. Latman	31	103	2	7	1	2.71
	LF	L. Maye	358	.288	9	36	145	4	8	0	1.6	.949	C. Raymond	62	92	7	5	16	3.13
	C	J. Bateman	433	.279	17	70	731	63	15	14	6.7	.981	J. Owens	40	50	4	7	2	4.68
	OF	D. Nicholson	280	.246	10	31	139	11	5	0	1.7	.968							
	OF	R. Davis	194	.247	2	19	98	9	2	1	2.3	.982							
	UT	B. Lillis	164	.232	0	11	99	109	10	24		.954							
	UT	F. Mantilla	151	.219	6	22	124	46	4	11		.977							
New York W-66 L-95 Wes Westrum	1B	E. Kranepool	464	.254	16	57	1161	85	10	100	9.5	.992	J. Fisher	38	230	11	14	0	3.68
	2B	R. Hunt	479	.288	3	33	295	384	21	81	5.7	.970	D. Ribant	39	188	11	9	3	3.20
	SS	E. Bressoud	405	.225	10	49	135	252	16	52	4.3	.960	B. Shaw	26	168	11	10	0	3.92
	3B	K. Boyer	496	.266	14	61	113	292	21	33	3.3	.951	J. Hamilton	57	149	6	13	13	3.93
	RF	A. Luplow	334	.251	7	31	147	4	2	1	1.5	.987	R. Gardner	41	134	4	8	1	5.12
	CF	C. Jones	495	.275	8	57	275	10	6	2	2.3	.979	B. Friend	22	86	5	8	1	4.40
	LF	R. Swoboda	342	.222	8	50	145	7	2	0	1.6	.987	D. Selma	30	81	4	6	1	4.24
	C	J. Grote	317	.237	3	31	516	55	11	7	5.1	.981	T. McGraw	15	62	2	9	0	5.34
	UT	C. Hiller	254	.280	2	14	110	153	5	32		.981							
	SS	R. McMillan	220	.214	1	12	112	203	8	35	4.5	.975							
	OF	L. Elliot	199	.246	5	32	73	10	8	0	1.7	.912							
	OF	J. Lewis	166	.193	5	20	77	2	1	1	1.6	.988							
Chicago W-59 L-103 Leo Durocher	1B	E. Banks	511	.272	15	75	1178	81	10	88	9.8	.992	D. Ellsworth	38	269	8	22	0	3.98
	2B	G. Beckert	656	.287	1	59	373	402	24	89	5.3	.970	K. Holtzman	34	221	11	16	0	3.79
	SS	D. Kessinger	533	.274	1	43	202	474	35	68	4.8	.951	F. Jenkins	60	182	6	8	5	3.31
	3B	R. Santo	561	.312	30	94	150	391	25	36	3.7	.956	B. Hands	41	159	8	13	2	4.58
	RF	B. Williams	648	.276	29	91	319	9	8	3	2.1	.976	C. Koonce	45	109	5	5	2	3.81
	CF	A. Phillips	416	.262	16	36	258	14	6	2	2.5	.978	B. Hendley	43	90	4	5	7	3.91
	LF	B. Browne	419	.243	16	51	200	3	7	0	1.8	.967	C. Simmons	19	77	4	7	0	4.07
	C	R. Hundley	526	.236	19	63	871	85	14	8	6.5	.986							
	O1	Boccabella	206	.228	6	25	230	18	1	13		.996							
	OF	G. Altman	185	.222	5	17	42	4	2	0	1.1	.958							

BATTING AND BASE RUNNING LEADERS

Batting Average
M. Alou, PIT — .342
F. Alou, ATL — .327
R. Carty, ATL — .326
D. Allen, PHI — .317
R. Clemente, PIT — .317

Total Bases
F. Alou, ATL — 355
R. Clemente, PIT — 342
D. Allen, PHI — 331
H. Aaron, ATL — 325
W. Mays, SF — 307

Hits
F. Alou, ATL — 218
P. Rose, CIN — 205
R. Clemente, PIT — 202
G. Beckert, CHI — 188

Runs Scored
F. Alou, ATL — 122
H. Aaron, ATL — 117
D. Allen, PHI — 112
R. Clemente, PIT — 105

Slugging Average
D. Allen, PHI — .632
W. McCovey, SF — .586
W. Stargell, PIT — .581
J. Torre, ATL — .560
W. Mays, SF — .556

Runs Batted In
H. Aaron, ATL — 127
R. Clemente, PIT — 119
D. Allen, PHI — 110
W. Mays, SF — 103
B. White, PHI — 103

Base on Balls
R. Santo, CHI — 95
J. Morgan, HOU — 89
W. McCovey, SF — 76
H. Aaron, ATL — 76

Doubles
J. Callison, PHI — 40
P. Rose, CIN — 38
V. Pinson, CIN — 35
F. Alou, ATL — 32

Home Runs
H. Aaron, ATL — 44
D. Allen, PHI — 40
W. Mays, SF — 37
W. McCovey, SF — 36
J. Torre, ATL — 36

Stolen Bases
L. Brock, STL — 74
S. Jackson, HOU — 49
M. Wills, LA — 38
A. Phillips, CHI, PHI — 32
T. Harper, CIN — 29

Home Run Percentage
D. Allen, PHI — 7.6
H. Aaron, ATL — 7.3
W. McCovey, SF — 7.2
W. Stargell, PIT — 6.8

Triples
T. McCarver, STL — 13
L. Brock, STL — 12
R. Clemente, PIT — 11
D. Allen, PHI — 10

Winning Percentage
J. Marichal, SF — .806
S. Koufax, LA — .750
G. Perry, SF — .724
C. Short, PHI — .667
J. Maloney, CIN — .667

Saves
P. Regan, LA — 21
B. McCool, CIN — 18
R. Face, PIT — 18
F. Linzy, SF — 16
C. Raymond, HOU — 16

Fewest Hits/9 Innings
J. Marichal, SF — 6.68
S. Koufax, LA — 6.72
B. Gibson, STL — 6.74
J. Maloney, CIN — 6.97

Most Strikeouts/9 Inn.
S. Koufax, LA — 8.83
J. Maloney, CIN — 8.65
D. Sutton, LA — 8.34
B. Veale, PIT — 7.68

PITCHING LEADERS

Earned Run Average
S. Koufax, LA — 1.73
M. Cuellar, HOU — 2.22
J. Marichal, SF — 2.23
J. Bunning, PHI — 2.41
B. Gibson, STL — 2.44

Strikeouts
S. Koufax, LA — 317
J. Bunning, PHI — 252
B. Veale, PIT — 229
B. Gibson, STL — 225
J. Marichal, SF — 222

Shutouts
5 tied with — 5

Innings
S. Koufax, LA — 323
J. Bunning, PHI — 314
J. Marichal, SF — 307
B. Gibson, STL — 280

Wins
S. Koufax, LA — 27
J. Marichal, SF — 25
G. Perry, SF — 21
B. Gibson, STL — 21
C. Short, PHI — 20

Complete Games
S. Koufax, LA — 27
J. Marichal, SF — 25
B. Gibson, STL — 20
C. Short, PHI — 19
J. Bunning, PHI — 16

Fewest Walks/9 Innings
J. Marichal, SF — 1.05
V. Law, PIT — 1.22
G. Perry, SF — 1.41
D. Drysdale, LA — 1.48

Games Pitched
C. Carroll, ATL — 73
P. Mikkelsen, PIT — 71
D. Knowles, PHI — 69
P. Regan, LA — 65

NATIONAL LEAGUE 1966, *cont.*

	W	L	PCT	GB	R	OR	2B	3B	HR	BA	SA	SB	E	DP	FA	CG	BB	SO	ShO	SV	ERA
							Batting						**Fielding**			**Pitching**					
Los Angeles	95	67	.586		606	490	201	27	108	.256	.362	94	133	128	.979	**52**	356	1084	**20**	35	2.62
San Francisco	93	68	.578	1.5	675	626	195	31	181	.248	.392	29	168	131	.974	52	359	973	14	27	3.24
Pittsburgh	92	70	.568	3	759	641	**238**	**66**	158	**.279**	**.428**	64	141	**215**	.978	35	463	898	12	**43**	3.52
Philadelphia	87	75	.537	8	696	640	224	49	117	.258	.378	56	**113**	147	**.982**	52	412	928	15	23	3.57
Atlanta	85	77	.525	10	**782**	683	220	32	**207**	.263	.424	59	154	139	.976	37	485	884	10	36	3.68
St. Louis	83	79	.512	12	571	577	196	61	108	.251	.368	**144**	145	166	.977	47	448	892	19	32	3.11
Cincinnati	76	84	.475	18	692	702	232	33	149	.260	.395	70	122	133	.980	28	490	1043	10	35	4.08
Houston	72	90	.444	23	612	695	203	35	112	.255	.365	90	174	126	.972	34	391	929	13	26	3.76
New York	66	95	.410	28.5	587	761	187	35	98	.239	.342	55	159	171	.975	37	521	773	9	22	4.17
Chicago	59	103	.364	36	644	809	203	43	140	.254	.380	76	166	132	.974	28	479	908	6	24	4.33
					6624	6624	2099	412	1378	.256	.384	737	1475	1488	.977	402	4404	9312	128	303	3.61

AMERICAN LEAGUE 1966

Baltimore — W-97 L-63 — Hank Bauer

POS	Player	AB	BA	HR	RBI	PO	A	E	DP	TC/G	FA	Pitcher	G	IP	W	L	SV	ERA
1B	B. Powell	491	.287	34	109	1094	68	13	96	8.6	.989	D. McNally	34	213	13	6	0	3.17
2B	D. Johnson	501	.257	7	56	288	347	**19**	75	5.2	.971	J. Palmer	30	208	15	10	0	3.46
SS	L. Aparicio	**659**	.276	6	41	**303**	441	17	104	5.0	**.978**	E. Watt	43	146	9	7	4	3.83
3B	B. Robinson	620	.269	23	100	174	**313**	12	26	3.2	.976	W. Bunker	29	143	10	6	0	4.29
RF	F. Robinson	576	**.316**	**49**	**122**	254	4	4	0	1.7	.985	S. Barber	25	133	10	5	0	2.30
CF	P. Blair	303	.277	6	33	204	4	2	2	1.7	.990	J. Miller	23	101	4	8	0	4.74
LF	R. Snyder	373	.306	3	41	209	6	3	2	2.1	.986	M. Drabowsky	44	96	6	0	7	2.81
C	Etchebarren	412	.221	11	50	799	65	10	7	7.2	.989	S. Miller	51	92	9	4	18	2.25
OF	C. Blefary	419	.255	23	64	159	5	4	0	1.5	.976	E. Fisher	44*	72	5	3	13	2.64
OF	S. Bowens	243	.210	6	20	114	7	5	2	1.9	.960	D. Hall	32	66	6	2	7	3.95

Minnesota — W-89 L-73 — Sam Mele

POS	Player	AB	BA	HR	RBI	PO	A	E	DP	TC/G	FA	Pitcher	G	IP	W	L	SV	ERA
1B	D. Mincher	431	.251	14	62	995	85	9	62	8.4	.992	J. Kaat	41	**305**	**25**	13	0	2.75
2B	B. Allen	319	.238	5	30	191	214	11	46	4.7	.974	M. Grant	35	249	13	13	0	3.25
SS	Z. Versalles	543	.249	7	36	195	377	**35**	69	4.5	.942	J. Perry	33	184	11	7	0	2.54
3B	H. Killebrew	569	.281	39	110	83	190	14	11	2.7	.951	D. Boswell	28	169	12	5	0	3.14
RF	T. Oliva	622	.307	25	87	335	9	**10**	3	2.2	.972	J. Merritt	31	144	7	14	3	3.38
CF	T. Uhlaender	367	.226	2	22	258	4	4	2	2.7	.985	C. Pascual	21	103	8	6	0	4.89
LF	J. Hall	356	.239	20	47	175	6	4	1	1.8	.978	Worthington	65	91	6	3	16	2.46
C	E. Battey	364	.255	4	34	705	45	4	9	6.7	.995	P. Cimino	35	65	2	5	4	2.92
UT	C. Tovar	465	.260	2	41	254	274	14	44		.974							
3B	R. Rollins	269	.245	10	40	54	107	8	13	2.6	.953							
OF	B. Allison	168	.220	8	19	86	3	3	0	1.6	.967							

Detroit — W-88 L-74 — Chuck Dressen (W-16 L-10), Bob Swift (W-32 L-25), Frank Skaff (W-40 L-39)

POS	Player	AB	BA	HR	RBI	PO	A	E	DP	TC/G	FA	Pitcher	G	IP	W	L	SV	ERA
1B	N. Cash	603	.279	32	93	1271	114	**17**	118	8.9	.988	D. McLain	38	264	20	14	0	3.92
2B	J. Lumpe	385	.231	1	26	202	223	4	51	4.5	.991	M. Lolich	40	204	14	14	3	4.77
SS	McAuliffe	430	.274	23	56	160	292	17	49	4.5	.964	E. Wilson	23	163	13	6	0	2.59
3B	D. Wert	559	.268	11	70	128	253	11	20	2.6	.972	Wickersham	38	141	8	3	1	3.20
RF	J. Northrup	419	.265	16	58	241	8	5	1	2.2	.980	O. Pena	54	108	4	2	7	3.08
CF	A. Kaline	479	.288	29	88	279	7	2	1	2.1	**.993**	J. Podres	36	108	4	5	3	3.43
LF	W. Horton	526	.262	27	100	233	4	5	1	1.8	.979	H. Aguirre	30	104	3	9	0	3.82
C	B. Freehan	492	.234	12	46	898	56	4	11	7.3	**.996**	Monbouquette	30	103	7	8	0	4.73
OF	M. Stanley	235	.289	3	19	163	6	0	2	2.1	1.000	L. Sherry	55	78	8	5	20	3.82
2B	J. Wood	230	.252	2	27	109	100	7	25	4.2	.968							
SS	R. Oyler	210	.171	1	9	107	194	11	42	4.5	.965							
OF	G. Brown	169	.266	7	27	46	4	1	1	1.2	.980							

Chicago — W-83 L-79 — Eddie Stanky

POS	Player	AB	BA	HR	RBI	PO	A	E	DP	TC/G	FA	Pitcher	G	IP	W	L	SV	ERA
1B	T. McCraw	389	.229	5	48	843	67	9	56	7.6	.990	T. John	34	223	14	11	0	2.62
2B	A. Weis	187	.155	0	9	130	173	4	44	3.2	.987	J. Horlen	37	211	10	13	1	2.43
SS	L. Elia	195	.205	3	22	103	186	14	39	4.0	.954	G. Peters	30	205	12	10	0	**1.98**
3B	D. Buford	607	.244	8	52	98	301	**26**	24	3.2	.939	J. Buzhardt	33	150	6	11	1	3.83
RF	F. Robinson	342	.237	5	35	148	2	6	0	1.4	.962	B. Howard	27	149	9	5	0	2.30
CF	T. Agee	629	.273	22	86	376	12	7	7	2.5	.982	J. Lamabe	34	121	7	9	0	3.93
LF	K. Berry	443	.271	8	34	208	10	2	1	1.6	.991	B. Locker	56	95	9	8	12	2.46
C	J. Romano	329	.231	15	47	622	46	4	7	6.6	.994	J. Pizarro	34	89	8	6	3	3.76
S2	J. Adair	370	.243	4	36	198	328	12	54		.978	H. Wilhelm	46	81	5	2	6	1.66
1B	B. Skowron	337	.249	6	29	722	60	7	75	8.1	.991	E. Fisher	23*	35	1	3	6	2.29
OF	P. Ward	251	.219	3	28	83	3	1	1	1.5	.989							
2B	W. Causey	164	.244	0	13	86	110	4	15	3.3	.980							
C	J. Martin	157	.255	2	20	243	23	4	3	4.3	.982							

Cleveland — W-81 L-81 — Birdie Tebbetts (W-66 L-57), George Strickland (W-15 L-24)

POS	Player	AB	BA	HR	RBI	PO	A	E	DP	TC/G	FA	Pitcher	G	IP	W	L	SV	ERA
1B	F. Whitfield	502	.241	27	78	1104	76	11	96	9.0	.991	G. Bell	40	254	14	15	0	3.22
2B	P. Gonzalez	352	.233	2	17	237	257	8	62	4.8	.984	S. Siebert	34	241	16	8	1	2.80
SS	L. Brown	340	.229	3	17	131	238	15	45	4.3	.961	S. McDowell	35	194	9	8	3	2.87
3B	M. Alvis	596	.245	17	55	**180**	280	20	24	3.1	.958	S. Hargan	38	192	13	10	0	2.48
RF	R. Colavito	533	.238	30	72	261	10	5	0	1.9	.982	L. Tiant	46	155	12	11	8	2.79
CF	V. Davalillo	344	.250	3	19	208	6	3	1	2.0	.986	O'Donoghue	32	108	6	8	0	3.83
LF	L. Wagner	549	.279	23	66	185	4	2	1	1.4	.990	T. Kelley	31	95	4	8	0	4.34
C	J. Azcue	302	.275	9	37	588	40	7	3	6.5	.989	D. Radatz	39	57	0	3	10	4.61
UT	C. Salmon	422	.256	7	40	315	225	19	53		.966							
OF	C. Hinton	348	.256	12	50	176	6	5	1	1.8	.973							

AMERICAN LEAGUE 1966, *cont.*

	POS	Player	AB	BA	HR	RBI	PO	A	E	DP	TC/G	FA	Pitcher	G	IP	W	L	SV	ERA
California W-80 L-82 Bill Rigney	1B	N. Siebern	336	.247	5	41	1014	65	7	96	11.0	.994	D. Chance	41	260	12	17	1	3.08
	2B	B. Knoop	590	.232	17	72	381	488	17	135	5.5	.981	G. Brunet	41	212	13	13	0	3.31
	SS	J. Fregosi	611	.252	13	67	297	531	35	125	5.3	.959	M. Lopez	37	199	7	14	1	3.93
	3B	P. Schaal	386	.244	6	24	97	249	19	21	2.8	.948	J. Sanford	50	108	13	7	5	3.83
	RF	Kirkpatrick	312	.192	9	44	151	4	1	1	1.5	.994	F. Newman	21	103	4	7	0	4.73
	CF	J. Cardenal	561	.276	16	48	351	10	3	4	2.5	.992	B. Lee	61	102	5	4	16	2.74
	LF	R. Reichardt	319	.288	16	44	153	8	4	1	1.9	.976	C. Wright	20	91	4	7	0	3.74
	C	B. Rodgers	454	.236	7	48	662	69	6	7	5.5	.992	M. Rojas	47	84	7	4	10	2.88
	OF	J. Johnstone	254	.264	3	17	114	2	3	1	2.0	.975	L. Burdette	54	80	7	2	5	3.39
	1B	J. Adcock	231	.273	18	48	565	39	2	60	8.5	.997							
	UT	T. Satriano	226	.239	0	24	283	58	6	13		.983							
	OF	W. Smith	195	.185	1	20	71	4	2	1	1.5	.974							
Kansas City W-74 L-86 Alvin Dark	1B	K. Harrelson	210	.224	5	22	485	48	8	42	9.3	.985	L. Krausse	36	178	14	9	3	2.99
	2B	D. Green	507	.250	9	62	300	389	15	86	5.1	.979	C. Hunter	30	177	9	11	0	4.02
	SS	Campaneris	573	.267	5	42	283	350	19	80	4.7	.971	J. Nash	18	127	12	1	1	2.06
	3B	E. Charles	385	.286	9	42	85	201	11	21	2.9	.963	P. Lindblad	38	121	5	10	1	4.17
	RF	Hershberger	538	.253	2	57	285	14	7	3	2.1	.977	J. Aker	66	113	8	4	32	1.99
	CF	J. Gosger	272	.224	5	27	158	3	1	0	2.1	.994	B. Odom	14	90	5	5	0	2.49
	LF	L. Stahl	312	.250	5	34	142	6	3	1	1.6	.980	C. Dobson	14	84	4	6	0	4.09
	C	P. Roof	369	.209	7	44	680	52	11	7	6.0	.985	R. Sheldon	14	69	4	7	0	3.13
	UT	D. Cater	425	.292	7	52	545	104	9	55		.986							
	O1	R. Repoz	319	.216	11	34	445	22	5	27		.989							
	OF	J. Nossek	230	.261	1	27	161	8	3	1	2.2	.983							
	UT	O. Chavarria	191	.241	2	10	105	86	7	23		.965							
Washington W-71 L-88 Gil Hodges	1B	D. Nen	235	.213	6	30	566	38	6	44	8.0	.990	P. Richert	36	246	14	14	0	3.37
	2B	B. Saverine	406	.251	5	24	149	169	9	35	4.7	.972	McCormick	41	216	11	14	0	3.46
	SS	E. Brinkman	582	.229	7	48	263	501	28	83	5.0	.965	P. Ortega	33	197	12	12	0	3.92
	3B	K. McMullen	524	.233	13	54	125	280	21	26	3.0	.951	J. Hannan	30	114	3	9	0	4.26
	RF	F. Valentine	508	.276	16	59	290	6	6	2	2.2	.980	C. Cox	66	113	4	5	7	3.50
	CF	D. Lock	386	.233	16	48	295	8	7	1	2.4	.977	B. Humphreys	58	112	7	3	3	2.82
	LF	D. Howard	493	.278	18	71	216	5	4	1	1.7	.982	R. Kline	63	90	6	4	23	2.39
	C	P. Casanova	429	.254	13	44	674	53	14	12	6.2	.981	D. Segui	21	72	3	7	0	5.00
	OF	J. King	310	.248	10	30	147	4	2	0	1.8	.987							
	1B	K. Harrelson	250	.248	7	28	641	38	6	53	9.8	.991							
	2B	Blasingame	200	.215	1	11	119	132	4	32	4.4	.984							
	OF	W. Kirkland	163	.190	6	17	56	3	1	0	.9	.983							
Boston W-72 L-90 Billy Herman W-64 L-82 Pete Runnels W-8 L-8	1B	G. Scott	601	.245	27	90	1362	112	14	130	9.4	.991	J. Lonborg	45	182	10	10	2	3.86
	2B	G. Smith	403	.213	8	37	239	287	17	76	5.0	.969	J. Santiago	35	172	12	13	2	3.66
	SS	Petrocelli	522	.238	18	59	206	381	28	69	4.8	.954	D. Brandon	40	158	8	8	2	3.31
	3B	J. Foy	554	.262	15	63	150	279	21	28	3.2	.953	L. Stange	28	153	7	9	3	3.35
	RF	Conigliaro	558	.265	28	93	244	8	7	1	1.8	.973	E. Wilson	15	101	5	5	0	3.84
	CF	D. Demeter	226	.292	9	29	109	3	2	0	2.0	.982	D. McMahon	49	78	8	7	9	2.65
	LF	Yastrzemski	594	.278	16	80	310	15	5	2	2.1	.985	J. Wyatt	42	72	3	4	8	3.14
	C	M. Ryan	369	.214	2	32	685	50	6	7	6.5	.985	K. Sanders	24	47	3	6	2	3.80
	2B	D. Jones	252	.234	4	23	129	121	10	26	3.7	.962							
	C	B. Tillman	204	.230	3	24	372	24	4	5	5.6	.990							
	OF	J. Tartabull	195	.277	0	11	90	1	1	0	2.0	.989							
	OF	G. Thomas	173	.237	5	20	84	4	0	0	1.8	1.000							
New York W-70 L-89 Johnny Keane W-4 L-16 Ralph Houk W-66 L-73	1B	J. Pepitone	585	.255	31	83	1044	92	6	92	9.6	.995	Stottlemyre	37	251	12	20	1	3.80
	2B	Richardson	610	.251	7	42	322	408	15	91	5.1	.980	F. Peterson	34	215	12	11	0	3.31
	SS	H. Clarke	312	.266	6	28	102	154	8	37	4.2	.980	A. Downing	30	200	10	11	0	3.56
	3B	C. Boyer	500	.240	14	57	87	226	11	12	3.8	.966	F. Talbot	23	124	7	7	0	4.15
	RF	R. Maris	348	.233	13	43	133	3	1	0	1.4	.993	J. Bouton	24	120	3	8	1	2.69
	CF	M. Mantle	333	.288	23	56	172	2	0	0	1.8	1.000	H. Reniff	56	95	3	7	9	3.21
	LF	T. Tresh	537	.233	27	68	181	12	3	3	2.0	.985	S. Hamilton	44	90	8	3	3	3.00
	C	E. Howard	410	.256	6	35	553	44	9	6	6.1	.985	P. Ramos	52	90	3	9	13	3.61
	OF	R. White	316	.225	7	20	153	3	7	0	2.0	.957	D. Womack	42	75	7	3	4	2.64
	C	J. Gibbs	182	.258	3	20	295	27	4	4	6.0	.988							
	OF	L. Clinton	159	.220	5	21	80	2	2	0	1.3	.976							

BATTING AND BASE RUNNING LEADERS / PITCHING LEADERS

Batting Average		Slugging Average		Home Runs		Winning Percentage		Earned Run Average		Wins	
F. Robinson, BAL	.316	F. Robinson, BAL	.637	F. Robinson, BAL	49	S. Siebert, CLE	.667	G. Peters, CHI	1.98	J. Kaat, MIN	25
T. Oliva, MIN	.307	H. Killebrew, MIN	.538	H. Killebrew, MIN	39	J. Kaat, MIN	.658	J. Horlen, CHI	2.43	D. McLain, DET	20
A. Kaline, DET	.288	A. Kaline, DET	.534	B. Powell, BAL	34	E. Wilson, BOS, DET	.621	S. Hargan, CLE	2.48	E. Wilson, BOS, DET	18
B. Powell, BAL	.287	B. Powell, BAL	.532	N. Cash, DET	32	J. Palmer, BAL	.600	J. Perry, MIN	2.54	S. Siebert, CLE	16
H. Killebrew, MIN	.281	T. Oliva, MIN	.502	J. Pepitone, NY	31	D. McLain, DET	.588	T. John, CHI	2.62	J. Palmer, BAL	15

AMERICAN LEAGUE 1966, *cont.*

BATTING AND BASE RUNNING LEADERS

Total Bases
F. Robinson, BAL	367
T. Oliva, MIN	312
H. Killebrew, MIN	306
N. Cash, DET	288
T. Agee, CHI	281

Runs Batted In
F. Robinson, BAL	122
H. Killebrew, MIN	110
B. Powell, BAL	109
W. Horton, DET	100
B. Robinson, BAL	100

Stolen Bases
Campaneris, KC	52
D. Buford, CHI	51
T. Agee, CHI	44
L. Aparicio, BAL	25
J. Cardenal, CAL	24

Hits
T. Oliva, MIN	191
F. Robinson, BAL	182
L. Aparicio, BAL	182
T. Agee, CHI	172

Base on Balls
H. Killebrew, MIN	103
J. Foy, BOS	91
F. Robinson, BAL	87
T. Tresh, NY	86

Home Run Percentage
F. Robinson, BAL	8.5
B. Powell, BAL	6.9
H. Killebrew, MIN	6.9
A. Kaline, DET	6.1

Runs Scored
F. Robinson, BAL	122
T. Oliva, MIN	99
N. Cash, DET	98
T. Agee, CHI	98

Doubles
Yastrzemski, BOS	39
B. Robinson, BAL	35
F. Robinson, BAL	34
J. Fregosi, CAL	32

Triples
B. Knoop, CAL	11
Campaneris, KC	10
E. Brinkman, WAS	9

PITCHING LEADERS

Saves
J. Aker, KC	32
R. Kline, WAS	23
L. Sherry, DET	20
E. Fisher, BAL, CHI	19
S. Miller, BAL	18

Strikeouts
S. McDowell, CLE	225
J. Kaat, MIN	205
E. Wilson, BOS, DET	200
P. Richert, WAS	195
G. Bell, CLE	194

Complete Games
J. Kaat, MIN	19
D. McLain, DET	14
E. Wilson, BOS, DET	13
G. Bell, CLE	12

Fewest Hits/9 Innings
S. McDowell, CLE	6.02
D. Boswell, MIN	6.38
G. Peters, CHI	6.86
D. McLain, DET	6.98

Shutouts
L. Tiant, CLE	5
S. McDowell, CLE	5
T. John, CHI	5
J. Buzhardt, CHI	4

Fewest Walks/9 Innings
J. Kaat, MIN	1.62
F. Peterson, NY	1.67
M. Grant, MIN	1.77
G. Peters, CHI	1.98

Most Strikeouts/9 Inn.
S. McDowell, CLE	10.42
D. Boswell, MIN	9.19
M. Lolich, DET	7.64
P. Richert, WAS	7.14

Innings
J. Kaat, MIN	305
D. McLain, DET	264
E. Wilson, BOS, DET	264
D. Chance, CAL	260

Games Pitched
E. Fisher, BAL, CHI	67
J. Aker, KC	66
C. Cox, WAS	66
Worthington, MIN	65

	W	L	PCT	GB	R	OR	2B	3B	HR	BA	SA	SB	E	DP	FA	CG	BB	SO	ShO	SV	ERA
Baltimore	97	63	.606		**755**	601	**243**	35	175	**.258**	**.409**	55	115	142	**.981**	23	514	1070	13	**51**	3.32
Minnesota	89	73	.549	9	663	581	219	33	144	.249	.382	67	139	118	.977	**52**	**392**	1015	11	28	3.13
Detroit	88	74	.543	10	719	698	224	45	179	.251	.406	41	120	142	.980	36	520	1026	11	38	3.85
Chicago	83	79	.512	15	574	**517**	193	40	87	.231	.331	153	159	149	.976	38	403	896	**22**	34	**2.68**
Cleveland	81	81	.500	17	574	586	156	25	155	.237	.360	53	138	132	.977	49	489	**1111**	15	28	3.23
California	80	82	.494	18	604	643	179	54	122	.232	.354	80	136	**186**	.979	31	511	836	12	40	3.56
Kansas City	74	86	.463	23	564	648	212	**56**	70	.236	.337	132	138	154	.977	19	630	854	11	47	3.70
Washington	71	88	.447	25.5	557	659	185	40	126	.234	.355	53	142	139	.977	25	448	866	6	35	3.92
Boston	72	90	.444	26	655	731	228	44	145	.240	.376	35	155	153	.975	32	577	977	10	31	3.42
New York	70	89	.440	26.5	611	612	182	36	162	.235	.374	49	142	142	.977	29	443	842	7	32	3.44
					6276	6276	2021	408	1365	.240	.369	718	1384	1457	.978	334	4927	9493	118	364	3.44

NATIONAL LEAGUE 1967

	POS	Player	AB	BA	HR	RBI	PO	A	E	DP	TC/G	FA	Pitcher	G	IP	W	L	SV	ERA
St. Louis W-101 L-60 Red Schoendienst	1B	O. Cepeda	563	.325	25	**111**	1304	90	10	103	9.3	.993	D. Hughes	37	222	16	6	3	2.67
	2B	J. Javier	520	.281	14	64	311	352	24	72	5.0	.965	S. Carlton	30	193	14	9	1	2.98
	SS	D. Maxvill	476	.227	1	41	236	470	19	74	4.9	.974	R. Washburn	27	186	10	7	0	3.53
	3B	M. Shannon	482	.245	12	77	88	239	29	18	2.9	.919	B. Gibson	24	175	13	7	0	2.98
	RF	R. Maris	410	.261	9	55	224	5	2	1	2.0	.991	N. Briles	49	155	14	5	6	2.43
	CF	C. Flood	514	.335	5	50	314	4	4	1	2.6	.988	L. Jaster	34	152	9	7	3	3.01
	LF	L. Brock	**689**	.299	21	76	272	12	13	2	1.9	.956	A. Jackson	38	107	9	4	1	3.95
	C	T. McCarver	471	.295	14	69	819	**67**	3	10	**6.8**	**.997**	R. Willis	65	81	6	5	10	2.67
	OF	B. Tolan	265	.253	6	32	118	4	1	1	1.5	.992	J. Hoerner	57	66	4	4	15	2.59
	UT	P. Gagliano	217	.221	2	21	115	99	8	16		.964	J. Lamabe	23	48	3	4	4	2.83
	OF	A. Johnson	175	.223	1	12	91	7	3	2	1.8	.970							
San Francisco W-91 L-71 Herman Franks	1B	W. McCovey	456	.276	31	91	1221	81	**15**	102	10.4	.989	G. Perry	39	293	15	17	1	2.61
	2B	T. Fuentes	344	.209	5	29	274	313	12	79	4.6	.980	McCormick	40	262	**22**	10	0	2.85
	SS	H. Lanier	525	.213	0	42	197	440	17	73	4.8	.974	J. Marichal	26	202	14	10	0	2.76
	3B	J. Hart	578	.289	29	99	60	177	16	10	2.8	.937	R. Sadecki	35	188	12	6	0	2.78
	RF	O. Brown	412	.267	13	53	190	5	3	0	1.7	.985	R. Herbel	42	126	4	5	1	3.08
	CF	W. Mays	486	.263	22	70	277	3	7	0	2.1	.976	B. Bolin	37	120	6	8	0	4.88
	LF	J. Alou	510	.292	5	30	195	5	11	2	1.7	.948	F. Linzy	57	96	7	7	17	1.51
	C	T. Haller	455	.251	14	49	797	64	3	5	6.4	.997	L. McDaniel	41	73	2	6	3	3.72
	UT	J. Davenport	295	.275	5	30	83	192	4	24		.986							
	OF	K. Henderson	179	.190	4	14	86	3	5	1	1.8	.947							
	1B	J. Hiatt	153	.275	6	26	288	17	3	25	8.6	.990							
Chicago W-87 L-74 Leo Durocher	1B	E. Banks	573	.276	23	95	**1383**	**91**	10	111	10.1	.993	F. Jenkins	38	289	20	13	0	2.80
	2B	G. Beckert	597	.280	5	40	327	422	**25**	89	5.4	.968	R. Nye	35	205	13	10	0	3.20
	SS	D. Kessinger	580	.231	0	42	215	457	19	77	4.8	.973	J. Niekro	36	170	10	7	0	3.34
	3B	R. Santo	586	.300	31	98	**187**	**393**	26	**33**	**3.8**	.957	R. Culp	30	153	8	11	0	3.89
	RF	T. Savage	225	.218	5	33	133	5	3	1	1.6	.979	B. Hands	49	150	7	8	6	2.46
	CF	A. Phillips	448	.268	17	70	340	13	7	0	2.6	.981	C. Simmons	17	82	3	7	0	4.94
	LF	B. Williams	634	.278	28	84	271	3	3	1	1.7	.989	Hartenstein	45	73	9	5	10	3.08
	C	R. Hundley	539	.267	14	60	**865**	59	4	7	6.1	.996	B. Stoneman	28	63	2	4	3	3.29
	OF	L. Thomas	191	.220	2	23	60	2	2	0	1.5	.969							

NATIONAL LEAGUE 1967, cont.

	POS	Player	AB	BA	HR	RBI	PO	A	E	DP	TC/G	FA	Pitcher	G	IP	W	L	SV	ERA
Cincinnati W-87 L-75 Dave Bristol	1B	L. May	438	.265	12	57	621	43	4	49	8.2	.994	G. Nolan	33	227	14	8	0	2.58
	2B	T. Helms	497	.274	2	35	185	224	9	50	4.8	.978	M. Pappas	34	218	16	13	0	3.35
	SS	L. Cardenas	379	.256	2	21	190	316	15	57	4.8	.971	J. Maloney	30	196	15	11	0	3.25
	3B	T. Perez	600	.290	26	102	113	221	13	13	2.5	.963	M. Queen	31	196	14	8	0	2.76
	RF	T. Harper	365	.225	7	22	208	6	1	0	2.2	.995	S. Ellis	32	176	8	11	0	3.84
	CF	V. Pinson	650	.288	18	66	341	4	5	1	2.2	.986	T. Abernathy	70	106	6	3	28	1.27
	LF	P. Rose	585	.301	12	76	211	5	4	0	1.8	.982	B. McCool	31	97	3	7	2	3.42
	C	J. Edwards	209	.206	2	20	454	30	5	4	6.7	.990	J. Arrigo	32	74	6	6	1	3.16
	1B	D. Johnson	361	.224	13	53	587	41	2	47	7.8	.997							
	UT	C. Ruiz	250	.220	0	13	131	168	10	33		.968							
	C	D. Pavletich	231	.238	6	34	383	31	6	5	6.4	.986							
Philadelphia W-82 L-80 Gene Mauch	1B	B. White	308	.250	8	33	775	52	6	85	8.8	.993	J. Bunning	40	302	17	15	0	2.29
	2B	C. Rojas	528	.259	4	45	282	360	15	92	4.8	.977	L. Jackson	40	262	13	15	0	3.10
	SS	B. Wine	363	.190	2	28	201	390	12	90	4.5	.980	C. Short	29	199	9	11	1	2.39
	3B	D. Allen	463	.307	23	77	95	249	35	23	3.1	.908	R. Wise	36	181	11	11	0	3.28
	RF	J. Callison	556	.261	14	64	286	12	7	1	2.1	.977	D. Ellsworth	32	125	6	7	0	4.38
	CF	J. Briggs	332	.232	9	30	182	2	4	0	2.0	.979	D. Farrell	50	92	9	6	12	2.05
	LF	T. Gonzalez	508	.339	9	59	260	10	2	1	1.9	.993	D. Hall	48	86	10	8	8	2.20
	C	C. Dalrymple	268	.172	3	21	558	59	4	7	6.4	.994	J. Boozer	28	75	5	4	1	4.10
	UT	T. Taylor	462	.238	2	34	524	182	9	73		.987							
	OF	D. Lock	313	.252	14	51	172	8	5	2	1.9	.973							
	C	G. Oliver	263	.224	7	34	425	30	6	3	5.8	.987							
	SS	Sutherland	231	.247	1	19	77	115	15	33	3.1	.928							
Pittsburgh W-81 L-81 Harry Walker W-42 L-42 Danny Murtaugh W-39 L-39	1B	D. Clendenon	478	.249	13	56	1199	89	15	122	10.6	.988	T. Sisk	37	208	13	13	1	3.34
	2B	B. Mazeroski	639	.261	9	77	417	498	18	131	5.7	.981	B. Veale	33	203	16	8	0	3.64
	SS	G. Alley	550	.287	6	55	257	500	26	105	5.4	.967	D. Ribant	38	172	9	8	0	4.08
	3B	M. Wills	616	.302	3	45	98	343	24	31	3.2	.948	A. McBean	51	131	7	4	2	2.54
	RF	R. Clemente	585	.357	23	110	273	17	9	4	2.1	.970	S. Blass	32	127	6	8	0	3.55
	CF	M. Alou	550	.338	2	28	249	9	3	3	1.9	.989	W. Fryman	28	113	3	8	1	4.05
	LF	W. Stargell	462	.271	20	73	140	12	10	1	1.7	.938	J. Pizarro	50	107	8	10	9	3.95
	C	J. May	325	.271	3	22	550	52	4	9	5.5	.993	B. O'Dell	27	87	5	6	5	5.82
	OF	M. Mota	349	.321	4	56	153	9	2	2	1.7	.988	R. Face	61	74	7	5	17	2.42
	UT	J. Pagan	211	.289	1	19	73	109	7	14		.963							
Atlanta W-77 L-85 Billy Hitchcock W-77 L-82 Ken Silvestri W-0 L-3	1B	F. Alou	574	.274	15	43	774	28	6	67	9.5	.993	D. Lemaster	31	215	9	9	0	3.34
	2B	W. Woodward	429	.226	0	25	270	339	11	81	5.2	.982	K. Johnson	29	210	13	9	0	2.74
	SS	D. Menke	418	.227	7	39	181	349	19	65	4.4	.965	P. Niekro	46	207	11	9	9	1.87
	3B	C. Boyer	572	.245	26	96	166	291	14	30	3.1	.970	P. Jarvis	32	194	15	10	0	3.66
	RF	H. Aaron	600	.307	39	109	321	12	7	3	2.2	.979	D. Kelley	39	98	2	9	2	3.77
	CF	M. Jones	454	.253	17	50	252	7	4	1	2.1	.985	C. Carroll	42	93	6	12	5	5.52
	LF	R. Carty	444	.255	15	64	203	7	9	3	2.0	.959	J. Ritchie	52	82	4	6	2	3.17
	C	J. Torre	477	.277	20	68	580	63	6	12	5.7	.991	T. Cloninger	16	77	4	7	0	5.17
	1B	T. Francona	254	.248	6	25	503	32	5	36	9.6	.991	C. Upshaw	30	45	2	3	8	2.58
Los Angeles W-73 L-89 Walter Alston	1B	W. Parker	413	.247	5	31	913	68	4	72	8.8	.996	C. Osteen	39	288	17	17	0	3.22
	2B	R. Hunt	388	.263	3	33	211	224	9	50	4.9	.980	D. Drysdale	38	282	13	16	0	2.74
	SS	G. Michael	223	.202	0	7	117	204	17	30	4.1	.950	D. Sutton	37	233	11	15	0	3.95
	3B	J. Lefebvre	494	.261	8	50	49	205	12	12	2.9	.955	B. Singer	32	204	12	8	0	2.64
	RF	R. Fairly	486	.220	10	55	129	8	2	1	1.4	.986	Perranoski	70	110	6	7	16	2.45
	CF	W. Davis	569	.257	6	41	300	6	9	2	2.3	.971	J. Brewer	30	101	5	4	1	2.68
	LF	L. Johnson	330	.270	11	41	153	7	4	0	1.8	.976	P. Regan	55	96	6	9	6	2.99
	C	J. Roseboro	334	.272	4	24	550	60	10	6	5.8	.984	B. Miller	52	86	2	9	0	4.31
	OF	A. Ferrara	347	.277	16	50	135	1	3	0	1.5	.978							
	3O	B. Bailey	322	.227	4	28	77	152	14	11		.942							
	OF	Gabrielson	238	.261	7	29	92	7	2	0	1.5	.980							
	SS	D. Schofield	232	.216	2	15	107	213	8	37	4.8	.976							
	2S	N. Oliver	232	.237	0	7	124	157	12	35		.959							
	C	J. Torborg	196	.214	2	12	413	30	5	3	6.0	.989							
Houston W-69 L-93 Grady Hatton	1B	E. Mathews	328	.238	10	38	572	40	8	50	7.8	.987	M. Cuellar	36	246	16	11	1	3.03
	2B	J. Morgan	494	.275	6	42	297	344	14	67	5.0	.979	D. Giusti	37	222	11	15	1	4.18
	SS	S. Jackson	520	.237	0	25	204	379	35	63	4.8	.943	D. Wilson	31	184	10	9	0	2.79
	3B	Aspromonte	486	.294	6	58	130	237	14	17	2.9	.963	B. Belinsky	27	115	3	9	0	4.68
	RF	R. Staub	546	.333	10	74	269	10	11	2	2.0	.962	L. Dierker	15	99	6	5	0	3.36
	CF	J. Wynn	594	.249	37	107	364	4	12	1	2.4	.968	Blasingame	15	77	4	7	0	5.96
	LF	R. Davis	285	.256	7	38	114	7	3	2	1.6	.976	D. Eilers	35	59	6	4	1	3.94
	C	J. Bateman	252	.190	2	17	483	46	6	5	7.5	.989	C. Sembera	45	60	2	6	3	4.83
	2S	J. Gotay	234	.282	2	15	91	137	8	27		.966							
	C	R. Brand	215	.242	0	18	397	36	1	3	6.5	.998							
	OF	N. Miller	190	.205	1	14	84	3	3	1	1.7	.967							
	1B	C. Harrison	177	.243	2	26	438	27	6	24	8.0	.987							
	1B	D. Rader	162	.333	2	26	263	18	8	26	8.0	.972							

NATIONAL LEAGUE 1967, *cont.*

	POS	Player	AB	BA	HR	RBI	PO	A	E	DP	TC/G	FA	Pitcher	G	IP	W	L	SV	ERA
New York	1B	E. Kranepool	469	.269	10	54	1137	87	10	103	8.9	.992	T. Seaver	35	251	16	13	0	2.76
	2B	J. Buchek	411	.236	14	41	203	255	11	54	4.9	.977	J. Fisher	39	220	9	18	0	4.70
W-61 L-101	SS	B. Harrelson	540	.254	1	28	254	467	32	88	5.1	.958	D. Cardwell	26	118	5	9	0	3.57
	3B	E. Charles	323	.238	3	31	85	201	17	16	3.4	.944	B. Shaw	23	99	3	9	0	4.29
Wes Westrum	RF	R. Swoboda	449	.281	13	53	190	8	9	0	1.9	.957	R. Taylor	50	73	4	6	8	2.34
W-57 L-94	CF	C. Jones	411	.246	5	30	210	5	5	3	1.9	.977	D. Shaw	40	51	4	5	2	2.98
	LF	T. Davis	577	.302	16	73	231	5	6	0	1.6	.975	H. Reniff	29	43	3	3	4	3.35
Salty Parker	C	J. Grote	344	.195	4	23	609	62	7	8	5.7	.990							
W-4 L-7	UT	B. Johnson	230	.348	5	27	222	105	7	37		.979							
	3B	K. Boyer	166	.235	3	13	27	84	6	7	2.7	.949							

BATTING AND BASE RUNNING LEADERS

Batting Average
R. Clemente, PIT	.357
T. Gonzalez, PHI	.339
M. Alou, PIT	.338
C. Flood, STL	.335
R. Staub, HOU	.333

Slugging Average
H. Aaron, ATL	.573
D. Allen, PHI	.566
R. Clemente, PIT	.554
W. McCovey, SF	.535
O. Cepeda, STL	.524

Home Runs
H. Aaron, ATL	39
J. Wynn, HOU	37
W. McCovey, SF	31
R. Santo, CHI	31
J. Hart, SF	29

Total Bases
H. Aaron, ATL	344
L. Brock, STL	325
R. Clemente, PIT	324
B. Williams, CHI	305
R. Santo, CHI	300

Runs Batted In
O. Cepeda, STL	111
R. Clemente, PIT	110
H. Aaron, ATL	109
J. Wynn, HOU	107
T. Perez, CIN	102

Stolen Bases
L. Brock, STL	52
J. Morgan, HOU	29
M. Wills, PIT	29
V. Pinson, CIN	26
A. Phillips, CHI	24

Hits
R. Clemente, PIT	209
L. Brock, STL	206
V. Pinson, CIN	187
M. Alou, PIT	186

Base on Balls
R. Santo, CHI	96
J. Morgan, HOU	81
A. Phillips, CHI	80
J. Hart, SF	77

Home Run Percentage
W. McCovey, SF	6.8
H. Aaron, ATL	6.5
J. Wynn, HOU	6.2
R. Santo, CHI	5.3

Runs Scored
H. Aaron, ATL	113
L. Brock, STL	113
R. Santo, CHI	107
R. Clemente, PIT	103

Doubles
R. Staub, HOU	44
O. Cepeda, STL	37
H. Aaron, ATL	37

Triples
V. Pinson, CIN	13
B. Williams, CHI	12
L. Brock, STL	12
J. Morgan, HOU	11

PITCHING LEADERS

Winning Percentage
D. Hughes, STL	.727
McCormick, SF	.688
B. Veale, PIT	.667
F. Jenkins, CHI	.606
P. Jarvis, ATL	.600

Earned Run Average
P. Niekro, ATL	1.87
J. Bunning, PHI	2.29
C. Short, PHI	2.39
G. Nolan, CIN	2.58
G. Perry, SF	2.61

Wins
McCormick, SF	22
F. Jenkins, CHI	20
J. Bunning, PHI	17
C. Osteen, LA	17

Saves
T. Abernathy, CIN	28
R. Face, PIT	17
F. Linzy, SF	17
Perranoski, LA	16
J. Hoerner, STL	15

Strikeouts
J. Bunning, PHI	253
F. Jenkins, CHI	236
G. Perry, SF	230
G. Nolan, CIN	206
M. Cuellar, HOU	203

Complete Games
F. Jenkins, CHI	20
J. Marichal, SF	18
T. Seaver, NY	18
G. Perry, SF	18
M. Cuellar, HOU	16
J. Bunning, PHI	16

Fewest Hits/9 Innings
D. Hughes, STL	6.64
D. Wilson, HOU	6.90
G. Perry, SF	7.10
M. Queen, CIN	7.13

Shutouts
J. Bunning, PHI	6
G. Nolan, CIN	5
McCormick, SF	5
C. Osteen, LA	5

Fewest Walks/9 Innings
M. Pappas, CIN	1.57
C. Osteen, LA	1.62
K. Johnson, ATL	1.63
J. Niekro, CHI	1.70

Most Strikeouts/9 Inn.
G. Nolan, CIN	8.18
B. Veale, PIT	7.94
S. Carlton, STL	7.83
D. Wilson, HOU	7.78

Innings
J. Bunning, PHI	302
G. Perry, SF	293
F. Jenkins, CHI	289
C. Osteen, LA	288

Games Pitched
Perranoski, LA	70
T. Abernathy, CIN	70
R. Willis, STL	65
R. Face, PIT	61

	W	L	PCT	GB	R	OR	2B	3B	HR	BA	SA	SB	E	DP	FA	CG	BB	SO	ShO	SV	ERA
St. Louis	101	60	.627		695	557	225	40	115	.263	.379	102	140	127	.978	44	431	956	17	45	3.05
San Francisco	91	71	.562	10.5	652	551	201	39	140	.245	.372	22	134	149	.979	64	453	990	17	25	2.92
Chicago	87	74	.540	14	702	624	211	49	128	.251	.378	63	121	143	.981	47	463	888	7	28	3.48
Cincinnati	87	75	.537	14.5	604	563	251	54	109	.248	.372	92	121	124	.980	34	498	1065	18	23	3.05
Philadelphia	82	80	.506	19.5	612	581	221	47	103	.242	.357	79	137	174	.978	46	403	967	17	23	3.10
Pittsburgh	81	81	.500	20.5	679	693	193	62	91	.277	.380	79	141	186	.978	35	561	820	5	35	3.74
Atlanta	77	85	.475	24.5	631	640	191	29	158	.240	.372	55	138	148	.978	35	449	862	5	32	3.47
Los Angeles	73	89	.451	28.5	519	595	203	38	82	.236	.332	56	160	144	.975	41	393	967	24	21	3.21
Houston	69	93	.426	32.5	626	742	259	46	93	.249	.364	88	159	120	.974	35	485	1060	8	21	4.03
New York	61	101	.377	40.5	498	672	178	23	83	.238	.325	58	157	147	.975	36	536	893	10	19	3.73
					6218	6218	2133	427	1102	.249	.363	694	1408	1462	.978	417	4672	9468	121	291	3.38

AMERICAN LEAGUE 1967

	POS	Player	AB	BA	HR	RBI	PO	A	E	DP	TC/G	FA	Pitcher	G	IP	W	L	SV	ERA
Boston	1B	G. Scott	565	.303	19	82	1321	94	19	115	9.4	.987	J. Lonborg	39	273	22	9	0	3.16
	2B	M. Andrews	494	.263	8	40	303	345	16	63	4.8	.976	L. Stange	35	182	8	10	1	2.77
W-92 L-70	SS	Petrocelli	491	.259	17	66	223	432	19	73	4.8	.972	G. Bell	29	165	12	8	3	3.16
	3B	J. Foy	446	.251	16	49	109	204	27	13	2.9	.921	D. Brandon	39	158	5	11	3	4.17
Dick Williams	RF	Conigliaro	349	.287	20	67	172	5	3	1	1.9	.983	J. Santiago	50	145	12	4	5	3.59
	CF	R. Smith	565	.246	15	61	335	10	6	3	2.4	.983	J. Wyatt	60	93	10	7	20	2.60
	LF	Yastrzemski	579	.326	44	121	297	13	7	1	2.0	.978							
	C	M. Ryan	226	.199	2	27	473	34	6	11	6.5	.988							
	UT	J. Adair	316	.291	3	26	105	175	8	30		.972							
	OF	J. Tartabull	247	.223	0	10	90	3	1	1	1.1	.989							
	32	D. Jones	159	.289	3	25	23	60	6	6		.933							

AMERICAN LEAGUE 1967, cont.

	POS	Player	AB	BA	HR	RBI	PO	A	E	DP	TC/G	FA	Pitcher	G	IP	W	L	SV	ERA
Detroit W-91 L-71 Mayo Smith	1B	N. Cash	488	.242	22	72	1135	**112**	6	89	8.6	.995	E. Wilson	39	264	**22**	11	0	3.27
	2B	McAuliffe	557	.239	22	65	270	307	21	74	4.1	.965	D. McLain	37	235	17	16	0	3.79
	SS	R. Oyler	367	.207	1	29	185	374	21	61	4.0	.964	J. Sparma	37	218	16	9	0	3.76
	3B	D. Wert	534	.257	6	40	112	280	9	21	2.9	.978	M. Lolich	31	204	14	13	0	3.04
	RF	A. Kaline	458	.308	25	78	217	14	4	2	1.8	.983	Wickersham	36	85	4	5	4	2.74
	CF	J. Northrup	495	.271	10	61	271	3	8	1	2.0	.972	F. Gladding	42	77	6	4	12	1.99
	LF	W. Horton	401	.274	19	67	165	5	5	2	1.6	.971	J. Hiller	23	65	4	3	2	2.63
	C	B. Freehan	517	.282	20	74	**950**	63	8	9	6.9	.992	M. Marshall	37	59	1	3	10	1.98
	OF	M. Stanley	333	.210	7	24	216	3	4	2	1.7	.982	F. Lasher	17	30	2	1	9	3.90
	2B	J. Lumpe	177	.232	4	17	70	85	4	12	3.0	.963							
Minnesota W-91 L-71 Sam Mele W-25 L-25 Cal Ermer W-66 L-46	1B	H. Killebrew	547	.269	**44**	113	1283	86	11	100	8.6	.992	D. Chance	41	**284**	20	14	1	2.73
	2B	R. Carew	514	.292	8	51	289	314	15	60	4.6	.976	J. Kaat	42	263	16	13	0	3.04
	SS	Z. Versalles	581	.200	6	50	229	454	**30**	81	4.5	.958	J. Merritt	37	228	13	7	0	2.53
	3B	R. Rollins	339	.245	6	39	83	153	9	13	2.5	.963	D. Boswell	37	223	14	12	0	3.27
	RF	T. Oliva	557	.289	17	83	286	8	4	2	2.0	.987	J. Perry	37	131	8	7	0	3.03
	CF	T. Uhlaender	415	.258	6	49	255	6	1	3	2.2	**.996**	M. Grant	27	95	5	6	0	4.72
	LF	B. Allison	496	.258	24	75	220	6	5	0	1.6	.978	Worthington	59	92	8	9	16	2.84
	C	J. Zimmerman	234	.167	1	12	572	44	5	7	6.0	.992	R. Kline	54	72	7	1	5	3.77
	UT	C. Tovar	649	.267	6	47	307	184	17	23		.967							
	C	R. Nixon	170	.235	1	22	308	26	2	1	4.9	.994							
	1B	R. Reese	101	.248	4	20	93	3	1	5	2.7	.990							
Chicago W-89 L-73 Eddie Stanky	1B	T. McCraw	453	.236	11	45	1167	110	11	92	10.5	.991	G. Peters	38	260	16	11	0	2.28
	2B	W. Causey	292	.226	1	28	153	199	8	36	3.8	.978	J. Horlen	35	258	19	7	0	**2.06**
	SS	R. Hansen	498	.233	8	51	243	**482**	27	91	4.8	.964	T. John	31	178	10	13	0	2.47
	3B	D. Buford	535	.241	4	32	95	250	19	16	3.0	.948	B. Locker	**77**	125	7	5	20	2.09
	RF	K. Berry	485	.241	7	41	233	9	2	1	1.7	.992	B. Howard	30	113	3	10	0	3.43
	CF	T. Agee	529	.234	14	52	337	9	**11**	2	2.3	.969	W. Wood	51	95	4	2	4	2.45
	LF	P. Ward	467	.233	18	62	107	3	1	0	1.2	.991	H. Wilhelm	49	89	8	3	12	1.31
	C	J. Martin	252	.234	4	22	478	39	7	3	5.5	.987	J. Buzhardt	28	89	3	9	0	3.96
	OF	W. Williams	275	.240	3	15	112	6	2	2	1.6	.983							
	OF	R. Colavito	190	.221	3	29	83	2	2	3	1.5	.977							
	C	D. Josephson	189	.238	1	9	292	24	0	3	5.4	1.000							
	31	K. Boyer	180	.261	4	21	154	79	5	16		.979							
California W-84 L-77 Bill Rigney	1B	D. Mincher	487	.273	25	76	1177	88	8	92	9.0	.994	G. Brunet	40	250	11	**19**	1	3.31
	2B	B. Knoop	511	.245	9	38	**376**	392	11	**91**	4.9	.986	McGlothlin	32	197	12	8	0	2.96
	SS	J. Fregosi	590	.290	9	56	258	435	25	73	4.8	.965	R. Clark	32	174	12	11	0	2.59
	3B	P. Schaal	272	.188	6	20	73	156	7	9	2.7	.970	M. Rojas	72	122	9	9	27	2.52
	RF	J. Hall	401	.249	16	55	197	6	2	1	1.7	.990	J. Hamilton	26	119	9	6	0	3.24
	CF	J. Cardenal	381	.236	6	27	195	10	3	0	2.1	.986	B. Kelso	69	112	5	3	11	2.97
	LF	R. Reichardt	498	.265	17	69	254	10	7	4	2.0	.974	C. Wright	20	77	5	5	0	3.26
	C	B. Rodgers	429	.219	6	41	728	**73**	7	11	6.0	.991							
	OF	J. Johnstone	230	.209	2	16	141	3	4	0	2.3	.973							
	UT	T. Satriano	201	.224	4	21	150	85	7	10		.971							
	OF	B. Morton	201	.313	0	32	83	1	0	0	1.4	1.000							
	OF	R. Repoz	176	.250	5	20	135	3	5	0	2.3	.965							
Baltimore W-76 L-85 Hank Bauer	1B	B. Powell	415	.234	13	55	903	64	14	82	8.6	.986	T. Phoebus	33	208	14	9	0	3.33
	2B	D. Johnson	510	.247	10	64	340	348	13	75	4.9	.981	P. Richert	26	132	7	10	2	2.99
	SS	L. Aparicio	546	.233	4	31	221	333	25	67	4.4	.957	B. Dillman	32	124	5	9	3	4.35
	3B	B. Robinson	610	.269	22	77	147	**405**	11	37	3.6	**.980**	D. McNally	24	119	7	7	0	4.54
	RF	F. Robinson	479	.311	30	94	191	7	2	2	1.6	.990	J. Hardin	19	111	8	3	2	2.27
	CF	P. Blair	552	.293	11	64	**369**	13	6	3	2.7	.985	E. Watt	49	104	3	5	8	2.26
	LF	C. Blefary	554	.242	22	81	170	13	6	5	1.8	.968	M. Drabowsky	43	95	7	5	12	1.60
	C	Etchebarren	330	.215	7	35	673	57	8	10	6.7	.989	G. Brabender	14	94	6	4	0	3.35
	OF	R. Snyder	275	.236	4	23	127	3	2	0	1.9	.985	W. Bunker	29	88	3	7	1	4.09
	S2	M. Belanger	184	.174	1	10	98	134	9	23		.963	S. Miller	42	81	3	10	8	2.55
	C	L. Haney	164	.268	3	8	311	31	3	3	6.1	.991	S. Barber	15	75	4	9	0	4.10
Washington W-76 L-85 Gil Hodges	1B	M. Epstein	284	.229	9	29	718	54	10	72	9.8	.987	P. Ortega	34	220	10	10	0	3.03
	2B	B. Allen	254	.193	3	18	177	200	4	57	5.1	.990	C. Pascual	28	165	12	10	0	3.28
	SS	E. Brinkman	320	.188	1	18	160	309	10	54	4.4	.979	B. Moore	27	144	7	11	0	3.76
	3B	K. McMullen	563	.245	16	67	153	348	18	**38**	3.6	.965	J. Coleman	28	134	8	9	0	4.63
	RF	C. Peterson	405	.240	8	46	190	5	6	1	2.0	.970	D. Knowles	61	113	6	8	14	2.70
	CF	F. Valentine	457	.234	11	44	258	7	3	0	2.0	.989	B. Priddy	46	110	3	7	4	3.44
	LF	F. Howard	519	.256	36	89	210	5	3	1	1.5	.986	B. Humphreys	48	106	6	2	4	4.17
	C	P. Casanova	528	.248	9	53	827	70	15	**19**	6.7	.984	F. Bertaina	18	96	6	5	0	2.92
	UT	T. Cullen	402	.236	2	31	219	361	20	67		.956	D. Lines	54	86	2	5	4	3.36
	OF	H. Allen	292	.233	3	17	148	1	3	1	1.5	.980	C. Cox	54	73	7	4	1	2.96
	1B	D. Nen	238	.218	6	29	516	42	3	49	8.6	.995	D. Baldwin	58	69	2	4	12	1.70
	2B	B. Saverine	233	.236	0	8	80	98	8	22	3.9	.957							
	OF	E. Stroud	204	.201	1	10	117	1	3	0	1.5	.983							

AMERICAN LEAGUE 1967, cont.

	POS	Player	AB	BA	HR	RBI	PO	A	E	DP	TC/G	FA	Pitcher	G	IP	W	L	SV	ERA
Cleveland	1B	T. Horton	363	.281	10	44	763	46	7	62	8.7	.991	S. McDowell	37	236	13	15	0	3.85
	2B	P. Gonzalez	189	.228	1	8	114	120	7	29	3.8	.971	S. Hargan	30	223	14	13	0	2.62
W-75 L-87	SS	L. Brown	485	.227	7	37	233	414	22	90	4.5	.967	L. Tiant	33	214	12	9	2	2.74
	3B	M. Alvis	637	.256	21	70	169	304	17	20	3.0	.965	S. Siebert	34	185	10	12	4	2.38
Joe Adcock	RF	C. Hinton	498	.245	10	37	239	5	6	0	1.8	.976	O'Donoghue	33	131	8	9	2	3.24
	CF	V. Davalillo	359	.287	2	22	202	5	3	1	1.7	.986	O. Pena	48	88	0	3	8	3.36
	LF	L. Wagner	433	.242	15	54	142	4	3	1	1.3	.980	S. Williams	16	79	6	4	1	2.62
	C	J. Azcue	295	.251	11	34	636	57	1	4	8.1	.999	G. Culver	53	75	7	3	3	3.96
	OF	L. Maye	297	.259	9	27	102	2	2	0	1.4	.981	B. Allen	47	54	0	5	5	2.98
	C	D. Sims	272	.202	12	37	561	56	7	7	7.3	.989							
	1B	F. Whitfield	257	.218	9	31	494	40	4	51	8.2	.993							
	2B	V. Fuller	206	.223	7	21	133	144	4	39	4.4	.986							
	UT	C. Salmon	203	.227	2	19	199	103	5	26		.984							
	OF	R. Colavito	191	.241	5	21	75	2	3	0	1.6	.963							
New York	1B	M. Mantle	440	.245	22	55	1089	91	8	82	9.1	.993	Stottlemyre	36	255	15	15	0	2.96
	2B	H. Clarke	588	.272	3	29	348	410	8	79	5.5	.990	A. Downing	31	202	14	10	0	2.63
W-72 L-90	SS	R. Amaro	417	.223	1	17	212	374	16	73	4.9	.973	F. Peterson	36	181	8	14	0	3.47
	3B	C. Smith	425	.224	9	38	92	283	21	22	3.4	.947	F. Talbot	29	139	6	8	0	4.22
Ralph Houk	RF	S. Whitaker	441	.243	11	50	202	12	4	6	1.9	.982	Monbouquette	33	133	6	5	1	2.36
	CF	J. Pepitone	501	.251	13	64	277	7	7	1	2.4	.976	T. Tillotson	43	98	3	9	2	4.03
	LF	T. Tresh	448	.219	14	53	198	9	6	1	1.8	.972	D. Womack	65	97	5	6	18	2.41
	C	J. Gibbs	374	.233	4	25	582	55	16	7	6.6	.975	S. Barber	17	98	6	9	0	4.05
	OF	B. Robinson	342	.196	7	29	169	10	6	1	1.8	.968	S. Hamilton	44	62	2	4	4	3.48
	O3	R. White	214	.224	2	18	79	29	10	1		.915							
	C	E. Howard	199	.196	3	17	289	26	5	5	6.7	.984							
	S3	J. Kennedy	179	.196	1	17	74	151	16	21		.934							
Kansas City	1B	R. Webster	360	.256	11	51	615	41	7	42	8.0	.989	C. Hunter	35	260	13	17	0	2.81
	2B	J. Donaldson	377	.276	0	28	210	230	8	40	4.4	.982	J. Nash	37	222	12	17	0	3.76
W-62 L-99	SS	Campaneris	601	.248	3	32	259	365	30	75	4.5	.954	C. Dobson	32	198	10	10	0	3.69
	3B	D. Green	349	.198	5	37	54	86	8	5	2.5	.946	L. Krausse	48	160	7	17	6	4.28
Alvin Dark	RF	Hershberger	480	.254	1	49	206	17	4	2	1.7	.982	P. Lindblad	46	116	5	8	6	3.58
W-52 L-69	CF	R. Monday	406	.251	14	58	260	14	8	6	2.5	.972	B. Odom	29	104	3	8	0	5.04
	LF	J. Gosger	356	.242	5	36	201	6	4	1	1.9	.981	T. Pierce	49	98	3	4	7	3.04
Luke Appling	C	P. Roof	327	.205	6	24	677	55	7	6	6.5	.991	J. Aker	57	88	3	8	12	4.30
W-10 L-30	UT	D. Cater	529	.270	4	46	424	109	13	35		.976							
	1B	K. Harrelson	174	.305	6	30	333	25	3	21	8.0	.992							
	OF	J. Nossek	166	.205	0	10	105	2	2	0	1.7	.982							

BATTING AND BASE RUNNING LEADERS

Batting Average
Yastrzemski, BOS .326
F. Robinson, BAL .311
A. Kaline, DET .308
G. Scott, BOS .303
P. Blair, BAL .293

Slugging Average
Yastrzemski, BOS .622
F. Robinson, BAL .576
H. Killebrew, MIN .558
A. Kaline, DET .541
F. Howard, WAS .511

Home Runs
H. Killebrew, MIN 44
Yastrzemski, BOS 44
F. Howard, WAS 36
F. Robinson, BAL 30
A. Kaline, DET 25
D. Mincher, CAL 25

Total Bases
Yastrzemski, BOS 360
H. Killebrew, MIN 305
F. Robinson, BAL 276
F. Howard, WAS 265
B. Robinson, BAL 265

Runs Batted In
Yastrzemski, BOS 121
H. Killebrew, MIN 113
F. Robinson, BAL 94
F. Howard, WAS 89
T. Oliva, MIN 83

Stolen Bases
Campaneris, KC 55
D. Buford, CHI 34
T. Agee, CHI 28
T. McCraw, CHI 24
H. Clarke, NY 21

Hits
Yastrzemski, BOS 189
C. Tovar, MIN 173
G. Scott, BOS 171
J. Fregosi, CAL 171

Base on Balls
H. Killebrew, MIN 131
M. Mantle, NY 107
McAuliffe, DET 105
Yastrzemski, BOS 91

Home Run Percentage
H. Killebrew, MIN 8.0
Yastrzemski, BOS 7.6
F. Howard, WAS 6.9
F. Robinson, BAL 6.3

Runs Scored
Yastrzemski, BOS 112
H. Killebrew, MIN 105
C. Tovar, MIN 98
A. Kaline, DET 94

Doubles
T. Oliva, MIN 34
C. Tovar, MIN 32
Yastrzemski, BOS 31
D. Johnson, BAL 30

Triples
P. Blair, BAL 12
D. Buford, CHI 9

PITCHING LEADERS

Winning Percentage
J. Horlen, CHI .731
J. Lonborg, BOS .710
E. Wilson, DET .667
J. Sparma, DET .640
G. Peters, CHI .593

Earned Run Average
J. Horlen, CHI 2.06
G. Peters, CHI 2.28
S. Siebert, CLE 2.38
T. John, CHI 2.47
J. Merritt, MIN 2.53

Wins
J. Lonborg, BOS 22
E. Wilson, DET 22
D. Chance, MIN 20
J. Horlen, CHI 19
D. McLain, DET 17

Saves
M. Rojas, CAL 27
J. Wyatt, BOS 20
B. Locker, CHI 20
D. Womack, NY 18
Worthington, MIN 16

Strikeouts
J. Lonborg, BOS 246
S. McDowell, CLE 236
D. Chance, MIN 220
L. Tiant, CLE 219
G. Peters, CHI 215

Complete Games
D. Chance, MIN 18
S. Hargan, CLE 15
J. Lonborg, BOS 15
J. Horlen, CHI 13
C. Hunter, KC 13
J. Kaat, MIN 13

Fewest Hits/9 Innings
G. Peters, CHI 6.47
D. Boswell, MIN 6.55
J. Horlen, CHI 6.56
S. Siebert, CLE 6.60

Shutouts
S. Hargan, CLE 6
T. John, CHI 6
McGlothlin, CAL 6
M. Lolich, DET 6

Fewest Walks/9 Innings
J. Merritt, MIN 1.19
J. Kaat, MIN 1.44
L. Stange, BOS 1.59
J. Horlen, CHI 2.02

Most Strikeouts/9 Inn.
L. Tiant, CLE 9.22
S. McDowell, CLE 8.99
D. Boswell, MIN 8.25
J. Lonborg, BOS 8.10

Innings
D. Chance, MIN 284
J. Lonborg, BOS 273
E. Wilson, DET 264
J. Kaat, MIN 263

Games Pitched
B. Locker, CHI 77
M. Rojas, CAL 72
B. Kelso, CAL 69
D. Womack, NY 65

AMERICAN LEAGUE 1967, *cont.*

	W	L	PCT	GB	R	OR	Batting 2B	3B	HR	BA	SA	SB	Fielding E	DP	FA	Pitching CG	BB	SO	ShO	SV	ERA
Boston	92	70	.568		722	614	216	39	158	.255	.395	68	142	142	.977	41	477	1010	9	44	3.36
Detroit	91	71	.562	1	683	587	192	36	152	.243	.376	37	131	126	.979	46	472	1038	17	40	3.32
Minnesota	91	71	.562	1	671	590	216	48	131	.240	.369	55	132	123	.978	58	396	1089	18	24	3.14
Chicago	89	73	.549	3	531	491	181	34	89	.225	.320	124	138	149	.979	36	465	927	24	39	2.45
California	84	77	.522	7.5	567	587	170	37	114	.238	.349	40	111	135	.982	19	525	892	14	46	3.19
Baltimore	76	85	.472	15.5	654	592	215	44	138	.240	.372	54	124	144	.980	29	566	1034	17	36	3.32
Washington	76	85	.472	15.5	550	637	168	25	115	.223	.326	53	144	167	.978	24	495	878	14	39	3.38
Cleveland	75	87	.463	17	559	613	213	35	131	.235	.359	53	117	138	.981	49	559	1189	14	27	3.25
New York	72	90	.444	20	522	621	166	17	100	.225	.317	63	154	144	.976	37	480	898	16	27	3.24
Kansas City	62	99	.385	29.5	533	660	212	50	69	.233	.330	132	132	120	.978	26	558	990	10	34	3.68
					5992	5992	1949	365	1197	.236	.351	679	1325	1388	.979	365	4993	9945	153	356	3.23

NATIONAL LEAGUE 1968

St. Louis
W-97 L-65
Red Schoendienst

POS	Player	AB	BA	HR	RBI	PO	A	E	DP	TC/G	FA	Pitcher	G	IP	W	L	SV	ERA
1B	O. Cepeda	600	.248	16	73	1362	90	17	109	9.5	.988	B. Gibson	34	305	22	9	0	1.12
2B	J. Javier	519	.260	4	52	304	339	16	68	4.7	.976	N. Briles	33	244	19	11	0	2.81
SS	D. Maxvill	459	.253	1	24	232	458	22	81	4.7	.969	S. Carlton	34	232	13	11	0	2.99
3B	M. Shannon	576	.266	15	79	110	310	21	25	2.8	.952	R. Washburn	31	215	14	8	0	2.26
RF	R. Maris	310	.255	5	45	169	4	3	1	2.1	.983	L. Jaster	31	154	9	13	0	3.51
CF	C. Flood	618	.301	5	60	386	11	7	4	2.7	.983	J. Hoerner	47	49	8	2	17	1.47
LF	L. Brock	660	.279	6	51	269	9	14	1	1.9	.952	W. Granger	34	44	4	2	4	2.25
C	T. McCarver	434	.253	5	48	708	54	11	6	7.1	.986							
OF	B. Tolan	278	.230	5	17	116	3	4	1	1.8	.967							
C	J. Edwards	230	.239	3	29	350	25	3	2	7.0	.992							

San Francisco
W-88 L-74
Herman Franks

POS	Player	AB	BA	HR	RBI	PO	A	E	DP	TC/G	FA	Pitcher	G	IP	W	L	SV	ERA
1B	W. McCovey	523	.293	36	105	1305	103	21	91	9.8	.985	J. Marichal	38	326	26	9	0	2.43
2B	R. Hunt	529	.250	2	28	289	410	20	66	4.9	.976	G. Perry	39	291	16	15	1	2.45
SS	H. Lanier	486	.206	0	27	282	496	20	72	5.3	.979	R. Sadecki	38	254	12	18	0	2.91
3B	J. Davenport	272	.224	1	17	49	120	7	12	2.1	.960	McCormick	38	198	12	14	1	3.58
RF	B. Bonds	307	.254	9	35	169	6	4	1	2.2	.978	B. Bolin	34	177	10	5	0	1.99
CF	W. Mays	498	.289	23	79	301	7	7	2	2.2	.978	F. Linzy	57	95	9	8	12	2.08
LF	J. Alou	419	.263	0	39	175	10	2	2	1.8	.989							
C	D. Dietz	301	.272	6	38	497	37	13	10	6.1	.976							
3O	J. Hart	480	.258	23	78	165	112	19	12		.936							
OF	T. Cline	291	.223	1	28	93	6	3	1	1.5	.971							
C	J. Hiatt	224	.232	4	34	328	31	2	4	6.2	.994							
OF	D. Marshall	174	.264	1	16	58	3	5	3	1.3	.924							
UT	F. Johnson	174	.190	1	7	61	83	9	6		.941							

Chicago
W-84 L-78
Leo Durocher

POS	Player	AB	BA	HR	RBI	PO	A	E	DP	TC/G	FA	Pitcher	G	IP	W	L	SV	ERA
1B	E. Banks	552	.246	32	83	1379	88	6	118	10.0	.996	F. Jenkins	40	308	20	15	0	2.63
2B	G. Beckert	643	.294	4	37	356	461	19	107	5.4	.977	B. Hands	38	259	16	10	0	2.89
SS	D. Kessinger	655	.240	1	32	263	573	33	97	5.5	.962	K. Holtzman	34	215	11	14	1	3.35
3B	R. Santo	577	.246	26	98	130	378	15	33	3.2	.971	J. Niekro	34	177	14	10	2	4.31
RF	J. Hickman	188	.223	5	23	115	4	3	0	1.8	.975	R. Nye	27	133	7	12	1	3.80
CF	A. Phillips	439	.241	13	33	311	11	7	3	2.3	.979	P. Regan	68	127	10	5	25	2.20
LF	B. Williams	642	.288	30	98	261	4	9	0	1.7	.967							
C	R. Hundley	553	.226	7	65	885	81	5	11	6.1	.995							
OF	L. Johnson	205	.244	1	14	97	0	3	0	1.8	.970							
OF	A. Spangler	177	.271	2	18	71	2	2	1	1.6	.973							
OF	W. Smith	142	.275	5	25	42	1	0	0	1.1	1.000							

Cincinnati
W-83 L-79
Dave Bristol

POS	Player	AB	BA	HR	RBI	PO	A	E	DP	TC/G	FA	Pitcher	G	IP	W	L	SV	ERA
1B	L. May	559	.290	22	80	1040	70	5	86	9.1	.996	G. Culver	42	226	11	16	2	3.23
2B	T. Helms	507	.288	2	47	322	370	15	82	5.6	.979	J. Maloney	33	207	16	10	0	3.61
SS	L. Cardenas	452	.235	7	41	221	388	29	66	4.7	.955	J. Arrigo	36	205	12	10	0	3.33
3B	T. Perez	625	.282	18	92	151	343	25	33	3.2	.952	G. Nolan	23	150	9	4	0	2.40
RF	P. Rose	626	.335	10	49	268	20	3	4	2.0	.990	T. Abernathy	78	135	10	7	13	2.46
CF	V. Pinson	499	.271	5	48	258	7	6	0	2.2	.978	C. Carroll	58	122	7	7	17	2.29
LF	A. Johnson	603	.312	2	58	243	8	14	2	1.9	.947							
C	J. Bench	564	.275	15	82	942	102	9	10	6.8	.991							
OF	M. Jones	234	.252	10	34	82	1	1	0	1.4	.988							
1B	F. Whitfield	171	.257	6	32	285	21	6	28	7.6	.981							

Atlanta
W-81 L-81
Lum Harris

POS	Player	AB	BA	HR	RBI	PO	A	E	DP	TC/G	FA	Pitcher	G	IP	W	L	SV	ERA
1B	D. Johnson	342	.208	8	33	738	46	3	66	8.1	.996	P. Niekro	37	257	14	12	2	2.59
2B	F. Millan	570	.289	1	33	330	438	16	91	5.4	.980	P. Jarvis	34	256	16	12	0	2.60
SS	S. Jackson	358	.226	1	19	132	307	22	35	4.7	.952	R. Reed	35	202	11	10	0	3.35
3B	C. Boyer	273	.227	4	17	74	135	4	17	3.1	.981	K. Johnson	31	135	5	8	0	3.47
RF	H. Aaron	606	.287	29	86	330	13	3	2	2.3	.991	M. Pappas	22	121	10	8	0	2.37
CF	F. Alou	662	.317	11	57	379	8	8	2	2.5	.980	C. Upshaw	52	117	8	7	13	2.47
LF	M. Lum	232	.224	3	21	115	7	3	0	1.3	.976	J. Britton	34	90	4	6	3	3.09
C	J. Torre	424	.271	10	55	492	37	2	7	5.8	.996	G. Stone	17	75	7	4	0	2.76
UT	M. Martinez	356	.230	0	12	169	264	18	44		.960	C. Raymond	36	60	3	5	10	2.83
O1	T. Francona	346	.286	2	47	382	12	4	18		.990							
O1	T. Aaron	283	.244	1	25	287	20	5	13		.984							
C	B. Tillman	236	.220	5	20	359	29	4	7	5.2	.990							
3B	B. Johnson	187	.262	0	11	45	101	8	9	3.2	.948							

NATIONAL LEAGUE 1968, *cont.*

	POS	Player	AB	BA	HR	RBI	PO	A	E	DP	TC/G	FA	Pitcher	G	IP	W	L	SV	ERA
Pittsburgh W-80 L-82 Larry Shepard	1B	D. Clendenon	584	.257	17	87	1587	128	17	134	11.2	.990	B. Veale	36	245	13	14	0	2.05
	2B	B. Mazeroski	506	.251	3	42	319	467	15	107	5.6	.981	S. Blass	33	220	18	6	0	2.12
	SS	G. Alley	474	.245	4	39	162	394	15	86	5.2	.974	A. McBean	36	198	9	12	0	3.58
	3B	M. Wills	627	.278	0	31	105	276	17	27	2.8	.957	B. Moose	38	171	8	12	3	2.74
	RF	R. Clemente	502	.291	18	57	297	9	5	1	2.4	.984	J. Bunning	27	160	4	14	0	3.88
	CF	M. Alou	558	.332	0	52	298	8	5	0	2.2	.984	R. Kline	56	113	12	5	7	1.68
	LF	W. Stargell	435	.237	24	67	144	12	9	1	1.5	.945	D. Ellis	26	104	6	5	0	2.50
	C	J. May	416	.219	1	33	752	70	10	10	6.2	.988	T. Sisk	33	96	5	5	1	3.28
	OF	M. Mota	331	.281	1	33	149	5	3	1	1.7	.981	R. Face	43	52	2	4	13	2.60
	SS	F. Patek	208	.255	2	18	80	164	6	23	4.8	.976							
	UT	J. Pagan	163	.221	4	21	40	65	7	7		.938							
Los Angeles W-76 L-86 Walter Alston	1B	W. Parker	468	.239	3	27	939	69	1	74	8.9	.999	B. Singer	37	256	13	17	0	2.88
	2B	P. Popovich	418	.232	2	25	172	229	7	48	4.6	.983	C. Osteen	39	254	12	18	0	3.08
	SS	Z. Versalles	403	.196	2	24	204	380	28	62	5.1	.954	D. Drysdale	31	239	14	12	0	2.15
	3B	B. Bailey	322	.227	8	39	81	164	12	14	2.9	.953	D. Sutton	35	208	11	15	1	2.60
	RF	R. Fairly	441	.234	4	43	159	13	2	7	1.7	.989	M. Kekich	25	115	2	10	0	3.91
	CF	W. Davis	643	.250	7	31	345	9	10	2	2.3	.973	M. Grant	37	95	6	4	3	2.08
	LF	Gabrielson	304	.270	10	35	114	6	3	1	1.4	.976	J. Brewer	54	76	8	3	14	2.49
	C	T. Haller	474	.285	4	53	863	81	6	23	6.8	.994	Billingham	50	71	3	0	8	2.14
	2B	J. Lefebvre	286	.241	5	31	126	137	6	29	4.3	.978							
	31	K. Boyer	221	.271	6	41	275	64	10	29		.971							
	OF	W. Crawford	175	.251	4	14	78	6	3	1	1.8	.966							
Philadelphia W-76 L-86 Gene Mauch W-27 L-27 George Myatt W-1 L-0 Bob Skinner W-48 L-59	1B	B. White	385	.239	9	40	982	77	6	94	9.6	.994	C. Short	42	270	19	13	1	2.94
	2B	C. Rojas	621	.232	9	48	365	424	10	110	5.3	.987	L. Jackson	34	244	13	17	0	2.77
	SS	R. Pena	500	.260	1	38	230	434	32	93	5.2	.954	W. Fryman	34	214	12	14	0	2.78
	3B	T. Taylor	547	.250	3	38	112	315	15	25	3.2	.966	R. Wise	30	182	9	15	0	4.54
	RF	J. Callison	398	.244	14	40	187	10	0	1	1.8	1.000	J. James	29	116	4	4	0	4.28
	CF	T. Gonzalez	416	.264	3	38	227	4	5	1	2.0	.979	D. Farrell	54	83	4	6	12	3.48
	LF	D. Allen	521	.263	33	90	208	5	6	0	1.6	.973	G. Wagner	44	78	4	4	8	3.00
	C	M. Ryan	296	.179	1	15	501	62	5	7	5.9	.991							
	O1	J. Briggs	338	.254	7	31	423	23	7	33		.985							
	OF	D. Lock	248	.210	8	34	145	2	7	1	2.0	.955							
	C	C. Dalrymple	241	.207	3	26	463	34	5	3	6.3	.990							
New York W-73 L-89 Gil Hodges	1B	E. Kranepool	373	.231	3	20	921	75	6	76	8.9	.994	T. Seaver	36	278	16	12	1	2.20
	2B	P. Linz	258	.209	1	17	136	162	10	36	4.8	.968	J. Koosman	35	264	19	12	0	2.08
	SS	B. Harrelson	402	.219	0	14	199	317	15	58	5.0	.972	D. Cardwell	29	180	7	13	1	2.95
	3B	E. Charles	369	.276	15	53	69	200	13	19	2.7	.954	D. Selma	33	170	9	10	0	2.75
	RF	R. Swoboda	450	.242	11	59	217	14	6	4	1.9	.975	N. Ryan	21	134	6	9	0	3.09
	CF	T. Agee	368	.217	5	17	216	6	5	2	1.8	.978	K. Koonce	55	97	6	4	11	2.42
	LF	C. Jones	509	.297	14	55	226	7	9	0	1.7	.963	A. Jackson	25	93	3	7	3	3.69
	C	J. Grote	404	.282	3	31	754	60	5	8	7.1	.994	J. McAndrew	12	79	4	7	0	2.28
	OF	A. Shamsky	345	.238	12	48	128	6	1	2	1.6	.993	R. Taylor	58	77	1	5	13	2.70
	2B	K. Boswell	284	.261	4	11	154	203	13	37	5.4	.965							
	S2	A. Weis	274	.172	1	14	138	242	14	43		.964							
	C	J. Martin	244	.225	3	31	334	24	2	4	6.8	.994							
	UT	J. Buchek	192	.182	1	11	57	91	7	11		.955							
	OF	L. Stahl	183	.235	3	10	110	5	2	1	2.5	.983							
Houston W-72 L-90 Grady Hatton W-23 L-38 Harry Walker W-49 L-52	1B	R. Staub	591	.291	6	72	1313	93	11	100	9.6	.992	D. Giusti	37	251	11	14	1	3.19
	2B	D. Menke	542	.249	6	56	269	285	10	47	4.7	.982	L. Dierker	32	234	12	15	0	3.31
	SS	H. Torres	466	.223	1	24	159	391	24	55	4.5	.958	D. Lemaster	33	224	10	15	0	2.81
	3B	D. Rader	333	.267	6	43	83	168	19	14	3.1	.930	D. Wilson	33	209	13	16	0	3.28
	RF	N. Miller	257	.237	6	28	131	1	4	1	1.8	.971	M. Cuellar	28	171	8	11	1	2.74
	CF	R. Davis	217	.212	1	12	131	4	4	0	2.7	.971	J. Buzhardt	39	84	4	4	5	3.12
	LF	J. Wynn	542	.269	26	67	298	20	4	8	2.1	.988	S. Shea	30	35	4	4	6	3.38
	C	J. Bateman	350	.249	4	33	690	49	11	6	6.9	.985							
	3O	Aspromonte	409	.225	1	46	110	153	10	9		.963							
	OF	L. Thomas	201	.194	1	11	67	5	2	0	1.5	.973							
	OF	D. Simpson	177	.186	3	11	63	2	2	1	1.4	.970							
	2B	J. Gotay	165	.248	1	11	116	103	4	28	4.6	.982							

BATTING AND BASE RUNNING LEADERS

Batting Average		Slugging Average		Home Runs		Winning Percentage		Earned Run Average		Wins	
P. Rose, CIN	.335	W. McCovey, SF	.545	W. McCovey, SF	36	S. Blass, PIT	.750	B. Gibson, STL	1.12	J. Marichal, SF	26
M. Alou, PIT	.332	D. Allen, PHI	.520	D. Allen, PHI	33	J. Marichal, SF	.743	B. Bolin, SF	1.99	B. Gibson, STL	22
F. Alou, ATL	.317	B. Williams, CHI	.500	E. Banks, CHI	32	B. Gibson, STL	.710	B. Veale, PIT	2.05	F. Jenkins, CHI	20
A. Johnson, CIN	.312	H. Aaron, ATL	.498	B. Williams, CHI	30	N. Briles, STL	.633	J. Koosman, NY	2.08	N. Briles, STL	19
C. Flood, STL	.301	W. Mays, SF	.488	H. Aaron, ATL	29	B. Hands, CHI	.615	S. Blass, PIT	2.12	J. Koosman, NY	19
						J. Maloney, CIN	.615			C. Short, PHI	19

PITCHING LEADERS

NATIONAL LEAGUE 1968, *cont.*

BATTING AND BASE RUNNING LEADERS

Total Bases			Runs Batted In			Stolen Bases			Saves		
B. Williams, CHI	321		W. McCovey, SF	105		L. Brock, STL	62		P. Regan, CHI, LA	25	
H. Aaron, ATL	302		R. Santo, CHI	98		M. Wills, PIT	52		J. Hoerner, STL	17	
P. Rose, CIN	294		B. Williams, CHI	98		W. Davis, LA	36		C. Carroll, ATL, CIN	17	
F. Alou, ATL	290		T. Perez, CIN	92		H. Aaron, ATL	28		J. Brewer, LA	14	
W. McCovey, SF	285		D. Allen, PHI	90		C. Jones, NY	23				

Hits			Base on Balls			Home Run Percentage			Fewest Hits/9 Innings		
P. Rose, CIN	210		R. Santo, CHI	96		W. McCovey, SF	6.9		B. Gibson, STL	5.85	
F. Alou, ATL	210		J. Wynn, HOU	90		D. Allen, PHI	6.3		B. Bolin, SF	6.52	
G. Beckert, CHI	189		R. Hunt, SF	78		E. Banks, CHI	5.8		B. Veale, PIT	6.86	
A. Johnson, CIN	188		D. Allen, PHI	74		J. Wynn, HOU	4.8		P. Jarvis, ATL	7.10	

Runs Scored			Doubles			Triples			Most Strikeouts/9 Inn.		
G. Beckert, CHI	98		L. Brock, STL	46		L. Brock, STL	14		B. Singer, LA	7.97	
P. Rose, CIN	94		P. Rose, CIN	42		R. Clemente, PIT	12		B. Gibson, STL	7.92	
T. Perez, CIN	93		J. Bench, CIN	40		W. Davis, LA	10		J. Maloney, CIN	7.87	
L. Brock, STL	92		R. Staub, HOU	37		D. Allen, PHI	9		F. Jenkins, CHI	7.60	

PITCHING LEADERS

Strikeouts			Complete Games		
B. Gibson, STL	268		J. Marichal, SF	30	
F. Jenkins, CHI	260		B. Gibson, STL	28	
B. Singer, LA	227		F. Jenkins, CHI	20	
J. Marichal, SF	218		G. Perry, SF	19	
R. Sadecki, SF	206		J. Koosman, NY	17	

Shutouts			Fewest Walks/9 Innings		
B. Gibson, STL	13		B. Hands, CHI	1.25	
D. Drysdale, LA	8		J. Marichal, SF	1.27	
S. Blass, PIT	7		T. Seaver, NY	1.55	
J. Koosman, NY	7		M. Pappas, ATL, CIN	1.57	

Innings			Games Pitched		
J. Marichal, SF	326		T. Abernathy, CIN	78	
F. Jenkins, CHI	308		P. Regan, CHI, LA	73	
B. Gibson, STL	305		C. Carroll, ATL, CIN	68	
G. Perry, SF	291		R. Taylor, NY	58	

	W	L	PCT	GB	R	OR	2B	3B	HR	BA	SA	SB	E	DP	FA	CG	BB	SO	ShO	SV	ERA
St. Louis	97	65	.599		583	472	227	48	73	.249	.346	110	140	135	.978	63	375	971	30	32	2.49
San Francisco	88	74	.543	9	599	529	162	33	108	.239	.341	50	162	125	.975	77	344	942	20	16	2.71
Chicago	84	78	.519	13	612	611	203	43	130	.242	.366	41	119	149	.981	46	392	894	12	32	3.41
Cincinnati	83	79	.512	14	690	673	281	36	106	.273	.389	59	144	144	.978	24	573	963	16	38	3.56
Atlanta	81	81	.500	16	514	549	179	31	80	.252	.339	83	125	139	.980	44	362	871	16	29	2.92
Pittsburgh	80	82	.494	17	583	532	180	44	80	.252	.343	130	139	162	.979	42	485	897	19	30	2.74
Los Angeles	76	86	.469	21	470	509	202	36	67	.230	.319	57	144	144	.977	38	414	994	23	31	2.69
Philadelphia	76	86	.469	21	543	615	178	30	100	.233	.333	58	127	163	.980	42	421	935	12	27	3.36
New York	73	89	.451	24	473	499	178	30	81	.228	.315	72	133	142	.979	45	430	1014	25	32	2.72
Houston	72	90	.444	25	510	588	205	28	66	.231	.317	44	156	129	.975	50	479	1021	12	23	3.26
					5577	5577	1995	359	891	.243	.341	704	1389	1432	.978	471	4275	9502	185	290	2.99

AMERICAN LEAGUE 1968

	POS	Player	AB	BA	HR	RBI	PO	A	E	DP	TC/G	FA	Pitcher	G	IP	W	L	SV	ERA
Detroit	1B	N. Cash	411	.263	25	63	924	88	8	66	8.7	.992	D. McLain	41	336	31	6	0	1.96
	2B	McAuliffe	570	.249	16	56	288	348	9	79	4.4	.986	E. Wilson	34	224	13	12	0	2.85
W-103 L-59	SS	R. Oyler	215	.135	1	12	139	207	8	31	3.2	.977	M. Lolich	39	220	17	9	1	3.19
	3B	D. Wert	536	.200	12	37	142	284	15	22	2.9	.966	J. Sparma	34	182	10	10	0	3.70
Mayo Smith	RF	J. Northrup	580	.264	21	90	321	7	7	1	2.2	.979	J. Hiller	39	128	9	6	2	2.39
	CF	M. Stanley	583	.259	11	60	297	7	0	2	2.3	1.000	P. Dobson	47	125	5	8	7	2.66
	LF	W. Horton	512	.285	36	85	212	6	6	2	1.6	.973	D. Patterson	38	68	2	3	7	2.12
	C	B. Freehan	540	.263	25	84	971	73	6	15	7.6	.994	F. Lasher	34	49	5	1	5	3.33
	OF	A. Kaline	327	.287	10	53	131	1	3	0	1.8	.978							
	SS	T. Matchick	227	.203	3	14	53	118	9	20	3.1	.950							
	UT	D. Tracewski	212	.156	4	15	82	157	5	27		.980							
Baltimore	1B	B. Powell	550	.249	22	85	1293	79	14	102	9.3	.990	D. McNally	35	273	22	10	0	1.95
	2B	D. Johnson	504	.242	9	56	260	330	13	67	4.7	.978	J. Hardin	35	244	18	13	0	2.51
W-91 L-71	SS	M. Belanger	472	.208	2	21	248	444	22	73	4.9	.969	T. Phoebus	36	241	15	15	0	2.62
	3B	B. Robinson	608	.253	17	75	168	353	16	31	3.3	.970	D. Leonhard	28	126	7	7	1	3.13
Hank Bauer	RF	F. Robinson	421	.268	15	52	173	5	7	0	1.6	.962	G. Brabender	37	125	6	7	3	3.32
W-43 L-37	CF	P. Blair	421	.211	7	38	271	10	2	2	2.1	.993	E. Watt	59	83	5	5	11	2.27
	LF	C. Blefary	451	.200	15	39	144	9	6	1	1.7	.962	P. Richert	36	62	6	3	6	3.47
Earl Weaver	C	Etchebarren	189	.233	5	20	414	29	1	3	6.3	.998	M. Drabowsky	45	61	4	4	7	1.91
W-48 L-34	O2	D. Buford	426	.282	15	46	239	111	8	22		.978							
	OF	C. Motton	217	.198	8	25	91	2	1	0	1.7	.989							
	C	E. Hendricks	183	.202	7	23	303	21	3	3	6.2	.991							
Cleveland	1B	T. Horton	477	.249	14	59	972	63	8	80	8.1	.992	S. McDowell	38	269	15	14	0	1.81
	2B	V. Fuller	244	.242	0	18	112	129	3	24	3.3	.988	L. Tiant	34	258	21	9	0	1.60
W-86 L-75	SS	L. Brown	495	.234	6	35	255	371	22	70	4.2	.966	S. Siebert	31	206	12	10	0	2.97
	3B	M. Alvis	452	.223	8	37	114	202	13	18	2.6	.960	S. Williams	44	194	13	11	9	2.50
Alvin Dark	RF	T. Harper	235	.217	6	26	121	0	2	0	1.1	.984	S. Hargan	32	158	8	15	0	4.15
	CF	J. Cardenal	583	.257	7	44	367	12	10	7	2.5	.974	E. Fisher	54	95	4	2	4	2.85
	LF	L. Maye	299	.281	4	26	123	4	2	0	1.6	.984	M. Paul	36	92	5	8	3	3.93
	C	J. Azcue	357	.280	4	42	699	50	3	11	7.8	.996	V. Romo	40	83	5	3	12	1.62
	C	D. Sims	361	.249	11	44	523	41	10	4	6.8	.983							
	UT	C. Salmon	276	.214	3	12	152	145	8	29		.974							
	OF	R. Snyder	217	.281	2	23	106	4	1	3	2.1	.991							
	OF	L. Johnson	202	.257	5	23	87	5	1	1	1.6	.989							
	2B	D. Nelson	189	.233	0	19	115	114	3	26	3.9	.987							
	OF	V. Davalillo	180	.239	2	13	84	4	3	1	1.9	.967							

AMERICAN LEAGUE 1968, *cont.*

Boston — W-86 L-76 — Dick Williams

POS	Player	AB	BA	HR	RBI	PO	A	E	DP	TC/G	FA	Pitcher	G	IP	W	L	SV	ERA
1B	G. Scott	350	.171	3	25	807	55	11	68	7.8	.987	R. Culp	35	216	16	6	0	2.91
2B	M. Andrews	536	.271	7	45	330	375	17	93	5.2	.976	G. Bell	35	199	11	11	1	3.12
SS	Petrocelli	406	.234	12	46	169	360	12	66	4.6	.978	D. Ellsworth	31	196	16	7	0	3.03
3B	J. Foy	515	.225	10	60	116	313	30	36	3.1	.935	J. Santiago	18	124	9	4	0	2.25
RF	K. Harrelson	535	.275	35	109	241	8	0	1	1.9	1.000	J. Lonborg	23	113	6	10	0	4.29
CF	R. Smith	558	.265	15	69	390	8	6	1	2.6	.985	J. Pizarro	19	108	6	8	2	3.59
LF	Yastrzemski	539	.301	23	74	301	12	3	3	2.0	.991	G. Waslewski	34	105	4	7	0	3.67
C	R. Gibson	231	.225	3	20	428	36	8	7	6.4	.983	L. Stange	50	103	5	5	12	3.93
12	D. Jones	354	.234	5	29	481	65	3	55		.995	Stephenson	23	69	2	8	0	5.64
UT	J. Adair	208	.216	2	12	90	139	8	22		.966	S. Lyle	49	66	6	1	11	2.74
C	E. Howard	203	.241	5	18	377	30	2	3	6.0	.995							

New York — W-83 L-79 — Ralph Houk

POS	Player	AB	BA	HR	RBI	PO	A	E	DP	TC/G	FA	Pitcher	G	IP	W	L	SV	ERA
1B	M. Mantle	435	.237	18	54	1195	76	15	91	9.8	.988	Stottlemyre	36	279	21	12	0	2.45
2B	H. Clarke	579	.230	2	26	357	444	13	80	5.9	.984	B. Bahnsen	37	267	17	12	0	2.05
SS	T. Tresh	507	.195	11	52	199	409	31	70	5.4	.951	F. Peterson	36	212	12	11	0	2.63
3B	B. Cox	437	.229	7	41	98	279	17	22	3.0	.957	S. Barber	20	128	6	5	0	3.23
RF	B. Robinson	342	.240	6	40	195	3	3	1	2.1	.985	F. Talbot	29	99	1	9	0	3.36
CF	J. Pepitone	380	.245	15	56	190	4	4	1	2.2	.980	J. Verbanic	40	97	6	7	4	3.15
LF	R. White	577	.267	17	62	283	14	1	4	1.9	.997	Monbouquette	17	89	5	7	0	4.43
C	J. Gibbs	423	.213	3	29	642	55	6	7	5.8	.991	D. Womack	45	62	3	7	2	3.21
OF	A. Kosco	466	.240	15	59	160	9	7	0	1.9	.960	L. McDaniel	24	51	4	1	10	1.75
C	F. Fernandez	135	.170	7	30	240	27	3	2	6.0	.989	S. Hamilton	40	51	2	2	11	2.13

Oakland — W-82 L-80 — Bob Kennedy

POS	Player	AB	BA	HR	RBI	PO	A	E	DP	TC/G	FA	Pitcher	G	IP	W	L	SV	ERA
1B	D. Cater	504	.290	6	62	985	68	5	89	8.7	.995	C. Hunter	36	234	13	13	1	3.35
2B	J. Donaldson	363	.220	2	27	169	263	13	48	4.5	.971	B. Odom	32	231	16	10	0	2.45
SS	Campaneris	642	.276	4	38	279	458	34	86	5.0	.956	J. Nash	34	229	13	13	0	2.28
3B	S. Bando	605	.251	9	67	188	272	17	27	2.9	.964	C. Dobson	35	225	12	14	0	3.00
RF	R. Jackson	553	.250	29	74	269	14	12	5	2.0	.959	L. Krausse	36	185	10	11	4	3.11
CF	R. Monday	482	.274	8	49	299	11	7	3	2.2	.978	D. Segui	52	83	6	5	6	2.39
LF	Hershberger	246	.272	5	32	128	5	3	0	1.5	.978	J. Aker	54	75	4	4	11	4.10
C	D. Duncan	246	.191	7	28	474	41	7	5	6.6	.987	E. Sprague	47	69	3	4	4	3.28
2B	D. Green	202	.233	6	18	124	170	8	35	5.0	.974							
C	Pagliaroni	199	.246	6	20	375	16	1	3	6.2	.997							
1B	R. Webster	196	.214	3	23	454	27	6	33	8.9	.988							
OF	J. Rudi	181	.177	1	12	77	1	1	0	1.4	.987							

Minnesota — W-79 L-83 — Cal Ermer

POS	Player	AB	BA	HR	RBI	PO	A	E	DP	TC/G	FA	Pitcher	G	IP	W	L	SV	ERA
1B	R. Reese	332	.259	4	28	620	38	6	36	7.6	.991	D. Chance	43	292	16	16	1	2.53
2B	R. Carew	461	.273	1	42	262	280	18	48	4.8	.968	J. Merritt	38	238	12	16	1	3.25
SS	J. Hernandez	199	.176	2	17	119	197	25	43	4.3	.927	J. Kaat	30	208	14	12	0	2.94
3B	C. Tovar	613	.272	6	47	48	147	14	8	2.8	.933	D. Boswell	34	190	10	13	0	3.32
RF	T. Oliva	470	.289	18	68	227	7	4	1	1.9	.983	J. Perry	32	139	8	6	1	2.27
CF	T. Uhlaender	488	.283	7	52	283	3	4	1	2.2	.986	Perranoski	66	87	8	7	6	3.10
LF	B. Allison	469	.247	22	52	166	4	6	0	1.5	.966	Worthington	54	76	4	5	18	2.71
C	J. Roseboro	380	.216	8	39	689	52	7	5	6.4	.991							
1B	H. Killebrew	295	.210	17	40	594	56	4	50	8.5	.994							
23	F. Quilici	229	.245	1	22	121	165	3	30		.990							
3S	R. Clark	227	.185	1	13	73	157	16	18		.935							
3B	R. Rollins	203	.241	6	30	28	93	9	4	2.3	.931							

California — W-67 L-95 — Bill Rigney

POS	Player	AB	BA	HR	RBI	PO	A	E	DP	TC/G	FA	Pitcher	G	IP	W	L	SV	ERA
1B	D. Mincher	399	.236	13	48	949	59	9	90	9.0	.991	G. Brunet	39	245	13	17	0	2.86
2B	B. Knoop	494	.249	3	39	350	425	15	94	5.2	.981	McGlothlin	40	208	10	15	3	3.54
SS	J. Fregosi	614	.244	9	49	273	454	29	92	4.8	.962	S. Ellis	42	164	9	10	2	3.95
3B	A. Rodriguez	223	.242	1	16	61	113	15	18	2.7	.921	C. Wright	41	126	10	6	3	3.94
RF	R. Repoz	375	.240	13	54	226	4	3	1	2.0	.987	T. Murphy	15	99	5	6	2	2.17
CF	V. Davalillo	339	.298	1	18	212	4	1	2	2.5	.995	R. Clark	21	94	1	11	0	3.53
LF	R. Reichardt	534	.255	21	73	267	9	3	2	1.9	.989	M. Pattin	52	84	4	4	3	2.79
C	B. Rodgers	258	.190	1	14	407	50	7	11	5.3	.985	Messersmith	28	81	4	2	4	2.21
C	T. Satriano	297	.253	8	35	404	40	5	6	5.3	.989	T. Burgmeier	56	73	1	4	5	4.33
UT	C. Hinton	267	.195	7	23	390	60	7	32		.985	M. Rojas	38	55	4	3	6	4.25
3B	P. Schaal	219	.210	2	16	61	142	9	13	3.7	.958							
OF	B. Morton	163	.270	1	18	64	1	1	1	1.3	.985							

Chicago — W-67 L-95 — Eddie Stanky W-34 L-45 · Les Moss W-0 L-2 · Al Lopez W-6 L-5 · Les Moss W-12 L-22 · Al Lopez W-15 L-21

POS	Player	AB	BA	HR	RBI	PO	A	E	DP	TC/G	FA	Pitcher	G	IP	W	L	SV	ERA
1B	T. McCraw	477	.235	9	44	1285	93	20	103	10.4	.986	J. Horlen	35	224	12	14	0	2.37
2B	S. Alomar	363	.253	0	12	188	221	18	48	4.3	.958	J. Fisher	35	181	8	13	0	2.99
SS	L. Aparicio	622	.264	4	36	269	535	19	92	5.3	.977	T. John	25	177	10	5	0	1.98
3B	P. Ward	399	.216	15	50	59	151	12	7	2.9	.946	G. Peters	31	163	4	13	1	3.76
RF	B. Bradford	281	.217	5	24	162	4	6	0	1.7	.965	W. Wood	88	159	13	12	16	1.87
CF	K. Berry	504	.252	7	32	352	11	7	2	2.5	.981	C. Carlos	29	122	4	14	0	3.90
LF	T. Davis	456	.268	8	50	171	8	7	2	1.6	.962	B. Priddy	35	114	3	11	0	3.63
C	D. Josephson	434	.247	6	45	641	86	7	15	6.0	.990	H. Wilhelm	72	94	4	4	12	1.73
C	McNertney	169	.219	3	18	299	39	5	8	5.4	.985	B. Locker	70	90	5	4	10	2.29
OF	B. Voss	167	.156	2	15	73	5	3	3	1.5	.963							
OF	L. Wagner	162	.284	1	18	48	0	3	0	1.1	.941							

AMERICAN LEAGUE 1968, cont.

	POS	Player	AB	BA	HR	RBI	PO	A	E	DP	TC/G	FA	Pitcher	G	IP	W	L	SV	ERA
Washington	1B	M. Epstein	385	.234	13	33	947	70	13	83	9.4	.987	J. Coleman	33	223	12	16	0	3.27
	2B	B. Allen	373	.241	6	40	263	271	5	63	4.9	.991	C. Pascual	31	201	13	12	0	2.69
W-65 L-96	SS	R. Hansen	275	.185	8	28	137	256	15	45	5.0	.963	J. Hannan	25	140	10	6	0	3.01
	3B	K. McMullen	557	.248	20	62	185	296	19	26	3.4	.962	D. Bosman	46	139	2	9	1	3.69
Jim Lemon	RF	E. Stroud	306	.239	4	23	139	2	3	1	1.7	.979	F. Bertaina	27	127	7	13	0	4.66
	CF	D. Unser	635	.230	1	30	388	22	5	10	2.7	.988	B. Moore	32	118	4	6	3	3.37
	LF	F. Howard	598	.274	44	106	160	11	8	1	1.7	.955	P. Ortega	31	116	5	12	0	4.98
	C	P. Casanova	322	.196	4	25	472	46	6	3	5.7	.989	D. Higgins	59	100	4	4	13	3.25
	OF	C. Peterson	226	.204	3	18	82	2	0	0	1.6	1.000	B. Humphreys	56	93	5	7	2	3.69
	SS	E. Brinkman	193	.187	0	6	97	197	10	28	4.1	.967							
	2B	F. Coggins	171	.175	0	7	122	122	12	33	4.9	.953							
	C	J. French	165	.194	1	10	268	42	5	2	5.9	.984							
	OF	B. Alyea	150	.267	6	23	76	0	0	0	1.9	1.000							

BATTING AND BASE RUNNING LEADERS

Batting Average
Yastrzemski, BOS	.301
D. Cater, OAK	.290
T. Oliva, MIN	.289
W. Horton, DET	.285
T. Uhlaender, MIN	.283

Slugging Average
F. Howard, WAS	.552
W. Horton, DET	.543
K. Harrelson, BOS	.518
Yastrzemski, BOS	.495
T. Oliva, MIN	.477

Home Runs
F. Howard, WAS	44
W. Horton, DET	36
K. Harrelson, BOS	35
R. Jackson, OAK	29
N. Cash, DET	25
B. Freehan, DET	25

Winning Percentage
D. McLain, DET	.838
R. Culp, BOS	.727
L. Tiant, CLE	.700
D. Ellsworth, BOS	.696
D. McNally, BAL	.688

Earned Run Average
L. Tiant, CLE	1.60
S. McDowell, CLE	1.81
D. McNally, BAL	1.95
D. McLain, DET	1.96
T. John, CHI	1.98

Wins
D. McLain, DET	31
D. McNally, BAL	22
L. Tiant, CLE	21
Stottlemyre, NY	21
J. Hardin, BAL	18

Total Bases
F. Howard, WAS	330
W. Horton, DET	278
K. Harrelson, BOS	277
Yastrzemski, BOS	267
J. Northrup, DET	259

Runs Batted In
K. Harrelson, BOS	109
F. Howard, WAS	106
J. Northrup, DET	90
W. Horton, DET	85
B. Powell, BAL	85

Stolen Bases
Campaneris, OAK	62
J. Cardenal, CLE	40
C. Tovar, MIN	35
D. Buford, BAL	27
J. Foy, BOS	26

Saves
Worthington, MIN	18
W. Wood, CHI	16
D. Higgins, WAS	13
L. Stange, BOS	12
V. Romo, CLE	12
H. Wilhelm, CHI	12

Strikeouts
S. McDowell, CLE	283
D. McLain, DET	280
L. Tiant, CLE	264
D. Chance, MIN	234
D. McNally, BAL	202

Complete Games
D. McLain, DET	28
L. Tiant, CLE	19
Stottlemyre, NY	19
D. McNally, BAL	18
J. Hardin, BAL	16

Hits
Campaneris, OAK	177
C. Tovar, MIN	167
F. Howard, WAS	164
L. Aparicio, CHI	164

Base on Balls
Yastrzemski, BOS	119
M. Mantle, NY	106
J. Foy, BOS	84
McAuliffe, DET	82

Home Run Percentage
F. Howard, WAS	7.4
W. Horton, DET	7.0
K. Harrelson, BOS	6.5
R. Jackson, OAK	5.2

Fewest Hits/9 Innings
L. Tiant, CLE	5.30
D. McNally, BAL	5.77
S. McDowell, CLE	6.06
S. Siebert, CLE	6.33

Shutouts
L. Tiant, CLE	9
R. Culp, BOS	6
J. Nash, OAK	6
Stottlemyre, NY	6

Fewest Walks/9 Innings
F. Peterson, NY	1.23
D. McLain, DET	1.69
D. Ellsworth, BOS	1.70
J. Kaat, MIN	1.73

Runs Scored
McAuliffe, DET	95
Yastrzemski, BOS	90
R. White, NY	89
C. Tovar, MIN	89

Doubles
R. Smith, BOS	37
B. Robinson, BAL	36
Yastrzemski, BOS	32
C. Tovar, MIN	31

Triples
J. Fregosi, CAL	13
T. McCraw, CHI	12
E. Stroud, WAS	10
McAuliffe, DET	10

Most Strikeouts/9 Inn.
S. McDowell, CLE	9.47
L. Tiant, CLE	9.20
M. Lolich, DET	8.06
R. Culp, BOS	7.90

Innings
D. McLain, DET	336
D. Chance, MIN	292
Stottlemyre, NY	279
D. McNally, BAL	273

Games Pitched
W. Wood, CHI	88
H. Wilhelm, CHI	72
B. Locker, CHI	70
Perranoski, MIN	66

	W	L	PCT	GB	R	OR	2B	3B	HR	BA	SA	SB	E	DP	FA	CG	BB	SO	ShO	SV	ERA
									Batting					**Fielding**			**Pitching**				
Detroit	103	59	.636		671	492	190	39	185	.235	.385	26	105	133	.983	59	486	1115	19	29	2.71
Baltimore	91	71	.562	12	579	497	215	28	133	.225	.352	78	120	131	.981	53	502	1044	16	31	2.66
Cleveland	86	75	.534	16.5	516	504	210	36	75	.234	.327	115	127	130	.979	48	540	1157	23	32	2.66
Boston	86	76	.531	17	614	611	207	17	125	.236	.352	76	128	147	.979	55	523	972	17	31	3.33
New York	83	79	.512	20	536	531	154	34	109	.214	.318	90	139	142	.979	45	424	831	14	27	2.79
Oakland	82	80	.506	21	569	544	192	40	94	.240	.343	147	145	136	.976	45	505	997	18	29	2.94
Minnesota	79	83	.488	24	562	546	207	41	105	.237	.350	98	170	117	.973	46	414	996	14	29	2.89
California	67	95	.414	36	498	615	170	33	83	.227	.318	62	140	156	.977	29	519	869	11	31	3.43
Chicago	67	95	.414	36	463	527	169	33	71	.228	.311	90	151	152	.977	20	451	834	11	40	2.75
Washington	65	96	.404	37.5	524	665	160	37	124	.224	.336	29	148	144	.976	26	517	826	11	28	3.64
					5532	5532	1874	338	1104	.230	.339	811	1373	1388	.978	426	4881	9641	154	307	2.98

NATIONAL LEAGUE 1969

	POS	Player	AB	BA	HR	RBI	PO	A	E	DP	TC/G	FA	Pitcher	G	IP	W	L	SV	ERA
East **New York**	1B	E. Kranepool	353	.238	11	49	809	64	6	76	8.3	.993	T. Seaver	36	273	25	7	0	2.21
	2B	K. Boswell	362	.279	3	32	190	229	18	51	4.6	.959	J. Koosman	32	241	17	9	0	2.28
W-100 L-62	SS	B. Harrelson	395	.248	0	24	243	347	19	70	5.1	.969	G. Gentry	35	234	13	12	0	3.43
	3B	W. Garrett	400	.218	1	39	40	115	8	10	2.3	.951	D. Cardwell	30	152	8	10	0	3.01
Gil Hodges	RF	R. Swoboda	327	.235	9	52	163	5	2	0	1.8	.988	J. McAndrew	27	135	6	7	0	3.47
	CF	T. Agee	565	.271	26	76	334	7	5	0	2.4	.986	T. McGraw	42	100	9	3	12	2.24
	LF	C. Jones	483	.340	12	75	223	4	2	0	1.9	.991	N. Ryan	25	89	6	3	1	3.53
	C	J. Grote	365	.252	6	40	718	63	7	11	7.0	.991	C. Koonce	40	83	6	3	7	4.99
	OF	A. Shamsky	303	.300	14	47	117	2	1	2	1.5	.992	R. Taylor	59	76	9	4	13	2.72
	S2	A. Weis	247	.215	2	23	138	218	13	50		.965							
	OF	R. Gaspar	215	.228	1	14	104	12	2	6	1.3	.983							
	3B	B. Pfeil	211	.232	0	10	32	88	3	8	2.5	.976							
	1B	D. Clendenon	202	.252	12	37	418	25	7	46	7.8	.984							
	C	J. Martin	177	.209	4	21	275	9	1	2	5.9	.996							
	3B	E. Charles	169	.207	3	18	37	86	7	9	2.5	.946							

NATIONAL LEAGUE 1969, *cont.*

	POS	Player	AB	BA	HR	RBI	PO	A	E	DP	TC/G	FA	Pitcher	G	IP	W	L	SV	ERA
Chicago	1B	E. Banks	565	.253	23	106	**1419**	87	4	116	9.9	**.997**	F. Jenkins	43	311	21	15	1	3.21
	2B	G. Beckert	543	.291	1	37	262	401	**24**	71	5.3	.965	B. Hands	41	300	20	14	0	2.49
W-92 L-70	SS	D. Kessinger	664	.273	4	53	**266**	**542**	20	**101**	5.3	**.976**	K. Holtzman	39	261	17	13	0	3.59
	3B	R. Santo	575	.289	29	123	144	334	27	23	3.2	.947	D. Selma	36	169	10	8	1	3.63
Leo Durocher	RF	J. Hickman	338	.237	21	54	153	6	3	0	1.3	.981	P. Regan	71	112	12	6	17	3.70
	CF	D. Young	272	.239	6	27	191	4	5	0	2.0	.975	T. Abernathy	56	85	4	3	3	3.18
	LF	B. Williams	642	.293	21	95	250	15	12	2	1.7	.957	R. Nye	34	69	3	5	3	5.09
	C	R. Hundley	522	.255	18	64	978	**79**	8	17	7.1	.992							
	OF	A. Spangler	213	.211	4	23	75	1	4	0	1.4	.950							
	O1	W. Smith	195	.246	9	25	185	9	3	14		.985							
Pittsburgh	1B	A. Oliver	463	.285	17	70	869	49	8	87	8.7	.991	B. Veale	34	226	13	14	0	3.23
	2B	B. Mazeroski	227	.229	3	25	134	192	4	46	5.1	.988	D. Ellis	35	219	11	17	0	3.58
W-88 L-74	SS	F. Patek	460	.239	5	32	227	399	30	81	4.5	.954	S. Blass	38	210	16	10	2	4.46
	3B	R. Hebner	459	.301	8	47	79	240	19	31	2.7	.944	B. Moose	44	170	14	3	2	2.91
Larry Shepard	RF	R. Clemente	507	.345	19	91	226	14	5	1	1.8	.980	J. Bunning	25	156	10	9	0	3.81
W-84 L-73	CF	M. Alou	**698**	.331	1	48	327	10	8	4	2.1	.977	L. Walker	31	119	4	6	0	3.63
	LF	W. Stargell	522	.307	29	92	159	4	5	1	1.4	.970	Hartenstein	56	96	5	4	10	3.94
Alex Grammas	C	Sanguillen	459	.303	5	57	825	71	**17**	11	8.1	.981	Dal Canton	57	86	8	2	5	3.35
W-4 L-1	2S	G. Alley	285	.246	8	32	145	213	11	56		.970	J. Gibbon	35	51	5	1	9	1.93
	3O	J. Pagan	274	.285	9	42	56	76	5	7		.964							
	O1	C. Taylor	221	.348	4	33	267	16	8	26		.973							
	C	J. May	190	.232	7	23	325	22	2	3	6.7	.994							
	UT	J. Martinez	168	.268	1	16	86	132	6	31		.973							
St. Louis	1B	J. Torre	602	.289	18	101	1270	83	6	117	9.4	.996	B. Gibson	35	314	20	13	0	2.18
	2B	J. Javier	493	.282	10	42	244	374	21	70	4.5	.967	S. Carlton	31	236	17	11	0	2.17
W-87 L-75	SS	D. Maxvill	372	.175	2	32	216	408	20	78	4.9	.969	N. Briles	36	228	15	13	0	3.51
	3B	M. Shannon	551	.254	12	55	123	258	22	22	2.7	.945	R. Washburn	28	132	3	8	1	3.07
Red Schoendienst	RF	V. Pinson	495	.255	10	70	218	6	1	2	1.8	**.996**	C. Taylor	27	127	7	5	2	2.55
	CF	C. Flood	606	.285	4	57	**362**	14	4	2	2.5	.989	M. Torrez	24	108	10	4	0	3.58
	LF	L. Brock	655	.298	12	47	255	7	14	2	1.8	.949	D. Giusti	22	100	3	7	0	3.60
	C	T. McCarver	515	.260	7	51	925	66	14	10	7.4	.986	M. Grant	30	63	7	5	7	4.12
Philadelphia	1B	D. Allen	438	.288	32	89	1024	54	16	100	9.4	.985	G. Jackson	38	253	14	18	1	3.34
	2B	C. Rojas	391	.228	4	30	259	229	10	68	5.2	.980	W. Fryman	36	228	12	15	0	4.42
W-63 L-99	SS	D. Money	450	.229	6	42	212	443	21	82	5.4	.969	R. Wise	33	220	15	13	0	3.23
	3B	T. Taylor	557	.262	3	30	57	150	7	8	3.0	.967	J. Johnson	33	147	6	13	1	4.29
Bob Skinner	RF	J. Callison	495	.265	16	64	273	12	3	3	2.2	.990	B. Champion	23	117	5	10	1	5.00
W-44 L-64	CF	L. Hisle	482	.266	20	56	324	11	8	2	2.5	.977	L. Palmer	26	90	2	8	0	5.20
	LF	J. Briggs	361	.238	12	46	197	6	6	1	1.9	.971	D. Farrell	46	74	3	4	3	4.01
George Myatt	C	M. Ryan	446	.204	12	44	769	**79**	8	13	6.5	.991	B. Wilson	37	62	2	5	6	3.34
W-19 L-35	UT	D. Johnson	475	.255	17	80	250	99	11	12		.969							
	3B	R. Joseph	264	.273	6	37	49	103	7	11	2.7	.956							
	OF	R. Stone	222	.239	1	24	85	6	3	0	1.3	.978							
	S2	T. Harmon	201	.239	0	16	94	168	7	42		.974							
Montreal	1B	B. Bailey	358	.265	9	53	704	67	6	77	9.1	.992	B. Stoneman	42	236	11	19	0	4.39
	2B	Sutherland	544	.239	3	35	318	381	21	110	5.2	.971	J. Robertson	38	180	5	16	1	3.96
W-52 L-110	SS	B. Wine	370	.200	3	25	208	367	**31**	96	5.1	.949	M. Wegener	32	166	5	14	0	4.40
	3B	C. Laboy	562	.258	18	83	115	307	25	28	2.9	.944	D. McGinn	74	132	7	10	6	3.94
Gene Mauch	RF	R. Staub	549	.302	29	79	265	16	10	2	1.9	.966	G. Waslewski	30	109	3	7	1	3.29
	CF	A. Phillips	199	.216	4	7	99	3	2	0	2.0	.981	H. Reed	31	106	6	7	4	4.84
	LF	M. Jones	455	.270	22	79	226	6	10	0	1.9	.959	S. Renko	18	103	6	7	0	4.02
	C	R. Brand	287	.258	0	32	492	44	8	7	6.5	.985	R. Face	44	59	4	2	5	3.94
	1B	R. Fairly	253	.289	12	39	409	36	4	53	8.6	.991							
	C	J. Bateman	235	.209	8	19	433	26	7	5	7.1	.985							
	OF	T. Cline	209	.239	2	12	77	2	1	1	2.0	.988							
	SS	M. Wills	189	.222	0	8	72	139	11	31	4.8	.950							
West Atlanta	1B	O. Cepeda	573	.257	22	88	1318	101	9	91	9.3	.994	P. Niekro	40	284	23	13	1	2.57
	2B	F. Millan	652	.267	6	57	**373**	**444**	17	72	5.1	**.980**	R. Reed	36	241	18	10	0	3.47
W-93 L-69	SS	S. Jackson	318	.239	1	27	161	254	17	48	4.5	.961	P. Jarvis	37	217	13	11	0	4.44
	3B	C. Boyer	496	.250	14	57	139	275	15	18	3.0	**.965**	G. Stone	36	165	13	10	3	3.65
Lum Harris	RF	H. Aaron	547	.300	44	97	267	11	5	3	2.0	.982	M. Pappas	26	144	6	10	0	3.63
	CF	F. Alou	476	.282	5	32	260	4	3	1	2.3	.989	C. Upshaw	62	105	6	4	27	2.91
	LF	T. Gonzalez	320	.294	10	50	173	1	2	0	2.1	.989	J. Britton	24	88	7	5	1	3.78
	C	B. Didier	352	.256	0	32	633	52	4	3	6.0	.994							
	OF	R. Carty	304	.342	16	58	118	0	6	0	1.6	.952							
	SS	G. Garrido	227	.220	0	10	99	192	6	32	3.7	.973							
	UT	Aspromonte	198	.253	3	24	74	46	8	2		.938							
	C	B. Tillman	190	.195	12	29	309	15	4	5	4.8	.988							
	OF	M. Lum	168	.268	1	22	119	2	1	1	1.4	.992							
	O1	T. Francona	88	.295	2	22	64	4	2	4		.971							

NATIONAL LEAGUE 1969, cont.

	POS	Player	AB	BA	HR	RBI	PO	A	E	DP	TC/G	FA	Pitcher	G	IP	W	L	SV	ERA
San Francisco	1B	W. McCovey	491	.320	**45**	**126**	1392	79	12	116	**10.0**	.992	G. Perry	40	**325**	19	14	0	2.49
	2B	R. Hunt	478	.262	3	41	254	356	13	67	5.0	.979	J. Marichal	37	300	21	11	0	**2.10**
W-90 L-72	SS	H. Lanier	495	.228	0	35	252	530	25	98	5.4	.969	McCormick	32	197	11	9	0	3.34
	3B	J. Davenport	303	.241	2	42	77	158	8	15	2.3	.967	B. Bolin	30	146	7	7	0	4.44
Clyde King	RF	B. Bonds	622	.259	32	90	339	9	8	2	2.3	.978	R. Sadecki	29	138	5	8	0	4.24
	CF	W. Mays	403	.283	13	58	199	4	5	0	1.9	.976	F. Linzy	58	116	14	9	11	3.65
	LF	K. Henderson	374	.225	6	44	175	10	6	2	1.7	.969							
	C	D. Dietz	244	.230	11	35	432	31	13	5	6.5	.973							
	OF	D. Marshall	267	.232	2	33	106	3	5	0	1.3	.956							
	23	D. Mason	250	.228	0	13	132	174	18	36		.944							
	OF	J. Hart	236	.254	3	26	80	2	5	1	1.3	.943							
	C	J. Hiatt	194	.196	7	34	335	30	3	6	6.1	.992							
	3S	T. Fuentes	183	.295	1	14	50	117	13	18		.928							
	1B	B. Burda	161	.230	6	27	206	12	1	15	4.9	.995							
Cincinnati	1B	L. May	607	.278	38	110	1387	102	11	**128**	9.6	.993	J. Merritt	42	251	17	9	0	4.37
	2B	T. Helms	480	.269	1	40	320	344	17	87	5.4	.975	T. Cloninger	35	190	11	17	0	5.02
W-89 L-73	SS	W. Woodward	241	.261	0	15	147	248	14	36	4.4	.966	J. Maloney	30	179	12	5	0	2.77
	3B	T. Perez	629	.294	37	122	136	**342**	32	35	3.2	.937	C. Carroll	71	151	12	6	7	3.52
Dave Bristol	RF	P. Rose	627	**.348**	16	82	316	10	4	3	2.1	.988	W. Granger	**90**	145	9	6	27	2.79
	CF	B. Tolan	637	.305	21	93	362	6	10	3	**2.5**	.974	J. Fisher	34	113	4	4	1	5.50
	LF	A. Johnson	523	.315	17	88	222	5	18	1	1.9	.927	G. Nolan	16	109	8	8	0	3.55
	C	J. Bench	532	.293	26	90	793	76	7	10	6.0	.992	G. Culver	32	101	5	7	4	4.28
													J. Arrigo	20	91	4	7	0	4.14
	OF	J. Stewart	221	.253	4	24	68	4	2	0	1.1	.973							
	SS	D. Chaney	209	.191	0	15	115	191	17	44	3.5	.947							
	UT	C. Ruiz	196	.245	0	13	120	147	12	36		.957							
Los Angeles	1B	W. Parker	471	.278	13	68	1189	79	6	87	10.0	.995	C. Osteen	41	321	20	15	0	2.66
	2B	T. Sizemore	590	.271	4	46	283	331	13	76	5.3	.979	B. Singer	41	316	20	12	1	2.34
W-85 L-77	SS	M. Wills	434	.297	4	39	168	357	17	61	5.2	.969	D. Sutton	41	293	17	18	0	3.47
	3B	B. Sudakis	462	.234	14	53	98	272	21	26	3.2	.946	A. Foster	24	103	3	9	0	4.27
Walter Alston	RF	A. Kosco	424	.248	19	74	153	6	3	2	1.5	.981	J. Brewer	59	88	7	6	20	2.56
	CF	W. Davis	498	.311	11	59	271	8	6	1	2.3	.979	P. Mikkelsen	48	81	7	5	4	2.78
	LF	W. Crawford	389	.247	11	41	177	5	5	0	1.7	.973	A. McBean	31	48	2	6	4	3.91
	C	T. Haller	445	.263	6	39	800	48	7	4	6.5	.992							
	OF	M. Mota	294	.323	3	30	118	8	4	2	1.6	.969							
	32	J. Lefebvre	275	.236	4	44	96	181	6	23		.979							
	OF	B. Russell	212	.226	5	15	132	4	3	1	1.6	.978							
	OF	Gabrielson	178	.270	1	18	50	1	1	0	1.1	.981							
Houston	1B	C. Blefary	542	.253	12	67	1235	**103**	17	117	8.9	.987	L. Dierker	39	305	20	13	0	2.33
	2B	J. Morgan	535	.236	15	43	303	328	18	79	4.9	.972	D. Lemaster	38	245	13	17	1	3.16
W-81 L-81	SS	D. Menke	553	.269	10	90	161	356	24	63	4.1	.956	D. Wilson	34	225	16	12	0	4.00
	3B	D. Rader	569	.246	11	83	126	307	25	34	3.0	.945	T. Griffin	31	188	11	10	0	3.54
Harry Walker	RF	N. Miller	409	.264	4	50	172	7	3	3	1.6	.984	J. Ray	40	115	8	2	0	3.91
	CF	J. Wynn	495	.269	33	87	318	9	5	3	2.2	.985	Billingham	52	83	6	7	2	4.23
	LF	J. Alou	452	.248	5	34	173	8	14	1	1.7	.928	F. Gladding	57	73	4	8	29	4.19
	C	J. Edwards	496	.232	6	50	**1135**	79	7	9	**8.1**	**.994**							
	UT	M. Martinez	198	.308	0	15	77	66	11	8		.929							
San Diego	1B	N. Colbert	483	.255	24	66	1217	87	13	96	9.8	.990	C. Kirby	35	216	7	**20**	0	3.79
	2B	J. Arcia	302	.215	0	10	162	176	8	33	5.1	.977	J. Niekro	37	202	8	17	0	3.70
W-52 L-110	SS	T. Dean	273	.176	2	9	139	255	9	41	4.2	.978	A. Santorini	32	185	8	14	0	3.94
	3B	E. Spiezio	355	.234	13	43	93	198	19	10	3.2	.939	T. Sisk	53	143	2	13	6	4.78
Preston Gomez	RF	O. Brown	568	.264	20	61	269	14	7	4	2.0	.976	D. Kelley	27	136	4	8	0	3.57
	CF	C. Gaston	391	.230	2	28	243	12	11	4	2.4	.959	G. Ross	46	110	3	12	3	4.19
	LF	A. Ferrara	366	.260	14	56	131	5	6	2	1.5	.958	J. Baldschun	61	77	7	2	1	4.79
	C	Cannizzaro	418	.220	4	33	644	69	9	8	5.5	.988	J. Podres	17	65	5	6	0	4.29
													B. McCool	54	59	3	5	7	4.27
	UT	R. Pena	472	.250	4	30	289	285	13	54		.978							
	OF	I. Murrell	247	.255	3	25	137	3	6	0	2.0	.959							
	2B	J. Sipin	229	.223	2	9	106	173	7	41	4.8	.976							
	3B	V. Kelly	209	.244	3	15	42	91	4	10	2.8	.971							
	OF	T. Gonzalez	182	.225	2	8	114	2	3	0	2.4	.975							
	OF	L. Stahl	162	.198	3	10	48	3	1	0	1.4	.981							

BATTING AND BASE RUNNING LEADERS

Batting Average		Slugging Average		Home Runs	
P. Rose, CIN	.348	W. McCovey, SF	.656	W. McCovey, SF	45
R. Clemente, PIT	.345	H. Aaron, ATL	.607	H. Aaron, ATL	44
C. Jones, NY	.340	D. Allen, PHI	.573	L. May, CIN	38
M. Alou, PIT	.331	W. Stargell, PIT	.556	T. Perez, CIN	37
W. McCovey, SF	.320	R. Clemente, PIT	.544	J. Wynn, HOU	33

PITCHING LEADERS

Winning Percentage		Earned Run Average		Wins	
T. Seaver, NY	.781	J. Marichal, SF	2.10	T. Seaver, NY	25
J. Marichal, SF	.656	S. Carlton, STL	2.17	P. Niekro, ATL	23
J. Merritt, CIN	.654	B. Gibson, STL	2.18	J. Marichal, SF	21
J. Koosman, NY	.654	T. Seaver, NY	2.21	F. Jenkins, CHI	21
R. Reed, ATL	.643	J. Koosman, NY	2.28		

NATIONAL LEAGUE 1969, *cont.*

BATTING AND BASE RUNNING LEADERS

Total Bases		Runs Batted In		Stolen Bases	
H. Aaron, ATL	332	W. McCovey, SF	126	L. Brock, STL	53
T. Perez, CIN	331	R. Santo, CHI	123	J. Morgan, HOU	49
W. McCovey, SF	322	T. Perez, CIN	122	B. Bonds, SF	45
L. May, CIN	321	L. May, CIN	110	M. Wills, LA, MON	40
P. Rose, CIN	321	E. Banks, CHI	106	B. Tolan, CIN	26

Hits		Base on Balls		Home Run Percentage	
M. Alou, PIT	231	J. Wynn, HOU	148	W. McCovey, SF	9.2
P. Rose, CIN	218	W. McCovey, SF	121	H. Aaron, ATL	8.0
L. Brock, STL	195	J. Morgan, HOU	110	D. Allen, PHI	7.3
B. Tolan, CIN	194	R. Staub, MON	110	J. Wynn, HOU	6.7

Runs Scored		Doubles		Triples	
B. Bonds, SF	120	M. Alou, PIT	41	R. Clemente, PIT	12
P. Rose, CIN	120	D. Kessinger, CHI	38	P. Rose, CIN	11
J. Wynn, HOU	113	P. Rose, CIN	33	B. Tolan, CIN	10
D. Kessinger, CHI	109	B. Williams, CHI	33	B. Williams, CHI	10

PITCHING LEADERS

Saves		Strikeouts		Complete Games	
F. Gladding, HOU	29	F. Jenkins, CHI	273	B. Gibson, STL	28
W. Granger, CIN	27	B. Gibson, STL	269	J. Marichal, SF	27
C. Upshaw, ATL	27	B. Singer, LA	247	G. Perry, SF	26
J. Brewer, LA	20	D. Wilson, HOU	235	F. Jenkins, CHI	23
P. Regan, CHI	17	G. Perry, SF	233	P. Niekro, ATL	21

Fewest Hits/9 Innings		Shutouts		Fewest Walks/9 Innings	
T. Seaver, NY	6.65	J. Marichal, SF	8	J. Marichal, SF	1.62
J. Maloney, CIN	6.79	C. Osteen, LA	7	P. Niekro, ATL	1.81
B. Singer, LA	6.95	F. Jenkins, CHI	7	F. Jenkins, CHI	2.05
J. Koosman, NY	6.98	J. Koosman, NY	6	J. Niekro, CHI, SD	2.07

Most Strikeouts/9 Inn.		Innings		Games Pitched	
D. Wilson, HOU	9.40	G. Perry, SF	325	W. Granger, CIN	90
B. Moose, PIT	8.74	C. Osteen, LA	321	D. McGinn, MON	74
D. Selma, CHI, SD	8.54	B. Singer, LA	316	C. Carroll, CIN	71
B. Veale, PIT	8.48	B. Gibson, STL	314	P. Regan, CHI	71

		W	L	PCT	GB	R	OR	2B	3B	HR	BA	SA	SB	E	DP	FA	CG	BB	SO	ShO	SV	ERA
East	New York	100	62	.617		632	541	184	41	109	.242	.351	66	122	146	.980	51	517	1012	**28**	35	2.99
	Chicago	92	70	.568	8	720	611	215	40	142	.253	.384	30	136	149	.979	58	475	1017	22	27	3.34
	Pittsburgh	88	74	.543	12	725	652	220	**52**	119	**.277**	.398	74	155	169	.975	39	553	1124	9	33	3.61
	St. Louis	87	75	.537	13	595	**540**	**228**	44	90	.253	.359	87	138	144	.978	63	511	1004	12	26	**2.94**
	Philadelphia	63	99	.389	37	645	745	227	35	137	.241	.372	73	136	157	.978	47	570	921	14	21	4.17
	Montreal	52	110	.321	48	582	791	202	33	125	.240	.359	52	184	**179**	.971	26	702	973	8	21	4.33
West	Atlanta	93	69	.574		691	631	195	22	141	.258	.380	59	**115**	114	**.981**	38	438	893	7	42	3.53
	San Francisco	90	72	.556	3	713	636	187	28	136	.242	.361	71	169	155	.974	**71**	461	906	15	17	3.25
	Cincinnati	89	73	.549	4	**798**	768	224	42	**171**	.277	**.422**	79	168	158	.973	23	611	818	11	**44**	4.13
	Los Angeles	85	77	.525	8	645	561	185	**52**	97	.254	.359	80	126	130	.980	47	**420**	975	20	31	3.09
	Houston	81	81	.500	12	676	668	208	40	104	.240	.352	**101**	153	136	.975	52	547	**1221**	11	34	3.60
	San Diego	52	110	.321	41	468	746	180	42	99	.225	.329	45	156	140	.975	16	592	764	9	25	4.24
						7890	7890	2455	471	1470	.250	.369	817	1758	1777	.977	531	6397	11628	166	356	3.60

AMERICAN LEAGUE 1969

		POS	Player	AB	BA	HR	RBI	PO	A	E	DP	TC/G	FA	Pitcher	G	IP	W	L	SV	ERA
East	**Baltimore**	1B	B. Powell	533	.304	37	121	1192	84	7	105	8.9	.995	M. Cuellar	39	291	23	11	0	2.38
		2B	D. Johnson	511	.280	7	57	355	369	12	93	5.2	.984	D. McNally	41	269	20	7	0	3.22
	W-109 L-53	SS	M. Belanger	530	.287	2	50	251	449	23	79	4.9	.968	T. Phoebus	35	202	14	7	0	3.52
		3B	B. Robinson	598	.234	23	84	163	**370**	13	37	3.5	**.976**	J. Palmer	26	181	16	4	0	2.34
	Earl Weaver	RF	F. Robinson	539	.308	32	100	226	9	3	2	1.8	.987	J. Hardin	30	138	6	7	1	3.60
		CF	P. Blair	625	.285	26	76	**407**	14	5	5	2.8	.988	D. Leonhard	37	94	7	4	1	2.49
		LF	D. Buford	554	.291	11	64	228	7	4	1	1.9	.983	E. Watt	56	71	5	2	16	1.65
		C	E. Hendricks	295	.244	12	38	479	40	1	2	6.0	**.998**	D. Hall	39	66	5	2	6	1.92
		C	Etchebarren	217	.249	3	26	380	27	4	1	5.7	.990	P. Richert	44	57	7	4	12	2.20
		OF	Rettenmund	190	.247	4	25	107	3	1	0	1.4	.991							
		OF	C. Motton	89	.303	6	21	26	0	0	0	1.3	1.000							
	Detroit	1B	N. Cash	483	.280	22	74	1016	96	7	99	8.4	.994	D. McLain	42	**325**	**24**	9	0	2.80
		2B	McAuliffe	271	.262	11	33	167	196	9	40	5.2	.976	M. Lolich	37	281	19	11	1	3.14
	W-90 L-72	SS	T. Tresh	331	.224	13	37	118	187	11	38	4.1	.965	E. Wilson	35	215	12	10	0	3.31
		3B	D. Wert	423	.225	14	50	114	259	13	20	3.0	.966	M. Kilkenny	39	128	8	6	2	3.37
	Mayo Smith	RF	A. Kaline	456	.272	21	69	192	9	7	4	1.8	.966	P. Dobson	49	105	5	10	9	3.60
		CF	J. Northrup	543	.295	25	66	323	8	5	2	2.3	.985	J. Hiller	40	99	4	4	4	3.99
		LF	W. Horton	508	.262	28	91	272	8	8	0	2.1	.972	J. Sparma	23	93	6	8	0	4.76
		C	B. Freehan	489	.262	16	49	**821**	49	7	7	**7.3**	.992	D. McMahon	34	37	3	5	11	3.89
		OS	M. Stanley	592	.235	16	70	300	130	12	22		.978							
		23	T. Matchick	298	.242	0	32	104	167	7	34		.975							
		C	J. Price	192	.234	9	28	337	18	4	4	7.0	.989							
		2B	I. Brown	170	.229	5	12	75	100	7	18	4.0	.962							
	Boston	1B	D. Jones	336	.220	3	33	692	54	6	61	9.3	.992	R. Culp	32	227	17	8	0	3.81
		2B	M. Andrews	464	.293	15	59	297	334	18	82	5.4	.972	M. Nagy	33	197	12	2	0	3.11
	W-87 L-75	SS	Petrocelli	535	.297	40	97	269	466	14	103	4.9	**.981**	S. Siebert	43	163	14	10	5	3.80
		3B	G. Scott	549	.253	16	52	106	203	15	29	3.0	.954	J. Lonborg	29	144	7	11	0	4.51
	Dick Williams	RF	Conigliaro	506	.255	20	82	207	4	4	1	1.6	.981	L. Stange	41	137	6	9	3	3.68
	W-82 L-71	CF	R. Smith	543	.309	25	93	321	8	**14**	1	2.5	.959	V. Romo	52	127	7	9	11	3.18
		LF	Yastrzemski	603	.255	40	111	246	17	4	2	1.9	.985	S. Lyle	71	103	8	3	17	2.54
	Eddie Popowski	C	R. Gibson	287	.251	3	27	466	41	11	2	6.2	.979	R. Jarvis	29	100	5	6	1	4.75
	W-5 L-4	UT	S. O'Brien	263	.243	9	29	65	143	15	30		.933	B. Landis	45	82	5	5	1	5.25
		UT	D. Schofield	226	.257	2	20	97	150	7	30		.972							
		OF	J. Lahoud	218	.188	9	21	91	3	2	0	1.5	.979							

AMERICAN LEAGUE 1969, *cont.*

	POS	Player	AB	BA	HR	RBI	PO	A	E	DP	TC/G	FA	Pitcher	G	IP	W	L	SV	ERA
Washington	1B	M. Epstein	403	.278	30	85	1035	69	11	99	9.4	.990	J. Coleman	40	248	12	13	1	3.27
	2B	B. Allen	365	.247	9	45	239	281	14	70	4.9	.974	D. Bosman	31	193	14	5	1	**2.19**
W-86 L-76	SS	E. Brinkman	576	.266	2	43	248	511	19	92	5.2	.976	C. Cox	52	172	12	7	0	2.78
	3B	K. McMullen	562	.272	19	87	185	347	13	35	3.5	.976	J. Hannan	35	158	7	6	0	3.64
Ted Williams	RF	H. Allen	271	.277	1	17	120	6	9	2	1.5	.933	B. Moore	31	134	9	8	0	4.30
	CF	D. Unser	581	.286	7	57	339	8	10	3	2.4	.972	D. Higgins	55	85	10	9	16	3.48
	LF	F. Howard	592	.296	48	111	147	3	4	0	1.4	.974	Shellenback	30	85	4	7	1	4.04
	C	P. Casanova	379	.216	4	37	583	59	5	5	5.3	.992	D. Knowles	53	84	9	2	13	2.24
	2B	T. Cullen	249	.209	1	15	166	188	7	44	3.4	.981	B. Humphreys	47	80	3	3	5	3.05
	OF	L. Maye	238	.290	9	26	100	1	6	1	1.6	.944	D. Baldwin	43	67	2	4	4	4.05
	OF	B. Alyea	237	.249	11	40	84	6	6	0	1.4	.938							
	OF	E. Stroud	206	.252	4	29	109	1	2	0	1.3	.982							
New York	1B	J. Pepitone	513	.242	27	70	**1254**	74	7	118	**10.1**	**.995**	Stottlemyre	39	303	20	14	0	2.82
	2B	H. Clarke	**641**	.285	4	48	373	429	15	112	5.2	.982	F. Peterson	37	272	17	16	0	2.55
W-80 L-81	SS	G. Michael	412	.272	2	31	205	365	19	64	5.0	.968	S. Bahnsen	40	221	9	16	1	3.83
	3B	J. Kenney	447	.257	2	34	63	207	7	20	3.3	.975	B. Burbach	31	141	6	8	0	3.65
Ralph Houk	RF	B. Murcer	564	.259	26	82	212	4	8	0	1.9	.964	A. Downing	30	131	7	5	0	3.38
	CF	B. Robinson	222	.171	3	21	99	5	4	0	1.7	.963	M. Kekich	28	105	4	6	1	4.54
	LF	R. White	448	.290	7	74	267	9	3	1	2.2	.989	L. McDaniel	51	84	5	6	5	3.55
	C	J. Gibbs	219	.224	0	18	364	31	4	6	6.0	.990	J. Aker	38	66	8	4	11	2.06
	C	F. Fernandez	229	.223	12	29	321	29	2	2	5.4	.994							
	OF	J. Hall	212	.236	3	26	78	1	3	0	1.6	.963							
	3B	B. Cox	191	.215	2	17	37	122	11	14	3.0	.935							
	OF	R. Woods	171	.175	1	7	129	2	0	0	2.0	1.000							
Cleveland	1B	T. Horton	625	.278	27	93	1179	100	14	130	8.2	.989	S. McDowell	39	285	18	14	1	2.94
	2B	V. Fuller	254	.236	4	22	217	192	9	53	4.1	.978	L. Tiant	38	250	9	**20**	0	3.71
W-62 L-99	SS	L. Brown	469	.239	4	24	172	276	19	59	4.6	.959	S. Williams	61	178	6	14	12	3.94
	3B	M. Alvis	191	.225	1	15	49	96	4	10	2.6	.973	S. Hargan	32	144	5	14	0	5.70
Alvin Dark	RF	K. Harrelson	519	.222	27	84	257	7	4	2	1.9	.985	D. Ellsworth	34	135	6	9	0	4.13
	CF	J. Cardenal	557	.257	11	45	327	9	6	2	2.4	.982	M. Paul	47	117	5	10	2	3.61
	LF	R. Snyder	266	.248	2	24	144	2	6	1	1.8	.961	J. Pizarro	48	83	3	3	4	3.16
	C	D. Sims	326	.236	18	45	634	51	6	8	6.8	.991							
	3B	L. Klimchock	258	.287	6	26	46	82	9	7	2.4	.934							
	23	Z. Versalles	217	.226	1	13	100	125	6	24		.974							
	SS	E. Leon	213	.239	3	19	114	185	15	43	4.9	.952							
	OF	Scheinblum	199	.186	1	13	71	4	2	1	1.5	.974							
	OF	F. Baker	172	.256	3	15	71	5	4	0	1.7	.950							
West **Minnesota**	1B	R. Reese	419	.322	16	69	924	56	7	97	8.4	.993	J. Perry	46	262	20	6	0	2.82
	2B	R. Carew	458	**.332**	8	56	244	302	17	80	4.8	.970	D. Boswell	39	256	20	12	0	3.23
W-97 L-65	SS	L. Cardenas	578	.280	10	70	310	570	32	126	5.7	.965	J. Kaat	40	242	14	13	1	3.49
	3B	H. Killebrew	555	.276	49	140	75	185	20	12	2.7	.929	T. Hall	31	141	8	7	3	3.33
Billy Martin	RF	T. Oliva	637	.309	24	101	311	14	6	3	2.2	.982	Perranoski	75	120	9	10	31	2.11
	CF	C. Tovar	535	.288	11	52	225	9	4	3	2.1	.983	B. Miller	48	119	5	5	3	3.02
	LF	T. Uhlaender	554	.273	8	62	278	8	1	1	1.9	.997	D. Woodson	44	110	7	5	1	3.67
	C	J. Roseboro	361	.263	3	32	585	52	13	16	5.9	.980							
	OF	G. Nettles	225	.222	7	26	76	2	1	0	1.5	.987							
	OF	B. Allison	189	.228	8	27	91	2	0	1	1.6	1.000							
	C	Mitterwald	187	.257	5	13	340	33	5	6	6.0	.987							
	OF	C. Manuel	164	.207	2	24	57	2	2	0	1.3	.967							
Oakland	1B	D. Cater	584	.262	10	76	1087	97	9	112	9.0	.992	C. Hunter	38	247	12	15	0	3.35
	2B	D. Green	483	.275	12	64	302	379	10	93	5.3	**.986**	C. Dobson	35	235	15	13	0	3.86
W-88 L-74	SS	Campaneris	547	.260	2	25	220	391	21	72	5.1	.967	B. Odom	32	231	15	6	0	2.92
	3B	S. Bando	609	.281	31	113	178	321	**24**	36	3.2	.954	L. Krausse	43	140	7	7	7	4.44
Hank Bauer	RF	R. Jackson	549	.275	47	118	278	14	11	2	2.0	.964	R. Fingers	60	119	6	7	12	3.71
W-80 L-69	CF	R. Monday	399	.271	12	54	262	3	10	0	2.3	.964	J. Nash	26	115	8	8	0	3.67
	LF	T. Reynolds	315	.257	2	20	184	5	4	2	2.2	.979	P. Lindblad	60	78	9	6	9	4.14
John McNamara	C	P. Roof	247	.235	2	19	493	40	9	4	5.1	.983							
W-8 L-5	S2	T. Kubiak	305	.249	2	27	153	215	10	41		.974							
	OF	J. Tartabull	266	.267	0	11	134	2	1	0	2.2	.993							
	C	D. Duncan	127	.126	3	22	209	15	4	1	4.1	.982							
	1B	T. Francona	85	.341	3	20	158	6	2	11	8.7	.988							
California	1B	J. Spencer	386	.254	10	31	926	66	9	81	9.4	.991	Messersmith	40	250	16	11	2	2.52
	2B	S. Alomar	559	.250	1	30	294	354	21*	94	5.0	.969	T. Murphy	36	216	10	16	0	4.21
W-71 L-91	SS	J. Fregosi	580	.260	12	47	255	465	21	88	4.6	.972	McGlothlin	37	201	8	16	0	3.18
	3B	A. Rodriguez	561	.232	7	49	145	352	**24**	42	3.3	.954	R. May	43	180	10	13	2	3.44
Bill Rigney	RF	B. Voss	349	.261	2	40	175	11	1	3	1.7	.995	G. Brunet	23	101	6	7	0	3.84
W-11 L-28	CF	J. Johnstone	540	.270	10	59	331	12	6	4	2.4	.983	K. Tatum	45	86	7	2	22	1.36
	LF	R. Reichardt	493	.254	13	68	244	13	5	4	1.9	.981	H. Wilhelm	44	66	5	7	10	2.47
Lefty Phillips	C	J. Azcue	248	.218	1	19	437	52*	4	10	9.0	.992							
W-60 L-63	O1	R. Repoz	219	.164	8	19	296	22	2	26		.994							
	OF	B. Morton	172	.244	7	32	70	5	0	1	1.5	1.000							

AMERICAN LEAGUE 1969, cont.

Kansas City
W-69 L-93

Joe Gordon

POS	Player	AB	BA	HR	RBI	PO	A	E	DP	TC/G	FA	Pitcher	G	IP	W	L	SV	ERA
1B	M. Fiore	339	.274	12	35	696	94	10	54	8.8	.988	W. Bunker	35	223	12	11	2	3.23
2B	J. Adair	432	.250	5	48	223	261	8	41	4.5	.984	D. Drago	41	201	11	13	1	3.77
SS	J. Hernandez	504	.222	4	40	306	375	33	60	5.0	.954	B. Butler	34	194	9	10	0	3.90
3B	J. Foy	519	.262	11	71	117	209	12	20	3.0	.964	R. Nelson	29	193	7	13	0	3.31
RF	B. Oliver	394	.254	13	43	199	11	5	4	2.2	.977	J. Rooker	28	158	4	16	0	3.75
CF	P. Kelly	417	.264	8	32	237	12	5	3	2.4	.980	M. Hedlund	34	125	3	6	2	3.24
LF	L. Piniella	493	.282	11	68	278	13	7	1	2.3	.977	M. Drabowsky	52	98	11	9	11	2.94
C	E. Rodriguez	267	.236	2	20	433	39	5	2	5.3	.990	Wickersham	34	50	2	3	5	3.96
OF	Kirkpatrick	315	.257	14	49	180	8	1	1	2.3	.995							
1B	C. Harrison	213	.221	3	18	415	36	3	27	8.3	.993							
C	B. Martinez	205	.229	4	23	290	25	9	7	5.9	.972							
3B	P. Schaal	205	.263	1	13	27	77	12	3	2.4	.897							
2S	J. Rios	196	.224	1	5	101	105	9	23		.958							
OF	J. Keough	166	.187	0	7	82	2	0	1	1.7	1.000							
OF	H. Taylor	89	.270	3	21	19	1	2	1	1.2	.909							

Chicago
W-68 L-94

Al Lopez
W-8 L-9

Don Gutteridge
W-60 L-85

POS	Player	AB	BA	HR	RBI	PO	A	E	DP	TC/G	FA	Pitcher	G	IP	W	L	SV	ERA
1B	G. Hopkins	373	.265	8	46	903	51	6	81	9.5	.994	J. Horlen	36	236	13	16	0	3.78
2B	B. Knoop	345	.229	6	41	271	320	9	76	5.8*	.985	T. John	33	232	9	11	0	3.25
SS	L. Aparicio	599	.280	5	51	248	563	20	94	5.4	.976	G. Peters	36	219	10	15	0	4.53
3B	B. Melton	556	.255	23	87	112	322	22	36	3.1	.952	B. Wynne	20	129	7	7	0	4.06
RF	W. Williams	471	.304	3	32	183	13	3	4	1.8	.985	W. Wood	76	120	10	11	15	3.01
CF	K. Berry	297	.232	4	18	215	7	0	1	1.9	1.000	D. Osinski	51	61	5	5	2	3.56
LF	C. May	367	.281	18	62	154	10	3	0	1.7	.982							
C	E. Herrmann	290	.231	8	31	420	41	8	7	5.1	.983							
OF	B. Bradford	273	.256	11	27	141	5	6	1	1.7	.961							
10	T. McCraw	240	.258	2	25	302	15	3	21		.991							
UT	P. Ward	199	.246	6	32	193	48	3	13		.988							
C	D. Pavletich	188	.245	6	33	195	26	6	3	4.5	.974							
UT	R. Hansen	185	.259	2	22	216	83	8	28		.974							
C	D. Josephson	162	.241	1	20	227	27	4	1	5.5	.984							

Seattle
W-64 L-98

Joe Schultz

POS	Player	AB	BA	HR	RBI	PO	A	E	DP	TC/G	FA	Pitcher	G	IP	W	L	SV	ERA
1B	D. Mincher	427	.246	25	78	1033	93	6	98	9.3	.995	G. Brabender	40	202	13	14	0	4.36
2B	J. Donaldson	338	.234	1	19	209	242	12	56	5.1	.974	M. Pattin	34	159	7	12	0	5.62
SS	R. Oyler	255	.165	7	22	143	266	15	47	4.0	.965	D. Segui	66	142	12	6	12	3.35
3B	T. Harper	537	.235	9	41	70	123	10	9	3.4	.951	F. Talbot	25	115	5	8	0	4.16
RF	S. Hovley	329	.277	3	20	175	8	2	3	2.2	.989	J. Gelnar	39	109	3	10	3	3.31
CF	W. Comer	481	.245	15	54	287	14	6	6	2.2	.980	M. Marshall	20	88	3	10	0	5.13
LF	T. Davis	454	.271	6	80	174	3	6	0	1.6	.967	S. Barber	25	86	4	7	0	4.80
C	McNertney	410	.241	8	55	697	67	9	13	6.3	.988	B. Locker	51	78	3	3	6	2.18
OF	M. Hegan	267	.292	8	37	100	7	5	1	1.8	.955	O'Donoghue	55	70	2	2	6	2.96
UT	G. Gil	221	.222	0	17	65	130	9	16		.956	G. Bell	13	61	2	6	2	4.70
3B	R. Rollins	187	.225	4	21	42	103	8	6	3.3	.948							
UT	R. Clark	163	.196	0	12	79	116	9	17		.956							
1B	G. Goossen	139	.309	10	24	265	23	2	15	9.4	.993							

BATTING AND BASE RUNNING LEADERS

Batting Average
R. Carew, MIN	.332
R. Smith, BOS	.309
T. Oliva, MIN	.309
F. Robinson, BAL	.308
B. Powell, BAL	.304

Slugging Average
R. Jackson, OAK	.608
Petrocelli, BOS	.589
H. Killebrew, MIN	.584
F. Howard, WAS	.574
B. Powell, BAL	.559

Home Runs
H. Killebrew, MIN	49
F. Howard, WAS	48
R. Jackson, OAK	47
Petrocelli, BOS	40
Yastrzemski, BOS	40

Winning Percentage
J. Palmer, BAL	.800
J. Perry, MIN	.769
D. McNally, BAL	.741
D. McLain, DET	.727
B. Odom, OAK	.714

Total Bases
F. Howard, WAS	340
R. Jackson, OAK	334
H. Killebrew, MIN	324
T. Oliva, MIN	316
Petrocelli, BOS	315

Runs Batted In
H. Killebrew, MIN	140
B. Powell, BAL	121
R. Jackson, OAK	118
S. Bando, OAK	113
F. Howard, WAS	111
Yastrzemski, BOS	111

Stolen Bases
T. Harper, SEA	73
Campaneris, OAK	62
C. Tovar, MIN	45
P. Kelly, KC	40
J. Foy, KC	37

Saves
Perranoski, MIN	31
K. Tatum, CAL	22
S. Lyle, BOS	17
D. Higgins, WAS	16
E. Watt, BAL	16

Hits
T. Oliva, MIN	197
H. Clarke, NY	183
P. Blair, BAL	178
F. Howard, WAS	175

Base on Balls
H. Killebrew, MIN	145
R. Jackson, OAK	114
S. Bando, OAK	111
F. Howard, WAS	102

Home Run Percentage
H. Killebrew, MIN	8.8
R. Jackson, OAK	8.6
F. Howard, WAS	8.1
Petrocelli, BOS	7.5

Fewest Hits/9 Innings
Messersmith, CAL	6.08
J. Palmer, BAL	6.51
M. Cuellar, BAL	6.59
M. Lolich, DET	6.85

Runs Scored
R. Jackson, OAK	123
F. Robinson, BAL	111
F. Howard, WAS	111
H. Killebrew, MIN	106

Doubles
T. Oliva, MIN	39
R. Jackson, OAK	36
D. Johnson, BAL	34
Petrocelli, BOS	32

Triples
D. Unser, WAS	8
R. Smith, BOS	7
H. Clarke, NY	7

Most Strikeouts/9 Inn.
S. McDowell, CLE	8.81
M. Lolich, DET	8.68
Messersmith, CAL	7.60
B. Butler, KC	7.24

PITCHING LEADERS

Earned Run Average
D. Bosman, WAS	2.19
J. Palmer, BAL	2.34
M. Cuellar, BAL	2.38
Messersmith, CAL	2.52
F. Peterson, NY	2.55

Wins
D. McLain, DET	24
M. Cuellar, BAL	23
J. Perry, MIN	20
D. McNally, BAL	20
D. Boswell, MIN	20
Stottlemyre, NY	20

Strikeouts
S. McDowell, CLE	279
M. Lolich, DET	271
Messersmith, CAL	211
D. Boswell, MIN	190
J. Coleman, WAS	182
M. Cuellar, BAL	182

Complete Games
Stottlemyre, NY	24
D. McLain, DET	23
S. McDowell, CLE	18
M. Cuellar, BAL	18
F. Peterson, NY	16

Shutouts
D. McLain, DET	9
J. Palmer, BAL	6
M. Cuellar, BAL	5

Fewest Walks/9 Innings
F. Peterson, NY	1.42
D. Bosman, WAS	1.82
D. McLain, DET	1.86
J. Perry, MIN	2.27

Innings
D. McLain, DET	325
Stottlemyre, NY	303
M. Cuellar, BAL	291
S. McDowell, CLE	285

Games Pitched
W. Wood, CHI	76
Perranoski, MIN	75
S. Lyle, BOS	71
B. Locker, CHI, SEA	68

AMERICAN LEAGUE 1969, *cont.*

		W	L	PCT	GB	R	OR	2B	3B	Batting HR	BA	SA	SB	E	Fielding DP	FA	CG	BB	Pitching SO	ShO	SV	ERA
East	Baltimore	109	53	.673		779	517	234	29	175	.265	.414	82	101	145	.984	50	498	897	20	36	2.83
	Detroit	90	72	.556	19	701	601	188	29	182	.242	.387	35	130	130	.979	55	586	1032	20	28	3.32
	Boston	87	75	.537	22	743	736	234	37	197	.251	.415	41	157	178	.975	30	685	935	7	41	3.93
	Washington	86	76	.531	23	694	644	171	40	148	.251	.378	52	140	159	.978	28	656	835	10	41	3.49
	New York	80	81	.497	28.5	562	587	210	44	94	.235	.344	119	131	158	.979	53	522	801	13	20	3.23
	Cleveland	62	99	.385	46.5	573	717	173	24	119	.237	.345	85	145	153	.976	35	681	1000	7	22	3.94
West	Minnesota	97	65	.599		790	618	246	32	163	.268	.408	115	150	177	.977	41	524	906	8	43	3.25
	Oakland	88	74	.543	9	740	678	210	28	148	.249	.376	100	137	162	.978	42	586	887	14	36	3.71
	California	71	91	.438	26	528	652	151	29	88	.230	.319	54	136	164	.978	25	517	885	9	39	3.55
	Kansas City	69	93	.426	28	586	688	179	32	98	.240	.338	129	157	114	.975	42	560	894	10	25	3.72
	Chicago	68	94	.420	29	625	723	210	27	112	.247	.357	54	122	163	.981	29	564	810	10	25	4.21
	Seattle	64	98	.395	33	639	799	179	27	125	.234	.346	167	167	149	.974	21	653	963	6	33	4.35
						7960	7960	2385	378	1649	.246	.369	1033	1673	1852	.978	451	7032	10845	134	389	3.63

NATIONAL LEAGUE 1970

		POS	Player	AB	BA	HR	RBI	PO	A	E	DP	TC/G	FA	Pitcher	G	IP	W	L	SV	ERA
East	**Pittsburgh**	1B	B. Robertson	390	.287	27	82	907	78	5	107	10.0	.995	D. Ellis	30	202	13	10	0	3.21
		2B	B. Mazeroski	367	.229	7	39	227	325	7	87	5.5	.987	B. Veale	34	202	10	15	0	3.92
	W-89 L-73	SS	G. Alley	426	.244	8	41	202	381	15	84	5.5	.975	S. Blass	31	197	10	12	0	3.52
		3B	R. Hebner	420	.290	11	46	64	235	19	24	2.7	.940	B. Moose	28	190	11	10	0	3.98
	Danny Murtaugh	RF	R. Clemente	412	.352	14	60	189	12	7	2	2.0	.966	L. Walker	42	163	15	6	3	3.04
		CF	M. Alou	677	.297	1	47	297	15	8	1	2.1	.975	D. Giusti	66	103	9	3	26	3.06
		LF	W. Stargell	474	.264	31	85	184	16	5	1	1.6	.976	Dal Canton	41	85	9	4	1	4.55
		C	Sanguillen	486	.325	7	61	775	66	10	12	6.8	.988							
		O1	A. Oliver	551	.270	12	83	718	52	9	69		.988							
		SS	F. Patek	237	.245	1	19	122	212	10	42	5.3	.971							
		3B	J. Pagan	230	.265	7	29	43	91	6	14	2.6	.957							
		2B	D. Cash	210	.314	1	28	147	156	8	46	5.7	.974							
	Chicago	1B	J. Hickman	514	.315	32	115	563	60	6	46	8.5	.990	F. Jenkins	40	313	22	16	0	3.39
		2B	G. Beckert	591	.288	3	36	302	412	22	88	5.3	.970	K. Holtzman	39	288	17	11	0	3.38
	W-84 L-78	SS	D. Kessinger	631	.266	1	39	257	501	22	86	5.1	.972	B. Hands	39	265	18	15	1	3.70
		3B	R. Santo	555	.267	26	114	143	320	27	36	3.2	.945	M. Pappas	21	145	10	8	0	2.68
	Leo Durocher	RF	J. Callison	477	.264	19	68	244	8	7	3	1.8	.973	J. Decker	24	109	2	7	0	4.62
		CF	C. James	176	.210	3	14	115	5	0	1	1.3	1.000	P. Regan	54	76	5	9	12	4.74
		LF	B. Williams	636	.322	42	129	259	13	3	1	1.9	.989							
		C	R. Hundley	250	.244	7	36	455	26	5	2	6.7	.990							
		1B	E. Banks	222	.252	12	44	528	35	4	53	9.1	.993							
		OF	J. Pepitone	213	.268	12	44	121	1	1	0	2.2	.992							
		UT	P. Popovich	186	.253	4	20	75	97	4	26		.977							
		C	J. Hiatt	178	.242	2	22	380	22	4	1	6.4	.990							
		1B	W. Smith	167	.216	5	24	318	11	2	32	7.7	.994							
	New York	1B	D. Clendenon	396	.288	22	97	722	62	7	72	7.9	.991	T. Seaver	37	291	18	12	0	2.81
		2B	K. Boswell	351	.254	5	44	204	244	2	49	4.5	.996	J. Koosman	30	212	12	7	0	3.14
	W-83 L-79	SS	B. Harrelson	564	.243	1	42	305	401	21	84	4.7	.971	G. Gentry	32	188	9	9	1	3.69
		3B	J. Foy	322	.236	6	37	90	179	18	20	3.0	.937	J. McAndrew	32	184	10	14	2	3.57
	Gil Hodges	RF	R. Swoboda	245	.233	9	40	117	3	2	1	1.2	.984	R. Sadecki	28	139	8	4	0	3.88
		CF	T. Agee	636	.286	24	75	374	4	13	3	2.6	.967	N. Ryan	27	132	7	11	1	3.41
		LF	C. Jones	506	.277	10	63	243	10	5	3	2.0	.981	T. McGraw	57	91	4	6	10	3.26
		C	J. Grote	415	.255	2	34	855	46	8	12	7.3	.991	D. Frisella	30	66	8	3	1	3.00
		O1	A. Shamsky	403	.293	11	49	482	37	2	30		.996	R. Taylor	57	66	5	4	13	3.95
		32	W. Garrett	366	.254	12	45	151	205	12	34		.967							
		OF	K. Singleton	198	.263	5	26	90	1	3	0	1.8	.968							
		OF	D. Marshall	189	.243	6	29	71	2	2	0	1.7	.973							
	St. Louis	1B	J. Hague	451	.271	14	68	672	48	4	65	8.8	.994	B. Gibson	34	294	23	7	0	3.12
		2B	J. Javier	513	.251	2	42	329	413	15	84	5.5	.980	S. Carlton	34	254	10	19	0	3.72
	W-76 L-86	SS	D. Maxvill	399	.201	0	28	216	426	12	80	4.8	.982	M. Torrez	30	179	8	10	0	4.22
		3B	J. Torre	624	.325	21	100	68	133	11	12	2.9	.948	J. Reuss	20	127	7	8	0	4.11
	Red Schoendienst	RF	L. Lee	264	.227	6	23	120	3	4	0	1.6	.969	C. Taylor	56	124	6	7	8	3.12
		CF	J. Cardenal	552	.293	10	74	276	6	9	0	2.2	.969	N. Briles	30	107	6	7	0	6.22
		LF	L. Brock	664	.304	13	57	247	9	10	2	1.8	.962	F. Linzy	47	61	3	5	2	3.67
		C	T. Simmons	284	.243	3	24	466	37	5	2	6.4	.990							
		13	D. Allen	459	.279	34	101	703	108	16	70		.981							
		OF	C. Taylor	245	.249	6	45	66	3	1	1	1.5	.986							
		OF	V. Davalillo	183	.311	1	33	67	3	2	1	1.3	.972							
		3B	M. Shannon	174	.213	0	22	32	59	8	4	1.9	.919							

NATIONAL LEAGUE 1970, cont.

	POS	Player	AB	BA	HR	RBI	PO	A	E	DP	TC/G	FA	Pitcher	G	IP	W	L	SV	ERA
Philadelphia W-73 L-88 Frank Lucchesi	1B	D. Johnson	574	.256	27	93	1178	73	6	104	8.2	.995	R. Wise	35	220	13	14	0	4.17
	2B	D. Doyle	413	.208	2	16	251	228	11	55	4.8	.978	J. Bunning	34	219	10	15	0	4.11
	SS	L. Bowa	547	.250	0	34	202	418	13	69	4.4	.979	C. Short	36	199	9	16	1	4.30
	3B	D. Money	447	.295	14	66	131	236	15	27	3.2	.961	G. Jackson	32	150	5	15	0	5.28
	RF	R. Stone	321	.262	3	39	148	5	5	0	1.6	.968	B. Lersch	42	138	6	3	3	3.26
	CF	L. Hisle	405	.205	10	44	262	5	6	0	2.3	.978	D. Selma	73	134	8	9	22	2.75
	LF	J. Briggs	341	.270	9	47	188	7	4	1	2.1	.980	W. Fryman	27	128	8	6	0	4.08
	C	T. McCarver	164	.287	4	14	314	18	3	2	7.6	.991	L. Palmer	38	102	1	2	0	5.47
	UT	T. Taylor	439	.301	9	55	220	215	5	48		.989	J. Hoerner	44	58	9	5	9	2.64
	OF	O. Gamble	275	.262	1	19	148	4	7	0	2.1	.956							
	OF	B. Browne	270	.248	10	36	150	4	4	1	1.8	.975							
Montreal W-73 L-89 Gene Mauch	1B	R. Fairly	385	.288	15	61	944	90	5	112	8.8	.995	C. Morton	43	285	18	11	0	3.60
	2B	Sutherland	359	.206	3	26	178	254	11	72	4.6	.975	S. Renko	41	223	13	11	1	4.32
	SS	B. Wine	501	.232	3	51	284	481	19	137	4.9	.976	B. Stoneman	40	208	7	15	0	4.59
	3B	C. Laboy	432	.199	5	53	105	194	17	19	2.4	.946	D. McGinn	52	131	7	10	0	5.43
	RF	R. Staub	569	.274	30	94	308	14	5	4	2.0	.985	M. Wegener	25	104	3	6	0	5.28
	CF	A. Phillips	214	.238	6	21	130	1	2	0	1.8	.985	H. Reed	57	89	6	5	5	3.13
	LF	M. Jones	271	.240	14	32	118	3	4	1	1.4	.968	C. Raymond	59	83	6	7	23	4.45
	C	J. Bateman	520	.237	15	68	824	62	15	19	6.6	.983	M. Marshall	24	65	3	7	3	3.48
	UT	B. Bailey	352	.287	28	84	179	86	8	18		.971							
	2B	M. Staehle	321	.218	0	26	152	208	14	53	4.1	.963							
	OF	J. Gosger	274	.263	5	37	124	5	0	1	1.8	1.000							
	OF	J. Fairey	211	.242	3	25	86	1	2	0	1.5	.978							

West

	POS	Player	AB	BA	HR	RBI	PO	A	E	DP	TC/G	FA	Pitcher	G	IP	W	L	SV	ERA
Cincinnati W-102 L-60 Sparky Anderson	1B	L. May	605	.253	34	94	1362	109	10	143	9.7	.993	G. Nolan	37	251	18	7	0	3.26
	2B	T. Helms	575	.237	1	45	350	410	13	107	4.8	.983	J. Merritt	35	234	20	12	0	4.08
	SS	Concepcion	265	.260	1	19	137	244	22	51	4.3	.945	McGlothlin	35	211	14	10	0	3.58
	3B	T. Perez	587	.317	40	129	131	286	35	34	3.0	.923	W. Simpson	26	176	14	3	0	3.02
	RF	P. Rose	649	.316	15	52	309	8	1	2	2.0	.997	T. Cloninger	30	148	9	7	1	3.83
	CF	B. Tolan	589	.316	16	80	349	7	8	0	2.4	.978	C. Carroll	65	104	9	4	16	2.60
	LF	B. Carbo	365	.310	21	63	177	8	4	2	1.6	.979	W. Granger	67	85	6	5	35	2.65
	C	J. Bench	605	.293	45	148	759	73	12	12	6.0	.986	D. Gullett	44	78	5	2	6	2.42
	SS	W. Woodward	264	.223	1	14	101	226	9	48	4.4	.973							
	OF	H. McRae	165	.248	8	23	52	1	1	0	1.2	.981							
Los Angeles W-87 L-74 Walter Alston	1B	W. Parker	614	.319	10	111	1498	125	7	116	10.1	.996	D. Sutton	38	260	15	13	0	4.08
	2B	T. Sizemore	340	.306	1	34	194	232	7	47	5.0	.984	C. Osteen	37	259	16	14	0	3.82
	SS	M. Wills	522	.270	0	34	171	396	24	58	4.7	.959	A. Foster	33	199	10	13	0	4.25
	3B	Grabarkewitz	529	.289	17	84	88	190	12	19	3.0	.959	J. Moeller	31	135	7	9	4	3.93
	RF	M. Mota	417	.305	3	37	172	8	5	3	1.7	.973	S. Vance	20	115	7	7	0	3.13
	CF	W. Davis	593	.305	8	93	342	12	3	4	2.5	.992	B. Singer	16	106	8	5	0	3.14
	LF	W. Crawford	299	.234	8	40	160	9	7	1	1.9	.960	J. Brewer	58	89	7	6	24	3.13
	C	T. Haller	325	.286	10	47	524	26	4	7	5.2	.993	P. Mikkelsen	33	62	4	2	6	2.76
	2B	J. Lefebvre	314	.252	4	44	142	177	4	34	4.6	.988	J. Pena	29	57	4	3	4	4.42
	OF	B. Russell	278	.259	0	28	167	8	3	1	2.3	.983							
	C3	B. Sudakis	269	.264	14	44	188	99	14	9		.953							
	OF	A. Kosco	224	.228	8	27	101	2	0		1.8	.981							
San Francisco W-86 L-76 Clyde King W-19 L-23 Charlie Fox W-67 L-53	1B	W. McCovey	495	.289	39	126	1217	134	15	117	9.4	.989	G. Perry	41	329	23	13	0	3.20
	2B	R. Hunt	367	.281	6	41	162	173	11	38	4.1	.968	J. Marichal	34	243	12	10	0	4.11
	SS	H. Lanier	438	.231	2	41	256	397	22	83	5.2	.967	R. Robertson	41	184	8	9	1	4.84
	3B	A. Gallagher	282	.266	4	28	70	128	6	12	2.2	.971	F. Reberger	45	152	7	8	2	5.57
	RF	B. Bonds	663	.302	26	78	326	14	11	7	2.2	.969	R. Bryant	34	96	5	8	0	4.78
	CF	W. Mays	478	.291	28	83	269	6	7	3	2.2	.975	D. McMahon	61	94	9	5	19	2.97
	LF	K. Henderson	554	.294	17	88	272	15	10	2	2.1	.966	S. Pitlock	18	87	5	5	0	4.66
	C	D. Dietz	493	.300	22	107	820	58	14	9	6.4	.984	J. Johnson	33	65	3	4	3	4.27
	UT	T. Fuentes	435	.267	2	32	202	324	19	57		.965							
	3B	J. Hart	255	.282	8	37	39	69	11	2	2.1	.908							
	O1	F. Johnson	161	.273	3	31	199	14	5	16		.977							
	S2	B. Heise	154	.234	1	22	78	124	13	24		.940							
Houston W-79 L-83 Harry Walker	1B	B. Watson	327	.272	11	61	695	39	6	54	8.9	.992	L. Dierker	37	270	16	12	1	3.87
	2B	J. Morgan	548	.268	8	52	349	430	17	98	5.6	.979	Billingham	46	188	13	9	0	3.97
	SS	D. Menke	562	.304	13	92	192	394	28	66	4.6	.954	D. Wilson	29	184	11	6	0	3.91
	3B	D. Rader	576	.252	25	87	147	357	18	39	3.4	.966	D. Lemaster	39	162	7	12	3	4.56
	RF	J. Alou	458	.306	1	44	169	6	7	2	1.7	.962	T. Griffin	23	111	3	13	0	5.76
	CF	C. Cedeno	355	.310	7	42	211	1	7	0	2.4	.968	J. Ray	52	105	6	3	5	3.26
	LF	J. Wynn	554	.282	27	88	293	14	4	4	2.1	.987	R. Cook	41	82	4	4	2	3.53
	C	J. Edwards	458	.221	7	49	854	74	5	11	6.7	.995	J. Bouton	29	73	4	6	0	5.42
	1O	J. Pepitone	279	.251	14	35	428	30	3	45		.993	F. Gladding	63	71	7	4	18	4.06
	OF	N. Miller	226	.239	4	29	101	6	6	1	1.6	.947							
	OF	T. Davis	213	.282	3	30	71	4	4	1	1.5	.949							

NATIONAL LEAGUE 1970, *cont.*

	POS	Player	AB	BA	HR	RBI	PO	A	E	DP	TC/G	FA	Pitcher	G	IP	W	L	SV	ERA
Atlanta	1B	O. Cepeda	567	.305	34	111	1288	112	12	100	9.5	.992	P. Jarvis	36	254	16	16	0	3.61
	2B	F. Millan	590	.310	2	37	337	359	15	83	5.0	.979	P. Niekro	34	230	12	18	0	4.27
W-76 L-86	SS	S. Jackson	328	.259	0	20	123	240	26	40	4.5	.933	J. Nash	34	212	13	9	0	4.08
	3B	C. Boyer	475	.246	16	62	107	268	18	21	3.1	.954	G. Stone	35	207	11	11	0	3.87
Lum Harris	RF	H. Aaron	516	.298	38	118	246	6	6	1	2.1	.977	R. Reed	21	135	7	10	0	4.40
	CF	T. Gonzalez	430	.265	7	55	235	1	3	0	2.0	.987	H. Wilhelm	50	78	6	4	13	3.10
	LF	R. Carty	478	**.366**	25	101	219	5	6	0	1.7	.974	B. Priddy	41	73	5	5	8	5.42
	C	B. Tillman	223	.238	11	30	404	22	5	0	6.2	.988							
	SS	G. Garrido	367	.264	1	19	119	233	9	36	4.5	.975							
	OF	M. Lum	291	.254	7	28	168	3	2	0	1.8	.988							
	C	H. King	204	.260	11	30	316	14	5	1	5.4	.985							
	C	B. Didier	168	.149	0	7	297	25	4	3	5.7	.988							
San Diego	1B	N. Colbert	572	.259	38	86	1406	90	14	126	9.9	.991	P. Dobson	40	251	14	15	1	3.76
	2B	D. Campbell	581	.219	12	40	**359**	**455**	**22**	96	5.5	.974	C. Kirby	36	215	10	16	0	4.52
W-63 L-99	SS	J. Arcia	229	.223	0	17	89	146	11	32	3.7	.955	D. Coombs	35	188	10	14	0	3.30
	3B	E. Spiezio	316	.285	12	42	66	178	12	10	2.8	.953	D. Roberts	43	182	8	14	1	3.81
Preston Gomez	RF	O. Brown	534	.292	23	89	258	12	10	3	2.0	.964	M. Corkins	24	111	5	6	0	4.62
	CF	C. Gaston	584	.318	29	93	310	7	8	0	2.3	.975	R. Herbel	64*	111	5	9	5	4.95
	LF	I. Murrell	347	.245	12	35	183	8	6	2	2.0	.970	A. Santorini	21	76	1	8	1	6.04
	C	Cannizzaro	341	.279	5	42	559	44	12	5	5.6	.980	T. Dukes	53	69	1	6	10	4.04
	OF	A. Ferrara	372	.277	13	51	119	2	4	0	1.3	.968							
	S3	S. Huntz	352	.219	11	37	118	257	20	39	5.5	.949							
	C	B. Barton	188	.218	4	16	347	28	2	5	6.4	.995							

BATTING AND BASE RUNNING LEADERS

PITCHING LEADERS

Batting Average
R. Carty, ATL	.366
J. Torre, STL	.325
Sanguillen, PIT	.325
B. Williams, CHI	.322
W. Parker, LA	.319

Slugging Average
W. McCovey, SF	.612
T. Perez, CIN	.589
J. Bench, CIN	.587
B. Williams, CHI	.586
R. Carty, ATL	.584

Home Runs
J. Bench, CIN	45
B. Williams, CHI	42
T. Perez, CIN	40
W. McCovey, SF	39
H. Aaron, ATL	38
N. Colbert, SD	38

Winning Percentage
B. Gibson, STL	.767
G. Nolan, CIN	.720
L. Walker, PIT	.714
G. Perry, SF	.639
J. Merritt, CIN	.625

Earned Run Average
T. Seaver, NY	2.81
W. Simpson, CIN	3.02
L. Walker, PIT	3.04
B. Gibson, STL	3.12
J. Koosman, NY	3.14

Wins
B. Gibson, STL	23
G. Perry, SF	23
F. Jenkins, CHI	22
J. Merritt, CIN	20

Total Bases
B. Williams, CHI	373
J. Bench, CIN	355
T. Perez, CIN	346
B. Bonds, SF	334
C. Gaston, SD	317

Runs Batted In
J. Bench, CIN	148
T. Perez, CIN	129
B. Williams, CHI	129
W. McCovey, SF	126
H. Aaron, ATL	118

Stolen Bases
B. Tolan, CIN	57
L. Brock, STL	51
B. Bonds, SF	48
J. Morgan, HOU	42
W. Davis, LA	38

Saves
W. Granger, CIN	35
D. Giusti, PIT	26
J. Brewer, LA	24
C. Raymond, MON	23
D. Selma, PHI	22

Strikeouts
T. Seaver, NY	283
B. Gibson, STL	274
F. Jenkins, CHI	274
G. Perry, SF	214
K. Holtzman, CHI	202

Complete Games
F. Jenkins, CHI	24
B. Gibson, STL	23
G. Perry, SF	23
T. Seaver, NY	19
L. Dierker, HOU	17

Hits
B. Williams, CHI	205
P. Rose, CIN	205
J. Torre, STL	203
L. Brock, STL	202

Base on Balls
W. McCovey, SF	137
R. Staub, MON	112
D. Dietz, SF	109
J. Wynn, HOU	106

Home Run Percentage
W. McCovey, SF	7.9
J. Bench, CIN	7.4
D. Allen, STL	7.4
H. Aaron, ATL	7.4

Fewest Hits/9 Innings
W. Simpson, CIN	6.39
T. Seaver, NY	7.11
L. Walker, PIT	7.12
G. Gentry, NY	7.42

Shutouts
G. Perry, SF	5
D. Ellis, PIT	4
C. Osteen, LA	4
C. Morton, MON	4

Fewest Walks/9 Innings
F. Jenkins, CHI	1.73
J. Marichal, SF	1.78
C. Osteen, LA	1.81
J. McAndrew, NY	1.86

Runs Scored
B. Williams, CHI	137
B. Bonds, SF	134
P. Rose, CIN	120
L. Brock, STL	114

Doubles
W. Parker, LA	47
W. McCovey, SF	39
P. Rose, CIN	37
D. Dietz, SF	36

Triples
W. Davis, LA	16
D. Kessinger, CHI	14
R. Clemente, PIT	10
B. Bonds, SF	10

Most Strikeouts/9 Inn.
T. Seaver, NY	8.75
B. Gibson, STL	8.39
B. Veale, PIT	7.93
F. Jenkins, CHI	7.88

Innings
G. Perry, SF	329
F. Jenkins, CHI	313
B. Gibson, STL	294
T. Seaver, NY	291

Games Pitched
R. Herbel, NY, SD	76
D. Selma, PHI	73
F. Linzy, SF, STL	67
W. Granger, CIN	67

		W	L	PCT	GB	R	OR	Batting 2B	3B	HR	BA	SA	SB	Fielding E	DP	FA	Pitching CG	BB	SO	ShO	SV	ERA
East	Pittsburgh	89	73	.549		729	664	235	**70**	130	.270	.406	66	137	**195**	.979	36	625	990	13	43	3.70
	Chicago	84	78	.519	5	806	679	228	44	179	.259	.415	39	137	146	.978	59	**475**	1000	9	25	3.76
	New York	83	79	.512	6	695	**630**	211	42	120	.249	.370	118	124	136	.979	47	575	**1064**	10	32	**3.46**
	St. Louis	76	86	.469	13	744	747	218	51	113	.263	.379	117	150	159	.979	51	632	960	11	20	4.05
	Philadelphia	73	88	.453	15.5	594	730	224	58	101	.238	.356	72	**114**	134	**.981**	24	538	1047	8	36	4.17
	Montreal	73	89	.451	16	687	807	211	35	136	.237	.365	65	141	193	.977	29	716	914	10	32	4.50
West	Cincinnati	102	60	.630		775	681	253	45	**191**	**.270**	**.436**	115	151	173	.976	32	592	843	15	**60**	3.71
	Los Angeles	87	74	.540	14.5	749	684	233	67	87	.270	.382	**138**	135	135	.978	37	496	880	**17**	42	3.82
	San Francisco	86	76	.531	16	**831**	826	**257**	35	165	.262	.409	83	170	153	.973	50	604	931	7	30	4.50
	Houston	79	83	.488	23	744	763	250	47	129	.259	.391	114	140	144	.978	36	577	942	6	35	4.23
	Atlanta	76	86	.469	26	736	772	215	24	160	.270	.404	58	141	118	.977	45	478	960	9	24	4.35
	San Diego	63	99	.389	39	681	788	208	36	172	.246	.391	60	158	159	.975	24	611	886	9	32	4.38
						8771	8771	2743	554	1683	.258	.392	1045	1698	1845	.977	470	6919	11417	124	411	4.05

AMERICAN LEAGUE 1970

East

Baltimore
W-108 L-54
Earl Weaver

POS	Player	AB	BA	HR	RBI	PO	A	E	DP	TC/G	FA	Pitcher	G	IP	W	L	SV	ERA
1B	B. Powell	526	.297	35	114	1209	89	10	107	9.0	.992	J. Palmer	39	305	20	10	0	2.71
2B	D. Johnson	530	.281	10	53	379	390	8	101	5.2	.990	M. Cuellar	40	298	24	8	0	3.47
SS	M. Belanger	459	.218	1	36	212	412	19	78	4.5	.970	D. McNally	40	296	24	9	0	3.22
3B	B. Robinson	608	.276	18	94	157	321	17	30	3.2	.966	J. Hardin	36	145	6	5	1	3.54
RF	F. Robinson	471	.306	25	78	221	9	3	3	1.9	.987	T. Phoebus	27	135	5	5	0	3.07
CF	P. Blair	480	.267	18	65	368	10	4	3	3.0	.990	D. Hall	32	61	10	5	3	3.10
LF	D. Buford	504	.272	17	66	221	13	3	3	1.8	.987	E. Watt	53	55	7	7	12	3.27
C	E. Hendricks	322	.242	12	41	509	35	8	6	5.8	.986	P. Richert	50	55	7	2	13	1.96
OF	Rettenmund	338	.322	18	58	201	6	5	1	2.3	.976							
C	Etchebarren	230	.243	4	28	392	29	7	3	5.6	.984							
UT	C. Salmon	172	.250	7	22	61	87	9	12		.943							
O1	T. Crowley	152	.257	5	20	138	6	2	9		.986							

New York
W-93 L-69
Ralph Houk

POS	Player	AB	BA	HR	RBI	PO	A	E	DP	TC/G	FA	Pitcher	G	IP	W	L	SV	ERA
1B	D. Cater	582	.301	6	76	981	70	8	79	8.1	.992	Stottlemyre	37	271	15	13	0	3.09
2B	H. Clarke	686	.251	4	46	379	478	18	95	5.6	.979	F. Peterson	39	260	20	11	0	2.91
SS	G. Michael	435	.214	2	38	248	379	28	78	5.3	.957	S. Bahnsen	36	233	14	11	0	3.32
3B	J. Kenney	404	.193	4	35	111	300	17	18	3.2	.960	L. McDaniel	62	112	9	5	29	2.01
RF	C. Blefary	269	.212	9	37	103	1	3	0	1.4	.972	S. Kline	16	100	6	6	0	3.42
CF	B. Murcer	581	.251	23	78	375	15	3	3	2.5	.992	Klimkowski	45	98	6	7	1	2.66
LF	R. White	609	.296	22	94	315	6	2	0	2.0	.994	J. Aker	41	70	4	2	16	2.06
C	T. Munson	453	.302	6	53	631	80	8	11	5.8	.989	S. Hamilton	35	45	4	3	3	2.78
1B	J. Ellis	226	.248	7	29	449	37	4	35	9.2	.992							
OF	R. Woods	225	.227	8	27	108	6	3	1	1.5	.974							
C	J. Gibbs	153	.301	8	26	208	19	3	1	5.2	.987							

Boston
W-87 L-75
Eddie Kasko

POS	Player	AB	BA	HR	RBI	PO	A	E	DP	TC/G	FA	Pitcher	G	IP	W	L	SV	ERA
1B	Yastrzemski	566	.329	40	102	696	61	8	62	8.1	.990	R. Culp	33	251	17	14	0	3.05
2B	M. Andrews	589	.253	17	65	342	350	19	74	4.8	.973	G. Siebert	33	223	15	8	0	3.43
SS	Petrocelli	583	.261	29	103	262	393	20	77	4.8	.970	G. Peters	34	222	16	11	0	4.05
3B	G. Scott	480	.296	16	63	71	113	13	13	2.9	.934	K. Brett	41	139	8	9	2	4.08
RF	Conigliaro	560	.266	36	116	252	7	6	1	1.8	.977	M. Nagy	23	129	6	5	0	4.47
CF	R. Smith	580	.303	22	74	361	15	9	1	2.7	.977	V. Romo	48	108	7	3	6	4.08
LF	Conigliaro	398	.271	18	58	201	8	7	0	2.0	.968	S. Lyle	63	67	1	7	20	3.90
C	G. Moses	315	.263	6	35	578	45	6	3	7.1	.990	G. Wagner	38	40	3	1	7	3.38
3S	L. Alvarado	183	.224	1	10	45	134	8	17		.957							
C	T. Satriano	165	.236	3	13	318	19	5	5	6.7	.985							

Detroit
W-79 L-83
Mayo Smith

POS	Player	AB	BA	HR	RBI	PO	A	E	DP	TC/G	FA	Pitcher	G	IP	W	L	SV	ERA
1B	N. Cash	370	.259	15	53	868	70	10	76	8.3	.989	M. Lolich	40	273	14	19	0	3.79
2B	McAuliffe	530	.234	12	50	280	333	16	75	5.0	.975	J. Niekro	38	213	12	13	0	4.06
SS	C. Gutierrez	415	.243	0	22	183	326	23	60	3.9	.957	L. Cain	29	181	12	7	0	3.83
3B	D. Wert	363	.218	6	33	94	191	14	20	2.6	.953	M. Kilkenny	36	129	7	6	0	5.16
RF	A. Kaline	467	.278	16	71	156	3	2	1	1.8	.988	J. Hiller	47	104	6	6	3	3.03
CF	M. Stanley	568	.252	13	47	317	3	0	0	2.4	1.000	E. Wilson	18	96	4	6	0	4.41
LF	J. Northrup	504	.262	24	80	284	4	2	1	2.1	.993	T. Timmerman	61	85	6	7	27	4.13
C	B. Freehan	395	.241	16	52	742	42	2	6	6.9	.997	D. Patterson	43	78	7	1	2	4.85
OF	W. Horton	371	.305	17	69	154	10	3	1	1.7	.982							
UT	E. Maddox	258	.248	3	24	104	100	14	10		.936							
UT	D. Jones	191	.220	6	21	111	99	4	26		.981							
OF	G. Brown	124	.226	3	24	37	1	2	0	1.5	.950							

Cleveland
W-76 L-86
Alvin Dark

POS	Player	AB	BA	HR	RBI	PO	A	E	DP	TC/G	FA	Pitcher	G	IP	W	L	SV	ERA
1B	T. Horton	413	.269	17	59	898	73	6	106	8.7	.994	S. McDowell	39	305	20	12	0	2.92
2B	E. Leon	549	.248	10	56	342	378	13	102	5.2	.982	R. Hand	35	160	6	13	3	3.83
SS	J. Heidemann	445	.211	6	37	216	354	23	79	4.5	.961	D. Chance	45	155	9	8	4	4.24
3B	G. Nettles	549	.235	26	62	134	358	17	40	3.3	.967	S. Hargan	23	143	11	3	0	2.90
RF	V. Pinson	574	.286	24	82	265	8	5	3	2.0	.982	S. Dunning	19	94	4	9	0	4.98
CF	T. Uhlaender	473	.268	11	46	225	5	2	1	1.7	.991	D. Higgins	58	90	4	6	11	4.00
LF	R. Foster	477	.268	23	60	188	6	7	0	1.5	.965	M. Paul	30	88	2	8	0	4.81
C	R. Fosse	450	.307	18	61	854	70	10	7	7.8	.989	P. Hennigan	42	72	6	3	3	4.00
UT	D. Sims	345	.264	23	56	505	34	8	18		.985	R. Austin	31	68	2	5	3	4.76
UT	C. Hinton	195	.318	9	29	229	15	2	14		.992	F. Lasher	43	58	1	7	5	4.58
OF	B. Bradford	163	.196	7	23	117	1	2	0	1.9	.983							

Washington
W-70 L-92
Ted Williams

POS	Player	AB	BA	HR	RBI	PO	A	E	DP	TC/G	FA	Pitcher	G	IP	W	L	SV	ERA
1B	M. Epstein	430	.256	20	56	1100	70	10	104	9.7	.992	D. Bosman	36	231	16	12	0	3.00
2B	T. Cullen	262	.214	1	18	211	262	3	65	4.3	.994	J. Coleman	39	219	8	12	0	3.58
SS	E. Brinkman	625	.262	1	40	301	569	23	103	5.7	.974	C. Cox	37	192	8	12	1	4.45
3B	A. Rodriguez	547	.247	19	76	97	343	18	36*	3.4	.961	J. Hannan	42	128	9	11	0	4.01
RF	E. Stroud	433	.266	5	32	271	8	2	3	2.4	.993	D. Knowles	71	119	2	14	27	2.04
CF	D. Unser	322	.258	5	30	173	8	3	2	1.8	.984	G. Brunet	24	118	8	6	0	4.42
LF	F. Howard	566	.283	44	126	172	6	5	4	1.5	.973	Shellenback	39	117	6	7	0	3.69
C	P. Casanova	328	.229	6	30	461	48	5	12	5.2	.988	J. Grzenda	49	85	3	6	6	4.98
OF	R. Reichardt	277	.253	15	46	134	0	2	0	1.7	.985	H. Pina	61	71	5	3	6	2.79
2B	B. Allen	261	.234	8	29	169	175	11	47	4.4	.969							
OF	L. Maye	255	.263	7	30	75	4	0	1	1.2	1.000							
C	J. French	166	.211	1	13	267	23	8	4	4.8	.973							

AMERICAN LEAGUE 1970, cont.

West — Minnesota
W-98 L-64 — Bill Rigney

POS	Player	AB	BA	HR	RBI	PO	A	E	DP	TC/G	FA	Pitcher	G	IP	W	L	SV	ERA
1B	R. Reese	501	.261	10	56	1118	82	10	94	8.3	.992	J. Perry	40	279	24	12	0	3.03
2B	D. Thompson	302	.219	0	22	144	204	5	35	4.4	.986	J. Kaat	45	230	14	10	0	3.56
SS	L. Cardenas	588	.247	11	65	280	487	17	91	4.9	.978	B. Blyleven	27	164	10	9	0	3.18
3B	H. Killebrew	527	.271	41	113	108	203	17	14	2.4	.948	T. Hall	52	155	11	6	4	2.55
RF	T. Oliva	628	.325	23	107	351	12	12	4	2.4	.968	B. Zepp	43	151	9	4	2	3.22
CF	C. Tovar	650	.300	10	54	370	12	9	1	2.6	.977	S. Williams	68	113	10	1	15	1.99
LF	J. Holt	319	.266	3	40	201	2	1	0	1.6	.995	Perranoski	67	111	7	8	34	2.43
C	Mitterwald	369	.222	15	46	740	62	3	8	6.9	.996	L. Tiant	18	93	7	3	0	3.39
OF	B. Alyea	258	.291	16	61	93	4	2	0	1.3	.980	D. Boswell	18	69	3	7	0	6.39
2B	R. Carew	191	.366	4	28	73	122	8	26	4.5	.961							
30	R. Renick	179	.229	7	25	52	54	2	5		.981							
C	P. Ratliff	149	.268	5	22	183	11	4	4	3.7	.980							

Oakland
W-89 L-73 — John McNamara

POS	Player	AB	BA	HR	RBI	PO	A	E	DP	TC/G	FA	Pitcher	G	IP	W	L	SV	ERA
1B	D. Mincher	463	.246	27	74	1109	91	12	107	8.8	.990	C. Dobson	41	267	16	15	0	3.74
2B	D. Green	384	.190	4	29	259	332	13	66	4.8	.978	C. Hunter	40	262	18	14	0	3.81
SS	Campaneris	603	.279	22	64	267	414	19	92	4.9	.973	D. Segui	47	162	10	10	2	2.56
3B	S. Bando	502	.263	20	75	158	258	20	22	2.9	.954	B. Odom	29	156	9	8	0	3.81
RF	R. Jackson	426	.237	23	66	251	8	12	0	1.9	.956	R. Fingers	45	148	7	9	2	3.65
CF	R. Monday	376	.290	10	37	257	3	5	2	2.4	.981	M. Grant	72	123	6	2	24	1.83
LF	F. Alou	575	.271	8	55	287	11	7	3	2.1	.977	P. Lindblad	62	63	8	2	3	2.71
C	F. Fernandez	252	.214	15	44	405	25	3	6	5.7	.993	B. Locker	38	56	3	3	4	2.88
O1	J. Rudi	350	.309	11	42	302	18	4	17		.988							
C	D. Duncan	232	.259	10	29	373	28	9	9	5.6	.978							
OF	T. Davis	200	.290	1	27	51	1	2	0	1.2	.963							
C	G. Tenace	105	.305	7	20	180	18	2	7	6.7	.990							

California
W-86 L-76 — Lefty Phillips

POS	Player	AB	BA	HR	RBI	PO	A	E	DP	TC/G	FA	Pitcher	G	IP	W	L	SV	ERA
1B	J. Spencer	511	.274	12	68	1212	85	7	131	9.2	.995	C. Wright	39	261	22	12	0	2.83
2B	S. Alomar	672	.251	2	36	375	460	18	119	5.6	.979	T. Murphy	39	227	16	13	0	4.24
SS	J. Fregosi	601	.278	22	82	264	468	20	99	5.0	.973	R. May	38	209	7	13	0	4.00
3B	K. McMullen	422	.232	14	61	128	266	17	32	3.4*	.959	Messersmith	37	195	11	10	5	3.00
RF	R. Repoz	407	.238	18	47	203	6	1	2	1.9	.989	E. Fisher	67	130	4	4	8	3.05
CF	J. Johnstone	320	.238	11	39	200	7	4	3	2.1	.981	K. Tatum	62	89	7	4	17	2.93
LF	A. Johnson	614	.329	14	86	269	11	12	0	1.9	.959	G. Garrett	32	75	5	6	0	2.64
C	J. Azcue	351	.242	2	25	587	51	6	10	5.8	.991	M. Queen	34	60	3	6	9	4.20
C	T. Egan	210	.238	4	20	367	31	5	4	5.1	.988							
OF	J. Tatum	181	.238	0	6	108	2	2	0	1.9	.982							
OF	B. Voss	181	.243	3	30	86	7	2	1	1.7	.979							
O1	B. Cowan	134	.276	5	25	95	6	2	7		.981							

Kansas City
W-65 L-97 — Charlie Metro W-19 L-33 — Bob Lemon W-46 L-64

POS	Player	AB	BA	HR	RBI	PO	A	E	DP	TC/G	FA	Pitcher	G	IP	W	L	SV	ERA
1B	B. Oliver	612	.260	27	99	1020	65	8	100	9.5	.993	D. Drago	35	240	9	15	0	3.75
2B	C. Rojas	384	.260	2	28	217	283	9	69	5.2	.982	B. Johnson	40	214	8	13	4	3.07
SS	J. Hernandez	238	.231	2	10	142	187	17	38	4.5	.951	J. Rooker	38	204	10	15	1	3.53
3B	P. Schaal	380	.268	5	35	69	159	15	12	2.5	.938	B. Butler	25	141	4	12	0	3.77
RF	P. Kelly	452	.235	6	38	254	8	10	2	2.3	.963	D. Morehead	28	122	3	5	1	3.61
CF	A. Otis	620	.284	11	58	388	15	4	6	2.6	.990		24	122	2	0	1	4.20
LF	L. Piniella	542	.301	11	88	247	6	4	2	1.8	.984	Fitzmorris	43	118	8	5	1	4.42
C	Kirkpatrick	424	.229	18	62	463	61	12	12	6.0	.978	T. Burgmeier	41	68	6	6	1	3.18
S2	R. Severson	240	.250	1	22	127	202	12	45		.965	T. Abernathy	36	56	9	3	12	2.57
C	E. Rodriguez	231	.225	0	15	451	32	6	5	6.5	.988							
O1	J. Keough	183	.322	4	21	176	13	4	13		.979							

Milwaukee
W-65 L-97 — Dave Bristol

POS	Player	AB	BA	HR	RBI	PO	A	E	DP	TC/G	FA	Pitcher	G	IP	W	L	SV	ERA
1B	M. Hegan	476	.244	11	52	1097	113	7	104	8.8	.994	M. Pattin	37	233	14	12	0	3.40
2B	T. Kubiak	540	.252	4	41	233	238	5	63	5.2	.989	L. Krausse	37	216	13	18	0	4.75
SS	R. Pena	416	.238	3	42	149	272	8	58	4.3	.981*	S. Lockwood	27	174	5	12	0	4.29
3B	T. Harper	604	.296	31	82	123	275	24	23	3.3	.943	B. Bolin	32	132	5	11	1	4.91
RF	D. May	342	.240	7	31	255	6	3	0	2.7	.989	G. Brabender	29	129	6	15	1	6.00
CF	R. Snyder	276	.232	4	31	140	1	5	0	1.4	.966	A. Downing	17	94	2	10	0	3.34
LF	D. Walton	397	.257	17	66	162	4	6	0	1.5	.965	K. Sanders	50	92	5	2	13	1.76
C	P. Roof	321	.227	13	37	596	47	8	6	6.1	.988	J. Gelnar	53	92	4	3	4	4.21
C	McNertney	296	.243	6	22	387	46	7	3	4.7	.984							
OF	T. Savage	276	.279	12	50	119	3	6	1	1.6	.953							
OF	B. Burda	222	.248	4	20	71	3	1	1	1.2	.987							

Chicago
W-56 L-106 — Don Gutteridge W-49 L-87 — Bill Adair W-4 L-6 — Chuck Tanner W-3 L-13

POS	Player	AB	BA	HR	RBI	PO	A	E	DP	TC/G	FA	Pitcher	G	IP	W	L	SV	ERA
1B	G. Hopkins	287	.286	6	29	629	42	9	67	8.8	.987	T. John	37	269	12	17	0	3.28
2B	B. Knoop	402	.229	5	36	276	403	11	102	5.5	.984	G. Janeski	35	206	10	17	0	4.76
SS	L. Aparicio	552	.313	5	43	251	483	18	99	5.2	.976	J. Horlen	28	172	6	16	0	4.87
3B	B. Melton	514	.263	33	96	47	179	18	19	3.5	.926	W. Wood	77	122	9	13	21	2.80
RF	W. Williams	315	.251	3	15	119	12	7	1	1.7	.949	J. Crider	32	91	4	7	4	4.45
CF	K. Berry	463	.276	7	50	331	9	4	2	2.5	.988	B. Johnson	18	90	4	7	0	4.80
LF	C. May	555	.285	12	68	203	12	2	2	1.5	.991	D. Murphy	51	81	2	3	5	5.67
C	E. Herrmann	297	.283	19	52	433	51	6	10	5.6	.988	B. Miller	15	70	4	6	0	5.01
32	S. O'Brien	441	.247	8	44	155	264	23	49		.948							
10	T. McCraw	332	.220	6	31	427	35	9	34		.981							
C	D. Josephson	285	.316	4	41	353	38	6	7	4.7	.985							

AMERICAN LEAGUE 1970, *cont.*

BATTING AND BASE RUNNING LEADERS

Batting Average
A. Johnson, CAL	.329
Yastrzemski, BOS	.329
T. Oliva, MIN	.325
L. Aparicio, CHI	.313
F. Robinson, BAL	.306

Slugging Average
Yastrzemski, BOS	.592
B. Powell, BAL	.549
H. Killebrew, MIN	.546
F. Howard, WAS	.546
T. Harper, MIL	.522

Home Runs
F. Howard, WAS	44
H. Killebrew, MIN	41
Yastrzemski, BOS	40
Conigliaro, BOS	36
B. Powell, BAL	35

Total Bases
Yastrzemski, BOS	335
T. Oliva, MIN	323
T. Harper, MIL	315
F. Howard, WAS	309
B. Powell, BAL	289

Runs Batted In
F. Howard, WAS	126
Conigliaro, BOS	116
B. Powell, BAL	114
H. Killebrew, MIN	113
T. Oliva, MIN	107

Stolen Bases
Campaneris, OAK	42
T. Harper, MIL	38
S. Alomar, CAL	35
P. Kelly, KC	34
A. Otis, KC	33

Hits
T. Oliva, MIN	204
A. Johnson, CAL	202
C. Tovar, MIN	195
Yastrzemski, BOS	186

Base on Balls
F. Howard, WAS	132
H. Killebrew, MIN	128
Yastrzemski, BOS	128
S. Bando, OAK	118

Home Run Percentage
H. Killebrew, MIN	7.8
F. Howard, WAS	7.8
Yastrzemski, BOS	7.1
B. Powell, BAL	6.7

Runs Scored
Yastrzemski, BOS	125
C. Tovar, MIN	120
R. Smith, BOS	109
R. White, NY	109

Doubles
A. Otis, KC	36
T. Oliva, MIN	36
C. Tovar, MIN	36
T. Harper, MIL	35

Triples
C. Tovar, MIN	13
M. Stanley, DET	11
A. Otis, KC	9

PITCHING LEADERS

Winning Percentage
M. Cuellar, BAL	.750
D. McNally, BAL	.727
J. Perry, MIN	.667
J. Palmer, BAL	.667
S. Siebert, BOS	.652

Earned Run Average
D. Segui, OAK	2.56
J. Palmer, BAL	2.71
C. Wright, CAL	2.83
F. Peterson, NY	2.91
S. McDowell, CLE	2.92

Wins
M. Cuellar, BAL	24
D. McNally, BAL	24
J. Perry, MIN	24
C. Wright, CAL	22

Saves
Perranoski, MIN	34
L. McDaniel, NY	29
T. Timmerman, DET	27
D. Knowles, WAS	27
M. Grant, OAK	24

Strikeouts
S. McDowell, CLE	304
M. Lolich, DET	230
B. Johnson, KC	206
J. Palmer, BAL	199
R. Culp, BOS	197

Complete Games
M. Cuellar, BAL	21
S. McDowell, CLE	19
J. Palmer, BAL	17
D. McNally, BAL	16
R. Culp, BOS	15

Fewest Hits/9 Innings
Messersmith, CAL	6.65
S. McDowell, CLE	6.96
D. Segui, OAK	7.22
B. Johnson, KC	7.49

Shutouts
J. Palmer, BAL	5
C. Dobson, OAK	5
G. Peters, BOS	4
M. Cuellar, BAL	4

Fewest Walks/9 Innings
F. Peterson, NY	1.38
J. Perry, MIN	1.84
C. Cox, WAS	2.06
M. Cuellar, BAL	2.08

Most Strikeouts/9 Inn.
S. McDowell, CLE	8.97
B. Johnson, KC	8.66
L. Cain, DET	7.76
M. Lolich, DET	7.58

Innings
S. McDowell, CLE	305
J. Palmer, BAL	305
M. Cuellar, BAL	298
D. McNally, BAL	296

Games Pitched
W. Wood, CHI	77
M. Grant, OAK	72
D. Knowles, WAS	71
S. Williams, MIN	68

		W	L	PCT	GB	R	OR	2B	3B	HR	BA	SA	SB	E	DP	FA	CG	BB	SO	ShO	SV	ERA
East	Baltimore	108	54	.667		792	574	213	25	179	.257	.401	84	117	148	.981	60	469	941	12	31	3.15
	New York	93	69	.574	15	680	612	208	41	111	.251	.365	105	130	146	.980	36	451	777	6	49	3.25
	Boston	87	75	.537	21	786	722	252	28	203	.262	.428	50	156	131	.974	38	594	1003	8	44	3.90
	Detroit	79	83	.488	29	666	731	207	38	148	.238	.374	29	133	142	.978	33	623	1045	9	39	4.09
	Cleveland	76	86	.469	32	649	675	197	23	183	.249	.394	25	133	168	.979	34	689	1076	8	35	3.91
	Washington	70	92	.432	38	626	689	184	28	138	.238	.358	72	116	173	.982	20	611	823	11	40	3.80
West	Minnesota	98	64	.605		744	605	230	41	153	.262	.403	57	123	130	.980	26	486	940	12	58	3.23
	Oakland	89	73	.549	9	678	593	208	24	171	.249	.392	131	141	152	.977	33	542	858	15	40	3.30
	California	86	76	.531	12	631	630	197	40	114	.251	.363	69	127	169	.980	21	559	922	10	49	3.48
	Kansas City	65	97	.401	33	611	705	202	41	97	.244	.348	97	152	142	.976	30	641	915	11	25	3.78
	Milwaukee	65	97	.401	33	613	751	202	24	126	.242	.358	91	136	142	.978	31	587	895	2	27	4.20
	Chicago	56	106	.346	42	633	822	192	20	123	.253	.362	54	165	187	.975	20	556	762	6	30	4.54
						8109	8109	2492	373	1746	.250	.379	864	1629	1850	.978	382	6808	10957	110	467	3.72

NATIONAL LEAGUE 1971

		POS	Player	AB	BA	HR	RBI	PO	A	E	DP	TC/G	FA	Pitcher	G	IP	W	L	SV	ERA
East	**Pittsburgh** W-97 L-65 Danny Murtaugh	1B	B. Robertson	469	.271	26	72	1089	128	9	107	9.7	.993	S. Blass	33	240	15	8	0	2.85
		2B	D. Cash	478	.289	2	34	228	304	7	80	5.1	.987	D. Ellis	31	227	19	9	0	3.05
		SS	G. Alley	348	.227	6	28	187	316	22	55	4.9	.958	B. Johnson	31	175	9	10	0	3.45
		3B	R. Hebner	388	.271	17	67	89	172	14	21	2.5	.949	L. Walker	28	160	10	8	0	3.54
		RF	R. Clemente	522	.341	13	86	267	11	2	4	2.3	.993	B. Moose	30	140	11	7	1	4.11
		CF	A. Oliver	529	.282	14	64	305	4	6	2	2.7	.981	N. Briles	37	136	8	4	1	3.04
		LF	W. Stargell	511	.295	48	125	237	8	4	1	1.8	.984	B. Kison	18	95	6	5	0	3.41
		C	Sanguillen	533	.319	7	81	712	72	5	12	5.8	.994	D. Giusti	58	86	5	6	30	2.93
		OF	V. Davalillo	295	.285	1	33	112	5	2	0	2.0	.983	M. Grant	42	75	5	3	7	3.60
		OF	G. Clines	273	.308	0	24	146	8	3	2	2.1	.981							
		SS	J. Hernandez	233	.206	3	26	105	235	18	42	4.8	.950							
		2B	B. Mazeroski	193	.254	1	16	95	121	3	22	4.8	.986							
		C	M. May	126	.278	6	25	168	12	0	3	5.8	1.000							
	St. Louis W-90 L-72 Red Schoendienst	1B	J. Hague	380	.226	16	54	618	50	3	63	7.4	.996	S. Carlton	37	273	20	9	0	3.56
		2B	T. Sizemore	478	.264	3	42	206	237	11	55	4.9	.976	B. Gibson	31	246	16	13	0	3.04
		SS	D. Maxvill	356	.225	0	24	188	413	13	71	4.4	.979	R. Cleveland	34	222	12	12	0	4.01
		3B	J. Torre	634	.363	24	137	136	271	21	22	2.7	.951	J. Reuss	36	211	14	14	0	4.78
		RF	M. Alou	609	.315	7	74	203	8	4	0	2.3	.981	C. Zachary	23	90	3	10	0	5.30
		CF	J. Cruz	292	.274	9	27	197	2	5	1	2.5	.975	M. Drabowsky	51	60	6	1	8	3.45
		LF	L. Brock	640	.313	7	61	262	7	14	3	1.8	.951	F. Linzy	50	59	4	3	6	2.14
		C	T. Simmons	510	.304	7	77	747	52	9	11	6.2	.989	D. Shaw	45	51	7	2	2	2.65
		OF	J. Cardenal	301	.243	7	48	181	9	6	1	2.4	.969							
		2B	J. Javier	259	.259	3	28	163	186	8	45	4.5	.978							
		OF	L. Melendez	173	.225	0	11	90	3	4	0	1.5	.959							
		1B	J. Beauchamp	162	.235	2	16	311	19	6	27	7.6	.982							
		C	McNertney	128	.289	4	22	192	7	3	1	5.6	.985							

NATIONAL LEAGUE 1971, *cont.*

Chicago
W-83 L-79
Leo Durocher

POS	Player	AB	BA	HR	RBI	PO	A	E	DP	TC/G	FA	Pitcher	G	IP	W	L	SV	ERA
1B	J. Pepitone	427	.307	16	61	872	64	9	75	9.9	.990	F. Jenkins	39	325	24	13	0	2.77
2B	G. Beckert	530	.342	2	42	275	382	9	76	5.2	.986	M. Pappas	35	261	17	14	0	3.52
SS	D. Kessinger	617	.258	2	38	263	512	27	97	5.2	.966	B. Hands	36	242	12	18	0	3.42
3B	R. Santo	555	.267	21	88	118	274	17	29	2.7	.958	K. Holtzman	30	195	9	15	0	4.48
RF	J. Callison	290	.210	8	38	158	3	3	0	1.8	.982	J. Pizarro	16	101	7	6	0	3.48
CF	B. Davis	301	.256	0	28	213	5	4	1	2.4	.982	P. Regan	48	73	5	5	6	3.95
LF	B. Williams	594	.301	28	93	284	8	7	3	1.9	.977							
C	Cannizzaro	197	.213	5	23	311	26	6	2	4.9	.983							
O1	J. Hickman	383	.256	19	60	470	34	3	28		.994							
2B	P. Popovich	226	.217	4	28	74	119	3	26	4.9	.985							
P	F. Jenkins	115	.243	6	20	31	48	7	1	2.2	.919							

New York
W-83 L-79
Gil Hodges

POS	Player	AB	BA	HR	RBI	PO	A	E	DP	TC/G	FA	Pitcher	G	IP	W	L	SV	ERA
1B	E. Kranepool	421	.280	14	58	786	61	2	67	7.9	.998	T. Seaver	36	286	20	10	0	1.76
2B	K. Boswell	392	.273	5	40	191	234	12	56	4.0	.973	G. Gentry	32	203	12	11	0	3.24
SS	B. Harrelson	547	.252	0	32	257	441	16	86	5.1	.978	J. Koosman	26	166	6	11	0	3.04
3B	Aspromonte	342	.225	5	33	76	145	8	10	2.4	.965	R. Sadecki	34	163	7	7	0	2.93
RF	K. Singleton	298	.245	13	46	143	5	4	0	1.6	.974	N. Ryan	30	152	10	14	0	3.97
CF	T. Agee	425	.285	14	50	265	7	6	0	2.6	.978	T. McGraw	51	111	11	4	8	1.70
LF	C. Jones	505	.319	14	69	248	4	5	1	1.9	.981	D. Frisella	53	91	8	5	12	1.98
C	J. Grote	403	.270	2	35	892	41	9	4	7.7	.990	C. Williams	31	90	5	6	0	4.80
UT	T. Foli	288	.226	0	24	150	199	12	43		.967							
1B	D. Clendenon	263	.247	11	37	505	37	8	49	7.6	.985							
OF	D. Marshall	214	.238	3	21	92	2	1	0	1.5	.989							
3B	W. Garrett	202	.213	1	11	30	89	4	7	2.3	.967							
OF	D. Hahn	178	.236	1	11	140	2	4	1	1.8	.973							
C	D. Dyer	169	.231	2	18	336	21	3	3	6.8	.992							

Montreal
W-71 L-90
Gene Mauch

POS	Player	AB	BA	HR	RBI	PO	A	E	DP	TC/G	FA	Pitcher	G	IP	W	L	SV	ERA
1B	R. Fairly	447	.257	13	71	1108	104	10	110	9.1	.992	B. Stoneman	39	295	17	16	0	3.14
2B	R. Hunt	520	.279	5	38	270	370	14	72	4.9	.979	S. Renko	40	276	15	14	0	3.75
SS	B. Wine	340	.200	1	19	221	321	10	76	4.6	.982	C. Morton	36	214	10	18	1	4.79
3B	B. Bailey	545	.251	14	83	69	194	11	14	2.3	.960	E. McAnally	31	178	11	12	0	3.89
RF	R. Staub	599	.311	19	97	290	20	18	5	2.0	.945	Strohmayer	27	114	7	5	1	4.34
CF	B. Day	371	.283	4	33	262	10	5	1	2.3	.982	M. Marshall	66	111	5	8	23	4.30
LF	J. Fairey	200	.245	1	19	85	7	3	1	1.6	.968							
C	J. Bateman	492	.242	10	56	726	56	12	12	5.8	.985							
2S	Sutherland	304	.257	4	26	154	249	21	59		.950							
C1	Boccabella	177	.220	3	15	334	33	4	30		.989							

Philadelphia
W-67 L-95
Frank Lucchesi

POS	Player	AB	BA	HR	RBI	PO	A	E	DP	TC/G	FA	Pitcher	G	IP	W	L	SV	ERA
1B	D. Johnson	582	.265	34	95	1219	88	7	124	9.7	.995	R. Wise	38	272	17	14	0	2.88
2B	D. Doyle	342	.231	3	24	241	264	17	62	5.7	.967	B. Lersch	38	214	5	14	0	3.79
SS	L. Bowa	650	.249	0	25	272	560	11	97	5.4	.987	C. Short	31	173	7	14	1	3.85
3B	J. Vukovich	217	.166	0	14	58	137	9	8	2.8	.956	K. Reynolds	35	162	5	9	0	4.50
RF	R. Freed	348	.221	6	37	184	4	2	1	1.8	.989	W. Fryman	37	149	10	7	2	3.38
CF	W. Montanez	599	.255	30	99	364	11	11	3	2.4	.971	J. Bunning	29	110	5	12	1	5.48
LF	O. Gamble	280	.221	6	23	125	4	4	1	1.7	.970	B. Champion	37	109	3	5	0	4.38
C	T. McCarver	474	.278	8	46	673	51	11	8	5.9	.985	D. Brandon	52	83	6	6	4	3.90
UT	D. Money	439	.223	7	38	167	197	11	21		.971	J. Hoerner	49	73	4	5	9	1.97
2B	T. Harmon	221	.204	0	12	122	166	4	39	5.0	.986	B. Wilson	38	59	4	6	7	3.05
OF	R. Stone	185	.227	2	23	76	5	3	0	1.6	.964							

West

San Francisco
W-90 L-72
Charlie Fox

POS	Player	AB	BA	HR	RBI	PO	A	E	DP	TC/G	FA	Pitcher	G	IP	W	L	SV	ERA
1B	W. McCovey	329	.277	18	70	828	63	15	80	9.5	.983	G. Perry	37	280	16	12	0	2.76
2B	T. Fuentes	630	.273	4	52	373	465	23	109	5.7	.973	J. Marichal	37	279	18	11	0	2.94
SS	C. Speier	601	.235	8	46	239	517	33	95	5.1	.958	Cumberland	45	185	9	6	2	2.92
3B	A. Gallagher	429	.277	5	57	88	204	15	18	2.4	.951	R. Bryant	27	140	7	10	0	3.79
RF	B. Bonds	619	.288	33	102	329	10	2	1	2.2	.994	S. Stone	24	111	5	9	0	4.14
CF	W. Mays	417	.271	18	61	192	2	6	1	2.4	.970	J. Johnson	67	109	12	9	18	2.97
LF	K. Henderson	504	.264	15	65	277	3	10	1	2.1	.966	D. McMahon	61	82	10	6	4	4.06
C	D. Dietz	453	.252	19	72	712	37	14	4	5.7	.982							
3B	H. Lanier	206	.233	1	13	33	79	5	6	1.4	.957							
OF	J. Rosario	192	.224	0	13	151	1	0	0	2.3	1.000							
10	D. Kingman	115	.278	6	24	168	9	4	9		.978							

Los Angeles
W-89 L-73
Walter Alston

POS	Player	AB	BA	HR	RBI	PO	A	E	DP	TC/G	FA	Pitcher	G	IP	W	L	SV	ERA
1B	W. Parker	533	.274	6	62	1215	97	5	113	8.9	.996	D. Sutton	38	265	17	12	1	2.55
2B	J. Lefebvre	388	.245	12	68	244	260	6	69	5.0	.988	A. Downing	37	262	20	9	0	2.68
SS	M. Wills	601	.281	3	44	220	484	16	86	5.0	.978	C. Osteen	38	259	14	11	0	3.51
3B	S. Garvey	225	.227	7	26	53	161	14	11	2.9	.939	B. Singer	31	203	10	17	0	4.17
RF	B. Buckner	358	.277	5	41	165	5	1	0	2.0	.994	D. Alexander	17	92	6	6	0	3.82
CF	W. Davis	641	.309	10	74	404	7	8	0	2.7	.981	J. Brewer	55	81	6	5	22	1.89
LF	W. Crawford	342	.281	9	40	146	5	3	1	1.6	.981	P. Mikkelsen	41	74	8	5	5	3.65
C	D. Sims	230	.274	6	25	345	33	3	5	5.1	.992							
UT	D. Allen	549	.295	23	90	382	151	21	38		.962							
UT	B. Valentine	281	.249	1	25	123	176	16	31		.949							
OF	M. Mota	269	.312	0	34	108	3	4	1	1.4	.965							
20	B. Russell	211	.227	2	15	130	109	7	21		.972							
C	T. Haller	202	.267	5	32	320	34	8	3	5.4	.978							

NATIONAL LEAGUE 1971, *cont.*

	POS	Player	AB	BA	HR	RBI	PO	A	E	DP	TC/G	FA	Pitcher	G	IP	W	L	SV	ERA
Atlanta W-82 L-80 Lum Harris	1B	H. Aaron	495	.327	47	118	629	38	3	56	9.4	.996	P. Niekro	42	269	15	14	2	2.98
	2B	F. Millan	577	.289	2	45	373	437	15	120	5.9	.982	R. Reed	32	222	13	14	0	3.73
	SS	M. Perez	410	.227	4	32	195	382	27	91	4.8	.955	G. Stone	27	173	6	8	0	3.59
	3B	D. Evans	260	.242	12	38	71	138	14	13	3.1	.937	P. Jarvis	35	162	6	14	1	4.11
	RF	M. Lum	454	.269	13	55	286	10	3	2	2.4	.990	T. Kelley	28	143	9	5	0	2.96
	CF	S. Jackson	547	.258	2	25	336	8	7	0	2.4	.980	J. Nash	32	133	9	7	2	4.94
	LF	R. Garr	639	.343	9	44	315	15	11	3	2.2	.968	C. Upshaw	49	82	11	6	17	3.51
	C	E. Williams	497	.260	33	87	375	35	8	4	5.8	.981	B. Priddy	40	64	4	9	4	4.22
	1B	O. Cepeda	250	.276	14	44	586	49	5	60	10.2	.992							
	C	H. King	198	.207	5	19	274	23	5	0	5.0	.983							
	3S	Z. Versalles	194	.191	5	22	61	105	13	13		.927							
Cincinnati W-79 L-83 Sparky Anderson	1B	L. May	553	.278	39	98	1261	78	8	118	9.4	.994	G. Nolan	35	245	12	15	0	3.16
	2B	T. Helms	547	.258	3	52	395	468	9	130	5.3	.990	D. Gullett	35	218	16	6	0	2.64
	SS	Concepcion	327	.205	1	20	160	294	12	62	4.2	.974	McGlothlin	30	171	8	12	0	3.21
	3B	T. Perez	609	.269	25	91	113	304	18	26	2.9	.959	R. Grimsley	26	161	10	7	0	3.58
	RF	P. Rose	632	.304	13	44	306	13	2	1	2.0	.994	W. Simpson	22	117	4	7	0	4.77
	CF	G. Foster	368	.234	10	50	267	8	4	3	2.7	.986	J. Merritt	28	107	1	11	0	4.37
	LF	H. McRae	337	.264	9	34	167	6	6	1	2.0	.966	W. Granger	70	100	7	6	11	3.33
	C	J. Bench	562	.238	27	61	687	59	9	9	5.4	.988	C. Carroll	61	94	10	4	15	2.49
	OF	B. Carbo	310	.219	5	20	154	7	3	0	1.8	.982	J. Gibbon	50	64	5	6	11	2.95
	S3	W. Woodward	273	.242	0	18	114	236	7	44		.980							
Houston W-79 L-83 Harry Walker	1B	D. Menke	475	.246	1	43	845	59	3	77	9.0	.997	D. Wilson	35	268	16	10	0	2.45
	2B	J. Morgan	583	.256	13	56	336	482	12	93	5.3	.986	Billingham	33	228	10	16	0	3.39
	SS	R. Metzger	562	.235	0	26	275	459	17	91	5.1	.977	K. Forsch	33	188	8	8	0	2.54
	3B	D. Rader	484	.244	12	56	93	275	21	28	2.9	.946	L. Dierker	24	159	12	6	0	2.72
	RF	J. Wynn	404	.203	7	45	232	9	3	5	2.1	.988	Blasingame	30	158	9	11	0	4.61
	CF	C. Cedeno	611	.264	10	81	345	6	4	0	2.3	.989	J. Ray	47	98	10	4	3	2.11
	LF	B. Watson	468	.288	9	67	131	2	2	0	1.6	.985	G. Culver	59	95	5	8	7	2.65
	C	J. Edwards	317	.233	1	23	555	48	3	7	5.8	.995	F. Gladding	48	51	4	5	12	2.12
	OF	J. Alou	433	.279	2	40	229	7	4	3	2.0	.983							
	C	J. Hiatt	174	.276	1	16	329	20	3	6	5.4	.991							
San Diego W-61 L-100 Preston Gomez	1B	N. Colbert	565	.264	27	84	1372	106	10	125	9.7	.993	D. Roberts	37	270	14	17	0	2.10
	2B	D. Mason	344	.212	2	11	188	231	15	47	4.8	.965	C. Kirby	38	267	15	13	0	2.83
	SS	E. Hernandez	549	.222	0	12	260	445	33	82	5.2	.955	S. Arlin	36	228	9	19	0	3.47
	3B	E. Spiezio	308	.231	7	36	57	168	9	12	2.6	.962	T. Phoebus	29	133	3	11	0	4.47
	RF	O. Brown	484	.273	9	55	263	9	5	2	2.1	.982	F. Norman	20	127	3	12	0	3.32
	CF	C. Gaston	518	.228	17	61	271	8	5	1	2.1	.982	Severinsen	59	70	2	5	8	3.47
	LF	L. Stahl	308	.253	8	36	141	11	2	4	2.1	.987	B. Miller	38	64	7	3	7	1.41
	C	B. Barton	376	.250	5	23	698	67	15	10	6.6	.981							
	23	D. Campbell	365	.227	7	29	169	254	17	48		.961							
	OF	L. Lee	256	.273	4	21	86	6	8	1	1.5	.920							
	OF	I. Murrell	255	.235	7	24	133	2	3	0	1.9	.978							
	32	G. Jestadt	189	.291	0	13	63	141	12	11		.944							

BATTING AND BASE RUNNING LEADERS

Batting Average
J. Torre, STL	.363
R. Garr, ATL	.343
G. Beckert, CHI	.342
R. Clemente, PIT	.341
H. Aaron, ATL	.327

Slugging Average
H. Aaron, ATL	.669
W. Stargell, PIT	.628
J. Torre, STL	.555
L. May, CIN	.532
B. Bonds, SF	.512

Home Runs
W. Stargell, PIT	48
H. Aaron, ATL	47
L. May, CIN	39
D. Johnson, PHI	34
E. Williams, ATL	33
B. Bonds, SF	33

Total Bases
J. Torre, STL	352
H. Aaron, ATL	331
W. Stargell, PIT	321
B. Bonds, SF	317
B. Williams, CHI	300

Runs Batted In
J. Torre, STL	137
W. Stargell, PIT	125
H. Aaron, ATL	118
B. Bonds, SF	102
W. Montanez, PHI	99

Stolen Bases
L. Brock, STL	64
J. Morgan, HOU	40
R. Garr, ATL	30
T. Agee, NY	28
B. Harrelson, NY	28
L. Bowa, PHI	28

Hits
J. Torre, STL	230
R. Garr, ATL	219
L. Brock, STL	200
W. Davis, LA	198

Base on Balls
W. Mays, SF	112
D. Dietz, SF	97
B. Bailey, MON	97
D. Allen, LA	93

Home Run Percentage
H. Aaron, ATL	9.5
W. Stargell, PIT	9.4
L. May, CIN	7.1
E. Williams, ATL	6.6

Runs Scored
L. Brock, STL	126
B. Bonds, SF	110
W. Stargell, PIT	104
R. Garr, ATL	101

Doubles
C. Cedeno, HOU	40
L. Brock, STL	37
R. Staub, MON	34
J. Torre, STL	34

Triples
R. Metzger, HOU	11
J. Morgan, HOU	11
W. Davis, LA	10
C. Gaston, SD	9

PITCHING LEADERS

Winning Percentage
D. Gullett, CIN	.727
S. Carlton, STL	.690
A. Downing, LA	.690
D. Ellis, PIT	.679
T. Seaver, NY	.667

Earned Run Average
T. Seaver, NY	1.76
D. Roberts, SD	2.10
D. Wilson, HOU	2.45
K. Forsch, HOU	2.54
D. Sutton, LA	2.55

Wins
F. Jenkins, CHI	24
S. Carlton, STL	20
A. Downing, LA	20
T. Seaver, NY	20
D. Ellis, PIT	19

Saves
D. Giusti, PIT	30
M. Marshall, MON	23
J. Brewer, LA	22
J. Johnson, SF	18
C. Upshaw, ATL	17

Strikeouts
T. Seaver, NY	289
F. Jenkins, CHI	263
B. Stoneman, MON	251
C. Kirby, SD	231
D. Sutton, LA	194

Complete Games
F. Jenkins, CHI	30
T. Seaver, NY	21
B. Gibson, STL	20
B. Stoneman, MON	20

Fewest Hits/9 Innings
D. Wilson, HOU	6.55
T. Seaver, NY	6.61
C. Kirby, SD	7.18
G. Gentry, NY	7.40

Shutouts
B. Gibson, STL	5
S. Blass, PIT	5
M. Pappas, CHI	5
A. Downing, LA	5

Fewest Walks/9 Innings
F. Jenkins, CHI	1.02
J. Marichal, SF	1.81
G. Stone, ATL	1.82
B. Hands, CHI	1.86

Most Strikeouts/9 Inn.
T. Seaver, NY	9.09
C. Kirby, SD	7.79
B. Stoneman, MON	7.66
F. Jenkins, CHI	7.28

Innings
F. Jenkins, CHI	325
B. Stoneman, MON	295
T. Seaver, NY	286
G. Perry, SF	280

Games Pitched
W. Granger, CIN	70
J. Johnson, SF	67
M. Marshall, MON	66
C. Carroll, CIN	61

NATIONAL LEAGUE 1971, cont.

		W	L	PCT	GB	R	OR	2B	3B	HR	BA	SA	SB	E	DP	FA	CG	BB	SO	ShO	SV	ERA
East	Pittsburgh	97	65	.599		788	599	223	61	154	.274	.416	65	133	164	.979	43	470	813	15	48	3.31
	St. Louis	90	72	.556	7	739	699	225	54	95	.275	.385	124	142	155	.978	56	576	911	14	22	3.87
	Chicago	83	79	.512	14	637	648	202	34	128	.258	.378	44	126	150	.980	75	411	900	17	13	3.61
	New York	83	79	.512	14	588	550	203	29	98	.249	.351	89	114	135	.981	42	529	1157	13	22	3.00
	Montreal	71	90	.441	25.5	622	729	197	29	88	.246	.343	51	150	164	.976	49	658	829	8	25	4.12
	Philadelphia	67	95	.414	30	558	688	209	35	123	.233	.350	63	122	158	.981	31	525	838	10	25	3.71
West	San Francisco	90	72	.556		706	644	224	36	140	.247	.378	101	179	153	.972	45	471	831	14	30	3.33
	Los Angeles	89	73	.549	1	663	587	213	38	95	.266	.370	76	131	159	.979	48	399	853	18	33	3.23
	Atlanta	82	80	.506	8	643	699	192	30	153	.257	.385	57	146	180	.977	40	485	823	11	31	3.75
	Cincinnati	79	83	.488	11	586	581	203	28	138	.241	.366	59	103	174	.984	27	501	750	11	38	3.35
	Houston	79	83	.488	11	585	567	230	52	71	.240	.340	101	106	152	.983	43	475	914	10	25	3.13
	San Diego	61	100	.379	28.5	486	610	184	31	96	.233	.332	70	161	144	.974	47	559	923	10	17	3.23
						7601	7601	2505	457	1379	.252	.366	900	1613	1888	.979	546	6059	10542	151	329	3.47

AMERICAN LEAGUE 1971

East — Baltimore
W-101 L-57 — Earl Weaver

POS	Player	AB	BA	HR	RBI	PO	A	E	DP	TC/G	FA	Pitcher	G	IP	W	L	SV	ERA
1B	B. Powell	418	.256	22	92	1031	67	5	97	8.9	.995	M. Cuellar	38	292	20	9	0	3.08
2B	D. Johnson	510	.282	18	72	361	367	12	103	5.3	.984	P. Dobson	38	282	20	8	1	2.90
SS	M. Belanger	500	.266	0	35	280	443	16	77	5.0	.978	J. Palmer	37	282	20	9	0	2.68
3B	B. Robinson	589	.272	20	92	131	354	16	35	3.2	.968	D. McNally	30	224	21	5	0	2.89
RF	Rettenmund	491	.318	11	75	292	7	7	4	2.3	.977	D. Hall	27	43	6	6	1	5.02
CF	P. Blair	516	.262	10	44	331	4	3	1	2.4	.991	E. Watt	35	40	3	1	11	1.80
LF	D. Buford	449	.290	19	54	217	6	3	0	2.0	.987	T. Dukes	28	38	1	5	4	3.55
C	E. Hendricks	316	.250	9	42	429	33	7	5	5.2	.985	P. Richert	35	36	3	5	4	3.50
OF	F. Robinson	455	.281	28	99	177	3	5	0	2.0	.973							
C	Etchebarren	222	.270	9	29	337	24	5	2	5.2	.986							

Detroit
W-91 L-71 — Billy Martin

POS	Player	AB	BA	HR	RBI	PO	A	E	DP	TC/G	FA	Pitcher	G	IP	W	L	SV	ERA
1B	N. Cash	452	.283	32	91	1020	75	9	105	8.4	.992	M. Lolich	45	376	25	14	0	2.92
2B	McAuliffe	477	.208	18	57	322	308	8	86	5.2	.987	J. Coleman	39	286	20	9	0	3.15
SS	E. Brinkman	527	.228	1	37	235	513	15	91	4.8	.980	L. Cain	26	145	10	9	0	4.34
3B	A. Rodriguez	604	.253	15	39	127	341	23	33	3.2	.953	J. Niekro	31	122	6	7	1	4.50
RF	A. Kaline	405	.294	15	54	207	6	0	0	1.7	1.000	F. Scherman	69	113	11	6	20	2.71
CF	M. Stanley	401	.292	7	41	315	10	4	3	2.4	.988	D. Chance	31	90	4	6	0	3.50
LF	W. Horton	450	.289	22	72	176	8	7	1	1.6	.963	M. Kilkenny	30	86	4	5	1	5.02
C	B. Freehan	516	.277	21	71	912	50	4	6	6.7	.996	T. Timmerman	52	84	7	6	4	3.86
OF	J. Northrup	459	.270	16	71	205	4	4	0		.981							
OF	G. Brown	195	.338	11	29	68	2	1	0	1.3	.986							
2B	T. Taylor	181	.287	3	19	114	107	1	29	4.4	.995							

Boston
W-85 L-77 — Eddie Kasko

POS	Player	AB	BA	HR	RBI	PO	A	E	DP	TC/G	FA	Pitcher	G	IP	W	L	SV	ERA
1B	G. Scott	537	.263	24	78	1256	75	11	122	9.4	.992	R. Culp	35	242	14	16	0	3.61
2B	D. Griffin	483	.244	3	27	311	344	9	90	5.4	.986	S. Siebert	32	235	16	10	0	2.91
SS	L. Aparicio	491	.232	4	45	194	338	16	56	4.5	.971	G. Peters	34	214	14	11	1	4.37
3B	Petrocelli	553	.251	28	89	118	334	11	37	3.0	.976	J. Lonborg	27	168	10	7	0	4.13
RF	R. Smith	618	.283	30	96	386	15	14	2	2.6	.966	B. Lee	47	102	9	2	0	2.74
CF	Conigliaro	351	.262	11	33	232	5	4	2	2.4	.983	B. Bolin	52	70	5	3	6	4.24
LF	Yastrzemski	508	.254	15	70	281	16	2	4	2.0	.993	K. Tatum	36	54	2	4	9	4.17
C	D. Josephson	306	.245	10	39	491	32	6	5	6.1	.989	S. Lyle	50	52	6	4	16	2.77
2S	J. Kennedy	272	.276	5	22	112	150	13	34		.953							
OF	J. Lahoud	256	.215	14	32	139	4	1	3	2.1	.993							
C	Montgomery	205	.239	2	24	361	15	4	3	5.8	.989							

New York
W-82 L-80 — Ralph Houk

POS	Player	AB	BA	HR	RBI	PO	A	E	DP	TC/G	FA	Pitcher	G	IP	W	L	SV	ERA
1B	D. Cater	428	.276	4	50	564	62	3	54	8.1	.995	F. Peterson	37	274	15	13	1	3.05
2B	H. Clarke	625	.250	2	41	386	455	16	97	5.5	.981	Stottlemyre	35	270	16	12	0	2.87
SS	G. Michael	456	.224	3	35	243	474	20	88	5.4	.973	S. Bahnsen	36	242	14	12	0	3.35
3B	J. Kenney	325	.262	0	20	69	237	15	20	2.9	.953	S. Kline	31	222	12	13	0	2.96
RF	F. Alou	461	.289	8	69	129	3	2	0	1.7	.985	M. Kekich	37	170	10	9	0	4.08
CF	B. Murcer	529	.331	25	94	317	10	5	1	2.3	.985	L. McDaniel	44	70	5	10	4	5.01
LF	R. White	524	.292	19	84	306	8	0	2	2.2	1.000	J. Aker	41	56	4	4	4	2.57
C	T. Munson	451	.251	10	42	547	67	1	4	5.3	.998							
1B	J. Ellis	238	.244	3	34	625	35	7	66	10.3	.990							
C	J. Gibbs	206	.218	5	21	229	12	3	1	4.8	.988							
OF	R. Blomberg	199	.322	7	31	96	1	3	1	1.8	.970							
3B	R. Hansen	145	.207	2	20	16	51	6	9	2.4	.918							
OF	R. Swoboda	138	.261	2	20	80	2	3	0	1.8	.965							

Washington
W-63 L-96 — Ted Williams

POS	Player	AB	BA	HR	RBI	PO	A	E	DP	TC/G	FA	Pitcher	G	IP	W	L	SV	ERA
1B	D. Mincher	323	.291	10	45	705	59	8	80	8.8	.990	D. Bosman	35	237	12	16	0	3.72
2B	T. Cullen	403	.191	2	26	165	213	1	47	4.9	.997	D. McLain	33	217	10	22	0	4.27
SS	T. Harrah	383	.230	2	22	181	307	23	69	4.4	.955	P. Broberg	18	125	5	9	0	3.46
3B	D. Nelson	329	.280	5	33	63	149	14	15	2.7	.938	Gogolewski	27	124	6	5	0	2.76
RF	D. Unser	581	.255	9	41	394	10	8	2	2.7	.981	C. Cox	54	124	5	7	7	3.99
CF	E. Maddox	258	.217	1	18	197	7	2	1	2.0	.990	Shellenback	40	120	3	11	0	3.53
LF	F. Howard	549	.279	26	83	141	7	1	0	1.5	.993	P. Lindblad	43	84	6	4	8	2.58
C	P. Casanova	311	.203	5	26	416	40	7	4	5.6	.985	J. Grzenda	46	70	5	2	5	1.93
CO	D. Billings	349	.246	6	48	378	37	4	5		.990							
23	B. Allen	229	.266	4	22	85	126	10	16		.955							
2B	L. Randle	215	.219	2	13	178	178	12	50	5.6	.967							
O1	T. McCraw	207	.213	7	25	134	2	5	3		.965							
OF	J. Burroughs	181	.232	5	25	82	3	3	0	1.8	.965							
OF	L. Biittner	171	.257	0	16	72	6	5	0	2.0	.940							

AMERICAN LEAGUE 1971, *cont.*

	POS	Player	AB	BA	HR	RBI	PO	A	E	DP	TC/G	FA	Pitcher	G	IP	W	L	SV	ERA
Cleveland W-60 L-102 Alvin Dark W-42 L-61 Johnny Lipon W-18 L-41	1B	C. Chambliss	415	.275	9	48	943	55	8	85	9.3	.992	S. McDowell	35	215	13	17	1	3.39
	2B	E. Leon	429	.261	4	35	235	271	9	71	4.8	.983	S. Dunning	31	184	8	14	1	4.50
	SS	J. Heidemann	240	.208	0	9	113	188	7	34	3.8	.977	A. Foster	36	182	8	12	0	4.15
	3B	G. Nettles	598	.261	28	86	159	412	16	54	3.7	.973	R. Lamb	43	158	6	12	1	3.36
	RF	V. Pinson	566	.263	11	35	305	11	7	2	2.3	.978	V. Colbert	50	143	7	6	2	3.97
	CF	T. Uhlaender	500	.288	2	47	245	6	2	0	1.9	.992	S. Hargan	37	113	1	13	1	6.21
	LF	R. Foster	396	.245	18	45	174	9	6	2	1.8	.968	P. Hennigan	57	82	4	3	14	4.94
	C	R. Fosse	486	.276	12	62	748	73	10	16	6.6	.988	E. Farmer	43	79	5	4	4	4.33
	OF	T. Ford	196	.194	2	14	107	4	0	0	2.0	1.000							
	OF	F. Baker	181	.210	1	23	65	2	1	1	1.3	.985							
West **Oakland** W-101 L-60 Dick Williams	1B	M. Epstein	329	.234	18	51	714	52	4	93*	8.0	.995	V. Blue	39	312	24	8	0	**1.82**
	2B	D. Green	475	.244	12	49	366	384	11	98	5.3	.986	C. Hunter	37	274	21	11	0	2.96
	SS	Campaneris	569	.251	5	47	231	303	26	85	4.2	.954	C. Dobson	30	189	15	5	0	3.81
	3B	S. Bando	538	.271	24	94	141	267	12	22	2.7	.971	D. Segui	26	146	10	8	0	3.14
	RF	R. Jackson	567	.277	32	80	285	15	7	3	2.1	.977	B. Odom	25	141	10	12	0	4.28
	CF	R. Monday	355	.245	18	56	238	6	4	1	2.2	.984	R. Fingers	48	129	4	6	17	3.00
	LF	J. Rudi	513	.267	10	52	249	5	1	1	2.1	.996	B. Locker	47	72	7	2	6	2.88
	C	D. Duncan	363	.253	15	40	678	41	12	3	7.2	.984	D. Knowles	43	53	5	2	7	3.59
	OF	A. Mangual	287	.286	4	30	163	3	2	1	2.1	.988							
	10	T. Davis	219	.324	3	42	274	30	5	24		.984							
	UT	L. Brown	189	.196	1	9	82	141	6	31		.974							
	C	G. Tenace	179	.274	7	25	300	20	2	3	6.2	.994							
Kansas City W-85 L-76 Bob Lemon	1B	G. Hopkins	295	.278	9	47	669	57	7	76	8.8	.990	D. Drago	35	241	17	11	0	2.99
	2B	C. Rojas	414	.300	6	59	252	293	5	76	5.0	**.991**	M. Hedlund	32	206	15	8	0	2.71
	SS	F. Patek	591	.267	6	36	301	459	25	107	5.3	.968	Splittorff	22	144	8	9	0	2.69
	3B	P. Schaal	548	.274	11	63	107	335	28	31	2.9	.940	Dal Canton	25	141	8	6	0	3.45
	RF	J. Keough	351	.248	3	30	164	4	3	1	1.7	.982	Fitzmorris	36	127	7	5	0	4.18
	CF	A. Otis	555	.301	15	79	404	10	4	4	2.9	.990	J. York	53	93	5	5	3	2.90
	LF	L. Piniella	448	.279	3	51	201	6	3	2	1.8	.986	T. Burgmeier	67	88	9	7	17	1.74
	C	J. May	218	.252	1	24	314	38	1	6	5.0	.997	T. Abernathy	63	81	4	6	23	2.56
	10	B. Oliver	373	.244	8	52	564	34	8	52		.987	K. Wright	21	78	3	6	1	3.69
	OC	Kirkpatrick	365	.219	9	46	412	30	8	6		.982							
	1B	C. Harrison	143	.217	2	21	335	24	3	31	9.3	.992							
Chicago W-79 L-83 Chuck Tanner	1B	C. May	500	.294	7	70	1189	71	18	90	**9.8**	.986	W. Wood	44	334	22	13	1	1.91
	2B	M. Andrews	330	.282	12	47	177	191	17	51	5.1	.956	T. Bradley	45	286	15	15	2	2.96
	SS	L. Alvarado	264	.216	0	8	89	189	12	34	4.1	.959	T. John	38	229	13	16	0	3.62
	3B	B. Melton	543	.269	33	86	116	371	16	26	3.4	.968	B. Johnson	53	178	12	10	14	2.93
	RF	W. Williams	361	.294	8	35	157	4	0	2	1.8	1.000	J. Horlen	34	137	8	9	2	4.27
	CF	J. Johnstone	388	.260	16	40	232	9	8	1	2.1	.984	S. Kealey	54	77	2	2	6	3.86
	LF	R. Reichardt	496	.278	19	62	283	4	4	0	2.3	.986	V. Romo	45	72	1	7	5	3.38
	C	E. Herrmann	294	.214	11	35	556	56	3	5	6.3	.995							
	20	R. McKinney	369	.271	8	46	192	160	10	34		.972							
	SS	L. Richard	260	.231	2	17	87	210	26	30	4.8	.920							
	C	T. Egan	251	.239	10	34	443	41	7	2	6.4	.986							
	OF	P. Kelly	213	.291	3	22	100	7	1	0	1.8	.991							
	SS	R. Morales	185	.243	2	14	66	138	6	14	3.7	.976							
	OF	Hershberger	177	.260	2	15	96	1	4	0	1.7	.960							
California W-76 L-86 Lefty Phillips	1B	J. Spencer	510	.237	18	59	**1296**	**93**	5	117	9.6	**.996**	Messersmith	38	277	20	13	0	2.99
	2B	S. Alomar	689	.260	4	42	350	432	9	100	5.8	.989	C. Wright	37	277	16	17	0	2.99
	SS	J. Fregosi	347	.233	5	33	93	237	22	31	4.8	.938	T. Murphy	37	243	6	17	0	3.78
	3B	K. McMullen	593	.250	21	68	137	344	17	27	3.2	.966	R. May	32	208	11	12	0	3.03
	RF	R. Repoz	297	.199	13	42	172	6	0	2	1.8	1.000	E. Fisher	57	119	10	8	3	2.72
	CF	K. Berry	298	.221	3	22	237	5	3	0	2.4	.988	L. Allen	54	94	4	6	15	2.49
	LF	T. Gonzalez	314	.245	3	38	146	4	2	1	1.7	.987	D. LaRoche	56	72	5	1	9	2.50
	C	Stephenson	279	.219	3	25	434	33	4	3	5.4	.992							
	OF	M. Rivers	268	.265	1	12	159	5	4	2	2.2	.976							
	OF	Conigliaro	266	.222	4	15	155	6	1	1	2.3	.994							
	SS	S. O'Brien	251	.199	5	21	87	136	9	30	4.5	.961							
	OF	A. Johnson	242	.260	2	21	84	3	7	0	1.5	.926							
	C	G. Moses	181	.227	4	15	299	38	8	3	5.5	.977							
	OF	B. Cowan	174	.276	4	20	69	1	0	0	1.8	1.000							
Minnesota W-74 L-86 Bill Rigney	1B	R. Reese	329	.219	10	39	673	43	4	71	7.6	.994	B. Blyleven	38	278	16	15	0	2.82
	2B	R. Carew	577	.307	2	48	321	329	16	76	4.7	.976	J. Perry	40	270	17	17	1	4.23
	SS	L. Cardenas	554	.264	18	75	266	445	11	89	4.7	**.985**	J. Kaat	39	260	13	14	0	3.32
	3B	S. Braun	343	.254	5	35	48	106	11	7	2.3	.933	R. Corbin	52	140	8	11	3	4.11
	RF	T. Oliva	487	**.337**	22	81	216	6	7	3	1.9	.969	T. Hall	48	130	4	7	9	3.32
	CF	J. Holt	340	.259	1	29	209	4	3	2	2.0	.986	S. Williams	46	78	4	5	4	4.15
	LF	C. Tovar	657	.311	1	45	348	14	5	3	2.4	.986	Perranoski	36	43	1	4	5	6.75
	C	Mitterwald	388	.250	13	44	656	53	10	7	6.0	.986							
	13	H. Killebrew	500	.254	28	119	700	149	13	55		.985							
	OF	J. Nettles	168	.250	6	24	139	3	2	1	2.3	.986							

AMERICAN LEAGUE 1971, *cont.*

	POS	Player	AB	BA	HR	RBI	PO	A	E	DP	TC/G	FA	Pitcher	G	IP	W	L	SV	ERA
Milwaukee	1B	J. Briggs	375	.264	21	59	458	40	5	53	8.4	.990	M. Pattin	36	265	14	14	0	3.12
	2B	R. Theobald	388	.276	1	23	233	311	15	81	5.0	.973	B. Parsons	36	245	13	17	0	3.20
W-69 L-92	SS	R. Auerbach	236	.203	1	9	120	193	12	31	4.2	.963	S. Lockwood	33	208	10	15	0	3.33
	3B	T. Harper	585	.258	14	52	71	115	13	10	2.8	.935	L. Krausse	43	180	8	12	0	2.95
Dave Bristol	RF	B. Voss	275	.251	10	30	151	1	2	1	1.9	.987	J. Slaton	26	148	10	8	0	3.77
	CF	D. May	501	.277	16	65	342	10	9	3	2.5	.975	K. Sanders	83	136	7	12	31	1.92
	LF	J. Cardenal	198	.258	3	32	133	6	3	0	2.7	.979							
	C	E. Rodriguez	319	.210	1	30	520	67	5	8	5.2	.992							
	UT	R. Pena	274	.237	3	28	290	112	4	38		.990							
	UT	A. Kosco	264	.227	10	39	264	25	3	23		.990							
	2S	T. Kubiak	260	.227	3	17	171	222	14	44		.966							
	SS	B. Heise	189	.254	0	7	85	138	9	36	4.5	.961							

BATTING AND BASE RUNNING LEADERS

Batting Average
T. Oliva, MIN	.337
B. Murcer, NY	.331
Rettenmund, BAL	.318
C. Tovar, MIN	.311
R. Carew, MIN	.307

Slugging Average
T. Oliva, MIN	.546
B. Murcer, NY	.543
N. Cash, DET	.531
F. Robinson, BAL	.510
R. Jackson, OAK	.508

Home Runs
B. Melton, CHI	33
N. Cash, DET	32
R. Jackson, OAK	32
R. Smith, BOS	30

Winning Percentage
D. McNally, BAL	.808
V. Blue, OAK	.750
C. Dobson, OAK	.750
P. Dobson, BAL	.714

Earned Run Average
V. Blue, OAK	1.82
W. Wood, CHI	1.91
J. Palmer, BAL	2.68
M. Hedlund, KC	2.71
B. Blyleven, MIN	2.82

Wins
M. Lolich, DET	25
V. Blue, OAK	24
W. Wood, CHI	22
D. McNally, BAL	21
C. Hunter, OAK	21

Total Bases
R. Smith, BOS	302
R. Jackson, OAK	288
B. Murcer, NY	287
B. Melton, CHI	267
T. Oliva, MIN	266

Runs Batted In
H. Killebrew, MIN	119
F. Robinson, BAL	99
R. Smith, BOS	96
B. Murcer, NY	94
S. Bando, OAK	94

Stolen Bases
A. Otis, KC	52
F. Patek, KC	49
S. Alomar, CAL	39
Campaneris, OAK	34
V. Pinson, CLE	25
T. Harper, MIL	25

Saves
K. Sanders, MIL	31
T. Abernathy, KC	23
F. Scherman, DET	20
T. Burgmeier, KC	17
R. Fingers, OAK	17

Strikeouts
M. Lolich, DET	308
V. Blue, OAK	301
J. Coleman, DET	236
B. Blyleven, MIN	224
W. Wood, CHI	210

Complete Games
M. Lolich, DET	29
V. Blue, OAK	24
W. Wood, CHI	22
M. Cuellar, BAL	21
J. Palmer, BAL	20

Hits
C. Tovar, MIN	204
S. Alomar, CAL	179
R. Carew, MIN	177
B. Murcer, NY	175

Base on Balls
H. Killebrew, MIN	114
Yastrzemski, BOS	106
P. Schaal, KC	103
B. Murcer, NY	91

Home Run Percentage
N. Cash, DET	7.1
F. Robinson, BAL	6.2
B. Melton, CHI	6.1
R. Jackson, OAK	5.6

Fewest Hits/9 Innings
V. Blue, OAK	6.03
S. McDowell, CLE	6.70
R. May, CAL	6.92
Messersmith, CAL	7.28

Shutouts
V. Blue, OAK	8
Stottlemyre, NY	7
W. Wood, CHI	7
T. Bradley, CHI	6

Fewest Walks/9 Innings
F. Peterson, NY	1.38
S. Kline, NY	1.50
J. Kaat, MIN	1.63
W. Wood, CHI	1.67

Runs Scored
D. Buford, BAL	99
B. Murcer, NY	94
C. Tovar, MIN	94
R. Carew, MIN	88

Doubles
R. Smith, BOS	33
P. Schaal, KC	31
T. Oliva, MIN	30
A. Rodriguez, DET	30

Triples
F. Patek, KC	11
R. Carew, MIN	10
P. Blair, BAL	8

Most Strikeouts/9 Inn.
V. Blue, OAK	8.68
S. McDowell, CLE	8.04
B. Johnson, CHI	7.74
J. Coleman, DET	7.43

Innings
M. Lolich, DET	376
W. Wood, CHI	334
V. Blue, OAK	312
M. Cuellar, BAL	292

Games Pitched
K. Sanders, MIL	83
F. Scherman, DET	69
T. Burgmeier, KC	67
T. Abernathy, KC	63

		W	L	PCT	GB	R	OR	2B	3B	HR	BA	SA	SB	E	DP	FA	CG	BB	SO	ShO	SV	ERA
										Batting					**Fielding**				**Pitching**			
East	Baltimore	101	57	.639		**742**	530	207	25	158	**.261**	.398	66	112	148	.981	**71**	**416**	793	15	22	**3.00**
	Detroit	91	71	.562	12	701	645	214	38	**179**	.254	**.405**	35	**106**	156	**.983**	53	609	**1000**	11	32	3.64
	Boston	85	77	.525	18	691	667	**246**	28	161	.252	.397	51	116	149	.981	44	535	871	11	35	3.83
	New York	82	80	.506	21	648	641	195	**43**	97	.254	.360	75	125	159	.981	67	423	707	15	12	3.45
	Washington	63	96	.396	38.5	537	660	189	30	86	.230	.326	68	141	170	.977	30	554	762	10	26	3.70
	Cleveland	60	102	.370	43	543	747	200	20	109	.238	.342	57	116	159	.981	21	770	937	7	32	4.28
West	Oakland	101	60	.627		691	564	195	25	160	.252	.384	80	117	157	.981	57	501	999	18	36	3.06
	Kansas City	85	76	.528	16	603	566	225	40	80	.250	.353	**130**	134	**178**	.978	34	496	775	15	**44**	3.25
	Chicago	79	83	.488	22.5	617	597	185	30	138	.250	.373	83	160	128	.975	46	468	976	19	32	3.13
	California	76	86	.469	25.5	511	576	213	18	96	.231	.329	72	131	159	.980	39	607	904	11	32	3.10
	Minnesota	74	86	.463	26.5	654	670	197	31	116	.260	.372	66	118	134	.980	43	529	895	9	25	3.82
	Milwaukee	69	92	.429	32	534	609	160	23	104	.229	.329	82	138	152	.977	32	569	795	**23**	32	3.38
						7472	7472	2426	351	1484	.247	.364	865	1514	1849	.980	537	6477	10414	164	360	3.47

NATIONAL LEAGUE 1972

	POS	Player	AB	BA	HR	RBI	PO	A	E	DP	TC/G	FA	Pitcher	G	IP	W	L	SV	ERA
East Pittsburgh	1B	W. Stargell	495	.293	33	112	881	40	**15**	96	9.3	.984	S. Blass	33	250	19	8	0	2.49
	2B	D. Cash	425	.282	3	30	260	342	5	81	6.3	.992	B. Moose	31	226	13	10	1	2.91
W-96 L-59	SS	G. Alley	347	.248	3	36	181	339	16	88	4.7	.970	N. Briles	28	196	14	11	0	3.08
	3B	R. Hebner	427	.300	19	72	76	210	9	17	2.4	.969	D. Ellis	25	163	15	7	0	2.70
Bill Virdon	RF	R. Clemente	378	.312	10	60	199	5	0	2	2.2	1.000	B. Kison	32	152	9	7	3	3.26
	CF	A. Oliver	565	.312	12	89	332	4	5	1	2.5	.985	B. Johnson	31	116	4	4	3	2.96
	LF	V. Davalillo	368	.318	4	28	181	4	4	0	1.9	.979	L. Walker	26	93	4	6	2	3.40
	C	Sanguillen	520	.298	7	71	721	50	9	4	6.1	.988	D. Giusti	54	75	7	4	22	1.93
	2O	R. Stennett	370	.286	3	30	192	164	9	43		.975	R. Hernandez	53	70	5	0	14	1.67
	OF	G. Clines	311	.334	0	17	131	7	6	0	1.7	.958	B. Miller	36	54	5	2	3	2.65
	1B	B. Robertson	306	.193	12	41	502	60	4	57	6.4	.993							
	SS	J. Hernandez	176	.188	1	14	110	180	22	34	4.6	.929							

NATIONAL LEAGUE 1972, *cont.*

	POS	Player	AB	BA	HR	RBI	PO	A	E	DP	TC/G	FA	Pitcher	G	IP	W	L	SV	ERA
Chicago	1B	J. Hickman	368	.272	17	64	670	70	6	61	9.7	.992	F. Jenkins	36	289	20	12	0	3.21
	2B	G. Beckert	474	.270	3	43	256	396	16	71	5.7	.976	B. Hooton	33	218	11	14	0	2.80
W-85 L-70	SS	D. Kessinger	577	.274	1	39	259	504	28	90	5.4	.965	M. Pappas	29	195	17	7	0	2.77
	3B	R. Santo	464	.302	17	74	108	274	21	19	3.1	.948	B. Hands	32	189	11	8	0	2.99
Leo Durocher	RF	J. Cardenal	533	.291	17	70	223	11	7	1	1.8	.971	R. Reuschel	21	129	10	8	0	2.93
W-46 L-44	CF	R. Monday	434	.249	11	42	268	6	1	2	2.1	.996	T. Phoebus	37	83	3	3	6	3.78
	LF	B. Williams	574	.333	37	122	233	9	4	0	1.7	.984	J. Aker	48	67	6	6	17	2.96
Whitey Lockman	C	R. Hundley	357	.218	5	30	569	53	3	7	5.5	.995	J. Pizarro	16	59	4	5	1	3.97
W-39 L-26	UT	C. Fanzone	222	.225	8	42	243	115	9	21		.975							
	1B	J. Pepitone	214	.262	8	21	552	31	2	51	8.9	.997							
New York	1B	E. Kranepool	327	.269	8	34	705	48	3	65	7.0	.996	T. Seaver	35	262	21	12	0	2.92
	2B	K. Boswell	355	.211	9	33	208	183	4	53	4.2	.990	J. Matlack	34	244	15	10	0	2.32
W-83 L-73	SS	B. Harrelson	418	.215	1	24	191	334	16	51	4.7	.970	G. Gentry	32	164	7	10	0	4.01
	3B	J. Fregosi	340	.232	5	32	71	144	15	9	2.7	.935	J. Koosman	34	163	11	12	1	4.14
Yogi Berra	RF	R. Staub	239	.293	9	38	108	4	2	2	1.8	.982	J. McAndrew	28	161	11	8	1	2.80
	CF	T. Agee	422	.227	13	47	273	6	11	1	2.7	.962	T. McGraw	54	106	8	6	27	1.70
	LF	C. Jones	375	.245	5	52	136	8	2	1	1.7	.986	D. Frisella	39	67	5	8	9	3.34
	C	D. Dyer	325	.231	8	36	690	61	5	12	8.3	.993							
	OF	J. Milner	362	.238	17	38	160	7	6	0	1.9	.965							
	UT	T. Martinez	330	.224	1	19	175	194	5	30		.987							
	3B	W. Garrett	298	.232	2	29	66	150	9	13	2.7	.960							
	C	J. Grote	205	.210	3	21	405	42	1	5	7.6	.998							
	OF	W. Mays	195	.267	8	19	109	3	3	1	2.3	.974							
St. Louis	1B	M. Alou	404	.314	3	31	535	40	7	53	8.8	.988	B. Gibson	34	278	19	11	0	2.46
	2B	T. Sizemore	439	.264	2	38	222	342	14	68	5.2	.976	R. Wise	35	269	16	16	0	3.11
W-75 L-81	SS	D. Maxvill	276	.221	1	23	145	243	8	56	4.2	.980	R. Cleveland	33	231	14	15	0	3.94
	3B	J. Torre	544	.289	11	81	102	182	11	17	2.5	.963	A. Santorini	30	134	8	11	0	4.11
Red Schoendienst	RF	L. Melendez	332	.238	5	28	206	5	9	0	2.1	.959	S. Spinks	16	118	5	5	0	2.67
	CF	J. Cruz	332	.235	2	23	220	9	5	5	2.3	.979	D. Segui	33	56	3	1	9	3.07
	LF	L. Brock	621	.311	3	42	253	6	13	1	1.8	.952							
	C	T. Simmons	594	.303	16	96	842	78	8	6	6.9	.991							
	OF	B. Carbo	302	.258	7	34	162	15*	6	3	2.0	.967							
	UT	E. Crosby	276	.217	0	19	130	197	10	42		.970							
Montreal	1B	M. Jorgensen	372	.231	13	47	757	56	4	66	10.8	.995	B. Stoneman	36	251	12	14	0	2.98
	2B	R. Hunt	443	.253	0	18	257	353	11	61	5.1	.982	M. Torrez	34	243	16	12	0	3.33
W-70 L-86	SS	T. Foli	540	.241	2	35	281	487	27	94	5.4	.966	C. Morton	27	172	7	13	0	3.92
	3B	B. Bailey	489	.233	16	57	83	250	22	21	2.6	.938	E. McAnally	29	170	6	15	0	3.81
Gene Mauch	RF	K. Singleton	507	.274	14	50	236	9	7	3	1.8	.972	B. Moore	22	148	9	9	0	3.47
	CF	B. Day	386	.233	10	30	225	7	5	3	2.0	.979	M. Marshall	65	116	14	8	18	1.78
	LF	R. Fairly	446	.278	17	68	125	8	2	2	1.9	.985	S. Renko	30	97	1	10	0	5.20
	C	Boccabella	207	.227	1	10	316	33	6	6	4.9	.983							
	CO	T. McCarver	239	.251	5	20	312	24	4	2		.988							
	OF	R. Woods	221	.258	10	31	110	2	1	0	1.5	.991							
	C	T. Humphrey	215	.186	1	9	322	37	5	4	5.6	.986							
	2B	H. Torres	181	.155	2	7	86	132	8	28	3.8	.965							
	OF	C. Mashore	176	.227	3	23	80	3	1	0	1.1	.988							
Philadelphia	1B	T. Hutton	381	.260	4	38	555	36	5	46	6.9	.992	S. Carlton	41	346	27	10	0	1.97
	2B	D. Doyle	442	.249	1	26	265	288	10	66	4.7	.982	K. Reynolds	33	154	2	15	0	4.26
W-59 L-97	SS	L. Bowa	579	.250	1	31	212	494	9	88	4.8	.987	W. Twitchell	49	140	5	9	1	4.06
	3B	D. Money	536	.222	15	52	139	316	10	31	3.1	.978	B. Champion	30	133	4	14	0	5.09
Frank Lucchesi	RF	B. Robinson	188	.239	8	21	109	2	2	1	1.6	.982	W. Fryman	23	120	4	10	1	4.36
W-26 L-50	CF	W. Montanez	531	.247	13	64	318	15	5	2	2.6	.985	D. Brandon	42	104	7	7	2	3.45
	LF	G. Luzinski	563	.281	18	68	255	9	11	2	1.9	.960	B. Lersch	36	101	4	6	0	3.04
Paul Owens	C	J. Bateman	252	.222	3	17	447	38	14*	6	6.2	.972	D. Selma	46	99	2	9	3	5.56
W-33 L-47	1B	D. Johnson	230	.213	9	31	479	24	9	43	8.3	.982							
	2B	T. Harmon	218	.284	2	13	106	136	1	31	4.9	.996							
West **Cincinnati**	1B	T. Perez	515	.283	21	90	1207	68	9	111	9.4	.993	Billingham	36	218	12	12	1	3.18
	2B	J. Morgan	552	.292	16	73	370	436	8	92	5.5	.990	R. Grimsley	30	198	14	8	1	3.05
W-95 L-59	SS	Concepcion	378	.209	2	29	194	365	16	75	5.1	.999	G. Nolan	25	176	15	5	0	1.99
	3B	D. Menke	447	.233	9	50	85	258	16	20	2.8	.955	McGlothlin	31	145	9	8	0	3.91
Sparky Anderson	RF	C. Geronimo	255	.275	4	29	150	10	3	1	1.5	.982	D. Gullett	31	135	9	10	2	3.94
	CF	B. Tolan	604	.283	8	82	401	9	4	3	2.8	.990	W. Simpson	24	130	8	5	0	4.14
	LF	P. Rose	645	.307	6	57	330	15	2	2	2.3	.994	T. Hall	47	124	10	1	8	2.61
	C	J. Bench	538	.270	40	125	742	56	6	9	6.2	.993	P. Borbon	62	122	8	3	11	3.17
	SS	D. Chaney	196	.250	2	19	83	149	9	24	3.8	.963	C. Carroll	65	96	6	4	37	2.25
	1O	J. Hague	138	.246	4	20	196	9	0	13		1.000							
	O3	H. McRae	97	.278	5	26	16	14	6	1		.833							

NATIONAL LEAGUE 1972, *cont.*

Houston
W-84 L-69

Harry Walker
W-67 L-54

Salty Parker
W-1 L-0

Leo Durocher
W-16 L-15

POS	Player	AB	BA	HR	RBI	PO	A	E	DP	TC/G	FA	Pitcher	G	IP	W	L	SV	ERA
1B	L. May	592	.284	29	98	1318	76	6	133	9.6	.996	D. Wilson	33	228	15	10	0	2.68
2B	T. Helms	518	.259	5	60	353	441	17	115	5.8	.979	L. Dierker	31	215	15	8	0	3.40
SS	R. Metzger	641	.222	2	38	238	504	22	101	5.0	.971	J. Reuss	33	192	9	13	1	4.17
3B	D. Rader	553	.237	22	90	119	340	20	31	3.2	.958	D. Roberts	35	192	12	7	2	4.50
RF	J. Wynn	542	.273	24	90	284	8	5	2	2.1	.983	K. Forsch	30	156	6	8	3	3.91
CF	C. Cedeno	559	.320	22	82	345	9	7	1	2.6	.981	G. Culver	45	97	6	2	2	3.05
LF	B. Watson	548	.312	16	86	218	6	5	0	1.6	.978	T. Griffin	39	94	5	4	3	3.24
C	J. Edwards	332	.268	5	40	645	41	8	8	6.6	.988	J. Ray	54	90	10	9	8	4.30

Los Angeles
W-85 L-70

Walter Alston

POS	Player	AB	BA	HR	RBI	PO	A	E	DP	TC/G	FA	Pitcher	G	IP	W	L	SV	ERA
1B	W. Parker	427	.279	4	59	1074	68	4	91	9.6	.997	D. Sutton	33	273	19	9	0	2.08
2B	L. Lacy	243	.259	0	12	125	161	8	38	5.1	.973	C. Osteen	33	252	20	11	0	2.64
SS	B. Russell	434	.272	4	34	197	439	34	69	5.5	.949	A. Downing	31	203	9	9	0	2.98
3B	S. Garvey	294	.269	9	30	71	187	28	18	3.4	.902	T. John	29	187	11	5	0	2.89
RF	F. Robinson	342	.251	19	59	168	6	6	2	1.9	.967	B. Singer	26	169	6	16	0	3.67
CF	W. Davis	615	.289	19	79	373	10	5	1	2.7	.987	J. Brewer	51	78	8	7	17	1.26
LF	M. Mota	371	.323	5	48	141	3	1	1	1.5	.993	P. Mikkelsen	33	58	5	5	4	4.06
C	Cannizzaro	200	.240	2	18	312	26	6	4	4.8	.983	P. Richert	37	52	2	3	6	2.25
UT	B. Valentine	391	.274	3	32	178	245	23	38		.948							
O1	B. Buckner	383	.319	5	37	434	22	4	28		.991							
OF	W. Crawford	243	.251	8	27	111	2	2	0	1.6	.983							
2B	J. Lefebvre	169	.201	5	24	66	82	2	21	4.5	.987							

Atlanta
W-70 L-84

Lum Harris
W-47 L-57

Eddie Mathews
W-23 L-27

POS	Player	AB	BA	HR	RBI	PO	A	E	DP	TC/G	FA	Pitcher	G	IP	W	L	SV	ERA
1B	H. Aaron	449	.265	34	77	968	66	14	75	9.6	.987	P. Niekro	38	282	16	12	0	3.06
2B	F. Millan	498	.257	1	38	273	339	8	67	5.2	.987	R. Reed	31	213	11	15	0	3.93
SS	M. Perez	479	.228	1	28	220	378	27	73	4.4	.957	R. Schueler	37	145	5	8	2	3.66
3B	D. Evans	418	.254	19	71	126	273	25	20	3.4	.941	T. Kelley	27	116	5	7	0	4.58
RF	M. Lum	369	.228	9	38	241	4	6	1	2.3	.976	G. Stone	31	111	6	11	1	5.51
CF	D. Baker	446	.321	17	76	344	8	4	1	2.9	.989	P. Jarvis	37	99	11	7	2	4.09
LF	R. Garr	554	.325	12	53	246	8	10	1	2.0	.962	C. Upshaw	42	54	3	5	13	3.67
C	E. Williams	565	.258	28	87	584	49	13	7	5.6	.980							
OF	R. Carty	271	.277	6	29	139	3	3	1	1.9	.979							
OF	O. Brown	164	.226	3	16	82	7	10	2	1.7	.899							

San Francisco
W-69 L-86

Charlie Fox

POS	Player	AB	BA	HR	RBI	PO	A	E	DP	TC/G	FA	Pitcher	G	IP	W	L	SV	ERA
1B	W. McCovey	263	.213	14	35	617	32	9	52	8.9	.986	R. Bryant	35	214	14	7	0	2.90
2B	T. Fuentes	572	.264	7	53	361	417	29	89	5.3	.964	J. Barr	44	179	8	10	2	2.87
SS	C. Speier	562	.269	15	71	243	517	20	69	5.2	.974	J. Marichal	25	165	6	16	0	3.71
3B	A. Gallagher	233	.223	2	18	64	120	5	7	2.7	.974	S. McDowell	28	164	10	8	0	4.34
RF	B. Bonds	626	.259	26	80	345	8	8	3	2.4	.978	S. Stone	27	124	6	8	0	2.98
CF	G. Maddox	458	.266	12	58	279	7	6	3	2.4	.979	Carrithers	25	90	4	8	1	5.80
LF	K. Henderson	439	.257	18	51	247	14	7	3	2.2	.974	Willoughby	11	88	6	4	0	2.35
C	D. Rader	459	.259	6	41	661	45	11	7	5.6	.985	J. Johnson	48	73	8	6	8	4.44
UT	D. Kingman	472	.225	29	83	496	159	22	49		.968	R. Moffitt	40	71	1	5	4	3.68
1B	E. Goodson	150	.280	6	30	299	27	3	28	7.8	.991	D. McMahon	44	63	3	3	5	3.71

San Diego
W-58 L-95

Preston Gomez
W-4 L-7

Don Zimmer
W-54 L-88

POS	Player	AB	BA	HR	RBI	PO	A	E	DP	TC/G	FA	Pitcher	G	IP	W	L	SV	ERA
1B	N. Colbert	563	.250	38	111	1290	103	6	119	9.3	.996	S. Arlin	38	250	10	21	0	3.60
2B	D. Thomas	500	.230	5	36	197	239	15	52	5.4	.967	C. Kirby	34	239	12	14	0	3.13
SS	E. Hernandez	329	.195	1	15	169	319	19	59	4.7	.963	F. Norman	42	212	9	11	2	3.44
3B	D. Roberts	418	.244	5	33	62	166	17	20	2.9	.931	M. Caldwell	42	164	7	11	2	4.01
RF	C. Gaston	379	.269	7	44	158	10	4	3	1.8	.977	M. Corkins	47	140	6	9	6	3.54
CF	J. Morales	347	.239	4	18	214	8	3	2	2.3	.987	B. Greif	34	125	5	16	2	5.60
LF	L. Lee	370	.300	12	47	186	6	5	2	2.1	.975	G. Ross	60	92	4	3	3	2.45
C	F. Kendall	273	.216	6	18	504	41	3	11	6.7	.995							
OF	J. Jeter	326	.221	7	21	222	1	3	0	2.5	.987							
OF	L. Stahl	297	.226	7	20	139	4	2	1	1.9	.986							
23	G. Jestadt	256	.246	6	22	104	131	13	27		.948							

BATTING AND BASE RUNNING LEADERS

Batting Average

B. Williams, CHI	.333
R. Garr, ATL	.325
C. Cedeno, HOU	.320
B. Watson, HOU	.312
A. Oliver, PIT	.312

Slugging Average

B. Williams, CHI	.606
W. Stargell, PIT	.558
J. Bench, CIN	.541
C. Cedeno, HOU	.537
H. Aaron, ATL	.514

Home Runs

J. Bench, CIN	40
N. Colbert, SD	38
B. Williams, CHI	37
H. Aaron, ATL	34
W. Stargell, PIT	33

Total Bases

B. Williams, CHI	348
C. Cedeno, HOU	300
J. Bench, CIN	291
L. May, HOU	290
N. Colbert, SD	286

Runs Batted In

J. Bench, CIN	125
B. Williams, CHI	122
W. Stargell, PIT	112
N. Colbert, SD	111
L. May, HOU	98

Stolen Bases

L. Brock, STL	63
J. Morgan, CIN	58
C. Cedeno, HOU	55
B. Bonds, SF	44
B. Tolan, CIN	42

PITCHING LEADERS

Winning Percentage

G. Nolan, CIN	.750
S. Carlton, PHI	.730
M. Pappas, CHI	.708
S. Blass, PIT	.704
D. Ellis, PIT	.682

Earned Run Average

S. Carlton, PHI	1.97
G. Nolan, CIN	1.99
D. Sutton, LA	2.08
J. Matlack, NY	2.32
B. Gibson, STL	2.46

Wins

S. Carlton, PHI	27
T. Seaver, NY	21
C. Osteen, LA	20
F. Jenkins, CHI	20

Saves

C. Carroll, CIN	37
T. McGraw, NY	27
D. Giusti, PIT	22
M. Marshall, MON	18
J. Brewer, LA	17
J. Aker, CHI	17

Strikeouts

S. Carlton, PHI	310
T. Seaver, NY	249
B. Gibson, STL	208
D. Sutton, LA	207
F. Jenkins, CHI	184

Complete Games

S. Carlton, PHI	30
B. Gibson, STL	23
F. Jenkins, CHI	23
R. Wise, STL	20
D. Sutton, LA	18

NATIONAL LEAGUE 1972, *cont.*

BATTING AND BASE RUNNING LEADERS

Hits			Base on Balls			Home Run Percentage	
P. Rose, CIN	198		J. Morgan, CIN	115		H. Aaron, ATL	7.6
L. Brock, STL	193		J. Wynn, HOU	103		J. Bench, CIN	7.4
B. Williams, CHI	191		J. Bench, CIN	100		N. Colbert, SD	6.7
R. Garr, ATL	180		H. Aaron, ATL	92		W. Stargell, PIT	6.7

Runs Scored			Doubles			Triples	
J. Morgan, CIN	122		W. Montanez, PHI	39		L. Bowa, PHI	13
B. Bonds, SF	118		C. Cedeno, HOU	39		P. Rose, CIN	11
J. Wynn, HOU	117		T. Simmons, STL	36		Sanguillen, PIT	8
P. Rose, CIN	107		B. Williams, CHI	34		C. Cedeno, HOU	8

PITCHING LEADERS

Fewest Hits/9 Innings			Shutouts			Fewest Walks/9 Innings	
D. Sutton, LA	6.14		D. Sutton, LA	9		M. Pappas, CHI	1.34
S. Carlton, PHI	6.68		S. Carlton, PHI	8		G. Nolan, CIN	1.53
B. Gibson, STL	7.32		F. Norman, SD	6		P. Niekro, ATL	1.69
T. Seaver, NY	7.39		L. Dierker, HOU	5		D. Ellis, PIT	1.82

Most Strikeouts/9 Inn.			Innings			Games Pitched	
T. Seaver, NY	8.55		S. Carlton, PHI	346		M. Marshall, MON	65
J. Reuss, HOU	8.16		F. Jenkins, CHI	289		C. Carroll, CIN	65
J. Koosman, NY	8.12		P. Niekro, ATL	282		P. Borbon, CIN	62
S. Carlton, PHI	8.06		B. Gibson, STL	278		G. Ross, SD	60

		W	L	PCT	GB	R	OR	2B	3B	HR	BA	SA	SB	E	DP	FA	CG	BB	SO	ShO	SV	ERA
East	Pittsburgh	96	59	.619		691	512	251	47	110	.274	.397	49	136	171	.978	39	433	838	15	48	2.81
	Chicago	85	70	.548	11	685	567	206	40	133	.257	.387	69	132	148	.979	54	421	824	19	32	3.22
	New York	83	73	.532	13.5	528	578	175	31	105	.225	.332	41	116	122	.980	32	486	1059	12	41	3.27
	St. Louis	75	81	.481	21.5	568	600	214	42	70	.260	.355	104	141	146	.977	64	531	912	13	13	3.42
	Montreal	70	86	.449	26.5	513	609	156	22	91	.234	.325	68	134	141	.978	39	579	888	11	23	3.60
	Philadelphia	59	97	.378	37.5	503	635	200	36	98	.236	.344	42	116	142	.978	43	536	927	13	15	3.67
West	Cincinnati	95	59	.617		707	557	214	44	124	.251	.380	140	110	143	.982	25	435	806	15	60	3.21
	Houston	84	69	.549	10.5	708	636	233	38	134	.258	.393	111	116	151	.980	38	498	971	14	31	3.77
	Los Angeles	85	70	.548	10.5	584	527	178	39	98	.256	.360	82	162	145	.974	50	429	856	23	29	2.78
	Atlanta	70	84	.455	25	628	730	186	17	144	.258	.382	47	156	130	.974	40	512	732	4	27	4.27
	San Francisco	69	86	.445	26.5	662	649	211	36	150	.244	.384	123	156	141	.974	44	507	771	8	23	3.70
	San Diego	58	95	.379	36.5	488	665	168	38	102	.227	.332	78	144	146	.976	39	618	960	17	19	3.78
						7265	7265	2392	430	1359	.248	.365	954	1619	1706	.978	507	5985	10544	164	361	3.46

AMERICAN LEAGUE 1972

		POS	Player	AB	BA	HR	RBI	PO	A	E	DP	TC/G	FA	Pitcher	G	IP	W	L	SV	ERA
East	**Detroit**	1B	N. Cash	440	.259	22	61	1060	70	8	102	8.5	.993	M. Lolich	41	327	22	14	0	2.50
		2B	McAuliffe	408	.240	8	30	266	249	13	63	4.6	.975	J. Coleman	40	280	19	14	0	2.80
	W-86 L-70	SS	E. Brinkman	516	.203	6	49	233	495	7	81	4.7	.990	T. Timmerman	34	150	8	10	0	2.88
		3B	A. Rodriguez	601	.236	13	56	150	348	16	33	3.4	.969	W. Fryman	16	114	10	3	0	2.05
	Billy Martin	RF	J. Northrup	426	.261	8	42	215	8	5	2	1.8	.978	C. Seelbach	61	112	9	8	14	2.89
		CF	M. Stanley	435	.234	14	55	309	9	2	1	2.9	.994	F. Scherman	57	94	7	3	12	3.64
		LF	W. Horton	333	.231	11	36	131	6	0	0	1.4	1.000	B. Slayback	23	82	5	6	0	3.18
		C	B. Freehan	374	.262	10	56	648	57	8	9	6.8	.989							
		OF	A. Kaline	278	.313	10	32	111	5	1	0	1.4	.991							
		OF	G. Brown	252	.230	10	31	122	5	3	1	1.8	.977							
		2B	T. Taylor	228	.303	1	20	121	108	8	25	3.5	.966							
	Boston	1B	D. Cater	317	.237	8	39	656	61	5	65	8.0	.993	M. Pattin	38	253	17	13	0	3.24
		2B	D. Griffin	470	.260	2	35	321	331	15	81	5.2	.978	S. Siebert	32	196	12	12	0	3.81
	W-85 L-70	SS	L. Aparicio	436	.257	3	39	183	304	16	54	4.6	.968	L. Tiant	43	179	15	6	3	1.91
		3B	Petrocelli	521	.240	15	75	146	278	13	38	3.0	.970	J. Curtis	26	154	11	8	0	3.74
	Eddie Kasko	RF	R. Smith	467	.270	21	74	247	8	5	2	2.0	.981	McGlothen	22	145	8	7	0	3.41
		CF	T. Harper	556	.254	14	49	321	4	5	4	2.3	.985	R. Culp	16	105	5	8	0	4.46
		LF	Yastrzemski	455	.264	12	68	141	10	4	1	1.9	.974	B. Lee	47	84	7	4	5	3.21
		C	C. Fisk	457	.293	22	61	846	72	15	10	7.1	.984	D. Newhauser	31	37	4	2	4	2.43
		OF	B. Oglivie	253	.241	8	30	98	5	2	2	1.6	.981							
		UT	J. Kennedy	212	.245	2	22	110	141	13	34		.951							
	Baltimore	1B	B. Powell	465	.252	21	81	1116	70	15	111	9.0	.988	J. Palmer	36	274	21	10	0	2.07
		2B	D. Johnson	376	.221	5	32	286	307	6	81	5.2	.990	P. Dobson	38	268	16	18	0	2.65
	W-80 L-74	SS	M. Belanger	285	.186	2	16	180	285	12	53	4.5	.975	M. Cuellar	35	248	18	12	0	2.58
		3B	B. Robinson	556	.250	8	64	129	333	11	27	3.1	.977	D. McNally	36	241	13	17	0	2.95
	Earl Weaver	RF	Rettenmund	301	.233	6	21	174	6	2	2	1.9	.989	D. Alexander	35	106	6	8	2	2.46
		CF	P. Blair	477	.233	8	49	337	10	3	1	2.5	.991	R. Harrison	39	94	3	4	4	2.30
		LF	D. Buford	408	.206	5	22	173	6	2	1	1.7	.989	E. Watt	38	46	2	3	7	2.15
		C	J. Oates	253	.261	4	21	391	31	2	4	5.2	.995	G. Jackson	32	41	1	1	8	2.63
		UT	B. Grich	460	.278	12	50	299	338	20	81		.970							
		OF	D. Baylor	320	.253	11	38	152	2	4	0	1.9	.975							
		OF	T. Crowley	247	.231	11	29	95	2	1	1	1.4	.990							
		C	Etchebarren	188	.202	2	21	334	22	3	2	5.1	.992							

AMERICAN LEAGUE 1972, *cont.*

New York — W-79 L-76 — Ralph Houk

POS	Player	AB	BA	HR	RBI	PO	A	E	DP	TC/G	FA
1B	R. Blomberg	299	.268	14	49	813	32	13	88	9.0	.985
2B	H. Clarke	547	.241	3	37	347	399	11	104	5.3	.985
SS	G. Michael	391	.233	1	32	218	437	21	89	5.6	.969
3B	C. Sanchez	250	.248	0	22	47	167	14	13	3.4	.939
RF	J. Callison	275	.258	9	34	127	4	1	1	1.8	.992
CF	B. Murcer	585	.292	33	96	382	11	3	1	2.6	.992
LF	R. White	556	.270	10	54	323	8	2	1	2.1	.994
C	T. Munson	511	.280	7	46	575	71	15	11	5.0	.977
1B	F. Alou	324	.278	6	37	648	54	7	69	7.5	.990
32	B. Allen	220	.227	9	21	75	132	9	26		.958
OF	R. Torres	199	.211	3	13	86	4	2	0	1.5	.978
C	J. Ellis	136	.294	5	25	127	11	5	1	5.7	.965

Pitcher	G	IP	W	L	SV	ERA
Stottlemyre	36	260	14	18	0	3.22
F. Peterson	35	250	17	15	0	3.24
S. Kline	32	236	16	9	0	2.40
M. Kekich	29	175	10	13	0	3.70
S. Lyle	59	108	9	5	35	1.92
R. Gardner	20	97	8	5	0	3.06

Cleveland — W-72 L-84 — Ken Aspromonte

POS	Player	AB	BA	HR	RBI	PO	A	E	DP	TC/G	FA
1B	C. Chambliss	466	.292	6	44	1109	56	8	109	9.9	.993
2B	J. Brohamer	527	.233	5	35	285	393	16	87	5.3	.977
SS	F. Duffy	385	.239	3	27	197	360	13	75	4.5	.977
3B	G. Nettles	557	.253	17	70	114	358	21	27	3.3	.957
RF	B. Bell	466	.255	9	36	274	10	3	4	2.3	.990
CF	D. Unser	383	.238	1	17	248	10	3	1	2.2	.989
LF	A. Johnson	356	.239	8	37	145	4	7	1	1.6	.955
C	R. Fosse	457	.241	10	41	713	70	12	9	6.4	.985
O1	T. McCraw	391	.258	7	33	504	28	3	29		.994
2S	E. Leon	225	.200	4	16	103	179	6	39		.979
OF	Lowenstein	151	.212	6	21	77	7	0	3	1.4	1.000

Pitcher	G	IP	W	L	SV	ERA
G. Perry	41	343	24	16	1	1.92
D. Tidrow	39	237	14	15	0	2.77
M. Wilcox	32	156	7	14	0	3.40
R. Lamb	34	108	5	6	0	3.08
S. Dunning	16	105	6	4	0	3.26
P. Hennigan	38	67	5	3	6	2.69
E. Farmer	46	61	2	5	7	4.43
S. Mingori	41	57	0	6	10	3.95

Milwaukee — W-65 L-91 — Dave Bristol W-10 L-20 — Roy McMillan W-1 L-1 — Del Crandall W-54 L-70

POS	Player	AB	BA	HR	RBI	PO	A	E	DP	TC/G	FA
1B	G. Scott	578	.266	20	88	1210	73	10	106	9.3	.992
2B	R. Theobald	391	.220	1	19	193	299	6	68	4.4	.988
SS	R. Auerbach	554	.218	2	30	256	452	30	90	4.8	.959
3B	M. Ferraro	381	.255	2	29	93	174	14	16	2.4	.950
RF	J. Lahoud	316	.237	12	34	189	2	5	0	2.0	.974
CF	D. May	500	.238	9	45	376	9	6	3	2.8	.985
LF	J. Briggs	418	.266	21	65	194	6	4	1	1.9	.980
C	E. Rodriguez	355	.285	2	35	542	54	10	6	5.3	.983
UT	B. Heise	271	.266	0	12	125	170	6	31		.980
OF	Conigliaro	191	.230	7	16	120	5	1	2	2.5	.992
OF	O. Brown	179	.279	3	25	116	8	1	3	2.2	.992

Pitcher	G	IP	W	L	SV	ERA
J. Lonborg	33	223	14	12	1	2.83
B. Parsons	33	214	13	13	0	3.91
S. Lockwood	29	170	8	15	0	3.60
J. Colborn	39	148	7	7	0	3.10
K. Brett	26	133	7	12	0	4.53
G. Ryerson	20	102	3	8	0	3.62
K. Sanders	62	92	2	9	17	3.13
F. Linzy	47	77	2	2	12	3.04

West

Oakland — W-93 L-62 — Dick Williams

POS	Player	AB	BA	HR	RBI	PO	A	E	DP	TC/G	FA
1B	M. Epstein	455	.270	26	70	1111	73	12	101	8.7	.990
2B	T. Cullen	142	.261	0	15	103	117	11	24	3.6	.952
SS	Campaneris	625	.240	8	32	283	494	18	93	5.4	.977
3B	S. Bando	535	.236	15	77	123	337	19	29	3.2	.960
RF	R. Jackson	499	.265	25	75	301	5	9	5	2.5	.971
CF	A. Mangual	272	.246	5	32	166	4	5	2	2.4	.971
LF	J. Rudi	593	.305	19	75	247	9	2	1	1.8	.992
C	D. Duncan	403	.218	19	59	661	43	5	9	6.3	.993
C	G. Tenace	227	.225	5	32	266	18	6	1	5.9	.979

Pitcher	G	IP	W	L	SV	ERA
C. Hunter	38	295	21	7	0	2.04
K. Holtzman	39	265	19	11	0	2.51
B. Odom	31	194	15	6	0	2.51
V. Blue	25	151	6	10	0	2.80
R. Fingers	65	111	11	9	21	2.51
D. Hamilton	25	101	6	6	0	2.94
B. Locker	56	78	6	4	10	2.65
D. Knowles	54	66	5	1	11	1.36

Chicago — W-87 L-67 — Chuck Tanner

POS	Player	AB	BA	HR	RBI	PO	A	E	DP	TC/G	FA
1B	D. Allen	506	.308	37	113	1234	67	7	94	9.1	.995
2B	M. Andrews	505	.220	7	50	354	325	19	69	4.8	.973
SS	R. Morales	287	.206	2	20	120	213	11	32	4.0	.968
3B	E. Spiezio	277	.238	2	22	67	172	12	11	3.4	.952
RF	P. Kelly	402	.261	5	24	173	8	6	3	1.7	.968
CF	R. Reichardt	291	.251	8	43	157	2	3	1	1.8	.981
LF	C. May	523	.308	12	68	215	13	4	2	1.6	.983
C	E. Herrmann	354	.249	10	40	641	69	8	10	6.4	.989
OF	J. Johnstone	261	.188	4	17	154	5	2	1	1.7	.988
SS	L. Alvarado	254	.213	2	29	98	213	14	28	4.0	.957
OF	W. Williams	221	.249	2	11	93	6	1	2	1.8	.990
3B	B. Melton	208	.245	7	30	47	125	12	12	3.3	.935

Pitcher	G	IP	W	L	SV	ERA
W. Wood	49	377	24	17	0	2.51
T. Bradley	40	260	15	14	0	2.98
S. Bahnsen	43	252	21	16	0	3.60
T. Forster	62	100	6	5	29	2.25
D. Lemonds	31	95	4	7	0	2.95
G. Gossage	36	80	7	1	2	4.28

Minnesota — W-77 L-77 — Bill Rigney W-36 L-34 — Frank Quilici W-41 L-43

POS	Player	AB	BA	HR	RBI	PO	A	E	DP	TC/G	FA
1B	H. Killebrew	433	.231	26	74	995	99	9	82	8.5	.992
2B	R. Carew	535	.318	0	51	331	378	16	85	5.2	.978
SS	D. Thompson	573	.276	4	48	247	468	32	76	5.2	.957
3B	E. Soderholm	287	.188	13	39	66	163	14	17	3.1	.942
RF	C. Tovar	548	.265	2	31	287	10	5	2	2.2	.983
CF	B. Darwin	513	.267	22	80	289	8	6	1	2.1	.980
LF	S. Brye	253	.241	0	12	170	9	1	1	1.9	.994
C	G. Borgmann	175	.234	3	14	304	31	12	4	6.2	.965
UT	S. Braun	402	.289	2	50	110	207	13	26		.961
OF	J. Nettles	235	.204	4	15	156	5	3	1	2.1	.982
1B	R. Reese	197	.218	5	26	392	30	5	55	4.4	.988
C	Mitterwald	163	.184	1	8	272	33	5	4	5.1	.984

Pitcher	G	IP	W	L	SV	ERA
B. Blyleven	39	287	17	17	0	2.73
D. Woodson	36	252	14	14	0	2.71
J. Perry	35	218	13	16	0	3.34
R. Corbin	31	162	8	9	0	2.61
J. Kaat	15	113	10	2	0	2.07
D. LaRoche	62	95	5	7	10	2.84
W. Granger	63	90	4	6	19	3.00

AMERICAN LEAGUE 1972, cont.

Kansas City — W-76 L-78 — Bob Lemon

POS	Player	AB	BA	HR	RBI	PO	A	E	DP	TC/G	FA	Pitcher	G	IP	W	L	SV	ERA
1B	J. Mayberry	503	.298	25	100	1338	82	7	141	9.8	.995	D. Drago	34	239	12	17	0	3.01
2B	C. Rojas	487	.261	3	53	265	360	9	82	4.8	.986	Splittorff	35	216	12	12	0	3.13
SS	F. Patek	518	.212	0	32	230	510	22	113	5.6	.971	R. Nelson	34	173	11	6	2	2.08
3B	P. Schaal	435	.228	6	41	77	245	18	16	2.8	.947	Dal Canton	35	132	6	6	2	3.41
RF	Scheinblum	450	.300	8	66	215	6	8	2	1.9	.965	M. Hedlund	29	113	5	7	0	4.78
CF	A. Otis	540	.293	11	54	351	6	3	3	2.6	.992	Fitzmorris	38	101	2	5	3	3.74
LF	L. Piniella	574	.312	11	72	275	8	7	2	1.9	.976	J. Rooker	18	72	5	6	0	4.38
C	Kirkpatrick	364	.275	9	43	590	49	6	5	6.0	.991	T. Abernathy	45	58	3	4	5	1.71
OF	S. Hovley	196	.270	3	24	103	6	2	0	1.6	.982	T. Burgmeier	51	55	5	2	9	4.25

California — W-75 L-80 — Del Rice

POS	Player	AB	BA	HR	RBI	PO	A	E	DP	TC/G	FA	Pitcher	G	IP	W	L	SV	ERA
1B	B. Oliver	509	.269	19	70	1079	54	7	93	9.0	.994	N. Ryan	39	284	19	16	0	2.28
2B	S. Alomar	610	.239	1	25	350	388	17	92	4.9	.977	C. Wright	35	251	18	11	0	2.98
SS	L. Cardenas	551	.223	6	42	241	471	22	84	4.9	.970	R. May	35	205	12	11	1	2.94
3B	K. McMullen	472	.269	9	34	89	267	11	26	2.7	.970	Messersmith	25	170	8	11	2	2.81
RF	L. Stanton	402	.251	12	39	225	6	4	2	1.9	.983	R. Clark	26	110	4	9	1	4.50
CF	K. Berry	409	.289	5	39	272	13	0	5	2.5	1.000	L. Allen	42	85	3	7	5	3.49
LF	V. Pinson	484	.275	7	49	205	11	2	3	1.6	.991	E. Fisher	43	81	4	5	3	3.76
C	A. Kusnyer	179	.207	2	13	362	33	10	3	6.4	.975	S. Barber	34	58	4	4	2	2.02
10	J. Spencer	212	.222	1	14	289	23	3	25		.990							

Texas — W-54 L-100 — Ted Williams

POS	Player	AB	BA	HR	RBI	PO	A	E	DP	TC/G	FA	Pitcher	G	IP	W	L	SV	ERA
1B	F. Howard	287	.244	9	31	441	27	9	39	7.2	.981	P. Broberg	39	176	5	12	1	4.30
2B	L. Randle	249	.193	2	21	151	166	16	38	5.1	.952	D. Bosman	29	173	8	10	0	3.64
SS	T. Harrah	374	.259	1	31	166	308	20	64	4.7	.960	R. Hand	30	171	10	14	0	3.32
3B	D. Nelson	499	.226	2	28	107	222	19	25	2.9	.945	M. Paul	49	162	8	9	1	2.17
RF	T. Ford	429	.235	14	50	242	11	6	2	2.2	.977	Gogolewski	36	151	4	11	2	4.23
CF	E. Maddox	294	.252	0	10	199	7	2	4	2.2	.990	D. Stanhouse	24	105	2	9	0	3.77
LF	J. Lovitto	330	.224	1	19	233	7	6	2	2.4	.976	P. Lindblad	66	100	5	8	9	2.61
C	D. Billings	469	.254	5	58	478	45	10	13	5.8	.981	J. Panther	58	94	5	9	0	4.12
O1	L. Biittner	382	.259	3	31	503	41	8	37		.986	H. Pina	60	76	2	7	15	3.20
1B	D. Mincher	191	.236	6	39	467	44	3	45	8.7	.994	C. Cox	35	65	3	5	4	4.41
2B	V. Harris	186	.140	0	10	110	132	10	29	4.3	.960							

BATTING AND BASE RUNNING LEADERS

Batting Average
R. Carew, MIN .318
L. Piniella, KC .312
D. Allen, CHI .308
C. May, CHI .308
J. Rudi, OAK .305

Slugging Average
D. Allen, CHI .603
C. Fisk, BOS .538
B. Murcer, NY .537
J. Mayberry, KC .507
M. Epstein, OAK .490

Home Runs
D. Allen, CHI 37
B. Murcer, NY 33
H. Killebrew, MIN 26
M. Epstein, OAK 26
R. Jackson, OAK 25
J. Mayberry, KC 25

Total Bases
B. Murcer, NY 314
D. Allen, CHI 305
J. Rudi, OAK 288
J. Mayberry, KC 255
L. Piniella, KC 253

Runs Batted In
D. Allen, CHI 113
J. Mayberry, KC 100
B. Murcer, NY 96
G. Scott, MIL 88
B. Powell, BAL 81

Stolen Bases
Campaneris, OAK 52
D. Nelson, TEX 51
F. Patek, KC 33
P. Kelly, CHI 32
A. Otis, KC 28

Hits
J. Rudi, OAK 181
L. Piniella, KC 179
B. Murcer, NY 171
R. Carew, MIN 170

Base on Balls
D. Allen, CHI 99
R. White, NY 99
H. Killebrew, MIN 94
C. May, CHI 79

Home Run Percentage
D. Allen, CHI 7.3
H. Killebrew, MIN 6.0
M. Epstein, OAK 5.7
B. Murcer, NY 5.6

Runs Scored
B. Murcer, NY 102
J. Rudi, OAK 94
T. Harper, BOS 92
D. Allen, CHI 90

Doubles
L. Piniella, KC 33
J. Rudi, OAK 32
B. Murcer, NY 30
T. Harper, BOS 29

Triples
C. Fisk, BOS 9
J. Rudi, OAK 9
P. Blair, BAL 8
P. Kelly, CHI 7

PITCHING LEADERS

Winning Percentage
C. Hunter, OAK .750
B. Odom, OAK .714
L. Tiant, BOS .714
J. Palmer, BAL .677
S. Kline, NY .640

Earned Run Average
L. Tiant, BOS 1.91
G. Perry, CLE 1.92
C. Hunter, OAK 2.04
J. Palmer, BAL 2.07
R. Nelson, KC 2.08

Wins
G. Perry, CLE 24
W. Wood, CHI 24
M. Lolich, DET 22
C. Hunter, OAK 21
J. Palmer, BAL 21
S. Bahnsen, CHI 21

Saves
S. Lyle, NY 35
T. Forster, CHI 29
R. Fingers, OAK 21
W. Granger, MIN 19
K. Sanders, MIL 17

Strikeouts
N. Ryan, CAL 329
M. Lolich, DET 250
G. Perry, CLE 234
B. Blyleven, MIN 228
J. Coleman, DET 222

Complete Games
G. Perry, CLE 29
M. Lolich, DET 23
N. Ryan, CAL 20
W. Wood, CHI 20
J. Palmer, BAL 18

Fewest Hits/9 Innings
N. Ryan, CAL 5.26
C. Hunter, OAK 6.10
R. Nelson, KC 6.23
L. Tiant, BOS 6.44

Shutouts
N. Ryan, CAL 9
W. Wood, CHI 8
Stottlemyre, NY 7
L. Tiant, BOS 6

Fewest Walks/9 Innings
F. Peterson, NY 1.58
R. Nelson, KC 1.61
S. Kline, NY 1.68
K. Holtzman, OAK 1.77

Most Strikeouts/9 Inn.
N. Ryan, CAL 10.43
Messersmith, CAL 7.52
R. May, CAL 7.42
T. Bradley, CHI 7.23

Innings
W. Wood, CHI 377
G. Perry, CLE 343
M. Lolich, DET 327
C. Hunter, OAK 295

Games Pitched
P. Lindblad, TEX 66
R. Fingers, OAK 65
W. Granger, MIN 63
T. Forster, CHI 62

		W	L	PCT	GB	R	OR	Batting 2B	3B	HR	BA	SA	SB	Fielding E	DP	FA	Pitching CG	BB	SO	ShO	SV	ERA
East	Detroit	86	70	.551		558	514	179	32	122	.237	.356	17	96	137	.984	46	465	952	11	33	2.96
	Boston	85	70	.548	.5	640	620	229	34	124	.248	.376	66	130	141	.978	48	512	918	20	25	3.47
	Baltimore	80	74	.519	5	519	430	193	29	100	.229	.339	78	100	150	.983	62	395	788	20	21	2.54
	New York	79	76	.510	6.5	557	527	201	24	103	.249	.357	71	134	179	.978	35	419	625	19	39	3.05
	Cleveland	72	84	.462	14	472	519	187	18	91	.234	.330	49	116	157	.981	47	534	846	13	25	2.97
	Milwaukee	65	91	.417	21	493	595	167	22	88	.235	.328	64	139	145	.977	37	486	740	14	32	3.45
West	Oakland	93	62	.600		604	457	195	29	134	.240	.366	87	130	146	.979	42	418	862	23	43	2.58
	Chicago	87	67	.565	5.5	566	538	170	28	108	.238	.346	100	135	136	.977	36	431	936	14	42	3.12
	Minnesota	77	77	.500	15.5	537	535	182	31	93	.244	.344	53	159	133	.974	37	444	838	17	34	2.86
	Kansas City	76	78	.494	16.5	580	545	220	26	78	.255	.353	85	120	164	.980	44	405	801	16	28	3.24
	California	75	80	.484	18	454	533	171	26	78	.242	.330	57	114	135	.981	57	620	1000	18	16	3.06
	Texas	54	100	.351	38.5	461	628	166	17	56	.217	.290	126	166	147	.972	11	613	868	8	34	3.53
						6441	6441	2260	316	1175	.239	.343	853	1539	1770	.979	502	5742	10174	193	372	3.07

NATIONAL LEAGUE 1973

East

New York
W-82 L-79
Yogi Berra

POS	Player	AB	BA	HR	RBI	PO	A	E	DP	TC/G	FA	Pitcher	G	IP	W	L	SV	ERA
1B	J. Milner	451	.239	23	72	771	47	9	66	8.7	.989	T. Seaver	36	290	19	10	0	2.08
2B	F. Millan	638	.290	3	37	410	411	9	99	5.4	.989	J. Koosman	35	263	14	15	0	2.84
SS	B. Harrelson	356	.258	0	20	153	315	10	49	4.6	.979	J. Matlack	34	242	14	16	0	3.20
3B	W. Garrett	504	.256	16	58	80	280	22	36	2.9	.942	G. Stone	27	148	12	3	1	2.80
RF	R. Staub	585	.279	15	76	297	17	7	5	2.1	.978	T. McGraw	60	119	5	6	25	3.87
CF	D. Hahn	262	.229	2	21	176	2	2	0	2.1	.989	R. Sadecki	31	117	5	4	1	3.39
LF	C. Jones	339	.260	11	48	168	6	6	0	2.0	.967	H. Parker	38	97	8	4	5	3.35
C	J. Grote	285	.256	1	32	545	34	3	6	7.2	.995	J. McAndrew	23	80	3	8	1	5.38
1O	E. Kranepool	284	.239	1	35	448	28	2	39		.996	B. Capra	24	42	2	7	4	3.86
UT	T. Martinez	263	.255	1	14	119	139	12	15		.956							
OF	W. Mays	209	.211	6	25	103	2	1	0	2.4	.991							
C	D. Dyer	189	.185	1	9	308	26	2	7	5.6	.994							

St. Louis
W-81 L-81
Red Schoendienst

POS	Player	AB	BA	HR	RBI	PO	A	E	DP	TC/G	FA	Pitcher	G	IP	W	L	SV	ERA
1B	J. Torre	519	.287	13	69	833	60	6	80	7.9	.993	R. Wise	35	259	16	12	0	3.37
2B	T. Sizemore	521	.282	1	54	312	463	15	83	5.7	.981	R. Cleveland	32	224	14	10	0	3.01
SS	M. Tyson	469	.243	1	33	202	352	33	68	4.6	.944	A. Foster	35	204	13	9	0	3.14
3B	K. Reitz	426	.235	6	42	85	211	8	19	2.3	.974	B. Gibson	25	195	12	10	0	2.77
RF	L. Melendez	341	.267	2	35	196	8	2	4	2.2	.990	D. Segui	65	100	7	6	17	2.78
CF	J. Cruz	406	.227	10	57	276	2	6	1	2.4	.979	T. Murphy	19	89	3	7	0	3.76
LF	L. Brock	650	.297	7	63	310	3	12	1	2.0	.963	R. Folkers	34	82	4	4	3	3.61
C	T. Simmons	619	.310	13	91	888	74	13	13	6.4	.987	O. Pena	42	62	4	4	6	2.18
1B	T. McCarver	331	.266	3	49	545	30	8	47	7.6	.986	A. Hrabosky	44	56	2	4	5	2.09
OF	B. Carbo	308	.286	8	40	171	11	4	3	2.0	.978	W. Granger	33	47	2	4	5	4.24

Pittsburgh
W-80 L-82
Bill Virdon
W-67 L-69
Danny Murtaugh
W-13 L-13

POS	Player	AB	BA	HR	RBI	PO	A	E	DP	TC/G	FA	Pitcher	G	IP	W	L	SV	ERA
1B	B. Robertson	397	.239	14	40	957	79	5	91	9.7	.995	N. Briles	33	219	14	13	0	2.84
2B	D. Cash	436	.271	2	31	227	276	11	46	5.6	.979	B. Moose	33	201	12	13	0	3.53
SS	D. Maxvill	217	.189	0	17	105	234	10	46	4.7	.971	D. Ellis	28	192	12	14	0	3.05
3B	R. Hebner	509	.271	25	74	92	260	23	19	2.7	.939	J. Rooker	41	170	10	6	5	2.85
RF	R. Zisk	333	.324	10	54	139	12	2	4	1.8	.987	L. Walker	37	122	7	12	1	4.65
CF	A. Oliver	654	.292	20	99	238	5	9	0	2.3	.964	D. Giusti	67	99	9	2	20	2.37
LF	W. Stargell	522	.299	44	119	261	14	7	1	2.0	.975	B. Johnson	50	92	4	2	4	3.62
C	Sanguillen	589	.282	12	65	493	35	9	9	6.0	.983	R. Hernandez	59	90	4	5	11	2.41
2S	R. Stennett	466	.242	10	55	277	348	14	84		.978	S. Blass	23	89	3	9	0	9.85
OF	G. Clines	304	.263	1	23	145	6	5	0	2.0	.968							
C	M. May	283	.269	7	31	402	36	12	4	5.7	.973							

Montreal
W-79 L-83
Gene Mauch

POS	Player	AB	BA	HR	RBI	PO	A	E	DP	TC/G	FA	Pitcher	G	IP	W	L	SV	ERA
1B	M. Jorgensen	413	.230	9	47	990	80	5	88	8.7	.995	S. Renko	36	250	15	11	1	2.81
2B	R. Hunt	401	.309	4	31	219	280	9	54	5.0	.982	M. Torrez	35	208	9	12	0	4.46
SS	T. Foli	458	.240	2	36	245	396	27	84	5.4	.960	M. Marshall	92	179	14	11	31	2.66
3B	B. Bailey	513	.273	26	86	93	275	17	25	2.6	.956	B. Moore	35	176	7	16	0	4.49
RF	K. Singleton	560	.302	23	103	278	20	5	3	1.9	.983	E. McAnally	27	147	7	9	0	4.04
CF	R. Woods	318	.230	3	31	208	7	5	1	1.9	.977	S. Rogers	17	134	10	5	0	1.54
LF	R. Fairly	413	.298	17	49	182	4	5	0	1.6	.974	B. Stoneman	29	97	4	8	1	6.80
C	Boccabella	403	.233	7	46	610	65	14	10	5.9	.980	T. Walker	54	92	7	5	4	3.63
1B	H. Breeden	258	.275	15	43	515	45	5	50	8.6	.991							
S2	P. Frias	225	.231	0	22	120	211	15	46		.957							
OF	B. Day	207	.275	4	28	86	2	0	0	1.7	1.000							

Chicago
W-77 L-84
Whitey Lockman

POS	Player	AB	BA	HR	RBI	PO	A	E	DP	TC/G	FA	Pitcher	G	IP	W	L	SV	ERA
1B	J. Hickman	201	.244	3	20	398	31	5	37	8.5	.988	F. Jenkins	38	271	14	16	0	3.89
2B	G. Beckert	372	.255	0	29	163	262	7	50	4.9	.984	B. Hooton	42	240	14	17	0	3.68
SS	D. Kessinger	577	.262	0	43	274	526	30	109	5.3	.964	R. Reuschel	36	237	14	15	0	3.00
3B	R. Santo	536	.267	20	77	107	271	20	17	2.7	.950	M. Pappas	30	162	7	12	0	4.28
RF	J. Cardenal	522	.303	11	68	234	13	5	2	1.8	.980	B. Bonham	44	152	7	5	3	3.02
CF	R. Monday	554	.267	26	56	317	9	9	2	2.3	.973	B. Locker	63	106	10	6	18	2.55
LF	B. Williams	576	.288	20	86	253	14	4	1	2.0	.985	J. Aker	47	64	4	5	12	4.08
C	R. Hundley	368	.226	10	43	648	59	5	7	5.8	.993							
2B	P. Popovich	280	.236	2	24	171	247	8	53	5.1	.981							
C	K. Rudolph	170	.206	2	17	259	28	9	4	4.6	.970							
UT	C. Fanzone	150	.273	6	22	193	41	8	13		.967							
1B	P. Bourque	139	.209	7	20	327	35	5	32	9.7	.986							

Philadelphia
W-71 L-91
Danny Ozark

POS	Player	AB	BA	HR	RBI	PO	A	E	DP	TC/G	FA	Pitcher	G	IP	W	L	SV	ERA
1B	W. Montanez	552	.263	11	65	785	52	5	87	8.5	.994	S. Carlton	40	293	13	20	0	3.90
2B	D. Doyle	370	.273	3	26	231	296	14	71	4.7	.974	W. Twitchell	34	223	13	9	0	2.50
SS	L. Bowa	446	.211	0	23	191	361	12	87	4.6	.979	K. Brett	31	212	13	9	0	3.44
3B	M. Schmidt	367	.196	18	52	101	251	17	30	3.0	.954	J. Lonborg	38	199	13	16	0	4.88
RF	B. Robinson	452	.288	25	65	227	8	5	1	2.1	.979	D. Ruthven	25	128	6	9	1	4.21
CF	D. Unser	440	.289	11	52	329	14	4	4	2.6	.988	B. Lersch	42	98	3	6	1	4.39
LF	G. Luzinski	610	.285	29	97	262	7	2	1	1.7	.993	M. Scarce	52	71	1	8	12	2.42
C	B. Boone	521	.261	10	61	868	89	10	16	6.7	.990							
UT	C. Tovar	328	.268	1	21	113	113	12	32		.950							
1B	T. Hutton	247	.263	5	29	527	43	1	61	8.0	.998							
OF	M. Anderson	193	.254	9	28	99	4	2	1	1.6	.981							

NATIONAL LEAGUE 1973, *cont.*

	POS	Player	AB	BA	HR	RBI	PO	A	E	DP	TC/G	FA	Pitcher	G	IP	W	L	SV	ERA
West **Cincinnati** W-99 L-63 Sparky Anderson	1B	T. Perez	564	.314	27	101	1318	85	13	131	9.4	.991	Billingham	40	293	19	10	0	3.04
	2B	J. Morgan	576	.290	26	82	417	440	9	106	5.6	.990	R. Grimsley	38	242	13	10	1	3.23
	SS	Concepcion	328	.287	8	46	165	292	12	56	5.3	.974	D. Gullett	45	228	18	8	2	3.51
	3B	D. Menke	241	.191	3	26	68	189	9	19	2.2	.966	F. Norman	24	166	12	6	0	3.30
	RF	C. Geronimo	324	.210	4	33	243	9	2	2	2.0	.992	P. Borbon	80	121	11	4	14	2.15
	CF	B. Tolan	457	.206	9	51	279	9	10	1	2.5	.966	T. Hall	54	104	8	5	8	3.47
	LF	P. Rose	680	.338	5	64	343	15	3	0	2.3	.992	C. Carroll	53	93	8	8	14	3.69
	C	J. Bench	557	.253	25	104	693	61	4	7	5.7	.995							
	3B	D. Driessen	366	.301	4	47	62	150	12	19	2.6	.946							
	SS	D. Chaney	227	.181	0	14	103	216	12	44	4.4	.964							
	OF	A. Kosco	118	.280	9	21	50	1	0	0	1.4	1.000							
Los Angeles W-95 L-66 Walter Alston	1B	B. Buckner	575	.275	8	46	888	50	2	93	10.1	.998	D. Sutton	33	256	18	10	0	2.42
	2B	D. Lopes	535	.275	6	37	319	379	11	90	5.3	.984	Messersmith	33	250	14	10	0	2.70
	SS	B. Russell	615	.265	4	56	243	560	31	106	5.1	.963	C. Osteen	33	237	16	11	0	3.31
	3B	R. Cey	507	.245	15	80	111	328	18	39	3.1	.961	T. John	36	218	16	7	0	3.10
	RF	W. Crawford	457	.295	14	66	250	13	6	4	1.9	.978	A. Downing	30	193	9	9	0	3.31
	CF	W. Davis	599	.285	16	77	344	6	7	0	2.4	.980	C. Hough	37	72	4	2	5	2.76
	LF	M. Mota	293	.314	0	23	96	4	0	0	1.4	1.000	J. Brewer	56	72	6	8	20	3.01
	C	J. Ferguson	487	.263	25	88	757	57	3	17	6.7	.996	P. Richert	39	51	3	3	7	3.18
	1B	S. Garvey	349	.304	8	50	718	26	5	58	9.9	.993	G. Culver	28	42	4	4	2	3.00
	OF	T. Paciorek	195	.262	5	18	92	2	2	0	1.2	.979							
San Francisco W-88 L-74 Charlie Fox	1B	W. McCovey	383	.266	29	75	930	76	12	89	8.7	.988	R. Bryant	41	270	24	12	0	3.54
	2B	T. Fuentes	656	.277	6	63	386	478	6	102	5.4	.993	J. Barr	41	231	11	17	2	3.82
	SS	C. Speier	542	.249	11	71	255	470	33	92	5.1	.956	T. Bradley	35	224	13	12	0	3.90
	3B	E. Goodson	384	.302	12	53	64	171	23	13	2.8	.911	J. Marichal	34	209	11	15	0	3.79
	RF	B. Bonds	643	.283	39	96	346	12	11	5	2.3	.970	Willoughby	39	123	4	5	1	4.70
	CF	G. Maddox	587	.319	11	76	370	4	12	0	2.8	.969	E. Sosa	71	107	10	4	18	3.28
	LF	G. Matthews	540	.300	12	58	277	11	5	0	2.0	.983	R. Moffitt	60	100	4	4	14	2.43
	C	D. Rader	462	.229	9	41	701	48	7	5	5.1	.991	D. McMahon	22	30	4	0	6	1.50
	31	D. Kingman	305	.203	24	55	313	146	22	30		.954							
	10	G. Thomasson	235	.285	4	30	312	15	6	15		.982							
Houston W-82 L-80 Leo Durocher	1B	L. May	545	.270	28	105	1220	78	9	112	9.1	.993	J. Reuss	41	279	16	13	0	3.74
	2B	T. Helms	543	.287	4	61	325	438	9	104	5.3	.988	D. Roberts	39	249	17	11	0	2.85
	SS	R. Metzger	580	.250	1	35	231	429	12	83	4.5	.982	D. Wilson	37	239	11	16	2	3.20
	3B	D. Rader	574	.254	21	89	134	296	25	24	3.0	.945	K. Forsch	46	201	9	12	4	4.20
	RF	J. Wynn	481	.220	20	55	270	9	4	1	1.9	.986	T. Griffin	25	100	4	6	0	4.15
	CF	C. Cedeno	525	.320	25	70	357	10	7	2	2.8	.981	J. Crawford	48	70	2	4	6	4.50
	LF	B. Watson	573	.312	16	94	271	8	9	0	2.0	.969	J. Ray	42	69	6	4	6	4.43
	C	S. Jutze	278	.223	0	18	450	31	8	4	5.7	.984	J. York	41	53	3	4	6	4.42
	C	J. Edwards	250	.244	5	27	435	22	5	3	6.1	.989							
	OF	T. Agee	204	.235	8	15	114	2	2	2	1.8	.983							
Atlanta W-76 L-85 Eddie Mathews	1B	M. Lum	513	.294	16	82	707	42	7	64	9.0	.991	C. Morton	38	256	15	10	0	3.41
	2B	D. Johnson	559	.270	43	99	383	464	30	106	5.7	.966	P. Niekro	42	245	13	10	4	3.31
	SS	M. Perez	501	.250	8	57	215	416	25	78	4.7	.962	R. Schueler	39	186	8	7	2	3.86
	3B	D. Evans	595	.281	41	104	124	325	22	33	3.2	.953	R. Harrison	38	177	11	8	5	4.16
	RF	H. Aaron	392	.301	40	96	206	5	5	0	2.1	.977	R. Reed	20	116	4	11	1	4.42
	CF	D. Baker	604	.288	21	99	390	10	7	1	2.6	.983	G. Gentry	16	87	4	6	1	3.41
	LF	R. Garr	668	.299	11	55	293	9	10	2	2.1	.968	T. House	52	67	4	2	4	4.70
	C	J. Oates	322	.248	4	27	409	57	9	6	5.5	.981	P. Dobson	12	58	3	7	0	4.97
	C	P. Casanova	236	.216	7	18	330	48	9	3	5.0	.977	D. Frisella	42	45	1	2	8	4.20
	OS	S. Jackson	206	.209	0	12	93	89	6	10		.968							
	1B	F. Tepedino	148	.304	4	29	331	28	3	30	6.2	.992							
	1C	D. Dietz	139	.295	3	24	325	29	6	19		.983							
San Diego W-60 L-102 Don Zimmer	1B	N. Colbert	529	.270	22	80	1300	98	11	124	9.8	.992	B. Greif	36	199	10	17	1	3.21
	2B	R. Morales	244	.164	0	16	176	239	5	45	5.3	.988	C. Kirby	34	192	8	18	0	4.79
	SS	D. Thomas	404	.238	0	22	115	227	32	39	5.1	.914	S. Arlin	34	180	11	14	0	5.10
	3B	D. Roberts	479	.286	21	64	77	245	20	25	3.1	.942	R. Troedson	50	152	7	9	1	4.25
	RF	C. Gaston	476	.250	16	57	198	16	12	4	1.9	.947	M. Caldwell	55	149	5	14	10	3.74
	CF	J. Grubb	389	.311	8	37	229	11	3	1	2.4	.988	R. Jones	20	140	7	6	0	3.16
	LF	J. Morales	388	.281	9	34	214	5	2	1	2.2	.991	M. Corkins	47	122	5	8	3	4.50
	C	F. Kendall	507	.282	10	59	749	64	13	7	6.0	.984	V. Romo	49	88	2	3	7	3.70
	OF	L. Lee	333	.237	3	30	154	7	5	0	2.0	.970							
	SS	E. Hernandez	247	.223	0	9	106	190	7	42	4.5	.977							
	32	D. Hilton	234	.197	5	16	79	141	6	19		.973							
	01	I. Murrell	210	.229	9	21	249	16	5	14		.981							
	OF	G. Locklear	154	.240	3	25	77	2	4	0	2.2	.952							

BATTING AND BASE RUNNING LEADERS

Batting Average		Slugging Average		Home Runs	
P. Rose, CIN	.338	W. Stargell, PIT	.646	W. Stargell, PIT	44
C. Cedeno, HOU	.320	D. Evans, ATL	.556	D. Johnson, ATL	43
G. Maddox, SF	.319	D. Johnson, ATL	.546	D. Evans, ATL	41
T. Perez, CIN	.314	C. Cedeno, HOU	.537	H. Aaron, ATL	40
B. Watson, HOU	.312	B. Bonds, SF	.530	B. Bonds, SF	39

PITCHING LEADERS

Winning Percentage		Earned Run Average		Wins	
T. John, LA	.696	T. Seaver, NY	2.08	R. Bryant, SF	24
D. Gullett, CIN	.692	W. Twitchell, PHI	2.50	T. Seaver, NY	19
R. Bryant, SF	.667	M. Marshall, MON	2.66	Billingham, CIN	19
T. Seaver, NY	.655	Messersmith, LA	2.70	D. Gullett, CIN	18
Billingham, CIN	.655	S. Renko, MON	2.81	D. Sutton, LA	18

NATIONAL LEAGUE 1973, *cont.*

BATTING AND BASE RUNNING LEADERS

Total Bases			Runs Batted In			Stolen Bases		
B. Bonds, SF	341		W. Stargell, PIT	119		L. Brock, STL	70	
W. Stargell, PIT	337		L. May, HOU	105		J. Morgan, CIN	67	
D. Evans, ATL	331		J. Bench, CIN	104		C. Cedeno, HOU	56	
D. Johnson, ATL	305		D. Evans, ATL	104		B. Bonds, SF	43	
A. Oliver, PIT	303		K. Singleton, MON	103		D. Lopes, LA	36	

Hits			Base on Balls			Home Run Percentage		
P. Rose, CIN	230		D. Evans, ATL	124		W. Stargell, PIT	8.4	
R. Garr, ATL	200		K. Singleton, MON	123		D. Johnson, ATL	7.7	
L. Brock, STL	193		J. Morgan, CIN	111		D. Evans, ATL	6.9	
T. Simmons, STL	192		W. McCovey, SF	105		B. Bonds, SF	6.1	

Runs Scored			Doubles			Triples		
B. Bonds, SF	131		W. Stargell, PIT	43		R. Metzger, HOU	14	
J. Morgan, CIN	116		A. Oliver, PIT	38		G. Matthews, SF	10	
P. Rose, CIN	115		R. Staub, NY	36		G. Maddox, SF	10	
D. Evans, ATL	114		T. Simmons, STL	36		W. Davis, LA	9	

PITCHING LEADERS

Saves			Strikeouts			Complete Games		
M. Marshall, MON	31		T. Seaver, NY	251		T. Seaver, NY		18
T. McGraw, NY	25		S. Carlton, PHI	223		S. Carlton, PHI		18
D. Giusti, PIT	20		J. Matlack, NY	205		Billingham, CIN		16
J. Brewer, LA	20		D. Sutton, LA	200		D. Sutton, LA		14
B. Locker, CHI	18		Messersmith, LA	177		R. Wise, STL		14
E. Sosa, SF	18		J. Reuss, HOU	177		J. Matlack, NY		14

Fewest Hits/9 Innings			Shutouts			Fewest Walks/9 Innings		
T. Seaver, NY	6.80		Billingham, CIN	7		J. Marichal, SF	1.59	
D. Sutton, LA	6.88		D. Roberts, HOU	6		F. Jenkins, CHI	1.89	
W. Twitchell, PHI	6.93		W. Twitchell, PHI	5		J. Barr, SF	1.91	
D. Wilson, HOU	7.03		R. Wise, STL	5		D. Sutton, LA	1.97	

Most Strikeouts/9 Inn.			Innings			Games Pitched		
T. Seaver, NY	7.79		S. Carlton, PHI	293		M. Marshall, MON	92	
B. Moore, MON	7.71		Billingham, CIN	293		P. Borbon, CIN	80	
J. Matlack, NY	7.62		T. Seaver, NY	290		E. Sosa, SF	71	
D. Sutton, LA	7.02		J. Reuss, HOU	279		D. Giusti, PIT	67	

		W	L	PCT	GB	R	OR	2B	3B	HR	BA	SA	SB	E	DP	FA	CG	BB	SO	ShO	SV	ERA
East	New York	82	79	.509		608	588	198	24	85	.246	.338	27	126	140	.980	47	490	1027	15	40	3.27
	St. Louis	81	81	.500	1.5	643	603	240	35	75	.259	.357	100	159	149	.975	42	486	867	14	36	3.25
	Pittsburgh	80	82	.494	2.5	704	693	257	44	154	.261	.405	23	151	156	.976	26	564	839	11	44	3.74
	Montreal	79	83	.488	3.5	668	702	190	23	125	.251	.364	77	163	156	.974	26	681	866	6	38	3.73
	Chicago	77	84	.478	5	614	655	201	21	117	.247	.357	65	157	155	.975	27	438	885	13	40	3.66
	Philadelphia	71	91	.438	11.5	642	717	218	29	134	.249	.371	51	134	179	.979	49	632	919	11	22	4.00
West	Cincinnati	99	63	.611		741	621	232	34	137	.254	.383	148	115	162	.982	39	518	801	17	43	3.43
	Los Angeles	95	66	.590	3.5	675	565	219	29	110	.263	.371	109	125	166	.981	45	461	961	15	38	3.00
	San Francisco	88	74	.543	11	739	702	212	52	161	.262	.407	112	163	138	.974	33	485	787	8	44	3.79
	Houston	82	80	.506	17	681	672	216	35	134	.251	.376	92	116	140	.981	45	575	907	14	26	3.78
	Atlanta	76	85	.472	22.5	799	774	219	34	206	.266	.427	84	166	142	.974	34	575	803	9	35	4.25
	San Diego	60	102	.370	39	548	770	198	26	112	.244	.351	88	170	152	.973	34	548	845	10	23	4.16
						8062	8062	2600	386	1550	.254	.376	976	1745	1835	.977	447	6453	10507	143	429	3.67

AMERICAN LEAGUE 1973

East

Baltimore

W-97 L-65

Earl Weaver

POS	Player	AB	BA	HR	RBI	PO	A	E	DP	TC/G	FA	Pitcher	G	IP	W	L	SV	ERA
1B	B. Powell	370	.265	11	54	988	77	12	95	9.7	.989	J. Palmer	38	296	22	9	1	2.40
2B	B. Grich	581	.251	12	50	431	509	5	130	5.8	.995	M. Cuellar	38	267	18	13	0	3.27
SS	M. Belanger	470	.226	0	27	241	530	23	100	5.2	.971	D. McNally	38	266	17	17	0	3.21
3B	B. Robinson	549	.257	9	72	129	354	15	25	3.2	.970	D. Alexander	29	175	12	8	0	3.86
RF	R. Coggins	389	.319	7	41	220	6	3	3	2.3	.987	B. Reynolds	42	111	7	5	9	1.95
CF	P. Blair	500	.280	10	64	369	14	4	4	2.7	.990	J. Jefferson	18	101	6	5	0	4.10
LF	D. Baylor	405	.286	11	51	204	5	4	0	1.9	.981	G. Jackson	45	80	8	0	9	1.90
C	E. Williams	459	.237	22	83	407	33	6	5	4.7	.987	E. Watt	30	71	3	4	5	3.30
DH	T. Davis	552	.306	7	89													
OF	A. Bumbry	356	.337	7	34	134	2	3	0	1.6	.978							
OF	Rettenmund	321	.262	9	44	196	4	3	1	2.3	.985							
C	Etchebarren	152	.257	2	23	201	14	2	5	4.3	.991							

Boston

W-89 L-73

Eddie Kasko
W-88 L-73

Eddie Popowski
W-1 L-0

POS	Player	AB	BA	HR	RBI	PO	A	E	DP	TC/G	FA	Pitcher	G	IP	W	L	SV	ERA
1B	Yastrzemski	540	.296	19	95	912	56	6	85	9.1	.994	B. Lee	38	285	17	11	1	2.75
2B	D. Griffin	396	.255	1	33	294	284	6	77	5.2	.990	L. Tiant	35	272	20	13	0	3.34
SS	L. Aparicio	499	.271	0	49	190	404	21	68	4.7	.966	J. Curtis	35	221	13	13	0	3.58
3B	Petrocelli	356	.244	13	45	73	224	6	22	3.1	.980	M. Pattin	34	219	15	15	1	4.31
RF	R. Smith	423	.303	21	69	275	8	5	1	2.8	.983	R. Moret	30	156	13	2	3	3.17
CF	R. Miller	441	.261	6	43	301	4	7	1	2.3	.978	B. Bolin	39	53	3	4	15	2.70
LF	T. Harper	566	.281	17	71	251	13	4	2	1.9	.985	B. Veale	32	36	2	3	11	3.47
C	C. Fisk	508	.246	26	71	739	50	14	8	6.1	.983							
DH	O. Cepeda	550	.289	20	86													
OF	D. Evans	282	.223	10	32	178	4	1	0	1.6	.995							
S2	M. Guerrero	219	.233	0	11	106	183	8	49		.973							
13	D. Cater	195	.313	1	24	303	56	6	45		.984							
C	Montgomery	128	.320	7	25	168	19	5	2	5.8	.974							

AMERICAN LEAGUE 1973, cont.

	POS	Player	AB	BA	HR	RBI	PO	A	E	DP	TC/G	FA	Pitcher	G	IP	W	L	SV	ERA
Detroit	1B	N. Cash	363	.262	19	40	856	64	8	72	8.1	.991	M. Lolich	42	309	16	15	0	3.82
	2B	McAuliffe	343	.274	12	47	217	265	7	62	4.8	.986	J. Coleman	40	288	23	15	0	3.53
W-85 L-77	SS	E. Brinkman	515	.237	7	40	249	480	24	89	4.6	.968	J. Perry	35	203	14	13	0	4.03
	3B	A. Rodriguez	555	.222	9	58	135	335	14	30	3.0	.971	W. Fryman	34	170	6	13	0	5.36
Billy Martin	RF	J. Northrup	404	.307	12	44	207	6	4	2	1.9	.982	J. Hiller	65	125	10	5	38	1.44
W-71 L-63	CF	M. Stanley	602	.244	17	57	420	10	3	3	2.8	.993							
	LF	W. Horton	411	.316	17	53	160	2	10	0	1.6	.942							
Joe Schultz	C	B. Freehan	380	.234	6	29	584	50	3	3	6.5	.995							
W-14 L-14	DH	G. Brown	377	.236	12	50													
	O1	A. Kaline	310	.255	10	45	347	13	1	32		.997							
	2B	T. Taylor	275	.229	5	24	134	165	4	37	4.2	.987							
	C	D. Sims	252	.242	8	30	375	39	9	7	6.2	.979							
	DH	F. Howard	227	.256	12	29													
	OF	D. Sharon	178	.242	7	16	124	5	4	1	1.5	.970							
New York	1B	F. Alou	280	.236	4	27	467	30	6	43	7.5	.988	Stottlemyre	38	273	16	16	0	3.07
	2B	H. Clarke	590	.263	2	35	378	442	18	107	5.7	.979	D. Medich	34	235	14	9	0	2.95
W-80 L-82	SS	G. Michael	418	.225	3	47	208	433	23	84	5.1	.965	F. Peterson	31	184	8	15	0	3.95
	3B	G. Nettles	552	.234	22	81	117	410	26	39	3.5	.953	L. McDaniel	47	160	12	6	10	2.86
Ralph Houk	RF	M. Alou	497	.296	2	28	146	6	4	2	1.8	.974	P. Dobson	22	142	9	8	0	4.17
	CF	B. Murcer	616	.304	22	95	380	14	6	2	2.5	.985	S. McDowell	16	96	5	8	0	3.95
	LF	R. White	639	.246	18	60	339	4	8	0	2.2	.977	S. Lyle	51	82	5	9	27	2.51
	C	T. Munson	519	.301	20	74	673	80	12	11	5.4	.984	S. Kline	14	74	4	7	0	4.01
	DH	J. Hart	339	.254	13	52													
	D1	R. Blomberg	301	.329	12	57	359	28	8	38	9.6	.980							
Milwaukee	1B	G. Scott	604	.306	24	107	1388	118	9	144	9.6	.994	J. Colborn	43	314	20	12	1	3.18
	2B	P. Garcia	580	.245	15	54	405	470	27	111	5.6	.970	J. Slaton	38	276	13	15	0	3.71
W-74 L-88	SS	T. Johnson	465	.213	0	32	253	381	25	88	4.9	.962	J. Bell	31	184	9	9	1	3.97
	3B	D. Money	556	.284	11	61	112	224	10	24	2.8	.971	S. Lockwood	37	155	5	12	0	3.90
Del Crandall	RF	B. Coluccio	438	.224	15	58	236	12	2	3	2.3	.992	B. Champion	37	136	5	8	1	3.70
	CF	D. May	624	.303	25	93	401	9	9	3	2.8	.979	E. Rodriguez	30	76	9	7	5	3.30
	LF	J. Briggs	488	.246	18	57	294	9	10	1	2.3	.968	C. Short	42	72	3	5	2	5.13
	C	D. Porter	350	.254	16	67	372	47	10	9	4.8	.977	F. Linzy	42	63	2	6	13	3.57
	DH	O. Brown	296	.280	7	32													
	C	E. Rodriguez	290	.269	0	30	324	40	5	5	4.9	.986							
	DO	J. Lahoud	225	.204	5	26	85	2	0	1	2.2	1.000							
	OD	B. Mitchell	130	.223	5	20	24	0	1	0	1.3	.960							
Cleveland	1B	C. Chambliss	572	.273	11	53	1437	114	14	153	10.2	.991	G. Perry	41	344	19	19	0	3.38
	2B	J. Brohamer	300	.220	4	29	215	279	15	67	5.2	.971	D. Tidrow	42	275	14	16	0	4.42
W-71 L-91	SS	F. Duffy	361	.263	8	50	198	377	8	82	5.1	.986	M. Wilcox	26	134	8	10	0	5.83
	3B	B. Bell	631	.268	14	59	144	363	22	44	3.4	.958	T. Timmerman	29	124	8	7	2	4.92
Ken Aspromonte	RF	R. Torres	312	.205	7	28	191	9	5	1	1.8	.976	B. Strom	27	123	2	10	0	4.61
	CF	G. Hendrick	440	.268	21	61	242	7	3	1	2.3	.988	Hilgendorf	48	95	5	3	3	3.14
	LF	C. Spikes	506	.237	23	73	202	13	8	0	2.0	.964	J. Johnson	39	60	5	6	5	6.18
	C	D. Duncan	344	.233	17	43	533	41	7	8	6.8	.988	K. Sanders	15	27	5	1	5	1.65
	DH	O. Gamble	390	.267	20	44													
	CD	J. Ellis	437	.270	14	68	370	27	8	5	5.6	.980							
	OF	W. Williams	350	.289	8	38	123	7	4	0	2.2	.970							
	UT	Lowenstein	305	.292	6	40	124	85	7	22		.968							
	SS	L. Cardenas	195	.215	0	12	87	154	9	33	3.7	.964							
	2B	T. Ragland	183	.257	0	12	136	166	5	43	4.7	.984							
West **Oakland**	1B	G. Tenace	510	.259	24	84	1095	61	13	104	8.7	.989	K. Holtzman	40	297	21	13	0	2.97
	2B	D. Green	332	.262	3	42	264	297	7	86	4.3	.988	V. Blue	37	264	20	9	0	3.28
	SS	Campaneris	601	.250	4	46	228	496	23	87	5.0	.969	C. Hunter	36	256	21	5	0	3.34
W-94 L-68	3B	S. Bando	592	.287	29	98	126	281	22	24	2.7	.949	B. Odom	30	150	5	12	0	4.49
	RF	R. Jackson	539	.293	32	117	302	4	9	0	2.2	.971	R. Fingers	62	127	7	8	22	1.92
Dick Williams	CF	B. North	554	.285	5	34	429	14	9	5	3.3	.980	D. Knowles	52	99	6	8	9	3.09
	LF	J. Rudi	437	.270	12	66	231	6	2	2	2.0	.992	H. Pina	47	88	6	3	8	2.76
	C	R. Fosse	492	.256	7	52	712	63	10	5	5.6	.987	D. Hamilton	16	70	6	4	0	4.39
	DH	D. Johnson	464	.246	19	81													
	OF	A. Mangual	192	.224	3	13	88	2	5	0	1.9	.947							
	2B	T. Kubiak	182	.220	3	17	89	129	6	28	2.7	.973							
Kansas City	1B	J. Mayberry	510	.278	26	100	1457	81	9	156	10.4	.994	Splittorff	38	262	20	11	0	3.98
	2B	C. Rojas	551	.276	6	69	302	424	13	114	5.4	.982	S. Busby	37	238	16	15	0	4.23
	SS	F. Patek	501	.234	5	45	242	503	26	115	5.7	.966	D. Drago	37	213	12	14	0	4.23
W-88 L-74	3B	P. Schaal	396	.288	8	42	77	237	30	14	2.8	.913	G. Garber	48	153	9	9	11	4.24
	RF	Kirkpatrick	429	.263	6	45	198	3	2	0	1.9	.990	D. Bird	54	102	4	4	20	2.99
Jack McKeon	CF	A. Otis	583	.300	26	93	330	10	5	4	2.6	.986	Dal Canton	32	97	4	3	3	4.82
	LF	L. Piniella	513	.250	9	69	196	9	3	3	1.6	.986	Fitzmorris	15	89	8	3	0	2.83
	C	F. Healy	279	.276	6	34	429	43	10	4	5.2	.979	K. Wright	25	81	6	5	0	4.91
	DH	H. McRae	338	.234	9	50													
	UT	K. Bevacqua	276	.257	2	40	120	90	9	20		.959							
	OF	S. Hovley	232	.254	2	24	114	4	3	1	1.5	.975							

AMERICAN LEAGUE 1973, *cont.*

	POS	Player	AB	BA	HR	RBI	PO	A	E	DP	TC/G	FA	Pitcher	G	IP	W	L	SV	ERA
Minnesota	1B	J. Lis	253	.245	9	25	626	48	9	59	7.1	.987	B. Blyleven	40	325	20	17	0	2.52
	2B	R. Carew	580	**.350**	6	62	383	413	13	96	5.5	.984	J. Kaat	29	182	11	12	0	4.41
W-81 L-81	SS	D. Thompson	347	.225	1	36	131	326	24	50	5.1	.950	J. Decker	29	170	10	10	0	4.17
	3B	S. Braun	361	.283	6	42	79	175	16	21	2.6	.941	R. Corbin	51	148	8	5	14	3.03
Frank Quilici	RF	J. Holt	441	.297	11	58	193	6	2	2	2.0	.990	B. Hands	39	142	7	10	2	3.49
	CF	B. Darwin	560	.252	18	90	233	13	5	1	1.8	.980	D. Woodson	23	141	10	8	0	3.95
	LF	L. Hisle	545	.272	15	64	337	11	9	0	2.5	.975	D. Goltz	32	106	6	4	1	5.25
	C	Mitterwald	432	.259	16	64	676	59	6	6	6.1	.992	B. Campbell	28	52	3	3	7	3.14
	DH	T. Oliva	571	.291	16	92							K. Sanders	27	44	2	4	8	6.09
	UT	J. Terrell	438	.265	1	32	170	298	18	55		.963							
	OF	S. Brye	278	.263	6	33	209	4	3	1	2.5	.986							
	1B	H. Killebrew	248	.242	5	32	431	45	1	42	8.4	.998							
California	1B	M. Epstein	312	.215	8	32	710	50	5	61	8.9	.993	N. Ryan	41	326	21	16	1	2.87
	2B	S. Alomar	470	.238	0	28	243	267	11	70	4.7	.979	B. Singer	40	316	20	14	0	3.22
W-79 L-83	SS	R. Meoli	305	.223	2	23	122	252	**27**	52	4.2	.933	C. Wright	37	257	11	19	0	3.68
	3B	A. Gallagher	311	.273	0	26	59	185	10	13	2.6	.961	R. May	34	185	7	17	0	4.38
Bobby Winkles	RF	L. Stanton	306	.235	8	34	160	5	6	2	1.6	.965	D. Sells	51	68	7	2	10	3.71
	CF	K. Berry	415	.284	3	36	309	5	1	0	2.4	.997							
	LF	V. Pinson	466	.260	8	57	210	11	8	2	1.9	.965							
	C	J. Torborg	255	.220	1	18	611	37	6	2	6.4	.991							
	DH	F. Robinson	534	.266	30	97													
	UT	B. Oliver	544	.265	18	89	396	121	11	26		.979							
	UT	T. McCraw	264	.265	3	24	268	25	1	28		.997							
	OF	Scheinblum	229	.328	3	21	92	3	3	0	1.8	.969							
	UT	W. Llenas	130	.269	1	25	42	37	1	3		.988							
Chicago	1B	T. Muser	309	.285	4	30	680	38	6	70	8.1	.992	W. Wood	49	359	**24**	20	0	3.46
	2B	J. Orta	425	.266	6	40	254	300	18	75	4.7	.969	S. Bahnsen	42	282	18	21	0	3.57
W-77 L-85	SS	E. Leon	399	.228	3	30	198	382	17	78	4.9	.972	S. Stone	36	176	6	11	1	4.24
	3B	B. Melton	560	.277	20	87	115	347	23	31	3.2	.953	T. Forster	51	173	6	11	16	3.23
Chuck Tanner	RF	P. Kelly	550	.280	1	44	254	9	6	2	1.9	.978	E. Fisher	26	111	6	7	0	4.88
	CF	J. Jeter	300	.240	7	26	144	3	7	0	2.1	.955	C. Acosta	48	97	10	6	18	2.23
	LF	B. Sharp	196	.276	4	22	146	10	3	2	2.3	.981							
	C	E. Herrmann	379	.224	10	38	617	70	11	**11**	6.1	.984							
	DH	C. May	553	.268	20	96													
	OD	K. Henderson	262	.260	6	32	102	1	3	0	2.4	.972							
	1B	D. Allen	250	.316	16	41	597	43	4	55	9.6	.994							
	UT	J. Hairston	210	.271	0	25	194	13	5	11		.976							
	UT	L. Alvarado	203	.232	0	20	120	158	9	31		.969							
	OF	B. Bradford	168	.238	8	15	114	9	1	2	2.4	.992							
Texas	1B	J. Spencer	352	.267	4	43	790	67	1	110	8.7	.999*	J. Bibby	26	180	9	10	1	3.24
	2B	D. Nelson	576	.286	7	48	327	364	11	98	5.0	.984	J. Merritt	35	160	5	13	1	4.05
W-57 L-105	SS	J. Mason	238	.206	3	19	113	206	18	43	4.6	.947	Gogolewski	49	124	3	6	6	4.22
	3B	T. Harrah	461	.260	10	50	39	79	8	4	2.4	.937	P. Broberg	22	119	5	9	0	5.61
Whitey Herzog	RF	J. Burroughs	526	.279	30	85	304	13	8	2	1.9	.975	S. Siebert	25	120	7	11	2	3.99
W-47 L-91	CF	V. Harris	555	.249	8	44	297	5	7	1	2.7	.977	D. Clyde	18	93	4	8	0	5.01
	LF	L. Biittner	258	.252	1	12	91	6	2	1	1.7	.980	M. Paul	36	87	5	4	2	4.95
Del Wilber	C	K. Suarez	278	.248	1	27	501	44	6	4	6.1	.989	J. Brown	25	67	5	5	2	3.92
W-1 L-0	DH	A. Johnson	624	.287	8	68							S. Foucault	32	56	2	4	8	3.88
	OD	R. Carty	306	.232	3	33	87	2	0	0	1.7	1.000							
Billy Martin	C	D. Billings	280	.179	3	32	356	32	10	3	5.5	.975							
W-9 L-14	UT	B. Sudakis	235	.255	15	43	216	62	5	21		.982							
	OF	E. Maddox	172	.238	1	17	144	7	3	1	1.7	.981							
	OF	T. Grieve	123	.309	7	21	68	0	0	0	1.2	1.000							

BATTING AND BASE RUNNING LEADERS

Batting Average		Slugging Average		Home Runs		Winning Percentage		Earned Run Average		Wins	
R. Carew, MIN	.350	R. Jackson, OAK	.531	R. Jackson, OAK	32	C. Hunter, OAK	.808	J. Palmer, BAL	2.40	W. Wood, CHI	24
G. Scott, MIL	.306	S. Bando, OAK	.498	J. Burroughs, TEX	30	J. Palmer, BAL	.710	B. Blyleven, MIN	2.52	J. Coleman, DET	23
T. Davis, BAL	.306	F. Robinson, CAL	.489	F. Robinson, CAL	30	V. Blue, OAK	.690	B. Lee, BOS	2.74	J. Palmer, BAL	22
B. Murcer, NY	.304	G. Scott, MIL	.488	S. Bando, OAK	29	Splittorff, KC	.645	N. Ryan, CAL	2.87	C. Hunter, OAK	21
D. May, MIL	.303	T. Munson, NY	.487			J. Colborn, MIL	.625	K. Holtzman, OAK	2.97	K. Holtzman, OAK	21
										N. Ryan, CAL	21

PITCHING LEADERS

Total Bases		Runs Batted In		Stolen Bases		Saves		Strikeouts		Complete Games	
G. Scott, MIL	295	R. Jackson, OAK	117	T. Harper, BOS	54	J. Hiller, DET	38	N. Ryan, CAL	383	G. Perry, CLE	29
D. May, MIL	295	G. Scott, MIL	107	B. North, OAK	53	S. Lyle, NY	27	B. Blyleven, MIN	258	N. Ryan, CAL	26
S. Bando, OAK	294	J. Mayberry, KC	100	D. Nelson, TEX	43	R. Fingers, OAK	22	B. Singer, CAL	241	B. Blyleven, MIN	25
R. Jackson, OAK	286	S. Bando, OAK	98	R. Carew, MIN	41	D. Bird, KC	20	G. Perry, CLE	238	L. Tiant, BOS	23
B. Murcer, NY	286	F. Robinson, CAL	97	F. Patek, KC	36	C. Acosta, CHI	18	M. Lolich, DET	214	J. Colborn, MIL	22

AMERICAN LEAGUE 1973, *cont.*

BATTING AND BASE RUNNING LEADERS

Hits		Base on Balls		Home Run Percentage		Fewest Hits/9 Innings	
R. Carew, MIN	203	J. Mayberry, KC	122	R. Jackson, OAK	5.9	J. Bibby, TEX	6.05
D. May, MIL	189	B. Grich, BAL	107	J. Burroughs, TEX	5.7	N. Ryan, CAL	6.57
B. Murcer, NY	187	Yastrzemski, BOS	105	F. Robinson, CAL	5.6	J. Palmer, BAL	6.84
G. Scott, MIL	185	G. Tenace, OAK	101	C. Fisk, BOS	5.1	L. Tiant, BOS	7.18

Runs Scored		Doubles		Triples		Most Strikeouts/9 Inn.	
R. Jackson, OAK	99	P. Garcia, MIL	32	A. Bumbry, BAL	11	N. Ryan, CAL	10.57
B. North, OAK	98	S. Bando, OAK	32	R. Carew, MIN	11	J. Bibby, TEX	7.75
R. Carew, MIN	98	C. Chambliss, CLE	30	J. Orta, CHI	10	B. Blyleven, MIN	7.14
G. Scott, MIL	98	R. Carew, MIN	30	R. Coggins, BAL	9	S. Stone, CHI	7.04

PITCHING LEADERS

Shutouts		Fewest Walks/9 Innings	
B. Blyleven, MIN	9	J. Kaat, CHI, MIN	1.73
G. Perry, CLE	7	B. Blyleven, MIN	1.86
J. Palmer, BAL	6	K. Holtzman, OAK	2.00
		W. Wood, CHI	2.28

Innings		Games Pitched	
W. Wood, CHI	359	J. Hiller, DET	65
G. Perry, CLE	344	R. Fingers, OAK	62
N. Ryan, CAL	326	D. Bird, KC	54
B. Blyleven, MIN	325	D. Knowles, OAK	52

		W	L	PCT	GB	R	OR	2B	3B	HR	BA	SA	SB	E	DP	FA	CG	BB	SO	ShO	SV	ERA
East	Baltimore	97	65	.599		754	561	229	48	119	.266	.389	146	119	184	.981	67	475	715	14	26	3.07
	Boston	89	73	.549	8	738	647	235	30	147	.267	.401	114	127	162	.979	67	499	808	10	33	3.65
	Detroit	85	77	.525	12	642	674	213	32	157	.254	.390	28	112	144	.982	39	493	911	11	46	3.90
	New York	80	82	.494	17	641	610	212	17	131	.261	.378	47	156	172	.976	47	457	708	16	39	3.34
	Milwaukee	74	88	.457	23	708	731	229	40	145	.253	.388	110	145	167	.977	50	623	671	11	28	3.98
	Cleveland	71	91	.438	26	680	826	205	29	158	.256	.387	60	139	174	.978	55	602	883	9	21	4.58
West	Oakland	94	68	.580		758	615	216	28	147	.260	.389	128	137	170	.978	46	494	797	16	41	3.29
	Kansas City	88	74	.543	6	755	752	239	40	114	.261	.381	105	167	192	.974	40	617	790	7	41	4.21
	Minnesota	81	81	.500	13	738	692	240	44	120	.270	.393	87	139	147	.978	48	519	880	18	34	3.77
	California	79	83	.488	15	629	657	183	29	93	.253	.348	59	156	153	.975	72	614	1010	13	19	3.86
	Chicago	77	85	.475	17	652	705	228	38	111	.256	.372	83	144	165	.977	48	574	848	15	35	3.86
	Texas	57	105	.352	37	619	844	195	29	110	.255	.361	91	161	164	.974	35	680	831	10	27	4.64
						8314	8314	2624	404	1552	.259	.381	1058	1702	1994	.977	614	6647	9852	150	390	3.82

NATIONAL LEAGUE 1974

		POS	Player	AB	BA	HR	RBI	PO	A	E	DP	TC/G	FA	Pitcher	G	IP	W	L	SV	ERA
East	**Pittsburgh** W-88 L-74 Danny Murtaugh	1B	B. Robertson	236	.229	16	48	494	37	5	44	8.5	.991	J. Rooker	33	263	15	11	0	2.77
		2B	R. Stennett	673	.291	7	56	441	475	19	115	6.1	.980	J. Reuss	35	260	16	11	0	3.50
		SS	F. Taveras	333	.246	0	26	170	321	31	60	4.2	.941	K. Brett	27	191	13	9	0	3.30
		3B	R. Hebner	550	.291	18	68	115	304	28	34	3.2	.937	D. Ellis	26	177	12	9	0	3.15
		RF	R. Zisk	536	.313	17	100	312	9	5	3	2.3	.985	B. Kison	40	129	9	8	2	3.49
		CF	A. Oliver	617	.321	11	85	284	3	4	1	3.0	.986	D. Giusti	64	106	7	5	12	3.31
		LF	W. Stargell	508	.301	25	96	253	8	9	1	3.0	.967	L. Demery	19	95	6	6	0	4.26
		C	Sanguillen	596	.287	7	68	713	76	12	8	5.3	.985							
		OF	G. Clines	276	.225	0	14	177	6	2	1	2.4	.989							
		1B	Kirkpatrick	271	.247	6	38	512	31	4	55	9.3	.993							
		OF	D. Parker	220	.282	4	29	101	5	4	1	2.2	.964							
		SS	M. Mendoza	163	.221	0	15	77	187	10	21	3.1	.964							
	St. Louis W-86 L-75 Red Schoendienst	1B	J. Torre	529	.282	11	70	1165	102	10	144	9.2	.992	B. Gibson	33	240	11	13	0	3.83
		2B	T. Sizemore	504	.250	2	47	335	412	15	109	6.0	.980	McGlothen	31	237	16	12	0	2.70
		SS	M. Tyson	422	.223	1	37	231	410	30	108	4.7	.955	J. Curtis	33	195	10	14	1	3.78
		3B	K. Reitz	579	.271	7	54	131	278	11	29	2.8	.974	A. Foster	31	162	7	10	0	3.89
		RF	R. Smith	517	.309	23	100	275	9	7	3	2.2	.976	S. Siebert	28	134	8	8	0	3.83
		CF	B. McBride	559	.309	6	56	395	9	4	1	2.8	.990	B. Forsch	19	100	7	4	0	2.97
		LF	L. Brock	635	.306	3	48	283	8	10	2	2.0	.967	R. Folkers	55	90	6	2	2	3.00
		C	T. Simmons	599	.272	20	103	717	82	11	13	5.7	.986	A. Hrabosky	65	88	8	1	9	2.97
		OF	J. Cruz	161	.261	5	20	76	2	2	1	1.5	.975	M. Garman	64	82	7	2	6	2.63
	Philadelphia W-80 L-82 Danny Ozark	1B	W. Montanez	527	.304	7	79	1216	79	10	126	9.5	.992	S. Carlton	39	291	16	13	0	3.22
		2B	D. Cash	687	.300	2	58	396	519	22	141	5.8	.977	J. Lonborg	39	283	17	13	0	3.21
		SS	L. Bowa	669	.275	1	36	256	462	12	104	4.5	.984	D. Ruthven	35	213	9	13	0	4.01
		3B	M. Schmidt	568	.282	36	116	134	404	26	40	3.5	.954	R. Schueler	44	203	11	16	1	3.72
		RF	M. Anderson	395	.251	5	34	238	12	5	3	1.9	.980	W. Twitchell	25	112	6	9	0	5.22
		CF	D. Unser	454	.264	11	61	300	13	6	0	2.4	.981	M. Scarce	58	70	3	8	5	5.01
		LF	G. Luzinski	302	.272	7	48	146	10	3	0	1.9	.981							
		C	B. Boone	488	.242	3	52	825	77	22	7	6.3	.976							
		OF	B. Robinson	280	.236	5	29	162	8	5	0	2.0	.971							
		1O	T. Hutton	208	.240	4	33	285	15	2	25		.993							
		OF	J. Johnstone	200	.295	6	30	88	4	3	1	1.6	.968							

NATIONAL LEAGUE 1974, *cont.*

	POS	Player	AB	BA	HR	RBI	PO	A	E	DP	TC/G	FA	Pitcher	G	IP	W	L	SV	ERA
Montreal	1B	M. Jorgensen	287	.310	11	59	606	51	1	47	7.2	.998	S. Rogers	38	254	15	**22**	0	4.46
	2B	J. Cox	236	.220	2	26	148	220	12	45	5.3	.968	S. Renko	37	228	12	16	0	4.03
W-79 L-82	SS	T. Foli	441	.254	0	39	220	412	19	85	5.4	.971	M. Torrez	32	186	15	8	0	3.58
	3B	R. Hunt	403	.268	0	26	37	140	11	14	2.5	.941	D. Blair	22	146	11	7	0	3.27
Gene Mauch	RF	K. Singleton	511	.276	9	74	224	7	11	0	1.7	.955	E. McAnally	25	129	6	13	0	4.47
	CF	W. Davis	611	.295	12	89	369	8	12	1	2.6	.969	C. Taylor	61	108	6	2	11	2.17
	LF	B. Bailey	507	.280	20	73	105	8	3	3	1.5	.974	T. Walker	33	92	4	5	2	3.82
	C	B. Foote	420	.262	11	60	640	83	12	12	6.0	.984	J. Montague	46	83	3	4	3	3.14
	2S	L. Lintz	319	.238	0	20	168	250	18	48		.959	D. Murray	32	70	1	1	10	1.03
	1B	R. Fairly	282	.245	12	43	572	42	7	41	9.3	.989							
	1B	H. Breeden	190	.247	2	20	422	31	6	43	8.2	.987							
New York	1B	J. Milner	507	.252	20	63	1147	77	7	103	9.3	.994	J. Matlack	34	265	13	15	0	2.41
	2B	F. Millan	518	.268	1	33	374	315	15	81	5.3	.979	J. Koosman	35	265	15	11	0	3.36
W-71 L-91	SS	B. Harrelson	331	.227	1	13	196	325	17	65	5.5	.968	T. Seaver	32	236	11	11	0	3.20
	3B	W. Garrett	522	.224	13	53	111	318	20	31	3.1	.955	H. Parker	40	131	4	12	4	3.92
Yogi Berra	RF	R. Staub	561	.258	19	78	262	19	5	5	1.9	.983	B. Apodaca	35	103	6	6	3	3.50
	CF	D. Hahn	323	.251	4	28	217	8	3	0	2.2	.987	R. Sadecki	34	100	8	8	0	3.48
	LF	C. Jones	461	.282	13	60	220	8	7	0	2.0	.970	T. McGraw	41	89	6	11	3	4.15
	C	J. Grote	319	.257	5	36	549	36	7	1	6.3	.988							
	UT	T. Martinez	334	.219	4	43	164	257	20	38		.955							
	OF	D. Schneck	254	.205	5	25	179	7	5	2	2.3	.974							
	UT	K. Boswell	222	.216	2	15	94	113	6	18		.972							
	O1	E. Kranepool	217	.300	4	24	207	9	5	18		.977							
Chicago	1B	A. Thornton	303	.261	10	46	760	70	7	61	9.3	.992	B. Bonham	44	243	11	**22**	1	3.85
	2B	V. Harris	200	.195	0	11	122	144	16	20	5.0	.943	R. Reuschel	41	241	13	12	0	4.29
W-66 L-96	SS	D. Kessinger	599	.259	1	42	259	476	32	87	5.1	.958	B. Hooton	48	176	7	11	1	4.81
	3B	B. Madlock	453	.313	9	54	84	229	18	14	2.7	.946	S. Stone	38	170	8	6	0	4.13
Whitey Lockman	RF	J. Cardenal	542	.293	13	72	262	15	10	4	2.1	.965	K. Frailing	55	125	6	9	1	3.89
W-41 L-52	CF	R. Monday	538	.294	20	58	302	10	5	5	2.3	.984	D. LaRoche	49	92	5	6	5	4.79
	LF	J. Morales	534	.273	15	82	266	5	7	2	1.9	.975	O. Zamora	56	84	3	9	10	3.11
Jim Marshall	C	S. Swisher	280	.214	5	27	493	50	7	8	6.1	.987	H. Pina	34	47	3	4	4	4.02
W-25 L-44	1O	B. Williams	404	.280	16	68	635	53	11	50		.984							
	C	Mitterwald	215	.251	7	28	335	40	10	4	5.7	.974							
	UT	C. Fanzone	158	.190	4	22	87	82	15	14		.918							
West Los Angeles	1B	S. Garvey	642	.312	21	111	1536	62	8	108	10.3	.995	Messersmith	39	292	20	6	0	2.59
	2B	D. Lopes	530	.266	10	35	309	360	24	71	4.8	.965	D. Sutton	40	276	19	9	0	3.23
W-102 L-60	SS	B. Russell	553	.269	5	65	194	491	39	68	4.5	.946	M. Marshall	106	208	15	12	21	2.42
	3B	R. Cey	577	.262	18	97	155	365	22	25	3.4	.959	D. Rau	36	198	13	11	0	3.73
Walter Alston	RF	W. Crawford	468	.295	11	61	225	3	8	1	1.8	.966	T. John	22	153	13	3	0	2.59
	CF	J. Wynn	535	.271	32	108	365	10	3	3	2.6	.992	A. Downing	21	98	5	6	0	3.67
	LF	B. Buckner	580	.314	7	58	235	4	6	0	1.8	.976	C. Hough	49	96	9	4	1	3.75
	C	S. Yeager	316	.266	12	41	552	58	5	4	6.6	.992							
	C	J. Ferguson	349	.252	16	57	436	40	6	2	5.9	.988							
	OF	T. Paciorek	175	.240	1	24	83	1	5	1	1.2	.944							
Cincinnati	1B	T. Perez	596	.265	28	101	1292	75	6	111	8.7	.996	D. Gullett	36	243	17	11	0	3.04
	2B	J. Morgan	512	.293	22	67	344	385	13	92	5.2	.982	C. Kirby	36	231	12	9	0	3.27
W-98 L-64	SS	Concepcion	594	.281	14	82	239	536	30	99	5.0	.963	Billingham	36	212	19	11	0	3.95
	3B	D. Driessen	470	.281	7	56	67	192	24	19	2.2	.915	F. Norman	35	186	13	12	0	3.15
Sparky Anderson	RF	C. Geronimo	474	.281	7	54	355	13	5	2	2.6	.987	P. Borbon	73	139	10	7	14	3.24
	CF	G. Foster	276	.264	7	41	172	2	2	1	1.8	.989	C. Carroll	57	101	12	5	6	2.14
	LF	P. Rose	652	.284	3	51	346	11	1	3	2.2	**.997**							
	C	J. Bench	621	.280	33	**129**	757	68	6	16	6.1	.993							
	OF	K. Griffey	227	.251	2	19	115	5	0	1	1.7	1.000							
	OF	Rettenmund	208	.216	6	28	103	3	0	0	1.5	1.000							
	OF	T. Crowley	125	.240	1	20	29	1	0	0	1.4	1.000							
Atlanta	1B	D. Johnson	454	.251	15	62	641	54	5	57	9.6	.993	P. Niekro	41	**302**	20	13	1	2.38
	2B	M. Perez	447	.260	2	34	225	311	8	64	5.3	.985	C. Morton	38	275	16	12	0	3.14
W-88 L-74	SS	C. Robinson	452	.230	0	29	238	395	29	73	4.7	.956	B. Capra	39	217	16	8	1	**2.28**
	3B	D. Evans	571	.240	25	79	185	367	26	45	3.6	.955	R. Reed	28	186	10	11	0	3.39
Eddie Mathews	RF	D. Baker	574	.256	20	69	359	10	7	2	2.5	.981	R. Harrison	20	126	6	11	0	4.71
W-50 L-49	CF	R. Office	248	.246	3	31	171	0	1	0	1.4	.994	T. House	56	103	6	2	11	1.92
	LF	R. Garr	606	.353	11	54	255	8	9	2	2.0	.967	M. Leon	34	75	4	7	3	2.64
Clyde King	C	J. Oates	291	.223	1	21	434	55	4	4	5.4	.992	D. Frisella	36	42	3	4	6	5.14
W-38 L-25	1O	M. Lum	361	.233	11	50	554	26	4	44		.993							
	OF	H. Aaron	340	.268	20	69	142	3	2	0	1.7	.986							
	C	V. Correll	202	.238	4	29	282	40	4	4	5.5	.988							
	1B	F. Tepedino	169	.231	0	16	307	26	4	35	7.3	.988							

NATIONAL LEAGUE 1974, *cont.*

Houston
W-81 L-81

Preston Gomez

POS	Player	AB	BA	HR	RBI	PO	A	E	DP	TC/G	FA	Pitcher	G	IP	W	L	SV	ERA
1B	L. May	556	.268	24	85	1253	88	8	116	9.3	.994	L. Dierker	33	224	11	10	0	2.89
2B	T. Helms	452	.279	5	50	308	360	10	99	5.1	.985	T. Griffin	34	211	14	10	0	3.54
SS	R. Metzger	572	.253	0	30	238	451	17	85	4.9	.976	D. Wilson	33	205	11	13	0	3.07
3B	D. Rader	533	.257	17	78	128	347	17	28	3.2	.965	D. Roberts	34	204	10	12	1	3.40
RF	G. Gross	589	.314	0	36	296	15	2	4	2.1	.994	C. Osteen	23	138	9	9	0	3.71
CF	C. Cedeno	610	.269	26	102	446	11	3	4	2.9	.993	K. Forsch	70	103	8	7	10	2.80
LF	B. Watson	524	.298	11	67	202	7	4	2	1.9	.981	M. Cosgrove	45	90	7	3	2	3.49
C	M. May	405	.289	7	54	525	63	4	10	5.1	.993	F. Scherman	53	61	2	5	4	4.13
C1	C. Johnson	171	.228	10	29	270	18	4	17		.986							

San Francisco
W-72 L-90

Charlie Fox
W-34 L-42

Wes Westrum
W-38 L-48

POS	Player	AB	BA	HR	RBI	PO	A	E	DP	TC/G	FA	Pitcher	G	IP	W	L	SV	ERA
1B	D. Kingman	350	.223	18	55	680	60	13	66	8.3	.983	J. Barr	44	240	13	9	2	2.74
2B	T. Fuentes	390	.249	2	49	238	287	11	70	5.2	.979	D'Acquisto	38	215	12	14	0	3.77
SS	C. Speier	501	.250	9	53	210	445	21	82	5.0	.969	M. Caldwell	31	189	14	5	0	2.95
3B	S. Ontiveros	343	.265	4	33	64	144	16	16	3.0	.929	T. Bradley	30	134	8	11	0	5.17
RF	B. Bonds	567	.256	21	71	305	11	11	3	2.2	.966	R. Bryant	41	127	3	15	0	5.60
CF	G. Maddox	538	.284	8	50	345	3	5	0	2.7	.986	R. Moffitt	61	102	5	7	15	4.50
LF	G. Matthews	561	.287	16	82	281	9	9	2	2.0	.970	E. Sosa	68	101	9	7	6	3.48
C	D. Rader	323	.291	1	26	461	38	8	4	4.7	.984	C. Williams	39	100	1	3	0	2.79
OF	G. Thomasson	315	.244	2	29	149	4	3	1	2.1	.981							
1B	E. Goodson	298	.272	6	48	593	30	2	52	8.6	.997							
UT	M. Phillips	283	.219	2	20	125	195	19	33		.944							
UT	B. Miller	198	.278	0	16	55	161	12	11		.947							
2B	C. Arnold	174	.241	1	26	64	86	4	16	5.0	.974							

San Diego
W-60 L-102

John McNamara

POS	Player	AB	BA	HR	RBI	PO	A	E	DP	TC/G	FA	Pitcher	G	IP	W	L	SV	ERA
1B	W. McCovey	344	.253	22	63	815	47	11	59	8.4	.987	B. Greif	43	226	9	19	1	4.66
2B	D. Thomas	523	.247	3	41	232	294	13	45	5.2	.976	Freisleben	33	212	9	14	0	3.65
SS	E. Hernandez	512	.232	0	34	229	449	24	64	4.8	.966	R. Jones	40	208	8	22	2	4.46
3B	D. Roberts	318	.167	5	18	83	170	12	15	2.6	.955	D. Spillner	30	148	9	11	0	4.01
RF	D. Winfield	498	.265	20	75	276	11	12	2	2.3	.960	L. Hardy	76	102	9	4	2	4.68
CF	J. Grubb	444	.286	8	42	321	8	8	1	2.8	.976	V. Romo	54	71	5	5	9	4.56
LF	B. Tolan	357	.266	8	40	161	5	5	0	1.9	.971							
C	F. Kendall	424	.231	8	45	631	64	12	12	5.3	.983							
1O	N. Colbert	368	.207	14	54	605	52	9	43		.986							
OF	C. Gaston	267	.213	6	33	119	7	1	1	2.0	.992							
3B	D. Hilton	217	.240	1	12	51	94	8	13	2.8	.948							
2B	G. Beckert	172	.256	0	7	70	80	10	16	4.4	.938							

BATTING AND BASE RUNNING LEADERS

Batting Average
R. Garr, ATL	.353
A. Oliver, PIT	.321
G. Gross, HOU	.314
B. Buckner, LA	.314
R. Zisk, PIT	.313

Slugging Average
M. Schmidt, PHI	.546
W. Stargell, PIT	.537
R. Smith, STL	.528
J. Bench, CIN	.507
R. Garr, ATL	.503

Home Runs
M. Schmidt, PHI	36
J. Bench, CIN	33
J. Wynn, LA	32
T. Perez, CIN	28
C. Cedeno, HOU	26

Total Bases
J. Bench, CIN	315
M. Schmidt, PHI	310
R. Garr, ATL	305
S. Garvey, LA	301
A. Oliver, PIT	293

Runs Batted In
J. Bench, CIN	129
M. Schmidt, PHI	116
S. Garvey, LA	111
J. Wynn, LA	108
T. Simmons, STL	103

Stolen Bases
L. Brock, STL	118
D. Lopes, LA	59
J. Morgan, CIN	58
C. Cedeno, HOU	57
L. Lintz, MON	50

Hits
R. Garr, ATL	214
D. Cash, PHI	206
S. Garvey, LA	200
A. Oliver, PIT	198

Base on Balls
D. Evans, ATL	126
J. Morgan, CIN	120
J. Wynn, LA	108
M. Schmidt, PHI	106

Home Run Percentage
M. Schmidt, PHI	6.3
J. Wynn, LA	6.0
J. Bench, CIN	5.3
W. Stargell, PIT	4.9

Runs Scored
P. Rose, CIN	110
M. Schmidt, PHI	108
J. Bench, CIN	108
J. Morgan, CIN	107

Doubles
P. Rose, CIN	45
A. Oliver, PIT	38
J. Bench, CIN	38
W. Stargell, PIT	37

Triples
R. Garr, ATL	17
A. Oliver, PIT	12
D. Cash, PHI	11
R. Metzger, HOU	10

PITCHING LEADERS

Winning Percentage
Messersmith, LA	.769
D. Sutton, LA	.679
B. Capra, ATL	.667
M. Torrez, MON	.652
Billingham, CIN	.633

Earned Run Average
B. Capra, ATL	2.28
P. Niekro, ATL	2.38
J. Matlack, NY	2.41
M. Marshall, LA	2.42
Messersmith, LA	2.59

Wins
Messersmith, LA	20
P. Niekro, ATL	20
D. Sutton, LA	19
Billingham, CIN	19
D. Gullett, CIN	17
J. Lonborg, PHI	17

Saves
M. Marshall, LA	21
R. Moffitt, SF	15
P. Borbon, CIN	14
D. Giusti, PIT	12
C. Taylor, MON	11
T. House, ATL	11

Strikeouts
S. Carlton, PHI	240
Messersmith, LA	221
T. Seaver, NY	201
J. Matlack, NY	195
P. Niekro, ATL	195

Complete Games
P. Niekro, ATL	18
S. Carlton, PHI	17
J. Lonborg, PHI	16
J. Rooker, PIT	15
J. Matlack, NY	14
J. Reuss, PIT	14

Fewest Hits/9 Innings
B. Capra, ATL	6.76
Messersmith, LA	7.00
P. Niekro, ATL	7.42
D. Gullett, CIN	7.44

Shutouts
J. Matlack, NY	7
P. Niekro, ATL	6
J. Barr, SF	5
B. Capra, ATL	5

Fewest Walks/9 Innings
J. Barr, SF	1.76
R. Reed, ATL	1.98
D. Ellis, PIT	2.08
J. Lonborg, PHI	2.23

Most Strikeouts/9 Inn.
T. Seaver, NY	7.67
S. Carlton, PHI	7.42
B. Bonham, CHI	7.07
D'Acquisto, SF	6.99

Innings
P. Niekro, ATL	302
Messersmith, LA	292
S. Carlton, PHI	291
J. Lonborg, PHI	283

Games Pitched
M. Marshall, LA	106
L. Hardy, SD	76
P. Borbon, CIN	73
K. Forsch, HOU	70

NATIONAL LEAGUE 1974, *cont.*

		W	L	PCT	GB	R	OR	2B	3B	HR	BA	SA	SB	E	DP	FA	CG	BB	SO	ShO	SV	ERA
East	Pittsburgh	88	74	.543		751	657	238	46	114	**.274**	.391	55	162	154	.975	**51**	543	721	9	17	3.49
	St. Louis	86	75	.534	1.5	677	643	216	46	83	.265	.365	**172**	147	**192**	.977	37	616	794	13	20	3.48
	Philadelphia	80	82	.494	8	676	701	233	**50**	95	.261	.373	115	148	168	.976	46	682	892	4	19	3.92
	Montreal	79	82	.491	8.5	662	657	201	29	86	.254	.350	124	153	157	.976	35	544	822	8	**27**	3.60
	New York	71	91	.438	17	572	646	183	22	96	.235	.329	43	158	150	.975	46	504	908	5	14	3.42
	Chicago	66	96	.407	22	669	826	221	42	110	.251	.365	78	199	141	.969	23	576	895	6	26	4.28
West	Los Angeles	102	60	.630		**798**	561	231	34	**139**	.272	**.401**	149	157	122	.975	33	**464**	**943**	19	23	**2.97**
	Cincinnati	98	64	.605	4	776	631	**271**	35	135	.260	.394	146	134	151	.979	34	536	875	11	**27**	3.42
	Atlanta	88	74	.543	14	661	563	202	37	120	.249	.363	72	132	161	.979	46	488	772	**21**	22	3.05
	Houston	81	81	.500	21	653	632	222	41	110	.263	.378	108	**113**	161	**.982**	36	601	738	18	18	3.48
	San Francisco	72	90	.444	30	634	723	228	38	93	.252	.358	107	175	153	.972	27	559	756	11	25	3.80
	San Diego	60	102	.370	42	541	830	196	27	99	.229	.330	85	170	126	.973	25	715	855	7	19	4.61
						8070	8070	2642	447	1280	.255	.367	1254	1848	1836	.976	439	6828	9971	142	257	3.62

AMERICAN LEAGUE 1974

East

Baltimore

W-91 L-71

Earl Weaver

POS	Player	AB	BA	HR	RBI	PO	A	E	DP	TC/G	FA	Pitcher	G	IP	W	L	SV	ERA
1B	B. Powell	344	.265	12	45	866	61	4	102	9.1	.996	R. Grimsley	40	296	18	13	1	3.07
2B	B. Grich	582	.263	19	82	**484**	**453**	20	**132**	6.0	.979	M. Cuellar	38	269	22	10	0	3.11
SS	M. Belanger	493	.225	5	36	243	**552**	13	100	5.2	**.984**	D. McNally	39	259	16	10	1	3.58
3B	B. Robinson	553	.288	7	59	115	**410**	11	44	3.5	.967	J. Palmer	26	179	7	12	0	3.27
RF	R. Coggins	411	.243	4	32	238	3	4	1	2.3	.984	D. Alexander	30	114	6	9	0	4.03
CF	P. Blair	552	.261	17	62	447	7	7	2	3.1	.985	W. Garland	20	91	5	5	1	2.97
LF	D. Baylor	489	.272	10	59	218	1	5	0	1.7	.978	B. Reynolds	54	69	7	5	7	2.74
C	E. Williams	413	.254	14	52	308	33	6	5	4.6	.983	G. Jackson	49	67	6	4	12	2.55
DH	T. Davis	626	.289	11	84													
OF	A. Bumbry	270	.233	1	19	115	7	6	0	1.9	.953							
OF	J. Fuller	189	.222	7	28	116	3	5	1	2.1	.960							
C	Etchebarren	180	.222	2	15	269	19	7	3	4.9	.976							
UT	E. Cabell	174	.241	3	17	223	45	4	18		.985							

New York

W-89 L-73

Bill Virdon

POS	Player	AB	BA	HR	RBI	PO	A	E	DP	TC/G	FA	Pitcher	G	IP	W	L	SV	ERA
1B	C. Chambliss	400	.243	6	43	873	78	8	93	9.0	.992	P. Dobson	39	281	19	15	0	3.07
2B	S. Alomar	279	.269	1	27	140	136	9	37	3.8	.968	D. Medich	38	280	19	15	0	3.60
SS	J. Mason	440	.250	5	37	241	430	25	87	4.6	.964	D. Tidrow	33	191	11	9	1	3.86
3B	G. Nettles	566	.246	22	75	**147**	377	21	29	3.5	.961	S. Lyle	66	114	9	3	15	1.66
RF	B. Murcer	606	.274	10	88	297	**21**	7	2	2.1	.978	R. May	17	114	8	4	0	2.29
CF	E. Maddox	466	.303	3	45	334	18	5	4	2.6	.986	Stottlemyre	16	113	6	7	0	3.58
LF	L. Piniella	518	.305	9	70	265	16	3	0	2.2	.989	C. Upshaw	36	60	1	5	0	3.00
C	T. Munson	517	.261	13	60	743	**75**	22	10	6.1	.974							
DH	R. White	473	.275	7	43													
DH	R. Blomberg	264	.311	10	48													
D1	B. Sudakis	259	.232	7	39	277	23	3	31	9.2	.990							
2S	G. Michael	177	.260	0	13	121	169	9	40		.970							

Boston

W-84 L-78

Darrell Johnson

POS	Player	AB	BA	HR	RBI	PO	A	E	DP	TC/G	FA	Pitcher	G	IP	W	L	SV	ERA
1B	Yastrzemski	515	.301	15	79	707	44	2	67	9.0	.997	L. Tiant	38	311	22	13	0	2.92
2B	D. Griffin	312	.266	0	33	178	242	9	53	4.7	.979	B. Lee	38	282	17	15	0	3.51
SS	M. Guerrero	284	.246	0	23	136	266	13	50	4.5	.969	R. Cleveland	41	221	12	14	0	4.32
3B	Petrocelli	454	.267	15	76	83	219	12	23	2.7	.962	D. Drago	33	176	7	10	3	3.48
RF	D. Evans	463	.281	10	70	294	8	3	2	2.5	.990	R. Moret	31	173	9	10	2	3.75
CF	R. Miller	280	.261	5	22	253	7	3	3	2.5	.989	D. Segui	58	108	6	8	10	4.00
LF	J. Beniquez	389	.267	5	33	264	4	6	2	2.8	.978							
C	Montgomery	254	.252	4	38	318	28	8	3	4.5	.977							
DH	T. Harper	443	.237	5	24													
1D	C. Cooper	414	.275	8	43	637	40	12	66	9.3	.983							
SS	R. Burleson	384	.284	4	44	142	249	18	41	4.6	.956							
OF	B. Carbo	338	.249	12	61	164	5	1	1	2.0	.994							
23	McAuliffe	272	.210	5	24	150	177	11	37		.967							
C	C. Fisk	187	.299	11	26	267	26	6	2	6.0	.980							
1D	D. Cater	126	.246	5	20	126	10	0	9	5.9	1.000							

Cleveland

W-77 L-85

Ken Aspromonte

POS	Player	AB	BA	HR	RBI	PO	A	E	DP	TC/G	FA	Pitcher	G	IP	W	L	SV	ERA
1B	J. Ellis	477	.285	10	64	667	37	6	57	10.3	.992	G. Perry	37	322	21	13	0	2.52
2B	J. Brohamer	315	.270	2	30	203	269	8	67	4.8	.987	J. Perry	36	252	17	12	0	2.96
SS	F. Duffy	549	.233	8	48	242	491	15	83	4.7	.980	F. Peterson	29	153	9	14	0	4.35
3B	B. Bell	423	.262	7	46	112	274	15	31	3.5	.963	D. Bosman	25	127	7	5	0	4.11
RF	C. Spikes	568	.271	22	80	284	16	10	3	2.8	.968	T. Buskey	51	93	2	6	17	3.19
CF	G. Hendrick	495	.279	19	67	355	9	4	2	2.8	.989	F. Beene	32	73	4	4	2	4.93
LF	Lowenstein	508	.242	8	48	200	6	3	1	2.1	.986	S. Kline	16	71	3	8	5	5.07
C	D. Duncan	425	.200	16	46	557	47	15	7	4.6	.976	Hilgendorf	35	48	4	3	3	4.88
DH	O. Gamble	454	.291	19	59													
OF	L. Lee	232	.233	5	25	131	5	6	1	2.3	.958							

AMERICAN LEAGUE 1974, *cont.*

	POS	Player	AB	BA	HR	RBI	PO	A	E	DP	TC/G	FA	Pitcher	G	IP	W	L	SV	ERA
Milwaukee W-76 L-86 Del Crandall	1B	G. Scott	604	.281	17	82	**1345**	114	12	**137**	9.9	**.992**	J. Slaton	40	250	13	16	0	3.92
	2B	P. Garcia	452	.199	12	54	382	365	23	102	5.5	.970	C. Wright	38	232	9	20	0	4.42
	SS	R. Yount	344	.250	3	26	148	327	19	55	4.6	.962	J. Colborn	33	224	10	13	0	4.06
	3B	D. Money	**629**	.283	15	65	131	336	5	42	3.0	**.989**	K. Kobel	34	169	6	14	0	3.99
	RF	B. Coluccio	394	.223	6	31	346	10	4	2	2.7	.989	B. Champion	31	162	11	4	0	3.61
	CF	D. May	477	.226	10	42	249	10	3	2	2.2	.989	T. Murphy	70	123	10	10	20	1.90
	LF	J. Briggs	554	.253	17	73	309	10	9	2	2.2	.973	E. Rodriguez	43	112	7	4	4	3.62
	C	D. Porter	432	.241	12	56	484	60	12	8	4.8	.978							
	DH	B. Mitchell	173	.243	5	20													
	OF	K. Berry	267	.240	1	24	187	8	1	1	2.4	.995							
	S2	T. Johnson	245	.245	0	25	138	230	9	51		.976							
	C	C. Moore	204	.245	0	19	229	28	4	5	4.3	.985							
	UT	M. Hegan	190	.237	7	32	136	5	1	12		.993							
Detroit W-72 L-90 Ralph Houk	1B	B. Freehan	445	.297	18	60	590	36	4	49	9.7	.994	M. Lolich	41	308	16	**21**	0	4.15
	2B	Sutherland	619	.254	5	49	337	360	17	101	4.9	.976	J. Coleman	41	286	14	12	0	4.31
	SS	E. Brinkman	502	.221	14	54	237	493	21	88	5.0	.972	L. LaGrow	37	216	8	19	0	4.67
	3B	A. Rodriguez	571	.222	5	49	132	389	21	40	3.4	.961	J. Hiller	59	150	17	14	13	2.64
	RF	J. Northrup	376	.237	11	42	209	5	6	0	2.3	.973	W. Fryman	27	142	6	9	0	4.31
	CF	M. Stanley	394	.221	8	34	252	4	2	2	2.8	.992	L. Walker	28	92	5	5	0	4.99
	LF	W. Horton	238	.298	15	47	106	2	6	0	1.8	.947							
	C	G. Moses	198	.237	4	19	377	26	6	6	5.5	.985							
	DH	A. Kaline	558	.262	13	64													
	OF	R. LeFlore	254	.260	2	13	151	8	**11**	3	2.9	.935							
	OF	B. Oglivie	252	.270	4	29	87	3	5	0	1.5	.947							

West

	POS	Player	AB	BA	HR	RBI	PO	A	E	DP	TC/G	FA	Pitcher	G	IP	W	L	SV	ERA
Oakland W-90 L-72 Alvin Dark	1B	G. Tenace	484	.211	26	73	816	41	4	80	8.1	.995	C. Hunter	41	318	**25**	12	0	**2.49**
	2B	D. Green	287	.213	2	22	233	243	8	67	4.8	.983	V. Blue	40	282	17	15	0	3.26
	SS	Campaneris	527	.290	2	41	207	423	22	76	4.9	.966	K. Holtzman	39	255	19	17	0	3.07
	3B	S. Bando	498	.243	22	103	113	287	23	28	3.0	.946	R. Fingers	76	119	9	5	18	2.65
	RF	R. Jackson	506	.289	29	93	296	8	10	2	2.5	.968	D. Hamilton	29	117	7	4	0	3.15
	CF	B. North	543	.260	4	33	437	9	4	2	**3.3**	.991	P. Lindblad	45	101	4	4	6	2.05
	LF	J. Rudi	593	.293	22	99	234	7	4	0	1.8	.984	G. Abbott	19	96	5	7	0	3.00
	C	R. Fosse	204	.196	4	23	299	28	9	6	4.9	.973							
	DH	J. Alou	220	.268	2	15													
	OD	A. Mangual	365	.233	9	43	142	5	6	0	2.1	.961							
	DO	Washington	221	.285	0	19	63	2	1	0	2.1	.985							
	UT	T. Kubiak	220	.209	0	18	129	175	6	38		.981							
	1D	D. Johnson	174	.195	7	23	211	9	2	15	7.9	.991							
Texas W-84 L-76 Billy Martin	1B	M. Hargrove	415	.323	4	66	631	72	9	57	7.8	.987	F. Jenkins	41	328	**25**	12	0	2.83
	2B	D. Nelson	474	.236	3	42	295	337	20	74	5.4	.969	J. Bibby	41	264	19	19	0	4.74
	SS	T. Harrah	573	.260	21	74	**281**	466	**29**	98	4.9	.963	J. Brown	35	217	13	12	0	3.57
	3B	L. Randle	520	.302	1	49	92	167	18	23	3.1	.935	S. Hargan	37	187	12	9	0	3.95
	RF	J. Burroughs	554	.301	25	**118**	231	10	7	5	1.7	.972	S. Foucault	69	144	8	9	12	2.25
	CF	J. Lovitto	283	.223	2	26	201	7	6	1	2.0	.972	D. Clyde	28	117	3	9	0	4.38
	LF	C. Tovar	562	.292	4	58	331	13	7	3	2.6	.980							
	C	J. Sundberg	368	.247	3	36	722	69	8	**15**	6.1	.990							
	DH	J. Spencer	352	.278	7	44													
	OF	A. Johnson	453	.291	4	41	168	6	8	2	2.2	.956							
	DO	T. Grieve	259	.255	9	32	62	5	0	1	1.8	1.000							
	13	J. Fregosi	230	.261	12	34	331	73	5	35		.988							
Minnesota W-82 L-80 Frank Quilici	1B	C. Kusick	201	.239	8	26	479	42	2	45	7.0	.996	B. Blyleven	37	281	17	17	0	2.66
	2B	R. Carew	599	**.364**	3	55	375	416	33	114	5.6	.960	J. Decker	37	249	16	14	0	3.29
	SS	D. Thompson	264	.250	4	25	127	183	12	39	3.7	.963	D. Goltz	28	174	10	10	1	3.26
	3B	E. Soderholm	464	.276	10	51	100	273	17	19	3.0	.956	V. Albury	32	164	8	9	0	4.12
	RF	S. Brye	488	.283	2	41	301	10	1	2	2.4	**.997**	B. Campbell	63	120	8	7	19	2.63
	CF	B. Darwin	575	.264	25	94	254	8	8	1	1.9	.970	B. Hands	35	115	4	5	3	4.46
	LF	L. Hisle	510	.286	19	79	279	4	6	1	2.1	.979	R. Corbin	29	112	7	6	0	5.30
	C	G. Borgmann	345	.252	3	45	652	52	2	4	5.5	**.997**	B. Butler	26	99	4	6	1	4.09
	DH	T. Oliva	459	.285	13	57							T. Burgmeier	50	92	5	3	4	4.50
	OF	S. Braun	453	.280	8	40	180	10	7	2	1.8	.964							
	D1	H. Killebrew	333	.222	13	54	218	22	7	21	7.3	.992							
	UT	J. Terrell	229	.245	0	19	114	179	9	35		.970							
	1B	J. Holt	197	.254	0	16	449	43	2	57	7.4	.996							
	SS	L. Gomez	168	.208	0	3	97	190	12	37	4.0	.960							
Chicago W-80 L-80 Chuck Tanner	1B	D. Allen	462	.301	**32**	88	998	49	**15**	112	8.5	.986	W. Wood	42	320	20	19	0	3.60
	2B	J. Orta	525	.316	10	67	297	313	18	93	5.1	.971	J. Kaat	42	277	21	13	0	2.92
	SS	B. Dent	496	.274	5	45	251	499	22	**108**	5.0	.972	S. Bahnsen	38	216	12	15	0	4.71
	3B	B. Melton	495	.242	21	63	100	272	**24**	29	3.2	.939	T. Forster	59	134	7	8	24	3.63
	RF	B. Sharp	320	.253	4	24	210	3	3	0	2.2	.986	B. Johnson	18	122	10	4	0	2.73
	CF	K. Henderson	602	.292	20	95	**462**	7	6	3	2.9	.987	S. Pitlock	40	106	3	3	1	4.42
	LF	C. May	551	.249	8	58	245	11	3	1	2.0	.988	G. Gossage	39	89	4	6	1	4.15
	C	E. Herrmann	367	.259	10	39	561	55	8	8	5.8	.987							
	DH	P. Kelly	424	.281	4	21													
	UT	R. Santo	375	.221	5	41	135	148	8	49		.973							
	CO	B. Downing	293	.225	10	39	337	30	2	5		.995							
	1B	T. Muser	206	.291	1	18	419	13	1	46	5.4	.998							

AMERICAN LEAGUE 1974, *cont.*

	POS	Player	AB	BA	HR	RBI	PO	A	E	DP	TC/G	FA	Pitcher	G	IP	W	L	SV	ERA
Kansas City	1B	J. Mayberry	427	.234	22	69	963	61	10	101	9.8	.990	S. Busby	38	292	22	14	0	3.39
	2B	C. Rojas	542	.271	6	60	292	368	9	94	4.7	**.987**	Splittorff	36	226	13	19	0	4.10
W-77 L-85	SS	F. Patek	537	.225	3	38	250	493	25	**108**	5.2	.967	Fitzmorris	34	190	13	6	1	2.79
	3B	G. Brett	457	.282	2	47	102	279	21	16	3.0	.948	Dal Canton	31	175	8	10	0	3.14
Jack McKeon	RF	J. Wohlford	501	.271	2	44	273	7	5	4	2.1	.982	M. Pattin	25	117	3	7	0	4.00
	CF	A. Otis	552	.284	12	73	425	8	6	3	3.1	.986	L. McDaniel	38	107	1	4	1	3.45
	LF	V. Pinson	406	.276	6	41	188	9	4	2	1.8	.980	N. Briles	18	103	5	7	0	4.02
	C	F. Healy	445	.252	9	53	620	64	16	4	5.1	.977	D. Bird	55	92	7	6	10	2.74
	DH	H. McRae	539	.310	15	88													
	OF	A. Cowens	269	.242	1	25	151	13	2	2	1.6	.988							
	1B	T. Solaita	239	.268	7	30	508	40	5	36	8.5	.991							
	UT	F. White	204	.221	1	18	119	189	12	40		.963							
California	1B	J. Doherty	223	.256	3	15	538	30	5	55	8.2	.991	N. Ryan	42	**333**	22	16	0	2.89
	2B	D. Doyle	511	.260	1	34	311	404	12	99	5.0	.983	F. Tanana	39	269	14	19	0	3.11
W-68 L-94	SS	D. Chalk	465	.252	5	31	168	269	**29**	55	4.7	.938	A. Hassler	23	162	7	11	1	2.61
	3B	P. Schaal	165	.248	2	20	24	78	11	9	2.2	.903	D. Lange	21	114	3	8	0	3.79
Bobby Winkles	RF	L. Stanton	415	.267	11	62	226	11	6	0	2.1	.975	B. Singer	14	109	7	4	0	2.97
W-30 L-44	CF	M. Rivers	466	.285	3	31	309	9	2	3	2.8	.994	E. Figueroa	25	105	2	8	0	3.69
	LF	J. Lahoud	325	.271	13	44	156	6	4	2	1.6	.976							
Whitey Herzog	C	E. Rodriguez	395	.253	7	36	**782**	75	7	7	**6.3**	.992							
W-2 L-2	DH	F. Robinson	427	.251	20	63													
	UT	B. Valentine	371	.261	3	39	160	116	17	10		.942							
Dick Williams	13	B. Oliver	359	.248	8	55	400	83	12	46		.976							
W-36 L-48	O1	B. Bochte	196	.270	5	26	248	9	5	16		.981							
	OF	M. Nettles	175	.274	0	8	99	0	1	0	1.9	.990							

BATTING AND BASE RUNNING LEADERS

PITCHING LEADERS

Batting Average
R. Carew, MIN	.364
J. Orta, CHI	.316
H. McRae, KC	.310
L. Piniella, NY	.305
E. Maddox, NY	.303

Slugging Average
D. Allen, CHI	.563
R. Jackson, OAK	.514
J. Burroughs, TEX	.504
J. Rudi, OAK	.484
H. McRae, KC	.475

Home Runs
D. Allen, CHI	32
R. Jackson, OAK	29
G. Tenace, OAK	26
J. Burroughs, TEX	25
B. Darwin, MIN	25

Winning Percentage
M. Cuellar, BAL	.688
C. Hunter, OAK	.676
F. Jenkins, TEX	.676
L. Tiant, BOS	.629
J. Kaat, CHI	.618
G. Perry, CLE	.618

Earned Run Average
C. Hunter, OAK	2.49
G. Perry, CLE	2.52
A. Hassler, CAL	2.61
B. Blyleven, MIN	2.66
Fitzmorris, KC	2.79

Wins
C. Hunter, OAK	25
F. Jenkins, TEX	25
M. Cuellar, BAL	22
L. Tiant, BOS	22
S. Busby, KC	22
N. Ryan, CAL	22

Total Bases
J. Rudi, OAK	287
K. Henderson, CHI	281
J. Burroughs, TEX	279
R. Carew, MIN	267
G. Scott, MIL	261
D. Money, MIL	261

Runs Batted In
J. Burroughs, TEX	118
S. Bando, OAK	103
J. Rudi, OAK	99
K. Henderson, CHI	95
B. Darwin, MIN	94

Stolen Bases
B. North, OAK	54
R. Carew, MIN	38
Lowenstein, CLE	36
Campaneris, OAK	34
F. Patek, KC	33

Saves
T. Forster, CHI	24
T. Murphy, MIL	20
B. Campbell, MIN	19
R. Fingers, OAK	18
T. Buskey, CLE, NY	18

Strikeouts
N. Ryan, CAL	367
B. Blyleven, MIN	249
F. Jenkins, TEX	225
G. Perry, CLE	216
M. Lolich, DET	202

Complete Games
F. Jenkins, TEX	29
G. Perry, CLE	28
M. Lolich, DET	27
N. Ryan, CAL	26
L. Tiant, BOS	25

Hits
R. Carew, MIN	218
T. Davis, BAL	181
D. Money, MIL	178
K. Henderson, CHI	176

Base on Balls
G. Tenace, OAK	110
Yastrzemski, BOS	104
J. Burroughs, TEX	91
B. Grich, BAL	90

Home Run Percentage
D. Allen, CHI	6.9
R. Jackson, OAK	5.7
G. Tenace, OAK	5.4
J. Mayberry, KC	5.2

Fewest Hits/9 Innings
N. Ryan, CAL	5.97
G. Perry, CLE	6.43
Dal Canton, KC	6.94
A. Hassler, CAL	7.33

Shutouts
L. Tiant, BOS	7
C. Hunter, OAK	6
F. Jenkins, TEX	6
M. Cuellar, BAL	5

Fewest Walks/9 Innings
F. Jenkins, TEX	1.23
C. Hunter, OAK	1.30
K. Holtzman, OAK	1.80
J. Kaat, CHI	2.05

Runs Scored
Yastrzemski, BOS	93
B. Grich, BAL	92
R. Jackson, OAK	90
A. Otis, KC	87

Doubles
J. Rudi, OAK	39
H. McRae, KC	36
G. Scott, MIL	36
K. Henderson, CHI	35

Triples
M. Rivers, CAL	11
A. Otis, KC	9
D. Evans, BOS	8
R. White, NY	8

Most Strikeouts/9 Inn.
N. Ryan, CAL	9.92
B. Blyleven, MIN	7.98
F. Jenkins, TEX	6.17
S. Busby, KC	6.10

Innings
N. Ryan, CAL	333
F. Jenkins, TEX	328
G. Perry, CLE	322
W. Wood, CHI	320

Games Pitched
R. Fingers, OAK	76
T. Murphy, MIL	70
S. Foucault, TEX	69
S. Lyle, NY	66

		W	L	PCT	GB	R	OR	2B	3B	HR	BA	SA	SB	E	DP	FA	CG	BB	SO	ShO	SV	ERA
East	Baltimore	91	71	.562		659	612	226	27	116	.256	.370	145	128	174	**.980**	57	480	701	**16**	25	3.27
	New York	89	73	.549	2	671	623	220	30	101	.263	.368	53	142	158	.977	53	528	829	13	24	3.32
	Boston	84	78	.519	7	**696**	661	**236**	31	109	.264	.377	104	145	156	.977	**71**	463	751	12	18	3.72
	Cleveland	77	85	.475	14	662	694	201	19	131	.255	.370	79	146	157	.977	45	479	650	8	27	3.80
	Milwaukee	76	86	.469	15	647	660	228	**49**	120	.244	.369	106	**127**	168	.980	43	493	621	11	24	3.77
	Detroit	72	90	.444	19	620	768	200	35	131	.247	.366	67	158	155	.975	54	621	869	7	15	4.17
West	Oakland	90	72	.556		689	**551**	205	37	132	.247	.373	164	141	154	.977	49	**430**	755	12	28	**2.95**
	Texas	84	76	.525	5	690	698	198	39	99	**.272**	.377	113	163	164	.974	62	449	871	**16**	12	3.82
	Minnesota	82	80	.506	8	673	669	190	37	111	**.272**	.378	74	151	164	.976	43	513	934	11	**29**	3.64
	Chicago	80	80	.500	9	684	721	225	23	**135**	.268	**.389**	64	147	168	.977	55	548	826	11	**29**	3.94
	Kansas City	77	85	.475	13	667	662	232	42	89	.259	.364	146	152	166	.976	54	482	731	14	17	3.51
	California	68	94	.420	22	618	657	203	31	95	.254	.356	119	147	150	.977	64	649	**986**	13	12	3.52
						7976	7976	2564	400	1369	.258	.371	1234	1747	1954	.977	650	6135	9524	144	260	3.62

NATIONAL LEAGUE 1975

		POS	Player	AB	BA	HR	RBI	PO	A	E	DP	TC/G	FA	Pitcher	G	IP	W	L	SV	ERA
East	**Pittsburgh**	1B	W. Stargell	461	.295	22	90	1121	54	10	112	9.7	.992	J. Reuss	32	237	18	11	0	2.54
		2B	R. Stennett	616	.286	7	62	379	463	18	98	6.0	.979	J. Rooker	28	197	13	11	0	2.97
	W-92 L-69	SS	F. Taveras	378	.212	0	23	200	369	28	74	4.5	.953	B. Kison	33	192	12	11	0	3.23
		3B	R. Hebner	472	.246	15	57	86	244	19	17	2.8	.946	D. Ellis	27	140	8	9	0	3.79
	Danny Murtaugh	RF	D. Parker	558	.308	25	101	311	7	9	2	2.3	.972	Candelaria	18	121	8	6	0	2.75
		CF	A. Oliver	628	.280	18	84	380	5	5	3	2.5	.987	K. Brett	23	118	9	5	0	3.36
		LF	R. Zisk	504	.290	20	75	264	7	7	1	2.0	.975	L. Demery	45	115	7	5	4	2.90
		C	Sanguillen	481	.328	9	58	650	53	9	4	5.4	.987	D. Giusti	61	92	5	4	17	2.93
		OF	B. Robinson	200	.280	6	33	107	3	1	1	1.9	.991	R. Hernandez	46	64	7	2	5	2.95
	Philadelphia	1B	D. Allen	416	.233	12	62	900	70	18	79	8.7	.982	S. Carlton	37	255	15	14	0	3.56
		2B	D. Cash	**699**	.305	4	57	**400**	481	17	**126**	5.5	.981	T. Underwood	35	219	14	13	0	4.15
	W-86 L-76	SS	L. Bowa	583	.305	2	38	227	403	25	82	4.9	.962	Christenson	29	172	11	6	0	3.66
		3B	M. Schmidt	562	.249	**38**	95	132	368	24	30	3.5	.954	J. Lonborg	27	159	8	6	0	4.13
	Danny Ozark	RF	M. Anderson	247	.259	4	28	161	6	4	0	1.6	.977	W. Twitchell	36	134	5	10	0	4.43
		CF	G. Maddox	374	.291	4	46	288	10	5	4	3.1*	.983	G. Garber	**71**	110	10	12	14	3.60
		LF	G. Luzinski	596	.300	34	**120**	248	10	9	0	1.7	.966	T. McGraw	56	103	9	6	14	2.97
		C	B. Boone	289	.246	2	20	456	44	5	7	5.5	.990	Hilgendorf	53	97	7	3	0	2.13
		OF	J. Johnstone	350	.329	7	54	152	10	4	3	1.6	.976							
		C	J. Oates	269	.286	1	25	429	44	5	10*	5.8	.990							
		1B	T. Hutton	165	.248	3	24	307	32	2	37	4.8	.994							
		OF	O. Brown	145	.303	6	26	67	0	0	0	1.8	1.000							
	New York	1B	E. Kranepool	325	.323	4	43	666	46	2	51	8.7	.997	T. Seaver	36	280	**22**	9	0	2.38
		2B	F. Millan	676	.283	1	56	379	420	23	95	5.1	.972	J. Koosman	36	240	14	13	2	3.41
	W-82 L-80	SS	M. Phillips	383	.256	1	28	185	334	31*	52	4.8	.944	J. Matlack	33	229	16	12	0	3.38
		3B	W. Garrett	274	.266	6	34	64	160	8	24	2.5	.966	R. Tate	26	138	5	13	0	4.43
	Yogi Berra	RF	R. Staub	574	.282	19	105	267	**15**	4	3	1.9	.986	H. Webb	29	115	7	6	0	4.07
	W-56 L-53	CF	D. Unser	531	.294	10	53	362	13	5	2	2.6	.987	R. Baldwin	54	97	3	5	6	3.34
		LF	D. Kingman	502	.231	36	88	134	3	6	0	2.0	.958	B. Apodaca	46	85	3	4	13	1.48
	Roy McMillan	C	J. Grote	386	.295	2	39	706	55	4	8	**6.9**	**.995**							
	W-26 L-27	3B	J. Torre	361	.247	6	35	61	148	11	14	2.7	.950							
		O1	J. Milner	220	.191	7	29	267	27	3	21		.990							
		OF	G. Clines	203	.227	0	10	98	9	2	2	1.8	.982							
		C	J. Stearns	169	.189	3	10	297	40	2	9	6.3	.994							
		OF	M. Vail	162	.302	3	17	92	9	3	1	2.9	.971							
	St. Louis	1B	R. Smith	477	.302	19	76	524	33	10	51	8.6	.982	McGlothen	35	239	15	13	0	3.92
		2B	T. Sizemore	562	.240	3	49	329	405	21	82	4.9	.972	B. Forsch	34	230	15	10	0	2.86
	W-82 L-80	SS	M. Tyson	368	.266	2	37	154	246	12	44	4.3	.971	R. Reed	24	176	9	8	0	3.23
		3B	K. Reitz	592	.269	5	63	124	279	23	21	2.7	.946	J. Curtis	39	147	8	9	1	3.43
	Red Schoendienst	RF	B. McBride	413	.300	5	36	289	4	3	1	2.8	.990	J. Denny	25	136	10	7	0	3.97
		CF	W. Davis	350	.291	6	50	187	5	6	2	2.2	.970	B. Gibson	22	109	3	10	2	5.04
		LF	L. Brock	528	.309	3	47	247	5	9	0	2.0	.966	A. Hrabosky	65	97	13	3	22	1.67
		C	T. Simmons	581	.332	18	100	803	62	**15**	5	5.7	.983	E. Rasmussen	14	81	5	5	0	3.78
		OF	L. Melendez	291	.265	2	27	169	3	3	1	2.0	.983	M. Garman	66	79	3	8	10	2.39
		1B	R. Fairly	229	.301	7	37	351	33	8	33	7.0	.980							
		1B	K. Hernandez	188	.250	3	20	469	36	2	34	9.1	.996							
		SS	M. Guerrero	184	.239	0	11	76	198	13	29	4.5	.955							
	Chicago	1B	A. Thornton	372	.293	18	60	982	77	13	88	9.5	.988	R. Burris	36	238	15	10	0	4.12
		2B	M. Trillo	545	.248	7	70	350	**509**	29	103	5.8	.967	R. Reuschel	38	234	11	**17**	1	3.73
	W-75 L-87	SS	D. Kessinger	601	.243	0	46	205	436	22	100	4.7	.967	B. Bonham	38	229	13	15	0	4.72
		3B	B. Madlock	514	**.354**	7	64	79	250	20	14	2.7	.943	S. Stone	33	214	12	8	0	3.95
	Jim Marshall	RF	J. Cardenal	574	.317	9	68	313	14	8	3	2.2	.976	D. Knowles	58	88	6	9	15	5.83
		CF	R. Monday	491	.267	17	60	315	6	9	4	2.5	.973	O. Zamora	52	71	5	2	10	5.07
		LF	J. Morales	578	.270	12	91	273	11	6	1	1.9	.979	G. Zahn	16	63	2	7	1	4.45
		C	S. Swisher	254	.213	1	22	426	36	10	5	5.1	.979							
		1O	P. LaCock	249	.229	6	30	479	45	6	39		.989							
		C	Mitterwald	200	.220	5	26	247	32	7	4	4.8	.976							
		C	T. Hosley	141	.255	6	20	254	16	9	3	5.3	.968							
	Montreal	1B	M. Jorgensen	445	.261	18	67	1150	91	7	123	9.4	.994	S. Rogers	35	252	11	12	0	3.29
		2B	P. Mackanin	448	.225	12	44	300	410	25	100	5.8	.966	S. Renko	31	170	6	12	1	4.08
	W-75 L-87	SS	T. Foli	572	.238	1	29	**260**	**497**	21	**104**	5.2	.973	D. Warthen	40	168	8	6	3	3.11
		3B	L. Parrish	532	.274	10	65	105	291	35	33	3.0	.919	D. Blair	30	163	8	15	0	3.81
	Gene Mauch	RF	L. Biittner	346	.315	3	28	166	8	5	0	1.9	.972	W. Fryman	38	157	9	12	3	3.32
		CF	P. Mangual	514	.245	9	45	308	8	9	2	2.4	.972	D. Murray	63	111	15	8	9	3.97
		LF	G. Carter	503	.270	17	68	150	1	4	1	1.7	.974	Carrithers	19	101	5	3	0	3.30
		C	B. Foote	387	.194	7	30	590	50	10	**10**	5.7	.985	D. DeMola	60	98	4	7	1	4.13
		OF	B. Bailey	227	.273	5	30	88	4	2	1	1.5	.979	C. Taylor	54	74	2	2	6	3.53
		OF	J. Dwyer	175	.286	3	20	86	8	4	1	1.9	.959							
		1B	J. Morales	163	.301	2	24	201	26	4	19	8.6	.983							

NATIONAL LEAGUE 1975, *cont.*

	POS	Player	AB	BA	HR	RBI	PO	A	E	DP	TC/G	FA	Pitcher	G	IP	W	L	SV	ERA
West **Cincinnati**	1B	T. Perez	511	.282	20	109	1192	72	9	113	9.6	.993	G. Nolan	32	211	15	9	0	3.16
	2B	J. Morgan	498	.327	17	94	356	425	11	96	5.6	**.986**	Billingham	33	208	15	10	0	4.11
W-108 L-54	SS	Concepcion	507	.274	5	49	238	445	16	102	**5.4**	.977	F. Norman	34	188	12	4	0	3.73
	3B	P. Rose	662	.317	7	74	106	230	13	21	2.5	.963	D. Gullett	22	160	15	4	0	2.42
Sparky Anderson	RF	K. Griffey	463	.305	4	46	202	6	7	0	1.8	.967	P. Darcy	27	131	11	5	1	3.57
	CF	C. Geronimo	501	.257	6	53	**408**	12	3	5	2.9	.993	P. Borbon	67	125	9	5	5	2.95
	LF	G. Foster	463	.300	23	78	299	11	3	3	2.5	.990	C. Kirby	26	111	10	6	0	4.70
	C	J. Bench	530	.283	28	110	568	51	7	9	5.2	.989	C. Carroll	56	96	7	5	7	2.63
	10	D. Driessen	210	.281	7	38	309	20	5	34		.985	W. McEnaney	70	91	5	2	15	2.47
	OF	Rettenmund	188	.239	2	19	99	1	0	1	1.6	1.000	R. Eastwick	58	90	5	3	22	2.60
	UT	D. Chaney	160	.219	2	26	77	164	7	27		.972							
	UT	D. Flynn	127	.268	1	20	57	118	2	20		.989							
Los Angeles	1B	S. Garvey	659	.319	18	95	**1500**	77	8	96	**9.9**	.995	Messersmith	42	**322**	19	14	1	2.29
	2B	D. Lopes	618	.262	8	41	307	377	15	58	5.1	.979	D. Rau	38	258	15	9	0	3.10
W-88 L-74	SS	B. Russell	252	.206	0	14	94	230	11	27	4.0	.967	D. Sutton	35	254	16	13	0	2.87
	3B	R. Cey	566	.283	25	101	144	309	19	23	3.0	.960	B. Hooton	31	224	18	7	0	2.82
Walter Alston	RF	W. Crawford	373	.263	9	46	201	2	2	0	1.8	.990	M. Marshall	57	109	9	14	13	3.30
	CF	J. Wynn	412	.248	18	58	282	6	5	2	2.4	.983	C. Hough	38	61	3	7	4	2.95
	LF	B. Buckner	288	.243	6	31	138	4	2	0	2.0	.986							
	C	S. Yeager	452	.228	12	54	806	62	7	4	6.5	.992							
	O2	L. Lacy	306	.314	7	40	151	75	13	11		.946							
	OF	J. Hale	204	.211	6	22	128	2	3	0	2.0	.977							
	CO	J. Ferguson	202	.208	5	23	215	20	2	4		.992							
	SS	R. Auerbach	170	.224	0	12	77	137	9	17	2.8	.960							
San Francisco	1B	W. Montanez	518	.305	8	85	1150	81*	8	114*	9.2	.994	Montefusco	35	244	15	9	0	2.88
	2B	D. Thomas	540	.276	6	48	348	372	19	100	5.2	.974	J. Barr	35	244	13	14	0	3.06
W-80 L-81	SS	C. Speier	487	.271	10	69	247	420	12	81	5.0	.982	P. Falcone	34	190	12	11	0	4.17
	3B	S. Ontiveros	325	.289	3	31	64	188	21	14	3.1	.923	M. Caldwell	38	163	7	13	1	4.80
Wes Westrum	RF	B. Murcer	526	.298	11	91	201	10	4	3	1.5	.981	E. Halicki	24	160	9	13	0	3.49
	CF	V. Joshua	507	.318	7	43	279	10	2	3	2.5	**.993**	C. Williams	55	98	5	3	3	3.49
	LF	G. Matthews	425	.280	12	58	225	11	8	2	2.2	.967	G. Lavelle	65	82	6	3	8	2.96
	C	D. Rader	292	.291	5	31	457	37	8	7	5.3	.984	R. Moffitt	55	74	4	5	11	3.89
	OF	G. Thomasson	326	.227	7	32	172	9	4	2	2.5	.978							
	3B	B. Miller	309	.239	1	31	66	120	10	11	2.9	.949							
	C	M. Hill	182	.214	5	23	282	27	2	7	5.2	.994							
San Diego	1B	W. McCovey	413	.252	23	68	979	73	15	94	9.3	.986	R. Jones	37	285	20	12	0	**2.24**
	2B	T. Fuentes	565	.280	4	43	389	448	26	105	6.1	.970	J. McIntosh	37	183	8	15	0	3.69
W-71 L-91	SS	E. Hernandez	344	.218	0	19	168	327	18	70	4.6	.965	Freisleben	36	181	5	14	0	4.28
	3B	T. Kubiak	196	.224	0	14	36	110	7	9	2.4	.954	D. Spillner	37	167	5	13	1	4.26
John McNamara	RF	D. Winfield	509	.267	15	76	302	9	9	1	2.3	.972	R. Folkers	45	142	6	11	0	4.18
	CF	J. Grubb	553	.269	4	38	334	3	3	0	2.4	.991	B. Strom	18	120	8	8	0	2.55
	LF	B. Tolan	506	.255	5	43	230	5	7	1	2.0	.971	D. Frisella	65	98	1	6	9	3.12
	C	F. Kendall	286	.199	0	24	337	38	9	6	4.5	.977	B. Greif	59	72	4	6	9	3.88
	13	M. Ivie	377	.249	8	46	539	138	23	54		.967							
	UT	H. Torres	352	.259	5	26	128	338	13	55		.973							
	OF	G. Locklear	237	.321	5	27	92	4	3	1	1.9	.970							
	C	R. Hundley	180	.206	2	14	237	20	8	3	5.2	.970							
	OF	D. Sharon	160	.194	4	20	91	1	5	0	1.7	.948							
Atlanta	1B	E. Williams	383	.240	11	50	844	50	10	77	10.0	.989	C. Morton	39	278	17	16	0	3.50
	2B	M. Perez	461	.275	2	34	259	341	9	74	5.3	.985	P. Niekro	39	276	15	15	1	3.20
W-67 L-94	SS	L. Blanks	471	.234	3	38	183	414	25	68	4.8	.960	T. House	58	79	7	7	11	3.19
	3B	D. Evans	567	.243	22	73	**161**	**381**	36	**41**	3.7	.938	B. Capra	12	78	4	7	0	4.27
Clyde King	RF	D. Baker	494	.261	19	72	287	10	3	0	2.2	.990	J. Easterly	21	69	2	9	0	4.96
W-58 L-76	CF	R. Office	355	.290	3	30	229	6	8	0	2.3	.967	Dal Canton	26	67	2	7	3	3.36
Connie Ryan	LF	R. Garr	625	.278	6	31	298	12	11	2	2.2	.966							
W-9 L-18	C	V. Correll	325	.215	11	39	413	63	13	2	5.0	.973							
	10	M. Lum	364	.228	8	36	657	34	5	41		.993							
	OF	D. May	203	.276	12	40	103	3	4	2	2.1	.964							
	2B	R. Gilbreath	202	.243	2	16	121	125	5	29	4.8	.980							
	C	B. Pocoroba	188	.255	1	22	237	25	8	2	4.4	.970							
Houston	1B	B. Watson	485	.324	18	85	1077	69	8	106	9.8	.993	L. Dierker	34	232	14	16	0	4.00
	2B	R. Andrews	277	.238	0	19	191	237	8	65	4.6	.982	J. Richard	33	203	12	10	0	4.39
W-64 L-97	SS	R. Metzger	450	.227	2	26	186	441	15	83	5.1	.977	D. Roberts	32	198	8	14	1	4.27
	3B	D. Rader	448	.223	12	48	111	257	11	24	3.1	**.971**	D. Konieczny	32	171	6	13	0	4.47
Preston Gomez	RF	J. Cruz	315	.257	9	49	187	6	4	0	2.1	.980	K. Forsch	34	109	4	8	2	3.22
W-47 L-80	CF	C. Cedeno	500	.288	13	63	322	8	6	2	2.6	.982	J. Niekro	40	88	6	4	4	3.07
	LF	G. Gross	483	.294	0	41	216	14	10	2	2.0	.958	J. Crawford	44	87	3	5	4	3.62
Bill Virdon	C	M. May	386	.241	4	52	568	**70**	9	8	6.3	.986	T. Griffin	17	79	3	8	0	5.35
W-17 L-17	OF	W. Howard	392	.283	0	21	194	7	1	0	2.1	.995	W. Granger	55	74	2	5	5	3.65
	UT	E. Cabell	348	.264	2	43	197	58	6	17		.977							
	1C	C. Johnson	340	.276	20	65	602	37	12	37		.982							
	23	K. Boswell	178	.242	0	21	54	103	6	13		.963							

NATIONAL LEAGUE 1975, cont.

BATTING AND BASE RUNNING LEADERS

Batting Average		Slugging Average		Home Runs		Winning Percentage		Earned Run Average		Wins	
B. Madlock, CHI	.354	D. Parker, PIT	.541	M. Schmidt, PHI	38	T. Seaver, NY	.710	R. Jones, SD	2.24	T. Seaver, NY	22
T. Simmons, STL	.332	G. Luzinski, PHI	.540	D. Kingman, NY	36	B. Hooton, CHI, LA	.667	Messersmith, LA	2.29	R. Jones, SD	20
Sanguillen, PIT	.328	M. Schmidt, PHI	.523	G. Luzinski, PHI	34	R. Jones, SD	.625	T. Seaver, NY	2.38	Messersmith, LA	19
J. Morgan, CIN	.327	J. Bench, CIN	.519	J. Bench, CIN	28	G. Nolan, CIN	.625	J. Reuss, PIT	2.54	B. Hooton, CHI, LA	18
B. Watson, HOU	.324	G. Foster, CIN	.518	D. Parker, PIT	25	Montefusco, SF	.625	B. Forsch, STL	2.86	J. Reuss, PIT	18
				R. Cey, LA	25	D. Rau, LA	.625				

Total Bases		Runs Batted In		Stolen Bases		Saves		Strikeouts		Complete Games	
G. Luzinski, PHI	322	G. Luzinski, PHI	120	D. Lopes, LA	77	A. Hrabosky, STL	22	T. Seaver, NY	243	Messersmith, LA	19
S. Garvey, LA	314	J. Bench, CIN	110	J. Morgan, CIN	67	R. Eastwick, CIN	22	Montefusco, SF	215	R. Jones, SD	18
D. Parker, PIT	302	T. Perez, CIN	109	L. Brock, STL	56	D. Giusti, PIT	17	Messersmith, LA	213	J. Reuss, PIT	15
M. Schmidt, PHI	294	R. Staub, NY	105	C. Cedeno, HOU	50	D. Knowles, CHI	15	S. Carlton, PHI	192	T. Seaver, NY	15
P. Rose, CIN	286			J. Cardenal, CHI	34	W. McEnaney, CIN	15	J. Richard, HOU	176	L. Dierker, HOU	14
										S. Carlton, PHI	14

Hits		Base on Balls		Home Run Percentage		Fewest Hits/9 Innings		Shutouts		Fewest Walks/9 Innings	
D. Cash, PHI	213	J. Morgan, CIN	132	D. Kingman, NY	7.2	Messersmith, LA	6.82	Messersmith, LA	7	G. Nolan, CIN	1.24
S. Garvey, LA	210	J. Wynn, LA	110	M. Schmidt, PHI	6.8	D. Warthen, MON	6.96	J. Reuss, PIT	6	R. Jones, SD	1.77
P. Rose, CIN	210	D. Evans, ATL	105	G. Luzinski, PHI	5.7	T. Seaver, NY	6.98	R. Jones, SD	6	R. Reed, ATL, STL	1.90
T. Simmons, STL	193	M. Schmidt, PHI	101	J. Bench, CIN	5.3	D. Sutton, LA	7.16	T. Seaver, NY	5	D. Rau, LA	2.13

Runs Scored		Doubles		Triples		Most Strikeouts/9 Inn.		Innings		Games Pitched	
P. Rose, CIN	112	P. Rose, CIN	47	R. Garr, ATL	11	Montefusco, SF	7.93	Messersmith, LA	322	G. Garber, PHI	71
D. Cash, PHI	111	D. Cash, PHI	40	G. Gross, HOU	10	T. Seaver, NY	7.81	R. Jones, SD	285	W. McEnaney, CIN	70
D. Lopes, LA	108	J. Bench, CIN	39	V. Joshua, SF	10	D. Warthen, MON	6.86	T. Seaver, NY	280	P. Borbon, CIN	67
J. Morgan, CIN	107	A. Oliver, PIT	39	D. Parker, PIT	10	S. Carlton, PHI	6.78	C. Morton, ATL	278	D. Tomlin, SD	67

PITCHING LEADERS

			W	L	PCT	GB	R	OR	2B	3B	HR	BA	SA	SB	E	DP	FA	CG	BB	SO	ShO	SV	ERA
East	Pittsburgh		92	69	.571		712	565	255	47	138	.263	.402	49	151	147	.976	43	551	768	14	31	3.02
	Philadelphia		86	76	.531	6.5	735	694	283	42	125	.269	.402	126	152	156	.976	33	546	897	11	30	3.82
	New York		82	80	.506	10.5	646	625	217	34	101	.256	.361	32	151	144	.976	40	568	989	14	31	3.39
	St. Louis		82	80	.506	10.5	662	689	239	46	81	.273	.375	116	171	140	.973	33	571	824	13	36	3.58
	Chicago		75	87	.463	17.5	712	827	229	41	95	.259	.368	67	179	152	.972	27	551	850	8	33	4.57
	Montreal		75	87	.463	17.5	601	690	216	31	98	.244	.348	108	180	179	.973	30	665	831	12	25	3.73
West	Cincinnati		108	54	.667		840	586	278	37	124	.271	.401	168	102	173	.984	22	487	663	8	50	3.37
	Los Angeles		88	74	.543	20	668	534	217	31	118	.248	.365	138	127	106	.979	51	448	894	18	21	2.92
	San Francisco		80	81	.497	27.5	659	671	235	45	84	.259	.365	99	146	164	.976	37	612	856	9	24	3.74
	San Diego		71	91	.438	37	552	683	215	22	78	.244	.335	85	188	163	.971	40	521	713	12	20	3.51
	Atlanta		67	94	.416	40.5	583	739	179	28	107	.244	.346	55	175	147	.972	32	519	669	4	25	3.93
	Houston		64	97	.398	43.5	664	711	218	54	84	.254	.359	133	137	166	.979	39	679	839	6	25	4.05
							8014	8014	2781	458	1233	.257	.369	1176	1859	1837	.976	427	6730	9793	129	351	3.63

AMERICAN LEAGUE 1975

		POS	Player	AB	BA	HR	RBI	PO	A	E	DP	TC/G	FA	Pitcher	G	IP	W	L	SV	ERA
East	**Boston**	1B	Yastrzemski	543	.269	14	60	1202	87	5	103	9.2	.996	B. Lee	41	260	17	9	0	3.95
		2B	D. Doyle	310	.310	4	36	141	193	9	35	4.1	.974	L. Tiant	35	260	18	14	0	4.02
	W-95 L-65	SS	R. Burleson	580	.252	6	62	267	498	29	102	5.0	.963	R. Wise	35	255	19	12	0	3.95
		3B	Petrocelli	402	.239	7	59	85	229	13	13	2.9	.960	R. Cleveland	31	171	13	9	0	4.42
	Darrell Johnson	RF	D. Evans	412	.274	13	56	281	15	4	8	2.6	.987	R. Moret	36	145	14	3	1	3.60
		CF	F. Lynn	528	.331	21	105	404	11	7	1	2.9	.983	D. Pole	18	90	4	6	0	4.40
		LF	J. Rice	564	.309	22	102	162	6	0	0	1.9	1.000	D. Drago	40	73	2	2	15	3.82
		C	C. Fisk	263	.331	10	52	347	30	8	2	5.4	.979	D. Segui	33	71	2	5	6	4.82
		DH	C. Cooper	305	.311	14	44							Willoughby	24	48	5	2	8	3.56
		OF	B. Carbo	319	.257	15	50	157	7	4	1	2.0	.976							
		2B	D. Griffin	287	.240	1	29	195	215	14	45	4.3	.967							
		UT	J. Beniquez	254	.291	2	17	110	17	1	2		.992							
		C	Montgomery	195	.226	2	26	210	23	3	6	4.5	.987							
		3B	B. Heise	126	.214	0	21	36	90	8	7	3.0	.940							
	Baltimore	1B	L. May	580	.262	20	99	1312	106	10	138	9.9	.993	J. Palmer	39	323	23	11	1	2.09
		2B	B. Grich	524	.260	13	57	423	484	21	122	6.2	.977	M. Torrez	36	271	20	9	0	3.06
	W-90 L-69	SS	M. Belanger	442	.226	3	27	259	508	17	105	5.2	.978	M. Cuellar	36	256	14	12	0	3.66
		3B	B. Robinson	482	.201	6	53	96	326	9	30	3.0	.979	R. Grimsley	35	197	10	13	0	4.07
	Earl Weaver	RF	K. Singleton	586	.300	15	55	283	9	3	2	1.9	.990	D. Alexander	32	133	8	8	1	3.05
		CF	P. Blair	440	.218	5	31	327	8	3	1	2.4	.991	W. Garland	29	87	2	5	4	3.72
		LF	D. Baylor	524	.282	25	76	268	8	5	0	2.1	.982	G. Jackson	41	48	4	3	7	3.38
		C	D. Duncan	307	.205	12	41	397	41	8	5	4.7	.982	D. Miller	30	46	6	3	8	2.74
		DH	T. Davis	460	.283	6	57													
		DO	A. Bumbry	349	.269	2	32	70	2	0	1	1.8	1.000							
		C	E. Hendricks	223	.215	8	38	332	36	2	3	4.5	.995							
		OF	J. Northrup	194	.273	5	29	91	2	2	0	1.6	.979							
		UT	D. DeCinces	167	.251	4	23	92	115	7	20		.967							

AMERICAN LEAGUE 1975, *cont.*

	POS	Player	AB	BA	HR	RBI	PO	A	E	DP	TC/G	FA	Pitcher	G	IP	W	L	SV	ERA
New York	1B	C. Chambliss	562	.304	9	72	1222	106	12	113	9.1	.991	C. Hunter	39	**328**	**23**	14	0	2.58
	2B	S. Alomar	489	.239	2	39	340	368	11	93	4.8	**.985**	D. Medich	38	272	16	16	0	3.50
W-83 L-77	SS	J. Mason	223	.152	2	16	134	209	16	45	3.9	.955	R. May	32	212	14	12	0	3.06
	3B	G. Nettles	581	.267	21	91	135	**379**	19	31	3.4	.964	P. Dobson	33	208	11	14	0	4.07
Bill Virdon	RF	B. Bonds	529	.270	32	85	287	12	4	6	2.3	.987	L. Gura	26	151	7	8	0	3.51
W-53 L-51	CF	E. Maddox	218	.307	1	23	157	5	0	3	2.9	1.000	S. Lyle	49	89	5	7	6	3.12
	LF	R. White	556	.290	12	59	303	11	5	0	2.4	.984	D. Tidrow	37	69	6	3	5	3.13
Billy Martin	C	T. Munson	597	.318	12	102	700	95	**23**	14	**6.3**	.972	T. Martinez	23	37	1	2	8	2.68
W-30 L-26	DH	E. Herrmann	200	.255	6	30													
	SS	F. Stanley	252	.222	0	15	105	189	7	36	3.6	.977							
	OF	L. Piniella	199	.196	0	22	65	5	1	0	1.5	.986							
	UT	W. Williams	185	.281	5	16	57	4	1	0		.984							
Cleveland	1B	B. Powell	435	.297	27	86	997	69	3	92	8.8	**.997**	D. Eckersley	34	187	13	7	2	2.60
	2B	D. Kuiper	346	.292	0	25	192	230	12	65	5.0	.972	F. Peterson	25	146	14	8	0	3.94
W-79 L-80	SS	F. Duffy	482	.243	1	47	225	464	16	85	4.9	.977	D. Hood	29	135	6	10	0	4.39
	3B	B. Bell	553	.271	10	59	**146**	330	25	29	3.3	.950	R. Harrison	19	126	7	7	0	4.79
Frank Robinson	RF	G. Hendrick	561	.258	24	86	338	4	6	1	2.4	.983	G. Perry	15	122	6	9	0	3.55
	CF	R. Manning	480	.285	3	35	331	12	9	2	3.0	.974	J. Bibby	24	113	5	9	1	3.20
	LF	C. Spikes	345	.229	11	33	176	13	5	5	1.9	.974	E. Raich	18	93	7	8	0	5.54
	C	A. Ashby	254	.224	5	32	441	43	5	6	5.6	.990	D. LaRoche	61	82	5	3	17	2.19
	DH	R. Carty	383	.308	18	64							T. Buskey	50	77	5	3	7	2.57
	C	J. Ellis	296	.230	7	32	396	44	11	3	5.4	.976							
	UT	Lowenstein	265	.242	12	33	61	16	2	1		.975							
	2B	J. Brohamer	217	.244	6	16	166	162	8	52	5.1	.976							
	DH	F. Robinson	118	.237	9	24													
Milwaukee	1B	G. Scott	617	.285	**36**	109	1202	**109**	14	118	9.2	.989	P. Broberg	38	220	14	16	0	4.13
	2B	P. Garcia	302	.225	6	38	230	293	8	67	5.6	.985	J. Slaton	37	217	11	18	0	4.52
W-68 L-94	SS	R. Yount	558	.267	8	52	273	402	**44**	80	5.0	.939	J. Colborn	36	206	11	13	2	4.27
	3B	D. Money	405	.277	15	43	95	179	14	22	2.9	.951	B. Travers	28	136	6	11	0	4.29
Del Crandall	RF	G. Thomas	240	.179	10	28	215	5	9	1	2.0	.961	T. Hausman	29	112	3	6	0	4.10
W-67 L-94	CF	S. Lezcano	429	.247	11	43	240	10	6	1	2.0	.977	B. Champion	27	110	6	6	0	5.89
	LF	B. Sharp	373	.255	1	34	294	12	2	4	2.5	.994	E. Rodriguez	43	88	7	0	7	3.49
Harvey Kuenn	C	D. Porter	409	.232	18	60	532	82	13	10	5.1	.979	T. Murphy	52	72	1	9	20	4.48
W-1 L-0	DH	H. Aaron	465	.234	12	60													
	32	K. Bevacqua	258	.229	2	24	145	159	12	32		.962							
	CO	C. Moore	241	.290	1	29	234	23	10	2		.963							
	OF	B. Mitchell	229	.249	9	41	128	2	1	1	1.8	.992							
	O1	M. Hegan	203	.251	5	22	241	21	2	19		.992							
	OF	B. Darwin	186	.247	8	23	82	5	2	1	2.1	.978							
	2B	B. Sheldon	181	.287	0	14	87	122	5	33	4.9	.977							
Detroit	1B	D. Meyer	470	.236	8	47	441	37	5	39	10.5	.990	M. Lolich	32	241	12	18	0	3.78
	2B	Sutherland	503	.258	6	39	278	365	21	83	5.2	.968	J. Coleman	31	201	10	18	0	5.55
W-57 L-102	SS	T. Veryzer	404	.252	5	48	215	358	24	62	4.7	.960	V. Ruhle	32	190	11	12	0	4.03
	3B	A. Rodriguez	507	.245	13	60	136	375	25	33	**3.5**	.953	L. LaGrow	32	164	7	14	0	4.38
Ralph Houk	RF	L. Roberts	447	.257	10	38	268	10	5	2	2.2	.982	R. Bare	29	151	8	13	0	4.48
	CF	R. LeFlore	550	.258	8	37	317	13	9	3	2.5	.973	T. Walker	36	115	3	8	0	4.45
	LF	B. Oglivie	332	.286	9	36	192	4	5	1	2.3	.975	D. Lemanczyk	26	109	2	7	0	4.46
	C	B. Freehan	427	.246	14	47	582	64	6	8	5.8	.991	J. Hiller	36	71	2	3	14	2.17
	DH	W. Horton	615	.275	25	92													
	1B	J. Pierce	170	.235	8	22	407	26	13	38	9.1	.971							
	UT	M. Stanley	164	.256	3	19	183	22	2	9		.990							

West

	POS	Player	AB	BA	HR	RBI	PO	A	E	DP	TC/G	FA	Pitcher	G	IP	W	L	SV	ERA
Oakland	1B	J. Rudi	468	.278	21	75	732	36	7	64	8.5	.991	V. Blue	39	278	22	11	1	3.01
	2B	P. Garner	488	.246	6	54	354	426	**26**	93	5.0	.968	K. Holtzman	39	266	18	14	0	3.14
W-98 L-64	SS	Campaneris	509	.265	4	46	199	378	23	58	4.4	.962	R. Fingers	**75**	127	10	6	24	2.98
	3B	S. Bando	562	.230	15	78	122	314	15	**36**	2.8	.967	J. Todd	58	122	8	3	12	2.29
Alvin Dark	RF	R. Jackson	593	.253	**36**	104	315	13	**12**	5	2.3	.965	P. Lindblad	68	122	9	1	7	2.72
	CF	B. North	524	.273	1	43	**420**	10	-11	1	3.2	.975	D. Bosman	22	123	11	4	0	3.52
	LF	Washington	590	.308	10	77	305	8	7	1	2.2	.978	G. Abbott	30	114	5	5	0	4.25
	C	G. Tenace	498	.255	29	87	541	63	10	10	4.9	.984	S. Bahnsen	21	100	6	7	0	3.24
	DH	B. Williams	520	.244	23	81													
Kansas City	1B	J. Mayberry	554	.291	34	106	1199	100	**16**	105	**10.0**	.988	S. Busby	34	260	18	12	0	3.08
	2B	C. Rojas	406	.254	2	37	233	303	11	65	4.7	.980	Fitzmorris	35	242	16	12	0	3.57
W-91 L-71	SS	F. Patek	483	.228	5	45	231	405	27	78	4.9	.959	D. Leonard	32	212	15	7	0	3.77
	3B	G. Brett	**634**	.308	11	89	131	355	**26**	27	3.2	.949	M. Pattin	44	177	10	10	5	3.25
Jack McKeon	RF	A. Cowens	328	.277	4	42	214	4	5	2	2.0	.978	Splittorff	35	159	9	10	1	3.17
W-50 L-46	CF	A. Otis	470	.247	9	46	310	9	4	3	2.5	.988	N. Briles	24	112	6	6	2	4.26
	LF	H. McRae	480	.306	5	71	207	7	3	2	1.9	.986	D. Bird	51	105	9	6	11	3.25
Whitey Herzog	C	B. Martinez	226	.226	3	23	361	39	8	4	5.2	.980							
W-41 L-25	DH	H. Killebrew	312	.199	14	44													
	OF	J. Wohlford	353	.255	0	30	175	9	9	1	1.9	.953							
	OF	V. Pinson	319	.223	4	22	144	6	1	0	1.8	.993							
	2S	F. White	304	.250	7	36	179	265	11	55		.976							
	D1	T. Solaita	231	.260	16	44	282	28	2	24	8.9	.994							
	C	F. Healy	188	.255	2	18	258	17	5	2	5.5	.982							

AMERICAN LEAGUE 1975, cont.

	POS	Player	AB	BA	HR	RBI	PO	A	E	DP	TC/G	FA	Pitcher	G	IP	W	L	SV	ERA
Texas W-79 L-83 Billy Martin W-44 L-51 Frank Lucchesi W-35 L-32	1B	J. Spencer	403	.266	11	47	844	70	5	92	9.3	.995	F. Jenkins	37	270	17	18	0	3.93
	2B	L. Randle	601	.276	4	57	205	232	12	61	5.7	.973	S. Hargan	33	189	9	10	0	3.80
	SS	T. Harrah	522	.293	20	93	198	375	22	68	5.0	.963	G. Perry	22	184	12	8	0	3.03
	3B	R. Howell	383	.251	10	51	80	214	21	32	2.7	.933	J. Umbarger	56	131	8	7	2	4.12
	RF	J. Burroughs	585	.226	29	94	249	10	9	2	1.8	.966	B. Hands	18	110	6	7	0	4.02
	CF	W. Davis	169	.249	5	17	100	1	1	1	2.4	.990	S. Foucault	59	107	8	4	10	4.12
	LF	M. Hargrove	519	.303	11	62	187	2	7	0	2.0	.964	C. Wright	25	93	4	6	0	4.44
	C	J. Sundberg	472	.199	6	36	791	101	17	11	5.9	.981	S. Thomas	46	81	4	4	3	3.10
	DH	C. Tovar	427	.258	3	28							J. Brown	17	70	5	5	0	4.22
	OD	T. Grieve	369	.276	14	61	93	3	1	0	1.5	.990							
	SS	R. Smalley	250	.228	3	33	80	175	16	30	4.6	.941							
	1B	J. Fregosi	191	.262	7	33	355	34	6	31	7.3	.985							
	OF	D. Moates	175	.274	3	14	114	6	2	1	2.4	.984							
	2B	M. Cubbage	143	.224	4	21	67	111	7	24	5.0	.962							
Minnesota W-76 L-83 Frank Quilici	1B	C. Kusick	156	.237	6	27	372	31	4	45	8.0	.990	B. Blyleven	35	276	15	10	0	3.00
	2B	R. Carew	535	**.359**	14	80	285	369	18	79	5.5	.973	J. Hughes	37	250	16	14	0	3.82
	SS	D. Thompson	355	.270	5	37	138	245	24	40	4.1	.941	D. Goltz	32	243	14	14	0	3.67
	3B	E. Soderholm	419	.286	11	58	94	277	12	14	3.4	.969	V. Albury	32	135	6	7	1	4.53
	RF	L. Bostock	369	.282	0	29	188	3	3	0	2.1	.985	B. Campbell	47	121	4	6	5	3.79
	CF	D. Ford	440	.280	15	59	246	3	3	2	1.8	.988	R. Corbin	18	90	5	7	0	5.12
	LF	S. Braun	453	.302	11	45	195	6	6	1	2.0	.971	T. Burgmeier	46	76	5	8	11	3.09
	C	G. Borgmann	352	.207	2	33	618	81	8	6	5.7	.989							
	DH	T. Oliva	455	.270	13	58													
	UT	J. Terrell	385	.286	1	36	267	232	14	60		.973							
	1O	J. Briggs	264	.231	7	39	483	55	8	38		.985							
	OF	L. Hisle	255	.314	11	51	118	2	3	0	2.1	.976							
	OF	S. Brye	246	.252	9	34	112	7	2	0	1.7	.983							
	OD	B. Darwin	169	.219	5	18	28	3	1	0	1.2	.969							
	C	P. Roof	126	.302	7	21	245	30	3	4	4.4	.989							
Chicago W-75 L-86 Chuck Tanner	1B	C. May	454	.271	8	53	508	46	6	54	8.9	.989	J. Kaat	43	304	20	14	0	3.11
	2B	J. Orta	542	.304	11	83	354	354	16	95	5.4	.978	W. Wood	43	291	16	**20**	0	4.11
	SS	B. Dent	602	.264	3	58	**279**	**543**	16	**105**	5.3	**.981**	C. Osteen	37	204	7	16	0	4.32
	3B	B. Melton	512	.240	15	70	131	313	26	23	3.4	.945	G. Gossage	62	142	9	8	26	1.84
	RF	P. Kelly	471	.274	9	45	222	4	2	1	2.0	**.991**	J. Jefferson	22	108	5	9	0	5.10
	CF	N. Nyman	327	.226	2	28	177	6	8	0	2.0	.958	D. Hamilton	30	70	6	5	6	2.84
	LF	K. Henderson	513	.251	9	53	394	7	4	0	3.0	.990	S. Bahnsen	12	67	4	6	0	6.01
	C	B. Downing	420	.240	7	41	730	84	8	5	6.0	.990	T. Forster	17	37	3	3	4	2.19
	DH	D. Johnson	555	.232	18	72													
	UT	B. Stein	226	.270	3	21	87	118	9	21		.958							
	OF	J. Hairston	219	.283	0	23	111	6	6	1	2.1	.951							
California W-72 L-89 Dick Williams	1B	B. Bochte	375	.285	3	48	850	51	12	90	8.7	.987	F. Tanana	34	257	16	9	0	2.62
	2B	J. Remy	569	.258	1	46	336	427	14	111	5.3	.982	E. Figueroa	33	245	16	13	0	2.91
	SS	M. Miley	224	.174	4	26	107	186	19	53	4.5	.939	N. Ryan	28	198	14	12	0	3.45
	3B	D. Chalk	513	.273	3	56	108	333	11	30	3.0	.976	B. Singer	29	179	7	15	1	4.98
	RF	L. Stanton	440	.261	14	82	230	**16**	10	2	2.0	.961	A. Hassler	30	133	3	12	0	5.94
	CF	M. Rivers	616	.284	1	53	371	13	9	3	2.6	.977	D. Lange	30	102	4	6	1	5.21
	LF	D. Collins	319	.266	3	29	159	3	2	2	2.2	.988	D. Kirkwood	44	84	6	5	7	3.11
	C	E. Rodriguez	226	.235	3	27	492	33	5	2	5.9	.991							
	DH	T. Harper	285	.239	3	31													
	DO	J. Lahoud	192	.214	6	33	41	1	0	0	1.4	1.000							

BATTING AND BASE RUNNING LEADERS

Batting Average
R. Carew, MIN .359
F. Lynn, BOS .331
T. Munson, NY .318
J. Rice, BOS .309
Washington, OAK .308

Slugging Average
F. Lynn, BOS .566
J. Mayberry, KC .547
G. Scott, MIL .515
B. Bonds, NY .512
R. Jackson, OAK .511

Home Runs
R. Jackson, OAK 36
G. Scott, MIL 36
J. Mayberry, KC 34
B. Bonds, NY 32
G. Tenace, OAK 29
J. Burroughs, TEX 29

Total Bases
G. Scott, MIL 318
J. Mayberry, KC 303
R. Jackson, OAK 303
F. Lynn, BOS 299
G. Brett, KC 289

Runs Batted In
G. Scott, MIL 109
J. Mayberry, KC 106
F. Lynn, BOS 105
R. Jackson, OAK 104
J. Rice, BOS 102
T. Munson, NY 102

Stolen Bases
M. Rivers, CAL 70
Washington, OAK 40
A. Otis, KC 39
R. Carew, MIN 35
J. Remy, CAL 34

Hits
G. Brett, KC 195
R. Carew, MIN 192
T. Munson, NY 190
Washington, OAK 182

Base on Balls
J. Mayberry, KC 119
K. Singleton, BAL 118
B. Grich, BAL 107
G. Tenace, OAK 106

Home Run Percentage
J. Mayberry, KC 6.1
R. Jackson, OAK 6.1
B. Bonds, NY 6.0
G. Scott, MIL 5.8

PITCHING LEADERS

Winning Percentage
M. Torrez, BAL .690
D. Leonard, KC .682
J. Palmer, BAL .676
V. Blue, OAK .667
B. Lee, BOS .654

Earned Run Average
J. Palmer, BAL 2.09
C. Hunter, NY 2.58
D. Eckersley, CLE 2.60
F. Tanana, CAL 2.62
E. Figueroa, CAL 2.91

Wins
J. Palmer, BAL 23
C. Hunter, NY 23
V. Blue, OAK 22
M. Torrez, BAL 20
J. Kaat, CHI 20

Saves
G. Gossage, CHI 26
R. Fingers, OAK 24
T. Murphy, MIL 20
D. LaRoche, CLE 17
D. Drago, BOS 15

Strikeouts
F. Tanana, CAL 269
B. Blyleven, MIN 233
G. Perry, CLE, TEX 233
J. Palmer, BAL 193
V. Blue, OAK 189

Complete Games
C. Hunter, NY 30
G. Perry, CLE, TEX 25
J. Palmer, BAL 25
F. Jenkins, TEX 22
B. Blyleven, MIN 20

Fewest Hits/9 Innings
C. Hunter, NY 6.80
N. Ryan, CAL 6.91
J. Palmer, BAL 7.05
D. Eckersley, CLE 7.09

Shutouts
J. Palmer, BAL 10
C. Hunter, NY 7
N. Ryan, CAL 5
F. Tanana, CAL 5

Fewest Walks/9 Innings
F. Jenkins, TEX 1.87
G. Perry, CLE, TEX 2.06
R. Grimsley, BAL 2.15
J. Palmer, BAL 2.23

AMERICAN LEAGUE 1975, *cont.*

BATTING AND BASE RUNNING LEADERS

Runs Scored
F. Lynn, BOS 103
J. Mayberry, KC 95
B. Bonds, NY 93
J. Rice, BOS 92

Doubles
F. Lynn, BOS 47
R. Jackson, OAK 39
H. McRae, KC 38
J. Mayberry, KC 38

Triples
M. Rivers, CAL 13
G. Brett, KC 13
J. Orta, CHI 10
A. Cowens, KC 8

PITCHING LEADERS

Most Strikeouts/9 Inn.
F. Tanana, CAL 9.41
N. Ryan, CAL 8.45
B. Blyleven, MIN 7.61
D. Eckersley, CLE 7.33

Innings
C. Hunter, NY 328
J. Palmer, BAL 323
G. Perry, CLE, TEX 306
J. Kaat, CHI 304

Games Pitched
R. Fingers, OAK 75
P. Lindblad, OAK 68
G. Gossage, CHI 62
D. LaRoche, CLE 61

		W	L	PCT	GB	R	OR	2B	3B	HR	BA	SA	SB	E	DP	FA	CG	BB	SO	ShO	SV	ERA
East	Boston	95	65	.594		796	709	284	44	134	.275	.417	66	139	142	.977	62	490	720	11	31	3.99
	Baltimore	90	69	.566	4.5	682	553	224	33	124	.252	.373	104	107	175	.983	70	500	717	19	21	3.17
	New York	83	77	.519	12	681	588	230	39	110	.264	.382	102	135	148	.978	70	502	809	11	20	3.29
	Cleveland	79	80	.497	15.5	688	703	201	25	153	.261	.392	106	134	156	.978	37	599	800	6	32	3.84
	Milwaukee	68	94	.420	28	675	793	242	34	146	.250	.389	65	180	162	.971	36	624	643	10	34	4.34
	Detroit	57	102	.358	37.5	570	786	171	39	125	.249	.366	63	173	141	.972	52	533	787	10	17	4.29
West	Oakland	98	64	.605		758	606	220	33	151	.254	.391	183	143	140	.977	36	523	784	10	44	3.29
	Kansas City	91	71	.562	7	710	649	263	58	118	.261	.394	155	154	151	.976	52	498	815	11	25	3.49
	Texas	79	83	.488	19	714	733	208	17	134	.256	.371	102	191	173	.971	60	518	792	16	17	3.90
	Minnesota	76	83	.478	20.5	724	736	215	28	121	.271	.386	81	170	147	.973	57	617	846	7	22	4.05
	Chicago	75	86	.466	22.5	655	707	209	38	94	.255	.358	101	140	155	.978	34	655	799	7	39	3.93
	California	72	89	.447	25.5	628	723	195	41	55	.246	.328	220	184	164	.971	59	613	975	19	16	3.89
						8281	8286	2662	429	1465	.258	.379	1348	1850	1854	.975	625	6672	9487	137	318	3.79

NATIONAL LEAGUE 1976

		POS	Player	AB	BA	HR	RBI	PO	A	E	DP	TC/G	FA	Pitcher	G	IP	W	L	SV	ERA
East	**Philadelphia**	1B	D. Allen	298	.268	15	49	671	44	8	71	8.5	.989	S. Carlton	35	253	20	7	0	3.13
		2B	D. Cash	666	.284	1	56	407	424	10	118	5.3	.988	J. Kaat	38	228	12	14	0	3.48
	W-101 L-61	SS	L. Bowa	624	.248	0	49	180	492	17	90	4.4	.975	J. Lonborg	33	222	18	10	1	3.08
		3B	M. Schmidt	584	.262	38	107	139	377	21	29	3.4	.961	Christenson	32	169	13	8	0	3.68
	Danny Ozark	RF	J. Johnstone	440	.318	5	53	266	8	5	1	2.3	.982	T. Underwood	33	156	10	5	2	3.53
		CF	G. Maddox	531	.330	6	68	441	10	5	0	3.2	.989	R. Reed	59	128	8	7	14	2.46
		LF	G. Luzinski	533	.304	21	95	204	8	8	0	1.5	.964	T. McGraw	58	97	7	6	11	2.50
		C	B. Boone	361	.271	4	54	557	36	4	5	5.5	.993	G. Garber	59	93	9	3	11	2.82
		10	B. Tolan	272	.261	5	35	395	14	5	36		.988							
		OF	O. Brown	209	.254	5	30	105	7	6	2	1.6	.949							
		C	T. McCarver	155	.277	3	29	254	9	0	1	6.4	1.000							
	Pittsburgh	1B	W. Stargell	428	.257	20	65	1037	53	13	76	9.9	.988	Candelaria	32	220	16	7	1	3.15
		2B	R. Stennett	654	.257	2	60	430	502	18	111	6.1	.981	J. Reuss	31	209	14	9	2	3.53
	W-92 L-70	SS	F. Taveras	519	.258	0	24	210	481	35	41	5.1	.952	J. Rooker	30	199	15	8	1	3.35
		3B	R. Hebner	434	.249	8	51	87	236	16	16	2.7	.953	B. Kison	31	193	14	9	1	3.08
	Danny Murtaugh	RF	D. Parker	537	.313	13	90	294	12	14	0	2.4	.956	D. Medich	29	179	8	11	0	3.51
		CF	A. Oliver	443	.323	12	61	301	4	5	0	2.9	.984	L. Demery	36	145	10	7	2	3.17
		LF	R. Zisk	581	.289	21	89	300	11	4	2	2.1	.987	K. Tekulve	64	103	5	3	9	2.45
		C	Sanguillen	389	.290	2	36	518	52	13	7	5.3	.978	B. Moose	53	88	3	9	10	3.70
		O3	B. Robinson	393	.303	21	64	164	53	8	7		.964	D. Giusti	40	58	5	4	6	4.32
		C	D. Dyer	184	.223	3	9	279	37	2	4	5.5	.994							
		1B	B. Robertson	129	.217	2	25	257	17	1	28	9.5	.996							
	New York	1B	E. Kranepool	415	.292	10	49	675	33	3	48	8.3	.996	T. Seaver	35	271	14	11	0	2.59
		2B	F. Millan	531	.282	1	35	311	315	15	68	4.7	.977	J. Matlack	35	262	17	10	0	2.95
	W-86 L-76	SS	B. Harrelson	359	.234	1	26	183	330	20	44	4.6	.962	J. Koosman	34	247	21	10	0	2.70
		3B	R. Staiger	304	.220	2	26	55	209	9	18	2.9	.967	M. Lolich	31	193	8	13	0	3.22
	Joe Frazier	RF	J. Milner	443	.271	15	78	195	7	3	2	1.8	.985	C. Swan	23	132	6	9	0	3.55
		CF	D. Unser	276	.228	5	25	180	5	1	0	2.4	.995	S. Lockwood	56	94	10	7	19	2.67
		LF	D. Kingman	474	.238	37	86	202	10	9	0	2.0	.959	B. Apodaca	43	90	3	7	5	2.80
		C	J. Grote	323	.272	4	28	617	49	5	6	7.1	.993							
		1B	J. Torre	310	.306	5	31	590	49	7	40	8.3	.989							
		OF	B. Boisclair	286	.287	2	13	156	3	3	1	1.9	.981							
		UT	M. Phillips	262	.256	4	29	115	191	11	26		.965							
		3B	W. Garrett	251	.223	4	26	47	137	10	12	3.0	.948							
		C	R. Hodges	155	.226	4	24	262	18	7	0	5.5	.976							
	Chicago	1B	P. LaCock	244	.221	8	28	435	30	12	47	8.8	.975	R. Reuschel	38	260	14	12	1	3.46
		2B	M. Trillo	582	.239	4	59	349	527	17	103	5.7	.981	R. Burris	37	249	15	13	0	3.11
	W-75 L-87	SS	M. Kelleher	337	.228	0	22	147	289	9	52	4.4	.980	B. Bonham	32	196	9	13	0	4.27
		3B	B. Madlock	514	.339	15	84	107	234	14	21	2.6	.961	S. Renko	28	163	8	11	0	3.86
	Jim Marshall	RF	J. Morales	537	.274	16	67	273	12	6	6	2.1	.983	B. Sutter	52	83	6	3	10	2.71
		CF	R. Monday	534	.272	32	77	278	4	0	0	2.8	.993	J. Coleman	39	79	2	8	4	4.10
		LF	J. Cardenal	521	.299	8	47	246	10	5	1	2.0	.981	D. Knowles	58	72	5	7	9	2.88
		C	S. Swisher	377	.236	5	42	574	49	11	6	5.9	.983	O. Zamora	40	55	5	3	3	5.24
		OF	J. Wallis	338	.254	5	21	193	11	5	3	2.3	.976							
		C	Mitterwald	303	.215	4	28	320	40	7	2	5.7	.981							
		SS	D. Rosello	227	.242	1	11	128	217	12	45	4.2	.966							
		10	L. Biittner	192	.245	0	17	266	34	4	20		.987							

NATIONAL LEAGUE 1976, cont.

	POS	Player	AB	BA	HR	RBI	PO	A	E	DP	TC/G	FA	Pitcher	G	IP	W	L	SV	ERA
St. Louis	1B	K. Hernandez	374	.289	7	46	862	107	10	87	8.9	.990	P. Falcone	32	212	12	16	0	3.23
	2B	M. Tyson	245	.286	3	28	158	237	12	54	5.5	.971	J. Denny	30	207	11	9	0	2.52
W-72 L-90	SS	D. Kessinger	502	.239	1	40	212	350	18	84	5.1	.969	McGlothen	33	205	13	15	0	3.91
	3B	H. Cruz	526	.228	13	71	100	270	26	19	2.7	.934	B. Forsch	33	194	8	10	0	3.94
Red Schoendienst	RF	W. Crawford	392	.304	9	50	209	6	4	1	2.0	.982	E. Rasmussen	43	150	6	12	0	3.53
	CF	J. Mumphrey	384	.258	1	26	261	6	2	1	2.9	.993	J. Curtis	37	134	6	11	1	4.50
	LF	L. Brock	498	.301	4	67	221	6	4	0	1.9	.983	A. Hrabosky	68	95	8	6	13	3.30
	C	T. Simmons	546	.291	5	75	493	66	4	4	5.0	.993	B. Greif	47	55	1	5	6	4.12
	OF	B. McBride	272	.335	3	24	201	5	4	0	3.2	.981							
	UT	V. Harris	259	.228	1	19	173	103	14	21		.952							
	SS	G. Templeton	213	.291	1	17	111	172	24	41	5.8	.922							
	OF	M. Anderson	199	.291	1	12	106	5	2	1	1.9	.982							
	C	J. Ferguson	189	.201	4	21	238	32	6	6	5.8	.978							
	UT	R. Smith	170	.218	8	23	184	44	2	18		.991							
	1B	R. Fairly	110	.264	0	21	174	21	1	19	7.3	.995							
Montreal	1B	M. Jorgensen	343	.254	6	23	599	57	7	59	8.2	.989	S. Rogers	33	230	7	17	1	3.21
	2B	P. Mackanin	380	.224	8	33	201	289	18	60	5.1	.965	W. Fryman	34	216	13	13	2	3.37
W-55 L-107	SS	T. Foli	546	.264	6	54	247	469	18	102	5.0	.975	D. Stanhouse	34	184	9	12	1	3.77
	3B	L. Parrish	543	.232	11	61	122	310	25	35	3.0	.945	Carrithers	34	140	6	12	0	4.43
Karl Kuehl	RF	E. Valentine	305	.279	7	39	162	12	5	4	2.0	.972	D. Murray	81	113	4	9	13	3.26
W-43 L-85	CF	P. Mangual	215	.260	3	16	146	3	5	1	2.5	.968	D. Warthen	23	90	2	10	0	5.30
	LF	J. White	278	.245	2	21	157	4	3	0	1.8	.982							
Charlie Fox	C	B. Foote	350	.234	7	27	476	59	6	13	5.6	.989							
W-12 L-22	CO	G. Carter	311	.219	6	38	364	42	2	8		.995							
	OF	D. Unser	220	.227	7	15	108	5	2	2	1.8	.983							
	1B	E. Williams	190	.237	8	29	377	41	8	37	9.1	.981							
	OF	B. Rivera	185	.276	2	19	89	7	5	3	1.8	.950							
	1B	A. Thornton	183	.191	9	24	326	26	2	43	8.2	.994							
	2B	W. Garrett	177	.243	2	11	121	157	5	32	5.2	.982							
	1C	J. Morales	158	.316	4	37	137	21	3	9		.981							
West **Cincinnati**	1B	T. Perez	527	.260	19	91	1158	73	5	110	9.1	.996	G. Nolan	34	239	15	9	0	3.46
	2B	J. Morgan	472	.320	27	111	342	335	13	85	5.2	.981	P. Zachry	38	204	14	7	0	2.74
W-102 L-60	SS	Concepcion	576	.281	9	69	304	506	27	93	5.6	.968	F. Norman	33	180	12	7	0	3.10
	3B	P. Rose	665	.323	10	63	115	293	13	25	2.6	.969	Billingham	34	177	12	10	1	4.32
Sparky Anderson	RF	K. Griffey	562	.336	6	74	270	10	6	2	2.0	.979	S. Alcala	30	132	11	4	0	4.70
	CF	C. Geronimo	486	.307	2	49	386	4	6	2	2.7	.985	D. Gullett	23	126	11	3	1	3.00
	LF	G. Foster	562	.306	29	121	322	9	2	3	2.3	.994	P. Borbon	69	121	4	3	8	3.35
	C	J. Bench	465	.234	16	74	651	60	2	11	5.6	.997	R. Eastwick	71	108	11	5	26	2.08
	1O	D. Driessen	219	.247	7	44	314	23	2	33		.994	W. McEnaney	55	72	2	6	7	4.88
	UT	D. Flynn	219	.283	1	20	107	152	4	33		.985							
	OF	M. Lum	136	.228	3	20	48	0	0	0	1.3	1.000							
	OF	B. Bailey	124	.298	6	23	35	2	1	1	1.2	.974							
Los Angeles	1B	S. Garvey	631	.317	13	80	1583	67	3	138	10.2	.998	D. Sutton	35	268	21	10	0	3.06
	2B	D. Lopes	427	.241	4	20	218	266	18	56	5.0	.964	D. Rau	34	231	16	12	0	2.57
W-92 L-70	SS	B. Russell	554	.274	5	65	251	476	28	90	5.1	.963	B. Hooton	33	227	11	15	0	3.26
	3B	R. Cey	502	.277	23	80	111	334	16	22	3.2	.965	T. John	31	207	10	10	0	3.09
Walter Alston	RF	R. Smith	225	.280	10	26	130	3	2	2	2.3	.985	R. Rhoden	27	181	12	3	0	2.98
W-90 L-68	CF	D. Baker	384	.242	4	39	254	3	1	1	2.4	.996	C. Hough	77	143	12	8	18	2.21
	LF	B. Buckner	642	.301	7	60	315	7	5	0	2.1	.985	M. Marshall	30	63	4	3	8	4.45
Tom Lasorda	C	S. Yeager	359	.214	11	35	522	77	9	9	5.3	.985							
W-2 L-2	2B	T. Sizemore	266	.241	0	18	168	191	5	51	5.1	.986							
	OC	J. Ferguson	185	.222	6	18	156	12	6	2		.966							
Houston	1B	B. Watson	585	.313	16	102	1395	96	15	126	9.7	.990	J. Richard	39	291	20	15	0	2.75
	2B	R. Andrews	410	.256	0	23	228	354	14	66	5.6	.977	L. Dierker	28	188	13	14	0	3.69
W-80 L-82	SS	R. Metzger	481	.210	0	29	253	462	10	93	4.8	.986	J. Andujar	28	172	9	10	0	3.61
	3B	E. Cabell	586	.273	2	43	128	263	17	24	2.9	.958	J. Niekro	36	118	4	8	0	3.36
Bill Virdon	RF	J. Cruz	439	.303	4	61	265	10	8	4	2.3	.972	D. Larson	13	92	5	8	0	3.03
	CF	C. Cedeno	575	.297	18	83	377	11	8	5	2.7	.980	K. Forsch	52	92	4	3	19	2.15
	LF	G. Gross	426	.286	0	27	208	13	5	4	2.0	.978	McLaughlin	17	79	4	5	1	2.85
	C	E. Herrmann	265	.204	3	25	412	37	6	5	5.8	.987	G. Pentz	40	64	3	3	5	2.95
	UT	C. Johnson	318	.226	10	49	468	35	9	10		.982							
	OF	L. Roberts	235	.289	7	33	99	1	2	0	1.7	.980							
	OF	W. Howard	191	.220	1	18	96	2	4	1	1.6	.961							
	UT	J. DaVanon	107	.290	1	20	53	94	7	16		.955							
San Francisco	1B	D. Evans	257	.222	10	36	681	68	7	53	9.1	.991	Montefusco	37	253	16	14	0	2.84
	2B	M. Perez	332	.259	2	26	189	273	10	51	5.3	.979	J. Barr	37	252	15	12	0	2.89
W-74 L-88	SS	C. Speier	495	.226	3	40	225	441	18	81	5.1	.974	E. Halicki	32	186	12	14	0	3.62
	3B	K. Reitz	577	.267	5	66	140	303	19	32	3.0	.959	G. Lavelle	65	110	10	6	12	2.69
Bill Rigney	RF	B. Murcer	533	.259	23	90	282	11	12	2	2.1	.961	R. Dressler	25	108	3	10	0	4.43
	CF	L. Herndon	337	.288	2	23	226	8	8	4	2.2	.967	M. Caldwell	50	107	1	7	4	4.86
	LF	G. Matthews	587	.279	20	84	265	8	7	0	1.8	.975	D'Acquisto	28	106	3	8	0	5.35
	C	D. Rader	255	.263	1	22	349	32	6	4	4.8	.984	R. Moffitt	58	103	6	6	14	2.27
	O1	G. Thomasson	328	.259	8	38	436	20	12	28		.974							
	2B	D. Thomas	272	.232	2	19	160	212	14	52	5.6	.964							
	1B	W. Montanez	230	.309	2	20	583	51*	7*	54*	11.1*	.989							

NATIONAL LEAGUE 1976, *cont.*

	POS	Player	AB	BA	HR	RBI	PO	A	E	DP	TC/G	FA	Pitcher	G	IP	W	L	SV	ERA
San Diego	1B	M. Ivie	405	.291	7	70	1020	70	5	89	8.1	.995	R. Jones	40	315	22	14	0	2.74
	2B	T. Fuentes	520	.263	2	36	339	387	22	91	5.9	.971	B. Strom	36	211	12	16	0	3.29
W-73 L-89	SS	E. Hernandez	340	.256	1	24	132	344	18	64	4.9	.964	Freisleben	34	172	10	13	1	3.51
	3B	D. Rader	471	.257	9	55	109	318	20	22	3.3	.955	B. Metzger	77	123	11	4	16	2.92
John McNamara	RF	J. Grubb	384	.284	5	27	183	3	5	0	1.9	.974	D. Spillner	32	107	2	11	0	5.06
	CF	W. Davis	493	.268	5	46	349	6	3	2	2.8	.992							
	LF	D. Winfield	492	.283	13	69	304	15	6	4	2.4	.982							
	C	F. Kendall	456	.246	2	39	582	54	4	6	4.4	.994							
	OF	J. Turner	281	.267	5	37	115	6	5	0	1.7	.960							
	SS	H. Torres	215	.195	4	15	64	160	12	29	3.7	.949							
	UT	T. Kubiak	212	.236	0	26	77	110	4	21		.979							
	1B	W. McCovey	202	.203	7	36	420	44	4	39	9.2	.991							
Atlanta	1B	W. Montanez	420	.321	9	64	986	56*	15*	87*	10.3*	.986	P. Niekro	38	271	17	11	0	3.29
	2B	R. Gilbreath	383	.251	1	32	239	311	14	76	5.4	.975	D. Ruthven	36	240	14	17	0	4.20
W-70 L-92	SS	D. Chaney	496	.252	1	50	243	466	37	88	4.9	.950	Messersmith	29	207	11	11	1	3.04
	3B	J. Royster	533	.248	5	45	156	306	18	35	3.2	.963	C. Morton	26	140	4	9	0	4.18
Dave Bristol	RF	K. Henderson	435	.262	13	61	219	3	3	0	1.8	.987	F. LaCorte	19	105	3	12	0	4.71
	CF	R. Office	359	.281	4	34	204	3	3	2	2.3	.986	A. Devine	48	73	5	6	9	3.21
	LF	J. Wynn	449	.207	17	66	287	17	9	2	2.3	.971	E. Sosa	21	35	4	4	3	5.35
	C	V. Correll	200	.225	5	16	319	36	7	1	5.6	.981							
	OF	T. Paciorek	324	.290	4	36	115	3	2	0	1.4	.983							
	OF	D. May	214	.215	3	23	98	5	3	1	1.8	.972							
	C1	E. Williams	184	.212	9	26	298	18	1	9		.997							
	2B	L. Lacy	180	.272	3	20	88	101	6	25	4.4	.969							
	C	B. Pocoroba	174	.241	0	14	273	39	7	5	5.9	.978							
	OF	C. Gaston	134	.291	4	25	42	1	1	0	1.6	.977							

BATTING AND BASE RUNNING LEADERS

PITCHING LEADERS

Batting Average
B. Madlock, CHI .339
K. Griffey, CIN .336
G. Maddox, PHI .330
P. Rose, CIN .323
J. Morgan, CIN .320

Slugging Average
J. Morgan, CIN .576
G. Foster, CIN .530
M. Schmidt, PHI .524
R. Monday, CHI .507
B. Madlock, CHI .500

Home Runs
M. Schmidt, PHI 38
D. Kingman, NY 37
R. Monday, CHI 32
G. Foster, CIN 29
J. Morgan, CIN 27

Winning Percentage
S. Carlton, PHI .741
Candelaria, PIT .696
D. Sutton, LA .677
J. Koosman, NY .677
J. Rooker, PIT .652

Earned Run Average
J. Denny, STL 2.52
D. Rau, LA 2.57
T. Seaver, NY 2.59
J. Koosman, NY 2.70
P. Zachry, CIN 2.74

Wins
R. Jones, SD 22
D. Sutton, LA 21
J. Koosman, NY 21
S. Carlton, PHI 20
J. Richard, HOU 20

Total Bases
M. Schmidt, PHI 306
P. Rose, CIN 299
G. Foster, CIN 298
S. Garvey, LA 284
J. Morgan, CIN 272
W. Montanez, ATL, SF 272

Runs Batted In
G. Foster, CIN 121
J. Morgan, CIN 111
M. Schmidt, PHI 107
B. Watson, HOU 102
G. Luzinski, PHI 95

Stolen Bases
D. Lopes, LA 63
J. Morgan, CIN 60
F. Taveras, PIT 58
C. Cedeno, HOU 58
L. Brock, STL 56

Saves
R. Eastwick, CIN 26
S. Lockwood, NY 19
K. Forsch, HOU 19
C. Hough, LA 18
B. Metzger, SD 16

Strikeouts
T. Seaver, NY 235
J. Richard, HOU 214
J. Koosman, NY 200
S. Carlton, PHI 195
P. Niekro, ATL 173

Complete Games
R. Jones, SD 25
J. Koosman, NY 17
J. Matlack, NY 16
D. Sutton, LA 15
J. Richard, HOU 14

Hits
P. Rose, CIN 215
W. Montanez, ATL, SF 206
S. Garvey, LA 200
B. Buckner, LA 193

Base on Balls
J. Wynn, ATL 127
J. Morgan, CIN 114
M. Schmidt, PHI 100
R. Cey, LA 89

Home Run Percentage
M. Schmidt, PHI 6.5
R. Monday, CHI 6.0
J. Morgan, CIN 5.7
G. Foster, CIN 5.2

Fewest Hits/9 Innings
J. Richard, HOU 6.84
T. Seaver, NY 7.01
Candelaria, PIT 7.08
Messersmith, ATL 7.22

Shutouts
J. Matlack, NY 6
Montefusco, SF 6
T. Seaver, NY 5
R. Jones, SD 5

Fewest Walks/9 Innings
G. Nolan, CIN 1.02
J. Kaat, PHI 1.26
R. Jones, SD 1.43
J. Matlack, NY 1.96

Runs Scored
P. Rose, CIN 130
J. Morgan, CIN 113
M. Schmidt, PHI 112
K. Griffey, CIN 111

Doubles
P. Rose, CIN 42
J. Johnstone, PHI 38
G. Maddox, PHI 37
S. Garvey, LA 37

Triples
D. Cash, PHI 12
C. Geronimo, CIN 11
W. Davis, SD 10
D. Parker, PIT 10

Most Strikeouts/9 Inn.
T. Seaver, NY 7.80
J. Koosman, NY 7.29
S. Carlton, PHI 6.95
J. Richard, HOU 6.62

Innings
R. Jones, SD 315
J. Richard, HOU 291
P. Niekro, ATL 271
T. Seaver, NY 271

Games Pitched
D. Murray, MON 81
C. Hough, LA 77
B. Metzger, SD 77
R. Eastwick, CIN 71

		W	L	PCT	GB	R	OR	2B	3B	HR	BA	SA	SB	E	DP	FA	CG	BB	SO	ShO	SV	ERA
East	Philadelphia	101	61	.623		770	557	259	45	110	.272	.395	127	115	148	.981	34	397	918	9	44	3.10
	Pittsburgh	92	70	.568	9	708	630	249	56	110	.267	.391	130	163	142	.975	45	460	762	12	35	3.37
	New York	86	76	.531	15	615	538	198	34	102	.246	.352	66	131	116	.979	53	419	1025	18	25	2.94
	Chicago	75	87	.463	26	611	728	216	24	105	.251	.356	74	140	145	.978	27	490	850	12	33	3.93
	St. Louis	72	90	.444	29	629	671	243	57	63	.260	.359	123	174	163	.973	35	581	731	15	26	3.61
	Montreal	55	107	.340	46	531	734	224	32	94	.235	.340	86	155	179	.976	26	659	783	10	21	3.99
West	Cincinnati	102	60	.630		857	633	271	63	141	.280	.424	210	102	157	.984	33	491	790	12	45	3.51
	Los Angeles	92	70	.568	10	608	543	200	34	91	.251	.349	144	128	154	.980	47	479	747	17	28	3.02
	Houston	80	82	.494	22	625	657	195	50	66	.256	.347	150	140	155	.978	42	662	780	17	29	3.55
	San Francisco	74	88	.457	28	595	686	211	37	85	.246	.345	88	186	153	.971	27	518	746	18	31	3.53
	San Diego	73	89	.451	29	570	662	216	37	64	.247	.337	92	141	148	.978	47	543	652	11	18	3.65
	Atlanta	70	92	.432	32	620	700	170	30	82	.245	.334	74	167	151	.973	33	564	818	13	27	3.87
						7739	7739	2652	499	1113	.255	.361	1364	1742	1811	.977	449	6263	9602	164	362	3.50

459

AMERICAN LEAGUE 1976

	POS	Player	AB	BA	HR	RBI	PO	A	E	DP	TC/G	FA	Pitcher	G	IP	W	L	SV	ERA
East																			
New York	1B	C. Chambliss	641	.293	17	96	1440	109	9	123	10.1	.994	C. Hunter	36	299	17	15	0	3.53
	2B	W. Randolph	430	.267	1	40	307	415	19	87	**6.0**	.974	E. Figueroa	34	257	19	10	0	3.02
W-97 L-62	SS	F. Stanley	260	.238	1	20	145	251	7	36	3.7	**.983**	D. Ellis	32	212	17	8	0	3.19
	3B	G. Nettles	583	.254	**32**	93	137	**383**	19	30	3.4	.965	K. Holtzman	21	149	9	7	0	4.17
Billy Martin	RF	O. Gamble	340	.232	17	57	199	10	4	3	2.0	.981	D. Alexander	19	137	10	5	0	3.29
	CF	M. Rivers	590	.312	8	67	407	6	6	0	**3.1**	.986	S. Lyle	64	104	7	8	23	2.26
	LF	R. White	626	.286	14	65	380	9	5	1	2.5	.987	D. Tidrow	47	92	4	5	10	2.63
	C	T. Munson	616	.302	17	105	537	78	12	8	5.2	.981							
	DH	C. May	288	.278	3	40													
	OD	L. Piniella	327	.281	3	38	106	4	2	0	2.3	.982							
	SS	J. Mason	217	.180	1	14	128	245	13	47	4.2	.966							
	UT	S. Alomar	163	.239	1	10	95	114	7	18		.968							
Baltimore	1B	T. Muser	326	.227	1	30	683	62	7	65	6.9	.991	J. Palmer	40	**315**	**22**	13	0	2.51
	2B	B. Grich	518	.266	13	54	**389**	400	12	91	5.7	.985	W. Garland	38	232	20	7	1	2.68
W-88 L-74	SS	M. Belanger	522	.270	1	40	239	**545**	14	97	5.2	.982	R. May	24	152	11	7	0	3.78
	3B	D. DeCinces	440	.234	11	42	96	208	19	9	3.0	.941	R. Grimsley	28	137	8	7	0	3.94
Earl Weaver	RF	R. Jackson	498	.277	27	91	284	8	**11**	3	2.5	.964	M. Cuellar	26	107	4	13	1	4.96
	CF	P. Blair	375	.197	3	16	327	6	7	1	2.4	.979	D. Miller	49	89	2	4	7	2.93
	LF	K. Singleton	544	.278	13	70	278	9	5	2	2.2	.983	T. Martinez	28	42	3	1	8	2.59
	C	D. Duncan	284	.204	4	17	371	35	6	9	4.4	.985							
	DH	L. May	530	.258	25	**109**													
	OF	A. Bumbry	450	.251	9	36	251	9	3	2	2.3	.989							
	DO	A. Mora	220	.218	6	25	55	3	3	0	2.0	.951							
	3B	B. Robinson	218	.211	3	11	59	126	6	11	2.7	.969							
	C	R. Dempsey	174	.213	0	10	269	34	4	8	5.2	.987							
Boston	1B	Yastrzemski	546	.267	21	102	829	52	2	78	9.4	.998	L. Tiant	38	279	21	12	0	3.06
	2B	D. Doyle	432	.250	0	26	209	311	12	67	4.7	.977	R. Wise	34	224	14	11	0	3.54
W-83 L-79	SS	R. Burleson	540	.291	7	42	274	478	34	88	5.2	.957	F. Jenkins	30	209	12	11	0	3.27
	3B	B. Hobson	269	.234	8	34	60	146	14	11	2.9	.936	R. Cleveland	41	170	10	9	2	4.31
Darrell Johnson	RF	D. Evans	501	.242	17	62	324	15	2	4	2.4	**.994**	D. Pole	31	121	6	5	0	4.31
W-41 L-45	CF	F. Lynn	507	.314	10	65	367	13	6	4	3.0	.984	R. Jones	24	104	5	3	0	3.36
	LF	J. Rice	581	.282	25	85	199	8	7	0	2.2	.967	Willoughby	54	99	3	12	10	2.82
Don Zimmer	C	C. Fisk	487	.255	17	58	649	73	12	9	5.5	.984	B. Lee	24	96	5	7	3	5.63
W-42 L-34	DH	C. Cooper	451	.282	15	78							T. Murphy	37	81	4	5	8	3.44
	OF	R. Miller	269	.283	0	27	220	4	2	1	2.8	.991							
	3B	Petrocelli	240	.213	3	24	57	120	6	11	2.5	.967							
	UT	S. Dillard	167	.275	1	15	58	102	11	21		.936							
Cleveland	1B	B. Powell	293	.215	9	33	698	61	10	76	8.6	.987	P. Dobson	35	217	16	12	0	3.48
	2B	D. Kuiper	506	.263	0	37	300	365	9	92	5.3	**.987**	D. Eckersley	36	199	13	12	1	3.44
W-81 L-78	SS	F. Duffy	392	.212	2	30	222	344	10	83	4.4	**.983**	J. Brown	32	180	9	11	0	4.25
	3B	B. Bell	604	.281	7	60	104	330	20	23	2.9	.956	J. Bibby	34	163	13	7	1	3.20
Frank Robinson	RF	R. Manning	552	.292	6	43	359	8	5	1	2.7	.987	R. Waits	26	124	7	9	0	3.99
	CF	G. Hendrick	551	.265	25	81	288	13	4	6	2.1	.987	J. Kern	50	118	10	7	15	2.36
	LF	C. Spikes	334	.237	3	31	185	7	3	0	2.0	.985	S. Thomas	37	106	4	4	6	2.29
	C	A. Ashby	247	.239	4	32	475	51	7	7	6.2	.987	D. LaRoche	61	96	1	4	21	2.25
	DH	R. Carty	552	.310	13	83							T. Buskey	39	94	5	4	1	3.64
	S2	L. Blanks	328	.280	5	41	152	213	11	53		.971							
	C	R. Fosse	276	.301	2	30	483	42	7	9	**6.3**	.987							
	OF	Lowenstein	229	.205	2	14	97	7	3	1	1.8	.972							
	OF	T. Smith	164	.256	2	12	90	4	7	0	1.9	.979							
Detroit	1B	J. Thompson	412	.218	17	54	1157	88	8	104	**10.7**	.994	D. Roberts	36	252	16	17	0	4.00
	2B	P. Garcia	227	.198	3	20	168	219	17	53	5.2	.958	M. Fidrych	31	250	19	9	0	**2.34**
W-74 L-87	SS	T. Veryzer	354	.234	1	25	164	313	17	53	5.1	.966	V. Ruhle	32	200	9	12	0	3.92
	3B	A. Rodriguez	480	.240	8	50	120	280	9	21	3.2	**.978**	R. Bare	30	134	7	8	0	4.63
Ralph Houk	RF	R. Staub	589	.299	15	96	218	8	7	3	1.8	.970	J. Hiller	56	121	12	8	13	2.38
	CF	R. LeFlore	544	.316	4	39	381	14	**11**	1	3.1	.973	J. Crawford	32	109	1	8	2	4.53
	LF	A. Johnson	429	.268	6	45	159	7	8	1	1.9	.954	D. Lemanczyk	20	81	4	6	0	5.11
	C	B. Freehan	237	.270	5	27	312	28	6	2	5.7	.983							
	DH	W. Horton	401	.262	14	56													
	OF	B. Oglivie	305	.285	15	47	136	7	2	0	2.3	.986							
	OF	D. Meyer	294	.252	2	16	76	4	1	1	1.7	.988							
	2S	C. Scrivener	222	.221	2	16	134	221	11	46		.970							
	UT	M. Stanley	214	.257	4	29	187	47	5	14		.979							
Milwaukee	1B	G. Scott	606	.274	18	77	1393	107	13	133	9.8	.991	J. Slaton	38	293	14	15	0	3.44
	2B	T. Johnson	273	.275	0	14	161	222	8	42	3.9	.980	B. Travers	34	240	15	16	0	2.81
W-66 L-95	SS	R. Yount	638	.252	2	54	**290**	510	31	104	5.2	.963	J. Colborn	32	226	9	15	0	3.71
	3B	D. Money	439	.267	12	62	96	202	13	21	3.0	.958	J. Augustine	39	172	9	12	0	3.30
Alex Grammas	RF	S. Lezcano	513	.285	7	56	345	10	10	3	2.6	.973	E. Rodriguez	45	136	5	13	8	3.64
	CF	V. Joshua	423	.267	5	28	268	10	5	4	2.7	.982	B. Castro	39	70	4	6	8	3.45
	LF	G. Thomas	227	.198	8	36	210	4	3	0	2.3	.986	D. Frisella	32	49	5	2	9	2.74
	C	D. Porter	389	.208	5	32	491	52	14	7	5.0	.975							
	DH	H. Aaron	271	.229	10	35													
	CO	C. Moore	241	.191	3	16	249	44	9	1		.970							
	UT	M. Hegan	218	.248	5	31	88	6	2	8		.979							
	OD	B. Carbo	183	.235	3	15	71	5	0	1	2.3	1.000							
	OF	B. Sharp	180	.244	0	11	108	7	3	2	2.1	.975							

AMERICAN LEAGUE 1976, cont.

		POS	Player	AB	BA	HR	RBI	PO	A	E	DP	TC/G	FA	Pitcher	G	IP	W	L	SV	ERA
West	**Kansas City**	1B	J. Mayberry	594	.232	13	95	1484	105	7	132	10.0	.996	D. Leonard	35	259	17	10	0	3.51
		2B	F. White	446	.229	2	46	255	387	18	75	5.1	.973	Fitzmorris	35	220	15	11	0	3.07
	W-90 L-72	SS	F. Patek	432	.241	1	43	233	426	26	87	4.8	.962	D. Bird	39	198	12	10	2	3.36
		3B	G. Brett	645	.333	7	67	140	335	26	22	3.2	.948	Splittorff	26	159	11	8	0	3.96
	Whitey Herzog	RF	A. Cowens	581	.265	3	59	329	13	5	3	2.3	.986	M. Pattin	44	141	8	14	5	2.49
		CF	A. Otis	592	.279	18	86	373	5	3	1	2.5	.992	M. Littell	60	104	8	4	16	2.08
		LF	T. Poquette	344	.302	2	34	188	1	4	0	2.0	.979	A. Hassler	19	100	5	6	0	2.89
		C	B. Martinez	267	.228	5	34	420	40	4	4	4.9	.991	S. Mingori	55	85	5	5	10	2.33
		DH	H. McRae	527	.332	8	73													
		OF	J. Wohlford	293	.249	1	24	189	6	5	0	2.2	.975							
		C	B. Stinson	209	.263	2	25	304	30	7	4	4.3	.979							
	Oakland	1B	D. Baylor	595	.247	15	68	629	44	9	40	9.9	.987	V. Blue	37	298	18	13	0	2.36
		2B	P. Garner	555	.261	8	74	378	465	22	91	5.4	.975	M. Torrez	39	266	16	12	0	2.50
	W-87 L-74	SS	Campaneris	536	.256	1	52	231	490	23	66	5.0	.969	S. Bahnsen	35	143	8	7	0	3.34
		3B	S. Bando	550	.240	27	84	125	304	17	26	2.9	.962	P. Mitchell	26	142	9	7	0	4.25
	Chuck Tanner	RF	Washington	490	.257	5	53	276	10	11	2	2.4	.963	R. Fingers	70	135	13	11	20	2.47
		CF	B. North	590	.276	2	31	397	8	9	1	2.9	.978	P. Lindblad	65	115	6	5	5	3.05
		LF	J. Rudi	500	.270	13	94	258	6	3	2	2.1	.989	D. Bosman	27	112	4	2	0	4.10
		C	L. Haney	177	.226	0	10	290	45	9	2	4.0	.974	J. Todd	49	83	7	8	4	3.80
		DH	B. Williams	351	.211	11	41													
		1C	G. Tenace	417	.249	22	66	840	56	8	50		.991							
		UT	K. McMullen	186	.220	5	23	222	39	2	20		.992							
	Minnesota	1B	R. Carew	605	.331	9	90	1394	108	16	149	10.0	.989	D. Goltz	36	249	14	14	0	3.36
		2B	B. Randall	475	.267	1	34	327	423	24	124	5.1	.969	J. Hughes	37	177	9	14	0	4.98
	W-85 L-77	SS	R. Smalley	384	.271	2	36	189	338	18	70	5.3	.967	B. Singer	26	172	9	9	0	3.77
		3B	M. Cubbage	342	.260	3	49	71	209	18	22	3.0	.940	B. Campbell	78	168	17	5	20	3.00
	Gene Mauch	RF	D. Ford	514	.267	20	86	267	6	9	1	2.0	.968	S. Luebber	38	119	4	5	2	4.01
		CF	L. Bostock	474	.323	4	60	320	10	4	2	2.7	.988	P. Redfern	23	118	8	8	0	3.51
		LF	L. Hisle	581	.272	14	96	361	16	6	1	2.5	.984	T. Burgmeier	57	115	8	1	1	2.50
		C	B. Wynegar	534	.260	10	69	650	78	16	6	5.4	.978	E. Bane	17	79	4	7	0	5.13
		DH	C. Kusick	266	.259	11	36													
		UT	S. Braun	417	.288	3	61	71	32	6	3		.945							
		OF	S. Brye	258	.264	2	23	147	1	2	0	1.9	.987							
		UT	J. Terrell	171	.246	0	8	82	122	8	27		.962							
	California	1B	B. Bochte	466	.258	2	49	489	39	5	37	9.0	.991	F. Tanana	34	288	19	10	0	2.44
		2B	J. Remy	502	.263	0	28	279	406	16	77	5.3	.977	N. Ryan	39	284	17	18	0	3.36
	W-76 L-86	SS	D. Chalk	438	.217	0	33	141	293	13	45	4.4	.971	G. Ross	34	225	8	16	0	3.00
		3B	R. Jackson	410	.227	8	40	85	222	16	19	2.8	.950	P. Hartzell	37	166	7	4	2	2.77
	Dick Williams	RF	R. Torres	264	.205	6	27	195	5	2	0	1.9	.990	D. Kirkwood	28	158	6	12	0	4.61
	W-39 L-57	CF	B. Bonds	378	.265	10	54	199	9	5	3	2.2	.977	S. Monge	32	118	6	7	0	3.36
		LF	D. Collins	365	.263	4	28	160	3	1	0	2.3	.994	D. Drago	43	79	7	8	6	2.70
	Norm Sherry	C	Etchebarren	247	.227	0	21	539	46	12	7	5.9	.980							
	W-37 L-29	DH	B. Melton	341	.208	6	42													
		S2	M. Guerrero	268	.284	1	18	129	172	14	32		.956							
		1O	D. Briggs	248	.214	1	14	358	26	5	33		.987							
		OF	L. Stanton	231	.190	2	25	128	1	2	0	1.7	.985							
		DH	T. Davis	219	.265	3	26													
		1B	T. Solaita	215	.270	9	33	451	54	1	32	9.4	.998							
		C	T. Humphrey	196	.245	1	19	397	42	9	4	6.3	.980							
		OF	B. Jones	166	.211	6	14	98	6	1	0	1.7	.990							
	Texas	1B	M. Hargrove	541	.287	7	58	1222	110	21	103	9.6	.984	G. Perry	32	250	15	14	0	3.24
		2B	L. Randle	539	.224	1	51	291	319	18	63	5.6	.971	N. Briles	32	210	11	9	1	3.26
	W-76 L-86	SS	T. Harrah	584	.260	15	67	290	473	36	81	5.5	.955	B. Singer	24	202	9	11	0	2.76
		3B	R. Howell	491	.253	8	53	103	245	28	20	2.9	.926	J. Umbarger	30	197	10	12	0	3.15
	Frank Lucchesi	RF	J. Burroughs	604	.237	18	86	289	12	4	3	2.0	.987	S. Hargan	35	124	8	8	1	3.63
		CF	J. Beniquez	478	.255	0	33	410	18	6	3	3.1	.986	S. Foucault	46	76	8	8	5	3.32
		LF	G. Clines	446	.276	0	38	215	9	3	1	2.2	.987	J. Hoerner	41	35	0	4	8	5.14
		C	J. Sundberg	448	.228	3	34	719	96	7	11	5.9	.991							
		DH	T. Grieve	546	.255	20	81													
		UT	D. Thompson	196	.214	1	13	60	117	4	12		.978							
	Chicago	1B	J. Spencer	518	.253	14	70	1206	112	2	116	9.2	.998	G. Gossage	31	224	9	17	1	3.94
		2B	J. Brohamer	354	.251	7	40	263	334	10	74	5.2	.984	B. Johnson	32	211	9	16	0	4.73
	W-64 L-97	SS	B. Dent	562	.246	2	52	279	468	18	96	4.8	.976	K. Brett	27	201	10	12	1	3.32
		3B	K. Bell	230	.248	5	20	70	124	6	10	3.0	.970	F. Barrios	35	142	5	9	3	4.31
	Paul Richards	RF	J. Orta	636	.274	14	72	156	9	5	1	2.2	.971	T. Forster	29	111	2	12	1	4.38
		CF	C. Lemon	451	.246	4	38	353	12	3	1	2.8	.992	P. Vuckovich	33	110	7	4	0	4.66
		LF	R. Garr	527	.300	4	36	254	7	6	2	2.1	.978	D. Hamilton	45	90	6	6	10	3.60
		C	B. Downing	317	.256	3	30	450	38	6	4	5.3	.988	C. Carroll	29	77	4	4	6	2.57
		DH	P. Kelly	311	.254	5	34													
		32	B. Stein	392	.268	4	36	153	241	19	39		.954							
		D1	L. Johnson	222	.320	4	33	210	18	4	20	6.8	.983							
		C	J. Essian	199	.246	0	21	319	53	10	10	5.0	.974							

AMERICAN LEAGUE 1976, *cont.*

BATTING AND BASE RUNNING LEADERS

Batting Average
G. Brett, KC	.333
H. McRae, KC	.332
R. Carew, MIN	.331
L. Bostock, MIN	.323
R. LeFlore, DET	.316

Slugging Average
R. Jackson, BAL	.502
J. Rice, BOS	.482
G. Nettles, NY	.475
F. Lynn, BOS	.467
R. Carew, MIN	.463

Home Runs
G. Nettles, NY	32
R. Jackson, BAL	27
S. Bando, OAK	27
L. May, BAL	25
G. Hendrick, CLE	25
J. Rice, BOS	25

Total Bases
G. Brett, KC	298
C. Chambliss, NY	283
J. Rice, BOS	280
R. Carew, MIN	280
G. Nettles, NY	277

Runs Batted In
L. May, BAL	109
T. Munson, NY	105
Yastrzemski, BOS	102
L. Hisle, MIN	96
R. Staub, DET	96
C. Chambliss, NY	96

Stolen Bases
B. North, OAK	75
R. LeFlore, DET	58
Campaneris, OAK	54
D. Baylor, OAK	52
F. Patek, KC	51

Hits
G. Brett, KC	215
R. Carew, MIN	200
C. Chambliss, NY	188
T. Munson, NY	186

Base on Balls
M. Hargrove, TEX	97
T. Harrah, TEX	91
B. Grich, BAL	86
R. Staub, DET	83

Home Run Percentage
G. Nettles, NY	5.5
R. Jackson, BAL	5.4
S. Bando, OAK	4.9
L. May, BAL	4.7

Runs Scored
R. White, NY	104
R. Carew, MIN	97
M. Rivers, NY	95
G. Brett, KC	94

Doubles
A. Otis, KC	40
D. Evans, BOS	34
H. McRae, KC	34
R. Carty, CLE	34

Triples
G. Brett, KC	14
P. Garner, OAK	12
R. Carew, MIN	12
T. Poquette, KC	10

PITCHING LEADERS

Winning Percentage
B. Campbell, MIN	.773
W. Garland, BAL	.741
D. Ellis, NY	.680
M. Fidrych, DET	.679
E. Figueroa, NY	.655
F. Tanana, CAL	.655

Earned Run Average
M. Fidrych, DET	2.34
V. Blue, OAK	2.36
F. Tanana, CAL	2.44
M. Torrez, OAK	2.50
J. Palmer, BAL	2.51

Wins
J. Palmer, BAL	22
L. Tiant, BOS	21
W. Garland, BAL	20
M. Fidrych, DET	19
E. Figueroa, NY	19
F. Tanana, CAL	19

Saves
S. Lyle, NY	23
D. LaRoche, CLE	21
B. Campbell, MIN	20
R. Fingers, OAK	20
M. Littell, KC	16

Strikeouts
N. Ryan, CAL	327
F. Tanana, CAL	261
B. Blyleven, MIN, TEX	219
D. Eckersley, CLE	200
C. Hunter, NY	173

Complete Games
M. Fidrych, DET	24
F. Tanana, CAL	23
J. Palmer, BAL	23
G. Perry, TEX	21
C. Hunter, NY	21
N. Ryan, CAL	21

Fewest Hits/9 Innings
N. Ryan, CAL	6.12
F. Tanana, CAL	6.62
D. Eckersley, CLE	7.01
J. Palmer, BAL	7.29

Shutouts
N. Ryan, CAL	7
B. Blyleven, MIN, TEX	6
V. Blue, OAK	6
J. Palmer, BAL	6

Fewest Walks/9 Innings
D. Bird, KC	1.41
F. Jenkins, BOS	1.85
G. Perry, TEX	1.87
V. Blue, OAK	1.90

Most Strikeouts/9 Inn.
N. Ryan, CAL	10.36
D. Eckersley, CLE	9.05
F. Tanana, CAL	8.16
B. Blyleven, MIN, TEX	6.62

Innings
J. Palmer, BAL	315
C. Hunter, NY	299
V. Blue, OAK	298
B. Blyleven, MIN, TEX	298

Games Pitched
B. Campbell, MIN	78
R. Fingers, OAK	70
P. Lindblad, OAK	65
S. Lyle, NY	64

		W	L	PCT	GB	R	OR	2B	3B	HR	BA	SA	SB	E	DP	FA	CG	BB	SO	ShO	SV	ERA
East	New York	97	62	.610		730	575	231	36	120	.269	.389	163	126	141	.980	62	448	674	15	37	3.19
	Baltimore	88	74	.543	10.5	619	598	213	28	119	.243	.358	150	118	157	.982	59	489	678	16	23	3.31
	Boston	83	79	.512	15.5	716	660	257	53	134	.263	.402	95	141	148	.978	49	409	673	13	27	3.52
	Cleveland	81	78	.509	16	615	615	189	38	85	.263	.359	75	121	159	.980	30	533	928	17	46	3.48
	Detroit	74	87	.460	24	609	709	207	38	101	.257	.365	107	168	161	.974	55	550	738	12	20	3.87
	Milwaukee	66	95	.410	32	570	655	170	38	88	.246	.340	62	152	160	.975	45	567	677	10	27	3.64
West	Kansas City	90	72	.556		713	611	259	57	65	.269	.371	218	139	147	.978	41	493	735	12	35	3.21
	Oakland	87	74	.540	2.5	686	598	208	33	113	.246	.361	341	144	130	.977	39	415	711	15	29	3.26
	Minnesota	85	77	.525	5	743	704	222	51	81	.274	.375	146	172	182	.973	29	610	762	11	23	3.72
	California	76	86	.469	14	550	631	210	23	63	.235	.318	126	150	139	.977	64	553	992	15	17	3.36
	Texas	76	86	.469	14	616	652	213	26	80	.250	.341	87	156	142	.976	63	461	773	15	15	3.47
	Chicago	64	97	.398	25.5	586	745	209	46	73	.255	.349	120	130	155	.979	54	600	802	10	22	4.25
						7753	7753	2588	467	1122	.256	.361	1690	1717	1821	.977	590	6128	9143	161	321	3.52

NATIONAL LEAGUE 1977

		POS	Player	AB	BA	HR	RBI	PO	A	E	DP	TC/G	FA	Pitcher	G	IP	W	L	SV	ERA
East	**Philadelphia** W-101 L-61 Danny Ozark	1B	R. Hebner	397	.285	18	62	927	65	9	91	9.7	.991	S. Carlton	36	283	23	10	0	2.64
		2B	T. Sizemore	519	.281	4	47	348	427	11	104	5.2	.986	Christenson	34	219	19	6	0	4.07
		SS	L. Bowa	624	.280	4	41	222	518	13	94	4.9	.983	R. Lerch	32	169	10	6	0	5.06
		3B	M. Schmidt	544	.274	38	101	106	396	19	33	3.5	.964	J. Kaat	35	160	6	11	0	5.40
		RF	B. McBride	280	.339	11	41	140	6	2	1	2.0	.962	J. Lonborg	25	158	11	4	0	4.10
		CF	G. Maddox	571	.292	14	74	383	7	9	2	2.9	.977	R. Reed	60	124	7	5	15	2.76
		LF	G. Luzinski	554	.309	39	130	205	11	8	2	1.5	.964	G. Garber	64	103	8	6	19	2.36
		C	B. Boone	440	.284	11	66	653	80	8	9	5.7	.989	T. McGraw	45	79	7	3	9	2.62
		OF	J. Johnstone	363	.284	15	59	163	9	0	1	1.9	1.000	W. Brusstar	46	71	7	2	3	2.66
		OF	J. Martin	215	.260	6	28	117	4	2	1	1.2	.984							
		C	T. McCarver	169	.320	6	30	233	14	3	3	6.0	.988							
		1B	D. Johnson	156	.321	8	36	291	14	0	26	7.1	1.000							
	Pittsburgh W-96 L-66 Chuck Tanner	1B	B. Robinson	507	.304	26	104	695	34	6	62	8.5	.992	Candelaria	33	231	20	5	0	2.34
		2B	R. Stennett	453	.336	5	51	269	315	11	70	5.9	.982	J. Reuss	33	208	10	13	0	4.11
		SS	F. Taveras	544	.252	1	29	178	449	25	62	4.5	.962	J. Rooker	30	204	14	9	0	3.09
		3B	P. Garner	585	.260	17	77	98	240	10	28	3.3	.971	B. Kison	33	193	9	10	0	4.90
		RF	D. Parker	637	.338	21	88	389	26	15	0	2.7	.965	G. Gossage	72	133	11	9	26	1.62
		CF	O. Moreno	492	.240	7	34	366	10	9	4	2.6	.977	O. Jones	34	108	3	7	0	5.08
		LF	A. Oliver	568	.308	19	82	305	6	6	1	2.1	.981	K. Tekulve	72	103	10	1	7	3.06
		C	D. Dyer	270	.241	3	19	502	41	2	10	5.9	.996	G. Jackson	49	91	5	3	4	3.86
		C	E. Ott	311	.264	7	38	455	49	9	6	5.7	.982	L. Demery	39	90	6	5	1	5.10
		1B	W. Stargell	186	.274	13	35	449	27	7	26	8.8	.986	T. Forster	33	87	6	4	1	4.45
		UT	F. Gonzalez	181	.276	4	27	43	66	2	6		.982							

NATIONAL LEAGUE 1977, cont.

St. Louis
W-83 L-79 — Vern Rapp

POS	Player	AB	BA	HR	RBI	PO	A	E	DP	TC/G	FA	Pitcher	G	IP	W	L	SV	ERA
1B	K. Hernandez	560	.291	15	91	1453	106	12	146	9.9	.992	E. Rasmussen	34	233	11	17	0	3.48
2B	M. Tyson	418	.246	7	57	267	423	15	99	5.2	.979	B. Forsch	35	217	20	7	0	3.48
SS	G. Templeton	621	.322	8	79	285	453	32	98	5.1	.958	J. Denny	26	150	8	8	0	4.50
3B	K. Reitz	587	.261	17	79	121	320	9	35	2.9	.980	J. Urrea	41	140	7	6	4	3.15
RF	H. Cruz	339	.236	6	42	154	9	6	1	1.6	.964	P. Falcone	27	124	4	8	1	5.44
CF	J. Mumphrey	463	.287	2	38	291	8	9	1	2.3	.971	T. Underwood	19	100	6	9	0	4.95
LF	L. Brock	489	.272	2	46	184	2	9	1	1.5	.954	B. Metzger	58	93	4	2	7	3.11
C	T. Simmons	516	.318	21	95	683	75	10	5	5.3	.987	C. Carroll	51	90	4	2	4	2.50
OF	T. Scott	292	.291	3	41	223	5	1	0	2.6	.996	A. Hrabosky	65	86	6	5	10	4.40
OF	B. McBride	122	.262	4	20	48	2	0	0	1.5	1.000	R. Eastwick	41	54	3	7	4	4.70
1B	R. Freed	83	.398	5	21	102	7	0	13	6.1	1.000							

Chicago
W-81 L-81 — Herman Franks

POS	Player	AB	BA	HR	RBI	PO	A	E	DP	TC/G	FA	Pitcher	G	IP	W	L	SV	ERA
1B	B. Buckner	426	.284	11	60	966	58	10	75	10.4	.990	R. Reuschel	39	252	20	10	1	2.79
2B	M. Trillo	504	.280	7	57	330	467	25	81	5.5	.970	R. Burris	39	221	14	16	0	4.72
SS	I. DeJesus	624	.266	3	40	234	595	33	94	5.6	.962	B. Bonham	34	215	10	13	0	4.35
3B	S. Ontiveros	546	.299	10	68	100	324	20	24	2.9	.955	M. Krukow	34	172	8	14	0	4.40
RF	B. Murcer	554	.265	27	89	237	11	5	5	1.7	.980	G. Hernandez	67	110	8	7	4	3.03
CF	J. Morales	490	.290	11	69	247	8	4	3	2.0	.985	B. Sutter	62	107	7	3	31	1.35
LF	G. Gross	239	.322	5	32	109	3	1	0	1.6	.991	P. Reuschel	69	107	5	6	4	4.37
C	Mitterwald	349	.238	9	43	621	78	8	13	6.5	.989							
1O	L. Biittner	493	.298	12	62	792	65	11	51		.987							
OF	G. Clines	239	.293	3	41	68	3	1	0	1.1	.986							
OF	J. Cardenal	226	.239	3	18	85	1	1	0	1.4	.989							
C	S. Swisher	205	.190	5	15	327	38	9	3	5.2	.976							

Montreal
W-75 L-87 — Dick Williams

POS	Player	AB	BA	HR	RBI	PO	A	E	DP	TC/G	FA	Pitcher	G	IP	W	L	SV	ERA
1B	T. Perez	559	.283	19	91	1312	110	11	88	9.7	.992	S. Rogers	40	302	17	16	0	3.10
2B	D. Cash	650	.289	0	43	343	443	11	73	5.2	.986	J. Brown	42	186	9	12	0	4.50
SS	C. Speier	531	.235	5	38	236	435	21	75	5.0	.970	D. Stanhouse	47	158	10	10	10	3.42
3B	L. Parrish	402	.246	11	46	81	225	21	11	2.8	.936	W. Twitchell	22	139	6	5	0	4.21
RF	E. Valentine	508	.293	25	76	232	9	7	1	2.0	.972	S. Bahnsen	23	127	8	9	0	4.82
CF	A. Dawson	525	.282	19	65	352	9	4	1	2.7	.989	S. Alcala	31	102	2	6	2	4.69
LF	W. Cromartie	620	.282	5	50	319	10	8	1	2.2	.976	J. Kerrigan	66	89	3	5	11	3.24
C	G. Carter	522	.284	31	84	811	101	9	14	6.3	.990	W. McEnaney	69	87	3	5	3	3.93
OF	D. Unser	289	.273	12	40	120	2	3	0	1.7	.976	B. Atkinson	55	83	7	2	7	3.36
3B	W. Garrett	159	.270	2	22	34	101	0	2	2.8	1.000							

New York
W-64 L-98 — Joe Frazier W-15 L-30 — Joe Torre W-49 L-68

POS	Player	AB	BA	HR	RBI	PO	A	E	DP	TC/G	FA	Pitcher	G	IP	W	L	SV	ERA
1B	J. Milner	388	.255	12	57	672	48	4	64	8.3	.994	J. Koosman	32	227	8	20	0	3.49
2B	F. Millan	314	.248	2	21	197	188	9	43	4.4	.977	N. Espinosa	32	200	10	13	0	3.42
SS	B. Harrelson	269	.178	1	12	141	239	6	41	3.9	.984	J. Matlack	26	169	7	15	0	4.21
3B	L. Randle	513	.304	5	27	98	221	13	25	3.0	.961	C. Swan	26	147	9	10	0	4.22
RF	M. Vail	279	.262	8	35	159	5	6	2	1.6	.965	P. Zachry	19	120	7	6	0	3.76
CF	L. Mazzilli	537	.250	6	46	386	9	3	1	2.6	.992	S. Lockwood	63	104	4	8	20	3.38
LF	S. Henderson	350	.297	12	65	189	4	4	1	2.0	.980	T. Seaver	13	96	7	3	0	3.00
C	J. Stearns	431	.251	12	55	742	76	15	12	6.6	.982	B. Apodaca	59	84	4	8	5	3.43
OF	B. Boisclair	307	.293	4	44	140	1	6	0	1.6	.959							
S2	D. Flynn	282	.191	0	14	155	203	13	38		.965							
O1	E. Kranepool	281	.281	10	40	347	30	4	21		.990							
OF	D. Kingman	211	.209	9	28	76	0	2	0	1.7	.974							
UT	Youngblood	182	.253	0	11	99	88	7	21		.964							

West

Los Angeles
W-98 L-64 — Tom Lasorda

POS	Player	AB	BA	HR	RBI	PO	A	E	DP	TC/G	FA	Pitcher	G	IP	W	L	SV	ERA
1B	S. Garvey	646	.297	33	115	1606	55	8	137	10.4	.995	D. Sutton	33	240	14	8	0	3.19
2B	D. Lopes	502	.283	11	53	287	380	14	74	5.2	.979	B. Hooton	32	223	12	7	1	2.62
SS	B. Russell	634	.278	4	51	234	523	29	102	5.1	.963	T. John	31	220	20	7	0	2.78
3B	R. Cey	564	.241	30	110	138	346	18	29	3.3	.964	R. Rhoden	31	216	16	10	0	3.75
RF	R. Smith	488	.307	32	87	240	7	5	0	1.8	.980	D. Rau	32	212	14	8	0	3.44
CF	R. Monday	392	.230	15	48	208	3	2	0	1.9	.991	C. Hough	70	127	6	12	22	3.33
LF	D. Baker	533	.291	30	86	227	8	3	2	1.6	.987	M. Garman	49	63	4	4	12	2.71
C	S. Yeager	387	.256	16	55	690	89	18	12	6.5	.977							
UT	L. Lacy	169	.266	6	21	56	69	4	11		.969							
OF	G. Burke	169	.254	1	13	98	1	3	0	1.4	.971							

Cincinnati
W-88 L-74 — Sparky Anderson

POS	Player	AB	BA	HR	RBI	PO	A	E	DP	TC/G	FA	Pitcher	G	IP	W	L	SV	ERA
1B	D. Driessen	536	.300	17	91	1182	75	7	116	8.5	.994	F. Norman	35	221	14	13	0	3.38
2B	J. Morgan	521	.288	22	78	351	359	5	100	4.7	.993	T. Seaver	20	165	14	3	0	2.34
SS	Concepcion	572	.271	8	64	280	490	11	101	5.0	.986	Billingham	36	162	10	10	0	5.22
3B	P. Rose	655	.311	9	64	98	268	16	18	2.4	.958	P. Borbon	73	127	10	5	18	3.19
RF	K. Griffey	585	.318	12	57	298	10	3	3	2.9	.990	P. Moskau	20	108	6	6	0	4.00
CF	C. Geronimo	492	.266	10	52	375	9	3	2	2.6	.992	D. Capilla	22	106	7	8	0	4.23
LF	G. Foster	615	.320	52	149	352	12	3	1	2.3	.992	D. Murray	61	102	7	2	4	4.94
C	J. Bench	494	.275	31	109	705	66	10	10	5.8	.987	P. Zachry	12	75	3	7	0	5.04

Houston
W-81 L-81 — Bill Virdon

POS	Player	AB	BA	HR	RBI	PO	A	E	DP	TC/G	FA	Pitcher	G	IP	W	L	SV	ERA
1B	B. Watson	554	.289	22	110	1331	118	9	100	10.0	.994	J. Richard	36	267	18	12	0	2.97
2B	A. Howe	413	.264	8	58	192	279	7	49	5.0	.985	Lemongello	34	215	9	14	0	3.47
SS	R. Metzger	269	.186	0	16	130	260	11	45	4.2	.973	J. Niekro	44	181	13	8	5	3.03
3B	E. Cabell	625	.282	16	68	140	280	23	17	3.1	.948	J. Andujar	26	159	11	8	0	3.68
RF	J. Cruz	579	.299	17	87	311	11	9	1	2.1	.973	F. Bannister	24	143	8	9	0	4.03
CF	C. Cedeno	530	.279	14	71	335	14	1	2	2.6	.997	J. Sambito	54	89	5	5	7	2.33
LF	T. Puhl	229	.301	0	10	119	3	1	0	2.1	.992	K. Forsch	42	86	5	8	8	2.72
C	J. Ferguson	421	.257	16	61	634	80	11	10	5.9	.985	McLaughlin	46	85	4	7	5	4.24
S2	J. Gonzalez	383	.245	1	27	154	293	27	56		.943							
OF	W. Howard	187	.257	2	13	100	2	1	1	1.7	.990							
OF	C. Johnson	144	.299	10	23	49	4	3	0	1.6	.946							

NATIONAL LEAGUE 1977, cont.

	POS	Player	AB	BA	HR	RBI	PO	A	E	DP	TC/G	FA	Pitcher	G	IP	W	L	SV	ERA
San Francisco	1B	W. McCovey	478	.280	28	86	1072	60	13	93	8.4	.989	E. Halicki	37	258	16	12	0	3.31
	2B	R. Andrews	436	.264	0	25	225	314	20	66	4.9	.964	J. Barr	38	234	12	16	0	4.77
W-75 L-87	SS	T. Foli	368	.228	4	27	184	302	13	72	4.9	.974	B. Knepper	27	166	11	9	0	3.36
	3B	B. Madlock	533	.302	12	46	96	220	17	16	2.6	.949	Montefusco	26	157	7	12	0	3.50
Joe Altobelli	RF	J. Clark	413	.252	13	51	226	11	6	2	2.1	.975	C. Williams	55	119	6	5	0	4.01
	CF	T. Whitfield	326	.285	7	36	167	4	5	0	2.1	.972	G. Lavelle	73	118	7	7	20	2.06
	LF	G. Thomasson	446	.256	17	71	255	2	11	1	2.4	.959	R. Moffitt	64	88	4	9	11	3.58
	C	M. Hill	320	.250	9	50	505	57	6	4	5.6	.989	McGlothen	21	80	2	9	0	5.63
	UT	D. Thomas	506	.267	8	44	307	158	14	24		.971							
	UT	D. Evans	461	.254	17	72	324	83	13	15		.969							
	OF	R. Elliott	167	.240	7	26	68	5	2	1	1.6	.973							
	UT	V. Harris	165	.261	2	14	69	96	8	21		.954							
	C	G. Alexander	119	.303	5	20	174	8	6	0	5.7	.968							
San Diego	1B	M. Ivie	489	.272	9	66	863	56	7	76	8.8	.992	B. Shirley	39	214	12	18	0	3.70
	2B	M. Champion	507	.229	1	43	301	348	17	82	4.5	.974	B. Owchinko	30	170	9	12	0	4.45
W-69 L-93	SS	B. Almon	613	.261	2	43	303	538	41	87	5.7	.954	T. Griffin	38	151	6	9	0	4.47
	3B	T. Ashford	249	.217	3	24	32	145	12	14	2.6	.937	R. Jones	27	147	6	12	0	4.59
John McNamara	RF	G. Richards	525	.290	5	32	193	13	8	0	2.0	.963	Freisleben	33	139	7	9	0	4.60
W-20 L-28	CF	G. Hendrick	541	.311	23	81	386	11	7	2	2.8	.983	R. Fingers	78	132	8	9	35	3.00
	LF	D. Winfield	615	.275	25	92	368	15	11	3	2.5	.972	D. Spillner	76	123	7	6	6	3.73
Bob Skinner	C	G. Tenace	437	.233	15	61	523	61	12	9	6.0	.980	R. Sawyer	56	111	7	6	0	5.84
W-1 L-0	OF	J. Turner	289	.246	10	48	114	10	7	2	1.9	.947	D. Tomlin	76	102	4	4	3	3.00
	C	D. Roberts	186	.220	1	23	254	24	5	2	4.5	.982							
Alvin Dark	3B	D. Rader	170	.271	5	27	43	104	6	9	3.0	.961							
W-48 L-65	O1	D. Kingman	168	.238	11	39	142	14	3	5		.981							
Atlanta	1B	W. Montanez	544	.287	20	68	1129	70	10	88	9.0	.992	P. Niekro	44	330	16	20	0	4.04
	2B	R. Gilbreath	407	.243	8	43	277	305	13	61	4.9	.978	D. Ruthven	25	151	7	13	0	4.23
W-61 L-101	SS	P. Rockett	264	.254	1	24	152	209	23	38	4.6	.937	B. Capra	45	139	6	11	0	5.37
	3B	J. Moore	361	.260	5	34	86	189	17	10	2.8	.942	Messersmith	16	102	5	4	0	4.41
Dave Bristol	RF	G. Matthews	555	.283	17	64	262	11	10	1	2.0	.965	E. Solomon	18	89	6	6	0	4.55
W-8 L-21	CF	R. Office	428	.241	5	39	249	8	3	3	2.5	.988	D. Campbell	65	89	0	6	13	3.03
	LF	J. Burroughs	579	.271	41	114	249	9	7	3	1.7	.974	R. Camp	54	79	6	3	10	3.99
Ted Turner	C	B. Pocoroba	321	.290	8	44	542	78	7	8	6.3	.989	D. Collins	40	71	3	9	2	5.07
W-0 L-1	UT	J. Royster	445	.216	6	28	182	267	28	40		.941							
	OF	B. Bonnell	360	.300	1	45	181	3	2	1	2.5	.989							
Vern Benson	S2	D. Chaney	209	.201	3	15	113	182	8	30		.974							
W-1 L-0	PH	C. Gaston	85	.271	3	21													
Dave Bristol																			
W-52 L-79																			

BATTING AND BASE RUNNING LEADERS

Batting Average
D. Parker, PIT	.338
G. Templeton, STL	.322
G. Foster, CIN	.320
K. Griffey, CIN	.318
T. Simmons, STL	.318

Slugging Average
G. Foster, CIN	.631
G. Luzinski, PHI	.594
R. Smith, LA	.576
M. Schmidt, PHI	.574
J. Bench, CIN	.540

Home Runs
G. Foster, CIN	52
J. Burroughs, ATL	41
G. Luzinski, PHI	39
M. Schmidt, PHI	38
S. Garvey, LA	33

Total Bases
G. Foster, CIN	388
D. Parker, PIT	338
G. Luzinski, PHI	329
S. Garvey, LA	322
M. Schmidt, PHI	312

Runs Batted In
G. Foster, CIN	149
G. Luzinski, PHI	130
S. Garvey, LA	115
J. Burroughs, ATL	114
B. Watson, HOU	110
R. Cey, LA	110

Stolen Bases
F. Taveras, PIT	70
C. Cedeno, HOU	61
G. Richards, SD	56
O. Moreno, PIT	53
J. Morgan, CIN	49

Hits
D. Parker, PIT	215
P. Rose, CIN	204
G. Templeton, STL	200
G. Foster, CIN	197

Base on Balls
G. Tenace, SD	125
J. Morgan, CIN	117
R. Smith, LA	104
M. Schmidt, PHI	104

Home Run Percentage
G. Foster, CIN	8.5
J. Burroughs, ATL	7.1
G. Luzinski, PHI	7.0
M. Schmidt, PHI	7.0

Runs Scored
G. Foster, CIN	124
K. Griffey, CIN	117
M. Schmidt, PHI	114
J. Morgan, CIN	113

Doubles
D. Parker, PIT	44
D. Cash, MON	42
K. Hernandez, STL	41
W. Cromartie, MON	41

Triples
G. Templeton, STL	18
G. Richards, SD	11
M. Schmidt, PHI	11
B. Almon, SD	11

PITCHING LEADERS

Winning Percentage
Candelaria, PIT	.800
T. Seaver, CIN, NY	.778
Christenson, PHI	.760
T. John, LA	.741
B. Forsch, STL	.741

Earned Run Average
Candelaria, PIT	2.34
T. Seaver, CIN, NY	2.58
B. Hooton, LA	2.62
S. Carlton, PHI	2.64
T. John, LA	2.78

Wins
S. Carlton, PHI	23
T. Seaver, CIN, NY	21
Candelaria, PIT	20
T. John, LA	20
B. Forsch, STL	20
R. Reuschel, CHI	20

Saves
R. Fingers, SD	35
B. Sutter, CHI	31
G. Gossage, PIT	26
C. Hough, LA	22
G. Lavelle, SF	20
S. Lockwood, NY	20

Strikeouts
P. Niekro, ATL	262
J. Richard, HOU	214
S. Rogers, MON	206
S. Carlton, PHI	198
T. Seaver, CIN, NY	196

Complete Games
P. Niekro, ATL	20
T. Seaver, CIN, NY	19
S. Carlton, PHI	17
S. Rogers, MON	17
J. Richard, HOU	13

Fewest Hits/9 Innings
T. Seaver, CIN, NY	6.85
J. Richard, HOU	7.15
S. Carlton, PHI	7.28
B. Hooton, LA	7.43

Shutouts
T. Seaver, CIN, NY	7
R. Reuschel, CHI	4
S. Rogers, MON	4

Fewest Walks/9 Innings
Candelaria, PIT	1.95
T. John, LA	2.05
D. Rau, LA	2.08
J. Barr, SF	2.15

Most Strikeouts/9 Inn.
J. Koosman, NY	7.61
J. Richard, HOU	7.21
P. Niekro, ATL	7.15
T. Seaver, CIN, NY	6.75

Innings
P. Niekro, ATL	330
S. Rogers, MON	302
S. Carlton, PHI	283
J. Richard, HOU	267

Games Pitched
R. Fingers, SD	78
D. Spillner, SD	76
D. Tomlin, SD	76
B. Metzger, SD, STL	75

NATIONAL LEAGUE 1977, *cont.*

		W	L	PCT	GB	R	OR	2B	3B	HR	BA	SA	SB	E	DP	FA	CG	BB	SO	ShO	SV	ERA
										Batting					**Fielding**				**Pitching**			
East	Philadelphia	101	61	.623		**847**	668	266	56	186	**.279**	**.448**	135	120	168	.981	31	482	856	4	**47**	3.71
	Pittsburgh	96	66	.593	5	734	665	278	57	133	.274	.413	**260**	145	137	.977	25	485	890	**15**	39	3.61
	St. Louis	83	79	.512	18	737	688	252	56	96	.270	.388	134	139	**174**	.978	26	532	768	10	31	3.81
	Chicago	81	81	.500	20	692	739	271	37	111	.266	.387	64	153	147	.977	16	489	**942**	10	44	4.01
	Montreal	75	87	.463	26	665	736	**294**	50	138	.260	.402	88	129	128	.980	31	579	856	11	33	4.01
	New York	64	98	.395	37	587	663	227	30	88	.244	.346	98	134	132	.978	27	490	911	12	28	3.77
West	Los Angeles	98	64	.605		769	582	223	28	**191**	.266	.418	114	124	160	.981	34	**438**	930	13	39	**3.22**
	Cincinnati	88	74	.543	10	802	725	269	42	181	.274	.436	170	**95**	154	**.984**	33	544	868	12	32	4.22
	Houston	81	81	.500	17	680	650	263	**60**	114	.254	.385	187	142	136	.978	**37**	545	871	11	28	3.54
	San Francisco	75	87	.463	23	673	711	227	41	134	.253	.383	90	179	136	.972	27	529	854	10	33	3.75
	San Diego	69	93	.426	29	692	834	245	49	120	.249	.375	133	189	142	.971	6	673	827	5	44	4.43
	Atlanta	61	101	.377	37	678	895	218	20	139	.254	.376	82	175	127	.972	28	701	915	5	31	4.85
						8556	8556	3033	526	1631	.262	.396	1555	1724	1741	.977	321	6487	10488	118	429	3.91

AMERICAN LEAGUE 1977

	POS	Player	AB	BA	HR	RBI	PO	A	E	DP	TC/G	FA	Pitcher	G	IP	W	L	SV	ERA
East **New York** W-100 L-62 Billy Martin	1B	C. Chambliss	600	.287	17	90	1368	98	16	129	9.4	.989	E. Figueroa	32	239	16	11	0	3.58
	2B	W. Randolph	551	.274	4	40	350	454	16	108	5.6	.980	M. Torrez	31	217	14	12	0	3.86
	SS	B. Dent	477	.247	8	49	250	434	18	90	4.5	.974	R. Guidry	31	211	16	7	1	2.82
	3B	G. Nettles	589	.255	37	107	132	321	12	31	3.0	.974	D. Gullett	22	158	14	4	0	3.59
	RF	R. Jackson	525	.286	32	110	236	7	13	0	2.0	.949	D. Tidrow	49	151	11	4	5	3.16
	CF	M. Rivers	565	.326	12	69	380	11	7	1	2.9	.982	C. Hunter	22	143	9	9	0	4.72
	LF	R. White	519	.268	14	52	301	7	6	**4**	2.3	.981	S. Lyle	**72**	137	13	5	26	2.17
	C	T. Munson	595	.308	18	100	657	73	12	4	5.5	.984							
	DH	L. Piniella	339	.330	12	45													
	DH	C. May	181	.227	2	16													
	OF	P. Blair	164	.262	4	25	125	1	4	0	1.6	.969							
	UT	C. Johnson	142	.296	12	31	145	14	1	13		.994							
Baltimore W-97 L-64 Earl Weaver	1B	L. May	585	.253	27	99	907	56	5	101	8.8	.995	J. Palmer	39	319	**20**	11	0	2.91
	2B	B. Smith	367	.215	5	29	260	272	5	78	5.2	.991	R. May	37	252	18	14	0	3.61
	SS	M. Belanger	402	.206	2	30	244	417	10	82	4.7	**.985**	M. Flanagan	36	235	15	10	1	3.64
	3B	D. DeCinces	522	.259	19	69	124	**330**	20	**34**	3.2	.958	R. Grimsley	34	218	14	10	0	3.96
	RF	K. Singleton	536	.328	24	99	278	8	4	2	1.9	.986	D. Martinez	42	167	14	7	4	4.10
	CF	A. Bumbry	518	.317	4	41	329	7	3	0	2.6	.991	S. McGregor	29	114	3	5	4	4.42
	LF	P. Kelly	360	.256	10	49	181	2	3	1	1.7	.984	T. Martinez	41	50	5	1	9	2.70
	C	R. Dempsey	270	.226	3	34	416	52	11	10	5.3	.977	D. Drago	36	40	6	3	3	3.63
	DH	E. Murray	611	.283	27	88													
	2B	R. Dauer	304	.243	5	25	179	213	7	55	4.8	.982							
	OF	A. Mora	233	.245	13	44	66	2	0	0	1.2	1.000							
	C	D. Skaggs	216	.287	1	24	344	34	2	4	4.8	.995							
Boston W-97 L-64 Don Zimmer	1B	G. Scott	584	.269	33	95	1446	115	**24**	150	10.1	.985	F. Jenkins	28	193	10	10	0	3.68
	2B	D. Doyle	455	.240	2	49	230	412	14	90	4.8	.979	R. Cleveland	36	190	11	8	2	4.26
	SS	R. Burleson	**663**	.293	3	52	**285**	482	24	111	5.1	.970	L. Tiant	32	189	12	8	0	4.53
	3B	B. Hobson	593	.265	30	112	128	272	23	27	2.7	.946	B. Stanley	41	151	8	7	3	3.99
	RF	D. Evans	230	.287	14	36	126	2	1	0	2.0	.992	B. Campbell	69	140	13	9	31	2.96
	CF	F. Lynn	497	.260	18	76	333	7	2	1	2.7	.994	B. Lee	27	128	9	5	1	4.77
	LF	Yastrzemski	558	.296	28	102	287	16	0	1	2.2	**1.000**	R. Wise	26	128	11	5	0	4.78
	C	C. Fisk	536	.315	26	102	779	69	11	7	5.7	.987	M. Paxton	29	108	10	5	0	3.83
	DH	J. Rice	644	.320	**39**	114							Willoughby	31	55	6	2	2	4.94
	OF	B. Carbo	228	.289	15	34	131	5	7	1	2.1	.951							
	OF	R. Miller	189	.254	0	24	118	5	1	3	1.6	.992							
Detroit W-74 L-88 Ralph Houk	1B	J. Thompson	585	.270	31	105	**1599**	97	16	135	**10.8**	.991	D. Rozema	28	218	15	7	0	3.10
	2B	T. Fuentes	615	.309	5	51	**379**	459	**26**	115	5.7	.970	F. Arroyo	38	209	8	18	0	4.18
	SS	T. Veryzer	350	.197	2	28	185	377	18	62	4.7	.969	B. Sykes	32	133	5	7	0	4.40
	3B	A. Rodriguez	306	.219	10	32	60	222	8	19	3.1	.972	D. Roberts	22	129	4	10	0	5.16
	RF	B. Oglivie	450	.262	21	61	236	10	6	3	2.1	.976	J. Crawford	37	126	7	8	1	4.79
	CF	R. LeFlore	652	.325	16	57	365	12	11	0	2.5	.972	J. Hiller	45	124	8	14	7	3.56
	LF	S. Kemp	552	.257	18	88	252	10	5	1	1.8	.981	M. Wilcox	20	106	6	2	0	3.65
	C	M. May	397	.249	12	46	551	78	9	**12**	5.7	.986	M. Fidrych	11	81	6	4	0	2.89
	DH	R. Staub	623	.278	22	101							S. Foucault	44	74	7	7	13	3.16
	3B	P. Mankowski	286	.276	3	27	73	196	10	15	3.3	.964							
	OF	M. Stanley	222	.230	8	23	101	2	3	0	1.9	.972							
	C	Wockenfuss	164	.274	9	25	175	20	3	2	5.4	.985							

AMERICAN LEAGUE 1977, cont.

	POS	Player	AB	BA	HR	RBI	PO	A	E	DP	TC/G	FA	Pitcher	G	IP	W	L	SV	ERA
Cleveland	1B	A. Thornton	433	.263	28	70	1026	71	6	97	9.4	.995	W. Garland	38	283	13	19	0	3.59
	2B	D. Kuiper	610	.277	1	50	334	449	12	104	5.4	.985	D. Eckersley	33	247	14	13	0	3.53
W-71 L-90	SS	F. Duffy	334	.201	4	31	145	301	15	62	3.8	.967	J. Bibby	37	207	12	13	2	3.57
	3B	B. Bell	479	.292	11	64	111	253	15	23	3.2	.960	R. Waits	37	135	9	7	2	4.00
Frank Robinson	RF	J. Norris	440	.270	2	37	320	9	6	1	2.7	.982	Fitzmorris	29	133	6	10	0	5.41
W-26 L-31	CF	R. Manning	252	.226	5	18	191	2	2	0	2.9	.990	P. Dobson	33	133	3	12	1	6.16
	LF	P. Dade	461	.291	3	45	167	10	2	2	1.8	.989	D. Hood	41	105	2	1	0	3.00
Jeff Torborg	C	F. Kendall	317	.249	3	39	506	35	5	5	5.4	.991	J. Kern	60	92	8	10	18	3.42
W-45 L-59	DH	R. Carty	461	.280	15	80													
	O1	B. Bochte	392	.304	5	43	438	28	9	18		.981							
	UT	L. Blanks	322	.286	6	38	100	181	11	27		.962							
	C	R. Fosse	238	.265	6	27	427	48	8	4	6.3	.983							
	OF	R. Pruitt	219	.288	2	32	104	2	3	0	1.6	.972							
Milwaukee	1B	C. Cooper	643	.300	20	78	1386	118	12	134	10.2	.992	J. Slaton	32	221	10	14	0	3.58
	2B	D. Money	570	.279	25	83	256	357	12	82	5.4	.981	J. Augustine	33	209	12	18	0	4.48
W-67 L-95	SS	R. Yount	605	.288	4	49	256	449	26	94	4.8	.964	M. Haas	32	198	10	12	0	4.32
	3B	S. Bando	580	.250	17	82	96	277	13	31	2.9	.966	E. Rodriguez	42	143	5	6	4	4.34
Alex Grammas	RF	S. Lezcano	400	.273	21	49	238	11	3	2	2.3	.988	L. Sorensen	23	142	7	10	0	4.37
	CF	V. Joshua	536	.261	9	49	311	8	10	0	2.4	.970	B. Travers	19	122	4	12	0	5.24
	LF	J. Wohlford	391	.248	2	36	246	6	5	1	2.1	.981	M. Caldwell	21	94	5	8	0	4.60
	C	C. Moore	375	.248	5	45	566	78	13	10	4.8	.980	B. Castro	51	69	8	6	13	4.17
	DH	J. Quirk	221	.217	3	13													
	OF	S. Brye	241	.249	7	28	166	8	0	1	2.1	1.000							
Toronto	1B	D. Ault	445	.245	11	64	1113	103	16	91	10.1	.987	D. Lemanczyk	34	252	13	16	0	4.25
	2B	S. Staggs	291	.258	2	28	169	194	13	35	5.2	.965	J. Garvin	34	245	10	18	0	4.19
W-54 L-107	SS	H. Torres	266	.241	5	26	82	165	5	29	3.7	.980	J. Jefferson	33	217	9	17	0	4.31
	3B	R. Howell	364	.316	10	44	81	165	12	12	3.0	.953	P. Vuckovich	53	148	7	7	8	3.47
Roy Hartsfield	RF	B. Bailor	496	.310	5	32	156	10	2	2	2.7	.988	M. Willis	43	107	2	6	5	3.95
	CF	G. Woods	227	.216	0	17	154	4	1	0	2.7	.994	J. Byrd	17	87	2	13	0	6.21
	LF	A. Woods	440	.284	6	35	215	6	7	1	2.0	.969	J. Johnson	43	86	2	4	5	4.40
	C	A. Ashby	396	.210	2	29	619	71	11	11	5.7	.984	J. Clancy	13	77	4	9	0	5.03
	DH	R. Fairly	458	.279	19	64							B. Singer	13	60	2	8	0	6.75
	OF	O. Velez	360	.256	16	62	140	5	4	1	1.9	.973							
	3D	D. Rader	313	.240	13	40	38	103	5	2	3.2	.966							
	UT	D. McKay	274	.197	3	22	141	205	14	36		.961							
	OD	S. Ewing	244	.287	4	34	65	1	3	0	1.5	.957							
	OF	J. Scott	233	.240	2	15	127	3	5	2	2.0	.963							
	OF	S. Bowling	194	.206	1	13	139	14	2	0	1.8	.987							
West **Kansas City**	1B	J. Mayberry	543	.230	23	82	1296	81	7	118	9.5	**.995**	D. Leonard	38	293	20	12	1	3.04
	2B	F. White	474	.245	5	50	310	434	8	86	4.9	**.989**	J. Colborn	36	239	18	14	0	3.62
W-102 L-60	SS	F. Patek	497	.262	5	60	252	413	29	70	4.5	.958	Splittorff	37	229	16	6	0	3.69
	3B	G. Brett	564	.312	22	88	115	325	20	33	3.4	.957	A. Hassler	29	156	9	6	0	4.21
Whitey Herzog	RF	A. Cowens	606	.312	23	112	307	14	6	2	2.1	.982	M. Pattin	31	128	10	3	0	3.59
	CF	A. Otis	478	.251	17	78	326	10	3	0	2.4	.991	D. Bird	53	118	11	4	14	3.89
	LF	T. Poquette	342	.292	2	33	177	4	0	1	1.9	1.000	L. Gura	52	106	8	5	10	3.14
	C	D. Porter	425	.275	16	60	663	61	13	4	5.9	.982	M. Littell	48	105	8	4	12	3.60
	DH	H. McRae	641	.298	21	92							S. Mingori	43	64	2	4	4	3.09
	UT	P. LaCock	218	.303	3	29	203	9	2	16		.991							
	OF	J. Zdeb	195	.297	2	23	93	4	3	0	1.1	.970							
	C	J. Wathan	119	.328	2	21	130	9	1	0	4.0	.993							
Texas	1B	M. Hargrove	525	.305	18	69	1393	100	11	134	9.9	.993	G. Perry	34	238	15	12	0	3.37
	2B	B. Wills	541	.287	9	62	321	492	15	89	5.5	.982	D. Alexander	34	237	17	11	0	3.65
W-94 L-68	SS	Campaneris	552	.254	5	46	269	483	25	91	5.2	.968	B. Blyleven	30	235	14	12	0	2.72
	3B	T. Harrah	539	.263	27	87	108	278	15	20	2.5	.963	D. Ellis	23	167	10	6	1	2.90
Frank Lucchesi	RF	Washington	521	.284	12	68	255	11	6	3	2.1	.978	N. Briles	30	168	6	4	1	4.07
W-31 L-31	CF	J. Beniquez	424	.269	10	42	311	10	4	1	2.6	.988	A. Devine	56	106	11	6	15	3.57
	LF	D. May	340	.241	7	42	181	8	6	2	1.8	.969	P. Lindblad	42	99	4	5	4	4.18
Eddie Stanky	C	J. Sundberg	453	.291	6	65	801	103	5	12	6.1	**.994**	R. Moret	18	72	3	3	4	3.75
W-1 L-0	DH	W. Horton	519	.289	15	75							D. Knowles	42	50	5	2	4	3.24
	OF	K. Henderson	244	.258	5	23	113	0	2	0	1.8	.983							
Connie Ryan	OF	T. Grieve	236	.225	7	30	77	5	2	1	1.4	.976							
W-2 L-4	UT	K. Bevacqua	96	.333	5	28	42	31	1	4		.986							
Billy Hunter																			
W-60 L-33																			
Chicago	1B	J. Spencer	470	.247	18	69	977	90	10	76	8.6	.991	F. Barrios	33	231	14	7	0	4.13
	2B	J. Orta	564	.282	11	84	287	335	19	64	4.6	.970	S. Stone	31	207	15	12	0	4.52
W-90 L-72	SS	A. Bannister	560	.275	3	57	259	325	**40**	51	4.7	.936	K. Kravec	26	167	11	8	0	4.10
	3B	E. Soderholm	460	.280	25	67	99	249	8	18	2.8	**.978**	C. Knapp	27	146	12	7	0	4.81
Bob Lemon	RF	R. Garr	543	.300	10	54	225	10	3	2	1.9	.987	W. Wood	24	123	7	8	0	4.98
	CF	C. Lemon	553	.273	19	67	512	12	12	2	3.6	.982	L. LaGrow	66	99	7	3	25	2.45
	LF	R. Zisk	531	.290	30	101	210	9	4	3	2.0	.982	B. Johnson	29	92	4	5	2	4.01
	C	J. Essian	322	.273	10	44	592	62	9	8	6.0	.986	K. Brett	13	83	6	4	0	5.01
	DH	O. Gamble	408	.297	31	83							D. Hamilton	55	67	4	5	9	3.63
	D1	L. Johnson	374	.302	18	65	346	32	4	31	8.5	.990							
	C	B. Downing	169	.284	4	25	320	28	6	5	5.8	.983							
	32	J. Brohamer	152	.257	2	20	54	100	8	15		.951							
	OF	W. Nordhagen	124	.315	4	22	50	1	3	0	1.2	.944							

AMERICAN LEAGUE 1977, *cont.*

	POS	Player	AB	BA	HR	RBI	PO	A	E	DP	TC/G	FA	Pitcher	G	IP	W	L	SV	ERA
Minnesota	1B	R. Carew	616	**.388**	14	100	1459	121	10	161	10.5	.994	D. Goltz	39	303	**20**	11	0	3.36
	2B	B. Randall	306	.239	0	22	222	297	8	74	5.2	.985	Thormodsgard	37	218	11	15	0	4.52
W-84 L-77	SS	R. Smalley	584	.231	6	56	255	**504**	33	116	5.3	.958	G. Zahn	34	198	12	14	0	4.68
	3B	M. Cubbage	417	.264	9	55	90	266	18	29	3.0	.952	T. Johnson	71	147	16	7	0	3.12
Gene Mauch	RF	D. Ford	453	.267	11	60	205	9	8	2	1.6	.964	P. Redfern	30	137	6	9	0	5.19
	CF	L. Hisle	546	.302	28	119	287	11	8	2	2.3	.974	R. Schueler	52	135	8	7	3	4.40
	LF	L. Bostock	593	.336	14	90	349	10	4	0	2.4	.989	T. Burgmeier	61	97	6	4	7	5.10
	C	B. Wynegar	532	.261	10	79	676	84	5	8	5.4	.993							
	DH	C. Kusick	268	.254	12	45													
	DO	G. Adams	269	.338	6	49	60	3	2	1	1.5	.969							
	DH	R. Chiles	261	.264	3	36													
	UT	J. Terrell	214	.224	1	20	58	129	6	20		.969							
	2B	R. Wilfong	171	.246	1	13	114	164	12	40	4.4	.959							
	OF	B. Gorinski	118	.195	3	22	44	0	3	0	1.3	.936							
California	1B	T. Solaita	324	.241	14	53	641	57	7	50	7.7	.990	N. Ryan	37	299	19	16	0	2.77
	2B	J. Remy	575	.252	4	44	307	420	19	90	4.9	.975	F. Tanana	31	241	15	9	0	**2.54**
W-74 L-88	SS	R. Mulliniks	271	.269	3	21	112	229	13	37	4.6	.963	P. Hartzell	41	189	8	12	0	3.57
	3B	D. Chalk	519	.277	3	45	114	266	21	21	2.8	.948	K. Brett	21	142	7	10	0	4.25
Norm Sherry	RF	B. Bonds	592	.264	37	115	272	5	4	0	2.0	.986	W. Simpson	27	122	6	12	0	5.83
W-39 L-42	CF	G. Flores	342	.278	1	26	177	5	4	2	2.2	.978	D. Miller	41	92	4	4	0	3.02
	LF	J. Rudi	242	.264	13	53	131	3	0	0	2.2	1.000	D. LaRoche	46	81	6	5	13	3.10
Dave Garcia	C	T. Humphrey	304	.227	2	34	661	63	8	10	6.0	.989							
W-35 L-46	DH	D. Baylor	561	.251	25	75													
	UT	R. Jackson	292	.243	8	28	314	75	6	33		.985							
	UT	M. Guerrero	244	.283	1	28	61	105	2	18		.988							
	OF	T. Bosley	212	.297	0	19	130	1	5	0	2.5	.963							
	SS	B. Grich	181	.243	7	23	88	141	4	23	4.5	.983							
Seattle	1B	D. Meyer	582	.273	22	90	1407	109	12	134	9.6	.992	G. Abbott	36	204	12	13	0	4.46
	2B	J. Baez	305	.259	1	17	151	250	11	54	5.4	.973	J. Montague	47	182	8	12	4	4.50
W-64 L-98	SS	C. Reynolds	420	.248	4	28	197	397	28	86	4.6	.955	D. Pole	25	122	7	12	0	5.16
	3B	B. Stein	556	.259	13	67	**146**	255	15	20	2.8	.964	E. Romo	58	114	8	10	16	2.84
Darrell Johnson	RF	C. Lopez	297	.283	8	34	160	11	5	3	2.0	.972	D. Segui	40	111	0	7	2	5.68
	CF	R. Jones	597	.263	24	76	465	11	9	3	3.1	.981	M. Kekich	41	90	5	4	5	5.60
	LF	S. Braun	451	.235	5	31	186	11	5	3	2.0	.975	T. House	26	89	4	5	1	3.93
	C	B. Stinson	297	.269	8	32	494	43	9	11	5.5	.984	G. Wheelock	17	88	6	9	0	4.91
	DH	D. Collins	402	.239	5	28													
	OF	L. Stanton	454	.275	27	90	175	9	9	2	2.1	.953							
	D3	J. Bernhardt	305	.243	7	30	18	37	1	1	2.7	.982							
	2S	L. Milbourne	242	.219	2	21	120	209	11	46		.968							
	2B	J. Cruz	199	.256	1	7	114	171	5	29	5.4	.983							
Oakland	1B	D. Allen	171	.240	5	31	389	37	7	36	8.7	.984	V. Blue	38	280	14	**19**	0	3.83
	2B	M. Perez	373	.231	2	23	192	287	13	48	4.7	.974	R. Langford	37	208	8	**19**	0	4.02
W-63 L-98	SS	R. Picciolo	419	.200	2	22	213	381	21	70	4.2	.966	D. Medich	26	148	10	6	0	4.69
	3B	W. Gross	485	.233	22	63	126	242	27	26	2.7	.932	J. Coleman	43	128	4	4	2	2.95
Jack McKeon	RF	J. Tyrone	294	.245	5	26	167	5	9	0	2.2	.950	B. Lacey	64	122	6	8	7	3.02
W-26 L-27	CF	T. Armas	363	.240	13	53	294	9	4	4	2.8	.981	P. Torrealba	41	117	4	6	2	2.62
	LF	M. Page	501	.307	21	75	279	11	14	0	2.3	.954	D. Bair	45	83	4	6	8	3.47
Bobby Winkles	C	J. Newman	162	.222	4	15	251	36	9	5	3.1	.970	D. Giusti	40	60	3	3	6	3.00
W-37 L-71	DH	Sanguillen	571	.275	6	58													
	2S	R. Scott	364	.261	0	20	198	270	21	49		.957							
	UT	E. Williams	348	.241	13	38	305	26	3	14		.991							
	1O	M. Jorgensen	203	.246	8	32	365	32	4	26		.990							
	UT	R. McKinney	198	.177	6	21	213	27	9	22		.964							
	OF	B. North	184	.261	1	9	112	1	2	0	2.2	.983							
	OF	L. Murray	162	.179	1	9	114	3	1	3	1.5	.992							

BATTING AND BASE RUNNING LEADERS

Batting Average		Slugging Average		Home Runs		Winning Percentage	
R. Carew, MIN	.388	J. Rice, BOS	.593	J. Rice, BOS	39	Splittorff, KC	.727
L. Bostock, MIN	.336	R. Carew, MIN	.570	G. Nettles, NY	37	R. Guidry, NY	.696
K. Singleton, BAL	.328	R. Jackson, NY	.550	B. Bonds, CAL	37	D. Rozema, DET	.682
M. Rivers, NY	.326	L. Hisle, MIN	.533	G. Scott, BOS	33	J. Palmer, BAL	.645
R. LeFlore, DET	.325	G. Brett, KC	.532	R. Jackson, NY	32	D. Goltz, MIN	.645

PITCHING LEADERS

Earned Run Average		Wins	
F. Tanana, CAL	2.54	J. Palmer, BAL	20
B. Blyleven, TEX	2.72	D. Goltz, MIN	20
N. Ryan, CAL	2.77	D. Leonard, KC	20
R. Guidry, NY	2.82	N. Ryan, CAL	19
J. Palmer, BAL	2.91	R. May, BAL	18
		J. Colborn, KC	18

Total Bases		Runs Batted In		Stolen Bases		Saves		Strikeouts		Complete Games	
J. Rice, BOS	382	L. Hisle, MIN	119	F. Patek, KC	53	B. Campbell, BOS	31	N. Ryan, CAL	341	N. Ryan, CAL	22
R. Carew, MIN	351	B. Bonds, CAL	115	M. Page, OAK	42	S. Lyle, NY	26	D. Leonard, KC	244	J. Palmer, BAL	22
H. McRae, KC	330	J. Rice, BOS	114	J. Remy, CAL	41	L. LaGrow, CHI	25	F. Tanana, CAL	205	D. Leonard, KC	21
A. Cowens, KC	318	B. Hobson, BOS	112	B. Bonds, CAL	41	J. Kern, CLE	18	J. Palmer, BAL	193	W. Garland, CLE	21
R. LeFlore, DET	310	A. Cowens, KC	112	R. LeFlore, DET	39	D. LaRoche, CAL, CLE	17	D. Eckersley, CLE	191	F. Tanana, CAL	20

AMERICAN LEAGUE 1977, *cont.*

BATTING AND BASE RUNNING LEADERS

Hits			Base on Balls			Home Run Percentage			Fewest Hits/9 Innings	
R. Carew, MIN	239		T. Harrah, TEX	109		A. Thornton, CLE		6.5	N. Ryan, CAL	5.96
R. LeFlore, DET	212		K. Singleton, BAL	107		G. Nettles, NY		6.3	B. Blyleven, TEX	6.93
J. Rice, BOS	206		M. Hargrove, TEX	103		B. Bonds, CAL		6.3	J. Palmer, BAL	7.42
L. Bostock, MIN	199		W. Gross, OAK	86		R. Jackson, NY		6.1	R. Guidry, NY	7.42

PITCHING LEADERS

Shutouts			Fewest Walks/9 Innings	
F. Tanana, CAL	7		D. Rozema, DET	1.40
R. Guidry, NY	5		F. Jenkins, BOS	1.68
B. Blyleven, TEX	5		P. Hartzell, CAL	1.81
D. Leonard, KC	5		D. Eckersley, CLE	1.97

Runs Scored			Doubles			Triples			Most Strikeouts/9 Inn.	
R. Carew, MIN	128		H. McRae, KC	54		R. Carew, MIN		16	N. Ryan, CAL	10.26
C. Fisk, BOS	106		R. Jackson, NY	39		J. Rice, BOS		15	F. Tanana, CAL	7.64
G. Brett, KC	105		C. Lemon, CHI	38		A. Cowens, KC		14	R. Guidry, NY	7.51
L. Bostock, MIN	104		R. Carew, MIN	38		G. Brett, KC		13	D. Leonard, KC	7.42

Innings			Games Pitched	
J. Palmer, BAL	319		S. Lyle, NY	72
D. Goltz, MIN	303		T. Johnson, MIN	71
N. Ryan, CAL	299		B. Campbell, BOS	69
D. Leonard, KC	296		B. McClure, MIL	68

		W	L	PCT	GB	R	OR	2B	3B	HR	BA	SA	SB	E	DP	FA	CG	BB	SO	ShO	SV	ERA
East	New York	100	62	.617		831	651	267	47	184	.281	.444	93	132	151	.979	52	486	758	16	34	3.61
	Baltimore	97	64	.602	2.5	719	653	231	25	148	.261	.393	90	106	189	.983	65	494	737	11	23	3.74
	Boston	97	64	.602	2.5	859	712	258	56	213	.281	.465	66	133	162	.978	40	378	758	13	40	4.16
	Detroit	74	88	.457	26	714	751	228	45	166	.264	.410	60	142	153	.978	44	470	784	3	23	4.13
	Cleveland	71	90	.441	28.5	676	739	221	46	100	.269	.380	87	130	145	.979	45	550	876	8	30	4.10
	Milwaukee	67	95	.414	33	639	765	255	46	125	.258	.389	85	139	165	.978	38	566	719	6	25	4.32
	Toronto	54	107	.335	45.5	605	822	230	41	100	.252	.365	65	164	133	.974	40	623	771	3	20	4.57
West	Kansas City	102	60	.630		822	651	299	77	146	.277	.436	170	137	145	.978	41	499	850	15	42	3.52
	Texas	94	68	.580	8	767	657	265	39	135	.270	.405	154	117	156	.982	49	471	864	17	31	3.56
	Chicago	90	72	.556	12	844	771	254	52	192	.278	.444	42	159	125	.974	34	516	842	3	40	4.25
	Minnesota	84	77	.522	17.5	867	776	273	60	123	.282	.417	105	143	184	.978	35	507	737	4	25	4.38
	California	74	88	.457	28	675	695	233	40	131	.255	.386	159	147	137	.976	53	572	965	13	26	3.76
	Seattle	64	98	.395	38	624	855	218	33	133	.256	.381	110	147	162	.976	18	578	785	1	31	4.83
	Oakland	63	98	.391	38.5	605	749	176	37	117	.240	.352	176	190	136	.970	32	560	788	4	26	4.05
						10247	10247	3408	644	2013	.266	.405	1462	1986	2143	.977	586	7270	11234	117	416	4.07

NATIONAL LEAGUE 1978

		POS	Player	AB	BA	HR	RBI	PO	A	E	DP	TC/G	FA	Pitcher	G	IP	W	L	SV	ERA
East	**Philadelphia**	1B	R. Hebner	435	.283	17	71	987	49	6	86	8.9	.994	S. Carlton	34	247	16	13	0	2.84
		2B	T. Sizemore	351	.219	0	25	232	302	12	61	5.1	.978	Christenson	33	228	13	14	0	3.24
		SS	L. Bowa	654	.294	3	43	224	502	10	87	4.7	.986	R. Lerch	33	184	11	8	0	3.96
	W-90 L-72	3B	M. Schmidt	513	.251	21	78	98	324	16	34	3.2	.963	D. Ruthven	20	151	13	5	0	2.99
		RF	B. McBride	472	.269	10	49	234	8	1	3	2.0	.996	J. Kaat	26	140	8	5	0	4.11
	Danny Ozark	CF	G. Maddox	598	.288	11	68	444	7	8	1	3.0	.983	J. Lonborg	22	114	8	10	0	5.21
		LF	G. Luzinski	540	.265	35	101	232	7	4	2	1.6	.984	R. Reed	66	109	3	4	17	2.23
		C	B. Boone	435	.283	12	62	619	55	6	6	5.3	.991	T. McGraw	55	90	8	7	9	3.20
		OF	J. Martin	266	.271	9	36	148	8	2	1	1.4	.987							
		1B	J. Cardenal	201	.249	4	33	360	17	4	39	7.6	.990							
	Pittsburgh	1B	W. Stargell	390	.295	28	97	875	57	6	76	8.4	.994	B. Blyleven	34	244	14	10	0	3.02
		2B	R. Stennett	333	.243	3	35	164	208	11	40	4.8	.971	D. Robinson	35	228	14	6	1	3.47
		SS	F. Taveras	654	.278	0	38	216	448	38	80	4.5	.946	Candelaria	30	189	12	11	1	3.24
	W-88 L-73	3B	P. Garner	528	.261	10	66	67	172	18	12	3.2	.930	J. Rooker	28	163	9	11	0	4.25
		RF	D. Parker	581	.334	30	117	302	12	13	3	2.2	.960	K. Tekulve	91	135	8	7	31	2.33
	Chuck Tanner	CF	O. Moreno	515	.235	2	33	409	9	7	2	2.8	.984	J. Bibby	34	107	8	7	1	3.53
		LF	B. Robinson	499	.246	14	80	235	8	3	2	1.9	.988	B. Kison	28	96	6	6	0	3.19
		C	E. Ott	379	.269	9	38	537	42	15	7	6.1	.975	G. Jackson	60	77	7	5	5	3.27
		OF	J. Milner	295	.271	6	38	118	1	0	0	1.7	1.000	E. Whitson	43	74	5	6	4	3.28
		1C	Sanguillen	220	.264	3	16	438	20	0	26		1.000							
		C	D. Dyer	175	.211	0	13	326	22	3	2	6.4	.991							
	Chicago	1B	B. Buckner	446	.323	5	74	1075	83	6	85	11.1	.995	R. Reuschel	35	243	14	15	0	3.41
		2B	M. Trillo	552	.261	4	55	354	505	19	99	5.9	.978	D. Lamp	37	224	7	15	0	3.29
		SS	I. DeJesus	619	.278	3	35	232	558	27	96	5.1	.967	R. Burris	40	199	7	13	1	4.75
	W-79 L-83	3B	S. Ontiveros	276	.243	1	22	57	194	9	16	3.4	.965	D. Roberts	35	142	6	8	1	5.26
		RF	B. Murcer	499	.281	9	64	225	8	5	0	1.7	.979	M. Krukow	27	138	9	3	0	3.91
	Herman Franks	CF	G. Gross	347	.265	1	39	182	6	4	1	1.7	.979	D. Moore	71	103	9	7	4	4.11
		LF	D. Kingman	395	.266	28	79	170	8	4	2	1.8	.979	B. Sutter	64	99	8	10	27	3.18
		C	D. Rader	305	.203	3	36	412	51	11	7	4.2	.977	G. Hernandez	54	60	8	2	3	3.75
		1O	L. Biittner	343	.257	4	50	601	53	9	53		.986							
		OF	G. Clines	229	.258	0	17	84	6	2	0	1.4	.978							
		3B	R. Scott	227	.282	0	15	43	101	11	15	2.6	.929							
		OF	M. Vail	180	.333	4	33	50	1	1	0	1.2	.981							

NATIONAL LEAGUE 1978, *cont.*

	POS	Player	AB	BA	HR	RBI	PO	A	E	DP	TC/G	FA	Pitcher	G	IP	W	L	SV	ERA
Montreal	1B	T. Perez	544	.290	14	78	1181	82	11	116	8.8	.991	R. Grimsley	36	263	20	11	0	3.05
	2B	D. Cash	658	.252	3	43	**362**	400	11	91	4.9	**.986**	S. Rogers	30	219	13	10	1	2.47
W-76 L-86	SS	C. Speier	501	.251	5	51	245	467	18	93	4.9	.975	Schatzeder	29	144	7	7	0	3.06
	3B	L. Parrish	520	.277	15	70	122	288	23	20	3.1	.947	R. May	27	144	8	10	0	3.88
Dick Williams	RF	E. Valentine	570	.289	25	76	296	**24**	10	3	2.3	.970	W. Twitchell	33	112	4	12	0	5.38
	CF	A. Dawson	609	.253	25	72	411	17	5	2	2.8	.988	H. Dues	25	99	5	6	1	2.36
	LF	W. Cromartie	607	.297	10	56	340	24	8	5	2.4	.978	W. Fryman	19	95	5	7	1	3.61
	C	G. Carter	533	.255	20	72	**781**	83	10	9	5.8	.989	S. Bahnsen	44	75	1	5	7	3.84
	10	D. Unser	179	.196	2	15	232	12	2	16		.992	D. Knowles	60	72	3	3	6	2.38
St. Louis	1B	K. Hernandez	542	.255	11	64	1436	96	10	124	9.8	.994	B. Forsch	34	234	11	17	0	3.69
	2B	M. Tyson	377	.233	3	26	246	306	13	78	4.6	.977	J. Denny	33	234	14	11	0	2.96
W-69 L-93	SS	G. Templeton	647	.280	2	47	**285**	523	40	108	5.5	.953	P. Vuckovich	45	198	12	12	1	2.55
	3B	K. Reitz	540	.246	10	75	111	314	12	18	2.9	**.973**	S. Martinez	22	138	9	8	0	3.65
Vern Rapp	RF	J. Morales	457	.239	4	46	254	5	6	0	2.1	.977	M. Littell	72	106	4	8	11	2.80
W-6 L-11	CF	G. Hendrick	382	.288	17	67	241	5	1	0	2.4	.996	J. Urrea	27	99	4	9	0	5.36
	LF	J. Mumphrey	367	.262	2	37	178	10	1	1	1.6	.995	B. Schultz	62	83	2	4	6	3.80
Jack Krol	C	T. Simmons	516	.287	22	80	670	**88**	9	6	5.7	.988							
W-1 L-1	OF	L. Brock	298	.221	0	12	114	2	3	0	1.5	.975							
	OF	T. Scott	219	.228	1	14	100	6	6	0	1.5	.946							
Ken Boyer	2B	M. Phillips	164	.268	1	28	93	110	6	24	3.8	.971							
W-62 L-81	1B	R. Freed	92	.239	2	20	110	10	1	13	8.1	.992							
New York	1B	W. Montanez	609	.256	17	96	1350	**104**	8	**138**	9.3	.995	J. Koosman	38	235	3	15	2	3.75
	2B	D. Flynn	532	.237	0	36	249	299	8	70	4.3	.986	C. Swan	29	207	9	6	0	**2.43**
W-66 L-96	SS	T. Foli	413	.257	1	27	190	314	18	78	4.7	.966	N. Espinosa	32	204	11	15	0	4.72
	3B	L. Randle	437	.233	2	35	108	215	11	21	2.7	.967	P. Zachry	21	138	10	6	0	3.33
Joe Torre	RF	E. Maddox	389	.257	2	39	155	8	2	3	2.3	.988	M. Bruhert	27	134	4	11	0	4.77
	CF	L. Mazzilli	542	.273	16	61	386	8	5	3	2.8	.987	K. Kobel	32	108	5	6	0	2.92
	LF	S. Henderson	587	.266	10	65	315	18	11	3	2.2	.968	S. Lockwood	57	91	7	13	15	3.56
	C	J. Stearns	477	.264	15	73	711	84	12	7	5.7	.985	D. Murray	53	86	8	5	5	3.65
	UT	Youngblood	266	.252	7	30	160	96	6	21		.977							
	OF	B. Boisclair	214	.224	4	15	114	3	2	0	1.7	.983							
West **Los Angeles**	1B	S. Garvey	639	.316	21	113	**1546**	74	9	121	**10.1**	.994	D. Sutton	34	238	15	11	0	3.55
	2B	D. Lopes	587	.278	17	58	337	424	20	88	5.3	.974	B. Hooton	32	236	19	10	0	2.71
W-95 L-67	SS	B. Russell	625	.286	3	46	245	533	31	91	5.2	.962	T. John	33	213	17	10	1	3.30
	3B	R. Cey	555	.270	23	84	116	336	16	26	3.0	.966	D. Rau	30	199	15	9	0	3.26
Tom Lasorda	RF	R. Smith	447	.295	29	93	220	8	12	4	1.9	.950	R. Rhoden	30	165	10	8	0	3.65
	CF	R. Monday	342	.254	19	57	209	3	1	0	2.1	.995	B. Welch	23	111	7	4	3	2.03
	LF	D. Baker	522	.262	11	66	250	13	4	1	1.8	.985	C. Hough	55	93	5	5	7	3.29
	C	S. Yeager	228	.193	4	23	373	55	5	3	4.8		T. Forster	47	65	5	4	22	1.94
	OF	B. North	304	.234	0	10	232	2	6	1	2.3	.975							
	UT	L. Lacy	245	.261	13	40	114	64	9	7		.952							
	C	J. Ferguson	198	.237	7	28	284	23	5	2	5.0	.984							
Cincinnati	1B	D. Driessen	524	.250	16	70	1264	93	6	92	9.0	**.996**	T. Seaver	36	260	16	14	0	2.87
	2B	J. Morgan	441	.236	13	75	252	290	11	49	4.5	.980	F. Norman	36	177	11	9	1	3.71
W-92 L-69	SS	Concepcion	565	.301	6	67	255	459	23	72	4.8	.969	T. Hume	42	174	8	11	1	4.14
	3B	P. Rose	655	.302	7	52	117	256	15	23	2.5	.961	P. Moskau	26	145	6	4	1	3.97
Sparky Anderson	RF	K. Griffey	614	.288	10	63	296	13	10	2	2.1	.969	B. Bonham	23	140	11	5	0	3.54
	CF	C. Geronimo	296	.226	5	27	259	4	5	1	2.3	.981	M. Sarmiento	63	127	9	7	5	4.39
	LF	G. Foster	604	.281	**40**	**120**	319	10	10	1	2.2	.971	D. Bair	70	100	7	6	28	1.98
	C	J. Bench	393	.260	23	73	605	48	7	6	**6.2**	.989	P. Borbon	62	99	8	2	4	5.00
	OF	M. Lum	146	.267	6	23	69	6	1	2	1.8	.987	M. LaCoss	16	96	4	8	0	4.50
San Francisco	1B	W. McCovey	351	.228	12	64	721	44	10	49	8.0	.987	B. Knepper	36	260	17	11	0	2.63
	2B	B. Madlock	447	.309	15	44	223	299	14	48	4.7	.974	V. Blue	35	258	18	10	0	2.79
W-89 L-73	SS	J. LeMaster	272	.235	1	14	135	260	14	40	4.3	.966	Montefusco	36	239	11	9	0	3.80
	3B	D. Evans	547	.243	20	78	**147**	348	25	25	3.4	.952	E. Halicki	29	199	9	10	1	2.85
Joe Altobelli	RF	J. Clark	592	.306	25	98	320	16	6	5	2.3	.982	J. Barr	32	163	8	11	1	3.53
	CF	L. Herndon	471	.259	1	32	369	3	10	0	2.6	.974	G. Lavelle	67	98	13	10	14	3.31
	LF	T. Whitfield	488	.289	10	32	249	7	3	2	1.8	.988	R. Moffitt	70	82	8	4	12	3.29
	C	M. Hill	358	.243	3	36	586	56	9	3	5.6	.986							
	1B	M. Ivie	318	.308	11	55	550	18	3	33	7.5	.995							
	SS	R. Metzger	235	.260	0	17	112	184	8	30	4.1	.974							
	OF	H. Cruz	197	.223	6	24	82	5	2	3	1.7	.978							
	2B	R. Andrews	177	.220	1	11	120	131	6	23	4.1	.977							
	O1	J. Dwyer	173	.225	5	22	197	14	2	14		.991							

NATIONAL LEAGUE 1978, *cont.*

	POS	Player	AB	BA	HR	RBI	PO	A	E	DP	TC/G	FA	Pitcher	G	IP	W	L	SV	ERA
San Diego	1B	G. Tenace	401	.224	16	61	668	37	5	61	8.9	.993	G. Perry	37	261	**21**	6	0	2.72
	2B	F. Gonzalez	320	.250	2	29	190	256	8	68	4.8	.982	R. Jones	37	253	13	14	0	2.88
W-84 L-78	SS	O. Smith	590	.258	1	46	264	548	25	98	5.3	.970	B. Owchinko	36	202	10	13	0	3.56
	3B	B. Almon	405	.252	0	21	72	221	21	20	2.8	.933	B. Shirley	50	166	8	11	5	3.69
Roger Craig	RF	O. Gamble	375	.275	7	47	172	12	4	3	1.8	.979	E. Rasmussen	27	146	12	10	0	4.06
	CF	G. Richards	555	.308	4	45	210	8	8	0	1.8	.965	R. Fingers	67	107	6	13	37	2.52
	LF	D. Winfield	587	.308	24	97	321	7	7	1	2.2	.979	D'Acquisto	45	93	4	3	10	2.13
	C	R. Sweet	226	.221	1	11	337	33	6	3	4.9	.984							
	UT	D. Thomas	352	.227	3	26	328	168	12	39		.976							
	OF	J. Turner	225	.280	8	37	91	5	3	0	1.7	.970							
	1B	B. Perkins	217	.240	2	33	538	41	4	56	9.9	.993							
	UT	T. Ashford	155	.245	3	26	108	53	6	22		.964							
Houston	1B	B. Watson	461	.289	14	79	974	95	9	63	8.4	.992	J. Richard	36	275	18	11	0	3.11
	2B	A. Howe	420	.293	7	55	224	289	12	51	4.9	.977	Lemongello	33	210	9	14	1	3.94
W-74 L-88	SS	R. Landestoy	218	.266	0	9	65	132	4	18	4.0	.980	J. Niekro	35	203	14	14	0	3.86
	3B	E. Cabell	**660**	.295	7	71	136	274	18	15	2.8	.958	T. Dixon	30	140	7	11	1	3.99
Bill Virdon	RF	J. Cruz	565	.315	10	83	311	4	8	0	2.1	.975	K. Forsch	52	133	10	5	1	2.71
	CF	C. Cedeno	192	.281	7	23	149	2	2	1	3.1	.987	J. Andujar	35	111	5	7	1	3.41
	LF	T. Puhl	585	.289	3	35	386	6	3	2	2.7	.992	F. Bannister	28	110	3	9	0	4.83
	C	L. Pujols	153	.131	1	11	271	33	6	2	5.6	.981	J. Sambito	62	88	4	9	11	3.07
	OF	D. Walling	247	.251	3	36	140	4	3	2	1.9	.980							
	2B	J. Gonzalez	223	.233	1	16	62	112	3	21	3.3	.983							
	1O	D. Bergman	186	.231	0	12	328	16	4	26		.989							
	C	J. Ferguson	150	.207	7	22	288	29	2	0	6.3	.994							
Atlanta	1B	D. Murphy	530	.226	23	79	1137	92	**20**	84	9.7	.984	P. Niekro	44	**334**	19	**18**	1	2.88
	2B	J. Royster	529	.259	2	35	186	193	10	39	5.2	.974	P. Hanna	29	140	7	13	0	5.14
W-69 L-93	SS	D. Chaney	245	.224	3	20	97	189	7	30	3.8	.976	M. Mahler	34	135	4	11	0	4.67
	3B	B. Horner	323	.266	23	63	81	199	13	17	3.3	.956	E. Solomon	37	106	4	6	2	4.08
Bobby Cox	RF	G. Matthews	474	.285	18	62	238	10	8	0	2.0	.969	McWilliams	15	99	9	3	0	2.82
	CF	R. Office	404	.250	9	40	291	4	3	2	2.2	.990	J. Easterly	37	78	3	6	1	5.65
	LF	J. Burroughs	488	.301	23	77	224	13	6	2	1.7	.975	G. Garber	43	78	4	4	22	2.53
	C	B. Pocoroba	289	.242	6	34	454	43	5	1	6.4	.990	A. Devine	31	65	5	4	3	5.95
	32	R. Gilbreath	326	.245	3	31	108	204	9	22		.972	T. Boggs	16	59	2	8	0	6.71
	OF	B. Bonnell	304	.240	1	16	172	7	3	1	1.7	.984							
	C	J. Nolan	213	.230	4	22	295	24	7	3	5.3	.979							
	1B	B. Beall	185	.243	1	16	275	24	4	23	7.6	.987							
	2B	G. Hubbard	163	.258	2	13	102	130	5	30	5.4	.979							

BATTING AND BASE RUNNING LEADERS

Batting Average
D. Parker, PIT .334
S. Garvey, LA .316
J. Cruz, HOU .315
D. Winfield, SD .308
G. Richards, SD .308

Slugging Average
D. Parker, PIT .585
R. Smith, LA .559
G. Foster, CIN .546
J. Clark, SF .537
J. Burroughs, ATL .529

Home Runs
G. Foster, CIN 40
G. Luzinski, PHI 35
D. Parker, PIT 30
R. Smith, LA 29
W. Stargell, PIT 28
D. Kingman, CHI 28

Total Bases
D. Parker, PIT 340
G. Foster, CIN 330
S. Garvey, LA 319
J. Clark, SF 318
D. Winfield, SD 293

Runs Batted In
G. Foster, CIN 120
D. Parker, PIT 117
S. Garvey, LA 113
G. Luzinski, PHI 101
J. Clark, SF 98

Stolen Bases
O. Moreno, PIT 71
F. Taveras, PIT 46
D. Lopes, LA 45
I. DeJesus, CHI 41
O. Smith, SD 40

Hits
S. Garvey, LA 202
P. Rose, CIN 198
E. Cabell, HOU 195
D. Parker, PIT 194

Base on Balls
J. Burroughs, ATL 117
D. Evans, SF 105
G. Tenace, SD 101
G. Luzinski, PHI 100

Home Run Percentage
G. Foster, CIN 6.6
R. Smith, LA 6.5
G. Luzinski, PHI 6.5
D. Parker, PIT 5.2

Runs Scored
I. DeJesus, CHI 104
P. Rose, CIN 103
D. Parker, PIT 102
G. Foster, CIN 97

Doubles
P. Rose, CIN 51
J. Clark, SF 46
T. Simmons, STL 40
L. Parrish, MON 39

Triples
G. Templeton, STL 13
G. Richards, SD 12
D. Parker, PIT 12

PITCHING LEADERS

Winning Percentage
G. Perry, SD .778
D. Robinson, PIT .700
B. Hooton, LA .655
R. Grimsley, MON .645
V. Blue, SF .643

Earned Run Average
C. Swan, NY 2.43
S. Rogers, MON 2.47
P. Vuckovich, STL 2.55
B. Knepper, SF 2.63
B. Hooton, LA 2.71

Wins
G. Perry, SD 21
R. Grimsley, MON 20
B. Hooton, LA 19
P. Niekro, ATL 19
V. Blue, SF 18
J. Richard, HOU 18

Saves
R. Fingers, SD 37
K. Tekulve, PIT 31
D. Bair, CIN 28
B. Sutter, CHI 27
G. Garber, ATL, PHI 25

Strikeouts
J. Richard, HOU 303
P. Niekro, ATL 248
T. Seaver, CIN 226
B. Blyleven, PIT 182
Montefusco, SF 177

Complete Games
P. Niekro, ATL 22
R. Grimsley, MON 19
B. Knepper, SF 16
J. Richard, HOU 16
S. Carlton, PHI 12
D. Sutton, LA 12

Fewest Hits/9 Innings
J. Richard, HOU 6.28
C. Swan, NY 7.13
B. Hooton, LA 7.47
E. Halicki, SF 7.51

Shutouts
B. Knepper, SF 6
E. Halicki, SF 4
B. Blyleven, PIT 4
V. Blue, SF 4

Fewest Walks/9 Innings
Christenson, PHI 1.86
J. Barr, SF 1.93
R. Reuschel, CHI 2.00
E. Halicki, SF 2.04

Most Strikeouts/9 Inn.
J. Richard, HOU 9.92
T. Seaver, CIN 7.82
P. Vuckovich, STL 6.77
B. Blyleven, PIT 6.71

Innings
P. Niekro, ATL 334
J. Richard, HOU 275
R. Grimsley, MON 263
G. Perry, SD 261

Games Pitched
K. Tekulve, PIT 91
M. Littell, STL 72
D. Moore, CHI 71
D. Bair, CIN 70

NATIONAL LEAGUE 1978, cont.

		W	L	PCT	GB	R	OR	2B	3B	HR	BA	SA	SB	E	DP	FA	CG	BB	SO	ShO	SV	ERA
									Batting						**Fielding**				**Pitching**			
East	Philadelphia	90	72	.556		708	586	248	32	133	.258	.388	152	**104**	155	**.983**	38	**393**	813	9	29	3.33
	Pittsburgh	88	73	.547	1.5	684	637	239	**54**	115	.257	.385	**213**	167	133	.973	30	499	880	13	44	3.41
	Chicago	79	83	.488	11	664	724	224	48	72	**.264**	.361	110	144	154	.978	24	539	768	7	38	4.05
	Montreal	76	86	.469	14	633	611	269	31	121	.254	.379	80	134	150	.979	42	572	740	7	33	3.42
	St. Louis	69	93	.426	21	600	657	263	44	79	.249	.358	97	136	155	.978	32	600	859	13	22	3.58
	New York	66	96	.407	24	607	690	227	47	86	.245	.352	100	132	159	.979	21	531	775	7	26	3.87
West	Los Angeles	95	67	.586		**727**	**573**	251	27	**149**	.264	**.402**	137	140	138	.978	46	440	800	16	38	**3.12**
	Cincinnati	92	69	.571	2.5	710	688	**270**	32	136	.256	.393	137	134	120	.978	16	567	908	10	46	3.81
	San Francisco	89	73	.549	6	613	594	240	41	117	.248	.374	87	146	118	.977	42	453	840	17	29	3.30
	San Diego	84	78	.519	11	591	598	208	42	75	.252	.348	152	160	**171**	.975	21	483	744	10	**55**	3.28
	Houston	74	88	.457	21	605	634	231	45	70	.258	.355	178	133	109	.978	**48**	578	**930**	17	23	3.63
	Atlanta	69	93	.426	26	600	750	191	39	123	.244	.363	90	153	126	.975	29	624	848	12	32	4.08
						7742	7742	2861	482	1276	.254	.372	1533	1683	1688	.978	389	6279	9905	144	414	3.58

AMERICAN LEAGUE 1978

		POS	Player	AB	BA	HR	RBI	PO	A	E	DP	TC/G	FA	Pitcher	G	IP	W	L	SV	ERA
East	**New York**	1B	C. Chambliss	625	.274	12	90	1366	111	4	119	9.6	**.997**	R. Guidry	35	274	**25**	3	0	**1.74**
	W-100 L-63	2B	W. Randolph	499	.279	3	42	296	400	16	80	5.3	.978	E. Figueroa	35	253	20	9	0	2.99
		SS	B. Dent	379	.243	5	40	178	341	10	56	4.3	.981	D. Tidrow	31	185	7	11	0	3.84
	Billy Martin	3B	G. Nettles	587	.276	27	93	109	326	11	30	2.8	.975	G. Gossage	63	134	10	11	27	2.01
	W-52 L-42	RF	R. Jackson	511	.274	27	97	212	6	3	1	2.1	.986	J. Beattie	25	128	6	9	0	3.73
	Dick Howser	CF	M. Rivers	559	.265	11	48	384	8	8	2	2.9	.980	C. Hunter	21	118	12	6	0	3.58
	W-0 L-1	LF	L. Piniella	472	.314	6	69	213	4	7	0	2.2	.969	S. Lyle	59	112	9	3	9	3.47
		C	T. Munson	617	.297	6	71	666	61	10	4	5.9	.986							
	Bob Lemon	DH	C. Johnson	174	.184	6	19													
	W-48 L-20	OF	R. White	346	.269	8	43	128	1	1	0	1.8	.992							
		DH	J. Spencer	150	.227	7	24													
		OF	G. Thomasson	116	.276	3	20	101	4	3	1	2.2	.972							
	Boston	1B	G. Scott	412	.233	12	54	1052	55	10	99	9.9	.991	D. Eckersley	35	268	20	8	0	2.99
		2B	J. Remy	583	.278	2	44	327	444	13	**114**	5.6	.983	M. Torrez	36	250	16	13	0	3.96
	W-99 L-64	SS	R. Burleson	626	.248	5	49	285	482	15	100	5.4	.981	L. Tiant	32	212	13	8	0	3.31
		3B	B. Hobson	512	.250	17	80	122	261	**43**	25	3.2	.899	B. Lee	28	177	10	10	0	3.46
	Don Zimmer	RF	D. Evans	497	.247	24	63	305	14	6	2	2.3	.982	B. Stanley	52	142	15	2	10	2.60
		CF	F. Lynn	541	.298	22	82	408	11	7	2	2.9	.984	J. Wright	24	116	8	4	0	3.57
		LF	J. Rice	677	.315	46	139	245	13	3	1	2.3	.989	D. Drago	37	77	4	4	7	3.03
		C	C. Fisk	571	.284	20	88	733	90	17	13	5.5	.980	B. Campbell	29	51	7	5	4	3.91
		DH	Yastrzemski	523	.277	17	81													
		UT	J. Brohamer	244	.234	1	25	64	103	5	18		.971							
	Milwaukee	1B	C. Cooper	407	.312	13	54	842	66	11	71	10.9	.988	M. Caldwell	37	293	22	9	1	2.36
		2B	P. Molitor	521	.273	6	45	197	283	12	57	5.4	.976	L. Sorensen	37	281	18	12	1	3.21
	W-93 L-69	SS	R. Yount	502	.293	9	71	246	453	30	78	**5.8**	.959	J. Augustine	35	188	13	12	0	4.54
		3B	S. Bando	540	.285	17	78	89	329	14	25	3.2	.968	B. Travers	28	176	12	11	0	4.41
	George Bamberger	RF	S. Lezcano	442	.292	15	61	262	**18**	6	5	2.3	.979	A. Replogle	32	149	9	5	0	3.93
		CF	G. Thomas	452	.246	32	86	345	5	6	0	2.6	.983	E. Rodriguez	32	105	5	5	3	3.93
		LF	L. Hisle	520	.290	34	115	172	6	4	2	2.1	.978	B. McClure	44	65	2	6	9	3.74
		C	C. Moore	268	.269	5	31	314	41	6	3	3.8	.983	B. Castro	42	50	5	4	8	1.81
		DH	D. Davis	218	.248	5	26													
		UT	D. Money	518	.293	14	54	705	216	9	88		.990							
		OF	B. Oglivie	469	.303	18	72	187	5	4	0	2.2	.980							
		C	B. Martinez	256	.219	1	20	327	32	8	7	4.1	.978							
	Baltimore	1B	E. Murray	610	.285	27	95	**1504**	106	5	143	10.3	.997	J. Palmer	38	**296**	21	12	0	2.46
		2B	R. Dauer	459	.264	6	46	193	239	1	60	5.0	.998	M. Flanagan	40	281	19	15	0	4.03
	W-90 L-71	SS	M. Belanger	348	.213	0	16	184	409	9	76	4.5	**.985**	D. Martinez	40	276	16	11	0	3.52
		3B	D. DeCinces	511	.286	28	80	111	280	10	27	3.1	.975	S. McGregor	35	233	15	13	1	3.32
	Earl Weaver	RF	K. Singleton	502	.293	20	81	244	1	6	0	1.8	.976	D. Stanhouse	56	75	6	9	24	2.89
		CF	L. Harlow	460	.243	8	26	313	7	7	2	2.4	.979	T. Martinez	42	69	3	3	5	4.83
		LF	C. Lopez	193	.238	4	20	151	7	2	2	1.4	.988							
		C	R. Dempsey	441	.259	6	32	636	79	11	**14**	5.4	.985							
		DH	L. May	556	.246	25	80													
		OF	P. Kelly	274	.274	11	40	123	3	4	1	1.6	.969							
		2B	B. Smith	250	.260	5	30	146	208	5	43	4.3	.986							
		OF	A. Mora	229	.214	8	14	129	4	3	0	2.0	.978							
		SS	K. Garcia	186	.263	0	13	86	173	15	35	3.7	.945							

AMERICAN LEAGUE 1978, *cont.*

Detroit — W-86 L-76 — Ralph Houk

POS	Player	AB	BA	HR	RBI	PO	A	E	DP	TC/G	FA	Pitcher	G	IP	W	L	SV	ERA
1B	J. Thompson	589	.287	26	96	1503	92	11	153	10.6	.993	J. Slaton	35	234	17	11	0	4.12
2B	L. Whitaker	484	.285	3	58	301	458	17	95	5.7	.978	M. Wilcox	29	215	13	12	0	3.76
SS	A. Trammell	448	.268	2	34	239	421	14	95	4.8	.979	D. Rozema	28	209	9	12	0	3.14
3B	A. Rodriguez	385	.265	7	43	79	228	4	20	2.4	.987	Billingham	30	202	15	8	0	3.88
RF	T. Corcoran	324	.265	1	27	186	6	3	4	1.8	.985	J. Morris	28	106	3	5	0	4.33
CF	R. LeFlore	666	.297	12	62	440	9	11	4	3.0	.976	K. Young	14	106	6	7	0	2.81
LF	S. Kemp	582	.277	15	79	325	11	8	2	2.2	.977	B. Sykes	22	94	6	6	2	3.94
C	M. May	352	.250	10	37	406	58	10	5	5.0	.979	J. Hiller	51	92	9	4	15	2.34
DH	R. Staub	642	.273	24	121							S. Foucault	24	37	2	4	4	3.16
C	L. Parrish	288	.219	14	41	353	39	5	5	5.0	.987							
3B	P. Mankowski	222	.275	4	20	42	129	5	17	2.2	.972							
OF	Wockenfuss	187	.283	7	22	89	2	2	0	1.6	.978							

Cleveland — W-69 L-90 — Jeff Torborg

POS	Player	AB	BA	HR	RBI	PO	A	E	DP	TC/G	FA	Pitcher	G	IP	W	L	SV	ERA
1B	A. Thornton	508	.262	33	105	1327	106	7	106	9.9	.995	R. Waits	34	230	13	15	0	3.20
2B	D. Kuiper	547	.283	0	43	341	408	16	91	5.1	.979	R. Wise	33	213	9	19	0	4.32
SS	T. Veryzer	421	.271	1	32	177	375	21	58	4.4	.963	M. Paxton	33	191	12	11	1	3.86
3B	B. Bell	556	.282	6	62	125	355	15	30	3.6	.970	D. Hood	36	155	5	6	0	4.47
RF	J. Grubb	378	.265	14	61	199	14	6	4	2.0	.973	D. Clyde	28	153	8	11	0	4.28
CF	R. Manning	566	.263	3	50	377	7	2	1	2.7	.995	J. Kern	58	99	10	10	13	3.08
LF	J. Norris	315	.283	2	27	153	6	2	2	2.1	.988	S. Monge	48	85	4	3	6	2.76
C	G. Alexander	324	.235	17	62	305	34	6	3	5.2	.983							
DH	B. Carbo	174	.287	4	16													
OF	P. Dade	307	.254	3	20	171	6	7	2	2.3	.962							
UT	T. Cox	227	.233	0	19	100	42	4	6		.973							
S2	L. Blanks	193	.254	2	20	81	138	13	25		.944							
CO	R. Pruitt	187	.235	6	17	199	15	4	4		.982							
DH	W. Horton	169	.249	5	22													

Toronto — W-59 L-102 — Roy Hartsfield

POS	Player	AB	BA	HR	RBI	PO	A	E	DP	TC/G	FA	Pitcher	G	IP	W	L	SV	ERA
1B	J. Mayberry	515	.250	22	70	1143	52	8	120	8.7	.993	J. Jefferson	31	212	7	16	0	4.38
2B	D. McKay	504	.238	7	45	310	408	12	96	5.2	.984	T. Underwood	31	198	6	14	0	4.10
SS	L. Gomez	413	.223	0	32	247	400	16	97	4.3	.976	J. Clancy	31	194	10	12	0	4.09
3B	R. Howell	551	.270	8	61	109	306	22	27	3.3	.950	B. Moore	37	144	6	9	0	4.68
RF	B. Bailor	621	.264	1	52	303	15	12	7	2.6	.964	J. Garvin	26	145	4	12	0	5.52
CF	R. Bosetti	568	.259	5	42	417	17	6	1	3.3	.986	D. Lemanczyk	29	137	4	14	0	6.26
LF	O. Velez	248	.266	9	38	150	10	3	4	2.2	.982	M. Willis	44	101	3	7	7	4.56
C	R. Cerone	282	.223	3	20	426	44	4	7	5.6	.992	T. Murphy	50	94	6	9	7	3.93
DH	R. Carty	387	.284	20	68							V. Cruz	32	47	7	3	9	1.71
C	A. Ashby	264	.261	9	29	399	38	6	6	5.5	.986							
UT	W. Upshaw	224	.237	1	17	131	4	7	5		.951							
OF	A. Woods	220	.241	3	25	131	2	3	0	2.3	.978							
OF	T. Hutton	173	.254	2	9	85	2	0	0	1.6	1.000							

West — Kansas City — W-92 L-70 — Whitey Herzog

POS	Player	AB	BA	HR	RBI	PO	A	E	DP	TC/G	FA	Pitcher	G	IP	W	L	SV	ERA
1B	P. LaCock	322	.295	5	48	700	39	5	67	7.0	.993	D. Leonard	40	295	21	17	0	3.33
2B	F. White	461	.275	7	50	325	385	16	96	5.2	.978	Splittorff	39	262	19	13	0	3.40
SS	F. Patek	440	.248	2	46	240	350	32	84	4.5	.949	L. Gura	35	222	16	4	0	2.72
3B	G. Brett	510	.294	9	62	104	289	16	25	3.2	.961	R. Gale	31	192	14	8	0	3.09
RF	A. Cowens	485	.274	5	63	275	10	3	5	2.3	.990	D. Bird	40	99	6	6	1	5.29
CF	A. Otis	486	.298	22	96	382	9	2	1	2.9	.995	M. Pattin	32	79	3	3	4	3.32
LF	T. Poquette	204	.216	4	30	144	5	7	0	2.5	.955	A. Hrabosky	58	75	8	7	20	2.88
C	D. Porter	520	.265	18	78	608	62	8	10	4.7	.988	S. Mingori	45	69	1	4	7	2.74
DH	H. McRae	623	.273	16	72													
O1	C. Hurdle	417	.264	7	56	544	30	12	48		.980							
OF	W. Wilson	198	.217	0	16	171	6	4	2	1.6	.978							
1C	J. Wathan	190	.300	2	28	385	28	2	20		.995							

California — W-87 L-75 — Dave Garcia W-25 L-20 — Jim Fregosi W-62 L-55

POS	Player	AB	BA	HR	RBI	PO	A	E	DP	TC/G	FA	Pitcher	G	IP	W	L	SV	ERA
1B	R. Fairly	235	.217	10	40	482	31	1	47	6.6	.998	F. Tanana	33	239	18	12	0	3.65
2B	B. Grich	487	.251	6	42	325	419	13	77	5.3	.983	N. Ryan	31	235	10	13	0	3.72
SS	D. Chalk	470	.253	1	34	168	237	19	46	4.4	.955	C. Knapp	30	188	14	8	0	4.21
3B	C. Lansford	453	.294	8	52	93	182	17	18	2.5	.942	D. Aase	29	179	11	8	0	4.03
RF	R. Miller	475	.263	1	37	353	9	4	5	2.8	.989	P. Hartzell	54	157	6	10	6	3.44
CF	L. Bostock	568	.296	5	71	366	7	4	2	2.6	.989	K. Brett	31	100	3	5	1	4.95
LF	J. Rudi	497	.256	17	79	231	4	2	1	2.1	.992	D. LaRoche	59	96	10	9	25	2.81
C	B. Downing	412	.255	7	46	681	82	5	6	6.0	.993							
DH	D. Baylor	591	.255	34	99													
13	R. Jackson	387	.297	6	57	605	88	7	56		.990							
OF	K. Landreaux	260	.223	5	23	138	6	2	0	1.8	.986							

Texas — W-87 L-75 — Billy Hunter W-86 L-75 — Pat Corrales W-1 L-0

POS	Player	AB	BA	HR	RBI	PO	A	E	DP	TC/G	FA	Pitcher	G	IP	W	L	SV	ERA
1B	M. Hargrove	494	.251	7	40	1221	116	17	90	9.7	.987	J. Matlack	35	270	15	13	1	2.27
2B	B. Wills	539	.250	9	57	350	526	17	84	5.7	.981	F. Jenkins	34	249	18	8	0	3.04
SS	Campaneris	269	.186	1	17	151	263	20	44	4.9	.954	D. Alexander	31	191	9	10	0	3.86
3B	T. Harrah	450	.229	12	59	54	167	8	15	2.5	.965	D. Medich	28	171	9	8	2	3.74
RF	B. Bonds	475	.265	29	82	213	13	7	5	2.1	.970	D. Ellis	22	141	9	7	0	4.20
CF	J. Beniquez	473	.260	11	50	309	8	9	1	2.6	.972	S. Comer	30	117	11	5	1	2.30
LF	A. Oliver	525	.324	14	89	219	8	3	1	2.1	.987	J. Umbarger	32	98	5	8	1	4.88
C	J. Sundberg	518	.278	6	58	769	91	3	14	5.8	.997	R. Cleveland	53	76	5	7	12	3.09
DH	R. Zisk	511	.262	22	85							L. Barker	29	52	1	5	4	4.82
UT	K. Bevacqua	248	.222	6	30	62	116	18	12		.908							
UT	Lowenstein	176	.222	5	21	34	42	6	2		.927							

AMERICAN LEAGUE 1978, *cont.*

Minnesota
W-73 L-89
Gene Mauch

POS	Player	AB	BA	HR	RBI	PO	A	E	DP	TC/G	FA	Pitcher	G	IP	W	L	SV	ERA
1B	R. Carew	564	.333	5	70	1362	105	16	134	10.0	.989	R. Erickson	37	266	14	13	0	3.96
2B	B. Randall	330	.270	0	21	231	345	10	81	5.1	.983	G. Zahn	35	252	14	14	0	3.03
SS	R. Smalley	586	.273	19	77	287	527	25	121	5.3	.970	D. Goltz	29	220	15	10	0	2.49
3B	M. Cubbage	394	.282	7	57	65	233	9	24	2.7	.971	G. Serum	34	184	9	9	1	4.10
RF	D. Ford	592	.274	11	82	376	6	9	2	2.6	.977	M. Marshall	54	99	10	12	21	2.36
CF	H. Powell	381	.247	3	31	219	9	4	2	2.0	.983	D. Jackson	19	92	4	6	0	4.48
LF	W. Norwood	428	.255	8	46	227	7	14	1	2.2	.944	Perzanowski	13	57	2	7	1	5.24
C	B. Wynegar	454	.229	4	45	582	70	8	12	5.0	.988							
DH	G. Adams	310	.258	7	35													
OF	B. Rivera	251	.271	3	23	162	5	3	0	1.8	.982							
DH	J. Morales	242	.314	2	38													
3B	L. Wolfe	235	.234	3	25	60	143	10	9	2.6	.953							
2B	R. Wilfong	199	.266	1	11	152	196	5	37	4.4	.986							
OF	R. Chiles	198	.268	1	22	108	3	4	0	1.9	.965							
UT	C. Kusick	191	.173	4	20	228	22	4	14		.984							

Chicago
W-71 L-90

Bob Lemon
W-34 L-40

Larry Doby
W-37 L-50

POS	Player	AB	BA	HR	RBI	PO	A	E	DP	TC/G	FA	Pitcher	G	IP	W	L	SV	ERA
1B	L. Johnson	498	.273	6	72	887	71	8	74	8.9	.992	S. Stone	30	212	12	12	0	4.37
2B	J. Orta	420	.274	13	53	275	290	9	62	5.0	.984	K. Kravec	30	203	11	16	0	4.08
SS	D. Kessinger	431	.255	1	31	171	321	13	60	4.1	.974	F. Barrios	33	196	9	15	0	4.05
3B	E. Soderholm	457	.258	20	67	128	245	14	17	3.0	.964	W. Wood	28	168	10	10	0	5.20
RF	Washington	314	.264	6	31	159	6	7	0	2.1	.959	Willoughby	59	93	1	6	13	3.86
CF	C. Lemon	357	.300	13	55	284	8	5	2	3.1	.983	L. LaGrow	52	88	6	5	16	4.40
LF	R. Garr	443	.275	3	29	205	5	9	2	2.0	.959							
C	B. Nahorodny	347	.236	8	35	486	53	11	6	5.3	.980							
DH	B. Molinaro	286	.262	6	27													
UT	G. Pryor	222	.261	2	15	100	202	11	31		.965							
OF	T. Bosley	219	.269	2	13	155	3	4	0	2.5	.975							
UT	W. Nordhagen	206	.301	5	35	87	12	6	2		.943							
DH	R. Blomberg	156	.231	5	22													
C	M. Colbern	141	.270	2	20	203	19	7	1	4.9	.969							

Oakland
W-69 L-93

Bobby Winkles
W-24 L-15

Jack McKeon
W-45 L-78

POS	Player	AB	BA	HR	RBI	PO	A	E	DP	TC/G	FA	Pitcher	G	IP	W	L	SV	ERA
1B	D. Revering	521	.271	16	46	1013	110	13	98	8.2	.989	M. Keough	32	197	8	15	0	3.24
2B	M. Edwards	414	.273	1	23	228	309	20	71	4.2	.964	J. Johnson	33	186	11	10	0	3.39
SS	M. Guerrero	505	.275	3	38	258	330	26	67	4.3	.958	R. Langford	37	176	7	13	0	3.43
3B	W. Gross	285	.200	7	23	72	150	20	22	2.3	.917	P. Broberg	35	166	10	12	0	4.62
RF	T. Armas	239	.213	2	13	214	3	2	0	2.6	.991	S. Renko	27	151	6	12	0	4.29
CF	M. Dilone	258	.229	1	14	195	3	3	1	2.0	.985	D. Heaverlo	69	130	3	6	10	3.63
LF	M. Page	516	.285	17	70	211	4	6	0	1.9	.973	B. Lacey	74	120	8	9	5	3.01
C	J. Essian	278	.223	3	26	431	78	10	12	4.4	.981	E. Sosa	68	109	8	2	14	2.64
DH	G. Alexander	174	.207	10	22							A. Wirth	16	81	5	6	0	3.43
3B	T. Duncan	319	.257	2	37	63	119	9	4	2.3	.953							
OF	J. Wallis	279	.237	6	26	187	7	4	5	2.5	.980							
C1	J. Newman	268	.239	9	32	399	41	12	20		.973							
OF	G. Burke	200	.235	1	14	152	1	2	0	2.3	.987							
OF	D. Alston	173	.208	1	10	86	0	4	0	1.8	.956							
DH	R. Carty	141	.277	11	31													

Seattle
W-56 L-104

Darrell Johnson

POS	Player	AB	BA	HR	RBI	PO	A	E	DP	TC/G	FA	Pitcher	G	IP	W	L	SV	ERA
1B	D. Meyer	444	.227	8	56	1104	79	13	119	9.9	.989	P. Mitchell	29	168	8	14	0	4.18
2B	J. Cruz	550	.235	1	25	286	472	10	101	5.4	.987	G. Abbott	29	155	7	15	0	5.27
SS	C. Reynolds	548	.292	5	44	243	461	29	102	5.0	.960	R. Honeycutt	26	134	5	11	0	4.89
3B	B. Stein	403	.261	4	37	72	244	24	21	3.1	.929	T. House	34	116	5	4	0	4.66
RF	B. Bochte	486	.263	11	51	172	7	3	2	2.0	.984	J. Colborn	20	114	3	10	0	5.37
CF	R. Jones	472	.235	6	46	393	10	6	2	3.2	.985	S. Rawley	52	111	4	9	4	4.12
LF	L. Roberts	472	.301	22	92	296	10	8	4	2.5	.975	E. Romo	56	107	11	7	10	3.69
C	B. Stinson	364	.258	11	55	472	60	7	7	4.4	.987	McLaughlin	56	107	4	8	0	4.37
DH	L. Stanton	302	.182	3	24							J. Todd	49	107	3	4	3	3.88
OF	T. Paciorek	251	.299	4	30	95	3	2	0	1.9	.980	D. Pole	21	99	4	11	0	6.48
UT	L. Milbourne	234	.226	2	20	92	169	9	27		.967							
OF	J. Hale	211	.171	4	22	160	1	2	0	1.7	.988							
D1	B. Robertson	174	.230	8	28	141	8	0	16	8.3	1.000							
13	J. Bernhardt	165	.230	2	12	263	63	6	21		.982							

BATTING AND BASE RUNNING LEADERS

Batting Average

R. Carew, MIN	.333
A. Oliver, TEX	.324
J. Rice, BOS	.315
L. Piniella, NY	.314
B. Oglivie, MIL	.303

Slugging Average

J. Hisle, MIL	.600
L. Hisle, MIL	.533
D. DeCinces, BAL	.526
A. Otis, KC	.525
A. Thornton, CLE	.516

Home Runs

J. Rice, BOS	46
L. Hisle, MIL	34
D. Baylor, CAL	34
A. Thornton, CLE	33
G. Thomas, MIL	32

PITCHING LEADERS

Winning Percentage

R. Guidry, NY	.893
B. Stanley, BOS	.882
L. Gura, KC	.800
D. Eckersley, BOS	.714
M. Caldwell, MIL	.710

Earned Run Average

R. Guidry, NY	1.74
J. Matlack, TEX	2.27
M. Caldwell, MIL	2.36
J. Palmer, BAL	2.46
D. Goltz, MIN	2.49

Wins

R. Guidry, NY	25
M. Caldwell, MIL	22
J. Palmer, BAL	21
D. Leonard, KC	21
D. Eckersley, BOS	20
E. Figueroa, NY	20

Total Bases

J. Rice, BOS	406
E. Murray, BAL	293
D. Baylor, CAL	279
R. Staub, DET	279
J. Thompson, DET	278

Runs Batted In

J. Rice, BOS	139
R. Staub, DET	121
L. Hisle, MIL	115
A. Thornton, CLE	105
R. Carty, OAK, TOR	99
D. Baylor, CAL	99

Stolen Bases

R. LeFlore, DET	68
J. Cruz, SEA	59
B. Wills, TEX	52
M. Dilone, OAK	50
W. Wilson, KC	46

Saves

G. Gossage, NY	27
D. LaRoche, CAL	25
D. Stanhouse, BAL	24
M. Marshall, MIN	21
A. Hrabosky, KC	20

Strikeouts

N. Ryan, CAL	260
R. Guidry, NY	248
D. Leonard, KC	183
M. Flanagan, BAL	167
D. Eckersley, BOS	162

Complete Games

M. Caldwell, MIL	23
D. Leonard, KC	20
J. Palmer, BAL	19
J. Matlack, TEX	18
L. Sorensen, MIL	17
M. Flanagan, BAL	17

AMERICAN LEAGUE 1978, cont.

BATTING AND BASE RUNNING LEADERS

Hits

J. Rice, BOS	213
R. LeFlore, DET	198
R. Carew, MIN	188
T. Munson, NY	183

Base on Balls

M. Hargrove, TEX	107
K. Singleton, BAL	98
S. Kemp, DET	97
A. Thornton, CLE	93

Home Run Percentage

G. Thomas, MIL	7.1
J. Rice, BOS	6.8
L. Hisle, MIL	6.5
A. Thornton, CLE	6.5

Runs Scored

R. LeFlore, DET	126
J. Rice, BOS	121
D. Baylor, CAL	103
A. Thornton, CLE	97

Doubles

G. Brett, KC	45
C. Fisk, BOS	39
H. McRae, KC	39
D. DeCinces, BAL	37

Triples

J. Rice, BOS	15
R. Carew, MIN	10
D. Ford, MIN	10
R. Garr, CHI	9

PITCHING LEADERS

Fewest Hits/9 Innings

R. Guidry, NY	6.15
N. Ryan, CAL	7.01
L. Gura, KC	7.43
J. Palmer, BAL	7.48

Shutouts

R. Guidry, NY	9
M. Caldwell, MIL	6
J. Palmer, BAL	6
L. Tiant, BOS	5

Fewest Walks/9 Innings

F. Jenkins, TEX	1.48
L. Sorensen, MIL	1.60
M. Caldwell, MIL	1.66
J. Matlack, TEX	1.70

Most Strikeouts/9 Inn.

N. Ryan, CAL	9.96
R. Guidry, NY	8.16
K. Kravec, CHI	6.83
T. Underwood, TOR	6.33

Innings

J. Palmer, BAL	296
D. Leonard, KC	295
M. Caldwell, MIL	293
M. Flanagan, BAL	281

Games Pitched

B. Lacey, OAK	74
D. Heaverlo, OAK	69
E. Sosa, OAK	68
G. Gossage, NY	63

		W	L	PCT	GB	R	OR	2B	3B	HR	BA	SA	SB	E	DP	FA	CG	BB	SO	ShO	SV	ERA
East	New York *	100	63	.613		735	582	228	38	125	.267	.388	98	113	136	.982	39	478	817	16	36	3.18
	Boston	99	64	.607	1	796	657	270	46	172	.267	.424	74	146	172	.977	57	464	706	15	26	3.54
	Milwaukee	93	69	.574	6.5	804	650	265	38	173	.276	.432	95	150	144	.977	62	398	577	19	33	3.65
	Baltimore	90	71	.559	9	659	633	248	19	154	.258	.396	75	110	166	.982	65	509	754	16	33	3.56
	Detroit	86	76	.531	13.5	714	653	218	34	129	.271	.392	90	118	177	.981	60	503	684	12	21	3.64
	Cleveland	69	90	.434	29	639	694	223	45	106	.261	.379	64	123	142	.980	36	568	739	6	28	3.97
	Toronto	59	102	.366	40	590	775	217	39	98	.250	.359	28	131	163	.979	35	614	758	5	23	4.55
West	Kansas City	92	70	.568		743	634	305	59	98	.268	.399	216	150	152	.976	53	478	657	14	33	3.44
	California	87	75	.537	5	691	666	226	28	108	.259	.370	86	136	136	.978	44	599	892	13	33	3.65
	Texas	87	75	.537	5	692	632	216	36	132	.253	.381	196	153	140	.976	54	421	776	12	25	3.42
	Minnesota	73	89	.451	19	666	678	259	47	82	.267	.375	99	146	171	.977	48	520	703	9	26	3.69
	Chicago	71	90	.441	20.5	634	731	221	41	106	.264	.379	83	139	130	.977	38	586	710	9	33	4.22
	Oakland	69	93	.426	23	532	690	200	31	100	.245	.351	144	179	142	.971	26	582	750	11	29	3.62
	Seattle	56	104	.350	35	614	834	229	37	97	.248	.359	123	141	172	.978	28	567	630	4	20	4.72
						9509	9509	3325	538	1680	.261	.385	1471	1935	2143	.978	645	7287	10153	161	390	3.77

* Defeated Boston in a 1 game playoff.

NATIONAL LEAGUE 1979

East — Pittsburgh
W-98 L-64
Chuck Tanner

POS	Player	AB	BA	HR	RBI	PO	A	E	DP	TC/G	FA	Pitcher	G	IP	W	L	SV	ERA
1B	W. Stargell	424	.281	32	82	949	47	3	102	8.8	.997	B. Blyleven	37	237	12	5	0	3.61
2B	P. Garner	549	.293	11	59	175	234	8	58	5.0	.981	Candelaria	33	207	14	9	0	3.22
SS	T. Foli	525	.291	1	65	255	404	15	97	5.1	.978	B. Kison	33	172	13	7	0	3.19
3B	B. Madlock	311	.328	7	44	63	153	7	12	2.6	.969	D. Robinson	29	161	8	8	0	3.86
RF	D. Parker	622	.310	25	94	341	15	15	1	2.3	.960	J. Bibby	34	138	12	4	0	2.80
CF	O. Moreno	695	.282	8	69	490	11	13	3	3.2	.975	K. Tekulve	94	134	10	8	31	2.75
LF	B. Robinson	421	.264	24	75	161	6	3	0	1.4	.982	E. Romo	84	129	10	5	5	3.00
C	E. Ott	403	.273	7	51	612	53	4	6	5.8	.994	J. Rooker	19	104	4	7	0	4.59
O1	J. Milner	326	.276	16	60	367	20	8	28		.980	G. Jackson	72	82	8	5	14	2.96
2B	R. Stennett	319	.238	0	24	172	282	12	63	4.6	.974							
C	S. Nicosia	191	.288	4	13	320	25	3	4	5.4	.991							
OF	L. Lacy	182	.247	5	15	70	3	2	0	1.8	.973							

Montreal
W-95 L-65
Dick Williams

POS	Player	AB	BA	HR	RBI	PO	A	E	DP	TC/G	FA	Pitcher	G	IP	W	L	SV	ERA
1B	T. Perez	489	.270	13	73	1114	65	11	81	9.2	.991	S. Rogers	37	249	13	12	0	3.00
2B	R. Scott	562	.238	3	42	301	324	13	71	5.6	.980	B. Lee	33	222	16	10	0	3.04
SS	C. Speier	344	.227	7	26	194	355	17	52	5.1	.970	S. Sanderson	34	168	9	8	1	3.43
3B	L. Parrish	544	.307	30	82	119	290	23	25	2.8	.947	Schatzeder	32	162	10	5	1	2.83
RF	E. Valentine	548	.276	21	82	281	10	5	2	2.1	.983	R. Grimsley	32	151	10	9	0	5.36
CF	A. Dawson	639	.275	25	92	394	7	5	1	2.7	.988	D. Palmer	36	123	10	2	2	2.63
LF	W. Cromartie	659	.275	8	46	343	16	9	4	2.3	.976	E. Sosa	62	97	8	7	18	1.95
C	G. Carter	505	.283	22	75	751	88	9	12	6.1	.989	R. May	33	94	10	3	0	2.30
2B	D. Cash	187	.321	2	19	88	110	6	18	4.3	.971	W. Fryman	44	58	3	6	10	2.79

St. Louis
W-86 L-76
Ken Boyer

POS	Player	AB	BA	HR	RBI	PO	A	E	DP	TC/G	FA	Pitcher	G	IP	W	L	SV	ERA
1B	K. Hernandez	610	.344	11	105	1489	146	8	145	10.3	.995	P. Vuckovich	34	233	15	10	0	3.59
2B	K. Oberkfell	369	.301	1	35	213	323	8	65	4.6	.985	B. Forsch	33	219	11	11	0	3.82
SS	G. Templeton	672	.314	9	62	292	525	34	102	5.7	.960	S. Martinez	32	207	15	8	0	3.26
3B	K. Reitz	605	.268	8	73	124	290	12	26	2.7	.972	J. Denny	31	206	8	11	0	4.85
RF	G. Hendrick	493	.300	16	75	254	20	2	7	2.0	.993	J. Fulgham	20	146	10	6	0	2.53
CF	T. Scott	587	.259	6	68	427	14	7	5	3.0	.984	M. Littell	63	82	9	4	13	2.20
LF	L. Brock	405	.304	5	38	152	7	7	2	1.7	.958	D. Knowles	48	49	2	5	6	4.04
C	T. Simmons	448	.283	26	87	606	69	10	10	5.6	.985	B. Schultz	31	42	4	3	3	4.50
OF	J. Mumphrey	339	.295	3	32	180	3	3	0	1.6	.984							
2B	M. Tyson	190	.221	5	20	125	184	8	42	4.5	.975							
OF	D. Iorg	179	.291	1	21	51	2	2	0	1.4	.964							

NATIONAL LEAGUE 1979, *cont.*

	POS	Player	AB	BA	HR	RBI	PO	A	E	DP	TC/G	FA	Pitcher	G	IP	W	L	SV	ERA
Philadelphia	1B	P. Rose	628	.331	4	59	1424	87	8	124	9.6	.995	S. Carlton	35	251	18	11	0	3.62
	2B	M. Trillo	431	.260	6	42	270	368	10	84	5.5	.985	R. Lerch	37	214	10	13	0	3.74
W-84 L-78	SS	L. Bowa	539	.241	0	31	229	448	6	80	4.7	.991	N. Espinosa	33	212	14	12	0	3.65
	3B	M. Schmidt	541	.253	45	114	114	361	23	36	3.2	.954	D. Ruthven	20	122	7	5	0	4.28
Danny Ozark	RF	B. McBride	582	.280	12	60	341	12	4	3	2.4	.989	Christenson	19	106	5	10	0	4.50
W-65 L-67	CF	G. Maddox	548	.281	13	61	433	13	2	2	3.2	.996	R. Reed	61	102	13	8	5	4.15
	LF	G. Luzinski	452	.252	18	81	156	3	9	1	1.3	.946	T. McGraw	65	84	4	3	16	5.14
Dallas Green	C	B. Boone	398	.286	9	58	527	65	7	8	5.1	.988	R. Eastwick	51	83	3	6	6	4.88
W-19 L-11	OF	G. Gross	174	.333	0	15	82	5	2	2	1.2	.978							
	O1	D. Unser	141	.298	6	29	118	5	3	6		.976							
Chicago	1B	B. Buckner	591	.284	14	66	1258	124	7	118	9.9	.995	R. Reuschel	36	239	18	12	0	3.62
	2B	T. Sizemore	330	.248	2	24	230	312	15	68	5.8	.973	McGlothen	42	212	13	14	2	4.12
W-80 L-82	SS	I. DeJesus	636	.283	5	52	235	507	32	97	4.8	.959	D. Lamp	38	200	11	10	0	3.51
	3B	S. Ontiveros	519	.285	4	57	98	268	23	27	2.7	.941	M. Krukow	28	165	9	9	0	4.20
Herman Franks	RF	S. Thompson	346	.289	2	29	161	7	5	3	1.7	.971	K. Holtzman	23	118	6	9	0	4.58
W-78 L-77	CF	J. Martin	534	.272	19	73	297	11	6	4	2.2	.981	D. Tidrow	63	103	11	5	4	2.71
	LF	D. Kingman	532	.288	48	115	240	11	12	3	1.9	.954	B. Sutter	62	101	6	6	37	2.23
Joey Amalfitano	C	B. Foote	429	.254	16	56	713	63	17	9	6.1	.979							
W-2 L-5	O1	L. Biittner	272	.290	3	50	282	23	6	24		.981							
	OF	B. Murcer	190	.258	7	22	110	4	0	0	2.1	1.000							
	OF	M. Vail	179	.335	7	35	51	3	2	0	1.4	.964							
	2B	S. Dillard	166	.283	5	24	111	132	3	31	4.1	.988							
New York	1B	W. Montanez	410	.234	5	47	905	76	11	95	9.2	.989	C. Swan	35	251	14	13	0	3.30
	2B	D. Flynn	555	.243	4	61	369	380	13	98	5.1	.983	P. Falcone	33	184	6	14	0	4.16
W-63 L-99	SS	F. Taveras	635	.263	1	33	270	438	25	88	4.8	.966	K. Kobel	30	162	6	8	0	3.50
	3B	R. Hebner	473	.268	10	79	99	246	22	26	2.7	.940	N. Allen	50	99	6	10	8	3.55
Joe Torre	RF	Youngblood	590	.275	16	60	308	18	5	3	2.3	.985	D. Murray	58	97	4	8	4	4.82
	CF	L. Mazzilli	597	.303	15	79	358	12	4	1	2.6	.989	D. Ellis	17	85	3	7	0	6.04
	LF	S. Henderson	350	.306	5	39	201	6	2	3	2.2	.990	A. Hassler	29	80	4	5	4	3.71
	C	J. Stearns	538	.243	9	66	628	85	12	11	6.0	.983	T. Hausman	19	79	2	6	2	2.73
	OF	E. Maddox	224	.268	1	12	129	5	2	1	2.1	.985	E. Glynn	46	60	1	4	7	3.00
	UT	A. Trevino	207	.271	0	20	229	71	9	14		.971	S. Lockwood	27	42	2	5	9	1.50
West **Cincinnati**	1B	D. Driessen	515	.250	18	75	1289	79	9	112	9.6	.993	T. Seaver	32	215	16	6	0	3.14
	2B	J. Morgan	436	.250	9	32	259	329	12	74	5.0	.980	M. LaCoss	35	206	14	8	0	3.50
W-90 L-71	SS	Concepcion	590	.281	16	84	284	495	27	102	5.4	.967	F. Norman	34	195	11	13	0	3.65
	3B	R. Knight	551	.318	10	79	120	262	15	26	2.7	.962	B. Bonham	29	176	9	7	0	3.78
John McNamara	RF	K. Griffey	380	.316	8	32	175	8	3	1	2.0	.984	T. Hume	57	163	10	9	17	2.76
	CF	C. Geronimo	356	.239	4	38	291	11	2	2	2.6	.993	P. Moskau	21	106	5	4	0	3.91
	LF	G. Foster	440	.302	30	98	214	7	4	1	1.9	.982	F. Pastore	30	95	6	7	4	4.26
	C	J. Bench	464	.276	22	80	619	68	10	11	5.5	.986	D. Bair	65	94	11	7	16	4.31
	OF	D. Collins	396	.318	3	35	159	2	4	2	1.8	.976							
	2B	J. Kennedy	220	.273	1	17	95	144	5	28	4.1	.980							
	OF	H. Cruz	182	.242	4	27	119	8	2	4	1.9	.984							
Houston	1B	C. Cedeno	470	.262	6	54	832	33	17	79	9.7	.981	J. Richard	38	292	18	13	0	**2.71**
	2B	R. Landestoy	282	.270	0	30	166	234	12	53	3.6	.971	J. Niekro	38	264	**21**	11	0	3.00
W-89 L-73	SS	C. Reynolds	555	.265	0	39	208	428	23	88	4.6	.965	J. Andujar	46	194	12	12	4	3.43
	3B	E. Cabell	603	.272	6	67	109	178	13	11	2.3	.957	K. Forsch	26	178	11	6	0	3.03
Bill Virdon	RF	J. Leonard	411	.290	0	47	227	6	10	1	2.0	.959	R. Williams	31	121	4	7	0	3.27
	CF	T. Puhl	600	.287	8	49	352	7	0	3	2.4	**1.000**	J. Sambito	63	91	8	7	22	1.78
	LF	J. Cruz	558	.289	9	72	320	7	14	0	2.2	.959							
	C	A. Ashby	336	.202	2	35	548	57	8	5	5.8	.987							
	23	A. Howe	355	.248	6	33	173	258	7	39		.984							
	UT	J. Gonzalez	181	.249	0	10	92	146	5	27		.979							
	1B	B. Watson	163	.239	3	18	371	33	3	23	9.3	.993							
	OF	D. Walling	147	.327	3	31	65	2	1	0	1.6	.985							
Los Angeles	1B	S. Garvey	648	.315	28	110	1402	93	7	101	9.3	.995	R. Sutcliffe	39	242	17	10	0	3.46
	2B	D. Lopes	582	.265	28	73	341	**384**	14	82	4.9	.981	D. Sutton	33	226	12	15	1	3.82
W-79 L-83	SS	B. Russell	627	.271	7	56	218	452	30	70	4.7	.957	B. Hooton	29	212	11	10	0	2.97
	3B	R. Cey	487	.281	28	81	123	265	9	25	2.6	**.977**	J. Reuss	39	160	7	14	3	3.54
Tom Lasorda	RF	G. Thomasson	315	.248	14	45	194	4	4	1	2.0	.980	C. Hough	42	151	7	5	0	4.77
	CF	D. Thomas	406	.256	5	44	269	10	1	4	2.4	.996	B. Welch	25	81	5	6	5	4.00
	LF	D. Baker	554	.274	23	88	289	14	3	4	2.0	.990	D. Patterson	36	53	4	1	6	5.26
	C	S. Yeager	310	.216	13	41	513	56	9	7	5.6	.984	L. LaGrow	31	37	5	1	4	3.41
	CO	J. Ferguson	363	.262	20	69	414	37	9	8		.980							
	OF	R. Smith	234	.274	10	32	159	5	2	0	2.7	.988							

NATIONAL LEAGUE 1979, *cont.*

	POS	Player	AB	BA	HR	RBI	PO	A	E	DP	TC/G	FA	Pitcher	G	IP	W	L	SV	ERA
San Francisco	1B	M. Ivie	402	.286	27	89	724	40	4	51	7.8	.995	V. Blue	34	237	14	14	0	5.01
	2B	J. Strain	257	.241	1	12	147	188	6	32	5.1	.982	B. Knepper	34	207	9	12	0	4.65
W-71 L-91	SS	J. LeMaster	343	.254	3	29	160	303	20	32	4.6	.959	Montefusco	22	137	3	8	0	3.94
	3B	D. Evans	562	.253	17	70	**129**	**369**	**30**	28	3.3	.943	E. Halicki	33	126	5	8	0	4.57
Joe Altobelli	RF	J. Clark	527	.273	26	86	261	13	5	**7**	2.0	.982	J. Curtis	27	121	10	9	0	4.17
W-61 L-79	CF	B. North	460	.259	5	30	300	8	4	2	2.4	.987	P. Nastu	25	100	3	4	0	4.32
	LF	L. Herndon	354	.257	7	36	196	10	8	2	1.8	.963	E. Whitson	18	100	5	8	0	3.95
Dave Bristol	C	Littlejohn	193	.197	1	13	366	43	6	7	6.6	.986	G. Lavelle	70	97	7	9	20	2.51
W-10 L-12	OF	T. Whitfield	394	.287	5	44	167	10	8	3	1.7	.957	T. Griffin	59	94	5	6	2	3.93
	1B	W. McCovey	353	.249	15	57	740	48	10	60	9.0	.987	G. Minton	46	80	4	3	4	1.80
	SS	R. Metzger	259	.251	0	31	108	219	15	34	4.4	.956	P. Borbon	30	46	4	3	3	4.89
	2B	B. Madlock	249	.261	7	41	137	144	7	32	4.6	.976							
	C	M. Hill	169	.207	3	15	283	31	3	4	5.5	.991							
San Diego	1B	D. Briggs	227	.207	8	30	326	28	5	20	7.2	.986	R. Jones	39	263	11	12	0	3.63
	2B	F. Gonzalez	323	.217	9	34	217	225	11	52	4.4	.976	G. Perry	32	233	12	11	0	3.05
W-68 L-93	SS	O. Smith	587	.211	0	27	256	555	20	86	5.4	.976	B. Shirley	49	205	8	16	0	3.38
	3B	P. Dade	283	.276	1	19	44	162	11	12	3.1	.949	E. Rasmussen	45	157	6	9	3	3.27
Roger Craig	RF	J. Turner	448	.248	9	61	197	7	9	2	1.9	.958	B. Owchinko	42	149	6	12	0	3.74
	CF	G. Richards	545	.279	4	41	320	7	9	2	2.5	.973	D'Acquisto	51	134	9	13	2	4.90
	LF	D. Winfield	597	.308	34	**118**	344	14	5	3	2.3	.986	R. Fingers	54	84	9	9	13	4.50
	C	G. Tenace	463	.263	20	67	413	51	1	10	4.9	**.998**	S. Mura	38	73	4	4	2	3.08
	UT	K. Bevacqua	297	.253	1	34	115	156	11	21		.961	M. Lee	46	65	2	4	5	4.29
	C	B. Fahey	209	.287	3	19	277	33	2	5	4.6	.994							
	O1	J. Johnstone	201	.294	0	32	185	18	4	10		.981							
	2B	B. Almon	198	.227	1	8	116	150	4	37	4.4	.985							
	3B	B. Evans	162	.216	1	14	30	108	7	12	2.7	.952							
Atlanta	1B	D. Murphy	384	.276	21	57	685	42	15	61	9.8	.980	P. Niekro	44	**342**	**21**	**20**	0	3.39
	2B	G. Hubbard	325	.231	3	29	193	268	**15**	57	5.2	.968	E. Solomon	31	186	7	14	0	4.21
W-66 L-94	SS	P. Frias	475	.259	1	44	229	432	32	79	5.1	.954	R. Matula	28	171	8	10	0	4.16
	3B	B. Horner	487	.314	33	98	56	143	15	11	2.6	.930	Brizzolara	20	107	6	9	0	5.30
Bobby Cox	RF	J. Burroughs	397	.224	11	47	175	8	7	1	1.7	.963	G. Garber	68	106	6	16	25	4.33
	CF	B. Bonnell	375	.259	12	45	220	8	4	2	1.9	.983	M. Mahler	26	100	5	11	0	5.85
	LF	G. Matthews	631	.304	27	90	292	12	8	4	2.0	.974	McLaughlin	37	69	5	3	5	2.48
	C	B. Benedict	204	.225	0	15	344	35	6	3	5.1	.984							
	32	J. Royster	601	.273	3	51	261	405	22	62		.968							
	OF	R. Office	277	.249	2	37	164	4	2	0	1.8	.988							
	C	J. Nolan	230	.248	4	21	328	27	6	2	4.9	.983							
	1B	M. Lum	217	.249	6	27	414	30	1	36	8.7	.998							
	OF	C. Spikes	93	.280	3	21	16	0	3	0	1.3	.842							

BATTING AND BASE RUNNING LEADERS

Batting Average
K. Hernandez, STL	.344
P. Rose, PHI	.331
R. Knight, CIN	.318
S. Garvey, LA	.315
B. Horner, ATL	.314

Slugging Average
D. Kingman, CHI	.613
M. Schmidt, PHI	.564
D. Winfield, SD	.558
B. Horner, ATL	.552
L. Parrish, MON	.551

Home Runs
D. Kingman, CHI	48
M. Schmidt, PHI	45
D. Winfield, SD	34
B. Horner, ATL	33
W. Stargell, PIT	32

Total Bases
D. Winfield, SD	333
D. Parker, PIT	327
D. Kingman, CHI	326
S. Garvey, LA	322
G. Matthews, ATL	317

Runs Batted In
D. Winfield, SD	118
D. Kingman, CHI	115
M. Schmidt, PHI	114
S. Garvey, LA	110
K. Hernandez, STL	105

Stolen Bases
O. Moreno, PIT	77
B. North, SF	58
D. Lopes, LA	44
F. Taveras, NY, PIT	44
R. Scott, MON	39

Hits
G. Templeton, STL	211
K. Hernandez, STL	210
P. Rose, PHI	208
S. Garvey, LA	204

Base on Balls
M. Schmidt, PHI	120
G. Tenace, SD	105
D. Lopes, LA	97
B. North, SF	96

Home Run Percentage
D. Kingman, CHI	9.0
M. Schmidt, PHI	8.3
B. Horner, ATL	6.8
T. Simmons, STL	5.8

Runs Scored
K. Hernandez, STL	116
O. Moreno, PIT	110
M. Schmidt, PHI	109
D. Lopes, LA	109

Doubles
K. Hernandez, STL	48
W. Cromartie, MON	46
D. Parker, PIT	45
K. Reitz, STL	41

Triples
G. Templeton, STL	19
B. McBride, PHI	12
A. Dawson, MON	12
O. Moreno, PIT	12

PITCHING LEADERS

Winning Percentage
T. Seaver, CIN	.727
J. Niekro, HOU	.656
S. Martinez, STL	.652
R. Sutcliffe, LA	.630
S. Carlton, PHI	.621

Earned Run Average
J. Richard, HOU	2.71
T. Hume, CIN	2.76
Schatzeder, MON	2.83
B. Hooton, LA	2.97
J. Niekro, HOU	3.00
S. Rogers, MON	3.00

Wins
J. Niekro, HOU	21
P. Niekro, ATL	21
S. Carlton, PHI	18
R. Reuschel, CHI	18
J. Richard, HOU	18

Saves
B. Sutter, CHI	37
K. Tekulve, PIT	31
G. Garber, ATL	25
J. Sambito, HOU	22
G. Lavelle, SF	20

Strikeouts
J. Richard, HOU	313
S. Carlton, PHI	213
P. Niekro, ATL	208
B. Blyleven, PIT	172
McGlothen, CHI	147

Complete Games
P. Niekro, ATL	23
J. Richard, HOU	19
S. Carlton, PHI	13
S. Rogers, MON	13
B. Hooton, LA	12

Fewest Hits/9 Innings
J. Richard, HOU	6.78
S. Carlton, PHI	7.24
J. Niekro, HOU	7.53
Schatzeder, MON	7.56

Shutouts
T. Seaver, CIN	5
S. Rogers, MON	5
J. Niekro, HOU	5
S. Carlton, PHI	4

Fewest Walks/9 Innings
K. Forsch, HOU	1.77
Candelaria, PIT	1.78
T. Hume, CIN	1.82
B. Lee, MON	1.86

Most Strikeouts/9 Inn.
J. Richard, HOU	9.65
S. Carlton, PHI	7.64
S. Sanderson, MON	7.39
B. Blyleven, PIT	6.53

Innings
P. Niekro, ATL	342
J. Richard, HOU	292
J. Niekro, HOU	264
R. Jones, SD	263

Games Pitched
K. Tekulve, PIT	94
E. Romo, PIT	84
G. Jackson, PIT	72
G. Lavelle, SF	70

NATIONAL LEAGUE 1979, cont.

		W	L	PCT	GB	R	OR	2B	3B	HR	BA	SA	SB	E	DP	FA	CG	BB	SO	ShO	SV	ERA
									(Batting)					(Fielding)			(Pitching)					
East	Pittsburgh	98	64	.605		775	643	264	52	148	.272	.416	180	134	163	.979	24	504	904	7	52	3.41
	Montreal	95	65	.594	2	701	581	273	42	143	.264	.408	121	131	123	.979	33	450	813	18	39	3.14
	St. Louis	86	76	.531	12	731	693	279	63	100	.278	.401	116	132	166	.980	38	501	788	10	25	3.72
	Philadelphia	84	78	.519	14	683	718	250	53	119	.266	.396	128	106	148	.983	33	477	787	14	29	4.16
	Chicago	80	82	.494	18	706	707	250	43	135	.269	.403	73	159	163	.975	20	521	933	11	44	3.88
	New York	63	99	.389	35	593	706	255	41	74	.250	.350	135	140	168	.978	16	607	819	10	36	3.84
West	Cincinnati	90	71	.559		731	644	266	31	132	.264	.396	99	124	152	.980	27	485	773	10	40	3.58
	Houston	89	73	.549	1.5	583	582	224	52	49	.256	.344	190	138	146	.978	55	504	854	19	31	3.19
	Los Angeles	79	83	.488	11.5	739	717	220	24	183	.263	.412	106	118	123	.981	30	555	811	6	34	3.83
	San Francisco	71	91	.438	19.5	672	751	192	36	125	.246	.365	140	163	138	.974	25	577	880	6	34	4.16
	San Diego	68	93	.422	22	603	681	193	53	93	.242	.348	100	141	154	.978	29	513	779	7	25	3.69
	Atlanta	66	94	.413	23.5	669	763	220	28	126	.256	.377	98	183	139	.970	32	494	779	3	34	4.18
						8186	8186	2886	518	1427	.261	.385	1486	1669	1783	.978	362	6188	9920	121	423	3.73

AMERICAN LEAGUE 1979

	POS	Player	AB	BA	HR	RBI	PO	A	E	DP	TC/G	FA	Pitcher	G	IP	W	L	SV	ERA
East — Baltimore W-102 L-57 Earl Weaver	1B	E. Murray	606	.295	25	99	1456	107	10	135	10.0	.994	D. Martinez	40	292	15	16	0	3.67
	2B	R. Dauer	479	.257	9	61	213	260	10	68	4.7	.979	M. Flanagan	39	266	23	9	0	3.08
	SS	K. Garcia	417	.247	5	24	173	271	21	66	4.1	.955	S. Stone	32	186	11	7	0	3.77
	3B	D. DeCinces	422	.230	16	61	99	247	13	21	3.0	.964	S. McGregor	27	175	13	6	0	3.34
	RF	K. Singleton	570	.295	35	111	247	8	5	2	1.8	.981	J. Palmer	23	156	10	6	0	3.29
	CF	A. Bumbry	569	.285	7	49	367	7	7	1	2.6	.982	S. Stewart	31	118	8	5	1	3.51
	LF	G. Roenicke	376	.261	25	64	246	10	5	1	2.0	.981	T. Martinez	39	78	10	3	3	2.88
	C	R. Dempsey	368	.239	6	41	615	81	7	13	5.7	.990	D. Stanhouse	52	73	7	3	21	2.84
	DH	L. May	456	.254	19	69													
	SS	M. Belanger	198	.167	0	9	110	195	3	38	3.1	.990							
	OF	Lowenstein	197	.254	11	34	120	4	1	2	1.7	.992							
	2B	B. Smith	189	.249	6	33	107	142	5	33	4.0	.980							
	OD	P. Kelly	153	.288	9	25	36	0	0	0	1.5	1.000							
Milwaukee W-95 L-66 George Bamberger	1B	C. Cooper	590	.308	24	106	1323	78	10	119	10.5	.993	L. Sorensen	34	235	15	14	0	3.98
	2B	P. Molitor	584	.322	9	62	289	413	15	81	5.9	.979	M. Caldwell	30	235	16	6	0	3.29
	SS	R. Yount	577	.267	8	51	267	517	25	97	5.4	.969	J. Slaton	32	213	15	9	0	3.63
	3B	S. Bando	476	.246	9	43	87	222	12	16	2.9	.963	B. Travers	30	187	14	8	0	3.90
	RF	S. Lezcano	473	.321	28	101	281	10	4	2	2.2	.986	M. Haas	29	185	11	11	0	4.77
	CF	G. Thomas	557	.244	45	123	435	4	4	0	2.9	.991	J. Augustine	43	86	9	6	5	3.45
	LF	B. Oglivie	514	.282	29	81	252	7	4	0	2.2	.985	R. Cleveland	29	55	1	5	4	6.71
	C	C. Moore	337	.300	5	38	414	58	10	7	4.5	.979	B. McClure	36	51	5	2	5	3.88
	DH	D. Davis	335	.266	12	41							B. Castro	39	44	3	1	6	2.05
	UT	D. Money	350	.237	6	38	240	117	2	33		.994							
	32	J. Gantner	208	.284	2	22	78	147	7	24		.970							
	C	B. Martinez	196	.270	4	26	198	39	8	2	3.6	.967							
	OF	J. Wohlford	175	.263	1	17	126	0	4	0	2.4	.969							
Boston W-91 L-69 Don Zimmer	1B	B. Watson	312	.337	13	53	525	47	7	58	10.0	.988	M. Torrez	36	252	16	13	0	4.50
	2B	J. Remy	306	.297	0	29	147	205	11	43	4.8	.970	D. Eckersley	33	247	17	10	0	2.99
	SS	R. Burleson	627	.278	5	60	272	523	16	109	5.3	.980	B. Stanley	40	217	16	12	1	3.98
	3B	B. Hobson	528	.261	28	93	110	251	25	17	2.7	.935	S. Renko	27	171	11	9	0	4.11
	RF	D. Evans	489	.274	21	58	307	15	4	5	2.2	.988	C. Rainey	20	104	8	5	1	3.81
	CF	F. Lynn	531	.333	39	122	381	10	5	4	2.8	.987	D. Drago	53	89	10	6	13	3.03
	LF	J. Rice	619	.325	39	130	241	8	4	1	2.0	.984	B. Campbell	41	55	3	4	9	4.25
	C	G. Allenson	241	.203	3	22	407	40	9	3	4.4	.980							
	DH	Yastrzemski	518	.270	21	87													
	DC	C. Fisk	320	.272	10	42	155	8	3	1	4.3	.982							
	23	J. Brohamer	192	.266	1	11	74	140	5	27		.977							
	1B	G. Scott	156	.224	4	23	400	25	6	40	10.5	.986							
	OF	T. Poquette	154	.331	2	23	73	2	4	1	1.8	.949							
New York W-89 L-71 Bob Lemon W-34 L-31 Billy Martin W-55 L-40	1B	C. Chambliss	554	.280	18	63	1299	95	7	135	10.5	.995	T. John	37	276	21	9	0	2.97
	2B	W. Randolph	574	.270	5	61	355	478	13	128	5.5	.985	R. Guidry	33	236	18	8	2	2.78
	SS	B. Dent	431	.230	2	32	219	512	17	107	5.3	.977	L. Tiant	30	196	13	8	0	3.90
	3B	G. Nettles	521	.253	20	73	110	339	16	30	3.2	.966	E. Figueroa	16	105	4	6	0	4.11
	RF	R. Jackson	465	.297	29	89	274	7	4	2	2.3	.986	C. Hunter	19	105	2	9	0	5.31
	CF	M. Rivers	286	.287	3	25	147	4	4	0	2.2	.974	R. Davis	44	85	14	2	9	2.86
	LF	L. Piniella	461	.297	11	69	204	13	4	1	2.0	.982	K. Clay	32	78	1	7	2	5.42
	C	T. Munson	382	.288	3	39	405	44	10	5	5.2	.978	G. Gossage	36	58	5	3	18	2.64
	DH	J. Spencer	295	.288	23	53													
	OF	B. Murcer	264	.273	8	33	169	4	3	0	2.5	.983							
	DO	R. White	205	.215	3	27	45	3	0	0	1.8	1.000							
	OD	O. Gamble	113	.389	11	32	47	3	2	2	2.0	.943							

AMERICAN LEAGUE 1979, cont.

Detroit
W-85 L-76

Les Moss
W-27 L-26

Dick Tracewski
W-2 L-0

Sparky Anderson
W-56 L-50

POS	Player	AB	BA	HR	RBI	PO	A	E	DP	TC/G	FA	Pitcher	G	IP	W	L	SV	ERA
1B	J. Thompson	492	.246	20	79	1176	91	8	135	9.1	.994	J. Morris	27	198	17	7	0	3.27
2B	L. Whitaker	423	.286	3	42	280	369	9	103	5.2	.986	M. Wilcox	33	196	12	10	0	4.36
SS	A. Trammell	460	.276	6	50	245	388	26	99	4.6	.961	Billingham	35	158	10	7	3	3.30
3B	A. Rodriguez	343	.254	5	36	72	211	13	23	2.8	.956	A. Lopez	61	127	10	5	21	2.41
RF	J. Morales	440	.211	14	56	206	6	3	2	1.8	.986	P. Underwood	27	122	6	4	0	4.57
CF	R. LeFlore	600	.300	9	57	293	6	3	3	2.7	.990	D. Petry	15	98	6	5	0	3.95
LF	S. Kemp	490	.318	26	105	229	12	6	2	2.1	.976	J. Hiller	43	79	4	7	9	5.24
C	L. Parrish	493	.276	19	65	707	79	9	10	5.6	.989	D. Tobik	37	69	3	5	3	4.30
DH	R. Staub	246	.236	9	40													
OF	C. Summers	246	.313	20	51	87	3	1	0	1.3	.989							
UT	Wockenfuss	231	.264	15	46	318	26	3	22		.991							
OF	L. Jones	213	.296	4	26	142	3	3	1	1.8	.980							
32	T. Brookens	190	.263	4	21	76	141	11	21		.952							

Cleveland
W-81 L-80

Jeff Torborg
W-43 L-52

Dave Garcia
W-38 L-28

POS	Player	AB	BA	HR	RBI	PO	A	E	DP	TC/G	FA	Pitcher	G	IP	W	L	SV	ERA
1B	A. Thornton	515	.233	26	93	1089	82	7	100	9.1	.994	R. Wise	34	232	15	10	0	3.72
2B	D. Kuiper	479	.255	0	39	345	380	9	89	5.2	**.988**	R. Waits	34	231	16	13	0	4.44
SS	T. Veryzer	449	.220	0	34	238	446	18	90	4.7	.974	M. Paxton	33	160	8	8	0	5.91
3B	T. Harrah	527	.279	20	77	91	160	16	19	2.1	.940	D. Spillner	49	158	9	5	1	4.61
RF	B. Bonds	538	.275	25	85	267	9	6	1	2.4	.979	L. Barker	29	137	6	6	0	4.93
CF	R. Manning	560	.259	3	51	417	9	6	2	3.1	.986	S. Monge	76	131	12	10	19	2.40
LF	J. Norris	353	.246	3	30	214	2	4	0	2.4	.982	W. Garland	18	95	4	10	0	5.21
C	G. Alexander	358	.229	15	54	404	40	18	5	5.1	.961	V. Cruz	61	79	3	9	10	4.22
DH	C. Johnson	240	.271	18	61													
O1	M. Hargrove	338	.325	10	56	356	16	2	23		.995							
C	R. Hassey	223	.287	4	32	345	29	3	4	5.5	.992							
3B	T. Cox	189	.212	4	22	29	78	4	11	2.1	.964							
OF	P. Dade	170	.282	3	18	73	4	3	1	2.2	.963							
UT	R. Pruitt	166	.283	2	21	66	5	2	1		.973							

Toronto
W-53 L-109

Roy Hartsfield

POS	Player	AB	BA	HR	RBI	PO	A	E	DP	TC/G	FA	Pitcher	G	IP	W	L	SV	ERA
1B	J. Mayberry	464	.274	21	74	1192	74	6	129	9.4	.995	T. Underwood	33	227	9	16	0	3.69
2B	D. Ainge	308	.237	2	19	198	261	11	67	5.5	.977	P. Huffman	31	173	6	18	0	5.77
SS	A. Griffin	624	.287	2	31	272	501	36	124	5.3	.956	D. Lemanczyk	22	143	8	10	0	3.71
3B	R. Howell	511	.247	15	72	108	290	20	28	3.1	.952	B. Moore	34	139	5	7	0	4.86
RF	B. Bailor	414	.229	1	38	210	16	3	2	1.9	.987	D. Stieb	18	129	8	8	0	4.33
CF	R. Bosetti	619	.260	8	65	**466**	18	13	4	**3.1**	.974	J. Jefferson	34	116	2	10	1	5.51
LF	A. Woods	436	.278	5	36	251	10	9	2	2.1	.967	Lemongello	18	83	1	9	0	6.29
C	R. Cerone	469	.239	7	61	560	68	13	10	4.7	.980	T. Buskey	44	79	6	10	7	3.42
DH	R. Carty	461	.256	12	55													
OF	O. Velez	274	.288	15	48	130	3	4	1	1.9	.971							
UT	L. Gomez	163	.239	0	11	70	116	3	25		.984							

West

California
W-88 L-74

Jim Fregosi

POS	Player	AB	BA	HR	RBI	PO	A	E	DP	TC/G	FA	Pitcher	G	IP	W	L	SV	ERA
1B	R. Carew	409	.318	3	44	804	55	10	101	8.4	.988	D. Frost	36	239	16	10	1	3.58
2B	B. Grich	534	.294	30	101	340	438	13	111	5.2	.984	N. Ryan	34	223	16	14	0	3.59
SS	J. Anderson	234	.248	3	23	126	189	17	42	4.0	.949	J. Barr	36	197	10	12	0	4.20
3B	C. Lansford	654	.287	19	79	135	263	7	29	2.6	**.983**	D. Aase	37	185	9	10	2	4.82
RF	D. Ford	569	.290	21	101	332	10	8	2	2.5	.977	M. Clear	52	109	11	5	14	3.63
CF	R. Miller	427	.293	2	28	349	3	4	1	3.0	.989	C. Knapp	20	98	5	5	0	5.51
LF	D. Baylor	628	.296	36	139	198	3	5	0	2.1	.976	F. Tanana	18	90	7	5	0	3.90
C	B. Downing	509	.326	12	75	669	35	11	5	5.5	.985	D. LaRoche	53	86	7	11	10	5.55
DH	W. Aikens	379	.280	21	81													
OF	J. Rudi	330	.242	11	61	174	5	2	2	2.3	.989							
SS	Campaneris	239	.234	0	15	136	220	16	69	4.5	.957							

Kansas City
W-85 L-77

Whitey Herzog

POS	Player	AB	BA	HR	RBI	PO	A	E	DP	TC/G	FA	Pitcher	G	IP	W	L	SV	ERA
1B	P. LaCock	408	.277	3	56	829	68	3	79	8.3	**.997**	Splittorff	36	240	15	17	0	4.24
2B	F. White	467	.266	10	48	317	332	12	78	5.3	.982	D. Leonard	32	236	14	12	0	4.08
SS	F. Patek	306	.252	1	37	153	249	19	54	4.0	.955	L. Gura	39	234	13	12	0	4.46
3B	G. Brett	645	.329	23	107	129	**373**	30	28	**3.6**	.944	R. Gale	34	182	9	10	0	5.64
RF	A. Cowens	516	.295	9	73	288	3	4	0	2.2	.986	S. Busby	22	94	6	6	0	3.64
CF	A. Otis	577	.295	18	90	385	11	3	5	2.7	**.992**	M. Pattin	31	94	5	2	3	4.60
LF	W. Wilson	588	.315	6	49	384	13	6	0	2.5	.985	A. Hrabosky	58	65	9	4	11	3.74
C	D. Porter	533	.291	20	112	628	68	13	15	5.0	.982	Quisenberry	32	40	3	2	5	3.15
DH	H. McRae	393	.288	10	74													
S2	Washington	268	.254	2	25	174	242	18	68		.959							
UT	J. Wathan	199	.206	2	28	336	24	3	30		.992							
OF	C. Hurdle	171	.240	3	30	88	2	3	0	1.9	.968							
1B	G. Scott	146	.267	1	20	335	21	4	27	8.8	.989							

Texas
W-83 L-79

Pat Corrales

POS	Player	AB	BA	HR	RBI	PO	A	E	DP	TC/G	FA	Pitcher	G	IP	W	L	SV	ERA
1B	P. Putnam	426	.277	18	64	832	62	5	65	9.4	.994	F. Jenkins	37	259	16	14	0	4.07
2B	B. Wills	543	.273	5	46	337	468	20	95	5.7	.976	S. Comer	36	242	17	12	0	3.68
SS	N. Norman	343	.222	0	21	177	302	24	64	3.5	.952	D. Medich	29	149	10	7	0	4.17
3B	B. Bell	670	.299	18	101	112	364	15	22	3.3	.969	J. Kern	71	143	13	5	29	1.57
RF	R. Zisk	503	.262	18	64	234	10	7	**6**	1.9	.972	D. Alexander	23	113	5	7	0	4.46
CF	A. Oliver	492	.323	12	76	260	9	7	2	2.3	.975	S. Lyle	67	95	5	8	13	3.13
LF	B. Sample	325	.292	5	35	173	7	0	1	1.7	1.000							
C	J. Sundberg	495	.275	5	64	**754**	75	4	13	5.6	**.995**							
DH	J. Ellis	316	.285	12	61													
OF	J. Grubb	289	.273	10	37	135	8	2	4	1.8	.986							
OF	M. Rivers	247	.300	6	25	153	4	3	1	2.8	.981							
DO	O. Gamble	161	.335	8	32	41	2	0	2	2.0	1.000							
1D	W. Montanez	144	.319	8	24	191	16	1	14	10.9	.995							

AMERICAN LEAGUE 1979, *cont.*

	POS	Player	AB	BA	HR	RBI	PO	A	E	DP	TC/G	FA	Pitcher	G	IP	W	L	SV	ERA
Minnesota	1B	R. Jackson	583	.271	14	68	1447	**137**	9	175	10.1	.994	J. Koosman	37	264	20	13	0	3.38
	2B	R. Wilfong	419	.313	9	59	287	379	14	92	5.1	.979	D. Goltz	36	251	14	13	0	4.16
W-82 L-80	SS	R. Smalley	621	.271	24	95	296	572	29	144	5.6	.968	G. Zahn	26	169	13	7	0	3.57
	3B	J. Castino	393	.285	5	52	85	277	14	31	2.6	.963	P. Hartzell	28	163	6	10	0	5.36
Gene Mauch	RF	B. Rivera	263	.281	2	31	169	12	2	0	1.7	.989	M. Marshall	90	143	10	15	32	2.64
	CF	K. Landreaux	564	.305	15	83	292	10	6	1	2.1	.981	R. Erickson	24	123	3	10	0	5.63
	LF	H. Powell	338	.293	2	36	165	6	4	3	1.9	.977	P. Redfern	40	108	7	3	1	3.50
	C	B. Wynegar	504	.270	7	57	653	65	6	10	5.0	.992							
	DH	J. Morales	191	.267	2	27													
	DO	G. Adams	326	.301	8	50	66	2	3	0	1.3	.958							
	OF	W. Norwood	270	.248	6	30	147	4	4	0	2.2	.974							
	3B	M. Cubbage	243	.276	2	23	34	94	10	9	2.2	.928							
	OF	D. Edwards	229	.249	8	35	165	7	3	0	2.0	.983							
	2B	B. Randall	199	.246	0	14	130	166	5	48	4.2	.983							
	DH	D. Goodwin	159	.289	5	27													
Chicago	1B	L. Johnson	479	.309	12	74	748	63	11	62	8.7	.987	K. Kravec	36	250	15	13	1	3.74
	2B	A. Bannister	506	.285	2	55	150	160	12	32	5.0	.963	R. Wortham	34	204	14	14	0	4.90
W-73 L-87	SS	G. Pryor	476	.275	3	49	161	362	21	54	4.6	.961	Baumgarten	28	191	13	8	0	3.53
	3B	K. Bell	200	.245	4	22	51	153	17	11	3.3	.923	S. Trout	34	155	11	8	0	3.89
Don Kessinger	RF	Washington	471	.280	13	66	256	7	7	3	2.2	.974	R. Scarbery	45	101	2	8	4	4.63
W-46 L-60	CF	C. Lemon	556	.318	17	86	411	10	10	2	2.9	.977	F. Barrios	15	95	8	3	0	3.60
	LF	R. Torres	170	.253	8	24	117	4	3	0	1.5	.976	M. Proly	38	88	3	8	9	3.89
Tony LaRussa	C	M. May	202	.252	7	28	277	27	6	1	4.8	.981	E. Farmer	42	81	3	7	14	2.44
W-27 L-27	DH	J. Orta	325	.262	11	46													
	OF	R. Garr	307	.280	9	39	94	3	5	1	1.5	.951							
	1B	M. Squires	295	.264	2	22	741	60	4	62	7.3	.995							
	23	J. Morrison	240	.275	14	35	121	185	9	38		.971							
	3B	E. Soderholm	210	.252	6	34	55	154	3	12	3.8	.986							
	OF	J. Moore	201	.264	1	23	83	3	3	0	1.5	.966							
	DH	W. Nordhagen	193	.280	7	25													
	C	B. Nahorodny	179	.257	6	29	223	25	7	3	4.3	.973							
Seattle	1B	B. Bochte	554	.316	16	100	1361	114	14	140	10.1	.991	M. Parrott	38	229	14	12	0	3.77
	2B	J. Cruz	414	.271	1	29	258	361	13	87	5.9	.979	R. Honeycutt	33	194	11	12	0	4.04
W-67 L-95	SS	M. Mendoza	373	.198	1	29	177	422	20	91	4.2	.968	F. Bannister	30	182	10	15	0	4.05
	3B	D. Meyer	525	.278	20	74	76	201	19	22	2.9	.936	McLaughlin	47	124	7	7	14	4.21
Darrell Johnson	RF	J. Simpson	265	.283	2	27	162	10	6	4	1.7	.966	O. Jones	25	119	3	11	0	6.05
	CF	R. Jones	622	.267	21	78	453	13	5	4	2.9	.989	G. Abbott	23	117	4	10	0	5.15
	LF	L. Roberts	450	.271	15	54	286	6	5	2	2.2	.983	J. Montague	41	116	6	4	1	5.59
	C	L. Cox	293	.215	4	36	408	49	9	6	4.7	.981	R. Dressler	21	104	3	2	0	4.93
	DH	W. Horton	646	.279	29	106							S. Rawley	48	84	5	9	11	3.86
	S2	L. Milbourne	356	.278	2	26	136	250	11	57		.972							
	OF	T. Paciorek	310	.287	6	42	137	2	0	0	1.9	1.000							
	3B	B. Stein	250	.248	7	27	45	120	7	13	2.6	.959							
	C	B. Stinson	247	.243	6	28	376	29	9	2	4.5	.978							
Oakland	1B	D. Revering	472	.288	19	77	828	80	13	77	8.9	.986	R. Langford	34	219	12	16	0	4.27
	2B	M. Edwards	400	.233	1	23	244	314	22	54	5.1	.962	S. McCatty	31	186	11	12	0	4.21
W-54 L-108	SS	R. Picciolo	348	.253	2	27	191	265	17	51	4.5	.964	M. Keough	30	177	2	17	0	5.03
	3B	W. Gross	442	.224	14	50	120	211	20	19	2.9	.943	M. Norris	29	146	5	8	0	4.81
Jim Marshall	RF	L. Murray	226	.186	2	20	173	7	7	2	2.1	.963	C. Minetto	36	118	1	5	0	5.57
	CF	D. Murphy	388	.255	11	40	322	10	4	0	2.8	.988	B. Kingman	18	113	8	7	0	4.30
	LF	R. Henderson	351	.274	1	26	215	5	6	0	2.6	.973	D. Heaverlo	62	86	4	11	9	4.19
	C	J. Newman	516	.231	22	71	378	53	10	7	5.4	.977	J. Johnson	14	85	2	8	0	4.34
	DH	M. Page	478	.247	9	42							D. Hamilton	40	83	3	4	5	3.69
	C	J. Essian	313	.243	8	40	348	57	8	5	5.9	.981	M. Morgan	13	77	2	10	0	5.96
	OF	T. Armas	278	.248	11	34	194	7	5	2	2.6	.976	B. Lacey	42	48	1	5	4	5.81
	UT	M. Heath	258	.256	3	27	167	32	5	2		.975							
	UT	D. Chalk	212	.222	2	13	122	151	11	31		.961							
	SS	M. Guerrero	166	.229	0	18	68	129	10	33	4.8	.952							

BATTING AND BASE RUNNING LEADERS

Batting Average
F. Lynn, BOS .333
G. Brett, KC .329
B. Downing, CAL .326
J. Rice, BOS .325
A. Oliver, TEX .323

Slugging Average
F. Lynn, BOS .637
J. Rice, BOS .596
S. Lezcano, MIL .573
G. Brett, KC .563
R. Jackson, NY .544

Home Runs
G. Thomas, MIL 45
F. Lynn, BOS 39
J. Rice, BOS 39
D. Baylor, CAL 36
K. Singleton, BAL 35

Total Bases
J. Rice, BOS 369
G. Brett, KC 363
F. Lynn, BOS 338
D. Baylor, CAL 333
K. Singleton, BAL 304

Runs Batted In
D. Baylor, CAL 139
J. Rice, BOS 130
G. Thomas, MIL 123
F. Lynn, BOS 122
D. Porter, KC 112

Stolen Bases
W. Wilson, KC 83
R. LeFlore, DET 78
J. Cruz, SEA 49
A. Bumbry, BAL 37
B. Wills, TEX 35

PITCHING LEADERS

Winning Percentage
M. Caldwell, MIL .727
M. Flanagan, BAL .719
J. Morris, DET .708
T. John, NY .700
R. Guidry, NY .692

Earned Run Average
R. Guidry, NY 2.78
T. John, NY 2.97
D. Eckersley, BOS 2.99
M. Flanagan, BAL 3.08
J. Morris, DET 3.27

Wins
M. Flanagan, BAL 23
T. John, NY 21
J. Koosman, MIN 20
R. Guidry, NY 18

Saves
M. Marshall, MIN 32
J. Kern, TEX 29
A. Lopez, DET 21
D. Stanhouse, BAL 21
S. Monge, CLE 19

Strikeouts
N. Ryan, CAL 223
R. Guidry, NY 201
M. Flanagan, BAL 190
F. Jenkins, TEX 164
J. Koosman, MIN 157

Complete Games
D. Martinez, BAL 18
D. Eckersley, BOS 17
N. Ryan, CAL 17
T. John, NY 17

AMERICAN LEAGUE 1979, *cont.*

BATTING AND BASE RUNNING LEADERS

Hits
G. Brett, KC	212
J. Rice, BOS	201
B. Bell, TEX	200
P. Molitor, MIL	188

Base on Balls
D. Porter, KC	121
K. Singleton, BAL	109
G. Thomas, MIL	98
W. Randolph, NY	95

Home Run Percentage
G. Thomas, MIL	8.1
F. Lynn, BOS	7.3
J. Rice, BOS	6.3
R. Jackson, NY	6.2

Runs Scored
D. Baylor, CAL	120
G. Brett, KC	119
J. Rice, BOS	117
F. Lynn, BOS	116

Doubles
C. Lemon, CHI	44
C. Cooper, MIL	44
F. Lynn, BOS	42
G. Brett, KC	42

Triples
G. Brett, KC	20
P. Molitor, MIL	16
W. Randolph, NY	13
W. Wilson, KC	13

PITCHING LEADERS

Fewest Hits/9 Innings
N. Ryan, CAL	6.82
K. Kravec, CHI	7.49
R. Guidry, NY	7.74
J. Morris, DET	8.14

Shutouts
D. Leonard, KC	5
N. Ryan, CAL	5
M. Flanagan, BAL	5
M. Caldwell, MIL	4

Fewest Walks/9 Innings
S. McGregor, BAL	1.18
M. Caldwell, MIL	1.49
L. Sorensen, MIL	1.61
B. Stanley, BOS	1.82

Most Strikeouts/9 Inn.
N. Ryan, CAL	9.00
R. Guidry, NY	7.67
M. Flanagan, BAL	6.43
F. Jenkins, TEX	5.70

Innings
D. Martinez, BAL	292
T. John, NY	276
M. Flanagan, BAL	266
J. Koosman, MIN	264

Games Pitched
M. Marshall, MIN	90
S. Monge, CLE	76
J. Kern, TEX	71
S. Lyle, TEX	67

		W	L	PCT	GB	R	OR	2B	3B	HR	BA	SA	SB	E	DP	FA	CG	BB	SO	ShO	SV	ERA
East	Baltimore	102	57	.642		757	582	258	24	181	.261	.419	99	125	161	.980	52	467	786	**12**	30	**3.26**
	Milwaukee	95	66	.590	8	807	722	291	41	185	.280	.448	100	127	153	.980	**61**	381	580	**12**	23	4.03
	Boston	91	69	.569	11.5	841	711	**310**	34	**194**	**.283**	**.456**	60	142	166	.977	47	463	731	11	29	4.03
	New York	89	71	.556	13.5	734	672	226	40	150	.266	.406	65	122	183	.981	43	455	731	10	37	3.83
	Detroit	85	76	.528	18	770	738	221	35	164	.269	.415	176	**120**	184	.981	25	547	802	5	37	4.28
	Cleveland	81	80	.503	22	760	805	206	29	138	.258	.384	143	134	149	.978	28	570	781	7	32	4.57
	Toronto	53	109	.327	50.5	613	862	253	34	95	.251	.363	75	159	187	.975	44	594	613	7	11	4.82
West	California	88	74	.543		**866**	768	242	43	164	.282	.429	100	135	172	.978	46	573	**820**	9	33	4.34
	Kansas City	85	77	.525	3	851	816	286	**79**	116	.282	.422	**207**	146	160	.977	42	536	640	7	27	4.45
	Texas	83	79	.512	5	750	698	252	26	140	.278	.409	79	130	151	.979	26	532	773	10	**42**	3.86
	Minnesota	82	80	.506	6	764	725	256	46	112	.278	.402	66	134	**203**	.979	31	452	721	6	33	4.13
	Chicago	73	87	.456	14	730	748	290	33	127	.275	.410	97	173	142	.972	28	618	675	9	37	4.10
	Seattle	67	95	.414	21	711	820	250	52	132	.269	.404	126	141	170	.978	37	571	736	7	26	4.58
	Oakland	54	108	.333	34	573	860	188	32	108	.239	.346	104	174	137	.972	41	654	726	4	20	4.75
						10527	10527	3529	548	2006	.270	.408	1497	1962	2318	.978	551	7413	10115	116	417	4.22

NATIONAL LEAGUE 1980

		POS	Player	AB	BA	HR	RBI	PO	A	E	DP	TC/G	FA	Pitcher	G	IP	W	L	SV	ERA
East	**Philadelphia** W-91 L-71 Dallas Green	1B	P. Rose	655	.282	1	64	1427	**123**	5	113	9.6	.997	S. Carlton	38	**304**	**24**	9	0	2.34
		2B	M. Trillo	531	.292	7	43	360	467	11	91	6.0	.987	D. Ruthven	33	223	17	10	0	3.55
		SS	L. Bowa	540	.267	2	39	225	449	17	70	4.7	.975	B. Walk	27	152	11	7	0	4.56
		3B	M. Schmidt	548	.286	**48**	**121**	98	**372**	27	31	3.3	.946	R. Lerch	30	150	4	14	0	5.16
		RF	B. McBride	554	.309	9	87	282	6	3	1	2.2	.990	T. McGraw	57	92	5	4	20	1.47
		CF	G. Maddox	549	.259	11	73	405	7	10	0	3.0	.976	R. Reed	55	91	7	5	9	4.05
		LF	G. Luzinski	368	.228	19	56	137	2	1	0	1.3	.993	D. Noles	48	81	1	4	6	3.89
		C	B. Boone	480	.229	9	55	741	88	18	7	6.1	.979	K. Saucier	40	50	7	3	0	3.42
		OF	L. Smith	298	.339	3	20	121	2	4	0	1.5	.969							
		C	K. Moreland	159	.314	4	29	183	21	7	7	5.4	.967							
	Montreal W-90 L-72 Dick Williams	1B	W. Cromartie	597	.288	14	70	1457	93	14	104	9.9	.991	S. Rogers	37	281	16	11	0	2.98
		2B	R. Scott	567	.224	0	46	287	380	12	73	5.3	.982	S. Sanderson	33	211	16	11	0	3.11
		SS	C. Speier	388	.265	1	32	187	396	21	62	4.8	.965	Gullickson	24	141	10	5	0	3.00
		3B	L. Parrish	452	.254	15	72	106	231	18	15	2.9	.949	D. Palmer	24	130	8	6	0	2.98
		RF	E. Valentine	311	.315	13	67	154	6	5	1	2.0	.970	B. Lee	24	118	4	6	0	4.96
		CF	A. Dawson	577	.308	17	87	410	14	6	3	2.9	.986	C. Lea	21	104	7	5	0	3.72
		LF	R. LeFlore	521	.257	4	39	233	14	11	1	2.0	.957	F. Norman	48	98	4	4	4	4.05
		C	G. Carter	549	.264	29	101	**822**	108	7	8	6.3	**.993**	E. Sosa	67	94	9	6	9	3.06
		OF	R. Office	292	.267	6	30	150	2	2	1	1.6	.987	S. Bahnsen	57	91	7	6	4	3.07
		OF	J. White	214	.262	7	23	101	5	6	1	1.3	.946	W. Fryman	61	80	7	4	17	2.25
		2S	T. Bernazard	183	.224	5	18	82	151	9	25		.963							
	Pittsburgh W-83 L-79 Chuck Tanner	1B	J. Milner	238	.244	8	34	502	32	5	48	7.7	.991	J. Bibby	35	238	19	6	0	3.33
		2B	P. Garner	548	.259	5	58	349	**499**	21	116	5.8	.976	Candelaria	35	233	11	14	1	4.02
		SS	T. Foli	495	.265	3	38	212	402	12	87	5.0	**.981**	B. Blyleven	34	217	8	13	0	3.82
		3B	B. Madlock	494	.277	10	53	86	214	14	18	2.5	.955	D. Robinson	29	160	7	10	1	3.99
		RF	D. Parker	518	.295	17	79	235	14	9	0	2.0	.965	R. Rhoden	20	127	7	5	0	3.83
		CF	O. Moreno	676	.249	2	36	479	15	5	2	3.1	.990	E. Romo	74	124	5	5	11	3.27
		LF	M. Easler	393	.338	21	74	201	6	3	1	1.8	.986	E. Solomon	26	100	7	3	0	2.70
		C	E. Ott	392	.260	8	41	569	73	11	5	5.6	.983	K. Tekulve	78	93	8	12	21	3.39
		OF	L. Lacy	278	.335	7	33	173	7	3	1	2.1	.984	G. Jackson	61	71	8	4	9	2.92
		1O	B. Robinson	272	.287	12	36	427	22	7	30		.985							
		3S	D. Berra	245	.220	6	31	82	167	11	23		.958							
		1B	W. Stargell	202	.262	11	38	460	33	4	54	9.2	.992							
		C	S. Nicosia	176	.216	1	22	284	25	5	4	5.4	.984							

NATIONAL LEAGUE 1980, *cont.*

St. Louis

W-74 L-88
Ken Boyer W-18 L-33
Jack Krol W-0 L-1
Whitey Herzog W-38 L-35
Red Schoendienst W-18 L-19

POS	Player	AB	BA	HR	RBI	PO	A	E	DP	TC/G	FA
1B	K. Hernandez	595	.321	16	99	1572	115	9	146	10.8	.995
2B	K. Oberkfell	422	.303	3	46	223	310	6	62	5.3	.989
SS	G. Templeton	504	.319	4	43	223	451	29	85	6.1	.959
3B	K. Reitz	523	.270	8	58	86	293	8	25	2.6	.979
RF	G. Hendrick	572	.302	25	109	322	10	2	2	2.2	.994
CF	T. Scott	415	.251	0	28	324	5	1	2	2.5	.997
LF	L. Durham	303	.271	8	42	136	14	2	2	1.9	.987
C	T. Simmons	495	.303	21	98	520	71	9	12	4.7	.985
OF	D. Iorg	251	.303	3	36	108	2	1	0	1.8	.991
CO	T. Kennedy	248	.254	4	34	231	22	7	3		.973
OF	B. Bonds	231	.203	5	24	114	5	4	2	1.8	.967
2B	T. Herr	222	.248	0	15	107	136	4	37	4.3	.984

Pitcher	G	IP	W	L	SV	ERA
P. Vuckovich	32	222	12	9	1	3.41
B. Forsch	31	215	11	10	0	3.77
J. Kaat	49	130	8	7	4	3.81
B. Sykes	27	126	6	10	0	4.64
S. Martinez	25	120	5	10	0	4.80
J. Fulgham	15	85	4	6	0	3.39
D. Hood	33	82	4	6	0	3.40
Littlefield	52	66	5	5	9	3.14

New York

W-67 L-95
Joe Torre

POS	Player	AB	BA	HR	RBI	PO	A	E	DP	TC/G	FA
1B	L. Mazzilli	578	.280	16	76	708	49	13	67	8.4	.983
2B	D. Flynn	443	.255	0	24	283	370	6	70	5.1	.991
SS	F. Taveras	562	.279	0	25	237	347	25	63	4.4	.959
3B	E. Maddox	411	.246	4	34	96	209	14	18	2.8	.956
RF	Washington	284	.275	10	42	123	12	3	1	2.0	.978
CF	Youngblood	514	.276	8	49	292	18	5	6	2.6	.984
LF	S. Henderson	513	.290	8	58	299	7	6	1	2.3	.981
C	A. Trevino	355	.256	0	37	443	63	12	5	6.0	.977
10	M. Jorgensen	321	.255	7	43	562	37	4	33		.993
C	J. Stearns	319	.285	0	45	432	41	7	6	6.5	.985
OF	J. Morales	193	.254	3	30	107	3	3	1	1.8	.973

Pitcher	G	IP	W	L	SV	ERA
R. Burris	29	170	7	13	0	4.02
P. Zachry	28	165	6	10	0	3.00
M. Bomback	36	163	10	8	0	4.09
P. Falcone	37	157	7	10	1	4.53
C. Swan	21	128	5	9	0	3.59
T. Hausman	55	122	6	5	1	3.98
J. Reardon	61	110	8	7	6	2.62
N. Allen	59	97	7	10	22	3.71

Chicago

W-64 L-98
Preston Gomez W-38 L-52
Joey Amalfitano W-26 L-46

POS	Player	AB	BA	HR	RBI	PO	A	E	DP	TC/G	FA
1B	B. Buckner	578	.324	10	68	826	73	6	67	9.6	.993
2B	M. Tyson	341	.238	3	23	222	329	18	69	4.9	.968
SS	I. DeJesus	618	.259	3	33	229	529	24	99	5.0	.969
3B	L. Randle	489	.276	5	39	76	225	23	7	2.9	.929
RF	S. Thompson	226	.212	2	13	100	4	4	2	1.6	.963
CF	J. Martin	494	.227	23	73	262	8	6	0	2.1	.978
LF	D. Kingman	255	.278	18	57	103	8	7	0	1.9	.941
C	T. Blackwell	320	.272	5	30	572	93	12	16	6.6	.982
OF	M. Vail	312	.298	6	47	126	5	5	1	1.8	.963
10	L. Biittner	273	.249	1	34	305	23	2	16		.994
32	S. Dillard	244	.225	4	27	89	169	14	19		.949
C	B. Foote	202	.238	6	28	317	36	3	5	6.5	.992
OF	J. Figueroa	198	.253	1	11	89	6	2	2	1.7	.979
1B	C. Johnson	196	.235	10	34	468	16	4	34	10.6	.992

Pitcher	G	IP	W	L	SV	ERA
R. Reuschel	38	257	11	13	0	3.40
M. Krukow	34	205	10	15	0	4.39
D. Lamp	41	203	10	14	0	5.19
McGlothen	39	182	12	14	0	4.80
B. Caudill	72	128	4	6	1	2.18
D. Tidrow	84	116	6	5	6	2.79
G. Hernandez	53	108	1	9	0	4.42
B. Sutter	60	102	5	8	28	2.65
D. Capilla	39	90	2	8	0	4.10

West

Houston

W-93 L-70
Bill Virdon

POS	Player	AB	BA	HR	RBI	PO	A	E	DP	TC/G	FA
1B	A. Howe	321	.283	10	46	580	49	9	47	8.3	.986
2B	J. Morgan	461	.243	11	49	244	348	7	68	4.6	.988
SS	C. Reynolds	381	.226	3	28	162	362	17	59	4.0	.969
3B	E. Cabell	604	.276	2	55	118	250	29	15	2.6	.927
RF	T. Puhl	535	.282	13	55	311	14	3	3	2.4	.991
CF	C. Cedeno	499	.309	10	73	338	9	8	3	2.6	.977
LF	J. Cruz	612	.302	11	91	323	16	11	1	2.2	.969
C	A. Ashby	352	.256	3	48	608	60	6	10	5.9	.991
2S	R. Landestoy	393	.247	1	27	184	291	9	67		.981
1B	D. Walling	284	.299	3	29	505	31	6	46	8.6	.989
C	L. Pujols	221	.199	2	20	348	35	4	5	5.2	.990
OF	J. Leonard	216	.213	3	20	87	6	2	0	1.7	.979

Pitcher	G	IP	W	L	SV	ERA
J. Niekro	37	256	20	12	0	3.55
N. Ryan	35	234	11	10	0	3.35
K. Forsch	32	222	12	13	0	3.20
V. Ruhle	28	159	12	4	0	2.38
J. Andujar	35	122	3	8	2	3.91
J. Richard	17	114	10	4	0	1.89
D. Smith	57	103	7	5	10	1.92
J. Sambito	64	90	8	4	17	2.20
F. LaCorte	55	83	8	5	11	2.82

Los Angeles

W-92 L-71
Tom Lasorda

POS	Player	AB	BA	HR	RBI	PO	A	E	DP	TC/G	FA
1B	S. Garvey	658	.304	26	106	1502	1†2	6	122	10.0	.996
2B	D. Lopes	553	.251	10	49	304	416	15	85	5.3	.980
SS	B. Russell	466	.264	3	34	179	387	19	57	4.5	.968
3B	R. Cey	551	.254	28	77	127	317	13	24	2.9	.972
RF	R. Smith	311	.322	15	55	153	15	1	5	2.0	.994
CF	R. Law	388	.260	1	23	233	6	3	3	2.3	.988
LF	D. Baker	579	.294	29	97	308	5	3	3	2.1	.991
C	S. Yeager	227	.211	2	20	382	36	7	5	4.5	.984
UT	D. Thomas	297	.266	1	22	203	175	14	39		.964
OF	J. Johnstone	251	.307	2	20	100	9	4	0	1.9	.965
OF	R. Monday	194	.268	10	25	92	1	3	0	1.9	.969
OF	P. Guerrero	183	.322	7	31	74	1	1	0	1.9	.987
C	J. Ferguson	172	.238	9	29	297	23	6	4	4.9	.982

Pitcher	G	IP	W	L	SV	ERA
J. Reuss	37	229	18	6	3	2.52
B. Welch	32	214	14	9	0	3.28
D. Sutton	32	212	13	5	1	2.21
B. Hooton	34	207	14	8	1	3.65
D. Goltz	35	171	7	11	1	4.32
R. Sutcliffe	42	110	3	9	5	5.56
B. Castillo	61	98	8	6	5	2.76
S. Howe	59	85	7	9	17	2.65
D. Stanhouse	21	25	2	2	7	5.04

Cincinnati

W-89 L-73
John McNamara

POS	Player	AB	BA	HR	RBI	PO	A	E	DP	TC/G	FA
1B	D. Driessen	524	.265	14	74	1349	85	7	115	9.5	.995
2B	J. Kennedy	337	.261	1	34	200	303	6	53	4.9	.988
SS	Concepcion	622	.260	5	77	265	451	16	98	4.9	.978
3B	R. Knight	618	.264	14	78	120	291	13	19	2.6	.969
RF	K. Griffey	544	.294	13	85	266	5	5	3	2.0	.978
CF	D. Collins	551	.303	3	35	337	5	5	1	2.5	.986
LF	G. Foster	528	.273	25	93	295	6	1	1	2.1	.997
C	J. Bench	360	.250	24	68	505	39	5	7	5.2	.991
2B	R. Oester	303	.277	2	20	144	194	7	42	4.4	.980
C	J. Nolan	154	.312	3	24	251	23	5	5	5.5	.982

Pitcher	G	IP	W	L	SV	ERA
M. Soto	53	190	10	8	4	3.08
F. Pastore	27	185	13	7	0	3.26
C. Leibrandt	36	174	10	9	0	4.24
M. LaCoss	34	169	10	12	0	4.63
T. Seaver	26	168	10	8	0	3.64
P. Moskau	33	153	9	7	2	4.00
T. Hume	78	137	9	10	25	2.56
J. Price	24	111	7	3	0	3.57
D. Bair	61	85	3	6	6	4.24

NATIONAL LEAGUE 1980, *cont.*

	POS	Player	AB	BA	HR	RBI	PO	A	E	DP	TC/G	FA	Pitcher	G	IP	W	L	SV	ERA
Atlanta	1B	C. Chambliss	602	.282	18	72	**1626**	101	12	140	11.0	.993	P. Niekro	40	275	15	**18**	1	3.63
	2B	G. Hubbard	431	.248	9	43	268	405	15	91	5.9	.978	D. Alexander	35	232	14	11	0	4.19
W-81 L-80	SS	L. Gomez	278	.191	0	24	135	319	15	55	3.9	.968	T. Boggs	32	192	12	9	0	3.42
	3B	B. Horner	463	.268	35	89	78	251	23	20	2.9	.935	R. Matula	33	177	11	13	0	4.58
Bobby Cox	RF	J. Burroughs	278	.263	13	51	129	0	3	0	1.8	.977	McWilliams	30	164	9	14	0	4.94
	CF	D. Murphy	569	.281	33	89	374	14	6	4	2.6	.985	R. Camp	77	108	6	4	22	1.92
	LF	G. Matthews	571	.278	19	75	258	8	11	0	1.9	.960	G. Garber	68	82	5	5	7	3.84
	C	B. Benedict	359	.253	2	34	502	76	7	6	4.9	.988	L. Bradford	56	55	3	4	4	2.45
	UT	J. Royster	392	.242	1	20	195	166	18	32		.953							
	S3	L. Blanks	221	.204	2	12	64	189	17	31		.937							
	OF	Asselstine	218	.284	3	25	102	0	4	0	1.7	.962							
	SS	R. Ramirez	165	.267	2	11	63	140	11	25	4.7	.949							
San Francisco	1B	M. Ivie	286	.241	4	25	669	32	5	46	9.8	.993	V. Blue	31	224	14	10	0	2.97
	2B	R. Stennett	397	.244	2	37	244	293	15	53	5.0	.973	B. Knepper	35	215	9	16	0	4.10
W-75 L-86	SS	J. LeMaster	405	.215	3	31	200	372	26	54	4.5	.957	E. Whitson	34	212	11	13	0	3.10
	3B	D. Evans	556	.264	20	78	113	328	25	26	3.3	.946	A. Ripley	23	113	9	10	0	4.14
Dave Bristol	RF	J. Clark	437	.284	22	82	229	7	8	1	2.0	.967	Montefusco	22	113	4	8	0	4.38
	CF	B. North	415	.251	1	19	313	6	6	1	2.8	.982	T. Griffin	42	108	5	1	0	2.75
	LF	L. Herndon	493	.258	8	49	247	8	11	4	2.6	.959	G. Lavelle	62	100	6	8	9	3.42
	C	M. May	358	.260	6	50	500	59	8	12	5.5	.986	G. Minton	68	91	4	6	19	2.47
	OF	T. Whitfield	321	.296	4	26	140	11	2	1	1.6	.987	A. Holland	54	82	5	3	7	1.76
	1B	R. Murray	194	.216	4	24	508	35	7	32	10.4	.987	Hargesheimer	15	75	4	6	0	4.32
	OF	J. Wohlford	193	.280	1	24	89	2	1	0	1.9	.989							
	UT	J. Pettini	190	.232	1	9	66	147	8	24		.964							
	2B	J. Strain	189	.286	0	16	85	102	2	15	4.5	.989							
San Diego	1B	W. Montanez	481	.274	6	63	1185	84	8	105	10.3	.994	J. Curtis	30	187	10	8	0	3.51
	2B	D. Cash	397	.227	1	23	290	326	8	72	5.1	.987	S. Mura	37	169	8	7	2	3.67
W-73 L-89	SS	O. Smith	609	.230	0	35	**288**	**621**	24	**113**	5.9	.974	R. Jones	24	154	5	13	0	3.92
	3B	A. Rodriguez	175	.200	2	13	38	128	6	12	2.0	.965	R. Wise	27	154	6	8	0	3.68
Jerry Coleman	RF	D. Winfield	558	.276	20	87	273	20	4	4	1.9	.987	G. Lucas	46	150	5	8	3	3.24
	CF	J. Mumphrey	564	.298	4	59	398	10	11	1	2.7	.974	B. Shirley	59	137	11	12	7	3.55
	LF	G. Richards	642	.301	4	41	307	21	7	4	2.1	.979	E. Rasmussen	40	111	4	11	1	4.38
	C	G. Tenace	316	.222	17	50	415	46	10	7	4.5	.979	R. Fingers	66	103	11	9	23	2.80
	23	T. Flannery	292	.240	0	25	140	204	8	34		.977	D. Kinney	50	83	4	6	1	4.23
	C	B. Fahey	241	.257	1	22	309	34	8	6	4.1	.977							
	3B	L. Salazar	169	.337	1	25	29	88	7	7	3.0	.944							

BATTING AND BASE RUNNING LEADERS

Batting Average
B. Buckner, CHI	.324
K. Hernandez, STL	.321
G. Templeton, STL	.319
B. McBride, PHI	.309
C. Cedeno, HOU	.309

Slugging Average
M. Schmidt, PHI	.624
J. Clark, SF	.517
D. Murphy, ATL	.510
T. Simmons, STL	.505
D. Baker, LA	.503

Home Runs
M. Schmidt, PHI	48
B. Horner, ATL	35
D. Murphy, ATL	33
G. Carter, MON	29
D. Baker, LA	29

Total Bases
M. Schmidt, PHI	342
S. Garvey, LA	307
K. Hernandez, STL	294
D. Baker, LA	291
D. Murphy, ATL	290

Runs Batted In
M. Schmidt, PHI	121
G. Hendrick, STL	109
S. Garvey, LA	106
G. Carter, MON	101
K. Hernandez, STL	99

Stolen Bases
R. LeFlore, MON	97
O. Moreno, PIT	96
D. Collins, CIN	79
R. Scott, MON	63
G. Richards, SD	61

Hits
S. Garvey, LA	200
G. Richards, SD	193
K. Hernandez, STL	191
B. Buckner, CHI	187

Base on Balls
J. Morgan, HOU	93
D. Driessen, CIN	93
G. Tenace, SD	92
M. Schmidt, PHI	89

Home Run Percentage
M. Schmidt, PHI	8.8
D. Murphy, ATL	5.8
G. Carter, MON	5.3
R. Cey, LA	5.1

Runs Scored
K. Hernandez, STL	111
M. Schmidt, PHI	104
D. Murphy, ATL	98
A. Dawson, MON	96

Doubles
P. Rose, PHI	42
A. Dawson, MON	41
B. Buckner, CHI	41
K. Hernandez, STL	39

Triples
R. Scott, MON	13
O. Moreno, PIT	13
L. Herndon, SF	11
R. LeFlore, MON	11

PITCHING LEADERS

Winning Percentage
J. Bibby, PIT	.760
J. Reuss, LA	.750
S. Carlton, PHI	.727
D. Ruthven, PHI	.630
J. Niekro, HOU	.625

Earned Run Average
D. Sutton, LA	2.21
S. Carlton, PHI	2.34
J. Reuss, LA	2.52
V. Blue, SF	2.97
S. Rogers, MON	2.98

Wins
S. Carlton, PHI	24
J. Niekro, HOU	20
J. Bibby, PIT	19
J. Reuss, LA	18
D. Ruthven, PHI	17

Saves
B. Sutter, CHI	28
T. Hume, CIN	25
R. Fingers, SD	23
N. Allen, NY	22
R. Camp, ATL	22

Strikeouts
S. Carlton, PHI	286
N. Ryan, HOU	200
M. Soto, CIN	182
P. Niekro, ATL	176
B. Blyleven, PIT	168

Complete Games
S. Rogers, MON	14
S. Carlton, PHI	13
J. Niekro, HOU	11
P. Niekro, ATL	11
J. Reuss, LA	10
V. Blue, SF	10

Fewest Hits/9 Innings
M. Soto, CIN	5.97
D. Sutton, LA	6.92
S. Carlton, PHI	7.19
T. Seaver, CIN	7.50

Shutouts
J. Reuss, LA	6
J. Richard, HOU	4
S. Rogers, MON	4

Fewest Walks/9 Innings
B. Forsch, STL	1.38
J. Reuss, LA	1.57
K. Forsch, HOU	1.66
Candelaria, PIT	1.93

Most Strikeouts/9 Inn.
M. Soto, CIN	8.62
S. Carlton, PHI	8.47
N. Ryan, HOU	7.69
B. Blyleven, PIT	6.97

Innings
S. Carlton, PHI	304
S. Rogers, MON	281
P. Niekro, ATL	275
R. Reuschel, CHI	257

Games Pitched
D. Tidrow, CHI	84
T. Hume, CIN	78
K. Tekulve, PIT	78
R. Camp, ATL	77

NATIONAL LEAGUE 1980, cont.

		W	L	PCT	GB	R	OR	2B	3B	HR	BA	SA	SB	E	DP	FA	CG	BB	SO	ShO	SV	ERA
								\	Batting	\				\	Fielding	\	\	\	Pitching	\	\	
East	Philadelphia	91	71	.562	—	728	639	272	54	117	.270	.400	140	136	136	.979	25	530	889	8	40	3.43
	Montreal	90	72	.556	1	694	629	250	61	114	.257	.388	237	144	126	.977	33	460	823	15	36	3.48
	Pittsburgh	83	79	.512	8	666	646	249	38	116	.266	.388	209	137	154	.978	25	451	832	8	43	3.58
	St. Louis	74	88	.457	17	738	710	300	49	101	.275	.400	117	122	174	.981	34	495	664	9	27	3.93
	New York	67	95	.414	24	611	702	218	41	61	.257	.345	158	154	132	.975	17	510	886	9	33	3.85
	Chicago	64	98	.395	27	614	728	251	35	107	.251	.365	93	174	149	.974	13	589	923	6	35	3.89
West	Houston *	93	70	.571	—	637	589	231	67	75	.261	.367	194	140	145	.978	31	466	929	18	41	3.10
	Los Angeles	92	71	.564	1	663	591	209	24	148	.263	.388	123	123	149	.981	24	480	835	19	42	3.24
	Cincinnati	89	73	.549	3.5	707	670	256	45	113	.262	.386	156	106	144	.983	30	506	833	12	37	3.85
	Atlanta	81	80	.503	11	630	660	226	22	144	.250	.380	73	162	156	.975	29	454	696	9	37	3.77
	San Francisco	75	86	.466	17	573	634	199	44	80	.244	.342	100	159	124	.975	27	492	811	10	35	3.46
	San Diego	73	89	.451	19.5	591	654	195	43	67	.255	.342	239	132	157	.980	19	536	728	9	39	3.65
						7852	7852	2856	523	1243	.259	.374	1839	1689	1746	.978	307	5969	9849	132	445	3.60

* Defeated Los Angeles in a 1 game playoff.

AMERICAN LEAGUE 1980

POS	Player	AB	BA	HR	RBI	PO	A	E	DP	TC/G	FA	Pitcher	G	IP	W	L	SV	ERA
East — New York W-103 L-59 Dick Howser																		
1B	B. Watson	469	.307	13	68	851	63	9	87	8.9	.990	T. John	36	265	22	9	0	3.43
2B	W. Randolph	513	.294	7	46	361	401	19	97	5.7	.976	R. Guidry	37	220	17	10	1	3.56
SS	B. Dent	489	.262	5	52	224	489	13	77	5.1	.982	T. Underwood	38	187	13	9	2	0.00
3B	G. Nettles	324	.244	16	45	58	182	10	18	2.8	.960	R. May	41	175	15	5	3	2.47
RF	R. Jackson	514	.300	41	111	174	3	7	0	2.0	.962	L. Tiant	25	136	8	9	0	4.90
CF	B. Brown	412	.260	14	47	303	7	9	0	2.4	.972	R. Davis	53	131	9	3	7	2.95
LF	L. Piniella	321	.287	2	27	157	8	5	1	1.6	.971	G. Gossage	64	99	6	2	33	2.27
C	R. Cerone	519	.277	14	85	800	73	9	9	6.0	.990							
DH	E. Soderholm	275	.287	11	35													
OF	R. Jones	328	.223	9	42	246	4	3	1	3.1	.988							
OD	B. Murcer	297	.269	13	57	82	2	4	0	1.5	.955							
1B	J. Spencer	259	.236	13	43	567	41	6	51	8.2	.990							
OF	O. Gamble	194	.278	14	50	65	2	0	1	1.4	1.000							
3B	A. Rodriguez	164	.220	3	14	26	77	5	5	2.2	.954							
OF	J. Lefebvre	150	.227	8	21	75	3	2	1	1.1	.975							
Baltimore W-100 L-62 Earl Weaver																		
1B	E. Murray	621	.300	32	116	1369	77	9	158	9.4	.994	S. McGregor	36	252	20	8	0	3.32
2B	R. Dauer	557	.284	2	63	320	368	6	110	5.1	.991	S. Stone	37	251	25	7	0	3.23
SS	K. Garcia	311	.199	1	27	135	240	10	52	4.0	.974	M. Flanagan	37	251	16	13	0	4.12
3B	D. DeCinces	489	.249	16	64	120	340	19	41	3.4	.960	J. Palmer	34	224	16	10	0	3.98
RF	K. Singleton	583	.304	24	104	248	3	4	1	1.7	.984	S. Stewart	33	119	7	7	3	3.55
CF	A. Bumbry	645	.318	9	53	488	7	5	1	3.1	.990	D. Martinez	25	100	6	4	1	3.96
LF	G. Roenicke	297	.239	10	28	197	8	0	1	1.8	1.000	T. Stoddard	64	86	5	3	26	2.51
C	R. Dempsey	362	.262	9	40	531	54	8	8	5.3	.987	T. Martinez	53	81	4	4	10	3.00
DH	T. Crowley	233	.288	12	50													
SS	M. Belanger	268	.228	0	22	133	258	10	49	3.7	.975							
C	D. Graham	266	.278	15	54	328	35	7	3	5.1	.981							
DH	L. May	222	.243	7	31													
OD	P. Kelly	200	.260	3	26	48	4	0	0	1.4	1.000							
OF	Lowenstein	196	.311	4	27	128	3	1	0	1.5	.992							
DO	B. Ayala	170	.265	10	33	20	2	0	1	1.2	1.000							
Milwaukee W-86 L-76 Buck Rodgers W-26 L-21 George Bamberger W-47 L-45 Buck Rodgers W-13 L-10																		
1B	C. Cooper	622	.352	25	122	1336	106	5	160	10.2	.997	M. Haas	33	252	16	15	0	3.11
2B	P. Molitor	450	.304	9	37	240	294	16	80	6.0	.971	M. Caldwell	34	225	13	11	1	4.04
SS	R. Yount	611	.293	23	87	239	455	28	89	5.4	.961	L. Sorensen	35	196	12	10	1	3.67
3B	J. Gantner	415	.282	4	40	41	126	11	15	2.6	.938	B. Travers	29	154	12	6	0	3.92
RF	S. Lezcano	411	.229	18	55	228	8	4	4	2.2	.983	R. Cleveland	45	154	11	9	4	3.74
CF	G. Thomas	628	.239	38	105	455	6	7	1	2.9	.985	B. McClure	52	91	5	8	10	3.07
LF	B. Oglivie	592	.304	41	118	384	18	9	3	2.7	.978	P. Mitchell	17	89	5	5	1	3.54
C	C. Moore	320	.291	2	30	319	28	4	3	3.3	.989	B. Castro	56	84	2	4	8	2.79
DH	D. Davis	365	.271	4	30													
UT	D. Money	289	.256	17	46	176	129	12	35		.962							
3B	S. Bando	254	.197	5	31	46	110	11	12	2.9	.934							
C	B. Martinez	219	.224	3	17	293	33	5	0	4.4	.985							
Boston W-83 L-77 Don Zimmer W-82 L-73 Johnny Pesky W-1 L-4																		
1B	T. Perez	585	.275	25	105	1301	87	10	150	10.2	.993	M. Torrez	36	207	9	16	0	5.09
2B	D. Stapleton	449	.321	7	45	178	327	11	90	5.5	.979	D. Eckersley	30	198	12	14	0	4.27
SS	R. Burleson	644	.278	8	51	301	528	22	147	5.5	.974	B. Stanley	52	175	10	8	14	3.39
3B	G. Hoffman	312	.285	4	42	72	193	15	17	2.5	.946	S. Renko	32	165	9	9	0	4.20
RF	D. Evans	463	.266	18	60	268	11	5	7	2.0	.982	D. Drago	43	133	7	7	3	4.13
CF	F. Lynn	415	.301	12	61	302	11	2	4	2.9	.994	T. Burgmeier	62	99	5	4	24	2.00
LF	J. Rice	504	.294	24	86	233	10	3	2	2.3	.988	J. Tudor	16	92	8	5	0	3.03
C	C. Fisk	478	.289	18	62	522	56	10	8	5.1	.983	C. Rainey	16	87	8	3	0	4.86
DH	Yastrzemski	364	.275	15	50													
3D	B. Hobson	324	.228	11	39	52	109	16	5	3.1	.910							
OF	J. Dwyer	260	.285	9	38	111	7	3	2	1.9	.975							
2B	J. Remy	230	.313	0	9	109	189	7	30	5.1	.977							

AMERICAN LEAGUE 1980, *cont.*

	POS	Player	AB	BA	HR	RBI	PO	A	E	DP	TC/G	FA	Pitcher	G	IP	W	L	SV	ERA
Detroit	1B	R. Hebner	341	.290	12	82	466	35	1	35	8.2	.998	J. Morris	36	250	16	15	0	4.18
	2B	L. Whitaker	477	.233	1	45	340	428	12	93	5.5	.985	M. Wilcox	32	199	13	11	0	4.48
W-84 L-78	SS	A. Trammell	560	.300	9	65	225	412	13	89	4.5	.980	Schatzeder	32	193	11	13	0	4.01
	3B	T. Brookens	509	.275	10	66	112	279	29	27	3.0	.931	D. Petry	27	165	10	9	0	3.93
Sparky Anderson	RF	A. Cowens	403	.280	5	42	199	8	3	2	2.0	.986	D. Rozema	42	145	6	9	4	3.91
	CF	R. Peters	477	.291	2	42	296	1	7	1	2.8	.977	A. Lopez	67	124	13	6	21	3.77
	LF	S. Kemp	508	.293	21	101	197	4	1	3	2.4	.995	P. Underwood	49	113	3	6	5	3.58
	C	L. Parrish	553	.286	24	82	557	66	6	8	5.2	.990							
	DH	C. Summers	347	.297	17	60													
	UT	Wockenfuss	372	.274	16	65	575	47	11	44		.983							
	OF	K. Gibson	175	.263	9	16	122	1	1	0	2.5	.992							
	1B	J. Thompson	126	.214	4	20	328	30	0	33	9.9	1.000							
Cleveland	1B	M. Hargrove	589	.304	11	85	**1391**	88	10	128	9.3	.993	L. Barker	36	246	19	12	0	4.17
	2B	A. Bannister	262	.328	1	32	77	106	6	20	4.6	.968	R. Waits	33	224	13	14	0	4.46
W-79 L-81	SS	T. Veryzer	358	.271	2	28	169	331	15	59	4.8	.971	D. Spillner	34	194	16	11	0	5.29
	3B	T. Harrah	561	.267	11	72	120	317	13	27	2.9	.971	W. Garland	25	150	6	9	0	4.62
Dave Garcia	RF	J. Orta	481	.291	10	64	269	10	5	1	2.4	.982	B. Owchinko	29	114	2	9	0	5.29
	CF	R. Manning	471	.234	3	52	379	7	4	1	2.8	.990	J. Denny	16	109	8	6	0	4.38
	LF	M. Dilone	528	.341	0	40	249	7	7	2	2.2	.973	S. Monge	67	94	3	5	14	3.64
	C	R. Hassey	390	.318	8	65	549	52	4	8	5.4	.993	V. Cruz	55	86	6	7	12	3.45
	DH	Charboneau	453	.289	23	87													
	S2	J. Dybzinski	248	.230	1	23	142	261	13	45		.969							
	C	B. Diaz	207	.227	3	32	317	35	4	4	4.7	.989							
	DH	G. Alexander	178	.225	5	31													
	DH	C. Johnson	174	.230	6	28													
Toronto	1B	J. Mayberry	501	.248	30	82	1243	79	8	138	9.8	.994	J. Clancy	34	251	13	16	0	3.30
	2B	D. Garcia	543	.278	4	46	316	471	16	112	**5.8**	.980	D. Stieb	34	243	12	15	0	3.70
W-67 L-95	SS	A. Griffin	653	.254	2	41	295	489	37	126	5.3	.955	McLaughlin	55	136	6	9	4	4.50
	3B	R. Howell	528	.269	10	57	105	257	16	24	2.7	.958	P. Mirabella	33	131	5	12	0	4.33
Bobby Mattick	RF	L. Moseby	389	.229	9	46	208	12	4	1	2.2	.982	J. Jefferson	29	122	4	13	0	5.46
	CF	B. Bonnell	463	.268	13	56	271	15	8	3	2.4	.973	J. Garvin	61	83	4	7	8	2.28
	LF	A. Woods	373	.300	15	47	205	5	2	1	2.4	.991	J. Kucek	23	68	3	8	1	6.75
	C	E. Whitt	295	.237	6	34	436	56	7	11	4.8	.986							
	DH	O. Velez	357	.269	20	62													
	OF	B. Bailor	347	.236	1	16	205	16	2	5	2.3	.991							
	UT	G. Iorg	222	.248	2	14	122	155	3	45		.989							
	C	B. Davis	218	.216	4	19	317	28	6	6	3.9	.983							
	OF	R. Bosetti	188	.213	4	18	124	4	2	0	2.5	.985							
West **Kansas City**	1B	W. Aikens	543	.278	20	98	1081	65	12	95	8.4	.990	L. Gura	36	283	18	10	0	2.96
	2B	F. White	560	.264	7	60	395	448	10	103	5.6	.988	D. Leonard	38	280	20	11	0	3.79
W-97 L-65	SS	Washington	549	.273	6	53	237	467	32	86	4.8	.957	Splittorff	34	204	14	11	0	4.15
	3B	G. Brett	449	**.390**	24	118	103	256	17	28	3.4	.955	R. Gale	32	191	13	9	1	3.91
Jim Frey	RF	C. Hurdle	395	.294	10	60	233	8	10	1	2.0	.960	R. Martin	32	137	10	10	2	4.40
	CF	A. Otis	394	.251	10	53	310	6	4	1	3.0	.988	Quisenberry	**75**	128	12	7	33	3.09
	LF	W. Wilson	705	.326	3	49	482	9	6	1	3.1	.988							
	C	D. Porter	418	.249	7	51	322	37	8	6	4.5	.978							
	DH	H. McRae	489	.297	14	83													
	CO	J. Wathan	453	.305	6	58	360	26	7	5		.982							
	UT	D. Chalk	167	.251	1	20	57	88	6	10		.960							
	3C	J. Quirk	163	.276	5	21	69	66	8	3		.944							
Oakland	1B	D. Revering	376	.290	15	62	724	67	9	56	8.4	.989	R. Langford	35	**290**	19	12	0	3.26
	2B	D. McKay	295	.244	1	29	99	151	6	24	4.1	.977	M. Norris	33	284	22	9	0	2.54
W-83 L-79	SS	M. Guerrero	381	.239	2	23	184	276	18	50	4.1	.962	M. Keough	34	250	16	13	0	2.92
	3B	W. Gross	366	.281	14	61	69	130	11	13	2.1	.948	S. McCatty	33	222	14	14	0	3.85
Billy Martin	RF	T. Armas	628	.279	35	109	374	17	10	2	2.5	.975	B. Kingman	32	211	8	**20**	0	3.84
	CF	D. Murphy	573	.274	13	68	**507**	13	5	0	**3.3**	.990	B. Lacey	47	80	3	2	6	2.93
	LF	R. Henderson	591	.303	9	53	407	15	7	1	2.7	.984							
	C	J. Essian	285	.232	5	29	333	46	5	5	5.6	.987							
	DH	M. Page	348	.244	17	51													
	1C	J. Newman	438	.233	15	56	675	54	15	28		.980							
	CD	M. Heath	305	.243	1	33	268	19	4	5	6.2	.986							
	S2	R. Picciolo	271	.240	5	18	163	208	6	39		.984							
	3B	M. Klutts	197	.269	4	21	46	80	7	3	2.1	.947							
	2B	J. Cox	169	.213	0	9	107	167	6	28	4.8	.979							
Minnesota	1B	R. Jackson	396	.265	5	42	983	74	10	105	9.0	.991	J. Koosman	38	243	16	13	2	4.04
	2B	R. Wilfong	416	.248	8	45	238	337	3	85	4.8	**.995**	G. Zahn	38	233	14	18	0	4.40
W-77 L-84	SS	R. Smalley	486	.278	12	63	210	446	17	100	5.4	.975	R. Erickson	32	191	7	13	0	3.25
	3B	J. Castino	546	.302	13	64	105	**340**	18	34	3.4	.961	D. Jackson	32	172	9	9	1	3.87
Gene Mauch	RF	H. Powell	485	.262	6	35	265	11	9	1	2.2	.968	D. Corbett	73	136	8	6	23	1.99
W-54 L-71	CF	K. Landreaux	484	.281	7	62	231	8	6	0	2.2	.976	P. Redfern	23	105	7	7	2	4.54
	LF	R. Sofield	417	.247	9	49	267	7	6	0	2.2	.979	J. Verhoeven	44	100	3	4	0	3.96
John Goryl	C	B. Wynegar	486	.255	5	57	670	72	9	**13**	5.3	.988	F. Arroyo	21	92	6	6	0	4.70
W-23 L-13	DH	J. Morales	241	.303	8	36													
	UT	P. Mackanin	319	.266	4	35	168	285	18	75		.962							
	13	M. Cubbage	285	.246	8	42	541	98	4	62		.994							
	DH	G. Adams	262	.286	6	38													
	OF	D. Edwards	200	.250	2	20	144	7	11	1	2.3	.932							

AMERICAN LEAGUE 1980, *cont.*

Texas — W-76 L-85 — Pat Corrales

POS	Player	AB	BA	HR	RBI	PO	A	E	DP	TC/G	FA	Pitcher	G	IP	W	L	SV	ERA
1B	P. Putnam	410	.263	13	55	979	80	9	107	7.8	.992	J. Matlack	35	235	10	10	1	3.68
2B	B. Wills	578	.263	5	58	340	473	13	112	5.7	.984	D. Medich	34	204	14	11	0	3.93
SS	P. Frias	227	.242	0	10	117	167	16	38	2.8	.947	F. Jenkins	29	198	12	12	0	3.77
3B	B. Bell	490	.329	17	83	125	282	8	26	3.4	.981	G. Perry	24	155	6	9	0	3.43
RF	J. Grubb	274	.277	9	32	112	6	6	1	1.6	.952	D. Darwin	53	110	13	4	8	2.62
CF	M. Rivers	630	.333	7	60	342	19	8	4	2.6	.978	S. Lyle	49	81	3	2	8	4.67
LF	A. Oliver	656	.319	19	117	314	9	9	2	2.1	.973	J. Kern	38	63	3	11	2	4.86
C	J. Sundberg	505	.273	10	63	853	76	7	7	6.2	.993							
DH	R. Zisk	448	.290	19	77													
UT	R. Staub	340	.300	9	55	262	14	6	28		.979							
UT	D. Roberts	235	.238	10	30	138	100	11	11		.956							
OF	B. Sample	204	.260	4	19	105	2	3	0	1.5	.973							
1D	J. Ellis	182	.236	1	23	240	12	2	22	6.5	.992							
SS	B. Harrelson	180	.272	1	9	118	220	17	57	4.1	.952							
OF	J. Norris	174	.247	0	16	73	3	0	0	.9	1.000							

Chicago — W-70 L-90 — Tony LaRussa

POS	Player	AB	BA	HR	RBI	PO	A	E	DP	TC/G	FA	Pitcher	G	IP	W	L	SV	ERA
1B	M. Squires	343	.283	2	33	904	68	5	79	8.6	.995	B. Burns	34	238	15	13	0	2.84
2B	J. Morrison	604	.283	15	57	422	481	29	117	5.8	.969	S. Trout	32	200	9	16	0	3.69
SS	T. Cruz	293	.232	2	18	138	298	20	62	5.1	.956	R. Dotson	33	198	12	10	0	4.27
3B	K. Bell	191	.178	1	11	35	151	15	12	2.4	.925	M. Proly	62	147	5	10	8	3.06
RF	H. Baines	491	.255	13	49	229	6	9	1	1.8	.963	Baumgarten	24	136	2	12	0	3.44
CF	C. Lemon	514	.292	11	51	347	11	7	2	2.6	.981	L. Hoyt	24	112	9	3	0	4.58
LF	W. Nordhagen	415	.277	15	59	120	6	4	1	1.8	.969	E. Farmer	64	100	7	9	30	3.33
C	B. Kimm	251	.243	0	19	375	26	6	2	4.2	.985	R. Wortham	41	92	4	7	1	5.97
DH	L. Johnson	541	.277	13	81													
OD	B. Molinaro	344	.291	5	36	85	3	4	0	1.9	.957							
S3	G. Pryor	338	.240	1	29	125	333	16	53		.966							

California — W-65 L-95 — Jim Fregosi

POS	Player	AB	BA	HR	RBI	PO	A	E	DP	TC/G	FA	Pitcher	G	IP	W	L	SV	ERA
1B	R. Carew	540	.331	3	59	897	57	6	82	9.3	.994	F. Tanana	32	204	11	12	0	4.15
2B	B. Grich	498	.271	14	62	326	463	9	101	5.5	.989	D. Aase	40	175	8	13	2	4.06
SS	F. Patek	273	.264	5	34	129	199	16	42	4.2	.953	F. Martinez	30	149	7	9	0	4.53
3B	C. Lansford	602	.261	15	80	151	250	19	29	2.8	.955	D. LaRoche	52	128	3	5	4	4.08
RF	L. Harlow	301	.276	4	27	234	11	6	5	2.7	.976	C. Knapp	32	117	2	11	1	6.15
CF	R. Miller	412	.274	2	38	299	11	5	3	2.7	.984	M. Clear	58	106	11	11	9	3.31
LF	J. Rudi	372	.237	16	53	220	5	2	1	2.5	.991	A. Hassler	41	83	5	1	10	2.49
C	T. Donohue	218	.188	2	14	330	29	5	5	4.3	.986	D. Frost	15	78	4	8	0	5.31
DH	J. Thompson	312	.317	17	70													
OD	D. Baylor	340	.250	5	51	119	4	4	0	2.4	.969							
UT	D. Thon	267	.255	0	15	70	128	10	28		.952							
OF	B. Clark	261	.230	5	23	213	6	4	2	2.9	.982							
OF	D. Ford	226	.279	7	26	75	3	5	0	1.8	.940							
SS	Campaneris	210	.252	2	18	108	157	12	41	4.3	.957							
CD	B. Downing	93	.290	2	25	69	6	0	0	4.7	1.000							

Seattle — W-59 L-103 — Darrell Johnson W-39 L-65 — Maury Wills W-20 L-38

POS	Player	AB	BA	HR	RBI	PO	A	E	DP	TC/G	FA	Pitcher	G	IP	W	L	SV	ERA
1B	B. Bochte	520	.300	13	78	1273	98	6	143	10.4	.996	F. Bannister	32	218	9	13	0	3.47
2B	J. Cruz	422	.209	2	16	269	355	11	85	5.5	.983	G. Abbott	31	215	12	12	0	4.10
SS	M. Mendoza	277	.245	2	14	149	290	19	68	4.0	.959	R. Honeycutt	30	203	10	17	0	3.95
3B	T. Cox	247	.243	2	23	47	142	11	20	2.5	.945	J. Beattie	33	187	5	15	0	4.86
RF	L. Roberts	374	.251	10	33	238	6	4	1	2.4	.984	R. Dressler	30	149	4	10	0	3.99
CF	J. Simpson	365	.249	3	34	205	10	5	1	1.8	.977	S. Rawley	59	114	7	7	13	3.32
LF	D. Meyer	531	.275	11	71	189	10	8	2	1.7	.961	M. Parrott	27	94	1	16	3	7.28
C	L. Cox	243	.202	4	20	412	45	3	5	4.4	.993	McLaughlin	45	91	3	6	2	6.82
DH	W. Horton	335	.221	8	36							D. Heaverlo	60	79	6	3	4	3.87
UT	T. Paciorek	418	.273	15	59	360	22	5	25		.987							
S3	J. Anderson	317	.227	8	30	118	253	22	45		.944							
UT	L. Milbourne	258	.264	0	26	103	195	8	50		.974							
OF	R. Craig	240	.238	3	20	155	2	2	1	2.5	.987							
OF	J. Beniquez	237	.228	6	21	176	3	8	0	2.9	.957							
UT	B. Stein	198	.268	5	27	119	115	4	21		.983							

BATTING AND BASE RUNNING LEADERS

Batting Average		Slugging Average		Home Runs		Winning Percentage	
G. Brett, KC	.390	G. Brett, KC	.664	R. Jackson, NY	41	S. Stone, BAL	.781
C. Cooper, MIL	.352	R. Jackson, NY	.597	B. Oglivie, MIL	41	R. May, NY	.750
M. Dilone, CLE	.341	B. Oglivie, MIL	.563	G. Thomas, MIL	38	S. McGregor, BAL	.714
M. Rivers, TEX	.333	C. Cooper, MIL	.539	T. Armas, OAK	35	T. John, NY	.710
R. Carew, CAL	.331	R. Yount, MIL	.519	E. Murray, BAL	32	M. Norris, OAK	.710

Total Bases		Runs Batted In		Stolen Bases		Saves	
C. Cooper, MIL	335	C. Cooper, MIL	122	R. Henderson, OAK	100	Quisenberry, KC	33
B. Oglivie, MIL	333	G. Brett, KC	118	W. Wilson, KC	79	G. Gossage, NY	33
E. Murray, BAL	322	B. Oglivie, MIL	118	M. Dilone, CLE	61	E. Farmer, CHI	30
R. Yount, MIL	317	A. Oliver, TEX	117	J. Cruz, SEA	45	T. Stoddard, BAL	26
A. Oliver, TEX	315	E. Murray, BAL	116	A. Bumbry, BAL	44	T. Burgmeier, BOS	24

PITCHING LEADERS

Earned Run Average		Wins		Strikeouts		Complete Games	
R. May, NY	2.47	S. Stone, BAL	25	L. Barker, CLE	187	R. Langford, OAK	28
M. Norris, OAK	2.54	T. John, NY	22	M. Norris, OAK	180	M. Norris, OAK	24
B. Burns, CHI	2.84	M. Norris, OAK	22	R. Guidry, NY	166	M. Keough, OAK	20
M. Keough, OAK	2.92	S. McGregor, BAL	20	F. Bannister, SEA	155	T. John, NY	16
L. Gura, KC	2.96	D. Leonard, KC	20	D. Leonard, KC	155	L. Gura, KC	16

AMERICAN LEAGUE 1980, *cont.*

BATTING AND BASE RUNNING LEADERS

Hits			Base on Balls			Home Run Percentage			Fewest Hits/9 Innings			Shutouts			Fewest Walks/9 Innings	
W. Wilson, KC	230		W. Randolph, NY	119		R. Jackson, NY	8.0		M. Norris, OAK	6.81		T. John, NY	6		J. Matlack, TEX	1.84
C. Cooper, MIL	219		R. Henderson, OAK	117		B. Oglivie, MIL	6.9		R. May, NY	7.41		G. Zahn, MIN	5		Splittorff, KC	1.90
M. Rivers, TEX	210		M. Hargrove, CLE	111		G. Thomas, MIL	6.1		J. Clancy, TOR	7.78		D. Stieb, TOR	4		T. John, NY	1.90
A. Oliver, TEX	209		D. Murphy, OAK	102		J. Mayberry, TOR	6.0		T. Underwood, NY	7.84		S. McGregor, BAL	4		F. Tanana, CAL	1.99

Runs Scored			Doubles			Triples			Most Strikeouts/9 Inn.			Innings			Games Pitched	
W. Wilson, KC	133		R. Yount, MIL	49		A. Griffin, TOR	15		L. Barker, CLE	6.84		R. Langford, OAK	290		Quisenberry, KC	75
R. Yount, MIL	121		A. Oliver, TEX	43		W. Wilson, KC	15		R. May, NY	6.84		M. Norris, OAK	284		D. Corbett, MIN	73
A. Bumbry, BAL	118		J. Morrison, CHI	40		K. Landreaux, MIN	11		R. Guidry, NY	6.79		L. Gura, KC	283		A. Lopez, DET	67
R. Henderson, OAK	111		H. McRae, KC	39		Washington, KC	11		F. Bannister, SEA	6.40		D. Leonard, KC	280		S. Monge, CLE	67

PITCHING LEADERS

		W	L	PCT	GB	R	OR	2B	3B	HR	BA	SA	SB	E	DP	FA	CG	BB	SO	ShO	SV	ERA
East	New York	103	59	.636		820	662	239	34	189	.267	.425	86	138	160	.978	29	463	845	**15**	**50**	3.58
	Baltimore	100	62	.617	3	805	**640**	258	29	156	.273	.413	111	**95**	178	**.985**	42	507	789	10	41	3.64
	Milwaukee	86	76	.531	17	811	682	**298**	36	**203**	.275	**.448**	131	147	189	.977	48	**420**	575	14	30	3.71
	Boston	83	77	.519	19	757	767	297	36	162	**.283**	.436	79	149	**206**	.977	30	481	696	8	43	4.38
	Detroit	84	78	.519	19	**830**	757	232	53	143	.273	.409	75	133	165	.979	40	558	741	9	30	4.25
	Cleveland	79	81	.494	23	738	807	221	40	89	.277	.381	118	105	143	.983	35	552	843	8	32	4.68
	Toronto	67	95	.414	36	624	762	249	53	126	.251	.383	67	133	**206**	.979	39	635	705	9	23	4.19
West	Kansas City	97	65	.599		809	694	266	59	115	**.286**	.413	**185**	141	150	.978	37	465	614	10	42	3.83
	Oakland	83	79	.512	14	686	642	212	35	137	.259	.385	175	130	115	.979	**94**	521	769	9	13	**3.46**
	Minnesota	77	84	.478	19.5	670	724	252	46	99	.265	.381	62	148	192	.977	35	468	744	9	30	3.93
	Texas	76	85	.472	20.5	756	752	263	27	124	.284	.405	91	147	169	.977	35	519	**890**	6	25	4.02
	Chicago	70	90	.438	26	587	722	255	38	91	.259	.370	68	171	162	.973	32	563	724	12	42	3.92
	California	65	95	.406	31	698	797	236	32	106	.265	.378	91	134	144	.978	22	529	725	6	30	4.52
	Seattle	59	103	.364	38	610	793	211	35	104	.248	.356	116	149	189	.977	31	540	703	7	26	4.38
						10201	10201	3489	553	1844	.269	.399	1455	1920	2368	.978	549	7221	10363	132	457	4.03

NATIONAL LEAGUE 1981

		POS	Player	AB	BA	HR	RBI	PO	A	E	DP	TC/G	FA	Pitcher	G	IP	W	L	SV	ERA
East	**St. Louis**	1B	K. Hernandez	376	.306	8	48	**1054**	86	3	**99**	**11.7**	.997	L. Sorensen	23	140	7	7	0	3.28
		2B	T. Herr	411	.268	0	46	211	**374**	5	74	5.7	**.992**	B. Forsch	20	124	10	5	0	3.19
		SS	G. Templeton	333	.288	1	33	160	272	18	54	5.9	.960	J. Martin	17	103	8	5	0	3.41
	W-59 L-43	3B	K. Oberkfell	376	.293	2	45	77	246	15	23	3.3	.956	B. Sutter	48	82	3	5	25	2.63
		RF	S. Lezcano	214	.266	5	28	103	5	3	1	1.7	.973	B. Shirley	28	79	6	4	1	4.10
	Whitey Herzog	CF	G. Hendrick	394	.284	18	61	227	6	4	0	2.3	.983	J. Kaat	41	53	6	6	4	3.40
		LF	D. Iorg	217	.327	2	39	78	0	3	0	1.4	.963							
		C	D. Porter	174	.224	6	31	206	31	5	2	4.7	.979							
		OF	T. Scott	176	.227	2	17	120	2	0	0	2.8	1.000							
		C	G. Tenace	129	.233	5	22	126	18	3	1	3.9	.980							
		SS	M. Ramsey	124	.258	0	9	52	118	6	20	5.0	.966							
		OF	T. Landrum	119	.261	0	10	72	6	0	1	1.2	1.000							
	Montreal	1B	W. Cromartie	358	.304	6	42	488	32	4	38	8.5	.992	S. Rogers	22	161	12	8	0	3.41
		2B	R. Scott	336	.205	0	26	187	278	8	41	5.1	.983	Gullickson	22	157	7	9	0	2.81
		SS	C. Speier	307	.225	2	25	175	280	17	57	4.9	.964	S. Sanderson	22	137	9	7	0	2.96
	W-60 L-48	3B	L. Parrish	349	.244	8	44	**91**	141	16	7	2.6	.935	R. Burris	22	136	9	7	0	3.04
		RF	J. White	119	.218	3	11	58	2	3	1	1.6	.952	B. Lee	31	89	5	6	6	2.93
	Dick Williams	CF	A. Dawson	394	.302	24	64	**327**	10	7	1	3.0	.980	W. Fryman	35	43	5	3	7	1.88
	W-44 L-37	LF	T. Raines	313	.304	5	37	160	6	4	0	2.1	.976							
		C	G. Carter	374	.251	16	68	**509**	58	4	11	5.7	.993							
	Jim Fanning	UT	T. Wallach	212	.236	4	13	207	31	1	9		.996							
	W-16 L-11																			
	Philadelphia	1B	P. Rose	431	.325	0	33	929	91	4	69	9.6	.996	S. Carlton	24	190	13	4	0	2.42
		2B	M. Trillo	349	.287	6	36	**245**	286	7	61	5.7	.987	D. Ruthven	23	147	12	7	0	5.14
		SS	L. Bowa	360	.283	0	31	117	309	11	50	4.3	.975	Christenson	20	107	4	7	1	3.53
	W-59 L-48	3B	M. Schmidt	354	.316	**31**	**91**	74	**249**	15	20	3.3	.956	S. Lyle	48	75	9	6	2	4.44
		RF	B. McBride	221	.271	2	21	76	2	1	1	1.4	.987	R. Reed	39	61	5	3	8	3.10
	Dallas Green	CF	G. Maddox	323	.263	5	40	251	8	6	4	2.8	.977	T. McGraw	34	44	2	4	10	2.66
		LF	G. Matthews	359	.301	9	67	170	11	7	1	1.9	.963							
		C	B. Boone	227	.211	4	24	365	32	6	5	5.4	.985							
		C	K. Moreland	196	.255	6	37	256	20	5	2	5.6	.982							
		OF	L. Smith	176	.324	2	11	89	10	3	2	2.0	.971							
		OF	G. Gross	102	.225	0	7	48	7	1	2	1.0	.982							

NATIONAL LEAGUE 1981, *cont.*

	POS	Player	AB	BA	HR	RBI	PO	A	E	DP	TC/G	FA	Pitcher	G	IP	W	L	SV	ERA
Pittsburgh	1B	J. Thompson	223	.242	15	42	590	46	7	65	8.2	.989	R. Rhoden	21	136	9	4	0	3.90
W-46 L-56	2B	P. Garner	181	.254	1	20	121	148	9	31	5.6	.968	E. Solomon	22	127	8	6	1	3.12
	SS	T. Foli	316	.247	0	20	140	247	14	52	5.0	.965	R. Scurry	27	74	4	5	7	3.77
Chuck Tanner	3B	B. Madlock	279	**.341**	6	45	50	147	9	17	2.6	.956	K. Tekulve	45	65	5	5	3	2.49
	RF	D. Parker	240	.258	9	48	110	1	7	0	2.2	.941	E. Romo	33	42	1	3	9	4.50
	CF	O. Moreno	434	.276	1	35	302	6	1	1	3.0	.997							
	LF	M. Easler	339	.286	7	42	188	13	4	2	2.3	.980							
	C	T. Pena	210	.300	2	17	286	41	5	10	5.2	.985							
	UT	D. Berra	232	.241	2	27	89	167	8	27		.970							
	OF	L. Lacy	213	.268	2	10	121	7	3	1	2.1	.977							
	C	S. Nicosia	169	.231	2	18	257	23	5	2	5.5	.982							
	2B	J. Ray	102	.245	0	6	52	96	2	22	4.8	.987							
New York	1B	D. Kingman	353	.221	22	59	462	31	13	39	9.0	.974	P. Zachry	24	139	7	**14**	0	4.14
W-41 L-62	2B	D. Flynn	325	.222	1	20	220	301	7	58	5.3	.987	M. Scott	23	136	5	10	0	3.90
	SS	F. Taveras	283	.230	0	11	120	202	24	44	4.4	.931	N. Allen	43	67	7	6	18	2.96
Joe Torre	3B	H. Brooks	358	.307	4	38	65	192	**21**	14	3.0	.924							
	RF	E. Valentine	169	.207	5	21	83	6	4	0	2.0	.957							
	CF	M. Wilson	328	.271	3	14	226	3	4	1	2.9	.983							
	LF	L. Mazzilli	324	.228	6	34	192	5	6	1	2.3	.970							
	C	J. Stearns	273	.271	1	24	302	38	6	7	5.2	.983							
	1B	R. Staub	161	.317	5	21	339	20	4	26	8.9	.989							
	C	A. Trevino	149	.262	0	10	211	22	9	1	5.4	.963							
	OF	Youngblood	143	.350	4	25	70	6	3	0	1.9	.962							
	10	M. Jorgensen	122	.205	3	15	143	9	1	8		.993							
Chicago	1B	B. Buckner	421	.311	10	75	996	81	**17**	92	10.4	.984	M. Krukow	25	144	9	9	0	3.69
	2B	P. Tabler	101	.188	1	5	70	93	3	17	4.7	.982	R. Martz	33	108	5	7	6	3.67
W-38 L-65	SS	I. DeJesus	403	.194	0	13	**221**	343	24	**81**	5.5	.959	R. Reuschel	13	86	4	7	0	3.45
	3B	K. Reitz	260	.215	2	28	57	157	5	11	2.7	**.977**	D. Tidrow	51	75	3	10	9	5.04
Joey Amalfitano	RF	L. Durham	328	.290	10	35	159	4	5	1	2.0	.970	L. Smith	40	67	3	6	1	3.49
	CF	S. Henderson	287	.293	5	35	152	4	**8**	2	2.1	.951							
	LF	J. Morales	245	.286	1	25	142	2	1	1	2.0	.986							
	C	J. Davis	180	.256	4	21	274	44	9	4	5.8	.972							
	OF	B. Bonds	163	.215	6	19	108	2	2	0	2.5	.982							
	C	T. Blackwell	158	.234	1	11	268	28	2	1	5.3	.993							
	2B	S. Dillard	119	.218	2	11	54	96	4	21	4.8	.974							
	OF	S. Thompson	115	.165	0	8	49	1	1	0	1.7	.980							
	30	H. Cruz	109	.229	7	15	33	26	3	0		.952							
West Cincinnati	1B	D. Driessen	233	.236	7	33	558	30	3	54	8.0	.995	M. Soto	25	175	12	9	0	3.29
	2B	R. Oester	354	.271	5	42	202	328	11	61	5.3	.980	T. Seaver	23	166	**14**	2	0	2.55
W-66 L-42	SS	Concepcion	421	.306	5	67	208	322	22	71	5.2	.960	F. Pastore	22	132	4	9	0	4.02
	3B	R. Knight	386	.259	6	34	69	176	11	18	2.4	.957	B. Berenyi	21	126	9	6	0	3.50
John McNamara	RF	D. Collins	360	.272	3	23	167	4	4	2	1.9	.977	M. LaCoss	20	78	4	7	1	6.12
	CF	K. Griffey	396	.311	2	34	268	8	3	1	2.8	.989	T. Hume	51	68	9	4	13	3.44
	LF	G. Foster	414	.295	22	90	224	8	2	1	2.2	.991	J. Price	41	54	6	1	4	2.50
	C	J. Nolan	236	.309	1	26	393	18	2	2	5.1	**.995**							
	1B	J. Bench	178	.309	8	25	334	23	6	35	9.6	.983							
	C	M. O'Berry	111	.180	1	5	208	22	4	2	4.3	.983							
Los Angeles	1B	S. Garvey	431	.283	10	64	1019	55	1	84	9.8	**.999**	Valenzuela	25	**192**	13	7	0	2.48
	2B	D. Lopes	214	.206	5	17	129	161	2	30	5.3	.993	J. Reuss	22	153	10	4	0	2.29
W-63 L-47	SS	B. Russell	262	.233	0	22	128	261	14	49	5.0	.973	B. Hooton	23	142	11	6	0	2.28
	3B	R. Cey	312	.288	13	50	71	184	16	15	3.2	.941	B. Welch	23	141	9	5	0	3.45
Tom Lasorda	RF	P. Guerrero	347	.300	12	48	145	4	4	0	2.0	.974	D. Goltz	26	77	2	7	1	4.09
	CF	K. Landreaux	390	.251	7	41	210	4	0	0	2.3	**1.000**	S. Howe	41	54	5	3	8	2.50
	LF	D. Baker	400	.320	9	49	181	8	2	1	1.9	.990	B. Castillo	34	51	2	4	5	5.29
	C	M. Scioscia	290	.276	2	29	493	48	7	4	6.0	.987	D. Stewart	32	43	4	3	6	2.51
	UT	D. Thomas	218	.248	4	24	133	144	14	30		.952							
	OF	R. Monday	130	.315	11	25	50	1	2	0	1.3	.962							
	2B	S. Sax	119	.277	2	9	64	93	4	22	5.6	.975							
Houston	1B	C. Cedeno	306	.271	5	34	428	27	4	27	10.0	.991	J. Niekro	24	166	9	9	0	2.82
	2B	J. Pittman	135	.281	0	7	56	89	3	14	4.2	.980	D. Sutton	23	159	11	9	0	2.60
W-61 L-49	SS	C. Reynolds	323	.260	4	31	139	261	11	36	4.8	.973	B. Knepper	22	157	9	5	0	2.18
	3B	A. Howe	361	.296	3	36	52	206	9	16	2.7	.966	N. Ryan	21	149	11	5	0	**1.69**
Bill Virdon	RF	T. Puhl	350	.251	3	28	185	5	0	1	2.2	**1.000**	V. Ruhle	20	102	4	6	1	2.91
	CF	T. Scott	225	.293	2	22	127	5	2	0	2.4	.985	D. Smith	42	75	5	3	8	2.76
	LF	J. Cruz	409	.267	13	55	237	5	4	2	2.3	.984	J. Sambito	49	64	5	5	10	1.83
	C	A. Ashby	255	.271	4	33	434	58	9	6	**6.2**	.982	F. LaCorte	37	42	4	2	5	3.64
	O1	D. Walling	158	.234	5	23	226	9	2	18		.992							
	UT	K. Garcia	136	.272	0	15	58	119	11	14		.941							
	C	L. Pujols	117	.239	1	14	192	14	1	1	5.3	.995							
	2B	P. Garner	113	.239	0	6	62	102	3	17	5.4	.982							
	OF	G. Woods	110	.209	0	12	61	1	1	0	1.6	.984							

NATIONAL LEAGUE 1981, cont.

	POS	Player	AB	BA	HR	RBI	PO	A	E	DP	TC/G	FA	Pitcher	G	IP	W	L	SV	ERA
San Francisco	1B	E. Cabell	396	.255	2	36	620	63	9	56	10.0	.987	D. Alexander	24	152	11	7	0	2.90
	2B	J. Morgan	308	.240	8	31	177	258	4	61	5.0	.991	T. Griffin	22	129	8	8	0	3.77
W-56 L-55	SS	J. LeMaster	324	.253	0	28	166	294	17	57	4.6	.964	V. Blue	18	125	8	6	0	2.45
	3B	D. Evans	357	.258	12	48	74	187	13	10	3.1	.953	E. Whitson	22	123	6	9	0	4.02
Frank Robinson	RF	J. Clark	385	.268	17	53	193	14	4	4	2.2	.981	A. Holland	47	101	7	5	7	2.41
	CF	J. Martin	241	.241	4	25	138	4	1	1	2.2	.993	G. Minton	55	84	4	5	21	2.89
	LF	L. Herndon	364	.288	5	41	207	8	5	1	2.4	.977	G. Lavelle	34	66	2	6	4	3.82
	C	M. May	316	.310	2	33	468	48	6	4	5.6	.989							
	10	D. Bergman	145	.255	3	13	252	24	3	21		.989							
	OF	B. North	131	.221	1	12	84	1	3	1	2.4	.966							
	1B	J. Leonard	127	.307	4	26	79	2	0	0	2.9	1.000							
Atlanta	1B	C. Chambliss	404	.272	8	51	1046	**94**	4	83	10.7	.997	G. Perry	23	151	8	9	0	3.93
	2B	G. Hubbard	361	.235	6	33	188	344	5	50	5.5	.991	T. Boggs	25	143	3	13	0	4.09
W-50 L-56	SS	R. Ramirez	307	.218	2	20	181	306	**30**	55	5.4	.942	P. Niekro	22	139	7	7	0	3.11
	3B	B. Horner	300	.277	15	42	51	129	12	6	2.4	.938	R. Mahler	34	112	8	6	2	2.81
Bobby Cox	RF	Washington	320	.291	5	37	145	5	1	0	1.9	.993	R. Camp	48	76	9	3	17	1.78
	CF	D. Murphy	369	.247	13	50	254	11	5	4	2.6	.981	G. Garber	35	59	4	6	2	2.59
	LF	R. Linares	253	.265	5	25	124	6	5	1	2.3	.963							
	C	B. Benedict	295	.264	5	35	404	**73**	7	7	5.4	.986							
	OF	E. Miller	134	.231	0	7	65	2	1	0	1.9	.985							
	OF	B. Butler	126	.254	0	4	76	2	1	0	2.1	.987							
	3B	B. Pocoroba	122	.180	0	8	15	30	3	4	2.3	.938							
San Diego	1B	B. Perkins	254	.280	2	40	598	38	2	56	8.0	.997	Eichelberger	25	141	8	8	0	3.51
	2B	J. Bonilla	369	.290	1	25	229	290	13	72	5.5	.976	S. Mura	23	139	5	**14**	0	4.27
W-41 L-69	SS	O. Smith	450	.222	0	21	220	**422**	16	72	**6.0**	**.976**	C. Welsh	22	124	6	7	0	3.77
	3B	L. Salazar	400	.303	3	38	63	189	12	16	2.8	.955	R. Wise	18	98	4	8	0	3.77
Frank Howard	RF	G. Richards	393	.288	3	42	178	**14**	5	1	1.9	.975	G. Lucas	**57**	90	7	7	13	2.00
	CF	R. Jones	397	.249	4	39	295	9	2	3	2.9	.993	T. Lollar	24	77	2	8	1	6.08
	LF	J. Lefebvre	246	.256	8	31	167	6	1	2	2.1	.994							
	C	T. Kennedy	382	.301	2	41	465	63	**20**	**12**	5.5	.964							
	1B	R. Bass	176	.210	4	20	390	35	3	38	8.6	.993							
	OF	D. Edwards	112	.214	2	13	59	6	2	2	1.4	.970							

BATTING AND BASE RUNNING LEADERS

Batting Average
B. Madlock, PIT	.341
P. Rose, PHI	.325
D. Baker, LA	.320
M. Schmidt, PHI	.316
B. Buckner, CHI	.311

Slugging Average
M. Schmidt, PHI	.644
A. Dawson, MON	.553
G. Foster, CIN	.519
B. Madlock, PIT	.495
G. Hendrick, STL	.485

Home Runs
M. Schmidt, PHI	31
A. Dawson, MON	24
D. Kingman, NY	22
G. Foster, CIN	22
G. Hendrick, STL	18

Total Bases
M. Schmidt, PHI	228
A. Dawson, MON	218
G. Foster, CIN	215
B. Buckner, CHI	202
G. Hendrick, STL	191

Runs Batted In
M. Schmidt, PHI	91
G. Foster, CIN	90
B. Buckner, CHI	75
G. Carter, MON	68
G. Matthews, PHI	67
Concepcion, CIN	67

Stolen Bases
T. Raines, MON	71
O. Moreno, PIT	39
R. Scott, MON	30
B. North, SF	26
D. Collins, CIN	26
A. Dawson, MON	26

Hits
P. Rose, PHI	140
B. Buckner, CHI	131
Concepcion, CIN	129
D. Baker, LA	128

Base on Balls
M. Schmidt, PHI	73
J. Morgan, SF	66
K. Hernandez, STL	61
J. Thompson, PIT	59

Home Run Percentage
M. Schmidt, PHI	8.8
D. Kingman, NY	6.2
A. Dawson, MON	6.1
G. Foster, CIN	5.3

Runs Scored
M. Schmidt, PHI	78
P. Rose, PHI	73
A. Dawson, MON	71
G. Hendrick, STL	67

Doubles
B. Buckner, CHI	35
R. Jones, SD	34
Concepcion, CIN	28
K. Hernandez, STL	27

Triples
C. Reynolds, HOU	12
G. Richards, SD	12
T. Herr, STL	9

PITCHING LEADERS

Winning Percentage
T. Seaver, CIN	.875
S. Carlton, PHI	.765
J. Reuss, LA	.714
N. Ryan, HOU	.688
B. Forsch, STL	.667

Earned Run Average
N. Ryan, HOU	1.69
B. Knepper, HOU	2.18
B. Hooton, LA	2.28
J. Reuss, LA	2.29
S. Carlton, PHI	2.42

Wins
T. Seaver, CIN	14
S. Carlton, PHI	13
Valenzuela, LA	13
D. Ruthven, PHI	12
S. Rogers, MON	12
M. Soto, CIN	12

Saves
B. Sutter, STL	25
G. Minton, SF	21
N. Allen, NY	18
R. Camp, ATL	17
T. Hume, CIN	13
G. Lucas, SD	13

Strikeouts
Valenzuela, LA	180
S. Carlton, PHI	179
M. Soto, CIN	151
N. Ryan, HOU	140
Gullickson, MON	115

Complete Games
Valenzuela, LA	11
S. Carlton, PHI	10
M. Soto, CIN	10
J. Reuss, LA	8
S. Rogers, MON	7

Fewest Hits/9 Innings
N. Ryan, HOU	5.98
T. Seaver, CIN	6.51
Valenzuela, LA	6.56
B. Berenyi, CIN	6.93

Shutouts
Valenzuela, LA	8
B. Knepper, HOU	5
B. Hooton, LA	4

Fewest Walks/9 Innings
G. Perry, ATL	1.43
J. Reuss, LA	1.59
D. Sutton, HOU	1.64
L. Sorensen, STL	1.67

Most Strikeouts/9 Inn.
S. Carlton, PHI	8.48
N. Ryan, HOU	8.46
Valenzuela, LA	8.44
M. Soto, CIN	7.77

Innings
Valenzuela, LA	192
S. Carlton, PHI	190
M. Soto, CIN	175
J. Niekro, HOU	166

Games Pitched
G. Lucas, SD	57
G. Minton, SF	55
D. Tidrow, CHI	51
T. Hume, CIN	51

NATIONAL LEAGUE 1981, *cont.*

		W	L	PCT	GB	R	OR	2B	3B	HR	BA	SA	SB	E	DP	FA	CG	BB	SO	ShO	SV	ERA
East	St. Louis	59	43	.578		464	417	158	45	50	.265	.377	88	82	108	.981	11	290	388	5	33	3.63
	Montreal	60	48	.556	2	443	394	146	28	81	.246	.370	138	81	88	.980	20	268	520	12	23	3.30
	Philadelphia	59	48	.551	2.5	491	472	165	25	69	.273	.389	103	86	90	.980	19	347	580	5	23	4.05
	Pittsburgh	46	56	.451	13	407	425	176	30	55	.257	.369	122	86	106	.979	11	346	492	5	29	3.56
	New York	41	62	.398	18.5	348	432	136	35	57	.248	.356	103	130	89	.968	7	336	490	3	24	3.55
	Chicago	38	65	.369	21.5	370	483	138	29	57	.236	.340	72	113	103	.974	6	388	532	2	20	4.01
West	Cincinnati	66	42	.611		464	440	190	24	64	.267	.385	58	80	99	.981	25	393	593	14	20	3.73
	Los Angeles	63	47	.573	4	450	356	133	20	82	.262	.374	73	87	101	.980	26	302	603	19	24	3.01
	Houston	61	49	.555	6	394	331	160	35	45	.257	.356	81	87	81	.980	23	300	610	19	25	2.66
	San Francisco	56	55	.505	11.5	427	414	161	26	63	.250	.357	89	102	102	.977	8	393	561	9	33	3.28
	Atlanta	50	56	.472	15	395	416	148	22	64	.243	.349	98	102	93	.976	11	330	471	4	24	3.45
	San Diego	41	69	.373	26	382	455	170	35	32	.256	.346	83	102	117	.977	9	414	492	6	23	3.72
						5035	5035	1881	354	719	.255	.364	1108	1138	1177	.978	176	4107	6332	103	301	3.49

First Half

East
	W	L	PCT	GB
PHI	34	21	.618	
STL	30	20	.600	1.5
MON	30	25	.545	4
PIT	25	23	.521	5.5
NY	17	34	.333	15
CHI	15	37	.288	17.5

*Defeated Philadelphia in playoff 3 games to 2.

West
	W	L	PCT	GB
LA*	36	21	.632	
CIN	35	21	.625	.5
HOU	28	29	.491	8
ATL	25	29	.463	9.5
SF	27	32	.458	10
SD	23	33	.411	12.5

*Defeated Houston in playoff 3 games to 2.

Second Half

East
	W	L	PCT	GB
MON*	30	23	.566	
STL	29	23	.558	.5
PHI	25	27	.481	4.5
NY	24	28	.462	5.5
CHI	23	28	.451	6
PIT	21	33	.389	9.5

West
	W	L	PCT	GB
HOU	33	20	.623	
CIN	31	23	.596	1.5
SF	29	23	.558	3.5
LA	27	26	.509	6
ATL	25	27	.481	7.5
SD	18	36	.333	15.5

AMERICAN LEAGUE 1981

East

Milwaukee — W-62 L-47 — Buck Rodgers

POS	Player	AB	BA	HR	RBI	PO	A	E	DP	TC/G	FA	Pitcher	G	IP	W	L	SV	ERA
1B	C. Cooper	416	.320	12	60	987	72	9	111	10.6	.992	P. Vuckovich	24	150	14	4	0	3.54
2B	J. Gantner	352	.267	2	33	251	352	10	95	5.7	.984	M. Caldwell	24	144	11	9	0	3.94
SS	R. Yount	377	.273	10	49	161	370	8	83	5.8	.985	M. Haas	24	137	11	7	0	4.47
3B	R. Howell	244	.238	6	33	38	98	6	9	2.7	.958	J. Slaton	24	117	5	7	0	4.38
RF	M. Brouhard	186	.274	2	20	92	7	1	2	2.0	.990	R. Lerch	23	111	7	9	0	4.57
CF	G. Thomas	363	.259	21	65	221	8	5	3	2.4	.979	R. Fingers	47	78	6	3	28	1.04
LF	B. Oglivie	400	.243	14	72	211	3	4	1	2.2	.982	J. Easterly	44	62	3	3	4	3.19
C	T. Simmons	380	.216	14	61	300	37	7	3	4.6	.980							
DH	P. Molitor	251	.267	2	19													
3B	D. Money	185	.216	2	14	27	100	3	8	2.3	.977							
C	C. Moore	156	.301	1	9	147	16	5	0	4.9	.970							
OF	T. Bosley	105	.229	0	3	55	1	2	0	1.6	.966							

Baltimore — W-59 L-46 — Earl Weaver

POS	Player	AB	BA	HR	RBI	PO	A	E	DP	TC/G	FA	Pitcher	G	IP	W	L	SV	ERA
1B	E. Murray	378	.294	22	78	899	91	1	98	10.0	.999	D. Martinez	25	179	14	5	0	3.32
2B	R. Dauer	369	.263	4	38	201	253	5	71	4.9	.989	S. McGregor	24	160	13	5	0	3.26
SS	M. Belanger	139	.165	1	10	86	162	7	21	4.0	.973	J. Palmer	22	127	7	8	0	3.76
3B	D. DeCinces	346	.263	13	55	86	191	17	31	2.9	.942	M. Flanagan	20	116	9	6	0	4.19
RF	K. Singleton	363	.278	13	49	125	2	0	2	1.8	1.000	S. Stewart	29	112	4	8	4	2.33
CF	A. Bumbry	392	.273	1	27	255	6	2	2	2.6	.992	S. Stone	15	63	4	7	0	4.57
LF	G. Roenicke	219	.269	3	20	175	2	3	1	2.2	.983	T. Martinez	37	59	3	3	11	2.90
C	R. Dempsey	251	.215	6	15	384	35	1	6	4.7	.998	T. Stoddard	31	37	4	2	7	3.89
DH	T. Crowley	134	.246	4	25													
OF	Lowenstein	189	.249	6	20	100	3	1	0	1.4	.990							
S2	L. Sakata	150	.227	5	15	82	148	7	33		.970							
C	D. Graham	142	.176	2	11	138	20	4	1	4.1	.975							
OF	J. Dwyer	134	.224	3	10	84	2	2	0	1.5	.977							

New York — W-59 L-48 — Gene Michael W-48 L-34 — Bob Lemon W-11 L-14

POS	Player	AB	BA	HR	RBI	PO	A	E	DP	TC/G	FA	Pitcher	G	IP	W	L	SV	ERA
1B	B. Watson	156	.212	6	12	367	25	1	42	7.9	.997	R. May	27	148	6	11	1	4.14
2B	W. Randolph	357	.232	2	24	205	268	11	74	5.2	.977	T. John	20	140	9	8	0	2.64
SS	B. Dent	227	.238	7	27	104	217	10	49	4.5	.970	R. Guidry	23	127	11	5	0	2.76
3B	G. Nettles	349	.244	15	46	63	214	8	14	2.9	.972	D. Righetti	15	105	8	4	0	2.06
RF	R. Jackson	334	.237	15	54	111	3	3	0	1.9	.974	R. Davis	43	73	4	5	6	2.71
CF	J. Mumphrey	319	.307	6	32	219	5	8	0	2.9	.966	G. Gossage	32	47	3	2	20	0.77
LF	D. Winfield	388	.294	13	68	196	1	3	0	2.0	.985							
C	R. Cerone	234	.244	2	21	353	26	3	1	5.5	.992							
DH	B. Murcer	117	.265	6	24													
OD	O. Gamble	189	.238	10	27	77	0	0	0	1.8	1.000							
UT	L. Milbourne	163	.313	1	12	74	121	8	26		.961							
OD	L. Piniella	159	.277	5	18	69	2	1	1	2.0	.986							
C	B. Foote	125	.208	6	10	227	14	1	3	7.1	.996							
1B	D. Revering	119	.235	2	7	276	30	2	24	7.0	.994							

AMERICAN LEAGUE 1981, *cont.*

	POS	Player	AB	BA	HR	RBI	PO	A	E	DP	TC/G	FA	Pitcher	G	IP	W	L	SV	ERA
Detroit	1B	R. Hebner	226	.226	5	28	531	29	3	36	9.2	.995	J. Morris	25	198	14	7	0	3.05
	2B	L. Whitaker	335	.263	5	36	227	354	9	77	5.5	.985	M. Wilcox	24	166	12	9	0	3.04
W-60 L-49	SS	A. Trammell	392	.258	2	31	181	347	9	65	5.1	.983	D. Petry	23	141	10	9	0	3.00
	3B	T. Brookens	239	.243	4	25	58	139	10	13	2.9	.952	D. Rozema	28	104	5	5	3	3.63
Sparky Anderson	RF	K. Gibson	290	.328	9	40	142	1	4	0	2.2	.973	A. Lopez	29	82	5	2	3	3.62
	CF	A. Cowens	253	.261	1	18	166	3	1	0	2.0	.994	Schatzeder	17	71	6	8	0	6.08
	LF	S. Kemp	372	.277	9	49	207	4	3	0	2.3	.986	K. Saucier	38	49	4	2	13	1.65
	C	L. Parrish	348	.244	10	46	407	40	3	6	5.0	.993							
	DH	C. Summers	165	.255	3	21													
	OD	R. Peters	207	.256	0	15	103	3	1	1	2.8	.991							
	OF	L. Jones	174	.259	2	19	85	5	1	2	1.5	.989							
	D1	Wockenfuss	172	.215	9	25	179	5	3	27	7.5	.984							
Boston	1B	T. Perez	306	.252	9	39	519	37	4	63	10.0	.993	D. Eckersley	23	154	9	8	0	4.27
	2B	J. Remy	358	.307	0	31	162	272	7	58	5.1	.984	F. Tanana	24	141	4	10	0	4.02
W-59 L-49	SS	G. Hoffman	242	.231	1	20	131	233	15	62	4.9	.960	M. Torrez	22	127	10	3	0	3.69
	3B	C. Lansford	399	.336	4	52	70	180	13	17	3.1	.951	B. Stanley	35	99	10	8	0	3.82
Ralph Houk	RF	D. Evans	412	.296	22	71	259	9	2	1	2.5	.993	M. Clear	34	77	8	3	9	4.09
	CF	R. Miller	316	.291	2	33	219	5	3	0	2.4	.987	T. Burgmeier	32	60	4	5	6	2.85
	LF	J. Rice	451	.284	17	62	237	9	3	1	2.3	.988							
	C	R. Gedman	205	.288	5	26	275	30	3	1	5.2	.990							
	DH	Yastrzemski	338	.246	7	53													
	UT	D. Stapleton	355	.285	10	42	260	204	17	50		.965							
	C	G. Allenson	139	.223	5	25	235	18	8	3	5.6	.969							
	DH	J. Rudi	122	.180	6	24													
Cleveland	1B	M. Hargrove	322	.317	2	49	766	76	9	67	9.7	.989	B. Blyleven	20	159	11	7	0	2.89
	2B	D. Kuiper	206	.257	0	14	118	174	5	24	4.1	.983	L. Barker	22	154	8	7	0	3.92
W-52 L-51	SS	T. Veryzer	221	.244	0	14	121	207	10	48	4.5	.970	J. Denny	19	146	10	6	0	3.14
	3B	T. Harrah	361	.291	5	44	63	179	13	12	2.5	.949	R. Waits	22	126	8	10	0	4.93
Dave Garcia	RF	J. Orta	338	.272	5	34	150	11	1	2	1.9	.994	D. Spillner	32	97	4	4	7	3.15
	CF	R. Manning	360	.244	4	33	305	6	4	3	3.1	.987	S. Monge	31	58	3	5	4	4.34
	LF	M. Dilone	269	.290	0	19	126	7	4	1	2.4	.971	W. Garland	12	56	3	7	0	5.79
	C	R. Hassey	190	.232	1	25	296	38	3	6	6.0	.991							
	DH	A. Thornton	226	.239	6	30													
	O2	A. Bannister	232	.263	1	17	121	76	2	14		.990							
	C	B. Diaz	182	.313	7	38	247	27	7	0	5.5	.975							
	OD	Charboneau	138	.210	4	18	51	1	2	0	2.0	.963							
	UT	V. Hayes	109	.257	1	17	30	4	3	1		.919							
Toronto	1B	J. Mayberry	290	.248	17	43	647	36	5	65	8.6	.993	D. Stieb	25	184	11	10	0	3.18
	2B	D. Garcia	250	.252	1	13	132	181	9	32	5.2	.972	L. Leal	29	130	7	13	1	3.67
W-37 L-69	SS	A. Griffin	388	.209	0	21	186	275	31	64	5.1	.937	J. Clancy	22	125	6	12	0	4.90
	3B	D. Ainge	246	.187	0	14	73	133	11	19	2.8	.949	M. Bomback	20	90	5	5	0	3.90
Bobby Mattick	RF	B. Bonnell	227	.220	4	28	148	5	4	1	2.4	.975	J. Berenguer	12	71	2	9*	0	4.31
	CF	L. Moseby	378	.233	9	43	259	4	3	0	2.7	.989	R. Jackson	39	62	1	2	7	2.61
	LF	A. Woods	288	.247	1	21	179	4	5	0	2.4	.973	McLaughlin	40	60	1	5	10	2.85
	C	E. Whitt	195	.236	1	16	297	46	3	5	4.8	.991							
	DH	O. Velez	240	.213	11	28													
	2B	G. Iorg	215	.242	0	10	82	152	9	29	5.3	.963							
	OF	G. Bell	163	.233	5	12	92	3	3	2	2.2	.969							
	C	B. Martinez	128	.227	4	21	192	22	2	3	4.8	.991							
	UT	W. Upshaw	111	.171	4	10	72	6	0	8		1.000							
West																			
Oakland	1B	J. Spencer	171	.205	2	9	344	36	1	30	7.9	.997	R. Langford	24	195	12	10	0	3.00
	2B	S. Babitt	156	.256	0	14	84	125	6	12	4.1	.972	S. McCatty	22	186	14	7	0	2.32
W-64 L-45	SS	R. Picciolo	179	.268	4	13	99	157	5	*30	3.2	.981	M. Norris	23	173	12	9	0	3.75
	3B	W. Gross	243	.206	10	31	65	127	11	7	2.8	.946	M. Keough	19	140	10	6	0	3.41
Billy Martin	RF	T. Armas	440	.261	22	76	259	8	2	2	2.5	.993	B. Kingman	18	100	3	6	0	3.96
	CF	D. Murphy	390	.251	15	60	326	6	5	0	3.2	.985							
	LF	R. Henderson	423	.319	6	35	327	7	7	0	3.2	.979							
	C	M. Heath	301	.236	8	30	391	45	10	6	5.7	.978							
	DH	C. Johnson	273	.260	17	59													
	32	D. McKay	224	.263	4	21	112	167	13	26		.955							
	C1	J. Newman	216	.231	3	15	367	28	2	14		.995							
	SS	F. Stanley	145	.193	0	7	94	118	3	25	3.5	.986							
Texas	1B	P. Putnam	.297	.266	8	35	769	64	6	65	8.9	.993	D. Darwin	22	146	9	9	0	3.64
	2B	B. Wills	410	.251	2	41	268	326	10	70	6.0	.983	D. Medich	20	143	10	6	0	3.08
W-57 L-48	SS	M. Mendoza	229	.231	0	22	114	270	12	47	4.5	.970	R. Honeycutt	20	128	11	6	0	3.30
	3B	B. Bell	360	.294	10	64	66	281	14	18	3.8	.961	F. Jenkins	19	106	5	8	0	4.50
Don Zimmer	RF	J. Grubb	199	.231	3	26	95	2	1	0	1.7	.990	J. Matlack	17	104	4	7	0	4.15
	CF	M. Rivers	399	.286	3	26	225	12	1	3	2.5	.996	S. Comer	36	77	8	2	6	2.57
	LF	B. Sample	230	.283	3	25	132	4	1	1	2.1	.993							
	C	J. Sundberg	339	.277	3	28	464	52	2	9	5.3	.996							
	DH	A. Oliver	421	.309	4	55													
	OF	L. Roberts	233	.279	4	31	130	2	1	0	1.9	.992							
	UT	B. Stein	115	.330	2	22	166	26	2	10		.990							

AMERICAN LEAGUE 1981, *cont.*

	POS	Player	AB	BA	HR	RBI	PO	A	E	DP	TC/G	FA	Pitcher	G	IP	W	L	SV	ERA
Chicago W-54 L-52 Tony LaRussa	1B	M. Squires	294	.265	0	25	729	58	6	68	9.0	.992	B. Burns	24	157	10	6	0	2.64
	2B	T. Bernazard	384	.276	6	34	228	320	7	66	5.3	.987	R. Dotson	24	141	9	8	0	3.77
	SS	B. Almon	349	.301	4	41	190	340	17	78	5.3	.969	D. Lamp	27	127	7	6	0	2.41
	3B	J. Morrison	290	.234	10	34	64	199	12	14	3.2	.956	S. Trout	20	125	8	7	0	3.46
	RF	H. Baines	280	.286	10	41	120	10	2	1	1.7	.985	Baumgarten	19	102	5	9	0	4.06
	CF	C. Lemon	328	.302	9	50	240	2	4	1	2.6	.984	L. Hoyt	43	91	9	3	10	3.56
	LF	R. LeFlore	337	.246	0	24	162	6	7	2	2.1	.960	E. Farmer	42	53	3	3	10	4.58
	C	C. Fisk	338	.263	7	45	470	44	5	10	5.5	.990							
	DH	G. Luzinski	378	.265	21	62													
	OF	W. Nordhagen	208	.308	6	33	85	4	5	1	1.6	.947							
	1B	L. Johnson	134	.276	1	15	264	15	3	31	7.8	.989							
Kansas City W-50 L-53 Jim Frey W-30 L-40 Dick Howser W-20 L-13	1B	W. Aikens	349	.266	17	53	844	56	7	79	9.2	.992	D. Leonard	26	202	13	11	0	2.99
	2B	F. White	364	.250	9	38	226	263	6	70	5.3	.988	L. Gura	23	172	11	8	0	2.72
	SS	Washington	339	.227	2	29	135	297	12	58	4.5	.973	R. Gale	19	102	6	6	0	5.38
	3B	G. Brett	347	.314	6	43	74	170	14	7	2.9	.946	Splittorff	21	99	5	5	0	4.36
	RF	D. Motley	125	.232	2	8	88	3	3	1	2.4	.968	Quisenberry	40	62	1	4	18	1.74
	CF	A. Otis	372	.269	9	57	294	6	2	1	3.1	.993	R. Martin	29	62	4	5	4	2.76
	LF	W. Wilson	439	.303	1	32	299	14	4	3	3.1	.987							
	C	J. Wathan	301	.252	1	19	300	26	7	1	4.6	.979							
	DH	H. McRae	389	.272	7	36													
	OF	C. Geronimo	118	.246	2	13	96	1	2	0	1.7	.980							
California W-51 L-59 Jim Fregosi W-22 L-25 Gene Mauch W-29 L-34	1B	R. Carew	364	.305	2	21	877	60	5	90	10.5	.995	G. Zahn	25	161	10	11	0	4.42
	2B	B. Grich	352	.304	22	61	230	349	10	85	5.9	.983	K. Forsch	20	153	11	7	0	2.88
	SS	R. Burleson	430	.293	5	33	208	394	13	88	5.6	.979	M. Witt	22	129	8	9	0	3.28
	3B	B. Hobson	268	.235	4	36	85	139	17	13	2.9	.929	S. Renko	22	102	8	4	1	3.44
	RF	D. Ford	375	.277	15	48	188	3	8	2	2.1	.960	A. Hassler	42	76	4	3	5	3.20
	CF	F. Lynn	256	.219	5	31	176	4	4	1	2.7	.978	D. Aase	39	65	4	4	11	2.35
	LF	B. Downing	317	.249	9	41	97	1	1	0	1.8	.990							
	C	E. Ott	258	.217	2	22	287	36	7	1	4.6	.979							
	DH	D. Baylor	377	.239	17	66													
	OF	J. Beniquez	166	.181	3	13	117	0	5	0	2.2	.959							
Seattle W-44 L-65 Maury Wills W-6 L-18 Rene Lachemann W-38 L-47	1B	B. Bochte	335	.260	6	30	745	49	4	70	9.7	.995	G. Abbott	22	130	4	9	0	3.95
	2B	J. Cruz	352	.256	2	24	239	294	10	72	5.9	.982	F. Bannister	21	121	9	9	0	4.46
	SS	J. Anderson	162	.204	2	19	88	181	15	44	4.2	.947	K. Clay	22	101	2	7	0	4.63
	3B	L. Randle	273	.231	4	25	38	105	2	8	2.5	.986	J. Gleaton	20	85	4	7	0	4.76
	RF	T. Paciorek	405	.326	14	66	253	10	7	1	2.6	.974	M. Parrott	24	85	3	6	1	5.08
	CF	J. Simpson	288	.222	2	30	219	5	5	1	2.6	.978	S. Rawley	46	68	4	6	8	3.97
	LF	J. Burroughs	319	.254	10	41	127	4	2	1	1.5	.985	L. Andersen	41	68	3	3	5	2.65
	C	J. Narron	203	.222	3	17	248	11	1	3	4.0	.996	D. Drago	39	54	4	6	5	5.50
	DH	R. Zisk	357	.311	16	43													
	3B	D. Meyer	252	.262	3	22	36	87	6	12	2.6	.961							
	1D	G. Gray	208	.245	13	31	275	16	2	34	8.6	.993							
	C	T. Bulling	154	.247	2	15	239	21	6	3	4.3	.977							
	OF	D. Henderson	126	.167	6	13	105	4	0	1	1.9	1.000							
Minnesota W-41 L-68 John Goryl W-11 L-25 Billy Gardner W-30 L-43	1B	D. Goodwin	151	.225	2	17	341	20	3	27	9.1	.992	A. Williams	23	150	6	10	0	4.08
	2B	R. Wilfong	305	.246	3	19	183	268	9	52	4.9	.980	P. Redfern	24	142	9	8	0	4.06
	SS	R. Smalley	167	.263	7	22	52	89	8	14	4.0	.946	F. Arroyo	23	128	7	10	0	3.94
	3B	J. Castino	381	.268	6	36	86	224	8	24	3.2	**.975**	J. Koosman	19	94	3	9*	5	4.21
	RF	D. Engle	248	.258	5	32	144	4	3	0	2.0	.980	R. Erickson	14	91	3	8	0	3.86
	CF	M. Hatcher	377	.255	3	37	239	3	2	0	2.7	.992	D. Corbett	54	88	2	6	17	2.56
	LF	G. Ward	295	.264	3	29	185	8	5	4	2.5	.975							
	C	S. Butera	167	.240	0	18	254	41	9	0	5.2	.970							
	DH	G. Adams	220	.209	2	24													
	OF	H. Powell	264	.239	2	25	122	6	4	1	2.1	.970							
	UT	P. Mackanin	225	.231	4	18	171	149	12	40		.964							
	UT	R. Jackson	175	.263	4	28	329	30	5	26		.986							
	C	B. Wynegar	150	.247	0	10	162	24	1	4	5.1	.995							
	OF	R. Sofield	102	.176	0	5	54	5	1	0	1.8	.983							

BATTING AND BASE RUNNING LEADERS

Batting Average
C. Lansford, BOS	.336
T. Paciorek, SEA	.326
C. Cooper, MIL	.320
R. Henderson, OAK	.319
M. Hargrove, CLE	.317

Slugging Average
B. Grich, CAL	.543
E. Murray, BAL	.534
D. Evans, BOS	.522
T. Paciorek, SEA	.509
C. Cooper, MIL	.495

Home Runs
B. Grich, CAL	22
E. Murray, BAL	22
D. Evans, BOS	22
T. Armas, OAK	22
G. Thomas, MIL	21
G. Luzinski, CHI	21

Total Bases
D. Evans, BOS	215
T. Armas, OAK	211
T. Paciorek, SEA	206
C. Cooper, MIL	206
E. Murray, BAL	202

Runs Batted In
E. Murray, BAL	78
T. Armas, OAK	76
B. Oglivie, MIL	72
D. Evans, BOS	71
D. Winfield, NY	68

Stolen Bases
R. Henderson, OAK	56
J. Cruz, SEA	43
R. LeFlore, CHI	36
W. Wilson, KC	34
M. Dilone, CLE	29

PITCHING LEADERS

Winning Percentage
P. Vuckovich, MIL	.778
M. Torrez, BOS	.769
D. Martinez, BAL	.737
S. McGregor, BAL	.722
R. Guidry, NY	.688

Earned Run Average
S. McCatty, OAK	2.32
S. Stewart, BAL	2.33
D. Lamp, CHI	2.41
T. John, NY	2.64
B. Burns, CHI	2.64

Wins
P. Vuckovich, MIL	14
D. Martinez, BAL	14
S. McCatty, OAK	14
J. Morris, DET	14
S. McGregor, BAL	13
D. Leonard, KC	13

Saves
R. Fingers, MIL	28
G. Gossage, NY	20
Quisenberry, KC	18
D. Corbett, MIN	17
K. Saucier, DET	13

Strikeouts
L. Barker, CLE	127
B. Burns, CHI	108
B. Blyleven, CLE	107
D. Leonard, KC	107
R. Guidry, NY	104

Complete Games
R. Langford, OAK	18
S. McCatty, OAK	16
J. Morris, DET	15
M. Norris, OAK	12
L. Gura, KC	12

AMERICAN LEAGUE 1981, cont.

BATTING AND BASE RUNNING LEADERS

Hits		Base on Balls		Home Run Percentage	
R. Henderson, OAK	135	D. Evans, BOS	85	B. Grich, CAL	6.3
C. Lansford, BOS	134	D. Murphy, OAK	73	J. Mayberry, TOR	5.9
C. Cooper, MIL	133	S. Kemp, DET	70	E. Murray, BAL	5.8
W. Wilson, KC	133	R. Henderson, OAK	64	G. Thomas, MIL	5.8

Runs Scored		Doubles		Triples	
R. Henderson, OAK	89	C. Cooper, MIL	35	J. Castino, MIN	9
D. Evans, BOS	84	A. Oliver, TEX	29	H. Baines, CHI	7
C. Cooper, MIL	70	T. Paciorek, SEA	28	G. Brett, KC	7
T. Harrah, CLE	64	G. Brett, KC	27	R. Henderson, OAK	7

PITCHING LEADERS

Fewest Hits/9 Innings		Shutouts		Fewest Walks/9 Innings	
S. McCatty, OAK	6.77	K. Forsch, CAL	4	R. Honeycutt, TEX	1.20
J. Morris, DET	6.95	D. Medich, TEX	4	K. Forsch, CAL	1.59
R. Guidry, NY	7.09	S. McCatty, OAK	4	D. Leonard, KC	1.83
D. Darwin, TEX	7.09	R. Dotson, CHI	4	L. Gura, KC	1.83

Most Strikeouts/9 Inn.		Innings		Games Pitched	
L. Barker, CLE	7.42	D. Leonard, KC	202	D. Corbett, MIN	54
R. Guidry, NY	7.37	J. Morris, DET	198	R. Fingers, MIL	47
F. Bannister, SEA	6.32	R. Langford, OAK	195	S. Rawley, SEA	46
B. Burns, CHI	6.19	S. McCatty, OAK	186	J. Easterly, MIL	44

		W	L	PCT	GB	R	OR	2B	3B	HR	BA	SA	SB	E	DP	FA	CG	BB	SO	ShO	SV	ERA
East	Milwaukee	62	47	.569		493	459	173	20	96	.257	.391	39	79	135	.982	11	352	448	4	35	3.91
	Baltimore	59	46	.562	1	429	437	165	11	88	.251	.379	41	68	114	.983	25	347	489	10	23	3.70
	New York	59	48	.551	2	421	343	148	22	100	.252	.391	47	72	100	.982	16	287	606	13	30	2.90
	Detroit	60	49	.550	2	427	404	148	29	65	.256	.368	61	67	109	.984	33	373	476	13	22	3.53
	Boston	59	49	.546	2.5	519	481	168	17	90	.275	.399	32	91	108	.979	19	354	536	4	24	3.81
	Cleveland	52	51	.505	7	431	442	150	21	39	.263	.351	119	87	91	.978	33	311	569	10	13	3.88
	Toronto	37	69	.349	23.5	329	466	137	23	61	.226	.330	66	105	102	.975	20	377	451	4	18	3.82
West	Oakland	64	45	.587		458	403	119	26	104	.247	.379	98	81	74	.980	60	370	505	11	10	3.30
	Texas	57	48	.543	5	452	389	178	15	49	.270	.369	46	69	102	.984	23	322	488	13	18	3.40
	Chicago	54	52	.509	8.5	476	423	135	27	76	.272	.387	86	87	113	.979	20	336	529	8	23	3.47
	Kansas City	50	53	.485	11	397	405	169	29	61	.267	.383	100	72	94	.982	24	273	404	8	24	3.56
	California	51	59	.464	13.5	476	453	134	16	97	.256	.380	44	101	120	.977	27	323	426	8	19	3.70
	Seattle	44	65	.404	20	426	521	148	13	89	.251	.368	100	91	122	.979	10	360	478	5	23	4.23
	Minnesota	41	68	.376	23	378	486	147	36	47	.240	.338	34	96	103	.978	13	376	500	6	22	3.98
						6112	6112	2119	305	1062	.256	.373	913	1166	1487	.980	334	4761	6905	117	304	3.66

		W	L	PCT	GB
First Half	East				
	NY*	34	22	.607	
	BAL	31	23	.574	2
	MIL	31	25	.554	3
	DET	31	26	.544	3.5
	BOS	30	26	.536	4
	CLE	26	24	.520	5
	TOR	16	42	.276	19

*Defeated Milwaukee in playoff 3 games to 2.

		W	L	PCT	GB
	West				
	OAK*	37	23	.617	
	TEX	33	22	.600	1.5
	CHI	31	22	.585	2.5
	CAL	31	29	.517	6
	KC	20	30	.400	12
	SEA	21	36	.368	14.5
	MIN	17	39	.304	18

*Defeated Kansas City in playoff 3 games to 0.

		W	L	PCT	GB
Second Half	East				
	MIL	31	22	.585	
	BOS	29	23	.558	1.5
	DET	29	23	.558	1.5
	BAL	28	23	.549	2
	CLE	26	27	.491	5
	NY	25	26	.490	5
	TOR	21	27	.438	7.5
	West				
	KC	30	23	.566	
	OAK	27	22	.551	1
	TEX	24	26	.480	4.5
	MIN	24	29	.453	6
	SEA	23	29	.442	6.5
	CHI	23	30	.434	7
	CAL	20	30	.400	8.5

NATIONAL LEAGUE 1982

East **St. Louis**

W-92 L-70

Whitey Herzog

POS	Player	AB	BA	HR	RBI	PO	A	E	DP	TC/G	FA	Pitcher	G	IP	W	L	SV	ERA
1B	K. Hernandez	579	.299	7	94	1586	135	11	140	11.0	.994	J. Andujar	38	266	15	10	0	2.47
2B	T. Herr	493	.266	0	36	263	427	9	97	5.5	.987	B. Forsch	36	233	15	9	1	3.48
SS	O. Smith	488	.248	2	43	279	535	13	101	5.9	.984	S. Mura	35	184	12	11	0	4.05
3B	K. Oberkfell	470	.289	2	34	78	304	11	23	2.9	.972	D. LaPoint	42	153	9	3	0	3.42
RF	G. Hendrick	515	.282	19	104	238	6	5	1	1.9	.980	J. Stuper	23	137	9	7	0	3.36
CF	W. McGee	422	.296	4	56	245	3	11	0	2.2	.958	B. Sutter	70	102	9	8	36	2.90
LF	L. Smith	592	.307	8	69	303	16	10	3	2.2	.970	D. Bair	63	92	5	3	8	2.55
C	D. Porter	373	.231	12	48	469	64	9	8	4.9	.983	J. Kaat	62	75	5	3	2	4.08
UT	M. Ramsey	256	.230	1	21	135	219	10	42		.973							
OF	D. Iorg	238	.294	0	34	99	2	3	0	1.7	.971							
OF	D. Green	166	.283	2	23	111	4	1	1	1.7	.991							

NATIONAL LEAGUE 1982, *cont.*

Philadelphia — W-89 L-73 — Pat Corrales

POS	Player	AB	BA	HR	RBI	PO	A	E	DP	TC/G	FA	Pitcher	G	IP	W	L	SV	ERA
1B	P. Rose	634	.271	3	54	1428	123	8	114	9.6	.995	S. Carlton	38	296	23	11	0	3.10
2B	M. Trillo	549	.271	0	39	343	441	5	101	5.3	.994	Christenson	33	223	9	10	0	3.47
SS	I. DeJesus	536	.239	3	59	216	469	19	80	4.6	.973	M. Krukow	33	208	13	11	0	3.12
3B	M. Schmidt	514	.280	35	87	110	324	23	28	3.1	.950	D. Ruthven	33	204	11	11	0	3.79
RF	G. Vukovich	335	.272	6	42	168	4	4	3	1.7	.977	R. Reed	57	98	5	5	14	2.66
CF	G. Maddox	412	.284	8	61	253	8	2	4	2.4	.992	M. Bystrom	19	89	5	6	0	4.85
LF	G. Matthews	616	.281	19	83	268	14	10	2	1.8	.966	E. Farmer	47	76	2	6	6	4.86
C	B. Diaz	525	.288	18	85	850	80	10	7	6.5	.989	S. Monge	47	72	7	1	2	3.75
OF	B. Dernier	370	.249	4	21	255	5	5	0	2.2	.981	T. McGraw	34	40	3	3	5	4.31

Montreal — W-86 L-76 — Jim Fanning

POS	Player	AB	BA	HR	RBI	PO	A	E	DP	TC/G	FA	Pitcher	G	IP	W	L	SV	ERA
1B	A. Oliver	617	.331	22	109	1286	92	19	96	8.8	.986	S. Rogers	35	277	19	8	0	2.40
2B	D. Flynn	193	.244	0	20	135	157	5	40	5.1	.983	Gullickson	34	237	12	14	0	3.57
SS	C. Speier	530	.257	7	60	291	405	13	76	4.6	.982	S. Sanderson	32	224	12	12	0	3.46
3B	T. Wallach	596	.268	28	97	132	287	23	23	2.8	.948	C. Lea	27	178	12	10	0	3.24
RF	W. Cromartie	497	.254	14	62	275	10	6	1	2.1	.979	R. Burris	37	124	4	14	2	4.73
CF	A. Dawson	608	.301	23	83	419	8	8	2	3.0	.982	J. Reardon	75	109	7	4	26	2.06
LF	T. Raines	647	.277	4	43	232	7	2	1	2.0	.992	D. Palmer	13	74	6	4	0	3.18
C	G. Carter	557	.293	29	97	954	104	10	6	7.0	.991	W. Fryman	60	70	9	4	12	3.75

Pittsburgh — W-84 L-78 — Chuck Tanner

POS	Player	AB	BA	HR	RBI	PO	A	E	DP	TC/G	FA	Pitcher	G	IP	W	L	SV	ERA
1B	J. Thompson	550	.284	31	101	1395	105	10	114	9.7	.993	R. Rhoden	35	230	11	14	0	4.14
2B	J. Ray	647	.281	7	63	381	512	21	89	5.6	.977	D. Robinson	38	227	15	13	0	4.28
SS	D. Berra	529	.263	10	61	238	498	30	77	5.0	.961	Candelaria	31	175	12	7	1	2.94
3B	B. Madlock	568	.319	19	95	92	266	18	23	2.6	.952	M. Sarmiento	35	165	9	4	1	3.39
RF	L. Lacy	359	.312	5	31	186	7	7	1	1.8	.965	K. Tekulve	85	129	12	8	20	2.87
CF	O. Moreno	645	.245	3	44	396	10	7	3	2.6	.983	McWilliams	19	122	6	5	1	3.11
LF	M. Easler	475	.276	15	58	243	8	7	2	1.9	.973	R. Scurry	76	104	4	5	14	1.74
C	T. Pena	497	.296	11	63	763	89	16	6	6.3	.982	E. Romo	45	87	9	3	1	4.36
OF	D. Parker	244	.270	6	29	108	2	5	1	1.8	.957							

Chicago — W-73 L-89 — Lee Elia

POS	Player	AB	BA	HR	RBI	PO	A	E	DP	TC/G	FA	Pitcher	G	IP	W	L	SV	ERA
1B	B. Buckner	657	.306	15	105	1547	159	12	89	10.7	.993	F. Jenkins	34	217	14	15	0	3.15
2B	B. Wills	419	.272	6	38	199	297	19	45	5.0	.963	D. Bird	35	191	9	14	0	5.14
SS	L. Bowa	499	.246	0	29	210	396	17	64	4.5	.973	D. Noles	31	171	10	13	0	4.42
3B	R. Sandberg	635	.271	7	54	79	278	11	19	2.8	.970	R. Martz	28	148	11	10	0	4.21
RF	J. Johnstone	269	.249	10	43	154	8	3	0	1.9	.982	A. Ripley	28	123	5	7	0	4.26
CF	L. Durham	539	.312	22	90	301	11	12	1	2.3	.963	L. Smith	72	117	2	5	17	2.69
LF	K. Moreland	476	.261	15	68	169	9	2	0	2.1	.989	D. Tidrow	65	104	8	3	6	3.39
C	J. Davis	418	.261	12	52	598	89	11	11	5.4	.984	B. Campbell	62	100	3	6	8	3.69
OF	S. Henderson	257	.233	2	29	126	5	6	0	2.0	.956	G. Hernandez	75	75	4	6	10	3.00
OF	G. Woods	245	.269	4	30	161	6	0	1	1.6	1.000							
2S	J. Kennedy	242	.219	2	25	137	220	12	35		.967							
OF	J. Morales	116	.284	4	30	72	5	0	1	1.9	1.000							

New York — W-65 L-97 — George Bamberger

POS	Player	AB	BA	HR	RBI	PO	A	E	DP	TC/G	FA	Pitcher	G	IP	W	L	SV	ERA
1B	D. Kingman	535	.204	37	99	1232	69	18	88	9.2	.986	C. Puleo	36	171	9	9	1	4.47
2B	W. Backman	261	.272	3	22	169	202	14	30	4.4	.964	P. Falcone	40	171	8	10	2	3.84
SS	Gardenhire	384	.240	3	33	234	398	29	68	4.9	.956	C. Swan	37	166	11	7	1	3.35
3B	H. Brooks	457	.249	2	40	89	237	24	17	2.8	.931	M. Scott	37	147	7	13	3	5.14
RF	E. Valentine	337	.288	8	48	159	10	3	4	1.8	.983	E. Lynch	43	139	4	8	2	3.55
CF	M. Wilson	639	.279	5	55	415	12	5	4	2.8	.988	P. Zachry	36	138	6	9	1	4.05
LF	G. Foster	550	.247	13	70	289	12	8	4	2.2	.974	J. Orosco	54	109	4	10	4	2.72
C	J. Stearns	352	.293	4	28	379	61	6	9	5.5	.987	R. Jones	28	108	7	10	0	4.60
UT	B. Bailor	376	.277	0	31	166	272	11	42		.976	N. Allen	50	65	3	7	19	3.06
C	R. Hodges	228	.246	5	27	362	35	8	5	5.5	.980							
O1	R. Staub	219	.242	3	27	172	19	2	12		.990							
OF	Youngblood	202	.257	3	21	88	5	3	1	1.5	.969							
OF	G. Rajsich	162	.259	2	12	60	0	0	1	1.7	1.000							

West

Atlanta — W-89 L-73 — Joe Torre

POS	Player	AB	BA	HR	RBI	PO	A	E	DP	TC/G	FA	Pitcher	G	IP	W	L	SV	ERA
1B	C. Chambliss	534	.270	20	86	1352	138	10	144	9.9	.993	P. Niekro	35	234	17	4	0	3.61
2B	G. Hubbard	532	.248	9	59	312	505	14	111	5.8	.983	R. Mahler	39	205	9	10	0	4.21
SS	R. Ramirez	609	.278	10	52	300	528	38	130	5.5	.956	R. Camp	51	165	11	13	5	3.65
3B	B. Horner	499	.261	32	97	102	217	10	20	2.4	.970	B. Walk	32	164	11	9	0	4.87
RF	Washington	563	.266	16	80	221	9	12	3	1.7	.950	S. Bedrosian	64	138	8	6	11	2.42
CF	D. Murphy	598	.281	36	109	407	6	9	2	2.6	.979	G. Garber	69	119	8	10	30	2.34
LF	B. Butler	240	.217	0	7	129	2	0	0	1.7	1.000	K. Dayley	20	71	5	6	0	4.54
C	B. Benedict	386	.246	3	44	602	73	5	9	5.8	.993							
UT	J. Royster	261	.295	2	25	105	112	11	20		.952							
OF	R. Linares	191	.298	2	17	92	4	0	1	1.8	1.000							
C	B. Pocoroba	120	.275	2	22	143	16	2	2	4.5	.988							
1B	B. Watson	114	.246	5	22	206	8	0	18	7.9	1.000							

Los Angeles — W-88 L-74 — Tom Lasorda

POS	Player	AB	BA	HR	RBI	PO	A	E	DP	TC/G	FA	Pitcher	G	IP	W	L	SV	ERA
1B	S. Garvey	625	.282	16	86	1539	111	8	132	10.5	.995	Valenzuela	37	285	19	13	0	2.87
2B	S. Sax	638	.282	4	47	347	452	19	83	5.5	.977	J. Reuss	39	255	18	11	0	3.11
SS	B. Russell	497	.274	3	46	216	502	29	64	5.0	.961	B. Welch	36	236	16	11	0	3.36
3B	R. Cey	556	.254	24	79	93	320	16	23	2.9	.963	D. Stewart	45	146	9	8	1	3.81
RF	P. Guerrero	575	.304	32	100	269	11	7	6	1.9	.976	B. Hooton	21	121	4	7	0	4.03
CF	K. Landreaux	461	.284	7	50	281	3	4	1	2.5	.986	S. Howe	66	99	7	5	13	2.08
LF	D. Baker	570	.300	23	88	226	7	6	1	1.9	.975	T. Forster	56	83	5	6	3	3.04
C	M. Scioscia	365	.219	5	38	631	57	10	10	5.7	.986	Niedenfuer	55	70	3	4	9	2.71
OF	R. Monday	210	.257	11	42	62	4	4	0	1.2	.943							
C	S. Yeager	196	.245	2	18	338	42	4	8	5.1	.990							

NATIONAL LEAGUE 1982, *cont.*

	POS	Player	AB	BA	HR	RBI	PO	A	E	DP	TC/G	FA	Pitcher	G	IP	W	L	SV	ERA
San Francisco	1B	R. Smith	349	.284	18	56	792	78	16	61	8.9	.982	B. Laskey	32	189	13	12	0	3.14
	2B	J. Morgan	463	.289	14	61	254	364	7	69	5.2	.989	A. Hammaker	29	175	12	8	0	4.11
W-87 L-75	SS	J. LeMaster	436	.216	2	30	223	382	23	63	4.8	.963	R. Gale	33	170	7	14	0	4.23
Frank Robinson	3B	D. Evans	465	.256	16	61	59	150	15	12	2.7	.933	F. Breining	54	143	11	6	0	3.08
	RF	J. Clark	563	.274	27	103	281	10	6	2	1.9	.980	R. Martin	29	141	7	10	0	4.66
	CF	C. Davis	641	.261	19	76	404	16	12	4	2.8	.972	A. Holland	58	130	7	3	5	3.33
	LF	J. Leonard	278	.259	9	49	135	2	6	0	1.9	.958	J. Barr	53	129	4	3	2	3.29
	C	M. May	395	.263	9	39	552	61	8	5	5.6	.987	G. Minton	78	123	10	4	30	1.83
	3B	T. O'Malley	291	.275	2	27	59	160	8	9	2.7	.965	G. Lavelle	68	105	10	7	8	2.67
	OF	J. Wohlford	250	.256	2	25	122	4	1	0	1.8	.992							
	2B	D. Kuiper	218	.280	0	17	101	124	5	24	4.5	.978							
	C	B. Brenly	180	.283	4	15	265	32	12	2	5.1	.961							
San Diego	1B	B. Perkins	347	.271	2	34	817	64	5	61	9.0	.994	T. Lollar	34	233	16	9	0	3.13
	2B	T. Flannery	379	.264	0	30	221	260	13	46	4.8	.974	Montefusco	32	184	10	11	0	4.00
W-81 L-81	SS	G. Templeton	563	.247	6	64	220	422	26	70	4.9	.961	Eichelberger	31	178	7	14	0	4.20
Dick Williams	3B	L. Salazar	524	.242	8	62	104	291	26	28	3.3	.938	E. Show	47	150	10	6	3	2.64
	RF	S. Lezcano	470	.289	16	84	275	16	3	8	2.2	.990	C. Welsh	28	139	8	8	0	4.91
	CF	R. Jones	424	.283	12	61	314	3	5	1	2.8	.984	J. Curtis	26	116	8	6	0	4.10
	LF	G. Richards	521	.286	3	28	200	8	5	1	2.1	.977	D. Dravecky	31	105	5	3	2	2.57
	C	T. Kennedy	562	.295	21	97	666	56	7	11	5.2	.990	L. DeLeon	61	102	9	5	15	2.03
	OF	A. Wiggins	254	.256	1	15	140	8	5	2	2.3	.967	G. Lucas	65	97	1	10	16	3.24
	3O	J. Lefebvre	239	.238	4	21	70	74	3	6		.980	F. Chiffer	51	79	4	3	4	2.95
	OF	T. Gwynn	190	.289	1	17	110	1	1	0	2.2	.991							
	2B	J. Bonilla	182	.280	0	8	99	134	6	26	5.3	.975							
	1B	K. Bevacqua	123	.252	0	24	253	16	3	13	9.1	.989							
Houston	1B	R. Knight	609	.294	6	70	945	55	10	76	10.5	.990	J. Niekro	35	270	17	12	0	2.47
	2B	P. Garner	588	.274	13	83	273	429	14	90	5.3	.980	N. Ryan	35	250	16	12	0	3.16
W-77 L-85	SS	D. Thon	496	.276	3	36	177	399	15	80	5.0	.975	D. Sutton	27	195	13	8	0	3.00
Bill Virdon	3B	A. Howe	365	.238	5	38	53	153	6	13	2.9	.972	B. Knepper	33	180	5	15	1	4.45
W-49 L-62	RF	T. Puhl	507	.262	8	50	257	4	3	3	1.9	.989	V. Ruhle	31	149	9	13	1	3.93
	CF	T. Scott	460	.239	1	29	262	7	5	0	2.1	.982	M. LaCoss	41	115	6	6	0	2.90
Bob Lillis	LF	J. Cruz	570	.275	9	68	340	9	13	3	2.3	.964	F. LaCorte	55	76	1	5	7	4.48
W-28 L-23	C	A. Ashby	339	.257	12	49	530	55	14	5	6.3	.977	D. Smith	49	63	5	4	11	3.84
	OF	D. Heep	198	.237	4	22	62	2	0	1	1.6	1.000							
	C	L. Pujols	176	.199	4	15	295	39	3	3	5.3	.991							
Cincinnati	1B	D. Driessen	516	.269	17	57	1239	78	3	123	9.2	.998	M. Soto	35	258	14	13	0	2.79
	2B	R. Oester	549	.260	9	47	258	325	17	72	5.1	.972	B. Berenyi	34	222	9	18	0	3.36
W-61 L-101	SS	Concepcion	572	.287	5	53	262	459	17	94	5.1	.977	F. Pastore	31	188	8	13	0	3.97
John McNamara	3B	J. Bench	399	.258	13	38	54	155	19	10	2.1	.917	B. Shirley	41	153	8	13	0	3.60
W-34 L-58	RF	Householder	417	.211	9	34	220	14	2	4	1.8	.992	T. Seaver	21	111	5	13	0	5.50
	CF	C. Cedeno	492	.289	8	57	301	4	3	2	2.4	.990	C. Leibrandt	36	108	5	7	2	5.10
Russ Nixon	LF	E. Milner	407	.268	4	31	215	8	3	1	2.1	.987	J. Kern	50	76	3	5	2	2.84
W-27 L-43	C	A. Trevino	355	.251	1	33	725	61	17	7	6.9	.979	J. Price	59	73	3	4	3	2.85
	OF	D. Walker	239	.218	5	22	110	7	1	1	1.7	.992	T. Hume	46	64	2	6	17	3.11
	OF	M. Vail	189	.254	4	29	72	7	1	0	1.5	.988							
	3B	Krenchicki	187	.283	2	21	35	93	6	7	1.9	.955							
	O1	L. Biittner	184	.310	2	24	170	14	2	13		.989							
	2B	T. Lawless	165	.212	0	4	87	136	5	35	4.9	.978							

BATTING AND BASE RUNNING LEADERS

Batting Average		Slugging Average		Home Runs		Winning Percentage	
A. Oliver, MON	.331	M. Schmidt, PHI	.547	D. Kingman, NY	37	P. Niekro, ATL	.810
B. Madlock, PIT	.319	P. Guerrero, LA	.536	D. Murphy, ATL	36	S. Rogers, MON	.704
L. Durham, CHI	.312	L. Durham, CHI	.521	M. Schmidt, PHI	35	M. Sarmiento, PIT	.692
L. Smith, STL	.307	A. Oliver, MON	.514	B. Horner, ATL	32	S. Carlton, PHI	.676
B. Buckner, CHI	.306	J. Thompson, PIT	.511	P. Guerrero, LA	32	T. Lollar, SD	.640

Total Bases		Runs Batted In		Stolen Bases		Saves	
A. Oliver, MON	317	D. Murphy, ATL	109	T. Raines, MON	78	B. Sutter, STL	36
P. Guerrero, LA	308	A. Oliver, MON	109	L. Smith, STL	68	G. Minton, SF	30
D. Murphy, ATL	303	B. Buckner, CHI	105	O. Moreno, PIT	60	G. Garber, ATL	30
A. Dawson, MON	303	G. Hendrick, STL	104	M. Wilson, NY	58	J. Reardon, MON	26
B. Buckner, CHI	290	J. Clark, SF	103	S. Sax, LA	49	K. Tekulve, PIT	20

Hits		Base on Balls		Home Run Percentage		Fewest Hits/9 Innings	
A. Oliver, MON	204	M. Schmidt, PHI	107	D. Kingman, NY	6.9	N. Ryan, HOU	7.05
B. Buckner, CHI	201	J. Thompson, PIT	101	M. Schmidt, PHI	6.8	M. Soto, CIN	7.06
A. Dawson, MON	183	K. Hernandez, STL	100	B. Horner, ATL	6.4	C. Lea, MON	7.35
L. Smith, STL	182	D. Murphy, ATL	93	D. Murphy, ATL	6.0	T. Lollar, SD	7.43

PITCHING LEADERS

Earned Run Average		Wins	
S. Rogers, MON	2.40	S. Carlton, PHI	23
J. Niekro, HOU	2.47	S. Rogers, MON	19
J. Andujar, STL	2.47	Valenzuela, LA	19
M. Soto, CIN	2.79	J. Reuss, LA	18
Valenzuela, LA	2.87	P. Niekro, ATL	17
		J. Niekro, HOU	17

Strikeouts		Complete Games	
S. Carlton, PHI	286	S. Carlton, PHI	19
M. Soto, CIN	274	Valenzuela, LA	18
N. Ryan, HOU	245	J. Niekro, HOU	16
Valenzuela, LA	199	S. Rogers, MON	14
S. Rogers, MON	179	M. Soto, CIN	13

Shutouts		Fewest Walks/9 Innings	
S. Carlton, PHI	6	D. Bird, CHI	1.41
J. Niekro, HOU	5	A. Hammaker, SF	1.44
J. Andujar, STL	5	J. Andujar, STL	1.69
S. Rogers, MON	4	J. Reuss, LA	1.77

NATIONAL LEAGUE 1982, *cont.*

BATTING AND BASE RUNNING LEADERS

Runs Scored		Doubles		Triples	
L. Smith, STL	120	A. Oliver, MON	43	D. Thon, HOU	10
D. Murphy, ATL	113	T. Kennedy, SD	42	T. Puhl, HOU	9
M. Schmidt, PHI	108	A. Dawson, MON	37	M. Wilson, NY	9
A. Dawson, MON	107	R. Knight, HOU	36	O. Moreno, PIT	9

PITCHING LEADERS

Most Strikeouts/9 Inn.		Innings		Games Pitched	
M. Soto, CIN	9.57	S. Carlton, PHI	296	K. Tekulve, PIT	85
N. Ryan, HOU	8.81	Valenzuela, LA	285	G. Minton, SF	78
S. Carlton, PHI	8.71	S. Rogers, MON	277	R. Scurry, PIT	76
Candelaria, PIT	6.85	J. Niekro, HOU	270	J. Reardon, MON	75

		W	L	PCT	GB	R	OR	2B	3B	HR	BA	SA	SB	E	DP	FA	CG	BB	SO	ShO	SV	ERA
										Batting					**Fielding**				**Pitching**			
East	St. Louis	92	70	.568		685	609	239	52	67	.264	.364	200	124	169	.981	25	502	689	10	47	3.37
	Philadelphia	89	73	.549	3	664	654	245	25	112	.260	.376	128	121	138	.981	38	472	1002	13	33	3.61
	Montreal	86	76	.531	6	697	616	270	38	133	.262	.396	156	122	117	.980	34	448	936	10	43	3.31
	Pittsburgh	84	78	.519	8	724	696	272	40	134	.273	.408	161	145	133	.977	19	521	933	7	39	3.81
	Chicago	73	89	.451	19	676	709	239	46	102	.260	.375	132	132	110	.979	9	452	764	7	43	3.92
	New York	65	97	.401	27	609	723	227	26	97	.247	.350	137	175	134	.972	15	582	759	5	37	3.88
West	Atlanta	89	73	.549		739	702	215	22	146	.256	.383	151	137	186	.979	15	502	813	11	51	3.82
	Los Angeles	88	74	.543	1	691	612	222	32	138	.264	.388	151	139	131	.979	37	468	932	16	28	3.26
	San Francisco	87	75	.537	2	673	687	213	30	133	.253	.376	130	173	125	.973	18	466	810	4	45	3.64
	San Diego	81	81	.500	8	675	658	217	52	81	.257	.359	165	152	142	.976	20	502	765	11	41	3.52
	Houston	77	85	.475	12	569	620	236	48	74	.247	.349	140	136	154	.978	37	479	899	16	31	3.41
	Cincinnati	61	101	.377	28	545	661	228	34	82	.251	.350	131	128	158	.980	22	570	998	7	31	3.66
						7947	7947	2823	445	1299	.258	.373	1782	1684	1697	.978	289	5964	10300	117	469	3.60

AMERICAN LEAGUE 1982

POS	Player	AB	BA	HR	RBI	PO	A	E	DP	TC/G	FA	Pitcher	G	IP	W	L	SV	ERA
	Milwaukee W-95 L-67 — Buck Rodgers W-23 L-24, Harvey Kuenn W-72 L-43																	
1B	C. Cooper	654	.313	32	121	1428	98	5	156	9.9	.997	M. Caldwell	35	258	17	13	0	3.91
2B	J. Gantner	447	.295	4	43	307	398	13	104	5.5	.982	P. Vuckovich	30	224	18	6	0	3.34
SS	R. Yount	635	.331	29	114	253	489	24	95	5.0	.969	M. Haas	32	193	11	8	1	4.47
3B	P. Molitor	666	.302	19	71	128	340	29	48	3.3	.942	B. McClure	34	173	12	7	0	4.22
RF	C. Moore	456	.254	6	45	231	13	3	6	2.1	.988	J. Slaton	39	118	10	6	0	3.29
CF	G. Thomas	567	.245	39	112	427	11	4	4	2.8	.991	R. Lerch	21	109	8	7	0	4.97
LF	B. Oglivie	602	.244	34	102	359	15	7	3	2.4	.982	D. Bernard	47	79	3	1	6	3.76
C	T. Simmons	539	.269	23	97	570	62	3	8	5.2	.995	R. Fingers	50	80	5	6	29	2.60
DH	R. Howell	300	.260	4	38													
DH	D. Money	275	.284	16	55													
OF	M. Edwards	178	.247	2	14	119	2	2	1	2.3	.984							
	Baltimore W-94 L-68 — Earl Weaver																	
1B	E. Murray	550	.316	32	110	1269	97	4	106	9.2	.997	D. Martinez	40	252	16	12	0	4.21
2B	R. Dauer	558	.280	8	57	261	268	7	67	4.4	.987	M. Flanagan	36	236	15	11	0	3.97
SS	C. Ripken	598	.264	28	93	155	289	13	47	4.9	.972	J. Palmer	36	227	15	5	1	3.13
3B	G. Gulliver	145	.200	1	5	34	97	4	6	2.7	.970	S. McGregor	37	226	14	12	0	4.61
RF	D. Ford	421	.235	10	43	263	6	7	2	2.3	.975	S. Stewart	38	139	10	9	5	4.14
CF	A. Bumbry	562	.262	5	40	404	9	6	1	2.9	.986	S. Davis	29	101	8	4	0	3.49
LF	Lowenstein	322	.320	24	66	202	2	0	0	1.8	1.000	T. Martinez	76	95	8	8	16	3.41
C	R. Dempsey	344	.256	5	36	491	46	5	4	4.4	.991	T. Stoddard	50	56	3	4	12	4.02
DH	K. Singleton	561	.251	14	77													
OF	G. Roenicke	393	.270	21	74	288	7	3		2.4	.990							
2S	L. Sakata	343	.259	6	31	182	299	16	61		.968							
C	J. Nolan	219	.233	6	35	292	22	7	2	4.5	.978							
OD	B. Ayala	128	.305	6	24	35	0	1		1.4	.972							
	Boston W-89 L-73 — Ralph Houk																	
1B	D. Stapleton	538	.264	14	65	964	77	9	98	9.9	.991	D. Eckersley	33	224	13	13	0	3.73
2B	J. Remy	636	.280	0	47	290	432	13	104	4.8	.982	J. Tudor	32	196	13	10	0	3.63
SS	G. Hoffman	469	.209	7	49	246	439	20	93	4.7	.972	M. Torrez	31	176	9	9	0	5.23
3B	C. Lansford	482	.301	11	63	83	216	10	19	2.7	.968	B. Stanley	48	168	12	7	14	3.10
RF	D. Evans	609	.292	32	98	346	9	10	3	2.3	.973	C. Rainey	27	129	7	5	0	5.02
CF	R. Miller	409	.254	4	38	277	6	5	2	2.3	.983	B. Hurst	28	117	3	7	0	5.77
LF	J. Rice	573	.309	24	97	273	10	9	3	2.0	.969	M. Clear	55	105	14	9	14	3.00
C	G. Allenson	264	.205	6	33	454	39	4	8	5.5	.992	T. Burgmeier	40	102	7	0	2	2.29
DH	Yastrzemski	459	.275	16	72							B. Ojeda	22	78	4	6	0	5.63
13	W. Boggs	338	.349	5	44	488	168	8	51		.988							
C	R. Gedman	289	.249	4	26	397	29	10	5	5.1	.977							
OF	R. Nichols	245	.302	7	33	169	9	2	4	2.2	.989							
DH	T. Perez	196	.260	6	31													
	Detroit W-83 L-79 — Sparky Anderson																	
1B	E. Cabell	464	.261	2	37	548	52	5	62	7.3	.992	J. Morris	37	266	17	16	0	4.06
2B	L. Whitaker	560	.286	15	65	331	470	10	120	5.4	.988	D. Petry	35	246	15	9	0	3.22
SS	A. Trammell	489	.258	9	57	259	459	16	97	4.7	.978	M. Wilcox	29	194	12	10	0	3.62
3B	T. Brookens	398	.231	9	58	72	206	18	20	2.6	.939	J. Ujdur	25	178	10	10	0	3.69
RF	C. Lemon	436	.266	19	52	242	11	4	2	2.1	.984	P. Underwood	33	99	4	8	3	4.73
CF	G. Wilson	322	.292	12	34	215	8	3	1	2.8	.987	D. Tobik	51	99	4	9	9	3.56
LF	L. Herndon	614	.292	23	88	328	11	6	3	2.2	.983	D. Rucker	27	64	5	6	3	3.38
C	L. Parrish	486	.284	32	87	627	76	8	8	5.4	.989	E. Sosa	38	61	3	3	4	4.43
DH	M. Ivie	259	.232	14	38													
OF	K. Gibson	266	.278	8	35	167	4	1	3	2.7	.994							
1B	R. Leach	218	.239	3	12	410	28	2	36	7.9	.995							
DH	J. Turner	210	.248	8	27													
UT	Wockenfuss	193	.301	8	32	228	14	2	9		.992							
1D	R. Hebner	179	.274	8	18	286	25	3	15	7.9	.990							

AMERICAN LEAGUE 1982, cont.

	POS	Player	AB	BA	HR	RBI	PO	A	E	DP	TC/G	FA	Pitcher	G	IP	W	L	SV	ERA
New York W-79 L-83 Bob Lemon W-6 L-8 Gene Michael W-44 L-42 Clyde King W-29 L-33	1B	J. Mayberry	215	.209	8	27	455	25	2	49	7.7	.996	R. Guidry	34	222	14	8	0	3.81
	2B	W. Randolph	553	.280	3	36	352	380	14	100	5.3	.981	T. John	30	187	10	10	0	3.66
	SS	R. Smalley	486	.257	20	67	109	238	8	42	4.0	.977	D. Righetti	33	183	11	10	1	3.79
	3B	G. Nettles	405	.232	18	55	73	255	23	23	3.1	.934	S. Rawley	47	164	11	10	3	4.06
	RF	K. Griffey	484	.277	12	54	282	8	5	2	2.4	.983	M. Morgan	30	150	7	11	0	4.37
	CF	J. Mumphrey	477	.300	9	68	336	5	5	2	2.8	.986	G. Frazier	63	112	4	4	1	3.47
	LF	D. Winfield	539	.280	37	106	279	17	8	2	2.3	.974	R. May	41	106	6	6	3	2.89
	C	R. Cerone	300	.227	5	28	509	25	6	5	6.1	.989	G. Gossage	56	93	4	5	30	2.23
	DH	O. Gamble	316	.272	18	57							R. Erickson	16	71	4	5	1	4.46
	O1	D. Collins	348	.253	3	25	498	28	7	30		.987							
	DO	L. Piniella	261	.307	6	37	68	2	0	1	1.8	1.000							
	C	B. Wynegar	191	.293	3	20	395	17	3	6	6.7*	.993							
	DH	B. Murcer	141	.227	7	30													
Cleveland W-78 L-84 Dave Garcia	1B	M. Hargrove	591	.271	4	65	1293	**123**	5	110	9.3	.996	L. Barker	33	245	15	11	0	3.90
	2B	J. Perconte	219	.237	0	15	131	199	8	23	4.1	.976	R. Sutcliffe	34	216	14	8	1	**2.96**
	SS	M. Fischlin	276	.268	0	21	136	253	12	42	4.0	.970	L. Sorensen	32	189	10	15	0	5.61
	3B	T. Harrah	602	.304	25	78	126	279	12	25	2.6	.971	J. Denny	21	138	6	11	0	5.01
	RF	V. Hayes	527	.250	14	82	306	9	6	4	2.3	.981	D. Spillner	65	134	12	10	21	2.49
	CF	R. Manning	562	.270	8	44	387	10	9	1	2.7	.978	R. Waits	25	115	2	13	0	5.40
	LF	M. Dilone	379	.235	3	25	187	3	7	1	2.0	.964	E. Whitson	40	108	4	2	2	3.26
	C	R. Hassey	323	.251	5	34	562	38	4	6	5.8	.993	E. Glynn	47	50	5	2	4	4.17
	DH	A. Thornton	589	.273	32	116													
	O2	A. Bannister	348	.267	4	41	206	124	10	22		.971							
	UT	L. Milbourne	291	.275	2	25	149	224	14	41		.964							
	SS	J. Dybzinski	212	.231	0	22	118	239	16	39	4.8	.957							
	C	C. Bando	184	.212	3	16	268	23	3	1	4.7	.990							
Toronto W-78 L-84 Bobby Cox	1B	W. Upshaw	580	.267	21	75	**1438**	101	17	123	10.0	.989	D. Stieb	38	**288**	17	14	0	3.25
	2B	D. Garcia	597	.310	5	42	273	461	15	94	5.3	.980	J. Clancy	40	267	16	14	0	3.71
	SS	A. Griffin	539	.241	1	48	**319**	479	**26**	92	**5.1**	.968	L. Leal	38	250	12	15	0	3.93
	3B	R. Mulliniks	311	.244	4	35	60	137	13	13	2.1	.938	J. Gott	30	136	5	10	0	4.43
	RF	J. Barfield	394	.246	18	58	217	15	9	4	1.8	.963	D. Murray	56	111	8	7	11	3.16
	CF	L. Moseby	487	.236	9	52	361	4	3	0	2.5	.992	R. Jackson	48	97	8	8	6	3.06
	LF	B. Bonnell	437	.293	6	49	232	3	5	0	1.9	.979	McLaughlin	44	70	8	6	8	3.21
	C	E. Whitt	284	.261	11	42	406	30	8	0	4.5	.982							
	DH	W. Nordhagen	185	.270	1	20													
	3B	G. Iorg	417	.285	1	36	57	155	12	13	2.2	.946							
	OF	H. Powell	265	.275	3	26	111	2	3	0	1.5	.974							
	C	B. Martinez	260	.242	10	37	382	35	5	8	4.5	.988							
	OF	A. Woods	201	.234	3	24	96	3	3	1	1.6	.970							
West **California** W-93 L-69 Gene Mauch	1B	R. Carew	523	.319	3	44	1339	94	12	115	**10.8**	.992	G. Zahn	34	229	18	8	0	3.73
	2B	B. Grich	506	.261	19	65	338	450	11	112	5.6	.986	K. Forsch	37	228	13	11	0	3.87
	SS	T. Foli	480	.252	3	56	235	432	10	87	4.9	**.985**	M. Witt	33	180	8	6	0	3.51
	3B	D. DeCinces	575	.301	30	97	112	**399**	21	41	3.5	.961	S. Renko	31	156	11	6	0	4.44
	RF	R. Jackson	530	.275	**39**	101	200	6	6	1	1.5	.972	B. Kison	33	142	10	5	1	3.17
	CF	F. Lynn	472	.299	21	86	317	6	3	3	2.5	.991	L. Sanchez	46	93	7	4	5	3.21
	LF	B. Downing	623	.281	28	84	321	9	0	0	2.1	**1.000**	D. Goltz	28	86	8	5	3	4.08
	C	B. Boone	472	.256	7	58	650	87	8	8	5.2	.989	D. Corbett	33	57	1	7	8	5.05
	DH	D. Baylor	608	.263	24	93							D. Aase	24	52	3	3	4	3.46
	OF	J. Beniquez	196	.265	3	24	113	4	2	1	1.1	.983	A. Moreno	13	49	3	7	1	4.74
Kansas City W-90 L-72 Dick Howser	1B	W. Aikens	466	.281	17	74	1048	75	7	95	8.8	.994	L. Gura	37	248	18	12	0	4.03
	2B	F. White	524	.298	11	56	**361**	389	**17**	99	5.3	.978	V. Blue	31	181	13	12	0	3.78
	SS	Washington	437	.286	10	60	173	371	22	63	4.8	.961	Splittorff	29	162	10	10	0	4.28
	3B	G. Brett	552	.301	21	82	107	294	17	22	3.1	.959	Quisenberry	72	137	9	7	35	2.57
	RF	J. Martin	519	.266	15	65	333	4	7	2	2.4	.980	D. Leonard	21	131	10	6	0	5.10
	CF	A. Otis	475	.286	11	88	308	5	1	1	2.5	.997	M. Armstrong	52	113	5	5	6	3.20
	LF	W. Wilson	585	**.332**	3	46	376	4	5	0	2.9	.987	B. Black	22	88	4	6	0	4.58
	C	J. Wathan	448	.270	3	51	463	38	10	3	4.3	.980	D. Frost	21	82	6	6	1	5.51
	DH	H. McRae	613	.308	27	**133**													
	S2	Concepcion	205	.234	0	15	92	168	11	28		.959							
	OF	C. Geronimo	119	.269	4	23	93	3	0	0	2.2	1.000							
Chicago W-87 L-75 Tony LaRussa	1B	M. Squires	195	.267	1	21	512	48	3	59	5.2	.995	L. Hoyt	39	240	**19**	15	0	3.53
	2B	T. Bernazard	540	.256	11	56	353	443	12	116	**5.9**	.985	R. Dotson	34	197	11	15	0	3.84
	SS	B. Almon	308	.256	4	26	164	317	**26**	72	4.7	.949	D. Lamp	44	190	11	8	5	3.99
	3B	A. Rodriguez	257	.241	3	31	78	204	9	19	2.6	.969	J. Koosman	42	173	11	7	3	3.84
	RF	H. Baines	608	.271	25	105	326	10	7	4	2.1	.980	B. Burns	28	169	13	5	0	4.04
	CF	R. Law	336	.318	3	32	215	2	6	0	2.4	.973	S. Trout	25	120	6	9	0	4.26
	LF	S. Kemp	580	.286	19	98	280	6	7	1	1.9	.976	S. Barojas	61	107	6	6	21	3.54
	C	C. Fisk	476	.267	14	65	639	62	4	7	5.3	.994	K. Hickey	60	78	4	4	6	3.00
	DH	G. Luzinski	583	.292	18	102													
	1B	T. Paciorek	382	.312	11	55	833	66	6	85	8.9	.993							
	S3	V. Law	359	.281	5	54	145	294	23	47		.950							
	OF	R. LeFlore	334	.287	4	25	179	7	**12**	1	2.4	.939							
	3B	J. Morrison	166	.223	7	19	19	87	10	10	2.3	.914							

AMERICAN LEAGUE 1982, *cont.*

	POS	Player	AB	BA	HR	RBI	PO	A	E	DP	TC/G	FA	Pitcher	G	IP	W	L	SV	ERA
Seattle	1B	G. Gray	269	.257	7	29	476	31	8	36	8.6	.984	F. Bannister	35	247	12	13	0	3.43
	2B	J. Cruz	549	.242	8	49	320	434	10	98	5.1	.987	G. Perry	32	217	10	12	0	4.40
W-76 L-86	SS	T. Cruz	492	.230	16	57	215	439	25	**98**	5.0	.963	J. Beattie	28	172	8	12	0	3.34
	3B	M. Castillo	506	.257	3	49	96	209	20	18	2.5	.938	M. Moore	28	144	7	14	0	5.36
Rene Lachemann	RF	A. Cowens	560	.270	20	78	280	14	4	1	2.1	.987	G. Nelson	22	123	6	9	0	4.62
	CF	J. Simpson	296	.257	2	23	177	7	3	0	1.9	.984	B. Clark	37	115	5	2	0	2.75
	LF	B. Bochte	509	.297	12	70	161	5	2	1	1.7	.988	B. Caudill	70	96	12	9	26	2.35
	C	R. Sweet	258	.256	4	24	431	26	3	6	5.5	.993	Vande Berg	**78**	76	9	4	5	2.37
	DH	R. Zisk	503	.292	21	62							M. Stanton	56	71	2	4	7	4.16
	OF	D. Henderson	324	.253	14	48	249	11	4	4	2.6	.985							
	OF	B. Brown	245	.241	4	17	148	5	5	1	2.3	.968							
	1B	J. Maler	221	.226	4	26	529	41	5	45	10.1	.991							
	UT	P. Serna	169	.225	3	8	63	126	9	23		.955							
	C	J. Essian	153	.275	3	20	282	26	2	1	6.5	.994							
Oakland	1B	D. Meyer	383	.240	8	59	373	31	4	38	7.0	.990	R. Langford	32	237	11	16	0	4.21
	2B	D. Lopes	450	.242	11	42	289	338	15	82	5.1	.977	M. Keough	34	209	11	**18**	0	5.72
W-68 L-94	SS	F. Stanley	228	.193	2	17	112	223	13	42	3.6	.963	M. Norris	28	166	7	11	0	4.76
	3B	W. Gross	386	.251	9	41	113	182	9	25	2.8	.970	T. Underwood	56	153	10	6	7	3.29
Billy Martin	RF	T. Armas	536	.233	28	89	333	9	6	1	2.6	.983	S. McCatty	21	129	6	3	0	3.99
	CF	D. Murphy	543	.238	27	94	**452**	14	8	3	**3.2**	.983	B. Kingman	23	123	4	12	1	4.48
	LF	R. Henderson	536	.267	10	51	379	2	9	0	2.7	.977	B. Owchinko	54	102	2	4	3	5.21
	C	M. Heath	318	.242	3	39	350	50	11	8	4.6	.973	D. Beard	54	92	10	9	11	3.44
	DH	J. Burroughs	285	.277	16	48													
	C	J. Newman	251	.199	6	30	320	27	4	5	5.2	.989							
	DH	C. Johnson	214	.238	7	31													
	2B	D. McKay	212	.198	4	17	99	116	7	22	3.8	.968							
	1B	J. Rudi	193	.212	5	18	398	20	4	37	8.6	.991							
Texas	1B	D. Hostetler	418	.232	22	67	1099	48	12	102	10.6	.990	C. Hough	34	228	16	13	0	3.95
	2B	M. Richardt	402	.241	3	43	234	278	6	68	5.3	.988	F. Tanana	30	194	7	**18**	0	4.21
W-64 L-98	SS	M. Wagner	179	.240	0	8	77	197	13	32	4.8	.955	R. Honeycutt	30	164	5	17	0	5.27
	3B	B. Bell	537	.296	13	67	131	396	13	35	**3.7**	.976	J. Matlack	33	148	7	7	1	3.53
Don Zimmer	RF	L. Parrish	440	.264	17	62	190	12	8	4	1.7	.962	D. Medich	21	123	7	11	0	5.06
W-38 L-58	CF	G. Wright	557	.264	11	50	398	14	8	3	2.8	.981	D. Schmidt	33	110	4	6	5	3.20
	LF	B. Sample	360	.261	10	29	196	6	4	1	2.3	.981	S. Comer	37	97	1	6	6	5.10
Darrell Johnson	C	J. Sundberg	470	.251	10	47	607	69	6	**15**	5.2	.991	D. Darwin	56	89	10	8	7	3.44
W-26 L-40	DH	L. Johnson	324	.259	7	38													
	OF	J. Grubb	308	.279	3	26	135	4	5	1	1.9	.965							
	2S	D. Flynn	270	.211	0	19	161	254	9	48		.979							
	OD	L. Mazzilli	195	.241	4	17	51	1	3	1	2.1	.945							
	UT	B. Stein	184	.239	1	16	72	122	6	28		.970							
Minnesota	1B	K. Hrbek	532	.301	23	92	1174	88	9	125	9.2	.993	B. Castillo	40	219	13	11	0	3.66
	2B	J. Castino	410	.241	6	37	193	228	2	63	4.4	.995	B. Havens	33	209	10	14	0	4.31
W-60 L-102	SS	Washington	451	.271	5	39	127	186	9	38	3.5	.972	A. Williams	26	154	9	7	0	4.22
	3B	G. Gaetti	508	.230	25	84	106	286	15	35	2.9	.963	F. Viola	22	126	4	10	0	5.21
Billy Gardner	RF	T. Brunansky	463	.272	20	46	343	8	5	0	2.8	.986	J. O'Connor	23	126	8	9	0	4.29
	CF	B. Mitchell	454	.249	2	28	350	8	1	3	3.0	.997	T. Felton	48	117	0	13	3	4.99
	LF	G. Ward	570	.289	28	91	343	13	4	3	2.4	.989	R. Davis	63	106	3	9	22	4.42
	C	T. Laudner	306	.255	7	33	454	41	**12**	5	5.5	.976	P. Redfern	27	94	5	11	0	6.58
	DH	R. Johnson	234	.248	10	33													
	OD	M. Hatcher	277	.249	3	33	78	7	1	0	1.8	.988							
	SS	L. Faedo	255	.243	3	22	129	218	12	52	4.1	.967							
	D1	J. Vega	199	.266	5	29	106	8	3	9	6.5	.974							
	OD	D. Engle	186	.226	4	16	63	3	1	2	2.0	.985							

BATTING AND BASE RUNNING LEADERS

Batting Average		Slugging Average		Home Runs	
W. Wilson, KC	.332	R. Yount, MIL	.578	R. Jackson, CAL	39
R. Yount, MIL	.331	D. Winfield, NY	.560	G. Thomas, MIL	39
R. Carew, CAL	.319	E. Murray, BAL	.549	D. Winfield, NY	37
E. Murray, BAL	.316	D. DeCinces, CAL	.548	B. Oglivie, MIL	34
C. Cooper, MIL	.313	H. McRae, KC	.542		

Total Bases		Runs Batted In		Stolen Bases	
R. Yount, MIL	367	H. McRae, KC	133	R. Henderson, OAK	130
C. Cooper, MIL	345	C. Cooper, MIL	121	D. Garcia, TOR	54
H. McRae, KC	332	A. Thornton, CLE	116	J. Cruz, SEA	46
D. Evans, BOS	325	R. Yount, MIL	114	P. Molitor, MIL	41
D. DeCinces, CAL	315	G. Thomas, MIL	112	W. Wilson, KC	37

PITCHING LEADERS

Winning Percentage		Earned Run Average		Wins	
P. Vuckovich, MIL	.750	R. Sutcliffe, CLE	2.96	L. Hoyt, CHI	19
J. Palmer, BAL	.750	B. Stanley, BOS	3.10	P. Vuckovich, MIL	18
B. Burns, CHI	.722	J. Palmer, BAL	3.13	G. Zahn, CAL	18
G. Zahn, CAL	.692	D. Petry, DET	3.22	L. Gura, KC	18
R. Guidry, NY	.636	D. Stieb, TOR	3.25		
R. Sutcliffe, CLE	.636				

Saves		Strikeouts		Complete Games	
Quisenberry, KC	35	F. Bannister, SEA	209	D. Stieb, TOR	19
G. Gossage, NY	30	L. Barker, CLE	187	J. Morris, DET	17
R. Fingers, MIL	29	D. Righetti, NY	163	R. Langford, OAK	15
B. Caudill, SEA	26	R. Guidry, NY	162	L. Hoyt, CHI	14
R. Davis, MIN	22	J. Tudor, BOS	146		

AMERICAN LEAGUE 1982, *cont.*

BATTING AND BASE RUNNING LEADERS

Hits		Base on Balls		Home Run Percentage		Fewest Hits/9 Innings	
R. Yount, MIL	210	R. Henderson, OAK	116	R. Jackson, CAL	7.4	R. Sutcliffe, CLE	7.25
C. Cooper, MIL	205	D. Evans, BOS	112	G. Thomas, MIL	6.9	J. Ujdur, DET	7.58
P. Molitor, MIL	201	A. Thornton, CLE	109	D. Winfield, NY	6.9	D. Righetti, NY	7.62
W. Wilson, KC	194	M. Hargrove, CLE	101	L. Parrish, DET	6.6	J. Palmer, BAL	7.73

Runs Scored		Doubles		Triples		Most Strikeouts/9 Inn.	
P. Molitor, MIL	136	H. McRae, KC	46	W. Wilson, KC	15	D. Righetti, NY	8.02
R. Yount, MIL	129	R. Yount, MIL	46	L. Herndon, DET	13	F. Bannister, SEA	7.62
D. Evans, BOS	122	F. White, KC	45	R. Yount, MIL	12	J. Beattie, SEA	7.31
R. Henderson, OAK	119	D. DeCinces, CAL	42	J. Mumphrey, NY	10	L. Barker, CLE	6.88

PITCHING LEADERS

Shutouts		Fewest Walks/9 Innings	
D. Stieb, TOR	5	T. John, CAL, NY	1.58
G. Zahn, CAL	4	D. Eckersley, BOS	1.73
K. Forsch, CAL	4	L. Hoyt, CHI	1.80
		M. Haas, MIL	1.82

Innings		Games Pitched	
D. Stieb, TOR	288	Vande Berg, SEA	78
J. Clancy, TOR	267	T. Martinez, BAL	76
J. Morris, DET	266	Quisenberry, KC	72
M. Caldwell, MIL	258	B. Caudill, SEA	70

		W	L	PCT	GB	R	OR	2B	3B	HR	BA	SA	SB	E	DP	FA	CG	BB	SO	ShO	SV	ERA
East	Milwaukee	95	67	.586		891	717	277	41	216	.279	.455	84	125	184	.980	34	511	717	6	47	3.98
	Baltimore	94	68	.580	1	774	687	259	27	179	.266	.419	49	101	140	.984	38	488	719	8	34	3.99
	Boston	89	73	.549	6	753	713	271	31	136	.274	.407	42	121	172	.981	23	478	816	11	33	4.03
	Detroit	83	79	.512	12	729	685	237	40	177	.266	.418	93	117	164	.981	45	491	740	5	27	3.80
	New York	79	83	.488	16	709	716	225	37	161	.256	.398	69	128	157	.979	24	491	939	4	39	3.99
	Cleveland	78	84	.481	17	683	748	225	32	109	.262	.373	151	123	127	.980	31	589	882	9	30	4.11
	Toronto	78	84	.481	17	651	701	262	45	106	.262	.383	118	136	146	.978	41	493	776	13	25	3.95
West	California	93	69	.574		814	670	268	26	186	.274	.433	55	108	171	.983	40	482	728	10	27	3.82
	Kansas City	90	72	.556	3	784	717	295	58	132	.285	.428	133	127	140	.979	16	471	650	12	45	4.08
	Chicago	87	75	.537	6	786	710	266	52	136	.273	.413	136	154	173	.978	30	460	753	10	41	3.87
	Seattle	76	86	.469	17	651	712	259	33	130	.254	.381	131	139	157	.978	23	547	1002	11	39	3.88
	Oakland	68	94	.420	25	691	819	211	27	149	.236	.367	232	160	135	.974	42	648	697	6	22	4.54
	Texas	64	98	.395	29	590	749	204	26	115	.249	.359	63	121	148	.981	32	483	690	5	24	4.28
	Minnesota	60	102	.370	33	657	819	234	44	148	.257	.396	38	108	162	.982	26	643	812	7	30	4.72
						10163	10163	3493	519	2080	.264	.402	1394	1768	2196	.980	445	7338	10921	121	463	4.07

NATIONAL LEAGUE 1983

		POS	Player	AB	BA	HR	RBI	PO	A	E	DP	TC/G	FA	Pitcher	G	IP	W	L	SV	ERA
East	**Philadelphia**	1B	P. Rose	493	.245	0	45	786	74	9	57	7.8	.990	S. Carlton	37	284	15	16	0	3.11
		2B	J. Morgan	404	.230	16	59	231	331	17	63	4.9	.971	J. Denny	36	243	19	6	0	2.37
	W-90 L-72	SS	I. DeJesus	497	.254	4	45	214	438	23	64	4.3	.966	C. Hudson	26	169	8	8	0	3.35
		3B	M. Schmidt	534	.255	40	109	107	332	19	29	3.0	.959	M. Bystrom	24	119	6	9	0	4.60
	Pat Corrales	RF	V. Hayes	351	.265	6	32	165	7	5	0	1.7	.972	K. Gross	17	96	4	6	0	3.56
	W-43 L-42	CF	G. Maddox	324	.275	4	32	216	1	5	0	2.3	.977	G. Hernandez	63	96	8	4	7	3.29
		LF	G. Matthews	446	.258	10	50	174	11	5	2	1.6	.974	R. Reed	61	96	9	1	8	3.48
	Paul Owens	C	B. Diaz	471	.236	15	64	903	97	14	7	7.6	.986	A. Holland	68	92	8	4	25	2.26
	W-47 L-30																			
		OF	J. Lefebvre	258	.310	8	38	92	4	1	0	1.3	.990							
		1B	T. Perez	253	.241	6	43	514	40	1	36	8.0	.998							
		OF	G. Gross	245	.302	0	29	104	1	1	0	1.0	.991							
		OF	B. Dernier	221	.231	1	15	164	3	2	1	1.6	.988							
		C	O. Virgil	140	.214	6	23	228	24	9	2	5.1	.966							
	Pittsburgh	1B	J. Thompson	517	.259	18	76	1266	89	9	131	9.0	.993	R. Rhoden	36	244	13	13	1	3.09
		2B	J. Ray	576	.283	5	53	319	452	13	102	5.2	.983	McWilliams	35	238	15	8	0	3.25
		SS	D. Berra	537	.251	10	52	286	505	30	103	5.1	.963	Candelaria	33	198	15	8	0	3.23
	W-84 L-78	3B	B. Madlock	473	.323	12	68	59	193	11	20	2.1	.958	L. Tunnell	35	178	11	6	0	3.65
		RF	D. Parker	552	.279	12	69	282	3	8	2	2.1	.973	J. DeLeon	15	108	7	3	0	2.83
	Chuck Tanner	CF	M. Wynne	366	.243	7	26	223	3	4	2	2.3	.983	C. Guante	49	100	2	6	9	3.32
		LF	M. Easler	381	.307	10	54	158	6	6	1	1.6	.965	K. Tekulve	76	99	7	5	18	1.64
		C	T. Pena	542	.301	15	70	976	90	9	9	7.2	.992	M. Sarmiento	52	84	3	5	4	2.99
		OF	L. Lacy	288	.302	4	13	167	2	0	0	1.7	1.000	J. Bibby	29	78	5	12	2	6.69
		OF	L. Mazzilli	246	.240	5	24	130	3	2	1	2.4	.985	R. Scurry	61	68	4	9	7	5.56
		3B	R. Hebner	162	.265	5	26	16	43	2	1	1.5	.967							
		UT	J. Morrison	158	.304	6	25	55	99	7	21		.957							
		OF	B. Harper	131	.221	7	20	40	0	0	0	1.1	1.000							
	Montreal	1B	A. Oliver	614	.300	8	84	1207	118	13	93	8.7	.990	S. Rogers	36	273	17	12	0	3.23
		2B	D. Flynn	452	.237	0	26	205	290	7	57	4.7	.986	Gullickson	34	242	17	12	0	3.75
		SS	C. Speier	261	.257	2	22	107	196	12	31	4.3	.962	C. Lea	33	222	16	11	0	3.12
	W-82 L-80	3B	T. Wallach	581	.269	19	70	151	265	19	25	2.8	.956	B. Smith	49	155	6	11	3	2.49
		RF	W. Cromartie	360	.278	3	43	208	12	6	2	2.2	.973	R. Burris	40	154	4	7	0	3.68
	Bill Virdon	CF	A. Dawson	633	.299	32	113	435	6	9	2	2.9	.980	J. Reardon	66	92	7	9	21	3.03
		LF	T. Raines	615	.298	11	71	307	21	4	3	2.2	.988	S. Sanderson	18	81	6	7	1	4.65
		C	G. Carter	541	.270	17	79	847	107	5	14	6.7	.995							
		S2	B. Little	350	.260	1	36	181	248	9	44		.979							
		O1	T. Francona	230	.257	3	22	172	10	3	10		.984							

NATIONAL LEAGUE 1983, *cont.*

	POS	Player	AB	BA	HR	RBI	PO	A	E	DP	TC/G	FA	Pitcher	G	IP	W	L	SV	ERA
St. Louis	1B	G. Hendrick	529	.318	18	97	819	77	7	72	9.8	.992	J. Andujar	39	225	6	16	1	4.16
	2B	T. Herr	313	.323	2	31	178	245	6	60	5.0	.986	J. Stuper	40	198	12	11	1	3.68
W-79 L-83	SS	O. Smith	552	.243	3	50	304	519	21	100	5.3	.975	D. LaPoint	37	191	12	9	0	3.95
	3B	K. Oberkfell	488	.293	3	38	79	231	13	27	2.5	.960	B. Forsch	34	187	10	12	0	4.28
Whitey Herzog	RF	D. Green	422	.284	8	69	214	10	7	2	1.7	.970	N. Allen	25	122	10	6	0	3.70
	CF	W. McGee	601	.286	5	75	385	7	5	1	2.7	.987	B. Sutter	60	89	9	10	21	4.23
	LF	L. Smith	492	.321	8	45	225	14	15	4	2.0	.941							
	C	D. Porter	443	.262	15	66	578	70	7	8	4.9	.989							
	O3	A. Van Slyke	309	.262	8	38	132	54	4	3		.979							
	1B	K. Hernandez	218	.284	3	26	581*	51	6*	62*	11.8*	.991							
	2S	M. Ramsey	175	.263	1	16	91	140	8	31		.967							
Chicago	1B	B. Buckner	626	.280	16	66	1366	161	13	132	10.7	.992	C. Rainey	34	191	14	13	0	4.48
	2B	R. Sandberg	633	.261	8	48	330	571	13	126	5.8	.986	S. Trout	34	180	10	14	0	4.65
W-71 L-91	SS	L. Bowa	499	.267	2	43	230	464	11	102	4.9	.984	F. Jenkins	33	167	6	9	0	4.30
	3B	R. Cey	581	.275	24	90	90	270	17	12	2.4	.955	D. Ruthven	25	149	12	9	0	4.10
Lee Elia	RF	K. Moreland	533	.302	16	70	236	7	6	1	1.6	.976	B. Campbell	82	122	6	8	8	4.49
W-54 L-69	CF	M. Hall	410	.283	17	56	239	8	3	2	2.2	.988	D. Noles	24	116	5	10	0	4.72
	LF	L. Durham	337	.258	12	55	168	2	6	0	1.9	.966	L. Smith	66	103	4	10	29	1.65
Charlie Fox	C	J. Davis	510	.271	24	84	730	75	13	7	5.5	.984							
W-17 L-22	OF	G. Woods	190	.242	4	22	97	4	3	0	1.4	.971							
	OF	J. Johnstone	140	.257	6	22	55	3	4	1	1.4	.935							
New York	1B	K. Hernandez	320	.306	9	37	837*	96	7*	85*	10.4*	.993	T. Seaver	34	231	9	14	0	3.55
	2B	B. Giles	400	.245	2	27	299	380	14	87	5.0	.980	M. Torrez	39	222	10	17	0	4.37
W-68 L-94	SS	J. Oquendo	328	.213	1	17	182	326	21	65	4.6	.960	E. Lynch	30	175	10	10	0	4.28
	3B	H. Brooks	586	.251	5	58	107	289	21	25	2.9	.957	W. Terrell	21	134	8	8	0	3.57
George Bamberger	RF	Strawberry	420	.257	26	74	232	8	4	0	2.1	.984	J. Orosco	62	110	13	7	17	1.47
W-16 L-30	CF	M. Wilson	638	.276	7	51	422	5	7	1	2.9	.984	D. Sisk	67	104	5	4	11	2.24
	LF	G. Foster	601	.241	28	90	314	12	4	3	2.2	.988	S. Holman	35	101	1	7	0	3.74
Frank Howard	C	R. Hodges	250	.260	0	21	360	45	12	4	4.3	.971	C. Swan	27	96	2	8	1	5.51
W-52 L-64	S2	B. Bailor	340	.250	1	30	157	282	16	60		.965	N. Allen	21	54	2	7	2	4.50
	OF	D. Heep	253	.253	8	21	90	4	0	1	1.5	1.000							
	1B	D. Kingman	248	.198	13	29	443	28	3	43	9.5	.994							
	C	J. Ortiz	185	.254	0	12	273	31	11	2	4.7	.965							
	PH	R. Staub	115	.296	3	28													
West **Los Angeles**	1B	G. Brock	455	.224	20	66	1162	106	12	94	9.1	.991	Valenzuela	35	257	15	10	0	3.75
	2B	S. Sax	623	.281	5	41	331	399	30	74	5.0	.961	J. Reuss	32	223	12	11	0	2.94
W-91 L-71	SS	B. Russell	451	.246	1	30	192	392	22	61	4.8	.964	B. Welch	31	204	15	12	0	2.65
	3B	P. Guerrero	584	.298	32	103	123	305	30	22	2.9	.934	A. Pena	34	177	12	9	1	2.75
Tom Lasorda	RF	M. Marshall	465	.284	17	65	160	3	4	1	1.5	.976	B. Hooton	33	160	9	8	0	4.22
	CF	K. Landreaux	481	.281	17	66	299	4	3	1	2.2	.990	Niedenfuer	66	95	8	3	11	1.90
	LF	D. Baker	531	.260	15	73	249	4	5	2	1.8	.981	D. Stewart	46	76	5	2	8	2.96
	C	S. Yeager	335	.203	15	41	579	63	10	10	5.8	.985	S. Howe	46	69	4	7	18	1.44
	OF	D. Thomas	192	.250	2	8	97	3	1	0	1.2	.990							
	OF	R. Monday	178	.247	6	20	62	1	2	0	1.5	.969							
	C	J. Fimple	148	.250	2	22	336	32	4	2	6.9	.989							
Atlanta	1B	C. Chambliss	447	.280	20	78	1092	89	5	117	9.4	.996	C. McMurtry	36	225	15	9	0	3.08
	2B	G. Hubbard	517	.263	12	70	313	484	12	103	5.5	.985	P. Perez	33	215	15	8	0	3.43
W-88 L-74	SS	R. Ramirez	622	.297	7	58	232	490	39	116	5.0	.949	P. Niekro	34	202	11	10	0	3.97
	3B	B. Horner	386	.303	20	68	76	153	10	18	2.3	.958	R. Camp	40	140	10	9	0	3.79
Joe Torre	RF	Washington	496	.278	9	44	218	8	6	3	1.8	.974	S. Bedrosian	70	120	9	10	19	3.60
	CF	D. Murphy	589	.302	36	121	373	10	6	0	2.4	.985	P. Falcone	33	107	9	4	0	3.63
	LF	B. Butler	549	.281	5	37	284	13	4	4	2.1	.987	K. Dayley	24	105	5	8	0	4.30
	C	B. Benedict	423	.298	2	43	738	91	7	12	6.2	.992	T. Forster	56	79	3	2	13	2.16
	UT	J. Royster	268	.235	3	30	112	156	10	29		.964	D. Moore	43	69	2	3	6	3.67
	OF	T. Harper	201	.264	3	26	95	5	5	0	1.8	.952	G. Garber	43	61	4	5	9	4.60
	1B	B. Watson	149	.309	6	37	280	19	5	23	8.9	.984							
Houston	1B	R. Knight	507	.304	9	70	1285	73	9	131	9.6	.993	J. Niekro	38	264	15	14	0	3.48
	2B	B. Doran	535	.271	8	39	347	461	17	109	5.4	.979	B. Knepper	35	203	6	13	0	3.19
W-85 L-77	SS	D. Thon	619	.286	20	79	258	533	28	114	5.3	.966	N. Ryan	29	196	14	9	0	2.98
	3B	P. Garner	567	.238	14	79	100	311	24	22	2.8	.945	M. Scott	24	145	10	6	0	3.72
Bob Lillis	RF	T. Puhl	465	.292	8	44	220	4	2	1	1.8	.991	M. LaCoss	38	138	5	7	1	4.43
	CF	O. Moreno	405	.242	0	25	251	8	6	3	2.7	.977	V. Ruhle	41	115	8	5	3	3.69
	LF	J. Cruz	594	.318	14	92	322	9	7	1	2.1	.979	M. Madden	28	95	9	5	0	3.14
	C	A. Ashby	275	.229	8	34	435	56	13	2	5.9	.974	B. Dawley	48	80	6	6	14	2.82
	OF	K. Bass	195	.236	2	18	68	1	4	1	1.4	.945	D. Smith	42	73	3	1	6	3.10
	OF	T. Scott	186	.226	2	17	89	2	0	1	1.5	1.000	F. DiPino	53	71	3	4	20	2.65

NATIONAL LEAGUE 1983, cont.

	POS	Player	AB	BA	HR	RBI	PO	A	E	DP	TC/G	FA	Pitcher	G	IP	W	L	SV	ERA
San Diego	1B	S. Garvey	388	.294	14	59	888	49	6	69	9.4	.994	E. Show	35	201	15	12	0	4.17
	2B	J. Bonilla	556	.237	4	45	335	414	11	90	5.1	.986	D. Dravecky	28	184	14	10	0	3.58
W-81 L-81	SS	G. Templeton	460	.263	3	40	219	355	24	66	4.9	.960	T. Lollar	30	176	7	12	0	4.61
	3B	L. Salazar	481	.258	14	45	102	250	19	17	3.1	.949	E. Whitson	31	144	5	7	1	4.30
Dick Williams	RF	S. Lezcano	317	.233	8	49	171	8	6	1	2.0	.968	A. Hawkins	21	120	5	7	0	2.93
	CF	R. Jones	335	.233	12	49	249	3	5	2	2.3	.981	M. Thurmond	21	115	7	3	0	2.65
	LF	A. Wiggins	503	.276	0	22	242	6	2	1	2.4	.992	L. DeLeon	63	111	6	6	13	2.68
	C	T. Kennedy	549	.284	17	98	782	79	12	8	6.1	.986	Montefusco	31	95	9	4	4	3.30
	OF	T. Gwynn	304	.309	1	37	163	9	1	1	2.1	.994	G. Lucas	62	91	5	8	17	2.87
	OF	G. Richards	233	.275	3	22	96	2	2	0	1.9	.980	S. Monge	47	69	7	3	7	3.15
	OF	B. Brown	225	.267	5	22	103	1	4	0	2.0	.963							
	32	T. Flannery	214	.234	3	19	58	148	4	19		.981							
	UT	K. Bevacqua	156	.244	2	24	207	28	2	16		.992							
San Francisco	1B	D. Evans	523	.277	30	82	979	88	7	60	9.5	.993	F. Breining	32	203	11	12	0	3.82
	2B	B. Wellman	182	.214	1	16	91	160	9	26	3.5	.965	M. Krukow	31	184	11	11	0	3.95
W-79 L-83	SS	J. LeMaster	534	.240	6	30	215	402	23	58	4.6	.964	A. Hammaker	23	172	10	9	0	2.25
	3B	T. O'Malley	410	.259	5	45	70	213	18	12	2.6	.940	B. Laskey	25	148	13	10	0	4.19
Frank Robinson	RF	J. Clark	492	.268	20	66	249	17	9	3	2.1	.967	McGaffigan	43	134	3	9	2	4.29
	CF	C. Davis	486	.233	11	59	357	7	9	1	2.8	.976	M. Davis	20	111	6	4	0	3.49
	LF	J. Leonard	516	.279	21	87	253	17	7	2	2.0	.975	G. Minton	73	107	7	11	22	3.54
	C	B. Brenly	281	.224	7	34	403	70	8	9	5.3	.983	J. Barr	53	93	5	3	2	3.98
	UT	Youngblood	373	.292	17	53	147	182	19	28		.945	G. Lavelle	56	87	7	4	20	2.59
	OF	M. Venable	228	.219	6	27	141	5	1	0	2.2	.993							
	C	M. May	186	.247	6	20	285	32	6	5	5.8	.981							
	2B	D. Kuiper	176	.250	0	14	107	140	3	17	3.9	.988							
	1B	D. Bergman	140	.286	6	24	291	27	2	20	6.4	.994							
Cincinnati	1B	D. Driessen	386	.277	12	57	917	71	4	73	8.9	.996	M. Soto	34	274	17	13	0	2.70
	2B	R. Oester	549	.264	11	58	315	413	17	80	4.8	.977	B. Berenyi	32	186	9	14	0	3.86
W-74 L-88	SS	Concepcion	528	.233	1	47	225	376	13	67	4.4	.977	F. Pastore	36	184	9	12	0	4.88
	3B	N. Esasky	302	.265	12	46	53	133	13	11	2.4	.935	J. Price	21	144	10	6	0	2.88
Russ Nixon	RF	Householder	380	.255	6	43	221	5	2	0	2.0	.991	C. Puleo	27	144	6	12	0	4.89
	CF	E. Milner	502	.261	9	33	392	9	4	0	2.9	.990	T. Power	49	111	5	6	2	4.54
	LF	G. Redus	453	.247	17	51	235	11	7	0	2.1	.972	B. Scherrer	73	92	2	3	10	2.74
	C	Bilardello	298	.238	9	38	494	72	5	4	5.4	.991	R. Gale	33	90	4	6	1	5.82
	OF	C. Cedeno	332	.232	9	39	138	5	1	1	2.0	.993	B. Hayes	60	69	4	6	7	6.49
	31	J. Bench	310	.255	12	54	275	72	9	26		.975	T. Hume	48	66	3	5	9	4.77
	OF	D. Walker	225	.236	2	29	104	4	5	0	1.9	.956							
	C	A. Trevino	167	.216	1	13	359	28	5	2	6.2	.987							

BATTING AND BASE RUNNING LEADERS

Batting Average		Slugging Average		Home Runs		Winning Percentage	
B. Madlock, PIT	.323	D. Murphy, ATL	.540	M. Schmidt, PHI	40	J. Denny, PHI	.760
L. Smith, STL	.321	A. Dawson, MON	.539	D. Murphy, ATL	36	Candelaria, PIT	.652
J. Cruz, HOU	.318	P. Guerrero, LA	.531	P. Guerrero, LA	32	McWilliams, PIT	.652
G. Hendrick, STL	.318	M. Schmidt, PHI	.524	A. Dawson, MON	32	P. Perez, ATL	.652
R. Knight, HOU	.304	D. Evans, SF	.516	D. Evans, SF	30	L. Tunnell, PIT	.647

Total Bases		Runs Batted In		Stolen Bases		Saves	
A. Dawson, MON	341	D. Murphy, ATL	121	T. Raines, MON	90	L. Smith, CHI	29
D. Murphy, ATL	318	A. Dawson, MON	113	A. Wiggins, SD	66	A. Holland, PHI	25
P. Guerrero, LA	310	M. Schmidt, PHI	109	S. Sax, LA	56	G. Minton, SF	22
D. Thon, HOU	283	P. Guerrero, LA	103	M. Wilson, NY	54	B. Sutter, STL	21
M. Schmidt, PHI	280	T. Kennedy, SD	98	L. Smith, STL	43	J. Reardon, MON	21

Hits		Base on Balls		Home Run Percentage		Fewest Hits/9 Innings	
J. Cruz, HOU	189	M. Schmidt, PHI	128	M. Schmidt, PHI	7.5	N. Ryan, HOU	6.14
A. Dawson, MON	189	J. Thompson, PIT	99	D. Murphy, ATL	6.1	M. Soto, CIN	6.81
R. Ramirez, ATL	185	T. Raines, MON	97	D. Evans, SF	5.7	B. Welch, LA	7.24
A. Oliver, MON	184	D. Murphy, ATL	90	P. Guerrero, LA	5.5	A. Hammaker, SF	7.68

Runs Scored		Doubles		Triples		Most Strikeouts/9 Inn.	
T. Raines, MON	133	J. Ray, PIT	38	B. Butler, ATL	13	S. Carlton, PHI	8.72
D. Murphy, ATL	131	A. Oliver, MON	38	O. Moreno, HOU	11	N. Ryan, HOU	8.39
M. Schmidt, PHI	104	B. Buckner, CHI	38	D. Green, STL	10	M. Soto, CIN	7.96
A. Dawson, MON	104	G. Carter, MON	37	A. Dawson, MON	10	McWilliams, PIT	7.53

PITCHING LEADERS

Earned Run Average		Wins	
A. Hammaker, SF	2.25	J. Denny, PHI	19
J. Denny, PHI	2.37	Gullickson, MON	17
B. Welch, LA	2.65	S. Rogers, MON	17
M. Soto, CIN	2.70	M. Soto, CIN	17
A. Pena, LA	2.75	C. Lea, MON	16

Strikeouts		Complete Games	
S. Carlton, PHI	275	M. Soto, CIN	18
M. Soto, CIN	242	S. Rogers, MON	13
McWilliams, PIT	199	Gullickson, MON	10
Valenzuela, LA	189	D. Dravecky, SD	9
N. Ryan, HOU	183	Valenzuela, LA	9
		J. Niekro, HOU	9

Shutouts		Fewest Walks/9 Innings	
S. Rogers, MON	5	A. Hammaker, SF	1.67
C. Lea, MON	4	D. Ruthven, CHI, PHI	1.87
McWilliams, PIT	4	J. Denny, PHI	1.97
Valenzuela, LA	4	J. Reuss, LA	2.01

Innings		Games Pitched	
S. Carlton, PHI	284	B. Campbell, CHI	82
M. Soto, CIN	274	K. Tekulve, PIT	76
S. Rogers, MON	273	G. Hernandez, CHI, PHI	74
J. Niekro, HOU	264	G. Minton, SF	73

NATIONAL LEAGUE 1983, *cont.*

		W	L	PCT	GB	R	OR	2B	3B	HR	BA	SA	SB	E	DP	FA	CG	BB	SO	ShO	SV	ERA
										Batting					**Fielding**				**Pitching**			
East	Philadelphia	90	72	.556		696	635	209	45	125	.249	.373	143	152	117	.976	20	**464**	**1092**	10	41	3.34
	Pittsburgh	84	78	.519	6	659	648	238	29	121	.264	.383	124	115	165	.982	25	563	1061	14	41	3.55
	Montreal	82	80	.506	8	677	646	297	41	102	.264	.386	138	116	130	.981	**38**	479	899	**15**	34	3.58
	St. Louis	79	83	.488	11	679	710	262	**63**	83	.270	.384	**207**	152	173	.976	22	525	709	10	27	3.79
	Chicago	71	91	.438	19	701	719	272	42	140	.261	**.401**	84	115	164	**.982**	9	498	807	10	42	4.07
	New York	68	94	.420	22	575	680	172	26	112	.241	.344	141	151	171	.976	18	615	717	7	33	3.68
West	Los Angeles	91	71	.562		654	**609**	197	34	**146**	.250	.379	166	168	132	.974	27	495	1000	12	40	**3.10**
	Atlanta	88	74	.543	3	**746**	640	218	45	130	**.272**	**.400**	146	137	**176**	.978	18	540	895	4	**48**	3.67
	Houston	85	77	.525	6	643	646	239	60	97	.257	.375	164	147	165	.977	22	570	904	14	**48**	3.45
	San Diego	81	81	.500	10	653	653	207	34	93	.250	.351	179	129	135	.979	23	528	850	5	44	3.62
	San Francisco	79	83	.488	12	687	697	206	30	142	.247	.375	140	171	109	.973	20	520	881	9	47	3.70
	Cincinnati	74	88	.457	17	623	710	236	35	107	.239	.356	154	**114**	121	.981	34	627	934	5	29	3.98
						7993	7993	2753	484	1398	.255	.376	1786	1667	1758	.978	276	6424	10749	115	474	3.63

AMERICAN LEAGUE 1983

		POS	Player	AB	BA	HR	RBI	PO	A	E	DP	TC/G	FA	Pitcher	G	IP	W	L	SV	ERA
East	**Baltimore**	1B	E. Murray	582	.306	33	111	1393	114	10	136	**9.9**	.993	S. McGregor	36	260	18	7	0	3.18
		2B	R. Dauer	459	.235	5	41	273	322	7	78	4.6	.988	S. Davis	34	200	13	7	0	3.59
	W-98 L-64	SS	C. Ripken	**663**	.318	27	102	272	**534**	25	113	5.1	.970	M. Boddicker	27	179	16	8	0	2.77
		3B	T. Cruz	221	.208	3	27	49	162	13	19	2.8	.942	D. Martinez	32	153	7	16	0	5.53
	Joe Altobelli	RF	D. Ford	407	.280	9	55	218	2	3	0	2.2	.987	S. Stewart	58	144	9	4	7	3.62
		CF	J. Shelby	325	.258	5	27	200	9	4	3	1.9	.981	M. Flanagan	20	125	12	4	0	3.30
		LF	Lowenstein	310	.281	15	60	155	8	3	1	1.6	.982	T. Martinez	65	103	9	3	21	2.35
		C	R. Dempsey	347	.231	4	32	591	65	2	7	5.1	**.997**	T. Stoddard	47	58	4	3	9	6.09
		DH	K. Singleton	507	.276	18	84													
		OF	A. Bumbry	378	.275	3	31	235	3	3	1	2.3	.988							
		OF	G. Roenicke	323	.260	19	64	159	7	3	0	1.7	.982							
		3B	L. Hernandez	203	.246	6	26	44	109	13	3	2.6	.922							
		OF	J. Dwyer	196	.286	8	38	85	1	3	1	1.6	.966							
		C	J. Nolan	184	.277	5	24	223	16	5	2	3.8	.980							
	Detroit	1B	E. Cabell	392	.311	5	46	830	79	3	76	8.6	.997	J. Morris	37	**294**	20	13	0	3.34
		2B	L. Whitaker	643	.320	12	72	299	447	13	92	4.7	.983	D. Petry	38	266	19	11	0	3.92
	W-92 L-70	SS	A. Trammell	505	.319	14	66	236	367	13	71	4.4	.979	M. Wilcox	26	186	11	10	0	3.97
		3B	T. Brookens	332	.214	6	32	54	164	17	21	2.3	.928	J. Berenguer	37	158	9	5	1	3.14
	Sparky Anderson	RF	G. Wilson	503	.268	11	65	225	12	3	2	1.7	.988	A. Lopez	57	115	9	8	18	2.81
		CF	C. Lemon	491	.255	24	69	406	6	5	3	2.9	.988	D. Rozema	29	105	8	3	2	3.43
		LF	L. Herndon	603	.302	20	92	283	6	**15**	1	2.3	.951	H. Bailey	33	72	5	5	4	4.88
		C	L. Parrish	605	.269	27	114	695	73	4	8	**5.9**	.995	D. Bair	27	56	7	3	4	3.88
		DH	K. Gibson	401	.227	15	51													
		UT	Wockenfuss	245	.269	9	44	225	21	2	10		.992							
		1B	R. Leach	242	.248	3	26	447	45	3	37	6.8	.994							
		OD	J. Grubb	134	.254	4	22	34	1	0	0	1.3	1.000							
	New York	1B	K. Griffey	458	.306	11	46	830	57	7	82	8.9	.992	R. Guidry	31	250	21	9	0	3.42
		2B	W. Randolph	420	.279	2	38	265	298	12	77	5.5	.979	S. Rawley	34	238	14	14	1	3.78
	W-91 L-71	SS	R. Smalley	451	.275	18	62	125	230	15	40	4.1	.959	D. Righetti	31	217	14	8	0	3.44
		3B	G. Nettles	462	.266	20	75	78	273	16	18	2.9	.956	G. Frazier	61	115	4	4	8	3.43
	Billy Martin	RF	S. Kemp	373	.241	12	49	215	5	3	3	2.2	.987	B. Shirley	25	108	5	8	0	5.08
		CF	J. Mumphrey	267	.262	7	36	227	7	4	1	2.9	.983	R. Fontenot	15	97	8	2	0	3.33
		LF	D. Winfield	598	.283	32	116	313	5	7	2	2.2	.978	G. Gossage	57	87	13	5	22	2.27
		C	B. Wynegar	301	.296	6	42	480	29	8	4	5.6	.985							
		DH	D. Baylor	534	.303	21	85													
		SS	A. Robertson	322	.248	1	22	91	242	14	49	4.4	.960							
		O1	D. Mattingly	279	.283	4	32	350	15	3	31		.992							
		C	R. Cerone	246	.220	2	22	412	18	4	2	5.6	.991							
		OD	O. Gamble	180	.261	7	26	64	1	4	1	2.2	.942							
	Toronto	1B	W. Upshaw	579	.306	27	104	1294	117	**21**	131	9.0	.985	D. Stieb	36	278	17	12	0	3.04
		2B	D. Garcia	525	.307	3	38	266	360	12	75	4.9	.981	J. Clancy	34	223	15	11	0	3.91
	W-89 L-73	SS	A. Griffin	528	.250	4	47	**280**	413	25	84	4.6	.965	L. Leal	35	217	13	12	0	4.31
		3B	R. Mulliniks	364	.275	10	49	70	161	7	12	2.1	.971	J. Gott	34	177	9	14	0	4.74
	Bobby Cox	RF	J. Barfield	388	.253	27	68	213	16	8	4	2.0	.966	D. Alexander	17	117	7	6	0	3.93
		CF	L. Moseby	539	.315	18	81	399	10	7	1	2.8	.983	R. Jackson	49	92	8	3	7	4.50
		LF	D. Collins	402	.271	1	34	251	8	3	1	2.3	.989	McLaughlin	50	65	7	4	9	4.45
		C	E. Whitt	344	.256	17	56	554	50	5	4	5.1	.992	R. Moffitt	45	57	6	2	10	3.77
		DH	C. Johnson	407	.265	22	76													
		OF	B. Bonnell	377	.318	10	54	212	7	3	0	1.9	.986							
		32	G. Iorg	375	.275	2	39	105	223	9	31		.973							
		DH	J. Orta	245	.237	10	38													
		C	B. Martinez	221	.253	10	33	331	25	4	3	4.2	.989							

AMERICAN LEAGUE 1983, *cont.*

	POS	Player	AB	BA	HR	RBI	PO	A	E	DP	TC/G	FA	Pitcher	G	IP	W	L	SV	ERA
Milwaukee W-87 L-75 Harvey Kuenn	1B	C. Cooper	661	.307	30	**126**	**1452**	87	11	**144**	9.8	.993	M. Caldwell	32	228	12	11	0	4.53
	2B	J. Gantner	603	.282	11	74	374	512	14	**128**	5.7	.984	D. Sutton	31	220	8	13	0	4.08
	SS	R. Yount	578	.308	17	80	256	420	19	86	5.0	.973	M. Haas	25	179	13	3	0	3.27
	3B	P. Molitor	608	.270	15	47	105	343	16	37	3.2	.966	B. McClure	24	142	9	9	0	4.50
	RF	C. Moore	529	.284	2	49	301	9	7	1	2.1	.978	C. Porter	25	134	7	9	0	4.50
	CF	R. Manning	375	.229	3	33	325*	1	3	0	3.0		J. Slaton	46	112	14	6	5	4.33
	LF	B. Oglivie	411	.280	13	66	259	8	4	1	2.4	.985	T. Tellmann	44	100	9	4	8	2.80
	C	T. Simmons	600	.308	13	108	395	41	11	4	5.2	.975	P. Ladd	44	49	3	4	25	2.55
	DH	R. Howell	194	.278	4	25													
	C	N. Yost	196	.224	6	28	252	16	8	2	4.5	.971							
	OF	M. Brouhard	185	.276	7	23	112	1	1	0	2.7	.991							
	OF	G. Thomas	164	.183	5	18	126	0	1	0	2.8	.992							
Boston W-78 L-84 Ralph Houk	1B	D. Stapleton	542	.247	10	66	1242	95	9	129	9.3	.993	J. Tudor	34	242	13	12	0	4.09
	2B	J. Remy	592	.275	0	43	295	376	7	104	4.7	.990	B. Hurst	33	211	12	12	0	4.09
	SS	G. Hoffman	473	.260	4	41	240	417	26	82	4.8	.962	D. Eckersley	28	176	9	13	0	5.61
	3B	W. Boggs	582	**.361**	5	74	118	368	**27**	40	3.4	.947	B. Ojeda	29	174	12	7	0	4.04
	RF	D. Evans	470	.238	22	58	222	6	3	1	2.3	.987	B. Stanley	64	145	8	10	33	2.85
	CF	T. Armas	574	.218	36	107	326	5	5	0	2.9	.985	M. Brown	19	104	6	6	0	4.67
	LF	J. Rice	626	.305	**39**	**126**	339	21	6	5	2.4	.984	O. Boyd	15	99	4	8	0	3.28
	C	G. Allenson	230	.230	3	30	393	29	7	6	5.1	.984	M. Clear	48	96	4	5	6	6.28
	DH	Yastrzemski	380	.266	10	56							L. Aponte	34	62	5	4	3	3.63
	OF	R. Nichols	274	.285	6	22	168	4	1	1	2.4	.994							
	OF	R. Miller	262	.286	2	21	141	4	1	1	2.2	.993							
	C	R. Gedman	204	.294	2	18	274	26	6	5	4.4	.980							
Cleveland W-70 L-92 Mike Ferraro W-40 L-60 Pat Corrales W-30 L-32	1B	M. Hargrove	469	.286	3	57	1098	115	7	131	9.3	.994	R. Sutcliffe	36	243	17	11	0	4.29
	2B	M. Trillo	320	.272	1	29	172	269	5	58	5.1	.989	L. Sorensen	36	223	12	11	0	4.24
	SS	J. Franco	560	.273	8	80	247	438	28	92	4.8	.961	B. Blyleven	24	156	7	10	0	3.91
	3B	T. Harrah	526	.266	9	53	101	273	11	32	2.8	**.971**	N. Heaton	39	149	11	7	7	4.16
	RF	G. Vukovich	312	.247	3	44	203	3	3	0	1.7	.986	L. Barker	24	150	8	13	0	5.11
	CF	G. Thomas	371	.221	17	51	313	7	6	2	3.1	.982	Eichelberger	28	134	4	11	0	4.90
	LF	A. Bannister	377	.265	5	45	148	7	5	2	1.8	.969	D. Spillner	60	92	2	9	8	5.07
	C	R. Hassey	341	.270	6	42	514	43	3	4	5.0	.995	B. Anderson	39	68	1	6	7	4.08
	DH	A. Thornton	508	.281	17	77													
	OF	P. Tabler	430	.291	6	65	180	4	10	0	2.4	.948							
	OF	B. McBride	230	.291	1	18	81	4	2	1	1.9	.977							
	2B	M. Fischlin	225	.209	2	23	151	179	12	46	4.8	.965							
	OF	R. Manning	194	.278	1	10	146*	1	2	0	3.0								
	UT	B. Perkins	184	.272	0	24	148	6	2	12		.987							
West **Chicago** W-99 L-63 Tony LaRussa	1B	M. Squires	153	.222	1	11	515	40	2	55	4.5	**.996**	L. Hoyt	36	261	**24**	10	0	3.66
	2B	J. Cruz	334	.251	1	40	213	298	9	71	5.4	.983	R. Dotson	35	240	22	7	0	3.23
	SS	J. Dybzinski	256	.230	1	32	140	252	14	47	3.4	.966	F. Bannister	34	217	16	10	0	3.35
	3B	V. Law	408	.243	4	42	91	309	14	28	3.0	.966	B. Burns	29	174	10	11	0	3.58
	RF	H. Baines	596	.280	20	99	312	10	9	3	2.1	.973	J. Koosman	37	170	11	7	2	4.77
	CF	R. Law	501	.283	3	34	302	5	2	2	2.3	**.994**	D. Lamp	49	116	7	7	15	3.71
	LF	R. Kittle	520	.254	35	100	234	7	9	1	1.8	.964	D. Tidrow	50	92	2	4	7	4.22
	C	C. Fisk	488	.289	26	86	**709**	46	7	5	5.7	.991	S. Barojas	52	87	3	3	12	2.47
	DH	G. Luzinski	502	.255	32	95							J. Agosto	39	42	2	2	7	4.10
	1O	T. Paciorek	420	.307	9	63	629	38	1	42		.999							
	1B	G. Walker	307	.270	10	55	426	19	7	40	7.7	.985							
	SS	S. Fletcher	262	.237	3	31	107	275	14	52	4.0	.965							
	2B	T. Bernazard	233	.262	2	26	96	189	7	38	4.9	.976							
	OF	J. Hairston	126	.294	5	22	29	1	1	0	1.0	.968							
Kansas City W-79 L-83 Dick Howser	1B	W. Aikens	410	.302	23	72	884	64	11	101	8.6	.989	L. Gura	34	200	11	**18**	0	4.90
	2B	F. White	549	.260	11	77	390	442	8	123	5.8	**.990**	B. Black	24	161	10	7	0	3.79
	SS	Washington	547	.236	5	41	201	448	**36**	91	4.9	.947	Splittorff	27	156	13	8	0	3.63
	3B	G. Brett	464	.310	25	93	85	188	24	25	2.9	.919	Quisenberry	69	139	5	3	45	1.94
	RF	A. Otis	356	.261	4	41	233	6	1	1	2.5	.996	S. Renko	25	121	6	11	1	4.30
	CF	W. Wilson	576	.276	2	33	354	3	9	0	2.5	.975	M. Armstrong	58	103	10	7	3	3.86
	LF	P. Sheridan	333	.270	7	36	237	6	3	2	2.5	.988							
	C	J. Wathan	437	.245	2	32	360	32	6	5	4.3	.985							
	DH	H. McRae	589	.311	12	82													
	C	D. Slaught	276	.312	0	28	299	18	12	7	4.2	.964							
	UT	Concepcion	219	.242	0	20	92	175	15	35		.947							
	OF	L. Roberts	213	.258	8	24	139	3	3	0	1.9	.979							
Texas W-77 L-85 Doug Rader	1B	P. O'Brien	524	.237	8	53	1144	**120**	9	104	9.6	.993	C. Hough	34	252	15	13	0	3.18
	2B	W. Tolleson	470	.260	3	20	246	315	16	69	5.2	.972	M. Smithson	33	223	10	14	0	3.91
	SS	B. Dent	417	.237	2	34	150	369	11	71	4.1	**.979**	D. Darwin	28	183	8	13	0	3.49
	3B	B. Bell	618	.277	14	66	123	**383**	17	29	**3.4**	.967	R. Honeycutt	25	175	14	8	0	**2.42**
	RF	L. Parrish	555	.272	26	88	215	11	9	1	1.8	.962	F. Tanana	29	159	7	9	0	3.16
	CF	G. Wright	634	.276	18	80	460	6	7	1	2.9	.985	J. Butcher	36	123	6	6	5	3.51
	LF	B. Sample	554	.274	12	57	329	8	4	0	2.3	.988	O. Jones	42	67	3	6	10	3.09
	C	J. Sundberg	378	.201	2	28	618	56	5	2	5.2	.993	D. Tobik	27	44	2	1	9	3.68
	DH	D. Hostetler	304	.220	11	46													
	DO	M. Rivers	309	.285	1	20	48	1	1	0	2.2	.980							
	UT	B. Stein	232	.310	2	33	222	103	5	40		.985							
	C	B. Johnson	175	.211	5	16	252	15	0	4	4.3	1.000							

AMERICAN LEAGUE 1983, *cont.*

	POS	Player	AB	BA	HR	RBI	PO	A	E	DP	TC/G	FA	Pitcher	G	IP	W	L	SV	ERA
Oakland	1B	W. Gross	339	.233	12	44	426	21	2	41	6.1	.996	C. Codiroli	37	206	12	12	1	4.46
	2B	D. Lopes	494	.277	17	67	254	278	9	81	4.4	.983	S. McCatty	38	167	6	9	5	3.99
W-74 L-88	SS	T. Phillips	412	.248	4	35	112	257	23	59	3.9	.941	T. Conroy	39	162	7	10	0	3.94
	3B	C. Lansford	299	.308	10	45	60	163	10	19	3.0	.957	T. Underwood	51	145	9	7	4	4.04
Steve Boros	RF	M. Davis	443	.275	8	62	278	16	8	4	2.5	.974	B. Krueger	17	110	7	6	0	3.61
	CF	D. Murphy	471	.227	17	75	365	7	8	0	3.1	.979	T. Burgmeier	49	96	6	7	4	2.81
	LF	R. Henderson	513	.292	9	48	349	9	3	1	2.5	.992	K. Atherton	29	68	2	5	4	2.77
	C	B. Kearney	298	.255	8	32	437	41	9	5	4.8	.982	D. Beard	43	61	5	5	10	5.61
	DH	J. Burroughs	401	.269	10	56							S. Baker	35	54	3	3	5	4.33
	UT	B. Almon	451	.266	4	63	327	176	20	33		.962							
	C	M. Heath	345	.281	6	33	316	47	10	6	4.7	.973							
	O1	G. Hancock	256	.273	8	30	249	10	4	17		.985							
	OF	R. Peters	178	.287	0	20	141	3	2	1	3.1	.986							
	UT	D. Meyer	169	.189	1	13	305	16	4	28		.988							
California	1B	R. Carew	472	.339	2	44	890	42	6	94	10.5	.994	T. John	34	235	11	13	0	4.33
	2B	B. Grich	387	.292	16	62	270	415	22	94	6.0	.969	K. Forsch	31	219	11	12	0	4.06
W-70 L-92	SS	T. Foli	330	.252	2	29	115	274	10	51	5.4	.975	G. Zahn	29	203	9	11	0	3.33
	3B	D. DeCinces	370	.281	18	65	79	216	14	26	3.7	.955	M. Witt	43	154	7	14	5	4.91
John McNamara	RF	E. Valentine	271	.240	13	43	152	5	6	1	1.9	.963	B. Kison	26	127	11	5	2	4.05
	CF	F. Lynn	437	.272	22	74	274	8	2	4	2.5	.993	L. Sanchez	56	98	10	8	7	3.66
	LF	B. Downing	403	.246	19	53	160	9	1	0	2.0	.994							
	C	B. Boone	468	.256	9	52	606	83	14	12	5.0	.980							
	DH	R. Jackson	397	.194	14	49													
	UT	R. Jackson	348	.230	8	39	402	114	13	43		.975							
	OF	J. Beniquez	315	.305	3	34	174	8	6	1	2.2	.968							
	1D	D. Sconiers	314	.274	8	46	473	23	7	46	8.8	.986							
	OF	B. Clark	212	.231	5	21	122	0	0	0	1.7	1.000							
	UT	R. Wilfong	177	.254	2	17	107	144	2	33		.992							
Minnesota	1B	K. Hrbek	515	.297	16	84	1151	89	13	125	9.1	.990	F. Viola	35	210	7	15	0	5.49
	2B	J. Castino	563	.277	11	57	301	406	7	94	5.4	.990	K. Schrom	33	196	15	8	0	3.71
W-70 L-92	SS	Washington	317	.246	4	26	121	204	13	49	4.2	.962	A. Williams	36	193	11	14	1	4.14
	3B	G. Gaetti	584	.245	21	78	131	360	17	46	3.3	.967	B. Castillo	27	158	8	12	0	4.77
Billy Gardner	RF	T. Brunansky	542	.227	28	82	375	16	6	8	2.7	.985	R. Lysander	61	125	5	12	3	3.38
	CF	D. Brown	309	.272	0	22	188	2	1	0	2.4	.995	R. Davis	66	89	5	8	30	3.34
	LF	G. Ward	623	.278	19	88	374	24	9	6	2.7	.978	B. Havens	16	80	5	8	0	8.18
	C	D. Engle	374	.305	8	43	299	26	9	3	4.6	.973	Whitehouse	60	74	7	1	2	4.15
	DH	R. Bush	373	.249	11	56													
	OD	M. Hatcher	375	.317	9	47	137	4	3	1	2.6	.979							
	SS	L. Faedo	173	.277	1	18	53	133	9	22	3.8	.954							
	C	T. Laudner	168	.185	6	18	259	22	4	5	5.0	.986							
Seattle	1B	P. Putnam	469	.269	19	67	1067	85	7	105	9.3	.994	M. Young	33	204	11	15	0	3.27
	2B	T. Bernazard	300	.267	6	30	166	233	12	51	5.2	.971	J. Beattie	30	197	10	15	0	3.84
W-60 L-102	SS	S. Owen	306	.196	2	21	122	233	11	45	4.6	.970	B. Stoddard	35	176	9	17	0	4.41
	3B	J. Allen	273	.223	4	21	55	155	9	16	2.7	.959	B. Clark	41	162	7	10	0	3.94
Rene Lachemann	RF	R. Nelson	291	.254	5	36	122	10	4	1	1.5	.971	M. Moore	22	128	6	8	0	4.71
W-26 L-47	CF	D. Henderson	484	.269	17	55	304	17	6	4	2.5	.982	G. Perry	16	102	3	10	0	4.94
	LF	S. Henderson	436	.294	10	54	182	15	6	2	1.8	.970	B. Caudill	63	73	2	8	26	4.71
Del Crandall	C	R. Sweet	249	.221	1	22	413	34	6	6	5.3	.987	M. Stanton	50	65	2	3	7	3.32
W-34 L-55	DH	R. Zisk	285	.242	12	36							Vande Berg	68	64	2	4	5	3.36
	OD	A. Cowens	356	.205	7	35	124	7	2	1	1.9	.985							
	SS	T. Cruz	216	.190	7	21	97	224	12	42	5.3	.964							
	3B	M. Castillo	203	.207	0	24	35	101	4	9	2.5	.971							
	OF	R. Roenicke	198	.253	4	23	124	12	1	3	2.5	.993							
	2B	J. Cruz	181	.254	2	12	131	173	5	41	5.2	.984							
	C	O. Mercado	178	.197	1	16	342	27	2	2	5.7	.995							

BATTING AND BASE RUNNING LEADERS

Batting Average
W. Boggs, BOS	.361
R. Carew, CAL	.339
L. Whitaker, DET	.320
A. Trammell, DET	.319
C. Ripken, BAL	.318

Slugging Average
G. Brett, KC	.563
J. Rice, BOS	.550
E. Murray, BAL	.538
C. Fisk, CHI	.518
C. Ripken, BAL	.517

Home Runs
J. Rice, BOS	39
T. Armas, BOS	36
R. Kittle, CHI	35
E. Murray, BAL	33
G. Luzinski, CHI	32
D. Winfield, NY	32

Winning Percentage
M. Haas, MIL	.813
R. Dotson, CHI	.759
S. McGregor, BAL	.720
L. Hoyt, CHI	.706
R. Guidry, NY	.700

PITCHING LEADERS

Earned Run Average
R. Honeycutt, TEX	2.42
M. Boddicker, BAL	2.77
D. Stieb, TOR	3.04
C. Hough, TEX	3.18
S. McGregor, BAL	3.18

Wins
L. Hoyt, CHI	24
R. Dotson, CHI	22
R. Guidry, NY	21
J. Morris, DET	20
D. Petry, DET	19

Total Bases
J. Rice, BOS	344
C. Ripken, BAL	343
C. Cooper, MIL	336
E. Murray, BAL	313
D. Winfield, NY	307

Runs Batted In
J. Rice, BOS	126
C. Cooper, MIL	126
D. Winfield, NY	116
L. Parrish, DET	114
E. Murray, BAL	111

Stolen Bases
R. Henderson, OAK	108
R. Law, CHI	77
W. Wilson, KC	59
J. Cruz, CHI, SEA	57
B. Sample, TEX	44

Saves
Quisenberry, KC	45
B. Stanley, BOS	33
R. Davis, MIN	30
B. Caudill, SEA	26
P. Ladd, MIL	25

Strikeouts
J. Morris, DET	232
F. Bannister, CHI	193
D. Stieb, TOR	187
D. Righetti, NY	169
R. Sutcliffe, CLE	160

Complete Games
R. Guidry, NY	21
J. Morris, DET	20
D. Stieb, TOR	14
S. Rawley, NY	13
S. McGregor, BAL	12

AMERICAN LEAGUE 1983, *cont.*

BATTING AND BASE RUNNING LEADERS

Hits			Base on Balls			Home Run Percentage			Fewest Hits/9 Innings			Shutouts			Fewest Walks/9 Innings		
C. Ripken, BAL	211		R. Henderson, OAK	103		R. Kittle, CHI	6.7		M. Boddicker, BAL	7.09		M. Boddicker, BAL	5		L. Hoyt, CHI	1.07
W. Boggs, BOS	210		K. Singleton, BAL	99		G. Luzinski, CHI	6.4		D. Stieb, TOR	7.22		B. Burns, CHI	4		S. McGregor, BAL	1.56
L. Whitaker, DET	206		W. Boggs, BOS	92		T. Armas, BOS	6.3		T. Conroy, OAK	7.82		D. Stieb, TOR	4		T. John, CAL	1.88
C. Cooper, MIL	203		A. Thornton, CLE	87		J. Rice, BOS	6.2		C. Hough, TEX	7.82					R. Honeycutt, TEX	1.91

Runs Scored			Doubles			Triples			Most Strikeouts/9 Inn.			Innings			Games Pitched		
C. Ripken, BAL	121		C. Ripken, BAL	47		R. Yount, MIL	10		F. Bannister, CHI	7.99		J. Morris, DET	294		Quisenberry, KC	69
E. Murray, BAL	115		W. Boggs, BOS	44		K. Gibson, DET	9		J. Morris, DET	7.11		D. Stieb, TOR	278		Vande Berg, SEA	68
C. Cooper, MIL	106		R. Yount, MIL	42		A. Griffin, TOR	9		D. Righetti, NY	7.01		D. Petry, DET	266		R. Davis, MIN	66
R. Henderson, OAK	105		L. Parrish, DET	42		L. Herndon, DET	9		T. Conroy, OAK	6.21		L. Hoyt, CHI	261		T. Martinez, BAL	65

		W	L	PCT	GB	R	OR	2B	3B	HR	BA	SA	SB	E	DP	FA	CG	BB	SO	ShO	SV	ERA
										Batting					**Fielding**			**Pitching**				
East	Baltimore	98	64	.605		799	652	283	27	**168**	.269	.421	61	121	159	.981	36	452	774	**15**	38	3.63
	Detroit	92	70	.568	6	789	679	283	53	156	.274	.427	93	125	142	.980	42	522	875	9	28	3.80
	New York	91	71	.562	7	770	703	269	40	153	.273	.416	84	139	157	.978	**47**	455	892	12	32	3.85
	Toronto	89	73	.549	9	795	726	268	**58**	167	**.277**	**.436**	131	115	148	.981	43	517	835	8	32	4.12
	Milwaukee	87	75	.537	11	764	708	281	57	132	.277	.418	101	**113**	162	.982	35	491	689	10	43	4.02
	Boston	78	84	.481	20	724	775	**287**	32	142	.270	.409	30	130	168	.979	29	493	767	7	42	4.34
	Cleveland	70	92	.432	28	704	785	249	31	86	.265	.369	109	122	174	.980	34	529	794	8	25	4.43
West	Chicago	99	63	.611		**800**	650	270	42	157	.262	.413	165	120	158	.981	35	**447**	877	12	48	3.67
	Kansas City	79	83	.488	20	696	767	273	54	109	.271	.397	182	165	178	.974	19	471	593	9	**49**	4.25
	Texas	77	85	.475	22	639	**609**	242	33	106	.255	.366	119	**113**	150	**.982**	43	471	826	11	32	**3.31**
	Oakland	74	88	.457	25	708	782	237	28	121	.262	.381	**235**	157	157	.974	22	626	719	12	33	4.35
	California	70	92	.432	29	722	779	241	22	154	.260	.393	41	154	**190**	.977	39	496	668	7	23	4.31
	Minnesota	70	92	.432	29	709	822	280	41	141	.261	.401	44	121	170	.980	20	580	748	5	39	4.67
	Seattle	60	102	.370	39	558	740	247	31	111	.240	.360	144	136	159	.978	25	544	**910**	9	39	4.12
						10177	10177	3710	549	1903	.266	.401	1539	1831	2272	.979	469	7094	10967	133	503	4.06

NATIONAL LEAGUE 1984

		POS	Player	AB	BA	HR	RBI	PO	A	E	DP	TC/G	FA	Pitcher	G	IP	W	L	SV	ERA
East	**Chicago**	1B	L. Durham	473	.279	23	96	1162	96	7	96	9.7	.994	S. Trout	32	190	13	7	0	3.41
		2B	R. Sandberg	636	.314	19	84	314	**550**	6	102	5.6	**.993**	D. Eckersley	24	160	10	8	0	3.03
	W-96 L-65	SS	L. Bowa	391	.223	0	17	217	378	16	64	4.6	.974	R. Sutcliffe	20	150	16	1	0	2.69
		3B	R. Cey	505	.240	25	97	97	230	11	22	2.3	.967	S. Sanderson	24	141	8	5	0	3.14
	Jim Frey	RF	K. Moreland	495	.279	16	80	154	6	4	0	1.6	.976	D. Ruthven	23	127	6	10	0	5.04
		CF	B. Dernier	536	.278	3	32	355	5	5	1	2.6	.986	L. Smith	69	101	9	7	33	3.65
		LF	G. Matthews	491	.291	14	82	224	7	11	0	1.7	.955	R. Reuschel	19	92	5	5	0	5.17
		C	J. Davis	523	.256	19	94	811	89	**15**	9	6.3	.984	T. Stoddard	58	92	10	6	7	3.82
		OF	M. Hall	150	.280	4	22	69	5	3	2	1.7	.961	C. Rainey	17	88	5	7	0	4.28
	New York	1B	K. Hernandez	550	.311	15	94	1214	**142**	8	**127**	8.9	.994	D. Gooden	31	218	17	9	0	2.60
		2B	W. Backman	436	.280	1	26	218	295	10	72	4.5	.981	W. Terrell	33	215	11	12	0	3.52
	W-90 L-72	SS	J. Oquendo	189	.222	0	10	95	152	7	33	3.8	.972	R. Darling	33	206	12	9	0	3.81
		3B	H. Brooks	561	.283	16	73	79	211	22	22	2.4	.929	E. Lynch	40	124	9	8	2	4.50
	Davey Johnson	RF	Strawberry	522	.251	26	97	276	11	6	3	2.0	.980	B. Berenyi	19	115	9	6	0	3.76
		CF	M. Wilson	587	.276	10	54	396	8	4	6	2.8	.990	S. Fernandez	15	90	6	6	0	3.50
		LF	G. Foster	553	.269	24	86	278	6	7	1	2.1	.976	J. Orosco	60	87	10	6	31	2.59
		C	Fitzgerald	360	.242	2	33	715	47	4	6	**7.2**	**.995**	D. Sisk	50	78	1	3	15	2.09
		S2	Gardenhire	207	.246	1	10	96	143	10	20		.960							
		OF	D. Heep	199	.231	1	12	86	1	3	1	1.9	.967							
		2B	K. Chapman	197	.289	3	23	104	130	5	32	4.3	.979							
	St. Louis	1B	D. Green	452	.268	15	65	1088	69	10	98	**10.0**	.991	J. Andujar	36	**261**	**20**	14	0	3.34
		2B	T. Herr	558	.276	4	49	328	452	6	**106**	5.5	.992	D. LaPoint	33	193	12	10	0	3.96
	W-84 L-78	SS	O. Smith	412	.257	1	44	233	437	12	**94**	5.5	**.982**	D. Cox	29	156	9	11	0	4.03
		3B	T. Pendleton	262	.324	1	33	59	155	13	10	3.4	.943	R. Horton	37	126	9	4	1	3.44
	Whitey Herzog	RF	G. Hendrick	441	.277	9	69	188	9	2	1	1.7	.990	B. Sutter	71	123	5	7	45	1.54
		CF	W. McGee	571	.291	6	50	374	10	6	4	2.8	.985	N. Allen	57	119	9	6	3	3.55
		LF	L. Smith	504	.250	6	49	184	**18**	11	0	1.5	.948	K. Kepshire	17	109	6	5	0	3.30
		C	D. Porter	422	.232	11	68	620	58	11	6	5.6	.984							
		UT	A. Van Slyke	361	.244	7	50	357	82	8	40		.982							
		OF	T. Landrum	173	.272	3	26	93	1	2	0	1.1	.979							

NATIONAL LEAGUE 1984, *cont.*

	POS	Player	AB	BA	HR	RBI	PO	A	E	DP	TC/G	FA	Pitcher	G	IP	W	L	SV	ERA
Philadelphia	1B	L. Matuszek	262	.248	12	43	643	55	7	40	8.7	.990	S. Carlton	33	229	13	7	0	3.58
	2B	J. Samuel	701	.272	15	69	388	438	33	77	5.4	.962	J. Koosman	36	224	14	15	0	3.25
W-81 L-81	SS	I. DeJesus	435	.257	0	35	166	400	29	57	4.2	.951	C. Hudson	30	174	9	11	0	4.04
	3B	M. Schmidt	528	.277	36	106	85	329	26	19	3.0	.941	J. Denny	22	154	7	7	0	2.45
Paul Owens	RF	S. Lezcano	256	.277	14	40	151	3	3	0	1.8	.981	K. Gross	44	129	8	5	1	4.12
	CF	V. Hayes	561	.292	16	67	341	2	4	1	2.3	.988	S. Rawley	18	120	10	6	0	3.81
	LF	G. Wilson	341	.240	6	31	147	4	5	0	1.4	.968	A. Holland	68	98	5	10	29	3.39
	C	O. Virgil	456	.261	18	68	722	58	6	6	5.7	.992	L. Andersen	64	91	3	7	4	2.38
	OF	G. Maddox	241	.282	5	19	160	3	0	1	2.4	1.000	B. Campbell	57	81	6	5	1	3.43
	1B	T. Corcoran	208	.341	5	36	318	21	1	20	6.7	.997							
	O1	G. Gross	202	.322	0	16	195	13	2	9		.990							
	OF	J. Stone	185	.362	1	15	75	1	7	0	1.8	.916							
	1C	Wockenfuss	180	.289	6	24	323	20	7	21		.980							
Montreal	1B	T. Francona	214	.346	1	18	427	49	3	43	9.6	.994	Gullickson	32	227	12	9	0	3.61
	2B	D. Flynn	366	.243	0	17	148	223	8	47	4.3	.979	C. Lea	30	224	15	10	0	2.89
W-78 L-83	SS	A. Salazar	174	.155	0	12	88	155	10	35	3.2	.960	B. Smith	28	179	12	13	0	3.32
	3B	T. Wallach	582	.246	18	72	162	332	21	29	3.2	.959	S. Rogers	31	169	6	15	0	4.31
Bill Virdon	RF	A. Dawson	533	.248	17	86	297	11	8	2	2.4	.975	Schatzeder	36	136	7	7	1	2.71
W-64 L-67	CF	T. Raines	622	.309	8	60	420	8	5	1	2.7	.988	D. Palmer	20	105	7	3	0	3.84
	LF	J. Wohlford	213	.300	5	29	85	3	1	1	1.5	.989	B. James	62	96	6	6	10	3.66
Jim Fanning	C	G. Carter	596	.294	27	106	772	65	6	6	5.9	.993	J. Reardon	68	87	7	7	23	2.90
W-14 L-16	10	P. Rose	278	.259	0	23	349	44	6	22		.985	G. Lucas	55	53	0	3	8	2.72
	2B	B. Little	266	.244	0	9	137	197	6	44	4.4	.982							
	UT	D. Thomas	243	.255	0	20	118	135	10	33		.962							
	OF	M. Stenhouse	175	.183	4	16	67	4	1	2	1.5	.986							
	1B	D. Driessen	169	.254	9	32	363	23	2	38	8.6	.995							
	OF	M. Dilone	169	.278	1	10	76	1	1	0	1.9	.987							
Pittsburgh	1B	J. Thompson	543	.254	17	74	1337	74	14	111	9.4	.990	R. Rhoden	33	238	14	9	0	2.72
	2B	J. Ray	555	.312	6	67	331	400	12	90	5.0	.984	McWilliams	34	227	12	11	1	2.93
W-75 L-87	SS	D. Berra	450	.222	9	52	186	449	30	65	4.9	.955	J. Tudor	32	212	12	11	0	3.27
	3B	B. Madlock	403	.253	4	44	66	176	15	17	2.6	.942	J. DeLeon	30	192	7	13	0	3.74
Chuck Tanner	RF	L. Lacy	474	.321	12	70	268	15	1	4	2.2	.996	Candelaria	33	185	12	11	2	2.72
	CF	M. Wynne	653	.266	0	39	373	8	4	1	2.5	.990	D. Robinson	51	122	5	6	10	3.02
	LF	L. Mazzilli	266	.237	4	21	92	2	1	0	1.3	.989	K. Tekulve	72	88	3	9	13	2.66
	C	T. Pena	546	.286	15	78	895	95	9	15	6.8	.991	R. Scurry	43	46	5	6	4	2.53
	32	J. Morrison	304	.286	11	45	81	163	10	21		.961							
	OF	D. Frobel	276	.203	12	28	188	9	9	3	1.8	.956							
West **San Diego**	1B	S. Garvey	617	.284	8	86	1232	87	0	117	8.2	1.000	E. Show	32	207	15	9	0	3.40
	2B	A. Wiggins	596	.258	3	34	391	410	32	95	5.3	.962	T. Lollar	31	196	11	13	0	3.91
W-92 L-70	SS	G. Templeton	493	.258	2	35	225	407	26	79	4.5	.960	E. Whitson	31	189	14	8	0	3.24
	3B	G. Nettles	395	.228	20	65	93	201	20	14	2.6	.936	M. Thurmond	32	179	14	8	0	2.97
Dick Williams	RF	T. Gwynn	606	.351	5	71	345	11	4	4	2.3	.989	D. Dravecky	50	157	9	8	8	2.93
	CF	McReynolds	525	.278	20	75	422	10	4	1	3.0	.991	A. Hawkins	36	146	8	9	0	4.68
	LF	C. Martinez	488	.250	13	66	312	15	8	4	2.4	.976	C. Lefferts	62	106	3	4	10	2.13
	C	T. Kennedy	530	.240	14	57	708	54	14	6	5.3	.982	G. Gossage	62	102	10	6	25	2.90
	30	L. Salazar	228	.241	3	17	84	92	6	5		.967							
	OF	B. Brown	171	.251	3	29	100	2	3	0	2.0	.971							
Atlanta	1B	C. Chambliss	389	.257	9	44	996	70	8	84	9.9	.993	R. Mahler	38	222	13	10	0	3.12
	2B	G. Hubbard	397	.234	9	43	237	405	8	78	5.6	.988	P. Perez	30	212	14	8	0	3.74
W-80 L-82	SS	R. Ramirez	591	.266	2	48	251	443	30	94	5.0	.959	C. McMurtry	37	183	9	17	0	4.32
	3B	R. Johnson	294	.279	5	30	44	171	14	14	2.8	.939	R. Camp	31	149	8	6	0	3.27
Joe Torre	RF	Washington	416	.286	17	61	170	4	6	0	1.7	.967	L. Barker	21	126	7	8	0	3.85
	CF	D. Murphy	607	.290	36	100	369	10	5	1	2.4	.987	P. Falcone	35	120	5	7	2	4.13
	LF	G. Perry	347	.265	7	47	74	2	6	0	1.5	.927	G. Garber	62	106	3	6	11	3.06
	C	B. Benedict	300	.223	4	25	504	37	5	2	5.7	.991	S. Bedrosian	40	84	9	6	11	2.37
	OF	B. Komminsk	301	.203	8	36	135	2	1	0	1.7	.993	J. Dedmon	54	81	4	3	4	3.78
	C	A. Trevino	266	.244	3	28	399	60	5	5	5.9	.989	D. Moore	47	64	4	5	16	2.94
	UT	J. Royster	227	.207	1	21	99	162	9	23		.967							
	3B	K. Oberkfell	172	.233	1	10	31	77	4	8	2.5	.964							
Houston	1B	E. Cabell	436	.310	8	44	971	66	7	97	9.3	.993	J. Niekro	38	248	16	12	0	3.04
	2B	B. Doran	548	.261	4	41	261	419	10	83	5.0	.986	B. Knepper	35	234	15	10	0	3.20
W-80 L-82	SS	C. Reynolds	527	.260	6	60	212	472	25	91	5.0	.965	N. Ryan	30	184	12	11	0	3.04
	3B	P. Garner	374	.278	4	45	71	163	5	16	2.9	.979	M. Scott	31	154	5	11	0	4.68
Bob Lillis	RF	T. Puhl	449	.301	9	55	213	6	3	4	1.8	.986	M. LaCoss	39	132	7	5	3	4.02
	CF	J. Mumphrey	524	.290	9	83	317	5	4	2	2.4	.988	B. Dawley	60	98	11	4	5	1.93
	LF	J. Cruz	600	.312	12	95	310	11	8	1	2.1	.976	V. Ruhle	40	90	1	9	2	4.58
	C	M. Bailey	344	.212	9	34	629	56	12	4	6.5	.983	D. Smith	53	77	5	4	5	2.21
	OF	K. Bass	331	.260	2	29	149	4	4	2	1.9	.975	F. DiPino	57	75	4	9	14	3.35
	31	R. Knight	278	.223	2	29	236	95	7	22		.979							
	3B	D. Walling	249	.281	3	31	30	100	6	14	2.6	.956							
	C	A. Ashby	191	.262	4	27	303	42	5	3	5.6	.986							

NATIONAL LEAGUE 1984, *cont.*

Los Angeles
W-79 L-83

Tom Lasorda

POS	Player	AB	BA	HR	RBI	PO	A	E	DP	TC/G	FA	Pitcher	G	IP	W	L	SV	ERA
1B	G. Brock	271	.225	14	34	703	65	4	61	9.3	.995	Valenzuela	34	261	12	17	0	3.03
2B	S. Sax	569	.243	1	35	318	450	21	99	5.6	.973	A. Pena	28	199	12	6	0	2.48
SS	D. Anderson	374	.251	3	34	169	334	18	63	4.7	.965	O. Hershiser	45	190	11	8	2	2.66
3B	P. Guerrero	535	.303	16	72	36	141	16	12	2.5	.917	R. Honeycutt	29	184	10	9	0	2.84
RF	C. Maldonado	254	.268	5	28	124	4	6	0	1.3	.955	B. Welch	31	179	13	13	0	3.78
CF	K. Landreaux	438	.251	11	47	212	3	3	2	1.7	.986	B. Hooton	54	110	3	6	4	3.44
LF	M. Marshall	495	.257	21	65	200	9	4	1	1.8	.981	J. Reuss	30	99	5	7	1	3.82
C	M. Scioscia	341	.273	5	38	701	64	12	8	6.9	.985	P. Zachry	58	83	5	6	2	3.81
SS	B. Russell	262	.267	0	19	81	165	9	29	3.9	.965	K. Howell	32	51	5	5	6	3.33
OF	R. Reynolds	240	.258	2	24	104	4	3	1	1.8	.973	Niedenfuer	33	47	2	5	11	2.47
3B	G. Rivera	227	.260	2	17	55	167	15	12	2.6	.937							
1B	F. Stubbs	217	.194	8	17	395	37	3	31	8.5	.993							
C	S. Yeager	197	.228	4	29	317	30	2	1	5.4	.994							
OF	T. Whitfield	180	.244	4	18	76	4	1	0	1.4	.988							

Cincinnati
W-70 L-92

Vern Rapp
W-51 L-70

Pete Rose
W-19 L-22

POS	Player	AB	BA	HR	RBI	PO	A	E	DP	TC/G	FA	Pitcher	G	IP	W	L	SV	ERA
1B	D. Driessen	218	.280	7	28	507	29	5	31	7.7	.991	M. Soto	33	237	18	7	0	3.53
2B	R. Oester	553	.242	3	38	357	388	15	75	5.2	.980	J. Russell	33	182	6	18	0	4.26
SS	Concepcion	531	.245	4	58	156	247	9	41	4.0	.978	J. Price	30	172	7	13	0	4.19
3B	N. Esasky	322	.193	10	45	51	130	18	8	2.4	.910	T. Hume	54	113	4	13	3	5.64
RF	D. Parker	607	.285	16	94	296	6	8	1	2.1	.974	T. Power	78	109	9	7	11	2.82
CF	E. Milner	336	.232	7	29	285	8	5	4	2.8	.983	J. Tibbs	14	101	6	2	0	2.86
LF	G. Redus	394	.254	7	22	200	6	7	3	1.9	.967	F. Pastore	24	98	3	8	0	6.50
C	B. Gulden	292	.226	4	33	485	53	14	8	5.5	.975	B. Owchinko	49	94	3	5	2	4.12
O1	C. Cedeno	380	.276	10	47	355	21	7	16		.982	J. Franco	54	79	6	2	4	2.61
SS	T. Foley	277	.253	5	27	104	197	11	31	3.8	.965	B. Berenyi	13	51	3	7	0	6.00
OF	D. Walker	195	.292	10	28	110	3	6	0	1.8	.950							
C	Bilardello	182	.209	2	10	323	34	3	3	5.3	.992							
3B	Krenchicki	181	.298	6	22	25	91	4	5	1.9	.967							
OF	E. Davis	174	.224	10	30	125	4	1	2	2.5	.992							

San Francisco
W-66 L-96

Frank Robinson
W-42 L-64

Danny Ozark
W-24 L-32

POS	Player	AB	BA	HR	RBI	PO	A	E	DP	TC/G	FA	Pitcher	G	IP	W	L	SV	ERA
1B	S. Thompson	245	.306	1	31	555	36	1	48	6.8	.998	B. Laskey	35	208	9	14	0	4.33
2B	M. Trillo	401	.254	4	36	215	287	6	67	5.3	.988	M. Krukow	35	199	11	12	1	4.56
SS	J. LeMaster	451	.217	4	32	222	391	23	70	4.9	.964	M. Davis	46	175	5	17	0	5.36
3B	Youngblood	469	.254	10	51	87	195	36	11	2.7	.887	J. Robinson	34	172	7	15	0	4.56
RF	C. Davis	499	.315	21	81	292	9	9	2	2.5	.971	G. Minton	74	124	4	9	19	3.76
CF	D. Gladden	342	.351	4	31	232	8	3	1	2.9	.988	F. Williams	61	106	9	4	3	3.55
LF	J. Leonard	514	.302	21	86	247	14	8	4	2.1	.970	G. Lavelle	77	101	5	4	12	2.76
C	B. Brenly	506	.291	20	80	635	69	10	4	5.6	.986	R. Lerch	37	72	5	3	2	4.23
1B	A. Oliver	339	.298	0	34	665	55	11	50	8.9	.985							
UT	B. Wellman	265	.226	2	25	151	258	11	37		.974							
OF	D. Baker	243	.292	3	32	112	1	3	0	1.9	.974							
OF	J. Clark	203	.320	11	44	94	3	1	0	1.8	.990							

BATTING AND BASE RUNNING LEADERS

Batting Average

T. Gwynn, SD	.351
L. Lacy, PIT	.321
C. Davis, SF	.315
R. Sandberg, CHI	.314
J. Ray, PIT	.312

Slugging Average

D. Murphy, ATL	.547
M. Schmidt, PHI	.536
R. Sandberg, CHI	.520
C. Davis, SF	.507
L. Durham, CHI	.505

Home Runs

M. Schmidt, PHI	36
D. Murphy, ATL	36
G. Carter, MON	27
Strawberry, NY	26
R. Cey, CHI	25

Total Bases

D. Murphy, ATL	332
R. Sandberg, CHI	331
J. Samuel, PHI	310
G. Carter, MON	290
M. Schmidt, PHI	283

Runs Batted In

M. Schmidt, PHI	106
G. Carter, MON	106
D. Murphy, ATL	100
R. Cey, CHI	97
Strawberry, NY	97

Stolen Bases

T. Raines, MON	75
J. Samuel, PHI	72
A. Wiggins, SD	70
L. Smith, STL	50
G. Redus, CIN	48
V. Hayes, PHI	48

Hits

T. Gwynn, SD	213
R. Sandberg, CHI	200
T. Raines, MON	192
J. Samuel, PHI	191

Base on Balls

G. Matthews, CHI	103
K. Hernandez, NY	97
M. Schmidt, PHI	92
J. Thompson, PIT	87

Home Run Percentage

M. Schmidt, PHI	6.8
D. Murphy, ATL	5.9
Strawberry, NY	5.0
R. Cey, CHI	5.0

Runs Scored

R. Sandberg, CHI	114
A. Wiggins, SD	106
T. Raines, MON	106
J. Samuel, PHI	105

Doubles

J. Ray, PIT	38
T. Raines, MON	38
R. Sandberg, CHI	36
J. Samuel, PHI	36

Triples

R. Sandberg, CHI	19
J. Samuel, PHI	19
J. Cruz, HOU	13

PITCHING LEADERS

Winning Percentage

M. Soto, CIN	.720
A. Pena, LA	.667
D. Gooden, NY	.654
S. Carlton, PHI	.650
S. Trout, CHI	.650

Earned Run Average

A. Pena, LA	2.48
D. Gooden, NY	2.60
O. Hershiser, LA	2.66
R. Rhoden, PIT	2.72
Candelaria, PIT	2.72

Wins

J. Andujar, STL	20
M. Soto, CIN	18
D. Gooden, NY	17
R. Sutcliffe, CHI	16
J. Niekro, HOU	16

Saves

B. Sutter, STL	45
L. Smith, CHI	33
J. Orosco, NY	31
A. Holland, PHI	29
G. Gossage, SD	25

Strikeouts

D. Gooden, NY	276
Valenzuela, LA	240
N. Ryan, HOU	197
M. Soto, CIN	185
S. Carlton, PHI	163

Complete Games

M. Soto, CIN	13
Valenzuela, LA	12
J. Andujar, STL	12
B. Knepper, HOU	11
R. Mahler, ATL	9

Fewest Hits/9 Innings

D. Gooden, NY	6.65
M. Soto, CIN	6.86
J. DeLeon, PIT	6.88
N. Ryan, HOU	7.01

Shutouts

O. Hershiser, LA	4
A. Pena, LA	4
J. Andujar, STL	4

Fewest Walks/9 Innings

Gullickson, MON	1.47
Candelaria, PIT	1.65
E. Whitson, SD	2.00
A. Pena, LA	2.08

Most Strikeouts/9 Inn.

D. Gooden, NY	11.39
N. Ryan, HOU	9.65
Valenzuela, LA	8.28
B. Berenyi, CIN, NY	7.26

Innings

J. Andujar, STL	261
Valenzuela, LA	261
J. Niekro, HOU	248
R. Rhoden, PIT	238

Games Pitched

T. Power, CIN	78
G. Lavelle, SF	77
G. Minton, SF	74
K. Tekulve, PIT	72

NATIONAL LEAGUE 1984, *cont.*

		W	L	PCT	GB	R	OR	2B	3B	HR	BA	SA	SB	E	DP	FA	CG	BB	SO	ShO	SV	ERA
										Batting					Fielding				Pitching			
East	Chicago	96	65	.596		**762**	658	239	47	136	.260	.397	154	121	137	.981	19	**442**	879	8	50	3.75
	New York	90	72	.556	6.5	652	676	235	25	107	.257	.369	149	129	154	.979	12	573	1028	15	50	3.60
	St. Louis	84	78	.519	12.5	652	645	225	44	75	.252	.351	**220**	118	184	.982	19	494	808	12	**51**	3.58
	Philadelphia	81	81	.500	15.5	720	690	**248**	51	**147**	**.266**	**.407**	186	161	112	.975	11	448	904	6	48	3.62
	Montreal	78	83	.484	18	593	585	242	36	96	.251	.362	131	132	147	.978	19	474	861	10	48	3.31
	Pittsburgh	75	87	.463	21.5	615	**567**	237	33	98	.255	.363	96	128	142	.980	27	502	995	13	34	**3.11**
West	San Diego	92	70	.568		686	634	207	42	109	.259	.371	152	138	144	.978	13	563	812	**17**	44	3.48
	Atlanta	80	82	.494	12	632	655	234	27	111	.247	.361	140	139	153	.978	17	525	859	7	49	3.57
	Houston	80	82	.494	12	693	630	222	**67**	79	.264	.371	105	133	160	.979	24	502	950	13	29	3.32
	Los Angeles	79	83	.488	13	580	600	213	23	102	.244	.348	109	163	146	.975	**39**	499	**1033**	16	27	3.17
	Cincinnati	70	92	.432	22	627	747	238	30	106	.244	.356	160	139	116	.977	25	578	946	6	25	4.16
	San Francisco	66	96	.407	26	682	807	229	26	112	.265	.375	126	173	134	.973	9	549	854	7	38	4.39
						7894	7894	2769	451	1278	.255	.369	1728	1674	1729	.978	234	6149	10929	130	480	3.59

AMERICAN LEAGUE 1984

		POS	Player	AB	BA	HR	RBI	PO	A	E	DP	TC/G	FA	Pitcher	G	IP	W	L	SV	ERA
East	**Detroit**	1B	D. Bergman	271	.273	7	44	657	75	8	63	6.5	.989	J. Morris	35	241	19	11	0	3.65
		2B	L. Whitaker	558	.289	13	56	290	405	15	83	5.0	.979	D. Petry	35	233	18	8	0	3.24
	W-104 L-58	SS	A. Trammell	555	.314	14	69	180	314	10	71	4.4	.980	M. Wilcox	33	194	17	8	0	4.00
		3B	H. Johnson	355	.248	12	50	58	143	12	16	2.0	.944	J. Berenguer	31	168	11	10	0	3.48
	Sparky Anderson	RF	K. Gibson	531	.282	27	91	245	4	**12**	2	1.9	.954	G. Hernandez	**80**	140	9	3	32	1.92
		CF	C. Lemon	509	.287	20	76	427	6	2	1	3.1	.995	A. Lopez	71	138	10	1	14	2.94
		LF	L. Herndon	407	.280	7	43	199	7	3	0	1.8	.986	D. Rozema	29	101	7	6	0	3.74
		C	L. Parrish	578	.237	33	98	720	67	7	**11**	6.3	.991	D. Bair	47	94	5	3	4	3.75
		DH	D. Evans	401	.232	16	63													
		UT	B. Garbey	327	.287	5	52	411	58	12	53		.975							
		UT	T. Brookens	224	.246	5	26	98	187	12	35		.960							
		OF	R. Jones	215	.284	12	37	150	4	0	1	2.1	1.000							
		OD	J. Grubb	176	.267	8	17	47	0	0	0	1.3	1.000							
		OF	R. Kuntz	140	.286	2	22	74	2	1	1	1.1	.987							
	Toronto	1B	W. Upshaw	569	.278	19	84	1246	103	14	133	9.0	.990	D. Stieb	35	**267**	16	8	0	2.83
		2B	D. Garcia	633	.284	5	46	267	427	14	95	4.8	.980	D. Alexander	36	262	17	6	0	3.13
	W-89 L-73	SS	A. Griffin	419	.241	4	30	189	269	18	65	4.1	.962	L. Leal	35	222	13	8	0	3.89
		3B	R. Mulliniks	343	.324	3	42	65	148	7	8	1.8	**.968**	J. Clancy	36	220	13	15	0	5.12
	Bobby Cox	RF	G. Bell	606	.292	26	87	289	11	9	1	2.1	.971	J. Gott	35	110	7	6	2	4.02
		CF	L. Moseby	592	.280	18	92	473	8	5	2	3.1	.990	R. Jackson	54	86	7	8	10	3.56
		LF	D. Collins	441	.308	2	44	203	8	2	3	2.0	.991	D. Lamp	56	85	8	8	9	4.55
		C	E. Whitt	315	.238	15	46	583	40	4	8	5.3	.994	J. Key	63	62	4	5	10	4.65
		DH	C. Johnson	359	.304	16	61													
		OF	J. Barfield	320	.284	14	49	190	9	10	5	2.4	.952							
		3B	G. Iorg	247	.227	1	25	62	110	10	15	1.6	.945							
		DH	W. Aikens	234	.205	11	26													
		SS	T. Fernandez	233	.270	3	19	116	178	8	40	4.1	.974							
		C	B. Martinez	232	.220	5	37	360	34	2	5	4.0	.995							
	New York	1B	D. Mattingly	603	**.343**	23	110	1107	124	5	135	9.3	**.996**	P. Niekro	32	216	16	8	0	3.09
		2B	W. Randolph	564	.287	2	31	334	419	13	**112**	5.4	.983	R. Guidry	29	196	10	11	0	4.51
	W-87 L-75	SS	B. Meacham	360	.253	2	25	136	269	19	52	4.4	.955	R. Fontenot	33	169	8	9	0	3.61
		3B	T. Harrah	253	.217	1	27	51	128	6	17	2.5	.968	D. Rasmussen	24	148	9	6	0	4.57
	Yogi Berra	RF	D. Winfield	567	.340	19	100	306	3	2	1	2.2	.994	B. Shirley	41	114	3	3	0	3.38
		CF	O. Moreno	355	.259	4	38	262	9	4	2	2.5	.985	J. Howell	61	104	9	4	7	2.69
		LF	S. Kemp	313	.291	7	41	138	2	4	0	1.9	.972	D. Righetti	64	96	5	6	31	2.34
		C	B. Wynegar	442	.267	6	45	757	59	6	9	6.5	.993	J. Cowley	16	83	9	2	0	3.56
		DH	D. Baylor	493	.262	27	89							J. Rijo	24	62	2	8	2	4.76
		OF	K. Griffey	399	.273	7	56	181	6	5	0	2.3	.974							
		UT	R. Smalley	209	.239	7	26	66	99	12	17		.932							
		3B	Pagliarulo	201	.239	7	34	44	106	7	16	2.3	.955							
		UT	T. Foli	163	.252	0	16	88	122	6	32		.972							
		OF	B. Dayett	127	.244	4	23	80	3	1	0	1.4	.988							
		DO	O. Gamble	125	.184	10	27	15	1	0	0	1.3	1.000							
	Boston	1B	B. Buckner	439	.278	11	67	974	96	**15**	75	9.6	.986	B. Hurst	33	218	12	12	0	3.92
		2B	M. Barrett	475	.303	3	45	245	417	9	67	4.9	**.987**	B. Ojeda	33	217	12	12	0	3.99
	W-86 L-76	SS	J. Gutierrez	449	.263	2	29	228	347	31	60	4.0	.949	O. Boyd	29	198	12	12	0	4.37
		3B	W. Boggs	625	.325	6	55	141	330	**20**	30	3.2	.959	A. Nipper	29	183	11	6	0	3.89
	Ralph Houk	RF	D. Evans	630	.295	32	104	311	7	2	2	2.2	.994	R. Clemens	21	133	9	4	0	4.32
		CF	T. Armas	639	.268	**43**	**123**	329	4	9	2	2.7	.974	B. Stanley	57	107	9	10	22	3.54
		LF	J. Rice	657	.280	28	122	336	12	4	3	2.2	.989	M. Clear	47	67	8	3	8	4.03
		C	R. Gedman	449	.269	24	72	693	58	**18**	5	6.2	.977							
		DH	M. Easler	601	.313	27	91													

AMERICAN LEAGUE 1984, *cont.*

		POS	Player	AB	BA	HR	RBI	PO	A	E	DP	TC/G	FA	Pitcher	G	IP	W	L	SV	ERA
	Baltimore	1B	E. Murray	588	.306	29	110	**1538**	**143**	13	152	10.7	.992	M. Boddicker	34	261	**20**	11	0	**2.79**
		2B	R. Dauer	397	.254	2	24	225	325	11	76	4.6	.980	M. Flanagan	34	227	13	13	0	3.53
	W-85 L-77	SS	C. Ripken	641	.304	27	86	**297**	**583**	26	122	5.6	.971	S. Davis	35	225	14	9	1	3.12
		3B	W. Gross	342	.216	22	64	64	205	18	13	2.5	.937	S. McGregor	30	196	15	12	0	3.94
	Joe Altobelli	RF	M. Young	401	.252	17	52	216	4	4	0	1.9	.982	D. Martinez	34	142	6	9	0	5.02
		CF	J. Shelby	383	.209	6	30	261	9	2	1	2.2	.993	S. Stewart	60	93	7	4	13	3.29
		LF	G. Roenicke	326	.224	10	44	197	6	1	0	1.7	.995	T. Martinez	55	90	4	9	17	3.91
		C	R. Dempsey	330	.230	11	34	453	43	4	5	4.6	.992							
		DH	K. Singleton	363	.215	6	36													
		OF	A. Bumbry	344	.270	3	24	230	7	3	1	2.4	.988							
		OF	Lowenstein	270	.237	8	28	94	5	3	0	1.5	.971							
		C	F. Rayford	250	.256	4	27	287	35	3	2	4.9	.991							
		OF	J. Dwyer	161	.255	2	21	83	3	3	1	1.7	.966							
		DH	B. Ayala	118	.212	4	24													
	Cleveland	1B	M. Hargrove	352	.267	2	44	790	83	8	86	7.1	.991	B. Blyleven	33	245	19	7	0	2.87
		2B	T. Bernazard	439	.221	2	38	264	397	20	85	5.0	.971	N. Heaton	38	199	12	15	0	5.21
	W-75 L-87	SS	J. Franco	658	.286	3	79	280	481	36	116	5.0	.955	S. Comer	22	117	4	8	0	5.68
		3B	B. Jacoby	439	.264	7	40	86	187	14	17	2.3	.951	S. Farr	31	116	3	11	1	4.58
	Pat Corrales	RF	G. Vukovich	437	.304	9	60	316	13	2	5	2.5	.994	E. Camacho	69	100	5	9	23	2.43
		CF	B. Butler	602	.269	3	49	448	13	4	3	3.0	.991	T. Waddell	58	97	7	4	6	3.06
		LF	M. Hall	257	.257	7	30	143	3	1	0	2.1	.993	R. Smith	22	86	5	5	0	4.59
		C	J. Willard	246	.224	10	37	335	35	7	7	5.0	.981							
		DH	A. Thornton	587	.271	33	99													
		UT	P. Tabler	473	.290	10	68	532	89	7	54		.989							
		OF	J. Carter	244	.275	13	41	122	9	6	0	2.3	.956							
		C	C. Bando	220	.291	12	41	305	30	6	4	5.4	.982							
		OF	C. Castillo	211	.261	10	36	123	2	9	0	1.9	.933							
	Milwaukee	1B	C. Cooper	603	.275	11	67	1061	98	10	106	9.6	.991	D. Sutton	33	213	14	12	0	3.77
		2B	J. Gantner	613	.282	3	56	**362**	469	13	111	5.5	.985	M. Haas	31	189	9	11	0	3.99
	W-67 L-94	SS	R. Yount	624	.298	16	80	199	402	18	80	5.2	.971	J. Cocanower	33	175	8	16	0	4.02
		3B	E. Romero	357	.252	1	31	38	111	9	13	2.7	.943	B. McClure	39	140	4	8	1	4.38
	Rene Lachemann	RF	D. James	387	.295	1	30	252	7	3	1	2.2	.989	M. Caldwell	26	126	6	13	0	4.64
		CF	R. Manning	341	.249	7	31	231	2	3	2	2.1	.987	P. Ladd	54	91	4	9	3	5.24
		LF	B. Oglivie	461	.262	12	60	256	6	8	1	1.9	.970	C. Porter	17	81	6	4	0	3.87
		C	J. Sundberg	348	.261	7	43	556	55	3	6	5.6	**.995**	T. Tellmann	50	81	6	3	4	2.78
		DH	T. Simmons	497	.221	4	52							R. Fingers	33	46	1	2	23	1.96
		C	B. Schroeder	210	.257	14	25	274	24	4	2	5.2	.987							
		OF	M. Brouhard	197	.239	6	22	107	6	2	2	2.2	.983							
		OF	C. Moore	188	.234	2	17	119	2	2	0	2.0	.984							
		OF	B. Clark	169	.260	2	16	106	0	2	0	1.9	.981							
		3B	R. Howell	164	.232	4	17	21	67	9	7	2.1	.907							
		3B	W. Lozado	107	.271	1	20	23	51	6	7	2.2	.925							
West	**Kansas City**	1B	S. Balboni	438	.244	28	77	1102	79	15	102	9.6	.987	B. Black	35	257	17	12	0	3.12
		2B	F. White	479	.271	17	56	299	425	11	97	5.7	.985	M. Gubicza	29	189	10	14	0	4.05
	W-84 L-78	SS	Concepcion	287	.282	1	23	105	280	11	53	4.7	.972	L. Gura	31	169	12	9	0	5.18
		3B	G. Brett	377	.284	13	69	59	201	14	18	2.7	.949	Saberhagen	38	158	10	11	1	3.48
	Dick Howser	RF	P. Sheridan	481	.283	8	53	273	8	4	1	1.9	.986	C. Leibrandt	23	144	11	7	0	3.63
		CF	W. Wilson	541	.301	2	44	383	6	4	2	3.1	.990	Quisenberry	72	129	6	3	44	2.64
		LF	D. Motley	522	.284	15	70	301	7	5	2	2.3	.984	J. Beckwith	49	101	8	4	2	3.40
		C	D. Slaught	409	.264	4	42	547	44	11	8	4.9	.982							
		DH	H. McRae	317	.303	3	42													
		DH	J. Orta	403	.298	9	50													
		3B	G. Pryor	270	.263	4	25	59	138	6	13	1.9	.970							
		1O	D. Iorg	235	.255	5	30	399	22	3	33		.993							
		C1	J. Wathan	171	.181	2	10	304	31	6	10		.982							
		SS	Washington	170	.224	1	10	81	166	10	40	4.2	.961							
	California	1B	R. Carew	329	.295	3	31	724	59	15	73	9.6	.981	M. Witt	34	247	15	11	0	3.47
		2B	R. Wilfong	307	.248	6	33	161	266	11	48	4.5	.975	R. Romanick	33	230	12	12	0	3.76
	W-81 L-81	SS	D. Schofield	400	.193	4	21	218	420	12	95	4.6	**.982**	G. Zahn	28	199	13	10	0	3.12
		3B	D. DeCinces	547	.269	20	82	107	266	14	22	2.8	.964	T. John	32	181	7	13	0	4.52
	John McNamara	RF	F. Lynn	517	.271	23	79	321	12	6	5	2.4	.982	J. Slaton	32	163	7	10	0	4.97
		CF	G. Pettis	397	.227	2	29	337	11	6	4	2.6	.983	D. Corbett	45	85	5	1	4	2.12
		LF	B. Downing	539	.275	23	91	272	5	0	0	2.1	**1.000**	L. Sanchez	49	84	9	7	11	3.33
		C	B. Boone	450	.202	3	32	660	**71**	12	10	5.4	.984	B. Kison	20	65	4	5	2	5.37
		DH	R. Jackson	525	.223	25	81							D. Aase	23	39	4	1	8	1.62
		UT	B. Grich	363	.256	18	58	311	282	12	84		.980							
		OF	J. Beniquez	354	.336	8	39	197	5	6	1	2.1	.971							
		OF	M. Brown	148	.284	7	22	57	4	2	0	1.4	.968							

AMERICAN LEAGUE 1984, *cont.*

Minnesota
W-81 L-81

Billy Gardner

POS	Player	AB	BA	HR	RBI	PO	A	E	DP	TC/G	FA	Pitcher	G	IP	W	L	SV	ERA
1B	K. Hrbek	559	.311	27	107	1320	99	14	113	9.7	.990	F. Viola	35	258	18	12	0	3.21
2B	T. Teufel	568	.262	14	61	315	485	13	81	5.2	.984	M. Smithson	36	252	15	13	0	3.68
SS	H. Jimenez	298	.201	0	19	145	273	18	59	4.1	.959	J. Butcher	34	225	13	11	0	3.44
3B	G. Gaetti	588	.262	5	65	142	334	20	26	3.2	.960	K. Schrom	25	137	5	11	0	4.47
RF	T. Brunansky	567	.252	32	85	304	13	5	6	2.1	.984	P. Filson	55	119	6	5	1	4.10
CF	K. Puckett	557	.296	0	31	438	16	3	4	3.6	.993	E. Hodge	25	100	4	3	0	4.77
LF	M. Hatcher	576	.302	5	69	249	11	7	1	2.7	.974	R. Davis	64	83	7	11	29	4.55
C	D. Engle	391	.266	4	38	376	34	8	3	4.9	.981	R. Lysander	36	57	4	3	5	3.65
DH	R. Bush	311	.225	11	43													
C	T. Laudner	262	.206	10	35	362	38	9	2	5.0	.978							
OF	D. Brown	260	.273	1	19	144	4	1	0	2.7	.993							
SS	Washington	197	.294	3	23	60	114	4	19	2.5	.978							

Oakland
W-77 L-85

Steve Boros
W-20 L-24

Jackie Moore
W-57 L-61

POS	Player	AB	BA	HR	RBI	PO	A	E	DP	TC/G	FA	Pitcher	G	IP	W	L	SV	ERA
1B	B. Bochte	469	.264	5	52	1048	66	8	119	7.8	.993	R. Burris	34	212	13	10	0	3.15
2B	J. Morgan	365	.244	6	43	201	229	10	62	4.4	.977	L. Sorensen	46	183	6	13	1	4.91
SS	T. Phillips	451	.266	4	37	133	235	23	54	4.3	.941	S. McCatty	33	180	8	14	0	4.76
3B	C. Lansford	597	.300	14	74	137	268	18	27	2.8	.957	B. Krueger	26	142	10	10	0	4.75
RF	M. Davis	382	.230	9	46	287	6	12	4	2.4	.961	C. Young	20	109	9	4	0	4.06
CF	D. Murphy	559	.256	33	88	474	14	6	2	3.2	.988	K. Atherton	57	104	7	6	2	4.33
LF	R. Henderson	502	.293	16	58	341	7	11	1	2.6	.969	B. Caudill	68	96	9	7	36	2.71
C	M. Heath	475	.248	13	64	423	54	7	7	4.5	.986	C. Codiroli	28	89	6	4	1	5.84
DH	D. Kingman	549	.268	35	118													
UT	D. Lopes	230	.257	9	36	99	47	6	10		.961							
UT	B. Almon	211	.223	7	16	255	15	2	19		.993							
SS	D. Hill	174	.230	2	16	99	125	12	28	3.6	.949							

Chicago
W-74 L-88

Tony LaRussa

POS	Player	AB	BA	HR	RBI	PO	A	E	DP	TC/G	FA	Pitcher	G	IP	W	L	SV	ERA
1B	G. Walker	442	.294	24	75	791	51	4	66	8.4	.995	R. Dotson	32	246	14	15	0	3.59
2B	J. Cruz	415	.222	5	43	273	452	18	92	5.3	.976	T. Seaver	34	237	15	11	0	3.95
SS	S. Fletcher	456	.250	3	35	193	381	16	75	4.4	.973	L. Hoyt	34	236	13	18	0	4.47
3B	V. Law	481	.252	17	59	79	199	13	24	2.1	.955	F. Bannister	34	218	14	11	0	4.83
RF	H. Baines	569	.304	29	94	307	8	6	1	2.2	.981	B. Burns	34	117	4	12	3	5.00
CF	R. Law	487	.251	6	37	322	5	5	2	2.6	.985	R. Reed	51	73	0	6	12	3.08
LF	R. Kittle	466	.215	32	74	226	14	7	2	2.0	.972	J. Agosto	49	55	2	1	7	3.09
C	C. Fisk	359	.231	21	43	421	38	6	4	5.2	.987							
DH	G. Luzinski	412	.238	13	58													
10	T. Paciorek	363	.256	4	29	596	25	6	50		.990							
OD	J. Hairston	227	.260	5	19	57	2	2	0	1.6	.967							
C	M. Hill	193	.233	5	20	308	17	3	4	4.6	.991							

Seattle
W-74 L-88

Del Crandall
W-59 L-76

Chuck Cottier
W-15 L-12

POS	Player	AB	BA	HR	RBI	PO	A	E	DP	TC/G	FA	Pitcher	G	IP	W	L	SV	ERA
1B	A. Davis	567	.284	27	116	1271	94	11	108	9.4	.992	M. Langston	35	225	17	10	0	3.40
2B	J. Perconte	612	.294	0	31	303	438	14	90	5.0	.981	M. Moore	34	212	7	17	0	4.97
SS	S. Owen	530	.245	3	43	245	463	17	86	4.8	.977	J. Beattie	32	211	12	16	0	3.41
3B	J. Presley	251	.227	10	36	48	113	7	12	2.4	.958	Vande Berg	50	130	8	12	7	4.76
RF	A. Cowens	524	.277	15	78	228	8	3	0	1.8	.987	M. Young	22	113	6	8	0	5.72
CF	D. Henderson	350	.280	14	43	242	11	3	3	2.6	.988	S. Barojas	19	95	6	5	1	3.98
LF	S. Henderson	325	.262	10	35	84	4	6	0	1.8	.936	D. Beard	43	76	3	2	5	5.80
C	B. Kearney	431	.225	7	43	823	63	11	9	6.7	.988	E. Nunez	37	68	2	2	7	3.18
DH	K. Phelps	290	.241	24	51							P. Mirabella	52	68	2	5	3	4.37
OF	B. Bonnell	363	.264	8	48	153	8	1	0	1.7	.994	M. Stanton	54	61	4	4	8	3.54
OF	P. Bradley	322	.301	0	24	235	3	2	1	2.1	.992							
UT	L. Milbourne	211	.265	1	22	53	86	12	14		.921							

Texas
W-69 L-92

Doug Rader

POS	Player	AB	BA	HR	RBI	PO	A	E	DP	TC/G	FA	Pitcher	G	IP	W	L	SV	ERA
1B	P. O'Brien	520	.287	18	80	1270	105	11	103	9.8	.992	C. Hough	36	266	16	14	0	3.76
2B	W. Tolleson	338	.213	0	9	191	276	10	61	4.4	.979	F. Tanana	35	246	15	15	0	3.25
SS	C. Wilkerson	484	.248	1	26	151	285	26	50	4.0	.944	D. Darwin	35	224	8	12	0	3.94
3B	B. Bell	553	.315	11	83	129	323	20	28	3.2	.958	D. Stewart	32	192	7	14	0	4.73
RF	G. Ward	602	.284	21	79	376	11	5	1	2.6	.987	M. Mason	36	184	9	13	0	3.61
CF	G. Wright	383	.243	9	48	175	3	3	0	2.3	.983	D. Schmidt	43	70	6	6	12	2.56
LF	B. Sample	489	.247	5	33	285	3	4	2	2.4	.986	D. Tobik	24	42	1	6	5	3.61
C	D. Scott	235	.221	3	20	400	41	12	9	5.7	.974							
DH	L. Parrish	613	.285	22	101													
DO	M. Rivers	313	.300	4	33	49	3	0	2	1.7	1.000							
C	N. Yost	242	.182	6	25	368	20	2	1	5.0	.995							
O1	B. Jones	143	.259	4	22	139	7	1	8		.993							

BATTING AND BASE RUNNING LEADERS

Batting Average		Slugging Average		Home Runs	
D. Mattingly, NY	.343	H. Baines, CHI	.541	T. Armas, BOS	43
D. Winfield, NY	.340	D. Mattingly, NY	.537	D. Kingman, OAK	35
W. Boggs, BOS	.325	D. Evans, BOS	.532	D. Murphy, OAK	33
B. Bell, TEX	.315	T. Armas, BOS	.531	L. Parrish, DET	33
A. Trammell, DET	.314	K. Hrbek, MIN	.522	A. Thornton, CLE	33

PITCHING LEADERS

Winning Percentage		Earned Run Average		Wins	
D. Alexander, TOR	.739	M. Boddicker, BAL	2.79	M. Boddicker, BAL	20
B. Blyleven, CLE	.731	D. Stieb, TOR	2.83	B. Blyleven, CLE	19
D. Petry, DET	.692	B. Blyleven, CLE	2.87	J. Morris, DET	19
M. Wilcox, DET	.680	P. Niekro, NY	3.09	D. Petry, DET	18
P. Niekro, NY	.667	G. Zahn, CAL	3.12	F. Viola, MIN	18
D. Stieb, TOR	.667				

AMERICAN LEAGUE 1984, *cont.*

BATTING AND BASE RUNNING LEADERS

Total Bases
T. Armas, BOS	339
D. Evans, BOS	335
C. Ripken, BAL	327
D. Mattingly, NY	324
M. Easler, BOS	310

Runs Batted In
T. Armas, BOS	123
J. Rice, BOS	122
D. Kingman, OAK	118
A. Davis, SEA	116
E. Murray, BAL	110
D. Mattingly, NY	110

Stolen Bases
R. Henderson, OAK	66
D. Collins, TOR	60
B. Butler, CLE	52
G. Pettis, CAL	48
W. Wilson, KC	47

Hits
D. Mattingly, NY	207
W. Boggs, BOS	203
C. Ripken, BAL	195
D. Winfield, NY	193

Base on Balls
E. Murray, BAL	107
A. Davis, SEA	97
D. Evans, BOS	96
A. Thornton, CLE	91

Home Run Percentage
R. Kittle, CHI	6.9
T. Armas, BOS	6.7
D. Kingman, OAK	6.4
D. Murphy, OAK	5.9

Runs Scored
D. Evans, BOS	121
R. Henderson, OAK	113
W. Boggs, BOS	109
B. Butler, CLE	108

Doubles
D. Mattingly, NY	44
L. Parrish, TEX	42
G. Bell, TOR	39
D. Evans, BOS	37

Triples
D. Collins, TOR	15
L. Moseby, TOR	15
K. Gibson, DET	10
H. Baines, CHI	10

PITCHING LEADERS

Saves
Quisenberry, KC	44
B. Caudill, OAK	36
G. Hernandez, DET	32
D. Righetti, NY	31
R. Davis, MIN	29

Strikeouts
M. Langston, SEA	204
D. Stieb, TOR	198
M. Witt, CAL	196
B. Blyleven, CLE	170
C. Hough, TEX	165

Complete Games
C. Hough, TEX	17
M. Boddicker, BAL	16
R. Dotson, CHI	14
B. Blyleven, CLE	12
J. Beattie, SEA	12

Fewest Hits/9 Innings
D. Stieb, TOR	7.25
B. Blyleven, CLE	7.49
M. Boddicker, BAL	7.51
M. Langston, SEA	7.52

Shutouts
G. Zahn, CAL	5
B. Ojeda, BOS	5
B. Blyleven, CLE	4
T. Seaver, CHI	4

Fewest Walks/9 Innings
L. Hoyt, CHI	1.64
M. Smithson, MIN	1.93
R. Guidry, NY	2.02
D. Alexander, TOR	2.03

Most Strikeouts/9 Inn.
M. Langston, SEA	8.16
M. Witt, CAL	7.15
M. Moore, SEA	6.71
D. Stieb, TOR	6.67

Innings
D. Stieb, TOR	267
C. Hough, TEX	266
D. Alexander, TOR	262
M. Boddicker, BAL	261

Games Pitched
G. Hernandez, DET	80
Quisenberry, KC	72
A. Lopez, DET	71
E. Camacho, CLE	69

	Team	W	L	PCT	GB	R	OR	2B	3B	HR	BA	SA	SB	E	DP	FA	CG	BB	SO	ShO	SV	ERA
East	Detroit	104	58	.642	—	829	643	254	46	187	.271	.432	106	127	162	.979	19	489	914	8	51	3.49
	Toronto	89	73	.549	15	750	696	275	68	143	.273	.421	193	123	166	.980	34	528	875	10	33	3.86
	New York	87	75	.537	17	758	679	276	32	130	.276	.405	62	142	177	.977	15	518	992	12	43	3.78
	Boston	86	76	.531	18	810	764	259	45	181	.283	.441	37	143	127	.977	40	517	927	12	32	4.18
	Baltimore	85	77	.525	19	681	667	234	23	160	.252	.391	51	123	166	.981	48	512	713	13	32	3.72
	Cleveland	75	87	.463	29	761	766	222	39	123	.265	.384	126	146	163	.977	21	545	803	7	35	4.25
	Milwaukee	67	94	.416	36.5	641	734	232	36	96	.262	.370	52	136	156	.978	13	480	785	7	41	4.06
West	Kansas City	84	78	.519	—	673	686	268	52	117	.268	.399	106	131	157	.979	18	433	724	9	50	3.91
	California	81	81	.500	3	696	697	211	30	150	.249	.381	79	128	170	.980	36	474	754	12	26	3.96
	Minnesota	81	81	.500	3	673	675	259	33	114	.265	.385	39	120	133	.980	32	463	713	9	38	3.86
	Oakland	77	85	.475	7	738	796	257	29	158	.259	.404	145	146	159	.975	15	592	695	6	44	4.49
	Chicago	74	88	.457	10	679	736	225	38	172	.247	.395	109	122	160	.981	43	483	840	9	32	4.13
	Seattle	74	88	.457	10	682	774	244	34	129	.258	.384	116	128	141	.979	26	619	972	4	35	4.31
	Texas	69	92	.429	14.5	656	714	227	29	120	.261	.377	80	138	137	.977	38	518	864	6	21	3.91
						10027	10027	3443	534	1980	.264	.398	1301	1853	2174	.979	398	7171	11571	124	513	3.99

NATIONAL LEAGUE 1985

		POS	Player	AB	BA	HR	RBI	PO	A	E	DP	TC/G	FA	Pitcher	G	IP	W	L	SV	ERA
East	**St. Louis** W-101 L-61 Whitey Herzog	1B	J. Clark	442	.281	22	87	1116	66	14	102	9.9	.988	J. Tudor	36	275	21	8	0	1.93
		2B	T. Herr	596	.302	8	110	337	448	12	120	5.0	.985	J. Andujar	38	270	21	12	0	3.40
		SS	O. Smith	537	.276	6	54	264	549	14	111	5.2	.983	D. Cox	35	241	18	9	0	2.88
		3B	T. Pendleton	559	.240	5	69	129	361	18	26	3.4	.965	K. Kepshire	32	153	10	9	0	4.75
		RF	A. Van Slyke	424	.259	13	55	234	13	1	4	1.7	.996	B. Forsch	34	136	9	6	2	3.90
		CF	W. McGee	612	.353	10	82	382	11	9	2	2.7	.978	J. Lahti	52	68	5	2	19	1.84
		LF	V. Coleman	636	.267	1	40	305	16	7	1	2.2	.979	K. Dayley	57	65	4	4	11	2.76
		C	T. Nieto	253	.225	0	34	384	28	4	3	4.4	.990	B. Campbell	50	64	5	3	4	3.50
		C	D. Porter	240	.221	10	34	386	26	4	4	5.1	.990							
		OF	T. Landrum	161	.280	4	21	91	2	0	1	1.3	1.000							
	New York W-98 L-64 Davey Johnson	1B	K. Hernandez	593	.309	10	91	1310	139	4	113	9.3	.997	D. Gooden	35	277	24	4	0	1.53
		2B	W. Backman	520	.273	1	38	272	370	7	76	4.6	.989	R. Darling	36	248	16	6	0	2.90
		SS	R. Santana	529	.257	1	29	301	396	25	81	4.7	.965	E. Lynch	31	191	10	8	0	3.44
		3B	H. Johnson	389	.242	11	46	67	171	15	21	2.2	.941	S. Fernandez	26	170	9	9	0	2.80
		RF	Strawberry	393	.277	29	79	211	5	2	2	2.0	.991	R. McDowell	62	127	6	5	17	2.83
		CF	M. Wilson	337	.276	6	26	216	0	8	0	2.7	.964	R. Aguilera	21	122	10	7	0	3.24
		LF	G. Foster	452	.263	21	77	198	7	5	2	1.7	.976	J. Orosco	54	79	8	6	17	2.73
		C	G. Carter	555	.281	32	100	956	67	8	11	7.2	.992	D. Sisk	42	73	4	5	2	5.30
		OF	D. Heep	271	.280	7	42	126	1	3	0	1.7	.977							
		3B	R. Knight	271	.218	6	36	52	109	7	5	2.3	.958							
		OF	L. Dykstra	236	.254	1	19	165	6	1	2	2.3	.994							
	Montreal W-84 L-77 Buck Rodgers	1B	D. Driessen	312	.250	6	25	804	64	3	79	9.9	.997	B. Smith	32	222	18	5	0	2.91
		2B	V. Law	519	.266	10	52	276	367	10	86	5.2	.985	Gullickson	29	181	14	12	0	3.52
		SS	H. Brooks	605	.269	13	100	203	441	28	81	4.3	.958	J. Hesketh	25	155	10	5	0	2.49
		3B	T. Wallach	569	.260	22	81	148	383	18	34	3.6	.967	D. Palmer		136	7	10	0	3.71
		RF	A. Dawson	529	.255	23	91	248	9	7	1	2.0	.973	T. Burke	78	120	9	4	8	2.39
		CF	Winningham	312	.237	3	21	229	6	4	2	2.1	.983	Schatzeder	24	104	3	5	0	3.80
		LF	T. Raines	575	.320	11	41	284	8	2	4	2.0	.993	J. Reardon	63	88	2	8	41	3.18
		C	Fitzgerald	295	.207	5	34	542	46	8	7	5.5	.987	G. Lucas	49	68	6	2	2	3.19
		10	T. Francona	281	.267	2	31	431	37	6	32		.987							
		OF	M. Webster	212	.274	11	30	133	3	1	0	2.1	.993							
		2B	Washington	193	.249	1	17	70	104	4	22	4.1	.978							

NATIONAL LEAGUE 1985, cont.

Chicago

W-77 L-84

Jim Frey

POS	Player	AB	BA	HR	RBI	PO	A	E	DP	TC/G	FA	Pitcher	G	IP	W	L	SV	ERA
1B	L. Durham	542	.282	21	75	1421	107	7	121	10.2	.995	D. Eckersley	25	169	11	7	0	3.08
2B	R. Sandberg	609	.305	26	83	353	500	12	99	5.7	.986	R. Fontenot	38	155	6	10	0	4.36
SS	S. Dunston	250	.260	4	18	144	248	17	39	5.6	.958	S. Trout	24	141	9	7	0	3.39
3B	R. Cey	500	.232	22	63	75	273	21	21	2.6	.943	R. Sutcliffe	20	130	8	8	0	3.18
RF	K. Moreland	587	.307	14	106	233	10	6	2	1.7	.976	S. Sanderson	19	121	5	6	0	3.12
CF	B. Dernier	469	.254	1	21	310	4	9	1	2.8	.972	L. Smith	65	98	7	4	33	3.04
LF	G. Matthews	298	.235	13	40	119	7	3	2	1.5	.977	D. Ruthven	20	87	4	7	0	4.53
C	J. Davis	482	.232	17	58	694	84	8	7	5.7	.990	L. Sorensen	45	82	3	7	0	4.26
OF	D. Lopes	275	.284	11	44	113	2	1	0	1.5	.991	G. Frazier	51	76	7	8	2	6.39
UT	C. Speier	218	.243	4	24	87	177	11	43		.960	W. Brusstar	51	74	4	3	4	6.05
SS	L. Bowa	195	.246	0	13	91	197	9	34	4.5	.970							
OF	T. Bosley	180	.328	7	27	84	0	1	0	1.5	.988							
OF	B. Hatcher	163	.245	2	10	77	2	1	0	1.8	.988							
13	R. Hebner	120	.217	3	22	110	24	4	15		.971							

Philadelphia

W-75 L-87

John Felske

POS	Player	AB	BA	HR	RBI	PO	A	E	DP	TC/G	FA	Pitcher	G	IP	W	L	SV	ERA
1B	M. Schmidt	549	.277	33	93	880	83	7	89	9.2	.993	J. Denny	33	231	11	14	0	3.82
2B	J. Samuel	663	.264	19	74	389	463	15	88	5.5	.983	K. Gross	38	206	15	13	0	3.41
SS	S. Jeltz	196	.189	0	12	106	215	14	38	3.9	.958	S. Rawley	36	199	13	8	0	3.31
3B	R. Schu	416	.252	7	24	86	191	20	19	2.7	.933	C. Hudson	38	193	8	13	0	3.78
RF	G. Wilson	608	.275	14	102	343	18	12	4	2.4	.968	J. Koosman	19	99	6	4	0	4.62
CF	V. Hayes	570	.263	13	70	368	9	6	1	2.6	.984	D. Carman	71	86	9	4	7	2.08
LF	J. Stone	264	.265	3	11	82	4	3	0	1.3	.966	K. Tekulve	58	72	4	10	14	2.99
C	O. Virgil	426	.246	19	55	667	52	4	11	6.0	.994							
OF	G. Maddox	218	.239	4	23	143	3	3	0	1.6	.980							
OF	J. Russell	216	.218	9	23	56	4	0	1	1.2	1.000							
1B	T. Corcoran	182	.214	0	22	386	25	3	27	7.0	.993							
OF	G. Gross	169	.260	0	14	48	4	0	0	1.0	1.000							
SS	L. Aguayo	165	.279	6	21	61	117	8	21	3.1	.957							

Pittsburgh

W-57 L-104

Chuck Tanner

POS	Player	AB	BA	HR	RBI	PO	A	E	DP	TC/G	FA	Pitcher	G	IP	W	L	SV	ERA
1B	J. Thompson	402	.241	12	61	995	82	9	69	9.5	.992	R. Rhoden	35	213	10	15	0	4.47
2B	J. Ray	594	.274	7	70	305	423	18	89	4.9	.976	R. Reuschel	31	194	14	8	1	2.27
SS	S. Khalifa	320	.238	2	31	156	316	16	45	5.1	.967	J. DeLeon	31	163	2	19	3	4.70
3B	B. Madlock	399	.251	10	41	46	175	14	10	2.4	.940	L. Tunnell	24	132	4	10	0	4.01
RF	G. Hendrick	256	.230	2	25	133	2	4	0	2.1	.971	McWilliams	30	126	7	9	0	4.70
CF	M. Wynne	337	.205	2	18	229	7	3	1	2.4	.987	C. Guante	63	109	4	6	5	2.72
LF	S. Kemp	236	.250	2	21	105	1	0	0	1.7	1.000	D. Robinson	44	95	5	11	3	3.87
C	T. Pena	546	.249	10	59	922	100	12	9	7.1	.988	Candelaria	37	54	2	4	9	3.64
OF	J. Orsulak	397	.300	0	21	229	10	6	1	2.1	.976							
3B	J. Morrison	244	.254	4	22	39	84	5	9	2.2	.961							
UT	B. Almon	244	.270	6	29	104	108	5	22		.977							
OF	M. Brown	205	.332	5	33	87	3	6	1	1.7	.938							

West

Los Angeles

W-95 L-67

Tom Lasorda

POS	Player	AB	BA	HR	RBI	PO	A	E	DP	TC/G	FA	Pitcher	G	IP	W	L	SV	ERA
1B	G. Brock	438	.251	21	66	1113	84	7	86	9.9	.994	Valenzuela	35	272	17	10	0	2.45
2B	S. Sax	488	.279	1	42	330	357	22	84	5.3	.969	O. Hershiser	36	240	19	3	0	2.03
SS	M. Duncan	562	.244	6	39	174	386	27	57	4.8	.954	J. Reuss	34	213	14	10	0	2.92
3B	D. Anderson	221	.199	4	18	28	107	6	10	2.8	.957	B. Welch	23	167	14	4	0	2.31
RF	M. Marshall	518	.293	28	95	206	9	2	2	1.7	.991	R. Honeycutt	31	142	8	12	1	3.42
CF	K. Landreaux	482	.268	12	50	267	4	7	1	2.0	.975	Niedenfuer	64	106	7	9	19	2.71
LF	P. Guerrero	487	.320	33	87	141	7	4	2	1.9	.974	K. Howell	56	86	4	7	12	3.77
C	M. Scioscia	429	.296	7	53	818	66	13	8	6.5	.986							
OF	C. Maldonado	213	.225	5	19	121	6	2	0	1.1	.984							
OF	R. Reynolds	207	.266	0	25	94	3	3	0	1.9	.970							
31	E. Cabell	192	.292	0	22	140	75	9	11		.960							
UT	B. Russell	169	.260	0	21	60	82	10	11		.934							

Cincinnati

W-89 L-72

Pete Rose

POS	Player	AB	BA	HR	RBI	PO	A	E	DP	TC/G	FA	Pitcher	G	IP	W	L	SV	ERA
1B	P. Rose	405	.264	2	46	870	73	5	80	8.6	.995	T. Browning	38	261	20	9	0	3.55
2B	R. Oester	526	.295	1	34	366	457	9	100	5.6	.989	M. Soto	36	257	12	15	0	3.58
SS	Concepcion	560	.252	7	48	212	404	24	64	4.2	.963	J. Tibbs	35	218	10	16	0	3.92
3B	B. Bell	247	.219	6	36	54	105	9	13	2.5	.946	R. Robinson	33	108	7	7	1	3.99
RF	D. Parker	635	.312	34	125	329	12	10	1	2.2	.972	J. Franco	67	99	12	3	12	2.18
CF	E. Milner	453	.254	3	33	340	12	6	3	2.7	.983	J. Stuper	33	99	8	5	0	4.55
LF	N. Esasky	413	.262	21	66	91	4	0	1	1.8	1.000	T. Power	64	80	8	6	27	2.70
C	B. Diaz	161	.261	3	15	301	32	4	8	6.6	.988	T. Hume	56	80	3	5	3	3.26
OF	G. Redus	246	.252	6	28	140	3	2	0	1.7	.986							
O1	C. Cedeno	220	.241	3	30	206	9	2	11		.991							
1B	T. Perez	183	.328	6	33	340	22	2	34	7.3	.995							
3B	Krenchicki	173	.272	4	25	34	84	4	9	2.3	.967							
C	A. Knicely	158	.253	5	26	231	13	6	1	5.5	.968							
C	Van Gorder	151	.238	2	24	255	11	3	2	3.8	.989							

Houston

W-83 L-79

Bob Lillis

POS	Player	AB	BA	HR	RBI	PO	A	E	DP	TC/G	FA	Pitcher	G	IP	W	L	SV	ERA
1B	G. Davis	350	.271	20	64	749	57	12	76	9.2	.985	B. Knepper	37	241	15	13	0	3.55
2B	B. Doran	578	.287	14	59	345	440	16	108	5.4	.980	N. Ryan	35	232	10	12	0	3.80
SS	C. Reynolds	379	.272	4	32	158	318	11	65	4.8	.977	M. Scott	36	222	18	8	0	3.29
3B	P. Garner	463	.268	6	51	75	197	20	14	2.4	.932	J. Niekro	32	213	9	12	0	3.72
RF	J. Mumphrey	444	.277	8	61	248	6	8	1	2.1	.969	B. Dawley	49	81	5	3	2	3.56
CF	K. Bass	539	.269	16	68	328	10	1	1	2.4	.997	D. Smith	64	79	9	5	27	2.27
LF	J. Cruz	544	.300	9	79	257	12	8	3	2.0	.971	F. DiPino	54	76	3	7	6	4.03
C	M. Bailey	332	.265	10	45	565	51	13	6	5.7	.979	J. Calhoun	44	64	2	5	4	2.54
UT	D. Walling	345	.270	7	45	326	124	12	31		.974							
SS	D. Thon	251	.251	6	29	106	218	11	48	4.2	.967							
OF	T. Puhl	194	.284	2	23	92	3	0	1	1.8	1.000							
C	A. Ashby	189	.280	8	25	312	37	8	1	6.0	.978							
O2	J. Pankovits	172	.244	4	14	80	37	1	8		.992							

NATIONAL LEAGUE 1985, cont.

	POS	Player	AB	BA	HR	RBI	PO	A	E	DP	TC/G	FA	Pitcher	G	IP	W	L	SV	ERA
San Diego	1B	S. Garvey	654	.281	17	81	**1442**	92	5	**138**	9.5	.997	E. Show	35	233	12	11	0	3.09
	2B	T. Flannery	384	.281	1	40	261	287	13	72	4.6	.977	A. Hawkins	33	229	18	8	0	3.15
W-83 L-79	SS	G. Templeton	546	.282	6	55	245	460	23	96	4.9	.968	D. Dravecky	34	215	13	11	0	2.93
	3B	G. Nettles	440	.261	15	61	122	229	15	16	2.8	.959	L. Hoyt	31	210	16	8	0	3.47
Dick Williams	RF	T. Gwynn	622	.317	6	46	337	14	4	2	2.3	.989	M. Thurmond	36	138	7	11	2	3.97
	CF	McReynolds	564	.234	15	75	**430**	12	3	3	3.0	.993	C. Lefferts	60	83	7	6	2	3.35
	LF	C. Martinez	514	.253	21	72	298	13	7	3	2.1	.978	G. Gossage	50	79	5	3	26	1.82
	C	T. Kennedy	532	.261	10	74	654	67	10	**12**	5.2	.986							
	23	J. Royster	249	.281	5	31	125	189	8	34		.975							
	3B	K. Bevacqua	138	.239	3	25	32	56	5	7	2.8	.946							
Atlanta	1B	B. Horner	483	.267	27	89	892	58	0	105	10.9	1.000	R. Mahler	39	267	17	15	0	3.48
	2B	G. Hubbard	439	.232	5	39	339	**539**	10	**127**	6.3	.989	S. Bedrosian	37	207	7	15	0	3.83
W-66 L-96	SS	R. Ramirez	568	.248	5	58	214	451	**32**	115	5.2	.954	Z. Smith	42	147	9	10	0	3.80
	3B	K. Oberkfell	412	.272	3	35	70	220	11	19	2.6	.963	R. Camp	66	128	4	6	3	3.95
Eddie Haas	RF	Washington	398	.276	15	43	122	3	5	1	1.3	.962	G. Garber	59	97	6	6	1	3.61
W-50 L-71	CF	D. Murphy	616	.300	**37**	111	334	8	7	4	2.2	.980	P. Perez	22	95	1	13	0	6.14
	LF	T. Harper	492	.264	17	72	215	10	5	0	1.8	.978	B. Sutter	58	88	7	7	23	4.48
Bobby Wine	C	R. Cerone	282	.216	3	25	384	48	6	4	4.8	.986	L. Barker	20	74	2	9	0	6.35
W-16 L-25	OF	B. Komminsk	300	.227	4	21	161	2	7	0	1.8	.959							
	1B	G. Perry	238	.214	3	13	541	37	9	48	10.7	.985							
	C	B. Benedict	208	.202	0	20	314	35	4	1	5.0	.989							
	2S	P. Zuvella	190	.253	0	4	112	169	8	38		.972							
	OF	M. Thompson	182	.302	0	6	78	2	3	0	1.7	.964							
	1B	C. Chambliss	170	.235	3	21	299	25	1	31	8.3	.997							
San Francisco	1B	D. Green	294	.248	5	20	628	42	9	54	8.7	.987	D. LaPoint	31	207	7	17	0	3.57
	2B	M. Trillo	451	.224	3	25	262	357	12	73	5.3	.981	M. Krukow	28	195	8	11	0	3.38
W-62 L-100	SS	J. Uribe	476	.237	3	26	209	438	26	77	4.6	.961	A. Hammaker	29	171	5	12	0	3.74
	3B	C. Brown	432	.271	16	61	94	243	10	15	2.9	**.971**	J. Gott	26	148	7	10	0	3.88
Jim Davenport	RF	C. Davis	481	.270	13	56	279	10	6	2	2.3	.980	V. Blue	33	131	8	8	0	4.47
W-56 L-88	CF	D. Gladden	502	.243	7	41	273	3	7	0	2.3	.975	B. Laskey	19	114	5	11	0	3.55
	LF	J. Leonard	507	.241	17	62	203	10	5	0	1.7	.977	M. Davis	77	114	5	12	7	3.54
Roger Craig	C	B. Brenly	440	.220	19	56	662	62	12	8	6.7	.984	S. Garrelts	74	106	9	6	13	2.30
W-6 L-12	OF	Youngblood	230	.270	4	24	103	4	5	0	2.0	.955	G. Minton	68	97	5	4	4	3.54
	1B	D. Driessen	181	.232	3	12	399	27	1	32	8.7	.998							
	23	B. Wellman	174	.236	0	16	65	105	8	13		.955							
	OF	R. Deer	162	.185	8	20	54	1	1	0	1.5	.982							

BATTING AND BASE RUNNING LEADERS

Batting Average
W. McGee, STL .353
P. Guerrero, LA .320
T. Raines, MON .320
T. Gwynn, SD .317
D. Parker, CIN .312

Slugging Average
P. Guerrero, LA .577
D. Parker, CIN .551
D. Murphy, ATL .539
M. Schmidt, PHI .532
M. Marshall, LA .515

Home Runs
D. Murphy, ATL 37
D. Parker, CIN 34
P. Guerrero, LA 33
M. Schmidt, PHI 33
G. Carter, NY 32

Total Bases
D. Parker, CIN 350
D. Murphy, ATL 332
W. McGee, STL 308
R. Sandberg, CHI 307
M. Schmidt, PHI 292

Runs Batted In
D. Parker, CIN 125
D. Murphy, ATL 111
T. Herr, STL 110
K. Moreland, CHI 106
G. Wilson, PHI 102

Stolen Bases
V. Coleman, STL 110
T. Raines, MON 70
W. McGee, STL 56
R. Sandberg, CHI 54
J. Samuel, PHI 53

Hits
W. McGee, STL 216
D. Parker, CIN 198
T. Gwynn, SD 197
R. Sandberg, CHI 186

Base on Balls
D. Murphy, ATL 90
C. Martinez, SD 87
M. Schmidt, PHI 87
P. Rose, CIN 86

Home Run Percentage
P. Guerrero, LA 6.8
M. Schmidt, PHI 6.0
D. Murphy, ATL 6.0
G. Carter, NY 5.8

Runs Scored
D. Murphy, ATL 118
T. Raines, MON 115
W. McGee, STL 114
R. Sandberg, CHI 113

Doubles
D. Parker, CIN 42
G. Wilson, PHI 39
T. Herr, STL 38
T. Wallach, MON 36

Triples
W. McGee, STL 18
T. Raines, MON 13
J. Samuel, PHI 13
P. Garner, HOU 10

PITCHING LEADERS

Winning Percentage
O. Hershiser, LA .864
D. Gooden, NY .857
B. Smith, MON .783
B. Welch, LA .778
R. Darling, NY .727

Earned Run Average
D. Gooden, NY 1.53
J. Tudor, STL 1.93
O. Hershiser, LA 2.03
R. Reuschel, PIT 2.27
B. Welch, LA 2.31

Wins
D. Gooden, NY 24
J. Tudor, STL 21
J. Andujar, STL 21
T. Browning, CIN 20
O. Hershiser, LA 19

Saves
J. Reardon, MON 41
L. Smith, CHI 33
D. Smith, HOU 27
T. Power, CIN 27
G. Gossage, SD 26

Strikeouts
D. Gooden, NY 268
M. Soto, CIN 214
N. Ryan, HOU 209
Valenzuela, LA 208
S. Fernandez, NY 180

Complete Games
D. Gooden, NY 16
Valenzuela, LA 14
J. Tudor, STL 14
D. Cox, STL 10
J. Andujar, STL 10

Fewest Hits/9 Innings
S. Fernandez, NY 5.71
D. Gooden, NY 6.44
O. Hershiser, LA 6.72
J. Tudor, STL 6.84

Shutouts
J. Tudor, STL 10
D. Gooden, NY 8
O. Hershiser, LA 5
Valenzuela, LA 5

Fewest Walks/9 Innings
L. Hoyt, SD 0.86
D. Eckersley, CHI 1.01
E. Lynch, NY 1.27
J. Tudor, STL 1.60

Most Strikeouts/9 Inn.
S. Fernandez, NY 9.51
D. Gooden, NY 8.72
J. DeLeon, PIT 8.24
N. Ryan, HOU 8.11

Innings
D. Gooden, NY 277
J. Tudor, STL 275
Valenzuela, LA 272
J. Andujar, STL 270

Games Pitched
T. Burke, MON 78
M. Davis, SF 77
S. Garrelts, SF 74
D. Carman, PHI 71

NATIONAL LEAGUE 1985, cont.

		W	L	PCT	GB	R	OR	Batting 2B	3B	HR	BA	SA	SB	Fielding E	DP	FA	Pitching CG	BB	SO	ShO	SV	ERA
East	St. Louis	101	61	.623		**747**	572	245	**59**	87	**.264**	.379	**314**	**108**	166	**.983**	**37**	453	798	20	44	3.10
	New York	98	64	.605	3	695	**568**	239	35	134	.257	.385	117	115	138	.982	32	515	**1039**	19	37	3.11
	Montreal	84	77	.522	16.5	633	636	242	49	118	.247	.375	169	121	152	.981	13	509	870	13	**54**	3.55
	Chicago	77	84	.478	23.5	686	729	239	28	**150**	.254	**.390**	182	134	150	.979	20	519	820	8	42	4.16
	Philadelphia	75	87	.463	26	667	673	238	47	141	.245	.383	122	139	142	.978	24	596	899	9	30	3.68
	Pittsburgh	57	104	.354	43.5	568	708	252	28	80	.247	.347	110	133	127	.979	15	584	962	6	29	3.97
West	Los Angeles	95	67	.586		682	579	226	28	129	.261	.382	136	166	131	.974	**37**	462	979	**21**	36	**2.96**
	Cincinnati	89	72	.553	5.5	677	666	249	34	114	.255	.376	159	122	142	.980	24	535	910	11	45	3.71
	Houston	83	79	.512	12	706	691	**261**	42	121	.261	.388	96	152	159	.976	17	543	909	9	42	3.66
	San Diego	83	79	.512	12	650	622	241	28	109	.255	.368	60	124	158	.980	26	**443**	727	19	44	3.41
	Atlanta	66	96	.407	29	632	781	213	28	126	.246	.363	72	159	**197**	.976	9	642	776	9	29	4.19
	San Francisco	62	100	.383	33	556	674	217	31	115	.233	.348	99	148	134	.976	13	572	985	5	24	3.61
						7899	7899	2862	437	1424	.252	.374	1636	1621	1796	.979	267	6373	10674	149	456	3.59

AMERICAN LEAGUE 1985

		POS	Player	AB	BA	HR	RBI	PO	A	E	DP	TC/G	FA	Pitcher	G	IP	W	L	SV	ERA
East	**Toronto**	1B	W. Upshaw	501	.275	15	65	1157	104	10	111	8.6	.992	D. Stieb	36	265	14	13	0	**2.48**
		2B	D. Garcia	600	.282	8	65	302	371	13	88	4.8	.981	D. Alexander	36	261	17	10	0	3.45
	W-99 L-62	SS	T. Fernandez	564	.289	2	51	283	**478**	30	109	**4.9**	.962	J. Key	35	213	14	6	0	3.00
		3B	R. Mulliniks	366	.295	10	56	75	162	7	16	2.1	**.971**	J. Clancy	23	129	9	6	0	3.78
	Bobby Cox	RF	J. Barfield	539	.289	27	84	349	**22**	4	**8**	2.4	.989	D. Lamp	53	106	11	0	2	3.32
		CF	L. Moseby	584	.259	18	71	394	7	8	1	2.7	.980	J. Acker	61	86	7	2	10	3.23
		LF	G. Bell	607	.275	28	95	320	13	**11**	3	2.2	.968	G. Lavelle	69	73	5	7	8	3.10
		C	E. Whitt	412	.245	19	64	649	38	8	6	5.2	.988	B. Caudill	67	69	4	6	14	2.99
		DH	A. Oliver	187	.251	5	23							T. Henke	28	40	3	3	13	2.03
		3B	G. Iorg	288	.313	7	37	39	137	9	13	1.8	.951							
		DH	J. Burroughs	191	.257	6	28													
	New York	1B	D. Mattingly	652	.324	35	145	1318	87	7	**154**	8.9	**.995**	R. Guidry	34	259	**22**	6	0	3.27
		2B	W. Randolph	497	.276	5	40	303	425	11	104	5.2	.985	P. Niekro	33	220	16	12	0	4.09
	W-97 L-64	SS	B. Meacham	481	.218	1	47	236	390	24	103	4.2	.963	J. Cowley	30	160	12	6	0	3.95
		3B	Pagliarulo	380	.239	19	62	67	187	13	15	2.0		E. Whitson	30	159	10	8	0	4.88
	Yogi Berra	RF	D. Winfield	633	.275	26	114	316	13	3	3	2.2	.991	B. Shirley	48	109	5	5	2	2.64
	W-6 L-10	CF	R. Henderson	547	.314	24	72	439	7	9	3	3.2	.980	D. Righetti	74	107	12	7	29	2.78
		LF	K. Griffey	438	.274	10	69	222	8	7	3	2.2	.970	D. Rasmussen	22	102	3	5	0	3.98
	Billy Martin	C	B. Wynegar	309	.223	5	32	547	34	6	7	6.1	.990	B. Fisher	55	98	4	4	14	2.38
	W-91 L-54	DH	D. Baylor	477	.231	23	91							R. Bordi	51	98	6	8	2	3.21
		C	R. Hassey	267	.296	13	42	402	20	7	2	6.2	.984							
		OF	D. Pasqua	148	.209	9	25	72	2	0	0	2.0	1.000							
	Detroit	1B	D. Evans	505	.248	**40**	94	827	114	15	80	8.5	.984	J. Morris	35	257	16	11	0	3.33
		2B	L. Whitaker	608	.280	21	73	314	414	11	101	4.9	.985	D. Petry	34	239	15	13	0	3.36
		SS	A. Trammell	605	.258	13	57	225	400	15	89	4.3	.977	W. Terrell	34	229	15	10	0	3.85
	W-84 L-77	3B	T. Brookens	485	.237	7	47	123	261	**23**	26	2.7	.943	F. Tanana	20	137	10	7	0	3.34
		RF	K. Gibson	581	.287	29	97	286	1	11	0	2.1	.963	G. Hernandez	74	107	8	10	31	2.70
	Sparky Anderson	CF	C. Lemon	517	.265	18	68	411	6	4	3	2.9	.990	J. Berenguer	31	95	5	6	0	5.59
		LF	L. Herndon	443	.244	12	37	273	7	7	4	2.1	.976	R. O'Neal	28	94	5	5	1	3.24
		C	L. Parrish	549	.273	28	98	695	53	5	9	6.3	.993	A. Lopez	51	86	3	7	5	4.80
		DH	N. Simmons	251	.239	10	33													
		UT	B. Garbey	237	.257	6	29	228	20	3	24		.988							
		DO	J. Grubb	155	.245	5	25	23	0	0	0	1.3	1.000							
	Baltimore	1B	E. Murray	583	.297	31	124	1338	152	19	154	9.8	.987	S. McGregor	35	204	14	14	0	4.81
		2B	A. Wiggins	298	.285	0	21	148	186	14	58	4.6	.960	M. Boddicker	32	203	12	17	0	4.07
	W-83 L-78	SS	C. Ripken	642	.282	26	110	**286**	474	26	**123**	4.9	.967	D. Martinez	33	180	13	11	0	5.15
		3B	F. Rayford	359	.306	18	48	62	145	6	13	2.7	.972	S. Davis	31	175	10	8	0	4.53
	Joe Altobelli	RF	L. Lacy	492	.293	9	48	231	9	4	0	2.1	.984	K. Dixon	34	162	8	4	1	3.67
	W-29 L-26	CF	F. Lynn	448	.263	23	68	314	6	2	2	2.6	.994	S. Stewart	56	130	5	7	9	3.61
		LF	M. Young	450	.273	28	81	190	6	5	0	2.2	.975	N. Snell	43	100	3	2	5	2.69
	Cal Ripken	C	R. Dempsey	362	.254	12	52	575	49	8	5	4.8	.987	D. Aase	54	88	10	6	14	3.78
	W-1 L-0	DH	L. Sheets	328	.262	17	50							T. Martinez	49	70	3	3	4	5.40
		OF	J. Dwyer	233	.249	7	36	131	4	1	0	1.7	.993							
	Earl Weaver	OF	G. Roenicke	225	.218	15	43	134	6	1	0	1.6	.993							
	W-53 L-52	3B	W. Gross	217	.235	11	18	41	98	10	14	2.2	.933							
		2B	R. Dauer	208	.202	2	14	117	181	3	44	4.1	.990							
		OF	J. Shelby	205	.283	7	27	148	3	3	0	2.6	.981							

AMERICAN LEAGUE 1985, cont.

	POS	Player	AB	BA	HR	RBI	PO	A	E	DP	TC/G	FA	Pitcher	G	IP	W	L	SV	ERA
Boston	1B	B. Buckner	673	.299	16	110	1384	184	12	140	9.8	.992	O. Boyd	35	272	15	13	0	3.70
	2B	M. Barrett	534	.266	5	56	355	479	11	110	5.5	.987	B. Hurst	35	229	11	13	0	4.51
W-81 L-81	SS	J. Gutierrez	275	.218	2	21	143	238	23	47	4.1	.943	A. Nipper	25	162	9	12	0	4.06
	3B	W. Boggs	653	.368	8	78	134	335	17	30	3.0	.965	B. Ojeda	39	158	9	11	1	4.00
John McNamara	RF	D. Evans	617	.263	29	78	291	9	3	1	2.0	.990	R. Clemens	15	98	7	5	0	3.29
	CF	S. Lyons	371	.264	5	30	253	4	7	0	2.3	.973	S. Crawford	44	91	6	5	12	3.76
	LF	J. Rice	546	.291	27	103	236	8	9	1	1.9	.964	B. Stanley	48	88	6	6	10	2.87
	C	R. Gedman	498	.295	18	80	768	78	15	13	6.2	.983	T. Lollar	16	67	5	5	1	4.57
	DH	M. Easler	568	.262	16	74													
	OF	T. Armas	385	.265	23	64	173	3	3	1	2.3	.983							
	SS	G. Hoffman	279	.276	6	34	155	231	10	61	4.3	.975							
Milwaukee	1B	C. Cooper	631	.293	16	99	1087	94	17	101	9.7	.986	D. Darwin	39	218	8	18	2	3.80
	2B	J. Gantner	523	.254	5	44	262	402	8	89	5.4	.988	T. Higuera	32	212	15	8	0	3.90
W-71 L-90	SS	E. Riles	448	.286	5	45	183	310	22	62	4.5	.957	R. Burris	29	170	9	13	0	4.81
	3B	P. Molitor	576	.297	10	48	126	263	19	30	3.0	.953	M. Haas	27	162	8	8	0	3.84
George Bamberger	RF	B. Oglivie	341	.290	10	61	190	4	7	0	2.2	.965	J. Cocanower	24	116	6	8	0	4.33
	CF	R. Manning	216	.218	2	18	160	2	4	0	2.2	.976	P. Vuckovich	22	113	6	10	0	5.51
	LF	R. Yount	466	.277	15	68	258	4	8	2	2.5	.970	B. Gibson	41	92	6	7	11	3.90
	C	C. Moore	349	.232	0	31	504	54	13	7	5.6	.977	R. Fingers	47	55	1	6	17	5.04
	DH	T. Simmons	528	.273	12	76													
	OF	Householder	299	.258	11	34	202	5	3	0	2.3	.986							
	UT	E. Romero	251	.251	0	21	157	219	8	53		.979							
	C	B. Schroeder	194	.242	8	25	211	23	3	4	4.9	.987							
	OF	R. Ready	181	.265	1	21	85	5	1	1	2.5	.989							
Cleveland	1B	P. Tabler	404	.275	5	59	739	72	14	77	9.0	.983	N. Heaton	36	208	9	17	0	4.90
	2B	T. Bernazard	500	.274	11	59	311	399	16	86	4.9	.978	B. Blyleven	23	180*	9	11	0	3.26
W-60 L-102	SS	J. Franco	636	.288	6	90	238	419	35	95	4.6	.949	V. Ruhle	42	125	2	10	3	4.32
	3B	B. Jacoby	606	.274	20	87	114	319	19	26	2.8	.958	T. Waddell	49	113	8	6	9	4.87
Pat Corrales	RF	G. Vukovich	434	.244	8	45	250	4	3	0	1.9	.988	D. Schulze	19	94	4	10	0	6.01
	CF	B. Butler	591	.311	5	50	437	19	1	5	3.0	.998	R. Thompson	57	80	3	8	5	6.30
	LF	J. Carter	489	.262	15	59	278	11	5	2	2.2	.983	J. Reed	33	72	3	5	8	4.11
	C	J. Willard	300	.270	7	36	427	52	5	11	5.0	.990	C. Wardle	15	66	7	6	0	6.68
	DH	A. Thornton	461	.236	22	88													
	1B	M. Hargrove	284	.285	1	27	595	66	6	66	7.9	.991							
	OF	C. Castillo	184	.245	11	25	101	0	5	0	2.1	.953							
	C	C. Bando	173	.139	0	13	251	28	4	3	4.2	.986							
	OF	O. Nixon	162	.235	3	9	129	5	4	1	1.7	.971							
Kansas City	1B	S. Balboni	600	.243	36	88	1573	101	12	138	10.5	.993	C. Leibrandt	33	238	17	9	0	2.69
	2B	F. White	563	.249	22	69	342	490	17	101	5.7	.980	Saberhagen	32	235	20	6	0	2.87
W-91 L-71	SS	Concepcion	314	.204	2	20	127	367	21	63	4.0	.959	D. Jackson	32	208	14	12	0	3.42
	3B	G. Brett	550	.335	30	112	107	339	15	33	3.0	.967	B. Black	33	206	10	15	0	4.33
Dick Howser	RF	D. Motley	383	.222	17	49	198	4	7	1	1.8	.967	M. Gubicza	29	177	14	10	0	4.06
	CF	W. Wilson	605	.278	4	43	378	4	2	1	2.7	.995	Quisenberry	84	129	8	9	37	2.37
	LF	L. Smith	448	.257	6	41	195	10	9	3	1.6	.958							
	C	J. Sundberg	367	.245	10	35	572	41	5	10	5.5	.992							
	DH	H. McRae	320	.259	14	70													
	DH	J. Orta	300	.267	4	45													
	OF	P. Sheridan	206	.228	3	17	116	3	2	0	1.8	.983							
	OF	D. Iorg	130	.223	1	21	41	0	0	0	1.3	1.000							
California	1B	R. Carew	443	.280	2	39	1055	65	7	121	9.7	.994	M. Witt	35	250	15	9	0	3.56
	2B	B. Grich	479	.242	13	53	224	380	2	99	5.2	.997	R. Romanick	31	195	14	9	0	4.11
W-90 L-72	SS	D. Schofield	438	.219	8	41	261	397	25	108	4.6	.963	McCaskill	30	190	12	12	0	4.70
	3B	D. DeCinces	427	.244	20	78	95	202	13	27	2.8	.958	J. Slaton	29	148	6	10	1	4.37
Gene Mauch	RF	R. Jackson	460	.252	27	85	112	6	7	1	1.5	.944	D. Moore	65	103	8	8	31	1.92
	CF	G. Pettis	443	.257	1	32	368	13	4	5	3.2	.990	S. Cliburn	44	99	9	3	6	2.09
	LF	B. Downing	520	.263	20	85	244	5	2	0	2.1	.992	Candelaria	13	71	7	3	0	3.80
	C	B. Boone	460	.248	5	55	670	71	10	15	5.1	.987							
	DH	R. Jones	389	.231	21	67													
	UT	J. Beniquez	411	.304	8	42	439	26	4	42		.991							
	2B	R. Wilfong	217	.189	4	13	124	216	5	45	5.0	.986							
	OF	M. Brown	153	.268	4	20	78	3	0	1	1.7	1.000							
Chicago	1B	G. Walker	601	.258	24	92	1217	97	8	116	8.8	.994	T. Seaver	35	239	16	11	0	3.17
	2B	J. Cruz	234	.197	0	15	158	220	7	59	4.4	.982	B. Burns	36	227	18	11	0	3.96
W-85 L-77	SS	O. Guillen	491	.273	1	33	220	382	12	80	4.1	.980	F. Bannister	34	211	10	14	0	4.87
	3B	T. Hulett	395	.268	5	36	69	210	23	22	2.6	.924	G. Nelson	46	146	10	10	2	4.26
Tony LaRussa	RF	H. Baines	640	.309	22	113	318	8	2	2	2.1	.994	B. James	69	110	8	7	32	2.13
	CF	D. Boston	232	.228	3	15	179	7	2	1	2.0	.989							
	LF	R. Law	390	.259	4	35	226	7	3	3	2.0	.987							
	C	C. Fisk	543	.238	37	107	801	60	10	13	6.7	.989							
	DH	R. Kittle	379	.230	26	58													
	UT	L. Salazar	327	.245	10	45	180	57	10	13		.960							
	UT	S. Fletcher	301	.256	2	31	123	208	8	36		.976							
	2B	B. Little	188	.250	2	27	100	164	3	33	3.9	.989							
	DH	O. Gamble	148	.203	4	20													
	DH	J. Hairston	140	.243	2	20													

West (Kansas City, California, Chicago)

AMERICAN LEAGUE 1985, cont.

Minnesota

W-77 L-85

Billy Gardner
W-27 L-35

Ray Miller
W-50 L-50

POS	Player	AB	BA	HR	RBI	PO	A	E	DP	TC/G	FA	Pitcher	G	IP	W	L	SV	ERA
1B	K. Hrbek	593	.278	21	93	1339	114	8	114	9.4	.995	M. Smithson	37	257	15	14	0	4.34
2B	T. Teufel	434	.260	10	50	237	352	12	67	4.4	.980	F. Viola	36	251	18	14	0	4.09
SS	G. Gagne	293	.225	2	23	149	269	14	48	4.1	.968	J. Butcher	34	208	11	14	0	4.98
3B	G. Gaetti	560	.246	20	63	146	316	18	31	3.1	.963	K. Schrom	29	161	9	12	0	4.99
RF	T. Brunansky	567	.242	27	90	300	14	5	2	2.1	.984	B. Blyleven	14	114*	8	5	0	3.00
CF	K. Puckett	691	.288	4	74	465	19	8	5	3.1	.984	P. Filson	40	96	4	5	2	3.67
LF	M. Hatcher	444	.282	3	49	215	6	2	2	2.3	.991	R. Davis	57	65	2	6	25	3.48
C	M. Salas	360	.300	9	41	529	39	5	10	5.0	.991							
DH	R. Smalley	388	.258	12	45													
OD	R. Bush	234	.239	10	35	63	0	2	0	1.6	.969							
UT	M. Stenhouse	179	.223	5	21	83	10	3	4		.969							
DC	D. Engle	172	.256	7	25	58	3	1	1	3.6	.984							
C	T. Laudner	164	.238	7	19	233	19	8	3	3.8	.969							

Oakland

W-77 L-85

Jackie Moore

POS	Player	AB	BA	HR	RBI	PO	A	E	DP	TC/G	FA	Pitcher	G	IP	W	L	SV	ERA
1B	B. Bochte	424	.295	14	60	942	60	10	83	7.9	.990	C. Codiroli	37	226	14	14	0	4.46
2B	D. Hill	393	.285	3	48	228	320	15	56	4.6	.973	D. Sutton	29	194	13	8	0	3.89
SS	A. Griffin	614	.270	2	64	278	440	30	87	4.6	.960	B. Krueger	32	151	9	10	0	4.52
3B	C. Lansford	401	.277	13	46	85	119	5	11	2.2	.976	T. Birtsas	29	141	10	6	0	4.01
RF	M. Davis	547	.287	24	82	370	6	8	1	2.5	.979	K. Atherton	56	105	4	7	3	4.30
CF	D. Murphy	523	.233	20	59	432	6	5	1	3.0	.989	J. Howell	63	98	9	8	29	2.85
LF	D. Collins	379	.251	4	29	221	1	5	0	2.5	.978	S. Ontiveros	39	75	1	3	8	1.93
C	M. Heath	436	.250	13	55	483	44	10	9	4.8	.981	J. Rijo	12	64	6	4	0	3.53
DH	D. Kingman	592	.238	30	91													
UT	D. Baker	343	.268	14	52	465	29	5	33		.990							
C	M. Tettleton	211	.251	3	15	344	24	4	9	4.9	.989							
OF	S. Henderson	193	.301	3	31	79	3	4	0	1.5	.953							

Seattle

W-74 L-88

Chuck Cottier

POS	Player	AB	BA	HR	RBI	PO	A	E	DP	TC/G	FA	Pitcher	G	IP	W	L	SV	ERA
1B	A. Davis	578	.287	18	78	1438	103	13	131	10.1	.992	M. Moore	35	247	17	10	0	3.46
2B	J. Perconte	485	.264	2	23	244	381	9	91	5.1	.986	M. Young	37	218	12	19	1	4.91
SS	S. Owen	352	.259	6	37	196	361	14	76	4.9	.975	M. Langston	24	127	7	14	0	5.47
3B	J. Presley	570	.275	28	84	82	335	17	24	2.8	.961	F. Wills	24	123	5	11	1	6.00
RF	A. Cowens	452	.265	14	69	198	10	7	2	2.0	.967	B. Swift	23	121	6	10	0	4.77
CF	D. Henderson	502	.241	14	68	335	8	5	3	2.5	.986	E. Nunez	70	90	7	3	16	3.09
LF	P. Bradley	641	.300	26	88	336	10	5	3	2.2	.986	J. Beattie	18	70	5	6	0	7.29
C	B. Kearney	305	.243	6	27	529	50	3	7	5.4	.995							
DH	G. Thomas	484	.215	32	87													
OF	I. Calderon	210	.286	8	28	100	5	2	2	2.0	.981							
C	D. Scott	185	.222	4	23	277	31	6	1	4.2	.981							
UT	D. Ramos	168	.196	1	15	87	119	10	26		.954							
DH	K. Phelps	116	.207	9	24													

Texas

W-62 L-99

Doug Rader
W-9 L-23

Bobby Valentine
W-53 L-76

POS	Player	AB	BA	HR	RBI	PO	A	E	DP	TC/G	FA	Pitcher	G	IP	W	L	SV	ERA
1B	P. O'Brien	573	.267	22	92	1457	98	8	125	9.8	.995	C. Hough	34	250	14	16	0	3.31
2B	T. Harrah	396	.270	9	44	212	351	6	71	4.7	.989	M. Mason	38	179	8	15	0	4.83
SS	C. Wilkerson	360	.244	0	22	125	274	18	50	3.8	.957	B. Hooton	29	124	5	8	0	5.23
3B	B. Bell	313	.236	4	32	70	192	16	22	3.3	.942	G. Harris	58	113	5	4	11	2.47
RF	L. Parrish	346	.249	17	51	111	4	1	0	1.7	.991	D. Noles	28	110	4	8	1	5.06
CF	O. McDowell	406	.239	18	42	282	9	2	2	2.8	.993	D. Rozema	34	88	3	7	7	4.19
LF	G. Ward	593	.287	15	70	304	11	10	2	2.1	.969	D. Schmidt	51	86	7	6	5	3.15
C	D. Slaught	343	.280	8	35	550	33	6	4	5.8	.990	D. Stewart	42	81	0	6	4	5.42
DH	C. Johnson	296	.257	12	56													
OF	G. Wright	363	.190	2	18	213	8	2	2	2.2	.991							
UT	W. Tolleson	323	.313	1	18	149	255	14	48		.967							
3B	S. Buechele	219	.219	6	21	52	137	6	17	2.8	.969							
OD	B. Jones	134	.224	5	23	30	0	0	0	1.0	1.000							

BATTING AND BASE RUNNING LEADERS

Batting Average
W. Boggs, BOS	.368
G. Brett, KC	.335
D. Mattingly, NY	.324
R. Henderson, NY	.314
B. Butler, CLE	.311

Slugging Average
G. Brett, KC	.585
D. Mattingly, NY	.567
J. Barfield, TOR	.536
E. Murray, BAL	.523
D. Evans, DET	.519

Home Runs
D. Evans, DET	40
C. Fisk, CHI	37
S. Balboni, KC	36
D. Mattingly, NY	35
G. Thomas, SEA	32

Total Bases
D. Mattingly, NY	370
G. Brett, KC	322
P. Bradley, SEA	319
W. Boggs, BOS	312
E. Murray, BAL	305

Runs Batted In
D. Mattingly, NY	145
E. Murray, BAL	124
D. Winfield, NY	114
H. Baines, CHI	113
G. Brett, KC	112

Stolen Bases
R. Henderson, NY	80
G. Pettis, CAL	56
B. Butler, CLE	47
W. Wilson, KC	43
L. Smith, KC	40

Hits
W. Boggs, BOS	240
D. Mattingly, NY	211
B. Buckner, BOS	201
K. Puckett, MIN	199

Base on Balls
D. Evans, BOS	114
T. Harrah, TEX	113
G. Brett, KC	103
R. Henderson, NY	99

Home Run Percentage
D. Evans, DET	7.9
C. Fisk, CHI	6.8
G. Thomas, SEA	6.6
S. Balboni, KC	6.0

PITCHING LEADERS

Winning Percentage
R. Guidry, NY	.786
Saberhagen, KC	.769
J. Key, TOR	.700
K. Dixon, BAL	.667
C. Leibrandt, KC	.654

Earned Run Average
D. Stieb, TOR	2.48
C. Leibrandt, KC	2.69
Saberhagen, KC	2.87
J. Key, TOR	3.00
B. Blyleven, CLE, MIN	3.16

Wins
R. Guidry, NY	22
Saberhagen, KC	20
B. Burns, CHI	18
F. Viola, MIN	18

Saves
Quisenberry, KC	37
B. James, CHI	32
D. Moore, CAL	31
G. Hernandez, DET	31
D. Righetti, NY	29
J. Howell, OAK	29

Strikeouts
B. Blyleven, CLE, MIN	206
F. Bannister, CHI	198
J. Morris, DET	191
B. Hurst, BOS	189
M. Witt, CAL	180

Complete Games
B. Blyleven, CLE, MIN	24
C. Hough, TEX	14
M. Moore, SEA	14
J. Morris, DET	13
O. Boyd, BOS	13

Fewest Hits/9 Innings
D. Stieb, TOR	7.00
C. Hough, TEX	7.12
D. Petry, DET	7.16
J. Morris, DET	7.42

Shutouts
B. Blyleven, CLE, MIN	5
B. Burns, CHI	4
J. Morris, DET	4

Fewest Walks/9 Innings
Saberhagen, KC	1.45
R. Guidry, NY	1.46
J. Butcher, MIN	1.86
J. Key, TOR	2.12

AMERICAN LEAGUE 1985, *cont.*

BATTING AND BASE RUNNING LEADERS

Runs Scored		Doubles		Triples	
R. Henderson, NY	146	D. Mattingly, NY	48	W. Wilson, KC	21
C. Ripken, BAL	116	B. Buckner, BOS	46	B. Butler, CLE	14
E. Murray, BAL	111	W. Boggs, BOS	42	K. Puckett, MIN	13
D. Evans, BOS	110	C. Cooper, MIL	39	T. Fernandez, TOR	10

PITCHING LEADERS

Most Strikeouts/9 Inn.		Innings		Games Pitched	
F. Bannister, CHI	8.46	B. Blyleven, CLE, MIN	294	Quisenberry, KC	84
B. Hurst, BOS	7.42	O. Boyd, BOS	272	Vande Berg, SEA	76
B. Burns, CHI	6.82	D. Stieb, TOR	265	D. Righetti, NY	74
J. Morris, DET	6.69	D. Alexander, TOR	261	G. Hernandez, DET	74

		W	L	PCT	GB	R	OR	2B	3B	HR	BA	SA	SB	E	DP	FA	CG	BB	SO	ShO	SV	ERA
East	Toronto	99	62	.615		759	588	281	53	158	.269	.425	143	125	164	.980	18	484	823	9	47	3.31
	New York	97	64	.602	2	839	660	272	31	176	.267	.425	155	126	172	.979	25	518	907	9	49	3.69
	Detroit	84	77	.522	15	729	688	254	45	202	.253	.424	75	143	152	.977	31	556	943	11	40	3.78
	Baltimore	83	78	.516	16	818	764	234	22	214	.263	.430	69	129	168	.979	32	568	793	6	33	4.38
	Boston	81	81	.500	18.5	800	720	292	31	162	.282	.429	66	145	161	.977	35	540	913	6	29	4.06
	Milwaukee	71	90	.441	28	690	802	250	44	101	.263	.379	69	142	153	.977	34	499	777	6	37	4.39
	Cleveland	60	102	.370	39.5	729	861	254	31	116	.265	.385	132	141	161	.977	24	547	702	7	28	4.91
West	Kansas City	91	71	.562		687	639	261	49	154	.252	.401	128	127	160	.980	27	463	846	11	41	3.49
	California	90	72	.556	1	732	703	215	31	153	.251	.386	106	112	202	.982	22	514	767	8	41	3.91
	Chicago	85	77	.525	6	736	720	247	37	146	.253	.392	108	111	152	.982	20	569	1023	8	39	4.07
	Minnesota	77	85	.475	14	705	782	282	41	141	.264	.407	68	120	139	.980	41	462	767	7	34	4.48
	Oakland	77	85	.475	14	757	787	230	34	155	.255	.412	116	140	137	.977	10	607	785	6	41	4.41
	Seattle	74	88	.457	17	719	818	277	38	171	.255	.412	94	122	156	.980	23	637	868	8	30	4.68
	Texas	62	99	.385	28.5	617	785	213	41	129	.253	.381	130	120	145	.980	18	501	863	5	33	4.56
						10317	10317	3562	528	2178	.261	.406	1459	1803	2222	.979	360	7465	11777	109	522	4.15

NATIONAL LEAGUE 1986

East — New York
W-108 L-54 — Davey Johnson

POS	Player	AB	BA	HR	RBI	PO	A	E	DP	TC/G	FA	Pitcher	G	IP	W	L	SV	ERA
1B	K. Hernandez	551	.310	13	83	1199	149	5	115	9.1	.996	D. Gooden	33	250	17	6	0	2.84
2B	W. Backman	387	.320	1	27	186	290	17	56	4.4	.966	R. Darling	34	237	15	6	0	2.81
SS	R. Santana	394	.218	1	28	203	369	16	68	4.3	.973	B. Ojeda	32	217	18	5	0	2.57
3B	R. Knight	486	.298	11	76	88	204	16	17	2.3	.948	S. Fernandez	32	204	16	6	1	3.52
RF	Strawberry	475	.259	27	93	226	10	6	3	1.8	.975	R. Aguilera	28	142	10	7	0	3.88
CF	L. Dykstra	431	.295	8	45	283	8	3	2	2.1	.990	R. McDowell	75	128	14	9	22	3.02
LF	M. Wilson	381	.289	9	45	228	7	5	2	2.1	.979	J. Orosco	58	81	8	6	21	2.33
C	G. Carter	490	.255	24	105	869	62	8	13	7.7	.991							
OS	K. Mitchell	328	.277	12	43	145	59	8	8		.962							
2B	T. Teufel	279	.247	4	31	133	173	9	28	3.8	.971							
OF	G. Foster	233	.227	13	38	96	4	4	1	1.7	.962							
3S	H. Johnson	220	.245	10	39	50	136	20	24		.903							
OF	D. Heep	195	.282	5	33	83	2	1	1	1.5	.988							

Philadelphia
W-86 L-75 — John Felske

POS	Player	AB	BA	HR	RBI	PO	A	E	DP	TC/G	FA	Pitcher	G	IP	W	L	SV	ERA
1B	V. Hayes	610	.305	19	98	1182	96	13	105	9.6	.990	K. Gross	37	242	12	12	0	4.02
2B	J. Samuel	591	.266	16	78	290	440	25	83	5.3	.967	S. Rawley	23	158	11	7	0	3.54
SS	S. Jeltz	439	.219	0	36	229	406	22	81	4.7	.967	B. Ruffin	21	146	9	4	0	2.46
3B	M. Schmidt	552	.290	37	119	78	220	6	27	2.5	.980	C. Hudson	33	144	7	10	0	4.94
RF	G. Wilson	584	.271	15	84	331	20	4	5	2.3	.989	D. Carman	50	134	10	5	1	3.22
CF	M. Thompson	299	.251	6	23	212	1	2	1	2.4	.991	K. Tekulve	73	110	11	5	4	2.54
LF	G. Redus	340	.247	11	33	185	8	4	2	2.2	.980	S. Bedrosian	68	90	8	6	29	3.39
C	J. Russell	315	.241	13	60	498	39	13	10	6.2	.976	S. Carlton	16	83	4	8	0	6.18
OF	R. Roenicke	275	.247	5	42	181	3	2	0	2.2	.989	M. Maddux	16	78	3	7	0	5.42
OF	J. Stone	249	.277	6	19	103	8	2	1	1.9	.982							
3B	R. Schu	208	.274	8	25	42	94	13	6	2.6	.913							
C	D. Daulton	138	.225	8	21	244	21	4	6	5.6	.985							

St. Louis
W-79 L-82 — Whitey Herzog

POS	Player	AB	BA	HR	RBI	PO	A	E	DP	TC/G	FA	Pitcher	G	IP	W	L	SV	ERA
1B	J. Clark	232	.237	9	23	623	35	3	66	10.3	.995	B. Forsch	33	230	14	10	0	3.25
2B	T. Herr	559	.252	2	61	352	414	9	121	5.1	.988	D. Cox	23	220	12	13	0	2.90
SS	O. Smith	514	.280	0	54	229	453	15	96	4.8	.978	J. Tudor	30	219	13	7	0	2.92
3B	T. Pendleton	578	.239	1	59	133	371	20	36	3.4	.962	G. Mathews	23	145	11	8	0	3.65
RF	A. Van Slyke	418	.270	13	61	211	11	7	2	2.1	.969	T. Conroy	25	115	5	11	0	5.23
CF	W. McGee	497	.256	7	48	325	9	3	0	2.8	.991	T. Worrell	74	104	9	10	36	2.08
LF	V. Coleman	600	.232	0	29	300	12	9	2	2.2	.972	R. Horton	42	100	4	3	3	2.24
C	LaValliere	303	.234	3	30	468	47	6	8	4.8	.988							
OF	C. Ford	214	.248	2	29	109	7	3	5	1.9	.975							
OF	T. Landrum	205	.210	2	17	131	6	1	1	1.8	.993							
C	M. Heath	190	.205	4	25	259	30	10	4	4.7	.967							

NATIONAL LEAGUE 1986, cont.

	POS	Player	AB	BA	HR	RBI	PO	A	E	DP	TC/G	FA	Pitcher	G	IP	W	L	SV	ERA
Montreal W-78 L-83 Buck Rodgers	1B	A. Galarraga	321	.271	10	42	805	40	4	59	8.3	.995	F. Youmans	33	219	13	12	0	3.53
	2B	V. Law	360	.225	5	44	170	284	3	50	4.9	.993	J. Tibbs	35	190	7	9	0	3.97
	SS	H. Brooks	306	.340	14	58	116	222	15	37	4.4	.958	B. Smith	30	187	10	8	0	3.94
	3B	T. Wallach	480	.233	18	71	94	270	16	26	2.9	.958	McGaffigan	48	143	10	5	2	2.65
	RF	A. Dawson	496	.284	20	78	200	11	3	2	1.7	.986	T. Burke	68	101	9	7	4	2.93
	CF	M. Webster	576	.290	8	49	325	12	8	3	2.4	.977	B. Sebra	17	91	5	5	0	3.55
	LF	T. Raines	580	**.334**	9	62	270	13	6	1	2.0	.979	J. Reardon	62	89	7	9	35	3.94
	C	Bilardello	191	.194	4	17	391	38	8	3	5.7	.982	J. Hesketh	15	83	6	5	0	5.01
	13	Krenchicki	221	.240	2	23	325	58	6	26		.985	B. McClure	52	63	2	5	6	3.02
	C	Fitzgerald	209	.282	6	37	415	35	3	5	6.4	.993							
	UT	T. Foley	202	.257	1	18	81	147	4	18		.983							
	2B	A. Newman	185	.200	1	8	76	127	7	25	3.6	.967							
	OF	Winningham	185	.216	4	11	97	2	2	1	1.5	.980							
	SS	L. Rivera	166	.205	0	13	64	119	9	24	3.5	.953							
Chicago W-70 L-90 Jim Frey W-23 L-33 John Vukovich W-1 L-1 Gene Michael W-46 L-56	1B	L. Durham	484	.262	20	65	1231	80	7	101	9.3	.995	D. Eckersley	33	201	6	11	0	4.57
	2B	R. Sandberg	627	.284	14	76	309	**492**	5	86	5.3	**.994**	R. Sutcliffe	28	177	5	14	0	4.64
	SS	S. Dunston	581	.250	17	68	320	465	32	96	5.5	.961	S. Sanderson	37	170	9	11	1	4.19
	3B	R. Cey	256	.273	13	36	41	118	8	7	2.2	.952	S. Trout	37	161	5	7	0	4.75
	RF	K. Moreland	586	.271	12	79	181	13	4	3	1.6	.980	E. Lynch	23	100	7	5	0	3.79
	CF	B. Dernier	324	.225	4	18	222	3	3	2	2.2	.987	L. Smith	66	90	9	9	31	3.09
	LF	G. Matthews	370	.259	21	46	137	5	**9**	1	1.4	.940	J. Moyer	16	87	7	4	0	5.05
	C	J. Davis	528	.250	21	74	**885**	105	8	14	6.9	.992	R. Fontenot	42	56	3	5	2	3.86
	OF	J. Mumphrey	309	.304	5	32	161	3	3	3	1.8	.982	J. Baller	36	54	2	4	5	5.37
	3O	D. Lopes	157	.299	6	22	51	54	8	3		.929							
	3S	C. Speier	155	.284	6	23	53	88	3	14		.979							
Pittsburgh W-64 L-98 Jim Leyland	1B	S. Bream	522	.268	16	77	1320	**166**	**17**	107	9.8	.989	R. Rhoden	34	254	15	12	0	2.84
	2B	J. Ray	579	.301	7	78	280	479	5	89	5.1	.993	R. Reuschel	35	216	9	16	0	3.96
	SS	R. Belliard	309	.233	0	31	117	269	12	42	4.1	.970	M. Bielecki	31	149	6	11	0	4.66
	3B	J. Morrison	537	.274	23	88	92	257	20	12	2.4	.946	B. Walk	44	142	7	8	2	3.75
	RF	J. Orsulak	401	.249	2	19	193	11	4	2	1.7	.981	McWilliams	49	122	3	11	0	5.15
	CF	B. Bonds	413	.223	16	48	280	9	5	2	2.7	.983	B. Kipper	20	114	6	8	0	4.03
	LF	R. Reynolds	402	.269	9	48	190	2	**9**	0	1.8	.955	J. Winn	50	88	3	5	3	3.58
	C	T. Pena	510	.288	10	52	810	99	**18**	13	6.7	.981	C. Guante	52	78	5	2	4	3.35
	OF	M. Brown	243	.218	4	26	107	3	3	3		.973	D. Robinson	50	69	3	4	14	3.38
	O1	M. Diaz	209	.268	12	36	201	6	3	9	1.6	.986	B. Jones	26	37	3	4	3	2.89
	UT	B. Almon	196	.219	7	27	80	45	8	4		.940							
	OF	B. Bonilla	192	.240	1	17	73	3	2	1	1.5	.974							
West **Houston** W-96 L-66 Hal Lanier	1B	G. Davis	574	.265	31	101	1253	111	11	90	8.8	.992	M. Scott	37	**275**	18	10	0	**2.22**
	2B	B. Doran	550	.276	6	37	262	329	16	62	4.2	.974	B. Knepper	40	258	17	12	0	3.14
	SS	D. Thon	278	.248	3	21	142	210	10	39	3.5	.972	N. Ryan	30	178	12	8	0	3.34
	3B	D. Walling	382	.312	13	58	59	156	9	6	2.2	.960	J. Deshaies	26	144	12	5	0	3.25
	RF	K. Bass	591	.311	20	79	303	12	5	4	2.1	.984	C. Kerfeld	61	94	11	2	7	2.59
	CF	B. Hatcher	419	.258	6	36	226	7	4	0	2.0	.983	A. Lopez	45	78	3	3	7	3.46
	LF	J. Cruz	479	.278	10	72	237	5	4	1	1.8	.984	D. Smith	54	56	4	7	33	2.73
	C	A. Ashby	315	.257	7	38	632	43	10	2	6.7	.985							
	3B	P. Garner	313	.265	9	41	58	141	23	13	2.6	.896							
	SS	C. Reynolds	313	.249	6	41	106	206	7	38	3.3	.978							
	OF	T. Puhl	172	.244	3	14	65	0	0	0	1.4	1.000							
Cincinnati W-86 L-76 Pete Rose	1B	N. Esasky	330	.230	12	41	512	30	5	12	7.8	.991	Gullickson	37	245	15	12	0	3.38
	2B	R. Oester	523	.258	8	44	**367**	475	19	100	**5.7**	.978	T. Browning	39	243	14	13	0	3.81
	SS	K. Stillwell	279	.229	0	26	107	205	16	40	4.1	.951	J. Denny	27	171	11	10	0	4.20
	3B	B. Bell	568	.278	20	75	105	290	10	28	2.7	.975	C. Welsh	24	139	6	9	0	4.78
	RF	D. Parker	637	.273	31	116	278	9	**9**	2	1.9	.970	T. Power	56	129	10	6	1	3.70
	CF	E. Milner	424	.259	15	47	292	6	3	0	2.4	.990	R. Robinson	70	117	10	3	14	3.24
	LF	E. Davis	415	.277	27	71	274	2	7	0	2.3	.975	M. Soto	19	105	5	10	0	4.71
	C	B. Diaz	474	.272	10	56	732	83	13	10	6.2	.984	J. Franco	74	101	6	6	29	2.94
	UT	Concepcion	311	.260	3	30	153	223	10	53		.974							
	1B	P. Rose	237	.219	0	25	523	43	6	54	9.4	.990							
	1B	T. Perez	200	.255	2	29	398	29	7	46	7.9	.984							
	OF	K. Daniels	181	.320	6	23	88	0	3	0	1.9	.967							
San Francisco W-83 L-79 Roger Craig	1B	W. Clark	408	.287	11	41	942	72	11	76	10.0	.989	M. Krukow	34	245	20	9	0	3.05
	2B	R. Thompson	549	.271	7	47	255	450	17	97	4.8	.976	M. LaCoss	37	204	10	13	0	3.57
	SS	J. Uribe	453	.223	3	43	249	444	16	95	4.5	.977	S. Garrelts	53	174	13	9	10	3.11
	3B	C. Brown	416	.317	7	49	73	177	18	17	2.4	.933	V. Blue	28	157	10	10	0	3.27
	RF	C. Davis	526	.278	13	70	303	9	**9**	2	2.2	.972	J. Robinson	64	104	6	3	8	3.36
	CF	D. Gladden	351	.276	4	29	226	7	3	2	2.7	.987	M. Davis	67	84	5	7	4	2.99
	LF	J. Leonard	341	.279	6	42	158	4	5	1	1.9	.970	G. Minton	48	69	4	4	5	3.93
	C	B. Brenly	472	.246	16	62	518	55	3	4	5.7	**.995**							
	OF	C. Maldonado	405	.252	18	85	161	10	3	0	1.7	.983							
	C	B. Melvin	268	.224	5	25	442	59	6	7	6.0	.988							
	10	M. Aldrete	216	.250	2	25	317	36	1	34		.997							
	OF	R. Kutcher	186	.237	7	16	99	3	1	1	2.0	.990							
	OF	Youngblood	184	.255	5	28	49	2	0	1	1.1	1.000							
	1B	H. Spilman	94	.287	2	22	138	15	1	8	8.1	.994							

NATIONAL LEAGUE 1986, *cont.*

POS	Player	AB	BA	HR	RBI	PO	A	E	DP	TC/G	FA	Pitcher	G	IP	W	L	SV	ERA
San Diego												A. Hawkins	37	209	10	8	0	4.30
1B	S. Garvey	557	.255	21	81	1160	53	7	94	8.2	.994	D. Dravecky	26	161	9	11	0	3.07
2B	T. Flannery	368	.280	3	28	209	246	3	52	4.2	.993	L. Hoyt	35	159	8	11	0	5.15
W-74 L-88	SS	G. Templeton	510	.247	2	44	207	358	20	60	4.1	.966	McCullers	70	136	10	10	5	2.78
3B	G. Nettles	354	.218	16	55	83	174	16	14	2.4	.941	E. Show	24	136	9	5	0	2.97
Steve Boros	RF	T. Gwynn	642	.329	14	59	337	19	4	3	2.3	.989	C. Lefferts	83	108	9	8	4	3.09
CF	McReynolds	560	.288	26	96	332	9	8	4	2.3	.977	M. Thurmond	17	71	3	7	0	6.50
LF	J. Kruk	278	.309	4	38	102	4	2	0	1.5	.981	G. Gossage	45	65	5	7	21	4.45
C	T. Kennedy	432	.264	12	57	692	70	8	13	6.3	.990							
OF	M. Wynne	288	.264	7	37	203	3	3	2	1.7	.986							
UT	J. Royster	257	.257	5	26	87	166	14	23		.948							
O1	C. Martinez	244	.238	9	25	142	14	2	4		.987							
2B	B. Roberts	241	.253	1	12	166	172	10	33	4.0	.971							
C	B. Bochy	127	.252	8	22	202	22	2	3	4.7	.991							
Los Angeles												Valenzuela	34	269	21	11	0	3.14
1B	G. Brock	325	.234	16	52	726	87	3	46	8.2	.996	B. Welch	33	236	7	13	0	3.28
2B	S. Sax	633	.332	6	56	367	432	16	71	5.3	.980	O. Hershiser	35	231	14	14	0	3.85
W-73 L-89	SS	M. Duncan	407	.229	8	30	172	317	25	46	4.8	.951	R. Honeycutt	32	171	11	9	0	3.32
3B	B. Madlock	379	.280	10	60	72	170	24	7	2.6	.910	K. Howell	62	98	6	12	12	3.87
Tom Lasorda	RF	M. Marshall	330	.233	19	53	149	8	6	1	1.7	.963	Niedenfuer	60	80	6	6	11	3.71
CF	R. Williams	303	.277	4	32	179	5	3	2	1.5	.984							
LF	F. Stubbs	420	.226	23	58	206	10	7	2	1.8	.969							
C	M. Scioscia	374	.251	5	26	756	64	15	4	7.0	.982							
OF	K. Landreaux	283	.261	4	29	145	5	7	0	1.8	.955							
1B	E. Cabell	277	.256	2	29	360	32	5	29	6.5	.987							
3S	D. Anderson	216	.245	1	15	73	152	11	21		.953							
UT	B. Russell	216	.250	0	18	103	84	5	17		.974							
C	A. Trevino	202	.262	4	26	304	45	11	4	5.7	.969							
O1	L. Matuszek	199	.261	9	28	235	22	5	18		.981							
Atlanta												R. Mahler	39	238	14	18	0	4.88
1B	B. Horner	517	.273	27	87	1378	102	8	138	10.7	.995	D. Palmer	35	210	11	10	0	3.65
2B	G. Hubbard	408	.230	4	36	282	487	19	120	5.5	.976	Z. Smith	38	205	8	16	1	4.05
W-72 L-89	SS	A. Thomas	323	.251	6	32	143	290	19	62	4.7	.958	D. Alexander	17	117	6	6	0	3.84
3B	K. Oberkfell	503	.270	5	48	65	258	8	24	2.5	.976	J. Dedmon	57	100	6	6	3	2.98
Chuck Tanner	RF	O. Moreno	359	.234	4	27	151	8	5	3	1.7	.970	J. Acker	21	95	3	8	0	3.79
CF	D. Murphy	614	.265	29	83	303	6	6	1	2.0	.981	J. Johnson	17	87	6	7	0	4.97
LF	K. Griffey	292	.308	12	32	136	1	2	0	1.8	.986	G. Garber	61	78	5	5	24	2.54
C	O. Virgil	359	.223	15	48	682	93	13	9	7.1	.984	Assenmacher	61	68	7	3	7	2.50
S3	R. Ramirez	496	.240	8	33	155	371	29	68		.948							
OF	T. Harper	265	.257	8	30	92	5	3	0	1.2	.970							
OF	B. Sample	200	.285	6	14	69	1	1	1	1.3	.986							
UT	T. Simmons	127	.252	4	25	167	18	6	13		.969							

BATTING AND BASE RUNNING LEADERS

Batting Average
T. Raines, MON	.334
S. Sax, LA	.332
T. Gwynn, SD	.329
K. Bass, HOU	.311
K. Hernandez, NY	.310

Slugging Average
M. Schmidt, PHI	.547
Strawberry, NY	.507
McReynolds, SD	.504
G. Davis, HOU	.493
K. Bass, HOU	.486

Home Runs
M. Schmidt, PHI	37
G. Davis, HOU	31
D. Parker, CIN	31
D. Murphy, ATL	29

Total Bases
D. Parker, CIN	304
M. Schmidt, PHI	302
T. Gwynn, SD	300
V. Hayes, PHI	293
D. Murphy, ATL	293

Runs Batted In
M. Schmidt, PHI	119
D. Parker, CIN	116
G. Carter, NY	105
G. Davis, HOU	101
V. Hayes, PHI	98

Stolen Bases
V. Coleman, STL	107
E. Davis, CIN	80
T. Raines, MON	70
M. Duncan, LA	48
B. Doran, HOU	42
J. Samuel, PHI	42

Hits
T. Gwynn, SD	211
S. Sax, LA	210
T. Raines, MON	194
V. Hayes, PHI	186

Base on Balls
K. Hernandez, NY	94
M. Schmidt, PHI	89
C. Davis, SF	84
K. Oberkfell, ATL	83

Home Run Percentage
M. Schmidt, PHI	6.7
Strawberry, NY	5.7
G. Davis, HOU	5.4
B. Horner, ATL	5.2

Runs Scored
V. Hayes, PHI	107
T. Gwynn, SD	107
E. Davis, CIN	97
M. Schmidt, PHI	97

Doubles
V. Hayes, PHI	46
S. Sax, LA	43
S. Bream, PIT	37
S. Dunston, CHI	36

Triples
M. Webster, MON	13
J. Samuel, PHI	12
T. Raines, MON	10
V. Coleman, STL	8

PITCHING LEADERS

Winning Percentage
B. Ojeda, NY	.783
D. Gooden, NY	.739
S. Fernandez, NY	.727
R. Darling, NY	.714
M. Krukow, SF	.690

Earned Run Average
M. Scott, HOU	2.22
B. Ojeda, NY	2.57
R. Darling, NY	2.81
R. Rhoden, PIT	2.84
D. Gooden, NY	2.84

Wins
Valenzuela, LA	21
M. Krukow, SF	20
B. Ojeda, NY	18
M. Scott, HOU	18
D. Gooden, NY	17
B. Knepper, HOU	17

Saves
T. Worrell, STL	36
J. Reardon, MON	35
D. Smith, HOU	33
L. Smith, CHI	31
S. Bedrosian, PHI	29
J. Franco, CIN	29

Strikeouts
M. Scott, HOU	306
Valenzuela, LA	242
F. Youmans, MON	202
S. Fernandez, NY	200
D. Gooden, NY	200

Complete Games
Valenzuela, LA	20
D. Gooden, NY	12
R. Rhoden, PIT	12
M. Krukow, SF	10

Fewest Hits/9 Innings
M. Scott, HOU	5.95
F. Youmans, MON	5.96
N. Ryan, HOU	6.02
S. Fernandez, NY	7.09

Shutouts
M. Scott, HOU	5
B. Knepper, HOU	5
B. Welch, LA	3
Valenzuela, LA	3

Fewest Walks/9 Innings
D. Eckersley, CHI	1.93
S. Sanderson, CHI	1.96
M. Krukow, SF	2.02
B. Welch, LA	2.10

Most Strikeouts/9 Inn.
M. Scott, HOU	10.00
N. Ryan, HOU	9.81
S. Fernandez, NY	8.81
F. Youmans, MON	8.30

Innings
M. Scott, HOU	275
Valenzuela, LA	269
B. Knepper, HOU	258
R. Rhoden, PIT	254

Games Pitched
C. Lefferts, SD	83
R. McDowell, NY	75
T. Worrell, STL	74
J. Franco, CIN	74

NATIONAL LEAGUE 1986, cont.

		W	L	PCT	GB	R	OR	Batting 2B	3B	HR	BA	SA	SB	Fielding E	DP	FA	Pitching CG	BB	SO	ShO	SV	ERA
East	New York	108	54	.667		**783**	578	261	31	148	**.263**	**.401**	118	138	145	.978	27	509	1083	11	46	**3.11**
	Philadelphia	86	75	.534	21.5	739	713	266	39	154	.253	.400	153	137	157	.978	22	553	874	11	39	3.85
	St. Louis	79	82	.491	28.5	601	611	216	48	58	.236	.327	**262**	**123**	178	**.981**	17	**485**	761	4	46	3.37
	Montreal	78	83	.484	29.5	637	688	255	**50**	110	.254	.379	193	133	132	.979	15	566	1051	9	50	3.78
	Chicago	70	90	.438	37	680	781	257	27	**155**	.256	.397	132	124	147	.980	11	557	962	6	42	4.49
	Pittsburgh	64	98	.395	44	663	700	**273**	33	111	.250	.374	152	143	134	.978	17	570	924	9	30	3.90
West	Houston	96	66	.593		654	**569**	244	32	125	.255	.381	163	130	108	.979	18	523	**1160**	**19**	**51**	3.15
	Cincinnati	86	76	.531	10	732	717	237	35	144	.254	.387	177	140	160	.978	14	524	924	8	45	3.91
	San Francisco	83	79	.512	13	698	618	269	29	114	.253	.375	148	143	149	.977	18	591	992	10	35	3.33
	San Diego	74	88	.457	22	656	723	239	25	136	.261	.388	96	137	135	.978	13	607	934	7	32	3.99
	Los Angeles	73	89	.451	23	638	679	232	14	130	.251	.370	155	181	118	.971	**35**	499	1051	14	25	3.76
	Atlanta	72	89	.447	23.5	615	719	241	24	138	.250	.381	93	141	**181**	.978	17	576	932	5	39	3.97
						8096	8096	2990	387	1523	.253	.380	1842	1670	1744	.978	224	6560	11648	113	480	3.72

AMERICAN LEAGUE 1986

		POS	Player	AB	BA	HR	RBI	PO	A	E	DP	TC/G	FA	Pitcher	G	IP	W	L	SV	ERA
East	**Boston** W-95 L-66 John McNamara	1B	B. Buckner	629	.267	18	102	1067	**157**	14	104	9.0	.989	R. Clemens	33	254	**24**	4	0	**2.48**
		2B	M. Barrett	625	.286	4	60	303	**450**	14	101	4.9	.982	O. Boyd	30	214	16	10	0	3.78
		SS	E. Romero	233	.210	2	23	102	132	10	29	3.3	.959	B. Hurst	25	174	13	8	0	2.99
		3B	W. Boggs	580	**.357**	8	71	121	267	19	30	2.7	.953	A. Nipper	26	159	10	12	0	5.38
		RF	D. Evans	529	.259	26	97	280	10	5	3	2.0	.983	T. Seaver	16	104	5	7	0	3.80
		CF	T. Armas	425	.264	11	58	247	4	8	0	2.2	.969	J. Sellers	14	82	3	7	0	4.94
		LF	J. Rice	618	.324	20	110	330	16	8	0	2.3	.977	B. Stanley	66	82	6	6	16	4.37
		C	R. Gedman	462	.258	16	65	**866**	65	6	10	**7.0**	.994	C. Schiraldi	25	51	4	2	9	1.41
		DH	D. Baylor	585	.238	31	94							J. Sambito	53	45	2	0	12	4.84
		SS	R. Quinones	190	.237	2	15	86	150	15	26	4.0	.940							
	New York W-90 L-72 Lou Piniella	1B	D. Mattingly	677	.352	31	113	**1377**	100	6	132	9.3	**.996**	D. Rasmussen	31	202	18	6	0	3.88
		2B	W. Randolph	492	.276	5	50	313	381	20	94	5.1	.972	R. Guidry	30	192	9	12	0	3.98
		SS	B. Meacham	161	.224	0	10	70	149	12	31	4.1	.948	D. Drabek	27	132	7	8	0	4.10
		3B	Pagliarulo	504	.238	28	71	103	283	19	25	2.8	.953	B. Tewksbury	23	130	9	5	0	3.31
		RF	D. Winfield	565	.262	24	104	292	9	5	5	2.1	.984	J. Niekro	25	126	9	10	0	4.87
		CF	R. Henderson	608	.263	28	74	426	4	6	0	3.0	.986	D. Righetti	74	107	8	8	46	2.45
		LF	D. Pasqua	280	.293	16	45	148	4	2	1	1.9	.987	B. Shirley	39	105	0	4	3	5.04
		C	B. Wynegar	194	.206	7	29	325	22	2	1	6.1	.994	B. Fisher	62	97	9	5	6	4.93
		DH	M. Easler	490	.302	14	78													
		SS	W. Tolleson	215	.284	0	14	87	177	5	35	4.8	.981							
		OF	K. Griffey	198	.303	9	26	96	5	3	2	2.0	.971							
		C	R. Hassey	191	.298	6	29	251	9	4	4	5.2	.985							
		C	J. Skinner	166	.259	1	17	280	22	6	5	5.7	.981							
	Detroit W-87 L-75 Sparky Anderson	1B	D. Evans	507	.241	29	85	808	108	2	85	8.7	.998	J. Morris	35	267	21	8	0	3.27
		2B	L. Whitaker	584	.269	20	73	276	421	11	98	5.0	.984	W. Terrell	34	217	15	12	0	4.56
		SS	A. Trammell	574	.277	21	75	238	445	22	99	4.7	.969	F. Tanana	32	188	12	9	0	4.16
		3B	D. Coles	521	.273	20	86	107	242	23	23	2.8	.938	E. King	33	138	11	4	3	3.51
		RF	K. Gibson	441	.268	28	86	190	2	2	1	1.7	.990	R. O'Neal	37	123	3	7	2	4.33
		CF	C. Lemon	403	.251	12	53	316	6	5	1	2.6	.985	D. Petry	20	116	5	10	0	4.66
		LF	D. Collins	419	.270	1	27	211	2	1	1	2.3	.995	G. Hernandez	64	89	8	7	24	3.55
		C	L. Parrish	327	.257	22	62	483	48	6	5	6.3	.989	B. Campbell	34	56	3	6	3	3.88
		DH	J. Grubb	210	.333	13	51													
		OF	L. Herndon	283	.247	8	37	156	2	2	0	1.9	.988							
		UT	T. Brookens	281	.270	3	25	106	144	7	26		.973							
		OF	P. Sheridan	236	.237	6	19	172	1	4	0	2.0	.977							
	Toronto W-86 L-76 Jimy Williams	1B	W. Upshaw	573	.251	9	60	1314	131	12	118	9.5	.992	J. Key	36	232	14	11	0	3.57
		2B	D. Garcia	424	.281	6	46	224	286	8	66	4.9	.985	J. Clancy	34	219	14	14	0	3.94
		SS	T. Fernandez	**687**	.310	10	65	**294**	445	13	103	4.6	**.983**	D. Stieb	37	205	7	12	1	4.74
		3B	R. Mulliniks	348	.259	11	45	60	176	6	13	2.2	**.975**	M. Eichhorn	69	157	14	6	10	1.72
		RF	J. Barfield	589	.289	**40**	108	368	**20**	3	**8**	2.5	.992	J. Cerutti	34	145	9	4	1	4.15
		CF	L. Moseby	589	.253	21	86	371	6	6	1	2.6	.984	D. Alexander	17	111	5	4	0	4.46
		LF	G. Bell	641	.309	31	108	269	17	10	1	2.0	.966	T. Henke	63	91	9	5	27	3.35
		C	E. Whitt	395	.268	16	56	709	41	7	7	5.9	.991	D. Lamp	40	73	2	6	2	5.05
		DH	C. Johnson	336	.250	15	55													
		32	G. Iorg	327	.260	3	44	91	185	12	16		.958							
		DO	R. Leach	246	.309	5	39	44	0	1	0	1.2	.978							
	Cleveland W-84 L-78 Pat Corrales	1B	P. Tabler	473	.326	6	48	846	84	9	87	8.8	.990	T. Candiotti	36	252	16	12	0	3.57
		2B	T. Bernazard	562	.301	17	73	**351**	442	17	95	5.5	.979	P. Niekro	34	210	11	11	0	4.32
		SS	J. Franco	599	.306	10	74	231	374	18	81	4.6	.971	K. Schrom	34	206	14	7	0	4.54
		3B	B. Jacoby	583	.288	17	80	109	292	25	24	2.7	.941	S. Bailes	62	113	10	10	7	4.95
		RF	J. Carter	663	.302	29	**121**	241	8	6	2	2.5	.976	E. Camacho	51	57	2	4	20	4.08
		CF	B. Butler	587	.278	4	51	434	9	3	3	2.8	.993	F. Wills	26	40	4	4	4	4.91
		LF	M. Hall	442	.296	18	77	233	7	7	1	2.0	.972							
		C	A. Allanson	293	.225	1	29	446	33	**20**	4	5.0	.960							
		OS	C. Snyder	416	.272	24	69	203	70	10	21		.965							
		DH	A. Thornton	401	.229	17	66													
		C	C. Bando	254	.268	2	26	359	30	4	3	4.6	.990							
		OD	C. Castillo	205	.278	8	32	58	4	4	1	1.8	.939							

AMERICAN LEAGUE 1986, *cont.*

	POS	Player	AB	BA	HR	RBI	PO	A	E	DP	TC/G	FA	Pitcher	G	IP	W	L	SV	ERA
Milwaukee	1B	C. Cooper	542	.258	12	75	697	61	9	78	8.5	.988	T. Higuera	34	248	20	11	0	2.79
	2B	J. Gantner	497	.274	7	38	304	347	10	87	4.9	.985	B. Wegman	35	198	5	12	0	5.13
W-77 L-84	SS	E. Riles	524	.252	9	47	212	327	20	76	3.9	.964	T. Leary	33	188	12	12	0	4.21
	3B	P. Molitor	437	.281	9	55	82	170	15	25	2.9	.944	J. Nieves	35	185	11	12	0	4.92
George Bamberger	RF	R. Deer	466	.232	33	86	286	8	8	1	2.3	.974	D. Darwin	27	130	6	8	0	3.52
W-71 L-81	CF	R. Yount	522	.312	9	46	352	9	1	4	2.8	**.997**	D. Plesac	51	91	10	7	14	2.97
	LF	G. Braggs	215	.237	4	18	116	5	12	0	2.4	.910	M. Clear	59	74	5	5	16	2.20
Tom Trebelhorn	C	C. Moore	235	.260	3	39	425	43	4	6	6.6	.992							
W-6 L-3	DH	B. Oglivie	346	.283	5	53													
	3B	D. Sveum	317	.246	7	35	45	122	**26**	8	3.0	.865							
	UT	B. Schroeder	217	.212	7	19	307	25	1	13		.997							
	C	R. Cerone	216	.259	4	18	391	44	4	2	6.5	.991							
	OF	R. Manning	205	.254	8	27	155	3	2	0	1.9	.988							
	1B	B. Robidoux	181	.227	1	21	326	29	5	35	8.4	.986							
Baltimore	1B	E. Murray	495	.305	17	84	1045	88	13	100	9.6	.989	M. Boddicker	33	218	14	12	0	4.70
	2B	J. Bonilla	284	.243	1	18	122	140	5	38	3.8	.981	S. McGregor	34	203	11	15	0	4.52
W-73 L-89	SS	C. Ripken	627	.282	25	81	240	**482**	13	105	4.5	.982	K. Dixon	35	202	11	13	0	4.58
	3B	F. Rayford	210	.176	8	19	40	115	15	15	2.4	.912	M. Flanagan	29	172	7	11	0	4.24
Earl Weaver	RF	L. Lacy	491	.287	11	47	239	8	2	4	2.1	.992	S. Davis	25	154	9	12	0	3.62
	CF	F. Lynn	397	.287	23	67	244	2	4	1	2.3	.984	R. Bordi	52	107	6	4	3	4.46
	LF	M. Young	369	.252	9	42	149	1	6	0	2.3	.962	D. Aase	66	82	6	7	34	2.98
	C	R. Dempsey	327	.208	13	29	659	53	7	9	5.9	.990							
	DH	L. Sheets	338	.272	18	60													
	OF	J. Shelby	404	.228	11	49	222	5	5	2	1.9	.978							
	UT	J. Beniquez	343	.300	6	36	211	56	13	15		.954							
	2B	A. Wiggins	239	.251	0	11	121	151	6	40	4.2	.978							
	UT	J. Traber	212	.255	13	44	243	23	5	28		.982							
	3B	T. O'Malley	181	.254	1	18	37	98	9	8	2.6	.938							
	DO	J. Dwyer	160	.244	8	31	33	3	0	1	1.5	1.000							
West **California**	1B	W. Joyner	593	.290	22	100	1222	139	15	128	9.1	.989	M. Witt	34	269	18	10	0	2.84
	2B	R. Wilfong	288	.219	3	33	135	257	7	48	4.4	.982	McCaskill	34	246	17	10	0	3.36
W-92 L-70	SS	D. Schofield	458	.249	13	57	246	389	18	103	4.8	.972	D. Sutton	34	207	15	11	0	3.74
	3B	D. DeCinces	512	.256	26	96	119	216	12	19	2.6	.965	R. Romanick	18	106	5	8	0	5.50
Gene Mauch	RF	R. Jones	393	.229	17	49	205	5	4	0	1.8	.981	Candelaria	16	92	10	2	0	2.55
	CF	G. Pettis	539	.258	5	58	**462**	9	7	3	**3.1**	.985	D. Corbett	46	79	4	2	10	3.66
	LF	B. Downing	513	.267	20	95	267	5	3	0	2.0	.989	J. Slaton	14	73	4	6	0	5.65
	C	B. Boone	442	.222	7	49	812	**84**	11	16	6.3	.988	D. Moore	49	73	4	5	21	2.97
	DH	R. Jackson	419	.241	18	58							T. Forster	41	41	4	1	5	3.51
	2B	B. Grich	313	.268	9	30	127	221	7	49	4.1	.980							
	OF	G. Hendrick	283	.272	14	47	144	6	5	2	1.7	.968							
	UT	R. Burleson	271	.284	5	29	62	90	3	15		.981							
	3B	J. Howell	151	.272	4	21	28	56	2	4	2.2	.977							
Texas	1B	P. O'Brien	551	.290	23	90	1224	115	11	123	8.7	.992	C. Hough	33	230	17	10	0	3.79
	2B	T. Harrah	289	.218	7	41	166	211	7	49	4.1	.982	E. Correa	32	202	12	14	0	4.23
W-87 L-75	SS	S. Fletcher	530	.300	3	50	196	354	15	86	4.2	.973	J. Guzman	29	172	9	15	0	4.54
	3B	S. Buechele	461	.243	18	54	111	226	11	17	2.5	.968	B. Witt	31	158	11	9	0	5.48
Bobby Valentine	RF	Incaviglia	540	.250	30	88	157	6	**14**	1	1.6	.921	M. Mason	27	135	7	3	0	4.33
	CF	O. McDowell	572	.266	18	49	325	13	3	3	2.3	.991	G. Harris	73	111	10	8	20	2.83
	LF	G. Ward	380	.316	5	51	237	8	1	3	2.4	.996	M. Williams	80	98	8	6	8	3.58
	C	D. Slaught	314	.264	13	46	533	40	4	1	6.3	.993	D. Mohorcic	58	79	2	4	7	2.51
	DH	L. Parrish	464	.276	28	94													
	OF	R. Sierra	382	.264	16	55	200	7	6	1	2.0	.972							
	2S	C. Wilkerson	236	.237	0	15	125	199	13	56		.961							
	UT	T. Paciorek	213	.286	4	22	178	45	4	16		.982							
	CD	D. Porter	155	.265	12	29	165	9	1	2	7.0	.994							
Kansas City	1B	S. Balboni	512	.229	29	88	1236	98	**18**	115	**9.9**	.987	C. Leibrandt	35	231	14	11	0	4.09
	2B	F. White	566	.272	22	84	316	439	10	91	5.1	.987	D. Leonard	33	193	8	13	0	4.44
W-76 L-86	SS	A. Salazar	298	.245	0	24	121	283	9	50	3.6	.978	D. Jackson	32	186	11	12	1	3.20
	3B	G. Brett	441	.290	16	73	97	218	16	17	2.9	.952	M. Gubicza	35	181	12	6	0	3.64
Dick Howser	RF	D. Motley	217	.203	7	20	92	2	2	1	1.5	.979	Saberhagen	30	156	7	12	0	4.15
W-40 L-48	CF	W. Wilson	631	.269	9	44	408	4	3	2	2.7	.993	S. Bankhead	24	121	8	9	0	4.61
	LF	L. Smith	508	.287	8	44	245	5	9	1	2.2	.965	B. Black	56	121	5	10	9	3.20
Mike Ferraro	C	J. Sundberg	429	.212	12	42	686	46	4	11	5.5	**.995**	S. Farr	56	109	8	4	8	3.13
W-36 L-38	DH	J. Orta	336	.277	9	46							Quisenberry	62	81	3	7	12	2.77
	OF	R. Law	307	.261	1	36	145	2	2	0	1.9	.987							
	DH	H. McRae	278	.252	7	37													
	CS	J. Quirk	219	.215	8	26	260	58	4	9		.988							
	OF	M. Kingery	209	.258	3	14	102	6	3	2	1.9	.973							
	SS	Biancalana	190	.242	2	8	102	177	16	40	3.3	.946							

AMERICAN LEAGUE 1986, *cont.*

Oakland
W-76 L-86
Jackie Moore W-29 L-44
Jeff Newman W-2 L-8
Tony LaRussa W-45 L-34

POS	Player	AB	BA	HR	RBI	PO	A	E	DP	TC/G	FA	Pitcher	G	IP	W	L	SV	ERA
1B	B. Bochte	407	.256	6	43	912	88	9	79	8.8	.991	C. Young	29	198	13	9	0	3.45
2B	T. Phillips	441	.256	5	52	160	290	11	40	5.2	.976	J. Rijo	39	194	9	11	1	4.65
SS	A. Griffin	594	.285	4	51	282	421	25	85	4.5	.966	J. Andujar	28	155	12	7	1	3.82
3B	C. Lansford	591	.284	19	72	67	147	4	13	2.2	.982	D. Stewart	29	149	9	5	0	3.74
RF	M. Davis	489	.268	19	55	310	9	9	2	2.4	.973	E. Plunk	26	120	4	7	0	5.31
CF	D. Murphy	329	.252	9	39	276	6	2	3	2.9	.993	B. Mooneyham	45	100	4	5	2	4.52
LF	J. Canseco	600	.240	33	117	319	4	14	1	2.2	.958	C. Codiroli	16	92	5	8	0	4.03
C	M. Tettleton	211	.204	10	35	463	32	8	6	5.7	.984	S. Ontiveros	46	73	2	2	10	4.71
DH	D. Kingman	561	.210	35	94							R. Langford	16	55	1	10	0	7.36
23	D. Hill	339	.283	4	29	104	213	9	31		.972	J. Howell	38	53	3	6	16	3.38
OF	D. Baker	242	.240	4	19	80	4	0	1	1.5	1.000							
C	J. Willard	161	.267	4	26	300	12	2	1	4.4	.994							

Chicago
W-72 L-90
Tony LaRussa W-26 L-38
Doug Rader W-1 L-1
Jim Fregosi W-45 L-51

POS	Player	AB	BA	HR	RBI	PO	A	E	DP	TC/G	FA	Pitcher	G	IP	W	L	SV	ERA
1B	G. Walker	282	.277	13	51	670	57	5	57	9.5	.993	R. Dotson	34	197	10	17	0	5.48
2B	J. Cruz	209	.215	0	19	132	205	5	45	4.4	.985	F. Bannister	28	165	10	14	0	3.54
SS	O. Guillen	547	.250	2	47	261	459	22	93	4.7	.970	J. Cowley	27	162	11	11	0	3.88
3B	T. Hulett	520	.231	17	44	70	144	11	10	2.5	.951	G. Nelson	54	115	6	6	0	3.85
RF	H. Baines	570	.296	21	88	295	15	5	5	2.2	.984	N. Allen	22	113	7	2	0	3.82
CF	D. Boston	199	.266	5	22	152	3	5	1	3.0	.969	J. Davis	19	105	4	5	0	4.70
LF	J. Cangelosi	438	.235	2	32	276	7	9	1	2.3	.969	D. Schmidt	49	92	3	6	8	3.31
C	C. Fisk	457	.221	14	63	389	39	4	3	6.1	.991	B. James	49	58	5	4	14	5.25
DH	R. Kittle	296	.213	17	48													
3B	W. Tolleson	260	.250	3	29	37	113	7	9	2.4	.955							
O1	B. Bonilla	234	.269	2	26	361	22	2	26		.995							
UT	J. Hairston	225	.271	5	26	132	9	0	11		1.000							
DH	R. Hassey	150	.353	3	20													
C	J. Skinner	149	.201	4	20	227	15	3	4	4.1	.988							

Minnesota
W-71 L-91
Ray Miller W-59 L-80
Tom Kelly W-12 L-11

POS	Player	AB	BA	HR	RBI	PO	A	E	DP	TC/G	FA	Pitcher	G	IP	W	L	SV	ERA
1B	K. Hrbek	550	.267	29	91	1218	104	10	137	9.1	.992	B. Blyleven	36	272	17	14	0	4.01
2B	Lombardozzi	453	.227	8	33	289	407	6	102	4.5	.991	F. Viola	37	246	16	13	0	4.51
SS	G. Gagne	472	.250	12	54	228	377	26	96	4.1	.959	M. Smithson	34	198	13	14	0	4.77
3B	G. Gaetti	596	.287	34	108	118	334	21	36	3.0	.956	N. Heaton	21	124	4	9	1	3.98
RF	T. Brunansky	593	.256	23	75	315	10	6	1	2.2	.982	M. Portugal	27	113	6	10	1	4.31
CF	K. Puckett	680	.328	31	96	429	8	6	3	2.8	.986	A. Anderson	21	84	3	6	1	5.55
LF	R. Bush	357	.269	7	45	167	2	4	0	1.7	.977	K. Atherton	47	82	5	8	10	3.75
C	M. Salas	258	.233	8	33	358	32	8	5	5.8	.980	R. Davis	36	39	2	6	2	9.08
DH	R. Smalley	459	.246	20	57													
UT	M. Hatcher	317	.278	3	32	220	16	4	16		.983							
C	T. Laudner	193	.244	10	29	299	13	5	3	4.7	.984							
OF	B. Beane	183	.213	3	15	118	0	0	0	1.8	1.000							
C	J. Reed	165	.236	2	9	332	19	2	5	5.5	.994							

Seattle
W-67 L-95
Chuck Cottier W-9 L-19
Marty Martinez W-0 L-1
Dick Williams W-58 L-75

POS	Player	AB	BA	HR	RBI	PO	A	E	DP	TC/G	FA	Pitcher	G	IP	W	L	SV	ERA
1B	A. Davis	479	.271	18	72	880	82	14	112	9.7	.986	M. Moore	38	266	11	13	1	4.30
2B	H. Reynolds	445	.222	1	24	278	415	16	111	5.6	.977	M. Langston	37	239	12	14	0	4.85
SS	S. Owen	402	.246	0	35	209	372	17	99*	5.3*	.972	M. Morgan	37	216	11	17	1	4.53
3B	J. Presley	616	.265	27	107	110	308	15	31	2.8	.965	B. Swift	29	115	2	9	0	5.46
RF	D. Tartabull	511	.270	25	96	157	7	8	0	1.7	.953	M. Young	65	104	8	6	13	3.82
CF	J. Moses	399	.256	3	34	211	9	3	1	2.4	.987	M. Huismann	36	80	3	3	4	3.71
LF	P. Bradley	526	.310	12	50	250	11	1	0	1.9	.996	P. Ladd	52	71	8	6	6	3.82
C	B. Kearney	204	.240	6	25	419	46	5	3	5.9	.989							
DH	K. Phelps	344	.247	24	64													
OF	D. Henderson	337	.276	14	44	182	9	4	1	2.4	.979							
C	S. Bradley	199	.302	5	28	281	21	3	5	5.2	.990							
DH	G. Thomas	170	.194	10	26													

BATTING AND BASE RUNNING LEADERS

Batting Average
W. Boggs, BOS	.357
D. Mattingly, NY	.352
K. Puckett, MIN	.328
J. Rice, BOS	.324
R. Yount, MIL	.312

Slugging Average
D. Mattingly, NY	.573
J. Barfield, TOR	.559
K. Puckett, MIN	.537
G. Bell, TOR	.532
G. Gaetti, MIN	.518

Home Runs
J. Barfield, TOR	40
D. Kingman, OAK	35
G. Gaetti, MIN	34
R. Deer, MIL	33
J. Canseco, OAK	33

Winning Percentage
R. Clemens, BOS	.857
D. Rasmussen, NY	.750
J. Morris, DET	.724
K. Schrom, CLE	.667
M. Gubicza, KC	.667

PITCHING LEADERS

Earned Run Average
R. Clemens, BOS	2.48
T. Higuera, MIL	2.79
M. Witt, CAL	2.84
B. Hurst, BOS	2.99
D. Jackson, KC	3.20

Wins
R. Clemens, BOS	24
J. Morris, DET	21
T. Higuera, MIL	20
D. Rasmussen, NY	18
M. Witt, CAL	18

Total Bases
D. Mattingly, NY	388
K. Puckett, MIN	365
G. Bell, TOR	341
J. Carter, CLE	341
J. Barfield, TOR	329

Runs Batted In
J. Carter, CLE	121
J. Canseco, OAK	117
D. Mattingly, NY	113
J. Rice, BOS	110

Stolen Bases
R. Henderson, NY	87
J. Cangelosi, CHI	50
G. Pettis, CAL	50
K. Gibson, DET	34
W. Wilson, KC	34

Saves
D. Righetti, NY	46
D. Aase, BAL	34
T. Henke, TOR	27
G. Hernandez, DET	24
D. Moore, CAL	21

Strikeouts
M. Langston, SEA	245
R. Clemens, BOS	238
J. Morris, DET	223
B. Blyleven, MIN	215
M. Witt, CAL	208

Complete Games
T. Candiotti, CLE	17
B. Blyleven, MIN	16
T. Higuera, MIL	15
J. Morris, DET	15
M. Witt, CAL	14

Hits
D. Mattingly, NY	238
K. Puckett, MIN	223
T. Fernandez, TOR	213
W. Boggs, BOS	207

Base on Balls
W. Boggs, BOS	105
D. Evans, BOS	97
W. Randolph, NY	94
R. Jackson, CAL	92

Home Run Percentage
R. Deer, MIL	7.1
J. Barfield, TOR	6.8
K. Gibson, DET	6.3
D. Kingman, OAK	6.2

Fewest Hits/9 Innings
R. Clemens, BOS	6.34
D. Rasmussen, NY	7.13
M. Witt, CAL	7.29
C. Hough, TEX	7.35

Shutouts
J. Morris, DET	6
B. Hurst, BOS	4
T. Higuera, MIL	4

Fewest Walks/9 Innings
R. Guidry, NY	1.78
O. Boyd, BOS	1.89
B. Blyleven, MIN	1.92
B. Wegman, MIL	1.95

AMERICAN LEAGUE 1986, *cont.*

BATTING AND BASE RUNNING LEADERS

Runs Scored		Doubles		Triples		Most Strikeouts/9 Inn.	
R. Henderson, NY	130	D. Mattingly, NY	53	B. Butler, CLE	14	M. Langston, SEA	9.21
K. Puckett, MIN	119	W. Boggs, BOS	47	R. Sierra, TEX	10	B. Hurst, BOS	8.62
D. Mattingly, NY	117	J. Rice, BOS	39	J. Carter, CLE	9	R. Clemens, BOS	8.43
J. Carter, CLE	108	M. Barrett, BOS	39	T. Fernandez, TOR	9	E. Correa, TEX	8.41

PITCHING LEADERS

Innings		Games Pitched	
B. Blyleven, MIN	272	M. Williams, TEX	80
M. Witt, CAL	269	D. Righetti, NY	74
J. Morris, DET	267	G. Harris, TEX	73
M. Moore, SEA	266	M. Eichhorn, TOR	69

		W	L	PCT	GB	R	OR	2B	3B	HR	BA	SA	SB	E	DP	FA	CG	BB	SO	ShO	SV	ERA
East	Boston	95	66	.590		794	696	**320**	21	144	.271	.415	41	129	146	.979	36	**474**	1033	6	41	3.93
	New York	90	72	.556	5.5	797	738	275	23	188	.271	**.430**	139	127	153	.979	13	492	878	8	**58**	4.11
	Detroit	87	75	.537	8.5	798	714	234	30	**198**	.263	.424	138	108	163	.982	33	571	880	12	38	4.02
	Toronto	86	76	.531	9.5	809	733	285	35	181	.269	.427	110	**100**	150	**.984**	16	487	1002	12	44	4.08
	Cleveland	84	78	.519	11.5	**831**	841	270	**45**	157	**.284**	.430	141	157	148	.975	31	605	744	7	34	4.57
	Milwaukee	77	84	.478	18	667	734	255	38	127	.255	.385	100	146	146	.976	29	494	952	12	32	4.01
	Baltimore	73	89	.451	22.5	708	760	223	13	169	.258	.395	64	135	163	.978	17	535	954	6	39	4.30
West	California	92	70	.568		786	684	236	36	167	.255	.404	109	107	156	.983	29	478	955	12	40	3.84
	Texas	87	75	.537	5	771	743	248	43	184	.267	.428	103	122	160	.980	15	736	**1059**	8	41	4.11
	Kansas City	76	86	.469	16	654	**673**	264	**45**	137	.252	.390	97	123	153	.980	24	479	888	**13**	31	**3.82**
	Oakland	76	86	.469	16	731	760	213	25	163	.252	.390	139	135	120	.978	22	667	937	8	37	4.31
	Chicago	72	90	.444	20	644	699	197	34	121	.247	.363	115	117	142	.981	18	561	895	8	38	3.93
	Minnesota	71	91	.438	21	741	839	257	39	196	.261	.428	81	118	168	.980	**39**	503	937	6	24	4.77
	Seattle	67	95	.414	25	718	835	243	41	158	.253	.399	93	156	**191**	.975	33	585	944	5	27	4.65
						10449	10449	3520	468	2290	.262	.408	1470	1780	2159	.979	355	7667	13058	123	524	4.18

Column group headers: **Batting** (2B, 3B, HR, BA, SA), **Fielding** (E, DP, FA), **Pitching** (CG, BB, SO, ShO, SV).

NATIONAL LEAGUE 1987

		POS	Player	AB	BA	HR	RBI	PO	A	E	DP	TC/G	FA	Pitcher	G	IP	W	L	SV	ERA
East	**St. Louis**	1B	J. Clark	419	.286	35	106	1151	77	14	116	9.9	.989	D. Cox	31	199	11	9	0	3.88
		2B	T. Herr	510	.263	2	83	306	350	7	103	4.8	.989	G. Mathews	32	198	11	11	0	3.73
	W-95 L-67	SS	O. Smith	600	.303	0	75	245	**516**	10	**111**	4.9	**.987**	B. Forsch	33	179	11	7	0	4.32
		3B	T. Pendleton	583	.286	12	96	117	**369**	26	27	**3.2**	.949	J. Magrane	27	170	9	7	0	3.54
	Whitey Herzog	RF	C. Ford	228	.285	3	26	157	2	3	0	2.2	.981	R. Horton	67	125	8	3	7	3.82
		CF	W. McGee	620	.285	11	105	353	9	7	1	2.4	.981	B. Dawley	60	97	5	8	2	4.47
		LF	V. Coleman	623	.289	3	43	274	16	9	3	2.0	.970	J. Tudor	16	96	10	2	0	3.84
		C	T. Pena	384	.214	5	44	615	51	8	8	6.0	.988	T. Worrell	75	95	8	6	33	2.66
		UT	J. Oquendo	248	.286	1	24	149	133	4	31		.986	K. Dayley	53	61	9	5	4	2.66
		OF	J. Lindeman	207	.208	8	28	78	4	2	3	1.7	.976							
		C	S. Lake	179	.251	2	19	253	21	1	2	4.7	.996							
		OF	J. Morris	157	.261	3	23	86	0	1	0	1.2	.989							
	New York	1B	K. Hernandez	587	.290	18	89	1298	**149**	10	110	9.5	.993	R. Darling	32	208	12	8	0	4.29
		2B	T. Teufel	299	.308	14	61	138	213	10	43	3.9	.972	D. Gooden	25	180	15	7	0	3.21
	W-92 L-70	SS	R. Santana	439	.255	5	44	213	396	17	82	4.5	.973	S. Fernandez	28	156	12	8	0	3.81
		3B	H. Johnson	554	.265	36	99	82	235	21	15	2.4	.938	T. Leach	44	131	11	1	0	3.22
	Davey Johnson	RF	Strawberry	532	.284	39	104	272	6	8	3	1.9	.972	R. Aguilera	18	115	11	3	0	3.60
		CF	L. Dykstra	431	.285	10	43	239	4	3	1	2.1	.988	J. Mitchell	20	112	3	6	0	4.11
		LF	McReynolds	590	.276	29	95	286	8	4	0	2.0	.987	D. Cone	21	99	5	6	1	3.71
		C	G. Carter	523	.235	20	83	874	70	9	**13**	7.1	.991	R. McDowell	56	89	7	5	25	4.16
		OF	M. Wilson	385	.299	9	34	205	3	8	2	2.0	.963	J. Orosco	58	77	3	9	16	4.44
		2B	W. Backman	300	.250	1	23	131	210	4	44	4.0	.983	R. Myers	54	75	3	6	6	3.96
		3B	D. Magadan	192	.318	3	24	17	85	2	5	2.1	.981							
		C	B. Lyons	130	.254	4	24	223	17	4	0	5.0	.984							
		O1	L. Mazzilli	124	.306	3	24	82	3	0	1		1.000							
	Montreal	1B	A. Galarraga	551	.305	13	90	**1300**	103	10	96	9.7	.993	N. Heaton	32	193	13	10	0	4.52
		2B	V. Law	436	.273	12	56	158	276	9	47	4.2	.980	B. Sebra	36	177	6	15	0	4.42
	W-91 L-71	SS	H. Brooks	430	.263	14	72	131	271	20	53	3.9	.953	B. Smith	26	150	10	9	0	4.37
		3B	T. Wallach	593	.298	26	123	**128**	292	21	21	2.9	.952	D. Martinez	22	145	11	4	0	3.30
	Buck Rodgers	RF	M. Webster	588	.281	15	63	266	8	5	0	1.8	.982	McGaffigan	69	120	5	2	12	2.39
		CF	Winningham	347	.239	4	41	225	5	6	1	1.8	.975	F. Youmans	23	116	9	8	0	4.64
		LF	T. Raines	530	.330	18	68	297	9	4	1	2.2	.987	T. Burke	55	91	7	0	18	1.19
		C	Fitzgerald	287	.240	3	36	602	27	12	2	6.2	.981	St. Claire	44	67	3	3	7	4.03
		UT	C. Candaele	449	.272	1	23	237	176	8	28		.981	J. Parrett	45	62	7	6	6	4.21
		S2	T. Foley	280	.293	5	24	133	186	9	43		.973	B. McClure	52	52	6	1	5	3.44
		C	J. Reed	207	.213	1	21	357	36	12	6	5.5	.970							
		OF	R. Nichols	147	.265	4	20	97	4	1	0	1.7	.990							

NATIONAL LEAGUE 1987, *cont.*

Philadelphia

W-80 L-82

John Felske
W-29 L-32

Lee Elia
W-51 L-50

POS	Player	AB	BA	HR	RBI	PO	A	E	DP	TC/G	FA	Pitcher	G	IP	W	L	SV	ERA
1B	V. Hayes	556	.277	21	84	1164	78	12	100	8.7	.990	S. Rawley	36	230	17	11	0	4.39
2B	J. Samuel	655	.272	28	100	374	434	18	99	5.2	.978	D. Carman	35	211	13	11	0	4.22
SS	S. Jeltz	293	.232	0	12	191	271	14	55	4.2	.971	B. Ruffin	35	205	11	14	0	4.35
3B	M. Schmidt	522	.293	35	113	87	315	12	28	3.0	.971	K. Gross	34	201	9	16	0	4.35
RF	G. Wilson	569	.264	14	54	315	18	11	2	2.2	.968	M. Jackson	55	109	3	10	1	4.20
CF	M. Thompson	527	.302	7	43	354	4	4	1	2.5	.989	K. Tekulve	90	105	6	4	3	3.09
LF	C. James	358	.293	17	54	198	5	2	1	1.9	.990	S. Bedrosian	65	89	5	3	40	2.83
C	L. Parrish	466	.245	17	67	724	66	9	1	6.3	.989							
SS	L. Aguayo	209	.206	12	21	81	154	7	29	3.1	.971							
31	R. Schu	196	.235	7	23	193	71	10	11		.964							

Pittsburgh

W-80 L-82

Jim Leyland

POS	Player	AB	BA	HR	RBI	PO	A	E	DP	TC/G	FA	Pitcher	G	IP	W	L	SV	ERA
1B	S. Bream	516	.275	13	65	1236	127	17	109	9.6	.988	B. Fisher	37	185	11	9	0	4.52
2B	J. Ray	472	.273	5	54	248	358	12	84	5.2	.981	R. Reuschel	25	177	8	6	0	2.75
SS	A. Pedrique	246	.301	1	27	115	185	10	43	4.1	.968	D. Drabek	29	176	11	12	0	3.88
3B	B. Bonilla	466	.300	15	77	53	138	14	12	2.3	.932	M. Dunne	23	163	13	6	0	3.03
RF	R. Reynolds	335	.260	7	51	134	7	1	2	1.4	.993	B. Walk	39	117	8	2	0	3.31
CF	A. Van Slyke	564	.293	21	82	328	10	4	6	2.3	.988	B. Kipper	24	111	5	9	0	5.94
LF	B. Bonds	551	.261	25	59	330	15	5	3	2.4	.986	J. Smiley	63	75	5	5	4	5.76
C	LaValliere	340	.300	1	36	584	70	5	11	5.9	.992	D. Robinson	42	65	6	6	12	3.86
3B	J. Morrison	348	.264	9	46	46	151	5	11	2.5	.975	J. Gott	25	31	0	2	13	1.45
UT	M. Diaz	241	.241	16	48	303	23	6	14		.982							
SS	R. Belliard	203	.207	1	15	104	176	6	29	4.0	.979							
C	J. Ortiz	192	.271	1	22	313	39	9	2	5.0	.975							
OF	J. Cangelosi	182	.275	4	18	74	3	3	0	1.7	.963							
OF	D. Coles	119	.227	6	24	28	1	0	0	1.1	1.000							

Chicago

W-76 L-85

Gene Michael
W-68 L-68

Frank Lucchesi
W-8 L-17

POS	Player	AB	BA	HR	RBI	PO	A	E	DP	TC/G	FA	Pitcher	G	IP	W	L	SV	ERA
1B	L. Durham	439	.273	27	63	1049	57	11	90	9.1	.990	R. Sutcliffe	34	237	18	10	0	3.68
2B	R. Sandberg	523	.294	16	59	294	375	10	84	5.2	.985	J. Moyer	35	201	12	15	0	5.10
SS	S. Dunston	346	.246	5	22	160	271	14	54	4.7	.969	G. Maddux	30	156	6	14	0	5.61
3B	K. Moreland	563	.266	27	88	99	300	28	27	2.8	.934	S. Sanderson	32	145	8	9	2	4.29
RF	A. Dawson	621	.287	49	137	271	12	4	0	1.9	.986	L. Lancaster	27	132	8	3	0	4.90
CF	D. Martinez	459	.292	8	36	283	10	6	1	2.2	.980	E. Lynch	58	110	2	9	4	5.38
LF	J. Mumphrey	309	.333	13	44	124	5	1	0	1.5	.992	L. Smith	62	84	4	10	36	3.12
C	J. Davis	428	.248	19	51	749	79	9	11	6.8	.989	F. DiPino	69	80	3	3	4	3.15
OF	R. Palmeiro	221	.276	14	30	64	1	0	1	1.4	1.000							
UT	M. Trillo	214	.294	8	26	301	53	4	35		.989							
OF	B. Dernier	199	.317	8	21	86	2	1	1	1.3	.989							
2S	P. Noce	180	.228	3	14	116	157	5	39		.982							
OF	B. Dayett	177	.277	5	25	72	2	0	0	.9	1.000							

West

San Francisco

W-90 L-72

Roger Craig

POS	Player	AB	BA	HR	RBI	PO	A	E	DP	TC/G	FA	Pitcher	G	IP	W	L	SV	ERA
1B	W. Clark	529	.308	35	91	1253	103	13	130	9.8	.991	K. Downs	41	186	12	9	1	3.63
2B	R. Thompson	420	.262	10	44	246	341	17	99	4.8	.972	M. LaCoss	39	171	13	10	0	3.68
SS	J. Uribe	309	.291	5	30	145	286	13	62	4.7	.971	A. Hammaker	31	168	10	10	0	3.58
3B	K. Mitchell	268	.306	15	44	44	131	7	10	2.7	.962	M. Krukow	30	163	5	6	0	4.80
RF	C. Maldonado	442	.292	20	85	176	7	5	0	1.6	.973	D. Dravecky	18	112	7	5	0	3.20
CF	C. Davis	500	.250	24	76	265	6	7	2	1.5	.975	S. Garrelts	64	106	11	7	12	3.22
LF	J. Leonard	503	.280	19	63	193	7	7	2	1.6	.966	J. Robinson	63	97	6	8	10	2.79
C	B. Brenly	375	.267	18	51	642	83	9	10	6.8	.988	C. Lefferts	44	47	3	3	4	3.23
OF	M. Aldrete	357	.325	9	51	141	3	2	1	1.8	.986	D. Robinson	25	43	5	1	7	2.74
UT	C. Speier	317	.249	11	39	118	229	4	41		.989							
C	B. Melvin	246	.199	11	31	407	43	1	7	5.8	.998							
SS	M. Williams	245	.188	8	21	104	210	8	49	4.6	.975							
OF	E. Milner	214	.252	4	19	135	0	1	0	1.6	.993							

Cincinnati

W-84 L-78

Pete Rose

POS	Player	AB	BA	HR	RBI	PO	A	E	DP	TC/G	FA	Pitcher	G	IP	W	L	SV	ERA
1B	N. Esasky	346	.272	22	59	772	40	5	72	8.8	.994	T. Power	34	204	10	13	0	4.50
2B	R. Oester	237	.253	2	23	183	186	10	37	5.5	.974	T. Browning	32	183	10	13	0	5.02
SS	B. Larkin	439	.244	12	43	168	358	19	72	4.6	.965	Gullickson	27	165	10	11	0	4.85
3B	B. Bell	522	.284	17	70	93	241	7	17	2.4	.979	G. Hoffman	36	159	9	10	0	4.37
RF	D. Parker	589	.253	26	97	278	13	10	3	2.1	.967	R. Robinson	48	154	7	5	4	3.68
CF	E. Davis	474	.293	37	100	380	10	4	4	3.1	.990	F. Williams	85	106	4	0	2	2.30
LF	K. Daniels	368	.334	26	64	178	5	6	0	2.0	.968	R. Murphy	87	101	8	5	3	3.04
C	B. Diaz	496	.270	15	82	747	70	7	6	6.0	.992	J. Franco	68	82	8	5	32	2.52
UT	K. Stillwell	395	.258	4	33	144	247	23	38		.944							
OF	T. Jones	359	.290	10	44	189	2	2	0	2.0	.990							
UT	Concepcion	279	.319	1	33	250	169	5	43		.988							
1B	T. Francona	207	.227	3	12	373	45	2	38	7.4	.995							
OF	P. O'Neill	160	.256	7	28	73	2	4	0	1.9	.949							

Houston

W-76 L-86

Hal Lanier

POS	Player	AB	BA	HR	RBI	PO	A	E	DP	TC/G	FA	Pitcher	G	IP	W	L	SV	ERA
1B	G. Davis	578	.251	27	93	1283	112	12	89	9.3	.991	M. Scott	36	248	16	13	0	3.23
2B	B. Doran	625	.283	16	79	300	431	6	70	4.5	.992	N. Ryan	34	212	8	16	0	2.76
SS	C. Reynolds	374	.254	4	28	160	290	14	43	3.6	.970	D. Darwin	33	196	9	10	0	3.59
3B	D. Walling	325	.283	5	33	72	109	10	13	2.4	.948	B. Knepper	33	178	8	17	0	5.27
RF	K. Bass	592	.284	19	85	287	11	4	2	1.9	.987	J. Deshaies	26	152	11	6	0	4.62
CF	B. Hatcher	564	.296	11	63	276	16	4	6	2.1	.986	L. Andersen	67	102	9	5	5	3.45
LF	J. Cruz	365	.241	11	38	178	5	3	3	1.9	.984	D. Smith	50	60	2	3	24	1.65
C	A. Ashby	386	.288	14	63	778	46	6	6	7.5	.993							
OF	G. Young	274	.321	1	15	143	5	3	1	2.3	.980							
3B	K. Caminiti	203	.246	3	23	50	98	8	11	2.6	.949							

NATIONAL LEAGUE 1987, *cont.*

	POS	Player	AB	BA	HR	RBI	PO	A	E	DP	TC/G	FA	Pitcher	G	IP	W	L	SV	ERA
Los Angeles	1B	F. Stubbs	386	.233	16	52	802	78	5	65	8.0	.994	O. Hershiser	37	265	16	16	1	3.06
	2B	S. Sax	610	.280	6	46	342	420	14	92	5.1	.982	Valenzuela	34	251	14	14	0	3.98
W-73 L-89	SS	M. Duncan	261	.215	6	18	90	191	21	37	4.5	.930	B. Welch	35	252	15	9	0	3.22
	3B	M. Hatcher	287	.282	7	42	37	81	9	7	2.6	.929	R. Honeycutt	27	116	2	12	0	4.59
Tom Lasorda	RF	M. Marshall	402	.294	16	72	147	4	2	0	1.5	.987	T. Leary	39	108	3	11	1	4.76
	CF	J. Shelby	476	.277	21	69	269	9	8	3	2.4	.972	A. Pena	37	87	2	7	11	3.50
	LF	P. Guerrero	545	.338	27	89	163	6	5	0	1.6	.971	M. Young	47	54	5	8	11	4.47
	C	M. Scioscia	461	.265	6	38	925	80	11	11	7.4	.989							
	S3	D. Anderson	265	.234	1	13	102	202	7	33		.977							
	OF	K. Landreaux	182	.203	6	23	72	5	4	3	1.3	.951							
Atlanta	1B	G. Perry	533	.270	12	74	1288	72	14	118	10.1	.990	Z. Smith	36	242	15	10	0	4.09
	2B	G. Hubbard	443	.264	5	38	284	478	11	114	5.6	.986	R. Mahler	39	197	8	13	0	4.98
W-69 L-92	SS	A. Thomas	324	.231	5	39	128	276	20	56	5.2	.953	D. Palmer	28	152	8	11	0	4.90
	3B	K. Oberkfell	508	.280	3	48	76	248	7	20	2.6	.979	C. Puleo	35	123	6	8	0	4.23
Chuck Tanner	RF	D. Murphy	566	.295	44	105	325	14	8	1	2.2	.977	D. Alexander	16	118	5	10	0	4.13
	CF	D. James	494	.312	10	61	262	4	1	1	2.1	.996	J. Acker	68	115	4	9	14	4.16
	LF	K. Griffey	399	.286	14	64	181	7	1	1	1.8	.995	J. Dedmon	53	90	3	4	4	3.91
	C	O. Virgil	429	.247	27	72	654	74	8	12	6.0	.989	G. Garber	49	69	8	10	10	4.41
	OF	A. Hall	292	.284	3	33	148	5	3	1	2.3	.981							
	SS	R. Ramirez	179	.263	1	21	59	99	9	30	4.4	.946							
	1C	T. Simmons	177	.277	4	30	280	33	5	25		.984							
	3B	G. Nettles	177	.209	5	33	12	46	3	6	1.5	.951							
	SS	J. Blauser	165	.242	2	15	65	166	9	28	4.8	.963							
	OF	G. Roenicke	151	.219	9	28	60	0	2	0	1.4	.968							
San Diego	1B	J. Kruk	447	.313	20	91	870	75	4	74	9.4	.996	E. Show	34	206	8	16	0	3.84
	2B	T. Flannery	276	.228	0	20	139	207	5	40	4.2	.986	E. Whitson	36	206	10	13	0	4.73
W-65 L-97	SS	G. Templeton	510	.222	5	48	253	447	20	77	4.9	.972	J. Jones	30	146	9	7	0	4.14
	3B	R. Ready	350	.309	12	54	30	95	12	11	2.6	.912	McCullers	78	123	8	10	16	3.72
Larry Bowa	RF	T. Gwynn	589	.370	7	54	298	13	6	1	2.0	.981	A. Hawkins	24	118	3	10	0	5.05
	CF	S. Jefferson	422	.230	8	29	232	3	3	1	2.2	.987	M. Grant	17	102	6	7	0	4.66
	LF	C. Martinez	447	.273	15	70	116	6	4	0	1.6	.968	D. Dravecky	30	79	3	7	0	3.76
	C	B. Santiago	546	.300	18	79	817	80	22	12	6.3	.976	M. Davis	43	62	5	3	2	3.18
	2B	J. Cora	241	.237	0	13	118	192	8	31	4.8	.975	G. Gossage	40	52	5	4	11	3.12
	OF	S. Mack	238	.239	4	25	159	1	3	0	1.8	.982							
	3B	K. Mitchell	196	.245	7	26	29	108	8	9	2.8	.945							
	UT	L. Salazar	189	.254	3	17	56	95	9	11		.944							
	OF	M. Wynne	188	.250	2	24	100	2	2	0	1.5	.981							
	3B	C. Brown	155	.232	6	23	27	70	6	12	2.4	.942							

BATTING AND BASE RUNNING LEADERS

Batting Average
T. Gwynn, SD	.370
P. Guerrero, LA	.338
T. Raines, MON	.330
J. Kruk, SD	.313
D. James, ATL	.312

Slugging Average
J. Clark, STL	.597
E. Davis, CIN	.593
Strawberry, NY	.583
W. Clark, SF	.580
D. Murphy, ATL	.580

Home Runs
A. Dawson, CHI	49
D. Murphy, ATL	44
Strawberry, NY	39
E. Davis, CIN	37
H. Johnson, NY	36

PITCHING LEADERS

Winning Percentage
M. Dunne, PIT	.684
D. Gooden, NY	.682
R. Sutcliffe, CHI	.643
B. Welch, LA	.625
B. Forsch, STL	.611

Earned Run Average
N. Ryan, HOU	2.76
M. Dunne, PIT	3.03
O. Hershiser, LA	3.06
R. Reuschel, PIT, SF	3.09
D. Gooden, NY	3.21

Wins
R. Sutcliffe, CHI	18
S. Rawley, PHI	17
M. Scott, HOU	16
O. Hershiser, LA	16

Total Bases
A. Dawson, CHI	353
J. Samuel, PHI	329
D. Murphy, ATL	328
Strawberry, NY	310
W. Clark, SF	307

Runs Batted In
A. Dawson, CHI	137
T. Wallach, MON	123
M. Schmidt, PHI	113
J. Clark, STL	106
D. Murphy, ATL	105
W. McGee, STL	105

Stolen Bases
V. Coleman, STL	109
T. Gwynn, SD	56
B. Hatcher, HOU	53
E. Davis, CIN	50
T. Raines, MON	50

Saves
S. Bedrosian, PHI	40
L. Smith, CHI	36
T. Worrell, STL	33
J. Franco, CIN	32
R. McDowell, NY	25

Strikeouts
N. Ryan, HOU	270
M. Scott, HOU	233
B. Welch, LA	196
Valenzuela, LA	190
O. Hershiser, LA	190

Complete Games
R. Reuschel, PIT, SF	12
Valenzuela, LA	12
O. Hershiser, LA	10
Z. Smith, ATL	9
M. Scott, HOU	8

Hits
T. Gwynn, SD	218
P. Guerrero, LA	184
O. Smith, STL	182
V. Coleman, STL	180

Base on Balls
J. Clark, STL	136
V. Hayes, PHI	121
D. Murphy, ATL	115
Strawberry, NY	97

Home Run Percentage
J. Clark, STL	8.4
A. Dawson, CHI	7.9
E. Davis, CIN	7.8
D. Murphy, ATL	7.8

Fewest Hits/9 Innings
N. Ryan, HOU	6.55
M. Scott, HOU	7.23
B. Welch, LA	7.30
M. Dunne, PIT	7.88

Shutouts
R. Reuschel, PIT, SF	4
B. Welch, LA	4

Fewest Walks/9 Innings
R. Reuschel, PIT, SF	1.67
N. Heaton, MON	1.72
Gullickson, CIN	2.13
B. Forsch, STL	2.26

Runs Scored
T. Raines, MON	123
V. Coleman, STL	121
E. Davis, CIN	120
T. Gwynn, SD	119

Doubles
T. Wallach, MON	42
A. Galarraga, MON	40
O. Smith, STL	40

Triples
J. Samuel, PHI	15
T. Gwynn, SD	13
A. Van Slyke, PIT	11
W. McGee, STL	11

Most Strikeouts/9 Inn.
N. Ryan, HOU	11.48
M. Scott, HOU	8.47
B. Sebra, MON	7.92
D. Gooden, NY	7.41

Innings
O. Hershiser, LA	265
B. Welch, LA	252
Valenzuela, LA	251
M. Scott, HOU	248

Games Pitched
K. Tekulve, PHI	90
R. Murphy, CIN	87
F. Williams, CIN	85
J. Robinson, PIT, SF	81

NATIONAL LEAGUE 1987, cont.

		W	L	PCT	GB	R	OR	Batting 2B	3B	HR	BA	SA	SB	Fielding E	DP	FA	Pitching CG	BB	SO	ShO	SV	ERA
East	St. Louis	95	67	.586		798	693	252	49	94	.263	.378	**248**	**116**	172	**.982**	10	533	873	4	48	3.91
	New York	92	70	.568	3	**823**	698	287	34	192	**.268**	**.434**	159	137	137	.978	16	510	1032	5	**51**	3.84
	Montreal	91	71	.562	4	741	720	**310**	39	120	.265	.401	166	147	122	.976	16	**446**	1012	6	50	3.92
	Philadelphia	80	82	.494	15	702	749	248	**51**	169	.254	.410	111	121	137	.980	13	587	877	5	48	4.18
	Pittsburgh	80	82	.494	15	723	744	282	45	131	.264	.403	140	123	147	.980	25	562	914	**10**	39	4.20
	Chicago	76	85	.472	18.5	720	801	244	33	**209**	.264	.432	109	130	154	.979	11	628	1024	4	48	4.55
West	San Francisco	90	72	.556		783	**669**	274	32	205	.260	.430	126	129	**183**	.980	19	547	1038	8	38	**3.68**
	Cincinnati	84	78	.519	6	783	752	262	29	192	.266	.427	169	130	137	.979	7	485	919	2	44	4.25
	Houston	76	86	.469	14	648	678	238	28	122	.253	.373	162	**116**	113	.981	13	525	**1137**	4	33	3.84
	Los Angeles	73	89	.451	17	635	675	236	23	125	.252	.371	128	155	144	.975	**29**	565	1097	7	32	3.72
	Atlanta	69	92	.429	20.5	747	829	284	24	152	.258	.403	135	**116**	170	.982	16	587	837	4	32	4.63
	San Diego	65	97	.401	25	668	763	209	48	113	.260	.378	198	147	135	.976	14	602	897	6	33	4.27
						8771	8771	3126	435	1824	.261	.404	1851	1567	1751	.979	189	6577	11657	65	496	4.08

AMERICAN LEAGUE 1987

POS	Player	AB	BA	HR	RBI	PO	A	E	DP	TC/G	FA	Pitcher	G	IP	W	L	SV	ERA
East **Detroit** W-98 L-64 Sparky Anderson																		
1B	D. Evans	499	.257	34	99	810	100	3	86	8.7	.997	J. Morris	34	266	18	11	0	3.38
2B	L. Whitaker	604	.265	16	59	275	416	17	99	4.8	.976	W. Terrell	35	245	17	10	0	4.05
SS	A. Trammell	597	.343	28	105	222	421	19	94	4.4	.971	F. Tanana	34	219	15	10	0	3.91
3B	T. Brookens	444	.241	13	59	85	208	14	15	2.5	.954	D. Petry	30	135	9	7	0	5.61
RF	P. Sheridan	421	.259	6	49	236	6	6	1	1.8	.976	J. Robinson	29	127	9	6	0	5.37
CF	C. Lemon	470	.277	20	75	350	4	3	1	2.5	.992	E. King	55	116	6	9	9	4.89
LF	K. Gibson	487	.277	24	79	253	6	7	0	2.2	.974	M. Henneman	55	97	11	3	7	2.98
C	M. Nokes	461	.289	32	87	595	32	5	2	5.8	.992	G. Hernandez	45	49	3	4	8	3.67
DH	B. Madlock	326	.279	14	50													
UT	M. Heath	270	.281	8	33	384	43	5	8		.988							
OF	L. Herndon	225	.324	9	47	82	4	1	1	1.5	.989							
1B	D. Bergman	172	.273	6	22	353	29	3	33	5.9	.992							
Toronto W-96 L-66 Jimy Williams																		
1B	W. Upshaw	512	.244	15	58	1169	127	9	114	8.9	.993	J. Key	36	261	17	8	0	**2.76**
2B	G. Iorg	310	.210	4	30	139	195	6	33	3.7	.982	J. Clancy	37	241	15	11	0	3.54
SS	T. Fernandez	578	.322	5	67	**270**	396	14	88	4.7	.979	D. Stieb	33	185	13	9	0	4.09
3B	K. Gruber	341	.235	12	36	52	168	12	11	1.9	.948	J. Cerutti	44	151	11	4	0	4.40
RF	J. Barfield	590	.263	28	84	341	**17**	3	4	2.3	.992	M. Eichhorn	89	128	10	6	4	3.17
CF	L. Moseby	592	.282	26	96	294	7	6	1	2.0	.980	T. Henke	72	94	0	6	34	2.49
LF	G. Bell	610	.308	47	**134**	248	14	11	1	1.8	.960	J. Musselman	68	89	12	5	3	4.15
C	E. Whitt	446	.269	19	75	**803**	55	5	10	6.6	.994							
3B	R. Mulliniks	332	.310	11	44	29	137	13	14	1.9	.927							
DH	F. McGriff	295	.247	20	43													
OD	R. Leach	195	.282	3	25	51	1	1	0	1.2	.981							
DH	C. Fielder	175	.269	14	32													
DO	J. Beniquez	81	.284	5	21	7	0	1	0	1.1	.875							
Milwaukee W-91 L-71 Tom Trebelhorn																		
1B	G. Brock	532	.299	13	85	1065	109	8	111	8.4	.993	T. Higuera	35	262	18	10	0	3.85
2B	J. Castillo	321	.224	3	28	181	219	11	54	4.2	.973	B. Wegman	34	225	12	11	0	4.24
SS	D. Sveum	535	.252	25	95	221	361	21	82	4.2	.965	J. Nieves	34	196	14	8	0	4.88
3B	E. Riles	276	.261	4	38	41	103	10	11	2.4	.935	C. Bosio	46	170	11	8	2	5.24
RF	G. Braggs	505	.269	13	77	301	6	9	1	2.6	.972	C. Crim	53	130	6	8	12	3.67
CF	R. Yount	635	.312	21	103	380	5	5	2	2.6	.987	D. Plesac	57	79	5	6	23	2.61
LF	R. Deer	474	.238	28	80	256	10	7	**1**	2.2	.974	M. Clear	58	78	8	5	6	4.48
C	B. Surhoff	395	.299	7	68	645	49	11	10	**7.2**	.984							
UT	P. Molitor	465	.353	16	75	60	113	5	24		.972							
OF	M. Felder	289	.266	2	31	188	7	5	3	2.0	.975							
23	J. Gantner	265	.272	4	30	119	193	6	44		.981							
C	B. Schroeder	250	.332	14	42	363	26	2	4	5.8	.995							
DH	C. Cooper	250	.248	6	36													
New York W-89 L-73 Lou Piniella																		
1B	D. Mattingly	569	.327	30	115	1239	91	5	122	9.5	**.996**	T. John	33	188	13	6	0	4.03
2B	W. Randolph	449	.305	7	67	286	338	12	89	5.3	.981	R. Rhoden	30	182	16	10	0	3.86
SS	W. Tolleson	349	.221	1	22	162	321	15	64	4.2	.970	C. Hudson	35	155	11	7	0	3.61
3B	Pagliarulo	522	.234	32	87	96	297	17	35	2.8	.959	D. Rasmussen	26	146	9	7	0	4.75
RF	D. Winfield	575	.275	27	97	253	6	3	1	1.8	.989	R. Guidry	22	118	5	8	0	3.67
CF	Washington	312	.279	9	44	166	3	2	1	2.4	.988	D. Righetti	60	95	8	6	31	3.51
LF	D. Pasqua	318	.233	17	42	132	2	2	0	1.8	.985	T. Stoddard	57	93	4	3	8	3.50
C	R. Cerone	284	.243	4	23	538	38	1	6	5.2	**.998**	P. Clements	55	80	3	3	7	4.95
UT	G. Ward	529	.248	16	78	318	10	3	11		.991							
OF	R. Henderson	358	.291	17	37	189	3	4	1	2.8	.980							
S2	B. Meacham	203	.271	5	21	110	184	10	36		.967							
DO	M. Easler	167	.281	4	21	24	1	0	0	1.7	1.000							
DH	R. Kittle	159	.277	12	28													
OF	H. Cotto	149	.235	5	20	89	2	1	0	1.6	.989							

AMERICAN LEAGUE 1987, *cont.*

Boston — W-78 L-84 — John McNamara

POS	Player	AB	BA	HR	RBI	PO	A	E	DP	TC/G	FA	Pitcher	G	IP	W	L	SV	ERA
1B	B. Buckner	286	.273	2	42	605	58	6	53	9.0	.991	R. Clemens	36	282	**20**	9	0	2.97
2B	M. Barrett	559	.293	3	43	320	438	9	108	5.6	.988	B. Hurst	33	239	15	13	0	4.41
SS	S. Owen	437	.259	2	48	176	336	13	69	4.0	.975	A. Nipper	30	174	11	12	0	5.43
3B	W. Boggs	551	**.363**	24	89	111	277	14	37	2.8	.965	B. Stanley	34	153	4	15	0	5.01
RF	D. Evans	541	.305	34	123	134	5	1	0	1.8	.993	J. Sellers	25	140	7	8	0	5.28
CF	E. Burks	558	.272	20	59	320	15	4	2	2.6	.988	W. Gardner	49	90	3	6	10	5.42
LF	J. Rice	404	.277	13	62	155	12	4	2	1.8	.977	C. Schiraldi	62	84	8	5	6	4.41
C	M. Sullivan	160	.169	2	10	303	29	2	6	5.6	.994							
OF	M. Greenwell	412	.328	19	89	162	8	5	0	1.9	.971							
DH	D. Baylor	339	.239	16	57													
UT	E. Romero	235	.272	0	14	122	151	6	28		.978							
OF	T. Benzinger	223	.278	8	43	146	6	2	2	2.5	.987							
OF	D. Henderson	184	.234	8	25	114	0	5	0	1.9	.958							
C	J. Marzano	168	.244	5	24	337	24	5	7	7.0	.986							
DH	S. Horn	158	.278	14	34													

Baltimore — W-67 L-95 — Cal Ripken

POS	Player	AB	BA	HR	RBI	PO	A	E	DP	TC/G	FA	Pitcher	G	IP	W	L	SV	ERA
1B	E. Murray	618	.277	30	91	1371	145	10	**146**	**9.8**	.993	M. Boddicker	33	226	10	12	0	4.18
2B	B. Ripken	234	.308	2	20	133	162	3	53	5.1	.990	E. Bell	33	165	10	13	0	5.45
SS	C. Ripken	624	.252	27	98	240	**480**	20	103	4.6	.973	Williamson	61	125	8	9	3	4.03
3B	R. Knight	563	.256	14	65	110	282	18	28	3.2	.956	D. Schmidt	35	124	10	5	1	3.77
RF	L. Lacy	258	.244	7	28	135	11	4	2	1.9	.973	J. Habyan	27	116	6	7	1	4.80
CF	F. Lynn	396	.253	23	60	229	2	2	1	2.3	.991	K. Dixon	34	105	7	10	5	6.43
LF	L. Sheets	469	.316	31	94	229	5	6	2	1.9	.975	J. Ballard	14	70	2	8	0	6.59
C	T. Kennedy	512	.250	18	62	750	58	6	11	5.7	.993	Niedenfuer	45	52	3	5	13	4.99
OD	M. Young	363	.240	16	39	117	0	3	0	2.0	.975							
D2	A. Wiggins	306	.232	1	15	78	98	3	21	5.4	.983							
OF	K. Gerhart	284	.243	14	34	174	3	5	0	2.0	.973							
DO	J. Dwyer	241	.274	15	39	57	1	0	0	1.9	1.000							
2B	R. Burleson	206	.209	2	14	112	145	6	39	4.8	.977							

Cleveland — W-61 L-101 — Pat Corrales W-31 L-56 — Doc Edwards W-30 L-45

POS	Player	AB	BA	HR	RBI	PO	A	E	DP	TC/G	FA	Pitcher	G	IP	W	L	SV	ERA
1B	J. Carter	588	.264	32	106	644	45	**12**	61	8.3	.983	T. Candiotti	32	202	7	18	0	4.78
2B	T. Bernazard	293	.239	11	30	153	200	6	39	4.6	.983	K. Schrom	32	154	6	13	0	6.50
SS	J. Franco	495	.319	8	52	157	285	17	53	4.1	.963	P. Niekro	22	124	7	11	0	5.89
3B	B. Jacoby	540	.300	32	69	**134**	254	**22**	19	2.8	.946	S. Bailes	39	120	7	8	6	4.64
RF	C. Snyder	577	.236	33	82	283	16	9	3	2.2	.971	S. Carlton	23	109	5	9	1	5.37
CF	B. Butler	522	.295	9	41	393	4	4	2	2.9	.990	G. Swindell	16	102	3	8	0	5.10
LF	M. Hall	485	.280	18	76	264	3	3	2	2.2	.989	R. Yett	37	98	3	9	1	5.25
C	C. Bando	211	.218	5	16	351	34	4	8	4.5	.990	D. Jones	49	91	6	5	8	3.15
1D	P. Tabler	553	.307	11	86	650	75	12	49	9.0	.984							
2B	T. Hinzo	257	.265	3	21	115	204	9	44	4.9	.973							
DO	C. Castillo	220	.250	11	31	29	3	0	0	1.4	1.000							

West

Minnesota — W-85 L-77 — Tom Kelly

POS	Player	AB	BA	HR	RBI	PO	A	E	DP	TC/G	FA	Pitcher	G	IP	W	L	SV	ERA
1B	K. Hrbek	477	.285	34	90	1179	68	5	112	9.1	.996	B. Blyleven	37	267	15	12	0	4.01
2B	Lombardozzi	432	.238	8	38	245	356	14	77	4.6	.977	F. Viola	36	252	17	10	0	2.90
SS	G. Gagne	437	.265	10	40	194	391	18	75	4.4	.970	L. Straker	31	154	8	10	0	4.37
3B	G. Gaetti	584	.257	31	109	**134**	261	11	28	2.7	.973	J. Berenguer	47	112	8	1	4	3.94
RF	T. Brunansky	532	.259	32	85	273	10	3	1	2.1	.990	M. Smithson	21	109	4	7	0	5.94
CF	K. Puckett	624	.332	28	99	341	8	5	2	2.4	.986	J. Niekro	19	96	4	9	0	6.26
LF	D. Gladden	438	.249	8	38	223	9	3	2	2.1	.987	G. Frazier	54	81	5	5	2	4.98
C	T. Laudner	288	.191	16	43	517	28	7	2	5.5	.987	J. Reardon	63	80	8	8	31	4.48
DH	R. Smalley	309	.275	8	34							K. Atherton	59	79	7	5	2	4.54
UT	A. Newman	307	.221	0	29	120	225	5	44		.986							
OF	R. Bush	293	.253	11	46	107	1	2	0	1.5	.982							
D1	G. Larkin	233	.266	4	28	165	10	2	12	6.8	.989							

Kansas City — W-83 L-79 — Billy Gardner W-62 L-64 — John Wathan W-21 L-15

POS	Player	AB	BA	HR	RBI	PO	A	E	DP	TC/G	FA	Pitcher	G	IP	W	L	SV	ERA
1B	G. Brett	427	.290	22	78	798	50	6	69	10.3	.993	Saberhagen	33	257	18	10	0	3.36
2B	F. White	563	.245	17	78	320	458	10	89	5.2	.990	M. Gubicza	35	242	13	18	0	3.98
SS	A. Salazar	317	.205	2	21	134	332	9	56	4.1	.981	C. Leibrandt	35	240	16	11	0	3.41
3B	K. Seitzer	641	.323	15	83	105	292	**22**	32	3.0	.947	D. Jackson	36	224	9	18	0	4.02
RF	D. Tartabull	582	.309	34	101	228	11	6	1	1.6	.976	B. Black	29	122	8	6	1	3.60
CF	W. Wilson	610	.279	4	30	342	3	1	1	2.4	**.997**	J. Gleaton	48	51	4	4	5	4.26
LF	B. Jackson	396	.235	22	53	180	9	9	1	1.8	.955	Quisenberry	47	49	4	1	8	2.76
C	J. Quirk	296	.236	5	33	532	40	8	3	5.4	.986							
1D	S. Balboni	386	.207	24	60	521	41	6	39	10.3	.989							
UT	J. Beniquez	174	.236	3	26	83	5	1	6		.989							
OD	L. Smith	167	.251	3	8	52	2	5	0	1.8	.915							
C	L. Owen	164	.189	5	14	370	38	7	4	5.5	.983							
DH	Eisenreich	105	.238	4	21													

Oakland — W-81 L-81 — Tony LaRussa

POS	Player	AB	BA	HR	RBI	PO	A	E	DP	TC/G	FA	Pitcher	G	IP	W	L	SV	ERA
1B	M. McGwire	557	.289	**49**	118	1173	90	10	91	8.8	.992	D. Stewart	37	261	**20**	13	0	3.68
2B	T. Phillips	379	.240	10	46	160	260	11	40	5.0	.974	C. Young	31	203	13	7	0	4.08
SS	A. Griffin	494	.263	3	60	245	386	24	72	4.8	.963	S. Ontiveros	35	151	10	8	1	4.00
3B	C. Lansford	554	.289	19	76	98	249	7	15	2.5	**.980**	G. Nelson	54	124	6	5	3	3.93
RF	M. Davis	494	.265	22	72	210	3	**13**	1	1.9	.942	D. Eckersley	54	116	6	8	16	3.03
CF	D. Murphy	219	.233	8	35	185	1	3	0	2.4	.984	E. Plunk	32	95	4	6	2	4.74
LF	J. Canseco	630	.257	31	113	263	12	7	3	2.2	.975	J. Howell	36	44	3	4	16	5.89
C	T. Steinbach	391	.284	16	56	640	40	10	6	6.4	.986							
OF	L. Polonia	435	.287	4	49	235	2	5	1	2.3	.979							
DH	R. Jackson	336	.220	15	43													
2B	T. Bernazard	214	.266	3	19	90	135	11	22	4.0	.953							
C	M. Tettleton	211	.194	8	26	433	28	6	1	5.8	.987							

AMERICAN LEAGUE 1987, *cont.*

Seattle
W-78 L-84
Dick Williams

POS	Player	AB	BA	HR	RBI	PO	A	E	DP	TC/G	FA	Pitcher	G	IP	W	L	SV	ERA
1B	A. Davis	580	.295	29	100	1386	96	9	133	9.5	.994	M. Langston	35	272	19	13	0	3.84
2B	H. Reynolds	530	.275	1	35	347	507	20	111	5.5	.977	M. Moore	33	231	9	19	0	4.71
SS	R. Quinones	478	.276	12	56	204	384	25	76	4.5	.959	M. Morgan	34	207	12	17	0	4.65
3B	J. Presley	575	.247	24	88	113	311	21	28	3.0	.953	S. Bankhead	27	149	9	8	0	5.42
RF	M. Kingery	354	.280	9	52	226	15	2	3	2.1	.992	Guetterman	25	113	11	4	0	3.81
CF	J. Moses	390	.246	3	38	220	5	3	0	2.3	.987	J. Reed	39	82	1	2	7	3.42
LF	P. Bradley	603	.297	14	67	273	13	5	1	1.8	.983	B. Wilkinson	56	76	3	4	10	3.66
C	S. Bradley	342	.278	5	43	433	29	8	4	5.7	.983	E. Nunez	48	47	3	4	12	3.80
OF	M. Brantley	351	.302	14	54	163	3	3	1	2.1	.982							
DH	K. Phelps	332	.259	27	68													
C	D. Valle	324	.256	12	53	420	34	5	2	6.1	.989							

Chicago
W-77 L-85
Jim Fregosi

POS	Player	AB	BA	HR	RBI	PO	A	E	DP	TC/G	FA	Pitcher	G	IP	W	L	SV	ERA
1B	G. Walker	566	.256	27	94	1402	80	9	135	9.7	.994	F. Bannister	34	229	16	11	0	3.58
2B	F. Manrique	298	.258	4	29	147	234	6	58	4.2	.984	R. Dotson	31	211	11	12	0	4.17
SS	O. Guillen	560	.279	2	51	266	475	19	105	5.1	.975	J. DeLeon	33	206	11	12	0	4.02
3B	T. Hulett	240	.217	7	28	44	118	8	15	2.8	.953	B. Long	29	169	8	8	1	4.37
RF	I. Calderon	542	.293	28	83	295	8	5	3	2.2	.984	J. Winn	56	94	4	6	4	4.79
CF	K. Williams	391	.281	11	50	303	5	6	2	2.3	.981	B. Thigpen	51	89	7	5	16	2.73
LF	G. Redus	475	.236	12	48	262	13	6	4	2.3	.979	S. Nielsen	19	66	3	5	2	6.24
C	C. Fisk	454	.256	23	71	550	57	6	15	5.0	.990	B. James	43	54	4	6	10	4.67
DH	H. Baines	505	.293	20	93													
2B	D. Hill	410	.239	9	46	153	223	5	47	4.5	.987							
OF	D. Boston	337	.258	10	29	207	3	2	3	2.3	.991							
3B	S. Lyons	193	.280	1	19	35	99	4	11	2.7	.971							
UT	J. Royster	154	.240	7	23	56	47	2	5		.981							
UT	J. Hairston	126	.230	5	20	82	5	1	7		.989							

California
W-75 L-87
Gene Mauch

POS	Player	AB	BA	HR	RBI	PO	A	E	DP	TC/G	FA	Pitcher	G	IP	W	L	SV	ERA
1B	W. Joyner	564	.285	34	117	1276	92	10	133	9.2	.993	M. Witt	36	247	16	14	0	4.01
2B	M. McLemore	433	.236	3	41	291	358	17	96	5.0	.974	D. Sutton	35	192	11	11	0	4.70
SS	D. Schofield	479	.251	9	46	204	348	9	76	4.3	.984	W. Fraser	36	177	10	10	1	3.92
3B	D. DeCinces	453	.234	16	63	83	226	17	24	2.5	.948	J. Lazorko	26	118	5	6	0	4.59
RF	D. White	639	.263	24	87	424	16	9	3	2.5	.980	Candelaria	20	117	8	6	0	4.71
CF	G. Pettis	394	.208	1	17	344	2	7	2	2.7	.980	D. Buice	57	114	6	7	17	3.39
LF	R. Jones	192	.245	8	28	81	1	3	0	1.3	.965	G. Minton	41	76	5	4	10	3.08
C	B. Boone	389	.242	3	33	684	56	13	11	5.9	.983	McCaskill	14	75	4	6	0	5.67
DH	B. Downing	567	.272	29	77													
O3	J. Howell	449	.245	23	64	181	89	6	13		.978							
DH	B. Buckner	183	.306	3	32													
OF	G. Hendrick	162	.241	5	25	58	1	2	0	1.4	.967							

Texas
W-75 L-87
Bobby Valentine

POS	Player	AB	BA	HR	RBI	PO	A	E	DP	TC/G	FA	Pitcher	G	IP	W	L	SV	ERA
1B	P. O'Brien	569	.286	23	88	1233	146	11	118	8.8	.992	C. Hough	40	285	18	13	0	3.79
2B	J. Browne	454	.271	1	38	258	338	12	66	4.7	.980	J. Guzman	37	208	14	14	0	4.67
SS	S. Fletcher	588	.287	5	63	249	413	23	98	4.4	.966	B. Witt	26	143	8	10	0	4.91
3B	S. Buechele	363	.237	13	50	68	175	9	13	2.0	.964	G. Harris	42	141	5	10	0	4.86
RF	R. Sierra	643	.263	30	109	272	17	11	6	1.9	.963	M. Williams	85	109	8	6	6	3.23
CF	O. McDowell	407	.241	14	52	263	5	3	1	2.2	.989	D. Mohorcic	74	99	7	6	16	2.99
LF	Incaviglia	509	.271	27	80	216	8	13	0	1.8	.945	J. Russell	52	97	5	4	3	4.44
C	D. Slaught	237	.224	8	16	429	39	7	5	5.6	.985							
DH	L. Parrish	557	.268	32	100													
OF	B. Brower	303	.261	14	46	183	2	7	0	1.8	.964							
C	M. Stanley	216	.273	6	37	330	17	7	1	5.8	.980							
UT	G. Petralli	202	.302	7	31	370	34	5	4		.988							
DH	D. Porter	130	.238	7	21													

BATTING AND BASE RUNNING LEADERS

Batting Average
W. Boggs, BOS .363
P. Molitor, MIL .353
A. Trammell, DET .343
K. Puckett, MIN .332
D. Mattingly, NY .327

Slugging Average
M. McGwire, OAK .618
G. Bell, TOR .605
W. Boggs, BOS .588
D. Evans, BOS .569
P. Molitor, MIL .566

Home Runs
M. McGwire, OAK 49
G. Bell, TOR 47

Total Bases
G. Bell, TOR 369
M. McGwire, OAK 344
K. Puckett, MIN 333
A. Trammell, DET 329
W. Boggs, BOS 324

Runs Batted In
G. Bell, TOR 134
D. Evans, BOS 123
M. McGwire, OAK 118
W. Joyner, CAL 117
D. Mattingly, NY 115

Stolen Bases
H. Reynolds, SEA 60
W. Wilson, KC 59
G. Redus, CHI 52
P. Molitor, MIL 45
R. Henderson, NY 41

Hits
K. Puckett, MIN 207
K. Seitzer, KC 207
A. Trammell, DET 205
W. Boggs, BOS 200

Base on Balls
D. Evans, BOS 106
B. Downing, CAL 106
W. Boggs, BOS 105
D. Evans, DET 100

Home Run Percentage
M. McGwire, OAK 8.8
G. Bell, TOR 7.7
K. Hrbek, MIN 7.1
D. Evans, DET 6.8

PITCHING LEADERS

Winning Percentage
R. Clemens, BOS .690
T. John, NY .684
J. Key, TOR .680
C. Young, OAK .650
Saberhagen, KC .643
T. Higuera, MIL .643

Saves
T. Henke, TOR 34
J. Reardon, MIN 31
D. Righetti, NY 31
D. Plesac, MIL 23
D. Buice, CAL 17

Fewest Hits/9 Innings
J. Key, TOR 7.24
C. Hough, TEX 7.51
J. Morris, DET 7.68
D. Stewart, OAK 7.71

Earned Run Average
J. Key, TOR 2.76
F. Viola, MIN 2.90
R. Clemens, BOS 2.97
Saberhagen, KC 3.36
J. Morris, DET 3.38

Strikeouts
M. Langston, SEA 262
R. Clemens, BOS 256
T. Higuera, MIL 240
C. Hough, TEX 223
J. Morris, DET 208

Shutouts
R. Clemens, BOS 7
Saberhagen, KC 4

Wins
R. Clemens, BOS 20
D. Stewart, OAK 20
M. Langston, SEA 19

Complete Games
R. Clemens, BOS 18
B. Hurst, BOS 15
Saberhagen, KC 15
M. Langston, SEA 14
T. Higuera, MIL 14

Fewest Walks/9 Innings
B. Long, CHI 1.49
Saberhagen, KC 1.86
D. Sutton, CAL 1.93
F. Bannister, CHI 1.93

AMERICAN LEAGUE 1987, *cont.*

BATTING AND BASE RUNNING LEADERS

Runs Scored		Doubles		Triples		Most Strikeouts/9 Inn.	
P. Molitor, MIL	114	P. Molitor, MIL	41	W. Wilson, KC	15	M. Langston, SEA	8.67
G. Bell, TOR	111	W. Boggs, BOS	40	L. Polonia, OAK	10	T. Higuera, MIL	8.25
B. Downing, CAL	110	I. Calderon, CHI	38	P. Bradley, SEA	10	R. Clemens, BOS	8.18
L. Whitaker, DET	110	D. Mattingly, NY	38	R. Yount, MIL	9	C. Bosio, MIL	7.94

PITCHING LEADERS

Innings		Games Pitched	
C. Hough, TEX	285	M. Eichhorn, TOR	89
R. Clemens, BOS	282	M. Williams, TEX	85
M. Langston, SEA	272	D. Mohorcic, TEX	74
B. Blyleven, MIN	267	T. Henke, TOR	72

		W	L	PCT	GB	R	OR	2B	3B	HR	BA	SA	SB	E	DP	FA	CG	BB	SO	ShO	SV	ERA
East	Detroit	98	64	.605		**896**	735	274	32	**225**	.272	**.451**	106	122	147	.980	33	563	976	8	31	4.02
	Toronto	96	66	.593	2	845	**655**	277	38	215	.269	.446	126	111	148	.982	18	567	1064	3	43	**3.74**
	Milwaukee	91	71	.562	7	862	817	272	46	163	.276	.428	176	145	155	.976	28	529	1039	5	45	4.62
	New York	89	73	.549	9	788	758	239	16	196	.262	.418	105	102	155	.983	19	542	900	3	**47**	4.36
	Boston	78	84	.481	20	842	825	273	26	174	**.278**	.430	77	110	158	.982	**47**	517	1034	**13**	16	4.77
	Baltimore	67	95	.414	31	729	880	219	20	211	.258	.418	69	111	**174**	.982	17	547	870	5	30	5.01
	Cleveland	61	101	.377	37	742	957	267	30	187	.263	.422	140	153	128	.975	24	606	849	4	25	5.28
West	Minnesota	85	77	.525		786	806	258	35	196	.261	.430	113	**98**	147	**.984**	16	564	990	2	39	4.63
	Kansas City	83	79	.512	2	715	691	239	40	168	.262	.412	125	131	151	.979	44	548	923	11	26	3.86
	Oakland	81	81	.500	4	806	789	263	33	199	.260	.428	140	142	122	.977	18	531	1042	2	40	4.32
	Seattle	78	84	.481	7	760	801	282	**48**	161	.272	.428	174	122	150	.980	39	**497**	919	6	33	4.48
	Chicago	77	85	.475	8	748	746	**283**	36	173	.258	.415	138	116	**174**	.981	29	537	792	8	37	4.29
	California	75	87	.463	10	770	803	257	26	172	.252	.401	125	117	162	.981	20	504	941	3	36	4.38
	Texas	75	87	.463	10	823	849	264	35	194	.266	.430	120	151	148	.976	20	760	**1103**		27	4.63
						11112	11112	3667	461	2634	.265	.425	1734	1731	2119	.980	372	7812	13442	73	475	4.46

NATIONAL LEAGUE 1988

		POS	Player	AB	BA	HR	RBI	PO	A	E	DP	TC/G	FA	Pitcher	G	IP	W	L	SV	ERA
East	**New York**	1B	K. Hernandez	348	.276	11	55	734	77	2	63	8.7	.998	D. Gooden	34	248	18	9	0	3.19
		2B	W. Backman	294	.303	0	17	128	219	4	36	3.8	.989	R. Darling	34	241	17	9	0	3.25
	W-100 L-60	SS	K. Elster	406	.214	9	37	196	345	13	61	3.7	.977	D. Cone	35	231	20	3	0	2.22
		3B	H. Johnson	495	.230	24	68	65	187	13	16	2.0	.951	B. Ojeda	29	190	10	13	0	2.88
	Davey Johnson	RF	Strawberry	543	.269	**39**	101	297	4	9	3	2.1	.971	S. Fernandez	31	187	12	10	0	3.03
		CF	L. Dykstra	429	.270	8	33	270	3	1	0	2.4	.996	T. Leach	52	92	7	2	3	2.54
		LF	McReynolds	552	.288	27	99	252	**18**	4	**5**	1.9	.985	R. McDowell	62	89	5	5	16	2.63
		C	G. Carter	455	.242	11	46	**797**	54	9	5	**7.2**	.990	R. Myers	55	68	7	3	26	1.72
		OF	M. Wilson	378	.296	8	41	200	4	5	1	2.0	.976							
		13	D. Magadan	314	.277	1	35	459	99	10	42		.982							
		2B	T. Teufel	273	.234	4	31	153	212	7	48	4.4	.981							
	Pittsburgh	1B	S. Bream	462	.264	10	65	1118	**140**	6	88	9.2	.995	D. Drabek	33	219	15	7	0	3.08
		2B	J. Lind	611	.262	2	49	333	473	11	73	5.3	.987	B. Walk	32	213	12	10	0	2.71
		SS	R. Belliard	286	.213	0	11	131	258	9	50	3.4	**.977**	J. Smiley	34	205	13	11	0	3.25
	W-85 L-75	3B	B. Bonilla	584	.274	24	100	121	**336**	32	17	**3.1**	.935	M. Dunne	30	170	7	11	0	3.92
		RF	R. Reynolds	323	.248	6	51	142	7	4	2	1.6	.974	B. Fisher	33	146	8	10	1	4.61
	Jim Leyland	CF	A. Van Slyke	587	.288	25	100	**406**	12	4	2	**2.8**	.991	J. Robinson	75	125	11	5	9	3.03
		LF	B. Bonds	538	.283	24	58	292	5	6	0	2.2	.980	J. Gott	67	77	6	6	34	3.49
		C	LaValliere	352	.261	2	47	565	55	8	6	5.5	.987							
		OF	D. Coles	211	.232	5	36	98	0	1	0	1.8	.990							
	Montreal	1B	A. Galarraga	609	.302	29	92	1464	103	15	124	10.1	.991	D. Martinez	34	235	15	13	0	2.72
		2B	T. Foley	377	.265	5	43	164	255	12	46	4.8	.972	B. Smith	32	198	12	10	0	3.00
		SS	L. Rivera	371	.224	4	30	160	301	18	69	4.1	.962	P. Perez	27	188	12	8	0	2.44
	W-81 L-81	3B	T. Wallach	592	.257	12	69	**123**	328	18	**31**	3.1	.962	J. Dopson	26	169	3	11	0	3.04
		RF	H. Brooks	588	.279	20	90	261	8	9	1	1.9	.968	B. Holman	18	100	4	8	0	3.23
	Buck Rodgers	CF	M. Webster	259	.255	2	13	153	2	1	0	2.2	.994	N. Heaton	32	97	3	10	2	4.99
		LF	T. Raines	429	.270	12	48	235	5	3	1	2.3	.988	J. Parrett	61	92	12	4	6	2.65
		C	Santovenia	309	.236	8	41	457	63	9	7	6.2	.983	McGaffigan	63	91	6	0	4	2.76
		OF	O. Nixon	271	.244	0	15	176	2	1	1	2.2	.994	T. Burke	61	82	3	5	18	3.40
		2S	R. Hudler	216	.273	4	14	113	168	10	30		.966	J. Hesketh	60	73	4	3	9	2.85
		OF	D. Martinez	191	.257	2	12	119	2	1	1	2.0	.992							
		C	Fitzgerald	155	.271	5	23	258	21	6	2	6.1	.979							
	Chicago	1B	M. Grace	486	.296	7	57	1182	87	**17**	91	9.7	.987	G. Maddux	34	249	18	8	0	3.18
		2B	R. Sandberg	618	.264	19	69	291	**522**	11	79	5.4	.987	R. Sutcliffe	32	226	13	14	0	3.86
		SS	S. Dunston	575	.249	9	56	**257**	455	20	76	4.8	.973	J. Moyer	34	202	9	15	0	3.48
	W-77 L-85	3B	V. Law	556	.293	11	78	111	272	19	22	2.7	.953	C. Schiraldi	29	166	9	13	1	4.38
		RF	A. Dawson	591	.303	24	79	267	7	3	1	1.9	.989	J. Pico	29	113	6	7	1	4.15
	Don Zimmer	CF	D. Martinez	256	.254	4	34	162	2	5	0	2.3	.970	F. DiPino	63	90	2	3	6	4.98
		LF	R. Palmeiro	580	.307	8	53	30	5	0	1	7.0	1.000	L. Lancaster	44	86	4	6	5	3.78
		C	D. Berryhill	309	.259	7	38	448	54	9	5	5.7	.982	G. Gossage	46	44	4	4	13	4.33
		OF	M. Webster	264	.265	4	26	169	1	5	0	2.7	.971							
		C	J. Davis	249	.229	6	33	383	32	2	1	5.6	.995							
		OF	D. Jackson	188	.266	6	20	116	1	2	0	1.6	.983							
		UT	M. Trillo	164	.250	1	14	177	81	3	19		.989							

NATIONAL LEAGUE 1988, *cont.*

	POS	Player	AB	BA	HR	RBI	PO	A	E	DP	TC/G	FA	Pitcher	G	IP	W	L	SV	ERA
St. Louis	1B	B. Horner	206	.257	3	33	463	40	5	39	8.9	.990	J. DeLeon	34	225	13	10	0	3.67
	2B	L. Alicea	297	.212	1	24	206	240	14	52	5.1	.970	J. Magrane	24	165	5	9	0	**2.18**
W-76 L-86	SS	O. Smith	575	.270	3	51	234	519	22	79	**5.2**	.972	J. Tudor	21	145	6	5	0	2.29
	3B	T. Pendleton	391	.253	6	53	75	239	12	13	3.2	.963	McWilliams	42	136	6	9	1	3.90
Whitey Herzog	RF	T. Brunansky	523	.245	22	79	267	10	1	0	1.9	**.996**	S. Terry	51	129	9	6	3	2.92
	CF	W. McGee	562	.292	3	50	348	9	9	0	2.7	.975	B. Forsch	30	109	9	4	0	3.73
	LF	V. Coleman	616	.260	3	38	290	14	9	1	2.1	.971	T. Worrell	68	90	5	9	32	3.00
	C	T. Pena	505	.263	10	51	777	70	5	8	6.0	**.994**	D. Cox	13	86	3	8	0	3.98
	UT	J. Oquendo	451	.277	7	46	268	315	11	61		.981	G. Mathews	13	68	4	6	0	4.24
	C1	T. Pagnozzi	195	.282	0	15	340	28	4	11		.989	K. Dayley	54	55	2	7	5	2.77
	1B	P. Guerrero	149	.268	5	30	348	22	0	18	10.0	1.000							
Philadelphia	1B	V. Hayes	367	.272	6	45	712	55	8	66	9.1	.990	K. Gross	33	232	12	14	0	3.69
	2B	J. Samuel	629	.243	12	67	343	385	14	92	4.9	.978	D. Carman	36	201	10	14	0	4.29
W-65 L-96	SS	S. Jeltz	379	.187	0	27	195	368	14	73	3.9	.976	S. Rawley	32	198	8	16	0	4.18
	3B	M. Schmidt	390	.249	12	62	73	222	19	17	3.0	.939	B. Ruffin	55	144	6	10	3	4.43
Lee Elia	RF	C. James	566	.242	19	66	256	7	3	3	2.3	.989	D. Palmer	22	129	7	9	0	4.47
W-60 L-92	CF	M. Thompson	378	.288	2	33	278	5	5	1	2.6	.983	G. Harris	66	107	4	6	1	2.36
	LF	P. Bradley	569	.264	11	56	298	14	3	2	2.1	.990	K. Tekulve	70	80	3	7	4	3.60
John Vukovich	C	L. Parrish	424	.215	15	60	639	73	9	11	6.2	.988	S. Bedrosian	57	74	6	6	28	3.75
W-5 L-4	1B	R. Jordan	273	.308	11	43	579	35	5	41	9.0	.992							
	OF	B. Dernier	166	.289	1	10	98	2	2	0	1.9	.980							
	OF	R. Jones	124	.290	8	26	70	1	0	0	2.2	1.000							
West																			
Los Angeles	1B	F. Stubbs	242	.223	8	34	521	57	13	41	7.0	.978	O. Hershiser	35	**267**	**23**	8	1	2.26
	2B	S. Sax	**632**	.277	5	57	276	429	14	69	4.6	.981	T. Leary	35	229	17	11	0	2.91
W-94 L-67	SS	A. Griffin	316	.199	1	27	145	264	15	44	4.6	.965	T. Belcher	36	180	12	6	4	2.91
	3B	J. Hamilton	309	.236	6	33	67	157	14	8	2.3	.941	Valenzuela	23	142	5	8	1	4.24
Tom Lasorda	RF	M. Marshall	542	.277	20	82	468	45	2	31	9.7	.996	A. Pena	60	94	6	7	12	1.91
	CF	J. Shelby	494	.263	10	64	329	7	6	1	2.4	.982	B. Holton	45	85	7	3	1	1.70
	LF	K. Gibson	542	.290	25	76	311	6	12	3	2.2	.964	J. Howell	50	65	5	3	21	2.08
	C	M. Scioscia	408	.257	3	35	748	63	7	10	6.7	.991	J. Orosco	55	53	3	2	9	2.72
	SS	D. Anderson	285	.249	2	20	128	225	5	49	4.4	.986							
	OF	M. Davis	281	.196	2	17	121	3	5	2	1.7	.961							
	3B	P. Guerrero	215	.298	5	35	21	64	10	2	2.1	.895							
	O1	M. Hatcher	191	.293	1	25	188	17	3	7		.986							
	31	T. Woodson	173	.249	3	15	160	60	6	13		.973							
	C	R. Dempsey	167	.251	7	30	333	29	4	4	4.9	.989							
Cincinnati	1B	N. Esasky	391	.243	15	62	982	52	6	70	9.0	.994	D. Jackson	35	261	**23**	8	0	2.73
	2B	J. Treadway	301	.252	2	23	188	252	7	49	4.6	.984	T. Browning	36	251	18	5	0	3.41
W-87 L-74	SS	B. Larkin	588	.296	12	56	231	470	29	67	4.9	.960	J. Rijo	49	162	13	8	0	2.39
	3B	C. Sabo	538	.271	11	44	75	318	14	**31**	3.0	**.966**	M. Soto	14	87	3	7	0	4.66
Pete Rose	RF	P. O'Neill	485	.252	16	73	173	8	2	14	8.7	.989	J. Franco	70	86	6	6	39	1.57
W-11 L-12	CF	E. Davis	472	.273	26	93	300	2	6	0	2.4	.981	R. Robinson	17	79	3	7	0	4.12
	LF	K. Daniels	495	.291	18	64	256	10	5	2	2.0	.982	J. Armstrong	14	65	4	7	0	5.79
Tommy Helms	C	B. Diaz	315	.219	10	35	468	44	5	9	5.9	.990							
W-12 L-15	UT	Concepcion	197	.198	0	8	151	131	2	36		.993							
Pete Rose	OF	D. Collins	174	.236	0	14	53	2	2	0	1.6	.965							
W-64 L-47																			
San Diego	1B	K. Moreland	511	.256	5	64	637	52	4	55	9.5	.994	E. Show	32	235	16	11	0	3.26
	2B	R. Alomar	545	.266	9	41	319	459	16	88	5.6	.980	A. Hawkins	33	218	14	11	0	3.35
W-83 L-78	SS	G. Templeton	362	.249	3	36	168	316	16	62	4.8	.968	E. Whitson	34	205	13	11	0	3.77
	3B	C. Brown	247	.235	2	19	54	131	10	15	2.7	.949	J. Jones	29	179	9	14	0	4.12
Larry Bowa	RF	T. Gwynn	521	**.313**	7	70	264	8	5	1	2.1	.982	D. Rasmussen	20	148	14	4	0	2.55
W-16 L-30	CF	M. Wynne	333	.264	11	42	216	5	3	2	2.0	.987	M. Davis	62	98	5	10	28	2.01
	LF	C. Martinez	365	.236	18	65	143	6	1	2	2.3	.993	McCullers	60	98	3	6	10	2.49
Jack McKeon	C	B. Santiago	492	.248	10	46	725	**75**	12	11	6.0	.985	M. Grant	33	98	2	8	0	3.69
W-67 L-48	10	J. Kruk	378	.241	9	44	634	37	3	45		.996							
	UT	R. Ready	331	.266	7	39	112	153	11	22		.960							
	SS	D. Thon	258	.264	1	18	82	168	12	28	3.7	.954							
	3B	T. Flannery	170	.265	0	19	27	76	3	8	2.1	.972							
San Francisco	1B	W. Clark	575	.282	29	**109**	1492	104	12	**126**	**10.2**	.993	R. Reuschel	36	245	19	11	0	3.12
	2B	R. Thompson	477	.264	7	48	255	365	14	88	4.7	.978	D. Robinson	51	177	10	5	6	2.45
W-83 L-79	SS	J. Uribe	493	.252	3	35	212	404	19	77	4.5	.970	K. Downs	27	168	13	9	0	3.32
	3B	K. Mitchell	505	.251	19	80	61	203	16	18	2.7	.943	A. Hammaker	43	145	9	9	3	3.73
Roger Craig	RF	C. Maldonado	499	.255	12	68	251	5	10	1	1.9	.962	M. Krukow	20	125	7	4	0	3.54
	CF	B. Butler	568	.287	6	43	395	3	5	1	2.6	.988	M. LaCoss	19	114	7	7	0	3.62
	LF	M. Aldrete	389	.267	3	50	61	3	0	2	6.4	1.000	S. Garrelts	65	98	5	9	13	3.58
	C	B. Melvin	273	.234	8	27	403	31	7	4	5.0	.984	C. Lefferts	64	92	3	8	11	2.92
	C	B. Brenly	206	.189	5	22	334	27	6	2	5.3	.984	J. Price	38	62	1	6	4	3.94
	UT	E. Riles	187	.294	3	28	46	133	3	17		.984							
	UT	C. Speier	171	.216	3	18	70	142	3	26		.986							
	OF	J. Leonard	160	.256	2	20	74	0	1	0	1.7	.987							

NATIONAL LEAGUE 1988, *cont.*

	POS	Player	AB	BA	HR	RBI	PO	A	E	DP	TC/G	FA	Pitcher	G	IP	W	L	SV	ERA
Houston	1B	G. Davis	561	.271	30	99	1355	103	6	104	9.7	**.996**	N. Ryan	33	220	12	11	0	3.52
	2B	B. Doran	480	.248	7	53	260	371	8	73	4.9	.987	M. Scott	32	219	14	8	0	2.92
W-82 L-80	SS	R. Ramirez	566	.276	6	59	232	408	23	68	4.3	.965	J. Deshaies	31	207	11	14	0	3.00
	3B	B. Bell	269	.253	7	37	31	114	12	8	2.4	.924	D. Darwin	44	192	8	13	3	3.84
Hal Lanier	RF	K. Bass	541	.255	14	72	267	7	6	2	1.9	.979	B. Knepper	27	175	14	5	0	3.14
	CF	G. Young	576	.257	0	37	357	10	3	1	2.6	.992	J. Agosto	75	92	10	2	4	2.26
	LF	B. Hatcher	530	.268	7	52	280	7	5	2	2.1	.983	L. Andersen	53	83	2	4	5	2.94
	C	A. Trevino	193	.249	2	13	360	24	9	5	5.3	.977	D. Smith	51	57	4	5	27	2.67
	OF	T. Puhl	234	.303	3	19	116	2	2	0	1.5	.983							
	C	A. Ashby	227	.238	7	33	414	23	4	4	6.7	.991							
	3B	D. Walling	176	.244	1	20	33	99	7	14	2.7	.950							
Atlanta	1B	G. Perry	547	.300	8	74	1282	106	**17**	102	10.0	.988	R. Mahler	39	249	9	16	0	3.69
	2B	R. Gant	563	.259	19	60	295	378	**26**	82	**5.7**	.963	P. Smith	32	195	7	15	0	3.69
W-54 L-106	SS	A. Thomas	606	.252	13	68	230	456	**29**	**90**	4.8	.959	T. Glavine	34	195	7	**17**	0	4.56
	3B	K. Oberkfell	422	.277	3	40	83	207	15	21	2.7	.951	Z. Smith	23	140	5	10	0	4.30
Chuck Tanner	RF	D. Murphy	592	.226	24	77	340	15	3	4	2.3	.992	C. Puleo	53	106	5	5	1	3.47
W-12 L-27	CF	A. Hall	231	.247	1	15	137	7	4	1	2.3	.973	J. Alvarez	60	102	5	6	3	2.99
	LF	D. James	386	.256	3	30	222	5	3	0	1.9	.987	Assenmacher	64	79	8	7	5	3.06
Russ Nixon	C	O. Virgil	320	.256	9	31	448	45	5	3	5.2	.990	B. Sutter	38	45	1	4	14	4.76
W-42 L-79	C	B. Benedict	236	.242	0	15	384	54	5	3	5.0	.989							
	OF	T. Blocker	198	.212	2	10	164	1	1	0	2.7	.994							
	OF	K. Griffey	193	.249	2	19	61	2	2	0	1.5	.969							

BATTING AND BASE RUNNING LEADERS

Batting Average
T. Gwynn, SD	.313
R. Palmeiro, CHI	.307
A. Dawson, CHI	.303
A. Galarraga, MON	.302
G. Perry, ATL	.300

Slugging Average
Strawberry, NY	.545
A. Galarraga, MON	.540
W. Clark, SF	.508
A. Van Slyke, PIT	.506
A. Dawson, CHI	.504

Home Runs
Strawberry, NY	39
G. Davis, HOU	30
W. Clark, SF	29
A. Galarraga, MON	29
McReynolds, NY	27

Total Bases
A. Galarraga, MON	329
A. Dawson, CHI	298
A. Van Slyke, PIT	297
Strawberry, NY	296
W. Clark, SF	292

Runs Batted In
W. Clark, SF	109
Strawberry, NY	101
B. Bonilla, PIT	100
A. Van Slyke, PIT	100
McReynolds, NY	99
G. Davis, HOU	99

Stolen Bases
V. Coleman, STL	81
G. Young, HOU	65
O. Smith, STL	57
O. Nixon, MON	46
C. Sabo, CIN	46

Hits
A. Galarraga, MON	184
A. Dawson, CHI	179
R. Palmeiro, CHI	178
S. Sax, LA	175

Base on Balls
W. Clark, SF	100
B. Butler, SF	97
K. Daniels, CIN	87
H. Johnson, NY	86

Home Run Percentage
Strawberry, NY	7.2
E. Davis, CIN	5.5
G. Davis, HOU	5.3
W. Clark, SF	5.0

Runs Scored
B. Butler, SF	109
K. Gibson, LA	106
W. Clark, SF	102
Strawberry, NY	101

Doubles
A. Galarraga, MON	42
R. Palmeiro, CHI	41
C. Sabo, CIN	40
S. Bream, PIT	37

Triples
A. Van Slyke, PIT	15
V. Coleman, STL	10
B. Butler, SF	9
G. Young, HOU	9

PITCHING LEADERS

Winning Percentage
D. Cone, NY	.870
T. Browning, CIN	.783
O. Hershiser, LA	.742
D. Jackson, CIN	.742
B. Knepper, HOU	.737

Earned Run Average
J. Magrane, STL	2.18
D. Cone, NY	2.22
O. Hershiser, LA	2.26
J. Tudor, LA, STL	2.32
J. Rijo, CIN	2.39

Wins
O. Hershiser, LA	23
D. Jackson, CIN	23
D. Cone, NY	20
R. Reuschel, SF	19

Saves
J. Franco, CIN	39
J. Gott, PIT	34
T. Worrell, STL	32
S. Bedrosian, PHI	28
M. Davis, SD	28

Strikeouts
N. Ryan, HOU	228
D. Cone, NY	213
J. DeLeon, STL	208
M. Scott, HOU	190
S. Fernandez, NY	189

Complete Games
O. Hershiser, LA	15
D. Jackson, CIN	15
E. Show, SD	13
R. Sutcliffe, CHI	12
D. Gooden, NY	10

Fewest Hits/9 Innings
S. Fernandez, NY	6.11
P. Perez, MON	6.37
J. Rijo, CIN	6.67
M. Scott, HOU	6.67

Shutouts
O. Hershiser, LA	8
T. Leary, LA	6
D. Jackson, CIN	6
B. Ojeda, NY	5

Fewest Walks/9 Innings
B. Smith, MON	1.45
R. Mahler, ATL	1.52
R. Reuschel, SF	1.54
B. Ojeda, NY	1.56

Most Strikeouts/9 Inn.
N. Ryan, HOU	9.33
S. Fernandez, NY	9.10
J. Rijo, CIN	8.89
J. DeLeon, STL	8.31

Innings
O. Hershiser, LA	267
D. Jackson, CIN	261
T. Browning, CIN	251
R. Mahler, ATL	249

Games Pitched
R. Murphy, CIN	76
J. Robinson, PIT	75
J. Agosto, HOU	75
J. Franco, CIN	70

		W	L	PCT	GB	R	OR	2B	3B	HR	BA	SA	SB	E	DP	FA	CG	BB	SO	ShO	SV	ERA
											Batting				Fielding			Pitching				
East	New York	100	60	.625		**703**	532	251	24	**152**	.256	**.396**	140	**115**	127	.981	31	**404**	1100	17	46	**2.91**
	Pittsburgh	85	75	.531	15	651	616	240	45	110	.247	.369	119	125	128	.980	12	469	790	4	46	3.47
	Montreal	81	81	.500	20	628	592	260	**48**	107	.251	.373	189	142	145	.978	18	476	923	6	43	3.08
	Chicago	77	85	.475	24	660	694	**262**	46	113	**.261**	.383	120	125	128	.980	30	490	897	9	29	3.84
	St. Louis	76	86	.469	25	578	633	207	33	71	.249	.337	**234**	121	131	**.981**	17	486	881	7	42	3.47
	Philadelphia	65	96	.404	35.5	597	734	246	31	106	.239	.355	112	145	139	.976	16	628	859	3	36	4.14
West	Los Angeles	94	67	.584		628	544	217	25	99	.248	.352	131	142	126	.977	**32**	473	1029	15	**49**	2.97
	Cincinnati	87	74	.540	7	641	596	246	25	122	.246	.368	207	125	131	.980	24	504	934	10	43	3.35
	San Diego	83	78	.516	11	594	583	205	35	94	.247	.351	123	120	**147**	.981	30	439	885	4	39	3.28
	San Francisco	83	79	.512	11.5	670	626	227	44	113	.248	.368	121	129	145	.980	25	422	875	11	42	3.39
	Houston	82	80	.506	12.5	617	631	239	31	96	.244	.351	198	138	124	.978	21	478	1049	10	40	3.40
	Atlanta	54	106	.338	39.5	555	741	228	28	96	.242	.348	95	151	138	.976	14	524	810	3	25	4.09
						7522	7522	2828	415	1279	.248	.363	1789	1578	1609	.979	270	5793	11032	99	480	3.45

AMERICAN LEAGUE 1988

		POS	Player	AB	BA	HR	RBI	PO	A	E	DP	TC/G	FA	Pitcher	G	IP	W	L	SV	ERA
East	**Boston**	1B	T. Benzinger	405	.254	13	70	520	38	5	47	6.6	.991	R. Clemens	35	264	18	12	0	2.93
		2B	M. Barrett	612	.283	1	65	312	402	7	97	4.8	.990	B. Hurst	33	217	18	6	0	3.66
	W-89 L-73	SS	J. Reed	338	.293	1	28	123	242	11	49	4.0	.971	W. Gardner	36	149	8	6	2	3.50
		3B	W. Boggs	584	**.366**	5	58	**122**	250	11	17	2.5	.971	O. Boyd	23	130	9	7	0	5.34
	John McNamara	RF	D. Evans	559	.293	21	111	151	4	2	0	1.8	.987	M. Smithson	31	127	9	6	0	5.97
	W-43 L-42	CF	E. Burks	540	.294	18	92	370	9	9	0	2.7	.977	B. Stanley	57	102	6	4	5	3.19
		LF	M. Greenwell	590	.325	22	119	302	6	6	2	2.1	.981	M. Boddicker	15	89	7	3	0	2.63
	Joe Morgan	C	R. Gedman	299	.231	9	39	570	40	5	4	6.6	.992	L. Smith	64	84	4	5	29	2.80
	W-46 L-31	DH	J. Rice	485	.264	15	72							D. Lamp	46	83	7	6	0	3.48
		C	R. Cerone	264	.269	3	27	471	28	0	4	6.0	**1.000**							
		SS	S. Owen	257	.249	5	18	102	192	10	34	4.0	.967							
		1B	L. Parrish	158	.259	7	26	221	25	3	18	6.9	.988							
	Detroit	1B	D. Evans	437	.208	22	64	509	58	4	43	8.8	.993	J. Morris	34	235	15	13	0	3.94
		2B	L. Whitaker	403	.275	12	55	218	284	8	53	4.6	.984	D. Alexander	34	229	14	11	0	4.32
	W-88 L-74	SS	A. Trammell	466	.311	15	69	195	355	11	67	4.5	.980	W. Terrell	29	206	7	16	0	3.97
		3B	T. Brookens	441	.243	5	38	101	234	17	16	2.6	.952	F. Tanana	32	203	14	11	0	4.21
	Sparky Anderson	RF	C. Lemon	512	.264	17	64	296	8	8	3	2.2	.974	J. Robinson	24	172	13	6	0	2.98
		CF	G. Pettis	458	.210	3	36	361	5	5	0	2.9	.987	M. Henneman	65	91	9	6	22	1.87
		LF	P. Sheridan	347	.254	11	47	203	2	4	0	1.9	.981	G. Hernandez	63	68	6	5	10	3.06
		C	M. Nokes	382	.251	16	53	574	45	7	8	5.7	.989							
		UT	L. Salazar	452	.270	12	62	199	151	10	22		.972							
		1B	R. Knight	299	.217	3	33	432	33	4	40	7.3	.991							
		UT	D. Bergman	289	.294	5	35	386	37	4	31		.991							
		C	M. Heath	219	.247	5	18	357	24	6	3	5.2	.984							
		2B	Walewander	175	.211	0	6	114	144	6	36	4.3	.977							
		DH	L. Herndon	174	.224	4	20													
	Milwaukee	1B	G. Brock	364	.212	6	50	915	102	7	89	9.0	.993	T. Higuera	31	227	16	9	0	2.45
		2B	J. Gantner	539	.276	0	47	**325**	428	11	92	5.0	.986	B. Wegman	32	199	13	13	0	4.12
	W-87 L-75	SS	D. Sveum	467	.242	9	51	208	370	**27**	93	4.8	.955	C. Bosio	38	182	7	15	6	3.36
		3B	P. Molitor	609	.312	13	60	86	187	17	15	2.8	.941	D. August	24	148	13	7	0	3.09
	Tom Trebelhorn	RF	R. Deer	492	.252	23	85	284	10	3	3	2.2	.990	M. Birkbeck	23	124	10	8	0	4.72
		CF	R. Yount	621	.306	13	91	444	12	2	2	2.9	.996	J. Nieves	25	110	7	5	1	4.08
		LF	J. Leonard	374	.235	8	44	191	4	3	1	2.2	.985	C. Crim	**70**	105	7	6	9	2.91
		C	B. Surhoff	493	.245	5	38	525	42	6	2	5.4	.990	T. Filer	19	102	5	8	0	4.43
		D1	J. Meyer	327	.263	11	45	190	18	3	19	6.4	.986	D. Plesac	50	52	1	2	30	2.41
		OF	G. Braggs	272	.261	10	42	134	1	3	0	2.6	.978							
	Toronto	1B	F. McGriff	536	.282	34	82	1344	93	5	143	9.4	**.997**	M. Flanagan	34	211	13	13	0	4.18
		2B	M. Lee	381	.291	2	38	221	261	6	64	5.0	.988	D. Stieb	32	207	16	8	0	3.04
	W-87 L-75	SS	T. Fernandez	648	.287	5	70	247	470	14	106	4.7	.981	J. Clancy	36	196	11	13	1	4.49
		3B	K. Gruber	569	.278	16	81	114	**349**	14	31	**3.1**	.971	J. Key	21	131	12	5	0	3.29
	Jimy Williams	RF	J. Barfield	468	.244	18	56	325	12	4	4	2.5	.988	J. Cerutti	46	124	6	7	1	3.13
		CF	L. Moseby	472	.239	10	42	304	2	5	1	2.5	.984	D. Ward	64	112	9	3	15	3.30
		LF	G. Bell	614	.269	24	97	253	8	15	1	1.9	.946	Stottlemyre	28	98	4	8	0	5.69
		C	E. Whitt	398	.251	16	70	643	43	4	10	5.6	.994	T. Henke	52	68	4	4	25	2.91
		DH	R. Mulliniks	337	.300	12	48							D. Wells	41	64	3	5	4	4.62
		2B	N. Liriano	276	.264	3	23	121	177	12	48	3.9	.961							
		OD	R. Leach	199	.276	0	23	74	1	0	0	1.5	1.000							
		1B	C. Fielder	174	.230	9	23	99	10	1	10	6.5	.991							
		C	P. Borders	154	.273	5	21	205	14	6	0	5.2	.973							
	New York	1B	D. Mattingly	599	.311	18	88	1250	99	9	131	9.5	.993	R. Rhoden	30	197	12	12	0	4.29
		2B	W. Randolph	404	.230	2	34	254	339	7	83	**5.5**	.988	T. John	35	176	9	8	0	4.49
	W-85 L-76	SS	R. Santana	480	.240	4	38	202	421	22	96	4.4	.966	R. Dotson	32	171	12	9	0	5.00
		3B	Pagliarulo	444	.216	15	67	82	232	19	16	2.7	.943	Candelaria	25	157	13	7	1	3.38
	Billy Martin	RF	D. Winfield	559	.322	25	107	276	3	3	1	2.0	.989	N. Allen	41	117	5	3	0	3.84
	W-40 L-28	CF	Washington	455	.308	11	64	309	5	5	1	2.7	.984	C. Hudson	28	106	6	6	2	4.49
		LF	R. Henderson	554	.305	6	50	320	7	12	**5**	2.9	.965	D. Righetti	60	87	5	4	25	3.52
	Lou Piniella	C	D. Slaught	322	.283	9	43	496	24	**11**	4	5.6	.979	S. Shields	39	82	5	5	0	4.37
	W-45 L-48	DH	J. Clark	496	.242	27	93							C. Guante	56	75	5	6	11	2.88
		C	J. Skinner	251	.227	4	23	395	16	4	5	4.9	.990							
		OF	G. Ward	231	.225	4	24	130	0	1	0	2.4	.992							
		DH	K. Phelps	107	.224	10	22													
	Cleveland	1B	W. Upshaw	493	.245	11	50	1162	102	**12**	93	8.9	.991	G. Swindell	33	242	18	14	0	3.20
		2B	J. Franco	613	.303	10	54	310	434	14	87	5.0	.982	T. Candiotti	31	217	14	8	0	3.28
	W-78 L-84	SS	J. Bell	211	.218	2	21	103	170	10	37	3.9	.965	J. Farrell	31	210	14	10	0	4.24
		3B	B. Jacoby	552	.241	9	49	99	298	10	23	2.7	.975	S. Bailes	37	145	9	14	0	4.90
	Doc Edwards	RF	C. Snyder	511	.272	26	75	314	**16**	5	0	2.4	.985	R. Yett	23	134	9	6	0	4.62
		CF	J. Carter	621	.271	27	98	444	8	7	3	2.9	.985	D. Jones	51	83	3	4	37	2.27
		LF	M. Hall	515	.280	6	71	288	3	10	1	2.1	.967							
		C	A. Allanson	434	.263	5	50	**691**	60	**11**	11	5.7	.986							
		DH	R. Kittle	225	.258	18	43													
		SS	Washington	223	.256	2	21	83	141	16	26	4.4	.933							
		DH	T. Francona	212	.311	1	12													
		OF	C. Castillo	176	.273	4	14	69	1	5	0	1.7	.933							

AMERICAN LEAGUE 1988, *cont.*

	POS	Player	AB	BA	HR	RBI	PO	A	E	DP	TC/G	FA	Pitcher	G	IP	W	L	SV	ERA
Baltimore	1B	E. Murray	603	.284	28	84	867	106	11	101	9.6	.989	J. Bautista	33	172	6	15	0	4.30
	2B	B. Ripken	512	.207	2	34	309	440	12	110	5.1	.984	J. Tibbs	30	159	4	15	0	5.39
W-54 L-107	SS	C. Ripken	575	.264	23	81	**284**	480	21	119	4.9	.973	J. Ballard	25	153	8	12	0	4.40
	3B	R. Gonzales	237	.215	2	15	45	153	7	19	2.6	.966	M. Boddicker	21	147	6	12	0	3.86
Cal Ripken	RF	J. Orsulak	379	.288	8	27	228	6	5	2	2.0	.979	D. Schmidt	41	130	8	5	2	3.40
W-0 L-6	CF	F. Lynn	301	.252	18	37	216	1	2	0	2.6	.991	Williamson	37	118	5	8	2	4.90
	LF	P. Stanicek	261	.230	4	17	128	4	2	2	2.1	.985	O. Peraza	19	86	5	7	0	5.55
Frank Robinson	C	M. Tettleton	283	.261	11	37	361	31	3	1	4.9	.992	M. Thurmond	43	75	1	8	3	4.58
W-54 L-101																			
	OD	L. Sheets	452	.230	10	47	139	9	4	0	2.0	.974	Niedenfuer	52	59	3	4	18	3.51
	UT	J. Traber	352	.222	10	45	481	59	6	51		.989							
	3B	R. Schu	270	.256	4	20	56	108	11	7	2.4	.937							
	C	T. Kennedy	265	.226	3	16	332	23	2	3	4.5	.994							
	OF	K. Gerhart	262	.195	9	23	192	3	5	1	2.2	.975							
	OF	B. Anderson	177	.198	1	9	156	1	3	0	3.3	.981							
West **Oakland**	1B	M. McGwire	550	.260	32	99	1228	88	9	118	8.6	.993	D. Stewart	37	**276**	21	12	0	3.23
	2B	G. Hubbard	294	.255	3	33	195	267	6	60	4.5	.987	B. Welch	36	245	17	9	0	3.64
W-104 L-58	SS	W. Weiss	452	.250	3	39	254	431	15	83	4.8	.979	S. Davis	33	202	16	7	0	3.70
	3B	C. Lansford	556	.279	7	57	113	220	7	16	2.4	**.979**	C. Young	26	156	11	8	0	4.14
Tony LaRussa	RF	J. Canseco	610	.307	**42**	**124**	304	11	7	3	2.2	.978	G. Nelson	54	112	9	6	3	3.06
	CF	D. Henderson	507	.304	24	94	382	5	7	2	2.8	.982	T. Burns	17	103	8	2	1	3.16
	LF	L. Polonia	288	.292	2	27	155	3	2	1	2.1	.988	R. Honeycutt	55	80	3	2	7	3.50
	C	R. Hassey	323	.257	7	45	465	31	3	7	5.5	.994	E. Plunk	49	78	7	2	5	3.00
	OF	S. Javier	397	.257	2	35	240	6	5	2	2.2	.980	D. Eckersley	60	73	4	2	45	2.35
	DO	D. Parker	377	.257	12	55	58	3	3	0	1.9	.953	G. Cadaret	58	72	5	2	3	2.89
	C	T. Steinbach	351	.265	9	51	484	48	9	5	6.4	.983							
	UT	M. Gallego	277	.209	2	20	155	254	8	49		.981							
	DH	D. Baylor	264	.220	7	34													
	UT	T. Phillips	212	.203	2	17	84	80	10	18		.943							
Minnesota	1B	K. Hrbek	510	.312	25	76	842	57	3	92	8.6	.997	F. Viola	35	255	**24**	7	0	2.64
	2B	Lombardozzi	287	.209	3	27	140	211	5	47	4.0	.986	B. Blyleven	33	207	10	17	0	5.43
W-91 L-71	SS	G. Gagne	461	.236	14	48	200	373	18	79	4.0	.970	A. Anderson	30	202	16	9	0	**2.45**
	3B	G. Gaetti	468	.301	28	88	105	189	7	24	2.6	.977	C. Lea	24	130	7	7	0	4.85
Tom Kelly	RF	R. Bush	394	.261	14	51	19	2	0	1	3.5	1.000	F. Toliver	21	115	7	6	0	4.24
	CF	K. Puckett	**657**	.356	24	121	**450**	12	3	4	2.9	.994	J. Berenguer	57	100	8	4	2	3.96
	LF	D. Gladden	576	.269	11	62	0	0	0	**0**		.000	K. Atherton	49	74	7	5	3	3.41
	C	T. Laudner	375	.251	13	54	621	35	5	8	6.1	.992	J. Reardon	63	73	2	4	42	2.47
	D1	G. Larkin	505	.267	8	70	466	28	3	46	8.3	.994							
	2B	T. Herr	304	.263	1	21	140	195	4	54	4.6	.988							
	UT	A. Newman	260	.223	0	19	97	155	6	33		.977							
	OF	J. Moses	206	.316	2	12	123	1	0	0	1.5	1.000							
	C	B. Harper	166	.295	3	20	207	15	2	0	4.7	.991							
Kansas City	1B	G. Brett	589	.306	24	103	1126	70	10	105	9.7	.992	M. Gubicza	35	270	20	8	0	2.70
	2B	F. White	537	.235	8	58	293	426	4	88	4.9	**.994**	Saberhagen	35	261	14	16	0	3.80
W-84 L-77	SS	K. Stillwell	459	.251	10	53	170	349	13	60	4.3	.976	C. Leibrandt	35	243	13	12	0	3.19
	3B	K. Seitzer	559	.304	5	60	93	297	26	33	2.8	.938	F. Bannister	31	189	12	13	0	4.33
John Wathan	RF	D. Tartabull	507	.274	26	102	227	8	9	1	1.9	.963	S. Farr	62	83	5	4	20	2.50
	CF	W. Wilson	591	.262	1	37	365	1	4	0	2.6	.989	T. Power	22	80	5	6	0	5.94
	LF	B. Jackson	439	.246	25	68	246	11	7	2	2.2	.973	Montgomery	45	63	7	2	1	3.45
	C	J. Quirk	196	.240	8	25	409	31	8	5	5.7	.982	G. Garber	26	33	0	4	6	3.58
	OF	P. Tabler	301	.309	1	49	68	1	1	0	1.9	.986							
	D1	B. Buckner	242	.256	3	34	160	12	1	11	8.2	.994							
	C	Macfarlane	211	.265	4	26	309	18	2	3	4.8	.994							
	OF	Eisenreich	202	.218	1	19	109	0	4	0	1.8	.965							
	UT	B. Pecota	178	.208	1	15	98	145	6	25		.976							
California	1B	W. Joyner	597	.295	13	85	**1369**	143	8	**148**	**9.7**	.995	M. Witt	34	250	13	16	0	4.15
	2B	J. Ray	602	.306	6	83	194	328	15	64	5.2	.972	W. Fraser	34	195	12	13	0	5.41
W-75 L-87	SS	D. Schofield	527	.239	6	34	278	492	13	**125**	5.1	**.983**	C. Finley	31	194	9	15	0	4.17
	3B	J. Howell	500	.254	16	63	96	249	17	19	2.4	.953	McCaskill	23	146	8	6	0	4.31
Cookie Rojas	RF	C. Davis	600	.268	21	93	299	10	**19**	1	2.2	.942	D. Petry	22	140	3	9	0	4.38
W-75 L-79	CF	D. White	455	.259	11	51	364	7	9	2	**3.3**	.976	T. Clark	15	94	6	6	0	5.07
	LF	T. Armas	368	.272	13	49	212	5	3	1	1.9	.986	G. Minton	44	79	4	5	7	2.85
Larry Stubing	C	B. Boone	352	.295	5	39	506	**66**	8	9	4.8	.986	B. Harvey	50	76	7	5	17	2.13
W-0 L-8	DH	B. Downing	484	.242	25	64							D. Moore	27	33	5	2	4	4.91
	2B	M. McLemore	233	.240	2	16	107	171	6	52	4.5	.979							
Chicago	1B	G. Walker	377	.247	8	42	935	41	7	93	10.0	.993	M. Perez	32	197	12	10	0	3.79
	2B	F. Manrique	345	.235	5	37	228	308	8	77	4.2	.985	J. Reuss	32	183	13	9	0	3.44
W-71 L-90	SS	O. Guillen	566	.261	0	39	273	**570**	20	115	**5.5**	.977	B. Long	47	174	8	11	2	4.03
	3B	S. Lyons	472	.269	5	45	81	238	25	**36**	2.7	.927	D. LaPoint	25	161	10	11	0	3.40
Jim Fregosi	RF	I. Calderon	264	.212	14	35	141	5	7	1	2.3	.954	J. McDowell	26	159	5	10	0	3.97
	CF	D. Gallagher	347	.303	5	31	228	5	0	2	2.5	1.000	R. Horton	52	109	6	10	2	4.86
	LF	D. Pasqua	422	.227	20	50	316	14	2	13	2.8	**.993**	B. Thigpen	68	90	5	8	34	3.30
	C	C. Fisk	253	.277	19	50	338	36	2	7	5.1	.995							
	DH	H. Baines	599	.277	13	81													
	OF	D. Boston	281	.217	15	31	190	4	10	2	2.4	.951							
	OF	G. Redus	262	.263	6	34	140	7	2	1	2.2	.987							
	2B	D. Hill	221	.217	2	20	106	132	6	36	4.1	.975							
	O3	K. Williams	220	.159	8	28	87	69	17	4		.902							
	C	M. Salas	196	.250	3	9	251	35	6	4	4.2	.979							

AMERICAN LEAGUE 1988, *cont.*

	POS	Player	AB	BA	HR	RBI	PO	A	E	DP	TC/G	FA	Pitcher	G	IP	W	L	SV	ERA
Texas	1B	P. O'Brien	547	.272	16	71	1346	140	8	124	9.6	.995	C. Hough	34	252	15	16	0	3.32
	2B	C. Wilkerson	338	.293	0	28	153	240	12	52	4.7	.970	J. Guzman	30	207	11	13	0	3.70
W-70 L-91	SS	S. Fletcher	515	.276	0	47	215	414	11	90	4.6	.983	P. Kilgus	32	203	12	15	0	4.16
	3B	S. Buechele	503	.250	16	58	110	297	16	25	2.8	.962	J. Russell	34	189	10	9	0	3.82
Bobby Valentine	RF	R. Sierra	615	.254	23	91	310	11	7	3	2.1	.979	B. Witt	22	174	8	10	0	3.92
	CF	O. McDowell	437	.247	6	37	267	2	3	1	2.4	.989	M. Williams	67	68	2	7	18	4.63
	LF	Incaviglia	418	.249	22	54	172	12	2	1	2.0	.989	R. Hayward	12	63	4	6	0	5.46
	C	G. Petralli	351	.282	7	36	409	45	9	7	5.4	.981	D. Mohorcic	43	52	2	6	5	4.85
	OF	C. Espy	347	.248	2	39	196	10	6	0	2.2	.972							
	C	M. Stanley	249	.229	3	27	310	14	3	3	5.1	.991							
	DH	L. Parrish	248	.190	7	26													
	2B	J. Browne	214	.229	1	17	112	139	11	27	3.7	.958							
	OF	B. Brower	201	.224	1	11	104	2	3	1	1.8	.972							
Seattle	1B	A. Davis	478	.295	18	69	980	65	6	111	9.1	.994	M. Langston	35	261	15	11	0	3.34
	2B	H. Reynolds	598	.283	4	41	303	**471**	**18**	111	5.0	.977	M. Moore	37	229	9	15	1	3.78
W-68 L-93	SS	R. Quinones	499	.248	12	52	202	396	23	103	4.6	.963	B. Swift	38	175	8	12	0	4.59
	3B	J. Presley	544	.230	14	62	112	234	22	25	2.5	.940	S. Bankhead	21	135	7	9	0	3.07
Dick Williams	RF	G. Wilson	284	.250	3	17	140	4	3	1	2.0	.980	M. Campbell	20	115	6	10	0	5.89
W-23 L-33	CF	H. Cotto	386	.259	8	33	253	6	2	0	2.2	.992	M. Jackson	62	99	6	5	4	2.63
	LF	M. Brantley	577	.263	15	56	327	5	6	1	2.3	.982	S. Trout	15	56	4	7	0	7.83
Jimmy Snyder	C	S. Bradley	335	.257	4	33	524	37	5	6	**6.7**	.991	M. Schooler	40	48	5	8	15	3.54
W-45 L-60																			
	D1	S. Balboni	350	.251	21	61	334	25	2	34	9.0	.994							
	C	D. Valle	290	.231	10	50	484	47	6	7	6.4	.989							
	OF	D. Coles	195	.292	10	34	66	3	1	0	1.5	.986							
	OF	J. Buhner	192	.224	10	25	134	7	1	3	2.4	.993							
	DH	K. Phelps	190	.284	14	32													

BATTING AND BASE RUNNING LEADERS

Batting Average
W. Boggs, BOS	.366
K. Puckett, MIN	.356
M. Greenwell, BOS	.325
D. Winfield, NY	.322
P. Molitor, MIL	.312

Slugging Average
J. Canseco, OAK	.569
F. McGriff, TOR	.552
G. Gaetti, MIN	.551
K. Puckett, MIN	.545
M. Greenwell, BOS	.531

Home Runs
J. Canseco, OAK	42
F. McGriff, TOR	34
M. McGwire, OAK	32
G. Gaetti, MIN	28
E. Murray, BAL	28

Total Bases
K. Puckett, MIN	358
J. Canseco, OAK	347
M. Greenwell, BOS	313
G. Brett, KC	300
J. Carter, CLE	297

Runs Batted In
J. Canseco, OAK	124
K. Puckett, MIN	121
M. Greenwell, BOS	119
D. Evans, BOS	111
D. Winfield, NY	107

Stolen Bases
R. Henderson, NY	93
G. Pettis, DET	44
P. Molitor, MIL	41
J. Canseco, OAK	40
W. Wilson, KC	35
H. Reynolds, SEA	35

Hits
K. Puckett, MIN	234
W. Boggs, BOS	214
M. Greenwell, BOS	192
P. Molitor, MIL	190

Base on Balls
W. Boggs, BOS	125
J. Clark, NY	113
C. Ripken, BAL	102
A. Davis, SEA	95

Home Run Percentage
J. Canseco, OAK	6.9
F. McGriff, TOR	6.3
G. Gaetti, MIN	6.0
M. McGwire, OAK	5.8

Runs Scored
W. Boggs, BOS	128
J. Canseco, OAK	120
R. Henderson, NY	118
P. Molitor, MIL	115

Doubles
W. Boggs, BOS	45
G. Brett, KC	42
J. Ray, CAL	42
K. Puckett, MIN	42

Triples
W. Wilson, KC	11
H. Reynolds, SEA	11
R. Yount, MIL	11

PITCHING LEADERS

Winning Percentage
F. Viola, MIN	.774
B. Hurst, BOS	.750
M. Gubicza, KC	.714
S. Davis, OAK	.696
J. Robinson, DET	.684

Earned Run Average
A. Anderson, MIN	2.45
T. Higuera, MIL	2.45
F. Viola, MIN	2.64
M. Gubicza, KC	2.70
R. Clemens, BOS	2.93

Wins
F. Viola, MIN	24
D. Stewart, OAK	21
M. Gubicza, KC	20
B. Hurst, BOS	18
R. Clemens, BOS	18
G. Swindell, CLE	18

Saves
D. Eckersley, OAK	45
J. Reardon, MIN	42
D. Jones, CLE	37
B. Thigpen, CHI	34
D. Plesac, MIL	30

Strikeouts
R. Clemens, BOS	291
M. Langston, SEA	235
F. Viola, MIN	193
T. Higuera, MIL	192
D. Stewart, OAK	192

Complete Games
R. Clemens, BOS	14
D. Stewart, OAK	14
B. Witt, TEX	13
G. Swindell, CLE	12
M. Witt, CAL	12

Fewest Hits/9 Innings
J. Robinson, DET	6.33
T. Higuera, MIL	6.65
D. Stieb, TOR	6.82
B. Witt, TEX	6.92

Shutouts
R. Clemens, BOS	8
D. Stieb, TOR	4
G. Swindell, CLE	4
M. Gubicza, KC	4

Fewest Walks/9 Innings
A. Anderson, MIN	1.65
G. Swindell, CLE	1.67
D. Alexander, DET	1.81
C. Bosio, MIL	1.88

Most Strikeouts/9 Inn.
R. Clemens, BOS	9.92
M. Langston, SEA	8.09
B. Witt, TEX	7.64
T. Higuera, MIL	7.60

Innings
D. Stewart, OAK	276
M. Gubicza, KC	270
R. Clemens, BOS	264
M. Langston, SEA	261

Games Pitched
C. Crim, MIL	70
B. Thigpen, CHI	68
M. Williams, TEX	67
M. Henneman, DET	65

		W	L	PCT	GB	R	OR	2B	3B	HR	BA	SA	SB	E	DP	FA	CG	BB	SO	ShO	SV	ERA
East	Boston	89	73	.549		813	689	**310**	39	124	**.283**	.420	65	93	123	.984	26	493	**1085**	10	37	3.97
	Detroit	88	74	.543	1	703	658	213	28	143	.250	.378	87	109	129	.982	34	497	890	6	36	3.71
	Milwaukee	87	75	.537	2	682	616	258	26	113	.257	.375	159	120	146	.981	30	**437**	832	6	51	3.45
	Toronto	87	75	.537	2	763	680	271	**47**	**158**	.268	.419	107	110	170	.982	16	528	904	7	47	3.80
	New York	85	76	.528	3.5	772	748	272	12	148	.263	.395	146	134	161	.978	16	487	861	3	43	4.26
	Cleveland	78	84	.481	11	666	731	235	28	134	.261	.387	97	124	131	.980	35	442	812	7	46	4.16
	Baltimore	54	107	.335	34.5	550	789	199	20	137	.238	.359	69	119	172	.980	20	523	709	2	26	4.54
West	Oakland	104	58	.642		800	620	251	22	156	.263	.399	129	105	151	.983	22	553	983	4	**64**	**3.44**
	Minnesota	91	71	.562	13	759	672	294	31	151	.274	**.421**	107	**84**	155	**.986**	18	453	897	4	52	3.93
	Kansas City	84	77	.522	19.5	704	648	275	40	121	.259	.391	137	124	147	.980	29	465	886	9	52	3.66
	California	75	87	.463	29	714	771	258	31	124	.261	.385	86	135	175	.979	26	568	817	6	33	4.31
	Chicago	71	90	.441	32.5	631	757	224	35	132	.244	.370	98	154	**177**	.976	11	533	754	2	43	4.12
	Texas	70	91	.435	33.5	637	735	227	39	112	.252	.368	130	131	145	.979	**41**	**654**	912	8	31	4.05
	Seattle	68	93	.422	35.5	664	744	271	27	148	.257	.398	95	123	168	.980	28	558	981	8	28	4.15
						9858	9858	3558	425	1901	.259	.391	1512	1665	2150	.981	352	7191	12323	82	569	3.97

NATIONAL LEAGUE 1989

East — Chicago
W-93 L-69 — Don Zimmer

POS	Player	AB	BA	HR	RBI	PO	A	E	DP	TC/G	FA	Pitcher	G	IP	W	L	SV	ERA
1B	M. Grace	510	.314	13	79	1230	126	6	93	9.6	.996	G. Maddux	35	238	19	12	0	2.95
2B	R. Sandberg	606	.290	30	76	294	466	6	80	4.9	.992	R. Sutcliffe	35	229	16	11	0	3.66
SS	S. Dunston	471	.278	9	60	213	379	17	76	4.4	.972	M. Bielecki	33	212	18	7	0	3.14
3B	V. Law	408	.235	7	42	76	168	13	13	2.2	.949	S. Sanderson	37	146	11	9	0	3.94
RF	A. Dawson	416	.252	21	77	227	4	3	0	2.1	.987	P. Kilgus	35	146	6	10	2	4.39
CF	J. Walton	475	.293	5	46	289	2	3	1	2.6	.990	S. Wilson	53	86	6	4	2	4.20
LF	D. Smith	343	.324	9	52	188	7	5	3	2.0	.975	M. Williams	76	82	4	4	36	2.64
C	D. Berryhill	334	.257	5	41	473	41	4	4	5.8	.992	C. Schiraldi	54	79	3	6	4	3.78
OF	M. Webster	272	.257	3	19	161	3	6	0	2.3	.965	L. Lancaster	42	73	4	2	8	1.36
UT	McClendon	259	.286	12	40	310	18	6	21		.982							
S3	D. Ramos	179	.263	1	19	49	142	11	20		.946							

New York
W-87 L-75 — Davey Johnson

POS	Player	AB	BA	HR	RBI	PO	A	E	DP	TC/G	FA	Pitcher	G	IP	W	L	SV	ERA
1B	D. Magadan	374	.286	4	41	574	59	6	50	7.3	.991	D. Cone	34	220	14	8	0	3.52
2B	G. Jefferies	508	.258	12	56	223	254	12	41	4.0	.975	S. Fernandez	35	219	14	5	0	2.83
SS	K. Elster	458	.231	10	55	235	374	15	63	4.2	.976	R. Darling	33	217	14	14	0	3.52
3B	H. Johnson	571	.287	36	101	63	180	24	15	1.9	.910	B. Ojeda	31	192	13	11	0	3.47
RF	Strawberry	476	.225	29	77	272	4	8	2	2.2	.972	D. Gooden	19	118	9	4	1	2.89
CF	J. Samuel	333	.228	3	28	206	4	3	3	2.5	.986	F. Viola	12	85	5	5	0	3.38
LF	McReynolds	545	.272	22	85	307	10	10	3	2.3	.969	R. Myers	65	84	7	4	24	2.35
C	B. Lyons	235	.247	3	27	463	29	10	4	6.6	.980	R. Aguilera	36	69	6	6	7	2.34
OF	M. Wilson	249	.205	3	18	152	2	4	0	2.2	.975	R. McDowell	25	35	1	5	4	3.31
21	T. Teufel	219	.256	2	15	261	112	10	30		.974							
1B	K. Hernandez	215	.233	4	19	405	31	4	22	7.6	.991							
C	M. Sasser	182	.291	1	22	335	19	3	3	5.8	.992							

St. Louis
W-86 L-76 — Whitey Herzog

POS	Player	AB	BA	HR	RBI	PO	A	E	DP	TC/G	FA	Pitcher	G	IP	W	L	SV	ERA
1B	P. Guerrero	570	.311	17	117	1445	72	15	99	9.6	.990	J. DeLeon	36	245	16	12	0	3.05
2B	J. Oquendo	556	.291	1	48	346	500	5	106	5.5	.994	J. Magrane	34	235	18	9	0	2.91
SS	O. Smith	593	.273	2	50	209	483	17	73	4.6	.976	K. Hill	33	197	7	15	0	3.80
3B	T. Pendleton	613	.264	13	74	113	392	15	25	3.2	.971	S. Terry	31	149	8	10	2	3.57
RF	T. Brunansky	556	.239	20	85	291	9	7	2	2.0	.977	T. Power	23	97	7	7	0	3.71
CF	M. Thompson	545	.290	4	68	348	5	8	1	2.5	.978	Quisenberry	63	78	3	1	6	2.64
LF	V. Coleman	563	.254	2	28	247	5	10	1	1.8	.962	K. Dayley	71	75	4	3	12	2.87
C	T. Pena	424	.259	4	37	674	70	2	13	5.6	.997	J. Costello	48	62	5	4	3	3.32
OF	W. McGee	199	.236	3	17	118	2	3	2	2.6	.976	T. Worrell	47	52	3	5	20	2.96

Montreal
W-81 L-81 — Buck Rodgers

POS	Player	AB	BA	HR	RBI	PO	A	E	DP	TC/G	FA	Pitcher	G	IP	W	L	SV	ERA
1B	A. Galarraga	572	.257	23	85	1335	91	11	97	9.8	.992	D. Martinez	34	232	16	7	0	3.18
2B	T. Foley	375	.229	7	39	188	295	6	53	4.5	.988	B. Smith	33	216	10	11	0	2.84
SS	S. Owen	437	.233	6	41	232	388	13	65	4.5	.979	K. Gross	31	201	11	12	0	4.38
3B	T. Wallach	573	.277	13	77	113	302	18	20	2.8	.958	P. Perez	33	198	9	13	0	3.31
RF	H. Brooks	542	.268	14	70	234	6	9	2	1.8	.964	M. Langston	24	177	12	9	0	2.39
CF	D. Martinez	361	.274	3	27	199	7	7	1	1.8	.967	T. Burke	68	85	9	3	28	2.55
LF	T. Raines	517	.286	9	60	253	7	1	0	1.9	.996	McGaffigan	57	75	3	5	2	4.68
C	Santovenia	304	.250	5	31	561	66	12	7	7.2	.981	J. Hesketh	43	48	6	4	3	5.77
C	Fitzgerald	290	.238	7	42	459	35	8	5	6.5	.984							
OF	O. Nixon	258	.217	0	21	160	2	2	0	1.7	.988							
2B	D. Garcia	203	.271	3	18	86	157	7	25	4.0	.972							

Pittsburgh
W-74 L-88 — Jim Leyland

POS	Player	AB	BA	HR	RBI	PO	A	E	DP	TC/G	FA	Pitcher	G	IP	W	L	SV	ERA
1B	G. Redus	279	.283	6	33	567	54	8	42	8.7	.987	D. Drabek	35	244	14	12	0	2.80
2B	J. Lind	578	.232	2	48	309	438	18	81	5.1	.976	J. Smiley	28	205	12	8	0	2.81
SS	J. Bell	271	.258	2	27	109	197	10	41	4.1	.968	B. Walk	33	196	13	10	0	4.41
3B	B. Bonilla	616	.281	24	86	125	330	35	31	3.1	.929	N. Heaton	42	147	6	7	0	3.05
RF	G. Wilson	330	.282	9	49	163	4	4	0	2.0	.977	J. Robinson	50	141	7	13	4	4.58
CF	A. Van Slyke	476	.237	9	53	338	9	4	5	2.9	.989	R. Kramer	35	111	5	9	2	3.96
LF	B. Bonds	580	.248	19	58	365	14	6	1	2.5	.984	B. Kipper	52	83	3	4	4	2.93
C	J. Ortiz	230	.217	1	22	334	32	2	2	4.4	.995	B. Landrum	56	81	2	3	26	1.67
OF	R. Reynolds	363	.270	6	48	200	6	2	3	2.1	.990							
SS	R. Quinones	225	.209	3	29	94	174	19	24	4.2	.934							
UT	J. King	215	.195	5	19	403	59	4	36		.991							
C	LaValliere	190	.316	2	23	306	24	3	3	5.1	.991							

Philadelphia
W-67 L-95 — Nick Leyva

POS	Player	AB	BA	HR	RBI	PO	A	E	DP	TC/G	FA	Pitcher	G	IP	W	L	SV	ERA
1B	R. Jordan	523	.285	12	75	1271	61	9	99	9.6	.993	K. Howell	33	204	12	12	0	3.44
2B	T. Herr	561	.287	2	37	281	415	7	80	4.9	.990	D. Carman	49	149	5	15	0	5.24
SS	D. Thon	435	.271	15	60	174	380	16	65	4.4	.972	B. Ruffin	24	126	6	10	0	4.44
3B	C. Hayes	299	.258	8	43	49	173	22	15	3.0	.910	McWilliams	40	121	2	11	0	4.10
RF	V. Hayes	540	.259	26	78	236	9	5	1	2.0	.980	D. Cook	21	106	6	8	0	3.99
CF	L. Dykstra	352	.222	4	19	208	9	2	0	2.5	.991	J. Parrett	72	106	12	6	2	2.98
LF	J. Kruk	281	.331	5	38	111	5	2	2	1.6	.983	Mulholland	20	104	4	7	0	5.00
C	D. Daulton	368	.201	8	44	627	56	11	8	5.5	.984	R. McDowell	44	57	3	3	19	1.11
UT	S. Jeltz	263	.243	4	25	111	205	4	33		.981	S. Bedrosian	28	34	2	3	6	3.21
OF	J. Samuel	199	.246	8	20	133	2	1	0	2.7	.993							
UT	R. Ready	187	.267	8	21	64	36	7	9		.935							
OF	B. Dernier	187	.171	1	13	95	1	3	0	1.3	.970							
OF	C. James	179	.207	2	19	61	3	1	0	1.8	.985							
OF	D. Murphy	156	.218	9	27	69	1	1	1	1.4	.986							
3B	M. Schmidt	148	.203	6	28	18	71	8	8	2.3	.918							

NATIONAL LEAGUE 1989, cont.

West — San Francisco — W-92 L-70 — Roger Craig

POS	Player	AB	BA	HR	RBI	PO	A	E	DP	TC/G	FA	Pitcher	G	IP	W	L	SV	ERA
1B	W. Clark	588	.333	23	111	1445	111	10	117	9.9	.994	R. Reuschel	32	208	17	8	0	2.94
2B	R. Thompson	547	.241	13	50	307	425	8	88	5.0	.989	D. Robinson	34	197	12	11	0	3.43
SS	J. Uribe	453	.221	1	30	225	436	18	85	4.5	.973	S. Garrelts	30	193	14	5	0	2.28
3B	E. Riles	302	.278	7	40	45	107	6	13	1.9	.962	M. LaCoss	45	150	10	10	6	3.17
RF	C. Maldonado	345	.217	9	41	181	6	5	1	1.7	.974	C. Lefferts	70	107	2	4	20	2.69
CF	B. Butler	594	.283	4	36	407	11	6	3	2.8	.986	K. Downs	18	83	4	8	0	4.79
LF	K. Mitchell	543	.291	47	125	305	8	7	0	2.2	.978	A. Hammaker	28	77	6	6	0	3.76
C	T. Kennedy	355	.239	5	34	516	47	8	6	4.7	.986	S. Bedrosian	40	51	1	4	17	2.65
3B	M. Williams	292	.202	18	50	71	126	8	10	2.8	.961							
C	K. Manwaring	200	.210	0	18	289	32	6	3	4.0	.982							
OF	D. Nixon	166	.265	1	15	87	0	3	0	1.4	.967							

San Diego — W-89 L-73 — Jack McKeon

POS	Player	AB	BA	HR	RBI	PO	A	E	DP	TC/G	FA	Pitcher	G	IP	W	L	SV	ERA
1B	J. Clark	455	.242	26	94	1135	88	15	99	9.5	.988	B. Hurst	33	245	15	11	0	2.69
2B	R. Alomar	623	.295	7	56	341	472	28	91	5.4	.967	E. Whitson	33	227	16	11	0	2.66
SS	G. Templeton	506	.255	6	40	232	409	20	74	4.7	.970	D. Rasmussen	33	184	10	10	0	4.26
3B	L. Salazar	246	.268	8	22	37	116	5	10	2.2	.968	G. Harris	56	135	8	9	6	2.60
RF	T. Gwynn	604	.336	4	62	353	13	6	1	2.4	.984	W. Terrell	19	123	5	13	0	4.01
CF	M. Wynne	294	.252	6	35	160	7	5	2	1.8	.971	M. Grant	50	116	8	2	2	3.33
LF	C. Martinez	267	.221	6	39	103	5	2	1	1.7	.982	E. Show	16	106	8	6	0	4.23
C	B. Santiago	462	.236	16	62	685	81	20	10	6.2	.975	M. Davis	70	93	4	3	44	1.85
UT	B. Roberts	329	.301	3	25	134	113	9	17		.965							
OF	C. James	303	.264	11	46	145	3	2	0	1.9	.987							
C	M. Parent	141	.191	7	21	241	17	0	2	6.3	1.000							

Houston — W-86 L-76 — Art Howe

POS	Player	AB	BA	HR	RBI	PO	A	E	DP	TC/G	FA	Pitcher	G	IP	W	L	SV	ERA
1B	G. Davis	581	.269	34	89	1347	113	12	101	9.4	.992	M. Scott	33	229	20	10	0	3.10
2B	B. Doran	507	.219	8	58	254	345	12	64	4.4	.980	J. Deshaies	34	226	15	10	0	2.91
SS	R. Ramirez	537	.246	6	54	189	326	30	60	3.7	.945	J. Clancy	33	147	7	14	0	5.08
3B	K. Caminiti	585	.255	10	72	126	335	22	27	3.0	.954	D. Darwin	68	122	11	4	7	2.36
RF	T. Puhl	354	.271	0	27	204	3	0	0	2.0	1.000	B. Knepper	22	113	4	10	0	5.89
CF	G. Young	533	.233	0	38	412	15	1	5	3.0	.998	M. Portugal	20	108	7	1	0	2.75
LF	B. Hatcher	395	.228	3	44	223	1	2	1	2.2	.991	B. Forsch	37	108	4	5	0	5.32
C	C. Biggio	443	.257	13	60	728	56	8	6	6.3	.990	L. Andersen	60	88	4	4	3	1.54
OF	K. Bass	313	.300	5	44	186	6	3	0	2.3	.985	J. Agosto	71	83	4	5	1	2.93
UT	C. Reynolds	189	.201	2	14	86	136	8	24		.965	D. Smith	52	58	3	4	25	2.64

Los Angeles — W-77 L-83 — Tom Lasorda

POS	Player	AB	BA	HR	RBI	PO	A	E	DP	TC/G	FA	Pitcher	G	IP	W	L	SV	ERA
1B	E. Murray	594	.247	20	88	1316	137	6	122	9.2	.996	O. Hershiser	35	257	15	15	0	2.31
2B	W. Randolph	549	.282	2	36	260	412	9	85	4.9	.987	T. Belcher	39	230	15	12	1	2.82
SS	A. Griffin	506	.247	0	29	208	333	14	69	4.2	.975	Valenzuela	31	197	10	13	0	3.43
3B	J. Hamilton	548	.245	12	56	139	233	19	29	2.7	.951	M. Morgan	40	153	8	11	0	2.53
RF	M. Marshall	377	.260	11	42	179	2	4	0	1.8	.978	T. Leary	19	117	6	7	0	3.38
CF	J. Shelby	345	.183	1	12	220	3	2	1	2.3	.991	J. Wetteland	31	103	5	8	1	3.77
LF	K. Gibson	253	.213	9	28	146	3	3	2	2.2	.980	R. Martinez	15	99	6	4	0	3.19
C	M. Scioscia	408	.250	10	44	822	82	11	12	7.0	.988	J. Howell	56	80	5	3	28	1.58
OF	J. Gonzalez	261	.268	3	18	171	8	6	2	2.1	.968	A. Pena	53	76	4	3	5	2.13
O3	M. Hatcher	224	.295	2	25	73	19	4	4		.958							
OF	M. Davis	173	.249	5	19	74	1	1	1	1.6	.987							

Cincinnati — W-75 L-87 — Pete Rose W-61 L-66 — Tommy Helms W-14 L-21

POS	Player	AB	BA	HR	RBI	PO	A	E	DP	TC/G	FA	Pitcher	G	IP	W	L	SV	ERA
1B	T. Benzinger	628	.245	17	76	1417	73	7	96	9.5	.995	T. Browning	37	250	15	12	0	3.39
2B	R. Oester	305	.246	1	14	211	239	7	42	4.5	.985	R. Mahler	40	221	9	13	0	3.83
SS	B. Larkin	325	.342	4	36	142	267	10	31	5.1	.976	D. Jackson	20	116	6	11	0	5.60
3B	C. Sabo	304	.260	6	29	36	145	11	12	2.5	.943	J. Rijo	19	111	7	6	0	2.84
RF	P. O'Neill	428	.276	15	74	223	7	4	1	2.0	.983	S. Scudder	23	100	4	9	0	4.49
CF	E. Davis	462	.281	34	101	298	2	5	1	2.4	.984	R. Dibble	74	99	10	5	2	2.09
LF	K. Griffey	236	.263	8	30	76	2	1	1	1.4	.987	N. Charlton	69	95	8	3	0	2.93
C	J. Reed	287	.223	3	23	504	50	7	2	5.7	.988	J. Franco	60	81	4	8	32	3.12
23	L. Quinones	340	.244	12	34	112	206	10	25		.970							
OF	R. Roomes	315	.263	7	34	201	4	4	0	2.1	.981							
OF	Winningham	251	.251	3	13	146	3	3	0	1.8	.980							
UT	L. Harris	188	.223	2	11	92	134	13	23		.946							
SS	M. Duncan	174	.247	3	13	65	103	8	17	4.0	.955							
C	J. Oliver	151	.272	3	23	260	21	4	1	6.1	.986							

Atlanta — W-63 L-97 — Russ Nixon

POS	Player	AB	BA	HR	RBI	PO	A	E	DP	TC/G	FA	Pitcher	G	IP	W	L	SV	ERA
1B	G. Perry	266	.252	4	21	618	51	9	49	9.4	.987	J. Smoltz	29	208	12	11	0	2.94
2B	J. Treadway	473	.277	8	40	271	336	12	80	5.0	.981	T. Glavine	29	186	14	8	0	3.68
SS	A. Thomas	554	.213	13	57	231	400	29	81	4.8	.956	Lilliquist	32	166	8	10	0	3.97
3B	J. Blauser	456	.270	12	46	42	128	13	9	2.3	.929	P. Smith	28	142	5	14	0	4.75
RF	T. Gregg	276	.243	6	23	57	1	2	0	1.3	.967	M. Clary	18	109	4	3	0	3.15
CF	D. Murphy	574	.228	20	84	331	5	5	0	2.3	.985	Z. Smith	17	99	1	12	0	4.45
LF	L. Smith	482	.315	21	79	289	3	2	0	2.2	.993	J. Boever	66	82	4	11	21	3.94
C	J. Davis	231	.169	4	19	364	40	6	1	5.7	.985	M. Eichhorn	45	68	5	5	0	4.35
OF	O. McDowell	280	.304	7	24	179	2	4	0	2.7	.978							
13	D. Evans	276	.207	11	39	371	90	10	37		.979							
3B	R. Gant	260	.177	9	25	23	103	16	8	2.7	.887							
OF	D. James	170	.259	1	11	87	0	0	0	1.9	1.000							

NATIONAL LEAGUE 1989, *cont.*

BATTING AND BASE RUNNING LEADERS

Batting Average
T. Gwynn, SD	.336
W. Clark, SF	.333
L. Smith, ATL	.315
M. Grace, CHI	.314
P. Guerrero, STL	.311

Slugging Average
K. Mitchell, SF	.635
H. Johnson, NY	.559
W. Clark, SF	.546
E. Davis, CIN	.541
L. Smith, ATL	.533

Home Runs
K. Mitchell, SF	47
H. Johnson, NY	36
E. Davis, CIN	34
G. Davis, HOU	34
R. Sandberg, CHI	30

PITCHING LEADERS

Winning Percentage
S. Garrelts, SF	.737
S. Fernandez, NY	.737
M. Bielecki, CHI	.720
D. Martinez, MON	.696
R. Reuschel, SF	.680

Earned Run Average
S. Garrelts, SF	2.28
O. Hershiser, LA	2.31
M. Langston, MON	2.39
E. Whitson, SD	2.66
B. Hurst, SD	2.69

Wins
M. Scott, HOU	20
G. Maddux, CHI	19
M. Bielecki, CHI	18
J. Magrane, STL	18
R. Reuschel, SF	17

Total Bases
K. Mitchell, SF	345
W. Clark, SF	321
H. Johnson, NY	319
B. Bonilla, PIT	302
R. Sandberg, CHI	301

Runs Batted In
K. Mitchell, SF	125
P. Guerrero, STL	117
W. Clark, SF	111
E. Davis, CIN	101
H. Johnson, NY	101

Stolen Bases
V. Coleman, STL	65
J. Samuel, NY, PHI	42
R. Alomar, SD	42
T. Raines, MON	41
H. Johnson, NY	41

Saves
M. Davis, SD	44
M. Williams, CHI	36
J. Franco, CIN	32
T. Burke, MON	28
J. Howell, LA	28

Strikeouts
J. DeLeon, STL	201
T. Belcher, LA	200
S. Fernandez, NY	198
D. Cone, NY	190
B. Hurst, SD	179

Complete Games
T. Belcher, LA	10
B. Hurst, SD	10
M. Scott, HOU	9
J. Magrane, STL	9
T. Browning, CIN	9

Hits
T. Gwynn, SD	203
W. Clark, SF	196
R. Alomar, SD	184
P. Guerrero, STL	177

Base on Balls
J. Clark, SD	132
V. Hayes, PHI	101
T. Raines, MON	93
B. Bonds, PIT	93

Home Run Percentage
K. Mitchell, SF	8.7
E. Davis, CIN	7.4
H. Johnson, NY	6.3
Strawberry, NY	6.1

Fewest Hits/9 Innings
J. DeLeon, STL	6.36
S. Fernandez, NY	6.44
K. Howell, PHI	6.84
J. Smoltz, ATL	6.92

Shutouts
T. Belcher, LA	8
D. Drabek, PIT	5
M. Langston, MON	4
T. Glavine, ATL	4

Fewest Walks/9 Innings
D. Robinson, SF	1.69
Lilliquist, ATL	1.85
D. Martinez, MON	1.90
E. Whitson, SD	1.90

Runs Scored
H. Johnson, NY	104
W. Clark, SF	104
R. Sandberg, CHI	104
K. Mitchell, SF	100

Doubles
P. Guerrero, STL	42
T. Wallach, MON	42
H. Johnson, NY	41
W. Clark, SF	38

Triples
R. Thompson, SF	11
B. Bonilla, PIT	10
A. Van Slyke, PIT	9
V. Coleman, STL	9

Most Strikeouts/9 Inn.
M. Langston, MON	8.92
S. Fernandez, NY	8.12
T. Belcher, LA	7.83
D. Cone, NY	7.78

Innings
O. Hershiser, LA	257
T. Browning, CIN	250
J. DeLeon, STL	245
B. Hurst, SD	245

Games Pitched
M. Williams, CHI	76
R. Dibble, CIN	74
J. Parrett, PHI	72
J. Agosto, HOU	71

		W	L	PCT	GB	R	OR	2B	3B	HR	BA	SA	SB	E	DP	FA	CG	BB	SO	ShO	SV	ERA
East	Chicago	93	69	.574		702	623	235	45	124	.261	.387	136	124	130	.980	18	532	918	5	55	3.43
	New York	87	75	.537	6	683	595	280	21	147	.246	.385	158	144	110	.976	24	532	1108	7	38	3.29
	St. Louis	86	76	.531	7	632	608	263	47	73	.258	.363	155	112	134	.982	18	482	844	8	43	3.36
	Montreal	81	81	.500	12	632	630	267	30	100	.247	.361	160	136	126	.979	20	519	1059	10	35	3.48
	Pittsburgh	74	88	.457	19	637	680	263	53	95	.241	.359	155	160	130	.975	20	539	827	7	40	3.64
	Philadelphia	67	95	.414	26	629	735	215	36	123	.243	.364	106	133	136	.979	10	613	899	6	33	4.04
West	San Francisco	92	70	.568		699	600	241	52	141	.250	.390	87	114	135	.982	12	471	802	3	47	3.30
	San Diego	89	73	.549	3	642	626	215	32	120	.251	.369	136	154	147	.976	21	481	933	4	52	3.38
	Houston	86	76	.531	6	647	669	239	28	97	.239	.345	144	142	121	.977	19	551	965	6	38	3.65
	Los Angeles	77	83	.481	14	554	536	241	17	89	.240	.339	81	118	153	.981	25	504	1052	14	36	2.95
	Cincinnati	75	87	.463	17	632	691	243	28	128	.247	.370	128	121	108	.980	16	559	981	5	37	3.73
	Atlanta	63	97	.394	28	584	680	201	22	128	.234	.350	83	152	124	.976	15	468	966	6	33	3.70
						7673	7673	2903	411	1365	.246	.365	1529	1610	1554	.978	218	6251	11354	81	487	3.50

AMERICAN LEAGUE 1989

		POS	Player	AB	BA	HR	RBI	PO	A	E	DP	TC/G	FA	Pitcher	G	IP	W	L	SV	ERA
East	**Toronto** W-89 L-73 Jimy Williams W-12 L-24 Clarence Gaston W-77 L-49	1B	F. McGriff	551	.269	36	92	1460	115	17	148	10.0	.989	J. Key	33	216	13	14	0	3.88
		2B	N. Liriano	418	.263	5	53	267	330	12	76	5.0	.980	D. Stieb	33	207	17	8	0	3.35
		SS	T. Fernandez	573	.257	11	64	260	475	6	93	5.3	.992	J. Cerutti	33	205	11	11	0	3.07
		3B	K. Gruber	545	.290	18	73	86	291	22	15	3.4	.945	M. Flanagan	30	172	8	10	0	3.93
		RF	J. Felix	415	.258	9	46	243	9	9	0	2.4	.966	Stottlemyre	27	128	7	7	0	3.88
		CF	L. Moseby	502	.221	11	43	288	3	4	1	2.5	.986	D. Ward	66	115	4	10	15	3.77
		LF	G. Bell	613	.297	18	104	258	4	10*	1	2.0	.963	T. Henke	64	89	8	3	20	1.92
		C	E. Whitt	385	.262	11	53	550	43	5	5	5.2	.992	D. Wells	54	86	7	4	2	2.40
		DH	R. Mulliniks	273	.238	3	29													
		UT	M. Lee	300	.260	3	34	152	201	11	51		.970							
		C	P. Borders	241	.257	3	29	261	27	6	1	4.3	.980							
		OF	M. Wilson	238	.298	2	17	111	2	1	1	2.1	.991							
	Baltimore W-87 L-75 Frank Robinson	1B	R. Milligan	365	.268	12	45	914	83	5	92	8.6	.995	B. Milacki	37	243	14	12	0	3.74
		2B	B. Ripken	318	.239	2	26	255	335	9	81	5.3	.985	J. Ballard	35	215	18	8	0	3.43
		SS	C. Ripken	646	.257	21	93	276	531	8	119	5.0	.990	D. Schmidt	38	157	10	13	0	5.69
		3B	Worthington	497	.247	15	70	113	277	20	22	2.8	.951	B. Holton	39	116	5	7	0	4.02
		RF	J. Orsulak	390	.285	7	55	250	10	4	2	2.4	.985	Williamson	65	107	10	5	9	2.93
		CF	M. Devereaux	391	.266	8	46	288	1	5	0	2.6	.983	P. Harnisch	18	103	5	9	0	4.62
		LF	P. Bradley	545	.277	11	55	284	4	3	0	2.1	.990	M. Thurmond	49	90	2	4	4	3.90
		C	B. Melvin	278	.241	1	32	303	20	3	1	4.3	.991	D. Johnson	14	89	4	7	0	4.23
		DH	L. Sheets	304	.243	7	33							G. Olson	64	85	5	2	27	1.69
		CD	M. Tettleton	411	.258	26	65	297	42	2	1	4.5	.994							
		OF	B. Anderson	266	.207	4	16	191	3	3	0	2.5	.985							
		1B	J. Traber	234	.209	4	26	514	54	1	59	8.2	.998							
		OF	S. Finley	217	.249	2	25	144	1	2	0	1.9	.986							
		2B	R. Gonzales	166	.217	1	11	93	125	5	35	4.1	.978							
		OF	S. Jefferson	127	.260	4	20	79	3	1	1	2.6	.988							

AMERICAN LEAGUE 1989, *cont.*

	POS	Player	AB	BA	HR	RBI	PO	A	E	DP	TC/G	FA	Pitcher	G	IP	W	L	SV	ERA
Boston	1B	N. Esasky	564	.277	30	108	1317	107	6	129	9.3	.996	R. Clemens	35	253	17	11	0	3.13
	2B	M. Barrett	336	.256	1	27	152	245	10	53	5.1	.975	M. Boddicker	34	212	15	11	0	4.00
W-83 L-79	SS	L. Rivera	323	.257	5	29	126	240	16	59	4.2	.958	J. Dopson	29	169	12	8	0	3.99
	3B	W. Boggs	621	.330	3	54	**123**	264	17	**29**	2.7	.958	M. Smithson	40	144	7	14	2	4.95
Joe Morgan	RF	D. Evans	520	.285	20	100	153	5	3	1	2.1	.981	D. Lamp	42	112	4	2	2	2.32
	CF	E. Burks	399	.303	12	61	245	7	6	3	2.7	.977	R. Murphy	74	105	5	7	9	2.74
	LF	M. Greenwell	578	.308	14	95	220	11	8	1	1.7	.967	W. Gardner	22	86	3	7	0	5.97
	C	R. Cerone	296	.243	4	48	578	41	10	5	**6.5**	.984	B. Stanley	43	79	5	2	4	4.88
	DH	J. Rice	209	.234	3	28							L. Smith	64	71	6	1	25	3.57
	S2	J. Reed	524	.288	3	40	250	422	19	88		.973							
	OF	D. Heep	320	.300	5	49	92	2	1	1	1.3	.989							
	OF	K. Romine	274	.274	1	23	157	9	3	4	1.9	.982							
	C	R. Gedman	260	.212	4	16	486	36	10	6	5.8	.981							
Milwaukee	1B	G. Brock	373	.265	12	52	850	58	5	86	9.1	.995	C. Bosio	33	235	15	10	0	2.95
	2B	J. Gantner	409	.274	0	34	241	362	8	88	5.4	.987	D. August	31	142	12	12	0	5.31
W-81 L-81	SS	B. Spiers	345	.255	4	33	138	264	16	57	4.7	.962	T. Higuera	22	135	9	6	0	3.46
	3B	P. Molitor	615	.315	11	56	78	243	17	18	3.0	.950	M. Knudson	40	124	8	5	0	3.35
Tom Trebelhorn	RF	R. Deer	466	.210	26	65	267	10	8	1	2.3	.972	C. Crim	**76**	118	9	7	7	2.83
	CF	R. Yount	614	.318	21	103	361	8	7	2	2.6	.981	J. Navarro	19	110	7	8	0	3.12
	LF	G. Braggs	514	.247	15	66	267	6	8	1	2.1	.972	T. Filer	13	72	7	3	0	3.61
	C	B. Surhoff	436	.248	5	55	526	51	9	6	5.5	.985	D. Plesac	52	61	3	4	33	2.35
	SS	G. Sheffield	368	.247	5	32	85	194	12	40	4.2	.959							
	OF	M. Felder	315	.241	3	23	191	8	3	3	2.2	.985							
	UT	T. Francona	233	.232	3	23	339	26	4	32		.985							
	C	C. O'Brien	188	.234	6	35	314	36	5	5	5.7	.986							
	UT	G. Polidor	175	.194	0	14	78	123	12	20		.944							
	D1	J. Meyer	147	.224	7	29	100	7	2	14	6.1	.982							
	OD	G. Vaughn	113	.265	5	23	32	1	2	0	1.5	.943							
New York	1B	D. Mattingly	631	.303	23	113	1274	87	7	143	9.4	.995	A. Hawkins	34	208	15	15	0	4.80
	2B	S. Sax	**651**	.315	5	63	312	460	10	117	4.9	**.987**	C. Parker	22	120	4	5	0	3.68
W-74 L-87	SS	A. Espinoza	503	.282	0	41	237	471	22	114	5.0	.970	D. LaPoint	20	114	6	9	0	5.62
	3B	Pagliarulo	223	.197	4	16	25	122	10	6	2.3	.936	Guetterman	70	103	5	5	13	2.45
Dallas Green	RF	J. Barfield	441	.240	18	56	297	16*	9*	3	2.5	.972	G. Cadaret	20	92	5	5	0	4.58
W-56 L-65	CF	R. Kelly	441	.302	9	48	353	9	6	2	2.7	.984	McCullers	52	85	4	3	4	4.57
	LF	L. Polonia	227	.313	2	29	105	6	2	1	2.1	.982	W. Terrell	13	83	6	5	0	5.20
Bucky Dent	C	D. Slaught	350	.251	5	38	493	44	5	8	5.2	.991	E. Plunk	27	76	7	5	0	3.69
W-18 L-22	DH	S. Balboni	300	.237	17	59							D. Righetti	55	69	2	6	25	3.00
	OD	M. Hall	361	.260	17	58	141	3	1	2	1.9	.993							
	OF	R. Henderson	235	.247	3	22	144	3	1	0	2.3	.993							
	C	B. Geren	205	.288	9	27	308	24	3	4	5.6	.991							
	DH	K. Phelps	185	.249	7	29													
	3B	T. Brookens	168	.226	4	14	17	70	7	4	1.8	.926							
Cleveland	1B	P. O'Brien	554	.260	12	55	1359	114	9	111	9.6	.994	B. Black	33	222	12	11	0	3.36
	2B	J. Browne	598	.299	5	45	305	380	15	67	4.6	.979	J. Farrell	31	208	9	14	0	3.63
W-73 L-89	SS	F. Fermin	484	.238	0	21	247	512	**26**	84	5.1	.967	T. Candiotti	31	206	13	10	0	3.10
	3B	B. Jacoby	519	.272	13	64	92	268	17	15	2.6	.955	G. Swindell	28	184	13	6	0	3.37
Doc Edwards	RF	C. Snyder	489	.215	18	59	291	18	1	5	2.5	**.997**	S. Bailes	34	114	5	9	0	4.28
W-65 L-78	CF	J. Carter	651	.243	35	105	350	6	8	3	2.5	.978	R. Yett	32	99	5	6	0	5.00
	LF	O. McDowell	239	.222	3	22	124	5	1	1	2.0	.992	D. Jones	59	81	7	10	32	2.34
John Hart	C	A. Allanson	323	.232	3	17	570	53	9	4	5.7	.986	J. Orosco	69	78	3	4	2	2.08
W-8 L-11	DH	D. Clark	253	.237	8	29							R. Nichols	15	72	4	6	0	4.40
	OD	D. James	245	.306	4	29	82	1	2	0	2.3	.976							
	OF	J. Belle	218	.225	7	37	92	3	2	1	2.2	.979							
	OF	B. Komminsk	198	.237	8	33	181	3	1	1	2.7	.995							
	C	J. Skinner	178	.230	1	13	280	22	3	1	3.9	.990							
Detroit	1B	D. Bergman	385	.268	7	37	912	85	7	88	8.2	.993	F. Tanana	33	224	10	14	0	3.58
	2B	L. Whitaker	509	.251	28	85	**327**	393	11	99	5.0	.985	D. Alexander	33	223	6	**18**	0	4.44
W-59 L-103	SS	A. Trammell	449	.243	5	43	188	396	9	71	5.1	.985	J. Morris	24	170	6	14	0	4.86
	3B	R. Schu	266	.214	7	21	52	119	12	11	2.2	.934	P. Gibson	45	132	4	8	0	4.64
Sparky Anderson	RF	C. Lemon	414	.237	7	47	189	6	3	0	1.8	.985	M. Henneman	60	90	11	4	8	3.70
	CF	G. Pettis	444	.257	1	18	325	1	4	0	2.8	.988	K. Ritz	12	74	4	6	0	4.38
	LF	F. Lynn	353	.241	11	46	119	5	1	0	1.8	.992	G. Hernandez	32	31	2	2	15	5.74
	C	M. Heath	396	.263	10	43	582	**66**	9	**10**	5.6	.986							
	UT	K. Moreland	318	.299	5	35	243	32	4	23		.986							
	UT	G. Ward	275	.251	9	29	227	16	3	15		.988							
	CD	M. Nokes	268	.250	9	39	235	26	6	3	5.2	.978							
	OF	K. Williams	258	.205	6	23	180	11	4	3	2.2	.979							
	UT	M. Brumley	212	.198	1	11	80	160	12	24		.952							
	3B	D. Strange	196	.214	1	14	33	96	18	11	2.7	.878							
	OF	T. Jones	158	.259	3	26	72	0	1	0	2.0	.986							

AMERICAN LEAGUE 1989, cont.

West — Oakland — W-99 L-63 — Tony LaRussa

POS	Player	AB	BA	HR	RBI	PO	A	E	DP	TC/G	FA	Pitcher	G	IP	W	L	SV	ERA
1B	M. McGwire	490	.231	33	95	1170	114	6	122	9.1	.995	D. Stewart	36	258	21	9	0	3.32
2B	T. Phillips	451	.262	4	47	140	252	6	46	4.7	.985	M. Moore	35	242	19	11	0	2.61
SS	M. Gallego	357	.252	3	30	152	255	14	68	4.5	.967	B. Welch	33	210	17	8	0	3.00
3B	C. Lansford	551	.336	2	52	104	183	13	11	2.2	.957	S. Davis	31	169	19	7	0	4.36
RF	S. Javier	310	.248	1	28	219	4	2	0	2.1	.991	C. Young	25	111	5	9	0	3.73
CF	D. Henderson	579	.250	15	80	385	5	9	1	2.7	.977	T. Burns	50	96	6	5	8	2.24
LF	R. Henderson	306	.294	9	35	191	3	3	1	2.4	.985	G. Nelson	50	80	3	5	3	3.26
C	T. Steinbach	454	.273	7	42	529	43	9	6	5.6	.985	R. Honeycutt	64	77	2	2	12	2.35
DH	D. Parker	553	.264	22	97							D. Eckersley	51	58	4	0	33	1.56
C	R. Hassey	268	.228	5	23	421	25	4	4	5.8	.991							
SS	W. Weiss	236	.233	3	21	106	195	15	44	3.8	.953							
OF	J. Canseco	227	.269	17	57	119	5	3	2	2.3	.976							
OF	L. Polonia	206	.286	1	17	126	3	2	1	2.4	.985							

Kansas City — W-92 L-70 — John Wathan

POS	Player	AB	BA	HR	RBI	PO	A	E	DP	TC/G	FA	Pitcher	G	IP	W	L	SV	ERA
1B	G. Brett	457	.282	12	80	896	80	2	71	9.4	.998	Saberhagen	36	262	23	6	0	2.16
2B	F. White	418	.256	2	36	238	407	10	64	5.0	.985	M. Gubicza	36	255	15	11	0	3.04
SS	K. Stillwell	463	.261	7	54	179	334	16	65	4.1	.970	T. Gordon	49	163	17	9	1	3.64
3B	K. Seitzer	597	.281	4	48	112	272	20	28	2.5	.950	C. Leibrandt	33	161	5	11	0	5.14
RF	D. Tartabull	441	.268	18	62	108	3	2	0	1.6	.982	L. Aquino	34	141	6	8	0	3.50
CF	W. Wilson	383	.253	3	43	252	2	6	0	2.4	.977	Montgomery	63	92	7	3	18	1.37
LF	B. Jackson	515	.256	32	105	224	11	8	2	2.2	.967	T. Leach	30	74	5	6	0	4.15
C	B. Boone	405	.274	1	43	752	64	7	6	6.4	.991	S. Farr	51	63	2	5	18	4.12
OF	Eisenreich	475	.293	9	59	273	4	3	0	2.3	.989							
UT	P. Tabler	390	.259	2	42	217	25	4	11		.984							
2S	B. Wellman	178	.230	2	12	104	184	2	42		.993							
1D	B. Buckner	176	.216	1	16	181	13	3	19	8.2	.985							

California — W-91 L-71 — Doug Rader

POS	Player	AB	BA	HR	RBI	PO	A	E	DP	TC/G	FA	Pitcher	G	IP	W	L	SV	ERA
1B	W. Joyner	593	.282	16	79	1487	99	4	146	10.0	.997	B. Blyleven	33	241	17	5	0	2.73
2B	J. Ray	530	.289	5	62	279	403	11	98	5.3	.984	M. Witt	33	220	9	15	0	4.54
SS	D. Schofield	302	.228	4	26	118	276	7	56	4.5	.983	McCaskill	32	212	15	10	0	2.93
3B	J. Howell	474	.228	20	52	95	322	11	27	3.0	.974	C. Finley	29	200	16	9	0	2.57
RF	Washington	418	.273	13	42	187	6	5	2	2.0	.975	J. Abbott	29	181	12	12	0	3.92
CF	D. White	636	.245	12	56	430	10	5	3	2.9	.989	W. Fraser	44	92	4	7	3	3.24
LF	C. Davis	560	.271	22	90	270	5	6	0	1.9	.979	G. Minton	62	90	4	3	8	2.20
C	L. Parrish	433	.238	17	50	638	63	5	7	5.8	.993	B. Harvey	51	55	3	3	25	3.44
DH	B. Downing	544	.283	14	59							B. McClure	48	52	6	1	3	1.55
SS	K. Anderson	223	.229	0	17	96	215	9	52	4.6	.972							
OF	T. Armas	202	.257	11	30	97	4	1	1	2.2	.990							

Texas — W-83 L-79 — Bobby Valentine

POS	Player	AB	BA	HR	RBI	PO	A	E	DP	TC/G	FA	Pitcher	G	IP	W	L	SV	ERA
1B	R. Palmeiro	559	.275	8	64	1167	119	12	106	8.8	.991	N. Ryan	32	239	16	10	0	3.20
2B	J. Franco	548	.316	13	92	256	386	13	70	4.7	.980	B. Witt	31	194	12	13	0	5.14
SS	S. Fletcher	314	.239	0	22	124	190	13	45	4.0	.960	K. Brown	28	191	12	9	0	3.35
3B	S. Buechele	486	.235	16	59	106	264	12	22	2.6	.969	C. Hough	30	182	10	13	0	4.35
RF	R. Sierra	634	.306	29	119	313	13	9	2	2.1	.973	M. Jeffcoat	22	131	9	6	0	3.58
CF	C. Espy	475	.257	3	31	281	5	3	2	2.2	.990	J. Moyer	15	76	4	9	0	4.86
LF	Incaviglia	453	.236	21	81	213	7	6	2	1.8	.973	J. Russell	71	73	6	4	38	1.98
C	C. Kreuter	158	.152	5	9	453	26	4	4	5.7	.992	C. Guante	50	69	6	6	2	3.91
DH	H. Baines	172	.285	3	16													
UT	J. Kunkel	293	.270	8	29	143	168	22	27		.934							
DO	R. Leach	239	.272	1	23	57	1	3	0	1.5	.951							
S2	F. Manrique	191	.288	2	22	76	112	10	28		.949							
C	G. Petralli	184	.304	4	23	258	15	3	3	5.6	.989							

Minnesota — W-80 L-82 — Tom Kelly

POS	Player	AB	BA	HR	RBI	PO	A	E	DP	TC/G	FA	Pitcher	G	IP	W	L	SV	ERA
1B	K. Hrbek	375	.272	25	84	723	60	4	66	8.8	.995	A. Anderson	33	197	17	10	0	3.80
2B	A. Newman	446	.253	0	38	116	171	6	37	3.5	.980	F. Viola	24	176	8	12	0	3.79
SS	G. Gagne	460	.272	9	48	218	389	18	66	4.3	.971	R. Smith	32	172	10	6	1	3.92
3B	G. Gaetti	498	.251	19	75	104	251	10	23	2.9	.973	S. Rawley	27	145	5	12	0	5.21
RF	R. Bush	391	.263	14	54	200	7	3	1	1.9	.986	S. Rawley	27	145	5	12	0	5.21
CF	K. Puckett	635	.339	9	85	438	13	4	3	2.9	.991	J. Berenguer	56	106	9	3	3	3.48
LF	D. Gladden	461	.295	8	46	245	8	9	3	2.2	.966	J. Reardon	65	73	5	4	31	4.07
C	B. Harper	385	.325	8	57	456	35	11	7	5.0	.978	M. Dyer	16	71	4	7	0	4.82
DH	J. Dwyer	225	.316	3	23													
UT	G. Larkin	446	.267	6	46	524	28	4	45		.993							
2B	W. Backman	299	.231	1	26	146	187	6	37	4.0	.982							
OF	J. Moses	242	.281	1	31	156	3	2	0	1.5	.988							
UT	T. Laudner	239	.222	6	27	347	16	3	5		.992							
OF	C. Castillo	218	.257	3	33	119	3	1	1	1.9	.976							

Seattle — W-73 L-89 — Jim Lefebvre

POS	Player	AB	BA	HR	RBI	PO	A	E	DP	TC/G	FA	Pitcher	G	IP	W	L	SV	ERA
1B	A. Davis	498	.305	21	95	1106	81	10	119	9.6	.992	S. Bankhead	33	210	14	6	0	3.34
2B	H. Reynolds	613	.300	0	43	311	506	17	109	5.5	.980	B. Holman	23	160	8	10	0	3.44
SS	O. Vizquel	387	.220	1	20	208	388	18	102	4.3	.971	R. Johnson	22	131	7	9	0	4.40
3B	J. Presley	390	.236	12	41	54	154	17	13	2.5	.924	B. Swift	37	130	7	3	1	4.43
RF	D. Coles	535	.252	10	59	184	9	5	3	2.2	.975	E. Hanson	17	113	9	5	0	3.18
CF	K. Griffey	455	.264	16	61	302	12	10	6	2.6	.969	J. Reed	52	102	7	7	0	3.19
LF	G. Briley	394	.266	13	52	179	5	8	1	1.8	.958	M. Jackson	65	99	4	6	7	3.17
C	D. Valle	316	.237	7	34	496	52	4	3	5.9	.993	M. Dunne	15	85	2	9	0	5.27
DH	J. Leonard	566	.254	24	93							M. Schooler	67	77	1	7	33	2.81
OF	H. Cotto	295	.264	9	33	153	9	2	3	1.8	.988							
C	S. Bradley	270	.274	3	37	388	25	3	4	5.9	.993							
OF	J. Buhner	204	.275	9	33	106	6	4	3	2.0	.966							
3B	E. Martinez	171	.240	2	20	40	72	6	9	1.9	.949							

AMERICAN LEAGUE 1989, *cont.*

Chicago
W-69 L-92

Jeff Torborg

POS	Player	AB	BA	HR	RBI	PO	A	E	DP	TC/G	FA	Pitcher	G	IP	W	L	SV	ERA
1B	G. Walker	233	.210	5	26	373	17	5	38	8.2	.987	M. Perez	31	183	11	14	0	5.01
2B	S. Lyons	443	.264	2	50	142	185	6	46	4.8	.982	E. King	25	159	9	10	0	3.39
SS	O. Guillen	597	.253	1	54	272	512	22	106	5.2	.973	S. Rosenberg	38	142	4	13	0	4.94
3B	C. Martinez	350	.300	5	32	45	121	16	12	2.7	.912	G. Hibbard	23	137	6	7	0	3.21
RF	I. Calderon	622	.286	14	87	217	8	5	3	2.2	.978	S. Hillegas	50	120	7	11	3	4.74
CF	D. Gallagher	601	.266	1	46	390	8	3	4	2.5	.993	J. Reuss	23	107	8	5	0	5.06
LF	D. Boston	218	.252	5	23	134	2	4	0	1.9	.971	R. Dotson	17	100	3	7	0	3.88
C	C. Fisk	375	.293	13	68	419	37	3	1	5.1	.993	B. Long	30	99	5	5	1	3.92
DH	H. Baines	333	.321	13	56							D. Pall	53	87	4	5	6	3.31
OF	D. Pasqua	246	.248	11	47	149	3	1	2	2.3	.993	B. Thigpen	61	79	2	6	34	3.76
2B	S. Fletcher	232	.272	1	21	108	161	0	38	5.1	1.000							
3B	E. Williams	201	.274	3	10	37	123	16	21	2.7	.909							
2B	F. Manrique	187	.299	2	30	94	127	9	30	4.0	.961							
C	R. Karkovice	182	.264	3	24	299	47	5	6	5.2	.986							
OF	L. Johnson	180	.300	0	16	113	0	2	0	2.6	.983							
UT	R. Kittle	169	.302	11	37	216	12	4	28		.983							

BATTING AND BASE RUNNING LEADERS

Batting Average
K. Puckett, MIN — .339
C. Lansford, OAK — .336
W. Boggs, BOS — .330
R. Yount, MIL — .318
J. Franco, TEX — .316

Slugging Average
R. Sierra, TEX — .543
F. McGriff, TOR — .525
R. Yount, MIL — .511
N. Esasky, BOS — .500
A. Davis, SEA — .496

Home Runs
F. McGriff, TOR — 36
J. Carter, CLE — 35
M. McGwire, OAK — 33
B. Jackson, KC — 32
N. Esasky, BOS — 30

Winning Percentage
Saberhagen, KC — .793
B. Blyleven, CAL — .773
S. Davis, OAK — .731
D. Stewart, OAK — .700
S. Bankhead, SEA — .700

PITCHING LEADERS

Earned Run Average
Saberhagen, KC — 2.16
C. Finley, CAL — 2.57
M. Moore, OAK — 2.61
B. Blyleven, CAL — 2.73
McCaskill, CAL — 2.93

Wins
Saberhagen, KC — 23
D. Stewart, OAK — 21
S. Davis, OAK — 19
M. Moore, OAK — 19
J. Ballard, BAL — 18

Total Bases
R. Sierra, TEX — 344
R. Yount, MIL — 314
J. Carter, CLE — 303
D. Mattingly, NY — 301
K. Puckett, MIN — 295

Runs Batted In
R. Sierra, TEX — 119
D. Mattingly, NY — 113
N. Esasky, BOS — 108
B. Jackson, KC — 105
J. Carter, CLE — 105

Stolen Bases
R. Henderson, NY, OAK — 77
C. Espy, TEX — 45
D. White, CAL — 44
G. Pettis, DET — 43
S. Sax, NY — 43

Saves
J. Russell, TEX — 38
B. Thigpen, CHI — 34
D. Eckersley, OAK — 33
D. Plesac, MIL — 33
M. Schooler, SEA — 33

Strikeouts
N. Ryan, TEX — 301
R. Clemens, BOS — 230
Saberhagen, KC — 193
C. Bosio, MIL — 173
M. Gubicza, KC — 173

Complete Games
Saberhagen, KC — 12
J. Morris, DET — 10
C. Finley, CAL — 9

Hits
K. Puckett, MIN — 215
W. Boggs, BOS — 205
S. Sax, NY — 205
R. Yount, MIL — 195

Base on Balls
R. Henderson, NY, OAK — 126
F. McGriff, TOR — 119
W. Boggs, BOS — 107
K. Seitzer, KC — 102

Home Run Percentage
M. McGwire, OAK — 6.7
F. McGriff, TOR — 6.5
B. Jackson, KC — 6.2
R. Deer, MIL — 5.6

Fewest Hits/9 Innings
N. Ryan, TEX — 6.09
T. Gordon, KC — 6.74
D. Stieb, TOR — 7.14
Saberhagen, KC — 7.17

Shutouts
B. Blyleven, CAL — 5
McCaskill, CAL — 4
Saberhagen, KC — 4
B. Black, CLE — 3

Fewest Walks/9 Innings
J. Key, TOR — 1.13
Saberhagen, KC — 1.48
B. Blyleven, CAL — 1.64
C. Bosio, MIL — 1.84

Runs Scored
R. Henderson, NY, OAK — 113
W. Boggs, BOS — 113
R. Yount, MIL — 101
R. Sierra, TEX — 101

Doubles
W. Boggs, BOS — 51
K. Puckett, MIN — 45
J. Reed, BOS — 42
G. Bell, TOR — 41

Triples
R. Sierra, TEX — 14
D. White, CAL — 13
P. Bradley, BAL — 10

Most Strikeouts/9 Inn.
N. Ryan, TEX — 11.32
T. Gordon, KC — 8.45
R. Clemens, BOS — 8.17
B. Witt, TEX — 7.69

Innings
Saberhagen, KC — 262
D. Stewart, OAK — 258
M. Gubicza, KC — 255
R. Clemens, BOS — 253

Games Pitched
C. Crim, MIL — 76
R. Murphy, BOS — 74
K. Rogers, TEX — 73
J. Russell, TEX — 71

		W	L	PCT	GB	R	OR	2B	3B	HR	BA	SA	SB	E	DP	FA	CG	BB	SO	ShO	SV	ERA
								Batting						**Fielding**			**Pitching**					
East	Toronto	89	73	.549		731	651	265	40	142	.260	.398	144	127	164	.980	12	478	849	5	38	3.58
	Baltimore	87	75	.537	2	708	686	238	33	129	.252	.379	118	**87**	163	**.986**	16	486	676	3	44	4.00
	Boston	83	79	.512	6	**774**	735	**326**	30	108	**.277**	**.403**	56	127	162	.980	14	548	1054	6	42	4.01
	Milwaukee	81	81	.500	8	707	679	235	32	126	.259	.382	**165**	155	164	.975	16	457	812	4	45	3.80
	New York	74	87	.460	14.5	698	792	229	23	130	.269	.391	137	122	**183**	.980	15	521	787	4	44	4.50
	Cleveland	73	89	.451	16	604	654	221	26	127	.245	.365	74	118	126	.981	23	**452**	844	7	38	3.65
	Detroit	59	103	.364	30	617	816	198	24	116	.242	.351	103	130	153	.979	24	652	831	3	26	4.53
West	Oakland	99	63	.611		712	**576**	220	25	127	.261	.381	157	129	159	.979	17	510	930	3	**57**	3.09
	Kansas City	92	70	.568	7	690	635	227	41	101	.261	.373	154	114	139	.982	27	455	978	9	38	3.55
	California	91	71	.562	8	669	578	208	37	**145**	.256	.386	89	96	173	.985	**32**	465	897	**12**	38	3.28
	Texas	83	79	.512	16	695	714	260	**46**	122	.263	.394	101	136	137	.978	26	654	**1112**	6	44	3.91
	Minnesota	80	82	.494	19	740	738	278	35	117	.276	.402	111	107	141	.982	19	500	851	5	38	4.28
	Seattle	73	89	.451	26	694	728	237	29	134	.257	.384	81	143	168	.977	15	560	897	5	44	4.00
	Chicago	69	92	.429	29.5	693	750	262	36	94	.271	.383	97	151	176	.975	9	539	778	2	46	4.23
						9732	9732	3404	457	1718	.261	.384	1587	1742	2208	.980	265	7277	12296	71	582	3.88

PART FIVE

Home/Road Performance

Year-by-Year Breakdowns of Team Performance
At Home and on the Road for Wins and Losses,
Runs Scored and Allowed, and Home Runs
Hit and Allowed

Seasonal Winning and Losing Streaks

Days in First Place

Date of Clinching Title

Home/Road Performance

The Home/Road Performance section is a chronological listing of team performance at home and on the road for every team since 1900. Categories listed for each team are wins and losses at home and on the road; runs scored and allowed at home and on the road; and home runs hit and allowed at home and on the road.

In the twenty-one years since the publication of the first edition of *The Baseball Encyclopedia,* a wide range of new methods of analyzing player performance have emerged. Perhaps the most significant of these are the methods examining players in light of the characteristics of the parks in which they play the majority of their games. Baseball fans have known for years that some ball parks are good hitters' parks or good pitchers' parks. Few could have known, until recent research, just how large an effect the park can have on performance. In 1978, to take one example, the Atlanta Braves scored 364 runs in 81 games at home and 236 runs in 81 games on the road: a 54.2% increase in runs scored in their home games. That same year, the Houston Astros allowed 254 runs in 81 games at home, and 380 runs in 81 games on the road: a 33.1% difference. In evaluating the statistics for players on these two teams, it is important to note the advantages given to a hitter in Atlanta and the disadvantages faced by one in Houston.

Historical research has indicated that a normal home-field advantage will be 5% for both hitters and pitchers; in a theoretically neutral home park with no unusual configuration or visibility problems, a team should score 5% more runs in home games and allow 5% fewer. The task facing each team seeking to construct a team for its particular park is to improve on these theoretical advantages, or to ensure that its club is better able to take advantage of its park's oddities. In examining the statistics that follow, then, it is important to note those parks which have distinct pro-hitter or pro-pitcher tendencies, like Wrigley Field, Fenway Park, Yankee Stadium, or the Houston Astrodome, but also to note those teams which adapt particularly well to their parks, as reflected in a substantial increase in runs and decrease in runs allowed at home.

Finally, a new feature in this edition lists the number of days a particular team spent in first place in each season, plus each team's longest winning streak and losing streak. These new additions should add a greater appreciation of each club's performance throughout the course of the year.

We are indebted to Bob Tiemann for supplying us with this material.

| | Team | Home Games | | | Road Games | | | HR | Home Games OHR | R | OR | HR | Road Games OHR | R | OR | DIF | LDF | WS | LS |
		W	L	PCT	W	L	PCT												
1968 National League (4/10 - 9/28)	St. Louis	47	34	.580	50	31	.617	31	35	267	218	42	47	316	254	160	9/15	9	5
	San Francisco	42	39	.519	46	35	.568	60	32	299	242	48	54	300	287	11	5/31	5	3
	Chicago	47	34	.580	37	44	.457	83	83	363	332	47	55	249	279	0	—	6	7
	Cincinnati	40	41	.494	43	38	.531	55	66	377	400	51	48	313	273	1	4/10	7	7
	Atlanta	41	40	.506	40	41	.494	42	43	241	241	38	44	273	308	1	6/1	6	5
	Pittsburgh	40	41	.494	40	41	.494	33	30	289	268	47	43	294	264	0	—	9	10
	Los Angeles	41	40	.506	35	46	.432	25	24	212	215	42	41	258	294	0	—	7	8
	Philadelphia	38	43	.469	38	43	.469	52	46	274	297	48	45	269	318	1	4/10	7	9
	New York	32	49	.395	41	40	.506	49	50	224	270	32	37	249	229	0	—	4	6
	Houston	42	39	.519	30	51	.370	22	30	279	269	44	38	231	319	9	4/18	4	6

Team Information Explanation

The abbreviations for the teams appear as listed below:

ATL	Atlanta	CAL	California
BAL	Baltimore	CHI	Chicago
BOS	Boston	CIN	Cincinnati
BKN	Brooklyn	CLE	Cleveland
BUF	Buffalo	DET	Detroit

HOU	Houston	NY	New York
IND	Indianapolis	OAK	Oakland
KC	Kansas City	PHI	Philadelphia
LA	Los Angeles	PIT	Pittsburgh
MIL	Milwaukee	SD	San Diego
MIN	Minnesota	SEA	Seattle
MON	Montreal	SF	San Francisco
NWK	Newark	STL	St. Louis

TEX   Texas   WAS   Washington
TOR   Toronto

Within each league (or division) teams are listed in their order of standings for the year. For further details on a club's performance in that season, see The Teams and Their Players.

Column Headings Information

W   Wins
L   Losses
PCT   Winning Percentage
HR   Home Runs
OHR   Opposition Home Runs
R   Runs Scored
OR   Opposition Runs Scored
WS   Winning Streak
LS   Losing Streak
DIF   Days in First Place
LDF   Last Day in First Place

League Leaders. For each year, the leaders in a league are indicated, as in The Teams and Their Players, by listing that statistic in boldfaced type. Leaders are listed in the following categories:

Home Games:

Highest Winning
   Percentage
Most Home Runs
Fewest Home Runs
Most Opposition Home
   Runs

Fewest Opposition Home
   Runs
Most Runs
Fewest Runs
Most Opposition Runs
Fewest Opposition Runs

Road Games:
Highest Winning
   Percentage
Most Home Runs
Fewest Opposition Home
   Runs
Most Runs

Seasonal Leaders:
Longest Winning Streak
Longest Losing Streak
Most Days in First Place

Fewest Opposition Runs
Highest Run Factor
Highest Opposition Run
   Factor

Days in First Place. The DIF listing gives the number of days each club was in first place (either tied or alone) during the regular season, counting the standings at the end of each day's league play from Opening Day through the pennant winner's final game.

Last Date in First. The LDF listing indicates the latest date each club was in first place (either alone or tied). For the league or division champion, however, the date given in bold-face is the date the pennant was mathematically clinched. For the 1981 split season, the clinching date for the champion of each half is given.

Winning and Losing Streaks. WS and LS give the longest winning and losing streaks for each club during each season. Tie games and postponements are not counted, and suspended games are considered to be won or lost on the date the final lead change took place.

For years since 1968, the leading DIF figure and the pennant clinching date are highlighted for each division, while only the longest winning and losing streaks for the league as a whole are highlighted.

	Team	Home Games			Road Games			Home Games				Road Games				DIF	LDF	WS	LS
		W	L	PCT	W	L	PCT	HR	OHR	R	OR	HR	OHR	R	OR				
1900 National League (4/19 - 10/14)	Brooklyn	43	26	.623	39	28	**.582**	15	15	452	394	10	**15**	364	328	117	10/6	9	5
	Pittsburgh	42	28	.600	37	32	.536	14	7	359	315	12	17	374	**297**			8	7
	Philadelphia	45	23	**.662**	30	40	.429	13	7	434	353	15	22	376	438	61	6/20	6	6
	Boston	42	29	.592	24	43	.358	40	43	507	420	8	16	271	319			8	8
	Chicago	45	30	.600	20	45	.308	12	5	337	329	21	16	298	422	2	4/20	9	6
	St. Louis	40	31	.563	25	44	.362	23	13	382	316	13	19	361	431	4	4/29	5	8
	Cincinnati	27	34	.443	35	43	.449	12	9	**255**	309	18	19	**447**	436	2	4/28	5	7
	New York	38	31	.551	22	47	.319	13	8	393	375	10	18	320	448			4	12
1901 National League (4/18 - 10/6)	Pittsburgh	45	24	.652	45	25	**.643**	15	8	372	255	13	**12**	**404**	279	127	9/27	10	4
	Philadelphia	46	23	**.667**	37	34	.521	11	**6**	349	**247**	13	13	319	296			10	3
	Brooklyn	43	25	.632	36	32	.529	13	6	400	303	**19**	12	344	297	7	5/3	9	5
	St. Louis	40	31	.563	36	33	.522	21	19	392	338	18	19	400	351	2	4/30	6	6
	Boston	41	29	.586	28	40	.412	18	17	297	298	10	**12**	234	**258**	5	4/26	8	5
	Chicago	30	39	.435	23	47	.329	**7**	10	293	357	11	17	285	342	1	4/19	5	8
	New York	30	38	.441	22	47	.319	8	11	**255**	350	11	13	289	405	23	6/14	7	8
	Cincinnati	27	43	.386	25	44	.362	**23**	**33**	279	409	15	18	282	409	22	5/22	4	10
1901 American League (4/24 - 9/28)	Chicago	49	21	.700	34	32	**.515**	14	11	441	285	17	16	378	346	122	**9/23**	10	5
	Boston	49	20	.710	30	37	.448	**20**	16	383	**252**	16	16	376	356	14	7/17	9	5
	Detroit	42	27	.609	32	34	.485	15	10	438	369	14	12	303	325	26	5/22	7	6
	Philadelphia	42	24	.636	32	38	.457	15	9	410	352	**20**	11	**395**	409			9	10
	Baltimore	40	25	.615	28	40	.412	11	11	430	367	13	9	330	383	3	4/28	11	6
	Washington	31	35	.470	30	38	.441	17	**36**	333	375	17	15	345	392	6	5/1	6	8
	Cleveland	29	39	.426	26	43	.377	0	13	**317**	399	12	9	346	428			6	11
	Milwaukee	32	37	.464	16	52	.235	15	14	342	373	11	19	299	455			5	8
1902 National League (4/17 - 10/6)	Pittsburgh	56	15	**.789**	47	21	**.691**	9	**2**	410	207	10	**2**	365	233	170	**9/3**	10	2
	Brooklyn	45	23	.662	30	40	.429	8	**2**	277	210	**11**	8	287	309	2	4/18	8	7
	Boston	42	27	.609	31	37	.456	**13**	11	283	230	1	4	289	286			9	6
	Cincinnati	35	35	.500	35	35	.500	11	8	353	305	7	8	280	261			6	5
	Chicago	31	38	.449	37	31	.544	1	3	228	249	5	7	302	252	6	4/26	6	8
	St. Louis	28	38	.424	28	40	.412	3	7	262	336	7	9	255	359			6	8
	Philadelphia	29	39	.426	27	42	.391	1	6	264	**351**	4	6	220	298			6	7
	New York	24	44	.353	24	44	.353	7	7	**214**	297	1	9	187	293	1	4/17	7	13
1902 American League (4/19 - 9/29)	Philadelphia	56	17	**.767**	27	36	.429	19	12	**477**	330	**19**	21	298	**306**	62	**9/24**	10	4
	St. Louis	49	21	.700	29	37	.439	16	14	350	289	13	22	269	318	11	8/14	9	6
	Boston	43	27	.614	34	33	**.507**	24	15	348	284	18	12	316	316	4	4/22	8	6
	Chicago	48	19	.716	26	41	.388	**5**	**2**	371	**238**	9	28	304	364	77	8/12	8	6
	Cleveland	40	25	.615	29	42	.408	15	7	357	257	18	19	**329**	410			7	5
	Washington	40	28	.588	21	47	.309	**35**	**38**	407	341	12	18	300	449	4	4/27	5	6
	Detroit	35	33	.515	17	50	.254	13	8	**312**	286	9	12	254	371	18	5/25	5	11
	Baltimore	32	31	.508	18	57	.240	17	18	391	**369**	16	12	324	479			4	11
1903 National League (4/16 - 9/27)	Pittsburgh	46	24	**.657**	45	25	**.643**	17	5	393	327	**17**	**3**	**400**	286	112	**9/18**	15	4
	New York	41	27	.603	43	28	.606	9	10	368	296	11	10	361	271	42	6/18	8	5
	Chicago	45	28	.616	37	28	.569	2	7	345	285	7	6	350	314	11	6/5	8	4
	Cincinnati	41	35	.539	33	30	.524	12	7	440	389	16	8	325	**267**			8	6
	Brooklyn	40	33	.548	30	33	.476	8	9	359	361	7	9	308	321	1	4/17	6	4
	Boston	31	35	.470	27	45	.375	11	19	283	314	14	11	295	385	1	4/17	4	7
	Philadelphia	25	33	.431	24	53	.312	9	6	250	298	3	15	367	440			5	10
	St. Louis	22	45	.328	21	49	.300	7	13	**248**	393	1	13	257	402	1	4/16	4	11
1903 American League (4/20 - 9/29)	Boston	49	20	**.710**	42	27	**.609**	**35**	12	395	266	13	11	**313**	238	118	**9/16**	11	3
	Philadelphia	44	21	.677	31	39	.443	16	8	323	238	15	12	274	281	10	6/22	6	5
	Cleveland	49	25	.662	28	38	.424	11	5	364	256	**20**	11	275	323			8	4
	New York	41	26	.612	31	36	.463	10	6	301	269	8	13	278	304			6	6
	Detroit	37	28	.569	28	43	.394	**5**	7	279	222	7	12	288	317	13	5/24	4	6
	St. Louis	38	32	.543	27	42	.391	7	15	**250**	228	5	10	250	297			8	11
	Chicago	41	28	.594	19	49	.279	5	**2**	284	244	9	21	232	369	32	5/31	7	6
	Washington	29	40	.420	14	54	.206	15	**24**	275	349	2	14	162	342	1	4/22	4	9
1904 National League (4/14 - 10/9)	New York	56	26	**.683**	50	21	**.704**	23	30	397	258	8	6	**347**	218	168	**9/22**	18	6
	Chicago	49	27	.645	44	33	.571	6	10	303	**240**	16	6	296	277	9	6/5	8	6
	Cincinnati	49	27	.645	39	38	.506	12	7	**409**	295	9	7	286	252	8	5/26	8	4
	Pittsburgh	48	30	.615	39	36	.520	5	**2**	338	286	10	11	337	306	1	4/15	8	7
	St. Louis	39	36	.520	36	43	.456	14	15	298	280	10	8	304	315			8	7
	Brooklyn	31	44	.413	25	53	.321	3	11	**234**	287	12	16	263	327			5	8
	Boston	34	45	.430	21	53	.284	13	10	269	**363**	11	14	222	386			7	8
	Philadelphia	28	43	.394	24	57	.296	7	7	269	348	**16**	15	302	436	1	4/14	5	12

	Team	Home Games			Road Games			Home Games				Road Games				DIF	LDF	WS	LS
		W	L	PCT	W	L	PCT	HR	OHR	R	OR	HR	OHR	R	OR				
1904 American League (4/14 - 10/10)	Boston	49	30	.620	46	29	**.613**	18	18	325	240	8	13	283	**226**	132	10/10	8	6
	New York	46	29	.613	46	30	.605	**22**	**25**	321	288	5	**4**	277	238	39	10/7	6	4
	Chicago	50	27	**.649**	39	38	.506	0	**2**	297	**226**	**14**	11	303	256	7	8/21	7	5
	Cleveland	44	31	.587	42	34	.553	14	2	**329**	242	13	8	**318**	240	2	4/15	9	7
	Philadelphia	47	31	.603	34	39	.466	19	8	308	235	12	5	249	268	5	4/18	8	5
	St. Louis	32	43	.427	33	44	.429	2	14	231	288	8	11	250	316			4	7
	Detroit	34	40	.459	28	50	.359	3	4	237	295	8	12	268	332	3	4/16	6	11
	Washington	23	52	.307	15	61	.197	3	2	**221**	350	7	17	216	393			3	13
1905 National League (4/15 - 10/7)	New York	54	21	**.720**	51	27	**.654**	**33**	19	377	234	6	6	**401**	271	174	9/30	13	4
	Pittsburgh	49	28	.636	47	29	.618	4	1	362	287	**18**	11	330	283	4	4/22	11	5
	Chicago	54	25	.684	38	36	.514	7	5	365	212	5	10	302	**230**	1	4/14	7	4
	Philadelphia	39	36	.520	44	33	.571	8	9	353	314	8	12	355	288	7	4/21	9	7
	Cincinnati	50	28	.641	29	46	.387	12	2	**438**	330	15	20	297	368			8	8
	St. Louis	32	45	.416	26	51	.338	13	10	245	342	8	18	290	392			4	14
	Boston	29	46	.387	22	57	.278	14	14	**234**	344	3	22	234	387			4	8
	Brooklyn	29	47	.382	19	57	.250	16	16	273	**379**	13	8	233	428			6	10
1905 American League (4/14 - 10/7)	Philadelphia	50	23	**.685**	42	33	.560	12	12	**337**	247	12	9	286	245	82	10/6	7	3
	Chicago	50	29	.633	42	31	**.575**	5	2	300	**207**	6	9	**312**	244	24	7/31	7	5
	Detroit	45	30	.600	34	44	.436	5	5	267	275	8	6	245	327	2	4/26	5	6
	Boston	44	32	.579	34	42	.447	21	20	296	281	8	13	283	283			8	6
	Cleveland	40	37	.519	36	41	.468	5	13	290	284	**13**	10	277	303	73	8/1	8	10
	New York	40	35	.533	31	43	.419	15	15	316	303	8	11	270	319	10	5/1	**12**	6
	Washington	33	42	.440	31	45	.408	10	4	289	**340**	12	8	270	283	6	5/11	5	7
	St. Louis	34	42	.447	20	57	.260	5	7	**250**	267	11	12	261	341	1	4/14	4	8
1906 National League (4/12 - 10/7)	Chicago	56	21	**.727**	60	15	**.800**	7	6	345	214	13	6	**360**	167	147	9/19	14	3
	New York	51	24	.680	45	32	.584	9	8	309	239	6	5	316	271	25	5/27	10	4
	Pittsburgh	49	27	.645	44	33	.571	4	8	325	232	8	5	298	238	7	4/21	8	6
	Philadelphia	37	40	.481	34	42	.447	2	5	226	270	10	13	302	294	3	4/24	5	8
	Brooklyn	31	44	.413	35	42	.455	9	5	191	287	**16**	10	305	338			6	11
	Cincinnati	36	40	.474	28	47	.373	10	10	316	**333**	6	4	217	249			6	6
	St. Louis	28	48	.368	24	50	.324	6	10	241	313	4	7	229	294			6	10
	Boston	28	47	.373	21	55	.276	**11**	16	218	329	5	8	190	320	8	4/20	4	19
1906 American League (4/14 - 10/7)	Chicago	54	23	**.701**	39	35	.527	2	1	275	**180**	5	10	295	280	45	10/3	19	5
	New York	53	23	.697	37	38	.493	14	8	**398**	294	3	13	246	**249**	48	9/24	15	6
	Cleveland	47	30	.610	42	34	**.553**	4	8	351	229	8	8	**312**	253	22	7/5	6	6
	Philadelphia	48	23	.676	30	44	.405	21	4	285	211	11	5	276	331	78	8/11	11	8
	St. Louis	40	34	.541	36	39	.480	12	10	272	225	8	4	286	273			7	6
	Detroit	42	34	.553	29	44	.397	4	5	315	317	**6**	9	203	282			9	8
	Washington	33	41	.446	22	54	.289	7	5	260	288	19	10	258	376	6	5/6	6	8
	Boston	22	54	.289	27	51	.346	10	**22**	**230**	364	3	15	232	342			4	20
1907 National League (4/11 - 10/6)	Chicago	54	19	**.740**	53	26	**.671**	2	5	282	**198**	11	6	290	**192**	151	9/23	8	4
	Pittsburgh	47	29	.618	44	34	.564	7	3	**330**	258	**12**	9	**304**	252			8	5
	Philadelphia	45	30	.600	38	34	.528	2	4	265	247	10	9	247	229	4	4/14	7	5
	New York	45	30	.600	37	41	.474	19	19	317	250	4	6	257	260	25	5/29	17	7
	Brooklyn	37	38	.493	28	45	.384	9	10	223	232	9	6	223	290			6	12
	Cincinnati	43	36	.544	23	51	.311	3	5	287	227	12	11	239	292	5	4/15	7	6
	Boston	31	42	.425	27	48	.360	14	20	253	**304**	8	8	249	348	4	4/15	4	16
	St. Louis	31	47	.397	21	54	.280	9	10	**223**	289	10	10	196	317			9	12
1907 American League (4/11 - 10/6)	Detroit	50	27	**.649**	42	31	**.575**	3	5	**373**	265	8	4	**321**	267	32	10/5	10	4
	Philadelphia	50	20	**.714**	38	37	.507	14	6	324	235	8	6	258	276	45	9/26	7	6
	Chicago	48	29	.623	39	35	.527	0	5	316	**222**	5	8	272	**252**	102	8/25	6	5
	Cleveland	46	31	.597	39	36	.520	7	3	267	226	4	3	263	299	1	4/17	8	4
	New York	33	40	.452	37	38	.493	10	7	331	**372**	5	7	274	293	6	4/23	5	6
	St. Louis	36	40	.474	33	43	.434	5	**11**	261	262	4	6	281	293	2	4/12	7	6
	Boston	34	41	.453	25	49	.338	12	11	249	270	6	11	215	288	2	4/12	4	16
	Washington	27	47	.365	22	55	.286	1	3	**228**	310	11	7	278	381			4	8
1908 National League (4/14 - 10/8)	Chicago	47	30	.610	52	25	.675	9	15	294	264	10	5	330	**197**	90	10/8	9	5
	New York	52	25	**.675**	46	31	.597	10	11	**343**	235	10	15	309	221	44	10/7	11	4
	Pittsburgh	42	35	.545	56	21	**.727**	12	4	227	255	**13**	12	**358**	214	53	10/3	8	4
	Philadelphia	43	34	.558	40	37	.519	0	3	251	**213**	11	5	253	232			8	7
	Cincinnati	40	37	.519	33	44	.429	8	7	260	272	6	12	229	272			6	6
	Boston	35	42	.455	28	49	.364	13	20	295	328	4	9	242	294	2	4/15	4	7
	Brooklyn	27	50	.351	26	51	.338	**16**	3	179	243	12	14	198	273			5	9
	St. Louis	28	49	.364	21	56	.273	9	11	185	295	8	5	186	331			4	11

	Team	Home Games			Road Games			Home Games				Road Games				DIF	LDF	WS	LS
		W	L	PCT	W	L	PCT	HR	OHR	R	OR	HR	OHR	R	OR				
1908 American League (4/14 - 10/8)	Detroit	44	33	.571	46	30	**.605**	6	6	**315**	300	**13**	6	**332**	247	**85**	**10/6**	10	6
	Cleveland	51	26	.662	39	38	.506	8	6	305	223	10	9	263	**234**	17	9/26	9	5
	Chicago	51	25	**.671**	37	39	.487	1	4	271	**184**	2	7	266	286	19	6/24	**13**	7
	St. Louis	46	31	.597	37	38	.493	11	2	292	234	9	**5**	252	249	29	7/14	8	4
	Boston	37	40	.481	38	39	.494	9	9	273	249	5	9	291	264	3	4/16	5	7
	Philadelphia	46	30	.605	22	55	.286	11	5	294	272	10	6	192	290	5	6/6	7	10
	Washington	43	32	.573	24	53	.312	2	8	249	237	6	7	230	302			5	11
	New York	30	47	.390	21	56	.273	11	16	**234**	352	1	10	225	361	38	6/1	3	12
1909 National League (4/14 - 10/7)	Pittsburgh	56	21	**.727**	54	21	.720	10	6	**354**	237	15	6	345	210	155	9/28	16	4
	Chicago	47	29	.618	57	20	**.740**	8	**0**	281	**199**	12	6	**354**	191	6	5/1	10	4
	New York	44	33	.571	48	28	.632	19	23	298	294	7	6	325	252			9	4
	Cincinnati	39	38	.506	38	38	.500	5	2	282	299	**17**	**3**	324	300	6	4/25	7	6
	Philadelphia	40	37	.519	34	42	.447	6	10	266	279	6	13	250	239	3	5/4	7	8
	Brooklyn	34	45	.430	21	53	.284	12	9	238	311	4	22	206	316	1	4/15	4	10
	St. Louis	26	48	.351	28	50	.359	9	12	271	387	6	10	312	344			4	**15**
	Boston	27	47	.365	18	61	.228	11	9	**219**	326	4	14	216	357	10	5/3	5	15
1909 American League (4/12 - 10/3)	Detroit	57	19	**.750**	41	35	.539	13	**12**	**377**	246	6	7	289	247	161	9/30	14	5
	Philadelphia	49	27	.645	46	31	**.597**	8	4	293	**200**	**12**	5	**312**	**208**	18	8/24	8	4
	Boston	47	28	.627	41	35	.539	18	12	329	**295**	3	4	268	255	1	4/13	11	6
	Chicago	42	34	.553	36	40	.474	1	3	256	201	3	5	236	262			8	6
	New York	41	35	.539	33	42	.440	11	6	338	263	5	12	252	324	4	4/25	8	6
	Cleveland	39	37	.513	32	45	.416	2	**0**	262	259	8	10	231	273	2	4/15	7	**11**
	St. Louis	40	37	.519	21	52	.288	5	6	242	235	5	10	199	340			4	11
	Washington	27	48	.360	15	62	.195	5	3	**197**	271	4	10	183	385	2	4/13	3	11
1910 National League (4/14 - 10/15)	Chicago	58	19	**.753**	46	31	**.597**	18	9	354	**231**	16	**9**	358	268	144	10/2	11	5
	New York	52	26	.667	39	37	.513	20	17	352	255	11	13	**363**	312	10	5/7	9	5
	Pittsburgh	46	30	.605	40	37	.519	17	8	**365**	308	16	12	290	**268**	21	5/24	8	6
	Philadelphia	40	36	.526	38	39	.494	12	18	333	290	10	18	341	349	14	5/15	7	10
	Cincinnati	39	37	.513	36	42	.462	6	8	320	341	**17**	**19**	300	343	3	4/16	4	6
	Brooklyn	39	39	.500	25	51	.329	9	**5**	255	287	16	12	242	336	1	4/14	7	7
	St. Louis	35	41	.461	28	49	.364	**3**	14	312	316	12	16	327	402			8	**13**
	Boston	29	48	.377	24	52	.316	**25**	25	292	396	6	11	203	305	6	4/19	4	7
1910 American League (4/14 - 10/9)	Philadelphia	57	19	**.750**	45	29	**.608**	9	**0**	339	211	10	8	**334**	**230**	150	9/20	13	4
	New York	49	25	.662	39	38	.506	13	4	343	284	7	10	283	273	12	6/20	9	7
	Detroit	46	31	.597	40	37	.519	17	**23**	346	306	9	13	333	276	10	5/4	11	5
	Boston	51	28	.646	30	44	.405	**32**	21	338	262	**11**	8	300	302	3	4/21	9	6
	Cleveland	39	36	.520	32	45	.416	4	2	278	330	5	7	270	327	8	4/21	7	7
	Chicago	41	37	.526	27	48	.360	**2**	2	233	**198**	5	14	224	281	1	4/14	10	11
	Washington	38	35	.521	28	50	.359	3	7	265	252	6	12	236	298	4	4/18	4	10
	St. Louis	26	51	.338	21	56	.273	4	2	**229**	359	8	12	222	384			3	**12**
1911 National League (4/12 - 10/12)	New York	49	25	.662	50	29	**.633**	24	15	357	267	16	20	**399**	275	80	10/4	11	4
	Chicago	49	32	.605	43	30	.589	26	14	380	306	**29**	**13**	377	301	53	8/24	10	5
	Pittsburgh	48	29	.623	37	40	.481	27	**6**	**393**	**246**	21	29	351	311	4	8/9	**13**	6
	Philadelphia	42	34	.553	37	39	.487	**48**	26	352	357	12	17	306	312	51	7/21	6	7
	St. Louis	36	38	.486	39	36	.520	11	12	343	380	16	27	328	365	3	4/16	8	6
	Cincinnati	38	42	.475	32	41	.438	**5**	6	331	317	16	30	351	389			7	8
	Brooklyn	31	42	.425	33	44	.429	10	11	**247**	303	18	15	292	356			5	6
	Boston	19	54	.260	25	53	.321	28	**47**	391	536	9	28	308	485	1	4/12	3	**16**
1911 American League (4/12 - 10/8)	Philadelphia	54	20	**.730**	47	30	**.610**	11	**24**	384	**253**	5	12	477	348	66	9/26	10	6
	Detroit	51	25	.671	38	40	.487	**21**	9	**468**	403	15	13	363	373	112	8/3	9	4
	Cleveland	46	30	.605	34	43	.442	**7**	13	368	344	4	13	323	368			10	5
	Boston	39	37	.513	39	38	.506	20	15	328	312	16	6	352	331			6	7
	Chicago	40	37	.519	37	37	.500	8	12	341	299	13	9	378	325			5	6
	New York	36	40	.474	40	36	.526	14	11	365	**422**	14	11	319	**302**	6	4/17	7	6
	Washington	39	38	.506	25	52	.325	10	6	323	356	**21**	18	302	410	3	4/14	5	8
	St. Louis	25	53	.321	20	54	.270	9	8	**296**	396	10	18	271	416	2	4/13	4	**13**
1912 National League (4/11 - 10/6)	New York	49	25	**.662**	54	23	**.701**	**31**	21	387	302	16	15	**436**	269	151	9/26	16	4
	Pittsburgh	45	31	.592	48	27	.640	15	10	347	**275**	**24**	18	404	290			12	4
	Chicago	46	29	.613	45	30	.600	22	18	394	347	21	15	362	321			7	5
	Cincinnati	45	32	.584	30	46	.395	7	2	309	311	14	26	347	411	29	5/19	6	7
	Philadelphia	34	41	.453	39	38	.506	25	26	318	352	18	17	352	336			5	6
	St. Louis	37	40	.481	26	50	.342	14	9	354	414	13	22	305	416	6	4/17	6	9
	Brooklyn	33	43	.434	25	52	.325	17	20	**303**	368	15	25	348	386			5	7
	Boston	31	47	.397	21	54	.280	22	**28**	**407**	**471**	13	**15**	286	390	2	4/12	3	10

1912 American League (4/11 - 10/6)

Team	Home Games W	L	PCT	Road Games W	L	PCT	Home Games HR	OHR	R	OR	Road Games HR	OHR	R	OR	DIF	LDF	WS	LS
Boston	57	20	.740	48	27	.640	10	10	417	286	19	8	382	258	130	9/18	10	5
Washington	45	33	.577	46	28	.622	13	12	336	295	7	11	362	286			17	4
Philadelphia	45	32	.584	45	30	.600	11	6	381	342	11	6	398	316	5	4/15	7	4
Chicago	34	43	.442	44	33	.571	11	11	276	340	6	14	362	306	49	6/9	8	6
Cleveland	39	35	.527	36	43	.456	3	6	338	326	7	9	338	354	2	4/12	9	8
Detroit	37	39	.487	32	45	.416	8	6	344	370	11	10	376	407			5	7
St. Louis	27	50	.351	26	51	.338	6	11	287	379	13	6	265	385			7	7
New York	31	44	.413	19	58	.247	14	16	352	423	4	12	278	419			5	9

1913 National League (4/9 - 10/5)

Team	Home Games W	L	PCT	Road Games W	L	PCT	Home Games HR	OHR	R	OR	Road Games HR	OHR	R	OR	DIF	LDF	WS	LS
New York	54	23	.701	47	28	.627	23	22	367	250	8	16	317	265	102	9/27	14	5
Philadelphia	43	33	.566	45	30	.600	51	23	361	366	22	17	332	270	63	6/29	8	9
Chicago	51	25	.671	37	40	.481	37	19	372	273	22	19	348	352	6	5/3	7	6
Pittsburgh	41	35	.539	37	36	.507	13	6	324	277	22	20	349	308	1	4/12	8	7
Boston	34	40	.459	35	42	.455	14	12	298	337	18	26	343	353	7	4/16	5	7
Brooklyn	29	47	.382	36	37	.493	20	14	296	343	19	19	299	270	1	4/17	7	10
Cincinnati	32	44	.421	32	45	.416	15	13	307	380	12	27	300	337			5	7
St. Louis	25	48	.342	26	51	.338	8	20	239	346	6	37	284	409	5	4/17	5	8

1913 American League (4/10 - 10/5)

Team	Home Games W	L	PCT	Road Games W	L	PCT	Home Games HR	OHR	R	OR	Road Games HR	OHR	R	OR	DIF	LDF	WS	LS
Philadelphia	50	26	.658	46	31	.597	19	14	388	271	14	10	406	321	173	9/22	15	6
Washington	43	35	.551	47	29	.618	10	29	297	318	10	6	299	243	13	4/23	6	3
Cleveland	45	31	.592	41	35	.539	4	9	336	284	12	11	297	252	1	4/11	9	5
Boston	41	34	.547	38	37	.507	3	0	328	312	14	6	303	298			5	5
Chicago	40	37	.519	38	37	.507	6	4	216	233	17	6	272	265			5	7
Detroit	34	42	.447	32	45	.416	9	4	312	368	15	8	312	348			5	9
New York	27	47	.365	30	47	.390	5	20	265	339	4	12	264	329			4	13
St. Louis	31	46	.403	26	50	.342	13	11	247	309	5	10	281	333	3	4/12	3	9

1914 National League (4/14 - 10/6)

Team	Home Games W	L	PCT	Road Games W	L	PCT	Home Games HR	OHR	R	OR	Road Games HR	OHR	R	OR	DIF	LDF	WS	LS
Boston	51	25	.671	43	34	.558	17	16	339	279	18	22	318	269	34	9/28	9	7
New York	43	36	.544	41	34	.547	17	24	316	288	14	23	356	288	100	9/7	6	6
St. Louis	42	34	.553	39	38	.506	20	14	285	280	13	12	273	260	1	4/14	7	7
Chicago	46	30	.605	32	46	.410	22	20	318	281	20	17	287	357			9	7
Brooklyn	45	34	.570	30	45	.400	17	17	342	306	14	19	280	312	7	4/20	11	8
Philadelphia	48	30	.615	26	50	.342	50	16	377	321	12	11	274	366	7	4/20	8	8
Pittsburgh	39	36	.520	30	49	.380	3	6	234	214	15	21	269	326	39	5/29	8	12
Cincinnati	34	42	.447	26	52	.333	4	5	290	328	12	25	240	323	3	4/17	7	19

1914 American League (4/14 - 10/7)

Team	Home Games W	L	PCT	Road Games W	L	PCT	Home Games HR	OHR	R	OR	Road Games HR	OHR	R	OR	DIF	LDF	WS	LS
Philadelphia	51	24	.680	48	29	.623	17	13	354	247	12	5	395	282	130	9/27	12	5
Boston	44	31	.587	47	31	.603	3	5	270	247	15	13	318	264			6	5
Washington	40	33	.548	41	40	.506	8	7	282	246	10	13	290	273			7	7
Detroit	42	35	.545	38	38	.500	11	9	315	318	14	8	300	300	33	5/25	8	7
St. Louis	42	36	.538	29	46	.387	11	14	271	298	6	6	252	316			6	6
Chicago	43	37	.538	27	47	.365	7	4	271	285	12	11	216	275	14	4/27	7	8
New York	36	40	.474	34	44	.436	8	24	278	259	4	6	260	291	4	4/17	5	6
Cleveland	32	47	.405	19	55	.257	4	3	289	380	6	7	249	329			4	8

1914 Federal League (4/13 - 10/10)

Team	Home Games W	L	PCT	Road Games W	L	PCT	Home Games HR	OHR	R	OR	Road Games HR	OHR	R	OR	DIF	LDF	WS	LS
Indianapolis	53	23	.697	35	42	.455	14	8	439	339	19	21	323	283	50	10/7	15	6
Chicago	41	34	.547	46	33	.582	30	19	248	208	22	23	373	309	69	10/5	6	4
Baltimore	53	26	.671	31	44	.413	25	15	350	298	7	19	295	330	51	8/7	7	7
Buffalo	47	29	.618	33	42	.440	21	18	345	300	17	27	275	302	2	6/16	6	4
Brooklyn	47	32	.595	30	45	.400	27	13	358	335	15	18	304	342	7	4/20	7	9
Kansas City	38	37	.507	29	47	.382	28	21	322	306	11	16	322	377			5	7
Pittsburgh	37	37	.500	27	49	.355	11	10	297	307	23	29	308	391			5	6
St. Louis	31	44	.413	31	45	.408	12	23	304	368	13	15	261	329	13	5/13	8	7

1915 National League (4/14 - 10/7)

Team	Home Games W	L	PCT	Road Games W	L	PCT	Home Games HR	OHR	R	OR	Road Games HR	OHR	R	OR	DIF	LDF	WS	LS
Philadelphia	49	27	.645	41	35	.539	46	18	313	235	12	8	276	228	135	9/29	8	4
Boston	49	27	.645	34	42	.447	3	5	280	263	14	18	302	282			8	5
Brooklyn	51	26	.662	29	46	.387	9	14	299	263	5	15	237	297			8	8
Chicago	42	34	.553	31	46	.403	31	16	296	314	22	12	274	306	45	7/12	8	8
Pittsburgh	40	37	.519	33	44	.429	8	6	290	241	16	15	267	279	1	4/14	6	6
St. Louis	42	36	.538	30	45	.400	11	10	320	303	9	20	270	298			6	6
Cincinnati	39	37	.513	32	46	.410	6	7	265	295	9	21	251	290			6	7
New York	37	38	.493	32	45	.416	15	20	275	270	9	20	307	358	2	4/15	5	7

1915 American League (4/14 - 10/7)

Team	Home Games W	L	PCT	Road Games W	L	PCT	Home Games HR	OHR	R	OR	Road Games HR	OHR	R	OR	DIF	LDF	WS	LS
Boston	55	20	.733	46	30	.605	5	4	323	221	9	14	345	278	84	9/30	8	5
Detroit	50	26	.658	50	28	.641	11	7	410	314	12	7	368	283	23	6/7	9	4
Chicago	54	24	.692	39	37	.513	9	4	353	236	16	10	364	273	59	7/17	11	6
Washington	48	28	.632	37	40	.481	2	2	277	235	10	10	292	256	2	4/16	7	8
New York	37	44	.457	32	39	.451	28	32	310	309	3	9	274	279	11	5/21	7	8
St. Louis	35	38	.479	28	53	.346	6	7	237	315	13	14	284	364			7	8
Cleveland	27	50	.351	30	45	.400	7	9	277	362	13	10	262	308	2	4/16	6	7
Philadelphia	20	55	.267	23	54	.299	9	18	285	457	7	3	260	431	1	4/14	3	11

1915 Federal League (4/10 - 10/3)

Team	Home W	L	PCT	Road W	L	PCT	HR	OHR	R	OR	HR	OHR	R	OR	DIF	LDF	WS	LS
Chicago	44	32	.579	42	34	.553	21	10	310	252	29	23	330	286	38	10/3	6	6
St. Louis	43	34	.558	44	33	.571	12	15	334	280	11	7	300	247	18	7/14	12	4
Pittsburgh	45	31	.592	41	36	.532	4	10	292	269	16	27	300	255	69	10/1	7	4
Kansas City	46	31	.597	35	41	.461	15	19	274	249	13	10	273	302	45	8/21	5	5
Newark	40	39	.506	40	33	.548	4	2	267	271	13	13	318	291	17	8/23	8	6
Buffalo	37	40	.481	37	38	.493	21	21	290	324	19	14	284	310			8	6
Brooklyn	34	40	.459	36	42	.462	20	11	315	324	16	16	332	349	11	4/23	10	8
Baltimore	24	51	.320	23	56	.291	29	36	299	419	7	16	251	341			4	9

1916 National League (4/12 - 10/5)

Team	Home W	L	PCT	Road W	L	PCT	HR	OHR	R	OR	HR	OHR	R	OR	DIF	LDF	WS	LS
Brooklyn	50	27	.649	44	33	.571	19	9	300	233	9	15	285	238	152	10/3	8	5
Philadelphia	50	29	.633	41	33	.554	29	17	281	233	13	11	300	256	18	9/8	8	5
Boston	41	31	.569	48	32	.600	6	4	224	207	16	20	318	246	10	9/4	6	7
New York	47	30	.610	39	36	.520	21	23	291	229	21	18	306	275			26	8
Chicago	37	41	.474	30	45	.400	34	22	309	317	12	10	211	224	2	4/28	7	8
Pittsburgh	37	40	.481	28	49	.364	9	5	268	298	11	19	216	288			5	10
Cincinnati	32	44	.421	28	49	.364	4	10	242	312	10	25	263	305			4	8
St. Louis	36	40	.474	24	53	.312	12	15	251	295	13	16	225	334	1	4/12	5	14

1916 American League (4/12 - 10/4)

Team	Home W	L	PCT	Road W	L	PCT	HR	OHR	R	OR	HR	OHR	R	OR	DIF	LDF	WS	LS
Boston	49	28	.636	42	35	.545	1	1	252	205	13	9	298	275	73	10/1	7	4
Chicago	49	28	.636	40	37	.519	9	5	326	254	8	9	275	243	6	8/8	7	8
Detroit	49	28	.636	38	39	.494	7	8	350	313	10	4	320	282	6	9/17	9	5
New York	46	31	.597	34	43	.442	22	22	306	277	13	15	271	284	35	7/29	7	9
St. Louis	45	32	.584	34	43	.442	7	10	290	238	7	5	298	307	3	4/14	14	7
Cleveland	44	33	.571	33	44	.429	4	9	323	293	12	7	307	309	47	7/12	8	8
Washington	49	28	.636	27	49	.355	6	1	294	248	6	13	242	295	16	6/2	7	7
Philadelphia	23	53	.303	13	64	.169	15	17	231	399	4	9	216	377			2	20

1917 National League (4/11 - 10/4)

Team	Home W	L	PCT	Road W	L	PCT	HR	OHR	R	OR	HR	OHR	R	OR	DIF	LDF	WS	LS
New York	50	28	.641	48	28	.632	21	17	294	220	18	12	341	237	151	9/24	6	3
Philadelphia	46	29	.613	41	36	.532	26	20	297	270	12	5	281	230	23	6/26	6	6
St. Louis	38	38	.500	44	32	.579	15	15	266	302	11	14	265	265	1	5/6	7	4
Cincinnati	39	38	.506	39	38	.506	10	3	279	296	16	17	322	315	2	4/12	7	8
Chicago	35	42	.455	39	38	.506	11	14	273	305	6	20	279	262	10	5/21	10	6
Boston	35	42	.455	37	39	.487	13	3	240	269	9	16	296	283	1	4/20	5	5
Brooklyn	36	38	.486	34	43	.442	14	14	270	288	11	18	241	271			7	7
Pittsburgh	25	53	.321	26	50	.342	2	4	232	307	7	10	232	288			4	7

1917 American League (4/11 - 10/4)

Team	Home W	L	PCT	Road W	L	PCT	HR	OHR	R	OR	HR	OHR	R	OR	DIF	LDF	WS	LS
Chicago	56	21	.727	44	33	.571	7	3	327	204	11	7	329	260	126	9/21	9	4
Boston	45	33	.577	45	29	.608	3	4	293	245	11	8	262	209	53	8/17	10	4
Cleveland	43	34	.558	45	32	.584	5	8	317	314	8	9	267	229	5	4/15	10	4
Detroit	34	41	.453	44	34	.564	5	5	285	303	20	7	354	274			6	7
Washington	42	36	.538	32	43	.427	1	3	264	255	3	9	279	311	4	4/14	7	10
New York	35	40	.467	36	42	.462	19	24	269	292	8	4	255	266	2	5/19	5	8
St. Louis	31	46	.403	26	51	.338	7	11	252	337	8	8	258	350			3	8
Philadelphia	29	47	.382	26	51	.338	11	17	264	319	6	6	265	372			4	7

1918 National League (4/15 - 9/2)

Team	Home W	L	PCT	Road W	L	PCT	HR	OHR	R	OR	HR	OHR	R	OR	DIF	LDF	WS	LS
Chicago	50	26	.658	34	19	.642	9	5	300	235	12	8	238	158	89	8/24	9	4
New York	35	21	.625	36	32	.529	9	13	204	181	4	7	276	234	51	6/5	9	6
Cincinnati	46	24	.657	22	36	.379	9	5	298	256	6	14	232	240	1	4/16	8	9
Pittsburgh	41	27	.603	24	33	.421	9	4	270	232	6	9	196	180			8	7
Brooklyn	33	21	.611	24	48	.333	4	12	173	185	6	10	187	278			4	9
Philadelphia	27	29	.482	28	39	.418	19	13	220	261	6	9	210	246	1	4/16	5	9
Boston	23	29	.442	30	42	.417	5	2	163	183	8	12	261	286			5	6
St. Louis	32	40	.444	19	38	.333	14	7	241	280	13	9	213	247	2	4/17	4	6

1918 American League (4/15 - 9/2)

Team	Home W	L	PCT	Road W	L	PCT	HR	OHR	R	OR	HR	OHR	R	OR	DIF	LDF	WS	LS
Boston	49	21	.700	26	30	.464	2	3	272	165	13	6	202	215	129	8/31	6	6
Cleveland	38	22	.633	35	32	.522	1	4	274	219	8	6	230	228	8	7/5	7	3
Washington	41	32	.562	31	24	.564	2	6	268	238	3	4	193	174			7	4
New York	37	29	.561	23	34	.404	10	22	251	237	10	3	242	238	8	7/3	4	7
St. Louis	23	30	.434	35	34	.507	1	7	178	195	4	4	248	253	2	4/17	6	6
Chicago	30	26	.536	27	41	.397	4	4	216	194	5	5	241	252			5	8
Detroit	28	29	.491	27	42	.391	2	7	221	246	11	4	255	311			5	7
Philadelphia	35	32	.522	17	44	.279	15	8	256	273	7	5	156	265			5	8

1919 National League (4/19 - 9/28)

Team	Home W	L	PCT	Road W	L	PCT	HR	OHR	R	OR	HR	OHR	R	OR	DIF	LDF	WS	LS
Cincinnati	52	19	.732	44	25	.638	10	5	315	189	10	16	262	212	75	9/16	10	4
New York	46	23	.667	41	30	.577	28	17	310	209	12	17	295	261	76	7/31	7	4
Chicago	40	31	.563	35	34	.507	11	7	232	190	10	7	222	217	1	4/24	7	6
Pittsburgh	40	30	.571	31	38	.449	8	7	273	218	9	16	199	248			7	6
Brooklyn	36	33	.522	33	38	.465	12	10	243	227	13	11	282	286	21	5/15	6	10
Boston	29	38	.433	28	44	.389	11	9	231	265	13	20	234	298			4	9
St. Louis	34	35	.493	20	48	.294	9	10	240	244	9	15	223	308			7	9
Philadelphia	26	44	.371	21	46	.313	29	24	307	378	13	16	203	321			5	13

Team	Home Games			Road Games			Home Games				Road Games				DIF	LDF	WS	LS
	W	L	PCT	W	L	PCT	HR	OHR	R	OR	HR	OHR	R	OR				
1919 American League (4/23 - 9/29)																		
Chicago	48	22	.686	40	30	.571	5	11	344	279	20	14	323	255	134	9/24	10	4
Cleveland	44	25	.638	40	30	.571	12	4	340	276	13	15	296	261	2	6/19	10	6
New York	46	25	.648	34	34	.500	33	30	326	255	12	17	252	251	21	7/9	8	6
Detroit	46	24	.657	34	36	.486	10	14	307	243	13	21	311	335	1	4/25	8	6
Boston	35	30	.538	31	41	.431	10	3	233	241	23	13	331	311	6	4/28	9	6
St. Louis	40	30	.571	27	42	.391	19	23	280	249	12	12	253	318			6	9
Washington	32	40	.444	24	44	.353	2	5	265	282	22	15	268	288	1	4/23	4	11
Philadelphia	21	49	.300	15	55	.214	29	31	266	400	6	13	191	342			2	9
1920 National League (4/14 - 10/3)																		
Brooklyn	49	29	.628	44	32	.579	17	14	360	291	11	11	300	237	87	9/27	10	6
New York	45	35	.563	41	33	.554	31	33	334	282	15	11	348	261			6	5
Cincinnati	42	34	.553	40	37	.519	5	1	281	238	13	25	358	331	75	9/8	6	6
Pittsburgh	42	35	.545	37	40	.481	6	4	276	263	10	21	254	289	15	5/27	6	6
Chicago	43	34	.558	32	45	.416	19	15	322	302	15	22	297	333	4	5/31	9	10
St. Louis	38	38	.500	37	41	.474	10	10	330	332	22	20	345	350			7	7
Boston	36	37	.493	26	53	.329	5	11	271	292	18	28	252	378	4	4/17	7	10
Philadelphia	32	45	.416	30	46	.395	50	30	339	380	14	5	226	334	1	5/3	5	9
1920 American League (4/14 - 10/3)																		
Cleveland	51	27	.654	47	29	.618	20	10	441	330	15	21	416	312	134	10/2	7	5
Chicago	52	25	.675	44	33	.571	18	10	381	298	19	35	413	367	31	8/31	7	7
New York	49	28	.636	46	31	.597	71	36	424	308	44	12	414	321	9	9/15	10	4
St. Louis	40	38	.513	36	39	.480	31	33	473	415	19	20	324	351			10	7
Boston	41	35	.539	31	46	.403	3	14	327	300	19	25	323	398	14	5/27	6	5
Washington	37	38	.493	31	46	.403	5	7	343	386	31	44	380	416			7	10
Detroit	32	46	.410	29	47	.382	12	24	336	452	18	22	316	381			4	13
Philadelphia	25	50	.333	23	56	.291	35	40	254	401	9	16	304	433	1	4/14	3	18
1921 National League (4/13 - 10/2)																		
New York	53	26	.671	41	33	.554	47	46	407	321	28	33	433	316	32	9/28	10	6
Pittsburgh	45	31	.592	45	32	.584	13	10	343	295	24	27	349	300	140	9/10	9	6
St. Louis	48	29	.623	39	37	.513	43	25	397	307	40	36	412	374			10	6
Boston	42	32	.568	37	42	.468	20	18	332	292	41	36	389	405			8	7
Brooklyn	41	37	.526	36	38	.486	32	23	360	361	27	23	307	320	1	4/13	11	6
Cincinnati	40	36	.526	30	47	.390	5	2	321	306	15	35	297	343	1	4/13	5	6
Chicago	32	44	.421	32	45	.416	23	37	345	434	14	30	323	339	7	4/19	4	7
Philadelphia	29	47	.382	22	56	.282	67	49	326	485	21	30	291	434			4	7
1921 American League (4/13 - 10/2)																		
New York	53	25	.679	45	30	.600	83	34	500	355	51	17	448	353	54	10/1	9	5
Cleveland	51	26	.662	43	34	.558	15	10	467	330	27	33	458	382	115	9/19	8	5
St. Louis	43	34	.558	38	39	.494	42	43	423	434	25	28	412	411	4	4/13	8	4
Washington	46	30	.605	34	43	.442	14	13	358	332	28	38	346	406	4	4/30	11	10
Boston	41	36	.532	34	43	.442	3	16	332	333	14	37	336	363	1	4/13	5	8
Detroit	37	40	.481	34	42	.447	19	28	433	412	39	43	450	440	1	4/14	6	9
Chicago	37	40	.481	25	52	.325	13	20	378	399	22	32	305	459			5	11
Philadelphia	28	47	.373	25	53	.321	65	59	353	464	17	26	304	430			4	10
1922 National League (4/12 - 10/1)																		
New York	51	27	.654	42	34	.553	48	38	439	333	32	33	413	325	162	9/25	8	5
Cincinnati	48	29	.623	38	39	.494	8	13	378	297	37	36	388	380			7	8
Pittsburgh	45	33	.577	40	36	.526	22	16	439	390	30	35	426	346			13	6
St. Louis	42	35	.545	43	34	.558	59	31	446	414	48	34	417	405	11	8/11	8	5
Chicago	39	37	.513	41	37	.526	22	37	344	382	20	40	427	426	6	4/27	8	5
Brooklyn	44	34	.564	32	44	.421	25	35	380	326	31	39	363	428	1	4/12	8	8
Philadelphia	35	41	.461	22	55	.286	94	60	449	517	21	29	289	403	2	4/13	4	12
Boston	32	43	.427	21	57	.269	6	15	287	373	26	42	309	449			6	9
1922 American League (4/12 - 10/1)																		
New York	50	27	.649	44	33	.571	53	48	387	291	42	25	371	327	95	9/30	7	8
St. Louis	54	23	.701	39	38	.506	70	41	471	314	28	30	396	329	78	9/7	5	3
Detroit	43	34	.558	36	41	.468	15	32	426	370	39	30	402	421			8	6
Cleveland	44	35	.557	34	41	.453	12	20	423	424	20	38	345	393	10	4/21	12	6
Chicago	43	34	.558	34	43	.442	10	21	351	335	35	36	340	356			8	7
Washington	40	39	.506	29	46	.387	15	3	329	295	30	46	321	411	1	4/12	5	7
Philadelphia	38	39	.494	27	50	.351	80	82	388	437	31	25	317	393	1	4/12	4	7
Boston	31	42	.425	30	51	.370	6	17	280	344	39	31	318	425			5	9
1923 National League (4/17 - 10/7)																		
New York	47	30	.610	48	28	.632	41	53	408	362	44	29	446	317	174	9/28	11	6
Cincinnati	46	32	.590	45	31	.592	6	4	337	300	39	24	371	329	1	4/17	9	6
Pittsburgh	47	30	.610	40	37	.519	16	9	381	322	33	44	405	374	1	4/17	7	5
Chicago	46	31	.597	37	40	.481	63	57	402	354	27	29	354	350			7	6
St. Louis	42	35	.545	37	39	.487	22	27	335	320	41	43	411	412			6	6
Brooklyn	37	40	.481	39	38	.506	26	27	348	383	36	28	405	358	1	4/18	5	10
Boston	22	55	.286	32	45	.416	7	27	291	429	25	37	345	369			6	12
Philadelphia	20	55	.267	30	49	.380	76	77	418	597	36	23	330	411			3	7

	Team	Home Games			Road Games			Home Games				Road Games				DIF	LDF	WS	LS
		W	L	PCT	W	L	PCT	HR	OHR	R	OR	HR	OHR	R	OR				
1923 American League (4/18 - 10/7)	New York	46	30	.605	52	24	.684	62	50	407	329	43	18	416	293	161	9/20	9	3
	Detroit	45	32	.584	38	39	.494	21	31	400	351	20	27	431	390	5	5/4	5	3
	Cleveland	42	36	.538	40	35	.533	22	16	455	393	37	20	433	353	15	5/2	6	6
	Washington	43	34	.558	32	44	.421	7	16	363	339	19	40	357	408			6	7
	St. Louis	40	36	.526	34	42	.447	50	43	377	364	32	15	311	356			6	5
	Philadelphia	34	41	.453	35	42	.455	28	32	345	360	24	36	316	401	3	4/20	6	12
	Chicago	30	45	.400	39	40	.494	13	24	327	348	29	25	365	393			4	4
	Boston	37	40	.481	24	51	.320	11	15	327	402	23	33	257	407			5	5
1924 National League (4/15 - 9/29)	New York	51	26	.662	42	34	.553	51	40	385	272	44	37	472	369	153	9/27	10	5
	Brooklyn	46	31	.597	46	31	.597	26	30	342	338	46	28	375	337	1	4/15	15	3
	Pittsburgh	49	28	.636	41	35	.539	19	17	393	293	24	25	331	295			9	4
	Cincinnati	43	33	.566	40	37	.519	3	3	311	283	33	27	338	296	9	5/20	6	4
	Chicago	46	31	.597	35	41	.461	33	68	373	341	33	21	325	358	5	6/14	6	5
	St. Louis	40	37	.519	25	52	.325	32	37	419	359	35	32	321	391	1	4/15	7	7
	Philadelphia	26	49	.347	29	47	.382	58	64	369	483	36	20	307	366			5	10
	Boston	28	48	.368	25	52	.325	9	8	254	366	16	41	266	434	3	4/18	4	10
1924 American League (4/15 - 9/30)	Washington	47	30	.610	45	32	.584	1	7	371	280	21	27	384	333	52	9/29	10	6
	New York	45	32	.584	44	31	.587	57	46	397	324	41	13	401	343	97	9/18	8	6
	Detroit	45	33	.577	41	35	.539	17	28	427	393	18	27	422	403	27	8/12	8	5
	St. Louis	41	36	.532	33	42	.440	44	49	426	445	23	19	343	364	1	4/15	6	6
	Philadelphia	36	39	.480	35	42	.455	32	24	328	391	31	19	357	387			4	12
	Cleveland	37	38	.493	30	48	.385	13	18	374	375	28	25	381	439			5	9
	Boston	41	36	.532	26	51	.338	8	17	402	391	22	26	335	415	16	6/13	6	9
	Chicago	37	39	.487	29	48	.377	13	23	403	414	28	29	390	444	6	5/2	4	13
1925 National League (4/14 - 10/4)	Pittsburgh	52	25	.675	43	33	.566	27	31	481	342	51	50	431	373	93	9/23	9	4
	New York	47	29	.618	39	37	.513	55	39	362	334	59	34	374	368	75	8/1	8	6
	Cincinnati	44	32	.579	36	41	.468	10	5	334	285	34	30	356	358	6	4/19	9	5
	St. Louis	48	28	.632	29	48	.377	66	41	449	359	43	45	379	405			7	7
	Boston	37	39	.487	33	44	.429	15	14	315	383	26	53	393	419	2	4/15	5	5
	Brooklyn	40	37	.519	28	48	.368	25	41	383	407	39	34	403	459	2	4/15	6	12
	Philadelphia	38	39	.494	30	46	.395	73	74	488	547	27	43	324	383			5	11
	Chicago	37	40	.481	31	46	.403	57	63	367	359	29	39	356	414	2	4/17	5	6
1925 American League (4/14 - 10/4)	Washington	53	22	.707	43	33	.566	13	13	408	298	43	36	421	372	76	9/24	7	4
	Philadelphia	51	26	.662	37	38	.493	35	37	435	351	41	23	396	362	98	8/19	9	12
	St. Louis	45	32	.584	37	39	.487	73	73	503	501	37	26	397	405			6	6
	Detroit	43	34	.558	38	39	.494	18	36	451	399	32	34	452	430	1	4/14	10	7
	Chicago	44	33	.571	35	42	.455	13	32	366	378	25	37	445	392			7	5
	Cleveland	37	39	.487	33	45	.423	23	19	421	430	29	22	361	387	17	5/7	6	8
	New York	42	36	.538	27	49	.355	54	56	354	356	56	22	352	418	1	4/14	5	5
	Boston	28	47	.373	19	58	.247	10	28	309	441	31	39	330	481			3	9
1926 National League (4/13 - 9/29)	St. Louis	47	30	.610	42	35	.545	54	42	411	359	36	34	406	319	30	9/25	8	5
	Cincinnati	53	23	.697	34	44	.436	8	8	372	259	27	32	375	392	75	9/16	10	6
	Pittsburgh	49	28	.636	35	41	.461	17	16	446	374	27	35	323	315	38	8/30	5	7
	Chicago	49	28	.636	33	44	.429	38	17	377	295	28	21	305	307			8	5
	New York	43	33	.566	31	44	.413	45	43	333	317	28	27	330	351	11	4/29	7	6
	Brooklyn	38	38	.500	33	44	.429	23	26	314	331	17	24	309	374	16	5/14	6	9
	Boston	43	34	.558	23	52	.307	4	5	296	266	12	41	328	453			8	9
	Philadelphia	33	42	.440	25	51	.329	51	42	392	470	24	26	295	430	5	4/17	5	6
1926 American League (4/13 - 9/29)	New York	50	25	.667	41	38	.519	58	33	417	326	63	23	430	387	158	9/25	16	4
	Cleveland	49	31	.613	39	35	.527	11	19	376	301	16	30	362	311	13	5/11	9	6
	Philadelphia	44	27	.620	39	40	.494	34	27	365	314	27	11	312	256			9	7
	Washington	42	30	.583	39	39	.500	4	15	373	378	39	30	429	383	4	4/19	10	5
	Chicago	47	31	.603	34	41	.453	8	19	332	294	24	28	398	371	7	4/19	8	6
	Detroit	39	41	.488	40	34	.541	16	38	380	445	20	20	413	385	1	4/20	7	6
	St. Louis	40	39	.506	22	53	.293	53	64	375	429	19	22	307	416			5	7
	Boston	25	51	.329	21	56	.273	9	16	288	438	23	29	274	397			5	17
1927 National League (4/12 - 10/2)	Pittsburgh	48	31	.608	46	29	.613	25	23	406	345	29	35	411	314	104	10/1	11	3
	St. Louis	55	25	.688	37	36	.507	55	51	433	354	29	21	321	311	10	5/10	6	6
	New York	49	25	.662	43	37	.538	62	49	389	342	47	28	428	378	19	5/20	10	6
	Chicago	50	28	.641	35	40	.467	37	19	398	315	37	31	352	346	49	8/31	12	7
	Cincinnati	45	35	.563	30	43	.411	3	11	348	320	26	25	295	333			8	6
	Brooklyn	34	39	.466	31	49	.388	20	35	266	296	19	28	275	323	1	4/12	5	7
	Boston	32	41	.438	28	53	.346	5	10	296	339	32	33	355	432			4	15
	Philadelphia	34	43	.442	17	60	.221	32	46	375	429	25	38	303	474			4	14

Team	Home Games			Road Games			Home Games				Road Games				DIF	LDF	WS	LS
	W	L	PCT	W	L	PCT	HR	OHR	R	OR	HR	OHR	R	OR				

1927 American League (4/12 - 10/2)

Team	W	L	PCT	W	L	PCT	HR	OHR	R	OR	HR	OHR	R	OR	DIF	LDF	WS	LS
New York	57	19	.750	53	25	.679	83	30	479	267	75	12	496	332	173	9/13	9	4
Philadelphia	50	27	.649	41	36	.532	26	36	412	327	30	29	429	399	1	4/30	6	7
Washington	51	28	.646	34	41	.453	10	19	416	308	19	34	366	422	4	4/15	10	12
Detroit	44	32	.579	38	39	.494	25	28	467	433	26	24	378	372	2	4/20	13	8
Chicago	38	37	.507	32	46	.410	6	22	337	343	30	33	325	365			7	12
Cleveland	35	42	.455	31	45	.408	10	11	333	367	16	26	335	399	1	4/12	7	8
St. Louis	38	38	.500	21	56	.273	42	57	440	457	13	22	284	447	1	4/16	6	8
Boston	29	49	.372	22	54	.289	5	29	299	409	23	27	298	447			6	15

1928 National League (4/11 - 9/30)

Team	W	L	PCT	W	L	PCT	HR	OHR	R	OR	HR	OHR	R	OR	DIF	LDF	WS	LS
St. Louis	42	35	.545	53	24	.688	62	51	367	336	51	35	440	300	107	9/29	8	4
New York	51	26	.662	42	35	.545	80	46	411	315	38	31	396	338	32	8/21	9	8
Chicago	52	25	.675	39	38	.506	40	18	335	264	52	38	379	351	7	5/21	13	5
Pittsburgh	47	30	.610	38	37	.507	16	14	479	356	36	51	358	348			9	6
Cincinnati	44	33	.571	34	41	.453	3	17	324	318	29	41	324	368	30	6/14	7	8
Brooklyn	41	35	.539	36	41	.468	31	25	330	296	35	34	335	344	4	4/30	6	5
Boston	25	51	.329	25	52	.325	24	62	309	448	28	38	322	430			4	10
Philadelphia	26	49	.347	17	60	.221	54	67	360	521	31	42	300	436	2	4/12	4	12

1928 American League (4/10 - 9/30)

Team	W	L	PCT	W	L	PCT	HR	OHR	R	OR	HR	OHR	R	OR	DIF	LDF	WS	LS
New York	52	25	.675	49	28	.636	69	36	400	301	64	23	494	384	165	9/28	8	3
Philadelphia	52	25	.675	46	30	.605	54	33	430	295	35	33	399	320	2	9/8	10	6
St. Louis	44	33	.571	38	39	.494	51	64	398	389	12	29	374	353	5	4/15	5	9
Washington	37	43	.463	38	36	.514	16	12	363	378	24	28	355	327			6	9
Chicago	37	40	.481	35	42	.455	11	28	316	369	13	38	340	356			6	7
Detroit	36	41	.468	32	45	.416	33	26	382	400	29	32	362	404			5	7
Cleveland	29	48	.377	33	44	.429	10	15	366	443	24	37	308	387	12	4/28	4	11
Boston	26	47	.356	31	49	.388	10	15	283	363	28	34	306	407	1	4/10	6	7

1929 National League (4/16 - 10/6)

Team	W	L	PCT	W	L	PCT	HR	OHR	R	OR	HR	OHR	R	OR	DIF	LDF	WS	LS
Chicago	52	25	.675	46	29	.613	76	41	490	374	63	36	492	384	102	9/18	9	4
Pittsburgh	45	31	.592	43	34	.558	28	37	471	382	32	58	433	398	40	7/23	8	4
New York	39	37	.513	45	30	.600	79	59	418	374	57	43	479	335	7	4/25	6	5
St. Louis	43	32	.573	35	42	.455	48	50	414	386	52	51	417	420	19	6/18	7	11
Philadelphia	39	37	.513	32	45	.416	86	74	503	580	67	49	394	452			8	9
Brooklyn	42	35	.545	28	48	.368	53	48	371	413	46	44	384	475			5	9
Cincinnati	38	39	.494	28	49	.364	7	18	356	356	27	43	330	404	1	4/17	5	6
Boston	34	43	.442	22	55	.286	11	39	318	403	22	64	339	473	18	5/7	5	11

1929 American League (4/16 - 10/6)

Team	W	L	PCT	W	L	PCT	HR	OHR	R	OR	HR	OHR	R	OR	DIF	LDF	WS	LS
Philadelphia	57	16	.781	47	30	.610	72	47	484	302	50	26	417	313	159	9/14	11	4
New York	49	28	.636	39	38	.506	69	55	463	362	73	28	436	413	10	5/13	8	5
Cleveland	44	32	.579	37	39	.487	27	21	359	363	35	35	358	373	3	4/24	6	5
St. Louis	41	36	.532	38	37	.507	22	58	370	341	24	42	363	372	11	5/4	7	5
Washington	37	40	.481	34	41	.453	10	17	376	390	38	31	354	386			5	6
Detroit	38	39	.494	32	45	.416	57	33	476	453	53	40	450	475			6	7
Chicago	35	41	.461	24	52	.316	19	41	306	366	18	42	321	426			5	6
Boston	32	45	.416	26	51	.338	11	36	328	399	17	42	277	404			4	8

1930 National League (4/15 - 9/28)

Team	W	L	PCT	W	L	PCT	HR	OHR	R	OR	HR	OHR	R	OR	DIF	LDF	WS	LS
St. Louis	53	24	.688	39	38	.506	52	50	541	383	52	37	463	401	22	9/26	9	7
Chicago	51	26	.662	39	38	.506	93	62	538	454	78	49	460	416	40	9/12	9	4
New York	47	31	.603	40	36	.526	91	63	468	395	52	54	491	419	28	5/17	9	5
Brooklyn	49	27	.645	37	41	.474	73	66	438	336	49	49	433	402	76	9/15	11	7
Pittsburgh	42	35	.545	38	39	.494	26	51	433	454	60	77	458	474	6	5/3	7	5
Boston	39	38	.506	31	46	.403	29	51	329	401	37	66	364	434			4	7
Cincinnati	37	40	.481	22	55	.286	20	21	300	368	54	54	365	489			7	13
Philadelphia	35	42	.455	17	60	.221	72	72	543	644	54	70	401	555	4	4/18	3	11

1930 American League (4/14 - 9/28)

Team	W	L	PCT	W	L	PCT	HR	OHR	R	OR	HR	OHR	R	OR	DIF	LDF	WS	LS
Philadelphia	58	18	.763	44	34	.564	76	49	485	329	49	35	466	422	134	9/18	10	5
Washington	56	21	.727	38	39	.494	17	15	474	300	40	37	418	389	31	7/12	10	5
New York	47	29	.618	39	39	.500	69	54	471	390	83	39	591	508			6	7
Cleveland	44	33	.571	37	40	.481	34	46	494	469	38	39	396	446	6	6/14	7	7
Detroit	45	33	.577	30	46	.395	45	48	441	419	37	38	342	414	3	4/17	6	7
St. Louis	38	40	.487	26	50	.342	35	72	432	475	40	52	319	411			6	7
Chicago	34	44	.436	28	48	.368	25	42	393	457	38	32	336	427	2	4/18	4	6
Boston	30	46	.395	22	56	.282	15	31	287	354	32	44	325	460	1	4/14	5	14

1931 National League (4/14 - 9/27)

Team	W	L	PCT	W	L	PCT	HR	OHR	R	OR	HR	OHR	R	OR	DIF	LDF	WS	LS
St. Louis	54	24	.692	47	29	.618	31	29	439	320	29	36	376	294	164	9/16	8	4
New York	50	27	.649	37	38	.493	80	47	379	274	21	24	389	325	5	5/29	8	4
Chicago	50	27	.649	34	43	.442	40	22	414	311	44	32	414	399	5	4/30	8	8
Brooklyn	46	29	.613	33	44	.429	46	22	363	317	25	34	318	356			6	5
Pittsburgh	44	33	.571	31	46	.403	25	16	343	327	16	39	293	364			8	6
Philadelphia	40	36	.526	26	52	.333	53	33	391	423	28	42	293	405			5	10
Boston	36	41	.468	28	49	.364	16	24	278	318	18	42	255	362	7	4/27	4	9
Cincinnati	38	39	.494	20	57	.260	6	3	312	328	15	48	280	414			6	7

Team	Home Games W	L	PCT	Road Games W	L	PCT	Home Games HR	OHR	R	OR	Road Games HR	OHR	R	OR	DIF	LDF	WS	LS

1931 American League (4/14 - 9/27)

Team	W	L	PCT	W	L	PCT	HR	OHR	R	OR	HR	OHR	R	OR	DIF	LDF	WS	LS
Philadelphia	60	15	.800	47	30	.610	61	37	446	289	57	36	412	337	140	9/15	17	4
New York	51	25	.671	43	34	.558	84	39	545	337	71	28	522	423	14	5/11	10	4
Washington	55	22	.714	37	40	.481	13	24	453	308	36	49	390	383	4	4/21	12	4
Cleveland	45	31	.592	33	45	.423	38	32	503	405	33	32	382	428	18	5/8	10	12
St. Louis	39	38	.506	24	53	.312	42	48	407	425	34	36	315	445	3	4/18	8	9
Boston	39	40	.494	23	50	.315	11	29	332	362	26	25	293	438			5	8
Detroit	36	41	.468	25	52	.325	19	43	349	432	24	36	302	404			4	8
Chicago	31	45	.408	25	52	.325	11	45	341	421	16	37	363	518			5	10

1932 National League (4/12 - 9/25)

Team	W	L	PCT	W	L	PCT	HR	OHR	R	OR	HR	OHR	R	OR	DIF	LDF	WS	LS
Chicago	53	24	.688	37	40	.481	32	33	390	303	37	35	330	330	102	9/20	14	4
Pittsburgh	45	31	.592	41	37	.526	22	25	352	338	26	61	349	373	44	8/10	11	10
Brooklyn	44	34	.564	37	39	.487	59	31	378	353	51	41	374	394	1		6	5
Philadelphia	45	32	.584	33	44	.429	86	71	507	429	36	36	337	367	7	4/19	5	6
Boston	44	33	.571	33	44	.429	27	20	299	285	36	41	350	370	22	6/10	6	8
New York	37	40	.481	35	42	.455	78	71	362	359	38	41	393	347			6	7
St. Louis	42	35	.545	30	47	.390	36	38	354	357	40	38	330	360	2	4/13	6	8
Cincinnati	33	44	.429	27	50	.351	11	11	270	344	36	58	305	371	1	4/12	5	10

1932 American League (4/11 - 9/25)

Team	W	L	PCT	W	L	PCT	HR	OHR	R	OR	HR	OHR	R	OR	DIF	LDF	WS	LS
New York	62	15	.805	45	32	.584	81	44	482	300	79	49	520	424	141	9/13	9	3
Philadelphia	51	26	.662	43	34	.558	109	80	572	406	63	32	409	346	1	4/17	7	6
Washington	51	26	.662	42	35	.545	21	26	431	325	40	47	409	391	23	5/15	9	4
Cleveland	43	33	.566	44	32	.579	36	33	460	401	42	37	385	346	1	4/13	9	6
Detroit	42	34	.553	34	41	.453	29	50	423	399	51	39	376	388	9	4/26	6	4
St. Louis	33	42	.440	30	49	.380	47	56	385	428	20	47	351	470			5	11
Chicago	28	49	.364	21	53	.284	10	36	300	390	26	52	367	507	3	4/16	4	10
Boston	27	50	.351	16	61	.208	18	31	295	439	35	48	271	476			3	11

1933 National League (4/12 - 10/1)

Team	W	L	PCT	W	L	PCT	HR	OHR	R	OR	HR	OHR	R	OR	DIF	LDF	WS	LS
New York	48	27	.640	43	34	.558	55	44	298	241	27	17	338	274	126	9/19	8	7
Pittsburgh	50	27	.649	37	40	.481	12	13	332	272	27	41	335	347	44	5/31	8	7
Chicago	55	24	.696	31	44	.413	40	32	334	239	32	19	312	297	1	4/12	8	6
Boston	45	31	.592	38	40	.487	27	26	265	230	27	28	287	301			8	7
St. Louis	46	31	.597	36	40	.474	18	25	347	315	39	30	340	294	4	6/9	7	4
Brooklyn	36	41	.468	29	47	.382	33	29	306	352	29	22	311	343	2	4/14	5	6
Philadelphia	32	40	.444	28	52	.350	45	46	355	437	15	41	252	323			7	6
Cincinnati	37	42	.468	21	52	.288	5	10	264	321	29	37	232	322			5	10

1933 American League (4/12 - 10/1)

Team	W	L	PCT	W	L	PCT	HR	OHR	R	OR	HR	OHR	R	OR	DIF	LDF	WS	LS
Washington	46	30	.605	53	23	.697	14	16	358	338	46	48	492	327	102	9/21	13	4
New York	51	23	.689	40	36	.526	79	26	421	324	65	40	506	444	76	7/23	9	4
Philadelphia	46	29	.613	33	43	.434	82	50	414	387	57	27	461	466			7	6
Cleveland	45	32	.584	30	44	.405	22	24	353	341	28	36	301	328	9	5/15	7	6
Detroit	43	35	.551	32	44	.421	27	36	394	382	30	48	328	351			6	8
Chicago	35	41	.461	32	42	.432	20	42	355	426	23	43	328	388	3	4/14	6	9
Boston	32	40	.444	31	46	.403	23	35	341	377	27	40	359	381			6	9
St. Louis	30	46	.395	25	50	.333	43	68	389	480	21	28	280	340			3	7

1934 National League (4/17 - 9/30)

Team	W	L	PCT	W	L	PCT	HR	OHR	R	OR	HR	OHR	R	OR	DIF	LDF	WS	LS
St. Louis	48	29	.623	47	29	.618	56	43	451	363	48	34	348	293	13	9/30	7	5
New York	49	26	.653	44	34	.564	75	43	363	254	51	32	397	329	127	9/28	5	5
Chicago	47	30	.610	39	35	.527	53	44	347	301	48	36	358	338	25	5/21	8	5
Boston	40	35	.533	38	38	.500	36	27	280	280	47	51	403	434			7	6
Pittsburgh	45	32	.584	29	44	.397	22	38	421	369	30	40	314	344	10	5/27	7	9
Brooklyn	43	33	.566	28	48	.368	40	38	390	355	39	43	358	440	1	4/17	6	8
Philadelphia	35	36	.493	21	57	.269	28	72	384	400	28	54	291	394			5	7
Cincinnati	30	47	.390	22	52	.297	17	24	331	406	38	37	259	395			5	8

1934 American League (4/17 - 9/30)

Team	W	L	PCT	W	L	PCT	HR	OHR	R	OR	HR	OHR	R	OR	DIF	LDF	WS	LS
Detroit	54	26	.675	47	27	.635	28	32	479	345	46	54	479	363	100	9/24	14	4
New York	53	24	.688	41	36	.532	75	34	416	275	60	37	426	394	61	7/31	8	4
Cleveland	47	31	.603	38	38	.500	45	34	435	362	55	36	379	401	9	6/2	5	4
Boston	42	35	.545	34	41	.453	23	24	447	405	28	46	373	370			5	4
Philadelphia	34	40	.459	34	42	.447	81	48	371	410	63	36	393	428	1	4/17	7	6
St. Louis	36	39	.480	31	46	.403	35	60	356	405	27	34	318	395			7	6
Washington	34	40	.459	32	46	.410	14	26	368	397	37	48	361	409	2	4/18	6	5
Chicago	29	46	.387	24	53	.312	47	82	370	464	24	57	334	482			4	10

1935 National League (4/16 - 9/29)

Team	W	L	PCT	W	L	PCT	HR	OHR	R	OR	HR	OHR	R	OR	DIF	LDF	WS	LS
Chicago	56	21	.727	44	33	.571	43	40	426	264	45	45	421	333	18	9/27	21	4
St. Louis	53	24	.688	43	34	.558	39	27	441	298	47	41	388	327	20	9/13	14	5
New York	50	27	.649	41	35	.539	84	66	386	302	39	40	384	373	130	8/24	7	6
Pittsburgh	46	31	.597	40	36	.526	32	25	398	340	34	38	345	307	1	4/16	10	5
Brooklyn	38	38	.500	32	45	.416	32	43	349	346	27	45	362	421	10	4/26	7	7
Cincinnati	41	35	.539	27	50	.351	18	18	331	320	55	47	315	452	4	4/22	7	7
Philadelphia	35	43	.449	29	46	.387	52	68	416	499	40	38	269	372			3	9
Boston	25	50	.333	13	65	.167	34	41	309	381	41	40	266	471	3	4/18	4	15

	Team	Home Games			Road Games			Home Games				Road Games				DIF	LDF	WS	LS
		W	L	PCT	W	L	PCT	HR	OHR	R	OR	HR	OHR	R	OR				
1935 American League (4/16 - 9/29)	Detroit	53	25	.679	40	33	.548	45	38	467	304	61	40	452	361	66	9/21	10	6
	New York	41	33	.554	48	27	.640	60	51	341	294	44	40	477	338	57	7/25	7	4
	Cleveland	48	29	.623	34	42	.447	53	30	391	340	40	38	385	399	18	5/10	8	8
	Boston	41	37	.526	37	38	.493	26	29	393	404	43	38	325	328	6	4/24	4	4
	Chicago	42	34	.553	32	44	.421	50	61	418	396	24	44	320	354	23	5/29	7	7
	Washington	37	39	.487	30	47	.390	5	28	388	414	27	61	435	489	2	4/18	5	8
	St. Louis	31	44	.413	34	43	.442	36	49	374	513	37	43	344	417			5	10
	Philadelphia	30	42	.417	28	49	.364	63	39	369	414	49	34	341	455			5	13
1936 National League (4/14 - 9/27)	New York	52	26	.667	40	36	.526	68	54	378	296	29	21	364	325	55	9/24	15	6
	Chicago	50	27	.649	37	40	.481	34	41	404	290	42	35	351	313	31	8/11	15	6
	St. Louis	43	33	.566	44	34	.564	38	43	363	386	50	46	432	408	85	8/24	6	6
	Pittsburgh	46	30	.605	38	40	.487	23	25	375	342	37	49	429	376	2	4/15	7	5
	Cincinnati	42	34	.553	32	46	.410	24	21	358	350	58	30	364	410			7	9
	Boston	35	43	.449	36	40	.474	26	23	292	339	41	46	339	376			5	5
	Brooklyn	37	40	.481	30	47	.390	15	46	360	397	18	39	302	355			3	9
	Philadelphia	30	48	.385	24	52	.316	69	56	408	499	34	31	318	375	1	4/14	5	14
1936 American League (4/14 - 9/27)	New York	56	21	.727	46	30	.605	82	41	492	311	100	43	573	420	141	9/9	7	3
	Detroit	44	33	.571	39	38	.506	51	58	448	399	43	42	473	472	1	4/14	9	7
	Chicago	43	32	.573	38	38	.500	23	55	453	419	37	49	467	454	8	4/22	8	8
	Washington	42	35	.545	40	36	.526	16	27	433	380	46	46	456	419	2	4/15	8	8
	Cleveland	49	30	.620	31	44	.413	73	33	535	433	50	40	386	429	7	4/28	9	6
	Boston	47	29	.618	27	51	.346	38	31	437	360	48	47	338	404	17	5/9	5	7
	St. Louis	31	43	.419	26	52	.333	47	63	443	552	32	52	361	512			4	13
	Philadelphia	31	46	.403	22	54	.289	43	77	383	531	29	54	331	514			4	12
1937 National League (4/19 - 10/3)	New York	50	25	.667	45	32	.584	76	57	353	288	35	28	379	314	50	9/30	8	5
	Chicago	46	32	.590	47	29	.618	47	48	412	361	49	43	399	321	75	9/1	10	7
	Pittsburgh	46	32	.590	40	36	.526	13	28	360	332	34	43	344	314	42	6/4	8	5
	St. Louis	45	33	.577	36	40	.474	52	51	406	379	42	44	383	354	9	5/1	6	6
	Boston	43	33	.566	36	40	.474	26	15	252	224	37	45	327	332			7	11
	Brooklyn	36	39	.480	26	52	.333	20	30	336	389	17	38	280	383			4	14
	Philadelphia	29	45	.392	32	47	.405	65	69	379	481	38	47	345	388	4	4/22	6	7
	Cincinnati	28	51	.354	28	47	.373	13	14	268	347	60	24	344	360			4	14
1937 American League (4/19 - 10/3)	New York	57	20	.740	45	32	.584	94	41	520	298	80	51	459	373	143	9/23	9	4
	Detroit	49	28	.636	40	37	.519	91	58	521	448	59	44	414	393	10	5/8	6	5
	Chicago	47	30	.610	39	38	.506	39	62	397	365	28	53	383	365	2	6/9	10	7
	Cleveland	50	28	.641	33	43	.434	48	22	430	329	55	39	387	439	4	5/21	7	6
	Boston	44	29	.603	36	43	.456	53	43	420	368	47	49	401	407	6	5/7	12	5
	Washington	43	35	.551	30	45	.400	14	30	376	381	33	66	381	460			8	10
	Philadelphia	27	50	.351	27	47	.365	51	47	333	419	43	58	366	435	14	5/23	5	15
	St. Louis	25	51	.329	21	57	.269	39	74	385	513	32	69	330	510	1	4/21	3	12
1938 National League (4/19 - 10/2)	Chicago	44	33	.571	45	30	.600	24	41	349	326	41	30	364	272	10	10/1	10	6
	Pittsburgh	44	33	.571	42	31	.575	22	22	348	330	43	49	359	300	87	9/27	13	5
	New York	43	30	.589	40	37	.519	89	58	365	297	36	29	340	340	74	7/11	11	6
	Cincinnati	43	34	.558	39	34	.534	50	31	344	323	60	44	379	311			7	6
	Boston	45	30	.600	32	45	.416	12	19	233	241	42	47	328	377			7	7
	St. Louis	36	41	.468	35	39	.473	58	45	414	425	33	32	311	296			6	8
	Brooklyn	31	41	.431	38	39	.494	38	44	319	349	23	44	385	361	1	4/19	5	6
	Philadelphia	26	48	.351	19	57	.250	18	40	286	439	22	36	264	401			3	9
1938 American League (4/18 - 10/2)	New York	55	22	.714	44	31	.587	112	43	524	342	62	42	442	368	87	9/18	9	6
	Boston	52	23	.693	36	38	.486	67	52	481	356	31	50	421	395	8	5/18	8	6
	Cleveland	46	30	.605	40	36	.526	54	35	425	363	59	65	422	419	72	7/12	9	5
	Detroit	48	31	.608	36	39	.480	83	60	447	392	54	50	415	403			8	7
	Washington	44	33	.571	31	43	.419	33	27	412	413	52	65	402	460	10	5/13	7	5
	Chicago	33	39	.458	32	44	.421	24	41	326	364	43	60	383	388	3	4/22	4	10
	St. Louis	31	43	.419	24	54	.308	52	62	385	487	40	70	370	475	1	4/19	4	10
	Philadelphia	28	47	.373	25	52	.325	55	64	378	486	43	78	348	470			5	9
1939 National League (4/17 - 10/1)	Cincinnati	55	25	.688	42	32	.568	48	39	404	307	50	42	363	288	138	9/28	12	4
	St. Louis	51	27	.654	41	34	.547	63	42	431	317	35	34	348	316	19	5/25	10	5
	Brooklyn	51	27	.654	33	42	.440	41	49	385	329	37	44	323	316			6	6
	Chicago	44	34	.564	40	36	.526	44	35	379	343	47	39	345	335	6	4/27	6	4
	New York	41	33	.554	36	41	.468	84	58	360	315	32	28	343	370	2	4/19	9	9
	Pittsburgh	35	42	.455	33	43	.434	22	29	339	365	41	41	327	356	1	4/17	5	12
	Boston	37	35	.514	26	53	.329	13	14	254	272	43	49	318	387	9	5/5	6	7
	Philadelphia	29	44	.397	16	62	.205	19	49	288	384	30	57	265	472			4	11

		Home Games			Road Games			Home Games				Road Games							
	Team	W	L	PCT	W	L	PCT	HR	OHR	R	OR	HR	OHR	R	OR	DIF	LDF	WS	LS
1939 American League (4/17 - 10/1)	New York	52	25	.675	54	20	.730	84	48	382	261	82	37	585	295	159	9/16	12	6
	Boston	42	32	.568	47	30	.610	57	39	458	445	67	38	432	350	7	5/10	12	6
	Cleveland	44	33	.571	43	34	.558	30	33	363	347	55	42	434	353	2	4/22	7	5
	Chicago	50	27	.649	35	42	.455	38	51	414	366	26	48	341	371			6	4
	Detroit	42	35	.545	39	38	.506	66	65	461	434	58	39	388	328	3	4/20	9	7
	Washington	37	39	.487	28	48	.368	11	19	326	337	33	56	376	460			8	6
	Philadelphia	28	48	.368	27	49	.355	45	83	354	523	53	65	357	499	1	4/20	4	8
	St. Louis	18	59	.234	25	52	.325	47	80	372	561	44	53	361	474	1	4/22	2	11
1940 National League (4/16 - 9/29)	Cincinnati	55	21	.724	45	32	.584	47	36	352	240	42	37	355	288	139	9/18	11	3
	Brooklyn	41	37	.526	47	28	.627	40	55	369	358	53	46	328	263	50	7/6	9	6
	St. Louis	41	36	.532	43	33	.566	69	47	368	364	50	36	379	335			9	6
	Pittsburgh	40	34	.541	38	42	.475	26	22	390	354	50	50	419	429	8	4/23	8	9
	Chicago	40	37	.519	35	42	.455	40	32	333	316	46	42	348	320			7	6
	New York	33	43	.434	39	37	.513	61	75	323	339	30	35	340	320			8	11
	Boston	35	40	.467	30	47	.390	25	30	328	352	34	53	295	393			6	9
	Philadelphia	24	55	.304	26	48	.351	33	50	232	403	42	42	262	347	7	4/22	3	9
1940 American League (4/16 - 9/29)	Detroit	50	29	.633	40	35	.533	82	64	512	389	52	38	376	328	49	9/27	6	6
	Cleveland	51	30	.630	38	35	.521	37	27	350	281	64	59	360	356	73	9/19	8	6
	New York	52	24	.684	36	42	.462	83	63	414	284	72	56	403	387			8	8
	Boston	45	34	.570	37	38	.493	73	64	468	421	72	60	404	404	57	6/19	6	8
	Chicago	41	36	.532	41	36	.532	36	65	357	363	37	46	378	309			8	5
	St. Louis	37	39	.487	30	48	.385	68	68	419	460	50	45	338	422	2	4/17	6	14
	Washington	36	41	.468	28	49	.364	19	28	316	368	33	65	349	443			5	7
	Philadelphia	29	42	.408	25	58	.301	44	62	336	409	61	73	367	523	1	4/16	3	9
1941 National League (4/15 - 9/28)	Brooklyn	52	25	.675	48	29	.623	55	40	421	282	46	41	379	299	85	9/25	9	6
	St. Louis	53	24	.688	44	32	.579	37	53	405	324	33	32	329	265	81	9/3	11	5
	Cincinnati	45	34	.570	43	32	.573	27	27	308	273	37	34	308	291			8	5
	Pittsburgh	45	32	.584	36	41	.468	20	28	346	336	36	38	344	307			7	5
	New York	38	39	.494	36	40	.474	68	69	360	358	27	21	307	348	12	4/26	5	6
	Chicago	38	39	.494	32	45	.416	37	20	311	306	62	40	355	364	2	4/16	4	5
	Boston	32	44	.421	30	48	.385	17	28	276	321	31	47	316	399			5	8
	Philadelphia	23	52	.307	20	59	.253	34	37	255	384	30	42	246	409	1	4/15	3	9
1941 American League (4/14 - 9/28)	New York	51	26	.662	50	27	.649	76	44	396	295	75	37	434	336	99	9/4	14	5
	Boston	47	30	.610	37	40	.481	70	51	461	371	54	37	404	379	9	4/23	8	5
	Chicago	38	39	.494	39	38	.506	17	40	288	297	30	49	350	352	2	6/1	9	5
	Cleveland	42	35	.545	33	44	.429	45	35	340	322	58	36	337	346	60	6/27	11	8
	Detroit	43	34	.558	32	45	.416	51	43	381	377	30	37	305	366			5	8
	St. Louis	40	37	.519	30	47	.390	49	63	407	408	42	57	358	415	2	4/17	4	6
	Washington	40	37	.519	30	47	.390	13	19	367	387	39	50	361	411			6	12
	Philadelphia	36	41	.468	28	49	.364	43	75	373	432	42	61	340	408	2	4/16	5	8
1942 National League (4/14 - 9/27)	St. Louis	60	17	.779	46	31	.597	31	24	419	229	29	25	336	253	16	9/27	8	4
	Brooklyn	57	22	.722	47	28	.627	30	35	381	250	32	38	361	260	148	9/12	8	5
	New York	47	31	.603	38	36	.514	80	67	376	296	29	27	299	304			6	5
	Cincinnati	38	39	.494	38	37	.507	30	23	264	276	36	24	263	269			6	6
	Pittsburgh	41	34	.547	25	47	.347	15	21	333	301	39	41	252	330	4	4/19	7	10
	Chicago	36	41	.468	32	45	.416	36	27	298	318	39	43	293	347	1	4/14	5	4
	Boston	33	36	.478	26	53	.329	36	34	250	271	32	48	265	374	6	4/19	5	12
	Philadelphia	23	51	.311	19	58	.247	18	31	182	340	26	30	212	366			3	13
1942 American League (4/14 - 9/27)	New York	58	19	.753	45	32	.584	62	39	394	226	46	32	407	281	157	9/14	11	5
	Boston	53	24	.688	40	35	.533	54	33	403	299	49	32	358	295	8	4/22	9	5
	St. Louis	40	37	.519	42	32	.568	55	37	376	350	43	26	354	287	5	4/18	8	9
	Cleveland	39	39	.500	36	40	.474	20	24	266	308	30	37	324	351	12	5/5	13	6
	Detroit	43	34	.558	30	47	.390	50	40	344	302	26	20	245	285			5	7
	Chicago	35	35	.500	31	47	.397	6	31	256	275	19	43	282	334			9	7
	Washington	35	42	.455	27	47	.365	13	11	339	409	27	39	314	408			5	5
	Philadelphia	25	51	.329	30	48	.385	16	42	249	415	17	47	300	386			5	9
1943 National League (4/21 - 10/3)	St. Louis	58	21	.734	47	28	.627	33	17	355	243	37	16	324	232	121	9/18	12	4
	Cincinnati	48	29	.623	39	38	.506	17	15	282	280	26	23	326	263	3	4/23	10	5
	Brooklyn	46	31	.597	35	41	.461	21	30	389	323	18	29	327	351	44	6/4	10	10
	Pittsburgh	47	30	.610	33	44	.429	20	15	364	296	22	29	305	309	1	4/21	5	5
	Chicago	36	38	.486	38	41	.481	24	19	292	300	28	34	340	300			6	12
	Boston	38	39	.494	30	46	.395	25	34	247	327	14	32	218	285			7	6
	Philadelphia	33	43	.434	31	47	.397	29	18	269	314	37	41	302	362			7	8
	New York	34	43	.442	21	55	.276	63	52	291	326	18	28	267	387			4	7

	Team	Home Games			Road Games			Home Games				Road Games				DIF	LDF	WS	LS
		W	L	PCT	W	L	PCT	HR	OHR	R	OR	HR	OHR	R	OR				
1943 American League (4/20 - 10/3)	New York	54	23	.701	44	33	.571	60	33	321	241	40	27	348	301	158	9/25	9	5
	Washington	44	32	.579	40	37	.519	9	14	345	307	38	34	321	288	5	5/29	10	5
	Cleveland	44	33	.571	38	38	.500	16	21	269	247	39	31	331	330	7	5/28	8	4
	Chicago	40	36	.526	42	36	.538	20	25	264	311	13	29	309	283			7	6
	Detroit	45	32	.584	33	44	.429	45	26	345	284	32	25	287	276			5	5
	St. Louis	44	33	.571	28	47	.373	49	51	319	290	29	23	277	314	3	4/23	7	8
	Boston	39	36	.520	29	48	.377	29	25	293	312	28	36	270	295	1	4/22	4	8
	Philadelphia	27	51	.346	22	54	.289	14	36	261	387	12	37	236	330			4	20
1944 National League (4/18 - 10/1)	St. Louis	54	22	.711	51	27	.654	39	14	360	230	61	41	412	260	163	9/21	9	5
	Pittsburgh	49	28	.636	41	35	.539	23	31	399	357	47	34	345	305			11	4
	Cincinnati	45	33	.577	44	32	.579	14	23	253	252	37	37	320	285	2	5/6	6	4
	Chicago	35	42	.455	40	37	.519	33	40	346	342	38	35	356	327	1	4/18	11	13
	New York	39	36	.520	28	51	.354	75	86	372	382	18	30	310	391	11	4/28	7	13
	Boston	38	40	.487	27	49	.355	51	44	293	307	28	36	300	367			5	8
	Brooklyn	37	39	.487	26	52	.333	27	34	372	413	29	41	318	419			5	16
	Philadelphia	29	49	.372	32	43	.427	20	21	271	346	35	28	268	312	1	4/18	6	12
1944 American League (4/18 - 10/1)	St. Louis	54	23	.701	35	42	.455	45	24	368	272	27	34	316	315	128	10/1	10	4
	Detroit	43	34	.558	45	32	.584	38	21	325	318	22	18	333	263	14	9/30	9	5
	New York	47	31	.603	36	40	.474	58	45	388	307	38	37	286	310	32	9/15	6	7
	Boston	47	30	.610	30	47	.390	48	34	389	311	21	32	350	365			9	10
	Cleveland	39	38	.506	33	44	.429	27	16	345	328	43	24	298	349			4	6
	Philadelphia	39	37	.513	33	45	.423	18	28	277	270	18	30	248	324	2	4/19	6	8
	Chicago	41	36	.532	30	47	.390	11	24	302	304	12	44	241	358	2	4/20	8	5
	Washington	40	37	.519	24	53	.312	9	13	286	268	24	35	306	396			3	11
1945 National League (4/17 - 9/30)	Chicago	49	26	.653	49	30	.620	24	17	330	253	33	40	405	279	88	9/29	11	6
	St. Louis	48	29	.623	47	30	.610	28	29	368	286	36	41	388	297			7	4
	Brooklyn	48	30	.615	39	37	.513	29	34	387	347	28	40	408	377	22	7/7	11	6
	Pittsburgh	45	34	.570	37	38	.493	31	25	407	352	41	36	346	334	3	6/16	9	5
	New York	47	30	.610	31	44	.413	83	47	366	325	31	38	302	375	58	6/16	8	5
	Boston	36	38	.486	31	47	.397	68	63	411	395	33	36	310	333			9	10
	Cincinnati	36	41	.468	25	52	.325	25	23	267	307	31	47	269	387	2	4/18	9	13
	Philadelphia	22	55	.286	24	53	.312	23	28	261	450	33	33	287	415			5	9
1945 American League (4/17 - 9/30)	Detroit	50	26	.658	38	39	.494	43	28	333	285	34	20	300	280	113	9/30	6	4
	Washington	46	31	.597	41	36	.532	1	6	278	255	26	36	344	307	1	4/17	7	4
	St. Louis	47	27	.635	34	43	.442	32	33	353	291	31	26	244	257	1	4/17	5	6
	New York	48	28	.632	33	43	.434	65	51	395	297	28	15	281	309	25	6/27	8	9
	Cleveland	44	33	.571	29	39	.426	27	15	292	273	38	24	265	275			7	5
	Chicago	44	29	.603	27	49	.355	8	34	305	277	14	29	291	356	37	5/24	5	6
	Boston	42	35	.545	29	48	.377	22	28	306	299	28	30	293	375			5	8
	Philadelphia	39	35	.527	13	63	.171	16	21	265	270	17	34	229	368			5	14
1946 National League (4/16 - 10/3)	St. Louis	49	29	.628	49	29	.628	39	36	370	288	42	27	342	257	70	10/3	7	4
	Brooklyn	56	22	.718	40	38	.513	20	22	374	273	35	36	327	297	122	9/30	8	6
	Chicago	44	33	.571	38	38	.500	24	30	291	260	32	28	335	321	5	4/20	7	5
	Boston	45	31	.592	36	41	.468	14	31	300	268	30	45	330	324	1	4/16	6	6
	Philadelphia	41	36	.532	28	49	.364	38	34	280	335	42	39	280	370			6	5
	Cincinnati	35	42	.455	32	45	.416	37	39	267	289	28	31	256	281			4	9
	Pittsburgh	37	40	.481	26	51	.338	24	23	303	342	36	27	249	326	1	4/16	6	6
	New York	38	39	.494	23	54	.299	76	75	340	336	45	39	272	349	2	4/17	5	7
1946 American League (4/16 - 9/29)	Boston	61	16	.792	43	34	.558	65	44	469	315	44	45	323	279	164	9/13	15	6
	Detroit	48	30	.615	44	32	.579	75	46	391	300	33	29	313	267	2	4/25	10	7
	New York	47	30	.610	40	37	.519	68	34	342	262	68	32	342	285	5		5	5
	Washington	38	38	.500	38	40	.487	16	25	253	343	44	56	355	363			6	9
	Chicago	40	38	.513	34	42	.447	17	46	272	290	20	34	290	305			5	9
	Cleveland	36	41	.468	32	45	.416	25	36	231	264	54	48	306	374	4	4/19	5	7
	St. Louis	35	41	.461	31	47	.397	46	29	313	344	38	44	308	366			4	5
	Philadelphia	31	46	.403	18	59	.234	21	38	297	351	19	45	232	329			4	10
1947 National League (4/15 - 9/28)	Brooklyn	52	25	.675	42	35	.545	37	57	409	343	46	47	365	325	113	9/22	13	5
	St. Louis	46	31	.597	43	34	.558	45	49	400	331	70	57	380	303			9	9
	Boston	50	27	.649	36	41	.468	29	39	332	289	56	54	369	333	18	7/5	5	3
	New York	45	31	.592	36	42	.462	131	75	417	380	90	47	413	381	18	6/18	5	8
	Cincinnati	42	35	.545	31	46	.403	48	47	318	330	47	55	363	425	1	4/15	4	6
	Chicago	36	43	.456	33	42	.440	29	51	280	384	42	55	287	338	13	6/14	5	9
	Philadelphia	38	38	.500	24	54	.308	24	43	309	323	36	55	280	364	3	4/17	4	7
	Pittsburgh	32	45	.416	30	47	.390	95	87	384	437	61	68	360	380	11	4/25	4	6

Team	Home Games W	L	PCT	Road Games W	L	PCT	Home Games HR	OHR	R	OR	Road Games HR	OHR	R	OR	DIF	LDF	WS	LS

1947 American League (4/15 - 9/28)

Team	W	L	PCT	W	L	PCT	HR	OHR	R	OR	HR	OHR	R	OR	DIF	LDF	WS	LS
New York	55	22	.714	42	35	.545	54	49	392	242	61	46	402	326	112	9/15	19	3
Detroit	46	31	.597	39	38	.506	62	47	370	345	41	32	344	297	39	6/14	6	10
Boston	49	30	.620	34	41	.453	61	39	421	355	42	45	299	314	6	6/19	8	6
Cleveland	38	39	.494	42	35	.545	52	51	314	279	60	43	373	309	1	4/24	5	6
Philadelphia	39	38	.506	39	38	.506	33	41	296	324	28	44	337	290	2	4/16	4	7
Chicago	32	43	.427	38	41	.481	20	31	244	322	33	45	309	339	19	5/9	6	5
Washington	36	41	.468	28	49	.364	10	20	244	326	32	43	252	349			5	11
St. Louis	29	48	.377	30	47	.390	52	57	286	401	38	46	278	343			6	8

1948 National League (4/19 - 10/3)

Team	W	L	PCT	W	L	PCT	HR	OHR	R	OR	HR	OHR	R	OR	DIF	LDF	WS	LS
Boston	45	31	.592	46	31	.597	32	40	349	297	63	53	390	287	109	9/26	8	4
St. Louis	44	33	.571	41	36	.532	47	43	359	327	58	60	383	319	26	6/6	6	6
Brooklyn	36	41	.468	48	29	.623	43	68	352	386	48	51	392	281	8	9/2	7	8
Pittsburgh	47	31	.603	36	44	.474	69	64	384	370	39	56	322	329	8	6/16	7	6
New York	37	40	.481	41	36	.532	89	82	366	374	75	40	414	330	23	6/14	7	7
Philadelphia	32	44	.421	34	44	.436	32	44	276	332	59	51	315	397	5	4/24	5	10
Cincinnati	32	45	.416	32	44	.421	68	52	312	398	36	52	276	354	1	4/19	5	8
Chicago	35	42	.455	29	48	.377	38	34	282	323	49	55	315	383			4	10

1948 American League (4/19 - 10/4)

Team	W	L	PCT	W	L	PCT	HR	OHR	R	OR	HR	OHR	R	OR	DIF	LDF	WS	LS
Cleveland	48	30	.615	49	28	.636	77	41	398	272	78	41	442	296	115	10/4	8	5
Boston	55	23	.705	41	36	.532	60	43	481	336	61	40	426	384	40	10/3	13	5
New York	50	27	.649	44	33	.571	70	54	413	315	69	40	444	318	2	9/24	9	4
Philadelphia	36	41	.468	48	29	.623	33	47	347	396	35	39	382	339	23	8/13	10	8
Detroit	39	38	.506	39	38	.506	39	61	327	355	39	31	373	371	3	4/22	7	5
St. Louis	34	42	.447	25	52	.325	29	64	363	451	34	39	308	398			4	6
Washington	29	48	.377	27	49	.355	11	24	312	419	20	57	266	377			5	18
Chicago	27	48	.360	24	53	.312	21	36	278	378	34	53	281	436			3	9

1949 National League (4/18 - 10/2)

Team	W	L	PCT	W	L	PCT	HR	OHR	R	OR	HR	OHR	R	OR	DIF	LDF	WS	LS
Brooklyn	48	29	.623	49	28	.636	86	73	431	335	66	59	448	316	71	10/2	8	4
St. Louis	51	26	.662	45	32	.584	48	33	427	325	54	54	339	291	64	9/28	9	4
Philadelphia	40	37	.519	41	36	.532	61	35	336	326	61	69	326	342	1	4/18	7	5
Boston	43	34	.558	32	45	.416	40	40	344	328	63	70	362	391	30	6/4	5	9
New York	43	34	.558	30	47	.390	94	78	404	331	53	54	332	362	23	6/6	7	6
Pittsburgh	36	41	.468	35	42	.455	77	75	341	397	49	67	340	363	2	4/27	8	8
Cincinnati	35	42	.455	27	50	.351	50	54	326	349	36	70	301	421	4	4/30	4	7
Chicago	33	44	.429	28	49	.364	53	38	285	365	44	66	308	408			3	8

1949 American League (4/18 - 10/2)

Team	W	L	PCT	W	L	PCT	HR	OHR	R	OR	HR	OHR	R	OR	DIF	LDF	WS	LS
New York	54	23	.701	43	34	.558	72	53	419	304	43	45	410	333	164	10/2	6	4
Boston	61	16	.792	35	42	.455	71	43	514	310	60	39	382	357	7	10/1	11	8
Cleveland	49	28	.636	40	37	.519	61	42	319	263	51	40	356	311			7	6
Detroit	50	27	.649	37	40	.481	57	60	402	350	31	42	349	305	2	4/20	10	6
Philadelphia	52	25	.675	29	48	.377	42	42	389	326	40	63	337	399			6	6
Chicago	32	45	.416	31	46	.403	15	52	327	353	28	56	321	384			5	6
St. Louis	36	41	.468	17	60	.221	69	56	394	426	48	57	273	487	1	4/19	6	11
Washington	26	51	.338	24	53	.312	20	14	254	426	61	65	330	442		4/18	9	11

1950 National League (4/18 - 10/1)

Team	W	L	PCT	W	L	PCT	HR	OHR	R	OR	HR	OHR	R	OR	DIF	LDF	WS	LS
Philadelphia	47	30	.610	44	33	.571	58	53	348	279	67	69	374	345	104	10/1	6	5
Brooklyn	48	30	.615	41	35	.539	110	96	458	386	84	67	389	338	41	6/29	10	6
New York	44	32	.579	42	36	.538	84	69	362	290	49	73	373	353			9	7
Boston	46	31	.597	37	40	.481	59	45	343	294	89	84	442	442	6	7/18	6	5
St. Louis	47	29	.618	31	46	.403	50	43	389	303	52	76	304	367	30	7/24	7	7
Cincinnati	38	38	.500	28	49	.364	52	81	355	373	47	64	299	361			5	10
Chicago	35	42	.455	29	47	.382	79	63	352	411	82	67	291	361	10	4/27	5	7
Pittsburgh	33	44	.429	24	52	.316	81	79	370	447	57	73	311	410			6	9

1950 American League (4/18 - 10/1)

Team	W	L	PCT	W	L	PCT	HR	OHR	R	OR	HR	OHR	R	OR	DIF	LDF	WS	LS
New York	53	24	.688	45	32	.584	78	51	440	333	81	67	474	358	50	9/29	9	4
Detroit	50	30	.625	45	29	.608	60	72	405	346	54	69	432	367	120	9/21	7	4
Boston	55	22	.714	39	38	.506	100	67	625	427	61	54	402	377	2	5/10	11	5
Cleveland	49	28	.636	43	34	.558	102	57	386	297	62	63	420	357			8	6
Washington	35	42	.455	32	45	.416	18	28	347	407	58	71	343	406	1	4/18	4	7
Chicago	35	42	.455	25	52	.325	52	55	316	352	41	52	309	397			6	7
St. Louis	27	47	.365	31	49	.388	52	69	368	484	54	60	316	432	4	4/21	8	9
Philadelphia	29	48	.377	23	54	.299	45	67	314	406	55	71	356	507			3	10

1951 National League (4/16 - 10/3)

Team	W	L	PCT	W	L	PCT	HR	OHR	R	OR	HR	OHR	R	OR	DIF	LDF	WS	LS
New York	50	28	.641	48	31	.608	115	89	399	308	64	59	382	333	7	10/3	16	11
Brooklyn	49	29	.628	48	31	.608	100	81	412	316	84	69	443	356	147	10/2	10	4
St. Louis	44	34	.564	37	39	.487	44	56	370	323	51	63	313	348	10	5/7	7	5
Boston	42	35	.545	34	43	.442	59	37	367	310	71	59	356	352	10	5/12	6	6
Philadelphia	38	39	.494	35	42	.455	43	50	312	305	65	60	336	339	2	4/26	5	8
Cincinnati	35	42	.455	33	44	.429	44	46	289	320	44	73	270	347			7	7
Pittsburgh	32	45	.416	32	45	.416	72	84	388	465	65	73	301	380	5	4/20	4	8
Chicago	32	45	.416	30	47	.390	45	59	304	364	58	66	310	386	3	4/19	3	8

	Home Games			Road Games			Home Games				Road Games				DIF	LDF	WS	LS
Team	W	L	PCT	W	L	PCT	HR	OHR	R	OR	HR	OHR	R	OR				
1951 American League (4/17 - 9/30)																		
New York	56	22	.718	42	34	.553	72	43	366	258	68	49	432	363	79	9/28	8	4
Cleveland	53	24	.688	40	37	.519	76	42	324	249	64	44	372	345	43	9/15	13	6
Boston	50	25	.667	37	42	.468	80	65	460	348	47	35	344	377	10	7/21	10	9
Chicago	39	38	.506	42	35	.545	28	47	334	310	58	62	380	334	43	7/11	14	5
Detroit	36	41	.468	37	40	.481	58	60	358	402	46	42	327	339			5	7
Philadelphia	38	41	.481	32	43	.427	54	59	406	407	48	50	330	338			5	10
Washington	32	44	.421	30	48	.385	13	35	319	362	41	75	353	402	12	5/3	5	11
St. Louis	24	53	.312	28	49	.364	41	66	327	486	45	65	284	396			3	9
1952 National League (4/15 - 9/28)																		
Brooklyn	45	33	.577	51	24	.680	76	78	389	324	77	43	386	279	152	9/23	9	5
New York	50	27	.649	42	35	.545	103	74	369	327	48	47	353	312	20	5/31	7	6
St. Louis	48	29	.623	40	37	.519	46	59	343	291	51	60	334	339	2	4/16	10	6
Philadelphia	47	29	.618	40	38	.513	42	43	318	269	51	52	339	283			7	5
Chicago	42	35	.545	35	42	.455	51	40	329	316	56	61	299	315	2	4/16	5	9
Cincinnati	38	39	.494	31	46	.403	43	43	318	319	61	68	297	340			4	6
Boston	31	45	.408	33	44	.429	48	44	257	314	62	62	312	337			5	10
Pittsburgh	23	54	.299	19	58	.247	45	72	261	414	47	61	254	379			2	10
1952 American League (4/15 - 9/28)																		
New York	49	28	.636	46	31	.597	64	48	345	264	65	46	382	293	110	9/26	7	5
Cleveland	49	28	.636	44	33	.571	72	43	333	260	76	51	430	346	37	8/22	9	6
Chicago	44	33	.571	37	40	.481	42	39	305	276	38	47	305	292			6	6
Philadelphia	45	32	.584	34	43	.442	55	60	382	403	34	53	282	320			6	7
Washington	42	35	.545	36	41	.468	13	18	299	292	37	60	299	316			6	5
Boston	50	27	.649	26	51	.338	68	49	406	309	45	58	262	349	19	6/13	5	7
St. Louis	42	35	.545	22	55	.286	47	52	321	346	35	59	283	387	7	4/25	4	8
Detroit	32	45	.416	18	59	.234	65	59	284	366	38	52	273	372			4	8
1953 National League (4/13 - 9/27)																		
Brooklyn	60	17	.779	45	32	.584	110	82	517	333	98	87	438	356	112	9/12	13	4
Milwaukee	45	31	.592	47	31	.603	51	44	332	260	105	63	406	329	38	6/27	8	8
Philadelphia	48	29	.623	35	42	.455	63	65	363	304	52	73	353	362	27	5/22	8	5
St. Louis	48	30	.615	35	41	.461	65	58	420	321	75	81	348	392	1	4/22	5	6
New York	38	39	.494	32	45	.416	109	81	395	345	67	65	373	402	1	4/14	8	7
Cincinnati	38	39	.494	30	47	.390	89	96	367	391	77	83	347	397			6	8
Chicago	43	34	.558	22	55	.286	74	69	351	417	63	82	282	418	2	4/15	10	8
Pittsburgh	26	51	.338	24	53	.312	53	88	338	460	46	80	284	427			5	9
1953 American League (4/14 - 9/27)																		
New York	50	27	.649	49	25	.662	64	39	347	255	75	55	454	292	158	9/14	18	9
Cleveland	53	24	.688	39	38	.506	90	46	379	272	70	46	391	355	8	5/10	7	6
Chicago	41	36	.532	48	29	.623	30	56	349	328	44	57	367	264			8	6
Boston	38	38	.500	46	31	.597	57	59	335	354	44	33	321	278	1	4/16	6	8
Washington	39	36	.520	37	40	.481	10	31	305	283	59	81	382	331			6	8
Detroit	30	47	.390	30	47	.390	55	97	369	462	53	57	326	461			5	13
Philadelphia	27	50	.351	32	45	.416	49	74	299	447	67	47	333	352	1	4/14	7	8
St. Louis	23	54	.299	31	46	.403	58	64	281	447	54	37	274	331	6	4/20	5	14
1954 National League (4/13 - 9/26)																		
New York	53	23	.697	44	34	.564	120	67	387	254	66	46	345	296	110	9/20	8	6
Brooklyn	45	32	.584	47	30	.610	101	92	380	393	85	72	398	347	26	6/14	10	5
Milwaukee	43	34	.558	46	31	.597	43	29	285	251	96	77	385	305	11	6/1	10	5
Philadelphia	39	39	.500	36	40	.474	47	60	315	305	55	73	344	309	19	5/18	6	8
Cincinnati	41	36	.532	33	44	.429	94	105	380	407	53	64	349	356	15	5/7	6	5
St. Louis	33	44	.429	39	38	.506	57	90	386	431	62	80	413	359	4	5/22	5	7
Chicago	40	37	.519	24	53	.312	86	59	366	385	73	72	334	381	3	4/17	7	11
Pittsburgh	31	46	.403	22	55	.286	22	42	277	422	54	86	280	423	1	4/13	5	10
1954 American League (4/13 - 9/26)																		
Cleveland	59	18	.766	52	25	.675	78	57	376	252	78	32	370	252	134	9/18	11	4
New York	54	23	.701	49	28	.636	68	42	388	274	65	44	417	289	4	4/23	13	3
Chicago	45	32	.584	49	28	.636	39	51	327	294	55	43	384	227	22	6/11	8	5
Boston	38	39	.494	31	46	.403	69	70	357	384	54	48	343	344			6	8
Detroit	35	42	.455	33	44	.429	44	80	285	336	46	58	299	328	17	5/13	4	5
Washington	37	41	.474	29	47	.382	27	27	320	335	54	52	312	345	4	4/23	6	6
Baltimore	32	45	.416	22	55	.286	19	23	235	313	33	55	248	355	2	4/16	5	14
Philadelphia	29	47	.382	22	56	.282	44	85	260	467	50	56	282	408	2	5/10	5	10
1955 National League (4/11 - 9/25)																		
Brooklyn	56	21	.727	42	34	.553	119	85	461	318	82	83	396	332	166	9/8	11	5
Milwaukee	46	31	.597	39	38	.506	75	51	342	297	107	87	401	371	2	4/13	7	5
New York	44	35	.557	36	39	.480	95	91	362	327	74	64	340	346			11	13
Philadelphia	46	31	.597	31	46	.403	76	78	371	309	56	83	304	357	3	4/15	7	7
Cincinnati	46	31	.597	29	48	.377	102	91	425	341	79	70	336	343			7	7
Chicago	43	33	.566	29	48	.377	80	62	348	322	84	91	278	391	5	4/15	6	9
St. Louis	41	36	.532	27	50	.351	84	92	358	362	59	93	296	395			5	7
Pittsburgh	36	39	.480	24	55	.304	34	48	298	337	57	94	262	430			6	11

1955 American League (4/11 - 9/25)

Team	Home Games			Road Games			Home Games				Road Games				DIF	LDF	WS	LS
	W	L	PCT	W	L	PCT	HR	OHR	R	OR	HR	OHR	R	OR				
New York	52	25	.675	44	33	.571	89	44	378	248	86	64	384	321	93	9/23	8	4
Cleveland	49	28	.636	44	33	.571	84	58	343	318	64	53	355	283	43	9/15	6	4
Chicago	49	28	.636	42	35	.545	54	47	357	262	62	64	368	295	27	9/3	7	6
Boston	47	31	.603	37	39	.487	84	79	470	395	53	49	285	257	9	4/21	7	7
Detroit	46	31	.597	33	44	.429	81	59	386	301	49	67	389	357	3	5/5	7	6
Kansas City	33	43	.434	30	48	.385	70	110	333	477	51	65	305	434	1	4/12	5	10
Baltimore	30	47	.390	27	50	.351	15	42	249	335	39	61	291	419			5	9
Washington	28	49	.364	25	52	.325	20	25	282	357	60	74	316	432	2	4/12	7	12

1956 National League (4/17 - 9/30)

Team	W	L	PCT	W	L	PCT	HR	OHR	R	OR	HR	OHR	R	OR	DIF	LDF	WS	LS
Brooklyn	52	25	.675	41	36	.532	102	89	369	300	77	82	351	301	17	9/30	8	5
Milwaukee	47	29	.618	45	33	.577	77	53	344	265	100	80	365	304	126	9/28	11	5
Cincinnati	51	26	.662	40	37	.519	128	75	426	346	93	66	349	312	16	7/12	6	4
St. Louis	43	34	.558	33	44	.429	58	73	358	328	66	82	320	370	4	5/2	6	7
Philadelphia	40	37	.519	31	46	.403	61	74	337	335	60	98	331	403	2	4/18	6	10
New York	37	40	.481	30	47	.390	94	86	269	306	51	58	271	344	2	4/18	5	8
Pittsburgh	35	43	.449	31	45	.408	49	45	301	328	61	97	287	325	9	6/17	4	8
Chicago	39	38	.506	21	56	.273	78	77	335	328	64	84	262	380			4	7

1956 American League (4/17 - 9/30)

Team	W	L	PCT	W	L	PCT	HR	OHR	R	OR	HR	OHR	R	OR	DIF	LDF	WS	LS
New York	49	28	.636	48	29	.623	88	48	412	303	102	66	445	328	157	9/18	11	6
Cleveland	46	31	.597	42	35	.545	71	61	340	287	82	55	372	294	2	5/15	9	6
Chicago	46	31	.597	39	38	.506	69	47	403	320	59	71	373	314	11	5/4	9	11
Boston	43	34	.558	41	36	.532	68	64	408	388	71	66	372	363	3	4/19	6	5
Detroit	37	40	.481	45	32	.584	75	77	359	357	75	63	430	342			7	10
Baltimore	41	36	.532	28	49	.364	35	39	275	315	56	60	296	390			6	5
Washington	32	45	.416	27	50	.351	63	95	354	481	49	76	298	443			4	11
Kansas City	22	55	.286	30	47	.390	62	113	305	449	50	74	314	382	3	4/19	3	6

1957 National League (4/16 - 9/29)

Team	W	L	PCT	W	L	PCT	HR	OHR	R	OR	HR	OHR	R	OR	DIF	LDF	WS	LS
Milwaukee	45	32	.584	50	27	.649	75	51	312	289	124	73	460	324	110	9/23	10	3
St. Louis	42	35	.545	45	32	.584	64	70	356	348	68	70	381	318	26	8/5	8	9
Brooklyn	43	34	.558	41	36	.532	84	88	383	348	63	56	307	243	9	6/8	5	4
Cincinnati	45	32	.584	35	42	.455	118	101	417	410	69	78	330	371	34	7/4	12	10
Philadelphia	38	39	.494	39	38	.506	60	60	299	322	57	79	324	334	2	7/16	5	5
New York	37	40	.481	32	45	.416	99	86	353	341	58	64	290	360			5	6
Chicago	31	46	.403	31	46	.403	81	68	301	353	66	76	327	369			6	9
Pittsburgh	36	41	.468	26	51	.338	20	53	273	321	72	105	313	375	2	4/18	5	8

1957 American League (4/15 - 9/29)

Team	W	L	PCT	W	L	PCT	HR	OHR	R	OR	HR	OHR	R	OR	DIF	LDF	WS	LS
New York	48	29	.623	50	27	.649	60	51	316	241	85	59	407	293	108	9/23	10	3
Chicago	45	32	.584	45	32	.584	40	59	347	263	66	65	360	303	68	6/29	9	5
Boston	44	33	.571	38	39	.494	72	67	408	360	81	49	313	308	2	4/17	6	5
Detroit	45	32	.584	33	44	.429	71	86	351	304	45	61	263	310			5	6
Baltimore	42	33	.560	34	43	.442	36	30	283	248	51	65	314	340	1	4/15	5	5
Cleveland	40	37	.519	36	40	.474	71	74	348	384	69	56	334	338			5	7
Kansas City	37	40	.481	22	54	.289	91	77	294	344	75	76	269	366	2	4/17	5	11
Washington	28	49	.364	27	50	.351	60	79	304	415	51	70	299	393			4	10

1958 National League (4/15 - 9/28)

Team	W	L	PCT	W	L	PCT	HR	OHR	R	OR	HR	OHR	R	OR	DIF	LDF	WS	LS
Milwaukee	48	29	.623	44	33	.571	72	48	291	207	95	77	384	334	119	9/21	7	5
Pittsburgh	49	28	.636	35	42	.455	41	40	323	260	93	83	339	347	3	5/4	7	7
San Francisco	44	33	.571	36	41	.468	85	88	363	354	85	78	364	344	34	7/29	6	6
Cincinnati	40	37	.519	36	41	.468	71	86	364	337	52	62	331	284			6	7
Chicago	35	42	.455	37	40	.481	101	72	350	381	81	70	359	344	17	5/7	5	7
St. Louis	39	38	.506	33	44	.429	62	88	329	381	49	70	290	323			7	7
Los Angeles	39	38	.506	32	45	.416	92	101	359	405	80	72	309	356			4	6
Philadelphia	35	42	.455	34	43	.442	59	77	318	397	65	71	346	365	3	4/17	6	7

1958 American League (4/14 - 9/28)

Team	W	L	PCT	W	L	PCT	HR	OHR	R	OR	HR	OHR	R	OR	DIF	LDF	WS	LS
New York	44	33	.571	48	29	.623	78	62	362	318	86	54	397	259	165	9/14	10	6
Chicago	47	30	.610	35	42	.455	47	68	318	282	54	84	316	333			7	5
Boston	49	28	.636	30	47	.390	73	65	384	350	82	56	313	341			6	8
Cleveland	42	34	.553	35	42	.455	72	59	324	293	89	64	370	342			7	5
Detroit	43	34	.558	34	43	.442	59	79	348	306	50	54	311	300	2	4/16	6	9
Baltimore	46	31	.597	28	48	.368	46	36	248	256	62	70	273	319	3	4/17	7	11
Kansas City	43	34	.558	30	47	.390	88	96	365	363	50	54	277	350	2	4/16	6	6
Washington	33	44	.429	28	49	.364	49	80	269	373	72	76	284	374	1	4/14	4	13

1959 National League (4/9 - 9/29)

Team	W	L	PCT	W	L	PCT	HR	OHR	R	OR	HR	OHR	R	OR	DIF	LDF	WS	LS
Los Angeles	46	32	.590	42	36	.538	82	90	363	333	66	67	342	337	15	9/29	7	5
Milwaukee	49	29	.628	37	41	.474	83	64	350	274	94	64	374	349	89	9/27	7	7
San Francisco	42	35	.545	41	36	.532	80	63	339	271	87	76	366	342	79	9/19	4	5
Pittsburgh	47	30	.610	31	46	.403	47	53	348	334	65	81	303	346			5	9
Chicago	38	39	.494	36	41	.468	87	76	336	329	76	76	337	359	1	4/11	5	7
Cincinnati	43	34	.558	31	46	.403	101	84	423	367	60	78	341	371	2	5/9	4	6
St. Louis	42	35	.545	29	48	.377	64	64	366	359	54	73	275	366			4	7
Philadelphia	37	40	.481	27	50	.351	55	66	316	354	58	84	283	371	4	4/13	5	9

	Team	Home Games			Road Games			Home Games				Road Games				DIF	LDF	WS	LS
		W	L	PCT	W	L	PCT	HR	OHR	R	OR	HR	OHR	R	OR				
1959 American League (4/9 - 9/27)	Chicago	47	30	.610	47	30	.610	**44**	61	313	**272**	53	68	356	**316**	87	9/22	8	5
	Cleveland	43	34	.558	46	31	.597	84	74	346	316	83	74	**399**	330	90	7/27	8	7
	New York	40	37	.519	39	38	.506	63	**45**	293	305	**90**	75	394	342	4	4/15	6	5
	Detroit	41	36	.532	35	42	.455	**95**	105	401	**411**	65	72	312	321			5	6
	Boston	43	34	.558	32	45	.416	62	66	**404**	356	63	69	322	340			5	7
	Baltimore	38	39	.494	36	41	.468	53	50	**260**	299	56	61	291	322	1	6/9	4	6
	Kansas City	37	40	.481	29	48	.377	58	80	362	386	59	68	319	374			11	13
	Washington	34	43	.442	29	48	.377	83	68	307	360	80	**55**	312	341	5	4/13	4	18
1960 National League (4/12 - 10/2)	Pittsburgh	52	25	**.675**	43	34	**.558**	51	36	362	287	69	69	372	306	146	9/25	9	4
	Milwaukee	51	26	.662	37	40	.481	**90**	56	342	270	80	74	**382**	388	3	7/24	7	4
	St. Louis	51	26	.662	35	42	.455	78	64	361	308	60	63	278	308			7	8
	Los Angeles	42	35	.545	40	37	.519	89	97	379	334	37	57	283	**259**	9	4/20	5	4
	San Francisco	45	32	.584	34	43	.442	46	34	296	256	84	73	375	375	30	5/29	7	6
	Cincinnati	37	40	.481	30	47	.390	75	68	314	347	65	66	326	345	2	4/13	9	6
	Chicago	33	44	.429	27	50	.351	52	78	331	390	67	74	303	386	2	4/15	4	9
	Philadelphia	31	46	.403	28	49	.364	54	74	300	373	45	59	246	318			6	7
1960 American League (4/18 - 10/2)	New York	55	22	**.714**	42	35	.545	**92**	52	350	**273**	101	71	**396**	354	99	9/25	15	4
	Baltimore	44	33	.571	45	32	**.584**	50	52	332	313	73	65	350	**293**	29	9/9	8	5
	Chicago	51	26	.662	36	41	.468	57	54	**379**	298	55	73	362	319	31	8/14	8	5
	Cleveland	39	38	.506	37	40	.481	62	84	315	351	65	77	352	342	10	6/15	5	5
	Washington	32	45	.416	41	36	.532	75	74	336	366	72	**56**	336	330	1	4/18	5	7
	Detroit	40	37	.519	31	46	.403	78	**85**	322	323	72	**56**	311	321	11	4/29	7	10
	Boston	36	41	.468	29	48	.377	65	69	347	**413**	59	58	311	362			7	10
	Kansas City	34	43	.442	24	53	.312	58	79	327	369	52	81	288	387			5	10
1961 National League (4/11 - 10/1)	Cincinnati	47	30	.610	46	31	**.597**	70	75	345	355	88	72	365	**298**	113	9/26	8	8
	Los Angeles	45	32	.584	44	33	.571	83	**109**	373	358	74	**58**	362	339	28	8/15	8	10
	San Francisco	45	32	.584	40	37	.519	97	77	371	316	86	75	**402**	339	37	5/31	6	6
	Milwaukee	45	32	.584	38	39	.494	84	72	324	280	104	81	388	376	1	4/28	10	8
	St. Louis	48	29	**.623**	32	45	.416	54	69	**413**	362	49	67	290	306	4	4/21	8	6
	Pittsburgh	38	39	.494	37	40	.481	49	54	338	338	79	67	356	337	4	5/2	4	5
	Chicago	40	37	.519	24	53	.312	**102**	81	372	391	74	84	317	409			6	8
	Philadelphia	22	55	.286	25	52	.325	**43**	77	**256**	408	60	78	328	388			4	23
1961 American League (4/10 - 10/1)	New York	65	16	**.802**	44	37	.543	112	59	411	**251**	128	78	416	361	83	9/20	13	4
	Detroit	50	31	.617	51	30	**.630**	90	95	389	324	90	75	**452**	347	77	7/24	8	8
	Baltimore	48	33	.593	47	34	.580	61	46	320	283	88	63	371	**305**			7	5
	Chicago	53	28	.654	33	48	.407	80	55	411	320	58	103	354	406	4	4/13	12	5
	Cleveland	40	41	.494	38	42	.475	74	98	342	380	76	80	395	372	14	6/16	10	7
	Boston	50	31	.617	26	55	.321	63	91	401	386	49	76	328	406			6	6
	Minnesota	36	44	.450	34	46	.425	92	89	380	423	75	74	327	355	11	4/27	6	13
	Los Angeles	46	36	.561	24	55	.304	**122**	126	**447**	421	67	**54**	297	363	4	4/14	6	9
	Kansas City	33	47	.413	28	53	.346	**33**	61	365	**434**	57	80	318	429	4	4/14	4	6
	Washington	33	46	.418	28	54	.341	34	53	**288**	366	85	78	330	410			5	14
1962 National League (4/9 - 10/3)	San Francisco	61	21	**.744**	42	41	.506	**109**	74	**479**	299	95	74	399	391	54	10/3	10	6
	Los Angeles	54	29	.651	48	34	**.585**	47	**39**	409	289	93	76	**433**	408	111	10/2	13	5
	Cincinnati	58	23	.716	40	41	.494	95	68	456	294	72	81	346	391			9	4
	Pittsburgh	51	30	.630	42	38	.525	48	56	358	315	60	62	348	311	19	4/29	10	6
	Milwaukee	49	32	.605	37	44	.457	93	74	374	307	88	77	356	358			7	6
	St. Louis	44	37	.543	40	41	.494	64	83	407	362	73	66	367	**302**	12	4/28	7	8
	Philadelphia	46	34	.575	35	46	.432	70	66	341	346	72	89	364	413	1	4/9	6	8
	Houston	32	48	.400	32	48	.400	**44**	41	**268**	340	61	72	324	377	3	4/12	6	9
	Chicago	32	49	.395	27	54	.333	71	94	333	456	55	65	299	371			5	10
	New York	22	58	.275	18	62	.225	93	**120**	335	**510**	46	72	282	438			3	17
1962 American League (4/9 - 9/30)	New York	50	30	**.625**	46	36	.561	92	67	369	306	**107**	79	**448**	374	130	9/25	9	6
	Minnesota	45	36	.556	46	35	**.568**	97	97	417	378	88	69	381	335	1	6/11	6	5
	Los Angeles	40	41	.494	46	35	**.568**	50	**50**	357	368	87	68	361	338	5	7/5	6	6
	Detroit	49	33	.598	36	43	.456	**117**	91	**448**	368	92	78	310	**324**			5	7
	Chicago	43	38	.531	42	39	.519	**36**	58	315	319	56	**65**	392	339	5	4/20	6	5
	Cleveland	43	38	.531	37	44	.457	103	89	348	350	77	85	334	395	47	7/7	6	9
	Baltimore	44	38	.537	33	47	.413	66	65	328	**299**	90	82	324	381			5	6
	Boston	39	40	.494	37	44	.457	72	76	369	377	74	83	338	379			5	8
	Kansas City	39	42	.481	33	48	.407	64	**118**	387	**423**	52	81	358	414	1	4/10	6	7
	Washington	27	53	.338	33	48	.407	65	79	**293**	364	67	72	306	352	6	4/14	5	13
1963 National League (4/8 - 9/29)	Los Angeles	53	28	**.654**	46	35	**.568**	42	43	296	**248**	68	68	344	302	98	9/24	8	5
	St. Louis	53	28	**.654**	40	41	.494	79	70	**429**	311	49	54	318	317	32	7/1	10	8
	San Francisco	50	31	.617	38	43	.469	**101**	64	363	289	96	62	**362**	352	47	6/24	9	7
	Philadelphia	45	36	.556	42	39	.519	61	60	340	282	65	53	302	296	6	4/15	8	5
	Cincinnati	46	35	.568	40	41	.494	65	46	344	300	57	71	304	294	1	4/8	7	4
	Milwaukee	45	36	.556	39	42	.481	68	81	341	307	71	68	336	296	2	4/18	7	8
	Chicago	43	38	.531	39	42	.481	63	70	298	302	64	49	272	**276**	1	6/6	6	6
	Pittsburgh	42	39	.519	32	49	.395	47	42	275	295	61	57	292	300	9	5/6	5	6
	Houston	44	37	.543	22	59	.272	**25**	34	**236**	268	37	61	228	372			6	10
	New York	34	47	.420	17	64	.210	61	**93**	276	**381**	35	69	225	393			5	15

	Team	Home Games			Road Games			Home Games				Road Games				DIF	LDF	WS	LS
		W	L	PCT	W	L	PCT	HR	OHR	R	OR	HR	OHR	R	OR				
1963 American League (4/8 – 9/29)	New York	58	22	.725	46	35	.568	88	55	367	246	100	60	347	301	120	9/13	7	4
	Chicago	49	33	.598	45	35	.563	63	46	362	272	51	54	321	272	19	6/14	7	4
	Minnesota	48	33	.593	43	37	.538	112	99	377	306	113	63	390	296			10	5
	Baltimore	48	33	.593	38	43	.469	72	56	311	268	74	81	333	353	28	6/8	9	5
	Cleveland	41	40	.506	38	43	.469	88	87	308	341	81	89	327	361	1	4/9	7	9
	Detroit	47	34	.580	32	49	.395	94	109	395	339	54	86	305	364	4	4/18	8	10
	Boston	44	36	.550	32	49	.395	95	73	383	346	76	79	283	358	5	5/19	6	9
	Kansas City	36	45	.444	37	44	.457	52	87	326	390	43	69	289	314	11	5/6	5	6
	Los Angeles	39	42	.481	31	49	.388	24	44	264	306	71	76	333	354	1	4/9	5	10
	Washington	31	49	.388	25	57	.305	63	82	286	406	75	94	292	406			7	10
1964 National League (4/13 – 10/4)	St. Louis	48	33	.593	45	36	.556	59	81	386	378	50	52	329	274	6	10/4	8	5
	Cincinnati	47	34	.580	45	36	.556	62	59	331	294	68	53	329	272	4	10/3	9	4
	Philadelphia	46	35	.568	46	35	.568	59	61	352	298	71	68	341	334	133	9/26	5	10
	San Francisco	44	37	.543	46	35	.568	86	63	314	299	79	55	342	288	36	7/15	5	6
	Milwaukee	45	36	.556	43	38	.531	89	78	405	356	70	82	398	388			8	7
	Los Angeles	41	40	.506	39	42	.481	26	38	259	259	53	50	355	313	1	4/14	4	7
	Pittsburgh	42	39	.519	38	43	.469	55	31	340	315	66	61	323	321		0/	5	6
	Chicago	40	41	.494	36	45	.444	85	87	337	397	60	57	312	327	1	4/14	4	5
	Houston	41	40	.506	25	56	.309	29	44	246	290	41	61	249	338	3	4/15	6	8
	New York	33	48	.407	20	61	.247	58	61	298	363	45	69	271	413			5	8
1964 American League (4/13 – 10/4)	New York	50	31	.617	49	32	.605	69	56	363	290	93	73	367	287	33	10/3	11	6
	Chicago	52	29	.642	46	35	.568	43	42	306	213	63	82	336	288	41	9/16	9	6
	Baltimore	49	32	.605	48	33	.593	79	64	351	296	83	65	328	271	87	9/16	7	4
	Detroit	46	35	.568	39	42	.481	85	89	340	320	72	75	359	358	3	4/16	7	6
	Los Angeles	45	36	.556	37	44	.457	32	31	230	226	70	69	314	325	2	4/14	11	5
	Cleveland	41	40	.506	38	43	.469	84	82	365	351	80	72	324	342	16	5/16	8	7
	Minnesota	40	41	.494	39	42	.481	115	88	386	336	106	93	351	342	3	4/16	6	8
	Boston	45	36	.556	27	54	.333	100	87	393	382	86	91	295	411	2	4/17	5	7
	Washington	31	50	.383	31	50	.383	71	95	294	380	54	77	284	353			4	8
	Kansas City	26	55	.321	31	50	.383	107	132	330	455	59	88	291	381			5	7
1965 National League (4/12 – 10/3)	Los Angeles	50	31	.617	47	34	.580	26	41	268	218	52	86	340	303	136	10/2	13	4
	San Francisco	51	30	.630	44	37	.543	81	81	365	327	78	56	317	266	21	9/27	14	4
	Pittsburgh	49	32	.605	41	40	.506	37	38	334	284	74	51	341	296	4	4/20	12	8
	Cincinnati	49	32	.605	40	41	.494	108	69	450	352	75	67	375	352	16	9/1	4	6
	Milwaukee	44	37	.543	42	39	.519	98	75	366	331	98	48	342	302	3	8/20	10	6
	Philadelphia	45	35	.563	40	41	.494	77	55	312	300	67	61	342	367	3	4/14	6	5
	St. Louis	42	39	.519	38	42	.475	68	103	379	361	41	63	328	313			7	5
	Chicago	40	41	.494	32	49	.395	79	94	330	380	55	60	305	343	4	4/17	4	8
	Houston	36	45	.444	29	52	.358	25	32	250	313	72	91	319	398			10	8
	New York	29	52	.358	21	60	.259	50	81	258	380	57	66	237	372			4	11
1965 American League (4/12 – 10/3)	Minnesota	51	30	.630	51	30	.630	67	89	379	308	83	77	395	292	138	9/26	9	4
	Chicago	48	33	.593	47	34	.580	45	51	288	241	80	71	359	314	29	6/28	10	6
	Baltimore	46	33	.582	48	35	.578	62	71	302	282	63	49	339	296			9	3
	Detroit	47	34	.580	42	39	.519	96	85	362	310	66	52	318	292	8	5/1	8	5
	Cleveland	52	30	.634	35	45	.438	90	58	342	287	66	71	321	326	9	7/4	10	6
	New York	40	43	.482	37	42	.468	77	63	320	306	72	63	291	298			5	7
	California	46	34	.575	29	53	.354	36	35	265	254	56	56	262	315			5	5
	Washington	36	45	.444	34	47	.420	62	86	302	366	74	74	289	355			4	5
	Boston	34	47	.420	28	53	.346	94	88	375	433	71	70	294	358	4	4/20	4	8
	Kansas City	33	48	.407	26	55	.321	47	68	301	365	63	93	284	390			4	8
1966 National League (4/12 – 10/2)	Los Angeles	53	28	.654	42	39	.519	43	36	286	220	65	48	320	270	29	10/2	8	4
	San Francisco	47	34	.580	46	34	.575	91	77	317	312	90	63	358	314	87	9/1	12	4
	Pittsburgh	46	35	.568	46	35	.568	48	48	384	317	110	77	375	324	69	9/10	6	4
	Philadelphia	48	33	.593	39	42	.481	52	65	354	319	65	72	342	321	3	4/15	7	5
	Atlanta	43	38	.531	42	39	.519	119	82	394	335	88	47	388	348			8	7
	St. Louis	43	38	.531	40	41	.494	48	64	274	288	60	66	297	289			7	8
	Cincinnati	46	33	.582	30	51	.370	91	93	417	372	58	60	275	330			8	11
	Houston	45	36	.556	27	54	.333	48	48	318	317	64	82	294	378			5	9
	New York	32	49	.395	34	46	.425	51	94	276	372	47	72	311	389			7	7
	Chicago	32	49	.395	27	54	.333	80	100	342	410	60	84	302	399			4	6
1966 American League (4/11 – 10/2)	Baltimore	48	31	.608	49	32	.605	85	65	375	296	90	62	380	305	125	9/22	10	4
	Minnesota	49	32	.605	40	41	.494	94	83	375	311	50	56	288	270	3	4/14	6	7
	Detroit	42	39	.519	46	35	.568	97	101	360	374	82	84	359	324	5	4/16	6	6
	Chicago	45	36	.556	38	43	.469	31	36	273	217	56	65	301	300	2	4/13	8	5
	Cleveland	41	40	.506	40	41	.494	82	65	283	300	73	64	291	286	56	6/12	10	6
	California	42	39	.519	38	43	.469	54	67	303	315	68	69	301	328			7	6
	Kansas City	42	39	.519	32	47	.405	18	27	284	292	52	79	280	356			8	5
	Washington	42	36	.538	29	52	.358	62	84	273	292	64	70	284	367			5	8
	Boston	40	41	.494	32	49	.395	80	97	374	397	65	67	281	334			6	6
	New York	35	46	.432	35	43	.449	74	63	302	280	88	61	309	332			6	7

Team	Home Games W	L	PCT	Road Games W	L	PCT	Home Games HR	OHR	R	OR	Road Games HR	OHR	R	OR	DIF	LDF	WS	LS
1967 National League (4/10 - 10/1)																		
St. Louis	49	32	.605	52	28	**.650**	53	54	326	301	62	43	**369**	256	121	9/18	8	4
San Francisco	51	31	**.622**	40	40	.500	65	59	333	271	75	54	319	280			7	6
Chicago	49	34	.590	38	40	.487	70	90	366	**332**	58	52	336	292	5	7/24	7	7
Cincinnati	49	32	.605	38	43	.469	57	66	343	287	52	**35**	261	276	57	6/17	5	4
Philadelphia	45	35	.563	37	45	.451	48	44	320	292	55	42	292	289			8	5
Pittsburgh	49	32	.605	32	49	.395	43	49	370	321	48	59	309	372	2	4/12	5	5
Atlanta	48	33	.593	29	52	.358	**91**	74	352	316	67	44	279	324			5	6
Los Angeles	42	39	.519	31	50	.383	36	35	241	230	46	58	278	365			5	8
Houston	46	35	.568	23	58	.284	31	32	337	315	62	88	289	427	2	4/12	7	10
New York	36	42	.462	25	59	.298	44	61	258	307	39	63	240	365			5	7
1967 American League (4/10 - 10/1)																		
Boston	49	32	.605	43	38	**.531**	90	88	408	355	68	54	314	**259**	18	10/1	10	5
Detroit	52	29	**.642**	39	42	.481	83	79	360	272	69	72	323	315	26	9/18	7	7
Minnesota	52	29	**.642**	39	42	.481	70	63	372	292	61	52	299	298	39	9/30	8	6
Chicago	49	33	.598	40	40	.500	38	38	**243**	222	51	49	288	269	89	9/6	10	5
California	53	30	.639	31	47	.397	56	59	288	276	58	56	279	311	3	4/24	7	7
Baltimore	35	42	.455	41	43	.488	64	49	283	275	**74**	67	**371**	317	11	4/28	7	6
Washington	40	40	.500	36	45	.444	57	54	277	332	58	59	273	305			8	6
Cleveland	36	45	.444	39	42	.481	76	69	274	316	55	51	285	297	1	4/20	4	6
New York	43	38	.531	29	52	.358	60	47	268	271	40	63	254	350	6	4/29	4	6
Kansas City	37	44	.457	25	55	.313	**19**	38	288	320	50	87	245	340	3	4/13	5	**9**
1968 National League (4/10 - 9/29)																		
St. Louis	47	34	**.580**	50	31	**.617**	31	35	267	218	42	47	**316**	254	160	9/15	9	5
San Francisco	42	39	.519	46	35	.568	60	32	299	242	48	54	300	287	11	5/31	5	3
Chicago	47	34	**.580**	37	44	.457	**83**	83	363	332	47	55	249	279			6	7
Cincinnati	40	41	.494	43	38	.531	55	66	**377**	**400**	51	48	313	273	1	4/10	7	7
Atlanta	41	40	.506	40	41	.494	42	43	241	241	38	44	273	308	1	6/1	6	5
Pittsburgh	40	41	.494	40	41	.494	33	30	289	268	47	43	294	264			9	10
Los Angeles	41	40	.506	35	46	.432	25	24	**212**	215	42	41	258	294			7	8
Philadelphia	38	43	.469	38	43	.469	52	46	274	297	48	45	269	318	1	4/10	7	9
New York	32	49	.395	41	40	.506	49	50	224	270	32	37	249	**229**			4	6
Houston	42	39	.519	30	51	.370	**22**	30	279	269	44	38	231	319	9	4/18	4	6
1968 American League (4/10 - 9/29)																		
Detroit	56	25	**.691**	47	34	**.580**	107	75	348	254	**78**	54	323	238	158	9/17	11	4
Baltimore	47	33	.588	44	38	.537	57	54	288	**248**	76	47	291	249	11	5/9	8	7
Cleveland	43	37	.538	43	38	.531	36	56	246	262	39	42	270	242	1	4/10	6	7
Boston	46	35	.568	40	41	.494	58	61	325	299	67	54	289	312	1	4/10	8	4
New York	39	42	.481	44	37	.543	56	50	268	268	53	49	268	263	3	4/12	10	6
Oakland	44	38	.537	38	42	.475	38	58	296	258	56	66	273	286			4	7
Minnesota	41	40	.506	38	43	.469	50	51	299	290	55	**41**	263	256	10	4/19	6	6
California	32	49	.395	35	46	.432	49	66	229	299	34	65	269	316			4	6
Chicago	36	45	.444	31	50	.383	29	47	**225**	273	42	50	238	254			4	10
Washington	34	47	.420	31	49	.388	53	53	257	**300**	71	65	267	365			4	9
1969 National League (4/8 - 10/2)																		
East																		
New York	52	30	.634	48	32	**.600**	56	59	312	270	53	60	320	271	23	**9/24**	11	5
Chicago	49	32	.605	43	38	.531	84	64	387	321	58	**54**	333	290	155	9/9	7	8
Pittsburgh	47	34	.580	41	40	.506	**41**	33	324	322	78	63	**401**	330	6	4/13	8	7
St. Louis	42	38	.525	45	37	.549	**41**	43	273	273	49	56	322	**267**			6	4
Philadelphia	30	51	.370	33	48	.407	75	64	317	378	62	70	328	367			9	9
Montreal	24	57	.296	28	53	.346	73	87	288	421	52	58	294	370	1	4/9	4	**20**
West																		
Atlanta	50	31	.617	43	38	.531	77	84	360	321	64	60	331	310	**107**	**9/30**	10	5
San Francisco	52	29	**.642**	38	43	.469	77	61	362	317	59	59	351	319	29	9/22	9	5
Cincinnati	50	31	.617	39	42	.481	**97**	74	**407**	373	74	75	391	395	22	9/11	9	5
Los Angeles	50	31	.617	35	46	.432	**41**	55	325	**258**	56	67	320	303	33	8/20	7	8
Houston	52	29	**.642**	29	52	.358	47	43	371	313	57	56	305	355			10	8
San Diego	28	53	.346	24	57	.296	47	47	**239**	358	52	66	229	388	3	4/10	6	11
1969 American League (4/7 - 10/2)																		
East																		
Baltimore	60	21	**.741**	49	32	**.605**	82	51	402	251	93	66	377	**266**	169	9/13	8	5
Detroit	46	35	.568	44	37	.543	104	72	361	305	78	**56**	340	296	3	4/10	7	4
Boston	46	35	.568	41	40	.506	105	78	392	391	92	77	351	345	6	4/15	8	7
Washington	47	34	.580	39	42	.481	77	62	353	290	71	73	341	354	1	4/11	6	6
New York	48	32	.600	32	49	.395	44	51	284	**245**	50	67	278	342	2	4/8	8	7
Cleveland	33	48	.407	29	51	.363	56	60	**276**	341	63	74	297	376			5	10
West																		
Minnesota	57	24	.704	40	41	.494	79	61	**414**	298	84	58	376	320	138	9/22	9	5
Oakland	49	32	.605	39	42	.481	73	70	330	315	75	93	**410**	363	30	7/4	7	6
California	43	38	.531	28	53	.346	49	65	277	305	39	61	251	347	2	4/12	6	10
Kansas City	36	45	.444	33	48	.407	**39**	63	301	362	59	66	285	326	12	4/24	4	6
Chicago	41	40	.506	27	54	.333	61	80	352	387	51	66	273	336	4	4/26	5	8
Seattle	34	47	.420	30	51	.370	74	**93**	329	**399**	51	79	310	400	3	4/12	5	10

Team	Home Games W	L	PCT	Road Games W	L	PCT	Home Games HR	OHR	R	OR	Road Games HR	OHR	R	OR	DIF	LDF	WS	LS
1970 National League (4/6 - 10/1)																		
East																		
Pittsburgh	50	32	.610	39	41	.488	43	**41**	356	315	87	65	373	349	**85**	9/27	7	7
Chicago	46	34	.575	38	44	.463	109	92	471	394	70	**51**	335	**285**	64	6/23	11	12
New York	44	38	.537	39	41	.488	63	75	374	**314**	57	60	321	316	25	9/10	7	5
St. Louis	34	47	.420	42	39	.519	51	44	377	**418**	62	58	367	329	14	9/10	7	5
Philadelphia	40	40	.500	33	48	.407	48	63	**293**	337	53	69	301	393	7	4/21	6	8
Montreal	39	41	.488	34	48	.415	77	91	363	385	59	71	324	422			5	11
West																		
Cincinnati	57	24	**.704**	45	36	.556	100	58	416	334	91	60	359	347	178	9/17	8	4
Los Angeles	39	42	.481	48	32	**.600**	35	82	310	316	52	82	**439**	368			7	5
San Francisco	48	33	.593	38	43	.469	84	77	413	386	81	79	418	440	1	4/11	5	4
Houston	44	37	.543	35	46	.432	51	64	350	351	78	67	394	412	1	4/7	7	8
Atlanta	42	39	.519	34	47	.420	92	119	395	398	68	66	341	374			11	7
San Diego	31	50	.383	32	49	.395	68	56	312	393	104	93	369	395	1	4/7	5	8
1970 American League (4/6 - 10/1)																		
East																		
Baltimore	59	22	**.728**	49	32	**.605**	88	58	386	**256**	91	81	**406**	318	169	9/17	11	3
New York	53	28	.654	40	41	.494	60	**40**	317	257	51	90	363	355			6	5
Boston	52	29	.642	35	46	.432	117	75	**455**	382	86	81	331	340			7	5
Detroit	42	39	.519	37	44	.457	86	86	348	379	62	67	318	352	2	4/8	7	5
Cleveland	43	38	.531	33	48	.407	133	103	386	370	50	**60**	263	**305**	10	4/25	8	7
Washington	40	41	.494	30	51	.370	72	61	303	330	66	78	323	359			7	14
West																		
Minnesota	51	30	.630	47	34	.580	66	53	366	285	87	77	378	320	171	9/22	7	9
Oakland	49	32	.605	40	41	.494	83	56	337	265	88	78	341	328	1	4/7	8	6
California	43	38	.531	43	38	.531	41	59	**287**	274	73	95	344	356	16	5/15	5	9
Kansas City	35	44	.443	30	53	.361	46	48	305	331	51	90	306	374			4	7
Milwaukee	38	42	.475	27	55	.329	68	72	313	362	58	74	300	389			5	9
Chicago	31	53	.369	25	53	.321	78	97	346	**469**	45	67	287	353			4	8
1971 National League (4/6 - 9/30)																		
East																		
Pittsburgh	52	28	**.650**	45	37	.549	66	49	**393**	279	**88**	59	**395**	320	124	9/22	11	4
St. Louis	45	36	.556	45	36	.556	38	49	376	358	57	55	363	341	16	6/8	7	7
Chicago	44	37	.543	39	42	.481	74	70	363	342	54	62	274	306	1	4/6	7	5
New York	44	37	.543	39	42	.481	48	50	281	256	50	50	307	**294**	31	6/10	5	6
Montreal	36	44	.450	35	46	.432	50	68	304	366	38	65	318	363	10	5/1	8	6
Philadelphia	34	47	.420	33	48	.407	73	80	296	353	50	52	262	335			4	8
West																		
San Francisco	51	30	.630	39	42	.481	71	58	372	300	69	70	334	344	176	9/30	9	7
Los Angeles	42	39	.519	47	34	**.580**	43	56	324	286	52	54	339	301			8	6
Atlanta	43	39	.524	39	41	.488	96	90	366	**384**	57	62	277	315	7	4/11	6	5
Cincinnati	46	35	.568	33	48	.407	69	51	303	**251**	69	61	283	330			5	7
Houston	39	42	.481	40	41	.494	18	**27**	256	263	53	48	329	304	1	4/5	8	6
San Diego	33	48	.407	28	52	.350	42	43	**233**	296	54	50	253	314			4	8
1971 American League (4/5 - 9/30)																		
East																		
Baltimore	53	24	**.688**	48	33	.593	78	67	374	**254**	80	58	**368**	276	142	9/24	11	4
Detroit	54	27	.667	37	44	.457	90	70	352	289	**89**	56	349	356	3	4/8	7	3
Boston	47	33	.588	38	44	.463	88	75	**375**	338	73	61	316	329	39	6/4	7	7
New York	44	37	.543	38	43	.469	39	61	327	297	58	65	321	344			5	5
Washington	35	46	.432	28	50	.359	34	59	268	296	52	73	269	364	2	4/6	6	9
Cleveland	29	52	.358	31	50	.383	62	**99**	297	**400**	47	55	246	347			4	7
West																		
Oakland	46	35	.568	55	25	**.688**	84	74	325	300	76	57	366	**264**	164	9/15	7	4
Kansas City	44	37	.543	41	39	.513	23	**36**	296	277	57	48	307	289	1	4/6	6	8
Chicago	39	42	.481	40	41	.494	60	53	278	310	78	47	339	287	4	4/10	6	7
California	35	46	.432	41	40	.506	39	55	**233**	297	57	**46**	278	279	3	4/19	7	4
Minnesota	37	42	.468	37	44	.457	57	71	332	356	59	68	322	314	2	4/13	6	6
Milwaukee	34	48	.415	35	44	.443	46	64	282	319	58	66	252	290	4	4/15	3	8
1972 National League (4/15 - 10/4)																		
East																		
Pittsburgh	49	29	**.628**	47	30	.610	53	**34**	351	259	57	56	340	**253**	113	9/21	9	6
Chicago	46	31	.597	39	39	.500	83	63	**392**	305	50	49	293	262			7	8
New York	41	37	.526	42	36	.538	45	56	254	264	60	62	274	314	50	6/8	11	3
St. Louis	40	37	.519	35	44	.443	31	38	298	308	39	49	270	292			7	8
Montreal	35	43	.449	35	43	.449	50	56	252	324	41	47	261	285	14	5/1	5	8
Philadelphia	28	51	.354	31	46	.403	49	57	246	316	49	60	257	319	1	4/15	5	10
West																		
Cincinnati	42	34	.553	53	25	**.679**	58	59	300	266	66	70	**407**	291	115	9/22	9	4
Houston	41	36	.532	43	33	.566	58	56	367	355	**76**	58	341	281	31	6/24	9	6
Los Angeles	41	34	.547	44	36	.550	46	37	267	**221**	57	**46**	317	306	29	6/8	6	5
Atlanta	36	41	.468	34	43	.442	**86**	88	339	392	58	67	289	338			5	7
San Francisco	34	43	.442	35	43	.449	**86**	65	336	321	64	65	326	328	4	4/18	5	8
San Diego	26	54	.325	32	41	.438	41	64	**217**	315	61	57	271	350	2	4/17	5	10

	Home Games			Road Games			Home Games				Road Games				DIF	LDF	WS	LS
Team	W	L	PCT	W	L	PCT	HR	OHR	R	OR	HR	OHR	R	OR				
1972 American League (4/15 - 10/4)																		
East																		
Detroit	44	34	.564	42	36	.538	68	67	312	288	54	34	246	226	110	10/3	5	4
Boston	52	26	.667	33	44	.429	71	49	373	303	53	52	267	317	24	10/1	7	5
Baltimore	38	39	.494	42	35	.545	44	40	240	211	56	45	279	219	41	9/4	9	5
New York	46	31	.597	33	45	.423	53	37	270	219	50	50	287	308			6	5
Cleveland	43	34	.558	29	50	.367	59	79	263	261	32	44	209	258	15	5/27	6	8
Milwaukee	37	42	.468	28	49	.364	36	45	243	286	52	71	250	309	3	4/17	6	9
West																		
Oakland	48	29	.623	45	33	.577	68	52	287	210	66	44	317	247	132	9/28	8	4
Chicago	55	23	.705	32	44	.421	65	44	341	252	43	50	225	286	14	8/28	7	6
Minnesota	42	32	.568	35	45	.438	52	54	299	255	41	51	238	280	25	5/20	6	8
Kansas City	44	33	.571	32	45	.416	29	28	309	257	49	57	271	288	4	4/18	5	6
California	44	36	.550	31	44	.413	30	31	221	218	48	59	233	315	1	4/15	6	6
Texas	31	46	.403	23	54	.299	33	41	235	288	23	51	226	340			5	15
1973 National League (4/6 - 10/1)																		
East																		
New York	43	38	.531	39	41	.488	39	61	314	283	46	66	294	305	22	10/1	7	5
St. Louis	43	38	.531	38	43	.469	27	30	290	255	48	75	353	348	51	9/11	8	7
Pittsburgh	41	40	.506	39	42	.481	72	42	334	301	82	68	370	392	37	9/20	7	6
Montreal	43	38	.531	36	45	.444	63	70	364	353	62	58	304	349			7	7
Chicago	41	39	.513	36	45	.444	66	72	327	356	51	56	287	299	80	7/21	7	11
Philadelphia	38	43	.469	33	48	.407	78	80	358	381	56	51	284	336			5	7
West																		
Cincinnati	50	31	.617	49	32	.605	47	67	330	287	90	68	411	334	31	9/24	7	4
Los Angeles	50	31	.617	45	35	.563	63	62	338	271	47	67	337	294	79	9/3	7	9
San Francisco	47	34	.580	41	40	.506	85	79	395	363	76	66	344	339	66	6/16	7	5
Houston	41	40	.506	41	40	.506	58	53	315	322	76	58	366	350	9	5/25	9	4
Atlanta	40	40	.500	36	45	.444	118	87	460	437	88	57	339	337			6	7
San Diego	31	50	.383	29	52	.358	51	80	273	355	61	77	275	415	3	4/8	4	10
1973 American League (4/6 - 9/30)																		
East																		
Baltimore	50	31	.617	47	34	.580	63	60	408	284	56	64	346	277	77	9/22	14	5
Boston	48	33	.593	41	40	.506	83	83	390	339	64	75	348	308	12	7/9	8	5
Detroit	47	34	.580	38	43	.469	86	71	329	332	71	83	313	342	42	8/14	8	8
New York	50	31	.617	30	51	.370	74	42	359	263	57	67	282	347	46	7/31	8	8
Milwaukee	40	41	.494	34	47	.420	73	52	349	343	72	67	359	388	14	6/19	10	6
Cleveland	34	47	.420	37	44	.457	92	100	320	427	66	72	360	399	1	4/7	4	10
West																		
Oakland	50	31	.617	44	37	.543	70	70	313	253	77	73	445	362	81	9/23	9	5
Kansas City	48	33	.593	40	41	.494	54	61	422	404	60	53	333	348	29	8/15	7	5
Minnesota	37	44	.457	44	37	.543	56	60	357	386	64	55	381	306	10	7/2	5	7
California	43	38	.531	36	45	.444	41	49	316	294	52	55	313	363	3	6/27	5	5
Chicago	40	41	.494	37	44	.457	56	58	329	368	55	52	323	337	62	6/29	9	5
Texas	35	46	.432	22	59	.272	47	51	321	408	63	79	298	436			6	8
1974 National League (4/5 - 10/2)																		
East																		
Pittsburgh	52	29	.642	36	45	.444	47	32	380	303	67	61	371	354	28	10/2	8	6
St. Louis	44	37	.543	42	38	.525	45	46	356	329	38	51	321	314	83	9/30	6	7
Philadelphia	46	35	.568	34	47	.420	55	56	378	329	40	55	298	364	61	8/2	6	8
Montreal	42	38	.525	37	44	.457	50	49	356	329	36	50	306	328	22	5/16	8	7
New York	36	45	.444	35	46	.432	43	49	279	325	53	50	293	321			7	7
Chicago	32	49	.395	34	47	.420	67	72	344	424	43	50	325	402	2	4/10	6	8
West																		
Los Angeles	52	29	.642	50	31	.617	68	51	355	250	71	61	443	311	177	10/1	9	6
Cincinnati	50	31	.617	48	33	.593	74	62	389	295	61	64	387	336	2	4/6	7	4
Atlanta	46	35	.568	42	39	.519	65	44	337	290	55	53	324	273			6	4
Houston	46	35	.568	35	46	.432	58	35	330	293	52	49	323	339			6	10
San Francisco	37	44	.457	35	46	.432	50	61	340	398	43	55	294	325	9	4/13	4	6
San Diego	36	45	.444	24	57	.296	47	54	272	381	52	70	269	449			5	10
1974 American League (4/5 - 10/2)																		
East																		
Baltimore	46	35	.568	45	36	.556	48	46	281	293	68	55	378	319	25	10/1	10	5
New York	47	34	.580	42	39	.519	42	50	315	295	59	54	356	328	37	9/23	6	7
Boston	46	35	.568	38	43	.469	58	66	375	348	51	60	321	313	97	9/8	6	8
Cleveland	40	41	.494	37	44	.457	72	92	338	349	59	46	324	345	6	7/12	5	6
Milwaukee	40	41	.494	36	45	.444	58	69	342	329	62	57	305	331	23	6/8	5	6
Detroit	36	45	.444	36	45	.444	74	84	335	412	57	64	285	356	2	5/18	6	6
West																		
Oakland	49	32	.605	41	40	.506	69	43	345	265	63	47	344	286	142	9/27	6	4
Texas	42	38	.525	42	38	.525	43	57	321	340	56	69	369	358	17	5/8	5	6
Minnesota	48	33	.593	34	47	.420	60	56	365	317	51	59	308	352	3	4/23	5	4
Chicago	46	34	.575	34	46	.425	66	43	360	365	69	60	324	356	9	5/19	7	5
Kansas City	40	41	.494	37	44	.457	38	42	355	353	51	49	312	309			5	8
California	36	45	.444	32	49	.395	46	47	291	287	49	54	327	370	16	4/22	6	11

Team	Home Games			Road Games			Home Games				Road Games				DIF	LDF	WS	LS
	W	L	PCT	W	L	PCT	HR	OHR	R	OR	HR	OHR	R	OR				
1975 National League (4/7 - 9/28)																		
East																		
Pittsburgh	52	28	.650	40	41	.494	67	41	348	270	71	38	364	295	121	9/22	6	6
Philadelphia	51	30	.630	35	46	.432	72	47	401	326	53	64	334	368	1	8/18	7	6
New York	42	39	.519	40	41	.494	52	48	294	301	49	51	352	324	2	4/9	7	7
St. Louis	45	36	.556	37	44	.457	46	39	351	352	35	59	311	337			7	6
Chicago	42	39	.519	33	48	.407	54	71	392	427	41	59	320	400	51	6/5	7	5
Montreal	39	42	.481	36	45	.444	53	57	326	375	45	45	275	315	2	4/8	6	6
West																		
Cincinnati	64	17	.790	44	37	.543	70	52	457	275	54	60	383	311	122	9/7	10	6
Los Angeles	49	32	.605	39	42	.481	64	52	319	221	54	52	329	313	40	6/6	8	5
San Francisco	46	35	.568	34	46	.425	36	37	346	335	48	55	313	336			7	8
San Diego	38	43	.469	33	48	.407	33	38	279	338	45	61	273	345	13	4/26	5	7
Atlanta	37	43	.463	30	51	.370	58	63	280	350	49	38	303	389	1	4/17	4	6
Houston	37	44	.457	27	53	.338	40	43	313	338	44	63	351	373	1	4/7	5	9
1975 American League (4/8 - 9/28)																		
East																		
Boston	47	34	.580	48	31	.608	74	83	427	399	60	62	369	310	137	9/27	10	5
Baltimore	44	33	.571	46	36	.561	46	45	282	231	78	65	400	322	2	4/22	7	7
New York	43	35	.551	40	42	.488	50	56	323	276	60	48	358	312	4	6/28	8	7
Cleveland	41	39	.513	38	41	.481	79	85	331	367	74	51	357	336	3	4/10	6	7
Milwaukee	36	45	.444	32	49	.395	72	63	348	398	74	70	327	394	34	5/22	5	8
Detroit	31	49	.388	26	53	.329	63	83	301	421	62	54	269	365	9	5/1	9	19
West																		
Oakland	54	27	.667	44	37	.543	75	43	366	247	76	59	392	359	161	9/24	8	4
Kansas City	51	30	.630	40	41	.494	46	45	377	309	72	63	333	340	13	6/3	8	6
Texas	39	41	.488	40	42	.488	52	70	349	366	82	53	365	367	5	5/22	6	6
Minnesota	39	43	.476	37	40	.481	75	88	401	410	46	49	323	326	3	4/11	4	7
Chicago	42	39	.519	33	47	.413	42	54	350	359	52	53	305	344			9	6
California	35	46	.432	37	46	.463	24	52	294	349	31	71	334	374	3	4/30	4	7
1976 National League (4/9 - 10/3)																		
East																		
Philadelphia	53	28	.654	48	33	.593	63	49	424	277	47	49	346	280	156	9/25	6	9
Pittsburgh	47	34	.580	45	36	.556	54	44	366	302	56	51	342	328	15	4/25	10	4
New York	45	37	.549	41	39	.513	43	43	269	245	59	54	346	293	9	5/8	10	5
Chicago	42	39	.519	33	48	.407	71	84	355	385	34	39	256	343			5	9
St. Louis	37	44	.457	35	46	.432	27	40	335	346	36	51	294	325	1	4/9	4	5
Montreal	27	53	.338	28	54	.341	45	41	266	374	49	48	265	360			4	12
West																		
Cincinnati	49	32	.605	53	28	.654	73	46	426	337	68	54	431	296	155	9/21	7	4
Los Angeles	49	32	.605	43	38	.531	42	48	296	265	49	49	312	278	20	5/28	12	6
Houston	46	36	.561	34	46	.425	30	27	277	264	36	55	348	393	3	4/21	7	6
San Francisco	40	41	.494	34	47	.420	44	32	314	352	41	36	281	334	4	4/24	5	7
San Diego	42	38	.525	31	51	.378	30	38	254	271	34	49	316	391	1	4/9	5	8
Atlanta	34	47	.420	36	45	.444	43	56	338	401	39	30	282	299	7	4/26	6	13
1976 American League (4/8 - 10/3)																		
East																		
New York	45	35	.563	52	27	.658	67	51	349	294	53	46	381	281	172	9/25	7	6
Baltimore	42	39	.519	46	35	.568	58	38	280	306	61	42	339	292	2	4/10	7	9
Boston	46	35	.568	37	44	.457	71	61	408	352	63	48	308	308			7	10
Cleveland	44	35	.557	37	43	.463	40	43	311	295	45	37	304	320			5	5
Detroit	36	44	.450	38	43	.469	51	62	305	381	50	39	304	328	3	4/12	4	6
Milwaukee	36	45	.444	30	50	.375	45	43	292	321	43	56	278	334	5	5/3	5	7
West																		
Kansas City	49	32	.605	41	40	.506	37	35	368	287	28	48	345	324	139	10/1	7	6
Oakland	51	30	.630	36	44	.450	56	57	353	284	57	39	333	314	4	4/20	9	8
Minnesota	44	37	.543	41	40	.506	34	52	368	348	47	37	375	356			8	6
California	38	43	.469	38	43	.469	24	35	249	284	39	60	301	347			4	6
Texas	39	42	.481	37	44	.457	40	57	319	330	40	49	297	322	36	5/29	8	10
Chicago	35	45	.438	29	52	.358	31	34	300	369	42	53	286	376	8	4/19	10	10
1977 National League (4/7 - 10/2)																		
East																		
Philadelphia	60	21	.741	41	40	.506	101	63	453	299	85	71	394	369	59	9/27	13	5
Pittsburgh	58	23	.716	38	43	.469	64	76	396	315	69	73	338	350	29	5/27	11	7
St. Louis	52	31	.627	31	48	.392	41	53	379	314	55	86	358	374	21	5/1	6	7
Chicago	46	35	.568	35	46	.432	69	82	411	402	42	46	281	337	69	8/4	8	7
Montreal	38	43	.469	37	44	.457	66	65	329	362	72	70	336	374	4	4/19	7	11
New York	35	44	.443	29	54	.349	46	56	282	297	42	62	305	366	4	4/12	4	9
West																		
Los Angeles	51	30	.630	47	34	.580	96	65	386	273	95	54	383	309	175	9/20	8	4
Cincinnati	48	33	.593	40	41	.494	83	83	408	355	98	73	394	370	3	4/8	7	8
Houston	46	35	.568	35	46	.432	40	33	309	291	74	77	371	359	8	4/15	7	8
San Francisco	38	43	.469	37	44	.457	62	56	353	371	72	58	320	340			6	8
San Diego	35	46	.432	34	47	.420	53	70	299	368	67	90	393	466			5	8
Atlanta	40	41	.494	21	60	.259	97	111	416	488	42	58	262	407			5	17

	Team	Home Games			Road Games			Home Games				Road Games				DIF	LDF	WS	LS
		W	L	PCT	W	L	PCT	HR	OHR	R	OR	HR	OHR	R	OR				
1977 American League (4/7 - 10/2)	**East**																		
	New York	55	26	.679	45	36	.556	84	63	412	305	100	76	**419**	346	**70**	**10/1**	8	5
	Baltimore	54	27	.667	43	37	.538	74	62	356	**269**	74	62	363	384	35	8/1	7	6
	Boston	51	29	.638	46	35	.568	124	95	495	407	89	63	364	305	47	8/22	11	9
	Detroit	39	42	.481	35	46	.432	81	100	369	401	85	62	345	350			5	6
	Cleveland	37	44	.457	34	46	.425	54	66	339	357	46	70	337	382	8	4/15	9	7
	Milwaukee	37	44	.457	30	51	.370	49	54	305	365	76	82	334	400	21	5/6	5	5
	Toronto	25	55	.313	29	52	.358	**45**	94	**297**	**444**	55	58	308	378	3	4/11	3	11
	West																		
	Kansas City	55	26	**.679**	47	34	.580	56	**50**	408	320	90	60	414	331	52	**9/23**	16	4
	Texas	44	37	.543	50	31	**.617**	62	78	369	368	73	**56**	398	**289**	9	8/18	7	4
	Chicago	48	33	.593	42	39	.519	85	58	434	370	107	78	410	401	61	8/19	9	4
	Minnesota	48	32	.600	36	45	.444	61	79	469	376	62	72	398	400	59	8/16	5	6
	California	39	42	.481	35	46	.432	69	65	320	321	62	71	355	374	2	4/7	6	7
	Seattle	29	52	.358	35	46	.432	75	103	303	419	58	91	321	436			5	9
	Oakland	35	46	.432	28	52	.350	58	69	302	347	59	76	303	402	6	4/28	6	**14**
1978 National League (4/7 - 10/1)	**East**																		
	Philadelphia	54	28	.659	36	44	.450	80	70	**405**	279	53	48	303	307	**131**	**9/30**	8	5
	Pittsburgh	55	26	**.679**	33	47	.413	57	61	389	310	58	**42**	295	327	2	4/8	11	7
	Chicago	44	38	.537	35	45	.438	41	76	393	387	31	49	271	337	29	6/23	8	6
	Montreal	41	39	.513	35	47	.427	46	49	299	283	**75**	68	334	328	9	5/5	6	7
	St. Louis	37	44	.457	32	49	.395	**29**	32	**289**	307	50	62	311	350	3	4/13	5	11
	New York	33	47	.413	33	49	.402	37	60	295	340	49	54	312	350	7	4/22	5	6
	West																		
	Los Angeles	54	27	.667	41	40	.506	78	59	361	272	71	48	**366**	301	75	**9/24**	7	6
	Cincinnati	49	31	.613	43	38	**.531**	74	61	379	338	62	61	331	350	20	8/6	7	6
	San Francisco	50	31	.617	39	42	.481	47	30	291	**244**	70	54	322	350	93	8/15	8	7
	San Diego	50	31	.617	34	47	.420	31	**23**	291	245	44	51	300	353	1	4/7	10	5
	Houston	50	31	.617	24	57	.296	30	29	327	254	40	57	278	380			8	7
	Atlanta	39	42	.481	30	51	.370	**87**	**89**	364	**400**	36	43	236	350			5	7
1978 American League (4/7 - 10/2)	**East**																		
	New York	55	26	.679	45	37	**.549**	68	59	358	275	57	**52**	**377**	307	21	**10/2**	7	4
	Boston	59	23	**.720**	40	41	.494	**94**	72	445	334	78	65	351	323	**115**	10/1	9	5
	Milwaukee	54	27	.667	39	42	.481	**94**	50	446	318	79	59	358	332	9	4/15	13	8
	Baltimore	51	30	.630	39	41	.488	74	42	316	**258**	**80**	65	343	375			5	7
	Detroit	47	34	.580	39	42	.481	74	78	395	338	55	57	319	315	39	5/23	5	7
	Cleveland	42	36	.538	27	54	.333	50	**37**	319	287	56	63	320	407	1	4/8	4	6
	Toronto	37	44	.457	22	58	.275	50	75	334	366	48	74	256	409			5	9
	West																		
	Kansas City	56	25	.691	36	45	.444	**43**	44	434	264	55	64	309	370	**100**	**9/26**	10	5
	California	50	31	.617	37	44	.457	56	58	371	316	52	67	320	350	23	8/26	4	7
	Texas	52	30	.634	35	45	.438	62	49	348	289	70	59	344	343	9	7/2	7	8
	Minnesota	38	43	.469	35	46	.432	44	39	322	308	38	63	344	370	1	4/6	8	9
	Chicago	38	42	.475	33	48	.407	56	58	342	349	50	70	292	382	5	4/12	7	9
	Oakland	38	42	.475	31	51	.378	52	51	**281**	330	48	55	251	360	45	7/5	8	11
	Seattle	32	49	.395	24	55	.304	58	**93**	343	**423**	39	62	271	411	2	4/6	5	10
1979 National League (4/5 - 9/30)	**East**																		
	Pittsburgh	48	33	.593	50	31	**.617**	74	77	399	339	74	48	**376**	304	48	**9/30**	9	6
	Montreal	56	25	**.691**	39	40	.494	68	51	378	275	75	65	323	306	95	9/24	10	5
	St. Louis	42	39	.519	44	37	.543	48	65	379	372	52	62	352	321	10	6/12	7	6
	Philadelphia	43	38	.531	41	40	.506	52	72	332	342	67	63	351	376	32	5/27	7	6
	Chicago	45	36	.556	35	46	.432	79	72	**423**	370	56	55	283	337			6	7
	New York	28	53	.346	35	46	.432	30	58	**267**	354	44	62	326	352	5	4/9	6	9
	West																		
	Cincinnati	48	32	.600	42	39	.519	71	53	360	298	61	50	371	346	47	**9/28**	8	4
	Houston	52	29	.642	37	44	.457	**15**	**31**	269	**234**	34	59	314	348	**128**	9/10	7	7
	Los Angeles	46	35	.568	33	48	.407	**106**	55	389	341	**77**	**46**	350	376	1	4/9	8	6
	San Francisco	38	43	.469	33	48	.407	53	61	298	361	72	82	374	390	7	4/14	4	8
	San Diego	39	42	.481	29	51	.363	36	47	287	335	57	61	316	346	1	4/5	5	7
	Atlanta	34	45	.430	32	49	.395	73	80	359	**425**	53	52	310	338			6	6

Team	Home Games W	L	PCT	Road Games W	L	PCT	Home Games HR	OHR	R	OR	Road Games HR	OHR	R	OR	DIF	LDF	WS	LS

1979 American League
(4/5 - 9/30)

East
Baltimore	55	24	.696	47	33	.588	74	57	369	259	107	76	388	323	150	9/22	9	6
Milwaukee	52	29	.642	43	37	.538	91	81	401	362	94	81	406	360	15	4/19	10	5
Boston	51	29	.638	40	40	.500	121	59	470	357	73	74	371	354	23	6/5	7	4
New York	51	30	.630	38	41	.481	77	59	360	308	73	64	374	364			5	8
Detroit	46	34	.575	39	42	.481	101	74	394	323	63	93	376	415			6	5
Cleveland	47	34	.580	34	46	.425	87	72	428	409	51	66	332	396			10	10
Toronto	32	49	.395	21	60	.259	50	74	345	432	45	91	268	430			4	7

West
California	49	32	.605	39	42	.481	71	55	408	339	93	76	458	429	124	9/25	10	7
Kansas City	46	35	.568	39	42	.481	53	81	462	421	63	84	389	395	7	8/30	6	7
Texas	44	37	.543	39	42	.481	69	63	382	335	71	72	368	363	27	7/8	8	6
Minnesota	39	42	.481	43	38	.531	67	61	415	390	45	67	349	335	31	5/26	6	6
Chicago	33	46	.418	40	41	.494	56	60	349	401	71	54	381	347			5	7
Seattle	36	45	.444	31	50	.383	88	94	371	404	44	71	340	416	3	4/6	4	11
Oakland	31	50	.383	23	58	.284	46	65	262	371	62	82	311	489			4	8

1980 National League
(4/10 - 10/5)

East
Philadelphia	49	32	.605	42	39	.519	64	44	398	334	53	43	330	305	19	10/4	6	6
Montreal	51	29	.638	39	43	.476	51	40	357	286	63	60	337	343	82	10/2	10	4
Pittsburgh	47	34	.580	36	45	.444	63	53	355	322	53	57	311	324	81	8/31	8	8
St. Louis	41	40	.506	33	48	.407	41	42	396	357	60	48	342	353	1	4/10	6	10
New York	38	44	.463	29	51	.363	35	80	306	336	26	60	305	366	1	4/10	4	13
Chicago	37	44	.457	27	54	.333	54	62	338	385	53	47	276	343	2	5/3	4	7

West
Houston	55	26	.679	38	44	.463	26	22	329	255	49	47	308	334	112	10/6	10	5
Los Angeles	55	27	.671	37	44	.457	82	58	327	272	66	47	336	319	57	10/5	10	4
Cincinnati	44	37	.543	45	36	.556	66	70	356	349	47	43	351	321	27	8/14	8	5
Atlanta	50	30	.625	31	50	.383	84	79	352	297	60	52	278	363			7	7
San Francisco	44	37	.543	31	49	.388	24	41	283	293	56	51	290	341			7	6
San Diego	45	36	.556	28	53	.346	29	33	295	274	38	64	296	380	3	4/12	8	8

1980 American League
(4/9 - 10/5)

East
New York	53	28	.654	50	31	.617	91	47	409	315	98	55	411	347	156	10/4	9	3
Baltimore	50	31	.617	50	31	.617	75	81	397	319	81	53	408	321	2	4/18	10	6
Milwaukee	40	42	.488	46	34	.575	90	65	368	336	113	72	443	346	11	4/25	7	7
Boston	36	45	.444	47	32	.595	79	74	370	420	83	55	387	347	7	5/3	9	5
Detroit	43	38	.531	41	40	.506	77	95	440	404	66	57	390	353	1	4/10	9	7
Cleveland	44	35	.557	35	46	.432	55	66	400	389	34	71	338	418			8	7
Toronto	35	46	.432	32	49	.395	56	75	311	386	70	60	313	376	15	5/13	6	8

West
Kansas City	49	32	.605	48	33	.593	47	51	397	335	68	78	412	359	137	9/17	8	8
Oakland	46	35	.568	37	44	.457	58	57	337	277	79	85	349	365	21	5/17	7	7
Minnesota	44	36	.550	33	48	.407	51	63	392	361	48	57	278	363	1	4/10	12	9
Texas	39	41	.488	37	44	.457	58	57	380	365	66	62	376	387	7	4/19	5	8
Chicago	37	42	.468	33	48	.407	41	37	281	350	50	71	306	372	15	5/22	4	6
California	30	51	.370	35	44	.443	49	76	330	403	57	65	368	394	1	4/11	6	9
Seattle	36	45	.444	23	58	.284	74	99	340	389	30	60	270	404	4	4/14	6	12

1981 National League
(4/18 - 6/11)
(8/10 - 10/4)

East
St. Louis	32	21	.604	27	22	.551	22	26	244	218	28	26	220	199	77	9/30	8	5
Montreal	38	18	.679	22	30	.423	39	23	255	170	42	35	188	224	29	10/3	7	5
Philadelphia	36	19	.655	23	29	.442	41	39	295	261	28	33	196	211	11	6/10	6	6
Pittsburgh	22	28	.440	24	28	.462	29	29	189	207	26	31	218	218			4	7
New York	24	27	.471	17	35	.327	30	38	186	207	27	36	162	225	11	8/18	4	9
Chicago	27	30	.474	11	35	.239	41	38	239	254	16	21	131	229			4	12

West
Cincinnati	32	22	.593	34	20	.630	26	41	226	230	38	26	238	210	2	4/9	8	4
Los Angeles	33	23	.589	30	24	.556	37	34	221	171	45	20	229	185	69	6/10	7	5
Houston	31	20	.608	30	29	.508	16	9	166	106	29	31	228	225	42	10/2	9	4
San Francisco	29	24	.547	27	31	.466	28	19	218	204	35	38	209	210	1	8/30	5	6
Atlanta	22	27	.449	28	29	.491	37	41	182	195	27	21	213	221	18	8/30	6	5
San Diego	20	35	.364	21	34	.382	9	27	168	223	23	37	214	232	2	4/10	5	7

Team	Home Games W	L	PCT	Road Games W	L	PCT	Home Games HR	OHR	R	OR	Road Games HR	OHR	R	OR	DIF	LDF	WS	LS
1981 American League (4/9 - 6/11) (8/10 - 10/5)																		
East																		
Milwaukee	28	21	.571	34	26	**.567**	33	29	203	203	**63**	43	**290**	256	17	**10/3**	6	4
Baltimore	33	22	.600	26	24	.520	49	47	231	217	39	36	198	220	24	8/29	8	5
New York	32	19	**.627**	27	29	.482	47	**24**	203	**154**	53	40	218	**189**	12	**6/9**	9	4
Detroit	32	23	.582	28	26	.519	43	44	241	196	22	39	186	208	50	9/30	9	10
Boston	30	23	.566	29	26	.527	52	47	**278**	247	38	43	241	234	2	9/25	6	7
Cleveland	25	29	.463	27	22	.551	19	33	210	216	20	34	221	226	25	5/17	5	5
Toronto	17	36	.321	20	33	.377	34	41	172	272	27	31	157	194	2	8/15	4	**12**
West																		
Oakland	35	21	.625	29	24	.547	**57**	46	234	183	47	34	224	220	**77**	**6/11**	11	8
Texas	32	24	.571	25	24	.510	21	**24**	232	168	28	43	220	221	1	6/8	5	4
Chicago	25	24	.510	29	28	.509	31	33	215	198	45	40	261	225	13	8/30	6	6
Kansas City	19	28	.404	31	25	.554	**17**	27	**163**	197	44	48	234	208	29	**10/5**	6	4
California	26	28	.481	25	31	.446	48	39	244	233	49	42	232	220	1	4/9	5	8
Seattle	20	37	.351	24	28	.462	52	53	226	271	37	**23**	200	250	8	8/17	5	10
Minnesota	24	36	.400	17	32	.347	25	47	213	**292**	22	32	165	194	2	8/12	7	8
1982 National League (4/5 - 10/3)																		
East																		
St. Louis	46	35	.568	46	35	.568	**27**	48	338	325	40	46	347	284	131	9/27	12	4
Philadelphia	51	30	**.630**	38	43	.469	57	46	301	307	55	**40**	363	347	41	9/13	8	4
Montreal	40	41	.494	46	35	.568	59	65	335	352	74	45	362	**264**	7	6/24	8	5
Pittsburgh	42	39	.519	42	39	.519	77	65	**391**	**394**	57	53	333	302	1	4/10	6	4
Chicago	38	43	.469	35	46	.432	53	62	352	371	49	63	324	338	3	4/9	6	13
New York	33	48	.407	32	49	.395	48	60	307	357	49	59	302	366	4	4/13	4	15
West																		
Atlanta	42	39	.519	47	34	**.580**	**95**	**86**	388	387	51	**40**	351	315	**148**	**10/3**	13	11
Los Angeles	43	38	.531	45	36	.556	57	35	321	**283**	**81**	46	**370**	329	36	9/27	8	8
San Francisco	45	36	.556	42	39	.519	55	54	319	312	78	55	354	375			10	6
San Diego	43	38	.531	38	43	.469	33	76	316	286	48	63	359	372	1	4/27	11	6
Houston	43	38	.531	34	47	.420	31	**26**	**290**	294	43	61	279	326			4	6
Cincinnati	33	48	.407	28	53	.346	37	47	296	325	45	58	249	336			4	9
1982 American League (4/5 - 10/3)																		
East																		
Milwaukee	48	34	.585	47	33	**.588**	89	64	431	319	**127**	88	**460**	398	89	**10/3**	8	5
Baltimore	53	28	.654	41	40	.506	87	87	397	330	92	60	377	357	7	10/2	10	9
Boston	49	32	.605	40	41	.494	67	82	**434**	370	69	73	319	343	68	8/2	8	4
Detroit	47	34	.580	36	45	.444	**108**	100	378	328	69	72	351	357	25	6/10	8	10
New York	42	39	.519	37	44	.457	73	55	346	338	88	58	363	378	1	4/16	6	9
Cleveland	41	40	.506	37	44	.457	49	64	342	377	60	58	341	371	3	4/18	11	8
Toronto	44	37	.543	34	47	.420	62	70	353	379	44	77	298	**322**	2	4/17	6	6
West																		
California	52	29	.642	41	40	.506	99	69	414	322	87	**55**	400	348	**104**	**10/2**	7	8
Kansas City	56	25	**.691**	34	47	.420	61	64	431	**318**	71	99	353	399	52	9/19	8	7
Chicago	49	31	.613	38	44	.463	51	**43**	383	332	85	56	403	378	29	5/27	8	7
Seattle	42	39	.519	34	47	.420	78	104	356	388	52	69	295	324	2	4/7	5	7
Oakland	36	45	.444	32	49	.395	71	83	328	398	78	94	363	421	2	4/7	7	6
Texas	38	43	.469	26	55	.321	**43**	66	**286**	333	72	62	304	416	1	4/10	4	12
Minnesota	37	44	.457	23	58	.284	81	**110**	351	**401**	67	98	306	418	3	4/9	4	**14**
1983 National League (4/5 - 10/2)																		
East																		
Philadelphia	50	31	**.617**	40	41	.494	61	61	361	310	64	50	335	325	68	9/28	11	6
Pittsburgh	41	40	.506	43	38	**.531**	60	63	335	336	61	46	324	**312**	38	9/17	9	6
Montreal	46	35	.568	36	45	.444	40	56	341	325	62	64	336	321	37	9/13	5	6
St. Louis	44	37	.543	35	46	.432	38	58	334	350	45	57	345	360	56	7/19	7	8
Chicago	43	38	.531	28	53	.346	71	69	384	341	69	48	317	378			7	6
New York	41	41	.500	27	53	.338	63	53	300	329	49	**44**	275	351	4	4/8	4	5
West																		
Los Angeles	48	32	.600	43	39	.524	**74**	49	316	296	**72**	48	338	313	102	**9/30**	8	5
Atlanta	46	34	.575	42	40	.512	66	71	**394**	327	64	61	**352**	313	81	8/28	7	6
Houston	46	36	.561	39	41	.488	**26**	**28**	**294**	**278**	71	66	349	368			6	9
San Diego	47	34	.580	34	47	.420	53	**82**	350	299	40	62	303	354	4	4/8	6	5
San Francisco	43	38	.531	36	45	.444	73	67	346	356	69	60	341	341			6	4
Cincinnati	36	45	.444	38	43	.469	52	64	331	**360**	55	71	292	350	6	4/11	4	5

		Home Games			Road Games			Home Games				Road Games							
	Team	W	L	PCT	W	L	PCT	HR	OHR	R	OR	HR	OHR	R	OR	DIF	LDF	WS	LS
1983 American League (4/4 - 10/2)	**East**																		
	Baltimore	50	31	.617	48	33	.593	79	66	389	328	89	64	410	324	114	9/25	8	7
	Detroit	48	33	.593	44	37	.543	83	87	377	314	73	83	412	365	9	8/13	6	4
	New York	51	30	.630	40	41	.494	67	55	398	323	86	61	372	380	3	7/27	7	4
	Toronto	48	33	.593	41	40	.506	101	84	437	385	66	61	358	341	44	7/25	5	6
	Milwaukee	52	29	.642	35	46	.432	64	57	356	305	68	76	408	403	12	8/25	8	10
	Boston	38	43	.469	40	41	.494	65	76	373	390	77	82	351	385	18	6/5	5	7
	Cleveland	36	45	.444	34	47	.420	48	71	367	424	38	49	337	361	10	4/16	6	5
	West																		
	Chicago	55	26	.679	44	37	.543	84	64	432	306	73	64	368	344	77	9/17	8	5
	Kansas City	45	36	.556	34	47	.420	50	66	381	369	59	67	315	398	9	5/3	5	6
	Texas	44	37	.543	33	48	.407	45	33	326	294	61	64	313	315	43	7/17	6	8
	Oakland	42	39	.519	32	49	.395	60	54	348	367	61	81	360	415	8	5/2	5	6
	California	35	46	.432	35	46	.432	86	67	368	354	68	63	354	425	59	7/10	7	6
	Minnesota	37	44	.457	33	48	.407	56	91	389	427	85	72	320	395			5	8
	Seattle	30	51	.370	30	51	.370	64	80	281	369	47	65	277	371	2	4/6	4	8
1984 National League (4/2 - 9/30)	**East**																		
	Chicago	51	29	.638	45	36	.556	86	70	414	360	50	29	348	298	105	9/24	6	5
	New York	48	33	.593	42	39	.519	56	47	336	327	51	57	316	349	65	7/31	8	7
	St. Louis	44	37	.543	40	41	.494	29	42	327	310	46	52	325	335	3	4/6	6	7
	Philadelphia	39	42	.481	42	39	.519	79	45	353	369	68	56	367	321	26	6/30	10	9
	Montreal	39	42	.481	39	41	.488	45	56	266	260	51	58	327	325	3	4/7	6	6
	Pittsburgh	41	40	.506	34	47	.420	48	44	282	263	50	58	333	304			7	7
	West																		
	San Diego	48	33	.593	44	37	.543	60	61	344	300	49	61	342	334	145	9/20	6	7
	Atlanta	38	43	.469	42	39	.519	53	72	328	376	58	50	304	279	8	6/8	9	5
	Houston	43	38	.531	37	44	.457	18	29	309	292	61	62	384	338			9	5
	Los Angeles	40	41	.494	39	42	.481	49	40	287	321	53	36	293	279	29	6/1	6	7
	Cincinnati	39	42	.481	31	50	.383	58	73	356	381	48	55	271	366	2	4/3	7	8
	San Francisco	35	46	.432	31	50	.383	55	63	340	393	57	62	342	414			6	9
1984 American League (4/2 - 9/30)	**East**																		
	Detroit	53	29	.646	51	29	.638	85	69	406	295	102	61	423	348	181	9/18	9	4
	Toronto	49	32	.605	40	41	.494	59	78	387	339	84	62	363	357			7	6
	New York	51	30	.630	36	45	.444	62	49	372	292	68	71	386	387			8	5
	Boston	41	40	.506	45	36	.556	100	76	456	413	81	65	354	351			6	8
	Baltimore	44	37	.543	41	40	.506	82	59	319	306	78	78	362	361			6	5
	Cleveland	41	39	.513	34	48	.415	65	73	411	399	58	68	350	367	5	4/7	8	6
	Milwaukee	38	43	.469	29	51	.363	42	68	286	344	54	69	355	390			5	10
	West																		
	Kansas City	44	37	.543	40	41	.494	48	59	344	326	69	77	329	360	26	9/28	6	7
	California	37	44	.457	44	37	.543	79	83	341	364	71	60	355	333	77	8/4	5	7
	Minnesota	47	34	.580	34	47	.420	63	77	372	337	51	82	301	338	58	9/23	6	6
	Oakland	44	37	.543	33	48	.407	77	72	356	344	81	83	382	452	21	5/8	5	9
	Chicago	43	38	.531	31	50	.383	103	77	394	389	69	78	285	347	10	7/11	7	6
	Seattle	42	39	.519	32	49	.395	68	82	357	394	61	56	325	380	12	4/26	5	6
	Texas	34	46	.425	35	46	.432	55	70	327	357	65	78	329	357			6	7
1985 National League (4/8 - 10/6)	**East**																		
	St. Louis	54	27	.667	47	34	.580	36	39	358	255	51	59	389	317	88	10/5	7	4
	New York	51	30	.630	47	34	.580	58	58	344	254	76	53	351	314	74	9/15	9	6
	Montreal	44	37	.543	40	40	.500	45	45	300	289	73	54	333	347	10	6/28	6	6
	Chicago	41	39	.513	36	45	.444	98	104	399	423	52	52	287	306	35	6/15	6	13
	Philadelphia	41	40	.506	34	47	.420	72	57	350	338	69	58	317	335			6	11
	Pittsburgh	35	45	.438	22	59	.272	39	53	314	347	41	54	254	361			3	9
	West																		
	Los Angeles	48	33	.593	47	34	.580	47	54	310	258	82	48	372	321	91	10/2	8	4
	Cincinnati	47	34	.580	42	38	.525	49	65	347	359	65	66	330	307	8	4/24	7	4
	Houston	44	37	.543	39	42	.481	47	48	333	338	74	71	373	353	2	4/23	9	6
	San Diego	44	37	.543	39	42	.481	63	77	321	323	46	50	329	299	78	7/12	7	6
	Atlanta	32	49	.395	34	47	.420	65	80	336	431	61	54	296	350	8	4/16	5	6
	San Francisco	38	43	.469	24	57	.296	58	67	265	307	57	58	291	367	2	4/12	4	10

Team	Home Games			Road Games			Home Games				Road Games				DIF	LDF	WS	LS
	W	L	PCT	W	L	PCT	HR	OHR	R	OR	HR	OHR	R	OR				
1985 American League (4/8 - 10/6)																		
East																		
Toronto	54	26	.675	45	36	.556	75	78	396	264	83	69	363	324	152	10/5	9	6
New York	58	22	.725	39	42	.481	92	67	411	288	84	90	428	372			11	8
Detroit	44	37	.543	40	40	.500	108	93	386	368	94	48	343	320	20	4/29	6	8
Baltimore	45	36	.556	38	42	.475	103	87	414	374	111	73	404	390	21	5/19	6	6
Boston	43	37	.538	38	44	.463	73	64	415	357	89	66	385	363	6	4/13	8	6
Milwaukee	40	40	.500	31	50	.383	50	86	368	416	51	89	322	386			5	7
Cleveland	38	43	.469	22	59	.272	52	76	380	379	64	94	349	482			5	6
West																		
Kansas City	50	32	.610	41	39	.513	67	43	357	317	87	60	330	322	30	10/5	8	5
California	49	30	.620	41	42	.494	75	93	370	331	78	78	362	372	142	10/2	6	5
Chicago	45	36	.556	40	41	.494	74	83	359	361	72	78	377	359	11	6/20	5	7
Minnesota	49	35	.583	28	50	.359	71	83	407	393	70	81	298	389	2	4/10	10	10
Oakland	43	36	.544	34	49	.410	66	71	348	347	89	101	409	440	6	4/25	5	7
Seattle	42	41	.506	32	47	.405	92	78	360	389	79	76	359	429	13	4/21	8	8
Texas	37	43	.463	25	56	.309	76	102	356	406	53	71	261	379			5	7
1986 National League (4/7 - 10/5)																		
East																		
New York	55	26	.679	53	28	.654	77	47	379	251	71	56	404	327	170	9/17	11	4
Philadelphia	49	31	.613	37	44	.457	86	49	413	344	68	81	326	369			7	5
St. Louis	42	39	.519	37	43	.463	27	63	321	303	31	72	280	308	15	4/22	7	8
Montreal	36	44	.450	42	39	.519	42	56	296	347	68	63	341	341			8	6
Chicago	42	38	.525	28	52	.350	89	79	394	399	66	64	286	382			5	7
Pittsburgh	31	50	.383	33	48	.407	49	75	331	357	62	63	332	343			5	5
West																		
Houston	52	29	.642	44	37	.543	49	56	327	289	76	60	327	280	149	9/25	7	4
Cincinnati	43	38	.531	43	38	.531	86	73	383	377	58	63	349	340	2	4/8	6	9
San Francisco	46	35	.568	37	44	.457	50	61	345	275	64	60	353	343	37	7/20	6	6
San Diego	43	38	.531	31	50	.383	80	78	339	319	56	72	317	404	3	4/17	4	5
Los Angeles	46	35	.568	27	54	.333	57	46	326	290	73	69	312	389	1	4/7	8	6
Atlanta	41	40	.506	31	49	.388	77	71	331	360	61	46	284	359	2	4/9	7	6
1986 American League (4/7 - 10/5)																		
East																		
Boston	51	30	.630	44	36	.550	55	85	389	350	89	82	405	346	147	9/28	11	4
New York	41	39	.513	49	33	.598	93	96	384	396	95	79	413	342	29	5/14	6	5
Detroit	49	32	.605	38	43	.469	96	83	403	310	102	100	395	404	4	4/11	5	5
Toronto	42	39	.519	44	37	.543	87	89	415	389	94	75	394	344	1	4/11	9	5
Cleveland	45	35	.563	39	43	.476	80	80	403	415	77	87	428	426	7	5/8	10	6
Milwaukee	41	39	.513	36	45	.444	63	79	338	375	64	79	329	359	5	4/11	5	8
Baltimore	37	42	.468	36	47	.434	91	98	348	362	78	79	360	398			6	7
West																		
California	50	32	.610	42	38	.525	88	84	371	335	79	69	415	349	131	9/26	7	5
Texas	51	30	.630	36	45	.444	87	61	374	343	97	84	397	400	46	7/6	7	7
Kansas City	45	36	.556	31	50	.383	60	46	342	317	77	75	312	356	3	6/1	4	11
Oakland	47	36	.566	29	50	.367	75	81	363	349	88	85	368	411	4	5/10	7	9
Chicago	41	40	.506	31	50	.383	51	63	341	335	70	80	303	364			7	8
Minnesota	43	38	.531	28	53	.346	116	107	426	439	80	93	315	400	5	4/12	4	7
Seattle	41	41	.500	26	54	.325	97	99	410	427	61	72	308	408	6	4/15	4	9
1987 National League (4/6 - 10/4)																		
East																		
St. Louis	49	32	.605	46	35	.568	42	60	387	339	52	69	411	354	167	10/1	9	7
New York	49	32	.605	43	38	.531	93	63	407	335	99	73	416	363	15	4/25	7	4
Montreal	48	33	.593	43	38	.531	62	74	401	371	58	70	340	349			8	5
Philadelphia	43	38	.531	37	44	.457	80	78	385	373	89	89	317	376			5	6
Pittsburgh	47	34	.580	33	48	.407	71	84	404	363	60	80	319	381			7	7
Chicago	40	40	.500	36	45	.444	114	90	381	389	95	69	339	412	7	5/19	5	5
West																		
San Francisco	46	35	.568	44	37	.543	118	72	373	312	87	74	410	357	89	9/28	7	6
Cincinnati	42	39	.519	42	39	.519	94	97	396	401	98	73	387	351	111	8/20	6	7
Houston	47	34	.580	29	52	.358	51	46	334	268	71	95	314	410	9	4/23	7	7
Los Angeles	40	41	.494	33	48	.407	52	56	280	306	73	74	355	369			4	9
Atlanta	42	39	.519	27	53	.338	82	88	421	450	70	75	326	379	3	4/9	5	6
San Diego	37	44	.457	28	53	.346	60	97	338	357	53	78	330	406			7	9

		Home Games			Road Games			Home Games				Road Games							
	Team	W	L	PCT	W	L	PCT	HR	OHR	R	OR	HR	OHR	R	OR	DIF	LDF	WS	LS
1987 American League (4/6 - 10/4)	**East**																		
	Detroit	54	27	.667	44	37	**.543**	**125**	101	**442**	338	100	79	**454**	397	33	**10/4**	6	5
	Toronto	52	29	.642	44	37	**.543**	101	83	425	**319**	**114**	75	420	336	55	**10/2**	11	9
	Milwaukee	48	33	.593	43	38	.531	72	79	440	420	91	90	422	397	38	5/13	**13**	12
	New York	51	30	.630	38	43	.469	98	88	401	346	98	91	387	412	68	8/8	10	5
	Boston	50	30	.625	28	54	.341	86	75	436	383	88	115	406	442			5	6
	Baltimore	31	51	.378	36	44	.450	110	**125**	351	456	101	101	378	424	2	4/7	11	10
	Cleveland	35	46	.432	26	55	.321	94	118	373	**519**	93	101	369	438			4	8
	West																		
	Minnesota	56	25	**.691**	29	52	.358	106	92	411	348	90	118	375	458	138	**9/28**	7	6
	Kansas City	46	35	.568	37	44	.457	73	**57**	375	349	95	**71**	340	342	34	7/5	6	6
	Oakland	42	39	.519	39	42	.481	88	75	363	351	111	101	443	438	3	8/29	5	5
	Seattle	40	41	.494	38	43	.469	103	115	403	400	58	84	357	401	2	5/14	5	6
	Chicago	38	43	.469	39	42	.481	72	90	394	414	101	99	354	**332**	2	4/7	7	7
	California	38	43	.469	37	44	.457	88	116	377	405	84	96	393	398	13	5/11	8	9
	Texas	43	38	.531	32	49	.395	93	111	426	447	101	88	397	402			6	9
1988 National League (4/4 - 10/2)	**East**																		
	New York	56	24	**.700**	44	36	.550	67	**34**	313	**218**	**85**	**44**	390	314	158	**9/22**	8	5
	Pittsburgh	43	38	.531	42	37	.532	56	50	326	298	54	58	325	318	21	5/2	**9**	5
	Montreal	43	38	.531	38	43	.469	47	62	333	304	60	60	295	288			8	9
	Chicago	39	42	.481	38	43	.469	58	**71**	346	373	55	44	314	321	9	4/15	5	5
	St. Louis	41	40	.506	35	46	.432	**29**	39	314	318	42	52	264	315			7	8
	Philadelphia	38	42	.475	27	54	.333	62	64	327	361	44	54	270	373	1	4/9	4	8
	West																		
	Los Angeles	45	36	.556	49	31	**.613**	49	38	316	297	50	46	312	**247**	163	**9/26**	7	3
	Cincinnati	45	35	.563	42	39	.519	**75**	**71**	333	312	47	50	308	284	4	4/7	8	6
	San Diego	47	34	.580	36	44	.450	56	56	303	267	38	56	291	316			6	6
	San Francisco	45	36	.556	38	43	.469	58	42	318	284	55	57	352	342	2	4/9	6	6
	Houston	44	37	.543	38	43	.469	33	50	**293**	282	63	73	324	349	19	5/24	6	6
	Atlanta	28	51	.354	26	55	.321	48	64	295	391	48	44	260	350			3	10
1988 American League (4/4 - 10/2)	**East**																		
	Boston	53	28	**.654**	36	45	.444	68	73	**456**	360	56	70	357	329	30	**9/30**	12	4
	Detroit	50	31	.617	38	43	.469	83	76	328	303	60	74	375	355	**76**	9/4	5	6
	Milwaukee	47	34	.580	40	41	.494	60	65	354	310	53	**60**	328	**306**	4	4/7	10	7
	Toronto	45	36	.556	42	39	.519	78	73	371	344	80	70	392	336	3	4/6	6	6
	New York	46	34	.575	39	42	.481	77	75	378	345	71	82	394	403	65	7/27	6	6
	Cleveland	44	37	.543	34	47	.420	62	52	353	359	72	68	313	372	18	5/2	6	6
	Baltimore	34	46	.425	20	61	.247	70	77	**286**	354	67	76	264	435			3	**21**
	West																		
	Oakland	54	27	**.667**	50	31	**.617**	67	47	362	**294**	89	69	**438**	326	177	**9/18**	14	5
	Minnesota	47	34	.580	44	37	.543	76	79	402	354	75	67	357	318			8	6
	Kansas City	44	36	.550	40	41	.494	**55**	**37**	359	330	66	65	345	318	6	4/17	7	6
	California	35	46	.432	40	41	.494	58	71	333	368	66	64	381	403	1	4/17	7	12
	Chicago	40	41	.494	31	49	.388	**55**	64	311	373	77	74	320	384	7	4/19	5	7
	Texas	38	43	.469	32	48	.400	58	67	336	368	54	62	301	367	2	4/5	8	6
	Seattle	37	44	.457	31	49	.388	**97**	81	362	405	51	63	302	339			4	9
1989 National League (4/3 - 10/1)	**East**																		
	Chicago	48	33	.593	45	36	**.556**	61	64	**381**	334	63	42	321	**289**	108	**9/26**	7	7
	New York	51	30	.630	36	45	.444	**78**	54	333	275	69	61	**350**	320	25	6/25	6	7
	St. Louis	46	35	.568	40	41	.494	**27**	**36**	319	308	46	48	313	300	14	5/12	6	6
	Montreal	44	37	.543	37	44	.457	55	60	336	309	45	60	296	321	49	8/6	6	7
	Pittsburgh	39	42	.481	35	46	.432	45	60	296	313	50	61	341	367	1	4/5	6	6
	Philadelphia	38	42	.475	29	53	.354	63	67	321	376	60	60	308	359	12	4/25	4	**11**
	West																		
	San Francisco	53	28	**.654**	39	42	.481	62	61	368	255	**79**	59	331	345	140	**9/27**	7	3
	San Diego	46	35	.568	43	38	.531	66	**82**	324	312	54	51	318	314	1	4/11	6	7
	Houston	47	35	.573	39	41	.488	44	50	340	344	53	55	307	325	5	6/16	10	5
	Los Angeles	44	37	.543	33	46	.418	37	47	**253**	**244**	52	48	301	292			5	5
	Cincinnati	38	43	.469	37	44	.457	59	71	312	**377**	69	54	320	314	45	6/10	4	10
	Atlanta	33	46	.418	30	51	.370	55	61	309	334	73	53	275	346	4	4/9	7	8

		Home Games			Road Games			Home Games				Road Games							
Team		W	L	PCT	W	L	PCT	HR	OHR	R	OR	HR	OHR	R	OR	DIF	LDF	WS	LS
1989 American League (4/3 - 10/1)	East																		
	Toronto	46	35	.568	43	38	.531	64	50	330	308	**78**	49	**401**	343	35	**9/30**	6	5
	Baltimore	47	34	.580	40	41	.494	61	65	347	338	68	69	361	348	117	8/31	8	8
	Boston	46	35	.568	37	44	.457	52	70	**419**	374	56	61	355	361	21	5/25	**9**	8
	Milwaukee	45	36	.556	36	45	.444	69	54	344	321	57	75	363	358	6	4/28	8	6
	New York	41	40	.506	33	47	.413	64	**88**	373	**419**	66	62	325	373	5	5/16	**9**	7
	Cleveland	41	40	.506	32	49	.395	56	51	319	332	71	56	285	322	18	5/23	5	6
	Detroit	38	43	.469	21	60	.259	74	77	321	389	42	73	296	427			7	**12**
	West																		
	Oakland	54	27	.667	45	36	**.556**	65	51	370	**284**	62	52	342	**292**	109	9/27	7	4
	Kansas City	55	26	**.679**	37	44	.457	38	**26**	335	388	63	60	355	347	3	5/16	**9**	6
	California	52	29	.642	39	42	.481	73	75	317	285	72	**38**	352	293	49	8/20	7	7
	Texas	45	36	.556	38	43	.469	**75**	63	352	371	47	56	343	343	29	5/4	8	4
	Minnesota	45	36	.556	35	46	.432	59	69	387	404	58	70	353	334	2	4/8	6	8
	Seattle	40	41	.494	33	48	.407	68	67	353	386	66	47	341	342			6	**12**
	Chicago	35	45	.438	34	47	.420	**36**	58	**301**	365	58	86	392	385	3	4/8	8	7

PART SIX

Manager Register

Alphabetical List of Every Man Who Ever
Managed in the Major Leagues
And His Complete Managerial Record

Manager Register

The Manager Register is an alphabetical listing of every man who has managed a major league team from 1876 through today. Included are facts about the managers and their year-by-year managerial records and lifetime totals for the regular season and for Championship Series and World Series. All managers who played in the major leagues can also be found in the Player Register.

Managers included here are defined as men who were in charge of a team while the team was on the field. This definition includes interim managers (those who served between outgoing and incoming managers), but not "acting managers," men who took over a team while the regular manager was temporarily absent because of illness, injury, or suspension. All information and abbreviations that may appear unfamiliar are explained in the sample format presented below. The man, John Doe, used in the sample is fictitious and serves only to illustrate the information:

	G	W	L	T	ND	PCT	Standing

John Doe

DOE, JOHN LEE (Slim)
Born John Lee Doughnut.
Brother of Bill Doe.
B. Jan. 1, 1850, New York, N. Y.
D. July 1, 1955, New York, N.Y.
Hall of Fame 1946.

Year	Team	Lg	G	W	L	T	ND	PCT	Standing		
1908	BOS	N	100	70	30	0	0	.700	4	1	
1909	NY	N	155	90	64	0	0	.584	3		
1910			154	96	58	0	0	.623	1		
1911			105	60	45	0	0	.571	5	6	
1912	CHI	A	154	101	53	0	0	.656	1		
1913	STL	N	154	90	64	0	0	.584	2		
1914	CHI	F	25	8	17	0	0	.320	4	6	5
1915	NY	A	54	20	34	0	0	.370	6	4	
1915	CLE	A	100	65	35	0	0	.650	5	2	
8 yrs.			1001	600	400	0	0	.600 3rd			

LEAGUE CHAMPIONSHIP SERIES

Year	Team	Lg	G	W	L	T	ND	PCT
1974	OAK	A	4	3	1	0	0	.750
1975			3	0	3	0	0	.000
2 yrs.			7	3	4	0	0	.429

WORLD SERIES

Year	Team	Lg	G	W	L	T	ND	PCT
1962	SF	N	7	3	4	0	0	.429
1974	OAK	A	5	4	1	0	0	.800
2 yrs.			12	7	5	0	0	.583

Manager Information

John Doe

This shortened version of the manager's full name is the name most familiar to the fans. All managers in this section are alphabetically arranged by the last name part of this name.

Doe, John Lee

Manager's full name. The arrangement is last name first, then first and middle name(s).

(Slim)

Nickname. Any name appearing in parentheses is a nickname.

Born John Lee Doughnut

The name the manager was given at birth. A name shown in this form means that the man never used this name while he was a major league manager.

Brother of Bill Doe

The manager's brother. (Relatives indicated here are fathers, sons, and brothers who played or managed in the major leagues and the National Association.)

B. Jan. 1, 1850, New York, N.Y.

Date and place of birth.

D. July 1, 1955, New York, N.Y.

Date and place of death. (Some managers are listed simply as "deceased." Although no certification of death or other information is presently available, it is reasonably certain they are dead.)

Hall of Fame 1946

Doe was elected to the Hall of Fame in 1946.

Column Headings

	G	W	L	T	N	PCT	Standing

G	Games Managed
W	Wins
L	Losses
T	Ties
N	No Decisions
PCT	Winning Percentage
Standing	(explained under Statistical Information)

Bill Adair

ADAIR, MARION DANNE
B. Feb. 10, 1913, Mobile, Ala.

Year	Team	Lg	G	W	L	T	N	PCT	Standing		
1970	CHI	A	10	4	6	0	0	.400	6	6	6

Joe Adcock

ADCOCK, JOSEPH WILBUR
B. Oct. 30, 1927, Coushatta, La.

Year	Team	Lg	G	W	L	T	N	PCT	Standing
1967	CLE	A	162	75	87	0	0	.463	8

Bob Addy

ADDY, ROBERT EDWARD (The Magnet)
B. Feb., 1845, Rochester, N. Y.
D. Apr. 9, 1910, Pocatello, Ida.

Year	Team	Lg	G	W	L	T	N	PCT	Standing	
1877	CIN	N	44	12	31	1	0	.279	6	6

Bob Allen

ALLEN, ROBERT GILMAN
B. July 10, 1867, Marion, Ohio
D. May 4, 1943, Little Rock, Ark.

Year	Team	Lg	G	W	L	T	N	PCT	Standing		
1890	PHI	N	35	25	10	0	0	.714	3	2	3
1900	CIN	N	144	62	77	5	0	.446	7		
2 yrs.			179	87	87	5	0	.500			

Walter Alston

ALSTON, WALTER EMMONS (Smokey)
B. Dec. 1, 1911, Venice, Ohio
D. Oct. 1, 1984, Oxford, Ohio
Hall of Fame 1983.

Year	Team	Lg	G	W	L	T	N	PCT	Standing	
1954	BKN	N	154	92	62	0	0	.597	2	
1955			154	98	55	1	0	.641	1	
1956			154	93	61	0	0	.604	1	
1957			154	84	70	0	0	.545	3	
1958	LA	N	154	71	83	0	0	.461	7	
1959			156	88	68	0	0	.564	1	
1960			154	82	72	0	0	.532	4	
1961			154	89	65	0	0	.578	2	
1962			165	102	63	0	0	.618	2	
1963			163	99	63	1	0	.611	1	
1964			164	80	82	2	0	.494	6	
1965			162	97	65	0	0	.599	1	
1966			162	95	67	0	0	.586	1	
1967			162	73	89	0	0	.451	8	
1968			162	76	86	0	0	.469	7	
1969			162	85	77	0	0	.525	4	
1970			161	87	74	0	0	.540	2	
1971			162	89	73	0	0	.549	2	
1972			155	85	70	0	0	.548	3	
1973			162	95	66	1	0	.590	2	
1974			162	102	60	0	0	.630	1	
1975			162	88	74	0	0	.543	2	
1976			158	90	68	0	0	.570	2	2
23 yrs.			3658	2040	1613	5	0	.558		
			7th	5th	8th					

LEAGUE CHAMPIONSHIP SERIES

Year	Team	Lg	G	W	L	T	N	PCT
1974	LA	N	4	3	1	0	0	.750

WORLD SERIES

Year	Team	Lg	G	W	L	T	N	PCT
1955	BKN	N	7	4	3	0	0	.571
1956			7	3	4	0	0	.429
1959	LA	N	6	4	2	0	0	.667
1963			4	4	0	0	0	1.000
1965			7	4	3	0	0	.571
1966			4	0	4	0	0	.000
1974			5	1	4	0	0	.200
7 yrs.			40	20	20	0	0	.500
			5th	5th	3rd			9th

Joe Altobelli

ALTOBELLI, JOSEPH SALVATORE
B. May 26, 1932, Detroit, Mich.

Year	Team	Lg	G	W	L	T	N	PCT	Standing	
1977	SF	N	162	75	87	0	0	.463	4	
1978			162	89	73	0	0	.549	3	
1979			140	61	79	0	0	.436	4	4
1983	BAL	A	162	98	64	0	0	.605	1	
1984			162	85	77	0	0	.525	5	
1985			55	29	26	0	0	.527	4	4
6 yrs.			843	437	406	0	0	.518		

LEAGUE CHAMPIONSHIP SERIES

Year	Team	Lg	G	W	L	T	N	PCT
1983	BAL	A	4	3	1	0	0	.750

WORLD SERIES

Year	Team	Lg	G	W	L	T	N	PCT
1983	BAL	A	5	4	1	0	0	.800

Joey Amalfitano

AMALFITANO, JOHN JOSEPH
B. Jan. 23, 1934, San Pedro, Calif.

Year	Team	Lg	G	W	L	T	N	PCT	Standing	
1979	CHI	N	7	2	5	0	0	.286	5	5
1980			72	26	46	0	0	.361	6	6
1981			54	15	37	2	0	.288	6	(1st)
1981			52	23	28	1	0	.451	5	(2nd)
3 yrs.			185	66	116	3	0	.363		

Sparky Anderson

ANDERSON, GEORGE LEE
B. Feb. 22, 1934, Bridgewater, S. D.

Year	Team	Lg	G	W	L	T	N	PCT	Standing	
1970	CIN	N	162	102	60	0	0	.630	1	
1971			162	79	83	0	0	.488	4	
1972			154	95	59	0	0	.617	1	
1973			162	99	63	0	0	.611	1	
1974			163	98	64	1	0	.605	2	
1975			162	108	54	0	0	.667	1	
1976			162	102	60	0	0	.630	1	
1977			162	88	74	0	0	.543	2	
1978			161	92	69	0	0	.571	2	
1979	DET	A	106	56	50	0	0	.528	5	5
1980			163	84	78	1	0	.519	4	
1981			57	31	26	0	0	.544	4	(1st)
1981			52	29	23	0	0	.558	2	(2nd)
1982			162	83	79	0	0	.512	4	
1983			162	92	70	0	0	.568	2	
1984			162	104	58	0	0	.642	1	
1985			161	84	77	0	0	.522	3	
1986			162	87	75	0	0	.537	3	
1987			162	98	64	0	0	.605	1	
1988			162	88	74	0	0	.543	2	
1989			162	59	103	0	0	.364	7	
20 yrs.			3123	1758	1363	2	0	.563		
			10th							

LEAGUE CHAMPIONSHIP SERIES

Year	Team	Lg	G	W	L	T	N	PCT
1970	CIN	N	3	3	0	0	0	1.000
1972			5	3	2	0	0	.600
1973			5	2	3	0	0	.400
1975			3	3	0	0	0	1.000
1976			3	3	0	0	0	1.000
1984	DET	A	3	3	0	0	0	1.000
1987			5	1	4	0	0	.200
7 yrs.			27	18	9	0	0	.667
			3rd	1st	5th			3rd

WORLD SERIES

Year	Team	Lg	G	W	L	T	N	PCT
1970	CIN	N	5	1	4	0	0	.200
1972			7	3	4	0	0	.429
1975			7	4	3	0	0	.571
1976			4	4	0	0	0	1.000
1984	DET	A	5	4	1	0	0	.800
5 yrs.			28	16	12	0	0	.571
			7th	7th	10th			3rd

Cap Anson

ANSON, ADRIAN CONSTANTINE (Old Anse)
B. Apr. 11, 1852, Marshalltown, Iowa
D. Apr. 14, 1922, Chicago, Ill.
Hall of Fame 1939.

Year	Team	Lg	G	W	L	T	N	PCT	Standing		
1879	CHI	N	64	41	21	2	0	.661	4	4	
1880			86	67	17	2	0	.798	1		
1881			84	56	28	0	0	.667	1		
1882			84	55	29	0	0	.655	1		
1883			98	59	39	0	0	.602	2		
1884			113	62	50	1	0	.554	4		
1885			113	87	25	1	0	.777	1		
1886			126	90	34	2	0	.726	1		
1887			127	71	50	3	3	.587	3		
1888			136	77	58	1	0	.570	2		
1889			136	67	65	4	0	.508	3		
1890			139	84	53	2	0	.613	2		
1891			137	82	53	2	0	.607	2		
1892			147	70	76	1	0	.479	7		
1893			128	56	71	1	0	.441	9		
1894			137	57	75	3	2	.432	4		
1895			133	72	58	3	0	.554	4		
1896			132	71	57	4	0	.555	5		
1897			138	59	73	6	0	.447	9		
1898	NY	N	22	9	13	0	0	.409	6	7	7
20 yrs.			2280	1292	945	38	5	.578			
			10th								

Luke Appling

APPLING, LUCIUS BENJAMIN (Old Aches and Pains)
B. Apr. 2, 1909, High Point, N. C.
Hall of Fame 1964.

Year	Team	Lg	G	W	L	T	N	PCT	Standing	
1967	KC	A	40	10	30	0	0	.250	10	10

Bill Armour

ARMOUR, WILLIAM R.
B. Sept. 3, 1869, Homestead, Pa.
D. Dec. 2, 1922, Minneapolis, Minn.

Year	Team	Lg	G	W	L	T	N	PCT	Standing
1902	CLE	A	137	69	67	1	0	.507	5
1903			140	77	63	0	0	.550	3
1904			154	86	65	3	0	.570	4
1905	DET	A	154	79	74	1	0	.516	3
1906			151	71	78	2	0	.477	6
5 yrs.			736	382	347	7	0	.524	

Ken Aspromonte

ASPROMONTE, KENNETH JOSEPH
Brother of Bob Aspromonte.
B. Sept. 22, 1931, Brooklyn, N. Y.

Year	Team	Lg	G	W	L	T	N	PCT	Standing
1972	CLE	A	156	72	84	0	0	.462	5
1973			162	71	91	0	0	.438	6
1974			162	77	85	0	0	.475	4
3 yrs.			480	220	260	0	0	.458	

Jimmy Austin

AUSTIN, JAMES PHILIP (Pepper)
B. Dec. 8, 1879, Swansea, Wales
D. Mar. 6, 1965, Laguna Beach, Calif.

Year	Team	Lg	G	W	L	T	N	PCT	Standing		
1913	STL	A	8	2	6	0	0	.250	7	8	8
1918			16	7	9	0	0	.438	5	6	5
1923			51	22	29	0	0	.431	9		
3 yrs.			75	31	44	0	0	.413			

Del Baker

BAKER, DELMAR DAVID
B. May 3, 1892, Sherwood, Ore.
D. Sept. 11, 1973, San Antonio, Tex.

Year	Team	Lg	G	W	L	T	N	PCT	Standing		
1933	DET	A	2	2	0	0	0	1.000	5	5	
1937			54	34	20	0	0	.630	3	3	2

Del Baker continued

Year	Team	Lg	G	W	L	T	N	PCT	Standing
1938			57	37	19	1	0	.661	5 4
1939			155	81	73	1	0	.526	5
1940			155	90	64	1	0	.584	1
1941			155	75	79	1	0	.487	4
1942			156	73	81	2	0	.474	5
1960	BOS	A	7	2	5	0	0	.286	8 8 7
8 yrs.			741	394	341	6	0	.536	

WORLD SERIES

Year	Team	Lg	G	W	L	T	N	PCT	Standing
1940	DET	A	7	3	4	0	0	.429	

George Bamberger

BAMBERGER, GEORGE IRVIN
B. Aug. 1, 1925, Staten Island, N. Y.

Year	Team	Lg	G	W	L	T	N	PCT	Standing
1978	MIL	A	162	93	69	0	0	.574	3
1979			161	95	66	0	0	.590	2
1980			92	47	45	0	0	.511	2 4 3
1982	NY	N	162	65	97	0	0	.401	6
1983			46	16	30	0	0	.348	6 6
1985	MIL	A	161	71	90	0	0	.441	6
1986			152	71	81	0	0	.467	6 6
7 yrs.			936	458	478	0	0	.489	

Dave Bancroft

BANCROFT, DAVID JAMES (Beauty)
B. Apr. 20, 1891, Sioux City, Iowa
D. Oct. 9, 1972, Superior, Wis.
Hall of Fame 1971.

Year	Team	Lg	G	W	L	T	N	PCT	Standing
1924	BOS	N	66	27	38	1	0	.415	6 8
1924			50	15	35	0	0	.300	8 8
1925			153	70	83	0	0	.458	5
1926			153	66	86	1	0	.434	7
1927			155	60	94	1	0	.390	7
4 yrs.			577	238	336	3	0	.415	

Frank Bancroft

BANCROFT, FRANK CARTER
B. May 9, 1846, Lancaster, Mass.
D. Mar. 30, 1921, Cincinnati, Ohio

Year	Team	Lg	G	W	L	T	N	PCT	Standing
1880	WOR	N	85	40	43	2	0	.482	5
1881	DET	N	84	41	43	0	0	.488	4
1882			86	42	41	3	0	.506	6
1883	CLE	N	100	55	42	3	0	.567	4
1884	PRO	N	114	84	28	2	0	.750	1
1885			110	53	57	0	0	.482	4
1887	PHI	AA	55	26	29	0	0	.473	5
1889	IND	N	68	25	43	0	0	.368	7 7
1902	CIN	N	16	9	7	0	0	.563	7 5 4
9 yrs.			718	375	333	10	0	.530	

Sam Barkley

BARKLEY, SAMUEL E
B. May 24, 1858, Wheeling, W. Va.
D. Apr. 20, 1912, Wheeling, W. Va.

Year	Team	Lg	G	W	L	T	N	PCT	Standing
1888	KC	AA	57	21	36	0	0	.368	8 8 8

Billy Barnie

BARNIE, WILLIAM HARRISON (Bald Billy)
B. Jan. 26, 1853, New York, N. Y.
D. July 15, 1900, Hartford, Conn.

Year	Team	Lg	G	W	L	T	N	PCT	Standing
1883	BAL	AA	96	28	68	0	0	.292	8
1884			108	63	43	2	0	.594	6
1885			110	41	68	1	0	.376	8
1886			139	48	83	8	0	.366	8
1887			141	77	58	6	0	.570	3
1888			138	57	80	0	1	.416	5
1889			139	70	65	4	0	.519	5
1890			38	15	19	4	0	.441	6

Billy Barnie continued

Year	Team	Lg	G	W	L	T	N	PCT	Standing
1891			139	72	63	4	0	.533	4 3
1892	WAS	N	2	0	2	0	0	.000	11 10
1893	LOU	N	126	50	75	1	0	.400	11
1894			131	36	94	0	1	.277	12
1897	BKN	N	136	61	71	4	0	.462	6
1898			35	15	20	0	0	.429	9 10
14 yrs.			1478	633	809	34	2	.439	

Ed Barrow

BARROW, EDWARD GRANT (Cousin Ed)
B. May 10, 1868, Springfield, Ill.
D. Dec. 15, 1953, Port Chester, N. Y.
Hall of Fame 1953.

Year	Team	Lg	G	W	L	T	N	PCT	Standing
1903	DET	A	137	65	71	1	0	.478	5
1904			84	32	46	6	0	.410	7 7
1918	BOS	A	126	75	51	0	0	.595	1
1919			138	66	71	1	0	.482	6
1920			154	72	81	1	0	.471	5
5 yrs.			639	310	320	9	0	.492	

WORLD SERIES

Year	Team	Lg	G	W	L	T	N	PCT	Standing
1918	BOS	A	6	4	2	0	0	.667	

Jack Barry

BARRY, JOHN JOSEPH
B. Apr. 26, 1887, Meriden, Conn.
D. Apr. 23, 1961, Shrewsbury, Mass.

Year	Team	Lg	G	W	L	T	N	PCT	Standing
1917	BOS	A	157	90	62	5	0	.592	2

Joe Battin

BATTIN, JOSEPH V.
B. Nov. 11, 1851, Philadelphia, Pa.
D. Dec. 10, 1937, Akron, Ohio

Year	Team	Lg	G	W	L	T	N	PCT	Standing
1883	PIT	AA	13	2	11	0	0	.154	7 7
1884			13	6	7	0	0	.462	12 10 11
1884	PIT	U	6	1	5	0	0	.167	8 8
2 yrs.			32	9	23	0	0	.281	

Hank Bauer

BAUER, HENRY ALBERT
B. July 31, 1922, East St. Louis, Ill.

Year	Team	Lg	G	W	L	T	N	PCT	Standing
1961	KC	A	102	35	67	0	0	.343	8 9
1962			162	72	90	0	0	.444	9
1964	BAL	A	163	97	65	1	0	.599	3
1965			162	94	68	0	0	.580	3
1966			160	97	63	0	0	.606	1
1967			161	76	85	0	0	.472	6
1968			80	43	37	0	0	.538	3 2
1969	OAK	A	149	80	69	0	0	.537	2 2
8 yrs.			1139	594	544	1	0	.522	

WORLD SERIES

Year	Team	Lg	G	W	L	T	N	PCT	Standing
1966	BAL	A	4	4	0	0	0	1.000	

Vern Benson

BENSON, VERNON ADAIR
B. Sept. 19, 1924, Granite Quarry, N. C.

Year	Team	Lg	G	W	L	T	N	PCT	Standing
1977	ATL	N	1	1	0	0	0	1.000	6 6 6

Yogi Berra

BERRA, LAWRENCE PETER
Father of Dale Berra.
B. May 12, 1925, St. Louis, Mo.
Hall of Fame 1972.

Year	Team	Lg	G	W	L	T	N	PCT	Standing
1964	NY	A	164	99	63	2	0	.611	1
1972	NY	N	156	83	73	0	0	.532	3

Yogi Berra continued

Year	Team	Lg	G	W	L	T	N	PCT	Standing
1973			161	82	79	0	0	.509	1
1974			162	71	91	0	0	.438	5
1975			109	56	53	0	0	.514	3 3
1984	NY	A	162	87	75	0	0	.537	3
1985			16	6	10	0	0	.375	7 2
7 yrs.			930	484	444	2	0	.522	

LEAGUE CHAMPIONSHIP SERIES

Year	Team	Lg	G	W	L	T	N	PCT	Standing
1973	NY	N	5	3	2	0	0	.600	

WORLD SERIES

Year	Team	Lg	G	W	L	T	N	PCT	Standing
1964	NY	A	7	3	4	0	0	.429	
1973	NY	N	7	3	4	0	0	.429	
2 yrs.			14	6	8	0	0	.429	

Hugo Bezdek

BEZDEK, HUGO FRANCIS
B. Apr. 1, 1883, Prague, Austria-Hungary
D. Sept. 19, 1952, Atlantic City, N. J.

Year	Team	Lg	G	W	L	T	N	PCT	Standing
1917	PIT	N	91	30	59	2	0	.337	8 8
1918			126	65	60	1	0	.520	4
1919			139	71	68	0	0	.511	4
3 yrs.			356	166	187	3	0	.470	

Bickerson

BICKERSON,

Year	Team	Lg	G	W	L	T	N	PCT	Standing
1884	WAS	AA	1	0	1	0	0	.000	13 13

Joe Birmingham

BIRMINGHAM, JOSEPH LEO (Dode)
B. Aug. 6, 1884, Elmira, N. Y.
D. Apr. 24, 1946, Tampico, Mexico

Year	Team	Lg	G	W	L	T	N	PCT	Standing
1912	CLE	A	28	21	7	0	0	.750	6 5
1913			155	86	66	3	0	.566	3
1914			157	51	102	4	0	.333	8
1915			28	12	16	0	0	.429	6 7
4 yrs.			368	170	191	7	0	.471	

Del Bissonette

BISSONETTE, DELPHIA LOUIS
B. Sept. 6, 1899, Winthrop, Me.
D. June 9, 1972, Augusta, Me.

Year	Team	Lg	G	W	L	T	N	PCT	Standing
1945	BOS	N	60	25	34	1	0	.424	7 6

Lena Blackburne

BLACKBURNE, RUSSELL AUBREY (Slats)
B. Oct. 23, 1886, Clifton Heights, Pa.
D. Feb. 29, 1968, Riverside, N. J.

Year	Team	Lg	G	W	L	T	N	PCT	Standing
1928	CHI	A	80	40	40	0	0	.500	6 5
1929			152	59	93	0	0	.388	7
2 yrs.			232	99	133	0	0	.427	

Ray Blades

BLADES, FRANCIS RAYMOND
B. Aug. 6, 1896, Mt. Vernon, Ill.
D. May 18, 1979, Lincoln, Ill.

Year	Team	Lg	G	W	L	T	N	PCT	Standing
1939	STL	N	155	92	61	2	0	.601	2
1940			39	14	24	1	0	.368	6 3
1948	BKN	N	1	1	0	0	0	1.000	5 5 3
3 yrs.			195	107	85	3	0	.557	

		G	W	L	T	N	PCT	Standing	

Walter Blair

BLAIR, WALTER ALLEN (Heavy)
B. Oct. 13, 1883, Landrus, Pa.
D. Aug. 20, 1948, Lewisburg, Pa.

			G	W	L	T	N	PCT	Standing		
1915	BUF	F	2	1	1	0	0	.500	8	8	6

Ossie Bluege

BLUEGE, OSWALD LOUIS
Brother of Otto Bluege.
B. Oct. 24, 1900, Chicago, Ill.
D. Oct. 14, 1985, Edina, Minn.

			G	W	L	T	N	PCT	Standing
1943	WAS	A	153	84	69	0	0	.549	2
1944			154	64	90	0	0	.416	8
1945			156	87	67	2	0	.565	2
1946			155	76	78	1	0	.494	4
1947			154	64	90	0	0	.416	7
5 yrs.			772	375	394	3	0	.488	

Tommy Bond

BOND, THOMAS HENRY
B. Apr. 2, 1856, Granard, Ireland
D. Jan. 24, 1941, Boston, Mass.

			G	W	L	T	N	PCT	Standing		
1882	WOR	N	6	2	4	0	0	.333	8	8	8

Steve Boros

BOROS, STEPHEN
B. Sept. 3, 1936, Flint, Mich.

			G	W	L	T	N	PCT	Standing	
1983	OAK	A	162	74	88	0	0	.457	4	
1984			44	20	24	0	0	.455	4	4
1986	SD	N	162	74	88	0	0	.457	4	
3 yrs.			368	168	200	0	0	.457		

Jim Bottomley

BOTTOMLEY, JAMES LeROY (Sunny Jim)
B. Apr. 23, 1900, Oglesby, Ill.
D. Dec. 11, 1959, St. Louis, Mo.
Hall of Fame 1974.

			G	W	L	T	N	PCT	Standing	
1937	STL	A	78	21	56	1	0	.273	7	8

Lou Boudreau

BOUDREAU, LOUIS
B. July 17, 1917, Harvey, Ill.
Hall of Fame 1970.

			G	W	L	T	N	PCT	Standing	
1942	CLE	A	156	75	79	2	0	.487	4	
1943			153	82	71	0	0	.536	3	
1944			155	72	82	1	0	.468	5	
1945			147	73	72	2	0	.503	5	
1946			156	68	86	2	0	.442	6	
1947			157	80	74	3	0	.519	4	
1948			156	97	58	1	0	.626	1	
1949			154	89	65	0	0	.578	3	
1950			155	92	62	1	0	.597	4	
1952	BOS	A	154	76	78	0	0	.494	6	
1953			153	84	69	0	0	.549	4	
1954			156	69	85	2	0	.448	4	
1955	KC	A	155	63	91	1	0	.409	6	
1956			154	52	102	0	0	.338	8	
1957			104	36	67	1	0	.350	8	7
1960	CHI	N	139	54	83	2	0	.394	8	7
16 yrs.			2404	1162	1224	18	0	.487		

WORLD SERIES
			G	W	L	T	N	PCT	
1948	CLE	A	6	4	2	0	0	.667	

Larry Bowa

BOWA, LAWRENCE ROBERT
B. Dec. 6, 1945, Sacramento, Calif.

			G	W	L	T	N	PCT	Standing	
1987	SD	N	162	65	97	0	0	.401	6	
1988			46	16	30	0	0	.348	5	3
2 yrs.			208	81	127	0	0	.389		

Frank Bowerman

BOWERMAN, FRANK EUGENE (Mike)
B. Dec. 5, 1868, Romeo, Mich.
D. Nov. 30, 1948, Romeo, Mich.

			G	W	L	T	N	PCT	Standing	
1909	BOS	N	79	23	54	2	0	.299	8	8

Ken Boyer

BOYER, KENTON LLOYD
Brother of Cloyd Boyer.
Brother of Clete Boyer.
B. May 20, 1931, Liberty, Mo.
D. Sept. 7, 1982, St. Louis, Mo.

			G	W	L	T	N	PCT	Standing	
1978	STL	N	143	62	81	0	0	.434	6	5
1979			163	86	76	1	0	.531	3	
1980			51	18	33	0	0	.353	6	4
3 yrs.			357	166	190	1	0	.466		

Bill Bradley

BRADLEY, WILLIAM JOSEPH
B. Feb. 13, 1878, Cleveland, Ohio
D. Mar. 11, 1954, Cleveland, Ohio

			G	W	L	T	N	PCT	Standing	
1905	CLE	A	41	20	21	0	0	.488	1	2	5
1914	BKN	F	157	77	77	3	0	.500	5	
2 yrs.			198	97	98	3	0	.497		

Bobby Bragan

BRAGAN, ROBERT RANDALL
B. Oct. 30, 1917, Birmingham, Ala.

			G	W	L	T	N	PCT	Standing	
1956	PIT	N	157	66	88	3	0	.429	7	
1957			104	36	67	1	0	.350	8	7
1958	CLE	A	67	31	36	0	0	.463	5	4
1963	MIL	N	163	84	78	1	0	.519	6	
1964			162	88	74	0	0	.543	5	
1965			162	86	76	0	0	.531	5	
1966	ATL	N	112	52	59	1	0	.468	5	5
7 yrs.			927	443	478	6	0	.481		

Roger Bresnahan

BRESNAHAN, ROGER PHILIP (The Duke of Tralee)
B. June 11, 1879, Toledo, Ohio
D. Dec. 4, 1944, Toledo, Ohio
Hall of Fame 1945.

			G	W	L	T	N	PCT	Standing	
1909	STL	N	154	54	98	2	0	.355	7	
1910			153	63	90	0	0	.412	7	
1911			158	75	74	9	0	.503	5	
1912			153	63	90	0	0	.412	6	
1915	CHI	N	157	73	80	3	1	.477	4	
5 yrs.			775	328	432	14	1	.432		

Dave Bristol

BRISTOL, JAMES DAVID
B. June 23, 1933, Macon, Ga.

			G	W	L	T	N	PCT	Standing	
1966	CIN	N	77	39	38	0	0	.506	8	7
1967			162	87	75	0	0	.537	4	
1968			163	83	79	1	0	.512	4	
1969			163	89	73	1	0	.549	3	
1970	MIL	A	163	65	97	1	0	.401	5	
1971			161	69	92	0	0	.429	6	
1972			30	10	20	0	0	.333	6	6

Dave Bristol continued

			G	W	L	T	N	PCT	Standing	
1976	ATL	N	162	70	92	0	0	.432	6	
1977			29	8	21	0	0	.276	6	6
1977			131	52	79	0	0	.397	6	6
1979	SF	N	22	10	12	0	0	.455	4	4
1980			161	75	86	0	0	.466	5	
11 yrs.			1424	657	764	3	0	.462		

Freeman Brown

BROWN, FREEMAN
B. Jan. 31, 1845, Hubbardstown, Mass.
D. Dec. 27, 1916, Worcester, Mass.

			G	W	L	T	N	PCT	Standing	
1882	WOR	N	41	9	32	0	0	.220	8	8

Three Finger Brown

BROWN, MORDECAI PETER CENTENNIAL (Miner)
B. Oct. 19, 1876, Nyesville, Ind.
D. Feb. 14, 1948, Terre Haute, Ind.
Hall of Fame 1949.

			G	W	L	T	N	PCT	Standing	
1914	STL	F	114	50	63	1	0	.442	7	8

Tom Brown

BROWN, THOMAS T. (Handsome)
B. Sept. 21, 1860, Liverpool, England
D. Oct. 25, 1927, Washington, D. C.

			G	W	L	T	N	PCT	Standing	
1897	WAS	N	99	52	46	1	0	.531	11	6
1898			38	12	26	0	0	.316	11	11
2 yrs.			137	64	72	1	0	.471		

Earle Brucker

BRUCKER, EARLE FRANCIS, SR.
Father of Earle Brucker.
B. May 6, 1901, Albany, N. Y.
D. May 8, 1981, San Diego, Calif.

			G	W	L	T	N	PCT	Standing		
1952	CIN	N	5	3	2	0	0	.600	7	7	6

Al Buckenberger

BUCKENBERGER, ALBERT C.
B. Jan. 31, 1861, Detroit, Mich.
D. July 1, 1917, Syracuse, N. Y.

			G	W	L	T	N	PCT	Standing	
1889	COL	AA	140	60	78	2	0	.435	6	
1890			80	39	41	0	0	.488	5	2
1892	PIT	N	99	55	43	1	0	.561	6	6
1893			131	81	48	2	0	.628	2	
1894			110	53	55	1	1	.491	7	7
1895	STL	N	50	16	34	0	0	.320	11	11
1902	BOS	N	142	73	64	5	0	.533	3	
1903			140	58	80	2	0	.420	6	
1904			155	55	98	2	0	.359	7	
9 yrs.			1047	490	541	15	1	.475		

Charlie Buffinton

BUFFINTON, CHARLES G.
B. June 14, 1861, Fall River, Mass.
D. Sept. 23, 1907, Fall River, Mass.

			G	W	L	T	N	PCT	Standing	
1890	PHI	P	116	61	54	1	0	.530	5	5

Jack Burdock

BURDOCK, JOHN JOSEPH (Black Jack)
B. 1851, Brooklyn, N. Y.
D. Nov. 28, 1931, Brooklyn, N. Y.

			G	W	L	T	N	PCT	Standing	
1883	BOS	N	54	30	24	0	0	.556	4	1

581

Jimmy Burke

BURKE, JAMES TIMOTHY (Sunset Jimmy)
B. Oct. 12, 1874, St. Louis, Mo.
D. Mar. 26, 1942, St. Louis, Mo.

			G	W	L	T	N	PCT	Standing		
1905	STL	N	90	34	56	0	0	.378	7	6	6
1918	STL	A	61	29	31	1	0	.483	6	5	
1919			140	67	72	1	0	.482	5		
1920			154	76	77	1	0	.497	4		
4 yrs.			445	206	236	3	0	.466			

Watch Burnham

BURNHAM, GEORGE WALTER
B. May 20, 1860, Albion, Mich.
D. Nov. 18, 1902, Detroit, Mich.

			G	W	L	T	N	PCT	Standing		
1887	IND	N	28	6	22	0	0	.214	8	8	

Tom Burns

BURNS, THOMAS EVERETT
B. Mar. 30, 1857, Honesdale, Pa.
D. Mar. 19, 1902, Jersey City, N. J.

			G	W	L	T	N	PCT	Standing	
1892	PIT	N	56	25	30	1	0	.455	6	6
1898	CHI	N	152	85	65	2	0	.567	4	
1899			152	75	73	4	0	.507	8	
3 yrs.			360	185	168	7	0	.524		

Bill Burwell

BURWELL, WILLIAM EDWIN
B. Mar. 27, 1895, Jarbalo, Kans.
D. June 11, 1973, Ormond Beach, Fla.

			G	W	L	T	N	PCT	Standing	
1947	PIT	N	1	1	0	0	0	1.000	8	7

Donie Bush

BUSH, OWEN JOSEPH
B. Oct. 8, 1887, Indianapolis, Ind.
D. Mar. 28, 1972, Indianapolis, Ind.

			G	W	L	T	N	PCT	Standing	
1923	WAS	A	155	75	78	2	0	.490	4	
1927	PIT	N	156	94	60	2	0	.610	1	
1928			152	85	67	0	0	.559	4	
1929			119	67	51	1	0	.568	2	2
1930	CHI	A	154	62	92	0	0	.403	7	
1931			156	56	97	3	0	.366	8	
1933	CIN	N	153	58	94	1	0	.382	8	
7 yrs.			1045	497	539	9	0	.480		

WORLD SERIES

			G	W	L	T	N	PCT	
1927	PIT	N	4	0	4	0	0	.000	

Ormond Butler

BUTLER, ORMOND HOOK
B. Nov. 18, 1854, West Virginia
D. Sept. 12, 1915, Baltimore, Md.

			G	W	L	T	N	PCT	Standing		
1883	PIT	AA	53	17	36	0	0	.321	6	7	7

Charlie Byrne

BYRNE, CHARLES H.
B. Sept., 1843, New York, N. Y.
D. Jan. 4, 1898, New York, N. Y.

			G	W	L	T	N	PCT	Standing	
1885	BKN	AA	75	38	37	0	0	.507	7	5
1886			141	76	61	4	0	.555	3	
1887			138	60	74	4	0	.448	6	
3 yrs.			354	174	172	8	0	.503		

Nixey Callahan

CALLAHAN, JAMES JOSEPH (Cal)
B. Mar. 18, 1874, Fitchburg, Mass.
D. Oct. 4, 1934, Boston, Mass.

			G	W	L	T	N	PCT	Standing	
1903	CHI	A	138	60	77	1	0	.438	7	
1904			42	23	18	1	0	.561	4	3
1912			158	78	76	4	0	.506	4	
1913			153	78	74	1	0	.513	5	
1914			157	70	84	3	0	.455	6	
1916	PIT	N	157	65	89	3	0	.422	6	
1917			61	20	40	1	0	.333	8	8
7 yrs.			866	394	458	14	0	.462		

Bill Cammeyer

CAMMEYER, WILLIAM HENRY
B. Mar. 20, 1821, New York, N. Y.
D. Sept. 4, 1898, New York, N. Y.

			G	W	L	T	N	PCT	Standing
1876	NY	N	57	21	35	1	0	.375	6

Joe Cantillon

CANTILLON, JOSEPH D. (Pongo)
B. Aug. 19, 1861, Janesville, Wis.
D. Jan. 31, 1930, Hickman, Ky.

			G	W	L	T	N	PCT	Standing
1907	WAS	A	154	49	102	3	0	.325	8
1908			155	67	85	3	0	.441	7
1909			156	42	110	4	0	.276	8
3 yrs.			465	158	297	10	0	.347	

Max Carey

CAREY, MAX (Scoops)
Born Maximilian Carnarius.
B. Jan. 11, 1890, Terre Haute, Ind.
D. May 30, 1976, Miami, Fla.
Hall of Fame 1961.

			G	W	L	T	N	PCT	Standing
1932	BKN	N	154	81	73	0	0	.526	3
1933			157	65	88	4	0	.425	6
2 yrs.			311	146	161	4	0	.476	

Bill Carrigan

CARRIGAN, WILLIAM FRANCIS (Rough)
B. Oct. 22, 1883, Lewiston, Me.
D. July 8, 1969, Lewiston, Me.

			G	W	L	T	N	PCT	Standing	
1913	BOS	A	70	40	30	0	0	.571	5	4
1914			159	91	62	6	0	.595	2	
1915			155	101	50	4	0	.669	1	
1916			156	91	63	2	0	.591	1	
1927			154	51	103	0	0	.331	8	
1928			154	57	96	1	0	.373	8	
1929			155	58	96	1	0	.377	8	
7 yrs.			1003	489	500	14	0	.494		

WORLD SERIES

			G	W	L	T	N	PCT	
1915	BOS	A	5	4	1	0	0	.800	
1916			5	4	1	0	0	.800	
2 yrs.			10	8	2	0	0	.800	

Bob Caruthers

CARUTHERS, ROBERT LEE (Parisian Bob)
B. Jan. 5, 1864, Memphis, Tenn.
D. Aug. 5, 1911, Peoria, Ill.

			G	W	L	T	N	PCT	Standing	
1892	STL	N	50	16	32	2	0	.333	12	11

Phil Cavarretta

CAVARRETTA, PHILIP JOSEPH
B. July 19, 1916, Chicago, Ill.

			G	W	L	T	N	PCT	Standing	
1951	CHI	N	74	27	47	0	0	.365	7	8
1952			155	77	77	1	0	.500	5	
1953			155	65	89	1	0	.422	7	
3 yrs.			384	169	213	2	0	.442		

Ollie Caylor

CAYLOR, OLIVER PERRY
B. Dec. 14, 1849, Dayton, Ohio
D. Oct. 19, 1897, Winona, Minn.

			G	W	L	T	N	PCT	Standing	
1885	CIN	AA	112	63	49	0	0	.563	2	
1886			141	65	73	3	0	.471	5	
1887	NY	AA	100	35	60	5	0	.368	7	7
3 yrs.			353	163	182	8	0	.472		

Frank Chance

CHANCE, FRANK LEROY (Husk, The Peerless Leader)
B. Sept. 9, 1877, Fresno, Calif.
D. Sept. 15, 1924, Los Angeles, Calif.
Hall of Fame 1946.

			G	W	L	T	N	PCT	Standing	
1905	CHI	N	90	55	33	2	0	.625	4	3
1906			155	116	36	3	0	.763	1	
1907			155	107	45	3	0	.704	1	
1908			158	99	55	4	0	.643	1	
1909			155	104	49	2	0	.680	2	
1910			154	104	50	0	0	.675	1	
1911			158	92	62	3	1	.597	2	
1912			153	91	59	2	1	.607	3	
1913	NY	A	153	57	94	2	0	.377	7	
1914			137	60	74	3	0	.448	7	6
1923	BOS	A	154	61	91	2	0	.401	8	
11 yrs.			1622	946	648	26	2	.593		
									6th	

WORLD SERIES

			G	W	L	T	N	PCT		
1906	CHI	N	6	2	4	0	0	.333		
1907			5	4	0	1	0	1.000		
1908			5	4	1	0	0	.800		
1910			5	1	4	0	0	.200		
4 yrs.			21	11	9	1	0	.550		
								10th		5th

Ben Chapman

CHAPMAN, WILLIAM BENJAMIN
B. Dec. 25, 1908, Nashville, Tenn.

			G	W	L	T	N	PCT	Standing	
1945	PHI	N	87	28	57	2	0	.329	8	8
1946			155	69	85	1	0	.448	5	
1947			155	62	92	1	0	.403	7	
1948			79	37	42	0	0	.468	7	6
4 yrs.			476	196	276	4	0	.415		

Jack Chapman

CHAPMAN, JOHN CURTIS
B. May 8, 1843, Brooklyn, N. Y.
D. June 10, 1916, Brooklyn, N. Y.

			G	W	L	T	N	PCT	Standing	
1876	LOU	N	69	30	36	3	0	.455	5	
1877			61	35	25	1	0	.583	2	
1878	MIL	N	61	15	45	1	0	.250	6	
1882	WOR	N	37	7	30	0	0	.189	8	8
1883	DET	N	101	40	58	3	0	.408	7	
1884			114	28	84	2	0	.250	8	
1885	BUF	N	88	31	57	0	0	.352	7	6
1889	LOU	AA	7	1	6	0	0	.143	8	8
1890			136	88	44	4	0	.667	1	
1891			141	55	84	2	0	.396	7	
1892	LOU	N	58	23	35	0	0	.397	10	9
11 yrs.			873	353	504	16	0	.412		

	G	W	L	T	N	PCT	Standing

Hal Chase

CHASE, HAROLD HOMER (Prince Hal)
B. Feb. 13, 1883, Los Gatos, Calif.
D. May 18, 1947, Colusa, Calif.

		G	W	L	T	N	PCT	Standing
1910	NY A	14	10	4	0	0	.714	3	2
1911		153	76	76	1	0	.500	6
2 yrs.		167	86	80	1	0	.518

John Clapp

CLAPP, JOHN EDGAR
Brother of Aaron Clapp.
B. July 17, 1851, Ithaca, N. Y.
D. Dec. 18, 1904, Ithaca, N. Y.

		G	W	L	T	N	PCT	Standing
1878	IND N	63	24	36	3	0	.400	5
1879	BUF N	79	46	32	1	0	.590	3
1880	CIN N	83	21	59	3	0	.263	8
1883	NY N	98	46	50	2	0	.479	6
4 yrs.		323	137	177	9	0	.436

Fred Clarke

CLARKE, FRED CLIFFORD (Cap)
Brother of Josh Clarke.
B. Oct. 3, 1872, Winterset, Iowa
D. Aug. 14, 1960, Winfield, Kans.
Hall of Fame 1945.

		G	W	L	T	N	PCT	Standing
1897	LOU N	92	35	54	2	1	.393	9	11
1898		154	70	81	3	0	.464	9
1899		156	75	77	3	1	.493	9
1900	PIT N	140	79	60	1	0	.568	2
1901		140	90	49	1	0	.647	1
1902		142	103	36	3	0	.741	1
1903		141	91	49	1	0	.650	1
1904		156	87	66	3	0	.569	4
1905		155	96	57	2	0	.627	2
1906		154	93	60	1	0	.608	3
1907		157	91	63	3	0	.591	2
1908		155	98	56	1	0	.636	2
1909		154	110	42	1	1	.724	1
1910		154	86	67	1	0	.562	3
1911		156	85	69	1	1	.552	3
1912		153	93	58	1	1	.616	5
1913		155	78	71	6	0	.523	4
1914		158	69	85	4	0	.448	7
1915		157	73	81	2	1	.474	5
19 yrs.		2829	1602	1181	40	6	.576

WORLD SERIES

		G	W	L	T	N	PCT	Standing
1903	PIT N	8	3	5	0	0	.375
1909		7	4	3	0	0	.571
2 yrs.		15	7	8	0	0	.467

Jack Clements

CLEMENTS, JOHN J.
B. June 24, 1864, Philadelphia, Pa.
D. May 23, 1941, Philadelphia, Pa.

		G	W	L	T	N	PCT	Standing
1890	PHI N	19	13	6	0	0	.684	1	2	3

Ty Cobb

COBB, TYRUS RAYMOND (The Georgia Peach)
B. Dec. 18, 1886, Narrows, Ga.
D. July 17, 1961, Atlanta, Ga.
Hall of Fame 1936.

		G	W	L	T	N	PCT	Standing
1921	DET A	154	71	82	1	0	.464	6
1922		155	79	75	1	0	.513	3
1923		155	83	71	1	0	.539	2
1924		156	86	68	2	0	.558	3
1925		156	81	73	2	0	.526	4
1926		157	79	75	3	0	.513	6
6 yrs.		933	479	444	10	0	.519

Mickey Cochrane

COCHRANE, GORDON STANLEY (Black Mike)
B. Apr. 6, 1903, Bridgewater, Mass.
D. June 28, 1962, Lake Forest, Ill.
Hall of Fame 1947.

		G	W	L	T	N	PCT	Standing
1934	DET A	154	101	53	0	0	.656	1
1935		152	93	58	1	0	.616	1
1936		154	83	71	0	0	.539	2
1937		29	16	13	0	0	.552	3	2
1937		72	39	32	1	0	.549	3	2
1938		98	47	51	0	0	.480	5	4
5 yrs.		659	379	278	2	0	.577

WORLD SERIES

		G	W	L	T	N	PCT	Standing
1934	DET A	7	3	4	0	0	.429
1935		6	4	2	0	0	.667
2 yrs.		13	7	6	0	0	.538

Andy Cohen

COHEN, ANDREW HOWARD
Brother of Syd Cohen.
B. Oct. 25, 1904, Baltimore, Md.
D. Oct. 29, 1988, El Paso, Tex.

		G	W	L	T	N	PCT	Standing
1960	PHI N	1	1	0	0	0	1.000	8	4	8

Bob Coleman

COLEMAN, ROBERT HUNTER
B. Sept. 26, 1890, Huntingburg, Ind.
D. July 16, 1959, Boston, Mass.

		G	W	L	T	N	PCT	Standing
1943	BOS N	46	21	25	0	0	.457	6	6
1944		155	65	89	1	0	.422	6
1945		94	42	51	1	0	.452	7	6
3 yrs.		295	128	165	2	0	.437

Jerry Coleman

COLEMAN, GERALD FRANCIS
B. Sept. 14, 1924, San Jose, Calif.

		G	W	L	T	N	PCT	Standing
1980	SD N	163	73	89	1	0	.451	6

Eddie Collins

COLLINS, EDWARD TROWBRIDGE, SR. (Cocky)
Played as Eddie Sullivan In 1906.
Father of Eddie Collins.
B. May 2, 1887, Millerton, N. Y.
D. Mar. 25, 1951, Boston, Mass.
Hall of Fame 1939.

		G	W	L	T	N	PCT	Standing
1924	CHI A	27	14	13	0	0	.519	6	6	8
1925		154	79	75	0	0	.513	5
1926		155	81	72	2	0	.529	5
3 yrs.		336	174	160	2	0	.521

Jimmy Collins

COLLINS, JAMES JOSEPH
B. Jan. 16, 1870, Buffalo, N. Y.
D. Mar. 6, 1943, Buffalo, N. Y.
Hall of Fame 1945.

		G	W	L	T	N	PCT	Standing
1901	BOS A	138	79	57	2	0	.581	2
1902		138	77	60	1	0	.562	3
1903		141	91	47	3	0	.659	1
1904		157	95	59	3	0	.617	1
1905		153	78	74	1	0	.513	4
1906		115	35	79	1	0	.307	8	8
6 yrs.		842	455	376	11	0	.548

WORLD SERIES

		G	W	L	T	N	PCT	Standing
1903	BOS A	8	5	3	0	0	.625

Shano Collins

COLLINS, JOHN FRANCIS
B. Dec. 4, 1885, Charlestown, Mass.
D. Sept. 10, 1955, Newton, Mass.

		G	W	L	T	N	PCT	Standing
1931	BOS A	153	62	90	1	0	.408	6
1932		55	11	44	0	0	.200	8	8
2 yrs.		208	73	134	1	0	.353

Charlie Comiskey

COMISKEY, CHARLES ALBERT (Commy, The Old Roman)
B. Aug. 15, 1859, Chicago, Ill.
D. Oct. 26, 1931, Eagle River, Wis.
Hall of Fame 1939.

		G	W	L	T	N	PCT	Standing
1883	STL AA	19	12	7	0	0	.632	2	2
1884		25	16	7	2	0	.696	5	4
1885		112	79	33	0	0	.705	1
1886		139	93	46	0	0	.669	1
1887		138	95	40	3	0	.704	1
1888		137	92	45	2	0	.681	1
1889		141	90	45	6	0	.667	2
1890	CHI P	138	75	62	1	0	.547	4
1891	STL AA	141	86	52	2	1	.623	2
1892	CIN N	152	82	68	2	0	.547	5
1893		131	65	63	3	0	.508	6
1894		134	55	75	2	2	.423	10
12 yrs.		1407	840	541	23	3	.608
								3rd

Roger Connor

CONNOR, ROGER
Brother of Joe Connor.
B. July 1, 1857, Waterbury, Conn.
D. Jan. 4, 1931, Waterbury, Conn.
Hall of Fame 1976.

		G	W	L	T	N	PCT	Standing
1896	STL N	46	8	37	1	0	.178	11	11	11

Dusty Cooke

COOKE, ALLEN LINDSEY
B. June 23, 1907, Swepsonville, N. C.
D. Nov. 21, 1987, Raleigh, N. C.

		G	W	L	T	N	PCT	Standing
1948	PHI N	13	6	6	1	0	.500	7	6	6

Jack Coombs

COOMBS, JOHN WESLEY (Cy)
B. Nov. 18, 1882, LeGrand, Iowa
D. Apr. 15, 1957, Palestine, Tex.

		G	W	L	T	N	PCT	Standing
1919	PHI N	63	18	44	1	0	.290	8	8

Johnny Cooney

COONEY, JOHN WALTER
Son of Jimmy Cooney.
Brother of Jimmy Cooney.
B. Mar. 18, 1901, Cranston, R. I.
D. July 8, 1986, Sarasota, Fla.

		G	W	L	T	N	PCT	Standing
1949	BOS N	46	20	25	1	0	.444	4	4

Pat Corrales

CORRALES, PATRICK (Ike)
B. Mar. 20, 1941, Los Angeles, Calif.

		G	W	L	T	N	PCT	Standing
1978	TEX A	1	1	0	0	0	1.000	2	2
1979		162	83	79	0	0	.512	3
1980		163	76	85	2	0	.472	4
1982	PHI N	162	89	73	0	0	.549	2
1983		86	43	42	1	0	.506	1	1
1983	CLE A	62	30	32	0	0	.484	7	7

	G	W	L	T	N	PCT	Standing		

Pat Corrales *continued*

		G	W	L	T	N	PCT	Standing	
1984		163	75	87	1	0	.463	6	
1985		162	60	102	0	0	.370	7	
1986		163	84	78	1	0	.519	5	
1987		87	31	56	0	0	.356	7	7
9 yrs.		1211	572	634	5	0	.474		

Red Corriden

CORRIDEN, JOHN MICHAEL, SR.
Father of John Corriden.
B. Sept. 4, 1887, Logansport, Ind.
D. Sept. 28, 1959, Indianapolis, Ind.

		G	W	L	T	N	PCT	Standing	
1950	CHI A	125	52	72	1	0	.419	8	6

Chuck Cottier

COTTIER, CHARLES KEITH
B. Jan. 8, 1936, Delta, Colo.

		G	W	L	T	N	PCT	Standing	
1984	SEA A	27	15	12	0	0	.556	7	6
1985		162	74	88	0	0	.457	6	
1986		28	9	19	0	0	.321	6	7
3 yrs.		217	98	119	0	0	.452		

Bobby Cox

COX, ROBERT JOE
B. May 21, 1941, Tulsa, Okla.

		G	W	L	T	N	PCT	Standing	
1978	ATL N	162	69	93	0	0	.426	6	
1979		160	66	94	0	0	.413	6	
1980		161	81	80	0	0	.503	4	
1981		55	25	29	1	0	.463	4	(1st)
1981		52	25	27	0	0	.481	5	(2nd)
1982	TOR A	162	78	84	0	0	.481	6	
1983		162	89	73	0	0	.549	4	
1984		163	89	73	1	0	.549	2	
1985		161	99	62	0	0	.615	1	
8 yrs.		1238	621	615	2	0	.502		

LEAGUE CHAMPIONSHIP SERIES

		G	W	L	T	N	PCT		
1985	TOR A	7	3	4	0	0	.429		

Harry Craft

CRAFT, HARRY FRANCIS
B. Apr. 19, 1915, Ellisville, Miss.

		G	W	L	T	N	PCT	Standing		
1957	KC A	50	23	27	0	0	.460	8	7	
1958		156	73	81	2	0	.474	7		
1959		154	66	88	0	0	.429	7		
1961	CHI N	16	7	9	0	0	.438	7	7	7
1962	HOU N	162	64	96	2	0	.400	8		
1963		162	66	96	0	0	.407	9		
1964		149	61	88	0	0	.409	9	9	
7 yrs.		849	360	485	4	0	.426			

Roger Craig

CRAIG, ROGER LEE
B. Feb. 17, 1930, Durham, N.C.

		G	W	L	T	N	PCT	Standing	
1978	SD N	162	84	78	0	0	.519	4	
1979		161	68	93	0	0	.422	5	
1985	SF N	18	6	12	0	0	.333	6	6
1986		162	83	79	0	0	.512	3	
1987		162	90	72	0	0	.556	1	
1988		162	83	79	0	0	.512	4	
1989		162	92	70	0	0	.568	1	
7 yrs.		989	506	483	0	0	.512		

LEAGUE CHAMPIONSHIP SERIES

		G	W	L	T	N	PCT		
1987	SF N	7	3	4	0	0	.429		
1989		5	4	1	0	0	.800		
2 yrs.		12	7	5	0	0	.583		
			8th				**4th**		

Roger Craig *continued*

WORLD SERIES

		G	W	L	T	N	PCT		
1989	SF N	4	0	4	0	0	.000		

Del Crandall

CRANDALL, DELMAR WESLEY
B. Mar. 5, 1930, Ontario, Calif.

		G	W	L	T	N	PCT	Standing	
1972	MIL A	124	54	70	0	0	.435	6	6
1973		162	74	88	0	0	.457	5	
1974		162	76	86	0	0	.469	5	
1975		161	67	94	0	0	.416	5	5
1983	SEA A	89	34	55	0	0	.382	7	7
1984		135	59	76	0	0	.437	7	6
6 yrs.		833	364	469	0	0	.437		

Sam Crane

CRANE, SAMUEL NEWHALL
B. Jan. 2, 1854, Springfield, Mass.
D. June 26, 1925, New York, N.Y.

		G	W	L	T	N	PCT	Standing	
1880	BUF N	84	24	58	2	0	.293	7	
1884	CIN U	70	49	21	0	0	.700	5	3
2 yrs.		154	73	79	2	0	.480		

Gavvy Cravath

CRAVATH, CLIFFORD CARLTON
(Cactus)
B. Mar. 23, 1881, Escondido, Calif.
D. May 23, 1963, Laguna Beach, Calif.

		G	W	L	T	N	PCT	Standing	
1919	PHI N	75	29	46	0	0	.387	8	8
1920		153	62	91	0	0	.405	8	
2 yrs.		228	91	137	0	0	.399		

George Creamer

CREAMER, GEORGE W.
Born George W. Triebel.
B. 1855, Philadelphia, Pa.
D. June 27, 1886, Philadelphia, Pa.

		G	W	L	T	N	PCT	Standing		
1884	PIT AA	8	0	8	0	0	.000	10	12	11

Joe Cronin

CRONIN, JOSEPH EDWARD
B. Oct. 12, 1906, San Francisco, Calif.
D. Sept. 7, 1984, Osterville, Mass.
Hall of Fame 1956.

		G	W	L	T	N	PCT	Standing	
1933	WAS A	153	99	53	1	0	.651	1	
1934		155	66	86	3	0	.434	7	
1935	BOS A	154	78	75	1	0	.510	4	
1936		155	74	80	1	0	.481	6	
1937		154	80	72	2	0	.526	5	
1938		150	88	61	1	0	.591	2	
1939		152	89	62	1	0	.589	2	
1940		154	82	72	0	0	.532	4	
1941		155	84	70	1	0	.545	2	
1942		152	93	59	0	0	.612	2	
1943		155	68	84	3	0	.447	7	
1944		156	77	77	2	0	.500	4	
1945		157	71	83	3	0	.461	7	
1946		156	104	50	2	0	.675	1	
1947		157	83	71	3	0	.539	3	
15 yrs.		2315	1236	1055	24	0	.540		

WORLD SERIES

		G	W	L	T	N	PCT		
1933	WAS A	5	1	4	0	0	.200		
1946	BOS A	7	3	4	0	0	.429		
2 yrs.		12	4	8	0	0	.333		

Jack Crooks

CROOKS, JOHN CHARLES
B. Nov. 9, 1866, St. Paul, Minn.
D. Jan. 29, 1918, St. Louis, Mo.

		G	W	L	T	N	PCT	Standing		
1892	STL N	61	27	33	1	0	.450	11	**12**	11

Lave Cross

CROSS, LAFAYETTE NAPOLEON
Brother of Frank Cross.
Brother of Amos Cross.
B. May 12, 1866, Milwaukee, Wis.
D. Sept. 6, 1927, Toledo, Ohio

		G	W	L	T	N	PCT	Standing	
1899	CLE N	38	8	30	0	0	.211	12	12

Ed Curtis

CURTIS, EDWIN R.
Deceased.

		G	W	L	T	N	PCT	Standing	
1884	ALT U	25	6	19	0	0	.240	11	

Charlie Cushman

CUSHMAN, CHARLES H.
B. May 25, 1850, New York, N.Y.
D. June 29, 1909, Milwaukee, Wis.

		G	W	L	T	N	PCT	Standing	
1891	MIL AA	36	21	15	0	0	.583	3	

Ned Cuthbert

CUTHBERT, EDGAR EDWARD
B. June 20, 1845, Philadelphia, Pa.
D. Feb. 6, 1905, St. Louis, Mo.

		G	W	L	T	N	PCT	Standing	
1882	STL AA	80	37	43	0	0	.463	5	

Bill Dahlen

DAHLEN, WILLIAM FREDERICK (Bad Bill)
B. Jan. 5, 1870, Nelliston, N.Y.
D. Dec. 5, 1950, Brooklyn, N.Y.

		G	W	L	T	N	PCT	Standing	
1910	BKN N	156	64	90	2	0	.416	6	
1911		154	64	86	4	0	.427	7	
1912		153	58	95	0	0	.379	7	
1913		152	65	84	3	0	.436	6	
4 yrs.		615	251	355	9	0	.414		

Alvin Dark

DARK, ALVIN RALPH (Blackie)
B. Jan. 7, 1922, Comanche, Okla.

		G	W	L	T	N	PCT	Standing		
1961	SF N	155	85	69	1	0	.552	3		
1962		165	103	62	0	0	.624	1		
1963		162	88	74	0	0	.543	3		
1964		162	90	72	0	0	.556	4		
1966	KC A	160	74	86	0	0	.463	7		
1967		121	52	69	0	0	.430	10	10	
1968	CLE A	162	86	75	1	0	.534	3		
1969		161	62	99	0	0	.385	6		
1970		162	76	86	0	0	.469	5		
1971		103	42	61	0	0	.408	6	6	
1974	OAK A	162	90	72	0	0	.556	1		
1975		162	98	64	0	0	.605	1		
1977	SD N	113	48	65	0	0	.425	5	5	
13 yrs.		1950	994	954	2	0	.510			

LEAGUE CHAMPIONSHIP SERIES

		G	W	L	T	N	PCT		
1974	OAK A	4	3	1	0	0	.750		
1975		3	0	3	0	0	.000		
2 yrs.		7	3	4	0	0	.429		

	G	W	L	T	N	PCT	Standing		

Alvin Dark continued

WORLD SERIES

		G	W	L	T	N	PCT		
1962	SF N	7	3	4	0	0	.429		
1974	OAK A	5	4	1	0	0	.800		
2 yrs.		12	7	5	0	0	.583		

Jim Davenport

DAVENPORT, JAMES HOUSTON
B. Aug. 17, 1933, Siluria, Ala.

		G	W	L	T	N	PCT	Standing	
1985	SF N	144	56	88	0	0	.389	6	6

Mordecai Davidson

DAVIDSON, MORDECAI H.
B. Nov. 30, 1846, Port Washington, Ohio
D. Sept. 6, 1940, Louisville, Ky.

		G	W	L	T	N	PCT	Standing	
1888	LOU AA	3	1	2	0	0	.333	8	8	7
1888		90	34	52	4	0	.395	8	7

George Davis

DAVIS, GEORGE STACEY
B. Aug. 23, 1870, Cohoes, N. Y.
D. Oct. 17, 1940, Philadelphia, Pa.

		G	W	L	T	N	PCT	Standing	
1895	NY N	33	16	17	0	0	.485	8	9
1900		78	39	37	2	0	.513	8	8
1901		141	52	85	4	0	.380	7	
3 yrs.		252	107	139	6	0	.435		

Harry Davis

DAVIS, HARRY H. (Jasper)
B. July 19, 1873, Philadelphia, Pa.
D. Aug. 11, 1947, Philadelphia, Pa.

		G	W	L	T	N	PCT	Standing	
1912	CLE A	127	54	71	2	0	.432	6	5

Spud Davis

DAVIS, VIRGIL LAWRENCE
B. Dec. 20, 1904, Birmingham, Ala.
D. Aug. 14, 1984, Birmingham, Ala.

		G	W	L	T	N	PCT	Standing	
1946	PIT N	3	1	2	0	0	.333	7	7

John Day

DAY, JOHN B.
B. Sept. 23, 1847, Colchester, Mass.
D. Jan. 25, 1925, Cliffside, N. J.

		G	W	L	T	N	PCT	Standing	
1899	NY N	66	29	35	1	1	.453	9	10

Bucky Dent

DENT, RUSSELL EARL
Born Russell Earl O'Dey.
B. Nov. 25, 1951, Savannah, Ga.

		G	W	L	T	N	PCT	Standing	
1989	NY A	40	18	22	0	0	.450	6	5

Bill Dickey

DICKEY, WILLIAM MALCOLM
Brother of George Dickey.
B. June 6, 1907, Bastrop, La.
Hall of Fame 1954.

		G	W	L	T	N	PCT	Standing	
1946	NY A	105	57	48	0	0	.543	2	3	3

Harry Diddlebock

DIDDLEBOCK, HENRY H.
B. June 27, 1854, Philadelphia, Pa.
D. Feb. 5, 1900, Philadelphia, Pa.

		G	W	L	T	N	PCT	Standing	
1896	STL N	17	7	10	0	0	.412	10	11

Larry Doby

DOBY, LAWRENCE EUGENE
B. Dec. 13, 1924, Camden, S. C.

		G	W	L	T	N	PCT	Standing	
1978	CHI A	87	37	50	0	0	.425	5	5

Patsy Donovan

DONOVAN, PATRICK JOSEPH
B. Mar. 16, 1865, Queenstown, Ireland
D. Dec. 25, 1953, Lawrence, Mass.

		G	W	L	T	N	PCT	Standing	
1897	PIT N	135	60	71	4	0	.458	8	
1899		131	69	58	4	0	.543	10	7
1901	STL N	142	76	64	2	0	.543	4	
1902		140	56	78	6	0	.418	6	
1903		139	43	94	2	0	.314	8	
1904	WAS A	139	37	97	5	0	.276	8	8
1906	BKN N	153	66	86	1	0	.434	5	
1907		153	65	83	5	0	.439	5	
1908		154	53	101	0	0	.344	7	
1910	BOS A	158	81	72	5	0	.529	4	
1911		153	78	75	0	0	.510	5	
11 yrs.		1597	684	879	34	0	.438		

Wild Bill Donovan

DONOVAN, WILLIAM EDWARD
B. Oct. 13, 1876, Lawrence, Mass.
D. Dec. 9, 1923, Forsyth, N. Y.

		G	W	L	T	N	PCT	Standing	
1915	NY A	154	69	83	2	0	.454	5	
1916		156	80	74	2	0	.519	4	
1917		155	71	82	2	0	.464	6	
1921	PHI N	87	25	62	0	0	.287	8	8
4 yrs.		552	245	301	6	0	.449		

Red Dooin

DOOIN, CHARLES SEBASTIAN
B. June 12, 1879, Cincinnati, Ohio
D. May 12, 1952, Rochester, N. Y.

		G	W	L	T	N	PCT	Standing	
1910	PHI N	157	78	75	4	0	.510	4	
1911		153	79	73	1	0	.520	4	
1912		152	73	79	0	0	.480	5	
1913		159	88	63	8	0	.583	2	
1914		154	74	80	0	0	.481	6	
5 yrs.		775	392	370	13	0	.514		

Mike Dorgan

DORGAN, MICHAEL CORNELIUS
Brother of Jerry Dorgan.
B. Oct. 2, 1853, Middletown, Conn.
D. Apr. 26, 1909, Syracuse, N. Y.

		G	W	L	T	N	PCT	Standing	
1879	SYR N	43	17	26	0	0	.395	6	7
1880	PRO N	39	26	12	1	0	.684	3	2
1881	WOR N	56	24	32	0	0	.429	7	8
3 yrs.		138	67	70	1	0	.489		

Tommy Dowd

DOWD, THOMAS JEFFERSON
(Buttermilk Tommy)
B. Apr. 20, 1869, Holyoke, Mass.
D. July 2, 1933, Holyoke, Mass.

		G	W	L	T	N	PCT	Standing	
1896	STL N	63	25	38	0	0	.397	11	11

Tommy Dowd continued

		G	W	L	T	N	PCT	Standing	
1897		29	6	22	1	0	.214	12	12
2 yrs.		92	31	60	1	0	.341		

Jack Doyle

DOYLE, JOHN JOSEPH (Dirty Jack)
B. Oct. 25, 1869, Killorgin, Ireland
D. Dec. 31, 1958, Holyoke, Mass.

		G	W	L	T	N	PCT	Standing	
1895	NY N	64	32	31	1	0	.508	8	9	9
1898	WAS N	17	8	9	0	0	.471	11	10	11
2 yrs.		81	40	40	1	0	.500		

Chuck Dressen

DRESSEN, CHARLES WALTER
B. Sept. 20, 1898, Decatur, Ill.
D. Aug. 10, 1966, Detroit, Mich.

		G	W	L	T	N	PCT	Standing	
1934	CIN N	60	21	39	0	0	.350	8	8
1935		154	68	85	1	0	.444	6	
1936		154	74	80	0	0	.481	5	
1937		130	51	78	1	0	.395	8	8
1951	BKN N	158	97	60	1	0	.618	2	
1952		155	96	57	2	0	.627	1	
1953		155	105	49	1	0	.682	1	
1955	WAS A	154	53	101	0	0	.344	8	
1956		155	59	95	1	0	.383	7	
1957		20	4	16	0	0	.200	8	8
1960	MIL N	154	88	66	0	0	.571	2	
1961		130	71	58	1	0	.550	3	4
1963	DET A	102	55	47	0	0	.539	9	5
1964		163	85	77	1	0	.525	4	
1965		120	65	55	0	0	.542	3	4
1966		26	16	10	0	0	.615	3	3
16 yrs.		1990	1008	973	9	0	.509		

WORLD SERIES

		G	W	L	T	N	PCT		
1952	BKN N	7	3	4	0	0	.429		
1953		6	2	4	0	0	.333		
2 yrs.		13	5	8	0	0	.385		

Hugh Duffy

DUFFY, HUGH
B. Nov. 26, 1866, Cranston, R. I.
D. Oct. 19, 1954, Boston, Mass.
Hall of Fame 1945.

		G	W	L	T	N	PCT	Standing	
1901	MIL A	139	48	89	2	0	.350	8	
1904	PHI N	155	52	100	3	0	.342	8	
1905		155	83	69	3	0	.546	4	
1906		154	71	82	1	0	.464	4	
1910	CHI A	156	68	85	3	0	.444	6	
1911		154	77	74	3	0	.510	4	
1921	BOS A	154	75	79	0	0	.487	5	
1922		154	61	93	0	0	.396	8	
8 yrs.		1221	535	671	15	0	.444		

Fred Dunlap

DUNLAP, FREDERICK C. (Sure Shot)
B. May 21, 1859, Philadelphia, Pa.
D. Dec. 1, 1902, Philadelphia, Pa.

		G	W	L	T	N	PCT	Standing	
1882	CLE N	80	42	36	2	0	.538	8	5
1884	STL U	83	66	16	1	0	.805	1	1
1885	STL N	50	21	29	0	0	.420	5	8
1885		22	9	11	2	0	.450	8	8
1889	PIT N	17	7	10	0	0	.412	7	7	5
4 yrs.		252	145	102	5	0	.587		

Leo Durocher

DUROCHER, LEO ERNEST (The Lip)
B. July 27, 1905, W. Springfield, Mass.

		G	W	L	T	N	PCT	Standing	
1939	BKN N	157	84	69	4	0	.549	3	
1940		156	88	65	3	0	.575	2	

Leo Durocher *continued*

Year			G	W	L	T	N	PCT	Standing	
1941			157	100	54	3	0	.649	1	
1942			155	104	50	1	0	.675	2	
1943			153	81	72	0	0	.529	3	
1944			155	63	91	1	0	.409	7	
1945			155	87	67	1	0	.565	3	
1946			157	96	60	1	0	.615	2	
1948			73	35	37	1	0	.486	5	3
1948	NY	N	79	41	38	0	0	.519	4	5
1949			156	73	81	2	0	.474	5	
1950			154	86	68	0	0	.558	3	
1951			157	98	59	0	0	.624	1	
1952			154	92	62	0	0	.597	2	
1953			155	70	84	1	0	.455	5	
1954			154	97	57	0	0	.630	1	
1955			154	80	74	0	0	.519	3	
1966	CHI	N	162	59	103	0	0	.364	10	
1967			162	87	74	1	0	.540	3	
1968			163	84	78	1	0	.519	3	
1969			163	92	70	1	0	.568	2	
1970			162	84	78	0	0	.519	2	
1971			162	83	79	0	0	.512	3	
1972			91	46	44	1	0	.511	4	2
1972	HOU	N	31	16	15	0	0	.516	2	2
1973			162	82	80	0	0	.506	4	
24 yrs.			3739	2008	1709	22	0	.540		
				6th	6th	7th				

WORLD SERIES

Year			G	W	L	T	N	PCT	Standing
1941	BKN	N	5	1	4	0	0	.200	
1951	NY	N	6	2	4	0	0	.333	
1954			4	4	0	0	0	1.000	
3 yrs.			15	7	8	0	0	.467	

Frank Dwyer

DWYER, JOHN FRANCIS
B. Mar. 25, 1868, Lee, Mass.
D. Feb. 4, 1943, Pittsfield, Mass.

Year			G	W	L	T	N	PCT	Standing
1902	DET	A	137	52	83	2	0	.385	7

Eddie Dyer

DYER, EDWIN HAWLEY
B. Oct. 11, 1900, Morgan City, La.
D. Apr. 20, 1964, Houston, Tex.

Year			G	W	L	T	N	PCT	Standing
1946	STL	N	156	98	58	0	0	.628	1
1947			156	89	65	2	0	.578	2
1948			155	85	69	1	0	.552	2
1949			157	96	58	3	0	.623	2
1950			153	78	75	0	0	.510	5
5 yrs.			777	446	325	6	0	.578	

WORLD SERIES

Year			G	W	L	T	N	PCT	Standing
1946	STL	N	7	4	3	0	0	.571	

Jimmy Dykes

DYKES, JAMES JOSEPH
B. Nov. 10, 1896, Philadelphia, Pa.
D. June 15, 1976, Philadelphia, Pa.

Year			G	W	L	T	N	PCT	Standing	
1934	CHI	A	138	49	88	1	0	.358	8	8
1935			153	74	78	1	0	.487	5	
1936			153	81	70	2	0	.536	3	
1937			154	86	68	0	0	.558	3	
1938			149	65	83	1	0	.439	6	
1939			155	85	69	0	1	.552	4	
1940			155	82	72	0	1	.532	4	
1941			156	77	77	2	0	.500	3	
1942			148	66	82	0	0	.446	6	
1943			155	82	72	1	0	.532	4	
1944			154	71	83	0	0	.461	7	
1945			150	71	78	1	0	.477	6	
1946			30	10	20	0	0	.333	7	5
1951	PHI	A	154	70	84	0	0	.455	6	
1952			155	79	75	1	0	.513	4	
1953			157	59	95	3	0	.383	7	
1954	BAL	A	154	54	100	0	0	.351	7	
1958	CIN	N	41	24	17	0	0	.585	7	4

Jimmy Dykes *continued*

Year			G	W	L	T	N	PCT	Standing	
1959	DET	A	137	74	63	0	0	.540	8	4
1960			96	44	52	0	0	.458	6	6
1960	CLE	A	58	26	32	0	0	.448	4	4
1961			160	77	83	0	0	.481	5	5
21 yrs.			2962	1406	1541	13	2	.477		
									9th	

Charlie Ebbets

EBBETS, CHARLES HERCULES
B. Oct. 29, 1859, New York, N.Y.
D. Apr. 18, 1925, New York, N.Y.

Year			G	W	L	T	N	PCT	Standing	
1898	BKN	N	110	38	68	4	0	.358	9	10

Doc Edwards

EDWARDS, HOWARD RODNEY
B. Dec. 10, 1936, Red Jacket, W. Va.

Year			G	W	L	T	N	PCT	Standing	
1987	CLE	A	75	30	45	0	0	.400	7	7
1988			162	78	84	0	0	.481	6	
1989			143	65	78	0	0	.455	6	6
3 yrs.			380	173	207	0	0	.455		

Kid Elberfeld

ELBERFELD, NORMAN ARTHUR (The Tabasco Kid)
B. Apr. 13, 1875, Pomeroy, Ohio
D. Jan. 13, 1944, Chattanooga, Tenn.

Year			G	W	L	T	N	PCT	Standing	
1908	NY	A	98	27	71	0	0	.276	6	8

Lee Elia

ELIA, LEE CONSTANTINE
B. July 16, 1937, Philadelphia, Pa.

Year			G	W	L	T	N	PCT	Standing	
1982	CHI	N	162	73	89	0	0	.451	5	
1983			123	54	69	0	0	.439	5	5
1987	PHI	N	101	51	50	0	0	.505	5	4
1988			153	60	92	1	0	.395	6	6
4 yrs.			539	238	300	1	0	.442		

Joe Ellick

ELLICK, JOSEPH J.
B. Apr. 3, 1854, Cincinnati, Ohio
D. Apr. 21, 1923, Kansas City, Mo.

Year			G	W	L	T	N	PCT	Standing	
1884	PIT	U	13	6	6	1	0	.500	8	8

Bob Elliott

ELLIOTT, ROBERT IRVING
B. Nov. 26, 1916, San Francisco, Calif.
D. May 4, 1966, San Diego, Calif.

Year			G	W	L	T	N	PCT	Standing
1960	KC	A	155	58	96	1	0	.377	8

Jewel Ens

ENS, JEWEL WINKLEMEYER
Brother of Mutz Ens.
B. Aug. 24, 1889, St. Louis, Mo.
D. Jan. 17, 1950, Syracuse, N.Y.

Year			G	W	L	T	N	PCT	Standing	
1929	PIT	N	35	21	14	0	0	.600	2	2
1930			154	80	74	0	0	.519	5	
1931			155	75	79	1	0	.487	5	
3 yrs.			344	176	167	1	0	.513		

Cal Ermer

ERMER, CALVIN COOLIDGE
B. Nov. 10, 1923, Baltimore, Md.

Year			G	W	L	T	N	PCT	Standing	
1967	MIN	A	114	66	46	2	0	.589	6	2
1968			162	79	83	0	0	.488	7	
2 yrs.			276	145	129	2	0	.529		

Dude Esterbrook

ESTERBROOK, THOMAS JOHN
B. June 9, 1857, Staten Island, N.Y.
D. Apr. 30, 1901, Middletown, N.Y.

Year			G	W	L	T	N	PCT	Standing	
1889	LOU	AA	10	2	8	0	0	.200	8	8

Johnny Evers

EVERS, JOHN JOSEPH (The Trojan, The Crab)
Brother of Joe Evers.
B. July 22, 1883, Troy, N.Y.
D. Mar. 28, 1947, Albany, N.Y.
Hall of Fame 1946.

Year			G	W	L	T	N	PCT	Standing	
1913	CHI	N	155	88	65	2	0	.575	3	
1921			96	41	55	0	0	.427	6	7
1924	CHI	A	21	10	11	0	0	.476	6	8
1924			103	41	61	1	0	.402	6	8
3 yrs.			375	180	192	3	0	.484		

Buck Ewing

EWING, WILLIAM
Brother of John Ewing.
B. Oct. 17, 1859, Hoaglands, Ohio
D. Oct. 20, 1906, Cincinnati, Ohio
Hall of Fame 1939.

Year			G	W	L	T	N	PCT	Standing	
1890	NY	P	132	74	57	1	0	.565	3	
1895	CIN	N	132	66	64	2	0	.508	8	
1896			128	77	50	1	0	.606	3	
1897			134	76	56	2	0	.576	4	
1898			157	92	60	5	0	.605	3	
1899			157	83	67	6	1	.553	6	
1900	NY	N	63	21	41	1	0	.339	8	8
7 yrs.			903	489	395	18	1	.553		

Jay Faatz

FAATZ, JAYSON S.
B. Oct. 24, 1860, Weedsport, N.Y.
D. Apr. 10, 1923, Syracuse, N.Y.

Year			G	W	L	T	N	PCT	Standing		
1890	BUF	P	34	9	24	1	0	.273	8	8	8

Bibb Falk

FALK, BIBB AUGUST (Jockey)
Brother of Chet Falk.
B. Jan. 27, 1899, Austin, Tex.
D. June 8, 1989, Austin, Tex.

Year			G	W	L	T	N	PCT	Standing		
1933	CLE	A	1	1	0	0	0	1.000	5	5	4

Jim Fanning

FANNING, WILLIAM JAMES
B. Sept. 14, 1927, Chicago, Ill.

Year			G	W	L	T	N	PCT	Standing		
1981	MON	N	27	16	11	0	0	.593	2	1	(2nd)
1982			162	86	76	0	0	.531	3		
1984			30	14	16	0	0	.467	5	5	
3 yrs.			219	116	103	0	0	.530			

DIVISIONAL PLAYOFF SERIES

Year			G	W	L	T	N	PCT	Standing
1981	MON	N	5	3	2	0	0	.600	

	G	W	L	T	N	PCT	Standing

Jim Fanning *continued*

LEAGUE CHAMPIONSHIP SERIES

		G	W	L	T	N	PCT		
1981	MON N	5	2	3	0	0	.400		

Jack Farrell

FARRELL, JOHN A. (Moose)
B. July 5, 1857, Newark, N. J.
D. Feb. 10, 1914, Overbrook, N. J.

		G	W	L	T	N	PCT		
1881	PRO N	51	24	27	0	0	.471	4	2

Kerby Farrell

FARRELL, MAJOR KERBY
B. Sept. 3, 1913, Leapwood, Tenn.
D. Dec. 17, 1975, Nashville, Tenn.

		G	W	L	T	N	PCT	
1957	CLE A	153	76	77	0	0	.497	6

John Felske

FELSKE, JOHN FREDERICK
B. May 30, 1942, Chicago, Ill.

		G	W	L	T	N	PCT		
1985	PHI N	162	75	87	0	0	.463	5	
1986		161	86	75	0	0	.534	2	
1987		61	29	32	0	0	.475	5	4
3 yrs.		384	190	194	0	0	.495		

Bob Ferguson

FERGUSON, ROBERT V. (Death to Flying Things)
B. Jan. 31, 1845, Brooklyn, N. Y.
D. May 3, 1894, Brooklyn, N. Y.

		G	W	L	T	N	PCT			
1876	HAR N	69	47	21	1	0	.691	3		
1877		60	31	27	2	0	.534	3		
1878	CHI N	61	30	30	1	0	.500	4		
1879	TRO N	30	7	22	1	0	.241	8	8	
1880		83	41	42	0	0	.494	4		
1881		85	39	45	1	0	.464	5		
1882		85	35	48	2	0	.422	7		
1883	PHI N	17	4	13	0	0	.235	8	8	
1884	PIT AA	42	11	31	0	0	.262	9	12	11
1886	NY AA	120	48	70	2	0	.407	8	7	
1887		30	6	24	0	0	.200	8	7	
11 yrs.		682	299	373	10	0	.445			

Mike Ferraro

FERRARO, MICHAEL DENNIS
B. Aug. 14, 1944, Kingston, N. Y.

		G	W	L	T	N	PCT		
1983	CLE A	100	40	60	0	0	.400	7	7
1986	KC A	74	36	38	0	0	.486	4	3
2 yrs.		174	76	98	0	0	.437		

Wally Fessenden

FESSENDEN, WALLACE CLIFFORD
B. Watertown, Mass.

		G	W	L	T	N	PCT			
1890	SYR AA	11	4	7	0	0	.364	7	6	6

Freddie Fitzsimmons

FITZSIMMONS, FREDERICK LANDIS (Fat Freddie)
B. July 26, 1901, Mishawaka, Ind.
D. Nov. 18, 1979, Yucca Valley, Calif.

		G	W	L	T	N	PCT		
1943	PHI N	65	26	38	1	0	.406	5	7
1944		154	61	92	1	0	.399	8	
1945		69	18	51	0	0	.261	8	8
3 yrs.		288	105	181	2	0	.367		

Art Fletcher

FLETCHER, ARTHUR
B. Jan. 5, 1885, Collinsville, Ill.
D. Feb. 6, 1950, Los Angeles, Calif.

		G	W	L	T	N	PCT		
1923	PHI N	155	50	104	1	0	.325	8	
1924		152	55	96	1	0	.364	7	
1925		153	68	85	0	0	.444	6	
1926		152	58	93	1	0	.384	8	
1929	NY A	11	6	5	0	0	.545	2	2
5 yrs.		623	237	383	3	0	.382		

Silver Flint

FLINT, FRANK SYLVESTER
B. Aug. 3, 1855, Philadelphia, Pa.
D. Jan. 14, 1892, Chicago, Ill.

		G	W	L	T	N	PCT		
1879	CHI N	19	5	12	2	0	.294	4	4

Jim Fogarty

FOGARTY, JAMES G.
Brother of Joe Fogarty.
B. Feb. 12, 1864, San Francisco, Calif.
D. May 20, 1891, San Francisco, Calif.

		G	W	L	T	N	PCT		
1890	PHI P	16	7	9	0	0	.438	5	5

Horace Fogel

FOGEL, HORACE S.
B. Mar. 2, 1861, Macungie, Pa.
D. Nov. 15, 1928, Philadelphia, Pa.

		G	W	L	T	N	PCT		
1887	IND N	70	20	49	1	0	.290	8	8
1902	NY N	44	18	23	1	2	.439	4	8
2 yrs.		114	38	72	2	2	.345		

Lee Fohl

FOHL, LEO ALEXANDER
B. Nov. 28, 1870, Pittsburgh, Pa.
D. Oct. 30, 1965, Cleveland, Ohio

		G	W	L	T	N	PCT		
1915	CLE A	127	45	79	2	1	.363	6	7
1916		157	77	77	3	0	.500	6	
1917		156	88	66	2	0	.571	3	
1918		129	73	54	2	0	.575	2	
1919		78	44	34	0	0	.564	3	2
1921	STL A	154	81	73	0	0	.526	3	
1922		154	93	61	0	0	.604	3	
1923		103	52	49	2	0	.515	3	5
1924	BOS A	157	67	87	2	1	.435	7	
1925		152	47	105	0	0	.309	8	
1926		154	46	107	1	0	.301	8	
11 yrs.		1521	713	792	14	2	.474		

Lew Fonseca

FONSECA, LEWIS ALBERT
B. Jan. 21, 1899, Oakland, Calif.
D. Nov. 26, 1989, Ely, Iowa

		G	W	L	T	N	PCT		
1932	CHI A	152	49	102	1	0	.325	7	
1933		151	67	83	1	0	.447	6	
1934		15	4	11	0	0	.267	8	8
3 yrs.		318	120	196	2	0	.380		

Dave Foutz

FOUTZ, DAVID LUTHER (Scissors)
Brother of Frank Foutz.
B. Sept. 7, 1856, Carroll County, Md.
D. Mar. 5, 1897, Waverly, Md.

		G	W	L	T	N	PCT	
1893	BKN N	130	65	63	2	0	.508	6
1894		135	70	61	3	0	.534	5
1895		134	71	60	2	1	.542	5

Dave Foutz *continued*

		G	W	L	T	N	PCT	
1896		133	58	73	2	0	.443	9
4 yrs.		532	264	257	9	2	.507	

Charlie Fox

FOX, CHARLES FRANCIS (Irish)
B. Oct. 7, 1921, New York, N. Y.

		G	W	L	T	N	PCT		
1970	SF N	120	67	53	0	0	.558	4	3
1971		162	90	72	0	0	.556	1	
1972		155	69	86	0	0	.445	5	
1973		162	88	74	0	0	.543	3	
1974		76	34	42	0	0	.447	5	5
1976	MON N	34	12	22	0	0	.353	6	6
1983	CHI N	39	17	22	0	0	.436	5	5
7 yrs.		748	377	371	0	0	.504		

LEAGUE CHAMPIONSHIP SERIES

		G	W	L	T	N	PCT	
1971	SF N	4	1	3	0	0	.250	

Herman Franks

FRANKS, HERMAN LOUIS
B. Jan. 4, 1914, Price, Utah

		G	W	L	T	N	PCT		
1965	SF N	163	95	67	1	0	.586	2	
1966		161	93	68	0	0	.578	2	
1967		162	91	71	0	0	.562	2	
1968		163	88	74	1	0	.543	2	
1977	CHI N	162	81	81	0	0	.500	4	
1978		162	79	83	0	0	.488	3	
1979		155	78	77	0	0	.503	5	5
7 yrs.		1128	605	521	2	0	.537		

George Frazer

FRAZER, GEORGE KASSON
B. Jan. 7, 1861, Syracuse, N. Y.
D. Feb. 5, 1913, Philadelphia, Pa.

		G	W	L	T	N	PCT		
1890	SYR AA	71	31	40	0	0	.437	7	6
1890		46	20	25	1	0	.444	6	6

Joe Frazier

FRAZIER, JOSEPH FILMORE (Cobra Joe)
B. Oct. 6, 1922, Liberty, N. C.

		G	W	L	T	N	PCT		
1976	NY N	162	86	76	0	0	.531	3	
1977		45	15	30	0	0	.333	6	6
2 yrs.		207	101	106	0	0	.488		

Jim Fregosi

FREGOSI, JAMES LOUIS
B. Apr. 4, 1942, San Francisco, Calif.

		G	W	L	T	N	PCT			
1978	CAL A	117	62	55	0	0	.530	3	2	
1979		162	88	74	0	0	.543	1		
1980		160	65	95	0	0	.406	6		
1981		48	22	25	0	1	.468	4	4	(1st)
1986	CHI A	96	45	51	0	0	.469	5	5	
1987		162	77	85	0	0	.475	5		
1988		161	71	90	0	0	.441	5		
7 yrs.		906	430	475	0	1	.475			

LEAGUE CHAMPIONSHIP SERIES

		G	W	L	T	N	PCT	
1979	CAL A	4	1	3	0	0	.250	

Jim Frey

FREY, JAMES GOTTFRIED
B. May 26, 1931, Cleveland, Ohio

		G	W	L	T	N	PCT			
1980	KC A	162	97	65	0	0	.599	1		
1981		50	20	30	0	0	.400	5		(1st)
1981		20	10	10	0	0	.500	2	1	(2nd)

Jim Frey continued

			G	W	L	T	N	PCT	Standing	
1984	CHI	N	161	96	65	0	0	.596	1	
1985			162	77	84	1	0	.478	4	
1986			56	23	33	0	0	.411	5	5
5 yrs.			611	323	287	1	0	.530		

LEAGUE CHAMPIONSHIP SERIES

			G	W	L	T	N	PCT	
1980	KC	A	3	3	0	0	0	1.000	
1984	CHI	N	5	2	3	0	0	.400	
2 yrs.			8	5	3	0	0	.625	

WORLD SERIES

			G	W	L	T	N	PCT	
1980	KC	A	6	2	4	0	0	.333	

Frankie Frisch

FRISCH, FRANK FRANCIS (The Fordham Flash)
B. Sept. 9, 1898, Bronx, N. Y.
D. Mar. 12, 1973, Wilmington, Del.
Hall of Fame 1947.

			G	W	L	T	N	PCT	Standing	
1933	STL	N	63	36	26	1	0	.581	5	5
1934			154	95	58	1	0	.621	1	
1935			154	96	58	0	0	.623	2	
1936			155	87	67	1	0	.565	2	
1937			157	81	73	3	0	.526	4	
1938			139	63	72	4	0	.467	6	6
1940	PIT	N	156	78	76	2	0	.506	4	
1941			156	81	73	2	0	.526	4	
1942			151	66	81	4	0	.449	5	
1943			157	80	74	3	0	.519	4	
1944			158	90	63	5	0	.588	2	
1945			155	82	72	1	0	.532	4	
1946			152	62	89	1	0	.411	7	7
1949	CHI	N	104	42	62	0	0	.404	8	8
1950			154	64	89	1	0	.418	7	
1951			81	35	45	1	0	.438	7	8
16 yrs.			2246	1138	1078	30	0	.514		

WORLD SERIES

			G	W	L	T	N	PCT	
1934	STL	N	7	4	3	0	0	.571	

Judge Fuchs

FUCHS, EMIL EDWIN
B. Apr. 17, 1878, Hamburg, Germany
D. Dec. 5, 1961, Boston, Mass.

			G	W	L	T	N	PCT	Standing	
1929	BOS	N	154	56	98	0	0	.364	8	

John Gaffney

GAFFNEY, JOHN H. (Honest John, King of the Umpires)
B. June 29, 1855, Roxbury, Mass.
D. Aug. 8, 1913, New York, N. Y.

			G	W	L	T	N	PCT	Standing	
1886	WAS	N	43	15	25	3	0	.375	8	8
1887			126	46	76	4	0	.377	7	
2 yrs.			169	61	101	7	0	.377		

Pud Galvin

GALVIN, JAMES FRANCIS (Gentle Jeems, The Little Steam Engine)
B. Dec. 25, 1856, St. Louis, Mo.
D. Mar. 7, 1902, Pittsburgh, Pa.
Hall of Fame 1965.

			G	W	L	T	N	PCT	Standing	
1885	BUF	N	24	7	17	0	0	.292	7	6

John Ganzel

GANZEL, JOHN HENRY
Brother of Charlie Ganzel.
B. Apr. 7, 1874, Kalamazoo, Mich.
D. Jan. 14, 1959, Orlando, Fla.

			G	W	L	T	N	PCT	Standing	
1908	CIN	N	155	73	81	1	0	.474	5	
1915	BKN	F	35	17	18	0	0	.486	7	7
2 yrs.			190	90	99	1	0	.476		

Dave Garcia

GARCIA, DAVID
B. Sept. 15, 1920, East St. Louis, Ill.

			G	W	L	T	N	PCT	Standing	
1977	CAL	A	81	35	46	0	0	.432	5	5
1978			45	25	20	0	0	.556	3	2
1979	CLE	A	66	38	28	0	0	.576	6	6
1980			160	79	81	0	0	.494	6	
1981			50	26	24	0	0	.520	6	(1st)
1981			53	26	27	0	0	.491	5	(2nd)
1982			162	78	84	0	0	.481	6	
6 yrs.			617	307	310	0	0	.498		

Billy Gardner

GARDNER, WILLIAM FREDERICK (Shotgun)
B. July 19, 1927, Waterford, Conn.

			G	W	L	T	N	PCT	Standing	
1981	MIN	A	20	6	14	0	0	.300	5	(1st) 7
1981			53	24	29	0	0	.453	4	(2nd)
1982			162	60	102	0	0	.370	7	
1983			162	70	92	0	0	.432	5	
1984			162	81	81	0	0	.500	2	
1985			62	27	35	0	0	.435	6	4
1987	KC	A	126	62	64	0	0	.492	4	2
6 yrs.			747	330	417	0	0	.442		

Clarence Gaston

GASTON, CLARENCE EDWIN (Cito)
B. Mar. 17, 1944, San Antonio, Tex.

			G	W	L	T	N	PCT	Standing	
1989	TOR	A	126	77	49	0	0	.611	6	1

LEAGUE CHAMPIONSHIP SERIES

			G	W	L	T	N	PCT	
1989	TOR	A	5	1	4	0	0	.200	

Joe Gerhardt

GERHARDT, JOHN JOSEPH (Move Up Joe)
B. Feb. 14, 1855, Washington, D. C.
D. Mar. 11, 1922, Middletown, N. Y.

			G	W	L	T	N	PCT	Standing	
1883	LOU	AA	98	52	45	1	0	.536	5	

Doc Gessler

GESSLER, HARRY HOMER (Brownie)
B. Dec. 23, 1880, Indiana, Pa.
D. Dec. 26, 1924, Indiana, Pa.

			G	W	L	T	N	PCT	Standing	
1914	PIT	F	11	3	8	0	0	.273	8	7

George Gibson

GIBSON, GEORGE C. (Moon)
B. July 22, 1880, London, Ont., Canada
D. Jan. 25, 1967, London, Ont., Canada

			G	W	L	T	N	PCT	Standing	
1920	PIT	N	155	79	75	1	0	.513	4	
1921			154	90	63	1	0	.588	2	
1922			65	32	33	0	0	.492	5	3
1925	CHI	N	26	12	14	0	0	.462	8	8
1932	PIT	N	154	86	68	0	0	.558	2	
1933			154	87	67	0	0	.565	2	

George Gibson continued

			G	W	L	T	N	PCT	Standing	
1934			51	27	24	0	0	.529	4	5
7 yrs.			759	413	344	2	0	.546		

Jim Gifford

GIFFORD, JAMES H.
B. Oct. 18, 1845, Warren, N. Y.
D. Dec. 19, 1901, Columbus, Ohio

			G	W	L	T	N	PCT	Standing	
1884	IND	AA	86	25	59	2	0	.298	11	12
1885	NY	AA	108	44	64	0	0	.407	7	
1886			17	5	12	0	0	.294	8	7
3 yrs.			211	74	135	2	0	.354		

Jack Glasscock

GLASSCOCK, JOHN WESLEY (Old Battle Ax)
B. July 22, 1859, Wheeling, W. Va.
D. Feb. 24, 1947, Wheeling, W. Va.

			G	W	L	T	N	PCT	Standing	
1889	IND	N	67	34	32	1	0	.515	7	7
1892	STL	N	4	1	3	0	0	.250	10	11
2 yrs.			71	35	35	1	0	.500		

Kid Gleason

GLEASON, WILLIAM J. (Youngster)
Brother of Harry Gleason.
B. Oct. 26, 1866, Camden, N. J.
D. Jan. 2, 1933, Philadelphia, Pa.

			G	W	L	T	N	PCT	Standing	
1919	CHI	A	140	88	52	0	0	.629	1	
1920			154	96	58	0	0	.623	2	
1921			154	62	92	0	0	.403	7	
1922			155	77	77	1	0	.500	5	
1923			156	69	85	2	0	.448	7	
5 yrs.			759	392	364	3	0	.519		

WORLD SERIES

			G	W	L	T	N	PCT	
1919	CHI	A	8	3	5	0	0	.375	

Preston Gomez

GOMEZ, PRESTON
Born Pedro Gomez y Martinez.
B. Apr. 20, 1923, Central Preston, Cuba

			G	W	L	T	N	PCT	Standing	
1969	SD	N	162	52	110	0	0	.321	6	
1970			162	63	99	0	0	.389	6	
1971			161	61	100	0	0	.379	6	
1972			11	4	7	0	0	.364	4	6
1974	HOU	N	162	81	81	0	0	.500	4	
1975			127	47	80	0	0	.370	6	6
1980	CHI	N	90	38	52	0	0	.422	6	6
7 yrs.			875	346	529	0	0	.395		

Mike Gonzalez

GONZALEZ, MIGUEL ANGEL
Born Miguel Angel Gonzalez y Cordero.
B. Sept. 24, 1890, Havana, Cuba
D. Feb. 19, 1977, Havana, Cuba

			G	W	L	T	N	PCT	Standing	
1938	STL	N	17	8	8	1	0	.500	6	6
1940			6	1	5	0	0	.167	6	7	3
2 yrs.			23	9	13	1	0	.409		

Joe Gordon

GORDON, JOSEPH LOWELL (Flash)
B. Feb. 18, 1915, Los Angeles, Calif.
D. Apr. 14, 1978, Sacramento, Calif.

			G	W	L	T	N	PCT	Standing	
1958	CLE	A	86	46	40	0	0	.535	5	4
1959			154	89	65	0	0	.578	2	
1960			95	49	46	0	0	.516	4	4
1960	DET	A	57	26	31	0	0	.456	6	6

	G	W	L	T	N	PCT	Standing

Joe Gordon *continued*

		G	W	L	T	N	PCT	Standing	
1961	KC A	60	26	33	1	0	.441	8	9
1969		163	69	93	1	0	.426	4	
5 yrs.		615	305	308	2	0	.498		

George Gore

GORE, GEORGE F.
B. May 3, 1857, Saccarappa, Me.
D. Sept. 16, 1933, Utica, N. Y.

		G	W	L	T	N	PCT	Standing		
1892	STL N	16	6	9	1	0	.400	12	12	11

John Goryl

GORYL, JOHN ALBERT
B. Oct. 21, 1933, Cumberland, R. I.

		G	W	L	T	N	PCT	Standing	
1980	MIN A	36	23	13	0	0	.639	6	3
1981		37	11	25	0	1	.306	5	7	(1st)
2 yrs.		73	34	38	0	1	.472		

Charlie Gould

GOULD, CHARLES HARVEY
B. Aug. 21, 1847, Cincinnati, Ohio
D. Apr. 10, 1917, Flushing, N. Y.

		G	W	L	T	N	PCT	Standing
1876	CIN N	65	9	56	0	0	.138	8

Mase Graffen

GRAFFEN, SAMUEL MASON
B. 1845, Philadelphia, Pa.
D. Nov. 18, 1883, Silver City, N. M.

		G	W	L	T	N	PCT	Standing	
1876	STL N	56	39	17	0	0	.696	2	2

Alex Grammas

GRAMMAS, ALEXANDER PETER
B. Apr. 3, 1926, Birmingham, Ala.

		G	W	L	T	N	PCT	Standing	
1969	PIT N	5	4	1	0	0	.800	3	3
1976	MIL A	161	66	95	0	0	.410	6	
1977		162	67	95	0	0	.414	6	
3 yrs.		328	137	191	0	0	.418		

Dallas Green

GREEN, GEORGE DALLAS
B. Aug. 4, 1934, Newport, Del.

		G	W	L	T	N	PCT	Standing		
1979	PHI N	30	19	11	0	0	.633	5	4	
1980		162	91	71	0	0	.562	1		
1981		56	34	21	1	0	.618	1		(1st)
1981		53	25	27	1	0	.481	3		(2nd)
1989	NY A	121	56	65	0	0	.463	6	5	
4 yrs.		422	225	195	2	0	.536			

DIVISIONAL PLAYOFF SERIES

		G	W	L	T	N	PCT
1981	PHI N	5	2	3	0	0	.400

LEAGUE CHAMPIONSHIP SERIES

		G	W	L	T	N	PCT
1980	PHI N	5	3	2	0	0	.600

WORLD SERIES

		G	W	L	T	N	PCT
1980	PHI N	6	4	2	0	0	.667

Mike Griffin

GRIFFIN, MICHAEL JOSEPH
B. Mar. 20, 1865, Utica, N. Y.
D. Apr. 10, 1908, Utica, N. Y.

		G	W	L	T	N	PCT	Standing		
1898	BKN N	4	1	3	0	0	.250	9	9	10

Sandy Griffin

GRIFFIN, TOBIAS CHARLES
B. July 19, 1858, Fayetteville, N. Y.
D. June 5, 1926, Fayetteville, N. Y.

		G	W	L	T	N	PCT	Standing	
1891	WAS AA	6	2	4	0	0	.333	9	9

Clark Griffith

GRIFFITH, CLARK CALVIN (Griff, General)
B. Nov. 20, 1869, Clear Creek, Mo.
D. Oct. 27, 1955, Washington, D. C.
Hall of Fame 1946.

		G	W	L	T	N	PCT	Standing	
1901	CHI A	137	83	53	1	0	.610	1	
1902		138	74	60	4	0	.552	4	
1903	NY A	136	72	62	2	0	.537	4	
1904		155	92	59	4	0	.609	2	
1905		152	71	78	3	0	.477	6	
1906		155	90	61	4	0	.596	2	
1907		152	70	78	4	0	.473	5	
1908		57	24	32	1	0	.429	6	8
1909	CIN N	157	77	76	3	1	.503	4	
1910		156	75	79	2	0	.487	5	
1911		159	70	83	6	0	.458	6	
1912	WAS A	154	91	61	2	0	.599	2	
1913		155	90	64	1	0	.584	2	
1914		158	81	73	4	0	.526	3	
1915		155	85	68	2	0	.556	4	
1916		159	76	77	6	0	.497	7	
1917		158	74	79	4	1	.484	5	
1918		130	72	56	2	0	.563	3	
1919		142	56	84	2	0	.400	7	
1920		153	68	84	1	0	.447	6	
20 yrs.		2918	1491	1367	58	2	.522		

Burleigh Grimes

GRIMES, BURLEIGH ARLAND (Ol' Stubblebeard)
B. Aug. 9, 1893, Emerald, Wis.
D. Dec. 6, 1985, Clear Lake, Wis.
Hall of Fame 1964.

		G	W	L	T	N	PCT	Standing
1937	BKN N	155	62	91	2	0	.405	6
1938		151	69	80	2	0	.463	7
2 yrs.		306	131	171	4	0	.434	

Charlie Grimm

GRIMM, CHARLES JOHN (Jolly Cholly)
B. Aug. 25, 1896, St. Louis, Mo.
D. Nov. 15, 1983, Scottsdale, Ariz.

		G	W	L	T	N	PCT	Standing	
1932	CHI N	55	37	18	0	0	.673	2	1
1933		154	86	68	0	0	.558	3	
1934		152	86	65	1	0	.570	3	
1935		154	100	54	0	0	.649	1	
1936		154	87	67	0	0	.565	2	
1937		154	93	61	0	0	.604	2	
1938		81	45	36	0	0	.556	3	1
1944		146	74	69	3	0	.517	8	4
1945		155	98	56	1	0	.636	1	
1946		155	82	71	2	0	.536	3	
1947		155	69	85	1	0	.448	6	
1948		155	64	90	1	0	.416	8	
1949		50	19	31	0	0	.380	8	8
1952	BOS N	120	51	67	2	0	.432	6	7
1953	MIL N	157	92	62	3	0	.597	2	
1954		154	89	65	0	0	.578	3	
1955		154	85	69	0	0	.552	2	
1956		46	24	22	0	0	.522	5	2
1960	CHI N	17	6	11	0	0	.353	8	7
19 yrs.		2368	1287	1067	14	0	.547		

WORLD SERIES

		G	W	L	T	N	PCT
1932	CHI N	4	0	4	0	0	.000
1935		6	2	4	0	0	.333
1945		7	3	4	0	0	.429
3 yrs.		17	5	12	0	0	.294
				10th			

Heinie Groh

GROH, HENRY KNIGHT
Brother of Lew Groh.
B. Sept. 18, 1889, Rochester, N. Y.
D. Aug. 22, 1968, Cincinnati, Ohio

		G	W	L	T	N	PCT	Standing	
1918	CIN N	10	7	3	0	0	.700	4	3

Don Gutteridge

GUTTERIDGE, DONALD JOSEPH
B. June 19, 1912, Pittsburg, Kans.

		G	W	L	T	N	PCT	Standing	
1969	CHI A	145	60	85	0	0	.414	4	5
1970		136	49	87	0	0	.360	6	6
2 yrs.		281	109	172	0	0	.388		

Eddie Haas

HAAS, GEORGE EDWIN
B. May 26, 1935, Paducah, Ky.

		G	W	L	T	N	PCT	Standing	
1985	ATL N	121	50	71	0	0	.413	5	5

Stan Hack

HACK, STANLEY CAMFIELD (Smiling Stan)
B. Dec. 6, 1909, Sacramento, Calif.
D. Dec. 15, 1979, Dixon, Ill.

		G	W	L	T	N	PCT	Standing	
1954	CHI N	154	64	90	0	0	.416	7	
1955		154	72	81	1	0	.471	6	
1956		157	60	94	3	0	.390	8	
1958	STL N	10	3	7	0	0	.300	5	5
4 yrs.		475	199	272	4	0	.423		

Charlie Hackett

HACKETT, CHARLES M.
B. Holyoke, Mass.
D. Aug. 1, 1898, Holyoke, Mass.

		G	W	L	T	N	PCT	Standing	
1884	CLE N	113	35	77	1	0	.313	7	
1885	BKN AA	37	15	22	0	0	.405	7	5
2 yrs.		150	50	99	1	0	.336		

Bill Hallman

HALLMAN, WILLIAM WILSON
B. Mar. 31, 1867, Pittsburg, Pa.
D. Sept. 11, 1920, Philadelphia, Pa.

		G	W	L	T	N	PCT	Standing		
1897	STL N	50	13	36	0	1	.265	12	12	12

Fred Haney

HANEY, FRED GIRARD (Pudge)
B. Apr. 25, 1898, Albuquerque, N. M.
D. Nov. 9, 1977, Beverly Hills, Calif.

		G	W	L	T	N	PCT	Standing	
1939	STL A	156	43	111	2	0	.279	8	
1940		156	67	87	2	0	.435	6	
1941		44	15	29	0	0	.341	7	6
1953	PIT N	154	50	104	0	0	.325	8	
1954		154	53	101	0	0	.344	8	
1955		154	60	94	0	0	.390	8	
1956	MIL N	109	68	40	1	0	.630	5	2
1957		155	95	59	1	0	.617	1	
1958		154	92	62	0	0	.597	1	
1959		157	86	70	1	0	.551	2	
10 yrs.		1393	629	757	7	0	.454		

WORLD SERIES

		G	W	L	T	N	PCT
1957	MIL N	7	4	3	0	0	.571
1958		7	3	4	0	0	.429
2 yrs.		14	7	7	0	0	.500

| | G | W | L | T | N | PCT | Standing | | | G | W | L | T | N | PCT | Standing | | | G | W | L | T | N | PCT | Standing |

Ned Hanlon

HANLON, EDWARD HUGH
B. Aug. 22, 1857, Montville, Conn.
D. Apr. 14, 1937, Baltimore, Md.

		G	W	L	T	N	PCT	Standing
1889	PIT N	46	26	18	2	0	.591	7 5
1890	PIT P	131	60	68	0	3	.469	6
1891	PIT N	78	31	47	0	0	.397	8 8
1892	BAL N	130	45	85	0	0	.346	12 12
1893		130	60	70	0	0	.462	8
1894		129	89	39	1	0	.695	1
1895		132	87	43	2	0	.669	1
1896		132	90	39	3	0	.698	1
1897		136	90	40	6	0	.692	2
1898		154	96	53	5	0	.644	2
1899	BKN N	150	101	47	2	0	.682	1
1900		142	82	54	6	0	.603	1
1901		137	79	57	1	0	.581	3
1902		141	75	63	3	0	.543	2
1903		139	70	66	3	0	.515	5
1904		154	56	97	1	0	.366	6
1905		155	48	104	3	0	.316	8
1906	CIN N	155	64	87	4	0	.424	6
1907		156	66	87	3	0	.431	6
19 yrs.		2527	1315	1164	45	3	.530	

Mel Harder

HARDER, MELVIN LeROY (Chief, Wimpy)
B. Oct. 15, 1909, Beemer, Neb.

		G	W	L	T	N	PCT	Standing
1961	CLE A	1	1	0	0	0	1.000	5 5

Bucky Harris

HARRIS, STANLEY RAYMOND
B. Nov. 8, 1896, Port Jervis, N. Y.
D. Nov. 8, 1977, Bethesda, Md.
Hall of Fame 1975.

		G	W	L	T	N	PCT	Standing
1924	WAS A	156	92	62	2	0	.597	1
1925		152	96	55	1	0	.636	1
1926		152	81	69	2	0	.540	4
1927		157	85	69	3	0	.552	3
1928		155	75	79	1	0	.487	4
1929	DET A	155	70	84	1	0	.455	6
1930		154	75	79	0	0	.487	5
1931		154	61	93	0	0	.396	7
1932		153	76	75	1	1	.503	5
1933		153	73	79	1	0	.480	5 5
1934	BOS A	153	76	76	1	0	.500	4
1935	WAS A	154	67	86	1	0	.438	6
1936		153	82	71	0	0	.536	4
1937		158	73	80	5	0	.477	6
1938		152	75	76	1	0	.497	5
1939		153	65	87	0	1	.428	6
1940		154	64	90	0	0	.416	7
1941		156	70	84	2	0	.455	6
1942		151	62	89	0	0	.411	7
1943	PHI N	92	38	52	2	0	.422	5 7
1947	NY A	155	97	57	1	0	.630	1
1948		154	94	60	0	0	.610	3
1950	WAS A	155	67	87	1	0	.435	5
1951		154	62	92	0	0	.403	7
1952		157	78	76	3	0	.506	5
1953		152	76	76	0	0	.500	5
1954		155	66	88	1	0	.429	6
1955	DET A	154	79	75	0	0	.513	5
1956		155	82	72	1	0	.532	5
29 yrs.		4408	2157	2218	31	2	.493	
			3rd	**3rd**			**2nd**	

WORLD SERIES

		G	W	L	T	N	PCT	Standing
1924	WAS A	7	4	3	0	0	.571	
1925		7	3	4	0	0	.429	
1947	NY A	7	4	3	0	0	.571	
3 yrs.		21	11	10	0	0	.524	
			10th				**7th**	

Lum Harris

HARRIS, CHALMER LUMAN
B. Jan. 17, 1915, New Castle, Ala.

		G	W	L	T	N	PCT	Standing
1961	BAL A	27	17	10	0	0	.630	3 3
1964	HOU N	13	5	8	0	0	.385	9 9
1965		162	65	97	0	0	.401	9
1968	ATL N	163	81	81	1	0	.500	5
1969		162	93	69	0	0	.574	1
1970		162	76	86	0	0	.469	5
1971		162	82	80	0	0	.506	3
1972		105	47	57	1	0	.452	5 4
8 yrs.		956	466	488	2	0	.488	

LEAGUE CHAMPIONSHIP SERIES

		G	W	L	T	N	PCT	Standing
1969	ATL N	3	0	3	0	0	.000	

Jim Hart

HART, JAMES ARISTOTLE
B. July 10, 1855, Fairview, Pa.
D. July 18, 1919, Chicago, Ill.

		G	W	L	T	N	PCT	Standing
1885	LOU AA	112	53	59	0	0	.473	5
1886		138	66	70	2	0	.485	4
1889	BOS N	133	83	45	5	0	.648	2
3 yrs.		383	202	174	7	0	.537	

John Hart

HART, JOHN HENRY
Born John Henry Reen.
B. July 21, 1948, Tampa, Fla.

		G	W	L	T	N	PCT	Standing
1989	CLE A	19	8	11	0	0	.421	6 6

Gabby Hartnett

HARTNETT, CHARLES LEO
B. Dec. 20, 1900, Woonsocket, R. I.
D. Dec. 20, 1972, Park Ridge, Ill.
Hall of Fame 1955.

		G	W	L	T	N	PCT	Standing
1938	CHI N	73	44	27	2	0	.620	3 1
1939		156	84	70	2	0	.545	4
1940		154	75	79	0	0	.487	5
3 yrs.		383	203	176	4	0	.536	

WORLD SERIES

		G	W	L	T	N	PCT	Standing
1938	CHI N	4	0	4	0	0	.000	

Roy Hartsfield

HARTSFIELD, ROY THOMAS
B. Oct. 25, 1925, Chattahoochee, Ga.

		G	W	L	T	N	PCT	Standing
1977	TOR A	161	54	107	0	0	.335	7
1978		161	59	102	0	0	.366	7
1979		162	53	109	0	0	.327	7
3 yrs.		484	166	318	0	0	.343	

Grady Hatton

HATTON, GRADY EDGEBERT
B. Oct. 7, 1922, Beaumont, Tex.

		G	W	L	T	N	PCT	Standing
1966	HOU N	163	72	90	1	0	.444	8
1967		162	69	93	0	0	.426	9
1968		61	23	38	0	0	.377	10 10
3 yrs.		386	164	221	1	0	.426	

Guy Hecker

HECKER, GUY JACKSON (Blond Guy)
B. Apr. 3, 1856, Youngville, Pa.
D. Dec. 3, 1938, Wooster, Ohio

		G	W	L	T	N	PCT	Standing
1890	PIT N	138	23	113	2	0	.169	8

Don Heffner

HEFFNER, DONALD HENRY (Jeep)
B. Feb. 8, 1911, Rouzerville, Pa.
D. Aug. 1, 1989, Pasadena, Calif.

		G	W	L	T	N	PCT	Standing
1966	CIN N	83	37	46	0	0	.446	8 7

Louie Heilbroner

HEILBRONER, LOUIS WILBUR
B. July 4, 1861, Ft. Wayne, Ind.
D. Dec. 21, 1933, Ft. Wayne, Ind.

		G	W	L	T	N	PCT	Standing
1900	STL N	50	23	25	2	0	.479	7 5

Tommy Helms

HELMS, TOMMY VANN
B. May 5, 1941, Charlotte, N. C.

		G	W	L	T	N	PCT	Standing
1988	CIN N	27	12	15	0	0	.444	4 4 2
1989		35	14	21	0	0	.400	4 5
2 yrs.		62	26	36	0	0	.419	

Solly Hemus

HEMUS, SOLOMON JOSEPH
B. Apr. 17, 1923, Phoenix, Ariz.

		G	W	L	T	N	PCT	Standing
1959	STL N	154	71	83	0	0	.461	7
1960		155	86	68	1	0	.558	3
1961		75	33	41	1	0	.446	6 5
3 yrs.		384	190	192	2	0	.497	

Bill Henderson

HENDERSON, WILLIAM C.

		G	W	L	T	N	PCT	Standing
1884	BAL U	106	58	47	1	0	.552	4

Jack Hendricks

HENDRICKS, JOHN CHARLES
B. Apr. 9, 1875, Joliet, Ill.
D. May 13, 1943, Chicago, Ill.

		G	W	L	T	N	PCT	Standing
1918	STL N	133	51	78	2	2	.395	8
1924	CIN N	153	83	70	0	0	.542	4
1925		153	80	73	0	0	.523	3
1926		157	87	67	3	0	.565	2
1927		153	75	78	0	0	.490	5
1928		153	78	74	1	0	.513	5
1929		155	66	88	1	0	.429	7
7 yrs.		1057	520	528	7	2	.496	

Ed Hengle

HENGLE, EDWARD S.
B. Chicago, Ill.
Deceased.

		G	W	L	T	N	PCT	Standing
1884	CHI U	74	34	39	1	0	.466	6

Billy Herman

HERMAN, WILLIAM JENNINGS BRYAN
B. July 7, 1909, New Albany, Ind.
Hall of Fame 1975.

		G	W	L	T	N	PCT	Standing
1947	PIT N	155	61	92	2	0	.399	8 7
1964	BOS A	2	2	0	0	0	1.000	8 8
1965		162	62	100	0	0	.383	9
1966		146	64	82	0	0	.438	10 9
4 yrs.		465	189	274	2	0	.408	

Buck Herzog

HERZOG, CHARLES LINCOLN
B. July 9, 1885, Baltimore, Md.
D. Sept. 4, 1953, Baltimore, Md.

			G	W	L	T	N	PCT	Standing	
1914	CIN	N	157	60	94	3	0	.390	8	
1915			160	71	83	6	0	.461	7	
1916			84	34	49	1	0	.410	8	7
3 yrs.			401	165	226	10	0	.422		

Whitey Herzog

HERZOG, DORREL NORMAN ELVERT
(The White Rat)
B. Nov. 9, 1931, New Athens, Ill.

			G	W	L	T	N	PCT	Standing		
1973	TEX	A	138	47	91	0	0	.341	6	6	
1974	CAL	A	4	2	2	0	0	.500	6	6	6
1975	KC	A	66	41	25	0	0	.621	2	2	
1976			162	90	72	0	0	.556	1		
1977			162	102	60	0	0	.630	1		
1978			162	92	70	0	0	.568	1		
1979			162	85	77	0	0	.525	2		
1980	STL	N	73	38	35	0	0	.521	6	5	4
1981			51	30	20	1	0	.600	2	(1st)	
1981			52	29	23	0	0	.558	2	(2nd)	
1982			162	92	70	0	0	.568	1		
1983			162	79	83	0	0	.488	4		
1984			162	84	78	0	0	.519	3		
1985			162	101	61	0	0	.623	1		
1986			161	79	82	0	0	.491	3		
1987			162	95	67	0	0	.586	1		
1988			162	76	86	0	0	.469	5		
1989			162	86	76	0	0	.531	3		
17 yrs.			2327	1248	1078	1	0	.537			

LEAGUE CHAMPIONSHIP SERIES

			G	W	L	T	N	PCT	
1976	KC	A	5	2	3	0	0	.400	
1977			5	2	3	0	0	.400	
1978			4	1	3	0	0	.250	
1982	STL	N	3	3	0	0	0	1.000	
1985			6	4	2	0	0	.667	
1987			7	4	3	0	0	.571	
6 yrs.			30	16	14	0	0	.533	
				1st	2nd	1st			6th

WORLD SERIES

			G	W	L	T	N	PCT
1982	STL	N	7	4	3	0	0	.571
1985			7	3	4	0	0	.429
1987			7	3	4	0	0	.429
3 yrs.			21	10	11	0	0	.476

Walter Hewett

HEWETT, WALTER F.
B. 1861, Washington, D. C.
D. Oct. 7, 1944, Washington, D. C.

			G	W	L	T	N	PCT	Standing	
1888	WAS	N	40	10	29	1	0	.256	8	8

Pinky Higgins

HIGGINS, MICHAEL FRANKLIN
B. May 27, 1909, Red Oak, Tex.
D. Mar. 21, 1969, Dallas, Tex.

			G	W	L	T	N	PCT	Standing	
1955	BOS	A	154	84	70	0	0	.545	4	
1956			155	84	70	1	0	.545	4	
1957			154	82	72	0	0	.532	3	
1958			155	79	75	1	0	.513	3	
1959			73	31	42	0	0	.425	8	5
1960			105	48	57	0	0	.457	8	7
1961			163	76	86	1	0	.469	6	
1962			160	76	84	0	0	.475	8	
8 yrs.			1119	560	556	3	0	.502		

Vedie Himsl

HIMSL, AVITUS BERNARD
B. Apr. 2, 1917, Plevna, Mont.

			G	W	L	T	N	PCT	Standing	
1961	CHI	N	31	10	21	0	0	.323	7	7

Billy Hitchcock

HITCHCOCK, WILLIAM CLYDE
Brother of Jim Hitchcock.
B. July 31, 1916, Inverness, Ala.

			G	W	L	T	N	PCT	Standing		
1960	DET	A	1	1	0	0	0	1.000	6	6	6
1962	BAL	A	162	77	85	0	0	.475	7		
1963			162	86	76	0	0	.531	4		
1966	ATL	N	51	33	18	0	0	.647	5	5	
1967			159	77	82	0	0	.484	7	7	
5 yrs.			535	274	261	0	0	.512			

Gil Hodges

HODGES, GILBERT RAYMOND
Born Gilbert Ray Hodge.
B. Apr. 4, 1924, Princeton, Ind.
D. Apr. 2, 1972, West Palm Beach, Fla.

			G	W	L	T	N	PCT	Standing	
1963	WAS	A	121	42	79	0	0	.347	10	10
1964			162	62	100	0	0	.383	9	
1965			162	70	92	0	0	.432	8	
1966			159	71	88	0	0	.447	8	
1967			161	76	85	0	0	.472	6	
1968	NY	N	163	73	89	1	0	.451	9	
1969			162	100	62	0	0	.617	1	
1970			162	83	79	0	0	.512	3	
1971			162	83	79	0	0	.512	3	
9 yrs.			1414	660	753	1	0	.467		

LEAGUE CHAMPIONSHIP SERIES

			G	W	L	T	N	PCT
1969	NY	N	3	3	0	0	0	1.000

WORLD SERIES

			G	W	L	T	N	PCT
1969	NY	N	5	4	1	0	0	.800

Fred Hoey

HOEY, FREDERICK C.
B. New York, N. Y.
D. Dec. 7, 1933, Paris, France

			G	W	L	T	N	PCT	Standing	
1899	NY	N	87	31	55	1	0	.360	9	10

Bill Holbert

HOLBERT, WILLIAM H.
B. Mar. 14, 1855, Baltimore, Md.
D. Mar. 1, 1935, Laurel, Md.

			G	W	L	T	N	PCT	Standing		
1879	SYR	N	1	0	1	0	0	.000	6	6	7

Holly Hollingshead

HOLLINGSHEAD, JOHN SAMUEL
B. Jan. 17, 1853, Washington, D. C.
D. Oct. 6, 1926, Washington, D. C.

			G	W	L	T	N	PCT	Standing	
1884	WAS	AA	62	12	50	0	0	.194	13	13

Tommy Holmes

HOLMES, THOMAS FRANCIS (Kelly)
B. Mar. 29, 1917, Brooklyn, N. Y.

			G	W	L	T	N	PCT	Standing	
1951	BOS	N	95	48	47	0	0	.505	5	4
1952			35	13	22	0	0	.371	6	7
2 yrs.			130	61	69	0	0	.469		

Rogers Hornsby

HORNSBY, ROGERS (Rajah)
B. Apr. 27, 1896, Winters, Tex.
D. Jan. 5, 1963, Chicago, Ill.
Hall of Fame 1942.

			G	W	L	T	N	PCT	Standing	
1925	STL	N	115	64	51	0	0	.557	8	4
1926			156	89	65	2	0	.578	1	
1927	NY	N	33	22	10	1	0	.688	4	3
1928	BOS	N	122	39	83	0	0	.320	7	7
1930	CHI	N	4	4	0	0	0	1.000	2	2
1931			156	84	70	2	0	.545	3	
1932			99	53	46	0	0	.535	2	1
1933	STL	A	54	19	33	2	0	.365	8	8
1934			154	67	85	2	0	.441	6	
1935			155	65	87	3	0	.428	7	
1936			155	57	95	3	0	.375	7	
1937			78	25	52	1	0	.325	7	8
1952			51	22	29	0	0	.431	8	7
1952	CIN	N	51	27	24	0	0	.529	7	6
1953			147	64	82	1	0	.438	6	6
14 yrs.			1530	701	812	17	0	.463		

WORLD SERIES

			G	W	L	T	N	PCT
1926	STL	N	7	4	3	0	0	.571

Ralph Houk

HOUK, RALPH GEORGE (Major)
B. Aug. 9, 1919, Lawrence, Kans.

			G	W	L	T	N	PCT	Standing	
1961	NY	A	163	109	53	1	0	.673	1	
1962			162	96	66	0	0	.593	1	
1963			161	104	57	0	0	.646	1	
1966			140	66	73	1	0	.475	10	10
1967			163	72	90	1	0	.444	9	
1968			164	83	79	2	0	.512	5	
1969			162	80	81	1	0	.497	5	
1970			163	93	69	1	0	.574	2	
1971			162	82	80	0	0	.506	4	
1972			155	79	76	0	0	.510	4	
1973			162	80	82	0	0	.494	4	
1974	DET	A	162	72	90	0	0	.444	6	
1975			159	57	102	0	0	.358	6	
1976			161	74	87	0	0	.460	5	
1977			162	74	88	0	0	.457	4	
1978			162	86	76	0	0	.531	5	
1981	BOS	A	56	30	26	0	0	.536	5	(1st)
1981			52	29	23	0	0	.558	2	(2nd)
1982			162	89	73	0	0	.549	3	
1983			162	78	84	0	0	.481	6	
1984			162	86	76	0	0	.531	4	
20 yrs.			3157	1619	1531	7	0	.514		
									10th	10th

WORLD SERIES

			G	W	L	T	N	PCT	
1961	NY	A	5	4	1	0	0	.800	
1962			7	4	3	0	0	.571	
1963			4	0	4	0	0	.000	
3 yrs.			16	8	8	0	0	.500	
									9th

Frank Howard

**HOWARD, FRANK OLIVER (The Capital
Punisher, Hondo)**
B. Aug. 8, 1936, Columbus, Ohio

			G	W	L	T	N	PCT	Standing	
1981	SD	N	56	23	33	0	0	.411	6	(1st)
1981			54	18	36	0	0	.333	6	(2nd)
1983	NY	N	116	52	64	0	0	.448	6	6
2 yrs.			226	93	133	0	0	.412		

Art Howe

HOWE, ARTHUR HENRY JR.
B. Dec. 15, 1946, Pittsburgh, Pa.

			G	W	L	T	N	PCT	Standing
1989	HOU	N	162	86	76	0	0	.531	3

	G	W	L	T	N	PCT	Standing

Dan Howley

HOWLEY, DANIEL PHILIP (Dapper Dan)
B. Oct. 16, 1885, E. Weymouth, Mass.
D. Mar. 10, 1944, E. Weymouth, Mass.

		G	W	L	T	N	PCT	Standing
1927	STL A	155	59	94	2	0	.386	7
1928		154	82	72	0	0	.532	3
1929		154	79	73	2	0	.520	4
1930	CIN N	154	59	95	0	0	.383	7
1931		154	58	96	0	0	.377	8
1932		155	60	94	1	0	.390	8
6 yrs.		926	397	524	5	0	.431	

Dick Howser

HOWSER, RICHARD DALTON
B. May 14, 1936, Miami, Fla.
D. June 17, 1987, Kansas City, Mo.

		G	W	L	T	N	PCT	Standing		
1978	NY A	1	0	1	0	0	.000	3	3	1
1980		162	103	59	0	0	.636	1		
1981	KC A	33	20	13	0	0	.606	2	1	(2nd)
1982		162	90	72	0	0	.556	2		
1983		163	79	83	1	0	.488	2		
1984		162	84	78	0	0	.519	1		
1985		162	91	71	0	0	.562	1		
1986		88	40	48	0	0	.455	4	3	
8 yrs.		933	507	425	1	0	.544			

DIVISIONAL PLAYOFF SERIES

		G	W	L	T	N	PCT
1981	KC A	3	0	3	0	0	.000

LEAGUE CHAMPIONSHIP SERIES

		G	W	L	T	N	PCT
1980	NY A	3	0	3	0	0	.000
1984	KC A	3	0	3	0	0	.000
1985		7	4	3	0	0	.571
3 yrs.		13	4	9	0	0	.308
			8th	5th			

WORLD SERIES

		G	W	L	T	N	PCT
1985	KC A	7	4	3	0	0	.571

George Huff

HUFF, GEORGE A.
B. June 11, 1872, Champaign, Ill.
D. Oct. 1, 1936, Champaign, Ill.

		G	W	L	T	N	PCT	Standing		
1907	BOS A	8	2	6	0	0	.250	4	6	7

Miller Huggins

HUGGINS, MILLER JAMES (Hug, The Mighty Mite)
B. Mar. 27, 1879, Cincinnati, Ohio
D. Sept. 25, 1929, New York, N. Y.
Hall of Fame 1964.

		G	W	L	T	N	PCT	Standing		
1913	STL N	153	51	99	3	0	.340	8		
1914		157	81	72	4	0	.529	3		
1915		157	72	81	4	0	.471	6		
1916		153	60	93	0	0	.392	7		
1917		154	82	70	2	0	.539	3		
1918	NY A	126	60	63	3	0	.488	4		
1919		141	80	59	2	0	.576	3		
1920		154	95	59	0	0	.617	3		
1921		153	98	55	0	0	.641	1		
1922		154	94	60	0	0	.610	1		
1923		152	98	54	0	0	.645	1		
1924		153	89	63	1	0	.586	2		
1925		156	69	85	2	0	.448	7		
1926		155	91	63	1	0	.591	1		
1927		155	110	44	1	0	.714	1		
1928		154	101	53	0	0	.656	1		
1929		143	82	61	0	0	.573	2	2	
17 yrs.		2570	1413	1134	23	0	.555			

WORLD SERIES

		G	W	L	T	N	PCT
1921	NY A	8	3	5	0	0	.375
1922		5	0	4	1	0	.000
1923		6	4	2	0	0	.667

Miller Huggins *continued*

	G	W	L	T	N	PCT	Standing
1926	7	3	4	0	0	.429	
1927	4	4	0	0	0	1.000	
1928	4	4	0	0	0	1.000	
6 yrs.	34	18	15	1	0	.545	
		6th	6th	5th			6th

Billy Hunter

HUNTER, GORDON WILLIAM
B. June 4, 1928, Punxsutawney, Pa.

		G	W	L	T	N	PCT	Standing		
1977	TEX A	93	60	33	0	0	.645	4	2	
1978		161	86	75	0	0	.534	2	2	
2 yrs.		254	146	108	0	0	.575			

Tim Hurst

HURST, TIMOTHY CARROLL
B. June 30, 1865, Ashland, Pa.
D. June 4, 1915, Pottsville, Pa.

		G	W	L	T	N	PCT	Standing
1898	STL N	154	39	111	4	0	.260	12

Fred Hutchinson

HUTCHINSON, FREDERICK CHARLES
B. Aug. 12, 1919, Seattle, Wash.
D. Nov. 12, 1964, Bradenton, Fla.

		G	W	L	T	N	PCT	Standing		
1952	DET A	83	27	55	1	0	.329	8	8	
1953		158	60	94	4	0	.390	6		
1954		155	68	86	1	0	.442	5		
1956	STL N	156	76	78	2	0	.494	4		
1957		154	87	67	0	0	.565	2		
1958		144	69	75	0	0	.479	5	5	
1959	CIN N	74	39	35	0	0	.527	7	5	
1960		154	67	87	0	0	.435	6		
1961		154	93	61	0	0	.604	1		
1962		162	98	64	0	0	.605	3		
1963		162	86	76	0	0	.531	5		
1964		100	54	45	1	0	.545	3	2	
1964		10	6	4	0	0	.600	4	3	2
12 yrs.		1666	830	827	9	0	.501			

WORLD SERIES

		G	W	L	T	N	PCT
1961	CIN N	5	1	4	0	0	.200

Arthur Irwin

IRWIN, ARTHUR ALBERT
Brother of John Irwin.
B. Feb. 14, 1858, Toronto, Ont., Canada
D. July 16, 1921, Atlantic Ocean

		G	W	L	T	N	PCT	Standing		
1889	WAS N	76	28	45	3	0	.384	8	8	
1891	BOS AA	139	93	42	4	0	.689	1		
1892	WAS N	106	46	60	0	0	.434	11	11	10
1894	PHI N	132	71	57	1	3	.555	4		
1895		133	78	53	2	0	.595	3		
1896	NY N	90	36	53	1	0	.404	10	7	
1898	WAS N	30	10	19	1	0	.345	11	11	
1899		155	54	98	3	0	.355	11		
8 yrs.		861	416	427	15	3	.493			

Hughie Jennings

JENNINGS, HUGH AMBROSE (Hustling Hughie)
B. Apr. 2, 1869, Pittston, Pa.
D. Feb. 1, 1928, Scranton, Pa.
Hall of Fame 1945.

		G	W	L	T	N	PCT	Standing
1907	DET A	153	92	58	3	0	.613	1
1908		154	90	63	1	0	.588	1
1909		158	98	54	6	0	.645	1
1910		155	86	68	1	0	.558	3
1911		154	89	65	0	0	.578	2
1912		154	69	84	1	0	.451	6
1913		153	66	87	0	0	.431	6

Hughie Jennings *continued*

	G	W	L	T	N	PCT	Standing		
1914	157	80	73	4	0	.523	4		
1915	156	100	54	2	0	.649	2		
1916	155	87	67	1	0	.565	3		
1917	155	78	75	1	1	.510	4		
1918	128	55	71	2	0	.437	7		
1919	140	80	60	0	0	.571	4		
1920	155	61	93	1	0	.396	7		
1924	NY N 44	32	12	0	0	.727	3	1	1
15 yrs.	2171	1163	984	23	1	.542			

WORLD SERIES

		G	W	L	T	N	PCT
1907	DET A	4	0	4	0	0	.000
1908		5	1	4	0	0	.200
1909		7	3	4	0	0	.429
3 yrs.		16	4	12	0	0	.250
				10th			

Darrell Johnson

JOHNSON, DARRELL DEAN
B. Aug. 25, 1928, Horace, Neb.

		G	W	L	T	N	PCT	Standing		
1974	BOS A	162	84	78	0	0	.519	3		
1975		160	95	65	0	0	.594	1		
1976		86	41	45	0	0	.477	3	3	
1977	SEA A	162	64	98	0	0	.395	6		
1978		160	56	104	0	0	.350	7		
1979		162	67	95	0	0	.414	6		
1980		105	39	65	1	0	.375	7	7	
1982	TEX A	66	26	40	0	0	.394	6	6	
8 yrs.		1063	472	590	1	0	.444			

LEAGUE CHAMPIONSHIP SERIES

		G	W	L	T	N	PCT
1975	BOS A	3	3	0	0	0	1.000

WORLD SERIES

		G	W	L	T	N	PCT
1975	BOS A	7	3	4	0	0	.429

Davey Johnson

JOHNSON, DAVID ALLEN
B. Jan. 30, 1943, Orlando, Fla.

		G	W	L	T	N	PCT	Standing
1984	NY N	162	90	72	0	0	.556	2
1985		162	98	64	0	0	.605	2
1986		162	108	54	0	0	.667	1
1987		162	92	70	0	0	.568	2
1988		160	100	60	0	0	.625	1
1989		162	87	75	0	0	.537	2
6 yrs.		970	575	395	0	0	.593	

LEAGUE CHAMPIONSHIP SERIES

		G	W	L	T	N	PCT
1986	NY N	6	4	2	0	0	.667
1988		7	3	4	0	0	.429
2 yrs.		13	7	6	0	0	.538
			8th	8th			5th

WORLD SERIES

		G	W	L	T	N	PCT
1986	NY N	7	4	3	0	0	.571

Roy Johnson

JOHNSON, ROY CLEVELAND
Brother of Bob Johnson.
B. Feb. 23, 1903, Pryor, Okla.
D. Sept. 10, 1973, Tacoma, Wash.

		G	W	L	T	N	PCT	Standing		
1944	CHI N	1	0	1	0	0	.000	8	8	4

Walter Johnson

JOHNSON, WALTER PERRY (The Big Train, Barney)
B. Nov. 6, 1887, Humboldt, Kans.
D. Dec. 10, 1946, Washington, D. C.
Hall of Fame 1936.

		G	W	L	T	N	PCT	Standing
1929	WAS A	153	71	81	1	0	.467	5
1930		154	94	60	0	0	.610	2
1931		156	92	62	2	0	.597	3

	G	W	L	T	N	PCT	Standing

Walter Johnson *continued*

		G	W	L	T	N	PCT	Standing
1932		154	93	61	0	0	.604	3
1933	CLE A	99	48	51	0	0	.485	5 4
1934		154	85	69	0	0	.552	3
1935		96	46	48	2	0	.489	5 3
7 yrs.		966	529	432	5	0	.550	

Fielder Jones

JONES, FIELDER ALLISON
B. Aug. 13, 1871, Shinglehouse, Pa.
D. Mar. 13, 1934, Portland, Ore.

		G	W	L	T	N	PCT	Standing
1904	CHI A	114	66	47	1	0	.584	4 3
1905		158	92	60	6	0	.605	2
1906		154	93	58	3	0	.616	1
1907		157	87	64	6	0	.576	3
1908		156	88	64	4	0	.579	3
1914	STL F	40	12	26	2	0	.316	7 8
1915		159	87	67	5	0	.565	2
1916	STL A	158	79	75	4	0	.513	5
1917		155	57	97	1	0	.370	7
1918		46	22	24	0	0	.478	5 5
10 yrs.		1297	683	582	32	0	.540	

WORLD SERIES

		G	W	L	T	N	PCT	
1906	CHI A	6	4	2	0	0	.667	

Eddie Joost

JOOST, EDWIN DAVID
B. June 5, 1916, San Francisco, Calif.

		G	W	L	T	N	PCT	Standing
1954	PHI A	156	51	103	2	0	.331	8

Bill Joyce

JOYCE, WILLIAM MICHAEL (Scrappy Bill)
B. Sept. 21, 1865, St. Louis, Mo.
D. May 8, 1941, St. Louis, Mo.

		G	W	L	T	N	PCT	Standing
1896	NY N	43	28	14	1	0	.667	10 7
1897		138	83	48	6	1	.634	3
1898		43	22	21	0	0	.512	6 7
1898		92	46	39	7	0	.541	7 7
3 yrs.		316	179	122	14	1	.595	

Bill Jurges

JURGES, WILLIAM FREDERICK
B. May 9, 1908, Bronx, N. Y.

		G	W	L	T	N	PCT	Standing
1959	BOS A	80	44	36	0	0	.550	8 5
1960		42	15	27	0	0	.357	8 7
2 yrs.		122	59	63	0	0	.484	

Eddie Kasko

KASKO, EDWARD MICHAEL
B. June 27, 1932, Linden, N. J.

		G	W	L	T	N	PCT	Standing
1970	BOS A	162	87	75	0	0	.537	3
1971		162	85	77	0	0	.525	3
1972		155	85	70	0	0	.548	2
1973		161	88	73	0	0	.547	2 2
4 yrs.		640	345	295	0	0	.539	

Johnny Keane

KEANE, JOHN JOSEPH
B. Nov. 3, 1911, St. Louis, Mo.
D. Jan. 6, 1967, Houston, Tex.

		G	W	L	T	N	PCT	Standing
1961	STL N	80	47	33	0	0	.588	6 5
1962		163	84	78	1	0	.519	6
1963		162	93	69	0	0	.574	2
1964		162	93	69	0	0	.574	1
1965	NY A	162	77	85	0	0	.475	6

Johnny Keane *continued*

		G	W	L	T	N	PCT	Standing
1966		20	4	16	0	0	.200	10 10
6 yrs.		749	398	350	1	0	.532	

WORLD SERIES

		G	W	L	T	N	PCT	
1964	STL N	7	4	3	0	0	.571	

Joe Kelley

KELLEY, JOSEPH JAMES
B. Dec. 9, 1871, Cambridge, Mass.
D. Aug. 14, 1943, Baltimore, Md.
Hall of Fame 1971.

		G	W	L	T	N	PCT	Standing
1902	CIN N	60	34	26	0	0	.567	5 4
1903		141	74	65	2	0	.532	4
1904		157	88	65	4	0	.575	3
1905		155	79	74	2	0	.516	5
1908	BOS N	156	63	91	2	0	.409	6
5 yrs.		669	338	321	10	0	.513	

Honest John Kelly

KELLY, JOHN O.
B. Oct. 31, 1856, New York, N. Y.
D. Mar. 27, 1926, Malba, N. Y.

		G	W	L	T	N	PCT	Standing
1887	LOU AA	139	76	60	3	0	.559	4
1888		39	10	29	0	0	.256	8 7
2 yrs.		178	86	89	3	0	.491	

King Kelly

KELLY, MICHAEL JOSEPH
B. Dec. 31, 1857, Troy, N. Y.
D. Nov. 8, 1894, Boston, Mass.
Hall of Fame 1945.

		G	W	L	T	N	PCT	Standing
1887	BOS N	94	49	43	2	0	.533	5 5
1890	BOS P	133	81	48	1	3	.628	1
1891	CIN AA	102	43	57	1	1	.430	7
3 yrs.		329	173	148	4	4	.539	

Tom Kelly

KELLY, JAY THOMAS
B. Aug. 15, 1950, Graceville, Minn.

		G	W	L	T	N	PCT	Standing
1986	MIN A	23	12	11	0	0	.522	7 6
1987		162	85	77	0	0	.525	1
1988		162	91	71	0	0	.562	2
1989		162	80	82	0	0	.494	5
4 yrs.		509	268	241	0	0	.527	

LEAGUE CHAMPIONSHIP SERIES

		G	W	L	T	N	PCT	
1987	MIN A	5	4	1	0	0	.800	

WORLD SERIES

		G	W	L	T	N	PCT	
1987	MIN A	7	4	3	0	0	.571	

Bob Kennedy

KENNEDY, ROBERT DANIEL
Father of Terry Kennedy.
B. Aug. 18, 1920, Chicago, Ill.

		G	W	L	T	N	PCT	Standing
1963	CHI N	162	82	80	0	0	.506	7
1964		162	76	86	0	0	.469	8
1965		58	24	32	2	0	.429	9 8
1968	OAK A	163	82	80	1	0	.506	6
4 yrs.		545	264	278	3	0	.487	

Jim Kennedy

KENNEDY, JAMES C.
B. 1867, New York, N. Y.
D. Apr. 20, 1904, Brighton Beach, N. Y.

		G	W	L	T	N	PCT	Standing
1890	BKN AA	99	26	73	0	0	.263	9

John Kerins

KERINS, JOHN NELSON
B. July 15, 1858, Indianapolis, Ind.
D. Sept. 8, 1919, Louisville, Ky.

		G	W	L	T	N	PCT	Standing
1888	LOU AA	7	3	4	0	0	.429	8 8 7

Don Kessinger

KESSINGER, DONALD EULON
B. July 17, 1942, Forrest City, Ark.

		G	W	L	T	N	PCT	Standing
1979	CHI A	106	46	60	0	0	.434	5 5

Bill Killefer

KILLEFER, WILLIAM LAVIER (Reindeer Bill)
Brother of Red Killefer.
B. Oct. 10, 1887, Bloomingdale, Mich.
D. July 3, 1960, Elsmere, Del.

		G	W	L	T	N	PCT	Standing
1921	CHI N	57	23	34	0	0	.404	6 7
1922		156	80	74	2	0	.519	5
1923		154	83	71	0	0	.539	4
1924		154	81	72	0	1	.529	5
1925		75	33	42	0	0	.440	7 8
1930	STL A	154	64	90	0	0	.416	6
1931		154	63	91	0	0	.409	5
1932		154	63	91	0	0	.409	6
1933		91	34	57	0	0	.374	8
9 yrs.		1149	524	622	2	1	.457	

Clyde King

KING, CLYDE EDWARD
B. May 23, 1925, Goldsboro, N. C.

		G	W	L	T	N	PCT	Standing
1969	SF N	162	90	72	0	0	.556	2
1970		42	19	23	0	0	.452	4 3
1974	ATL N	64	38	25	1	0	.603	4 3
1975		134	58	76	0	0	.433	5 5
1982	NY A	62	29	33	0	0	.468	5 5
5 yrs.		464	234	229	1	0	.505	

Mal Kittridge

KITTRIDGE, MALACHI JEDDIDAH
B. Oct. 12, 1869, Clinton, Mass.
D. June 23, 1928, Gary, Ind.

		G	W	L	T	N	PCT	Standing
1904	WAS A	18	1	16	1	0	.059	8 8

Lou Klein

KLEIN, LOUIS FRANK
B. Oct. 22, 1918, New Orleans, La.
D. June 20, 1976, Metairie, La.

		G	W	L	T	N	PCT	Standing
1961	CHI N	12	5	7	0	0	.417	7 7
1962		30	12	18	0	0	.400	9 9 9
1965		106	48	58	0	0	.453	9 8
3 yrs.		148	65	83	0	0	.439	

Johnny Kling

KLING, JOHN (Noisy)
Brother of Bill Kling.
B. Feb. 25, 1875, Kansas City, Mo.
D. Jan. 31, 1947, Kansas City, Mo.

		G	W	L	T	N	PCT	Standing
1912	BOS N	155	52	101	2	0	.340	8

	G	W	L	T	N	PCT	Standing				G	W	L	T	N	PCT	Standing				G	W	L	T	N	PCT	Standing

Otto Knabe

KNABE, FRANZ OTTO (Dutch)
B. June 12, 1884, Carrick, Pa.
D. May 17, 1961, Philadelphia, Pa.

		G	W	L	T	N	PCT	Standing
1914	BAL F	160	84	70	6	0	.545	3
1915		155	47	107	0	1	.305	8
2 yrs.		315	131	177	6	1	.425	

Jack Krol

KROL, JOHN THOMAS
B. July 5, 1936, Chicago, Ill.

		G	W	L	T	N	PCT	Standing		
1978	STL N	2	1	1	0	0	.500	6	6	5
1980		1	0	1	0	0	.000	6	6	4
2 yrs.		3	1	2	0	0	.333			

Karl Kuehl

KUEHL, KARL OTTO
B. Sept. 5, 1937, Monterey Park, Calif.

		G	W	L	T	N	PCT	Standing	
1976	MON N	128	43	85	0	0	.336	6	6

Harvey Kuenn

KUENN, HARVEY EDWARD
B. Dec. 4, 1930, West Allis, Wis.
D. Feb. 28, 1988, Peoria, Ariz.

		G	W	L	T	N	PCT	Standing	
1975	MIL A	1	1	0	0	0	1.000	5	5
1982		116	72	43	1	0	.626	5	1
1983		162	87	75	0	0	.537	5	
3 yrs.		279	160	118	1	0	.576		

LEAGUE CHAMPIONSHIP SERIES

		G	W	L	T	N	PCT
1982	MIL A	5	3	2	0	0	.600

WORLD SERIES

		G	W	L	T	N	PCT
1982	MIL A	7	3	4	0	0	.429

Joe Kuhel

KUHEL, JOSEPH ANTHONY
B. June 25, 1906, Cleveland, Ohio.
D. Feb. 26, 1984, Kansas City, Kans.

		G	W	L	T	N	PCT	Standing
1948	WAS A	154	56	97	1	0	.366	7
1949		154	50	104	0	0	.325	8
2 yrs.		308	106	201	1	0	.345	

Rene Lachemann

LACHEMANN, RENE GEORGE
Brother of Marcel Lachemann.
B. May 4, 1945, Los Angeles, Calif.

		G	W	L	T	N	PCT	Standing		
1981	SEA A	33	15	18	0	0	.455	7	6	(1st)
1981		52	23	29	0	0	.442	5		(2nd)
1982		162	76	86	0	0	.469	4		
1983		73	26	47	0	0	.356	7	7	
1984	MIL A	161	67	94	0	0	.416	7		
4 yrs.		481	207	274	0	0	.430			

Nap Lajoie

LAJOIE, NAPOLEON (Larry)
B. Sept. 5, 1874, Woonsocket, R. I.
D. Feb. 7, 1959, Daytona Beach, Fla.
Hall of Fame 1937.

		G	W	L	T	N	PCT	Standing	
1905	CLE A	60	37	21	2	0	.638	1	5
1905		56	19	36	1	0	.345	2	5
1906		157	89	64	4	0	.582	3	
1907		158	85	67	6	0	.559	4	
1908		157	90	64	3	0	.584	2	
1909		114	57	57	0	0	.500	6	6
5 yrs.		702	377	309	16	0	.550		

Fred Lake

LAKE, FREDERICK LOVETT
B. Oct. 16, 1866, Nova Scotia, Canada
D. Nov. 24, 1931, Boston, Mass.

		G	W	L	T	N	PCT	Standing	
1908	BOS A	40	22	17	1	0	.564	6	5
1909		152	88	63	1	0	.583	3	
1910	BOS N	157	53	100	4	0	.346	8	
3 yrs.		349	163	180	6	0	.475		

Hal Lanier

LANIER, HAROLD CLIFTON
Son of Max Lanier.
B. July 4, 1942, Denton, N. C.

		G	W	L	T	N	PCT	Standing
1986	HOU N	162	96	66	0	0	.593	1
1987		162	76	86	0	0	.469	3
1988		162	82	80	0	0	.506	5
3 yrs.		486	254	232	0	0	.523	

LEAGUE CHAMPIONSHIP SERIES

		G	W	L	T	N	PCT
1986	HOU N	6	2	4	0	0	.333

Henry Larkin

LARKIN, HENRY E. (Ted)
B. Jan. 12, 1860, Reading, Pa.
D. Jan. 31, 1942, Reading, Pa.

		G	W	L	T	N	PCT	Standing	
1890	CLE P	79	34	45	0	0	.430	7	7

Tony LaRussa

LaRUSSA, ANTHONY
B. Oct. 4, 1944, Tampa, Fla.

		G	W	L	T	N	PCT	Standing		
1979	CHI A	54	27	27	0	0	.500	5	5	
1980		162	70	90	2	0	.438	5		
1981		53	31	22	0	0	.585	3		(1st)
1981		53	23	30	0	0	.434	6		(2nd)
1982		162	87	75	0	0	.537	3		
1983		162	99	63	0	0	.611	1		
1984		162	74	88	0	0	.457	5		
1985		163	85	77	1	0	.525	3		
1986		64	26	38	0	0	.406	6	5	
1986	OAK A	79	45	34	0	0	.570	7	3	
1987		162	81	81	0	0	.500	3		
1988		162	104	58	0	0	.642	1		
1989		162	99	63	0	0	.611	1		
11 yrs.		1600	851	746	3	0	.533			

LEAGUE CHAMPIONSHIP SERIES

		G	W	L	T	N	PCT
1983	CHI A	4	1	3	0	0	.250
1988	OAK A	4	4	0	0	0	1.000
1989		5	4	1	0	0	.800
3 yrs.		13	9	4	0	0	.692
		8th	5th				1st

WORLD SERIES

		G	W	L	T	N	PCT
1988	OAK A	5	1	4	0	0	.200
1989		4	4	0	0	0	1.000
2 yrs.		9	5	4	0	0	.556

Tom Lasorda

LASORDA, THOMAS CHARLES
B. Sept. 22, 1927, Norristown, Pa.

		G	W	L	T	N	PCT	Standing		
1976	LA N	4	2	2	0	0	.500	2	2	
1977		162	98	64	0	0	.605	1		
1978		162	95	67	0	0	.586	1		
1979		162	79	83	0	0	.488	3		
1980		163	92	71	0	0	.564	2		
1981		57	36	21	0	0	.632	1		(1st)
1981		53	27	26	0	0	.509	4		(2nd)
1982		162	88	74	0	0	.543	2		
1983		163	91	71	1	0	.562	1		
1984		162	79	83	0	0	.488	4		
1985		162	95	67	0	0	.586	1		
1986		162	73	89	0	0	.451	5		

Tom Lasorda *continued*

		G	W	L	T	N	PCT	Standing
1987		162	73	89	0	0	.451	4
1988		162	94	67	1	0	.584	1
1989		160	77	83	0	0	.481	4
14 yrs.		2058	1099	957	2	0	.535	

DIVISIONAL PLAYOFF SERIES

		G	W	L	T	N	PCT
1981	LA N	5	3	2	0	0	.600

LEAGUE CHAMPIONSHIP SERIES

		G	W	L	T	N	PCT
1977	LA N	4	3	1	0	0	.750
1978		4	3	1	0	0	.750
1981		5	3	2	0	0	.600
1983		4	1	3	0	0	.250
1985		6	2	4	0	0	.333
1988		7	4	3	0	0	.571
6 yrs.		30	16	14	0	0	.533
		1st	2nd	1st			6th

WORLD SERIES

		G	W	L	T	N	PCT
1977	LA N	6	2	4	0	0	.333
1978		6	2	4	0	0	.333
1981		6	4	2	0	0	.667
1988		5	4	1	0	0	.800
4 yrs.		23	12	11	0	0	.522
		10th	8th				8th

Arlie Latham

LATHAM, WALTER ARLINGTON (The Freshest Man on Earth)
B. Mar. 15, 1860, W. Lebanon, N. H.
D. Nov. 29, 1952, Garden City, N. Y.

		G	W	L	T	N	PCT	Standing		
1896	STL N	3	0	3	0	0	.000	10	10	11

Juice Latham

LATHAM, GEORGE WARREN (Jumbo)
B. Sept. 6, 1852, Utica, N. Y.
D. May 26, 1914, Utica, N. Y.

		G	W	L	T	N	PCT	Standing
1882	PHI AA	75	41	34	0	0	.547	2

Cookie Lavagetto

LAVAGETTO, HARRY ARTHUR
B. Dec. 1, 1912, Oakland, Calif.

		G	W	L	T	N	PCT	Standing		
1957	WAS A	134	51	83	0	0	.381	8	8	
1958		156	61	93	2	0	.396	8		
1959		154	63	91	0	0	.409	8		
1960		154	73	81	0	0	.474	5		
1961	MIN A	49	19	30	0	0	.388	8	7	
1961		10	4	6	0	0	.400	9	9	7
5 yrs.		657	271	384	2	0	.414			

Bob Leadley

LEADLEY, ROBERT H.
B. 1858, Brooklyn, N. Y.
Deceased.

		G	W	L	T	N	PCT	Standing	
1888	DET N	40	19	19	2	0	.500	3	5
1890	CLE N	58	23	33	2	0	.411	7	7
1891		68	34	34	0	0	.500	6	5
3 yrs.		166	76	86	4	0	.469		

Jim Lefebvre

LEFEBVRE, JAMES KENNETH (Frenchy)
B. Jan. 7, 1942, Inglewood, Calif.

		G	W	L	T	N	PCT	Standing
1989	SEA A	162	73	89	0	0	.451	6

		G	W	L	T	N	PCT	Standing

Bob Lemon

LEMON, ROBERT GRANVILLE
B. Sept. 22, 1920, San Bernardino, Calif.
Hall of Fame 1976.

			G	W	L	T	N	PCT	Standing	
1970	KC	A	110	46	64	0	0	.418	5	4
1971			161	85	76	0	0	.528	2	
1972			154	76	78	0	0	.494	4	
1977	CHI	A	162	90	72	0	0	.556	3	
1978			74	34	40	0	0	.459	5	5
1978	NY	A	68	48	20	0	0	.706	3	1
1979			65	34	31	0	0	.523	4	4
1981			25	11	14	0	0	.440	5	6	(2nd)
1982			14	6	8	0	0	.429	4	5
8 yrs.			833	430	403	0	0	.516		

DIVISIONAL PLAYOFF SERIES

			G	W	L	T	N	PCT
1981	NY	A	5	3	2	0	0	.600

LEAGUE CHAMPIONSHIP SERIES

			G	W	L	T	N	PCT
1978	NY	A	4	3	1	0	0	.750
1981			3	3	0	0	0	1.000
2 yrs.			7	6	1	0	0	.857

WORLD SERIES

			G	W	L	T	N	PCT
1978	NY	A	6	4	2	0	0	.667
1981			6	2	4	0	0	.333
2 yrs.			12	6	6	0	0	.500

Jim Lemon

LEMON, JAMES ROBERT
B. Mar. 23, 1928, Covington, Va.

			G	W	L	T	N	PCT	Standing
1968	WAS	A	161	65	96	0	0	.404	10

Jim Leyland

LEYLAND, JAMES RICHARD
B. Dec. 15, 1944, Toledo, Ohio

			G	W	L	T	N	PCT	Standing
1986	PIT	N	162	64	98	0	0	.395	6
1987			162	80	82	0	0	.494	4
1988			160	85	75	0	0	.531	2
1989			162	74	88	0	0	.457	5
4 yrs.			646	303	343	0	0	.469	

Nick Leyva

LEYVA, NICHOLAS TOMAS
B. Aug. 16, 1953, Ontario, Calif.

			G	W	L	T	N	PCT	Standing
1989	PHI	N	162	67	95	0	0	.414	6

Bob Lillis

LILLIS, ROBERT PERRY (Flea)
B. June 2, 1930, Altadena, Calif.

			G	W	L	T	N	PCT	Standing	
1982	HOU	N	51	28	23	0	0	.549	5	5
1983			162	85	77	0	0	.525	3	
1984			162	80	82	0	0	.494	2	
1985			162	83	79	0	0	.512	3	
4 yrs.			537	276	261	0	0	.514		

Johnny Lipon

LIPON, JOHN JOSEPH (Skids)
B. Nov. 10, 1922, Martin's Ferry, Ohio

			G	W	L	T	N	PCT	Standing	
1971	CLE	A	59	18	41	0	0	.305	6	6

Hans Lobert

LOBERT, JOHN BERNARD (Honus)
Brother of Frank Lobert.
B. Oct. 18, 1881, Wilmington, Del.
D. Sept. 14, 1968, Philadelphia, Pa.

			G	W	L	T	N	PCT	Standing	
1938	PHI	N	2	0	2	0	0	.000	8	8

Hans Lobert continued

		G	W	L	T	N	PCT	Standing
1942	151	42	109	0	0	.278	8	
2 yrs.	153	42	111	0	0	.275		

Whitey Lockman

LOCKMAN, CARROLL WALTER
B. July 25, 1926, Lowell, N. C.

			G	W	L	T	N	PCT	Standing	
1972	CHI	N	65	39	26	0	0	.600	4	2
1973			161	77	84	0	0	.478	5	
1974			93	41	52	0	0	.441	5	6
3 yrs.			319	157	162	0	0	.492		

Tom Loftus

LOFTUS, THOMAS JOSEPH
B. Nov. 15, 1856, St. Louis, Mo.
D. Apr. 16, 1910, Dubuque, Iowa

			G	W	L	T	N	PCT	Standing	
1884	MIL	U	12	8	4	0	0	.667	2	
1888	CLE	AA	71	30	38	3	0	.441	7	6
1889	CLE	N	136	61	72	3	0	.459	6	
1890	CIN	N	134	77	55	2	0	.583	4	
1891			138	56	81	1	0	.409	7	
1900	CHI	N	146	65	75	6	0	.464	5	
1901			140	53	86	1	0	.381	6	
1902	WAS	A	138	61	75	2	0	.449	6	
1903			140	43	94	3	0	.314	8	
9 yrs.			1055	454	580	21	0	.439		

Ed Lopat

LOPAT, EDMUND WALTER (Steady Eddie)
Born Edmund Walter Lopatynski.
B. June 21, 1918, New York, N. Y.

			G	W	L	T	N	PCT	Standing	
1963	KC	A	162	73	89	0	0	.451	8	
1964			52	17	35	0	0	.327	10	10
2 yrs.			214	90	124	0	0	.421		

Al Lopez

LOPEZ, ALFONSO RAYMOND
B. Aug. 20, 1908, Tampa, Fla.
Hall of Fame 1977.

			G	W	L	T	N	PCT	Standing	
1951	CLE	A	155	93	61	1	0	.604	2	
1952			155	93	61	1	0	.604	2	
1953			155	92	62	1	0	.597	2	
1954			156	111	43	2	0	.721	1	
1955			154	93	61	0	0	.604	2	
1956			155	88	66	1	0	.571	2	
1957	CHI	A	155	90	64	1	0	.584	2	
1958			155	82	72	1	0	.532	2	
1959			156	94	60	2	0	.610	1	
1960			154	87	67	0	0	.565	3	
1961			163	86	76	1	0	.531	4	
1962			162	85	77	0	0	.525	5	
1963			162	94	68	0	0	.580	2	
1964			162	98	64	0	0	.605	2	
1965			162	95	67	0	0	.586	2	
1968			11	6	5	0	0	.545	9	9	8
1968			36	15	21	0	0	.417	9	8
1969			17	8	9	0	0	.471	4	5
17 yrs.			2425	1410	1004	11	0	.584		
									8th	

WORLD SERIES

			G	W	L	T	N	PCT
1954	CLE	A	4	0	4	0	0	.000
1959	CHI	A	6	2	4	0	0	.333
2 yrs.			10	2	8	0	0	.200

Harry Lord

LORD, HARRY DONALD
B. Mar. 8, 1882, Porter, Me.
D. Aug. 9, 1948, Westbrook, Me.

			G	W	L	T	N	PCT	Standing	
1915	BUF	F	110	60	49	1	0	.550	8	6

Bobby Lowe

LOWE, ROBERT LINCOLN (Link)
B. July 10, 1868, Pittsburgh, Pa.
D. Dec. 8, 1951, Detroit, Mich.

			G	W	L	T	N	PCT	Standing	
1904	DET	A	78	30	44	4	0	.405	7	7

Frank Lucchesi

LUCCHESI, FRANK JOSEPH
B. Apr. 24, 1927, San Francisco, Calif.

			G	W	L	T	N	PCT	Standing	
1970	PHI	N	161	73	88	0	0	.453	5	
1971			162	67	95	0	0	.414	6	
1972			76	26	50	0	0	.342	6	6
1975	TEX	A	67	35	32	0	0	.522	4	3
1976			162	76	86	0	0	.469	5	
1977			62	31	31	0	0	.500	4	2
1987	CHI	N	25	8	17	0	0	.320	5	6
7 yrs.			715	316	399	0	0	.442		

Harry Lumley

LUMLEY, HARRY G
B. Sept. 29, 1880, Forest City, Pa.
D. May 22, 1938, Binghamton, N. Y.

			G	W	L	T	N	PCT	Standing
1909	BKN	N	155	55	98	2	0	.359	6

Ted Lyons

LYONS, THEODORE AMAR
B. Dec. 28, 1900, Lake Charles, La.
D. July 25, 1986, Sulphur, La.
Hall of Fame 1955.

			G	W	L	T	N	PCT	Standing	
1946	CHI	A	125	64	60	1	0	.516	7	5
1947			155	70	84	1	0	.455	6	
1948			154	51	101	2	0	.336	8	
3 yrs.			434	185	245	4	0	.430		

Connie Mack

MACK, CORNELIUS ALEXANDER (The Tall Tactician)
Born Cornelius Alexander McGillicuddy.
Father of Earle Mack.
B. Dec. 22, 1862, E. Brookfield, Mass.
D. Feb. 8, 1956, Germantown, Pa.
Hall of Fame 1937.

			G	W	L	T	N	PCT	Standing	
1894	PIT	N	23	12	10	1	0	.545	7	7
1895			135	71	61	2	1	.538	7	
1896			131	66	63	2	0	.512	6	
1901	PHI	A	137	74	62	1	0	.544	4	
1902			137	83	53	1	0	.610	1	
1903			137	75	60	2	0	.556	2	
1904			155	81	70	4	0	.536	5	
1905			152	92	56	4	0	.622	1	
1906			149	78	67	4	0	.538	4	
1907			150	88	57	5	0	.607	2	
1908			157	68	85	4	0	.444	6	
1909			153	95	58	0	0	.621	2	
1910			155	102	48	5	0	.680	1	
1911			152	101	50	1	0	.669	1	
1912			153	90	62	1	0	.592	3	
1913			153	96	57	0	0	.627	1	
1914			158	99	53	6	0	.651	1	
1915			154	43	109	2	0	.283	8	
1916			154	36	117	1	0	.235	8	
1917			154	55	98	1	0	.359	8	

	G	W	L	T	N	PCT	Standing	

Connie Mack *continued*

		G	W	L	T	N	PCT	Standing	
1918		130	52	76	2	0	.406	8	
1919		140	36	104	0	0	.257	8	
1920		156	48	106	2	0	.312	8	
1921		155	53	100	2	0	.346	8	
1922		155	65	89	1	0	.422	7	
1923		153	69	83	1	0	.454	6	
1924		152	71	81	0	0	.467	5	
1925		153	88	64	1	0	.579	2	
1926		150	83	67	0	0	.553	3	
1927		155	91	63	1	0	.591	2	
1928		153	98	55	0	0	.641	2	
1929		151	104	46	1	0	.693	1	
1930		154	102	52	0	0	.662	1	
1931		153	107	45	1	0	.704	1	
1932		154	94	60	0	0	.610	2	
1933		152	79	72	1	0	.523	3	
1934		153	68	82	3	0	.453	5	
1935		149	58	91	0	0	.389	8	
1936		154	53	100	1	0	.346	8	
1937		120	39	80	1	0	.328	7	7
1938		154	53	99	2	0	.349	8	
1939		62	25	37	0	0	.403	6	7
1940		154	54	100	0	0	.351	8	
1941		154	64	90	0	0	.416	8	
1942		154	55	99	0	0	.357	8	
1943		155	49	105	1	0	.318	8	
1944		155	72	82	1	0	.468	5	
1945		153	52	98	3	0	.347	8	
1946		155	49	105	1	0	.318	8	
1947		156	78	76	2	0	.506	5	
1948		154	84	70	0	0	.545	4	
1949		154	81	73	0	0	.526	5	
1950		154	52	102	0	0	.338	8	
53 yrs.		7755	3731	3948	75	1	.486		
			1st	**1st**			**1st**		

WORLD SERIES

		G	W	L	T	N	PCT	Standing
1905	PHI A	5	1	4	0	0	.200	
1910		5	4	1	0	0	.800	
1911		6	4	2	0	0	.667	
1913		5	4	1	0	0	.800	
1914		4	0	4	0	0	.000	
1929		5	4	1	0	0	.800	
1930		6	4	2	0	0	.667	
1931		7	3	4	0	0	.429	
8 yrs.		43	24	19	0	0	.558	
			3rd	**4th**	**4th**			**4th**

Denny Mack

MACK, DENNIS JOSEPH
Born Dennis Joseph McGee.
B. 1851, Easton, Pa.
D. Apr. 10, 1888, Wilkes-Barre, Pa.

		G	W	L	T	N	PCT	Standing
1882	LOU AA	80	42	38	0	0	.525	3

Earle Mack

MACK, EARLE THADDEUS
Born Earle Thaddeus McGillicuddy.
Son of Connie Mack.
B. Feb. 1, 1890, Spencer, Mass.
D. Feb. 4, 1967, Upper Darby, Pa.

		G	W	L	T	N	PCT	Standing	
1937	PHI A	34	15	17	2	0	.469	7	7
1939		91	30	60	1	0	.333	6	7
2 yrs.		125	45	77	3	0	.369		

Jimmy Macullar

MACULLAR, JAMES F. (Little Mac)
B. Jan. 16, 1855, Boston, Mass.
D. Apr. 8, 1924, Baltimore, Md.

		G	W	L	T	N	PCT	Standing	
1879	SYR N	27	5	21	1	0	.192	6	7

Lee Magee

MAGEE, LEO CHRISTOPHER
Born Leopold Christopher
Hoernschemeyer.
B. June 4, 1889, Cincinnati, Ohio
D. Mar. 14, 1966, Columbus, Ohio

		G	W	L	T	N	PCT	Standing	
1915	BKN F	118	53	64	1	0	.453	7	7

Fergy Malone

MALONE, FERGUSON G.
B. 1842, Ireland
D. Jan. 1, 1905, Seattle, Wash.

		G	W	L	T	N	PCT	Standing
1884	PHI U	67	21	46	0	0	.313	9

Jimmy Manning

MANNING, JAMES H.
B. Jan. 31, 1862, Fall River, Mass.
D. Oct. 22, 1929, Edinburg, Tex.

		G	W	L	T	N	PCT	Standing
1901	WAS A	138	61	73	4	0	.455	6

Rabbit Maranville

MARANVILLE, WALTER JAMES VINCENT
B. Nov. 11, 1891, Springfield, Mass.
D. Jan. 5, 1954, New York, N. Y.
Hall of Fame 1954.

		G	W	L	T	N	PCT	Standing		
1925	CHI N	53	23	30	0	0	.434	7	8	8

Marty Marion

MARION, MARTIN WHITFORD (Slats, The Octopus)
Brother of Red Marion.
B. Dec. 1, 1917, Richburg, S. C.

		G	W	L	T	N	PCT	Standing	
1951	STL N	155	81	73	1	0	.526	3	
1952	STL A	104	42	61	1	0	.408	8	7
1953		154	54	100	0	0	.351	8	
1954	CHI A	9	3	6	0	0	.333	3	3
1955		155	91	63	1	0	.591	3	
1956		154	85	69	0	0	.552	3	
6 yrs.		731	356	372	3	0	.489		

Jim Marshall

MARSHALL, RUFUS JAMES
B. May 25, 1931, Danville, Ill.

		G	W	L	T	N	PCT	Standing	
1974	CHI N	69	25	44	0	0	.362	5	6
1975		162	75	87	0	0	.463	5	
1976		162	75	87	0	0	.463	4	
1979	OAK A	162	54	108	0	0	.333	7	
4 yrs.		555	229	326	0	0	.413		

Billy Martin

MARTIN, ALFRED MANUEL (The Kid)
Born Alfred Manuel Pesano.
B. May 16, 1928, Berkeley, Calif.
D. Dec. 25, 1989, Johnson City, N. Y.

		G	W	L	T	N	PCT	Standing	
1969	MIN A	162	97	65	0	0	.599	1	
1971	DET A	162	91	71	0	0	.562	2	
1972		156	86	70	0	0	.551	1	
1973		134	71	63	0	0	.530	3	3
1973	TEX A	23	9	14	0	0	.391	6	6
1974		161	84	76	1	0	.525	2	
1975		95	44	51	0	0	.463	4	3
1975	NY A	56	30	26	0	0	.536	3	3
1976		159	97	62	0	0	.610	1	
1977		162	100	62	0	0	.617	1	
1978		94	52	42	0	0	.553	3	1

Billy Martin *continued*

		G	W	L	T	N	PCT	Standing		
1979		95	55	40	0	0	.579	4	**4**	
1980	OAK A	162	83	79	0	0	.512	2		
1981		60	37	23	0	0	.617	1		(1st)
1981		49	27	22	0	0	.551	2		(2nd)
1982		162	68	94	0	0	.420	5		
1983	NY A	162	91	71	0	0	.562	3		
1985		145	91	54	0	0	.628	7	**2**	
1988		68	40	28	0	0	.588	2	5	
16 yrs.		2267	1253	1013	1	0	.553			

DIVISIONAL PLAYOFF SERIES

		G	W	L	T	N	PCT	Standing
1981	OAK A	3	3	0	0	0	1.000	

LEAGUE CHAMPIONSHIP SERIES

		G	W	L	T	N	PCT	Standing
1969	MIN A	3	0	3	0	0	.000	
1972	DET A	5	2	3	0	0	.400	
1976	NY A	5	3	2	0	0	.600	
1977		5	3	2	0	0	.600	
1981	OAK A	3	0	3	0	0	.000	
5 yrs.		21	8	13	0	0	.381	
			5th	**7th**	**3rd**			

WORLD SERIES

		G	W	L	T	N	PCT	Standing
1976	NY A	4	0	4	0	0	.000	
1977		6	4	2	0	0	.667	
2 yrs.		10	4	6	0	0	.400	

Marty Martinez

MARTINEZ, ORLANDO
Born Orlando Martinez y Oliva.
B. Aug. 23, 1941, Havana, Cuba

		G	W	L	T	N	PCT	Standing		
1986	SEA A	1	0	1	0	0	.000	6	6	7

Charlie Mason

MASON, CHARLES E.
B. June 25, 1853, New Orleans, La.
D. Oct. 21, 1936, Philadelphia, Pa.

		G	W	L	T	N	PCT	Standing	
1884	PHI AA	51	28	23	0	0	.549	7	7

Eddie Mathews

MATHEWS, EDWIN LEE
B. Oct. 13, 1931, Texarkana, Tex.
Hall of Fame 1978.

		G	W	L	T	N	PCT	Standing	
1972	ATL N	50	23	27	0	0	.460	5	4
1973		162	76	85	1	0	.472	5	
1974		99	50	49	0	0	.505	4	3
3 yrs.		311	149	161	1	0	.481		

Christy Mathewson

MATHEWSON, CHRISTOPHER (Big Six, Matty)
Brother of Henry Mathewson.
B. Aug. 12, 1880, Factoryville, Pa.
D. Oct. 7, 1925, Saranac Lake, N. Y.
Hall of Fame 1936.

		G	W	L	T	N	PCT	Standing	
1916	CIN N	69	25	43	1	0	.368	8	7
1917		157	78	76	3	0	.506	4	
1918		120	61	57	1	1	.517	4	3
3 yrs.		346	164	176	5	1	.482		

Bobby Mattick

MATTICK, ROBERT JAMES
Son of Wally Mattick.
B. Dec. 5, 1915, Sioux City, Iowa

		G	W	L	T	N	PCT	Standing		
1980	TOR A	162	67	95	0	0	.414	7		
1981		59	16	42	0	1	.276	7		(1st)
1981		48	21	27	0	0	.438	7		(2nd)
2 yrs.		269	104	164	0	1	.388			

	G	W	L	T	N	PCT	Standing		

Gene Mauch

MAUCH, GENE WILLIAM (Skip)
B. Nov. 18, 1925, Salina, Kans.

			G	W	L	T	N	PCT	Standing		
1960	PHI	N	152	58	94	0	0	.382	4	8	
1961			155	47	107	1	0	.305	8		
1962			161	81	80	0	0	.503	7		
1963			162	87	75	0	0	.537	4		
1964			162	92	70	0	0	.568	2		
1965			162	85	76	1	0	.528	6		
1966			162	87	75	0	0	.537	4		
1967			162	82	80	0	0	.506	5		
1968			54	27	27	0	0	.500	6	8	
1969	MON	N	162	52	110	0	0	.321	6		
1970			162	73	89	0	0	.451	6		
1971			162	71	90	1	0	.441	5		
1972			156	70	86	0	0	.449	5		
1973			162	79	83	0	0	.488	4		
1974			161	79	82	0	0	.491	4		
1975			162	75	87	0	0	.463	5		
1976	MIN	A	162	85	77	0	0	.525	3		
1977			161	84	77	0	0	.522	4		
1978			162	73	89	0	0	.451	4		
1979			162	82	80	0	0	.506	4		
1980			125	54	71	0	0	.432	6	3	
1981	CAL	A	13	9	4	0	0	.692	4	4	(1st)
1981			50	20	30	0	0	.400	7		(2nd)
1982			162	93	69	0	0	.574	1		
1985			162	90	72	0	0	.556	2		
1986			162	92	70	0	0	.568	1		
1987			162	75	87	0	0	.463	6		
26 yrs.			3942	1902	2037	3	0	.483			
				4th	8th			3rd			

LEAGUE CHAMPIONSHIP SERIES

			G	W	L	T	N	PCT	
1982	CAL	A	5	2	3	0	0	.400	
1986			7	3	4	0	0	.429	
2 yrs.			12	5	7	0	0	.417	
				10th	9th			9th	

Jimmy McAleer

McALEER, JAMES ROBERT
B. July 10, 1864, Youngstown, Ohio
D. Apr. 29, 1931, Youngstown, Ohio

			G	W	L	T	N	PCT	Standing
1901	CLE	A	138	55	82	1	0	.401	7
1902	STL	A	140	78	58	4	0	.574	2
1903			139	65	74	0	0	.468	6
1904			156	65	87	4	0	.428	6
1905			156	54	99	3	0	.353	8
1906			154	76	73	5	0	.510	5
1907			155	69	83	3	0	.454	6
1908			155	83	69	3	0	.546	4
1909			154	61	89	4	0	.407	7
1910	WAS	A	157	66	85	6	0	.437	7
1911			154	64	90	0	0	.416	7
11 yrs.			1658	736	889	33	0	.453	

George McBride

McBRIDE, GEORGE FLORIAN
B. Nov. 20, 1880, Milwaukee, Wis.
D. July 2, 1973, Milwaukee, Wis.

			G	W	L	T	N	PCT	Standing
1921	WAS	A	154	80	73	1	0	.523	4

Jack McCallister

McCALLISTER, JOHN
B. Jan. 19, 1879, Marietta, Ohio
D. Oct. 18, 1946, Columbus, Ohio

			G	W	L	T	N	PCT	Standing
1927	CLE	A	153	66	87	0	0	.431	6

Joe McCarthy

McCARTHY, JOSEPH VINCENT (Marse Joe)
B. Apr. 21, 1887, Philadelphia, Pa.
D. Jan. 3, 1978, Buffalo, N. Y.
Hall of Fame 1957.

			G	W	L	T	N	PCT	Standing	
1926	CHI	N	155	82	72	1	0	.532	4	
1927			153	85	68	0	0	.556	4	
1928			154	91	63	0	0	.591	3	
1929			156	98	54	4	0	.645	1	
1930			152	86	64	2	0	.573	2	2
1931	NY	A	155	94	59	2	0	.614	2	
1932			156	107	47	1	1	.695	1	
1933			152	91	59	2	0	.607	2	
1934			154	94	60	0	0	.610	2	
1935			149	89	60	0	0	.597	2	
1936			155	102	51	2	0	.667	1	
1937			157	102	52	2	1	.662	1	
1938			157	99	53	5	0	.651	1	
1939			152	106	45	1	0	.702	1	
1940			155	88	66	0	1	.571	3	
1941			156	101	53	2	0	.656	1	
1942			154	103	51	0	0	.669	1	
1943			155	98	56	1	0	.636	1	
1944			154	83	71	0	0	.539	3	
1945			152	81	71	0	0	.533	4	
1946			35	22	13	0	0	.629	2	3
1948	BOS	A	155	96	59	0	0	.619	2	
1949			155	96	58	1	0	.623	2	
1950			59	31	28	0	0	.525	4	3
24 yrs.			3487	2125	1333	26	3	.615		
				9th	4th			1st		

WORLD SERIES

			G	W	L	T	N	PCT	
1929	CHI	N	5	1	4	0	0	.200	
1932	NY	A	4	4	0	0	0	1.000	
1936			6	4	2	0	0	.667	
1937			5	4	1	0	0	.800	
1938			4	4	0	0	0	1.000	
1939			4	4	0	0	0	1.000	
1941			5	4	1	0	0	.800	
1942			5	1	4	0	0	.200	
1943			5	4	1	0	0	.800	
9 yrs.			43	30	13	0	0	.698	
				3rd	2nd	8th		1st	

Tommy McCarthy

McCARTHY, THOMAS FRANCIS MICHAEL
B. July 24, 1863, Boston, Mass.
D. Aug. 5, 1922, Boston, Mass.
Hall of Fame 1946.

			G	W	L	T	N	PCT	Standing
1890	STL	AA	22	11	11	0	0	.500	4

John McCloskey

McCLOSKEY, JOHN JAMES (Honest John)
B. Apr. 4, 1862, Louisville, Ky.
D. Nov. 17, 1940, Louisville, Ky.

			G	W	L	T	N	PCT	Standing	
1895	LOU	N	133	35	96	2	0	.267	12	
1896			19	2	17	0	0	.105	12	12
1906	STL	N	154	52	98	4	0	.347	7	
1907			155	52	101	2	0	.340	8	
1908			154	49	105	0	0	.318	8	
5 yrs.			615	190	417	8	0	.313		

Jim McCormick

McCORMICK, JAMES
B. 1856, Glasgow, Scotland
D. Mar. 10, 1918, Paterson, N. J.

			G	W	L	T	N	PCT	Standing	
1879	CLE	N	82	27	55	0	0	.329	6	
1880			85	47	37	1	0	.560	3	
1881			74	32	41	1	0	.438	7	7

Jim McCormick *continued*

	G	W	L	T	N	PCT	Standing	
1882	4	0	4	0	0	.000	8	5
4 yrs.	245	106	137	2	0	.436		

Mel McGaha

McGAHA, FRED MELVIN
B. Sept. 26, 1926, Bastrop, La.

			G	W	L	T	N	PCT	Standing	
1962	CLE	A	162	80	82	0	0	.494	6	
1964	KC	A	111	40	70	1	0	.364	10	10
1965			26	5	21	0	0	.192	10	10
3 yrs.			299	125	173	1	0	.419		

Mike McGeary

McGEARY, MICHAEL HENRY
B. 1851, Philadelphia, Pa.
Deceased.

			G	W	L	T	N	PCT	Standing	
1880	PRO	N	16	8	7	1	0	.533	4	2
1881	CLE	N	11	4	7	0	0	.364	7	7
2 yrs.			27	12	14	1	0	.462		

John McGraw

McGRAW, JOHN JOSEPH (Little Napoleon)
B. Apr. 7, 1873, Truxton, N. Y.
D. Feb. 25, 1934, New Rochelle, N. Y.
Hall of Fame 1937.

			G	W	L	T	N	PCT	Standing	
1899	BAL	N	152	86	62	4	0	.581	4	
1901	BAL	A	135	68	65	2	0	.511	5	
1902			58	26	31	1	0	.456	7	8
1902	NY	N	65	25	38	2	0	.397	8	8
1903			142	84	55	3	0	.604	2	
1904			158	106	47	5	0	.693	1	
1905			155	105	48	2	0	.686	1	
1906			153	96	56	1	0	.632	2	
1907			155	82	71	2	0	.536	4	
1908			157	98	56	3	0	.636	2	
1909			158	92	61	5	0	.601	3	
1910			155	91	63	1	0	.591	2	
1911			154	99	54	1	0	.647	1	
1912			154	103	48	3	0	.682	1	
1913			156	101	51	4	0	.664	1	
1914			156	84	70	2	0	.545	2	
1915			155	69	83	3	0	.454	8	
1916			155	86	66	3	0	.566	4	
1917			158	98	56	4	0	.636	1	
1918			124	71	53	0	0	.573	2	
1919			140	87	53	0	0	.621	2	
1920			155	86	68	1	0	.558	2	
1921			153	94	59	0	0	.614	1	
1922			156	93	61	2	0	.604	1	
1923			153	95	58	0	0	.621	1	
1924			29	16	13	0	0	.552	3	1
1924			81	45	35	0	1	.563	1	1
1925			152	86	66	0	0	.566	2	
1926			151	74	77	0	0	.490	5	
1927			122	70	52	0	0	.574	4	3
1928			155	93	61	1	0	.604	2	
1929			152	84	67	1	0	.556	3	
1930			154	87	67	0	0	.565	3	
1931			153	87	65	1	0	.572	2	
1932			40	17	23	0	0	.425	8	6
33 yrs.			4801	2784	1959	57	1	.587		
				2nd	2nd	4th		7th	

WORLD SERIES

			G	W	L	T	N	PCT	
1905	NY	N	5	4	1	0	0	.800	
1911			6	2	4	0	0	.333	
1912			7	3	4	0	0	.429	
1913			5	1	4	0	0	.200	
1917			6	2	4	0	0	.333	
1921			8	5	3	0	0	.625	
1922			5	4	0	1	0	1.000	
1923			6	2	4	0	0	.333	
1924			7	3	4	0	0	.429	
9 yrs.			55	26	28	1	0	.481	
				2nd	3rd	1st			

597

Deacon McGuire

McGUIRE, JAMES THOMAS
B. Nov. 18, 1863, Youngstown, Ohio
D. Oct. 31, 1936, Albion, Mich.

		G	W	L	T	N	PCT	Standing		
1898	WAS N	70	21	47	2	0	.309	10	11	11
1907	BOS A	112	45	61	6	0	.425	8	7	
1908		115	53	62	0	0	.461	6	5	
1909	CLE A	41	14	25	2	0	.359	6	6	
1910		161	71	81	9	0	.467	5		
1911		17	6	11	0	0	.353	7	3	
6 yrs.		516	210	287	19	0	.423			

Bill McGunnigle

McGUNNIGLE, WILLIAM HENRY
(Gunner)
B. Jan. 1, 1855, Boston, Mass.
D. Mar. 9, 1899, Brockton, Mass.

		G	W	L	T	N	PCT	Standing	
1888	BKN AA	143	88	52	3	0	.629	2	
1889		140	93	44	3	0	.679	1	
1890	BKN N	129	86	43	0	0	.667	1	
1891	PIT N	59	24	33	2	0	.421	8	8
1896	LOU N	115	36	76	3	0	.321	12	12
5 yrs.		586	327	248	11	0	.569		

Stuffy McInnis

McINNIS, JOHN PHALEN
B. Sept. 19, 1890, Gloucester, Mass.
D. Feb. 16, 1960, Ipswich, Mass.

		G	W	L	T	N	PCT	Standing
1927	PHI N	155	51	103	1	0	.331	8

Bill McKechnie

McKECHNIE, WILLIAM BOYD (Deacon)
B. Aug. 7, 1886, Wilkinsburg, Pa.
D. Oct. 29, 1965, Bradenton, Fla.
Hall of Fame 1962.

		G	W	L	T	N	PCT	Standing	
1915	NWK F	102	54	45	3	0	.545	6	5
1922	PIT N	90	53	36	1	0	.596	5	3
1923		154	87	67	0	0	.565	3	
1924		153	90	63	0	0	.588	3	
1925		153	95	58	0	0	.621	1	
1926		157	84	69	4	0	.549	3	
1928	STL N	154	95	59	0	0	.617	1	
1929		63	34	29	0	0	.540	4	4
1930	BOS N	154	70	84	0	0	.455	6	
1931		156	64	90	2	0	.416	7	
1932		155	77	77	1	0	.500	5	
1933		156	83	71	2	0	.539	4	
1934		152	78	73	1	0	.517	4	
1935		153	38	115	0	0	.248	8	
1936		157	71	83	3	0	.461	6	
1937		152	79	73	0	0	.520	5	
1938	CIN N	151	82	68	1	0	.547	4	
1939		156	97	57	2	0	.630	1	
1940		155	100	53	2	0	.654	1	
1941		154	88	66	0	0	.571	3	
1942		154	76	76	2	0	.500	4	
1943		155	87	67	1	0	.565	2	
1944		155	89	65	1	0	.578	3	
1945		154	61	93	0	0	.396	7	
1946		156	67	87	2	0	.435	6	
25 yrs.		3651	1899	1724	28	0	.524		
								8th 9th 6th	

WORLD SERIES

		G	W	L	T	N	PCT	Standing
1925	PIT N	7	4	3	0	0	.571	
1928	STL N	4	0	4	0	0	.000	
1939	CIN N	4	0	4	0	0	.000	
1940		7	4	3	0	0	.571	
4 yrs.		22	8	14	0	0	.364	
								6th

Jack McKeon

McKEON, JOHN ALOYSIUS
B. Nov. 23, 1930, South Amboy, N. J.

		G	W	L	T	N	PCT	Standing	
1973	KC A	162	88	74	0	0	.543	2	
1974		162	77	85	0	0	.475	5	
1975		96	50	46	0	0	.521	2	2
1977	OAK A	53	26	27	0	0	.491	7	7
1978		123	45	78	0	0	.366	6	6
1988	SD N	115	67	48	0	0	.583	5	3
1989		162	89	73	0	0	.549	2	
7 yrs.		873	442	431	0	0	.506		

Alex McKinnon

McKINNON, ALEXANDER J.
B. Aug. 14, 1856, Boston, Mass.
D. July 24, 1887, Charlestown, Mass.

		G	W	L	T	N	PCT	Standing		
1885	STL N	39	6	32	1	0	.158	5	8	8

Denny McKnight

McKNIGHT, HENRY DENNIS
B. 1847, Pittsburgh, Pa.
D. May 5, 1900, Pittsburgh, Pa.

		G	W	L	T	N	PCT	Standing	
1884	PIT AA	12	4	8	0	0	.333	9	11

George McManus

McMANUS, GEORGE
B. Oct., 1846
D. Oct. 2, 1918, New York, N. Y.

		G	W	L	T	N	PCT	Standing	
1876	STL N	8	6	2	0	0	.750	2	2
1877		60	28	32	0	0	.467	4	
2 yrs.		68	34	34	0	0	.500		

Marty McManus

McMANUS, MARTIN JOSEPH
B. Mar. 14, 1900, Chicago, Ill.
D. Feb. 18, 1966, St. Louis, Mo.

		G	W	L	T	N	PCT	Standing	
1932	BOS A	99	32	67	0	0	.323	8	8
1933		149	63	86	0	0	.423	7	
2 yrs.		248	95	153	0	0	.383		

Roy McMillan

McMILLAN, ROY DAVID
B. July 17, 1930, Bonham, Tex.

		G	W	L	T	N	PCT	Standing		
1972	MIL A	2	1	1	0	0	.500	6	6	6
1975	NY N	53	26	27	0	0	.491	3	3	
2 yrs.		55	27	28	0	0	.491			

John McNamara

McNAMARA, JOHN FRANCIS
B. June 4, 1932, Sacramento, Calif.

		G	W	L	T	N	PCT	Standing		
1969	OAK A	13	8	5	0	0	.615	2	2	
1970		162	89	73	0	0	.549	2		
1974	SD N	162	60	102	0	0	.370	6		
1975		162	71	91	0	0	.438	4		
1976		162	73	89	0	0	.451	5		
1977		48	20	28	0	0	.417	5	5	
1979	CIN N	161	90	71	0	0	.559	1		
1980		163	89	73	1	0	.549	3		
1981		56	35	21	0	0	.625	2		(1st)
1981		52	31	21	0	0	.596	2		(2nd)
1982		92	34	58	0	0	.370	6	6	
1983	CAL A	162	70	92	0	0	.432	5		
1984		162	81	81	0	0	.500	2		
1985	BOS A	163	81	81	1	0	.500	5		
1986		161	95	66	0	0	.590	1		
1987		162	78	84	0	0	.481	5		

John McNamara continued

		G	W	L	T	N	PCT	Standing	
1988		85	43	42	0	0	.506	4	1
16 yrs.		2128	1048	1078	2	0	.493		

LEAGUE CHAMPIONSHIP SERIES

		G	W	L	T	N	PCT	Standing
1979	CIN N	3	0	3	0	0	.000	
1986	BOS A	7	4	3	0	0	.571	
2 yrs.		10	4	6	0	0	.400	
								10th

WORLD SERIES

		G	W	L	T	N	PCT	Standing
1986	BOS A	7	3	4	0	0	.429	

Bid McPhee

McPHEE, JOHN ALEXANDER
B. Nov. 1, 1859, Massena, N. Y.
D. Jan. 3, 1943, San Diego, Calif.

		G	W	L	T	N	PCT	Standing	
1901	CIN N	142	52	87	3	0	.374	8	
1902		65	27	37	1	0	.422	7	4
2 yrs.		207	79	124	4	0	.389		

Cal McVey

McVEY, CALVIN ALEXANDER
B. Aug. 30, 1850, Montrose, Iowa
D. Aug. 20, 1926, San Francisco, Calif.

		G	W	L	T	N	PCT	Standing	
1878	CIN N	61	37	23	1	0	.617	2	
1879		63	34	28	1	0	.548	5	5
2 yrs.		124	71	51	2	0	.582		

Sam Mele

MELE, SABATH ANTHONY
B. Jan. 21, 1923, Astoria, N. Y.

		G	W	L	T	N	PCT	Standing		
1961	MIN A	8	2	5	1	0	.286	8	9	7
1961		95	45	49	1	0	.479	9	7	
1962		163	91	71	1	0	.562	2		
1963		161	91	70	0	0	.565	3		
1964		163	79	83	1	0	.488	6		
1965		162	102	60	0	0	.630	1		
1966		162	89	73	0	0	.549	2		
1967		50	25	25	0	0	.500	6	2	
7 yrs.		964	524	436	4	0	.546			

WORLD SERIES

		G	W	L	T	N	PCT	Standing
1965	MIN A	7	3	4	0	0	.429	

Charlie Metro

METRO, CHARLES
Born Charles Moreskonich.
B. Apr. 28, 1919, Nanty-Glo, Pa.

		G	W	L	T	N	PCT	Standing	
1962	CHI A	112	43	69	0	0	.384	9	9
1970	KC A	52	19	33	0	0	.365	5	4
2 yrs.		164	62	102	0	0	.378		

Billy Meyer

MEYER, WILLIAM ADAM
B. Jan. 14, 1892, Knoxville, Tenn.
D. Mar. 31, 1957, Knoxville, Tenn.

		G	W	L	T	N	PCT	Standing
1948	PIT N	156	83	71	2	0	.539	4
1949		154	71	83	0	0	.461	6
1950		154	57	96	1	0	.373	8
1951		155	64	90	1	0	.416	7
1952		155	42	112	1	0	.273	8
5 yrs.		774	317	452	5	0	.412	

	G	W	L	T	N	PCT	Standing

Gene Michael

MICHAEL, EUGENE RICHARD (Stick)
B. June 2, 1938, Kent, Ohio

			G	W	L	T	N	PCT	Standing	
1981	NY	A	56	34	22	0	0	.607	1	(1st)
1981			26	14	12	0	0	.538	5 6	(2nd)
1982			86	44	42	0	0	.512	4 5	5
1986	CHI	N	102	46	56	0	0	.451	5 5	
1987			136	68	68	0	0	.500	5 6	
4 yrs.			406	206	200	0	0	.507		

Clyde Milan

MILAN, JESSE CLYDE (Deerfoot)
Brother of Horace Milan.
B. Mar. 25, 1887, Linden, Tenn.
D. Mar. 3, 1953, Orlando, Fla.

			G	W	L	T	N	PCT	Standing
1922	WAS	A	154	69	85	0	0	.448	6

George Miller

MILLER, GEORGE C.
B. Feb. 19, 1853, Newport, Ky.
D. July 24, 1929, Norwood, Ohio

			G	W	L	T	N	PCT	Standing
1894	STL	N	133	56	76	1	0	.424	9

Ray Miller

MILLER, RAYMOND ROGER
B. Apr. 30, 1945, Takoma Park, Md.

			G	W	L	T	N	PCT	Standing
1985	MIN	A	100	50	50	0	0	.500	6 4
1986			139	59	80	0	0	.424	7 6
2 yrs.			239	109	130	0	0	.456	

Buster Mills

MILLS, COLONEL BUSTER
B. Sept. 16, 1908, Ranger, Tex.

			G	W	L	T	N	PCT	Standing
1953	CIN	N	8	4	4	0	0	.500	6 6

Fred Mitchell

MITCHELL, FREDERICK FRANCIS
Born Frederick Francis Yapp.
B. June 5, 1878, Cambridge, Mass.
D. Oct. 13, 1970, Newton, Mass.

			G	W	L	T	N	PCT	Standing
1917	CHI	N	157	74	80	3	0	.481	5
1918			131	84	45	2	0	.651	1
1919			140	75	65	0	0	.536	3
1920			154	75	79	0	0	.487	5
1921	BOS	N	153	79	74	0	0	.516	4
1922			154	53	100	1	0	.346	8
1923			155	54	100	1	0	.351	7
7 yrs.			1044	494	543	7	0	.476	

WORLD SERIES

			G	W	L	T	N	PCT
1918	CHI	N	6	2	4	0	0	.333

Jackie Moore

MOORE, JACKIE SPENCER
B. Feb. 19, 1939, Jay, Fla.

			G	W	L	T	N	PCT	Standing
1984	OAK	A	118	57	61	0	0	.483	4 4
1985			162	77	85	0	0	.475	4
1986			73	29	44	0	0	.397	6 3
3 yrs.			353	163	190	0	0	.462	

Terry Moore

MOORE, TERRY BLUFORD
B. May 27, 1912, Vernon, Ala.

			G	W	L	T	N	PCT	Standing
1954	PHI	N	77	35	42	0	0	.455	3 4

Pat Moran

MORAN, PATRICK JOSEPH
B. Feb. 7, 1876, Fitchburg, Mass.
D. Mar. 7, 1924, Orlando, Fla.

			G	W	L	T	N	PCT	Standing
1915	PHI	N	153	90	62	1	0	.592	1
1916			154	91	62	1	0	.595	2
1917			155	87	65	2	1	.572	2
1918			125	55	68	2	0	.447	6
1919	CIN	N	140	96	44	0	0	.686	1
1920			154	82	71	1	0	.536	3
1921			153	70	83	0	0	.458	6
1922			156	86	68	2	0	.558	2
1923			154	91	63	0	0	.591	2
9 yrs.			1344	748	586	9	1	.561	

WORLD SERIES

			G	W	L	T	N	PCT
1915	PHI	N	5	1	4	0	0	.200
1919	CIN	N	8	5	3	0	0	.625
2 yrs.			13	6	7	0	0	.462

Joe Morgan

MORGAN, JOSEPH MICHAEL
B. Nov. 19, 1930, Walpole, Mass.

			G	W	L	T	N	PCT	Standing
1988	BOS	A	77	46	31	0	0	.597	4 1
1989			162	83	79	0	0	.512	3
2 yrs.			239	129	110	0	0	.540	

LEAGUE CHAMPIONSHIP SERIES

			G	W	L	T	N	PCT
1988	BOS	A	4	0	4	0	0	.000

George Moriarty

MORIARTY, GEORGE JOSEPH
Brother of Bill Moriarty.
B. July 7, 1884, Chicago, Ill.
D. Apr. 8, 1964, Miami, Fla.

			G	W	L	T	N	PCT	Standing
1927	DET	A	156	82	71	3	0	.536	4
1928			154	68	86	0	0	.442	6
2 yrs.			310	150	157	3	0	.489	

John Morrill

MORRILL, JOHN FRANCIS (Honest John)
B. Feb. 19, 1855, Boston, Mass.
D. Apr. 2, 1932, Boston, Mass.

			G	W	L	T	N	PCT	Standing	
1882	BOS	N	85	45	39	1	0	.536	3	
1883			44	33	11	0	0	.750	4	1
1884			116	73	38	5	0	.658	2	
1885			113	46	66	1	0	.411	5	
1886			118	56	61	1	0	.479	5	
1887			32	12	17	0	3	.414	5	5
1888			137	70	64	3	0	.522	4	
1889	WAS	N	51	13	38	0	0	.255	8	8
8 yrs.			696	348	334	11	3	.510		

Charlie Morton

MORTON, CHARLES HAZEN
B. Oct. 12, 1854, Kingsville, Ohio
D. Dec. 9, 1921, Massillon, Ohio

			G	W	L	T	N	PCT	Standing	
1884	TOL	AA	110	46	58	6	0	.442	8	
1885	DET	N	38	7	31	0	0	.184	7	6
1890	TOL	AA	134	68	64	2	0	.515	4	
3 yrs.			282	121	153	8	0	.442		

Felix Moses

MOSES, FELIX I.
B. Richmond, Va.
Deceased.

			G	W	L	T	N	PCT	Standing
1884	RIC	AA	46	12	30	4	0	.286	10

Les Moss

MOSS, JOHN LESTER
B. May 14, 1925, Tulsa, Okla.

			G	W	L	T	N	PCT	Standing	
1968	CHI	A	2	0	2	0	0	.000	9	9 8
1968			34	12	22	0	0	.353	9	9 8
1979	DET	A	53	27	26	0	0	.509	5 5	
2 yrs.			89	39	50	0	0	.438		

Tim Murnane

MURNANE, TIMOTHY HAYES
B. June 4, 1852, Naugatuck, Conn.
D. Feb. 7, 1917, Boston, Mass.

			G	W	L	T	N	PCT	Standing
1884	BOS	U	111	58	51	2	0	.532	5

Billy Murray

MURRAY, WILLIAM JEREMIAH
B. Apr. 13, 1864, Peabody, Mass.
D. Mar. 25, 1937, Youngstown, Ohio

			G	W	L	T	N	PCT	Standing
1907	PHI	N	149	83	64	2	0	.565	3
1908			155	83	71	1	0	.539	4
1909			154	74	79	1	0	.484	5
3 yrs.			458	240	214	4	0	.529	

Danny Murtaugh

MURTAUGH, DANIEL EDWARD
B. Oct. 8, 1917, Chester, Pa.
D. Dec. 2, 1976, Chester, Pa.

			G	W	L	T	N	PCT	Standing	
1957	PIT	N	51	26	25	0	0	.510	8	7
1958			154	84	70	0	0	.545	2	
1959			155	78	76	1	0	.506	4	
1960			155	95	59	1	0	.617	1	
1961			154	75	79	0	0	.487	6	
1962			161	93	68	0	0	.578	4	
1963			162	74	88	0	0	.457	8	
1964			162	80	82	0	0	.494	6	
1967			79	39	39	1	0	.500	6	6
1970			162	89	73	0	0	.549	1	
1971			162	97	65	0	0	.599	1	
1973			26	13	13	0	0	.500	2	3
1974			162	88	74	0	0	.543	1	
1975			161	92	69	0	0	.571	1	
1976			162	92	70	0	0	.568	2	
15 yrs.			2068	1115	950	3	0	.540		

LEAGUE CHAMPIONSHIP SERIES

			G	W	L	T	N	PCT
1970	PIT	N	3	0	3	0	0	.000
1971			4	3	1	0	0	.750
1974			4	1	3	0	0	.250
1975			3	0	3	0	0	.000
4 yrs.			14	4	10	0	0	.286
			7th			4th		

WORLD SERIES

			G	W	L	T	N	PCT
1960	PIT	N	7	4	3	0	0	.571
1971			7	4	3	0	0	.571
2 yrs.			14	8	6	0	0	.571

Jim Mutrie

MUTRIE, JAMES J. (Truthful Jim)
B. June 13, 1851, Chelsea, Mass.
D. Jan. 24, 1938, New York, N. Y.

			G	W	L	T	N	PCT	Standing
1883	NY	AA	97	54	42	1	0	.563	4
1884			112	75	32	5	0	.701	1
1885	NY	N	112	85	27	0	0	.759	2

Jim Mutrie *continued*

		G	W	L	T	N	PCT	Standing		
1886		124	75	44	5	0	.630	3		
1887		129	68	55	6	0	.553	4		
1888		138	84	47	7	0	.641	1		
1889		131	83	43	5	0	.659	1		
1890		135	63	68	4	0	.481	6		
1891		136	71	61	4	0	.538	3		
9 yrs.		1114	658	419	37	0	.611			
								2nd		

George Myatt

MYATT, GEORGE EDWARD (Mercury, Stud, Foghorn)
B. June 14, 1914, Denver, Colo.

			G	W	L	T	N	PCT	Standing		
1968	PHI	N	1	1	0	0	0	1.000	6	5	8
1969			54	19	35	0	0	.352	5	5	
2 yrs.			55	20	35	0	0	.364			

Henry Myers

MYERS, HENRY C.
B. May, 1858, Philadelphia, Pa.
D. Apr. 18, 1895, Philadelphia, Pa.

			G	W	L	T	N	PCT	Standing
1882	BAL	AA	74	19	54	1	0	.260	6

Billy Nash

NASH, WILLIAM MITCHELL
B. June 24, 1865, Richmond, Va.
D. Nov. 15, 1929, East Orange, N. J.

			G	W	L	T	N	PCT	Standing
1896	PHI	N	130	62	68	0	0	.477	8

Johnny Neun

NEUN, JOHN HENRY
B. Oct. 28, 1900, Baltimore, Md.

			G	W	L	T	N	PCT	Standing	
1946	NY	A	14	8	6	0	0	.571	3	3
1947	CIN	N	154	73	81	0	0	.474	5	
1948			100	44	56	0	0	.440	7	7
3 yrs.			268	125	143	0	0	.466		

Jeff Newman

NEWMAN, JEFFREY LYNN
B. Sept. 11, 1948, Ft. Worth, Tex.

			G	W	L	T	N	PCT	Standing		
1986	OAK	A	10	2	8	0	0	.200	6	7	3

Kid Nichols

NICHOLS, CHARLES AUGUSTUS (Nick)
B. Sept. 14, 1869, Madison, Wis.
D. Apr. 11, 1953, Kansas City, Mo.
Hall of Fame 1949.

			G	W	L	T	N	PCT	Standing	
1904	STL	N	155	75	79	1	0	.487	5	
1905			14	5	9	0	0	.357	7	6
2 yrs.			169	80	88	1	0	.476		

Hugh Nicol

NICOL, HUGH N.
B. Jan. 1, 1858, Campsie, Scotland
D. June 27, 1921, Lafayette, Ind.

			G	W	L	T	N	PCT	Standing		
1897	STL	N	40	8	32	0	0	.200	12	12	12

Russ Nixon

NIXON, RUSSELL EUGENE
B. Feb. 19, 1935, Cleves, Ohio

			G	W	L	T	N	PCT	Standing	
1982	CIN	N	70	27	43	0	0	.386	6	6
1983			162	74	88	0	0	.457	6	
1988	ATL	N	121	42	79	0	0	.347	6	6
1989			160	63	97	0	0	.394	6	
4 yrs.			513	206	307	0	0	.402		

Bill Norman

NORMAN, HENRY WILLIS PATRICK
B. July 16, 1910, St. Louis, Mo.
D. Apr. 21, 1962, Milwaukee, Wis.

			G	W	L	T	N	PCT	Standing	
1958	DET	A	105	56	49	0	0	.533	5	5
1959			17	2	15	0	0	.118	8	4
2 yrs.			122	58	64	0	0	.475		

Rebel Oakes

OAKES, ENNIS TELFAIR
B. Dec. 17, 1886, Homer, La.
D. Feb. 29, 1948, Rocky Springs, La.

			G	W	L	T	N	PCT	Standing	
1914	PIT	F	143	61	78	4	0	.439	8	7
1915			156	86	67	3	0	.562	4	
2 yrs.			299	147	145	7	0	.503		

Jack O'Connor

O'CONNOR, JOHN JOSEPH (Peach Pie)
B. June 2, 1869, St. Louis, Mo.
D. Nov. 14, 1937, St. Louis, Mo.

			G	W	L	T	N	PCT	Standing
1910	STL	A	158	47	107	4	0	.305	8

Hank O'Day

O'DAY, HENRY FRANCIS (Peep)
B. July 8, 1862, Chicago, Ill.
D. July 2, 1935, Chicago, Ill.

			G	W	L	T	N	PCT	Standing
1912	CIN	N	155	75	78	2	0	.490	4
1914	CHI	N	156	78	76	2	0	.506	4
2 yrs.			311	153	154	4	0	.498	

Bob O'Farrell

O'FARRELL, ROBERT ARTHUR
B. Oct. 19, 1896, Waukegan, Ill.
D. Feb. 20, 1988, Waukegan, Ill.

			G	W	L	T	N	PCT	Standing	
1927	STL	N	153	92	61	0	0	.601	2	
1934	CIN	N	91	30	60	1	0	.333	8	8
2 yrs.			244	122	121	1	0	.502		

Dan O'Leary

O'LEARY, DANIEL (Hustling Dan)
B. Oct. 22, 1856, Detroit, Mich.
D. June 24, 1922, Chicago, Ill.

			G	W	L	T	N	PCT	Standing	
1884	CIN	U	35	20	15	0	0	.571	5	3

Steve O'Neill

O'NEILL, STEPHEN FRANCIS
Brother of Jim O'Neill.
Brother of Jack O'Neill.
Brother of Mike O'Neill.
B. July 6, 1891, Minooka, Pa.
D. Jan. 26, 1962, Cleveland, Ohio

			G	W	L	T	N	PCT	Standing	
1935	CLE	A	60	36	23	1	0	.610	5	3
1936			157	80	74	3	0	.519	5	
1937			156	83	71	1	1	.539	4	
1943	DET	A	155	78	76	1	0	.506	5	

Steve O'Neill *continued*

			G	W	L	T	N	PCT	Standing	
1944			156	88	66	2	0	.571	2	
1945			155	88	65	2	0	.575	1	
1946			155	92	62	1	0	.597	2	
1947			158	85	69	4	0	.552	2	
1948			154	78	76	0	0	.506	5	
1950	BOS	A	95	63	32	0	0	.663	4	3
1951			154	87	67	0	0	.565	3	
1952	PHI	N	91	59	32	0	0	.648	6	4
1953			156	83	71	2	0	.539	3	
1954			77	40	37	0	0	.519	3	4
14 yrs.			1879	1040	821	17	1	.559		

WORLD SERIES

			G	W	L	T	N	PCT	Standing
1945	DET	A	7	4	3	0	0	.571	

Jack Onslow

ONSLOW, JOHN JAMES
Brother of Eddie Onslow.
B. Oct. 13, 1888, Scottdale, Pa.
D. Dec. 22, 1960, Concord, Mass.

			G	W	L	T	N	PCT	Standing	
1949	CHI	A	154	63	91	0	0	.409	6	
1950			31	8	22	1	0	.267	8	6
2 yrs.			185	71	113	1	0	.386		

Jim O'Rourke

O'ROURKE, JAMES HENRY (Orator Jim)
Brother of John O'Rourke.
B. Sept. 1, 1850, Bridgeport, Conn.
D. Jan. 8, 1919, Bridgeport, Conn.
Hall of Fame 1945.

			G	W	L	T	N	PCT	Standing
1881	BUF	N	83	45	38	0	0	.542	3
1882			84	45	39	0	0	.536	3
1883			98	52	45	1	0	.536	5
1884			114	64	47	3	0	.577	3
1893	WAS	N	130	40	89	1	0	.310	12
5 yrs.			509	246	258	5	0	.488	

Dave Orr

ORR, DAVID L.
B. Sept. 29, 1859, New York, N. Y.
D. June 3, 1915, Brooklyn, N. Y.

			G	W	L	T	N	PCT	Standing		
1887	NY	AA	8	3	5	0	0	.375	8	7	7

Mel Ott

OTT, MELVIN THOMAS (Master Melvin)
B. Mar. 2, 1909, Gretna, La.
D. Nov. 21, 1958, New Orleans, La.
Hall of Fame 1951.

			G	W	L	T	N	PCT	Standing	
1942	NY	N	154	85	67	2	0	.559	3	
1943			156	55	98	3	0	.359	8	
1944			155	67	87	1	0	.435	5	
1945			154	78	74	2	0	.513	5	
1946			154	61	93	0	0	.396	8	
1947			155	81	73	1	0	.526	4	
1948			76	37	38	1	0	.493	4	5
7 yrs.			1004	464	530	10	0	.467		

Paul Owens

OWENS, PAUL FRANCIS (The Pope)
B. Feb. 7, 1924, Salamanca, N. Y.

			G	W	L	T	N	PCT	Standing	
1972	PHI	N	80	33	47	0	0	.413	6	6
1983			77	47	30	0	0	.610	1	1
1984			162	81	81	0	0	.500	4	
3 yrs.			319	161	158	0	0	.505		

LEAGUE CHAMPIONSHIP SERIES

			G	W	L	T	N	PCT	Standing
1983	PHI	N	4	3	1	0	0	.750	

	G	W	L	T	N	PCT	Standing

Paul Owens *continued*

WORLD SERIES

			G	W	L	T	N	PCT	
1983	PHI	N	5	1	4	0	0	.200	

Danny Ozark

OZARK, DANIEL LEONARD (Ozark Ike)
B. Nov. 24, 1923, Buffalo, N. Y.

1973	PHI	N	162	71	91	0	0	.438	6
1974			162	80	82	0	0	.494	3
1975			162	86	76	0	0	.531	2
1976			162	101	61	0	0	.623	1
1977			162	101	61	0	0	.623	1
1978			162	90	72	0	0	.556	1
1979			133	65	67	1	0	.492	5 4
1984	SF	N	56	24	32	0	0	.429	6 6
8 yrs.			1161	618	542	1	0	.533	

LEAGUE CHAMPIONSHIP SERIES

1976	PHI	N	3	0	3	0	0	.000	
1977			4	1	3	0	0	.250	
1978			4	1	3	0	0	.250	
3 yrs.			11	2	9	0	0	.182	
								5th	

Salty Parker

PARKER, FRANCIS JAMES
B. July 8, 1913, East St. Louis, Ill.

1967	NY	N	11	4	7	0	0	.364	10 10
1972	HOU	N	1	1	0	0	0	1.000	3 2 2
2 yrs.			12	5	7	0	0	.417	

Roger Peckinpaugh

PECKINPAUGH, ROGER THORPE
B. Feb. 5, 1891, Wooster, Ohio
D. Nov. 17, 1977, Cleveland, Ohio

1914	NY	A	20	10	10	0	0	.500	7 6
1928	CLE	A	155	62	92	1	0	.403	7
1929			152	81	71	0	0	.533	3
1930			154	81	73	0	0	.526	4
1931			155	78	76	1	0	.506	4
1932			153	87	65	1	0	.572	4
1933			51	26	25	0	0	.510	5 4
1941			155	75	79	1	0	.487	4
8 yrs.			995	500	491	4	0	.505	

Johnny Pesky

PESKY, JOHN MICHAEL
Born John Michael Paveskovich.
B. Sept. 27, 1919, Portland, Ore.

1963	BOS	A	161	76	85	0	0	.472	7
1964			160	70	90	0	0	.438	8 8
1980			5	1	4	0	0	.200	4 4
3 yrs.			326	147	179	0	0	.451	

Fred Pfeffer

**PFEFFER, NATHANIEL FREDERICK
(Dandelion, Fritz)**
B. Mar. 17, 1860, Louisville, Ky.
D. Apr. 10, 1932, Chicago, Ill.

1892	LOU	N	94	40	54	0	0	.426	10 9

Lew Phelan

PHELAN, LEWIS G.
Deceased.

1895	STL	N	45	11	30	4	0	.268	11 11

Bill Phillips

**PHILLIPS, WILLIAM CORCORAN
(Whoa Bill, Silver Bill)**
B. Nov. 9, 1868, Allenport, Pa.
D. Oct. 25, 1941, Charleroi, Pa.

1914	IND	F	157	88	65	4	0	.575	1
1915	NWK	F	53	26	27	0	0	.491	6 5
2 yrs.			210	114	92	4	0	.553	

Horace Phillips

**PHILLIPS, HORACE B. (Hustling
Horace)**
B. May 14, 1853, Salem, Ohio
Deceased.

1879	TRO	N	47	12	34	1	0	.261	8 8
1883	COL	AA	97	32	65	0	0	.330	6
1884	PIT	AA	14	9	4	1	0	.692	12 11
1885			111	56	55	0	0	.505	3
1886			140	80	57	3	0	.584	2
1887	PIT	N	125	55	69	1	0	.444	6
1888			139	66	68	4	0	.493	6
1889			71	28	43	0	0	.394	7 5
8 yrs.			744	338	395	10	1	.461	

Lefty Phillips

PHILLIPS, HAROLD ROSS
B. May 16, 1919, Los Angeles, Calif.
D. June 10, 1972, Fullerton, Calif.

1969	CAL	A	124	60	63	1	0	.488	6 3
1970			162	86	76	0	0	.531	3
1971			162	76	86	0	0	.469	4
3 yrs.			448	222	225	1	0	.497	

Lip Pike

**PIKE, LIPMAN EMANUEL (The Iron
Batter)**
Brother of Jay Pike.
B. May 25, 1845, New York, N. Y.
D. Oct. 10, 1893, Brooklyn, N. Y.

1877	CIN	N	14	3	11	0	0	.214	6 6

Lou Piniella

PINIELLA, LOUIS VICTOR (Sweet Lou)
B. Aug. 28, 1943, Tampa, Fla.

1986	NY	A	162	90	72	0	0	.556	2
1987			162	89	73	0	0	.549	4
1988			93	45	48	0	0	.484	2 5
3 yrs.			417	224	193	0	0	.537	

Eddie Popowski

POPOWSKI, EDWARD JOSEPH (Pop)
B. Aug. 20, 1913, Sayreville, N. J.

1969	BOS	A	9	5	4	0	0	.556	3 3
1973			1	1	0	0	0	1.000	2 2
2 yrs.			10	6	4	0	0	.600	

Matt Porter

PORTER, MATTHEW S.
B. 1859, N. Y.

1884	KC	U	16	3	13	0	0	.188	12 12 12

Pat Powers

POWERS, PATRICK THOMAS
B. June 27, 1860, Trenton, N. J.
D. Aug. 29, 1925, Belmar, N. J.

1890	ROC	AA	133	63	63	7	0	.500	5
1892	NY	N	151	71	80	0	0	.470	8
2 yrs.			284	134	143	7	0	.484	

Al Pratt

PRATT, ALBERT G. (Uncle Al)
B. Nov. 19, 1847, Pittsburgh, Pa.
D. Nov. 21, 1937, Pittsburgh, Pa.

1882	PIT	AA	79	39	39	1	0	.500	4
1883			32	12	20	0	0	.375	6 7
2 yrs.			111	51	59	1	0	.464	

Jim Price

PRICE, JAMES LYMAN
B. 1847, New York, N. Y.
Deceased.

1884	NY	N	100	56	42	2	0	.571	4 4

Doc Prothro

PROTHRO, JAMES THOMPSON
B. July 16, 1893, Memphis, Tenn.
D. Oct. 14, 1971, Memphis, Tenn.

1939	PHI	N	152	45	106	1	0	.298	8
1940			153	50	103	0	0	.327	8
1941			155	43	111	1	0	.279	8
3 yrs.			460	138	320	2	0	.301	

Blondie Purcell

PURCELL, WILLIAM ALOYSIUS
B. Mar. 16, 1854, Paterson, N. J.
D. Feb. 20, 1912, Trenton N. J.,

1883	PHI	N	82	13	68	1	0	.160	8 8

Frank Quilici

QUILICI, FRANCIS RALPH (Guido)
B. May 11, 1939, Chicago, Ill.

1972	MIN	A	84	41	43	0	0	.488	3 3
1973			162	81	81	0	0	.500	3
1974			163	82	80	1	0	.506	3
1975			159	76	83	0	0	.478	4
4 yrs.			568	280	287	1	0	.494	

Joe Quinn

**QUINN, JOSEPH J. (Uncle Joe, Ol'
Reliable)**
B. Dec. 25, 1864, Sydney, Australia
D. Nov. 12, 1940, St. Louis, Mo.

1895	STL	N	40	11	28	0	1	.282	11 11 11
1899	CLE	N	116	12	104	0	0	.103	12 12
2 yrs.			156	23	132	0	1	.148	

Doug Rader

**RADER, DOUGLAS LEE (Rojo, The Red
Rooster)**
B. July 30, 1944, Chicago, Ill.

1983	TEX	A	163	77	85	1	0	.475	3
1984			161	69	92	0	0	.429	7
1985			32	9	23	0	0	.281	7 7
1986	CHI	A	2	1	1	0	0	.500	6 5 5

Doug Rader continued

			G	W	L	T	N	PCT	Standing	
1989	CAL	A	162	91	71	0	0	.562	3	
5 yrs.			520	247	272	1	0	.476		

Vern Rapp

RAPP, VERNON FRED
B. May 11, 1928, St. Louis, Mo.

			G	W	L	T	N	PCT	Standing	
1977	STL	N	162	83	79	0	0	.512	3	
1978			17	6	11	0	0	.353	6	5
1984	CIN	N	121	51	70	0	0	.421	5	5
3 yrs.			300	140	160	0	0	.467		

Al Reach

REACH, ALFRED JAMES
Brother of Bob Reach.
B. May 25, 1840, London, England
D. Jan. 14, 1928, Atlantic City, N. J.

			G	W	L	T	N	PCT	Standing		
1890	PHI	N	11	4	7	0	0	.364	2	3	3

Del Rice

RICE, DELBERT W.
B. Oct. 27, 1922, Portsmouth, Ohio
D. Jan. 26, 1983, Buena Park, Calif.

			G	W	L	T	N	PCT	Standing
1972	CAL	A	155	75	80	0	0	.484	5

Paul Richards

RICHARDS, PAUL RAPIER
B. Nov. 21, 1908, Waxahachie, Tex.
D. May 4, 1986, Waxahachie, Tex.

			G	W	L	T	N	PCT	Standing	
1951	CHI	A	155	81	73	1	0	.526	4	
1952			156	81	73	2	0	.526	3	
1953			156	89	65	2	0	.578	3	
1954			146	91	54	1	0	.628	3	3
1955	BAL	A	156	57	97	2	0	.370	7	
1956			154	69	85	0	0	.448	6	
1957			154	76	76	2	0	.500	5	
1958			154	74	79	1	0	.484	6	
1959			155	74	80	1	0	.481	6	
1960			154	89	65	0	0	.578	2	
1961	CHI	A	135	78	57	0	0	.578	3	3
1976	CHI	A	161	64	97	0	0	.398	6	
12 yrs.			1836	923	901	12	0	.506		

Danny Richardson

RICHARDSON, DANIEL
B. Jan. 25, 1863, Elmira, N. Y.
D. Sept. 12, 1926, New York, N. Y.

			G	W	L	T	N	PCT	Standing	
1892	WAS	N	43	12	31	0	0	.279	11	10

Branch Rickey

RICKEY, WESLEY BRANCH (The Mahatma)
B. Dec. 20, 1881, Stockdale, Ohio
D. Dec. 9, 1965, Columbia, Mo.
Hall of Fame 1967.

			G	W	L	T	N	PCT	Standing	
1913	STL	A	12	5	6	1	0	.455	8	8
1914			159	71	82	6	0	.464	5	
1915			159	63	91	5	0	.409	6	
1919	STL	N	138	54	83	1	0	.394	7	
1920			155	75	79	1	0	.487	5	
1921			154	87	66	1	0	.569	3	
1922			154	85	69	0	0	.552	3	
1923			154	79	74	1	0	.516	3	
1924			154	65	89	0	0	.422	6	
1925			38	13	25	0	0	.342	8	4
10 yrs.			1277	597	664	16	0	.473		

Bill Rigney

RIGNEY, WILLIAM JOSEPH (Specs, The Cricket)
B. Jan. 29, 1918, Alameda, Calif.

			G	W	L	T	N	PCT	Standing	
1956	NY	N	154	67	87	0	0	.435	6	
1957			154	69	85	0	0	.448	6	
1958	SF	N	154	80	74	0	0	.519	3	
1959			154	83	71	0	0	.539	3	
1960			58	33	25	0	0	.569	2	5
1961	LA	A	162	70	91	1	0	.435	8	
1962			162	86	76	0	0	.531	3	
1963			161	70	91	0	0	.435	9	
1964			162	82	80	0	0	.506	5	
1965	CAL	A	162	75	87	0	0	.463	7	
1966			162	80	82	0	0	.494	6	
1967			161	84	77	0	0	.522	5	
1968			162	67	95	0	0	.414	8	
1969			39	11	28	0	0	.282	6	3
1970	MIN	A	162	98	64	0	0	.605	1	
1971			160	74	86	0	0	.463	5	
1972			70	36	34	0	0	.514	3	3
1976	SF	N	162	74	88	0	0	.457	4	
18 yrs.			2561	1239	1321	1	0	.484		

LEAGUE CHAMPIONSHIP SERIES

			G	W	L	T	N	PCT
1970	MIN	A	3	0	3	0	0	.000

Cal Ripken

RIPKEN, CALVIN EDWIN, SR.
Father of Cal Ripken.
Father of Billy Ripken.
B. Dec. 17, 1935, Aberdeen, Md.

			G	W	L	T	N	PCT	Standing		
1985	BAL	A	1	1	0	0	0	1.000	4	4	4
1987			162	67	95	0	0	.414	6		
1988			6	0	6	0	0	.000	6	7	
3 yrs.			169	68	101	0	0	.402			

Frank Robinson

ROBINSON, FRANK
B. Aug. 31, 1935, Beaumont, Tex.
Hall of Fame 1982.

			G	W	L	T	N	PCT	Standing		
1975	CLE	A	159	79	80	0	0	.497	4		
1976			159	81	78	0	0	.509	4		
1977			57	26	31	0	0	.456	6	5	
1981	SF	N	59	27	32	0	0	.458	5		(1st)
1981			52	29	23	0	0	.558	3		(2nd)
1982			162	87	75	0	0	.537	3		
1983			162	79	83	0	0	.488	5		
1984			106	42	64	0	0	.396	6	6	
1988	BAL	A	155	54	101	0	0	.348	6	7	
1989			162	87	75	0	0	.537	2		
9 yrs.			1233	591	642	0	0	.479			

Wilbert Robinson

ROBINSON, WILBERT (Uncle Robbie)
Brother of Fred Robinson.
B. June 29, 1863, Bolton, Mass.
D. Aug. 8, 1934, Atlanta, Ga.
Hall of Fame 1945.

			G	W	L	T	N	PCT	Standing	
1902	BAL	A	83	24	57	2	0	.296	7	8
1914	BKN	N	154	75	79	0	0	.487	5	
1915			154	80	72	2	0	.526	3	
1916			156	94	60	2	0	.610	1	
1917			156	70	81	5	0	.464	7	
1918			127	57	69	0	1	.452	5	
1919			141	69	71	1	0	.493	5	
1920			155	93	61	1	0	.604	1	
1921			152	77	75	0	0	.507	5	
1922			155	76	78	1	0	.494	6	
1923			155	76	78	1	0	.494	6	
1924			154	92	62	0	0	.597	2	
1925			153	68	85	0	0	.444	6	
1926			155	71	82	2	0	.464	6	
1927			154	65	88	1	0	.425	6	
1928			155	77	76	2	0	.503	6	

Wilbert Robinson continued

			G	W	L	T	N	PCT	Standing
1929			153	70	83	0	0	.458	6
1930			154	86	68	0	0	.558	4
1931			153	79	73	1	0	.520	4
19 yrs.			2819	1399	1398	21	1	.500	

WORLD SERIES

			G	W	L	T	N	PCT
1916	BKN	N	5	1	4	0	0	.200
1920			7	2	5	0	0	.286
2 yrs.			12	3	9	0	0	.250

Matt Robison

ROBISON, MATTHEW STANLEY
B. Mar. 30, 1859, Pittsburgh, Pa.
D. Mar. 24, 1911, Cleveland, Ohio

			G	W	L	T	N	PCT	Standing	
1905	STL	N	50	19	31	0	0	.380	6	6

Buck Rodgers

RODGERS, ROBERT LEROY
B. Aug. 16, 1938, Delaware, Ohio

			G	W	L	T	N	PCT	Standing		
1980	MIL	A	47	26	21	0	0	.553	2	3	
1980			23	13	10	0	0	.565	4	3	
1981			56	31	25	0	0	.554	3		(1st)
1981			53	31	22	0	0	.585	1		(2nd)
1982			47	23	24	0	0	.489	5	1	
1985	MON	N	161	84	77	0	0	.522	3		
1986			161	78	83	0	0	.484	4		
1987			162	91	71	0	0	.562	3		
1988			163	81	81	1	0	.500	3		
1989			162	81	81	0	0	.500	4		
8 yrs.			1035	539	495	1	0	.521			

DIVISIONAL PLAYOFF SERIES

			G	W	L	T	N	PCT
1981	MIL	A	5	2	3	0	0	.400

Jim Rogers

ROGERS, JAMES F.
B. Apr. 9, 1872, Hartford, Conn.
D. Jan. 21, 1900, Bridgeport, Conn.

			G	W	L	T	N	PCT	Standing	
1897	LOU	N	44	17	24	2	1	.415	9	11

Cookie Rojas

ROJAS, OCTAVIO VICTOR
Born Octavio Victor Rojas y Rivas.
B. Mar. 6, 1939, Havana, Cuba

			G	W	L	T	N	PCT	Standing	
1988	CAL	A	154	75	79	0	0	.487	4	4

Red Rolfe

ROLFE, ROBERT ABIAL
B. Oct. 17, 1908, Penacook, N. H.
D. July 8, 1969, Gifford, N. H.

			G	W	L	T	N	PCT	Standing	
1949	DET	A	155	87	67	1	0	.565	4	
1950			157	95	59	3	0	.617	2	
1951			154	73	81	0	0	.474	5	
1952			73	23	49	1	0	.319	8	8
4 yrs.			539	278	256	5	0	.521		

Pete Rose

ROSE, PETER EDWARD (Charlie Hustle)
B. Apr. 14, 1941, Cincinnati, Ohio

			G	W	L	T	N	PCT	Standing	
1984	CIN	N	41	19	22	0	0	.463	5	5
1985			162	89	72	1	0	.553	2	
1986			162	86	76	0	0	.531	2	
1987			162	84	78	0	0	.519	2	
1988			23	11	12	0	0	.478	4	2
1988			111	64	47	0	0	.577	4	2

Pete Rose *continued*

			G	W	L	T	N	PCT	Standing	
1989			127	61	66	0	0	.480	4	5
6 yrs.			788	414	373	1	0	.526		

Dave Rowe

ROWE, DAVID (Eli)
Brother of Jack Rowe.
B. Feb., 1856, Jacksonville, Ill.
Deceased.

			G	W	L	T	N	PCT	Standing	
1886	KC	N	126	30	91	5	0	.248	7	
1888	KC	AA	50	14	36	0	0	.280	8	8
2 yrs.			176	44	127	5	0	.257		

Jack Rowe

ROWE, JOHN CHARLES
Brother of Dave Rowe.
B. Dec. 18, 1857, Harrisburg, Pa.
D. Apr. 25, 1911, St. Louis, Mo.

			G	W	L	T	N	PCT	Standing	
1890	BUF	P	87	28	58	1	0	.326	8	8
1890			19	5	14	0	0	.263	8	8

Pants Rowland

ROWLAND, CLARENCE HENRY
B. Feb. 12, 1879, Platteville, Wis.
D. May 17, 1969, Chicago, Ill.

			G	W	L	T	N	PCT	Standing
1915	CHI	A	156	93	61	1	1	.604	3
1916			155	89	65	1	0	.578	2
1917			156	100	54	2	0	.649	1
1918			124	57	67	0	0	.460	6
4 yrs.			591	339	247	4	1	.578	

WORLD SERIES

			G	W	L	T	N	PCT	Standing
1917	CHI	A	6	4	2	0	0	.667	

Dick Rudolph

RUDOLPH, RICHARD (Baldy)
B. Aug. 25, 1887, New York, N. Y.
D. Oct. 20, 1949, Bronx, N. Y.

			G	W	L	T	N	PCT	Standing		
1924	BOS	N	38	11	27	0	0	.289	6	8	8

Muddy Ruel

RUEL, HEROLD DOMINIC
B. Feb. 20, 1896, St. Louis, Mo.
D. Nov. 13, 1963, Palo Alto, Calif.

			G	W	L	T	N	PCT	Standing
1947	STL	A	154	59	95	0	0	.383	8

Pete Runnels

RUNNELS, JAMES EDWARD
Born James Edward Runnells.
B. Jan. 28, 1928, Lufkin, Tex.

			G	W	L	T	N	PCT	Standing	
1966	BOS	A	16	8	8	0	0	.500	10	9

Connie Ryan

RYAN, CORNELIUS JOSEPH
B. Feb. 27, 1920, New Orleans, La.

			G	W	L	T	N	PCT	Standing		
1975	ATL	N	27	9	18	0	0	.333	5	5	
1977	TEX	A	6	2	4	0	0	.333	2	4	2
2 yrs.			33	11	22	0	0	.333			

Eddie Sawyer

SAWYER, EDWIN MILBY
B. Sept. 10, 1910, Westerly, R. I.

			G	W	L	T	N	PCT	Standing	
1948	PHI	N	63	23	40	0	0	.365	6	6
1949			154	81	73	0	0	.526	3	
1950			157	91	63	3	0	.591	1	
1951			154	73	81	0	0	.474	5	
1952			63	28	35	0	0	.444	6	4
1958			70	30	40	0	0	.429	7	8
1959			155	64	90	1	0	.416	8	
1960			1	0	1	0	0	.000	8	8
8 yrs.			817	390	423	4	0	.480		

WORLD SERIES

			G	W	L	T	N	PCT	Standing
1950	PHI	N	4	0	4	0	0	.000	

Mike Scanlon

SCANLON, MICHAEL B.
B. 1847, Cork, Ireland
D. Jan. 18, 1929, Washington, D. C.

			G	W	L	T	N	PCT	Standing	
1884	WAS	U	114	47	65	2	0	.420	7	
1886	WAS	N	82	13	67	2	0	.163	8	8
2 yrs.			196	60	132	4	0	.313		

Ray Schalk

SCHALK, RAYMOND WILLIAM
(Cracker)
B. Aug. 12, 1892, Harvel, Ill.
D. May 19, 1970, Chicago, Ill.
Hall of Fame 1955.

			G	W	L	T	N	PCT	Standing	
1927	CHI	A	153	70	83	0	0	.458	5	
1928			75	32	42	1	0	.432	6	5
2 yrs.			228	102	125	1	0	.449		

Bob Scheffing

SCHEFFING, ROBERT BODEN
B. Aug. 11, 1913, Overland, Mo.
D. Oct. 26, 1985, Phoenix, Ariz.

			G	W	L	T	N	PCT	Standing	
1957	CHI	N	156	62	92	2	0	.403	7	
1958			154	72	82	0	0	.468	5	
1959			155	74	80	1	0	.481	5	
1961	DET	A	163	101	61	1	0	.623	2	
1962			161	85	76	0	0	.528	4	
1963			60	24	36	0	0	.400	9	5
6 yrs.			849	418	427	4	0	.495		

Harry Schlafly

SCHLAFLY, HARRY LINTON
B. Sept. 20, 1878, Port Washington, Ohio
D. June 27, 1919, Canton, Ohio

			G	W	L	T	N	PCT	Standing	
1914	BUF	F	156	80	71	4	1	.530	4	
1915			41	13	28	0	0	.317	8	6
2 yrs.			197	93	99	4	1	.484		

Gus Schmelz

SCHMELZ, GUSTAVUS HEINRICH
B. Sept. 26, 1850, Columbus, Ohio
D. Oct. 14, 1925, Columbus, Ohio

			G	W	L	T	N	PCT	Standing		
1884	COL	AA	110	69	39	2	0	.639	2		
1886	STL	N	126	43	79	4	0	.352	6		
1887	CIN	AA	136	81	54	1	0	.600	2		
1888			137	80	54	3	0	.597	4		
1889			141	76	63	2	0	.547	4		
1890	CLE	N	78	21	55	2	0	.276	7	7	
1890	COL	AA	57	38	13	6	0	.745	5	2	2
1891			138	61	76	1	0	.445	6		
1894	WAS	N	132	45	87	0	0	.341	11		
1895			133	43	85	4	1	.336	10		
1896			133	58	73	2	0	.443	9		

Gus Schmelz *continued*

			G	W	L	T	N	PCT	Standing	
1897			36	9	25	2	0	.265	11	6
11 yrs.			1357	624	703	29	1	.470		

Red Schoendienst

SCHOENDIENST, ALBERT FRED
B. Feb. 2, 1923, Germantown, Ill.
Hall of Fame 1989.

			G	W	L	T	N	PCT	Standing	
1965	STL	N	162	80	81	1	0	.497	7	
1966			162	83	79	0	0	.512	6	
1967			161	101	60	0	0	.627	1	
1968			162	97	65	0	0	.599	1	
1969			162	87	75	0	0	.537	4	
1970			162	76	86	0	0	.469	4	
1971			163	90	72	1	0	.556	2	
1972			156	75	81	0	0	.481	4	
1973			162	81	81	0	0	.500	2	
1974			161	86	75	0	0	.534	2	
1975			163	82	80	1	0	.506	3	
1976			162	72	90	0	0	.444	5	
1980			37	18	19	0	0	.486	5	4
13 yrs.			1975	1028	944	3	0	.521		

WORLD SERIES

			G	W	L	T	N	PCT	Standing
1967	STL	N	7	4	3	0	0	.571	
1968			7	3	4	0	0	.429	
2 yrs.			14	7	7	0	0	.500	

Joe Schultz

SCHULTZ, JOSEPH CHARLES, JR.
(Dode)
Son of Joe Schultz.
B. Aug. 29, 1918, Chicago, Ill.

			G	W	L	T	N	PCT	Standing	
1969	SEA	A	163	64	98	1	0	.395	6	
1973	DET	A	28	14	14	0	0	.500	3	3
2 yrs.			191	78	112	1	0	.411		

Frank Selee

SELEE, FRANK GIBSON
B. Oct. 26, 1859, Amherst, N. H.
D. July 5, 1909, Denver, Colo.

			G	W	L	T	N	PCT	Standing	
1890	BOS	N	134	76	57	1	0	.571	5	
1891			140	87	51	2	0	.630	1	
1892			151	102	48	1	0	.680	1	
1893			131	86	43	2	0	.667	1	
1894			133	83	49	1	0	.629	3	
1895			133	71	60	1	1	.542	5	
1896			132	74	57	1	0	.565	4	
1897			135	93	39	3	0	.705	1	
1898			152	102	47	3	0	.685	1	
1899			153	95	57	1	0	.625	2	
1900			142	66	72	4	0	.478	4	
1901			140	69	69	2	0	.500	5	
1902	CHI	N	143	68	69	4	2	.496	5	
1903			139	82	56	1	0	.594	3	
1904			156	93	60	3	0	.608	2	
1905			65	37	28	0	0	.569	4	3
16 yrs.			2179	1284	862	30	3	.598		
									4th	

Luke Sewell

SEWELL, JAMES LUTHER
Brother of Tommy Sewell.
Brother of Joe Sewell.
B. Jan. 5, 1901, Titus, Ala.
D. May 14, 1987, Akron, Ohio

			G	W	L	T	N	PCT	Standing	
1941	STL	A	113	55	55	3	0	.500	7	6
1942			151	82	69	0	0	.543	3	
1943			153	72	80	1	0	.474	6	
1944			154	89	65	0	0	.578	1	
1945			154	81	70	3	0	.536	3	
1946			125	53	71	1	0	.427	7	7

	G	W	L	T	N	PCT	Standing	

Luke Sewell *continued*

		G	W	L	T	N	PCT	Standing	
1949	CIN N	3	1	2	0	0	.333	7	7
1950		153	66	87	0	0	.431	6	
1951		155	68	86	1	0	.442	6	
1952		98	39	59	0	0	.398	7	6
10 yrs.		1259	606	644	9	0	.485		

WORLD SERIES

		G	W	L	T	N	PCT	
1944	STL A	6	2	4	0	0	.333	

Dan Shannon

SHANNON, DANIEL W.
B. Mar. 23, 1865, Bridgeport, Conn.
D. Oct. 25, 1913, Bridgeport, Conn.

		G	W	L	T	N	PCT	Standing	
1889	LOU AA	58	10	46	2	0	.179	8	8
1891	WAS AA	51	15	34	2	0	.306	7	9
2 yrs.		109	25	80	4	0	.238		

Bill Sharsig

SHARSIG, WILLIAM A.
B. 1855, Philadelphia, Pa.
D. Feb. 1, 1902, Philadelphia, Pa.

		G	W	L	T	N	PCT	Standing	
1884	PHI AA	57	33	23	1	0	.589	7	7
1886		41	22	17	2	0	.564	6	6
1888		137	81	52	3	1	.609	3	
1889		138	75	58	5	0	.564	3	
1890		136	54	78	4	0	.409	8	
1891		18	6	11	1	0	.353	7	5
6 yrs.		527	271	239	16	1	.531		

Bob Shawkey

SHAWKEY, JAMES ROBERT
B. Dec. 4, 1890, Sigel, Pa.
D. Dec. 31, 1980, Syracuse, N. Y.

		G	W	L	T	N	PCT	Standing	
1930	NY A	154	86	68	0	0	.558	3	

Tom Sheehan

SHEEHAN, THOMAS CLANCY
B. Mar. 31, 1894, Grand Ridge, Ill.
D. Oct. 29, 1982, Chillicothe, Ohio

		G	W	L	T	N	PCT	Standing	
1960	SF N	98	46	50	2	0	.479	2	5

Larry Shepard

SHEPARD, LAWRENCE WILLIAM
B. Apr. 3, 1919, Lakewood, Ohio

		G	W	L	T	N	PCT	Standing	
1968	PIT N	163	80	82	1	0	.494	6	
1969		157	84	73	0	0	.535	3	3
2 yrs.		320	164	155	1	0	.514		

Norm Sherry

SHERRY, NORMAN BURT
Brother of Larry Sherry.
B. July 16, 1931, New York, N. Y.

		G	W	L	T	N	PCT	Standing	
1976	CAL A	66	37	29	0	0	.561	4	4
1977		81	39	42	0	0	.481	5	5
2 yrs.		147	76	71	0	0	.517		

Bill Shettsline

SHETTSLINE, WILLIAM JOSEPH
(Shetts)
B. Oct. 25, 1863, Philadelphia, Pa.
D. Feb. 22, 1933, Philadelphia, Pa.

		G	W	L	T	N	PCT	Standing	
1898	PHI N	104	59	44	1	0	.573	8	6
1899		154	94	58	2	0	.618	3	

Bill Shettsline *continued*

		G	W	L	T	N	PCT	Standing	
1900		141	75	63	3	0	.543	3	
1901		140	83	57	0	0	.593	2	
1902		138	56	81	1	0	.409	7	
5 yrs.		677	367	303	7	0	.548		

Burt Shotton

SHOTTON, BURTON EDWIN (Barney)
B. Oct. 18, 1884, Brownhelm, Ohio
D. July 29, 1962, Lake Wales, Fla.

		G	W	L	T	N	PCT	Standing	
1928	PHI N	152	43	109	0	0	.283	8	
1929		154	71	82	1	0	.464	5	
1930		156	52	102	2	0	.338	8	
1931		155	66	88	1	0	.429	6	
1932		154	78	76	0	0	.506	4	
1933		152	60	92	0	0	.395	7	
1934	CIN N	1	1	0	0	0	1.000	8	8
1947	BKN N	153	92	60	1	0	.605	1	1
1948		81	48	33	0	0	.593	5	3
1949		156	97	57	2	0	.630	1	
1950		155	89	65	1	0	.578	2	
11 yrs.		1469	697	764	8	0	.477		

WORLD SERIES

		G	W	L	T	N	PCT	
1947	BKN N	7	3	4	0	0	.429	
1949		5	1	4	0	0	.200	
2 yrs.		12	4	8	0	0	.333	

Ken Silvestri

SILVESTRI, KENNETH JOSEPH (Hawk)
B. May 3, 1916, Chicago, Ill.

		G	W	L	T	N	PCT	Standing	
1967	ATL N	3	0	3	0	0	.000	7	7

Joe Simmons

SIMMONS, JOSEPH S.
B. June 13, 1845, New York, N. Y.
D. Dec. 10, 1888, Brooklyn, N. Y.

		G	W	L	T	N	PCT	Standing	
1884	WIL U	18	2	16	0	0	.111	13	

Lew Simmons

SIMMONS, LEWIS
B. Aug. 27, 1838, New Castle, Pa.
D. Sept. 2, 1911, Jamestown, Pa.

		G	W	L	T	N	PCT	Standing	
1883	PHI AA	98	66	32	0	0	.673	1	
1886		98	41	55	2	0	.427	6	6
2 yrs.		196	107	87	2	0	.552		

Dick Sisler

SISLER, RICHARD ALLAN
Son of George Sisler.
Brother of Dave Sisler.
B. Nov. 2, 1920, St. Louis, Mo.

		G	W	L	T	N	PCT	Standing	
1964	CIN N	6	3	3	0	0	.500	3	4	2
1964		47	29	18	0	0	.617	3	2
1965		162	89	73	0	0	.549	4	
2 yrs.		215	121	94	0	0	.563		

George Sisler

SISLER, GEORGE HAROLD (Gorgeous George)
Father of Dick Sisler.
Father of Dave Sisler.
B. Mar. 24, 1893, Manchester, Ohio
D. Mar. 26, 1973, Richmond Heights, Mo.
Hall of Fame 1939.

		G	W	L	T	N	PCT	Standing	
1924	STL A	153	74	78	0	1	.487	4	
1925		154	82	71	1	0	.536	3	

George Sisler *continued*

		G	W	L	T	N	PCT	Standing	
1926		155	62	92	1	0	.403	7	
3 yrs.		462	218	241	2	1	.475		

Frank Skaff

SKAFF, FRANCIS MICHAEL
B. Sept. 30, 1913, LaCrosse, Wis.
D. Apr. 12, 1988, Towson, Md.

		G	W	L	T	N	PCT	Standing	
1966	DET A	79	40	39	0	0	.506	3	3

Bob Skinner

SKINNER, ROBERT RALPH
Father of Joel Skinner.
B. Oct. 3, 1931, La Jolla, Calif.

		G	W	L	T	N	PCT	Standing	
1968	PHI N	107	48	59	0	0	.449	5	8
1969		108	44	64	0	0	.407	5	5
1977	SD N	1	1	0	0	0	1.000	5	5	5
3 yrs.		216	93	123	0	0	.431		

Jack Slattery

SLATTERY, JOHN TERRENCE
B. Jan. 6, 1878, South Boston, Mass.
D. July 17, 1949, Boston, Mass.

		G	W	L	T	N	PCT	Standing	
1928	BOS N	31	11	20	0	0	.355	7	7

Harry Smith

SMITH, HARRY THOMAS
B. Oct. 31, 1874, Yorkshire, England
D. Feb. 17, 1933, Salem, N. J.

		G	W	L	T	N	PCT	Standing	
1909	BOS N	76	22	54	0	0	.289	8	8

Heinie Smith

SMITH, GEORGE HENRY
B. Oct. 24, 1871, Pittsburgh, Pa.
D. June 25, 1939, Buffalo, N. Y.

		G	W	L	T	N	PCT	Standing	
1902	NY N	32	5	27	0	0	.156	4	8	8

Mayo Smith

SMITH, EDWARD MAYO
B. Jan. 17, 1915, New London, Mo.
D. Nov. 24, 1977, Boynton Beach, Fla.

		G	W	L	T	N	PCT	Standing	
1955	PHI N	154	77	77	0	0	.500	4	
1956		154	71	83	0	0	.461	5	
1957		156	77	77	2	0	.500	5	
1958		84	39	45	0	0	.464	7	8
1959	CIN N	80	35	45	0	0	.438	7	5
1967	DET A	163	91	71	1	0	.562	2	
1968		164	103	59	2	0	.636	1	
1969		162	90	72	0	0	.556	2	
1970		162	79	83	0	0	.488	4	
9 yrs.		1279	662	612	5	0	.520		

WORLD SERIES

		G	W	L	T	N	PCT	
1968	DET A	7	4	3	0	0	.571	

Jimmy Snyder

SNYDER, JAMES ROBERT
B. Aug. 15, 1932, Dearborn, Mich.

		G	W	L	T	N	PCT	Standing	
1988	SEA A	105	45	60	0	0	.429	6	7

	G	W	L	T	N	PCT	Standing

Pop Snyder

SNYDER, CHARLES N.
B. Oct. 6, 1854, Washington, D. C.
D. Oct. 29, 1924, Washington, D. C.

		G	W	L	T	N	PCT	Standing	
882	CIN AA	80	55	25	0	0	.688	1	
883		98	61	37	0	0	.622	3	
884		40	24	14	2	0	.632	5	5
891	WAS AA	70	23	46	1	0	.333	6	7 9
4 yrs.		288	163	122	3	0	.572		

Allen Sothoron

SOTHORON, ALLEN SUTTON
B. Apr. 27, 1893, Bradford, Ohio
D. June 17, 1939, St. Louis, Mo.

		G	W	L	T	N	PCT	Standing	
1933	STL A	8	2	6	0	0	.250	8	8 8

Billy Southworth

SOUTHWORTH, WILLIAM HARRISON
B. Mar. 9, 1893, Harvard, Neb.
D. Nov. 15, 1969, Columbus, Ohio

		G	W	L	T	N	PCT	Standing	
1929	STL N	90	43	45	2	0	.489	4	4
1940		111	69	40	2	0	.633	7	3
1941		155	97	56	2	0	.634	2	
1942		156	106	48	2	0	.688	1	
1943		157	105	49	3	0	.682	1	
1944		157	105	49	3	0	.682	1	
1945		155	95	59	1	0	.617	2	
1946	BOS N	154	81	72	1	0	.529	4	
1947		154	86	68	0	0	.558	3	
1948		154	91	62	1	0	.595	1	
1949		111	55	54	2	0	.505	4	4
1950		156	83	71	2	0	.539	4	
1951		60	28	31	1	0	.475	5	4
13 yrs.		1770	1044	704	22	0	.597		
								5th	

WORLD SERIES

		G	W	L	T	N	PCT	Standing	
1942	STL N	5	4	1	0	0	.800		
1943		5	1	4	0	0	.200		
1944		6	4	2	0	0	.667		
1948	BOS N	6	2	4	0	0	.333		
4 yrs.		22	11	11	0	0	.500		
								10th	9th

Al Spalding

SPALDING, ALBERT GOODWILL
B. Sept. 2, 1850, Byron, Ill.
D. Sept. 9, 1915, San Diego, Calif.
Hall of Fame 1939.

		G	W	L	T	N	PCT	Standing
1876	CHI N	66	52	14	0	0	.788	1
1877		60	26	33	1	0	.441	5
2 yrs.		126	78	47	1	0	.624	

Tris Speaker

SPEAKER, TRISTRAM E (The Grey Eagle, Spoke)
B. Apr. 4, 1888, Hubbard, Tex.
D. Dec. 8, 1958, Lake Whitney, Tex.
Hall of Fame 1937.

		G	W	L	T	N	PCT	Standing	
1919	CLE A	61	40	21	0	0	.656	3	2
1920		154	98	56	0	0	.636	1	
1921		154	94	60	0	0	.610	2	
1922		155	78	76	1	0	.506	4	
1923		153	82	71	0	0	.536	3	
1924		153	67	86	0	0	.438	6	
1925		155	70	84	1	0	.455	6	
1926		154	88	66	0	0	.571	2	
8 yrs.		1139	617	520	2	0	.543		

WORLD SERIES

		G	W	L	T	N	PCT	Standing
1920	CLE A	7	5	2	0	0	.714	

Harry Spence

SPENCE, HARRISON L.
B. 1858, Virginia
D. May 17, 1908, Chicago, Ill.

		G	W	L	T	N	PCT	Standing
1888	IND N	136	50	85	1	0	.370	7

Chick Stahl

STAHL, CHARLES SYLVESTER
B. Jan. 10, 1873, Avila, Ind.
D. Mar. 28, 1907, West Baden, Ind.

		G	W	L	T	N	PCT	Standing	
1906	BOS A	40	14	26	0	0	.350	8	8

Jake Stahl

STAHL, JACOB GARLAND
B. Apr. 13, 1879, Elkhart, Ill.
D. Sept. 18, 1922, Monrovia, Calif.

		G	W	L	T	N	PCT	Standing	
1905	WAS A	154	64	87	3	0	.424	7	
1906		151	55	95	1	0	.367	7	
1912	BOS A	154	105	47	2	0	.691	1	
1913		81	39	41	1	0	.488	5	4
4 yrs.		540	263	270	7	0	.493		

WORLD SERIES

		G	W	L	T	N	PCT	Standing
1912	BOS A	8	4	3	1	0	.571	

George Stallings

STALLINGS, GEORGE TWEEDY (The Miracle Man)
B. Nov. 17, 1867, Augusta, Ga.
D. May 13, 1929, Haddock, Ga.

		G	W	L	T	N	PCT	Standing	
1897	PHI N	134	55	77	2	0	.417	10	
1898		46	19	27	0	0	.413	8	6
1901	DET A	136	74	61	1	0	.548	3	
1909	NY A	153	74	77	2	0	.490	5	
1910		142	78	59	5	0	.569	3	2
1913	BOS N	154	69	82	3	0	.457	5	
1914		158	94	59	5	0	.614	1	
1915		157	83	69	5	0	.546	2	
1916		158	89	63	6	0	.586	3	
1917		158	72	81	4	1	.471	6	
1918		124	53	71	0	0	.427	7	
1919		140	57	82	1	0	.410	6	
1920		153	62	90	1	0	.408	7	
13 yrs.		1813	879	898	35	1	.495		

WORLD SERIES

		G	W	L	T	N	PCT	Standing
1914	BOS N	4	4	0	0	0	1.000	

Eddie Stanky

STANKY, EDWARD RAYMOND (The Brat, Muggsy)
B. Sept. 3, 1916, Philadelphia, Pa.

		G	W	L	T	N	PCT	Standing	
1952	STL N	154	88	66	0	0	.571	3	
1953		157	83	71	3	0	.539	3	
1954		154	72	82	0	0	.468	6	
1955		36	17	19	0	0	.472	5	7
1966	CHI A	163	83	79	1	0	.512	4	
1967		162	89	73	0	0	.549	4	
1968		79	34	45	0	0	.430	9	8
1977	TEX A	1	1	0	0	0	1.000	4	2 2
8 yrs.		906	467	435	4	0	.518		

Casey Stengel

STENGEL, CHARLES DILLON (The Old Professor)
B. July 30, 1890, Kansas City, Mo.
D. Sept. 29, 1975, Glendale, Calif.
Hall of Fame 1966.

		G	W	L	T	N	PCT	Standing
1934	BKN N	153	71	81	1	0	.467	6

Casey Stengel *continued*

		G	W	L	T	N	PCT	Standing	
1935		154	70	83	1	0	.458	5	
1936		156	67	87	2	0	.435	7	
1938	BOS N	153	77	75	1	0	.507	5	
1939		152	63	88	1	0	.417	7	
1940		152	65	87	0	0	.428	7	
1941		156	62	92	2	0	.403	7	
1942		150	59	89	2	0	.399	7	
1943		107	47	60	0	0	.439	6	6
1949	NY A	155	97	57	1	0	.630	1	
1950		155	98	56	1	0	.636	1	
1951		154	98	56	0	0	.636	1	
1952		154	95	59	0	0	.617	1	
1953		151	99	52	0	0	.656	1	
1954		155	103	51	1	0	.669	2	
1955		154	96	58	0	0	.623	1	
1956		154	97	57	0	0	.630	1	
1957		154	98	56	0	0	.636	1	
1958		155	92	62	1	0	.597	1	
1959		155	79	75	1	0	.513	3	
1960		155	97	57	1	0	.630	1	
1962	NY N	161	40	120	1	0	.250	10	
1963		162	51	111	0	0	.315	10	
1964		163	53	109	1	0	.327	10	
1965		96	31	64	1	0	.326	10	10
25 yrs.		3766	1905	1842	19	0	.508		
								5th 7th	5th

WORLD SERIES

		G	W	L	T	N	PCT	Standing
1949	NY A	5	4	1	0	0	.800	
1950		4	4	0	0	0	1.000	
1951		6	4	2	0	0	.667	
1952		7	4	3	0	0	.571	
1953		6	4	2	0	0	.667	
1955		7	3	4	0	0	.429	
1956		7	4	3	0	0	.571	
1957		7	3	4	0	0	.429	
1958		7	4	3	0	0	.571	
1960		7	3	4	0	0	.429	
10 yrs.		63	37	26	0	0	.587	
								1st 1st 2nd	2nd

George Stovall

STOVALL, GEORGE THOMAS (Firebrand)
Brother of Jesse Stovall.
B. Nov. 23, 1878, Independence, Mo.
D. Nov. 5, 1951, Burlington, Iowa

		G	W	L	T	N	PCT	Standing	
1911	CLE A	139	74	62	3	0	.544	7	3
1912	STL A	117	41	74	2	0	.357	8	7
1913		135	50	84	1	0	.373	8	8
1914	KC F	154	67	84	3	0	.444	6	
1915		153	81	72	0	0	.529	4	
5 yrs.		698	313	376	9	0	.454		

Harry Stovey

STOVEY, HARRY DUFFIELD
Born Harry Duffield Stowe.
B. Dec. 20, 1856, Philadelphia, Pa.
D. Sept. 20, 1937, New Bedford, Mass.

		G	W	L	T	N	PCT	Standing	
1881	WOR N	27	8	18	1	0	.308	7	8
1885	PHI AA	113	55	57	1	0	.491	4	
2 yrs.		140	63	75	2	0	.457		

Gabby Street

STREET, CHARLES EVARD (Old Sarge)
B. Sept. 30, 1882, Huntsville, Ala.
D. Feb. 6, 1951, Joplin, Mo.

		G	W	L	T	N	PCT	Standing	
1929	STL N	1	1	0	0	0	1.000	4	4 4
1930		154	92	62	0	0	.597	1	
1931		154	101	53	0	0	.656	1	
1932		156	72	82	2	0	.468	6	
1933		91	46	45	0	0	.505	5	5
1938	STL A	156	55	97	4	0	.362	7	
6 yrs.		712	367	339	6	0	.520		

	G	W	L	T	N	PCT	Standing

Gabby Street *continued*

WORLD SERIES

			G	W	L	T	N	PCT	
1930	STL	N	6	2	4	0	0	.333	
1931			7	4	3	0	0	.571	
2 yrs.			13	6	7	0	0	.462	

Cub Stricker

STRICKER, JOHN A.
Born John A. Streaker.
B. June 8, 1859, Philadelphia, Pa.
D. Nov. 19, 1937, Philadelphia, Pa.

			G	W	L	T	N	PCT		
1892	STL	N	23	6	17	0	0	.261	10	11 11

George Strickland

STRICKLAND, GEORGE BEVAN (Bo)
B. Jan. 10, 1926, New Orleans, La.

			G	W	L	T	N	PCT		
1964	CLE	A	73	33	39	1	0	.458	8	6
1966			39	15	24	0	0	.385	5	5
2 yrs.			112	48	63	1	0	.432		

Larry Stubing

STUBING, LAWRENCE GEORGE
(Moose)
B. Mar. 31, 1938, Bronx, N. Y.

			G	W	L	T	N	PCT		
1988	CAL	A	8	0	8	0	0	.000	4	4

Clyde Sukeforth

SUKEFORTH, CLYDE LeROY (Sukey)
B. Nov. 30, 1901, Washington, Me.

			G	W	L	T	N	PCT		
1947	BKN	N	2	2	0	0	0	1.000	1	1

Billy Sullivan

SULLIVAN, WILLIAM JOSEPH, SR.
Father of Billy Sullivan.
B. Feb. 1, 1875, Oakland, Wis.
D. Jan. 28, 1965, Newberg, Ore.

			G	W	L	T	N	PCT	
1909	CHI	A	159	78	74	7	0	.513	4

Haywood Sullivan

SULLIVAN, HAYWOOD COOPER
Father of Marc Sullivan.
B. Dec. 15, 1930, Donalsonville, Ga.

			G	W	L	T	N	PCT		
1965	KC	A	136	54	82	0	0	.397	10	10

Pat Sullivan

SULLIVAN, JAMES PATRICK
D. May 22, 1898

			G	W	L	T	N	PCT		
1890	COL	AA	3	2	1	0	0	.667	2	2

Ted Sullivan

SULLIVAN, THEODORE PAUL
B. 1851, County Clare, Ireland
D. July 5, 1929, Washington, D. C.

			G	W	L	T	N	PCT		
1883	STL	AA	79	53	26	0	0	.671	2	2
1884	STL	U	31	28	3	0	0	.903	1	1
1884	KC	U	62	13	46	3	0	.220	12	12
1888	WAS	N	96	38	57	1	0	.400	8	8
3 yrs.			268	132	132	4	0	.500		

Bob Swift

SWIFT, ROBERT VIRGIL
B. Mar. 6, 1915, Salina, Kans.
D. Oct. 17, 1966, Detroit, Mich.

			G	W	L	T	N	PCT			
1965	DET	A	42	24	18	0	0	.571	3	4	
1966			57	32	25	0	0	.561	3	3	3
2 yrs.			99	56	43	0	0	.566			

Chuck Tanner

TANNER, CHARLES WILLIAM
Father of Bruce Tanner.
B. July 4, 1929, New Castle, Pa.

			G	W	L	T	N	PCT			
1970	CHI	A	16	3	13	0	0	.188	6	6	
1971			162	79	83	0	0	.488	3		
1972			154	87	67	0	0	.565	2		
1973			162	77	85	0	0	.475	5		
1974			163	80	80	3	0	.500	4		
1975			161	75	86	0	0	.466	5		
1976	OAK	A	161	87	74	0	0	.540	2		
1977	PIT	N	162	96	66	0	0	.593	2		
1978			161	88	73	0	0	.547	2		
1979			163	98	64	1	0	.605	1		
1980			162	83	79	0	0	.512	3		
1981			49	25	23	1	0	.521	4		(1st)
1981			54	21	33	0	0	.389	6		(2nd)
1982			162	84	78	0	0	.519	4		
1983			162	84	78	0	0	.519	2		
1984			162	75	87	0	0	.463	6		
1985			161	57	104	0	0	.354	6		
1986	ATL	N	161	72	89	0	0	.447	6		
1987			161	69	92	0	0	.429	5		
1988			39	12	27	0	0	.308	6	6	
19 yrs.			2738	1352	1381	5	0	.495			

LEAGUE CHAMPIONSHIP SERIES

			G	W	L	T	N	PCT	
1979	PIT	N	3	3	0	0	0	1.000	

WORLD SERIES

			G	W	L	T	N	PCT	
1979	PIT	N	7	4	3	0	0	.571	

El Tappe

TAPPE, ELVIN WALTER
B. May 21, 1927, Quincy, Ill.

			G	W	L	T	N	PCT			
1961	CHI	N	96	42	53	1	0	.442	7	7	7
1962			20	4	16	0	0	.200	9	9	
2 yrs.			116	46	69	1	0	.400			

George Taylor

TAYLOR, GEORGE J.
B. Nov. 22, 1853, New York, N. Y.
Deceased.

			G	W	L	T	N	PCT	
1884	BKN	AA	109	40	64	5	0	.385	9

Zack Taylor

TAYLOR, JAMES WREN
B. July 27, 1898, Yulee, Fla.
D. Sept. 19, 1974, Orlando, Fla.

			G	W	L	T	N	PCT		
1946	STL	A	31	13	17	1	0	.433	7	7
1948			155	59	94	2	0	.386	6	
1949			155	53	101	1	0	.344	7	
1950			154	58	96	0	0	.377	7	
1951			154	52	102	0	0	.338	8	
5 yrs.			649	235	410	4	0	.364		

Birdie Tebbetts

TEBBETTS, GEORGE ROBERT
B. Nov. 10, 1912, Burlington, Vt.

			G	W	L	T	N	PCT	
1954	CIN	N	154	74	80	0	0	.481	5
1955			154	75	79	0	0	.487	5
1956			155	91	63	1	0	.591	3

Birdie Tebbetts *continued*

			G	W	L	T	N	PCT		
1957			154	80	74	0	0	.519	4	
1958			113	52	61	0	0	.460	7	4
1961	MIL	N	25	12	13	0	0	.480	3	4
1962			162	86	76	0	0	.531	5	
1963	CLE	A	162	79	83	0	0	.488	5	
1964			91	46	44	1	0	.511	8	6
1965			162	87	75	0	0	.537	5	
1966			123	66	57	0	0	.537	5	5
11 yrs.			1455	748	705	2	0	.515		

Patsy Tebeau

TEBEAU, OLIVER WENDELL
Brother of White Wings Tebeau.
B. Dec. 5, 1864, St. Louis, Mo.
D. May 15, 1918, St. Louis, Mo.

			G	W	L	T	N	PCT		
1890	CLE	P	52	21	30	1	0	.412	7	7
1891	CLE	N	76	34	40	2	0	.459	6	5
1892			150	93	56	1	0	.624	2	
1893			129	73	55	1	0	.570	3	
1894			130	68	61	1	0	.527	6	
1895			132	84	46	1	1	.646	2	
1896			135	80	48	7	0	.625	2	
1897			132	69	62	1	0	.527	5	
1898			156	81	68	7	0	.544	5	
1899	STL	N	155	84	67	4	0	.556	5	
1900			92	42	50	0	0	.457	7	5
11 yrs.			1339	729	583	26	1	.556		

Fred Tenney

TENNEY, FREDERICK
B. Nov. 26, 1871, Georgetown, Mass.
D. July 3, 1952, Boston, Mass.

			G	W	L	T	N	PCT	
1905	BOS	N	156	51	103	2	0	.331	7
1906			152	49	102	1	0	.325	8
1907			152	58	90	4	0	.392	7
1911			156	44	107	5	0	.291	8
4 yrs.			616	202	402	12	0	.334	

Bill Terry

TERRY, WILLIAM HAROLD (Memphis Bill)
B. Oct. 30, 1896, Atlanta, Ga.
D. Jan. 9, 1989, Jacksonville, Fla.
Hall of Fame 1954.

			G	W	L	T	N	PCT		
1932	NY	N	114	55	59	0	0	.482	8	6
1933			156	91	61	4	0	.599	1	
1934			153	93	60	0	0	.608	2	
1935			156	91	62	3	0	.595	3	
1936			154	92	62	0	0	.597	1	
1937			152	95	57	0	0	.625	1	
1938			152	83	67	2	0	.553	3	
1939			151	77	74	0	0	.510	5	
1940			152	72	80	0	0	.474	6	
1941			156	74	79	3	0	.484	5	
10 yrs.			1496	823	661	12	0	.555		

WORLD SERIES

			G	W	L	T	N	PCT	
1933	NY	N	5	4	1	0	0	.800	
1936			6	2	4	0	0	.333	
1937			5	1	4	0	0	.200	
3 yrs.			16	7	9	0	0	.438	

Fred Thomas

THOMAS, FREDERICK L.
B. Ind.
Deceased.

			G	W	L	T	N	PCT		
1887	IND	N	29	11	18	0	0	.379	8	8 8

	G	W	L	T	N	PCT	Standing		

Andrew Thompson

THOMPSON, ANDREW M.
B. 1846, Ill.

	G	W	L	T	N	PCT	Standing
1884 STP U	9	2	6	1	0	.250	10

Jack Tighe

TIGHE, JOHN THOMAS
B. Aug. 9, 1913, Kearny, N. J.

	G	W	L	T	N	PCT	Standing	
1957 DET A	154	78	76	0	0	.506	4	
1958	49	21	28	0	0	.429	5	5
2 yrs.	203	99	104	0	0	.488		

Joe Tinker

TINKER, JOSEPH BERT
B. July 27, 1880, Muscotah, Kans.
D. July 27, 1948, Orlando, Fla.
Hall of Fame 1946.

	G	W	L	T	N	PCT	Standing
1913 CIN N	156	64	89	3	0	.418	7
1914 CHI F	158	87	67	3	1	.565	2
1915	156	86	66	3	1	.566	1
1916 CHI N	156	67	86	3	0	.438	5
4 yrs.	626	304	308	12	2	.497	

Jeff Torborg

TORBORG, JEFFREY ALLEN
B. Nov. 26, 1941, Plainfield, N. J.

	G	W	L	T	N	PCT	Standing	
1977 CLE A	104	45	59	0	0	.433	6	5
1978	159	69	90	0	0	.434	6	
1979	95	43	52	0	0	.453	6	6
1989 CHI A	161	69	92	0	0	.429	7	
4 yrs.	519	226	293	0	0	.435		

Joe Torre

TORRE, JOSEPH PAUL
Brother of Frank Torre.
B. July 18, 1940, Brooklyn, N. Y.

	G	W	L	T	N	PCT	Standing	
1977 NY N	117	49	68	0	0	.419	6	6
1978	162	66	96	0	0	.407	6	
1979	163	63	99	1	0	.389	6	
1980	162	67	95	0	0	.414	5	
1981	52	17	34	1	0	.333	5	(1st)
1981	53	24	28	1	0	.462	4	(2nd)
1982 ATL N	162	89	73	0	0	.549	1	
1983	162	88	74	0	0	.543	2	
1984	162	80	82	0	0	.494	2	
8 yrs.	1195	543	649	3	0	.456		

LEAGUE CHAMPIONSHIP SERIES

	G	W	L	T	N	PCT
1982 ATL N	3	0	3	0	0	.000

Dick Tracewski

TRACEWSKI, RICHARD JOSEPH
B. Feb. 3, 1935, Eynon, Pa.

	G	W	L	T	N	PCT	Standing		
1979 DET A	2	2	0	0	0	1.000	5	5	5

Pie Traynor

TRAYNOR, HAROLD JOSEPH
B. Nov. 11, 1899, Framingham, Mass.
D. Mar. 16, 1972, Pittsburgh, Pa.
Hall of Fame 1948.

	G	W	L	T	N	PCT	Standing	
1934 PIT N	100	47	52	1	0	.475	4	5
1935	153	86	67	0	0	.562	4	
1936	156	84	70	2	0	.545	4	
1937	154	86	68	0	0	.558	3	
1938	152	86	64	2	0	.573	2	

Pie Traynor continued

	G	W	L	T	N	PCT	Standing
1939	153	68	85	0	0	.444	6
6 yrs.	868	457	406	5	0	.530	

Tom Trebelhorn

TREBELHORN, THOMAS LYNN
B. Jan. 27, 1948, Portland, Ore.

	G	W	L	T	N	PCT	Standing	
1986 MIL A	9	6	3	0	0	.667	6	6
1987	162	91	71	0	0	.562	3	
1988	162	87	75	0	0	.537	3	
1989	162	81	81	0	0	.500	4	
4 yrs.	495	265	230	0	0	.535		

Sam Trott

TROTT, SAMUEL W.
B. 1858, Washington, D. C.
D. June 5, 1925, Cantonsville, Md.

	G	W	L	T	N	PCT	Standing	
1891 WAS AA	12	4	7	1	0	.364	6	9

Ted Turner

TURNER, ROBERT EDWARD
B. Nov. 19, 1938, Cincinnati, Ohio

	G	W	L	T	N	PCT	Standing	
1977 ATL N	1	0	1	0	0	.000	6	6

Bob Unglaub

UNGLAUB, ROBERT ALEXANDER
B. July 31, 1881, Baltimore, Md.
D. Nov. 29, 1916, Baltimore, Md.

	G	W	L	T	N	PCT	Standing		
1907 BOS A	29	9	20	0	0	.310	6	8	7

Bobby Valentine

VALENTINE, ROBERT JOHN
B. May 13, 1950, Stamford, Conn.

	G	W	L	T	N	PCT	Standing	
1985 TEX A	129	53	76	0	0	.411	7	7
1986	162	87	75	0	0	.537	2	
1987	162	75	87	0	0	.463	6	
1988	161	70	91	0	0	.435	6	
1989	162	83	79	0	0	.512	4	
5 yrs.	776	368	408	0	0	.474		

George Van Haltren

VAN HALTREN, GEORGE EDWARD MARTIN
B. Mar. 30, 1866, St. Louis, Mo.
D. Sept. 29, 1945, Oakland, Calif.

	G	W	L	T	N	PCT	Standing	
1891 BAL AA	6	4	2	0	0	.667	4	3
1892 BAL N	15	1	14	0	0	.067	12	12
2 yrs.	21	5	16	0	0	.238		

Mickey Vernon

VERNON, JAMES BARTON
B. Apr. 22, 1918, Marcus Hook, Pa.

	G	W	L	T	N	PCT	Standing	
1961 WAS A	161	61	100	0	0	.379	9	
1962	162	60	101	1	0	.373	10	
1963	40	14	26	0	0	.350	10	10
3 yrs.	363	135	227	1	0	.373		

Bill Virdon

VIRDON, WILLIAM CHARLES
B. June 9, 1931, Hazel Park, Mich.

	G	W	L	T	N	PCT	Standing	
1972 PIT N	155	96	59	0	0	.619	1	
1973	136	67	69	0	0	.493	2	3

Bill Virdon continued

	G	W	L	T	N	PCT	Standing		
1974 NY A	162	89	73	0	0	.549	2		
1975	104	53	51	0	0	.510	3	3	
1975 HOU N	35	17	17	1	0	.500	6	6	
1976	162	80	82	0	0	.494	3		
1977	162	81	81	0	0	.500	3		
1978	162	74	88	0	0	.457	5		
1979	162	89	73	0	0	.549	2		
1980	163	93	70	0	0	.571	1		
1981	57	28	29	0	0	.491	3		(1st)
1981	53	33	20	0	0	.623	1		(2nd)
1982	111	49	62	0	0	.441	5	5	
1983 MON N	163	82	80	1	0	.506	3		
1984	131	64	67	0	0	.489	5	5	
13 yrs.	1918	995	921	2	0	.519			

DIVISIONAL PLAYOFF SERIES

	G	W	L	T	N	PCT
1981 HOU N	5	2	3	0	0	.400

LEAGUE CHAMPIONSHIP SERIES

	G	W	L	T	N	PCT
1972 PIT N	5	2	3	0	0	.400
1980 HOU N	5	2	3	0	0	.400
2 yrs.	10	4	6	0	0	.400
						10th

Ossie Vitt

VITT, OSCAR JOSEPH
B. Jan. 4, 1890, San Francisco, Calif.
D. Jan. 31, 1963, Oakland, Calif.

	G	W	L	T	N	PCT	Standing
1938 CLE A	153	86	66	1	0	.566	3
1939	154	87	67	0	0	.565	3
1940	155	89	65	1	0	.578	2
3 yrs.	462	262	198	2	0	.570	

Chris Von Der Ahe

VON DER AHE, CHRISTIAN FREDERICK WILHELM
B. Nov. 7, 1851, Hille, Germany
D. June 7, 1913, St. Louis, Mo.

	G	W	L	T	N	PCT	Standing		
1895 STL N	1	1	0	0	0	1.000	11	11	11
1896	2	0	2	0	0	.000	10	11	11
1897	14	2	12	0	0	.143	12	12	
3 yrs.	17	3	14	0	0	.176			

John Vukovich

VUKOVICH, JOHN CHRISTOPHER
B. July 31, 1947, Sacramento, Calif.

	G	W	L	T	N	PCT	Standing		
1986 CHI N	2	1	1	0	0	.500	5	5	5
1988 PHI N	9	5	4	0	0	.556	6	6	
2 yrs.	11	6	5	0	0	.545			

Heinie Wagner

WAGNER, CHARLES F.
B. Sept. 23, 1880, New York, N. Y.
D. Mar. 20, 1943, New Rochelle, N. Y.

	G	W	L	T	N	PCT	Standing
1930 BOS A	154	52	102	0	0	.338	8

Honus Wagner

WAGNER, JOHN PETER (The Flying Dutchman)
Brother of Butts Wagner.
B. Feb. 24, 1874, Mansfield, Pa.
D. Dec. 6, 1955, Carnegie, Pa.
Hall of Fame 1936.

	G	W	L	T	N	PCT	Standing		
1917 PIT N	5	1	4	0	0	.200	8	8	8

	G	W	L	T	N	PCT	Standing

Harry Walker

WALKER, HARRY WILLIAM (The Hat)
Son of Dixie Walker.
Brother of Dixie Walker.
B. Oct. 22, 1916, Pascagoula, Miss.

		G	W	L	T	N	PCT	Standing	
1955	STL N	118	51	67	0	0	.432	5	7
1965	PIT N	163	90	72	1	0	.556	3	
1966		162	92	70	0	0	.568	3	
1967		84	42	42	0	0	.500	6	6
1968	HOU N	101	49	52	0	0	.485	10	10
1969		162	81	81	0	0	.500	5	
1970		162	79	83	0	0	.488	4	
1971		162	79	83	0	0	.488	4	
1972		121	67	54	0	0	.554	3	2
9 yrs.		1235	630	604	1	0	.511		

Bobby Wallace

WALLACE, RHODERICK JOHN (Rhody)
B. Nov. 4, 1873, Pittsburgh, Pa.
D. Nov. 3, 1960, Torrance, Calif.
Hall of Fame 1953.

		G	W	L	T	N	PCT	Standing	
1911	STL A	152	45	107	0	0	.296	8	
1912		40	12	27	1	0	.308	8	7
1937	CIN N	25	5	20	0	0	.200	8	8
3 yrs.		217	62	154	1	0	.287		

Ed Walsh

WALSH, EDWARD AUGUSTINE (Big Ed)
Father of Ed Walsh.
B. May 14, 1881, Plains, Pa.
D. May 26, 1959, Pompano Beach, Fla.
Hall of Fame 1946.

		G	W	L	T	N	PCT	Standing		
1924	CHI A	3	1	2	0	0	.333	6	6	8

Mike Walsh

WALSH, MICHAEL JOHN
B. Apr. 29, 1850, Ireland
D. Feb. 2, 1929, Louisville, Ky.

		G	W	L	T	N	PCT	Standing
1884	LOU AA	110	68	40	2	0	.630	3

Bucky Walters

WALTERS, WILLIAM HENRY
B. Apr. 19, 1909, Philadelphia, Pa.

		G	W	L	T	N	PCT	Standing	
1948	CIN N	53	20	33	0	0	.377	7	7
1949		153	61	90	2	0	.404	7	7
2 yrs.		206	81	123	2	0	.397		

John Waltz

WALTZ, JOHN J.
Deceased.

		G	W	L	T	N	PCT	Standing		
1892	BAL N	8	2	6	0	0	.250	12	12	12

Monte Ward

WARD, JOHN MONTGOMERY
B. Mar. 3, 1860, Bellefonte, Pa.
D. Mar. 4, 1925, Augusta, Ga.
Hall of Fame 1964.

		G	W	L	T	N	PCT	Standing		
1880	PRO N	32	18	13	1	0	.581	4	3	2
1884	NY N	16	6	8	2	0	.429	4	4	
1890	BKN P	133	76	56	1	0	.576	2		
1891	BKN N	137	61	76	0	0	.445	6		
1892		155	95	59	1	0	.617	3		
1893	NY N	136	68	64	4	0	.515	5		
1894		139	88	44	5	2	.667	2		
7 yrs.		748	412	320	14	2	.563			

John Wathan

WATHAN, JOHN DAVID (Duke)
B. Oct. 4, 1949, Cedar Rapids, Iowa

		G	W	L	T	N	PCT	Standing	
1987	KC A	36	21	15	0	0	.583	4	2
1988		161	84	77	0	0	.522	3	
1989		162	92	70	0	0	.568	2	
3 yrs.		359	197	162	0	0	.549		

Bill Watkins

WATKINS, WILLIAM HENRY
B. May 5, 1858, Brantford, Ont., Canada
D. June 9, 1937, Port Huron, Mich.

		G	W	L	T	N	PCT	Standing	
1884	IND AA	24	4	19	1	0	.174	11	12
1885	DET N	70	34	36	0	0	.486	7	6
1886		126	87	36	3	0	.707	2	
1887		127	79	45	3	0	.637	1	
1888		94	49	44	1	0	.527	3	5
1888	KC AA	25	8	17	0	0	.320	8	8
1889		139	55	82	2	0	.401	7	
1893	STL N	135	57	75	3	0	.432	10	
1898	PIT N	152	72	76	4	0	.486	8	
1899		24	7	15	1	1	.318	10	7
9 yrs.		916	452	445	18	1	.504		

Harvey Watkins

WATKINS, HARVEY L.
Deceased.

		G	W	L	T	N	PCT	Standing	
1895	NY N	35	18	17	0	0	.514	9	9

Earl Weaver

WEAVER, EARL SIDNEY
B. Aug. 14, 1930, St. Louis, Mo.

		G	W	L	T	N	PCT	Standing		
1968	BAL A	82	48	34	0	0	.585	3	2	
1969		162	109	53	0	0	.673	1		
1970		162	108	54	0	0	.667	1		
1971		158	101	57	0	0	.639	1		
1972		154	80	74	0	0	.519	3		
1973		162	97	65	0	0	.599	1		
1974		162	91	71	0	0	.562	1		
1975		159	90	69	0	0	.566	2		
1976		162	88	74	0	0	.543	2		
1977		161	97	64	0	0	.602	2		
1978		161	90	71	0	0	.559	4		
1979		159	102	57	0	0	.642	1		
1980		162	100	62	0	0	.617	2		
1981		54	31	23	0	0	.574	2		(1st)
1981		51	28	23	0	0	.549	4		(2nd)
1982		163	94	68	1	0	.580	2		
1985		105	53	52	0	0	.505	4	4	
1986		162	73	89	0	0	.451	7		
17 yrs.		2541	1480	1060	1	0	.583			
								9th		

LEAGUE CHAMPIONSHIP SERIES

		G	W	L	T	N	PCT			
1969	BAL A	3	3	0	0	0	1.000			
1970		3	3	0	0	0	1.000			
1971		3	3	0	0	0	1.000			
1973		5	2	3	0	0	.400			
1974		4	1	3	0	0	.250			
1979		4	3	1	0	0	.750			
6 yrs.		22	15	7	0	0	.682			
		4th	4th	9th				2nd		

WORLD SERIES

		G	W	L	T	N	PCT		
1969	BAL A	5	1	4	0	0	.200		
1970		5	4	1	0	0	.800		
1971		7	3	4	0	0	.429		
1979		7	3	4	0	0	.429		
4 yrs.		24	11	13	0	0	.458		
		9th	10th	8th					

Wes Westrum

WESTRUM, WESLEY NOREEN
B. Nov. 28, 1922, Clearbrook, Minn.

		G	W	L	T	N	PCT	Standing	
1965	NY N	68	19	48	1	0	.284	10	10
1966		161	66	95	0	0	.410	9	
1967		151	57	94	0	0	.377	10	10
1974	SF N	86	38	48	0	0	.442	5	5
1975		161	80	81	0	0	.497	3	
5 yrs.		627	260	366	1	0	.415		

Harry Wheeler

WHEELER, HARRY EUGENE
B. Mar. 3, 1858, Versailles, Ind.
D. Oct. 9, 1900, Cincinnati, Ohio

		G	W	L	T	N	PCT	Standing	
1884	KC U	4	0	4	0	0	.000	12	12

Deacon White

WHITE, JAMES LAURIE
Brother of Will White.
B. Dec. 7, 1847, Caton, N. Y.
D. July 7, 1939, Aurora, Ill.

		G	W	L	T	N	PCT	Standing	
1879	CIN N	18	9	9	0	0	.500	5	5

Jo-Jo White

WHITE, JOYNER CLIFFORD
Father of Mike White.
B. June 1, 1909, Red Oak, Ga.
D. Oct. 9, 1986, Tacoma, Wash.

		G	W	L	T	N	PCT	Standing		
1960	CLE A	1	1	0	0	0	1.000	4	4	4

Will White

WHITE, WILLIAM HENRY (Whoop-La)
Brother of Deacon White.
B. Oct. 11, 1854, Caton, N. Y.
D. Aug. 31, 1911, Port Carling, Ont., Canada

		G	W	L	T	N	PCT	Standing	
1884	CIN AA	72	44	27	1	0	.620	5	5

Del Wilber

WILBER, DELBERT QUENTIN (Babe)
B. Feb. 24, 1919, Lincoln Park, Mich.

		G	W	L	T	N	PCT	Standing		
1973	TEX A	1	1	0	0	0	1.000	6	6	6

Kaiser Wilhelm

WILHELM, IRVIN KEY
B. Jan. 26, 1874, Wooster Ohio
D. May 21, 1936, Rochester, N. Y.

		G	W	L	T	N	PCT	Standing	
1921	PHI N	67	26	41	0	0	.388	8	8
1922		154	57	96	1	0	.373	7	
2 yrs.		221	83	137	1	0	.377		

Dick Williams

WILLIAMS, RICHARD HIRSCHFELD
B. May 7, 1928, St. Louis, Mo.

		G	W	L	T	N	PCT	Standing	
1967	BOS A	162	92	70	0	0	.568	1	
1968		162	86	76	0	0	.531	4	
1969		153	82	71	0	0	.536	3	3
1971	OAK A	161	101	60	0	0	.627	1	
1972		155	93	62	0	0	.600	1	
1973		162	94	68	0	0	.580	1	
1974	CAL A	84	36	48	0	0	.429	6	6
1975		161	72	89	0	0	.447	6	
1976		96	39	57	0	0	.406	4	4
1977	MON N	162	75	87	0	0	.463	5	

		G	W	L	T	N	PCT	Standing	

Dick Williams *continued*

			G	W	L	T	N	PCT			
1978			162	76	86	0	0	.469	4		
1979			160	95	65	0	0	.594	2		
1980			162	90	72	0	0	.556	2		
1981			55	30	25	0	0	.545	3		(1st)
1981			26	14	12	0	0	.538	2	1	(2nd)
1982	SD	N	162	81	81	0	0	.500	4		
1983			163	81	81	1	0	.500	4		
1984			162	92	70	0	0	.568	1		
1985			162	83	79	0	0	.512	3		
1986	SEA	A	133	58	75	0	0	.436	6	7	
1987			162	78	84	0	0	.481	4		
1988			56	23	33	0	0	.411	6	7	
21 yrs.			3023	1571	1451	1	0	.520			

LEAGUE CHAMPIONSHIP SERIES

			G	W	L	T	N	PCT	
1971	OAK	A	3	0	3	0	0	.000	
1972			5	3	2	0	0	.600	
1973			5	3	2	0	0	.600	
1984	SD	N	5	3	2	0	0	.600	
4 yrs.			18	9	9	0	0	.500	
			6th	5th	5th				8th

WORLD SERIES

			G	W	L	T	N	PCT	
1967	BOS	A	7	3	4	0	0	.429	
1972	OAK	A	7	4	3	0	0	.571	
1973			7	4	3	0	0	.571	
1984	SD	N	5	1	4	0	0	.200	
4 yrs.			26	12	14	0	0	.462	
			8th	8th	6th				

Jimmy Williams

WILLIAMS, JAMES ANDREWS
B. Jan. 3, 1848, Columbus, Ohio
D. Oct. 24, 1918, North Hempstead, N. Y.

			G	W	L	T	N	PCT		
1884	STL	AA	85	51	33	1	0	.607	5	4
1887	CLE	AA	133	39	92	2	0	.298	8	
1888			64	20	44	0	0	.313	7	6
3 yrs.			282	110	169	3	0	.394		

Jimy Williams

WILLIAMS, JAMES FRANCIS
B. Oct. 4, 1943, Santa Maria, Calif.

			G	W	L	T	N	PCT		
1986	TOR	A	163	86	76	1	0	.531	4	
1987			162	96	66	0	0	.593	2	
1988			162	87	75	0	0	.537	3	
1989			36	12	24	0	0	.333	6	1
4 yrs.			523	281	241	1	0	.538		

Ted Williams

WILLIAMS, THEODORE SAMUEL (The Splendid Splinter, The Thumper)
B. Aug. 30, 1918, San Diego, Calif.
Hall of Fame 1966.

			G	W	L	T	N	PCT	
1969	WAS	A	162	86	76	0	0	.531	4
1970			162	70	92	0	0	.432	6
1971			159	63	96	0	0	.396	5
1972	TEX	A	154	54	100	0	0	.351	6
4 yrs.			637	273	364	0	0	.429	

Maury Wills

WILLS, MAURICE MORNING
Father of Bump Wills.
B. Oct. 2, 1932, Washington, D. C.

			G	W	L	T	N	PCT			
1980	SEA	A	58	20	38	0	0	.345	7	7	
1981			24	6	18	0	0	.250	7	6	(1st)
2 yrs.			82	26	56	0	0	.317			

Jimmie Wilson

WILSON, JAMES (Ace)
B. July 23, 1900, Philadelphia, Pa.
D. May 31, 1947, Bradenton, Fla.

			G	W	L	T	N	PCT		
1934	PHI	N	149	56	93	0	0	.376	7	
1935			156	64	89	3	0	.418	7	
1936			154	54	100	0	0	.351	8	
1937			155	61	92	2	0	.399	7	
1938			149	45	103	1	0	.304	8	8
1941	CHI	N	155	70	84	1	0	.455	6	
1942			155	68	86	1	0	.442	6	
1943			154	74	79	1	0	.484	5	
1944			10	1	9	0	0	.100	8	4
9 yrs.			1237	493	735	9	0	.401		

Bobby Wine

WINE, ROBERT PAUL, SR.
Father of Robbie Wine.
B. Sept. 17, 1938, New York, N. Y.

			G	W	L	T	N	PCT		
1985	ATL	N	41	16	25	0	0	.390	5	5

Ivy Wingo

WINGO, IVEY BROWN
Brother of Al Wingo.
B. July 8, 1890, Gainesville, Ga.
D. Mar. 1, 1941, Norcross, Ga.

			G	W	L	T	N	PCT			
1916	CIN	N	2	1	1	0	0	.500	8	8	7

Bobby Winkles

WINKLES, BOBBY BROOKS (Winks)
B. Mar. 11, 1930, Tuckerman, Ark.

			G	W	L	T	N	PCT		
1973	CAL	A	162	79	83	0	0	.488	4	
1974			75	30	44	1	0	.405	6	6
1977	OAK	A	108	37	71	0	0	.343	7	7
1978			39	24	15	0	0	.615	6	6
4 yrs.			384	170	213	1	0	.444		

Chicken Wolf

WOLF, WILLIAM VAN WINKLE
B. May 12, 1862, Louisville, Ky.
D. May 16, 1903, Louisville, Ky.

			G	W	L	T	N	PCT			
1889	LOU	AA	65	14	51	0	0	.215	8	8	8

Harry Wolverton

WOLVERTON, HARRY STERLING
B. Dec. 6, 1873, Mt. Vernon, Ohio
D. Feb. 4, 1937, Oakland, Calif.

			G	W	L	T	N	PCT	
1912	NY	A	153	50	102	1	0	.329	8

George Wood

WOOD, GEORGE A. (Dandy)
B. Nov. 9, 1858, Boston, Mass.
D. Apr. 4, 1924, Harrisburg, Pa.

			G	W	L	T	N	PCT		
1891	PHI	AA	125	67	55	3	0	.549	7	5

Al Wright

WRIGHT, ALFRED HECTOR
B. Mar. 30, 1842, Cedar Grove, N. J.
D. Apr. 20, 1905

			G	W	L	T	N	PCT	
1876	PHI	N	60	14	45	1	0	.237	7

George Wright

WRIGHT, GEORGE
Brother of Harry Wright.
Brother of Sam Wright.
B. Jan. 28, 1847, Yonkers, N. Y.
D. Aug. 21, 1937, Boston, Mass.
Hall of Fame 1937.

			G	W	L	T	N	PCT	
1879	PRO	N	85	59	25	1	0	.702	1

Harry Wright

WRIGHT, WILLIAM HENRY
Brother of Sam Wright.
Brother of George Wright.
B. Jan. 10, 1835, Sheffield, England
D. Oct. 3, 1895, Atlantic City, N. J.
Hall of Fame 1953.

			G	W	L	T	N	PCT		
1876	BOS	N	70	39	31	0	0	.557	4	
1877			61	42	18	1	0	.700	1	
1878			60	41	19	0	0	.683	1	
1879			84	54	30	0	0	.643	2	
1880			86	40	44	2	0	.476	6	
1881			83	38	45	0	0	.458	6	
1882	PRO	N	84	52	32	0	0	.619	2	
1883			98	58	40	0	0	.592	3	
1884	PHI	N	113	39	73	1	0	.348	6	
1885			111	56	54	1	0	.509	3	
1886			119	71	43	5	0	.623	4	
1887			128	75	48	5	0	.610	2	
1888			132	69	61	1	1	.531	3	
1889			130	63	64	3	0	.496	4	
1890			22	14	8	0	0	.636	1	3
1890			46	22	23	1	0	.489	2	3
1891			138	68	69	1	0	.496	4	
1892			154	87	66	1	0	.569	4	
1893			133	72	57	4	0	.558	4	
18 yrs.			1852	1000	825	26	1	.548		

Rudy York

YORK, RUDOLPH PRESTON
B. Aug. 17, 1913, Ragland, Ala.
D. Feb. 5, 1970, Rome, Ga.

			G	W	L	T	N	PCT			
1959	BOS	A	1	0	1	0	0	.000	8	8	5

Tom York

YORK, THOMAS J.
B. July 13, 1851, Brooklyn, N. Y.
D. Feb. 17, 1936, New York, N. Y.

			G	W	L	T	N	PCT		
1878	PRO	N	62	33	27	2	0	.550	3	
1881			34	23	10	1	0	.697	4	2
2 yrs.			96	56	37	3	0	.602		

Eddie Yost

YOST, EDWARD FREDERICK (The Walking Man)
B. Oct. 13, 1926, Brooklyn, N. Y.

			G	W	L	T	N	PCT			
1963	WAS	A	1	0	1	0	0	.000	10	10	10

Cy Young

YOUNG, DENTON TRUE (Foxy Grandpa)
B. Mar. 29, 1867, Gilmore, Ohio
D. Nov. 4, 1955, Newcomerstown, Ohio
Hall of Fame 1937.

			G	W	L	T	N	PCT		
1907	BOS	A	6	3	3	0	0	.500	4	7

	G	W	L	T	N	PCT	Standing		G	W	L	T	N	PCT	Standing		G	W	L	T	N	PCT	Standing

Chief Zimmer

ZIMMER, CHARLES LOUIS
  B. Nov. 23, 1860, Marietta, Ohio
  D. Aug. 22, 1949, Cleveland, Ohio

1903	PHI	N	139	49	86	4	0	.363	7

Don Zimmer

ZIMMER, DONALD WILLIAM
  B. Jan. 17, 1931, Cincinnati, Ohio

1972	SD	N	142	54	88	0	0	.380	4	6	
1973			162	60	102	0	0	.370	6		
1976	BOS	A	76	42	34	0	0	.553	3	3	
1977			161	97	64	0	0	.602	2		
1978			163	99	64	0	0	.607	2		
1979			160	91	69	0	0	.569	3		
1980			155	82	73	0	0	.529	4	4	
1981	TEX	A	56	33	22	0	1	.600	2		(1st)
1981			50	24	26	0	0	.480	3		(2nd)
1982			96	38	58	0	0	.396	6	6	
1988	CHI	N	163	77	85	1	0	.475	4		
1989			162	93	69	0	0	.574	1		
11 yrs.			1546	790	754	1	1	.512			

LEAGUE CHAMPIONSHIP SERIES

1989	CHI	N	5	1	4	0	0	.200	

PART SEVEN

Player Register

Alphabetical List of Every Man
(Except Certain Pitchers)
Who Ever Played in the Major Leagues
With His Complete Batting and Fielding Records

Player Register

The Player Register is an alphabetical listing of every man who has played in the major leagues from 1876 through today, except those players who were primarily pitchers. However, pitchers who pinch hit and played in other positions for a total of 25 games or more are listed in this Player Register. Included are facts about the players and their year-by-year batting and fielding records and lifetime totals for the regular season, League Championship Series and World Series.

Much of this information has never been compiled, especially for the period 1876 through 1919. For certain other years some statistics are still missing or incomplete. Research in this area is still in progress, and the years that lack complete information are indicated. In fact, all information and abbreviations that may appear unfamiliar are explained in the sample format presented below. John Doe, the player used in the sample, is fictitious and serves only to illustrate the information.

Year	Team	Games	BA	SA	AB	H	2B	3B	HR	HR %	R	RBI	BB	SO	SB	Pinch Hit AB	Pinch Hit H	PO	A	E	DP	TC/G	FA	G by POS

John Doe

DOE, JOHN LEE (Slim)
Played as John Cherry part of 1900.
Born John Lee Doughnut. Brother of Bill Doe.
B. Jan. 1, 1850, New York, N. Y. D. July 1, 1955, New York, N. Y.
Manager 1908–15.
Hall of Fame 1946.

BR TR 6'2" 165 lbs.
BB 1884 BL 1906

Year	Team		Games	BA	SA	AB	H	2B	3B	HR	HR %	R	RBI	BB	SO	SB	PH AB	PH H	PO	A	E	DP	TC/G	FA	G by POS
1884	STL	U	125	.278	.345	435	121	18	1	3	0.7		44	37	42	7	9	2	118	267	46	16	3.4	.893	SS-99, P-26
1885	LOU	AA	155	.252	.320	547	138	22	3	3	0.6	50	58	42	48	8	8	4	94	266	44	23	2.6	.891	SS-115, P-40
1886	CLE	N	147	.276	.375	485	134	38	5	0	0.0	66	54	48	50	8	7	1	120	277	51	25	3.0	.886	SS-107, P-40
1887	BOS	N	129	.280	.337	418	117	15	3	1	0.2	38	52	32	37	1	1	0	136	310	59	29	3.9	.883	SS-102, P-27
1888	NY	N	144	.267	.362	506	135	26	2	6	1.2	50	63	43	50	1	10	8	136	245	72	20	3.1	.841	SS-105, P-39
1889	3 teams					DET N (10G - .300)		PIT N (32G - .241)			PHI N (41G - .364)														
"	total		83	.316	.671	237	75	31	16	7	3.0	90	42	25	35	3	6	3	91	156	35	14	4.3	.876	SS-61, P-22
1890	NY	P	123	.277	.370	430	119	27	5	1	0.2	63	59	39	39	2	12	10	137	331	65	44	3.5	.878	SS-85, P-38
1900	CHI	N	146	.233	.325	498	116	29	4	3	0.6	51	46	59	53	1	13	8	161	307	48	32	4.5	.907	SS-111, P-35
1901	NY	N	149	.272	.352	540	147	19	6	4	0.7	57	74	49	58	3	23	15	202	405	59	47	4.8	.911	SS-114, P-35
1906	BOS	N	144	.252	.333	567	143	26	4	4	0.7	70	43	37	54	1	7	1	244	393	54	35	4.8	.922	SS-113, P-31
1907			134	.272	.369	515	140	31	2	5	1.0	61	70	37	42	0	13	8	215	390	39	45	4.8	.939	SS-97, P-37
1908			106	.247	.317	372	92	10	2	4	1.1	36	40	4	55	1	1	0	227	352	35	33	5.8	.943	SS-105, P-1
1914	CHI	F	6	.000	.000	6	0	0	0	0	0.0	0	0	0	1	0	0	0	2	4	0	1	1.0	1.000	P-6
1915	NY	A	1	—	—	0	0	0	0	0	—	0	0	0	0	0	0	0	2	3	1	2	6.0	.833	SS-1
14 yrs.			1592	.266	.360	5556	1927	292	53	41	0.7	676	601	452	564	36	110	60	1185	3706	608	366	3.5	.889	SS-1215, P-377
									4th																
LEAGUE CHAMPIONSHIP SERIES																									
1908	BOS	N	3	.357	1.143	14	5	2	0	3	21.4	3	7	0	1	0	0	0	2	4	0	1	2.0	1.000	SS-3
WORLD SERIES																									
1906	BOS	N	7	.321	1.000	28	9	1	0	6	21.4	12	14	3	4	0	0	0	4	8	2	2	2.0	.857	SS-5, P-2
1908			5	.500	.900	10	5	1	0	1	10.0	3	2	0	2	0	2	0	3	6	1	2	2.0	.900	P-4, SS-1
2 yrs.			12	.368	.974	38	14	2	0	7	18.4	15	16	3	6	0	2	0	7	14	3	4	2.0	.875	SS-6, P-6
								5th					9th												

Player Information

John Doe
This shortened version of the player's full name is the name most familiar to the fans. All players in this section are alphabetically arranged by the last name part of this name.

DOE, JOHN LEE
Player's full name. The arrangement is last name first, then first and middle name(s).

(Slim)
Player's nickname. Any name appearing in parentheses is a nickname.

BR TR BB 1884 BL 1906
The player's main batting and throwing style. Doe, for instance, batted and threw right-handed. The information listed directly below the main batting information indicates that at various times in a player's career he changed his batting style. The "BB" for Doe in 1884 means he was a switch hitter that year, and the "BL" means he batted left-

handed in 1906. For the years that are not shown it can be assumed that Doe batted right, as his main batting information indicates.

6'2"
Player's height.

165 lbs
Player's average playing weight.

Played as John Cherry part of 1900
The player at one time in his major league career played under another name and can be found in box scores or newspaper stories only under that name.

Born John Lee Doughnut
The name the player was given at birth. (For the most part, the player never used this name while playing in the major leagues, but, if he did, it would be listed as "played as," which is explained above under the heading "Played as John Cherry part of 1900.")

Brother of Bill Doe
The player's brother. (Relatives indicated here are fathers, sons, and brothers who played or managed in the major leagues and the National Association.)

B. Jan. 1, 1850, New York, N.Y.
Date and place of birth.

D. July 1, 1955, New York, N.Y.
Date and place of death. (Some players are listed simply as "deceased." Although no certification of death or other information is available, it is reasonably certain they are dead.)

Manager 1908–15
Doe also served as a major league manager. All men who were managers can be found also in the Manager Register, where their complete managerial record is shown.

Hall of Fame 1946
Doe was elected to the Baseball Hall of Fame in 1946.

Column Headings Information

Year Team	Games	BA	SA	AB	H	2B	3B	HR	HR %	R	RBI	BB	SO	SB	Pinch Hit AB	H	PO	A	E	DP	TC/G	FA	G by POS

G	Games
AB	At Bats
BA	Batting Average
SA	Slugging Average
H	Hits
2B	Doubles
3B	Triples
HR	Home Runs
HR %	Home Run Percentage (the number of home runs per 100 times at bat)
R	Runs Scored
RBI	Runs Batted In
BB	Bases on Balls
SO	Strikeouts
SB	Stolen Bases

Pinch Hit

AB	Pinch Hit At Bats
H	Pinch Hits

Fielding

PO	Putouts
A	Assists
E	Errors
DP	Double Plays
TC/G	Total Chances Per Game
FA	Fielding Average
G by POS	Games by Position. (All fielding positions a man played within the given year are shown. The position where the most games were played is listed first. Any man who pitched, as Doe did, is listed also in the alphabetically arranged Pitcher Register, where his complete pitching record can be found.) If no fielding positions are shown in a particular year, it means the player only pinch-hit, pinch-ran, or was a "designated hitter." In the case of a designated hitter, the number of games he has played as a designated hitter will be shown alongside the letters DH.

Team and League Information

1884	STL	U																								
1885	LOU	AA																								
1886	CLE	N																								
1887	BOS	N																								
1888	NY	N																								
1889	3 teams		DET N (10G - .300)	PIT N (32G - .241)	PHI N (41G - .364)																				
"	total		83	.316	.671	237	75	31	16	7	3.0	90	42	25	35	3	6	3	91	156	35	14	4.3	.876	SS-61, P-22
1890	NY	P																								
1900	CHI	N																								
1901	NY	N																								
1906	BOS	N																								
1907																										
1908																										
1914	CHI	F																								
1915	NY	A																								
14 yrs.																										

Doe's record has been exaggerated so that his playing career spans all the years of the six different major leagues. Directly alongside the year and team information is the symbol for the league:

N   National League (1876 to date)

A   American League (1901 to date)

F   Federal League (1914–15)

AA   American Association (1882–91)

P   Players' League (1890)

U   Union Association (1884)

STL—The abbreviation of the city in which the team played. Doe, for example, played for St. Louis in 1884. All teams in this section are listed by an abbreviation of the city in which the team played. The abbreviations follow:

ALT	Altoona	COL	Columbus
ATL	Atlanta	DET	Detroit
BAL	Baltimore	HAR	Hartford
BOS	Boston	HOU	Houston
BKN	Brooklyn	IND	Indianapolis
BUF	Buffalo	KC	Kansas City
CAL	California	LA	Los Angeles
CHI	Chicago	LOU	Louisville
CIN	Cincinnati	MIL	Milwaukee
CLE	Cleveland	MIN	Minnesota
MON	Montreal	SF	San Francisco
NWK	Newark	STL	St. Louis
NY	New York	STP	St. Paul
OAK	Oakland	SYR	Syracuse
PHI	Philadelphia	TEX	Texas
PIT	Pittsburgh	TOL	Toledo
PRO	Providence	TOR	Toronto
RIC	Richmond	TRO	Troy
ROC	Rochester	WAS	Washington
SD	San Diego	WIL	Wilmington
SEA	Seattle	WOR	Worcester

Blank space appearing beneath a team and league indicates that the team and league are the same. Doe, for example, played for Boston in the National League from 1906 through 1908.

3 Teams Total. Indicates a player played for more than one team in the same year. Doe played for three teams in 1889. The number of games he played and his batting average for each team are also shown. Directly beneath this line, following the word "total," is Doe's combined record for all three teams for 1889.

Total Playing Years. This information, which appears as the first item on the player's lifetime total line, indicates the total number of years in which he played at least one game. Doe, for example, played in at least one game for 14 years.

Statistical Information

Year	Team		Games	BA	SA	AB	H	2B	3B	HR	HR %	R	RBI	BB	SO	SB	Pinch Hit AB	H	PO	A	E	DP	TC/G	FA	G by POS

John Doe

DOE, JOHN LEE (Slim)
Played as John Cherry part of 1900.
Born John Lee Doughnut. Brother of Bill Doe.
B. Jan. 1, 1850, New York, N. Y.   D. July 1, 1955, New York, N. Y.
Manager 1908–15.
Hall of Fame 1946.

BR TR   6'2"   165 lbs.
BB 1884   BL 1906

Year	Team		Games	BA	SA	AB	H	2B	3B	HR	HR %	R	RBI	BB	SO	SB	PH AB	H	PO	A	E	DP	TC/G	FA	G by POS
1884	STL	U	125	.278	.345	435	121	18	1	3	0.7		44	37	42	7	9	2	118	267	46	16	3.4	.893	SS-99, P-26
1885	LOU	AA	155	.252	.320	547	138	22	3	3	0.6	50	58	42	48	8	8	4	94	266	44	23	2.6	.891	SS-115, P-40
1886	CLE	N	147	.276	.375	485	134	38	5	0	0.0	66	54	48	50	8	7	1	120	277	51	25	3.0	.886	SS-107, P-40
1887	BOS	N	129	.280	.337	418	117	15	3	1	0.2	38	52	32	37	1	1	0	136	310	59	29	3.9	.883	SS-102, P-27
1888	NY	N	144	.267	.362	506	135	26	2	6	1.2	50	63	43	50	1	10	8	136	245	72	20	3.1	.841	SS-105, P-39
1889	3 teams	DET N (10G - .300) PIT N (32G - .241) PHI N (41G - .364)																							
"	total		83	.316	.671	237	75	31	16	7	3.0	90	42	25	35	3	6	3	91	156	35	14	4.3	.876	SS-61, P-22
1890	NY	P	123	.277	.370	430	119	27	5	1	0.2	63	59	39	39	2	12	10	137	331	65	44	3.5	.878	SS-85, P-38
1900	CHI	N	146	.233	.325	498	116	29	4	3	0.6	51	46	59	53	1	13	8	161	307	48	32	4.5	.907	SS-111, P-35
1901	NY	N	149	.272	.352	540	147	19	6	4	0.7	57	74	49	58	3	23	15	202	405	59	47	4.8	.911	SS-114, P-35
1906	BOS	N	144	.252	.333	567	143	26	4	4	0.7	70	43	37	54	1	7	1	244	393	54	35	4.8	.922	SS-113, P-31
1907			134	.272	.369	515	140	31	2	5	1.0	61	70	37	42	0	13	8	215	390	39	45	4.8	.939	SS-97, P-37
1908			106	.247	.317	372	92	10	2	4	1.1	36	40	4	55	1	1	0	227	352	35	33	5.8	.943	SS-105, P-1
1914	CHI	F	6	.000	.000	6	0	0	0	0	0.0	0	0	0	0	1	0	0	2	4	0	1	1.0	1.000	P-6
1915	NY	A	1	—	—	0	0	0	0	0	—	0	0	0	0	0	0	0	2	3	1	2	6.0	.833	SS-1
14 yrs.			1592	.266	.360	5556	1927	292	53	41	0.7	676	601	452	564	36	110	60	1185	3706	608	366	3.5	.889	SS-1215, P-377
									4th																

League Leaders. Statistics that appear in boldfaced print indicate the player led his league that year in a particular statistical category. Doe, for example, led the National League in doubles in 1889. When there is a tie for league lead, the figures for all the men who tied are shown in boldface.

All-Time Single Season Leaders. Indicated by the small number that appears next to the statistic. Doe, for example, is shown by a small number "1" next to his doubles total in 1889. This means he is first on the all-time major league list for hitting the most doubles in a single season. All players who tied for first are shown by the same number.

Lifetime Leaders. Indicated by the figure that appears beneath the line showing the player's lifetime totals. Doe has a "4th" shown below his lifetime triples total. This means that, lifetime, Doe ranks fourth among major league players for hitting the most triples. Once again, only the top ten are indicated, and players who are tied receive the same number.

Unavailable Information. Any time a blank space is shown in a particular statistical column, such as in Doe's 1884 RBI total, it indicates the information was unavailable or incomplete.

Meaningless Averages. Indicated by use of a dash (—). In the case of Doe, a dash is shown for his 1915 batting average. This means that, although he played one game, he had no official at bats. A batting average of .000 would mean he had at least one at bat with no hits.

League Leaders Qualifications. Throughout baseball there have been different rules used to determine the minimum appearances necessary to qualify for league leader in categories concerning averages (Batting Average, Earned Run Average, etc.). For the rules and the years they were in effect, see Appendix C.

World Series and Championship Playoffs

Year	Team		Games	BA	SA	AB	H	2B	3B	HR	HR %	R	RBI	BB	SO	SB	PH AB	H	PO	A	E	DP	TC/G	FA	G by POS
LEAGUE CHAMPIONSHIP SERIES																										
1908	BOS	N	3	.357	1.143	14	5	2	0	3	21.4	3	7	0	1	0	0	0	2	4	0	1	2.0	1.000	SS-3
WORLD SERIES																										
1906	BOS	N	7	.321	1.000	28	9	1	0	6	21.4	12	14	3	4	0	0	0	4	8	2	2	2.0	.857	SS-5, P-2
1908			5	.500	.900	10	5	1	0	1	10.0	3	2	0	2	0	2	0	3	6	1	2	2.0	.900	P-4, SS-1
2 yrs.			12	.368	.974	38	14	2	0	7	18.4	15	16	3	6	0	2	0	7	14	3	4	2.0	.875	SS-6, P-6
										5th		9th													

World Series Lifetime Leaders. Indicated by the figure that appears beneath the player's lifetime totals. Doe has a "5th" shown below his lifetime home run total. This means that, lifetime, Doe ranks fifth among major league players for hitting the most home runs in total World Series play. Play-ers who tied for a position in the top ten are shown by the same number, so that, if two men tied for fourth and fifth place, the appropriate information for both men would be followed by the small number "4," and the next man would be considered sixth in the ranking.

Year	Team		Games	BA	SA	AB	H	2B	3B	HR	HR%	R	RBI	BB	SO	SB	Pinch Hit AB	H	PO	A	E	DP	TC/G	FA	G by Pos

Hank Aaron

AARON, HENRY LOUIS
Brother of Tommie Aaron.
B. Feb. 5, 1934, Mobile, Ala.
Hall of Fame 1982.

BR TR 6' 180 lbs.

Year	Team		Games	BA	SA	AB	H	2B	3B	HR	HR%	R	RBI	BB	SO	SB	PH AB	PH H	PO	A	E	DP	TC/G	FA	G by Pos
1954	MIL	N	122	.280	.447	468	131	27	6	13	2.8	58	69	28	39	2	6	1	223	5	7	0	1.9	.970	OF-116
1955			153	.314	.540	602	189	37	9	27	4.5	105	106	49	61	3	2	1	340	93	15	25	2.9	.967	OF-126, 2B-27
1956			153	**.328**	.558	609	**200**	34	14	26	4.3	106	92	37	54	2	1	0	316	17	13	4	2.3	.962	OF-152
1957			151	.322	.600	615	198	27	6	**44**	7.2	118	**132**	57	58	1	0	0	346	9	6	0	2.4	.983	OF-150
1958			153	.326	.546	601	196	34	4	30	5.0	109	95	59	49	4	0	0	305	12	5	0	2.1	.984	OF-153
1959			154	**.355**	**.636**	629	**223**	46	7	39	6.2	116	123	51	54	8	0	0	263	22	5	3	1.9	.983	OF-152, 3B-5
1960			153	.292	.566	590	172	20	11	40	6.8	102	126	60	63	16	0	0	321	13	6	6	2.2	.982	OF-153, 2B-2
1961			155	.327	.594	603	197	**39**	10	34	5.6	115	120	56	64	21	1	0	379	15	7	3	2.6	.983	OF-154, 3B-2
1962			156	.323	.618	592	191	28	6	45	7.6	127	128	66	73	15	2	1	341	11	7	1	2.3	.981	OF-153, 1B-1
1963			161	.319	**.586**	631	201	29	4	**44**	7.0	121	**130**	78	94	31	0	0	267	10	6	1	1.8	.979	OF-161
1964			145	.328	.514	570	187	30	2	24	4.2	103	95	62	46	22	1	0	284	28	6	7	2.2	.981	OF-139, 2B-11
1965			150	.318	.560	570	181	**40**	1	32	5.6	109	89	60	81	24	2	1	298	9	4	2	2.1	.987	OF-148
1966	ATL	N	158	.279	.539	603	168	23	1	**44**	7.3	117	**127**	76	96	21	1	1	315	12	4	5	2.1	.979	OF-158, 2B-2
1967			155	.307	**.573**	600	184	37	3	**39**	6.5	**113**	109	63	97	17	3	0	322	12	7	3	2.2	.979	OF-152, 2B-1
1968			160	.287	.498	606	174	33	4	29	4.8	84	86	64	62	28	2	0	418	20	5	10	2.8	.989	OF-151, 1B-14
1969			147	.300	.607	547	164	30	3	44	8.0	100	97	87	47	9	0	0	299	13	5	6	2.2	.984	OF-144, 1B-4
1970			150	.298	.574	516	154	26	1	38	7.4	103	118	74	63	9	9	1	319	10	7	7	2.2	.979	OF-125, 1B-11
1971			139	.327	**.669**	495	162	22	3	47	**9.5**	95	118	71	58	1	8	2	733	40	5	56	5.6	**.994**	1B-71, OF-60
1972			129	.265	.514	449	119	10	0	34	7.6	75	77	92	55	4	5	2	996	70	17	75	8.4	.984	1B-109, OF-15
1973			120	.301	.643	392	118	12	1	40	10.2	84	96	68	51	1	11	3	206	5	5	0	1.8	.977	OF-105
1974			112	.268	.491	340	91	16	0	20	5.9	47	69	39	29	1	17	1	142	3	2	0	1.3	.986	OF-89
1975	MIL	A	137	.234	.355	465	109	16	2	12	2.6	45	60	70	51	0	5	1	2	0	0	0	0.0	1.000	DH-128, OF-3
1976			85	.229	.369	271	62	8	0	10	3.7	22	35	35	38	0	10	2	1	0	0	0	0.0	1.000	DH-74, OF-1
23 yrs.			3298	.305	.555	12364	3771	624	98	755	6.1	2174	2297	1402	1383	240	86	17	7436	429	144	214	2.4	.982	OF-2760, 1B-210, DH-202,
			3rd			2nd	3rd	8th		1st		2nd	1st												2B-43, 3B-7

LEAGUE CHAMPIONSHIP SERIES

Year	Team		Games	BA	SA	AB	H	2B	3B	HR	HR%	R	RBI	BB	SO	SB	PH AB	PH H	PO	A	E	DP	TC/G	FA	G by Pos
1969	ATL	N	3	.357	1.143	14	5	2	0	3	21.4	3	7	0	1	0	0	0	5	1	1	0	2.3	.857	OF-3

WORLD SERIES

Year	Team		Games	BA	SA	AB	H	2B	3B	HR	HR%	R	RBI	BB	SO	SB	PH AB	PH H	PO	A	E	DP	TC/G	FA	G by Pos
1957	MIL	N	7	.393	.786	28	11	0	1	3	10.7	5	7	1	6	0	0	0	11	0	0	0	1.6	1.000	OF-7
1958			7	.333	.407	27	9	2	0	0	0.0	3	2	4	6	0	0	0	14	0	0	0	2.0	1.000	OF-7
2 yrs.			14	.364	.600	55	20	2	1	3	5.5	8	9	5	12	0	0	0	25	0	0	0	1.8	1.000	OF-14
				5th																					

Tommie Aaron

AARON, TOMMIE LEE
Brother of Hank Aaron.
B. Aug. 5, 1939, Mobile, Ala. D. Aug. 16, 1984, Atlanta, Ga.

BR TR 6'3" 190 lbs.

Year	Team		Games	BA	SA	AB	H	2B	3B	HR	HR%	R	RBI	BB	SO	SB	PH AB	PH H	PO	A	E	DP	TC/G	FA	G by Pos
1962	MIL	N	141	.231	.374	334	77	20	2	8	2.4	54	38	41	58	6	11	3	572	48	10	56	4.5	.984	1B-110, OF-42, 3B-1, 2B-1
1963			72	.200	.281	135	27	6	1	1	0.7	6	15	11	27	0	16	2	221	18	1	28	3.3	.996	1B-45, OF-14, 2B-6, 3B-1
1965			8	.188	.188	16	3	0	0	0	0.0	1	1	1	2	0	2	1	45	4	2	3	6.4	.961	1B-6
1968	ATL	N	98	.244	.311	283	69	10	3	1	0.4	21	25	21	37	3	18	3	287	20	5	13	3.2	.984	OF-62, 1B-28, 3B-1
1969			49	.250	.333	60	15	2	0	1	1.7	13	5	6	6	0	23	4	65	2	0	5	1.4	1.000	1B-16, OF-8
1970			44	.206	.333	63	13	2	0	2	3.2	3	7	3	10	0	16	2	53	2	2	1	1.3	.965	1B-16, OF-12
1971			25	.226	.264	53	12	2	0	0	0.0	4	3	3	5	0	6	2	74	19	2	18	3.8	.979	1B-11, 3B-7
7 yrs.			437	.229	.327	944	216	42	6	13	1.4	102	94	86	145	9	92	17	1317	113	22	124	3.3	.985	1B-232, OF-138, 3B-10, 2B-7

LEAGUE CHAMPIONSHIP SERIES

Year	Team		Games	BA	SA	AB	H	2B	3B	HR	HR%	R	RBI	BB	SO	SB	PH AB	PH H	PO	A	E	DP	TC/G	FA	G by Pos
1969	ATL	N	1	.000	.000	1	0	0	0	0	0.0	0	0	0	0	0	1	0	0	0	0	0	0.0	—	

Ed Abbaticchio

ABBATICCHIO, EDWARD JAMES
B. Apr. 15, 1877, Latrobe, Pa. D. Jan. 6, 1957, Fort Lauderdale, Fla.

BR TR 5'11" 170 lbs.

Year	Team		Games	BA	SA	AB	H	2B	3B	HR	HR%	R	RBI	BB	SO	SB	PH AB	PH H	PO	A	E	DP	TC/G	FA	G by Pos
1897	PHI	N	3	.300	.300	10	3	0	0	0	0.0	0		0				0	7	1	0	2.7	.875	2B-3
1898			25	.228	.272	92	21	4	0	0	0.0	9	14	7		4	0	0	36	25	12	0	2.9	.836	3B-20, 2B-4, OF-1
1903	BOS	N	136	.227	.290	489	111	18	5	1	0.2	61	46	52		23	3	1	361	367	55	43	5.8	.926	2B-116, SS-17
1904			154	.256	.337	579	148	18	10	3	0.5	76	54	40		24	0	0	367	473	78	47	6.0	.915	SS-154
1905			153	.279	.374	**610**	170	25	12	3	0.5	70	41	35		30	0	0	387	468	75	53	6.1	.919	SS-152, OF-1
1907	PIT	N	147	.262	.331	496	130	14	7	2	0.4	63	82	65		35	0	0	320	380	36	37	5.0	.951	2B-147
1908			146	.250	.316	500	125	16	7	1	0.2	43	61	58		22	2	0	268	423	22	42	4.9	.969	2B-144
1909			36	.230	.264	87	20	0	0	1	1.1	13	16	19		2	11	2	57	74	10	6	3.9	.929	SS-18, 2B-4, OF-1
1910	2 teams		PIT N	(3G –	.000)		BOS N	(52G –	.247)																
"	total		55	.243	.287	181	44	4	2	0	0.0	20	10	12	16	2	7	0	77	151	23	19	4.6	.908	SS-47, 2B-1
9 yrs.			855	.254	.325	3044	772	99	43	11	0.4	355	324	289	16	142	23	3	1873	2368	315	247	5.3	.931	2B-419, SS-388, 3B-20, OF-3

WORLD SERIES

Year	Team		Games	BA	SA	AB	H	2B	3B	HR	HR%	R	RBI	BB	SO	SB	PH AB	PH H	PO	A	E	DP	TC/G	FA	G by Pos
1909	PIT	N	1	.000	.000	1	0	0	0	0	0.0	0	0	0	1	0	1	0	0	0	0	0	0.0	—	

Charlie Abbey

ABBEY, CHARLES S.
B. Oct., 1868, Falls City, Neb. Deceased.

BL 5'8½" 169 lbs.

Year	Team		Games	BA	SA	AB	H	2B	3B	HR	HR%	R	RBI	BB	SO	SB	PH AB	PH H	PO	A	E	DP	TC/G	FA	G by Pos
1893	WAS	N	31	.259	.336	116	30	1	4	0	0.0	11	12	12	6	9	0	0	68	6	5	1	2.5	.937	OF-31
1894			129	.314	.472	523	164	26	18	7	1.3	95	101	58	38	31	0	0	344	26	37	6	3.2	.909	OF-129
1895			132	.276	.389	511	141	14	10	8	1.6	102	84	43	41	28	0	0	275	32	33	7	2.6	.903	OF-132
1896			79	.262	.352	301	79	12	6	1	0.3	47	49	27	20	16	2	1	105	10	16	0	1.7	.878	OF-78, P-1
1897			80	.260	.390	300	78	14	8	3	1.0	52	34	27		9	0	0	126	14	8	1	1.9	.946	OF-80
5 yrs.			451	.281	.404	1751	492	67	46	19	1.1	307	280	167	105	93	2	1	918	88	99	15	2.5	.910	OF-450, P-1

Fred Abbott

ABBOTT, HARRY FREDERICK (Faithful Fred)
Born Harry Frederick Winbigler.
B. Oct. 22, 1874, Versailles, Ohio D. June 11, 1935, Los Angeles, Calif.

BR TR 5'10" 180 lbs.

Year	Team	Games	BA	SA	AB	H	2B	3B	HR	HR%	R	RBI	BB	SO	SB	Pinch Hit AB	Pinch Hit H	PO	A	E	DP	TC/G	FA	G by Pos

Fred Abbott *continued*

1903	CLE A	77	.235	.314	255	60	11	3	1	0.4	25	25	7		8	3	0	357	101	19	10	6.2	.960	C-71, 1B-3
1904		41	.169	.231	130	22	4	2	0	0.0	14	12	6		2	1	0	216	41	10	5	6.5	.963	C-33, 1B-7
1905	PHI N	42	.195	.258	128	25	6	1	0	0.0	9	12	6		4	2	0	195	43	11	11	5.9	.956	C-34, 1B-5
3 yrs.		160	.209	.279	513	107	21	6	1	0.2	48	49	19		14	6	0	768	185	40	26	6.2	.960	C-138, 1B-15

Ody Abbott

ABBOTT, ODY CLEON (Toby)
B. Sept. 5, 1888, New Eagle, Pa.   D. Apr. 13, 1933, Washington, D. C.

BR TR 6'2"   180 lbs.

| 1910 | STL N | 22 | .186 | .243 | 70 | 13 | 2 | 1 | 0 | 0.0 | 2 | 6 | 6 | 20 | 3 | 1 | 0 | 52 | 2 | 1 | 2 | 2.5 | .982 | OF-21 |

Cliff Aberson

ABERSON, CLIFFORD ALEXANDER
B. Aug. 28, 1921, Chicago, Ill.   D. June 23, 1973, Vallejo, Calif.

BR TR 6'   200 lbs.

1947	CHI N	47	.279	.450	140	39	6	3	4	2.9	24	20	20	32	0	6	2	62	7	6	1	1.6	.920	OF-40
1948		12	.188	.313	32	6	1	0	1	3.1	1	6	5	10	0	3	1	12	1	2	1	1.3	.867	OF-8
1949		4	.000	.000	7	0	0	0	0	0.0	0	0	0	2	0	3	0	2	0	0	0	0.5	1.000	OF-1
3 yrs.		63	.251	.408	179	45	7	3	5	2.8	25	26	25	44	0	12	3	76	8	8	2	1.5	.913	OF-49

Shawn Abner

ABNER, SHAWN WESLEY
B. June 17, 1966, Hamilton, Ohio

BR TR 6'1"   190 lbs.

1987	SD N	16	.277	.511	47	13	3	1	2	4.3	9	7	2	8	1	3	1	23	2	1	1	1.7	.926	OF-14
1988		37	.181	.289	83	15	3	0	2	2.4	6	5	4	19	0	0	0	55	1	1	1	1.5	.982	OF-35
1989		57	.176	.275	102	18	4	0	2	2.0	13	14	5	20	1	8	1	67	0	0	0	1.2	1.000	OF-51
3 yrs.		110	.198	.328	232	46	10	1	6	2.6	24	26	11	47	2	11	2	145	3	3	2	1.4	.980	OF-100

Cal Abrams

ABRAMS, CALVIN ROSS (Abie)
B. Mar. 2, 1924, Philadelphia, Pa.

BL TL 6'   180 lbs.

1949	BKN N	8	.083	.125	24	2	1	0	0	0.0	6	0	7	6	1	1	0	9	1	2	0	1.5	.833	OF-7
1950		38	.205	.227	44	9	1	0	0	0.0	5	4	9	13	0	20	4	17	0	0	0	0.4	1.000	OF-15
1951		67	.280	.393	150	42	8	0	3	2.0	27	19	36	26	3	22	5	64	3	4	1	1.1	.944	OF-34
1952	2 teams		BKN N	(10G – .200)			CIN N	(71G – .278)																
"	total	81	.274	.387	168	46	9	2	2	1.2	24	13	21	29	1	35	4	87	1	0	1	1.1	1.000	OF-46
1953	PIT N	119	.286	.435	448	128	10	6	15	3.3	66	43	58	70	4	7	2	205	13	6	3	1.9	.973	OF-112
1954	2 teams		PIT N	(17G – .143)			BAL A	(115G – .293)																
"	total	132	.280	.402	465	130	23	8	6	1.3	73	27	82	76	1	5	1	271	8	6	1	2.2	.979	OF-128
1955	BAL A	118	.243	.359	309	75	12	3	6	1.9	56	32	89	69	2	16	2	195	7	3	1	1.7	.985	OF-96, 1B-4
1956	CHI A	4	.333	.333	3	1	0	0	0	0.0	0	0	2	1	0	2	1	2	0	0	0	0.5	1.000	OF-2
8 yrs.		567	.269	.392	1611	433	64	19	32	2.0	257	138	304	290	12	108	21	850	33	21	7	1.6	.977	OF-440, 1B-4

Joe Abreu

ABREU, JOSEPH LAWRENCE (The Magician)
B. May 24, 1916, Oakland, Calif.

BR TR 5'8"   160 lbs.

| 1942 | CIN N | 9 | .214 | .357 | 28 | 6 | 0 | 1 | 1 | 3.6 | 3 | 4 | 4 | 4 | 0 | 1 | 0 | 9 | 15 | 1 | 0 | 2.8 | .960 | 3B-6, 2B-2 |

Bill Abstein

ABSTEIN, WILLIAM HENRY (Big Bill)
B. Feb. 2, 1885, St. Louis, Mo.   D. Apr. 8, 1940, St. Louis, Mo.

BR TR 6'   185 lbs.

1906	PIT N	8	.200	.200	20	4	0	0	0	0.0	2	3	0		2	3	0	5	8	3	0	2.0	.813	2B-3, OF-2
1909		137	.260	.344	512	133	20	10	1	0.2	51	70	27		16	2	0	1412	65	27	70	11.0	.982	1B-135
1910	STL A	25	.149	.172	87	13	2	0	0	0.0	1	3	2		3	2	0	268	20	11	13	12.0	.963	1B-23
3 yrs.		170	.242	.315	619	150	22	10	1	0.2	54	76	29		21	7	0	1685	93	41	83	10.7	.977	1B-158, 2B-3, OF-2

WORLD SERIES

| 1909 | PIT N | 7 | .231 | .308 | 26 | 6 | 2 | 0 | 0 | 0.0 | 3 | 2 | 3 | 10 | 1 | 0 | 0 | 70 | 4 | 5 | 3 | 11.3 | .937 | 1B-7 |

Merito Acosta

ACOSTA, BALDOMERO PEDRO
Brother of Jose Acosta.
B. May 19, 1896, Havana, Cuba   D. Nov. 17, 1963, Miami, Fla.

BL TL 5'7"   140 lbs.

1913	WAS A	9	.300	.400	20	6	0	1	0	0.0	3	1	2		2	1	1	5	0	2	0	0.8	.714	OF-7
1914		38	.257	.338	74	19	2	2	0	0.0	10	4	11	18	3	12	2	24	6	5	1	0.9	.857	OF-24
1915		72	.209	.245	163	34	4	1	0	0.0	20	18	28	15	8	15	4	75	4	3	2	1.1	.963	OF-53
1916		4	.143	.143	7	1	0	0	0	0.0	0	0	2		0	0	0	10	1	0	0	2.8	1.000	OF-4
1918	2 teams		WAS A	(3G – .000)			PHI A	(49G – .302)																
"	total	52	.298	.351	171	51	3	3	0	0.0	23	14	18	11	4	6	1	77	7	5	2	1.7	.944	OF-45
5 yrs.		175	.255	.308	435	111	9	7	0	0.0	56	37	63	46	17	35	8	191	18	15	5	1.3	.933	OF-133

Jerry Adair

ADAIR, KENNETH JERRY
B. Dec. 17, 1936, Sand Springs, Okla.   D. May 31, 1987, Tulsa, Okla.

BR TR 6'   175 lbs.

1958	BAL A	11	.105	.105	19	2	0	1	0	0.0	0	1	7		0	0	0	11	23	2	5	3.3	.944	SS-10, 2B-1
1959		12	.314	.371	35	11	0	1	0	0.0	3	2	1	5	0	0	0	26	19	4	5	4.1	.918	2B-11, SS-1
1960		3	.200	.800	5	1	0	0	1	20.0	1	1	0	0	0	0	0	3	4	0	2	2.3	1.000	2B-3
1961		133	.264	.394	386	102	21	1	9	2.3	41	37	35	51	5	0	0	259	299	11	62	4.3	.981	2B-107, SS-27, 3B-2
1962		139	.284	.414	538	153	29	4	11	2.0	67	48	27	77	7	4	0	295	362	20	89	4.9	.970	SS-113, 2B-34, 3B-1
1963		109	.228	.346	382	87	21	3	6	1.6	34	30	9	51	3	5	2	242	268	8	67	4.8	.985	2B-103
1964		155	.248	.341	569	141	20	3	9	1.6	56	47	28	72	3	2	1	395	422	5	107	5.3	.994	2B-153
1965		157	.259	.351	582	151	26	3	7	1.2	51	66	35	65	6	0	0	395	446	12	99	5.4	.986	2B-157
1966	2 teams		BAL A	(17G – .288)			CHI A	(105G – .243)																
"	total	122	.249	.332	422	105	19	2	4	0.9	30	39	21	52	3	4	1	228	361	14	61	4.9	.977	SS-75, 2B-63
1967	2 teams		CHI A	(28G – .204)			BOS A	(89G – .291)																
"	total	117	.271	.338	414	112	17	1	3	0.7	47	35	17	52	1	8	2	77	72	2	22	1.3	.987	2B-50, 3B-35, SS-30
1968	BOS A	74	.216	.250	208	45	1	0	2	1.0	18	12	9	28	0	13	3	90	139	8	22	3.2	.966	2B-46, 2B-12, 3B-7, 1B-1
1969	KC A	126	.250	.310	432	108	9	1	5	1.2	29	48	9	36	1	6	1	237	279	9	42	4.2	.983	2B-109, SS-8, 3B-1
1970		7	.148	.148	27	4	0	0	0	0.0	0	0	1	5	3	0	0	24	6	0	6	6.3	1.000	2B-7
13 yrs.		1165	.254	.347	4019	1022	163	19	57	1.4	378	366	208	499	29	42	10	2282	2714	95	589	4.4	.981	2B-810, SS-310, 3B-46, 1B-1

Year	Team		Games	BA	SA	AB	H	2B	3B	HR	HR%	R	RBI	BB	SO	SB	Pinch Hit AB	H	PO	A	E	DP	TC/G	FA	G by Pos

Jerry Adair *continued*
WORLD SERIES

Year	Team		Games	BA	SA	AB	H	2B	3B	HR	HR%	R	RBI	BB	SO	SB	PH AB	H	PO	A	E	DP	TC/G	FA	G by Pos
1967	BOS	A	5	.125	.125	16	2	0	0	0	0.0	0	1	0	3	1	0	0	7	11	0	1	3.6	1.000	2B-4

Jimmy Adair
ADAIR, JAMES AUDREY (Choppy)
B. Jan. 25, 1907, Waxahachie, Tex. D. Dec. 9, 1982, Dallas, Tex.
BR TR 5'10½" 154 lbs.

| 1931 | CHI | N | 18 | .276 | .342 | 76 | 21 | 3 | 1 | 0 | 0.0 | 9 | 3 | 1 | 8 | 1 | 0 | 0 | 37 | 55 | 5 | 9 | 5.4 | .948 | SS-18 |

Ricky Adams
ADAMS, RICKY LEE
B. Jan. 21, 1959, Upland, Calif.
BR TR 6'2" 180 lbs.

1982	CAL	A	8	.143	.143	14	2	0	0	0	0.0	1	0	0	2	1	1	1	6	12	1	4	2.4	.947	SS-8
1983			58	.250	.321	112	28	2	0	2	1.8	22	6	5	23	1	0	0	58	141	8	29	3.6	.961	SS-38, 3B-16, 2B-4
1985	SF	N	54	.190	.281	121	23	3	1	2	1.7	12	10	5	23	1	4	1	35	101	5	13	2.6	.965	SS-38, 3B-16, 2B-6
3 yrs.			120	.215	.291	247	53	5	1	4	1.6	35	16	10	37	3	5	2	99	254	14	46	3.1	.962	SS-71, 3B-32, 2B-10

Bert Adams
ADAMS, JOHN BERTRAM
B. June 21, 1891, Wharton, Tex. D. June 24, 1940, Los Angeles, Calif.
BB TR 6'1" 185 lbs.

1910	CLE	A	5	.231	.231	13	3	0	0	0	0.0	1	0	0		0	0	0	12	15	1	1	5.6	.964	C-5
1911			2	.200	.200	5	1	0	0	0	0.0	0	0	1		0	0	0	6	3	1	0	5.0	.900	C-2
1912			20	.204	.278	54	11	2	1	0	0.0	5	6	4		0	0	0	85	28	7	3	6.0	.942	C-20
1915	PHI	N	24	.111	.111	27	3	0	0	0	0.0	1	2	2	3	0	0	0	34	6	2	0	1.8	.952	C-23, 1B-1
1916			11	.231	.231	13	3	0	0	0	0.0	2	1	0	3	0	1	0	20	6	2	1	2.5	.929	C-11
1917			43	.206	.290	107	22	4	1	1	0.9	4	7	0	20	0	4	1	135	40	1	4	4.1	.994	C-38, 1B-1
1918			84	.176	.194	227	40	4	0	0	0.0	10	12	10	26	5	8	3	261	69	8	8	4.0	.976	C-76
1919			78	.233	.293	232	54	7	2	1	0.4	14	17	6	27	4	4	0	249	90	12	15	4.5	.966	C-73
8 yrs.			267	.202	.248	678	137	17	4	2	0.3	37	45	23	79	9	17	4	802	257	34	32	4.1	.969	C-248, 1B-2

Bob Adams
ADAMS, ROBERT MELVIN
B. Jan. 6, 1952, Pittsburgh, Pa.
BR TR 6'2" 200 lbs.

| 1977 | DET | A | 15 | .250 | .542 | 24 | 6 | 1 | 0 | 2 | 8.3 | 2 | 2 | 0 | 5 | 0 | 12 | 4 | 26 | 1 | 0 | 1 | 1.8 | 1.000 | 1B-2, C-1 |

Bobby Adams
ADAMS, ROBERT HENRY
Brother of Dick Adams. Father of Mike Adams.
B. Dec. 14, 1921, Tuolumne, Calif.
BR TR 5'10½" 160 lbs.

1946	CIN	N	94	.244	.344	311	76	13	3	4	1.3	35	24	18	32	16	13	4	192	252	15	67	4.9	.967	2B-74, OF-2, 3B-1
1947			81	.272	.396	217	59	11	2	4	1.8	39	20	25	23	9	1	1	172	177	12	46	4.5	.967	2B-69
1948			87	.298	.408	262	78	20	3	1	0.4	33	21	25	23	6	14	5	167	155	11	34	3.8	.967	2B-64, 3B-7
1949			107	.253	.325	277	70	16	2	0	0.0	32	25	26	36	4	23	6	176	160	7	29	3.2	.980	2B-63, 3B-4
1950			115	.282	.414	348	98	21	8	3	0.9	57	25	43	29	7	9	1	170	200	14	34	3.3	.964	2B-53, 3B-42
1951			125	.266	.357	403	107	12	5	5	1.2	57	24	43	40	4	30	10	184	215	18	33	3.3	.957	3B-60, 2B-42, OF-1
1952			154	.283	.363	637	180	25	4	6	0.9	85	48	49	67	11	0	0	176	328	20	28	3.4	.962	3B-154
1953			150	.275	.357	607	167	14	6	8	1.3	99	49	58	67	3	0	0	159	324	25	39	3.4	.951	3B-150
1954			150	.269	.387	390	105	25	6	3	0.8	69	23	55	46	2	11	4	134	189	16	25	3.1	.953	3B-93, 2B-2
1955	2 teams				CIN N (64G – .273)		CHI A (28G – .095)																			
"	total		92	.251	.386	171	43	11	3	2	1.2	31	23	24	25	2	20	5	47	105	5	13	1.7	.968	3B-51, 2B-6
1956	BAL	A	41	.225	.297	111	25	6	1	0	0.0	19	7	25	15	1	0	0	62	65	5	12	3.2	.962	3B-24, 2B-18
1957	CHI	N	60	.251	.342	187	47	10	2	1	0.5	21	10	17	28	0	8	1	44	68	6	5	2.0	.949	3B-47, 2B-1
1958			62	.281	.406	96	27	4	0	0	0.0	14	4	6	15	2	35	9	63	24	3	6	1.5	.967	1B-11, 3B-9, 2B-7
1959			3	.000	.000	2	0	0	0	0	0.0	0	0	0	0	0	1	0	2	0	1	0	1.0	.667	1B-1
14 yrs.			1281	.269	.368	4019	1082	188	49	37	0.9	591	303	414	447	67	166	46	1748	2262	158	371	3.3	.962	3B-652, 2B-399, 1B-12, OF-3

Buster Adams
ADAMS, ELVIN CLARK
B. June 24, 1915, Trinidad, Colo.
BR TR 6' 180 lbs.

1939	STL	N	2	.000	.000	1	0	0	0	0	0.0	1	0	1	0	0	1	0	0	0	0	0	0.0	–	
1943	2 teams	STL	N (8G – .091)		PHI	N (111G – .256)																				
"	total		119	.252	.347	429	108	15	4	4	0.9	49	39	43	71	2	1	0	309	6	5	8	2.7	.984	OF-113
1944	PHI	N	151	.283	.440	584	165	35	4	17	2.9	86	64	74	74	2	0	0	449	14	10	1	3.1	.979	OF-151
1945	2 teams	PHI	N (14G – .232)		STL	N (140G – .292)																				
"	total		154	.287	.440	634	182	29	4	22	3.5	104	109	62	80	3	0	0	408	9	9	3	2.8	.979	OF-153
1946	STL	N	81	.185	.306	173	32	6	0	5	2.9	21	22	29	27	3	21	6	95	1	1	1	1.2	.990	OF-58
1947	PHI	N	69	.247	.352	182	45	11	1	2	1.1	21	15	26	29	2	15	6	78	5	4	2	1.3	.954	OF-51
6 yrs.			576	.266	.400	2003	532	96	12	50	2.5	282	249	234	281	12	39	13	1339	35	29	15	2.4	.979	OF-526

Dick Adams
ADAMS, RICHARD LEROY
Brother of Bobby Adams.
B. Apr. 8, 1920, Tuolumne, Calif.
BR TL 6' 185 lbs.

| 1947 | PHI | A | 37 | .202 | .360 | 89 | 18 | 2 | 3 | 2 | 2.2 | 9 | 11 | 2 | 18 | 0 | 10 | 1 | 171 | 17 | 1 | 19 | 5.1 | .995 | 1B-24, OF-3 |

Doug Adams
ADAMS, HAROLD DOUGLAS
B. Jan. 27, 1943, Blue River, Wis.
BL TR 6'3" 185 lbs.

| 1969 | CHI | A | 8 | .214 | .214 | 14 | 3 | 0 | 0 | 0 | 0.0 | 1 | 1 | 1 | 3 | 0 | 5 | 2 | 9 | 2 | 0 | 0 | 1.4 | 1.000 | C-4 |

George Adams
ADAMS, GEORGE (Partridge)
B. Grafton, Mass. Deceased.

| 1879 | SYR | N | 4 | .231 | .231 | 13 | 3 | 0 | 0 | 0 | 0.0 | 0 | 0 | 1 | 1 | | 0 | 0 | 21 | 0 | 4 | 0 | 6.3 | .840 | OF-2, 1B-2 |

Glenn Adams
ADAMS, GLENN CHARLES
B. Oct. 4, 1947, Northbridge, Mass.
BL TR 6'1" 180 lbs.

| 1975 | SF | N | 61 | .300 | .478 | 90 | 27 | 2 | 1 | 4 | 4.4 | 10 | 15 | 11 | 25 | 1 | 33 | 12 | 31 | 1 | 2 | 0 | 0.6 | .941 | OF-25 |

Year	Team		Games	BA	SA	AB	H	2B	3B	HR	HR%	R	RBI	BB	SO	SB	Pinch Hit AB	Pinch Hit H	PO	A	E	DP	TC/G	FA	G by Pos

Glenn Adams *continued*

1976			69	.243	.297	74	18	4	0	0	0.0	2	3	1	12	1	59	13	3	0	0	0	0.0	1.000	OF-6
1977	MIN	A	95	.338	.468	269	91	17	0	6	2.2	32	49	18	30	0	11	6	60	3	2	1	0.7	.969	DH-47, OF-44
1978			116	.258	.390	310	80	18	1	7	2.3	27	35	17	32	0	23	8	5	0	0	0	1.000	DH-101, OF-5
1979			119	.301	.420	326	98	13	1	8	2.5	34	50	25	27	2	21	2	66	0	3	0	0.6	.958	DH-55, OF-53
1980			99	.286	.412	262	75	11	2	6	2.3	32	38	15	26	2	16	2	18	0	1	0	0.2	.947	DH-81, OF-12
1981			72	.209	.282	220	46	10	4	2	0.9	13	24	20	26	0	13	6	0	0	0	0	0.0	–	DH-62
1982	TOR	A	30	.258	.364	66	17	4	0	1	1.5	2	11	4	5	0	9	2	0	0	0	0	0.0	–	DH-27
8 yrs.			661	.280	.398	1617	452	79	5	34	2.1	152	225	111	183	6	185	51	183	6	8	1	0.3	.959	DH-373, OF-145

Herb Adams

ADAMS, HERBERT LOREN
B. Apr. 14, 1928, Hollywood, Calif.

BL TL 5'9" 160 lbs.

1948	CHI	A	5	.273	.364	11	3	1	0	0	0.0	1	1	0	0	0	0	0	10	2	0	0	2.4	1.000	OF-4
1949			56	.293	.346	208	61	5	3	0	0.0	26	16	9	16	1	5	1	112	4	3	1	2.1	.975	OF-48
1950			34	.203	.271	118	24	2	3	0	0.0	12	2	12	7	3	1	0	90	1	2	0	2.7	.978	OF-33
3 yrs.			95	.261	.320	337	88	8	6	0	0.0	39	18	22	24	4	6	1	212	7	5	1	2.4	.978	OF-85

Jim Adams

ADAMS, JOHN J.
B. 1868, East St. Louis, Ill.   Deceased.

TR

| 1890 | STL | AA | 1 | .250 | .250 | 4 | 1 | 0 | 0 | 0 | | 0 | | 0 | 0 | 0 | 0 | 0 | 4 | 1 | 0 | 0 | 5.0 | 1.000 | C-1 |

Mike Adams

ADAMS, ROBERT MICHAEL
Son of Bobby Adams.
B. July 22, 1948, Cincinnati, Ohio

BR TR 5'9" 180 lbs.

1972	MIN	A	3	.333	.333	6	2	0	0	0	0.0	0	1	0	1	0	1	0	1	0	0	0	0.3	1.000	OF-1
1973			55	.212	.379	66	14	2	0	3	4.5	21	6	17	18	2	1	0	45	0	1	0	0.8	.978	OF-24, DH-2
1976	CHI	N	25	.138	.207	29	4	2	0	0	0.0	1	2	8	7	0	16	1	4	0	0	0	0.2	1.000	OF-4, 3B-3, 2B-1
1977			2	.000	.000	2	0	0	0	0	0.0	0	0	0	1	0	1	0	0	0	0	0	0.0	–	OF-2
1978	OAK	A	15	.200	.267	15	3	1	0	0	0.0	5	1	7	2	0	5	0	7	6	0	2	0.9	1.000	2B-6, DH-3, 3B-3
5 yrs.			100	.195	.314	118	23	5	0	3	2.5	27	9	32	29	2	24	1	57	8	1	2	0.7	.985	OF-31, 2B-7, 3B-6, DH-5

Sparky Adams

ADAMS, EARL JOHN
B. Aug. 26, 1894, Zerbe, Pa.   D. Feb. 24, 1989, Pottsville, Pa.

BR TR 5'5½" 151 lbs.

1922	CHI	N	11	.250	.295	44	11	0	1	0	0.0	5	3	4	3	1	0	0	18	35	5	5	5.3	.914	2B-11
1923			95	.289	.367	311	90	12	0	4	1.3	40	35	26	10	20	10	4	156	249	28	45	4.6	.935	SS-79, OF-1
1924			117	.280	.337	418	117	11	5	1	0.2	66	27	40	20	15	7	2	224	343	31	79	5.1	.948	SS-88, 2B-19
1925			149	.287	.368	627	180	29	8	2	0.3	95	48	44	15	26	0		367	573	16	95	6.4	.983	2B-144, SS-5
1926			154	.309	.375	624	193	35	3	0	0.0	95	39	52	27	27	2	0	338	523	31	97	5.8	.965	2B-136, 3B-19, SS-2
1927			146	.292	.340	647	189	17	7	0	0.0	100	49	42	26	26	0		317	440	19	68	5.7	.976	2B-107, SS-27, OF-1
1928	PIT	N	135	.276	.325	539	149	14	6	0	0.0	91	38	64	18	8	1	0	75	130	17	14	3.0	.923	SS-30, 2B-20, 3B-15, OF-2
1929			74	.260	.311	196	51	8	0	0	0.0	37	11	15	5	3	4	2	140	264	16	46	3.1	.962	3B-104, 2B-25, SS-7
1930	STL	N	137	.314	.409	570	179	36	9	0	0.0	98	55	45	27	7	2	1	127	239	18	30	2.7	.953	3B-138, SS-6
1931			143	.293	.390	608	178	46	5	1	0.2	97	40	42	24	16	1	0	25	42	5	11	2.3	.931	3B-30
1932			31	.276	.315	127	35	3	1	0	0.0	22	13	14	5	0			25	42	5	11	2.3	.931	3B-30
1933	2 teams		STL N (8G – .167)		CIN N (137G – .262)																				
"	total		145	.257	.305	568	146	22	1	1	0.2	60	22	45	33	3	0	0	132	311	18	19	3.2	.961	3B-135, SS-13
1934	CIN	N	87	.252	.317	278	70	16	1	0	0.0	38	14	20	10	2	12	4	92	156	8	21	2.9	.969	3B-38, 2B-29
13 yrs.			1424	.286	.353	5557	1588	249	48	9	0.2	844	394	453	223	154	39	13	2287	3748	230	599	4.4	.963	2B-551, 3B-532, SS-297, OF-4

WORLD SERIES

1930	STL	N	6	.143	.143	21	3	0	0	0	0.0	0	1	0	4	0	0	0	4	7	0	1	1.8	1.000	3B-6
1931			2	.250	.250	4	1	0	0	0	0.0	0	0	0	1	0	0	0	0	1	0	0	0.5	1.000	3B-2
2 yrs.			8	.160	.160	25	4	0	0	0	0.0	0	1	0	5	0	0	0	4	8	0	1	1.5	1.000	3B-8

Spencer Adams

ADAMS, SPENCER DEWEY
B. July 21, 1898, Layton, Utah   D. Nov. 24, 1970, Salt Lake City, Utah

BL TR 5'9" 158 lbs.

1923	PIT	N	25	.250	.286	56	14	0	1	0	0.0	11	4	6	6	2	1	1	25	33	7	5	2.6	.892	2B-11, SS-6
1925	WAS	A	39	.273	.382	55	15	4	1	0	0.0	11	4	5	4	1	1	0	30	30	6	4	1.7	.909	2B-15, SS-8, 3B-3
1926	NY	A	28	.120	.160	25	3	1	0	0	0.0	7	1	3	7	1	10	0	11	10	0	2	0.8	1.000	2B-4, 3B-1
1927	STL	A	88	.266	.332	259	69	11	3	0	0.0	32	29	24	33	1	5	0	159	190	21	35	4.2	.943	2B-54, 3B-28
4 yrs.			180	.256	.322	395	101	16	5	0	0.0	61	38	38	50	5	17	1	225	263	34	46	2.9	.935	2B-84, 3B-32, SS-14

WORLD SERIES

1925	WAS	A	2	.000	.000	1	0	0	0	0	0.0	0	0	0	1	0	0	0	0	0	0	0	0.0	–	2B-1
1926	NY	A	2	–	–	0	0	0	0	0	–	0	0	0	0	0	0	0	0	0	0	0	0.0	–	2B-1
2 yrs.			4	.000	.000	1	0	0	0	0	0.0	0	0	0	1	0	0	0	0	0	0	0	0.0	–	2B-1

Joe Adcock

ADCOCK, JOSEPH WILBUR
B. Oct. 30, 1927, Coushatta, La.
Manager 1967.

BR TR 6'4" 210 lbs.

1950	CIN	N	102	.293	.406	372	109	16	1	8	2.2	46	55	24	24	2	4	0	346	17	8	16	3.6	.978	OF-75, 1B-24
1951			113	.243	.380	395	96	16	4	10	2.5	40	47	24	29	1	5	2	221	8	4	2	2.1	.983	OF-107
1952			117	.278	.460	378	105	22	4	13	3.4	43	52	23	38	1	14	4	306	8	3	8	2.7	.991	OF-85, 1B-17
1953	MIL	N	157	.285	.453	590	168	33	6	18	3.1	71	80	42	82	3	0	0	1389	96	13	146	9.5	.991	1B-157
1954			133	.308	.520	500	154	27	5	23	4.6	73	87	44	58	1	1	1	1229	67	6	125	9.8	.995	1B-133
1955			84	.264	.469	288	76	14	0	15	5.2	40	45	31	44	1	5	1	725	44	8	68	9.3	.990	1B-78
1956			137	.291	.597	454	132	23	1	38	8.4	76	103	32	86	1	8	2	1086	75	6	109	8.5	.995	1B-129
1957			65	.287	.541	209	60	13	2	12	5.7	31	38	20	51	0	6	1	477	30	2	60	7.8	.996	1B-56
1958			105	.275	.506	320	88	15	1	19	5.9	40	54	21	63	0	14	3	564	37	7	55	5.8	.988	1B-71, OF-22
1959			115	.292	.535	404	118	19	2	25	6.2	53	76	32	77	0	10	3	807	81	7	67	7.8	.992	1B-89, OF-25
1960			138	.298	.500	514	153	21	4	25	4.9	55	91	46	86	1	4	2	1229	104	9	105	9.7	.993	1B-136

Year Team	Games	BA	SA	AB	H	2B	3B	HR	HR%	R	RBI	BB	SO	SB	Pinch Hit AB	Pinch Hit H	PO	A	E	DP	TC/G	FA	G by Pos

Joe Adcock *continued*

Year Team	Games	BA	SA	AB	H	2B	3B	HR	HR%	R	RBI	BB	SO	SB	PH AB	PH H	PO	A	E	DP	TC/G	FA	G by Pos
1961	152	.285	.507	562	160	20	0	35	6.2	77	108	59	94	2	4	1	1471	102	11	133	10.4	.993	1B-148
1962	121	.248	.506	391	97	12	1	29	7.4	48	78	50	91	2	8	3	907	57	3	72	8.0	.997	1B-112
1963 CLE A	97	.251	.420	283	71	7	1	13	4.6	28	49	30	53	1	22	5	608	36	3	46	6.7	.995	1B-78
1964 LA A	118	.268	.475	366	98	13	0	21	5.7	39	64	48	61	0	11	4	959	54	7	94	8.6	.993	1B-105
1965 CAL A	122	.241	.401	349	84	14	0	14	4.0	30	47	37	74	2	23	4	789	45	3	68	6.9	.996	1B-97
1966	83	.273	.576	231	63	10	3	18	7.8	33	48	31	48	2	16	4	565	39	2	60	7.3	.997	1B-71
17 yrs.	1959	.277	.485	6606	1832	295	35	336	5.1	823	1122	594	1059	20	153	39	13678	900	102	1234	7.5	.993	1B-1501, OF-310

WORLD SERIES

Year Team	Games	BA	SA	AB	H	2B	3B	HR	HR%	R	RBI	BB	SO	SB	PH AB	PH H	PO	A	E	DP	TC/G	FA	G by Pos
1957 MIL N	5	.200	.200	15	3	0	0	0	0.0	1	2	0	2	0	1	0	38	2	1	2	8.2	.976	1B-5
1958	4	.308	.308	13	4	0	0	0	0.0	1	0	1	3	0	1	1	23	2	0	0	6.3	1.000	1B-4
2 yrs.	9	.250	.250	28	7	0	0	0	0.0	2	2	1	5	0	2	1	61	4	1	2	7.3	.985	1B-9

Bob Addis

ADDIS, ROBERT GORDON
B. Nov. 6, 1925, Mineral, Ohio
BL TR 6' 175 lbs.

Year Team	Games	BA	SA	AB	H	2B	3B	HR	HR%	R	RBI	BB	SO	SB	PH AB	PH H	PO	A	E	DP	TC/G	FA	G by Pos
1950 BOS N	16	.250	.286	28	7	1	0	0	0.0	7	2	3	5	1	10	1	7	0	0	0	0.4	1.000	OF-7
1951	85	.276	.327	199	55	7	0	1	0.5	23	24	9	10	3	36	12	107	1	2	1	1.3	.982	OF-46
1952 CHI N	93	.295	.363	292	86	13	2	1	0.3	38	20	23	30	4	15	4	160	8	2	2	1.8	.988	OF-76
1953 2 teams	CHI N (10G – .167)								PIT N (4G – .000)														
" total	14	.133	.200	15	2	1	0	0	0.0	2	1	2	2	0	8	1	7	1	0	1	0.6	1.000	OF-3
4 yrs.	208	.281	.341	534	150	22	2	2	0.4	70	47	37	47	8	69	18	281	10	4	4	1.4	.986	OF-132

Jim Adduci

ADDUCI, JAMES DAVID
B. Aug. 9, 1959, Chicago, Ill.
BL TL 6'5" 200 lbs.

Year Team	Games	BA	SA	AB	H	2B	3B	HR	HR%	R	RBI	BB	SO	SB	PH AB	PH H	PO	A	E	DP	TC/G	FA	G by Pos
1983 STL N	10	.050	.050	20	1	0	0	0	0.0	0	0	1	6	0	3	0	47	4	0	3	5.1	1.000	1B-6, OF-1
1986 MIL A	3	.091	.182	11	1	1	0	0	0.0	2	0	1	2	0	0	0	25	3	0	1	9.3	1.000	1B-3
1988	44	.266	.383	94	25	6	1	1	1.1	8	15	0	15	0	3	0	40	3	1	1	1.0	.977	OF-24, DH-12, 1B-3
1989 PHI N	13	.368	.421	19	7	1	0	0	0.0	1	0	0	4	0	8	3	25	3	0	1	2.2	1.000	1B-4, OF-1
4 yrs.	70	.236	.326	144	34	8	1	1	0.7	11	15	2	27	0	14	3	137	13	1	6	2.2	.993	OF-26, 1B-16, DH-12

Bob Addy

ADDY, ROBERT EDWARD (The Magnet)
B. Feb., 1845, Rochester, N. Y. D. Apr. 9, 1910, Pocatello, Ida.
Manager 1875, 1877.
BL TL 5'8" 160 lbs.

Year Team	Games	BA	SA	AB	H	2B	3B	HR	HR%	R	RBI	BB	SO	SB	PH AB	PH H	PO	A	E	DP	TC/G	FA	G by Pos
1876 CHI N	32	.282	.324	142	40	4	1	0	0.0	36	16	5	0	0	0	0	46	6	13	0	2.0	.800	OF-32
1877 CIN N	57	.278	.310	245	68	2	3	0	0.0	27	31	6	5	0	0	0	74	17	22	5	2.0	.805	OF-57
2 yrs.	89	.279	.315	387	108	6	4	0	0.0	63	47	11	5	0	0	0	120	23	35	5	2.0	.803	OF-89

Morrie Aderholt

ADERHOLT, MORRIS WOODROW
B. Sept. 13, 1915, Mt. Olive, N. C. D. Mar. 18, 1955, Sarasota, Fla.
BL TR 6'1" 188 lbs.

Year Team	Games	BA	SA	AB	H	2B	3B	HR	HR%	R	RBI	BB	SO	SB	PH AB	PH H	PO	A	E	DP	TC/G	FA	G by Pos
1939 WAS A	7	.200	.320	25	5	0	0	1	4.0	5	4	2	6	0	1	0	22	19	6	3	6.7	.872	2B-7
1940	1	.000	.000	2	0	0	0	0	0.0	0	0	0	0	0	0	0	2	1	0	1	3.0	1.000	2B-1
1941	11	.143	.143	14	2	0	0	0	0.0	3	1	1	3	0	5	1	8	4	3	1	1.4	.800	2B-2, 3B-1
1944 BKN N	17	.271	.407	59	16	2	3	0	0.0	9	10	4	4	0	3	0	26	1	4	0	1.8	.871	OF-13
1945 2 teams	BKN N (39G – .217)								BOS N (31G – .333)														
" total	70	.290	.358	162	47	5	0	2	1.2	19	17	12	16	3	36	8	67	1	1	0	1.0	.986	OF-32, 2B-1
5 yrs.	106	.267	.351	262	70	7	3	2	1.1	36	32	19	29	3	45	9	125	26	14	5	1.6	.915	OF-45, 2B-11, 3B-1

Dick Adkins

ADKINS, RICHARD EARL
B. Mar. 3, 1920, Electra, Tex. D. Sept. 12, 1955, Electra, Tex.
BR TR 5'10" 165 lbs.

Year Team	Games	BA	SA	AB	H	2B	3B	HR	HR%	R	RBI	BB	SO	SB	PH AB	PH H	PO	A	E	DP	TC/G	FA	G by Pos
1942 PHI A	3	.143	.143	7	1	0	0	0	0.0	2	0	0	2	0	0	0	2	5	1	1	2.7	.875	SS-3

Henry Adkinson

ADKINSON, HENRY MAGEE
B. Sept. 1, 1874, Chicago, Ill. D. May 1, 1923, Salt Lake City, Utah

Year Team	Games	BA	SA	AB	H	2B	3B	HR	HR%	R	RBI	BB	SO	SB	PH AB	PH H	PO	A	E	DP	TC/G	FA	G by Pos
1895 STL N	1	.400	.400	5	2	0	0	0	0.0	1	0	0	2	0	0	0	2	0	1	0	3.0	.667	OF-1

Dave Adlesh

ADLESH, DAVID GEORGE
B. July 15, 1943, Long Beach, Calif.
BR TR 6' 187 lbs.

Year Team	Games	BA	SA	AB	H	2B	3B	HR	HR%	R	RBI	BB	SO	SB	PH AB	PH H	PO	A	E	DP	TC/G	FA	G by Pos
1963 HOU N	6	.000	.000	8	0	0	0	0	0.0	0	0	0	4	0	2	0	8	0	1	0	1.5	.889	C-6
1964	3	.200	.200	10	2	0	0	0	0.0	0	0	0	5	0	0	0	11	2	0	0	4.3	1.000	C-3
1965	15	.147	.176	34	5	1	0	0	0.0	2	3	2	12	0	2	1	51	5	0	1	3.7	1.000	C-13
1966	3	.000	.000	6	0	0	0	0	0.0	0	0	0	4	0	3	0	11	0	0	0	3.7	1.000	C-1
1967	39	.181	.223	94	17	1	0	1	1.1	4	4	11	28	0	8	2	179	8	1	1	4.8	.995	C-31
1968	40	.183	.212	104	19	1	1	0	0.0	3	4	5	27	0	4	2	193	11	2	0	5.2	.990	C-36
6 yrs.	106	.168	.199	256	43	3	1	1	0.4	9	11	18	80	0	19	5	453	26	4	2	4.6	.992	C-90

Troy Afenir

AFENIR, MICHAEL TROY
B. Sept. 21, 1963, Escondido, Calif.
BR TR 6'4" 185 lbs.

Year Team	Games	BA	SA	AB	H	2B	3B	HR	HR%	R	RBI	BB	SO	SB	PH AB	PH H	PO	A	E	DP	TC/G	FA	G by Pos
1987 HOU N	10	.300	.350	20	6	1	0	0	0.0	1	1	0	12	0	1	0	35	2	1	1	3.8	.974	C-10

Tommie Agee

AGEE, TOMMIE LEE
B. Aug. 9, 1942, Magnolia, Ala.
BR TR 5'11" 195 lbs.

Year Team	Games	BA	SA	AB	H	2B	3B	HR	HR%	R	RBI	BB	SO	SB	PH AB	PH H	PO	A	E	DP	TC/G	FA	G by Pos
1962 CLE A	5	.214	.214	14	3	0	0	0	0.0	0	2	0	4	0	2	0	4	0	0	0	0.8	1.000	OF-3
1963	13	.148	.296	27	4	1	0	1	3.7	3	3	2	9	0	0	0	10	2	0	1	0.9	1.000	OF-13
1964	13	.167	.167	12	2	0	0	0	0.0	0	0	0	3	0	0	0	5	0	0	0	0.4	1.000	OF-12
1965 CHI A	10	.158	.211	19	3	1	0	0	0.0	2	3	2	6	0	1	0	13	0	0	0	1.3	1.000	OF-9
1966	160	.273	.447	629	172	27	8	22	3.5	98	86	41	127	44	0	0	376	12	7	7	2.5	.982	OF-159
1967	158	.234	.371	529	124	26	4	14	2.6	73	52	44	129	28	2	1	337	6	11	2	2.2	.969	OF-152
1968 NY N	132	.217	.307	368	80	12	3	5	1.4	30	17	15	103	13	3	1	216	6	5	2	1.7	.978	OF-127
1969	149	.271	.464	565	153	23	4	26	4.6	97	76	59	137	12	3	1	334	7	5	1	2.3	.986	OF-146
1970	153	.286	.469	636	182	30	7	24	3.8	107	75	55	156	31	3	1	374	4	13	3	2.6	.967	OF-150
1971	113	.285	.428	425	121	19	0	14	3.3	58	50	50	84	28	6	3	265	7	6	0	2.5	.978	OF-107

Year	Team	Games	BA	SA	AB	H	2B	3B	HR	HR%	R	RBI	BB	SO	SB	Pinch Hit AB	Pinch Hit H	PO	A	E	DP	TC/G	FA	G by Pos

Tommie Agee *continued*

1972		114	.227	.374	422	96	23	0	13	3.1	52	47	53	92	8	4	0	273	6	11	1	2.5	.962	OF-109
1973	2 teams	109	HOU N (83G – .235)		STL N	(26G – .177)																		
"	total	109	.222	.398	266	59	8	3	11	4.1	38	22	21	68	3	19	4	164	3	3	2	1.6	.982	OF-86
12 yrs.		1129	.255	.412	3912	999	170	27	130	3.3	558	433	342	918	167	43	11	2371	53	61	18	2.2	.975	OF-1073

LEAGUE CHAMPIONSHIP SERIES

| 1969 | NY N | 3 | .357 | .857 | 14 | 5 | 1 | 0 | 2 | 14.3 | 4 | 4 | 2 | 5 | 2 | 0 | 0 | 9 | 0 | 0 | 0 | 3.0 | 1.000 | OF-3 |

WORLD SERIES

| 1969 | NY N | 5 | .167 | .333 | 18 | 3 | 0 | 0 | 1 | 5.6 | 1 | 1 | 2 | 5 | 1 | 0 | 0 | 19 | 0 | 0 | 0 | 3.8 | 1.000 | OF-5 |

Harry Agganis

AGGANIS, HARRY (The Golden Greek)
B. Apr. 20, 1930, Lynn, Mass.   D. June 27, 1955, Cambridge, Mass.
BL TL 6'2"   200 lbs.

1954	BOS A	132	.251	.394	434	109	13	8	11	2.5	54	57	47	57	6	11	3	1064	89	12	101	8.8	.990	1B-119
1955		25	.313	.458	83	26	10	1	0	0.0	11	10	10	10	2	3	0	208	14	3	15	9.0	.987	1B-20
2 yrs.		157	.261	.404	517	135	23	9	11	2.1	65	67	57	67	8	14	3	1272	103	15	116	8.9	.989	1B-139

Joe Agler

AGLER, JOSEPH ABRAM
B. June 12, 1887, Coshocton, Ohio   D. Apr. 26, 1971, Massillon, Ohio
BL TL 5'11"   165 lbs.

1912	WAS A	1	.000	.000	1	0	0	0	0	0.0	0	0	0		0	0	0	0	0	0	0	0.0	–	
1914	BUF F	135	.272	.335	463	126	17	6	0	0.0	82	20	77		21	3	1	831	57	16	47	6.7	.982	1B-76, OF-54
1915	2 teams	97	BUF F	(25G – .178)	BAL F	(72G – .215)																		
"	total	97	.206	.251	287	59	5	4	0	0.0	39	16	54		17	7	0	626	54	15	44	7.2	.978	1B-59, OF-24, 2B-3
3 yrs.		233	.246	.302	751	185	22	10	0	0.0	121	36	131		38	11	1	1457	111	31	91	6.9	.981	1B-135, OF-78, 2B-3

Sam Agnew

AGNEW, SAMUEL LESTER
B. Apr. 12, 1887, Farmington, Mo.   D. July 19, 1951, Sonoma, Calif.
BR TR 5'11"   185 lbs.

1913	STL A	104	.208	.290	307	64	9	5	2	0.7	27	24	20	49	11	0	0	383	170	28	17	5.6	.952	C-103
1914		113	.212	.254	311	66	5	4	0	0.0	22	16	24	63	10	0	0	451	163	25	10	5.7	.961	C-113
1915		104	.203	.231	295	60	4	2	0	0.0	18	19	12	36	5	1	0	398	153	39	16	5.7	.934	C-102
1916	BOS A	40	.209	.269	67	14	2	1	0	0.0	4	7	6	4	0	2	0	110	47	8	4	4.1	.952	C-38
1917		85	.208	.246	260	54	6	2	0	0.0	17	16	19	30	2	0	0	297	88	14	5	4.7	.965	C-85
1918		72	.166	.196	199	33	8	0	0	0.0	11	6	11	26	0	0	0	254	104	13	10	5.2	.965	C-72
1919	WAS A	42	.235	.306	98	23	7	0	0	0.0	6	10	10	8	1	5	1	141	48	5	5	4.6	.974	C-36
7 yrs.		560	.204	.253	1537	314	41	14	2	0.1	105	98	102	216	29	8	1	2034	773	132	67	5.2	.955	C-549

WORLD SERIES

| 1918 | BOS A | 4 | .000 | .000 | 9 | 0 | 0 | 0 | 0 | 0.0 | 0 | 0 | 0 | 0 | 0 | 0 | 0 | 12 | 6 | 0 | 0 | 4.5 | 1.000 | C-4 |

Luis Aguayo

AGUAYO, LUIS
Born Luis Aguayo y Muriel.
B. Mar. 13, 1959, Vega Baja, Puerto Rico
BR TR 5'9"   173 lbs.

1980	PHI N	20	.277	.447	47	13	1	2	1	2.1	7	8	2	3	1	1	0	44	44	3	10	4.6	.967	2B-14, SS-5
1981		45	.214	.298	84	18	4	0	1	1.2	11	7	6	15	1	3	1	39	63	5	15	2.4	.953	2B-21, SS-21, 3B-3
1982		50	.268	.518	56	15	1	2	3	5.4	11	7	5	7	1	5	1	27	49	4	5	1.6	.950	2B-21, SS-15, 3B-5
1983		2	.250	.250	4	1	0	0	0	0.0	1	0	1	2	0	0	0	3	0	0	0	1.5	1.000	SS-2
1984		58	.278	.458	72	20	4	0	3	4.2	15	11	8	16	1	16	3	18	55	3	7	1.3	.961	3B-14, 2B-12, SS-10
1985		91	.279	.467	165	46	7	3	6	3.6	27	21	22	26	1	8	3	92	158	9	27	2.8	.965	SS-60, 2B-17, 3B-7
1986		62	.211	.361	133	28	6	1	4	3.0	17	13	8	26	1	14	7	57	90	5	19	2.5	.967	2B-31, SS-20, 3B-1
1987		94	.206	.431	209	43	9	1	12	5.7	25	21	15	54	0	18	2	86	172	7	30	2.8	.974	SS-78, 2B-6, 3B-2
1988	2 teams	99	PHI N	(49G – .247)	NY A	(50G – .250)																		
"	total	99	.249	.354	237	59	7	0	6	2.5	21	13	20	50	2	13	4	83	156	13	24	2.5	.948	3B-46, SS-33, 2B-15
1989	CLE A	47	.175	.268	97	17	4	1	1	1.0	7	8	7	19	0	5	0	34	80	5	11	2.5	.958	3B-19, SS-15, 2B-10, DH-2
10 yrs.		568	.236	.393	1104	260	43	10	37	3.4	142	109	94	220	7	83	21	483	867	54	148	2.5	.962	SS-259, 2B-147, 3B-97, DH-2

DIVISIONAL PLAYOFF SERIES

| 1981 | PHI N | 2 | – | – | 0 | 0 | 0 | 0 | 0 | – | 1 | 0 | 0 | 0 | 0 | 0 | 0 | 0 | 0 | 0 | 0 | 0.0 | – | |

Charlie Ahearn

AHEARN, CHARLES
B. Troy, N. Y.   Deceased.

| 1880 | TRO N | 1 | .250 | .250 | 4 | 1 | 0 | 0 | 0 | 0.0 | 1 | 0 | 0 | | 0 | 0 | 0 | 2 | 5 | 2 | 0 | 9.0 | .778 | C-1 |

Willie Aikens

AIKENS, WILLIE MAYS
B. Oct. 14, 1954, Seneca, S. C.
BL TR 6'3"   220 lbs.

1977	CAL A	42	.198	.242	91	18	4	0	0	0.0	5	6	10	23	1	15	1	94	8	3	10	2.5	.971	DH-13, 1B-13
1979		116	.280	.493	379	106	18	0	21	5.5	59	81	61	79	1	11	3	462	31	2	49	4.3	.996	1B-55, DH-51
1980	KC A	151	.278	.433	543	151	24	0	20	3.7	70	98	64	88	1	0	0	1081	65	12	95	7.7	.990	1B-138, DH-13
1981		101	.266	.458	349	93	16	0	17	4.9	45	53	62	47	0	2	0	844	56	7	79	9.0	.992	1B-99
1982		134	.281	.457	466	131	29	1	17	3.6	50	74	45	70	0	10	4	1048	75	7	95	8.4	.994	1B-128
1983		125	.302	.539	410	124	26	1	23	5.6	49	72	45	75	0	8	2	884	64	11	101	7.7	.989	1B-112, DH-6
1984	TOR A	93	.205	.376	234	48	7	0	11	4.7	21	26	21	56	0	15	3	12	1	0	0	0.1	1.000	DH-81, 1B-2
1985		12	.200	.400	20	4	1	0	1	5.0	2	5	3	6	0	6	1								DH-11
8 yrs.		774	.271	.455	2492	675	125	2	110	4.4	301	415	319	444	3	67	14	4425	300	42	430	6.2	.991	1B-547, DH-175

DIVISIONAL PLAYOFF SERIES

| 1981 | KC A | 3 | .333 | .333 | 9 | 3 | 0 | 0 | 0 | 0.0 | 0 | 0 | 0 | 3 | 0 | 0 | 0 | 0 | 0 | 0 | 0 | 0.0 | – | 1B-3 |

LEAGUE CHAMPIONSHIP SERIES

| 1980 | KC A | 3 | .364 | .364 | 11 | 4 | 0 | 0 | 0 | 0.0 | 0 | 2 | 1 | 0 | 0 | 0 | 0 | 22 | 1 | 0 | 2 | 7.7 | 1.000 | 1B-3 |

WORLD SERIES

| 1980 | KC A | 6 | .400 | 1.100 | 20 | 8 | 0 | 0 | 4 | 20.0 | 5 | 8 | 6 | 8 | 0 | 0 | 0 | 55 | 2 | 2 | 6 | 9.8 | .966 | 1B-6 |

Year	Team		Games	BA	SA	AB	H	2B	3B	HR	HR%	R	RBI	BB	SO	SB	Pinch Hit AB	H	PO	A	E	DP	TC/G	FA	G by Pos

Danny Ainge

AINGE, DANIEL RAE
B. Mar. 17, 1959, Eugene, Ore.   BR TR 6'4"   175 lbs.

Year	Team	Games	BA	SA	AB	H	2B	3B	HR	HR%	R	RBI	BB	SO	SB	PH AB	H	PO	A	E	DP	TC/G	FA	G by Pos
1979	TOR A	87	.237	.286	308	73	7	1	2	0.6	26	19	12	58	1	0	0	198	261	11	67	5.4	.977	2B-86, DH-1
1980		38	.243	.315	111	27	6	1	0	0.0	11	4	2	29	3	3	0	69	12	1	3	2.2	.988	OF-29, 3B-3, DH-2, 2B-1
1981		86	.187	.228	246	46	6	2	0	0.0	20	14	23	41	8	0	0	88	146	12	20	2.9	.951	3B-77, SS-6, OF-4, 2B-2, DH-1
3 yrs.		211	.220	.269	665	146	19	4	2	0.3	57	37	37	128	12	3	0	355	419	24	90	3.8	.970	2B-89, 3B-80, OF-33, SS-6, DH-4

Eddie Ainsmith

AINSMITH, EDWARD WILBUR
B. Feb. 4, 1892, Cambridge, Mass.   D. Sept. 6, 1981, Fort Lauderdale, Fla.   BR TR 5'11"   180 lbs.

Year	Team	Games	BA	SA	AB	H	2B	3B	HR	HR%	R	RBI	BB	SO	SB	PH AB	H	PO	A	E	DP	TC/G	FA	G by Pos
1910	WAS A	33	.192	.240	104	20	1	2	0	0.0	4	9	6		0	0	0	131	52	7	4	5.8	.963	C-30
1911		61	.221	.275	149	33	2	3	0	0.0	12	14	10		5	7	1	208	71	14	2	4.8	.952	C-49
1912		60	.226	.285	186	42	7	2	0	0.0	22	22	14		4	2	0	415	85	22	5	8.7	.958	C-58
1913		79	.214	.293	229	49	4	4	2	0.9	26	20	12	41	17	0	0	418	82	17	10	6.5	.967	C-79, P-1
1914		58	.225	.272	151	34	7	0	0	0.0	11	13	9	28	8	3	2	290	55	11	5	6.1	.969	C-51
1915		47	.200	.267	120	24	4	2	0	0.0	13	6	10	18	7	3	0	209	47	3	2	5.5	.988	C-42
1916		51	.170	.210	100	17	4	0	0	0.0	11	8	8	14	3	1	0	207	50	11	9	5.3	.959	C-46
1917		125	.191	.263	350	67	17	4	0	0.0	38	42	40	48	16	5	0	580	154	22	15	6.0	.971	C-119
1918		96	.212	.308	292	62	10	9	0	0.0	22	20	29	44	6	4	1	413	131	14	13	5.8	.975	C-89
1919	DET A	114	.272	.409	364	99	17	12	3	0.8	42	32	45	30	9	8	1	456	107	22	7	5.1	.962	C-106
1920		69	.231	.306	186	43	5	3	1	0.5	19	19	14	19	4	7	2	219	55	13	4	4.2	.955	C-61
1921	2 teams	DET A (35G – .276)			STL N	(27G – .290)																		
"	total	62	.281	.350	160	45	5	3	0	0.0	11	17	16	11	1	4	0	177	42	11	2	3.7	.952	C-57, 1B-1
1922	STL N	119	.293	.454	379	111	14	4	13	3.4	46	59	28	43	2	'2	1	428	99	20	14	4.6	.963	C-116
1923	2 teams	STL N (82G – .213)			BKN N	(2G – .200)																		
"	total	84	.212	.330	273	58	11	6	3	1.1	22	36	22	19	4	2	1	251	58	6	4	3.8	.981	C-82
1924	NY N	10	.600	.600	5	3	0	0	0	0.0	0	0	0	0	0	1	1	5	0	0	0	0.5	1.000	C-9
15 yrs.		1068	.232	.324	3048	707	108	54	22	0.7	299	317	263	315	86	49	10	4407	1088	193	96	5.3	.966	C-994, 1B-1, P-1

George Aiton

AITON, GEORGE WILSON (Bill)
B. Dec. 29, 1890, Kingman, Kans.   D. Aug. 16, 1976, Van Nuys, Calif.   BB TR 5'11½" 175 lbs.

Year	Team	Games	BA	SA	AB	H	2B	3B	HR	HR%	R	RBI	BB	SO	SB	PH AB	H	PO	A	E	DP	TC/G	FA	G by Pos
1912	STL A	8	.235	.235	17	4	0	0	0	0.0	1	1	4		0	1	0	10	1	1	0	1.5	.917	OF-6

John Ake

AKE, JOHN LECKIE
B. Aug. 29, 1861, Altoona, Pa.   D. May 11, 1887, La Crosse, Wis.   BR TR 6'1"   180 lbs.

Year	Team	Games	BA	SA	AB	H	2B	3B	HR	HR%	R	RBI	BB	SO	SB	PH AB	H	PO	A	E	DP	TC/G	FA	G by Pos
1884	BAL AA	13	.192	.231	52	10	0	1	0	0.0	1		0			0	0	10	15	10	2	2.7	.714	3B-9, OF-3, SS-1

Bill Akers

AKERS, WILLIAM G.
B. Dec. 25, 1904, Chattanooga, Tenn.   D. Apr. 13, 1962, Chattanooga, Tenn.   BR TR 5'11"   178 lbs.

Year	Team	Games	BA	SA	AB	H	2B	3B	HR	HR%	R	RBI	BB	SO	SB	PH AB	H	PO	A	E	DP	TC/G	FA	G by Pos
1929	DET A	24	.265	.373	83	22	4	1	1	1.2	15	9	10	9	2	0	0	43	57	7	13	4.5	.935	SS-24
1930		85	.279	.472	233	65	8	5	9	3.9	36	40	36	34	5	5	2	119	184	20	43	3.8	.938	SS-49, 3B-26
1931		29	.197	.288	66	13	2	2	0	0.0	5	3	7	6	0	5	2	46	42	7	8	3.3	.926	SS-21, 2B-2
1932	BOS N	36	.258	.344	93	24	3	1	1	1.1	8	17	10	15	0	6	1	27	46	7	4	2.2	.913	3B-20, SS-5, 2B-5
4 yrs.		174	.261	.404	475	124	17	9	11	2.3	64	69	63	64	7	16	5	235	329	41	68	3.5	.932	SS-99, 3B-46, 2B-7

Butch Alberts

ALBERTS, FRANCIS BURT
B. May 4, 1950, Williamsport, Pa.   BR TR 6'2"   205 lbs.

Year	Team	Games	BA	SA	AB	H	2B	3B	HR	HR%	R	RBI	BB	SO	SB	PH AB	H	PO	A	E	DP	TC/G	FA	G by Pos
1978	TOR A	6	.278	.333	18	5	1	0	0	0.0	1	0	2	2	0	2	0	0	0	0	0	0.0	–	DH-4

Gus Alberts

ALBERTS, AUGUSTUS PETER
B. 1861, Reading, Pa.   D. May 7, 1912, Idaho Springs, Colo.   BR TR 5'6½"   180 lbs.

Year	Team	Games	BA	SA	AB	H	2B	3B	HR	HR%	R	RBI	BB	SO	SB	PH AB	H	PO	A	E	DP	TC/G	FA	G by Pos
1884	2 teams	PIT AA (2G – .200)			WAS U	(4G – .250)																		
"	total	6	.238	.238	21	5	0	0	0	0.0	5		4			0	0	5	18	6	1	4.8	.793	SS-6
1888	CLE AA	102	.206	.275	364	75	10	6	1	0.3	51	48	41		26	0	0	126	277	57	24	4.5	.876	SS-53, 3B-49
1891	MIL AA	12	.098	.098	41	4	0	0	0	0.0	6	2	7	5	1	0	0	14	21	8	2	3.6	.814	3B-12
3 yrs.		120	.197	.256	426	84	10	6	1	0.2	62	50	52	5	27	0	0	145	316	71	27	4.4	.867	3B-61, SS-59

Jack Albright

ALBRIGHT, HAROLD JOHN
B. June 30, 1921, St. Petersburg, Fla.   BR TR 5'9"   175 lbs.

Year	Team	Games	BA	SA	AB	H	2B	3B	HR	HR%	R	RBI	BB	SO	SB	PH AB	H	PO	A	E	DP	TC/G	FA	G by Pos
1947	PHI N	41	.232	.333	99	23	4	0	2	2.0	9	5	10	11	1	2	0	48	85	8	15	3.4	.943	SS-33

Luis Alcaraz

ALCARAZ, ANGEL LUIS
Born Angel Luis Alcaraz y Acosta.
B. June 20, 1941, Humacao, Puerto Rico   BR TR 5'9"   165 lbs.

Year	Team	Games	BA	SA	AB	H	2B	3B	HR	HR%	R	RBI	BB	SO	SB	PH AB	H	PO	A	E	DP	TC/G	FA	G by Pos
1967	LA N	17	.233	.250	60	14	1	0	0	0.0	1	3	1	13	1	0	0	44	51	1	18	5.6	.990	2B-17
1968		41	.151	.217	106	16	1	0	2	1.9	4	5	9	23	1	5	1	57	71	7	9	3.3	.948	2B-20, 3B-13, SS-1
1969	KC A	22	.253	.342	79	20	2	1	1	1.3	15	7	7	9	0	1	0	43	50	1	5	4.3	.989	2B-19, 3B-2, SS-1
1970		35	.167	.250	120	20	5	1	1	0.8	10	14	4	13	0	3	1	65	68	1	12	3.8	.993	2B-31
4 yrs.		115	.192	.260	365	70	9	2	4	1.1	30	29	21	58	2	9	2	209	240	10	44	4.0	.978	2B-87, 3B-15, SS-2

Scotty Alcock

ALCOCK, JOHN FORBES
B. Nov. 29, 1885, Wooster, Ohio   D. Jan. 30, 1973, Wooster, Ohio   BR TR 5'9½"   160 lbs.

Year	Team	Games	BA	SA	AB	H	2B	3B	HR	HR%	R	RBI	BB	SO	SB	PH AB	H	PO	A	E	DP	TC/G	FA	G by Pos
1914	CHI A	54	.173	.224	156	27	4	2	0	0.0	12	7	14		1	3	0	61	96	16	11	3.2	.908	3B-48, 2B-1

Mike Aldrete

ALDRETE, MICHAEL PETER
B. Jan. 29, 1961, Carmel, Calif.   BL TL 5'11"   180 lbs.

Year	Team	Games	BA	SA	AB	H	2B	3B	HR	HR%	R	RBI	BB	SO	SB	PH AB	H	PO	A	E	DP	TC/G	FA	G by Pos
1986	SF N	84	.250	.389	216	54	18	3	2	0.9	27	25	33	34	1	16	4	317	36	1	34	4.2	.997	1B-37, OF-31
1987		126	.325	.462	357	116	18	2	9	2.5	50	51	43	50	6	25	6	328	18	3	21	2.8	.991	OF-79, 1B-33
1988		139	.267	.329	389	104	15	0	3	0.8	44	50	56	65	6	29	11	272	8	4	3	2.0	.986	OF-125

Year	Team		Games	BA	SA	AB	H	2B	3B	HR	HR%	R	RBI	BB	SO	SB	Pinch Hit AB	H	PO	A	E	DP	TC/G	FA	G by Pos

Mike Aldrete *continued*

| 1989 | MON | N | 76 | .221 | .316 | 136 | 30 | 8 | 1 | 1 | 0.7 | 12 | 12 | 19 | 30 | 1 | 26 | 8 | 109 | 9 | 1 | 8 | 1.6 | .992 | OF-37, 1B-10 |
| 4 yrs. | | | 425 | .277 | .383 | 1098 | 304 | 59 | 6 | 15 | 1.4 | 133 | 138 | 151 | 179 | 14 | 96 | 29 | 1026 | 71 | 9 | 66 | 2.6 | .992 | OF-272, 1B-80 |

LEAGUE CHAMPIONSHIP SERIES

| 1987 | SF | N | 5 | .100 | .100 | 10 | 1 | 0 | 0 | 0 | 0.0 | 0 | 1 | 0 | 2 | 0 | 2 | 0 | 5 | 0 | 0 | 0 | 1.0 | 1.000 | OF-3 |

Chuck Aleno

ALENO, CHARLES
B. Feb. 19, 1917, St. Louis, Mo.

BR TR 6'1½" 215 lbs.

1941	CIN	N	54	.243	.337	169	41	7	3	1	0.6	23	18	11	16	3	11	2	56	77	3	6	2.5	.978	3B-40, 1B-2
1942			7	.143	.214	14	2	1	0	0	0.0	1	0	3	3	0	3	0	4	11	3	2	2.6	.833	3B-2, 2B-1
1943			7	.300	.300	10	3	0	0	0	0.0	0	1	2	1	0	4	2	2	0	0	0	0.3	1.000	OF-2
1944			50	.165	.213	127	21	3	0	1	0.8	10	15	15	15	0	2	0	75	65	6	9	2.9	.959	3B-42, 1B-5, SS-3, 1B-3
4 yrs.			118	.209	.281	320	67	11	3	2	0.6	34	34	31	35	3	20	4	137	153	12	17	2.6	.960	3B-84, 1B-5, SS-3, OF-2, 2B-1

Dale Alexander

ALEXANDER, DAVID DOYLE (Moose)
B. Apr. 26, 1903, Greeneville, Tenn. D. Mar. 2, 1979, Greeneville, Tenn.

BR TR 6'3" 210 lbs.

1929	DET	A	155	.343	.580	626	215	43	15	25	4.0	110	137	56	63	5	0	0	1443	90	18	129	10.0	.988	1B-155
1930			154	.326	.507	602	196	33	8	20	3.3	86	135	42	56	6	0	0	1338	71	22	132	9.3	.985	1B-154
1931			135	.325	.445	517	168	47	3	3	0.6	75	87	64	35	5	6	0	1205	53	16	91	9.4	.987	1B-126, OF-4
1932	2 teams			DET A (23G – .250)			BOS A	(101G – .372)																		
"	total		124	.367	.513	392	144	27	3	8	2.0	58	60	61	21	4	15	4	1055	67	9	93	9.1	.992	1B-103
1933	BOS	A	94	.281	.383	313	88	14	1	5	1.6	40	40	25	22	0	15	4	728	47	6	51	8.3	.992	1B-79
5 yrs.			662	.331	.497	2450	811	164	30	61	2.5	369	459	248	197	20	36	8	5769	328	71	496	9.3	.988	1B-617, OF-4

Gary Alexander

ALEXANDER, GARY WAYNE
B. Mar. 27, 1953, Los Angeles, Calif.

BR TR 6'2" 195 lbs.

1975	SF	N	3	.000	.000	3	0	0	0	0	0.0	1	0	1	2	0	3	0	2	0	0	0	0.7	1.000	C-2
1976			23	.178	.301	73	13	1	1	2	2.7	12	7	10	16	1	10	0	92	16	4	0	4.9	.964	C-23
1977			51	.303	.496	119	36	4	2	5	4.2	17	20	20	33	3	17	7	174	8	6	0	3.7	.968	C-33, OF-1
1978	2 teams			OAK A (58G – .207)			CLE A	(90G – .235)																		
"	total		148	.225	.444	498	112	20	4	27	5.4	57	84	57	166	0	10	1	321	34	6	3	2.4	.983	DH-71, C-66, OF-6, 1B-1
1979	CLE	A	110	.229	.391	358	82	9	2	15	4.2	54	54	46	100	4	6	2	404	40	18	5	4.2	.961	C-91, DH-13, OF-2
1980			76	.225	.360	178	40	7	1	5	2.8	22	31	17	52	0	23	7	34	2	1	0	0.5	.973	DH-40, C-13, OF-2
1981	PIT	N	21	.213	.404	47	10	4	1	1	2.1	6	6	3	12	0	5	0	64	6	3	4	3.5	.959	1B-9, OF-8
7 yrs.			432	.230	.411	1276	293	45	11	55	4.3	169	202	154	381	8	64	17	1091	106	38	12	2.9	.969	C-228, DH-124, OF-19, 1B-10

Hugh Alexander

ALEXANDER, HUGH
B. July 10, 1917, Buffalo, Mo.

BR TR 6' 190 lbs.

| 1937 | CLE | A | 7 | .091 | .091 | 11 | 1 | 0 | 0 | 0 | 0.0 | 0 | 0 | 0 | 5 | 1 | 3 | 0 | 2 | 0 | 1 | 0 | 0.4 | .667 | OF-3 |

Matt Alexander

ALEXANDER, MATTHEW
B. Jan. 30, 1947, Shreveport, La.

BB TR 5'11" 168 lbs.

1973	CHI	N	12	.200	.200	5	1	0	0	0	0.0	4	1	1	1	2	1	0	2	0	0	0	0.2	1.000	OF-3
1974			45	.204	.278	54	11	2	1	0	0.0	15	0	12	12	8	11	3	13	24	3	3	0.9	.925	3B-19, OF-4, 2B-2
1975	OAK	A	63	.100	.100	10	1	0	0	0	0.0	16	0	1	1	17	2	0	7	2	1	1	0.2	.900	DH-17, OF-11, 2B-3, 3B-2
1976			61	.033	.033	30	1	0	0	0	0.0	16	0	4	5	20	1	0	23	0	0	0	0.4	1.000	OF-23, DH-19
1977			90	.238	.262	42	10	1	0	0	0.0	24	2	4	26	26	2	0	21	2	0	0	0.3	1.000	OF-31, DH-12, SS-12, 2B-4, 3B-1
1978	PIT	N	7	–	–	0	0	0	0	0	–	2	0	0	0	4	0	0	0	0	0	0	0.0	–	OF-11, SS-1
1979			44	.538	.692	13	7	0	1	0	0.0	16	1	0	13	13	1	0	8	1	0	0	0.2	1.000	OF-4, 2B-1
1980			37	.333	.667	3	1	1	0	0	0.0	13	0	0	0	10	0	0	6	0	0	0	0.2	1.000	OF-6
1981			15	.364	.364	11	4	0	0	0	0.0	5	0	0	1	3	4	0	8	0	0	0	0.5	1.000	OF-8
9 yrs.			374	.214	.262	168	36	4	2	0	0.0	111	4	18	26	103	20	3	88	29	4	4	0.3	.967	OF-93, DH-48, 3B-22, SS-13, 2B-10

LEAGUE CHAMPIONSHIP SERIES

| 1979 | PIT | N | 1 | – | – | 0 | 0 | 0 | 0 | 0 | – | 0 | 0 | 0 | 0 | 0 | 0 | 0 | 0 | 0 | 0 | 0 | 0.0 | – | |

WORLD SERIES

| 1979 | PIT | N | 1 | – | – | 0 | 0 | 0 | 0 | 0 | – | 0 | 0 | 0 | 0 | 0 | 0 | 0 | 0 | 0 | 0 | 0 | 0.0 | – | OF-1 |

Nin Alexander

ALEXANDER, WILLIAM HENRY
B. Nov. 24, 1858, Pana, Ill. D. Dec. 22, 1933, Pana, Ill.

BR TR 5'4½" 163 lbs.

| 1884 | 2 teams | | | KC U (19G – .138) | | | STL AA | (1G – .000) | | | | | | | | | | | | | | | | | | |
| " | total | | 20 | .130 | .130 | 69 | 9 | 0 | 0 | 0 | 0.0 | 2 | | 1 | | | 0 | 0 | 81 | 43 | 14 | 0 | 6.9 | .899 | C-18, OF-3, SS-2 |

Walt Alexander

ALEXANDER, WALTER ERNEST
B. Mar. 5, 1891, Atlanta, Ga. D. Dec. 29, 1978, Ft. Worth, Tex.

BR TR 5'10½" 165 lbs.

1912	STL	A	37	.175	.216	97	17	4	0	0	0.0	5	5	8		1	0	0	140	46	6	2	5.2	.969	C-37
1913			43	.136	.173	110	15	2	1	0	0.0	5	7	4	36	1	0	0	128	71	11	7	4.9	.948	C-43
1915	2 teams			STL A (1G – .000)			NY A	(25G – .250)																		
"	total		26	.246	.348	69	17	4	0	1	1.4	7	5	13	16	2	0	0	132	44	6	5	7.0	.967	C-25
1916	NY	A	36	.256	.359	78	20	6	1	0	0.0	8	3	13	20	1	0	0	100	43	6	2	4.1	.960	C-27
1917			20	.137	.216	51	7	2	1	0	0.0	1	4	4	11	0	0	0	82	16	5	2	5.2	.951	C-20
5 yrs.			162	.188	.254	405	76	18	3	1	0.2	26	24	42	83	5	8	2	582	220	34	18	5.2	.959	C-152

Luis Alicea

ALICEA, LUIS RENE
Born Luis Rene Alicea y DeJesus.
B. July 29, 1965, Santurce, Puerto Rico

BB TR 5'9" 165 lbs.

| 1988 | STL | N | 93 | .212 | .283 | 297 | 63 | 10 | 4 | 1 | 0.3 | 20 | 24 | 25 | 32 | 1 | 5 | 1 | 206 | 240 | 14 | 52 | 4.9 | .970 | 2B-91 |

Year	Team		Games	BA	SA	AB	H	2B	3B	HR	HR%	R	RBI	BB	SO	SB	Pinch Hit AB	Pinch Hit H	PO	A	E	DP	TC/G	FA	G by Pos

Andy Allanson

ALLANSON, ANDREW NEAL
B. Dec. 22, 1961, Richmond, Va.
BR TR 6'5" 220 lbs.

Year	Team		Games	BA	SA	AB	H	2B	3B	HR	HR%	R	RBI	BB	SO	SB	AB	H	PO	A	E	DP	TC/G	FA	G by Pos
1986	CLE	A	101	.225	.280	293	66	7	3	1	0.3	30	29	14	36	10	0	0	446	33	20	4	4.9	.960	C-99
1987			50	.266	.364	154	41	6	0	3	1.9	17	16	9	30	1	0	0	252	22	4	3	5.6	.986	C-50
1988			133	.263	.323	434	114	11	0	5	1.2	44	50	25	63	5	0	0	691	60	11	11	5.7	.986	C-133
1989			111	.232	.294	323	75	9	1	3	0.9	30	17	23	47	4	0	0	570	53	9	4	5.7	.986	C-111
4 yrs.			395	.246	.310	1204	296	33	4	12	1.0	121	112	71	176	20	0	0	1959	168	44	22	5.5	.980	C-393

Bernie Allen

ALLEN, BERNARD KEITH
B. Apr. 16, 1939, East Liverpool, Ohio
BL TR 6' 175 lbs.

Year	Team		Games	BA	SA	AB	H	2B	3B	HR	HR%	R	RBI	BB	SO	SB	AB	H	PO	A	E	DP	TC/G	FA	G by Pos
1962	MIN	A	159	.269	.403	573	154	27	7	12	2.1	79	64	62	82	0	1	1	357	394	13	109	4.8	.983	2B-158
1963			139	.240	.356	421	101	20	1	9	2.1	52	43	38	52	0	5	2	236	256	12	65	3.6	.976	2B-128
1964			74	.214	.329	243	52	8	1	6	2.5	28	20	33	30	1	3	0	161	173	7	40	4.6	.979	2B-71
1965			19	.231	.282	39	9	2	0	0	0.0	2	6	6	8	0	8	3	18	22	0	6	2.1	1.000	2B-10, 3B-1
1966			101	.238	.348	319	76	18	1	5	1.6	34	30	26	40	2	6	0	191	216	11	47	4.1	.974	2B-89, 3B-2
1967	WAS	A	87	.193	.256	254	49	5	1	3	1.2	13	18	18	43	1	12	1	177	200	4	57	4.4	.990	2B-75
1968			120	.241	.343	373	90	12	4	6	1.6	31	40	28	35	2	15	3	263	272	5	63	4.5	.991	2B-110, 3B-2
1969			122	.247	.389	365	90	17	4	9	2.5	33	45	50	35	5	13	5	243	286	15	70	4.5	.972	2B-110, 3B-6
1970			104	.234	.360	261	61	7	1	8	3.1	31	29	43	21	0	23	3	176	204	11	49	3.8	.972	2B-80, 3B-12
1971			97	.266	.376	229	61	11	1	4	1.7	18	22	33	27	2	32	7	85	126	10	16	2.3	.955	2B-41, 3B-34
1972	NY	A	84	.227	.391	220	50	9	0	9	4.1	26	21	20	42	0	20	0	75	132	9	26	2.6	.958	3B-44, 2B-20
1973	2 teams	NY A (17G – .228)				MON N (16G – .180)																			
"	total		33	.206	.299	107	22	4	0	2	1.9	10	13	10	9	0	3	0	49	66	3	10	3.6	.975	2B-22, 3B-8, DH-4
12 yrs.			1139	.239	.357	3404	815	140	21	73	2.1	357	351	370	424	13	141	25	2031	2347	100	558	3.9	.978	2B-914, 3B-109, DH-4

Bob Allen

ALLEN, ROBERT
B. 1896
BR TR 5'10" 180 lbs.

Year	Team		Games	BA	SA	AB	H	2B	3B	HR	HR%	R	RBI	BB	SO	SB	AB	H	PO	A	E	DP	TC/G	FA	G by Pos
1919	PHI	A	9	.136	.182	22	3	1	0	0	0.0	3	0	3	7	0	2	1	8	0	1	0	1.0	.889	OF-6

Bob Allen

ALLEN, ROBERT GILMAN
B. July 10, 1867, Marion, Ohio   D. May 4, 1943, Little Rock, Ark.
Manager 1890, 1900.
BR TR 5'11" 175 lbs.

Year	Team		Games	BA	SA	AB	H	2B	3B	HR	HR%	R	RBI	BB	SO	SB	AB	H	PO	A	E	DP	TC/G	FA	G by Pos
1890	PHI	N	133	.226	.320	456	103	15	11	2	0.4	69	57	87	54	13	0	0	337	500	69	68	6.8	.924	SS-133
1891			118	.221	.263	438	97	7	4	1	0.2	46	51	43	44	12	0	0	258	426	79	50	6.5	.896	SS-118
1892			152	.227	.323	563	128	20	14	2	0.4	77	64	61	60	15	0	0	331	537	77	67	6.2	.919	SS-152
1893			124	.268	.410	471	126	19	12	8	1.7	86	90	71	40	8	0	0	302	447	66	65	6.6	.919	SS-124
1894			40	.255	.362	149	38	10	3	0	0.0	26	19	17	11	4	0	0	87	129	20	15	5.9	.915	SS-40
1897	BOS	N	34	.319	.387	119	38	5	0	1	0.8	33	24	18		1	0	0	82	119	16	12	6.4	.926	SS-32, OF-1, 2B-1
1900	CIN	N	5	.133	.200	15	2	1	0	0	0.0	0	0	0	1	0	0	0	6	13	3	1	4.4	.864	SS-5
7 yrs.			606	.241	.334	2211	532	77	44	14	0.6	337	306	297	209	53	0	0	1403	2171	330	278	6.4	.915	SS-604, OF-1, 2B-1

Dick Allen

ALLEN, RICHARD ANTHONY
Also known as Richie Allen.   Brother of Hank Allen.
Brother of Ron Allen.
B. Mar. 8, 1942, Wampum, Pa.
BR TR 5'11" 187 lbs.

Year	Team		Games	BA	SA	AB	H	2B	3B	HR	HR%	R	RBI	BB	SO	SB	AB	H	PO	A	E	DP	TC/G	FA	G by Pos
1963	PHI	N	10	.292	.458	24	7	2	1	0	0.0	6	2	0	5	0	2	0	10	0	2	0	1.2	.833	OF-7, 3B-1
1964			162	.318	.557	632	201	38	13	29	4.6	125	91	67	138	3	0	0	154	325	41	30	3.2	.921	3B-162
1965			161	.302	.494	619	187	31	14	20	3.2	93	85	74	150	15	1	0	130	305	26	29	2.9	.944	3B-160, SS-2
1966			141	.317	.632	524	166	25	10	40	7.6	112	110	68	136	10	4	1	146	182	14	15	2.4	.959	3B-91, OF-47
1967			122	.307	.566	463	142	31	10	23	5.0	89	77	75	117	20	1	0	95	249	35	23	3.1	.908	3B-121, SS-1, 2B-1
1968			152	.263	.520	521	137	17	9	33	6.3	87	90	74	161	7	8	0	215	20	12	4	1.6	.951	OF-139, 3B-10
1969			118	.288	.573	438	126	23	3	32	7.3	79	89	64	144	9	1	1	1024	54	16	100	9.3	.985	1B-117
1970	STL	N	122	.279	.560	459	128	17	5	34	7.4	88	101	71	118	5	3	1	708	109	18	70	6.8	.978	1B-79, 3B-38, OF-3
1971	LA	N	155	.295	.468	549	162	24	1	23	4.2	82	90	93	113	8	3	0	382	151	21	38	3.6	.962	3B-67, OF-60, 1B-28
1972	CHI	A	148	.308	.603	506	156	28	5	37	7.3	90	113	99	126	19	7	1	1235	69	7	94	8.9	.995	1B-143, 3B-2
1973			72	.316	.612	250	79	20	3	16	6.4	39	41	33	51	7	3	0	601	46	4	55	9.0	.994	1B-67, 2B-2, DH-1
1974			128	.301	.563	462	139	23	1	32	6.9	84	88	57	89	7	4	0	998	50	16	112	8.3	.985	1B-125, DH-1, 2B-1
1975	PHI	N	119	.233	.385	416	97	21	3	12	2.9	54	62	58	109	11	5	0	900	70	18	79	8.3	.982	1B-113
1976			85	.268	.480	298	80	16	1	15	5.0	52	49	37	63	1	4	1	671	44	8	71	8.5	.989	1B-85
1977	OAK	A	54	.240	.351	171	41	4	0	5	2.9	19	31	24	36	1	2	0	389	37	7	36	8.0	.984	1B-50, DH-1
15 yrs.			1749	.292	.534	6332	1848	320	79	351	5.5	1099	1119	894	1556	133	46	5	7658	1711	245	756	5.5	.975	1B-807, 3B-652, OF-256, 2B-4, DH-3, SS-3

LEAGUE CHAMPIONSHIP SERIES

Year	Team		Games	BA	SA	AB	H	2B	3B	HR	HR%	R	RBI	BB	SO	SB	AB	H	PO	A	E	DP	TC/G	FA	G by Pos
1976	PHI	N	3	.222	.222	9	2	0	0	0	0.0	1	0	3	2	0	0	0	28	0	1	1	9.7	.966	1B-3

Ethan Allen

ALLEN, ETHAN NATHAN
B. Jan. 1, 1904, Cincinnati, Ohio
BR TR 6'1" 180 lbs.

Year	Team		Games	BA	SA	AB	H	2B	3B	HR	HR%	R	RBI	BB	SO	SB	AB	H	PO	A	E	DP	TC/G	FA	G by Pos
1926	CIN	N	18	.308	.385	13	4	1	0	0	0.0	3	0	0	3	0	2	0	9	0	0	0	0.5	1.000	OF-9
1927			111	.295	.407	359	106	26	4	2	0.6	54	20	14	23	12	2	1	250	6	3	3	2.3	.988	OF-98
1928			129	.305	.402	485	148	30	7	1	0.2	55	62	27	29	6	0	0	348	12	7	4	2.8	.981	OF-129
1929			143	.292	.416	538	157	27	11	6	1.1	69	64	20	21	21	2	0	393	12	5	2	2.9	.988	OF-137
1930	2 teams	CIN N (21G – .217)				NY N (76G – .307)																			
"	total		97	.292	.447	284	83	10	2	10	3.5	58	38	17	25	6	18	5	153	6	3	0	1.7	.981	OF-77
1931	NY	N	94	.329	.453	298	98	18	2	5	1.7	58	43	15	15	6	14	8	151	2	4	1	1.7	.975	OF-77
1932			54	.175	.301	103	18	6	2	1	1.0	13	7	11	12	0	22	1	44	1	2	0	0.9	.957	OF-24
1933	STL	N	91	.241	.291	261	63	7	0	0	0.0	25	36	13	22	3	21	3	179	8	3	1	2.1	.984	OF-67
1934	PHI	N	145	.330	.468	581	192	42	4	10	1.7	87	85	33	47	6	0	0	337	19	8	3	2.5	.978	OF-145
1935			156	.307	.419	645	198	46	1	8	1.2	90	63	43	54	5	0	0	412	26	9	6	2.9	.980	OF-156

Year	Team		Games	BA	SA	AB	H	2B	3B	HR	HR%	R	RBI	BB	SO	SB	Pinch Hit AB	Pinch Hit H	PO	A	E	DP	TC/G	FA	G by Pos

Ethan Allen *continued*

Year	Team		Games	BA	SA	AB	H	2B	3B	HR	HR%	R	RBI	BB	SO	SB	PH AB	PH H	PO	A	E	DP	TC/G	FA	G by Pos
1936	2 teams	PHI N (30G – .296)	CHI N (91G – .295)																						
"	total		121	.295	.390	498	147	21	7	4	0.8	68	48	17	38	16	0	0	273	3	8	2	2.3	.972	OF-119
1937	STL	A	103	.316	.378	320	101	18	1	0	0.0	39	31	21	17	3	23	8	186	8	4	1	1.9	.980	OF-78
1938			19	.303	.455	33	10	3	1	0	0.0	4	4	2	4	0	12	3	11	0	0	0	0.6	1.000	OF-7
13 yrs.			1281	.300	.410	4418	1325	255	45	47	1.1	623	501	223	310	84	116	29	2746	103	56	23	2.3	.981	OF-1123

Hank Allen

ALLEN, HAROLD ANDREW
Brother of Dick Allen. Brother of Ron Allen.
B. July 23, 1940, Wampum, Pa.

BR TR 6' 190 lbs.

Year	Team		Games	BA	SA	AB	H	2B	3B	HR	HR%	R	RBI	BB	SO	SB	PH AB	PH H	PO	A	E	DP	TC/G	FA	G by Pos
1966	WAS	A	9	.387	.484	31	12	0	0	1	3.2	2	6	3	6	0	0	0	22	0	2	0	2.7	.917	OF-9
1967			116	.233	.318	292	68	8	4	3	1.0	34	17	13	53	3	21	7	148	1	3	1	1.3	.980	OF-99
1968			68	.219	.289	128	28	2	2	1	0.8	16	9	7	16	0	22	5	51	41	7	6	1.5	.929	OF-25, 3B-16, 2B-11
1969			109	.277	.343	271	75	9	3	1	0.4	42	17	13	28	12	23	5	128	14	10	3	1.4	.934	OF-91, 3B-6, 2B-3
1970	2 teams	WAS A (22G – .211)	MIL A (28G – .230)																						
"	total		50	.222	.283	99	22	6	0	0	0.0	7	8	12	14	0	14	2	65	12	0	4	1.5	1.000	OF-31, 2B-5, 1B-4
1972	CHI	N	9	.143	.143	21	3	0	0	0	0.0	1	0	0	2	0	0	0	4	15	2	5	2.3	.905	3B-6
1973			28	.103	.154	39	4	0	0	0	0.0	2	0	1	9	0	5	0	42	12	1	0	2.0	.982	3B-9, 1B-8, OF-5, 2B-1, C-1
7 yrs.			389	.241	.312	881	212	27	9	6	0.7	104	57	49	128	15	85	19	460	95	25	20	1.5	.957	OF-260, 3B-37, 2B-20, 1B-12, C-1

Hezekiah Allen

ALLEN, HEZEKIAH (Ki)
B. Feb. 25, 1863, Westport, Conn. D. Sept. 21, 1916, Saugatuck, Conn.

5'11" 160 lbs.

Year	Team		Games	BA	SA	AB	H	2B	3B	HR	HR%	R	RBI	BB	SO	SB	PH AB	PH H	PO	A	E	DP	TC/G	FA	G by Pos
1884	PHI	N	1	.667	.667	3	2	0	0	0	0.0	0		0	0		0	0	2	0	0	1	2.0	1.000	C-1

Horace Allen

ALLEN, HORACE TANNER (Pug)
B. June 11, 1899, DeLand, Fla. D. July 5, 1981, Canton, N.C.

BL TR 6' 187 lbs.

Year	Team		Games	BA	SA	AB	H	2B	3B	HR	HR%	R	RBI	BB	SO	SB	PH AB	PH H	PO	A	E	DP	TC/G	FA	G by Pos
1919	BKN	N	4	.000	.000	7	0	0	0	0	0.0	0	0	0	2	0	1	0	2	1	0	0	0.8	1.000	OF-2

Jack Allen

ALLEN, CYRUS ALBAN
B. Oct. 2, 1855, Woodstock, Ill. D. Apr. 21, 1915, Girard, Pa.

Year	Team		Games	BA	SA	AB	H	2B	3B	HR	HR%	R	RBI	BB	SO	SB	PH AB	PH H	PO	A	E	DP	TC/G	FA	G by Pos
1879	2 teams	SYR N (11G – .188)	CLE N (16G – .117)																						
"	total		27	.148	.213	108	16	3	2	0	0.0	14	7	2	14	0		0	48	37	21	2	3.9	.802	3B-22, OF-5

Jamie Allen

ALLEN, JAMES BRADLEY
B. May 29, 1958, Yakima, Wash.

BR TR 6' 205 lbs.

Year	Team		Games	BA	SA	AB	H	2B	3B	HR	HR%	R	RBI	BB	SO	SB	PH AB	PH H	PO	A	E	DP	TC/G	FA	G by Pos
1983	SEA	A	86	.223	.304	273	61	10	0	4	1.5	23	21	33	52	6	3	1	55	155	9	16	2.5	.959	3B-82, DH-2

Kim Allen

ALLEN, KIM BRYANT
B. Apr. 5, 1953, Fontana, Calif.

BR TR 5'11" 175 lbs.

Year	Team		Games	BA	SA	AB	H	2B	3B	HR	HR%	R	RBI	BB	SO	SB	PH AB	PH H	PO	A	E	DP	TC/G	FA	G by Pos
1980	SEA	A	23	.235	.294	51	12	3	0	0	0.0	9	3	8	3	10	0	0	26	42	2	8	3.0	.971	2B-15, OF-4, SS-1
1981			19	.000	.000	3	0	0	0	0	0.0	1	0	0	2	2	2	0	1	0	0	0	0.1	1.000	DH-2, OF-2, 2B-2
2 yrs.			42	.222	.278	54	12	3	0	0	0.0	10	3	8	5	12	2	0	27	42	2	8	1.7	.972	2B-17, OF-6, DH-2, SS-1

Myron Allen

ALLEN, MYRON SMITH
B. Mar. 22, 1854, Kingston, N.Y. D. Mar. 8, 1924, Kingston, N.Y.

BR TR 5'8" 150 lbs.

Year	Team		Games	BA	SA	AB	H	2B	3B	HR	HR%	R	RBI	BB	SO	SB	PH AB	PH H	PO	A	E	DP	TC/G	FA	G by Pos
1883	NY	N	1	.000	.000	4	0	0	0	0	0.0	0		0	2		0	0	1	1	0	0	2.0	1.000	P-1
1886	BOS	N	1	.000	.000	3	0	0	0	0	0.0	0		0	1		0	0	2	2	0	0	4.0	1.000	2B-1
1887	CLE	AA	117	.276	.393	463	128	22	10	4	0.9	66		36		26			230	32	31	7	2.5	.894	OF-115, 3B-3, SS-2, P-2
1888	KC	AA	37	.213	.316	136	29	6	4	0	0.0	23		10	9	4			73	17	7	1	2.6	.928	OF-35, P-2
4 yrs.			156	.259	.371	606	157	28	14	4	0.7	89	10	45	3	30	0	0	306	52	38	8	2.5	.904	OF-150, P-5, 3B-3, SS-2, 2B-1

Nick Allen

ALLEN, ARTEMUS WARD
B. Sept. 14, 1888, Norton, Kans. D. Oct. 16, 1939, Hines, Ill.

BR TR 6' 180 lbs.

Year	Team		Games	BA	SA	AB	H	2B	3B	HR	HR%	R	RBI	BB	SO	SB	PH AB	PH H	PO	A	E	DP	TC/G	FA	G by Pos
1914	BUF	F	32	.238	.254	63	15	1	0	0	0.0	3	4	3		4	5	2	93	30	4	5	4.0	.969	C-26
1915			84	.205	.247	215	44	7	1	0	0.0	14	17	18		4	4	1	347	110	21	8	5.7	.956	C-80
1916	CHI	N	5	.063	.063	16	1	0	0	0	0.0	1	1	0	3		1	0	19	4	1	1	4.8	.958	C-4
1918	CIN	N	37	.260	.323	96	25	2	2	0	0.0	6	5	4	7	0	4	3	105	47	8	7	4.3	.950	C-31
1919			15	.320	.400	25	8	0	1	0	0.0	5	2	6		0	2	1	36	10	2	2	3.2	.958	C-12
1920			43	.271	.329	85	23	1	0	0	0.0	10	4	6	11	0	6	2	107	39	6	5	3.5	.961	C-36
6 yrs.			216	.232	.278	500	116	13	5	0	0.0	41	36	33	27	8	22	8	707	240	42	28	4.6	.958	C-189

Pete Allen

ALLEN, JESSE HALL
B. May 1, 1868, Columbiana, Ohio D. Apr. 16, 1946, Philadelphia, Pa.

BR TR 5'8½" 185 lbs.

Year	Team		Games	BA	SA	AB	H	2B	3B	HR	HR%	R	RBI	BB	SO	SB	PH AB	PH H	PO	A	E	DP	TC/G	FA	G by Pos
1893	CLE	N	1	.000	.000	4	0	0	0	0	0.0	0	0	0	0	0	0	0	1	0	0	0	1.0	1.000	C-1

Rod Allen

ALLEN, RODERICK BERNET
B. Oct. 5, 1959, Los Angeles, Calif.

BR TR 6'1" 185 lbs.

Year	Team		Games	BA	SA	AB	H	2B	3B	HR	HR%	R	RBI	BB	SO	SB	PH AB	PH H	PO	A	E	DP	TC/G	FA	G by Pos
1983	SEA	A	11	.167	.167	12	2	0	0	0	0.0	0	1	0	4	0	5	0	0	0		0.5	1.000	DH-3, OF-2
1984	DET	A	15	.296	.333	27	8	1	0	0	0.0	6	3	2	8	1	3	1	2	0	0	0	0.1	1.000	DH-11, OF-2
1988	CLE	A	5	.091	.182	11	1	1	0	0	0.0	1	0	2	2	1	0	0	0	0		0.0	–	DH-4
3 yrs.			31	.220	.260	50	11	2	0	0	0.0	8	3	2	11	1	9	1	7	0	0	0	0.2	1.000	DH-18, OF-4

Ron Allen

ALLEN, RONALD FREDERICK
Brother of Hank Allen. Brother of Dick Allen.
B. Dec. 23, 1943, Wampum, Pa.

BB TR 6'3" 205 lbs.

Year	Team		Games	BA	SA	AB	H	2B	3B	HR	HR%	R	RBI	BB	SO	SB	PH AB	PH H	PO	A	E	DP	TC/G	FA	G by Pos
1972	STL	N	7	.091	.364	11	1	0	0	1	9.1	2	1	3	5	0	0	0	29	1	1	1	4.4	.968	1B-5

Year Team	Games	BA	SA	AB	H	2B	3B	HR	HR%	R	RBI	BB	SO	SB	PH AB	PH H	PO	A	E	DP	TC/G	FA	G by Pos

Sled Allen
ALLEN, FLETCHER MANSON
B. Aug. 23, 1886, West Plains, Mo. D. Oct. 16, 1959, Lubbock, Tex.
BR TR 6'1" 180 lbs.

Year Team	Games	BA	SA	AB	H	2B	3B	HR	HR%	R	RBI	BB	SO	SB	PH AB	PH H	PO	A	E	DP	TC/G	FA	G by Pos
1910 STL A	14	.130	.174	23	3	1	0	0	0.0	3	1	1		0	1	0	21	7	3	0	2.2	.903	C-12, 1B-1

Gary Allenson
ALLENSON, GARY MARTIN (Hardrock)
B. Feb. 4, 1955, Culver City, Calif.
BR TR 5'11" 185 lbs.

Year Team	Games	BA	SA	AB	H	2B	3B	HR	HR%	R	RBI	BB	SO	SB	PH AB	PH H	PO	A	E	DP	TC/G	FA	G by Pos
1979 BOS A	108	.203	.299	241	49	16	2	3	1.2	27	22	20	42	1	0	0	410	42	9	4	4.3	.980	C-104, 3B-3
1980	36	.357	.443	70	25	6	0	1	1.4	9	10	13	11	2	1	0	100	8	2	1	3.1	.982	C-24, DH-6, 3B-5
1981	47	.223	.388	139	31	8	0	5	3.6	23	25	23	33	0	1	0	235	18	8	3	5.6	.969	C-47
1982	92	.205	.314	264	54	11	0	6	2.3	25	33	38	39	0	1	0	454	39	4	8	5.4	.992	C-91
1983	84	.230	.317	230	53	11	0	3	1.3	19	30	27	43	0	1	0	393	29	7	6	5.1	.984	C-84
1984	35	.229	.325	83	19	2	0	2	2.4	9	8	9	14	0	0	0	135	12	2	0	4.3	.987	C-35
1985 TOR A	14	.118	.147	34	4	1	0	0	0.0	2	3	0	10	0	0	0	39	2	0	0	2.9	1.000	C-14
7 yrs.	416	.221	.325	1061	235	49	2	19	1.8	114	131	130	192	3	3	0	1766	150	32	26	4.7	.984	C-399, 3B-8, DH-6

Gene Alley
ALLEY, LEONARD EUGENE
B. July 10, 1940, Richmond, Va.
BR TR 5'10" 160 lbs.

Year Team	Games	BA	SA	AB	H	2B	3B	HR	HR%	R	RBI	BB	SO	SB	PH AB	PH H	PO	A	E	DP	TC/G	FA	G by Pos
1963 PIT N	17	.216	.235	51	11	1	0	0	0.0	3	0	2	12	0	1	0	20	35	3	7	3.4	.948	3B-7, SS-4, 2B-4
1964	81	.211	.321	209	44	3	1	6	2.9	30	13	21	56	0	9	1	102	213	11	45	4.0	.966	SS-61, 3B-3, 2B-1
1965	153	.252	.348	500	126	21	6	5	1.0	47	47	32	82	7	2	0	243	516	26	113	5.1	.967	SS-110, 2B-40, 3B-1
1966	147	.299	.418	579	173	28	10	7	1.2	88	43	27	83	8	1	0	235	472	15	128	4.9	.979	SS-143
1967	152	.287	.391	550	158	25	7	6	1.1	59	55	36	70	10	4	0	257	500	26	105	5.2	.967	SS-146
1968	133	.245	.321	474	116	20	2	4	0.8	48	39	39	78	13	4	0	209	475	16	97	5.3	.977	SS-109, 2B-24
1969	82	.246	.354	285	70	3	2	8	2.8	28	32	19	48	4	1	0	146	220	12	56	4.6	.968	2B-53, SS-25, 3B-5
1970	121	.244	.362	426	104	16	5	8	1.9	46	41	31	70	7	5	0	216	412	15	88	5.3	.977	SS-108, 2B-8, 3B-2
1971	114	.227	.342	348	79	8	7	6	1.7	38	28	35	43	9	4	2	187	317	22	55	4.6	.958	SS-108, 3B-1
1972	119	.248	.320	347	86	12	2	3	0.9	30	36	38	52	4	5	3	181	340	16	88	4.5	.970	SS-114, 3B-4
1973	76	.203	.285	158	32	3	2	2	1.3	25	8	20	28	1	12	0	83	141	4	23	3.0	.982	SS-49, 3B-8
11 yrs.	1195	.254	.354	3927	999	140	44	55	1.4	442	342	300	622	63	48	6	1879	3641	166	805	4.8	.971	SS-977, 2B-130, 3B-31

LEAGUE CHAMPIONSHIP SERIES

Year Team	Games	BA	SA	AB	H	2B	3B	HR	HR%	R	RBI	BB	SO	SB	PH AB	PH H	PO	A	E	DP	TC/G	FA	G by Pos
1970 PIT N	2	.000	.000	7	0	0	0	0	0.0	0	0	1	2	0	1	0	6	7	0	3	6.5	1.000	SS-2
1971	1	.500	.500	2	1	0	0	0	0.0	1	0	0	0	0	0	0	1	1	0	1	2.0	1.000	SS-1
1972	5	.000	.000	16	0	0	0	0	0.0	1	0	0	3	0	0	0	10	4	2	0	3.2	.875	SS-5
3 yrs.	8	.040	.040	25	1	0	0	0	0.0	2	0	1	5	0	0	0	17	12	2	4	3.9	.935	SS-8

WORLD SERIES

Year Team	Games	BA	SA	AB	H	2B	3B	HR	HR%	R	RBI	BB	SO	SB	PH AB	PH H	PO	A	E	DP	TC/G	FA	G by Pos
1971 PIT N	2	.000	.000	2	0	0	0	0	0.0	0	0	1	0	0	0	0	1	4	0	0	2.5	1.000	SS-2

Gair Allie
ALLIE, GAIR ROOSEVELT
B. Oct. 29, 1931, Statesville, N. C.
BR TR 6'1" 190 lbs.

Year Team	Games	BA	SA	AB	H	2B	3B	HR	HR%	R	RBI	BB	SO	SB	PH AB	PH H	PO	A	E	DP	TC/G	FA	G by Pos
1954 PIT N	121	.199	.268	418	83	8	6	3	0.7	38	30	56	84	1	4	0	211	295	26	59	4.4	.951	SS-95, 3B-19

Bob Allietta
ALLIETTA, ROBERT GEORGE
B. May 1, 1952, New Bedford, Mass.
BR TR 6' 190 lbs.

Year Team	Games	BA	SA	AB	H	2B	3B	HR	HR%	R	RBI	BB	SO	SB	PH AB	PH H	PO	A	E	DP	TC/G	FA	G by Pos
1975 CAL A	21	.178	.267	45	8	1	0	1	2.2	4	2	1	6	0	0	0	92	6	0	0	4.7	1.000	C-21

Art Allison
ALLISON, ARTHUR ALGERNON
Brother of Doug Allison.
B. Jan. 29, 1849, Philadelphia, Pa. D. Feb. 25, 1916, Washington, D. C.
5'8" 150 lbs.

Year Team	Games	BA	SA	AB	H	2B	3B	HR	HR%	R	RBI	BB	SO	SB	PH AB	PH H	PO	A	E	DP	TC/G	FA	G by Pos
1876 LOU N	31	.208	.238	130	27	2	1	0	0.0	9	10	2	6		0	0	124	12	16	3	4.9	.895	OF-23, 1B-8

Bob Allison
ALLISON, WILLIAM ROBERT
B. July 11, 1934, Raytown, Mo.
BR TR 6'3" 205 lbs.

Year Team	Games	BA	SA	AB	H	2B	3B	HR	HR%	R	RBI	BB	SO	SB	PH AB	PH H	PO	A	E	DP	TC/G	FA	G by Pos
1958 WAS A	11	.200	.229	35	7	1	0	0	0.0	1	0	2	5	0	0	0	24	0	0	0	2.2	1.000	OF-11
1959	150	.261	.482	570	149	18	9	30	5.3	83	85	60	92	13	1	0	333	8	9	1	2.3	.974	OF-149
1960	144	.251	.413	501	126	30	3	15	3.0	79	69	92	94	11	4	0	311	13	11	4	2.3	.967	OF-140, 1B-4
1961 MIN A	159	.245	.450	556	136	21	3	29	5.2	83	105	103	100	2	0	0	417	18	10	12	2.8	.978	OF-150, 1B-18
1962	149	.266	.511	519	138	24	8	29	5.6	102	102	84	115	8	0	0	287	10	7	1	2.0	.977	OF-147
1963	148	.271	.533	527	143	25	4	35	6.6	99	91	90	109	6	1	0	326	11	10	4	2.3	.971	OF-147
1964	149	.287	.553	492	141	27	4	32	6.5	90	86	92	99	10	8	1	829	58	12	64	6.0	.987	1B-93, OF-61
1965	135	.233	.445	438	102	14	5	23	5.3	71	78	73	114	10	14	2	247	12	7	5	2.0	.974	OF-122, 1B-3
1966	70	.220	.411	168	37	6	1	8	4.8	34	19	30	34	6	11	5	86	3	3	0	1.3	.967	OF-56
1967	153	.258	.470	496	128	21	6	24	4.8	73	75	74	114	6	6	4	220	6	5	0	1.5	.978	OF-145
1968	145	.247	.456	469	116	16	8	22	4.7	63	52	52	98	9	13	2	316	16	8	14	2.3	.976	OF-117, 1B-17
1969	81	.228	.418	189	43	8	2	8	4.2	18	27	29	39	2	20	4	96	3	0	1	1.2	1.000	OF-58, 1B-3
1970	47	.208	.319	72	15	5	0	1	1.4	15	7	14	20	1	20	7	54	4	0	1	1.3	.967	OF-17, 1B-7
13 yrs.	1541	.255	.471	5032	1281	216	53	256	5.1	811	796	795	1033	84	98	25	3546	162	84	108	2.5	.978	OF-1320, 1B-145

LEAGUE CHAMPIONSHIP SERIES

Year Team	Games	BA	SA	AB	H	2B	3B	HR	HR%	R	RBI	BB	SO	SB	PH AB	PH H	PO	A	E	DP	TC/G	FA	G by Pos
1969 MIN A	2	.000	.000	8	0	0	0	0	0.0	0	1	0	0	0	0	0	6	0	0	0	3.0	1.000	OF-2
1970	3	.000	.000	2	0	0	0	0	0.0	0	0	1	1	0	2	0	0	0	0	0	0.0	—	OF-2
2 yrs.	5	.000	.000	10	0	0	0	0	0.0	0	1	1	1	0	2	0	6	0	0	0	1.2	1.000	OF-2

WORLD SERIES

Year Team	Games	BA	SA	AB	H	2B	3B	HR	HR%	R	RBI	BB	SO	SB	PH AB	PH H	PO	A	E	DP	TC/G	FA	G by Pos
1965 MIN A	5	.125	.375	16	2	1	0	1	6.3	3	2	2	9	1	0	0	11	0	0	0	2.2	1.000	OF-5

Doug Allison
ALLISON, DOUGLAS L.
Brother of Art Allison.
B. 1846, Philadelphia, Pa. D. Dec. 19, 1916, Washington, D. C.
BR TR 5'10½" 160 lbs.

Year Team	Games	BA	SA	AB	H	2B	3B	HR	HR%	R	RBI	BB	SO	SB	PH AB	PH H	PO	A	E	DP	TC/G	FA	G by Pos
1876 HAR N	44	.264	.288	163	43	4	0	0	0.0	19	15	3	9		0	0	206	43	34	2	6.4	.880	C-40, OF-6
1877	29	.148	.165	115	17	2	0	0	0.0	14	6	3	7		0	0	127	36	19	4	6.3	.896	C-29

Year	Team		Games	BA	SA	AB	H	2B	3B	HR	HR%	R	RBI	BB	SO	SB	Pinch Hit AB	H	PO	A	E	DP	TC/G	FA	G by Pos

Doug Allison *continued*

Year	Team		Games	BA	SA	AB	H	2B	3B	HR	HR%	R	RBI	BB	SO	SB	AB	H	PO	A	E	DP	TC/G	FA	G by Pos
1878	PRO	N	19	.289	.316	76	22	2	0	0	0.0	9	7	1	8		0	0	96	27	12	1	7.1	.911	C-19, P-1
1879			1	.000	.000	5	0	0	0	0	0.0	0	0	0	1		0	0	9	1	2	0	12.0	.833	C-1
1883	BAL	AA	1	.667	.667	3	2	0	0	0	0.0	2		0			0	0	1	2	0	0	3.0	1.000	OF-1, C-1
5 yrs.			94	.232	.254	362	84	8	0	0	0.0	44	28	7	25		0	0	439	109	67	7	6.5	.891	C-90, OF-7, P-1

Milo Allison

ALLISON, MILO HENRY (Pete)
B. Oct. 16, 1890, Elk Rapids, Mich.   D. June 18, 1957, Kenosha, Wis.

BL TR 6'   163 lbs.

Year	Team		Games	BA	SA	AB	H	2B	3B	HR	HR%	R	RBI	BB	SO	SB	AB	H	PO	A	E	DP	TC/G	FA	G by Pos
1913	CHI	N	2	.333	.333	6	2	0	0	0	0.0	1	0	0	1	1	0	0	3	0	0	0	1.5	1.000	OF-1
1914			1	1.000	1.000	1	1	0	0	0	0.0	0	0	0	0	0	1	1	0	0	0	0	0.0	–	
1916	CLE	A	14	.278	.278	18	5	0	0	0	0.0	10	0	6	1	0	1	0	5	0	0	0	0.4	1.000	OF-5
1917			32	.143	.143	35	5	0	0	0	0.0	4	0	9	7	3	14	0	12	1	0	0	0.4	1.000	OF-11
4 yrs.			49	.217	.217	60	13	0	0	0	0.0	15	0	15	9	4	16	1	20	1	0	0	0.4	1.000	OF-17

Beau Allred

ALLRED, DALE LeBEAU
B. June 4, 1965, Mesa, Ariz.

BL TL 6'   190 lbs.

Year	Team		Games	BA	SA	AB	H	2B	3B	HR	HR%	R	RBI	BB	SO	SB	AB	H	PO	A	E	DP	TC/G	FA	G by Pos
1989	CLE	A	13	.250	.375	24	6	3	0	0	0.0	0	1	2	10	0	8	2	11	1	0	1	0.9	1.000	OF-5, DH-2

Mel Almada

ALMADA, BALDOMERO MELO
B. Feb. 7, 1913, Hwatabampo, Mexico   D. Aug. 13, 1988, Hermosillo, Mexico

BL TL 6'   170 lbs.

Year	Team		Games	BA	SA	AB	H	2B	3B	HR	HR%	R	RBI	BB	SO	SB	AB	H	PO	A	E	DP	TC/G	FA	G by Pos
1933	BOS	A	14	.341	.409	44	15	0	1	1	2.3	11	3	11	3	3	1	0	27	1	0	0	2.0	1.000	OF-13
1934			23	.233	.278	90	21	2	1	0	0.0	7	10	6	8	3	0	0	60	4	1	0	2.8	.985	OF-23
1935			151	.290	.379	607	176	27	9	3	0.5	85	59	55	34	20	0	0	354	23	12	4	2.6	.969	OF-149, 1B-3
1936			96	.253	.338	320	81	16	4	1	0.3	40	21	24	15	2	13	5	144	9	2	2	1.6	.987	OF-81
1937	2 teams		BOS A (32G – .236)			WAS A (100G – .309)																			
"	total		132	.295	.394	543	160	27	6	5	0.9	91	42	53	27	12	0	0	376	17	17	6	3.1	.959	OF-127, 1B-4
1938	2 teams		WAS A (47G – .244)			STL A (102G – .342)																			
"	total		149	.311	.395	633	197	29	6	4	0.6	101	52	46	38	13	1	0	394	16	14	2	2.8	.967	OF-148
1939	2 teams		STL A (42G – .239)			BKN N (39G – .214)																			
"	total		81	.228	.272	246	56	6	1	1	0.4	28	10	19	25	3	8	3	159	4	3	1	2.0	.982	OF-66
7 yrs.			646	.284	.367	2483	706	107	27	15	0.6	363	197	214	150	56	23	8	1514	74	49	15	2.5	.970	OF-607, 1B-7

Rafael Almeida

ALMEIDA, RAFAEL D.
B. July 30, 1887, Havana, Cuba   D. Mar., 1968, Havana, Cuba

BR TR 5'9"   164 lbs.

Year	Team		Games	BA	SA	AB	H	2B	3B	HR	HR%	R	RBI	BB	SO	SB	AB	H	PO	A	E	DP	TC/G	FA	G by Pos
1911	CIN	N	36	.313	.385	96	30	5	1	0	0.0	9	15	9	16	3	4	1	36	45	10	2	2.5	.890	3B-27, SS-1, 2B-1
1912			16	.220	.390	59	13	4	3	0	0.0	9	10	5	8	0	1	0	13	28	5	2	2.9	.891	3B-16
1913			50	.262	.392	130	34	4	2	3	2.3	14	21	11	16	4	7	1	49	72	11	8	2.6	.917	3B-37, OF-3, SS-2, 2B-1
3 yrs.			102	.270	.389	285	77	13	6	3	1.1	32	46	25	40	7	12	2	98	145	26	12	2.6	.903	3B-80, OF-3, SS-3, 2B-2

Bill Almon

ALMON, WILLIAM FRANCIS
B. Nov. 21, 1952, Providence, R. I.

BR TR 6'3"   180 lbs.

Year	Team		Games	BA	SA	AB	H	2B	3B	HR	HR%	R	RBI	BB	SO	SB	AB	H	PO	A	E	DP	TC/G	FA	G by Pos
1974	SD	N	16	.316	.342	38	12	1	0	0	0.0	4	3	1	9	1	0	0	13	30	4	4	2.9	.915	SS-14
1975			6	.400	.400	10	4	0	0	0	0.0	0	0	0	1	0	1	0	6	5	0	0	1.8	1.000	SS-2
1976			14	.246	.351	57	14	3	0	1	1.8	6	6	2	9	3	0	0	23	52	3	8	5.6	.962	SS-14
1977			155	.261	.336	613	160	18	11	2	0.3	75	43	37	114	20	0	0	303	538	41	87	5.7	.954	SS-155
1978			138	.252	.309	405	102	19	2	0	0.0	39	21	33	74	17	4	1	102	255	23	26	2.8	.939	3B-114, SS-15, 2B-7
1979			100	.227	.258	198	45	3	0	1	0.5	20	8	21	48	6	3	0	142	193	7	48	3.4	.980	2B-61, SS-25, OF-1
1980	2 teams		MON N (18G – .263)			NY N (48G – .170)																			
"	total		66	.193	.260	150	29	4	3	0	0.0	15	7	9	32	2	4	0	79	134	12	25	3.4	.947	SS-34, 2B-19, 3B-9
1981	CHI	A	103	.301	.375	349	105	10	2	4	1.1	46	41	21	60	16	0	0	190	340	17	78	5.3	.969	SS-103
1982			111	.256	.354	308	79	10	4	4	1.3	40	26	25	49	10	1	0	164	317	26	72	4.6	.949	SS-108, DH-1
1983	OAK	A	143	.266	.361	451	120	29	1	4	0.9	45	63	26	67	26	14	3	327	176	20	33	3.7	.962	SS-52, 3B-40, 1B-38, OF-23, 2B-5, DH-4
1984			106	.223	.374	211	47	11	0	7	3.3	24	24	10	42	5	15	3	255	15	2	19	2.6	.993	OF-48, 1B-44, DH-12, 3B-4, SS-1, C-1
1985	PIT	N	88	.270	.414	244	66	17	0	6	2.5	33	29	22	61	10	14	5	104	108	5	22	2.5	.977	SS-43, OF-32, 3B-7, 1B-7
1986			102	.219	.383	196	43	7	2	7	3.6	29	27	30	38	11	28	5	80	45	8	4	1.3	.940	OF-54, 3B-28, SS-19, 1B-4
1987	2 teams		PIT N (19G – .200)			NY N (49G – .241)																			
"	total		68	.230	.284	74	17	4	0	0	0.0	13	5	9	21	1	22	4	26	42	3	7	1.0	.958	SS-26, 2B-10, OF-3, 1B-2, 3B-1
1988	PHI	N	20	.115	.192	26	3	2	0	0	0.0	1	1	1	11	0	6	0	20	15	2	2	1.9	.946	3B-9, SS-5, 1B-1
15 yrs.			1236	.254	.343	3330	846	138	25	36	1.1	390	296	250	636	128	112	21	1834	2265	173	435	3.5	.960	SS-616, 3B-212, OF-161, 2B-102, 1B-96, DH-17, C-1

Roberto Alomar

ALOMAR, ROBERTO
Born Roberto Alomar y Velasquez.   Son of Sandy Alomar.
Brother of Sandy Alomar.
B. Feb. 5, 1968, Ponce, Puerto Rico

BB TR 6'   184 lbs.

Year	Team		Games	BA	SA	AB	H	2B	3B	HR	HR%	R	RBI	BB	SO	SB	AB	H	PO	A	E	DP	TC/G	FA	G by Pos
1988	SD	N	143	.266	.382	545	145	24	6	9	1.7	84	41	47	83	24	0	0	319	459	16	88	5.6	.980	2B-143
1989			158	.295	.376	623	184	27	1	7	1.1	82	56	53	76	42	1	0	341	472	28	91	5.3	.967	2B-157
2 yrs.			301	.282	.378	1168	329	51	7	16	1.4	166	97	100	159	66	1	0	660	931	44	179	5.4	.973	2B-300

Sandy Alomar

ALOMAR, SANTOS, SR.
Born Santos Alomar y Conde.   Father of Sandy Alomar.
Father of Roberto Alomar.
B. Oct. 19, 1943, Salinas, Puerto Rico

BB TR 5'9"   140 lbs.
BR 1964-66

Year	Team		Games	BA	SA	AB	H	2B	3B	HR	HR%	R	RBI	BB	SO	SB	AB	H	PO	A	E	DP	TC/G	FA	G by Pos
1964	MIL	N	19	.245	.264	53	13	1	0	0	0.0	3	6	0	11	1	0	0	27	60	3	8	4.7	.967	SS-19
1965			67	.241	.269	108	26	1	1	0	0.0	16	8	4	12	12	0	0	68	114	5	19	2.8	.973	SS-39, 2B-19
1966	ATL	N	31	.091	.114	44	4	1	0	0	0.0	4	2	1	10	0	1	0	30	34	1	11	2.1	.985	2B-21, SS-5

Year	Team		Games	BA	SA	AB	H	2B	3B	HR	HR%	R	RBI	BB	SO	SB	Pinch Hit AB	Pinch Hit H	PO	A	E	DP	TC/G	FA	G by Pos

Sandy Alomar *continued*

Year	Team		Games	BA	SA	AB	H	2B	3B	HR	HR%	R	RBI	BB	SO	SB	AB	H	PO	A	E	DP	TC/G	FA	G by Pos
1967 2 teams	NY	N (15G – .000)	CHI	A	(12G – .200)																				
" total	27		.081	.081	37	3	0	0	0	0.0	5	0	2	6	2	1	0	27	32	1	9	2.2	.983	SS-18, 2B-4, 3B-3
1968 CHI A	133		.253	.287	363	92	8	2	0	0.0	41	12	20	42	21	4	2	210	264	20	55	3.7	.960	2B-99, 3B-27, SS-9, OF-1
1969 2 teams	CHI	A (22G – .224)	CAL	A	(134G – .250)																				
" total	156		.248	.279	617	153	12	2	1	0.2	68	34	40	54	20	0	0	344	401	23	109	4.9	.970	2B-156
1970 CAL A	162		.251	.293	672	169	18	2	2	0.3	82	36	49	65	35	0	0	391	481	20	124	5.5	.978	2B-153, SS-10, 3B-1
1971	162		.260	.321	689	179	24	3	4	0.6	77	42	41	60	39	0	0	393	530	17	115	5.8	.982	2B-137, SS-28
1972	155		.239	.287	610	146	20	3	1	0.2	65	25	47	55	20	0	0	353	394	17	93	4.9	.978	2B-154, SS-4
1973	136		.238	.257	470	112	7	1	0	0.0	45	28	34	44	25	0	0	290	355	17	86	4.9	.974	2B-110, SS-31
1974 2 teams	CAL	A (46G – .222)	NY	A	(76G – .269)																				
" total	122		.261	.300	333	87	8	1	1	0.3	47	28	15	33	8	3	1	222	241	11	56	3.9	.977	2B-91, SS-19, 3B-5, DH-1, OF-1
1975 NY A	151		.239	.305	489	117	18	4	2	0.4	61	39	26	58	28	0	0	341	370	11	94	4.8	.985	2B-150, SS-1
1976	67		.239	.282	163	39	4	0	1	0.6	20	10	13	12	12	2	0	95	114	7	18	3.2	.968	2B-38, DH-9, SS-6, 3B-3, OF-1, 1B-1
1977 TEX A	69		.265	.337	83	22	3	0	1	1.2	21	11	8	13	4	7	2	52	52	3	13	1.6	.972	DH-26, 2B-18, SS-6, OF-5, 1B-4, 3B-1
1978	24		.207	.241	29	6	1	0	0	0.0	3	1	1	7	0	0	0	45	21	2	7	2.8	.971	1B-9, 2B-6, DH-3, 3B-3, SS-2
15 yrs.	1481		.245	.288	4760	1168	126	19	13	0.3	558	282	301	482	227	18	5	2888	3463	158	817	4.4	.976	2B-1156, SS-197, 3B-43, DH-39, 1B-14, OF-8

LEAGUE CHAMPIONSHIP SERIES

Year	Team		Games	BA	SA	AB	H	2B	3B	HR	HR%	R	RBI	BB	SO	SB	AB	H	PO	A	E	DP	TC/G	FA	G by Pos
1976 NY A	2		.000	.000	1	0	0	0	0	0.0	0	0	0	0	0	1	0	0	0	0	0	0.0	–	DH-1

Sandy Alomar

ALOMAR, SANTOS, JR.
Born Santos Alomar y Velasquez. Son of Sandy Alomar.
Brother of Roberto Alomar.
B. June 18, 1966, Salinas, Puerto Rico

BR TR 6'5" 200 lbs.

Year	Team		Games	BA	SA	AB	H	2B	3B	HR	HR%	R	RBI	BB	SO	SB	AB	H	PO	A	E	DP	TC/G	FA	G by Pos
1988 SD N	1		.000	.000	1	0	0	0	0	0.0	0	0	0	1	0	1	0	0	0	0	0	0.0	–	
1989	7		.211	.421	19	4	1	0	1	5.3	1	6	3	3	0	1	0	33	1	0	1	4.9	1.000	C-6
2 yrs.	8		.200	.400	20	4	1	0	1	5.0	1	6	3	4	0	1	0	33	1	0	1	4.3	1.000	C-6

Felipe Alou

ALOU, FELIPE
Born Felipe Rojas y Alou. Brother of Jesus Alou.
Brother of Matty Alou.
B. May 12, 1935, Santo Domingo, Dominican Republic

BR TR 6' 195 lbs.

Year	Team		Games	BA	SA	AB	H	2B	3B	HR	HR%	R	RBI	BB	SO	SB	AB	H	PO	A	E	DP	TC/G	FA	G by Pos
1958 SF N	75		.253	.390	182	46	9	2	4	2.2	21	16	19	34	4	5	1	126	2	2	1	1.7	.985	OF-70
1959	95		.275	.466	247	68	13	2	10	4.0	38	33	17	38	5	21	5	111	2	3	0	1.2	.974	OF-69
1960	106		.264	.410	322	85	17	3	8	2.5	48	44	16	42	10	9	0	156	5	7	0	1.6	.958	OF-95
1961	132		.289	.465	415	120	19	0	18	4.3	59	52	26	41	11	11	2	196	10	2	1	1.6	.990	OF-122
1962	154		.316	.513	561	177	30	3	25	4.5	96	98	33	66	10	4	0	262	7	8	3	1.8	.971	OF-150
1963	157		.281	.474	565	159	31	9	20	3.5	75	82	27	87	11	8	4	279	9	4	2	1.9	.986	OF-153
1964 MIL N	121		.253	.395	415	105	26	3	9	2.2	60	51	30	41	5	18	5	329	12	5	12	2.9	.986	OF-91, 1B-69, 3B-2, SS-1
1965	143		.297	.481	555	165	29	2	23	4.1	80	78	31	63	8	9	3	626	43	6	39	4.7	.991	1B-90, OF-79, 3B-3, SS-1
1966 ATL N	154		.327	.533	666	218	32	6	31	4.7	122	74	24	51	5	0	0	935	64	13	63	6.6	.987	1B-85, OF-56
1967	140		.274	.408	574	157	26	3	15	2.6	76	43	32	50	6	3	1	864	34	9	67	6.5	.990	1B-85, OF-56
1968	160		.317	.438	662	210	37	5	11	1.7	72	57	48	56	12	3	0	379	8	8	2	2.5	.980	OF-158
1969	123		.282	.345	476	134	13	1	5	1.1	54	32	23	23	4	2	2	260	4	3	1	2.2	.989	OF-116
1970 OAK A	154		.271	.367	575	156	25	3	8	1.4	70	55	32	31	10	9	1	290	11	7	4	2.0	.977	OF-145, 1B-1
1971 2 teams	OAK	A (2G – .250)	NY	A	(131G – .289)																				
" total	133		.288	.409	469	135	21	6	8	1.7	52	69	32	25	5	19	7	513	23	4	23	4.1	.993	OF-82, 1B-42
1972 NY A	120		.278	.395	324	90	18	1	6	1.9	33	37	22	27	1	29	10	669	54	7	69	6.1	.990	1B-95, OF-15
1973 2 teams	NY	A (93G – .236)	MON	N	(19G – .208)																				
" total	112		.232	.317	328	76	13	0	5	1.5	29	31	11	29	0	21	5	542	34	7	43	5.2	.988	1B-68, OF-37
1974 MIL N	3		.000	.000	3	0	0	0	0	0.0	0	0	0	2	0	3	0	0	0	1	0	0.3	–	OF-1
17 yrs.	2082		.286	.433	7339	2101	359	49	206	2.8	985	852	423	706	107	174	46	6537	322	96	330	3.3	.986	OF-1531, 1B-468, 3B-5, SS-2

LEAGUE CHAMPIONSHIP SERIES

Year	Team		Games	BA	SA	AB	H	2B	3B	HR	HR%	R	RBI	BB	SO	SB	AB	H	PO	A	E	DP	TC/G	FA	G by Pos
1969 ATL N	1		.000	.000	1	0	0	0	0	0.0	0	0	0	0	0	1	0	0	0	0	0	0.0	–	

WORLD SERIES

Year	Team		Games	BA	SA	AB	H	2B	3B	HR	HR%	R	RBI	BB	SO	SB	AB	H	PO	A	E	DP	TC/G	FA	G by Pos
1962 SF N	7		.269	.385	26	7	1	1	0	0.0	2	1	1	4	0	0	0	8	0	1	0	1.3	.889	OF-7

Jesus Alou

ALOU, JESUS MARIA (Jay)
Born Jesus Maria Rojas y Alou. Brother of Matty Alou.
Brother of Felipe Alou.
B. Mar. 24, 1942, Haina, Dominican Republic

BR TR 6'2" 190 lbs.

Year	Team		Games	BA	SA	AB	H	2B	3B	HR	HR%	R	RBI	BB	SO	SB	AB	H	PO	A	E	DP	TC/G	FA	G by Pos
1963 SF N	16		.250	.292	24	6	1	0	0	0.0	3	5	0	3	0	4	0	7	0	1	0	0.5	.875	OF-12
1964	115		.274	.327	376	103	11	0	3	0.8	42	28	13	35	6	13	4	172	8	5	2	1.6	.973	OF-108
1965	143		.298	.398	543	162	19	4	9	1.7	76	52	13	40	8	8	4	238	7	5	0	1.7	.980	OF-136
1966	110		.259	.308	370	96	13	1	1	0.3	41	20	9	22	5	13	3	141	4	5	1	1.4	.967	OF-100
1967	129		.292	.367	510	149	15	4	5	1.0	55	30	14	39	1	6	2	195	5	11	2	1.6	.948	OF-123
1968	120		.263	.317	419	110	15	4	0	0.0	26	39	9	23	1	18	4	175	10	2	2	1.6	.989	OF-105
1969 HOU N	115		.248	.341	452	112	19	4	5	1.1	49	34	15	30	4	0	0	173	8	14	1	1.7	.928	OF-112
1970	117		.306	.384	458	140	27	3	1	0.2	59	44	21	15	3	11	2	169	6	7	2	1.6	.962	OF-108
1971	122		.279	.360	433	121	21	4	2	0.5	41	40	13	17	5	17	5	229	7	4	3	2.0	.983	OF-109
1972	52		.312	.376	93	29	4	1	0	0.0	8	11	7	5	0	31	8	32	0	1	0	0.6	.970	OF-23
1973 2 teams	HOU	N (28G – .236)	OAK	A	(36G – .306)																				
" total	64		.282	.350	163	46	5	0	2	1.2	17	19	3	12	0	22	5	16	0	1	0	0.3	.941	OF-35, DH-6
1974 OAK A	96		.268	.332	220	59	8	0	2	0.9	13	15	5	9	0	41	7	35	3	0	1	0.4	1.000	DH-41, OF-25
1975 NY N	62		.265	.294	102	27	3	0	0	0.0	8	11	4	5	0	39	14	23	1	0	0	0.4	.963	OF-20
1978 HOU N	77		.324	.417	139	45	5	1	2	1.4	7	19	6	5	0	44	16	40	1	0	1	0.5	.976	OF-28

Year	Team		Games	BA	SA	AB	H	2B	3B	HR	HR%	R	RBI	BB	SO	SB	Pinch Hit AB	Pinch Hit H	PO	A	E	DP	TC/G	FA	G by Pos

Jesus Alou *continued*

Year	Team		Games	BA	SA	AB	H	2B	3B	HR	HR%	R	RBI	BB	SO	SB	AB	H	PO	A	E	DP	TC/G	FA	G by Pos
1979			42	.256	.349	43	11	4	0	0	0.0	3	10	6	7	0	34	8	8	0	0	1	0.2	1.000	OF-6, 1B-1
15 yrs.			1380	.280	.353	4345	1216	170	26	32	0.7	448	377	138	267	31	301	82	1653	62	58	15	1.3	.967	OF-1050, DH-47, 1B-1

LEAGUE CHAMPIONSHIP SERIES

Year	Team		Games	BA	SA	AB	H	2B	3B	HR	HR%	R	RBI	BB	SO	SB	AB	H	PO	A	E	DP	TC/G	FA	G by Pos
1973	OAK	A	4	.333	.333	6	2	0	0	0	0.0	0	1	0	1	0	3	1	0	0	0	0	0.0	–	DH-1
1974			1	1.000	1.000	1	1	0	0	0	0.0	0	0	0	0	0	1	1	0	0	0	0	0.0	–	
2 yrs.			5	.429	.429	7	3	0	0	0	0.0	0	1	0	1	0	4	2	0	0	0	0	0.0	–	DH-1

WORLD SERIES

Year	Team		Games	BA	SA	AB	H	2B	3B	HR	HR%	R	RBI	BB	SO	SB	AB	H	PO	A	E	DP	TC/G	FA	G by Pos
1973	OAK	A	7	.158	.211	19	3	1	0	0	0.0	0	3	0	0	0	1	0	5	0	0	0	0.7	1.000	OF-6
1974			1	.000	.000	1	0	0	0	0	0.0	0	0	0	1	0	1	0	0	0	0	0	0.0	–	
2 yrs.			8	.150	.200	20	3	1	0	0	0.0	0	3	0	1	0	2	0	5	0	0	0	0.6	1.000	OF-6

Matty Alou

ALOU, MATEO
Born Mateo Rojas y Alou.   Brother of Jesus Alou.
Brother of Felipe Alou.
B. Dec. 22, 1938, Haina, Dominican Republic

BL TL 5'9" 160 lbs.

Year	Team		Games	BA	SA	AB	H	2B	3B	HR	HR%	R	RBI	BB	SO	SB	AB	H	PO	A	E	DP	TC/G	FA	G by Pos
1960	SF	N	4	.333	.333	3	1	0	0	0	0.0	1	0	0	0	0	3	1	1	0	0	0	0.3	1.000	OF-1
1961			81	.310	.455	200	62	7	2	6	3.0	38	24	15	18	3	22	5	85	2	2	0	1.1	.978	OF-58
1962			78	.292	.390	195	57	8	1	3	1.5	28	14	14	17	3	24	9	80	3	2	0	1.1	.976	OF-57
1963			63	.145	.158	76	11	1	0	0	0.0	4	2	2	13	0	45	8	19	1	1	0	0.3	.952	OF-20
1964			110	.264	.308	250	66	4	2	1	0.4	28	14	11	25	5	30	4	120	2	3	1	1.1	.976	OF-80
1965			117	.231	.299	324	75	12	2	2	0.6	37	18	17	28	10	19	1	139	6	2	1	1.3	.986	OF-103, P-1
1966	PIT	N	141	.342	.421	535	183	18	9	2	0.4	86	27	24	44	23	7	4	264	11	8	3	2.0	.972	OF-136
1967			139	.338	.413	550	186	21	7	2	0.4	87	28	24	42	16	10	2	252	9	3	3	1.9	.989	OF-134, 1B-1
1968			146	.332	.396	558	185	28	4	0	0.0	59	27	27	26	18	2	1	298	8	5	0	2.1	.984	OF-144
1969			162	.331	.411	698	231	41	6	1	0.1	105	48	42	35	22	0	0	327	10	8	4	2.1	.977	OF-162
1970			155	.297	.356	677	201	21	8	1	0.1	97	47	30	18	19	2	0	297	15	8	1	2.1	.975	OF-153
1971	STL	N	149	.315	.415	609	192	28	6	7	1.1	85	74	34	27	19	6	2	710	35	9	42	5.1	.988	OF-94, 1B-57
1972	2 teams		STL	N	(108G – .314)		OAK	A	(32G – .281)																
"	total		140	.307	.379	525	161	22	2	4	0.8	57	47	35	35	13	9	1	595	44	7	53	4.6	.989	OF-71, 1B-67
1973	2 teams		NY	A	(123G – .296)		STL	N	(11G – .273)																
"	total		134	.295	.354	508	150	22	1	2	0.4	60	29	31	43	5	10	3	525	27	12	46	4.2	.979	OF-86, 1B-41, DH-1
1974	SD	N	48	.198	.235	81	16	3	0	0	0.0	8	3	5	6	0	30	5	33	0	1	0	0.7	.971	OF-13, 1B-2
15 yrs.			1667	.307	.381	5789	1777	236	50	31	0.5	780	427	311	377	156	219	46	3745	173	71	154	2.4	.982	OF-1312, 1B-168, DH-1, P-1

LEAGUE CHAMPIONSHIP SERIES

Year	Team		Games	BA	SA	AB	H	2B	3B	HR	HR%	R	RBI	BB	SO	SB	AB	H	PO	A	E	DP	TC/G	FA	G by Pos
1970	PIT	N	3	.250	.333	12	3	1	0	0	0.0	1	0	2	1	0	0	0	6	0	0	0	2.0	1.000	OF-3
1972	OAK	A	5	.381	.571	21	8	4	0	0	0.0	2	2	0	2	1	0	0	8	0	0	0	1.6	1.000	OF-5
2 yrs.			8	.333	.485	33	11	5	0	0	0.0	3	2	2	3	1	0	0	14	0	0	0	1.8	1.000	OF-8

WORLD SERIES

Year	Team		Games	BA	SA	AB	H	2B	3B	HR	HR%	R	RBI	BB	SO	SB	AB	H	PO	A	E	DP	TC/G	FA	G by Pos
1962	SF	N	6	.333	.417	12	4	1	0	0	0.0	2	1	0	0	0	3	2	3	0	0	0	0.5	1.000	OF-4
1972	OAK	A	7	.042	.042	24	1	0	0	0	0.0	0	0	3	1	0	0	0	11	1	1	1	1.9	.923	OF-7
2 yrs.			13	.139	.167	36	5	1	0	0	0.0	2	1	3	1	0	3	2	14	1	1	1	1.2	.938	OF-11

Whitey Alperman

ALPERMAN, CHARLES AUGUSTUS
B. Nov. 11, 1879, Etna, Pa.   D. Dec. 25, 1942, Pittsburgh, Pa.

BR TR 5'10" 180 lbs.

Year	Team		Games	BA	SA	AB	H	2B	3B	HR	HR%	R	RBI	BB	SO	SB	AB	H	PO	A	E	DP	TC/G	FA	G by Pos
1906	BKN	N	128	.252	.338	441	111	15	7	3	0.7	38	46	6		13	1	0	312	388	47	29	5.8	.937	2B-104, SS-24, 3B-1
1907			141	.233	.342	558	130	23	16	2	0.4	44	39	13		5	3	1	339	437	45	45	5.8	.945	2B-115, 3B-14, SS-12
1908			70	.197	.235	213	42	3	1	1	0.5	17	15	9		2	11	1	96	135	22	8	3.6	.913	2B-42, 3B-9, OF-5, SS-2
1909			111	.248	.357	420	104	19	12	1	0.2	35	41	2		7	3	0	266	297	42	32	5.5	.931	2B-108
4 yrs.			450	.237	.331	1632	387	60	36	7	0.4	134	141	30		27	18	2	1013	1257	156	114	5.4	.936	2B-369, SS-38, 3B-24, OF-5

Dell Alston

ALSTON, WENDELL
B. Sept. 22, 1952, Valhalla, N. Y.

BL TR 6' 180 lbs.

Year	Team		Games	BA	SA	AB	H	2B	3B	HR	HR%	R	RBI	BB	SO	SB	AB	H	PO	A	E	DP	TC/G	FA	G by Pos
1977	NY	A	22	.325	.500	40	13	4	0	1	2.5	10	4	3	4	3	8	3	2	1	0	0	0.1	1.000	DH-10, OF-2
1978	2 teams		NY	A	(3G – .000)		OAK	A	(58G – .208)																
"	total		61	.205	.233	176	36	2	0	1	0.6	17	10	10	23	11	7	1	106	0	4	2	1.8	.964	OF-50, 1B-9, DH-3
1979	CLE	A	54	.290	.403	62	18	0	2	1	1.6	10	12	10	10	4	11	1	29	2	1	0	0.6	.969	OF-30, DH-7
1980			52	.222	.315	54	12	1	2	0	0.0	11	9	5	7	2	7	1	35	1	2	0	0.7	.947	OF-26, DH-6
4 yrs.			189	.238	.310	332	79	7	4	3	0.9	48	35	28	44	20	33	6	172	4	7	2	1.0	.962	OF-108, DH-26, 1B-9

Tom Alston

ALSTON, THOMAS EDISON
B. Jan. 31, 1931, Greensboro, N. C.

BL TR 6'5" 210 lbs.

Year	Team		Games	BA	SA	AB	H	2B	3B	HR	HR%	R	RBI	BB	SO	SB	AB	H	PO	A	E	DP	TC/G	FA	G by Pos
1954	STL	N	66	.246	.369	244	60	14	2	4	1.6	28	34	24	41	3	2	1	552	72	7	57	9.6	.989	1B-65
1955			13	.125	.125	8	1	0	0	0	0.0	0	0	0	0	0	6	1	14	1	0	1	1.2	1.000	1B-7
1956			3	.000	.000	2	0	0	0	0	0.0	0	0	0	0	0	0	0	4	1	0	1	1.7	1.000	1B-3
1957			9	.294	.353	17	5	1	0	0	0.0	2	2	1	5	0	3	2	35	1	2	4	4.2	.947	1B-6
4 yrs.			91	.244	.358	271	66	15	2	4	1.5	30	36	25	46	3	11	4	605	75	9	63	7.6	.987	1B-81

Walter Alston

ALSTON, WALTER EMMONS (Smokey)
B. Dec. 1, 1911, Venice, Ohio   D. Oct. 1, 1984, Oxford, Ohio
Manager 1954-76.
Hall of Fame 1983.

BR TR 6'2" 195 lbs.

Year	Team		Games	BA	SA	AB	H	2B	3B	HR	HR%	R	RBI	BB	SO	SB	AB	H	PO	A	E	DP	TC/G	FA	G by Pos
1936	STL	N	1	.000	.000	1	0	0	0	0	0.0	0	0	0	1	0	0	0	0	1	1	0	2.0	.500	1B-1

Jesse Altenburg

ALTENBURG, JESSE HOWARD (Chip)
B. Jan. 2, 1893, Ashley, Mich.   D. Mar. 12, 1973, Lansing, Mich.

BL TR 5'9" 158 lbs.

Year	Team		Games	BA	SA	AB	H	2B	3B	HR	HR%	R	RBI	BB	SO	SB	AB	H	PO	A	E	DP	TC/G	FA	G by Pos
1916	PIT	N	8	.429	.643	14	6	1	1	0	0.0	2	0	1	1	0	1	0	5	0	0	0	0.6	1.000	OF-8

Year	Team		Games	BA	SA	AB	H	2B	3B	HR	HR%	R	RBI	BB	SO	SB	Pinch Hit AB	Pinch Hit H	PO	A	E	DP	TC/G	FA	G by Pos

Jesse Altenburg *continued*

| 1917 | | | 11 | .176 | .176 | 17 | 3 | 0 | 0 | 0 | 0.0 | 1 | 3 | 0 | 4 | 0 | 6 | 0 | 4 | 0 | 0 | 0 | 0.4 | 1.000 | OF-4 |
| 2 yrs. | | | 19 | .290 | .387 | 31 | 9 | 1 | 1 | 0 | 0.0 | 3 | 3 | 1 | 5 | 0 | 7 | 0 | 9 | 0 | 0 | 0 | 0.5 | 1.000 | OF-12 |

Dave Altizer

ALTIZER, DAVID TILDEN (Filipino)
B. Nov. 6, 1876, Pearl, Ill. D. May 14, 1964, Pleasant Hill, Ill.   BL TR 5'10½" 160 lbs.

1906	WAS	A	115	.256	.307	433	111	9	5	1	0.2	56	27	35			37	0	0	263	324	43	31	5.5	.932	SS-113, OF-2
1907			147	.269	.320	540	145	15	5	1	0.2	60	42	34			38	0	0	790	297	50	41	7.7	.956	SS-71, 1B-50, OF-26
1908	2 teams			WAS A	(67G – .224)			CLE A	(29G – .213)																	
"	total		96	.221	.248	294	65	2	3	0	0.0	30	23	20			15	7	1	169	162	19	15	3.6	.946	2B-38, OF-24, 3B-16, SS-4, 1B-4
1909	CHI	A	116	.233	.293	382	89	6	7	1	0.3	47	20	39			27	7	1	540	45	10	25	5.1	.983	OF-62, 1B-45
1910	CIN	N	3	.600	.600	10	6	0	0	0	0.0	3	0	3	0		0	0	0	7	7	1	5	5.0	.933	SS-3
1911			37	.227	.307	75	17	4	1	0	0.0	8	4	9	5		2	4	1	43	61	10	6	3.1	.912	SS-23, OF-1, 2B-1, 1B-1
6 yrs.			514	.250	.300	1734	433	36	21	3	0.2	204	116	140	5		119	18	3	1812	896	133	119	5.5	.953	SS-214, OF-115, 1B-100, 2B-39, 3B-16

George Altman

ALTMAN, GEORGE LEE
B. Mar. 20, 1933, Goldsboro, N. C.   BL TR 6'4" 200 lbs.

1959	CHI	N	135	.245	.383	420	103	14	4	12	2.9	54	47	34	80	1	15	4	278	7	3	2	2.1	.990	OF-121
1960			119	.266	.455	334	89	16	4	13	3.9	50	51	32	67	4	20	8	308	16	2	15	2.7	.994	OF-79, 1B-21
1961			138	.303	.560	518	157	28	12	27	5.2	77	96	40	92	6	6	0	278	12	6	5	2.1	.980	OF-130, 1B-3
1962			147	.318	.511	534	170	27	5	22	4.1	74	74	62	89	19	6	1	355	16	7	16	2.6	.981	OF-129, 1B-16
1963	STL	N	135	.274	.401	464	127	18	7	9	1.9	62	47	47	93	13	12	3	220	8	5	1	1.7	.979	OF-124
1964	NY	N	124	.230	.332	422	97	14	1	9	2.1	48	47	18	70	4	18	6	202	12	7	3	1.8	.968	OF-109
1965	CHI	N	90	.235	.342	196	46	7	1	4	2.0	24	23	19	36	3	43	6	78	0	4	1	0.9	.951	OF-45, 1B-2
1966			88	.222	.335	185	41	6	0	5	2.7	19	17	14	37	2	44	9	69	6	2	1	0.9	.974	OF-42, 1B-4
1967			15	.111	.222	18	2	2	0	0	0.0	1	2	2	8	0	9	2	4	0	0	1	0.3	1.000	OF-4, 1B-1
9 yrs.			991	.269	.432	3091	832	132	34	101	3.3	409	403	268	572	52	173	39	1792	77	36	45	1.9	.981	OF-783, 1B-47

Joe Altobelli

ALTOBELLI, JOSEPH SALVATORE
B. May 26, 1932, Detroit, Mich.   BL TL 6' 185 lbs.
Manager 1977-79, 1983-85.

1955	CLE	A	42	.200	.320	75	15	3	0	2	2.7	8	5	5	14		1	0	224	11	2	14	5.6	.992	1B-40
1957			83	.207	.287	87	18	3	2	0	0.0	9	9	5	14	3	22	4	158	9	1	16	2.0	.994	1B-56, OF-7
1961	MIN	A	41	.221	.358	95	21	2	1	3	3.2	10	14	13	14	0	12	4	54	1	2	0	1.4	.965	OF-25, 1B-2
3 yrs.			166	.210	.323	257	54	8	3	5	1.9	27	28	23	42	3	35	8	436	21	5	30	2.8	.989	1B-98, OF-32

George Alusik

ALUSIK, GEORGE JOSEPH (Turk, Glider)
B. Feb. 11, 1935, Ashley, Pa.   BR TR 6'3½" 175 lbs.

1958	DET	A	2	.000	.000	2	0	0	0	0	0.0	0	0	0	1		1	0	1	0	0	0	0.5	1.000	OF-1
1961			15	.143	.143	14	2	0	0	0	0.0	0	2	1	4		12	2	0	0	0	0	0.0	—	OF-1
1962	2 teams			DET A	(2G – .000)			KC A	(90G – .273)																	
"	total		92	.270	.483	211	57	10	1	11	5.2	29	35	16	29	1	38	11	89	3	3	0	1.0	.968	OF-50, 1B-1
1963	KC	A	87	.267	.439	221	59	11	0	9	4.1	28	37	26	33	0	19	9	98	5	0	1	1.2	1.000	OF-63
1964			102	.240	.343	204	49	10	1	3	1.5	18	19	30	36	0	40	6	150	6	2	10	1.5	.987	OF-44, 1B-12
5 yrs.			298	.256	.416	652	167	31	2	23	3.5	75	93	73	103	1	110	28	338	14	5	11	1.2	.986	OF-159, 1B-13

Luis Alvarado

ALVARADO, LUIS CESAR (Pimba)
Born Luis Cesar Alvarado y Martinez.   BR TR 5'9" 162 lbs.
B. Jan. 15, 1949, La Jas, Puerto Rico

1968	BOS	A	11	.130	.174	46	6	2	0	0	0.0	3	1	1	11	0	0	0	14	26	1	6	3.7	.976	SS-11
1969			6	.000	.000	5	0	0	0	0	0.0	0	0	0	2	0	1	0	4	6	0	2	1.7	1.000	SS-5
1970			59	.224	.301	183	41	11	0	1	0.5	19	10	9	30	1	1	0	45	134	8	17	3.2	.957	3B-29, SS-27
1971	CHI	A	99	.216	.277	264	57	14	1	0	0.0	22	8	11	34	1	9	0	120	238	13	46	3.7	.965	SS-71, 2B-16
1972			103	.213	.283	254	54	4	1	4	1.6	30	29	13	36	2	7	2	107	234	15	30	3.5	.958	SS-81, 2B-16, 3B-2
1973			80	.232	.286	203	47	7	2	0	0.0	21	20	4	20	6	7	4	120	158	9	31	3.6	.969	2B-45, SS-18, 3B-10
1974	3 teams			CHI A	(8G – .100)			CLE A	(61G – .219)		STL N	(17G – .139)													
"	total		86	.194	.219	160	31	4	0	0	0.0	16	13	8	21	1	5	1	104	147	11	34	3.0	.958	2B-47, SS-28, DH-3, 3B-1
1976	STL	N	16	.286	.310	42	12	1	0	0	0.0	5	3	3	6	0	0	0	22	23	3	3	2.9	.936	2B-16
1977	2 teams			DET A	(2G – .000)			NY N	(1G – .000)																	
"	total		3	.000	.000	3	0	0	0	0	0.0	0	0	0	0	0	1	0	2	0	0	0	1.0	1.000	3B-2, 2B-1
9 yrs.			463	.214	.271	1160	248	43	4	5	0.4	116	84	49	160	11	30	7	537	967	60	169	3.4	.962	SS-241, 2B-141, 3B-44, DH-3

Orlando Alvarez

ALVAREZ, JESUS MANUEL ORLANDO
Born Jesus Manuel Orlano Alvarez y Monge.   BR TR 6' 165 lbs.
B. Feb. 28, 1952, Rio Grande, Puerto Rico

1973	LA	N	4	.250	.500	4	1	1	0	0	0.0	0	0	0	0	0	4	1	0	0	0	0	0.0	—	
1974			2	.000	.000	1	0	0	0	0	0.0	0	0	0	1	0	1	0	0	0	0	0	0.5	1.000	OF-1
1975			4	.000	.000	4	0	0	0	0	0.0	0	0	0	1	0	5	0	1	0	0	0	0.0	—	
1976	CAL	A	15	.167	.333	42	7	1	0	2	4.8	4	8	0	3	0	5	0	12	1	0	1	0.9	1.000	OF-11, DH-2
4 yrs.			25	.157	.314	51	8	2	0	2	3.9	4	8	0	5	0	14	1	13	1	0	1	0.6	1.000	OF-12, DH-2

Ossie Alvarez

ALVAREZ, OSWALDO
Born Oswaldo Alvarez y Gonzalez.   BR TR 5'10" 165 lbs.
B. Oct. 19, 1933, Matanzas, Cuba

1958	WAS	A	87	.209	.224	196	41	3	0	0	0.0	20	5	16	26	1	3	0	126	183	10	38	3.7	.969	SS-64, 2B-14, 3B-3
1959	DET	A	8	.500	.500	2	1	0	0	0	0.0	0	0	0	1	0	2	1	0	0	0	0	0.0	—	
2 yrs.			95	.212	.227	198	42	3	0	0	0.0	20	5	16	27	1	5	1	126	183	10	38	3.4	.969	SS-64, 2B-14, 3B-3

Year	Team		Games	BA	SA	AB	H	2B	3B	HR	HR%	R	RBI	BB	SO	SB	Pinch Hit AB	Pinch Hit H	PO	A	E	DP	TC/G	FA	G by Pos

Rogelio Alvarez

ALVAREZ, ROGELIO (Borrego)
Born Rogelio Alvarez y Hernandez.
B. Apr. 18, 1938, Pinar Del Rio, Cuba

BR TR 5'11" 183 lbs.

Year	Team		Games	BA	SA	AB	H	2B	3B	HR	HR%	R	RBI	BB	SO	SB	AB	H	PO	A	E	DP	TC/G	FA	G by Pos
1960	CIN	N	3	.111	.111	9	1	0	0	0	0.0	1	0	0	3	0	1	0	21	0	0	1	7.0	1.000	1B-2
1962			14	.214	.214	28	6	0	0	0	0.0	1	2	1	10	0	2	0	69	4	2	8	5.4	.973	1B-13
2 yrs.			17	.189	.189	37	7	0	0	0	0.0	2	2	1	13	0	3	0	90	4	2	9	5.6	.979	1B-15

Max Alvis

ALVIS, ROY MAXWELL
B. Feb. 2, 1938, Jasper, Tex.

BR TR 5'11" 185 lbs.

Year	Team		Games	BA	SA	AB	H	2B	3B	HR	HR%	R	RBI	BB	SO	SB	AB	H	PO	A	E	DP	TC/G	FA	G by Pos
1962	CLE	A	12	.216	.255	51	11	2	0	0	0.0	1	3	2	11	3	0	0	13	16	2	1	2.6	.935	3B-12
1963			158	.274	.460	602	165	32	7	22	3.7	81	67	36	109	9	0	0	170	285	28	32	3.1	.942	3B-158
1964			107	.252	.446	381	96	14	3	18	4.7	51	53	29	77	5	1	1	83	191	13	18	2.7	.955	3B-105
1965			159	.247	.397	604	149	24	2	21	3.5	88	61	47	121	12	2	1	169	264	19	17	2.8	.958	3B-156
1966			157	.245	.378	596	146	22	3	17	2.9	67	55	50	98	4	0	0	180	280	20	24	3.1	.958	3B-157
1967			161	.256	.403	637	163	23	4	21	3.3	66	70	38	107	3	0	0	169	304	17	20	3.0	.965	3B-161
1968			131	.223	.327	452	101	17	3	8	1.8	38	37	41	91	5	6	1	114	202	13	18	2.5	.960	3B-128
1969			66	.225	.272	191	43	6	0	1	0.5	13	15	14	26	1	9	0	49	96	4	10	2.3	.973	3B-58, SS-1
1970	MIL	A	62	.183	.278	115	21	2	0	3	2.6	16	12	5	20	1	15	3	15	55	7	4	1.2	.909	3B-36
9 yrs.			1013	.247	.390	3629	895	142	22	111	3.1	421	373	262	662	43	33	6	962	1693	123	144	2.7	.956	3B-971, SS-1

Billy Alvord

ALVORD, WILLIAM CHARLES (Uncle Bill)
B. Aug., 1863, St. Louis, Mo.   D. 1908, Buffalo N. Y.,

5'10" 187 lbs.

Year	Team		Games	BA	SA	AB	H	2B	3B	HR	HR%	R	RBI	BB	SO	SB	AB	H	PO	A	E	DP	TC/G	FA	G by Pos
1885	STL	N	2	.000	.000	5	0	0	0	0	0.0	0	0	1	2		0	0	4	1	2	0	3.5	.714	3B-2
1889	KC	AA	50	.231	.371	186	43	8	9	0	0.0	23	18	10	35	3	0	0	66	140	43	17	5.0	.827	3B-34, SS-8, 2B-8
1890	TOL	AA	116	.273	.376	495	135	13	16	2	0.4	69		22		21	0	0	203	252	67	13	4.5	.872	3B-116
1891	2 teams			CLE	N	(13G – .288)		WAS	AA	(81G – .234)															
"	total		94	.243	.305	371	90	10	5	1	0.3	35	37	11	45	3	0	0	167	238	68	11	5.0	.856	3B-94
1893	CLE	N	3	.167	.167	12	2	0	0	0	0.0	2	2	0	1	0	0	0	5	2	1	0	2.7	.875	3B-3
5 yrs.			265	.253	.346	1069	270	31	30	3	0.3	129	57	44	83	27	0	0	445	633	181	41	4.8	.856	3B-249, SS-8, 2B-8

Brant Alyea

ALYEA, GARRABRANT RYERSON
B. Dec. 8, 1940, Passaic, N. J.

BR TR 6'3" 215 lbs.

Year	Team		Games	BA	SA	AB	H	2B	3B	HR	HR%	R	RBI	BB	SO	SB	AB	H	PO	A	E	DP	TC/G	FA	G by Pos
1965	WAS	A	8	.231	.692	13	3	0	0	2	15.4	3	6	1	4	0	5	1	17	0	0	0	2.1	1.000	1B-3, OF-1
1968			53	.267	.473	150	40	11	1	6	4.0	18	23	10	39	0	18	3	76	0	0	0	1.4	1.000	OF-39
1969			104	.249	.405	237	59	4	0	11	4.6	29	40	34	67	1	41	8	90	6	6	0	1.0	.941	OF-69, 1B-3
1970	MIN	A	94	.291	.531	258	75	12	1	16	6.2	34	61	28	51	3	18	7	93	4	2	0	1.1	.980	OF-75
1971			79	.177	.241	158	28	4	0	2	1.3	13	15	24	38	1	25	4	47	3	2	0	0.7	.962	OF-48
1972	2 teams			OAK	A	(20G – .194)		STL	N	(13G – .158)															
"	total		33	.180	.280	50	9	2	0	1	2.0	3	3	3	11	0	20	3	25	4	0	1	0.9	1.000	OF-11
6 yrs.			371	.247	.421	866	214	33	2	38	4.4	100	148	100	210	5	127	26	348	17	10	1	1.0	.973	OF-243, 1B-6
LEAGUE CHAMPIONSHIP SERIES																									
1970	MIN	A	3	.000	.000	7	0	0	0	0	0.0	1	0	2	3	0	1	0	0	0	0	0	0.0	–	OF-2

Joey Amalfitano

AMALFITANO, JOHN JOSEPH
B. Jan. 23, 1934, San Pedro, Calif.
Manager 1979-81.

BR TR 5'11" 175 lbs.

Year	Team		Games	BA	SA	AB	H	2B	3B	HR	HR%	R	RBI	BB	SO	SB	AB	H	PO	A	E	DP	TC/G	FA	G by Pos
1954	NY	N	9	.000	.000	5	0	0	0	0	0.0	2	0	0	4	0	0	0	2	5	0	1	0.8	1.000	3B-4, 2B-1
1955			36	.227	.364	22	5	1	1	0	0.0	8	1	2	2	0	4	0	12	19	3	3	0.9	.912	SS-5, 3B-2
1960	SF	N	106	.277	.351	328	91	15	3	1	0.3	47	27	26	31	2	13	5	103	187	14	24	2.9	.954	3B-63, 2B-33, SS-3, OF-1
1961			109	.255	.320	384	98	11	4	2	0.5	64	23	44	59	7	12	4	204	236	13	48	4.2	.971	2B-95, 3B-6
1962	HOU	N	117	.237	.303	380	90	12	5	1	0.3	44	27	45	43	4	2	1	231	270	18	72	4.4	.965	2B-110, 3B-5
1963	SF	N	54	.175	.219	137	24	3	0	1	0.7	11	7	12	18	2	18	1	61	92	3	13	2.9	.981	2B-37, 3B-7
1964	CHI	N	100	.241	.373	324	78	19	6	4	1.2	51	27	40	42	2	10	3	201	254	17	47	4.7	.964	2B-86, SS-1, 1B-1
1965			67	.271	.313	96	26	4	0	0	0.0	13	8	12	14	2	37	8	31	67	2	9	1.5	.980	2B-24, SS-4
1966			41	.158	.211	38	6	2	0	0	0.0	4	3	4	10	0	9	2	23	19	1	5	1.0	.977	2B-12, 3B-3, SS-2
1967			4	.000	.000	1	0	0	0	0	0.0	0	0	0	1	0	1	0	0	0	0	0	0.0	–	
10 yrs.			643	.244	.321	1715	418	67	19	9	0.5	248	123	185	224	19	106	24	868	1149	71	222	3.2	.966	2B-398, 3B-90, SS-15, OF-1, 1B-1

Ruben Amaro

AMARO, RUBEN
Born Ruben Amaro y Mora.
B. Jan. 6, 1936, Veracruz, Mexico

BR TR 5'11" 170 lbs.

Year	Team		Games	BA	SA	AB	H	2B	3B	HR	HR%	R	RBI	BB	SO	SB	AB	H	PO	A	E	DP	TC/G	FA	G by Pos
1958	STL	N	40	.224	.276	76	17	2	1	0	0.0	8	0	5	8	0	0	1	45	66	6	18	2.9	.949	SS-36, 2B-1
1960	PHI	N	92	.231	.273	264	61	9	1	0	0.0	25	16	21	32	0	0	0	153	230	14	47	4.3	.965	SS-92
1961			135	.257	.349	381	98	14	9	1	0.3	34	32	53	59	1	0	0	254	380	19	92	4.8	.971	SS-132, 1B-3, 2B-1
1962			79	.243	.288	226	55	10	0	0	0.0	24	19	30	28	5	0	0	144	224	12	50	4.8	.968	SS-78, 1B-1
1963			115	.217	.304	217	47	9	2	2	0.9	25	19	19	31	0	7	0	111	169	13	29	2.5	.956	SS-63, 3B-45, 1B-5
1964			129	.264	.341	299	79	11	0	4	1.3	31	34	16	37	1	9	1	298	203	11	55	4.0	.979	SS-79, 1B-58, 3B-3, 2B-3, OF-1
1965			118	.212	.250	184	39	7	0	0	0.0	26	15	27	22	1	37	8	187	134	11	34	2.8	.967	SS-60, 1B-60, 2B-6
1966	NY	A	14	.217	.217	23	5	0	0	0	0.0	4	0	3	2	0	0	0	17	25	1	8	3.1	.977	SS-14
1967			130	.223	.259	417	93	12	0	1	0.2	31	17	43	49	3	2	0	228	379	18	75	4.8	.971	SS-123, 3B-3, 1B-2
1968			47	.122	.146	41	5	1	0	0	0.0	3	0	9	6	0	1	0	54	37	2	11	2.0	.978	SS-23, 1B-22
1969	CAL	A	41	.222	.222	27	6	0	0	0	0.0	4	1	4	6	0	5	1	41	17	1	2	1.4	.983	1B-18, 2B-9, SS-5, 3B-2
11 yrs.			940	.234	.292	2155	505	75	13	8	0.4	211	156	227	280	11	32	2	1532	1864	108	421	3.7	.969	SS-705, 1B-169, 3B-53, 2B-20, OF-1

Wayne Ambler

AMBLER, WAYNE HARPER
B. Nov. 8, 1915, Abington, Pa.

BR TR 5'8½" 165 lbs.

Year	Team		Games	BA	SA	AB	H	2B	3B	HR	HR%	R	RBI	BB	SO	SB	AB	H	PO	A	E	DP	TC/G	FA	G by Pos
1937	PHI	A	56	.216	.247	162	35	5	0	0	0.0	3	11	13	8	1	0	0	107	149	12	34	4.8	.955	2B-56
1938			120	.234	.298	393	92	21	2	0	0.0	42	38	48	31	2	0	0	221	326	32	58	4.8	.945	SS-116, 2B-4

Year	Team		Games	BA	SA	AB	H	2B	3B	HR	HR%	R	RBI	BB	SO	SB	Pinch Hit AB	Pinch Hit H	PO	A	E	DP	TC/G	FA	G by Pos

Wayne Ambler *continued*

Year	Team		Games	BA	SA	AB	H	2B	3B	HR	HR%	R	RBI	BB	SO	SB	AB	H	PO	A	E	DP	TC/G	FA	G by Pos
1939			95	.211	.269	227	48	13	0	0	0.0	15	24	22	25	1	0	0	150	208	18	34	4.0	.952	SS-77, 2B-19
3 yrs.			271	.224	.279	782	175	39	2	0	0.0	60	73	83	64	4	0	0	478	683	62	126	4.5	.949	SS-193, 2B-79

Ed Amelung

AMELUNG, EDWARD ALLEN
B. Apr. 13, 1959, Fullerton, Calif. BL TL 5'11" 180 lbs.

Year	Team		Games	BA	SA	AB	H	2B	3B	HR	HR%	R	RBI	BB	SO	SB	AB	H	PO	A	E	DP	TC/G	FA	G by Pos
1984	LA	N	34	.217	.217	46	10	0	0	0	0.0	7	4	2	4	3	11	1	31	0	0	0	0.9	1.000	OF-23
1986			8	.091	.091	11	1	0	0	0	0.0	0	0	0	4	0	4	0	5	0	0	0	0.6	1.000	OF-4
2 yrs.			42	.193	.193	57	11	0	0	0	0.0	7	4	2	8	3	15	1	36	0	0	0	0.9	1.000	OF-27

Sandy Amoros

AMOROS, EDMUNDO
Born Edmundo Amoros y Isasi.
B. Jan. 30, 1930, Havana, Cuba BL TL 5'7½" 170 lbs.

Year	Team		Games	BA	SA	AB	H	2B	3B	HR	HR%	R	RBI	BB	SO	SB	AB	H	PO	A	E	DP	TC/G	FA	G by Pos
1952	BKN	N	20	.250	.364	44	11	3	1	0	0.0	10	3	5	14	1	11	0	18	0	0	0	0.9	1.000	OF-10
1954			79	.274	.490	263	72	18	6	9	3.4	44	34	31	24	1	8	2	149	6	2	1	2.0	.987	OF-70
1955			119	.247	.402	388	96	16	7	10	2.6	59	51	55	45	10	9	3	201	10	6	1	1.8	.972	OF-109
1956			114	.260	.517	292	76	11	8	16	5.5	53	58	59	51	3	23	6	123	3	6	0	1.2	.955	OF-86
1957			106	.277	.403	238	66	7	1	7	2.9	40	26	46	42	3	28	4	122	2	2	0	1.2	.984	OF-66
1959	LA	N	5	.200	.200					0		1	1	0	1	0	5	1	0	0	0	0	0.0	–	
1960	2 teams		LA	N	(9G –	.143)			DET	A	(65G –	.149)													
"	total		74	.148	.185	81	12	0	0	1	1.2	8	7	15	12	0	48	8	22	1	0	0	0.3	1.000	OF-13
7 yrs.			517	.255	.430	1311	334	55	23	43	3.3	215	180	211	189	18	131	21	635	22	16	2	1.3	.976	OF-354

WORLD SERIES

Year	Team		Games	BA	SA	AB	H	2B	3B	HR	HR%	R	RBI	BB	SO	SB	AB	H	PO	A	E	DP	TC/G	FA	G by Pos
1952	BKN	N	1	–	–	0	0	0	0	0	–	0	0	0	0	0	0	0	0	0	0	0	0.0	–	
1955			5	.333	.583	12	4	0	0	1	8.3	3	3	4	4	0	0	0	9	2	0	1	2.2	1.000	OF-5
1956			6	.053	.053	19	1	0	0	0	0.0	1	1	2	4	0	0	0	10	0	0	0	1.7	1.000	OF-6
3 yrs.			12	.161	.258	31	5	0	0	1	3.2	4	4	6	8	0	0	0	19	2	0	1	1.8	1.000	OF-11

Alf Anderson

ANDERSON, ALFRED WALTON
B. Jan. 28, 1914, Gainesville, Ga. D. June 23, 1985, Albany, Ga. BR TR 5'11" 165 lbs.

Year	Team		Games	BA	SA	AB	H	2B	3B	HR	HR%	R	RBI	BB	SO	SB	AB	H	PO	A	E	DP	TC/G	FA	G by Pos
1941	PIT	N	70	.215	.278	223	48	7	2	1	0.4	32	10	14	30	2	5	1	97	161	19	29	4.0	.931	SS-58
1942			54	.271	.307	166	45	4	1	0	0.0	24	7	18	19	4	4	1	77	103	11	17	3.5	.942	SS-48
1946			2	.000	.000	1	0	0	0	0	0.0	0	0	1	0	0	1	0	0	0	0	0	0.0	–	
3 yrs.			126	.238	.290	390	93	11	3	1	0.3	56	17	33	49	6	10	2	174	264	30	46	3.7	.936	SS-106

Andy Anderson

ANDERSON, ANDY HOLM
B. Nov. 13, 1922, Bremerton, Wash. D. July 18, 1982, Seattle, Wash. BR TR 5'11" 172 lbs.

Year	Team		Games	BA	SA	AB	H	2B	3B	HR	HR%	R	RBI	BB	SO	SB	AB	H	PO	A	E	DP	TC/G	FA	G by Pos
1948	STL	A	51	.276	.391	87	24	5	1	1	1.1	13	12	8	15	0	21	5	44	54	9	14	2.1	.916	2B-21, SS-10, 1B-2
1949			71	.125	.169	136	17	3	0	1	0.7	10	5	14	21	0	12	1	74	98	6	24	2.5	.966	SS-44, 3B-8, 2B-5
2 yrs.			122	.184	.256	223	41	8	1	2	0.9	23	17	22	36	0	33	6	118	152	15	38	2.3	.947	SS-54, 2B-29, 3B-8, 1B-2

Brady Anderson

ANDERSON, BRADY KEVIN
B. Jan. 18, 1964, Silver Spring, Md. BL TL 6'1" 170 lbs.

Year	Team		Games	BA	SA	AB	H	2B	3B	HR	HR%	R	RBI	BB	SO	SB	AB	H	PO	A	E	DP	TC/G	FA	G by Pos
1988	2 teams		BOS	A	(41G –	.230)			BAL	A	(53G –	.198)													
"	total		94	.212	.286	325	69	13	4	1	0.3	31	21	23	75	10	7	0	243	4	4	1	2.7	.984	OF-90
1989	BAL	A	94	.207	.312	266	55	12	2	4	1.5	44	16	43	45	16	6	1	191	3	3	0	2.1	.985	OF-79, DH-8
2 yrs.			188	.210	.298	591	124	25	6	5	0.8	75	37	66	120	26	13	1	434	7	7	1	2.4	.984	OF-169, DH-8

Dave Anderson

ANDERSON, DAVID CARTER
B. Aug. 1, 1960, Louisville, Ky. BR TR 6'2" 185 lbs.

Year	Team		Games	BA	SA	AB	H	2B	3B	HR	HR%	R	RBI	BB	SO	SB	AB	H	PO	A	E	DP	TC/G	FA	G by Pos
1983	LA	N	61	.165	.261	115	19	4	2	1	0.9	12	9	12	15	6	2	1	56	100	5	19	2.6	.969	SS-53, 3B-1
1984			121	.251	.329	374	94	16	2	3	0.8	51	34	45	55	15	5	0	176	359	19	67	4.6	.966	SS-111, 3B-11
1985			77	.199	.281	221	44	6	0	4	1.8	24	18	35	42	5	4	2	61	187	9	20	3.3	.965	3B-51, SS-25, 2B-2
1986			92	.245	.301	216	53	9	0	1	0.5	31	15	22	39	5	4	1	77	159	11	21	2.7	.955	3B-51, SS-34, 2B-5
1987			108	.234	.313	265	62	12	3	1	0.4	32	13	24	43	9	6	2	103	207	7	33	2.7	.978	SS-65, 3B-35, 2B-5
1988			116	.249	.319	285	71	10	2	2	0.7	31	20	32	45	4	7	2	139	244	5	53	3.3	.987	SS-82, 3B-12, 2B-11
1989			87	.229	.264	140	32	2	0	1	0.7	15	14	17	26	2	25	4	61	73	1	15	1.6	.993	SS-33, 3B-18, 2B-7
7 yrs.			662	.232	.304	1616	375	59	9	13	0.8	196	116	187	265	46	53	12	673	1329	57	228	3.1	.972	SS-403, 3B-179, 2B-30

LEAGUE CHAMPIONSHIP SERIES

Year	Team		Games	BA	SA	AB	H	2B	3B	HR	HR%	R	RBI	BB	SO	SB	AB	H	PO	A	E	DP	TC/G	FA	G by Pos
1985	LA	N	4	.000	.000	5	0	0	0	0	0.0	1	0	3	1	0	0	0	3	4	0	0	1.8	1.000	SS-3, 3B-1

WORLD SERIES

Year	Team		Games	BA	SA	AB	H	2B	3B	HR	HR%	R	RBI	BB	SO	SB	AB	H	PO	A	E	DP	TC/G	FA	G by Pos
1988	LA	N	1	.000	.000	1	0	0	0	0	0.0	0	0	0	1	0	1	0	0	0	0	0	0.0	–	DH-1

Dwain Anderson

ANDERSON, DWAIN CLEAVEN
B. Nov. 23, 1947, Oakland, Calif. BR TR 5'11" 165 lbs.

Year	Team		Games	BA	SA	AB	H	2B	3B	HR	HR%	R	RBI	BB	SO	SB	AB	H	PO	A	E	DP	TC/G	FA	G by Pos
1971	OAK	A	16	.270	.378	37	10	2	1	0	0.0	3	3	5	9	0	0	0	20	26	4	4	3.1	.920	SS-10, 2B-5, 3B-1
1972	2 teams		OAK	A	(3G –	.000)			STL	N	(57G –	.267)													
"	total		60	.254	.317	142	36	4	1	1	0.7	14	8	9	27	0	1	0	71	101	8	18	3.0	.956	SS-44, 3B-14, 2B-1
1973	2 teams		STL	N	(18G –	.118)			SD	N	(53G –	.121)													
"	total		71	.121	.121	124	15	0	0	0	0.0	16	3	18	33	2	15	1	46	93	13	15	2.1	.914	SS-42, 3B-6, OF-2
1974	CLE	A	2	.333	.333	3	1	0	0	0	0.0	0	0	0	1	0	0	0	1	0	0	0	0.5	1.000	2B-1
4 yrs.			149	.203	.245	306	62	6	2	1	0.3	33	14	32	70	2	16	1	138	220	25	37	2.6	.935	SS-96, 3B-21, 2B-7, OF-2

Ferrell Anderson

ANDERSON, FERRELL JACK
B. Jan. 9, 1918, Maple City, Kans. D. Mar. 12, 1978, Joplin, Mo. BR TR 6'1" 200 lbs.

Year	Team		Games	BA	SA	AB	H	2B	3B	HR	HR%	R	RBI	BB	SO	SB	AB	H	PO	A	E	DP	TC/G	FA	G by Pos
1946	BKN	N	79	.256	.337	199	51	10	6	2	1.0	19	14	18	21	1	8	2	258	35	11	5	3.8	.964	C-70
1953	STL	N	18	.286	.343	35	10	2	0	0	0.0	1	1	0	4	0	7	0	32	4	0	0	2.0	1.000	C-12
2 yrs.			97	.261	.338	234	61	12	6	2	0.9	20	15	18	25	1	15	2	290	39	11	5	3.5	.968	C-82

Year	Team		Games	BA	SA	AB	H	2B	3B	HR	HR%	R	RBI	BB	SO	SB	Pinch Hit AB	Pinch Hit H	PO	A	E	DP	TC/G	FA	G by Pos

George Anderson

ANDERSON, GEORGE JENDRUS BL TR 5'8½" 160 lbs.
Born George Andrew Jendrus
B. Sept. 26, 1889, Cleveland, Ohio D. May 28, 1962, Cleveland, Ohio

Year	Team		Games	BA	SA	AB	H	2B	3B	HR	HR%	R	RBI	BB	SO	SB	AB	H	PO	A	E	DP	TC/G	FA	G by Pos
1914	BKN	F	98	.316	.393	364	115	13	3	3	0.8	58	24	31		16	5	0	176	15	11	2	2.1	.946	OF-92
1915			136	.264	.356	511	135	23	9	2	0.4	70	39	52		20	1	0	200	16	10	5	1.7	.956	OF-134
1918	STL	N	35	.295	.402	132	39	4	5	0	0.0	20	6	15	7	0	0	0	62	3	3	1	1.9	.956	OF-35
3 yrs.			269	.287	.375	1007	289	40	17	5	0.5	148	69	98	7	36	6	0	438	34	24	8	1.8	.952	OF-261

Goat Anderson

ANDERSON, EDWARD JOHN TR
B. Jan. 13, 1880, Cleveland, Ohio D. Mar. 15, 1923, South Bend, Ind.

Year	Team		Games	BA	SA	AB	H	2B	3B	HR	HR%	R	RBI	BB	SO	SB	AB	H	PO	A	E	DP	TC/G	FA	G by Pos
1907	PIT	N	127	.206	.225	413	85	3	1	1	0.2	73	12	80		27	5	1	215	23	13	5	2.0	.948	OF-117, 2B-5

Hal Anderson

ANDERSON, HAROLD BR TR 5'11" 160 lbs.
B. Feb. 10, 1904, St. Louis, Mo. D. May 1, 1974, St. Louis, Mo.

Year	Team		Games	BA	SA	AB	H	2B	3B	HR	HR%	R	RBI	BB	SO	SB	AB	H	PO	A	E	DP	TC/G	FA	G by Pos
1932	CHI	A	9	.250	.250	32	8	0	0	0	0.0	4	2	0	1	0	0	0	21	1	0	1	2.4	1.000	OF-9

Harry Anderson

ANDERSON, HARRY WALTER BL TR 6'3" 205 lbs.
B. Sept. 10, 1931, North East, Md.

Year	Team		Games	BA	SA	AB	H	2B	3B	HR	HR%	R	RBI	BB	SO	SB	AB	H	PO	A	E	DP	TC/G	FA	G by Pos
1957	PHI	N	118	.268	.453	400	107	15	4	17	4.3	53	61	36	61	2	11	3	213	5	3	1	1.9	.986	OF-109
1958			140	.301	.524	515	155	34	6	23	4.5	80	97	59	95	0	10	1	552	33	13	40	4.3	.978	OF-87, 1B-49
1959			142	.240	.402	508	122	28	6	14	2.8	50	63	43	95	1	6	1	283	17	6	4	2.2	.980	OF-137
1960	2 teams		PHI N (38G – .247)			CIN N (42G – .167)																			
"	total		80	.214	.358	159	34	5	0	6	3.8	16	21	21	39	1	29	1	203	14	2	9	2.7	.991	1B-27, OF-20
1961	CIN	N	4	.250	.250	4	1	0	0	0	0.0	0	0	0	1	0	4	1	0	0	0	0	0.0	—	
5 yrs.			484	.264	.450	1586	419	82	16	60	3.8	199	242	159	291	3	60	7	1251	69	24	54	2.8	.982	OF-353, 1B-76

Jim Anderson

ANDERSON, JAMES LEA BR TR 6' 170 lbs.
B. Feb. 23, 1957, Los Angeles, Calif.

Year	Team		Games	BA	SA	AB	H	2B	3B	HR	HR%	R	RBI	BB	SO	SB	AB	H	PO	A	E	DP	TC/G	FA	G by Pos
1978	CAL	A	48	.194	.259	108	21	7	0	0	0.0	6	7	11	16	0	0	0	72	99	8	21	3.7	.955	SS-47, 2B-1
1979			96	.248	.350	234	58	13	1	3	1.3	33	23	17	31	3	0	0	141	205	17	44	3.8	.953	SS-82, 3B-10, 2B-6, C-3
1980	SEA	A	116	.227	.325	317	72	7	0	8	2.5	46	30	27	39	2	8	2	120	255	22	45	3.4	.945	SS-65, 3B-33, DH-5, 2B-2, C-1
1981			70	.204	.284	162	33	7	0	2	1.2	12	19	17	29	3	0	0	88	183	15	45	4.1	.948	SS-68, 3B-2
1983	TEX	A	50	.216	.245	102	22	1	1	0	0.0	8	6	5	8	1	1	0	46	102	5	13	3.1	.967	SS-27, 2B-17, OF-3, 3B-3, DH-2, C-1
1984			39	.106	.106	47	5	0	0	0	0.0	2	1	4	7	0	0	0	37	58	1	13	2.5	.990	SS-31, 3B-6, 2B-1
6 yrs.			419	.218	.298	970	211	35	2	13	1.3	107	86	81	130	9	8	2	504	902	68	181	3.5	.954	SS-320, 3B-54, 2B-27, DH-7, C-5, OF-3

LEAGUE CHAMPIONSHIP SERIES

Year	Team		Games	BA	SA	AB	H	2B	3B	HR	HR%	R	RBI	BB	SO	SB	AB	H	PO	A	E	DP	TC/G	FA	G by Pos
1979	CAL	A	4	.091	.091	11	1	0	0	0	0.0	0	0	0	1	0	0	0	4	11	0	2	3.8	1.000	SS-4

John Anderson

ANDERSON, JOHN JOSEPH (Terrible Swede) BB TR 6'2" 180 lbs.
B. Dec. 14, 1873, Sasbourg, Norway D. July 23, 1949, Worcester, Mass.

Year	Team		Games	BA	SA	AB	H	2B	3B	HR	HR%	R	RBI	BB	SO	SB	AB	H	PO	A	E	DP	TC/G	FA	G by Pos
1894	BKN	N	17	.302	.460	63	19	1	1	1	1.6	14	19	3	3	7	0	0	22	1	6	0	1.7	.793	OF-16, 3B-1
1895			102	.286	.444	419	120	11	14	9	2.1	76	87	12	29	24	0	0	205	11	29	4	2.4	.882	OF-101
1896			108	.314	.453	430	135	23	17	1	0.2	70	55	18	23	37	1	0	538	28	16	30	5.4	.973	OF-68, 1B-42
1897			117	.325	.455	492	160	28	12	4	0.8	93	85	17		29	0	0	279	12	21	3	2.7	.933	OF-115, 1B-3
1898	2 teams		BKN N (25G – .244)			WAS N (110G – .305)																			
"	total		135	.294	.494	520	153	33	22	9	1.7	82	81	29		20	1	0	407	33	22	19	3.4	.952	OF-115, 1B-19
1899	BKN	N	117	.269	.362	439	118	18	7	3	0.7	65	92	27		25	3	0	537	30	19	27	5.0	.968	OF-76, 1B-41
1901	MIL	A	138	.330	.476	576	190	46	7	8	1.4	90	99	24		35	0	0	1350	67	26	81	10.5	.982	1B-125, OF-13
1902	STL	A	126	.284	.385	524	149	29	6	4	0.8	60	85	21		15	0	0	1363	47	22	78	11.4	.985	1B-126, OF-3
1903			138	.284	.385	550	156	34	8	2	0.4	65	78	23		16	0	0	1423	92	22	71	11.1	.986	1B-133, OF-7
1904	NY	A	143	.278	.385	558	155	27	12	3	0.5	62	82	23		20	1	1	554	42	15	22	4.3	.975	OF-111, 1B-33
1905	2 teams		NY A (32G – .232)			WAS A (93G – .290)																			
"	total		125	.279	.361	499	139	24	7	1	0.2	62	52	30		31	7	1	266	15	13	1	2.4	.956	OF-111, 1B-7
1906	WAS	A	151	.271	.343	583	158	25	4	3	0.5	62	70	19		39	0	0	286	19	15	2	2.1	.953	OF-151
1907			87	.288	.348	333	96	12	4	0	0.0	33	44	34		19	0	0	671	34	13	13	8.3	.982	1B-61, OF-26
1908	CHI	A	123	.262	.315	355	93	17	1	0	0.0	36	47	30		21	25	5	176	13	5	11	1.6	.974	OF-90, 1B-9
14 yrs.			1627	.290	.404	6341	1841	328	124	48	0.8	870	976	310	55	338	38	7	8077	444	244	362	5.4	.972	OF-1003, 1B-599, 3B-1

Kent Anderson

ANDERSON, KENT McKAY BR TR 6'1" 180 lbs.
Brother of Mike Anderson.
B. Aug. 12, 1963, Florence, S. C.

Year	Team		Games	BA	SA	AB	H	2B	3B	HR	HR%	R	RBI	BB	SO	SB	AB	H	PO	A	E	DP	TC/G	FA	G by Pos
1989	CAL	A	86	.229	.265	223	51	6	0	0	0.0	27	17	17	42	1	3	0	102	233	10	56	4.0	.971	SS-70, 2B-7, 3B-5, OF-2, DH-1

Mike Anderson

ANDERSON, MICHAEL ALLEN BR TR 6'2" 200 lbs.
Brother of Kent Anderson.
B. June 22, 1951, Florence, S. C.

Year	Team		Games	BA	SA	AB	H	2B	3B	HR	HR%	R	RBI	BB	SO	SB	AB	H	PO	A	E	DP	TC/G	FA	G by Pos
1971	PHI	N	26	.247	.393	89	22	5	1	2	2.2	11	5	13	28	0	1	0	67	1	1	0	2.7	.986	OF-26
1972			36	.194	.320	103	20	5	1	2	1.9	8	5	19	36	1	0	0	68	6	1	1	2.1	.987	OF-35
1973			87	.254	.451	193	49	9	1	9	4.7	32	28	19	53	0	26	4	99	4	2	1	1.2	.981	OF-67
1974			145	.251	.354	395	99	22	2	6	1.3	35	34	37	75	2	19	5	240	12	5	3	1.8	.981	OF-133, 1B-3
1975			115	.259	.372	247	64	10	3	4	1.6	24	28	17	66	1	16	5	170	6	4	1	1.6	.978	OF-105, 1B-3
1976	STL	N	86	.291	.357	199	58	8	1	1	0.5	17	12	26	30	1	21	7	136	7	3	4	1.7	.979	OF-58, 1B-5
1977			94	.221	.338	154	34	4	1	4	2.6	18	17	14	31	2	20	5	96	4	2	0	1.1	.980	OF-77
1978	BAL	A	53	.094	.156	32	3	0	1	0	0.0	4	3	3	10	0	6	0	25	0	1	0	0.5	.962	OF-47
1979	PHI	N	79	.231	.321	78	18	4	0	1	1.3	12	2	13	14	1	11	0	68	3	2	1	0.9	.973	OF-70, P-1
9 yrs.			721	.246	.362	1490	367	67	11	28	1.9	159	134	161	343	8	119	26	969	43	21	11	1.4	.980	OF-618, 1B-9, P-1

Year	Team		Games	BA	SA	AB	H	2B	3B	HR	HR%	R	RBI	BB	SO	SB	Pinch Hit AB	H	PO	A	E	DP	TC/G	FA	G by Pos

Sparky Anderson
ANDERSON, GEORGE LEE
B. Feb. 22, 1934, Bridgewater, S. D.
Manager 1970-89.
BR TR 5'9" 170 lbs.

Year	Team		Games	BA	SA	AB	H	2B	3B	HR	HR%	R	RBI	BB	SO	SB	Pinch Hit AB	H	PO	A	E	DP	TC/G	FA	G by Pos
1959	PHI	N	152	.218	.249	477	104	9	3	0	0.0	42	34	42	53	6	0	0	343	403	12	70	5.0	.984	2B-152

Ernie Andres
ANDRES, ERNEST HENRY (Junie)
B. Jan. 11, 1918, Jeffersonville, Ind.
BR TR 6'1" 200 lbs.

Year	Team		Games	BA	SA	AB	H	2B	3B	HR	HR%	R	RBI	BB	SO	SB	Pinch Hit AB	H	PO	A	E	DP	TC/G	FA	G by Pos
1946	BOS	A	15	.098	.146	41	4	2	0	0	0.0	0	1	3	5	0	0	0	8	25	0	1	2.2	1.000	3B-15

Kim Andrew
ANDREW, KIM DARNELL
B. Nov. 14, 1953, Glendale, Calif.
BR TR 5'10" 160 lbs.

Year	Team		Games	BA	SA	AB	H	2B	3B	HR	HR%	R	RBI	BB	SO	SB	Pinch Hit AB	H	PO	A	E	DP	TC/G	FA	G by Pos
1975	BOS	A	2	.500	.500	2	1	0	0	0	0.0	0	0	0	0	0	0	0	1	1	0	0	1.0	1.000	2B-2

Ed Andrews
ANDREWS, GEORGE EDWARD
B. Apr. 5, 1859, Painesville, Ohio   D. Aug. 12, 1934, West Palm Beach, Fla.
BR TR 5'8" 160 lbs.

Year	Team		Games	BA	SA	AB	H	2B	3B	HR	HR%	R	RBI	BB	SO	SB	Pinch Hit AB	H	PO	A	E	DP	TC/G	FA	G by Pos
1884	PHI	N	109	.221	.281	420	93	21	2	0	0.0	74		9	42		0	0	239	326	69	37	5.8	.891	2B-109
1885			103	.266	.316	421	112	15	3	0	0.0	77		32	25		0	0	184	24	22	4	2.2	.904	OF-99, 2B-5
1886			107	.249	.316	437	109	15	4	2	0.5	93	28	31	35		0	0	196	31	26	3	2.4	.897	OF-104, 2B-3
1887			104	.325	.422	464	151	19	7	4	0.9	110	67	21	21	57	0	0	221	28	31	2	2.7	.889	OF-99, 2B-7, 1B-1
1888			124	.239	.297	528	126	14	4	3	0.6	75	44	21	41	35	0	0	210	23	25	5	2.1	.903	OF-124
1889	2 teams	PHI	N	(10G –	.282)	IND	N	(40G –	.306)																
"	total		50	.302	.358	212	64	12	0	0	0.0	42	29	7	14	14	0	0	91	12	16	1	2.4	.866	OF-49, 2B-2
1890	BKN	P	94	.253	.322	395	100	14	2	3	0.8	84	38	40	32	21	0	0	220	17	23	3	2.8	.912	OF-94
1891	CIN	AA	83	.211	.253	356	75	7	4	0	0.0	47	26	33	35	22	0	0	173	25	8	4	2.5	.961	OF-83
8 yrs.			774	.257	.320	3233	830	117	26	12	0.4	602	232	194	245	149	0	0	1534	486	220	59	2.9	.902	OF-652, 2B-126, 1B-1

Fred Andrews
ANDREWS, FRED
B. May 4, 1952, Lafayette, La.
BR TR 5'8" 163 lbs.

Year	Team		Games	BA	SA	AB	H	2B	3B	HR	HR%	R	RBI	BB	SO	SB	Pinch Hit AB	H	PO	A	E	DP	TC/G	FA	G by Pos
1976	PHI	N	4	.667	.667	6	4	0	0	0	0.0	1	0	2	0	1	0	0	7	3	0	1	2.5	1.000	2B-4
1977			12	.174	.261	23	4	0	1	0	0.0	3	2	1	5	1	5	2	16	18	0	6	2.8	1.000	2B-7
2 yrs.			16	.276	.345	29	8	0	1	0	0.0	4	2	3	5	2	5	2	23	21	0	7	2.8	1.000	2B-11

Jim Andrews
ANDREWS, JAMES PRATT
B. June 5, 1865, Shelburne Falls, Mass.   D. Dec. 27, 1907, Chicago, Ill.

Year	Team		Games	BA	SA	AB	H	2B	3B	HR	HR%	R	RBI	BB	SO	SB	Pinch Hit AB	H	PO	A	E	DP	TC/G	FA	G by Pos
1890	CHI	N	53	.188	.272	202	38	4	2	3	1.5	32	17	23	41	11	0	0	80	10	10	1	1.9	.900	OF-53

Mike Andrews
ANDREWS, MICHAEL JAY
Brother of Rob Andrews.
B. July 9, 1943, Los Angeles, Calif.
BR TR 6'3" 195 lbs.

Year	Team		Games	BA	SA	AB	H	2B	3B	HR	HR%	R	RBI	BB	SO	SB	Pinch Hit AB	H	PO	A	E	DP	TC/G	FA	G by Pos
1966	BOS	A	5	.167	.167	18	3	0	0	0	0.0	1	0	0	2	0	0	0	11	18	0	2	5.8	1.000	2B-5
1967			142	.263	.352	494	130	20	0	8	1.6	79	40	62	72	7	2	0	305	346	17	63	4.7	.975	2B-139, SS-6
1968			147	.271	.354	536	145	22	1	7	1.3	77	45	81	57	3	5	1	339	383	18	94	5.0	.976	2B-139, SS-4, 3B-1
1969			121	.293	.455	464	136	26	2	15	3.2	79	59	71	53	1	1	0	297	334	18	82	5.4	.972	2B-120
1970			151	.253	.390	589	149	28	1	17	2.9	91	65	81	63	2	3	0	342	350	19	74	4.7	.973	2B-148
1971	CHI	A	109	.282	.439	330	93	16	0	12	3.6	45	47	67	36	3	12	4	374	202	21	68	5.5	.965	2B-76, 1B-25
1972			148	.220	.297	505	111	18	0	7	1.4	58	50	70	78	2	1	1	387	327	19	76	5.0	.974	2B-145, 1B-5
1973	2 teams	CHI	A	(52G –	.201)	OAK	A	(18G –	.190)																
"	total		70	.200	.256	180	36	10	0	0	0.0	11	10	26	29	0	15	1	92	18	1	5	1.6	.991	DH-32, 2B-15, 1B-9, 3B-5
8 yrs.			893	.258	.369	3116	803	140	4	66	2.1	441	316	458	390	18	39	7	2147	1978	113	464	4.7	.973	2B-787, 1B-39, DH-32, SS-10, 3B-6

LEAGUE CHAMPIONSHIP SERIES

Year	Team		Games	BA	SA	AB	H	2B	3B	HR	HR%	R	RBI	BB	SO	SB	Pinch Hit AB	H	PO	A	E	DP	TC/G	FA	G by Pos
1973	OAK	A	2	.000	.000	1	0	0	0	0	0.0	0	0	0	0	0	0	0	1	0	0	0	0.5	1.000	DH-1, 1B-1

WORLD SERIES

Year	Team		Games	BA	SA	AB	H	2B	3B	HR	HR%	R	RBI	BB	SO	SB	Pinch Hit AB	H	PO	A	E	DP	TC/G	FA	G by Pos
1967	BOS	A	5	.308	.308	13	4	0	0	0	0.0	2	1	0	1	0	2	1	2	6	0	1	1.6	1.000	2B-3
1973	OAK	A	2	.000	.000	3	0	0	0	0	0.0	0	0	1	1	0	2	0	1	0	2	0	1.5	.333	2B-1
2 yrs.			7	.250	.250	16	4	0	0	0	0.0	2	1	1	2	0	4	1	3	6	2	0	1.6	.818	2B-4

Rob Andrews
ANDREWS, ROBERT PATRICK
Brother of Mike Andrews.
B. Dec. 11, 1952, Santa Monica, Calif.
BR TR 6' 185 lbs.

Year	Team		Games	BA	SA	AB	H	2B	3B	HR	HR%	R	RBI	BB	SO	SB	Pinch Hit AB	H	PO	A	E	DP	TC/G	FA	G by Pos
1975	HOU	N	103	.238	.285	277	66	5	4	0	0.0	29	19	31	34	12	1	0	193	249	10	67	4.4	.978	2B-94, SS-6
1976			109	.256	.300	410	105	8	5	0	0.0	42	23	33	27	7	0	0	228	356	14	66	5.5	.977	2B-107, SS-3
1977	SF	N	127	.264	.303	436	115	11	3	0	0.0	60	25	56	33	5	9	1	225	314	20	66	4.4	.964	2B-115
1978			79	.220	.288	177	39	3	1	1	0.6	21	11	20	18	5	12	2	123	135	6	23	3.3	.977	2B-62, SS-1
1979			75	.260	.318	154	40	3	2	2	1.3	22	13	8	9	4	22	5	97	102	9	21	2.8	.957	2B-53, 3B-3
5 yrs.			493	.251	.298	1454	365	30	15	3	0.2	174	91	148	121	33	44	8	866	1156	59	243	4.2	.972	2B-431, SS-10, 3B-3

Stan Andrews
ANDREWS, STANLEY JOSEPH (Polo)
Born Stanley Joseph Andruskewicz.
B. Apr. 17, 1917, Lynn, Mass.
BR TR 5'11" 178 lbs.

Year	Team		Games	BA	SA	AB	H	2B	3B	HR	HR%	R	RBI	BB	SO	SB	Pinch Hit AB	H	PO	A	E	DP	TC/G	FA	G by Pos
1939	BOS	N	13	.231	.231	26	6	0	0	0	0.0	0	1	1	2	0	3	1	22	2	4	0	2.2	.857	C-10
1940			19	.182	.182	33	6	0	0	0	0.0	1	2	0	3	1	5	1	29	5	2	0	1.9	.944	C-14
1944	BKN	N	4	.125	.125	8	1	0	0	0	0.0	1	1	1	2	0	0	0	10	1	0	0	2.8	1.000	C-4
1945	2 teams	BKN	N	(21G –	.163)	PHI	N	(13G –	.333)																
"	total		34	.232	.317	82	19	2	1	1	1.2	8	8	6	9	1	1	0	93	18	6	2	3.4	.949	C-33
4 yrs.			70	.215	.262	149	32	2	1	1	0.7	11	12	8	16	2	9	2	154	26	12	2	2.7	.938	C-61

Wally Andrews
ANDREWS, WILLIAM WALTER
B. Sept. 18, 1859, Philadelphia, Pa.   D. Jan. 20, 1940, Indianapolis, Ind.
BR TR 6'3" 170 lbs.

Year	Team		Games	BA	SA	AB	H	2B	3B	HR	HR%	R	RBI	BB	SO	SB	Pinch Hit AB	H	PO	A	E	DP	TC/G	FA	G by Pos
1884	LOU	AA	14	.204	.347	49	10	5	1	0	0.0	10		4			0	0	98	12	10	3	8.6	.917	1B-9, 3B-3, OF-1, SS-1

Wally Andrews *continued*

Year Team	Games	BA	SA	AB	H	2B	3B	HR	HR%	R	RBI	BB	SO	SB	PH AB	PH H	PO	A	E	DP	TC/G	FA	G by Pos
1885 PRO N	1	.000	.000	4	0	0	0	0	0.0	0	0	0	1		0	0	2	3	0	0	5.0	1.000	3B-1
1888 LOU AA	26	.194	.323	93	18	6	3	0	0.0	12	6	13		5	0	0	283	10	1	16	11.3	.997	1B-26
3 yrs.	41	.192	.322	146	28	11	4	0	0.0	22	6	17	1	5	0	0	383	25	11	19	10.2	.974	1B-35, 3B-4, OF-1, SS-1

Bill Andrus

ANDRUS, WILLIAM MORGAN
B. July 25, 1907, Beaumont, Tex. D. Mar. 12, 1982, Washington, D. C.

BR TR 6' 185 lbs.

Year Team	Games	BA	SA	AB	H	2B	3B	HR	HR%	R	RBI	BB	SO	SB	PH AB	PH H	PO	A	E	DP	TC/G	FA	G by Pos
1931 WAS A	3	.000	.000	7	0	0	0	0	0.0	0	0	1	0		1	0	2	1	1		1.3	.750	3B-2
1937 PHI N	3	.000	.000	2	0	0	0	0	0.0	0	0	0	2		2	0	0	0	0	0	0.0	–	3B-1
2 yrs.	6	.000	.000	9	0	0	0	0	0.0	0	1	0	3		3	0	1	2	1	1	0.7	.750	3B-3

Fred Andrus

ANDRUS, FREDERICK HOTHAM
B. Aug. 23, 1850, Washington, Mich. D. Nov. 10, 1937, Detroit, Mich.

BR TR 6'2" 185 lbs.

Year Team	Games	BA	SA	AB	H	2B	3B	HR	HR%	R	RBI	BB	SO	SB	PH AB	PH H	PO	A	E	DP	TC/G	FA	G by Pos
1876 CHI N	8	.306	.389	36	11	3	0	0	0.0	6	2	0	5		0	0	5	0	2	0	0.9	.714	OF-8
1884	1	.200	.200	5	1	0	0	0	0.0	3		1	0		0	0	0	3	0	0	3.0	1.000	P-1
2 yrs.	9	.293	.366	41	12	3	0	0	0.0	9	2	1	5		0	0	5	3	2	0	1.1	.800	OF-8, P-1

Wyman Andrus

ANDRUS, WYMAN W.
B. Oct. 14, 1858, Orono Ont., Canada D. June 17, 1935, Miles City, Mont.

Year Team	Games	BA	SA	AB	H	2B	3B	HR	HR%	R	RBI	BB	SO	SB	PH AB	PH H	PO	A	E	DP	TC/G	FA	G by Pos
1885 PRO N	1	.000	.000	4	0	0	0	0	0.0	0	0	0			0	0	2	3	0	0	5.0	1.000	3B-1

Tom Angley

ANGLEY, THOMAS SAMUEL
B. Oct. 2, 1904, Baltimore, Md. D. Oct. 26, 1952, Wichita, Kans.

BL TR 5'8" 190 lbs.

Year Team	Games	BA	SA	AB	H	2B	3B	HR	HR%	R	RBI	BB	SO	SB	PH AB	PH H	PO	A	E	DP	TC/G	FA	G by Pos
1929 CHI N	5	.250	.313	16	4	1	0	0	0.0	1	6	2	2	0	0	0	23	7	1	0	6.2	.968	C-5

Pat Ankenman

ANKENMAN, FREDERICK NORMAN
B. Dec. 23, 1912, Houston, Tex. D. Jan. 13, 1989, Houston, Tex.

BR TR 5'4" 125 lbs.

Year Team	Games	BA	SA	AB	H	2B	3B	HR	HR%	R	RBI	BB	SO	SB	PH AB	PH H	PO	A	E	DP	TC/G	FA	G by Pos
1936 STL N	1	.000	.000	3	0	0	0	0	0.0	0	0	0	0		0	0	2	1	2	0	5.0	.600	SS-1
1943 BKN N	1	.500	.500	2	1	0	0	0	0.0	1	0	0	0		0	0	2	2	0	1	4.0	1.000	SS-1
1944	13	.250	.292	24	6	1	0	0	0.0	3		0	2	1	0	1	0	11	23	1	2	2.7	.971	2B-11, SS-2
3 yrs.	15	.241	.276	29	7	1	0	0	0.0	2	3	0	5	1	0	1	0	15	26	3	3	2.9	.932	2B-11, SS-4

Bill Annis

ANNIS, WILLIAM PERLEY
B. May 24, 1857, Stoneham, Mass. D. June 10, 1923, Kennebunkport, Me.

BR 5'7" 150 lbs.

Year Team	Games	BA	SA	AB	H	2B	3B	HR	HR%	R	RBI	BB	SO	SB	PH AB	PH H	PO	A	E	DP	TC/G	FA	G by Pos
1884 BOS N	27	.177	.198	96	17	2	0	0	0.0	17		0	8		0	0	22	5	3	1	1.1	.900	OF-27

Cap Anson

ANSON, ADRIAN CONSTANTINE (Old Anse)
B. Apr. 11, 1852, Marshalltown, Iowa D. Apr. 14, 1922, Chicago, Ill.
Manager 1875, 1879-98.
Hall of Fame 1939.

BR TR 6' 227 lbs.

Year Team	Games	BA	SA	AB	H	2B	3B	HR	HR%	R	RBI	BB	SO	SB	PH AB	PH H	PO	A	E	DP	TC/G	FA	G by Pos
1876 CHI N	66	.356	.440	309	110	9	7	1	0.3	63	59	12	8		0	0	137	147	50	8	5.1	.850	3B-66, C-2
1877	59	.337	.420	255	86	19	1	0	0.0	52	32	9	3		0	7	177	118	42	14	5.7	.875	3B-40, C-31
1878	60	.341	.402	261	89	12	2	0	0.0	55	40	13	1		0	0	94	42	25	7	2.7	.845	OF-48, 2B-9, 3B-3, C-3
1879	51	.317	.414	227	72	20	1	0	0.0	40	34	2	2		0	0	620	8	16	26	12.6	.975	1B-51
1880	86	.337	.419	356	120	24	1	1	0.3	54	74	14	12		0	0	849	30	25	29	10.5	.972	1B-81, SS-1, 2B-1
1881	84	.399	.510	343	137	21	7	1	0.3	67	82	26	4		0	0	894	43	24	48	11.4	.975	1B-84, C-2, SS-1
1882	82	.362	.500	348	126	29	8	1	0.3	69	83	20	7		0	0	813	27	46	42	10.8	.948	1B-82, C-1
1883	98	.308	.419	413	127	36	5	0	0.0	70		18	9		0	0	1034	42	42	59	11.4	.962	1B-98, P-2, OF-1, C-1
1884	112	.335	.543	475	159	30	3	21	4.4	108		29	13		0	0	1216	48	62	66	11.8	.953	1B-112, C-3, SS-1, P-1
1885	112	.310	.461	464	144	35	7	7	1.5	100	114	34	13		0	0	1255	39	57	62	12.1	.958	1B-112, C-1
1886	125	.371	.544	504	187	35	11	10	2.0	117	147	55	19	29	0	0	1220	84	53	70	10.9	.961	1B-125, C-12
1887	122	.347	.517	472	164	33	13	7	1.5	107	102	60	18	27	0	0	1233	70	37	75	11.0	.972	1B-122, C-1
1888	134	.344	.499	515	177	20	12	12	2.3	101	84	47	24	28	0	0	1314	65	20	85	10.4	.986	1B-134
1889	134	.311	.440	518	161	32	7	7	1.4	100	117	86	19	27	0	0	1409	79	27	73	11.3	.982	1B-134
1890	139	.312	.401	504	157	14	5	7	1.4	95	107	113	23	29	0	0	1361	56	32	61	10.4	.978	1B-135, 2B-2
1891	136	.291	.409	540	157	24	8	8	1.5	81	120	75	29	17	0	0	1409	80	29	86	11.2	.981	1B-136, C-2
1892	146	.272	.354	559	152	25	9	1	0.2	62	74	67	30	13	0	0	1491	67	44	62	11.0	.973	1B-146
1893	103	.314	.384	398	125	24	2	0	0.0	70	91	68	12	13	1	1	997	44	20	59	10.3	.981	1B-101
1894	83	.395	.542	347	137	28	4	5	1.4	82	99	40	15	17	0	0	743	48	8	52	9.6	.990	1B-82, 2B-1
1895	122	.335	.422	474	159	23	6	2	0.4	87	91	55	23	12	0	0	1176	60	19	82	10.3	.985	1B-122
1896	108	.331	.400	402	133	18	2	2	0.5	72	90	49	10	24	1	0	901	62	20	67	9.1	.980	1B-98, C-10
1897	114	.285	.361	424	121	17	3	3	0.7	67	75	60		11	0	0	969	75	27	69	9.4	.975	1B-103, C-11
22 yrs.	2276	.329	.446	9108	3000	528	124	96	1.1	1719	1715	952	294	247	2	1	21312	1334	725	1222	10.3	.969	1B-2058, 3B-118, C-83, OF-49, 2B-13, SS-3, P-3

Eric Anthony

ANTHONY, ERIC TODD
B. Nov. 8, 1967, San Diego, Calif.

BL TL 6'2" 195 lbs.

Year Team	Games	BA	SA	AB	H	2B	3B	HR	HR%	R	RBI	BB	SO	SB	PH AB	PH H	PO	A	E	DP	TC/G	FA	G by Pos
1989 HOU N	25	.180	.410	61	11	2	0	4	6.6	7	7	9	16	0	5	2	34	1	0	0	1.4	1.000	OF-21

Joe Antolick

ANTOLICK, JOSEPH
B. Apr. 11, 1916, Hokendauqua, Pa.

BR TR 6' 185 lbs.

Year Team	Games	BA	SA	AB	H	2B	3B	HR	HR%	R	RBI	BB	SO	SB	PH AB	PH H	PO	A	E	DP	TC/G	FA	G by Pos
1944 PHI N	4	.333	.333	6	2	0	0	0	0.0	1	0	1	0		0	0	9	1	0	1	2.5	1.000	C-3

John Antonelli

ANTONELLI, JOHN LAWRENCE
B. July 15, 1915, Memphis, Tenn.

BR TR 5'10½" 165 lbs.

Year Team	Games	BA	SA	AB	H	2B	3B	HR	HR%	R	RBI	BB	SO	SB	PH AB	PH H	PO	A	E	DP	TC/G	FA	G by Pos
1944 STL N	8	.190	.238	21	4	1	0	0	0.0	0	1	0	4		0	0	28	10	0	2	4.8	1.000	3B-3, 1B-3, 2B-2

Year	Team	Games	BA	SA	AB	H	2B	3B	HR	HR%	R	RBI	BB	SO	SB	Pinch Hit AB	Pinch Hit H	PO	A	E	DP	TC/G	FA	G by Pos

John Antonelli *continued*

Year	Team	Games	BA	SA	AB	H	2B	3B	HR	HR%	R	RBI	BB	SO	SB	PH AB	PH H	PO	A	E	DP	TC/G	FA	G by Pos
1945	2 teams	STL N (2G – .000)			PHI N (125G – .256)																			
"	total	127	.254	.321	507	129	27	2	1	0.2	50	28	24	25	1	2	0	181	251	20	32	3.6	.956	3B-109, 2B-23, SS-1, 1B-1
2 yrs.		135	.252	.318	528	133	28	2	1	0.2	50	29	24	29	1	2	0	209	261	20	34	3.6	.959	3B-112, 2B-25, 1B-4, SS-1

Bill Antonello

ANTONELLO, WILLIAM JAMES
B. May 19, 1927, Brooklyn, N. Y.

BR TR 5'11" 185 lbs.

Year	Team	Games	BA	SA	AB	H	2B	3B	HR	HR%	R	RBI	BB	SO	SB	PH AB	PH H	PO	A	E	DP	TC/G	FA	G by Pos
1953	BKN N	40	.163	.302	43	7	1	1	1	2.3	9	4	2	11	0	8	0	27	0	1	0	0.7	.964	OF-25

Luis Aparicio

APARICIO, LUIS ERNESTO (Little Looie)
Born Luis Ernesto Aparicio y Montiel.
B. Apr. 29, 1934, Maracaibo, Venezuela
Hall of Fame 1984.

BR TR 5'9" 160 lbs.

Year	Team	Games	BA	SA	AB	H	2B	3B	HR	HR%	R	RBI	BB	SO	SB	PH AB	PH H	PO	A	E	DP	TC/G	FA	G by Pos
1956	CHI A	152	.266	.341	533	142	19	6	3	0.6	69	56	34	63	21	0	0	250	474	35	91	5.0	.954	SS-152
1957		143	.257	.332	575	148	22	6	3	0.5	82	41	52	55	28	1	0	246	449	20	85	5.0	.972	SS-142
1958		145	.266	.345	557	148	20	9	2	0.4	76	40	35	38	29	0	0	289	463	21	90	5.3	.973	SS-145
1959		152	.257	.332	612	157	18	5	6	1.0	98	51	53	40	56	0	0	282	460	23	87	5.0	.970	SS-152
1960		153	.277	.343	600	166	20	7	2	0.3	86	61	43	39	51	0	0	305	551	18	117	5.7	.979	SS-153
1961		156	.272	.352	625	170	24	4	6	1.0	90	45	38	33	53	0	0	264	487	30	86	5.0	.962	SS-156
1962		153	.241	.334	581	140	23	5	7	1.2	72	40	32	36	31	1	0	280	452	20	102	4.9	.973	SS-152
1963	BAL A	146	.250	.331	601	150	18	8	5	0.8	73	45	36	35	40	0	0	275	403	12	76	4.7	.983	SS-145
1964		146	.266	.363	578	154	20	3	10	1.7	93	37	49	51	57	1	0	260	437	15	98	4.9	.979	SS-145
1965		144	.225	.339	564	127	20	10	8	1.4	67	40	46	56	26	1	0	238	439	20	87	4.8	.971	SS-141
1966		151	.276	.366	659	182	25	8	6	0.9	97	41	33	42	25	0	0	303	441	17	104	5.0	.978	SS-151
1967		134	.233	.313	546	127	22	5	4	0.7	55	31	29	44	18	2	0	221	333	25	67	4.3	.957	SS-131
1968	CHI A	155	.264	.334	622	164	24	4	4	0.6	55	36	33	43	17	2	0	269	535	19	92	5.3	.977	SS-154
1969		156	.280	.362	599	168	24	5	5	0.8	77	51	66	29	24	1	0	248	563	20	94	5.3	.976	SS-154
1970		146	.313	.404	552	173	29	3	5	0.9	86	43	53	34	8	3	2	251	483	18	99	5.2	.976	SS-146
1971	BOS A	125	.232	.303	491	114	23	0	4	0.8	56	45	35	43	6	2	1	194	338	16	56	4.4	.971	SS-121
1972		110	.257	.351	436	112	26	3	3	0.7	47	39	26	28	3	1	0	183	304	16	54	4.6	.968	SS-109
1973		132	.271	.309	499	135	17	1	0	0.0	56	49	43	33	13	0	0	190	404	21	68	4.7	.966	SS-132
18 yrs.		2599	.262	.343	10230	2677	394	92	83	0.8	1335	791	736	742	506	15	3	4548	8016	366	1553	5.0	.972	SS-2581
					10th																			

WORLD SERIES

Year	Team	Games	BA	SA	AB	H	2B	3B	HR	HR%	R	RBI	BB	SO	SB	PH AB	PH H	PO	A	E	DP	TC/G	FA	G by Pos
1959	CHI A	6	.308	.346	26	8	1	0	0	0.0	1	0	2	3	1	0	0	10	16	2	2	4.7	.929	SS-6
1966	BAL A	4	.250	.313	16	4	1	0	0	0.0	0	2	0	0	0	0	0	9	8	0	2	4.3	1.000	SS-4
2 yrs.		10	.286	.333	42	12	2	0	0	0.0	1	2	2	3	1	0	0	19	24	2	4	4.5	.956	SS-10

Luke Appling

APPLING, LUCIUS BENJAMIN (Old Aches and Pains)
B. Apr. 2, 1909, High Point, N. C.
Manager 1967.
Hall of Fame 1964.

BR TR 5'10" 183 lbs.

Year	Team	Games	BA	SA	AB	H	2B	3B	HR	HR%	R	RBI	BB	SO	SB	PH AB	PH H	PO	A	E	DP	TC/G	FA	G by Pos
1930	CHI A	6	.308	.385	26	8	2	0	0	0.0	2	2	0	0	2	0	0	12	17	4	1	5.5	.879	SS-6
1931		96	.232	.313	297	69	13	4	1	0.3	36	28	29	27	9	12	3	151	233	43	39	4.4	.899	SS-76, 2B-1
1932		139	.274	.374	489	134	20	10	3	0.6	66	63	40	36	9	7	3	270	419	49	84	5.3	.934	SS-85, 2B-30, 3B-14
1933		151	.322	.443	612	197	36	10	6	1.0	90	85	56	29	6	0	0	314	534	55	107	6.0	.939	SS-151
1934		118	.303	.405	452	137	28	6	2	0.4	75	61	59	27	3	0	0	264	357	35	59	5.6	.947	SS-110, 2B-8
1935		153	.307	.389	525	161	28	6	1	0.2	94	71	122	40	12	0	0	335	556	39	93	6.1	.958	SS-153
1936		138	.388	.508	526	204	31	7	6	1.1	111	128	85	25	10	1	0	320	471	41	119	6.0	.951	SS-137
1937		154	.317	.439	574	182	42	8	4	0.7	98	77	86	28	18	0	0	280	541	49	111	5.6	.944	SS-154
1938		81	.303	.350	294	89	14	0	0	0.0	41	44	42	17	1	2	1	149	258	20	37	5.3	.953	SS-78
1939		148	.314	.368	516	162	16	6	0	0.0	82	56	105	37	16	0	0	289	461	39	78	5.3	.951	SS-148
1940		150	.348	.442	566	197	27	13	0	0.0	96	79	69	35	3	0	0	307	436	37	83	5.2	.953	SS-150
1941		154	.314	.390	592	186	26	8	1	0.2	93	57	82	32	12	0	0	294	473	42	95	5.3	.948	SS-154
1942		142	.262	.341	543	142	26	4	3	0.6	78	53	63	23	17	0	0	269	418	38	77	5.1	.948	SS-141
1943		155	.328	.407	585	192	33	2	3	0.5	63	80	90	29	27	0	0	300	500	36	115	5.4	.957	SS-155
1945		18	.362	.517	58	21	2	2	1	1.7	12	10	12	7	1	1	0	37	56	7	7	5.6	.930	SS-17
1946		149	.309	.378	582	180	27	5	1	0.2	59	55	71	41	6	0	0	252	505	39	99	5.3	.951	SS-149
1947		139	.306	.412	503	154	29	0	8	1.6	67	49	64	28	8	7	0	233	423	35	86	5.0	.949	SS-129, 3B-2
1948		139	.314	.354	497	156	16	2	0	0.0	63	47	94	35	10	3	1	217	373	35	63	4.5	.944	3B-72, SS-64
1949		142	.301	.394	492	148	21	5	5	1.0	82	58	121	24	7	1	0	253	450	26	95	5.1	.964	SS-141
1950		50	.234	.320	128	30	3	4	0	0.0	11	13	12	8	2	15	1	128	62	3	29	3.9	.984	SS-20, 1B-13, 2B-1
20 yrs.		2422	.310	.398	8857	2749	440	102	45	0.5	1319	1116	1302	528	179	49	9	4674	7543	672	1477	5.3	.948	SS-2218, 3B-88, 2B-40, 1B-13

Angel Aragon

ARAGON, ANGEL VALDES, SR. (Pete, Bing)
Born Angel Aragon y Valdes. Father of Jack Aragon.
B. Aug. 2, 1893, Havana, Cuba D. Jan. 24, 1952, New York, N. Y.

BR TR 5'5" 150 lbs.

Year	Team	Games	BA	SA	AB	H	2B	3B	HR	HR%	R	RBI	BB	SO	SB	PH AB	PH H	PO	A	E	DP	TC/G	FA	G by Pos
1914	NY A	6	.143	.143	7	1	0	0	0	0.0	1	0	1	2	0	5	1	0	0	0	0	0.0	–	OF-1
1916		13	.185	.185	27	5	0	0	0	0.0	3	3	2	1	0	5	0	7	18	3	0	2.2	.893	3B-8, OF-3
1917		14	.067	.089	45	3	1	0	0	0.0	2	2	2	5	1	0	0	22	13	1	2	2.6	.972	OF-6, 3B-4, SS-2
3 yrs.		33	.114	.127	79	9	1	0	0	0.0	6	5	5	8	1	10	2	29	31	4	2	1.9	.938	3B-12, OF-10, SS-2

Jack Aragon

ARAGON, ANGEL VALDES, JR.
Born Angel Valdes Aragon y Reyes. Son of Angel Aragon.
B. Nov. 20, 1915, Havana, Cuba D. Apr. 4, 1988, Clearwater, Fla.

BR TR 5'10" 176 lbs.

Year	Team	Games	BA	SA	AB	H	2B	3B	HR	HR%	R	RBI	BB	SO	SB	PH AB	PH H	PO	A	E	DP	TC/G	FA	G by Pos
1941	NY N	1	–	–	0	0	0	0	0	–	0	0	0	0	0	0	0	0	0	0	0	0.0	–	

Maurice Archdeacon

ARCHDEACON, MAURICE JOHN (Flash, Comet)
B. Dec. 14, 1898, St. Louis, Mo. D. Sept. 5, 1954, St. Louis, Mo.

BL TL 5'8" 153 lbs.

Year	Team		Games	BA	SA	AB	H	2B	3B	HR	HR%	R	RBI	BB	SO	SB	Pinch Hit AB	Pinch Hit H	PO	A	E	DP	TC/G	FA	G by Pos

Maurice Archdeacon *continued*

Year	Team		Games	BA	SA	AB	H	2B	3B	HR	HR%	R	RBI	BB	SO	SB	AB	H	PO	A	E	DP	TC/G	FA	G by Pos
1923	CHI	A	22	.402	.483	87	35	5	1	0	0.0	23	4	6	8	2	1	0	44	1	4	0	2.2	.918	OF-20
1924			95	.319	.372	288	92	9	3	0	0.0	59	25	40	30	11	14	5	173	8	8	2	2.0	.958	OF-77
1925			10	.111	.111	9	1	0	0	0	0.0	2	0	2	1	0	8	1	2	0	0	0	0.2	1.000	OF-1
3 yrs.			127	.333	.391	384	128	14	4	0	0.0	84	29	48	39	13	23	6	219	9	12	2	1.9	.950	OF-98

Jimmy Archer

ARCHER, JAMES PETER
B. May 13, 1883, Dublin, Ireland   D. Mar. 29, 1958, Milwaukee, Wis.

BR TR 5'10"   168 lbs.

Year	Team		Games	BA	SA	AB	H	2B	3B	HR	HR%	R	RBI	BB	SO	SB	AB	H	PO	A	E	DP	TC/G	FA	G by Pos
1904	PIT	N	7	.150	.150	20	3	0	0	0	0.0	1	1	0		0	0	0	25	9	3	0	5.3	.919	C-7, OF-1
1907	DET	A	18	.119	.119	42	5	0	0	0	0.0	6	0	4		0	0	0	64	20	3	0	4.8	.966	C-17, 2B-1
1909	CHI	N	80	.230	.291	261	60	9	2	1	0.4	31	30	12		5	0	0	408	97	21	7	6.6	.960	C-80
1910			98	.259	.371	313	81	17	6	2	0.6	36	41	14	49	6	8	3	620	97	20	31	7.5	.973	C-49, 1B-40
1911			116	.253	.357	387	98	18	5	4	1.0	41	41	18	43	5	3	0	560	128	15	17	6.1	.979	C-102, 1B-10, 2B-1
1912			120	.283	.384	385	109	20	2	5	1.3	35	58	22	36	7	1	0	504	149	23	15	5.6	.966	C-118
1913			110	.267	.360	367	98	14	7	2	0.5	38	44	19	27	4	3	1	512	143	21	10	6.1	.969	C-103, 1B-8
1914			79	.258	.310	248	64	9	2	0	0.0	17	19	9	9	1	3	1	367	105	13	8	6.1	.973	C-76
1915			97	.243	.320	309	75	11	5	1	0.3	21	27	11	38	5	5	2	447	126	13	11	6.0	.978	C-88
1916			77	.220	.283	205	45	6	2	1	0.5	11	30	12	24	3	16	2	236	84	7	5	4.2	.979	C-65, 3B-1
1917			2	.000	.000	2	0	0	0	0	0.0	0	0	0	1	0	2	0	0	0	0	0	0.0	–	
1918	3 teams		PIT N	(24G –	.155)			BKN	N	(9G –	.273)			CIN	N	(9G –	.269)								
"	total		42	.208	.283	106	22	3	0	0	0.0	10	5	3	14	0	5	1	117	54	3	8	4.1	.983	C-35, 1B-2
12 yrs.			846	.250	.333	2645	660	106	34	16	0.6	247	296	124	241	36	46	10	3860	1012	142	112	5.9	.972	C-740, 1B-60, 2B-2, OF-1, 3B-1

WORLD SERIES

Year	Team		Games	BA	SA	AB	H	2B	3B	HR	HR%	R	RBI	BB	SO	SB	AB	H	PO	A	E	DP	TC/G	FA	G by Pos
1907	DET	A	1	.000	.000	3	0	0	0	0	0.0	0	0	0	1	0	0	0	4	1	0	0	5.0	1.000	C-1
1910	CHI	N	3	.182	.273	11	2	1	0	0	0.0	1	0	0	4	0	0	0	36	7	0	2	14.3	1.000	C-2, 1B-1
2 yrs.			4	.143	.214	14	2	1	0	0	0.0	1	0	0	5	0	0	0	40	8	0	2	12.0	1.000	C-3, 1B-1

George Archie

ARCHIE, GEORGE ALBERT
B. Apr. 27, 1914, Nashville, Tenn.

BR TR 6'   170 lbs.

Year	Team		Games	BA	SA	AB	H	2B	3B	HR	HR%	R	RBI	BB	SO	SB	AB	H	PO	A	E	DP	TC/G	FA	G by Pos
1938	DET	A	3	.000	.000	2	0	0	0	0	0.0	0	0	0	1	0	2	0	0	0	0	0	0.0	–	
1941	2 teams		WAS A	(105G –	.269)			STL	A	(9G –	.379)														
"	total		114	.277	.375	408	113	23	4	3	0.7	48	53	37	45	10	9	1	341	174	19	36	4.7	.964	3B-73, 1B-31
1946	STL	A	4	.182	.273	11	2	1	0	0	0.0	1	0	0	1	0	0	0	34	6	0	6	10.0	1.000	1B-3
3 yrs.			121	.273	.371	421	115	24	4	3	0.7	49	53	37	47	10	11	1	375	180	19	42	4.7	.967	3B-73, 1B-34

Jose Arcia

ARCIA, JOSE RAIMUNDO (Flaco)
Born Jose Raimundo Arcia y Orta.
B. Aug. 22, 1943, Havana, Cuba

BR TR 6'3"   170 lbs.

Year	Team		Games	BA	SA	AB	H	2B	3B	HR	HR%	R	RBI	BB	SO	SB	AB	H	PO	A	E	DP	TC/G	FA	G by Pos
1968	CHI	N	59	.190	.274	84	16	4	0	1	1.2	15	8	3	24	1	5	1	49	34	2	3	1.4	.976	OF-17, 2B-10, SS-7, 3B-1
1969	SD	N	120	.215	.272	302	65	11	3	0	0.0	35	10	14	47	14	0	0	194	237	15	44	3.7	.966	2B-68, SS-37, 3B-8, OF-4, 1B-1
1970			114	.223	.288	229	51	9	3	0	0.0	28	17	12	36	3	1	0	137	189	15	47	3.0	.956	SS-67, 2B-20, 3B-9, OF-7
3 yrs.			293	.215	.278	615	132	24	6	1	0.2	78	35	29	107	17	6	1	380	460	32	94	3.0	.963	SS-111, 2B-98, OF-28, 3B-18, 1B-1

Dan Ardell

ARDELL, DANIEL MIERS
B. May 27, 1941, Seattle, Wash.

BL TL 6'2"   190 lbs.

Year	Team		Games	BA	SA	AB	H	2B	3B	HR	HR%	R	RBI	BB	SO	SB	AB	H	PO	A	E	DP	TC/G	FA	G by Pos
1961	LA	A	7	.250	.250	4	1	0	0	0	0.0	0	1	2	0	0	1	2	0	13	0	0	1	1.9	1.000	1B-1

Joe Ardner

ARDNER, JOSEPH A. (Old Hoss)
B. Feb. 27, 1858, Mt. Vernon, Ohio   D. Sept. 15, 1935, Cleveland, Ohio

BR TR

Year	Team		Games	BA	SA	AB	H	2B	3B	HR	HR%	R	RBI	BB	SO	SB	AB	H	PO	A	E	DP	TC/G	FA	G by Pos
1884	CLE	N	26	.174	.207	92	16	1	1	0	0.0	6	4	1	24		0	0	55	71	20	6	5.6	.863	2B-25, 3B-1
1890			84	.223	.269	323	72	13	1	0	0.0	28	35	17	40	9	0	0	205	257	40	42	6.0	.920	2B-84
2 yrs.			110	.212	.255	415	88	14	2	0	0.0	34	39	18	64	9	0	0	260	328	60	48	5.9	.907	2B-109, 3B-1

Hank Arft

ARFT, HENRY IRVEN (Bow Wow)
B. Jan. 28, 1922, Manchester, Mo.

BL TL 5'10½"   190 lbs.

Year	Team		Games	BA	SA	AB	H	2B	3B	HR	HR%	R	RBI	BB	SO	SB	AB	H	PO	A	E	DP	TC/G	FA	G by Pos
1948	STL	A	69	.238	.363	248	59	10	3	5	2.0	25	38	45	43	1	0	0	598	43	3	81	9.3	.995	1B-69
1949			6	.200	.400	5	1	1	0	0	0.0	1	2	0	1	0	5	1	0	0	0	0	0.0	–	
1950			98	.268	.364	280	75	16	4	1	0.4	45	32	46	48	3	13	3	701	51	4	59	7.7	.995	1B-84
1951			112	.261	.397	345	90	16	5	7	2.0	44	42	41	34	4	15	5	820	86	10	100	8.2	.989	1B-97
1952			15	.143	.321	28	4	3	1	0	0.0	1	4	5	7	0	5	0	63	4	1	11	4.5	.985	1B-10
5 yrs.			300	.253	.375	906	229	46	13	13	1.4	116	118	137	133	8	38	9	2182	184	18	251	7.9	.992	1B-260

Buzz Arlett

ARLETT, RUSSELL LORIS
B. Jan. 3, 1899, Elmhurst, Calif.   D. May 16, 1964, Minneapolis, Minn.

BB TR 6'3½"   225 lbs.

Year	Team		Games	BA	SA	AB	H	2B	3B	HR	HR%	R	RBI	BB	SO	SB	AB	H	PO	A	E	DP	TC/G	FA	G by Pos
1931	PHI	N	121	.313	.538	418	131	26	7	18	4.3	65	72	45	39	3	14	4	303	21	13	11	2.8	.961	OF-94, 1B-13

Tony Armas

ARMAS, ANTONIO RAFAEL
Born Antonio Rafael Armas y Machado.
B. July 2, 1953, Anzoatequi, Venezuela

BR TR 5'11"   182 lbs.

Year	Team		Games	BA	SA	AB	H	2B	3B	HR	HR%	R	RBI	BB	SO	SB	AB	H	PO	A	E	DP	TC/G	FA	G by Pos
1976	PIT	N	4	.333	.333	6	2	0	0	0	0.0	0	1	0	2	0	2	0	3	0	0	0	0.8	1.000	OF-2
1977	OAK	A	118	.240	.380	363	87	8	2	13	3.6	26	53	20	99	1	7	0	294	9	6	4	2.6	.981	OF-112, SS-1
1978			91	.213	.272	239	51	6	1	2	0.8	17	13	10	62	1	4	0	214	3	2	0	2.4	.991	OF-85, DH-3
1979			80	.248	.421	278	69	9	3	11	4.0	29	34	16	67	1	0	0	194	7	5	2	2.6	.976	OF-80
1980			158	.279	.500	628	175	18	8	35	5.6	87	109	29	128	5	0	0	374	17	10	2	2.5	.975	OF-158
1981			109	.261	.480	440	115	24	3	**22**	5.0	51	76	19	**115**	5	0	0	259	8	2	4	2.5	.993	OF-109
1982			138	.233	.433	536	125	19	2	28	5.2	58	89	33	128	2	2	0	333	9	6	1	2.5	.983	OF-135, DH-1
1983	BOS	A	145	.218	.453	574	125	23	2	36	6.3	77	107	29	131	0	5	0	326	5	5	0	2.3	.985	OF-116, DH-27

Year	Team	Games	BA	SA	AB	H	2B	3B	HR	HR%	R	RBI	BB	SO	SB	PH AB	PH H	PO	A	E	DP	TC/G	FA	G by Pos

Tony Armas *continued*

Year	Team	Games	BA	SA	AB	H	2B	3B	HR	HR%	R	RBI	BB	SO	SB	PH AB	PH H	PO	A	E	DP	TC/G	FA	G by Pos
1984		157	.268	.531	639	171	29	5	**43**	6.7	107	**123**	32	**156**	1	0	0	329	4	9	2	2.2	.974	OF-126, DH-31
1985		103	.265	.514	385	102	17	5	23	6.0	50	64	18	90	0	5	1	173	3	3	1	1.7	.983	OF-79, DH-19
1986		121	.264	.409	425	112	21	4	11	2.6	40	58	24	77	0	4	1	247	4	8	0	2.1	.969	OF-117, DH-1
1987	CAL A	28	.198	.370	81	16	3	1	3	3.7	9	9	1	11	1	6	2	36	0	0	0	1.3	1.000	OF-27
1988		120	.272	.443	368	100	20	2	13	3.5	42	49	22	87	1	9	2	212	5	3	1	1.8	.986	OF-113, DH-5
1989		60	.257	.465	202	52	7	1	11	5.4	22	30	7	48	0	9	2	101	5	2	3	1.8	.981	OF-47, DH-6, 1B-2
14 yrs.		1432	.252	.453	5164	1302	204	39	251	4.9	614	815	260	1201	18	50	8	3095	79	61	18	2.3	.981	OF-1306, DH-93, 1B-2, SS-1

DIVISIONAL PLAYOFF SERIES

Year	Team	Games	BA	SA	AB	H	2B	3B	HR	HR%	R	RBI	BB	SO	SB	PH AB	PH H	PO	A	E	DP	TC/G	FA	G by Pos
1981	OAK A	3	.545	.727	11	6	2	0	0	0.0	1	3	1	1	0	0	0	0	0	1	0	0.3	–	OF-3

LEAGUE CHAMPIONSHIP SERIES

Year	Team	Games	BA	SA	AB	H	2B	3B	HR	HR%	R	RBI	BB	SO	SB	PH AB	PH H	PO	A	E	DP	TC/G	FA	G by Pos
1981	OAK A	3	.167	.167	12	2	0	0	0	0.0	0	0	0	5	0	0	0	0	0	0	0	0.0	–	OF-3
1986	BOS A	5	.125	.188	16	2	1	0	0	0.0	1	0	0	2	0	0	0	12	0	0	0	2.4	1.000	OF-5
2 yrs.		8	.143	.179	28	4	1	0	0	0.0	1	0	0	7	0	0	0	12	0	0	0	1.5	1.000	OF-8

WORLD SERIES

Year	Team	Games	BA	SA	AB	H	2B	3B	HR	HR%	R	RBI	BB	SO	SB	PH AB	PH H	PO	A	E	DP	TC/G	FA	G by Pos
1986	BOS A	1	.000	.000	1	0	0	0	0	0.0	0	0	0	1	0	1	0	0	0	0	0	0.0	–	

Ed Armbrister

ARMBRISTER, EDISON ROSANDA
B. July 4, 1948, Nassau, Bahamas   BR TR 5'11" 160 lbs.

Year	Team	Games	BA	SA	AB	H	2B	3B	HR	HR%	R	RBI	BB	SO	SB	PH AB	PH H	PO	A	E	DP	TC/G	FA	G by Pos
1973	CIN N	18	.216	.432	37	8	3	1	1	2.7	5	5	2	8	0	5	1	21	1	2	0	1.3	.917	OF-14
1974		9	.286	.286	7	2	0	0	0	0.0	0	0	1	1	0	5	2	1	0	0	0	0.1	1.000	OF-4
1975		59	.185	.200	65	12	1	0	0	0.0	9	2	5	19	3	28	7	13	0	2	0	0.3	.867	OF-19
1976		73	.295	.462	78	23	3	2	2	2.6	20	7	6	22	7	27	7	31	4	1	1	0.5	.972	OF-32
1977		65	.256	.423	78	20	4	3	1	1.3	12	5	10	21	5	24	5	25	3	3	1	0.5	.903	OF-27
5 yrs.		224	.245	.377	265	65	11	6	4	1.5	46	19	24	71	15	89	22	91	8	8	2	0.5	.925	OF-96

LEAGUE CHAMPIONSHIP SERIES

Year	Team	Games	BA	SA	AB	H	2B	3B	HR	HR%	R	RBI	BB	SO	SB	PH AB	PH H	PO	A	E	DP	TC/G	FA	G by Pos
1973	CIN N	3	.167	.167	6	1	0	0	0	0.0	0	0	0	5	0	0	0	3	0	0	0	1.0	1.000	OF-1
1975		1	–	–	0	0	0	0	0	–	0	1	0	0	0	0	0	0	0	0	0	0.0	–	
1976		1	–	–	0	0	0	0	0	–	0	0	0	0	0	0	0	0	0	0	0	0.0	–	
3 yrs.		5	.167	.167	6	1	0	0	0	0.0	0	1	0	5	0	2	0	3	0	0	0	0.6	1.000	OF-1

WORLD SERIES

Year	Team	Games	BA	SA	AB	H	2B	3B	HR	HR%	R	RBI	BB	SO	SB	PH AB	PH H	PO	A	E	DP	TC/G	FA	G by Pos
1975	CIN N	5	.000	.000	1	0	0	0	0	0.0	1	0	2	0	0	1	0	0	0	0	0	0.0	–	

Charlie Armbruster

ARMBRUSTER, CHARLES A.
B. Aug. 30, 1880, Cincinnati, Ohio   D. Oct. 7, 1964, Grants Pass, Ore.   BR TR 5'9" 180 lbs.

Year	Team	Games	BA	SA	AB	H	2B	3B	HR	HR%	R	RBI	BB	SO	SB	PH AB	PH H	PO	A	E	DP	TC/G	FA	G by Pos
1905	BOS A	35	.198	.242	91	18	4	0	0	0.0	13	6	18		3	0	0	154	30	11	0	5.6	.944	C-35
1906		72	.144	.184	201	29	6	1	0	0.0	9	6	25		2	4	0	270	100	17	6	5.4	.956	C-66, 1B-1
1907	2 teams	BOS A (23G – .100)			CHI A (1G – .000)																			
"	total	24	.095	.111	63	6	1	0	0	0.0	2	0	9		1	1	0	89	37	8	4	5.6	.940	C-22
3 yrs.		131	.149	.186	355	53	11	1	0	0.0	24	12	52		6	5	0	513	167	36	10	5.5	.950	C-123, 1B-1

Harry Armbruster

ARMBRUSTER, HARRY (Buster)
B. Mar. 20, 1882, Cincinnati, Ohio   D. Dec. 10, 1953, Cincinnati, Ohio   BL TL 190 lbs.

Year	Team	Games	BA	SA	AB	H	2B	3B	HR	HR%	R	RBI	BB	SO	SB	PH AB	PH H	PO	A	E	DP	TC/G	FA	G by Pos
1906	PHI A	91	.238	.306	265	63	6	3	2	0.8	40	24	43		13	12	3	124	9	4	–	1.5	.971	OF-74

George Armstrong

ARMSTRONG, GEORGE NOBLE (Dodo)
B. June 3, 1924, Orange, N. J.   BR TR 5'10" 190 lbs.

Year	Team	Games	BA	SA	AB	H	2B	3B	HR	HR%	R	RBI	BB	SO	SB	PH AB	PH H	PO	A	E	DP	TC/G	FA	G by Pos
1946	PHI A	8	.167	.333	6	1	1	0	0	0.0	0	0	1	1	0	4	1	4	1	0	1	0.6	1.000	C-4

Harry Arndt

ARNDT, HARRY J.
B. Feb. 12, 1879, South Bend, Ind.   D. Mar. 24, 1921, South Bend, Ind.   TR

Year	Team	Games	BA	SA	AB	H	2B	3B	HR	HR%	R	RBI	BB	SO	SB	PH AB	PH H	PO	A	E	DP	TC/G	FA	G by Pos
1902	2 teams	DET A (10G – .147)			BAL A (68G – .254)																			
"	total	78	.241	.323	282	68	7	2	2	0.7	45	35	41		9	0	0	136	25	18	1	2.3	.899	OF-72, 2B-4, 3B-2, SS-1, 1B-1
1905	STL N	113	.243	.313	415	101	11	6	2	0.5	41	36	24		13	2	1	206	285	23	26	4.5	.955	2B-90, OF-9, 3B-7, SS-5
1906		69	.270	.391	256	69	7	9	2	0.8	30	26	19		5	1	0	116	139	9	16	3.8	.966	3B-65, OF-1, 1B-1
1907		11	.188	.219	32	6	1	0	0	0.0	3	2	1		0	4	1	36	9	1	3	4.2	.978	1B-4, 3B-3
4 yrs.		271	.248	.333	985	244	26	20	6	0.6	119	99	85		27	7	2	494	458	51	46	3.7	.949	2B-94, OF-82, 3B-77, SS-6, 1B-6

Larry Arndt

ARNDT, LARRY WAYNE
B. Feb. 25, 1963, Fremont, Ohio   BR TR 6'1" 195 lbs.

Year	Team	Games	BA	SA	AB	H	2B	3B	HR	HR%	R	RBI	BB	SO	SB	PH AB	PH H	PO	A	E	DP	TC/G	FA	G by Pos
1989	OAK A	2	.167	.167	6	1	0	0	0	0.0	1	0	0	1	0	0	0	8	2	0	3	5.0	1.000	3B-1, 1B-1

Chris Arnold

ARNOLD, CHRISTOPHER PAUL
B. Nov. 6, 1947, Long Beach, Calif.   BR TR 5'10" 160 lbs.

Year	Team	Games	BA	SA	AB	H	2B	3B	HR	HR%	R	RBI	BB	SO	SB	PH AB	PH H	PO	A	E	DP	TC/G	FA	G by Pos
1971	SF N	6	.231	.462	13	3	0	0	1	7.7	2	3	1	2	0	4	1	4	7	1	0	2.0	.917	2B-3
1972		51	.226	.321	84	19	3	1	1	1.2	8	4	8	12	0	21	4	24	50	2	5	1.5	.974	3B-17, 2B-7, SS-4
1973		49	.296	.389	54	16	2	0	1	1.9	7	13	8	11	0	36	12	16	2	1	0	0.4	.947	C-9, 3B-1, 2B-1
1974		78	.241	.333	174	42	7	3	1	0.6	22	26	15	27	1	38	9	72	94	5	19	2.2	.971	2B-31, 3B-7, SS-1
1975		29	.195	.195	41	8	0	0	0	0.0	4	0	4	8	0	17	3	10	8	1	5	0.7	.947	OF-4, 2B-4
1976		60	.217	.246	69	15	0	1	0	0.0	4	5	6	16	0	45	14	14	29	1	4	0.7	.977	2B-8, 3B-4, SS-1, 1B-1
6 yrs.		273	.237	.315	435	103	12	5	4	0.9	47	51	42	76	1	161	41	140	190	11	33	1.2	.968	2B-54, 3B-29, C-9, SS-6, OF-4, 1B-1

Morrie Arnovich

ARNOVICH, MORRIS (Snooker)
B. Nov. 16, 1910, Superior, Wis.   D. July 20, 1959, Superior, Wis.   BR TR 5'10" 168 lbs.

Year	Team		Games	BA	SA	AB	H	2B	3B	HR	HR%	R	RBI	BB	SO	SB	Pinch Hit AB	H	PO	A	E	DP	TC/G	FA	G by Pos

Morrie Arnovich *continued*

Year	Team		Games	BA	SA	AB	H	2B	3B	HR	HR%	R	RBI	BB	SO	SB	AB	H	PO	A	E	DP	TC/G	FA	G by Pos
1936	PHI	N	13	.313	.438	48	15	3	0	1	2.1	4	7	1	3	0	0	0	37	1	0	0	2.9	1.000	OF-13
1937			117	.290	.449	410	119	27	4	10	2.4	60	60	34	32	5	9	2	237	10	7	5	2.2	.972	OF-107
1938			139	.275	.357	502	138	29	4	4	0.8	47	72	42	37	2	6	0	327	18	6	0	2.5	.983	OF-133
1939			134	.324	.413	491	159	25	2	5	1.0	68	67	58	28	7	2	1	335	10	6	0	2.6	.983	OF-132
1940	2 teams	PHI N (39G – .199)				CIN N (62G – .284)																			
"	total		101	.250	.301	352	88	12	3	0	0.0	30	33	27	25	1	4	0	93	3	4	0	1.0	.960	OF-97
1941	NY	N	85	.280	.377	207	58	8	3	2	1.0	25	22	23	14	2	20	5	103	5	2	0	1.3	.982	OF-61
1946			1	.000	.000	3	0	0	0	0	0.0	0	0	0	0	0	0	0	1	0	0	0	1.0	1.000	OF-1
7 yrs.			590	.287	.383	2013	577	104	12	22	1.1	234	261	185	139	17	41	9	1133	47	25	5	2.0	.979	OF-544

WORLD SERIES

1940	CIN	N	1	.000	.000	1	0	0	0	0	0.0	0	0	0	0	0	1	0	2	0	0	0	2.0	1.000	OF-1

Tug Arundel

ARUNDEL, JOHN THOMAS
B. June 30, 1862, Auburn, N. Y. D. Sept. 5, 1912, Auburn, N. Y.

1882	PHI	AA	1	.000	.000	5	0	0	0	0	0.0	0		0		0	0	0	6	2	2	0	10.0	.800	C-1
1884	TOL	AA	15	.085	.085	47	4	0	0	0	0.0	6		3		0	0	0	113	26	8	2	9.8	.946	C-15
1887	IND	N	43	.197	.223	157	31	4	0	0	0.0	13	13	8	12	8	0	0	157	66	36	5	6.0	.861	C-42, OF-2, 1B-1
1888	WAS	N	17	.196	.235	51	10	0	1	0	0.0	2	3	5	10	1	0	0	63	16	15	1	5.5	.840	C-17
4 yrs.			76	.173	.196	260	45	4	1	0	0.0	21	16	16	22	9	0	0	339	110	61	8	6.7	.880	C-75, OF-2, 1B-1

Randy Asadoor

ASADOOR, RANDALL CARL   BR TR 6'1" 185 lbs.
B. Oct. 20, 1962, Fresno, Calif.

1986	SD	N	15	.364	.455	55	20	5	0	0	0.0	9	7	3	13	1	0	0	12	31	5	1	3.2	.896	3B-15, 2B-2

Jim Asbell

ASBELL, JAMES MARION   BR TR 6' 195 lbs.
B. June 22, 1914, Dallas, Tex. D. July 6, 1967, San Mateo, Calif.

1938	CHI	N	17	.182	.242	33	6	2	0	0	0.0	6	3	3	9	0	6	3	14	1	0	1	0.9	1.000	OF-17

Asby Asbjornson

ASBJORNSON, ROBERT ANTHONY   BR TR 6'1" 196 lbs.
B. June 19, 1909, Concord, Mass. D. Jan. 21, 1970, Williamsport, Pa.

1928	BOS	A	6	.188	.250	16	3	1	0	0	0.0	0	1	1	1	0	0	0	8	3	1	0	2.0	.917	C-6
1929			17	.103	.103	29	3	0	0	0	0.0	1	0	1	6	0	0	0	21	5	3	1	1.7	.897	C-15
1931	CIN	N	45	.305	.381	118	36	7	1	0	0.0	13	22	7	23	0	14	3	82	24	2	2	2.4	.981	C-31
1932			29	.172	.259	58	10	2	0	1	1.7	5	4	0	15	0	13	0	45	4	2	2	1.8	.961	C-16
4 yrs.			97	.235	.303	221	52	10	1	1	0.5	19	27	9	45	0	28	3	156	36	8	5	2.1	.960	C-68

Richie Ashburn

ASHBURN, DON RICHARD (Whitey)   BL TR 5'10" 170 lbs.
B. Mar. 19, 1927, Tilden, Neb.

1948	PHI	N	117	.333	.400	463	154	17	4	2	0.4	78	40	60	22	32	1	0	344	14	7	2	3.1	.981	OF-116
1949			154	.284	.349	662	188	18	11	1	0.2	84	37	58	38	9	0	0	514	13	11	3	3.5	.980	OF-154
1950			151	.303	.402	594	180	25	14	2	0.3	84	41	63	32	14	2	0	405	8	5	2	2.8	.988	OF-147
1951			154	.344	.426	643	221	31	5	4	0.6	92	63	50	37	29	0	0	538	15	7	6	3.6	.988	OF-154
1952			154	.282	.357	613	173	31	6	1	0.2	93	42	75	30	16	1	1	428	23	9	5	3.0	.980	OF-154
1953			156	.330	.408	622	205	25	9	2	0.3	110	57	61	35	14	0	0	496	18	5	4	3.3	.990	OF-156
1954			153	.313	.376	559	175	16	8	1	0.2	111	41	125	46	11	0	0	483	12	8	2	3.3	.984	OF-153
1955			140	.338	.448	533	180	32	9	3	0.6	91	40	105	36	12	1	1	387	10	7	3	2.9	.983	OF-140
1956			154	.303	.384	628	190	26	8	3	0.5	94	50	79	45	10	0	0	503	11	9	3	3.4	.983	OF-154
1957			156	.297	.364	626	186	26	8	0	0.0	93	33	94	44	13	0	0	502	18	7	7	3.4	.987	OF-156
1958			152	.350	.441	615	215	24	13	2	0.3	98	33	97	48	30	0	0	495	8	8	2	3.4	.984	OF-152
1959			153	.266	.307	564	150	16	2	1	0.2	86	20	79	42	9	4	1	359	4	11	1	2.4	.971	OF-149
1960	CHI	N	151	.291	.338	547	159	16	5	0	0.0	99	40	116	50	16	6	1	317	11	8	2	2.2	.976	OF-146
1961			109	.257	.306	307	79	7	4	0	0.0	49	19	55	27	7	34	10	131	4	3	0	1.3	.978	OF-76
1962	NY	N	135	.306	.393	389	119	7	3	7	1.8	60	28	81	39	12	31	13	192	13	6	2	1.6	.972	OF-97, 2B-2
15 yrs.			2189	.308	.382	8365	2574	317	109	29	0.3	1322	586	1198	571	234	80	27	6094	182	111	44	2.9	.983	OF-2104, 2B-2

WORLD SERIES

1950	PHI	N	4	.176	.235	17	3	1	0	0	0.0	0	1	0	4	0	0	0	9	0	0	0	2.3	1.000	OF-4

Alan Ashby

ASHBY, ALAN DEAN   BB TR 6'2" 185 lbs.
B. July 8, 1951, Long Beach, Calif.

1973	CLE	A	11	.172	.310	29	5	1	0	1	3.4	4	3	2	11	0	1	0	45	0	1	0	4.2	.978	C-11
1974			10	.143	.143	7	1	0	0	0	0.0	1	0	2	2	0	1	1	12	0	0	0	1.2	1.000	C-9
1975			90	.224	.331	254	57	10	1	5	2.0	32	32	30	42	3	1	0	450	43	6	7	5.5	.988	C-87, 1B-2, DH-1, 3B-1
1976			89	.239	.316	247	59	5	1	4	1.6	26	32	27	49	0	5	0	476	52	7	7	6.0	.987	C-86, 1B-2, 3B-1
1977	TOR	A	124	.210	.280	396	83	16	3	2	0.5	25	29	50	51	0	0	0	619	71	11	11	5.7	.984	C-124
1978			81	.261	.420	264	69	15	4	9	3.4	27	29	28	32	1	0	0	399	38	6	6	5.5	.986	C-81
1979	HOU	N	108	.202	.277	336	68	15	2	2	0.6	25	35	26	70	0	3	1	548	57	8	5	5.7	.987	C-105
1980			116	.256	.347	352	90	19	2	3	0.9	30	48	35	40	0	5	1	608	60	6	10	5.8	.991	C-114
1981			83	.271	.369	255	69	13	0	4	1.6	20	33	35	33	2	1	2	434	58	9	6	6.0	.982	C-81
1982			100	.257	.416	339	87	14	2	12	3.5	40	49	27	53	2	6	3	530	55	14	5	6.0	.977	C-95
1983			87	.229	.389	275	63	18	2	8	2.9	31	34	31	38	0	5	2	435	56	13	2	5.8	.974	C-85
1984			66	.262	.361	191	50	7	2	4	2.1	16	27	20	22	0	4	2	303	42	5	3	5.3	.986	C-63
1985			65	.280	.450	189	53	8	0	8	4.2	20	25	24	27	0	4	1	312	37	8	1	5.5	.978	C-60
1986			120	.257	.371	315	81	15	0	7	2.2	24	38	39	56	1	20	3	632	43	10	2	5.7	.985	C-103
1987			125	.288	.438	386	111	16	0	14	3.6	53	63	50	52	0	16	1	778	56	6	3	6.6	.993	C-110
1988			73	.238	.374	227	54	10	0	7	3.1	19	33	29	36	0	10	2	414	23	4	4	6.0	.991	C-66
1989			22	.164	.213	61	10	1	0	0	0.0	4	3	7	8	0	2	1	101	4	0	0	4.8	1.000	C-19
17 yrs.			1370	.245	.361	4123	1010	183	13	90	2.2	397	513	461	622	7	87	20	7096	685	114	75	5.8	.986	C-1299, 1B-4, 3B-2, DH-1

DIVISIONAL PLAYOFF SERIES

1981	HOU	N	3	.111	.444	9	1	0	0	1	11.1	1	2	2	0	0	0	0	0	0	0	0	0.0	—	C-3

Year	Team	Games	BA	SA	AB	H	2B	3B	HR	HR%	R	RBI	BB	SO	SB	Pinch Hit AB	Pinch Hit H	PO	A	E	DP	TC/G	FA	G by Pos

Alan Ashby *continued*
LEAGUE CHAMPIONSHIP SERIES

Year	Team	Games	BA	SA	AB	H	2B	3B	HR	HR%	R	RBI	BB	SO	SB	AB	H	PO	A	E	DP	TC/G	FA	G by Pos
1980	HOU N	2	.125	.125	8	1	0	0	0	0.0	0	1	0	0	0	1	1	11	2	0	0	6.5	1.000	C-2
1986		6	.130	.304	23	3	1	0	1	4.3	2	2	2	1	0	0	0	58	1	0	0	9.8	1.000	C-6
2 yrs.		8	.129	.258	31	4	1	0	1	3.2	2	3	2	1	0	1	1	69	3	0	0	9.0	1.000	C-8

Tucker Ashford
ASHFORD, THOMAS STEVEN
B. Dec. 4, 1954, Memphis, Tenn.
BR TR 6'1" 195 lbs.

Year	Team	Games	BA	SA	AB	H	2B	3B	HR	HR%	R	RBI	BB	SO	SB	AB	H	PO	A	E	DP	TC/G	FA	G by Pos
1976	SD N	4	.600	.800	5	3	0	0	0	0.0	1	0	2	1	2	1	1	1	2	0	0	0.8	1.000	3B-1
1977		81	.217	.325	249	54	18	0	3	1.2	25	24	21	35	2	1	0	49	159	15	16	2.8	.933	3B-74, SS-10, 2B-4
1978		75	.245	.374	155	38	11	0	3	1.9	11	26	14	31	1	18	7	108	53	6	22	2.2	.964	3B-32, 2B-18, 1B-14
1980	TEX A	15	.125	.125	32	4	0	0	0	0.0	2	3	3	3	0	0	0	10	25	2	1	2.5	.946	3B-12, SS-2
1981	NY A	3	–	–	0	0	0	0	0	–	0	0	0	0	0	0	0	0	0	0	0	0.0	–	2B-2
1983	NY A	35	.179	.214	56	10	1	0	0	0.0	3	2	7	4	0	10	1	14	31	1	6	1.3	.978	3B-15, 2B-13, C-1
1984	KC A	9	.154	.231	13	2	1	0	0	0.0	1	0	1	2	0	0	0	2	8	1	1	1.2	.909	3B-9
7 yrs.		222	.218	.318	510	111	31	1	6	1.2	42	55	47	75	5	31	9	184	278	25	46	2.2	.949	3B-143, 2B-37, 1B-14, SS-12, C-1

Tom Asmussen
ASMUSSEN, THOMAS WILLIAM
B. Sept. 26, 1876, Chicago, Ill. D. Aug. 21, 1963, Arlington Heights, Ill.
TR

Year	Team	Games	BA	SA	AB	H	2B	3B	HR	HR%	R	RBI	BB	SO	SB	AB	H	PO	A	E	DP	TC/G	FA	G by Pos
1907	BOS N	2	.000	.000	5	0	0	0	0	0.0	0	0	0		0	0	0	3	2	0	0	2.5	1.000	C-2

Bob Aspromonte
ASPROMONTE, ROBERT THOMAS
Brother of Ken Aspromonte.
B. June 19, 1938, Brooklyn, N. Y.
BR TR 6'2" 170 lbs.

Year	Team	Games	BA	SA	AB	H	2B	3B	HR	HR%	R	RBI	BB	SO	SB	AB	H	PO	A	E	DP	TC/G	FA	G by Pos
1956	BKN N	1	.000	.000	1	0	0	0	0	0.0	0	0	0	1	0	1	0	0	0	0	0	0.0	–	
1960	LA N	21	.182	.255	55	10	1	0	1	1.8	1	6	0	6	1	5	1	16	25	4	5	2.1	.911	SS-15, 3B-4
1961		47	.241	.293	58	14	3	0	0	0.0	7	2	4	12	0	31	9	8	18	1	0	0.6	.963	3B-9, SS-4, 2B-2
1962	HOU N	149	.266	.376	534	142	18	4	11	2.1	59	59	46	54	4	1	0	168	257	15	25	3.0	.966	3B-142, SS-11, 2B-1
1963		136	.214	.306	468	100	9	5	8	1.7	42	49	40	57	3	5	0	137	213	23	4	2.7	.938	3B-131, 1B-1
1964		157	.280	.392	553	155	20	3	12	2.2	51	69	35	54	6	2	0	133	261	11	10	2.6	.973	3B-155
1965		152	.263	.322	578	152	15	2	5	0.9	53	52	38	54	2	1	1	178	292	18	30	3.2	.963	3B-146, 1B-6, SS-4
1966		152	.252	.334	560	141	16	3	8	1.4	55	52	35	63	0	3	0	154	264	18	19	2.9	.959	3B-149, SS-2, 1B-2
1967		137	.294	.401	486	143	24	5	6	1.2	51	58	45	44	2	4	2	130	237	14	17	2.8	.963	3B-133
1968		124	.225	.264	409	92	9	2	1	0.2	25	46	35	57	1	12	3	116	155	10	9	2.3	.964	3B-75, OF-36, SS-1, 1B-1
1969	ATL N	82	.253	.348	198	50	8	1	3	1.5	16	24	13	19	0	26	5	74	46	8	2	1.6	.938	OF-24, 3B-23, SS-18, 2B-2
1970		62	.213	.236	127	27	3	0	0	0.0	5	7	13	13	0	27	5	29	53	5	5	1.4	.943	3B-30, SS-4, OF-1, 1B-1
1971	NY N	104	.225	.301	342	77	9	1	5	1.5	21	33	29	25	0	7	1	76	145	8	10	2.2	.965	3B-97
13 yrs.		1324	.252	.336	4369	1103	135	26	60	1.4	386	457	333	459	19	125	27	1219	1966	135	136	2.5	.959	3B-1094, OF-61, SS-59, 1B-11, 2B-5

LEAGUE CHAMPIONSHIP SERIES

Year	Team	Games	BA	SA	AB	H	2B	3B	HR	HR%	R	RBI	BB	SO	SB	AB	H	PO	A	E	DP	TC/G	FA	G by Pos
1969	ATL N	3	.000	.000	3	0	0	0	0	0.0	0	0	0	0	0	3	0	0	0	0	0	0.0	–	

Ken Aspromonte
ASPROMONTE, KENNETH JOSEPH
Brother of Bob Aspromonte.
B. Sept. 22, 1931, Brooklyn, N. Y.
Manager 1972-74.
BR TR 6' 180 lbs.

Year	Team	Games	BA	SA	AB	H	2B	3B	HR	HR%	R	RBI	BB	SO	SB	AB	H	PO	A	E	DP	TC/G	FA	G by Pos
1957	BOS A	24	.269	.333	78	21	5	0	0	0.0	9	4	17	10	0	0	0	46	65	4	14	4.8	.965	2B-24
1958	2 teams		BOS A (6G – .125)			WAS A (92G – .225)																		
"	total	98	.219	.316	269	59	9	1	5	1.9	15	27	28	29	1	9	2	159	204	13	53	3.8	.965	2B-78, 3B-11, SS-1
1959	WAS A	70	.244	.324	225	55	12	0	2	0.9	31	14	26	39	2	5	0	127	164	13	30	4.3	.957	2B-52, SS-12, OF-1, 1B-1
1960	2 teams		WAS A (4G – .000)			CLE A (117G – .290)																		
"	total	121	.288	.400	462	133	20	1	10	2.2	65	48	53	34	4	6	0	238	268	22	71	4.4	.958	2B-80, 3B-36
1961	2 teams		LA A (66G – .223)			CLE A (22G – .229)																		
"	total	88	.224	.302	308	69	16	1	2	0.6	34	19	39	24	0	3	1	185	246	14	63	5.1	.969	2B-83
1962	2 teams		CLE A (20G – .143)			MIL N (34G – .291)																		
"	total	54	.252	.290	107	27	4	0	0	0.0	15	8	12	10	0	21	5	46	52	2	10	1.9	.980	2B-18, 3B-9
1963	CHI N	20	.147	.235	34	5	3	0	0	0.0	2	4	4	4	0	8	0	19	26	2	4	2.4	.957	2B-7, 1B-2
7 yrs.		475	.249	.338	1483	369	69	3	19	1.3	171	124	179	150	7	52	8	820	1025	70	245	4.0	.963	2B-342, 3B-56, SS-13, 1B-3, OF-1

Brian Asselstine
ASSELSTINE, BRIAN HANLY
B. Sept. 23, 1953, Santa Barbara, Calif.
BL TR 6'1" 175 lbs.

Year	Team	Games	BA	SA	AB	H	2B	3B	HR	HR%	R	RBI	BB	SO	SB	AB	H	PO	A	E	DP	TC/G	FA	G by Pos
1976	ATL N	11	.212	.303	33	7	0	1	1	3.0	2	3	1	2	0	2	0	19	0	0	0	1.7	1.000	OF-9
1977		83	.210	.355	124	26	6	0	4	3.2	12	17	9	10	1	47	10	57	1	1	0	0.7	.983	OF-35
1978		39	.272	.417	103	28	3	3	2	1.9	11	13	11	16	2	6	1	60	1	2	0	1.6	.968	OF-35
1979		8	.100	.100	10	1	0	0	0	0.0	1	0	1	2	0	6	0	1	0	0	0	0.1	1.000	OF-1
1980		87	.284	.394	218	62	13	1	3	1.4	18	25	11	37	1	23	3	102	0	4	0	1.2	.962	OF-61
1981		56	.256	.384	86	22	5	0	2	2.3	8	10	5	7	1	36	9	22	1	1	1	0.4	.958	OF-16
6 yrs.		284	.254	.378	574	146	27	4	12	2.1	52	68	38	74	5	119	23	261	3	8	1	1.0	.971	OF-157

Joe Astroth
ASTROTH, JOSEPH HENRY
B. Sept. 1, 1922, East Alton, Ill.
BR TR 5'9" 187 lbs.

Year	Team	Games	BA	SA	AB	H	2B	3B	HR	HR%	R	RBI	BB	SO	SB	AB	H	PO	A	E	DP	TC/G	FA	G by Pos
1945	PHI A	10	.059	.059	17	1	0	0	0	0.0	1	1	0	1	0	2	0	20	4	4	0	2.8	.857	C-8
1946		4	.143	.143	7	1	0	0	0	0.0	1	1	0	1	0	0	0	7	1	1	0	2.3	.889	C-4
1949		55	.243	.284	148	36	4	1	0	0.0	18	12	21	13	1	8	2	163	24	4	4	3.5	.979	C-44
1950		39	.327	.400	110	36	3	1	1	0.9	11	18	18	3	0	0	0	123	9	2	3	3.4	.985	C-38
1951		64	.246	.353	187	46	10	2	2	1.1	30	27	18	13	0	6	1	228	18	2	2	3.9	.992	C-57
1952		104	.249	.291	337	84	7	2	1	0.3	24	36	25	27	2	1	0	436	36	4	9	4.6	.992	C-102
1953		82	.296	.404	260	77	15	4	3	1.2	28	24	27	12	1	3	0	341	47	5	13	4.8	.987	C-79
1954		77	.221	.279	226	50	8	1	1	0.4	22	23	21	19	0	6	2	300	39	4	5	4.5	.988	C-71

Year	Team		Games	BA	SA	AB	H	2B	3B	HR	HR%	R	RBI	BB	SO	SB	Pinch Hit AB	Pinch Hit H	PO	A	E	DP	TC/G	FA	G by Pos

Joe Astroth *continued*

Year	Team		Games	BA	SA	AB	H	2B	3B	HR	HR%	R	RBI	BB	SO	SB	AB	H	PO	A	E	DP	TC/G	FA	G by Pos
1955	KC	A	101	.252	.328	274	69	4	1	5	1.8	29	23	47	33	2	2	1	420	50	5	9	4.7	.989	C-100
1956			8	.077	.077	13	1	0	0	0	0.0	0	0	0	1	0	0	0	19	5	0	1	3.0	1.000	C-8
10 yrs.			544	.254	.324	1579	401	51	10	13	0.8	163	156	177	124	6	28	6	2057	233	31	46	4.3	.987	C-511

Charlie Atherton

ATHERTON, CHARLES MORGAN HERBERT (Prexy)
B. Oct. 19, 1873, New Brunswick N. J.   D. Dec. 19, 1934, Vienna, Austria   BR TR 5'10"   160 lbs.

Year	Team		Games	BA	SA	AB	H	2B	3B	HR	HR%	R	RBI	BB	SO	SB	AB	H	PO	A	E	DP	TC/G	FA	G by Pos
1899	WAS	N	65	.248	.318	242	60	5	6	0	0.0	28	23	21		2	1	1	91	119	26	7	3.6	.890	3B-63, OF-1

Lefty Atkinson

ATKINSON, HUBERT BURLEY
B. June 4, 1904, Chicago, Ill.   D. Feb. 12, 1961, Chicago, Ill.   BL TL 5'6½"   149 lbs.

Year	Team		Games	BA	SA	AB	H	2B	3B	HR	HR%	R	RBI	BB	SO	SB	AB	H	PO	A	E	DP	TC/G	FA	G by Pos
1927	WAS	A	1	.000	.000	1	0	0	0	0	0.0	1	0	0	0	0	0	0	0	0	0	0	0.0	—	

Dick Attreau

ATTREAU, RICHARD GILBERT
B. Apr. 8, 1897, Chicago, Ill.   D. July 5, 1964, Chicago, Ill.   BL TL 6'   160 lbs.

Year	Team		Games	BA	SA	AB	H	2B	3B	HR	HR%	R	RBI	BB	SO	SB	AB	H	PO	A	E	DP	TC/G	FA	G by Pos
1926	PHI	N	17	.230	.279	61	14	1	1	0	0.0	9	5	6	5	0	0	0	173	6	2	12	10.6	.989	1B-17
1927			44	.205	.277	83	17	1	1	1	1.2	17	11	14	18	1	10	0	174	8	2	13	4.2	.989	1B-26
2 yrs.			61	.215	.278	144	31	2	2	1	0.7	26	16	20	23	1	10	0	347	14	4	25	6.0	.989	1B-43

Toby Atwell

ATWELL, MAURICE DAILEY
B. Mar. 8, 1924, Leesburg, Va.   BL TR 5'9½"   185 lbs.

Year	Team		Games	BA	SA	AB	H	2B	3B	HR	HR%	R	RBI	BB	SO	SB	AB	H	PO	A	E	DP	TC/G	FA	G by Pos
1952	CHI	N	107	.290	.367	362	105	16	3	2	0.6	36	31	40	22	2	5	0	451	50	12	2	4.8	.977	C-101
1953	2 teams	CHI N (24G – .230)	PIT N (53G – .245)																						
"	total		77	.239	.291	213	51	8	0	1	0.5	21	25	33	19	0	11	2	295	37	15	2	4.5	.957	C-68
1954	PIT	N	96	.289	.376	287	83	8	4	3	1.0	36	26	43	21	2	8	4	360	39	4	4	4.2	.990	C-88
1955			71	.213	.266	207	44	8	0	1	0.5	21	18	40	16	0	6	0	334	24	3	3	5.1	.992	C-67
1956	2 teams	PIT N (12G – .111)	MIL N (15G – .167)																						
"	total		27	.146	.292	48	7	1	0	2	4.2	2	10	5	6	0	7	0	59	6	0	1	2.4	1.000	C-19
5 yrs.			378	.260	.333	1117	290	41	7	9	0.8	116	110	161	84	4	37	6	1499	156	34	12	4.5	.980	C-343

Bill Atwood

ATWOOD, WILLIAM FRANKLIN
B. Sept. 25, 1911, Rome, Ga.   BR TR 5'11½"   190 lbs.

Year	Team		Games	BA	SA	AB	H	2B	3B	HR	HR%	R	RBI	BB	SO	SB	AB	H	PO	A	E	DP	TC/G	FA	G by Pos
1936	PHI	N	71	.302	.401	192	58	9	2	2	1.0	21	29	11	15	0	15	4	184	27	6	3	3.1	.972	C-53
1937			87	.244	.326	279	68	15	1	2	0.7	27	32	30	27	3	6	1	290	48	11	5	4.0	.968	C-80
1938			102	.196	.263	281	55	8	1	3	1.1	27	28	25	26	0	5	2	350	53	13	12	4.1	.969	C-94
1939			4	.000	.000	6	0	0	0	0	0.0	0	1	2	3	1	0	0	7	0	1	1	1.8	1.000	C-2
1940			78	.192	.236	203	39	9	0	0	0.0	7	22	25	18	0	6	1	238	43	3	3	3.6	.989	C-69
5 yrs.			342	.229	.302	961	220	41	4	7	0.7	82	112	93	89	4	32	8	1069	171	33	24	3.7	.974	C-298

Jake Atz

ATZ, JOHN JACOB
Born John Jacob Zimmerman.
B. July 1, 1879, Washington, D. C.   D. May 22, 1945, New Orleans, La.   BR TR 5'9½"   160 lbs.

Year	Team		Games	BA	SA	AB	H	2B	3B	HR	HR%	R	RBI	BB	SO	SB	AB	H	PO	A	E	DP	TC/G	FA	G by Pos
1902	WAS	A	3	.100	.100	10	1	0	0	0	0.0	1	0	0		0	0	0	2	11	0	1	4.3	1.000	2B-3
1907	CHI	A	3	.143	.143	7	1	0	0	0	0.0	0	0	0		0	1	0	0	8	0	1	2.7	1.000	3B-2
1908			83	.194	.209	206	40	3	0	0	0.0	24	27	31		9	17	4	100	188	17	15	3.7	.944	2B-46, SS-18, 3B-1
1909			119	.236	.299	381	90	18	3	0	0.0	39	22	38		14	1	0	208	315	25	41	4.6	.954	2B-118, OF-3, SS-1
4 yrs.			208	.219	.263	604	132	21	3	0	0.0	64	49	69		23	19	4	310	522	42	58	4.2	.952	2B-167, SS-19, OF-3, 3B-3

Harry Aubrey

AUBREY, HARRY HERBERT
B. July 5, 1880, St. Joseph, Mo.   D. Sept. 18, 1953, Baltimore, Md.   TR

Year	Team		Games	BA	SA	AB	H	2B	3B	HR	HR%	R	RBI	BB	SO	SB	AB	H	PO	A	E	DP	TC/G	FA	G by Pos
1903	BOS	N	96	.212	.249	325	69	8	2	0	0.0	26	27	18		7	0	0	185	301	74	20	5.8	.868	SS-94, OF-1, 2B-1

Rick Auerbach

AUERBACH, FREDERICK STEVEN
B. Feb. 15, 1950, Woodland Hills, Calif.   BR TR 6'   165 lbs.

Year	Team		Games	BA	SA	AB	H	2B	3B	HR	HR%	R	RBI	BB	SO	SB	AB	H	PO	A	E	DP	TC/G	FA	G by Pos
1971	MIL	A	79	.203	.258	236	48	10	0	1	0.4	22	9	20	40	3	0	0	120	193	12	31	4.1	.963	SS-78
1972			153	.218	.269	554	121	16	3	2	0.4	50	30	43	62	24	1	0	256	452	30	90	4.8	.959	SS-153
1973			6	.100	.200	10	1	1	0	0	0.0	2	0	1	1	0	1	0	4	6	2	0	2.0	.833	SS-2
1974	LA	N	45	.342	.384	73	25	0	0	1	1.4	12	4	8	9	4	4	1	38	60	8	6	2.4	.925	SS-19, 2B-16, 3B-3
1975			85	.224	.276	170	38	9	0	0	0.0	18	12	18	22	3	0	0	82	137	9	18	2.7	.961	SS-81, 3B-1, 1B-1
1976			36	.128	.128	47	6	0	0	0	0.0	7	1	6	6	0	2	0	41	50	6	13	2.7	.938	SS-12, 3B-8, 2B-7
1977	CIN	N	33	.156	.200	45	7	2	0	0	0.0	5	3	4	7	0	2	0	37	46	5	7	2.7	.943	2B-19, SS-12
1978			63	.327	.545	55	18	6	0	2	3.6	17	5	7	12	1	13	7	29	47	3	9	1.3	.962	SS-26, 2B-10, 3B-3
1979			62	.210	.340	100	21	8	1	1	1.0	17	12	14	19	0	23	5	31	54	5	7	1.5	.944	3B-18, SS-16, 2B-3
1980			24	.333	.515	33	11	1	1	1	3.0	5	4	3	5	0	17	3	4	14	1	1	0.8	.947	SS-3, 3B-3, 2B-1
1981	SEA	A	38	.155	.226	84	13	3	0	1	1.2	12	6	4	15	1	0	0	44	99	3	26	3.8	.979	SS-38
11 yrs.			624	.220	.286	1407	309	56	5	9	0.6	167	86	127	198	36	63	16	686	1158	84	208	3.1	.956	SS-440, 2B-56, 3B-36, 1B-1

LEAGUE CHAMPIONSHIP SERIES

Year	Team		Games	BA	SA	AB	H	2B	3B	HR	HR%	R	RBI	BB	SO	SB	AB	H	PO	A	E	DP	TC/G	FA	G by Pos
1974	LA	N	1	1.000	2.000	1	1	1	0	0	0.0	0	0	0	0	0	1	1	0	0	0	0	0.0	—	
1979	CIN	N	2	.000	.000	2	0	0	0	0	0.0	0	0	0	1	0	2	0	0	0	0	0	0.0	—	
2 yrs.			3	.333	.667	3	1	1	0	0	0.0	0	0	0	1	0	3	1	0	0	0	0	0.0	—	

WORLD SERIES

Year	Team		Games	BA	SA	AB	H	2B	3B	HR	HR%	R	RBI	BB	SO	SB	AB	H	PO	A	E	DP	TC/G	FA	G by Pos
1974	LA	N	1	—	—	0	0	0	0	0	—	0	0	0	0	0	0	0	0	0	0	0	0.0	—	

Dave Augustine

AUGUSTINE, DAVID RALPH
B. Nov. 28, 1949, Follansbee, W. Va.   BB TR 6'2"   174 lbs.

Year	Team		Games	BA	SA	AB	H	2B	3B	HR	HR%	R	RBI	BB	SO	SB	AB	H	PO	A	E	DP	TC/G	FA	G by Pos
1973	PIT	N	11	.286	.429	7	2	1	0	0	0.0	1	0	0	1	0	0	0	4	0	0	0	0.5	1.000	OF-9
1974			18	.182	.182	22	4	0	0	0	0.0	3	0	0	5	0	0	0	20	2	0	0	1.2	1.000	OF-11
2 yrs.			29	.207	.241	29	6	1	0	0	0.0	4	0	0	6	0	0	0	24	3	0	0	0.9	1.000	OF-20

Year	Team		Games	BA	SA	AB	H	2B	3B	HR	HR%	R	RBI	BB	SO	SB	Pinch Hit AB	H	PO	A	E	DP	TC/G	FA	G by Pos

Doyle Aulds

AULDS, LEYCESTER DOYLE (Tex)
B. Dec. 28, 1920, Farmerville, La.
BR TR 6'2" 185 lbs.

Year	Team		Games	BA	SA	AB	H	2B	3B	HR	HR%	R	RBI	BB	SO	SB	AB	H	PO	A	E	DP	TC/G	FA	G by Pos
1947	BOS	A	3	.250	.250	4	1	0	0	0	0.0	0	0	0	1	0	0	0	7	0	0	0	2.3	1.000	C-3

Doug Ault

AULT, DOUGLAS REAGAN
B. Mar. 9, 1950, Beaumont, Tex.
BR TL 6'3" 200 lbs.

Year	Team		Games	BA	SA	AB	H	2B	3B	HR	HR%	R	RBI	BB	SO	SB	AB	H	PO	A	E	DP	TC/G	FA	G by Pos
1976	TEX	A	9	.300	.350	20	6	1	0	0	0.0	0	0	1	3	0	3	1	23	0	0	1	2.6	1.000	1B-4, DH-3
1977	TOR	A	129	.245	.382	445	109	22	3	11	2.5	44	64	39	68	4	8	4	1113	103	16	91	9.6	.987	1B-122, DH-4
1978			54	.240	.356	104	25	1	1	3	2.9	10	7	17	14	0	20	5	190	10	6	13	3.8	.971	1B-25, OF-7, DH-5
1980			64	.194	.306	144	28	5	1	3	2.1	12	15	14	23	0	14	5	200	20	0	21	3.4	1.000	1B-32, DH-21, OF-1
4 yrs.			256	.236	.362	713	168	29	5	17	2.4	66	86	71	108	4	45	15	1526	133	22	126	6.6	.987	1B-183, DH-33, OF-8

Jimmy Austin

AUSTIN, JAMES PHILIP (Pepper)
B. Dec. 8, 1879, Swansea, Wales D. Mar. 6, 1965, Laguna Beach, Calif.
Manager 1913, 1918, 1923.
BB TR 5'7½" 155 lbs.

Year	Team		Games	BA	SA	AB	H	2B	3B	HR	HR%	R	RBI	BB	SO	SB	AB	H	PO	A	E	DP	TC/G	FA	G by Pos
1909	NY	A	136	.231	.286	437	101	11	5	1	0.2	37	39	32		30	1	1	225	301	44	27	4.2	.923	3B-111, SS-23, 2B-1
1910			133	.218	.275	432	94	11	4	2	0.5	46	36	47		22	0	0	204	284	30	10	3.9	.942	3B-133
1911	STL	A	148	.261	.359	541	141	25	11	2	0.4	84	45	69		26	0	0	228	337	42	27	4.1	.931	3B-148
1912			149	.252	.319	536	135	14	8	2	0.4	57	44	38		28	0	0	219	292	50	22	3.8	.911	3B-149
1913			142	.266	.339	489	130	18	6	2	0.4	56	42	45	51	37	0	0	216	288	30	21	3.8	.944	3B-142
1914			130	.238	.290	466	111	16	4	0	0.0	55	30	40	59	20	2	0	183	249	30	18	3.6	.935	3B-127
1915			141	.266	.310	477	127	6	6	1	0.2	61	30	64	60	18	0	0	188	264	41	32	3.5	.917	3B-141
1916			129	.207	.280	411	85	15	6	1	0.2	55	28	74	59	19	3	0	128	274	26	21	3.3	.939	3B-124
1917			127	.240	.314	455	109	18	8	0	0.0	61	19	50	46	13	0	0	169	273	26	25	3.7	.944	3B-121, SS-6
1918			110	.264	.324	367	97	14	4	0	0.0	42	20	53	32	18	4	2	173	241	30	20	4.0	.932	SS-57, 3B-48
1919			106	.237	.313	396	94	9	4	1	0.3	54	21	42	31	8	6	2	161	207	24	15	3.7	.939	3B-98
1920			83	.271	.343	280	76	11	3	1	0.4	38	32	31	15	2	7	1	108	171	17	14	3.6	.943	3B-75
1921			27	.273	.333	66	18	2	1	0	0.0	8	2	4	7	2	2	1	43	46	4	4	3.4	.957	SS-14, 2B-6, 3B-2
1922			15	.290	.452	31	9	3	1	0	0.0	6	1	3	2	0	4	0	13	9	1	1	1.5	.957	3B-11, 2B-2
1923			1	–	–	0	0	0	0	0	–	0	0	0	0	0	0	0	0	0	0	0	0.0	–	C-1
1925			1	.000	.000	1	0	0	0	0	0.0	0	0	0	0	0	0	0	1	0	0	0	1.0	1.000	3B-1
1926			1	.500	1.000	2	1	1	0	0	0.0	1	1	0	0	0	1	0	1	1	0	1	2.0	1.000	3B-1
1929			1	.000	.000	1	0	0	0	0	0.0	0	0	0	1	0	0	0	2	0	0	0	2.0	1.000	3B-1
18 yrs.			1580	.246	.314	5388	1328	174	76	13	0.2	661	390	592	363	244	29	7	2260	3239	395	258	3.7	.933	3B-1433, SS-100, 2B-9, C-1

Chick Autry

AUTRY, WILLIAM ASKEW
B. Jan. 2, 1885, Humboldt, Tenn. D. Jan. 16, 1976, Santa Rosa, Calif.
BL TL 5'11" 168 lbs.

Year	Team		Games	BA	SA	AB	H	2B	3B	HR	HR%	R	RBI	BB	SO	SB	AB	H	PO	A	E	DP	TC/G	FA	G by Pos
1907	CIN	N	7	.200	.200	25	5	0	0	0	0.0	3	0	1		0	0	0	13	0	1	0	2.0	.929	OF-7
1909	2 teams		CIN	N	(9G – .182)		BOS	N	(65G – .196)																
"	total		74	.194	.220	232	45	6	0	0	0.0	19	17	23		6	0	0	701	45	8	30	10.2	.989	1B-70, OF-4
2 yrs.			81	.195	.218	257	50	6	0	0	0.0	22	17	24		6	0	0	714	45	9	30	9.5	.988	1B-70, OF-11

Martin Autry

AUTRY, MARTIN GORDON (Chick)
B. Mar. 5, 1903, Martindale, Tex. D. Jan. 26, 1950, Savannah, Ga.
BR TR 6' 180 lbs.

Year	Team		Games	BA	SA	AB	H	2B	3B	HR	HR%	R	RBI	BB	SO	SB	AB	H	PO	A	E	DP	TC/G	FA	G by Pos
1924	NY	A	2	–	–	0	0	0	0	0	–	1	0	0	0	0	0	0	1	0	0	0	0.5	1.000	C-2
1926	CLE	A	3	.143	.143	7	1	0	0	0	0.0	1	0	1	0	0	0	0	4	2	0	0	2.0	1.000	C-3
1927			16	.256	.395	43	11	4	1	0	0.0	5	7	0	6	0	1	0	42	14	4	1	3.8	.933	C-14
1928			22	.300	.483	60	18	6	1	1	1.7	6	7	9	7	0	4	0	61	8	2	3	3.2	.972	C-18
1929	CHI	A	43	.208	.302	96	20	6	0	1	1.0	7	12	1	8	0	11	3	64	14	5	1	1.9	.940	C-30
1930			34	.254	.296	71	18	1	1	0	0.0	1	5	4	8	0	5	1	96	22	1	1	3.5	.992	C-29
6 yrs.			120	.245	.350	277	68	17	3	2	0.7	21	25	15	29	0	21	4	268	60	12	6	2.8	.965	C-96

Earl Averill

AVERILL, EARL DOUGLAS
Son of Earl Averill.
B. Sept. 9, 1931, Cleveland, Ohio
BR TR 5'10" 185 lbs.

Year	Team		Games	BA	SA	AB	H	2B	3B	HR	HR%	R	RBI	BB	SO	SB	AB	H	PO	A	E	DP	TC/G	FA	G by Pos
1956	CLE	A	42	.237	.398	93	22	6	0	3	3.2	12	14	14	25	0	8	2	157	15	1	2	4.1	.994	C-34
1958			17	.182	.309	55	10	1	0	2	3.6	2	7	4	7	1	0	0	10	34	7	3	3.0	.863	3B-17
1959	CHI	N	74	.237	.452	186	44	10	0	10	5.4	23	34	15	39	0	25	10	197	49	13	4	3.5	.950	C-32, 3B-13, OF-5, 2B-2
1960	2 teams		CHI	N	(52G – .235)		CHI	A	(10G – .214)																
"	total		62	.233	.293	116	27	4	0	1	0.9	16	15	15	18	1	30	6	155	10	3	1	2.7	.982	C-39, OF-1, 3B-1
1961	LA	A	115	.266	.489	323	86	9	0	21	6.5	56	59	62	70	1	21	7	548	38	5	6	5.1	.992	C-88, OF-9, 2B-1
1962			92	.219	.332	187	41	9	0	4	2.1	21	22	43	47	0	34	7	85	7	0	0	1.0	1.000	OF-49, C-6
1963	PHI	N	47	.268	.423	71	19	2	0	3	4.2	8	8	9	14	0	24	4	89	12	5	0	2.3	.953	C-20, OF-8, 3B-1, 1B-1
7 yrs.			449	.242	.409	1031	249	41	0	44	4.3	137	159	162	220	3	142	36	1241	165	34	16	3.2	.976	C-219, OF-72, 3B-32, 2B-3, 1B-1

Earl Averill

AVERILL, HOWARD EARL
Father of Earl Averill.
B. May 21, 1902, Snohomish, Wash. D. Aug. 16, 1983, Everett, Wash.
Hall of Fame 1975.
BL TR 5'9½" 172 lbs.

Year	Team		Games	BA	SA	AB	H	2B	3B	HR	HR%	R	RBI	BB	SO	SB	AB	H	PO	A	E	DP	TC/G	FA	G by Pos
1929	CLE	A	152	.331	.535	602	199	43	13	18	3.0	110	97	64	53	13	0	0	388	14	14	3	2.7	.966	OF-152
1930			139	.339	.537	534	181	33	8	19	3.6	102	119	56	48	10	5	2	345	11	19	5	2.7	.949	OF-134
1931			155	.333	.576	627	209	36	10	32	5.1	140	143	68	38	9	0	0	398	9	10	3	2.7	.976	OF-155
1932			153	.314	.569	631	198	37	14	32	5.1	116	124	75	40	5	0	0	412	12	16	3	2.9	.964	OF-153
1933			151	.301	.474	599	180	39	16	11	1.8	83	92	54	29	3	2	1	390	8	12	3	2.7	.971	OF-149
1934			154	.313	.569	598	187	48	6	31	5.2	128	113	99	44	4	0	0	410	12	13	3	2.8	.970	OF-154
1935			140	.288	.496	563	162	34	13	19	3.4	109	79	70	58	8	1	0	371	6	7	2	2.7	.982	OF-139
1936			152	.378	.627	614	232	39	15	28	4.6	136	126	65	35	3	2	1	369	11	12	2	2.6	.969	OF-150
1937			156	.299	.493	609	182	33	11	21	3.4	121	92	88	65	5	0	0	362	11	9	3	2.6	.976	OF-156
1938			134	.330	.535	482	159	27	15	14	2.9	101	93	81	48	5	0	0	331	14	9	2	2.6	.975	OF-131

Year	Team	Games	BA	SA	AB	H	2B	3B	HR	HR%	R	RBI	BB	SO	SB	Pinch Hit AB	Pinch Hit H	PO	A	E	DP	TC/G	FA	G by Pos

Earl Averill *continued*

Year	Team		Games	BA	SA	AB	H	2B	3B	HR	HR%	R	RBI	BB	SO	SB	PH AB	PH H	PO	A	E	DP	TC/G	FA	G by Pos
1939	2 teams	CLE A (24G – .273)	DET A (87G – .262)																						
"	total		111	.264	.464	364	96	28	6	11	3.0	66	65	49	42	4	19	6	169	3	4	0	1.6	.977	OF-91
1940	DET A		64	.280	.381	118	33	4	1	2	1.7	10	20	5	14	0	38	12	23	2	1	0	0.4	.962	OF-22
1941	BOS N		8	.118	.118	17	2	0	0	0	0.0	2	2	1	4	0	3	0	5	2	0	0	0.9	1.000	OF-4
13 yrs.			1669	.318	.533	6358	2020	401	128	238	3.7	1224	1165	775	518	69	73	22	3973	115	126	29	2.5	.970	OF-1590

WORLD SERIES

| 1940 | DET A | | 3 | .000 | .000 | 3 | 0 | 0 | 0 | 0 | 0.0 | 0 | 0 | 0 | 0 | 0 | 3 | 0 | 0 | 0 | 0 | 0 | 0.0 | – | |

Bobby Avila

AVILA, ROBERTO FRANCISCO (Beto)
Born Roberto Francisco Avila y Gonzalez.
B. Apr. 2, 1924, Veracruz, Mexico
BR TR 5'10" 175 lbs.

Year	Team		Games	BA	SA	AB	H	2B	3B	HR	HR%	R	RBI	BB	SO	SB	PH AB	PH H	PO	A	E	DP	TC/G	FA	G by Pos
1949	CLE A		31	.214	.214	14	3	0	0	0	0.0	3	3	1	3	0	9	2	5	7	0	1	0.4	1.000	2B-5
1950			80	.299	.383	201	60	10	2	1	0.5	39	21	29	17	5	6	2	157	137	5	47	3.7	.983	2B-62, SS-2
1951			141	.304	.410	542	165	21	3	10	1.8	76	58	60	31	14	4	1	349	417	14	87	5.5	.982	2B-136
1952			150	.300	.415	597	179	26	11	7	1.2	102	45	67	36	12	1	0	355	431	28	81	5.4	.966	2B-149
1953			141	.286	.379	559	160	23	3	8	1.4	85	55	58	27	10	2	0	346	445	11	114	5.7	.986	2B-140
1954			143	.341	.477	555	189	27	2	15	2.7	112	67	59	31	9	1	0	361	410	21	102	5.5	.973	2B-141, SS-7
1955			141	.272	.400	537	146	22	4	13	2.4	83	61	82	47	1	1	1	348	342	13	108	5.0	.982	2B-141
1956			138	.224	.318	513	115	14	2	10	1.9	74	54	70	68	17	5	1	322	351	16	83	5.0	.977	2B-135
1957			129	.268	.354	463	124	19	3	5	1.1	60	48	46	47	2	8	1	293	270	11	74	4.4	.981	2B-107, 3B-16
1958			113	.253	.365	375	95	21	3	5	1.3	54	30	56	45	5	15	5	193	225	9	68	3.8	.979	2B-82, 3B-33
1959	3 teams	BAL A (20G – .170)	BOS A (22G – .244)		MIL N (51G – .238)																			
"	total		93	.227	.322	264	60	3	2	6	2.3	37	23	34	47	3	14	2	143	162	10	31	3.4	.968	2B-70, OF-10, 3B-1
11 yrs.			1300	.281	.388	4620	1296	185	35	80	1.7	725	465	562	399	78	66	15	2872	3197	138	796	4.8	.978	2B-1168, 3B-50, OF-10, SS-9

WORLD SERIES

| 1954 | CLE A | | 4 | .133 | .133 | 15 | 2 | 0 | 0 | 0 | 0.0 | 1 | 0 | 2 | 1 | 0 | 0 | 0 | 12 | 10 | 0 | 1 | 5.5 | 1.000 | 2B-4 |

Ramon Aviles

AVILES, RAMON ANTONIO
Born Ramon Antonio Aviles y Miranda.
B. Jan. 22, 1952, Manati, Puerto Rico
BR TR 5'9" 155 lbs.

Year	Team	Games	BA	SA	AB	H	2B	3B	HR	HR%	R	RBI	BB	SO	SB	PH AB	PH H	PO	A	E	DP	TC/G	FA	G by Pos
1977	BOS A	1			0	0	0	0	0	–	0	0	0	0	0	0	0	0	1	0	0	1.0	1.000	2B-1
1979	PHI N	27	.279	.311	61	17	2	0	0	0.0	7	12	8	8	0	3	1	40	44	2	8	3.2	.977	2B-27
1980		51	.277	.396	101	28	6	0	2	2.0	12	9	10	9	0	6	2	60	74	8	21	2.8	.944	SS-29, 2B-15
1981		38	.214	.250	28	6	1	0	0	0.0	2	3	3	5	0	4	0	16	30	1	4	1.2	.979	2B-20, 3B-13, SS-5
4 yrs.		117	.268	.347	190	51	9	0	2	1.1	21	24	21	22	0	13	3	116	149	11	33	2.4	.960	2B-63, SS-34, 3B-13

DIVISIONAL PLAYOFF SERIES

| 1981 | PHI N | 1 | – | – | 0 | 0 | 0 | 0 | 0 | – | 0 | 0 | 1 | 0 | 0 | 0 | 0 | 0 | 0 | 0 | 0 | 0.0 | – | |

LEAGUE CHAMPIONSHIP SERIES

| 1980 | PHI N | 1 | – | – | 0 | 0 | 0 | 0 | – | | 1 | 0 | 0 | 0 | 0 | 0 | 0 | 0 | 0 | 0 | 0 | 0.0 | – | |

Benny Ayala

AYALA, BENIGNO FELIX
Born Benigno Ayala y Felix.
B. Feb. 7, 1951, Yauco, Puerto Rico
BR TR 6'1" 185 lbs.

Year	Team	Games	BA	SA	AB	H	2B	3B	HR	HR%	R	RBI	BB	SO	SB	PH AB	PH H	PO	A	E	DP	TC/G	FA	G by Pos
1974	NY N	23	.235	.338	68	16	1	0	2	2.9	9	8	7	17	0	4	0	37	1	3	1	1.8	.927	OF-20
1976		22	.115	.231	26	3	0	0	1	3.8	2	2	2	6	0	15	2	7	1	1	0	0.4	.889	OF-7
1977	STL N	1	.333	.333	3	1	0	0	0	0.0	0	0	0	1	0	0	0	6	1	0	1	7.0	1.000	OF-1
1979	BAL A	42	.256	.523	86	22	5	0	6	7.0	15	13	6	9	0	13	3	38	0	1	0	0.9	.974	OF-24, DH-10
1980		76	.265	.500	170	45	8	1	10	5.9	28	33	19	21	0	28	5	20	2	0	1	0.3	1.000	DH-41, OF-19
1981		44	.279	.407	86	24	2	0	3	3.5	12	13	11	9	0	16	5	3	0	0	0	0.1	1.000	DH-27, OF-4
1982		64	.305	.492	128	39	6	0	6	4.7	17	24	5	14	1	24	9	59	0	1	2	0.9	.983	OF-25, DH-17, 1B-3
1983		47	.221	.404	104	23	7	0	4	3.8	12	13	9	18	0	14	4	41	0	0	0	0.9	.953	OF-24, DH-11
1984		60	.212	.364	118	25	6	0	4	3.4	9	24	8	24	1	29	9	10	0	0	0	0.2	1.000	DH-34, OF-13
1985	CLE A	46	.250	.421	76	19	7	0	2	2.6	10	15	4	17	0	22	4	21	1	2	0	0.5	.917	OF-20, DH-3
10 yrs.		425	.251	.434	865	217	42	1	38	4.4	114	145	71	136	2	165	41	242	8	10	5	0.6	.962	OF-157, DH-143, 1B-3

LEAGUE CHAMPIONSHIP SERIES

| 1983 | BAL A | 1 | – | – | 0 | 0 | 0 | 0 | 0 | – | 0 | 0 | 0 | 0 | 0 | 0 | 0 | 0 | 0 | 0 | 0 | 0.0 | – | DH-1 |

WORLD SERIES

1979	BAL A	4	.333	.833	6	2	0	0	1	16.7	1	2	1	0	0	0	0	4	0	0	0	1.0	1.000	OF-3
1983		1	1.000	1.000	1	1	0	0	0	0.0	1	1	0	0	0	1	1	0	0	0	0	0.0	–	
2 yrs.		5	.429	.857	7	3	0	0	1	14.3	2	3	1	0	0	1	1	4	0	0	0	0.8	1.000	OF-3

Dick Aylward

AYLWARD, RICHARD JOHN
B. June 4, 1925, Baltimore, Md. D. June 11, 1983, Spring Valley, Calif.
BR TR 6' 190 lbs.

Year	Team	Games	BA	SA	AB	H	2B	3B	HR	HR%	R	RBI	BB	SO	SB	PH AB	PH H	PO	A	E	DP	TC/G	FA	G by Pos
1953	CLE A	4	.000	.000	3	0	0	0	0	0.0	0	0	0	1	0	0	0	4	0	0	0	1.0	1.000	C-4

Joe Azcue

AZCUE, JOSE JOAQUIN (The Immortal Azcue)
Born Jose Joaquin Azcue y Lopez.
B. Aug. 18, 1939, Cienfuegos, Cuba
BR TR 6' 190 lbs.

Year	Team		Games	BA	SA	AB	H	2B	3B	HR	HR%	R	RBI	BB	SO	SB	PH AB	PH H	PO	A	E	DP	TC/G	FA	G by Pos
1960	CIN N		14	.097	.097	31	3	0	0	0	0.0	1	3	2	6	0	2	0	66	6	0	0	5.1	1.000	C-14
1962	KC A		72	.229	.305	223	51	9	1	2	0.9	18	25	17	27	1	2	0	363	42	6	5	5.7	.985	C-70
1963	2 teams	KC A (2G – .000)	CLE A (94G – .284)																						
"	total		96	.281	.460	324	91	16	0	14	4.3	26	46	15	47	1	8	2	569	42	5	13	6.4	.992	C-92
1964	CLE A		83	.273	.358	271	74	9	1	4	1.5	20	34	16	38	0	7	1	510	36	4	2	6.6	.993	C-76
1965			111	.230	.269	335	77	7	0	2	0.6	16	35	27	54	2	10	3	714	53	5	2	7.0	.994	C-108
1966			98	.275	.404	302	83	10	1	9	3.0	22	37	20	22	0	3	1	588	40	7	3	6.5	.989	C-97
1967			86	.251	.437	295	74	12	5	11	3.7	33	34	22	35	0	2	1	636	57	1	4	8.1	.999	C-86

Year Team	Games	BA	SA	AB	H	2B	3B	HR	HR%	R	RBI	BB	SO	SB	Pinch Hit AB	Pinch Hit H	PO	A	E	DP	TC/G	FA	G by Pos

Joe Azcue *continued*

Year Team	Games	BA	SA	AB	H	2B	3B	HR	HR%	R	RBI	BB	SO	SB	AB	H	PO	A	E	DP	TC/G	FA	G by Pos
1968	115	.280	.342	357	100	10	0	4	1.1	23	42	28	33	1	17	4	699	50	3	11	6.5	.996	C-97
1969 3 teams	CLE A (7G – .292)			BOS A (19G – .216)				CAL A (80G – .218)															
" total	106	.223	.266	323	72	8	0	2	0.6	23	23	35	36	0	4	0	573	70	7	15	6.1	.989	C-80
1970 CAL A	114	.242	.302	351	85	13	1	2	0.6	19	25	24	40	0	4	1	587	51	6	10	5.6	.991	C-112
1972 2 teams	CAL A (3G – .000)			MIL A (11G – .143)																			
" total	14	.125	.125	16	2	0	0	0	0.0	0	0	1	6	0	3	1	24	5	0	2	2.1	1.000	C-11
11 yrs.	909	.252	.344	2828	712	94	9	50	1.8	201	304	207	344	5	62	16	5329	452	44	67	6.4	.992	C-843

Charlie Babb

BABB, CHARLES AMOS
B. Feb. 20, 1873, Milwaukie, Ore. D. Mar. 20, 1954, Portland, Ore. BB TR 5'10½" 165 lbs.

Year Team	Games	BA	SA	AB	H	2B	3B	HR	HR%	R	RBI	BB	SO	SB	AB	H	PO	A	E	DP	TC/G	FA	G by Pos
1903 NY N	121	.248	.321	424	105	15	8	0	0.0	68	46	45			22	0	0	250	363	60	37	5.6	.911	SS-113, 3B-8
1904 BKN N	151	.265	.311	521	138	18	3	0	0.0	49	53	53			34	0	0	370	459	65	44	5.9	.927	SS-151
1905	75	.187	.238	235	44	8	2	0	0.0	27	17	27			10	1	0	401	141	27	34	7.6	.953	SS-36, 1B-31, 3B-5, 2B-2
3 yrs.	347	.243	.300	1180	287	41	13	0	0.0	144	116	125			66	1	0	1021	963	152	115	6.2	.929	SS-300, 1B-31, 3B-13, 2B-2

Loren Babe

BABE, LOREN ROLLAND (Bee Bee)
B. Jan. 11, 1928, Pisgah, Iowa D. Feb. 14, 1984, Omaha, Neb. BL TR 5'10" 180 lbs.

Year Team	Games	BA	SA	AB	H	2B	3B	HR	HR%	R	RBI	BB	SO	SB	AB	H	PO	A	E	DP	TC/G	FA	G by Pos
1952 NY A	12	.095	.143	21	2	1	0	0	0.0	1	0	4	4	1	2	0	4	16	2	3	1.8	.909	3B-9
1953 2 teams	NY A (5G – .333)			PHI A (103G – .224)																			
" total	108	.230	.305	361	83	17	2	2	0.6	36	26	35	22	0	12	3	122	207	18	27	3.2	.948	3B-98, SS-1
2 yrs.	120	.223	.296	382	85	18	2	2	0.5	37	26	39	26	1	14	3	126	223	20	30	3.1	.946	3B-107, SS-1

Charlie Babington

BABINGTON, CHARLES PERCY
B. May 4, 1895, Cranston, R. I. D. Mar. 22, 1957, Providence, R. I. BR TR 6' 170 lbs.

Year Team	Games	BA	SA	AB	H	2B	3B	HR	HR%	R	RBI	BB	SO	SB	AB	H	PO	A	E	DP	TC/G	FA	G by Pos
1915 NY N	28	.242	.394	33	8	3	1	0	0.0	5	2	4	1	1	10	2	10	0	1	0	0.4	.909	OF-12, 1B-1

Shooty Babitt

BABITT, MACK NEAL II
B. Mar. 9, 1959, Oakland, Calif. BR TR 5'8" 174 lbs.

Year Team	Games	BA	SA	AB	H	2B	3B	HR	HR%	R	RBI	BB	SO	SB	AB	H	PO	A	E	DP	TC/G	FA	G by Pos
1981 OAK A	54	.256	.301	156	40	1	0	0	0.0	10	14	13	13	5	2	0	84	125	6	12	4.0	.972	2B-52

Wally Backman

BACKMAN, WALTER WAYNE
B. Sept. 22, 1959, Hillsboro, Ore. BB TR 5'9" 160 lbs.

Year Team	Games	BA	SA	AB	H	2B	3B	HR	HR%	R	RBI	BB	SO	SB	AB	H	PO	A	E	DP	TC/G	FA	G by Pos
1980 NY N	27	.323	.355	93	30	1	1	0	0.0	12	9	11	14	2	0	0	62	55	1	11	4.4	.992	2B-20, SS-8
1981	26	.278	.333	36	10	2	0	0	0.0	5	4	7	1	15	3	1	14	21	2	2	1.4	.946	2B-11, 3B-1
1982	96	.272	.372	261	71	13	2	3	1.1	37	22	49	47	8	5	0	173	209	16	30	4.1	.960	2B-88, 3B-6, SS-1
1983	26	.167	.214	42	7	0	1	0	0.0	6	3	2	8	0	16	3	16	15	2	2	1.3	.939	2B-14, 3B-2
1984	128	.280	.339	436	122	19	2	1	0.2	68	26	56	63	32	11	3	223	307	10	73	4.2	.981	2B-115, SS-7
1985	145	.273	.344	520	142	24	5	1	0.2	77	38	36	72	30	15	6	273	370	7	76	4.5	.989	2B-140, SS-1
1986	124	.320	.385	387	124	18	2	1	0.3	67	27	36	32	13	15	5	186	290	17	56	4.0	.966	2B-113
1987	94	.250	.287	300	75	6	1	1	0.3	43	23	25	43	11	12	2	131	210	6	44	3.7	.983	2B-87
1988	99	.303	.344	294	89	12	0	0	0.0	44	17	41	49	9	6	1	128	219	4	36	3.5	.989	2B-92
1989 MIN A	87	.231	.284	299	69	9	2	1	0.3	33	26	32	45	1	4	0	146	187	6	37	3.9	.982	2B-84, DH-1
10 yrs.	852	.277	.337	2668	739	104	16	8	0.3	392	191	292	380	107	99	23	1352	1883	71	367	3.9	.979	2B-764, SS-17, 3B-9, DH-1

LEAGUE CHAMPIONSHIP SERIES

Year Team	Games	BA	SA	AB	H	2B	3B	HR	HR%	R	RBI	BB	SO	SB	AB	H	PO	A	E	DP	TC/G	FA	G by Pos
1986 NY N	6	.238	.238	21	5	0	0	0	0.0	5	2	2	4	1	0	0	9	18	0	4	4.5	1.000	2B-6
1988	7	.273	.318	22	6	1	0	0	0.0	2	2	2	5	1	0	0	7	19	2	1	4.0	.929	2B-7
2 yrs.	13	.256	.279	43	11	1	0	0	0.0	7	4	4	9	2	0	0	16	37	2	5	4.2	.964	2B-13

WORLD SERIES

Year Team	Games	BA	SA	AB	H	2B	3B	HR	HR%	R	RBI	BB	SO	SB	AB	H	PO	A	E	DP	TC/G	FA	G by Pos
1986 NY N	6	.333	.333	18	6	0	0	0	0.0	4	1	4	2	1	0	0	9	13	0	1	3.7	1.000	2B-6

Eddie Bacon

BACON, EDGAR SUTER
B. Apr. 8, 1895, Franklin County, Ky. D. Oct. 2, 1963, Frankfort, Ky.

Year Team	Games	BA	SA	AB	H	2B	3B	HR	HR%	R	RBI	BB	SO	SB	AB	H	PO	A	E	DP	TC/G	FA	G by Pos
1917 PHI A	4	.500	.667	6	3	1	0	0	0.0	1	2	0	0	0	3	1	1	7	0	0	2.0	1.000	P-1

Art Bader

BADER, ARTHUR HERMAN
B. Sept. 21, 1886, St. Louis, Mo. D. Apr. 5, 1957, St. Louis, Mo. BR TR 5'10" 170 lbs.

Year Team	Games	BA	SA	AB	H	2B	3B	HR	HR%	R	RBI	BB	SO	SB	AB	H	PO	A	E	DP	TC/G	FA	G by Pos
1904 STL A	2	.000	.000	3	0	0	0	0	0.0	0	0	1		0	1	0	1	1	0	0	1.0	1.000	OF-1

Red Badgro

BADGRO, MORRIS HIRAM
B. Dec. 1, 1902, Orilla, Wash. BL TR 6' 190 lbs.

Year Team	Games	BA	SA	AB	H	2B	3B	HR	HR%	R	RBI	BB	SO	SB	AB	H	PO	A	E	DP	TC/G	FA	G by Pos
1929 STL A	54	.284	.385	148	42	12	0	1	0.7	27	18	11	15	1	15	4	58	1	1	1	1.1	.983	OF-37
1930	89	.239	.355	234	56	18	3	1	0.4	30	27	13	27	3	24	9	112	8	6	3	1.4	.952	OF-61
2 yrs.	143	.257	.366	382	98	30	3	2	0.5	57	45	24	42	4	39	13	170	9	7	4	1.3	.962	OF-98

Jose Baez

BAEZ, JOSE ANTONIO
Born Jose Antonio Mota y Baez.
B. Dec. 31, 1953, San Cristobal, Dominican Republic BR TR 5'8" 160 lbs.

Year Team	Games	BA	SA	AB	H	2B	3B	HR	HR%	R	RBI	BB	SO	SB	AB	H	PO	A	E	DP	TC/G	FA	G by Pos
1977 SEA A	91	.259	.321	305	79	14	1	1	0.3	39	17	19	20	6	7	1	152	253	11	54	4.6	.974	2B-77, DH-3, 3B-1
1978	23	.160	.200	50	8	0	1	0	0.0	8	2	6	7	1	3	0	39	55	2	17	4.2	.979	2B-14, 3B-3, DH-1
2 yrs.	114	.245	.304	355	87	14	2	1	0.3	47	19	25	27	7	10	1	191	308	13	71	4.5	.975	2B-91, DH-4, 3B-4

Bill Bagwell

BAGWELL, WILLIAM MALLORY (Big Bill)
B. Feb. 24, 1896, Choudrant, La. D. Oct. 5, 1976, Choudrant, La. BL TL 6'1" 175 lbs.

Year Team	Games	BA	SA	AB	H	2B	3B	HR	HR%	R	RBI	BB	SO	SB	AB	H	PO	A	E	DP	TC/G	FA	G by Pos
1923 BOS N	56	.290	.441	93	27	4	2	2	2.2	8	10	6	12	0	32	6	33	1	0	1	0.6	1.000	OF-22
1925 PHI A	36	.300	.380	50	15	2	1	0	0.0	4	10	2	2	0	31	7	2	0	1	0	0.1	.667	OF-4
2 yrs.	92	.294	.420	143	42	6	3	2	1.4	12	20	8	14	0	63	13	35	1	1	1	0.4	.973	OF-26

Year	Team	Games	BA	SA	AB	H	2B	3B	HR	HR%	R	RBI	BB	SO	SB	Pinch Hit AB	Pinch Hit H	PO	A	E	DP	TC/G	FA	G by Pos

Frank Bahret

BAHRET, FRANK J.
B. Baltimore, Md.   Deceased.

| 1884 | BAL U | 2 | .000 | .000 | 8 | 0 | 0 | 0 | 0 | 0.0 | 0 | | 0 | | | 0 | 0 | 4 | 0 | 0 | 0 | 2.0 | 1.000 | OF-2 |

Bill Bailey

BAILEY, HARRY LEWIS
B. Nov. 19, 1881, Shawnee, Ohio   D. Oct. 27, 1967, Seattle, Wash.

BL TR 5'10½" 170 lbs.

| 1911 | NY A | 5 | .111 | .111 | 9 | 1 | 0 | 0 | 0 | 0.0 | 1 | 0 | 0 | | | 0 | 0 | 0 | 3 | 0 | 0 | 0.6 | 1.000 | OF-2, 3B-1 |

Bob Bailey

BAILEY, ROBERT SHERWOOD
B. Oct. 13, 1942, Long Beach, Calif.

BR TR 6'1" 180 lbs.

1962	PIT N	14	.167	.262	42	7	1	0	0	0.0	6	6	6	10	1	2	0	10	25	3	2	2.7	.921	3B-12
1963		154	.228	.328	570	130	15	3	12	2.1	60	45	58	98	10	1	1	118	337	33	40	3.2	.932	3B-153, SS-3
1964		143	.281	.404	530	149	26	3	11	2.1	73	51	44	78	10	13	3	117	224	23	19	2.5	.937	3B-105, OF-35, SS-2
1965		159	.256	.363	626	160	28	3	11	1.8	87	49	70	93	10	2	0	119	247	23	25	2.4	.941	3B-142, OF-28
1966		126	.279	.447	380	106	19	3	13	3.4	51	46	47	65	5	11	4	81	202	12	20	2.3	.959	3B-96, OF-22
1967	LA N	116	.227	.301	322	73	8	2	4	1.2	21	28	40	50	5	19	3	94	154	16	12	2.3	.939	3B-65, OF-27, 1B-4, SS-1
1968		105	.227	.348	322	73	9	3	8	2.5	24	39	38	69	1	16	2	81	164	13	14	2.5	.950	3B-90, OF-1, SS-1
1969	MON N	111	.265	.419	358	95	16	6	9	2.5	46	53	40	76	3	15	4	715	67	8	77	7.1	.990	1B-85, OF-12, 3B-1
1970		131	.287	.597	352	101	19	3	28	8.0	77	84	72	70	5	36	12	179	86	8	18	2.1	.971	3B-48, OF-44, 1B-18
1971		157	.251	.382	545	137	21	4	14	2.6	65	83	97	105	13	0	0	177	204	14	16	2.5	.965	3B-120, OF-51, 1B-9
1972		143	.233	.368	489	114	10	4	16	3.3	55	57	59	112	6	7	3	95	251	22	21	2.6	.940	3B-134, OF-5, 1B-3
1973		151	.273	.489	513	140	25	4	26	5.1	77	86	88	99	5	5	0	94	275	17	25	2.6	.956	3B-146, OF-2
1974		152	.280	.446	507	142	20	2	20	3.9	69	73	100	107	4	8	2	139	125	10	10	1.8	.963	OF-78, 3B-68
1975		106	.273	.361	227	62	5	0	5	2.2	23	30	46	38	4	40	11	89	10	2	2	1.0	.980	OF-61, 3B-3
1976	CIN N	69	.298	.508	124	37	6	1	6	4.8	17	23	16	26	0	27	10	39	14	3	2	0.8	.946	OF-31, 3B-10
1977	2 teams	CIN	N (49G – .253)		BOS	A	(2G – .000)																	
"	total	51	.247	.370	81	20	2	1	2	2.5	9	11	12	11	0	27	6	109	10	3	11	2.4	.975	1B-19, OF-3
1978	BOS A	43	.191	.351	94	18	3	0	4	4.3	12	9	19	19	2	13	1	2	2	0	0	0.1	1.000	DH-34, OF-1, 3B-1
17 yrs.		1931	.257	.403	6082	1564	234	43	189	3.1	772	773	852	1126	85	242	62	2258	2397	210	314	2.5	.957	3B-1194, OF-401, 1B-138, DH-34, SS-7

Ed Bailey

BAILEY, LONAS EDGAR
Brother of Jim Bailey.
B. Apr. 15, 1931, Strawberry Plains, Tenn.

BL TR 6'2" 205 lbs.

1953	CIN N	2	.375	.500	8	3	1	0	0	0.0	1	1	1	3	0	0	0	6	0	0	0	3.0	1.000	C-2
1954		73	.197	.388	183	36	2	3	9	4.9	21	20	35	34	1	12	0	194	20	6	2	3.0	.973	C-61
1955		21	.205	.359	39	8	1	1	1	2.6	3	4	4	10	0	9	3	42	8	2	3	2.5	.962	C-11
1956		118	.300	.551	383	115	8	2	28	7.3	59	75	52	50	2	13	8	511	52	9	10	4.8	.984	C-106
1957		122	.261	.463	391	102	15	2	20	5.1	54	48	73	69	5	6	2	542	41	5	5	4.8	.991	C-115
1958		112	.250	.411	360	90	23	1	11	3.1	39	59	47	61	2	11	1	438	44	6	6	4.4	.988	C-99
1959		121	.264	.393	379	100	13	0	12	3.2	43	40	62	53	2	8	2	549	64	6	6	5.1	.990	C-117
1960		133	.261	.406	441	115	19	3	13	2.9	52	67	59	70	1	9	2	621	52	7	8	5.1	.990	C-129
1961	2 teams	CIN	N (12G – .302)		SF	N	(107G – .238)																	
"	total	119	.245	.386	383	94	13	1	13	3.4	43	53	45	46	1	9	1	684	45	12	4	6.2	.984	C-115, OF-1
1962	SF N	96	.232	.476	254	59	9	1	17	6.7	32	45	42	42	1	18	6	419	25	6	3	4.7	.987	C-75
1963		105	.263	.494	308	81	8	0	21	6.8	41	68	50	64	0	16	3	560	44	8	3	5.8	.987	C-88
1964	MIL N	95	.262	.362	271	71	10	1	5	1.8	30	34	34	39	2	14	3	416	28	8	3	4.8	.982	C-80
1965	2 teams	SF	N (24G – .107)		CHI	N	(66G – .253)																	
"	total	90	.230	.348	178	41	6	0	5	2.8	14	26	40	35	0	22	2	302	29	6	5	3.7	.982	C-66, 1B-5
1966	CAL N	5	.000	.000	3	0	0	0	0	0.0	0	0	1	1	0	3	0	0	0	0	0	0.0	—	—
14 yrs.		1212	.256	.429	3581	915	128	15	155	4.3	432	540	545	577	17	150	37	5284	452	81	58	4.8	.986	C-1064, 1B-5, OF-1

WORLD SERIES

| 1962 | SF N | 6 | .071 | .286 | 14 | 1 | 0 | 0 | 1 | 7.1 | 1 | 2 | 0 | 3 | 0 | 2 | 0 | 15 | 0 | 0 | 0 | 2.5 | 1.000 | C-3 |

Fred Bailey

BAILEY, FREDERICK MIDDLETON (Penny)
B. Aug. 16, 1895, Mt. Hope, W. Va.   D. Aug. 16, 1972, Huntington, W. Va.

BL TL 5'11" 150 lbs.

1916	BOS N	6	.100	.100	10	1	0	0	0	0.0	0	1	0	3	0	5	1	1	0	0	0	0.2	1.000	OF-2
1917		50	.191	.255	110	21	2	1	1	0.9	9	5	9	25	3	18	4	46	5	2	0	1.1	.962	OF-31
1918		4	.250	.250	4	1	0	0	0	0.0	1	0	0	1	0	4	1	0	0	0	0	0.0	—	—
3 yrs.		60	.185	.242	124	23	2	1	1	0.8	10	6	9	29	3	27	6	47	5	2	0	0.9	.963	OF-33

Gene Bailey

BAILEY, ARTHUR EUGENE
B. Nov. 25, 1893, Pearsall, Tex.   D. Nov. 14, 1973, Houston, Tex.

BR TR 5'8" 160 lbs.

1917	PHI A	5	.083	.083	12	1	0	0	0	0.0	1	0	1	1	0	0	0	5	0	0	1	1.2	.833	OF-4
1919	BOS N	4	.333	.333	6	2	0	0	0	0.0	0	1	0	2	1	1	1	5	0	0	0	1.3	1.000	OF-3
1920	2 teams	BOS	N (13G – .083)		BOS	A	(46G – .230)																	
"	total	59	.208	.220	159	33	2	0	0	0.0	16	5	12	18	2	3	0	79	4	2	0	1.4	.976	OF-48
1923	BKN N	127	.265	.333	411	109	11	7	1	0.2	71	42	43	34	9	12	3	291	14	12	2	2.5	.962	OF-100, 1B-5
1924		18	.239	.370	46	11	3	0	1	2.2	7	4	7	6	1	0	0	39	2	0	1	2.3	1.000	OF-17
5 yrs.		213	.246	.303	634	156	16	7	2	0.3	95	52	63	61	13	16	4	419	20	15	3	2.1	.967	OF-172, 1B-5

Mark Bailey

BAILEY, JOHN MARK
B. Nov. 14, 1961, Springfield, Mo.

BB TR 6'5" 195 lbs.

1984	HOU N	108	.212	.343	344	73	16	1	9	2.6	38	34	53	71	0	0	0	629	56	12	4	6.5	.983	C-108
1985		114	.265	.398	332	88	14	0	10	3.0	47	45	67	70	0	2	1	566	52	13	6	5.5	.979	C-110, 1B-2
1986		57	.176	.288	153	27	5	0	4	2.6	9	15	28	45	1	5	2	322	33	4	3	6.3	.989	C-53, 1B-1
1987		35	.203	.219	64	13	1	0	0	0.0	3	2	10	21	1	8	3	126	7	2	0	3.9	.985	C-27
1988		8	.130	.130	23	3	0	0	0	0.0	1	0	5	6	0	0	0	48	3	1	0	6.5	.981	C-8
5 yrs.		322	.223	.340	916	204	36	1	23	2.5	100	97	163	213	2	15	6	1691	151	32	13	5.8	.983	C-306, 1B-3

Bob Bailor

BAILOR, ROBERT MICHAEL
B. Mar. 10, 1951, Connellsville, Pa.

BR TR 5'11" 170 lbs.

Year	Team	Games	BA	SA	AB	H	2B	3B	HR	HR%	R	RBI	BB	SO	SB	Pinch Hit AB	Pinch Hit H	PO	A	E	DP	TC/G	FA	G by Pos

Bob Bailor *continued*

Year	Team	Games	BA	SA	AB	H	2B	3B	HR	HR%	R	RBI	BB	SO	SB	PH AB	PH H	PO	A	E	DP	TC/G	FA	G by Pos
1975	BAL A	5	.143	.143	7	1	0	0	0	0.0	0	0	1	0	0	0	0	5	9	0	1	2.8	1.000	SS-2, 2B-1
1976		9	.333	.667	6	2	0	1	0	0.0	2	0	0	0	0	1	0	0	0	0	0	0.0	–	DH-1, SS-1
1977	TOR A	122	.310	.403	496	154	21	5	5	1.0	62	32	17	26	15	3	2	235	165	12	27	3.4	.971	OF-63, SS-53, DH-7
1978		154	.264	.338	621	164	29	7	1	0.2	74	52	38	21	5	3	2	329	82	15	15	2.8	.965	OF-125, 3B-28, SS-4
1979		130	.229	.287	414	95	11	5	1	0.2	50	38	36	27	14	4	1	217	33	3	2	1.9	.988	OF-118, 2B-9, DH-1
1980		117	.236	.297	347	82	14	2	1	0.3	44	16	36	33	12	1	0	233	61	2	14	2.5	.993	OF-98, SS-12, 3B-11, P-3, DH-1, 2B-1
1981	NY N	51	.284	.346	81	23	3	1	0	0.0	11	8	8	11	2	3	0	43	60	4	9	2.1	.963	SS-22, OF-13, 2B-13, 3B-1
1982		110	.277	.319	376	104	14	1	0	0.0	44	31	20	17	20	13	6	166	272	11	42	4.1	.976	SS-60, 2B-56, 3B-21, OF-4
1983		118	.250	.282	340	85	8	0	1	0.3	33	30	20	23	18	9	1	171	296	16	65	4.1	.967	SS-75, 2B-50, 3B-11, OF-3
1984	LA N	65	.275	.305	131	36	4	0	0	0.0	11	8	8	1	3	7	2	59	117	6	19	2.8	.967	2B-23, 3B-17, SS-16
1985		74	.246	.288	118	29	3	1	0	0.0	8	7	3	5	1	6	3	35	103	3	12	1.9	.979	3B-45, 2B-16, SS-5, OF-1
11 yrs.		955	.264	.325	2937	775	107	23	9	0.3	339	222	187	164	90	50	17	1493	1197	72	206	2.9	.974	OF-425, SS-250, 2B-169, 3B-134, DH-10, P-3

LEAGUE CHAMPIONSHIP SERIES

| 1985 | LA N | 2 | .000 | .000 | 1 | 0 | 0 | 0 | 0 | 0.0 | 0 | 0 | 0 | 0 | 0 | 0 | 0 | 0 | 1 | 0 | 0 | 0.5 | 1.000 | 3B-2 |

Harold Baines

BAINES, HAROLD DOUGLAS
B. Mar. 15, 1959, Easton, Md.

BL TL 6'2" 175 lbs.

Year	Team	Games	BA	SA	AB	H	2B	3B	HR	HR%	R	RBI	BB	SO	SB	PH AB	PH H	PO	A	E	DP	TC/G	FA	G by Pos
1980	CHI A	141	.255	.405	491	125	23	6	13	2.6	55	49	19	65	2	9	1	229	6	9	1	1.7	.963	OF-137, DH-1
1981		82	.286	.482	280	80	11	7	10	3.6	42	41	12	41	6	5	1	120	10	2	1	1.6	.985	OF-80, DH-1
1982		161	.271	.469	608	165	29	8	25	4.1	89	105	49	95	10	1	0	326	10	7	4	2.1	.980	OF-161
1983		156	.280	.443	596	167	33	2	20	3.4	76	99	49	85	7	1	1	312	10	9	3	2.1	.973	OF-155
1984		147	.304	**.541**	569	173	28	10	29	5.1	72	94	54	75	1	1	0	307	8	6	1	2.2	.981	OF-147
1985		160	.309	.467	640	198	29	3	22	3.4	86	113	42	89	1	1	0	318	8	2	2	2.1	.994	OF-159, DH-1
1986		145	.296	.465	570	169	29	2	21	3.7	72	88	38	89	2	1	0	295	15	5	5	2.2	.984	OF-141, DH-3
1987		132	.293	.479	505	148	26	4	20	4.0	59	93	46	82	0	9	3	13	0	0	0	0.1	1.000	DH-117, OF-8
1988		158	.277	.411	599	166	39	1	13	2.2	55	81	67	109	0	4	2	14	1	2	0	0.1	.882	DH-147, OF-9
1989	2 teams		CHI A	(96G – .321)		TEX A	(50G – .285)																	
"	total	146	.309	.465	505	156	29	1	16	3.2	73	72	73	79	0	8	1	54	0	2	0	0.4	.964	DH-116, OF-26
10 yrs.		1428	.288	.462	5363	1547	276	44	189	3.5	679	835	449	809	29	40	9	1988	68	44	17	1.5	.979	OF-1023, DH-386

LEAGUE CHAMPIONSHIP SERIES

| 1983 | CHI A | 4 | .125 | .125 | 16 | 2 | 0 | 0 | 0 | 0.0 | 0 | 0 | 1 | 3 | 0 | 0 | 0 | 6 | 1 | 0 | 0 | 1.8 | 1.000 | OF-4 |

Al Baird

BAIRD, ALBERT WELLS
B. June 2, 1895, Cleburne, Tex. D. Nov. 27, 1976, Shreveport, La.

BR TR 5'9" 160 lbs.

Year	Team	Games	BA	SA	AB	H	2B	3B	HR	HR%	R	RBI	BB	SO	SB	PH AB	PH H	PO	A	E	DP	TC/G	FA	G by Pos
1917	NY N	10	.292	.292	24	7	0	0	0	0.0	1	4	2	2	2	0	0	20	22	1	1	4.3	.977	2B-7, SS-3
1919		38	.241	.253	83	20	1	0	0	0.0	8	5	5	9	3	0	0	42	94	13	11	3.9	.913	2B-24, SS-9, 3B-5
2 yrs.		48	.252	.262	107	27	1	0	0	0.0	9	9	7	11	5	0	0	62	116	14	12	4.0	.927	2B-31, SS-12, 3B-5

Doug Baird

BAIRD, HOWARD DOUGLAS
B. Sept. 27, 1891, St. Charles, Mo. D. June 13, 1967, Thomasville, Ga.

BR TR 5'9½" 148 lbs.

Year	Team	Games	BA	SA	AB	H	2B	3B	HR	HR%	R	RBI	BB	SO	SB	PH AB	PH H	PO	A	E	DP	TC/G	FA	G by Pos
1915	PIT N	145	.219	.322	512	112	26	12	1	0.2	49	53	37	**88**	29	2	0	196	235	25	13	3.1	.945	3B-131, OF-20, 2B-3
1916		128	.216	.279	430	93	10	7	1	0.2	41	28	24	49	20	3	0	183	215	27	22	3.3	.936	3B-80, 2B-29, OF-16
1917	2 teams		PIT N	(43G – .259)		STL N	(104G – .253)																	
"	total	147	.255	.357	499	127	25	13	0	0.0	55	42	43	71	26	0	0	167	334	33	27	3.6	.938	3B-144, OF-2, 2B-2
1918	STL N	82	.247	.354	316	78	12	8	2	0.6	41	25	25	42	25	0	0	101	219	11	12	4.0	.967	3B-81, OF-1, SS-1
1919	3 teams		PHI N	(66G – .252)		STL N	(16G – .212)		BKN N	(20G – .183)														
"	total	102	.236	.322	335	79	13	5	2	0.6	43	42	25	41	18	5	1	122	195	19	19	3.3	.943	3B-91, OF-1, 2B-1
1920	2 teams		BKN N	(6G – .333)		NY N	(7G – .125)																	
"	total	13	.214	.214	14	3	0	0	0	0.0	1	1	3	4	0	3	1	5	8	1	1	1.1	.929	3B-6
6 yrs.		617	.234	.326	2106	492	86	45	6	0.3	230	191	157	295	118	13	2	774	1206	116	94	3.4	.945	3B-533, OF-40, 2B-35, SS-1

Bill Baker

BAKER, WILLIAM PRESLEY
B. Feb. 22, 1911, Paw Creek, N. C.

BR TR 6' 200 lbs.

Year	Team	Games	BA	SA	AB	H	2B	3B	HR	HR%	R	RBI	BB	SO	SB	PH AB	PH H	PO	A	E	DP	TC/G	FA	G by Pos
1940	CIN N	27	.217	.261	69	15	1	1	0	0.0	5	7	4	8	2	3	0	87	9	0	1	3.6	1.000	C-24
1941	2 teams		CIN N	(2G – .000)		PIT N	(35G – .224)																	
"	total	37	.221	.265	68	15	3	0	0	0.0	5	6	12	1	0	3	0	75	14	3	1	2.5	.967	C-34
1942	PIT N	18	.118	.118	17	2	0	0	0	0.0	1	2	1	0	0	7	0	19	1	0	0	1.1	1.000	C-11
1943		63	.273	.360	172	47	6	3	1	0.6	12	26	22	6	3	7	1	157	29	4	3	3.0	.979	C-56
1946		53	.239	.301	113	27	4	0	1	0.9	7	8	12	6	0	9	2	97	14	4	2	2.2	.965	C-41, 1B-1
1948	STL N	45	.294	.395	119	35	10	1	0	0.0	13	15	15	7	1	7	2	152	15	1	3	3.7	.994	C-36
1949		20	.133	.167	30	4	1	0	0	0.0	2	4	2	2	0	10	0	16	1	0	1	0.9	1.000	C-10
7 yrs.		263	.247	.316	588	145	25	5	2	0.3	45	68	68	30	6	46	7	603	83	12	11	2.7	.983	C-212, 1B-1

WORLD SERIES

| 1940 | CIN N | 3 | .250 | .250 | 4 | 1 | 0 | 0 | 0 | 0.0 | 1 | 0 | 1 | 0 | 1 | 0 | 7 | 0 | 1 | 1 | 2.7 | .875 | C-3 |

Charlie Baker

BAKER, CHARLES A.
B. Jan. 15, 1856, Stirling, Mass. D. Jan. 15, 1937, Manchester, N. H.

Year	Team	Games	BA	SA	AB	H	2B	3B	HR	HR%	R	RBI	BB	SO	SB	PH AB	PH H	PO	A	E	DP	TC/G	FA	G by Pos
1884	2 teams		CHI U	(12G – .156)		PIT U	(3G – .083)																	
"	total	15	.140	.228	57	8	2	0	1	1.8	5		0			0	0	15	10	9	1	2.3	.735	OF-11, SS-3, 2B-1

Chuck Baker

BAKER, CHARLES JOSEPH
B. Dec. 6, 1952, Seattle, Wash.

BR TR 5'11" 180 lbs.

Year	Team	Games	BA	SA	AB	H	2B	3B	HR	HR%	R	RBI	BB	SO	SB	PH AB	PH H	PO	A	E	DP	TC/G	FA	G by Pos
1978	SD N	44	.207	.224	58	12	1	0	0	0.0	8	3	2	15	0	6	1	42	70	6	16	2.7	.949	2B-24, SS-12
1980		9	.136	.182	22	3	1	0	0	0.0	0	0	0	4	0	1	0	3	23	1	3	3.0	.963	SS-8
1981	MIN A	40	.182	.273	66	12	0	3	0	0.0	6	6	1	8	0	5	2	35	72	4	13	2.8	.964	SS-31, 2B-3, DH-1, 3B-1
3 yrs.		93	.185	.240	146	27	2	3	0	0.0	14	9	3	27	0	12	3	80	165	11	32	2.8	.957	SS-51, 2B-27, DH-1, 3B-1

Year	Team	Games	BA	SA	AB	H	2B	3B	HR	HR%	R	RBI	BB	SO	SB	Pinch Hit AB	Pinch Hit H	PO	A	E	DP	TC/G	FA	G by Pos

Dave Baker

BAKER, DAVID GLENN
B. Nov. 25, 1956, Lacona, Iowa

BL TR 6' 185 lbs.

Year	Team	Games	BA	SA	AB	H	2B	3B	HR	HR%	R	RBI	BB	SO	SB	PH AB	PH H	PO	A	E	DP	TC/G	FA	G by Pos
1982	TOR A	9	.250	.300	20	5	1	0	0	0.0	3	2	3	3	0	0	0	5	16	5	2	2.9	.808	3B-8

Del Baker

BAKER, DELMAR DAVID
B. May 3, 1892, Sherwood, Ore.   D. Sept. 11, 1973, San Antonio, Tex.
Manager 1933, 1937-42, 1960.

BR TR 5'11½" 176 lbs.

Year	Team	Games	BA	SA	AB	H	2B	3B	HR	HR%	R	RBI	BB	SO	SB	PH AB	PH H	PO	A	E	DP	TC/G	FA	G by Pos
1914	DET A	43	.214	.271	70	15	2	1	0	0.0	4	1	6	9	0	3	0	79	25	9	3	2.6	.920	C-38
1915		68	.246	.313	134	33	3	3	0	0.0	16	15	15	15	3	3	0	184	53	15	8	3.7	.940	C-61
1916		61	.153	.194	98	15	4	0	0	0.0	7	6	11	8	2	1	0	164	29	5	4	3.2	.975	C-59
3 yrs.		172	.209	.265	302	63	9	4	0	0.0	27	22	32	32	5	7	0	427	107	29	15	3.3	.948	C-158

Doug Baker

BAKER, DOUGLAS LEE
B. Apr. 3, 1961, Fullerton, Calif.

BB TR 5'9" 160 lbs.

Year	Team	Games	BA	SA	AB	H	2B	3B	HR	HR%	R	RBI	BB	SO	SB	PH AB	PH H	PO	A	E	DP	TC/G	FA	G by Pos
1984	DET A	43	.185	.241	108	20	4	1	0	0.0	15	11	7	22	3	1	1	56	86	5	20	3.4	.966	SS-39, 2B-5
1985		15	.185	.222	27	5	1	0	0	0.0	4	1	0	9	0	3	0	12	12	1	2	1.7	.960	SS-12, 2B-1
1986		13	.125	.167	24	3	1	0	0	0.0	1	0	2	7	0	1	0	17	21	1	5	3.0	.974	SS-10, 2B-2, DH-1
1987		8	.000	.000	1	0	0	0	0	0.0	0	0	0	1	0	1	0	2	8	0	1	1.3	1.000	SS-6, 3B-1, 2B-1
1988	MIN A	11	.000	.000	7	0	0	0	0	0.0	1	0	0	5	0	0	0	5	7	0	3	1.1	1.000	SS-9, 3B-1, 2B-1
1989		43	.295	.385	78	23	5	1	0	0.0	17	9	9	18	0	4	1	42	63	2	9	2.5	.981	2B-25, SS-19, DH-1
6 yrs.		133	.208	.269	245	51	11	2	0	0.0	38	21	18	62	3	10	2	134	197	9	40	2.6	.974	SS-95, 2B-35, DH-2, 3B-2

LEAGUE CHAMPIONSHIP SERIES

Year	Team	Games	BA	SA	AB	H	2B	3B	HR	HR%	R	RBI	BB	SO	SB	PH AB	PH H	PO	A	E	DP	TC/G	FA	G by Pos
1984	DET A	1	–	–	0	0	0	0	0	–	0	0	0	0	0	0	0	0	0	0	0	0.0	–	SS-1

Dusty Baker

BAKER, JOHNNIE B., JR.
B. June 15, 1949, Riverside, Calif.

BR TR 6'2" 183 lbs.

Year	Team	Games	BA	SA	AB	H	2B	3B	HR	HR%	R	RBI	BB	SO	SB	PH AB	PH H	PO	A	E	DP	TC/G	FA	G by Pos
1968	ATL N	6	.400	.400	5	2	0	0	0	0.0	0	0	0	1	0	3	1	0	0	0	0	0.0	–	OF-3
1969		3	.000	.000	7	0	0	0	0	0.0	0	0	0	3	0	0	0	2	0	0	0	0.7	1.000	OF-3
1970		13	.292	.292	24	7	0	0	0	0.0	3	4	2	4	0	1	0	11	1	3	0	1.2	.800	OF-11
1971		29	.226	.258	62	14	2	0	0	0.0	2	4	1	14	0	13	2	29	1	0	0	1.0	1.000	OF-18
1972		127	.321	.504	446	143	27	2	17	3.8	62	76	45	68	4	4	1	344	8	4	1	2.8	.989	OF-123
1973		159	.288	.454	604	174	29	4	21	3.5	101	99	67	72	24	1	1	390	10	7	1	2.6	.983	OF-156
1974		149	.256	.422	574	147	35	0	20	3.5	80	69	71	87	18	1	0	359	10	7	2	2.5	.981	OF-148
1975		142	.261	.421	494	129	18	2	19	3.8	63	72	67	57	12	6	2	287	10	3	0	2.1	.990	OF-136
1976	LA N	112	.242	.307	384	93	13	0	4	1.0	36	39	31	54	2	8	4	254	3	1	1	2.3	.996	OF-106
1977		153	.291	.512	533	155	26	0	30	5.6	86	86	58	89	2	2	0	227	8	3	2	1.6	.987	OF-152
1978		149	.262	.375	522	137	24	1	11	2.1	62	66	47	66	12	5	0	250	13	4	1	1.8	.985	OF-145
1979		151	.274	.455	554	152	29	1	23	4.2	86	88	56	70	11	2	0	289	14	3	4	2.0	.990	OF-150
1980		153	.294	.503	579	170	26	4	29	5.0	80	97	43	66	12	3	0	308	5	3	3	2.1	.991	OF-151
1981		103	.320	.445	400	128	17	3	9	2.3	48	49	29	43	10	1	1	181	8	2	1	1.9	.990	OF-101
1982		147	.300	.458	570	171	19	1	23	4.0	80	88	56	62	17	4	1	226	7	6	1	1.6	.975	OF-144
1983		149	.260	.395	531	138	25	1	15	2.8	71	73	72	59	7	6	1	249	4	5	2	1.7	.981	OF-143
1984	SF N	100	.292	.374	243	71	7	2	3	1.2	31	32	40	27	4	30	7	112	1	3	0	1.2	.974	OF-62
1985	OAK A	111	.268	.440	343	92	15	1	14	4.1	48	52	50	47	2	17	7	465	29	5	33	4.5	.990	1B-58, OF-35, DH-13
1986		83	.240	.322	242	58	8	0	4	1.7	25	19	27	37	0	15	3	90	4	0	1	1.1	1.000	OF-55, DH-15, 1B-3
19 yrs.		2039	.278	.432	7117	1981	320	23	242	3.4	964	1013	762	926	137	125	31	4073	136	59	53	2.1	.986	OF-1842, 1B-61, DH-28

DIVISIONAL PLAYOFF SERIES

Year	Team	Games	BA	SA	AB	H	2B	3B	HR	HR%	R	RBI	BB	SO	SB	PH AB	PH H	PO	A	E	DP	TC/G	FA	G by Pos
1981	LA N	5	.167	.222	18	3	0	0	0	0.0	2	1	2	1	0	0	0	0	0	0	0	0.0	–	OF-5

LEAGUE CHAMPIONSHIP SERIES

Year	Team	Games	BA	SA	AB	H	2B	3B	HR	HR%	R	RBI	BB	SO	SB	PH AB	PH H	PO	A	E	DP	TC/G	FA	G by Pos
1977	LA N	4	.357	.857	14	5	1	0	2	14.3	4	8	2	3	0	0	0	3	0	0	0	0.8	1.000	OF-4
1978		4	.467	.600	15	7	2	0	0	0.0	1	1	3	0	0	0	0	5	0	0	0	1.3	1.000	OF-4
1981		5	.316	.368	19	6	1	0	0	0.0	3	3	1	0	0	0	0	0	0	1	0	0.2	–	OF-5
1983		4	.357	.643	14	5	1	0	1	7.1	4	1	2	0	0	0	0	9	0	0	0	2.3	1.000	OF-4
4 yrs.		17	.371	.597	62	23	5	0	3	4.8	12	13	8	3	0	0	0	17	0	1	0	1.1	.944	OF-17

WORLD SERIES

Year	Team	Games	BA	SA	AB	H	2B	3B	HR	HR%	R	RBI	BB	SO	SB	PH AB	PH H	PO	A	E	DP	TC/G	FA	G by Pos
1977	LA N	6	.292	.417	24	7	0	0	1	4.2	4	5	0	4	0	0	0	11	0	1	0	2.0	.917	OF-6
1978		6	.238	.381	21	5	0	0	1	4.8	2	1	1	3	0	0	0	12	0	0	0	2.0	1.000	OF-6
1981		6	.167	.167	24	4	0	0	0	0.0	3	1	1	6	0	0	0	13	0	0	0	2.2	1.000	OF-6
3 yrs.		18	.232	.319	69	16	0	0	2	2.9	9	7	2	11	0	0	0	36	0	1	0	2.1	.973	OF-18

Floyd Baker

BAKER, FLOYD WILSON
B. Oct. 10, 1916, Luray, Va.

BL TR 5'9" 160 lbs.

Year	Team	Games	BA	SA	AB	H	2B	3B	HR	HR%	R	RBI	BB	SO	SB	PH AB	PH H	PO	A	E	DP	TC/G	FA	G by Pos
1943	STL A	22	.174	.217	46	8	2	0	0	0.0	5	4	6	4	0	11	2	24	27	2	7	2.4	.962	SS-10, 3B-1
1944		44	.175	.206	97	17	3	0	0	0.0	10	5	11	5	2	11	4	41	68	5	9	2.6	.956	2B-17, SS-16
1945	CHI A	82	.250	.288	208	52	8	0	0	0.0	22	19	23	12	3	16	1	51	127	5	10	2.2	.973	3B-58, 2B-11
1946		9	.250	.292	24	6	1	0	0	0.0	2	3	2	3	0	3	0	10	15	1	1	2.9	.962	3B-6
1947		105	.264	.313	371	98	12	3	0	0.0	61	22	66	28	9	0	0	88	258	7	29	3.4	.980	3B-101, SS-1, 2B-1
1948		104	.215	.257	335	72	8	3	0	0.0	47	18	73	26	4	11	4	131	226	13	34	3.6	.965	3B-71, 2B-18, SS-1
1949		125	.260	.327	388	101	15	4	1	0.3	38	40	84	32	3	0	0	111	280	9	32	3.2	.978	3B-122, SS-3, 2B-1
1950		83	.317	.355	186	59	7	0	0	0.0	26	11	32	10	1	24	6	53	105	2	9	1.9	.988	3B-53, 2B-3, OF-2
1951		82	.263	.323	133	35	6	1	0	0.0	24	14	25	12	0	33	9	40	58	6	8	1.3	.942	3B-44, 2B-5, SS-3
1952	WAS A	79	.262	.293	263	69	8	0	0	0.0	27	33	30	17	1	4	0	166	196	6	42	4.7	.984	2B-68, SS-7, 3B-1
1953 2 teams					WAS A (9G – .000)								BOS A (81G – .273)											
" total		90	.263	.307	179	47	4	2	0	0.0	22	24	25	10	0	31	3	67	93	5	18	1.8	.970	3B-38, 2B-16
1954 2 teams					BOS A (21G – .200)								PHI N (23G – .227)											
" total		44	.214	.262	42	9	2	0	0	0.0	1	3	5	5	0	25	7	15	18	1	2	0.8	.971	3B-14, 2B-3
1955	PHI N	5	.000	.000	8	0	0	0	0	0.0	0	0	0	1	0	4	0	5	3	0	0	1.6	1.000	3B-1
13 yrs.		874	.251	.297	2280	573	76	13	1	0.0	285	196	382	165	23	173	36	802	1474	62	201	2.7	.973	3B-510, 2B-143, SS-41, OF-2

WORLD SERIES

Year	Team	Games	BA	SA	AB	H	2B	3B	HR	HR%	R	RBI	BB	SO	SB	PH AB	PH H	PO	A	E	DP	TC/G	FA	G by Pos
1944	STL A	2	.000	.000	2	0	0	0	0	0.0	0	0	0	2	0	2	0	1	0	0	0	0.5	1.000	2B-2

Year	Team		Games	BA	SA	AB	H	2B	3B	HR	HR%	R	RBI	BB	SO	SB	Pinch Hit AB	Pinch Hit H	PO	A	E	DP	TC/G	FA	G by Pos

Frank Baker

BAKER, FRANK
B. Jan. 11, 1944, Bartow, Fla.
BL TR 5'10" 180 lbs.

Year	Team		Games	BA	SA	AB	H	2B	3B	HR	HR%	R	RBI	BB	SO	SB	AB	H	PO	A	E	DP	TC/G	FA	G by Pos
1969	CLE	A	52	.256	.372	172	44	5	3	3	1.7	21	15	14	34	2	7	1	71	5	4	0	1.5	.950	OF-46
1971			73	.210	.304	181	38	12	1	1	0.6	18	23	12	34	1	23	3	65	2	1	1	0.9	.985	OF-51
2 yrs.			125	.232	.337	353	82	17	4	4	1.1	39	38	26	68	3	30	4	136	7	5	1	1.2	.966	OF-97

Frank Baker

BAKER, FRANK WATTS
B. Oct. 29, 1946, Meridian, Miss.
BL TR 6'2" 178 lbs.

Year	Team		Games	BA	SA	AB	H	2B	3B	HR	HR%	R	RBI	BB	SO	SB	AB	H	PO	A	E	DP	TC/G	FA	G by Pos
1970	NY	A	35	.231	.282	117	27	4	1	0	0.0	6	11	14	26	1	0	0	62	118	5	22	5.3	.973	SS-35
1971			43	.139	.165	79	11	2	0	0	0.0	9	2	16	22	3	1	0	53	97	8	28	3.7	.949	SS-38
1973	BAL		44	.190	.317	63	12	1	2	1	1.6	10	11	7	7	0	2	1	44	65	5	17	2.6	.956	SS-32, 2B-7, 3B-1, 1B-1
1974			24	.172	.207	29	5	1	0	0	0.0	3	0	3	5	0	0	0	16	31	9	5	2.3	.839	SS-17, 2B-3, 3B-1
4 yrs.			146	.191	.250	288	55	8	3	1	0.3	28	24	40	60	4	3	1	175	311	27	72	3.5	.947	SS-122, 2B-10, 3B-2, 1B-1

LEAGUE CHAMPIONSHIP SERIES

Year	Team		Games	BA	SA	AB	H	2B	3B	HR	HR%	R	RBI	BB	SO	SB	AB	H	PO	A	E	DP	TC/G	FA	G by Pos
1973	BAL	A	2	–	–	0	0	0	0	0	–	0	0	0	0	0	0	0	0	0	0	0	0.0	–	SS-2
1974			2	–	–	0	0	0	0	0	–	0	0	0	0	0	0	0	1	1	1	0	1.5	.667	SS-2
2 yrs.			4	–	–	0	0	0	0	0	–	0	0	0	0	0	0	0	1	1	1	0	0.8	.667	SS-4

Frank Baker

BAKER, JOHN FRANKLIN (Home Run)
B. Mar. 13, 1886, Trappe, Md. D. June 28, 1963, Trappe, Md.
Hall of Fame 1955.
BL TR 5'11" 173 lbs.

Year	Team		Games	BA	SA	AB	H	2B	3B	HR	HR%	R	RBI	BB	SO	SB	AB	H	PO	A	E	DP	TC/G	FA	G by Pos
1908	PHI	A	9	.290	.387	31	9	3	0	0	0.0	5	2	0		0	0	0	12	22	0	0	3.8	1.000	3B-9
1909			148	.305	.447	541	165	27	19	4	0.7	73	85	26		20	2	0	209	277	42	16	3.6	.920	3B-146
1910			146	.283	.392	561	159	25	15	2	0.4	83	74	34		21	0	0	207	313	45	35	3.9	.920	3B-146
1911			148	.334	.505	592	198	40	14	11	1.9	96	115	40		38	0	0	217	274	30	26	3.5	.942	3B-148
1912			149	.347	.541	577	200	40	21	10	1.7	116	133	50		40	0	0	217	321	34	25	3.8	.941	3B-149
1913			149	.336	.492	565	190	34	9	12	2.1	116	126	63	31	34	0	0	233	280	44	19	3.7	.921	3B-149
1914			150	.319	.442	570	182	23	10	9	1.6	84	97	53	37	19	1	0	221	292	24	20	3.6	.955	3B-149
1916	NY	A	100	.269	.428	360	97	23	2	10	2.8	46	52	36	30	15	3	0	133	210	22	16	3.7	.940	3B-96
1917			146	.282	.365	553	156	24	2	6	1.1	57	71	48	27	18	0	0	202	317	28	21	3.7	.949	3B-146
1918			126	.306	.409	504	154	24	5	6	1.2	65	68	38	13	8	0	0	175	282	13	30	3.7	.972	3B-126
1919			141	.293	.388	567	166	22	1	10	1.8	70	83	44	18	13	0	0	176	286	22	28	3.4	.955	3B-141
1921			94	.294	.436	330	97	16	2	9	2.7	46	71	26	12	8	9	0	84	173	11	16	2.9	.959	3B-83
1922			69	.278	.444	234	65	12	3	7	3.0	30	36	15	14	1	8	1	68	108	7	7	2.7	.962	3B-60
13 yrs.			1575	.307	.442	5985	1838	313	103	96	1.6	887	1013	473	182	235	23	1	2154	3155	322	259	3.6	.943	3B-1548

WORLD SERIES

Year	Team		Games	BA	SA	AB	H	2B	3B	HR	HR%	R	RBI	BB	SO	SB	AB	H	PO	A	E	DP	TC/G	FA	G by Pos
1910	PHI	A	5	.409	.545	22	9	3	0	0	0.0	6	4	2	1	0	0	0	9	11	3	2	4.6	.870	3B-5
1911			6	.375	.708	24	9	2	0	2	8.3	7	5	1	5	0	0	0	10	10	2	2	3.7	.909	3B-6
1913			5	.450	.600	20	9	0	0	1	5.0	2	7	0	2	1	0	0	6	6	1	0	2.6	.923	3B-5
1914			4	.250	.375	16	4	2	0	0	0.0	0	2	1	3	0	0	0	10	15	0	1	6.3	1.000	3B-4
1921	NY	A	4	.250	.250	8	2	0	0	0	0.0	0	1	1	0	0	2	0	2	3	0	0	1.3	1.000	3B-2
1922			1	.000	.000	1	0	0	0	0	0.0	0	0	0	1	0	1	0	0	0	0	0	0.0	–	
6 yrs.			25	.363	.538	91	33	7	0	3	3.3	15	18	5	11	1	3	0	37	45	6	5	3.5	.932	3B-22
				6th			9th																			

Gene Baker

BAKER, EUGENE WALTER
B. June 15, 1925, Davenport, Iowa
BR TR 6'1" 170 lbs.

Year	Team		Games	BA	SA	AB	H	2B	3B	HR	HR%	R	RBI	BB	SO	SB	AB	H	PO	A	E	DP	TC/G	FA	G by Pos
1953	CHI	N	7	.227	.273	22	5	1	0	0	0.0	1	0	1	4	1	1	0	11	11	2	3	3.4	.917	2B-6
1954			135	.275	.425	541	149	32	5	13	2.4	68	61	47	55	4	0	0	355	385	25	102	5.7	.967	2B-134
1955			154	.268	.392	609	163	29	7	11	1.8	82	52	49	57	9	0	0	432	444	30	114	5.9	.967	2B-154
1956			140	.258	.377	546	141	23	3	12	2.2	65	57	39	54	4	0	0	362	426	25	99	5.8	.969	2B-140
1957	2 teams		CHI N (12G – .250)			PIT N (111G – .266)																			
"	total		123	.264	.364	409	108	22	5	3	0.7	40	46	35	32	3	16	3	140	234	24	36	3.2	.940	3B-72, SS-28, 2B-13
1958	PIT	N	29	.250	.321	56	14	2	1	0	0.0	3	7	8	6	0	14	0	19	28	0	2	1.6	1.000	3B-11, 2B-3
1960			33	.243	.243	37	9	0	0	0	0.0	5	4	2	9	0	18	4	7	9	0	2	0.5	1.000	3B-7, 2B-1
1961			9	.100	.100	10	1	0	0	0	0.0	1	0	3	2	0	3	0	6	0	0	0	0.7	1.000	3B-3
8 yrs.			630	.265	.385	2230	590	109	21	39	1.7	265	227	184	219	21	52	13	1326	1543	106	358	4.7	.964	2B-451, 3B-93, SS-28

WORLD SERIES

Year	Team		Games	BA	SA	AB	H	2B	3B	HR	HR%	R	RBI	BB	SO	SB	AB	H	PO	A	E	DP	TC/G	FA	G by Pos
1960	PIT	N	3	.000	.000	3	0	0	0	0	0.0	0	0	0	1	0	3	0	0	0	0	0	0.0	–	

George Baker

BAKER, GEORGE F.
B. 1859, St. Louis, Mo. Deceased.

Year	Team		Games	BA	SA	AB	H	2B	3B	HR	HR%	R	RBI	BB	SO	SB	AB	H	PO	A	E	DP	TC/G	FA	G by Pos
1883	BAL	AA	7	.227	.227	22	5	0	0	0	0.0	0		0			0	0	13	6	7	2	3.7	.731	SS-4, C-3, OF-1
1884	STL	U	80	.164	.183	317	52	6	0	0	0.0	39		5			0	0	451	138	73	14	8.3	.890	C-68, OF-5, 2B-4, 3B-3, SS-2
1885	STL	N	38	.122	.122	131	16	0	0	0	0.0	5	5	9	28		0	0	153	34	32	2	5.8	.854	C-32, 3B-3, OF-2, 2B-1
1886	KC	N	1	.250	.250	4	1	0	0	0	0.0	1	0	0	1		0	0	5	3	1	0	9.0	.889	C-1
4 yrs.			126	.156	.169	474	74	6	0	0	0.0	45	5	14	29		0	0	622	181	113	18	7.3	.877	C-104, OF-8, SS-6, 3B-6, 2B-5

Howard Baker

BAKER, HOWARD FRANCIS
B. Mar. 1, 1888, Bridgeport, Conn. D. Jan. 16, 1964, Bridgeport, Conn.
BR TR 5'11" 175 lbs.

Year	Team		Games	BA	SA	AB	H	2B	3B	HR	HR%	R	RBI	BB	SO	SB	AB	H	PO	A	E	DP	TC/G	FA	G by Pos
1912	CLE	A	11	.167	.167	30	5	0	0	0	0.0	1	2	5		0	1	0	15	12	1	0	2.5	.964	3B-10
1914	CHI	A	15	.277	.340	47	13	1	0	0	0.0	4	5	3	8	2	0	0	7	22	4	1	2.2	.879	3B-15
1915	2 teams		CHI A (2G – .000)			NY N (1G – .000)																			
"	total		3	.000	.000	5	0	0	0	0	0.0	0	0	0	2	0	2	0	1	2	0	0	1.0	1.000	3B-1
3 yrs.			29	.220	.256	82	18	1	0	0	0.0	5	7	8	10	2	3	0	23	36	5	1	2.2	.922	3B-26

Jack Baker

BAKER, JACK EDWARD
B. May 4, 1950, Birmingham, Ala.
BR TR 6'5" 225 lbs.

Year	Team		Games	BA	SA	AB	H	2B	3B	HR	HR%	R	RBI	BB	SO	SB	AB	H	PO	A	E	DP	TC/G	FA	G by Pos
1976	BOS	A	12	.130	.261	23	3	0	0	1	4.3	1	2	1	5	0	4	0	48	3	1	6	4.3	.981	1B-8, DH-1

Year	Team		Games	BA	SA	AB	H	2B	3B	HR	HR%	R	RBI	BB	SO	SB	Pinch Hit AB	H	PO	A	E	DP	TC/G	FA	G by Pos

Jack Baker *continued*

| 1977 | | | 2 | .000 | .000 | 3 | 0 | 0 | 0 | 0 | 0.0 | 0 | 0 | 0 | 1 | 0 | 1 | 0 | 5 | 1 | 1 | 0 | 3.5 | .857 | 1B-1 |
| 2 yrs. | | | 14 | .115 | .231 | 26 | 3 | 0 | 0 | 1 | 3.8 | 1 | 2 | 1 | 6 | 0 | 5 | 0 | 53 | 4 | 2 | 6 | 4.2 | .966 | 1B-9, DH-1 |

Jesse Baker

BAKER, JESSE (Tiny)
Born Michael Myron Silverman.
B. Mar. 4, 1895, Cleveland, Ohio D. July 29, 1976, West Los Angeles, Calif.
BR TR 5'4" 140 lbs.

| 1919 | WAS | A | 1 | – | – | 0 | 0 | 0 | 0 | 0 | – | 0 | 0 | 0 | 0 | 0 | 0 | 0 | 0 | 1 | 0 | 0 | 1.0 | 1.000 | SS-1 |

Phil Baker

BAKER, PHILIP
B. Sept. 19, 1856, Philadelphia, Pa. D. June 4, 1940, Washington, D. C.
BL TL 5'8" 152 lbs.

1883	BAL	AA	28	.273	.331	121	33	2	1	1	0.8	22		8		0	0	113	14	21	2	5.3	.858	C-19, OF-14, SS-1
1884	WAS	U	86	.288	.356	371	107	12	5	1	0.3	75		11		0	0	515	40	34	16	6.8	.942	1B-39, OF-32, C-27
1886	WAS	N	81	.222	.280	325	72	6	5	1	0.3	37	34	20	32	0	0	602	15	21	30	7.9	.967	1B-56, OF-21, C-16
3 yrs.			195	.259	.322	817	212	20	11	3	0.4	134	34	39	32	0	0	1230	69	76	48	7.1	.945	1B-95, OF-67, C-62, SS-1

Tracy Baker

BAKER, TRACY LEE
B. Nov. 7, 1891, Pendleton, Ore. D. Mar. 14, 1975, Placerville, Calif.
BR TR 6'1" 180 lbs.

| 1911 | BOS | A | 1 | – | – | 0 | 0 | 0 | 0 | 0 | – | 0 | 0 | 0 | 0 | 0 | 0 | 0 | 4 | 0 | 0 | 0 | 4.0 | 1.000 | 1B-1 |

John Balaz

BALAZ, JOHN LAWRENCE
B. Nov. 24, 1950, Toronto, Ontario, Canada
BR TR 6'3" 180 lbs.

1974	CAL	A	14	.238	.310	42	10	0	0	1	2.4	4	5	2	10	0	1	1	17	0	0	0	1.2	1.000	OF-12
1975			45	.242	.350	120	29	8	1	1	0.8	10	10	5	25	0	7	2	40	3	0	1	1.0	1.000	OF-27, DH-11
2 yrs.			59	.241	.340	162	39	8	1	2	1.2	14	15	7	35	0	8	3	57	3	0	1	1.0	1.000	OF-39, DH-11

Steve Balboni

BALBONI, STEPHEN CHARLES (Bye-Bye)
B. Jan. 16, 1957, Brockton, Mass.
BR TR 6'3" 225 lbs.

1981	NY	A	4	.286	.714	7	2	1	0	0	0.0	2	2	1	4	0	1	0	14	1	0	2	3.8	1.000	1B-3, DH-1
1982			33	.187	.280	107	20	2	1	2	1.9	8	4	6	34	0	5	1	194	13	2	23	6.3	.990	1B-26, DH-5
1983			32	.233	.430	86	20	2	0	5	5.8	8	17	8	23	0	3	1	178	9	3	19	5.9	.984	1B-23, DH-4
1984	KC	A	126	.244	.498	438	107	23	2	28	6.4	58	77	45	139	0	1	0	1102	79	15	102	9.5	.987	1B-125, DH-1
1985			160	.243	.477	600	146	28	2	36	6.0	74	88	52	166	1	1	0	1573	101	12	138	10.5	.993	1B-160
1986			138	.229	.451	512	117	25	1	29	5.7	54	88	43	146	0	2	0	1236	98	18	115	9.8	.987	1B-137
1987			121	.207	.427	386	80	11	1	24	6.2	44	60	34	97	0	15	4	521	41	6	39	4.7	.989	1B-55, DH-52
1988	2 teams	KC A (21G – .143)				SEA A (97G – .251)																			
"	total		118	.235	.448	413	97	17	1	23	5.6	46	66	24	87	0	9	2	428	30	4	45	3.9	.991	DH-62, 1B-53
1989	NY	A	110	.237	.460	300	71	12	2	17	5.7	33	59	25	67	0	25	6	150	7	1	15	1.4	.994	DH-82, 1B-20
9 yrs.			842	.232	.455	2849	660	121	11	164	5.8	327	461	238	763	1	62	14	5396	379	61	498	6.9	.990	1B-602, DH-207

LEAGUE CHAMPIONSHIP SERIES

1984	KC	A	3	.100	.100	10	1	0	0	0	0.0	1	4	1	4	0	0	0	20	3	1	2	8.0	.958	1B-3
1985			7	.120	.120	25	3	0	0	0	0.0	0	1	2	8	0	0	0	71	7	2	5	11.4	.975	1B-7
2 yrs.			10	.114	.114	35	4	0	0	0	0.0	1	1	3	12	0	0	0	91	10	3	7	10.4	.971	1B-10

WORLD SERIES

| 1985 | KC | A | 7 | .320 | .320 | 25 | 8 | 0 | 0 | 0 | 0.0 | 3 | 5 | 4 | 6 | 0 | 0 | 1 | 70 | 3 | 0 | 1 | 10.4 | 1.000 | 1B-7 |

Bobby Balcena

BALCENA, ROBERT RUDOLPH
B. Aug. 1, 1928, San Pedro, Calif.
BR TL 5'7" 160 lbs.

| 1956 | CIN | N | 7 | .000 | .000 | 2 | 0 | 0 | 0 | 0 | 0.0 | 2 | 0 | 0 | 1 | 0 | 2 | 0 | 1 | 0 | 0 | 0 | 0.1 | 1.000 | OF-2 |

Billy Baldwin

BALDWIN, ROBERT HARVEY
B. June 9, 1951, Tazewell, Va.
BL TL 6' 175 lbs.

1975	DET	A	30	.221	.379	95	21	3	0	4	4.2	8	8	5	14	2	0	0	53	4	1	1	1.9	.983	OF-25, DH-1
1976	NY	N	9	.273	.545	22	6	1	1	1	4.5	4	5	1	2	0	3	1	12	1	1	1	1.6	.929	OF-5
2 yrs.			39	.231	.410	117	27	4	1	5	4.3	12	13	6	16	2	3	1	65	5	2	2	1.8	.972	OF-30, DH-1

Frank Baldwin

BALDWIN, FRANK DeWITT
B. Dec. 25, 1928, High Bridge, N. J.
BR TR 5'11" 195 lbs.

| 1953 | CIN | N | 16 | .100 | .100 | 20 | 2 | 0 | 0 | 0 | 0.0 | 0 | 1 | 0 | 9 | 0 | 11 | 2 | 9 | 0 | 0 | 0 | 0.6 | 1.000 | C-6 |

Henry Baldwin

BALDWIN, HENRY CLAY (Ted)
B. June 13, 1894, Chadds Ford, Pa. D. Feb. 24, 1964, West Chester, Pa.
BR TR 5'11" 180 lbs.

| 1927 | PHI | N | 6 | .313 | .313 | 16 | 5 | 0 | 0 | 0 | 0.0 | 1 | 1 | 1 | 2 | 0 | 1 | 1 | 4 | 6 | 1 | 1 | 1.8 | .909 | SS-3, 3B-2 |

Kid Baldwin

BALDWIN, CLARENCE GEOGHAN
B. Nov. 1, 1864, Newport, Ky. D. July 12, 1897, Cincinnati, Ohio
BR TR 5'6" 147 lbs.

1884	2 teams	KC U (50G – .194)				PIT U (1G – 1.000)																			
"	total		51	.198	.271	192	38	5	3	1	0.5	19		4		0	0	220	92	41	4	6.9	.884	C-45, OF-10, 3B-1, 2B-1
1885	CIN	AA	34	.135	.167	126	17	1	0	1	0.8	9		3		0	0	142	37	34	4	6.3	.840	C-25, OF-6, 2B-2, P-2, 3B-1
1886			87	.229	.327	315	72	8	7	3	1.0	41		8		0	0	369	118	67	13	6.4	.879	C-71, 3B-13, OF-6
1887			96	.253	.351	388	98	15	10	1	0.3	46		6		13	0	0	381	165	79	9	6.5	.874	C-96, OF-2
1888			67	.218	.292	271	59	11	3	1	0.4	27	25	3		0	0	355	108	41	6	7.5	.919	C-65, OF-2, 1B-1
1889			60	.247	.341	223	55	14	2	1	0.4	34	34	7		32	0	0	288	93	38	5	7.0	.909	C-55, OF-4, 3B-1, 1B-1
1890	2 teams	CIN N (22G – .153)				PHI AA (24G – .233)																			
"	total		46	.198	.228	162	32	1	2	0	0.0	10	10	7	6	4	0	0	201	75	35	7	6.8	.887	C-39, 3B-5, OF-2
7 yrs.			441	.221	.301	1677	371	55	27	8	0.5	186	69	36	38	28	0	0	1956	688	335	48	6.8	.888	C-396, OF-32, 3B-21, 2B-3, 1B-2, P-2

Reggie Baldwin

BALDWIN, REGINALD CONRAD
B. Aug. 19, 1954, River Rouge, Mich.
BR TR 6'1" 195 lbs.

Year Team	Games	BA	SA	AB	H	2B	3B	HR	HR%	R	RBI	BB	SO	SB	PH AB	PH H	PO	A	E	DP	TC/G	FA	G by Pos
1978 HOU N	38	.254	.373	67	17	5	0	1	1.5	5	11	3	3	0	18	5	76	8	4	1	2.3	.955	C-17
1979	14	.200	.250	20	4	1	0	0	0.0	0	1	0	1	0	12	3	10	1	0	0	0.8	1.000	C-3, 1B-1
2 yrs.	52	.241	.345	87	21	6	0	1	1.1	5	12	3	4	0	30	8	86	9	4	1	1.9	.960	C-20, 1B-1

Mike Balenti

BALENTI, MICHAEL RICHARD
B. July 3, 1886, Calumet, Okla. D. Aug. 4, 1955, Altus, Okla.
BR TR 5'11" 175 lbs.

Year Team	Games	BA	SA	AB	H	2B	3B	HR	HR%	R	RBI	BB	SO	SB	PH AB	PH H	PO	A	E	DP	TC/G	FA	G by Pos
1911 CIN N	8	.250	.250	8	2	0	0	0	0.0	2	0	0	1	3	0	0	2	4	1	1	0.9	.857	SS-2, OF-1
1913 STL A	70	.180	.227	211	38	2	4	0	0.0	17	11	6	32	3	4	1	124	170	23	26	4.5	.927	SS-56, OF-8
2 yrs.	78	.183	.228	219	40	2	4	0	0.0	19	11	6	33	6	4	1	126	174	24	27	4.2	.926	SS-58, OF-9

Lee Bales

BALES, WESLEY OWEN
B. Dec. 4, 1944, Los Angeles, Calif.
BB TR 5'10½" 165 lbs.

Year Team	Games	BA	SA	AB	H	2B	3B	HR	HR%	R	RBI	BB	SO	SB	PH AB	PH H	PO	A	E	DP	TC/G	FA	G by Pos
1966 ATL N	12	.063	.063	16	1	0	0	0	0.0	4	0	0	5	0	0		12	17	0	2	2.4	1.000	2B-7, 3B-3
1967 HOU N	19	.111	.111	27	3	0	0	0	0.0	4	2	8	7	1	6	0	9	13	1	2	1.2	.957	2B-6, SS-1
2 yrs.	31	.093	.093	43	4	0	0	0	0.0	8	2	8	12	1	6	0	21	30	1	4	1.7	.981	2B-13, 3B-3, SS-1

Art Ball

BALL, ARTHUR
B. 1873, Ind. D. Dec. 26, 1915, Chicago, Ill.
TR

Year Team	Games	BA	SA	AB	H	2B	3B	HR	HR%	R	RBI	BB	SO	SB	PH AB	PH H	PO	A	E	DP	TC/G	FA	G by Pos
1894 STL N	1	.333	.333	3	1	0	0	0	0.0	0	0	0	1	0			2	0	1	0	3.0	.667	2B-1
1898 BAL N	32	.185	.210	81	15	2	0	0	0.0	7	8	7		2	0	0	38	74	8	6	3.8	.933	3B-15, SS-14, 2B-2, OF-1
2 yrs.	33	.190	.214	84	16	2	0	0	0.0	7	8	7	1	2	0	0	40	74	9	6	3.7	.927	3B-15, SS-14, 2B-3, OF-1

Jim Ball

BALL, JAMES CHANDLER
B. Feb. 22, 1884, Harford County, Md. D. Apr. 7, 1963, Glendale, Calif.
BR TR 5'11" 175 lbs.

Year Team	Games	BA	SA	AB	H	2B	3B	HR	HR%	R	RBI	BB	SO	SB	PH AB	PH H	PO	A	E	DP	TC/G	FA	G by Pos
1907 BOS N	10	.167	.222	36	6	2	0	0	0.0	3	3	2			0	0	37	15	2	2	5.4	.963	C-10
1908	6	.067	.067	15	1	0	0	0	0.0	1	1	1	1		0	0	14	8	2	0	4.0	.917	C-6
2 yrs.	16	.137	.176	51	7	2	0	0	0.0	4	4	3	1	0	0	0	51	23	4	2	4.9	.949	C-16

Neal Ball

BALL, CORNELIUS
B. Apr. 22, 1881, Grand Haven, Mich. D. Oct. 15, 1957, Bridgeport, Conn.
BR TR 5'7" 145 lbs.

Year Team	Games	BA	SA	AB	H	2B	3B	HR	HR%	R	RBI	BB	SO	SB	PH AB	PH H	PO	A	E	DP	TC/G	FA	G by Pos
1907 NY A	15	.205	.273	44	9	1	1	0	0.0	5	4	1			1	0	29	36	13	3	5.2	.833	SS-11, 2B-5
1908	132	.247	.291	446	110	16	2	0	0.0	34	38	21		32	1	1	270	438	81	28	6.0	.897	SS-130, 2B-1
1909 2 teams										NY A (8G – .207)		CLE A (96G – .256)											
" total	104	.252	.317	353	89	14	1	1	0.3	34	28	20		19		0	213	307	49	43	5.5	.914	SS-95, 2B-8
1910 CLE A	53	.210	.252	119	25	3	1	0	0.0	12	12	9		4	3	0	73	95	11	10	3.4	.939	SS-27, OF-6, 2B-6, 3B-3
1911	116	.296	.396	412	122	14	9	3	0.7	45	45	27		21	1	0	228	329	36	41	5.1	.939	2B-95, 3B-17, SS-1
1912 2 teams										CLE A (37G – .227)		BOS A (18G – .200)											
" total	55	.220	.266	177	39	6	1	0	0.0	22	20	12		12	1	1	93	88	12	12	3.5	.938	2B-54
1913 BOS A	21	.172	.207	58	10	2	0	0	0.0	9	4	9	13	3	2	0	30	49	11	5	4.3	.878	2B-10, SS-8, 3B-1
7 yrs.	496	.251	.314	1609	404	56	17	4	0.2	161	151	99	13	92	8	2	936	1342	213	142	5.0	.914	SS-272, 2B-179, 3B-21, OF-6

WORLD SERIES

Year Team	Games	BA	SA	AB	H	2B	3B	HR	HR%	R	RBI	BB	SO	SB	PH AB	PH H	PO	A	E	DP	TC/G	FA	G by Pos
1912 BOS A	1	.000	.000	1	0	0	0	0	0.0	0	0	0	1	0	1	0	0	0	0	0	0.0	—	—

Pelham Ballenger

BALLENGER, PELHAM ASHBY
B. Feb. 6, 1894, Gilreath Mill, S. C. D. Dec. 8, 1948, Greenville County, S. C.
BR TR 5'11" 160 lbs.

Year Team	Games	BA	SA	AB	H	2B	3B	HR	HR%	R	RBI	BB	SO	SB	PH AB	PH H	PO	A	E	DP	TC/G	FA	G by Pos
1928 WAS A	3	.111	.111	9	1	0	0	0	0.0	0	0	0	1	0	0	0	1	8	0	1	3.0	1.000	3B-3

Hal Bamberger

BAMBERGER, HAROLD EARL (Dutch)
B. Oct. 29, 1924, Lebanon, Pa.
BL TR 6' 173 lbs.

Year Team	Games	BA	SA	AB	H	2B	3B	HR	HR%	R	RBI	BB	SO	SB	PH AB	PH H	PO	A	E	DP	TC/G	FA	G by Pos
1948 NY N	7	.083	.083	12	1	0	0	0	0.0	0	0	1	2	0	3	0	6	0	0	0	0.9	1.000	OF-3

Dave Bancroft

BANCROFT, DAVID JAMES (Beauty)
B. Apr. 20, 1891, Sioux City, Iowa D. Oct. 9, 1972, Superior, Wis.
Manager 1924-27.
Hall of Fame 1971.
BB TR 5'9½" 160 lbs.

Year Team	Games	BA	SA	AB	H	2B	3B	HR	HR%	R	RBI	BB	SO	SB	PH AB	PH H	PO	A	E	DP	TC/G	FA	G by Pos
1915 PHI N	153	.254	.330	563	143	18	2	7	1.2	85	30	77	62	15	0	0	336	492	64	60	5.8	.928	SS-153
1916	142	.212	.252	477	101	10	3	3	0.6	53	33	74	57	15	0	0	326	510	60	64	6.3	.933	SS-142
1917	127	.243	.335	478	116	22	5	4	0.8	56	43	44	42	14	1	0	289	445	52	58	6.2	.934	SS-120, 2B-3, OF-2
1918	125	.265	.319	499	132	19	4	0	0.0	69	26	54	36	11	0	0	371	457	64	57	7.1	.928	SS-125
1919	92	.272	.352	335	91	13	7	0	0.0	45	25	31	30	8	4	1	242	306	28	43	6.3	.951	SS-88
1920 2 teams										PHI N (42G – .298)		NY N (108G – .299)											
" total	150	.299	.387	613	183	36	9	0	0.0	102	36	42	44	8	0	0	362	598	45	95	6.7	.955	SS-150
1921 NY N	153	.318	.441	606	193	26	15	6	1.0	121	67	66	23	17	0	0	396	546	39	105	6.4	.960	SS-153
1922	156	.321	.418	651	209	41	5	4	0.6	117	60	79	27	16	0	0	405	579	62	93	6.7	.941	SS-156
1923	107	.304	.399	444	135	33	3	1	0.2	80	31	62	23	8	0	0	280	416	62	62	6.9	.938	SS-96, 2B-11
1924 BOS N	79	.279	.339	319	89	11	1	2	0.6	49	21	37	24	4	0	0	186	259	18	57	5.9	.961	SS-79
1925	128	.319	.426	479	153	29	8	2	0.4	75	49	64	24	7	3	1	300	459	44	81	6.3	.945	SS-125
1926	127	.311	.384	453	141	18	6	1	0.2	70	44	64	29	3	1	0	318	400	33	75	5.9	.956	SS-123, 3B-2
1927	111	.243	.307	375	91	13	4	1	0.3	44	31	43	36	5	5	1	275	329	39	66	5.8	.939	SS-104, 3B-1
1928 BKN N	149	.247	.303	515	127	19	5	0	0.0	47	51	59	20	7	0	0	350	484	46	66	5.9	.948	SS-149
1929	104	.277	.332	358	99	11	3	1	0.3	35	44	29	11	7	2	0	224	309	25	45	5.4	.955	SS-102
1930 NY N	10	.059	.118	17	1	1	0	0	0.0	2	1	2	1	0	1	0	13	15	1	0	2.9	.966	SS-8
16 yrs.	1913	.279	.358	7182	2004	320	77	32	0.4	1048	591	827	487	145	17	3	4673	6604	666	1027	6.2	.944	SS-1873, 2B-14, 3B-3, OF-2

WORLD SERIES

Year Team	Games	BA	SA	AB	H	2B	3B	HR	HR%	R	RBI	BB	SO	SB	PH AB	PH H	PO	A	E	DP	TC/G	FA	G by Pos
1915 PHI N	5	.294	.294	17	5	0	0	0	0.0	2	1	2	2	1	0	0	13	10	1	2	4.8	.958	SS-5
1921 NY N	8	.152	.182	33	5	1	0	0	0.0	3	3	1	5	0	1	0	16	17	1	1	4.3	.971	SS-8
1922	5	.211	.211	19	4	0	0	0	0.0	4	2	1	2	0	1	0	9	17	1	2	5.4	.963	SS-5

Year Team	Games	BA	SA	AB	H	2B	3B	HR	HR%	R	RBI	BB	SO	SB	Pinch Hit AB	Pinch Hit H	PO	A	E	DP	TC/G	FA	G by Pos

Dave Bancroft *continued*

Year Team	Games	BA	SA	AB	H	2B	3B	HR	HR%	R	RBI	BB	SO	SB	AB	H	PO	A	E	DP	TC/G	FA	G by Pos
1923	6	.083	.083	24	2	0	0	0	0.0	1	1	1	2	1	0	0	11	24	0	6	5.8	1.000	SS-6
4 yrs.	24	.172	.183	93	16	1	0	0	0.0	10	7	6	10	1	0	0	49	68	3	11	5.0	.975	SS-24

Chris Bando

BANDO, CHRISTOPHER MICHAEL
Brother of Sal Bando.
B. Feb. 4, 1956, Cleveland, Ohio

BB TR 6' 195 lbs.

Year Team	Games	BA	SA	AB	H	2B	3B	HR	HR%	R	RBI	BB	SO	SB	AB	H	PO	A	E	DP	TC/G	FA	G by Pos
1981 CLE A	21	.213	.277	47	10	3	0	0	0.0	3	6	2	9	0	0	0	53	5	2	0	2.9	.967	C-15, DH-2
1982	66	.212	.304	184	39	6	1	3	1.6	13	16	24	30	0	12	4	268	23	3	1	4.5	.990	C-63, 3B-2
1983	48	.256	.380	121	31	3	0	4	3.3	15	15	15	19	0	9	2	170	19	1	2	4.0	.995	C-43
1984	75	.291	.505	220	64	11	0	12	5.5	38	41	33	35	1	11	2	307	30	6	4	4.6	.983	C-63, DH-1, 3B-1, 1B-1
1985	73	.139	.173	173	24	4	1	0	0.0	11	13	22	21	0	8	2	251	28	4	3	3.9	.986	C-67
1986	92	.268	.327	254	68	9	0	2	0.8	28	26	22	49	0	13	2	359	30	4	3	4.3	.990	C-86
1987	89	.218	.332	211	46	9	0	5	2.4	20	16	12	28	0	5	0	351	34	4	8	4.4	.990	C-86
1988 2 teams	CLE A (32G – .125)					DET A	(1G – .000)																
" total	33	.125	.181	72	9	1	0	1	1.4	6	8	8	12	0	2	0	123	14	3	2	4.2	.979	C-33
1989 OAK A	1	.500	.500	2	1	0	0	0	0.0	0	1	0	0	0	0	0	8	0	0	0	8.0	1.000	C-1
9 yrs.	498	.227	.329	1284	292	46	2	27	2.1	134	142	138	197	1	69	12	1890	183	27	23	4.2	.987	C-457, DH-3, 3B-3, 1B-1

Sal Bando

BANDO, SALVATORE LEONARD
Brother of Chris Bando.
B. Feb. 13, 1944, Cleveland, Ohio

BR TR 6' 195 lbs.

Year Team	Games	BA	SA	AB	H	2B	3B	HR	HR%	R	RBI	BB	SO	SB	AB	H	PO	A	E	DP	TC/G	FA	G by Pos
1966 KC A	11	.292	.417	24	7	1	1	0	0.0	1	1	1	3	0	4	2	5	23	2	1	2.7	.933	3B-7
1967	47	.192	.246	130	25	3	2	1	0.8	11	6	16	24	1	4	0	43	96	6	7	3.1	.959	3B-44
1968 OAK A	162	.251	.354	605	152	25	5	9	1.5	67	67	51	78	13	0	0	188	272	17	27	2.9	.964	3B-162, OF-1
1969	162	.281	.484	609	171	25	3	31	5.1	106	113	111	82	1	0	0	178	321	24	36	3.2	.954	3B-162
1970	155	.263	.430	502	132	20	2	20	4.0	93	75	118	88	6	1	0	158	258	20	22	2.8	.954	3B-152
1971	153	.271	.452	538	146	23	1	24	4.5	75	94	86	55	3	0	0	141	267	12	22	2.7	.971	3B-153
1972	152	.236	.368	535	126	20	3	15	2.8	64	77	78	55	3	1	0	124	337	20	29	3.2	.958	3B-151, 2B-1
1973	162	.287	.498	592	170	32	3	29	4.9	97	98	82	84	4	0	0	126	281	22	24	2.6	.949	3B-159, DH-3
1974	146	.243	.426	498	121	21	2	22	4.4	84	103	86	79	2	4	2	113	287	23	28	2.9	.946	3B-141, DH-3
1975	160	.230	.356	562	129	24	1	15	2.7	64	78	87	80	7	1	0	122	314	15	36	2.8	.967	3B-160
1976	158	.240	.427	550	132	18	2	27	4.9	75	84	76	74	20	0	0	127	310	17	27	2.9	.963	3B-155, SS-5, DH-2
1977 MIL A	159	.250	.395	580	145	27	3	17	2.9	65	82	75	89	4	0	0	98	283	13	32	2.5	.967	3B-135, DH-24, SS-1, 2B-1
1978	152	.285	.439	540	154	20	6	17	3.1	85	78	72	52	3	4	0	132	332	15	29	3.2	.969	3B-134, DH-12, 1B-5
1979	130	.246	.345	476	117	14	3	9	1.9	57	43	57	42	2	1	1	106	225	12	19	2.6	.965	3B-109, DH-19, 1B-4, 2B-1, P-1
1980	78	.197	.311	254	50	12	1	5	2.0	28	31	29	35	5	6	0	62	112	12	14	2.4	.935	3B-57, DH-15, 1B-7
1981	32	.200	.354	65	13	4	0	2	3.1	10	9	6	3	1	6	1	65	15	1	9	2.8	.989	3B-15, 1B-9, DH-2
16 yrs.	2019	.254	.408	7060	1790	289	38	242	3.4	982	1039	1031	923	75	32	6	1788	3743	231	362	2.9	.960	3B-1896, DH-80, 1B-25, SS-6, 2B-3, OF-1, P-1

DIVISIONAL PLAYOFF SERIES

Year Team	Games	BA	SA	AB	H	2B	3B	HR	HR%	R	RBI	BB	SO	SB	AB	H	PO	A	E	DP	TC/G	FA	G by Pos
1981 MIL A	5	.294	.471	17	5	3	0	0	0.0	1	1	2	1	0	0	0	0	0	0	0	0.0	–	3B-5

LEAGUE CHAMPIONSHIP SERIES

Year Team	Games	BA	SA	AB	H	2B	3B	HR	HR%	R	RBI	BB	SO	SB	AB	H	PO	A	E	DP	TC/G	FA	G by Pos
1971 OAK A	3	.364	.818	11	4	0	1	1	9.1	3	1	1	0	0	0	0	6	2	0	2	2.7	1.000	3B-3
1972	5	.200	.200	20	4	0	0	0	0.0	0	0	0	3	0	0	0	6	16	0	1	4.4	1.000	3B-5
1973	5	.167	.500	18	3	0	0	2	11.1	2	3	3	4	0	0	0	7	10	0	0	3.4	1.000	3B-5
1974	4	.231	.692	13	3	0	0	2	15.4	4	2	4	0	0	0	0	3	8	0	2	2.8	1.000	3B-4
1975	3	.500	.667	12	6	2	0	0	0.0	1	2	0	1	0	0	0	3	11	1	0	5.0	.933	3B-3
5 yrs.	20	.270	.527	74	20	4	1	5	6.8	10	8	8	12	0	0	0	25	47	1	5	3.7	.986	3B-20

WORLD SERIES

Year Team	Games	BA	SA	AB	H	2B	3B	HR	HR%	R	RBI	BB	SO	SB	AB	H	PO	A	E	DP	TC/G	FA	G by Pos
1972 OAK A	7	.269	.308	26	7	1	0	0	0.0	2	1	2	5	0	0	0	3	12	1	0	2.3	.938	3B-7
1973	7	.231	.346	26	6	1	1	0	0.0	5	1	4	7	0	0	0	6	14	1	2	3.0	.952	3B-7
1974	5	.063	.063	16	1	0	0	0	0.0	3	2	2	5	0	0	0	2	10	0	0	2.4	1.000	3B-5
3 yrs.	19	.206	.265	68	14	2	1	0	0.0	10	4	8	17	0	0	0	11	36	2	2	2.6	.959	3B-19

Ernie Banks

BANKS, ERNEST
B. Jan. 31, 1931, Dallas, Tex.
Hall of Fame 1977.

BR TR 6'1" 180 lbs.

Year Team	Games	BA	SA	AB	H	2B	3B	HR	HR%	R	RBI	BB	SO	SB	AB	H	PO	A	E	DP	TC/G	FA	G by Pos
1953 CHI N	10	.314	.571	35	11	1	1	2	5.7	3	6	4	5	0	0	0	19	33	1	9	5.3	.981	SS-10
1954	154	.275	.427	593	163	19	7	19	3.2	70	79	40	50	6	0	0	312	475	34	105	5.3	.959	SS-154
1955	154	.295	.596	596	176	29	9	44	7.4	98	117	45	72	9	0	0	290	482	22	102	5.2	.972	SS-154
1956	139	.297	.530	538	160	25	8	28	5.2	82	85	52	62	6	0	0	279	357	25	92	4.8	.962	SS-139
1957	156	.285	.579	594	169	34	6	43	7.2	113	102	70	85	8	0	0	241	348	14	71	3.9	.977	SS-100, 3B-58
1958	154	.313	.614	617	193	23	11	47	7.6	119	129	52	87	4	0	0	292	468	32	100	5.1	.960	SS-154
1959	155	.304	.596	589	179	25	6	45	7.6	97	143	64	72	2	1	0	271	519	12	95	5.2	.985	SS-154
1960	156	.271	.554	597	162	32	7	41	6.9	94	117	71	69	1	0	0	283	488	18	94	5.1	.977	SS-156
1961	138	.278	.507	511	142	22	4	29	5.7	75	80	54	75	1	4	1	273	370	21	76	4.8	.968	SS-104, OF-23, 1B-7
1962	154	.269	.503	610	164	20	6	37	6.1	87	104	30	71	5	4	2	1462	107	11	135	10.3	.993	1B-149, 3B-3
1963	130	.227	.408	432	98	20	1	18	4.2	41	64	39	73	0	5	1	1178	78	9	97	9.7	.993	1B-125
1964	157	.264	.450	591	156	29	6	23	3.9	67	95	36	84	1	0	0	1565	132	10	122	10.9	.994	1B-157
1965	163	.265	.453	612	162	25	3	28	4.6	79	106	55	64	3	2	1	1682	93	15	143	11.0	.992	1B-162
1966	141	.272	.432	511	139	23	7	15	2.9	52	75	29	59	0	8	4	1183	92	13	88	9.1	.990	1B-130, 3B-8
1967	151	.276	.455	573	158	26	4	23	4.0	68	95	27	93	2	5	1	1383	91	10	111	9.8	.993	1B-147
1968	150	.246	.469	552	136	27	0	32	5.8	71	83	27	67	2	4	1	1379	88	6	118	9.8	.996	1B-147
1969	155	.253	.416	565	143	19	2	23	4.1	60	106	42	101	0	2	0	1419	87	4	116	9.7	.997	1B-153
1970	72	.252	.459	222	56	6	2	12	5.4	25	44	20	33	0	9	2	528	35	4	53	7.9	.993	1B-72
1971	39	.193	.325	83	16	2	0	3	3.6	4	6	6	14	0	18	2	167	12	0	15	4.6	1.000	1B-20
19 yrs.	2528	.274	.500	9421	2583	407	90	512	5.4	1305	1636	763	1236	50	62	14	14206	4355	261	1742	7.4	.986	1B-1259, SS-1125, 3B-69, OF-23

Year	Team	Games	BA	SA	AB	H	2B	3B	HR	HR%	R	RBI	BB	SO	SB	Pinch Hit AB	Pinch Hit H	PO	A	E	DP	TC/G	FA	G by Pos

George Banks

BANKS, GEORGE EDWARD
B. Sept. 24, 1938, Pacolet Mills, S. C.   D. Mar. 1, 1985, Spartanburg, S. C.

BR TR 5'11" 185 lbs.

Year	Team	Games	BA	SA	AB	H	2B	3B	HR	HR%	R	RBI	BB	SO	SB	Pinch Hit AB	Pinch Hit H	PO	A	E	DP	TC/G	FA	G by Pos
1962	MIN A	63	.252	.408	103	26	0	2	4	3.9	22	15	21	27	0	28	5	26	11	2	1	0.6	.949	OF-17, 3B-6
1963		25	.155	.338	71	11	4	0	3	4.2	5	8	9	21	0	3	0	22	39	6	4	2.7	.910	3B-21
1964	2 teams		MIN A (1G – .000)		CLE A (9G – .294)																			
"	total	10	.278	.667	18	5	1	0	2	11.1	6	3	6	7	0	5	1	7	2	0	0	0.9	1.000	OF-3, 3B-1, 2B-1
1965	CLE A	4	.200	.400	5	1	0	0	0	0.0	0	0	1	3	0	3	0	0	2	0	1	0.5	1.000	3B-1
1966		4	.250	.250	4	1	0	0	0	0.0	0	1	0	1	0	4	1	0	0	0	0	0.0	–	
5 yrs.		106	.219	.403	201	44	6	2	9	4.5	33	27	37	59	0	43	7	55	54	8	6	1.1	.932	3B-29, OF-20, 2B-1

Bill Bankston

BANKSTON, WILBORN EVERETT
B. May 25, 1893, Barnesville, Ga.   D. Feb. 26, 1970, Griffin, Ga.

BL TR 5'11" 180 lbs.

Year	Team	Games	BA	SA	AB	H	2B	3B	HR	HR%	R	RBI	BB	SO	SB	Pinch Hit AB	Pinch Hit H	PO	A	E	DP	TC/G	FA	G by Pos
1915	PHI A	11	.139	.306	36	5	1	1	1	2.8	6	2	2	5	1	2	1	14	1	2	0	1.5	.882	OF-8

Jim Banning

BANNING, JAMES M.
B. 1866, New York, N. Y.

BL TR 5'6" 150 lbs.

Year	Team	Games	BA	SA	AB	H	2B	3B	HR	HR%	R	RBI	BB	SO	SB	Pinch Hit AB	Pinch Hit H	PO	A	E	DP	TC/G	FA	G by Pos
1888	WAS N	1	–	–	0	0	0	0	0	–	0	0	0	0	0	0	0	1	0	0	0	1.0	1.000	C-1
1889		2	.000	.000	1	0	0	0	0	0.0	0	0	0	0	0	0	0	2	2	0	0	2.0	1.000	C-2
2 yrs.		3	.000	.000	1	0	0	0	0	0.0	0	0	0	0	0	0	0	3	2	0	0	1.7	1.000	C-3

Alan Bannister

BANNISTER, ALAN
B. Sept. 3, 1951, Montebello, Calif.

BR TR 5'11" 170 lbs.

Year	Team	Games	BA	SA	AB	H	2B	3B	HR	HR%	R	RBI	BB	SO	SB	Pinch Hit AB	Pinch Hit H	PO	A	E	DP	TC/G	FA	G by Pos
1974	PHI N	26	.120	.120	25	3	0	0	0	0.0	4	1	3	7	0	7	0	10	0	0	0	0.4	1.000	OF-8, SS-2
1975		24	.262	.344	61	16	3	1	0	0.0	10	0	1	9	2	1	0	54	4	2	0	2.5	.967	OF-18, SS-1, 2B-1
1976	CHI A	73	.248	.317	145	36	6	2	0	0.0	19	8	14	21	12	2	0	92	36	5	7	1.8	.962	OF-43, SS-14, DH-4, 2B-4, 3B-1
1977		139	.275	.338	560	154	20	3	3	0.5	87	57	54	49	4	1	0	265	331	40	52	4.6	.937	SS-133, OF-3, 2B-3
1978		49	.224	.290	107	24	3	2	0	0.0	16	8	11	12	3	10	0	34	16	2	3	1.1	.962	DH-19, OF-15, SS-8, 2B-2
1979		136	.285	.383	506	144	28	8	2	0.4	71	55	43	40	22	0	0	250	187	21	37	3.4	.954	2B-65, OF-47, 3B-12, DH-9, 1B-1
1980	2 teams		CHI A (45G – .192)		CLE A (81G – .328)																			
"	total	126	.283	.370	392	111	23	4	1	0.3	57	41	40	41	14	12	0	189	153	14	27	2.8	.961	OF-63, 2B-41, 3B-20, SS-2
1981	CLE A	68	.263	.332	232	61	11	1	1	0.4	36	17	16	19	16	11	4	129	76	3	14	3.1	.986	OF-35, 3B-30, 1B-2, SS-1
1982		101	.267	.353	348	93	16	1	4	1.1	40	41	42	41	18	6	1	207	124	10	22	3.4	.971	OF-55, 2B-48, SS-2, DH-1, 3B-1
1983		117	.265	.393	377	100	25	4	5	1.3	51	41	31	43	5	10	5	186	66	7	14	2.2	.973	OF-91, 3B-27, DH-3, 1B-3
1984	2 teams		HOU N (9G – .200)		TEX A (47G – .300)																			
"	total	56	.285	.377	130	37	4	1	2	1.5	22	9	23	19	2	17	4	71	38	5	5	2.0	.956	2B-25, DH-9, OF-4, SS-4, 3B-1, 1B-1
1985	TEX A	57	.262	.336	122	32	4	1	1	0.8	17	6	14	17	8	14	6	46	18	1	4	1.1	.985	DH-21, OF-14, 2B-10, 3B-5, 1B-4
12 yrs.		972	.270	.355	3005	811	143	28	19	0.6	430	288	292	318	107	91	20	1533	1049	110	185	2.8	.959	OF-396, 2B-256, SS-167, DH-66, 3B-40, 1B-11

Jimmy Bannon

BANNON, JAMES HENRY (Foxy Grandpa)
Brother of Tom Bannon.
B. May 5, 1871, Amesbury, Mass.   D. Mar. 24, 1948, Glen Rock, N. J.

BR TR 5'5" 160 lbs.

Year	Team	Games	BA	SA	AB	H	2B	3B	HR	HR%	R	RBI	BB	SO	SB	Pinch Hit AB	Pinch Hit H	PO	A	E	DP	TC/G	FA	G by Pos
1893	STL N	26	.336	.439	107	36	3	4	1	0.0	9	15	4	5	8	0	0	31	10	15	2	2.2	.732	OF-24, SS-2, P-1
1894	BOS N	128	.336	.514	494	166	29	10	13	2.6	130	114	62	42	47	0	0	241	43	41	12	2.5	.874	OF-128, P-1
1895		123	.350	.479	489	171	35	5	6	1.2	101	74	54	31	28	1	0	209	31	33	3	2.2	.879	OF-122, P-1
1896		89	.251	.306	343	86	9	5	0	0.0	52	50	32	23	16	1	0	164	57	29	7	2.8	.884	OF-76, 2B-6, SS-5, 3B-3
4 yrs.		366	.320	.447	1433	459	76	24	19	1.3	292	253	152	101	99	2	0	645	141	118	24	2.5	.869	OF-350, SS-7, 2B-6, 3B-3, P-3

Tom Bannon

BANNON, THOMAS EDWARD (Uncle Tom)
Brother of Jimmy Bannon.
B. May 8, 1869, Amesbury, Mass.   D. Jan. 26, 1950, Lynn, Mass.

BR TR 5'8" 175 lbs.

Year	Team	Games	BA	SA	AB	H	2B	3B	HR	HR%	R	RBI	BB	SO	SB	Pinch Hit AB	Pinch Hit H	PO	A	E	DP	TC/G	FA	G by Pos
1895	NY N	37	.270	.333	159	43	6	2	0	0.0	33	8	7	8	20	0	0	198	18	19	16	6.4	.919	OF-21, 1B-16
1896		2	.143	.286	7	1	1	0	0	0.0	1	0	1	1	0	0	0	1	0	1	0	1.0	.500	OF-2
2 yrs.		39	.265	.331	166	44	7	2	0	0.0	34	8	8	9	20	0	0	199	18	20	16	6.1	.916	OF-23, 1B-16

Walter Barbare

BARBARE, WALTER LAWRENCE (Dinty)
B. Aug. 11, 1891, Greenville, S. C.   D. Oct. 28, 1965, Greenville, S. C.

BR TR 6' 162 lbs.

Year	Team	Games	BA	SA	AB	H	2B	3B	HR	HR%	R	RBI	BB	SO	SB	Pinch Hit AB	Pinch Hit H	PO	A	E	DP	TC/G	FA	G by Pos
1914	CLE A	15	.308	.423	52	16	2	2	0	0.0	6	5	2	5	1	0	0	13	31	4	4	3.2	.917	3B-14, SS-1
1915		77	.191	.211	246	47	3	1	0	0.0	15	11	10	27	6	5	1	101	141	10	12	3.3	.960	3B-68, 1B-1
1916		13	.229	.250	48	11	1	0	0	0.0	3	3	4	9	1	0	1	12	30	1	2	3.3	.977	3B-12
1918	BOS A	13	.172	.276	29	5	3	0	0	0.0	6	5	0	3	1	1	0	6	14	4	1	1.8	.833	3B-11, SS-1
1919	PIT N	85	.273	.355	293	80	11	5	1	0.3	34	34	18	18	11	3	1	111	137	10	11	3.0	.961	3B-80, 1B-1
1920		57	.274	.323	186	51	5	2	0	0.0	9	12	9	11	5	7	2	79	161	13	21	4.4	.949	SS-34, 2B-12, 3B-5
1921	BOS N	134	.302	.367	550	166	22	7	0	0.0	66	49	24	28	11	2	0	311	421	32	63	5.7	.958	SS-121, 2B-8, 3B-2
1922		106	.231	.265	373	86	5	4	0	0.0	38	40	21	22	3	11	3	241	238	14	44	4.7	.972	2B-45, 3B-38, 1B-14
8 yrs.		500	.260	.315	1777	462	52	21	1	0.1	173	156	88	121	37	30	9	874	1173	88	158	4.3	.959	3B-230, SS-157, 2B-66, 1B-15

Red Barbary

BARBARY, DONALD ODELL
B. June 20, 1920, Simpsonville, S. C.

BR TR 6'3" 190 lbs.

Year	Team	Games	BA	SA	AB	H	2B	3B	HR	HR%	R	RBI	BB	SO	SB	Pinch Hit AB	Pinch Hit H	PO	A	E	DP	TC/G	FA	G by Pos
1943	WAS A	1	.000	.000	1	0	0	0	0	0.0	0	0	0	0	0	1	0	0	0	0	0	0.0	–	

Jap Barbeau

BARBEAU, WILLIAM JOSEPH
B. June 10, 1882, New York, N. Y.   D. Sept. 10, 1969, Milwaukee, Wis.

BR TR 5'5" 140 lbs.

Year	Team	Games	BA	SA	AB	H	2B	3B	HR	HR%	R	RBI	BB	SO	SB	Pinch Hit AB	Pinch Hit H	PO	A	E	DP	TC/G	FA	G by Pos
1905	CLE A	11	.270	.351	37	10	1	1	0	0.0	1	1	1	0	1	0	0	24	33	6	6	5.7	.905	2B-11
1906		42	.194	.279	129	25	5	3	0	0.0	8	12	9		5	3	0	41	68	21	5	3.1	.838	3B-32, SS-6

Year	Team		Games	BA	SA	AB	H	2B	3B	HR	HR%	R	RBI	BB	SO	SB	Pinch Hit AB	Pinch Hit H	PO	A	E	DP	TC/G	FA	G by Pos

Jap Barbeau *continued*

Year	Team		Games	BA	SA	AB	H	2B	3B	HR	HR%	R	RBI	BB	SO	SB	PH AB	PH H	PO	A	E	DP	TC/G	FA	G by Pos
1909	2 teams	PIT N	(91G – .220)			STL	N	(47G – .251)																	
"	total		138	.230	.278	525	121	19	3	0	0.0	83	30	65		33	7	0	155	211	43	15	3.0	.895	3B-131
1910	STL	N	7	.190	.286	21	4	0	1	0	0.0	4	2	3	3	0	0	0	6	19	2	1	3.9	.926	3B-6, 2B-1
4 yrs.			198	.225	.282	712	160	25	8	0	0.0	96	46	78	3	39	10	0	226	331	72	27	3.2	.886	3B-169, 2B-12, SS-6

Dave Barbee

BARBEE, DAVID MONROE   BR TR 5'11½" 178 lbs.
B. May 7, 1905, Greensboro, N. C.   D. July 1, 1968, Albemarle, N. C.

Year	Team		Games	BA	SA	AB	H	2B	3B	HR	HR%	R	RBI	BB	SO	SB	PH AB	PH H	PO	A	E	DP	TC/G	FA	G by Pos
1926	PHI	A	19	.170	.298	47	8	1	1	1	2.1	7	5	2	4	0	8	0	18	1	0	0	1.0	1.000	OF-10
1932	PIT	N	97	.257	.407	327	84	22	6	5	1.5	37	55	18	38	1	19	8	190	5	5	2	2.1	.975	OF-78
2 yrs.			116	.246	.393	374	92	23	7	6	1.6	44	60	20	42	1	27	8	208	6	5	2	1.9	.977	OF-88

Charlie Barber

BARBER, CHARLES D.   BR TR
B. 1854, Philadelphia, Pa.   D. Nov. 23, 1910, Philadelphia, Pa.

Year	Team		Games	BA	SA	AB	H	2B	3B	HR	HR%	R	RBI	BB	SO	SB	PH AB	PH H	PO	A	E	DP	TC/G	FA	G by Pos
1884	CIN	U	55	.201	.245	204	41	1	4	0	0.0	38		11			0	0	68	112	35	4	3.9	.837	3B-55

Turner Barber

BARBER, TYRUS TURNER   BL TR 5'11" 170 lbs.
B. July 9, 1893, Lavinia, Tenn.   D. Oct. 20, 1968, Milan, Tenn.

Year	Team		Games	BA	SA	AB	H	2B	3B	HR	HR%	R	RBI	BB	SO	SB	PH AB	PH H	PO	A	E	DP	TC/G	FA	G by Pos
1915	WAS	A	20	.302	.358	53	16	1	1	0	0.0	9	6	6	7	0	1	0	17	3	1	1	1.1	.952	OF-19
1916			15	.212	.364	33	7	0	1	1	3.0	3	5	2	3	0	3	1	10	0	2	0	0.8	.833	OF-9
1917	CHI	N	7	.214	.250	28	6	1	0	0	0.0	2	2	2	8	1	0	0	13	2	0	0	2.1	1.000	OF-7
1918			55	.236	.293	123	29	3	2	0	0.0	11	10	9	16	3	20	4	82	5	4	3	1.7	.956	OF-27, 1B-4
1919			76	.313	.387	230	72	9	4	0	0.0	26	21	14	17	7	6	1	123	7	7	1	1.8	.949	OF-68
1920			94	.265	.324	340	90	10	5	0	0.0	27	50	9	26	5	5	2	767	32	10	40	8.6	.988	1B-69, OF-17, 2B-2
1921			127	.314	.369	452	142	14	4	1	0.2	73	54	41	24	5	2	1	234	23	8	4	2.1	.970	OF-123
1922			84	.310	.376	226	70	7	4	0	0.0	35	29	30	9	7	19	2	242	8	4	12	3.0	.984	OF-47, 1B-16
1923	BKN	N	13	.217	.261	46	10	2	0	0	0.0	3	8	2	2	0	1	1	20	1	0	1	1.6	1.000	OF-12
9 yrs.			491	.289	.351	1531	442	47	21	2	0.1	189	185	115	112	28	57	12	1508	81	36	62	3.3	.978	OF-329, 1B-89, 2B-2

WORLD SERIES

Year	Team		Games	BA	SA	AB	H	2B	3B	HR	HR%	R	RBI	BB	SO	SB	PH AB	PH H	PO	A	E	DP	TC/G	FA	G by Pos
1918	CHI	N	3	.000	.000	2	0	0	0	0	0.0	0	0	0	0	0	2	0	0	0	0	0	0.0	–	

Jim Barbieri

BARBIERI, JAMES PATRICK   BL TR 5'7" 155 lbs.
B. Sept. 15, 1941, Schenectady, N. Y.

Year	Team		Games	BA	SA	AB	H	2B	3B	HR	HR%	R	RBI	BB	SO	SB	PH AB	PH H	PO	A	E	DP	TC/G	FA	G by Pos
1966	LA	N	39	.280	.341	82	23	6	0	0	0.0	9	3	9	7	2	17	4	29	2	2	1	0.8	.939	OF-20

WORLD SERIES

Year	Team		Games	BA	SA	AB	H	2B	3B	HR	HR%	R	RBI	BB	SO	SB	PH AB	PH H	PO	A	E	DP	TC/G	FA	G by Pos
1966	LA	N	1	.000	.000	1	0	0	0	0	0.0	0	0	0	1	0	1	0	0	0	0	0	0.0	–	

George Barclay

BARCLAY, GEORGE OLIVER (Deerfoot)   TR 5'10" 162 lbs.
B. May 16, 1876, Millville, Pa.   D. Apr. 3, 1909, Philadelphia, Pa.

Year	Team		Games	BA	SA	AB	H	2B	3B	HR	HR%	R	RBI	BB	SO	SB	PH AB	PH H	PO	A	E	DP	TC/G	FA	G by Pos
1902	STL	N	137	.300	.350	543	163	14	2	3	0.6	79	53	31		30	0	0	247	16	28	3	2.1	.904	OF-137
1903			108	.248	.310	419	104	10	8	0	0.0	37	42	15		12	0	0	187	13	22	0	2.1	.901	OF-107
1904	2 teams	STL	N	(103G – .200)			BOS	N	(24G – .226)																
"	total		127	.205	.254	468	96	10	5	1	0.2	46	38	14		17	0	0	197	9	12	3	1.7	.945	OF-127
1905	BOS	N	29	.176	.185	108	19	1	0	0	0.0	5	7	2		2	1	0	39	2	7	1	1.7	.854	OF-28
4 yrs.			401	.248	.298	1538	382	35	15	4	0.3	167	140	62		61	1	0	670	40	69	7	1.9	.911	OF-399

Jesse Barfield

BARFIELD, JESSE LEE   BR TR 6'1" 200 lbs.
B. Oct. 29, 1959, Joliet, Ill.

Year	Team		Games	BA	SA	AB	H	2B	3B	HR	HR%	R	RBI	BB	SO	SB	PH AB	PH H	PO	A	E	DP	TC/G	FA	G by Pos
1981	TOR	A	25	.232	.368	95	22	3	2	2	2.1	7	9	4	19	4	0	0	71	2	0	1	2.9	1.000	OF-25
1982			139	.246	.426	394	97	13	2	18	4.6	54	58	42	79	1	21	6	217	15	9	4	1.7	.963	OF-137, DH-1
1983			128	.253	.510	388	98	13	3	27	7.0	58	68	22	110	2	16	6	213	16	8	4	1.9	.966	OF-120, DH-5
1984			110	.284	.466	320	91	14	1	14	4.4	51	49	35	81	8	20	8	190	9	10	5	1.9	.952	OF-88, DH-9
1985			155	.289	.536	539	156	34	9	27	5.0	94	84	66	143	22	1	0	349	22	4	8	2.4	.989	OF-154
1986			158	.289	.559	589	170	35	2	**40**	6.8	107	108	69	146	8	1	0	368	20	3	6	2.5	.992	OF-157
1987			159	.263	.458	590	155	25	3	28	4.7	89	84	58	141	3	4	1	341	17	3	4	2.3	.992	OF-158
1988			137	.244	.425	468	114	21	5	18	3.8	62	56	41	108	7	4	1	325	12	4	4	2.5	.988	OF-136, DH-1
1989	2 teams	TOR	A	(21G – .200)			NY	A	(129G – .240)																
"	total		150	.234	.415	521	122	23	1	23	4.4	79	67	87	150	5	2	0	340	20	10	4	2.5	.973	OF-150
9 yrs.			1161	.263	.475	3904	1025	181	28	197	5.0	601	583	424	977	60	69	22	2414	133	51	42	2.2	.980	OF-1125, DH-16

LEAGUE CHAMPIONSHIP SERIES

Year	Team		Games	BA	SA	AB	H	2B	3B	HR	HR%	R	RBI	BB	SO	SB	PH AB	PH H	PO	A	E	DP	TC/G	FA	G by Pos
1985	TOR	A	7	.280	.440	25	7	1	0	1	4.0	3	4	3	7	1	0	0	21	0	1	0	3.1	.955	OF-7

Cy Barger

BARGER, EROS BOLIVAR   BL TR 6' 160 lbs.
B. May 18, 1885, Jamestown, Ky.   D. Sept. 23, 1964, Columbia, Ky.

Year	Team		Games	BA	SA	AB	H	2B	3B	HR	HR%	R	RBI	BB	SO	SB	PH AB	PH H	PO	A	E	DP	TC/G	FA	G by Pos
1906	NY	A	2	.333	.333	3	1	0	0	0	0.0	0	0	0		0	0	0	0	1	0	0	0.5	1.000	P-2
1907			1	.000	.000	2	0	0	0	0	0.0	0	0	0		0	0	0	0	1	0	0	1.0	–	P-1
1910	BKN	N	35	.231	.298	104	24	3	2	0	0.0	7	7	5	14	0	6	3	9	87	1	2	2.8	.990	P-35
1911			57	.228	.248	145	33	1	1	0	0.0	16	9	5	20	2	10	2	34	68	5	2	1.9	.953	P-30, OF-11, 1B-1
1912			17	.189	.216	37	7	1	0	0	0.0	3	3	3	7	1	1	0	2	29	2	0	1.9	.939	P-16
1914	PIT	F	38	.205	.265	83	17	1	2	0	0.0	4	9	2			0	0	9	61	2	0	1.9	.972	P-33, SS-1
1915			36	.278	.315	54	15	2	0	0	0.0	3	3	1			0	0	4	42	0	1	1.3	1.000	P-34
7 yrs.			186	.227	.269	428	97	8	5	0	0.0	33	31	16	41	3	17	5	58	288	11	5	1.9	.969	P-151, OF-11, SS-1, 1B-1

Ray Barker

BARKER, RAYMOND HERRELL (Buddy)   BL TR 6' 192 lbs.
B. Mar. 12, 1936, Martinsburg, W. Va.

Year	Team		Games	BA	SA	AB	H	2B	3B	HR	HR%	R	RBI	BB	SO	SB	PH AB	PH H	PO	A	E	DP	TC/G	FA	G by Pos
1960	BAL	A	5	.000	.000	6	0	0	0	0	0.0	0	0	0	3	0	5	0	0	0	0	0	0.0	–	OF-1

Year	Team	Games	BA	SA	AB	H	2B	3B	HR	HR%	R	RBI	BB	SO	SB	Pinch Hit AB	Pinch Hit H	PO	A	E	DP	TC/G	FA	G by Pos

Ray Barker *continued*

1965	2 teams	CLE A	(11G – .000)		NY	A	(98G – .254)																	
"	total	109	.246	.398	211	52	11	0	7	3.3	21	31	22	48	1	44	11	400	49	4	41	4.2	.991	1B-64, 3B-3
1966	NY	A	61	.187	.373	75	14	5	0	3	4.0	11	13	4	20	0	11	0	196	25	3	11	3.7	.987	1B-47
1967		17	.077	.077	26	2	0	0	0	0.0	2	0	3	5	0	4	0	66	8	3	5	4.5	.961	1B-13
4 yrs.		192	.214	.358	318	68	16	0	10	3.1	34	44	29	76	1	64	11	662	82	10	57	3.9	.987	1B-124, 3B-3, OF-1

Red Barkley

BARKLEY, JOHN DUNCAN
B. Sept. 19, 1913, Childress, Tex.   BR TR 5'11" 160 lbs.

1937	STL	A	31	.267	.327	101	27	6	0	0	0.0	9	14	14	17	1	0	0	75	81	5	20	5.2	.969	2B-31
1939	BOS	N	12	.000	.000	11	0	0	0	0	0.0	1	0	1	2	0	1	0	4	18	3	2	2.1	.880	SS-7, 3B-4
1943	BKN	N	20	.314	.373	51	16	3	0	0	0.0	6	7	4	7	1	0	0	22	37	7	9	3.3	.894	SS-18
3 yrs.		63	.264	.319	163	43	9	0	0	0.0	16	21	19	26	2	1	0	101	136	15	31	4.0	.940	2B-31, SS-25, 3B-4

Sam Barkley

BARKLEY, SAMUEL E
B. May 24, 1858, Wheeling, W. Va.   D. Apr. 20, 1912, Wheeling, W. Va.   TR 5'11½"
Manager 1888.

1884	TOL	AA	104	.306	.444	435	133	39	9	1	0.2	71		22			0	0	326	358	53	46	7.1	.928	2B-103, C-2
1885	STL	AA	106	.268	.373	418	112	18	10	2	0.5	67		25			0	0	411	331	55	46	7.5	.931	2B-96, 1B-11
1886	PIT	AA	122	.266	.366	478	127	32	8	0	0.0	77		58			0	0	391	329	47	53	6.3	.939	2B-112, OF-8, 1B-2
1887	PIT	N	89	.224	.285	340	76	10	4	1	0.3	44	35	30	24	6	0	0	664	129	37	38	9.3	.955	1B-53, 2B-36
1888	KC	AA	116	.216	.303	482	104	21	6	3	0.6	67	51	26		15	0	0	341	314	43	44	6.0	.938	2B-116
1889			45	.284	.341	176	50	6	2	0	0.0	36	23	15	20	8	0	0	116	104	17	21	5.3	.928	2B-41, 1B-4
6 yrs.		582	.258	.355	2329	602	126	39	7	0.3	362	109	176	44	29	0	0	2249	1565	252	248	7.0	.938	2B-504, 1B-70, OF-8, C-2

Bruce Barmes

BARMES, BRUCE RAYMOND (Squeaky)
B. Oct. 23, 1929, Vincennes, Ind.   BL TR 5'8" 165 lbs.

| 1953 | WAS | A | 5 | .200 | .200 | 5 | 1 | 0 | 0 | 0 | 0.0 | 1 | 0 | 0 | 0 | 0 | 4 | 1 | 2 | 0 | 0 | 0 | 0.4 | 1.000 | OF-1 |

Babe Barna

BARNA, HERBERT PAUL
B. Mar. 2, 1915, Clarksburg, W. Va.   D. May 18, 1972, Charleston, W. Va.   BL TR 6'2" 210 lbs.

1937	PHI	A	14	.389	.611	36	14	2	0	2	5.6	10	9	2	6	1	3	1	17	2	2	3	1.5	.905	OF-9, 1B-1
1938		9	.133	.133	30	4	0	0	0	0.0	4	2	3	5	0	2	0	10	1	1	0	1.3	.917	OF-7
1941	NY	N	10	.214	.357	42	9	3	0	1	2.4	5	5	2	6	0	0	0	16	2	0	1	1.8	1.000	OF-10
1942		104	.257	.378	331	85	8	7	6	1.8	39	58	38	48	3	13	5	169	4	3	0	1.7	.983	OF-89
1943	2 teams	NY	N	(40G – .204)		BOS	A	(30G – .170)																	
"	total	70	.187	.284	225	42	9	2	3	1.3	30	22	31	33	5	9	2	102	5	4	1	1.6	.964	OF-60
5 yrs.		207	.232	.346	664	154	22	9	12	1.8	88	96	76	98	9	27	8	314	14	10	5	1.6	.970	OF-175, 1B-1

Bill Barnes

BARNES, WILLIAM H.
B. Indianapolis, Ind.   Deceased.

| 1884 | STP | U | 8 | .200 | .233 | 30 | 6 | 1 | 0 | 0 | 0.0 | 2 | | 0 | | | 0 | 0 | 8 | 0 | 3 | 1 | 1.4 | .727 | OF-8 |

Eppie Barnes

BARNES, EVERETT DUANE
B. Dec. 1, 1900, Ossining, N. Y.   D. Nov. 17, 1980, Mineola, N. Y.   BL TL 5'9" 175 lbs.

1923	PIT	N	2	.500	.500	2	1	0	0	0	0.0	0	0	0	0	0	0	0	2	1	0	1	1.5	1.000	1B-1
1924		2	.000	.000	5	0	0	0	0	0.0	0	0	0	1	0	1	0	8	1	0	0	4.5	1.000	1B-1
2 yrs.		4	.143	.143	7	1	0	0	0	0.0	0	0	0	1	0	1	0	10	2	0	1	3.0	1.000	1B-2

Honey Barnes

BARNES, JOHN FRANCIS
B. Jan. 29, 1900, Fulton, N. Y.   D. June 18, 1981, Lockport, N. Y.   BL TR 5'10" 175 lbs.

| 1926 | NY | A | 1 | – | – | 0 | 0 | 0 | 0 | 0 | – | 0 | 0 | 1 | 0 | 0 | 0 | 0 | 0 | 0 | 0 | 0 | 0.0 | – | C-1 |

Lute Barnes

BARNES, LUTHER OWENS
B. Apr. 28, 1947, Forest City, Iowa   BR TR 5'10" 160 lbs.

1972	NY	N	24	.236	.319	72	17	2	2	0	0.0	5	6	6	4	0	3	0	40	50	3	13	3.9	.968	2B-14, SS-6
1973		3	.500	.500	2	1	0	0	0	0.0	2	1	0	1	0	2	1	0	0	0	0	0.0	–	
2 yrs.		27	.243	.324	74	18	2	2	0	0.0	7	7	6	5	0	5	1	40	50	3	13	3.4	.968	2B-14, SS-6

Red Barnes

BARNES, EMILE DEERING
B. Dec. 25, 1903, Suggsville, Ala.   D. July 3, 1959, Mobile, Ala.   BL TR 5'10½" 158 lbs.

1927	WAS	A	3	.364	.455	11	4	0	0	0	0.0	5	0	1	0	0	0	0	3	1	0	1	1.3	1.000	OF-3
1928		114	.302	.470	417	126	22	15	6	1.4	82	51	55	38	7	7	2	255	16	6	2	2.4	.978	OF-104
1929		72	.200	.292	130	26	5	2	1	0.8	16	15	13	12	1	36	8	48	2	7	0	0.8	.877	OF-30
1930	2 teams	WAS	A	(12G – .167)		CHI	A	(85G – .248)																	
"	total	97	.245	.353	278	68	13	7	1	0.4	49	31	26	23	4	22	3	179	6	12	3	2.0	.939	OF-72
4 yrs.		286	.268	.403	836	224	41	24	8	1.0	152	97	95	76	12	65	13	485	25	25	6	1.9	.953	OF-209

Ross Barnes

BARNES, ROSCOE CHARLES
B. May 8, 1850, Mount Morris, N. Y.   D. Feb. 5, 1915, Chicago, Ill.   BR TR 5'8½" 145 lbs.

1876	CHI	N	66	.429	.590	322	138	21	14	1	0.3	126	59	20	8		0	0	167	199	36	22	6.1	.910	2B-66, P-1
1877		22	.272	.283	92	25	1	0	0	0.0	16	5	7	4		0	0	49	70	23	5	6.5	.838	2B-22
1879	CIN	N	77	.266	.316	323	86	9	2	1	0.3	55	30	16	25		0	0	137	261	71	19	6.1	.849	SS-61, 2B-16
1881	BOS	N	69	.271	.325	295	80	14	1	0	0.0	42	17	16	16		0	0	110	235	59	20	5.9	.854	SS-63, 2B-7
4 yrs.		234	.319	.401	1032	329	45	17	2	0.2	239	111	59	53		0	0	463	765	189	66	6.1	.867	SS-124, 2B-111, P-1

Sam Barnes

BARNES, SAMUEL THOMAS
B. Dec. 18, 1899, Suggsville, Ala.   D. Feb. 19, 1981, Montgomery, Ala.   BL TR 5'8" 150 lbs.

| 1921 | DET | A | 7 | .182 | .273 | 11 | 2 | 1 | 0 | 0 | 0.0 | 2 | 0 | 2 | 1 | 0 | 2 | 0 | 6 | 11 | 1 | 0 | 2.6 | .944 | 2B-2 |

Year	Team		Games	BA	SA	AB	H	2B	3B	HR	HR%	R	RBI	BB	SO	SB	Pinch Hit AB	Pinch Hit H	PO	A	E	DP	TC/G	FA	G by Pos

Skeeter Barnes
BARNES, WILLIAM HENRY BR TR 5'11" 170 lbs.
B. Mar. 3, 1957, Cincinnati, Ohio

Year	Team		Games	BA	SA	AB	H	2B	3B	HR	HR%	R	RBI	BB	SO	SB	AB	H	PO	A	E	DP	TC/G	FA	G by Pos
1983	CIN	N	15	.206	.294	34	7	0	0	1	2.9	5	4	7	3	2	2	0	45	11	1	7	3.8	.982	3B-7, 1B-7
1984			32	.119	.190	42	5	0	0	1	2.4	5	3	4	6	0	16	1	7	15	0	1	0.7	1.000	3B-11, OF-3
1985	MON	N	19	.154	.192	26	4	1	0	0	0.0	0	0	0	2	0	10	1	13	6	0	1	1.0	1.000	3B-4, OF-3, 1B-1
1987	STL	N	4	.250	1.000	4	1	0	0	1	25.0	1	3	0	0	0	3	0	0	0	0	0	0.0	—	3B-1
1989	CIN	N	5	.000	.000	3	0	0	0	0	0.0	1	0	0	0	0	3	0	0	0	0	0	0.0	—	
5 yrs.			75	.156	.248	109	17	1	0	3	2.8	12	10	11	11	2	34	2	65	32	1	8	1.3	.990	3B-23, 1B-8, OF-6

Ed Barney
BARNEY, EDMUND J. BL TR 5'10½" 178 lbs.
B. Jan. 23, 1890, Amery, Wis. D. Oct. 4, 1967, Rice Lake, Wis.

Year	Team		Games	BA	SA	AB	H	2B	3B	HR	HR%	R	RBI	BB	SO	SB	AB	H	PO	A	E	DP	TC/G	FA	G by Pos
1915	2 teams	NY A (11G – .194)							PIT N		(32G – .273)														
"	total		43	.252	.289	135	34	1	2	0	0.0	17	13	14	18	9	6	2	88	3	2	2	2.2	.978	OF-36
1916	PIT	N	45	.197	.226	137	27	4	0	0	0.0	16	9	23	15	8	4	1	103	5	4	3	2.5	.964	OF-40
2 yrs.			88	.224	.257	272	61	5	2	0	0.0	33	22	37	33	17	10	3	191	8	6	5	2.3	.971	OF-76

Clyde Barnhart
BARNHART, CLYDE LEE (Pooch) BR TR 5'10" 155 lbs.
Father of Vic Barnhart.
B. Dec. 29, 1895, Buck Valley, Pa. D. Jan. 21, 1980, Hagerstown, Md.

Year	Team		Games	BA	SA	AB	H	2B	3B	HR	HR%	R	RBI	BB	SO	SB	AB	H	PO	A	E	DP	TC/G	FA	G by Pos
1920	PIT	N	12	.326	.500	46	15	4	2	0	0.0	5	5	1	2	1	0	0	10	23	1	3	2.8	.971	3B-12
1921			124	.258	.370	449	116	15	13	3	0.7	66	62	32	36	3	6	1	101	204	14	19	2.6	.956	3B-118
1922			75	.330	.426	209	69	7	5	1	0.5	30	38	25	7	3	16	4	76	34	8	4	1.6	.932	3B-30, OF-26
1923			114	.324	.563	327	106	25	13	9	2.8	60	72	47	21	5	17	4	179	14	3	1	1.7	.985	OF-92
1924			102	.276	.384	344	95	6	11	3	0.9	49	51	30	17	8	12	2	186	8	6	3	2.0	.970	OF-88
1925			142	.325	.447	539	175	32	11	4	0.7	85	114	59	25	9	3	1	295	11	12	2	2.2	.962	OF-138
1926			76	.192	.207	203	39	3	0	0	0.0	26	10	23	13	1	15	2	101	5	1	1	1.4	.991	OF-61
1927			108	.319	.442	360	115	25	5	3	0.8	66	54	37	19	2	11	1	222	5	5	2	2.1	.978	OF-94
1928			61	.296	.408	196	58	6	2	4	2.0	18	30	11	9	3	10	2	96	3	3	0	1.7	.971	OF-48, 3B-1
9 yrs.			814	.295	.418	2673	788	123	62	27	1.0	405	436	265	149	35	90	17	1266	307	53	35	2.0	.967	OF-547, 3B-161

WORLD SERIES

Year	Team		Games	BA	SA	AB	H	2B	3B	HR	HR%	R	RBI	BB	SO	SB	AB	H	PO	A	E	DP	TC/G	FA	G by Pos
1925	PIT	N	7	.250	.286	28	7	1	0	0	0.0	1	5	3	5	1	0	0	12	1	0	0	1.9	1.000	OF-7
1927			4	.313	.375	16	5	1	0	0	0.0	0	4	0	0	0	0	0	6	1	0	0	1.8	1.000	OF-4
2 yrs.			11	.273	.318	44	12	2	0	0	0.0	1	9	3	5	1	0	0	18	2	0	0	1.8	1.000	OF-11

Vic Barnhart
BARNHART, VICTOR DEE BR TR 6' 188 lbs.
Son of Clyde Barnhart.
B. Sept. 1, 1922, Hagerstown, Md.

Year	Team		Games	BA	SA	AB	H	2B	3B	HR	HR%	R	RBI	BB	SO	SB	AB	H	PO	A	E	DP	TC/G	FA	G by Pos
1944	PIT	N	1	.500	.500	2	1	0	0	0	0.0	0	0	1	1	0	0	0	2	6	1	0	9.0	.889	SS-1
1945			71	.269	.303	201	54	7	0	0	0.0	21	19	9	11	2	2	2	108	174	22	32	4.3	.928	SS-60, 3B-4
1946			2	.000	.000	1	0	0	0	0	0.0	0	0	0	0	0	1	0	0	0	0	0	0.0	—	
3 yrs.			74	.270	.304	204	55	7	0	0	0.0	21	19	10	12	2	3	2	110	180	23	32	4.2	.927	SS-61, 3B-4

Billy Barnie
BARNIE, WILLIAM HARRISON (Bald Billy) 5'7" 157 lbs.
B. Jan. 26, 1853, New York, N. Y. D. July 15, 1900, Hartford, Conn.
Manager 1883-94, 1897-98.

Year	Team		Games	BA	SA	AB	H	2B	3B	HR	HR%	R	RBI	BB	SO	SB	AB	H	PO	A	E	DP	TC/G	FA	G by Pos
1883	BAL	AA	17	.200	.200	55	11	0	0	0	0.0	7		2			0	0	71	23	18	2	6.6	.839	C-13, OF-6, SS-1
1886			2	.000	.000	6	0	0	0	0	0.0	0		1			0	0	5	2	1	0	4.0	.875	OF-1, C-1
2 yrs.			19	.180	.180	61	11	0	0	0	0.0	7		3			0	0	76	25	19	2	6.3	.842	C-14, OF-7, SS-1

Dick Barone
BARONE, RICHARD ANTHONY BR TR 5'9" 165 lbs.
B. Oct. 13, 1932, San Jose, Calif.

Year	Team		Games	BA	SA	AB	H	2B	3B	HR	HR%	R	RBI	BB	SO	SB	AB	H	PO	A	E	DP	TC/G	FA	G by Pos
1960	PIT	N	3	.000	.000	6	0	0	0	0	0.0	0	0	0	1	0	0	0	4	3	1	0	2.7	.875	SS-2

Bob Barr
BARR, ROBERT McCLELLAND BR TR 6'1" 192 lbs.
B. 1856, Washington, D. C. D. Mar. 11, 1930, Washington, D. C.

Year	Team		Games	BA	SA	AB	H	2B	3B	HR	HR%	R	RBI	BB	SO	SB	AB	H	PO	A	E	DP	TC/G	FA	G by Pos
1883	PIT	AA	37	.246	.317	142	35	4	3	0	0.0	12		5			0	0	62	43	17	2	3.3	.861	P-26, OF-14, 1B-4, 3B-1
1884	2 teams	WAS AA (39G – .148)							IND AA		(18G – .185)														
"	total		57	.160	.250	200	32	6	3	2	1.0	21		8			0	0	33	80	36	3	2.6	.758	P-48, OF-7, 1B-2
1886	WAS	N	22	.165	.190	79	13	2	0	0	0.0	6	2	4	23		0	0	6	36	9	1	2.3	.824	P-22
1890	ROC	AA	57	.179	.219	201	36	2	0	2	1.0	22		13		1	0	0	20	111	10	2	2.5	.929	P-57
1891	NY	N	5	.091	.091	11	1	0	0	0	0.0	0		2	3		0	0	1	6	1	1	1.6	.875	P-5
5 yrs.			178	.185	.245	633	117	14	6	4	0.6	61	2	32	26	1	0	0	122	276	73	9	2.6	.845	P-158, OF-21, 1B-6, 3B-1

Scotty Barr
BARR, HYDER EDWARD BR TR 6' 175 lbs.
B. Oct. 6, 1886, Bristol, Tenn. D. Dec. 2, 1934, Fort Worth, Tex.

Year	Team		Games	BA	SA	AB	H	2B	3B	HR	HR%	R	RBI	BB	SO	SB	AB	H	PO	A	E	DP	TC/G	FA	G by Pos
1908	PHI	A	19	.143	.179	56	8	2	0	0	0.0	4	1	3			1	0	28	27	5	1	3.2	.917	2B-11, 3B-4, 1B-2
1909			22	.078	.098	51	4	1	0	0	0.0	5	1	11		2	1	0	69	1	6	0	3.5	.921	OF-15, 1B-7
2 yrs.			41	.112	.140	107	12	3	0	0	0.0	9	2	14		2	1	0	97	28	11	1	3.3	.919	OF-15, 2B-11, 1B-9, 3B-4

Cuno Barragan
BARRAGAN, FACUNDO ANTHONY BR TR 5'11" 180 lbs.
B. June 20, 1932, Sacramento, Calif.

Year	Team		Games	BA	SA	AB	H	2B	3B	HR	HR%	R	RBI	BB	SO	SB	AB	H	PO	A	E	DP	TC/G	FA	G by Pos
1961	CHI	N	10	.214	.321	28	6	0	0	1	3.6	3	2	2	7	0	0	0	35	4	0	1	3.9	1.000	C-10
1962			58	.201	.261	134	27	6	0	0	0.0	11	12	21	28	0	7	0	207	27	7	2	4.2	.971	C-55
1963			1	.000	.000	1	0	0	0	0	0.0	0	0	0	1	0	0	0	1	0	0	0	1.0	1.000	C-1
3 yrs.			69	.202	.270	163	33	6	1	1	0.6	14	14	23	36	0	7	0	243	31	7	3	4.1	.975	C-66

German Barranca
BARRANCA, GERMAN BL TR 6' 160 lbs.
Born German Barranca y Costales.
B. Oct. 19, 1956, Veracruz, Mexico

Year	Team		Games	BA	SA	AB	H	2B	3B	HR	HR%	R	RBI	BB	SO	SB	AB	H	PO	A	E	DP	TC/G	FA	G by Pos
1979	KC	A	5	.600	.800	5	3	1	0	0	0.0	3	0	0	0	3	0	0	4	7	0	3	2.2	1.000	DH-1, 3B-1, 2B-1

Year	Team	Games	BA	SA	AB	H	2B	3B	HR	HR%	R	RBI	BB	SO	SB	PH AB	PH H	PO	A	E	DP	TC/G	FA	G by Pos

German Barranca *continued*

Year	Team	Games	BA	SA	AB	H	2B	3B	HR	HR%	R	RBI	BB	SO	SB	PH AB	PH H	PO	A	E	DP	TC/G	FA	G by Pos
1980		7	–	–	0	0	0	0	0	–	3	0	0	0	0	0	0	0	0	0	0	0.0	–	
1981	CIN N	9	.333	.333	6	2	0	0	0	0.0	2	1	0	0	0	6	2	0	0	0	0	0.0	–	
1982		46	.255	.392	51	13	1	3	0	0.5	11	2	2	9	2	39	9	5	9	3	1	0.4	.824	2B-6
4 yrs		67	.290	.419	62	18	2	3	0	0.0	19	3	2	9	5	45	11	9	16	3	4	0.4	.893	2B-7, DH-1, 3B-1

Bill Barrett

BARRETT, WILLIAM JOSEPH (Whispering Bill)
B. May 28, 1900, Cambridge, Mass.   D. Jan. 26, 1951, Cambridge, Mass.

BR TR 6' 175 lbs.

Year	Team	Games	BA	SA	AB	H	2B	3B	HR	HR%	R	RBI	BB	SO	SB	PH AB	PH H	PO	A	E	DP	TC/G	FA	G by Pos
1921	PHI A	14	.233	.367	30	7	2	1	0	0.0	3	3	0	5	0	0	0	13	32	3	1	3.4	.938	SS-7, P-4, 3B-2, 1B-1
1923	CHI A	42	.272	.377	162	44	7	2	2	1.2	17	23	9	24	12	1	0	91	8	6	1	2.5	.943	OF-40, 3B-1
1924		119	.271	.355	406	110	18	5	2	0.5	52	56	30	38	15	7	2	223	220	45	42	4.1	.908	SS-77, OF-27, 3B-8
1925		81	.363	.518	245	89	23	3	3	1.2	44	40	24	27	5	7	1	132	131	19	24	3.5	.933	2B-41, OF-27, SS-4, 3B-4
1926		111	.307	.462	368	113	31	4	6	1.6	46	61	25	26	9	6	3	190	9	8	3	1.9	.961	OF-102, 1B-2
1927		147	.286	.403	556	159	35	9	4	0.7	62	83	52	46	20	0	0	289	22	12	6	2.2	.963	OF-147
1928		76	.277	.379	235	65	11	2	3	1.3	34	26	14	30	8	9	2	122	62	5	7	2.5	.974	OF-37, 2B-26
1929 2 teams	CHI A (3G – .000)				BOS A (111G – .270)																			
" total		114	.270	.377	371	100	23	4	3	0.8	57	35	55	38	11	1	0	204	17	6	4	2.0	.974	OF-109, 3B-1
1930 2 teams	BOS A (6G – .167)				WAS A (6G – .000)																			
" total		12	.136	.182	22	3	1	0	0	0.0	3	1	2	5	0	5	0	6	0	0	0	0.5	1.000	OF-6
9 yrs		716	.288	.405	2395	690	151	30	23	1.0	318	328	211	239	80	36	8	1270	501	104	88	2.6	.945	OF-495, SS-88, 2B-67, 3B-16, P-4, 1B-3

Bob Barrett

BARRETT, ROBERT SCHLEY (Jumbo)
B. Jan. 27, 1899, Atlanta, Ga.   D. Jan. 18, 1982, Atlanta, Ga.

BR TR 5'11" 175 lbs.

Year	Team	Games	BA	SA	AB	H	2B	3B	HR	HR%	R	RBI	BB	SO	SB	PH AB	PH H	PO	A	E	DP	TC/G	FA	G by Pos
1923	CHI N	3	.333	.333	3	1	0	0	0	0.0	0	0	0	0	0	3	1	0	0	0	0	0.0	–	
1924		54	.241	.414	133	32	2	3	5	3.8	12	21	7	29	1	10	2	123	80	13	20	4.0	.940	2B-25, 1B-10, 3B-8
1925 2 teams	CHI N (14G – .313)				BKN N (1G – .000)																			
" total		15	.303	.333	33	10	1	0	0	0.0	1	8	1	4	1	5	1	13	9	0	3	1.5	1.000	3B-6, 2B-4
1927	BKN N	99	.259	.341	355	92	10	2	5	1.4	29	38	14	22	1	3	0	76	167	21	12	2.7	.920	3B-96
1929	BOS A	68	.270	.349	126	34	10	0	0	0.0	15	19	10	6	3	23	7	53	64	6	4	1.8	.951	3B-34, 1B-4, 2B-2, OF-1
5 yrs		239	.260	.357	650	169	23	5	10	1.5	57	86	32	61	6	44	12	265	320	40	39	2.6	.936	3B-144, 2B-31, 1B-14, OF-1

Jimmy Barrett

BARRETT, JAMES ERIGENA
B. Mar. 28, 1875, Athol, Mass.   D. Oct. 24, 1921, Detroit, Mich.

BL TR 5'9" 170 lbs.

Year	Team	Games	BA	SA	AB	H	2B	3B	HR	HR%	R	RBI	BB	SO	SB	PH AB	PH H	PO	A	E	DP	TC/G	FA	G by Pos
1899	CIN N	26	.370	.478	92	34	2	4	0	0.0	30	10	18		4	0		42	2	3	0	1.8	.936	OF-26
1900		137	.316	.389	545	172	11	7	5	0.9	114	42	72		44	0		287	25	24	6	2.5	.929	OF-137
1901	DET A	135	.293	.378	542	159	16	9	4	0.7	110	65	76		26	0		300	31	21	7	2.6	.940	OF-135
1902		136	.303	.387	509	154	19	6	4	0.8	93	44	74		24	0		326	22	14	6	2.7	.961	OF-136
1903		136	.315	.391	517	163	13	10	2	0.4	95	31	**74**		27	0		303	19	15	7	2.5	.955	OF-136
1904		162	.268	.300	624	167	10	5	0	0.0	83	31	79		15	0		339	29	11	6	2.3	.971	OF-162
1905		20	.254	.269	67	17	1	0	0	0.0	2	3	6		0	2		29	0	0	1	1.5	1.000	OF-18
1906	CIN N	5	.000	.000	12	0	0	0	0	0.0	1	0	2		0	1		3	1	0	1	0.8	1.000	OF-4
1907	BOS A	106	.244	.310	390	95	11	6	1	0.3	52	38	38		3	7		183	14	7	5	1.9	.966	OF-99
1908		2	.125	.125	8	1	0	0	0	0.0	0	1	1		0	0		2	0	0	0	1.0	1.000	OF-2
10 yrs		865	.291	.359	3306	962	83	47	16	0.5	580	255	440		143	10	3	1814	143	95	38	2.4	.954	OF-855

Johnny Barrett

BARRETT, JOHN JOSEPH
B. Dec. 18, 1915, Lowell, Mass.   D. Aug. 17, 1974, Seabrook Beach, N. H.

BL TL 5'10½" 170 lbs.

Year	Team	Games	BA	SA	AB	H	2B	3B	HR	HR%	R	RBI	BB	SO	SB	PH AB	PH H	PO	A	E	DP	TC/G	FA	G by Pos
1942	PIT N	111	.247	.316	332	82	11	6	0	0.0	56	26	48	42	10	13	4	202	11	6	4	2.0	.973	OF-94
1943		130	.231	.303	290	67	12	3	1	0.3	41	32	32	23	5	27	11	165	6	2	0	1.3	.988	OF-99
1944		149	.269	.415	568	153	24	19	7	1.2	99	83	86	56	**28**	2	1	373	12	11	4	2.7	.972	OF-147
1945		142	.256	.418	507	130	29	4	15	3.0	97	67	79	68	25	6	3	318	8	8	0	2.4	.976	OF-132
1946 2 teams	PIT N (32G – .169)				BOS N (24G – .233)																			
" total		56	.193	.246	114	22	6	0	0	0.0	10	12	20	12	1	16	4	57	2	4	1	1.1	.937	OF-38
5 yrs		588	.251	.369	1811	454	82	32	23	1.3	303	220	265	201	69	64	23	1115	39	31	9	2.0	.974	OF-510

Marty Barrett

BARRETT, MARTIN F.
B. Nov., 1860, Port Huron, Mich.   D. Jan. 29, 1910, Holyoke, Mass.

BR TR 5'9" 170 lbs.

Year	Team	Games	BA	SA	AB	H	2B	3B	HR	HR%	R	RBI	BB	SO	SB	PH AB	PH H	PO	A	E	DP	TC/G	FA	G by Pos
1884 2 teams	BOS N (3G – .000)				IND AA (5G – .077)																			
" total		8	.053	.105	19	1	1	0	0	0.0	1		1	4		0	0	23	7	6	0	4.5	.833	C-7, OF-1

Marty Barrett

BARRETT, MARTIN GLENN
Brother of Tom Barrett.
B. June 23, 1958, Arcadia, Calif.

BR TR 5'11" 175 lbs.

Year	Team	Games	BA	SA	AB	H	2B	3B	HR	HR%	R	RBI	BB	SO	SB	PH AB	PH H	PO	A	E	DP	TC/G	FA	G by Pos
1982	BOS A	8	.056	.056	18	1	0	0	0	0.0	0	0	0	1	0	0	0	11	21	0	4	4.0	1.000	2B-7
1983		33	.227	.295	44	10	1	1	0	0.0	7	2	3	1	0	0	0	32	28	1	8	1.8	.984	2B-23, DH-5
1984		139	.303	.383	475	144	23	4	3	0.6	56	45	42	25	4	1	0	245	417	9	67	4.8	.987	2B-136
1985		156	.266	.343	534	142	26	0	5	0.9	59	56	56	50	7	1	0	303	479	11	110	5.4	.987	2B-155
1986		158	.286	.381	625	179	39	4	4	0.6	94	60	65	31	15	0	0	303	450	14	101	4.9	.982	2B-158
1987		137	.293	.351	559	164	23	3	3	0.5	72	43	51	38	15	0	0	320	438	9	108	5.6	.988	2B-137
1988		150	.283	.337	612	173	28	1	1	0.2	83	65	40	35	7	1	0	312	402	7	97	4.8	.990	2B-150
1989		86	.256	.318	336	86	18	0	1	0.3	31	27	32	12	4	2	1	152	245	10	53	4.7	.975	2B-80, DH-4
8 yrs		867	.281	.352	3203	899	158	9	17	0.5	402	298	289	193	52	5	1	1730	2480	61	548	4.9	.986	2B-846, DH-9

LEAGUE CHAMPIONSHIP SERIES

Year	Team	Games	BA	SA	AB	H	2B	3B	HR	HR%	R	RBI	BB	SO	SB	PH AB	PH H	PO	A	E	DP	TC/G	FA	G by Pos
1986	BOS A	7	.367	.433	30	11	2	0	0	0.0	4	5	2	2	0	0	0	19	21	0	4	5.7	1.000	2B-7
1988		4	.067	.067	15	1	0	0	0	0.0	2	0	1	0	0	0	0	6	8	0	1	3.5	1.000	2B-4
2 yrs		11	.267	.311	45	12	2	0	0	0.0	6	5	3	2	0	0	0	25	29	0	5	4.9	1.000	2B-11

WORLD SERIES

Year	Team	Games	BA	SA	AB	H	2B	3B	HR	HR%	R	RBI	BB	SO	SB	PH AB	PH H	PO	A	E	DP	TC/G	FA	G by Pos
1986	BOS A	7	.433	.500	30	13	0	0	0	0.0	1	4	5	2	0	0	0	13	25	0	5	5.4	1.000	2B-7

Year	Team		Games	BA	SA	AB	H	2B	3B	HR	HR%	R	RBI	BB	SO	SB	Pinch Hit AB	Pinch Hit H	PO	A	E	DP	TC/G	FA	G by Pos

Tom Barrett

BARRETT, THOMAS LOREN
Brother of Marty Barrett.
B. Apr. 2, 1960, San Fernando, Calif.

BB TR 5'9" 157 lbs.

Year	Team		Games	BA	SA	AB	H	2B	3B	HR	HR%	R	RBI	BB	SO	SB	PH AB	PH H	PO	A	E	DP	TC/G	FA	G by Pos
1988	PHI	N	36	.204	.222	54	11	1	0	0	0.0	5	3	7	8	0	21	8	16	31	2	6	1.4	.959	2B-10
1989			14	.222	.222	27	6	0	0	0	0.0	3	1	1	7	0	2	0	26	18	1	9	3.2	.978	2B-9
2 yrs.			50	.210	.222	81	17	1	0	0	0.0	8	4	8	15	0	23	8	42	49	3	15	1.9	.968	

Jose Barrios

BARRIOS, JOSE MANUEL
B. June 26, 1957, New York, N. Y.

BR TR 6'4" 195 lbs.

Year	Team		Games	BA	SA	AB	H	2B	3B	HR	HR%	R	RBI	BB	SO	SB	PH AB	PH H	PO	A	E	DP	TC/G	FA	G by Pos
1982	SF	N	19	.158	.158	19	3	0	0	0	0.0	2	0	1	4	0	3	0	47	0	0	4	2.5	1.000	1B-7

Red Barron

BARRON, DAVID IRENUS
B. June 21, 1900, Clarksville, Ga. D. Oct. 4, 1982, Atlanta, Ga.

BR TR 5'11½" 185 lbs.

Year	Team		Games	BA	SA	AB	H	2B	3B	HR	HR%	R	RBI	BB	SO	SB	PH AB	PH H	PO	A	E	DP	TC/G	FA	G by Pos
1929	BOS	N	10	.190	.238	21	4	1	0	0	0.0	3	1	4	2	1	0	1	12	1	1	1	1.4	.929	OF-6

Cuke Barrows

BARROWS, ROLAND
B. Oct. 20, 1883, Gray, Me. D. Feb. 10, 1955, Gorham, Me.

BR TL 5'8" 158 lbs.

Year	Team		Games	BA	SA	AB	H	2B	3B	HR	HR%	R	RBI	BB	SO	SB	PH AB	PH H	PO	A	E	DP	TC/G	FA	G by Pos
1909	CHI	A	5	.150	.150	20	3	0	0	0	0.0	1	2	0			0	0	10	2	1	1	2.6	.923	OF-5
1910			6	.200	.200	20	4	0	0	0	0.0	0	1	3			0	0	7	0	1	0	1.3	.875	OF-6
1911			13	.196	.239	46	9	2	0	0	0.0	5	4	7			2	0	17	0	1	0	1.4	.944	OF-13
1912			8	.231	.231	13	3	0	0	0	0.0	0	2	2			1	4	1	1	0	0	0.3	1.000	OF-3
4 yrs.			32	.192	.212	99	19	2	0	0	0.0	6	9	12			3	4	35	3	3	1	1.3	.927	OF-27

Jack Barry

BARRY, JOHN JOSEPH
B. Apr. 26, 1887, Meriden, Conn. D. Apr. 23, 1961, Shrewsbury, Mass.
Manager 1917.

BR TR 5'9" 158 lbs.

Year	Team		Games	BA	SA	AB	H	2B	3B	HR	HR%	R	RBI	BB	SO	SB	PH AB	PH H	PO	A	E	DP	TC/G	FA	G by Pos
1908	PHI	A	40	.222	.296	135	30	4	3	0	0.0	13	8	10		5	3	1	54	86	10	3	3.8	.933	2B-20, SS-14, 3B-3
1909			124	.215	.259	409	88	11	2	1	0.2	56	23	44		17	0	0	196	351	43	40	4.8	.927	SS-124
1910			145	.259	.337	487	126	19	5	3	0.6	64	60	52		14	0	0	279	406	63	54	5.2	.916	SS-145
1911			127	.265	.344	442	117	18	7	1	0.2	73	63	38		30	0	0	268	384	39	49	5.4	.944	SS-127
1912			139	.261	.337	483	126	19	9	0	0.0	76	55	47		22	0	0	238	438	55	55	5.3	.925	SS-139
1913			134	.275	.365	455	125	20	6	3	0.7	62	85	44	32	15	0	0	248	403	32	60	5.1	.953	SS-134
1914			140	.242	.268	467	113	12	0	0	0.0	57	42	53	34	22	0	0	244	447	39	61	5.2	.947	SS-140
1915 2 teams	PHI	A (54G – .222)				BOS	A	(78G – .262)																	
" total			132	.244	.305	442	108	19	4	0	0.0	46	41	39	20	6	0	0	116	159	14	22	2.2	.952	2B-78, SS-54
1916	BOS	A	94	.203	.227	330	67	6	1	0	0.0	28	20	17	24	8	0	0	200	282	13	30	5.3	.974	2B-94
1917			116	.214	.253	388	83	9	0	2	0.5	45	30	47	27	12	0	0	196	339	14	40	4.7	.974	2B-116
1919			31	.241	.306	108	26	5	1	0	0.0	13	2	5	5	2	0	0	54	88	12	13	5.0	.922	2B-31
11 yrs.			1222	.243	.303	4146	1009	142	38	10	0.2	533	429	396	142	153	3	1	2093	3383	334	427	4.8	.943	SS-877, 2B-339, 3B-3

WORLD SERIES

Year	Team		Games	BA	SA	AB	H	2B	3B	HR	HR%	R	RBI	BB	SO	SB	PH AB	PH H	PO	A	E	DP	TC/G	FA	G by Pos
1910	PHI	A	5	.235	.353	17	4	2	0	0	0.0	3	3	1	3	0	0	0	8	12	0	1	4.0	1.000	SS-5
1911			6	.368	.579	19	7	4	0	0	0.0	2	2	0	1	2	0	0	9	13	3	0	4.2	.880	SS-6
1913			5	.300	.450	20	6	3	0	0	0.0	3	2	0	0	0	0	0	9	16	1	5	5.2	.962	SS-5
1914			4	.071	.071	14	1	0	0	0	0.0	1	0	1	3	0	0	0	5	21	0	2	6.5	1.000	SS-4
1915	BOS	A	5	.176	.176	17	3	0	0	0	0.0	1	1	1	2	0	0	0	10	9	1	1	4.0	.950	2B-5
5 yrs.			25	.241	.345	87	21	9	0	0	0.0	10	8	3	9	3	0	0	41	71	5	9	4.7	.957	SS-20, 2B-5

3rd

Rich Barry

BARRY, RICHARD DONOVAN
B. Sept. 12, 1940, Berkeley, Calif.

BR TR 6'4" 205 lbs.

Year	Team		Games	BA	SA	AB	H	2B	3B	HR	HR%	R	RBI	BB	SO	SB	PH AB	PH H	PO	A	E	DP	TC/G	FA	G by Pos
1969	PHI	N	20	.188	.219	32	6	1	0	0	0.0	4	0	5	6	0	11	2	15	0	1	0	0.8	.938	OF-9

Shad Barry

BARRY, JOHN C.
B. Sept. 23, 1876, Newburgh, N. Y. D. Nov. 27, 1936, Los Angeles, Calif.

BR TR

Year	Team		Games	BA	SA	AB	H	2B	3B	HR	HR%	R	RBI	BB	SO	SB	PH AB	PH H	PO	A	E	DP	TC/G	FA	G by Pos
1899	WAS	N	78	.287	.368	247	71	7	5	1	0.4	31	33	12		11	3	0	254	65	19	13	4.3	.944	OF-23, 1B-22, SS-13, 3B-13, 2B-7
1900	BOS	N	81	.260	.366	254	66	10	7	1	0.4	40	37	13		9	14	3	199	82	23	13	3.8	.924	OF-24, SS-18, 2B-16, 1B-10, 3B-1
1901 2 teams	BOS	N (11G – .175)				PHI	N	(67G – .246)																	
" total			78	.236	.288	292	69	12	0	1	0.3	38	28	17		14	4	0	146	124	33	8	3.9	.891	2B-35, OF-24, 3B-16, SS-1
1902	PHI	N	138	.287	.363	543	156	20	6	3	0.6	65	57	44		14	0	0	193	15	13	3	1.6	.941	OF-137, 1B-1
1903			138	.276	.344	550	152	24	5	1	0.2	75	60	30		26	0	0	503	28	16	12	4.0	.971	OF-107, 1B-30, 3B-1
1904 2 teams	PHI	N (35G – .205)				CHI	N	(73G – .262)																	
" total			108	.244	.286	385	94	9	2	1	0.3	44	29	28		14	3	0	350	89	25	21	4.3	.946	OF-62, 1B-18, 3B-17, SS-8, 2B-2
1905 2 teams	CHI	N (27G – .212)				CIN	N	(125G – .324)																	
" total			152	.304	.371	598	182	13	12	1	0.2	100	66	38		21	1	0	1474	79	28	17	10.4	.982	1B-149, OF-2
1906 2 teams	CIN	N (73G – .287)				STL	N	(62G – .249)																	
" total			135	.269	.335	516	139	19	6	1	0.2	64	45	41		17	0	0	746	61	20	33	6.1	.976	OF-65, 1B-64, 3B-6
1907	STL	N	81	.247	.277	292	72	5	2	0	0.0	30	19	28		4	0	0	94	11	4	0	1.3	.963	OF-81
1908 2 teams	STL	N (74G – .228)				NY	N	(37G – .149)																	
" total			111	.212	.251	335	71	9	2	0	0.0	29	16	28		10	7	1	146	12	8	1	1.5	.952	OF-100, SS-2
10 yrs.			1100	.267	.330	4012	1072	128	47	10	0.2	516	390	279		140	32	4	4105	566	189	121	4.4	.961	OF-625, 1B-294, 2B-60, 3B-54, SS-42

Dick Bartell

BARTELL, RICHARD WILLIAM (Rowdy Richard)
B. Nov. 22, 1907, Chicago, Ill.

BR TR 5'9" 160 lbs.

Year	Team		Games	BA	SA	AB	H	2B	3B	HR	HR%	R	RBI	BB	SO	SB	PH AB	PH H	PO	A	E	DP	TC/G	FA	G by Pos
1927	PIT	N	1	.000	.000	2	0	0	0	0	0.0	0	0	0	0	0	2	0	3	2	0	1	5.0	1.000	SS-1
1928			72	.305	.386	233	71	8	4	1	0.4	27	36	21	18	4	2	0	158	199	16	40	5.2	.957	2B-39, SS-27, 3B-1
1929			143	.302	.420	610	184	40	13	2	0.3	101	57	40	29	11	0	0	392	458	33	66	6.2	.963	SS-97, 2B-70
1930			129	.320	.467	475	152	32	13	4	0.8	69	75	39	34	8	3	0	304	458	48	111	6.3	.941	SS-126
1931	PHI	N	135	.289	.392	554	160	43	7	0	0.0	88	34	27	38	6	0	0	319	442	42	98	5.9	.948	SS-133, 2B-3

Year	Team		Games	BA	SA	AB	H	2B	3B	HR	HR%	R	RBI	BB	SO	SB	Pinch Hit AB	Pinch Hit H	PO	A	E	DP	TC/G	FA	G by Pos

Dick Bartell *continued*

Year	Team		Games	BA	SA	AB	H	2B	3B	HR	HR%	R	RBI	BB	SO	SB	AB	H	PO	A	E	DP	TC/G	FA	G by Pos
1932			154	.308	.414	614	189	48	7	1	0.2	118	53	64	47	8	0	0	359	529	34	83	6.0	.963	SS-154
1933			152	.271	.336	587	159	25	5	1	0.2	78	37	56	46	6	0	0	381	493	45	100	6.0	.951	SS-152
1934			146	.310	.373	604	187	30	4	0	0.0	102	37	64	59	13	0	0	350	483	40	93	6.0	.954	SS-146
1935	NY	N	137	.262	.406	539	141	28	4	14	2.6	60	53	37	52	5	0	0	339	424	37	71	5.8	.954	SS-137
1936			145	.298	.418	510	152	31	3	8	1.6	71	42	40	36	6	0	0	317	559	40	106	6.3	.956	SS-144
1937			128	.306	.469	516	158	38	2	14	2.7	91	62	40	38	5	0	0	281	476	33	96	6.2	.958	SS-128
1938			127	.262	.376	481	126	26	1	9	1.9	67	49	55	60	4	0	0	288	447	37	85	6.1	.952	SS-127
1939	CHI	N	105	.238	.348	336	80	24	2	3	0.9	37	34	42	25	6	3	1	241	307	33	62	5.5	.943	SS-101, 3B-1
1940	DET	A	139	.233	.330	528	123	24	3	7	1.3	76	53	76	53	12	0	0	295	394	34	74	5.2	.953	SS-139
1941 2 teams	DET	A		(5G – .167)																					
" total	NY	N	109	(104G – .303)		385	115	21	0	5	1.3	44	36	54	31	6	3	0	134	225	15	23	3.4	.960	3B-84, SS-26
1942	NY	N	90	.244	.342	316	77	10	3	5	1.6	53	24	44	34	4	8	1	135	191	14	23	3.8	.959	3B-52, SS-31
1943			99	.270	.356	337	91	14	0	5	1.5	48	28	47	27	5	10	1	128	258	11	19	4.0	.972	3B-54, SS-33
1946			5	.000	.000	2	0	0	0	0	0.0	0	0	0	0	0	0	0	1	3	0	1	0.8	1.000	3B-4, 2B-2
18 yrs.			2016	.284	.391	7629	2165	442	71	79	1.0	1130	710	748	627	109	29	3	4425	6348	512	1156	5.6	.955	SS-1702, 3B-196, 2B-114

WORLD SERIES

Year	Team		Games	BA	SA	AB	H	2B	3B	HR	HR%	R	RBI	BB	SO	SB	AB	H	PO	A	E	DP	TC/G	FA	G by Pos
1936	NY	N	6	.381	.667	21	8	3	0	1	4.8	5	3	4	4	0	0	0	8	13	1	4	3.7	.955	SS-6
1937			5	.238	.286	21	5	1	0	0	0.0	3	1	0	3	0	0	0	13	11	3	3	5.4	.889	SS-5
1940	DET	A	7	.269	.346	26	7	2	0	0	0.0	2	3	3	3	0	0	0	12	12	1	2	3.6	.960	SS-7
3 yrs.			18	.294	.426	68	20	6	0	1	1.5	10	7	7	10	0	0	0	33	36	5	9	4.1	.932	SS-18

Tony Bartirome

BARTIROME, ANTHONY JOSEPH
B. May 9, 1932, Pittsburgh, Pa.   BL TL 5'10" 155 lbs.

1952	PIT	N	124	.220	.265	355	78	10	3	0	0.0	32	16	26	37	3	1	0	909	72	11	91	8.0	.989	1B-118

Boyd Bartley

BARTLEY, BOYD OWEN
B. Feb. 11, 1920, Chicago, Ill.   BR TR 5'8½" 165 lbs.

1943	BKN	N	9	.048	.048	21	1	0	0	0	0.0	1	1	3	0	0	0	14	21	4	3	4.3	.897	SS-9

Irv Bartling

BARTLING, IRVING HENRY
B. June 27, 1914, Bay City, Mich.   D. June 12, 1973, Westland, Mich.   BR TR 6' 175 lbs.

1938	PHI	A	14	.174	.239	46	8	1	1	0	0.0	5	5	3	7	0	0	0	29	35	6	8	5.0	.914	SS-13, 3B-1

Bob Barton

BARTON, ROBERT WILBUR
B. July 30, 1941, Norwood, Ohio   BR TR 6' 175 lbs.

1965	SF	N	4	.571	.571	7	4	0	0	0	0.0			0	2	1			13	0	0	0	3.3	1.000	C-2
1966			43	.176	.220	91	16	2	1	0	0.0	1	3	5	5	0	4	0	161	19	1	4	4.2	.994	C-39
1967			7	.211	.211	19	4	0	0	0	0.0	1	0	2	0	0	0	0	33	3	0	0	5.1	1.000	C-7
1968			46	.261	.283	92	24	2	0	0	0.0	4	5	7	18	0	2	0	194	23	1	4	4.7	.995	C-45
1969			49	.170	.189	106	18	2	0	0	0.0	5	1	9	19	0	2	0	186	9	3	3	4.0	.985	C-49
1970	SD	N	61	.218	.314	188	41	6	0	4	2.1	15	16	15	37	1	2	0	347	28	2	5	6.2	.995	C-59
1971			121	.250	.346	376	94	17	2	5	1.3	23	23	35	49	0	3	1	698	67	15	10	6.4	.981	C-119
1972			29	.193	.205	88	17	1	0	0	0.0	1	9	2	19	2	0	0	170	13	2	1	6.4	.989	C-29
1973	CIN	N	3	.000	.000	4	0	0	0	0	0.0	0	0	1	1	0	1	0	5	0	0	0	1.7	1.000	C-2
1974	SD	N	30	.235	.247	81	19	1	0	0	0.0	4	7	13	19	0	0	1	179	23	4	3	6.9	.981	C-29
10 yrs.			393	.226	.287	1049	237	31	3	9	0.9	54	66	87	168	3	15	3	1986	185	28	30	5.6	.987	C-380

Harry Barton

BARTON, HARRY LAMB
B. Jan. 20, 1875, Chester, Pa.   D. Jan. 25, 1955, Upland, Pa.   BB TR 5'6½" 155 lbs.

1905	PHI	A	29	.167	.233	60	10	2	1	0	0.0	5	3	3		2	10	1	56	16	4	0	2.6	.947	C-13, 3B-2, 1B-2, OF-1

Vince Barton

BARTON, VINCENT DAVID
B. Feb. 1, 1908, Edmonton, Alta., Canada   D. Sept. 13, 1973, Toronto, Ont., Canada   BL TR 6' 180 lbs.

1931	CHI	N	66	.238	.452	239	57	10	1	13	5.4	45	50	21	40	1	4	1	133	2	5	0	2.1	.964	OF-61
1932			36	.224	.351	134	30	2	3	3	2.2	19	15	8	22	0	2	0	64	3	0	1	1.9	1.000	OF-34
2 yrs.			102	.233	.416	373	87	12	4	16	4.3	64	65	29	62	1	6	1	197	5	5	1	2.0	.976	OF-95

Dave Bartosch

BARTOSCH, DAVID ROBERT
B. Mar. 24, 1917, St. Louis, Mo.   BR TR 6'1" 190 lbs.

1945	STL	N	24	.255	.277	47	12	1	0	0	0.0	9	1	6	3	0	13	5	26	1	1	0	1.2	.964	OF-11

Monty Basgall

BASGALL, ROMANUS
B. Feb. 8, 1922, Pfeifer, Kans.   BR TR 5'10½" 175 lbs.

1948	PIT	N	38	.216	.353	51	11	1	0	2	3.9	12	6	3	5	0	5	1	37	35	0	4	1.9	1.000	2B-22
1949			107	.218	.273	308	67	9	1	2	0.6	25	26	31	32	1	4	1	224	225	13	58	4.3	.972	2B-98, 3B-3
1951			55	.209	.268	153	32	5	2	0	0.0	15	9	12	14	0	0	0	140	144	9	39	5.3	.969	2B-55
3 yrs.			200	.215	.279	512	110	15	3	4	0.8	52	41	46	51	1	9	2	401	404	22	101	4.1	.973	2B-175, 3B-3

Al Bashang

BASHANG, ALBERT C.
B. Aug. 22, 1888, Cincinnati, Ohio   D. June 23, 1967, Cincinnati, Ohio   BB TR 5'8" 150 lbs.

1912	DET	A	5	.083	.083	12	1	0	0	0	0.0	3		0	3		0	0	6	0	0	0	1.2	1.000	OF-5
1918	BKN	N	2	.200	.200	5	1	0	0	0	0.0	0	0	3	0	1	1	0	0	1	0	0	0.5	1.000	OF-1
2 yrs.			7	.118	.118	17	2	0	0	0	0.0	3	0	3	3	1	1	0	6	1	0	0	1.0	1.000	OF-6

Walt Bashore

BASHORE, WALTER FRANKLIN
Born Walter Franklin Beshore.
B. Oct. 6, 1909, Harrisburg, Pa.   D. Sept. 26, 1984, Sebring, Fla.   BR TR 6' 170 lbs.

1936	PHI	N	10	.200	.200	10	2	0	0	0	0.0	1	0	1	3	0	2	0	2	0	0	0	0.2	1.000	OF-6, 3B-1

Year	Team		Games	BA	SA	AB	H	2B	3B	HR	HR%	R	RBI	BB	SO	SB	Pinch Hit AB	Pinch Hit H	PO	A	E	DP	TC/G	FA	G by Pos

Eddie Basinski

BASINSKI, EDWIN FRANK (Fiddler)
B. Nov. 4, 1922, Buffalo, N. Y.
BR TR 6'1" 172 lbs.

Year	Team		Games	BA	SA	AB	H	2B	3B	HR	HR%	R	RBI	BB	SO	SB	AB	H	PO	A	E	DP	TC/G	FA	G by Pos
1944	BKN	N	39	.257	.314	105	27	4	1	0	0.0	13	9	6	10	1	1	0	86	87	8	15	4.6	.956	2B-37, SS-3
1945			108	.262	.313	336	88	9	4	0	0.0	30	33	11	33	0	2	0	177	267	35	62	4.4	.927	SS-101, 2B-6
1947	PIT	N	56	.199	.335	161	32	6	2	4	2.5	15	17	18	27	0	0	0	116	130	7	34	4.5	.972	2B-56
3 yrs.			203	.244	.319	602	147	19	7	4	0.7	58	59	35	70	1	3	0	379	484	50	111	4.5	.945	SS-104, 2B-99

Doc Bass

BASS, WILLIAM CAPERS
B. Dec. 4, 1899, Macon, Ga.   D. Jan. 12, 1970, Macon, Ga.
5'10" 165 lbs.

Year	Team		Games	BA	SA	AB	H	2B	3B	HR	HR%	R	RBI	BB	SO	SB	AB	H	PO	A	E	DP	TC/G	FA	G by Pos
1918	BOS	N	1	1.000	1.000	1	1	0	0	0	0.0	1	0	0	0	1	1	1	0	0	0	0	0.0	—	

John Bass

BASS, JOHN E.
B. 1850, Baltimore, Md.   Deceased.
5'6" 150 lbs.

Year	Team		Games	BA	SA	AB	H	2B	3B	HR	HR%	R	RBI	BB	SO	SB	AB	H	PO	A	E	DP	TC/G	FA	G by Pos
1877	HAR	N	1	.250	.250	4	1	0	0	0	0.0	0	0	0	0		0	0	0	0	0	0	0.0	—	OF-1

Kevin Bass

BASS, KEVIN CHARLES
B. May 12, 1959, Redwood City, Calif.
BB TR 6' 183 lbs.

Year	Team		Games	BA	SA	AB	H	2B	3B	HR	HR%	R	RBI	BB	SO	SB	AB	H	PO	A	E	DP	TC/G	FA	G by Pos
1982	2 teams			MIL A	(18G – .000)		HOU N	(12G – .042)																		
"	total		30	.030	.030	33	1	0	0	0	0.0	6	1	1	9	0	1	0	18	0	1	0	0.6	.947	OF-21, DH-2
1983	HOU	N	88	.236	.333	195	46	7	3	2	1.0	25	18	6	27	5	43	13	68	1	4	1	0.8	.945	OF-52
1984			121	.260	.360	331	86	17	5	2	0.6	33	29	6	57	5	44	13	149	4	4	2	1.3	.975	OF-81
1985			150	.269	.427	539	145	27	5	16	3.0	72	68	31	63	19	12	4	328	10	1	1	2.3	.997	OF-141
1986			157	.311	.486	591	184	33	5	20	3.4	83	79	38	72	22	2	2	303	12	5	4	2.0	.984	OF-155
1987			157	.284	.449	592	168	31	5	19	3.2	83	85	53	77	21	2	1	287	11	4	2	1.9	.987	OF-155
1988			157	.255	.390	541	138	27	2	14	2.6	57	72	42	65	31	16	6	267	7	6	2	1.8	.979	OF-147
1989			87	.300	.435	313	94	19	4	5	1.6	42	44	29	44	11	2	1	186	6	3	0	2.2	.985	OF-84
8 yrs.			947	.275	.419	3135	862	161	29	78	2.5	401	396	206	414	111	122	38	1606	51	28	12	1.8	.983	OF-836, DH-2

LEAGUE CHAMPIONSHIP SERIES

Year	Team		Games	BA	SA	AB	H	2B	3B	HR	HR%	R	RBI	BB	SO	SB	AB	H	PO	A	E	DP	TC/G	FA	G by Pos
1986	HOU	N	6	.292	.375	24	7	2	0	0	0.0	0	0	4	4	2	0	0	16	0	1	0	2.8	.941	OF-6

Randy Bass

BASS, RANDY WILLIAM
B. Mar. 13, 1954, Lawton, Okla.
BL TR 6'1" 210 lbs.

Year	Team		Games	BA	SA	AB	H	2B	3B	HR	HR%	R	RBI	BB	SO	SB	AB	H	PO	A	E	DP	TC/G	FA	G by Pos
1977	MIN	A	9	.105	.105	19	2	0	0	0	0.0	0	0	0	5	0	4	0	0	0	0	0	0.0	—	DH-6
1978	KC	A	2	.000	.000	2	0	0	0	0	0.0	0	0	0	2	0	0	0	0	0	0	0	0.0	—	1B-1
1979	MON	N	2	.000	.000	1	0	0	0	0	0.0	0	0	0	1	0	1	0	1	0	0	0	0.5	1.000	1B-1
1980	SD	N	19	.286	.510	49	14	0	1	3	6.1	5	8	7	7	0	3	0	127	6	2	10	7.1	.985	1B-15
1981			69	.210	.313	176	37	4	1	4	2.3	13	20	20	28	0	19	5	390	35	3	38	6.2	.993	1B-50
1982	2 teams			SD N	(13G – .200)		TEX A	(16G – .208)																		
"	total		29	.205	.308	78	16	2	0	2	2.6	6	14	3	11	0	5	1	121	7	0	16	4.4	1.000	1B-15, DH-7
6 yrs.			130	.212	.326	325	69	6	2	9	2.8	24	42	30	51	0	34	6	639	48	5	64	5.3	.993	1B-81, DH-13

Charley Bassett

BASSETT, CHARLES EDWIN
B. Feb. 9, 1863, Central Falls, R. I.   D. May 28, 1942, Pawtucket, R. I.
BR TR 5'10" 150 lbs.

Year	Team		Games	BA	SA	AB	H	2B	3B	HR	HR%	R	RBI	BB	SO	SB	AB	H	PO	A	E	DP	TC/G	FA	G by Pos
1884	PRO	N	27	.139	.190	79	11	2	1	0	0.0	10		4	15		0	0	23	47	15	1	3.1	.824	3B-13, SS-7, OF-2, 2B-1
1885			82	.144	.186	285	41	8	2	0	0.0	21	16	19	60		0	0	141	248	39	24	5.2	.909	2B-39, SS-23, 3B-20, C-1
1886	KC	N	90	.260	.380	342	89	19	8	2	0.6	41	32	36	43		0	0	131	290	55	25	5.3	.884	SS-82, 3B-8
1887	IND	N	119	.230	.294	452	104	14	6	1	0.2	41	47	25	31	25	0	0	273	444	53	62	6.5	.931	2B-119
1888			128	.241	.308	481	116	20	3	2	0.4	58	60	32	41	24	0	0	250	423	57	44	5.7	.922	2B-128
1889			127	.245	.317	477	117	12	5	4	0.8	64	68	37	38	15	0	0	322	451	52	67	6.5	.937	2B-127
1890	NY	N	100	.239	.310	410	98	13	8	0	0.0	52	54	29	25	14	0	0	201	332	27	43	5.6	.952	3B-100
1891			130	.260	.349	524	136	19	8	4	0.8	60	68	36	29	16	0	0	166	308	47	23	4.0	.910	3B-121, 2B-9
1892	2 teams			NY N	(35G – .208)		LOU N	(79G – .214)																		
"	total		114	.212	.278	443	94	7	8	2	0.5	45	51	21	29	16	0	0	162	313	59	24	4.7	.890	3B-78, 2B-36
9 yrs.			917	.231	.304	3493	806	114	49	15	0.4	392	396	239	311	110	0	0	1669	2856	404	313	5.4	.918	2B-559, 3B-240, SS-112, OF-2, C-1

Johnny Bassler

BASSLER, JOHN LANDIS
B. June 3, 1895, Lancaster, Pa.   D. June 29, 1979, Santa Monica, Calif.
BL TR 5'9" 170 lbs.

Year	Team		Games	BA	SA	AB	H	2B	3B	HR	HR%	R	RBI	BB	SO	SB	AB	H	PO	A	E	DP	TC/G	FA	G by Pos
1913	CLE	A	1	.000	.000	2	0	0	0	0	0.0	0	0	0	0		0	0	1	0	1	0	2.0	.500	C-1
1914			43	.182	.221	77	14	1	1	0	0.0	5	6	15	8	3	10	1	99	42	8	3	3.5	.946	C-25, OF-1, 3B-1
1921	DET	A	119	.307	.379	388	119	18	5	0	0.0	37	56	58	16	2	3	1	433	113	14	7	4.7	.975	C-115
1922			121	.323	.360	372	120	14	0	0	0.0	41	41	62	12	2	2	0	421	113	11	12	4.5	.980	C-118
1923			135	.298	.345	383	114	12	3	0	0.0	45	49	76	13	2	5	2	447	133	7	8	4.3	.988	C-128
1924			124	.346	.422	379	131	20	3	1	0.3	43	68	62	11	2	3	1	402	103	11	11	4.2	.979	C-122
1925			121	.279	.352	344	96	19	3	0	0.0	40	52	74	6	1	3	0	375	87	8	14	3.9	.983	C-118
1926			66	.305	.362	174	53	8	1	0	0.0	20	22	45	6	0	2	0	223	61	0	6	4.3	1.000	C-63
1927			81	.285	.320	200	57	7	0	0	0.0	19	24	45	9	1	12	2	206	56	7	8	3.3	.974	C-67
9 yrs.			811	.304	.361	2319	704	99	16	1	0.0	250	318	437	81	13	40	7	2607	708	67	69	4.2	.980	C-757, OF-1, 3B-1

Charlie Bastian

BASTIAN, CHARLES J.
B. July 4, 1860, Philadelphia, Pa.   D. Jan. 18, 1932, Pennsauken, N. J.
BR TR 5'6½" 145 lbs.

Year	Team		Games	BA	SA	AB	H	2B	3B	HR	HR%	R	RBI	BB	SO	SB	AB	H	PO	A	E	DP	TC/G	FA	G by Pos
1884	2 teams			WIL U	(17G – .200)		KC U	(11G – .196)																		
"	total		28	.198	.377	106	21	4	3	3	2.8	12		7			0	0	67	95	14	9	6.3	.920	2B-27, SS-1, P-1
1885	PHI	N	103	.167	.252	389	65	11	5	4	1.0	63		35	82		0	0	164	337	62	34	5.5	.890	SS-103
1886			105	.217	.316	373	81	9	11	2	0.5	46	38	33	73		0	0	175	326	34	23	5.1	.936	2B-87, SS-10, 3B-8
1887			60	.213	.285	221	47	11	1	1	0.5	33	21	19	29	11	0	0	110	170	25	21	5.1	.918	2B-39, SS-18, 3B-4
1888			80	.193	.225	275	53	4	1	1	0.4	30	17	27	41	12	0	0	162	277	27	16	5.8	.942	2B-65, 3B-14, SS-1
1889	CHI	N	46	.135	.135	155	21	0	0	0	0.0	19	10	25	46	1	0	0	67	163	19	10	5.4	.924	SS-45, 2B-1
1890	CHI	P	80	.191	.261	283	54	10	5	0	0.0	38	29	33	37	4	0	0	129	231	44	28	5.1	.891	SS-64, 2B-12, 3B-4

Year	Team	Games	BA	SA	AB	H	2B	3B	HR	HR%	R	RBI	BB	SO	SB	Pinch Hit AB	Pinch Hit H	PO	A	E	DP	TC/G	FA	G by Pos

Charlie Bastian *continued*

Year	Team	Games	BA	SA	AB	H	2B	3B	HR	HR%	R	RBI	BB	SO	SB	AB	H	PO	A	E	DP	TC/G	FA	G by Pos
1891	2 teams	CIN AA (1G – .000)			PHI N (1G – .000)																			
"	total	2	.000	.000	4	0	0	0	0	0.0	0	0	0	0	0	0	0	4	5	0	1	4.5	1.000	SS-1, 2B-1
8 yrs.		504	.189	.264	1806	342	49	26	11	0.6	241	115	179	308	28	0	0	878	1604	225	142	5.4	.917	SS-243, 2B-232, 3B-30, P-1

Emil Batch

BATCH, EMIL (Heinie)
B. Jan. 21, 1880, Brooklyn, N. Y.   D. Aug. 23, 1926, Brooklyn, N. Y.   BR TR 5'7"   170 lbs.

Year	Team	Games	BA	SA	AB	H	2B	3B	HR	HR%	R	RBI	BB	SO	SB	AB	H	PO	A	E	DP	TC/G	FA	G by Pos
1904	BKN N	28	.255	.372	94	24	1	2	2	2.1	9	7	1		6	0	0	26	55	11	3	3.3	.880	3B-28
1905		145	.252	.352	568	143	20	11	5	0.9	64	49	26		21	0	0	203	246	57	22	3.5	.887	3B-145
1906		59	.256	.350	203	52	7	6	0	0.0	23	11	15		3	6	1	104	7	5	0	2.0	.957	OF-50, 3B-2
1907		116	.247	.289	388	96	10	3	0	0.0	38	31	23		7	8	1	182	17	15	4	1.8	.930	OF-102, 3B-2, SS-1, 2B-1
4 yrs.		348	.251	.334	1253	315	38	22	7	0.6	134	98	65		37	14	2	515	325	88	29	2.7	.905	3B-177, OF-152, SS-1, 2B-1

John Bateman

BATEMAN, JOHN ALVIN
B. July 21, 1942, Killeen, Tex.   BR TR 6'3"   210 lbs.

Year	Team	Games	BA	SA	AB	H	2B	3B	HR	HR%	R	RBI	BB	SO	SB	AB	H	PO	A	E	DP	TC/G	FA	G by Pos
1963	HOU N	128	.210	.334	404	85	8	6	10	2.5	23	59	13	103	0	13	2	690	81	23	7	6.2	.971	C-115
1964		74	.190	.294	221	42	8	0	5	2.3	18	19	17	48	0	2	0	400	43	6	4	6.1	.987	C-72
1965		45	.197	.380	142	28	3	1	7	4.9	15	14	12	37	0	5	0	234	26	4	3	5.9	.985	C-39
1966		131	.279	.467	433	121	24	3	17	3.9	39	70	20	74	0	11	2	731	63	15	14	6.2	.981	C-121
1967		76	.190	.250	252	48	9	0	2	0.8	16	17	17	53	0	4	1	483	46	6	5	7.0	.989	C-71
1968		111	.249	.337	350	87	19	0	4	1.1	28	33	23	46	1	2	1	690	49	11	6	6.8	.985	C-108
1969	MON N	74	.209	.328	235	49	4	0	8	3.4	16	19	12	44	0	7	2	433	26	7	5	6.3	.985	C-66
1970		139	.237	.383	520	123	21	5	15	2.9	51	68	28	75	8	2	0	824	62	15	19	6.5	.983	C-137
1971		139	.242	.350	492	119	17	3	10	2.0	34	56	19	87	1	4	1	726	56	12	12	5.7	.985	C-137
1972	2 teams	MON N (18G – .241)			PHI N (82G – .222)																			
"	total	100	.224	.292	281	63	10	0	3	1.1	10	20	11	43	0	14	2	475	39	14	6	5.3	.973	C-87
10 yrs.		1017	.230	.350	3330	765	123	18	81	2.4	250	375	172	610	10	64	11	5686	491	113	81	6.2	.982	C-953

Billy Bates

BATES, WILLIAM DERRICK
B. Dec. 7, 1963   BB TR 5'7"   155 lbs.

Year	Team	Games	BA	SA	AB	H	2B	3B	HR	HR%	R	RBI	BB	SO	SB	AB	H	PO	A	E	DP	TC/G	FA	G by Pos
1989	MIL A	7	.214	.214	14	3	0	0	0	0.0	3	0	0	1	2	1	1	14	16	2	7	4.6	.938	2B-7

Bud Bates

BATES, HUBERT EDGAR
B. Mar. 16, 1912, Los Angeles, Calif.   D. Apr. 29, 1987, Long Beach, Calif.   BR TR 6'   165 lbs.

Year	Team	Games	BA	SA	AB	H	2B	3B	HR	HR%	R	RBI	BB	SO	SB	AB	H	PO	A	E	DP	TC/G	FA	G by Pos
1939	PHI N	15	.259	.345	58	15	2	0	1	1.7	8	2	8		1	0	0	44	1	1	1	3.1	.978	OF-14

Charlie Bates

BATES, CHARLES WILLIAM
B. Sept. 17, 1907, Philadelphia, Pa.   D. Jan. 29, 1980, Topeka, Kans.   BR TR 5'10"   165 lbs.

Year	Team	Games	BA	SA	AB	H	2B	3B	HR	HR%	R	RBI	BB	SO	SB	AB	H	PO	A	E	DP	TC/G	FA	G by Pos
1927	PHI A	9	.237	.395	38	9	2	2	0	0.0	5	2	3	5	3	0	0	17	1	3	0	2.3	.857	OF-9

Del Bates

BATES, DELBERT OAKLEY JR.
B. June 12, 1940, Seattle, Wash.   BL TR 6'2"   195 lbs.

Year	Team	Games	BA	SA	AB	H	2B	3B	HR	HR%	R	RBI	BB	SO	SB	AB	H	PO	A	E	DP	TC/G	FA	G by Pos
1970	PHI N	22	.133	.167	60	8	2	0	0	0.0	1	1	6	15	0	5	0	116	8	1	0	5.7	.992	C-20

Johnny Bates

BATES, JOHN WILLIAM
B. Aug. 21, 1882, Steubenville, Ohio   D. Feb. 10, 1949, Steubenville, Ohio   BL TL 5'7"   168 lbs.

Year	Team	Games	BA	SA	AB	H	2B	3B	HR	HR%	R	RBI	BB	SO	SB	AB	H	PO	A	E	DP	TC/G	FA	G by Pos
1906	BOS N	140	.252	.349	504	127	21	5	6	1.2	52	54	36		9	0	0	238	12	11	4	1.9	.958	OF-140
1907		126	.260	.367	447	116	18	12	2	0.4	52	49	39		11	5	1	171	18	4	5	1.5	.979	OF-120
1908		127	.258	.324	445	115	14	6	1	0.2	48	29	35		25	10	0	205	15	12	2	1.8	.948	OF-117
1909	2 teams	BOS N (63G – .288)			PHI N (77G – .293)																			
"	total	140	.291	.371	502	146	26	4	2	0.4	70	38	48		37	5	1	253	27	14	3	2.1	.952	OF-133
1910	PHI N	135	.305	.420	498	152	26	11	3	0.6	91	61	61	49	31	4	0	308	24	16	8	2.6	.954	OF-131
1911	CIN N	148	.292	.394	518	151	24	13	1	0.2	89	61	103	59	33	1	0	352	21	13	4	2.6	.966	OF-147
1912		81	.289	.410	239	69	12	7	1	0.4	45	29	47	16	10	12	3	157	15	9	4	2.2	.950	OF-65
1913		131	.278	.388	407	113	13	7	6	1.5	63	51	67	30	21	17	6	192	19	12	6	1.7	.946	OF-112
1914	3 teams	CIN N (67G – .245)			CHI N (9G – .125)				BAL F (59G – .305)															
"	total	135	.274	.380	361	99	13	8	3	0.8	62	45	68	19	10	8	1	204	11	15	1	1.7	.935	OF-119
9 yrs.		1163	.277	.376	3921	1088	167	73	25	0.6	572	417	504	173	187	62	12	2080	162	106	37	2.0	.955	OF-1084

Ray Bates

BATES, RAYMOND
B. Feb. 8, 1890, Paterson, N. J.   D. Aug. 15, 1970, Tucson, Ariz.   BR TR 6'   165 lbs.

Year	Team	Games	BA	SA	AB	H	2B	3B	HR	HR%	R	RBI	BB	SO	SB	AB	H	PO	A	E	DP	TC/G	FA	G by Pos
1913	CLE A	20	.167	.300	30	5	0	2	0	0.0	4	4	3	9	3	1	0	6	13	2	2	1.1	.905	3B-12, OF-2
1917	PHI A	127	.237	.320	485	115	20	7	2	0.4	47	66	21	39	12	3	0	168	267	31	17	3.7	.933	3B-124
2 yrs.		147	.233	.318	515	120	20	9	2	0.4	51	70	24	48	15	4	0	174	280	33	19	3.3	.932	3B-136, OF-2

Bill Bathe

BATHE, WILLIAM DAVID
B. Oct. 14, 1960, Downey, Calif.   BR TR 6'2"   200 lbs.

Year	Team	Games	BA	SA	AB	H	2B	3B	HR	HR%	R	RBI	BB	SO	SB	AB	H	PO	A	E	DP	TC/G	FA	G by Pos
1986	OAK A	39	.184	.359	103	19	3	0	5	4.9	9	11	2	20	0	0	0	211	11	2	1	5.7	.991	C-39
1989	SF N	30	.281	.313	32	9	1	0	0	0.0	3	6	0	7	0	26	6	13	0	0	0	0.4	1.000	C-7
2 yrs.		69	.207	.348	135	28	4	0	5	3.7	12	17	2	27	0	26	6	224	11	2	1	3.4	.992	C-46

LEAGUE CHAMPIONSHIP SERIES

Year	Team	Games	BA	SA	AB	H	2B	3B	HR	HR%	R	RBI	BB	SO	SB	AB	H	PO	A	E	DP	TC/G	FA	G by Pos
1989	SF N	2	.000	.000	1	0	0	0	0	0.0	0	0	0	1	0	1	0	0	0	0	0	0.0	–	

WORLD SERIES

Year	Team	Games	BA	SA	AB	H	2B	3B	HR	HR%	R	RBI	BB	SO	SB	AB	H	PO	A	E	DP	TC/G	FA	G by Pos
1989	SF N	2	.500	2.000	2	1	0	0	1	50.0	1	3	0	0	0	2	1	0	0	0	0	0.0	–	

Rafael Batista

BATISTA, RAFAEL
Born Rafael Batista y Sanchez.
B. Oct. 20, 1947, San Pedro de Macoris, Dominican Republic   BL TL 6'1"   195 lbs.

Year	Team	Games	BA	SA	AB	H	2B	3B	HR	HR%	R	RBI	BB	SO	SB	Pinch Hit AB	H	PO	A	E	DP	TC/G	FA	G by Pos

Rafael Batista *continued*

Year	Team	Games	BA	SA	AB	H	2B	3B	HR	HR%	R	RBI	BB	SO	SB	PH AB	H	PO	A	E	DP	TC/G	FA	G by Pos
1973	HOU N	12	.267	.267	15	4	0	0	0	0.0	2	2	1	6	0	6	0	26	1	0	1	2.3	1.000	1B-8
1975		10	.300	.400	10	3	1	0	0	0.0	0	0	0	4	0	10	3	0	0	0	0	0.0	–	1B-8
2 yrs.		22	.280	.320	25	7	1	0	0	0.0	2	2	1	10	0	16	3	26	1	0	1	1.2	1.000	1B-8

Kevin Batiste

BATISTE, KEVIN WADE
B. Oct. 21, 1966, Galveston, Tex.   BB TR 6'2" 178 lbs.

1989	TOR A	6	.250	.250	8	2	0	0	0	0.0	1	0	0	5	0	0	0	7	0	0	0	1.2	1.000	OF-5

Bill Batsch

BATSCH, WILLIAM McKINLEY
B. May 18, 1892, Mingo Junction, Ohio   D. Dec. 31, 1963, Canton, Ohio   BR TR 5'10½" 168 lbs.

1916	PIT N	1	–	–	0	0	0	0	0	–	0	0	1	0	0	0	0	0	0	0	0	0.0	–	

Larry Battam

BATTAM, LAWRENCE
B. May 1, 1878, Brooklyn, N. Y.   D. Jan. 27, 1938, Brooklyn, N. Y.   5'11"

1895	NY N	2	.250	.250	4	1	0	0	0	0.0	0	2	1	0	0	0	0	0	2	1	0	1.5	.667	3B-2

George Batten

BATTEN, GEORGE BURNETT
B. Oct. 7, 1891, Haddonfield, N. J.   D. Aug. 4, 1972, New Port Ritchey, Fla.   BR TR 5'11" 165 lbs.

1912	NY A	1	.000	.000	3	0	0	0	0	0.0	0	0	0	0	0	0	0	1	1	1	0	3.0	.667	2B-1

Earl Battey

BATTEY, EARL JESSE
B. Jan. 5, 1935, Los Angeles, Calif.   BR TR 6'1" 205 lbs.

Year	Team	Games	BA	SA	AB	H	2B	3B	HR	HR%	R	RBI	BB	SO	SB	PH AB	H	PO	A	E	DP	TC/G	FA	G by Pos
1955	CHI A	5	.286	.286	7	2	0	0	0	0.0	1	0	1	1	0	1	0	19	2	0	1	4.2	1.000	C-5
1956		4	.250	.250	4	1	0	0	0	0.0	0	1	1	1	0	0	0	4	0	1	0	1.3	.800	C-3
1957		48	.174	.322	115	20	2	3	3	2.6	12	6	11	38	0	4	3	165	19	2	2	3.9	.989	C-43
1958		68	.226	.417	168	38	8	0	8	4.8	24	26	24	34	1	17	1	220	27	3	6	3.7	.988	C-49
1959		26	.219	.391	64	14	1	2	2	3.1	9	7	8	13	0	5	0	92	10	1	1	4.0	.990	C-20
1960	WAS A	137	.270	.427	466	126	24	2	15	3.2	49	60	48	68	4	4	2	749	65	15	10	6.1	.982	C-136
1961	MIN A	133	.302	.470	460	139	24	1	17	3.7	70	55	53	66	3	2	0	812	60	6	9	6.6	.993	C-131
1962		148	.280	.393	522	146	20	3	11	2.1	58	57	57	48	0	1	0	872	82	9	9	6.5	.991	C-147
1963		147	.285	.476	508	145	17	1	26	5.1	64	84	61	75	0	2	0	861	66	6	11	6.3	.994	C-146
1964		131	.272	.407	405	110	17	1	12	3.0	33	52	51	49	1	8	2	813	52	9	4	6.7	.990	C-125
1965		131	.297	.409	394	117	22	2	6	1.5	36	60	50	23	0	5	0	652	56	10	10	5.5	.986	C-128
1966		115	.255	.327	364	93	12	1	4	1.1	30	34	43	30	4	2	1	705	45	4	9	6.6	.995	C-113
1967		48	.165	.211	109	18	3	1	0	0.0	6	8	13	24	0	9	3	212	17	3	2	4.8	.987	C-41
13 yrs.		1141	.270	.409	3586	969	150	17	104	2.9	393	449	421	470	13	60	12	6176	501	69	73	5.9	.990	C-1087

WORLD SERIES

1965	MIN A	7	.120	.200	25	3	0	1	0	0.0	1	2	0	5	0	0	0	31	6	0	2	5.3	1.000	C-7

Joe Battin

BATTIN, JOSEPH V.
B. Nov. 11, 1851, Philadelphia, Pa.   D. Dec. 10, 1937, Akron, Ohio
Manager 1883-84.   BR TR

Year	Team	Games	BA	SA	AB	H	2B	3B	HR	HR%	R	RBI	BB	SO	SB	PH AB	H	PO	A	E	DP	TC/G	FA	G by Pos
1876	STL N	64	.300	.367	283	85	11	4	0	0.0	34	46	6	6		0	0	118	146	40	8	4.8	.868	3B-63, 2B-1
1877		57	.199	.288	226	45	3	7	1	0.4	28	22	6	17		0	0	117	136	55	10	5.4	.821	3B-32, 2B-21, OF-5, P-1
1882	PIT AA	34	.211	.286	133	28	5	1	1	0.8	13		3			0	0	62	108	24	5	5.7	.876	3B-34
1883		98	.214	.276	388	83	9	6	1	0.3	42		11			0	0	151	258	50	12	4.7	.891	3B-98, P-2
1884	3 teams	PIT AA (43G – .177)			PIT U (18G – .188)			BAL U (17G – .102)																
"	total	78	.164	.192	286	47	4	2	0	0.0	21		3			0	0	101	178	33	8	4.0	.894	3B-78
1890	SYR AA	29	.210	.244	119	25	2	1	0	0.0	15		8		8	0	0	44	60	27	2	4.5	.794	3B-29
6 yrs.		360	.218	.277	1435	313	34	21	3	0.2	153	68	37	23	8	0	0	593	886	229	45	4.7	.866	3B-334, 2B-22, OF-5, P-3

Jim Battle

BATTLE, JAMES MILTON
B. Mar. 26, 1901, Bailey, Tex.   D. Sept. 30, 1965, Chico, Calif.   BR TR 6'1" 170 lbs.

1927	CHI A	6	.375	.625	8	3	0	1	0	0.0	1	0	0	1	0	0	0	5	2	0	0	1.2	1.000	3B-4, SS-2

Matt Batts

BATTS, MATTHEW DANIEL
B. Oct. 16, 1921, San Antonio, Tex.   BR TR 5'11" 200 lbs.

Year	Team	Games	BA	SA	AB	H	2B	3B	HR	HR%	R	RBI	BB	SO	SB	PH AB	H	PO	A	E	DP	TC/G	FA	G by Pos
1947	BOS A	7	.500	.750	16	8	1	0	1	6.3	3	5	1	1	0	1	0	15	2	0	1	2.4	1.000	C-6
1948		46	.314	.441	118	37	12	0	1	0.8	13	24	15	9	0	6	1	118	18	2	3	3.0	.986	C-41
1949		60	.242	.369	157	38	9	1	3	1.9	23	31	25	22	1	11	1	193	23	5	2	3.7	.977	C-50
1950		75	.273	.412	238	65	15	3	4	1.7	27	34	18	19	0	2	1	306	29	2	3	4.5	.994	C-73
1951	2 teams	BOS A (11G – .138)			STL A (79G – .302)																			
"	total	90	.285	.412	277	79	18	1	5	1.8	27	33	22	23	2	11	1	291	37	13	6	3.8	.962	C-75
1952	DET A	56	.237	.324	173	41	4	1	3	1.7	11	13	14	22	1	2	0	262	36	5	4	5.4	.983	C-55
1953		116	.278	.406	374	104	24	1	6	1.6	38	42	24	36	2	12	4	463	44	7	7	4.4	.986	C-103
1954	2 teams	DET A (12G – .286)			CHI A (55G – .228)																			
"	total	67	.235	.341	179	42	8	1	3	1.7	17	24	19	19	0	17	4	249	24	3	4	4.1	.989	C-50
1955	CIN N	26	.254	.338	71	18	4	1	0	0.0	4	13	8	11	0	5	1	65	8	1	2	2.8	.986	C-21
1956		3	.000	.000	2	0	0	0	0	0.0	0	0	1	1	0	0	0	0	0	0	0	0.0	–	
10 yrs.		546	.269	.391	1605	432	95	11	26	1.6	163	219	143	163	6	69	13	1962	221	38	32	4.1	.983	C-474

Hank Bauer

BAUER, HENRY ALBERT
B. July 31, 1922, East St. Louis, Ill.
Manager 1961-62, 1964-69.   BR TR 6' 192 lbs.

1948	NY A	19	.180	.300	50	9	1	1	1	2.0	6	9	6	13	1	2	0	26	1	0	1	1.5	.964	OF-14
1949		103	.272	.432	301	82	6	6	10	3.3	56	45	37	42	2	5	2	156	11	4	3	1.7	.977	OF-95
1950		113	.320	.463	415	133	16	2	13	3.1	72	70	35	41	2	2	1	228	8	3	3	2.1	.987	OF-110
1951		118	.296	.454	348	103	19	3	10	2.9	53	54	42	39	5	13	5	188	7	2	1	1.7	.990	OF-107
1952		141	.293	.463	553	162	31	6	17	3.1	86	74	50	61	5	4	2	233	16	4	2	1.8	.984	OF-139

Year	Team	Games	BA	SA	AB	H	2B	3B	HR	HR%	R	RBI	BB	SO	SB	Pinch Hit AB	Pinch Hit H	PO	A	E	DP	TC/G	FA	G by Pos

Hank Bauer *continued*

Year	Team	Games	BA	SA	AB	H	2B	3B	HR	HR%	R	RBI	BB	SO	SB	PH AB	PH H	PO	A	E	DP	TC/G	FA	G by Pos
1953		133	.304	.446	437	133	20	6	10	2.3	77	57	59	45	2	16	3	230	13	2	3	1.8	.992	OF-126
1954		114	.294	.459	377	111	16	5	12	3.2	73	54	40	42	4	9	4	179	6	2	1	1.6	.989	OF-108
1955		139	.278	.461	492	137	20	5	20	4.1	97	53	56	65	8	6	1	248	13	5	3	1.9	.981	OF-133, C-1
1956		147	.241	.445	539	130	18	7	26	4.8	96	84	59	72	4	7	4	242	10	8	2	1.8	.969	OF-135
1957		137	.259	.455	479	124	22	9	18	3.8	70	65	42	64	7	4	1	200	7	3	1	1.5	.986	OF-135
1958		128	.268	.423	452	121	22	6	12	2.7	62	50	32	56	3	6	2	186	7	4	0	1.5	.980	OF-123
1959		114	.238	.375	341	81	20	0	9	2.6	44	39	33	54	4	7	1	139	2	4	0	1.3	.972	OF-111
1960	KC A	95	.275	.369	255	70	15	0	3	1.2	30	31	21	36	1	33	10	85	4	2	1	1.0	.978	OF-67
1961		43	.264	.396	106	28	3	1	3	2.8	11	18	9	8	1	9	1	44	2	2	0	1.1	.958	OF-35
14 yrs.		1544	.277	.439	5145	1424	229	57	164	3.2	833	703	521	638	50	121	36	2384	107	46	20	1.6	.982	OF-1449, C-1

WORLD SERIES

Year	Team	Games	BA	SA	AB	H	2B	3B	HR	HR%	R	RBI	BB	SO	SB	PH AB	PH H	PO	A	E	DP	TC/G	FA	G by Pos
1949	NY A	3	.167	.167	6	1	0	0	0	0.0	0	0	0	0	0	1	0	3	0	0	0	1.0	1.000	OF-3
1950		4	.133	.133	15	2	0	0	0	0.0	0	1	0	0	0	0	0	8	0	0	0	2.0	1.000	OF-4
1951		6	.167	.278	18	3	0	1	0	0.0	0	3	1	1	0	0	0	7	0	0	0	1.2	1.000	OF-6
1952		7	.056	.056	18	1	0	0	0	0.0	2	1	4	3	0	1	0	10	0	0	0	1.4	1.000	OF-7
1953		6	.261	.348	23	6	0	1	0	0.0	6	1	2	4	0	0	0	14	0	0	0	2.3	1.000	OF-6
1955		6	.429	.429	14	6	0	0	0	0.0	1	1	0	1	0	1	0	7	0	0	0	1.2	1.000	OF-5
1956		7	.281	.375	32	9	0	0	1	3.1	3	3	0	5	1	0	0	14	1	1	0	2.3	.938	OF-7
1957		7	.258	.581	31	8	2	1	2	6.5	3	6	1	6	0	0	0	10	0	0	0	1.4	1.000	OF-7
1958		7	.323	.710	31	10	0	0	4	12.9	6	8	0	6	0	0	0	7	0	0	0	1.0	1.000	OF-7
9 yrs.		53	.245	.399	188	46	2	3	7	3.7	21	24	8	25	1	3	0	80	1	1	0	1.5	.988	OF-52
			4th			6th	5th		4th	10th		10th	8th		7th									

Paddy Baumann

BAUMANN, CHARLES JOHN
B. Dec. 20, 1885, Indianapolis, Ind.   D. Nov. 20, 1969, Indianapolis, Ind.
BR TR 5'9" 160 lbs.

Year	Team	Games	BA	SA	AB	H	2B	3B	HR	HR%	R	RBI	BB	SO	SB	PH AB	PH H	PO	A	E	DP	TC/G	FA	G by Pos
1911	DET A	26	.255	.362	94	24	2	4	0	0.0	8	11	6		1	0	0	68	71	6	6	5.6	.959	2B-23, OF-3
1912		13	.262	.286	42	11	1	0	0	0.0	3	7	6		4	1	0	19	23	9	1	3.9	.824	3B-6, 2B-5, OF-1
1913		49	.298	.393	191	57	7	4	1	0.5	31	22	16	18	4	0	0	97	136	14	15	5.0	.943	2B-49
1914		3	.000	.000	11	0	0	0	0	0.0	1	0	2	1	0	0	0	5	8	0	1	4.3	1.000	2B-3
1915	NY A	76	.292	.388	219	64	13	1	2	0.9	30	28	28	32	9	10	2	129	140	6	20	3.6	.978	2B-43, 3B-19
1916		79	.287	.346	237	68	5	3	1	0.4	35	25	19	16	10	14	5	93	64	8	8	2.1	.952	OF-28, 3B-26, 2B-9
1917		49	.218	.255	110	24	2	1	0	0.0	10	8	4	9	2	21	6	37	32	4	8	1.5	.945	2B-18, OF-7, 3B-1
7 yrs.		295	.274	.350	904	248	30	13	4	0.4	118	101	81	76	30	46	13	448	474	47	59	3.3	.951	2B-150, 3B-52, OF-39

Jim Baumer

BAUMER, JAMES SLOAN
B. Jan. 29, 1931, Tulsa, Okla.
BR TR 6'2" 185 lbs.

Year	Team	Games	BA	SA	AB	H	2B	3B	HR	HR%	R	RBI	BB	SO	SB	PH AB	PH H	PO	A	E	DP	TC/G	FA	G by Pos
1949	CHI A	8	.400	.700	10	4	1	1	0	0.0	2	2	2	1	0	0	0	3	12	1	4	2.0	.938	SS-7
1961	CIN N	10	.125	.125	24	3	0	0	0	0.0	0	0	0	9	0	0	0	18	14	0	2	3.2	1.000	2B-9
2 yrs.		18	.206	.294	34	7	1	1	0	0.0	2	2	2	10	0	0	0	21	26	1	6	2.7	.979	2B-9, SS-7

John Baumgartner

BAUMGARTNER, JOHN EDWARD
B. May 29, 1931, Birmingham, Ala.
BR TR 6'1" 190 lbs.

Year	Team	Games	BA	SA	AB	H	2B	3B	HR	HR%	R	RBI	BB	SO	SB	PH AB	PH H	PO	A	E	DP	TC/G	FA	G by Pos
1953	DET A	7	.185	.185	27	5	0	0	0	0.0	3	2	0	5	0	0	0	10	11	2	2	3.3	.913	3B-7

Frankie Baumholtz

BAUMHOLTZ, FRANK CONRAD
B. Oct. 7, 1918, Midvale, Ohio
BL TL 5'10½" 175 lbs.

Year	Team	Games	BA	SA	AB	H	2B	3B	HR	HR%	R	RBI	BB	SO	SB	PH AB	PH H	PO	A	E	DP	TC/G	FA	G by Pos
1947	CIN N	151	.283	.384	643	182	32	9	5	0.8	96	45	56	53	6	1	1	282	18	7	2	2.0	.977	OF-150
1948		128	.296	.395	415	123	19	5	4	1.0	57	30	27	32	8	15	7	216	11	3	2	1.8	.987	OF-110
1949	2 teams			CIN N (27G – .235)			CHI N (58G – .226)																	
"	total	85	.229	.331	245	56	9	5	2	0.8	27	23	15	29	2	20	6	120	4	3	3	1.5	.976	OF-63
1951	CHI N	146	.284	.380	560	159	28	10	2	0.4	62	50	49	36	5	4	2	307	6	8	2	2.2	.975	OF-140
1952		103	.325	.416	409	133	17	4	4	1.0	59	35	27	27	5	2	0	248	10	7	3	2.6	.974	OF-101
1953		133	.306	.419	520	159	36	7	3	0.6	75	25	42	36	3	3	0	290	6	6	0	2.3	.980	OF-130
1954		90	.297	.416	303	90	12	6	4	1.3	38	22	20	15	1	17	2	168	2	2	0	1.9	.988	OF-71
1955		105	.289	.379	280	81	12	5	1	0.4	23	27	16	24	0	37	15	131	3	1	1	1.3	.993	OF-15
1956	PHI N	76	.270	.270	100	27	0	0	0	0.0	13	9	6	6	0	52	14	23	2	1	0	0.3	.962	OF-15
1957		2	.000	.000	2	0	0	0	0	0.0	0	0	0	0	0	2	0	0	0	0	0	0.0	–	
10 yrs.		1019	.290	.389	3477	1010	165	51	25	0.7	450	272	258	258	30	153	47	1785	62	38	13	1.8	.980	OF-843

Jim Baxes

BAXES, DIMITRIOS SPEROS
Brother of Mike Baxes.
B. July 5, 1928, San Francisco, Calif.
BR TR 6'1" 190 lbs.

Year	Team	Games	BA	SA	AB	H	2B	3B	HR	HR%	R	RBI	BB	SO	SB	PH AB	PH H	PO	A	E	DP	TC/G	FA	G by Pos
1959	2 teams			LA N (11G – .303)			CLE A (77G – .239)																	
"	total	88	.246	.471	280	69	12	6	17	6.1	39	39	25	54	1	12	3	134	177	17	33	3.7	.948	2B-48, 3B-32

Mike Baxes

BAXES, MICHAEL
Brother of Jim Baxes.
B. Dec. 18, 1930, San Francisco, Calif.
BR TR 5'10" 175 lbs.

Year	Team	Games	BA	SA	AB	H	2B	3B	HR	HR%	R	RBI	BB	SO	SB	PH AB	PH H	PO	A	E	DP	TC/G	FA	G by Pos
1956	KC A	73	.226	.302	106	24	3	1	1	0.9	9	5	18	15	0	9	1	57	113	11	17	2.5	.939	SS-62, 2B-1
1958		73	.212	.264	231	49	10	1	0	0.0	31	8	21	24	1	4	0	135	157	9	40	4.1	.970	2B-61, SS-4
2 yrs.		146	.217	.276	337	73	13	2	1	0.3	40	13	39	39	1	13	1	192	270	20	57	3.3	.959	SS-66, 2B-62

John Baxter

BAXTER, JOHN MOORE
B. Spokane, Wash.
6'3"

Year	Team	Games	BA	SA	AB	H	2B	3B	HR	HR%	R	RBI	BB	SO	SB	PH AB	PH H	PO	A	E	DP	TC/G	FA	G by Pos
1907	STL N	6	.190	.190	21	4	0	0	0	0.0	1	0	0		0	0	0	54	4	5	1	10.5	.921	1B-6

Harry Bay

BAY, HARRY ELBERT (Deerfoot)
B. Jan. 17, 1878, Pontiac, Ill.   D. Mar. 20, 1952, Peoria, Ill.
BL TL 5'8" 138 lbs.

Year	Team	Games	BA	SA	AB	H	2B	3B	HR	HR%	R	RBI	BB	SO	SB	PH AB	PH H	PO	A	E	DP	TC/G	FA	G by Pos
1901	CIN N	41	.210	.261	157	33	1	2	1	0.6	25	3	13		4	1	1	78	3	4	3	2.1	.953	OF-40

Year	Team	Games	BA	SA	AB	H	2B	3B	HR	HR%	R	RBI	BB	SO	SB	Pinch Hit AB	Pinch Hit H	PO	A	E	DP	TC/G	FA	G by Pos

Harry Bay *continued*

Year	Team	Games	BA	SA	AB	H	2B	3B	HR	HR%	R	RBI	BB	SO	SB	AB	H	PO	A	E	DP	TC/G	FA	G by Pos
1902	2 teams	CIN N (6G – .375)			CLE A (108G – .290)																			
"	total	114	.293	.335	471	138	10	5	0	0.0	74	24	38		22	4	0	248	14	9	3	2.4	.967	OF-110
1903	CLE A	140	.292	.364	579	169	15	12	1	0.2	94	35	29		45	0	0	293	13	16	3	2.3	.950	OF-140
1904		132	.261	.338	506	132	12	9	3	0.6	69	36	43		38	0	0	281	15	4	6	2.3	.987	OF-132
1905		143	.298	.367	550	164	18	10	0	0.0	90	22	36		36	0	0	303	14	10	4	2.3	.969	OF-143
1906		68	.275	.325	280	77	8	3	0	0.0	47	14	26		17	0	0	131	8	3	2	2.1	.979	OF-68
1907		34	.179	.211	95	17	1	1	0	0.0	14	7	10		7	3	1	55	5	2	1	1.8	.968	OF-31
1908		1	–	–	0	0	0	0	0		0	0	0		0	0	0	0	0	0	0	0.0	–	
8 yrs.		673	.277	.339	2638	730	65	42	5	0.2	413	141	195		169	8	2	1389	72	48	22	2.2	.968	OF-664

Dick Bayless

BAYLESS, HARRY OWEN
B. Sept. 6, 1883, Joplin, Mo.   D. Dec. 16, 1920, Santa Rita, N. M.

BL TR 5'9"   178 lbs.

| 1908 | CIN N | 19 | .225 | .282 | 71 | 16 | 1 | 0 | 1 | 1.4 | 7 | 3 | 6 | | 0 | 0 | 0 | 29 | 6 | 2 | 2 | 1.9 | .946 | OF-19 |

Don Baylor

BAYLOR, DON EDWARD
B. June 28, 1949, Austin, Tex.

BR TR 6'1"   190 lbs.

1970	BAL A	8	.235	.235	17	4	0	0	0	0.0	4	4	2	3	1	0	0	15	0	0	0	1.9	1.000	OF-6
1971		1	.000	.000	2	0	0	0	0	0.0	0	1	2	1	0	0	0	4	0	0	0	4.0	1.000	OF-1
1972		102	.253	.416	320	81	13	3	11	3.4	33	38	29	50	24	16	5	206	4	5	5	2.1	.977	OF-84, 1B-9
1973		118	.286	.437	405	116	20	4	11	2.7	64	51	35	48	32	12	2	228	10	6	2	2.1	.975	OF-110, 1B-6, DH-1
1974		137	.272	.382	489	133	22	1	10	2.0	66	59	43	56	29	5	3	260	2	5	2	1.9	.981	OF-129, 1B-8, DH-1
1975		145	.282	.489	524	148	21	6	25	4.8	79	76	53	64	32	1	1	286	8	5	1	2.1	.983	OF-135, DH-7, 1B-2
1976	OAK A	157	.247	.368	595	147	25	1	15	2.5	85	68	58	72	52	2	0	781	45	12	40	5.3	.986	OF-76, DH-23
1977	CAL A	154	.251	.433	561	141	27	0	25	4.5	87	75	62	76	26	1	0	280	16	7	14	2.0	.977	OF-77, DH-61, 1B-18
1978		158	.255	.472	591	151	26	0	34	5.8	103	99	56	71	22	0	0	194	9	6	6	1.3	.971	DH-100, OF-39, 1B-17
1979		162	.296	.530	628	186	33	3	36	5.7	120	139	71	51	22	0	0	203	3	5	1	1.3	.976	OF-97, DH-65, 1B-1
1980		90	.250	.341	340	85	12	2	5	1.5	39	51	24	32	6	0	0	119	4	4	0	1.4	.969	OF-54, DH-36
1981		103	.239	.427	377	90	18	1	17	4.5	52	66	42	51	3	1	1	38	3	0	2	0.4	1.000	DH-97, 1B-4, OF-1
1982		157	.263	.424	608	160	24	1	24	3.9	80	93	57	69	10	0	0	0	0	0	0	0.0	–	DH-155
1983	NY A	144	.303	.494	534	162	33	2	21	3.9	82	85	40	53	17	9	2	23	0	1	0	0.2	.962	DH-136, OF-5, 1B-1
1984		134	.262	.489	493	129	29	1	27	5.5	84	89	39	67	1	10	2	8	0	1	0	0.1	.889	DH-127, 1B-5
1985		142	.231	.430	477	110	24	1	23	4.8	70	91	52	90	0	13	5	0	0	0	0	0.0	–	DH-140
1986	BOS A	160	.238	.439	585	139	23	1	31	5.3	93	94	62	111	3	0	0	71	4	1	7	0.5	.987	DH-143, 1B-13, OF-3
1987	2 teams	BOS A (108G – .239)			MIN A (20G – .286)																			
"	total	128	.245	.392	388	95	9	0	16	4.1	67	63	45	59	5	17	6	0	0	0	0	0.0	–	DH-117
1988	OAK A	92	.220	.326	264	58	7	0	7	2.7	28	34	34	44	0	12	1	0	0	0	0	0.0	–	DH-80
19 yrs.		2292	.260	.436	8198	2135	366	28	338	4.1	1236	1276	806	1068	285	99	28	2716	110	58	80	1.3	.980	DH-1289, OF-817, 1B-153

LEAGUE CHAMPIONSHIP SERIES

1973	BAL A	4	.273	.273	11	3	0	0	0	0.0	3	1	3	5	0	0	0	7	0	0	0	1.8	1.000	OF-3
1974		4	.267	.267	15	4	0	0	0	0.0	0	0	0	2	0	0	0	9	0	0	0	2.3	1.000	OF-4
1979	CAL A	4	.188	.375	16	3	0	0	1	6.3	2	2	1	2	0	0	0	4	0	0	0	1.0	1.000	DH-3, OF-1
1982		5	.294	.647	17	5	1	1	1	5.9	2	10	2	0	0	0	0	0	0	0	0	0.0	–	DH-5
1986	BOS A	7	.346	.577	26	9	3	0	1	3.8	6	2	4	5	0	0	0	0	0	0	0	0.0	–	DH-7
1987	MIN A	2	.400	.400	5	2	0	0	0	0.0	1	0	0	1	0	1	0	0	0	0	0	0.0	–	DH-2
1988	OAK A	2	.000	.000	6	0	0	0	0	0.0	0	1	1	2	0	0	0	0	0	0	0	0.0	–	DH-2
7 yrs.		28	.271	.427	96	26	4	1	3	3.1	13	17	11	16	0	1	0	20	0	0	0	0.7	1.000	DH-19, OF-8

WORLD SERIES

1986	BOS A	4	.182	.273	11	2	1	0	0	0.0	1	1	1	3	0	0	0	0	0	0	0	0.0	–	DH-3
1987	MIN A	5	.385	.615	13	5	0	0	1	7.7	3	3	1	1	0	2	1	0	0	0	0	0.0	–	DH-3
1988	OAK A	1	.000	.000	1	0	0	0	0	0.0	0	0	0	1	0	0	0	0	0	0	0	0.0	–	DH-6
3 yrs.		10	.280	.440	25	7	1	0	1	4.0	4	4	2	5	0	4	1	0	0	0	0	0.0	–	DH-6

Jack Beach

BEACH, JACKSON STONEWALL
B. 1862, Alexandria, Va.   D. July 23, 1896, Alexandria, Va.

| 1884 | WAS AA | 8 | .097 | .161 | 31 | 3 | 2 | 0 | 0 | 0.0 | 3 | | 0 | | 0 | 0 | 0 | 10 | 2 | 6 | 1 | 2.3 | .667 | OF-8 |

Bob Beall

BEALL, ROBERT BROOKS
B. Apr. 24, 1948, Portland, Ore.

BB TL 5'11"   180 lbs.

1975	ATL N	20	.226	.290	31	7	2	0	0	0.0	2	1	6	9	0	9	0	57	4	1	6	3.1	.984	1B-8
1978		108	.243	.303	185	45	8	0	1	0.5	29	16	36	27	4	50	10	282	24	4	23	2.9	.987	1B-40, OF-8
1979		17	.133	.267	15	2	2	0	0	0.0	1	1	3	4	0	9	1	9	1	0	0	0.6	1.000	1B-3
1980	PIT N	3	.000	.000	3	0	0	0	0	0.0	0	0	0	1	0	3	0	0	0	0	0	0.0	–	
4 yrs.		148	.231	.295	234	54	12	0	1	0.4	32	18	45	41	4	71	11	348	29	5	29	2.6	.987	1B-51, OF-8

Johnny Beall

BEALL, JOHN WOOLF
B. Mar. 12, 1882, Beltsville, Md.   D. June 14, 1926, Beltsville, Md.

BL TR 6'   180 lbs.

1913	2 teams	CLE A (6G – .167)			CHI A (17G – .267)																			
"	total	23	.258	.379	66	17	0	1	2	3.0	10	4	0	2	1	6	1	38	3	2	0	1.9	.953	OF-17
1915	CIN N	10	.235	.265	34	8	1	0	0	0.0	3	3	5	10	0	0	0	22	2	1	1	2.5	.960	OF-10
1916		6	.333	.571	21	7	2	0	1	4.8	3	4	3	7	1	1	0	9	2	0	0	1.8	1.000	OF-6
1918	STL N	19	.224	.245	49	11	1	0	0	0.0	2	6	3	6	0	5	2	26	2	0	1	1.5	1.000	OF-18
4 yrs.		58	.253	.341	170	43	4	1	3	1.8	18	17	11	25	2	12	3	95	9	3	2	1.8	.972	OF-51

Tommy Beals

BEALS, THOMAS L.
B. Hartford, Conn.   D. Oct. 2, 1915, San Francisco, Calif.

BR 5'5"   144 lbs.

| 1880 | CHI N | 13 | .152 | .152 | 46 | 7 | 0 | 0 | 0 | 0.0 | 4 | 3 | 1 | 6 | | 0 | 0 | 14 | 3 | 5 | 1 | 1.7 | .773 | OF-10, 2B-3 |

Charlie Beamon

BEAMON, CHARLES ALFONZO, JR.
Son of Charlie Beamon.
B. Dec. 4, 1953, Oakland, Calif.

BL TL 6'1"   183 lbs.

Year Team	Games	BA	SA	AB	H	2B	3B	HR	HR%	R	RBI	BB	SO	SB	Pinch Hit AB	H	PO	A	E	DP	TC/G	FA	G by Pos

Charlie Beamon *continued*

Year Team	Games	BA	SA	AB	H	2B	3B	HR	HR%	R	RBI	BB	SO	SB	PH AB	H	PO	A	E	DP	TC/G	FA	G by Pos
1978 SEA A	10	.182	.182	11	2	0	0	0	0.0	2	0	1	1	0	1	0	20	4	0	2	2.4	1.000	DH-6, 1B-2
1979	27	.200	.240	25	5	1	0	0	0.0	5	0	0	5	1	14	3	15	2	0	0	0.6	1.000	1B-7, DH-5, OF-2
1981 TOR A	8	.200	.267	15	3	1	0	0	0.0	1	0	2	2	0	3	0	6	0	0	0	0.8	1.000	DH-4, 1B-1
3 yrs.	45	.196	.235	51	10	2	0	0	0.0	8	0	3	8	1	18	3	41	6	0	2	1.0	1.000	DH-15, 1B-10, OF-2

Billy Bean
BEAN, WILLIAM DARO B. May 11, 1964, Santa Ana, Calif.   BL TL 6' 185 lbs.

Year Team	Games	BA	SA	AB	H	2B	3B	HR	HR%	R	RBI	BB	SO	SB	PH AB	H	PO	A	E	DP	TC/G	FA	G by Pos
1987 DET A	26	.258	.288	66	17	2	0	0	0.0	6	4	5	11	1	5	0	54	1	0	0	2.1	1.000	OF-24
1988	10	.182	.364	11	2	0	1	0	0.0	2	0	0	2	0	4	2	8	1	0	0	0.9	1.000	OF-4, 1B-2, DH-1
1989 2 teams				DET A (9G – .000)				LA N (51G – .197)															
" total	60	.171	.220	82	14	4	0	0	0.0	7	3	6	13	0	7	1	61	0	2	1	1.1	.968	OF-50, 1B-2
3 yrs.	96	.208	.258	159	33	6	1	0	0.0	15	7	11	26	1	16	3	123	2	2	3	1.3	.984	OF-78, 1B-4, DH-1

Joe Bean
BEAN, JOSEPH WILLIAM B. Mar. 18, 1874, Boston, Mass. D. Feb. 15, 1961, Atlanta, Ga.   BR TR 5'8" 138 lbs.

Year Team	Games	BA	SA	AB	H	2B	3B	HR	HR%	R	RBI	BB	SO	SB	PH AB	H	PO	A	E	DP	TC/G	FA	G by Pos
1902 NY N	48	.222	.244	176	39	2	1	0	0.0	13	5	5		9	0	0	71	153	28	19	5.3	.889	SS-48

Billy Beane
BEANE, WILLIAM LAMAR B. Mar. 29, 1962, Orlando, Fla.   BR TR 6'4" 195 lbs.

Year Team	Games	BA	SA	AB	H	2B	3B	HR	HR%	R	RBI	BB	SO	SB	PH AB	H	PO	A	E	DP	TC/G	FA	G by Pos
1984 NY N	5	.100	.100	10	1	0	0	0	0.0	0	0	0	2	0	2	0	2	0	0	0	0.4	1.000	OF-5
1985	8	.250	.375	8	2	1	0	0	0.0	0	1	0	3	0	4	2	1	0	0	0	0.1	1.000	OF-2
1986 MIN A	80	.213	.295	183	39	6	0	3	1.6	20	15	11	54	2	11	1	118	0	0	0	1.5	1.000	OF-67, DH-5
1987	12	.267	.400	15	4	2	0	0	0.0	1	1	0	6	0	3	0	8	0	0	0	0.7	1.000	OF-7
1988 DET A	6	.167	.167	6	1	0	0	0	0.0	1	1	0	2	0	0	0	5	0	0	0	0.8	1.000	OF-6
1989 OAK A	37	.241	.304	79	19	5	0	0	0.0	8	11	0	13	3	7	3	58	3	1	1	1.7	.984	OF-25, DH-4, 1B-4, 3B-1, C-1
6 yrs.	148	.219	.296	301	66	14	0	3	1.0	30	29	11	80	5	27	6	192	3	1	1	1.3	.995	OF-112, DH-9, 1B-4, 3B-1, C-1

Ollie Beard
BEARD, OLIVER PERRY B. May 2, 1862, Lexington, Ky. D. May 28, 1929, Cincinnati, Ohio   BR TR 5'11" 180 lbs.

Year Team	Games	BA	SA	AB	H	2B	3B	HR	HR%	R	RBI	BB	SO	SB	PH AB	H	PO	A	E	DP	TC/G	FA	G by Pos
1889 CIN AA	141	.285	.364	558	159	13	14	1	0.2	96	77	35	39	36	0	0	214	537	87	63	5.9	.896	SS-141
1890 CIN N	122	.268	.382	492	132	17	15	3	0.6	64	72	44	13	30	0	0	155	445	71	45	5.5	.894	SS-113, 3B-9
1891 LOU AA	68	.241	.296	257	62	4	5	0	0.0	35	24	33	9	7	0	0	91	172	36	17	4.4	.880	3B-61, SS-7
3 yrs.	331	.270	.357	1307	353	34	34	4	0.3	195	173	112	61	73	0	0	460	1154	194	125	5.5	.893	SS-261, 3B-70

Ted Beard
BEARD, CRAMER THEODORE B. Jan. 7, 1921, Woodsboro, Md.   BL TL 5'8" 165 lbs.

Year Team	Games	BA	SA	AB	H	2B	3B	HR	HR%	R	RBI	BB	SO	SB	PH AB	H	PO	A	E	DP	TC/G	FA	G by Pos
1948 PIT N	25	.198	.284	81	16	1	3	0	0.0	15	7	12	18	5	2	1	66	0	0	0	2.6	1.000	OF-22
1949	14	.083	.083	24	2	0	0	0	0.0	1	1	2	2	0	3	0	9	0	1	0	0.7	.900	OF-10
1950	61	.232	.356	177	41	6	2	4	2.3	32	12	27	45	3	12	3	112	4	2	0	1.9	.983	OF-49
1951	22	.188	.271	48	9	1	0	1	2.1	7	3	6	14	1	6	2	23	2	0	0	1.1	1.000	OF-22
1952	15	.182	.273	44	8	2	1	0	0.0	5	3	7	9	2	1	0	27	1	0	0	1.9	1.000	OF-13
1957 CHI A	38	.205	.218	78	16	1	0	0	0.0	15	7	18	14	3	3	1	33	5	1	0	1.0	.974	OF-28
1958	19	.091	.227	22	2	0	0	1	4.5	5	2	6	5	3	3	0	15	0	0	0	0.8	1.000	OF-15
7 yrs.	194	.198	.285	474	94	11	6	6	1.3	80	35	78	107	16	30	7	285	12	4	0	1.6	.987	OF-159

Lew Beasley
BEASLEY, LEWIS PAIGE B. Aug. 27, 1948, Sparta, Va.   BL TR 5'10" 172 lbs.

Year Team	Games	BA	SA	AB	H	2B	3B	HR	HR%	R	RBI	BB	SO	SB	PH AB	H	PO	A	E	DP	TC/G	FA	G by Pos
1977 TEX A	25	.219	.250	32	7	1	0	0	0.0	5	3	2	2	1	2	0	10	0	2	0	0.5	.833	OF-18, DH-1, SS-1

Dave Beatle
BEATLE, DAVID B. 1861, New York, N.Y. Deceased.   6'2" 200 lbs.

Year Team	Games	BA	SA	AB	H	2B	3B	HR	HR%	R	RBI	BB	SO	SB	PH AB	H	PO	A	E	DP	TC/G	FA	G by Pos
1884 DET N	1	.000	.000	3	0	0	0	0	0.0	0		0	2		0	0	3	1	3	0	7.0	.571	OF-1, C-1

Des Beatty
BEATTY, ALOYSIUS DESMOND (Desperate) B. Apr. 7, 1893, Baltimore, Md. D. Oct. 6, 1969, Norway, Me.   BR TR 5'8½" 158 lbs.

Year Team	Games	BA	SA	AB	H	2B	3B	HR	HR%	R	RBI	BB	SO	SB	PH AB	H	PO	A	E	DP	TC/G	FA	G by Pos
1914 NY N	2	.000	.000	3	0	0	0	0	0.0	0	1	0	0	0	0	0	2	3	3	0	4.0	.625	SS-1, 3B-1

Jim Beauchamp
BEAUCHAMP, JAMES EDWARD B. Aug. 21, 1939, Vinita, Okla.   BR TR 6'2" 190 lbs.

Year Team	Games	BA	SA	AB	H	2B	3B	HR	HR%	R	RBI	BB	SO	SB	PH AB	H	PO	A	E	DP	TC/G	FA	G by Pos
1963 STL N	4	.000	.000	3	0	0	0	0	0.0	0	0	0	2	0	3	0	0	0	0	0	0.0	—	
1964 HOU N	23	.164	.309	55	9	2	0	2	3.6	6	4	5	16	0	6	1	27	1	2	1	1.3	.933	OF-15, 1B-2
1965 2 teams				HOU N (24G – .189)				MIL N (4G – .000)															
" total	28	.179	.196	56	10	1	0	0	0.0	5	4	6	12	0	13	2	49	7	1	2	2.0	.982	OF-9, 1B-5
1967 ATL N	4	.000	.000	3	0	0	0	0	0.0	0	1	0	0	0	3	0	0	0	0	0	0.0	—	
1968 CIN N	31	.263	.404	57	15	2	0	2	3.5	10	14	4	19	0	17	2	34	1	0	1	1.1	1.000	OF-13, 1B-1
1969	43	.250	.317	60	15	1	0	1	1.7	8	8	5	13	0	32	7	38	2	1	2	1.0	.976	OF-9, 1B-3
1970 2 teams				HOU N (31G – .192)				STL N (44G – .259)															
" total	75	.238	.333	84	20	2	0	2	2.4	11	10	11	18	2	37	9	49	4	0	2	0.7	1.000	OF-26, 1B-5
1971 STL N	77	.235	.358	162	38	8	3	2	1.2	24	16	9	26	3	32	8	311	19	6	27	4.4	.982	1B-44, OF-1
1972 NY N	58	.242	.375	120	29	1	0	5	4.2	10	19	7	33	0	21	6	188	9	5	16	3.5	.975	1B-35, OF-3
1973	50	.279	.328	61	17	1	1	0	0.0	5	14	7	11	1	34	9	59	3	2	1	1.3	.969	1B-11
10 yrs.	393	.231	.334	661	153	18	4	14	2.1	79	90	54	150	6	198	46	755	46	17	58	2.1	.979	1B-106, OF-76

WORLD SERIES

Year Team	Games	BA	SA	AB	H	2B	3B	HR	HR%	R	RBI	BB	SO	SB	PH AB	H	PO	A	E	DP	TC/G	FA	G by Pos
1973 NY N	4	.000	.000	4	0	0	0	0	0.0	0	0	0	1	0	4	0	0	0	0	0	0.0	—	

Ginger Beaumont
BEAUMONT, CLARENCE HOWETH B. July 23, 1876, Rochester, Wis. D. Apr. 10, 1956, Burlington, Wis.   BL TR 5'8" 190 lbs.

Year	Team		Games	BA	SA	AB	H	2B	3B	HR	HR%	R	RBI	BB	SO	SB	Pinch Hit AB	Pinch Hit H	PO	A	E	DP	TC/G	FA	G by Pos

Ginger Beaumont *continued*

1899	PIT	N	111	.352	.444	437	154	15	8	3	0.7	90	38	41		31	6	3	250	21	23	7	2.6	.922	OF-102, 1B-2
1900			138	.279	.356	567	158	14	9	4	0.7	107	50	40		27	0	0	274	10	17	3	2.2	.944	OF-138
1901			133	.332	.418	558	185	14	5	8	1.4	120	72	44		36	0	0	289	8	18	2	2.4	.943	OF-133
1902			131	.357	.417	544	194	21	6	0	0.0	101	67	39		33	0	0	260	15	7	8	2.2	.975	OF-130
1903			141	.341	.444	613	209	30	6	7	1.1	137	68	44		23	0	0	258	15	15	2	2.0	.948	OF-141
1904			153	.301	.374	615	185	12	12	3	0.5	97	54	34		28	0	0	287	14	10	6	2.0	.968	OF-153
1905			103	.328	.424	384	126	12	8	3	0.8	60	40	22		21	4	1	200	12	6	5	2.1	.972	OF-97
1906			80	.265	.332	310	82	9	3	2	0.6	48	32	19		1	1	0	148	6	9	2	2.0	.945	OF-78
1907	BOS	N	150	.322	.424	580	187	19	14	4	0.7	67	62	37		25	1	1	296	30	13	12	2.3	.962	OF-149
1908			125	.267	.347	476	127	20	6	2	0.4	66	52	42		13	4	1	259	17	10	3	2.3	.965	OF-121
1909			123	.263	.310	407	107	11	4	0	0.0	35	60	35		12	14	5	234	15	8	3	2.1	.969	OF-111
1910	CHI	N	56	.267	.343	172	46	5	1	2	1.2	30	22	28	14	4	13	3	107	5	5	0	2.1	.957	OF-56
12 yrs.			1444	.311	.392	5663	1760	182	82	38	0.7	958	617	425	14	254	43	14	2862	168	141	53	2.2	.956	OF-1409, 1B-2

WORLD SERIES

1903	PIT	N	8	.265	.324	34	9	0	1	0	0.0	6	0	2	4	2	0	0	22	0	0	0	2.8	1.000	OF-8
1910	CHI	N	3	.000	.000	2	0	0	0	0	0.0	1	0	1	1	0	2	0	0	0	0	0	0.0	—	
2 yrs.			11	.250	.306	36	9	0	1	0	0.0	7	0	3	5	2	2	0	22	0	0	0	2.0	1.000	OF-8

George Bechtel   BECHTEL, GEORGE A.
B. Sept. 2, 1848, Philadelphia, Pa.   Deceased.   5'11"   165 lbs.

| 1876 | 2 teams | | LOU | N | (14G – .182) | | NY | N | (2G – .300) | | | | | | | | | | | | | | | | |
| " | total | | 16 | .200 | .215 | 65 | 13 | 1 | 0 | 0 | 0.0 | 4 | 2 | 0 | 1 | | 0 | 0 | 17 | 1 | 7 | 0 | 1.6 | .720 | OF-16 |

Clyde Beck   BECK, CLYDE EUGENE (Jersey)
B. Jan. 6, 1900, Bassett, Calif.   D. July 17, 1988, Temple City, Calif.   BR TR 5'10"   150 lbs.

1926	CHI	N	30	.198	.235	81	16	0	1	1	1.2	10	4	7	15	0	0	0	68	80	1	19	5.0	.993	2B-27
1927			117	.258	.350	391	101	20	5	2	0.5	44	44	43	37	0	0	0	267	402	24	67	5.9	.965	2B-99, 3B-17, SS-1
1928			131	.257	.329	483	124	18	4	3	0.6	72	52	58	58	3	1	1	167	299	18	53	3.7	.963	3B-87, SS-47, 2B-1
1929			54	.211	.247	190	40	7	0	0	0.0	28	9	19	24	3	5	1	42	118	6	20	3.1	.964	3B-33, SS-14
1930			83	.213	.316	244	52	7	0	6	2.5	32	34	36	32	2	0	0	149	236	20	54	4.9	.951	SS-57, 2B-24, 3B-2
1931	CIN	N	53	.154	.213	136	21	4	2	0	0.0	17	19	21	14	1	8	2	41	65	5	12	2.1	.955	3B-38, SS-6
6 yrs.			468	.232	.307	1525	354	56	11	12	0.8	203	162	184	180	9	14	4	734	1200	74	225	4.3	.963	3B-177, 2B-151, SS-125

Erve Beck   BECK, ERVIN THOMAS (Dutch)
B. July 19, 1878, Toledo, Ohio   D. Dec. 23, 1916, Toledo, Ohio   BR TR 5'10"   168 lbs.

1899	BKN	N	8	.167	.250	24	4	2	0	0	0.0	2	2	0		0	0	0	8	22	4	1	4.3	.882	2B-6, SS-2
1901	CLE	A	135	.289	.401	539	156	26	8	6	1.1	78	79	23		7	3	1	310	404	56	44	5.7	.927	2B-132
1902	2 teams		CIN	N	(48G – .305)		DET	A	(41G – .296)																
"	total		89	.301	.384	349	105	14	3	3	0.9	42	42	7		5	4	1	491	124	24	40	7.2	.962	1B-42, 2B-32, OF-11
3 yrs.			232	.291	.390	912	265	42	11	9	1.0	122	123	30		12	7	2	809	550	84	85	6.2	.942	2B-170, 1B-42, OF-11, SS-2

Fred Beck   BECK, FREDERICK THOMAS
B. Nov. 17, 1886, Havana, Ill.   D. Mar. 12, 1962, Havana, Ill.   BL TL 6'1"   180 lbs.

1909	BOS	N	96	.198	.272	334	66	4	6	3	0.9	20	27	17		5	8	0	464	26	14	18	5.3	.972	OF-57, 1B-33
1910			154	.275	.415	571	157	32	9	10	1.8	52	64	19	55	8	1	0	479	28	17	20	3.4	.968	OF-134, 1B-19
1911	2 teams		CIN	N	(41G – .184)		PHI	N	(66G – .281)																
"	total		107	.253	.367	297	75	9	5	5	1.7	33	45	18	34	5	21	4	129	10	5	6	1.3	.965	OF-77, 1B-6
1914	CHI	F	157	.279	.355	555	155	23	4	11	2.0	51	77	44		9	0	0	1614	55	31	86	10.8	.982	1B-157
1915			121	.223	.303	373	83	9	3	5	1.3	35	38	24		4	4	0	1073	42	9	57	9.3	.992	1B-117
5 yrs.			635	.252	.361	2130	536	77	27	34	1.6	191	251	122	89	31	34	4	3759	161	76	187	6.3	.981	1B-332, OF-268

Zinn Beck   BECK, ZINN BERTRAM
B. Sept. 30, 1885, Steubenville, Ohio   D. Mar. 19, 1981, West Palm Beach, Fla.   BR TR 5'10½" 160 lbs.

1913	STL	N	10	.167	.200	30	5	1	0	0	0.0	4	2	4	10	1	0	0	11	29	5	2	4.5	.889	SS-5, 3B-5
1914			137	.232	.333	457	106	15	11	3	0.7	42	45	28	32	14	0	0	182	318	35	30	3.9	.935	3B-122, SS-16
1915			70	.233	.309	223	52	9	4	0	0.0	21	15	12	31	3	2	0	63	137	16	10	3.1	.926	3B-60, SS-4, 2B-2
1916			62	.223	.272	184	41	7	1	0	0.0	8	10	14	21	3	9	2	46	86	13	8	2.3	.910	3B-52, 2B-1, 1B-1
1918	NY	A	11	.000	.000	8	0	0	0	0	0.0	0	1	0		0	4	0	16	2	0	2	1.6	1.000	1B-5
5 yrs.			290	.226	.307	902	204	32	16	3	0.3	75	73	58	95	21	15	2	318	572	69	52	3.3	.928	3B-239, SS-25, 1B-6, 2B-3

Heinie Beckendorf   BECKENDORF, HENRY WARD
B. June 15, 1884, New York, N. Y.   D. Sept. 15, 1949, Jackson Heights, N. Y.   BR TR 5'9"   174 lbs.

1909	DET	A	15	.259	.296	27	7	1	0	0	0.0	1	1	2		0	0	0	36	9	2	4	3.1	.957	C-15
1910	2 teams		DET	A	(3G – .231)		WAS	A	(37G – .155)																
"	total		40	.164	.173	110	18	0	0	0	0.0	8	12	6		0	2	1	206	37	3	3	6.2	.988	C-38
2 yrs.			55	.182	.197	137	25	2	0	0	0.0	9	13	8		0	2	1	242	46	5	7	5.3	.983	C-53

Beals Becker   BECKER, DAVID BEALS
B. July 5, 1886, El Dorado, Kans.   D. Aug. 16, 1943, Huntington Park, Calif.   BL TL 5'9"   170 lbs.

1908	2 teams		PIT	N	(20G – .154)		BOS	N	(43G – .275)																
"	total		63	.242	.271	236	57	3	2	0	0.0	17	7	9		9	3	1	57	12	3	1	1.1	.958	OF-60
1909	BOS	N	152	.246	.326	562	138	15	6	6	1.1	60	24	47		21	0	0	222	26	18	8	1.8	.932	OF-152
1910	NY	N	80	.286	.437	126	36	2	4	3	2.4	18	24	14	25	11	30	5	68	7	2	0	1.0	.974	OF-45, 1B-1
1911			88	.262	.355	172	45	11	1	1	0.6	28	20	26	22	19	26	3	72	7	2	0	0.9	.975	OF-55
1912			125	.264	.393	402	106	18	6	6	1.5	66	58	54	35	30	5	1	230	20	11	4	2.1	.958	OF-117
1913	2 teams		CIN	N	(30G – .296)		PHI	N	(88G – .324)																
"	total		118	.316	.502	414	131	24	13	9	2.2	64	58	28	42	11	11	4	243	11	6	3	2.2	.977	OF-105, 1B-1
1914	PHI	N	138	.325	.446	514	167	25	5	9	1.8	76	66	37	59	16	12	3	270	17	16	3	2.1	.947	OF-126

Year	Team		Games	BA	SA	AB	H	2B	3B	HR	HR%	R	RBI	BB	SO	SB	Pinch Hit AB	Pinch Hit H	PO	A	E	DP	TC/G	FA	G by Pos

Beals Becker *continued*

| 1915 | | | 112 | .246 | .414 | 338 | 83 | 16 | 4 | 11 | 3.3 | 38 | 35 | 26 | 48 | 12 | 13 | 2 | 177 | 5 | 11 | 0 | 1.7 | .943 | OF-95 |
| 8 yrs. | | | 876 | .276 | .397 | 2764 | 763 | 114 | 43 | 45 | 1.6 | 367 | 292 | 241 | 231 | 129 | 100 | 18 | 1339 | 105 | 69 | 19 | 1.7 | .954 | OF-755, 1B-2 |

WORLD SERIES

1911	NY	N	3	.000	.000	3	0	0	0	0	0.0	0	0	0	0	0	3	0	0	0	0	0	0.0	–	
1912			2	.000	.000	4	0	0	0	0	0.0	1	0	2	0	0	0	0	0	1	0	0	0.5	1.000	OF-1
1915	PHI	N	2	–	–	0	0	0	0	0	–	0	0	0	0	0	0	0	0	0	0	0	0.0	–	OF-2
3 yrs.			7	.000	.000	7	0	0	0	0	0.0	1	0	2	0	0	3	0	0	1	0	0	0.1	1.000	OF-3

Heinz Becker

BECKER, HEINZ REINHARD (Dutch)
B. Aug. 26, 1915, Berlin, Germany

BB TR 6'2" 200 lbs.
BL 1947

1943	CHI	N	24	.145	.145	69	10	0	0	0	0.0	5	2	9	6	0	3	0	161	15	3	9	7.5	.983	1B-18
1945			67	.286	.421	133	38	8	2	2	1.5	25	27	17	16	0	36	5	222	12	0	21	3.5	1.000	1B-28
1946	2 teams	CHI	N (9G – .286)			CLE	A	(50G – .299)																	
"	total		59	.299	.377	154	46	10	0	0	0.0	15	18	24	19	1	11	3	347	26	2	34	6.4	.995	1B-44
1947	CLE	A	2	.000	.000	2	0	0	0	0	0.0	0	0	0	1	0	2	0	0	0	0	0	0.0	–	
4 yrs.			152	.263	.346	358	94	18	2	2	0.6	45	47	50	42	1	52	8	730	53	5	64	5.2	.994	1B-90

WORLD SERIES

| 1945 | CHI | N | 3 | .500 | .500 | 2 | 1 | 0 | 0 | 0 | 0.0 | 0 | 0 | 1 | 1 | 0 | 2 | 1 | 0 | 0 | 0 | 0 | 0.0 | – | |

Joe Becker

BECKER, JOSEPH EDWARD
B. June 25, 1908, St. Louis, Mo.

BR TR 6'1" 180 lbs.

1936	CLE	A	22	.180	.340	50	9	3	1	1	2.0	5	11	5	4	0	7	0	40	3	1	0	2.0	.977	C-15
1937			18	.333	.455	33	11	2	1	0	0.0	3	2	3	4	0	6	2	29	8	2	0	2.2	.949	C-12
2 yrs.			40	.241	.386	83	20	5	2	1	1.2	8	13	8	8	0	13	2	69	11	3	0	2.1	.964	C-27

Marty Becker

BECKER, MARTIN HENRY
B. Dec. 25, 1893, Tiffin, Ohio   D. Sept. 25, 1957, Cincinnati, Ohio

BB TL 5'8½" 155 lbs.

| 1915 | NY | N | 17 | .250 | .288 | 52 | 13 | 2 | 0 | 0 | 0.0 | 5 | 3 | 2 | 9 | 3 | 1 | 0 | 29 | 4 | 3 | 1 | 2.1 | .917 | OF-16 |

Glenn Beckert

BECKERT, GLENN ALFRED
B. Oct. 12, 1940, Pittsburgh, Pa.

BR TR 6'1" 190 lbs.

1965	CHI	N	154	.239	.298	614	147	21	3	3	0.5	73	30	28	52	6	2	2	326	494	23	101	5.5	.973	2B-153
1966			153	.287	.348	656	188	23	7	1	0.2	73	59	26	36	10	1	0	373	403	24	89	5.2	.970	2B-152, SS-1
1967			146	.280	.369	597	167	32	3	5	0.8	91	40	30	25	10	1	0	327	422	25	89	5.3	.968	2B-144
1968			155	.294	.369	643	189	28	4	4	0.6	98	37	31	20	8	0	0	356	461	19	107	5.4	.977	2B-155
1969			131	.291	.341	543	158	22	1	1	0.2	69	37	24	24	6	1	0	262	401	24	71	5.2	.965	2B-129
1970			143	.288	.349	591	170	15	6	3	0.5	99	36	32	22	4	3	0	303	412	22	88	5.2	.970	2B-138, OF-1
1971			131	.342	.406	530	181	18	5	2	0.4	80	42	24	24	3	2	1	275	382	9	76	5.1	.986	2B-129
1972			120	.270	.344	474	128	22	2	3	0.6	51	43	23	17	2	2	1	256	396	16	71	5.6	.976	2B-118
1973			114	.255	.290	372	95	13	0	0	0.0	38	29	30	15	0	25	6	163	262	7	50	3.8	.984	2B-88
1974	SD	N	64	.256	.262	172	44	1	0	0	0.0	11	7	11	8	0	26	4	71	80	10	17	2.5	.938	2B-36, 3B-1
1975			9	.375	.438	16	6	1	0	0	0.0	2	0	1	0	0	5	1	0	6	0	0	0.7	1.000	3B-4
11 yrs.			1320	.283	.345	5208	1473	196	31	22	0.4	685	360	260	243	49	68	15	2712	3719	179	759	5.0	.973	2B-1242, 3B-5, OF-1, SS-1

Jake Beckley

BECKLEY, JACOB PETER (St. Jacob)
B. Aug. 4, 1867, Hannibal, Mo.   D. June 25, 1918, Kansas City, Mo.
Hall of Fame 1971.

BL TL 5'10" 200 lbs.

1888	PIT	N	71	.343	.417	283	97	15	3	0	0.0	35	27	7	22	20	0	0	744	19	16	38	11.0	.979	1B-71
1889			123	.301	.437	522	157	24	10	9	1.7	91	97	29	29	18	0	0	1236	54	24	73	10.7	.982	1B-122, OF-1
1890	PIT	P	121	.324	.541	516	167	38	22	10	1.9	109	120	42	32	18	0	0	1256	58	32	61	11.1	.976	1B-121
1891	PIT	N	133	.292	.422	554	162	20	20	4	0.7	94	73	44	46	13	0	0	1250	87	24	63	10.2	.982	1B-133
1892			151	.236	.381	614	145	21	19	10	1.6	102	96	31	44	30	0	0	1523	132	38	88	11.2	.978	1B-151
1893			131	.303	.459	542	164	32	19	5	0.9	106	106	54	26	15	0	0	1360	95	21	83	11.3	.986	1B-131
1894			131	.343	.520	533	183	36	17	8	1.5	121	120	43	16	21	0	0	1227	84	30	80	10.2	.978	1B-131
1895			131	.328	.487	530	174	31	19	5	0.9	104	110	24	20	20	0	0	1340	54	31	76	11.0	.978	1B-129
1896	2 teams	PIT	N (59G – .253)			NY	N	(46G – .302)																	
"	total		105	.276	.419	399	110	15	9	8	2.0	81	70	31	35	19	0	0	981	53	20	60	10.0	.981	1B-101, OF-5, 2B-1
1897	2 teams	NY	N (17G – .250)			CIN	N	(97G – .345)																	
"	total		114	.330	.485	433	143	19	12	8	1.8	84	87	20			25	0	0	996	60	24	68	9.5	.978	1B-114
1898	CIN	N	118	.294	.416	459	135	20	12	4	0.9	86	72	28			6	0	0	1167	53	21	76	10.5	.983	1B-118
1899			134	.333	.466	513	171	27	16	3	0.6	87	99	40			20	0	0	1291	72	19	74	10.3	.986	1B-134
1900			141	.341	.434	558	190	26	10	2	0.4	98	94	40			23	0	0	1389	93	30	91	10.7	.980	1B-140
1901			140	.307	.434	580	178	39	13	3	0.5	78	79	28			4	0	0	1366	71	34	79	10.5	.977	1B-140
1902			129	.331	.429	532	176	23	7	5	0.9	82	69	34			15	0	0	1269	66	23	84	10.5	.983	1B-129, P-1
1903			120	.327	.447	550	150	29	10	2	0.4	85	81	42			23	1	1	1127	78	30	56	10.0	.976	1B-119
1904	STL	N	142	.325	.403	551	179	22	9	1	0.2	72	67	35			17	0	0	1526	64	20	65	11.3	.988	1B-142
1905			134	.286	.370	514	147	20	10	1	0.2	48	57	30			12	0	0	1442	69	28	56	11.5	.982	1B-134
1906			87	.247	.334	320	79	16	6	0	0.0	29	44	13			3	2	1	928	43	13	38	11.3	.987	1B-85
1907			32	.209	.235	115	24	3	0	0	0.0	6	7	1			0	0	0	303	13	4	17	10.0	.988	1B-32
20 yrs.			2386	.308	.436	9527	2931	476	243	88	0.9	1600	1575	616	270	315	4	2	23721	1318	482	1326	10.7	.981	1B-2377, OF-6, 2B-1, P-1
									4th																

Julio Becquer

BECQUER, JULIO
Born Julio Becquer y Villegas.
B. Dec. 20, 1931, Havana, Cuba

BL TL 5'11½" 178 lbs.

1955	WAS	A	10	.214	.214	14	3	0	0	0	0.0	1	1	0	1	0	8	1	15	2	0	2	1.7	1.000	1B-2
1957			105	.226	.312	186	42	6	2	2	1.1	14	22	10	29	3	65	18	300	19	0	29	3.0	1.000	1B-43
1958			86	.238	.256	164	39	3	0	0	0.0	10	12	8	21	1	41	11	320	34	2	26	4.1	.994	1B-42, OF-1
1959			108	.268	.382	220	59	12	5	1	0.5	20	26	16	35	3	56	12	454	32	5	38	4.5	.990	1B-53
1960			110	.252	.389	298	75	15	7	4	1.3	41	35	12	35	1	39	8	611	38	7	59	6.0	.989	1B-77, P-1

Year	Team		Games	BA	SA	AB	H	2B	3B	HR	HR%	R	RBI	BB	SO	SB	Pinch Hit AB	Pinch Hit H	PO	A	E	DP	TC/G	FA	G by Pos

Julio Becquer *continued*

1961	2 teams	LA A (11G – .000)				MIN A (57G – .238)																				
"	total		68	.217	.435	92	20	1	2	5	5.4	13	18	3	17	0	47	11	73	5	0	8	1.1	1.000	1B-23, OF-5, P-1
1963	MIN	A	1	–	–	0	0	0	0	0	–	1	0	0	0	0	0	0	0	0	0	0	0.0	–	
7 yrs.			488	.244	.352	974	238	37	16	12	1.2	100	114	41	120	8	256	63	1773	130	14	162	3.9	.993	1B-240, OF-6, P-2

Howie Bedell

BEDELL, HOWARD WILLIAM
B. Sept. 29, 1935, Clearfield, Pa.

BL TR 6'1" 185 lbs.

1962	MIL	N	58	.196	.232	138	27	1	2	0	0.0	15	2	11	22	1	11	1	63	0	3	0	1.1	.955	OF-45
1968	PHI	N	9	.143	.143	7	1	0	0	0	0.0	0	1	1	0	0	7	1	0	0	0	0	0.0	–	
2 yrs.			67	.193	.228	145	28	1	2	0	0.0	15	3	12	22	1	18	2	63	0	3	0	1.0	.955	OF-45

Gene Bedford

BEDFORD, WILLIAM EUGENE
B. Dec. 2, 1896, Dallas, Tex.   D. Oct. 6, 1977, San Antonio, Tex.

BB TR 5'8" 170 lbs.

| 1925 | CLE | A | 2 | .000 | .000 | 3 | 0 | 0 | 0 | 0 | 0.0 | 1 | 0 | 0 | 1 | 0 | 0 | 0 | 0 | 1 | 0 | 0 | 0.5 | 1.000 | 2B-2 |

Ed Beecher

BEECHER, EDWARD (Scrap Iron)
B. May, 1876, Indiana   Deceased.

1897	STL	N	3	.333	.333	12	4	0	0	0	0.0	1	1	0		1	0	0	6	0	0	0	2.0	1.000	OF-3
1898	CLE	N	8	.200	.280	25	5	2	0	0	0.0	1	0	0		0	0	0	10	1	2	0	1.6	.846	OF-8
2 yrs.			11	.243	.297	37	9	2	0	0	0.0	2	1	0		1	0	0	16	1	2	0	1.7	.895	OF-11

Ed Beecher

BEECHER, EDWARD H.
B. July 2, 1860, Guilford, Conn.   D. Sept. 12, 1935, Hartford, Conn.

BL TL 5'10" 185 lbs.

1887	PIT	N	41	.243	.325	169	41	8	0	2	1.2	15	22	7	8	8	0	0	85	12	9	1	2.6	.915	OF-41
1889	WAS	N	42	.296	.346	179	53	9	0	2	1.1	20	30	5	4	3	0	0	88	7	13	3	2.6	.880	OF-39, 1B-3
1890	BUF	P	126	.297	.392	536	159	22	10	3	0.6	69	90	29	23	14	0	0	211	24	55	4	2.3	.810	OF-126, P-1
1891	2 teams	WAS AA (58G – .243)				PHI AA (16G – .211)																				
"	total		74	.235	.343	306	72	13	7	2	0.7	44	35	30	13	24	0	0	127	15	26	4	2.3	.845	OF-74
4 yrs.			283	.273	.363	1190	325	52	17	7	0.6	148	177	71	48	49	0	0	511	58	103	12	2.4	.847	OF-280, 1B-3, P-1

Jodie Beeler

BEELER, JOSEPH SAM
B. Nov. 26, 1921, Dallas, Tex.

BR TR 6' 170 lbs.

| 1944 | CIN | N | 3 | .000 | .000 | 3 | 0 | 0 | 0 | 0 | 0.0 | 0 | 0 | 0 | 2 | 0 | 0 | 0 | 0 | 0 | 2 | 0 | 0.7 | – | 3B-1, 2B-1 |

Gene Begley

BEGLEY, EUGENE T.
B. June 7, 1861, Brooklyn, N. Y.   Deceased.

| 1886 | NY | N | 5 | .125 | .125 | 16 | 2 | 0 | 0 | 0 | 0.0 | 1 | 1 | 1 | 3 | | 0 | 0 | 14 | 7 | 3 | 0 | 4.8 | .875 | C-3, OF-2 |

Jim Begley

BEGLEY, JAMES LAWRENCE (Imp)
B. Sept. 19, 1902, San Francisco, Calif.   D. Feb. 20, 1957, San Francisco, Calif.

BR TR 5'6" 145 lbs.

| 1924 | CIN | N | 2 | .200 | .200 | 5 | 1 | 0 | 0 | 0 | 0.0 | 1 | 2 | 0 | 0 | 0 | 0 | 0 | 5 | 9 | 1 | 0 | 7.5 | .933 | 2B-2 |

Steve Behel

BEHEL, STEPHEN ARNOLD DOUGLAS
B. Nov. 6, 1860, Earlville, Ill.   D. Feb. 15, 1945, Los Angeles, Calif.

1884	MIL	U	9	.242	.273	33	8	1	0	0	0.0	5		3			0	0	4	1	0	0	0.6	1.000	OF-9
1886	NY	AA	59	.205	.246	224	46	5	2	0	0.0	32		22			0	0	84	7	15	0	1.8	.858	OF-59
2 yrs.			68	.210	.249	257	54	6	2	0	0.0	37		25			0	0	88	8	15	0	1.6	.865	OF-68

Ollie Bejma

BEJMA, ALOYSIUS FRANK
Born Alojzy Frank Bejma.
B. Sept. 12, 1907, South Bend, Ind.

BR TR 5'10" 115 lbs.

1934	STL	A	95	.271	.378	262	71	16	3	2	0.8	39	29	40	36	3	22	6	129	145	11	27	3.0	.961	SS-32, 2B-14, 3B-13, OF-9
1935			64	.192	.283	198	38	8	2	2	1.0	18	26	27	21	1	7	2	122	178	15	34	4.9	.952	2B-47, SS-8, 3B-2
1936			67	.259	.360	139	36	2	3	2	1.4	19	18	27	21	0	21	6	74	82	8	9	2.4	.951	2B-32, 3B-7, SS-1
1939	CHI	A	90	.251	.378	307	77	9	3	8	2.6	52	44	36	27	1	6	1	174	201	7	36	4.2	.982	2B-81, SS-1, 3B-1
4 yrs.			316	.245	.354	906	222	35	11	14	1.5	128	117	130	105	5	56	15	499	606	41	106	3.6	.964	2B-174, SS-42, 3B-23, OF-9

Mark Belanger

BELANGER, MARK HENRY
B. June 8, 1944, Pittsfield, Mass.

BR TR 6'1" 170 lbs.

1965	BAL	A	11	.333	.333	3	1	0	0	0	0.0	1	0	0	0	0	0	0	1	1	0	2	0.2	1.000	SS-4
1966			8	.158	.211	19	3	1	0	0	0.0	2	0	0	3	0	0	0	9	20	0	3	3.6	1.000	SS-6
1967			69	.174	.217	184	32	5	0	1	0.5	19	10	12	46	2	0	0	100	138	9	24	3.6	.964	SS-38, 2B-26, 3B-2
1968			145	.208	.248	472	98	13	0	2	0.4	40	21	40	114	10	0	0	248	444	22	73	4.9	.969	SS-145
1969			150	.287	.345	530	152	17	4	2	0.4	76	50	53	54	14	3	1	251	449	23	79	4.8	.968	SS-148
1970			145	.218	.259	459	100	6	5	1	0.2	53	36	52	65	13	3	0	212	419	19	78	4.4	.970	SS-143
1971			150	.266	.320	500	133	19	4	0	0.0	67	35	73	48	10	1	0	280	443	16	77	4.9	.978	SS-149
1972			113	.186	.246	285	53	9	1	0	0.0	36	16	18	53	6	1	0	180	285	12	53	4.2	.975	SS-105
1973			154	.226	.262	470	106	15	1	0	0.0	60	27	49	54	13	0	0	241	530	23	100	5.2	.971	SS-154
1974			155	.225	.300	493	111	14	4	5	1.0	54	36	51	69	17	0	0	243	552	13	100	5.2	.984	SS-155
1975			152	.226	.276	442	100	11	1	3	0.7	44	27	36	53	16	0	0	259	508	17	105	5.2	.978	SS-152
1976			153	.270	.326	522	141	22	2	1	0.2	66	40	51	64	27	0	0	239	545	14	97	5.2	.982	SS-153
1977			144	.206	.274	402	83	13	4	2	0.5	39	30	43	68	15	0	0	244	417	10	82	4.7	.985	SS-142
1978			135	.213	.250	348	74	13	0	0	0.0	39	16	40	55	6	1	0	184	409	9	76	4.5	.985	SS-134
1979			101	.167	.217	198	33	6	0	0	0.0	28	9	29	33	5	1	1	110	195	3	38	3.0	.990	SS-98
1980			113	.228	.276	268	61	7	3	0	0.0	37	22	12	25	6	2	0	133	258	10	49	3.5	.975	SS-109
1981			64	.165	.237	139	23	3	2	1	0.7	9	10	12	25	2	1	0	86	162	7	21	4.0	.973	SS-63

Year	Team	Games	BA	SA	AB	H	2B	3B	HR	HR%	R	RBI	BB	SO	SB	Pinch Hit AB	Pinch Hit H	PO	A	E	DP	TC/G	FA	G by Pos

Mark Belanger *continued*

Year	Team	Games	BA	SA	AB	H	2B	3B	HR	HR%	R	RBI	BB	SO	SB	PH AB	PH H	PO	A	E	DP	TC/G	FA	G by Pos
1982	LA N	54	.240	.260	50	12	1	0	0	0.0	6	4	5	10	1	4	1	20	63	4	4	1.6	.954	SS-44, 2B-1
18 yrs.		2016	.228	.280	5784	1316	175	33	20	0.3	676	389	576	839	167	19	3	3040	5831	211	1061	4.5	.977	SS-1942, 2B-27, 3B-2

LEAGUE CHAMPIONSHIP SERIES

Year	Team	Games	BA	SA	AB	H	2B	3B	HR	HR%	R	RBI	BB	SO	SB	PH AB	PH H	PO	A	E	DP	TC/G	FA	G by Pos
1969	BAL A	3	.267	.600	15	4	0	1	1	6.7	4	1	0	0	0	0	0	4	9	0	1	4.3	1.000	SS-3
1970		3	.333	.333	12	4	0	0	0	0.0	5	1	1	0	0	0	0	6	14	0	3	6.7	1.000	SS-3
1971		3	.250	.250	8	2	0	0	0	0.0	1	1	3	2	0	0	0	6	11	0	3	5.7	1.000	SS-3
1973		5	.125	.125	16	2	0	0	0	0.0	0	1	1	1	0	0	0	8	17	0	1	5.0	1.000	SS-5
1974		4	.000	.000	9	0	0	0	0	0.0	0	0	1	3	0	0	0	7	12	1	2	5.0	.950	SS-4
1979		3	.200	.200	5	1	0	0	0	0.0	0	1	0	2	0	0	0	0	6	0	0	2.0	1.000	SS-3
6 yrs.		21	.200	.277	65	13	0	1	1	1.5	10	5	6	8	0	0	0	31	69	1	10	4.8	.990	SS-21

WORLD SERIES

Year	Team	Games	BA	SA	AB	H	2B	3B	HR	HR%	R	RBI	BB	SO	SB	PH AB	PH H	PO	A	E	DP	TC/G	FA	G by Pos
1969	BAL A	5	.200	.200	15	3	0	0	0	0.0	2	1	2	2	0	0	0	8	14	0	3	4.4	1.000	SS-5
1970		5	.105	.105	19	2	0	0	0	0.0	0	1	1	2	0	0	0	11	14	1	1	5.2	.962	SS-5
1971		7	.238	.333	21	5	0	1	0	0.0	4	0	5	2	1	0	0	10	20	3	1	4.7	.909	SS-7
1979		5	.000	.000	6	0	0	0	0	0.0	1	0	1	1	0	0	0	3	7	1	2	2.2	.909	SS-4
4 yrs.		22	.164	.197	61	10	0	1	0	0.0	7	2	9	6	1	0	0	32	55	5	7	4.2	.946	SS-21

Wayne Belardi

BELARDI, CARROLL WAYNE (Footsie)
B. Sept. 5, 1930, Calistoga, Calif. BL TL 6'1" 185 lbs.

Year	Team	Games	BA	SA	AB	H	2B	3B	HR	HR%	R	RBI	BB	SO	SB	PH AB	PH H	PO	A	E	DP	TC/G	FA	G by Pos
1950	BKN N	10	.000	.000	10	0	0	0	0	0.0	0	0	0	4	0	9	0	2	0	0	0	0.2	1.000	1B-1
1951		3	.333	1.000	3	1	0	0	0	0.0	1	0	0	2	0	3	1	0	0	0	0	0.0	—	
1953		69	.239	.485	163	39	3	2	11	6.7	19	34	16	40	0	28	9	283	23	5	34	4.5	.984	1B-38
1954	2 teams		BKN N (11G – .222)		DET A (88G – .232)																			
"	total	99	.232	.394	259	60	7	1	11	4.2	27	25	35	37	1	21	4	636	51	8	54	7.0	.988	1B-79
1955	DET A	3	.000	.000	3	0	0	0	0	0.0	0	0	0	1	0	3	0	0	0	0	0	0.0	—	
1956		79	.279	.429	154	43	3	1	6	3.9	24	15	15	13	0	37	8	243	17	5	21	3.4	.981	1B-31, OF-2
6 yrs.		263	.242	.422	592	143	13	5	28	4.7	71	74	66	97	1	101	22	1164	91	18	109	4.8	.986	1B-149, OF-2

WORLD SERIES

Year	Team	Games	BA	SA	AB	H	2B	3B	HR	HR%	R	RBI	BB	SO	SB	PH AB	PH H	PO	A	E	DP	TC/G	FA	G by Pos
1953	BKN N	2	.000	.000	2	0	0	0	0	0.0	0	0	0	1	0	2	0	0	0	0	0	0.0	—	

Ira Belden

BELDEN, IRA ALLISON
B. Apr. 16, 1874, Cleveland, Ohio D. July 15, 1916, Lakewood, Ohio BL TR 5'11" 175 lbs.

Year	Team	Games	BA	SA	AB	H	2B	3B	HR	HR%	R	RBI	BB	SO	SB	PH AB	PH H	PO	A	E	DP	TC/G	FA	G by Pos
1897	CLE N	8	.267	.400	30	8	0	2	0	0.0	5	4	2	0	0	0	0	17	2	0	0	2.4	1.000	OF-8

Beau Bell

BELL, ROY CHESTER
B. Aug. 20, 1907, Bellville, Tex. D. Sept. 14, 1977, College Station, Tex. BR TR 6'2" 185 lbs.

Year	Team	Games	BA	SA	AB	H	2B	3B	HR	HR%	R	RBI	BB	SO	SB	PH AB	PH H	PO	A	E	DP	TC/G	FA	G by Pos
1935	STL A	76	.250	.345	220	55	8	2	3	1.4	20	17	16	16	1	24	4	187	9	10	11	2.7	.951	OF-37, 1B-15, 3B-3
1936		155	.344	.502	616	212	40	12	11	1.8	100	123	60	55	4	0	0	425	19	13	20	2.9	.972	OF-142, 1B-17
1937		156	.340	.509	642	218	51	8	14	2.2	82	117	53	54	2	0	0	462	42	10	24	3.3	.981	OF-131, 1B-26, 3B-2
1938		147	.262	.414	526	138	35	3	13	2.5	91	84	71	46	1	8	3	290	12	6	7	2.1	.981	OF-132, 1B-4
1939	2 teams		STL A (11G – .219)		DET A (54G – .239)																			
"	total	65	.235	.307	166	39	5	2	1	0.6	18	29	28	19	0	17	3	93	4	0	1	1.5	.990	OF-46
1940	CLE A	120	.279	.365	444	124	22	2	4	0.9	55	58	34	41	2	9	0	309	13	8	17	2.8	.976	OF-97, 1B-14
1941		48	.192	.288	104	20	4	3	0	0.0	12	9	10	8	1	23	3	106	4	0	9	2.3	1.000	OF-14, 1B-10
7 yrs.		767	.297	.432	2718	806	165	32	46	1.7	378	437	272	239	11	81	13	1872	103	47	89	2.6	.977	OF-599, 1B-86, 3B-5

Buddy Bell

BELL, DAVID GUS
Son of Gus Bell.
B. Aug. 27, 1951, Pittsburgh, Pa. BR TR 6'1" 180 lbs.

Year	Team	Games	BA	SA	AB	H	2B	3B	HR	HR%	R	RBI	BB	SO	SB	PH AB	PH H	PO	A	E	DP	TC/G	FA	G by Pos
1972	CLE A	132	.255	.363	466	119	21	1	9	1.9	49	36	34	29	5	3	1	284	23	3	6	2.3	.990	OF-123, 3B-6
1973		156	.268	.393	631	169	23	7	14	2.2	86	59	49	47	7	1	0	146	363	22	44	3.4	.959	3B-154, OF-2
1974		116	.262	.352	423	111	15	1	7	1.7	51	46	35	29	1	1	0	112	274	15	31	3.5	.963	3B-115, DH-1
1975		153	.271	.376	553	150	20	4	10	1.8	66	59	51	72	6	0	0	146	330	25	29	3.3	.950	3B-153
1976		159	.281	.366	604	170	26	2	7	1.2	75	60	44	49	3	1	1	109	331	20	23	2.9	.957	3B-158, 1B-2
1977		129	.292	.426	479	140	23	4	11	2.3	64	64	45	63	1	3	1	134	253	16	23	3.1	.960	3B-118, OF-11
1978		142	.282	.392	556	157	27	8	6	1.1	71	62	39	43	1	3	1	125	355	15	30	3.5	.970	3B-139, DH-1
1979	TEX A	162	.299	.451	670	200	42	3	18	2.7	89	101	30	45	5	0	0	147	429	17	31	3.7	.971	3B-147, SS-33
1980		129	.329	.498	490	161	24	4	17	3.5	76	83	40	39	3	9	2	125	282	8	26	3.2	.981	3B-123, SS-3
1981		97	.294	.428	360	106	16	1	10	2.8	44	64	42	30	3	1	0	67	284	14	19	3.8	.962	3B-96, SS-1
1982		148	.296	.426	537	159	27	2	13	2.4	62	67	70	50	5	1	0	131	397	13	35	3.4	.976	3B-145, SS-4
1983		156	.277	.411	618	171	35	3	14	2.3	75	66	50	48	3	2	0	123	383	17	29	3.4	.967	3B-154
1984		148	.315	.458	553	174	36	5	11	2.0	87	83	63	54	2	1	0	129	323	20	28	3.2	.958	3B-147
1985	2 teams		TEX A (84G – .236)		CIN N (67G – .219)																			
"	total	151	.229	.350	560	128	28	5	10	1.8	61	68	67	48	3	2	1	124	297	25	35	3.0	.944	3B-150
1986	CIN N	155	.278	.445	568	158	29	3	20	3.5	89	75	73	49	2	4	2	105	291	10	28	2.6	.975	3B-151, 2B-1
1987		143	.284	.425	522	148	19	2	17	3.3	74	70	71	39	4	1	0	93	241	7	17	2.4	.979	3B-142
1988	2 teams		CIN N (21G – .185)		HOU N (74G – .253)																			
"	total	95	.241	.344	323	78	10	1	7	2.2	27	40	26	32	1	9	0	88	140	15	14	2.6	.938	3B-79, 1B-9
1989	TEX A	34	.183	.232	82	15	4	0	0	0.0	4	3	7	10	0	8	1	10	13	0	0	0.7	1.000	DH-22, 3B-9, 1B-1
18 yrs.		2405	.279	.406	8995	2514	425	56	201	2.2	1150	1106	836	776	55	48	10	2198	5009	262	448	3.1	.965	3B-2186, OF-136, SS-41, DH-24, 1B-12, 2B-1

Fern Bell

BELL, FERN LEE (Danny)
B. Jan. 21, 1913, Ada, Okla. BR TR 6' 180 lbs.

Year	Team	Games	BA	SA	AB	H	2B	3B	HR	HR%	R	RBI	BB	SO	SB	PH AB	PH H	PO	A	E	DP	TC/G	FA	G by Pos
1939	PIT N	83	.286	.389	262	75	5	8	2	0.8	44	34	42	18	2	8	1	154	7	7	0	2.0	.958	OF-67, 3B-1
1940		6	.000	.000	3	0	0	0	0	0.0	0	1	1	1	0	3	0	0	0	0	0	0.0	—	
2 yrs.		89	.283	.385	265	75	5	8	2	0.8	44	35	43	19	2	11	1	154	7	7	0	1.9	.958	OF-67, 3B-1

Frank Bell

BELL, FRANK GUSTAV
Brother of Charlie Bell.
B. 1863, Cincinnati, Ohio D. Apr. 14, 1891, Cincinnati, Ohio

Year	Team	Games	BA	SA	AB	H	2B	3B	HR	HR%	R	RBI	BB	SO	SB	Pinch Hit AB	Pinch Hit H	PO	A	E	DP	TC/G	FA	G by Pos

Frank Bell *continued*

Year	Team	Games	BA	SA	AB	H	2B	3B	HR	HR%	R	RBI	BB	SO	SB	AB	H	PO	A	E	DP	TC/G	FA	G by Pos
1885	BKN AA	10	.172	.241	29	5	0	1	0	0.0	5		0			0	0	27	5	9	0	4.1	.780	C-5, OF-4, 3B-2

George Bell

BELL, JORGE ANTONIO
Born Jorge Antonio Bell y Mathey.   Brother of Juan Bell.
B. Oct. 21, 1959, San Pedro de Macoris, Dominican Republic

BR TR 6'1"   190 lbs.

Year	Team	Games	BA	SA	AB	H	2B	3B	HR	HR%	R	RBI	BB	SO	SB	AB	H	PO	A	E	DP	TC/G	FA	G by Pos
1981	TOR A	60	.233	.350	163	38	2	1	5	3.1	19	12	5	27	3	5	3	92	3	3	2	1.6	.969	OF-44, DH-8
1983		39	.268	.438	112	30	5	4	2	1.8	5	17	4	17	1	3	1	61	1	3	0	1.7	.954	OF-34, DH-2
1984		159	.292	.498	606	177	39	4	26	4.3	85	87	24	86	11	8	3	289	13	9	1	2.0	.971	OF-147, DH-7, 3B-3
1985		157	.275	.479	607	167	28	6	28	4.6	87	95	43	90	21	1	0	320	14	11	3	2.2	.968	OF-157, 3B-2
1986		159	.309	.532	641	198	38	6	31	4.8	101	108	41	62	7	1	1	270	17	10	1	1.9	.966	OF-147, DH-11, 3B-1
1987		156	.308	.605	610	188	32	4	47	7.7	111	134	39	75	5	1	0	249	14	11	1	1.8	.960	OF-148, 3B-1, 2B-1
1988		156	.269	.446	614	165	27	5	24	3.9	78	97	34	66	4	2	0	253	8	15	1	1.8	.946	OF-149, DH-7
1989		153	.297	.458	613	182	41	2	18	2.9	88	104	33	60	4	0	0	258	4	10	1	1.8	.963	OF-134, DH-19
8 yrs.		1039	.289	.495	3966	1145	212	32	181	4.6	574	654	223	483	56	20	8	1792	74	72	10	1.9	.963	OF-960, DH-54, 3B-7, 2B-1

LEAGUE CHAMPIONSHIP SERIES

Year	Team	Games	BA	SA	AB	H	2B	3B	HR	HR%	R	RBI	BB	SO	SB	AB	H	PO	A	E	DP	TC/G	FA	G by Pos
1985	TOR A	7	.321	.429	28	9	3	0	0	0.0	4	1	0	4	0	0	0	13	0	0	0	1.9	1.000	OF-7
1989		5	.200	.350	20	4	0	0	1	5.0	2	2	0	3	0	0	0	3	1	0	0	0.8	1.000	DH-3, OF-2
2 yrs.		12	.271	.396	48	13	3	0	1	2.1	6	3	0	7	0	0	0	16	1	0	0	1.4	1.000	OF-9, DH-3

Gus Bell

BELL, DAVID RUSSELL
Father of Buddy Bell.
B. Nov. 15, 1928, Louisville, Ky.

BL TR 6'1½"   190 lbs.

Year	Team	Games	BA	SA	AB	H	2B	3B	HR	HR%	R	RBI	BB	SO	SB	AB	H	PO	A	E	DP	TC/G	FA	G by Pos
1950	PIT N	111	.282	.443	422	119	22	11	8	1.9	62	53	28	46	4	6	1	203	10	5	3	2.0	.977	OF-104
1951		149	.278	.443	600	167	27	12	16	2.7	80	89	42	41	1	2	1	267	18	4	4	1.9	.986	OF-145
1952		131	.250	.419	468	117	21	5	16	3.4	53	59	36	72	1	8	0	202	8	6	2	1.6	.972	OF-123
1953	CIN N	151	.300	.525	610	183	37	5	30	4.9	102	105	48	72	0	1	1	447	16	11	5	3.1	.977	OF-151
1954		153	.299	.465	619	185	38	7	17	2.7	104	101	48	58	5	1	0	406	12	6	2	2.8	.986	OF-153
1955		154	.308	.510	610	188	30	6	27	4.4	88	104	54	57	4	0	0	364	4	5	0	2.4	.987	OF-154
1956		150	.292	.501	603	176	31	4	29	4.8	82	84	50	66	6	1	0	330	12	5	4	2.3	.986	OF-149
1957		121	.292	.420	510	149	20	3	13	2.5	65	61	30	54	0	0	0	311	7	4	1	2.7	.988	OF-121
1958		112	.252	.382	385	97	16	2	10	2.6	42	46	36	40	2	7	1	235	7	1	2	2.2	.996	OF-107
1959		148	.293	.445	580	170	27	2	19	3.3	59	115	29	44	2	5	2	269	15	1	1	1.9	.996	OF-145
1960		143	.262	.388	515	135	19	5	12	2.3	65	62	29	65	4	13	3	239	13	3	1	1.8	.988	OF-131
1961		103	.255	.345	235	60	10	1	3	1.3	27	33	18	21	1	36	11	112	1	1	0	1.1	.991	OF-75
1962	2 teams	NY N (30G – .149)		MIL N (79G – .285)																				
"	total	109	.241	.359	315	76	13	3	6	1.9	36	30	22	24	0	26	4	115	10	2	3	1.2	.984	OF-84
1963	MIL N	3	.333	.333	3	1	0	0	0	0.0	0	0	0	0	0	3	1	0	0	0	0	0.0	—	
1964		3	.000	.000	3	0	0	0	0	0.0	0	0	0	1	0	3	0	0	0	0	0	0.0	—	
15 yrs.		1741	.281	.445	6478	1823	311	66	206	3.2	865	942	470	636	30	112	25	3500	133	54	28	2.1	.985	OF-1642

WORLD SERIES

Year	Team	Games	BA	SA	AB	H	2B	3B	HR	HR%	R	RBI	BB	SO	SB	AB	H	PO	A	E	DP	TC/G	FA	G by Pos
1961	CIN N	3	.000	.000	3	0	0	0	0	0.0	0	0	0	0	0	3	0	0	0	0	0	0.0	—	

Jay Bell

BELL, JAY STUART
B. Dec. 11, 1965, Pensacola, Fla.

BR TR 6'1"   180 lbs.

Year	Team	Games	BA	SA	AB	H	2B	3B	HR	HR%	R	RBI	BB	SO	SB	AB	H	PO	A	E	DP	TC/G	FA	G by Pos
1986	CLE A	5	.357	.714	14	5	2	1	1	7.1	3	4	2	3	0	1	0	1	6	2	1	1.8	.778	DH-2, 2B-2
1987		38	.216	.352	125	27	9	1	2	1.6	14	13	8	31	2	0	0	67	93	9	22	4.4	.947	SS-38
1988		73	.218	.280	211	46	5	1	2	0.9	23	21	21	53	4	0	0	103	170	10	37	3.9	.965	SS-72
1989	PIT N	78	.258	.351	271	70	13	3	2	0.7	33	27	19	47	5	3	1	109	197	10	41	4.1	.968	SS-78
4 yrs.		194	.238	.335	621	148	29	5	7	1.1	73	65	50	134	11	4	1	280	466	31	101	4.0	.960	SS-188, DH-2, 2B-2

John Bell

BELL, JOHN
Born Rudolph Fred Baerwald.
B. Jan. 1, 1881, Wausau, Wis.   D. July 28, 1955, Albuquerque, N. M.

BR TR 5'8½"   158 lbs.

Year	Team	Games	BA	SA	AB	H	2B	3B	HR	HR%	R	RBI	BB	SO	SB	AB	H	PO	A	E	DP	TC/G	FA	G by Pos
1907	NY A	17	.212	.288	52	11	2	1	0	0.0	4	3	3		4	0	0	35	0	4	0	2.3	.897	OF-17

Juan Bell

BELL, JUAN
Born Juan Bell y Mathey.   Brother of George Bell.
B. Mar. 29, 1968, San Pedro deMacoris, Dominican Republic

BR TR 5'11"   172 lbs.

Year	Team	Games	BA	SA	AB	H	2B	3B	HR	HR%	R	RBI	BB	SO	SB	AB	H	PO	A	E	DP	TC/G	FA	G by Pos
1989	BAL A	8	.000	.000	4	0	0	0	0	0.0	2	0	0	1	1	0	0	2	6	0	1	1.0	1.000	DH-4, SS-2, 2B-2

Kevin Bell

BELL, KEVIN ROBERT
B. July 13, 1955, Los Angeles, Calif.

BR TR 6'   195 lbs.

Year	Team	Games	BA	SA	AB	H	2B	3B	HR	HR%	R	RBI	BB	SO	SB	AB	H	PO	A	E	DP	TC/G	FA	G by Pos
1976	CHI A	68	.248	.396	230	57	7	6	5	2.2	24	20	18	56	2	1	0	70	124	6	10	2.9	.970	3B-67, DH-1
1977		9	.179	.321	28	5	1	0	1	3.6	4	6	3	8	0	0	0	12	21	2	8	3.9	.943	SS-5, 3B-4, OF-1
1978		54	.191	.279	68	13	0	0	2	2.9	9	5	5	19	1	2	0	23	64	5	6	1.7	.946	3B-52, DH-1
1979		70	.245	.355	200	49	8	1	4	2.0	20	22	15	43	2	2	0	51	154	17	11	3.2	.923	3B-68, SS-2
1980		92	.178	.241	191	34	5	2	1	0.5	16	11	29	37	0	3	2	36	153	16	13	2.2	.922	3B-83, DH-3, SS-3
1982	OAK A	4	.333	.444	9	3	1	0	0	0.0	1	0	0	2	0	0	0	3	3	1	1	1.8	.857	3B-3, DH-1
6 yrs.		297	.222	.331	726	161	22	9	13	1.8	74	64	70	165	5	8	2	195	519	47	49	2.6	.938	3B-277, SS-10, DH-6, OF-1

Les Bell

BELL, LESTER ROWLAND
B. Dec. 14, 1901, Harrisburg, Pa.   D. Dec. 26, 1985, Hershey, Pa.

BR TR 5'11"   165 lbs.

Year	Team	Games	BA	SA	AB	H	2B	3B	HR	HR%	R	RBI	BB	SO	SB	AB	H	PO	A	E	DP	TC/G	FA	G by Pos
1923	STL N	15	.373	.451	51	19	1	0	0	0.0	5	9	9	7	1	0	0	35	53	8	9	6.4	.917	SS-15
1924		17	.246	.421	57	14	3	2	1	1.8	5	5	3	7	0	0	0	44	42	9	8	5.6	.905	SS-17
1925		153	.285	.422	586	167	29	9	11	1.9	80	88	43	47	4	0	0	151	285	36	39	3.1	.924	3B-153, SS-1
1926		155	.325	.518	581	189	33	14	17	2.9	85	100	54	62	9	0	0	165	254	22	25	2.8	.950	3B-155
1927		115	.259	.426	390	101	26	6	9	2.3	48	65	34	63	5	5	0	101	183	30	21	2.7	.904	3B-100, SS-10
1928	BOS N	153	.277	.413	591	164	36	7	10	1.7	58	91	40	45	1	0	0	177	314	27	37	3.4	.948	3B-153

Year	Team		Games	BA	SA	AB	H	2B	3B	HR	HR%	R	RBI	BB	SO	SB	Pinch Hit AB	H	PO	A	E	DP	TC/G	FA	G by Pos

Les Bell *continued*

Year	Team		Games	BA	SA	AB	H	2B	3B	HR	HR%	R	RBI	BB	SO	SB	AB	H	PO	A	E	DP	TC/G	FA	G by Pos
1929			139	.298	.422	483	144	23	5	9	1.9	58	72	50	42	4	9	2	111	201	17	15	2.4	.948	3B-127, SS-1, 2B-1
1930	CHI	N	74	.278	.431	248	69	15	4	5	2.0	35	47	24	27	1	2	0	81	105	9	15	2.6	.954	3B-70, 1B-2
1931			75	.282	.405	252	71	17	1	4	1.6	30	32	19	22	0	5	1	66	118	11	18	2.6	.944	3B-70
9 yrs.			896	.290	.438	3239	938	184	49	66	2.0	404	509	276	322	25	21	3	931	1555	169	187	3.0	.936	3B-828, SS-44, 1B-2, 2B-1
WORLD SERIES																									
1926	STL	N	7	.259	.407	27	7	1	0	1	3.7	4	6	2	5	0	0	0	7	17	2	0	3.7	.923	3B-7

Terry Bell

BELL, TERENCE WILLIAM
B. Oct. 27, 1962, Dayton, Ohio
BR TR 6' 195 lbs.

Year	Team		Games	BA	SA	AB	H	2B	3B	HR	HR%	R	RBI	BB	SO	SB	AB	H	PO	A	E	DP	TC/G	FA	G by Pos
1986	KC	A	8	.000	.000	3	0	0	0	0	0.0	0	0	2	1	0	0	0	7	0	0	0	0.9	1.000	C-8
1987	ATL	N	1	.000	.000	1	0	0	0	0	0.0	0	0	0	1	0	1	0	0	0	0	0	0.0	—	C-8
2 yrs.			9	.000	.000	4	0	0	0	0	0.0	0	0	2	2	0	1	0	7	0	0	0	0.8	1.000	C-8

Zeke Bella

BELLA, JOHN
B. Aug. 23, 1930, Greenwich, Conn.
BR TL 5'11" 185 lbs.

Year	Team		Games	BA	SA	AB	H	2B	3B	HR	HR%	R	RBI	BB	SO	SB	AB	H	PO	A	E	DP	TC/G	FA	G by Pos
1957	NY	A	5	.100	.100	10	1	0	0	0	0.0	0	0	1	2	0	1	0	7	1	0	0	1.6	1.000	OF-4
1959	KC	A	47	.207	.293	82	17	2	1	1	1.2	10	9	9	14	0	22	5	23	2	0	1	0.5	1.000	OF-25, 1B-1
2 yrs.			52	.196	.272	92	18	2	1	1	1.1	10	9	10	16	0	23	5	30	3	0	1	0.6	1.000	OF-29, 1B-1

Joey Belle

BELLE, ALBERT JOJUAN
B. Aug. 25, 1966, Shreveport, La.
BR TR 6'1" 190 lbs.

Year	Team		Games	BA	SA	AB	H	2B	3B	HR	HR%	R	RBI	BB	SO	SB	AB	H	PO	A	E	DP	TC/G	FA	G by Pos
1989	CLE	A	62	.225	.394	218	49	8	4	7	3.2	22	37	12	55	2	2	1	92	3	2	1	1.6	.979	OF-44, DH-17

Rafael Belliard

BELLIARD, RAFAEL LEONIDAS
Born Rafael Leonidas Belliard y Matias.
B. Oct. 24, 1961, Puerto Nuevo Mao, Dominican Republic
BR TR 5'9" 139 lbs.
BB 1982

Year	Team		Games	BA	SA	AB	H	2B	3B	HR	HR%	R	RBI	BB	SO	SB	AB	H	PO	A	E	DP	TC/G	FA	G by Pos
1982	PIT	N	9	.500	.500	2	1	0	0	0	0.0	3	0	0	0	1	1	1	2	2	0	0	0.4	1.000	SS-4
1983			4	.000	.000	1	0	0	0	0	0.0	1	0	0	1	0	0	0	1	3	0	1	1.0	1.000	SS-3
1984			20	.227	.227	22	5	0	0	0	0.0	3	0	0	1	4	1	0	12	13	3	4	1.4	.893	SS-12, 2B-1
1985			17	.200	.200	20	4	0	0	0	0.0	1	1	0	5	0	2	0	13	23	2	3	2.2	.947	SS-12
1986			117	.233	.262	309	72	5	2	0	0.0	33	31	26	54	12	4	0	147	317	12	50	4.1	.975	SS-96, 2B-23
1987			81	.207	.271	203	42	4	3	1	0.5	26	15	20	25	5	1	0	113	191	6	31	3.8	.981	SS-71, 2B-7
1988			122	.213	.241	286	61	0	4	0	0.0	28	11	26	47	7	1	0	134	261	9	51	3.3	.978	SS-117, 2B-3
1989			67	.214	.240	154	33	4	0	0	0.0	10	8	8	22	5	1	0	71	138	3	20	3.2	.986	SS-40, 2B-20, 3B-6
8 yrs.			437	.219	.253	997	218	13	9	1	0.1	105	66	80	155	34	10	1	493	948	35	160	3.4	.976	SS-355, 2B-54, 3B-6

John Bellman

BELLMAN, JOHN HUTCHINS
B. Mar. 4, 1864, Louisville, Ky. D. Dec. 8, 1931, Louisville, Ky.

Year	Team		Games	BA	SA	AB	H	2B	3B	HR	HR%	R	RBI	BB	SO	SB	AB	H	PO	A	E	DP	TC/G	FA	G by Pos
1889	STL	AA	1	.500	.500	2	1	0	0	0	0.0	1	0	1	0	0	0	0	1	1	0	0	2.0	1.000	C-1

Bob Belloir

BELLOIR, ROBERT EDWARD
B. July 13, 1948, Heidelberg, Germany
BR TR 5'10" 155 lbs.

Year	Team		Games	BA	SA	AB	H	2B	3B	HR	HR%	R	RBI	BB	SO	SB	AB	H	PO	A	E	DP	TC/G	FA	G by Pos
1975	ATL	N	43	.219	.257	105	23	2	1	0	0.0	11	9	7	8	0	2	0	39	106	13	17	3.7	.918	SS-38, 2B-1
1976			30	.200	.233	60	12	2	0	0	0.0	5	4	5	7	0	3	0	25	41	4	8	2.3	.943	SS-12, 3B-10, 2B-5
1977			6	.000	.000	1	0	0	0	0	0.0	2	0	0	0	0	1	0	1	2	0	0	0.5	1.000	SS-3
1978			2	1.000	2.000	1	1	1	0	0	0.0	0	0	0	0	0	1	1	0	1	0	0	0.5	1.000	SS-1, 3B-1
4 yrs.			81	.216	.257	167	36	5	1	0	0.0	18	13	12	15	0	7	1	65	150	17	25	2.9	.927	SS-54, 3B-11, 2B-6

Harry Bemis

BEMIS, HARRY PARKER
B. Feb. 1, 1874, Farmington, N. H. D. May 23, 1947, Cleveland, Ohio
BR TR 5'6½" 155 lbs.

Year	Team		Games	BA	SA	AB	H	2B	3B	HR	HR%	R	RBI	BB	SO	SB	AB	H	PO	A	E	DP	TC/G	FA	G by Pos
1902	CLE	A	93	.312	.404	317	99	12	7	1	0.3	42	29	19		3	3	1	334	121	17	2	5.1	.964	C-87, OF-2, 2B-1
1903			92	.261	.354	314	82	20	3	1	0.3	31	41	8		5	8	3	414	86	6	9	5.5	.988	C-74, 1B-10, 2B-1
1904			97	.226	.295	336	76	11	6	0	0.0	35	25	8		6	4	1	497	90	26	14	6.3	.958	C-79, 1B-13, 2B-1
1905			69	.292	.376	226	66	13	3	0	0.0	27	28	13		3	4	1	268	72	9	4	5.1	.974	C-58, 2B-4, 3B-2, 1B-1
1906			93	.276	.374	297	82	13	5	2	0.7	28	30	12		8	12	2	340	73	16	7	4.6	.963	C-81
1907			65	.250	.291	172	43	7	0	0	0.0	12	19	7		5	12	4	206	42	10	6	4.0	.961	C-51, 1B-2
1908			91	.224	.264	277	62	9	1	0	0.0	23	33	7		14	12	1	337	75	15	5	4.7	.965	C-76, 1B-2
1909			42	.187	.252	123	23	2	3	0	0.0	4	13	0		2	5	2	167	33	6	0	4.9	.971	C-36
1910			61	.216	.275	167	36	5	1	1	0.6	11	16	5		3	12	3	186	63	10	4	4.2	.961	C-46
9 yrs.			703	.255	.329	2229	569	92	29	5	0.2	213	234	79		49	72	18	2749	655	115	51	5.0	.967	C-588, 1B-28, 2B-7, OF-2, 3B-2

Johnny Bench

BENCH, JOHNNY LEE
B. Dec. 7, 1947, Oklahoma City, Okla.
Hall of Fame 1989.
BR TR 6'1" 197 lbs.

Year	Team		Games	BA	SA	AB	H	2B	3B	HR	HR%	R	RBI	BB	SO	SB	AB	H	PO	A	E	DP	TC/G	FA	G by Pos
1967	CIN	N	26	.163	.256	86	14	3	1	1	1.2	7	6	5	19	0	0	0	175	16	1	0	7.4	.995	C-26
1968			154	.275	.433	564	155	40	2	15	2.7	67	82	31	96	1	2	0	942	102	9	10	6.8	.991	C-154
1969			148	.293	.487	532	156	23	1	26	4.9	83	90	49	86	6	10	2	793	76	7	10	5.9	.992	C-147
1970			158	.293	.587	605	177	35	4	45	7.4	97	148	54	102	5	4	1	854	78	15	19	6.0	.984	C-140, OF-23, 1B-12, 3B-1
1971			149	.238	.423	562	134	19	2	27	4.8	80	61	49	83	2	2	0	735	67	10	16	5.4	.988	C-141, OF-12, 1B-12, 3B-3
1972			147	.270	.541	538	145	22	2	40	7.4	87	125	100	84	6	0	0	791	63	10	10	5.9	.988	C-130, OF-17, 1B-6, 3B-4
1973			152	.253	.429	557	141	17	3	25	4.5	83	104	83	83	4	1	0	757	63	6	10	5.4	.991	C-134, OF-23, 1B-4, 3B-1
1974			160	.280	.507	621	174	38	2	33	5.3	108	129	80	90	5	1	0	794	123	9	18	5.8	.990	C-137, 3B-36, 1B-5
1975			142	.283	.519	530	150	39	1	28	5.3	83	110	65	108	11	5	1	646	52	8	11	5.0	.989	C-121, OF-19, 1B-9
1976			135	.234	.394	465	109	24	1	16	3.4	62	74	81	95	13	8	1	655	60	4	11	5.3	.994	C-128, OF-5, 1B-1
1977			142	.275	.540	494	136	34	2	31	6.3	67	109	58	95	2	2	0	735	69	12	13	5.7	.985	C-135, OF-8, 1B-4, 3B-1
1978			120	.260	.483	393	102	17	1	23	5.9	52	73	50	83	4	11	2	680	53	9	13	6.2	.988	C-107, 1B-11, OF-2
1979			130	.276	.459	464	128	19	0	22	4.7	73	80	67	73	4	0	0	632	69	10	12	5.5	.986	C-126, 1B-2
1980			114	.250	.483	360	90	12	0	24	6.7	52	68	41	64	4	13	2	505	39	5	7	4.8	.991	C-105

Year	Team	Games	BA	SA	AB	H	2B	3B	HR	HR%	R	RBI	BB	SO	SB	Pinch Hit AB	Pinch Hit H	PO	A	E	DP	TC/G	FA	G by Pos

Johnny Bench *continued*

Year	Team	Games	BA	SA	AB	H	2B	3B	HR	HR%	R	RBI	BB	SO	SB	PH-AB	PH-H	PO	A	E	DP	TC/G	FA	G by Pos
1981		52	.309	.489	178	55	8	0	8	4.5	14	25	17	21	0	8	3	375	28	7	35	7.9	.983	1B-38, C-7-
1982		119	.258	.396	399	103	16	0	13	3.3	44	38	37	58	1	9	1	108	159	19	17	2.4	.934	3B-107, 1B-8, C-1
1983		110	.255	.432	310	79	15	2	12	3.9	32	54	24	38	0	34	9	292	74	10	26	3.4	.973	3B-42, 1B-32, C-5, OF-1
17 yrs.		2158	.267	.476	7658	2048	381	24	389	5.1	1091	1376	891	1278	68	114	22	10469	1191	151	238	5.5	.987	C-1744, 3B-195, 1B-144, OF-110

LEAGUE CHAMPIONSHIP SERIES

Year	Team	Games	BA	SA	AB	H	2B	3B	HR	HR%	R	RBI	BB	SO	SB	PH-AB	PH-H	PO	A	E	DP	TC/G	FA	G by Pos
1970	CIN N	3	.222	.556	9	2	0	0	1	11.1	2	1	3	1	0	0	0	20	3	0	0	7.7	1.000	C-3
1972		5	.333	.667	18	6	1	1	1	5.6	3	2	1	3	2	0	0	28	3	1	1	6.4	.969	C-5
1973		5	.263	.526	19	5	2	0	1	5.3	1	1	2	3	0	0	0	31	2	0	0	6.6	1.000	C-5
1975		3	.077	.077	13	1	0	0	0	0.0	1	0	1	6	1	0	0	18	4	0	0	7.3	1.000	C-3
1976		3	.333	.667	12	4	1	0	1	8.3	3	1	1	2	0	0	0	11	4	0	1	5.0	1.000	C-3
1979		3	.250	.667	12	3	0	1	1	8.3	1	1	2	1	0	0	0	17	2	0	0	6.3	1.000	C-3
6 yrs.		22	.253	.530	83	21	4	2	5	6.0	11	6	10	16	4	0	0	125	18	1	2	6.5	.993	C-22

WORLD SERIES

Year	Team	Games	BA	SA	AB	H	2B	3B	HR	HR%	R	RBI	BB	SO	SB	PH-AB	PH-H	PO	A	E	DP	TC/G	FA	G by Pos
1970	CIN N	5	.211	.368	19	4	0	0	1	5.3	3	3	1	2	0	0	0	36	3	0	1	7.8	1.000	C-5
1972		7	.261	.435	23	6	1	0	1	4.3	4	1	5	5	2	0	0	41	7	1	2	7.0	.980	C-7
1975		7	.207	.379	29	6	2	0	1	3.4	5	4	2	4	0	0	0	44	6	0	3	7.1	1.000	C-7
1976		4	.533	1.133	15	8	1	1	2	13.3	4	6	0	1	0	0	0	18	2	0	0	5.0	1.000	C-4
4 yrs.		23	.279	.523	86	24	4	1	5	5.8	16	14	8	12	2	0	0	139	18	1	6	6.9	.994	C-23

Chief Bender

BENDER, CHARLES ALBERT
B. May 5, 1884, Crow Wing County, Minn. D. May 22, 1954, Philadelphia, Pa.
Hall of Fame 1953.

BR TR 6'2" 185 lbs.

Year	Team	Games	BA	SA	AB	H	2B	3B	HR	HR%	R	RBI	BB	SO	SB	PH-AB	PH-H	PO	A	E	DP	TC/G	FA	G by Pos
1903	PHI A	43	.183	.233	120	22	4	1	0	0.0	10	8	3		3	3	2	37	80	10	2	3.0	.921	P-36, 1B-3, OF-1
1904		31	.228	.316	79	18	3	2	0	0.0	8	5	5		3	1	0	13	48	7	0	2.2	.897	P-29
1905		38	.217	.293	92	20	3	2	0	0.0	11	14	3		3	3	0	14	77	3	2	2.5	.968	P-35
1906		44	.253	.384	99	25	4	0	3	3.0	9	13	9		2	2	0	32	54	8	1	2.1	.915	P-36, OF-4
1907		45	.230	.310	100	23	6	1	0	0.0	10	8	5		2	7	1	32	57	8	2	2.2	.918	P-33, 1B-2, OF-1, 2B-1
1908		20	.220	.240	50	11	1	0	0	0.0	5	2	10		1			25	31	3	1	3.0	.949	P-18, 1B-1
1909		40	.215	.269	93	20	5	0	0	0.0	6	9	5		1	5	1	13	78	4	1	2.4	.958	P-34
1910		36	.269	.344	93	25	3	2	0	0.0	6	16	0		6	1		13	85	3	3	2.8	.970	P-30
1911		32	.165	.165	79	13	0	0	0	0.0	9	8	2		2	1		11	58	0	4	2.2	1.000	P-31
1912		27	.150	.200	60	9	1	1	0	0.0	5	4	6		2	0		6	36	2	2	1.6	.955	P-27
1913		48	.154	.218	78	12	3	1	0	0.0	7	10	6	17	1			8	55	2	1	1.4	.969	P-48
1914		28	.145	.210	62	9	1	0	1	1.6	4	4	4	13	0			7	47	2	0	2.0	.964	P-28
1915	BAL F	26	.267	.350	60	16	2	0	1	1.7	7	2	6		0			12	45	3	2	2.3	.934	P-26
1916	PHI N	28	.279	.372	43	12	4	0	0	0.0	2	5	3	9	0			9	40	2	1	1.8	.961	P-27, 3B-1
1917		20	.205	.282	39	8	0	0	1	2.6	3	4	2	3	0			5	22	1	4	1.4	.964	P-20
1925	CHI A	1	—	—	0	0	0	0	0	0.0	0	0	0		0			0	0	0	0		—	P-1
16 yrs.		507	.212	.280	1147	243	40	10	6	0.5	102	116	75	42	20	29	5	237	813	59	27	2.2	.947	P-459, OF-6, 1B-6, 3B-1, 2B-1

WORLD SERIES

Year	Team	Games	BA	SA	AB	H	2B	3B	HR	HR%	R	RBI	BB	SO	SB	PH-AB	PH-H	PO	A	E	DP	TC/G	FA	G by Pos
1905	PHI A	2	.000	.000	5	0	0	0	0	0.0	0		1	1	0			1	6	0	0	3.5	1.000	P-2
1910		2	.333	.333	6	2	0	0	0	0.0	1	1	1	0				1	2	0	1	1.5	1.000	P-2
1911		3	.091	.091	11	1	0	0	0	0.0	0	0	1	0				1	6	0	0	2.3	1.000	P-3
1913		2	.000	.000	8	0	0	0	0	0.0	0	1	0	1	0			1	5	0	0	2.5	1.000	P-2
1914		1	.000	.000	2	0	0	0	0	0.0	0	0	0	0				1	3	0	2	4.0	1.000	P-1
5 yrs.		10	.094	.094	32	3	0	0	0	0.0	1	2	1	4	0			4	22	0	3	2.6	1.000	P-10

Art Benedict

BENEDICT, ARTHUR MELVILLE
B. Mar. 31, 1862, Cornwall, Ill. D. Jan. 20, 1948, Denver, Colo.

BR TR

Year	Team	Games	BA	SA	AB	H	2B	3B	HR	HR%	R	RBI	BB	SO	SB	PH-AB	PH-H	PO	A	E	DP	TC/G	FA	G by Pos
1883	PHI N	3	.267	.333	15	4	1	0	0	0.0	3		0	4		0	0	3	5	6	0	4.7	.571	2B-3

Bruce Benedict

BENEDICT, BRUCE EDWIN
B. Aug. 18, 1955, Birmingham, Ala.

BR TR 6'1" 175 lbs.

Year	Team	Games	BA	SA	AB	H	2B	3B	HR	HR%	R	RBI	BB	SO	SB	PH-AB	PH-H	PO	A	E	DP	TC/G	FA	G by Pos
1978	ATL N	22	.250	.288	52	13	2	0	0	0.0	3	1	6	6	0	0	0	81	14	1	1	4.4	.990	C-22
1979		76	.225	.279	204	46	11	0	0	0.0	14	15	33	18	1	1	0	344	35	6	3	5.1	.984	C-76
1980		120	.253	.315	359	91	14	1	0	0.0	18	34	28	36	3	0	0	502	76	7	6	4.9	.988	C-120
1981		90	.264	.363	295	78	12	1	5	1.7	26	35	33	21	1	0	0	404	73	7	7	5.4	.986	C-90
1982		118	.246	.303	386	95	11	1	3	0.8	34	44	37	40	4	1	0	602	73	5	9	5.8	.993	C-118
1983		134	.298	.348	423	126	13	1	2	0.5	43	43	61	24	1	0	0	738	91	7	12	6.2	.992	C-134
1984		95	.223	.297	300	67	8	1	4	1.3	26	25	34	25	1	0	0	504	37	5	2	5.7	.991	C-95
1985		70	.202	.231	208	42	6	0	0	0.0	12	20	22	12	0	0	0	314	35	4	1	5.0	.989	C-70
1986		64	.225	.300	160	36	10	1	0	0.0	11	13	15	10	1	7	4	252	28	2	4	4.4	.993	C-57
1987		37	.147	.189	95	14	1	0	1	1.1	4	5	17	15	0	2	0	165	21	2	3	5.1	.989	C-35
1988		90	.242	.271	236	57	7	0	0	0.0	11	19	19	26	0	0	0	384	54	5	3	4.9	.989	C-89
1989		66	.194	.231	160	31	3	0	1	0.6	12	6	23	18	0	1	0	361	40	2	2	6.1	.995	C-65
12 yrs.		982	.242	.299	2878	696	98	6	18	0.6	214	260	328	251	12	15	5	4651	577	53	50	5.4	.990	C-971

LEAGUE CHAMPIONSHIP SERIES

Year	Team	Games	BA	SA	AB	H	2B	3B	HR	HR%	R	RBI	BB	SO	SB	PH-AB	PH-H	PO	A	E	DP	TC/G	FA	G by Pos
1982	ATL N	3	.250	.375	8	2	1	0	0	0.0	1	0	2	1	0	0	0	0	0	0	0	0.0	—	C-3

Joe Benes

BENES, JOSEPH ANTHONY (Bananas)
B. Jan. 8, 1901, Long Island City, N.Y. D. Mar. 7, 1975, Elmhurst, N.Y.

BR TR 5'8½" 158 lbs.

Year	Team	Games	BA	SA	AB	H	2B	3B	HR	HR%	R	RBI	BB	SO	SB	PH-AB	PH-H	PO	A	E	DP	TC/G	FA	G by Pos
1931	STL N	10	.167	.167	12	2	0	0	0	0.0	1	0	2	1	0	0	0	8	13	1	1	2.2	.955	SS-6, 2B-2, 3B-1

Benny Bengough

BENGOUGH, BERNARD OLIVER
B. July 27, 1898, Niagara Falls, N.Y. D. Dec. 22, 1968, Philadelphia, Pa.

BR TR 5'7½" 168 lbs.

Year	Team	Games	BA	SA	AB	H	2B	3B	HR	HR%	R	RBI	BB	SO	SB	PH-AB	PH-H	PO	A	E	DP	TC/G	FA	G by Pos
1923	NY A	19	.132	.170	53	7	2	0	0	0.0	1	3	4	2	0	0	0	58	14	2	2	3.9	.973	C-19
1924		11	.313	.500	16	5	1	1	0	0.0	4	3	2	0	0	0	0	34	3	0	3	3.4	1.000	C-11

Year	Team	Games	BA	SA	AB	H	2B	3B	HR	HR%	R	RBI	BB	SO	SB	Pinch Hit AB	Pinch Hit H	PO	A	E	DP	TC/G	FA	G by Pos

Benny Bengough *continued*

Year	Team	Games	BA	SA	AB	H	2B	3B	HR	HR%	R	RBI	BB	SO	SB	PH AB	PH H	PO	A	E	DP	TC/G	FA	G by Pos
1925		95	.258	.322	283	73	14	2	0	0.0	17	23	19	9	0	1	0	325	83	3	12	4.3	.993	C-94
1926		36	.381	.452	84	32	6	0	0	0.0	9	14	7	4	1	1	0	107	36	4	2	4.1	.973	C-35
1927		31	.247	.353	85	21	3	3	0	0.0	6	10	4	4	0	1	0	114	31	2	0	4.7	.986	C-30
1928		58	.267	.298	161	43	3	1	0	0.0	12	9	7	8	0	0	0	206	37	2	7	4.2	.992	C-58
1929		23	.194	.258	62	12	2	1	0	0.0	5	7	0	2	0	0	0	47	8	1	1	2.4	.982	C-23
1930		44	.235	.314	102	24	4	2	0	0.0	10	12	3	8	1	0	0	171	18	2	2	4.3	.990	C-44
1931	STL A	40	.250	.293	140	35	4	1	0	0.0	6	12	4	4	0	3	0	119	26	2	6	3.7	.986	C-37
1932		54	.252	.317	139	35	7	1	0	0.0	13	15	12	4	0	5	0	153	30	2	7	3.4	.989	C-47
10 yrs.		411	.255	.317	1125	287	46	12	0	0.0	83	108	62	45	2	11	1	1334	286	20	42	4.0	.988	C-398

WORLD SERIES

Year	Team	Games	BA	SA	AB	H	2B	3B	HR	HR%	R	RBI	BB	SO	SB	PH AB	PH H	PO	A	E	DP	TC/G	FA	G by Pos
1927	NY A	2	.000	.000	4	0	0	0	0	0.0	1	1	1	0	0	0	0	4	0	0	0	2.0	1.000	C-2
1928		4	.231	.231	13	3	0	0	0	0.0	1	1	1	1	0	0	0	33	2	0	0	8.8	1.000	C-4
2 yrs.		6	.176	.176	17	3	0	0	0	0.0	2	2	2	1	0	0	0	37	2	0	0	6.5	1.000	C-6

Juan Beniquez

BENIQUEZ, JUAN JOSE
Born Juan Jose Beniquez y Torres.
B. May 13, 1950, San Sebastian, Puerto Rico

BR TR 5'11" 150 lbs.

Year	Team	Games	BA	SA	AB	H	2B	3B	HR	HR%	R	RBI	BB	SO	SB	PH AB	PH H	PO	A	E	DP	TC/G	FA	G by Pos
1971	BOS A	16	.298	.333	57	17	0	0	0	0.0	8	4	3	4	3	0	0	24	27	6	5	3.6	.895	SS-15
1972		33	.242	.333	99	24	4	1	1	1.0	10	8	7	11	2	3	1	38	88	14	19	4.2	.900	SS-27
1974		106	.267	.357	389	104	14	3	5	1.3	60	33	25	61	19	8	0	264	4	6	2	2.6	.978	OF-97, DH-4
1975		78	.291	.402	254	74	14	4	2	0.8	43	17	25	26	7	8	5	110	17	1	2	1.6	.992	OF-44, DH-20, 3B-14
1976	TEX A	145	.255	.301	478	122	14	4	0	0.0	49	33	39	56	17	4	1	411	18	7	3	3.0	.984	OF-141, 2B-1
1977		123	.269	.413	424	114	19	6	10	2.4	56	50	43	43	26	0	0	311	10	4	1	2.6	.988	OF-123
1978		127	.260	.378	473	123	17	3	11	2.3	61	50	20	59	10	2	0	309	8	9	1	2.6	.972	OF-126
1979	NY A	62	.254	.394	142	36	6	1	4	2.8	19	17	9	17	3	1	0	100	15	2	0	1.9	.983	OF-60, 3B-3
1980	SEA A	70	.228	.346	237	54	10	0	6	2.5	26	21	17	25	2	5	0	176	3	8	0	2.7	.957	OF-65, DH-1
1981	CAL A	58	.181	.265	166	30	5	0	3	1.8	18	13	15	16	2	2	0	117	0	5	0	2.1	.959	OF-55, DH-1
1982		112	.265	.388	196	52	11	2	3	1.5	25	24	15	21	3	3	1	113	4	2	1	1.1	.981	OF-107
1983		92	.305	.381	315	96	15	0	3	1.0	44	34	15	29	4	3	1	174	8	6	1	2.0	.968	OF-84, DH-6
1984		110	.336	.452	354	119	17	0	8	2.3	60	39	18	43	10	3	1	197	5	6	1	1.9	.971	OF-98
1985		132	.304	.418	411	125	13	5	8	1.9	54	42	34	47	4	24	5	439	26	4	42	3.6	.991	OF-71, 1B-46, DH-14, SS-1, 3B-1
1986	BAL A	113	.300	.397	343	103	15	0	6	1.7	48	36	40	49	2	19	9	211	56	13	15	2.5	.954	OF-54, 3B-25, DH-16, 1B-14
1987	2 teams	KC A	(57G – .236)		TOR A	(39G – .284)																		
"	total	96	.251	.400	255	64	12	1	8	3.1	20	47	16	39	0	23	6	97	5	2	6	1.1	.981	OF-29, DH-15, 1B-8, 3B-6
1988	TOR A	27	.293	.379	58	17	2	0	1	1.7	9	8	8	6	0	8	2	0	0	0	0	0.0	–	DH-19, OF-1
17 yrs.		1500	.274	.379	4651	1274	190	30	79	1.7	610	476	349	552	104	123	34	3091	294	95	99	2.3	.973	OF-1155, DH-96, 1B-68, 3B-49, SS-43, 2B-1

LEAGUE CHAMPIONSHIP SERIES

Year	Team	Games	BA	SA	AB	H	2B	3B	HR	HR%	R	RBI	BB	SO	SB	PH AB	PH H	PO	A	E	DP	TC/G	FA	G by Pos
1975	BOS A	3	.250	.250	12	3	0	0	0	0.0	2	1	0	1	2	0	0	0	0	0	0	0.0	–	DH-3
1982	CAL A	2	–	–	0	0	0	0	0	–	0	0	0	0	0	0	0	0	0	0	0	0.0	–	OF-2
2 yrs.		5	.250	.250	12	3	0	0	0	0.0	2	1	0	1	2	0	0	0	0	0	0	0.0	–	DH-3, OF-2

WORLD SERIES

Year	Team	Games	BA	SA	AB	H	2B	3B	HR	HR%	R	RBI	BB	SO	SB	PH AB	PH H	PO	A	E	DP	TC/G	FA	G by Pos
1975	BOS A	3	.125	.125	8	1	0	0	0	0.0	1	0	1	1	0	1	0	6	1	0	0	2.3	1.000	OF-2

Mike Benjamin

BENJAMIN, MICHAEL PAUL
B. Nov. 22, 1965, Euclid, Ohio

BR TR 6'3" 195 lbs.

Year	Team	Games	BA	SA	AB	H	2B	3B	HR	HR%	R	RBI	BB	SO	SB	PH AB	PH H	PO	A	E	DP	TC/G	FA	G by Pos
1989	SF N	14	.167	.167	6	1	0	0	0	0.0	6	0	0	1	1	1	1	4	4	0	0	0.6	1.000	SS-8

Stan Benjamin

BENJAMIN, ALFRED STANLEY
B. May 20, 1914, Framingham, Mass.

BR TR 6'2" 194 lbs.

Year	Team	Games	BA	SA	AB	H	2B	3B	HR	HR%	R	RBI	BB	SO	SB	PH AB	PH H	PO	A	E	DP	TC/G	FA	G by Pos
1939	PHI N	13	.140	.220	50	7	2	1	0	0.0	4	2	1	6	1	0	0	18	12	4	1	2.6	.882	OF-7, 3B-5
1940		8	.222	.222	9	2	0	0	0	0.0	1	1	1	1	0	4	1	3	1	0	0	0.5	1.000	OF-2
1941		129	.235	.325	480	113	20	7	3	0.6	47	27	20	81	17	9	1	254	18	5	8	2.1	.982	OF-110, 1B-8, 2B-2, 3B-1
1942		78	.224	.319	210	47	8	3	2	1.0	24	8	10	27	5	15	4	174	13	5	12	2.5	.974	OF-45, 1B-15
1945	CLE A	14	.333	.429	21	7	2	0	0	0.0	1	3	0	0	0	10	3	9	2	0	0	0.8	1.000	OF-4
5 yrs.		242	.229	.318	770	176	32	11	5	0.6	77	41	32	115	23	38	9	458	46	14	21	2.1	.973	OF-168, 1B-23, 3B-6, 2B-2

Ike Benners

BENNERS, ISAAC B. (Windy)
B. 1856, Philadelphia, Pa. Deceased.

BL 175 lbs.

Year	Team	Games	BA	SA	AB	H	2B	3B	HR	HR%	R	RBI	BB	SO	SB	PH AB	PH H	PO	A	E	DP	TC/G	FA	G by Pos
1884	2 teams	BKN AA	(49G – .201)		WIL U	(6G – .045)																		
"	total	55	.185	.299	211	39	11	5	1	0.5	25		8			0	0	76	2	18	1	1.7	.813	OF-54, 1B-1

Charlie Bennett

BENNETT, CHARLES WESLEY
B. Nov. 21, 1854, New Castle, Pa. D. Feb. 24, 1927, Detroit, Mich.

BR TR 5'11" 180 lbs.

Year	Team	Games	BA	SA	AB	H	2B	3B	HR	HR%	R	RBI	BB	SO	SB	PH AB	PH H	PO	A	E	DP	TC/G	FA	G by Pos
1878	MIL N	49	.245	.310	184	45	9	0	1	0.5	16	12	10	26		0	0	197	33	51	4	5.7	.819	C-35, OF-20
1880	WOR N	51	.228	.306	193	44	9	3	0	0.0	20	18	10	30		0	0	291	47	32	4	7.3	.914	C-46, OF-6
1881	DET N	76	.301	.478	299	90	18	7	7	2.3	44	64	18	37		0	0	432	102	25	8	7.4	.955	C-70, 3B-5, OF-3
1882		84	.301	.450	342	103	16	10	5	1.5	43	51	20	33		0	0	493	111	39	12	7.7	.939	C-65, 3B-11, 2B-7, SS-1, 1B-1
1883		92	.305	.474	371	113	34	7	5	1.3	56		26	59		0	0	382	124	38	17	5.9	.930	C-72, 2B-15, OF-12
1884		90	.264	.378	341	90	18	6	3	0.9	37		36	40		0	0	468	114	62	10	7.2	.904	C-80, OF-5, SS-4, 3B-1, 2B-1, 1B-1
1885		91	.269	.456	349	94	24	13	5	1.4	49	60	47	37		0	0	379	106	49	13	5.9	.908	C-62, OF-19, 3B-10
1886		72	.243	.396	235	57	13	4	5	2.1	37	34	48	29		0	0	432	86	24	14	7.5	.956	C-69, OF-4, SS-1
1887		46	.244	.400	160	39	6	5	3	1.9	26	20	30	22	7	0	0	201	58	13	11	5.9	.952	C-45, OF-1, 1B-1
1888		74	.264	.399	258	68	12	4	5	1.9	32	29	31	40	4	0	0	428	94	18	10	7.3	.967	C-73, 1B-1
1889	BOS N	82	.231	.328	247	57	8	2	4	1.6	42	28	21	43	7	0	0	419	74	23	9	6.3	.955	C-82
1890		85	.214	.320	281	60	17	2	3	1.1	59	40	72	56	6	0	0	448	90	23	8	6.6	.959	C-85

Year	Team	Games	BA	SA	AB	H	2B	3B	HR	HR%	R	RBI	BB	SO	SB	Pinch Hit AB	Pinch Hit H	PO	A	E	DP	TC/G	FA	G by Pos

Charlie Bennett *continued*

Year	Team	Games	BA	SA	AB	H	2B	3B	HR	HR%	R	RBI	BB	SO	SB	AB	H	PO	A	E	DP	TC/G	FA	G by Pos
1891		75	.215	.332	256	55	9	3	5	2.0	35	39	42	61	3	0	0	383	75	19	10	6.4	.960	C-75
1892		35	.202	.263	114	23	4	0	1	0.9	19	16	27	23	6	0	0	169	31	11	3	6.0	.948	C-35
1893		60	.209	.304	191	40	6	0	4	2.1	34	27	40	36	5	0	0	204	40	12	1	4.3	.953	C-60
15 yrs.		1062	.256	.388	3821	978	203	66	56	1.5	549	438	478	572	38	0	0	5326	1185	439	134	6.5	.937	C-954, OF-70, 3B-27, 2B-23, SS-6, 1B-4

Fred Bennett

BENNETT, JAMES FRED (Red)
B. Mar. 15, 1902, Atkins, Ark.   D. May 12, 1957, Atkins, Ark.

BR TR 5'9" 185 lbs.

Year	Team	Games	BA	SA	AB	H	2B	3B	HR	HR%	R	RBI	BB	SO	SB	AB	H	PO	A	E	DP	TC/G	FA	G by Pos
1928 STL	A	7	.250	.375	8	2	1	0	0	0.0	0	0	0	2	0	6	1	2	0	0	0	0.3	1.000	OF-1
1931 PIT	N	32	.281	.371	89	25	5	0	1	1.1	6	7	7	4	0	9	2	36	3	2	0	1.3	.951	OF-21
2 yrs.		39	.278	.371	97	27	6	0	1	1.0	6	7	7	6	0	15	3	38	3	2	0	1.1	.953	OF-22

Herschel Bennett

BENNETT, HERSCHEL EMMETT
B. Sept. 21, 1896, Elwood, Mo.   D. Sept. 9, 1964, Springfield, Mo.

BL TR 5'9½" 160 lbs.

Year	Team	Games	BA	SA	AB	H	2B	3B	HR	HR%	R	RBI	BB	SO	SB	AB	H	PO	A	E	DP	TC/G	FA	G by Pos
1923 STL	A	5	.000	.000	4	0	0	0	0	0.0	0	0	1	1	0	3	0	1	0	0	0	0.2	1.000	OF-1
1924		41	.330	.468	94	31	4	3	1	1.1	16	11	3	6	1	18	6	26	2	1	0	0.7	.966	OF-21
1925		98	.279	.376	298	83	11	6	2	0.7	46	37	18	16	4	16	9	140	12	14	1	1.7	.916	OF-73
1926		80	.267	.360	225	60	14	2	1	0.4	33	26	22	21	2	28	12	106	9	6	3	1.5	.950	OF-50
1927		93	.266	.363	256	68	12	2	3	1.2	40	30	14	21	6	30	5	118	5	7	1	1.4	.946	OF-55
5 yrs.		317	.276	.376	877	242	41	13	7	0.8	135	104	58	65	13	95	32	391	28	28	5	1.4	.937	OF-200

Joe Bennett

BENNETT, JOSEPH ROSENBLUM
B. July 2, 1900, New York, N. Y.   D. July 11, 1987, Morro Bay, Calif.

BR TR 5'9" 168 lbs.

Year	Team	Games	BA	SA	AB	H	2B	3B	HR	HR%	R	RBI	BB	SO	SB	AB	H	PO	A	E	DP	TC/G	FA	G by Pos
1923 PHI	N	1	—	—	0	0	0	0	0	–	0	0	0	0	0	0	0	0	1	0	0	1.0	1.000	3B-1

Pug Bennett

BENNETT, JUSTIN TITUS
B. Feb. 20, 1874, Ponca, Neb.   D. Sept. 12, 1935, Kirkland, Wash.

BR TR 5'11" 165 lbs.

Year	Team	Games	BA	SA	AB	H	2B	3B	HR	HR%	R	RBI	BB	SO	SB	AB	H	PO	A	E	DP	TC/G	FA	G by Pos
1906 STL	N	153	.262	.318	595	156	16	7	1	0.2	66	34	56		20	0	0	295	447	41	43	5.1	.948	2B-153
1907		87	.222	.259	324	72	8	2	0	0.0	20	21	21		7	1	0	178	214	25	27	4.8	.940	2B-83, 3B-3
2 yrs.		240	.248	.297	919	228	24	9	1	0.1	86	55	77		27	1	0	473	661	66	70	5.0	.945	2B-236, 3B-3

Vern Benson

BENSON, VERNON ADAIR
B. Sept. 19, 1924, Granite Quarry, N. C.
Manager 1977.

BL TR 5'10" 160 lbs.

Year	Team	Games	BA	SA	AB	H	2B	3B	HR	HR%	R	RBI	BB	SO	SB	AB	H	PO	A	E	DP	TC/G	FA	G by Pos
1943 PHI	A	2	.000	.000	2	0	0	0	0	0.0	0	0	0	2	0	0	0	0	0	0	0	0.0	—	OF-2
1946		7	.000	.000	5	0	0	0	0	0.0	1	0	1	3	0	0	0	4	0	0	0	0.6	1.000	3B-9, OF-4
1951 STL	N	13	.261	.435	46	12	3	1	1	2.2	8	7	6	8	0	0	0	10	19	2	3	2.4	.935	3B-15
1952		20	.191	.362	47	9	2	0	2	4.3	6	5	5	9	0	5	2	5	24	3	0	1.8	.889	3B-15
1953		13	.000	.000	4	0	0	0	0	0.0	2	0	1	0	0	0	0	0	0	0	0	0.0	—	
5 yrs.		55	.202	.356	104	21	5	1	3	2.9	17	12	13	22	0	11	2	19	46	6	6	1.3	.915	3B-24, OF-6

Jack Bentley

BENTLEY, JOHN NEEDLES
B. Mar. 8, 1895, Sandy Springs, Md.   D. Oct. 24, 1969, Olney, Md.

BL TL 5'11½" 200 lbs.

Year	Team	Games	BA	SA	AB	H	2B	3B	HR	HR%	R	RBI	BB	SO	SB	AB	H	PO	A	E	DP	TC/G	FA	G by Pos
1913 WAS	A	3	.000	.000	3	0	0	0	0	0.0	0	0	0	0	0	0	0	5	0	0	0	1.7	1.000	P-3
1914		30	.275	.325	40	11	2	0	0	0.0	7	4	0	5	0	0	0	9	33	3	1	1.5	.933	P-30
1915		4	.000	.000	2	0	0	0	0	0.0	0	0	0	1	0	0	0	1	2	1	0	1.0	.750	P-4
1916		2	—	—	0	0	0	0	0	–	0	0	0	0	0	0	0	1	0	0	0	0.5	1.000	P-2
1923 NY	N	52	.427	.573	89	38	6	2	1	1.1	9	14	3	4	0	20	10	5	38	1	1	0.8	.977	P-31
1924		46	.265	.337	98	26	5	1	0	0.0	12	6	3	13	0	18	4	3	43	1	3	1.0	.979	P-28
1925		64	.303	.485	99	30	5	2	3	3.0	10	18	9	11	0	28	9	13	33	3	2	0.8	.939	P-28, OF-3, 1B-1
1926 2 teams			PHI N (75G – .258)			NY N (3G – .250)																		
" total		78	.258	.357	244	63	12	3	2	0.8	19	27	5	4	0	16	2	516	33	4	41	7.1	.993	1B-56, P-8
1927 NY	N	8	.222	.556	9	2	0	0	1	11.1	1	2	1	1	0	1	0	10	2	1	0	1.6	.923	P-4, 1B-2
9 yrs.		287	.291	.406	584	170	30	9	7	1.2	58	71	21	39	0	83	25	557	190	14	48	2.7	.982	P-138, 1B-59, OF-3

WORLD SERIES

Year	Team	Games	BA	SA	AB	H	2B	3B	HR	HR%	R	RBI	BB	SO	SB	AB	H	PO	A	E	DP	TC/G	FA	G by Pos
1923 NY	N	5	.600	.800	5	3	1	0	0	0.0	0	0	0	3	0	2	1	0	2	0	0	0.4	1.000	P-2
1924		5	.286	.714	7	2	0	0	1	14.3	1	2	1	1	0	1	0	1	3	0	0	0.8	1.000	P-3
2 yrs.		10	.417	.750	12	5	1	0	1	8.3	1	2	1	4	0	2	1	1	5	0	0	0.6	1.000	P-5

Butch Benton

BENTON, ALFRED LEE
B. Aug. 24, 1957, Tampa, Fla.

BR TR 6'1" 190 lbs.

Year	Team	Games	BA	SA	AB	H	2B	3B	HR	HR%	R	RBI	BB	SO	SB	AB	H	PO	A	E	DP	TC/G	FA	G by Pos
1978 NY	N	4	.500	.500	4	2	0	0	0	0.0	0	0	0	0	0	0	0	4	0	0	0	1.0	1.000	C-1
1980		12	.048	.048	21	1	0	0	0	0.0	0	0	2	4	0	4	0	27	2	2	0	2.6	.935	C-8
1982 CHI	N	4	.143	.143	7	1	0	0	0	0.0	0	0	0	0	0	0	0	20	1	0	0	5.3	1.000	C-4
1985 CLE	A	31	.179	.239	67	12	4	0	0	0.0	5	7	3	9	0	1	0	75	13	4	1	3.0	.957	C-26
4 yrs.		51	.162	.202	99	16	4	0	0	0.0	6	10	5	14	0	9	1	126	16	6	1	2.9	.959	C-39

Stan Benton

BENTON, STANLEY W. (Rabbit)
B. Sept. 29, 1901, Cannel City, Ky.   D. June 7, 1984, Mesquite, Tex.

BR TR 5'7" 150 lbs.

Year	Team	Games	BA	SA	AB	H	2B	3B	HR	HR%	R	RBI	BB	SO	SB	AB	H	PO	A	E	DP	TC/G	FA	G by Pos
1922 PHI	N	6	.211	.263	19	4	1	0	0	0.0	1	3	2	1	0	0	0	14	18	4	0	6.0	.889	2B-5

Todd Benzinger

BENZINGER, TODD ERIC
B. Feb. 11, 1963, Dayton, Ky.

BB TR 6'1" 185 lbs.

Year	Team	Games	BA	SA	AB	H	2B	3B	HR	HR%	R	RBI	BB	SO	SB	AB	H	PO	A	E	DP	TC/G	FA	G by Pos
1987 BOS	A	73	.278	.444	223	62	11	1	8	3.6	36	43	22	41	5	8	2	155	7	2	2	2.2	.988	OF-61, 1B-2
1988		120	.254	.425	405	103	28	1	13	3.2	47	70	22	80	2	7	3	602	38	6	47	5.4	.991	1B-85, OF-48, DH-1
1989 CIN	N	161	.245	.381	628	154	28	3	17	2.7	79	76	44	120	3	3	1	1417	73	7	96	9.3	.995	1B-158
3 yrs.		354	.254	.406	1256	319	67	5	38	3.0	162	189	88	241	10	18	6	2174	118	15	145	6.5	.993	1B-245, OF-109, DH-1

LEAGUE CHAMPIONSHIP SERIES

Year	Team	Games	BA	SA	AB	H	2B	3B	HR	HR%	R	RBI	BB	SO	SB	AB	H	PO	A	E	DP	TC/G	FA	G by Pos
1988 BOS	A	4	.091	.091	11	1	0	0	0	0.0	0	0	1	3	0	1	0	21	1	0	2	5.5	1.000	1B-3

Johnny Berardino

BERARDINO, JOHN
B. May 1, 1917, Los Angeles, Calif. — BR TR 5'11½" 175 lbs.

Year	Team	Games	BA	SA	AB	H	2B	3B	HR	HR%	R	RBI	BB	SO	SB	PH AB	PH H	PO	A	E	DP	TC/G	FA	G by Pos
1939	STL A	126	.256	.361	468	120	24	5	5	1.1	42	58	37	36	6	2	1	325	363	33	71	5.7	.954	2B-114, 3B-8, SS-2
1940		142	.258	.424	523	135	31	4	16	3.1	71	85	32	46	6	8	2	297	399	42	96	5.2	.943	SS-112, 2B-13, 3B-9
1941		128	.271	.384	469	127	30	4	5	1.1	48	89	41	27	3	4	0	262	305	27	81	4.6	.955	SS-123, 3B-1
1942		29	.284	.405	74	21	6	0	1	1.4	11	10	4	2	3	8	1	65	32	4	13	3.5	.960	SS-6, 3B-6, 1B-5, 2B-4
1946		144	.265	.357	582	154	29	5	5	0.9	70	68	34	58	2	1	0	374	414	23	96	5.6	.972	2B-143
1947		90	.261	.350	306	80	22	1	1	0.3	29	20	44	26	6	2	0	242	221	11	61	5.3	.977	2B-86
1948	CLE A	66	.190	.279	147	28	5	1	2	1.4	19	10	27	16	0	11	2	199	85	3	34	4.3	.990	2B-20, 1B-18, SS-12, 3B-3
1949		50	.198	.267	116	23	6	1	0	0.0	11	13	14	14	0	14	2	38	68	6	7	2.2	.946	3B-25, 2B-8, SS-3
1950	2 teams	CLE A (4G – .400) PIT N (40G – .206)																						
"	total	44	.213	.272	136	29	6	1	1	0.7	13	15	20	11	0	3	2	94	118	7	29	5.0	.968	2B-37, 3B-4
1951	STL A	39	.227	.303	119	27	7	1	0	0.0	13	13	17	18	1	3	0	47	47	9	6	2.6	.913	3B-31, 2B-2, OF-1, 1B-1
1952	2 teams	CLE A (35G – .094) PIT N (19G – .143)																						
"	total	54	.125	.170	88	11	4	0	0	0.0	7	6	14	14	0	8	0	50	83	5	15	2.6	.964	2B-26, SS-8, 3B-4, 1B-2
11 yrs.		912	.249	.355	3028	755	167	23	36	1.2	334	387	284	268	27	64	10	1993	2135	170	509	4.7	.960	2B-453, SS-266, 3B-91, 1B-26, OF-1

Lou Berberet

BERBERET, LOUIS JOSEPH
B. Nov. 20, 1929, Long Beach, Calif. — BL TR 5'11" 200 lbs.

Year	Team	Games	BA	SA	AB	H	2B	3B	HR	HR%	R	RBI	BB	SO	SB	PH AB	PH H	PO	A	E	DP	TC/G	FA	G by Pos
1954	NY A	5	.400	.400	5	2	0	0	0	0.0	1	3	1	1	0	2	1	12	0	0	0	2.4	1.000	C-3
1955		2	.400	.400	5	2	0	0	0	0.0	1	2	1	0	0	1	1	10	0	0	0	5.0	1.000	C-1
1956	WAS A	95	.261	.377	207	54	6	3	4	1.9	25	27	46	33	0	33	6	266	28	1	6	3.1	.997	C-59
1957		99	.261	.398	264	69	11	2	7	2.7	24	36	41	38	0	16	3	349	48	0	8	4.0	1.000	C-77
1958	2 teams	WAS A (5G – .167) BOS A (57G – .210)																						
"	total	62	.208	.306	173	36	5	3	2	1.2	11	18	35	33	0	8	0	242	21	5	3	4.3	.981	C-51
1959	DET A	100	.216	.367	338	73	8	2	13	3.8	38	44	35	59	0	3	0	511	39	6	4	5.6	.989	C-95
1960		85	.194	.276	232	45	4	0	5	2.2	18	23	41	31	2	4	1	396	36	3	4	5.1	.993	C-81
7 yrs.		448	.230	.350	1224	281	34	10	31	2.5	118	153	200	195	2	67	12	1786	172	15	25	4.4	.992	C-367

Moe Berg

BERG, MORRIS
B. Mar. 2, 1902, New York, N.Y. D. May 29, 1972, Belleville, N.J. — BR TR 6'1" 185 lbs.

Year	Team	Games	BA	SA	AB	H	2B	3B	HR	HR%	R	RBI	BB	SO	SB	PH AB	PH H	PO	A	E	DP	TC/G	FA	G by Pos
1923	BKN N	49	.186	.240	129	24	3	2	0	0.0	9	5	2	5	1	0	1	86	126	22	20	4.8	.906	SS-47, 2B-1
1926	CHI A	41	.221	.274	113	25	6	0	0	0.0	4	7	6	9	0	6	1	60	89	8	21	3.8	.949	SS-31, 2B-2, 3B-1
1927		35	.246	.304	69	17	4	0	0	0.0	4	4	4	10	0	6	1	39	41	9	4	2.5	.899	2B-10, C-10, SS-6, 3B-3
1928		76	.246	.317	224	55	16	0	0	0.0	25	29	14	25	2	3	1	256	52	3	8	4.1	.990	C-73
1929		106	.288	.308	351	101	7	0	0	0.0	32	47	17	16	5	0	0	290	86	7	12	3.6	.982	C-106
1930		20	.115	.164	61	7	3	0	0	0.0	4	7	1	5	0	1	0	55	14	1	1	3.5	.986	C-20
1931	CLE A	10	.077	.154	13	1	1	0	0	0.0	1	0	1	1	0	1	0	12	4	2	1	1.8	.889	C-8
1932	WAS A	75	.236	.303	195	46	8	1	1	0.5	16	26	8	13	1	0	0	229	35	0	9	3.5	1.000	C-75
1933		40	.185	.323	65	12	3	0	2	3.1	8	9	4	5	0	4	0	76	10	0	2	2.2	1.000	C-35
1934	2 teams	WAS A (33G – .244) CLE A (29G – .258)																						
"	total	62	.251	.301	183	46	7	1	0	0.0	9	15	7	11	2	3	0	214	21	4	2	3.9	.983	C-62
1935	BOS A	38	.286	.398	98	28	5	0	2	2.0	13	12	5	3	0	1	0	99	15	1	2	3.0	.991	C-37
1936		39	.240	.288	125	30	4	1	0	0.0	9	19	2	6	0	0	0	175	29	3	3	5.3	.986	C-39
1937		47	.255	.291	141	36	3	1	0	0.0	13	20	5	4	0	0	0	208	24	5	2	5.0	.979	C-47
1938		10	.333	.333	12	4	0	0	0	0.0	0	1	0	1	0	1	0	14	1	0	2	1.5	1.000	C-7, 1B-1
1939		14	.273	.394	33	9	1	0	1	3.0	3	5	2	3	0	1	0	45	10	2	1	4.1	.965	C-13
15 yrs.		662	.243	.299	1812	441	71	6	6	0.3	150	206	78	117	11	28	5	1858	557	67	91	3.7	.973	C-532, SS-84, 2B-13, 3B-4, 1B-1

Augie Bergamo

BERGAMO, AUGUST SAMUEL
B. Feb. 14, 1917, Detroit, Mich. D. Aug. 19, 1974, Grosse Pointe, Mich. — BL TL 5'9" 165 lbs.

Year	Team	Games	BA	SA	AB	H	2B	3B	HR	HR%	R	RBI	BB	SO	SB	PH AB	PH H	PO	A	E	DP	TC/G	FA	G by Pos
1944	STL N	80	.286	.380	192	55	6	3	2	1.0	35	19	35	23	0	26	4	87	0	1	0	1.1	.989	OF-50, 1B-2
1945		94	.316	.414	304	96	17	2	3	1.0	51	44	43	21	0	15	4	160	9	5	4	1.9	.971	OF-77, 1B-2
2 yrs.		174	.304	.401	496	151	23	5	5	1.0	86	63	78	44	0	41	8	247	9	6	4	1.5	.977	OF-127, 1B-4

WORLD SERIES

Year	Team	Games	BA	SA	AB	H	2B	3B	HR	HR%	R	RBI	BB	SO	SB	PH AB	PH H	PO	A	E	DP	TC/G	FA	G by Pos
1944	STL N	3	.000	.000	6	0	0	0	0	0.0	0	1	2	3	0	0	0	1	0	0	0	0.3	1.000	OF-2

Bill Bergen

BERGEN, WILLIAM ALOYSIUS
Brother of Marty Bergen.
B. June 13, 1878, N. Brookfield, Mass. D. Dec. 19, 1943, Worcester, Mass. — BR TR 6' 184 lbs.

Year	Team	Games	BA	SA	AB	H	2B	3B	HR	HR%	R	RBI	BB	SO	SB	PH AB	PH H	PO	A	E	DP	TC/G	FA	G by Pos
1901	CIN N	87	.179	.234	308	55	6	4	1	0.3	15	17	8		2	0	0	406	117	16	8	6.2	.970	C-87
1902		89	.180	.224	322	58	8	3	0	0.0	19	36	14		2	0	0	406	137	23	13	6.4	.959	C-89, P-2
1903		58	.227	.266	207	47	4	2	0	0.0	21	19	7		2	0	0	251	85	7	3	5.9	.959	C-58
1904	BKN N	96	.182	.207	329	60	4	2	0	0.0	17	12	9		3	0	0	415	151	24	10	6.1	.959	C-93, 1B-1
1905		79	.190	.219	247	47	3	2	0	0.0	12	22	7		4	3	0	371	127	24	8	6.6	.954	C-76
1906		103	.159	.184	353	56	3	3	0	0.0	9	19	7		2	0	0	485	149	15	9	6.3	.977	C-103
1907		51	.159	.181	138	22	3	0	0	0.0	9	14	1		1	0	0	175	67	8	3	4.9	.968	C-51
1908		99	.175	.215	302	53	8	2	0	0.0	8	15	5		1	0	0	470	137	7	9	6.2	.989	C-99
1909		112	.139	.156	346	48	1	1	0	0.3	16	15	10		4	0	0	436	202	18	18	5.9	.972	C-112
1910		89	.161	.177	249	40	2	1	0	0.0	11	14	6	39	2	0	0	346	151	10	15	6.0	.981	C-89
1911		84	.132	.154	227	30	3	1	0	0.0	8	10	14	42	2	0	0	346	121	9	10	5.7	.981	C-84
11 yrs.		947	.170	.201	3028	516	45	21	2	0.1	138	193	88	81	23	3	0	4134	1444	161	106	6.1	.972	C-941, P-2, 1B-1

Marty Bergen

BERGEN, MARTIN
Brother of Bill Bergen.
B. Oct. 25, 1871, N. Brookfield, Mass. D. Jan. 19, 1900, N. Brookfield, Mass. — TR 5'10" 170 lbs.

Year	Team	Games	BA	SA	AB	H	2B	3B	HR	HR%	R	RBI	BB	SO	SB	PH AB	PH H	PO	A	E	DP	TC/G	FA	G by Pos
1896	BOS N	65	.269	.376	245	66	6	4	4	1.6	39	37	11	22	6	1	0	213	70	25	6	4.7	.919	C-63, 1B-1
1897		87	.248	.318	327	81	11	3	2	0.6	47	45	18		5	0	0	353	66	17	4	5.0	.961	C-85, OF-1
1898		120	.280	.359	446	125	16	5	3	0.7	62	60	13		9	1	0	511	109	24	6	5.4	.963	C-117, 1B-2

Year Team	Games	BA	SA	AB	H	2B	3B	HR	HR%	R	RBI	BB	SO	SB	Pinch Hit AB	H	PO	A	E	DP	TC/G	FA	G by Pos

Marty Bergen *continued*

Year Team	Games	BA	SA	AB	H	2B	3B	HR	HR%	R	RBI	BB	SO	SB	AB	H	PO	A	E	DP	TC/G	FA	G by Pos
1899	72	.258	.335	260	67	11	3	1	0.4	32	34	10		4	0	0	253	89	16	4	5.0	.955	C-72
4 yrs.	344	.265	.347	1278	339	44	15	10	0.8	180	176	52	22	24	2	1	1330	334	82	20	5.1	.953	C-337, 1B-3, OF-1

Boze Berger

BERGER, LOUIS WILLIAM B. May 13, 1910, Baltimore, Md.   BR TR 6'2" 180 lbs.

Year Team	Games	BA	SA	AB	H	2B	3B	HR	HR%	R	RBI	BB	SO	SB	AB	H	PO	A	E	DP	TC/G	FA	G by Pos
1932 CLE A	1	.000	.000	1	0	0	0	0	0.0	0	0	0	1	0	0	0	0	0	0	0	0.0	–	SS-1
1935	124	.258	.371	461	119	27	5	5	1.1	62	43	34	97	7	0	0	325	425	29	93	6.3	.963	2B-120, SS-3, 1B-2, 3B-1
1936	28	.173	.212	52	9	2	0	0	0.0	1	3	1	14	0	1	0	67	33	9	11	3.9	.917	2B-8, 1B-8, 3B-7, SS-2
1937 CHI A	52	.238	.392	130	31	5	0	5	3.8	19	13	15	24	1	6	2	37	76	10	9	2.4	.919	3B-40, SS-1, 2B-1
1938	118	.217	.281	470	102	15	3	3	0.6	60	36	43	80	4	0	0	239	353	39	79	5.3	.938	SS-67, 2B-42, 3B-9
1939 BOS A	20	.300	.367	30	9	2	0	0	0.0	4	2	1	10	0	3	1	12	21	1	2	1.7	.971	SS-10, 3B-5, 2B-2
6 yrs.	343	.236	.329	1144	270	51	8	13	1.1	146	97	94	226	12	10	3	680	908	88	194	4.9	.947	2B-173, SS-84, 3B-62, 1B-10

Clarence Berger

BERGER, CLARENCE EDWARD B. Nov. 1, 1894, East Cleveland, Ohio   D. June 30, 1959, Washington, D. C.   BL TR 6' 185 lbs.

Year Team	Games	BA	SA	AB	H	2B	3B	HR	HR%	R	RBI	BB	SO	SB	AB	H	PO	A	E	DP	TC/G	FA	G by Pos
1914 PIT N	6	.077	.077	13	1	0	0	0	0.0	2	0	1	4	0	1	0	2	0	0	0	0.3	1.000	OF-5

Joe Berger

BERGER, JOSEPH AUGUST (Fats) B. Dec. 20, 1886, St. Louis, Mo.   D. Mar. 5, 1956, Rock Island, Ill.   BR TR 5'10½" 170 lbs.

Year Team	Games	BA	SA	AB	H	2B	3B	HR	HR%	R	RBI	BB	SO	SB	AB	H	PO	A	E	DP	TC/G	FA	G by Pos
1913 CHI A	77	.215	.287	223	48	6	2	2	0.9	27	20	36	28	5	2	0	114	223	15	19	4.6	.957	2B-69, SS-4, 1B-1
1914	47	.155	.189	148	23	3	1	0	0.0	11	3	13	9	2	1	0	76	113	15	11	4.3	.926	SS-27, 2B-12, 3B-7
2 yrs.	124	.191	.248	371	71	9	3	2	0.5	38	23	49	37	7	3	0	190	336	30	30	4.5	.946	2B-81, SS-31, 3B-8

Johnny Berger

BERGER, JOHN HENNE B. Aug. 27, 1901, Philadelphia, Pa.   D. May 7, 1979, Lake Charles, La.   BR TR 5'9" 165 lbs.

Year Team	Games	BA	SA	AB	H	2B	3B	HR	HR%	R	RBI	BB	SO	SB	AB	H	PO	A	E	DP	TC/G	FA	G by Pos
1922 PHI A	2	1.000	1.000	1	1	0	0	0	0.0	0	0	0	0	0	1	0	4	0	0	0	2.0	1.000	C-2
1927 WAS A	9	.267	.267	15	4	0	0	0	0.0	1	1	2	3	0	0	0	25	0	2	1	3.0	.926	C-9
2 yrs.	11	.313	.313	16	5	0	0	0	0.0	1	1	2	3	0	1	0	29	0	2	1	2.8	.935	C-11

Tun Berger

BERGER, JOHN HENRY B. Dec. 6, 1867, Pittsburgh, Pa.   D. June 10, 1907, Pittsburgh, Pa.   TR 204 lbs.

Year Team	Games	BA	SA	AB	H	2B	3B	HR	HR%	R	RBI	BB	SO	SB	AB	H	PO	A	E	DP	TC/G	FA	G by Pos
1890 PIT N	104	.266	.332	391	104	18	4	0	0.0	64	40	35	23	11	0	0	224	168	56	11	4.3	.875	OF-41, SS-33, C-21, 2B-6, 3B-1
1891	43	.239	.291	134	32	2	1	1	0.7	15	14	12	10	4	0	0	116	64	30	2	4.9	.857	C-18, 2B-17, SS-6, OF-2
1892 WAS N	26	.144	.186	97	14	2	1	0	0.0	9	3	7	9	3	0	0	56	52	14	3	4.7	.885	SS-18, C-9
3 yrs.	173	.241	.301	622	150	22	6	1	0.2	88	57	54	42	18	0	0	396	284	100	16	4.5	.872	SS-57, C-48, OF-43, 2B-23, 3B-1

Wally Berger

BERGER, WALTER ANTONE B. Oct. 10, 1905, Chicago, Ill.   D. Nov. 30, 1988, Redondo Beach, Calif.   BR TR 6'2" 198 lbs.

Year Team	Games	BA	SA	AB	H	2B	3B	HR	HR%	R	RBI	BB	SO	SB	AB	H	PO	A	E	DP	TC/G	FA	G by Pos
1930 BOS N	151	.310	.614	555	172	27	14	38	6.8	98	119	54	69	3	6	1	307	10	11	3	2.2	.966	OF-145
1931	156	.323	.512	617	199	44	8	19	3.1	94	84	55	70	13	0	0	459	16	11	5	3.1	.977	OF-156, 1B-1
1932	145	.307	.468	602	185	34	6	17	2.8	90	73	33	66	5	1	0	498	14	3	11	3.6	.994	OF-134, 1B-11
1933	137	.313	.566	528	165	37	8	27	5.1	84	106	41	77	2	1	1	382	6	9	4	2.9	.977	OF-136
1934	150	.298	.546	615	183	35	8	34	5.5	92	121	49	65	2	0	0	385	9	9	2	2.7	.978	OF-150
1935	150	.295	.548	589	174	39	4	34	5.8	91	130	50	80	3	1	0	458	8	17	1	3.2	.965	OF-149
1936	138	.288	.483	534	154	23	3	25	4.7	88	91	53	84	1	5	1	384	10	14	1	3.0	.966	OF-133
1937 2 teams	BOS N (30G – .274)				NY N (59G – .291)																		
" total	89	.285	.532	312	89	20	3	17	5.4	54	65	29	63	3	9	1	158	5	4	0	1.9	.976	OF-80
1938 2 teams	NY N (16G – .188)				CIN N (99G – .307)																		
" total	115	.298	.478	439	131	23	4	16	3.6	76	60	31	48	2	5	2	221	7	7	2	2.0	.970	OF-107
1939 CIN N	97	.258	.438	329	85	15	1	14	4.3	36	44	36	63	1	2	0	158	6	5	0	1.7	.970	OF-95
1940 2 teams	CIN N (2G – .000)				PHI N (20G – .317)																		
" total	22	.302	.419	43	13	2	0	1	2.3	3	3	5	4	1	9	0	20	1	0	1	1.0	.952	OF-11, 1B-1
11 yrs.	1350	.300	.522	5163	1550	299	59	242	4.7	806	898	435	694	36	39	6	3430	91	91	29	2.7	.975	OF-1296, 1B-13

WORLD SERIES

Year Team	Games	BA	SA	AB	H	2B	3B	HR	HR%	R	RBI	BB	SO	SB	AB	H	PO	A	E	DP	TC/G	FA	G by Pos
1937 NY N	3	.000	.000	3	0	0	0	0	0.0	0	0	0	1	0	0	3	0	0	0	0	0.0	–	
1939 CIN N	4	.000	.000	15	0	0	0	0	0.0	0	0	1	4	0	0	0	8	0	0	0	2.0	1.000	OF-4
2 yrs.	7	.000	.000	18	0	0	0	0	0.0	0	0	1	5	0	0	3	8	0	0	0	1.1	1.000	OF-4

John Bergh

BERGH, JOHN BAPTIST B. Oct. 8, 1857, Boston, Mass.   D. Apr. 16, 1883, Boston, Mass.

Year Team	Games	BA	SA	AB	H	2B	3B	HR	HR%	R	RBI	BB	SO	SB	AB	H	PO	A	E	DP	TC/G	FA	G by Pos
1876 PHI N	1	.000	.000	4	0	0	0	0	0.0	0	0	0	2	0	0	0	3	2	1	0	6.0	.833	OF-1, C-1
1880 BOS N	11	.200	.275	40	8	3	0	0	0.0	2	0	2	5	0	0	0	54	11	12	0	7.0	.844	C-11
2 yrs.	12	.182	.250	44	8	3	0	0	0.0	2	0	2	7	0	0	0	57	13	13	0	6.9	.843	C-12, OF-1

Marty Berghammer

BERGHAMMER, MARTIN ANDREW B. Jan. 18, 1888, Elliot, Pa.   D. Dec. 21, 1957, Pittsburgh, Pa.   BL TR 5'9" 172 lbs.

Year Team	Games	BA	SA	AB	H	2B	3B	HR	HR%	R	RBI	BB	SO	SB	AB	H	PO	A	E	DP	TC/G	FA	G by Pos
1911 CHI A	2	.000	.000	5	0	0	0	0	0.0	0	0	0	0	0	0	0	5	2	0	0	3.5	1.000	2B-2
1913 CIN N	74	.218	.266	188	41	4	1	1	0.5	25	13	10	29	16	0	0	111	172	29	20	4.2	.907	SS-53, 2B-13
1914	77	.223	.241	112	25	2	0	0	0.0	15	6	10	18	4	13	2	93	88	10	9	1.9	.930	SS-33, 2B-13
1915 PIT F	132	.243	.290	469	114	10	6	0	0.0	96	33	83		26	0	0	286	359	39	55	5.2	.943	SS-132
4 yrs.	285	.233	.275	774	180	16	7	1	0.1	136	52	103	47	46	13	2	447	621	78	84	4.0	.932	SS-218, 2B-28

Al Bergman

BERGMAN, ALFRED HENRY (Dutch) B. Sept. 27, 1890, Peru, Ind.   D. June 20, 1961, Fort Wayne, Ind.   BR TR 5'7" 155 lbs.

Year Team	Games	BA	SA	AB	H	2B	3B	HR	HR%	R	RBI	BB	SO	SB	AB	H	PO	A	E	DP	TC/G	FA	G by Pos
1916 CLE A	8	.214	.357	14	3	0	1	0	0.0	2	0	2	4	0	3	0	2	6	1	0	1.1	.889	2B-3

Year	Team		Games	BA	SA	AB	H	2B	3B	HR	HR%	R	RBI	BB	SO	SB	Pinch Hit AB	Pinch Hit H	PO	A	E	DP	TC/G	FA	G by Pos

Dave Bergman

BERGMAN, DAVID BRUCE
B. June 6, 1953, Evanston, Ill.

BL TL 6'1½" 185 lbs.

Year	Team		Games	BA	SA	AB	H	2B	3B	HR	HR%	R	RBI	BB	SO	SB	AB	H	PO	A	E	DP	TC/G	FA	G by Pos
1975	NY	A	7	.000	.000	17	0	0	0	0	0.0	0	0	2	4	0	0	0	10	1	1	1	1.7	.917	OF-6
1977			5	.250	.250	4	1	0	0	0	0.0	1	1	0	0	0	0	0	8	0	0	0	1.6	1.000	OF-3, 1B-2
1978	HOU	N	104	.231	.269	186	43	5	1	0	0.0	15	12	39	32	2	16	2	328	16	4	26	3.3	.989	1B-66, OF-29
1979			13	.400	.600	15	6	0	0	1	6.7	4	2	0	3	0	10	5	8	0	0	1	0.6	1.000	1B-4
1980			90	.256	.359	78	20	6	1	0	0.0	12	3	10	10	1	24	0	187	16	1	23	2.3	.995	1B-59, OF-5
1981	2 teams	HOU N (6G – .167)			SF	N	(63G – .255)																		
"	total		69	.252	.391	151	38	9	0	4	2.6	17	14	19	18	2	23	4	255	25	3	21	4.1	.989	1B-34, OF-15
1982	SF	N	100	.273	.413	121	33	3	1	4	3.3	22	14	18	11	3	21	5	321	20	4	18	3.5	.988	1B-69, OF-6
1983			90	.286	.457	140	40	4	1	6	4.3	16	24	24	21	2	31	11	299	27	2	20	3.6	.994	1B-50, OF-6
1984	DET	A	120	.273	.417	271	74	8	5	7	2.6	42	44	33	40	3	21	6	658	75	8	63	6.2	.989	1B-114, OF-2
1985			69	.179	.257	140	25	2	0	3	2.1	8	7	14	15	0	24	6	306	25	3	25	4.8	.991	1B-44, DH-5, OF-1
1986			65	.231	.315	130	30	6	1	1	0.8	14	9	21	16	0	22	5	255	29	4	30	4.4	.986	1B-41, DH-8, OF-2
1987			91	.273	.453	172	47	7	3	6	3.5	25	22	30	23	0	21	4	357	29	3	33	4.3	.992	1B-65, DH-7, OF-7
1988			116	.294	.394	289	85	14	0	5	1.7	37	35	38	34	0	24	3	386	37	4	31	3.7	.991	1B-64, DH-30, OF-13
1989			137	.268	.361	385	103	13	1	7	1.8	38	37	44	44	1	18	1	912	85	7	88	7.3	.993	1B-123, DH-7, OF-1
14 yrs.			1076	.260	.373	2099	545	77	14	44	2.1	251	224	292	271	14	255	56	4290	385	44	380	4.4	.991	1B-735, OF-96, DH-57

LEAGUE CHAMPIONSHIP SERIES

Year	Team		Games	BA	SA	AB	H	2B	3B	HR	HR%	R	RBI	BB	SO	SB	AB	H	PO	A	E	DP	TC/G	FA	G by Pos
1980	HOU	N	4	.333	1.000	3	1	0	1	0	0.0	0	2	0	0	0	0	0	8	2	1	0	2.8	.909	1B-4
1984	DET	A	2	1.000	1.000	1	1	0	0	0	0.0	1	0	0	0	1	0	0	5	0	0	0	2.5	1.000	1B-1
1987			4	.250	.250	4	1	0	0	0	0.0	0	2	0	4	0	2	1	6	0	0	0	1.5	1.000	DH-1, 1B-1
3 yrs.			10	.375	.625	8	3	0	1	0	0.0	1	4	0	4	1	2	1	19	2	1	0	2.2	.955	1B-6, DH-1

WORLD SERIES

Year	Team		Games	BA	SA	AB	H	2B	3B	HR	HR%	R	RBI	BB	SO	SB	AB	H	PO	A	E	DP	TC/G	FA	G by Pos
1984	DET	A	5	.000	.000	5	0	0	0	0	0.0	0	0	0	1	0	0	0	22	4	0	0	5.2	1.000	1B-5

Frank Berkelbach

BERKELBACH, FRANCIS P.
B. Philadelphia, Pa. Deceased.

6' 182 lbs.

Year	Team		Games	BA	SA	AB	H	2B	3B	HR	HR%	R	RBI	BB	SO	SB	AB	H	PO	A	E	DP	TC/G	FA	G by Pos
1884	CIN	AA	6	.240	.320	25	6	1	0	0	0.0	3		0			0	0	6	0	3	0	1.5	.667	OF-6

Bob Berman

BERMAN, ROBERT LEON
B. Jan. 24, 1899, New York, N. Y. D. Aug. 2, 1988, Bridgeport, Conn.

BR TR 5'8" 147 lbs.

Year	Team		Games	BA	SA	AB	H	2B	3B	HR	HR%	R	RBI	BB	SO	SB	AB	H	PO	A	E	DP	TC/G	FA	G by Pos
1918	WAS	A	2	–	–	0	0	0	0	0	–	0	0	0	0	0	0	0	2	0	0	0	1.0	1.000	C-1

Curt Bernard

BERNARD, CURTIS HENRY
B. Feb. 18, 1878, Parkersburg, W. Va. D. Apr. 10, 1955, Culver City, Calif.

BL TR 5'10½" 150 lbs.

Year	Team		Games	BA	SA	AB	H	2B	3B	HR	HR%	R	RBI	BB	SO	SB	AB	H	PO	A	E	DP	TC/G	FA	G by Pos
1900	NY	N	20	.254	.282	71	18	2	0	0	0.0	9	8	6		1	0	0	26	6	2	0	1.7	.941	OF-19, SS-1
1901			23	.224	.276	76	17	0	2	0	0.0	11	6	7		2	1	0	31	14	11	1	2.4	.804	OF-15, 2B-4, SS-2, 3B-1
2 yrs.			43	.238	.279	147	35	2	2	0	0.0	20	14	13		3	1	0	57	20	13	1	2.1	.856	OF-34, 2B-4, SS-3, 3B-1

Tony Bernazard

BERNAZARD, ANTONIO
Born Antonio Bernazard y Garcia.
B. Aug. 24, 1956, Caguas, Puerto Rico

BB TR 5'9" 150 lbs.

Year	Team		Games	BA	SA	AB	H	2B	3B	HR	HR%	R	RBI	BB	SO	SB	AB	H	PO	A	E	DP	TC/G	FA	G by Pos
1979	MON	N	22	.300	.425	40	12	2	0	1	2.5	11	8	15	12	1	2	0	22	34	1	4	2.6	.982	2B-14
1980			82	.224	.355	183	41	7	1	5	2.7	26	18	17	41	9	22	4	82	151	9	25	3.0	.963	2B-39, SS-22
1981	CHI	A	106	.276	.380	384	106	14	4	6	1.6	53	34	54	66	4	2	0	228	321	7	66	5.2	.987	2B-104, SS-1
1982			137	.256	.396	540	138	25	9	11	2.0	90	56	67	88	11	0	0	353	443	12	116	5.9	.985	2B-137
1983	2 teams	CHI A (59G – .262)			SEA	A	(80G – .267)																		
"	total		139	.265	.385	533	141	34	3	8	1.5	65	56	55	97	23	2	0	262	422	19	89	5.1	.973	2B-138
1984	CLE	A	140	.221	.287	439	97	15	4	2	0.5	44	38	43	70	20	3	0	264	397	20	85	4.9	.971	2B-136, DH-1
1985			153	.274	.404	500	137	26	3	11	2.2	73	59	69	72	17	9	4	313	399	16	87	4.8	.978	2B-147, SS-1
1986			146	.301	.456	562	169	28	4	17	3.0	88	73	53	77	17	1	1	351	442	17	95	5.5	.979	2B-146
1987	2 teams	CLE A (79G – .239)			OAK	A	(61G – .266)																		
"	total		140	.250	.393	507	127	26	2	14	2.8	73	49	55	79	11	3	1	243	335	17	61	4.3	.971	2B-137, DH-3
9 yrs.			1065	.262	.388	3688	968	177	30	75	2.0	523	391	428	602	113	44	10	2118	2944	118	628	4.9	.977	2B-998, SS-24, DH-4

Juan Bernhardt

BERNHARDT, JUAN ROMAN
Born Juan Ramon Bernhardt y Coradin.
B. Aug. 31, 1953, San Pedro de Macoris, Dominican Republic

BR TR 5'11" 160 lbs.

Year	Team		Games	BA	SA	AB	H	2B	3B	HR	HR%	R	RBI	BB	SO	SB	AB	H	PO	A	E	DP	TC/G	FA	G by Pos
1976	NY	A	10	.190	.238	21	4	1	0	0	0.0	0	1	1	4	0	5	0	4	1	1	0	0.6	.833	OF-4, DH-2, 3B-1
1977	SEA	A	89	.243	.354	305	74	9	2	7	2.3	32	30	5	26	2	12	2	69	42	2	7	1.3	.982	DH-54, 3B-21, 1B-8
1978			54	.230	.321	165	38	9	0	2	1.2	13	12	9	10	1	5	1	263	63	6	21	6.1	.982	1B-25, 3B-22, DH-2
1979			1	1.000	1.000	1	1	0	0	0	0.0	0	0	0	0	0	1	1	0	0	0	0	0.0		
4 yrs.			154	.238	.339	492	117	19	2	9	1.8	46	43	14	40	3	23	4	336	106	9	28	2.9	.980	DH-58, 3B-44, 1B-33, OF-4

Carlos Bernier

BERNIER, CARLOS
Born Carlos Bernier y Rodriguez.
B. Jan. 28, 1929, Juana Diaz, Puerto Rico D. Apr. 6, 1989, Juana Diaz, Puerto Rico

BR TR 5'9" 180 lbs.

Year	Team		Games	BA	SA	AB	H	2B	3B	HR	HR%	R	RBI	BB	SO	SB	AB	H	PO	A	E	DP	TC/G	FA	G by Pos
1953	PIT	N	105	.213	.316	310	66	7	8	3	1.0	48	31	51	53	15	16	3	220	8	7	1	2.2	.970	OF-87

Johnny Bero

BERO, JOHN GEORGE
B. Dec. 22, 1922, Gary, W. Va. D. May 11, 1985, Gardena, Calif.

BL TR 6' 170 lbs.

Year	Team		Games	BA	SA	AB	H	2B	3B	HR	HR%	R	RBI	BB	SO	SB	AB	H	PO	A	E	DP	TC/G	FA	G by Pos
1948	DET	A	4	.000	.000	9	0	0	0	0	0.0	2	0	1	1	0	1	0	5	3	0	0	2.0	1.000	2B-2
1951	STL	A	61	.213	.338	160	34	5	0	5	3.1	24	17	26	30	1	7	2	91	137	11	30	3.9	.954	SS-55, 2B-1
2 yrs.			65	.201	.320	169	34	5	0	5	3.0	26	17	27	31	1	8	2	96	140	11	30	3.8	.955	SS-55, 2B-3

Dale Berra

BERRA, DALE ANTHONY
Son of Yogi Berra.
B. Dec. 13, 1956, Ridgewood, N. J.

BR TR 6' 180 lbs.

Year	Team		Games	BA	SA	AB	H	2B	3B	HR	HR%	R	RBI	BB	SO	SB	AB	H	PO	A	E	DP	TC/G	FA	G by Pos
1977	PIT	N	17	.175	.200	40	7	1	0	0	0.0	0	3	1	8	0	2	0	14	22	1	1	2.2	.973	3B-14

Dale Berra *continued*

Year	Team	Games	BA	SA	AB	H	2B	3B	HR	HR%	R	RBI	BB	SO	SB	Pinch Hit AB	Pinch Hit H	PO	A	E	DP	TC/G	FA	G by Pos
1978		56	.207	.356	135	28	2	0	6	4.4	16	14	13	20	3	0	0	31	84	11	11	2.3	.913	3B-55, SS-2
1979		44	.211	.325	123	26	5	0	3	2.4	11	15	11	17	0	0	0	43	86	12	14	3.2	.915	SS-22, 3B-22
1980		93	.220	.343	245	54	8	2	6	2.4	21	31	16	52	2	4	1	88	171	11	23	2.9	.959	3B-48, SS-45, 2B-4
1981		81	.241	.319	232	56	12	0	2	0.9	21	27	17	34	11	3	0	89	167	8	27	3.3	.970	3B-42, SS-30, 2B-18
1982		156	.263	.386	529	139	25	5	10	1.9	64	61	33	83	6	0	0	286	505	30	103	5.1	.963	SS-161
1983		161	.251	.358	537	135	25	1	10	1.9	51	52	61	84	8	0	0	186	449	30	65	4.9	.955	SS-135, 3B-1
1984		136	.222	.318	450	100	16	0	9	2.0	31	52	34	78	1	1	1	22	74	9	9	2.2	.914	3B-41, SS-6
1985	NY A	48	.229	.321	109	25	5	1	1	0.9	8	8	7	20	1	7	2	40	67	4	11	2.6	.964	SS-19, 3B-18, DH-4
1986		42	.231	.352	108	25	7	0	2	1.9	10	13	9	14	0	3	1	14	40	2	4	2.9	.964	SS-18, 2B-3
1987	HOU N	19	.178	.244	45	8	3	0	0	0.0	3	2	8	12	0	1	0							
11 yrs.		853	.236	.344	2553	603	109	9	49	1.9	236	278	210	422	32	21	5	1054	2170	148	345	4.0	.956	SS-591, 3B-247, 2B-25, DH-4

Yogi Berra

BERRA, LAWRENCE PETER
Father of Dale Berra.
B. May 12, 1925, St. Louis, Mo.
Manager 1964, 1972-75, 1984-85.
Hall of Fame 1972.

BL TR 5'7½" 185 lbs.

Year	Team	Games	BA	SA	AB	H	2B	3B	HR	HR%	R	RBI	BB	SO	SB	Pinch Hit AB	Pinch Hit H	PO	A	E	DP	TC/G	FA	G by Pos
1946	NY A	7	.364	.682	22	8	1	0	2	9.1	3	4	1	1	0	1	0	28	6	0	2	4.9	1.000	C-6
1947		83	.280	.464	293	82	15	3	11	3.8	41	54	13	12	0	8	2	307	18	9	5	4.0	.973	C-51, OF-24
1948		125	.305	.488	469	143	24	10	14	3.0	70	98	25	24	3	10	5	390	40	9	7	3.5	.979	C-71, OF-50
1949		116	.277	.480	415	115	20	2	20	4.8	59	91	22	25	2	7	3	544	60	7	18	5.3	.989	C-109
1950		151	.322	.533	597	192	30	6	28	4.7	116	124	55	12	4	3	1	777	64	13	16	5.7	.985	C-148
1951		141	.294	.492	547	161	19	4	27	4.9	92	88	44	20	5	0	0	693	82	13	25	5.6	.984	C-141
1952		142	.273	.478	534	146	17	1	30	5.6	97	98	66	24	2	3	0	700	73	6	10	5.5	.992	C-140
1953		137	.296	.523	503	149	23	5	27	5.4	80	108	50	32	0	10	4	566	64	9	9	4.7	.986	C-133
1954		151	.307	.488	584	179	28	6	22	3.8	88	125	56	29	0	1	0	718	64	8	14	5.2	.990	C-149, 3B-1
1955		147	.272	.470	541	147	20	3	27	5.0	84	108	60	20	1	4	1	721	54	13	10	5.4	.984	C-145
1956		140	.298	.534	521	155	29	2	30	5.8	93	105	65	29	3	4	0	733	57	11	15	5.7	.986	C-135, OF-1
1957		134	.251	.438	482	121	14	2	24	5.0	74	82	57	25	1	10	1	707	61	4	12	5.8	.995	C-121, OF-6
1958		122	.266	.471	433	115	17	3	22	5.1	60	90	35	35	3	10	3	558	44	2	11	5.0	.997	C-85, OF-21, 1B-2
1959		131	.284	.462	472	134	25	1	19	4.0	64	69	43	38	1	11	3	706	62	4	10	5.9	.995	C-116, OF-7
1960		120	.276	.446	359	99	14	1	15	4.2	46	62	38	23	2	24	5	312	24	5	6	2.8	.985	C-63, OF-36
1961		119	.271	.466	395	107	11	0	22	5.6	62	61	35	28	2	19	5	237	15	2	2	2.1	.992	OF-87, C-15
1962		86	.224	.388	232	52	8	0	10	4.3	25	35	24	18	0	23	6	238	17	6	6	3.0	.977	C-31, OF-28
1963		64	.293	.497	147	43	6	0	8	5.4	20	28	15	17	1	28	5	244	13	3	5	4.1	.988	C-35
1965	NY N	4	.222	.222	9	2	0	0	0	0.0	1	0	1	3	0	2	0	15	1	1	0	4.3	.941	C-2
19 yrs.		2120	.285	.482	7555	2150	321	49	358	4.7	1175	1430	704	415	30	178	44	9194	819	125	183	4.8	.988	C-1696, OF-260, 1B-2, 3B-1

WORLD SERIES

Year	Team	Games	BA	SA	AB	H	2B	3B	HR	HR%	R	RBI	BB	SO	SB	Pinch Hit AB	Pinch Hit H	PO	A	E	DP	TC/G	FA	G by Pos
1947	NY A	6	.158	.316	19	3	0	0	1	5.3	2	2	1	2	0	1	1	21	2	2	0	4.2	.920	C-4, OF-2
1949		4	.063	.063	16	1	0	0	0	0.0	2	1	1	3	0	0	0	37	3	0	1	10.0	1.000	C-4
1950		4	.200	.400	15	3	0	0	1	6.7	2	2	2	1	0	0	0	30	1	0	1	7.8	1.000	C-4
1951		6	.261	.304	23	6	1	0	0	0.0	4	0	2	1	0	0	0	27	3	1	0	5.2	.968	C-6
1952		7	.214	.464	28	6	1	0	2	7.1	2	3	2	4	0	0	0	59	7	1	1	9.6	.985	C-7
1953		6	.429	.619	21	9	1	0	1	4.8	3	4	3	1	0	0	0	36	3	0	1	6.5	1.000	C-6
1955		7	.417	.583	24	10	1	0	1	4.2	5	2	3	1	0	0	0	40	4	0	1	6.3	1.000	C-7
1956		7	.360	.800	25	9	2	0	3	12.0	5	10	2	0	0	0	0	50	3	1	0	7.6	.979	C-7
1957		7	.320	.480	25	8	1	0	1	4.0	5	2	4	0	0	0	0	44	2	1	0	6.7	.979	C-7
1958		7	.222	.333	27	6	0	0	0	0.0	3	2	1	0	0	0	0	60	6	0	1	9.4	1.000	C-7
1960		7	.318	.455	22	7	0	0	1	4.5	6	8	2	0	0	0	0	10	0	0	0	1.4	1.000	OF-4, C-3
1961		4	.273	.545	11	3	0	0	1	9.1	2	3	5	1	0	0	0	11	0	1	0	3.0	.917	OF-4
1962		2	.000	.000	2	0	0	0	0	0.0	0	0	2	0	0	0	0	6	1	0	0	3.5	1.000	C-1
1963		1	.000	.000	2	0	0	0	0	0.0	0	0	0	1	0	0	0					0.0	–	
14 yrs.		75	.274	.452	259	71	10	0	12	4.6	41	39	32	17	0	3	1	431	35	6	6	6.3	.987	C-63, OF-10
		1st			**1st**	**1st**	**1st**		**3rd**		**2nd**	**2nd**	**3rd**											

Denny Berran

BERRAN, DENNIS MARTIN
B. Oct. 8, 1887, Merrimac, Mass.   D. Apr. 28, 1943, Boston, Mass.

BL TL

Year	Team	Games	BA	SA	AB	H	2B	3B	HR	HR%	R	RBI	BB	SO	SB	Pinch Hit AB	Pinch Hit H	PO	A	E	DP	TC/G	FA	G by Pos
1912	CHI A	2	.250	.250	4	1	0	0	0	0.0	0		0	0	0	0	0	1	0	0	0	0.5	1.000	OF-2

Ray Berres

BERRES, RAYMOND FREDERICK
B. Aug. 31, 1907, Kenosha, Wis.

BR TR 5'9" 170 lbs.

Year	Team	Games	BA	SA	AB	H	2B	3B	HR	HR%	R	RBI	BB	SO	SB	Pinch Hit AB	Pinch Hit H	PO	A	E	DP	TC/G	FA	G by Pos
1934	BKN N	39	.215	.266	79	17	4	0	0	0.0	7	3	1	16	0	1	0	79	14	3	0	2.5	.969	C-37
1936		105	.240	.296	267	64	10	1	1	0.4	16	13	14	35	1	0	0	436	59	6	7	4.8	.988	C-105
1937	PIT N	2	.167	.167	6	1	0	0	0	0.0	0	0	0	0	0	0	0	9	2	0	0	5.5	1.000	C-2
1938		40	.230	.250	100	23	2	0	0	0.0	7	6	8	10	0	0	0	128	21	1	0	3.8	.993	C-40
1939		81	.229	.264	231	53	6	1	0	0.0	22	16	11	25	1	1	1	269	36	2	4	3.8	.993	C-80
1940	2 teams	PIT N (21G – .188)			BOS N (85G – .192)																				
"	total	106	.192	.215	261	50	4	1	0	0.0	14	16	19	20	0	0	0	294	65	7	8	3.5	.981	C-106
1941	BOS N	120	.201	.247	279	56	10	0	1	0.4	21	19	17	20	2	0	0	356	64	2	3	3.5	.995	C-120
1942	NY N	12	.188	.188	32	6	0	0	0	0.0	0	1	2	3	0	0	0	34	2	1	1	3.1	.973	C-12
1943		20	.143	.179	28	4	1	0	0	0.0	1	0	1	2	0	0	0	43	9	1	1	2.7	.981	C-12
1944		16	.471	.647	17	8	0	0	1	5.9	4	2	1	0	0	0	0	13	4	0	1	1.1	1.000	C-12
1945		20	.167	.167	30	5	0	0	0	0.0	4	2	1	3	0	0	0	43	2	0	0	2.3	1.000	C-20
11 yrs.		561	.216	.255	1330	287	37	3	3	0.2	96	78	76	134	4	5	2	1704	278	23	25	3.6	.989	C-551

Geronimo Berroa

BERROA, GERONIMO EMILIANO
B. Mar. 18, 1965, Santo Domingo, Dominican Republic

BR TR 6' 165 lbs.

Year	Team	Games	BA	SA	AB	H	2B	3B	HR	HR%	R	RBI	BB	SO	SB	Pinch Hit AB	Pinch Hit H	PO	A	E	DP	TC/G	FA	G by Pos
1989	ATL N	81	.265	.338	136	36	4	0	2	1.5	7	9	7	32	0	47	11	67	1	2	0	0.9	.971	OF-34

Year	Team		Games	BA	SA	AB	H	2B	3B	HR	HR%	R	RBI	BB	SO	SB	Pinch Hit AB	Pinch Hit H	PO	A	E	DP	TC/G	FA	G by Pos

Charlie Berry

BERRY, CHARLES FRANCIS
Son of Charlie Berry.
B. Oct. 18, 1902, Phillipsburg, N. J.   D. Sept. 6, 1972, Evanston, Ill.

BR TR 6'   185 lbs.

Year	Team		Games	BA	SA	AB	H	2B	3B	HR	HR%	R	RBI	BB	SO	SB	AB	H	PO	A	E	DP	TC/G	FA	G by Pos
1925	PHI	A	10	.214	.286	14	3	1	0	0	0.0	1	3		0		6	1	9	0	1	0	1.0	.900	C-4
1928	BOS	A	80	.260	.350	177	46	7	3	1	0.6	18	19	21	19	1	14	4	153	34	8	2	2.4	.959	C-63
1929			77	.242	.348	207	50	11	4	1	0.5	19	21	15	29	2	4	3	236	51	5	8	3.8	.983	C-72
1930			88	.289	.441	256	74	9	6	6	2.3	31	35	16	22	2	3	2	279	56	4	4	3.9	.988	C-85
1931			111	.283	.389	357	101	16	2	6	1.7	41	49	29	38	4	9	2	312	78	6	8	3.6	.985	C-102
1932 2 teams	BOS	A	(10G – .188)		CHI	A	(72G – .305)																		
" total			82	.291	.453	258	75	18	4	4	1.6	33	37	24	25	3	2	0	240	58	7	8	3.7	.977	C-80
1933	CHI	A	86	.255	.328	271	69	8	3	2	0.7	25	28	17	16	0	3	0	260	39	4	1	3.5	.987	C-83
1934	PHI	A	99	.268	.320	269	72	10	2	0	0.0	14	34	22	23	1	0	0	339	48	5	9	4.0	.987	C-99
1935			62	.253	.368	190	48	7	3	3	1.6	14	29	10	20	0	6	1	189	37	3	7	3.7	.987	C-56
1936			13	.059	.118	17	1	1	0	0	0.0	0	1	6	2	0	1	0	29	4	1	0	2.6	.971	C-12
1938			1	.000	.000	2	0	0	0	0	0.0	0	0	0	0	0	0	0	2	1	0	1	2.0	1.000	C-1
11 yrs.			709	.267	.374	2018	539	88	29	23	1.1	196	256	160	196	13	48	13	2047	406	44	48	3.5	.982	C-657

Charlie Berry

BERRY, CHARLES JOSEPH
Father of Charlie Berry.
B. Sept. 6, 1860, Elizabeth, N. J.   D. Jan. 22, 1940, Phillipsburg, N. J.

BR TR 5'11"   175 lbs.

Year	Team		Games	BA	SA	AB	H	2B	3B	HR	HR%	R	RBI	BB	SO	SB	AB	H	PO	A	E	DP	TC/G	FA	G by Pos
1884 4 teams	ALT	U	(7G – .240)		KC	U	(29G – .246)		CHI	U	(5G – .118)		PIT	U	(2G – .100)									
" total			43	.224	.300	170	38	8	1	1	0.6	21		1			0	0	115	89	30	7	5.4	.872	2B-36, OF-8, 3B-1

Claude Berry

BERRY, CLAUDE ELZY (Admiral)
B. Feb. 14, 1880, Losantville, Ind.   D. Feb. 1, 1974, Richmond, Ind.

BR TR 5'7"   165 lbs.

Year	Team		Games	BA	SA	AB	H	2B	3B	HR	HR%	R	RBI	BB	SO	SB	AB	H	PO	A	E	DP	TC/G	FA	G by Pos
1904	CHI	A	3	.000	.000	1	0	0	0	0	0.0	1	0	1			0	0	5	1	0	0	2.0	1.000	C-3
1906	PHI	A	10	.233	.233	30	7	0	0	0	0.0	2	2	2			1	0	52	24	5	0	8.1	.938	C-10
1907			8	.211	.316	19	4	2	0	0	0.0	2	1	2			0	0	29	5	2	0	4.5	.944	C-8
1914	PIT	F	124	.238	.341	411	98	18	9	2	0.5	35	36	26			6	1	550	202	23	18	6.3	.970	C-122
1915			100	.192	.247	292	56	11	1	1	0.3	32	26	29			7	0	384	144	11	8	5.4	.980	C-99
5 yrs.			245	.219	.299	753	165	31	10	3	0.4	72	65	60			14	1	1020	376	41	26	5.9	.971	C-242

Joe Berry

BERRY, JOSEPH HOWARD, SR. (Hodge)
Father of Joe Berry.
B. Sept. 10, 1872, Wheeling, W. Va.   D. Mar. 13, 1961, Allenwood, N. J.

BB TR 5'9"   172 lbs.

Year	Team		Games	BA	SA	AB	H	2B	3B	HR	HR%	R	RBI	BB	SO	SB	AB	H	PO	A	E	DP	TC/G	FA	G by Pos
1902	PHI	N	1	.250	.250	4	1	0	0	0	0.0	1	1	1			0	0	3	0	0	0	3.0	1.000	C-1

Joe Berry

BERRY, JOSEPH HOWARD, JR. (Nig)
Son of Joe Berry.
B. Dec. 31, 1894, Philadelphia, Pa.   D. Apr. 29, 1976, Philadelphia, Pa.

BR TR 5'10½" 159 lbs.
BB 1922

Year	Team		Games	BA	SA	AB	H	2B	3B	HR	HR%	R	RBI	BB	SO	SB	AB	H	PO	A	E	DP	TC/G	FA	G by Pos
1921	NY	N	9	.333	.667	6	2	1	0	0	0.0	1		1	0	2	1	1	0	7	1	0	0.9	.875	2B-7
1922			6	–	–	0	0	0	0	0	0.0	0	0	0	0	0	0	0	0	0	0	0	0.0	–	2B-6
2 yrs.			15	.333	.667	6	2	1	0	0	0.0	1		1	0	2	1	1	0	7	1	0	0.5	.875	2B-13

Ken Berry

BERRY, ALLEN KENT
B. May 10, 1941, Kansas City, Mo.

BR TR 6'   175 lbs.

Year	Team		Games	BA	SA	AB	H	2B	3B	HR	HR%	R	RBI	BB	SO	SB	AB	H	PO	A	E	DP	TC/G	FA	G by Pos
1962	CHI	A	3	.333	.333	6	2	0	0	0	0.0	0	0	0	1	1	4	1	0	1	1.7	1.000	OF-2
1963			4	.200	.200	5	1	0	0	0	0.0	2	0	1	1	0	0	0	6	0	0	0	1.8	.857	OF-2, 2B-1
1964			12	.375	.500	32	12	1	0	1	3.1	4	4	5	3	0	0	0	15	0	0	0	1.3	1.000	OF-12
1965			157	.218	.347	472	103	17	4	12	2.5	51	42	28	96	4	1	0	331	6	7	1	2.2	.980	OF-156
1966			147	.271	.379	443	120	20	2	8	1.8	50	34	28	63	7	3	0	208	10	2	1	1.5	.991	OF-141
1967			147	.241	.330	485	117	14	4	7	1.4	49	41	46	68	9	4	0	233	9	2	1	1.7	.992	OF-143
1968			153	.252	.343	504	127	21	2	7	1.4	49	32	25	64	6	2	1	352	11	7	2	2.4	.981	OF-151
1969			130	.232	.327	297	69	12	2	4	1.3	25	18	24	50	1	2	0	215	7	0	1	1.7	1.000	OF-120
1970			141	.276	.356	463	128	12	2	7	1.5	45	50	43	61	6	2	1	331	4	4	2	2.4	.988	OF-138
1971	CAL	A	111	.221	.309	298	66	17	0	3	1.0	29	22	18	33	3	10	5	237	5	3	0	2.2	.988	OF-101
1972			119	.289	.377	409	118	15	3	5	1.2	41	39	35	47	5	4	1	272	13	0	5	2.4	1.000	OF-116
1973			136	.284	.342	415	118	11	2	3	0.7	48	36	26	50	1	3	0	309	5	1	0	2.3	.997	OF-129
1974	MIL	A	98	.240	.300	267	64	9	2	1	0.4	21	24	18	26	1	9	1	187	8	1	1	2.0	.995	OF-82, DH-13
1975	CLE	A	25	.200	.225	40	8	1	0	0	0.0	6	1	1	7	0	9	1	24	1	2	0	1.1	.926	OF-18, DH-5
14 yrs.			1383	.255	.344	4136	1053	150	23	58	1.4	422	343	298	569	45	42	10	2724	85	30	15	2.1	.989	OF-1311, DH-18, 2B-1

Neil Berry

BERRY, CORNELIUS JOHN
B. Jan. 11, 1922, Kalamazoo, Mich.

BR TR 5'10"   168 lbs.

Year	Team		Games	BA	SA	AB	H	2B	3B	HR	HR%	R	RBI	BB	SO	SB	AB	H	PO	A	E	DP	TC/G	FA	G by Pos
1948	DET	A	87	.266	.305	256	68	8	1	0	0.0	46	16	37	23	1	5	1	138	199	17	46	4.1	.952	SS-41, 2B-26
1949			109	.237	.271	329	78	9	1	0	0.0	38	18	27	24	4	4	0	227	237	14	56	4.4	.971	2B-95, SS-4
1950			39	.250	.275	40	10	1	0	0	0.0	9	7	9	11	0	4	0	21	35	3	14	1.5	.949	SS-11, 2B-2, 3B-1
1951			67	.229	.287	157	36	5	2	0	0.0	17	9	10	15	4	4	0	78	127	12	22	3.2	.945	SS-38, 2B-10, 3B-7
1952			73	.228	.280	189	43	4	3	0	0.0	22	13	22	19	1	1	1	91	160	9	26	3.6	.965	SS-66, 3B-2
1953 2 teams	STL	A	(57G – .283)		CHI	A	(5G – .125)																		
" total			62	.271	.318	107	29	1	1	0	0.0	15	11	10	11	0	6	1	50	69	10	12	2.1	.922	3B-18, 2B-18, SS-6
1954	BAL	A	5	.111	.111	9	1	0	0	0	0.0	1	0	1	2	0	0	0	6	7	0	2	2.6	1.000	SS-5
7 yrs.			442	.244	.286	1087	265	28	9	0	0.0	148	74	113	105	11	24	3	611	834	65	178	3.4	.957	SS-171, 2B-151, 3B-28

Damon Berryhill

BERRYHILL, DAMON SCOTT
B. Dec. 3, 1963, South Laguna, Calif.

BR TR 6'   205 lbs.

Year	Team		Games	BA	SA	AB	H	2B	3B	HR	HR%	R	RBI	BB	SO	SB	AB	H	PO	A	E	DP	TC/G	FA	G by Pos
1987	CHI	N	12	.179	.214	28	5	0	0	0	0.0	2	1	3	5	0	1	0	37	3	4	0	3.7	.909	C-11
1988			95	.259	.395	309	80	19	1	7	2.3	19	38	17	56	1	6	1	448	54	9	5	5.4	.982	C-90
1989			91	.257	.341	334	86	13	0	5	1.5	37	41	16	54	1	6	2	473	41	4	4	5.7	.992	C-89
3 yrs.			198	.255	.361	671	171	33	1	12	1.8	58	80	36	115	2	13	3	958	98	17	9	5.4	.984	C-190

Year	Team		Games	BA	SA	AB	H	2B	3B	HR	HR%	R	RBI	BB	SO	SB	Pinch Hit AB	Pinch Hit H	PO	A	E	DP	TC/G	FA	G by Pos

Harry Berte

BERTE, HARRY THOMAS
B. May 10, 1872, Covington, Ky.   D. May 6, 1952, Los Angeles, Calif.   TR

Year	Team		Games	BA	SA	AB	H	2B	3B	HR	HR%	R	RBI	BB	SO	SB	PH AB	PH H	PO	A	E	DP	TC/G	FA	G by Pos
1903	STL	N	4	.333	.333	15	5	0	0	0	0.0	1	1	1		0	0	0	3	6	4	1	3.3	.692	2B-3, SS-1

Dick Bertell

BERTELL, RICHARD GEORGE
B. Nov. 21, 1935, Oak Park, Ill.   BR TR 6'½" 200 lbs.

Year	Team		Games	BA	SA	AB	H	2B	3B	HR	HR%	R	RBI	BB	SO	SB	PH AB	PH H	PO	A	E	DP	TC/G	FA	G by Pos
1960	CHI	N	5	.133	.133	15	2	0	0	0	0.0	0	2	3	1	0	0	0	18	6	0	0	4.8	1.000	C-5
1961			92	.273	.330	267	73	7	1	2	0.7	20	33	15	33	0	6	2	396	49	8	10	4.9	.982	C-90
1962			77	.302	.377	215	65	6	2	2	0.9	19	18	13	30	0	5	1	306	36	5	0	4.5	.986	C-76
1963			100	.233	.286	322	75	7	2	2	0.6	15	14	24	41	0	1	0	549	84	8	15	6.4	.988	C-99
1964			112	.238	.320	353	84	11	3	4	1.1	29	35	33	67	2	3	0	531	52	11	3	5.3	.981	C-110
1965	2 teams																								
"	total	CHI N (34G – .214) SF N (22G – .188)	56	.205	.227	132	27	3	0	0	0.0	7	10	18	15	0	0	0	241	35	4	4	5.0	.986	C-56
1967	CHI	N	2	.167	.500	6	1	0	1	0	0.0	1	0	0	1	0	0	0	12	1	0	0	6.5	1.000	C-2
7 yrs.			444	.250	.312	1310	327	34	9	10	0.8	91	112	106	188	2	15	3	2053	263	36	32	5.3	.985	C-438

Reno Bertoia

BERTOIA, RENO PETER
B. Jan. 8, 1935, St. Vito Udine, Italy   BR TR 5'11½" 185 lbs.

Year	Team		Games	BA	SA	AB	H	2B	3B	HR	HR%	R	RBI	BB	SO	SB	PH AB	PH H	PO	A	E	DP	TC/G	FA	G by Pos
1953	DET	A	1	.000	.000	1	0	0	0	0	0.0	0	0	1	0	0	0	0	1	0	1	0	2.0	.500	2B-1
1954			54	.162	.297	37	6	2	0	1	2.7	13	2	5	9	1	2	0	27	41	3	7	1.3	.958	2B-15, 3B-8, SS-3
1955			38	.206	.309	68	14	2	1	1	1.5	13	10	5	11	0	6	0	23	52	4	8	2.1	.949	3B-14, 2B-6, SS-5
1956			22	.182	.258	66	12	2	0	1	1.5	7	5	6	12	0	0	0	54	61	2	19	5.3	.983	2B-18, 3B-2
1957			97	.275	.383	295	81	16	2	4	1.4	28	28	19	43	2	9	0	79	128	10	8	2.2	.954	3B-83, SS-7, 2B-2
1958			86	.233	.333	240	56	6	0	6	2.5	28	27	20	35	5	5	0	72	142	12	13	2.6	.947	3B-68, SS-5, OF-1
1959	WAS	A	90	.237	.347	308	73	10	0	8	2.6	33	29	29	48	2	14	3	145	207	10	41	4.0	.972	2B-71, SS-14, 3B-1
1960			121	.265	.359	460	122	17	7	4	0.9	44	45	26	58	3	5	3	120	247	14	27	3.1	.963	3B-112, 2B-21
1961	3 teams	MIN A (35G – .212) KC A (39G – .242) DET A (24G – .217)	98	.226	.267	270	61	5	0	2	0.7	35	25	32	35	3	6	2	78	166	17	19	2.7	.935	3B-74, 2B-13, SS-1
1962	DET	A	5	–	–	0	0	0	0	0	–	0	3	0	0	0	0	0	2	0	0	0	0.4	1.000	SS-1, 3B-1, 2B-1
10 yrs.			612	.244	.336	1745	425	60	10	27	1.5	204	171	142	252	16	47	8	599	1046	73	142	2.8	.958	3B-367, 2B-148, SS-23, OF-1

Bob Bescher

BESCHER, ROBERT HENRY
B. Feb. 25, 1884, London, Ohio   D. Nov. 29, 1942, London, Ohio   BB TL 6'1" 200 lbs.

Year	Team		Games	BA	SA	AB	H	2B	3B	HR	HR%	R	RBI	BB	SO	SB	PH AB	PH H	PO	A	E	DP	TC/G	FA	G by Pos
1908	CIN	N	32	.272	.404	114	31	5	5	0	0.0	16	17	9		10	0	0	84	2	0	2	2.7	1.000	OF-32
1909			124	.240	.312	446	107	17	6	1	0.2	73	34	56		54	6	1	247	14	13	4	2.2	.953	OF-117
1910			150	.250	.338	589	147	20	10	4	0.7	95	48	81	75	70	0	0	339	16	20	4	2.5	.947	OF-150
1911			153	.275	.367	599	165	32	10	1	0.2	106	45	102	78	81	0	0	267	21	14	2	2.0	.954	OF-153
1912			145	.281	.396	548	154	29	11	4	0.7	120	38	83	61	67	2	1	347	15	14	4	2.6	.963	OF-143
1913			141	.258	.350	511	132	22	11	1	0.2	86	37	94	68	38	2	0	283	22	10	2	2.2	.968	OF-138
1914	NY	N	135	.270	.365	512	138	23	4	6	1.2	82	35	45	48	36	8	3	298	14	13	7	2.4	.960	OF-126
1915	STL	N	130	.263	.348	486	128	15	7	4	0.8	71	34	52	53	27	0	0	257	12	8	1	2.1	.971	OF-130
1916			151	.235	.339	561	132	24	8	6	1.1	78	43	60	50	39	0	0	284	18	15	2	2.1	.953	OF-151
1917			42	.155	.209	110	17	1	1	1	0.9	10	4	20	13	1	0	0	61	0	1	0	1.5	.984	OF-32
1918	CLE	A	25	.333	.400	60	20	1	1	0	0.0	12	6	17	6	5	3	4	28	3	1	0	1.3	.969	OF-17
11 yrs.			1228	.258	.351	4536	1171	190	74	28	0.6	749	345	619	451	428	30	8	2495	137	109	28	2.2	.960	OF-1189

Jim Beswick

BESWICK, JAMES WILLIAM
B. Feb. 12, 1958, Wilkensburg, Pa.   BB TR 6'1" 180 lbs.

Year	Team		Games	BA	SA	AB	H	2B	3B	HR	HR%	R	RBI	BB	SO	SB	PH AB	PH H	PO	A	E	DP	TC/G	FA	G by Pos
1978	SD	N	17	.050	.050	20	1	0	0	0	0.0	2	0	1	7	0	7	1	8	0	0	0	0.5	1.000	OF-6

Frank Betcher

BETCHER, FRANKLIN LYLE
Born Franklin Lyle Bettger.
B. Feb. 15, 1888, Philadelphia, Pa.   D. Nov. 27, 1981, Wynnewood, Pa.   BB TR 5'11" 173 lbs.

Year	Team		Games	BA	SA	AB	H	2B	3B	HR	HR%	R	RBI	BB	SO	SB	PH AB	PH H	PO	A	E	DP	TC/G	FA	G by Pos
1910	STL	N	35	.202	.225	89	18	2	0	0	0.0	7	6	7	14	1	8	2	37	61	8	5	3.0	.925	SS-12, 3B-7, 2B-6, OF-2

Bill Bethea

BETHEA, WILLIAM LAMAR (Spot)
B. Jan. 1, 1942, Houston, Tex.   BR TR 6' 175 lbs.

Year	Team		Games	BA	SA	AB	H	2B	3B	HR	HR%	R	RBI	BB	SO	SB	PH AB	PH H	PO	A	E	DP	TC/G	FA	G by Pos
1964	MIN	A	10	.167	.200	30	5	1	0	0	0.0	4	2	4	4	0	0	0	16	16	0	6	3.2	1.000	2B-7, SS-3

Larry Bettencourt

BETTENCOURT, LAWRENCE JOSEPH
B. Sept. 22, 1905, Newark, Calif.   D. Sept. 15, 1978, New Orleans, La.   BR TR 5'11" 195 lbs.

Year	Team		Games	BA	SA	AB	H	2B	3B	HR	HR%	R	RBI	BB	SO	SB	PH AB	PH H	PO	A	E	DP	TC/G	FA	G by Pos
1928	STL	A	67	.283	.465	159	45	9	4	4	2.5	30	24	22	19	2	17	2	42	68	6	4	1.7	.948	3B-41, OF-2, C-1
1931			74	.257	.364	206	53	9	2	3	1.5	27	26	31	35	4	14	2	99	6	4	1	1.5	.963	OF-58
1932			27	.133	.267	30	4	1	0	1	3.3	4	3	7	6	1	17	2	9	2	0	0	0.4	1.000	OF-4, 3B-2
3 yrs.			168	.258	.397	395	102	19	6	8	2.0	61	53	60	60	7	48	6	150	76	10	5	1.4	.958	OF-64, 3B-43, C-1

Bruno Betzel

BETZEL, CHRISTIAN FREDERICK ALBERT JOHN HENRY DAVID
B. Dec. 6, 1894, Chattanooga, Tenn.   D. Feb. 7, 1965, West Hollywood, Fla.   BR TR 5'9" 158 lbs.

Year	Team		Games	BA	SA	AB	H	2B	3B	HR	HR%	R	RBI	BB	SO	SB	PH AB	PH H	PO	A	E	DP	TC/G	FA	G by Pos
1914	STL	N	7	.000	.000	9	0	0	0	0	0.0	0	0	2	0	0	0	0	4	11	0	0	2.1	1.000	2B-4, 3B-1
1915			117	.251	.305	367	92	12	4	0	0.0	42	27	18	48	10	3	1	109	228	25	11	3.1	.931	3B-105, 2B-3, SS-2
1916			142	.233	.312	510	119	15	11	1	0.2	49	37	39	77	22	0	0	319	435	40	67	5.6	.950	2B-113, 3B-33, OF-7
1917			106	.216	.256	328	71	4	3	1	0.3	24	17	20	47	9	3	2	193	225	17	42	4.1	.961	2B-75, OF-23, 3B-4
1918			76	.222	.309	230	51	6	7	0	0.0	18	13	12	16	8	6	2	100	103	17	10	2.9	.923	3B-34, OF-21, 2B-10
5 yrs.			448	.231	.295	1444	333	37	25	2	0.1	135	94	90	189	49	14	5	725	1002	99	130	4.1	.946	2B-205, 3B-177, OF-51, SS-2

Kurt Bevacqua

BEVACQUA, KURT ANTHONY
B. Jan. 23, 1947, Miami Beach, Fla.   BR TR 6' 180 lbs.

Year	Team		Games	BA	SA	AB	H	2B	3B	HR	HR%	R	RBI	BB	SO	SB	PH AB	PH H	PO	A	E	DP	TC/G	FA	G by Pos
1971	CLE	A	55	.204	.307	137	28	6	0	3	2.2	9	13	4	28	0	15	3	77	72	5	11	2.8	.968	2B-36, OF-5, 3B-3, SS-2
1972			19	.114	.200	35	4	0	0	1	2.9	2	1	3	10	0	6	1	11	5	1	1	0.9	.941	OF-11, 3B-1

Year	Team		Games	BA	SA	AB	H	2B	3B	HR	HR%	R	RBI	BB	SO	SB	Pinch Hit AB	Pinch Hit H	PO	A	E	DP	TC/G	FA	G by Pos

Kurt Bevacqua *continued*

Year	Team		Games	BA	SA	AB	H	2B	3B	HR	HR%	R	RBI	BB	SO	SB	AB	H	PO	A	E	DP	TC/G	FA	G by Pos
1973	KC	A	99	.257	.330	276	71	8	3	2	0.7	39	40	25	42	2	14	6	120	90	9	20	2.2	.959	3B-40, 2B-16, OF-10, 1B-9
1974	2 teams											PIT N (18G – .114)					KC A (39G – .211)								
"	total		57	.184	.192	125	23	1	0	0	0.0	11	3	11	30	1	15	2	98	42	6	20	2.6	.959	3B-21, 1B-14, 2B-7, DH-3, SS-2, OF-1
1975	MIL	A	104	.229	.306	258	59	14	0	2	0.8	30	24	26	45	1	5	1	157	168	13	35	3.3	.962	3B-60, 2B-32, SS-5, 1B-3, DH-1
1976			12	.143	.143	7	1	0	0	0	0.0	3	0	0	0	0	2	0	0	6	0	0	0.5	1.000	2B-2
1977	TEX	A	39	.333	.604	96	32	7	2	5	5.2	13	28	6	13	0	14	5	42	31	1	4	1.9	.986	OF-14, 3B-11, 2B-5, 1B-5, DH-3
1978			90	.222	.343	248	55	12	0	6	2.4	21	30	18	31	1	16	1	62	116	18	12	2.2	.908	3B-49, DH-16, 2B-13, 1B-1
1979	SD	N	114	.253	.330	297	75	12	4	1	0.3	23	34	38	25	2	29	6	115	156	11	21	2.5	.961	3B-64, 1B-16, OF-8, 1B-8
1980	2 teams											SD N (62G – .268)					PIT N (22G – .163)								
"	total		84	.228	.307	114	26	7	1	0	0.0	5	16	12	8	1	56	17	32	31	2	0	0.8	.969	3B-22, OF-4, 1B-3, 2B-2
1981	PIT	N	29	.259	.407	27	7	1	0	1	3.7	2	4	4	6	0	19	5	7	10	1	3	0.6	.944	2B-4, 3B-2
1982	SD	N	64	.252	.325	123	31	9	0	0	0.0	15	24	17	22	2	26	9	256	16	3	13	4.3	.989	1B-30, OF-3, 3B-1
1983			74	.244	.327	156	38	7	0	2	1.3	17	24	18	33	0	34	14	207	28	2	16	3.2	.992	1B-27, OF-12, 3B-12
1984			59	.200	.275	80	16	3	0	1	1.3	7	9	14	19	0	30	7	73	15	1	10	1.5	.989	1B-20, 3B-10, OF-3
1985			71	.239	.348	138	33	6	0	3	2.2	17	25	25	17	0	26	5	49	60	7	8	1.6	.940	3B-33, 1B-9, OF-1
15 yrs.			970	.236	.327	2117	499	90	11	27	1.3	214	275	221	329	12	307	82	1306	846	80	176	2.3	.964	3B-329, 2B-133, 1B-129, OF-72, DH-23, SS-9

LEAGUE CHAMPIONSHIP SERIES

Year	Team		Games	BA	SA	AB	H	2B	3B	HR	HR%	R	RBI	BB	SO	SB	AB	H	PO	A	E	DP	TC/G	FA	G by Pos
1984	SD	N	2	.000	.000	2	0	0	0	0	0.0	0	0	0	0	0	2	0	0	0	0	0	0.0	–	

WORLD SERIES

Year	Team		Games	BA	SA	AB	H	2B	3B	HR	HR%	R	RBI	BB	SO	SB	AB	H	PO	A	E	DP	TC/G	FA	G by Pos
1984	SD	N	5	.412	.882	17	7	2	0	2	11.8	4	4	1	2	0	0	0	0	0	0	0	0.0	–	DH-5

Hal Bevan

BEVAN, JOSEPH HAROLD
B. Nov. 15, 1930, New Orleans, La. D. Oct. 5, 1968, New Orleans, La.   BR TR 6'2" 198 lbs.

Year	Team		Games	BA	SA	AB	H	2B	3B	HR	HR%	R	RBI	BB	SO	SB	AB	H	PO	A	E	DP	TC/G	FA	G by Pos
1952	2 teams											BOS A (1G – .000)					PHI A (8G – .353)								
"	total		9	.333	.333	18	6	0	0	0	0.0	1	4	0	1	2	0	0	5	9	0	0	1.6	1.000	3B-7
1955	KC	A	3	.000	.000	3	0	0	0	0	0.0	0	0	0	0	0	2	0	1	0	0	0	0.3	1.000	3B-1
1961	CIN	N	3	.333	1.333	3	1	0	0	1	33.3	1	1	0	2	0	3	1	0	0	0	0	0.0	–	
3 yrs.			15	.292	.417	24	7	0	0	1	4.2	2	5	0	3	2	5	1	6	9	0	0	1.0	1.000	3B-8

Monte Beville

BEVILLE, HENRY MONTE
B. Feb. 24, 1875, Dublin, Ind. D. Jan. 24, 1955, Grand Rapids, Mich.   BL TR 5'11" 180 lbs.

Year	Team		Games	BA	SA	AB	H	2B	3B	HR	HR%	R	RBI	BB	SO	SB	AB	H	PO	A	E	DP	TC/G	FA	G by Pos
1903	NY	A	82	.194	.256	258	50	14	1	0	0.0	23	29	16		4	4	1	314	69	15	7	4.9	.962	C-75, 1B-3
1904	2 teams											NY A (9G – .273)					DET A (54G – .207)								
"	total		63	.214	.260	196	42	7	1	0	0.0	16	15	10		2	4	0	394	45	21	11	7.3	.954	C-33, 1B-28
2 yrs.			145	.203	.258	454	92	21	2	0	0.0	39	44	26		6	8	1	708	114	36	18	5.9	.958	C-108, 1B-31

Buddy Biancalana

BIANCALANA, ROLAND AMERICO
B. Feb. 2, 1960, Greenbrae, Calif.   BB TR 5'11" 155 lbs.

Year	Team		Games	BA	SA	AB	H	2B	3B	HR	HR%	R	RBI	BB	SO	SB	AB	H	PO	A	E	DP	TC/G	FA	G by Pos
1982	KC	A	3	.500	1.500	2	1	0	1	0	0.0	0	0	1	0	0	0	0	2	8	0	1	3.3	1.000	SS-3
1983			6	.200	.200	15	3	0	0	0	0.0	2	0	0	7	1	0	0	11	21	3	3	5.8	.914	SS-6
1984			66	.194	.299	134	26	6	1	2	1.5	18	9	6	44	1	2	2	62	144	8	28	3.2	.963	SS-33, 2B-29, DH-1
1985			81	.188	.261	138	26	5	1	1	0.7	21	6	17	34	1	0	0	83	169	10	32	3.2	.962	SS-74, 2B-4, DH-2
1986			100	.242	.337	190	46	4	4	2	1.1	24	8	15	50	5	0	0	108	190	16	41	3.1	.949	SS-89, 2B-12
1987	2 teams											KC A (37G – .213)					HOU N (18G – .042)								
"	total		55	.155	.211	71	11	1	0	1	1.4	5	7	2	22	0	3	0	30	63	8	13	1.8	.921	SS-38, 2B-15
6 yrs.			311	.205	.293	550	113	16	7	6	1.1	70	30	41	157	8	5	2	296	595	45	118	3.0	.952	SS-243, 2B-60, DH-3

LEAGUE CHAMPIONSHIP SERIES

Year	Team		Games	BA	SA	AB	H	2B	3B	HR	HR%	R	RBI	BB	SO	SB	AB	H	PO	A	E	DP	TC/G	FA	G by Pos
1984	KC	A	2	.000	.000	1	0	0	0	0	0.0	0	0	0	1	0	0	0	1	2	0	0	1.5	1.000	SS-2
1985			7	.222	.278	18	4	1	0	0	0.0	1	1	1	6	0	0	0	10	20	0	5	4.3	1.000	SS-7
2 yrs.			9	.211	.263	19	4	1	0	0	0.0	2	1	1	7	0	0	0	11	22	0	5	3.7	1.000	SS-9

WORLD SERIES

Year	Team		Games	BA	SA	AB	H	2B	3B	HR	HR%	R	RBI	BB	SO	SB	AB	H	PO	A	E	DP	TC/G	FA	G by Pos
1985	KC	A	7	.278	.278	18	5	0	0	0	0.0	2	2	5	4	0	0	0	6	20	0	1	3.7	1.000	SS-7

Tommy Bianco

BIANCO, THOMAS ANTHONY
B. Dec. 16, 1952, Rockville Center, N. Y.   BB TR 5'11" 190 lbs.

Year	Team		Games	BA	SA	AB	H	2B	3B	HR	HR%	R	RBI	BB	SO	SB	AB	H	PO	A	E	DP	TC/G	FA	G by Pos
1975	MIL	A	18	.176	.206	34	6	1	0	0	0.0	6	0	3	7	0	5	0	16	13	1	0	1.7	.967	3B-7, 1B-5, DH-2

Hank Biasetti

BIASETTI, HENRY ARCADO
B. Jan. 14, 1922, Beano, Italy   BL TL 5'11" 175 lbs.

Year	Team		Games	BA	SA	AB	H	2B	3B	HR	HR%	R	RBI	BB	SO	SB	AB	H	PO	A	E	DP	TC/G	FA	G by Pos
1949	PHI	A	21	.083	.167	24	2	2	0	0	0.0	6	2	8	5	0	9	0	44	2	1	4	2.2	.979	1B-8

Dante Bichette

BICHETTE, ALPHONSE DANTE
B. Nov. 18, 1963, West Palm Beach, Fla.   BR TR 6'3" 215 lbs.

Year	Team		Games	BA	SA	AB	H	2B	3B	HR	HR%	R	RBI	BB	SO	SB	AB	H	PO	A	E	DP	TC/G	FA	G by Pos
1988	CAL	A	21	.261	.304	46	12	2	0	0	0.0	1	8	0	7	0	0	0	44	2	1	0	2.2	.979	OF-21
1989			48	.210	.326	138	29	7	0	3	2.2	13	15	6	24	3	9	0	95	6	1	2	2.1	.990	OF-40, DH-1
2 yrs.			69	.223	.321	184	41	9	0	3	1.6	14	23	6	31	3	9	0	139	8	2	2	2.2	.987	OF-61, DH-1

Oscar Bielaski

BIELASKI, OSCAR
B. Mar. 21, 1847, Washington, D. C. D. Nov. 8, 1911, Washington, D. C.   BR TR

Year	Team		Games	BA	SA	AB	H	2B	3B	HR	HR%	R	RBI	BB	SO	SB	AB	H	PO	A	E	DP	TC/G	FA	G by Pos
1876	CHI	N	32	.209	.230	139	29	3	0	0	0.0	24	10	2		0			41	4	14	1	1.8	.763	OF-32

Lou Bierbauer

BIERBAUER, LOUIS W.
Also appeared in box score as Bauer
B. Sept. 28, 1865, Erie, Pa. D. Jan. 31, 1926, Erie, Pa.   BL TR 5'8" 140 lbs.

Year	Team		Games	BA	SA	AB	H	2B	3B	HR	HR%	R	RBI	BB	SO	SB	Pinch Hit AB	Pinch Hit H	PO	A	E	DP	TC/G	FA	G by Pos

Lou Bierbauer *continued*

Year	Team		Games	BA	SA	AB	H	2B	3B	HR	HR%	R	RBI	BB	SO	SB	AB	H	PO	A	E	DP	TC/G	FA	G by Pos
1886	PHI	AA	137	.226	.289	522	118	17	5	2	0.4	56		21			40	0	0	406	435	89	55	6.8	.904	2B-133, C-4, SS-2, P-2
1887			126	.272	.340	530	144	19	7	1	0.2	74		13				0	0	332	378	61	45	6.1	.921	2B-126, P-1
1888			134	.267	.338	535	143	20	9	0	0.0	83	80	25		34		0	0	364	423	70	41	6.4	.918	2B-121, 3B-13, P-1
1889			130	.304	.417	549	167	27	7	7	1.3	80	105	29	30	17		0	0	472	406	55	80	7.2	.941	2B-130, C-1
1890	BKN	P	133	.306	.431	589	180	31	11	7	1.2	128	99	40	15	16		0	0	372	468	62	77	6.8	.931	2B-133
1891	PIT	N	121	.206	.262	500	103	13	6	1	0.2	60	47	28	19	12		0	0	331	384	55	42	6.4	.929	2B-121
1892			152	.236	.331	649	153	20	9	8	1.2	81	65	25	29	11		0	0	385	555	49	66	6.5	.950	2B-152
1893			128	.284	.384	528	150	19	11	4	0.8	84	94	36	12	11		0	0	352	441	34	71	6.5	.959	2B-128
1894			130	.303	.406	525	159	19	13	3	0.6	86	107	26	9	19		0	0	309	453	50	58	6.2	.938	2B-130
1895			117	.258	.333	466	120	13	11	0	0.0	53	69	19	8	18		0	0	284	400	39	52	6.2	.946	2B-117
1896			59	.287	.372	258	74	10	6	0	0.0	33	39	5	7	7		0	0	140	206	12	32	6.1	.966	2B-59
1897	STL	N	12	.217	.217	46	10	0	0	0	0.0	1	1	0		2		0	0	25	33	5	4	5.3	.921	2B-12
1898			4	.000	.000	9	0	0	0	0	0.0	0	0	1		0		0	0	3	10	4	0	4.3	.765	2B-2, SS-1, 3B-1
13 yrs.			1383	.267	.354	5706	1521	208	95	33	0.6	819	706	268	129	187		0	0	3775	4592	585	623	6.5	.935	2B-1364, 3B-14, C-5, P-4, SS-3

Carson Bigbee

BIGBEE, CARSON LEE (Skeeter)
Brother of Lyle Bigbee.
B. Mar. 31, 1895, Waterloo, Ore.   D. Oct. 17, 1964, Portland, Ore.

BL TR 5'9"   157 lbs.

Year	Team		Games	BA	SA	AB	H	2B	3B	HR	HR%	R	RBI	BB	SO	SB	AB	H	PO	A	E	DP	TC/G	FA	G by Pos
1916	PIT	N	43	.250	.341	164	41	3	6	0	0.0	17	3	7	14	8		0	0	81	55	10	7	3.4	.932	2B-23, OF-19, 3B-1
1917			133	.239	.288	469	112	11	6	0	0.0	46	21	37	16	19	5	2		272	56	15	10	2.6	.956	OF-107, 2B-16, SS-2
1918			92	.255	.319	310	79	11	3	1	0.3	47	19	42	10	19	4	2		168	13	8	1	2.1	.958	OF-92
1919			125	.276	.328	478	132	11	4	2	0.4	61	27	37	26	31	1	0		343	21	11	5	3.0	.971	OF-124
1920			137	.280	.391	550	154	19	15	4	0.7	78	32	45	28	31	0	0		289	16	9	4	2.3	.971	OF-133
1921			147	.323	.427	632	204	23	17	3	0.5	100	42	41	19	21	1	0		351	27	9	6	2.6	.977	OF-146
1922			150	.350	.471	614	215	29	15	5	0.8	113	99	56	13	24	0	0		345	27	17	5	2.6	.956	OF-150
1923			123	.299	.363	499	149	18	7	0	0.0	79	54	43	15	10	1	1		283	12	3	3	2.4	.990	OF-122
1924			89	.262	.284	282	74	4	1	0	0.0	42	15	26	12	15	8	4		155	9	10	2	2.0	.943	OF-75
1925			66	.238	.294	126	30	7	0	0	0.0	31	8	7	8	2	13	3		62	3	4	1	1.0	.942	OF-42
1926			42	.221	.382	68	15	3	1	2	2.9	15	4	3	0	2	10	3		26	2	1	0	0.7	.966	OF-21
11 yrs.			1147	.287	.369	4192	1205	139	75	17	0.4	629	324	344	161	182	43	15	2375	241	97	44	2.4	.964	OF-1031, 2B-39, SS-2, 3B-1

WORLD SERIES

Year	Team		Games	BA	SA	AB	H	2B	3B	HR	HR%	R	RBI	BB	SO	SB	AB	H	PO	A	E	DP	TC/G	FA	G by Pos
1925	PIT	N	4	.333	.667	3	1	1	0	0	0.0	1	1	0	0	1	3	1	0	0	0	0	0.0	—	OF-1

Lyle Bigbee

BIGBEE, LYLE RANDOLPH (Al)
Brother of Carson Bigbee.
B. Aug. 22, 1893, Sweet Home, Ore.   D. Aug. 5, 1942, Portland, Ore.

BL TR 6'   180 lbs.

Year	Team		Games	BA	SA	AB	H	2B	3B	HR	HR%	R	RBI	BB	SO	SB	AB	H	PO	A	E	DP	TC/G	FA	G by Pos
1920	PHI	A	37	.186	.243	70	13	1	0	1	1.4	4	8	8	10	1	10	3	23	12	4	0	1.1	.897	OF-13, P-12
1921	PIT	N	5	.000	.000	2	0	0	0	0	0.0	0	0	0	1	0	0	0	0	2	0	0	0.4	1.000	P-5
2 yrs.			42	.181	.236	72	13	1	0	1	1.4	4	8	8	11	1	10	3	23	14	4	0	1.0	.902	P-17, OF-13

Elliott Bigelow

BIGELOW, ELLIOTT ALLARDICE (Gilly)
B. Oct. 13, 1897, Tarpon Springs, Fla.   D. Aug. 10, 1933, Tampa, Fla.

BL TL 5'11"   185 lbs.

Year	Team		Games	BA	SA	AB	H	2B	3B	HR	HR%	R	RBI	BB	SO	SB	AB	H	PO	A	E	DP	TC/G	FA	G by Pos
1929	BOS	A	100	.284	.374	211	60	16	0	1	0.5	23	26	23	18	1	35	6	63	5	4	1	0.7	.944	OF-58

Craig Biggio

BIGGIO, CRAIG ALAN
B. Dec. 14, 1965, Smithtown, N. Y.

BR TR 5'11"   185 lbs.

Year	Team		Games	BA	SA	AB	H	2B	3B	HR	HR%	R	RBI	BB	SO	SB	AB	H	PO	A	E	DP	TC/G	FA	G by Pos
1988	HOU	N	50	.211	.350	123	26	6	1	3	2.4	14	5	7	29	6	0	0	292	28	3	0	6.5	.991	C-50
1989			134	.257	.402	443	114	21	2	13	2.9	64	60	49	64	21	4	3	742	56	9	6	6.0	.989	C-125, OF-5
2 yrs.			184	.247	.390	566	140	27	3	16	2.8	78	65	56	93	27	4	3	1034	84	12	6	6.1	.989	C-175, OF-5

George Bignell

BIGNELL, GEORGE WILLIAM
B. July 18, 1858, Taunton, Mass.   D. Jan. 16, 1925, Providence, R. I.

Year	Team		Games	BA	SA	AB	H	2B	3B	HR	HR%	R	RBI	BB	SO	SB	AB	H	PO	A	E	DP	TC/G	FA	G by Pos
1884	MIL	U	4	.222	.222	9	2	0	0	0	0.0	4		1		0	0	0	47	11	3	2	15.3	.951	C-4

Larry Biittner

BIITTNER, LAWRENCE DAVID
B. July 27, 1945, Pocahontas, Iowa

BL TL 6'2"   205 lbs.

Year	Team		Games	BA	SA	AB	H	2B	3B	HR	HR%	R	RBI	BB	SO	SB	AB	H	PO	A	E	DP	TC/G	FA	G by Pos
1970	WAS	A	2	.000	.000	2	0	0	0	0	0.0	0	0	0	0	0	2	0	0	0	0	0	0.0	—	
1971			66	.257	.292	171	44	4	1	0	0.0	12	16	16	20	1	19	7	83	7	6	1	1.5	.938	OF-41, 1B-3
1972	TEX	A	137	.259	.335	382	99	18	1	3	0.8	34	31	29	37	1	17	4	503	41	8	37	4.0	.986	OF-65, 1B-65
1973			83	.252	.310	258	65	8	2	1	0.4	19	12	20	21	1	7	1	234	20	2	17	3.1	.992	OF-57, 1B-20, DH-3
1974	MON	N	18	.269	.308	26	7	1	0	0	0.0	2	3	0	2	0	15	4	7	1	0	0	0.4	1.000	1B-4
1975			121	.315	.408	346	109	13	5	3	0.9	34	28	34	33	2	28	7	166	8	5	0	1.5	.972	OF-93
1976	2 teams	MON N (11G – .188)				CHI N (78G – .245)																			
"	total		89	.237	.308	224	53	14	1	0	0.0	23	18	10	9	0	32	6	283	35	5	20	3.6	.985	1B-33, OF-31
1977	CHI	N	138	.298	.432	493	147	28	1	12	2.4	74	62	35	36	2	15	5	792	65	11	51	6.3	.987	1B-80, OF-52, P-1
1978			120	.257	.341	343	88	15	1	4	1.2	32	50	23	37	0	33	11	601	53	9	53	5.5	.986	1B-62, OF-29
1979			111	.290	.393	272	79	13	3	3	1.1	35	50	21	23	1	42	13	282	23	6	24	2.8	.981	OF-44, 1B-32
1980			127	.249	.319	273	68	12	2	1	0.4	21	34	18	33	1	52	11	305	23	2	16	2.6	.994	1B-41, OF-38
1981	CIN	N	42	.213	.279	61	13	4	0	0	0.0	1	8	4	4	0	29	7	57	5	0	3	1.5	1.000	1B-8, OF-3
1982			97	.310	.413	184	57	9	2	2	1.1	18	24	17	16	1	49	10	170	14	2	13	1.9	.989	OF-31, 1B-15
1983	TEX	A	66	.276	.336	116	32	5	1	0	0.0	5	18	9	16	0	31	8	140	15	2	13	2.4	.987	1B-22, DH-9, OF-2
14 yrs.			1217	.273	.359	3151	861	144	20	29	0.9	310	354	236	287	10	370	95	3623	310	58	248	3.3	.985	OF-486, 1B-385, DH-12, P-1

Dann Bilardello

BILARDELLO, DANN JAMES
B. May 26, 1959, Santa Cruz, Calif.

BR TR 6'   185 lbs.

Year	Team		Games	BA	SA	AB	H	2B	3B	HR	HR%	R	RBI	BB	SO	SB	AB	H	PO	A	E	DP	TC/G	FA	G by Pos
1983	CIN	N	109	.238	.389	298	71	18	0	9	3.0	27	38	15	49	2	5	0	494	72	5	4	5.2	.991	C-105

Year	Team	Games	BA	SA	AB	H	2B	3B	HR	HR%	R	RBI	BB	SO	SB	Pinch Hit AB	H	PO	A	E	DP	TC/G	FA	G by Pos

Dann Bilardello *continued*

Year	Team	Games	BA	SA	AB	H	2B	3B	HR	HR%	R	RBI	BB	SO	SB	PH AB	PH H	PO	A	E	DP	TC/G	FA	G by Pos
1984		68	.209	.280	182	38	7	0	2	1.1	16	10	19	34	0	5	2	323	34	3	3	5.3	.992	C-68
1985		42	.167	.196	102	17	0	0	1	1.0	6	9	4	15	0	1	0	198	20	3	1	5.3	.986	C-42
1986	MON N	79	.194	.283	191	37	5	0	4	2.1	12	17	14	32	1	2	1	391	38	8	3	5.5	.982	C-77
1989	PIT N	33	.225	.375	80	18	6	0	2	2.5	11	8	2	18	1	0	0	150	14	5	1	5.1	.970	C-33
5 yrs.		331	.212	.318	853	181	36	0	18	2.1	72	82	54	148	4	13	3	1556	178	24	12	5.3	.986	C-325

Steve Bilko

BILKO, STEVEN THOMAS
B. Nov. 13, 1928, Nanticoke, Pa. D. Mar. 7, 1978, Wilkes-Barre, Pa. BR TR 6'1" 230 lbs.

Year	Team	Games	BA	SA	AB	H	2B	3B	HR	HR%	R	RBI	BB	SO	SB	PH AB	PH H	PO	A	E	DP	TC/G	FA	G by Pos
1949	STL N	6	.294	.412	17	5	2	0	0	0.0	3	2	5	6	0	1	0	42	3	0	1	7.5	1.000	1B-5
1950		10	.182	.212	33	6	1	0	0	0.0	1	2	4	10	0	1	1	81	7	1	8	8.9	.989	1B-9
1951		21	.222	.361	72	16	4	0	2	2.8	5	12	9	10	0	2	1	170	13	3	18	8.9	.984	1B-19
1952		20	.264	.417	72	19	6	1	1	1.4	7	6	4	15	0	1	0	177	24	1	14	10.1	.995	1B-20
1953		154	.251	.412	570	143	23	3	21	3.7	72	84	70	**125**	0	0	0	1446	124	15	145	10.3	.991	1B-154
1954	2 teams	STL N (8G – .143)		CHI N (47G – .239)																				
"	total	55	.226	.434	106	24	8	1	4	3.8	12	13	14	25	0	24	6	203	35	0	20	4.3	1.000	1B-28
1958	2 teams	CIN N (31G – .264)		LA N (47G – .208)																				
"	total	78	.234	.479	188	44	5	1	11	5.9	25	35	18	57	0	27	5	345	28	2	39	4.8	.995	1B-46
1960	DET A	78	.207	.396	222	46	11	2	9	4.1	20	25	27	31	0	17	1	501	36	5	47	6.9	.991	1B-62
1961	LA A	114	.279	.544	294	82	16	1	20	6.8	49	59	58	81	1	24	8	579	61	7	56	5.7	.989	1B-86, OF-3
1962		64	.287	.500	164	47	9	1	8	4.9	26	38	25	35	1	14	3	371	28	2	36	6.3	.995	1B-50
10 yrs.		600	.249	.444	1738	432	85	13	76	4.4	220	276	234	395	2	110	25	3915	359	36	384	7.2	.992	1B-479, OF-3

Dick Billings

BILLINGS, RICHARD ARLIN
B. Dec. 4, 1942, Detroit, Mich. BR TR 6'1" 195 lbs.

Year	Team	Games	BA	SA	AB	H	2B	3B	HR	HR%	R	RBI	BB	SO	SB	PH AB	PH H	PO	A	E	DP	TC/G	FA	G by Pos
1968	WAS A	12	.182	.303	33	6	1	0	1	3.0	3	3	5	13	0	3	1	14	6	1	0	1.8	.952	OF-8, 3B-4
1969		27	.135	.135	37	5	0	0	0	0.0	3	0	6	8	0	15	1	9	4	0	1	0.5	1.000	OF-6, 3B-1
1970		11	.250	.458	24	6	2	0	1	4.2	3	1	2	3	0	3	0	25	3	0	0	2.5	1.000	C-8
1971		116	.246	.338	349	86	14	0	6	1.7	32	48	21	54	2	24	8	379	37	4	5	3.6	.990	C-62, OF-32, 3B-2
1972	TEX A	133	.254	.322	469	119	15	1	5	1.1	41	58	29	77	1	10	1	547	64	16	13	4.7	.974	C-92, OF-41, 3B-5, 1B-1
1973		81	.179	.250	280	50	11	0	3	1.1	17	32	20	43	1	5	1	376	34	13	4	5.2	.969	C-72, OF-4, 1B-3, DH-2
1974	2 teams	TEX A (16G – .226)		STL N (1G – .200)																				
"	total	17	.222	.250	36	8	1	0	0	0.0	2	0	4	7	2	1	0	64	2	0	1	3.9	1.000	C-14, DH-1, OF-1
1975	STL N	3	.000	.000	3	0	0	0	0	0.0	0	0	0	2	0	0	0	0	0	0	0	0.0	—	
8 yrs.		400	.227	.304	1231	280	44	1	16	1.3	101	142	87	207	6	64	12	1414	150	34	24	4.0	.979	C-248, OF-92, 3B-12, 1B-4, DH-3

Josh Billings

BILLINGS, JOHN AUGUSTUS
B. Nov. 30, 1891, Grantville, Kans. D. Dec. 30, 1981, Santa Monica, Calif. BR TR 5'11" 165 lbs.

Year	Team	Games	BA	SA	AB	H	2B	3B	HR	HR%	R	RBI	BB	SO	SB	PH AB	PH H	PO	A	E	DP	TC/G	FA	G by Pos
1913	CLE A	1	.000	.000	3	0	0	0	0	0.0	0	0	0	3	0	0	0	4	2	1	0	7.0	.857	C-1
1914		8	.250	.375	8	2	1	0	0	0.0	0	1	1	2	0	1	0	10	3	3	0	2.0	.813	C-3
1915		8	.190	.238	21	4	1	0	0	0.0	2	0	0	6	1	0	0	30	6	0	0	4.5	1.000	C-7, OF-1
1916		22	.161	.161	31	5	0	0	0	0.0	2	1	2	11	0	9	1	38	13	1	3	2.4	.981	C-12
1917		66	.178	.233	129	23	3	2	0	0.0	8	9	8	21	2	17	4	134	51	5	2	2.9	.974	C-48
1918		2	.333	.333	3	1	0	0	0	0.0	0	0	0	0	0	1	0	2	0	0	0	1.0	1.000	C-1
1919	STL A	38	.197	.237	76	15	1	1	0	0.0	9	3	9	12	0	7	1	76	35	4	2	3.0	.965	C-27, 1B-1
1920		66	.277	.335	155	43	5	2	0	0.0	19	11	11	10	1	22	9	138	36	6	1	2.7	.967	C-40
1921		20	.217	.217	46	10	0	0	0	0.0	2	4	0	7	0	1	0	45	9	1	0	2.8	.982	C-12
1922		5	.429	.571	7	3	1	0	0	0.0	0	1	0	0	0	1	0	5	1	0	0	1.2	1.000	C-3
1923		4	.000	.000	9	0	0	0	0	0.0	0	0	0	1	0	0	0	8	3	1	1	3.0	.917	C-4
11 yrs.		240	.217	.262	488	106	12	5	0	0.0	44	29	23	73	5	66	15	490	159	22	9	2.8	.967	C-158, OF-1, 1B-1

George Binks

BINKS, GEORGE ALVIN (Bingo)
Born George Alvin Binkowski
B. July 11, 1916, Chicago, Ill. BL TL 6' 175 lbs.

Year	Team	Games	BA	SA	AB	H	2B	3B	HR	HR%	R	RBI	BB	SO	SB	PH AB	PH H	PO	A	E	DP	TC/G	FA	G by Pos
1944	WAS A	5	.250	.250	12	3	0	0	0	0.0	0	0	0	1	0	1	0	4	0	0	0	0.8	1.000	OF-3
1945		145	.278	.391	550	153	32	6	6	1.1	62	81	34	52	11	1	1	485	25	9	17	3.6	.983	OF-128, 1B-20
1946		65	.194	.216	134	26	3	0	0	0.0	13	12	6	16	1	**35**	7	68	1	0	0	1.1	1.000	OF-28
1947	PHI A	104	.258	.357	333	86	19	4	2	0.6	33	34	23	36	8	15	4	239	15	7	5	2.5	.973	OF-75, 1B-13
1948	2 teams	PHI A (17G – .098)		STL A (15G – .217)																				
"	total	32	.141	.156	64	9	1	0	0	0.0	4	3	4	3	1	9	1	35	1	0	1	1.1	1.000	OF-19, 1B-4
5 yrs.		351	.253	.344	1093	277	55	10	8	0.7	112	130	67	108	21	61	13	831	42	16	23	2.5	.982	OF-253, 1B-37

Steve Biras

BIRAS, STEPHEN ALEXANDER
B. Feb. 26, 1922, East St. Louis, Ill. D. Apr. 21, 1965, St. Louis, Mo. BR TR 5'11" 185 lbs.

Year	Team	Games	BA	SA	AB	H	2B	3B	HR	HR%	R	RBI	BB	SO	SB	PH AB	PH H	PO	A	E	DP	TC/G	FA	G by Pos
1944	CLE A	2	1.000	1.000	2	2	0	0	0	0.0	0	2	0	0	0	1	1	1	1	1	0	1.5	.667	2B-1

Jud Birchall

BIRCHALL, ADONIRAM JUDSON
B. 1858, Germantown, Pa. D. Dec. 22, 1887, Philadelphia, Pa.

Year	Team	Games	BA	SA	AB	H	2B	3B	HR	HR%	R	RBI	BB	SO	SB	PH AB	PH H	PO	A	E	DP	TC/G	FA	G by Pos
1882	PHI AA	75	.263	.305	338	89	12	1	0	0.0	65		8			0	0	138	18	24	0	2.4	.867	OF-74, 2B-1
1883		96	.241	.274	**449**	108	10	1	1	0.2	95		19			0	0	168	22	45	0	2.4	.809	OF-96
1884		54	.258	.285	221	57	2	2	0	0.0	36		4			0	0	82	15	17	1	2.1	.851	OF-52, 3B-2
3 yrs.		225	.252	.287	1008	254	24	4	1	0.1	196		31			0	0	388	55	86	1	2.4	.837	OF-222, 3B-2, 2B-1

Frank Bird

BIRD, FRANK ZEPHERIN (Dodo)
B. Mar. 10, 1869, Spencer, Mass. D. May 20, 1958, Worcester, Mass. BR TR 5'10" 195 lbs.

Year	Team	Games	BA	SA	AB	H	2B	3B	HR	HR%	R	RBI	BB	SO	SB	PH AB	PH H	PO	A	E	DP	TC/G	FA	G by Pos
1892	STL N	17	.200	.360	50	10	3	1	1	2.0	9	1	6	11	2	0	0	52	17	6	1	4.4	.920	C-17

Joe Birmingham

BIRMINGHAM, JOSEPH LEO (Dode)
B. Aug. 6, 1884, Elmira, N. Y. D. Apr. 24, 1946, Tampico, Mexico BR TR 5'10" 185 lbs.
Manager 1912-15.

Year	Team	Games	BA	SA	AB	H	2B	3B	HR	HR%	R	RBI	BB	SO	SB	PH AB	PH H	PO	A	E	DP	TC/G	FA	G by Pos
1906	CLE A	10	.297	.432	37	11	3	1	0	0.0	4	6	1			2	0	16	3	0	0	1.9	1.000	OF-10

Year	Team	Games	BA	SA	AB	H	2B	3B	HR	HR%	R	RBI	BB	SO	SB	Pinch Hit AB	Pinch Hit H	PO	A	E	DP	TC/G	FA	G by Pos

Joe Birmingham *continued*

Year	Team	Games	BA	SA	AB	H	2B	3B	HR	HR%	R	RBI	BB	SO	SB	PH AB	PH H	PO	A	E	DP	TC/G	FA	G by Pos
1907		138	.235	.300	476	112	10	9	1	0.2	55	33	16		23	1	0	277	35	17	11	2.4	.948	OF-134, SS-3
1908		122	.213	.257	413	88	10	1	2	0.5	32	38	19		15	0	0	250	23	12	6	2.3	.958	OF-121, SS-1
1909		100	.289	.356	343	99	10	5	1	0.3	29	38	19		12	2	1	203	15	12	2	2.3	.948	OF-98
1910		104	.231	.272	364	84	11	2	0	0.0	41	35	23		18	0	0	224	29	10	8	2.5	.962	OF-103, 3B-1
1911		125	.304	.380	447	136	18	5	2	0.4	55	51	15		16	6	1	253	55	14	10	2.6	.957	OF-101, 3B-16
1912		107	.255	.322	369	94	19	3	0	0.0	49	45	26		15	2	0	264	27	14	11	2.9	.954	OF-96, 1B-9
1913		47	.282	.366	131	37	9	1	0	0.0	16	15	8	22	7	10	0	73	2	2	0	1.6	.974	OF-37
1914		19	.128	.128	47	6	0	0	0	0.0	2	4	2	5	4	0	0	14	1	0	0	0.8	1.000	OF-14
9 yrs.		772	.254	.316	2627	667	90	27	6	0.2	283	265	129	27	108	25	2	1574	190	81	48	2.4	.956	OF-714, 3B-17, 1B-9, SS-4

John Bischooff

BISCHOOFF, JOHN GEORGE (Smiley)
B. Oct. 28, 1894, Edwardsville, Ill. D. Dec. 28, 1981, Granite City, Ill. BR TR 5'7" 165 lbs.

Year	Team	Games	BA	SA	AB	H	2B	3B	HR	HR%	R	RBI	BB	SO	SB	PH AB	PH H	PO	A	E	DP	TC/G	FA	G by Pos
1925	2 teams	CHI A (7G – .091)			BOS A (41G – .278)																			
"	total	48	.264	.361	144	38	9	1	1	0.7	14	16	7	16	1	3	0	108	39	7	1	3.2	.955	C-44
1926	BOS A	59	.260	.378	127	33	11	2	0	0.0	6	19	15	16	1	12	2	121	27	4	8	2.6	.974	C-46
2 yrs.		107	.262	.369	271	71	20	3	1	0.4	20	35	22	32	2	15	2	229	66	11	9	2.9	.964	C-90

Frank Bishop

BISHOP, FRANK H
B. Sept. 21, 1860, Belvedere, Ill. D. June 18, 1929, Chicago, Ill.

Year	Team	Games	BA	SA	AB	H	2B	3B	HR	HR%	R	RBI	BB	SO	SB	PH AB	PH H	PO	A	E	DP	TC/G	FA	G by Pos
1884	CHI U	4	.188	.250	16	3	1	0	0	0.0	1		0		0	0	0	6	4	5	0	3.8	.667	3B-3, SS-1

Max Bishop

BISHOP, MAX FREDERICK (Tilly, Camera Eye)
B. Sept. 5, 1899, Waynesboro, Pa. D. Feb. 24, 1962, Waynesboro, Pa. BL TR 5'8½" 165 lbs.

Year	Team	Games	BA	SA	AB	H	2B	3B	HR	HR%	R	RBI	BB	SO	SB	PH AB	PH H	PO	A	E	DP	TC/G	FA	G by Pos
1924	PHI A	91	.255	.333	294	75	13	2	2	0.7	52	21	54	30	4	5	1	189	273	15	50	5.2	.969	2B-80
1925		105	.280	.383	368	103	13	4	4	1.1	66	27	87	37	5	1	0	233	352	26	53	5.8	.957	2B-104
1926		122	.265	.325	400	106	20	2	0	0.0	77	33	116	41	4	2	0	235	365	8	55	5.0	.987	2B-119
1927		117	.277	.323	372	103	15	1	0	0.0	80	22	105	28	8	7	1	211	342	19	48	4.9	.967	2B-106
1928		126	.316	.432	472	149	27	5	6	1.3	104	50	97	36	9	0	0	284	371	15	62	5.3	.978	2B-125
1929		129	.232	.316	475	110	19	6	3	0.6	102	36	**128**	44	1	0	0	301	371	21	58	5.4	.970	2B-129
1930		130	.252	.408	441	111	27	6	10	2.3	117	38	128	60	3	3	2	267	418	17	61	5.4	.976	2B-127
1931		130	.294	.400	497	146	30	4	5	1.0	115	37	112	51	3	0	0	314	414	12	84	5.7	.984	2B-130
1932		114	.254	.359	409	104	24	2	5	1.2	89	37	110	43	2	6	0	232	340	7	68	5.1	.988	2B-106
1933		117	.294	.399	391	115	27	1	4	1.0	80	42	106	46	1	2	0	254	359	16	52	5.4	.975	2B-113
1934	BOS A	97	.261	.332	253	66	13	1	1	0.4	65	22	82	32	3	20	2	293	164	4	48	4.8	.991	2B-57, 1B-15
1935		60	.230	.295	122	28	3	1	1	0.8	19	14	28	14	0	8	1	114	94	4	12	3.5	.981	2B-34, 1B-11, SS-2
12 yrs.		1338	.271	.366	4494	1216	236	35	41	0.9	966	379	1153	452	43	54	2	2927	3863	164	651	5.2	.976	2B-1230, 1B-26, SS-2

WORLD SERIES

Year	Team	Games	BA	SA	AB	H	2B	3B	HR	HR%	R	RBI	BB	SO	SB	PH AB	PH H	PO	A	E	DP	TC/G	FA	G by Pos
1929	PHI A	5	.190	.190	21	4	0	0	0	0.0	2	1	2	3	0	0	0	9	12	0	2	4.2	1.000	2B-5
1930		6	.222	.222	18	4	0	0	0	0.0	5	0	7	3	0	0	0	8	9	0	4	2.8	1.000	2B-6
1931		7	.148	.148	27	4	0	0	0	0.0	4	0	3	5	0	0	0	12	18	0	4	4.3	1.000	2B-7
3 yrs.		18	.182	.182	66	12	0	0	0	0.0	11	1	12	11	0	0	0	29	39	0	6	3.8	1.000	2B-18

Mike Bishop

BISHOP, MICHAEL DAVID
B. Nov. 5, 1958, Santa Maria, Calif. BR TR 6'2" 185 lbs.

Year	Team	Games	BA	SA	AB	H	2B	3B	HR	HR%	R	RBI	BB	SO	SB	PH AB	PH H	PO	A	E	DP	TC/G	FA	G by Pos
1983	NY N	3	.125	.250	8	1	1	0	0	0.0	2	0	3	4	0	0	0	16	1	1	0	6.0	.944	C-3

Rivington Bisland

BISLAND, RIVINGTON MARTIN
B. Feb. 17, 1890, New York, N.Y. D. Jan. 11, 1973, Salzburg, Austria BR TR 5'9" 155 lbs.

Year	Team	Games	BA	SA	AB	H	2B	3B	HR	HR%	R	RBI	BB	SO	SB	PH AB	PH H	PO	A	E	DP	TC/G	FA	G by Pos
1912	PIT N	1	.000	.000	1	0	0	0	0	0.0	0	0	0	1	0	1	0	0	0	0	0	0.0	–	
1913	STL A	12	.136	.136	44	6	0	0	0	0.0	3	3	2	5	0	0	0	21	31	2	3	4.5	.963	SS-12
1914	CLE A	18	.105	.123	57	6	1	0	0	0.0	9	2	6	2	1	0	0	31	45	3	6	4.4	.962	SS-15, 3B-1
3 yrs.		31	.118	.127	102	12	1	0	0	0.0	12	5	8	7	1	1	0	52	76	5	9	4.3	.962	SS-27, 3B-1

Del Bissonette

BISSONETTE, DELPHIA LOUIS
B. Sept. 6, 1899, Winthrop, Me. D. June 9, 1972, Augusta, Me.
Manager 1945. BL TL 5'11" 180 lbs.

Year	Team	Games	BA	SA	AB	H	2B	3B	HR	HR%	R	RBI	BB	SO	SB	PH AB	PH H	PO	A	E	DP	TC/G	FA	G by Pos
1928	BKN N	155	.320	.543	587	188	30	13	25	4.3	90	106	70	75	5	0	0	1482	77	20	95	10.2	.987	1B-155
1929		116	.281	.476	431	121	28	10	12	2.8	68	75	46	58	2	3	0	1093	47	15	70	10.0	.987	1B-113
1930		146	.336	.523	572	192	33	13	16	2.8	102	113	56	66	4	0	0	1427	72	20	142	10.4	.987	1B-146
1931		152	.290	.431	587	170	19	14	12	2.0	90	87	59	53	4	0	0	1460	66	16	136	10.1	.990	1B-152
1933		35	.246	.307	114	28	7	0	0	0.0	9	10	2	17	2	3	1	298	19	4	25	9.2	.988	1B-32
5 yrs.		604	.305	.485	2291	699	117	50	65	2.8	359	391	233	269	17	6	1	5760	281	75	468	10.1	.988	1B-598

Red Bittmann

BITTMANN, HENRY PETER
B. July 22, 1862, Cincinnati, Ohio D. Nov. 8, 1929, Cincinnati, Ohio

Year	Team	Games	BA	SA	AB	H	2B	3B	HR	HR%	R	RBI	BB	SO	SB	PH AB	PH H	PO	A	E	DP	TC/G	FA	G by Pos
1889	KC AA	4	.286	.286	14	4	0	0	0	0.0	2	2	1	1	1	0	0	9	12	0	2	5.3	1.000	2B-4

George Bjorkman

BJORKMAN, GEORGE ANTON
B. Aug. 26, 1956, Ontario, Calif. BR TR 6'2" 190 lbs.

Year	Team	Games	BA	SA	AB	H	2B	3B	HR	HR%	R	RBI	BB	SO	SB	PH AB	PH H	PO	A	E	DP	TC/G	FA	G by Pos
1983	HOU N	29	.227	.360	75	17	4	0	2	2.7	8	14	16	29	0	0	0	136	16	1	0	5.3	.993	C-29

Bill Black

BLACK, JOHN WILLIAM (Jigger)
B. Aug. 12, 1899, Philadelphia, Pa. D. Jan. 14, 1968, Philadelphia, Pa. BL TR 5'11" 168 lbs.

Year	Team	Games	BA	SA	AB	H	2B	3B	HR	HR%	R	RBI	BB	SO	SB	PH AB	PH H	PO	A	E	DP	TC/G	FA	G by Pos
1924	CHI A	6	.200	.200	5	1	0	0	0	0.0	0	0	0	0	0	0	0	0	0	0	0	0.0	–	2B-1

Bob Black

BLACK, ROBERT BENJAMIM
B. Dec. 10, 1862, Cincinnati, Ohio D. Mar. 21, 1933, Sioux City, Iowa

Year	Team	Games	BA	SA	AB	H	2B	3B	HR	HR%	R	RBI	BB	SO	SB	PH AB	PH H	PO	A	E	DP	TC/G	FA	G by Pos
1884	KC U	38	.247	.390	146	36	14	2	1	0.7	25		10		0	0	0	58	50	20	4	3.4	.844	OF-19, P-16, 2B-6, SS-1

Jack Black

BLACK, JOHN FALCONER
Born John Falconer Haddow.
B. Feb. 23, 1890, Covington, Ky. D. Mar. 20, 1962, Rutherford, N. J.
BR TR 6'1" 185 lbs.

Year Team	Games	BA	SA	AB	H	2B	3B	HR	HR%	R	RBI	BB	SO	SB	Pinch Hit AB	Pinch Hit H	PO	A	E	DP	TC/G	FA	G by Pos
1911 STL A	54	.151	.172	186	28	4	0	0	0.0	13	7	10		4	0	0	519	37	16	31	10.6	.972	1B-54

Ethan Blackaby

BLACKABY, ETHAN ALLAN
B. July 24, 1940, Cincinnati, Ohio
BL TL 5'11" 190 lbs.

Year Team	Games	BA	SA	AB	H	2B	3B	HR	HR%	R	RBI	BB	SO	SB	Pinch Hit AB	Pinch Hit H	PO	A	E	DP	TC/G	FA	G by Pos
1962 MIL N	6	.154	.231	13	2	1	0	0	0.0	0	0	1	8	0	3	1	3	0	0	0	0.5	1.000	OF-3
1964	9	.083	.083	12	1	0	0	0	0.0	0	1	1	2	0	4	0	1	0	1	0	0.2	.500	OF-5
2 yrs.	15	.120	.160	25	3	1	0	0	0.0	0	1	2	10	0	7	1	4	0	1	0	0.3	.800	OF-8

Earl Blackburn

BLACKBURN, EARL STUART
B. Nov. 1, 1892, Leesville, Ohio D. Aug. 3, 1966, Mansfield, Ohio
BR TR 5'11" 180 lbs.

Year Team	Games	BA	SA	AB	H	2B	3B	HR	HR%	R	RBI	BB	SO	SB	Pinch Hit AB	Pinch Hit H	PO	A	E	DP	TC/G	FA	G by Pos
1912 2 teams	PIT N (1G – .000)			CIN N (1G – .000)																			
" total	2	–	–	0	0	0	0	0	–	0	0	1	0	0	0	0	6	0	0	0	3.0	1.000	C-2
1913 CIN N	17	.259	.259	27	7	0	0	0	0.0	1	3	2	5	2	5	1	30	9	7	1	2.7	.848	C-12
1915 BOS N	3	.167	.167	6	1	0	0	0	0.0	0	0	2	1	0	0	0	8	3	0	1	3.7	1.000	C-3
1916	47	.273	.382	110	30	4	4	0	0.0	12	7	9	21	2	3	1	166	45	6	2	4.6	.972	C-44
1917 CHI N	2	.000	.000	2	0	0	0	0	0.0	0	0	0	0	0	2	0	0	0	0	0	0.0	–	
5 yrs.	71	.262	.345	145	38	4	4	0	0.0	13	10	14	27	4	10	2	210	57	13	4	3.9	.954	C-61

Lena Blackburne

BLACKBURNE, RUSSELL AUBREY (Slats)
B. Oct. 23, 1886, Clifton Heights, Pa. D. Feb. 29, 1968, Riverside, N. J.
Manager 1928-29.
BR TR 5'11" 160 lbs.

Year Team	Games	BA	SA	AB	H	2B	3B	HR	HR%	R	RBI	BB	SO	SB	Pinch Hit AB	Pinch Hit H	PO	A	E	DP	TC/G	FA	G by Pos
1910 CHI A	75	.174	.194	242	42	3	1	0	0.0	16	10	19		4	0	0	173	265	43	29	6.4	.911	SS-74
1912	3	.000	.000	1	0	0	0	0	0.0	0	0	1		1	0	0	3	2	1	1	2.0	.833	SS-2, 3B-1
1914	144	.222	.270	474	105	10	5	1	0.2	52	35	66	58	25	1	0	239	433	26	28	4.8	.963	2B-143
1915	96	.216	.240	283	61	5	1	0	0.0	33	25	35	34	13	2	1	99	153	15	16	2.8	.944	3B-83, SS-9
1918 CIN N	125	.228	.299	435	99	8	10	1	0.2	35	45	25	30	6	0	0	319	413	48	69	6.2	.938	SS-125
1919 2 teams	BOS N (31G – .263)			PHI N (72G – .199)																			
" total	103	.213	.296	371	79	13	6	2	0.5	37	23	16	29	5	4	1	129	213	22	15	3.5	.940	3B-96, SS-2, 2B-2, 1B-2
1927 CHI A	1	1.000	1.000	1	1	0	0	0	0.0	1	1	0	0	0	1	1	0	0	0	0	0.0	–	
1929	1	–	–	0	0	0	0	0	–	0	0	0	0	0	0	0	0	0	0	0	0.0	–	P-1
8 yrs.	548	.214	.268	1807	387	39	23	4	0.2	174	139	162	151	54	8	3	962	1479	155	158	4.7	.940	SS-212, 3B-180, 2B-145, 1B-2, P-1

George Blackerby

BLACKERBY, GEORGE FRANKLIN
B. Nov. 18, 1903, Gluther, Okla.
BR TR 6'1" 176 lbs.

Year Team	Games	BA	SA	AB	H	2B	3B	HR	HR%	R	RBI	BB	SO	SB	Pinch Hit AB	Pinch Hit H	PO	A	E	DP	TC/G	FA	G by Pos
1928 CHI A	30	.253	.253	83	21	0	0	0	0.0	8	12	4	10	2	10	4	40	1	2	0	1.4	.953	OF-20

Fred Blackwell

BLACKWELL, FREDERICK WILLIAM
B. Sept. 7, 1891, Bowling Green, Ky. D. Dec. 8, 1975, Morgantown, Ky.
BL TR 5'10½" 160 lbs.

Year Team	Games	BA	SA	AB	H	2B	3B	HR	HR%	R	RBI	BB	SO	SB	Pinch Hit AB	Pinch Hit H	PO	A	E	DP	TC/G	FA	G by Pos
1917 PIT N	3	.200	.200	10	2	0	0	0	0.0	1	2	0	3	0	0	0	14	3	0	0	5.7	1.000	C-3
1918	8	.154	.154	13	2	0	0	0	0.0	1	4	3	4	0	0	0	19	6	2	0	3.4	.926	C-8
1919	24	.215	.262	65	14	3	0	0	0.0	3	4	3	9	0	2	1	87	19	4	1	4.6	.964	C-22
3 yrs.	35	.205	.239	88	18	3	0	0	0.0	5	10	6	16	0	2	1	120	28	6	1	4.4	.961	C-33

Tim Blackwell

BLACKWELL, TIMOTHY P.
B. Aug. 19, 1952, San Diego, Calif.
BB TR 5'11" 170 lbs.

Year Team	Games	BA	SA	AB	H	2B	3B	HR	HR%	R	RBI	BB	SO	SB	Pinch Hit AB	Pinch Hit H	PO	A	E	DP	TC/G	FA	G by Pos
1974 BOS A	44	.246	.270	122	30	1	1	0	0.0	9	8	10	21	1	0	0	182	21	6	5	4.8	.971	C-44
1975	59	.197	.250	132	26	3	2	0	0.0	15	6	19	13	0	0	0	230	23	4	3	4.4	.984	C-57, DH-2
1976 PHI N	4	.250	.250	8	2	0	0	0	0.0	0	1	0	1	0	2	1	17	0	0	0	4.3	1.000	C-4
1977 2 teams	PHI N (1G – .000)			MON N (16G – .091)																			
" total	17	.091	.136	22	2	1	0	0	0.0	4	0	2	7	0	2	0	37	2	3	1	2.5	.929	C-15
1978 CHI N	49	.223	.252	103	23	3	0	0	0.0	8	7	23	17	0	0	0	213	20	3	3	4.8	.987	C-49
1979	63	.164	.205	122	20	3	1	0	0.0	8	12	32	25	0	1	0	245	28	7	3	4.4	.975	C-63
1980	103	.272	.394	320	87	16	4	5	1.6	24	30	41	62	0	0	0	572	93	12	16	6.6	.982	C-103
1981	58	.234	.342	158	37	10	2	1	0.6	21	11	23	23	2	2	0	268	28	2	1	5.1	.993	C-56
1982 MON N	23	.190	.286	42	8	2	1	0	0.0	2	3	3	11	0	6	1	58	9	1	1	3.0	.985	C-18
1983	6	.200	.267	15	3	1	0	0	0.0	0	2	1	3	0	1	0	28	1	2	0	5.2	.935	C-5
10 yrs.	426	.228	.305	1044	238	40	11	6	0.6	91	80	154	183	3	14	2	1850	225	40	33	5.0	.981	C-414, DH-2

Ray Blades

BLADES, FRANCIS RAYMOND
B. Aug. 6, 1896, Mt. Vernon, Ill. D. May 18, 1979, Lincoln, Ill.
Manager 1939-40, 1948.
BR TR 5'7½" 163 lbs.

Year Team	Games	BA	SA	AB	H	2B	3B	HR	HR%	R	RBI	BB	SO	SB	Pinch Hit AB	Pinch Hit H	PO	A	E	DP	TC/G	FA	G by Pos
1922 STL N	37	.300	.446	130	39	2	4	3	2.3	27	21	25	21	3	0	0	67	20	11	2	2.6	.888	OF-29, SS-4, 3B-1
1923	98	.246	.391	317	78	21	5	5	1.6	48	44	37	46	4	4	1	194	12	7	2	2.2	.967	OF-83, 3B-4
1924	131	.311	.487	456	142	21	13	11	2.4	86	68	35	38	7	2	1	275	30	13	3	2.4	.959	OF-109, 3B-7, 2B-7
1925	122	.342	.535	462	158	37	8	12	2.6	112	57	59	47	6	4	2	267	13	6	4	2.3	.979	OF-114, 3B-1
1926	107	.305	.462	416	127	17	12	8	1.9	81	43	62	57	6	1	0	229	10	5	1	2.3	.980	OF-105
1927	61	.317	.450	180	57	8	5	2	1.1	33	29	28	22	3	9	4	64	0	6	0	1.1	.914	OF-50
1928	51	.235	.376	85	20	7	1	1	1.2	9	19	20	26	0	24	4	34	1	1	1	0.7	.972	OF-19
1930	45	.396	.614	101	40	6	2	4	4.0	26	25	21	15	1	7	2	66	1	3	0	1.6	.957	OF-32
1931	35	.284	.388	67	19	4	0	1	1.5	10	5	10	7	1	14	4	26	1	4	0	0.9	.871	OF-20
1932	80	.229	.333	201	46	10	1	3	1.5	35	29	34	31	2	16	2	117	2	3	0	1.5	.975	OF-62, 3B-1
10 yrs.	767	.301	.460	2415	726	133	51	50	2.1	467	340	331	310	33	81	20	1339	90	59	13	1.9	.960	OF-623, 3B-14, 2B-7, SS-4

WORLD SERIES

Year Team	Games	BA	SA	AB	H	2B	3B	HR	HR%	R	RBI	BB	SO	SB	Pinch Hit AB	Pinch Hit H	PO	A	E	DP	TC/G	FA	G by Pos
1928 STL N	1	.000	.000	1	0	0	0	0	0.0	0	0	0	1	0	1	0	0	0	0	0	0.0	–	
1930	5	.111	.111	9	1	0	0	0	0.0	2	0	2	2	0	1	0	10	0	0	0	2.0	1.000	OF-3
1931	2	.000	.000	2	0	0	0	0	0.0	0	0	0	2	0	2	0	0	0	0	0	0.0	–	
3 yrs.	8	.083	.083	12	1	0	0	0	0.0	2	0	2	5	0	4	0	10	0	0	0	1.3	1.000	OF-3

Year	Team	Games	BA	SA	AB	H	2B	3B	HR	HR%	R	RBI	BB	SO	SB	Pinch Hit AB	Pinch Hit H	PO	A	E	DP	TC/G	FA	G by Pos

Rick Bladt

BLADT, RICHARD ALAN
B. Dec. 9, 1946, Santa Cruz, Calif.   BR TR 6'1'' 160 lbs.

Year	Team	Games	BA	SA	AB	H	2B	3B	HR	HR%	R	RBI	BB	SO	SB	AB	H	PO	A	E	DP	TC/G	FA	G by Pos
1969	CHI N	10	.154	.154	13	2	0	0	0	0.0	1	0	5	0	0	1	0	12	1	0	0	1.3	1.000	1B-7
1975	NY A	52	.222	.291	117	26	3	1	1	0.9	13	11	11	8	6	1	1	103	4	3	1	2.1	.973	OF-51
2 yrs.		62	.215	.277	130	28	3	1	1	0.8	14	12	11	13	6	2	1	115	5	3	1	2.0	.976	OF-51, 1B-7

Rae Blaemire

BLAEMIRE, RAE BERTRUM
B. Feb. 8, 1911, Gary, Ind.   D. Dec. 23, 1975, Champaign, Ill.   BR TR 6' 178 lbs.

Year	Team	Games	BA	SA	AB	H	2B	3B	HR	HR%	R	RBI	BB	SO	SB	AB	H	PO	A	E	DP	TC/G	FA	G by Pos
1941	NY N	2	.400	.400	5	2	0	0	0	0.0	0	0	0	0	0	0	0	5	0	0	0	2.5	1.000	C-2

Buddy Blair

BLAIR, LOUIS NATHAN
B. Sept. 10, 1910, Columbia, Miss.   BL TR 6' 186 lbs.

Year	Team	Games	BA	SA	AB	H	2B	3B	HR	HR%	R	RBI	BB	SO	SB	AB	H	PO	A	E	DP	TC/G	FA	G by Pos
1942	PHI A	137	.279	.397	484	135	26	8	5	1.0	48	66	30	30	1	12	2	143	234	28	21	3.0	.931	3B-126

Footsie Blair

BLAIR, CLARENCE VICK
B. July 13, 1900, Interprise, Okla.   D. July 1, 1982, Texarkana, Tex.   BL TR 6'1'' 180 lbs.

Year	Team	Games	BA	SA	AB	H	2B	3B	HR	HR%	R	RBI	BB	SO	SB	AB	H	PO	A	E	DP	TC/G	FA	G by Pos
1929	CHI N	26	.319	.431	72	23	5	0	1	1.4	10	8	3	4	1	3	2	82	23	3	6	4.2	.972	3B-8, 1B-7, 2B-2
1930		134	.273	.388	578	158	24	12	6	1.0	97	59	20	58	9	6	1	266	456	34	85	5.6	.955	2B-115, 3B-13
1931		86	.258	.404	240	62	19	5	2	0.8	31	29	14	26	1	16	2	245	120	13	28	4.4	.966	2B-44, 1B-23, 3B-1
3 yrs.		246	.273	.396	890	243	48	17	9	1.0	138	96	37	88	11	25	5	593	599	50	119	5.0	.960	2B-161, 1B-30, 3B-22

WORLD SERIES

Year	Team	Games	BA	SA	AB	H	2B	3B	HR	HR%	R	RBI	BB	SO	SB	AB	H	PO	A	E	DP	TC/G	FA	G by Pos
1929	CHI N	1	.000	.000	1	0	0	0	0	0.0	0	0	0	0	0	1	0	0	0	0	0	0.0	—	

Paul Blair

BLAIR, PAUL L. D. (Motormouth)
B. Feb. 1, 1944, Cushing, Okla.   BR TR 6' 168 lbs.

Year	Team	Games	BA	SA	AB	H	2B	3B	HR	HR%	R	RBI	BB	SO	SB	AB	H	PO	A	E	DP	TC/G	FA	G by Pos
1964	BAL A	8	.000	.000	1	0	0	0	0	0.0	0	0	0	0	0	0	0	2	0	0	0	0.3	1.000	OF-6
1965		119	.234	.338	364	85	19	2	5	1.4	49	25	32	52	8	0	0	241	5	2	0	2.1	.992	OF-116
1966		133	.277	.416	303	84	20	2	6	2.0	35	33	15	36	5	5	1	204	4	2	2	1.6	.990	OF-127
1967		151	.293	.446	552	162	27	**12**	11	2.0	72	64	50	68	8	5	1	369	13	6	3	2.6	.985	OF-146
1968		141	.211	.318	421	89	22	1	7	1.7	48	38	37	60	4	11	2	272	11	3	3	2.0	.990	OF-132, 3B-1
1969		150	.285	.477	625	178	32	5	26	4.2	102	76	40	72	20	1	0	407	14	5	5	2.8	.988	OF-150
1970		133	.267	.438	480	128	24	2	18	3.8	79	65	56	93	24	6	0	368	10	5	3	2.9	.987	OF-128, 3B-1
1971		141	.262	.397	516	135	24	8	10	1.9	75	44	32	94	14	4	1	331	4	3	1	2.4	.991	OF-138
1972		142	.233	.358	477	111	20	4	8	1.7	47	49	25	78	7	11	3	337	10	3	1	2.5	.991	OF-139
1973		146	.280	.402	500	140	25	3	10	2.0	73	64	43	72	18	8	0	369	14	4	4	2.7	.990	OF-144, DH-1
1974		151	.261	.417	552	144	27	4	17	3.1	77	62	43	59	27	4	0	447	7	7	2	3.1	.985	OF-151
1975		140	.218	.300	440	96	13	4	5	1.1	51	31	25	82	17	5	2	327	8	3	1	2.4	.991	OF-138, DH-1, 1B-1
1976		145	.197	.264	375	74	16	0	3	0.8	29	16	22	49	15	11	2	327	6	7	1	2.3	.979	OF-139, DH-1
1977	NY A	83	.262	.396	164	43	4	3	4	2.4	20	25	9	16	3	3	1	125	1	4	0	1.6	.969	OF-79, DH-1
1978		75	.176	.264	125	22	5	0	2	1.6	10	13	9	17	1	16	5	90	5	2	1	1.3	.979	OF-64, 2B-5, SS-4, 3B-3
1979	2 teams		NY A (2G – .200)		CIN N	(75G – .150)																		OF-69
"	total	77	.152	.234	145	22	4	1	2	1.4	7	15	11	28	0	8	0	123	3	1	0	1.6	.992	OF-69
1980	NY A	12	.000	.000	2	0	0	0	0	0.0	2	0	0	0	0	2	0	8	0	0	0	0.7	1.000	OF-12
17 yrs.		1947	.250	.382	6042	1513	282	55	134	2.2	776	620	449	877	171	98	18	4347	115	57	27	2.3	.987	OF-1878, 3B-5, 2B-5, DH-4, SS-4, 1B-1

LEAGUE CHAMPIONSHIP SERIES

Year	Team	Games	BA	SA	AB	H	2B	3B	HR	HR%	R	RBI	BB	SO	SB	AB	H	PO	A	E	DP	TC/G	FA	G by Pos
1969	BAL A	3	.400	.733	15	6	2	0	1	6.7	1	6	2	2	0	0	0	8	0	0	0	2.7	1.000	OF-3
1970		3	.077	.077	13	1	0	0	0	0.0	0	1	4	4	0	0	0	4	0	0	0	1.3	1.000	OF-3
1971		3	.333	.444	9	3	1	0	0	0.0	1	2	0	3	0	0	0	5	0	0	0	1.7	1.000	OF-3
1973		5	.167	.167	18	3	0	0	0	0.0	0	1	5	0	0	0	0	8	0	0	0	1.6	1.000	OF-5
1974		4	.286	.500	14	4	0	0	1	7.1	3	2	2	2	0	0	0	7	0	0	0	1.8	1.000	OF-4
1977	NY A	3	.400	.400	5	2	0	0	0	0.0	0	0	0	1	0	0	0	5	0	0	0	1.7	1.000	OF-3
1978		4	.000	.000	6	0	0	0	0	0.0	1	0	0	1	0	2	0	5	0	0	0	2.0	1.000	OF-3, 2B-1
7 yrs.		25	.238	.350	80	19	3	0	1	1.3	9	10	6	17	0	2	0	42	0	0	0	1.7	1.000	OF-24, 2B-1

WORLD SERIES

Year	Team	Games	BA	SA	AB	H	2B	3B	HR	HR%	R	RBI	BB	SO	SB	AB	H	PO	A	E	DP	TC/G	FA	G by Pos
1966	BAL A	4	.167	.667	6	1	0	0	1	16.7	2	1	0	1	0	0	0	9	0	0	0	2.3	1.000	OF-4
1969		5	.100	.100	20	2	0	0	0	0.0	1	0	2	5	1	0	0	7	0	0	0	1.4	1.000	OF-5
1970		5	.474	.526	19	9	1	0	0	0.0	5	3	2	4	0	0	0	18	0	1	0	3.8	.947	OF-5
1971		4	.333	.444	9	3	1	0	0	0.0	2	0	0	1	0	0	0	6	2	1	0	2.3	.889	OF-3
1977	NY A	4	.250	.250	4	1	0	0	0	0.0	0	1	0	0	0	1	0	1	0	0	0	0.3	1.000	OF-3
1978		6	.375	.500	8	3	1	0	0	0.0	2	0	1	4	0	4	2	5	0	0	0	0.8	1.000	OF-3, 2B-1
6 yrs.		28	.288	.379	66	19	3	0	1	1.5	12	5	6	14	1	2	1	46	2	2	0	1.8	.960	OF-23, 2B-1

Walter Blair

BLAIR, WALTER ALLEN (Heavy)
B. Oct. 13, 1883, Landrus, Pa.   D. Aug. 20, 1948, Lewisburg, Pa.   BR TR 6' 185 lbs.
Manager 1915.

Year	Team	Games	BA	SA	AB	H	2B	3B	HR	HR%	R	RBI	BB	SO	SB	AB	H	PO	A	E	DP	TC/G	FA	G by Pos
1907	NY A	7	.182	.182	22	4	0	0	0	0.0	1	1	2		0	0	0	36	11	4	0	7.3	.922	C-7
1908		76	.190	.237	211	40	5	1	1	0.5	9	13	11		4	3	1	246	59	15	4	4.2	.953	C-60, OF-9, 1B-3
1909		42	.209	.264	110	23	2	2	0	0.0	5	11	7		2	0	0	151	37	7	2	4.6	.964	C-42
1910		6	.227	.318	22	5	0	1	0	0.0	2	2	0		0	0	0	22	10	1	2	5.5	.970	C-6
1911		85	.194	.252	222	43	9	2	0	0.0	18	26	16		2	0	0	386	102	16	12	5.9	.968	C-84, 1B-1
1914	BUF F	128	.243	.283	378	92	11	2	0	0.0	22	33	32		6	0	0	604	194	13	17	6.3	.984	C-128
1915		98	.224	.317	290	65	13	3	2	0.7	23	20	18		4	1	0	404	150	11	15	5.8	.981	C-97
7 yrs.		442	.217	.275	1255	272	42	11	3	0.2	80	106	86		18	4	1	1849	563	67	52	5.6	.973	C-424, OF-9, 1B-4

Harry Blake

BLAKE, HARRY COOPER (Dude)
B. June 16, 1874, Portsmouth, Ohio   D. Oct. 14, 1919, Chicago, Ill.   BR TR 5'7'' 165 lbs.

Year	Team	Games	BA	SA	AB	H	2B	3B	HR	HR%	R	RBI	BB	SO	SB	AB	H	PO	A	E	DP	TC/G	FA	G by Pos
1894	CLE N	73	.264	.351	296	78	15	4	1	0.3	51	51	30	22	1	0	0	120	16	10	4	2.0	.932	OF-73
1895		84	.276	.343	315	87	10	1	3	1.0	50	45	30	33	11	1	0	119	13	15	3	1.8	.898	OF-83
1896		104	.240	.305	383	92	12	5	1	0.3	66	43	46	30	10	0	0	186	21	15	5	2.1	.932	OF-103, SS-1

Year	Team		Games	BA	SA	AB	H	2B	3B	HR	HR%	R	RBI	BB	SO	SB	Pinch Hit AB	Pinch Hit H	PO	A	E	DP	TC/G	FA	G by Pos

Harry Blake *continued*

Year	Team		Games	BA	SA	AB	H	2B	3B	HR	HR%	R	RBI	BB	SO	SB	PH AB	PH H	PO	A	E	DP	TC/G	FA	G by Pos
1897			32	.256	.325	117	30	3	1	1	0.9	17	15	12		5	0	0	87	3	1	2	2.8	.989	OF-32
1898			136	.245	.312	474	116	18	7	0	0.0	65	58	69		12	0	0	239	25	13	4	2.0	.953	OF-136, 1B-2
1899	STL	N	97	.240	.318	292	70	9	4	2	0.7	50	41	43		16	4	2	203	27	10	6	2.5	.958	OF-87, 2B-4, SS-1, 1B-1, C-1
6 yrs.			526	.252	.324	1877	473	67	22	8	0.4	299	253	230	85	55	5	0	954	105	64	24	2.1	.943	OF-514, 2B-4, 1B-3, SS-2, C-1

Link Blakely

BLAKELY, LINCOLN HOWARD
B. Feb. 12, 1912, Oakland, Calif.   D. Sept. 28, 1976, Oakland, Calif.

BR TR 6'   180 lbs.

Year	Team		Games	BA	SA	AB	H	2B	3B	HR	HR%	R	RBI	BB	SO	SB	PH AB	PH H	PO	A	E	DP	TC/G	FA	G by Pos
1934	CIN	N	34	.225	.255	102	23	1	1	0	0.0	11	10	5	14	1	1	0	72	4	1	2	2.3	.987	OF-28

Bob Blakiston

BLAKISTON, ROBERT J.
Born Robert J. Blackstone.
B. Oct. 2, 1855, San Francisco, Calif.   D. Dec. 25, 1918, San Francisco, Calif.

5'8½"   180 lbs.

Year	Team		Games	BA	SA	AB	H	2B	3B	HR	HR%	R	RBI	BB	SO	SB	PH AB	PH H	PO	A	E	DP	TC/G	FA	G by Pos
1882	PHI	AA	72	.228	.249	281	64	4	1	0	0.0	40		9			0	0	84	94	45	3	3.1	.798	OF-38, 3B-34, 2B-1
1883			44	.246	.299	167	41	3	3	0	0.0	26		9			0	0	77	17	15	0	2.5	.862	OF-37, 1B-6, 3B-5
1884	2 teams					PHI AA (32G – .258)						IND AA (6G – .222)													
"	total		38	.253	.301	146	37	7	0	0	0.0	21		12			0	0	101	13	16	1	3.4	.877	OF-29, 1B-6, 3B-2, SS-1, 2B-1
3 yrs.			154	.239	.276	594	142	14	4	0	0.0	87		30			0	0	262	124	76	4	3.0	.835	OF-104, 3B-41, 1B-12, 2B-2, SS-1

Johnny Blanchard

BLANCHARD, JOHN EDWIN
B. Feb. 26, 1933, Minneapolis, Minn.

BL TR 6'1"   193 lbs.

Year	Team		Games	BA	SA	AB	H	2B	3B	HR	HR%	R	RBI	BB	SO	SB	PH AB	PH H	PO	A	E	DP	TC/G	FA	G by Pos
1955	NY	A	1	.000	.000	3	0	0	0	0	0.0	0	0	0	0	0	0	0	7	0	0	0	7.0	1.000	C-1
1959			49	.169	.288	59	10	1	0	2	3.4	6	4	7	12	0	28	2	36	1	2	1	0.8	.949	C-12, OF-8, 1B-1
1960			53	.242	.414	99	24	3	1	4	4.0	8	14	6	17	0	23	4	151	7	2	0	3.0	.988	C-28
1961			93	.305	.613	243	74	10	1	21	8.6	38	54	27	28	1	26	7	292	18	3	2	3.4	.990	C-48, OF-15
1962			93	.232	.419	246	57	7	0	13	5.3	33	39	28	32	0	25	3	159	3	6	0	1.8	.964	OF-47, C-15, 1B-2
1963			76	.225	.463	218	49	4	0	16	7.3	22	45	26	30	0	14	1	76	2	1	0	1.0	.987	OF-64
1964			77	.255	.435	161	41	3	0	7	4.3	18	28	24	24	1	31	8	166	11	2	6	2.3	.989	C-25, OF-14, 1B-3
1965	3 teams			NY A (12G – .147)			KC A (52G – .200)						MIL N (10G – .100)												
"	total		74	.183	.274	164	30	3	0	4	2.4	12	16	17	20	0	30	4	144	12	4	1	2.2	.975	C-26, OF-21
8 yrs.			516	.239	.441	1193	285	36	2	67	5.6	137	200	136	163	2	177	29	1031	54	20	10	2.1	.982	OF-169, C-155, 1B-6

WORLD SERIES

Year	Team		Games	BA	SA	AB	H	2B	3B	HR	HR%	R	RBI	BB	SO	SB	PH AB	PH H	PO	A	E	DP	TC/G	FA	G by Pos
1960	NY	A	5	.455	.636	11	5	2	0	0	0.0	2	2	0	0	0	3	1	5	2	0	1	1.4	1.000	C-2
1961			4	.400	1.100	10	4	1	0	2	20.0	4	3	2	0	0	2	1	2	1	0	0	0.8	1.000	OF-2
1962			1	.000	.000	1	0	0	0	0	0.0	0	0	0	1	0	1	0	0	0	0	0	0.0	–	
1963			1	.000	.000	3	0	0	0	0	0.0	0	0	0	1	0	0	0	0	0	0	0	0.0	–	
1964			4	.250	.500	4	1	0	0	0	0.0	0	0	0	1	0	4	1	0	0	0	0	0.0	–	OF-1
5 yrs.			15	.345	.690	29	10	4	0	2	6.9	6	5	2	3	0	10	3	7	3	0	1	0.7	1.000	OF-3, C-2
														1st	1st										

Damaso Blanco

BLANCO, DAMASO
Born Damaso Blanco y Caripe.
B. Dec. 11, 1941, Curiepe, Venezuela

BR TR 5'10"   165 lbs.

Year	Team		Games	BA	SA	AB	H	2B	3B	HR	HR%	R	RBI	BB	SO	SB	PH AB	PH H	PO	A	E	DP	TC/G	FA	G by Pos
1972	SF	N	39	.350	.400	20	7	1	0	0	0.0	5	2	4	3	2	0	0	14	22	2	3	1.0	.947	3B-19, SS-8, 2B-3
1973			28	.000	.000	12	0	0	0	0	0.0	4	0	1	2	0	6	0	6	4	0	0	0.4	1.000	3B-7, SS-5, 2B-3
1974			5	.000	.000	1	0	0	0	0	0.0	0	0	0	1	1	1	0	0	0	0	0	0.0	–	
3 yrs.			72	.212	.242	33	7	1	0	0	0.0	9	2	5	6	3	7	0	20	26	2	3	0.7	.958	3B-26, SS-13, 2B-6

Ossie Blanco

BLANCO, OSWALDO CARLOS
Born Oswaldo Carlos Blanco y Diaz.
B. Sept. 8, 1945, Caracas, Venezuela

BR TR 6'   185 lbs.

Year	Team		Games	BA	SA	AB	H	2B	3B	HR	HR%	R	RBI	BB	SO	SB	PH AB	PH H	PO	A	E	DP	TC/G	FA	G by Pos
1970	CHI	A	34	.197	.197	66	13	0	0	0	0.0	4	8	3	14	0	16	3	144	8	1	9	4.5	.993	1B-22, OF-1
1974	CLE	A	18	.194	.194	36	7	0	0	0	0.0	1	2	7	4	0	0	0	127	4	1	11	7.3	.992	1B-16, DH-1
2 yrs.			52	.196	.196	102	20	0	0	0	0.0	5	10	10	18	0	16	3	271	12	2	20	5.5	.993	1B-38, DH-1, OF-1

Coonie Blank

BLANK, FRANK IGNATZ
B. Oct. 18, 1892, St. Louis, Mo.   D. Dec. 8, 1961, St. Louis, Mo.

BR TR 5'11"   165 lbs.

Year	Team		Games	BA	SA	AB	H	2B	3B	HR	HR%	R	RBI	BB	SO	SB	PH AB	PH H	PO	A	E	DP	TC/G	FA	G by Pos
1909	STL	N	1	.000	.000	2	0	0	0	0	0.0	0	0	0	0	0	0	0	2	0	0	0	2.0	1.000	C-1

Cliff Blankenship

BLANKENSHIP, CLIFFORD DOUGLAS
B. Apr. 10, 1880, Columbus, Ga.   D. Apr. 26, 1956, Oakland, Calif.

BR TR 5'10½"   165 lbs.

Year	Team		Games	BA	SA	AB	H	2B	3B	HR	HR%	R	RBI	BB	SO	SB	PH AB	PH H	PO	A	E	DP	TC/G	FA	G by Pos
1905	CIN	N	19	.196	.250	56	11	1	1	0	0.0	8	7	1		0	3	0	139	4	6	7	7.8	.960	1B-15
1907	WAS	A	37	.225	.245	102	23	2	0	0	0.0	4	6	3		1	3	0	167	35	8	3	5.7	.962	C-22, 1B-9
1909			39	.250	.250	60	15	0	0	0	0.0	4	9	0		2	16	3	38	12	6	1	1.4	.893	C-17, OF-4
3 yrs.			95	.225	.248	218	49	3	1	0	0.0	16	22	7		6	24	5	344	51	20	11	4.4	.952	C-39, 1B-24, OF-4

Lance Blankenship

BLANKENSHIP, LANCE ROBERT
B. Dec. 6, 1963, Portland, Ore.

BR TR 6'   190 lbs.

Year	Team		Games	BA	SA	AB	H	2B	3B	HR	HR%	R	RBI	BB	SO	SB	PH AB	PH H	PO	A	E	DP	TC/G	FA	G by Pos
1988	OAK	A	10	.000	.000	3	0	0	0	0	0.0	0	1	0	2	0	1	0	1	1	0	0	0.2	1.000	2B-4
1989			58	.232	.312	125	29	5	1	1	0.8	22	4	8	31	5	4	0	69	49	1	11	2.1	.992	OF-25, 2B-24, DH-10
2 yrs.			68	.227	.305	128	29	5	1	1	0.8	23	4	8	32	5	6	0	70	50	1	11	1.8	.992	2B-28, OF-25, DH-10

LEAGUE CHAMPIONSHIP SERIES

Year	Team		Games	BA	SA	AB	H	2B	3B	HR	HR%	R	RBI	BB	SO	SB	PH AB	PH H	PO	A	E	DP	TC/G	FA	G by Pos
1989	OAK	A	1	–	–	0	0	0	0	0	–	0	0	0	0	0	0	0	1	0	0	0	1.0	1.000	2B-1

WORLD SERIES

Year	Team		Games	BA	SA	AB	H	2B	3B	HR	HR%	R	RBI	BB	SO	SB	PH AB	PH H	PO	A	E	DP	TC/G	FA	G by Pos
1989	OAK	A	1	.500	.500	2	1	0	0	0	0.0	0	0	0	1	0	1	1	1	0	0	0	1.0	1.000	2B-1

Larvell Blanks

BLANKS, LARVELL (Sugar Bear)
B. Jan. 28, 1950, Del Rio, Tex. — BR TR 5'8" 167 lbs.

Year	Team	Games	BA	SA	AB	H	2B	3B	HR	HR%	R	RBI	BB	SO	SB	PH AB	PH H	PO	A	E	DP	TC/G	FA	G by Pos
1972	ATL N	33	.329	.424	85	28	5	0	1	1.2	10	7	7	12	0	7	3	49	74	0	12	3.7	1.000	2B-18, SS-4, 3B-2
1973		17	.222	.222	18	4	0	0	0	0.0	1	1	1	3	0	10	3	1	3	0	0	0.2	1.000	3B-3, SS-2, 2B-2
1974		3	.250	.250	8	2	0	0	0	0.0	0	1	0	0	0	1	1	1	7	1	0	3.0	.889	SS-2
1975		141	.234	.293	471	110	13	3	3	0.6	49	38	38	43	4	2	0	212	438	27	75	4.8	.960	SS-129, 2B-12
1976	CLE A	104	.280	.393	328	92	8	7	5	1.5	45	41	30	31	1	14	4	152	214	11	53	3.6	.971	SS-56, 2B-46, 3B-2
1977		105	.286	.398	322	92	10	4	6	1.9	43	38	19	37	3	24	6	100	181	11	27	2.8	.962	SS-66, 3B-18, 2B-12, DH-3
1978		70	.254	.337	193	49	10	0	2	1.0	19	20	10	16	0	12	2	83	144	13	25	3.4	.946	SS-43, 2B-17, 3B-3, DH-1
1979	TEX A	68	.200	.267	120	24	5	0	1	0.8	13	15	11	9	0	12	2	65	90	3	22	2.3	.981	SS-49, 2B-16, DH-1
1980	ATL N	88	.204	.258	221	45	6	0	2	0.9	23	12	16	27	1	10	1	65	189	17	31	3.1	.937	SS-56, 3B-43, 2B-1
9 yrs.		629	.253	.335	1766	446	57	14	20	1.1	203	172	132	178	9	92	22	728	1340	83	245	3.4	.961	SS-407, 2B-124, 3B-71, DH-8

Don Blasingame

BLASINGAME, DON LEE (The Blazer)
B. Mar. 16, 1932, Corinth, Miss. — BL TR 5'10" 160 lbs.

Year	Team	Games	BA	SA	AB	H	2B	3B	HR	HR%	R	RBI	BB	SO	SB	PH AB	PH H	PO	A	E	DP	TC/G	FA	G by Pos
1955	STL N	5	.375	.438	16	6	1	0	0	0.0	4	0	6	0	1	0	0	10	19	2	2	6.2	.935	2B-3, SS-2
1956		150	.261	.322	587	153	22	7	0	0.0	94	27	72	52	8	2	0	373	442	21	120	5.6	.975	2B-98, SS-49, 3B-2
1957		154	.271	.368	650	176	25	7	8	1.2	108	58	71	49	21	0	0	372	512	14	128	5.4	.984	2B-154
1958		143	.274	.356	547	150	19	10	2	0.4	71	36	57	47	20	4	0	312	380	26	97	5.0	.964	2B-137
1959		150	.289	.359	615	178	26	7	1	0.2	90	24	67	42	15	1	0	362	439	17	104	5.5	.979	2B-150
1960	SF N	136	.235	.300	523	123	12	8	2	0.4	72	31	49	53	14	3	0	318	329	14	66	4.9	.979	2B-133
1961	2 teams	SF N (3G – .000)		CIN N (123G – .222)																				
"	total	126	.222	.286	451	100	9	7	1	0.2	60	21	41	39	4	8	2	5	4	0	0	0.1	1.000	2B-116
1962	CIN N	141	.281	.340	494	139	9	7	2	0.4	77	35	63	44	4	4	2	334	352	17	66	5.0	.976	2B-137
1963	2 teams	CIN N (18G – .161)		WAS A (69G – .256)																				
"	total	87	.246	.323	285	70	17	2	2	0.7	33	12	31	23	3	9	2	184	194	4	58	4.4	.977	2B-75, 3B-2
1964	WAS A	143	.267	.314	506	135	17	2	1	0.2	56	34	40	44	8	17	0	259	336	14	70	4.3	.977	2B-135
1965		129	.223	.290	403	90	8	8	1	0.2	47	18	35	45	5	13	2	235	248	8	68	3.8	.984	2B-110
1966	2 teams	WAS A (68G – .215)		KC A (12G – .158)																				
"	total	80	.210	.265	219	46	9	0	1	0.5	19	12	20	24	2	10	1	124	141	4	34	3.4	.985	2B-62, SS-1
12 yrs.		1444	.258	.327	5296	1366	178	62	21	0.4	731	308	552	462	105	73	9	2888	3396	141	813	4.4	.978	2B-1310, SS-52, 3B-4

WORLD SERIES

Year	Team	Games	BA	SA	AB	H	2B	3B	HR	HR%	R	RBI	BB	SO	SB	PH AB	PH H	PO	A	E	DP	TC/G	FA	G by Pos
1961	CIN N	3	.143	.143	7	1	0	0	0	0.0	1	0	0	3	0	0	0	5	4	0	0	3.0	1.000	2B-3

Johnny Blatnik

BLATNIK, JOHN LOUIS (Chief)
B. Mar. 10, 1921, Bridgeport, Conn. Deceased. — BR TR 6' 195 lbs.

Year	Team	Games	BA	SA	AB	H	2B	3B	HR	HR%	R	RBI	BB	SO	SB	PH AB	PH H	PO	A	E	DP	TC/G	FA	G by Pos
1948	PHI N	121	.260	.407	415	108	27	8	6	1.4	56	45	31	77	3	15	4	220	9	13	1	2.0	.946	OF-105
1949		6	.125	.125	8	1	0	0	0	0.0	3	0	4	1	0	3	1	3	0	0	0	0.5	1.000	OF-2
1950	2 teams	PHI N (4G – .250)		STL N (7G – .150)																				
"	total	11	.167	.167	24	4	0	0	0	0.0	0	1	5	5	0	4	1	8	1	1	0	0.9	.900	OF-8
3 yrs.		138	.253	.389	447	113	27	8	6	1.3	59	46	40	83	3	22	6	231	10	14	1	1.8	.945	OF-115

Buddy Blattner

BLATTNER, ROBERT GARNETT
B. Feb. 8, 1920, St. Louis, Mo. — BR TR 6'½" 180 lbs.

Year	Team	Games	BA	SA	AB	H	2B	3B	HR	HR%	R	RBI	BB	SO	SB	PH AB	PH H	PO	A	E	DP	TC/G	FA	G by Pos
1942	STL N	19	.043	.043	23	1	0	0	0	0.0	3	1	3	6	0	2	0	14	18	3	3	1.8	.914	SS-13, 2B-3
1946	NY N	126	.255	.405	420	107	18	6	11	2.6	63	49	56	52	12	2	0	286	315	15	62	4.9	.976	2B-114, 1B-1
1947		55	.261	.346	153	40	9	2	0	0.0	28	13	21	19	4	2	0	86	106	11	15	3.7	.946	2B-34, 3B-4
1948		8	.200	.250	20	4	1	0	0	0.0	3	2	2	2	0	0	0	8	22	0	4	3.8	1.000	2B-7
1949	PHI N	64	.247	.464	97	24	6	0	5	5.2	15	21	19	17	0	29	7	35	38	2	7	1.1	.973	3B-62, 2B-15, SS-7
5 yrs.		272	.247	.384	713	176	34	8	16	2.2	112	84	102	96	18	35	7	429	499	31	91	3.5	.968	2B-173, 3B-66, SS-20, 1B-1

Jeff Blauser

BLAUSER, JEFFREY SCOTT
B. Nov. 8, 1965, Los Gatos, Calif. — BR TR 6' 170 lbs.

Year	Team	Games	BA	SA	AB	H	2B	3B	HR	HR%	R	RBI	BB	SO	SB	PH AB	PH H	PO	A	E	DP	TC/G	FA	G by Pos
1987	ATL N	51	.242	.352	165	40	6	3	2	1.2	11	15	18	34	7	1	0	65	166	9	28	4.7	.963	SS-50
1988		18	.239	.403	67	16	3	1	2	3.0	7	7	2	11	0	1	0	35	59	4	8	5.4	.959	2B-9, SS-8
1989		142	.270	.410	456	123	24	2	12	2.6	63	46	38	101	5	9	4	137	254	21	28	2.9	.949	3B-78, 2B-39, SS-30, OF-2
3 yrs.		211	.260	.395	688	179	33	6	16	2.3	81	68	58	146	12	11	4	237	479	34	64	3.6	.955	SS-88, 3B-78, 2B-48, OF-2

Marv Blaylock

BLAYLOCK, MARVIN EDWARD
B. Sept. 30, 1929, Fort Smith, Ark. — BL TL 6'1½" 175 lbs.

Year	Team	Games	BA	SA	AB	H	2B	3B	HR	HR%	R	RBI	BB	SO	SB	PH AB	PH H	PO	A	E	DP	TC/G	FA	G by Pos
1950	NY N	1	.000	.000	1	0	0	0	0	0.0	0	0	0	0	0			0	0	0	0	0.0		
1955	PHI N	113	.208	.324	259	54	7	7	3	1.2	30	24	31	43	6	27	5	537	48	5	36	5.2	.992	1B-77, OF-6
1956		136	.254	.385	460	117	14	8	10	2.2	61	50	50	86	5	8	0	950	72	8	86	7.6	.992	1B-124, OF-1
1957		37	.154	.385	26	4	0	0	2	7.7	5	4	3	8	0	19	4	22	1	0	0	0.6	1.000	1B-12, OF-1
4 yrs.		287	.235	.363	746	175	21	15	15	2.0	96	78	84	137	11	55	9	1509	121	13	122	5.7	.992	1B-213, OF-8

Curt Blefary

BLEFARY, CURTIS LeROY
B. July 5, 1943, Brooklyn, N.Y. — BL TR 6'2" 195 lbs.

Year	Team	Games	BA	SA	AB	H	2B	3B	HR	HR%	R	RBI	BB	SO	SB	PH AB	PH H	PO	A	E	DP	TC/G	FA	G by Pos
1965	BAL A	144	.260	.470	462	120	23	4	22	4.8	72	70	88	73	4	9	1	227	10	5	3	1.7	.979	OF-136
1966		131	.255	.470	419	107	14	3	23	5.5	73	64	73	56	1	13	3	274	17	5	9	2.3	.983	OF-109, 1B-20
1967		155	.242	.413	554	134	19	5	22	4.0	69	81	73	94	4	6	1	583	63	11	39	4.2	.983	OF-103, 1B-52
1968		137	.200	.322	451	90	8	1	15	3.3	50	39	65	66	6	6	2	437	35	11	11	3.5	.977	OF-92, C-40, 1B-12
1969	HOU N	155	.253	.393	542	137	26	7	12	2.2	66	67	77	79	4	6	0	1238	103	17	117	8.8	.987	1B-152, OF-1
1970	NY A	99	.212	.335	269	57	6	0	9	3.3	34	37	43	37	1	12	3	159	3	3	9	1.7	.982	OF-79, 1B-6
1971	2 teams	NY A (21G – .194)		OAK A (50G – .218)																				
"	total	71	.212	.365	137	29	3	0	6	4.4	19	14	18	20	0	27	4	135	22	4	1	2.3	.975	OF-20, C-14, 3B-5, 1B-4, 2B-2
1972	2 teams	OAK A (8G – .455)		SD N (74G – .196)																				
"	total	82	.221	.345	113	25	5	0	3	2.7	11	10	19	19	0	56	11	89	8	2	3	1.2	.980	C-12, 1B-7, OF-4, 3B-3, 2B-1
8 yrs.		974	.237	.400	2947	699	104	20	112	3.8	394	382	456	444	24	131	25	3142	261	58	192	3.6	.983	OF-544, 1B-253, C-66, 3B-8, 2B-3

Year	Team		Games	BA	SA	AB	H	2B	3B	HR	HR%	R	RBI	BB	SO	SB	Pinch Hit AB	Pinch Hit H	PO	A	E	DP	TC/G	FA	G by Pos

Curt Blefary continued

LEAGUE CHAMPIONSHIP SERIES

| 1971 | OAK | A | 1 | .000 | .000 | 1 | 0 | 0 | 0 | 0 | 0.0 | 0 | 0 | 0 | 1 | 0 | 1 | 0 | 0 | 0 | 0 | 0 | 0.0 | — | |

WORLD SERIES

| 1966 | BAL | A | 4 | .077 | .077 | 13 | 1 | 0 | 0 | 0 | 0.0 | 0 | 0 | 2 | 3 | 0 | 0 | 0 | 7 | 0 | 0 | 0 | 1.8 | 1.000 | OF-4 |

Ike Blessitt

BLESSITT, ISAIAH
B. Sept. 30, 1949, Detroit, Mich.   BR TR 5'11" 185 lbs.

| 1972 | DET | A | 4 | .000 | .000 | 5 | 0 | 0 | 0 | 0 | 0.0 | 0 | 2 | 0 | 3 | 0 | 2 | 0 | 0 | 0 | 0 | 0 | 0.5 | 1.000 | OF-1 |

Ned Bligh

BLIGH, EDWIN FORREST
B. June 30, 1864, Brooklyn, N. Y.   D. Apr. 18, 1892, Brooklyn, N. Y.   BR TR 5'11" 172 lbs.

1886	BAL	AA	3	.000	.000	9	0	0	0	0	0.0	0							10	5	3	0	6.0	.833	C-3
1888	CIN	AA	3	.000	.000	5	0	0	0	0	0.0	0	1						5	1	0	1	2.0	1.000	C-2, OF-1
1889	COL	AA	28	.140	.172	93	13	1	1	0	0.0	6	5	4	14	2	0	0	121	45	13	2	6.4	.927	C-28
1890	2 teams		COL AA (8G – .207)			LOU AA (24G – .205)																			
"	total		32	.206	.255	102	21	2	0	1	1.0	11		11		1	0	0	152	44	16	2	6.6	.925	C-32
4 yrs.			66	.163	.201	209	34	3	1	1	0.5	17	5	16	14	3	0	0	288	95	32	5	6.3	.923	C-65, OF-1

Elmer Bliss

BLISS, ELMER WARD
B. Mar. 9, 1875, Penfield, Pa.   D. Mar. 18, 1962, Bradford, Pa.   BL TR 6' 180 lbs.

1903	NY	A	1	.000	.000	3	0	0	0	0	0.0	0	0	0	0	0	0	0	0	0	0	0	0.0	—	P-1
1904			1	.000	.000	1	0	0	0	0	0.0	0	0	0	0	0	0	0	0	0	0	0	0.0	—	OF-1
2 yrs.			2	.000	.000	4	0	0	0	0	0.0	0	0	0	0	0	0	0	0	0	0	0	0.0	—	OF-1, P-1

Frank Bliss

BLISS, HOWARD FESTUS
B. Feb. 15, 1844, Mt. Carroll, Ill.   D. July 25, 1919, Janesville, Wis.   5'9" 155 lbs.

| 1878 | MIL | N | 2 | .125 | .125 | 8 | 1 | 0 | 0 | 0 | 0.0 | 1 | 0 | 0 | 0 | | | | 9 | 3 | 1 | 0 | 6.5 | .923 | 3B-1, C-1 |

Jack Bliss

BLISS, JOHN JOSEPH ALBERT
B. Jan. 9, 1882, Vancouver, Wash.   D. Oct. 23, 1968, Temple City, Calif.   BR TR 5'9" 185 lbs.

1908	STL	N	44	.213	.265	136	29	4	0	1	0.7	9	5	8		3	2	1	194	59	2	6	5.8	.992	C-43
1909			35	.221	.283	113	25	2	1	1	0.9	12	8	12		2	9	1	138	37	9	10	5.3	.951	C-32
1910			16	.061	.061	33	2	0	0	0	0.0	2	3	4	8	0	3	0	39	10	1	0	3.1	.980	C-13
1911			97	.229	.295	258	59	6	4	1	0.4	36	27	42	25	5	8	1	332	104	22	9	4.7	.952	C-84, SS-1
1912			49	.246	.289	114	28	3	1	0	0.0	11	18	19	14	3	6	3	140	42	5	7	3.8	.973	C-41
5 yrs.			241	.219	.274	654	143	15	6	3	0.5	70	61	85	47	13	28	6	843	252	39	32	4.7	.966	C-213, SS-1

Bruno Block

BLOCK, JOHN JAMES
Born John James Blochowitz.
B. Mar. 13, 1885, Wisconsin Rapids, Wis.   D. Aug. 6, 1937, S. Milwaukee, Wis.   BR TR 5'9" 185 lbs.

1907	WAS	A	24	.140	.211	57	8	2	1	0	0.0	3	2	2					59	16	4	1	3.3	.949	C-21
1910	CHI	A	55	.211	.230	152	32	1	1	0	0.0	12	9	13		3	6	0	244	77	12	8	6.1	.964	C-47
1911			39	.304	.400	115	35	6	1	1	0.9	11	18	6		0	1	0	201	40	7	2	6.4	.972	C-38
1912			46	.257	.382	136	35	5	6	0	0.0	8	26	7		1	0	0	222	65	6	4	6.4	.980	C-46
1914	CHI	F	43	.190	.250	100	19	4	1	0	0.0	8	13	11		1	10	2	126	37	6	7	3.9	.964	C-33
5 yrs.			207	.230	.304	560	129	18	10	1	0.2	42	68	39		5	20	2	852	235	35	22	5.4	.969	C-185

Cy Block

BLOCK, SEYMOUR
B. May 4, 1919, Brooklyn, N. Y.   BR TR 6' 180 lbs.

1942	CHI	N	9	.364	.455	33	12	1	0	0	0.0	6	4	3	3	2	0	0	12	15	2	2	3.2	.931	3B-8, 2B-1
1945			2	.143	.143	7	1	0	0	0	0.0	1	1	0	0	0	0	0	3	7	0	0	5.0	1.000	3B-1, 2B-1
1946			6	.231	.231	13	3	0	0	0	0.0	2	0	4	0	0	1	0	4	7	0	3	1.8	1.000	3B-4
3 yrs.			17	.302	.358	53	16	1	0	0	0.0	9	5	7	3	2	1	0	19	29	2	5	2.9	.960	3B-13, 2B-2

WORLD SERIES

| 1945 | CHI | N | 1 | — | — | 0 | 0 | 0 | 0 | 0 | — | 0 | 0 | 0 | 0 | 0 | 0 | 0 | 0 | 0 | 0 | 0 | 0.0 | — | |

Terry Blocker

BLOCKER, TERRY FENNELL
B. Aug. 18, 1959, Columbia, S. C.   BL TL 6'2" 195 lbs.

1985	NY	N	18	.067	.067	15	1	0	0	0	0.0	1	0	1	2	0	5	0	4	0	0	0	0.2	1.000	OF-5
1988	ATL	N	66	.212	.283	198	42	4	2	2	1.0	13	10	10	20	1	4	0	164	1	1	0	2.5	.994	OF-61
1989			26	.226	.258	31	7	1	0	0	0.0	1	1	1	5	1	18	3	7	0	0	0	0.3	1.000	OF-8, P-1
3 yrs.			110	.205	.266	244	50	5	2	2	0.8	15	11	12	27	2	27	3	175	1	1	0	1.6	.994	OF-74, P-1

Ron Blomberg

BLOMBERG, RONALD MARK
B. Aug. 23, 1948, Atlanta, Ga.   BL TR 6'1½" 195 lbs.

1969	NY	A	4	.500	.500	6	3	0	0	0	0.0	1	0	0	1	0	2	0	0	0	0	0.5	1.000	OF-2
1971			64	.322	.477	199	64	6	2	7	3.5	30	31	14	23	2	11	2	96	1	3	1	1.6	.970	OF-57
1972			107	.268	.488	299	80	22	1	14	4.7	36	49	38	26	0	15	5	813	32	13	88	8.0	.985	1B-95
1973			100	.329	.498	301	99	13	1	12	4.0	45	57	34	25	2	10	2	359	28	8	38	4.0	.980	DH-55, OF-19
1974			90	.311	.481	264	82	11	2	10	3.8	39	48	29	33	2	10	5	32	2	0	0	0.4	1.000	DH-58, OF-19
1975			34	.255	.481	106	27	8	2	4	3.8	18	17	13	10	0	5	2	2	0	0	0	0.1	1.000	DH-27, OF-1
1976			1	.000	.000	2	0	0	0	0	0.0	0	0	0	0	0	0	0	0	0	0	0	0.0	—	DH-1
1978	CHI	A	61	.231	.372	156	36	9	1	5	3.2	16	22	11	17	0	16	2	70	3	1	2	1.2	.986	DH-36, 1B-7
8 yrs.			461	.293	.473	1333	391	67	6	52	3.9	184	224	140	134	6	65	19	1374	66	25	129	3.2	.983	DH-177, 1B-143, OF-79

Joe Blong

BLONG, JOSEPH MYLES
B. Sept. 17, 1853, St. Louis, Mo.   D. Sept. 22, 1892, St. Louis, Mo.   BR TR

| 1876 | STL | N | 62 | .235 | .292 | 264 | 62 | 7 | 4 | 0 | 0.0 | 30 | 30 | 2 | 9 | | 0 | 0 | 64 | 15 | 9 | 2 | 1.4 | .898 | OF-62, P-1 |

Year	Team		Games	BA	SA	AB	H	2B	3B	HR	HR%	R	RBI	BB	SO	SB	Pinch Hit AB	Pinch Hit H	PO	A	E	DP	TC/G	FA	G by Pos

Joe Blong *continued*

Year	Team		Games	BA	SA	AB	H	2B	3B	HR	HR%	R	RBI	BB	SO	SB	AB	H	PO	A	E	DP	TC/G	FA	G by Pos
1877			58	.216	.280	218	47	8	3	0	0.0	17	13	4	22		0	0	73	30	18	0	2.1	.851	OF-40, P-25
2 yrs.			120	.226	.286	482	109	15	7	0	0.0	47	43	6	31		0	0	137	45	27	2	1.7	.871	OF-102, P-26

Wes Blong

BLONG, WESLEY C.
B. 1855, Norfolk, Va.   D. Mar. 10, 1897

Year	Team		Games	BA	SA	AB	H	2B	3B	HR	HR%	R	RBI	BB	SO	SB	AB	H	PO	A	E	DP	TC/G	FA	G by Pos
1883	PIT	AA	9	.147	.147	34	5	0	0	0	0.0	0	0	0	0		0	0	36	6	7	0	5.4	.857	C-6, OF-3

Jimmy Bloodworth

BLOODWORTH, JAMES HENRY   BR TR 5'11" 180 lbs.
B. July 26, 1917, Tallahassee, Fla.

Year	Team		Games	BA	SA	AB	H	2B	3B	HR	HR%	R	RBI	BB	SO	SB	AB	H	PO	A	E	DP	TC/G	FA	G by Pos
1937	WAS	A	15	.220	.300	50	11	2	1	0	0.0	3	8	5	8	0	1	0	28	42	4	9	4.9	.946	2B-14
1939			83	.289	.409	318	92	24	1	4	1.3	34	40	10	26	3	5	2	237	220	13	66	5.7	.972	2B-73, OF-5
1940			119	.245	.386	469	115	17	8	11	2.3	47	70	16	71	3	0	0	456	304	15	94	6.5	.981	2B-96, 1B-17, 3B-6
1941			142	.245	.346	506	124	24	3	7	1.4	59	66	41	58	1	4	0	386	446	25	108	6.0	.971	2B-132, 3B-6, SS-1
1942	DET	A	137	.242	.362	533	129	23	1	13	2.4	62	57	35	63	2	1	0	336	431	22	66	5.8	.972	2B-134, SS-2
1943			129	.241	.344	474	114	23	4	6	1.3	41	52	29	59	4	0	0	349	393	21	74	5.9	.972	2B-129
1946			76	.245	.345	249	61	8	1	5	2.0	25	36	12	26	3	4	0	157	184	9	46	4.6	.974	2B-71
1947	PIT	N	88	.250	.345	316	79	9	0	7	2.2	27	48	16	39	1	1	0	222	206	9	56	5.0	.979	2B-87
1949	CIN	N	134	.261	.385	452	118	27	1	9	2.0	40	59	27	36	1	14	8	447	262	11	75	5.4	.985	2B-92, 1B-23, 3B-8
1950	2 teams		CIN N	(4G – .214)		PHI N	(54G – .229)																			
"	total		58	.227	.255	110	25	3	0	0	0.0	7	14	8	12	0	16	4	79	59	0	14	2.4	1.000	2B-31, 1B-7, 3B-2
1951	PHI	N	21	.143	.143	42	6	0	0	0	0.0	2	3	1	9	1	7	3	38	26	0	4	3.0	1.000	2B-8, 1B-6
11 yrs.			1002	.248	.358	3519	874	160	20	62	1.8	347	453	200	407	19	53	17	2735	2573	129	612	5.4	.976	2B-867, 1B-53, 3B-22, OF-5, SS-3

WORLD SERIES

Year	Team		Games	BA	SA	AB	H	2B	3B	HR	HR%	R	RBI	BB	SO	SB	AB	H	PO	A	E	DP	TC/G	FA	G by Pos
1950	PHI	N	1	–	–	0	0	0	0	0	–	0	0	0	0	0	0	0	0	0	0	0	0.0	–	2B-1

Clyde Bloomfield

BLOOMFIELD, CLYDE STALCUP (Bud)   BR TR 5'11½" 175 lbs.
B. Jan. 5, 1936, Oklahoma City, Okla.

Year	Team		Games	BA	SA	AB	H	2B	3B	HR	HR%	R	RBI	BB	SO	SB	AB	H	PO	A	E	DP	TC/G	FA	G by Pos
1963	STL	N	1			0	0	0	0	0	–	0	0	0	0	0	0	0	0	0	0	0	0.0	–	3B-1
1964	MIN	A	7	.143	.143	7	1	0	0	0	0.0	1	0	0	0	0	0	0	5	5	0	2	1.4	1.000	2B-3, SS-2
2 yrs.			8	.143	.143	7	1	0	0	0	0.0	1	0	0	0	0	0	0	5	5	0	2	1.3	1.000	2B-3, SS-2, 3B-1

Jack Blott

BLOTT, JOHN LEONARD   BR TR 6' 210 lbs.
B. Aug. 24, 1902, Girard, Ohio   D. June 11, 1964, Ann Arbor, Mich.

Year	Team		Games	BA	SA	AB	H	2B	3B	HR	HR%	R	RBI	BB	SO	SB	AB	H	PO	A	E	DP	TC/G	FA	G by Pos
1924	CIN	N	2	.000	.000	1	0	0	0	0	0.0	0	0	0	0	0	1	0	1	0	0	0	0.5	1.000	C-1

Mike Blowers

BLOWERS, MICHAEL ROY   BR TR 6'2" 190 lbs.
B. Apr. 24, 1965, Wurzburg, West Germany

Year	Team		Games	BA	SA	AB	H	2B	3B	HR	HR%	R	RBI	BB	SO	SB	AB	H	PO	A	E	DP	TC/G	FA	G by Pos
1989	NY	A	13	.263	.263	38	10	0	0	0	0.0	3	3	13	0	1	0	9	14	4	3	2.1	.852	3B-13

Bert Blue

BLUE, BIRD WAYNE   BR TR 6'3" 200 lbs.
B. Dec. 14, 1876, Bettsville, Ohio   D. Dec. 14, 1928, Detroit, Mich.

Year	Team		Games	BA	SA	AB	H	2B	3B	HR	HR%	R	RBI	BB	SO	SB	AB	H	PO	A	E	DP	TC/G	FA	G by Pos
1908	2 teams		STL A	(11G – .360)		PHI A	(6G – .158)																			
"	total		17	.273	.455	44	12	1	2	1	2.3	4	2	3		0	3	0	74	15	3	1	5.4	.967	C-14

Lu Blue

BLUE, LUZERNE ATWELL   BB TL 5'10" 165 lbs.
B. Mar. 5, 1897, Washington, D. C.   D. July 28, 1958, Alexandria, Va.

Year	Team		Games	BA	SA	AB	H	2B	3B	HR	HR%	R	RBI	BB	SO	SB	AB	H	PO	A	E	DP	TC/G	FA	G by Pos
1921	DET	A	153	.308	.427	585	180	33	11	5	0.9	103	75	103	47	13	1	0	1478	85	16	75	10.3	.990	1B-152
1922			145	.300	.414	584	175	31	9	6	1.0	131	45	82	48	8	1	1	1506	75	15	107	11.0	.991	1B-144
1923			129	.284	.371	504	143	27	7	1	0.2	100	46	96	40	9	0	0	1347	93	12	74	11.3	.992	1B-129
1924			108	.311	.428	395	123	26	7	2	0.5	81	50	64	26	9	0	0	1099	85	17	72	11.1	.986	1B-108
1925			150	.306	.391	532	163	18	9	3	0.6	91	94	83	29	19	2	0	1480	101	19	115	10.7	.988	1B-148
1926			128	.287	.415	429	123	24	14	1	0.2	92	52	90	18	13	12	5	1156	57	19	95	9.6	.985	1B-109, OF-1
1927			112	.260	.364	365	95	17	9	1	0.3	71	42	71	28	13	5	2	1019	68	18	99	9.9	.984	1B-104
1928	STL	A	154	.281	.455	549	154	32	11	14	2.6	116	80	105	43	12	0	0	1472	107	17	121	10.4	.989	1B-154
1929			151	.293	.429	573	168	40	10	6	1.0	111	61	126	32	12	0	0	1491	88	10	127	10.5	.994	1B-151
1930			117	.235	.351	425	100	27	5	4	0.9	85	42	81	44	12	4	1	1110	68	16	91	10.2	.987	1B-111
1931	CHI	A	155	.304	.399	589	179	23	15	1	0.2	119	62	127	60	13	0	0	1452	81	16	105	10.0	.990	1B-155
1932			112	.249	.316	373	93	21	2	0	0.0	51	43	64	21	17	6	1	1014	88	16	106	10.0	.986	1B-105
1933	BKN	N	1	.000	.000	1	0	0	0	0	0.0	0	0	0	0	0	0	0	2	0	0	0	2.0	1.000	1B-1
13 yrs.			1615	.287	.401	5904	1696	319	109	44	0.7	1151	692	1092	436	150	31	10	15626	996	191	1187	10.4	.989	1B-1571, OF-1

Ossie Bluege

BLUEGE, OSWALD LOUIS   BR TR 5'11" 162 lbs.
Brother of Otto Bluege.
B. Oct. 24, 1900, Chicago, Ill.   D. Oct. 14, 1985, Edina, Minn.
Manager 1943-47.

Year	Team		Games	BA	SA	AB	H	2B	3B	HR	HR%	R	RBI	BB	SO	SB	AB	H	PO	A	E	DP	TC/G	FA	G by Pos
1922	WAS	A	19	.197	.213	61	12	1	0	0	0.0	5	2	7	7	1	1	0	18	33	4	3	2.9	.927	3B-17, SS-2
1923			109	.245	.338	379	93	15	7	2	0.5	48	42	48	53	5	0	0	131	251	25	31	3.7	.939	3B-107, 2B-2
1924			117	.281	.353	402	113	15	4	2	0.5	59	49	39	36	7	1	1	118	231	20	15	3.2	.946	3B-102, 2B-10, SS-4
1925			145	.287	.377	522	150	27	4	4	0.8	77	79	59	56	16	0	0	160	290	22	29	3.3	.953	3B-144, SS-8
1926			139	.271	.361	487	132	19	8	3	0.6	69	65	70	46	12	0	0	146	270	22	18	3.2	.950	3B-134, SS-8
1927			146	.274	.362	503	138	21	10	1	0.2	71	66	56	47	15	0	0	185	337	21	20	3.7	.961	3B-146
1928			146	.297	.400	518	154	33	7	2	0.4	78	75	46	27	18	1	1	150	330	20	34	3.4	.960	3B-144
1929			64	.295	.400	220	65	6	1	5	2.3	35	31	19	15	6	4	0	74	145	6	24	3.5	.973	3B-34, 2B-14, SS-10
1930			134	.290	.395	476	138	27	7	3	0.6	64	69	51	40	15	0	0	138	258	15	20	3.1	.964	3B-134
1931			152	.272	.382	570	155	25	7	8	1.4	82	98	50	39	16	0	0	151	286	18	24	3.0	.960	3B-152, SS-1
1932			149	.258	.347	507	131	22	4	5	1.0	64	64	84	41	9	0	0	158	295	14	28	3.1	.970	3B-149
1933			140	.261	.325	501	131	14	0	6	1.2	63	71	55	34	6	0	0	116	247	13	25	2.7	.965	3B-138

Year	Team	Games	BA	SA	AB	H	2B	3B	HR	HR%	R	RBI	BB	SO	SB	Pinch Hit AB	Pinch Hit H	PO	A	E	DP	TC/G	FA	G by Pos

Ossie Bluege *continued*

Year	Team	Games	BA	SA	AB	H	2B	3B	HR	HR%	R	RBI	BB	SO	SB	PH AB	PH H	PO	A	E	DP	TC/G	FA	G by Pos
1934		99	.246	.291	285	70	9	2	0	0.0	39	11	23	15	2	13	4	114	202	10	28	3.3	.969	3B-41, SS-30, OF-5, 2B-5
1935		100	.263	.325	320	84	14	3	0	0.0	44	34	37	21	2	7	2	148	238	17	39	4.0	.958	SS-58, 3B-25, 2B-4
1936		90	.288	.342	319	92	12	1	1	0.3	38	16	5	0	5	0	177	258	5	46	4.9	.989	2B-52, SS-23, 3B-15
1937		42	.283	.370	127	36	4	2	1	0.8	12	13	13	19	1	7	2	78	95	8	19	4.3	.956	SS-28, 3B-2, 1B-2
1938		58	.261	.337	184	48	12	1	0	0.0	25	21	21	11	3	8	1	100	144	5	33	4.3	.980	2B-38, SS-10, 3B-1, 1B-1
1939		18	.153	.153	59	9	0	0	0	0.0	5	3	7	2	1	1	0	103	22	3	13	7.1	.977	1B-11, SS-2, 3B-2, 2B-2
18 yrs.		1867	.272	.356	6440	1751	276	68	43	0.7	883	848	724	525	140	45	12	2265	3932	248	449	3.5	.962	3B-1487, SS-180, 2B-127, 1B-14, OF-5

WORLD SERIES

Year	Team	Games	BA	SA	AB	H	2B	3B	HR	HR%	R	RBI	BB	SO	SB	PH AB	PH H	PO	A	E	DP	TC/G	FA	G by Pos
1924	WAS A	7	.192	.192	26	5	0	0	0	0.0	2	3	3	4	1	0	0							
1925		5	.278	.333	18	5	1	0	0	0.0	2	2	1	4	0	0	0	8	24	3	6	5.0	.914	SS-5, 3B-4
1933		5	.125	.188	16	2	1	0	0	0.0	1	0	1	6	0	0	0	1	14	0	1	3.0	1.000	3B-5
3 yrs.		17	.200	.233	60	12	2	0	0	0.0	5	5	5	14	1	0	0	3	13	0	0	3.2	1.000	3B-5
																		12	51	3	7	3.9	.955	3B-14, SS-5

Otto Bluege

BLUEGE, OTTO ADAM (Squeaky)
Brother of Ossie Bluege.
B. July 20, 1909, Chicago, Ill. D. June 28, 1977, Chicago, Ill.

BR TR 5'10" 154 lbs.

Year	Team	Games	BA	SA	AB	H	2B	3B	HR	HR%	R	RBI	BB	SO	SB	PH AB	PH H	PO	A	E	DP	TC/G	FA	G by Pos
1932	CIN N	1	–	–	0	0	0	0	0	–	1	0	0	0	0	0	0	0	0	0	0	0.0	–	
1933		108	.213	.247	291	62	6	2	0	0.0	17	18	26	29	0	0	0	176	272	29	50	4.4	.939	SS-95, 2B-10, 3B-1
2 yrs.		109	.213	.247	291	62	6	2	0	0.0	18	18	26	29	0	0	0	176	272	29	50	4.4	.939	SS-95, 2B-10, 3B-1

Red Bluhm

BLUHM, HARVEY FRED
B. June 27, 1894, Cleveland, Ohio D. May 7, 1952, Flint, Mich.

BR TR 5'11" 165 lbs.

Year	Team	Games	BA	SA	AB	H	2B	3B	HR	HR%	R	RBI	BB	SO	SB	PH AB	PH H	PO	A	E	DP	TC/G	FA	G by Pos
1918	BOS A	1	.000	.000	1	0	0	0	0	0.0	0	0	0	0	0	1	0	0	0	0	0	0.0	–	

Chet Boak

BOAK, CHESTER ROBERT
B. June 19, 1935, New Castle, Pa. D. Nov. 28, 1983, Emporium, Pa.

BR TR 6' 180 lbs.

Year	Team	Games	BA	SA	AB	H	2B	3B	HR	HR%	R	RBI	BB	SO	SB	PH AB	PH H	PO	A	E	DP	TC/G	FA	G by Pos
1960	KC A	5	.154	.154	13	2	0	0	0	0.0	0	0	0	0	0	0	0	11	11	1	4	4.6	.957	2B-5
1961	WAS A	5	.000	.000	7	0	0	0	0	0.0	1	1	1	4	0	1	0	1	2	0	0	0.6	1.000	2B-1
2 yrs.		10	.100	.100	20	2	0	0	0	0.0	1	1	1	4	0	1	0	12	13	1	4	2.6	.962	2B-6

Randy Bobb

BOBB, MARK RANDALL
B. Jan. 1, 1948, Los Angeles, Calif. D. June 13, 1982, Carnelian Bay, Calif.

BR TR 6'1" 195 lbs.

Year	Team	Games	BA	SA	AB	H	2B	3B	HR	HR%	R	RBI	BB	SO	SB	PH AB	PH H	PO	A	E	DP	TC/G	FA	G by Pos
1968	CHI N	7	.125	.125	8	1	0	0	0	0.0	0	0	1	2	0	0	0	14	2	0	0	2.3	1.000	C-7
1969		3	.000	.000	2	0	0	0	0	0.0	0	0	0	1	0	0	0	4	0	0	0	1.3	1.000	C-2
2 yrs.		10	.100	.100	10	1	0	0	0	0.0	0	0	1	3	0	0	0	18	2	0	0	2.0	1.000	C-9

John Boccabella

BOCCABELLA, JOHN DOMINIC
B. June 29, 1941, San Francisco, Calif.

BR TR 6'1" 195 lbs.

Year	Team	Games	BA	SA	AB	H	2B	3B	HR	HR%	R	RBI	BB	SO	SB	PH AB	PH H	PO	A	E	DP	TC/G	FA	G by Pos
1963	CHI N	24	.189	.311	74	14	4	1	1	1.4	7	5	6	21	0	1	0	234	12	1	29	10.3	.996	1B-24
1964		9	.391	.565	23	9	2	1	0	0.0	4	6	0	3	0	3	1	41	3	0	3	4.9	1.000	1B-5, OF-2
1965		6	.333	.833	12	4	0	0	2	16.7	2	4	1	2	0	3	1	12	1	1	0	2.3	.929	1B-2, OF-1
1966		75	.228	.359	206	47	9	0	6	2.9	22	25	14	39	0	16	2	255	20	1	13	3.7	.996	OF-33, 1B-30, C-5
1967		25	.171	.257	35	6	1	1	0	0.0	0	8	3	7	0	11	2	35	1	0	3	1.4	1.000	OF-9, 1B-3, C-1
1968		7	.071	.071	14	1	0	0	0	0.0	0	1	2	2	0	2	0	27	0	0	0	3.9	1.000	C-4, OF-1
1969	MON N	40	.105	.163	86	9	2	0	1	1.2	4	6	6	30	0	7	1	137	19	0	0	3.9	1.000	C-32
1970		61	.269	.407	145	39	3	1	5	3.4	18	17	11	24	0	8	2	314	44	3	25	5.0	.992	1B-33, C-24, 3B-1
1971		74	.220	.333	177	39	11	1	3	1.7	15	15	14	26	0	5	0	335	33	4	30	5.0	.989	1B-37, C-37, 3B-2
1972		83	.227	.290	207	47	8	1	1	0.5	14	10	9	29	1	3	0	367	39	6	12	5.0	.986	C-73, 1B-7, 3B-1
1973		118	.233	.318	403	94	13	0	7	1.7	25	46	26	57	1	1	0	610	65	14	10	5.8	.980	C-117, 1B-1
1974	SF N	29	.138	.175	80	11	3	0	0	0.0	6	5	4	6	0	4	0	110	6	1	1	4.0	.991	C-26
12 yrs.		551	.219	.317	1462	320	56	5	26	1.8	117	148	96	246	3	63	9	2477	243	31	126	5.0	.989	C-319, 1B-142, OF-46, 3B-4

Milt Bocek

BOCEK, MILTON FRANK
B. July 16, 1912, Chicago, Ill.

BR TR 6'1" 185 lbs.

Year	Team	Games	BA	SA	AB	H	2B	3B	HR	HR%	R	RBI	BB	SO	SB	PH AB	PH H	PO	A	E	DP	TC/G	FA	G by Pos
1933	CHI A	11	.364	.545	22	8	1	0	1	4.5	3	3	4	6	0	5	0	6	0	0	0	0.5	1.000	OF-6
1934		19	.211	.237	38	8	1	0	0	0.0	3	3	5	5	0	6	0	25	2	0	1	1.4	1.000	OF-10
2 yrs.		30	.267	.350	60	16	2	0	1	1.7	6	6	9	11	0	11	1	31	2	0	1	1.1	1.000	OF-16

Bruce Bochte

BOCHTE, BRUCE ANTON
B. Nov. 12, 1950, Pasadena, Calif.

BL TL 6'3" 195 lbs.

Year	Team	Games	BA	SA	AB	H	2B	3B	HR	HR%	R	RBI	BB	SO	SB	PH AB	PH H	PO	A	E	DP	TC/G	FA	G by Pos
1974	CAL A	57	.270	.378	196	53	4	1	5	2.6	24	26	18	23	6	1	0	248	9	5	16	4.6	.981	OF-39, 1B-24
1975		107	.285	.376	375	107	19	3	3	0.8	41	48	45	43	3	1	0	850	51	12	90	8.5	.987	1B-105, DH-1
1976		146	.258	.311	466	120	17	1	2	0.4	53	49	64	53	4	8	3	651	42	7	38	4.7	.990	OF-86, 1B-59, DH-1
1977	2 teams		CAL A (25G – .290)		CLE A (112G – .304)																			
"	total	137	.301	.394	492	148	23	4	7	1.4	64	51	47	42	6	1	0	486	33	9	19	3.9	.983	OF-100, 1B-36, DH-2
1978	SEA A	140	.263	.395	486	128	25	3	11	2.3	58	51	60	47	3	5	3	180	7	3	2	1.4	.984	OF-91, DH-43, 1B-1
1979		150	.316	.493	554	175	38	6	16	2.9	81	100	67	64	0	4	2	1361	114	14	140	9.9	.991	1B-147
1980		148	.300	.456	520	156	34	4	13	2.5	62	78	72	81	2	6	1	1273	98	6	143	9.3	.996	1B-133, DH-11
1981		99	.260	.361	335	87	16	0	6	1.8	39	30	47	53	1	8	2	766	49	4	70	8.3	.995	1B-82, OF-14, DH-1
1982		144	.297	.409	509	151	21	0	12	2.4	58	70	67	71	8	4	2	428	26	3	39	3.2	.993	OF-99, 1B-34, DH-12
1984	OAK A	148	.264	.345	469	124	23	0	6	1.1	58	52	52	59	2	11	4	1048	66	8	119	7.6	.993	1B-144, DH-2
1985		137	.295	.439	424	125	17	1	14	3.3	48	60	49	58	3	9	3	942	60	10	83	7.4	.990	1B-128
1986		125	.256	.337	407	104	13	1	6	1.5	57	43	57	43	4	9	2	912	88	9	79	8.1	.991	1B-115, DH-1
12 yrs.		1538	.282	.396	5233	1478	250	21	100	1.9	643	658	653	662	43	69	25	9145	643	90	838	6.4	.991	1B-1008, OF-429, DH-74

Bruce Bochy

BOCHY, BRUCE DOUGLAS
B. Apr. 16, 1955, Landes De Bussac, France

BR TR 6'3" 205 lbs.

Year	Team		Games	BA	SA	AB	H	2B	3B	HR	HR%	R	RBI	BB	SO	SB	Pinch Hit AB	Pinch Hit H	PO	A	E	DP	TC/G	FA	G by Pos

Bruce Bochy *continued*

1978	HOU	N	54	.266	.377	154	41	8	0	3	1.9	8	15	11	35	0	3	0	268	35	8	5	5.8	.974	C-53
1979			56	.217	.271	129	28	4	0	1	0.8	11	6	13	25	0	3	0	198	29	7	4	4.2	.970	C-55
1980			22	.182	.227	22	4	1	0	0	0.0	0	0	5	7	0	9	1	19	1	0	0	0.9	1.000	C-10, 1B-1
1982	NY	N	17	.306	.510	49	15	4	0	2	4.1	4	8	0	9	0	12	4	51	5	0	0	2.4	1.000	C-11
1983	SD	N	23	.214	.286	42	9	1	1	0	0.0	2	3	0	9	0	1	0	147	12	2	2	4.4	.988	C-36
1984			37	.228	.435	92	21	5	1	4	4.3	10	15	3	21	0	8	1	148	11	2	2	3.4	.988	C-46
1985			48	.268	.446	112	30	2	0	6	5.4	16	13	6	30	0	20	7	202	22	2	3	3.6	.991	C-48
1986			63	.252	.512	127	32	9	0	8	6.3	16	22	14	23	1	12	1	95	7	4	0	2.8	.962	C-23
1987			38	.160	.280	75	12	3	0	2	2.7	8	11	11	21	0	12	1							
	9 yrs.		358	.239	.388	802	192	37	2	26	3.2	75	93	67	177	1	68	14	1220	130	29	17	3.9	.979	C-298, 1B-2

LEAGUE CHAMPIONSHIP SERIES

| 1980 | HOU | N | 1 | .000 | .000 | 1 | 0 | 0 | 0 | 0 | 0.0 | 0 | 0 | 0 | 0 | 0 | 0 | 0 | 5 | 1 | 0 | 1 | 6.0 | 1.000 | C-1 |

WORLD SERIES

| 1984 | SD | N | 1 | 1.000 | 1.000 | 1 | 1 | 0 | 0 | 0 | 0.0 | 0 | 0 | 0 | 0 | 0 | 1 | 1 | 0 | 0 | 0 | 0 | 0.0 | — | |

Eddie Bockman

BOCKMAN, JOSEPH EDWARD
B. July 26, 1920, Santa Ana, Calif.   BR TR 5'9" 175 lbs.

1946	NY	A	4	.083	.167	12	1	1	0	0	0.0	2	0	1	4	0	0	0	8	6	1	3	3.8	.933	3B-4
1947	CLE	A	96	.258	.394	66	17	2	1	1	1.5	8	14	5	17	0	20	5	22	33	3	8	0.6	.948	3B-12, 2B-4, OF-1, SS-1
1948	PIT	N	70	.239	.358	176	42	7	1	4	2.3	23	23	17	35	2	11	2	51	100	6	9	2.2	.962	3B-51, 2B-1
1949			79	.223	.341	220	49	6	1	6	2.7	21	19	23	31	3	5	2	62	128	8	14	2.5	.960	3B-68, 2B-5
	4 yrs.		249	.230	.350	474	109	16	4	11	2.3	54	56	46	87	5	36	9	143	267	18	34	1.7	.958	3B-135, 2B-10, OF-1, SS-1

Ping Bodie

BODIE, FRANK STEPHAN
Born Francesco Stephano Pezzolo.
B. Oct. 8, 1887, San Francisco, Calif.   D. Dec. 17, 1961, San Francisco, Calif.   BR TR 5'8" 195 lbs.

1911	CHI	A	145	.289	.407	551	159	27	13	4	0.7	75	97	49		14	1	0	287	64	16	13	2.5	.956	OF-128, 2B-16
1912			137	.294	.407	472	139	24	7	5	1.1	58	72	43		12	7	3	208	11	7	3	1.6	.969	OF-130
1913			127	.264	.397	406	107	14	8	8	2.0	43	48	35	57	5	6	0	226	14	8	1	2.0	.968	OF-119
1914			107	.229	.315	327	75	9	5	3	0.9	21	29	21	35	12	10	2	175	14	8	2	1.8	.959	OF-95
1917	PHI	A	148	.291	.418	557	162	28	11	7	1.3	51	74	53	40	13	2	0	267	32	11	8	2.1	.965	OF-145, 1B-1
1918	NY	A	91	.256	.358	324	83	12	6	3	0.9	36	46	27	24	6	1	0	181	17	6	3	2.2	.971	OF-90
1919			134	.278	.406	475	132	27	8	6	1.3	45	59	36	46	15	0	0	293	19	13	6	2.4	.960	OF-134
1920			129	.295	.446	471	139	26	12	7	1.5	63	79	40	30	6	0	0	264	12	9	2	2.2	.968	OF-129
1921			31	.172	.241	87	15	2	2	0	0.0	5	12	8		6	0	0	32	2	2	1	1.1	.944	OF-25
	9 yrs.		1049	.275	.396	3670	1011	169	72	43	1.2	397	516	312	240	83	33	5	1933	185	80	39	2.1	.964	OF-995, 2B-16, 1B-1

Tony Boeckel

BOECKEL, NORMAN DOXIE (Elmer)
B. Aug. 25, 1892, Los Angeles, Calif.   D. Feb. 16, 1924, Torrey Pines, Calif.   BR TR 5'10½" 175 lbs.

1917	PIT	N	64	.265	.324	219	58	11	1	0	0.0	16	23	8	31	6	2	0	71	116	13	9	3.1	.935	3B-62
1919	2 teams			PIT	N	(45G –	.250)					BOS	N	(95G –	.249)										
"	total		140	.250	.321	517	129	20	7	1	0.2	60	42	53	33	21	2	1	141	265	21	13	3.1	.951	3B-138
1920	BOS	N	153	.268	.349	582	156	28	5	3	0.5	70	62	38	50	18	0	0	229	273	33	31	3.5	.938	3B-151, SS-3, 2B-1
1921			153	.313	.441	592	185	20	13	10	1.7	93	84	52	41	20	0	0	184	276	33	19	3.2	.933	3B-153
1922			119	.289	.410	402	116	19	6	6	1.5	61	47	35	32	14	13	4	128	168	15	13	2.6	.952	3B-106
1923			148	.298	.405	568	169	32	4	7	1.2	72	79	51	31	11	0	0	170	267	28	27	3.1	.940	3B-147, SS-1
	6 yrs.		777	.282	.381	2880	813	130	36	27	0.9	372	337	237	218	90	17	5	923	1365	143	112	3.1	.941	3B-757, SS-4, 2B-1

Len Boehmer

BOEHMER, LEONARD JOSEPH STEPHEN
B. June 28, 1941, Flint Hill, Mo.   BR TR 6'1" 192 lbs.

1967	CIN	N	2	.000	.000	3	0	0	0	0	0.0	0	0	0	0	0	0	0	0	1	0	0	0.5	1.000	2B-1
1969	NY	A	45	.176	.213	108	19	4	0	0	0.0	5	7	8	10	0	15	1	194	32	3	16	5.1	.987	1B-21, 3B-8, SS-1, 2B-1
1971			3	.000	.000	5	0	0	0	0	0.0	0	0	0	0	0	2	0	1	1	0	0	0.7	1.000	3B-1
	3 yrs.		50	.164	.198	116	19	4	0	0	0.0	5	7	8	10	0	17	1	195	34	3	16	4.6	.987	1B-21, 3B-9, 2B-2, SS-1

Terry Bogener

BOGENER, TERRY WAYNE
B. Sept. 28, 1955, Hannibal, Mo.   BL TL 6' 193 lbs.

| 1982 | TEX | A | 24 | .217 | .333 | 60 | 13 | 2 | 1 | 1 | 1.7 | 6 | 4 | 4 | 8 | 2 | 3 | 0 | 22 | 0 | 0 | 0 | 0.9 | 1.000 | OF-16, DH-4 |

Wade Boggs

BOGGS, WADE ANTHONY
B. June 15, 1958, Omaha, Neb.   BL TR 6'2" 190 lbs.

1982	BOS	A	104	.349	.441	338	118	14	1	5	1.5	51	44	35	21	1	13	4	489	168	8	51	6.4	.988	1B-49, 3B-44, DH-3, OF-1
1983			153	.361	.486	582	210	44	7	5	0.9	100	74	92	36	3	0	0	118	368	27	40	3.4	.947	3B-153
1984			158	.325	.416	625	203	31	4	6	1.0	109	55	89	44	3	1	0	141	330	20	30	3.1	.959	3B-155, DH-2
1985			161	.368	.478	653	240	42	3	8	1.2	107	78	96	61	2	0	0	134	335	17	30	3.0	.965	3B-161
1986			149	.357	.486	580	207	47	2	8	1.4	107	71	105	44	0	0	0	121	267	19	30	2.7	.953	3B-149
1987			147	.363	.588	551	200	40	6	24	4.4	108	89	105	48	1	1	0	112	277	14	37	2.7	.965	3B-145, DH-1, 1B-1
1988			155	.366	.490	584	214	45	6	5	0.9	128	58	125	34	2	1	1	122	250	11	17	2.5	.971	3B-151, DH-3
1989			156	.330	.449	621	205	51	7	3	0.5	113	54	107	51	2	1	0	123	264	17	29	2.6	.958	3B-152, DH-3
	8 yrs.		1183	.352	.480	4534	1597	314	36	64	1.4	823	523	754	339	14	17	5	1360	2259	133	264	3.2	.965	3B-1110, 1B-50, DH-12, OF-1
				4th																					

LEAGUE CHAMPIONSHIP SERIES

1986	BOS	A	7	.233	.333	30	7	1	1	0	0.0	3	2	4	4	0	0	0	7	14	2	1	3.3	.913	3B-7
1988			4	.385	.385	13	5	0	0	0	0.0	2	3	3	4	0	0	0	6	6	0	1	3.0	1.000	3B-4
	2 yrs.		11	.279	.349	43	12	1	1	0	0.0	5	5	7	5	0	0	0	13	20	2	2	3.2	.943	3B-11

WORLD SERIES

| 1986 | BOS | A | 7 | .290 | .387 | 31 | 9 | 3 | 0 | 0 | 0.0 | 3 | 3 | 3 | 2 | 0 | 0 | 0 | 4 | 15 | 0 | 1 | 2.7 | 1.000 | 3B-7 |

Year	Team		Games	BA	SA	AB	H	2B	3B	HR	HR%	R	RBI	BB	SO	SB	Pinch Hit AB	Pinch Hit H	PO	A	E	DP	TC/G	FA	G by Pos

Charlie Bohn

BOHN, CHARLES
B. 1857, Cleveland, Ohio   D. Aug. 1, 1903, Cleveland, Ohio

Year	Team		Games	BA	SA	AB	H	2B	3B	HR	HR%	R	RBI	BB	SO	SB	AB	H	PO	A	E	DP	TC/G	FA	G by Pos
1882	LOU	AA	4	.154	.154	13	2	0	0	0	0.0	0		0			0	0	5	9	4	0	4.5	.778	OF-2, P-2

Sammy Bohne

BOHNE, SAMUEL ARTHUR
Born Samuel Arthur Cohen.
B. Oct. 22, 1896, San Francisco, Calif.   D. May 23, 1977, Palo Alto, Calif.

BR TR 5'8½" 175 lbs.

Year	Team		Games	BA	SA	AB	H	2B	3B	HR	HR%	R	RBI	BB	SO	SB	AB	H	PO	A	E	DP	TC/G	FA	G by Pos
1916	STL	N	14	.237	.237	38	9	0	0	0	0.0	3	0	4	6	3	0	0	15	32	7	3	3.9	.870	SS-14
1921	CIN	N	153	.285	.398	613	175	28	16	3	0.5	98	44	54	38	26	0	0	313	450	26	73	5.2	.967	2B-102, 3B-53
1922			112	.274	.360	383	105	14	5	3	0.8	53	51	39	18	13	2	0	226	391	31	60	5.8	.952	2B-85, SS-22
1923			139	.252	.340	539	136	18	10	3	0.6	77	47	48	37	16	0	0	299	442	25	55	5.5	.967	2B-96, 3B-35, SS-9, 1B-1
1924			100	.255	.384	349	89	15	9	4	1.1	42	46	18	24	9	0	0	194	294	23	40	5.1	.955	2B-48, SS-40, 3B-12
1925			73	.257	.336	214	55	9	1	2	0.9	24	24	14	14	6	3	1	131	163	16	27	4.2	.948	SS-49, 2B-10, OF-4, 3B-2, 1B-2
1926	2 teams			CIN	N	(25G – .204)		BKN	N	(47G – .200)															
"	total		72	.201	.279	179	36	3	4	1	0.6	12	16	16	17	2	0	0	104	167	12	17	3.9	.958	2B-31, SS-20, 3B-15
7 yrs.			663	.261	.359	2315	605	87	45	16	0.7	309	228	193	154	75	5	1	1282	1939	140	275	5.1	.958	2B-372, SS-154, 3B-117, OF-4, 1B-3

Bruce Boisclair

BOISCLAIR, BRUCE ARMAND
B. Dec. 9, 1952, Putnam, Conn.

BL TL 6'2" 185 lbs.

Year	Team		Games	BA	SA	AB	H	2B	3B	HR	HR%	R	RBI	BB	SO	SB	AB	H	PO	A	E	DP	TC/G	FA	G by Pos
1974	NY	N	7	.250	.333	12	3	1	0	0	0.0	0	1	1	4	0	0	0	10	2	1	0	1.9	.923	OF-5
1976			110	.287	.374	286	82	13	3	2	0.7	42	13	28	55	9	21	12	156	3	3	1	1.5	.981	OF-87
1977			127	.293	.407	307	90	21	1	4	1.3	41	44	31	57	6	30	9	159	2	6	1	1.3	.964	OF-91, 1B-9
1978			107	.224	.322	214	48	7	1	4	1.9	24	15	23	43	3	47	12	115	3	2	0	1.1	.983	OF-69, 1B-1
1979			59	.184	.255	98	18	5	1	0	0.0	7	4	3	24	0	35	5	36	2	0	0	0.6	1.000	OF-24, 1B-1
5 yrs.			410	.263	.360	917	241	47	6	10	1.1	114	77	86	183	18	133	38	476	12	12	2	1.2	.976	OF-276, 1B-11

Bob Boken

BOKEN, ROBERT ANTHONY
B. Feb. 23, 1908, Maryville, Ill.   D. Oct. 6, 1988, Las Vegas, Nev.

BR TR 6'2" 165 lbs.

Year	Team		Games	BA	SA	AB	H	2B	3B	HR	HR%	R	RBI	BB	SO	SB	AB	H	PO	A	E	DP	TC/G	FA	G by Pos
1933	WAS	A	55	.278	.414	133	37	5	2	3	2.3	19	26	9	16	1	0	7	72	91	7	13	3.1	.959	2B-31, 3B-19, SS-10
1934	2 teams			WAS	A	(11G – .222)		CHI	A	(81G – .236)															
"	total		92	.235	.306	324	76	10	2	3	0.9	35	46	18	33	4	5	2	173	259	37	47	5.1	.921	2B-58, SS-22, 3B-6
2 yrs.			147	.247	.337	457	113	15	4	6	1.3	54	72	27	49	4	12	4	245	350	44	60	4.3	.931	2B-89, SS-32, 3B-25

Ed Boland

BOLAND, EDWARD JOHN
B. Apr. 18, 1908, Long Island City, N. Y.

BL TL 5'10" 165 lbs.

Year	Team		Games	BA	SA	AB	H	2B	3B	HR	HR%	R	RBI	BB	SO	SB	AB	H	PO	A	E	DP	TC/G	FA	G by Pos
1934	PHI	N	8	.300	.400	30	9	1	1	0	0.0	2	5	0	2	1	1	0	6	1	2	0	1.1	.778	OF-7
1935			30	.213	.213	47	10	0	0	0	0.0	5	4	4	6	1	17	2	15	0	3	0	0.6	.833	OF-10
1944	WAS	A	19	.271	.339	59	16	4	0	0	0.0	4	14	0	6	0	5	1	22	2	3	0	1.4	.889	OF-14
3 yrs.			57	.257	.309	136	35	5	1	0	0.0	11	23	4	14	2	23	3	43	3	8	0	0.9	.852	OF-31

Charlie Bold

BOLD, CHARLES DICKENS (Dutch)
B. Oct. 27, 1894, Karlskrona, Sweden   D. July 29, 1978, Chelsea, Mass.

BR TR 6'2" 185 lbs.

Year	Team		Games	BA	SA	AB	H	2B	3B	HR	HR%	R	RBI	BB	SO	SB	AB	H	PO	A	E	DP	TC/G	FA	G by Pos
1914	STL	A	2	.000	.000	1	0	0	0	0	0.0	0	0	0	1	0	0	0	1	0	1	0	1.0	.500	1B-1

Carl Boles

BOLES, CARL THEODORE
B. Oct. 31, 1934, Center Point, Ark.

BR TR 5'11" 185 lbs.

Year	Team		Games	BA	SA	AB	H	2B	3B	HR	HR%	R	RBI	BB	SO	SB	AB	H	PO	A	E	DP	TC/G	FA	G by Pos
1962	SF	N	19	.375	.375	24	9	0	0	0	0.0	0	6	0	11	4	5	0	1	0	0.3	.833	OF-7

Joe Boley

BOLEY, JOHN PETER
Born John Peter Bolinsky.
B. July 19, 1896, Mahoney City, Pa.   D. Dec. 30, 1962, Mahoney City, Pa.

BR TR 5'11" 170 lbs.

Year	Team		Games	BA	SA	AB	H	2B	3B	HR	HR%	R	RBI	BB	SO	SB	AB	H	PO	A	E	DP	TC/G	FA	G by Pos
1927	PHI	A	116	.311	.411	370	115	18	8	1	0.3	49	52	26	14	8	1	0	182	318	26	49	4.5	.951	SS-114
1928			132	.264	.325	425	112	20	3	0	0.0	49	49	32	11	5	0	0	244	320	30	51	4.5	.949	SS-132
1929			91	.251	.366	303	76	17	6	2	0.7	36	47	24	16	1	0	0	162	229	15	50	4.5	.963	SS-88, 3B-1
1930			121	.276	.367	420	116	22	2	4	1.0	41	55	32	26	0	1	0	221	296	16	62	4.4	.970	SS-120
1931			67	.228	.295	224	51	9	3	0	0.0	26	20	15	13	1	4	1	102	150	12	31	3.9	.955	SS-62, 2B-1
1932	2 teams			PHI	A	(10G – .206)		CLE	A	(1G – .250)															
"	total		11	.211	.263	38	8	2	0	0	0.0	2	4	1	4	0	0	0	11	20	3	2	3.1	.912	SS-11
6 yrs.			538	.269	.354	1780	478	88	22	7	0.4	203	227	130	84	15	6	1	922	1333	102	245	4.4	.957	SS-527, 3B-1, 2B-1

WORLD SERIES

Year	Team		Games	BA	SA	AB	H	2B	3B	HR	HR%	R	RBI	BB	SO	SB	AB	H	PO	A	E	DP	TC/G	FA	G by Pos
1929	PHI	A	5	.235	.235	17	4	0	0	0	0.0	1	1	0	3	0	0	0	4	13	0	1	3.4	1.000	SS-5
1930			6	.095	.095	21	2	0	0	0	0.0	1	1	0	1	0	0	0	9	13	1	0	3.8	.957	SS-6
1931			1	.000	.000	1	0	0	0	0	0.0	0	0	0	1	0	0	0	0	0	0	0	0.0	–	
3 yrs.			12	.154	.154	39	6	0	0	0	0.0	2	2	0	5	0	1	0	13	26	1	1	3.3	.975	SS-11

Jim Bolger

BOLGER, JAMES CYRIL (Dutch)
B. Feb. 23, 1932, Cincinnati, Ohio

BR TR 6'2" 180 lbs.

Year	Team		Games	BA	SA	AB	H	2B	3B	HR	HR%	R	RBI	BB	SO	SB	AB	H	PO	A	E	DP	TC/G	FA	G by Pos
1950	CIN	N	2	.000	.000	1	0	0	0	0	0.0	0	0	0	0	0	0	0	0	0	0	0	0.0	–	OF-2
1951			2	–	–	0	0	0	0	0	–	0	0	0	0	0	0	0	0	0	0	0	0.0	–	
1954	CHI	N	5	.333	.333	3	1	0	0	0	0.0	1	0	0	1	0	2	0	0	0	0	0	0.0	–	OF-2
1955			64	.206	.288	160	33	5	4	0	0.0	19	7	9	17	2	1	1	125	1	6	0	2.1	.955	OF-51
1957			112	.275	.352	273	75	4	1	5	1.8	28	29	10	36	0	**48**	**17**	154	7	4	1	1.5	.976	OF-63, 3B-3
1958			84	.225	.300	120	27	4	1	1	0.8	15	11	9	20	0	51	10	46	1	3	0	0.6	.940	OF-37
1959	2 teams			CLE	A	(8G – .000)		PHI	N	(35G – .083)															
"	total		43	.073	.091	55	4	1	0	0	0.0	1	1	4	9	0	32	4	15	0	1	0	0.4	.938	OF-9
7 yrs.			312	.229	.301	612	140	14	6	6	1.0	65	48	32	83	3	134	32	340	9	14	1	1.2	.961	OF-164, 3B-3

Year	Team		Games	BA	SA	AB	H	2B	3B	HR	HR%	R	RBI	BB	SO	SB	Pinch Hit AB	Pinch Hit H	PO	A	E	DP	TC/G	FA	G by Pos

Frank Bolling

BOLLING, FRANK ELMORE
Brother of Milt Bolling.
B. Nov. 16, 1931, Mobile, Ala.

BR TR 6'1" 175 lbs.

Year	Team		Games	BA	SA	AB	H	2B	3B	HR	HR%	R	RBI	BB	SO	SB	PH AB	PH H	PO	A	E	DP	TC/G	FA	G by Pos
1954	DET	A	117	.236	.337	368	87	15	2	6	1.6	46	38	36	51	3	3	0	248	232	13	54	4.2	.974	2B-113
1956			102	.281	.434	366	103	21	7	7	1.9	53	45	42	51	6	0	0	223	260	11	72	4.8	.978	2B-102
1957			146	.259	.405	576	149	27	6	15	2.6	72	40	57	64	4	0	0	394	401	16	112	5.6	.980	2B-146
1958			154	.269	.392	610	164	25	4	14	2.3	91	75	54	54	6	0	0	342	445	12	109	5.2	.985	2B-154
1959			127	.266	.403	459	122	18	3	13	2.8	56	55	45	37	2	1	0	281	340	8	81	5.0	.987	2B-126
1960			139	.254	.356	536	136	20	4	9	1.7	64	59	40	48	7	1	0	375	377	17	93	5.5	.978	2B-138
1961	MIL	N	148	.262	.379	585	153	16	4	15	2.6	86	56	57	62	7	0	0	326	489	10	112	5.6	.988	2B-148
1962			122	.271	.399	406	110	17	4	9	2.2	45	43	35	45	2	5	1	252	298	6	70	4.6	.989	2B-119
1963			142	.244	.312	542	132	18	2	5	0.9	73	43	41	47	2	0	0	326	379	14	107	5.1	.981	2B-141
1964			120	.199	.278	352	70	11	1	5	1.4	35	34	21	44	0	7	0	212	255	7	68	4.0	.985	2B-117
1965			148	.264	.363	535	141	26	3	7	1.3	55	50	24	41	0	1	0	310	393	17	90	4.9	.976	2B-147
1966	ATL	N	75	.211	.256	227	48	7	0	1	0.4	16	18	10	14	1	11	1	134	150	5	35	3.9	.983	2B-67
12 yrs.			1540	.254	.366	5562	1415	221	40	106	1.9	692	556	462	558	40	29	2	3423	4019	136	1003	4.9	.982	2B-1518

Jack Bolling

BOLLING, JOHN EDWARD
B. Feb. 20, 1917, Mobile, Ala.

BL TL 5'11" 168 lbs.

Year	Team		Games	BA	SA	AB	H	2B	3B	HR	HR%	R	RBI	BB	SO	SB	PH AB	PH H	PO	A	E	DP	TC/G	FA	G by Pos
1939	PHI	N	69	.289	.384	211	61	11	0	3	1.4	27	13	11	10	6	17	4	392	38	8	35	6.3	.982	1B-48
1944	BKN	N	56	.351	.496	131	46	14	1	1	0.8	21	25	14	4	0	24	6	206	20	2	7	4.1	.991	1B-27
2 yrs.			125	.313	.427	342	107	25	1	4	1.2	48	38	25	14	6	41	10	598	58	10	42	5.3	.985	1B-75

Milt Bolling

BOLLING, MILTON JOSEPH
Brother of Frank Bolling.
B. Aug. 9, 1930, Mississippi City, Miss.

BR TR 6'1" 177 lbs.

Year	Team		Games	BA	SA	AB	H	2B	3B	HR	HR%	R	RBI	BB	SO	SB	PH AB	PH H	PO	A	E	DP	TC/G	FA	G by Pos
1952	BOS	A	11	.222	.333	36	8	1	0	1	2.8	4	3	3	5	0	0	0	22	41	6	6	5.8	.984	SS-11
1953			109	.263	.353	323	85	12	1	5	1.5	30	28	24	41	1	1	0	174	321	23	71	4.8	.956	SS-109
1954			113	.249	.368	370	92	20	3	6	1.6	42	36	47	55	2	1	0	191	377	33	73	5.3	.945	SS-107, 3B-5
1955			6	.200	.200	5	1	0	0	0	0.0	0	0	0	1	0	2	0	1	3	1	0	0.8	.800	SS-2
1956			45	.212	.347	118	25	3	2	3	2.5	19	8	18	20	0	4	0	38	81	9	13	2.8	.930	SS-26, 3B-11, 2B-1
1957	2 teams				BOS	A	(1G – .000)			WAS	A	(91G – .227)													
"	total		92	.227	.320	278	63	12	1	4	1.4	29	19	18	59	2	4	0	168	232	12	53	4.5	.971	2B-53, SS-37, 3B-1
1958	DET	A	24	.194	.258	31	6	2	0	0	0.0	3	0	5	7	0	4	0	15	24	2	7	1.7	.951	SS-13, 3B-1, 2B-1
7 yrs.			400	.241	.345	1161	280	50	7	19	1.6	127	94	115	188	5	17	2	609	1079	81	223	4.4	.954	SS-305, 2B-55, 3B-18

Don Bollweg

BOLLWEG, DONALD RAYMOND
B. Feb. 12, 1921, Wheaton, Ill.

BL TL 6'1" 190 lbs.

Year	Team		Games	BA	SA	AB	H	2B	3B	HR	HR%	R	RBI	BB	SO	SB	PH AB	PH H	PO	A	E	DP	TC/G	FA	G by Pos
1950	STL	N	4	.182	.182	11	2	0	0	0	0.0	1	1	1	1	0	0	0	26	0	0	3	6.5	1.000	1B-4
1951			6	.111	.222	9	1	1	0	0	0.0	1	2	0	1	0	4	1	16	0	1	2	2.8	.941	1B-2
1953	NY	A	70	.297	.503	155	46	6	4	5	3.9	24	24	21	31	1	21	5	323	15	6	37	4.9	.983	1B-43
1954	PHI	A	103	.224	.358	268	60	15	3	5	1.9	35	24	35	33	1	29	6	530	51	13	55	5.8	.978	1B-71
1955	KC	A	12	.111	.111	9	1	0	0	0	0.0	1	2	3	2	0	9	1	8	0	0	3	0.7	1.000	1B-3
5 yrs.			195	.243	.396	452	110	22	7	11	2.4	62	53	60	68	2	63	13	903	66	20	100	5.1	.980	1B-123

WORLD SERIES

Year	Team		Games	BA	SA	AB	H	2B	3B	HR	HR%	R	RBI	BB	SO	SB	PH AB	PH H	PO	A	E	DP	TC/G	FA	G by Pos
1953	NY	A	3	.000	.000	2	0	0	0	0	0.0	0	0	0	2	0	0	0	0	0	0	0	0.0	–	1B-1

Cecil Bolton

BOLTON, CECIL GLANFORD (Lefty)
B. Feb. 13, 1904, Booneville, Miss.

BL TL 6'4" 195 lbs.

Year	Team		Games	BA	SA	AB	H	2B	3B	HR	HR%	R	RBI	BB	SO	SB	PH AB	PH H	PO	A	E	DP	TC/G	FA	G by Pos
1928	CLE	A	4	.154	.462	13	2	0	2	0	0.0	1	0	2	2	0	0	0	41	1	2	3	11.0	.955	1B-4

Cliff Bolton

BOLTON, WILLIAM CLIFTON
B. Apr. 10, 1907, High Point, N. C.   D. Apr. 21, 1979, Lexington, N. C.

BL TR 5'9" 160 lbs.

Year	Team		Games	BA	SA	AB	H	2B	3B	HR	HR%	R	RBI	BB	SO	SB	PH AB	PH H	PO	A	E	DP	TC/G	FA	G by Pos
1931	WAS	A	23	.256	.326	43	11	1	1	0	0.0	3	6	1	5	0	10	1	15	3	1	0	0.8	.947	C-13
1933			33	.410	.487	39	16	1	0	0	0.0	4	6	6	3	0	22	9	16	2	2	1	0.6	.900	C-9, OF-1
1934			42	.270	.365	148	40	9	1	1	0.7	12	17	11	9	2	3	2	134	20	3	4	3.7	.981	C-39
1935			110	.304	.427	375	114	18	11	2	0.5	47	55	56	13	0	3	0	356	52	12	8	3.9	.971	C-106
1936			86	.291	.401	289	84	18	4	2	0.7	41	51	25	12	1	5	1	287	44	7	4	3.9	.979	C-83
1937	DET	A	27	.263	.351	57	15	2	0	1	1.8	6	7	8	6	0	13	3	47	9	1	2	2.1	.982	C-13
1941	WAS	A	14	.000	.000	11	0	0	0	0	0.0	0	1	1	2	0	10	0	2	0	0	0	0.1	1.000	C-3
7 yrs.			335	.291	.398	962	280	49	18	6	0.6	113	143	108	50	3	66	21	857	130	26	19	3.0	.974	C-266, OF-1

WORLD SERIES

Year	Team		Games	BA	SA	AB	H	2B	3B	HR	HR%	R	RBI	BB	SO	SB	PH AB	PH H	PO	A	E	DP	TC/G	FA	G by Pos
1933	WAS	A	2	.000	.000	2	0	0	0	0	0.0	0	0	0	0	0	2	0	0	0	0	0	0.0	–	

Tommy Bond

BOND, THOMAS HENRY
B. Apr. 2, 1856, Granard, Ireland   D. Jan. 24, 1941, Boston, Mass.
Manager 1882.

BR TR 5'7½" 160 lbs.

Year	Team		Games	BA	SA	AB	H	2B	3B	HR	HR%	R	RBI	BB	SO	SB	PH AB	PH H	PO	A	E	DP	TC/G	FA	G by Pos
1876	HAR	N	45	.275	.319	182	50	8	0	0	0.0	18	21	0	4		0	0	25	93	15	0	3.0	.887	P-45
1877	BOS	N	61	.228	.266	259	59	4	3	0	0.0	32	30	1	15		0	0	30	104	9	2	2.3	.937	P-58, OF-3
1878			59	.212	.237	236	50	4	1	0	0.0	22	23	0	9		0	0	27	117	9	4	2.6	.941	P-59, OF-2
1879			65	.241	.261	257	62	3	1	0	0.0	35	21	6	8		0	0	36	144	9	7	2.9	.952	P-64, OF-5, 1B-1
1880			76	.220	.241	282	62	4	1	0	0.0	27	24	5	14		0	0	61	153	16	8	3.0	.930	P-63, OF-26, 3B-1, 1B-1
1881			3	.200	.200	10	2	0	0	0	0.0	1	0	0	0		0	0	2	7	0	0	3.0	1.000	P-3
1882	WOR	N	8	.133	.133	30	4	0	0	0	0.0	1	2	2	3		0	0	11	1	4	0	2.0	.750	OF-8, P-2
1884	2 teams				BOS	U	(37G – .296)			IND	AA	(7G – .130)													
"	total		44	.276	.335	185	51	9	1	0	0.0	21		4			0	0	27	62	17	3	2.4	.840	P-28, OF-19, 3B-1
8 yrs.			361	.236	.268	1441	340	32	7	0	0.0	156	121	21	53		0	0	219	681	79	24	2.7	.919	P-322, OF-63, 3B-2, 1B-2

Walt Bond

BOND, WALTER FRANKLIN
B. Oct. 19, 1937, Denmark, Tenn.   D. Sept. 14, 1967, Houston, Tex.

BL TR 6'7" 228 lbs.

Year	Team		Games	BA	SA	AB	H	2B	3B	HR	HR%	R	RBI	BB	SO	SB	Pinch Hit AB	Pinch Hit H	PO	A	E	DP	TC/G	FA	G by Pos

Walt Bond *continued*

Year	Team		Games	BA	SA	AB	H	2B	3B	HR	HR%	R	RBI	BB	SO	SB	AB	H	PO	A	E	DP	TC/G	FA	G by Pos
1960	CLE	A	40	.221	.366	131	29	2	1	5	3.8	19	18	13	14	4	5	0	76	2	0	1	2.0	1.000	OF-36
1961			38	.173	.346	52	9	1	1	2	3.8	7	7	6	10	1	23	2	17	1	0	0	0.5	1.000	OF-12
1962			12	.380	.800	50	19	3	0	6	12.0	10	17	4	9	1	0	0	25	0	0	0	2.1	1.000	OF-12
1964	HOU	N	148	.254	.420	543	138	16	7	20	3.7	63	85	38	90	2	2	0	796	41	13	46	5.7	.985	1B-76, OF-71
1965			117	.263	.366	407	107	17	2	7	1.7	46	47	42	51	2	7	1	704	49	14	52	6.6	.982	1B-74, OF-38
1967	MIN	A	10	.313	.563	16	5	1	0	1	6.3	4	5	3	1	0	5	2	7	0	1	0	0.8	.875	OF-3
6 yrs.			365	.256	.410	1199	307	40	11	41	3.4	149	179	106	175	10	42	5	1625	93	28	99	4.8	.984	OF-172, 1B-150

Barry Bonds

BONDS, BARRY LAMAR
Son of Bobby Bonds.
B. July 24, 1964, Riverside, Calif.

BL TL 6'1" 185 lbs.

Year	Team		Games	BA	SA	AB	H	2B	3B	HR	HR%	R	RBI	BB	SO	SB	AB	H	PO	A	E	DP	TC/G	FA	G by Pos
1986	PIT	N	113	.223	.416	413	92	26	3	16	3.9	72	48	65	102	36	3	1	280	9	5	2	2.6	.983	OF-110
1987			150	.261	.492	551	144	34	9	25	4.5	99	59	54	88	32	7	1	330	15	5	3	2.3	.986	OF-145
1988			144	.283	.491	538	152	30	5	24	4.5	97	58	72	82	17	11	2	292	5	6	0	2.1	.980	OF-136
1989			159	.248	.426	580	144	34	6	19	3.3	96	58	93	93	32	8	3	365	14	6	1	2.4	.984	OF-156
4 yrs.			566	.256	.458	2082	532	124	23	84	4.0	364	223	284	365	117	29	7	1267	43	22	6	2.4	.983	OF-547

Bobby Bonds

BONDS, BOBBY LEE
Father of Barry Bonds.
B. Mar. 15, 1946, Riverside, Calif.

BR TR 6'1" 190 lbs.

Year	Team		Games	BA	SA	AB	H	2B	3B	HR	HR%	R	RBI	BB	SO	SB	AB	H	PO	A	E	DP	TC/G	FA	G by Pos
1968	SF	N	81	.254	.407	307	78	10	5	9	2.9	55	35	38	84	16	0	0	169	6	4	1	2.2	.978	OF-80
1969			158	.259	.473	622	161	25	6	32	5.1	120	90	81	187	45	1	0	339	9	8	2	2.3	.978	OF-155
1970			157	.302	.504	663	200	36	10	26	3.9	134	78	77	189[1]	48	2	0	326	14	11	7	2.2	.969	OF-157
1971			155	.288	.512	619	178	32	4	33	5.3	110	102	62	137	26	3	1	329	10	2	1	2.2	.994	OF-154
1972			153	.259	.446	626	162	29	5	26	4.2	118	80	60	137	44	0	0	345	8	8	3	2.4	.978	OF-153
1973			160	.283	.530	643	182	34	4	39	6.1	131	96	87	148	43	2	1	346	11	11	5	2.3	.970	OF-158
1974			150	.256	.434	567	145	22	8	21	3.7	97	71	95	134	41	3	1	305	11	11	3	2.2	.966	OF-148
1975	NY	A	145	.270	.512	529	143	26	4	32	6.0	93	85	89	137	30	4	1	287	12	4	5	2.1	.987	OF-129, DH-12
1976	CAL	A	99	.265	.386	378	100	10	3	10	2.6	48	54	41	90	30	1	0	199	9	5	3	2.2	.977	OF-98, DH-1
1977			158	.264	.520	592	156	23	9	37	6.3	103	115	74	141	41	1	0	272	6	5	4	1.8	.986	OF-140, DH-18
1978	2 teams			CHI A (26G – .278)			TEX A (130G – .265)																			
"	total		156	.267	.480	565	151	19	4	31	5.5	93	90	79	120	43	2	0	253	16	9	6	1.8	.968	OF-133, DH-21
1979	CLE	A	146	.275	.463	538	148	24	4	25	4.6	93	85	74	135	34	1	0	267	9	6	1	1.9	.979	OF-116, DH-29
1980	STL	N	86	.203	.316	231	47	5	3	5	2.2	37	24	33	74	15	15	2	114	5	4	2	1.4	.967	OF-70
1981	CHI	N	45	.215	.380	163	35	7	1	6	3.7	26	19	24	44	5	0	0	108	2	2	0	2.5	.982	OF-45
14 yrs.			1849	.268	.471	7043	1886	302	66	332	4.7	1258	1024	914	1757	461	35	7	3659	128	89	40	2.1	.977	OF-1736, DH-81
															6th										

LEAGUE CHAMPIONSHIP SERIES

Year	Team		Games	BA	SA	AB	H	2B	3B	HR	HR%	R	RBI	BB	SO	SB	AB	H	PO	A	E	DP	TC/G	FA	G by Pos
1971	SF	N	3	.250	.250	8	2	0	0	0	0.0	0	0	2	4	0	0	0	3	0	1	0	1.3	.750	OF-3

George Bone

BONE, GEORGE DRUMMOND
B. Aug. 28, 1876, New Haven, Conn.   D. May 26, 1918, West Haven, Conn.

BB TR 5'7" 152 lbs.

Year	Team		Games	BA	SA	AB	H	2B	3B	HR	HR%	R	RBI	BB	SO	SB	AB	H	PO	A	E	DP	TC/G	FA	G by Pos
1901	MIL	A	12	.302	.349	43	13	2	0	0	0.0	6	6	4		0	0	0	24	29	8	6	5.1	.869	SS-12

Nino Bongiovanni

BONGIOVANNI, ANTHONY THOMAS
B. Dec. 21, 1911, Pike's Peak, La.

BL TL 5'10" 175 lbs.

Year	Team		Games	BA	SA	AB	H	2B	3B	HR	HR%	R	RBI	BB	SO	SB	AB	H	PO	A	E	DP	TC/G	FA	G by Pos
1938	CIN	N	2	.286	.429	7	2	0	0	0	0.0	0	0	0	0	0	0	0	6	0	0	0	3.0	1.000	OF-2
1939			66	.258	.296	159	41	6	0	0	0.0	17	16	9	8	0	27	7	89	1	1	1	1.4	.989	OF-39
2 yrs.			68	.259	.301	166	43	7	0	0	0.0	17	16	9	8	0	27	7	95	1	1	1	1.4	.990	OF-41

WORLD SERIES

Year	Team		Games	BA	SA	AB	H	2B	3B	HR	HR%	R	RBI	BB	SO	SB	AB	H	PO	A	E	DP	TC/G	FA	G by Pos
1939	CIN	N	1	.000	.000	1	0	0	0	0	0.0	0	0	0	0	0	1	0	0	0	0	0	0.0	—	—

Bobby Bonilla

BONILLA, ROBERTO MARTIN ANTONIO
B. Feb. 23, 1963, New York, N.Y.

BB TR 6'3" 210 lbs.

Year	Team		Games	BA	SA	AB	H	2B	3B	HR	HR%	R	RBI	BB	SO	SB	AB	H	PO	A	E	DP	TC/G	FA	G by Pos
1986	2 teams			CHI A (75G – .269)			PIT N (63G – .240)																			
"	total		138	.256	.333	426	109	16	4	3	0.7	55	43	62	88	8	19	2	451	38	5	29	3.6	.990	OF-94, 1B-34, 3B-8
1987	PIT	N	141	.300	.481	466	140	33	3	15	3.2	58	77	39	64	3	17	6	142	139	16	13	2.1	.946	3B-89, OF-46, 1B-6
1988			159	.274	.476	584	160	32	7	24	4.1	87	100	85	82	3	0	0	121	336	32	17	3.1	.935	3B-159
1989			163	.281	.490	616	173	37	10	24	3.9	96	86	76	93	8	1	0	190	334	35	37	3.4	.937	3B-159
4 yrs.			601	.278	.452	2092	582	118	24	66	3.2	296	306	262	327	22	37	8	904	847	88	96	3.1	.952	3B-408, OF-141, 1B-48

Juan Bonilla

BONILLA, JUAN GUILLERMO
Born Juan Guillermo Bonilla y Urania.
B. Jan. 12, 1956, Santurce, Puerto Rico

BR TR 5'9" 170 lbs.

Year	Team		Games	BA	SA	AB	H	2B	3B	HR	HR%	R	RBI	BB	SO	SB	AB	H	PO	A	E	DP	TC/G	FA	G by Pos
1981	SD	N	99	.290	.344	369	107	13	2	1	0.3	30	25	25	23	4	0	0	229	290	13	72	5.4	.976	2B-97
1982			45	.280	.335	182	51	6	2	0	0.0	21	8	11	15	0	0	0	99	134	6	26	5.3	.975	2B-45
1983			152	.237	.304	556	132	17	4	4	0.7	55	45	50	40	3	4	1	335	414	11	90	5.0	.986	2B-149
1985	NY	A	8	.125	.188	16	2	1	0	0	0.0	0	2	1	3	0	2	0	7	14	1	3	2.8	.955	2B-7
1986	BAL	A	102	.243	.296	284	69	10	1	1	0.4	33	18	25	21	0	7	2	143	175	10	48	3.2	.970	2B-70, 3B-33, DH-2
1987	NY	A	23	.255	.364	55	14	3	0	1	1.8	6	3	5	6	0	1	1	40	44	3	10	3.8	.966	2B-22, 3B-1
6 yrs.			429	.256	.317	1462	375	50	9	7	0.5	145	101	116	108	7	14	4	853	1071	44	249	4.6	.978	2B-390, 3B-34, DH-2

Luther Bonin

BONIN, ERNEST LUTHER
B. Jan. 13, 1888, Green Hill, Ind.   D. Jan. 3, 1965, Sycamore, Ohio

BL TR 5'9½" 178 lbs.

Year	Team		Games	BA	SA	AB	H	2B	3B	HR	HR%	R	RBI	BB	SO	SB	AB	H	PO	A	E	DP	TC/G	FA	G by Pos
1913	STL	A	1	.000	.000	1	0	0	0	0	0.0	0	0	0	0	0	1	0	0	0	0	0	0.0	—	—
1914	BUF	F	20	.184	.263	76	14	4	1	0	0.0	6	4	7		3	0	0	28	4	1	1	1.7	.970	OF-20
2 yrs.			21	.182	.260	77	14	4	1	0	0.0	6	4	7		3	1	0	28	4	1	1	1.6	.970	OF-20

Year	Team	Games	BA	SA	AB	H	2B	3B	HR	HR%	R	RBI	BB	SO	SB	Pinch Hit AB	H	PO	A	E	DP	TC/G	FA	G by Pos

Barry Bonnell

BONNELL, ROBERT BARRY
B. Oct. 27, 1953, Clermont County, Ohio
BR TR 6'3" 190 lbs.

1977	ATL N	100	.300	.339	360	108	11	0	1	0.3	41	45	37	32	7	7	1	203	65	8	1	2.8	.971	OF-75, 3B-32
1978		117	.240	.306	304	73	11	3	1	0.3	36	16	20	30	12	1	0	187	35	6	3	1.9	.974	OF-105, 3B-15
1979		127	.259	.424	375	97	20	3	12	3.2	47	45	26	55	8	4	1	221	8	4	2	1.8	.983	OF-124, 3B-1
1980	TOR A	130	.268	.417	463	124	22	4	13	2.8	55	56	37	59	3	5	1	271	15	8	3	2.3	.973	OF-122, DH-3
1981		66	.220	.339	227	50	7	4	4	1.8	21	28	12	25	4	2	0	148	5	4	1	2.4	.975	OF-66
1982		140	.293	.407	437	128	26	2	6	1.4	59	49	32	51	14	22	4	234	7	5	1	1.8	.980	OF-125, 3B-9, DH-6
1983		121	.318	.469	377	120	21	3	10	2.7	49	54	33	52	9	7	2	213	13	3	1	1.9	.987	OF-117, 3B-4, DH-1
1984	SEA A	110	.264	.394	363	96	15	4	8	2.2	42	48	25	51	5	8	1	171	23	6	1	1.8	.970	OF-94, 3B-10, 1B-5
1985		48	.243	.342	111	27	8	0	1	0.9	9	10	6	19	1	18	4	61	2	1	3	1.3	.984	OF-22, 1B-5, DH-2
1986		17	.196	.235	51	10	2	0	0	0.0	4	4	1	13	1	3	0	46	6	2	1	3.2	.963	OF-9, 1B-8, DH-2
10 yrs.		976	.272	.389	3068	833	143	24	56	1.8	363	355	229	387	63	77	14	1755	179	47	17	2.0	.976	OF-859, 3B-71, 1B-18, DH-14

Bob Bonner

BONNER, ROBERT AVERILL
B. Aug. 12, 1956, Uvalde, Tex.
BR TR 6' 185 lbs.

1980	BAL A	4	.000	.000	4	0	0	0	0	0.0	1	0	0	0	0	0	0	2	6	1	1	2.3	.889	SS-3
1981		10	.296	.370	27	8	2	0	0	0.0	6	2	1	4	1	0	0	15	26	1	8	4.2	.976	2B-9
1982		41	.169	.234	77	13	3	1	0	0.0	8	5	3	12	0	0	0	33	61	4	9	2.4	.959	SS-38, 2B-3
1983		6	—	—	0	0	0	0	0	—	0	0	0	0	0	0	0	1	0	0	0	0.2	1.000	2B-5, DH-1
4 yrs.		61	.194	.259	108	21	5	1	0	0.0	15	8	4	16	1	0	0	51	93	6	18	2.5	.960	SS-41, 2B-17, DH-1

Frank Bonner

BONNER, FRANK J (The Human Flea)
B. Aug. 20, 1869, Lowell, Mass.   D. Dec. 31, 1905, Kansas City, Mo.
BR TR 5'7½" 169 lbs.

1894	BAL N	33	.322	.441	118	38	10	2	0	0.0	27	24	17	5	12	1	0	67	65	14	9	4.4	.904	2B-27, OF-4, 3B-2, SS-1
1895	2 teams	26																BAL N (11G – .333)				STL N (15G – .136)		
"	total	26	.218	.297	101	22	1	2	1	1.0	12	15	6	9	6	0	0	27	28	19	2	2.8	.743	3B-21, OF-5, C-1
1896	BKN N	9	.176	.235	34	6	2	0	0	0.0	8	5	2	8	1	0	0	8	35	4	3	5.2	.915	2B-9
1899	WAS N	85	.274	.372	347	95	20	4	2	0.6	41	44	18		6	0	0	192	264	29	34	5.7	.940	2B-85
1902	2 teams	45																CLE A (34G – .280)				PHI A (11G – .182)		
"	total	45	.256	.290	176	45	1	0	0	0.0	16	17	5		1	0	0	92	123	20	9	5.2	.915	2B-45
1903	BOS N	48	.220	.266	173	38	5	0	1	0.6	11	10	7		2	2	1	104	116	15	19	4.9	.936	2B-24, SS-22
6 yrs.		246	.257	.333	949	244	44	8	4	0.4	115	115	55	22	28	3	1	490	631	101	76	5.0	.917	2B-190, SS-23, 3B-23, OF-9, C-1

Zeke Bonura

BONURA, HENRY JOHN
B. Sept. 20, 1908, New Orleans, La.   D. Mar. 9, 1987, New Orleans, La.
BR TR 6' 210 lbs.

1934	CHI A	127	.302	.545	510	154	35	4	27	5.3	86	110	64	31	0	0	0	1239	77	5	94	10.4	.996	1B-127
1935		138	.295	.485	550	162	34	4	21	3.8	107	92	57	28	4	0	0	1421	83	9	109	11.0	.994	1B-138
1936		148	.330	.482	587	194	39	7	12	2.0	120	138	94	29	4	1	0	1500	107	7	150	10.9	.996	1B-146
1937		116	.345	.573	447	154	41	2	19	4.3	79	100	49	24	5	1	0	1114	63	13	123	10.3	.989	1B-115
1938	WAS A	137	.289	.472	540	156	27	3	22	4.1	72	114	44	29	2	8	2	1209	93	9	132	9.6	.993	1B-129
1939	NY N	123	.321	.477	455	146	26	6	11	2.4	75	85	46	22	1	0	0	1205	90	11	110	10.6	.992	1B-122
1940	2 teams	128																WAS A (79G – .273)				CHI N (49G – .264)		
"	total	128	.270	.385	493	133	30	3	7	1.4	61	65	50	17	3	5	1	1120	82	18	104	9.5	.985	1B-123
7 yrs.		917	.307	.487	3582	1099	232	29	119	3.3	600	704	404	180	19	15	3	8808	595	72	822	10.3	.992	1B-900

Everitt Booe

BOOE, EVERITT LITTLE
B. Sept. 28, 1891, Mocksville, N. C.   D. Mar. 21, 1969, Kenedy, Tex.
BL TR 5'8½" 165 lbs.

1913	PIT N	29	.200	.250	80	16	0	2	0	0.0	9	2	6	2	6	1	0	37	4	0	1	1.4	1.000	OF-22
1914	2 teams	96																IND F (20G – .226)				BUF F (76G – .224)		
"	total	96	.224	.276	272	61	10	2	0	0.0	34	20	28		12	14	3	107	45	17	9	1.8	.899	OF-63, SS-11, 3B-2, 2B-1
2 yrs.		125	.219	.270	352	77	10	4	0	0.0	43	22	34		14	20	4	144	49	17	10	1.7	.919	OF-85, SS-11, 3B-2, 2B-1

Buddy Booker

BOOKER, RICHARD LEE
B. May 28, 1942, Lynchburg, Va.
BL TR 5'10" 170 lbs.

1966	CLE A	18	.214	.464	28	6	1	0	2	7.1	6	5	2	6	0	2	1	25	2	1	0	1.6	.964	C-12
1968	CHI A	5	.000	.000	5	0	0	0	0	0.0	0	1	2	2	0	4	0	2	0	0	0	0.4	1.000	C-3
2 yrs.		23	.182	.394	33	6	1	0	2	6.1	6	5	3	8	0	12	0	27	2	1	0	1.3	.967	C-15

Rod Booker

BOOKER, RODERICK STEWART
B. Sept. 4, 1958, Los Angeles, Calif.
BL TR 6' 175 lbs.

1987	STL N	44	.277	.340	47	13	1	1	0	0.0	9	8	7	7	2	18	4	25	28	2	5	1.3	.964	2B-18, 3B-4, SS-1
1988		18	.343	.429	35	12	3	0	0	0.0	6	3	4	2	2	6	2	3	15	2	1	1.1	.900	3B-13, 2B-1
1989		10	.250	.250	8	2	0	0	0	0.0	1	0	0	2	0	2	0	4	9	2	1	1.5	.867	2B-5, 3B-1
3 yrs.		72	.300	.367	90	27	4	1	0	0.0	16	11	11	11	4	26	6	32	52	6	7	1.3	.933	2B-24, 3B-18, SS-1

Al Bool

BOOL, ALBERT J.
B. Aug. 24, 1897, Lincoln, Neb.   D. Sept. 27, 1981, Lincoln, Neb.
BR TR 5'11" 180 lbs.

1928	WAS A	2	.143	.143	7	1	0	0	0	0.0	1	0	0	0	0	0	0	8	2	0	0	5.0	1.000	C-2
1930	PIT N	78	.259	.449	216	56	12	4	7	3.2	30	46	25	29	0	11	3	190	42	8	4	3.1	.967	C-65
1931	BOS N	49	.188	.200	85	16	1	0	0	0.0	5	6	9	13	0	11	1	73	14	1	4	1.8	.989	C-37
3 yrs.		129	.237	.373	308	73	13	4	7	2.3	35	53	34	42	0	22	4	271	58	9	8	2.6	.973	C-104

Bob Boone

BOONE, ROBERT RAYMOND
Son of Ray Boone.
B. Nov. 19, 1947, San Diego, Calif.
BR TR 6'2½" 195 lbs.

1972	PHI N	16	.275	.353	51	14	1	0	1	2.0	4	4	5	7	1	3	0	66	7	5	1	4.9	.936	C-14
1973		145	.261	.365	521	136	20	2	10	1.9	42	61	41	36	3	0	0	868	89	10	16	6.7	.990	C-145
1974		146	.242	.322	488	118	24	3	3	0.6	41	52	35	29	3	1	1	825	77	22	7	6.3	.976	C-146
1975		97	.246	.329	289	71	14	2	2	0.7	28	20	32	14	1	6	1	459	48	5	7	5.3	.990	C-92, 3B-3

Year	Team	Games	BA	SA	AB	H	2B	3B	HR	HR%	R	RBI	BB	SO	SB	Pinch Hit AB	Pinch Hit H	PO	A	E	DP	TC/G	FA	G by Pos

Bob Boone *continued*

Year	Team	Games	BA	SA	AB	H	2B	3B	HR	HR%	R	RBI	BB	SO	SB	PH AB	PH H	PO	A	E	DP	TC/G	FA	G by Pos
1976		121	.271	.366	361	98	18	2	4	1.1	40	54	45	44	2	12	4	587	39	6	5	5.2	.991	C-108, 1B-4
1977		132	.284	.436	440	125	26	4	11	2.5	55	66	42	54	5	1	0	654	83	8	9	5.6	.989	C-131, 3B-2
1978		132	.283	.425	435	123	18	4	12	2.8	48	62	46	37	2	5	1	650	55	8	7	5.4	.989	C-129, 1B-3, OF-1
1979		119	.286	.422	398	114	21	3	9	2.3	38	58	49	33	1	1	0	527	66	8	8	5.1	.987	C-117, 3B-2
1980		141	.229	.338	480	110	23	1	9	1.9	34	55	48	41	3	4	1	741	88	18	7	6.0	.979	C-138
1981		76	.211	.295	227	48	7	0	4	1.8	19	24	22	16	2	4	0	365	32	6	1	5.3	.985	C-75
1982	CAL A	143	.256	.337	472	121	17	0	7	1.5	42	58	39	34	0	0	0	650	87	8	8	5.2	.989	C-143
1983		142	.256	.353	468	120	18	0	9	1.9	46	52	24	42	4	0	0	606	83	14	8	5.0	.980	C-142
1984		139	.202	.262	450	91	16	1	3	0.7	33	32	25	45	3	2	2	660	71	12	10	5.3	.984	C-137
1985		150	.248	.317	460	114	17	0	5	1.1	37	55	37	35	1	2	2	670	71	10	15	5.0	.987	C-147
1986		144	.222	.305	442	98	12	2	7	1.6	48	49	43	30	1	0	0	812	84	11	16	6.3	.988	C-144
1987		128	.242	.311	389	94	18	0	3	0.8	42	33	35	36	0	1	1	684	56	13	11	5.9	.983	C-121, DH-1
1988		122	.295	.386	352	104	17	0	5	1.4	38	39	29	26	2	1	1	506	66	9	8	4.8	.986	C-121
1989	KC	131	.274	.323	405	111	13	2	1	0.2	33	43	49	37	3	1	0	752	64	7	6	6.3	.991	C-129
18 yrs.		2224	.254	.348	7128	1810	300	26	105	1.5	668	817	646	596	37	44	14	11082	1166	179	155	5.6	.986	C-2185, 3B-7, 1B-7, DH-1, OF-1

DIVISIONAL PLAYOFF SERIES

Year	Team	Games	BA	SA	AB	H	2B	3B	HR	HR%	R	RBI	BB	SO	SB	PH AB	PH H	PO	A	E	DP	TC/G	FA	G by Pos
1981	PHI N	3	.000	.000	5	0	0	0	0	0.0	0	0	0	0	0	0	0	0	0	0	0	0.0	–	C-3

LEAGUE CHAMPIONSHIP SERIES

Year	Team	Games	BA	SA	AB	H	2B	3B	HR	HR%	R	RBI	BB	SO	SB	PH AB	PH H	PO	A	E	DP	TC/G	FA	G by Pos
1976	PHI N	3	.286	.286	7	2	0	0	0	0.0	1	1	0	0	0	0	0	8	2	0	0	3.3	1.000	C-3
1977		4	.400	.400	10	4	0	0	0	0.0	1	0	0	0	0	0	0	18	2	0	1	5.0	1.000	C-4
1978		3	.182	.182	11	2	0	0	0	0.0	0	0	0	1	0	0	0	16	2	1	0	6.3	.947	C-3
1980		5	.222	.222	18	4	0	0	0	0.0	1	2	1	2	0	0	0	22	3	0	1	5.0	1.000	C-5
1982	CAL A	5	.250	.438	16	4	0	0	1	6.3	3	4	0	2	0	0	0	0	0	0	0	0.0	–	C-5
1986		7	.455	.591	22	10	0	0	1	4.5	4	2	1	3	0	0	0	35	4	0	0	5.6	1.000	C-7
6 yrs.		27	.310	.381	84	26	0	0	2	2.4	9	9	3	8	0	0	0	99	13	1	2	4.2	.991	C-27

WORLD SERIES

Year	Team	Games	BA	SA	AB	H	2B	3B	HR	HR%	R	RBI	BB	SO	SB	PH AB	PH H	PO	A	E	DP	TC/G	FA	G by Pos
1980	PHI N	6	.412	.529	17	7	2	0	0	0.0	3	4	4	0	0	0	0	49	3	0	0	8.7	1.000	C-6

Ike Boone

BOONE, ISAAC MORGAN
Brother of Danny Boone.
B. Feb. 17, 1897, Samantha, Ala.   D. Aug. 1, 1958, Northport, Ala.

BL TR 6'   195 lbs.

Year	Team	Games	BA	SA	AB	H	2B	3B	HR	HR%	R	RBI	BB	SO	SB	PH AB	PH H	PO	A	E	DP	TC/G	FA	G by Pos
1922	NY N	2	.500	.500	2	1	0	0	0	0.0	0	0	0	1	0	0	0	0	0	0	0	0.0	–	
1923	BOS A	5	.267	.400	15	4	0	1	0	0.0	1	2	1	0	0	0	0	13	0	1	0	2.8	.929	OF-4
1924		128	.333	.486	486	162	29	3	13	2.7	71	96	55	32	2	4	1	189	17	5	3	1.6	.976	OF-123
1925		133	.330	.479	476	157	34	5	9	1.9	79	68	60	19	1	11	3	198	9	13	1	1.7	.941	OF-118
1927	CHI A	29	.226	.358	53	12	4	0	1	1.9	10	11	3	4	0	16	3	15	0	0	0	0.5	1.000	OF-11
1930	BKN N	40	.297	.495	101	30	9	1	3	3.0	13	13	14	9	3	14	4	47	1	2	0	1.3	.960	OF-27
1931		6	.200	.200	5	1	0	0	0	0.0	0	0	2	2	0	5	1	0	0	0	0	0.0	–	
1932		13	.143	.190	21	3	1	0	0	0.0	2	2	5	2	0	5	0	8	1	0	1	0.7	1.000	OF-8
8 yrs.		356	.319	.470	1159	370	77	10	26	2.2	176	192	140	68	3	53	12	470	28	21	5	1.5	.960	OF-291

Luke Boone

BOONE, LUTE JOSEPH (Danny)
B. May 6, 1890, Pittsburgh, Pa.   D. July 29, 1982, Pittsburgh, Pa.

BR TR 5'9"   160 lbs.

Year	Team	Games	BA	SA	AB	H	2B	3B	HR	HR%	R	RBI	BB	SO	SB	PH AB	PH H	PO	A	E	DP	TC/G	FA	G by Pos
1913	NY A	5	.333	.333	12	4	0	0	0	0.0	3	1	3	1	0	1	0	8	10	3	0	4.2	.857	SS-4
1914		106	.222	.254	370	82	8	2	0	0.0	34	21	31	41	10	5	0	249	310	25	33	5.5	.957	2B-90, 3B-9
1915		130	.204	.276	431	88	12	2	5	1.2	44	43	41	53	14	0	0	271	419	24	61	5.5	.966	2B-115, SS-12, 3B-3
1916		46	.185	.242	124	23	4	0	1	0.8	14	8	8	10	7	0	0	58	108	13	11	3.9	.927	3B-25, SS-12, 2B-7
1918	PIT N	27	.198	.231	91	18	3	0	0	0.0	7	3	8	6	1	0	0	56	85	12	6	5.7	.922	SS-26, 2B-1
5 yrs.		314	.209	.261	1028	215	27	4	6	0.6	102	76	91	111	32	6	0	642	932	77	111	5.3	.953	2B-213, SS-54, 3B-37

Ray Boone

BOONE, RAYMOND OTIS (Ike)
Father of Bob Boone.
B. July 27, 1923, San Diego, Calif.

BR TR 6'   172 lbs.

Year	Team	Games	BA	SA	AB	H	2B	3B	HR	HR%	R	RBI	BB	SO	SB	PH AB	PH H	PO	A	E	DP	TC/G	FA	G by Pos
1948	CLE A	6	.400	.600	5	2	1	0	0	0.0	0	1	0	1	0	1	0	3	5	1	0	1.5	.889	SS-4
1949		86	.252	.345	258	65	4	4	4	1.6	39	26	38	17	0	7	1	162	210	21	58	4.6	.947	SS-76
1950		109	.301	.430	365	110	14	6	7	1.9	53	58	56	27	4	6	0	178	267	26	64	4.3	.945	SS-102
1951		151	.233	.329	544	127	14	1	12	2.2	65	51	48	36	5	0	0	311	425	33	108	5.1	.957	SS-151
1952		103	.263	.367	316	83	8	2	7	2.2	57	45	53	33	0	4	0	180	254	28	57	4.5	.939	SS-96, 3B-2, 2B-1
1953	2 teams																							
"	total	CLE A (34G – .241)			DET A (101G – .312)																			
"	total	135	.296	.519	497	147	17	8	26	5.2	94	114	72	68	3	4	1	179	313	23	58	3.8	.955	3B-97, SS-34
1954	DET A	148	.295	.466	543	160	19	7	20	3.7	76	85	71	53	4	4	0	170	332	19	22	3.6	.964	3B-148, SS-1
1955		135	.284	.476	500	142	22	7	20	4.0	61	**116**	50	49	1	8	2	135	252	19	33	3.0	.953	3B-126
1956		131	.308	.518	481	148	14	6	25	5.2	77	81	77	46	0	0	0	151	243	17	23	3.1	.959	3B-130
1957		129	.273	.418	462	126	25	3	12	2.6	48	65	57	47	1	5	1	977	57	12	103	8.1	.989	1B-117, 3B-4
1958	2 teams	DET A (39G – .237)			CHI A (77G – .244)																			
"	total	116	.242	.406	360	87	16	4	13	3.6	41	61	32	46	1	21	2	747	49	11	71	7.0	.986	1B-95
1959	3 teams	CHI A (9G – .238)			KC A (61G – .273)			MIL N (13G – .200)																
"	total	83	.262	.369	168	44	6	0	4	2.4	25	19	38	24	2	37	11	333	35	7	26	4.5	.981	1B-47, 3B-3
1960	2 teams	MIL N (7G – .250)			BOS A (34G – .205)																			
"	total	41	.211	.267	90	19	2	0	1	1.1	9	15	16	16	0	15	3	199	14	1	22	5.2	.995	1B-26
13 yrs.		1373	.275	.429	4589	1260	162	46	151	3.3	645	737	608	463	21	108	21	3725	2456	218	645	4.7	.966	3B-510, SS-464, 1B-285, 2B-1

WORLD SERIES

Year	Team	Games	BA	SA	AB	H	2B	3B	HR	HR%	R	RBI	BB	SO	SB	PH AB	PH H	PO	A	E	DP	TC/G	FA	G by Pos
1948	CLE A	1	.000	.000	1	0	0	0	0	0.0	0	0	0	1	0	1	0	0	0	0	0	0.0	–	

Amos Booth

BOOTH, AMOS SMITH (The Darling)
B. Sept. 4, 1852, Cincinnati, Ohio   D. July 1, 1921, Miamisburg, Ohio

BR TR

Year	Team	Games	BA	SA	AB	H	2B	3B	HR	HR%	R	RBI	BB	SO	SB	PH AB	PH H	PO	A	E	DP	TC/G	FA	G by Pos
1876	CIN N	63	.261	.272	272	71	3	0	0	0.0	31	14	9	11				138	117	76	10	5.3	.770	3B-24, C-24, SS-22, OF-3, P-3

Year	Team		Games	BA	SA	AB	H	2B	3B	HR	HR%	R	RBI	BB	SO	SB	Pinch Hit AB	Pinch Hit H	PO	A	E	DP	TC/G	FA	G by Pos

Amos Booth *continued*

Year	Team		Games	BA	SA	AB	H	2B	3B	HR	HR%	R	RBI	BB	SO	SB	AB	H	PO	A	E	DP	TC/G	FA	G by Pos
1877			44	.172	.197	157	27	2	1	0	0.0	16	13	12	10		0	0	77	101	36	6	4.9	.832	SS-13, C-12, P-12, 2B-10, 3B-3, OF-1
1880			1	.000	.000	2	0	0	0	0	0.0	0	0	0	0		0	0	0	0	0	0	0.0	—	3B-1
1882	2 teams		BAL AA (1G – .000)		LOU AA (1G – .000)																				
"	total		2	.000	.000	7	0	0	0	0	0.0	0		0			0	0	3	3	0	0	3.0	1.000	3B-1, 2B-1
4 yrs.			110	.224	.240	438	98	5	1	0	0.0	47	27	21	21		0	0	218	221	112	16	5.0	.797	C-36, SS-35, 3B-29, P-15, 2B-11, OF-4

Eddie Booth

BOOTH, EDWARD H.
B. Brooklyn, N. Y.

Year	Team		Games	BA	SA	AB	H	2B	3B	HR	HR%	R	RBI	BB	SO	SB	AB	H	PO	A	E	DP	TC/G	FA	G by Pos
1876	NY	N	57	.215	.232	228	49	2	1	0	0.0	17	7	2	4		0	0	88	18	31	1	2.4	.774	OF-53, 2B-5, P-1

Frenchy Bordagaray

BORDAGARAY, STANLEY GEORGE
B. Jan. 3, 1910, Coalinga, Calif.   BR TR 5'7½" 175 lbs.

Year	Team		Games	BA	SA	AB	H	2B	3B	HR	HR%	R	RBI	BB	SO	SB	AB	H	PO	A	E	DP	TC/G	FA	G by Pos
1934	CHI	A	29	.322	.379	87	28	3	1	0	0.0	12	2	3	8	1	12	8	28	2	2	0	1.1	.938	OF-17
1935	BKN	N	120	.282	.363	422	119	19	6	1	0.2	69	39	17	29	18	9	2	227	14	5	2	2.1	.980	OF-105
1936			125	.315	.419	372	117	21	3	4	1.1	63	31	17	42	12	6	2	230	39	8	3	2.2	.971	OF-92, 2B-11
1937	STL	N	96	.293	.367	300	88	11	4	1	0.3	43	37	15	25	11	16	1	105	72	9	2	1.9	.952	3B-50, OF-28
1938			81	.282	.327	156	44	5	1	0	0.0	19	21	8	9	2	**43**	**20**	72	9	6	0	1.1	.931	OF-29, 3B-4
1939	CIN	N	63	.197	.254	122	24	5	1	0	0.0	19	12	9	10	3	11	0	67	7	1	2	1.2	.987	OF-43, 2B-2
1941	NY	A	36	.260	.274	73	19	1	0	0	0.0	10	4	6	8	1	13	4	28	1	1	1	0.8	.967	OF-19
1942	BKN	N	48	.241	.276	58	14	2	0	0	0.0	11	5	3	3	2	15	4	22	0	0	0	0.5	1.000	OF-17
1943			89	.302	.384	268	81	18	2	0	0.0	47	19	30	15	6	6	2	115	32	8	2	1.7	.948	OF-53, 3B-25
1944			130	.281	.385	501	141	26	4	6	1.2	85	51	36	22	2	10	3	180	151	17	14	2.7	.951	3B-98, OF-25
1945			113	.256	.355	273	70	9	6	2	0.7	32	49	29	15	7	32	8	86	93	19	7	1.8	.904	3B-57, OF-22
11 yrs.			930	.283	.366	2632	745	120	28	14	0.5	410	270	173	186	65	173	54	1160	420	76	33	1.8	.954	OF-450, 3B-234, 2B-13

WORLD SERIES

Year	Team		Games	BA	SA	AB	H	2B	3B	HR	HR%	R	RBI	BB	SO	SB	AB	H	PO	A	E	DP	TC/G	FA	G by Pos
1939	CIN	N	2	—	—	0	0	0	0	0	—	0	0	0	0	0	0	0	0	0	0	0	0.0	—	
1941	NY	A	1	—	—	0	0	0	0	0	—	0	0	0	0	0	0	0	0	0	0	0	0.0	—	
2 yrs.			3	—	—	0	0	0	0	0	—	0	0	0	0	0	0	0	0	0	0	0	0.0	—	

Pat Borders

BORDERS, PATRICK LANCE
B. May 14, 1963, Columbus, Ohio   BR TR 6'2" 190 lbs.

Year	Team		Games	BA	SA	AB	H	2B	3B	HR	HR%	R	RBI	BB	SO	SB	AB	H	PO	A	E	DP	TC/G	FA	G by Pos
1988	TOR	A	56	.273	.448	154	42	6	3	5	3.2	15	21	3	24	0	15	5	205	19	7	0	4.1	.970	C-43, 3B-1, 2B-1
1989			94	.257	.349	241	62	11	1	3	1.2	22	29	11	45	2	20	5	261	27	6	1	3.1	.980	C-68, DH-18
2 yrs.			150	.263	.387	395	104	17	4	8	2.0	37	50	14	69	2	35	10	466	46	13	1	3.5	.975	C-111, DH-18, 3B-1, 2B-1

LEAGUE CHAMPIONSHIP SERIES

Year	Team		Games	BA	SA	AB	H	2B	3B	HR	HR%	R	RBI	BB	SO	SB	AB	H	PO	A	E	DP	TC/G	FA	G by Pos
1989	TOR	A	1	1.000	1.000	1	1	0	0	0	0.0	0	1	0	0	0	1	1	1	0	0	0	1.0	1.000	C-1

Glenn Borgmann

BORGMANN, GLENN DENNIS
B. May 25, 1950, Paterson, N. J.   BR TR 6'4" 210 lbs.

Year	Team		Games	BA	SA	AB	H	2B	3B	HR	HR%	R	RBI	BB	SO	SB	AB	H	PO	A	E	DP	TC/G	FA	G by Pos
1972	MIN	A	56	.234	.309	175	41	4	0	3	1.7	11	14	25	25	0	0	0	304	31	12	4	6.2	.965	C-56
1973			12	.265	.324	34	9	2	0	0	0.0	7	9	6	10	0	0	0	55	2	0	0	4.8	1.000	C-12
1974			128	.252	.307	345	87	8	1	3	0.9	33	45	39	44	2	4	0	652	52	2	4	5.5	.997	C-128
1975			125	.207	.278	352	73	15	2	2	0.6	34	33	47	59	0	2	0	618	81	8	6	5.7	.989	C-125
1976			24	.246	.338	65	16	3	0	1	1.5	10	6	19	7	1	1	1	110	13	3	1	5.3	.976	C-24
1977			17	.256	.419	43	11	1	0	2	4.7	12	7	11	9	0	0	0	70	8	0	1	4.6	1.000	C-17
1978			49	.211	.333	123	26	4	1	3	2.4	16	15	18	17	0	3	1	185	20	2	6	4.2	.990	C-46, DH-1
1979			31	.200	.243	70	14	3	0	0	0.0	4	8	12	11	1	0	0	129	11	1	0	4.5	.993	C-31
1980	CHI	A	32	.218	.310	87	19	2	0	2	2.3	10	14	14	9	0	1	0	134	18	0	1	4.8	1.000	C-32
9 yrs.			474	.229	.304	1294	296	42	4	16	1.2	137	151	191	191	4	11	2	2257	236	28	23	5.3	.989	C-471, DH-1

Bob Borkowski

BORKOWSKI, ROBERT VILARIAN (Bush)
B. Jan. 27, 1926, Dayton, Ohio   BR TR 6' 182 lbs.

Year	Team		Games	BA	SA	AB	H	2B	3B	HR	HR%	R	RBI	BB	SO	SB	AB	H	PO	A	E	DP	TC/G	FA	G by Pos
1950	CHI	N	85	.273	.379	256	70	7	4	4	1.6	27	29	16	30	1	14	2	155	4	4	1	1.9	.975	OF-65, 1B-1
1951			58	.157	.169	89	14	1	0	0	0.0	9	10	3	16	0	23	3	41	1	3	0	0.8	.933	OF-25
1952	CIN	N	126	.252	.334	377	95	11	4	4	1.1	42	24	26	53	1	18	3	258	8	3	4	2.1	.989	OF-103, 1B-5
1953			94	.269	.406	249	67	11	1	7	2.8	32	29	21	41	0	27	9	114	3	3	1	1.3	.975	OF-67, 1B-2
1954			73	.265	.370	162	43	12	1	1	0.6	13	19	8	18	0	33	8	82	3	0	1	1.2	1.000	OF-36, 1B-3
1955	2 teams		CIN N (25G – .167)		BKN N (9G – .105)																				
"	total		34	.135	.162	37	5	1	0	0	0.0	3	1	2	8	0	9	2	18	1	1	1	0.6	.950	OF-20, 1B-1
6 yrs.			470	.251	.346	1170	294	43	10	16	1.4	126	112	76	166	2	124	27	668	20	14	8	1.5	.980	OF-316, 1B-12

Red Borom

BOROM, EDWARD JONES
B. Oct. 30, 1915, Spartanburg, S. C.   BL TR 5'11" 180 lbs.

Year	Team		Games	BA	SA	AB	H	2B	3B	HR	HR%	R	RBI	BB	SO	SB	AB	H	PO	A	E	DP	TC/G	FA	G by Pos
1944	DET	A	7	.071	.071	14	1	0	0	0	0.0	1	1	2	2	0	2	0	6	14	2	1	3.1	.909	2B-4, SS-1
1945			55	.269	.300	130	35	4	0	0	0.0	19	9	7	8	4	12	2	66	93	6	16	3.0	.964	2B-28, 3B-4, SS-2
2 yrs.			62	.250	.278	144	36	4	0	0	0.0	20	10	9	10	4	14	2	72	107	8	17	3.0	.957	2B-32, 3B-4, SS-3

WORLD SERIES

Year	Team		Games	BA	SA	AB	H	2B	3B	HR	HR%	R	RBI	BB	SO	SB	AB	H	PO	A	E	DP	TC/G	FA	G by Pos
1945	DET	A	2	.000	.000	1	0	0	0	0	0.0	0	0	0	0	0	1	0	0	0	0	0	0.0	—	

Steve Boros

BOROS, STEPHEN
B. Sept. 3, 1936, Flint, Mich.
Manager 1983-84, 1986.   BR TR 6' 185 lbs.

Year	Team		Games	BA	SA	AB	H	2B	3B	HR	HR%	R	RBI	BB	SO	SB	AB	H	PO	A	E	DP	TC/G	FA	G by Pos
1957	DET	A	24	.146	.171	41	6	1	0	0	0.0	4	2	1	4	0	4	0	8	27	3	1	1.6	.921	3B-9, SS-5
1958			6	.000	.000	2	0	0	0	0	0.0	0	0	0	0	0	0	0	2	0	0	0	0.3	1.000	2B-1
1961			116	.270	.364	396	107	18	2	5	1.3	51	62	68	42	4	0	0	115	192	15	15	2.8	.953	3B-116
1962			116	.228	.407	356	81	14	1	16	4.5	46	47	53	62	3	8	0	118	163	21	19	2.6	.930	3B-105, 2B-6
1963	CHI	N	41	.211	.389	90	19	5	1	3	3.3	9	7	12	19	0	17	2	126	7	4	7	3.3	.971	1B-14, OF-11

Year	Team		Games	BA	SA	AB	H	2B	3B	HR	HR%	R	RBI	BB	SO	SB	Pinch Hit AB	Pinch Hit H	PO	A	E	DP	TC/G	FA	G by Pos

Steve Boros *continued*

Year	Team		Games	BA	SA	AB	H	2B	3B	HR	HR%	R	RBI	BB	SO	SB	PH AB	PH H	PO	A	E	DP	TC/G	FA	G by Pos
1964	CIN	N	117	.257	.322	370	95	12	3	2	0.5	31	31	47	43	4	1	0	95	204	12	18	2.7	.961	3B-114
1965			2	–	–	0	0	0	0	0	–	0	0	0	0	0	0	0	0	1	0	0	0.5	1.000	3B-2
7 yrs.			422	.245	.359	1255	308	50	7	26	2.1	141	149	181	174	11	30	2	464	594	55	60	2.6	.951	3B-346, 1B-14, OF-11, 2B-7, SS-5

Babe Borton

BORTON, WILLIAM BAKER
B. Aug. 14, 1888, Marion, Ill. D. July 29, 1954, Berkeley, Calif.
BL TL 6' 178 lbs.

Year	Team		Games	BA	SA	AB	H	2B	3B	HR	HR%	R	RBI	BB	SO	SB	PH AB	PH H	PO	A	E	DP	TC/G	FA	G by Pos
1912	CHI	A	31	.371	.419	105	39	3	1	0	0.0	15	17	8		1	1	1	312	16	1	14	10.6	.997	1B-30
1913	2 teams		CHI	A	(28G – .275)		NY	A	(33G – .130)																
"	total		61	.191	.239	188	36	6	0	1	0.5	17	24	41	24	2	2	0	632	44	11	35	11.3	.984	1B-59
1915	STL	F	159	.286	.390	549	157	20	14	3	0.5	97	83	92		17	0	0	1571	58	12	91	10.3	.993	1B-159
1916	STL	A	66	.224	.306	98	22	1	2	1	1.0	10	12	19	13	1	35	6	205	8	2	7	3.3	.991	1B-22
4 yrs.			317	.270	.354	940	254	30	17	5	0.5	139	136	160	37	21	38	7	2720	126	26	147	9.1	.991	1B-270

Don Bosch

BOSCH, DONALD JOHN
B. July 15, 1942, San Francisco, Calif.
BB TR 5'10" 160 lbs.

Year	Team		Games	BA	SA	AB	H	2B	3B	HR	HR%	R	RBI	BB	SO	SB	PH AB	PH H	PO	A	E	DP	TC/G	FA	G by Pos
1966	PIT	N	3	.000	.000	2	0	0	0	0	0.0	0	0	0	0	0	1	0	0	0	0	0	0.0	–	OF-1
1967	NY	N	44	.140	.161	93	13	0	1	0	0.0	7	2	5	24	3	3	0	55	2	0	0	1.3	1.000	OF-39
1968			50	.171	.261	111	19	1	0	3	2.7	14	7	9	33	0	9	1	73	3	2	1	1.6	.974	OF-33
1969	MON	N	49	.179	.250	112	20	5	0	1	0.9	13	4	8	20	1	15	2	52	1	2	0	1.1	.964	OF-32
4 yrs.			146	.164	.226	318	52	6	1	4	1.3	34	13	22	77	4	28	3	180	6	4	1	1.3	.979	OF-105

Rick Bosetti

BOSETTI, RICHARD ALAN
B. Aug. 5, 1953, Redding, Calif.
BR TR 5'11" 185 lbs.

Year	Team		Games	BA	SA	AB	H	2B	3B	HR	HR%	R	RBI	BB	SO	SB	PH AB	PH H	PO	A	E	DP	TC/G	FA	G by Pos
1976	PHI	N	13	.278	.333	18	5	1	0	0	0.0	6	0	1	3	3	1	0	9	1	0	0	0.8	1.000	OF-6
1977	STL	N	41	.232	.232	69	16	0	0	0	0.0	12	3	6	11	4	2	0	42	3	0	0	1.1	1.000	OF-35
1978	TOR	A	136	.259	.347	568	147	25	5	5	0.9	61	42	30	65	6	0	0	417	17	6	1	3.2	.986	OF-135
1979			162	.260	.362	619	161	35	2	8	1.3	59	65	22	70	13	0	0	466	18	13	4	3.1	.974	OF-162
1980			53	.213	.324	188	40	7	1	4	2.1	24	18	15	29	4	1	0	124	2	2	0	2.5	.985	OF-51
1981	2 teams		TOR	A	(25G – .234)		OAK	A	(9G – .105)																
"	total		34	.197	.227	66	13	2	0	0	0.0	9	5	5	9	0	3	1	40	0	0	0	1.2	1.000	OF-24, DH-3
1982	OAK	A	6	.200	.200	15	3	0	0	0	0.0	1	0	0	1	0	0	0	14	2	0	0	2.7	1.000	OF-6
7 yrs.			445	.250	.338	1543	385	70	8	17	1.1	172	133	79	188	30	7	1	1112	45	21	5	2.6	.982	OF-419, DH-3

DIVISIONAL PLAYOFF SERIES

Year	Team		Games	BA	SA	AB	H	2B	3B	HR	HR%	R	RBI	BB	SO	SB	PH AB	PH H	PO	A	E	DP	TC/G	FA	G by Pos
1981	OAK	A	1	–	–	0	0	0	0	0	–	0	0	0	0	0	0	0	0	0	0	0	0.0	–	OF-1

LEAGUE CHAMPIONSHIP SERIES

Year	Team		Games	BA	SA	AB	H	2B	3B	HR	HR%	R	RBI	BB	SO	SB	PH AB	PH H	PO	A	E	DP	TC/G	FA	G by Pos
1981	OAK	A	2	.250	.500	4	1	1	0	0	0.0	1	0	0	1	0	1	0	0	0	0	0	0.0	–	DH-1, OF-1

Thad Bosley

BOSLEY, THADDIS
B. Sept. 17, 1956, Oceanside, Calif.
BL TL 6'3" 175 lbs.

Year	Team		Games	BA	SA	AB	H	2B	3B	HR	HR%	R	RBI	BB	SO	SB	PH AB	PH H	PO	A	E	DP	TC/G	FA	G by Pos
1977	CAL	A	58	.297	.363	212	63	10	2	0	0.0	19	19	16	32	5	4	1	130	1	5	0	2.3	.963	OF-55
1978	CHI	A	66	.269	.329	219	59	5	2	2	0.9	25	13	13	32	12	1	0	155	3	4	0	2.5	.975	OF-64
1979			36	.312	.390	77	24	1	1	1	1.3	13	8	9	14	4	7	1	57	2	2	1	1.7	.967	OF-28, DH-1
1980			70	.224	.279	147	33	2	0	2	1.4	12	14	10	27	3	25	8	91	1	4	0	1.4	.958	OF-52
1981	MIL	A	42	.229	.248	105	24	2	0	0	0.0	11	3	6	13	2	4	0	55	1	2	0	1.4	.966	OF-37, DH-1
1982	SEA	A	22	.174	.196	46	8	1	0	0	0.0	3	2	4	8	3	3	0	12	0	0	0	0.6	1.000	OF-19
1983	CHI	N	43	.292	.458	72	21	4	1	2	2.8	12	12	10	12	1	18	4	27	1	0	1	0.7	1.000	OF-20
1984			55	.296	.418	98	29	2	2	2	2.0	17	14	13	22	5	23	6	39	2	1	0	0.8	.976	OF-33
1985			108	.328	.511	180	59	6	3	7	3.9	25	27	20	29	5	60	20	84	0	1	0	0.8	.988	OF-55
1986			87	.275	.350	120	33	4	1	1	0.8	15	9	18	24	3	51	16	31	0	1	0	0.4	.969	OF-41
1987	KC	A	80	.279	.357	140	39	6	1	1	0.7	13	16	9	26	1	42	12	28	0	1	0	0.4	.966	OF-28, DH-13
1988	2 teams		KC	A	(15G – .190)		CAL	A	(35G – .280)																
"	total		50	.260	.313	96	25	5	0	0	0.0	10	9	8	18	1	10	3	59	0	2	0	1.2	.967	OF-32, DH-6
1989	TEX	A	37	.225	.350	40	9	2	0	1	2.5	5	9	3	11	2	28	7	12	1	0	1	0.4	1.000	OF-8, DH-5
13 yrs.			754	.274	.359	1552	426	50	12	19	1.2	180	155	139	268	46	276	79	780	13	23	3	1.1	.972	OF-472, DH-26

DIVISIONAL PLAYOFF SERIES

Year	Team		Games	BA	SA	AB	H	2B	3B	HR	HR%	R	RBI	BB	SO	SB	PH AB	PH H	PO	A	E	DP	TC/G	FA	G by Pos
1981	MIL	A	1	–	–	0	0	0	0	0	–	0	0	0	0	0	0	0	0	0	0	0	0.0	–	DH-1

LEAGUE CHAMPIONSHIP SERIES

Year	Team		Games	BA	SA	AB	H	2B	3B	HR	HR%	R	RBI	BB	SO	SB	PH AB	PH H	PO	A	E	DP	TC/G	FA	G by Pos
1984	CHI	N	2	.000	.000	2	0	0	0	0	0.0	0	0	0	2	0	2	0	0	0	0	0	0.0	–	

Harley Boss

BOSS, ELMER HARLEY (Lefty)
B. Nov. 19, 1908, Hodge, La. D. May 15, 1964, Nashville, Tenn.
BL TL 5'11½" 185 lbs.

Year	Team		Games	BA	SA	AB	H	2B	3B	HR	HR%	R	RBI	BB	SO	SB	PH AB	PH H	PO	A	E	DP	TC/G	FA	G by Pos
1928	WAS	A	12	.250	.250	12	3	0	0	0	0.0	1	2	3	1	0	4	0	32	0	1	2	2.8	.970	1B-5
1929			28	.273	.333	66	18	2	1	0	0.0	9	6	2	6	0	9	1	119	9	3	13	4.7	.977	1B-18
1930			3	.000	.000	3	0	0	0	0	0.0	0	0	0	0	0	2	0	2	0	0	0	0.7	1.000	1B-1
1933	CLE	A	112	.269	.347	438	118	17	7	1	0.2	54	53	25	27	2	3	0	1062	71	7	89	10.2	.994	1B-110
4 yrs.			155	.268	.341	519	139	19	8	1	0.2	64	61	30	34	2	18	1	1215	80	11	104	8.4	.992	1B-134

Henry Bostick

BOSTICK, HENRY LANDERS
Born Henry Landers Lifsit.
B. Jan. 12, 1895, Boston, Mass. D. Sept. 16, 1968, Denver, Colo.
BR TR

Year	Team		Games	BA	SA	AB	H	2B	3B	HR	HR%	R	RBI	BB	SO	SB	PH AB	PH H	PO	A	E	DP	TC/G	FA	G by Pos
1915	PHI	A	2	.000	.000	7	0	0	0	0	0.0	0	2	1	1	0	0	0	0	2	0	0	1.0	1.000	3B-2

Lyman Bostock

BOSTOCK, LYMAN WESLEY
B. Nov. 22, 1950, Birmingham, Ala. D. Sept. 23, 1978, Gary, Ind.
BL TR 6'1" 180 lbs.

Year	Team		Games	BA	SA	AB	H	2B	3B	HR	HR%	R	RBI	BB	SO	SB	PH AB	PH H	PO	A	E	DP	TC/G	FA	G by Pos
1975	MIN	A	98	.282	.366	369	104	21	5	0	0.0	52	29	28	42	2	2	0	188	3	3	0	2.0	.985	OF-92, DH-1
1976			128	.323	.430	474	153	21	9	4	0.8	75	60	33	37	12	9	4	320	10	4	2	2.6	.988	OF-124
1977			153	.336	.508	593	199	36	12	14	2.4	104	90	51	59	16	10	1	349	10	4	0	2.4	.989	OF-149

Year	Team		Games	BA	SA	AB	H	2B	3B	HR	HR%	R	RBI	BB	SO	SB	Pinch Hit AB	H	PO	A	E	DP	TC/G	FA	G by Pos

Lyman Bostock *continued*

Year	Team		Games	BA	SA	AB	H	2B	3B	HR	HR%	R	RBI	BB	SO	SB	AB	H	PO	A	E	DP	TC/G	FA	G by Pos
1978	CAL	A	147	.296	.379	568	168	24	4	5	0.9	74	71	59	36	15	1	0	366	7	4	2	2.6	.989	OF-146, DH-1
4 yrs.			526	.311	.427	2004	624	102	30	23	1.1	305	250	171	174	45	22	5	1223	30	15	4	2.4	.988	OF-511, DH-2

Daryl Boston

BOSTON, DARYL LAMONT
B. Jan. 4, 1963, Cincinnati, Ohio   BL TL 6'3"   185 lbs.

Year	Team		Games	BA	SA	AB	H	2B	3B	HR	HR%	R	RBI	BB	SO	SB	AB	H	PO	A	E	DP	TC/G	FA	G by Pos
1984	CHI	A	35	.169	.229	83	14	3	1	0	0.0	8	3	4	20	6	2	1	59	2	6	1	1.9	.910	OF-34, DH-1
1985			95	.228	.332	232	53	13	1	3	1.3	20	15	14	44	8	5	1	179	7	2	1	2.0	.989	OF-93, DH-2
1986			56	.266	.427	199	53	11	3	5	2.5	29	22	21	33	9	1	0	152	3	5	1	2.9	.969	OF-53, DH-1
1987			103	.258	.421	337	87	21	2	10	3.0	51	29	25	68	12	10	2	207	3	2	3	2.1	.991	OF-92, DH-5
1988			105	.217	.434	281	61	12	2	15	5.3	37	31	21	44	9	13	3	190	4	10	2	1.9	.951	OF-85, DH-5
1989			101	.252	.372	218	55	3	4	5	2.3	34	23	24	31	7	16	4	134	2	4	0	1.4	.971	OF-75, DH-9
6 yrs.			495	.239	.390	1350	323	63	13	38	2.8	179	123	109	240	51	47	11	921	21	29	8	2.0	.970	OF-432, DH-23

Ken Boswell

BOSWELL, KENNETH GEORGE
B. Feb. 23, 1946, Austin, Tex.   BL TR 6'   170 lbs.

Year	Team		Games	BA	SA	AB	H	2B	3B	HR	HR%	R	RBI	BB	SO	SB	AB	H	PO	A	E	DP	TC/G	FA	G by Pos
1967	NY	N	11	.225	.375	40	9	3	0	1	2.5	2	4	1	5	0	1	0	12	34	1	5	4.3	.979	2B-6, 3B-4
1968			75	.261	.342	284	74	7	2	4	1.4	37	11	16	27	7	6	1	154	203	13	37	4.9	.965	2B-69
1969			102	.279	.381	362	101	14	7	3	0.8	48	32	36	47	7	10	1	190	229	18	51	4.3	.959	2B-96
1970			105	.254	.345	351	89	13	2	5	1.4	32	44	41	32	5	7	2	204	244	2	49	4.3	.996	2B-101
1971			116	.273	.367	392	107	20	1	5	1.3	46	40	36	31	5	7	0	191	234	12	56	3.8	.973	2B-109
1972			100	.211	.318	355	75	9	1	9	2.5	35	33	32	35	2	7	1	208	183	4	53	4.0	.990	2B-94
1973			76	.227	.318	110	25	2	1	2	1.8	12	14	12	11	0	51	12	15	33	2	3	0.7	.960	3B-17, 2B-3
1974			96	.216	.279	222	48	6	1	2	0.9	19	15	18	19	0	42	9	94	113	6	18	2.2	.972	2B-28, 3B-20, OF-7
1975	HOU	N	86	.242	.309	178	43	8	2	0	0.0	16	21	30	12	0	35	6	54	103	6	13	1.9	.963	2B-31, 3B-23
1976			91	.262	.341	126	33	8	1	0	0.0	12	18	8	8	1	65	20	8	21	2	4	0.3	.935	3B-16, 2B-3, OF-1
1977			72	.216	.247	97	21	1	1	0	0.0	7	12	10	12	0	53	14	33	35	0	9	0.9	1.000	2B-26, 3B-2
11 yrs.			930	.248	.337	2517	625	91	19	31	1.2	266	244	240	239	27	284	66	1163	1432	66	298	2.9	.975	2B-566, 3B-82, OF-8

LEAGUE CHAMPIONSHIP SERIES

Year	Team		Games	BA	SA	AB	H	2B	3B	HR	HR%	R	RBI	BB	SO	SB	AB	H	PO	A	E	DP	TC/G	FA	G by Pos
1969	NY	N	3	.333	.833	12	4	0	0	2	16.7	4	5	1	2	0	0	0	3	2	1	1	2.0	.833	2B-3
1973			1	.000	.000	1	0	0	0	0	0.0	0	0	0	0	0	1	0	0	0	0	0	0.0	—	
2 yrs.			4	.308	.769	13	4	0	0	2	15.4	4	5	1	2	0	1	0	3	2	1	1	1.5	.833	2B-3

WORLD SERIES

Year	Team		Games	BA	SA	AB	H	2B	3B	HR	HR%	R	RBI	BB	SO	SB	AB	H	PO	A	E	DP	TC/G	FA	G by Pos
1969	NY	N	1	.333	.333	3	1	0	0	0	0.0	1	0	0	0	0	0	0	0	1	0	0	1.0	1.000	2B-1
1973			3	1.000	1.000	3	3	0	0	0	0.0	1	0	0	0	0	3	3	0	0	0	0	0.0	—	
2 yrs.			4	.667	.667	6	4	0	0	0	0.0	2	0	0	0	0	3	3	0	1	0	0	0.3	1.000	2B-1

1st

John Bottarini

BOTTARINI, JOHN CHARLES
B. Sept. 14, 1908, Crockett, Calif.   D. Oct. 8, 1976, Jemez Springs, N. M.   BR TR 6'   190 lbs.

Year	Team		Games	BA	SA	AB	H	2B	3B	HR	HR%	R	RBI	BB	SO	SB	AB	H	PO	A	E	DP	TC/G	FA	G by Pos
1937	CHI	N	26	.275	.425	40	11	3	0	1	2.5	3	7	5	10	0	7	2	44	9	0	0	2.0	1.000	C-18, OF-1

Jim Bottomley

BOTTOMLEY, JAMES LeROY (Sunny Jim)
B. Apr. 23, 1900, Oglesby, Ill.   D. Dec. 11, 1959, St. Louis, Mo.   BL TL 6'   180 lbs.
Manager 1937.
Hall of Fame 1974.

Year	Team		Games	BA	SA	AB	H	2B	3B	HR	HR%	R	RBI	BB	SO	SB	AB	H	PO	A	E	DP	TC/G	FA	G by Pos
1922	STL	N	37	.325	.543	151	49	8	5	5	3.3	29	35	6	13	3	3	1	346	12	5	20	9.8	.986	1B-34
1923			134	.371	.535	523	194	34	14	8	1.5	79	94	45	44	4	4	1	1264	43	18	95	9.9	.986	1B-130
1924			137	.316	.500	528	167	31	12	14	2.7	87	111	35	35	5	3	1	1297	49	24	110	10.0	.982	1B-133, 2B-1
1925			153	.367	.578	619	227	44	12	21	3.4	92	128	47	36	3	0	0	1466	74	21	133	10.2	.987	1B-153
1926			154	.299	.506	603	180	40	14	19	3.2	98	120	58	52	4	0	0	1607	54	19	118	10.9	.989	1B-154
1927			152	.303	.509	574	174	31	15	19	3.3	95	124	74	49	8	0	0	1656	70	20	149	11.5	.989	1B-152
1928			149	.325	.628	576	187	42	20	31	5.4	123	136	71	54	10	0	0	1454	52	20	113	10.2	.987	1B-148
1929			146	.314	.568	560	176	31	12	29	5.2	108	137	70	54	3	1	0	1347	75	13	122	9.8	.991	1B-145
1930			131	.304	.493	487	148	33	7	15	3.1	92	97	44	36	5	7	2	1164	41	12	127	9.3	.990	1B-124
1931			108	.348	.534	382	133	34	5	9	2.4	73	75	34	24	3	14	3	897	43	12	95	8.8	.987	1B-93
1932			91	.296	.473	311	92	16	3	11	3.5	45	48	25	32	2	16	7	662	41	10	67	7.8	.986	1B-74
1933	CIN	N	145	.250	.395	549	137	23	9	13	2.4	57	83	42	28	3	0	0	1511	72	15	112	11.0	.991	1B-145
1934			142	.284	.439	556	158	31	11	11	2.0	72	78	33	40	1	3	0	1303	77	15	106	9.8	.989	1B-139
1935			107	.258	.323	399	103	21	1	1	0.3	44	49	18	24	1	3	0	934	53	8	74	9.3	.992	1B-97
1936	STL	A	140	.298	.476	544	162	39	11	12	2.2	72	95	44	55	0	0	0	1250	47	10	103	9.3	.992	1B-140
1937			65	.239	.330	109	26	7	0	1	0.9	11	12	18	15	1	38	7	179	12	1	16	3.0	.995	1B-24
16 yrs.			1991	.310	.500	7471	2313	465	151	219	2.9	1177	1422	664	591	58	99	27	18337	815	223	1560	9.7	.988	1B-1885, 2B-1

WORLD SERIES

Year	Team		Games	BA	SA	AB	H	2B	3B	HR	HR%	R	RBI	BB	SO	SB	AB	H	PO	A	E	DP	TC/G	FA	G by Pos
1926	STL	N	7	.345	.448	29	10	3	0	0	0.0	4	5	1	2	0	0	0	79	1	0	5	11.4	1.000	1B-7
1928			4	.214	.571	14	3	0	1	1	7.1	2	3	2	6	0	0	0	36	2	0	2	9.5	1.000	1B-4
1930			6	.045	.091	22	1	1	0	0	0.0	1	0	2	9	0	0	0	58	0	0	3	9.7	1.000	1B-6
1931			7	.160	.200	25	4	1	0	0	0.0	2	2	2	5	0	0	0	61	2	1	7	9.1	.984	1B-7
4 yrs.			24	.200	.311	90	18	5	1	1	1.1	9	10	7	22	0	0	0	234	7	1	17	10.1	.996	1B-24

Ed Bouchee

BOUCHEE, EDWARD FRANCIS
B. Mar. 7, 1933, Livingston, Mont.   BL TL 6'   200 lbs.

Year	Team		Games	BA	SA	AB	H	2B	3B	HR	HR%	R	RBI	BB	SO	SB	AB	H	PO	A	E	DP	TC/G	FA	G by Pos
1956	PHI	N	9	.273	.364	22	6	2	0	0	0.0	0	1	5	6	0	2	0	54	3	0	6	6.3	1.000	1B-6
1957			154	.293	.470	574	168	35	8	17	3.0	78	76	84	91	1	0	0	1182	125	16	93	8.6	.988	1B-154
1958			89	.257	.425	334	86	19	5	9	2.7	55	39	51	74	1	0	0	690	58	5	59	8.5	.993	1B-89
1959			136	.285	.449	499	142	29	4	15	3.0	75	74	70	74	0	2	1	1127	95	17	96	9.1	.986	1B-134
1960	2 teams		PHI	N (22G – .262)			CHI	N	(98G – .237)																	
"	total		120	.242	.330	364	88	15	1	5	1.4	34	52	54	62	2	17	1	867	71	8	68	7.9	.992	1B-102
1961	CHI	N	112	.248	.417	319	79	12	3	12	3.8	49	38	58	77	1	12	1	852	76	16	97	8.4	.983	1B-107

Year Team	Games	BA	SA	AB	H	2B	3B	HR	HR%	R	RBI	BB	SO	SB	Pinch Hit AB	H	PO	A	E	DP	TC/G	FA	G by Pos

Ed Bouchee *continued*

Year Team	Games	BA	SA	AB	H	2B	3B	HR	HR%	R	RBI	BB	SO	SB	AB	H	PO	A	E	DP	TC/G	FA	G by Pos
1962 NY N	50	.161	.287	87	14	2	0	3	3.4	7	10	18	17	0	28	5	137	23	4	16	3.3	.976	1B-19
7 yrs.	670	.265	.419	2199	583	114	21	61	2.8	298	290	340	401	5	61	8	4909	451	66	435	8.1	.988	1B-611

Al Boucher

BOUCHER, ALEXANDER FRANCIS (Bo)
B. Nov. 13, 1881, Franklin, Mass. D. June 23, 1974, Torrance, Calif.   BR TR 5'8½" 156 lbs.

Year Team	Games	BA	SA	AB	H	2B	3B	HR	HR%	R	RBI	BB	SO	SB	AB	H	PO	A	E	DP	TC/G	FA	G by Pos
1914 STL F	147	.231	.308	516	119	26	4	2	0.4	62	49	52		13	0	0	193	263	42	18	3.4	.916	3B-147

Medric Boucher

BOUCHER, MEDRIC CHARLES FRANCIS (Bush)
B. Mar. 12, 1886, St. Louis, Mo. D. Mar. 12, 1974, Martinez, Calif.   BR TR 5'10" 165 lbs.

Year Team	Games	BA	SA	AB	H	2B	3B	HR	HR%	R	RBI	BB	SO	SB	AB	H	PO	A	E	DP	TC/G	FA	G by Pos
1914 2 teams		BAL F	(16G – .313)				PIT F	(1G – .000)															
" total	17	.294	.471	17	5	1	0	0	0.0	2	2	1		0	6	2	24	2	1	1	1.6	.963	C-7, OF-1, 1B-1

Lou Boudreau

BOUDREAU, LOUIS
B. July 17, 1917, Harvey, Ill.
Manager 1942-50, 1952-57, 1960.
Hall of Fame 1970.   BR TR 5'11" 185 lbs.

Year Team	Games	BA	SA	AB	H	2B	3B	HR	HR%	R	RBI	BB	SO	SB	AB	H	PO	A	E	DP	TC/G	FA	G by Pos
1938 CLE A	1	.000	.000	1	0	0	0	0	0.0	0	0	1	0	0	0	0	0	0	0	0	0.0	–	3B-1
1939	53	.258	.360	225	58	15	4	0	0.0	42	19	28	24	2	0	0	103	184	14	31	5.7	.953	SS-53
1940	155	.295	.443	627	185	46	10	9	1.4	97	101	73	39	6	0	0	277	454	24	116	4.9	.968	SS-155
1941	148	.257	.415	579	149	45	8	10	1.7	95	56	85	57	9	0	0	296	444	26	97	5.2	.966	SS-147
1942	147	.283	.370	506	143	18	10	2	0.4	57	58	75	39	7	1	0	281	426	26	107	5.0	.965	SS-146
1943	152	.286	.388	539	154	32	7	3	0.6	69	67	90	31	4	1	0	331	489	25	122	5.6	.970	SS-152, C-1
1944	150	.327	.437	584	191	45	5	3	0.5	91	67	73	39	11	1	0	340	517	19	134	5.8	.978	SS-149, C-1
1945	97	.306	.408	346	106	24	1	3	0.9	50	48	35	20	6	1	0	217	289	9	73	5.3	.983	SS-97
1946	140	.293	.410	515	151	30	6	6	1.2	51	62	40	14	6	1	0	315	405	22	94	5.3	.970	SS-139
1947	150	.307	.424	538	165	45	3	4	0.7	79	67	67	10	1	1	1	305	475	14	120	5.3	.982	SS-148
1948	152	.355	.534	560	199	34	6	18	3.2	116	106	98	9	3	1	1	297	483	20	119	5.3	.975	SS-151, C-1
1949	134	.284	.364	475	135	20	3	4	0.8	53	60	70	10	0	4	1	253	353	12	95	4.6	.981	SS-88, 3B-38, 1B-6, 2B-1
1950	81	.269	.346	260	70	13	2	1	0.4	23	29	31	5	1	9	2	156	176	4	46	4.1	.988	SS-61, 1B-8, 3B-2, 2B-2
1951 BOS A	82	.267	.396	273	73	18	1	5	1.8	37	47	30	12	1	11	1	94	181	15	51	3.5	.948	SS-52, 3B-15, 1B-2
1952	4	.000	.000	2	0	0	0	0	0.0	1	0	2	0	0	2	0	1	0	0	1	0.3	1.000	SS-1, 3B-1
15 yrs.	1646	.295	.415	6030	1779	385	66	68	1.1	861	789	796	309	51	32	6	3265	4877	230	1205	5.1	.973	SS-1539, 3B-57, 1B-16, 2B-3, C-3

WORLD SERIES

Year Team	Games	BA	SA	AB	H	2B	3B	HR	HR%	R	RBI	BB	SO	SB	AB	H	PO	A	E	DP	TC/G	FA	G by Pos
1948 CLE A	6	.273	.455	22	6	4	0	0	0.0	1	3	1	1	0	0	0	11	14	0	5	4.2	1.000	SS-6

Chris Bourjos

BOURJOS, CHRISTOPHER
B. Oct. 16, 1954, Chicago, Ill.   BR TR 6' 185 lbs.

Year Team	Games	BA	SA	AB	H	2B	3B	HR	HR%	R	RBI	BB	SO	SB	AB	H	PO	A	E	DP	TC/G	FA	G by Pos
1980 SF N	13	.227	.409	22	5	1	0	1	4.5	4	2	2	7	0	7	2	5	0	0	0	0.4	1.000	OF-6

Pat Bourque

BOURQUE, PATRICK DANIEL
B. Mar. 23, 1947, Worcester, Mass.   BL TL 6' 210 lbs.

Year Team	Games	BA	SA	AB	H	2B	3B	HR	HR%	R	RBI	BB	SO	SB	AB	H	PO	A	E	DP	TC/G	FA	G by Pos
1971 CHI N	14	.189	.324	37	7	0	1	1	2.7	3	3	3	9	0	3	1	75	13	4	6	6.6	.957	1B-11
1972	11	.259	.296	27	7	1	0	0	0.0	3	5	2	2	0	4	0	57	6	0	8	5.7	1.000	1B-7
1973 2 teams		CHI N	(57G – .209)				OAK A	(23G – .190)															
" total	80	.204	.420	181	37	10	1	9	5.0	19	29	31	31	1	20	4	327	35	5	32	4.6	.986	1B-43, DH-15
1974 2 teams		OAK A	(73G – .229)				MIN A	(23G – .219)															
" total	96	.225	.300	160	36	6	0	2	1.3	11	24	22	31	0	35	7	291	26	4	33	3.3	.988	1B-60, DH-8
4 yrs.	201	.215	.356	405	87	17	2	12	3.0	36	61	58	73	1	62	12	750	80	13	79	4.2	.985	1B-121, DH-23

LEAGUE CHAMPIONSHIP SERIES

Year Team	Games	BA	SA	AB	H	2B	3B	HR	HR%	R	RBI	BB	SO	SB	AB	H	PO	A	E	DP	TC/G	FA	G by Pos
1973 OAK A	2	.000	.000	1	0	0	0	0	0.0	0	1	1	1	0	0	0	0	0	0	0	0.0	–	DH-2

WORLD SERIES

Year Team	Games	BA	SA	AB	H	2B	3B	HR	HR%	R	RBI	BB	SO	SB	AB	H	PO	A	E	DP	TC/G	FA	G by Pos
1973 OAK A	2	.500	.500	2	1	0	0	0	0.0	0	0	0	0	0	1	0	3	1	0	0	2.0	1.000	1B-2

Larry Bowa

BOWA, LAWRENCE ROBERT
B. Dec. 6, 1945, Sacramento, Calif.
Manager 1987-88.   BB TR 5'10" 155 lbs.

Year Team	Games	BA	SA	AB	H	2B	3B	HR	HR%	R	RBI	BB	SO	SB	AB	H	PO	A	E	DP	TC/G	FA	G by Pos
1970 PHI N	145	.250	.303	547	137	17	6	0	0.0	50	34	21	48	24	0	0	202	418	13	69	4.4	.979	SS-143, 2B-1
1971	159	.249	.292	650	162	18	5	0	0.0	74	25	36	61	28	0	0	272	560	11	97	5.3	.987	SS-157
1972	152	.250	.320	579	145	11	13	1	0.2	67	31	32	51	17	0	0	212	494	9	88	4.7	.987	SS-150
1973	122	.211	.249	446	94	11	3	0	0.0	42	23	24	31	10	0	0	191	361	12	87	4.6	.979	SS-122
1974	162	.275	.338	669	184	19	10	1	0.1	97	36	23	52	39	0	0	256	462	12	104	4.5	.984	SS-162
1975	136	.305	.377	583	178	18	9	2	0.3	79	38	24	32	24	0	0	227	403	25	82	4.8	.962	SS-135
1976	156	.248	.301	624	155	15	9	0	0.0	71	49	32	31	30	0	0	180	492	17	90	4.4	.975	SS-156
1977	154	.280	.340	624	175	19	3	4	0.6	93	41	32	32	32	0	0	222	518	13	94	4.9	.983	SS-154
1978	156	.294	.370	654	192	31	5	3	0.5	78	43	24	40	27	0	0	224	502	10	87	4.7	.986	SS-156
1979	147	.241	.314	539	130	17	11	0	0.0	74	31	61	32	20	0	0	229	448	6	80	4.6	.991	SS-146
1980	147	.267	.322	540	144	16	4	2	0.4	57	39	24	28	21	0	0	225	449	17	70	4.7	.975	SS-147
1981	103	.283	.339	360	102	14	3	0	0.0	34	31	26	17	16	1	0	117	309	11	50	4.2	.975	SS-102
1982 CHI N	142	.246	.305	499	123	15	7	2	0.4	50	29	39	38	8	2	1	210	396	17	64	4.4	.973	SS-140
1983	147	.267	.339	499	133	20	5	2	0.4	73	43	35	30	7	4	1	230	464	11	102	4.8	.984	SS-145
1984	133	.223	.269	391	87	14	2	0	0.0	33	17	28	24	10	2	2	217	378	16	64	4.6	.974	SS-132
1985 2 teams		CHI N	(72G – .246)				NY N	(14G – .105)															
" total	86	.234	.304	214	50	7	4	0	0.0	15	15	13	22	5	3	0	109	210	11	39	3.8	.967	SS-75, 2B-4
16 yrs.	2247	.260	.320	8418	2191	262	99	15	0.2	987	525	474	569	318	12	3	3323	6864	211	1267	4.6	.980	SS-2222, 2B-5

DIVISIONAL PLAYOFF SERIES

Year Team	Games	BA	SA	AB	H	2B	3B	HR	HR%	R	RBI	BB	SO	SB	AB	H	PO	A	E	DP	TC/G	FA	G by Pos
1981 PHI N	5	.176	.235	17	3	1	0	0	0.0	0	1	0	0	0	0	0	0	0	0	0	0.2	–	SS-5

Year	Team	Games	BA	SA	AB	H	2B	3B	HR	HR%	R	RBI	BB	SO	SB	Pinch Hit AB	Pinch Hit H	PO	A	E	DP	TC/G	FA	G by Pos

Larry Bowa *continued*

LEAGUE CHAMPIONSHIP SERIES

Year	Team	Games	BA	SA	AB	H	2B	3B	HR	HR%	R	RBI	BB	SO	SB	AB	H	PO	A	E	DP	TC/G	FA	G by Pos
1976	PHI	N	3	.125	.250	8	1	1	0	0	0.0	1	1	3	0	0	0	0	2	11	0	1	4.3	1.000	SS-3
1977			4	.118	.118	17	2	0	0	0	0.0	2	1	1	0	0	0	0	0	17	0	2	4.3	1.000	SS-4
1978			4	.333	.333	18	6	0	0	0	0.0	2	0	1	2	0	0	0	5	16	0	4	5.3	1.000	SS-4
1980			5	.316	.316	19	6	0	0	0	0.0	2	0	3	3	1	0	0	4	11	1	4	3.2	.938	SS-5
1984	CHI	N	5	.200	.267	15	3	1	0	0	0.0	1	1	1	0	0	0	0	8	15	0	6	4.6	1.000	SS-5
5 yrs.			21	.234	.260	77	18	2	0	0	0.0	8	3	9	5	1	0	0	19	70	1	17	4.3	.989	SS-21

WORLD SERIES

Year	Team	Games	BA	SA	AB	H	2B	3B	HR	HR%	R	RBI	BB	SO	SB	AB	H	PO	A	E	DP	TC/G	FA	G by Pos
1980	PHI	N	6	.375	.417	24	9	1	0	0	0.0	3	2	0	0	3	0	0	5	18	0	7	3.8	1.000	SS-6

Benny Bowcock

BOWCOCK, BENJAMIN JAMES
B. Oct. 28, 1879, Fall River, Mass. D. June 16, 1961, New Bedford, Mass.

BR TR 5'7" 150 lbs.

Year	Team	Games	BA	SA	AB	H	2B	3B	HR	HR%	R	RBI	BB	SO	SB	AB	H	PO	A	E	DP	TC/G	FA	G by Pos
1903	STL	A	14	.320	.480	50	16	3	1	1	2.0	7	10	3		1	0	0	22	32	7	4	4.4	.885	2B-14

Tim Bowden

BOWDEN, DAVID TIMON
B. Aug. 15, 1891, McDonough, Ga. D. Oct. 25, 1949, Emory, Ga.

BL TR 5'10" 175 lbs.

Year	Team	Games	BA	SA	AB	H	2B	3B	HR	HR%	R	RBI	BB	SO	SB	AB	H	PO	A	E	DP	TC/G	FA	G by Pos
1914	STL	A	7	.222	.222	9	2	0	0	0	0.0	0	0	1	6	0	3	1	4	0	0	0	0.6	1.000	OF-4

Chick Bowen

BOWEN, EMMONS JOSEPH
B. July 26, 1897, New Haven, Conn. D. Aug. 9, 1948, New Haven, Conn.

BR TR 5'7" 165 lbs.

Year	Team	Games	BA	SA	AB	H	2B	3B	HR	HR%	R	RBI	BB	SO	SB	AB	H	PO	A	E	DP	TC/G	FA	G by Pos
1919	NY	N	3	.200	.200	5	1	0	0	0	0.0	0	1	1	2	0	0	0	4	0	0	0	1.3	1.000	OF-2

Sam Bowen

BOWEN, SAMUEL THOMAS
B. Sept. 18, 1952, Brunswick, Ga.

BR TR 5'9" 170 lbs.

Year	Team	Games	BA	SA	AB	H	2B	3B	HR	HR%	R	RBI	BB	SO	SB	AB	H	PO	A	E	DP	TC/G	FA	G by Pos
1977	BOS	A	3	.000	.000	2	0	0	0	0	0.0	0	0	0	0	0	0	0	3	0	0	0	1.0	1.000	OF-3
1978			6	.143	.571	7	1	0	0	1	14.3	3	1	1	2	0	0	0	2	0	0	0	0.3	1.000	OF-4
1980			7	.154	.154	13	2	0	0	0	0.0	0	0	2	3	1	0	0	17	1	0	0	2.6	1.000	OF-6
3 yrs.			16	.136	.273	22	3	0	0	1	4.5	3	1	3	7	1	0	0	22	1	0	0	1.4	1.000	OF-13

Sam Bowens

BOWENS, SAMUEL EDWARD
B. Mar. 23, 1939, Wilmington, N. C.

BR TR 6'1½" 188 lbs.

Year	Team	Games	BA	SA	AB	H	2B	3B	HR	HR%	R	RBI	BB	SO	SB	AB	H	PO	A	E	DP	TC/G	FA	G by Pos
1963	BAL	A	15	.333	.500	48	16	3	1	1	2.1	8	9	4	5	1	2	0	20	0	1	0	1.4	.952	OF-13
1964			139	.263	.453	501	132	25	2	22	4.4	58	71	42	99	4	5	0	249	8	5	1	1.9	.981	OF-135
1965			84	.163	.296	203	33	4	1	7	3.4	16	20	10	41	7	13	2	108	3	2	1	1.3	.982	OF-68
1966			89	.210	.329	243	51	9	1	6	2.5	26	20	17	52	9	22	6	114	7	5	2	1.4	.960	OF-68
1967			62	.183	.342	120	22	2	1	5	4.2	13	12	11	43	1	26	6	41	2	1	0	0.7	.977	OF-32
1968	WAS	A	57	.191	.330	115	22	4	0	4	3.5	14	7	11	39	2	29	6	42	2	2	0	0.8	.957	OF-27
1969			33	.193	.211	57	11	1	0	0	0.0	6	4	5	14	1	3	0	32	1	1	0	1.0	.971	OF-30
7 yrs.			479	.223	.375	1287	287	48	6	45	3.5	141	143	100	293	25	100	20	606	23	17	4	1.3	.974	OF-373

Frank Bowerman

BOWERMAN, FRANK EUGENE (Mike)
B. Dec. 5, 1868, Romeo, Mich. D. Nov. 30, 1948, Romeo, Mich.
Manager 1909.

BR TR 6'2" 190 lbs.

Year	Team	Games	BA	SA	AB	H	2B	3B	HR	HR%	R	RBI	BB	SO	SB	AB	H	PO	A	E	DP	TC/G	FA	G by Pos
1895	BAL	N	1	.000	.000	1	0	0	0	0	0.0	0	0	0	0	0	0	0	2	0	0	0	2.0	1.000	C-1
1896			4	.125	.125	16	2	0	0	0	0.0	0	4	1	0	0	0	0	21	6	2	1	7.3	.931	C-3, 1B-1
1897			38	.315	.377	130	41	5	0	1	0.8	16	21	1		3	2	0	155	29	10	1	5.1	.948	C-36
1898	2 teams		74	BAL N (5G – .438)		PIT N (69G – .274)																			
"	total		74	.284	.335	257	73	7	3	0	0.0	22	30	9		5	2	0	300	86	18	14	5.5	.955	C-63, 1B-9
1899	PIT	N	109	.259	.366	424	110	16	10	3	0.7	49	53	11		10	2	0	535	144	32	21	6.5	.955	C-79, 1B-28
1900	NY	N	80	.241	.293	270	65	5	3	1	0.4	25	42	6		10	2	0	235	144	33	17	5.2	.920	C-75, SS-2
1901			59	.199	.257	191	38	5	3	0	0.0	20	14	7		3	4	1	281	95	24	6	6.8	.940	C-46, SS-3, 3B-2, 2B-3, 1B-1
1902			107	.253	.322	367	93	13	6	0	0.0	38	26	13		12	5	0	445	144	26	10	5.7	.958	C-98, 1B-3
1903			64	.276	.338	210	58	6	2	1	0.5	22	31	6		5	4	3	348	67	9	9	6.6	.979	C-55, 1B-4, OF-1
1904			93	.232	.318	289	67	11	4	2	0.7	38	27	16		7	3	0	495	103	13	14	6.6	.979	C-79, 1B-9, 2B-1, P-1
1905			98	.269	.333	297	80	8	1	3	1.0	37	41	12		6	7	3	528	76	13	12	6.3	.979	C-72, 1B-17, 2B-1
1906			103	.228	.284	285	65	7	3	1	0.4	23	42	15		5	5	2	477	92	8	10	5.6	.986	C-67, 1B-20
1907			96	.260	.299	311	81	8	2	0	0.0	31	32	17		11	5	1	606	79	6	14	7.2	.991	C-62, 1B-29
1908	BOS	N	86	.228	.280	254	58	8	1	1	0.4	16	25	13		4	12	4	329	77	12	14	4.9	.971	C-63, 1B-11
1909			33	.212	.232	99	21	2	0	0	0.0	6	4	2		0	6	0	122	33	12	6	5.1	.928	C-27
15 yrs.			1045	.251	.314	3401	852	101	38	13	0.4	343	392	129		81	59	14	4879	1175	218	149	6.0	.965	C-826, 1B-132, 2B-6, SS-5, 3B-3, OF-1, P-1

Billy Bowers

BOWERS, GROVER BILL
B. Mar. 25, 1923, Parkin, Ark.

BL TR 5'9½" 176 lbs.

Year	Team	Games	BA	SA	AB	H	2B	3B	HR	HR%	R	RBI	BB	SO	SB	AB	H	PO	A	E	DP	TC/G	FA	G by Pos
1949	CHI	A	26	.192	.244	78	15	2	1	0	0.0	5	6	4	5	1	6	0	46	2	1	0	1.9	.980	OF-20

Frank Bowes

BOWES, FRANK M.
B. 1865, Bath, N. Y. D. Jan. 21, 1895, Brooklyn, N. Y.

TR 5'9" 160 lbs.

Year	Team	Games	BA	SA	AB	H	2B	3B	HR	HR%	R	RBI	BB	SO	SB	AB	H	PO	A	E	DP	TC/G	FA	G by Pos
1890	BKN	AA	61	.220	.259	232	51	6	2	0	0.0	28		7		11	0	0	164	67	35	8	4.4	.868	C-25, OF-19, 3B-13, 1B-3, SS-2

Hoss Bowlin

BOWLIN, LOIS WELDON
B. Dec. 10, 1940, Paragould, Ark.

BR TR 5'9" 155 lbs.

Year	Team	Games	BA	SA	AB	H	2B	3B	HR	HR%	R	RBI	BB	SO	SB	AB	H	PO	A	E	DP	TC/G	FA	G by Pos
1967	KC	A	2	.200	.200	5	1	0	0	0	0.0	0	0	0	0	0	0	0	0	4	0	0	2.0	1.000	3B-2

Steve Bowling

BOWLING, STEPHEN SHADDON
B. June 26, 1952, Tulsa, Okla.

BR TR 6' 185 lbs.

Year	Team		Games	BA	SA	AB	H	2B	3B	HR	HR%	R	RBI	BB	SO	SB	Pinch Hit AB	Pinch Hit H	PO	A	E	DP	TC/G	FA	G by Pos

Steve Bowling *continued*

Year	Team		Games	BA	SA	AB	H	2B	3B	HR	HR%	R	RBI	BB	SO	SB	AB	H	PO	A	E	DP	TC/G	FA	G by Pos
1976	MIL	A	14	.167	.214	42	7	2	0	0	0.0	4	2	2	5	0	1	0	38	1	1	1	2.9	.975	OF-13, DH-1
1977	TOR	A	89	.206	.273	194	40	8	1	1	0.5	19	13	37	42	2	2	0	139	14	2	0	1.7	.987	OF-87
2 yrs.			103	.199	.263	236	47	10	1	1	0.4	23	15	39	47	2	3	0	177	15	3	1	1.9	.985	OF-100, DH-1

Bill Bowman

BOWMAN, WILLIAM GEORGE
B. 1869, Chicago, Ill.   D. Apr. 6, 1918, Arlington Heights, Ill.   5'11"   180 lbs.

Year	Team		Games	BA	SA	AB	H	2B	3B	HR	HR%	R	RBI	BB	SO	SB	AB	H	PO	A	E	DP	TC/G	FA	G by Pos
1891	CHI	N	15	.089	.111	45	4	1	0	0	0.0	2	5	5	9	0	0	0	41	13	5	1	3.9	.915	C-15

Bob Bowman

BOWMAN, ROBERT LEROY
B. May 10, 1931, Laytonville, Calif.   BR TR 6'1"   195 lbs.

Year	Team		Games	BA	SA	AB	H	2B	3B	HR	HR%	R	RBI	BB	SO	SB	AB	H	PO	A	E	DP	TC/G	FA	G by Pos
1955	PHI	N	3	.000	.000	3	0	0	0	0	0.0	0	0	0	0	0	0	0	3	0	0	0	1.0	1.000	OF-2
1956			6	.188	.500	16	3	0	1	1	6.3	2	2	0	6	0	0	0	5	0	1	0	1.0	.833	OF-5
1957			99	.266	.392	237	63	8	2	6	2.5	31	23	27	50	0	15	1	123	8	10	2	1.4	.929	OF-81
1958			91	.288	.500	184	53	11	2	8	4.3	31	24	16	30	0	31	5	82	1	1	0	0.9	.988	OF-57
1959			57	.127	.203	79	10	0	0	2	2.5	7	5	5	23	0	32	7	30	2	0	1	0.6	1.000	OF-20, P-5
5 yrs.			256	.249	.403	519	129	19	5	17	3.3	71	54	48	109	0	79	21	243	11	12	3	1.0	.955	OF-165, P-5

El Bowman

BOWMAN, ELMARI WILHELM (Big Bow)
Also known as Elmari Wilhelm Wilhelm.
B. Mar. 19, 1897, Proctor, Vt.   D. Dec. 17, 1985, Los Angeles, Calif.   BR TR 6'½"   193 lbs.

Year	Team		Games	BA	SA	AB	H	2B	3B	HR	HR%	R	RBI	BB	SO	SB	AB	H	PO	A	E	DP	TC/G	FA	G by Pos
1920	WAS	A	2	.000	.000	1	0	0	0	0	0.0	1	0	1	0	0	1	0	0	0	0	0	0.0	—	

Ernie Bowman

BOWMAN, ERNEST FERRELL
B. July 28, 1935, Johnson City, Tenn.   BR TR 5'10"   160 lbs.

Year	Team		Games	BA	SA	AB	H	2B	3B	HR	HR%	R	RBI	BB	SO	SB	AB	H	PO	A	E	DP	TC/G	FA	G by Pos
1961	SF	N	38	.211	.316	38	8	0	2	0	0.0	10	2	1	8	2	3	1	19	32	5	3	1.5	.911	2B-13, SS-12, 3B-7
1962			46	.190	.286	42	8	1	0	1	2.4	9	4	1	10	0	3	0	22	30	0	2	1.1	1.000	2B-17, 3B-11, SS-10
1963			81	.184	.208	125	23	3	0	0	0.0	10	4	0	15	1	1	0	70	101	8	17	2.2	.955	SS-40, 2B-26, 3B-12
3 yrs.			165	.190	.244	205	39	4	2	1	0.5	29	10	2	33	3	7	1	111	163	13	22	1.7	.955	SS-62, 2B-56, 3B-30

WORLD SERIES

Year	Team		Games	BA	SA	AB	H	2B	3B	HR	HR%	R	RBI	BB	SO	SB	AB	H	PO	A	E	DP	TC/G	FA	G by Pos
1962	SF	N	2	.000	.000	1	0	0	0	0	0.0	1	0	0	0	0	0	0	5	0	0	2.5	1.000	SS-1

Joe Bowman

BOWMAN, JOSEPH EMIL
B. June 17, 1910, Argentine, Kans.   BL TR 6'2"   190 lbs.

Year	Team		Games	BA	SA	AB	H	2B	3B	HR	HR%	R	RBI	BB	SO	SB	AB	H	PO	A	E	DP	TC/G	FA	G by Pos
1932	PHI	A	7	1.000	1.000	1	1	0	0	0	0.0	0	0	0	0	0	0	0	1	6	0	1	1.1	.875	P-7
1934	NY	N	31	.172	.241	29	5	0	1	0	0.0	4	4	2	3	0	0	0	6	20	0	0	0.8	1.000	P-30
1935	PHI	N	49	.194	.284	67	13	1	1	1	1.5	6	7	4	7	1	13	3	9	28	0	0	0.8	1.000	P-33, OF-1
1936			44	.195	.208	77	15	1	0	0	0.0	9	6	6	14	0	4	2	7	32	5	4	1.0	.886	P-40
1937	PIT	N	35	.213	.234	47	10	1	0	0	0.0	3	4	5	9	0	2	0	14	24	0	3	1.1	1.000	P-30
1938			18	.333	.429	21	7	0	1	0	0.0	5	1	3	0	0	2	8	1	2	0.6	.909	P-17
1939			70	.344	.448	96	33	8	1	0	0.0	9	18	5	9	0	29	6	6	39	0	1	0.6	1.000	P-37
1940			57	.244	.356	90	22	5	1	1	1.1	11	14	14	14	0	17	4	15	36	1	0	0.9	.981	P-32
1941	BOS	A	22	.258	.290	31	8	1	0	0	0.0	4	1	4	2	0	4	1	5	13	0	0	0.8	1.000	P-18
1944			59	.200	.290	100	20	5	1	0	0.0	7	16	5	19	1	31	7	9	20	2	3	0.5	.935	P-26
1945 2 teams	BOS A	(9G – .222)					CIN N	(29G – .070)																	
" total			38	.088	.138	80	7	0	0	0	0.0	4	4	3	10	1	9	1	12	28	3	0	1.1	.930	P-28
11 yrs.			430	.221	.293	639	141	24	8	2	0.3	62	75	46	90	3	109	24	86	254	15	17	0.8	.958	P-298, OF-1

Red Bowser

BOWSER, JAMES H.
B. 1886, Greensburg, Pa.

Year	Team		Games	BA	SA	AB	H	2B	3B	HR	HR%	R	RBI	BB	SO	SB	AB	H	PO	A	E	DP	TC/G	FA	G by Pos
1910	CHI	A	1	.000	.000	2	0	0	0	0	0.0	0	0	0	0	0	0	0	0	0	0	0	0.0	—	OF-1

Bob Boyd

BOYD, ROBERT RICHARD (The Rope)
B. Oct. 1, 1926, Potts Camp, Miss.   BL TL 5'10"   170 lbs.

Year	Team		Games	BA	SA	AB	H	2B	3B	HR	HR%	R	RBI	BB	SO	SB	AB	H	PO	A	E	DP	TC/G	FA	G by Pos
1951	CHI	A	12	.167	.278	18	3	0	1	0	0.0	3	4	3	3	0	5	1	36	1	0	8	3.1	1.000	1B-6
1953			55	.297	.412	165	49	6	2	3	1.8	20	23	13	11	1	8	4	301	16	1	25	5.8	.997	1B-29, OF-16
1954			29	.179	.232	56	10	3	0	0	0.0	10	5	4	3	2	2	0	71	3	2	3	2.6	.974	OF-13, 1B-12
1956	BAL	A	70	.311	.400	225	70	8	3	2	0.9	28	11	30	14	0	10	3	474	24	5	46	7.2	.990	1B-60, OF-8
1957			141	.318	.408	485	154	16	8	4	0.8	73	34	55	31	2	15	6	1073	70	10	107	8.2	.991	1B-132, OF-1
1958			125	.309	.439	401	124	21	5	7	1.7	58	36	25	24	1	32	4	757	53	5	85	6.5	.994	1B-99
1959			128	.265	.345	415	110	20	2	3	0.7	42	41	29	14	2	20	4	927	46	15	88	7.7	.985	1B-109
1960			71	.317	.427	82	26	5	2	0	0.0	9	6	5	5	0	56	10	64	4	0	9	1.0	1.000	1B-17
1961 2 teams	KC A	(26G – .229)					MIL N	(36G – .244)																	
" total			62	.236	.258	89	21	2	0	0	0.0	10	12	6	9	1	49	9	64	7	0	7	1.1	1.000	1B-11
9 yrs.			693	.293	.388	1936	567	81	23	19	1.0	253	175	167	114	9	197	48	3767	224	38	378	5.8	.991	1B-475, OF-38

Frank Boyd

BOYD, FRANK JAY
B. Apr. 2, 1868, West Middletown, Pa.   D. Dec. 16, 1937, Oil City, Pa.   BR TR

Year	Team		Games	BA	SA	AB	H	2B	3B	HR	HR%	R	RBI	BB	SO	SB	AB	H	PO	A	E	DP	TC/G	FA	G by Pos
1893	CLE	N	2	.200	.400	5	1	1	0	0	0.0	3	3	1	0	0	0	0	2	2	0	0	2.0	1.000	C-2

Jake Boyd

BOYD, JACOB HENRY
B. Jan. 19, 1874, Martinsburg, W. Va.   D. Aug. 12, 1932, Gettysburg, Pa.   TL   160 lbs.

Year	Team		Games	BA	SA	AB	H	2B	3B	HR	HR%	R	RBI	BB	SO	SB	AB	H	PO	A	E	DP	TC/G	FA	G by Pos
1894	WAS	N	6	.143	.143	21	3	0	0	0	0.0	1	1	1		4			4	8	2	0	2.3	.857	OF-3, P-3
1895			51	.268	.331	157	42	1	1	1	0.6	29	16	20	28	2	0	0	50	55	24	5	2.5	.814	OF-21, P-14, 2B-10, SS-8, 3B-1
1896			4	.077	.077	13	1	0	0	0	0.0	1	1	1		0			1	9	1	0	2.8	.909	P-4
3 yrs.			61	.241	.293	191	46	1	1	1	0.5	31	18	22	33	4	0	0	55	72	27	5	2.5	.825	OF-24, P-21, 2B-10, SS-8, 3B-1

Year Team	Games	BA	SA	AB	H	2B	3B	HR	HR%	R	RBI	BB	SO	SB	Pinch Hit AB	Pinch Hit H	PO	A	E	DP	TC/G	FA	G by Pos

Clete Boyer

BOYER, CLETIS LEROY
Brother of Ken Boyer. Brother of Cloyd Boyer.
B. Feb. 8, 1937, Cassville, Mo.
BR TR 6' 165 lbs.

Year Team	Games	BA	SA	AB	H	2B	3B	HR	HR%	R	RBI	BB	SO	SB	PH AB	PH H	PO	A	E	DP	TC/G	FA	G by Pos
1955 KC A	47	.241	.253	79	19	1	0	0	0.0	3	6	3	17	0	9	0	32	41	3	6	1.6	.961	SS-12, 3B-11, 2B-10
1956	67	.217	.279	129	28	3	1	1	0.8	15	4	11	24	1	5	1	100	124	6	34	3.4	.974	2B-51, 3B-7
1957	10	—	—	0	0	0	0	0	—	0	0	0	0	0	0	0	0	0	0	0	0.0	—	3B-1, 2B-1
1959 NY A	47	.175	.193	114	20	2	0	0	0.0	4	3	6	23	1	6	0	49	90	2	14	3.0	.986	SS-26, 3B-16
1960	124	.242	.405	393	95	20	1	14	3.6	54	46	23	85	2	2	0	157	297	17	44	3.8	.964	3B-99, SS-33
1961	148	.224	.347	504	113	19	5	11	2.2	61	55	63	83	1	0	0	170	373	17	41	3.8	.970	3B-141, SS-12, OF-1
1962	158	.272	.413	566	154	24	1	18	3.2	85	68	51	106	3	0	0	187	396	22	41	3.8	.964	3B-157
1963	152	.251	.363	557	140	20	3	12	2.2	59	54	33	91	4	0	0	184	344	25	40	3.6	.955	3B-141, SS-9, 2B-1
1964	147	.218	.304	510	111	10	5	8	1.6	43	52	36	93	6	3	0	164	339	16	41	3.5	.969	3B-123, SS-21
1965	148	.251	.424	514	129	23	6	18	3.5	69	58	39	79	4	1	0	137	354	16	46	3.4	.968	3B-147, SS-2
1966	144	.240	.384	500	120	22	4	14	2.8	59	57	46	48	6	0	0	201	396	18	38	4.3	.971	3B-85, SS-59
1967 ATL N	154	.245	.423	572	140	18	3	26	4.5	63	96	39	81	6	2	0	177	309	15	35	3.3	.970	3B-150, SS-6
1968	71	.227	.311	273	62	7	2	4	1.5	19	17	16	32	2	2	0	74	135	4	17	3.0	.981	3B-69
1969	144	.250	.371	496	124	16	1	14	2.8	57	57	55	87	3	3	0	139	275	15	18	3.0	.965	3B-141
1970	134	.246	.381	475	117	14	1	16	3.4	44	62	41	71	2	2	1	113	280	19	22	3.1	.954	3B-126, SS-5
1971	30	.245	.439	98	24	1	0	6	6.1	10	19	8	11	0	3	1	18	57	3	6	2.6	.962	3B-25, SS-1
16 yrs.	1725	.242	.372	5780	1396	200	33	162	2.8	645	654	470	931	41	38	3	1902	3810	198	443	3.4	.966	3B-1439, SS-186, 2B-63, OF-1

LEAGUE CHAMPIONSHIP SERIES

Year Team	Games	BA	SA	AB	H	2B	3B	HR	HR%	R	RBI	BB	SO	SB	PH AB	PH H	PO	A	E	DP	TC/G	FA	G by Pos
1969 ATL N	3	.111	.111	9	1	0	0	0	0.0	0	3	2	3	0	0	0	4	8	1	1	4.3	.923	3B-3

WORLD SERIES

Year Team	Games	BA	SA	AB	H	2B	3B	HR	HR%	R	RBI	BB	SO	SB	PH AB	PH H	PO	A	E	DP	TC/G	FA	G by Pos
1960 NY A	4	.250	.583	12	3	2	1	0	0.0	1	1	0	1	0	0	0	0	8	0	2	2.0	1.000	3B-4, SS-1
1961	5	.267	.400	15	4	2	0	0	0.0	0	3	4	0	0	0	0	6	12	1	0	3.8	.947	3B-5
1962	7	.318	.500	22	7	1	0	1	4.5	2	4	1	3	0	0	0	9	16	2	2	3.9	.926	3B-7
1963	4	.077	.077	13	1	0	0	0	0.0	0	0	1	6	0	0	0	2	8	0	0	2.5	1.000	3B-4
1964	7	.208	.375	24	5	1	0	1	4.2	2	3	1	5	1	0	0	5	22	2	0	4.1	.931	3B-7
5 yrs.	27	.233	.395	86	20	6	1	2	2.3	5	11	7	15	1	0	0	22	66	5	4	3.4	.946	3B-27, SS-1

Ken Boyer

BOYER, KENTON LLOYD
Brother of Cloyd Boyer. Brother of Clete Boyer.
B. May 20, 1931, Liberty, Mo. D. Sept. 7, 1982, St. Louis, Mo.
Manager 1978-80.
BR TR 6'1½" 190 lbs.

Year Team	Games	BA	SA	AB	H	2B	3B	HR	HR%	R	RBI	BB	SO	SB	PH AB	PH H	PO	A	E	DP	TC/G	FA	G by Pos
1955 STL N	147	.264	.425	530	140	27	2	18	3.4	78	62	37	67	22	1	0	155	295	21	34	3.2	.955	3B-139, SS-18
1956	150	.306	.494	595	182	30	2	26	4.4	91	98	38	65	8	1	0	130	309	18	37	3.0	.961	3B-149
1957	142	.265	.414	544	144	18	3	19	3.5	79	62	44	77	12	1	0	316	95	14	8	3.0	.967	OF-105, 3B-41
1958	150	.307	.496	570	175	21	9	23	4.0	101	90	49	53	11	1	0	168	350	20	41	3.6	.963	3B-144, OF-6, SS-1
1959	149	.309	.508	563	174	18	5	28	5.0	86	94	67	77	12	1	0	143	310	22	33	3.2	.954	3B-143, SS-12
1960	151	.304	.562	552	168	26	10	32	5.8	95	97	56	77	8	5	1	140	300	19	37	3.0	.959	3B-146
1961	153	.329	.533	589	194	26	11	24	4.1	109	95	68	91	6	0	0	117	346	24	23	3.2	.951	3B-153
1962	160	.291	.470	611	178	27	5	24	3.9	92	98	75	104	12	0	0	158	318	22	34	3.1	.956	3B-160
1963	159	.285	.454	617	176	28	2	24	3.9	86	111	70	90	1	0	0	129	293	34	23	2.9	.925	3B-159
1964	162	.295	.489	628	185	30	10	24	3.8	100	119	70	85	3	0	0	131	337	24	30	3.0	.951	3B-162
1965	144	.260	.374	535	139	18	2	13	2.4	71	75	57	73	2	3	0	113	250	12	18	2.6	.968	3B-143
1966 NY N	136	.266	.415	496	132	28	2	14	2.8	62	61	30	64	4	7	3	125	294	21	34	3.2	.952	3B-130, 1B-2
1967 2 teams	NY N (56G – .235)			CHI A (57G – .261)																			
" total	113	.249	.361	346	86	12	3	7	2.0	34	34	33	47	2	15	4	233	166	11	28	3.6	.973	3B-77, 1B-26
1968 2 teams	CHI A (10G – .125)			LA N (83G – .271)																			
" total	93	.257	.376	245	63	7	2	6	2.4	20	41	17	40	2	29	6	287	72	11	31	4.0	.970	3B-39, 1B-33
1969 LA N	25	.206	.265	34	7	2	0	0	0.0	4	2	7	10	0	19	4	31	2	1	6	1.4	.971	1B-4
15 yrs.	2034	.287	.462	7455	2143	318	68	282	3.8	1104	1141	713	1017	105	83	18	2376	3737	274	417	3.1	.957	3B-1785, OF-111, 1B-65, SS-31

WORLD SERIES

Year Team	Games	BA	SA	AB	H	2B	3B	HR	HR%	R	RBI	BB	SO	SB	PH AB	PH H	PO	A	E	DP	TC/G	FA	G by Pos
1964 STL N	7	.222	.481	27	6	1	0	2	7.4	5	6	1	5	0	0	0	9	16	1	0	3.7	.962	3B-7

Doe Boyland

BOYLAND, DORIAN SCOTT
B. Jan. 6, 1955, Chicago, Ill.
BL TL 6'4" 200 lbs.

Year Team	Games	BA	SA	AB	H	2B	3B	HR	HR%	R	RBI	BB	SO	SB	PH AB	PH H	PO	A	E	DP	TC/G	FA	G by Pos
1978 PIT N	6	.250	.250	8	2	0	0	0	0.0	1	1	0	1	0	5	1	8	0	0	0	1.3	1.000	1B-1
1979	4	.000	.000	3	0	0	0	0	0.0	0	0	0	2	0	3	0	0	0	0	0	0.0	—	
1981	11	.000	.000	8	0	0	0	0	0.0	0	0	1	3	0	8	0	0	0	0	0	0.0	—	
3 yrs.	21	.105	.105	19	2	0	0	0	0.0	1	1	1	6	0	16	1	8	0	0	0	0.4	1.000	1B-1

Buzz Boyle

BOYLE, RALPH FRANCIS
Brother of Jim Boyle.
B. Feb. 9, 1908, Cincinnati, Ohio D. Nov. 12, 1978, Cincinnati, Ohio
BL TL 5'11½" 170 lbs.

Year Team	Games	BA	SA	AB	H	2B	3B	HR	HR%	R	RBI	BB	SO	SB	PH AB	PH H	PO	A	E	DP	TC/G	FA	G by Pos
1929 BOS N	17	.263	.386	57	15	2	1	1	1.8	8	2	6	11	2	0	0	32	1	0	0	1.9	1.000	OF-17
1930	1	.000	.000	1	0	0	0	0	0.0	0	0	0	0	0	0	0	0	0	0	0	0.0	—	OF-1
1933 BKN N	93	.299	.361	338	101	13	4	0	0.0	38	31	16	24	7	3	1	195	2	5	0	2.2	.975	OF-90
1934	128	.305	.447	472	144	26	10	7	1.5	88	48	51	44	8	6	2	275	20	9	1	2.4	.970	OF-121
1935	127	.272	.371	475	129	17	9	4	0.8	51	44	43	45	7	2	0	244	18	10	5	2.1	.963	OF-124
5 yrs.	366	.290	.395	1343	389	58	24	12	0.9	185	125	116	125	24	11	3	746	41	24	6	2.2	.970	OF-353

Eddie Boyle

BOYLE, EDWARD J.
Brother of Jack Boyle.
B. May 8, 1874, Cincinnati, Ohio D. Feb. 9, 1941, Cincinnati, Ohio
BR TR 6'3" 200 lbs.

Year	Team		Games	BA	SA	AB	H	2B	3B	HR	HR%	R	RBI	BB	SO	SB	Pinch Hit AB	Pinch Hit H	PO	A	E	DP	TC/G	FA	G by Pos

Eddie Boyle *continued*

Year	Team		Games	BA	SA	AB	H	2B	3B	HR	HR%	R	RBI	BB	SO	SB	AB	H	PO	A	E	DP	TC/G	FA	G by Pos
1896	2 teams	LOU N (3G – .000)				PIT N (2G – .000)																			
"	total		5	.000	.000	14	0	0	0	0	0.0	0	0	2	3	0	0	0	16	4	2	0	4.4	.909	C-5

Henry Boyle

BOYLE, HENRY J. (Handsome Henry)
B. Sept. 20, 1860, Philadelphia, Pa.   D. May 25, 1932, Philadelphia, Pa.   TR

Year	Team		Games	BA	SA	AB	H	2B	3B	HR	HR%	R	RBI	BB	SO	SB	AB	H	PO	A	E	DP	TC/G	FA	G by Pos
1884	STL	U	65	.260	.366	262	68	10	3	4	1.5	41		9			0	0	85	49	19	7	2.4	.876	OF-43, P-19, 3B-4, SS-1, 2B-1, 1B-1
1885	STL	N	72	.202	.256	258	52	9	1	1	0.4	24	21	13	38		0	0	94	76	19	4	2.6	.899	P-42, OF-31, 2B-2
1886			30	.250	.333	108	27	2	2	1	0.9	8	13	5	19		0	0	18	39	9	1	2.2	.864	P-25, OF-6
1887	IND	N	41	.191	.312	141	27	9	1	2	1.4	17	13	9	18	2	0	0	12	42	10	2	1.6	.844	P-38, OF-4
1888			37	.144	.184	125	18	2	0	1	0.8	13	6	6	31	1	0	0	14	84	7	1	2.8	.933	P-37, 1B-1
1889			46	.245	.329	155	38	10	0	1	0.6	17	17	9	23	4	0	0	17	51	3	0	1.5	.958	P-46, 3B-1
6 yrs.			291	.219	.301	1049	230	42	7	10	1.0	120	70	51	129	7	0	0	240	341	67	15	2.2	.897	P-207, OF-84, 3B-5, 2B-3, 1B-2, SS-1

Jack Boyle

BOYLE, JOHN ANTHONY (Honest Jack)
Brother of Eddie Boyle.
B. Mar. 22, 1866, Cincinnati, Ohio   D. Jan. 7, 1913, Cincinnati, Ohio   BL TR 6'4" 190 lbs.

Year	Team		Games	BA	SA	AB	H	2B	3B	HR	HR%	R	RBI	BB	SO	SB	AB	H	PO	A	E	DP	TC/G	FA	G by Pos
1886	CIN	AA	1	.200	.200	5	1	0	0	0	0.0	0		0			0	0	8	2	3	0	13.0	.769	C-1
1887	STL	AA	88	.189	.220	350	66	3	1	2	0.6	48		20		7	0	0	352	116	57	8	6.0	.891	C-86, OF-2, 1B-2, 3B-1
1888			71	.241	.292	257	62	8	1	1	0.4	33	23	13		11	0	0	382	123	37	11	7.6	.932	C-70, OF-1
1889			99	.245	.334	347	85	11	4	4	1.2	54	42	21	42	5	0	0	409	135	33	14	5.8	.943	C-80, 3B-12, OF-5, 1B-4, 2B-1
1890	CHI	P	100	.260	.320	369	96	9	5	1	0.3	56	49	44	29	11	0	0	335	154	61	16	5.5	.889	C-50, 3B-30, SS-16, 1B-7, OF-2
1891	STL	AA	123	.280	.392	439	123	18	8	5	1.1	78	79	47	36	19	0	0	498	163	54	17	5.8	.924	C-91, SS-26, 3B-8, OF-3, 2B-3, 1B-3
1892	NY	N	120	.183	.239	436	80	8	8	0	0.0	52	32	36	40	10	0	0	787	152	60	34	8.3	.940	C-79, 1B-40, OF-2, SS-2
1893	PHI	N	116	.286	.403	504	144	29	9	4	0.8	105	81	41	30	22	0	0	1085	82	15	71	10.2	.987	1B-112, C-6, 3B-2
1894			114	.301	.408	495	149	21	10	4	0.8	98	88	45	26	21	0	0	952	63	19	76	9.1	.982	1B-114, 3B-1, 2B-1
1895			133	.253	.297	565	143	17	4	0	0.0	90	67	35	23	13	0	0	1245	61	36	69	10.1	.973	1B-133
1896			40	.297	.359	145	43	4	1	1	0.7	17	28	6	7	3	0	0	196	22	12	10	5.8	.948	C-28, 1B-12
1897			75	.253	.313	288	73	9	1	2	0.7	37	36	19		3	2	1	373	51	12	10	5.8	.972	C-50, 1B-24
1898			6	.091	.182	22	2	0	1	0	0.0	0	3	1			0	0	40	6	6	3	8.7	.885	1B-4, C-3
13 yrs.			1086	.253	.327	4222	1067	137	53	24	0.6	668	528	328	233	125	2	1	6662	1130	405	339	7.5	.951	C-544, 1B-455, 3B-52, SS-44, OF-15, 2B-7

Jack Boyle

BOYLE, JOHN BELLEW
B. July 9, 1889, Morris, Ill.   D. Apr. 3, 1971, Ft. Lauderdale, Fla.   BL TR 5'11½" 165 lbs.

Year	Team		Games	BA	SA	AB	H	2B	3B	HR	HR%	R	RBI	BB	SO	SB	AB	H	PO	A	E	DP	TC/G	FA	G by Pos
1912	PHI	N	15	.280	.320	25	7	1	0	0	0.0	4	2	1	5	0	5	2	6	23	2	2	2.1	.935	3B-6, SS-2

Jim Boyle

BOYLE, JAMES JOHN
Brother of Buzz Boyle.
B. Jan. 19, 1904, Cincinnati, Ohio   D. Dec. 24, 1958, Cincinnati, Ohio   BR TR 6' 180 lbs.

Year	Team		Games	BA	SA	AB	H	2B	3B	HR	HR%	R	RBI	BB	SO	SB	AB	H	PO	A	E	DP	TC/G	FA	G by Pos
1926	NY	N	1	–	–	0	0	0	0	0	–	0	0	0	0	0	0	0	0	0	0	0	0.0	–	C-1

Gib Brack

BRACK, GILBERT HERMAN (Gibby)
B. Mar. 29, 1908, Chicago, Ill.   D. Jan. 20, 1960, Greenville, Tex.   BR TR 5'9" 170 lbs.

Year	Team		Games	BA	SA	AB	H	2B	3B	HR	HR%	R	RBI	BB	SO	SB	AB	H	PO	A	E	DP	TC/G	FA	G by Pos
1937	BKN	N	112	.274	.435	372	102	27	9	5	1.3	60	38	44	93	9	6	1	208	10	7	0	2.0	.969	OF-101
1938	2 teams	BKN N (40G – .214)				PHI N (72G – .287)																			
"	total		112	.275	.414	338	93	22	5	5	1.5	50	34	22	44	3	14	6	182	8	6	3	1.8	.969	OF-81
1939	PHI	N	91	.289	.463	270	78	21	4	6	2.2	40	41	26	49	1	19	5	247	11	8	12	2.9	.970	OF-48, 1B-19
3 yrs.			315	.279	.436	980	273	70	18	16	1.6	150	113	92	186	13	39	12	637	29	21	15	2.2	.969	OF-230, 1B-19

Buddy Bradford

BRADFORD, CHARLES WILLIAM
B. July 25, 1944, Mobile, Ala.   BR TR 5'11" 170 lbs.

Year	Team		Games	BA	SA	AB	H	2B	3B	HR	HR%	R	RBI	BB	SO	SB	AB	H	PO	A	E	DP	TC/G	FA	G by Pos
1966	CHI	A	14	.143	.143	28	4	0	0	0	0.0	3	0	2	6	0	0	0	5	0	1	0	0.4	.833	OF-9
1967			24	.100	.150	20	2	1	0	0	0.0	6	1	1	7	3	1	0	9	0	1	0	0.4	.900	OF-14
1968			103	.217	.310	281	61	11	0	5	1.8	32	24	23	67	8	6	1	162	4	6	0	1.7	.965	OF-99
1969			93	.256	.421	273	70	8	2	11	4.0	36	27	34	75	5	5	0	141	5	6	1	1.6	.961	OF-88
1970	2 teams	CHI A (32G – .187)				CLE A (75G – .196)																			
"	total		107	.193	.343	254	49	9	1	9	3.5	33	31	31	73	1	18	3	163	2	3	0	1.6	.982	OF-91, 3B-1
1971	2 teams	CLE A (20G – .158)				CIN N (79G – .200)																			
"	total		99	.188	.283	138	26	5	1	2	1.4	21	15	20	33	4	14	2	106	3	4	1	1.1	.965	OF-84
1972	CHI	A	35	.271	.438	48	13	2	0	2	4.2	13	8	4	13	3	10	4	32	1	0	0	0.9	1.000	OF-28
1973			53	.238	.411	168	40	3	1	8	4.8	24	15	17	43	4	5	0	114	9	1	2	2.3	.992	OF-51
1974			39	.333	.510	96	32	2	0	5	5.2	16	10	13	11	1	7	2	47	2	1	0	1.3	.980	OF-32, DH-1
1975	2 teams	CHI A (25G – .155)				STL N (50G – .272)																			
"	total		75	.223	.396	139	31	4	1	6	4.3	20	30	20	46	3	27	6	69	2	4	0	1.0	.947	OF-43, DH-4
1976	CHI	A	55	.219	.350	160	35	5	2	4	2.5	20	14	19	37	6	9	0	91	0	2	0	1.7	.978	OF-48, DH-3
11 yrs.			697	.226	.364	1605	363	50	8	52	3.2	224	175	184	411	36	104	19	939	28	29	4	1.4	.971	OF-587, DH-8, 3B-1

Vic Bradford

BRADFORD, HENRY VICTOR
B. Mar. 5, 1915, Brownsville, Tenn.   BR TR 6'2" 190 lbs.

Year	Team		Games	BA	SA	AB	H	2B	3B	HR	HR%	R	RBI	BB	SO	SB	AB	H	PO	A	E	DP	TC/G	FA	G by Pos
1943	NY	N	6	.200	.200	5	1	0	0	0	0.0	1	1	1	1	0	1	0	3	0	0	0	0.5	1.000	OF-1

Bradley

BRADLEY,   5'10" 185 lbs.

Year	Team		Games	BA	SA	AB	H	2B	3B	HR	HR%	R	RBI	BB	SO	SB	AB	H	PO	A	E	DP	TC/G	FA	G by Pos
1884	WAS	U	1	.000	.000	3	0	0	0	0	0.0	0		2			0	0	3	0	0	0	3.0	1.000	OF-1

Year	Team		Games	BA	SA	AB	H	2B	3B	HR	HR%	R	RBI	BB	SO	SB	Pinch Hit AB	Pinch Hit H	PO	A	E	DP	TC/G	FA	G by Pos

Bill Bradley

BRADLEY, WILLIAM JOSEPH
B. Feb. 13, 1878, Cleveland, Ohio D. Mar. 11, 1954, Cleveland, Ohio
Manager 1905, 1914.

BR TR 6' 185 lbs.

Year	Team		Games	BA	SA	AB	H	2B	3B	HR	HR%	R	RBI	BB	SO	SB	AB	H	PO	A	E	DP	TC/G	FA	G by Pos
1899	CHI	N	35	.310	.419	129	40	6	1	2	1.6	26	18	12		4	0	0	61	82	23	8	4.7	.861	3B-30, SS-5
1900			122	.282	.399	444	125	21	8	5	1.1	63	49	27		14	1	1	292	304	63	21	5.4	.904	3B-106, 1B-15
1901	CLE	A	133	.293	.403	516	151	28	13	1	0.2	95	55	26		15	0	0	192	298	37	25	4.0	.930	3B-133, P-1
1902			137	.340	.515	550	187	39	12	11	2.0	104	77	27		11	0	0	188	324	43	21	4.1	.923	3B-137
1903			137	.315	.495	543	171	36	22	6	1.1	103	68	25		21	0	0	151	299	37	18	3.6	.924	3B-137
1904			154	.300	.402	607	182	31	8	5	0.8	94	83	26		27	0	0	178	308	23	18	3.3	.955	3B-154
1905			145	.268	.354	537	144	34	6	0	0.0	63	51	27		22	0	0	187	312	29	17	3.6	.945	3B-145
1906			82	.275	.358	302	83	15	2	2	0.7	32	25	18		13	0	0	107	177	10	6	3.6	.966	3B-82
1907			139	.223	.267	498	111	20	1	0	0.0	48	34	35		20	0	0	164	278	29	18	3.4	.938	3B-139
1908			148	.243	.318	548	133	24	7	1	0.2	70	46	29		18	0	0	192	296	30	16	3.5	.942	3B-116, SS-32
1909			95	.186	.222	334	62	6	3	0	0.0	30	22	19		8	2	1	126	162	13	17	3.2	.957	3B-87, 2B-3, 1B-3
1910			61	.196	.210	214	42	3	0	0	0.0	12	12	10		6	0	0	89	126	10	8	3.7	.956	3B-61
1914	BKN	F	7	.500	.667	6	3	1	0	0	0.0	1	3	0		0	6	3	0	0	0	0	0.0	—	
1915	KC	F	66	.187	.241	203	38	9	1	0	0.0	15	9	9		6	5	0	55	95	8	4	2.4	.949	3B-61
14 yrs.			1461	.271	.370	5431	1472	273	84	33	0.6	756	552	290		185	14	5	1982	3061	355	197	3.7	.934	3B-1388, SS-37, 1B-18, 2B-3, P-1

George Bradley

BRADLEY, GEORGE WASHINGTON (Grin)
B. July 13, 1852, Reading, Pa. D. Oct. 2, 1931, Philadelphia, Pa.

BR TR 5'10½" 175 lbs.

Year	Team		Games	BA	SA	AB	H	2B	3B	HR	HR%	R	RBI	BB	SO	SB	AB	H	PO	A	E	DP	TC/G	FA	G by Pos
1876	STL	N	64	.249	.321	265	66	7	6	0	0.0	29	28	3	12		0	0	50	87	12	4	2.3	.919	P-64
1877	CHI	N	55	.243	.304	214	52	7	3	0	0.0	31	12	6	19		0	0	48	89	18	2	2.8	.884	P-50, 3B-16, 1B-3, OF-1
1879	TRO	N	63	.247	.323	251	62	9	5	0	0.0	36	23	1	20		0	0	62	154	33	1	4.0	.867	P-54, 3B-5, 1B-3, OF-1, SS-1
1880	PRO	N	82	.227	.288	309	70	7	6	0	0.0	32	23	5	38		0	0	104	214	55	10	4.5	.853	3B-57, P-28, OF-7, 1B-2
1881	2 teams		DET N (1G – .000)			CLE N (60G – .249)																			
"	total		61	.245	.318	245	60	10	1	2	0.8	21	18	4	25		0	0	89	106	39	9	3.8	.833	3B-48, SS-7, P-6, OF-1
1882	CLE	N	30	.183	.226	115	21	5	0	0	0.0	16	6	4	16		0	0	82	47	13	8	4.7	.908	P-18, OF-9, 1B-6
1883	2 teams		CLE N (4G – .313)			PHI AA (76G – .234)																			
"	total		80	.238	.308	328	78	8	6	1	0.3	47		8	1		0	0	92	160	68	10	4.0	.788	3B-44, P-26, OF-11, SS-4, 1B-2
1884	CIN	U	58	.190	.270	226	43	4	7	0	0.0	31		7			0	0	82	94	24	4	3.4	.880	P-41, OF-16, SS-5, 1B-2
1886	PHI	AA	13	.083	.125	48	4	0	1	0	0.0	1		1			0	0	14	48	11	2	5.6	.849	SS-13
1888	BAL	AA	1	.000	.000	3	0	0	0	0	0.0	0	0	0		0	0	0	2	1	2	0	5.0	.600	SS-1
10 yrs.			507	.228	.295	2004	456	57	35	3	0.1	244	110	39	131		0	0	625	1000	275	50	3.7	.855	P-287, 3B-170, OF-46, SS-31, 1B-18

George Bradley

BRADLEY, GEORGE WASHINGTON
B. Apr. 1, 1914, Greenwood, Ark. D. Oct. 19, 1982, Lawrenceburg, Tenn.

BR TR 6'1½" 185 lbs.

Year	Team		Games	BA	SA	AB	H	2B	3B	HR	HR%	R	RBI	BB	SO	SB	AB	H	PO	A	E	DP	TC/G	FA	G by Pos
1946	STL	A	4	.167	.250	12	2	1	0	0	0.0	2	3	0	1		0	0	5	0	0	0	1.3	1.000	OF-3

Hugh Bradley

BRADLEY, HUGH FREDERICK (Corns)
B. May 23, 1885, Grafton, Mass. D. Jan. 26, 1949, Worcester, Mass.

BR TR 5'10" 175 lbs.

Year	Team		Games	BA	SA	AB	H	2B	3B	HR	HR%	R	RBI	BB	SO	SB	AB	H	PO	A	E	DP	TC/G	FA	G by Pos
1910	BOS	A	32	.169	.289	83	14	6	2	0	0.0	8	7	5		2	1	2	196	7	1	9	6.4	.995	1B-21, C-3, OF-1
1911			12	.317	.439	41	13	2	0	1	2.4	9	4	2		1	0	0	128	8	1	7	11.4	.993	1B-12
1912			40	.190	.307	137	26	11	1	1	0.7	16	19	15		3	0	0	354	21	4	13	9.5	.989	1B-40
1914	PIT	F	118	.307	.382	427	131	20	6	0	0.0	41	61	27		7	0	0	1132	60	12	52	10.2	.990	1B-118
1915	3 teams		PIT F (26G – .273)			BKN F (37G – .246)						NWK F (12G – .152)													
"	total		75	.240	.298	225	54	7	3	0	0.0	10	26	10		10	18	3	347	23	3	11	5.0	.992	1B-34, OF-22, C-1
5 yrs.			277	.261	.344	913	238	46	12	2	0.2	84	117	59		23	25	5	2157	119	21	92	8.3	.991	1B-225, OF-23, C-4

Jack Bradley

BRADLEY, JOHN THOMAS
B. Sept. 20, 1893, Denver, Colo. D. Mar. 18, 1969, Tulsa, Okla.

BR TR 5'11" 175 lbs.

Year	Team		Games	BA	SA	AB	H	2B	3B	HR	HR%	R	RBI	BB	SO	SB	AB	H	PO	A	E	DP	TC/G	FA	G by Pos
1916	CLE	A	2	.000	.000	3	0	0	0	0	0.0	0	0	0	1		1	0	2	0	0	0	1.0	1.000	C-1

Mark Bradley

BRADLEY, MARK ALLEN
B. Dec. 3, 1956, Elizabethtown, Ky.

BR TR 6'1" 180 lbs.

Year	Team		Games	BA	SA	AB	H	2B	3B	HR	HR%	R	RBI	BB	SO	SB	AB	H	PO	A	E	DP	TC/G	FA	G by Pos
1981	LA	N	9	.167	.333	6	1	1	0	0	0.0	0	1	0	2	0	2	0	3	0	0	0	0.4	1.000	OF-6
1982			8	.333	.333	3	1	0	0	0	0.0	1	0	0	1	0	1	0	1	0	0	0	0.1	1.000	OF-3
1983	NY	N	73	.202	.327	104	21	4	0	3	2.9	10	5	11	35	4	34	6	41	2	0	1	0.6	1.000	OF-35
3 yrs.			90	.204	.327	113	23	5	0	3	2.7	13	5	11	36	4	37	6	45	3	0	1	0.5	1.000	OF-44

Phil Bradley

BRADLEY, PHILIP POOLE
B. Mar. 11, 1959, Bloomington, Ind.

BR TR 6' 185 lbs.

Year	Team		Games	BA	SA	AB	H	2B	3B	HR	HR%	R	RBI	BB	SO	SB	AB	H	PO	A	E	DP	TC/G	FA	G by Pos
1983	SEA	A	23	.269	.299	67	18	2	0	0	0.0	8	5	8	5	3	3	0	36	1	1	0	1.7	.974	OF-21, DH-1
1984			124	.301	.363	322	97	12	4	0	0.0	49	24	34	61	21	3	0	235	3	2	1	1.9	.992	OF-117, DH-3
1985			159	.300	.498	641	192	33	8	26	4.1	100	88	55	129	22	0	0	336	10	5	3	2.2	.986	OF-159
1986			143	.310	.445	526	163	27	4	12	2.3	88	50	77	134	21	2	0	250	11	1	0	1.8	.996	OF-140
1987			158	.297	.463	603	179	38	10	14	2.3	101	67	84	119	40	0	0	273	13	5	1	1.8	.983	OF-158
1988	PHI	N	154	.264	.392	569	150	30	5	11	1.9	77	56	54	106	11	2	0	298	14	3	2	2.0	.990	OF-153
1989	BAL	A	144	.277	.417	545	151	23	10	11	2.0	83	55	70	103	20	4	0	284	4	3	0	2.0	.990	OF-140, DH-2
7 yrs.			905	.290	.434	3273	950	165	41	74	2.3	506	345	382	657	138	14	0	1712	56	20	7	2.0	.989	OF-888, DH-6

Scott Bradley

BRADLEY, SCOTT WILLIAM
B. Mar. 22, 1960, Glen Ridge, N.J.

BL TR 5'11" 175 lbs.

Year	Team		Games	BA	SA	AB	H	2B	3B	HR	HR%	R	RBI	BB	SO	SB	AB	H	PO	A	E	DP	TC/G	FA	G by Pos
1984	NY	A	9	.286	.333	21	6	1	0	0	0.0	3	2	1	1	0	1	0	10	0	0	0	1.1	1.000	OF-5, C-3
1985			19	.163	.245	49	8	2	1	0	0.0	4	1	1	5	0	7	1	12	0	1	0	0.7	.923	DH-9, C-3

Year Team	Games	BA	SA	AB	H	2B	3B	HR	HR%	R	RBI	BB	SO	SB	Pinch Hit AB	Pinch Hit H	PO	A	E	DP	TC/G	FA	G by Pos

Scott Bradley *continued*

Year Team	Games	BA	SA	AB	H	2B	3B	HR	HR%	R	RBI	BB	SO	SB	AB	H	PO	A	E	DP	TC/G	FA	G by Pos
1986 2 teams	CHI A (9G – .286)			SEA A (68G – .302)																			
" total	77	.300	.432	220	66	8	3	5	2.3	20	28	13	7	1	17	5	281	21	3	5	4.0	.990	C-59, DH-9, OF-1
1987 SEA A	102	.278	.371	342	95	15	1	5	1.5	34	43	15	18	0	12	4	438	39	8	4	4.8	.984	C-82, 3B-8, OF-2
1988	103	.257	.349	335	86	17	1	4	1.2	45	33	17	16	1	12	2	543	42	6	7	5.7	.990	C-85, DH-4, OF-4, 3B-3, 1B-2
1989	103	.274	.367	270	74	16	0	3	1.1	21	37	21	23	1	25	9	400	26	4	6	4.2	.991	C-70, DH-6, 1B-2, OF-1
6 yrs.	413	.271	.369	1237	335	59	6	17	1.4	127	144	68	70	3	74	21	1684	128	22	22	4.4	.988	C-302, DH-28, OF-13, 3B-11, 1B-4

Dallas Bradshaw

BRADSHAW, DALLAS CARL (Rabbit, Windy)
B. Nov. 23, 1895, Wolf Creek, Ill.   D. Dec. 11, 1939, Herrin, Ill.

BL TR 5'7"   145 lbs.

Year Team	Games	BA	SA	AB	H	2B	3B	HR	HR%	R	RBI	BB	SO	SB	AB	H	PO	A	E	DP	TC/G	FA	G by Pos
1917 PHI A	2	.000	.000	4	0	0	0	0	0.0	0	0	0	1	0	1	0	5	2	0	1	3.5	1.000	2B-1

George Bradshaw

BRADSHAW, GEORGE THOMAS
B. Sept. 12, 1924, Salisbury, N. C.

BR TR 6'2"   185 lbs.

Year Team	Games	BA	SA	AB	H	2B	3B	HR	HR%	R	RBI	BB	SO	SB	AB	H	PO	A	E	DP	TC/G	FA	G by Pos
1952 WAS A	10	.217	.304	23	5	2	0	0	0.0	3	6	1	2	0	1	0	21	1	2	0	2.4	.917	C-9

Bob Brady

BRADY, ROBERT JAY
B. Nov. 8, 1922, Lewistown, Pa.

BL TR 6'1"   175 lbs.

Year Team	Games	BA	SA	AB	H	2B	3B	HR	HR%	R	RBI	BB	SO	SB	AB	H	PO	A	E	DP	TC/G	FA	G by Pos
1946 BOS N	3	.200	.200	5	1	0	0	0	0.0	0	0	1	1	0	2	1	4	2	1	0	2.3	.857	C-1
1947	1	.000	.000	1	0	0	0	0	0.0	0	0	0	0	0	1	0	0	0	0	0	0.0	–	
2 yrs.	4	.167	.167	6	1	0	0	0	0.0	0	0	1	1	0	3	1	4	2	1	0	1.8	.857	C-1

Brian Brady

BRADY, BRIAN PHELAN
B. July 11, 1962, Queens, N. Y.

BL TL 5'11"   185 lbs.

Year Team	Games	BA	SA	AB	H	2B	3B	HR	HR%	R	RBI	BB	SO	SB	AB	H	PO	A	E	DP	TC/G	FA	G by Pos
1989 CAL A	2	.500	1.000	2	1	0	0	0	0.0	0	1	0	0	0	2	1	0	0	0	0	0.0	–	OF-1

Cliff Brady

BRADY, CLIFFORD FRANCIS
B. Mar. 6, 1897, St. Louis, Mo.   D. Sept. 25, 1974, Belleville, Ill.

BR TR 5'5½"   140 lbs.

Year Team	Games	BA	SA	AB	H	2B	3B	HR	HR%	R	RBI	BB	SO	SB	AB	H	PO	A	E	DP	TC/G	FA	G by Pos
1920 BOS A	53	.228	.267	180	41	5	1	0	0.0	16	12	13	12	0	0	0	111	193	8	21	5.9	.974	2B-53

Fred Brady

Playing record listed under Larry Kopf

Steve Brady

BRADY, STEPHEN A.
Brother of Tom Brady.
B. July 14, 1851, Worcester, Mass.   D. Nov. 1, 1917, Hartford, Conn.

5'9½"   165 lbs.

Year Team	Games	BA	SA	AB	H	2B	3B	HR	HR%	R	RBI	BB	SO	SB	AB	H	PO	A	E	DP	TC/G	FA	G by Pos
1883 NY AA	97	.271	.326	432	117	12	6	0	0.0	69		11			0	0	844	31	37	32	9.4	.959	1B-81, OF-16
1884	112	.252	.287	485	122	11	3	0	0.0	102		21			0	0	189	27	18	2	2.1	.923	OF-110, 1B-5, 2B-1
1885	108	.295	.371	434	128	14	5	3	0.7	60		25			0	0	198	18	29	5	2.3	.882	OF-105, 1B-4, 2B-2, 3B-1
1886	124	.240	.279	466	112	8	5	0	0.0	56		35			0	0	177	26	38	2	1.9	.842	OF-123, 1B-1
4 yrs.	441	.264	.314	1817	479	45	19	3	0.2	287		92			0	0	1408	102	122	41	3.7	.925	OF-354, 1B-91, 2B-3, 3B-1

Bobby Bragan

BRAGAN, ROBERT RANDALL
B. Oct. 30, 1917, Birmingham, Ala.
Manager 1956-58, 1963-66.

BR TR 5'10½" 175 lbs.

Year Team	Games	BA	SA	AB	H	2B	3B	HR	HR%	R	RBI	BB	SO	SB	AB	H	PO	A	E	DP	TC/G	FA	G by Pos
1940 PHI N	132	.222	.300	474	105	14	1	7	1.5	36	44	28	34	2	0	0	268	443	49	83	5.8	.936	SS-132, 3B-2
1941	154	.251	.318	557	140	19	3	4	0.7	37	69	26	29	7	0	0	324	438	45	86	5.2	.944	SS-154, 2B-2, 3B-1
1942	109	.218	.284	335	73	12	2	2	0.6	17	15	20	21	0	2	0	242	263	27	55	4.9	.949	SS-78, C-22, 2B-4, 3B-3
1943 BKN N	74	.264	.341	220	58	7	2	2	0.9	17	24	15	16	0	1	0	264	55	10	9	4.4	.970	SS-51, C-35, 2B-1
1944	94	.267	.327	266	71	8	4	0	0.0	26	17	13	14	2	3	1	207	130	12	21	3.7	.966	SS-57, 3B-12, SS-5
1947	25	.194	.250	36	7	2	0	0	0.0	3	3	7	3	1	4	1	56	5	0	1	2.4	1.000	C-24
1948	9	.167	.167	12	2	0	0	0	0.0	0	0	1	0	0	4	0	11	0	0	0	1.3	1.000	C-5
7 yrs.	597	.240	.309	1900	456	62	12	15	0.8	136	172	110	117	12	14	2	1372	1335	143	255	4.8	.950	SS-420, C-143, 3B-18, 2B-7

WORLD SERIES

Year Team	Games	BA	SA	AB	H	2B	3B	HR	HR%	R	RBI	BB	SO	SB	AB	H	PO	A	E	DP	TC/G	FA	G by Pos
1947 BKN N	1	1.000	2.000	1	1	1	0	0	0.0	0	1	0	0	0	1	1	0	0	0	0	0.0	–	

Glenn Braggs

BRAGGS, GLENN ERICK
B. Oct. 17, 1962, San Bernardino, Calif.

BR TR 6'3"   210 lbs.

Year Team	Games	BA	SA	AB	H	2B	3B	HR	HR%	R	RBI	BB	SO	SB	AB	H	PO	A	E	DP	TC/G	FA	G by Pos
1986 MIL A	58	.237	.349	215	51	8	2	4	1.9	19	18	11	47	1	0	0	116	5	12	0	2.3	.910	OF-56, DH-2
1987	132	.269	.430	505	136	28	7	13	2.6	67	77	47	96	12	3	0	301	6	9	1	2.4	.972	OF-126, DH-8
1988	72	.261	.423	272	71	14	0	10	3.7	30	42	14	60	6	0	0	134	1	3	0	1.9	.978	OF-54, DH-18
1989	144	.247	.370	514	127	12	3	15	2.9	77	66	42	111	17	1	0	267	6	8	1	2.0	.972	OF-132, DH-13
4 yrs.	406	.256	.396	1506	385	62	12	42	2.8	193	203	114	314	36	4	0	818	18	32	2	2.1	.963	OF-365, DH-41

Dave Brain

BRAIN, DAVID LEONARD
B. Jan. 24, 1879, Hereford, England   D. May 25, 1959, Los Angeles, Calif.

BR TR 5'10"   170 lbs.

Year Team	Games	BA	SA	AB	H	2B	3B	HR	HR%	R	RBI	BB	SO	SB	AB	H	PO	A	E	DP	TC/G	FA	G by Pos
1901 CHI A	5	.350	.400	20	7	0	0	0	0.0	2	5	1			0	0	14	16	3	4	6.6	.909	2B-5
1903 STL N	119	.231	.319	464	107	8	15	1	0.2	44	60	25			21	0	233	350	63	43	5.4	.902	SS-72, 3B-46
1904	127	.266	.408	488	130	24	12	7	1.4	57	72	17			18	2	259	308	45	26	4.8	.926	SS-59, 3B-30, OF-19, 2B-13, 1B-4
1905 2 teams	STL N (44G – .228)			PIT N (85G – .257)																			
" total	129	.247	.366	465	115	21	11	4	0.9	42	63	23			12	3	170	274	35	19	3.7	.927	3B-84, SS-33, OF-6
1906 BOS N	139	.250	.333	525	131	19	5	5	1.0	43	45	29			11	0	208	321	48	26	4.2	.917	3B-139
1907	133	.279	.420	509	142	24	9	10	2.0	60	56	29			10	0	198	325	47	27	4.3	.918	3B-130, OF-3

Dave Brain *continued*

Year	Team		Games	BA	SA	AB	H	2B	3B	HR	HR%	R	RBI	BB	SO	SB	Pinch Hit AB	Pinch Hit H	PO	A	E	DP	TC/G	FA	G by Pos
1908	2 teams	CIN N (16G – .109)				NY N (11G – .176)																			
"	total		27	.125	.125	72	9	0	0	0	0.0	6	2	10		1	2	0	44	10	6	0	2.2	.900	OF-19, 2B-3, 3B-2, SS-1
7 yrs.			679	.252	.363	2543	641	97	52	27	1.1	254	303	134		73	7	1	1126	1604	247	145	4.4	.917	3B-431, SS-165, OF-47, 2B-21, 1B-4

Fred Brainerd

BRAINERD, FREDERICK F.
B. Feb. 17, 1892, Champaign, Ill.   D. Apr. 17, 1959, Galveston, Tex.   BR TR 6' 176 lbs.

Year	Team	Games	BA	SA	AB	H	2B	3B	HR	HR%	R	RBI	BB	SO	SB	Pinch Hit AB	Pinch Hit H	PO	A	E	DP	TC/G	FA	G by Pos
1914	NY N	2	.200	.200	5	1	0	0	0	0.0	1	0	1	0	0	0	0	6	6	1	1	6.5	.923	2B-2
1915		91	.201	.257	249	50	7	2	1	0.4	31	21	21	44	6	20	3	443	94	18	37	6.1	.968	1B-45, 3B-16, SS-9, OF-1, 2B-1
1916		2	.000	.000	7	0	0	0	0	0.0	0	0	0	0	0	0	0	3	2	3	0	4.0	.625	3B-2
3 yrs.		95	.195	.249	261	51	7	2	1	0.4	32	21	22	44	6	20	3	452	102	22	38	6.1	.962	1B-45, 3B-18, SS-9, 2B-3, OF-1

Erv Brame

BRAME, ERVIN BECKHAM
B. Oct. 12, 1901, Big Rock, Tenn.   D. Nov. 22, 1949, Hopkinsville, Ky.   BL TR 6'2" 190 lbs.

Year	Team	Games	BA	SA	AB	H	2B	3B	HR	HR%	R	RBI	BB	SO	SB	Pinch Hit AB	Pinch Hit H	PO	A	E	DP	TC/G	FA	G by Pos
1928	PIT N	35	.265	.408	49	13	4	0	1	2.0	6	11	4	3	0	9	1	2	18	1	0	0.6	.952	P-24
1929		59	.310	.500	116	36	8	1	4	3.4	9	25	2	7	0	21	10	7	36	3	0	0.8	.935	P-37
1930		50	.353	.474	116	41	5	0	3	2.6	20	22	0	2	0	16	6	1	39	2	0	0.8	.952	P-32
1931		48	.274	.337	95	26	4	1	0	0.0	6	15	4	16	0	21	7	1	34	1	2	0.8	.972	P-26
1932		26	.250	.250	20	5	0	0	0	0.0	2	2	0	4	0	3	1	0	9	0	1	0.3	1.000	P-23
5 yrs.		218	.306	.429	396	121	21	2	8	2.0	43	75	10	32	0	70	25	11	136	7	3	0.7	.955	P-142

Art Bramhall

BRAMHALL, ARTHUR WASHINGTON
B. Feb. 22, 1909, Oak Park, Ill.   D. Sept. 4, 1985, Madison, Wis.   BR TR 5'11" 170 lbs.

Year	Team	Games	BA	SA	AB	H	2B	3B	HR	HR%	R	RBI	BB	SO	SB	Pinch Hit AB	Pinch Hit H	PO	A	E	DP	TC/G	FA	G by Pos
1935	PHI N	2	.000	.000	1	0	0	0	0	0.0	0	0	0	0	0	0	0	2	2	0	0	2.0	1.000	SS-1, 3B-1

Al Brancato

BRANCATO, ALBERT
B. May 29, 1919, Philadelphia, Pa.   BR TR 5'9½" 188 lbs.

Year	Team	Games	BA	SA	AB	H	2B	3B	HR	HR%	R	RBI	BB	SO	SB	Pinch Hit AB	Pinch Hit H	PO	A	E	DP	TC/G	FA	G by Pos
1939	PHI A	21	.206	.324	68	14	5	0	1	1.5	12	8	8	4	1	0	0	20	42	4	2	3.1	.939	3B-20, SS-1
1940		107	.191	.252	298	57	11	2	1	0.3	42	23	28	36	3	2	0	160	231	23	39	3.9	.944	SS-80, 3B-25
1941		144	.234	.317	530	124	20	9	2	0.4	60	49	59	49	1	1	0	267	403	61	82	5.1	.917	SS-139, 3B-7
1945		10	.118	.147	34	4	1	0	0	0.0	3	0	1	3	0	0	0	22	25	2	5	4.9	.959	SS-10
4 yrs.		282	.214	.290	930	199	37	11	4	0.4	117	80	96	92	5	3	0	469	701	90	128	4.5	.929	SS-230, 3B-52

Ron Brand

BRAND, RONALD GEORGE
B. Jan. 13, 1940, Los Angeles, Calif.   BR TR 5'7½" 167 lbs.

Year	Team	Games	BA	SA	AB	H	2B	3B	HR	HR%	R	RBI	BB	SO	SB	Pinch Hit AB	Pinch Hit H	PO	A	E	DP	TC/G	FA	G by Pos
1963	PIT N	46	.288	.364	66	19	2	0	1	1.5	8	7	10	11	0	5	0	141	13	5	4	3.5	.969	C-33, 3B-2, 2B-2
1965	HOU N	117	.235	.281	391	92	6	3	2	0.5	27	37	19	34	10	6	0	598	60	8	11	5.7	.988	C-102, 3B-6, OF-5
1966		56	.244	.260	123	30	2	0	0	0.0	12	10	9	13	0	20	3	150	29	3	6	3.3	.984	C-25, 2B-9, OF-3, 3B-1
1967		84	.242	.288	215	52	8	1	0	0.0	22	18	23	17	4	14	2	397	37	1	3	5.2	.998	C-67, OF-1, 2B-1
1968		43	.160	.185	81	13	2	0	0	0.0	7	4	9	11	1	7	1	154	14	0	3	3.9	1.000	C-84, OF-2
1969	MON N	103	.258	.300	287	74	12	0	0	0.0	19	20	30	19	2	13	3	492	44	8	7	5.3	.985	SS-19, 3B-12, C-9, OF-5, 2B-3
1970		72	.238	.302	126	30	2	3	0	0.0	10	9	9	16	2	35	7	60	57	7	8	1.7	.944	SS-22, OF-4, 3B-4, 2B-1, C-1
1971		47	.214	.214	56	12	0	0	0	0.0	3	1	3	5	1	15	3	28	44	3	10	1.6	.960	
8 yrs.		568	.239	.282	1345	322	34	7	3	0.2	108	106	112	126	20	115	19	2020	298	35	52	4.1	.985	C-350, SS-41, 3B-26, OF-21, 2B-16

Jackie Brandt

BRANDT, JOHN GEORGE
B. Apr. 28, 1934, Omaha, Neb.   BR TR 5'11" 165 lbs.

Year	Team		Games	BA	SA	AB	H	2B	3B	HR	HR%	R	RBI	BB	SO	SB	Pinch Hit AB	Pinch Hit H	PO	A	E	DP	TC/G	FA	G by Pos
1956	2 teams	STL N (27G – .286)				NY N (98G – .299)																			
"	total		125	.298	.478	393	117	19	8	12	3.1	54	50	21	36	3	4	2	198	9	2	1	1.7	.990	OF-122
1958	SF N		18	.250	.269	52	13	1	0	0	0.0	7	3	6	5	1	5	1	28	0	0	0	1.6	1.000	OF-14
1959			137	.270	.415	429	116	16	5	12	2.8	63	57	35	69	11	16	4	204	39	12	4	1.9	.953	OF-116, 3B-18, 1B-3, 2B-1
1960	BAL A		145	.254	.413	511	130	24	6	15	2.9	73	65	47	69	5	4	0	285	10	6	2	2.1	.980	OF-142, 3B-2, 1B-1
1961			139	.297	.444	516	153	18	5	16	3.1	93	72	62	51	10	0	0	293	6	8	2	2.2	.974	OF-138, 3B-2
1962			143	.255	.446	505	129	29	5	19	3.8	76	75	55	64	9	6	1	310	10	8	2	2.3	.976	OF-138, 3B-1
1963			142	.248	.404	451	112	15	5	15	3.3	49	61	34	85	4	8	1	272	11	4	1	2.0	.986	OF-134, 3B-1
1964			137	.243	.369	523	127	25	1	13	2.5	66	47	45	104	1	4	0	345	14	7	2	2.7	.981	OF-134
1965			96	.243	.412	243	59	17	0	8	3.3	35	24	21	40	1	14	2	143	6	6	0	1.6	.961	OF-84
1966	PHI N		82	.250	.317	164	41	6	1	1	0.6	16	15	17	36	0	15	4	78	5	1	0	1.0	.988	OF-71
1967	2 teams	PHI N (16G – .105)				HOU N (41G – .236)																			
"	total		57	.213	.306	108	23	5	1	1	0.9	8	16	8	15	0	33	9	106	7	1	5	2.0	.991	1B-14, OF-9, 3B-1
11 yrs.			1221	.262	.412	3895	1020	175	37	112	2.9	540	485	351	574	45	109	24	2262	115	55	19	2.0	.977	OF-1100, 3B-25, 1B-18, 2B-1

Otis Brannan

BRANNAN, OTIS OWEN
B. Mar. 13, 1899, Greenbrier, Ark.   D. June 6, 1967, Little Rock, Ark.   BL TR 5'9" 160 lbs.

Year	Team	Games	BA	SA	AB	H	2B	3B	HR	HR%	R	RBI	BB	SO	SB	Pinch Hit AB	Pinch Hit H	PO	A	E	DP	TC/G	FA	G by Pos
1928	STL A	135	.244	.356	483	118	18	3	10	2.1	68	66	60	19	3	0	0	272	434	26	74	5.4	.964	2B-135
1929		23	.275	.353	51	14	1	0	1	2.0	4	8	4	4	0	4	1	31	47	2	6	3.5	.975	2B-19
2 yrs.		158	.247	.356	534	132	19	3	11	2.1	72	74	64	23	3	4	1	303	481	28	80	5.1	.966	2B-154

Dudley Branom

BRANOM, EDGAR DUDLEY
B. Nov. 30, 1897, Sulphur Springs, Tex.   D. Feb. 4, 1980, Sun City, Ariz.   BL TL 6'1" 190 lbs.

Year	Team	Games	BA	SA	AB	H	2B	3B	HR	HR%	R	RBI	BB	SO	SB	Pinch Hit AB	Pinch Hit H	PO	A	E	DP	TC/G	FA	G by Pos
1927	PHI A	30	.234	.245	94	22	1	0	0	0.0	8	13	2	5	2	4	2	231	17	7	18	8.5	.973	1B-26

Kitty Bransfield

BRANSFIELD, WILLIAM EDWARD
B. Jan. 7, 1875, Worcester, Mass.   D. May 1, 1947, Worcester, Mass.   BR TR 5'11" 207 lbs.

Year	Team		Games	BA	SA	AB	H	2B	3B	HR	HR%	R	RBI	BB	SO	SB	Pinch Hit AB	H	PO	A	E	DP	TC/G	FA	G by Pos

Kitty Bransfield *continued*

Year	Team		Games	BA	SA	AB	H	2B	3B	HR	HR%	R	RBI	BB	SO	SB	AB	H	PO	A	E	DP	TC/G	FA	G by Pos
1898	BOS	N	5	.222	.444	9	2	0	1	0	0.0	2	1	0		0	0	0	12	0	1	0	2.6	.923	C-4, 1B-1
1901	PIT	N	139	.295	.398	566	167	26	16	0	0.0	92	91	29		23	0	0	1374	52	28	72	10.5	.981	1B-139
1902			102	.305	.396	417	127	21	7	1	0.2	50	69	17		23	1	0	1064	41	18	40	11.0	.984	1B-101
1903			127	.265	.350	505	134	23	7	2	0.4	69	57	33		13	0	0	1347	88	25	82	11.5	.981	1B-127
1904			139	.223	.290	520	116	17	9	0	0.0	47	60	22		11	0	0	1454	89	30	70	11.3	.981	1B-139
1905	PHI	N	151	.259	.345	580	150	23	9	3	0.5	55	76	27		27	0	0	1398	92	23	75	10.0	.985	1B-151
1906			140	.275	.353	524	144	28	5	1	0.2	47	60	16		12	1	0	1318	88	29	57	10.3	.980	1B-139
1907			94	.233	.287	348	81	15	2	0	0.0	25	38	14		8	2	0	862	53	21	46	10.0	.978	1B-92
1908			144	.304	.395	527	160	25	7	3	0.6	53	71	23		30	1	1	1472	89	22	67	11.0	.986	1B-143
1909			140	.292	.372	527	154	27	6	1	0.2	47	59	18		17	2	0	1377	89	16	71	10.6	.989	1B-138
1910			123	.239	.319	427	102	17	4	3	0.7	39	52	20	34	10	12	2	1026	51	20	82	8.9	.982	1B-110
1911	2 teams		PHI N (23G – .256)			CHI N (3G – .400)																			
"	total		26	.283	.377	53	15	3	1	0	0.0	4	3	2	7	1	15	1	101	5	1	8	4.1	.991	1B-11
	12 yrs.		1330	.270	.353	5003	1352	225	74	14	0.3	530	637	221	41	175	34	4	12805	737	237	670	10.4	.983	1B-1291, C-4

WORLD SERIES

| 1903 | PIT | N | 8 | .200 | .333 | 30 | 6 | 0 | 2 | 0 | 0.0 | 3 | 1 | 1 | 6 | 1 | 0 | 0 | 80 | 6 | 2 | 5 | 11.0 | .977 | 1B-8 |

Marshall Brant

BRANT, MARSHALL LEE
B. Sept. 17, 1955, Garberville, Calif.   BR TR 6'5" 185 lbs.

1980	NY	A	3	.000	.000	6	0	0	0	0	0.0	0	0	0	3	0	1	0	9	1	0	1	3.3	1.000	1B-2, DH-1
1983	OAK	A	5	.143	.143	14	2	0	0	0	0.0	0	2	0	3	0	2	0	19	0	2	4	4.2	.905	1B-3, DH-1
	2 yrs.		8	.100	.100	20	2	0	0	0	0.0	0	2	0	6	0	3	0	28	1	2	5	3.9	.935	1B-5, DH-2

Mickey Brantley

BRANTLEY, MICHAEL CHARLES
B. June 17, 1961, Catskill, N.Y.   BR TR 5'10" 180 lbs.

1986	SEA	A	27	.196	.353	102	20	3	2	3	2.9	12	7	10	21	1	2	0	54	3	1	1	2.1	.983	OF-25
1987			92	.302	.499	351	106	23	2	14	4.0	52	54	24	44	13	4	1	163	3	3	1	1.8	.982	OF-82, DH-8
1988			149	.263	.399	577	152	25	4	15	2.6	76	56	26	64	18	1	1	327	5	6	1	2.3	.982	OF-147
1989			34	.157	.204	108	17	5	0	0	0.0	14	8	7	7	2	3	0	50	1	0	0	1.5	1.000	OF-23, DH-7
	4 yrs.		302	.259	.407	1138	295	56	8	32	2.8	154	125	67	136	34	10	2	594	12	10	3	2.0	.984	OF-277, DH-15

Kitty Brashear

BRASHEAR, NORMAN C.
Brother of Roy Brashear.
B. Aug. 27, 1877, Mansfield, Ohio   D. Dec. 22, 1934, Los Angeles, Calif.   BR TR 5'11" 205 lbs.

| 1902 | STL | N | 110 | .276 | .314 | 388 | 107 | 8 | 2 | 1 | 0.3 | 36 | 40 | 32 | | 9 | 3 | 1 | 828 | 97 | 24 | 54 | 8.6 | .975 | 1B-67, 2B-21, OF-16, SS-3 |

Roy Brashear

BRASHEAR, ROY PARKS
Brother of Kitty Brashear.
B. Jan. 3, 1874, Ashtabula, Ohio   D. Apr. 20, 1951, Los Angeles, Calif.   BR TR

1899	LOU	N	3	.500	.500	2	1	0	0	0	0.0	0	0	0		0	0	0	0	3	0	0	1.0	1.000	P-3
1903	PHI	N	20	.227	.267	75	17	3	0	0	0.0	9	4	6		2	0	0	60	40	9	8	5.5	.917	2B-18, 1B-2
	2 yrs.		23	.234	.273	77	18	3	0	0	0.0	9	4	6		2	0	0	60	43	9	8	4.9	.920	2B-18, P-3, 1B-2

Joe Bratcher

BRATCHER, JOSEPH WARWICK (Goobers)
B. July 22, 1898, Grand Saline, Tex.   D. Oct. 13, 1977, Fort Worth, Tex.   BL TR 5'8½" 140 lbs.

| 1924 | STL | N | 4 | .000 | .000 | 1 | 0 | 0 | 0 | 0 | 0.0 | 1 | 0 | 0 | | 0 | 1 | 0 | 0 | 0 | 0 | 0 | 0.0 | – | OF-1 |

Fritz Bratschi

BRATSCHI, FREDERICK OSCAR
B. Jan. 16, 1892, Alliance, Ohio   D. Jan. 10, 1962, Massillon, Ohio   BR TR 5'10" 170 lbs.

1921	CHI	A	16	.286	.321	28	8	1	0	0	0.0	0	3	0	2	0	10	3	7	2	0	0	0.6	1.000	OF-5
1926	BOS	A	72	.275	.347	167	46	10	1	0	0.0	12	19	14	15	0	30	7	55	1	3	0	0.8	.949	OF-37
1927			1	.000	.000	1	0	0	0	0	0.0	0	0	0	0	0	1	0	0	0	0	0	0.0		
	3 yrs.		89	.276	.342	196	54	11	1	0	0.0	12	22	14	17	0	41	10	62	3	3	0	0.8	.956	OF-42

Steve Braun

BRAUN, STEPHEN RUSSELL
B. May 8, 1948, Trenton, N.J.   BL TR 5'10" 180 lbs.

1971	MIN	A	128	.254	.344	343	87	12	2	5	1.5	51	35	48	50	8	26	7	107	193	13	24	2.4	.958	3B-73, 2B-28, SS-10, OF-2
1972			121	.289	.356	402	116	21	0	2	0.5	40	50	45	38	4	14	4	110	207	13	26	2.7	.961	3B-74, 2B-20, SS-11, OF-9
1973			115	.283	.438	361	102	28	5	6	1.7	46	42	74	48	4	5	1	86	175	16	21	2.4	.942	3B-102, OF-6
1974			129	.280	.364	453	127	12	1	8	1.8	53	40	56	51	4	6	1	195	47	12	8	2.0	.953	OF-108, 3B-17
1975			136	.302	.428	453	137	18	1	11	2.4	70	45	66	55	0	11	6	271	14	10	4	2.2	.966	OF-106, DH-9, 1B-9, 3B-2, 2B-1
1976			122	.288	.353	417	120	12	3	3	0.7	73	61	67	43	12	9	5	71	32	6	3	0.9	.945	DH-71, OF-32, 3B-16
1977	SEA	A	139	.235	.315	451	106	19	1	5	1.1	51	31	80	59	8	11	0	186	11	6	3	1.5	.970	OF-100, DH-32, 3B-1
1978	2 teams		SEA A (32G – .230)			KC A (64G – .263)																			
"	total		96	.251	.370	211	53	14	1	3	1.4	27	29	37	21	4	38	11	10	0	0	0	0.1	1.000	OF-37, DH-14, 3B-11
1979	KC	A	58	.267	.388	116	31	2	0	4	3.4	15	10	22	11	0	28	9	26	4	0	0	0.5	1.000	OF-18, DH-11, 3B-2
1980	2 teams		KC A (14G – .043)			TOR A (37G – .273)																			
"	total		51	.205	.269	78	16	2	0	1	1.3	4	10	10	7	0	35	10	2	1	0	0	0.1	1.000	DH-14, OF-5, 3B-1
1981	STL	N	44	.196	.283	46	9	2	0	0	0.0	4	10	15	7	1	25	5	6	2	0	1	0.4	1.000	OF-12, 3B-1
1982			58	.274	.339	62	17	4	0	0	0.0	6	4	11	10	0	41	12	6	1	1	0	0.2	.917	OF-8, 3B-5
1983			78	.272	.413	92	25	3	0	3	3.3	8	7	21	7	0	48	15	26	3	0	0	0.4	1.000	OF-22, 3B-4
1984			86	.276	.327	98	27	3	1	0	0.0	6	16	17	17	0	60	17	10	1	0	0	0.1	1.000	OF-19, 3B-1
1985			64	.239	.343	67	16	4	0	1	1.5	7	6	10	9	0	45	11	14	1	0	0	0.2	1.000	OF-14
	15 yrs.		1425	.271	.367	3650	989	155	19	52	1.4	466	388	579	433	45	402	113	1135	697	77	92	1.3	.960	OF-498, 3B-310, DH-151, 2B-49, SS-21, 1B-9
																	7th								

LEAGUE CHAMPIONSHIP SERIES

| 1978 | KC | A | 2 | .000 | .000 | 5 | 0 | 0 | 0 | 0 | 0.0 | 0 | 1 | 1 | 1 | 0 | 1 | 0 | 5 | 0 | 0 | 0 | 2.5 | 1.000 | OF-1 |
| 1982 | STL | N | 1 | .000 | .000 | 1 | 0 | 0 | 0 | 0 | 0.0 | 0 | 0 | 1 | 0 | 0 | 1 | 0 | 0 | 0 | 0 | 0 | 0.0 | – | |

Year	Team	Games	BA	SA	AB	H	2B	3B	HR	HR%	R	RBI	BB	SO	SB	Pinch Hit AB	Pinch Hit H	PO	A	E	DP	TC/G	FA	G by Pos

Steve Braun *continued*

Year	Team	Games	BA	SA	AB	H	2B	3B	HR	HR%	R	RBI	BB	SO	SB	AB	H	PO	A	E	DP	TC/G	FA	G by Pos
1985		2	.000	.000	2	0	0	0	0	0.0	0	0	0	0	0	2	0	0	0	0	0	0.0	–	
3 yrs.		5	.000	.000	8	0	0	0	0	0.0	1	1	0	0	0	4	0	5	0	0	0	1.0	1.000	OF-1

WORLD SERIES

Year	Team	Games	BA	SA	AB	H	2B	3B	HR	HR%	R	RBI	BB	SO	SB	AB	H	PO	A	E	DP	TC/G	FA	G by Pos
1982	STL N	2	.500	.500	2	1	0	0	0	0.0	0	2	1	0	0	1	0	0	0	0	0	0.0	–	DH-2
1985		1	.000	.000	1	0	0	0	0	0.0	0	0	0	0	0	1	0	0	0	0	0	0.0	–	
2 yrs.		3	.333	.333	3	1	0	0	0	0.0	0	2	1	0	0	2	0	0	0	0	0	0.0	–	DH-2

Angel Bravo

BRAVO, ANGEL ALFONSO
Born Angel Alfonso Bravo y Urdaneta.
B. Aug. 4, 1942, Maracaibo, Venezuela

BL TL 5'8" 150 lbs.

Year	Team	Games	BA	SA	AB	H	2B	3B	HR	HR%	R	RBI	BB	SO	SB	AB	H	PO	A	E	DP	TC/G	FA	G by Pos
1969	CHI A	27	.289	.411	90	26	4	2	1	1.1	10	3	5	2	2	0		44	0	1	0	1.7	.978	OF-25
1970	CIN N	65	.277	.323	65	18	1	1	0	0.0	10	9	9	13	0	42	13	17	1	1	0	0.3	.947	OF-22
1971	2 teams	CIN N (5G – .200)	SD N (52G – .155)																					
"	total	57	.159	.190	63	10	2	0	0	0.0	6	6	8	13	0	40	7	5	0	1	0	0.1	.833	OF-9
3 yrs.		149	.248	.321	218	54	7	3	1	0.5	26	12	20	31	2	84	20	66	1	3	0	0.5	.957	OF-56

LEAGUE CHAMPIONSHIP SERIES

Year	Team	Games	BA	SA	AB	H	2B	3B	HR	HR%	R	RBI	BB	SO	SB	AB	H	PO	A	E	DP	TC/G	FA	G by Pos
1970	CIN N	1	.000	.000	1	0	0	0	0	0.0	0	0	0	0	0	1	0	0	0	0	0	0.0	–	

WORLD SERIES

Year	Team	Games	BA	SA	AB	H	2B	3B	HR	HR%	R	RBI	BB	SO	SB	AB	H	PO	A	E	DP	TC/G	FA	G by Pos
1970	CIN N	4	.000	.000	2	0	0	0	0	0.0	0	1	1	0	0	2	0	0	0	0	0	0.0	–	

Buster Bray

BRAY, CLARENCE WILBUR
B. Apr. 1, 1913, Birmingham, Ala.   D. Sept. 4, 1982, Evansville, Ind.

BL TL 6' 170 lbs.

Year	Team	Games	BA	SA	AB	H	2B	3B	HR	HR%	R	RBI	BB	SO	SB	AB	H	PO	A	E	DP	TC/G	FA	G by Pos
1941	BOS N	4	.091	.182	11	1	1	0	0	0.0	2	1	1	2	0	0	0	6	0	0	0	1.5	1.000	OF-3

Frank Brazill

BRAZILL, FRANK LEO
B. Aug. 11, 1899, Spangler, Pa.   D. Nov. 3, 1976, Oakland, Calif.

BL TR 5'11½" 175 lbs.

Year	Team	Games	BA	SA	AB	H	2B	3B	HR	HR%	R	RBI	BB	SO	SB	AB	H	PO	A	E	DP	TC/G	FA	G by Pos
1921	PHI A	66	.271	.299	177	48	3	1	0	0.0	17	19	23	21	2	19	5	350	42	9	30	6.1	.978	1B-36, 3B-9
1922		6	.077	.077	13	1	0	0	0	0.0	0	1	0	1	0	4	0	1	2	1	0	0.7	.750	3B-2
2 yrs.		72	.258	.284	190	49	3	1	0	0.0	17	20	23	22	2	23	5	351	44	10	30	5.6	.975	1B-36, 3B-11

Sid Bream

BREAM, SIDNEY EUGENE
B. Aug. 3, 1960, Carlisle, Pa.

BL TL 6'4" 215 lbs.

Year	Team	Games	BA	SA	AB	H	2B	3B	HR	HR%	R	RBI	BB	SO	SB	AB	H	PO	A	E	DP	TC/G	FA	G by Pos
1983	LA N	15	.182	.182	11	2	0	0	0	0.0	2	2	2	0	0	10	2	8	0	0	1	0.5	1.000	1B-4
1984		27	.184	.245	49	9	3	0	0	0.0	2	6	6	9	1	11	1	95	11	0	9	3.9	1.000	1B-14
1985	2 teams	LA N (24G – .132)	PIT N (26G – .284)																					
"	total	50	.230	.399	148	34	7	0	6	4.1	18	21	18	24	0	10	2	367	35	3	29	8.1	.993	1B-41
1986	PIT N	154	.268	.450	522	140	37	5	16	3.1	73	77	60	73	13	5	1	1320	166	17	107	9.8	.989	1B-153, OF-2
1987		149	.275	.411	516	142	25	3	13	2.5	64	65	49	69	9	7	2	1236	127	17	109	9.3	.988	1B-144
1988		148	.264	.409	462	122	37	0	10	2.2	50	65	47	64	9	16	6	1118	140	6	88	8.5	.995	1B-138
1989		19	.222	.306	36	8	3	0	0	0.0	3	4	12	10	0	2	0	111	7	1	5	6.3	.992	1B-13
7 yrs.		562	.262	.413	1744	457	112	8	45	2.6	210	240	194	251	32	61	14	4255	486	44	348	8.5	.991	1B-507, OF-2

Jim Breazeale

BREAZEALE, JAMES LEO
B. Oct. 3, 1949, Houston, Tex.

BL TR 6'2" 210 lbs.

Year	Team	Games	BA	SA	AB	H	2B	3B	HR	HR%	R	RBI	BB	SO	SB	AB	H	PO	A	E	DP	TC/G	FA	G by Pos
1969	ATL N	2	.000	.000	1	0	0	0	0	0.0	0	0	2	0	0	0	0	5	0	1	0	3.0	.833	1B-1
1971		10	.190	.333	21	4	0	0	1	4.8	1	3	0	3	0	5	3	31	0	0	3	3.3	1.000	1B-4
1972		52	.247	.447	85	21	2	0	5	5.9	10	17	6	12	0	33	10	121	3	0	11	2.4	1.000	1B-16, 3B-1
1978	CHI A	25	.208	.375	72	15	3	0	3	4.2	8	13	8	10	0	2	1	124	5	1	10	5.1	.992	1B-19, DH-4
4 yrs.		89	.223	.402	179	40	5	0	9	5.0	20	33	16	25	0	40	14	281	8	2	24	3.3	.993	1B-40, DH-4, 3B-1

Danny Breeden

BREEDEN, DANNY RICHARD
Brother of Hal Breeden.
B. June 27, 1942, Albany, Ga.

BR TR 5'11½" 185 lbs.

Year	Team	Games	BA	SA	AB	H	2B	3B	HR	HR%	R	RBI	BB	SO	SB	AB	H	PO	A	E	DP	TC/G	FA	G by Pos
1969	CIN N	3	.125	.125	8	1	0	0	0	0.0	0	1	0	3	0	0	0	12	4	1	0	5.7	.941	C-3
1971	CHI N	25	.154	.169	65	10	1	0	0	0.0	3	4	9	18	0	0	0	150	7	4	2	6.4	.975	C-25
2 yrs.		28	.151	.164	73	11	1	0	0	0.0	3	5	9	21	0	0	0	162	11	5	2	6.4	.972	C-28

Hal Breeden

BREEDEN, HAROLD NOEL
Brother of Danny Breeden.
B. June 28, 1944, Albany, Ga.

BR TL 6'2" 200 lbs.

Year	Team	Games	BA	SA	AB	H	2B	3B	HR	HR%	R	RBI	BB	SO	SB	AB	H	PO	A	E	DP	TC/G	FA	G by Pos
1971	CHI N	23	.139	.250	36	5	1	0	1	2.8	1	2	2	7	0	14	0	48	7	1	2	2.4	.982	1B-8
1972	MON N	42	.230	.356	87	20	2	0	3	3.4	6	10	7	15	0	17	5	159	10	1	12	4.0	.994	1B-26, OF-10
1973		105	.275	.535	258	71	10	6	15	5.8	36	43	29	45	0	43	12	515	45	5	50	5.4	.991	1B-66
1974		79	.247	.347	190	47	13	0	2	1.1	14	20	24	35	0	25	6	422	31	6	43	5.8	.987	1B-56
1975		24	.135	.189	37	5	2	0	0	0.0	4	1	7	5	0	12	3	84	4	1	5	3.7	.989	1B-12
5 yrs.		273	.243	.413	608	148	28	6	21	3.5	61	76	69	107	0	111	26	1228	97	14	112	4.9	.990	1B-168, OF-10

Marv Breeding

BREEDING, MARVIN EUGENE
B. Mar. 8, 1934, Decatur, Ala.

BR TR 6' 175 lbs.

Year	Team	Games	BA	SA	AB	H	2B	3B	HR	HR%	R	RBI	BB	SO	SB	AB	H	PO	A	E	DP	TC/G	FA	G by Pos
1960	BAL A	152	.267	.336	551	147	25	2	3	0.5	69	43	35	80	10	0	0	359	422	18	116	5.3	.977	2B-152
1961		90	.209	.254	244	51	8	0	1	0.4	32	16	14	33	5	3	0	179	179	11	53	4.1	.970	2B-80
1962		95	.246	.321	240	59	10	1	2	0.8	27	18	9	41	2	10	1	146	196	9	47	3.7	.974	2B-73, SS-1, 3B-1
1963	2 teams	WAS A (58G – .274)	LA A (20G – .167)																					
"	total	78	.258	.318	233	60	7	1	1	0.4	26	15	9	26	2	10	4	92	134	13	15	3.1	.946	2B-39, 3B-30, SS-3
4 yrs.		415	.250	.314	1268	317	50	5	7	0.6	154	92	66	180	19	23	5	776	931	51	231	4.2	.971	2B-344, 3B-31, SS-4

Ted Breitenstein

BREITENSTEIN, THEODORE P.
B. June 1, 1869, St. Louis, Mo.   D. May 3, 1935, St. Louis, Mo.

BL TL 5'9" 167 lbs.

Year	Team		Games	BA	SA	AB	H	2B	3B	HR	HR%	R	RBI	BB	SO	SB	Pinch Hit AB	Pinch Hit H	PO	A	E	DP	TC/G	FA	G by Pos

Ted Breitenstein *continued*

Year	Team		Games	BA	SA	AB	H	2B	3B	HR	HR%	R	RBI	BB	SO	SB	AB	H	PO	A	E	DP	TC/G	FA	G by Pos
1891	STL	AA	6	.000	.000	12	0	0	0	0	0.0	2	0	2	0	1	0	0	2	3	0	0	0.8	1.000	P-6, OF-1
1892	STL	N	47	.122	.145	131	16	1	1	0	0.0	16	6	16	20	4	0	0	33	69	6	3	2.3	.944	P-39, OF-10
1893			49	.181	.219	160	29	1	1	1	0.6	20	14	18	15	3	0	0	43	82	8	4	2.7	.940	P-48, OF-2
1894			63	.220	.280	182	40	7	2	0	0.0	27	13	31	19	3	0	0	47	83	10	4	2.2	.929	P-56, OF-7
1895			72	.193	.202	218	42	2	0	0	0.0	25	18	29	22	5	1	1	63	98	17	1	2.5	.904	P-54, OF-16
1896			51	.259	.315	162	42	5	2	0	0.0	21	12	13	26	8	1	1	46	89	8	4	2.8	.944	P-44, OF-8
1897	CIN	N	41	.266	.395	124	33	4	6	0	0.0	16	23	6		5	1	0	16	65	3	3	2.0	.964	P-40
1898			41	.215	.248	121	26	2	1	0	0.0	16	17	16		1	0	0	22	89	4	3	2.8	.965	P-39, OF-2
1899			33	.352	.438	105	37	4	1	1	1.0	18	11	10		1	0	0	25	50	5	1	2.4	.938	P-26, OF-7
1900			41	.190	.262	126	24	1	0	2	1.6	12	12	9		0	5	1	29	62	7	0	2.4	.929	P-24, OF-12
1901	STL	N	3	.333	.333	6	2	0	0	0	0.0	1	0	0		0	0	0	2	7	0	2	3.0	1.000	P-3
11 yrs.			447	.216	.267	1347	291	27	15	4	0.3	174	126	150	102	30	8	3	328	697	68	25	2.4	.938	P-379, OF-65

Herb Bremer

BREMER, HERBERT FREDERICK (Butch)
B. Oct. 25, 1913, Chicago, Ill. D. Nov. 28, 1979, Columbus, Ga. BR TR 6' 195 lbs.

Year	Team		Games	BA	SA	AB	H	2B	3B	HR	HR%	R	RBI	BB	SO	SB	AB	H	PO	A	E	DP	TC/G	FA	G by Pos
1937	STL	N	11	.212	.242	33	7	1	0	0	0.0	2	3	2	4	0	0	0	40	6	1	2	4.3	.979	C-10
1938			50	.219	.305	151	33	5	1	2	1.3	14	14	9	36	1	0	0	186	30	5	2	4.4	.977	C-50
1939			9	.111	.111	9	1	0	0	0	0.0	0	1	0	2	0	1	0	13	0	0	0	1.4	1.000	C-8
3 yrs.			70	.212	.285	193	41	6	1	2	1.0	16	18	11	42	1	1	0	239	36	6	4	4.0	.979	C-68

Sam Brenegan

BRENEGAN, OLAF SELMER
B. Sept. 1, 1890, Galesville, Wis. D. Apr. 20, 1956, Galesville, Wis. BL TR 6'2" 185 lbs.

Year	Team		Games	BA	SA	AB	H	2B	3B	HR	HR%	R	RBI	BB	SO	SB	AB	H	PO	A	E	DP	TC/G	FA	G by Pos
1914	PIT	N	1	–	–	0	0	0	0	0	–	0	0	0	0	0	0	0	0	0	0	0	–	C-1

Bob Brenly

BRENLY, ROBERT EARL
B. Feb. 25, 1954, Coshocton, Ohio BR TR 6'2" 210 lbs.

Year	Team		Games	BA	SA	AB	H	2B	3B	HR	HR%	R	RBI	BB	SO	SB	AB	H	PO	A	E	DP	TC/G	FA	G by Pos
1981	SF	N	19	.333	.489	45	15	2	1	1	2.2	5	4	6	4	0	1	0	52	6	4	2	3.3	.935	C-14, 3B-3, OF-1
1982			65	.283	.383	180	51	4	1	4	2.2	26	15	18	26	6	9	3	265	32	12	2	4.8	.961	C-61, 3B-1
1983			104	.224	.356	281	63	12	2	7	2.5	36	34	37	48	10	13	2	465	73	9	15	5.3	.984	C-90, 1B-10, OF-2
1984			145	.291	.464	506	147	28	0	20	4.0	74	80	48	52	6	6	1	807	76	13	21	6.2	.985	C-127, 1B-22, OF-3
1985			133	.220	.391	440	97	16	1	19	4.3	41	56	57	62	1	7	1	719	85	17	16	6.2	.979	C-110, 3B-17, 1B-10
1986			149	.246	.403	472	116	26	0	16	3.4	60	62	74	97	10	8	0	688	118	16	20	5.5	.981	C-101, 3B-45, 1B-19
1987			123	.267	.467	375	100	19	1	18	4.8	55	51	47	85	10	8	2	685	86	9	14	6.3	.988	C-108, 1B-6, 3B-2
1988			73	.189	.296	122	39	7	0	5	2.4	13	22	20	40	1	5	0	334	27	6	2	5.0	.984	C-69
1989	2 teams		TOR A	(48G – .170)		SF N	(12G – .182)																			
"	total		60	.173	.264	110	19	5	1	1	0.9	11	9	11	24	1	16	6	92	10	1	1	1.7	.990	DH-28, C-25, 1B-5
9 yrs.			871	.247	.403	2615	647	119	7	91	3.5	321	333	318	438	45	73	15	4107	513	87	93	5.4	.982	C-705, 1B-72, 3B-68, DH-28, OF-6

LEAGUE CHAMPIONSHIP SERIES

Year	Team		Games	BA	SA	AB	H	2B	3B	HR	HR%	R	RBI	BB	SO	SB	AB	H	PO	A	E	DP	TC/G	FA	G by Pos
1987	SF	N	6	.235	.471	17	4	1	0	1	5.9	3	2	3	7	0	1	0	28	2	0	0	5.0	1.000	C-6

Jim Brennan

BRENNAN, JAMES AUGUSTUS (Old Sport)
B. 1862, St. Louis, Mo. D. Oct. 18, 1904, Philadelphia, Pa.

Year	Team		Games	BA	SA	AB	H	2B	3B	HR	HR%	R	RBI	BB	SO	SB	AB	H	PO	A	E	DP	TC/G	FA	G by Pos
1884	STL	U	56	.216	.251	231	50	6	1	0	0.0	38		12			0	0	172	92	40	4	5.4	.868	C-33, OF-16, 3B-7, SS-1
1885	STL	N	3	.100	.100	10	1	0	0	0	0.0	1		1	1		0	0	3	1	3	0	2.3	.571	OF-2, 3B-1
1888	KC	AA	34	.169	.186	118	20	2	0	0	0.0	5	6	3			3	0	111	62	27	5	5.9	.865	C-25, OF-5, 3B-5
1889	PHI	AA	31	.221	.257	113	25	4	0	0	0.0	12	15	10	15		1	0	53	55	22	5	4.2	.831	C-13, OF-7, 2B-7, 3B-4
1890	CLE	P	59	.253	.326	233	59	3	7	0	0.0	32	26	13	29	8	0	0	153	77	47	8	4.7	.830	C-42, 3B-14, OF-6
5 yrs.			183	.220	.264	705	155	15	8	0	0.0	87	48	39	45	12	0	0	492	287	139	22	5.0	.849	C-113, OF-36, 3B-31, 2B-7, SS-1

Bill Brenzel

BRENZEL, WILLIAM RICHARD
B. Mar. 3, 1910, Oakland, Calif. D. June 12, 1979, Oakland, Calif. BR TR 5'10" 173 lbs.

Year	Team		Games	BA	SA	AB	H	2B	3B	HR	HR%	R	RBI	BB	SO	SB	AB	H	PO	A	E	DP	TC/G	FA	G by Pos
1932	PIT	N	9	.042	.083	24	1	1	0	0	0.0	2	4	0	0	0	0	0	35	2	0	1	4.1	1.000	C-9
1934	CLE	A	15	.216	.275	51	11	3	0	0	0.0	4	3	2	1	0	0	0	67	10	0	1	5.1	1.000	C-15
1935			52	.218	.268	142	31	5	1	0	0.0	12	14	6	10	2	0	0	135	18	4	3	3.0	.975	C-51
3 yrs.			76	.198	.249	217	43	9	1	0	0.0	16	19	8	15	2	0	0	237	30	4	5	3.6	.985	C-75

Roger Bresnahan

BRESNAHAN, ROGER PHILIP (The Duke of Tralee)
B. June 11, 1879, Toledo, Ohio D. Dec. 4, 1944, Toledo, Ohio
Manager 1909-12, 1915.
Hall of Fame 1945. BR TR 5'9" 200 lbs.

Year	Team		Games	BA	SA	AB	H	2B	3B	HR	HR%	R	RBI	BB	SO	SB	AB	H	PO	A	E	DP	TC/G	FA	G by Pos
1897	WAS	N	6	.375	.375	16	6	0	0	0	0.0	1	3	1		0	0	0	2	7	0	0	1.5	1.000	P-6, OF-1
1900	CHI	N	2	.000	.000	2	0	0	0	0	0.0	0	0	0		0	0	0	0	0	0	0	0.0	–	C-1
1901	BAL	A	86	.268	.369	295	79	9	9	1	0.3	40	32	23		10	1	0	219	71	27	4	3.7	.915	C-69, OF-8, 3B-4, 2B-2, P-2
1902	2 teams		BAL A	(65G – .272)		NY N	(51G – .292)																			
"	total		116	.281	.414	413	116	22	9	5	1.2	47	56	37		18	2	2	290	120	35	12	3.8	.921	OF-42, C-38, 3B-31, SS-4, 1B-4
1903	NY	N	113	.350	.493	406	142	30	8	4	1.0	87	55	61		34	1	1	300	46	21	11	3.2	.943	OF-84, 1B-13, C-11, 3B-4
1904			109	.284	.410	402	114	22	7	5	1.2	81	33	58		13	3	1	241	30	15	13	2.6	.948	OF-93, 1B-10, SS-4, 3B-1, 2B-1
1905			104	.302	.375	331	100	18	3	0	0.0	58	46	50		11	6	0	503	115	19	15	6.1	.970	C-87, OF-8
1906			124	.281	.356	405	114	22	4	0	0.0	69	43	81		25	1	0	478	131	17	8	5.0	.973	C-82, OF-40
1907			110	.253	.360	328	83	9	7	4	1.2	57	38	61		15	6	2	547	101	13	12	5.0	.980	C-95, 1B-6, OF-2, 3B-1
1908			140	.283	.359	449	127	25	3	1	0.2	70	54	**83**		14	1	1	657	140	12	12	5.8	.985	C-139
1909	STL	N	72	.244	.269	234	57	4	1	0	0.0	27	23	46		11	2	0	224	105	16	9	4.8	.954	C-59, OF-2, 3B-1
1910			88	.278	.368	234	65	15	3	0	0.0	35	27	55	17	13	5	0	296	103	16	12	4.7	.961	C-77, OF-2, P-1
1911			81	.278	.463	227	63	17	8	3	1.3	22	41	45	19	4	3	1	325	103	14	9	5.5	.968	C-77, 2B-2
1912			48	.333	.463	108	36	7	2	1	0.9	8	15	14	11	3	14	7	138	49	5	4	4.0	.974	C-28
1913	CHI	N	68	.230	.304	161	37	5	2	1	0.6	20	21	21	11	7	9	4	194	67	10	7	4.0	.963	C-58

Year	Team	Games	BA	SA	AB	H	2B	3B	HR	HR%	R	RBI	BB	SO	SB	Pinch Hit AB	Pinch Hit H	PO	A	E	DP	TC/G	FA	G by Pos

Roger Bresnahan *continued*

Year	Team	Games	BA	SA	AB	H	2B	3B	HR	HR%	R	RBI	BB	SO	SB	PH AB	PH H	PO	A	E	DP	TC/G	FA	G by Pos
1914		86	.278	.351	248	69	10	4	0	0.0	42	24	49	20	14	4	1	377	131	12	6	6.0	.977	C-85, 2B-14, OF-1
1915		77	.204	.262	221	45	8	1	1	0.5	19	19	29	23	19	6	0	345	95	8	9	5.8	.982	C-68
17 yrs		1430	.280	.379	4480	1253	223	71	26	0.6	683	530	714	99	212	63	20	5136	1414	240	138	4.7	.965	C-974, OF-281, 3B-42, 1B-33, 2B-28, P-9, SS-8

WORLD SERIES

| 1905 | NY N | 5 | .313 | .438 | 16 | 5 | 2 | 0 | 0 | 0.0 | 3 | 1 | 4 | 0 | 1 | 0 | 0 | 27 | 7 | 0 | 0 | 6.8 | 1.000 | C-5 |

Rube Bressler

BRESSLER, RAYMOND BLOOM
B. Oct. 23, 1894, Coder, Pa. D. Nov. 7, 1966, Mt. Washington, Ohio
BR TL 6' 187 lbs.

Year	Team	Games	BA	SA	AB	H	2B	3B	HR	HR%	R	RBI	BB	SO	SB	PH AB	PH H	PO	A	E	DP	TC/G	FA	G by Pos
1914	PHI A	29	.216	.275	51	11	1	1	0	0.0	6	4	6	7	0	0	0	6	26	2	2	1.2	.941	P-29
1915		33	.145	.236	55	8	0	1	1	1.8	9	4	9	13	0	1	0	7	56	7	0	2.1	.900	P-32
1916		4	.200	.600	5	1	0	1	0	0.0	1	1	0	0	0	0	0	0	2	0	0	0.5	1.000	P-4
1917	CIN N	3	.200	.200	5	1	0	0	0	0.0	0	0	0	2	0	1	0	1	1	0	0	0.7	1.000	P-2
1918		23	.274	.355	62	17	5	0	0	0.0	10	6	5	4	0	1	0	10	51	1	2	2.7	.984	P-17, OF-3
1919		61	.206	.309	165	34	3	4	2	1.2	22	17	23	15	2	1	0	107	19	5	1	2.1	.962	OF-48, P-13
1920		21	.267	.300	30	8	1	0	0	0.0	4	3	1	4	1	6	0	25	7	4	2	1.7	.889	P-10, OF-3, 1B-2
1921		109	.307	.409	323	99	18	6	1	0.3	41	54	39	20	5	12	4	202	7	8	5	2.0	.963	OF-85, 1B-6
1922		52	.264	.340	53	14	0	2	0	0.0	7	8	4	4	1	**43**	**13**	16	0	1	0	0.3	.941	1B-3, OF-2
1923		54	.277	.319	119	33	3	1	0	0.0	25	18	20	4	3	24	9	227	9	4	12	4.4	.983	1B-22, OF-6
1924		115	.347	.483	383	133	14	13	4	1.0	41	49	22	20	9	16	3	561	35	9	36	5.3	.985	1B-50, OF-49
1925		97	.348	.476	319	111	17	6	4	1.3	43	61	40	16	9	6	3	602	23	12	46	6.6	.981	1B-52, OF-38
1926		86	.357	.478	297	106	15	9	0	0.3	58	51	37	20	3	4	0	183	5	5	2	2.2	.974	OF-80, 1B-4
1927		124	.291	.375	467	136	14	8	3	0.6	43	77	32	22	4	3	0	261	15	8	5	2.3	.972	OF-120
1928	BKN N	145	.295	.429	501	148	29	13	4	0.8	78	70	80	33	2	7	3	254	7	4	0	1.8	.985	OF-137
1929		136	.318	.461	456	145	22	8	9	2.0	72	77	67	27	4	12	3	263	7	13	0	2.1	.954	OF-122
1930		109	.299	.409	335	100	12	8	3	0.9	53	52	51	19	4	8	0	262	11	1	8	2.5	.996	OF-90, 1B-7
1931		67	.281	.373	153	43	4	5	0	0.0	22	26	11	10	0	29	2	66	2	1	0	1.0	.986	OF-35, 1B-1
1932 2 teams	PHI N (27G – .229)				STL N (10G – .158)																			
" total		37	.216	.294	102	22	6	1	0	0.0	9	8	2	6	0	14	5	51	4	0	1	1.5	1.000	OF-22
19 yrs		1305	.301	.413	3881	1170	164	87	32	0.8	544	586	449	246	47	188	45	3104	287	85	122	2.7	.976	OF-840, 1B-147, P-107

Ed Bressoud

BRESSOUD, EDWARD FRANCIS
B. May 2, 1932, Los Angeles, Calif.
BR TR 6'1" 175 lbs.

Year	Team	Games	BA	SA	AB	H	2B	3B	HR	HR%	R	RBI	BB	SO	SB	PH AB	PH H	PO	A	E	DP	TC/G	FA	G by Pos
1956	NY N	49	.227	.276	163	37	4	2	0	0.0	15	9	12	20	1	1	0	67	125	10	26	4.1	.950	SS-48
1957		49	.268	.433	127	34	2	2	5	3.9	11	10	4	19	0	2	0	67	97	13	16	3.6	.927	SS-33, 3B-12
1958	SF N	66	.263	.343	137	36	5	3	0	0.0	19	8	14	22	0	0	0	105	106	8	26	3.3	.963	2B-57, 3B-6, SS-4
1959		104	.251	.403	315	79	17	2	9	2.9	36	26	28	55	0	5	0	153	270	13	38	4.2	.970	SS-92, 3B-1, 2B-1, 1B-1
1960		116	.225	.376	386	87	19	6	9	2.3	37	43	35	72	1	1	0	191	339	22	53	4.8	.960	SS-115
1961		59	.211	.342	114	24	6	0	3	2.6	14	11	11	23	1	20	4	51	61	4	12	2.0	.966	SS-34, 3B-3, 2B-1
1962	BOS A	153	.277	.444	599	166	40	4	14	2.3	79	68	46	118	2	0	0	291	482	28	107	5.2	.965	SS-153
1963		140	.260	.451	497	129	23	6	20	4.0	61	60	52	93	1	2	0	260	351	24	76	4.5	.962	SS-137
1964		158	.293	.456	566	166	41	3	15	2.7	86	55	72	99	1	0	0	248	411	19	78	4.3	.972	SS-158
1965		107	.226	.351	296	67	11	1	8	2.7	29	25	29	77	0	21	7	147	196	13	46	3.3	.963	SS-86, 3B-2, OF-1
1966	NY N	133	.225	.360	405	91	15	5	10	2.5	48	49	47	107	2	12	2	213	343	23	67	4.4	.960	SS-94, 3B-32, 1B-9, 2B-7
1967	STL N	52	.134	.224	67	9	1	1	1	1.5	8	1	9	18	0	3	1	34	58	7	12	1.9	.929	SS-48, 3B-1
12 yrs		1186	.252	.401	3672	925	184	40	94	2.6	443	365	359	723	9	67	14	1827	2839	184	557	4.1	.962	SS-1002, 2B-66, 3B-57, 1B-10, OF-1

WORLD SERIES

| 1967 | STL N | 2 | – | – | 0 | 0 | 0 | 0 | 0 | – | 0 | 0 | 0 | 0 | 0 | 0 | 0 | 0 | 0 | 0 | 0 | 0.0 | – | SS-2 |

Jim Breton

BRETON, JOHN FREDERICK
B. July 15, 1891, Chicago, Ill. D. May 30, 1973, Beloit, Wis.
BR TR 5'10½" 178 lbs.

Year	Team	Games	BA	SA	AB	H	2B	3B	HR	HR%	R	RBI	BB	SO	SB	PH AB	PH H	PO	A	E	DP	TC/G	FA	G by Pos
1913	CHI A	10	.167	.267	30	5	1	1	0	0.0	1	2	1	5	0	0	0	8	30	3	2	4.1	.927	SS-7, 3B-3
1914		81	.212	.260	231	49	7	2	0	0.0	21	24	24	42	9	0	0	84	159	24	6	3.3	.910	3B-79
1915		16	.139	.167	36	5	1	0	0	0.0	3	1	5	9	2	0	0	15	19	4	2	2.4	.895	3B-14, SS-1, 2B-1
3 yrs		107	.199	.249	297	59	9	3	0	0.0	25	27	30	56	11	0	0	107	208	31	10	3.2	.910	3B-96, SS-8, 2B-1

George Brett

BRETT, GEORGE HOWARD
Brother of Ken Brett.
B. May 15, 1953, Glen Dale, W. Va.
BL TR 6' 185 lbs.

Year	Team	Games	BA	SA	AB	H	2B	3B	HR	HR%	R	RBI	BB	SO	SB	PH AB	PH H	PO	A	E	DP	TC/G	FA	G by Pos
1973	KC A	13	.125	.175	40	5	2	0	0	0.0	2	0	0	5	0	1	0	9	28	1	2	2.9	.974	3B-13
1974		133	.282	.363	457	129	21	5	2	0.4	49	47	21	38	8	2	0	102	279	21	16	3.0	.948	3B-132, SS-1
1975		159	.308	.456	634	195	35	13	11	1.7	84	89	46	49	13	0	0	132	356	26	27	3.2	.949	3B-159
1976		159	**.333**	.462	645	**215**	34	**14**	7	1.1	94	67	49	36	21	0	0	146	350	26	23	3.3	.950	3B-157, SS-1
1977		139	.312	.532	564	176	32	13	22	3.9	105	88	55	24	14	3	1	115	325	21	33	3.3	.954	3B-135, DH-3, SS-1
1978		128	.294	.467	510	150	**45**	8	9	1.8	79	62	39	35	23	2	0	104	289	16	25	3.2	.961	3B-128, SS-1
1979		154	.329	.563	645	212	42	**20**	23	3.6	119	107	51	36	17	0	0	176	378	31	34	3.8	.947	3B-149, 1B-8, DH-1
1980		117	**.390**	**.664**	449	175	33	9	24	5.3	87	118	58	22	15	3	1	107	256	17	29	3.2	.955	3B-112, 1B-1
1981		89	.314	.484	347	109	27	7	6	1.7	42	43	27	23	14	0	0	74	170	14	7	2.9	.946	3B-88
1982		144	.301	.505	552	166	32	9	21	3.8	101	82	71	51	6	0	0	130	295	17	23	3.1	.962	3B-134, OF-12
1983		123	.310	**.563**	464	144	38	2	25	5.4	90	93	57	39	0	1	1	210	192	25	34	3.1	.941	3B-102, 1B-14, OF-13, DH-1
1984		104	.284	.459	377	107	21	3	13	3.4	42	69	38	37	0	3	1	59	201	14	18	2.6	.949	3B-101
1985		155	.335	**.585**	550	184	38	5	30	5.5	108	112	103	49	9	2	0	107	339	15	33	3.0	.967	3B-152, DH-1
1986		124	.290	.481	441	128	28	4	16	3.6	70	73	80	45	1	1	0	97	218	16	17	2.7	.952	3B-115, DH-7, SS-2
1987		115	.290	.496	427	124	18	2	22	5.2	71	78	72	47	6	0	0	805	69	9	72	7.7	.990	1B-83, DH-21, 3B-11
1988		157	.306	.509	589	180	42	3	24	4.1	90	103	82	51	14	0	0	1126	70	10	105	7.7	.992	1B-124, DH-33, SS-1
1989		124	.282	.431	457	129	26	3	12	2.6	67	80	59	47	14	3	0	898	80	2	71	7.9	.998	1B-104, DH-17, OF-2
17 yrs		2137	.310	.501	8148	2528	514	120	267	3.3	1300	1311	908	634	175	19	4	4397	3895	281	569	4.0	.967	3B-1688, 1B-334, DH-84, OF-27, SS-11

Year	Team	Games	BA	SA	AB	H	2B	3B	HR	HR%	R	RBI	BB	SO	SB	Pinch Hit AB	Pinch Hit H	PO	A	E	DP	TC/G	FA	G by Pos

George Brett *continued*

DIVISIONAL PLAYOFF SERIES

Year	Team	Games	BA	SA	AB	H	2B	3B	HR	HR%	R	RBI	BB	SO	SB	PH AB	PH H	PO	A	E	DP	TC/G	FA	G by Pos
1981	KC A	3	.167	.167	12	2	0	0	0	0.0	0	0	0	0	0	0	0	0	0	1	0	0.3	–	3B-3

LEAGUE CHAMPIONSHIP SERIES

Year	Team	Games	BA	SA	AB	H	2B	3B	HR	HR%	R	RBI	BB	SO	SB	PH AB	PH H	PO	A	E	DP	TC/G	FA	G by Pos
1976	KC A	5	.444	.778	18	8	1	1	1	5.6	4	5	2	1	0	0	0	3	7	3	1	2.6	.769	3B-5
1977		5	.300	.500	20	6	0	2	0	0.0	2	2	1	0	0	0	0	5	12	2	2	3.8	.895	3B-5
1978		4	.389	1.056	18	7	1	1	3	16.7	7	3	0	1	0	0	0	3	8	1	1	3.0	.917	3B-4
1980		3	.273	.909	11	3	1	0	2	18.2	3	4	1	0	0	0	0	2	7	0	0	3.0	1.000	3B-3
1984		3	.231	.231	13	3	0	0	0	0.0	0	0	0	2	0	0	0	2	7	0	1	3.0	1.000	3B-3
1985		7	.348	.826	23	8	2	0	3	13.0	6	5	7	5	0	0	0	7	8	2	0	2.4	.882	3B-7
6 yrs.		27	.340	.728	103	35	5	4	9	8.7	22	19	11	9	0	0	0	22	49	8	5	2.9	.899	3B-27

WORLD SERIES

Year	Team	Games	BA	SA	AB	H	2B	3B	HR	HR%	R	RBI	BB	SO	SB	PH AB	PH H	PO	A	E	DP	TC/G	FA	G by Pos
1980	KC A	6	.375	.667	24	9	2	1	1	4.2	3	3	2	4	1	0	0	4	17	1	1	3.7	.955	3B-6
1985		7	.370	.407	27	10	1	0	0	0.0	5	1	4	7	1	0	0	10	19	1	1	4.3	.967	3B-7
2 yrs.		13	.373	.529	51	19	3	1	1	2.0	8	4	6	11	2	0	0	14	36	2	2	4.0	.962	3B-13
			4th																					

Ken Brett

BRETT, KENNETH ALVEN
Brother of George Brett.
B. Sept. 18, 1948, Brooklyn, N. Y.

BL TL 6'   190 lbs.

Year	Team	Games	BA	SA	AB	H	2B	3B	HR	HR%	R	RBI	BB	SO	SB	PH AB	PH H	PO	A	E	DP	TC/G	FA	G by Pos
1967	BOS A	1	–	–	0	0	0	0	0	–	0	0	0	0	0	0	0	0	0	0	0	0.0	–	P-1
1969		8	.300	.700	10	3	1	0	1	10.0	1	3	1	1	0	0	0	2	6	0	0	1.0	1.000	P-8
1970		41	.317	.537	41	13	3	0	2	4.9	8	3	2	7	0	0	0	9	20	2	0	0.8	.935	P-41
1971		29	.200	.200	10	2	0	0	0	0.0	0	0	0	2	0	0	0	0	8	0	0	0.3	1.000	P-29
1972	MIL A	31	.227	.250	44	10	1	0	0	0.0	6	1	2	10	0	1	0	6	15	3	1	0.8	.875	P-26
1973	PHI N	37	.250	.463	80	20	5	0	4	5.0	6	16	4	17	0	2	0	13	39	0	4	1.4	1.000	P-31
1974	PIT N	43	.310	.448	87	27	4	1	2	2.3	13	15	4	20	0	15	3	12	28	0	1	0.9	1.000	P-27
1975		26	.231	.365	52	12	4	0	1	1.9	5	4	1	7	0	3	0	13	18	1	0	1.2	.969	P-23
1976	2 teams		NY A (2G – .000)				CHI A (33G – .083)																	
"	total	35	.083	.083	12	1	0	0	0	0.0	0	0	0	1	0	6	1	11	35	3	0	1.4	.939	P-29
1977	2 teams		CHI A (13G – .000)				CAL A (21G – .000)																	
"	total	34	–	–	0	0	0	0	0	–	0	0	0	0	0	0	0	11	48	2	6	1.8	.967	P-34
1978	CAL A	31	–	–	0	0	0	0	0	–	0	0	0	0	0	0	0	12	20	2	4	1.1	.941	P-31
1979	2 teams		MIN A (9G – .000)				LA N (30G – .273)																	
"	total	39	.273	.273	11	3	0	0	0	0.0	0	0	0	2	0	0	0	10	17	0	1	0.7	1.000	P-39
1980	KC A	8	–	–	0	0	0	0	0	–	0	0	0	0	0	0	0	0	3	0	0	0.4	1.000	P-8
1981		22	–	–	0	0	0	0	0	–	0	0	0	0	0	0	0	5	6	1	1	0.5	1.000	P-22
14 yrs.		385	.262	.406	347	91	18	1	10	2.9	39	44	14	67	0	27	4	104	263	13	18	1.0	.966	P-349

LEAGUE CHAMPIONSHIP SERIES

Year	Team	Games	BA	SA	AB	H	2B	3B	HR	HR%	R	RBI	BB	SO	SB	PH AB	PH H	PO	A	E	DP	TC/G	FA	G by Pos
1974	PIT N	1	.000	.000	1	0	0	0	0	0.0	0	0	0	1	0	0	0	0	1	0	0	1.0	1.000	P-1
1975		2	–	–	0	0	0	0	0	–	0	0	0	0	0	0	0	0	0	0	0	0.0	–	P-2
2 yrs.		3	.000	.000	1	0	0	0	0	0.0	0	0	0	1	0	0	0	0	1	0	0	0.3	1.000	P-3

WORLD SERIES

Year	Team	Games	BA	SA	AB	H	2B	3B	HR	HR%	R	RBI	BB	SO	SB	PH AB	PH H	PO	A	E	DP	TC/G	FA	G by Pos
1967	BOS A	2	–	–	0	0	0	0	0	–	0	0	0	0	0	0	0	0	0	0	0	0.0	–	P-2

Mike Brewer

BREWER, MICHAEL QUINN
Brother of Tony Brewer.
B. Oct. 24, 1959, Shreveport, La.

BR TR 6'5"   190 lbs.

Year	Team	Games	BA	SA	AB	H	2B	3B	HR	HR%	R	RBI	BB	SO	SB	PH AB	PH H	PO	A	E	DP	TC/G	FA	G by Pos
1986	KC A	12	.167	.222	18	3	1	0	0	0.0	0	0	2	6	0	1	0	9	0	0	0	0.8	1.000	OF-9, DH-1

Tony Brewer

BREWER, ANTHONY BRUCE
Brother of Mike Brewer.
B. Nov. 25, 1957, Coushatta, La.

BR TR 5'11"   190 lbs.

Year	Team	Games	BA	SA	AB	H	2B	3B	HR	HR%	R	RBI	BB	SO	SB	PH AB	PH H	PO	A	E	DP	TC/G	FA	G by Pos
1984	LA N	24	.108	.216	37	4	1	0	1	2.7	3	4	4	9	1	14	1	9	0	0	0	0.4	1.000	OF-10

Charlie Brewster

BREWSTER, CHARLES LAWRENCE
B. Dec. 27, 1916, Marthaville, La.

BR TR 5'8½"   175 lbs.

Year	Team	Games	BA	SA	AB	H	2B	3B	HR	HR%	R	RBI	BB	SO	SB	PH AB	PH H	PO	A	E	DP	TC/G	FA	G by Pos
1943	2 teams		CIN N (7G – .125)				PHI N (49G – .220)																	
"	total	56	.216	.228	167	36	2	0	0	0.0	13	12	10	20	1	2	0	76	112	20	19	3.7	.904	SS-46, 2B-2
1944	CHI N	10	.250	.295	44	11	2	0	0	0.0	4	2	5	7	0	0	0	27	29	6	9	6.2	.903	SS-10
1946	CLE A	3	.000	.000	2	0	0	0	0	0.0	0	0	1	1	0	1	0	0	1	0	0	0.3	1.000	SS-1
3 yrs.		69	.221	.239	213	47	4	0	0	0.0	17	14	16	28	1	3	0	103	142	26	28	3.9	.904	SS-57, 2B-2

Fred Brickell

BRICKELL, GEORGE FREDERICK
Father of Fritzie Brickell.
B. Nov. 9, 1906, Saffordville, Kans.   D. Apr. 8, 1961, Wichita, Kans.

BL TR 5'7"   160 lbs.

Year	Team	Games	BA	SA	AB	H	2B	3B	HR	HR%	R	RBI	BB	SO	SB	PH AB	PH H	PO	A	E	DP	TC/G	FA	G by Pos
1926	PIT N	24	.345	.436	55	19	3	1	0	0.0	11	4	3	6	0	4	2	20	3	2	1	1.0	.920	OF-14
1927		32	.286	.476	21	6	1	0	1	4.8	6	4	1	0	0	15	4	5	0	0	0	0.2	1.000	OF-3
1928		81	.322	.426	202	65	4	4	3	1.5	34	41	20	18	5	24	7	107	6	5	1	1.5	.958	OF-50
1929		60	.314	.381	118	37	4	2	0	0.0	13	17	7	12	3	29	6	54	3	0	0	1.0	1.000	OF-27
1930	2 teams		PIT N (68G – .297)				PHI N (53G – .246)																	
"	total	121	.270	.362	459	124	21	9	1	0.2	69	31	28	41	4	5	2	285	9	13	1	2.5	.958	OF-114
1931	PHI N	130	.253	.305	514	130	14	5	1	0.2	77	31	42	39	5	5	2	341	8	8	2	2.7	.978	OF-122
1932		45	.333	.455	66	22	6	1	0	0.0	9	2	4	5	2	20	5	27	2	2	1	0.7	.935	OF-12
1933		8	.308	.538	13	4	1	1	0	0.0	0	0	0	2	0	0	0	10	1	0	0	1.4	1.000	OF-4
8 yrs.		501	.281	.363	1448	407	54	23	6	0.4	221	131	106	121	19	104	28	849	32	30	6	1.8	.967	OF-346

WORLD SERIES

Year	Team	Games	BA	SA	AB	H	2B	3B	HR	HR%	R	RBI	BB	SO	SB	PH AB	PH H	PO	A	E	DP	TC/G	FA	G by Pos
1927	PIT N	2	.000	.000	2	0	0	0	0	0.0	1	0	0	0	0	2	0	0	0	0	0	0.0	–	

Year	Team		Games	BA	SA	AB	H	2B	3B	HR	HR%	R	RBI	BB	SO	SB	AB	H	PO	A	E	DP	TC/G	FA	G by Pos

Fritzie Brickell
BRICKELL, FRITZ DARRELL   BR TR 5'5½" 157 lbs.
    Son of Fred Brickell.
    B. Mar. 19, 1935, Wichita, Kans. D. Oct. 15, 1965, Wichita, Kans.

Year	Team		Games	BA	SA	AB	H	2B	3B	HR	HR%	R	RBI	BB	SO	SB	AB	H	PO	A	E	DP	TC/G	FA	G by Pos
1958	NY	A	2	–	–	0	0	0	0	0	–	0	0	0	0	0	0	0	0	1	0	0	0.5	1.000	2B-2
1959			18	.256	.359	39	10	1	0	1	2.6	4	4	1	10	0	0	0	16	35	4	3	3.1	.927	SS-15, 2B-3
1961	LA	A	21	.122	.122	49	6	0	0	0	0.0	3	3	6	9	0	3	0	30	34	7	11	3.4	.901	SS-17
3 yrs.			41	.182	.227	88	16	1	0	1	1.1	7	7	7	19	0	3	0	46	70	11	14	3.1	.913	SS-32, 2B-5

George Brickley
BRICKLEY, GEORGE VINCENT   BR TR 5'9" 180 lbs.
    B. July 19, 1894, Everett, Mass. D. Feb. 23, 1947, Everett, Mass.

Year	Team		Games	BA	SA	AB	H	2B	3B	HR	HR%	R	RBI	BB	SO	SB	AB	H	PO	A	E	DP	TC/G	FA	G by Pos
1913	PHI	A	5	.167	.333	12	2	0	1	0	0.0	0	0	0	4	0	1	0	2	0	0	0	0.4	1.000	OF-4

Jim Brideweser
BRIDEWESER, JAMES EHRENFELD   BR TR 6' 165 lbs.
    B. Feb. 13, 1927, Lancaster, Ohio D. Aug. 25, 1989, El Toro, Calif.

Year	Team		Games	BA	SA	AB	H	2B	3B	HR	HR%	R	RBI	BB	SO	SB	AB	H	PO	A	E	DP	TC/G	FA	G by Pos
1951	NY	A	2	.375	.375	8	3	0	0	0	0.0	1	0	1	0	0	0	0	4	5	2	3	5.5	.818	SS-2
1952			42	.263	.263	38	10	0	0	0	0.0	12	2	3	5	0	9	1	13	23	4	4	1.0	.900	SS-22, 2B-4, 3B-1
1953			7	1.000	1.667	3	3	0	1	0	0.0	3	3	1	0	0	2	2	5	0	1	0	0.9	.833	SS-3
1954	BAL	A	73	.265	.319	204	54	7	2	0	0.0	18	12	15	27	1	11	2	106	140	16	30	3.6	.939	SS-48, 2B-19
1955	CHI	A	34	.207	.328	58	12	3	2	0	0.0	6	4	3	7	0	1	0	30	51	4	13	2.5	.953	SS-26, 3B-3, 2B-2
1956	2 teams	CHI A (10G – .182)				DET A (70G – .218)																			
"	total		80	.216	.246	167	36	5	0	0	0.0	23	11	20	22	1	1	0	117	150	6	34	3.4	.978	SS-42, 2B-31, 3B-4
1957	BAL	A	91	.268	.345	142	38	6	1	1	0.7	16	18	21	16	2	5	1	93	146	14	33	2.8	.945	SS-74, 3B-3, 2B-1
7 yrs.			329	.252	.310	620	156	21	6	1	0.2	79	50	63	78	6	29	7	368	515	47	117	2.8	.949	SS-217, 2B-57, 3B-11

Rocky Bridges
BRIDGES, EVERETT LAMAR   BR TR 5'8" 170 lbs.
    B. Aug. 7, 1927, Refugio, Tex.

Year	Team		Games	BA	SA	AB	H	2B	3B	HR	HR%	R	RBI	BB	SO	SB	AB	H	PO	A	E	DP	TC/G	FA	G by Pos
1951	BKN	N	63	.254	.328	134	34	7	1	1	0.7	13	15	10	10	0	2	1	48	94	15	15	2.5	.904	3B-40, 2B-10, SS-9
1952			51	.196	.250	56	11	3	0	0	0.0	9	2	7	9	0	3	1	44	53	3	12	2.0	.970	2B-24, SS-13, 3B-6
1953	CIN	N	122	.227	.273	432	98	13	2	1	0.2	52	21	37	42	6	4	0	335	328	16	95	2.0	.976	2B-115, SS-6, 3B-3
1954			53	.231	.250	52	12	1	0	0	0.0	4	2	7	7	0	1	0	45	60	2	13	2.0	.981	SS-20, 2B-19, 3B-13
1955			95	.286	.387	168	48	4	0	1	0.6	20	18	15	19	1	0	0	69	117	6	14	2.0	.969	3B-59, SS-26, 2B-9
1956			71	.211	.211	19	4	0	0	0	0.0	9	1	4	3	1	2	0	25	24	1	1	0.7	.980	3B-51, 2B-8, SS-7, OF-1
1957	2 teams	CIN N (5G – .000)				WAS A (120G – .228)																			
"	total		125	.227	.304	392	89	17	2	3	0.8	41	47	41	33	0	0	0	261	422	20	84	5.6	.972	SS-109, 2B-16, 3B-3
1958	WAS	A	116	.263	.355	377	99	14	3	5	1.3	38	28	27	32	0	4	0	194	333	13	73	4.7	.976	SS-112, 3B-3, 2B-3
1959	DET	A	116	.268	.349	381	102	16	3	3	0.8	38	35	30	35	1	2	0	195	308	24	70	4.5	.954	SS-110, 2B-5
1960	3 teams	DET A (10G – .200)				CLE A (10G – .333)							STL N (3G – .000)												
"	total		23	.313	.313	32	10	0	0	0	0.0	1	2	1	3	1	2	0	20	36	3	6	2.6	.949	SS-10, 3B-10, 2B-3
1961	LA	A	84	.240	.297	229	55	5	1	2	0.9	20	15	26	37	1	1	0	145	197	6	35	4.1	.983	2B-58, SS-25, 3B-4
11 yrs.			919	.247	.313	2272	562	80	11	16	0.7	245	187	205	229	10	19	1	1381	1972	109	418	3.8	.969	SS-447, 2B-270, 3B-191, OF-1

Al Bridwell
BRIDWELL, ALBERT HENRY   BL TR 5'9" 170 lbs.
    B. Jan. 4, 1884, Friendship, Ohio D. Jan. 23, 1969, Portsmouth, Ohio

Year	Team		Games	BA	SA	AB	H	2B	3B	HR	HR%	R	RBI	BB	SO	SB	AB	H	PO	A	E	DP	TC/G	FA	G by Pos
1905	CIN	N	82	.252	.272	254	64	3	1	0	0.0	17	17	19		8	7	3	104	118	17	15	2.9	.929	3B-43, OF-18, 2B-7, SS-5, 1B-1
1906	BOS	N	120	.227	.251	459	104	9	1	0	0.0	41	22	44		6	0	0	322	390	54	43	6.4	.930	SS-119, OF-1
1907			140	.218	.242	509	111	8	2	0	0.0	49	26	61		17	0	0	325	437	47	57	5.8	.942	SS-140
1908	NY	N	147	.285	.319	467	133	14	1	0	0.0	53	46	52		20	0	0	277	486	55	39	5.6	.933	SS-147
1909			145	.294	.338	476	140	11	5	0	0.0	59	55	67		32	0	0	268	439	45	55	5.2	.940	SS-144
1910			142	.276	.335	492	136	15	7	0	0.0	74	48	73	23	14	1	0	304	417	41	52	5.4	.946	SS-141
1911	2 teams	NY N (76G – .270)				BOS N (51G – .291)																			
"	total		127	.279	.317	445	124	15	1	0	0.0	57	41	66	18	10	0	0	207	398	46	45	5.1	.929	SS-127
1912	BOS	N	31	.236	.302	106	25	5	1	0	0.0	6	14	7	6	2	0	0	52	80	9	14	4.5	.936	SS-31
1913	CHI	N	135	.240	.291	405	97	6	6	1	0.2	35	37	74	28	12	0	0	282	399	37	46	5.3	.948	SS-135
1914	STL	F	117	.236	.286	381	90	6	5	1	0.3	46	33	71		9	3	0	240	316	31	37	5.0	.947	SS-103, 2B-11
1915			65	.229	.269	175	40	3	2	0	0.0	20	9	25		6	6	2	77	130	12	16	3.4	.945	2B-42, 3B-15, 1B-1
11 yrs.			1251	.255	.295	4169	1064	95	32	2	0.0	457	348	559	75	136	17	5	2458	3610	394	413	5.2	.939	SS-1092, 2B-60, 3B-58, OF-19, 1B-2

Bunny Brief
BRIEF, ANTHONY VINCENT   BR TR 6' 185 lbs.
    Born Antonio Bordetzki.
    B. July 3, 1892, Remus, Mich. D. Feb. 10, 1963, Milwaukee, Wis.

Year	Team		Games	BA	SA	AB	H	2B	3B	HR	HR%	R	RBI	BB	SO	SB	AB	H	PO	A	E	DP	TC/G	FA	G by Pos
1912	STL	A	15	.310	.381	42	13	3	0	0	0.0	9	5	6		2	0	0	48	2	4	3	3.6	.926	OF-9, 1B-4
1913			84	.217	.318	258	56	11	6	1	0.4	24	26	21	46	3	14	1	640	35	10	41	8.2	.985	1B-62, OF-8
1915	CHI	A	48	.214	.318	154	33	6	2	2	1.3	13	17	16	28	8	2	0	458	23	7	21	10.2	.986	1B-46
1917	PIT	N	36	.217	.330	115	25	5	1	2	1.7	15	11	15	21	4	4	2	309	22	4	23	9.3	.988	1B-34
4 yrs.			183	.223	.325	569	127	25	9	5	0.9	61	59	58	95	17	20	3	1455	82	25	88	8.5	.984	1B-146, OF-17

Charlie Briggs
BRIGGS, CHARLES R.   5'7" 170 lbs.
    B. 1861, Batavia, Ill.

Year	Team		Games	BA	SA	AB	H	2B	3B	HR	HR%	R	RBI	BB	SO	SB	AB	H	PO	A	E	DP	TC/G	FA	G by Pos
1884	CHI	U	49	.170	.253	182	31	8	2	1	0.5	29		11			0	0	68	30	24	6	2.5	.803	OF-37, 2B-12, SS-2

Dan Briggs
BRIGGS, DAN LEE   BL TL 6' 180 lbs.
    B. Nov. 18, 1952, Scotia, Calif.

Year	Team		Games	BA	SA	AB	H	2B	3B	HR	HR%	R	RBI	BB	SO	SB	AB	H	PO	A	E	DP	TC/G	FA	G by Pos
1975	CAL	A	13	.226	.355	31	7	1	0	1	3.2	3	3	3	2	0	1	0	49	1	2	4	4.0	.962	1B-6, OF-5, DH-2
1976			77	.214	.294	248	53	13	2	1	0.4	19	14	13	47	0	4	2	358	26	5	33	5.1	.987	1B-44, OF-40, DH-1
1977			59	.162	.230	74	12	2	0	1	1.4	6	4	8	14	0	3	0	154	14	2	10	2.9	.988	1B-45, OF-13
1978	CLE	A	15	.163	.265	49	8	0	1	1	2.0	4	4	9	0	0	0	0	38	1	0	1	2.6	1.000	OF-15
1979	SD	N	104	.207	.357	227	47	4	3	8	3.5	34	30	18	45	2	29	3	393	31	7	21	4.1	.984	1B-50, OF-44
1981	MON	N	9	.091	.091	11	1	0	0	0	0.0	0	0	0	3	0	3	0	16	2	0	1	2.0	1.000	OF-3, 1B-3

Year	Team		Games	BA	SA	AB	H	2B	3B	HR	HR%	R	RBI	BB	SO	SB	Pinch Hit AB	Pinch Hit H	PO	A	E	DP	TC/G	FA	G by Pos

Dan Briggs *continued*

Year	Team		Games	BA	SA	AB	H	2B	3B	HR	HR%	R	RBI	BB	SO	SB	PH AB	PH H	PO	A	E	DP	TC/G	FA	G by Pos
1982	CHI	N	48	.125	.125	48	6	0	0	0	0.0	1	1	0	9	0	37	4	14	2	1	1	0.4	.941	OF-10, 1B-4
7 yrs.			325	.195	.294	688	134	20	6	12	1.7	67	53	45	133	2	77	9	1022	77	17	71	3.4	.985	1B-152, OF-130, DH-3

Grant Briggs

BRIGGS, GRANT
B. Mar. 16, 1865, Pittsburgh, Pa.   D. May 31, 1928, Pittsburgh, Pa.

Year	Team		Games	BA	SA	AB	H	2B	3B	HR	HR%	R	RBI	BB	SO	SB	PH AB	PH H	PO	A	E	DP	TC/G	FA	G by Pos
1890	SYR	AA	86	.180	.231	316	57	6	5	0	0.0	44		16		7	0	0	273	94	27	8	4.6	.931	C-46, OF-33, 3B-5, SS-4
1891	LOU	AA	1	.250	.250	4	1	0	0	0	0.0	0	0	0	0	0	0	0	3	1	0	0	4.0	1.000	C-1
1892	STL	N	23	.070	.088	57	4	1	0	0	0.0	2	1	6	16	3	0	0	46	13	9	0	3.0	.868	C-15, OF-9
1895	LOU	N	1	.000	.000	3	0	0	0	0	0.0	0	0	0	1	0	0	0	1	0	0	0	1.0	1.000	C-1
4 yrs.			111	.163	.208	380	62	7	5	0	0.0	46	1	22	17	10	0	0	323	108	36	8	4.2	.923	C-63, OF-42, 3B-5, SS-4

John Briggs

BRIGGS, JOHN EDWARD
B. Mar. 10, 1944, Paterson, N. J.   BL TL 6'1" 190 lbs.

Year	Team		Games	BA	SA	AB	H	2B	3B	HR	HR%	R	RBI	BB	SO	SB	PH AB	PH H	PO	A	E	DP	TC/G	FA	G by Pos
1964	PHI	N	61	.258	.333	66	17	2	0	1	1.5	16	6	9	12	1	29	7	22	1	1	0	0.4	.958	OF-19, 1B-1
1965			93	.236	.362	229	54	9	4	4	1.7	47	23	42	44	3	32	7	110	2	2	0	1.2	.982	OF-66
1966			81	.282	.490	255	72	13	5	10	3.9	43	23	41	55	3	17	2	126	3	3	0	1.6	.977	OF-69
1967			106	.232	.373	332	77	12	4	9	2.7	47	30	41	72	3	13	2	182	2	4	0	1.8	.979	OF-94
1968			110	.254	.361	338	86	13	1	7	2.1	36	31	58	72	8	14	7	423	23	7	33	4.1	.985	OF-65, 1B-36
1969			124	.238	.410	361	86	20	3	12	3.3	51	46	64	78	9	16	3	213	6	6	2	1.8	.973	OF-108, 1B-2
1970			110	.270	.434	341	92	15	7	9	2.6	43	47	39	65	5	15	6	188	7	4	1	1.8	.980	OF-95
1971	2 teams		135	PHI N (10G – .182)						MIL A	(125G – .264)														
"	total		135	.259	.453	397	103	12	1	21	5.3	54	62	77	81	1	10	1	578	45	12	54	4.7	.981	OF-73, 1B-60
1972	MIL	A	135	.266	.455	418	111	14	1	21	5.0	58	65	54	67	1	10	4	414	18	5	21	3.2	.989	OF-106, 1B-28
1973			142	.246	.426	488	120	20	7	18	3.7	78	57	87	83	15	2	0	294	9	10	1	2.2	.968	OF-137, DH-1
1974			154	.253	.428	554	140	30	8	17	3.1	72	73	71	102	9	4	1	309	10	9	2	2.1	.973	OF-149, DH-2
1975	2 teams		115	MIL A (28G – .297)						MIN A	(87G – .231)														
"	total		115	.246	.376	392	107	15	4	10	3.0	56	44	80	54	6	8	1	530	58	10	38	5.2	.983	OF-56, 1B-49, DH-3
12 yrs.			1366	.253	.416	4117	1041	170	43	139	3.4	601	507	663	785	64	170	41	3389	184	73	152	2.7	.980	OF-1037, 1B-176, DH-6

Harry Bright

BRIGHT, HARRY JAMES
B. Sept. 22, 1929, Kansas City, Mo.   BR TR 6' 190 lbs.

Year	Team		Games	BA	SA	AB	H	2B	3B	HR	HR%	R	RBI	BB	SO	SB	PH AB	PH H	PO	A	E	DP	TC/G	FA	G by Pos
1958	PIT	N	15	.250	.417	24	6	1	0	1	4.2	4	3	1	6	0	4	1	4	11	0	0	1.0	1.000	3B-7
1959			40	.250	.458	48	12	1	0	3	6.3	4	8	5	10	0	31	7	6	5	0	0	0.3	1.000	OF-4, 3B-3, 2B-1
1960			4	.000	.000	4	0	0	0	0	0.0	0	0	0	2	0	4	0	0	0	0	0	0.0	–	
1961	WAS	A	72	.240	.339	183	44	6	0	4	2.2	20	21	19	23	0	23	3	71	101	11	15	2.5	.940	3B-40, C-8, 2B-1
1962			113	.273	.462	392	107	15	4	17	4.3	55	67	26	51	2	15	4	802	72	11	83	7.8	.988	1B-99, C-3, 3B-1
1963	2 teams		61	CIN N (1G – .000)						NY	A	(60G – .236)														
"	total		61	.234	.411	158	37	7	0	7	4.4	15	23	13	32	0	12	2	2	0	0	0	0.0	1.000	1B-36, 3B-12
1964	NY	A	4	.200	.200	5	1	0	0	0	0.0	0	0	1	1	0	1	0	9	0	0	0	2.3	1.000	1B-2
1965	CHI	N	27	.280	.320	25	7	1	0	0	0.0	1	4	0	8	0	25	7	0	0	0	0	0.0	–	
8 yrs.			336	.255	.416	839	214	31	4	32	3.8	99	126	65	133	2	115	24	894	189	22	98	3.3	.980	1B-137, 3B-63, C-11, OF-4, 2B-2

WORLD SERIES

Year	Team		Games	BA	SA	AB	H	2B	3B	HR	HR%	R	RBI	BB	SO	SB	PH AB	PH H	PO	A	E	DP	TC/G	FA	G by Pos
1963	NY	A	2	.000	.000	2	0	0	0	0	0.0	0	0	0	2	0	2	0	0	0	0	0	0.0	–	

Greg Briley

BRILEY, GREGORY
B. May 24, 1965, Greenville, N. C.   BL TR 5'9" 175 lbs.

Year	Team		Games	BA	SA	AB	H	2B	3B	HR	HR%	R	RBI	BB	SO	SB	PH AB	PH H	PO	A	E	DP	TC/G	FA	G by Pos
1988	SEA	A	13	.250	.389	36	9	2	0	1	2.8	6	4	5	6	0	0	0	13	0	1	0	1.1	.929	OF-11
1989			115	.266	.442	394	105	22	4	13	3.3	52	52	39	82	11	11	3	197	38	9	7	2.1	.963	OF-105, 2B-10, DH-2
2 yrs.			128	.265	.437	430	114	24	4	14	3.3	58	56	44	88	11	14	3	210	38	10	7	2.0	.961	OF-116, 2B-10, DH-2

Bill Brinker

BRINKER, WILLIAM HUTCHINSON (Dode)
B. Aug. 30, 1883, Warrensburg, Mo.   D. Feb. 5, 1965, Arcadia, Calif.   BB TR 6'1" 190 lbs.

Year	Team		Games	BA	SA	AB	H	2B	3B	HR	HR%	R	RBI	BB	SO	SB	PH AB	PH H	PO	A	E	DP	TC/G	FA	G by Pos
1912	PHI	N	9	.222	.278	18	4	1	0	0	0.0	1	2	3		0	3	0	7	4	2	0	1.4	.846	OF-2, 3B-2

Chuck Brinkman

BRINKMAN, CHARLES ERNEST
Brother of Ed Brinkman.
B. Sept. 16, 1944, Cincinnati, Ohio   BR TR 6'1" 185 lbs.

Year	Team		Games	BA	SA	AB	H	2B	3B	HR	HR%	R	RBI	BB	SO	SB	PH AB	PH H	PO	A	E	DP	TC/G	FA	G by Pos
1969	CHI	A	14	.067	.067	15	1	0	0	0	0.0	0	1	1	5	0	1	0	28	2	0	1	2.1	1.000	C-14
1970			9	.250	.300	20	5	1	0	0	0.0	4	0	3	3	0	0	0	32	5	1	1	4.2	.974	C-9
1971			15	.200	.200	20	4	0	0	0	0.0	1	3	3	5	0	0	0	45	4	0	0	3.3	1.000	C-14
1972			35	.135	.135	52	7	0	0	0	0.0	1	0	4	7	0	3	1	118	11	2	3	3.7	.985	C-33
1973			63	.187	.252	123	23	6	0	1	0.7	13	10	11	37	0	0	0	262	36	4	5	4.8	.987	C-63
1974	2 teams		12	CHI A (8G – .143)						PIT	N	(4G – .143)														
"	total		12	.143	.143	21	3	0	0	0	0.0	2	1	1	3	0	0	0	28	1	0	0	2.4	1.000	C-12
6 yrs.			148	.172	.210	267	46	7	0	1	0.4	22	12	23	60	0	5	1	513	59	7	10	3.9	.988	C-145

Ed Brinkman

BRINKMAN, EDWIN ALBERT
Brother of Chuck Brinkman.
B. Dec. 8, 1941, Cincinnati, Ohio   BR TR 6' 170 lbs.

Year	Team		Games	BA	SA	AB	H	2B	3B	HR	HR%	R	RBI	BB	SO	SB	PH AB	PH H	PO	A	E	DP	TC/G	FA	G by Pos
1961	WAS	A	4	.091	.091	11	1	0	0	0	0.0	1	0	1	0	0	2	6	1	1	2.3	.889	3B-3			
1962			54	.165	.233	133	22	7	1	0	0.0	8	4	11	28	1	0	0	71	96	9	22	3.3	.949	SS-38, 3B-10
1963			145	.228	.319	514	117	20	3	7	1.4	44	45	31	86	5	2	1	241	462	37	97	5.1	.950	SS-143
1964			132	.224	.336	447	100	20	3	8	1.8	44	34	26	99	2	7	1	234	364	19	75	4.7	.969	SS-125
1965			154	.185	.257	444	82	13	2	5	1.1	35	28	38	82	1	3	0	292	369	25	76	4.5	.964	SS-150
1966			158	.229	.326	582	133	18	9	7	1.2	42	48	29	105	7	0	0	263	501	28	83	5.0	.965	SS-158
1967			109	.188	.238	320	60	9	2	1	0.3	21	18	24	58	1	0	0	160	309	10	54	4.4	.979	SS-109
1968			77	.187	.202	193	36	0	0	0	0.0	12	6	19	31	0	0	0	97	198	11	28	4.0	.964	SS-74, 2B-2, OF-1
1969			151	.266	.325	576	153	18	5	2	0.3	71	43	50	42	2	1	1	248	511	19	92	5.2	.976	SS-150
1970			158	.262	.301	625	164	17	2	1	0.2	63	40	60	41	8	2	1	301	569	23	103	5.7	.974	SS-157

Year	Team		Games	BA	SA	AB	H	2B	3B	HR	HR%	R	RBI	BB	SO	SB	Pinch Hit AB	H	PO	A	E	DP	TC/G	FA	G by Pos

Ed Brinkman *continued*

Year	Team		Games	BA	SA	AB	H	2B	3B	HR	HR%	R	RBI	BB	SO	SB	AB	H	PO	A	E	DP	TC/G	FA	G by Pos
1971	DET	A	159	.228	.275	527	120	18	2	1	0.2	40	37	44	54	1	0	0	235	513	15	91	4.8	.980	SS-159
1972			156	.203	.279	516	105	19	1	6	1.2	42	49	38	51	0	0	0	233	495	7	81	4.7	.990	SS-156
1973			162	.237	.324	515	122	16	4	7	1.4	55	40	34	79	0	0	0	249	480	24	89	4.6	.968	SS-162
1974			153	.221	.347	502	111	15	3	14	2.8	55	54	29	71	2	0	0	239	498	21	89	5.0	.972	SS-151, 3B-2
1975	3 teams		STL N	(28G – .240)		TEX A	(1G – .000)			NY	A	(44G – .175)													
"	total		73	.207	.300	140	29	8	1	1	0.7	8	8	10	17	0	4	1	71	129	12	28	2.9	.943	SS-63, 3B-4, 2B-3
	15 yrs.		1845	.224	.300	6045	1355	201	38	60	1.0	550	461	444	845	30	22	5	2936	5500	261	1009	4.7	.970	SS-1795, 3B-19, 2B-5, OF-1

LEAGUE CHAMPIONSHIP SERIES

| 1972 | DET | A | 1 | .250 | .500 | 4 | 1 | 1 | 0 | 0 | 0.0 | 0 | 0 | 0 | 0 | 0 | 0 | 0 | 1 | 2 | 0 | 0 | 3.0 | 1.000 | SS-1 |

Leon Brinkopf

BRINKOPF, LEON CLARENCE
B. Oct. 20, 1926, Cape Girardeau, Mo.   BR TR 5'11½" 185 lbs.

| 1952 | CHI | N | 9 | .182 | .182 | 22 | 4 | 0 | 0 | 0 | 0.0 | 1 | 2 | 4 | 5 | 0 | 2 | 1 | 4 | 17 | 1 | 1 | 2.4 | .955 | SS-6 |

Fatty Briody

BRIODY, CHARLES F. (Alderman)
B. Aug. 13, 1858, Lansingburg, N.Y.   D. June 22, 1903, Chicago, Ill.   TR 5'8½" 190 lbs.

1880	TRO	N	1	.000	.000	4	0	0	0	0	0.0	0		0			0	0	4	3	3	0	10.0	.700	C-1
1882	CLE	N	53	.258	.325	194	50	13	0	0	0.0	30	13	9	13		0	0	251	89	37	6	7.1	.902	C-53
1883			40	.234	.283	145	34	5	1	0	0.0	23		3	13		0	0	191	56	25	8	6.8	.908	C-33, 2B-4, 1B-2, 3B-1
1884	2 teams		CLE N	(43G – .169)		CIN U	(22G – .337)																		
"	total		65	.232	.295	237	55	8	1	1	0.4	28	12	7	19		0	0	437	112	41	6	9.1	.931	C-64, OF-1
1885	STL	N	62	.195	.251	215	42	9	0	1	0.5	14	17	12	23		0	0	245	87	39	3	6.0	.895	C-60, OF-1, 3B-1, 2B-1
1886	KC	N	56	.237	.312	215	51	10	3	0	0.0	14	29	3	35		0	0	269	95	32	4	7.1	.919	C-54, OF-2, 1B-1
1887	DET	N	33	.227	.336	128	29	6	1	2	1.6	24	26	9	10	6	0	0	144	61	21	4	6.8	.907	C-33
1888	KC	AA	13	.208	.229	48	10	1	0	0	0.0	0	1	1	8	1	0	0	52	17	8	3	5.9	.896	C-13
	8 yrs.		323	.228	.294	1186	271	52	7	4	0.3	134	105	44	113	6	0	0	1593	520	206	34	7.2	.911	C-311, 2B-5, OF-4, 1B-3, 3B-2

George Bristow

BRISTOW, GEORGE T.
B. May, 1870, Paw Paw, Ill. Deceased.   BR 5'10" 170 lbs.

| 1899 | CLE | N | 3 | .125 | .250 | 8 | 1 | 1 | 0 | 0 | 0.0 | 0 | 0 | 0 | | 0 | 0 | 0 | 4 | 1 | 0 | 0 | 1.7 | 1.000 | OF-3 |

Gus Brittain

BRITTAIN, AUGUST SCHUSTER
B. Nov. 29, 1909, Wilmington, N.C.   D. Feb. 16, 1974, Wilmington, N.C.   BR TR 5'10" 192 lbs.

| 1937 | CIN | N | 3 | .167 | .167 | 6 | 1 | 0 | 0 | 0 | 0.0 | 0 | 0 | 0 | 3 | 0 | 2 | 0 | 3 | 1 | 0 | 0 | 1.3 | 1.000 | C-1 |

Gil Britton

BRITTON, STEPHEN GILBERT
B. Sept. 21, 1891, Parsons, Kans.   D. June 20, 1983, Parsons, Kans.   BR TR 5'10" 160 lbs.

| 1913 | PIT | N | 3 | .000 | .000 | 12 | 0 | 0 | 0 | 0 | 0.0 | 0 | 0 | 0 | | 0 | 0 | 0 | 5 | 9 | 3 | 2 | 5.7 | .824 | SS-3 |

Greg Brock

BROCK, GREGORY ALLEN
B. June 14, 1957, McMinnville, Ore.   BL TR 6'3" 200 lbs.

1982	LA	N	18	.118	.176	17	2	1	0	0	0.0	1	0	1	5	0	13	2	9	0	0	0	0.5	1.000	1B-3
1983			146	.224	.396	455	102	14	2	20	4.4	64	66	83	81	5	6	1	1162	106	12	94	8.8	.991	1B-140
1984			88	.225	.402	271	61	6	0	14	5.2	33	34	39	37	8	8	0	703	65	4	61	8.8	.995	1B-83
1985			129	.251	.438	438	110	19	0	21	4.8	64	66	54	72	4	9	2	1113	84	7	86	9.3	.994	1B-122
1986			115	.234	.422	325	76	13	0	16	4.9	33	52	37	60	2	23	4	726	87	3	46	7.1	.996	1B-99
1987	MIL	A	141	.299	.438	532	159	29	3	13	2.4	81	85	57	63	5	0	0	1065	109	8	111	8.4	.993	1B-141
1988			115	.212	.310	364	77	16	1	6	1.6	53	50	63	48	6	1	1	915	102	7	89	8.9	.993	1B-114, DH-1
1989			107	.265	.405	373	99	16	0	12	3.2	40	52	43	49	6	1	1	850	58	5	86	8.5	.995	1B-100, DH-7
	8 yrs.		859	.247	.403	2775	686	114	6	102	3.7	369	406	377	415	36	61	10	6543	611	46	573	8.4	.994	1B-802, DH-8

LEAGUE CHAMPIONSHIP SERIES

1983	LA	N	3	.000	.000	9	0	0	0	0	0.0	1	0	1	3	0	1	0	13	0	0	3	4.3	1.000	1B-3
1985			5	.083	.333	12	1	0	0	1	8.3	2	2	1	2	0	1	0	35	4	0	2	7.8	1.000	1B-4
	2 yrs.		8	.048	.190	21	1	0	0	1	4.8	3	2	2	5	0	1	0	48	4	0	5	6.5	1.000	1B-7

John Brock

BROCK, JOHN ROY
B. Oct. 16, 1896, Hamilton, Ill.   D. Oct. 27, 1951, Clayton, Mo.   BR TR 5'6½" 165 lbs.

1917	STL	N	7	.400	.467	15	6	1	0	0	0.0	4	2	0	2	2	3	1	13	4	1	0	2.6	.944	C-4
1918			27	.212	.250	52	11	2	0	0	0.0	9	4	3	10	5	7	2	38	20	3	1	2.3	.951	C-18, OF-1
	2 yrs.		34	.254	.299	67	17	3	0	0	0.0	13	6	3	12	7	10	3	51	24	4	1	2.3	.949	C-22, OF-1

Lou Brock

BROCK, LOUIS CLARK
B. June 18, 1939, El Dorado, Ark.
Hall of Fame 1985.   BL TL 5'11½" 170 lbs.

1961	CHI	N	4	.091	.091	11	1	0	0	0	0.0	1	0	1	3	0	0	0	6	0	2	0	2.0	.750	OF-3
1962			123	.263	.412	434	114	24	7	9	2.1	73	35	35	96	16	15	2	243	7	9	2	2.1	.965	OF-106
1963			148	.258	.382	547	141	19	11	9	1.6	79	37	31	122	24	10	2	269	17	8	7	2.0	.973	OF-140
1964	2 teams		CHI N	(52G – .251)		STL N	(103G – .348)																		
"	total		155	.315	.464	634	200	30	11	14	2.2	111	58	40	127	43	1	0	266	15	14	1	1.9	.953	OF-154
1965	STL	N	155	.288	.445	631	182	35	8	16	2.5	107	69	45	116	63	1	0	272	11	12	1	1.9	.959	OF-153
1966			156	.285	.429	643	183	24	12	15	2.3	94	46	31	134	74	1	0	269	9	19	1	1.9	.936	OF-154
1967			159	.299	.472	689	206	32	12	21	3.0	113	76	24	109	52	4	0	272	12	13	2	1.9	.956	OF-157
1968			159	.279	.418	660	184	46	14	6	0.9	92	51	46	124	62	3	1	269	9	14	1	1.8	.952	OF-156
1969			157	.298	.434	655	195	33	10	12	1.8	97	47	50	115	53	2	1	255	7	14	2	1.8	.949	OF-157
1970			155	.304	.422	664	202	29	5	13	2.0	114	57	60	99	51	3	2	247	9	10	2	1.7	.962	OF-152
1971			157	.313	.425	640	200	37	7	7	1.1	126	61	76	107	64	2	1	262	7	14	3	1.8	.951	OF-157
1972			153	.311	.393	621	193	26	8	3	0.5	81	42	47	93	63	4	1	253	6	13	1	1.8	.952	OF-149

Year	Team		Games	BA	SA	AB	H	2B	3B	HR	HR%	R	RBI	BB	SO	SB	Pinch Hit AB	Pinch Hit H	PO	A	E	DP	TC/G	FA	G by Pos

Lou Brock *continued*

Year	Team		Games	BA	SA	AB	H	2B	3B	HR	HR%	R	RBI	BB	SO	SB	AB	H	PO	A	E	DP	TC/G	FA	G by Pos
1973			160	.297	.398	650	193	29	8	7	1.1	110	63	71	112	**70**	1	0	310	3	12	1	2.0	.963	OF-159
1974			153	.306	.381	635	194	25	7	3	0.5	105	48	61	88	**118**	3	1	283	8	10	2	2.0	.967	OF-152
1975			136	.309	.400	528	163	27	6	3	0.6	78	47	38	64	56	8	3	247	5	9	0	1.9	.966	OF-128
1976			133	.301	.394	498	150	24	5	4	0.8	73	67	35	75	56	12	3	221	6	4	0	1.7	.983	OF-123
1977			141	.272	.354	489	133	22	6	2	0.4	69	46	30	74	35	18	7	184	2	9	1	1.4	.954	OF-130
1978			92	.221	.252	298	66	9	0	0	0.0	31	12	17	29	17	15	4	114	2	3	0	1.3	.975	OF-79
1979			120	.304	.398	405	123	15	4	5	1.2	56	38	23	43	21	22	5	152	7	7	2	1.4	.958	OF-98
19 yrs.			2616	.293	.410	10332	3023	486	141	149	1.4	1610	900	761	1730	938	125	33	4394	142	196	29	1.8	.959	OF-2507
						9th									7th	1st									

WORLD SERIES

Year	Team		Games	BA	SA	AB	H	2B	3B	HR	HR%	R	RBI	BB	SO	SB	AB	H	PO	A	E	DP	TC/G	FA	G by Pos
1964	STL	N	7	.300	.467	30	9	2	0	1	3.3	2	5	0	3	0	0	0	8	1	1	0	1.4	.900	OF-7
1967			7	.414	.655	29	12	2	1	1	3.4	8	3	2	3	7	0	0	13	0	0	0	1.9	1.000	OF-7
1968			7	.464	.857	28	13	3	1	2	7.1	6	5	3	4	7	0	0	13	0	1	0	2.0	.929	OF-7
3 yrs.			21	.391	.655	87	34	7	2	4	4.6	16	13	5	10	14	0	0	34	1	2	0	1.8	.946	OF-21
				2nd	6th		9th									1st									

Matt Broderick

BRODERICK, MATTHEW THOMAS   BR TR 5'6½" 135 lbs.
B. Dec. 2, 1876, Lattimer Mines, Pa.   D. Feb. 22, 1941, Freeland, Pa.

Year	Team		Games	BA	SA	AB	H	2B	3B	HR	HR%	R	RBI	BB	SO	SB	AB	H	PO	A	E	DP	TC/G	FA	G by Pos
1903	BKN	N	2	.000	.000	2	0	0	0	0	0.0	0	0	0		0	1	0	1	0	0	1	0.5	1.000	2B-1

Steve Brodie

BRODIE, WALTER SCOTT   BL TR 5'11" 180 lbs.
B. Sept. 11, 1868, Warrenton, Va.   D. Oct. 30, 1935, Baltimore, Md.

Year	Team		Games	BA	SA	AB	H	2B	3B	HR	HR%	R	RBI	BB	SO	SB	AB	H	PO	A	E	DP	TC/G	FA	G by Pos
1890	BOS	N	132	.296	.368	514	152	19	9	0	0.0	77	67	66	20	29	0	0	225	19	12	6	1.9	.953	OF-132
1891			133	.260	.319	523	136	13	6	2	0.4	84	78	63	39	25	0	0	268	25	15	9	2.3	.951	OF-133
1892	STL	N	154	.252	.319	602	152	10	9	4	0.7	85	60	52	31	28	0	0	326	59	26	12	2.7	.937	OF-137, 2B-16, 3B-2
1893	2 teams		STL N (107G – .318)			BAL N	(25G – .361)																			
"	total		132	.325	.412	566	184	23	10	2	0.4	89	98	45	18	49	0	0	323	23	17	7	2.8	.953	OF-132
1894	BAL	N	129	.366	.464	573	210	25	11	3	0.5	134	113	18	8	42	0	0	310	14	17	4	2.6	.950	OF-129
1895			131	.348	.449	528	184	27	10	2	0.4	85	134	26	15	35	0	0	307	23	12	2	2.6	.951	OF-131
1896			132	.297	.388	516	153	19	11	2	0.4	98	87	36	17	25	0	0	320	22	10	6	2.7	.972	OF-132
1897	PIT	N	100	.292	.392	370	108	7	12	2	0.5	47	53	25		11	0	0	218	11	4	1	2.3	.983	OF-100
1898	2 teams		PIT N	(42G – .263)		BAL N	(23G – .306)																			
"	total		65	.280	.327	254	71	8	2	0	0.0	27	40	11		6	0	0	165	9	10	1	2.8	.946	OF-65
1899	BAL	N	137	.309	.379	531	164	26	1	3	0.6	82	87	31		19	0	0	310	15	7	5	2.4	.979	OF-137
1901	BAL	A	83	.310	.389	306	95	6	6	2	0.7	41	41	25		9	0	0	178	4	7	0	2.3	.963	OF-83
1902	NY	N	109	.281	.332	416	117	8	2	3	0.7	37	42	22		11	0	0	219	22	12	7	2.3	.953	OF-109
12 yrs.			1437	.303	.381	5699	1726	191	89	25	0.4	886	900	420	148	289	0	0	3169	246	149	60	2.5	.958	OF-1420, 2B-16, 3B-2

Jack Brohamer

BROHAMER, JOHN ANTHONY   BL TR 5'10" 165 lbs.
B. Feb. 26, 1950, Maywood, Calif.

Year	Team		Games	BA	SA	AB	H	2B	3B	HR	HR%	R	RBI	BB	SO	SB	AB	H	PO	A	E	DP	TC/G	FA	G by Pos
1972	CLE	A	136	.233	.294	527	123	13	2	5	0.9	49	35	27	46	3	6	1	285	395	16	87	5.1	.977	2B-132, 3B-1
1973			102	.220	.307	300	66	12	1	4	1.3	29	29	32	23	0	10	3	215	279	15	67	5.0	.971	2B-97
1974			101	.270	.330	315	85	11	1	2	0.6	33	30	26	22	2	9	4	203	269	6	67	4.7	.987	2B-99
1975			69	.244	.350	217	53	5	0	6	2.8	15	16	14	14	2	3	1	166	162	8	52	4.9	.976	2B-66
1976	CHI	A	119	.251	.356	354	89	12	2	7	2.0	33	40	44	28	1	1	0	265	338	10	75	5.2	.984	2B-117, 3B-1
1977			59	.257	.401	152	39	10	3	2	1.3	26	20	21	8	0	2	0	54	100	8	15	2.7	.951	3B-38, 2B-18, DH-1
1978	BOS	A	81	.234	.311	244	57	14	1	1	0.4	34	25	25	13	1	11	3	64	103	5	18	2.1	.971	3B-30, DH-25, 2B-23
1979			64	.266	.328	192	51	7	1	1	0.5	25	11	15	15	0	8	1	74	140	5	27	3.4	.977	2B-36, 3B-22
1980	2 teams		BOS A	(21G – .316)		CLE A	(53G – .225)																			
"	total		74	.251	.327	199	50	7	1	2	1.0	18	21	18	9	0	15	3	89	142	7	30	3.2	.971	2B-51, 3B-13, DH-4
9 yrs.			805	.245	.327	2500	613	91	12	30	1.2	262	227	222	178	9	65	16	1415	1928	80	438	4.3	.977	2B-639, 3B-105, DH-30

Herman Bronkie

BRONKIE, HERMAN CHARLES (Dutch)   BR TR 5'9" 165 lbs.
B. Mar. 30, 1885, S. Manchester, Conn.   D. May 27, 1968, Somers, Conn.

Year	Team		Games	BA	SA	AB	H	2B	3B	HR	HR%	R	RBI	BB	SO	SB	AB	H	PO	A	E	DP	TC/G	FA	G by Pos
1910	CLE	A	4	.222	.222	9	2	0	0	0	0.0	1	0	1		1	0	0	4	4	4	0	3.0	.667	3B-3, SS-1
1911			2	.167	.167	6	1	0	0	0	0.0	0	0	0		0	0	0	3	1	0	0	2.0	1.000	3B-2
1912			6	.000	.000	16	0	0	0	0	0.0	1	0	1		0	0	0	7	15	2	1	4.0	.917	3B-6
1914	CHI	N	1	1.000	2.000	1	1	1	0	0	0.0	1	1	0		0	0	0	0	1	0	1	1.0	–	3B-1
1918	STL	N	18	.221	.309	68	15	3	0	1	1.5	7	7	2	4	0	0	0	18	43	1	2	3.4	.984	3B-18
1919	STL	A	67	.255	.327	196	50	6	4	0	0.0	23	14	23	23	2	12	3	90	115	12	16	3.2	.945	3B-34, 2B-16, 1B-2
1922			23	.281	.375	64	18	4	1	0	0.0	7	2	6	7	0	4	1	24	31	5	7	2.6	.917	3B-18
7 yrs.			121	.242	.317	360	87	14	5	1	0.3	40	24	33	34	3	16	4	146	209	25	26	3.1	.934	3B-82, 2B-16, 1B-2, SS-1

Tom Brookens

BROOKENS, THOMAS DALE   BR TR 5'10" 165 lbs.
B. Aug. 10, 1953, Chambersburg, Pa.

Year	Team		Games	BA	SA	AB	H	2B	3B	HR	HR%	R	RBI	BB	SO	SB	AB	H	PO	A	E	DP	TC/G	FA	G by Pos
1979	DET	A	60	.263	.374	190	50	5	2	4	2.1	23	21	11	40	10	0	0	76	141	11	21	3.8	.952	3B-42, 2B-19, DH-1
1980			151	.275	.418	509	140	25	9	10	2.0	64	66	32	71	13	4	1	127	307	29	38	3.1	.937	3B-138, 2B-9, DH-1, SS-1
1981			71	.243	.343	239	58	10	1	4	1.7	19	25	14	43	5	1	0	58	139	10	13	2.9	.952	3B-71
1982			140	.231	.352	398	92	15	3	9	2.3	40	58	27	63	5	6	2	119	276	20	27	3.0	.952	3B-113, 2B-26, SS-9, OF-1
1983			138	.214	.325	332	71	13	3	6	1.8	50	32	29	46	10	10	1	97	254	22	34	2.7	.941	3B-103, SS-30, 2B-10, DH-1
1984			113	.246	.397	224	55	11	4	5	2.2	32	26	19	33	6	3	2	98	187	12	35	2.6	.960	3B-68, SS-28, 2B-26, DH-1
1985			156	.237	.375	485	115	34	6	7	1.4	54	47	27	78	14	1	1	135	277	24	28	2.8	.945	3B-151, SS-8, 2B-3, DH-1, C-1
1986			98	.270	.356	281	76	11	2	3	1.1	42	25	20	42	11	7	1	106	144	7	26	2.6	.973	3B-35, 2B-31, DH-14, SS-14, OF-3
1987			143	.241	.376	444	107	15	3	13	2.9	59	59	33	63	7	1	0	119	256	19	33	2.8	.952	3B-122, SS-16, 2B-11
1988			136	.243	.351	441	107	23	5	5	1.1	62	38	44	74	4	5	1	101	235	17	16	2.6	.952	3B-136, SS-3, 2B-2
1989	NY	A	66	.226	.333	168	38	6	0	4	2.4	14	14	11	27	1	11	3	27	85	7	7	1.8	.941	3B-51, SS-7, 2B-5, DH-3, OF-3
11 yrs.			1272	.245	.367	3711	909	168	38	70	1.9	459	411	267	580	86	50	12	1063	2301	178	278	2.8	.950	3B-1030, 2B-141, SS-116, DH-22, OF-7, C-1

Year	Team		Games	BA	SA	AB	H	2B	3B	HR	HR%	R	RBI	BB	SO	SB	Pinch Hit AB	H	PO	A	E	DP	TC/G	FA	G by Pos

Tom Brookens *continued*

LEAGUE CHAMPIONSHIP SERIES

Year	Team		Games	BA	SA	AB	H	2B	3B	HR	HR%	R	RBI	BB	SO	SB	PH AB	H	PO	A	E	DP	TC/G	FA	G by Pos
1984	DET	A	2	.000	.000	2	0	0	0	0	0.0	0	0	0	1	0	0	0	0	2	1	0	1.5	.667	3B-1, 2B-1
1987			5	.000	.000	13	0	0	0	0	0.0	0	0	0	3	0	0	0	3	15	0	0	3.6	1.000	3B-5
2 yrs.			7	.000	.000	15	0	0	0	0	0.0	0	0	0	4	0	0	0	3	17	1	0	3.0	.952	3B-6, 2B-1

WORLD SERIES

| 1984 | DET | A | 3 | .000 | .000 | 3 | 0 | 0 | 0 | 0 | 0.0 | 0 | 0 | 0 | 1 | 0 | 2 | 0 | 0 | 3 | 0 | 0 | 1.0 | 1.000 | 3B-3 |

Bobby Brooks

BROOKS, ROBERT, JR.
B. Nov. 1, 1945, Los Angeles, Calif. BR TR 5'8½" 165 lbs.

Year	Team		Games	BA	SA	AB	H	2B	3B	HR	HR%	R	RBI	BB	SO	SB	PH AB	H	PO	A	E	DP	TC/G	FA	G by Pos
1969	OAK	A	29	.241	.418	79	19	5	0	3	3.8	13	10	20	24	0	4	1	35	3	0	0	1.3	1.000	OF-21
1970			7	.333	.722	18	6	1	0	2	11.1	2	5	1	7	0	3	0	4	0	0	0	0.6	1.000	OF-5
1972			15	.179	.179	39	7	0	0	0	0.0	4	5	8	8	0	4	1	40	0	3	0	2.9	.930	OF-11
1973	CAL	A	4	.143	.143	7	1	0	0	0	0.0	0	0	0	3	0	3	0	0	0	0	0	0.0	–	OF-1
4 yrs.			55	.231	.378	143	33	6	0	5	3.5	19	20	29	42	0	14	2	79	3	3	0	1.5	.964	OF-38

Hubie Brooks

BROOKS, HUBERT, JR.
B. Sept. 24, 1956, Los Angeles, Calif. BR TR 6' 178 lbs.

Year	Team		Games	BA	SA	AB	H	2B	3B	HR	HR%	R	RBI	BB	SO	SB	PH AB	H	PO	A	E	DP	TC/G	FA	G by Pos
1980	NY	N	24	.309	.395	81	25	1	0	1	1.2	8	10	5	9	1	1	0	16	40	2	2	2.4	.966	3B-23
1981			98	.307	.411	358	110	21	2	4	1.1	34	38	23	65	9	2	0	67	193	21	14	2.9	.925	3B-93, OF-3, SS-1
1982			126	.249	.317	457	114	21	2	2	0.4	40	40	28	76	6	1	0	89	237	24	17	2.8	.931	3B-126
1983			150	.251	.321	586	147	18	4	5	0.9	53	58	24	96	6	2	1	116	303	21	28	2.9	.952	3B-145, 2B-7
1984			153	.283	.417	561	159	23	2	16	2.9	61	73	48	79	6	0	0	112	284	29	41	2.8	.932	3B-129, SS-26
1985	MON	N	156	.269	.413	605	163	34	7	13	2.1	67	100	34	79	6	2	1	203	441	28	81	4.3	.958	SS-155
1986			80	.340	.569	306	104	18	5	14	4.6	50	58	25	60	4	0	0	116	222	15	37	4.4	.958	SS-80
1987			112	.263	.426	430	113	22	3	14	3.3	57	72	24	72	4	3	2	131	271	20	53	3.8	.953	SS-109
1988			151	.279	.447	588	164	35	2	20	3.4	61	90	35	108	7	2	1	261	8	9	1	1.8	.968	OF-149
1989			148	.268	.404	542	145	30	1	14	2.6	56	70	39	108	6	8	0	234	6	9	2	1.7	.964	OF-140
10 yrs.			1198	.276	.407	4514	1244	224	29	103	2.3	487	609	285	752	55	21	5	1345	2005	178	276	2.9	.950	3B-516, SS-371, OF-292, 2B-7

Mandy Brooks

BROOKS, JONATHAN JOSEPH
Born Jonathan Joseph Brozek.
B. Aug. 18, 1897, Milwaukee, Wis. D. June 17, 1962, Kirkwood, Mo. BR TR 5'9" 165 lbs.

Year	Team		Games	BA	SA	AB	H	2B	3B	HR	HR%	R	RBI	BB	SO	SB	PH AB	H	PO	A	E	DP	TC/G	FA	G by Pos
1925	CHI	N	90	.281	.504	349	98	25	7	13	3.7	55	72	19	28	10	1	0	249	9	6	2	2.9	.977	OF-89
1926			26	.188	.271	48	9	1	0	1	2.1	7	6	5	5	0	6	1	23	2	0	2	1.0	1.000	OF-18
2 yrs.			116	.270	.476	397	107	26	7	14	3.5	62	78	24	33	10	7	1	272	11	6	4	2.5	.979	OF-107

Siggy Broskie

BROSKIE, SIGMUND THEODORE (Chops)
B. Mar. 23, 1911, Iselin, Pa. D. May 17, 1975, Canton, Ohio BR TR 5'11½" 200 lbs.

| 1940 | BOS | N | 11 | .273 | .318 | 22 | 6 | 1 | 0 | 0 | 0.0 | 1 | 4 | 1 | 2 | 0 | 0 | 0 | 23 | 6 | 2 | 1 | 2.8 | .935 | C-11 |

Tony Brottem

BROTTEM, ANTON CHRISTIAN
B. Apr. 30, 1892, Halstead, Minn. D. Aug. 5, 1929, Chicago, Ill. BR TR 6'½" 176 lbs.

Year	Team		Games	BA	SA	AB	H	2B	3B	HR	HR%	R	RBI	BB	SO	SB	PH AB	H	PO	A	E	DP	TC/G	FA	G by Pos
1916	STL	N	26	.182	.212	33	6	1	0	0	0.0	3	4	3	10	1	7	4	25	13	2	1	1.5	.950	C-15, OF-2
1918			2	.000	.000	4	0	0	0	0	0.0	0	0	1	0	0	1	0	11	3	0	0	7.0	1.000	1B-2
1921	2 teams	WAS A (4G – .143)				PIT	N	(30G – .242)																	
"	total		34	.235	.255	98	23	2	0	0	0.0	7	9	5	12	0	1	0	101	29	2	1	3.9	.985	C-33
3 yrs.			62	.215	.237	135	29	3	0	0	0.0	10	13	9	22	1	9	4	137	45	4	2	3.0	.978	C-48, OF-2, 1B-2

Cal Broughton

BROUGHTON, CECIL CALVERT
B. Dec. 28, 1860, Magnolia, Wis. D. Mar. 15, 1939, Evansville, Wis. BR TR

Year	Team		Games	BA	SA	AB	H	2B	3B	HR	HR%	R	RBI	BB	SO	SB	PH AB	H	PO	A	E	DP	TC/G	FA	G by Pos
1883	2 teams	CLE N (4G – .200)				BAL	AA	(9G – .188)																	
"	total		13	.190	.190	42	8	0	0	0	0.0	3		3	2				56	16	12	0	6.5	.857	C-12, OF-1
1884	MIL	U	11	.308	.436	39	12	5	0	0	0.0	5		0			0	0	72	12	5	0	8.1	.944	C-7, OF-5
1885	2 teams	STL AA (4G – .059)				NY	AA	(11G – .146)																	
"	total		15	.121	.138	58	7	1	0	0	0.0	2		1			0	0	80	24	16	1	8.0	.867	C-15
1888	DET	N	1	.000	.000	4	0	0	0	0	0.0	0	0	0	0		0	0	6	3	0	0	9.0	1.000	C-1
4 yrs.			40	.189	.231	143	27	6	0	0	0.0	10	0	4	2		0	0	214	55	33	1	7.6	.891	C-35, OF-6

Mark Brouhard

BROUHARD, MARK STEVEN
B. May 22, 1956, Burbank, Calif. BR TR 6'1" 210 lbs.

Year	Team		Games	BA	SA	AB	H	2B	3B	HR	HR%	R	RBI	BB	SO	SB	PH AB	H	PO	A	E	DP	TC/G	FA	G by Pos
1980	MIL	A	45	.232	.400	125	29	6	0	5	4.0	17	16	7	24	1	8	0	77	4	1	3	1.8	.988	DH-21, OF-12, 1B-10
1981			60	.274	.371	186	51	6	3	2	1.1	19	20	7	41	1	4	1	92	7	1	2	1.7	.990	OF-51, DH-7
1982			40	.269	.435	108	29	4	1	4	3.7	16	10	9	17	0	7	0	69	2	1	0	1.8	.986	OF-30, DH-7
1983			56	.276	.454	185	51	10	1	7	3.8	25	23	9	39	0	6	2	112	1	1	0	2.0	.991	OF-42, DH-11
1984			66	.239	.365	197	47	7	0	6	3.0	20	22	16	37	0	7	0	107	6	2	2	1.7	.983	OF-52, DH-8
1985			37	.259	.389	108	28	7	2	1	0.9	11	13	5	26	0	7	0	53	0	2	0	1.5	.964	OF-29, DH-1
6 yrs.			304	.259	.400	909	235	40	7	25	2.8	108	104	53	184	2	39	3	510	20	8	7	1.8	.985	OF-216, DH-55, 1B-10

LEAGUE CHAMPIONSHIP SERIES

| 1982 | MIL | A | 1 | .750 | 1.750 | 4 | 3 | 1 | 0 | 1 | 25.0 | 3 | 3 | 0 | 0 | 0 | 0 | 0 | 0 | 0 | 0 | 0 | 0.0 | – | OF-1 |

Art Brouthers

BROUTHERS, ARTHUR H.
B. Nov. 25, 1882, Montgomery, Ala. D. Sept. 28, 1959, Charleston, S. C. TR 6'1"

| 1906 | PHI | A | 36 | .208 | .257 | 144 | 30 | 5 | 1 | 0 | 0.0 | 18 | 14 | 5 | | 4 | 1 | 0 | 42 | 57 | 11 | 3 | 3.1 | .900 | 3B-33 |

Dan Brouthers

BROUTHERS, DENNIS JOSEPH (Big Dan)
B. May 8, 1858, Sylvan Lake, N. Y. D. Aug. 2, 1932, East Orange, N. J.
Hall of Fame 1945. BL TL 6'2" 207 lbs.

Year	Team	Games	BA	SA	AB	H	2B	3B	HR	HR%	R	RBI	BB	SO	SB	Pinch Hit AB	Pinch Hit H	PO	A	E	DP	TC/G	FA	G by Pos

Dan Brouthers *continued*

Year	Team	Games	BA	SA	AB	H	2B	3B	HR	HR%	R	RBI	BB	SO	SB	AB	H	PO	A	E	DP	TC/G	FA	G by Pos
1879	TRO N	39	.274	.429	168	46	12	1	4	2.4	17	17	1	18		0	0	406	7	34	11	11.5	.924	1B-37, P-3
1880		3	.167	.167	12	2	0	0	0	0.0	0	0	1	0		0	0	25	0	3	1	9.3	.893	1B-3
1881	BUF N	65	.319	.541	270	86	18	9	8	3.0	60	45	18	22		0	0	377	18	33	18	6.6	.923	OF-35, 1B-30
1882		84	.368	.547	351	129	23	11	6	1.7	71		21	7		0	0	882	19	24	35	11.0	.974	1B-84
1883		98	.374	.572	425	159	41	17	3	0.7	85		16	17		0	0	1041	40	44	40	11.5	.961	1B-97, 3B-1, P-1
1884		94	.327	.563	398	130	22	15	14	3.5	82		33	20		0	0	958	30	39	38	10.9	.962	1B-93, 3B-1
1885		98	.359	.543	407	146	32	11	7	1.7	87	60	34	10		0	0	996	25	26	54	10.7	.975	1B-98
1886	DET N	121	.370	.581	489	181	40	15	11	2.2	66	16	66	16		0	0	1256	27	42	64	11.0	.968	1B-121
1887		123	.338	.562	500	169	36	20	12	2.4	153	101	71	9	34	0	0	1141	35	38	67	9.9	.969	1B-123
1888		129	.307	.464	522	160	33	11	9	1.7	118	66	68	13	34	0	0	1345	48	42	56	11.1	.971	1B-129
1889	BOS N	126	.373	.507	485	181	26	9	7	1.4	105	118	66	6	22	0	0	1243	58	35	78	10.6	.974	1B-126
1890	BOS P	123	.330	.454	460	152	36	9	1	0.2	117	97	99	17	28	0	0	1187	73	49	78	10.6	.963	1B-123
1891	BOS AA	130	.350	.512	486	170	26	19	5	1.0	117	108	87	20	31	0	0	1313	34	30	82	10.6	.978	1B-130
1892	BKN N	152	.335	.480	588	197	30	20	5	0.9	121	124	84	30	31	0	0	1498	105	29	69	10.7	.982	1B-152
1893		77	.337	.511	282	95	21	11	2	0.7	57	59	52	10	9	0	0	736	47	11	51	10.3	.986	1B-77
1894	BAL N	123	.347	.560	525	182	39	23	9	1.7	137	128	67	9	38	0	0	1184	65	31	83	10.4	.976	1B-123
1895	2 teams	BAL	N (5G – .261)		LOU	N	(24G – .309)																	
"	total	29	.300	.467	120	36	12	1	2	1.7	15	20	12	3	1	0	0	254	13	11	22	9.6	.960	1B-29
1896	PHI N	57	.344	.445	218	75	13	3	1	0.5	42	41	44	11	7	0	0	566	23	10	44	10.5	.983	1B-57
1904	NY N	2	.000	.000	5	0	0	0	0	0.0	0	0	0		0	1	0	6	0	0	0	3.0	1.000	1B-1
19 yrs.		1673	.342 10th	.519	6711	2296	460	205	106	1.6	1523 8th	1057	840	238	235	1	0	16414	667	531	891	10.5	.970	1B-1633, OF-35, P-4, 3B-2

Joe Brovia

BROVIA, JOSEPH JOHN (Ox)
B. Feb. 18, 1922, Davenport, Calif.　　　　　　　　　　BL TR 6'3" 195 lbs.

Year	Team	Games	BA	SA	AB	H	2B	3B	HR	HR%	R	RBI	BB	SO	SB	AB	H	PO	A	E	DP	TC/G	FA	G by Pos
1955	CIN N	21	.111	.111	18	2	0	0	0	0.0	0	4	1	6	0	18	2	0	0	0	0	0.0	–	

Bob Brower

BROWER, ROBERT RICHARD
B. Jan. 10, 1960, Jamaica, N. Y.　　　　　　　　　　BR TR 5'11" 185 lbs.

Year	Team	Games	BA	SA	AB	H	2B	3B	HR	HR%	R	RBI	BB	SO	SB	AB	H	PO	A	E	DP	TC/G	FA	G by Pos
1986	TEX A	21	.111	.222	9	1	1	0	0	0.0	3	0	0	3	1	1	0	9	0	0	0	0.4	1.000	OF-17, DH-1
1987		127	.261	.452	303	79	10	3	14	4.6	63	46	36	66	15	9	1	183	2	7	0	1.5	.964	OF-106, DH-7
1988		82	.224	.274	201	45	7	0	1	0.5	29	11	27	38	10	6	1	104	2	3	1	1.3	.972	OF-59, DH-13
1989	NY A	26	.232	.362	69	16	3	0	2	2.9	9	3	6	11	3	1	1	62	2	2	1	2.5	.970	OF-25, DH-1
4 yrs.		256	.242	.376	582	141	21	3	17	2.9	104	60	69	118	29	17	3	358	6	12	2	1.5	.968	OF-207, DH-22

Frank Brower

BROWER, FRANK WILLARD (Turkeyfoot)
B. Mar. 26, 1893, Gainesville, Va.　　D. Nov. 20, 1960, Baltimore, Md.　　　　BL TR 6'2" 180 lbs.

Year	Team	Games	BA	SA	AB	H	2B	3B	HR	HR%	R	RBI	BB	SO	SB	AB	H	PO	A	E	DP	TC/G	FA	G by Pos
1920	WAS A	36	.311	.429	119	37	7	2	1	0.8	21	13	9	11		5	2	131	10	5	7	4.1	.966	OF-20, 1B-9, 3B-1
1921		83	.261	.365	203	53	12	3	1	0.5	31	35	18	7	1	27	6	108	12	9	4	1.6	.930	OF-46, 1B-4
1922		139	.293	.418	471	138	20	6	9	1.9	61	71	52	25	8	9	1	269	14	5	5	2.1	.983	OF-121, 1B-7
1923	CLE A	126	.285	.509	397	113	25	8	16	4.0	77	66	62	32	6	6	2	1047	66	13	87	8.9	.988	1B-112, OF-2
1924		66	.280	.477	107	30	10	1	3	2.8	16	20	27	9	1	24	5	188	18	2	11	3.2	.990	1B-26, P-4, OF-3
5 yrs.		450	.286	.443	1297	371	74	20	30	2.3	206	205	168	84	17	71	16	1743	120	34	114	4.2	.982	OF-192, 1B-158, P-4, 3B-1

Lou Brower

BROWER, LOUIS LESTER
B. July 1, 1900, Cleveland, Ohio　　　　　　　　　　BR TR 5'10" 155 lbs.

Year	Team	Games	BA	SA	AB	H	2B	3B	HR	HR%	R	RBI	BB	SO	SB	AB	H	PO	A	E	DP	TC/G	FA	G by Pos
1931	DET A	21	.161	.177	62	10	1	0	0	0.0	3	6	8	5	1	0	0	40	40	10	11	4.3	.889	SS-20, 2B-2

Bill Brown

BROWN, WILLIAM VERNA
B. July 8, 1893, Coleman, Tex.　　D. May 13, 1965, Lubbock, Tex.　　　　BL TL 5'8" 185 lbs.

Year	Team	Games	BA	SA	AB	H	2B	3B	HR	HR%	R	RBI	BB	SO	SB	AB	H	PO	A	E	DP	TC/G	FA	G by Pos
1912	STL A	9	.200	.200	20	4	0	0	0	0.0	0	1	0		0	2	1	10	0	1	0	1.2	.909	OF-7

Bobby Brown

BROWN, ROBERT WILLIAM
B. Oct. 25, 1924, Seattle, Wash.　　　　　　　　　　BL TR 6'1" 180 lbs.

Year	Team	Games	BA	SA	AB	H	2B	3B	HR	HR%	R	RBI	BB	SO	SB	AB	H	PO	A	E	DP	TC/G	FA	G by Pos
1946	NY A	7	.333	.375	24	8	1	0	0	0.0	1	1	4	0	0	0	0	9	12	0	1	3.0	1.000	SS-5, 3B-2
1947		69	.300	.373	150	45	6	1	1	0.7	21	18	21	9	0	27	9	35	54	7	8	1.4	.927	3B-27, SS-11, OF-3
1948		113	.300	.405	363	109	19	5	3	0.8	62	48	48	16	0	22	4	130	173	18	33	2.8	.944	3B-41, SS-26, 2B-17, OF-4
1949		104	.283	.399	343	97	14	4	6	1.7	61	61	38	18	4	16	5	89	158	13	17	2.5	.950	3B-86, OF-3
1950		95	.267	.339	277	74	4	2	4	1.4	33	37	39	18	3	14	3	63	140	9	13	2.2	.958	3B-82
1951		103	.268	.387	313	84	15	2	6	1.9	44	51	47	18	1	10	1	80	151	11	14	2.3	.955	3B-90
1952		29	.247	.303	89	22	2	0	1	1.1	6	14	9	6	1	4	0	23	61	10	4	3.2	.894	3B-24
1954		28	.217	.283	60	13	1	0	1	1.7	5	7	8	3	0	9	3	15	31	0	2	1.6	1.000	3B-17
8 yrs.		548	.279	.376	1619	452	62	14	22	1.4	233	237	214	88	9	102	25	444	780	68	92	2.4	.947	3B-369, SS-42, 2B-17, OF-10

WORLD SERIES

Year	Team	Games	BA	SA	AB	H	2B	3B	HR	HR%	R	RBI	BB	SO	SB	AB	H	PO	A	E	DP	TC/G	FA	G by Pos
1947	NY A	4	1.000	1.667	3	3	2	0	0	0.0	2	3	1	0	0	3	3	0	0	0	0	0.0	–	
1949		4	.500	.917	12	6	1	2	0	0.0	4	5	2	2	0	1	0	0	6	0	0	1.5	1.000	3B-3
1950		4	.333	.583	12	4	1	1	0	0.0	2	1	0	0	0	1	0	1	1	1	0	0.5	.500	3B-4
1951		5	.357	.429	14	5	1	0	0	0.0	1	0	2	1	0	1	0	0	8	0	0	1.8	1.000	3B-4
4 yrs.		17	.439 4th	.707	41	18	5	3	0	0.0	9	9	5	3	0	6	3 1st	1	15	1	0	1.0	.941	3B-11

Bobby Brown

BROWN, ROGERS LEE
B. May 25, 1954, Norfolk, Va.　　　　　　　　　　BB TR 6'2" 190 lbs.

Year	Team	Games	BA	SA	AB	H	2B	3B	HR	HR%	R	RBI	BB	SO	SB	AB	H	PO	A	E	DP	TC/G	FA	G by Pos
1979	2 teams	TOR	A (4G – .000)		NY	A	(30G – .250)																	
"	total	34	.218	.282	78	17	3	1	0	0.0	8	5	4	18	2	2	0	64	0	3	0	2.0	.955	OF-31, DH-1
1980	NY A	137	.260	.415	412	107	12	5	14	3.4	65	47	29	82	27	5	0	303	9	9	0	2.3	.972	OF-131, DH-1
1981		31	.226	.242	62	14	1	0	0	0.0	5	6	5	15	4	1	0	54	2	3	4	1.9	.949	OF-29, DH-2
1982	SEA A	79	.241	.327	245	59	7	1	4	1.6	29	17	17	32	28	7	2	148	5	5	1	2.0	.968	OF-68, DH-3
1983	SD N	57	.267	.382	225	60	5	3	5	2.2	40	22	23	38	27	2	1	103	1	4	0	1.9	.963	OF-54

Year	Team		Games	BA	SA	AB	H	2B	3B	HR	HR%	R	RBI	BB	SO	SB	Pinch Hit AB	Pinch Hit H	PO	A	E	DP	TC/G	FA	G by Pos

Bobby Brown *continued*

Year	Team		Games	BA	SA	AB	H	2B	3B	HR	HR%	R	RBI	BB	SO	SB	AB	H	PO	A	E	DP	TC/G	FA	G by Pos
1984			85	.251	.368	171	43	7	2	3	1.8	28	29	11	33	16	24	9	100	2	3	0	1.2	.971	OF-53
1985			79	.155	.190	84	13	3	0	0	0.0	8	6	5	20	6	44	8	20	2	0	2	0.3	1.000	OF-28
7 yrs.			502	.245	.355	1277	313	38	12	26	2.0	183	130	94	238	110	85	20	792	19	27	7	1.7	.968	OF-394, DH-7

DIVISIONAL PLAYOFF SERIES

| 1981 | NY | A | 1 | – | – | 0 | 0 | 0 | 0 | 0 | – | 0 | 0 | 0 | 0 | 0 | 0 | 0 | 0 | 0 | 0 | 0 | 0.0 | – | |

LEAGUE CHAMPIONSHIP SERIES

1980	NY	A	3	.000	.000	10	0	0	0	0	0.0	1	0	1	2	0	0	0	7	0	0	0	2.3	1.000	OF-3
1981			3	1.000	1.000	1	1	0	0	0	0.0	2	0	0	0	0	0	0	0	0	0	0	0.0	–	OF-2
1984	SD	N	3	.000	.000	4	0	0	0	0	0.0	1	0	1	2	1	1	0	3	0	0	0	1.0	1.000	OF-3
3 yrs.			9	.067	.067	15	1	0	0	0	0.0	4	0	2	4	1	1	0	10	0	0	0	1.1	1.000	OF-8

WORLD SERIES

1981	NY	A	4	.000	.000	1	0	0	0	0	0.0	1	0	0	1	0	0	0	1	0	0	0	0.3	1.000	OF-2
1984	SD	N	5	.067	.067	15	1	0	0	0	0.0	1	2	0	4	0	1	0	13	0	0	0	2.6	1.000	OF-5
2 yrs.			9	.063	.063	16	1	0	0	0	0.0	2	2	0	5	0	1	0	14	0	0	0	1.6	1.000	OF-7

Chris Brown

BROWN, JOHN CHRISTOPHER
B. Aug. 15, 1961, Jackson, Miss.

BR TR 6' 185 lbs.

Year	Team		Games	BA	SA	AB	H	2B	3B	HR	HR%	R	RBI	BB	SO	SB	AB	H	PO	A	E	DP	TC/G	FA	G by Pos
1984	SF	N	23	.286	.405	84	24	7	0	1	1.2	6	11	9	19	2	0	0	23	40	7	3	3.0	.900	3B-23
1985			131	.271	.442	432	117	20	3	16	3.7	50	61	38	78	2	9	3	94	243	10	15	2.6	.971	3B-120
1986			116	.317	.421	416	132	16	3	7	1.7	57	49	33	43	13	1	0	73	181	18	17	2.3	.934	3B-111, SS-2
1987	2 teams			SF	N	(38G – .242)			SD	N	(44G – .232)														
"	total		82	.237	.394	287	68	9	0	12	4.2	34	40	20	46	4	3	2	60	132	16	17	2.5	.923	3B-80, SS-1
1988	SD	N	80	.235	.283	247	58	6	0	2	0.8	14	19	19	49	0	5	0	54	131	10	15	2.4	.949	3B-72
1989	DET	A	17	.193	.246	57	11	3	0	0	0.0	3	4	1	17	0	0	0	15	25	4	4	2.6	.909	3B-17
6 yrs.			449	.269	.392	1523	410	61	6	38	2.5	164	184	120	252	21	18	5	319	752	65	71	2.5	.943	3B-423, SS-3

Curt Brown

BROWN, CURTIS JR.
B. Sept. 14, 1945, Sacramento, Calif.

BR TR 5'11" 180 lbs.

Year	Team		Games	BA	SA	AB	H	2B	3B	HR	HR%	R	RBI	BB	SO	SB	AB	H	PO	A	E	DP	TC/G	FA	G by Pos
1973	MON	N	1	.000	.000	4	0	0	0	0	0.0	0	0	0	0	0	0	0	3	0	0	0	3.0	1.000	OF-1

Darrell Brown

BROWN, DARRELL WAYNE
B. Oct. 29, 1955, Oklahoma City, Okla.

BB TR 6' 180 lbs.

Year	Team		Games	BA	SA	AB	H	2B	3B	HR	HR%	R	RBI	BB	SO	SB	AB	H	PO	A	E	DP	TC/G	FA	G by Pos
1981	DET	A	16	.250	.250	4	1	0	0	0	0.0	4	0	1	1	1	2	1	2	0	0	0	0.1	1.000	OF-6, DH-4
1982	OAK	A	8	.333	.444	18	6	0	1	0	0.0	2	3	1	2	1	0	0	9	0	0	0	1.1	1.000	OF-7, DH-1
1983	MIN	A	91	.272	.304	309	84	6	2	0	0.0	40	22	10	28	3	6	0	188	2	1	0	2.1	.995	OF-81, DH-3
1984			95	.273	.342	260	71	9	3	1	0.4	36	19	14	16	4	35	10	144	4	1	0	1.6	.993	OF-55, DH-13
4 yrs.			210	.274	.325	591	162	15	6	1	0.2	82	44	25	47	9	43	11	343	6	2	0	1.7	.994	OF-149, DH-21

Delos Brown

BROWN, DELOS HIGHT
B. Oct. 4, 1892, Anna, Ill. D. Dec. 21, 1964, Carbondale, Ill.

BR TR 5'9" 160 lbs.

Year	Team		Games	BA	SA	AB	H	2B	3B	HR	HR%	R	RBI	BB	SO	SB	AB	H	PO	A	E	DP	TC/G	FA	G by Pos
1914	CHI	A	1	.000	.000	1	0	0	0	0	0.0	0	0	0	1	0	1	0	0	0	0	0	0.0	–	

Dick Brown

BROWN, RICHARD ERNEST
Brother of Larry Brown.
B. Jan. 17, 1935, Shinnston, W. Va. D. Apr. 12, 1970, Baltimore, Md.

BR TR 6'2" 176 lbs.

Year	Team		Games	BA	SA	AB	H	2B	3B	HR	HR%	R	RBI	BB	SO	SB	AB	H	PO	A	E	DP	TC/G	FA	G by Pos
1957	CLE	A	34	.263	.404	114	30	4	0	4	3.5	10	22	4	23	1	1	0	190	18	3	4	6.2	.986	C-33
1958			68	.237	.387	173	41	5	0	7	4.0	20	20	12	27	1	6	0	278	23	4	6	4.5	.987	C-62
1959			48	.220	.376	141	31	7	0	5	3.5	15	16	11	39	0	2	0	245	20	1	5	5.5	.996	C-48
1960	CHI	A	16	.163	.372	43	7	0	0	3	7.0	4	5	3	11	0	2	1	66	7	1	1	4.6	.986	C-14
1961	DET	A	98	.266	.474	308	82	12	2	16	5.2	32	45	22	57	0	3	2	460	38	5	7	5.1	.990	C-91
1962			134	.241	.353	431	104	12	0	12	2.8	40	40	21	66	0	1	0	742	42	5	8	5.9	.994	C-132
1963	BAL	A	59	.246	.322	171	42	7	0	2	1.2	13	13	15	35	1	1	1	317	23	5	7	5.8	.986	C-58
1964			88	.257	.387	230	59	6	0	8	3.5	24	32	12	45	2	7	0	380	29	5	4	4.7	.988	C-84
1965			96	.231	.333	255	59	9	1	5	2.0	17	30	17	53	2	7	1	466	40	9	6	5.4	.983	C-92
9 yrs.			641	.244	.380	1866	455	62	3	62	3.3	175	223	117	356	7	32	6	3144	240	38	48	5.3	.989	C-614

Don Brown

BROWN, JAMES DONALDSON (Moose)
B. Mar. 31, 1897, Laurel, Md.

BR TR 6' 178 lbs.

Year	Team		Games	BA	SA	AB	H	2B	3B	HR	HR%	R	RBI	BB	SO	SB	AB	H	PO	A	E	DP	TC/G	FA	G by Pos
1915	STL	N	1	.500	.500	2	1	0	0	0	0.0	0	0	2	1	0	0	0	1	0	0	0	1.0	1.000	OF-1
1916	PHI	A	14	.238	.405	42	10	2	1	1	2.4	6	5	4	9	0	2	0	15	2	2	0	1.4	.895	OF-12
2 yrs.			15	.250	.409	44	11	2	1	1	2.3	6	5	6	10	0	2	0	16	2	2	0	1.3	.900	OF-13

Drummond Brown

BROWN, DRUMMOND NICHOL
B. Jan. 31, 1885, Los Angeles, Calif. D. Jan. 27, 1927, Platte County, Mo.

BR TR 6' 180 lbs.

Year	Team		Games	BA	SA	AB	H	2B	3B	HR	HR%	R	RBI	BB	SO	SB	AB	H	PO	A	E	DP	TC/G	FA	G by Pos
1913	BOS	N	15	.324	.441	34	11	1	0	1	2.9	3	2	2	9	0	3	0	41	17	2	0	4.0	.967	C-12
1914	KC	F	31	.190	.241	58	11	3	0	0	0.0	4	5	7		1	4	0	94	33	6	5	4.3	.955	C-23, 1B-2
1915			77	.242	.308	227	55	10	1	1	0.4	13	26	12		3	11	2	276	104	15	4	5.1	.962	C-65, 1B-1
3 yrs.			123	.241	.310	319	77	14	1	2	0.6	20	33	21	9	4	18	2	411	154	23	9	4.8	.961	C-100, 1B-3

Ed Brown

BROWN, EDWARD P.
B. Chicago, Ill. Deceased.
Manager 1882.

TR

Year	Team		Games	BA	SA	AB	H	2B	3B	HR	HR%	R	RBI	BB	SO	SB	AB	H	PO	A	E	DP	TC/G	FA	G by Pos
1882	STL	AA	17	.183	.183	60	11	0	0	0	0.0	4		4			0	0	21	6	6	0	1.9	.818	OF-15, 2B-2, P-1
1884	TOL	AA	42	.176	.196	153	27	3	0	0	0.0	13		2			0	0	45	56	24	1	3.0	.808	3B-39, OF-2, 2B-1, C-1, P-1
2 yrs.			59	.178	.192	213	38	3	0	0	0.0	17		6			0	0	66	62	30	1	2.7	.810	3B-39, OF-17, 2B-3, P-2, C-1

Eddie Brown

BROWN, EDWARD WILLIAM (Glass Arm Eddie)
B. July 17, 1891, Milligan, Neb. D. Sept. 10, 1956, Vallejo, Calif. BR TR 6'3" 190 lbs.

Year	Team	Games	BA	SA	AB	H	2B	3B	HR	HR%	R	RBI	BB	SO	SB	Pinch Hit AB	H	PO	A	E	DP	TC/G	FA	G by Pos
1920	NY N	3	.125	.250	8	1	1	0	0	0.0	1	0	0	3	0	1	0	6	0	0	0	2.0	1.000	OF-2
1921		70	.281	.359	128	36	6	2	0	0.0	16	12	4	11	1	37	11	63	2	3	0	1.0	.956	OF-30
1924	BKN N	114	.308	.424	455	140	30	4	5	1.1	56	78	26	15	3	0	0	311	3	8	0	2.8	.975	OF-114
1925		153	.306	.429	618	189	39	11	5	0.8	88	99	22	18	3	0	0	449	7	13	3	3.1	.972	OF-153
1926	BOS N	153	.328	.415	612	201	31	8	2	0.3	71	84	23	20	5	0	0	401	10	15	2	2.8	.965	OF-153
1927		155	.306	.401	558	171	35	6	2	0.4	64	75	28	20	11	4	2	347	10	7	1	2.3	.981	OF-150, 1B-1
1928		142	.268	.340	523	140	28	2	2	0.4	45	59	24	22	6	10	4	309	6	13	3	2.3	.960	OF-129, 1B-1
7 yrs.		790	.303	.400	2902	878	170	33	16	0.6	341	407	127	109	29	52	17	1886	38	59	9	2.5	.970	OF-731, 1B-2

Fred Brown

BROWN, FRED HERBERT
B. Apr. 12, 1879, Ossipee, N. H. D. Feb. 3, 1955, Somersworth, N. H. BR TR 5'10½" 190 lbs.

Year	Team	Games	BA	SA	AB	H	2B	3B	HR	HR%	R	RBI	BB	SO	SB	Pinch Hit AB	H	PO	A	E	DP	TC/G	FA	G by Pos
1901	BOS N	7	.143	.143	14	2	0	0	0	0.0	1	2	0		2	1		8	1	0	0	1.3	1.000	OF-5
1902		2	.333	.500	6	2	1	0	0	0.0	1	0	0		0	0	1	0	1	0	0	0.5	1.000	OF-2
2 yrs.		9	.200	.250	20	4	1	0	0	0.0	2	2	0		2	1		8	2	0	0	1.1	1.000	OF-7

Gates Brown

BROWN, WILLIAM JAMES
B. May 2, 1939, Crestline, Ohio BL TR 5'11" 220 lbs.

Year	Team	Games	BA	SA	AB	H	2B	3B	HR	HR%	R	RBI	BB	SO	SB	Pinch Hit AB	H	PO	A	E	DP	TC/G	FA	G by Pos
1963	DET A	55	.268	.402	82	22	3	1	2	2.4	16	14	8	13	2	30	6	35	3	0	1	0.7	1.000	OF-16
1964		123	.272	.458	426	116	22	6	15	3.5	65	54	31	53	11	19	4	205	4	4	0	1.7	.981	OF-106
1965		96	.256	.467	227	58	14	2	10	4.4	33	43	17	33	6	34	9	108	1	3	0	1.2	.973	OF-56
1966		88	.266	.432	169	45	5	1	7	4.1	27	27	18	19	3	40	13	46	4	1	1	0.6	.980	OF-43
1967		51	.187	.286	91	17	1	1	2	2.2	17	9	13	15	0	26	4	22	1	0	0	0.5	1.000	OF-20
1968		67	.370	.685	92	34	7	2	6	6.5	15	15	12	4	0	39	18	21	1	0	0	0.3	1.000	OF-17, 1B-1
1969		60	.204	.290	93	19	1	2	1	1.1	13	6	5	17	0	39	8	28	1	3	0	0.5	.906	OF-14
1970		81	.226	.323	124	28	3	0	3	2.4	18	24	20	14	0	41	10	37	1	2	0	0.5	.950	OF-26
1971		82	.338	.549	195	66	2	3	11	5.6	37	29	21	17	4	26	9	68	2	1	0	0.9	.986	OF-56
1972		103	.230	.369	252	58	5	0	10	4.0	33	31	26	28	3	28	4	122	5	3	1	1.3	.977	OF-72
1973		125	.236	.366	377	89	11	1	12	3.2	48	50	52	41	1	4	0	1	0	0	0	0.0	1.000	DH-119, OF-2
1974		73	.242	.384	99	24	2	0	4	4.0	7	17	10	15	0	53	16	0	0	0	0	0.0		DH-13
1975		47	.171	.314	35	6	2	0	1	2.9	1	3	9	6	0	35	6	0	0	0	0	0.0		
13 yrs.		1051	.257	.420	2262	582	78	19	84	3.7	330	322	242	275	30	414	107	693	23	17	3	0.7	.977	OF-428, DH-132, 1B-1
														9th	9th									

LEAGUE CHAMPIONSHIP SERIES

| 1972 | DET A | 3 | .000 | .000 | 2 | 0 | 0 | 0 | 0 | 0.0 | | 1 | 0 | | 1 | 0 | | 2 | 0 | 0 | 0 | 0 | 0.0 | |

WORLD SERIES

| 1968 | DET A | 1 | .000 | .000 | 1 | 0 | 0 | 0 | 0 | 0.0 | 0 | 0 | 0 | 0 | 0 | 1 | 0 | 0 | 0 | 0 | 0 | 0.0 | |

Ike Brown

BROWN, ISAAC
B. Apr. 13, 1942, Memphis, Tenn. BR TR 6' 190 lbs.

Year	Team	Games	BA	SA	AB	H	2B	3B	HR	HR%	R	RBI	BB	SO	SB	Pinch Hit AB	H	PO	A	E	DP	TC/G	FA	G by Pos
1969	DET A	70	.229	.376	170	39	4	3	5	2.9	24	12	26	43	2	12	0	87	116	9	18	3.0	.958	2B-45, 3B-12, OF-3, SS-1
1970		56	.287	.468	94	27	5	0	4	4.3	17	15	13	26	0	21	7	49	33	8	8	1.6	.911	2B-23, OF-4, 3B-1
1971		59	.255	.482	110	28	1	0	8	7.3	20	19	19	25	0	19	6	133	27	3	10	2.8	.982	1B-17, OF-9, 2B-8, 3B-4, SS-1
1972		51	.250	.357	84	21	3	0	2	2.4	12	10	17	23	1	12	1	122	11	1	7	2.6	.993	OF-22, 1B-13, 2B-3, SS-1, 3B-1
1973		42	.289	.382	76	22	2	1	1	1.3	12	9	15	13	0	7	1	117	12	2	9	3.1	.985	1B-21, OF-12, DH-2, 3B-2
1974		2	.000	.000	2	0	0	0	0	0.0	0	0	0	0	0	0	0	2	0	0	0	1.5	1.000	3B-2
6 yrs.		280	.256	.410	536	137	15	4	20	3.7	85	65	90	130	3	71	15	510	200	23	52	2.6	.969	2B-79, 1B-51, OF-50, 3B-22, SS-3, DH-2

LEAGUE CHAMPIONSHIP SERIES

| 1972 | DET A | 1 | .500 | .500 | 2 | 1 | 0 | 0 | 0 | 0.0 | 0 | 2 | 0 | 0 | 0 | 0 | 0 | 2 | 0 | 0 | 0 | 2.0 | 1.000 | 1B-1 |

Jake Brown

BROWN, JERALD RAY
B. Mar. 3, 1948, Sumrall, Miss. D. Dec. 18, 1981, Houston, Tex. BR TR 6'2" 200 lbs.

Year	Team	Games	BA	SA	AB	H	2B	3B	HR	HR%	R	RBI	BB	SO	SB	Pinch Hit AB	H	PO	A	E	DP	TC/G	FA	G by Pos
1975	SF N	41	.209	.279	43	9	3	0	0	0.0	6	4	5	13	0	22	4	11	1	2	0	0.3	.857	OF-14

Jimmy Brown

BROWN, JAMES ROBERTSON
B. Apr. 25, 1910, Jamesville, N. C. D. Dec. 29, 1977, Bath, N. C. BB TR 5'8½" 165 lbs.

Year	Team	Games	BA	SA	AB	H	2B	3B	HR	HR%	R	RBI	BB	SO	SB	Pinch Hit AB	H	PO	A	E	DP	TC/G	FA	G by Pos
1937	STL N	138	.276	.360	525	145	20	9	2	0.4	86	53	27	29	10	6	1	277	415	31	67	5.2	.957	2B-112, SS-25, 3B-1
1938		108	.301	.364	382	115	12	6	0	0.0	50	38	27	9	7	9	3	195	264	21	55	4.4	.956	2B-49, SS-30, 3B-24
1939		147	.298	.384	645	192	31	8	3	0.5	88	51	32	18	4	1	0	328	492	35	92	5.8	.959	SS-104, 2B-50
1940		107	.280	.335	454	127	17	4	0	0.0	56	30	24	15	9	1	0	198	243	22	42	4.3	.952	2B-48, 3B-41, SS-28
1941		132	.306	.406	549	168	28	9	3	0.5	81	56	45	22	2	1	1	157	304	17	31	3.6	.964	3B-123, 2B-11
1942		145	.256	.320	606	155	28	4	1	0.2	75	71	52	11	4	0	0	299	329	26	74	4.5	.960	2B-82, 3B-66, SS-12
1943		34	.182	.255	110	20	4	2	0	0.0	6	8	6	1	0	1	0	65	76	2	14	4.2	.986	2B-19, 3B-9, SS-6
1946	PIT N	79	.241	.266	241	58	6	0	0	0.0	23	12	18	5	3	20	7	127	168	16	28	3.9	.949	SS-30, 2B-21, 3B-9
8 yrs.		890	.279	.352	3512	980	146	42	9	0.3	465	319	231	110	39	39	12	1646	2291	170	395	4.6	.959	2B-392, 3B-273, SS-235

WORLD SERIES

| 1942 | STL N | 5 | .300 | .300 | 20 | 6 | 0 | 0 | 0 | 0.0 | 2 | 1 | 3 | 0 | 0 | 0 | 0 | 6 | 16 | 3 | 2 | 5.0 | .880 | 2B-5 |

Larry Brown

BROWN, LARRY LESLIE
Brother of Dick Brown.
B. Mar. 1, 1940, Shinnston, W. Va. BR TR 5'10" 160 lbs.

Year	Team	Games	BA	SA	AB	H	2B	3B	HR	HR%	R	RBI	BB	SO	SB	Pinch Hit AB	H	PO	A	E	DP	TC/G	FA	G by Pos
1963	CLE A	74	.255	.340	247	63	6	0	5	2.0	28	18	22	27	4	5	1	113	176	14	25	4.1	.954	SS-46, 2B-27
1964		115	.230	.379	335	77	12	1	12	3.6	33	40	24	55	4	12	1	189	275	9	56	4.1	.981	2B-49, SS-30, 3B-1
1965		124	.253	.368	438	111	22	2	8	1.8	52	40	38	62	1	5	1	195	310	15	66	4.2	.971	2B-103, SS-4
1966		105	.229	.291	340	78	12	0	3	0.9	29	17	36	58	0	6	2	153	264	19	52	4.2	.956	SS-95, 2B-10

Year	Team	Games	BA	SA	AB	H	2B	3B	HR	HR%	R	RBI	BB	SO	SB	Pinch Hit AB	Pinch Hit H	PO	A	E	DP	TC/G	FA	G by Pos

Larry Brown *continued*

Year	Team	Games	BA	SA	AB	H	2B	3B	HR	HR%	R	RBI	BB	SO	SB	PH AB	PH H	PO	A	E	DP	TC/G	FA	G by Pos
1967		152	.227	.311	485	110	16	2	7	1.4	38	37	53	62	4	1	0	233	414	22	90	4.4	.967	SS-150
1968		154	.234	.319	495	116	18	3	6	1.2	43	35	43	46	1	1	0	255	371	22	70	4.2	.966	SS-154
1969		132	.239	.294	469	112	10	2	4	0.9	48	24	44	43	5	6	2	200	315	20	63	4.1	.963	SS-101, 3B-29, 2B-5
1970		72	.258	.316	155	40	5	2	0	0.0	17	15	20	14	1	22	5	72	105	8	23	2.6	.957	SS-27, 3B-17, 2B-16
1971	2 teams		CLE A (13G – .220)			OAK A (70G – .196)																		
"	total	83	.201	.234	239	48	3	1	1	0.4	18	14	10	22	1	8	0	106	166	7	35	3.4	.975	SS-44, 2B-23, 3B-10
1972	OAK A	47	.183	.197	142	26	2	0	0	0.0	11	4	13	8	0	0	0	110	112	6	31	4.9	.974	2B-46, 3B-1
1973	BAL A	17	.250	.357	28	7	0	0	1	3.6	4	5	5	4	0	3	0	10	13	3	2	1.5	.885	3B-15, 2B-1
1974	TEX A	54	.197	.224	76	15	2	0	0	0.0	10	5	9	13	0	2	1	29	64	5	12	1.8	.949	3B-47, 2B-8, SS-1
12 yrs.		1129	.233	.313	3449	803	108	13	47	1.4	331	254	317	414	22	71	13	1665	2585	150	525	3.9	.966	SS-712, 2B-265, 3B-119

LEAGUE CHAMPIONSHIP SERIES

Year	Team	Games	BA	SA	AB	H	2B	3B	HR	HR%	R	RBI	BB	SO	SB	PH AB	PH H	PO	A	E	DP	TC/G	FA	G by Pos
1973	BAL A	1	–	–	0	0	0	0	0	–	0	0	0	0	0	0	0	0	0	0	0	0.0	–	3B-1

Leon Brown

BROWN, LEON (Brownie)
B. Nov. 16, 1949, Sacramento, Calif.   BR TR 6'   185 lbs.

Year	Team	Games	BA	SA	AB	H	2B	3B	HR	HR%	R	RBI	BB	SO	SB	PH AB	PH H	PO	A	E	DP	TC/G	FA	G by Pos
1976	NY N	64	.214	.257	70	15	3	0	0	0.0	11	2	4	4	2	7	1	46	3	0	1	0.8	1.000	OF-43

Lew Brown

BROWN, LEWIS J. (Blower)
B. Feb. 1, 1858, Leominster, Mass.   D. Jan. 16, 1889, Boston, Mass.   BR TR 5'10½" 185 lbs.

Year	Team	Games	BA	SA	AB	H	2B	3B	HR	HR%	R	RBI	BB	SO	SB	PH AB	PH H	PO	A	E	DP	TC/G	FA	G by Pos
1876	BOS N	45	.210	.333	195	41	6	6	2	1.0	23	21	3	22			0	0	193	45	40	4	6.2	.856	C-45, OF-1
1877		58	.253	.394	221	56	12	8	1	0.5	27	31	6	33			0	0	387	67	49	5	8.7	.903	C-55, 1B-4
1878	PRO N	58	.305	.453	243	74	21	6	1	0.4	44	43	7	37			0	0	410	88	54	18	9.5	.902	C-45, 1B-15, OF-1, P-1
1879	2 teams		PRO N (53G – .258)			CHI N (6G – .286)																		
"	total	59	.260	.372	250	65	14	4	2	0.8	25	41	5	28			0	0	362	66	68	10	8.4	.863	C-48, OF-6, 1B-6
1881	2 teams		DET N (27G – .241)			PRO N (18G – .240)																		
"	total	45	.240	.344	183	44	6	2	3	1.6	25	24	7	29			0	0	313	10	15	24	7.5	.956	1B-32, OF-13
1883	2 teams		BOS N (14G – .241)			LOU AA (14G – .183)																		
"	total	28	.211	.298	114	24	6	2	0	0.0	11	9	4	6			0	0	281	7	26	13	11.2	.917	1B-28, C-1
1884	BOS U	85	.231	.314	325	75	18	3	1	0.3	50		13				0	0	737	128	72	15	11.0	.923	C-54, 1B-33, OF-2, P-1
7 yrs.		378	.248	.362	1531	379	83	31	10	0.7	205	169	45	155			0	0	2683	411	324	89	9.0	.905	C-248, 1B-118, OF-23, P-2

Lindsay Brown

BROWN, JOHN LINDSAY (Red)
B. July 22, 1911, Mason, Tex.   D. Jan. 1, 1967, San Antonio, Tex.   BR TR 5'10" 160 lbs.

Year	Team	Games	BA	SA	AB	H	2B	3B	HR	HR%	R	RBI	BB	SO	SB	PH AB	PH H	PO	A	E	DP	TC/G	FA	G by Pos
1937	BKN N	48	.270	.313	115	31	3	1	0	0.0	16	6	3	17	1	0	0	73	106	12	26	4.0	.937	SS-45

Marty Brown

BROWN, MARTY LEO
B. Jan. 23, 1963, Lawton, Okla.   BR TR 6'1" 190 lbs.

Year	Team	Games	BA	SA	AB	H	2B	3B	HR	HR%	R	RBI	BB	SO	SB	PH AB	PH H	PO	A	E	DP	TC/G	FA	G by Pos
1988	CIN N	10	.188	.250	16	3	1	0	0	0.0	0	2	1	2	0	4	1	9	0	1	1.0	1.000	3B-8
1989		16	.167	.200	30	5	1	0	0	0.0	2	4	4	9	0	3	0	2	19	2	2	1.4	.913	3B-11
2 yrs.		26	.174	.217	46	8	2	0	0	0.0	2	6	5	11	0	7	1	3	28	2	2	1.3	.939	3B-19

Mike Brown

BROWN, MICHAEL CHARLES
B. Dec. 29, 1959, San Francisco, Calif.   BR TR 6'2" 190 lbs.

Year	Team	Games	BA	SA	AB	H	2B	3B	HR	HR%	R	RBI	BB	SO	SB	PH AB	PH H	PO	A	E	DP	TC/G	FA	G by Pos
1983	CAL A	31	.231	.385	104	24	5	1	3	2.9	12	9	7	20	1	0	0	52	4	3	1	1.9	.949	OF-31
1984		62	.284	.520	148	42	8	3	7	4.7	19	22	13	23	0	14	3	57	4	2	0	1.0	.968	OF-44, DH-3
1985	2 teams		CAL A (60G – .268)			PIT N (57G – .332)																		
"	total	117	.304	.472	358	109	27	3	9	2.5	52	53	29	48	2	11	3	165	6	6	2	1.5	.966	OF-104, DH-7
1986	PIT N	87	.218	.296	243	53	7	0	4	1.6	18	26	27	32	2	20	4	107	3	3	2	1.3	.973	OF-71
1988	CAL A	18	.220	.260	50	11	2	0	0	0.0	4	3	1	12	0	2	0	33	2	2	0	2.1	.946	OF-18
5 yrs.		315	.265	.411	903	239	49	7	23	2.5	105	113	77	135	5	47	10	414	19	16	5	1.4	.964	OF-268, DH-10

Ollie Brown

BROWN, OLLIE LEE (Downtown)
Brother of Oscar Brown.
B. Feb. 11, 1944, Tuscaloosa, Ala.   BR TR 6'2" 178 lbs.

Year	Team	Games	BA	SA	AB	H	2B	3B	HR	HR%	R	RBI	BB	SO	SB	PH AB	PH H	PO	A	E	DP	TC/G	FA	G by Pos
1965	SF N	6	.200	.300	10	2	1	0	0	0.0	0	0	0	2	0	1	0	4	0	0	0	0.7	1.000	OF-4
1966		115	.233	.319	348	81	7	1	7	2.0	32	33	33	66	2	3	0	163	12	4	1	1.6	.978	OF-114
1967		120	.267	.396	412	110	12	1	13	3.2	44	53	25	65	0	4	1	190	5	3	0	1.7	.985	OF-115
1968		40	.232	.274	95	22	4	0	0	0.0	7	11	3	23	1	6	1	32	1	0	0	0.8	1.000	OF-35
1969	SD N	151	.264	.412	568	150	18	3	20	3.5	76	61	44	97	1	1	1	269	14	7	4	1.9	.976	OF-148
1970		139	.292	.489	534	156	34	6	23	4.3	79	89	34	78	5	3	0	258	12	10	3	2.0	.964	OF-137
1971		145	.273	.362	484	132	16	6	9	1.9	36	55	52	74	3	11	3	263	9	5	2	1.9	.982	OF-134
1972	3 teams		SD N (23G – .171)			OAK A (20G – .241)			MIL A (66G – .279)															
"	total	109	.248	.323	303	75	11	0	4	1.3	29	29	28	47	1	24	1	181	9	1	0	1.8	.995	OF-89, 3B-1
1973	MIL A	97	.280	.392	296	83	10	1	7	2.4	28	32	33	53	4	9	0	1	0	0	0	0.0	1.000	DH-82, OF-4
1974	2 teams		HOU N (27G – .217)			PHI N (43G – .242)																		
"	total	70	.232	.417	168	39	6	2	7	4.2	19	19	10	35	0	29	11	73	1	3	0	1.1	.961	OF-53
1975	PHI N	84	.303	.510	145	44	12	0	6	4.1	19	26	15	29	1	30	8	67	0	0	0	0.8	1.000	OF-38
1976		92	.254	.383	209	53	10	1	5	2.4	30	30	33	33	2	26	9	105	7	6	2	1.3	.949	OF-75
1977		50	.243	.357	70	17	3	1	1	1.4	5	13	4	14	1	31	7	16	1	0	0	0.3	1.000	OF-21
13 yrs.		1218	.265	.394	3642	964	144	11	102	2.8	404	454	314	616	30	178	42	1622	71	39	15	1.4	.977	OF-967, DH-82, 3B-1

LEAGUE CHAMPIONSHIP SERIES

Year	Team	Games	BA	SA	AB	H	2B	3B	HR	HR%	R	RBI	BB	SO	SB	PH AB	PH H	PO	A	E	DP	TC/G	FA	G by Pos
1976	PHI N	1	.000	.000	2	0	0	0	0	0.0	0	1	0	1	0	2	0	2	0	0	0	2.0	1.000	OF-1
1977		2	.000	.000	2	0	0	0	0	0.0	0	0	1	1	0	2	0	0	0	0	0	0.0	–	
2 yrs.		3	.000	.000	4	0	0	0	0	0.0	0	1	1	2	0	4	0	2	0	0	0	0.7	1.000	OF-1

Oscar Brown

BROWN, OSCAR LEE
Brother of Ollie Brown.
B. Feb. 8, 1946, Long Beach, Calif.   BR TR 6' 175 lbs.

Year	Team	Games	BA	SA	AB	H	2B	3B	HR	HR%	R	RBI	BB	SO	SB	PH AB	PH H	PO	A	E	DP	TC/G	FA	G by Pos
1969	ATL N	7	.250	.250	4	1	0	0	0	0.0	2	0	0	1	0	2	0	2	0	0	0	0.3	1.000	OF-3
1970		28	.383	.532	47	18	2	1	1	2.1	6	7	7	7	0	3	2	24	0	1	0	0.9	.960	OF-25

Year	Team	Games	BA	SA	AB	H	2B	3B	HR	HR%	R	RBI	BB	SO	SB	Pinch Hit AB	H	PO	A	E	DP	TC/G	FA	G by Pos

Oscar Brown *continued*

Year	Team	Games	BA	SA	AB	H	2B	3B	HR	HR%	R	RBI	BB	SO	SB	AB	H	PO	A	E	DP	TC/G	FA	G by Pos
1971		27	.209	.302	43	9	4	0	0	0.0	4	5	3	8	0	10	1	20	1	0	0	0.8	1.000	OF-15
1972		76	.226	.323	164	37	5	1	3	1.8	19	16	4	29	0	15	1	82	7	10	2	1.3	.899	OF-59
1973		22	.207	.259	58	12	3	0	0	0.0	3	0	3	10	0	9	1	32	0	0	0	1.5	1.000	OF-13
5 yrs.		160	.244	.339	316	77	14	2	4	1.3	34	28	17	55	0	38	5	160	9	11	2	1.1	.939	OF-115

Randy Brown

BROWN, EDWIN RANDOLPH
B. Aug. 29, 1944, Leesburg, Fla.

BL TR 5'7" 170 lbs.

Year	Team	Games	BA	SA	AB	H	2B	3B	HR	HR%	R	RBI	BB	SO	SB	AB	H	PO	A	E	DP	TC/G	FA	G by Pos
1969	CAL A	13	.160	.200	25	4	1	0	0	0.0	3	0	6	1	0	3	0	41	4	0	2	3.5	1.000	C-10, OF-1
1970		5	.000	.000	4	0	0	0	0	0.0	0	0	0	0	0	0	0	5	1	0	0	1.2	1.000	C-5
2 yrs.		18	.138	.172	29	4	1	0	0	0.0	3	0	6	1	0	3	0	46	5	0	2	2.8	1.000	C-15, OF-1

Sam Brown

BROWN, SAMUEL WAKEFIELD
B. May 21, 1878, Webster, Pa. D. Nov. 8, 1931, Mount Pleasant, Pa.

BR TR

Year	Team	Games	BA	SA	AB	H	2B	3B	HR	HR%	R	RBI	BB	SO	SB	AB	H	PO	A	E	DP	TC/G	FA	G by Pos
1906	BOS N	71	.208	.242	231	48	6	1	0	0.0	12	20	13		4	5	1	235	88	13	5	4.7	.961	C-35, OF-13, 3B-12, 1B-3, 2B-2
1907		70	.192	.221	208	40	6	0	0	0.0	17	14	12		0	4	1	288	93	11	14	5.6	.972	C-63, 1B-2
2 yrs.		141	.200	.232	439	88	12	1	0	0.0	29	34	25		4	9	2	523	181	24	19	5.2	.967	C-98, OF-13, 3B-12, 1B-5, 2B-2

Tom Brown

BROWN, THOMAS T. (Handsome)
B. Sept. 21, 1860, Liverpool, England D. Oct. 25, 1927, Washington, D. C.
Manager 1897-98.

BL TR 5'10" 168 lbs.

Year	Team	Games	BA	SA	AB	H	2B	3B	HR	HR%	R	RBI	BB	SO	SB	AB	H	PO	A	E	DP	TC/G	FA	G by Pos
1882	BAL AA	45	.304	.370	181	55	5	2	1	0.6	30		6			0	0	59	16	28	1	2.3	.728	OF-45, P-2
1883	COL AA	97	.274	.371	420	115	12	7	5	1.2	69		20			0	0	153	22	49	3	2.3	.781	OF-96, P-3
1884		107	.273	.375	451	123	9	11	5	1.1	93		24			0	0	165	18	35	5	2.0	.839	OF-107, P-4
1885	PIT AA	108	.307	.426	437	134	16	12	4	0.9	81		34			0	0	186	21	44	2	2.3	.825	OF-108, P-2
1886		115	.285	.363	460	131	11	11	1	0.2	106		56			0	0	185	32	42	12	2.3	.838	OF-115, P-1
1887	2 teams				PIT N	(47G – .245)				IND N	(36G – .179)													
"	total	83	.217	.277	332	72	6	4	2	0.6	50	15	19	65	25	0	0	188	17	36	2	2.9	.851	OF-83
1888	BOS N	107	.248	.369	420	104	10	7	9	2.1	62	49	30	68	46	0	0	172	18	23	3	2.0	.896	OF-107
1889		90	.232	.304	362	84	10	5	2	0.6	93	24	59	56	63	0	0	169	13	20	1	2.2	.901	OF-90
1890	BOS P	128	.276	.392	543	150	23	14	4	0.7	146	61	86	84	79	0	0	276	32	30	8	2.6	.911	OF-128
1891	BOS AA	137	.321	.469	589	189	30	21	5	0.8	177	71	70	96	106	0	0	228	23	35	7	2.1	.878	OF-137
1892	LOU N	153	.227	.285	660	150	16	8	2	0.3	105	45	47	94	78	0	0	351	37	34	8	2.8	.919	OF-153
1893		122	.240	.323	529	127	15	7	5	0.9	104	54	56	63	66	0	0	339	39	29	13	3.3	.929	OF-122
1894		129	.254	.397	536	136	22	14	9	1.7	122	57	60	73	66	0	0	331	21	34	8	3.0	.912	OF-129
1895	2 teams				STL N	(83G – .217)				WAS N	(34G – .239)													
"	total	117	.223	.310	484	108	19	7	2	0.6	97	47	66	60	42	0	0	274	16	18	5	2.6	.942	OF-117
1896	WAS N	116	.294	.375	435	128	17	6	2	0.5	87	59	58	49	28	0	0	262	7	21	2	2.5	.928	OF-116
1897		116	.292	.369	469	137	17	2	5	1.1	91	45	52		25	0	0	252	17	21	5	2.5	.928	OF-115
1898		16	.164	.182	55	9	1	0	0	0.0	8	2	5		3	0	0	36	1	3	0	2.5	.925	OF-15
17 yrs.		1786	.265	.361	7363	1952	239	138	64	0.9	1521	529	748	708	627	0	0	3626	350	501	85	2.5	.888	OF-1783, P-12

Tom Brown

BROWN, THOMAS WILLIAM
B. Dec. 12, 1940, Laureldale, Pa.

BB TL 6'1" 190 lbs.

Year	Team	Games	BA	SA	AB	H	2B	3B	HR	HR%	R	RBI	BB	SO	SB	AB	H	PO	A	E	DP	TC/G	FA	G by Pos
1963	WAS A	61	.147	.207	116	17	4	0	1	0.9	8	4	11	45	2	22	4	120	0	0	9	2.1	1.000	OF-16, 1B-14

Tommy Brown

BROWN, THOMAS MICHAEL (Buckshot)
B. Dec. 6, 1927, Brooklyn, N. Y.

BR TR 6'1" 170 lbs.

Year	Team	Games	BA	SA	AB	H	2B	3B	HR	HR%	R	RBI	BB	SO	SB	AB	H	PO	A	E	DP	TC/G	FA	G by Pos
1944	BKN N	46	.164	.192	146	24	4	0	0	0.0	17	8	8	17	0	0	0	89	109	16	24	4.7	.925	SS-46
1945		57	.245	.332	196	48	3	4	2	1.0	13	19	6	16	3	1	0	93	164	23	27	4.9	.918	SS-55, OF-1
1947		15	.235	.265	34	8	1	0	0	0.0	3	2	1	6	0	4	1	12	15	2	2	1.9	.931	3B-6, OF-3, SS-1
1948		54	.241	.310	145	35	4	0	2	1.4	18	20	7	17	1	9	1	44	60	7	7	2.1	.937	3B-43, 1B-1
1949		41	.303	.427	89	27	2	0	3	3.4	14	18	6	8	0	13	4	53	1	4	0	1.4	.931	OF-27
1950		48	.291	.616	86	25	2	1	8	9.3	15	20	11	9	0	29	7	31	2	3	0	0.8	.917	OF-16
1951	2 teams		BKN N	(11G – .160)					PHI N	(78G – .219)														
"	total	89	.213	.376	221	47	4	1	10	4.5	26	33	17	25	1	26	4	183	37	9	15	2.6	.961	OF-37, 2B-14, 1B-12, 3B-1
1952	2 teams		PHI N	(18G – .160)					CHI N	(61G – .320)														
"	total	79	.302	.409	225	68	12	0	4	1.8	26	26	16	27	1	15	3	144	112	17	24	3.5	.938	SS-39, 2B-10, 1B-8, OF-3
1953	CHI N	65	.196	.304	138	27	7	1	2	1.4	19	13	13	17	1	30	5	48	70	13	13	2.0	.901	SS-25, OF-6
9 yrs.		494	.241	.355	1280	309	39	7	31	2.4	151	159	85	142	7	127	25	697	570	94	112	2.8	.931	SS-166, OF-93, 3B-50, 2B-24, 1B-21

WORLD SERIES

Year	Team	Games	BA	SA	AB	H	2B	3B	HR	HR%	R	RBI	BB	SO	SB	AB	H	PO	A	E	DP	TC/G	FA	G by Pos
1949	BKN N	2	.000	.000	2	0	0	0	0	0.0	0	0	0	1	0	2	0	0	0	0	0	0.0	—

Willard Brown

BROWN, WILLARD (Big Bill, California Brown)
B. 1866, San Francisco, Calif. D. Dec. 20, 1897, San Francisco, Calif.

BR TR 6'2" 190 lbs.

Year	Team	Games	BA	SA	AB	H	2B	3B	HR	HR%	R	RBI	BB	SO	SB	AB	H	PO	A	E	DP	TC/G	FA	G by Pos
1887	NY N	49	.218	.259	170	37	3	2	0	0.0	17	25	10	15	10	0	0	231	71	31	5	6.8	.907	C-46, 3B-3, OF-2
1888		20	.271	.288	59	16	1	0	0	0.0	4	6	1	8	1	0	0	134	24	19	0	8.9	.893	C-20
1889		40	.259	.353	139	36	10	0	1	0.7	16	29	9	9	6	0	0	146	39	32	3	5.4	.853	C-37, OF-3
1890	NY P	60	.278	.400	230	64	8	4	4	1.7	47	43	13	13	5	0	0	241	49	26	5	5.3	.918	C-34, OF-13, 1B-9, 3B-3, 2B-2
1891	PHI N	115	.243	.306	441	107	20	4	0	0.0	62	50	34	35	11	0	0	1059	68	18	62	10.0	.984	1B-97, C-19, OF-2
1893	2 teams		BAL N	(7G – .125)					LOU N	(111G – .304)														
"	total	118	.292	.379	493	144	26	7	1	0.2	85	90	51	35	11	0	0	1145	54	14	79	10.3	.988	1B-118, C-1
1894	2 teams		LOU N	(13G – .208)					STL N	(3G – .111)														
"	total	16	.193	.228	57	11	2	0	0	0.0	5	9	5	9	1	0	0	141	19	3	8	10.2	.982	1B-16
7 yrs.		418	.261	.338	1589	415	70	17	6	0.4	236	252	123	124	39	0	0	3097	324	143	162	8.5	.960	1B-240, C-157, OF-20, 3B-6, 2B-2

Year	Team	Games	BA	SA	AB	H	2B	3B	HR	HR%	R	RBI	BB	SO	SB	Pinch Hit AB	Pinch Hit H	PO	A	E	DP	TC/G	FA	G by Pos

Willard Brown

BROWN, WILLARD JESSIE
B. June 26, 1911, Shreveport, La.

BR TR 5'11½" 200 lbs.

Year	Team	Games	BA	SA	AB	H	2B	3B	HR	HR%	R	RBI	BB	SO	SB	PH AB	PH H	PO	A	E	DP	TC/G	FA	G by Pos
1947	STL A	21	.179	.269	67	12	3	0	1	1.5	4	6	0	7	2	3	1	41	0	0	0	2.0	1.000	OF-18

Byron Browne

BROWNE, BYRON ELLIS
B. Dec. 27, 1942, St. Joseph, Mo.

BR TR 6'2" 190 lbs.

Year	Team	Games	BA	SA	AB	H	2B	3B	HR	HR%	R	RBI	BB	SO	SB	PH AB	PH H	PO	A	E	DP	TC/G	FA	G by Pos
1965	CHI N	4	.000	.000	6	0	0	0	0	0.0	0	2	0	1	0	1	0	2	0	1	0	0.8	.667	OF-4
1966		120	.243	.427	419	102	15	7	16	3.8	46	51	40	143	3	5	0	200	3	7	0	1.8	.967	OF-114
1967		10	.158	.263	19	3	0	0	0	0.0	3	2	4	4	1	2	0	12	0	0	0	1.2	1.000	OF-8
1968	HOU N	10	.231	.231	13	3	0	0	0	0.0	0	1	4	6	1	1	0	7	1	0	1	0.8	1.000	OF-2
1969	STL N	22	.226	.321	53	12	0	1	1	1.9	9	7	11	14	0	7	0	35	3	0	1	1.7	1.000	OF-16
1970	PHI N	104	.248	.437	270	67	17	2	10	3.7	29	36	33	72	1	18	4	150	4	4	1	1.5	.975	OF-88
1971		58	.206	.382	68	14	3	0	3	4.4	5	5	8	23	0	27	7	21	0	0	0	0.4	1.000	OF-30
1972		21	.190	.190	21	4	0	0	0	0.0	2	0	1	8	0	14	3	2	0	0	0	0.1	1.000	OF-9
8 yrs.		349	.236	.405	869	205	37	10	30	3.5	94	102	101	273	5	80	15	429	11	12	3	1.3	.973	OF-271

Earl Browne

BROWNE, EARL JAMES (Snitz)
B. Mar. 5, 1911, Louisville, Ky.

BL TL 6' 175 lbs.

Year	Team	Games	BA	SA	AB	H	2B	3B	HR	HR%	R	RBI	BB	SO	SB	PH AB	PH H	PO	A	E	DP	TC/G	FA	G by Pos
1935	PIT N	9	.250	.313	32	8	2	0	0	0.0	6	6	2	8	0	0	0	76	5	0	4	9.0	1.000	1B-9
1936		8	.304	.522	23	7	1	2	0	0.0	7	3	1	4	0	3	1	16	2	1	2	2.4	.947	OF-4, 1B-1
1937	PHI N	105	.292	.422	332	97	19	3	6	1.8	42	52	21	41	4	26	7	305	29	5	31	3.2	.985	OF-54, 1B-23
1938		21	.257	.311	74	19	4	0	0	0.0	4	8	5	11	0	3	1	131	10	3	11	6.9	.979	1B-16, OF-2
4 yrs.		143	.284	.401	461	131	26	5	6	1.3	59	69	29	64	4	32	9	528	46	9	47	4.1	.985	OF-60, 1B-49

George Browne

BROWNE, GEORGE EDWARD
B. Jan. 12, 1876, Richmond, Va.   D. Dec. 9, 1920, Hyde Park, N. Y.

BL TR 5'10½" 160 lbs.

Year	Team	Games	BA	SA	AB	H	2B	3B	HR	HR%	R	RBI	BB	SO	SB	PH AB	PH H	PO	A	E	DP	TC/G	FA	G by Pos
1901	PHI N	8	.192	.231	26	5	1	0	0	0.0	2	4	1		2	0	0	13	0	0	0	1.6	1.000	OF-8
1902	2 teams		PHI N (70G – .260)			NY N (53G – .319)																		
"	total	123	.286	.342	497	142	16	6	0	0.0	71	40	25		24	0	0	262	21	30	3	2.5	.904	OF-123
1903	NY N	141	.313	.372	591	185	20	3	3	0.5	105	45	43		27	0	0	212	13	20	4	1.7	.918	OF-141
1904		150	.284	.347	596	169	16	5	4	0.7	99	39	39		24	1	0	201	20	18	7	1.6	.925	OF-149
1905		127	.293	.397	536	157	16	14	4	0.7	95	43	20		26	0	0	175	9	17	1	1.6	.915	OF-127
1906		122	.264	.302	477	126	10	4	0	0.0	61	38	27		32	1	0	153	17	12	3	1.5	.934	OF-121
1907		127	.260	.360	458	119	11	10	5	1.1	54	37	31		15	4	0	146	14	10	5	1.3	.941	OF-121
1908	BOS N	138	.228	.274	536	122	10	6	1	0.2	61	34	36		17	3	1	248	20	14	8	2.0	.950	OF-138
1909	2 teams		CHI N (12G – .205)			WAS A (103G – .272)																		
"	total	115	.266	.336	432	115	15	6	1	0.2	47	17	22		16	2	0	163	13	12	3	1.6	.936	OF-113
1910	2 teams		WAS A (7G – .182)			CHI A (30G – .241)																		
"	total	37	.231	.276	134	31	4	0	0	0.0	18	4	13		5	3	0	42	2	4	1	1.3	.917	OF-34
1911	BKN N	8	.333	.333	12	4	0	0	0	0.0	1	2	1		1	2	0	4	0	0	0	0.5	1.000	OF-2
1912	PHI N	6	.200	.200	5	1	0	0	0	0.0	0	0	0		0	4	1	0	0	0	0	–		3B-1
12 yrs.		1102	.273	.339	4300	1176	119	55	18	0.4	614	303	259		190	22	2	1619	129	137	35	1.7	.927	OF-1077, 3B-1

WORLD SERIES

Year	Team	Games	BA	SA	AB	H	2B	3B	HR	HR%	R	RBI	BB	SO	SB	PH AB	PH H	PO	A	E	DP	TC/G	FA	G by Pos
1905	NY N	5	.182	.182	22	4	0	0	0	0.0	2	1	0		2	0	0	3	0	0	0	0.6	1.000	OF-5

Jerry Browne

BROWNE, JEROME AUSTIN
B. Feb. 13, 1966, Christiansted, Virgin Islands

BB TR 5'10" 140 lbs.

Year	Team	Games	BA	SA	AB	H	2B	3B	HR	HR%	R	RBI	BB	SO	SB	PH AB	PH H	PO	A	E	DP	TC/G	FA	G by Pos
1986	TEX A	11	.417	.500	24	10	2	0	0	0.0	6	3	1	4	0	1	0	9	15	4	4	2.4	.923	2B-8
1987		132	.271	.339	454	123	16	6	1	0.2	63	38	61	50	27	5	0	258	338	12	66	4.6	.980	2B-130, DH-1
1988		73	.229	.304	214	49	9	2	1	0.5	26	17	25	32	7	3	0	112	139	11	27	3.6	.958	2B-70, DH-1
1989	CLE A	153	.299	.390	598	179	31	4	5	0.8	83	45	68	64	14	2	0	305	380	15	67	4.6	.979	2B-151, DH-2
4 yrs.		369	.280	.360	1290	361	58	12	7	0.5	178	103	155	150	48	11	0	684	872	42	164	4.3	.975	2B-359, DH-4

Pidge Browne

BROWNE, PRENTICE ALMONT
B. Mar. 21, 1929, Peekskill, N. Y.

BL TL 6'1" 190 lbs.

Year	Team	Games	BA	SA	AB	H	2B	3B	HR	HR%	R	RBI	BB	SO	SB	PH AB	PH H	PO	A	E	DP	TC/G	FA	G by Pos
1962	HOU N	65	.210	.320	100	21	4	2	1	1.0	8	10	13	9	0	36	8	155	15	3	11	2.7	.983	1B-26

Pete Browning

BROWNING, LOUIS ROGERS (The Gladiator)
B. June 17, 1861, Louisville, Ky.   D. Sept. 10, 1905, Louisville, Ky.

BR TR 6' 180 lbs.

Year	Team	Games	BA	SA	AB	H	2B	3B	HR	HR%	R	RBI	BB	SO	SB	PH AB	PH H	PO	A	E	DP	TC/G	FA	G by Pos
1882	LOU AA	69	.378	.510	288	109	17	3	5	1.7	67		26			0	0	200	221	63	31	7.0	.870	2B-42, SS-18, 3B-13
1883		84	.338	.458	358	121	15	11	2	0.6	95		23			0	0	137	94	48	9	3.3	.828	OF-48, SS-26, 3B-10, 2B-3, 1B-1
1884		103	.336	.472	447	150	33	8	4	0.9	101		13			0	0	393	86	52	23	5.2	.902	3B-52, OF-24, 1B-23, 2B-4, P-1
1885		112	.362	.530	481	174	34	10	9	1.9	98		25			0	0	214	20	26	4	2.3	.900	OF-112
1886		112	.340	.441	467	159	29	6	2	0.4	86		30			0	0	153	14	44	1	1.9	.791	OF-112
1887		134	.402	.547	547	220	35	16	4	0.7	137		55		103	0	0	281	21	46	7	2.6	.868	OF-134
1888		99	.313	.436	383	120	22	8	3	0.8	58	72	37	36	36	0	0	174	16	24	8	2.2	.888	OF-99
1889		83	.256	.364	324	83	19	5	2	0.6	39	32	34	30	21	0	0	152	12	22	4	2.2	.882	OF-83
1890	CLE P	118	.373	.517	493	184	40	8	5	1.0	112	93	75	36	35	0	0	248	18	32	4	2.5	.893	OF-118
1891	2 teams		PIT N (50G – .291)			CIN N (55G – .343)																		
"	total	105	.317	.422	419	133	24	4	4	1.0	64	61	51	54	16	0	0	218	14	22	2	2.4	.913	OF-105
1892	2 teams		LOU N (21G – .247)			CIN N (83G – .303)																		
"	total	104	.292	.383	384	112	16	5	3	0.8	57	56	52	32	13	0	0	203	14	19	2	2.3	.919	OF-103, 1B-2
1893	LOU N	57	.355	.445	220	78	11	3	1	0.5	38	37	44	15	8	0	0	114	5	16	1	2.4	.881	OF-57
1894	2 teams		STL N (2G – .143)			BKN N (1G – 1.000)																		
"	total	3	.333	.333	9	3	0	0	0	0.0	2	2	1	0	0	0	0	3	0	0	0	1.0	1.000	OF-3
13 yrs.		1183	.341	.466	4820	1646	295	87	44	0.9	954	353	466	167	232	0	0	2490	535	414	96	2.9	.880	OF-998, 3B-75, 2B-49, SS-44, 1B-26, P-1

Bill Brubaker

BRUBAKER, WILBUR LEE
B. Nov. 7, 1910, Cleveland, Ohio   D. Dec. 2, 1978, Laguna Beach, Calif.

BR TR 6'2" 185 lbs.

Year	Team	Lg	Games	BA	SA	AB	H	2B	3B	HR	HR%	R	RBI	BB	SO	SB	PH AB	PH H	PO	A	E	DP	TC/G	FA	G by Pos

Bill Brubaker *continued*

Year	Team	Lg	Games	BA	SA	AB	H	2B	3B	HR	HR%	R	RBI	BB	SO	SB	PH AB	PH H	PO	A	E	DP	TC/G	FA	G by Pos
1932	PIT	N	7	.417	.542	24	10	3	0	0	0.0	3	4	3	4	1	0	0	7	13	2	2	3.1	.909	3B-7
1933			2	.000	.000	2	0	0	0	0	0.0	0	0	0	0	0	1	0	0	1	0	0	0.5	1.000	3B-1
1934			3	.333	.500	6	2	1	0	0	0.0	0	1	1	0	0	1	0	1	5	0	1	2.0	1.000	3B-3
1935			6	.000	.000	11	0	0	0	0	0.0	0	0	2	5	0	1	0	3	5	1	0	1.5	.889	3B-5
1936			145	.289	.384	554	160	27	4	6	1.1	77	102	50	**96**	5	0	0	134	209	22	8	2.5	.940	3B-145
1937			120	.254	.366	413	105	20	4	6	1.5	57	48	47	51	2	0	0	108	225	17	17	2.9	.951	3B-115, SS-3, 1B-1
1938			45	.295	.420	112	33	5	0	3	2.7	18	19	9	14	2	9	3	111	36	9	10	3.5	.942	3B-18, 1B-9, SS-3, OF-1
1939			100	.232	.365	345	80	23	1	7	2.0	41	43	29	51	3	5	1	183	290	27	47	5.0	.946	2B-65, 3B-32, SS-1
1940			38	.192	.256	78	15	3	1	0	0.0	8	7	8	16	0	4	1	52	46	3	5	2.7	.970	3B-19, SS-8, 1B-4
1943	BOS	N	13	.421	.579	19	8	3	0	0	0.0	3	1	2	2	0	3	2	9	6	2	2	1.3	.882	3B-5, 1B-3
10 yrs.			479	.264	.373	1564	413	85	10	22	1.4	208	225	151	239	13	23	7	608	836	83	92	3.2	.946	3B-350, 2B-65, 1B-17, SS-15, OF-1

Lou Bruce

BRUCE, LOUIS R.
B. Jan. 16, 1877, St. Regis, N. Y.   D. Feb. 9, 1968, Ilion, N. Y.
BL TR 5'5"   145 lbs.

Year	Team	Lg	Games	BA	SA	AB	H	2B	3B	HR	HR%	R	RBI	BB	SO	SB	PH AB	PH H	PO	A	E	DP	TC/G	FA	G by Pos
1904	PHI	A	30	.267	.297	101	27	3	0	0	0.0	9	8	5	2	3	1		30	11	3	2	1.5	.932	OF-25, P-2, 3B-1, 2B-1

Earle Brucker

BRUCKER, EARLE FRANCIS, JR.
Son of Earle Brucker.
B. Aug. 29, 1925, Los Angeles, Calif.
BL TR 6'2"   210 lbs.

Year	Team	Lg	Games	BA	SA	AB	H	2B	3B	HR	HR%	R	RBI	BB	SO	SB	PH AB	PH H	PO	A	E	DP	TC/G	FA	G by Pos
1948	PHI	A	2	.167	.333	6	1	1	0	0	0.0	0	0	1	1	0	0	0	6	1	0	0	3.5	1.000	C-2

Earle Brucker

BRUCKER, EARLE FRANCIS, SR.
Father of Earle Brucker.
B. May 6, 1901, Albany, N. Y.   D. May 8, 1981, San Diego, Calif.
Manager 1952.
BR TR 5'11"   175 lbs.

Year	Team	Lg	Games	BA	SA	AB	H	2B	3B	HR	HR%	R	RBI	BB	SO	SB	PH AB	PH H	PO	A	E	DP	TC/G	FA	G by Pos
1937	PHI	A	102	.259	.397	317	82	16	5	6	1.9	40	37	48	30	1	9	0	323	48	11	13	3.7	.971	C-92
1938			53	.374	.561	171	64	21	1	3	1.8	26	35	19	16	1	7	2	188	20	3	1	4.0	.986	C-44, 1B-1
1939			62	.291	.442	172	50	15	1	3	1.7	18	31	24	16	0	13	4	150	18	0	5	2.7	1.000	C-47
1940			23	.196	.261	46	9	1	0	0	0.0	3	2	6	3	0	9	2	47	9	2	1	2.5	.966	C-13
1943			1	.000	.000	1	0	0	0	0	0.0	0	0	0	0	0	1	0	0	0	0	0	0.0		
5 yrs.			241	.290	.438	707	205	53	8	12	1.7	87	105	97	65	2	39	8	708	95	16	20	3.4	.980	C-196, 1B-1

Frank Bruggy

BRUGGY, FRANK LEO
B. May 4, 1891, Elizabeth, N. J.   D. Apr. 5, 1959, Elizabeth, N. J.
BR TR 5'11"   195 lbs.

Year	Team	Lg	Games	BA	SA	AB	H	2B	3B	HR	HR%	R	RBI	BB	SO	SB	PH AB	PH H	PO	A	E	DP	TC/G	FA	G by Pos
1921	PHI	N	86	.310	.419	277	86	11	2	5	1.8	28	28	23	37	6	12	4	236	73	15	16	3.8	.954	C-86, 1B-2
1922	PHI	A	53	.279	.342	111	31	7	0	0	0.0	10	9	6	11	1	21	4	73	25	8	2	2.0	.925	C-31
1923			54	.210	.267	105	22	3	0	1	1.0	4	6	4	9	1	13	1	88	24	5	2	2.2	.957	C-34, 1B-5
1924			50	.265	.319	113	30	6	0	0	0.0	9	8	8	15	4	7	0	91	25	9	0	2.5	.928	C-44
1925	CIN	N	6	.214	.214	14	3	0	0	0	0.0	1	2	0	0	0	0	0	17	3	3	0	3.8	.870	C-6
5 yrs.			249	.277	.356	620	172	27	2	6	1.0	53	52	43	72	12	53	9	505	150	40	20	2.8	.942	C-201, 1B-7

Mike Brumley

BRUMLEY, ANTHONY MICHAEL
Son of Mike Brumley.
B. Apr. 9, 1963, Oklahoma City, Okla.
BB TR 5'10"   165 lbs.

Year	Team	Lg	Games	BA	SA	AB	H	2B	3B	HR	HR%	R	RBI	BB	SO	SB	PH AB	PH H	PO	A	E	DP	TC/G	FA	G by Pos
1987	CHI	N	39	.202	.288	104	21	2	2	1	1.0	8	9	10	30	7	3	0	43	93	5	24	3.6	.965	SS-34, 2B-1
1989	DET	A	92	.198	.255	212	42	5	2	1	0.5	33	11	14	45	8	3	0	80	160	12	24	2.7	.952	SS-42, 2B-24, 3B-11, DH-8, OF-4
2 yrs.			131	.199	.266	316	63	7	4	2	0.6	41	20	24	75	15	6	0	123	253	17	48	3.0	.957	SS-76, 2B-25, 3B-11, DH-8, OF-4

Mike Brumley

BRUMLEY, TONY MIKE
Father of Mike Brumley.
B. July 10, 1938, Granite, Okla.
BL TR 5'10"   195 lbs.

Year	Team	Lg	Games	BA	SA	AB	H	2B	3B	HR	HR%	R	RBI	BB	SO	SB	PH AB	PH H	PO	A	E	DP	TC/G	FA	G by Pos
1964	WAS	A	136	.244	.312	426	104	19	2	2	0.5	36	35	40	54	1	14	3	628	44	6	4	5.0	.991	C-132
1965			79	.208	.269	216	45	4	2	3	1.4	15	15	20	33	1	15	3	376	25	4	2	5.1	.990	C-66
1966			9	.111	.167	18	2	1	0	0	0.0	1	0	0	2	0	2	0	19	4	0	0	2.6	1.000	C-7
3 yrs.			224	.229	.294	660	151	24	2	5	0.8	52	50	60	89	2	31	6	1023	73	10	6	4.9	.991	C-205

Glenn Brummer

BRUMMER, GLENN EDWARD
B. Nov. 23, 1954, Olney, Ill.
BR TR 6'   200 lbs.

Year	Team	Lg	Games	BA	SA	AB	H	2B	3B	HR	HR%	R	RBI	BB	SO	SB	PH AB	PH H	PO	A	E	DP	TC/G	FA	G by Pos
1981	STL	N	21	.200	.233	30	6	1	0	0	0.0	2	2	1	2	0	2	0	43	3	0	1	2.2	1.000	C-19
1982			35	.234	.297	64	15	4	0	0	0.0	4	8	0	12	2	1	1	88	8	3	1	2.8	.970	C-32
1983			45	.276	.356	87	24	7	0	0	0.0	7	9	10	11	1	5	0	122	11	3	2	3.0	.978	C-41
1984			28	.207	.259	58	12	0	0	1	1.7	3	3	3	7	0	2	0	101	9	3	0	4.0	.973	C-26
1985	TEX	A	49	.278	.315	108	30	4	0	0	0.0	7	5	11	22	1	1	0	183	5	2	2	3.9	.989	C-47, DH-1, OF-1
5 yrs.			178	.251	.305	347	87	16	0	1	0.3	23	27	25	54	4	11	1	537	36	11	6	3.3	.981	C-165, DH-1, OF-1

WORLD SERIES

Year	Team	Lg	Games	BA	SA	AB	H	2B	3B	HR	HR%	R	RBI	BB	SO	SB	PH AB	PH H	PO	A	E	DP	TC/G	FA	G by Pos
1982	STL	N	1	-	-	0	0	0	0	0	-	0	0	0	0	0	0	0	0	0	0	0	0.0	-	C-1

Tom Brunansky

BRUNANSKY, THOMAS ANDREW (Bruno)
B. Aug. 20, 1960, Covina, Calif.
BR TR 6'4"   205 lbs.

Year	Team	Lg	Games	BA	SA	AB	H	2B	3B	HR	HR%	R	RBI	BB	SO	SB	PH AB	PH H	PO	A	E	DP	TC/G	FA	G by Pos
1981	CAL	A	11	.152	.424	33	5	0	0	3	9.1	7	6	8	10	1	0	0	27	3	2	1	2.9	.938	OF-11
1982	MIN	A	127	.272	.471	463	126	30	1	20	4.3	77	46	71	101	1	0	0	343	8	5	0	2.8	.986	OF-127
1983			151	.227	.445	542	123	24	5	28	5.2	70	82	61	95	2	2	0	375	16	6	8	2.6	.985	OF-146, DH-4
1984			155	.252	.459	567	143	21	0	32	5.6	75	85	57	94	4	2	0	304	13	5	6	2.1	.984	OF-153, DH-1
1985			157	.242	.448	567	137	28	4	27	4.8	71	90	71	86	5	3	1	300	14	5	2	2.0	.984	OF-155
1986			157	.256	.423	593	152	28	1	23	3.9	69	75	53	98	12	5	1	315	10	6	1	2.1	.982	OF-152, DH-2
1987			155	.259	.489	532	138	22	2	32	6.0	83	85	74	104	11	1	1	273	10	3	1	1.8	.990	OF-138, DH-17

Year Team	Games	BA	SA	AB	H	2B	3B	HR	HR%	R	RBI	BB	SO	SB	Pinch Hit AB	Pinch Hit H	PO	A	E	DP	TC/G	FA	G by Pos

Tom Brunansky *continued*

Year Team	Games	BA	SA	AB	H	2B	3B	HR	HR%	R	RBI	BB	SO	SB	AB	H	PO	A	E	DP	TC/G	FA	G by Pos
1988 2 teams	MIN A (14G – .184)			STL N	(143G – .245)																		
" total	157	.240	.414	572	137	23	4	23	4.0	74	85	86	93	17	0	0	286	10	4	0	1.9	.987	OF-156, DH-1
1989 STL N	158	.239	.410	556	133	29	3	20	3.6	67	85	59	107	5	6	0	291	9	7	2	1.9	.977	OF-155, 1B-1
9 yrs.	1228	.247	.444	4425	1094	205	20	208	4.7	593	639	540	788	58	19	3	2514	93	43	21	2.2	.984	OF-1193, DH-25, 1B-1

LEAGUE CHAMPIONSHIP SERIES

Year Team	Games	BA	SA	AB	H	2B	3B	HR	HR%	R	RBI	BB	SO	SB	AB	H	PO	A	E	DP	TC/G	FA	G by Pos
1987 MIN A	5	.412	1.000	17	7	4	0	2	11.8	5	9	4	3	0	0	0	10	0	0	0	2.0	1.000	OF-5

WORLD SERIES

Year Team	Games	BA	SA	AB	H	2B	3B	HR	HR%	R	RBI	BB	SO	SB	AB	H	PO	A	E	DP	TC/G	FA	G by Pos
1987 MIN A	7	.200	.200	25	5	0	0	0	0.0	5	2	4	4	1	0	0	14	0	0	0	2.0	1.000	OF-7

Arlo Brunsberg

BRUNSBERG, ARLO ADOLPH
B. Aug. 15, 1940, Fertile, Minn.

BL TR 6' 195 lbs.

Year Team	Games	BA	SA	AB	H	2B	3B	HR	HR%	R	RBI	BB	SO	SB	AB	H	PO	A	E	DP	TC/G	FA	G by Pos
1966 DET A	2	.333	.667	3	1	1	0	0	0.0	1	0	0	0	0	0	0	4	0	0	0	2.0	1.000	C-2

Bob Brush

BRUSH, ROBERT
B. Mar. 8, 1875, Osage, Iowa D. Apr. 2, 1944, San Bernardino, Calif.

Year Team	Games	BA	SA	AB	H	2B	3B	HR	HR%	R	RBI	BB	SO	SB	AB	H	PO	A	E	DP	TC/G	FA	G by Pos
1907 BOS N	2	.000	.000	2	0	0	0	0	0.0	0	0	0		0	1	0	2	0	0	0	1.0	1.000	1B-1

Bill Bruton

BRUTON, WILLIAM HARON
B. Dec. 22, 1925, Panola, Ala.

BL TR 6'½" 169 lbs.

Year Team	Games	BA	SA	AB	H	2B	3B	HR	HR%	R	RBI	BB	SO	SB	AB	H	PO	A	E	DP	TC/G	FA	G by Pos
1953 MIL N	151	.250	.330	613	153	18	14	1	0.2	82	41	44	100	26	1	0	397	15	9	5	2.8	.979	OF-150
1954	142	.284	.365	567	161	20	7	4	0.7	89	30	40	78	34	3	2	350	14	7	3	2.6	.981	OF-141
1955	149	.275	.403	636	175	30	12	9	1.4	106	47	43	72	25	2	0	412	17	14	6	3.0	.968	OF-149
1956	147	.272	.419	525	143	23	15	8	1.5	73	56	26	63	8	4	0	391	10	13	1	2.8	.969	OF-145
1957	79	.278	.438	306	85	16	9	5	1.6	41	30	19	35	11	1	0	206	5	4	2	2.7	.981	OF-79
1958	100	.280	.360	325	91	11	3	3	0.9	47	28	27	37	4	5	0	203	6	5	0	2.1	.977	OF-96
1959	133	.289	.397	478	138	22	6	6	1.3	72	41	35	54	13	6	2	309	6	3	2	2.4	.991	OF-133
1960	151	.286	.428	629	180	27	13	12	1.9	112	54	41	97	22	3	0	351	10	5	3	2.4	.986	OF-149
1961 DET A	160	.257	.384	596	153	15	5	17	2.9	99	63	61	66	22	6	1	410	4	5	2	2.6	.988	OF-155
1962	147	.278	.430	561	156	27	5	16	2.9	90	74	55	67	14	5	1	394	5	7	2	2.8	.983	OF-145
1963	145	.256	.372	524	134	21	4	8	1.5	84	48	39	70	14	11	6	339	6	3	3	2.4	.991	OF-138
1964	106	.277	.399	296	82	11	5	5	1.7	42	33	32	54	14	26	6	143	7	2	3	1.4	.987	OF-81
12 yrs.	1610	.273	.393	6056	1651	241	102	94	1.6	937	545	482	793	207	73	18	3905	105	77	32	2.5	.981	OF-1561

WORLD SERIES

Year Team	Games	BA	SA	AB	H	2B	3B	HR	HR%	R	RBI	BB	SO	SB	AB	H	PO	A	E	DP	TC/G	FA	G by Pos
1958 MIL N	7	.412	.588	17	7	0	0	1	5.9	2	2	5	5	0	1	0	12	0	1	0	1.9	.923	OF-7

Ed Bruyette

BRUYETTE, EDWARD T.
B. Aug. 31, 1874, Manawa, Wis. D. Aug. 5, 1940, Peshastin, Wash.

BL TR 5'10" 170 lbs.

Year Team	Games	BA	SA	AB	H	2B	3B	HR	HR%	R	RBI	BB	SO	SB	AB	H	PO	A	E	DP	TC/G	FA	G by Pos
1901 MIL A	26	.183	.220	82	15	3	0	0	0.0	7	4	12		1	0	0	35	14	9	1	2.2	.845	OF-21, 2B-3, SS-1, 3B-1

Billy Bryan

BRYAN, WILLIAM RONALD
B. Dec. 4, 1938, Morgan, Ga.

BL TR 6'4" 200 lbs.

Year Team	Games	BA	SA	AB	H	2B	3B	HR	HR%	R	RBI	BB	SO	SB	AB	H	PO	A	E	DP	TC/G	FA	G by Pos
1961 KC A	9	.158	.316	19	3	0	1	1	5.3	2	2	2	7	0	5	1	16	1	0	0	1.9	1.000	C-4
1962	25	.149	.284	74	11	2	1	2	2.7	5	7	5	32	0	3	0	117	4	3	0	5.0	.976	C-22
1963	24	.169	.354	65	11	1	1	3	4.6	11	7	9	22	0	0	0	147	4	3	0	6.4	.981	C-24
1964	93	.241	.477	220	53	9	2	13	5.9	19	36	16	69	0	36	11	317	22	3	5	3.7	.991	C-65
1965	108	.252	.446	325	82	11	5	14	4.3	36	51	29	87	0	14	1	527	44	9	6	5.4	.984	C-95
1966 2 teams	KC A (32G – .132)			NY A	(27G – .217)																		
" total	59	.172	.297	145	25	6	0	4	2.8	5	12	11	36	0	22	3	214	23	6	8	4.1	.975	C-35, 1B-6
1967 NY A	16	.167	.417	12	2	0	0	1	8.3	1	2	5	3	0	10	1	5	1	0	1	0.4	1.000	C-1
1968 WAS A	40	.204	.315	108	22	3	0	3	2.8	7	8	14	27	0	12	1	155	15	3	1	4.3	.983	C-28
8 yrs.	374	.216	.395	968	209	32	9	41	4.2	86	125	91	283	0	102	18	1498	114	27	21	4.4	.984	C-274, 1B-6

Derek Bryant

BRYANT, DEREK ROSZELL
B. Oct. 9, 1951, Lexington, Ky.

BR TR 5'11" 185 lbs.

Year Team	Games	BA	SA	AB	H	2B	3B	HR	HR%	R	RBI	BB	SO	SB	AB	H	PO	A	E	DP	TC/G	FA	G by Pos
1979 OAK A	39	.179	.217	106	19	2	1	0	0.0	8	13	10	10	0	2	0	55	2	0	0	1.5	1.000	OF-33, DH-2

Don Bryant

BRYANT, DONALD RAY
B. July 13, 1941, Jasper, Fla.

BR TR 6'5" 200 lbs.

Year Team	Games	BA	SA	AB	H	2B	3B	HR	HR%	R	RBI	BB	SO	SB	AB	H	PO	A	E	DP	TC/G	FA	G by Pos
1966 CHI N	13	.308	.385	26	8	2	0	0	0.0	2	4	1	4	1	3	0	42	3	1	2	3.5	.978	C-10
1969 HOU N	31	.186	.254	59	11	1	0	1	1.7	2	6	4	13	0	2	1	141	7	1	2	4.8	.993	C-28
1970	15	.208	.208	24	5	0	0	0	0.0	2	3	1	8	0	3	0	42	2	2	0	3.1	.957	C-13
3 yrs.	59	.220	.275	109	24	3	0	1	0.9	6	13	6	25	1	8	1	225	12	4	4	4.1	.983	C-51

George Bryant

BRYANT, GEORGE
D. Mar. 14, 1898, Martinsville, Ind.

Year Team	Games	BA	SA	AB	H	2B	3B	HR	HR%	R	RBI	BB	SO	SB	AB	H	PO	A	E	DP	TC/G	FA	G by Pos
1885 DET N	1	.000	.000	4	0	0	0	0	0.0	0	1	0	2		0	0	1	1	0	1	2.0	1.000	2B-1

Ralph Bryant

BRYANT, RALPH WENDELL
B. May 20, 1961, Fort Gaines, Ga.

BL TR 6'2" 200 lbs.

Year Team	Games	BA	SA	AB	H	2B	3B	HR	HR%	R	RBI	BB	SO	SB	AB	H	PO	A	E	DP	TC/G	FA	G by Pos
1985 LA N	6	.333	.333	6	2	0	0	0	0.0	2	0	4	1	0	0	0	0	0	0	0	0.0	–	OF-3
1986	27	.253	.600	75	19	4	2	6	8.0	15	13	5	25	0	3	2	39	2	2	0	1.6	.953	OF-26
1987	46	.246	.391	69	17	2	1	2	2.9	7	10	10	24	2	29	6	22	0	2	0	0.5	.917	OF-19
3 yrs.	79	.253	.493	150	38	6	3	8	5.3	22	24	15	51	2	36	9	61	2	4	0	0.8	.940	OF-48

Steve Brye

BRYE, STEPHEN ROBERT
B. Feb. 4, 1949, Alameda, Calif.

BR TR 6' 190 lbs.

Year Team	Games	BA	SA	AB	H	2B	3B	HR	HR%	R	RBI	BB	SO	SB	AB	H	PO	A	E	DP	TC/G	FA	G by Pos
1970 MIN A	9	.182	.273	11	2	1	0	0	0.0	1	2	4	0	1	0	0	4	0	0	0	0.4	1.000	OF-6

Year	Team		Games	BA	SA	AB	H	2B	3B	HR	HR%	R	RBI	BB	SO	SB	Pinch Hit AB	Pinch Hit H	PO	A	E	DP	TC/G	FA	G by Pos

Steve Brye *continued*

Year	Team		Games	BA	SA	AB	H	2B	3B	HR	HR%	R	RBI	BB	SO	SB	AB	H	PO	A	E	DP	TC/G	FA	G by Pos
1971			28	.224	.318	107	24	1	0	3	2.8	10	11	7	15	3	0	0	53	4	2	0	2.1	.966	OF-28
1972			100	.241	.300	253	61	9	3	0	0.0	18	12	17	38	3	10	5	170	4	2	0	1.8	.994	OF-93
1973			92	.263	.396	278	73	9	5	6	2.2	39	33	35	43	3	2	0	209	4	3	1	2.3	.986	OF-87, DH-1
1974			135	.283	.365	488	138	32	1	2	0.4	52	41	22	59	3	5	1	301	10	1	2	2.3	.997	OF-129
1975			86	.252	.423	246	62	13	1	9	3.7	41	34	21	37	2	10	5	112	7	2	0	1.4	.983	OF-72, DH-6
1976			87	.264	.329	258	68	11	0	2	0.8	33	23	13	31	1	12	2	147	1	2	0	1.7	.987	OF-78, DH-3
1977	MIL	A	94	.249	.419	241	60	14	3	7	2.9	27	28	16	39	1	14	1	166	8	0	1	1.9	1.000	OF-83, DH-6
1978	PIT	N	66	.235	.322	115	27	7	0	1	0.9	16	9	11	10	2	21	3	57	2	1	0	0.9	.983	OF-47
9 yrs.			697	.258	.365	1997	515	97	13	30	1.5	237	193	144	276	16	75	17	1219	45	12	5	1.8	.991	OF-623, DH-16

Hal Bubser

BUBSER, HAROLD FRED
B. Sept. 28, 1895, Chicago, Ill. D. June 22, 1959, Melrose Park, Ill. BR TR 5'11" 170 lbs.

Year	Team		Games	BA	SA	AB	H	2B	3B	HR	HR%	R	RBI	BB	SO	SB	AB	H	PO	A	E	DP	TC/G	FA	G by Pos
1922	CHI	A	3	.000	.000	3	0	0	0	0	0.0	0	0	0	2	0	3	0	0	0	0	0	0.0	—	

Johnny Bucha

BUCHA, JOHN GEORGE
B. Jan. 22, 1925, Allentown, Pa. BR TR 5'11" 190 lbs.

Year	Team		Games	BA	SA	AB	H	2B	3B	HR	HR%	R	RBI	BB	SO	SB	AB	H	PO	A	E	DP	TC/G	FA	G by Pos
1948	STL	N	2	.000	.000	1	0	0	0	0	0.0	1	0	0	1	0	1	0	1	0	0	0	0.5	1.000	C-1
1950			22	.139	.167	36	5	1	0	0	0.0	1	1	4	7	0	5	2	42	5	2	0	2.2	.959	C-17
1953	DET	A	60	.222	.297	158	35	9	0	1	0.6	17	14	20	14	1	2	0	218	22	4	4	4.1	.984	C-56
3 yrs.			84	.205	.272	195	40	10	0	1	0.5	18	15	25	21	1	8	2	261	27	6	4	3.5	.980	C-74

Jerry Buchek

BUCHEK, GERALD PETER
B. May 9, 1942, St. Louis, Mo. BR TR 5'11" 185 lbs.

Year	Team		Games	BA	SA	AB	H	2B	3B	HR	HR%	R	RBI	BB	SO	SB	AB	H	PO	A	E	DP	TC/G	FA	G by Pos
1961	STL	N	31	.133	.156	90	12	1	0	0	0.0	6	0	0	28	0	0	0	42	62	10	20	3.7	.912	SS-31
1963			3	.250	.250	4	1	0	0	0	0.0	0	0	0	2	0	2	0	1	1	0	1	0.7	1.000	SS-1
1964			35	.200	.333	30	6	0	2	0	0.0	7	1	3	11	0	2	0	24	35	5	5	1.8	.922	SS-20, 2B-9, 3B-1
1965			55	.247	.386	166	41	8	3	3	1.8	17	21	13	46	1	5	0	93	154	5	38	4.6	.980	2B-33, SS-18, 3B-1
1966			100	.236	.342	284	67	10	4	4	1.4	23	25	23	71	0	9	1	151	228	19	52	4.0	.952	2B-49, SS-48, 3B-4
1967	NY	N	124	.236	.375	411	97	11	2	14	3.4	35	41	26	101	3	9	2	226	300	12	59	4.3	.978	2B-95, 3B-17, SS-9
1968			73	.182	.219	192	35	4	0	1	0.5	8	11	10	53	1	18	3	57	91	7	11	2.1	.955	3B-37, 2B-12, OF-9
7 yrs.			421	.220	.325	1177	259	35	11	22	1.9	96	108	75	312	5	45	6	594	871	58	186	3.6	.962	2B-198, SS-127, 3B-60, OF-9

WORLD SERIES

Year	Team		Games	BA	SA	AB	H	2B	3B	HR	HR%	R	RBI	BB	SO	SB	AB	H	PO	A	E	DP	TC/G	FA	G by Pos
1964	STL	N	4	1.000	1.000	1	1	0	0	0	0.0	1	0	0	0	0	0	0	0	1	0	0	0.3	1.000	2B-4

Jim Bucher

BUCHER, JAMES QUINTER
B. Mar. 11, 1911, Manassas, Va. BL TR 5'11" 170 lbs.

Year	Team		Games	BA	SA	AB	H	2B	3B	HR	HR%	R	RBI	BB	SO	SB	AB	H	PO	A	E	DP	TC/G	FA	G by Pos
1934	BKN	N	47	.226	.333	84	19	5	2	0	0.0	12	8	4	7	1	18	8	38	48	9	10	2.0	.905	2B-20, 3B-6
1935			123	.302	.397	473	143	22	1	7	1.5	72	58	10	33	4	12	0	194	188	18	29	3.3	.955	2B-41, 3B-39, OF-37
1936			110	.251	.343	370	93	12	8	2	0.5	49	41	29	27	5	10	3	145	138	19	15	2.7	.937	3B-39, 2B-32, OF-30
1937			125	.253	.324	380	96	11	2	4	1.1	44	37	20	18	5	23	3	173	192	23	35	3.1	.941	2B-49, 3B-43, OF-6
1938	STL	N	17	.228	.316	57	13	3	1	0	0.0	7	7	2	2	0	2	1	33	31	3	9	3.9	.955	2B-14, 3B-1
1944	BOS	A	80	.274	.365	277	76	9	2	4	1.4	39	31	19	13	3	15	5	99	138	11	25	3.1	.956	3B-44, 2B-21
1945			52	.225	.291	151	34	4	3	0	0.0	19	11	7	13	1	17	2	27	69	6	8	2.0	.941	3B-32, 2B-2
7 yrs.			554	.265	.351	1792	474	66	19	17	0.9	242	193	91	113	19	97	22	709	804	89	131	2.9	.944	3B-204, 2B-179, OF-73

Dick Buckley

BUCKLEY, RICHARD D.
B. Sept. 21, 1858, Troy, N. Y. D. Dec. 12, 1929, Pittsburgh, Pa. TR 5'10"

Year	Team		Games	BA	SA	AB	H	2B	3B	HR	HR%	R	RBI	BB	SO	SB	AB	H	PO	A	E	DP	TC/G	FA	G by Pos
1888	IND	N	71	.273	.388	260	71	9	3	5	1.9	28	22	6	24	4	0	0	238	89	43	9	5.2	.884	C-51, 3B-22, OF-1, 1B-1
1889			68	.258	.392	260	67	11	0	8	3.1	35	41	15	32	5	0	0	194	82	38	4	4.6	.879	C-55, 3B-12, OF-1, 1B-1
1890	NY	N	70	.256	.320	266	68	11	0	2	0.8	39	26	23	35	3	0	0	368	104	39	4	7.3	.924	C-62, 3B-8
1891			75	.217	.308	253	55	9	1	4	1.6	23	31	11	30	3	0	0	447	85	23	7	7.4	.959	C-74, 3B-1
1892	STL	N	121	.227	.324	410	93	17	4	5	1.2	43	52	22	34	7	0	0	535	124	43	15	5.8	.939	C-119, 1B-2
1893			9	.174	.217	23	4	1	0	0	0.0	2	1	0	0	0	0	0	26	6	3	2	3.9	.914	C-9
1894	2 teams	STL	N	(29G – .180)			PHI	N	(43G – .294)																
"	total		72	.253	.349	249	63	5	2	0	0.8	23	29	12	16	1	1	0	258	69	25	4	4.8	.956	C-69, 1B-2
1895	PHI	N	38	.250	.321	112	28	6	1	0	0.0	20	14	9	17	2	0	0	152	29	16	5	5.2	.919	C-38
8 yrs.			524	.245	.342	1833	449	72	14	26	1.4	213	216	98	188	25	1	0	2218	588	220	50	5.8	.927	C-477, 3B-43, 1B-6, OF-2

Kevin Buckley

BUCKLEY, KEVIN JOHN
B. Jan. 16, 1959, Quincy, Mass. BR TR 6'1" 195 lbs.

Year	Team		Games	BA	SA	AB	H	2B	3B	HR	HR%	R	RBI	BB	SO	SB	AB	H	PO	A	E	DP	TC/G	FA	G by Pos
1984	TEX	A	5	.286	.429	7	2	1	0	0	0.0	1	0	2	4	0	2	0	0	0	0	0	0.0	—	DH-3

Bill Buckner

BUCKNER, WILLIAM JOSEPH (Billy Bucks)
B. Dec. 14, 1949, Vallejo, Calif. BL TL 6' 185 lbs.

Year	Team		Games	BA	SA	AB	H	2B	3B	HR	HR%	R	RBI	BB	SO	SB	AB	H	PO	A	E	DP	TC/G	FA	G by Pos
1969	LA	N	1	.000	.000	1	0	0	0	0	0.0	0	0	0	1	0	1	0	0	0	0	0	0.0	—	
1970			28	.191	.265	68	13	3	1	0	0.0	6	4	3	7	0	8	2	37	1	0	1	1.4	1.000	OF-20, 1B-1
1971			108	.277	.366	358	99	15	1	5	1.4	37	41	11	18	4	17	3	235	11	1	4	2.3	.996	OF-86, 1B-11
1972			105	.319	.410	383	122	14	3	5	1.3	47	37	17	13	10	11	3	434	22	4	28	4.4	.991	OF-61, 1B-35
1973			140	.275	.351	575	158	20	0	8	1.4	68	46	17	34	12	9	2	981	50	3	93	7.4	.997	1B-93, OF-48
1974			145	.314	.412	580	182	30	3	7	1.2	83	58	30	24	31	9	1	284	5	7	2	2.0	.976	OF-137, 1B-6
1975			92	.243	.358	288	70	11	2	6	2.1	30	31	17	15	8	19	3	138	4	2	0	1.6	.986	OF-72
1976			154	.301	.389	642	193	28	4	7	1.1	76	60	26	26	28	1	1	315	7	5	0	2.1	.985	OF-153, 1B-1
1977	CHI	N	122	.284	.425	426	121	27	0	11	2.6	40	60	21	23	7	22	7	966	58	10	75	8.5	.990	1B-99
1978			117	.323	.419	446	144	26	1	5	1.1	47	74	18	17	7	12	2	1075	83	6	85	9.9	.995	1B-105
1979			149	.284	.437	591	168	34	7	14	2.4	72	66	30	28	9	8	3	1258	124	7	118	9.3	.995	1B-140
1980			145	**.324**	.457	578	187	41	3	10	1.7	69	68	30	18	1	6	0	916	78	8	69	6.9	.992	1B-94, OF-50
1981			106	.311	.480	421	131	**35**	3	10	2.4	45	75	26	15	5	2	1	996	81	17	92	10.3	.984	1B-105
1982			161	.306	.441	**657**	201	34	5	15	2.3	93	105	36	26	15	0	0	1547	159	12	89	10.7	.993	1B-161

Year	Team	Games	BA	SA	AB	H	2B	3B	HR	HR%	R	RBI	BB	SO	SB	Pinch Hit AB	Pinch Hit H	PO	A	E	DP	TC/G	FA	G by Pos

Bill Buckner *continued*

1983		153	.280	.436	626	175	**38**	6	16	2.6	79	66	25	30	12	2	1	1391	161	13	132	10.2	.992	1B-144, OF-15
1984	2 teams				CHI N (21G – .209)				BOS A (114G – .278)															
"	total	135	.272	.392	482	131	21	2	11	2.3	54	69	25	39	2	12	3	1045	102	15	80	8.6	.987	1B-120, OF-2
1985	BOS A	162	.299	.447	673	201	46	3	16	2.4	89	110	30	36	18	0	0	1384	184	12	140	9.8	.992	1B-162
1986		153	.267	.421	629	168	39	2	18	2.9	73	102	40	25	6	0	0	1067	157	14	104	8.1	.989	1B-138, DH-15
1987	2 teams				BOS A (75G – .273)				CAL A (57G – .306)															
"	total	132	.286	.365	469	134	18	2	5	1.1	39	74	22	26	2	15	8	640	60	6	54	5.3	.992	1B-79, DH-39
1988	2 teams				CAL A (19G – .209)				KC A (89G – .256)															
"	total	108	.249	.330	285	71	14	0	3	1.1	19	43	17	19	5	28	8	161	.13	1	12	1.6	.994	DH-53, 1B-22
1989	KC A	79	.216	.267	176	38	4	1	1	0.6	7	16	6	11	1	**38**	10	181	13	3	19	2.5	.985	1B-24, DH-19
21 yrs.		2495	.289	.409	9354	2707	498	49	173	1.8	1073	1205	447	451	183	220	58	15051	1373	146	1197	6.6	.991	1B-1540, OF-644, DH-126

LEAGUE CHAMPIONSHIP SERIES

1974	LA N	4	.167	.222	18	3	1	0	0	0.0	0	0	0	2	0	0	0	6	0	0	0	1.5	1.000	OF-4
1986	BOS A	7	.214	.250	28	6	1	0	0	0.0	3	3	0	2	0	0	0	51	5	0	4	8.0	1.000	1B-7
2 yrs.		11	.196	.239	46	9	2	0	0	0.0	3	3	0	4	0	0	0	57	5	0	4	5.6	1.000	1B-7, OF-4

WORLD SERIES

1974	LA N	5	.250	.450	20	5	1	0	1	5.0	1	1	0	1	0	0	0	11	0	0	0	2.2	1.000	OF-5
1986	BOS A	7	.188	.188	32	6	0	0	0	0.0	2	1	1	3	0	0	0	53	7	1	5	8.7	.984	1B-7
2 yrs.		12	.212	.288	52	11	1	0	1	1.9	3	2	1	4	0	0	0	64	7	1	5	6.0	.986	1B-7, OF-5

Mark Budaska

BUDASKA, MARK DAVID
B. Dec. 27, 1952, Sharon, Pa.   BB TL 6'   180 lbs.

1978	OAK A	4	.250	.500	4	1	1	0	0	0.0	0	0	1	2	0	0	1	1	0	1	0	0.5	.500	OF-2
1981		9	.156	.188	32	5	1	0	0	0.0	3	2	4	10	0	0	0	0	0	0	0	0.0	–	DH-9
2 yrs.		13	.167	.222	36	6	2	0	0	0.0	3	2	5	12	0	2	1	1	0	1	0	0.2	.500	DH-9, OF-2

Budd

BUDD
B. Cleveland, Ohio

| 1890 | CLE P | 1 | .000 | .000 | 4 | 0 | 0 | 0 | 0 | 0.0 | 0 | 0 | 0 | 3 | 0 | 0 | 0 | 2 | 0 | 0 | 0 | 2.0 | 1.000 | OF-1 |

Don Buddin

BUDDIN, DONALD THOMAS
B. May 5, 1934, Turbeville, S. C.   BR TR 5'11"   178 lbs.

1956	BOS A	114	.239	.342	377	90	24	0	5	1.3	49	37	65	62	2	1	0	213	370	29	98	5.4	.953	SS-113
1958		136	.237	.368	497	118	25	2	12	2.4	74	43	82	106	0	0	0	269	445	31	102	5.5	.958	SS-136
1959		151	.241	.357	485	117	24	1	10	2.1	75	53	92	99	6	0	0	235	412	35	89	4.5	.949	SS-150
1960		124	.245	.360	428	105	21	5	6	1.4	62	36	62	59	4	0	0	230	356	30	79	5.0	.951	SS-124
1961		115	.263	.398	339	89	22	3	6	1.8	58	42	72	45	2	4	1	204	294	23	70	4.5	.956	SS-109
1962	2 teams				HOU N (40G – .163)				DET A (31G – .229)															
"	total	71	.196	.288	163	32	7	1	2	1.2	24	14	37	33	1	12	3	92	128	10	28	3.2	.957	SS-46, 3B-11, 2B-5
6 yrs.		711	.241	.359	2289	551	123	12	41	1.8	342	225	410	404	15	17	4	1243	2005	158	466	4.8	.954	SS-678, 3B-11, 2B-5

Steve Buechele

BUECHELE, STEVEN BERNARD
B. Sept. 26, 1961, Lancaster, Calif.   BR TR 6'2"   190 lbs.

1985	TEX A	69	.219	.356	219	48	6	6	6	2.7	22	21	14	38	3	0	0	52	138	6	17	2.8	.969	3B-69, 2B-1
1986		153	.243	.410	461	112	19	2	18	3.9	54	54	35	98	5	2	1	174	292	12	42	3.1	.975	3B-137, 2B-33, OF-2
1987		136	.237	.399	363	86	20	0	13	3.6	45	50	28	66	2	2	1	89	211	9	20	2.3	.971	3B-123, 2B-18, OF-2
1988		155	.250	.404	503	126	21	4	16	3.2	68	58	65	79	2	2	2	114	300	16	25	2.8	.963	3B-153, 2B-2
1989		155	.235	.387	486	114	22	2	16	3.3	60	59	36	107	1	1	0	128	288	12	29	2.8	.972	3B-145, 2B-18, DH-1, SS-1
5 yrs.		668	.239	.395	2032	486	88	11	69	3.4	249	242	178	388	13	7	2	557	1229	55	133	2.8	.970	3B-627, 2B-72, OF-4, DH-1, SS-1

Charlie Buelow

BUELOW, CHARLES JOHN
B. Jan. 12, 1877, Dubuque, Iowa   D. May 4, 1951, Dubuque, Iowa   BR TR

| 1901 | NY N | 22 | .111 | .167 | 72 | 8 | 4 | 0 | 0 | 0.0 | 3 | 4 | 2 | | 0 | 3 | 0 | 20 | 43 | 11 | 2 | 3.4 | .851 | 3B-17, 2B-2 |

Fritz Buelow

BUELOW, FREDERICK WILLIAM
B. Feb. 13, 1876, Berlin, Germany   D. Dec. 27, 1933, Detroit, Mich.   BR TR 5'10½" 170 lbs.

1899	STL N	7	.467	.733	15	7	0	1	0	0.0	2	2			0	0	1	12	1	1	0	2.0	.929	C-4, OF-2
1900		6	.235	.235	17	4	0	0	0	0.0	2	3	0		0	1	1	13	6	3	0	3.7	.864	C-4, OF-1
1901	DET A	70	.225	.316	231	52	5	5	2	0.9	28	29	11		2	1	0	213	84	10	4	4.4	.967	C-69
1902		66	.223	.290	224	50	5	2	0	0.0	23	29	9		3	0	0	190	81	20	7	4.4	.931	C-63, 1B-2
1903		63	.214	.307	192	41	3	6	1	0.5	24	13	6		4	0	0	278	67	13	7	5.7	.964	C-60, 1B-2
1904	2 teams				DET A (42G – .110)				CLE A (42G – .176)															
"	total	84	.141	.176	255	36	6	0	0	0.0	17	10	19		4	0	0	378	88	11	5	5.7	.977	C-84
1905	CLE A	74	.174	.212	236	41	4	1	1	0.4	11	18	6		7	2	1	294	76	13	5	5.2	.966	C-59, OF-8, 1B-3, 3B-2
1906		34	.163	.186	86	14	2	0	0	0.0	7	7	9		0	0	0	122	39	10	5	5.0	.942	C-33, 1B-1
1907	STL A	26	.147	.160	75	11	1	0	0	0.0	9	1	7		0	1	0	77	36	2	4	4.4	.983	C-25
9 yrs.		430	.192	.252	1331	256	25	18	6	0.5	125	112	69		20	6	2	1577	478	83	37	5.0	.961	C-401, OF-11, 1B-8, 3B-2

Art Bues

BUES, ARTHUR FREDERICK
B. Mar. 3, 1888, Milwaukee, Wis.   D. Nov. 7, 1954, Whitefish Bay, Wis.   BR TR 5'11" 184 lbs.

1913	BOS N	2	.000	.000	1	0	0	0	0	0.0	0	0	0	1	0	0	0	0	0	0	0	0.0	–	3B-1, 2B-1
1914	CHI N	14	.222	.289	45	10	1	1	0	0.0	3	4	5	6	1	2	0	14	16	1	0	2.2	.968	3B-12
2 yrs.		16	.217	.283	46	10	1	1	0	0.0	3	4	5	7	1	2	0	14	16	1	0	1.9	.968	3B-13, 2B-1

Charlie Buffinton

BUFFINTON, CHARLES G.
B. June 14, 1861, Fall River, Mass.   D. Sept. 23, 1907, Fall River, Mass.   BR TR 6'1"   180 lbs.
Manager 1890.

| 1882 | BOS N | 15 | .260 | .280 | 50 | 13 | 1 | 0 | 0 | 0.0 | 5 | 4 | 2 | 3 | | 0 | 0 | 34 | 12 | 7 | 0 | 3.5 | .868 | OF-7, P-5, 1B-4 |
| 1883 | | 86 | .238 | .287 | 341 | 81 | 8 | 3 | 1 | 0.3 | 28 | 26 | 6 | 24 | | 0 | 0 | 84 | 69 | 33 | 6 | 2.2 | .823 | OF-51, P-43, 1B-2 |

Year Team	Games	BA	SA	AB	H	2B	3B	HR	HR%	R	RBI	BB	SO	SB	Pinch Hit AB	H	PO	A	E	DP	TC/G	FA	G by Pos

Charlie Buffinton *continued*

Year Team	Games	BA	SA	AB	H	2B	3B	HR	HR%	R	RBI	BB	SO	SB	AB	H	PO	A	E	DP	TC/G	FA	G by Pos
1884	87	.267	.344	352	94	18	3	1	0.3	48		16	12		0	0	146	118	24	6	3.3	.917	P-67, OF-13, 1B-11
1885	82	.240	.302	338	81	12	3	1	0.3	26	33	3	26		0	0	196	121	27	11	4.2	.922	P-51, OF-18, 1B-15
1886	44	.290	.341	176	51	4	1	1	0.6	27	30	6	12		0	0	181	35	11	8	5.2	.952	1B-19, P-18
1887 PHI N	66	.268	.331	269	72	12	1	1	0.4	34	46	11	3	8	0	0	124	93	23	8	3.6	.904	P-40, OF-22, 1B-10
1888	46	.181	.219	160	29	4	1	0	0.0	14	12	7	5	1	0	0	31	122	10	3	3.5	.939	P-46, OF-1
1889	47	.208	.221	154	32	2	0	0	0.0	16	21	9	5	0	0	0	18	80	9	4	2.3	.916	P-47, OF-1
1890 PHI P	42	.273	.340	150	41	3	2	1	0.7	24	24	9	3	1	0	0	50	81	16	6	3.5	.891	P-36, OF-5, 1B-3
1891 BOS AA	58	.188	.227	181	34	2	1	1	0.6	16	16	19	15	0	0	0	43	119	13	5	3.0	.926	P-48, OF-10, 1B-4
1892 BAL N	13	.349	.419	43	15	1	1	0	0.0	7	4	3	6	1	0	0	3	30	4	1	2.8	.892	P-13
11 yrs.	586	.245	.299	2214	543	67	16	7	0.3	245	216	91	114	11	0	0	910	880	177	58	3.4	.910	P-414, OF-128, 1B-68

Don Buford

BUFORD, DONALD ALVIN
B. Feb. 2, 1937, Linden, Tex.

BB TR 5'7'' 160 lbs.

Year Team	Games	BA	SA	AB	H	2B	3B	HR	HR%	R	RBI	BB	SO	SB	AB	H	PO	A	E	DP	TC/G	FA	G by Pos
1963 CHI A	12	.286	.405	42	12	1	2	0	0.0	9	5	5	7	1	1	0	13	12	2	1	2.3	.926	3B-9, 2B-2
1964	135	.262	.348	442	116	14	6	4	0.9	62	30	46	62	12	10	1	226	261	16	65	3.7	.968	2B-92, 3B-37
1965	155	.283	.389	586	166	22	5	10	1.7	93	47	67	76	17	8	2	339	416	14	102	5.0	.982	3B-139, 2B-41
1966	163	.244	.349	607	148	26	7	8	1.3	85	52	69	71	51	1	0	199	383	34	42	3.8	.945	3B-133, 2B-37, OF-11
1967	156	.241	.316	535	129	10	9	4	0.7	61	32	65	51	34	3	1	198	349	27	46	3.7	.953	3B-121, 2B-51, OF-1
1968 BAL A	130	.282	.437	426	120	13	4	15	3.5	65	46	57	46	27	20	6	239	111	8	22	2.8	.978	OF-65, 2B-58, 3B-2
1969	144	.291	.417	554	161	31	3	11	2.0	99	64	96	62	19	5	1	255	38	6	5	2.1	.980	OF-128, 2B-10, 3B-6
1970	144	.272	.411	504	137	15	2	17	3.4	99	66	109	55	16	10	2	224	19	4	3	1.7	.984	OF-130, 3B-3, 2B-3
1971	122	.290	.477	449	130	19	4	19	4.2	99	54	89	62	15	8	2	217	6	3	0	1.9	.987	OF-115
1972	125	.206	.267	408	84	6	2	5	1.2	46	22	69	83	8	19	2	173	6	2	1	1.4	.989	OF-105
10 yrs.	1286	.264	.379	4553	1203	157	44	93	2.0	718	418	672	575	200	85	17	2083	1601	116	287	3.0	.969	OF-555, 2B-392, 3B-352

LEAGUE CHAMPIONSHIP SERIES

Year Team	Games	BA	SA	AB	H	2B	3B	HR	HR%	R	RBI	BB	SO	SB	AB	H	PO	A	E	DP	TC/G	FA	G by Pos
1969 BAL A	3	.286	.357	14	4	1	0	0	0.0	3	1	3	0	0	0	0	8	0	0	0	2.7	1.000	OF-3
1970	2	.429	1.000	7	3	1	0	1	14.3	2	3	2	0	0	0	0	2	0	0	0	1.0	1.000	OF-2
1971	2	.429	.714	7	3	0	1	0	0.0	1	0	2	1	0	0	0	1	0	0	0	0.5	1.000	OF-2
3 yrs.	7	.357	.607	28	10	2	1	1	3.6	6	4	7	1	0	0	0	11	0	0	0	1.6	1.000	OF-7

WORLD SERIES

Year Team	Games	BA	SA	AB	H	2B	3B	HR	HR%	R	RBI	BB	SO	SB	AB	H	PO	A	E	DP	TC/G	FA	G by Pos
1969 BAL A	5	.100	.300	20	2	1	0	1	5.0	1	2	2	4	0	0	0	8	0	0	0	1.6	1.000	OF-5
1970	4	.267	.467	15	4	0	0	1	6.7	3	1	3	2	0	0	0	6	0	0	0	1.5	1.000	OF-4
1971	6	.261	.565	23	6	1	0	2	8.7	3	4	3	3	0	0	0	13	1	0	0	2.3	1.000	OF-6
3 yrs.	15	.207	.448	58	12	2	0	4	6.9	7	7	8	9	0	0	0	27	1	0	0	1.9	1.000	OF-15

Jay Buhner

BUHNER, JAY CAMPBELL
B. Aug. 13, 1964, Louisville, Ky.

BR TR 6'3'' 205 lbs.

Year Team	Games	BA	SA	AB	H	2B	3B	HR	HR%	R	RBI	BB	SO	SB	AB	H	PO	A	E	DP	TC/G	FA	G by Pos
1987 NY A	7	.227	.318	22	5	2	0	0	0.0	0	1	1	6	0	1	0	11	1	0	1	1.7	1.000	OF-7
1988 2 teams		NY A (25G – .188)					SEA A (60G – .224)																
" total	85	.215	.421	261	56	13	1	13	5.0	36	38	28	93	1	4	1	186	9	3	3	2.3	.985	OF-81
1989 SEA A	58	.275	.490	204	56	15	1	9	4.4	27	33	19	55	1	0	0	106	6	4	3	2.0	.966	OF-57
3 yrs.	150	.240	.446	487	117	30	2	22	4.5	63	72	48	154	2	4	1	303	16	7	7	2.2	.979	OF-145

Harry Buker

BUKER, HENRY L. (Happy)
B. 1859, Chicago, Ill.   D. Aug. 10, 1899, Chicago, Ill.

Year Team	Games	BA	SA	AB	H	2B	3B	HR	HR%	R	RBI	BB	SO	SB	AB	H	PO	A	E	DP	TC/G	FA	G by Pos
1884 DET N	30	.135	.144	111	15	1	0	0	0.0	5		4	15		0	0	35	65	14	5	3.8	.877	SS-19, OF-11

George Bullard

BULLARD, GEORGE DONALD (Curly)
B. Oct. 24, 1928, Lynn, Mass.

BR TR 5'9½'' 165 lbs.

Year Team	Games	BA	SA	AB	H	2B	3B	HR	HR%	R	RBI	BB	SO	SB	AB	H	PO	A	E	DP	TC/G	FA	G by Pos
1954 DET A	4	.000	.000	1	0	0	0	0	0.0	0	0	0	0	0	0	0	2	1	1	0	1.3	.800	SS-1

Sim Bullas

BULLAS, SIMEON EDWARD (Derby)
B. Apr. 10, 1861, Cleveland, Ohio   D. Jan. 14, 1908, Cleveland, Ohio

BR TR 5'7½'' 150 lbs.

Year Team	Games	BA	SA	AB	H	2B	3B	HR	HR%	R	RBI	BB	SO	SB	AB	H	PO	A	E	DP	TC/G	FA	G by Pos
1884 TOL AA	13	.089	.133	45	4	0	1	0	0.0	4		1			0	0	55	17	7	0	6.1	.911	C-12, OF-2

Terry Bulling

BULLING, TERRY CHARLES (Bud)
B. Dec. 15, 1952, Lynwood, Calif.

BR TR 6'1'' 200 lbs.

Year Team	Games	BA	SA	AB	H	2B	3B	HR	HR%	R	RBI	BB	SO	SB	AB	H	PO	A	E	DP	TC/G	FA	G by Pos
1977 MIN A	15	.156	.188	32	5	1	0	0	0.0	2	5	5	5	0	0	0	37	3	2	0	2.8	.952	C-10, DH-3
1981 SEA A	62	.247	.305	154	38	3	0	2	1.3	15	15	21	20	0	4	0	239	21	6	3	4.3	.977	C-62
1982	56	.221	.286	154	34	7	0	1	0.6	17	8	19	16	2	1	0	304	24	3	5	5.9	.991	C-56
1983	5	.000	.000	5	0	0	0	0	0.0	0	0	0	0	0	0	0	17	0	0	0	3.4	1.000	C-5
4 yrs.	138	.223	.281	345	77	11	0	3	0.9	34	28	45	41	2	6	0	597	48	11	8	4.8	.983	C-133, DH-3

Eric Bullock

BULLOCK, ERIC GERALD
B. Feb. 16, 1960, Los Angeles, Calif.

BL TL 5'11'' 185 lbs.

Year Team	Games	BA	SA	AB	H	2B	3B	HR	HR%	R	RBI	BB	SO	SB	AB	H	PO	A	E	DP	TC/G	FA	G by Pos
1985 HOU N	18	.280	.360	25	7	2	0	0	0.0	3	2	1	3	0	12	6	6	0	2	0	0.4	.750	OF-7
1986	6	.048	.048	21	1	0	0	0	0.0	0	1	0	3	2	0	0	7	0	1	0	1.3	.875	OF-6
1988 MIN A	16	.294	.294	17	5	0	0	0	0.0	3	3	3	1	1	10	3	7	0	1	0	0.5	.875	OF-4, DH-2
1989 PHI N	6	.000	.000	4	0	0	0	0	0.0	1	0	0	2	0	3	0	2	0	0	0	0.3	1.000	OF-3
4 yrs.	46	.194	.224	67	13	2	0	0	0.0	7	6	4	9	3	25	6	22	0	4	0	0.6	.846	OF-20, DH-2

Al Bumbry

BUMBRY, ALONZA BENJAMIN
Born Alonza Benjamin Bumbrey.
B. Apr. 21, 1947, Fredericksburg, Va.

BL TR 5'8'' 170 lbs.

Year Team	Games	BA	SA	AB	H	2B	3B	HR	HR%	R	RBI	BB	SO	SB	AB	H	PO	A	E	DP	TC/G	FA	G by Pos
1972 BAL A	9	.364	.545	11	4	0	1	0	0.0	5	0	0	0	1	3	0	4	0	0	0	0.4	1.000	OF-2
1973	110	.337	.500	356	120	15	11	7	2.0	73	34	34	49	23	8	5	134	2	3	0	1.3	.978	OF-86, DH-7
1974	94	.233	.304	270	63	10	3	1	0.4	35	19	21	46	12	7	1	115	7	6	0	1.4	.953	OF-67, DH-7
1975	114	.269	.364	349	94	19	4	2	0.6	47	32	32	81	16	20	4	70	2	0	1	0.6	1.000	DH-48, OF-39, 3B-1
1976	133	.251	.376	450	113	15	7	9	2.0	71	36	43	76	42	7	1	251	9	3	2	2.0	.989	OF-116, DH-10

Year	Team		Games	BA	SA	AB	H	2B	3B	HR	HR%	R	RBI	BB	SO	SB	Pinch Hit AB	Pinch Hit H	PO	A	E	DP	TC/G	FA	G by Pos

Al Bumbry *continued*

Year	Team		Games	BA	SA	AB	H	2B	3B	HR	HR%	R	RBI	BB	SO	SB	PH AB	PH H	PO	A	E	DP	TC/G	FA	G by Pos
1977			133	.317	.411	518	164	31	3	4	0.8	74	41	45	88	19	2	2	329	7	3	0	2.5	.991	OF-130
1978			33	.237	.368	114	27	5	2	2	1.8	21	6	17	15	5	5	1	62	2	1	0	2.0	.985	OF-28
1979			148	.285	.376	569	162	29	1	7	1.2	80	49	43	74	37	8	3	367	7	7	1	2.6	.982	OF-146
1980			160	.318	.433	645	205	29	9	9	1.4	118	53	78	75	44	1	0	488	7	5	1	3.1	.990	OF-160
1981			101	.273	.337	392	107	18	2	1	0.3	61	27	51	51	22	2	0	255	6	2	2	2.6	.992	OF-100
1982			150	.262	.338	562	147	20	4	5	0.9	77	40	44	77	10	7	0	404	9	6	1	2.8	.986	OF-147, DH-1
1983			124	.275	.357	378	104	14	4	3	0.8	63	31	31	33	12	12	3	235	3	3	1	1.9	.988	OF-104, DH-11
1984			119	.270	.337	344	93	12	1	3	0.9	47	24	25	35	9	12	2	230	7	3	1	2.0	.988	OF-99, DH-9
1985	SD	N	68	.200	.263	95	19	3	0	1	1.1	6	10	7	9	2	47	5	31	0	2	0	0.5	.939	OF-17
14 yrs.			1496	.281	.378	5053	1422	220	52	54	1.1	778	402	471	709	254	141	27	2975	68	44	10	2.1	.986	OF-1241, DH-93, 3B-1

LEAGUE CHAMPIONSHIP SERIES

Year	Team		Games	BA	SA	AB	H	2B	3B	HR	HR%	R	RBI	BB	SO	SB	PH AB	PH H	PO	A	E	DP	TC/G	FA	G by Pos
1973	BAL	A	2	.000	.000	7	0	0	0	0	0.0	1	0	2	2	0	1	0	4	1	1	0	3.0	.833	OF-2
1974			2	.000	.000	1	0	0	0	0	0.0	0	0	0	1	0	1	0	0	0	0	0	0.0	–	
1979			4	.250	.375	16	4	0	1	0	0.0	5	0	4	3	2	0	0	10	0	1	0	2.8	.909	OF-4
1983			3	.125	.250	8	1	1	0	0	0.0	0	1	0	2	0	0	0	3	0	0	0	1.0	1.000	OF-3
4 yrs.			11	.156	.250	32	5	1	1	0	0.0	6	1	6	8	2	1	0	17	1	2	0	1.8	.900	OF-9

WORLD SERIES

Year	Team		Games	BA	SA	AB	H	2B	3B	HR	HR%	R	RBI	BB	SO	SB	PH AB	PH H	PO	A	E	DP	TC/G	FA	G by Pos
1979	BAL	A	7	.143	.143	21	3	0	0	0	0.0	3	1	2	1	0	0	0	14	1	1	0	2.3	.938	OF-7
1983			4	.091	.182	11	1	1	0	0	0.0	0	1	0	1	0	0	0	12	0	0	0	3.0	1.000	OF-4
2 yrs.			11	.125	.156	32	4	1	0	0	0.0	3	2	2	2	0	0	0	26	1	1	0	2.5	.964	OF-11

Josh Bunce

BUNCE, JOSHUA
B. May 10, 1847, Brooklyn, N. Y.   D. Apr. 28, 1912, Brooklyn, N. Y.

Year	Team		Games	BA	SA	AB	H	2B	3B	HR	HR%	R	RBI	BB	SO	SB	PH AB	PH H	PO	A	E	DP	TC/G	FA	G by Pos
1877	HAR	N	1	.000	.000	4	0	0	0	0	0.0	0	0	0	0		0	0	1	0	0	0	1.0	1.000	OF-1

Nels Burbrink

BURBRINK, NELSON EDWARD
B. Dec. 28, 1921, Cincinnati, Ohio

BR TR 5'10" 195 lbs.

Year	Team		Games	BA	SA	AB	H	2B	3B	HR	HR%	R	RBI	BB	SO	SB	PH AB	PH H	PO	A	E	DP	TC/G	FA	G by Pos
1955	STL	N	58	.276	.335	170	47	8	1	0	0.0	11	15	14	13	1	3	2	261	24	6	4	5.0	.979	C-55

Al Burch

BURCH, ALBERT WILLIAM
B. Oct. 7, 1883, Albany, N. Y.   D. Oct. 5, 1926, Brooklyn, N. Y.

BL TR 5'8½" 160 lbs.

Year	Team		Games	BA	SA	AB	H	2B	3B	HR	HR%	R	RBI	BB	SO	SB	PH AB	PH H	PO	A	E	DP	TC/G	FA	G by Pos
1906	STL	N	91	.266	.287	335	89	5	1	0	0.0	40	11	37		15	0	0	155	15	12	6	2.0	.934	OF-91
1907	2 teams		STL	N	(48G – .227)		BKN	N	(40G – .292)																
"	total		88	.255	.296	274	70	5	3	0	0.0	30	17	28		12	3	0	150	24	7	4	2.2	.911	OF-84, 2B-1
1908	BKN	N	123	.243	.292	456	111	8	4	2	0.4	45	18	33		15	6	1	242	24	8	6	2.2	.971	OF-116
1909			152	.271	.329	601	163	20	6	1	0.2	80	30	51		38	0	0	335	23	16	5	2.5	.957	OF-151, 1B-1
1910			103	.236	.284	352	83	8	3	1	0.3	41	20	22	30	13	18	7	246	18	10	15	2.7	.964	OF-70, 1B-13
1911			54	.228	.275	167	38	2	3	0	0.0	18	7	15	22	3	6	0	104	13	3	3	2.2	.975	OF-43, 2B-3
6 yrs.			611	.254	.299	2185	554	48	20	4	0.2	254	103	186	52	96	33	8	1232	118	66	39	2.3	.953	OF-555, 1B-14, 2B-4

Ernie Burch

BURCH, EARNEST W.
B. 1856, DeKalb County, Ill.

BL

Year	Team		Games	BA	SA	AB	H	2B	3B	HR	HR%	R	RBI	BB	SO	SB	PH AB	PH H	PO	A	E	DP	TC/G	FA	G by Pos
1884	CLE	N	32	.210	.242	124	26	4	0	0	0.0	9	7	5	24		0	0	52	10	7	1	2.2	.899	OF-32
1886	BKN	AA	113	.261	.349	456	119	22	6	2	0.4	78		39		15	0	0	142	10	20	3	1.5	.884	OF-113
1887			49	.293	.388	188	55	4	4	2	1.1	47		29		15	0	0	90	8	11	1	2.2	.899	OF-49
3 yrs.			194	.260	.341	768	200	30	10	4	0.5	134	7	73	24	15	0	0	284	28	38	5	1.8	.891	OF-194

Bob Burda

BURDA, EDWARD ROBERT
B. July 16, 1938, St. Louis, Mo.

BL TL 5'11" 174 lbs.

Year	Team		Games	BA	SA	AB	H	2B	3B	HR	HR%	R	RBI	BB	SO	SB	PH AB	PH H	PO	A	E	DP	TC/G	FA	G by Pos
1962	STL	N	7	.071	.071	14	1	0	0	0	0.0	0	0	3	1	1	1	0	11	0	1	0	1.7	.917	OF-6
1965	SF	N	31	.111	.111	27	3	0	0	0	0.0	0	5	5	6	0	12	1	34	0	1	1	1.1	.971	1B-7, OF-4
1966			37	.163	.233	43	7	3	0	0	0.0	3	2	2	5	0	25	4	28	2	0	0	0.8	1.000	1B-7, OF-4
1969			97	.230	.391	161	37	9	0	6	3.7	20	27	21	12	0	35	8	234	14	3	15	2.6	.988	1B-45, OF-19
1970	2 teams		SF	N	(28G – .261)		MIL	A	(78G – .248)																
"	total		106	.249	.335	245	61	9	4	4	1.6	20	23	21	19	1	27	8	111	4	2	4	1.1	.983	OF-65, 1B-15
1971	STL	N	65	.296	.338	71	21	0	1	1	1.4	6	12	10	11	0	48	14	62	6	0	4	1.0	1.000	1B-13, OF-1
1972	BOS	A	45	.164	.260	73	12	1	0	2	2.7	4	9	8	11	0	27	2	124	7	1	13	2.9	.992	1B-15, OF-1
7 yrs.			388	.224	.319	634	142	21	0	13	2.1	53	78	70	65	2	175	37	604	33	8	37	1.7	.988	1B-106, OF-97

Jack Burdock

BURDOCK, JOHN JOSEPH (Black Jack)
B. 1851, Brooklyn, N. Y.   D. Nov. 28, 1931, Brooklyn, N. Y.
Manager 1883.

BR TR 5'9½" 158 lbs.

Year	Team		Games	BA	SA	AB	H	2B	3B	HR	HR%	R	RBI	BB	SO	SB	PH AB	PH H	PO	A	E	DP	TC/G	FA	G by Pos
1876	HAR	N	69	.259	.294	309	80	9	1	0	0.0	66	23	13	16		0	0	211	175	45	19	6.2	.896	2B-69, 3B-1
1877			58	.260	.282	277	72	6	0	0	0.0	35	9	2	16		0	0	190	201	44	25	7.5	.899	2B-55, 3B-3
1878	BOS	N	60	.260	.358	246	64	12	6	0	0.0	37	25	3	17		0	0	245	212	41	34	8.3	.918	2B-60
1879			84	.240	.284	359	86	10	4	0	0.0	64	36	9	28		0	0	303	300	59	43	7.9	.911	2B-84
1880			86	.253	.340	356	90	17	4	2	0.6	58	35	8	26		0	0	328	275	50	39	7.6	.923	2B-86
1881			73	.238	.319	282	67	12	4	1	0.4	36	24	7	18		0	0	202	208	40	35	6.2	.911	2B-72, SS-1
1882			83	.238	.301	319	76	6	7	0	0.0	36	27	9	24		0	0	223	256	35	28	6.2	.932	2B-83
1883			96	.330	.475	400	132	27	8	5	1.3	80	88	14	35		0	0	224	290	44	39	5.8	.921	2B-87, 3B-1
1884			87	.269	.380	361	97	14	4	6	1.7	65		15	52		0	0	183	278	39	39	5.7	.922	2B-87
1885			45	.142	.172	169	24	5	0	0	0.0	18	7	8	18		0	0	99	134	21	16	5.6	.917	2B-45
1886			59	.217	.253	221	48	6	1	0	0.0	26	25	11	27		0	0	145	165	33	22	5.8	.904	2B-59
1887			65	.257	.283	237	61	6	0	0	0.0	36	29	18	22	19	0	0	117	188	41	34	5.8	.882	2B-65
1888	2 teams		BOS	N	(22G – .203)		BKN	AA	(70G – .122)																
"	total		92	.142	.166	325	46	1	2	1	0.3	20	12	10	5	10	0	0	225	291	55	32	6.2	.904	2B-92
1891	BKN	N	3	.083	.083	12	1	0	0	0	0.0	1	1	1	1		0	0	4	9	0	1	4.3	1.000	2B-3
14 yrs.			960	.244	.310	3873	944	131	40	15	0.4	578	341	128	305	29	0	0	2699	2982	547	390	6.5	.912	2B-956, 3B-5, SS-1

Year	Team		Games	BA	SA	AB	H	2B	3B	HR	HR%	R	RBI	BB	SO	SB	Pinch Hit AB	H	PO	A	E	DP	TC/G	FA	G by Pos

Pete Burg

BURG, JOHN PETER
B. June 4, 1882, Chicago, Ill. D. Apr. 28, 1969, Joliet, Ill. BR TR 5'1" 150 lbs.

| 1910 | BOS | N | 13 | .326 | .370 | 46 | 15 | 0 | 1 | 0 | 0.0 | 7 | 10 | 7 | 12 | 5 | 0 | 0 | 16 | 33 | 8 | 3 | 4.4 | .860 | 3B-12, SS-1 |

Smoky Burgess

BURGESS, FORREST HARRILL
B. Feb. 6, 1927, Caroleen, N. C. BL TR 5'8½" 185 lbs.

1949	CHI	N	46	.268	.321	56	15	0	0	1	1.8	4	12	4	4	0	37	12	21	6	0	2	0.6	1.000	C-8
1951			94	.251	.315	219	55	4	2	2	0.9	21	20	21	12	2	30	5	210	35	5	6	2.7	.980	C-64
1952	PHI	N	110	.296	.429	371	110	27	2	6	1.6	49	56	49	21	3	6	3	439	47	11	6	4.5	.978	C-104
1953			102	.292	.417	312	91	17	5	4	1.3	31	36	37	17	3	9	3	395	23	3	8	4.1	.993	C-95
1954			108	.368	.510	345	127	27	5	4	1.2	41	46	42	11	1	17	6	356	30	10	4	3.7	.975	C-91
1955	2 teams		123	PHI N (7G – .190)		CIN N (116G – .306)																			
"	total		123	.301	.495	442	133	17	3	21	4.8	71	78	50	36	1	9	3	492	36	7	6	4.3	.987	C-113
1956	CIN	N	90	.275	.476	229	63	10	0	12	5.2	28	39	26	18	0	29	7	257	18	0	2	3.1	1.000	C-55
1957			90	.283	.566	205	58	14	1	14	6.8	29	39	24	16	0	39	11	223	15	3	0	2.7	.988	C-45
1958			99	.283	.410	251	71	12	1	6	2.4	28	31	22	20	0	40	11	297	21	4	2	3.3	.988	C-58
1959	PIT	N	114	.297	.485	377	112	28	5	11	2.9	41	59	31	16	0	17	7	441	39	8	4	4.3	.984	C-101
1960			110	.294	.412	337	99	15	2	7	2.1	33	39	35	13	0	20	9	485	38	3	7	4.8	.994	C-89
1961			100	.303	.486	323	98	17	3	12	3.7	37	52	30	16	1	14	4	426	27	4	4	4.6	.991	C-92
1962			130	.328	.500	360	118	19	2	13	3.6	38	61	31	19	0	5	1	550	45	7	5	4.6	.988	C-101
1963			91	.280	.394	264	74	10	1	6	2.3	20	37	24	14	0	18	6	364	40	4	4	4.5	.990	C-72
1964	2 teams		75	PIT N (68G – .246)		CHI N (7G – .200)																			
"	total		75	.244	.324	176	43	1	1	3	1.7	10	18	15	14	2	26	8	237	18	2	3	3.4	.992	C-44
1965	CHI	A	80	.286	.416	77	22	4	0	2	2.6	2	24	11	7	0	65	20	17	3	0	0	0.3	1.000	C-5
1966			79	.313	.388	67	21	5	0	0	0.0	0	15	11	8	0	66	21	4	0	0	0	0.1	1.000	C-2
1967			77	.133	.250	60	8	1	0	2	3.3	2	11	14	8	0	60	8	0	0	0	0	0.0	–	
	18 yrs.		1718	.295	.446	4471	1318	230	33	126	2.8	485	673	477	270	13	507 2nd	145 2nd	5214	441	71	63	3.3	.988	C-1139

WORLD SERIES

| 1960 | PIT | N | 5 | .333 | .389 | 18 | 6 | 1 | 0 | 0 | 0.0 | 2 | 0 | 2 | 1 | 0 | 0 | 0 | 27 | 2 | 0 | 0 | 5.8 | 1.000 | C-5 |

Tom Burgess

BURGESS, THOMAS ROLAND (Tim)
B. Sept. 1, 1927, London Ont., Canada BL TL 6' 180 lbs.

1954	STL	N	17	.048	.095	21	1	1	0	0	0.0	2	1	3	9	0	11	0	3	0	1	0	0.2	.750	OF-4
1962	LA	A	87	.196	.301	143	28	7	1	2	1.4	17	13	36	20	2	43	7	286	15	1	27	3.5	.997	1B-35, OF-2
	2 yrs.		104	.177	.274	164	29	8	1	2	1.2	19	14	39	29	2	54	7	289	15	2	27	2.9	.993	1B-35, OF-6

Bill Burgo

BURGO, WILLIAM ROSS
B. Nov. 5, 1919, Johnstown, Pa. BR TR 5'8" 185 lbs.

1943	PHI	A	17	.371	.529	70	26	4	1	1	1.4	12	9	4	1	0			45	2	1	1	2.8	.979	OF-17
1944			27	.239	.295	88	21	2	0	1	1.1	6	3	7	3	1	3	0	62	1	3	0	2.4	.955	OF-22
	2 yrs.		44	.297	.399	158	47	6	2	2	1.3	18	12	11	4	1	3	0	107	3	4	1	2.6	.965	OF-39

Bill Burich

BURICH, WILLIAM MAX
B. May 29, 1918, Calumet, Mich. BR TR 6' 180 lbs.

1942	PHI	N	25	.288	.300	80	23	1	0	0	0.0	3	7	6	13	2	3	0	49	49	8	6	4.2	.925	SS-19, 3B-3
1946			2	.000	.000	1	0	0	0	0	0.0	1	0	0	0	0	0	0	0	0	0	0	0.0	–	3B-1
	2 yrs.		27	.284	.296	81	23	1	0	0	0.0	4	7	6	13	2	3	0	49	49	8	6	3.9	.925	SS-19, 3B-4

Mack Burk

BURK, MACK EDWIN
B. Apr. 21, 1935, Nacogdoches, Tex. BR TR 6'4" 180 lbs.

1956	PHI	N	15	1.000	1.000	1	1	0	0	0	0.0	3	0	0	1	1	1	1	1	0	0	0	0.1	1.000	C-1
1958			1	.000	.000	1	0	0	0	0	0.0	0	0	0	1	0	1	0	0	0	0	0	0.0	–	
	2 yrs.		16	.500	.500	2	1	0	0	0	0.0	3	0	0	2	1	2	1	1	0	0	0	0.1	1.000	C-1

Bob Burkam

BURKAM, CHAUNCEY DePEW (Chris)
B. Oct. 13, 1892, Benton Harbor, Mich. D. May 9, 1964, Kalamazoo, Mich. BL TR 5'11" 175 lbs.

| 1915 | STL | A | 1 | .000 | .000 | 1 | 0 | 0 | 0 | 0 | 0.0 | 0 | 0 | 1 | 0 | 0 | 0 | 0 | 0 | 0 | 0 | 0 | 0.0 | – | |

Dan Burke

BURKE, DANIEL L.
B. Oct. 25, 1868, Abington, Mass. D. Mar. 20, 1933, Taunton, Mass. BR TR 5'10" 190 lbs.

1890	2 teams		41	ROC AA (32G – .216)		SYR AA (9G – .000)																			
"	total		41	.180	.189	122	22	1	0	0	0.0	15		22		2	0	0	105	18	13	2	3.3	.904	OF-29, C-13, 1B-2
1892	BOS	N	1	.000	.000	4	0	0	0	0	0.0	0		0		0	0	0	8	1	1	1	10.0	.900	C-1
	2 yrs.		42	.175	.183	126	22	1	0	0	0.0	15		22		2	0	0	113	19	14	3	3.5	.904	OF-29, C-14, 1B-2

Eddie Burke

BURKE, EDWARD D.
B. Oct. 6, 1866, Northumberland, Pa. D. Nov. 26, 1907, Utica, N. Y. BR TR 5'6" 161 lbs.

1890	2 teams		131	PHI N (100G – .263)		PIT N (31G – .210)																			
"	total		131	.251	.363	554	139	21	13	5	0.9	102	57	63	49	44	0	0	294	34	36	7	2.8	.901	OF-127, 2B-4
1891	MIL	AA	35	.236	.319	144	34	1	0	1	0.7	31	21	12	19	7	0	0	70	8	7	3	2.4	.918	OF-35
1892	2 teams		104	CIN N (15G – .146)		NY N (89G – .259)																			
"	total		104	.248	.344	404	100	11	5	6	1.5	87	45	55	41	44	0	0	206	188	61	20	4.4	.866	2B-59, OF-44, 3B-1
1893	NY	N	135	.279	.410	537	150	23	10	9	1.7	122	80	51	32	54	0	0	278	19	29	2	2.4	.911	OF-135
1894			136	.304	.410	566	172	23	11	5	0.9	121	77	37	35	34	0	0	260	17	20	3	2.2	.933	OF-136
1895	2 teams		96	NY N (40G – .257)		CIN N (56G – .268)																			
"	total		96	.263	.354	395	104	14	8	2	0.5	90	40	29	23	33	0	0	212	16	24	4	2.6	.905	OF-95
1896	CIN	N	122	.340	.426	521	177	24	9	1	0.2	120	52	41	29	53	0	0	290	13	21	3	2.7	.935	OF-122
1897			95	.266	.323	387	103	17	3	1	0.3	71	41	29		22	0	0	224	11	15	4	2.6	.940	OF-95
	8 yrs.		854	.279	.378	3508	979	142	57	30	0.9	744	413	317	228	291	0	0	1834	306	213	46	2.8	.909	OF-789, 2B-63, 3B-1

Year	Team	Games	BA	SA	AB	H	2B	3B	HR	HR%	R	RBI	BB	SO	SB	Pinch Hit AB	H	PO	A	E	DP	TC/G	FA	G by Pos

Frank Burke

BURKE, FRANK ALOYSIUS
B. Feb. 16, 1880, Carbon County, Pa. D. Sept. 17, 1946, Los Angeles, Calif. — TR

Year	Team	Games	BA	SA	AB	H	2B	3B	HR	HR%	R	RBI	BB	SO	SB	PH AB	PH H	PO	A	E	DP	TC/G	FA	G by Pos
1906	NY N	8	.333	.667	9	3	1	1	0	0.0	2	1	1		1	3	1	2	0	1	0	0.4	.667	OF-4
1907	BOS N	43	.178	.194	129	23	0	1	0	0.0	6	8	11		3	6	1	60	3	3	0	1.5	.955	OF-36
2 yrs.		51	.188	.225	138	26	1	2	0	0.0	8	9	12		4	9	2	62	3	4	0	1.4	.942	OF-40

Glenn Burke

BURKE, GLENN LAWRENCE
B. Nov. 16, 1952, Oakland, Calif. — BR TR 6' 195 lbs.

Year	Team	Games	BA	SA	AB	H	2B	3B	HR	HR%	R	RBI	BB	SO	SB	PH AB	PH H	PO	A	E	DP	TC/G	FA	G by Pos
1976	LA N	25	.239	.283	46	11	2	0	0	0.0	9	5	3	8	3	3	0	33	0	1	0	1.4	.971	OF-20
1977		83	.254	.320	169	43	8	0	1	0.6	16	13	5	22	13	9	0	98	1	3	0	1.2	.971	OF-74
1978	2 teams	LA N (16G – .211)			OAK A (78G – .235)																			
"	total	94	.233	.283	219	51	6	1	1	0.5	21	16	10	30	16	2	0	163	1	2	0	1.8	.988	OF-82, DH-2, 1B-1
1979	OAK A	23	.213	.258	89	19	2	1	0	0.0	4	4	4	10	3	0	0	46	2	0	0	2.1	1.000	OF-23
4 yrs.		225	.237	.291	523	124	18	2	2	0.4	50	38	22	70	35	12	0	340	4	6	0	1.6	.983	OF-199, DH-2, 1B-1

LEAGUE CHAMPIONSHIP SERIES

| 1977 | LA N | 4 | .000 | .000 | 7 | 0 | 0 | 0 | 0 | 0.0 | 0 | 0 | 0 | 3 | 0 | 0 | 0 | 3 | 0 | 0 | 0 | 0.8 | 1.000 | OF-4 |

WORLD SERIES

| 1977 | LA N | 3 | .200 | .200 | 5 | 1 | 0 | 0 | 0 | 0.0 | 0 | 0 | 0 | 1 | 0 | 0 | 0 | 10 | 0 | 0 | 0 | 3.3 | 1.000 | OF-3 |

Jimmy Burke

BURKE, JAMES TIMOTHY (Sunset Jimmy)
B. Oct. 12, 1874, St. Louis, Mo. D. Mar. 26, 1942, St. Louis, Mo. — BR TR 5'7" 160 lbs.
Manager 1905, 1918-20.

Year	Team	Games	BA	SA	AB	H	2B	3B	HR	HR%	R	RBI	BB	SO	SB	PH AB	PH H	PO	A	E	DP	TC/G	FA	G by Pos
1898	CLE N	13	.105	.132	38	4	1	0	0	0.0	1	1	2		1	0	0	8	21	5	0	2.6	.853	3B-13
1899	STL N	2	.333	.333	6	2	0	0	0	0.0	1	0	1		0	0	0	4	8	1	2	6.5	.923	2B-2
1901	3 teams	MIL A (64G – .206)			CHI A (42G – .264)				PIT N (14G – .196)															
"	total	120	.225	.255	432	97	13	0	0	0.0	48	51	33		17	0	0	172	291	73	18	4.5	.864	3B-89, SS-31
1902	PIT N	60	.296	.374	203	60	12	2	0	0.0	24	26	17		9	2	0	90	120	23	8	3.9	.901	2B-27, OF-18, 3B-9, SS-4
1903	STL N	115	.285	.329	431	123	13	3	0	0.0	55	42	23		28	1	0	170	257	40	14	4.1	.914	3B-93, 2B-15, OF-5
1904		118	.227	.266	406	92	10	3	0	0.0	37	37	15		17	0	0	148	217	42	10	3.4	.897	3B-118
1905		122	.225	.276	431	97	9	5	1	0.2	34	30	21		15	0	0	174	238	34	13	3.7	.924	3B-122
7 yrs.		550	.244	.289	1947	475	58	13	1	0.1	200	187	112		87	0	0	766	1152	218	65	3.9	.898	3B-444, 2B-44, SS-35, OF-23

Joe Burke

BURKE, JOSEPH A.
B. Cincinnati, Ohio Deceased. — 5'7" 160 lbs.

Year	Team	Games	BA	SA	AB	H	2B	3B	HR	HR%	R	RBI	BB	SO	SB	PH AB	PH H	PO	A	E	DP	TC/G	FA	G by Pos
1890	STL AA	2	.667	.667	6	4	0	0	0	0.0	3		0		0	0	0	0	6	2	0	4.0	.750	3B-2
1891	CIN AA	1	.250	.250	4	1	0	0	0	0.0	0	1	0	2	0	0	0	4	5	0	0	9.0	1.000	2B-1
2 yrs.		3	.500	.500	10	5	0	0	0	0.0	3	1	1	2	0	0	0	4	11	2	0	5.7	.882	3B-2, 2B-1

John Burke

BURKE, JOHN PATRICK
B. Jan. 27, 1877, Hazleton, Pa. D. Aug. 4, 1950, Jersey City, N. J. — BR TR

Year	Team	Games	BA	SA	AB	H	2B	3B	HR	HR%	R	RBI	BB	SO	SB	PH AB	PH H	PO	A	E	DP	TC/G	FA	G by Pos
1902	NY N	4	.154	.154	13	2	0	0	0	0.0	0	0	0		0	0	0	5	3	0	0	2.0	1.000	OF-2, P-2

Leo Burke

BURKE, LEO PATRICK
B. May 6, 1934, Hagerstown, Md. — BR TR 5'11" 185 lbs.

Year	Team	Games	BA	SA	AB	H	2B	3B	HR	HR%	R	RBI	BB	SO	SB	PH AB	PH H	PO	A	E	DP	TC/G	FA	G by Pos
1958	BAL A	7	.455	.818	11	5	1	0	1	9.1	4	4	1	2	0	3	1	2	0	1	0	0.4	.667	OF-3, 3B-1
1959		5	.200	.200	10	2	0	0	0	0.0	1	0	1	5	0	2	0	4	4	0	0	1.6	1.000	3B-2, 2B-2
1961	LA A	6	.000	.000	5	0	0	0	0	0.0	0	0	0	5	0	5	0	0	0	0	0	0.0	—	
1962		19	.266	.469	64	17	1	0	4	6.3	8	14	5	11	0	2	0	27	8	4	2	2.1	.897	OF-12, 3B-4, SS-1
1963	2 teams	STL N (30G – .204)			CHI N (27G – .184)																			
"	total	57	.194	.327	98	19	2	1	3	3.1	10	12	8	25	0	28	8	72	35	7	7	2.0	.939	OF-11, 2B-10, 3B-5, 1B-4
1964	CHI N	59	.262	.340	103	27	3	1	1	1.0	11	14	7	31	0	34	10	46	11	2	2	1.0	.966	OF-18, 2B-5, 3B-4, 1B-2, C-1
1965		12	.200	.200	10	2	0	0	0	0.0	0	0	0	4	0	9	1	2	0	0	0	0.2	1.000	C-2, OF-1
7 yrs.		165	.239	.365	301	72	7	2	9	3.0	33	45	21	79	0	83	20	153	58	14	11	1.4	.938	OF-45, 2B-17, 3B-16, 1B-6, C-3, SS-1

Les Burke

BURKE, LESLIE KINGSTON (Buck)
B. Dec. 18, 1902, Lynn, Mass. D. May 6, 1975, Danvers, Mass. — BL TR 5'9" 168 lbs.

Year	Team	Games	BA	SA	AB	H	2B	3B	HR	HR%	R	RBI	BB	SO	SB	PH AB	PH H	PO	A	E	DP	TC/G	FA	G by Pos
1923	DET A	7	.100	.100	10	1	0	0	0	0.0	2	1	2		0	1	0	1	3	2	0	0.9	.667	3B-2, 2B-1, C-1
1924		72	.253	.328	241	61	10	4	0	0.0	30	17	22	20	2	7	4	133	184	15	32	4.6	.955	2B-58, SS-6
1925		77	.289	.356	180	52	6	3	0	0.0	32	24	17	8	4	22	4	100	130	9	27	3.1	.962	2B-52
1926		38	.227	.240	75	17	1	0	0	0.0	9	4	7	3	1	13	1	35	54	6	8	2.5	.937	2B-15, 3B-7, SS-1
4 yrs.		194	.259	.320	506	131	17	7	0	0.0	73	47	46	32	7	43	9	269	371	32	67	3.5	.952	2B-126, 3B-9, SS-7, C-1

Mike Burke

BURKE, MICHAEL E.
B. 1855, Cincinnati, Ohio D. June 9, 1889, Albany, N. Y. — BR TR 6' 190 lbs.

Year	Team	Games	BA	SA	AB	H	2B	3B	HR	HR%	R	RBI	BB	SO	SB	PH AB	PH H	PO	A	E	DP	TC/G	FA	G by Pos
1879	CIN N	28	.222	.248	117	26	3	0	0	0.0	13	8	2		0	0	0	36	62	32	3	4.6	.754	SS-19, OF-5, 3B-5

Pat Burke

BURKE, PATRICK EDWARD
B. May 13, 1901, St. Louis, Mo. D. July 7, 1965, St. Louis, Mo. — BR TR 5'10½" 170 lbs.

Year	Team	Games	BA	SA	AB	H	2B	3B	HR	HR%	R	RBI	BB	SO	SB	PH AB	PH H	PO	A	E	DP	TC/G	FA	G by Pos
1924	STL A	1	.000	.000	3	0	0	0	0	0.0	1	0	1		0	0	0	0	0	0	0	0.0	—	3B-1

Jesse Burkett

BURKETT, JESSE CAIL (The Crab)
B. Dec. 4, 1868, Wheeling, W. Va. D. May 27, 1953, Worcester, Mass. — BL TL 5'8" 155 lbs.
Hall of Fame 1946.

Year	Team	Games	BA	SA	AB	H	2B	3B	HR	HR%	R	RBI	BB	SO	SB	PH AB	PH H	PO	A	E	DP	TC/G	FA	G by Pos
1890	NY N	101	.309	.461	401	124	23	13	4	1.0	67	60	33	52	14	0	0	111	56	36	5	2.0	.823	OF-90, P-21
1891	CLE N	42	.269	.359	167	45	7	4	0	0.0	29	13	23	19	1	0	0	53	5	7	1	1.5	.892	OF-42
1892		145	.275	.375	608	167	15	14	6	1.0	119	66	67	59	36	0	0	271	20	31	7	2.2	.904	OF-145
1893		125	.348	.491	511	178	25	15	6	1.2	145	82	98	23	39	0	0	239	19	46	5	2.4	.849	OF-125

Year	Team		Games	BA	SA	AB	H	2B	3B	HR	HR%	R	RBI	BB	SO	SB	Pinch Hit AB	Pinch Hit H	PO	A	E	DP	TC/G	FA	G by Pos

Jesse Burkett *continued*

Year	Team		Games	BA	SA	AB	H	2B	3B	HR	HR%	R	RBI	BB	SO	SB	AB	H	PO	A	E	DP	TC/G	FA	G by Pos
1894			125	.358	.509	523	187	27	14	8	1.5	138	94	84	27	28	0	0	242	17	24		2.3	.915	OF-125, P-1
1895			131	.409	.524	550	225	22	13	5	0.9	153	83	74	31	41	0	0	273	17	38	4	2.5	.884	OF-132
1896			133	.410	.541	586	240	27	16	6	1.0	160	72	49	19	34	0	0	269	18	23	4	2.3	.926	OF-133
1897			128	.383	.476	517	198	28	7	2	0.4	129	60	76		28	0	0	226	18	13	3	2.0	.949	OF-127
1898			150	.341	.399	624	213	18	9	0	0.0	114	42	69		19	0	0	268	17	19	3	2.0	.938	OF-150
1899	STL	N	141	.396	.500	558	221	21	8	7	1.3	116	71	67		25	0	0	298	23	23	3	2.4	.933	OF-140, 2B-1
1900			141	.363	.474	559	203	11	15	7	1.3	88	68	62		32	0	0	337	17	25	6	2.7	.934	OF-141
1901			142	.382	.524	597	228	21	17	10	1.7	139	75	59		27	0	0	307	17	27	4	2.5	.923	OF-142
1902	STL	A	137	.306	.419	549	168	29	7	5	0.9	97	52	71		23	0	0	301	20	26	6	2.5	.925	OF-137, SS-1, 3B-1, P-1
1903			133	.296	.379	514	152	20	7	3	0.6	74	40	52		17	0	0	230	10	15	4	1.9	.941	OF-132
1904			147	.273	.340	576	157	15	9	2	0.3	72	27	78		12	0	0	266	24	18	4	2.1	.942	OF-147
1905	BOS	A	149	.257	.346	573	147	13	13	4	0.7	78	47	67		13	0	0	276	11	22	0	2.1	.929	OF-149
16 yrs.			2070	.339	.448	8413	2853	322	183	75	0.9	1718	952	1029	230	389	0	0	3967	309	393	64	2.3	.916	OF-2057, P-23, SS-1, 3B-1, 2B-1

Ellis Burks

BURKS, ELLIS RENA
B. Sept. 11, 1964, Vicksburg, Miss.

BR TR 6'2" 175 lbs.

Year	Team		Games	BA	SA	AB	H	2B	3B	HR	HR%	R	RBI	BB	SO	SB	AB	H	PO	A	E	DP	TC/G	FA	G by Pos
1987	BOS	A	133	.272	.441	558	152	30	2	20	3.6	94	59	41	98	27	0	0	320	15	4	2	2.5	.988	OF-132
1988			144	.294	.481	540	159	37	5	18	3.3	93	92	62	89	25	0	0	370	9	9	0	2.7	.977	OF-142, DH-2
1989			97	.303	.471	399	121	19	6	12	3.0	73	61	36	52	21	0	0	245	7	6	3	2.7	.977	OF-95, DH-1
3 yrs.			374	.289	.464	1497	432	86	13	50	3.3	260	212	139	239	73	0	0	935	31	19	5	2.6	.981	OF-369, DH-3

LEAGUE CHAMPIONSHIP SERIES

Year	Team		Games	BA	SA	AB	H	2B	3B	HR	HR%	R	RBI	BB	SO	SB	AB	H	PO	A	E	DP	TC/G	FA	G by Pos
1988	BOS	A	4	.235	.294	17	4	1	0	0	0.0	2	1	0	3	0	0	0	10	0	0	0	2.5	1.000	OF-4

Rick Burleson

BURLESON, RICHARD PAUL (Rooster)
B. Apr. 29, 1951, Lynwood, Calif.

BR TR 5'10" 165 lbs.

Year	Team		Games	BA	SA	AB	H	2B	3B	HR	HR%	R	RBI	BB	SO	SB	AB	H	PO	A	E	DP	TC/G	FA	G by Pos
1974	BOS	A	114	.284	.372	384	109	22	1	4	1.0	36	44	21	34	3	1	0	209	329	21	65	4.9	.962	SS-88, 2B-31, 3B-2
1975			158	.252	.329	580	146	25	1	6	1.0	66	62	45	44	8	0	0	267	498	29	102	5.0	.963	SS-158
1976			152	.291	.383	540	157	27	1	7	1.3	75	42	60	37	14	0	0	274	478	34	88	5.2	.957	SS-152
1977			154	.293	.382	663	194	36	7	3	0.5	80	52	47	69	13	0	0	285	482	24	111	5.1	.970	SS-154
1978			145	.248	.339	626	155	32	5	5	0.8	75	49	40	71	8	0	0	285	482	15	100	5.4	.981	SS-144
1979			153	.278	.368	627	174	32	5	5	0.8	93	60	35	54	9	0	0	272	523	16	109	5.3	.980	SS-153
1980			155	.278	.366	644	179	29	2	8	1.2	89	51	62	51	12	0	0	301	528	22	147	5.5	.974	SS-155
1981	CAL	A	109	.293	.372	430	126	17	1	5	1.2	53	33	42	38	4	0	0	208	394	13	88	5.6	.979	SS-109
1982			11	.156	.178	45	7	1	0	0	0.0	4	2	6	3	0	0	0	19	51	1	12	6.5	.986	SS-11
1983			33	.286	.345	119	34	7	0	0	0.0	22	11	12	12	2	1	0	54	102	5	16	4.9	.969	SS-31
1984			7	.000	.000	4	0	0	0	0	0.0	2	0	0	2	0	0	0	0	0	0	0	0.0	—	
1986			93	.284	.391	271	77	14	0	5	1.8	35	29	33	32	1	11	3	62	90	3	15	1.7	.981	DH-38, SS-37, 2B-6, 3B-4
1987	BAL	A	62	.209	.316	206	43	14	1	2	1.0	26	14	17	30	0	2	0	112	145	6	39	4.2	.977	2B-55, DH-7
13 yrs.			1346	.273	.361	5139	1401	256	23	50	1.0	656	449	420	477	72	21	4	2348	4102	189	892	4.9	.972	SS-1192, 2B-92, DH-45, 3B-6

LEAGUE CHAMPIONSHIP SERIES

Year	Team		Games	BA	SA	AB	H	2B	3B	HR	HR%	R	RBI	BB	SO	SB	AB	H	PO	A	E	DP	TC/G	FA	G by Pos
1975	BOS	A	3	.444	.667	9	4	2	0	0	0.0	2	1	0	0	0	0	0	4	12	1	1	5.7	.941	SS-3
1986	CAL	A	4	.273	.273	11	3	0	0	0	0.0	0	0	1	1	1	1	0	3	5	0	0	2.0	1.000	2B-2, DH-1
2 yrs.			7	.350	.450	20	7	2	0	0	0.0	2	1	1	1	1	1	0	7	17	1	1	3.6	.960	SS-3, 2B-2, DH-1

WORLD SERIES

Year	Team		Games	BA	SA	AB	H	2B	3B	HR	HR%	R	RBI	BB	SO	SB	AB	H	PO	A	E	DP	TC/G	FA	G by Pos
1975	BOS	A	7	.292	.333	24	7	1	0	0	0.0	1	2	4	2	0	0	0	9	19	1	4	4.1	.966	SS-7

Hercules Burnett

BURNETT, HERCULES H.
B. Aug. 13, 1869, Louisville, Ky.   D. Oct. 4, 1936, Louisville, Ky.

BR

Year	Team		Games	BA	SA	AB	H	2B	3B	HR	HR%	R	RBI	BB	SO	SB	AB	H	PO	A	E	DP	TC/G	FA	G by Pos
1888	LOU	AA	1	.000	.000	4	0	0	0	0	0.0	1											3.0	.667	OF-1
1895	LOU	N	5	.412	.882	17	7	0	1	2	11.8	6	3	2	2	0			18	1	3	1	4.4	.864	OF-4, 1B-1
2 yrs.			6	.333	.714	21	7	0	1	2	9.5	7	3	2	2	0			20	1	4	1	4.2	.840	OF-5, 1B-1

Jack Burnett

BURNETT, JOHN P.
B. Dec. 2, 1889, Mo.,   D. Sept. 8, 1929, Taft, Calif.

Year	Team		Games	BA	SA	AB	H	2B	3B	HR	HR%	R	RBI	BB	SO	SB	AB	H	PO	A	E	DP	TC/G	FA	G by Pos
1907	STL	N	59	.238	.316	206	49	8	4	0	0.0	18	12	15		5	0	0	98	8	5	1	1.9	.955	OF-59

Johnny Burnett

BURNETT, JOHN HENDERSON
B. Nov. 1, 1904, Bartow, Fla.   D. Aug. 13, 1959, Tampa, Fla.

BL TR 5'11" 175 lbs.

Year	Team		Games	BA	SA	AB	H	2B	3B	HR	HR%	R	RBI	BB	SO	SB	AB	H	PO	A	E	DP	TC/G	FA	G by Pos
1927	CLE	A	17	.000	.000	8	0	0	0	0	0.0	5	0	0	3	1	6	0	2	3	1	0	0.4	.833	2B-2
1928			3	.500	.500	10	5	0	0	0	0.0	3	1	0		1			6	7	2	3	5.0	.867	SS-2
1929			19	.152	.182	33	5	1	0	0	0.0	2	2	1	1	0	1	1	30	38	6	3	3.9	.919	SS-10, 2B-4
1930			54	.312	.388	170	53	13	0	0	0.0	28	20	17	8	2	8	3	44	105	11	14	3.0	.931	3B-27, SS-19
1931			111	.300	.389	427	128	25	5	1	0.2	85	52	39	25	1			194	296	34	52	4.7	.935	SS-63, 2B-35, 3B-21, OF-1
1932			129	.297	.385	512	152	23	5	4	0.8	81	53	46	27	2	1	1	232	373	37	62	5.0	.943	SS-103, 2B-26
1933			83	.272	.341	261	71	11	2	1	0.4	39	29	23	14	3	12	1	124	198	23	31	4.2	.933	SS-41, 2B-17, 3B-12
1934			72	.293	.409	208	61	11	2	3	1.4	28	30	18	11	1	14	3	73	93	9	12	2.4	.949	3B-42, SS-9, 2B-3, OF-2
1935	STL	A	70	.223	.282	206	46	10	1	0	0.0	17	26	19	16	1	16	4	71	136	13	18	3.1	.941	3B-31, SS-18, 2B-12
9 yrs.			558	.284	.366	1835	521	94	15	9	0.5	288	213	163	107	15	61	14	776	1249	136	196	3.9	.937	SS-265, 3B-133, 2B-99, OF-3

Charlie Burns

BURNS, CHARLES BIRMINGHAM
B. May 15, 1879, Bay View, Md.   D. June 6, 1968, Havre de Grace, Md.

BR TR 6' 175 lbs.

Year	Team		Games	BA	SA	AB	H	2B	3B	HR	HR%	R	RBI	BB	SO	SB	AB	H	PO	A	E	DP	TC/G	FA	G by Pos
1902	BAL	A	1	1.000	1.000	1	1	0	0	0	0.0	0	0	0		0	1	1	0	0	0	0	0.0	—	

Dick Burns

BURNS, RICHARD SIMON
B. Dec. 26, 1863, Holyoke, Mass.   D. Nov. 11, 1937, Holyoke, Mass.

BL TL 140 lbs.

Year	Team		Games	BA	SA	AB	H	2B	3B	HR	HR%	R	RBI	BB	SO	SB	Pinch Hit AB	Pinch Hit H	PO	A	E	DP	TC/G	FA	G by Pos

Dick Burns *continued*

Year	Team		Games	BA	SA	AB	H	2B	3B	HR	HR%	R	RBI	BB	SO	SB	AB	H	PO	A	E	DP	TC/G	FA	G by Pos
1883	DET	N	37	.186	.250	140	26	7	1	0	0.0	11		2	22		0	0	22	32	14	2	1.8	.794	OF-24, P-17
1884	CIN	U	79	.306	.457	350	107	17	12	4	1.1	84		5			0	0	87	81	26	1	2.5	.866	OF-44, P-40, SS-2
1885	STL	N	14	.222	.296	54	12	2	1	0	0.0	2	4	3	8		0	0	13	5	7	1	1.8	.720	OF-14, P-1
3 yrs.			130	.267	.388	544	145	26	14	4	0.7	97	4	10	30		0	0	122	118	47	4	2.2	.836	OF-82, P-58, SS-2

Ed Burns

BURNS, EDWARD JAMES
B. Oct. 31, 1888, San Francisco, Calif. D. June 1, 1942, Monterey, Calif.

BR TR 5'6" 165 lbs.

Year	Team		Games	BA	SA	AB	H	2B	3B	HR	HR%	R	RBI	BB	SO	SB	AB	H	PO	A	E	DP	TC/G	FA	G by Pos
1912	STL	N	1	.000	.000	1	0	0	0	0	0.0	0	1	0	0	0	0	0	0	0	0	0	0.0	–	C-1
1913	PHI	N	17	.200	.300	30	6	3	0	0	0.0	3	3	6	3	2	1	0	38	10	1	2	2.9	.980	C-15
1914			70	.259	.338	139	36	3	4	0	0.0	8	16	20	12	5	14	3	180	72	14	5	3.8	.947	C-55
1915			67	.241	.270	174	42	5	0	0	0.0	11	16	20	12	1	5	2	241	61	6	6	4.6	.981	C-67
1916			78	.233	.279	219	51	8	1	0	0.0	14	14	16	18	3	2	0	285	87	8	5	4.9	.979	C-75, OF-1, SS-1
1917			20	.204	.224	49	10	1	0	0	0.0	2	6	1	5	2	5	0	47	20	2	0	3.5	.971	C-15
1918			68	.207	.223	184	38	1	1	0	0.0	10	9	20	9	1	0	0	184	77	5	3	3.9	.981	C-68
7 yrs.			321	.230	.271	796	183	21	6	0	0.0	48	65	83	59	14	27	5	975	327	36	21	4.2	.973	C-296, OF-1, SS-1
WORLD SERIES																									
1915	PHI	N	5	.188	.188	16	3	0	0	0	0.0	1	0	1	2	0	0	0	27	9	1	2	7.4	.973	C-5

George Burns

BURNS, GEORGE HENRY (Tioga George)
B. Jan. 31, 1893, Niles, Ohio D. Jan. 7, 1978, Kirkland, Wash.

BR TR 6'1½" 180 lbs.

Year	Team		Games	BA	SA	AB	H	2B	3B	HR	HR%	R	RBI	BB	SO	SB	AB	H	PO	A	E	DP	TC/G	FA	G by Pos
1914	DET	A	137	.291	.389	478	139	22	5	5	1.0	55	57	32	56	23	0	0	1576	79	30	72	12.3	.982	1B-137
1915			105	.253	.352	392	99	18	3	5	1.3	49	50	22	51	9	1	0	1155	57	17	65	11.7	.986	1B-104
1916			135	.286	.382	479	137	22	6	4	0.8	60	73	22	30	12	11	3	1355	54	22	71	10.6	.985	1B-124
1917	PHI	A	119	.226	.317	407	92	14	10	1	0.2	42	40	15	33	3	15	2	1127	57	12	44	10.1	.990	1B-104
1918		A	130	.352	.467	505	178	22	9	6	1.2	61	70	23	25	8	0	0	1389	104	27	109	11.7	.982	1B-128, OF-2
1919			126	.296	.447	470	139	29	9	8	1.7	63	57	19	18	15	5	0	971	75	24	46	8.5	.978	1B-86, OF-34
1920 2 teams	PHI	A	(22G – .233)			CLE	A	(44G – .268)																	
" total			66	.250	.353	116	29	7	1	1	0.9	8	20	10	10	5	39	11	58	4	2	2	1.0	.969	OF-13, 1B-12
1921	CLE	A	84	.361	.480	244	88	21	4	0	0.0	52	48	13	19	2	10	2	534	41	6	40	6.9	.990	1B-73
1922	BOS	A	147	.306	.446	558	171	32	5	12	2.2	71	73	20	28	8	6	2	1412	94	20	103	10.4	.987	1B-140
1923			146	.328	.470	551	181	47	5	7	1.3	91	82	45	33	9	0	0	1485	92	16	103	10.9	.990	1B-146
1924	CLE	A	129	.310	.437	462	143	37	5	4	0.9	64	66	29	27	14	2	0	1227	110	18	85	10.5	.987	1B-127
1925			127	.336	.473	488	164	41	4	6	1.2	69	79	24	24	16	1	1	1195	82	14	94	10.2	.989	1B-126
1926			151	.358	.494	603	216	64	3	4	0.7	97	114	28	33	13	0	0	1499	99	19	122	10.7	.988	1B-151
1927			140	.319	.435	549	175	51	2	3	0.5	84	78	42	27	13	1	0	1362	102	15	111	10.6	.990	1B-139
1928 2 teams	CLE	A	(82G – .249)			NY	A	(4G – .500)																	
" total			86	.254	.390	213	54	12	1	5	2.3	30	30	17	12	2	30	6	477	38	8	44	6.1	.985	1B-55
1929 2 teams	NY	A	(9G – .000)			PHI	A	(29G – .265)																	
" total			38	.224	.362	58	13	5	0	1	1.7	5	11	2	7	1	17	0	99	5	0	9	2.7	1.000	1B-19
16 yrs.			1866	.307	.429	6573	2018	444	72	72	1.1	901	948	363	433	153	138	27	16921	1093	250	1120	9.8	.986	1B-1671, OF-49
WORLD SERIES																									
1920	CLE	A	5	.300	.400	10	3	0	0	0	0.0	1	3	3	0	0	1	1	38	1	1	2	8.0	.975	1B-4
1929	PHI	A	1	.000	.000	2	0	0	0	0	0.0	0	0	0	1	0	2	0	0	0	0	0	0.0	–	
2 yrs.			6	.250	.333	12	3	0	0	0	0.0	1	3	3	4	0	3	1	38	1	1	2	6.7	.975	1B-4

George Burns

BURNS, GEORGE JOSEPH
B. Nov. 24, 1889, Utica, N.Y. D. Aug. 15, 1966, Gloversville, N.Y.

BR TR 5'7" 160 lbs.

Year	Team		Games	BA	SA	AB	H	2B	3B	HR	HR%	R	RBI	BB	SO	SB	AB	H	PO	A	E	DP	TC/G	FA	G by Pos
1911	NY	N	6	.059	.059	17	1	0	0	0	0.0	2		0	1	0	0	0	7	0	0	0	1.2	1.000	OF-6
1912			29	.294	.373	51	15	4	0	0	0.0	11	3	8	8	7	2	1	24	3	0	1	0.9	1.000	OF-23
1913			150	.286	.370	605	173	37	4	2	0.3	81	54	58	74	40	0	0	321	22	13	4	2.4	.963	OF-150
1914			154	.303	.417	561	170	35	10	3	0.5	100	60	89	53	62	0	0	326	19	18	5	2.4	.950	OF-154
1915			155	.272	.375	622	169	27	14	3	0.5	83	51	56	57	27	0	0	278	13	12	4	2.0	.960	OF-155
1916			155	.279	.368	623	174	24	8	5	0.8	105	41	63	47	37	0	0	289	19	12	3	2.1	.963	OF-155
1917			152	.302	.412	597	180	25	13	5	0.8	103	45	75	55	40	0	0	325	16	9	4	2.3	.974	OF-152
1918			119	.290	.389	465	135	22	6	4	0.9	80	51	43	37	40	0	0	292	10	11	1	2.6	.965	OF-119
1919			139	.303	.404	534	162	30	9	2	0.4	86	46	82	37	40	0	0	290	15	3	4	2.2	.990	OF-139
1920			154	.287	.399	631	181	35	9	6	1.0	115	46	76	48	22	0	0	336	11	6	5	2.3	.983	OF-154
1921			149	.299	.395	605	181	28	9	4	0.7	111	61	80	24	19	0	0	360	17	11	2	2.6	.972	OF-149, 3B-1
1922	CIN	N	156	.285	.353	631	180	20	10	2	0.3	104	53	78	38	30	0	0	386	20	10	3	2.7	.976	OF-156
1923			154	.274	.375	614	168	27	13	3	0.5	99	45	101	46	12	0	0	327	11	14	3	2.3	.960	OF-154
1924			93	.256	.342	336	86	19	2	2	0.6	43	33	29	21	3	3	2	168	13	7	4	2.0	.963	OF-90
1925	PHI	N	88	.292	.390	349	102	29	1	1	0.3	65	22	33	20	4	0	0	189	9	2	2	2.3	.990	OF-88
15 yrs.			1853	.287	.384	7241	2077	362	108	41	0.6	1188	611	872	565	383	5	3	3918	198	128	43	2.3	.970	OF-1844, 3B-1
WORLD SERIES																									
1913	NY	N	5	.158	.263	19	3	2	0	0	0.0	2	1	1	5	1	0	0	14	0	1	0	3.0	.933	OF-5
1917			6	.227	.227	22	5	0	0	0	0.0	3	2	3	6	1	0	0	10	0	0	0	1.7	1.000	OF-6
1921			8	.333	.515	33	11	4	1	0	0.0	2	3	3	5	1	0	0	9	0	0	0	1.1	1.000	OF-8
3 yrs.			19	.257	.365	74	19	6	1	0	0.0	7	7	16	3	0	0	33	0	1	0	1.8	.971	OF-19

Jack Burns

BURNS, JOHN IRVING (Slug)
B. Aug. 31, 1907, Cambridge, Mass. D. Apr. 18, 1975, Brighton, Mass.

BL TL 5'10½" 175 lbs.

Year	Team		Games	BA	SA	AB	H	2B	3B	HR	HR%	R	RBI	BB	SO	SB	AB	H	PO	A	E	DP	TC/G	FA	G by Pos
1930	STL	A	8	.300	.400	30	9	3	0	0	0.0	5	2	5	5	0	0	0	70	6	0	10	9.5	1.000	1B-8
1931			144	.260	.353	570	148	27	7	4	0.7	75	70	42	58	19	1	0	1346	125	11	131	10.3	.993	1B-143
1932			150	.305	.438	617	188	33	8	11	1.8	111	70	61	43	17	0	0	1399	101	12	130	10.1	.992	1B-150
1933			144	.288	.417	556	160	43	4	7	1.3	89	71	56	51	11	1	0	1336	81	12	129	9.9	.992	1B-143
1934			154	.257	.392	612	157	28	8	13	2.1	86	73	62	47	9	0	0	1365	81	12	132	9.5	.992	1B-154
1935			143	.286	.368	549	157	28	1	5	0.9	77	67	68	49	3	0	0	1239	57	11	115	9.1	.992	1B-141

Year Team	Games	BA	SA	AB	H	2B	3B	HR	HR%	R	RBI	BB	SO	SB	Pinch Hit AB	Pinch Hit H	PO	A	E	DP	TC/G	FA	G by Pos

Jack Burns *continued*

Year Team	Games	BA	SA	AB	H	2B	3B	HR	HR%	R	RBI	BB	SO	SB	PH AB	PH H	PO	A	E	DP	TC/G	FA	G by Pos
1936 2 teams		STL A (9G – .214)			DET A (138G – .283)																		
" total	147	.281	.378	572	161	37	3	4	0.7	98	64	82	46	4	6	3	1308	74	8	129	9.5	.994	1B-140
7 yrs.	890	.280	.392	3506	980	199	31	44	1.3	541	417	376	299	63	8	3	8063	525	66	776	9.7	.992	1B-879

Jim Burns

BURNS, JAMES M.
B. Quincy, Ill. Deceased.

5'7" 168 lbs.

Year Team	Games	BA	SA	AB	H	2B	3B	HR	HR%	R	RBI	BB	SO	SB	PH AB	PH H	PO	A	E	DP	TC/G	FA	G by Pos
1888 KC AA	15	.303	.303	66	20	0	0	0	0.0	13	4	1		6	0	0	25	4	5	2	2.3	.853	OF-15
1889	134	.304	.408	579	176	23	11	5	0.9	103	97	20	68	56	0	0	323	12	33	4	2.7	.910	OF-134, 3B-1
1891 WAS AA	20	.317	.390	82	26	6	0	0	0.0	15	10	6	10	2	0	0	27	6	11	0	2.2	.750	OF-20, SS-1
3 yrs.	169	.305	.396	727	222	29	11	5	0.7	131	111	27	78	64	0	0	375	22	49	6	2.6	.890	OF-169, SS-1, 3B-1

Joe Burns

BURNS, JOSEPH FRANCIS
B. Mar. 26, 1889, Ipswich, Mass. D. July 12, 1987, Beverly, Mass.

BL TL 5'11" 170 lbs.

Year Team	Games	BA	SA	AB	H	2B	3B	HR	HR%	R	RBI	BB	SO	SB	PH AB	PH H	PO	A	E	DP	TC/G	FA	G by Pos
1910 CIN N	1	1.000	1.000	1	1	0	0	0	0.0	0		0			0	0	0	0	0	0	0.0	–	
1913 DET A	4	.385	.385	13	5	0	0	0	0.0	0	1	2	4	1	0	0	7	0	0	0	1.8	1.000	OF-4
2 yrs.	5	.429	.429	14	6	0	0	0	0.0	0	1	2	4	1	0	0	7	0	0	0	1.4	1.000	OF-4

Joe Burns

BURNS, JOSEPH FRANCIS
B. Feb. 25, 1900, Trenton, N. J. D. Jan. 7, 1986, Trenton, N. J.

BR TR 6' 175 lbs.

Year Team	Games	BA	SA	AB	H	2B	3B	HR	HR%	R	RBI	BB	SO	SB	PH AB	PH H	PO	A	E	DP	TC/G	FA	G by Pos
1924 CHI A	8	.105	.105	19	2	0	0	0	0.0	1	0	0	2	0	2	0	12	2	1	1	1.9	.933	C-6

Joe Burns

BURNS, JOSEPH JAMES
B. June 17, 1916, Bryn Mawr, Pa. D. June 24, 1974, Bryn Mawr, Pa.

BR TR 5'10½" 175 lbs.

Year Team	Games	BA	SA	AB	H	2B	3B	HR	HR%	R	RBI	BB	SO	SB	PH AB	PH H	PO	A	E	DP	TC/G	FA	G by Pos
1943 BOS N	52	.207	.252	135	28	3	0	1	0.7	12	5	8	25	2	10	1	37	66	7	6	2.1	.936	3B-34, OF-4
1944 PHI A	28	.240	.307	75	18	2	0	1	1.3	5	8	4	8	0	2	1	28	37	7	5	2.6	.903	3B-17, 2B-9
1945	31	.256	.289	90	23	1	1	0	0.0	7	3	4	17	0	6	2	32	7	2	1	1.3	.951	OF-13, 3B-5, 1B-1
3 yrs.	111	.230	.277	300	69	6	1	2	0.7	24	16	16	50	2	18	4	97	110	16	12	2.0	.928	3B-56, OF-23, 2B-9, 1B-1

John Burns

BURNS, JOHN JOSEPH
B. May 13, 1880, Avoca, Pa. D. June 24, 1957, Waterford, Conn.

BR TR 5'10" 160 lbs.

Year Team	Games	BA	SA	AB	H	2B	3B	HR	HR%	R	RBI	BB	SO	SB	PH AB	PH H	PO	A	E	DP	TC/G	FA	G by Pos
1903 DET A	11	.270	.270	37	10	0	0	0	0.0	2	3	1		0	0	0	19	33	1	5	4.8	.981	2B-11
1904	4	.125	.125	16	2	0	0	0	0.0	3	1	1		1	0	0	11	9	1	1	5.3	.952	2B-4
2 yrs.	15	.226	.226	53	12	0	0	0	0.0	5	4	2		1	0	0	30	42	2	6	4.9	.973	2B-15

Oyster Burns

BURNS, THOMAS P.
B. Sept. 6, 1864, Philadelphia, Pa. D. Nov. 11, 1928, Brooklyn, N. Y.

BR TR 5'8" 183 lbs.

Year Team	Games	BA	SA	AB	H	2B	3B	HR	HR%	R	RBI	BB	SO	SB	PH AB	PH H	PO	A	E	DP	TC/G	FA	G by Pos
1884 2 teams		WIL U (2G – .143)			BAL AA (35G – .298)																		
" total	37	.290	.536	138	40	2	7	6	4.3	34		8			0	0	51	41	15	2	2.9	.860	OF-24, 2B-10, SS-2, P-2, 3B-1
1885 BAL AA	78	.231	.349	321	74	11	6	5	1.6	47		16			0	0	121	83	27	12	3.0	.883	OF-45, P-15, SS-10, 3B-6, 2B-6, 1B-1
1887	140	.341	.519	551	188	33	19	9	1.6	122		63		58	0	0	205	326	101	23	4.5	.840	SS-98, 3B-42, P-3, 2B-1
1888 2 teams		BAL AA (79G – .298)			BKN AA (52G – .284)																		
" total	131	.293	.440	529	155	30	15	6	1.1	94	67	38		44	0	0	226	182	69	16	3.6	.855	OF-70, SS-59, P-5, 2B-4, 3B-2
1889 BKN AA	131	.304	.423	504	153	19	13	5	1.0	105	100	68	26	32	0	0	160	83	24	9	2.0	.910	OF-113, SS-19
1890 BKN N	119	.284	.464	472	134	22	12	13	**2.8**	102	**128**	51	42	21	0	0	142	28	10	5	1.5	.944	OF-116, 3B-3
1891	123	.285	.417	470	134	24	13	4	0.9	75	83	53	30	21	0	0	187	49	30	6	2.2	.887	OF-113, SS-6, 3B-5
1892	141	.315	.454	542	171	27	18	4	0.7	91	96	65	42	33	0	0	183	34	23	6	1.7	.904	OF-129, 3B-7, SS-5
1893	109	.270	.412	415	112	22	8	7	1.7	68	60	36	16	14	0	0	159	20	14	4	1.8	.927	OF-108, SS-1
1894	126	.361	.507	513	185	32	14	5	1.0	107	109	44	18	30	0	0	208	15	12	4	1.9	.949	OF-125
1895 2 teams		BKN N (20G – .184)			NY N (33G – .307)																		
" total	53	.258	.342	190	49	5	4	1	0.5	28	32	22	8	10	0	0	94	9	11	3	2.2	.904	OF-51, 1B-1
11 yrs.	1188	.300	.447	4645	1395	227	129	65	1.4	873	675	464	182	263	1	0	1736	870	336	91	2.5	.886	OF-894, SS-200, 3B-66, P-25, 2B-21, 1B-2

Pat Burns

BURNS, PATRICK
Deceased.

Year Team	Games	BA	SA	AB	H	2B	3B	HR	HR%	R	RBI	BB	SO	SB	PH AB	PH H	PO	A	E	DP	TC/G	FA	G by Pos
1884 2 teams		BAL AA (6G – .200)			BAL U (1G – .500)																		
" total	7	.241	.379	29	7	1	0	0	0.0	3		3			0	0	71	1	4	3	10.9	.947	1B-7

Tom Burns

BURNS, THOMAS EVERETT
B. Mar. 30, 1857, Honesdale, Pa. D. Mar. 19, 1902, Jersey City, N. J.
Manager 1892, 1898-99.

BR TR 5'7" 152 lbs.

Year Team	Games	BA	SA	AB	H	2B	3B	HR	HR%	R	RBI	BB	SO	SB	PH AB	PH H	PO	A	E	DP	TC/G	FA	G by Pos
1880 CHI N	85	.309	.378	333	103	17	3	0	0.0	47	43	12	23		0	0	73	202	46	9	3.8	.857	SS-79, 3B-9, C-2, P-1
1881	84	.278	.389	342	95	20	3	4	1.2	41	42	14	22		0	0	116	263	56	22	5.2	.871	SS-80, 3B-3, 2B-3
1882	84	.248	.346	355	88	23	6	0	0.0	55	48	15	28		0	0	189	258	65	30	6.1	.873	2B-43, SS-41
1883	97	.294	.435	405	119	37	7	2	0.5	69		15	31		0	0	180	317	84	30	6.0	.855	SS-79, 3B-19, OF-1
1884	83	.245	.359	343	84	14	2	7	2.0	54		13	50		0	0	102	259	69	21	5.2	.840	SS-80, 3B-3
1885	111	.272	.411	445	121	23	9	7	1.6	82	70	16	48		0	0	151	370	96	35	5.6	.844	SS-111, 2B-1
1886	112	.276	.382	445	123	18	10	3	0.7	64	65	14	40		0	0	149	247	49	12	4.0	.890	3B-112
1887	115	.264	.380	424	112	20	10	3	0.7	57	60	34	32	32	0	0	184	248	61	25	4.3	.876	3B-107, OF-8
1888	134	.238	.306	483	115	12	6	3	0.6	60	70	26	49	34	0	0	194	273	49	16	3.9	.905	3B-134
1889	136	.242	.339	525	127	27	6	4	0.8	64	66	32	57	18	0	0	225	301	72	30	4.4	.880	3B-136
1890	139	.277	.362	538	149	16	5	6	1.1	86	86	57	45	44	0	0	188	290	54	25	3.8	.898	3B-139
1891	59	.226	.280	243	55	8	1	1	0.4	36	17	21	21	18	0	0	106	118	28	12	4.3	.889	3B-53, SS-4, OF-2
1892 PIT N	12	.205	.205	39	8	0	0	0	0.0	7	4	7	4	3	0	0	11	11	10	0	2.7	.688	3B-8, OF-3
13 yrs.	1251	.264	.364	4920	1299	235	69	40	0.8	722	571	270	454	147	1	0	1868	3157	739	267	4.6	.872	3B-704, SS-474, 2B-66, OF-14, C-2, P-1

Year	Team		Games	BA	SA	AB	H	2B	3B	HR	HR%	R	RBI	BB	SO	SB	Pinch Hit AB	H	PO	A	E	DP	TC/G	FA	G by Pos

Alex Burr

BURR, ALEXANDER THOMSON
B. Nov. 1, 1893, Chicago, Ill. D. Nov. 1, 1918, France
BR TR 6'3½" 190 lbs.

Year	Team		Games	BA	SA	AB	H	2B	3B	HR	HR%	R	RBI	BB	SO	SB	AB	H	PO	A	E	DP	TC/G	FA	G by Pos
1914	NY	A	1	–	–	0	0	0	0	0	0.0	0	0	0	0	0	0	0	0	0	0	0	0.0	–	OF-1

Buster Burrell

BURRELL, FRANK ANDREW
B. Dec. 22, 1866, E. Weymouth, Mass. D. May 8, 1962, East Weymouth, Mass.
BR TR 5'10" 165 lbs.

Year	Team		Games	BA	SA	AB	H	2B	3B	HR	HR%	R	RBI	BB	SO	SB	AB	H	PO	A	E	DP	TC/G	FA	G by Pos
1891	NY	N	15	.094	.094	53	5	0	0	0	0.0	1	1	3	12	2	0	0	67	16	15	1	6.5	.847	C-15, OF-1
1895	BKN	N	12	.143	.250	28	4	0	0	1	3.6	7	5	4	3	0	0	0	24	7	6	1	3.1	.838	C-12
1896			62	.301	.383	206	62	11	3	0	0.0	19	23	15	13	1	2	0	176	42	17	3	3.8	.928	C-60
1897			33	.243	.320	103	25	2	0	2	1.9	15	18	10		1	2	1	117	25	13	1	4.7	.916	C-27, 1B-4
4 yrs.			122	.246	.318	390	96	13	3	3	0.8	42	47	32	28	4	4	1	384	90	51	6	4.3	.903	C-114, 1B-4, OF-1

Larry Burright

BURRIGHT, LARRY ALLEN (Possum)
B. July 10, 1937, Roseville, Ill.
BR TR 5'11" 170 lbs.

Year	Team		Games	BA	SA	AB	H	2B	3B	HR	HR%	R	RBI	BB	SO	SB	AB	H	PO	A	E	DP	TC/G	FA	G by Pos
1962	LA	N	115	.205	.317	249	51	6	5	4	1.6	35	30	21	67	4	1	0	176	207	15	35	3.5	.962	2B-109, SS-1
1963	NY	N	41	.220	.260	100	22	2	1	0	0.0	9	3	8	25	1	2	0	70	111	9	21	4.6	.953	SS-19, 2B-15, 3B-1
1964			3	.000	.000	7	0	0	0	0	0.0	0	0	0	0	0	0	0	10	12	0	3	7.3	1.000	2B-3
3 yrs.			159	.205	.295	356	73	8	6	4	1.1	44	33	29	92	5	3	0	256	330	24	59	3.8	.961	2B-127, SS-20, 3B-1

Paul Burris

BURRIS, PAUL ROBERT
B. July 21, 1923, Hickory, N. C.
BR TR 6' 190 lbs.

Year	Team		Games	BA	SA	AB	H	2B	3B	HR	HR%	R	RBI	BB	SO	SB	AB	H	PO	A	E	DP	TC/G	FA	G by Pos
1948	BOS	N	2	.500	.500	4	2	0	0	0	0.0	0	0	0	0	0	0	0	6	1	0	0	3.5	1.000	C-2
1950			10	.174	.217	23	4	1	0	0	0.0	1	3	1	2	0	2	1	39	0	0	0	3.9	1.000	C-8
1952			55	.220	.280	168	37	4	0	2	1.2	14	21	7	19	0	5	1	208	16	0	3	4.1	1.000	C-50
1953	MIL	N	2	.000	.000	1	0	0	0	0	0.0	0	0	0	0	0	0	0	1	0	0	0	0.5	1.000	C-2
4 yrs.			69	.219	.276	196	43	5	0	2	1.0	15	24	8	21	0	7	2	254	17	0	3	3.9	1.000	C-62

Jeff Burroughs

BURROUGHS, JEFFREY ALAN
B. Mar. 7, 1951, Long Beach, Calif.
BR TR 6'1" 200 lbs.

Year	Team		Games	BA	SA	AB	H	2B	3B	HR	HR%	R	RBI	BB	SO	SB	AB	H	PO	A	E	DP	TC/G	FA	G by Pos
1970	WAS	A	6	.167	.167	12	2	0	0	0	0.0	1	1	2	5	0	4	1	5	0	0	0	0.8	1.000	OF-3
1971			59	.232	.365	181	42	9	0	5	2.8	20	25	22	55	1	8	2	82	3	3	0	1.5	.966	OF-50
1972	TEX	A	22	.185	.246	65	12	1	0	1	1.5	4	3	5	22	0	5	1	33	2	2	1	1.7	.946	OF-19, 1B-1
1973			151	.279	.487	526	147	17	1	30	5.7	71	85	67	88	0	5	0	320	14	8	3	2.3	.977	OF-148, 1B-1, DH-1
1974			152	.301	.504	554	167	33	2	25	4.5	84	118	91	104	2	0	0	242	11	8	6	1.7	.969	OF-150, 1B-2, DH-1
1975			152	.226	.409	585	132	20	0	29	5.0	81	94	79	155	4	2	1	249	10	9	2	1.8	.966	OF-148, DH-3
1976			158	.237	.369	604	143	22	2	18	3.0	71	86	69	93	0	0	0	289	12	4	3	1.9	.987	OF-155, DH-3
1977	ATL	N	154	.271	.520	579	157	19	1	41	7.1	91	114	86	126	4	0	0	249	9	7	3	1.7	.974	OF-154
1978			153	.301	.529	488	147	30	6	23	4.7	72	77	117	92	1	3	1	224	13	6	2	1.6	.975	OF-147
1979			116	.224	.348	397	89	14	1	11	2.8	49	47	73	75	2	5	1	175	8	7	1	1.6	.963	OF-110
1980			99	.263	.453	278	73	14	0	13	4.7	35	51	35	57	1	24	9	129	0	3	0	1.3	.977	OF-73
1981	SEA	A	89	.254	.395	319	81	13	1	10	3.1	32	41	41	64	0	1	0	127	4	2	1	1.5	.985	OF-87, DH-1
1982	OAK	A	113	.277	.505	285	79	13	2	16	5.6	42	48	45	61	1	33	11	52	0	1	0	0.5	.981	DH-48, OF-34
1983			121	.269	.387	401	108	15	1	10	2.5	43	56	47	79	0	13	5	0	0	0	0	0.0		DH-114
1984			58	.211	.310	71	15	1	0	2	2.8	5	8	18	23	0	33	4	1	0	0	0	0.0	1.000	DH-23, OF-4
1985	TOR	A	86	.257	.429	191	49	9	3	6	3.1	19	28	34	36	0	29	3	0	0	0	0	0.0		DH-75
16 yrs.			1689	.261	.439	5536	1443	230	20	240	4.3	720	882	831	1135	16	165	39	2177	86	60	22	1.4	.974	OF-1282, DH-269, 1B-6

LEAGUE CHAMPIONSHIP SERIES

Year	Team		Games	BA	SA	AB	H	2B	3B	HR	HR%	R	RBI	BB	SO	SB	AB	H	PO	A	E	DP	TC/G	FA	G by Pos
1985	TOR	A	1	.000	.000	1	0	0	0	0	0.0	0	0	0	0	0	1	0	0	0	0	0	0.0	–	

Dick Burrus

BURRUS, MAURICE LENNON
B. Jan. 29, 1898, Hatteras, N. C. D. Feb. 2, 1972, Elizabeth City, N. C.
BL TL 5'11" 175 lbs.

Year	Team		Games	BA	SA	AB	H	2B	3B	HR	HR%	R	RBI	BB	SO	SB	AB	H	PO	A	E	DP	TC/G	FA	G by Pos
1919	PHI	A	70	.258	.314	194	50	3	4	0	0.0	17	8	9	25	2	21	4	347	22	10	17	5.4	.974	1B-38, OF-10
1920			71	.185	.244	135	25	8	0	0	0.0	11	10	5	7	0	37	7	252	16	4	22	3.8	.985	1B-31, OF-2
1925	BOS	N	152	.340	.449	588	200	41	4	5	0.9	82	87	51	29	8	1	0	1416	85	15	110	10.0	.990	1B-151
1926			131	.270	.383	486	131	21	1	3	0.6	59	61	37	16	4	3	0	1153	103	12	97	9.7	.991	1B-130
1927			72	.318	.382	220	70	8	3	0	0.0	22	32	17	10	3	10	4	505	44	16	51	7.8	.972	1B-61
1928			64	.270	.380	137	37	6	0	3	2.2	15	13	19	8	1	23	7	286	15	7	29	4.8	.977	1B-32
6 yrs.			560	.291	.373	1760	513	87	12	11	0.6	206	211	138	95	18	95	22	3959	285	64	326	7.7	.985	1B-443, OF-12

Frank Burt

BURT, FRANK J.
B. Camden, N. J. Deceased.

Year	Team		Games	BA	SA	AB	H	2B	3B	HR	HR%	R	RBI	BB	SO	SB	AB	H	PO	A	E	DP	TC/G	FA	G by Pos
1882	BAL	AA	10	.111	.222	36	4	2	1	0	0.0	2		1		0	0	0	21	5	1	5	2.7	.815	OF-10

Ellis Burton

BURTON, ELLIS NARRINGTON
B. Aug. 12, 1936, Los Angeles, Calif.
BB TR 5'11" 160 lbs.

Year	Team		Games	BA	SA	AB	H	2B	3B	HR	HR%	R	RBI	BB	SO	SB	AB	H	PO	A	E	DP	TC/G	FA	G by Pos
1958	STL	N	8	.233	.500	30	7	0	1	2	6.7	5	4	3	8	0	1	0	12	0	0	0	1.5	1.000	OF-7
1960			29	.214	.250	28	6	1	0	0	0.0	5	2	4	14	0	5	2	8	0	0	0	0.3	1.000	OF-23
1963	2 teams			CLE A (26G – .194)			CHI N (93G – .230)																			
"	total		119	.227	.397	353	80	19	1	13	3.7	51	42	40	63	6	9	2	159	7	4	2	1.4	.976	OF-106
1964	CHI	N	42	.190	.314	105	20	3	2	2	1.9	12	7	17	22	4	12	2	51	0	1	0	1.2	.981	OF-29
1965			17	.175	.200	40	7	1	0	0	0.0	6	4	1	10	1	8	2	19	1	0	0	1.2	1.000	OF-12
5 yrs.			215	.216	.365	556	120	24	4	17	3.1	79	59	65	117	11	35	8	249	8	5	2	1.2	.981	OF-177

Jim Busby

BUSBY, JAMES FRANKLIN
B. Jan. 8, 1927, Kenedy, Tex.
BR TR 6'1" 175 lbs.

Year	Team		Games	BA	SA	AB	H	2B	3B	HR	HR%	R	RBI	BB	SO	SB	AB	H	PO	A	E	DP	TC/G	FA	G by Pos
1950	CHI	A	18	.208	.208	48	10	0	0	0	0.0	5	4	1	5	0	0	0	25	2	1	1	1.6	.964	OF-12
1951			143	.283	.354	477	135	15	2	5	1.0	59	68	40	46	26	3	0	360	16	7	4	2.7	.982	OF-139
1952	2 teams			CHI A (16G – .128)			WAS A (129G – .244)																			
"	total		145	.236	.305	551	130	24	4	2	0.4	63	47	24	55	5	1	0	472	4	3	0	3.3	.994	OF-144
1953	WAS	A	150	.312	.415	586	183	28	7	6	1.0	68	82	38	45	13	0	0	482	15	6	4	3.4	.988	OF-150
1954			155	.298	.389	628	187	28	7	7	1.1	83	54	43	56	17	0	0	491	6	6	1	3.2	.988	OF-155

Year	Team	Games	BA	SA	AB	H	2B	3B	HR	HR%	R	RBI	BB	SO	SB	Pinch Hit AB	Pinch Hit H	PO	A	E	DP	TC/G	FA	G by Pos

Jim Busby *continued*

Year	Team	Games	BA	SA	AB	H	2B	3B	HR	HR%	R	RBI	BB	SO	SB	AB	H	PO	A	E	DP	TC/G	FA	G by Pos
1955	2 teams	WAS A (47G – .230)			CHI A (99G – .243)																			
"	total	146	.239	.337	528	126	19	6	7	1.3	61	41	38	59	12	0	0	375	7	5	3	2.7	.987	OF-146
1956	CLE A	135	.235	.354	494	116	17	3	12	2.4	72	50	43	47	8	5	1	344	3	4	0	2.6	.989	OF-133
1957	2 teams	CLE A (30G – .189)			BAL A (86G – .250)																			
"	total	116	.238	.323	362	86	12	2	5	1.4	40	23	24	44	6	8	2	277	9	5	2	2.5	.983	OF-111
1958	BAL A	113	.237	.330	215	51	7	2	3	1.4	32	19	24	37	6	6	1	196	1	1	0	1.8	.995	OF-103, 3B-1
1959	BOS A	61	.225	.333	102	23	8	0	1	1.0	16	5	5	18	0	18	1	49	1	1	0	0.8	.980	OF-34
1960	BOS A (1G – .000)				BAL A (79G – .258)																			
"	total	80	.258	.314	159	41	7	1	0	0.0	25	12	20	14	2	3	1	133	2	2	1	1.7	.985	OF-72
1961	BAL A	75	.258	.315	89	23	3	1	0	0.0	15	6	8	10	2	4	1	76	2	1	0	1.1	.987	OF-71
1962	HOU N	15	.182	.182	11	2	0	0	0	0.0	2	1	2	3	0	3	1	4	0	0	0	0.3	1.000	OF-10, C-1
13 yrs.		1352	.262	.350	4250	1113	162	35	48	1.1	541	438	310	439	97	51	8	3284	68	42	16	2.5	.988	OF-1280, 3B-1, C-1

Paul Busby

BUSBY, PAUL MILLER (Red)   BL TR 6'1"   175 lbs.
B. Aug. 25, 1918, Waynesboro, Miss.

Year	Team	Games	BA	SA	AB	H	2B	3B	HR	HR%	R	RBI	BB	SO	SB	AB	H	PO	A	E	DP	TC/G	FA	G by Pos
1941	PHI N	10	.313	.313	16	5	0	0	0	0.0	3	2	0	1	0	6	1	3	0	0	0	0.3	1.000	OF-3
1943		26	.250	.275	40	10	1	0	0	0.0	13	5	2	1	2	11	3	25	0	0	0	1.0	1.000	OF-10
2 yrs.		36	.268	.286	56	15	1	0	0	0.0	16	7	2	2	2	17	4	28	0	0	0	0.8	1.000	OF-13

Ed Busch

BUSCH, EDGAR JOHN   BR TR 5'10"   175 lbs.
B. Nov. 16, 1917, Lebanon, Ill.   D. Jan. 17, 1987, St. Clair County, Ill.

Year	Team	Games	BA	SA	AB	H	2B	3B	HR	HR%	R	RBI	BB	SO	SB	AB	H	PO	A	E	DP	TC/G	FA	G by Pos
1943	PHI A	4	.294	.294	17	5	0	0	0	0.0	2	0	1	2	0	0	0	10	6	1	1	4.3	.941	SS-4
1944		140	.271	.306	484	131	11	3	0	0.0	41	40	29	17	5	1	0	257	393	41	62	4.9	.941	SS-111, 2B-27, 3B-4
1945		126	.250	.288	416	104	10	3	0	0.0	37	35	32	9	2	2	0	221	379	31	70	5.0	.951	SS-116, 3B-5, 2B-2, 1B-1
3 yrs.		270	.262	.298	917	240	21	6	0	0.0	80	75	62	28	7	3	0	488	778	73	133	5.0	.945	SS-231, 2B-29, 3B-9, 1B-1

Donie Bush

BUSH, OWEN JOSEPH   BB TR 5'6"   140 lbs.
B. Oct. 8, 1887, Indianapolis, Ind.   D. Mar. 28, 1972, Indianapolis, Ind.
Manager 1923, 1927-31, 1933.

Year	Team	Games	BA	SA	AB	H	2B	3B	HR	HR%	R	RBI	BB	SO	SB	AB	H	PO	A	E	DP	TC/G	FA	G by Pos
1908	DET A	20	.294	.338	68	20	1	1	0	0.0	13	4	7		2	0	0	42	63	7	9	5.6	.938	SS-20
1909		157	.273	.314	532	145	18	2	0	0.0	114	33	88		53	0	0	308	567	71	38	6.0	.925	SS-157
1910		142	.262	.323	496	130	13	4	3	0.6	90	34	78		49	0	0	310	489	51	31	6.0	.940	SS-141, 3B-1
1911		150	.232	.287	561	130	18	5	1	0.2	126	36	98		40	0	0	372	556	75	42	6.7	.925	SS-150
1912		144	.231	.301	511	118	14	8	2	0.4	107	38	117		35	0	0	317	547	66	45	6.5	.929	SS-144
1913		153	.251	.322	593	149	19	10	1	0.0	98	40	80	32	44	0	0	331	510	56	61	5.9	.938	SS-153
1914		157	.252	.295	596	150	18	4	0	0.0	97	32	112	54	35	0	0	425	544	58	64	6.5	.944	SS-157
1915		155	.228	.283	561	128	12	8	1	0.2	99	44	118	44	35	0	0	340	504	57	61	5.8	.937	SS-155
1916		145	.225	.267	550	124	5	9	0	0.0	73	34	75	42	19	0	0	278	435	34	41	5.2	.954	SS-144
1917		147	.281	.322	581	163	18	3	0	0.0	112	24	80	40	34	0	0	281	423	51	41	5.1	.932	SS-147
1918		128	.234	.266	500	117	10	3	0	0.0	74	22	79	31	9	0	0	280	364	48	29	5.4	.931	SS-128
1919		129	.244	.289	509	124	11	6	0	0.0	82	26	75	36	22	0	0	290	376	40	38	5.5	.943	SS-129
1920		141	.263	.324	506	133	18	5	1	0.2	85	33	73	32	15	1	1	258	421	45	39	5.1	.938	SS-140
1921	2 teams	DET A (104G – .281)			WAS A (23G – .214)																			
"	total	127	.270	.305	486	131	7	5	0	0.0	87	29	57	27	10	2	1	251	391	37	46	5.3	.946	SS-102, 2B-23
1922	WAS A	41	.239	.284	134	32	4	1	0	0.0	17	7	21	7	1	3	0	31	81	5	12	2.9	.957	3B-37, 2B-1
1923		10	.409	.409	22	9	0	0	0	0.0	6	0	1	0	1	0	1	5	15	3	0	2.3	.870	3B-6, 2B-1
16 yrs.		1946	.250	.300	7206	1803	186	74	9	0.1	1280	436	1158	346	403	7	2	4119	6286	704	597	5.7	.937	SS-1867, 3B-44, 2B-25

WORLD SERIES

Year	Team	Games	BA	SA	AB	H	2B	3B	HR	HR%	R	RBI	BB	SO	SB	AB	H	PO	A	E	DP	TC/G	FA	G by Pos
1909	DET A	7	.261	.304	23	6	1	0	0	0.0	5	2	5	3	1	0	0	10	18	5	3	4.7	.848	SS-7

Joe Bush

BUSH, LESLIE AMBROSE (Bullet Joe)   BR TR 5'9"   173 lbs.
B. Nov. 27, 1892, Brainerd, Minn.   D. Nov. 1, 1974, Ft. Lauderdale, Fla.

Year	Team	Games	BA	SA	AB	H	2B	3B	HR	HR%	R	RBI	BB	SO	SB	AB	H	PO	A	E	DP	TC/G	FA	G by Pos
1912	PHI A	1	.500	1.000	4	2	0	1	0	0.0	1	3	0		0	0	0	1	1	1	1	3.0	.667	P-1
1913		39	.157	.229	70	11	3	1	0	0.0	8	1	2	21	0	0	0	15	75	2	4	2.4	.978	P-39
1914		38	.189	.284	74	14	4	0	1	1.4	6	8	2	25	0	0	0	8	55	3	1	1.7	.955	P-38
1915		25	.143	.143	49	7	0	0	0	0.0	2	0	1	22	0	0	0	7	39	3	3	2.0	.939	P-25
1916		41	.140	.180	100	14	4	0	0	0.0	4	6	0	23	0	0	0	19	94	6	8	2.9	.950	P-40
1917		37	.200	.250	80	16	2	1	0	0.0	9	4	5	12	0	0	0	20	61	6	0	2.4	.931	P-37
1918	BOS A	36	.276	.347	98	27	3	2	0	0.0	8	14	6	11	0	0	0	16	81	2	5	2.8	.980	P-36
1919		6	.400	.400	5	2	0	0	0	0.0	0	2	0	1	0	1	0	0	2	0	1	0.3	1.000	P-3
1920		45	.245	.265	102	25	2	0	0	0.0	14	7	9	15	0	5	1	25	66	4	7	2.1	.958	P-35, OF-2
1921		51	.325	.433	120	39	5	4	0	0.0	19	14	3	14	2	8	2	15	64	1	0	1.6	.988	P-37, OF-4
1922	NY A	39	.326	.432	95	31	6	2	0	0.0	15	12	3	11	0	0	0	16	61	0	4	2.0	1.000	P-39
1923		38	.274	.425	113	31	5	3	2	1.8	12	19	3	8	0	1	0	15	74	3	3	2.4	.967	P-37
1924		60	.339	.484	124	42	9	3	1	0.8	13	14	7	6	0	16	6	24	60	1	4	1.4	.988	P-39
1925	STL A	57	.255	.431	102	26	12	0	2	2.0	10	18	6	8	2	21	4	17	54	0	5	1.2	1.000	P-33, OF-1
1926	2 teams	WAS A (17G – .233)			PIT N (28G – .265)																			
"	total	45	.253	.342	79	20	4	0	1	1.3	6	10	4	12	0	10	1	9	39	2	3	1.1	.960	P-31, OF-1
1927	2 teams	PIT N (7G – .600)			NY N (3G – .500)																			
"	total	10	.556	.556	9	5	0	0	0	0.0	0	2	1	1	0	1	0	4	0	0	0	0.4	1.000	P-8
1928	PHI A	15	.067	.067	15	1	0	0	0	0.0	0	0	1	2	0	1	0	5	10	0	1	1.0	1.000	P-11, OF-1
17 yrs.		583	.253	.345	1239	313	59	17	7	0.6	128	134	53	192	4	64	15	212	840	34	50	1.9	.969	P-489, OF-9

WORLD SERIES

Year	Team	Games	BA	SA	AB	H	2B	3B	HR	HR%	R	RBI	BB	SO	SB	AB	H	PO	A	E	DP	TC/G	FA	G by Pos
1913	PHI A	1	.250	.250	4	1	0	0	0	0.0	0	0	0	0	0	0	0	1	0	1	1.0	1.000	P-1
1914		1	.000	.000	5	0	0	0	0	0.0	0	0	0	2	0	0	0	1	5	1	0	6.0	.833	P-1
1918	BOS A	2	.000	.000	4	0	0	0	0	0.0	0	1	0	0	0	0	0	3	0	0	1.5	1.000	P-2
1922	NY A	2	.167	.167	6	1	0	0	0	0.0	0	1	0	1	0	0	0	1	3	0	2	2.0	1.000	P-2
1923		4	.429	.571	7	3	1	0	0	0.0	2	1	1	1	0	0	0	2	3	0	0	1.3	1.000	P-3
5 yrs.		10	.208	.250	24	5	1	0	0	0.0	2	2	2	4	0	0	0	3	15	1	3	1.9	.947	P-9

Year	Team		Games	BA	SA	AB	H	2B	3B	HR	HR%	R	RBI	BB	SO	SB	Pinch Hit AB	H	PO	A	E	DP	TC/G	FA	G by Pos

Randy Bush

BUSH, ROBERT RANDALL
B. Oct. 5, 1958, Dover, Del.   BL TL 6'1"   190 lbs.

Year	Team		Games	BA	SA	AB	H	2B	3B	HR	HR%	R	RBI	BB	SO	SB	PH AB	PH H	PO	A	E	DP	TC/G	FA	G by Pos
1982	MIN	A	55	.244	.412	119	29	6	1	4	3.4	13	13	8	28	0	25	3	7	0	0	0	0.1	1.000	DH-26, OF-6
1983			124	.249	.418	373	93	24	3	11	2.9	43	56	34	51	0	19	4	21	3	0	1	0.2	1.000	DH-103, 1B-3
1984			113	.225	.392	311	70	17	1	11	3.5	46	43	31	60	1	20	8	5	0	0	1	0.0	1.000	DH-89, 1B-2
1985			97	.239	.449	234	56	13	3	10	4.3	26	35	24	30	3	32	4	79	0	2	1	0.8	.975	OF-41, DH-28, 1B-1
1986			130	.269	.420	357	96	19	7	7	2.0	50	45	39	63	5	30	13	182	2	4	2	1.4	.979	OF-102, DH-6, 1B-3
1987			122	.253	.413	293	74	10	2	11	3.8	46	46	43	49	10	30	7	164	5	4	4	1.4	.977	OF-75, DH-9, 1B-9
1988			136	.261	.434	394	103	20	3	14	3.6	51	51	58	49	8	19	6	206	5	4	1	1.6	.981	OF-115, DH-17
1989			141	.263	.435	391	103	17	4	14	3.6	60	54	48	73	5	18	1	339	14	3	14	2.5	.992	OF-109, 1B-25, DH-5
8 yrs.			918	.252	.422	2472	624	126	24	82	3.3	335	343	285	403	32	193	46	1003	29	17	24	1.1	.984	OF-448, DH-283, 1B-43

LEAGUE CHAMPIONSHIP SERIES

| 1987 | MIN | A | 4 | .250 | .417 | 12 | 3 | 0 | 1 | 0 | 0.0 | 4 | 2 | 3 | 2 | 3 | 0 | 0 | 0 | 0 | 0 | 0 | 0.0 | – | DH-4 |

WORLD SERIES

| 1987 | MIN | A | 4 | .167 | .333 | 6 | 1 | 1 | 0 | 0 | 0.0 | 1 | 2 | 0 | 1 | 0 | 3 | 0 | 0 | 0 | 0 | 0 | 0.0 | – | DH-2 |

Doc Bushong

BUSHONG, ALBERT JOHN
B. Sept. 15, 1856, Philadelphia, Pa.   D. Aug. 19, 1908, Brooklyn, N. Y.   BR TR 5'11"   165 lbs.

Year	Team		Games	BA	SA	AB	H	2B	3B	HR	HR%	R	RBI	BB	SO	SB	PH AB	PH H	PO	A	E	DP	TC/G	FA	G by Pos
1876	PHI	N	5	.048	.048	21	1	0	0	0	0.0	4	1	0	0		0	0	24	6	9	0	7.8	.769	C-5
1880	WOR	N	41	.171	.192	146	25	3	0	0	0.0	13	19	1	16		0	0	261	76	30	6	9.0	.918	C-40, OF-1, 3B-1
1881			76	.233	.287	275	64	7	4	0	0.0	35	21	21	23		0	0	368	124	44	10	7.1	.918	C-76
1882			69	.158	.194	253	40	4	1	0	0.4	20	15	5	17		0	0	308	101	47	8	6.6	.897	C-69
1883	CLE	N	63	.172	.195	215	37	5	0	0	0.0	15		7	19		0	0	370	88	46	8	8.0	.909	C-63
1884			62	.236	.276	203	48	6	1	0	0.0	24	10	17	11		0	0	356	98	58	11	8.3	.887	C-62, OF-1
1885	STL	AA	85	.267	.343	300	80	13	5	0	0.0	42		11			0	0	429	122	40	10	7.0	.932	C-85, 3B-1
1886			107	.223	.251	386	86	8	0	1	0.3	56		31			0	0	653	134	48	14	7.8	.943	C-106, 1B-1
1887			53	.254	.274	201	51	4	0	0	0.0	35		11		14	0	0	204	93	23	8	6.0	.928	C-52, OF-2, 3B-2
1888	BKN	AA	69	.209	.237	253	53	5	1	0	0.0	23	16	5		9	0	0	347	105	42	8	7.2	.915	C-69
1889			25	.155	.167	84	13	1	0	0	0.0	15	8	9	7	2	0	0	85	41	15	5	5.6	.894	C-25
1890	BKN	N	16	.236	.273	55	13	2	0	0	0.0	5	7	6	4	2	0	0	82	13	9	1	6.5	.913	C-15, OF-1
12 yrs.			671	.214	.250	2392	511	58	12	2	0.1	287	97	124	97	27	0	0	3487	1001	411	81	7.3	.916	C-667, OF-5, 3B-4, 1B-1

Joe Buskey

BUSKEY, JOSEPH HENRY (Jazzbow)
B. Dec. 18, 1902, Cumberland, Md.   D. Apr. 11, 1949, Cumberland, Md.   BR TR 5'10"   175 lbs.

| 1926 | PHI | N | 5 | .000 | .000 | 8 | 0 | 0 | 0 | 0 | 0.0 | 1 | 0 | 1 | 1 | 0 | 0 | 0 | 8 | 9 | 4 | 1 | 4.2 | .810 | SS-5 |

Mike Buskey

BUSKEY, MICHAEL THOMAS
B. Jan. 13, 1949, San Francisco, Calif.   BR TR 5'11"   160 lbs.

| 1977 | PHI | N | 6 | .286 | .571 | 7 | 2 | 0 | 1 | 0 | 0.0 | 1 | 1 | 0 | 1 | 0 | 0 | 0 | 7 | 8 | 2 | 3 | 2.8 | .882 | SS-6 |

Ray Busse

BUSSE, RAYMOND EDWARD
B. Sept. 25, 1948, Daytona Beach, Fla.   BR TR 6'4"   175 lbs.

1971	HOU	N	10	.147	.235	34	5	3	0	0	0.0	2	4	2	9	0	2	0	7	15	2	0	2.4	.917	SS-5, 3B-3
1973	2 teams		STL N	(24G –	.143)	HOU N	(15G –	.059)																	
"	total		39	.126	.287	87	11	4	2	2	2.3	7	5	6	33	0	2	0	35	75	11	18	3.1	.909	SS-28, 3B-3
1974	HOU	N	19	.206	.235	34	7	1	0	0	0.0	3	0	3	12	0	11	1	2	17	3	1	1.2	.864	3B-8
3 yrs.			68	.148	.265	155	23	8	2	2	1.3	12	9	11	54	0	19	1	44	107	16	19	2.5	.904	SS-33, 3B-14

Hank Butcher

BUTCHER, HENRY JOSEPH
B. July 12, 1886, Chicago, Ill.   D. Dec. 28, 1979, Hazel Crest, Ill.   BR TR 5'10"   180 lbs.

1911	CLE	A	38	.241	.361	133	32	7	3	1	0.8	21	11	11		9	4	1	57	5	1	2	1.7	.984	OF-34
1912			24	.195	.305	82	16	4	1	1	1.2	9	10	6		1	4	0	43	3	4	1	2.1	.920	OF-20
2 yrs.			62	.223	.340	215	48	11	4	2	0.9	30	21	17		10	8	1	100	8	5	3	1.8	.956	OF-54

Sal Butera

BUTERA, SALVATORE PHILIP
B. Sept. 25, 1952, Richmond Hill, N. Y.   BR TR 6'   190 lbs.

1980	MIN	A	34	.271	.282	85	23	1	0	0	0.0	4	2	3	6	0	2	0	106	9	6	0	3.6	.950	C-32, DH-2
1981			62	.240	.293	167	40	7	1	0	0.0	13	18	22	14	0	1	0	256	41	9	4	4.9	.971	C-59, DH-1, 1B-1
1982			54	.254	.270	126	32	2	0	0	0.0	9	8	17	12	0	0	0	230	26	3	5	4.8	.988	C-53
1983	DET	A	4	.200	.200	5	1	0	0	0	0.0	1	0	1	0	0	0	0	12	1	1	0	3.5	.929	C-4
1984	MON	N	3	.000	.000	3	0	0	0	0	0.0	0	0	1	0	0	0	0	9	0	0	0	3.0	1.000	C-2
1985			67	.200	.283	120	24	1	0	3	2.5	11	12	13	12	0	1	0	227	20	4	5	3.7	.984	C-66, P-1
1986	CIN	N	16	.239	.363	113	27	6	1	2	1.8	14	16	21	10	0	2	0	215	17	5	2	4.2	.979	C-53, P-1
1987	2 teams		CIN N	(5G –	.182)	MIN A	(51G –	.171)																	
"	total		56	.172	.262	122	21	5	0	2	1.6	8	14	8	22	0	1	0	25	4	2	0	0.6	.935	C-56
1988	TOR	A	23	.233	.350	60	14	2	1	1	1.7	3	6	1	9	0	1	0	97	10	1	1	4.7	.991	C-23
9 yrs.			359	.227	.295	801	182	24	3	8	1.0	63	76	86	85	0	7	0	1177	128	31	13	3.7	.977	C-348, DH-3, P-2, 1B-1

LEAGUE CHAMPIONSHIP SERIES

| 1987 | MIN | A | 1 | .667 | .667 | 3 | 2 | 0 | 0 | 0 | 0.0 | 0 | 0 | 0 | 0 | 0 | 0 | 0 | 6 | 0 | 0 | 0 | 6.0 | 1.000 | C-1 |

WORLD SERIES

| 1987 | MIN | A | | – | – | 0 | 0 | 0 | 0 | 0 | 0.0 | 0 | 0 | 0 | 0 | 0 | 0 | 0 | 0 | 0 | 0 | 0 | 0.0 | – | C-1 |

Ed Butka

BUTKA, EDWARD LUKE (Babe)
B. Jan. 7, 1916, Canonsburg, Pa.   BR TR 6'3"   193 lbs.

1943	WAS	A	3	.333	.444	9	3	1	0	0	0.0	0	1	0	3	0	1	1	17	3	0	1	6.7	1.000	1B-3
1944			15	.195	.220	41	8	1	0	0	0.0	1	1	2	11	0	1	0	98	7	3	8	7.2	.972	1B-14
2 yrs.			18	.220	.260	50	11	2	0	0	0.0	1	2	2	14	0	2	1	115	10	3	9	7.1	.977	1B-17

Year	Team		Games	BA	SA	AB	H	2B	3B	HR	HR%	R	RBI	BB	SO	SB	Pinch Hit AB	H	PO	A	E	DP	TC/G	FA	G by Pos

Art Butler

BUTLER, ARTHUR EDWARD
Born Arthur Edward Bouthillier.
B. Dec. 19, 1887, Fall River, Mass.   D. Oct. 7, 1984, Fall River, Mass.
BR TR 5'9"   160 lbs.

Year	Team		Games	BA	SA	AB	H	2B	3B	HR	HR%	R	RBI	BB	SO	SB	AB	H	PO	A	E	DP	TC/G	FA	G by Pos
1911	BOS	N	27	.176	.206	68	12	2	0	0	0.0	11	2	6	6	0	7	1	19	32	7	1	2.1	.879	3B-14, 2B-4, SS-1
1912	PIT	N	43	.273	.344	154	42	4	2	1	0.6	19	17	15	11	2	0	0	71	99	7	12	4.1	.960	2B-43
1913			82	.280	.350	214	60	9	3	0	0.0	40	20	32	14	9	18	6	127	144	26	14	3.6	.912	2B-27, SS-24, OF-2, 3B-2
1914	STL	N	86	.201	.277	274	55	12	3	1	0.4	29	24	39	23	14	2	0	155	228	30	24	4.8	.927	SS-84, OF-1
1915			130	.254	.307	469	119	12	5	1	0.2	73	31	47	34	26	2	0	235	351	53	43	4.9	.917	SS-130
1916			86	.209	.255	110	23	5	0	0	0.0	9	7	7	12	3	54	13	23	10	3	3	0.4	.917	OF-15, 2B-8, SS-1, 3B-1
6 yrs.			454	.241	.303	1289	311	44	13	3	0.2	181	101	146	100	54	83	20	630	864	126	97	3.6	.922	SS-240, 2B-82, OF-18, 3B-17

Bill Butler

BUTLER, WILLIAM J.
B. 1861, New Orleans, La.   Deceased.

Year	Team		Games	BA	SA	AB	H	2B	3B	HR	HR%	R	RBI	BB	SO	SB	AB	H	PO	A	E	DP	TC/G	FA	G by Pos
1884	IND	AA	9	.226	.452	31	7	3	2	0	0.0	7		1			0	0	5	2	3	0	1.1	.700	OF-9

Brett Butler

BUTLER, BRETT MORGAN
B. June 15, 1957, Los Angeles, Calif.
BL TL 5'10"   160 lbs.

Year	Team		Games	BA	SA	AB	H	2B	3B	HR	HR%	R	RBI	BB	SO	SB	AB	H	PO	A	E	DP	TC/G	FA	G by Pos
1981	ATL	N	40	.254	.317	126	32	2	3	0	0.0	17	4	19	17	9	2	1	76	2	1	0	2.0	.987	OF-37
1982			89	.217	.225	240	52	2	0	0	0.0	35	7	25	35	21	6	1	129	2	0	0	1.5	1.000	OF-77
1983			151	.281	.393	549	154	21	13	5	0.9	84	37	54	56	39	6	1	284	13	4	4	2.0	.987	OF-143
1984	CLE	A	159	.269	.355	602	162	25	9	3	0.5	108	49	86	62	52	3	0	448	13	4	3	2.9	.991	OF-156
1985			152	.311	.431	591	184	28	14	5	0.8	106	50	63	42	47	1	0	437	19	1	5	3.0	.998	OF-150, DH-1
1986			161	.278	.375	587	163	17	14	4	0.7	92	51	70	65	32	1	0	434	9	3	3	2.8	.993	OF-159
1987			137	.295	.425	522	154	25	8	9	1.7	91	41	91	55	33	0	0	393	4	4	2	2.9	.990	OF-136
1988	SF	N	157	.287	.398	568	163	27	9	6	1.1	109	43	97	64	43	2	0	395	3	5	1	2.6	.988	OF-155
1989			154	.283	.354	594	168	22	4	4	0.7	100	36	59	69	31	0	0	407	11	6	3	2.8	.986	OF-152
9 yrs.			1200	.281	.378	4379	1232	169	74	36	0.8	742	318	564	465	307	21	3	3003	76	28	21	2.6	.991	OF-1165, DH-1

LEAGUE CHAMPIONSHIP SERIES

Year	Team		Games	BA	SA	AB	H	2B	3B	HR	HR%	R	RBI	BB	SO	SB	AB	H	PO	A	E	DP	TC/G	FA	G by Pos
1982	ATL	N	2	.000	.000	1	0	0	0	0	0.0	0	0	0	0	0	0	0	0	0	0	0	0.0	—	OF-1
1989	SF	N	5	.211	.211	19	4	0	0	0	0.0	6	0	3	3	0	0	0	9	0	0	0	1.8	1.000	OF-5
2 yrs.			7	.200	.200	20	4	0	0	0	0.0	6	0	3	3	0	0	0	9	0	0	0	1.3	1.000	OF-6

WORLD SERIES

Year	Team		Games	BA	SA	AB	H	2B	3B	HR	HR%	R	RBI	BB	SO	SB	AB	H	PO	A	E	DP	TC/G	FA	G by Pos
1989	SF	N	4	.286	.357	14	4	1	0	0	0.0	1	1	2	1	2	0	0	9	0	0	0	2.3	1.000	OF-4

Dick Butler

BUTLER, RICHARD H.
B. Brooklyn, N. Y.   Deceased.

Year	Team		Games	BA	SA	AB	H	2B	3B	HR	HR%	R	RBI	BB	SO	SB	AB	H	PO	A	E	DP	TC/G	FA	G by Pos
1897	LOU	N	10	.184	.184	38	7	0	0	0	0.0	3		1		1	0	0	25	11	8	0	4.4	.818	C-10
1899	WAS	N	12	.278	.333	36	10	0	1	0	0.0	4	1	2		1	1	0	19	14	4	0	3.1	.892	C-11
2 yrs.			22	.230	.257	74	17	0	1	0	0.0	7	3	2		2	1	0	44	25	12	0	3.7	.852	C-21

Frank Butler

BUTLER, FRANK DEAN (Stuffy)
B. July 18, 1860, Savannah, Ga.   D. July 18, 1945, Jacksonville, Fla.
BL TL

Year	Team		Games	BA	SA	AB	H	2B	3B	HR	HR%	R	RBI	BB	SO	SB	AB	H	PO	A	E	DP	TC/G	FA	G by Pos
1895	NY	N	5	.273	.318	22	6	1	0	0	0.0	5	2	1		0	0	0	9	0	0	0	1.8	1.000	OF-5

Frank Butler

BUTLER, FRANK EDWARD (Kid)
B. 1862, Boston, Mass.   D. Apr. 9, 1921, South Boston, Mass.

Year	Team		Games	BA	SA	AB	H	2B	3B	HR	HR%	R	RBI	BB	SO	SB	AB	H	PO	A	E	DP	TC/G	FA	G by Pos
1884	BOS	U	71	.169	.227	255	43	15	0	0	0.0	36		12					99	45	29	1	2.4	.832	OF-53, 2B-12, SS-6, 3B-2

John Butler

BUTLER, JOHN ALBERT
Played as Fred King in 1901.
B. July 26, 1879, Boston, Mass.   D. Feb. 2, 1950, Boston, Mass.
BR TR 5'7"   170 lbs.

Year	Team		Games	BA	SA	AB	H	2B	3B	HR	HR%	R	RBI	BB	SO	SB	AB	H	PO	A	E	DP	TC/G	FA	G by Pos
1901	MIL	A	1	.000	.000	3	0	0	0	0	0.0	0	0	0		0	0	0	2	0	0	0	2.0	1.000	C-1
1904	STL	N	12	.162	.189	37	6	1	0	0	0.0	0	1	4		0	0	0	49	11	2	2	5.2	.968	C-12
1906	BKN	N	1	—	—	0	0	0	0	0	—	0	0	0		0	0	0	1	1	0	0	2.0	1.000	C-1
1907			30	.127	.139	79	10	1	0	0	0.0	6	2	9		0	1	0	106	34	8	4	4.9	.946	C-28, OF-1
4 yrs.			44	.134	.151	119	16	2	0	0	0.0	6	3	13		0	1	0	158	46	10	6	4.9	.953	C-42, OF-1

Johnny Butler

BUTLER, JOHN STEPHEN (Trolley Line)
B. Mar. 20, 1893, Fall River, Kans.   D. Apr. 29, 1967, Seal Beach, Calif.
BR TR 6'   175 lbs.

Year	Team		Games	BA	SA	AB	H	2B	3B	HR	HR%	R	RBI	BB	SO	SB	AB	H	PO	A	E	DP	TC/G	FA	G by Pos
1926	BKN	N	147	.269	.349	501	135	27	5	1	0.2	54	68	54	44	6	0	0	298	407	34	48	5.0	.954	SS-102, 3B-42, 2B-8
1927			149	.238	.298	521	124	13	6	2	0.4	39	57	34	33	9	1	0	279	356	27	56	4.4	.959	SS-90, 3B-60
1928	CHI	N	62	.270	.310	174	47	7	0	0	0.0	17	16	19	7	2	1	0	53	124	10	10	3.0	.947	3B-59, SS-2
1929	STL	N	17	.164	.218	55	9	1	1	0	0.0	5	5	4	5	0	0	0	30	33	2	2	3.8	.969	3B-9, SS-8
4 yrs.			375	.252	.317	1251	315	48	12	3	0.2	115	146	111	89	17	2	0	660	920	73	116	4.4	.956	SS-202, 3B-170, 2B-8

Kid Butler

BUTLER, WILLIS EVERETT
B. Aug. 9, 1887, Franklin, Pa.   D. Feb. 22, 1964, Richmond, Calif.
BR TR 5'11"   155 lbs.

Year	Team		Games	BA	SA	AB	H	2B	3B	HR	HR%	R	RBI	BB	SO	SB	AB	H	PO	A	E	DP	TC/G	FA	G by Pos
1907	STL	A	20	.220	.254	59	13	2	0	0	0.0	4	6	2		1	3	0	18	43	3	3	3.2	.953	2B-11, 3B-5, SS-1

Joe Buzas

BUZAS, JOSEPH JOHN
B. Oct. 2, 1919, Alpha, N. J.
BR TR 6'1"   180 lbs.

Year	Team		Games	BA	SA	AB	H	2B	3B	HR	HR%	R	RBI	BB	SO	SB	AB	H	PO	A	E	DP	TC/G	FA	G by Pos
1945	NY	A	30	.262	.323	65	17	2	1	0	0.0	8	6	2	5	2	16	3	17	36	6	6	2.0	.898	SS-12

Bill Byers

BYERS, JAMES WILLIAM (Big Bill)
B. Oct. 3, 1877, Bridgetown, Ind.   D. Sept. 8, 1948, Baltimore, Md.
BR TR 5'7"

Year	Team		Games	BA	SA	AB	H	2B	3B	HR	HR%	R	RBI	BB	SO	SB	AB	H	PO	A	E	DP	TC/G	FA	G by Pos
1904	STL	N	19	.217	.217	60	13	0	0	0	0.0	3	4	1		0	2	1	90	15	4	1	5.7	.963	C-16, 1B-1

Year	Team	Games	BA	SA	AB	H	2B	3B	HR	HR%	R	RBI	BB	SO	SB	Pinch AB	Pinch H	PO	A	E	DP	TC/G	FA	G by Pos

Burley Byers

BYERS, BURLEY
Born Christopher A. Bayer.
B. Dec. 19, 1875, Louisville, Ky. D. May 30, 1933, Louisville, Ky.   175 lbs.

Year	Team	Games	BA	SA	AB	H	2B	3B	HR	HR%	R	RBI	BB	SO	SB	Pinch AB	Pinch H	PO	A	E	DP	TC/G	FA	G by Pos
1899	LOU N	1	.000	.000	3	0	0	0	0	0.0	0	0	0		0	0	0	2	1	2	0	5.0	.600	SS-1

Randell Byers

BYERS, RANDELL PARKER
B. Oct. 2, 1964, Bridgeton, N. J.   BL TR 6'2" 180 lbs.

Year	Team	Games	BA	SA	AB	H	2B	3B	HR	HR%	R	RBI	BB	SO	SB	Pinch AB	Pinch H	PO	A	E	DP	TC/G	FA	G by Pos
1987	SD N	10	.313	.375	16	5	1	0	0	0.0	1	1	1	5	1	3	0	6	1	0	0	0.7	1.000	OF-5
1988		11	.200	.300	10	2	1	0	0	0.0	0	0	0	5	0	10	2	0	0	0	0	0.0	–	OF-2
2 yrs.		21	.269	.346	26	7	2	0	0	0.0	1	1	1	10	1	13	2	6	1	0	0	0.3	1.000	OF-7

Sammy Byrd

BYRD, SAMUEL DEWEY (Babe Ruth's Legs)
B. Oct. 15, 1907, Bremen, Ga. D. May 11, 1981, Mesa, Ariz.   BR TR 5'10½" 175 lbs.

Year	Team	Games	BA	SA	AB	H	2B	3B	HR	HR%	R	RBI	BB	SO	SB	Pinch AB	Pinch H	PO	A	E	DP	TC/G	FA	G by Pos
1929	NY A	62	.312	.471	170	53	12	0	5	2.9	32	28	28	18	1	8	0	108	6	6	2	1.9	.950	OF-54
1930		92	.284	.440	218	62	12	2	6	2.8	46	31	30	18	5	4	2	119	2	1	0	1.3	.992	OF-85
1931		115	.270	.395	248	67	18	2	3	1.2	51	32	29	26	5	25	5	148	3	4	1	1.3	.974	OF-88
1932		104	.297	.478	209	62	12	1	8	3.8	49	30	30	20	1	9	4	129	4	5	1	1.3	.964	OF-90
1933		85	.280	.411	107	30	6	1	2	1.9	26	11	15	12	0	9	2	75	1	1	0	0.9	.987	OF-71
1934		106	.246	.335	191	47	8	0	3	1.6	32	23	18	22	1	1	0	156	2	2	1	1.5	.988	OF-104
1935	CIN N	121	.262	.406	416	109	25	4	9	2.2	51	52	37	51	4	6	4	284	10	9	1	2.5	.970	OF-115
1936		59	.248	.348	141	35	8	0	2	1.4	17	13	11	11	0	19	4	86	1	1	1	1.5	.989	OF-37
8 yrs.		744	.274	.412	1700	465	101	10	38	2.2	304	220	198	178	17	81	21	1105	29	29	7	1.6	.975	OF-644

WORLD SERIES

Year	Team	Games	BA	SA	AB	H	2B	3B	HR	HR%	R	RBI	BB	SO	SB	Pinch AB	Pinch H	PO	A	E	DP	TC/G	FA	G by Pos
1932	NY A	1	–	–	0	0	0	0	0	–	0	0	0	0	0	0	0	0	0	0	0	0.0	–	OF-1

Bobby Byrne

BYRNE, ROBERT MATTHEW
B. Dec. 31, 1884, St. Louis, Mo. D. Dec. 31, 1964, Wayne, Pa.   BR TR 5'7½" 145 lbs.

Year	Team	Games	BA	SA	AB	H	2B	3B	HR	HR%	R	RBI	BB	SO	SB	Pinch AB	Pinch H	PO	A	E	DP	TC/G	FA	G by Pos
1907	STL N	148	.256	.294	558	143	11	5	0	0.0	55	29	35		21	0	0	215	353	50	24	4.2	.919	3B-148, SS-1
1908		127	.191	.212	439	84	7	1	0	0.0	27	14	23		16	1	0	187	258	40	15	3.8	.918	3B-122, SS-4
1909	2 teams	STL N (105G – .214)			PIT N (46G – .256)																			
"	total	151	.226	.290	589	133	19	8	1	0.2	92	40	78		29	0	0	175	269	36	12	3.2	.925	3B-151
1910	PIT N	148	.296	.417	602	178	43	12	2	0.3	101	52	66	27	36	0	0	167	289	35	11	3.3	.929	3B-148
1911		153	.259	.366	598	155	24	17	2	0.3	96	52	67	41	23	1	0	181	282	35	21	3.3	.930	3B-152
1912		130	.288	.405	528	152	31	11	3	0.6	99	35	54	40	20	0	0	144	187	18	14	2.7	.948	3B-130
1913	2 teams	PIT N (113G – .270)			PHI N (19G – .224)																			
"	total	132	.265	.322	506	134	23	0	2	0.4	63	51	34	31	12	5	1	174	208	23	14	3.1	.943	3B-125
1914	PHI N	126	.272	.302	467	127	12	1	0	0.0	61	26	45	44	9	4	2	222	349	43	23	4.9	.930	2B-101, 3B-22
1915		105	.209	.245	387	81	6	4	0	0.0	50	21	39	28	4	0	0	98	183	9	9	2.8	.969	3B-105
1916		48	.234	.319	141	33	10	1	0	0.0	22	9	14	7	6	6	1	46	79	9	8	2.8	.933	3B-40
1917	2 teams	PHI N (13G – .357)			CHI A (1G – .000)																			
"	total	14	.333	.333	15	5	0	0	0	0.0	1	0	1	2	1	9	2	2	2	0	0	0.3	1.000	3B-4, 2B-1
11 yrs.		1282	.254	.323	4830	1225	186	60	10	0.2	667	329	456	220	176	26	6	1611	2459	298	151	3.4	.932	3B-1147, 2B-102, SS-5

WORLD SERIES

Year	Team	Games	BA	SA	AB	H	2B	3B	HR	HR%	R	RBI	BB	SO	SB	Pinch AB	Pinch H	PO	A	E	DP	TC/G	FA	G by Pos
1909	PIT N	7	.250	.292	24	6	1	0	0	0.0	5	0	1	4	1	0	0	11	17	1	1	4.1	.966	3B-7
1915	PHI N	1	.000	.000	1	0	0	0	0	0.0	0	0	0	0	0	0	0	0	0	0	0	0.0	–	
2 yrs.		8	.240	.280	25	6	1	0	0	0.0	5	0	1	4	1	0	0	11	17	1	1	3.6	.966	3B-7

Tommy Byrne

BYRNE, THOMAS JOSEPH
B. Dec. 31, 1919, Baltimore, Md.   BL TL 6'1" 182 lbs.

Year	Team	Games	BA	SA	AB	H	2B	3B	HR	HR%	R	RBI	BB	SO	SB	Pinch AB	Pinch H	PO	A	E	DP	TC/G	FA	G by Pos
1943	NY A	13	.091	.091	11	1	0	0	0	0.0	0	0	2	3	0	1	0	2	8	1	0	0.8	.909	P-11
1946		14	.222	.222	9	2	0	0	0	0.0	2	0	1	0	0	6	1	1	2	0	0	1.0	1.000	P-4
1947		4	–	–	0	0	0	0	0	–	0	0	1	0	0	0	0	0	1	0	0	0.3	1.000	P-4
1948		31	.326	.500	46	15	3	1	1	2.2	8	7	1	7	0	0	0	2	17	0	2	0.6	1.000	P-31
1949		35	.193	.289	83	16	4	2	0	0.0	8	13	2	20	0	1	0	7	19	3	4	0.8	.897	P-32
1950		34	.272	.407	81	22	3	1	2	2.5	14	16	4	15	1	1	0	9	23	0	2	0.9	1.000	P-31
1951	2 teams	NY A (9G – .222)			STL A (34G – .281)																			
"	total	43	.273	.409	66	18	3	0	2	3.0	9	15	4	10	1	13	2	6	20	1	2	0.6	.963	P-28
1952	STL A	40	.250	.369	84	21	5	1	1	1.2	9	12	5	18	0	9	0	10	15	2	1	0.7	.926	P-29
1953	2 teams	CHI A (18G – .167)			WAS A (14G – .059)																			
"	total	32	.114	.200	35	4	0	0	1	2.9	2	5	5	13	0	18	1	4	11	2	0	0.5	.882	P-12
1954	NY A	7	.368	.684	19	7	4	1	0	0.0	2	6	0	3	0	2	0	0	8	1	1	1.3	.889	P-5
1955		45	.205	.282	78	16	1	1	1	1.3	6	6	8	15	0	14	0	4	22	2	3	0.6	.929	P-27
1956		44	.269	.500	52	14	1	0	3	5.8	8	10	2	11	0	8	0	8	18	1	4	0.6	.963	P-37
1957		35	.189	.486	37	7	2	0	3	8.1	5	8	3	11	0	7	2	6	9	1	0	0.5	.938	P-30
13 yrs.		377	.238	.378	601	143	26	8	14	2.3	73	98	38	126	1	80	6	59	173	14	19	0.7	.943	P-281

WORLD SERIES

Year	Team	Games	BA	SA	AB	H	2B	3B	HR	HR%	R	RBI	BB	SO	SB	Pinch AB	Pinch H	PO	A	E	DP	TC/G	FA	G by Pos
1949	NY A	1	1.000	1.000	1	1	0	0	0	0.0	0	0	0	0	0	0	0	0	0	0	0	0.0	–	P-1
1955		3	.167	.167	6	1	0	0	0	0.0	0	0	1	0	0	2	0	0	2	0	0	0.7	1.000	P-2
1956		2	.000	.000	2	0	0	0	0	0.0	0	0	0	1	0	0	0	0	0	0	0	0.0	–	P-1
1957		2	.500	.500	2	1	0	0	0	0.0	0	2	0	2	0	0	0	0	0	0	0	0.0	–	P-2
4 yrs.		8	.300	.300	10	3	0	0	0	0.0	0	2	1	3	0	2	0	0	2	0	0	0.3	1.000	P-6

Jim Byrnes

BYRNES, JAMES JOSEPH
B. Jan. 5, 1880, San Francisco, Calif. D. July 31, 1941, San Francisco, Calif.   BR TR 5'9" 150 lbs.

Year	Team	Games	BA	SA	AB	H	2B	3B	HR	HR%	R	RBI	BB	SO	SB	Pinch AB	Pinch H	PO	A	E	DP	TC/G	FA	G by Pos
1906	PHI A	9	.174	.261	23	4	1	0	0	0.0	2	0	0		0	1	0	30	10	5	1	5.0	.889	C-8

Milt Byrnes

BYRNES, MILTON JOHN (Skippy)
B. Nov. 15, 1916, St. Louis, Mo. D. Feb. 1, 1979, St. Louis, Mo.   BL TL 5'10½" 170 lbs.

Year	Team	Games	BA	SA	AB	H	2B	3B	HR	HR%	R	RBI	BB	SO	SB	Pinch AB	Pinch H	PO	A	E	DP	TC/G	FA	G by Pos
1943	STL A	129	.280	.406	429	120	28	7	4	0.9	58	50	54	49	1	14	1	289	13	1	3	2.3	.997	OF-114
1944		128	.295	.393	407	120	20	4	4	1.0	63	45	68	50	1	5	3	282	7	7	1	2.3	.976	OF-122

Year	Team	Games	BA	SA	AB	H	2B	3B	HR	HR%	R	RBI	BB	SO	SB	Pinch Hit AB	Pinch Hit H	PO	A	E	DP	TC/G	FA	G by Pos

Milt Byrnes *continued*

Year	Team	Games	BA	SA	AB	H	2B	3B	HR	HR%	R	RBI	BB	SO	SB	PH AB	PH H	PO	A	E	DP	TC/G	FA	G by Pos
1945		133	.249	.387	442	110	29	4	8	1.8	53	59	78	84	1	7	2	333	13	4	0	2.6	.989	OF-125, 1B-2
3 yrs.		390	.274	.395	1278	350	77	15	16	1.3	174	154	200	183	3	26	6	904	33	12	4	2.4	.987	OF-361, 1B-2

WORLD SERIES

Year	Team	Games	BA	SA	AB	H	2B	3B	HR	HR%	R	RBI	BB	SO	SB	PH AB	PH H	PO	A	E	DP	TC/G	FA	G by Pos
1944	STL A	3	.000	.000	2	0	0	0	0	0.0	0	0	1	2	0	2	0	0	0	0	0	0.0	—	

Putsy Caballero

CABALLERO, RALPH JOSEPH
B. Nov. 5, 1927, New Orleans, La.
BR TR 5'10" 170 lbs.

Year	Team	Games	BA	SA	AB	H	2B	3B	HR	HR%	R	RBI	BB	SO	SB	PH AB	PH H	PO	A	E	DP	TC/G	FA	G by Pos
1944	PHI N	4	.000	.000	4	0	0	0	0	0.0	0	0	0	1	0	0	0	4	4	1	0	2.3	.889	3B-2
1945		9	.000	.000	1	0	0	0	0	0.0	1	1	0	0	0	0	0	4	2	1	1	0.8	.857	3B-5
1947		2	.143	.143	7	1	0	0	0	0.0	2	0	1	0	0	0	0	3	6	1	1	4.5	.900	3B-2, 2B-1
1948		113	.245	.285	351	86	12	1	0	0.0	33	19	24	18	7	11	3	145	200	18	23	3.2	.950	3B-79, 2B-23
1949		29	.279	.324	68	19	3	0	0	0.0	8	3	0	3	0	4	1	60	48	2	13	3.8	.982	2B-21, SS-1
1950		46	.167	.167	24	4	0	0	0	0.0	12	0	2	2	1	5	2	14	8	1	2	0.5	.957	2B-5, SS-2
1951		84	.186	.248	161	30	3	2	1	0.6	15	11	12	7	1	3	0	133	124	4	37	3.1	.985	2B-57, SS-3, 3B-3
1952		35	.238	.310	42	10	3	0	0	0.0	10	6	2	3	1	1	1	24	23	4	5	1.5	.922	SS-8, 3B-7, 2B-7
8 yrs.		322	.228	.274	658	150	21	3	1	0.2	81	40	41	34	10	24	7	387	415	31	82	2.6	.963	2B-115, 3B-101, SS-14

WORLD SERIES

Year	Team	Games	BA	SA	AB	H	2B	3B	HR	HR%	R	RBI	BB	SO	SB	PH AB	PH H	PO	A	E	DP	TC/G	FA	G by Pos
1950	PHI N	3	.000	.000	1	0	0	0	0	0.0	0	0	0	1	0	1	0	0	0	0	0	0.0	—	

Enos Cabell

CABELL, ENOS MILTON
B. Oct. 8, 1949, Fort Riley, Kans.
BR TR 6'4" 170 lbs.

Year	Team	Games	BA	SA	AB	H	2B	3B	HR	HR%	R	RBI	BB	SO	SB	PH AB	PH H	PO	A	E	DP	TC/G	FA	G by Pos
1972	BAL A	3	.000	.000	5	0	0	0	0	0.0	0	0	0	1	0	1	0	7	0	0	1	2.3	1.000	1B-1
1973		32	.213	.319	47	10	2	0	1	2.1	12	3	3	7	1	4	1	111	4	1	14	3.6	.991	1B-23, 3B-1
1974		80	.241	.339	174	42	4	2	3	1.7	24	17	7	20	5	4	0	223	45	4	18	3.4	.985	1B-28, OF-22, 3B-19, 2B-1
1975	HOU N	117	.264	.365	348	92	17	6	2	0.6	43	43	18	53	12	17	7	197	58	6	17	2.2	.977	1B-25, 3B-22
1976		144	.273	.329	586	160	13	7	2	0.3	85	43	29	79	35	1	0	131	263	17	24	2.9	.959	3B-143, 1B-3
1977		150	.282	.438	625	176	36	7	16	2.6	101	68	27	55	42	3	0	176	288	24	19	3.3	.951	3B-144, 1B-8, SS-1
1978		162	.295	.398	660	195	31	8	7	1.1	92	71	22	80	33	0	0	211	277	18	19	3.1	.964	3B-153, 1B-14, SS-1
1979		155	.272	.368	603	164	30	5	6	1.0	60	67	21	68	37	0	0	396	199	14	31	3.9	.977	3B-132, 1B-51
1980		152	.276	.351	604	167	23	8	2	0.3	69	55	26	84	21	1	1	118	250	29	15	2.6	.927	3B-150, 1B-1
1981	SF N	96	.255	.326	396	101	20	1	2	0.5	41	36	10	47	6	6	1	634	90	16	58	7.7	.978	1B-69, 3B-32
1982	DET A	125	.261	.323	464	121	17	3	2	0.4	45	37	15	48	15	10	2	592	143	16	69	6.0	.979	1B-83, 3B-59, OF-3
1983		121	.311	.434	392	122	23	5	5	1.3	62	46	16	41	4	11	4	830	79	3	76	7.5	.997	1B-106, DH-8, 3B-4, SS-1
1984	HOU N	127	.310	.417	436	135	17	3	8	1.8	52	44	21	47	21	17	5	971	66	7	97	8.2	.993	1B-112
1985	2 teams	HOU N (60G – .245)		LA N	(57G – .292)																			
"	total	117	.272	.352	335	91	19	1	2	0.6	40	30	30	36	9	31	0	456	97	11	41	4.8	.980	1B-70, 3B-32, OF-4
1986	LA N	107	.256	.318	277	71	11	0	2	0.7	27	29	14	26	10	34	4	389	49	9	31	4.2	.980	1B-61, OF-16, 3B-7
15 yrs.		1688	.277	.370	5952	1647	263	56	60	1.0	753	596	259	691	238	140	35	5442	1908	175	530	4.5	.977	3B-888, 1B-655, OF-112, DH-8, SS-3, 2B-1

LEAGUE CHAMPIONSHIP SERIES

Year	Team	Games	BA	SA	AB	H	2B	3B	HR	HR%	R	RBI	BB	SO	SB	PH AB	PH H	PO	A	E	DP	TC/G	FA	G by Pos
1974	BAL A	3	.250	.250	4	1	0	0	0	0.0	0	0	0	1	0	0	0	2	0	0	0	0.7	1.000	OF-1
1980	HOU N	5	.238	.286	21	5	1	0	0	0.0	1	0	1	3	0	0	0	1	9	0	1	2.0	1.000	3B-5
1985	LA N	5	.077	.077	13	1	0	0	0	0.0	0	0	0	3	0	1	0	19	3	0	1	4.4	1.000	1B-3
3 yrs.		13	.184	.211	38	7	1	0	0	0.0	1	0	1	7	0	1	0	22	12	0	2	2.6	1.000	3B-5, 1B-3, OF-1

Al Cabrera

CABRERA, ALFREDO A.
B. 1883, Canary Islands, Spain   D. Havana, Cuba
TR

Year	Team	Games	BA	SA	AB	H	2B	3B	HR	HR%	R	RBI	BB	SO	SB	PH AB	PH H	PO	A	E	DP	TC/G	FA	G by Pos
1913	STL N	1	.000	.000	2	0	0	0	0	0.0	0	0	0	0	0	0	0	0	0	0	0	0.0	—	SS-1

Francisco Cabrera

CABRERA, FRANCISCO
Born Francisco Cabrera y Paulino.
B. Oct. 10, 1966, Santo Domingo, Dominican Republic
BR TR 6'4" 195 lbs.

Year	Team	Games	BA	SA	AB	H	2B	3B	HR	HR%	R	RBI	BB	SO	SB	PH AB	PH H	PO	A	E	DP	TC/G	FA	G by Pos
1989	2 teams	TOR A (3G – .167)		ATL N	(4G – .214)																			
"	total	7	.192	.308	26	5	3	0	0	0.0	1	0	1	6	0	1	0	27	1	1	1	4.1	.966	DH-3, 1B-2, C-1

Craig Cacek

CACEK, CRAIG THOMAS
B. Sept. 10, 1954, Hollywood, Calif.
BR TR 6'1" 200 lbs.

Year	Team	Games	BA	SA	AB	H	2B	3B	HR	HR%	R	RBI	BB	SO	SB	PH AB	PH H	PO	A	E	DP	TC/G	FA	G by Pos
1977	HOU N	7	.050	.050	20	1	0	0	0	0.0	0	1	1	3	0	2	0	52	1	1	6	7.7	.981	1B-6

Charlie Cady

CADY, CHARLES B.
B. Dec., 1865, Chicago, Ill.   D. June 7, 1909, Kankakee, Ill.
5'11" 180 lbs.

Year	Team	Games	BA	SA	AB	H	2B	3B	HR	HR%	R	RBI	BB	SO	SB	PH AB	PH H	PO	A	E	DP	TC/G	FA	G by Pos
1883	CLE N	3	.000	.000	11	0	0	0	0	0.0	0		1		0	5		0	1	0	0	0.7	1.000	OF-2, P-1
1884	2 teams	CHI U (6G – .100)		KC U	(2G – .000)																			
"	total	8	.087	.217	23	2	0	1	0	0.0	4		1			0		7	8	7	0	2.8	.682	P-4, OF-2, 2B-1, C-1
2 yrs.		11	.059	.147	34	2	1	1	0	0.0	4		2	5		0		8	9	7	0	2.2	.708	P-5, OF-4, 2B-1, C-1

Hick Cady

CADY, FORREST LeROY
B. Jan. 26, 1886, Bishop Hill, Ill.   D. Mar. 3, 1946, Cedar Rapids, Iowa
BR TR 6'2" 179 lbs.

Year	Team	Games	BA	SA	AB	H	2B	3B	HR	HR%	R	RBI	BB	SO	SB	PH AB	PH H	PO	A	E	DP	TC/G	FA	G by Pos
1912	BOS A	47	.259	.385	135	35	13	2	0	0.0	19	9	10		0	0	0	280	57	3	6	7.2	.991	C-43, 1B-4
1913		39	.250	.344	96	24	5	2	0	0.0	10	6	5	14	1	1	0	198	44	2	3	6.3	.992	C-38
1914		61	.258	.308	159	41	6	1	0	0.0	14	8	12	22	2	3	0	217	80	9	1	5.0	.971	C-58
1915		78	.278	.346	205	57	10	2	0	0.0	25	17	19	25	0	1	0	313	79	8	12	5.1	.980	C-77
1916		78	.191	.265	162	31	6	3	0	0.0	5	13	15	16	0	1	0	195	51	8	4	3.3	.969	C-63, 1B-3
1917		17	.152	.217	46	7	1	0	0	0.0	2	6	1	6	0	3	1	54	17	3	2	4.4	.959	C-14
1919	PHI N	34	.214	.306	98	21	6	0	1	1.0	6	19	4	8	1	2	0	85	35	2	2	3.6	.984	C-29
7 yrs.		354	.240	.320	901	216	47	11	1	0.1	83	74	66	91	4	25	7	1342	363	35	30	4.9	.980	C-322, 1B-7

WORLD SERIES

Year	Team	Games	BA	SA	AB	H	2B	3B	HR	HR%	R	RBI	BB	SO	SB	PH AB	PH H	PO	A	E	DP	TC/G	FA	G by Pos
1912	BOS A	7	.136	.136	22	3	0	0	0	0.0	1	1	0	3	0	0	0	35	9	1	0	6.4	.978	C-7

Year	Team		Games	BA	SA	AB	H	2B	3B	HR	HR%	R	RBI	BB	SO	SB	Pinch Hit AB	Pinch Hit H	PO	A	E	DP	TC/G	FA	G by Pos

Hick Cady *continued*

1915			4	.333	.333	6	2	0	0	0	0.0	0	0	1	2	0	0	0	14	4	0	0	4.5	1.000	C-4
1916			2	.250	.250	4	1	0	0	0	0.0	1	0	3	0	0	0	0	11	1	0	1	6.0	1.000	C-2
3 yrs.			13	.188	.188	32	6	0	0	0	0.0	2	1	4	5	0	0	0	60	14	1	1	5.8	.987	C-13

Tom Cafego

CAFEGO, THOMAS   BL TR 5'10" 160 lbs.
B. Aug. 21, 1911, Whipple, W. Va.   D. Oct. 29, 1961, Detroit, Mich.

| 1937 | STL | A | 4 | .000 | .000 | 4 | 0 | 0 | 0 | 0 | 0.0 | 1 | 0 | 1 | 0 | 1 | 0 | 1 | 1 | 0 | 1 | 0 | 0.5 | .500 | OF-1 |

Joe Caffie

CAFFIE, JOSEPH CLIFFORD (Rabbit)   BL TR 5'10½" 180 lbs.
B. Feb. 14, 1931, Ramer, Ala.

1956	CLE	A	12	.342	.342	38	13	0	0	0	0.0	7	4	8	3	1	1	21	1	0	0	1.8	1.000	OF-10
1957			32	.270	.416	89	24	2	1	3	3.4	14	10	4	11	0	9	0	40	0	1	0	1.3	.976	OF-19
2 yrs.			44	.291	.394	127	37	2	1	3	2.4	21	11	8	19	3	10	1	61	1	1	0	1.4	.984	OF-29

Ben Caffyn

CAFFYN, BENJAMIN THOMAS   BL TL
B. Feb. 10, 1880, Peoria, Ill.   D. Nov. 22, 1942, Peoria, Ill.

| 1906 | CLE | A | 30 | .194 | .233 | 103 | 20 | 4 | 0 | 0 | 0.0 | 16 | 3 | 12 | | 2 | 1 | 0 | 38 | 2 | 4 | 2 | 1.5 | .909 | OF-29 |

Wayne Cage

CAGE, WAYNE LEVELL   BL TL 6'4" 205 lbs.
B. Nov. 23, 1951, Monroe, La.

1978	CLE	A	36	.245	.449	98	24	6	1	4	4.1	11	13	9	28	1	6	0	73	8	1	10	2.3	.988	DH-20, 1B-11
1979			29	.232	.321	56	13	2	0	1	1.8	6	6	5	16	0	12	1	37	4	0	3	1.4	1.000	DH-9, 1B-7
2 yrs.			65	.240	.403	154	37	8	1	5	3.2	17	19	14	44	1	18	1	110	12	1	13	1.9	.992	DH-29, 1B-18

John Cahill

CAHILL, JOHN PATRICK FRANCIS (Patsy)   BR TR 5'7½" 168 lbs.
B. 1864, San Francisco, Calif.   D. Nov. 1, 1901, Pleasanton, Calif.

1884	COL	AA	59	.219	.262	210	46	3	3	0	0.0	28		6			0	0	71	28	19	2	2.0	.839	OF-54, SS-5, P-2
1886	STL	N	125	.199	.268	463	92	17	6	1	0.2	43	32	9	79		0	0	166	39	36	5	1.9	.851	OF-124, P-2, SS-1, 3B-1
1887	IND	N	68	.205	.243	263	54	4	3	0	0.0	22	26	9	5	34	0	0	90	28	28	3	2.1	.808	OF-56, 3B-9, P-6, SS-1
3 yrs.			252	.205	.260	936	192	24	12	1	0.1	93	58	24	84	34	0	0	327	95	83	10	2.0	.836	OF-234, 3B-10, P-10, SS-7

Tom Cahill

CAHILL, THOMAS H.
B. Oct., 1868, Fall River, Mass.   D. Dec. 25, 1894, Scranton, Pa.

| 1891 | LOU | AA | 120 | .256 | .351 | 433 | 111 | 18 | 7 | 3 | 0.7 | 70 | 47 | 41 | 51 | 39 | 0 | 0 | 389 | 242 | 69 | 32 | 5.8 | .901 | C-56, SS-49, OF-12, 2B-6, 3B-2 |

George Caithamer

CAITHAMER, GEORGE THEODORE   BR TR 5'7½" 160 lbs.
B. July 22, 1910, Chicago, Ill.   D. June 1, 1954, Chicago, Ill.

| 1934 | CHI | A | 5 | .316 | .368 | 19 | 6 | 1 | 0 | 0 | 0.0 | 1 | 3 | 1 | 5 | 0 | 0 | 0 | 21 | 2 | 1 | 1 | 4.8 | .958 | C-5 |

Ivan Calderon

CALDERON, IVAN   BR TR 5'11" 160 lbs.
Born Ivan Calderon y Perez.
B. Mar. 19, 1962, Fajardo, Puerto Rico

1984	SEA	A	11	.208	.375	24	5	1	0	1	4.2	2	1	2	5	1	0	0	22	0	0	0	2.0	1.000	OF-11
1985			67	.286	.514	210	60	16	4	8	3.8	37	28	19	45	4	10	3	108	5	2	3	1.7	.983	OF-53, DH-3, 1B-2
1986	2 teams					SEA A	(37G – .237)			CHI A	(13G – .303)														
"	total		50	.250	.341	164	41	7	0	2	1.2	16	15	9	39	3	7	2	64	4	5	1	1.5	.932	OF-37, DH-6
1987	CHI	A	144	.293	.526	542	159	38	2	28	5.2	93	83	60	109	10	1	0	295	8	5	3	2.1	.984	OF-139, DH-3
1988			73	.212	.424	264	56	14	0	14	5.3	40	35	34	66	4	1	0	141	5	7	1	2.1	.954	OF-67, DH-3
1989			157	.286	.437	622	178	34	9	14	2.3	83	87	43	94	7	2	0	384	17	9	24	2.6	.978	OF-103, DH-36, 1B-26
6 yrs.			502	.273	.461	1826	499	110	16	67	3.7	271	249	167	358	29	21	5	1014	39	28	32	2.2	.974	OF-410, DH-51, 1B-28

Sammy Calderone

CALDERONE, SAMUEL FRANCIS   BR TR 5'10½" 185 lbs.
B. Feb. 6, 1926, Beverly, N. J.

1950	NY	N	34	.299	.358	67	20	1	0	1	1.5	9	12	2	5	0	1	0	63	6	2	1	2.1	.972	C-33
1953			35	.222	.267	45	10	2	0	0	0.0	4	8	1	4	0	6	0	50	6	2	2	1.7	.966	C-31
1954	MIL	N	22	.379	.448	29	11	2	0	0	0.0	3	5	4	4	0	7	2	45	4	0	3	2.2	1.000	C-16
3 yrs.			91	.291	.348	141	41	5	0	1	0.7	16	25	7	13	0	14	2	158	16	4	6	2.0	.978	C-80

Bruce Caldwell

CALDWELL, BRUCE   BR TR 6' 195 lbs.
B. Feb. 8, 1906, Ashton, R. I.   D. Feb. 15, 1959, West Haven, Conn.

1928	CLE	A	18	.222	.333	27	6	1	0	0	0.0	2	3	2	2	1	7	0	15	1	0	1	0.9	1.000	OF-10, 1B-1
1932	BKN	N	7	.091	.091	11	1	0	0	0	0.0	2	2	2	2	0	1	1	14	0	2	1	2.3	.875	1B-6
2 yrs.			25	.184	.263	38	7	1	0	0	0.0	4	5	4	4	1	8	1	29	1	2	2	1.3	.938	OF-10, 1B-7

Ray Caldwell

CALDWELL, RAYMOND BENJAMIN (Slim)   BL TR 6'2" 190 lbs.
B. Apr. 26, 1888, Croydon, Pa.   D. Aug. 17, 1967, Salamanca, N. Y.

1910	NY	A	6	.000	.000	6	0	0	0	0	0.0	0	0	0			0	0	1	4	0	0	0.8	1.000	P-6
1911			58	.272	.313	147	40	4	1	0	0.0	14	17	11	0	5	4	1	27	56	6	2	1.5	.933	P-41, OF-11
1912			41	.237	.303	76	18	1	2	0	0.0	18	6	5		4	7	2	2	59	4	2	1.6	.938	P-30
1913			55	.289	.361	97	28	3	2	0	0.0	10	11	3	15	3	19	4	8	42	0	1	0.9	1.000	P-27, OF-3
1914			59	.195	.230	113	22	4	0	0	0.0	9	10	7	24	2	21	4	56	46	6	3	1.8	.944	P-31, 1B-6
1915			72	.243	.368	144	35	4	1	4	2.8	27	20	9	32	4	**33**	9	12	72	1	5	1.2	.988	P-36
1916			45	.204	.226	93	19	2	0	0	0.0	4	2	4	17	1	19	3	4	45	3	2	1.2	.942	P-21, OF-3
1917			63	.258	.371	124	32	6	1	2	1.6	12	12	16	15	2	15	5	23	60	2	1	1.3	.976	P-32, OF-8
1918			65	.291	.377	151	44	10	0	1	0.7	14	19	13	23	2	19	6	52	38	3	2	1.4	.968	P-24, OF-19

Year	Team		Games	BA	SA	AB	H	2B	3B	HR	HR%	R	RBI	BB	SO	SB	Pinch Hit AB	Pinch Hit H	PO	A	E	DP	TC/G	FA	G by Pos

Ray Caldwell *continued*

Year	Team		Games	BA	SA	AB	H	2B	3B	HR	HR%	R	RBI	BB	SO	SB	AB	H	PO	A	E	DP	TC/G	FA	G by Pos
1919	2 teams	BOS A (33G – .271)				CLE A (6G – .348)																			
"	total		39	.296	.394	71	21	5	1	0	0.0	9	6	0	13	0	12	2	6	26	2	0	0.9	.941	P-24, OF-2
1920	CLE	A	41	.213	.247	89	19	3	0	0	0.0	17	7	10	13	0	4	0	6	49	5	0	1.5	.917	P-34
1921			38	.208	.340	53	11	4	0	1	1.9	2	3	2	5	0	1	0	5	35	3	1	1.1	.930	P-37
12 yrs.			582	.248	.322	1164	289	46	8	8	0.7	138	114	78	158	23	154	36	202	532	35	19	1.3	.954	P-343, OF-46, 1B-6

WORLD SERIES

Year	Team		Games	BA	SA	AB	H	2B	3B	HR	HR%	R	RBI	BB	SO	SB	AB	H	PO	A	E	DP	TC/G	FA	G by Pos
1920	CLE	A	1	–	–	0	0	0	0	0	–	0	0	0	0	0	0	0	0	0	0	0	0.0	–	P-1

Bill Calhoun

CALHOUN, WILLIAM DAVITTE (Mary)
B. June 23, 1890, Rockmart, Ga. D. Feb. 11, 1955, Sandersville, Ga. BL TL 6' 180 lbs.

Year	Team	Games	BA	SA	AB	H	2B	3B	HR	HR%	R	RBI	BB	SO	SB	AB	H	PO	A	E	DP	TC/G	FA	G by Pos
1913	BOS N	6	.077	.077	13	1	0	0	0	0.0	0	0	0	3	0	3	1	31	1	1	1	5.5	.970	1B-3

John Calhoun

CALHOUN, JOHN CHARLES (Red)
B. Dec. 14, 1879, Pittsburgh, Pa. D. Feb. 27, 1947, Cincinnati, Ohio BR TR 6' 185 lbs.

Year	Team	Games	BA	SA	AB	H	2B	3B	HR	HR%	R	RBI	BB	SO	SB	AB	H	PO	A	E	DP	TC/G	FA	G by Pos
1902	STL N	20	.156	.219	64	10	2	1	0	0.0	3	8	8		1	2	0	60	22	4	4	4.3	.953	3B-12, 1B-5, OF-1

Marty Callaghan

CALLAGHAN, MARTIN FRANCIS
B. June 9, 1900, Norwood, Mass. D. June 23, 1975, Norfolk, Mass. BL TL 5'10" 157 lbs.

Year	Team	Games	BA	SA	AB	H	2B	3B	HR	HR%	R	RBI	BB	SO	SB	AB	H	PO	A	E	DP	TC/G	FA	G by Pos
1922	CHI N	74	.257	.343	175	45	7	4	0	0.0	31	20	17	17	2	17	3	85	2	5	0	1.2	.946	OF-53
1923		61	.225	.279	129	29	1	4	0	0.0	18	14	8	18	2	16	3	60	3	2	0	1.1	.969	OF-38
1928	CIN N	81	.290	.370	238	69	11	4	0	0.0	29	24	27	10	5	7	1	140	5	3	2	1.8	.980	OF-69
1930		79	.276	.333	225	62	9	2	0	0.0	28	16	19	25	1	23	3	142	3	2	1	1.9	.986	OF-54
4 yrs.		295	.267	.338	767	205	28	13	0	0.0	106	74	71	70	10	63	10	427	13	12	3	1.5	.973	OF-214

Dave Callahan

CALLAHAN, DAVID JOSEPH
B. July 20, 1888, Ottawa, Ill. D. Oct. 28, 1969, Ottawa, Ill. BL TR 5'10" 165 lbs.

Year	Team	Games	BA	SA	AB	H	2B	3B	HR	HR%	R	RBI	BB	SO	SB	AB	H	PO	A	E	DP	TC/G	FA	G by Pos
1910	CLE A	13	.182	.205	44	8	1	0	0	0.0	6	2	4		5	1	0	28	0	0	0	2.2	1.000	OF-12
1911		5	.333	.500	12	4	0	1	0	0.0	1	0	1		0	2	1	4	2	0	1	1.2	1.000	OF-3
2 yrs.		18	.214	.268	56	12	1	1	0	0.0	7	2	5		5	3	1	32	2	0	1	1.9	1.000	OF-15

Ed Callahan

CALLAHAN, EDWARD J.
B. Boston, Mass. Deceased.

Year	Team		Games	BA	SA	AB	H	2B	3B	HR	HR%	R	RBI	BB	SO	SB	AB	H	PO	A	E	DP	TC/G	FA	G by Pos
1884	3 teams	STL U (1G – .000)				KC U (3G – .364)							BOS U (4G – .385)												
"	total		8	.333	.333	27	9	0	0	0	0.0	2		1			0	0	7	12	5	1	3.0	.792	OF-5, SS-3

Leo Callahan

CALLAHAN, LEO DAVID
B. Aug. 9, 1890, Jamaica Plain, Mass. D. May 2, 1982, Erie, Pa. BL TL 5'8" 142 lbs.

Year	Team	Games	BA	SA	AB	H	2B	3B	HR	HR%	R	RBI	BB	SO	SB	AB	H	PO	A	E	DP	TC/G	FA	G by Pos
1913	BKN N	33	.171	.293	41	7	3	1	0	0.0	6	3	4	5	1	24	5	12	0	2	0	0.4	.857	OF-8
1919	PHI N	81	.230	.336	235	54	14	4	1	0.4	26	9	29	19	5	21	3	102	13	6	1	1.5	.950	OF-58
2 yrs.		114	.221	.330	276	61	17	5	1	0.4	32	12	33	24	5	45	8	114	13	8	1	1.2	.941	OF-66

Nixey Callahan

CALLAHAN, JAMES JOSEPH (Cal)
B. Mar. 18, 1874, Fitchburg, Mass. D. Oct. 4, 1934, Boston, Mass. BR TR 5'10½" 180 lbs.
Manager 1903-04, 1912-14, 1916-17.

Year	Team	Games	BA	SA	AB	H	2B	3B	HR	HR%	R	RBI	BB	SO	SB	AB	H	PO	A	E	DP	TC/G	FA	G by Pos
1894	PHI N	9	.238	.238	21	5	0	0	0	0.0	4	0	0		7	0	0	4	8	1	0	1.4	.923	P-9
1897	CHI N	94	.292	.400	360	105	18	6	3	0.8	60	47	10		12	2	0	147	201	42	25	4.1	.892	2B-30, P-23, OF-21, SS-18, 3B-2
1898		43	.262	.366	164	43	7	5	0	0.0	27	22	4		3	0	0	42	67	11	3	2.8	.908	P-31, OF-9, SS-1, 2B-1, 1B-1
1899		47	.260	.327	150	39	4	3	0	0.0	21	18	8		9	1	0	40	103	14	4	3.3	.911	P-35, OF-9, SS-2, 2B-1
1900		32	.235	.296	115	27	3	2	0	0.0	16	9	6		5	0	0	21	94	3	2	3.7	.975	P-32
1901	CHI A	45	.331	.466	118	39	7	3	1	0.8	15	19	10		10	10	3	27	93	10	5	2.9	.923	P-27, 3B-6, 2B-2
1902		70	.234	.284	218	51	7	2	0	0.0	27	13	6		4	12	2	57	108	9	7	2.5	.948	P-35, OF-23, SS-1
1903		118	.292	.387	439	128	26	5	2	0.5	47	56	20		24	5	3	131	216	38	5	3.3	.901	3B-102, OF-8, P-3
1904		132	.261	.317	482	126	23	2	0	0.0	66	54	39		29	1	0	207	79	14	5	2.3	.953	OF-104, 2B-28
1905		96	.272	.368	345	94	18	6	1	0.3	50	43	29		26	3	1	120	10	6	0	1.4	.956	OF-93
1911		120	.281	.350	466	131	13	5	3	0.6	64	60	15		45	5	1	173	10	7	2	1.6	.963	OF-114
1912		111	.272	.336	408	111	9	7	1	0.2	45	52	12		19	4	1	166	3	11	0	1.6	.939	OF-107
1913		6	.222	.222	9	2	0	0	0	0.0	1	1	2		0	5	1	2	0	0	0	0.3	1.000	OF-1
13 yrs.		923	.273	.352	3295	901	135	46	11	0.3	442	394	159	9	186	48	12	1137	992	166	58	2.5	.928	OF-489, P-195, 3B-110, 2B-62, SS-22, 1B-1

Pat Callahan

CALLAHAN, PATRICK HENRY
B. Oct. 15, 1866, Cleveland, Ohio D. Feb. 4, 1940, Louisville, Ky.

Year	Team	Games	BA	SA	AB	H	2B	3B	HR	HR%	R	RBI	BB	SO	SB	AB	H	PO	A	E	DP	TC/G	FA	G by Pos
1884	IND AA	61	.260	.353	258	67	8	5	2	0.8	38		8			0	0	66	94	37	5	3.2	.812	3B-61

Red Callahan

CALLAHAN, JAMES TIMOTHY (Red)
Born James Timothy Callaghan.
B. Jan. 12, 1879, Allegheny County, Pa. D. Mar. 9, 1968, Carnegie, Pa. BR TR 5'9" 145 lbs.

Year	Team	Games	BA	SA	AB	H	2B	3B	HR	HR%	R	RBI	BB	SO	SB	AB	H	PO	A	E	DP	TC/G	FA	G by Pos
1902	NY N	1	.000	.000	4	0	0	0	0	0.0	0	0	1		0	0	0	0	0	0	0	0.0	–	OF-1

Wes Callahan

CALLAHAN, WESLEY LeROY
B. July 3, 1888, Lyons, Ind. D. Sept. 13, 1953, Dayton, Ohio BR TR 5'7½" 155 lbs.

Year	Team	Games	BA	SA	AB	H	2B	3B	HR	HR%	R	RBI	BB	SO	SB	AB	H	PO	A	E	DP	TC/G	FA	G by Pos
1913	STL N	7	.286	.286	14	4	0	0	0	0.0	0	1	2	2	1	1	0	8	15	2	2	3.6	.920	SS-6

Frank Callaway

CALLAWAY, FRANK BURNETT
B. Feb. 26, 1898, Knoxville, Tenn. D. Aug. 21, 1987, Knoxville, Tenn. BR TR 6' 170 lbs.

Year	Team	Games	BA	SA	AB	H	2B	3B	HR	HR%	R	RBI	BB	SO	SB	AB	H	PO	A	E	DP	TC/G	FA	G by Pos
1921	PHI A	14	.240	.300	50	12	1	1	0	0.0	7	2	2	11	0	0	0	22	43	9	2	5.3	.878	SS-14

Year	Team		Games	BA	SA	AB	H	2B	3B	HR	HR%	R	RBI	BB	SO	SB	Pinch Hit AB	H	PO	A	E	DP	TC/G	FA	G by Pos

Frank Callaway *continued*

Year	Team		Games	BA	SA	AB	H	2B	3B	HR	HR%	R	RBI	BB	SO	SB	AB	H	PO	A	E	DP	TC/G	FA	G by Pos
1922			29	.271	.354	48	13	0	2	0	0.0	5	4	0	13	0	4	0	19	38	6	5	2.2	.905	2B-11, 3B-5, SS-4
2 yrs.			43	.255	.327	98	25	1	3	0	0.0	12	6	2	24	1	4	0	41	81	15	7	3.2	.891	SS-18, 2B-11, 3B-5

Johnny Callison

CALLISON, JOHN WESLEY
B. Mar. 12, 1939, Qualls, Okla.

BL TR 5'10" 175 lbs.

Year	Team		Games	BA	SA	AB	H	2B	3B	HR	HR%	R	RBI	BB	SO	SB	AB	H	PO	A	E	DP	TC/G	FA	G by Pos
1958	CHI	A	18	.297	.469	64	19	4	2	1	1.6	10	12	6	14	1	0	0	39	2	1	1	2.3	.976	OF-18
1959			49	.173	.288	104	18	3	0	3	2.9	12	12	13	20	0	4	0	54	3	1	0	1.2	.983	OF-41
1960	PHI	N	99	.260	.427	288	75	11	5	9	3.1	36	30	45	70	0	15	3	176	7	2	4	1.9	.989	OF-86
1961			138	.266	.418	455	121	20	11	9	2.0	74	47	69	76	10	14	3	227	10	8	2	1.8	.967	OF-124
1962			157	.300	.491	603	181	26	10	23	3.8	107	83	54	96	10	9	4	327	24	7	7	2.3	.980	OF-152
1963			157	.284	.502	626	178	36	11	26	4.2	96	78	50	111	8	2	0	298	26	2	4	2.1	.994	OF-157
1964			162	.274	.492	654	179	30	10	31	4.7	101	104	36	95	6	2	1	319	19	4	3	2.1	.988	OF-162
1965			160	.262	.509	619	162	25	16	32	5.2	93	101	57	117	6	6	0	313	21	6	2	2.1	.982	OF-159
1966			155	.276	.418	612	169	40	7	11	1.8	93	55	56	83	8	3	1	275	12	3	2	1.9	.990	OF-154
1967			149	.261	.408	556	145	30	5	14	2.5	62	64	55	63	6	3	0	286	12	7	1	2.0	.977	OF-147
1968			121	.244	.415	398	97	18	4	14	3.5	46	40	42	70	4	11	3	187	10	0	1	1.6	1.000	OF-109
1969			134	.265	.440	495	131	29	5	16	3.2	66	64	49	73	2	6	1	273	12	3	3	2.1	.990	OF-129
1970	CHI	N	147	.264	.440	477	126	23	2	19	4.0	65	68	60	63	7	3	1	244	8	7	3	1.8	.973	OF-144
1971			103	.210	.341	290	61	12	1	8	2.8	27	38	36	55	2	14	1	158	3	3	0	1.6	.982	OF-89
1972	NY	A	92	.258	.393	275	71	10	0	9	3.3	28	34	18	34	3	19	4	127	4	1	1	1.4	.992	OF-74
1973			45	.176	.228	136	24	0	1	1	0.7	10	10	4	24	1	5	2	46	2	2	0	1.1	.960	OF-32, DH-10
16 yrs.			1886	.264	.441	6652	1757	321	89	226	3.4	926	840	650	1064	74	116	24	3349	175	57	34	1.9	.984	OF-1777, DH-10

Jack Calvo

CALVO, JACINTO
Born Jacinto Calvo y Gonzalez.
B. June 11, 1894, Havana, Cuba D. June 15, 1965, Miami, Fla.

BL TL 5'10" 156 lbs.

Year	Team		Games	BA	SA	AB	H	2B	3B	HR	HR%	R	RBI	BB	SO	SB	AB	H	PO	A	E	DP	TC/G	FA	G by Pos
1913	WAS	A	16	.242	.333	33	8	0	1	1	3.0	5	2	1	4	0	2	0	7	2	1	0	0.6	.900	OF-12
1920			17	.043	.130	23	1	0	1	0	0.0	5	2	2	2	0	7	1	6	0	0	0	0.4	1.000	OF-10
2 yrs.			33	.161	.250	56	9	0	1	1	1.8	10	4	3	6	0	9	1	13	2	1	0	0.5	.938	OF-22

Hank Camelli

CAMELLI, HENRY RICHARD
B. Dec. 12, 1914, Gloucester, Mass.

BR TR 5'11" 190 lbs.

Year	Team		Games	BA	SA	AB	H	2B	3B	HR	HR%	R	RBI	BB	SO	SB	AB	H	PO	A	E	DP	TC/G	FA	G by Pos
1943	PIT	N	1	.000	.000	3	0	0	0	0	0.0	1	0	1	0	0	0	0	4	0	0	0	5.0	1.000	C-1
1944			63	.296	.376	125	37	5	1	1	0.8	14	10	18	12	0	1	1	170	16	8	0	3.1	.959	C-61
1945			1	.000	.000	2	0	0	0	0	0.0	0	0	1	0	0	0	0	4	0	0	0	4.0	1.000	C-1
1946			42	.208	.271	96	20	2	0	0	0.0	8	5	8	9	0	2	0	117	18	4	2	3.3	.971	C-34
1947	BOS	N	52	.193	.280	150	29	8	1	1	0.7	10	11	18	18	0	1	1	194	20	5	3	4.2	.977	C-51
5 yrs.			159	.229	.306	376	86	15	4	2	0.5	33	26	46	39	0	4	2	489	55	17	5	3.5	.970	C-148

John Cameron

CAMERON, JOHN S. (Happy Jack)
B. 1885, Canada D. Aug. 17, 1951, Boston, Mass.

Year	Team		Games	BA	SA	AB	H	2B	3B	HR	HR%	R	RBI	BB	SO	SB	AB	H	PO	A	E	DP	TC/G	FA	G by Pos
1906	BOS	N	18	.180	.180	61	11	0	0	0	0.0	3	4	2			0	0	20	5	4	1	1.6	.862	OF-16, P-2

Dolf Camilli

CAMILLI, ADOLF LOUIS
Father of Doug Camilli.
B. Apr. 23, 1907, San Francisco, Calif.

BL TL 5'10" 185 lbs.

Year	Team		Games	BA	SA	AB	H	2B	3B	HR	HR%	R	RBI	BB	SO	SB	AB	H	PO	A	E	DP	TC/G	FA	G by Pos
1933	CHI	N	16	.224	.397	58	13	2	1	2	3.4	8	7	4	11	3	0	0	163	14	1	21	11.1	.994	1B-16
1934	CHI	N (32G – .275)																							
"	PHI	N (102G – .265)																							
"	total		134	.267	.432	498	133	28	4	16	3.2	69	87	53	94	4	0	0	1176	79	18	129	9.5	.986	1B-134
1935	PHI	N	156	.261	.440	602	157	23	5	25	4.2	88	83	65	113	9	0	0	1442	96	20	118	10.2	.987	1B-156
1936			151	.315	.577	530	167	29	13	28	5.3	106	102	116	84	5	1	1	1446	79	18	122	10.2	.988	1B-150
1937			131	.339	.587	475	161	23	7	27	5.7	101	80	90	82	6	0	0	1256	99	8	104	10.4	.994	1B-131
1938	BKN	N	146	.251	.485	509	128	25	11	24	4.7	106	100	119	101	6	0	0	1356	95	8	129	10.0	.995	1B-145
1939			157	.290	.524	565	164	30	12	26	4.6	105	104	110	107	1	0	0	1515	129	17	138	10.6	.990	1B-157
1940			142	.287	.529	512	147	29	13	23	4.5	92	96	89	83	9	1	0	1299	79	11	85	9.8	.992	1B-140
1941			149	.285	.556	529	151	29	6	34	6.4	92	120	104	115	3	1	0	1379	98	16	107	10.0	.989	1B-148
1942			150	.252	.484	524	132	23	7	26	5.0	89	109	97	85	10	0	0	1334	85	12	123	9.5	.992	1B-150
1943			95	.246	.374	353	87	15	6	6	1.7	56	43	65	48	2	0	0	853	60	7	78	9.7	.992	1B-95
1945	BOS	A	63	.212	.288	198	42	5	2	2	1.0	24	19	35	38	2	8	1	505	44	5	62	8.8	.991	1B-54
12 yrs.			1490	.277	.492	5353	1482	261	86	239	4.5	936	950	947	961	60	11	2	13724	957	141	1216	9.9	.990	1B-1476

WORLD SERIES

Year	Team		Games	BA	SA	AB	H	2B	3B	HR	HR%	R	RBI	BB	SO	SB	AB	H	PO	A	E	DP	TC/G	FA	G by Pos
1941	BKN	N	5	.167	.222	18	3	1	0	0	0.0	1	1	1	6	0	0	0	45	5	0	4	10.0	1.000	1B-5

Doug Camilli

CAMILLI, DOUGLAS JOSEPH
Son of Dolf Camilli.
B. Sept. 22, 1936, Philadelphia, Pa.

BR TR 5'11" 195 lbs.

Year	Team		Games	BA	SA	AB	H	2B	3B	HR	HR%	R	RBI	BB	SO	SB	AB	H	PO	A	E	DP	TC/G	FA	G by Pos
1960	LA	N	6	.333	.542	24	8	2	0	1	4.2	4	5	1	4	0	1	0	46	3	1	1	8.3	.980	C-6
1961			13	.133	.433	30	4	0	0	3	10.0	3	4	1	9	0	4	0	64	5	1	1	5.4	.986	C-12
1962			45	.284	.523	88	25	5	2	4	4.5	16	22	12	21	0	6	3	162	8	3	1	3.8	.983	C-39
1963			49	.162	.265	117	19	1	1	3	2.6	9	10	11	22	0	4	0	285	15	7	1	6.3	.977	C-47
1964			50	.179	.203	123	22	3	0	0	0.0	1	10	8	19	0	3	0	266	19	3	0	5.8	.990	C-46
1965	WAS	A	75	.192	.280	193	37	6	1	3	1.6	13	18	16	34	0	14	2	319	23	7	2	4.7	.980	C-59
1966			44	.206	.299	107	22	4	2	2	1.9	5	8	3	19	0	3	1	180	21	2	2	4.6	.990	C-39
1967			30	.183	.268	82	15	1	0	2	2.4	5	5	4	16	0	6	2	128	10	1	2	4.6	.993	C-24
1969			1	.333	.333	3	1	0	0	0	0.0	0	0	0	0	0	0	0	1	0	0	0	3.0	1.000	C-1
9 yrs.			313	.199	.309	767	153	22	4	18	2.3	56	80	56	146	0	40	9	1452	105	25	10	5.1	.984	C-273

Lou Camilli

CAMILLI, LOUIS STEVEN
B. Sept. 24, 1946, El Paso, Tex.

BB TR 5'10" 170 lbs.

Year Team	Games	BA	SA	AB	H	2B	3B	HR	HR%	R	RBI	BB	SO	SB	Pinch Hit AB	Pinch Hit H	PO	A	E	DP	TC/G	FA	G by Pos

Lou Camilli *continued*

Year Team	Games	BA	SA	AB	H	2B	3B	HR	HR%	R	RBI	BB	SO	SB	PH AB	PH H	PO	A	E	DP	TC/G	FA	G by Pos
1969 CLE A	13	.000	.000	14	0	0	0	0	0.0	0	0	0	3	0	0	0	13	11	0	1	1.8	1.000	3B-13
1970	16	.000	.000	15	0	0	0	0	0.0	0	0	2	2	0	12	0	4	4	0	0	0.5	1.000	SS-3, 2B-2, 3B-1
1971	39	.198	.222	81	16	2	0	0	0.0	5	0	8	10	0	4	0	39	74	4	9	3.0	.966	SS-23, 2B-16
1972	39	.146	.195	41	6	2	0	0	0.0	2	3	3	8	0	29	5	6	10	0	2	0.4	1.000	SS-8, 2B-2
4 yrs.	107	.146	.172	151	22	4	0	0	0.0	7	3	13	23	0	45	5	62	99	4	12	1.5	.976	SS-34, 2B-20, 3B-14

Ken Caminiti

CAMINITI, KENNETH GENE
B. Apr. 21, 1963, Hanford, Calif.

BB TR 6'3" 200 lbs.

Year Team	Games	BA	SA	AB	H	2B	3B	HR	HR%	R	RBI	BB	SO	SB	PH AB	PH H	PO	A	E	DP	TC/G	FA	G by Pos
1987 HOU N	63	.246	.335	203	50	7	1	3	1.5	10	23	12	44	0	9	2	50	98	8	11	2.5	.949	3B-61
1988	30	.181	.241	83	15	2	0	1	1.2	5	7	5	18	0	5	0	12	43	3	2	1.9	.948	3B-28
1989	161	.255	.369	585	149	31	3	10	1.7	71	72	51	93	4	2	0	126	335	22	27	3.0	.954	3B-160
3 yrs.	254	.246	.349	871	214	40	4	14	1.6	86	102	68	155	4	16	2	188	476	33	40	2.7	.953	3B-249

Howie Camp

CAMP, HOWARD LEE (Red)
B. July 1, 1893, Munford, Ala. D. May 8, 1960, Eastaboga, Ala.

BL TR 5'9" 169 lbs.

Year Team	Games	BA	SA	AB	H	2B	3B	HR	HR%	R	RBI	BB	SO	SB	PH AB	PH H	PO	A	E	DP	TC/G	FA	G by Pos
1917 NY A	5	.286	.333	21	6	1	0	0	0.0	3	0	1	2	0	0	0	10	2	2	0	2.8	.857	OF-5

Llewellan Camp

CAMP, LLEWELLAN ROBERT
Brother of Kid Camp.
B. Feb. 22, 1868, Columbus, Ohio D. Oct. 1, 1948, Omaha, Neb.

BL TR 6' 175 lbs.

Year Team	Games	BA	SA	AB	H	2B	3B	HR	HR%	R	RBI	BB	SO	SB	PH AB	PH H	PO	A	E	DP	TC/G	FA	G by Pos
1892 STL N	42	.207	.283	145	30	3	1	2	1.4	19	13	17	27	12	0	0	42	62	30	4	3.2	.776	3B-39, OF-3
1893 CHI N	38	.263	.436	156	41	7	7	2	1.3	37	17	19	19	30	0	0	55	66	18	7	3.7	.871	3B-16, OF-11, 2B-9, SS-3
1894	8	.182	.242	33	6	2	0	0	0.0	1	1	1	6	0	0	0	26	18	9	4	6.6	.830	2B-8
3 yrs.	88	.231	.350	334	77	12	8	4	1.2	57	31	37	52	42	0	0	123	146	57	15	3.7	.825	3B-55, 2B-17, OF-14, SS-3

Roy Campanella

CAMPANELLA, ROY
B. Nov. 19, 1921, Philadelphia, Pa.
Hall of Fame 1969.

BR TR 5'9½" 190 lbs.

Year Team	Games	BA	SA	AB	H	2B	3B	HR	HR%	R	RBI	BB	SO	SB	PH AB	PH H	PO	A	E	DP	TC/G	FA	G by Pos
1948 BKN N	83	.258	.416	279	72	11	3	9	3.2	32	45	36	45	3	4	1	413	45	9	12	5.6	.981	C-78
1949	130	.287	.498	436	125	22	2	22	5.0	65	82	67	36	3	3	1	684	55	11	5	5.8	.985	C-127
1950	126	.281	.551	437	123	19	3	31	7.1	70	89	55	51	1	3	2	683	54	11	14	5.9	.985	C-123
1951	143	.325	.590	505	164	33	1	33	6.5	90	108	53	51	1	5	2	722	72	11	12	5.6	.986	C-140
1952	128	.269	.453	468	126	18	1	22	4.7	73	97	57	59	8	6	1	662	55	4	7	5.6	.994	C-122
1953	144	.312	.611	519	162	26	3	41	7.9	103	142	67	58	4	9	5	807	57	10	9	6.1	.989	C-140
1954	111	.207	.401	397	82	14	3	19	4.8	43	51	42	49	1	1	0	600	58	7	7	6.0	.989	C-111
1955	123	.318	.583	446	142	20	1	32	7.2	81	107	56	41	2	3	2	672	54	6	8	6.0	.992	C-121
1956	124	.219	.394	388	85	6	1	20	5.2	39	73	66	61	1	7	0	659	49	11	3	5.8	.985	C-121
1957	103	.242	.388	330	80	9	0	13	3.9	31	62	34	50	1	4	1	618	51	5	5	6.5	.993	C-100
10 yrs.	1215	.276	.500	4205	1161	178	18	242	5.8	627	856	533	501	25	45	15	6520	550	85	82	5.9	.988	C-1183

WORLD SERIES

Year Team	Games	BA	SA	AB	H	2B	3B	HR	HR%	R	RBI	BB	SO	SB	PH AB	PH H	PO	A	E	DP	TC/G	FA	G by Pos
1949 BKN N	5	.267	.533	15	4	1	0	1	6.7	2	2	3	1	0	0	0	32	2	0	1	6.8	1.000	C-5
1952	7	.214	.214	28	6	0	0	0	0.0	0	1	1	6	0	0	0	39	5	0	0	6.3	1.000	C-7
1953	6	.273	.409	22	6	0	0	1	4.5	6	2	2	3	0	0	0	47	9	0	1	9.3	1.000	C-6
1955	7	.259	.593	27	7	3	0	2	7.4	4	4	3	3	0	0	0	42	3	1	1	6.6	.978	C-7
1956	7	.182	.227	22	4	1	0	0	0.0	2	3	3	7	0	0	0	49	3	0	1	7.4	1.000	C-7
5 yrs.	32	.237	.386	114	27	5	0	4	3.5	14	12	12	20	0	0	0	209	22	1	4	7.3	.996	C-32

Bert Campaneris

CAMPANERIS, DAGOBERTO
Born Dagoberto Campaneris y Blanco.
B. Mar. 9, 1942, Pueblo Nuevo, Cuba

BR TR 5'10" 160 lbs.

Year Team	Games	BA	SA	AB	H	2B	3B	HR	HR%	R	RBI	BB	SO	SB	PH AB	PH H	PO	A	E	DP	TC/G	FA	G by Pos
1964 KC A	67	.257	.375	269	69	14	3	4	1.5	27	22	15	41	10	1	0	102	108	8	16	3.3	.963	SS-38, OF-27, 3B-6
1965	144	.270	.382	578	156	23	12	6	1.0	67	42	41	71	51	2	1	258	276	35	53	4.0	.938	SS-109, OF-39, 3B-1, 2B-1, 1B-1, C-1, P-1
1966	142	.267	.379	573	153	29	10	5	0.9	82	42	25	72	52	2	0	283	350	19	80	4.6	.971	SS-138
1967	147	.248	.331	601	149	29	6	3	0.5	85	32	36	82	55	1	0	259	365	30	75	4.4	.954	SS-145
1968 OAK A	159	.276	.361	642	177	25	9	4	0.6	87	38	50	69	62	1	0	283	458	34	86	4.9	.956	SS-155, OF-3
1969	135	.260	.305	547	142	15	2	2	0.4	71	25	30	62	62	4	1	220	391	21	72	4.7	.967	SS-125
1970	147	.279	.448	603	168	28	4	22	3.6	97	64	36	73	42	5	2	267	414	19	92	4.8	.973	SS-143
1971	134	.251	.323	569	143	18	4	5	0.9	80	47	29	64	34	1	1	231	303	26	85	4.2	.954	SS-133
1972	149	.240	.325	625	150	25	2	8	1.3	85	32	32	88	52	0	0	283	494	18	93	5.3	.977	SS-148
1973	151	.250	.318	601	150	17	6	4	0.7	89	46	50	79	34	0	0	228	496	23	87	4.9	.969	SS-149
1974	134	.290	.366	527	153	18	8	2	0.4	77	41	47	81	34	0	0	207	423	22	76	4.9	.966	SS-133, DH-1
1975	137	.265	.330	509	135	15	3	4	0.8	69	46	50	71	24	0	0	199	378	23	58	4.4	.962	SS-137
1976	149	.256	.291	536	137	14	1	1	0.2	67	52	63	80	54	0	0	231	490	23	66	5.0	.969	SS-149
1977 TEX A	150	.254	.341	552	140	19	7	5	0.9	77	46	47	86	27	1	0	269	483	25	91	5.2	.968	SS-149
1978	98	.186	.238	269	50	5	3	1	0.4	30	17	20	36	22	1	0	151	263	20	44	4.4	.954	SS-89, DH-4
1979 2 teams		TEX A (8G – .111)		CAL A (85G – .234)																			
" total	93	.230	.278	248	57	4	4	0	0.0	29	15	20	35	13	0	0	12	13	1	5	0.3	.962	SS-90, DH-1
1980 CAL A	77	.252	.329	210	53	8	1	2	1.0	32	18	14	33	10	3	0	108	157	12	41	3.6	.957	SS-64, DH-2, 2B-1
1981	55	.256	.341	82	21	2	1	1	1.2	11	10	5	10	5	1	1	10	49	6	7	1.2	.908	3B-45, SS-3, 2B-2
1983 NY A	60	.322	.357	143	46	5	0	0	0.0	19	11	8	9	6	2	0	52	96	7	19	2.6	.955	2B-32, 3B-24
19 yrs.	2328	.259	.342	8684	2249	313	86	79	0.9	1181	646	618	1142	649	25	6	3653	6007	372	1146	4.3	.963	SS-2097, 3B-76, OF-69, 2B-36, DH-8, 1B-1, C-1, P-1
														8th									

LEAGUE CHAMPIONSHIP SERIES

Year Team	Games	BA	SA	AB	H	2B	3B	HR	HR%	R	RBI	BB	SO	SB	PH AB	PH H	PO	A	E	DP	TC/G	FA	G by Pos
1971 OAK A	3	.167	.250	12	2	1	0	0	0.0	0	0	0	1	0	0	0	3	6	0	1	3.0	1.000	SS-3
1972	2	.429	.429	7	3	0	0	0	0.0	3	0	1	0	2	0	0	3	7	0	1	5.0	1.000	SS-2
1973	5	.333	.667	21	7	1	0	2	9.5	3	3	2	3	2	0	0	6	15	1	1	4.4	.955	SS-5
1974	4	.176	.176	17	3	0	0	0	0.0	3	0	3	0	1	0	0	3	17	0	1	5.0	1.000	SS-4
1975	3	.000	.000	11	0	0	0	0	0.0	1	1	1	1	0	0	0	2	10	0	3	4.0	1.000	SS-3

Year Team	Games	BA	SA	AB	H	2B	3B	HR	HR%	R	RBI	BB	SO	SB	Pinch Hit AB	Pinch Hit H	PO	A	E	DP	TC/G	FA	G by Pos

Bert Campaneris *continued*

Year Team	Games	BA	SA	AB	H	2B	3B	HR	HR%	R	RBI	BB	SO	SB	AB	H	PO	A	E	DP	TC/G	FA	G by Pos
1979 CAL A	1	–	–	0	0	0	0	0	–	0	0	0	0	0	0	0	0	0	0	0	0.0	–	SS-1
6 yrs.	18	.221	.338	68	15	2	0	2	2.9	7	6	4	7	6	0	0	17	55	1	7	4.1	.986	SS-18

WORLD SERIES

Year Team	Games	BA	SA	AB	H	2B	3B	HR	HR%	R	RBI	BB	SO	SB	AB	H	PO	A	E	DP	TC/G	FA	G by Pos
1972 OAK A	7	.179	.179	28	5	0	0	0	0.0	1	0	1	4	0	0	0	17	15	1	2	4.7	.970	SS-7
1973	7	.290	.452	31	9	0	1	1	3.2	6	3	1	7	3	0	0	10	28	1	3	5.6	.974	SS-7
1974	5	.353	.471	17	6	2	0	0	0.0	1	2	0	2	1	0	0	6	16	2	5	4.8	.917	SS-5
3 yrs.	19	.263	.355	76	20	2	1	1	1.3	8	5	2	13	4	0	0	33	59	4	10	5.1	.958	SS-19

Al Campanis

CAMPANIS, ALEXANDER SEBASTIAN
Born Alessandro Campani. Father of Jim Campanis.
B. Nov. 2, 1916, Kos, Greece

BB TR 6' 185 lbs.

Year Team	Games	BA	SA	AB	H	2B	3B	HR	HR%	R	RBI	BB	SO	SB	AB	H	PO	A	E	DP	TC/G	FA	G by Pos
1943 BKN N	7	.100	.100	20	2	0	0	0	0.0	3	0	4	5	0	0	0	25	20	0	5	6.4	1.000	2B-7

Jim Campanis

CAMPANIS, JAMES ALEXANDER
Son of Al Campanis.
B. Feb. 9, 1944, New York, N. Y.

BR TR 6' 195 lbs.

Year Team	Games	BA	SA	AB	H	2B	3B	HR	HR%	R	RBI	BB	SO	SB	AB	H	PO	A	E	DP	TC/G	FA	G by Pos
1966 LA N	1	.000	.000	1	0	0	0	0	0.0	0	0	0	0	0	1	0	2	0	0	0	2.0	1.000	C-1
1967	41	.161	.274	62	10	1	0	2	3.2	3	2	9	14	0	24	5	90	6	1	2	2.4	.990	C-23
1968	4	.091	.091	11	1	0	0	0	0.0	0	0	1	2	0	0	0	18	6	1	0	6.3	.960	C-4
1969 KC A	30	.157	.217	83	13	5	0	0	0.0	4	5	5	19	0	7	1	155	7	3	2	5.5	.982	C-26
1970	31	.130	.241	54	7	0	0	2	3.7	6	2	4	14	0	16	1	64	7	1	1	2.3	.986	C-13, OF-1
1973 PIT N	6	.167	.167	6	1	0	0	0	0.0	0	0	0	0	0	6	1	0	0	0	0	0.0	–	
6 yrs.	113	.147	.230	217	32	6	0	4	1.8	13	9	19	49	0	54	8	329	26	6	5	3.2	.983	C-67, OF-1

Count Campau

CAMPAU, CHARLES COLUMBUS
B. Oct. 17, 1863, Detroit, Mich.   D. Apr. 3, 1938, New Orleans, La.
Manager 1890.

BL TR 5'11" 160 lbs.

Year Team	Games	BA	SA	AB	H	2B	3B	HR	HR%	R	RBI	BB	SO	SB	AB	H	PO	A	E	DP	TC/G	FA	G by Pos
1888 DET N	70	.203	.259	251	51	5	3	1	0.4	28	18	19	36	27	0	0	101	10	8	3	1.7	.933	OF-70
1890 STL AA	75	.322	.516	314	101	9	11	10	3.2	68		26		36	0	0	118	16	9	1	1.9	.937	OF-74, 3B-1, 1B-1
1894 WAS N	2	.143	.143	7	1	0	0	0	0.0	1	0	1	4	0	0	0	4	0	0	0	2.0	1.000	OF-2
3 yrs.	147	.267	.399	572	153	14	14	11	1.9	97	18	46	40	63	0	0	223	26	17	4	1.8	.936	OF-146, 3B-1, 1B-1

Bruce Campbell

CAMPBELL, BRUCE DOUGLAS
B. Oct. 20, 1909, Chicago, Ill.

BL TR 6'1" 185 lbs.

Year Team	Games	BA	SA	AB	H	2B	3B	HR	HR%	R	RBI	BB	SO	SB	AB	H	PO	A	E	DP	TC/G	FA	G by Pos
1930 CHI A	5	.500	.800	10	5	1	1	0	0.0	4	5	1	2	0	1	1	8	0	0	0	1.6	1.000	OF-4
1931	4	.412	.882	17	7	2	0	2	11.8	4	5	0	4	0	0	0	9	0	1	0	2.5	.900	OF-4
1932 2 teams		CHI A	(7G – .222)		STL	A	(139G – .285)																	
" total	146	.283	.447	611	173	36	11	14	2.3	86	87	40	104	7	3	0	306	13	22	4	2.3	.935	OF-143
1933 STL A	148	.277	.457	567	157	38	8	16	2.8	87	106	69	77	10	4	1	250	18	14	4	1.9	.950	OF-144
1934	138	.279	.412	481	134	25	6	9	1.9	62	74	51	64	5	14	4	230	14	17	3	1.9	.935	OF-123
1935 CLE A	80	.325	.497	308	100	26	3	7	2.3	56	54	31	33	2	4	1	129	2	1	1	1.7	.992	OF-75
1936	76	.372	.587	172	64	15	2	6	3.5	35	30	19	17	2	25	9	68	4	3	2	1.0	.960	OF-47
1937	134	.301	.471	448	135	42	11	4	0.9	82	61	67	49	4	11	5	204	14	5	5	1.7	.978	OF-123
1938	133	.290	.460	511	148	27	12	12	2.3	90	72	53	57	11	11	2	220	13	8	3	1.8	.967	OF-122
1939	130	.287	.449	450	129	23	13	8	1.8	84	72	67	48	7	14	2	200	12	13	3	1.7	.942	OF-115
1940 DET A	103	.283	.448	297	84	15	5	8	2.7	56	44	45	28	2	23	9	133	6	6	0	1.4	.959	OF-74
1941	141	.275	.457	512	141	28	10	15	2.9	72	93	68	67	3	5	2	241	5	6	1	1.8	.976	OF-133
1942 WAS A	122	.278	.389	378	105	17	5	5	1.3	41	63	37	34	0	29	5	188	4	9	1	1.6	.955	OF-87
13 yrs.	1360	.290	.455	4762	1382	295	87	106	2.2	759	766	548	584	53	144	41	2186	105	105	27	1.8	.956	OF-1194

WORLD SERIES

Year Team	Games	BA	SA	AB	H	2B	3B	HR	HR%	R	RBI	BB	SO	SB	AB	H	PO	A	E	DP	TC/G	FA	G by Pos
1940 DET A	7	.360	.520	25	9	1	0	1	4.0	4	5	4	4	0	0	0	17	0	0	0	2.4	1.000	OF-7

Dave Campbell

CAMPBELL, DAVID WILSON
B. Jan. 14, 1942, Manistee, Mich.

BR TR 6'1" 180 lbs.

Year Team	Games	BA	SA	AB	H	2B	3B	HR	HR%	R	RBI	BB	SO	SB	AB	H	PO	A	E	DP	TC/G	FA	G by Pos
1967 DET A	2	.000	.000	2	0	0	0	0	0.0	0	0	0	1	0	1	0	1	0	1	0	1.0	.500	1B-1
1968	9	.125	.500	8	1	0	0	1	12.5	1	2	1	3	0	3	0	4	3	0	1	0.8	1.000	2B-5
1969	32	.103	.128	39	4	1	0	0	0.0	4	2	4	15	0	14	2	38	9	2	5	1.5	.959	1B-13, 2B-5, 3B-1
1970 SD N	154	.219	.336	581	127	28	2	12	2.1	71	40	40	115	18	1	0	359	455	22	96	5.4	.974	2B-153
1971	108	.227	.334	365	83	14	2	7	1.9	38	29	37	75	9	1	0	179	264	18	50	4.3	.961	2B-69, 3B-40, SS-4, OF-2, 1B-2
1972	33	.240	.290	100	24	5	0	0	0.0	6	3	11	12	0	0	0	25	67	1	3	2.8	.989	3B-31, 2B-1
1973 3 teams	55	SD	N	(33G – .224)		STL	N	(13G – .000)		HOU	N	(9G – .267)											
" total	55	.194	.224	134	26	5	0	0	0.0	4	11	8	25	1	10	0	88	106	5	22	3.6	.975	2B-33, 3B-7, 1B-5, OF-1
1974 HOU N	35	.087	.130	23	2	1	0	0	0.0	4	2	1	8	1	13	0	20	17	2	5	1.1	.949	2B-9, 1B-6, 3B-2, OF-1
8 yrs.	428	.213	.311	1252	267	54	4	20	1.6	128	89	102	254	29	43	2	714	921	51	182	3.9	.970	2B-275, 3B-81, 1B-27, OF-4, SS-4

Gilly Campbell

CAMPBELL, WILLIAM GILTHORPE
B. Feb. 13, 1908, Kansas City, Kans.   D. Feb. 21, 1973, Los Angeles, Calif.

BL TR 5'7½" 182 lbs.

Year Team	Games	BA	SA	AB	H	2B	3B	HR	HR%	R	RBI	BB	SO	SB	AB	H	PO	A	E	DP	TC/G	FA	G by Pos
1933 CHI N	46	.281	.371	89	25	3	1	1	1.1	11	10	7	4	0	23	6	66	9	4	1	1.7	.949	C-20
1935 CIN N	88	.257	.330	218	56	7	0	3	1.4	26	30	42	7	3	15	4	278	37	4	4	3.6	.987	C-66, 1B-5, OF-1
1936	89	.268	.345	235	63	13	1	1	0.4	28	40	43	14	2	14	3	260	49	5	11	3.5	.984	C-71, 1B-1
1937	18	.275	.325	40	11	2	0	0	0.0	3	2	5	1	0	6	1	51	7	2	0	3.3	.967	C-17
1938 BKN N	54	.246	.286	126	31	5	0	0	0.0	10	11	19	9	0	10	2	139	22	7	2	3.1	.958	C-44
5 yrs.	295	.263	.332	708	186	30	2	5	0.7	78	93	116	35	5	63	15	794	124	22	18	3.2	.977	C-218, 1B-6, OF-1

Jim Campbell

CAMPBELL, JAMES ROBERT
B. June 24, 1937, Palo Alto, Calif.

BR TR 6' 190 lbs.

Year Team	Games	BA	SA	AB	H	2B	3B	HR	HR%	R	RBI	BB	SO	SB	AB	H	PO	A	E	DP	TC/G	FA	G by Pos
1962 HOU N	27	.221	.372	86	19	4	0	3	3.5	6	8	6	23	0	2	1	174	20	6	1	7.4	.970	C-25

Year	Team		Games	BA	SA	AB	H	2B	3B	HR	HR%	R	RBI	BB	SO	SB	Pinch Hit AB	Pinch Hit H	PO	A	E	DP	TC/G	FA	G by Pos

Jim Campbell *continued*

Year	Team		Games	BA	SA	AB	H	2B	3B	HR	HR%	R	RBI	BB	SO	SB	AB	H	PO	A	E	DP	TC/G	FA	G by Pos
1963			55	.222	.316	158	35	3	0	4	2.5	9	19	10	40	0	12	2	246	28	6	4	5.1	.979	C-42
2 yrs.			82	.221	.336	244	54	7	0	7	2.9	15	25	16	63	0	14	3	420	48	12	5	5.9	.975	C-67

Jim Campbell

CAMPBELL, JAMES ROBERT JR
B. Jan. 10, 1943, Hartsville, S. C.   BL TR 6'   205 lbs.

| 1970 | STL | N | 13 | .231 | .231 | 13 | 3 | 0 | 0 | 0 | 0.0 | 0 | 1 | 0 | 3 | 0 | 13 | 3 | 0 | 0 | 0 | 0 | 0.0 | – | |

Joe Campbell

CAMPBELL, JOSEPH EARL
B. Mar. 10, 1944, Louisville, Ky.   BR TR 6'1"   175 lbs.

| 1967 | CHI | N | 1 | .000 | .000 | 3 | 0 | 0 | 0 | 0 | 0.0 | 0 | 0 | 0 | 3 | 0 | 0 | 0 | 0 | 0 | 0 | 0 | 0.0 | – | OF-1 |

Marc Campbell

CAMPBELL, MARC THADDEUS (Hutch)
B. Nov. 29, 1884, Punxsutawney, Pa. D. Feb. 13, 1946, New Bethlehem, Pa.   BL TR 5'10"   155 lbs.

| 1907 | PIT | N | 2 | .250 | .250 | 4 | 1 | 0 | 0 | 0 | 0.0 | 0 | 1 | 1 | | 0 | 0 | 0 | 2 | 6 | 1 | 0 | 4.5 | .889 | SS-2 |

Paul Campbell

CAMPBELL, PAUL McLAUGHLIN
B. Sept. 1, 1917, Paw Creek, N. C.   BL TL 5'10"   185 lbs.

1941	BOS	A	1	–	–	0	0	0	0	0		0	0	0	0	0	0	0	0	0	0	0	0.0	–	
1942			26	.067	.067	15	1	0	0	0	0.0	4	0	1	5	1	13	1	1	0	0	0	0.0		
1946			28	.115	.154	26	3	1	0	0	0.0	3	0	2	7	0	14	2	34	1	0	2	1.3	1.000	1B-5
1948	DET	A	59	.265	.337	83	22	1	1	1	1.2	15	11	1	10	0	13	1	172	18	6	11	3.3	.969	1B-27
1949			87	.278	.404	255	71	15	4	3	1.2	38	30	24	32	3	9	5	461	38	7	67	5.8	.986	1B-74
1950			3	.000	.000	1	0	0	0	0	0.0	1	0	0	0	0	1	0	0	0	0	0	0.0		
6 yrs.			204	.255	.358	380	97	17	5	4	1.1	61	41	28	54	4	50	9	668	57	13	80	3.6	.982	1B-106, OF-4

WORLD SERIES

| 1946 | BOS | A | 1 | – | – | 0 | 0 | 0 | 0 | 0 | | 0 | 0 | 0 | 0 | 0 | 0 | 0 | 0 | 0 | 0 | 0 | 0.0 | – | |

Ron Campbell

CAMPBELL, RONALD THOMAS
B. Apr. 5, 1940, Chattanooga, Tenn.   BR TR 6'1"   180 lbs.

1964	CHI	N	26	.272	.391	92	25	6	1	1	1.1	7	10	1	21	0	0	0	64	95	10	15	6.5	.941	2B-26
1965			2	.000	.000	2	0	0	0	0	0.0	0	0	0	0	0	2	0	0	0	0	0	0.0	–	
1966			24	.217	.233	60	13	1	0	0	0.0	4	4	6	5	1	5	1	17	53	2	9	3.0	.972	SS-11, 3B-7
3 yrs.			52	.247	.325	154	38	7	1	1	0.6	11	14	7	26	1	7	1	81	148	12	24	4.6	.950	2B-26, SS-11, 3B-7

Sam Campbell

CAMPBELL, SAMUEL
B. Philadelphia, Pa. Deceased.

| 1890 | PHI | AA | 2 | .000 | .000 | 5 | 0 | 0 | 0 | 0 | 0.0 | 0 | 1 | 0 | | 0 | 0 | 0 | 4 | 1 | 1 | 0 | 3.0 | .833 | 2B-2 |

Soup Campbell

CAMPBELL, CLARENCE
B. Mar. 7, 1915, Sparta, Va.   BL TR 6'1"   188 lbs.

1940	CLE	A	35	.226	.242	62	14	1	0	0	0.0	8	2	7	12	0	19	5	32	0	0	0	0.9	1.000	OF-16
1941			104	.250	.332	328	82	10	4	3	0.9	36	35	31	21	1	24	4	202	6	4	0	2.0	.981	OF-78
2 yrs.			139	.246	.318	390	96	11	4	3	0.8	44	37	38	33	1	43	9	234	6	4	0	1.8	.984	OF-94

Vin Campbell

CAMPBELL, ARTHUR VINCENT
B. Jan. 30, 1888, St. Louis, Mo. D. Nov. 16, 1969, Towson, Md.   BL TR 6'   185 lbs.

1908	CHI	N	1	.000	.000	1	0	0	0	0	0.0	0	0	0		0	1	0	0	0	0	0	0.0	–	
1910	PIT	N	97	.326	.436	282	92	9	5	4	1.4	42	21	26	23	17	18	5	145	8	18	2	1.8	.895	OF-74
1911			42	.312	.366	93	29	3	1	0	0.0	12	10	8	7	6	17	4	35	1	3	0	0.9	.923	OF-21
1912	BOS	N	145	.296	.391	624	185	32	9	3	0.5	102	48	32	44	19	1	0	340	20	24	6	2.6	.938	OF-144
1914	IND	F	134	.318	.439	544	173	23	11	7	1.3	92	44	37		26	1	0	218	18	19	6	1.9	.925	OF-132
1915	NWK	F	127	.310	.389	525	163	18	10	1	0.2	78	44	29		24	1	0	200	15	12	3	1.8	.947	OF-126
6 yrs.			546	.310	.408	2069	642	85	36	15	0.7	326	167	132	74	92	39	9	938	62	76	17	2.0	.929	OF-497

Frank Campos

CAMPOS, FRANCISCO JOSE
Born Francisco Jose Campos y Lopez.
B. May 11, 1924, Havana, Cuba   BL TL 5'11"   180 lbs.

1951	WAS	A	8	.423	.615	26	11	3	1	0	0.0	4	3	0	1	0	1	0	6	0	0	0	0.8	1.000	OF-7
1952			53	.259	.330	112	29	6	1	0	0.0	9	8	1	13	0	27	2	45	0	1	0	0.9	.978	OF-23
1953			10	.111	.111	9	1	0	0	0	0.0	0	2	1	0	0	9	1	0	0	0	0	0.0		
3 yrs.			71	.279	.367	147	41	9	2	0	0.0	13	13	2	14	0	37	3	51	0	1	0	0.7	.981	OF-30

Sil Campusano

CAMPUSANO, SILVESTRE
Born Silvestre Campusano y Diaz.
B. Dec. 31, 1965, Santo Domingo, Dominican Republic   BR TR 6'   160 lbs.

| 1988 | TOR | A | 73 | .218 | .359 | 142 | 31 | 10 | 2 | 2 | 1.4 | 14 | 12 | 9 | 33 | 0 | 2 | 0 | 111 | 2 | 8 | 0 | 1.7 | .934 | OF-69, DH-2 |

George Canale

CANALE, GEORGE ANTHONY
B. Aug. 11, 1965, Memphis, Tenn.   BL TR 6'1"   190 lbs.

| 1989 | MIL | A | 13 | .192 | .346 | 26 | 5 | 1 | 0 | 1 | 3.8 | 5 | 3 | 2 | 3 | 0 | 0 | 0 | 86 | 4 | 1 | 4 | 7.0 | .989 | 1B-11 |

Jimmy Canavan

CANAVAN, JAMES EDWARD
B. Nov. 26, 1866, New Bedford, Mass. D. May 27, 1949, New Bedford, Mass.   BR TR 5'8"   160 lbs.

1891	2 teams		CIN AA (101G – .228)			MIL AA (35G – .268)																			
"	total		136	.238	.380	568	135	15	18	10	1.8	107	87	43	54	28	0	0	282	415	113	36	6.0	.860	SS-112, 2B-24
1892	CHI	N	118	.166	.239	439	73	10	11	0	0.0	48	32	48	48	33	0	0	294	355	54	41	6.0	.923	2B-112, OF-4, SS-2
1893	CIN	N	121	.226	.317	461	104	13	7	5	1.1	65	64	51	20	31	0	0	255	33	21	0	2.6	.932	OF-116, 2B-5, 3B-1
1894			101	.272	.478	356	97	16	9	13	3.7	77	70	62	25	13	1	0	205	29	27	8	2.6	.897	OF-95, SS-3, 3B-2, 2B-1, 1B-1

Year	Team		Games	BA	SA	AB	H	2B	3B	HR	HR%	R	RBI	BB	SO	SB	Pinch Hit AB	Pinch Hit H	PO	A	E	DP	TC/G	FA	G by Pos

Jimmy Canavan *continued*

| 1897 | BKN | N | 63 | .217 | .304 | 240 | 52 | 9 | 3 | 2 | 0.8 | 25 | 34 | 26 | | 9 | 0 | 0 | 157 | 162 | 32 | 18 | 5.6 | .909 | 2B-63 |
| 5 yrs. | | | 539 | .223 | .344 | 2064 | 461 | 63 | 48 | 30 | 1.5 | 322 | 287 | 230 | 147 | 114 | 2 | 0 | 1193 | 994 | 247 | 103 | 4.5 | .899 | OF-215, 2B-205, SS-117, 3B-3, 1B-1 |

Casey Candaele

CANDAELE, CASEY TODD
B. Jan. 12, 1961, Lompoc, Calif.
BB TR 5'9" 160 lbs.

1986	MON	N	30	.231	.288	104	24	4	1	0	0.0	9	6	5	15	3	3	1	45	74	2	13	4.0	.983	2B-24, 3B-4
1987			138	.272	.347	449	122	23	4	1	0.2	62	23	38	28	7	12	3	237	176	8	28	3.1	.981	2B-68, OF-67, SS-25, 1B-1
1988	2 teams		MON N	(36G – .172)		HOU N	(21G – .161)																		
"	total		57	.170	.238	147	25	8	1	0	0.0	11	5	11	17	1	7	1	79	126	2	21	3.6	.990	2B-45, OF-5, 3B-1
3 yrs.			225	.244	.316	700	171	35	6	1	0.1	82	34	54	60	11	22	5	361	376	12	62	3.3	.984	2B-137, OF-72, SS-25, 3B-5, 1B-1

John Cangelosi

CANGELOSI, JOHN ANTHONY
B. Mar. 10, 1963, Brooklyn, N. Y.
BB TL 5'8" 150 lbs.

1985	CHI	A	5	.000	.000	2	0	0	0	0	0.0	2	0	0	1	0	1	0	1	0	0	0	0.2	1.000	OF-3, DH-2
1986			137	.235	.299	438	103	16	3	2	0.5	65	32	71	61	50	1	0	276	7	9	1	2.1	.969	OF-129, DH-3
1987	PIT	N	104	.275	.418	182	50	8	3	4	2.2	44	18	46	33	21	50	10	74	3	3	0	0.8	.963	OF-47
1988			75	.254	.305	118	30	4	1	0	0.0	18	8	17	16	9	42	12	52	0	2	0	0.7	.963	OF-24, P-1
1989			112	.219	.269	160	35	4	2	0	0.0	18	9	35	20	11	68	12	71	1	2	0	0.7	.973	OF-46
5 yrs.			433	.242	.318	900	218	32	9	6	0.7	147	67	169	131	91	161	34	474	11	16	1	1.2	.968	OF-249, DH-5, P-1

Rip Cannell

CANNELL, VIRGIN WIRT
B. Jan. 23, 1880, S. Bridgton, Me. D. Aug. 26, 1948, Bridgton, Me.
BL TR 5'10½" 180 lbs.

1904	BOS	N	100	.234	.254	346	81	5	1	0	0.0	32	18	23		10	6	1	135	5	16	1	1.6	.897	OF-93
1905			154	.247	.286	567	140	14	4	0	0.0	52	36	51		17	0	0	315	14	23	6	2.3	.935	OF-154
2 yrs.			254	.242	.274	913	221	19	5	0	0.0	84	54	74		27	6	1	450	19	39	7	2.0	.923	OF-247

Chris Cannizzaro

CANNIZZARO, CHRISTOPHER JOHN
B. May 3, 1938, Oakland, Calif.
BR TR 6' 190 lbs.

1960	STL	N	7	.222	.222	9	2	0	0	0	0.0	0	1	1	3	0	0	0	19	3	0	1	3.1	1.000	C-6
1961			6	.500	.500	2	1	0	0	0	0.0	0	0	0	0	0	1	1	5	0	0	0	0.8	1.000	C-5
1962	NY	N	59	.241	.271	133	32	2	1	0	0.0	9	9	19	26	1	3	1	219	34	7	3	4.4	.973	C-56, OF-1
1963			16	.242	.273	33	8	1	0	0	0.0	4	4	1	8	0	1	1	49	6	0	0	3.4	1.000	C-15
1964			60	.311	.372	164	51	10	0	0	0.0	11	10	14	28	0	5	1	225	28	3	6	4.3	.988	C-53
1965			114	.183	.231	251	46	8	2	0	0.0	17	7	28	60	0	2	0	435	69	12	8	4.5	.977	C-112
1968	PIT	N	25	.241	.397	58	14	2	2	1	1.7	5	7	9	13	0	0	0	111	10	3	1	5.0	.976	C-25
1969	SD	N	134	.220	.297	418	92	14	3	4	1.0	23	33	42	81	0	2	0	644	69	9	8	5.4	.988	C-132
1970			111	.279	.389	341	95	13	3	5	1.5	27	42	48	49	2	2	0	559	44	12	5	5.4	.980	C-110
1971	2 teams		SD N	(21G – .190)		CHI N	(71G – .213)																		
"	total		92	.208	.319	260	54	9	1	6	2.3	20	31	39	34	0	2	0	425	32	7	4	5.0	.985	C-89
1972	LA	N	73	.240	.300	200	48	6	0	2	1.0	14	18	31	38	0	5	2	312	26	6	4	4.7	.983	C-72
1973			17	.190	.190	21	4	0	0	0	0.0	0	3	3	3	0	3	0	33	0	0	0	1.9	1.000	C-13
1974	SD	N	26	.183	.200	60	11	1	0	0	0.0	2	4	6	11	0	0	0	126	12	3	2	5.4	.979	C-26
13 yrs.			740	.235	.309	1950	458	66	12	18	0.9	132	169	241	354	3	26	6	3162	333	62	42	4.8	.983	C-714, OF-1

Joe Cannon

CANNON, JOSEPH JEROME
B. July 13, 1953, Camp Lejeune, N. C.
BL TR 6'3" 193 lbs.

1977	HOU	N	9	.118	.235	17	2	2	0	0	0.0	3	1	0	5	1	4	1	7	0	0	0	0.8	1.000	OF-3
1978			8	.222	.222	18	4	0	0	0	0.0	1	1	0	3	0	3	0	7	0	2	0	1.1	.778	OF-5
1979	TOR	A	61	.211	.254	142	30	1	1	1	0.7	14	5	1	34	12	0	0	81	5	1	1	1.4	1.000	OF-50
1980			70	.080	.080	50	4	0	0	0	0.0	16	4	0	14	2	4	0	29	1	0	0	0.4	.968	OF-33, DH-1
4 yrs.			148	.176	.211	227	40	3	1	1	0.4	34	11	1	54	15	11	1	124	6	3	1	0.9	.977	OF-91, DH-1

Jose Canseco

CANSECO, JOSE
Born Jose Canseco y Capas.
B. July 2, 1964, Havana, Cuba
BR TR 6'3" 185 lbs.

1985	OAK	A	29	.302	.490	96	29	3	0	5	5.2	16	13	4	31	1	4	1	56	2	3	1	2.1	.951	OF-26
1986			157	.240	.457	600	144	29	1	33	5.5	85	117	65	175	15	1	1	319	4	14	1	2.1	.958	OF-155, DH-1
1987			159	.257	.470	630	162	35	3	31	4.9	81	113	50	157	15	1	0	263	12	7	3	1.8	.975	OF-130, DH-30
1988			158	.307	**.569**	610	187	34	0	**42**	6.9	120	**124**	78	128	40	1	0	304	11	7	3	2.0	.978	OF-144, DH-13
1989			65	.269	.542	227	61	9	1	17	7.5	40	57	23	69	6	3	1	119	5	3	2	2.0	.976	OF-56, DH-5
5 yrs.			568	.270	.503	2163	583	110	5	128	5.9	342	424	220	560	77	10	3	1061	34	34	10	2.0	.970	OF-511, DH-49

LEAGUE CHAMPIONSHIP SERIES

1988	OAK	A	4	.313	.938	16	5	1	0	3	18.8	4	4	1	2	1	0	0	6	0	0	0	1.5	1.000	OF-4
1989			5	.294	.471	17	5	0	0	1	5.9	1	3	3	7	0	1	0	6	1	1	0	1.6	.875	OF-5
2 yrs.			9	.303	.697	33	10	1	0	4	12.1	5	7	4	9	1	1	0	12	1	1	0	1.6	.929	OF-9

WORLD SERIES

1988	OAK	A	5	.053	.211	19	1	0	0	1	5.3	1	5	2	5	1	0	0	8	0	0	0	1.6	1.000	OF-5
1989			4	.357	.571	14	5	0	0	1	7.1	5	3	4	3	1	0	0	6	0	0	0	1.5	1.000	OF-4
2 yrs.			9	.182	.364	33	6	0	0	2	6.1	6	8	6	8	2	0	0	14	0	0	0	1.6	1.000	OF-9

Bart Cantz

CANTZ, BARTHOLOMEW L.
B. Jan. 29, 1860, Philadelphia, Pa. D. Feb. 12, 1943, Philadelphia, Pa.
TR

1888	BAL	AA	37	.167	.198	126	21	2	1	0	0.0	7	9	2		0	0	0	158	50	23	1	6.2	.900	C-33, OF-4
1889			20	.174	.203	69	12	2	0	0	0.0	6	8	4	14	2	0	0	80	15	15	2	5.5	.864	C-18, OF-2
1890	PHI	AA	5	.045	.045	22	1	0	0	0	0.0	1	0	0		0	0	0	15	10	3	1	5.6	.893	C-5
			62	.157	.184	217	34	4	1	0	0.0	14	17	6	14	2	0	0	253	75	41	4	6.0	.889	C-56, OF-6

Nick Capra

CAPRA, NICK LEE
B. Mar. 8, 1958, Denver, Colo. BR TR 5'8" 164 lbs.

Year Team	Games	BA	SA	AB	H	2B	3B	HR	HR%	R	RBI	BB	SO	SB	Pinch Hit AB	Pinch Hit H	PO	A	E	DP	TC/G	FA	G by Pos
1982 TEX A	13	.267	.467	15	4	0	0	1	6.7	2	1	3	4	2	0	0	14	2	0	1	1.2	1.000	OF-9
1983	8	.000	.000	2	0	0	0	0	0.0	2	0	0	0	0	2	0	0	0	0	0	0.0	—	OF-4
1985	8	.125	.125	8	1	0	0	0	0.0	1	0	0	0	0	0	0	11	0	0	0	1.4	1.000	OF-8
1988 KC A	14	.138	.172	29	4	1	0	0	0.0	3	0	2	3	1	1	0	15	0	0	0	1.1	1.000	OF-11
4 yrs.	43	.167	.241	54	9	1	0	1	1.9	8	1	5	7	3	3	0	40	2	0	1	1.0	1.000	OF-32

Pat Capri

CAPRI, PATRICK NICHOLAS
B. Nov. 27, 1918, New York, N. Y. D. June 14, 1989, New York, N. Y. BR TR 6'½" 170 lbs.

Year Team	Games	BA	SA	AB	H	2B	3B	HR	HR%	R	RBI	BB	SO	SB	Pinch Hit AB	Pinch Hit H	PO	A	E	DP	TC/G	FA	G by Pos
1944 BOS N	7	.000	.000	1	0	0	0	0	0.0	1	0	0	1	0	0	0	0	2	0	1	0.3	1.000	2B-1

Ralph Capron

CAPRON, RALPH EARL (Cape)
B. June 16, 1889, Minneapolis, Minn. D. Sept. 19, 1980, Los Angeles, Calif. BL TR 5'11½" 165 lbs.

Year Team	Games	BA	SA	AB	H	2B	3B	HR	HR%	R	RBI	BB	SO	SB	Pinch Hit AB	Pinch Hit H	PO	A	E	DP	TC/G	FA	G by Pos
1912 PIT N	1	—	—	0	0	0	0	0	—	0	0	0	0	0	0	0	0	0	0	0	0.0	—	
1913 PHI N	2	.000	.000	1	0	0	0	0	0.0	1	0	0	0	0	0	0	0	0	0	0	0.0	—	OF-1
2 yrs.	3	.000	.000	1	0	0	0	0	0.0	1	0	0	0	0	0	0	0	0	0	0	0.0	—	OF-1

John Carbine

CARBINE, JOHN C.
B. Oct. 12, 1855, Syracuse, N. Y. D. Sept. 11, 1915, Forest Park, Ill. 6' 187 lbs.

Year Team	Games	BA	SA	AB	H	2B	3B	HR	HR%	R	RBI	BB	SO	SB	Pinch Hit AB	Pinch Hit H	PO	A	E	DP	TC/G	FA	G by Pos
1876 LOU N	7	.160	.160	25	4	0	0	0	0.0	3	1	0	0		0	0	72	2	10	5	12.0	.881	1B-6, OF-1

Bernie Carbo

CARBO, BERNARD
B. Aug. 5, 1947, Detroit, Mich. BL TR 5'11" 173 lbs.

Year Team	Games	BA	SA	AB	H	2B	3B	HR	HR%	R	RBI	BB	SO	SB	Pinch Hit AB	Pinch Hit H	PO	A	E	DP	TC/G	FA	G by Pos
1969 CIN N	4	.000	.000	3	0	0	0	0	0.0	0	0	0	2	0	3	0	0	0	0	0	0.0	—	
1970	125	.310	.551	365	113	19	3	21	5.8	54	63	94	77	10	7	3	177	8	4	2	1.5	.979	OF-119
1971	106	.219	.339	310	68	20	1	5	1.6	33	20	54	56	2	12	3	154	7	3	0	1.5	.982	OF-90
1972 2 teams CIN N (19G – .143) STL N (99G – .258)																							
" total	118	.251	.362	323	81	13	1	7	2.2	44	34	63	59	2	17	1	171	16	6	3	1.6	.969	OF-96, 3B-1
1973 STL N	111	.286	.422	308	88	18	0	8	2.6	42	40	58	52	2	17	5	171	11	4	3	1.7	.978	OF-94
1974 BOS A	117	.249	.414	338	84	20	0	12	3.6	40	61	58	90	4	12	6	164	5	1	1	1.5	.994	OF-87, DH-15
1975	107	.257	.483	319	82	21	3	15	4.7	64	50	83	69	2	8	2	157	7	4	1	1.6	.976	OF-85, DH-13
1976 2 teams BOS A (17G – .236) MIL A (69G – .235)																							
" total	86	.235	.345	238	56	11	0	5	2.1	25	25	41	72	1	12	2	72	5	0	1	0.9	1.000	DH-39, OF-34
1977 BOS A	86	.289	.522	228	66	6	1	15	6.6	36	34	47	72	1	14	4	131	5	7	1	1.7	.951	OF-67, DH-7
1978 2 teams BOS A (17G – .261) CLE A (60G – .287)																							
" total	77	.282	.400	220	62	11	0	5	2.3	28	22	39	39	2	8	0	27	0	0	0	0.4	1.000	DH-57, OF-13
1979 STL N	52	.281	.438	64	18	1	0	3	4.7	6	12	10	22	1	32	6	10	0	0	0	0.2	1.000	OF-17
1980 2 teams STL N (14G – .182) PIT N (7G – .333)																							
" total	21	.235	.235	17	4	0	0	0	0.0	0	1	2	1	0	17	0	0	0	0	0	0.0	—	
12 yrs.	1010	.264	.427	2733	722	140	9	96	3.5	372	358	538	611	26	159	36	1234	64	29	12	1.3	.978	OF-702, DH-131, 3B-1

LEAGUE CHAMPIONSHIP SERIES

Year Team	Games	BA	SA	AB	H	2B	3B	HR	HR%	R	RBI	BB	SO	SB	Pinch Hit AB	Pinch Hit H	PO	A	E	DP	TC/G	FA	G by Pos
1970 CIN N	2	.000	.000	6	0	0	0	0	0.0	0	0	1	3	0	0	0	0	0	0	0	0.0	—	OF-2

WORLD SERIES

Year Team	Games	BA	SA	AB	H	2B	3B	HR	HR%	R	RBI	BB	SO	SB	Pinch Hit AB	Pinch Hit H	PO	A	E	DP	TC/G	FA	G by Pos
1970 CIN N	4	.000	.000	8	0	0	0	0	0.0	0	0	2	3	0	2	0	4	0	0	0	1.0	1.000	OF-2
1975 BOS A	4	.429	1.429	7	3	1	0	2	28.6	3	4	1	1	0	3	2	1	0	0	0	0.5	1.000	OF-2
2 yrs.	8	.200	.667	15	3	1	0	2	13.3	3	4	3	4	0	5	2	5	1	0	0	0.8	1.000	OF-4

Jose Cardenal

CARDENAL, JOSE ROSARIO
Born Jose Rosario Domec y Cardenal.
B. Oct. 7, 1943, Matanzas, Cuba. BR TR 5'10" 150 lbs.

Year Team	Games	BA	SA	AB	H	2B	3B	HR	HR%	R	RBI	BB	SO	SB	Pinch Hit AB	Pinch Hit H	PO	A	E	DP	TC/G	FA	G by Pos
1963 SF N	9	.200	.200	5	1	0	0	0	0.0	1	2	1	4	1	0	0	0	0	0	0	0.0	—	OF-2
1964	20	.000	.000	15	0	0	0	0	0.0	3	0	2	3	2	2	0	8	2	1	0	0.6	.909	OF-16
1965 CAL A	134	.250	.367	512	128	23	2	11	2.1	58	57	27	72	37	1	1	287	13	11	2	2.3	.965	OF-129, 3B-2, 2B-1
1966	154	.276	.399	561	155	15	3	16	2.9	67	48	34	69	24	10	2	351	10	3	4	2.4	.992	OF-146
1967	108	.236	.344	381	90	13	5	6	1.6	40	27	15	63	10	8	0	195	10	3	0	1.9	.986	OF-101
1968 CLE A	157	.257	.353	583	150	21	7	7	1.2	78	44	39	74	40	7	1	367	12	10	7	2.5	.974	OF-153
1969	146	.257	.373	557	143	26	3	11	2.0	75	45	49	58	36	4	1	329	12	6	2	2.4	.983	OF-142, 3B-5
1970 STL N	148	.293	.428	552	162	32	6	10	1.8	73	74	45	70	26	16	8	276	6	9	0	2.0	.969	OF-134
1971 2 teams STL N (89G – .243) MIL A (53G – .258)																							
" total	142	.248	.369	499	124	22	4	10	2.0	57	80	42	55	21	5	9	314	15	9	1	2.4	.973	OF-135
1972 CHI N	143	.291	.454	533	155	24	6	17	3.2	96	70	55	58	25	5	2	223	11	7	1	1.7	.971	OF-135
1973	145	.303	.437	522	158	33	2	11	2.1	80	68	58	62	19	2	1	234	13	5	2	1.7	.980	OF-137
1974	143	.293	.441	542	159	35	3	13	2.4	75	72	56	67	23	2	3	262	15	10	4	2.0	.965	OF-142
1975	154	.317	.423	574	182	30	2	9	1.6	85	68	77	68	34	5	1	313	14	8	3	2.2	.976	OF-136
1976	136	.299	.401	521	156	25	2	8	1.5	64	47	32	39	23	8	1	246	10	5	1	1.9	.981	OF-151
1977	100	.239	.341	226	54	12	1	5	2.2	33	18	28	30	5	31	10	85	1	2	0	0.9	.977	OF-128
1978 PHI N	87	.249	.368	201	50	12	0	4	2.0	27	33	23	16	2	33	9	365	17	5	39	4.4	.987	OF-62, 3B-1, 2B-1
1979 2 teams PHI N (29G – .208) NY N (11G – .297)																							
" total	40	.247	.400	85	21	7	0	2	2.4	12	13	14	11	2	17	4	49	0	0	3	1.2	1.000	1B-50, OF-13
1980 2 teams NY N (26G – .167) KC A (25G – .340)																							
" total	51	.263	.295	95	25	3	0	0	0.0	12	9	11	9	0	17	1	37	1	0	1	0.7	1.000	OF-21, 1B-3
18 yrs.	2017	.275	.395	6964	1913	333	46	138	2.0	936	775	608	807	329	187	50	3941	162	94	70	2.1	.978	OF-1777, 1B-58, 3B-8, 2B-2

LEAGUE CHAMPIONSHIP SERIES

Year Team	Games	BA	SA	AB	H	2B	3B	HR	HR%	R	RBI	BB	SO	SB	Pinch Hit AB	Pinch Hit H	PO	A	E	DP	TC/G	FA	G by Pos
1978 PHI N	2	.167	.167	6	1	0	0	0	0.0	0	0	1	1	0	0	0	21	3	0	1	10.5	1.000	1B-2

WORLD SERIES

Year Team	Games	BA	SA	AB	H	2B	3B	HR	HR%	R	RBI	BB	SO	SB	Pinch Hit AB	Pinch Hit H	PO	A	E	DP	TC/G	FA	G by Pos
1980 KC A	4	.200	.200	10	2	0	0	0	0.0	0	0	0	3	0	1	0	7	0	0	0	1.8	1.000	OF-4

Year	Team		Games	BA	SA	AB	H	2B	3B	HR	HR%	R	RBI	BB	SO	SB	Pinch Hit AB	H	PO	A	E	DP	TC/G	FA	G by Pos

Leo Cardenas

CARDENAS, LEONARDO LAZARO (Chico)
Born Leonardo Lazaro Cardenas y Alfonso.
B. Dec. 17, 1938, Matanzas, Cuba

BR TR 5'11" 150 lbs.

Year	Team		Games	BA	SA	AB	H	2B	3B	HR	HR%	R	RBI	BB	SO	SB	AB	H	PO	A	E	DP	TC/G	FA	G by Pos
1960	CIN	N	48	.232	.324	142	33	2	4	1	0.7	13	12	6	32	0	1	0	76	128	9	32	4.4	.958	SS-47
1961			74	.308	.485	198	61	18	1	5	2.5	23	24	15	39	1	12	1	83	133	6	21	3.0	.973	SS-63
1962			153	.294	.411	589	173	31	4	10	1.7	77	60	39	99	2	3	1	273	443	21	84	4.8	.972	SS-149
1963			158	.235	.326	565	133	22	4	7	1.2	42	48	23	101	3	2	1	270	420	20	84	4.5	.972	SS-157
1964			163	.251	.357	597	150	32	2	9	1.5	61	69	41	110	4	0	0	336	436	32	87	4.9	.960	SS-163
1965			156	.287	.431	557	160	25	11	11	2.0	65	57	60	100	1	1	0	292	440	19	92	4.8	.975	SS-155
1966			160	.255	.419	568	145	25	4	20	3.5	59	81	45	87	9	0	0	279	446	15	87	4.6	.980	SS-160
1967			108	.256	.325	379	97	14	3	2	0.5	30	21	34	77	4	0	0	190	316	15	57	4.8	.971	SS-108
1968			137	.235	.319	452	106	13	2	7	1.5	45	41	36	83	2	1	0	221	388	29	66	4.7	.955	SS-136
1969	MIN	A	160	.280	.388	578	162	24	4	10	1.7	67	70	66	96	5	0	0	310	570	32	126	5.7	.965	SS-160
1970			160	.247	.374	588	145	34	4	11	1.9	67	65	42	101	2	0	0	280	487	17	91	4.9	.978	SS-160
1971			153	.264	.421	554	146	25	4	18	3.2	59	75	51	69	3	1	0	266	445	11	89	4.7	.985	SS-153
1972	CAL	A	150	.223	.283	551	123	11	2	6	1.1	25	42	35	73	1	0	0	241	471	22	82	4.9	.970	SS-150
1973	CLE	A	72	.215	.236	195	42	4	0	0	0.0	9	12	13	42	1	0	0	90	167	11	37	3.7	.959	SS-67, 3B-5
1974	TEX	A	34	.272	.304	92	25	3	0	0	0.0	5	7	2	14	1	1	0	26	54	2	3	2.4	.976	3B-21, SS-10, DH-4
1975			55	.235	.284	102	24	2	0	1	1.0	15	5	14	12	0	9	1	38	85	5	12	2.3	.961	3B-43, SS-5, 2B-3
16 yrs.			1941	.257	.367	6707	1725	285	49	118	1.8	662	689	522	1135	39	31	4	3271	5429	266	1050	4.6	.970	SS-1843, 3B-69, DH-4, 2B-3

LEAGUE CHAMPIONSHIP SERIES

1969	MIN	A	3	.154	.308	13	2	0	1	0	0.0	0	0	0	7	0	0	0	14	12	1	3	9.0	.963	SS-3
1970			3	.182	.182	11	2	0	0	0	0.0	1	1	1	1	0	0	0	6	11	2	3	6.3	.895	SS-3
2 yrs.			6	.167	.250	24	4	0	1	0	0.0	1	1	1	8	0	0	0	20	23	3	6	7.7	.935	SS-6

WORLD SERIES

1961	CIN	N	3	.333	.667	3	1	1	0	0	0.0	0	0	0	1	0	3	1	0	0	0	0	0.0	—	

Rod Carew

CAREW, RODNEY CLINE
Born Rodney Cline Carew y Scott.
B. Oct. 1, 1945, Gatun, Canal Zone

BL TR 6' 170 lbs.

Year	Team		Games	BA	SA	AB	H	2B	3B	HR	HR%	R	RBI	BB	SO	SB	AB	H	PO	A	E	DP	TC/G	FA	G by Pos
1967	MIN	A	137	.292	.409	514	150	22	7	8	1.6	66	51	37	91	5	1	1	289	314	15	60	4.5	.976	2B-134
1968			127	.273	.347	461	126	27	2	1	0.2	46	42	26	71	12	9	2	266	285	18	50	4.5	.968	2B-117, SS-4
1969			123	.332	.467	458	152	30	4	8	1.7	79	56	37	72	19	7	4	244	302	17	80	4.6	.970	2B-118
1970			51	.366	.524	191	70	12	3	4	2.1	27	28	11	28	4	5	0	79	122	8	26	4.1	.962	2B-45, 1B-1
1971			147	.307	.380	577	177	16	10	2	0.3	88	48	45	81	6	3	1	324	331	16	76	4.6	.976	2B-142, 3B-2
1972			142	.318	.379	535	170	21	6	0	0.0	61	51	43	60	12	5	1	331	378	16	85	5.1	.978	2B-139
1973			149	.350	.471	580	203	30	11	6	1.0	98	62	62	55	41	3	0	383	413	13	96	5.4	.984	2B-147
1974			153	.364	.446	599	218	30	5	3	0.5	86	55	74	49	38	5	1	375	416	33	114	5.4	.960	2B-148
1975			143	.359	.497	535	192	24	4	14	2.6	89	80	64	40	35	5	2	408	377	21	89	5.6	.974	1B-123, 2B-14, DH-2
1976			156	.331	.463	605	200	29	12	9	1.5	97	90	67	52	49	5	3	1398	110	16	149	9.8	.990	1B-152, 2B-7
1977			155	.388	.570	616	239	38	16	14	2.3	128	100	69	55	23	6	3	1463	124	10	161	10.3	.994	1B-151, 2B-4, DH-1
1978			152	.333	.441	564	188	26	10	5	0.9	85	70	78	62	27	10	4	1363	105	16	134	9.8	.989	1B-148, 2B-4, OF-1
1979	CAL	A	110	.318	.391	409	130	15	3	3	0.7	78	44	73	46	18	0	0	804	55	10	101	7.9	.988	1B-103, DH-6
1980			144	.331	.437	540	179	34	7	3	0.6	74	59	59	38	23	11	4	897	57	6	82	6.7	.994	1B-103, DH-32
1981			93	.305	.374	364	111	17	1	2	0.5	57	21	45	45	16	2	1	877	60	5	90	10.1	.995	1B-90, DH-2
1982			138	.319	.403	523	167	25	5	3	0.6	88	44	67	49	10	5	1	1339	94	12	115	10.5	.992	1B-134
1983			129	.339	.411	472	160	24	2	2	0.4	66	44	57	48	6	17	6	891	42	6	94	7.3	.994	1B-89, DH-24, 2B-2
1984			93	.295	.353	329	97	8	1	3	0.9	42	31	40	39	4	12	4	724	59	15	73	8.6	.981	1B-83, DH-1
1985			127	.280	.345	443	124	17	3	2	0.5	69	39	64	47	5	13	2	1055	65	7	121	8.9	.994	1B-116
19 yrs.			2469	.328	.429	9315	3053	445	112	92	1.0	1424	1015	1018	1028	353	124	40	13510	3709	260	1796	7.1	.985	1B-1184, 2B-1130, DH-68, SS-4, 3B-2, OF-1

LEAGUE CHAMPIONSHIP SERIES

1969	MIN	A	3	.071	.071	14	1	0	0	0	0.0	0	0	1	4	0	0	0	5	3	1	1	3.0	.889	2B-3
1970			2	.000	.000	2	0	0	0	0	0.0	0	0	0	1	0	2	0	0	0	0	0	0.0	—	
1979	CAL	A	4	.412	.588	17	7	3	0	0	0.0	4	1	0	0	1	0	0	34	1	0	6	8.8	1.000	1B-4
1982			5	.176	.235	17	3	1	0	0	0.0	2	0	4	4	1	0	0	0	0	0	0	0.0	—	1B-5
4 yrs.			14	.220	.300	50	11	4	0	0	0.0	6	1	5	9	2	2	0	39	4	1	7	3.1	.977	1B-9, 2B-3

Andy Carey

CAREY, ANDREW ARTHUR
Born Andrew Arthur Nordstrom.
B. Oct. 18, 1931, Oakland, Calif.

BR TR 6'1½" 190 lbs.

Year	Team		Games	BA	SA	AB	H	2B	3B	HR	HR%	R	RBI	BB	SO	SB	AB	H	PO	A	E	DP	TC/G	FA	G by Pos
1952	NY	A	16	.150	.150	40	6	0	0	0	0.0	6	1	3	10	0	0	0	13	23	6	4	2.6	.857	3B-14, SS-1
1953			51	.321	.531	81	26	5	0	4	4.9	14	8	9	12	2	7	1	34	56	2	8	1.8	.978	3B-40, SS-2, 2B-1
1954			122	.302	.423	411	124	14	6	8	1.9	60	65	43	38	5	3	0	154	283	15	32	3.7	.967	3B-120
1955			135	.257	.378	510	131	19	11	7	1.4	73	47	44	51	3	0	0	154	301	22	37	3.5	.954	3B-135
1956			132	.237	.339	422	100	18	2	7	1.7	54	50	45	53	9	1	0	114	265	21	26	3.0	.948	3B-131
1957			85	.255	.393	247	63	6	5	6	2.4	30	33	15	42	2	6	1	66	147	5	9	2.6	.977	3B-81
1958			102	.286	.486	315	90	19	4	12	3.8	39	45	34	43	1	0	0	99	195	12	22	3.0	.961	3B-99
1959			41	.257	.356	101	26	1	0	3	3.0	11	9	7	17	1	8	3	39	48	8	10	2.3	.916	3B-34
1960	2 teams	NY A (4G – .333)	KC A (102G – .233)																						
"	total		106	.234	.402	346	81	14	4	12	3.5	31	54	26	53	0	15	1	95	181	7	26	2.7	.975	3B-93, OF-1
1961	2 teams	KC A (39G – .244)	CHI A (56G – .266)																						
"	total		95	.256	.395	266	68	18	5	3	1.1	41	25	26	47	0	1	0	58	143	10	16	2.2	.953	3B-93
1962	LA	N	53	.234	.351	111	26	5	1	2	1.8	12	13	16	23	0	13	2	28	54	6	4	1.7	.932	3B-42
11 yrs.			938	.260	.396	2850	741	119	38	64	2.2	371	350	268	389	23	61	10	854	1696	114	194	2.8	.957	3B-882, SS-3, OF-1, 2B-1

WORLD SERIES

1955	NY	A	2	.500	1.500	2	1	0	0	0	0.0	0	0	0	0	0	2	1	0	0	0	0	0.0	—	
1956			7	.158	.158	19	3	0	0	0	0.0	2	0	1	6	0	0	0	6	10	2	0	2.6	.889	3B-7
1957			2	.286	.429	7	2	1	0	0	0.0	1	0	1	0	0	0	0	3	6	0	0	4.5	1.000	3B-2

Year	Team		Games	BA	SA	AB	H	2B	3B	HR	HR%	R	RBI	BB	SO	SB	Pinch Hit AB	Pinch Hit H	PO	A	E	DP	TC/G	FA	G by Pos

Andy Carey *continued*

1958			5	.083	.083	12	1	0	0	0	0.0	1	0	0	3	0	0	0	2	6	0	0	1.6	1.000	3B-5
4 yrs.			16	.175	.250	40	7	1	0	0	0.0	3	2	2	9	0	2	1	11	22	2	0	2.2	.943	3B-14

Max Carey

CAREY, MAX (Scoops)
Born Maximilian Carnarius.
B. Jan. 11, 1890, Terre Haute, Ind.   D. May 30, 1976, Miami, Fla.
Manager 1932-33.
Hall of Fame 1961.

BB TR 5'11½" 170 lbs.

Year	Team		Games	BA	SA	AB	H	2B	3B	HR	HR%	R	RBI	BB	SO	SB	PH AB	PH H	PO	A	E	DP	TC/G	FA	G by Pos
1910	PIT	N	2	.500	.833	6	3	0	1	0	0.0	2	2	2	1	0	0	0	10	1	0	0	5.5	1.000	OF-2
1911			129	.258	.375	427	110	15	10	5	1.2	77	43	44	75	27	5	1	304	11	8	5	2.5	.975	OF-122
1912			150	.302	.394	587	177	23	8	5	0.9	114	66	61	79	45	0	0	369	19	13	10	2.7	.968	OF-150
1913			154	.277	.371	620	172	23	10	5	0.8	99	49	55	67	61	0	0	363	28	16	6	2.6	.961	OF-154
1914			156	.243	.347	593	144	25	17	1	0.2	76	31	59	56	38	1	1	318	23	12	3	2.3	.966	OF-154
1915			140	.254	.333	564	143	26	5	3	0.5	76	27	57	58	36	1	0	307	21	6	5	2.4	.982	OF-140
1916			154	.264	.374	599	158	23	11	7	1.2	90	42	59	58	63	0	0	419	32	8	10	3.0	.983	OF-154
1917			155	.296	.378	588	174	21	12	1	0.2	82	51	58	38	46	2	2	440	28	10	8	3.1	.979	OF-153
1918			126	.274	.348	468	128	14	6	3	0.6	70	48	62	25	58	0	0	359	25	17	9	3.2	.958	OF-126
1919			66	.307	.365	244	75	10	2	0	0.0	41	9	25	24	18	2	1	173	5	10	1	2.8	.947	OF-63
1920			130	.289	.348	485	140	18	4	1	0.2	74	35	59	31	52	2	1	345	10	12	0	2.8	.967	OF-129
1921			140	.309	.430	521	161	34	4	7	1.3	85	56	70	30	37	1	0	431	15	20	6	3.3	.957	OF-139
1922			155	.329	.459	629	207	28	12	10	1.6	140	70	80	26	51	0	0	449	22	15	4	3.1	.969	OF-155
1923			153	.308	.452	610	188	32	19	6	1.0	120	63	73	28	51	0	0	450	28	19	4	3.2	.962	OF-153
1924			149	.297	.412	599	178	30	9	7	1.2	113	55	58	17	49	0	0	428	16	16	3	3.1	.965	OF-149
1925			133	.343	.491	542	186	39	13	5	0.9	109	44	66	19	46	2	0	363	20	20	2	3.0	.950	OF-130
1926	2 teams		PIT	N	(86G – .222)		BKN	N	(27G – .260)																
"	total		113	.231	.300	424	98	17	6	0	0.0	64	35	38	19	10	3	3	295	8	19	3	2.8	.941	OF-109
1927	BKN	N	144	.266	.364	538	143	30	10	1	0.2	70	54	64	18	32	2	1	331	19	11	6	2.5	.970	OF-141
1928			108	.247	.304	296	73	11	0	2	0.7	41	19	47	24	18	10	3	202	8	3	1	2.0	.986	OF-95
1929			19	.304	.304	23	7	0	0	0	0.0	2	1	3	2	0	11	4	7	0	0	0	0.4	1.000	OF-4
20 yrs.			2476	.285	.385	9363	2665	419	159	69	0.7	1545	800	1040	695	738	42	17	6363	339	235	86	2.8	.966	OF-2422
																5th									

WORLD SERIES

| 1925 | PIT | N | 7 | .458 | .625 | 24 | 11 | 4 | 0 | 0 | 0.0 | 6 | 2 | 2 | 3 | 3 | 0 | 0 | 14 | 0 | 1 | 0 | 2.1 | .933 | OF-7 |

Roger Carey

CAREY, ROGER J.
B. Unknown.

| 1887 | NY | N | 1 | .000 | .000 | 4 | 0 | 0 | 0 | 0 | 0.0 | 0 | | 0 | 2 | 0 | 1 | 0 | 0 | 0 | 2 | 6 | 2 | 1 | 10.0 | .800 | 2B-1 |

Scoops Carey

CAREY, GEORGE C.
B. Dec. 4, 1870, East Liverpool, Ohio   D. Dec. 17, 1916, East Liverpool, Ohio

BR TR 175 lbs.

1895	BAL	N	123	.261	.335	490	128	21	6	1	0.2	59	75	27	32	2	0	0	1137	46	15	73	9.7	.987	1B-123, OF-1, SS-1, 3B-1
1898	LOU	N	8	.188	.281	32	6	1	1	0	0.0	1	1	1			0	0	0	94	5	4	5	12.9	.961	1B-8
1902	WAS	A	120	.314	.440	452	142	35	11	0	0.0	46	60	20		3	0	0	1190	69	14	54	10.6	.989	1B-120
1903			48	.202	.240	183	37	3	2	0	0.0	8	23	4		0	1	0	435	23	11	18	9.8	.977	1B-47
4 yrs.			299	.271	.360	1157	313	60	20	1	0.1	114	159	52	32	5	1	0	2856	143	44	150	10.2	.986	1B-298, OF-1, SS-1, 3B-1

Tom Carey

CAREY, THOMAS FRANCIS ALOYSIUS (Scoops)
B. Oct. 11, 1906, Hoboken, N. J.   D. Feb. 21, 1970, Rochester, N. Y.

BR TR 5'8½" 170 lbs.

1935	STL	A	76	.291	.378	296	86	18	4	0	0.0	29	42	13	11	1	0	0	189	253	18	52	6.1	.961	2B-76
1936			134	.273	.359	488	133	27	6	1	0.0	58	57	27	25	2	6	2	308	435	25	82	5.7	.967	2B-128, SS-1
1937			130	.275	.335	487	134	24	1	1	0.2	54	40	21	26	1	0	0	293	397	15	83	5.4	.979	2B-87, SS-44, 3B-1
1939	BOS	A	54	.242	.304	161	39	6	2	0	0.0	17	20	3	9	0	7	2	93	116	2	22	3.9	.991	2B-35, SS-10
1940			43	.323	.387	62	20	4	0	0	0.0	4	7	2	1	0	10	3	24	49	3	14	1.8	.961	SS-20, 3B-4, 2B-4
1941			24	.200	.200	20	4	0	0	0	0.0	7	2	0	2	0	3	1	14	14	0	3	1.2	1.000	2B-9, SS-8
1942			1	1.000	1.000	1	1	0	0	0	0.0	0	1	0	0	0	0	0	1	0	0	0	1.0	1.000	2B-1
1946			3	.200	.200	5	1	0	0	0	0.0	0	0	0	1	0	0	0	3	6	1	2	3.3	.900	2B-3
8 yrs.			465	.275	.348	1520	418	79	13	2	0.1	169	169	66	75	3	26	8	925	1270	64	258	4.9	.972	2B-343, SS-83, 3B-5

Tom Carey

CAREY, THOMAS JOHN
Born J. J. Norton.
B. 1849, Brooklyn, N. Y.   D. Feb. 13, 1899, Los Angeles Calif.,
Manager 1873-74.

BR TR 5'8" 145 lbs.

1876	HAR	N	68	.270	.294	289	78	7	0	0	0.0	51	26	3	4		0	0	74	218	39	9	4.9	.882	SS-68
1877			60	.255	.292	274	70	3	2	1	0.4	38	20	0	9		0	0	49	203	53	11	5.1	.826	SS-60
1878	PRO	N	61	.237	.300	253	60	10	3	0	0.0	33	24	0	14		0	0	56	207	38	8	4.9	.874	SS-61
1879	CLE	N	80	.239	.287	335	80	14	1	0	0.0	30	32	5	20		0	0	79	263	54	13	5.0	.864	SS-80
4 yrs.			269	.250	.293	1151	288	34	6	1	0.1	152	102	8	47		0	0	258	891	184	41	5.0	.862	SS-269

Bobby Cargo

CARGO, ROBERT J.
B. 1871, Pittsburgh, Pa.   D. Apr. 27, 1904, Pittsburgh, Pa.

BR TR

| 1892 | PIT | N | 2 | .250 | .250 | 4 | 1 | 0 | 0 | 0 | 0.0 | 0 | 0 | 0 | 0 | 0 | 0 | 0 | 2 | 5 | 4 | 2 | 5.5 | .636 | SS-2 |

Fred Carisch

CARISCH, FREDERICK BEHLMER
B. Nov. 14, 1881, Fountain City, Wis.   D. Apr. 19, 1977, San Gabriel, Calif.

BR TR 5'10½" 174 lbs.

1903	PIT	N	5	.333	.722	18	6	4	0	1	5.6	4	5	0			0	1	0	24	7	1	0	6.4	.969	C-4
1904			37	.248	.288	125	31	3	1	0	0.0	9	8	9			3	1	0	237	44	5	6	7.7	.983	C-22, 1B-14
1905			32	.206	.262	107	22	0	3	0	0.0	7	8	2			1	2	0	137	42	5	3	5.8	.973	C-30
1906			4	.083	.083	12	1	0	0	0	0.0	0	0	1			0	0	0	15	5	2	0	5.5	.909	C-4
1912	CLE	A	26	.271	.343	70	19	3	1	0	0.0	4	5	1			3	2	0	100	40	7	5	5.7	.952	C-23

Year	Team		Games	BA	SA	AB	H	2B	3B	HR	HR%	R	RBI	BB	SO	SB	Pinch Hit AB	Pinch Hit H	PO	A	E	DP	TC/G	FA	G by Pos

Fred Carisch *continued*

Year	Team		Games	BA	SA	AB	H	2B	3B	HR	HR%	R	RBI	BB	SO	SB	AB	H	PO	A	E	DP	TC/G	FA	G by Pos
1913			81	.216	.252	222	48	4	2	0	0.0	11	26	21	19	6	2	0	391	114	15	10	6.4	.971	C-79
1914			40	.216	.284	102	22	3	2	0	0.0	8	5	12	18	2	2	0	183	44	9	5	5.9	.962	C-38
1923	DET	A	2	–	–	0	0	0	0	0	–	0	0	0	0	0	0	0	1	0	0	0	0.5	1.000	C-2
8 yrs.			227	.227	.285	656	149	17	9	1	0.2	43	57	46	37	16	10	0	1088	296	44	29	6.3	.969	C-202, 1B-14

Fred Carl

CARL, FREDERICK E.
B. 1858, Washington, D. C.   D. July 30, 1897, Washington, D. C.   TL   5'6"   158 lbs.

Year	Team		Games	BA	SA	AB	H	2B	3B	HR	HR%	R	RBI	BB	SO	SB	AB	H	PO	A	E	DP	TC/G	FA	G by Pos
1889	LOU	AA	25	.202	.263	99	20	2	2	0	0.0	13	13	16	22	0	0	0	38	29	13	9	3.2	.838	OF-18, 2B-6, 3B-1

Jim Carlin

CARLIN, JAMES ARTHUR
B. Feb. 23, 1918, Wylam, Ala.   BL   TR   5'11"   165 lbs.

Year	Team		Games	BA	SA	AB	H	2B	3B	HR	HR%	R	RBI	BB	SO	SB	AB	H	PO	A	E	DP	TC/G	FA	G by Pos
1941	PHI	N	16	.143	.333	21	3	1	0	1	4.8	2	2	3	4	0	4	0	4	1	0	0	0.3	1.000	OF-9, 3B-2

Walter Carlisle

CARLISLE, WALTER G. (Rosy)
B. July 6, 1883, Yorkshire, England   D. May 27, 1945, Los Angeles, Calif.   BB   TR   5'9"   154 lbs.

Year	Team		Games	BA	SA	AB	H	2B	3B	HR	HR%	R	RBI	BB	SO	SB	AB	H	PO	A	E	DP	TC/G	FA	G by Pos
1908	BOS	A	3	.100	.100	10	1	0	0	0	0.0	0		1		1	0	0	5	1	0	0	2.0	1.000	OF-3

Swede Carlstrom

CARLSTROM, ALBIN OSCAR
B. Oct. 26, 1886, Elizabeth, N. J.   D. Apr. 23, 1935, Elizabeth, N. J.   BR   TR   6'   167 lbs.

Year	Team		Games	BA	SA	AB	H	2B	3B	HR	HR%	R	RBI	BB	SO	SB	AB	H	PO	A	E	DP	TC/G	FA	G by Pos
1911	BOS	A	2	.167	.167	6	1	0	0	0	0.0	0	0	0	0	0	0	0	3	6	0	1	4.5	1.000	SS-2

Cleo Carlyle

CARLYLE, HIRAM CLEO
Brother of Roy Carlyle.
B. Sept. 7, 1902, Fairburn, Ga.   D. Nov. 12, 1967, Los Angeles, Calif.   BL   TR   6'   170 lbs.

Year	Team		Games	BA	SA	AB	H	2B	3B	HR	HR%	R	RBI	BB	SO	SB	AB	H	PO	A	E	DP	TC/G	FA	G by Pos
1927	BOS	A	95	.234	.345	278	65	12	8	1	0.4	31	28	36	40	4	10	3	127	10	5	0	1.5	.965	OF-83

Roy Carlyle

CARLYLE, ROY EDWARD (Dizzy)
Brother of Cleo Carlyle.
B. Dec. 10, 1900, Buford, Ga.   D. Nov. 22, 1956, Norcross, Ga.   BL   TR   6'2½"   195 lbs.

Year	Team		Games	BA	SA	AB	H	2B	3B	HR	HR%	R	RBI	BB	SO	SB	AB	H	PO	A	E	DP	TC/G	FA	G by Pos
1925	2 teams		WAS	A	(1G – .000)		BOS	A	(93G – .326)																
"	total		94	.325	.495	277	90	20	3	7	2.5	36	49	16	30	1	22	8	122	5	13	0	1.5	.907	OF-67
1926	2 teams		BOS	A	(45G – .287)		NY	A	(35G – .377)																
"	total		80	.309	.415	217	67	11	3	2	0.9	25	27	8	27	0	25	10	77	5	8	0	1.1	.911	OF-53
2 yrs.			174	.318	.460	494	157	31	6	9	1.8	61	76	24	57	1	47	18	199	10	21	0	1.3	.909	OF-120

George Carman

CARMAN, GEORGE WARTMAN
B. Mar. 29, 1866, Philadelphia, Pa.   D. June 16, 1929, Lancaster, Pa.

Year	Team		Games	BA	SA	AB	H	2B	3B	HR	HR%	R	RBI	BB	SO	SB	AB	H	PO	A	E	DP	TC/G	FA	G by Pos
1890	PHI	AA	28	.175	.196	97	17	2	0	0	0.0	9		8		5	0	0	34	48	26	4	3.9	.759	SS-15, OF-10, 2B-2, 3B-1

Duke Carmel

CARMEL, LEON JAMES
B. Apr. 23, 1937, New York, N. Y.   BL   TL   6'3"   202 lbs.

Year	Team		Games	BA	SA	AB	H	2B	3B	HR	HR%	R	RBI	BB	SO	SB	AB	H	PO	A	E	DP	TC/G	FA	G by Pos
1959	STL	N	10	.130	.174	23	3	1	0	0	0.0	2	3	0	6	0	0	0	15	0	0	0	1.5	1.000	OF-10
1960			4	.000	.000	3	0	0	0	0	0.0	0	0	1	1	0	1	0	10	2	0	1	3.0	1.000	1B-2, OF-1
1963	2 teams		STL	N	(57G – .227)		NY	N	(47G – .235)																
"	total		104	.233	.358	193	45	6	3	4	2.1	20	20	25	48	2	19	4	270	11	6	13	2.8	.979	OF-59, 1B-19
1965	NY	A	6	.000	.000	8	0	0	0	0	0.0	0	0	0	5	0	4	0	7	1	0	0	1.3	1.000	1B-2
4 yrs.			124	.211	.322	227	48	7	3	4	1.8	22	23	27	60	3	23	4	302	14	6	14	2.6	.981	OF-70, 1B-23

Eddie Carnett

CARNETT, EDWIN ELLIOTT (Lefty)
B. Oct. 21, 1916, Springfield, Mo.   BL   TL   6'   185 lbs.

Year	Team		Games	BA	SA	AB	H	2B	3B	HR	HR%	R	RBI	BB	SO	SB	AB	H	PO	A	E	DP	TC/G	FA	G by Pos
1941	BOS	N	2	–	–	0	0	0	0	0	–	0	0	0	0	0	0	0	0	0	0	0	0.0	–	P-2
1944	CHI	A	126	.276	.357	457	126	18	8	1	0.2	51	60	26	35	5	10	1	425	17	12	16	3.6	.974	OF-88, 1B-25, P-2
1945	CLE	A	30	.219	.315	73	16	7	0	0	0.0	5	7	2	9	0	11	3	33	1	1	1	1.2	.971	OF-16, P-2
3 yrs.			158	.268	.351	530	142	25	8	1	0.2	56	67	28	44	5	21	4	458	18	13	17	3.1	.973	OF-104, 1B-25, P-6

Bill Carney

CARNEY, WILLIAM JOHN
B. Mar. 25, 1874, St. Paul, Minn.   D. July 31, 1938, Hopkins, Minn.   BB   TR   5'10"

Year	Team		Games	BA	SA	AB	H	2B	3B	HR	HR%	R	RBI	BB	SO	SB	AB	H	PO	A	E	DP	TC/G	FA	G by Pos
1904	CHI	N	2	.000	.000	7	0	0	0	0	0.0	0	0	1		0	0	0	0	1	0	0	0.5	1.000	OF-2

Jack Carney

CARNEY, JOHN JOSEPH (Handsome Jack)
B. Nov. 10, 1866, Salem, Mass.   D. Oct. 19, 1925, Litchfield, N. H.   BR   TR   5'10"   175 lbs.

Year	Team		Games	BA	SA	AB	H	2B	3B	HR	HR%	R	RBI	BB	SO	SB	AB	H	PO	A	E	DP	TC/G	FA	G by Pos
1889	WAS	N	69	.231	.267	273	63	7	0	1	0.4	25	29	14	14	12	0	0	541	18	30	30	8.5	.949	1B-53, OF-16
1890	2 teams		BUF	P	(28G – .271)		CLE	P	(25G – .348)																
"	total		53	.306	.378	196	60	8	0	0	0.0	26	34	21	19	8	0	0	296	14	15	22	6.1	.954	1B-30, OF-23
1891	2 teams		CIN	AA	(99G – .278)		MIL	AA	(31G – .300)																
"	total		130	.283	.394	477	135	15	10	6	1.3	69	66	48	26	20	0	0	1308	65	33	58	10.8	.977	1B-130
3 yrs.			252	.273	.354	946	258	30	13	7	0.7	120	129	83	59	40	0	0	2145	97	78	110	9.2	.966	1B-213, OF-39

Pat Carney

CARNEY, PATRICK JOSEPH (Doc)
B. Aug. 7, 1876, Holyoke, Mass.   D. Jan. 9, 1953, Worcester, Mass.   BL   TL   6'   200 lbs.

Year	Team		Games	BA	SA	AB	H	2B	3B	HR	HR%	R	RBI	BB	SO	SB	AB	H	PO	A	E	DP	TC/G	FA	G by Pos
1901	BOS	N	13	.291	.364	55	16	2	1	0	0.0	6	6	3		0	0	0	14	0	1	0	1.2	.933	OF-13
1902			137	.270	.330	522	141	17	4	2	0.4	75	65	42		27	0	0	153	19	13	7	1.4	.930	OF-137, P-2
1903			110	.240	.298	392	94	12	4	1	0.3	37	49	28		10	8	0	116	29	7	4	1.4	.954	OF-92, P-10, 1B-1
1904			78	.204	.237	279	57	5	2	0	0.0	24	11	12		6	0	0	92	18	5	5	1.5	.957	OF-71, P-4, 1B-1
4 yrs.			338	.247	.300	1248	308	36	11	3	0.2	142	131	85		43	9	0	375	66	26	16	1.4	.944	OF-313, P-16, 1B-2

Hick Carpenter

CARPENTER, WARREN WILLIAM
B. Aug. 16, 1855, Grafton, Mass.   D. Apr. 18, 1937, San Diego, Calif.   BR   TL   5'11"   186 lbs.

Year	Team		Games	BA	SA	AB	H	2B	3B	HR	HR%	R	RBI	BB	SO	SB	Pinch Hit AB	H	PO	A	E	DP	TC/G	FA	G by Pos

Hick Carpenter *continued*

Year	Team		Games	BA	SA	AB	H	2B	3B	HR	HR%	R	RBI	BB	SO	SB	Pinch Hit AB	H	PO	A	E	DP	TC/G	FA	G by Pos
1879	SYR	N	65	.203	.226	261	53	6	0	0	0.0	30	20	2	15		0	0	355	49	39	12	6.8	.912	1B-34, 3B-18, OF-11, 2B-3
1880	CIN	N	77	.240	.287	300	72	6	4	0	0.0	32	23	2	15		0	0	213	128	50	12	5.1	.872	3B-67, 1B-9, SS-1
1881	WOR	N	83	.216	.280	347	75	12	2	2	0.6	40	31	3	19		0	0	141	172	56	14	4.4	.848	3B-83
1882	CIN	AA	80	.342	.422	351	120	15	5	1	0.3	78		10			0	0	137	167	60	7	4.6	.835	3B-80
1883			95	.296	.376	436	129	18	4	3	0.7	99		18			0	0	133	181	47	6	3.8	.870	3B-95
1884			108	.255	.323	474	121	16	2	4	0.8	80		6			0	0	157	168	44	16	3.4	.881	3B-108, OF-1
1885			112	.277	.349	473	131	12	8	2	0.4	89		9			0	0	153	191	56	17	3.6	.860	3B-112
1886			111	.221	.273	458	101	8	5	2	0.4	67		18			0	0	127	221	66	23	3.7	.841	3B-111
1887			127	.249	.303	498	124	12	6	1	0.2	70		19		44	0	0	144	242	70	17	3.6	.846	3B-127
1888			136	.267	.327	551	147	14	5	3	0.5	68	67	5		59	0	0	142	286	66	15	3.6	.866	3B-136
1889			123	.261	.333	486	127	23	6	0	0.0	67	63	18	41	47	0	0	161	208	69	19	3.6	.842	3B-121, 1B-2
1892	STL	N	1	.333	.333	3	1	0	0	0	0.0	0	0	1	1	0	0	0	2	3	2	0	7.0	.714	3B-1
12 yrs.			1118	.259	.321	4638	1201	142	47	18	0.4	720	204	111	91	150	0	0	1865	2016	625	158	4.0	.861	3B-1059, 1B-45, OF-12, 2B-3, SS-1

Charlie Carr

CARR, CHARLES CARBITT
B. Dec. 27, 1876, Coatesville, Pa. D. Nov. 25, 1932, Memphis, Tenn.
BR TR 6'2" 195 lbs.

Year	Team		Games	BA	SA	AB	H	2B	3B	HR	HR%	R	RBI	BB	SO	SB	Pinch Hit AB	H	PO	A	E	DP	TC/G	FA	G by Pos
1898	WAS	N	20	.192	.219	73	14	2	0	0	0.0	6	4	2			2	0	200	8	11	15	11.0	.950	1B-20
1901	PHI	A	2	.125	.125	8	1	0	0	0	0.0	0	0	0			0	0	23	2	2	0	13.5	.926	1B-2
1903	DET	A	135	.281	.374	548	154	23	11	2	0.4	59	79	10			10	0	1276	111	25	60	10.5	.982	1B-135
1904	2 teams		DET	A	(92G – .214)			CLE	A	(32G – .225)															
"	total		124	.217	.271	480	104	18	4	0	0.0	38	47	18			6	0	1233	121	27	59	11.1	.980	1B-124
1905	CLE	A	89	.235	.310	306	72	12	4	1	0.3	29	31	13			12	2	940	50	9	33	11.2	.991	1B-87
1906	CIN	N	22	.191	.277	94	18	2	3	0	0.0	9	10	2			0	0	221	16	4	16	11.0	.983	1B-22
1914	IND	F	115	.293	.383	441	129	11	10	3	0.7	44	69	26			19	0	1088	59	11	67	10.1	.991	1B-115
7 yrs.			507	.252	.329	1950	492	68	32	6	0.3	185	240	71			49	2	4981	367	89	250	10.7	.984	1B-505

Lew Carr

CARR, LEWIS SMITH
B. Aug. 15, 1872, Union Springs, N. Y. D. June 15, 1954, Moravia, N. Y.
BR TR 6'2" 200 lbs.

Year	Team		Games	BA	SA	AB	H	2B	3B	HR	HR%	R	RBI	BB	SO	SB	Pinch Hit AB	H	PO	A	E	DP	TC/G	FA	G by Pos
1901	PIT	N	9	.250	.357	28	7	1	1	0	0.0	2	4	2			0	0	12	19	5	3	4.0	.861	SS-9, 3B-1

Chico Carrasquel

CARRASQUEL, ALFONSO
Born Alfonso Carrasquel y Colon.
B. Jan. 23, 1926, Caracas, Venezuela
BR TR 6' 170 lbs.

Year	Team		Games	BA	SA	AB	H	2B	3B	HR	HR%	R	RBI	BB	SO	SB	Pinch Hit AB	H	PO	A	E	DP	TC/G	FA	G by Pos
1950	CHI	A	141	.282	.365	524	148	21	5	4	0.8	72	46	66	46	0	0	0	234	458	28	113	5.1	.961	SS-141
1951			147	.264	.331	538	142	22	4	2	0.4	41	58	46	39	14	0	0	306	477	20	107	5.5	.975	SS-147
1952			100	.248	.298	359	89	7	4	1	0.3	36	42	33	27	2	1	1	176	248	16	50	4.4	.964	SS-99
1953			149	.279	.359	552	154	30	4	2	0.4	72	47	38	47	5	0	0	278	462	18	87	5.1	.976	SS-149
1954			155	.255	.368	620	158	28	3	12	1.9	106	62	85	67	7	0	0	280	492	20	102	5.1	.975	SS-155
1955			145	.256	.348	523	134	11	2	11	2.1	83	52	61	59	1	4	1	222	424	18	81	4.6	.973	SS-144
1956	CLE	A	141	.243	.323	474	115	15	1	7	1.5	60	48	52	61	0	0	0	240	354	20	70	4.4	.967	SS-141, 3B-1
1957			125	.276	.378	392	108	14	1	8	2.0	37	57	41	53	0	3	1	212	357	24	75	4.7	.960	SS-122
1958	2 teams		CLE	A	(49G – .256)			KC	A	(59G – .213)															
"	total		108	.234	.313	316	74	11	4	4	1.3	33	34	35	27	0	11	4	107	181	12	33	2.8	.960	SS-54, 3B-46
1959	BAL	A	114	.223	.295	346	77	13	0	4	1.2	28	28	34	41	2	6	2	157	271	13	68	3.9	.971	SS-89, 2B-22, 3B-2, 1B-1
10 yrs.			1325	.258	.342	4644	1199	172	25	55	1.2	568	474	491	467	31	25	9	2212	3724	189	786	4.6	.969	SS-1241, 3B-49, 2B-22, 1B-1

Camilo Carreon

CARREON, CAMILO
Father of Mark Carreon.
B. Aug. 6, 1937, Colton, Calif. D. Sept. 2, 1987, Tucson, Ariz.
BR TR 6'1½" 190 lbs.

Year	Team		Games	BA	SA	AB	H	2B	3B	HR	HR%	R	RBI	BB	SO	SB	Pinch Hit AB	H	PO	A	E	DP	TC/G	FA	G by Pos
1959	CHI	A	1	.000	.000	1	0	0	0	0	0.0	0	0	0	0	0	0	0	3	0	0	0	3.0	1.000	C-1
1960			8	.235	.235	17	4	0	0	0	0.0	2	2	1	3	0	1	0	22	2	0	0	3.0	1.000	C-7
1961			78	.271	.354	229	62	5	1	4	1.7	32	27	21	24	0	7	2	395	25	2	6	5.4	.995	C-71
1962			106	.256	.361	313	80	19	1	4	1.3	31	37	33	37	1	11	5	519	30	3	5	5.2	.995	C-93
1963			101	.274	.341	270	74	10	1	2	0.7	28	35	23	32	1	7	3	429	36	6	7	4.7	.987	C-92
1964			37	.274	.326	95	26	6	0	0	0.0	12	4	7	10	0	3	0	134	13	2	2	4.6	.987	C-34
1965	CLE	A	19	.231	.365	52	12	2	1	1	1.9	6	7	9	6	1	0	0	122	9	0	1	6.9	1.000	C-19
1966	BAL	A	4	.222	.444	9	2	2	0	0	0.0	2	2	3	2	0	1	1	24	0	0	0	6.0	1.000	C-3
8 yrs.			354	.264	.349	986	260	43	4	11	1.1	113	114	97	117	3	30	11	1648	115	13	21	5.0	.993	C-320

Mark Carreon

CARREON, MARK STEVEN
Son of Camilo Carreon.
B. July 19, 1963, Chicago, Ill.
BR TL 6' 170 lbs.

Year	Team		Games	BA	SA	AB	H	2B	3B	HR	HR%	R	RBI	BB	SO	SB	Pinch Hit AB	H	PO	A	E	DP	TC/G	FA	G by Pos
1987	NY	N	9	.250	.250	12	3	0	0	0	0.0	1	1	1	1	0	5	1	4	0	1	0	0.6	.800	OF-5
1988			7	.556	1.111	9	5	2	0	1	11.1	5	1	2	1	0	2	0	1	0	0	0	0.1	1.000	OF-4
1989			68	.308	.489	133	41	6	0	6	4.5	20	16	12	17	2	27	10	57	0	1	0	0.9	.983	OF-39
3 yrs.			84	.318	.506	154	49	8	0	7	4.5	25	18	15	19	2	34	11	62	0	2	0	0.8	.969	OF-48

Bill Carrigan

CARRIGAN, WILLIAM FRANCIS (Rough)
B. Oct. 22, 1883, Lewiston, Me. D. July 8, 1969, Lewiston, Me.
Manager 1913-16, 1927-29.
BR TR 5'9" 175 lbs.

Year	Team		Games	BA	SA	AB	H	2B	3B	HR	HR%	R	RBI	BB	SO	SB	Pinch Hit AB	H	PO	A	E	DP	TC/G	FA	G by Pos
1906	BOS	A	37	.211	.211	109	23	0	0	0	0.0	5	10	5			3	2	139	48	12	2	5.4	.940	C-35
1908			57	.235	.295	149	35	5	2	0	0.0	13	14	3			1	7	223	75	13	6	5.5	.958	C-47, 1B-3
1909			94	.296	.368	280	83	13	2	1	0.4	27	36	17			2	6	411	118	13	14	5.8	.976	C-77, 1B-8
1910			114	.249	.313	342	85	11	2	3	0.9	36	53	23			10	4	495	134	25	12	5.7	.962	C-110
1911			72	.289	.336	232	67	6	1	1	0.4	29	30	26			5	4	374	94	13	13	6.7	.973	C-62, 1B-6
1912			87	.263	.297	266	70	7	1	0	0.0	34	24	38			7	0	413	102	16	7	6.1	.970	C-87
1913			85	.242	.340	256	62	15	5	0	0.0	17	28	27	26		6	2	383	127	11	8	6.1	.979	C-81
1914			81	.253	.309	178	45	5	1	1	0.6	18	22	40	18		6	1	350	84	7	8	5.4	.984	C-78

Year	Team	Games	BA	SA	AB	H	2B	3B	HR	HR%	R	RBI	BB	SO	SB	Pinch Hit AB	H	PO	A	E	DP	TC/G	FA	G by Pos

Bill Carrigan *continued*

1915		46	.200	.232	95	19	3	0	0	0.0	10	7	16	12	0	2	0	183	54	6	3	5.3	.975	C-44
1916		33	.270	.333	63	17	2	1	0	0.0	7	11	11	3	2	5	1	122	27	0	1	4.5	1.000	C-27
10 yrs.		706	.257	.314	1970	506	67	14	6	0.3	196	235	206	59	37	36	6	3093	863	116	74	5.8	.972	C-648, 1B-17

WORLD SERIES

1912	BOS A	2	.000	.000	7	0	0	0	0	0.0	0	0	0	0	0	0	0	9	5	0	0	7.0	1.000	C-2
1915		1	.000	.000	2	0	0	0	0	0.0	0	0	1	0	0	1	0	8	0	0	0	8.0	1.000	C-1
1916		1	.667	.667	3	2	0	0	0	0.0	0	1	0	1	0	0	0	3	1	0	0	4.0	1.000	C-1
3 yrs.		4	.167	.167	12	2	0	0	0	0.0	0	1	1	2	0	1	0	20	6	0	0	6.5	1.000	C-4

Chick Carroll

CARROLL, EDWARD
B. 1868, Arkansas D. July 13, 1908, Chicago, Ill.

| 1884 | WAS U | 4 | .250 | .250 | 16 | 4 | 0 | 0 | 0 | 0.0 | 1 | | 0 | | | 0 | 0 | 3 | 1 | 4 | 0 | 2.0 | .500 | OF-4 |

Cliff Carroll

CARROLL, SAMUEL CLIFFORD BB TR 5'8" 163 lbs.
B. Oct. 18, 1859, Clay Grove, Iowa D. June 12, 1923, Portland, Ore.

1882	PRO N	10	.122	.122	41	5	0	0	0	0.0	4		0	4		0	0	17	2	0	2	1.9	1.000	OF-10
1883		58	.265	.353	238	63	12	3	1	0.4	37		4	28		0	0	109	11	13	4	2.3	.902	OF-58
1884		113	.261	.334	452	118	16	4	3	0.7	90		29	39		0	0	206	11	23	1	2.1	.904	OF-113
1885	WAS N	104	.232	.282	426	99	12	3	1	0.2	62	40	29	29		0	0	153	22	28	4	1.8	.862	OF-104
1886	WAS N	111	.229	.296	433	99	11	6	2	0.5	73	22	44	26		0	0	146	19	18	6	1.8	.902	OF-111
1887		103	.248	.336	420	104	17	4	4	1.0	79	37	17	30		0	0	5	1	3	0	1.8	.667	OF-103
1888	PIT N	5	.000	.000	20	0	0	0	0	0.0	1	0	0	8	2	0	0	265	28	20	7	2.3	.936	OF-5
1890	CHI N	136	.285	.369	582	166	16	6	7	1.2	134	65	53	34	34	0	0	168	15	17	5	1.5	.915	OF-136
1891		130	.256	.367	515	132	20	8	7	1.4	87	80	50	42	31	0	0	181	19	22	1	2.2	.901	OF-130
1892	STL N	101	.273	.376	407	111	14	8	4	1.0	82	49	47	22	30	0	0	226	18	22	5	2.2	.917	OF-101
1893	BOS N	120	.224	.276	438	98	7	5	2	0.5	80	54	88	28	29	0	0	1683	156	194	37	2.1	.905	OF-991
11 yrs.		991	.251	.329	3972	995	125	47	31	0.8	729	347	361	290	166	0	0							

Dixie Carroll

CARROLL, DORSEY LEE BL TR 5'11" 165 lbs.
B. May 9, 1891, Paducah, Ky. D. Oct. 13, 1984, Jacksonville, Fla.

| 1919 | BOS N | 15 | .265 | .367 | 49 | 13 | 3 | 1 | 0 | 0.0 | 10 | 7 | 7 | 1 | 5 | 1 | 1 | 30 | 5 | 3 | 1 | 2.5 | .921 | OF-13 |

Doc Carroll

CARROLL, RALPH ARTHUR (Red) BR TR 6' 170 lbs.
B. Dec. 28, 1891, Worcester, Mass. D. June 27, 1983, Worcester, Mass.

| 1916 | PHI A | 10 | .091 | .091 | 22 | 2 | 0 | 0 | 0 | 0.0 | 1 | 0 | 1 | 8 | 0 | 0 | 0 | 35 | 14 | 3 | 1 | 5.2 | .942 | C-10 |

Fred Carroll

CARROLL, FREDERICK HERBERT BR TR 5'11" 185 lbs.
B. July 2, 1864, Sacramento, Calif. D. Nov. 7, 1904, San Rafael, Calif.

1884	COL AA	69	.278	.440	252	70	13	5	6	2.4	46		13			0	0	406	92	37	3	7.8	.931	C-54, OF-15
1885	PIT AA	71	.268	.371	280	75	13	8	0	0.0	45		7			0	0	348	102	43	3	6.9	.913	C-60, OF-12
1886		122	.288	.422	486	140	28	11	5	1.0	92		52			0	0	753	106	68	26	7.6	.927	C-70, OF-27, 1B-25, SS-1
1887	PIT N	102	.328	.499	421	138	24	15	6	1.4	71	54	36	21	23	0	0	451	56	62	9	5.6	.891	OF-46, C-40, 1B-17, SS-1
1888		97	.249	.331	366	91	14	5	2	0.5	62	48	32	31	18	0	0	366	68	50	10	5.0	.897	C-54, OF-38, 1B-5, 3B-1
1889		91	.330	.484	318	105	21	11	2	0.6	80	51	85	26	19	0	0	299	61	28	6	4.3	.928	C-43, OF-41, 1B-7, 3B-1
1890	PIT P	111	.298	.394	416	124	20	7	2	0.5	95	71	75	22	35	0	0	380	55	56	7	4.4	.886	C-56, OF-49, 1B-7
1891	PIT N	91	.218	.312	353	77	13	4	4	1.1	55	48	48	36	22	0	0	160	12	16	2	2.1	.915	OF-91
8 yrs.		754	.284	.408	2892	820	146	66	27	0.9	546	272	348	136	117	0	0	3163	552	360	66	5.4	.912	C-377, OF-319, 1B-61, SS-2, 3B-2

Pat Carroll

CARROLL, PATRICK
B. Philadelphia, Pa. D. Feb. 14, 1916, Philadelphia, Pa.

| 1884 | 2 teams | ALT U (11G – .265) | | | PHI U (5G – .158) | | | | | | | | | | | | | | | | | | | |
| " | total | 16 | .235 | .265 | 68 | 16 | 2 | 0 | 0 | 0.0 | 5 | | | | | 0 | 0 | 64 | 21 | 13 | 0 | 6.1 | .867 | C-13, OF-3 |

Scrappy Carroll

CARROLL, JOHN E. 5'7½"
B. Aug. 27, 1860, Buffalo, N. Y. D. Nov. 14, 1942, Buffalo, N. Y.

1884	STP U	9	.097	.129	31	3	1	0	0	0.0	3		2			0	0	11	7	5	1	2.6	.783	OF-8, 3B-2
1885	BUF N	13	.075	.075	40	3	0	0	0	0.0	1	1	2	8		0	0	18	4	2	0	1.8	.917	OF-13
1887	CLE AA	57	.199	.231	216	43	5	1	0	0.0	30		15		19	0	0	81	14	19	1	2.0	.833	OF-54, 3B-3, 2B-1
3 yrs.		79	.171	.199	287	49	6	1	0	0.0	34		19		19	0	0	110	25	26	2	2.0	.839	OF-75, 3B-5, 2B-1

Tommy Carroll

CARROLL, THOMAS EDWARD BR TR 6'3" 186 lbs.
B. Sept. 17, 1936, Jamaica, N. Y.

1955	NY A	14	.333	.333	6	2	0	0	0	0.0	3	0	0	2	0	0	0	2	5	1	0	0.6	.875	SS-4
1956		36	.353	.353	17	6	0	0	0	0.0	11	0	1	3	1	3	2	0	13	2	3	0.4	.867	3B-11, SS-1
1959	KC A	14	.143	.143	7	1	0	0	0	0.0	1	1	0	1	0	0	0	7	11	1	1	1.4	.947	SS-9, 3B-3
3 yrs.		64	.300	.300	30	9	0	0	0	0.0	15	1	1	6	1	3	2	9	29	4	4	0.7	.905	SS-14, 3B-14

WORLD SERIES

| 1955 | NY A | 2 | – | – | 0 | 0 | 0 | 0 | 0 | – | 0 | 0 | 0 | 0 | 0 | 0 | 0 | 0 | 0 | 0 | 0 | 0.0 | – | |

Kid Carsey

CARSEY, WILFRED BL TR 5'7" 168 lbs.
B. Oct. 22, 1870, New York, N. Y. D. Mar. 29, 1960, Miami, Fla.

1891	WAS AA	61	.150	.198	187	28	5	2	0	0.0	25	15	19	38	2	0	0	25	126	14	5	2.7	.915	P-54, OF-7, SS-2
1892	PHI N	44	.153	.207	131	20	2	1	0	0.0	8	10	9	24	1	0	0	20	85	14	3	2.7	.882	P-43, OF-2
1893		39	.186	.207	145	27	1	1	0	0.0	12	10	5	14	2	0	0	17	81	8	1	2.7	.925	P-39
1894		35	.272	.320	125	34	2	2	0	0.0	30	18	16	11	3	0	0	15	59	5	4	2.3	.937	P-35
1895		44	.291	.305	141	41	2	0	0	0.0	24	20	15	12	1	0	0	9	77	12	2	2.2	.878	P-44
1896		27	.222	.296	81	18	2	0	0	0.0	13	7	11	12	1	0	0	9	50	6	3	2.4	.908	P-27

Year	Team	Games	BA	SA	AB	H	2B	3B	HR	HR%	R	RBI	BB	SO	SB	Pinch Hit AB	H	PO	A	E	DP	TC/G	FA	G by Pos

Kid Carsey *continued*

Year	Team	Games	BA	SA	AB	H	2B	3B	HR	HR%	R	RBI	BB	SO	SB	AB	H	PO	A	E	DP	TC/G	FA	G by Pos
1897	2 teams	PHI N (4G – .231)			STL	N	(13G – .302)																	
"	total	17	.286	.393	56	16	2	2	0	0.0	3	6	1		1	1	1	8	32	3	0	2.5	.930	P-16
1898	STL N	38	.200	.248	105	21	0	1	1	1.0	8	10	10		3	0	0	29	65	13	3	2.8	.879	P-20, 2B-10, OF-8
1899	3 teams	CLE N (11G – .278)			WAS	N	(4G – .000)			NY	N	(5G – .333)											
"	total	20	.246	.262	65	16	1	0	0	0.0	8	5	5		2	0	0	18	53	10	4	4.1	.877	P-14, SS-3, 3B-3
1901	BKN N	2	.000	.000	2	0	0	0	0	0.0	0	0	0		0	0	0	0	1	0	0	0.5	1.000	P-2
	10 yrs.	327	.213	.256	1038	221	17	11	2	0.2	131	101	91	111	17	1	1	150	629	85	25	2.6	.902	P-294, OF-17, 2B-10, SS-5, 3B-3

Kit Carson

CARSON, WALTER LLOYD
B. Nov. 15, 1912, Colton, Calif.   D. June 21, 1983, Long Beach, Calif.   BL TL 6'   180 lbs.

Year	Team	Games	BA	SA	AB	H	2B	3B	HR	HR%	R	RBI	BB	SO	SB	AB	H	PO	A	E	DP	TC/G	FA	G by Pos
1934	CLE A	5	.278	.500	18	5	1	0	0	0.0	4	1	2	3	0	1	1	2	0	0	0	0.4	1.000	OF-4
1935		16	.227	.318	22	5	2	0	0	0.0	1	1	2	6	0	10	2	7	0	0	0	0.4	1.000	OF-4
	2 yrs.	21	.250	.400	40	10	4	1	0	0.0	5	2	4	9	0	11	3	9	0	0	0	0.4	1.000	OF-8

Frank Carswell

CARSWELL, FRANK WILLIS (Tex, Wheels)
B. Nov. 6, 1919, Palestine, Tex.   BR TR 6'   195 lbs.

Year	Team	Games	BA	SA	AB	H	2B	3B	HR	HR%	R	RBI	BB	SO	SB	AB	H	PO	A	E	DP	TC/G	FA	G by Pos
1953	DET A	16	.267	.267	15	4	0	0	0	0.0	2	2	3	1	0	12	4	1	0	0	0	0.1	1.000	OF-3

Blackie Carter

CARTER, OTIS LEONARD
B. Sept. 30, 1902, Langley, S. C.   D. Sept. 10, 1976, Greenville, S. C.   BR TR 5'10"   175 lbs.

Year	Team	Games	BA	SA	AB	H	2B	3B	HR	HR%	R	RBI	BB	SO	SB	AB	H	PO	A	E	DP	TC/G	FA	G by Pos
1925	NY N	1	.000	.000	4	0	0	0	0	0.0	0	0	0	1	0	0	0	1	1	0	0	2.0	1.000	OF-1
1926		5	.235	.471	17	4	1	0	1	5.9	4	1	1	0	0	1	0	11	0	1	0	2.4	.917	OF-4
	2 yrs.	6	.190	.381	21	4	1	0	1	4.8	4	1	1	1	0	1	0	12	1	1	0	2.3	.929	OF-5

Gary Carter

CARTER, GARY EDMUND (Kid)
B. Apr. 8, 1954, Culver City, Calif.   BR TR 6'2"   205 lbs.

Year	Team	Games	BA	SA	AB	H	2B	3B	HR	HR%	R	RBI	BB	SO	SB	AB	H	PO	A	E	DP	TC/G	FA	G by Pos
1974	MON N	9	.407	.593	27	11	0	1	1	3.7	5	6	1	2	2	1	1	28	4	0	1	3.6	1.000	C-6, OF-2
1975		144	.270	.416	503	136	20	1	17	3.4	58	68	72	83	5	5	1	430	38	9	7	3.3	.981	OF-92, C-66, 3B-1
1976		91	.219	.309	311	68	8	1	6	1.9	31	38	30	43	0	2	0	364	42	2	8	4.5	.995	C-60, OF-36
1977		154	.284	.525	522	148	29	2	31	5.9	86	84	58	103	5	6	3	813	101	9	14	6.0	.990	C-146, OF-1
1978		157	.255	.422	533	136	27	1	20	3.8	76	72	62	70	10	6	0	787	83	10	9	5.6	.989	C-152, 1B-1
1979		141	.283	.485	505	143	26	5	22	4.4	74	75	40	62	3	3	0	751	88	9	12	6.0	.989	C-138
1980		154	.264	.486	549	145	25	5	29	5.3	76	101	58	78	3	4	0	822	108	7	8	6.1	.993	C-149
1981		100	.251	.444	374	94	20	2	16	4.3	48	68	35	35	1	0	0	515	58	4	12	5.8	.993	C-100, 1B-1
1982		154	.293	.510	557	163	32	1	29	5.2	91	97	78	64	2	3	0	954	104	10	6	6.9	.991	C-153
1983		145	.270	.444	541	146	37	3	17	3.1	63	79	51	57	1	2	0	855	108	5	15	6.7	.995	C-144, 1B-1
1984		159	.294	.487	596	175	32	1	27	4.5	75	106	64	57	2	2	0	990	78	7	25	6.8	.993	C-143, 1B-25
1985	NY N	149	.281	.488	555	156	17	1	32	5.8	83	100	69	46	1	2	0	987	70	8	13	7.1	.992	C-143, 1B-6, OF-1
1986		132	.255	.439	490	125	14	2	24	4.9	81	105	62	63	1	1	0	943	70	9	18	7.7	.991	C-122, 1B-9, OF-4, 3B-1
1987		139	.235	.392	523	123	18	2	20	3.8	55	83	42	73	0	4	0	886	70	9	11	6.9	.991	C-135, 1B-4, OF-1
1988		130	.242	.358	455	110	16	2	11	2.4	39	46	34	52	0	7	4	842	58	10	8	7.0	.989	C-119, 1B-10, 3B-1
1989		50	.183	.275	153	28	8	0	2	1.3	14	15	12	15	0	4	1	266	31	6	6	6.1	.980	C-47, 1B-1
	16 yrs.	2008	.265	.446	7194	1907	329	30	304	4.2	955	1143	768	903	36	52	10	11233	1111	114	176	6.2	.991	C-1823, OF-137, 1B-58, 3B-3

DIVISIONAL PLAYOFF SERIES

Year	Team	Games	BA	SA	AB	H	2B	3B	HR	HR%	R	RBI	BB	SO	SB	AB	H	PO	A	E	DP	TC/G	FA	G by Pos
1981	MON N	5	.421	.895	19	8	3	0	2	10.5	3	6	1	1	0	0	0	0	0	0	0	0.0	–	C-5

LEAGUE CHAMPIONSHIP SERIES

Year	Team	Games	BA	SA	AB	H	2B	3B	HR	HR%	R	RBI	BB	SO	SB	AB	H	PO	A	E	DP	TC/G	FA	G by Pos
1981	MON N	5	.438	.500	16	7	1	0	0	0.0	3	0	4	2	0	0	0	0	0	0	0	0.0	–	C-5
1986	NY N	6	.148	.185	27	4	1	0	0	0.0	1	2	2	5	0	0	0	0	0	0	0	0.0	–	C-6
1988		7	.222	.333	27	6	1	1	0	0.0	0	4	1	3	0	0	0	58	1	0	0	8.4	1.000	C-7
	3 yrs.	18	.243	.314	70	17	3	1	0	0.0	4	6	7	10	0	0	0	58	1	0	0	3.3	1.000	C-18

WORLD SERIES

Year	Team	Games	BA	SA	AB	H	2B	3B	HR	HR%	R	RBI	BB	SO	SB	AB	H	PO	A	E	DP	TC/G	FA	G by Pos
1986	NY N	7	.276	.552	29	8	2	0	2	6.9	4	9	0	4	0	0	0	57	1	0	0	8.3	1.000	C-7

Howard Carter

CARTER, JOHN HOWARD (Nick)
B. Oct. 13, 1904, New York, N. Y.   BR TR 5'10"   154 lbs.

Year	Team	Games	BA	SA	AB	H	2B	3B	HR	HR%	R	RBI	BB	SO	SB	AB	H	PO	A	E	DP	TC/G	FA	G by Pos
1926	CIN N	5	.000	.000	1	0	0	0	0	0.0	0	0	0	0	0	0	0	0	3	0	0	0.6	1.000	2B-3, SS-1

Joe Carter

CARTER, JOSEPH CHRIS
B. Mar. 7, 1960, Oklahoma City, Okla.   BR TR 6'3"   210 lbs.

Year	Team	Games	BA	SA	AB	H	2B	3B	HR	HR%	R	RBI	BB	SO	SB	AB	H	PO	A	E	DP	TC/G	FA	G by Pos
1983	CHI N	23	.176	.235	51	9	0	1	0	0.0	6	1	0	21	1	5	1	26	0	0	0	1.1	1.000	OF-16
1984	CLE A	66	.275	.467	244	67	6	1	13	5.3	32	41	11	48	2	7	5	169	11	6	4	2.8	.968	OF-59, 1B-7
1985		143	.262	.409	489	128	27	0	15	3.1	64	59	25	74	24	4	0	311	17	6	4	2.3	.982	OF-135, 1B-11, DH-7, 3B-1, 2B-1
1986		162	.302	.514	663	200	36	9	29	4.4	108	121	32	95	29	1	1	800	55	10	52	5.3	.988	OF-104, 1B-70
1987		149	.264	.480	588	155	27	2	32	5.4	83	106	27	105	31	2	0	782	46	17	61	5.7	.980	1B-84, OF-62, DH-5
1988		157	.271	.478	621	168	36	6	27	4.3	85	98	35	82	27	1	0	444	8	7	3	2.9	.985	OF-156
1989		162	.243	.465	651	158	32	4	35	5.4	84	105	39	112	13	0	0	443	20	9	7	2.9	.981	OF-146, 1B-11, DH-8
	7 yrs.	862	.268	.468	3307	885	165	23	151	4.6	462	531	169	537	127	20	7	2975	157	55	131	3.7	.983	OF-678, 1B-183, DH-20, 3B-1, 2B-1

Steve Carter

CARTER, STEVEN JEROME
B. Dec. 3, 1964, Charlottesville, Va.   BL TR 6'4"   201 lbs.

Year	Team	Games	BA	SA	AB	H	2B	3B	HR	HR%	R	RBI	BB	SO	SB	AB	H	PO	A	E	DP	TC/G	FA	G by Pos
1989	PIT N	9	.125	.375	16	2	1	0	1	6.3	2	3	2	5	0	2	0	4	0	0	0	0.4	1.000	OF-5

Ed Cartwright

CARTWRIGHT, EDWARD CHARLES (Jumbo)
B. Oct. 6, 1859, Johnstown, Pa.   D. Sept. 3, 1933, St. Petersburg, Fla.   BR TR 5'10"   220 lbs.

Year	Team	Games	BA	SA	AB	H	2B	3B	HR	HR%	R	RBI	BB	SO	SB	Pinch Hit AB	Pinch Hit H	PO	A	E	DP	TC/G	FA	G by Pos

Ed Cartwright *continued*

Year	Team	Games	BA	SA	AB	H	2B	3B	HR	HR%	R	RBI	BB	SO	SB	PH AB	PH H	PO	A	E	DP	TC/G	FA	G by Pos
1890	STL AA	75	.300	.447	300	90	12	4	8	2.7	70		29		26	0	0	706	25	18	37	10.0	.976	1B-75
1894	WAS N	132	.294	.485	507	149	35	13	12	2.4	88	106	57	43	31	0	0	1219	71	36	63	10.0	.973	1B-132
1895		122	.331	.494	472	156	34	17	3	0.6	95	90	54	41	50	0	0	1102	95	19	69	10.0	.984	1B-122
1896		133	.277	.353	499	138	15	10	1	0.2	76	62	54	44	28	0	0	1276	71	30	76	10.4	.978	1B-133
1897		33	.234	.266	124	29	4	0	0	0.0	19	15	8		9	0	0	285	26	12	17	9.8	.963	1B-33
5 yrs.		495	.295	.432	1902	562	100	44	24	1.3	348	273	202	128	144	0	0	4588	288	115	262	10.1	.977	1B-495

Rico Carty

CARTY, RICARDO ADOLFO
Born Ricardo Adolfo Jacobo y Carty.
B. Sept. 1, 1939, San Pedro de Macoris, Dominican Republic

BR TR 6'3" 200 lbs.

Year	Team	Games	BA	SA	AB	H	2B	3B	HR	HR%	R	RBI	BB	SO	SB	PH AB	PH H	PO	A	E	DP	TC/G	FA	G by Pos
1963	MIL N	2	.000	.000	2	0	0	0	0	0.0	0	0	0	2	0	2	0	0	0	0	0	0.0	—	
1964		133	.330	.554	455	150	28	4	22	4.8	72	88	43	78	1	12	3	176	5	4	1	1.4	.978	OF-121
1965		83	.310	.494	271	84	18	1	10	3.7	37	35	17	44	1	11	3	112	3	5	1	1.4	.958	OF-73
1966	ATL N	151	.326	.468	521	170	25	2	15	2.9	73	76	60	74	4	12	2	318	16	10	1	2.3	.971	OF-126, C-17, 1B-2, 3B-1
1967		134	.255	.401	444	113	16	2	15	3.4	41	64	49	70	4	14	2	267	9	11	6	2.1	.962	OF-112, 1B-9
1969		104	.342	.549	304	104	15	0	16	5.3	47	58	32	28	0	22	9	118	0	6	0	1.2	.952	OF-79
1970		136	**.366**	.584	478	175	23	3	25	5.2	84	101	77	46	0	3	1	219	5	6	0	1.7	.974	OF-133
1972		86	.277	.402	271	75	12	2	6	2.2	31	29	44	33	0	8	2	139	3	3	1	1.7	.979	OF-78
1973	3 teams	TEX A (86G – .232)				CHI N (22G – .214)					OAK A (7G – .250)													
"	total	115	.229	.302	384	88	13	0	5	1.3	29	42	44	50	2	7	2	123	2	2	0	1.1	.984	OF-72, DH-32
1974	CLE A	33	.363	.451	91	33	5	0	1	1.1	6	16	5	9	0	11	2	64	1	1	9	2.0	.985	DH-14, 1B-8
1975		118	.308	.504	383	118	19	1	18	4.7	57	64	45	31	2	8	6	209	15	3	21	1.9	.987	DH-72, 1B-26, OF-12
1976		152	.310	.442	552	171	34	0	13	2.4	67	83	67	45	1	1	1	81	3	0	8	0.6	1.000	DH-137, 1B-12, OF-1
1977		127	.280	.432	461	129	23	1	15	3.3	50	80	56	51	1	2	1	20	3	0	4	0.2	1.000	DH-123, 1B-2
1978	2 teams	TOR A (104G – .284)				OAK A (41G – .277)																		
"	total	145	.282	.502	528	149	21	1	31	5.9	70	99	57	57	1	4	0	0	0	0	0	0.0	—	DH-142
1979	TOR A	132	.256	.390	461	118	26	0	12	2.6	48	55	46	45	3	9	4	0	0	0	0	0.0	—	DH-129
15 yrs.		1651	.299	.464	5606	1677	278	17	204	3.6	712	890	642	663	21	126	38	1846	65	51	52	1.2	.974	OF-807, DH-649, 1B-59, C-17, 3B-1

LEAGUE CHAMPIONSHIP SERIES

Year	Team	Games	BA	SA	AB	H	2B	3B	HR	HR%	R	RBI	BB	SO	SB	PH AB	PH H	PO	A	E	DP	TC/G	FA	G by Pos
1969	ATL N	3	.300	.500	10	3	2	0	0	0.0	4	0	3	1	0	0	0	2	0	0	0	0.7	1.000	OF-3

Bob Caruthers

CARUTHERS, ROBERT LEE (Parisian Bob)
B. Jan. 5, 1864, Memphis, Tenn. D. Aug. 5, 1911, Peoria, Ill.
Manager 1892.

BL TR 5'7" 138 lbs.

Year	Team	Games	BA	SA	AB	H	2B	3B	HR	HR%	R	RBI	BB	SO	SB	PH AB	PH H	PO	A	E	DP	TC/G	FA	G by Pos
1884	STL AA	23	.256	.354	82	21	2	0	2	2.4	15		4			0	0	14	10	5	0	1.3	.828	OF-16, P-13
1885		60	.225	.302	222	50	10	2	1	0.5	37		20			0	0	33	86	15	4	2.2	.888	P-53, OF-7
1886		87	.334	.527	317	106	21	14	4	1.3	91		64			0	0	72	76	19	5	1.9	.886	P-44, OF-43, 2B-2
1887		98	.357	.547	364	130	23	11	8	2.2	102		66		49	0	0	182	105	18	4	3.1	.941	OF-54, P-39, 1B-7
1888	BKN AA	94	.230	.334	335	77	10	5	5	1.5	58	53	45		23	0	0	127	97	26	5	2.7	.896	OF-51, P-44
1889		59	.250	.366	172	43	8	3	2	1.2	45	31	44	17	9	0	0	33	95	6	4	2.3	.955	P-56, OF-3, 1B-2
1890	BKN N	71	.265	.340	238	63	7	4	1	0.4	46	29	47	18	13	0	0	65	83	20	2	2.4	.881	OF-39, P-37
1891		56	.281	.380	171	48	5	3	2	1.2	24	23	25	13	4	1	0	29	69	11	2	1.9	.899	P-38, OF-17, 2B-1
1892	STL N	143	.277	.357	513	142	16	8	3	0.6	76	69	86	29	24	0	0	209	61	29	10	2.1	.903	OF-122, P-16, 2B-6, 1B-4
1893	2 teams	CHI N (1G – .000)				CIN N (13G – .292)																		
"	total	14	.275	.373	51	14	2	0	1	2.0	14	8	16	2	4	0	0	24	1	4	0	2.1	.862	OF-14
10 yrs.		705	.282	.400	2465	694	104	50	29	1.2	508	213	417	79	126	1	0	788	683	153	36	2.3	.906	OF-366, P-340, 1B-13, 2B-9

Paul Casanova

CASANOVA, PAULINO
Born Paulino Casanova y Ortiz.
B. Dec. 21, 1941, Colon, Cuba

BR TR 6'4" 180 lbs.

Year	Team	Games	BA	SA	AB	H	2B	3B	HR	HR%	R	RBI	BB	SO	SB	PH AB	PH H	PO	A	E	DP	TC/G	FA	G by Pos
1965	WAS A	5	.308	.385	13	4	1	0	0	0.0	2	1	1	3	0	0	0	15	0	1	0	3.2	.938	C-4
1966		122	.254	.406	429	109	16	5	13	3.0	45	44	14	78	1	3	0	674	53	14	12	6.1	.981	C-119
1967		141	.248	.339	528	131	19	1	9	1.7	47	53	17	65	1	8	1	827	70	15	19	6.5	.984	C-137
1968		96	.196	.252	322	63	6	0	4	1.2	19	25	7	52	0	7	1	472	46	6	3	5.5	.989	C-92
1969		124	.216	.282	379	82	9	2	4	1.1	26	37	18	52	0	5	1	583	59	5	5	5.2	.992	C-122
1970		104	.229	.354	328	75	17	3	6	1.8	25	30	10	47	0	9	1	461	48	6	12	5.0	.988	C-100
1971		94	.203	.286	311	63	9	1	5	1.6	19	26	14	52	0	8	1	416	40	7	4	4.9	.985	C-83
1972	ATL N	49	.206	.272	136	28	3	0	2	1.5	8	10	4	28	0	6	0	139	16	4	3	3.2	.975	C-43
1973		82	.216	.335	236	51	7	0	7	3.0	18	18	11	36	0	4	1	330	48	9	3	4.7	.977	C-78
1974		42	.202	.202	104	21	0	0	0	0.0	5	8	5	17	0	4	1	123	15	2	4	3.3	.986	C-33
10 yrs.		859	.225	.319	2786	627	87	12	50	1.8	214	252	101	430	2	59	10	4040	395	69	65	5.2	.985	C-811

George Case

CASE, GEORGE WASHINGTON
B. Nov. 11, 1915, Trenton, N. J. D. Jan. 23, 1989, Trenton, N. J.

BR TR 6' 183 lbs.

Year	Team	Games	BA	SA	AB	H	2B	3B	HR	HR%	R	RBI	BB	SO	SB	PH AB	PH H	PO	A	E	DP	TC/G	FA	G by Pos
1937	WAS A	22	.289	.400	90	26	6	2	0	0.0	14	11	3	5	2	0	0	51	1	3	0	2.5	.945	OF-22
1938		107	.305	.395	433	132	27	3	2	0.5	69	40	39	28	11	8	1	207	7	8	2	2.1	.964	OF-101
1939		128	.302	.377	530	160	20	7	2	0.4	103	35	56	36	**51**	0	0	332	7	16	2	2.8	.955	OF-123
1940		154	.293	.375	656	192	29	5	5	0.8	109	56	52	39	**35**	0	0	384	10	12	0	2.6	.970	OF-154
1941		153	.271	.354	649	176	32	8	2	0.3	95	53	51	37	**33**	2	0	362	21	10	3	2.6	.975	OF-151
1942		125	.320	.407	513	164	26	2	5	1.0	101	43	44	30	**44**	1	0	270	4	14	1	2.3	.951	OF-120
1943		141	.294	.374	613	180	36	5	1	0.2	**102**	52	40	27	**61**	0	0	318	8	5	2	2.3	.985	OF-140
1944		119	.249	.301	465	116	14	2	1	0.2	63	32	49	27	49	0	0	288	7	9	2	2.6	.970	OF-114
1945		123	.294	.357	504	148	19	5	1	0.2	72	31	49	27	30	0	0	316	17	7	1	2.8	.979	OF-123
1946	CLE A	118	.225	.295	484	109	23	4	1	0.2	46	22	34	38	**28**	0	0	226	5	4	0	2.0	.983	OF-118
1947	WAS A	36	.150	.163	80	12	1	0	0	0.0	11	2	8	8	5	3	0	51	1	2	0	1.5	.963	OF-21
11 yrs.		1226	.282	.358	5017	1415	233	43	21	0.4	785	377	425	297	349	16	1	2805	88	90	15	2.4	.970	OF-1187

Bob Casey

CASEY, ORRIN ROBINSON
B. Jan. 26, 1859, Adolphustown Ont., Canada D. Nov. 28, 1936, Syracuse, N. Y.

5'11" 190 lbs.

Year	Team		Games	BA	SA	AB	H	2B	3B	HR	HR%	R	RBI	BB	SO	SB	Pinch Hit AB	Pinch Hit H	PO	A	E	DP	TC/G	FA	G by Pos

Bob Casey *continued*

| 1882 | DET | N | 9 | .231 | .410 | 39 | 9 | 2 | 1 | 1 | 2.6 | 5 | 7 | 0 | 15 | | 0 | 0 | 10 | 10 | 12 | 0 | 3.6 | .625 | 3B-8, 2B-1 |

Dennis Casey

CASEY, DENNIS PATRICK
Brother of Dan Casey.
B. Mar. 30, 1858, Binghamton, N. Y.   D. Jan. 19, 1909, Binghamton, N. Y.

BL TR 5'9"   164 lbs.

1884	2 teams			WIL	U (2G – .250)		BAL	AA	(37G – .248)																
"	total		39	.248	.408	157	39	8	4	3	1.9	21		5			0	0	51	5	6	2	1.6	.903	OF-39
1885	BAL	AA	63	.288	.398	264	76	10	5	3	1.1	50		21			0	0	100	10	24	0	2.1	.821	OF-63
	2 yrs.		102	.273	.401	421	115	18	9	6	1.4	71		26			0	0	151	15	30	2	1.9	.847	OF-102

Doc Casey

CASEY, JAMES PATRICK
B. Mar. 15, 1870, Lawrence, Mass.   D. Dec. 30, 1936, Detroit, Mich.

BL TR 5'6"

1898	WAS	N	28	.277	.295	112	31	2	0	0	0.0	13	15	3		15	0	0	38	62	14	5	4.1	.877	3B-22, SS-4, C-3
1899	2 teams		143					WAS	N	(9G – .118)		BKN	N	(134G – .269)											
"	total		143	.259	.322	559	145	16	8	1	0.2	78	45	27		28	0	0	174	275	56	23	3.5	.889	3B-143
1900	BKN	N	1	.333	.333	3	1	0	0	0	0.0	0	1	0		0	0	0	1	2	0	0	3.0	1.000	3B-1
1901	DET	A	128	.283	.357	540	153	16	9	2	0.4	105	46	32		34	1	0	133	324	58	25	4.0	.887	3B-127
1902			132	.273	.352	520	142	18	7	3	0.6	69	55	44		22	0	0	174	309	51	17	4.0	.904	3B-132
1903	CHI	N	112	.290	.329	435	126	8	3	1	0.2	56	40	19		11	0	0	143	190	31	5	3.3	.915	3B-112
1904			136	.268	.325	548	147	20	4	1	0.2	71	43	18		21	0	0	163	244	39	11	3.3	.913	3B-134, C-2
1905			144	.232	.316	526	122	21	10	1	0.2	66	56	41		22	2	0	162	254	22	7	3.0	.950	3B-142, SS-1
1906	BKN	N	149	.233	.291	571	133	17	8	0	0.0	71	34	52		22	0	0	172	272	39	11	3.2	.919	3B-149
1907			141	.231	.279	527	122	19	3	0	0.0	55	19	34		16	3	0	176	274	21	16	3.3	.955	3B-138
	10 yrs.		1114	.258	.320	4341	1122	137	52	9	0.2	584	354	270		191	6	0	1336	2206	331	120	3.5	.915	3B-1100, SS-5, C-5

Joe Casey

CASEY, JOSEPH FELIX
B. Aug. 15, 1887, Boston, Mass.   D. June 2, 1966, Melrose, Mass.

BR TR 5'9"   180 lbs.

1909	DET	A	3	.000	.000	5	0	0	0	0	0.0	1	0	1		0	0	0	9	5	0	1	4.7	1.000	C-3
1910			23	.194	.242	62	12	3	0	0	0.0	3	2	2		1	0	0	101	33	5	2	6.0	.964	C-22
1911			15	.152	.152	33	5	0	0	0	0.0	2	3	3		0	0	0	35	10	3	1	3.2	.938	C-12, OF-3
1918	WAS	A	9	.235	.235	17	4	0	0	0	0.0	3	2	2	2	0	0	0	34	5	0	0	4.3	1.000	C-8
	4 yrs.		50	.179	.205	117	21	3	0	0	0.0	9	7	8	2	1	0	0	179	53	8	4	4.8	.967	C-45, OF-3

Dave Cash

CASH, DAVID, JR.
B. June 11, 1948, Utica, N. Y.

BR TR 5'11"   170 lbs.

1969	PIT	N	18	.279	.361	61	17	3	1	0	0.0	9	4	9	9	2	0	0	37	60	1	9	5.4	.990	2B-17
1970			64	.314	.419	210	66	7	6	1	0.5	30	28	17	25	5	4	1	147	156	8	46	4.9	.974	2B-55
1971			123	.289	.354	478	138	17	4	2	0.4	79	34	46	33	13	4	2	254	333	10	82	4.9	.983	2B-105, 3B-24, SS-3
1972			99	.282	.374	425	120	22	4	3	0.7	58	30	22	31	9	3	1	260	342	5	81	6.1	.992	2B-97
1973			116	.271	.342	436	118	21	2	2	0.5	59	31	38	36	2	14	4	244	311	12	49	4.9	.979	2B-92, 3B-17
1974	PHI	N	162	.300	.378	687	206	26	11	2	0.3	89	58	46	33	20	0	0	396	519	22	141	5.8	.977	2B-162
1975			162	.305	.388	699	213	40	3	4	0.6	111	57	56	34	13	0	0	400	481	17	126	5.5	.981	2B-162
1976			160	.284	.345	666	189	14	12	1	0.2	92	56	54	13	10	1	0	407	424	10	118	5.3	.988	2B-158
1977	MON	N	153	.289	.375	650	188	42	7	0	0.0	91	43	52	33	21	0	0	343	443	11	73	5.2	.986	2B-153
1978			159	.252	.315	658	166	26	3	3	0.5	66	43	37	29	12	0	0	362	400	11	91	4.9	.986	2B-159
1979			76	.321	.422	187	60	11	1	2	1.1	24	19	12	12	7	30	10	88	110	6	18	2.7	.971	2B-47
1980	SD	N	130	.227	.280	397	90	14	2	1	0.3	25	23	35	21	6	7	1	290	326	8	72	4.8	.987	2B-123
	12 yrs.		1422	.283	.358	5554	1571	243	56	21	0.4	732	426	424	309	120	63	19	3228	3905	121	906	5.1	.983	2B-1330, 3B-41, SS-3

LEAGUE CHAMPIONSHIP SERIES

1970	PIT	N	2	.125	.250	8	1	1	0	0	0.0	1	0	1	1	0	0	0	6	8	0	3	7.0	1.000	2B-2
1971			4	.421	.526	19	8	2	0	0	0.0	5	1	0	1	0	0	0	11	11	1	3	5.8	.957	2B-4
1972			5	.211	.211	19	4	0	0	0	0.0	0	3	0	0	0	0	0	5	10	1	1	3.2	.938	2B-5
1976	PHI	N	3	.308	.385	13	4	1	0	0	0.0	1	1	0	0	0	0	0	8	8	0	2	5.3	1.000	2B-3
	4 yrs.		14	.288	.356	59	17	4	0	0	0.0	7	5	1	2	1	0	0	30	37	2	9	4.9	.971	2B-14

WORLD SERIES

| 1971 | PIT | N | 7 | .133 | .167 | 30 | 4 | 1 | 0 | 0 | 0.0 | 2 | 1 | 3 | 1 | 1 | 0 | 0 | 20 | 23 | 0 | 6 | 6.1 | 1.000 | 2B-7 |

Norm Cash

CASH, NORMAN DALTON
B. Nov. 10, 1934, Justiceburg, Tex.   D. Oct. 12, 1986, Beaver Island, Mich.

BL TL 6'   185 lbs.

1958	CHI	A	13	.250	.250	8	2	0	0	0	0.0	2	0	0	1	0	5	1	2	0	0	0	0.2	1.000	OF-4
1959			58	.240	.375	104	25	0	1	4	3.8	16	16	18	9	1	19	5	231	14	4	19	4.3	.984	1B-31
1960	DET	A	121	.286	.501	353	101	16	3	18	5.1	64	63	65	58	4	23	9	743	59	7	68	6.7	.991	1B-99, OF-4
1961			159	.361	.662	535	193	22	8	41	7.7	119	132	124	85	11	1	0	1231	127	11	121	8.6	.992	1B-157
1962			148	.243	.513	507	123	16	2	39	7.7	94	89	104	82	6	2	1	1091	116	9	94	8.2	.992	1B-146, OF-3
1963			147	.270	.471	493	133	19	1	26	5.3	67	79	89	76	2	7	0	1161	99	7	93	8.6	.994	1B-142
1964			144	.257	.453	479	123	15	5	23	4.8	63	83	70	66	2	10	1	1105	92	4	97	8.3	.997	1B-137
1965			142	.266	.512	467	124	23	1	30	6.4	79	82	77	62	6	5	0	1091	97	9	96	8.4	.992	1B-139
1966			160	.279	.478	603	168	18	3	32	5.3	98	93	66	91	2	3	1	1271	114	17	118	8.8	.988	1B-158
1967			152	.242	.430	488	118	16	5	22	4.5	64	72	81	100	3	7	1	1135	112	6	88	8.2	.995	1B-146
1968			127	.263	.487	411	108	15	1	25	6.1	50	63	39	70	1	15	2	924	88	8	66	8.0	.992	1B-117
1969			142	.280	.464	483	135	15	4	22	4.6	81	74	63	80	2	9	2	1016	96	7	99	7.9	.994	1B-134
1970			130	.259	.441	370	96	18	2	15	4.1	58	53	72	58	0	17	6	868	70	10	76	7.3	.989	1B-114
1971			135	.283	.531	452	128	10	3	32	7.1	72	91	59	86	1	7	1	1020	75	9	105	8.2	.992	1B-131
1972			137	.259	.445	440	114	16	0	22	5.0	51	61	50	64	0	11	0	1060	70	8	102	8.3	.993	1B-134
1973			121	.262	.471	363	95	19	0	19	5.2	51	40	47	73	1	8	2	856	64	8	72	7.7	.991	1B-114, DH-3
1974			53	.228	.416	149	34	3	2	7	4.7	19	12	19	30	1	9	3	368	24	6	32	7.5	.985	1B-44
	17 yrs.		2089	.271	.488	6705	1820	241	41	377	5.6	1046	1103	1043	1091	43	158	35	15173	1317	131	1347	8.0	.992	1B-1943, OF-11, DH-3

LEAGUE CHAMPIONSHIP SERIES

| 1972 | DET | A | 5 | .267 | .467 | 15 | 4 | 0 | 0 | 1 | 6.7 | 1 | 2 | 2 | 3 | 0 | 1 | 0 | 39 | 3 | 0 | 2 | 8.4 | 1.000 | 1B-5 |

Year	Team		Games	BA	SA	AB	H	2B	3B	HR	HR%	R	RBI	BB	SO	SB	Pinch Hit AB	Pinch Hit H	PO	A	E	DP	TC/G	FA	G by Pos

Norm Cash *continued*

WORLD SERIES

Year	Team		Games	BA	SA	AB	H	2B	3B	HR	HR%	R	RBI	BB	SO	SB	Pinch Hit AB	Pinch Hit H	PO	A	E	DP	TC/G	FA	G by Pos
1959	CHI	A	4	.000	.000	4	0	0	0	0	0.0	0	0	0	2	0	4	0	0	0	0	0	0.0	–	
1968	DET	A	7	.385	.500	26	10	0	0	1	3.8	5	5	3	5	0	0	0	59	6	2	3	9.6	.970	1B-7
2 yrs.			11	.333	.433	30	10	0	0	1	3.3	5	5	3	7	0	4	0	59	6	2	3	6.1	.970	1B-7

Ron Cash

CASH, RONALD FORREST
B. Nov. 20, 1949, Atlanta, Ga. — BR TR 6' 180 lbs.

Year	Team		Games	BA	SA	AB	H	2B	3B	HR	HR%	R	RBI	BB	SO	SB	Pinch Hit AB	Pinch Hit H	PO	A	E	DP	TC/G	FA	G by Pos
1973	DET	A	14	.410	.487	39	16	1	1	0	0.0	8	6	5	5	0	0	0	13	10	1	0	1.7	.958	OF-7, 3B-6
1974			20	.226	.258	62	14	2	0	0	0.0	6	5	0	11	0	1	0	139	9	4	12	7.6	.974	1B-15, 3B-4
2 yrs.			34	.297	.347	101	30	3	1	0	0.0	14	11	5	16	0	1	0	152	19	5	12	5.2	.972	1B-15, 3B-10, OF-7

Jay Cashion

CASHION, JAY CARL
B. June 6, 1891, Mecklenburg, N. C. D. Nov. 17, 1935, Lake Millicent, Wis. — BL TR 6'2" 200 lbs.

Year	Team		Games	BA	SA	AB	H	2B	3B	HR	HR%	R	RBI	BB	SO	SB	Pinch Hit AB	Pinch Hit H	PO	A	E	DP	TC/G	FA	G by Pos
1911	WAS	A	21	.324	.351	37	12	1	0	0	0.0	3	4	1		0	9	2	3	22	0	0	1.2	1.000	P-11
1912			43	.214	.340	103	22	5	1	2	1.9	7	12	8		2	8	1	27	41	1	1	1.6	.986	P-26, OF-9
1913			7	.250	.250	12	3	0	0	0	0.0	1	2	1		0	0	0	4	5	2	1	1.6	.818	P-4, OF-3
1914			2	.000	.000	1	0	0	0	0	0.0	0	0	0		0	0	0	1	3	1	1	2.5	.800	P-2
4 yrs.			73	.242	.333	153	37	6	1	2	1.3	11	18	10	2	2	17	3	35	71	4	3	1.5	.964	P-43, OF-12

Ed Caskin

CASKIN, EDWARD JAMES
B. Dec. 30, 1851, Danvers, Mass. D. Oct. 9, 1924, Danvers, Mass. — BR TR 5'9½" 165 lbs.

Year	Team		Games	BA	SA	AB	H	2B	3B	HR	HR%	R	RBI	BB	SO	SB	Pinch Hit AB	Pinch Hit H	PO	A	E	DP	TC/G	FA	G by Pos
1879	TRO	N	70	.257	.313	304	78	13	2	0	0.0	32	21	2	14			0	0	170	225	50	12	6.4	.888	SS-42, C-22, 2B-6
1880			82	.225	.264	333	75	5	4	0	0.0	36	28	7	24			0	0	97	297	51	16	5.4	.885	SS-82, C-2
1881			63	.226	.265	234	53	7	1	0	0.0	33	21	13	29			0	0	85	205	30	18	5.1	.906	SS-63
1883	NY	N	95	.238	.285	383	91	11	2	1	0.3	47		14	25			0	0	194	277	80	19	5.8	.855	SS-81, 2B-13, C-1
1884			100	.231	.282	351	81	10	1	2	0.6	49		34	55			0	0	149	293	59	28	5.0	.882	SS-96, C-6
1885	STL	N	71	.179	.191	262	47	3	0	0	0.0	31	12	12	22			0	0	88	146	35	5	3.8	.870	3B-69, C-2, SS-1
1886	NY	N	1	.500	.500	4	2	0	0	0	0.0	1	1	0	1			0	0	3	0	0	0	3.0	1.000	SS-1
7 yrs.			482	.228	.270	1871	427	49	10	3	0.2	229	83	82	170			0	0	786	1443	305	98	5.3	.880	SS-366, 3B-69, C-33, 2B-19

Harry Cassady

CASSADY, HARRY DELBERT
B. July 20, 1880, Bellflower, Ill. D. Apr. 22, 1969, Fresno, Calif. — BL TL 5'8" 145 lbs.

Year	Team		Games	BA	SA	AB	H	2B	3B	HR	HR%	R	RBI	BB	SO	SB	Pinch Hit AB	Pinch Hit H	PO	A	E	DP	TC/G	FA	G by Pos
1904	PIT	N	12	.205	.205	44	9	0	0	0	0.0	8	3	2		2	0	0	10	3	2	0	1.3	.867	OF-12
1905	WAS	A	9	.133	.133	30	4	0	0	0	0.0	2	1	0		0	0	0	14	1	0	0	1.7	1.000	OF-9
2 yrs.			21	.176	.176	74	13	0	0	0	0.0	10	4	2		2	0	0	24	4	2	0	1.4	.933	OF-21

Joe Cassidy

CASSIDY, JOSEPH PHILLIP
B. Feb. 8, 1883, Chester, Pa. D. Mar. 25, 1906, Chester, Pa. — BR TR

Year	Team		Games	BA	SA	AB	H	2B	3B	HR	HR%	R	RBI	BB	SO	SB	Pinch Hit AB	Pinch Hit H	PO	A	E	DP	TC/G	FA	G by Pos
1904	WAS	A	152	.241	.332	581	140	12	19	1	0.2	63	33	15		17	0	0	336	362	51	42	4.9	.932	SS-99, OF-32, 3B-23
1905			151	.215	.262	576	124	16	4	1	0.2	67	43	25		23	0	0	308	520	66	50	5.9	.926	SS-151
2 yrs.			303	.228	.297	1157	264	28	23	2	0.2	130	76	40		40	0	0	644	882	117	92	5.4	.929	SS-250, OF-32, 3B-23

John Cassidy

CASSIDY, JOHN P.
B. 1855, Brooklyn, N. Y. D. July 2, 1891, Brooklyn, N. Y. — BR TL 5'8" 168 lbs.

Year	Team		Games	BA	SA	AB	H	2B	3B	HR	HR%	R	RBI	BB	SO	SB	Pinch Hit AB	Pinch Hit H	PO	A	E	DP	TC/G	FA	G by Pos
1876	HAR	N	12	.277	.319	47	13	2	0	0	0.0	6	8	1	0			0	0	41	4	2	3	3.9	.957	OF-8, 1B-4
1877			60	.378	.458	251	95	10	5	0	0.0	43	27	3	3			0	0	42	18	23	2	1.4	.723	OF-58, P-2
1878	CHI	N	60	.266	.301	256	68	7	1	0	0.0	33	29	9	11			0	0	91	31	28	6	2.5	.813	OF-60, C-1
1879	TRO	N	9	.189	.216	37	7	1	0	0	0.0	4	1	2	4			0	0	24	2	4	2	3.3	.867	OF-8, 1B-2
1880			83	.253	.338	352	89	14	8	0	0.0	40	29	12	34			0	0	130	18	22	1	2.0	.871	OF-82, 2B-1
1881			85	.222	.281	370	82	13	3	1	0.3	57	11	18	21			0	0	144	24	25	1	2.3	.870	OF-84, SS-1
1882			29	.174	.215	121	21	3	1	0	0.0	14	9	3	16			0	0	35	23	25	1	2.9	.699	OF-16, 3B-13
1883	PRO	N	89	.238	.309	366	87	16	5	0	0.0	46		9	38			0	0	132	29	26	2	2.1	.861	OF-88, 2B-1, 1B-1
1884	BKN	AA	106	.252	.319	433	109	11	6	2	0.5	57		19				0	0	131	31	34	5	1.8	.827	OF-100, 3B-5, SS-1
1885			54	.213	.271	221	47	6	2	1	0.5	36		8				0	0	62	7	12	3	1.5	.852	OF-54
10 yrs.			587	.252	.316	2454	618	83	31	4	0.2	336	114	84	127			0	0	832	187	201	26	2.1	.835	OF-558, 3B-18, 1B-7, SS-2, 2B-2, P-2, C-1

Pete Cassidy

CASSIDY, PETER FRANCIS
B. Apr. 8, 1873, Wilmington, Del. D. July 9, 1929, Wilmington, Del. — BR TR 5'10" 165 lbs.

Year	Team		Games	BA	SA	AB	H	2B	3B	HR	HR%	R	RBI	BB	SO	SB	Pinch Hit AB	Pinch Hit H	PO	A	E	DP	TC/G	FA	G by Pos
1896	LOU	N	49	.212	.228	184	39	1	1	0	0.0	16	12	7	7	5	0	0	368	48	24	18	9.0	.945	1B-38, SS-11
1899	2 teams			BKN	N	(6G – .150)				WAS	N	(46G – .315)														
"	total		52	.298	.414	198	59	14	6	3	1.5	23	36	10		6	0	0	360	45	21	26	8.2	.951	1B-37, 3B-9, SS-5
2 yrs.			101	.257	.325	382	98	15	1	3	0.8	39	48	17	7	11	1	0	728	93	45	44	8.6	.948	1B-75, SS-16, 3B-9

Jack Cassini

CASSINI, JACK DEMPSEY (Scat)
B. Oct. 26, 1919, Dearborn, Mich. — BR TR 5'10" 175 lbs.

Year	Team		Games	BA	SA	AB	H	2B	3B	HR	HR%	R	RBI	BB	SO	SB	Pinch Hit AB	Pinch Hit H	PO	A	E	DP	TC/G	FA	G by Pos
1949	PIT	N	8	–	–	0	0	0	0	0	–	3	0	0	0	0	0	0	0	0	0	0	0.0	–	

Jim Castiglia

CASTIGLIA, JAMES VINCENT
B. Sept. 30, 1918, Passaic, N. J. — BL TR 5'11" 200 lbs.

Year	Team		Games	BA	SA	AB	H	2B	3B	HR	HR%	R	RBI	BB	SO	SB	Pinch Hit AB	Pinch Hit H	PO	A	E	DP	TC/G	FA	G by Pos
1942	PHI	A	16	.389	.389	18	7	0	0	0	0.0	2	2	1	3	0	13	4	6	1	1	0	0.5	.875	C-3

Pete Castiglione

CASTIGLIONE, PETER PAUL
B. Feb. 13, 1921, Greenwich, Conn. — BR TR 5'11" 175 lbs.

Year	Team		Games	BA	SA	AB	H	2B	3B	HR	HR%	R	RBI	BB	SO	SB	Pinch Hit AB	Pinch Hit H	PO	A	E	DP	TC/G	FA	G by Pos
1947	PIT	N	13	.280	.280	50	14	0	0	0	0.0	6	1	2	5	0	0	0	26	39	2	6	5.2	.970	SS-13
1948			4	.000	.000	2	0	0	0	0	0.0	0	0	0	1	0	1	0	0	1	0	0	0.3	1.000	SS-1
1949			118	.268	.362	448	120	20	2	6	1.3	57	43	20	43	2	5	1	115	236	14	32	3.1	.962	3B-98, SS-17, OF-2
1950			94	.255	.350	263	67	10	3	3	1.1	29	22	23	23	1	22	7	116	125	10	23	2.7	.960	3B-35, SS-29, 2B-9, 1B-3

Year	Team	Games	BA	SA	AB	H	2B	3B	HR	HR%	R	RBI	BB	SO	SB	Pinch Hit AB	Pinch Hit H	PO	A	E	DP	TC/G	FA	G by Pos

Pete Castiglione *continued*

Year	Team	Games	BA	SA	AB	H	2B	3B	HR	HR%	R	RBI	BB	SO	SB	PH AB	PH H	PO	A	E	DP	TC/G	FA	G by Pos
1951		132	.261	.361	482	126	19	4	7	1.5	62	42	34	28	2	9	2	148	292	21	36	3.5	.954	3B-99, SS-28
1952		67	.266	.374	214	57	9	1	4	1.9	27	18	17	8	3	9	2	69	129	10	7	3.1	.952	3B-57, OF-1, 1B-1
1953 2 teams	PIT N (45G – .208)				STL N (67G – .173)																			
" total		112	.199	.284	211	42	4	1	4	1.9	23	24	7	19	1	8	4	68	132	7	14	1.8	.966	3B-94, 2B-9, SS-3
1954	STL N	5	—	—	0	0	0	0	0	—	1	0	0	0	0	0	0	0	1	0	0	0.2	1.000	3B-5
8 yrs.		545	.255	.349	1670	426	62	11	24	1.4	205	150	103	126	10	54	16	542	955	64	118	2.9	.959	3B-388, SS-91, 2B-18, 1B-4, OF-3

Carmen Castillo

CASTILLO, MONTE CARMELO
B. June 8, 1958, San Pedro de Macoris, Dominican Republic

BR TR 6'1" 180 lbs.

Year	Team	Games	BA	SA	AB	H	2B	3B	HR	HR%	R	RBI	BB	SO	SB	PH AB	PH H	PO	A	E	DP	TC/G	FA	G by Pos
1982	CLE A	47	.208	.292	120	25	4	0	2	1.7	11	11	6	17	0	3	0	91	0	2	0	2.0	.978	OF-43, DH-2
1983		23	.278	.472	36	10	2	1	1	2.8	9	3	4	6	1	2	0	23	3	2	1	1.2	.929	OF-19, DH-1
1984		87	.261	.464	211	55	9	2	10	4.7	36	36	21	32	1	18	3	123	2	9	0	1.5	.933	OF-70, DH-2
1985		67	.245	.462	184	45	5	1	11	6.0	27	25	11	40	3	9	1	101	0	5	0	1.6	.953	OF-51, DH-9
1986		85	.278	.439	205	57	9	0	8	3.9	34	32	9	48	2	21	3	58	4	4	1	0.8	.939	OF-37, DH-35
1987		89	.250	.477	220	55	17	0	11	5.0	27	31	16	52	1	29	5	29	3	0	0	0.4	1.000	DH-43, OF-23
1988		66	.273	.386	176	48	8	0	4	2.3	12	14	5	31	6	16	4	69	1	5	0	1.1	.933	OF-45, DH-9
1989	MIN A	94	.257	.454	218	56	13	3	8	3.7	23	33	15	40	1	29	8	119	3	3	1	1.3	.976	OF-67, DH-16
8 yrs.		558	.256	.436	1370	351	67	7	55	4.0	179	185	87	266	15	127	24	613	16	30	3	1.2	.954	OF-355, DH-117

Juan Castillo

CASTILLO, JUAN
Born Juan Castillo y Brayas.
B. Jan. 25, 1962, San Pedro de Macoris, Dominican Republic

BB TR 5'11" 162 lbs.

Year	Team	Games	BA	SA	AB	H	2B	3B	HR	HR%	R	RBI	BB	SO	SB	PH AB	PH H	PO	A	E	DP	TC/G	FA	G by Pos
1986	MIL A	26	.167	.204	54	9	0	1	0	0.0	6	5	5	12	1	0	0	41	46	4	10	3.5	.956	2B-17, SS-4, DH-2, 3B-2, OF-1
1987		116	.224	.312	321	72	11	4	3	0.9	44	28	33	76	15	7	2	190	251	12	59	3.9	.974	2B-97, SS-13, 3B-7
1988		54	.222	.222	90	20	0	0	0	0.0	10	2	3	14	2	0	0	24	82	7	13	2.1	.938	2B-18, 3B-17, SS-13, DH-3, OF-1
1989		3	.000	.000	4	0	0	0	0	0.0	0	3	0	2	0	0	0	6	5	0	1	3.7	1.000	2B-3
4 yrs.		199	.215	.279	469	101	11	5	3	0.6	60	38	41	104	18	7	2	261	384	23	83	3.4	.966	2B-135, SS-30, 3B-26, DH-5, OF-2

Manny Castillo

CASTILLO, ESTEBAN MANUEL ANTONIO
Born Esteban Manuel Antonio Castillo y Cabrera.
B. Apr. 1, 1957, Santo Domingo, Dominican Republic

BB TR 5'9" 160 lbs.

Year	Team	Games	BA	SA	AB	H	2B	3B	HR	HR%	R	RBI	BB	SO	SB	PH AB	PH H	PO	A	E	DP	TC/G	FA	G by Pos
1980	KC A	7	.200	.200	10	2	0	0	0	0.0	0	0	0	0	2	1	0	2	8	0	0	1.4	1.000	3B-3, DH-2, 2B-1
1982	SEA A	138	.257	.336	506	130	29	1	3	0.6	49	49	22	35	2	11	1	109	220	21	24	2.5	.940	3B-130, 2B-9
1983		91	.207	.266	203	42	6	3	0	0.0	13	24	7	20	1	29	7	78	118	6	17	2.2	.970	3B-55, 1B-11, DH-6, 2B-5, P-1
3 yrs.		236	.242	.314	719	174	35	4	3	0.4	63	73	29	55	3	42	9	189	346	27	41	2.4	.952	3B-188, 2B-15, 1B-11, DH-8, P-1

Marty Castillo

CASTILLO, MARTIN HORACE
B. Jan. 16, 1957, Long Beach, Calif.

BR TR 6'1" 190 lbs.

Year	Team	Games	BA	SA	AB	H	2B	3B	HR	HR%	R	RBI	BB	SO	SB	PH AB	PH H	PO	A	E	DP	TC/G	FA	G by Pos
1981	DET A	6	.125	.125	8	1	0	0	0	0.0	1	0	0	2	0	0	0	5	8	0	3	2.2	1.000	3B-4, OF-1, C-1
1982		1	—	—	0	0	0	0	0	0.0	0	0	0	0	0	0	0	1	0	0	0	1.0	1.000	C-1
1983		67	.193	.277	119	23	4	0	2	1.7	10	10	7	22	2	2	0	73	69	1	6	2.1	.993	3B-58, C-10
1984		70	.234	.383	141	33	5	2	4	2.8	16	17	10	33	1	1	0	161	37	7	3	2.9	.966	C-36, 3B-33, DH-1
1985		57	.119	.214	84	10	2	0	2	2.4	4	5	2	19	0	0	0	123	31	4	2	2.8	.975	C-32, 3B-25
5 yrs.		201	.190	.301	352	67	11	2	8	2.3	31	32	19	76	3	3	0	363	145	12	14	2.6	.977	3B-120, C-80, DH-1, OF-1

LEAGUE CHAMPIONSHIP SERIES

Year	Team	Games	BA	SA	AB	H	2B	3B	HR	HR%	R	RBI	BB	SO	SB	PH AB	PH H	PO	A	E	DP	TC/G	FA	G by Pos
1984	DET A	3	.250	.250	8	2	0	0	0	0.0	0	0	0	1	0	0	0	3	4	0	0	2.3	1.000	3B-3

WORLD SERIES

Year	Team	Games	BA	SA	AB	H	2B	3B	HR	HR%	R	RBI	BB	SO	SB	PH AB	PH H	PO	A	E	DP	TC/G	FA	G by Pos
1984	DET A	3	.333	.667	9	3	0	0	1	11.1	2	2	1	0	0	0	0	3	4	0	0	2.0	1.000	3B-3

Tony Castillo

CASTILLO, ANTHONY
B. June 14, 1957, San Jose, Calif.

BR TR 6'4" 190 lbs.

Year	Team	Games	BA	SA	AB	H	2B	3B	HR	HR%	R	RBI	BB	SO	SB	PH AB	PH H	PO	A	E	DP	TC/G	FA	G by Pos
1978	SD N	5	.125	.125	8	1	0	0	0	0.0	0	1	0	2	0	0	0	16	3	1	0	4.0	.950	C-5

John Castino

CASTINO, JOHN ANTHONY
B. Oct. 23, 1954, Evanston, Ill.

BR TR 5'11" 175 lbs.

Year	Team	Games	BA	SA	AB	H	2B	3B	HR	HR%	R	RBI	BB	SO	SB	PH AB	PH H	PO	A	E	DP	TC/G	FA	G by Pos
1979	MIN A	148	.285	.397	393	112	13	8	5	1.3	49	52	27	72	5	8	3	91	286	15	34	2.6	.962	3B-143, SS-5
1980		150	.302	.430	546	165	17	7	13	2.4	67	64	29	67	7	1	0	128	395	22	48	3.6	.960	3B-138, SS-18
1981		101	.268	.396	381	102	13	9	6	1.6	41	36	18	52	4	0	0	96	236	9	29	3.4	.974	3B-98, 2B-4
1982		117	.241	.344	410	99	12	6	6	1.5	48	37	36	51	2	0	0	230	278	4	69	4.4	.992	2B-96, 3B-21, OF-6, DH-1
1983		142	.277	.403	563	156	30	4	11	2.0	83	57	62	54	4	2	0	316	430	8	95	5.3	.989	2B-132, 3B-8, DH-1
1984		8	.444	.481	27	12	1	0	0	0.0	5	3	5	2	0	0	0	8	12	0	1	2.5	1.000	3B-8
6 yrs.		666	.278	.398	2320	646	86	34	41	1.8	293	249	177	298	22	11	3	869	1637	58	276	3.8	.977	3B-416, 2B-232, SS-23, OF-6, DH-2

Vince Castino

CASTINO, VINCENT CHARLES
B. Oct. 11, 1917, Willisville, Ill. D. Mar. 6, 1967, Sacramento, Calif.

BR TR 5'9" 175 lbs.

Year	Team	Games	BA	SA	AB	H	2B	3B	HR	HR%	R	RBI	BB	SO	SB	PH AB	PH H	PO	A	E	DP	TC/G	FA	G by Pos
1943	CHI A	33	.228	.297	101	23	1	0	2	2.0	14	16	12	11	0	3	0	90	9	3	3	3.1	.971	C-30
1944		29	.231	.295	78	18	5	0	0	0.0	8	3	10	13	0	2	1	85	16	1	4	3.5	.990	C-26
1945		26	.216	.243	37	8	1	0	0	0.0	2	4	3	7	0	1	0	32	7	2	1	1.6	.951	C-25
3 yrs.		88	.227	.287	216	49	7	0	2	0.9	24	23	25	31	0	6	1	207	32	6	8	2.8	.976	C-81

Don Castle

CASTLE, DONALD HARDY
B. Feb. 1, 1950, Kokomo, Ind.

BL TL 6'1" 205 lbs.

Year	Team	Games	BA	SA	AB	H	2B	3B	HR	HR%	R	RBI	BB	SO	SB	Pinch Hit AB	Pinch Hit H	PO	A	E	DP	TC/G	FA	G by Pos

Don Castle *continued*

Year	Team	Games	BA	SA	AB	H	2B	3B	HR	HR%	R	RBI	BB	SO	SB	PH AB	PH H	PO	A	E	DP	TC/G	FA	G by Pos
1973	TEX A	4	.308	.385	13	4	1	0	0	0.0	0	2	1	3	0	1	0	0	0	0	0	0.0	–	DH-3

John Castle

CASTLE, JOHN FRANCIS   5'10½"
B. June 1, 1883, Honey Brook, Pa.   D. Apr. 13, 1929, Philadelphia, Pa.

| 1910 | PHI N | 3 | .250 | .250 | 4 | 1 | 0 | 0 | 0 | 0.0 | 1 | 0 | 0 | 0 | 1 | 0 | 0 | 0 | 0 | 0 | 0 | 0.0 | – | OF-2 |

Foster Castleman

CASTLEMAN, FOSTER EPHRAIM   BR TR 6' 175 lbs.
B. Jan. 1, 1931, Nashville, Tenn.

1954	NY N	13	.250	.250	12	3	0	0	0	0.0	0	1	0	3	0	11	3	0	0	0	0	0.0	–	2B-2
1955		15	.214	.464	28	6	1	0	2	7.1	3	4	2	4	0	7	1	14	10	0	2	1.6	1.000	2B-6, 3B-3
1956		124	.226	.392	385	87	16	3	14	3.6	33	45	15	50	2	17	3	91	213	17	10	2.6	.947	3B-107, SS-2, 2B-1
1957		18	.162	.297	37	6	2	0	1	2.7	7	1	2	8	0	9	1	6	12	2	1	1.1	.900	3B-7, SS-1, 2B-1
1958	BAL A	98	.170	.240	200	34	5	0	3	1.5	15	14	16	34	2	2	0	113	174	11	40	3.0	.963	SS-91, 3B-4, 2B-4, OF-1
5 yrs.		268	.205	.341	662	136	24	3	20	3.0	58	65	35	99	4	46	8	224	409	30	53	2.5	.955	3B-119, SS-94, 2B-14, OF-1

Louis Castro

CASTRO, LOUIS R. (Jud)   BR TR 5'7"
B. 1877, Cartagena, Colombia   D. Venezuela

| 1902 | PHI A | 42 | .245 | .336 | 143 | 35 | 8 | 1 | 0 | 0.7 | 18 | 15 | 4 | | 2 | 2 | 0 | 75 | 86 | 17 | 10 | 4.2 | .904 | 2B-36, OF-3, SS-1 |

Danny Cater

CATER, DANNY ANDERSON   BR TR 6' 170 lbs.
B. Feb. 25, 1940, Austin, Tex.

1964	PHI N	60	.296	.388	152	45	9	1	1	0.7	13	13	7	15	1	18	6	110	7	3	7	2.0	.975	OF-39, 1B-7, 3B-1
1965	CHI A	142	.270	.403	514	139	18	4	14	2.7	74	55	33	65	3	7	2	189	21	6	3	1.5	.972	OF-127, 3B-11, 1B-3
1966	2 teams		CHI A (21G – .183)				KC A (116G – .292)																	
"	total	137	.278	.373	485	135	17	4	7	1.4	50	56	28	47	5	5	1	565	104	11	55	5.0	.984	1B-53, 3B-42, OF-40
1967	KC A	142	.270	.340	529	143	17	4	4	0.8	55	46	34	56	4	2	1	424	109	13	35	3.8	.976	3B-56, OF-55, 1B-44
1968	OAK A	147	.290	.393	504	146	28	3	6	1.2	53	62	35	43	8	11	4	1007	69	5	89	7.4	.995	1B-121, OF-20, 2B-1
1969		152	.262	.361	584	153	24	2	10	1.7	64	76	28	40	1	8	1	1125	108	9	113	8.2	.993	1B-132, OF-20, 2B-4
1970	NY A	155	.301	.393	582	175	26	5	6	1.0	64	76	34	44	4	3	0	1016	153	16	89	7.6	.986	1B-131, 3B-42, OF-7
1971		121	.276	.364	428	118	16	5	4	0.9	39	50	19	25	0	10	3	605	173	13	61	6.5	.984	1B-78, 3B-52
1972	BOS A	92	.237	.372	317	75	17	1	8	2.5	32	39	15	33	0	6	1	656	61	5	65	7.8	.993	1B-90
1973		63	.313	.390	195	61	12	0	1	0.5	30	24	10	22	0	7	2	303	56	6	45	5.8	.984	1B-37, 3B-21, DH-3
1974		56	.246	.405	126	31	5	0	5	4.0	14	20	10	13	1	18	5	126	10	0	9	2.4	1.000	1B-23, DH-14
1975	STL N	22	.229	.286	35	8	2	0	0	0.0	3	2	1	3	0	13	2	49	4	1	4	2.5	.981	1B-12
12 yrs.		1289	.276	.377	4451	1229	191	29	66	1.5	491	519	254	406	26	108	28	6175	875	88	575	5.5	.988	1B-731, OF-308, 3B-225, DH-17, 2B-5

Eli Cates

CATES, ELI ELDO   BR TR 5'9½" 175 lbs.
B. Jan. 26, 1877, Greensfork, Ind.   D. May 29, 1964, Richmond, Ind.

| 1908 | WAS A | 40 | .186 | .237 | 59 | 11 | 1 | 1 | 0 | 0.0 | 5 | 3 | 6 | | 0 | 16 | 1 | 8 | 38 | 5 | 1 | 1.3 | .902 | P-19, 2B-3 |

Ted Cather

CATHER, THODORE P.   BR TR 5'10½" 178 lbs.
B. May 20, 1889, Chester, Pa.   D. Apr. 9, 1945, Elkton, Md.

1912	STL N	5	.421	.579	19	8	1	1	0	0.0	4	2	0	4	1	0	0	15	2	1	0	3.6	.944	OF-5
1913		67	.213	.301	183	39	8	4	0	0.0	16	12	9	24	7	7	3	71	8	7	0	1.3	.919	OF-57, 1B-1, P-1
1914	2 teams		STL N (39G – .273)				BOS N (50G – .297)																	
"	total	89	.287	.377	244	70	18	2	0	0.0	30	40	10	43	11	12	1	51	4	1	0	0.6	.982	OF-76
1915	BOS N	40	.206	.314	102	21	3	1	2	2.0	10	18	15	19	2	7	1	35	2	4	1	1.0	.902	OF-40
4 yrs.		201	.252	.347	548	138	30	8	2	0.4	60	72	34	90	21	26	5	172	16	13	1	1.0	.935	OF-178, 1B-1, P-1

WORLD SERIES

| 1914 | BOS N | 1 | .000 | .000 | 5 | 0 | 0 | 0 | 0 | 0.0 | 0 | 0 | 0 | 1 | 0 | 0 | 0 | 2 | 0 | 0 | 0 | 2.0 | 1.000 | OF-1 |

Buster Caton

CATON, JAMES HOWARD   BR TR 5'6" 165 lbs.
B. July 16, 1896, Zanesville, Ohio   D. Jan. 8, 1948, Zanesville, Ohio

1917	PIT N	14	.211	.298	57	12	1	2	0	0.0	6	4	6	7	0	0	0	21	47	8	5	5.4	.895	SS-14
1918		80	.234	.297	303	71	5	7	0	0.0	37	17	32	16	12	1	0	136	276	32	35	5.6	.928	SS-79
1919		39	.176	.225	102	18	1	2	0	0.0	13	5	12	10	2	6	1	38	52	6	3	2.5	.938	SS-17, 3B-11, OF-1
1920		98	.236	.295	352	83	11	5	0	0.0	29	27	33	19	4	1	1	191	296	37	40	5.3	.929	SS-96
4 yrs.		231	.226	.287	814	184	18	16	0	0.0	85	53	83	52	18	8	2	386	671	83	83	4.9	.927	SS-206, 3B-11, OF-1

Tom Catterson

CATTERSON, THOMAS HENRY   BL TL 5'10" 170 lbs.
B. Aug. 25, 1884, Warwick, R. I.   D. Feb. 5, 1920, Portland, Me.

1908	BKN N	19	.191	.279	68	13	1	1	1	1.5	5	2	5		0	1	0	39	1	1	0	2.2	.976	OF-18
1909		9	.222	.222	18	4	0	0	0	0.0	0	1	3		0	1	0	5	0	1	0	0.7	.833	OF-6
2 yrs.		28	.198	.267	86	17	1	1	1	1.2	5	3	8		0	2	0	44	1	2	0	1.7	.957	OF-24

John Caulfield

CAULFIELD, JOHN JOSEPH (Jake)   BR TR 5'11" 170 lbs.
B. Nov. 23, 1917, Los Angeles, Calif.   D. Dec. 16, 1986, San Francisco, Calif.

| 1946 | PHI A | 44 | .277 | .362 | 94 | 26 | 8 | 0 | 0 | 0.0 | 13 | 10 | 4 | 11 | 0 | 2 | 0 | 49 | 55 | 8 | 13 | 2.5 | .929 | SS-31, 3B-1 |

Wayne Causey

CAUSEY, JAMES WAYNE   BL TR 5'10½" 175 lbs.
B. Dec. 26, 1936, Ruston, La.

1955	BAL A	68	.194	.234	175	34	2	1	0	0.6	14	9	17	25	0	8	0	30	85	12	11	1.9	.906	3B-55, 2B-7, SS-1
1956		53	.170	.227	88	15	0	1	1	1.1	7	4	8	23	0	16	5	26	52	2	4	1.5	.975	3B-30, 2B-7
1957		14	.200	.200	10	2	0	0	0	0.0	2	1	5	2	0	3	0	14	13	1	2	2.0	.964	2B-6, 3B-5
1961	KC A	104	.276	.404	312	86	14	4	8	2.6	37	49	37	28	0	2	0	133	228	16	25	3.6	.958	3B-88, SS-11, 2B-9
1962		117	.252	.344	305	77	14	1	4	1.3	40	38	41	30	2	28	2	143	200	14	25	3.1	.961	SS-51, 3B-26, 2B-9
1963		139	.280	.395	554	155	32	4	8	1.4	72	44	56	54	4	2	0	267	405	15	81	4.9	.978	SS-135, 3B-2

Year	Team	Games	BA	SA	AB	H	2B	3B	HR	HR%	R	RBI	BB	SO	SB	Pinch Hit AB	Pinch Hit H	PO	A	E	DP	TC/G	FA	G by Pos

Wayne Causey *continued*

Year	Team	Games	BA	SA	AB	H	2B	3B	HR	HR%	R	RBI	BB	SO	SB	AB	H	PO	A	E	DP	TC/G	FA	G by Pos
1964		157	.281	.386	604	170	31	4	8	1.3	82	49	88	65	0	3	2	323	423	25	92	4.9	.968	SS-131, 2B-17, 3B-9
1965		144	.261	.343	513	134	17	8	3	0.6	48	34	61	48	1	8	1	221	313	15	60	3.8	.973	
1966	2 teams				KC	A	(28G	–	.228)		CHI	A	(78G	–	.244)									
"	total	106	.239	.288	243	58	8	2	0	0.0	24	18	31	19	3	19	7	115	150	11	21	2.6	.960	2B-60, 3B-16, SS-11
1967	CHI A	124	.226	.291	292	66	10	3	1	0.3	21	28	32	35	2	34	10	153	200	8	36	2.9	.978	2B-96, SS-2
1968	3 teams		CHI	A	(59G	–	.180)		CAL	A	(4G	–	.000)		ATL	N	(16G	–	.108)					
"	total	79	.149	.196	148	22	2	1		0.7	10	11	14	12	0	36	6	62	76	4	17	1.8	.972	2B-51, SS-2, 3B-2
11 yrs.		1105	.252	.341	3244	819	130	26	35	1.1	357	285	390	341	12	158	41	1487	2145	123	374	3.4	.967	SS-406, 2B-307, 3B-268

John Cavanaugh

CAVANAUGH, JOHN J.
B. June 5, 1900, Reading, Pa.   D. Jan. 14, 1961, New Brunswick, N. J.
BR TR 5'9" 158 lbs.

Year	Team	Games	BA	SA	AB	H	2B	3B	HR	HR%	R	RBI	BB	SO	SB	AB	H	PO	A	E	DP	TC/G	FA	G by Pos
1919	PHI N	1	.000	.000	1	0	0	0	0	0.0	0	0	0	1	0	0	0	0	0	0	0	0.0	–	3B-1

Phil Cavarretta

CAVARRETTA, PHILIP JOSEPH
B. July 19, 1916, Chicago, Ill.
Manager 1951-53.
BL TL 5'11½" 175 lbs.

Year	Team	Games	BA	SA	AB	H	2B	3B	HR	HR%	R	RBI	BB	SO	SB	AB	H	PO	A	E	DP	TC/G	FA	G by Pos
1934	CHI N	7	.381	.619	21	8	0	1	1	4.8	5	6	2	3	1	2	0	53	5	0	6	8.3	1.000	1B-5
1935		146	.275	.404	589	162	28	12	8	1.4	85	82	39	61	4	1	0	1347	98	20	129	10.0	.986	1B-145
1936		124	.273	.376	458	125	18	1	9	2.0	55	56	17	36	8	8	4	980	71	14	93	8.6	.987	1B-115
1937		106	.286	.429	329	94	18	5	5	1.5	43	56	32	35	7	11	4	454	40	10	28	4.8	.980	OF-53, 1B-43
1938		92	.239	.321	268	64	11	4	1	0.4	29	28	14	27	4	13	1	277	21	4	14	3.3	.987	OF-52, 1B-28
1939		22	.273	.364	55	15	3	1	0	0.0	4	0	4	3	2	7	3	106	6	1	10	5.1	.991	1B-10, OF-1
1940		65	.280	.409	193	54	11	4	2	1.0	34	22	31	18	3	10	0	524	30	5	62	8.6	.991	1B-52
1941		107	.286	.413	346	99	18	4	6	1.7	46	40	53	28	2	5	2	463	15	5	20	4.5	.990	OF-66, 1B-33
1942		136	.270	.363	482	130	28	4	3	0.6	59	54	71	42	7	6	0	744	49	7	49	5.9	.991	OF-70, 1B-61
1943		143	.291	.421	530	154	27	9	8	1.5	93	73	75	42	3	2	0	1305	67	18	103	9.7	.987	1B-134, OF-7
1944		152	.321	.451	614	**197**	35	15	5	0.8	106	82	67	42	4	0	0	1363	78	13	121	9.6	.991	1B-139, OF-13
1945		132	**.355**	.500	498	177	34	10	6	1.2	94	97	81	34	5	0	0	1172	78	9	83	9.5	.993	1B-120, OF-11
1946		139	.294	.435	510	150	28	10	8	1.6	89	78	88	54	2	2	0	646	47	11	28	5.1	.984	OF-86, 1B-51
1947		127	.314	.397	459	144	22	5	2	0.4	56	63	58	35	2	3	2	420	24	8	26	3.6	.982	OF-100, 1B-24
1948		111	.278	.383	334	93	16	5	3	0.9	41	40	35	29	4	23	3	446	32	3	46	4.3	.994	1B-41, OF-40
1949		105	.294	.444	360	106	22	4	8	2.2	46	49	45	31	2	9	2	712	67	5	59	7.5	.994	1B-70, OF-25
1950		82	.273	.441	256	70	11	1	10	3.9	49	31	40	31	1	9	2	609	47	9	55	8.6	.986	1B-67, OF-3
1951		89	.311	.442	206	64	7	1	6	2.9	24	28	27	28	0	33	12	444	42	3	51	5.5	.994	1B-53
1952		41	.238	.333	63	15	1	1	1	1.6	7	8	9	3	0	26	5	98	10	1	13	2.7	.991	1B-13
1953		27	.286	.429	21	6	3	0	0	0.0	3	3	6	3	0	21	6	0	0	0	0	0.0	–	
1954	CHI A	71	.316	.411	158	50	6	0	3	1.9	21	24	26	12	4	16	2	269	17	3	29	4.1	.990	1B-44, OF-9
1955		6	.000	.000	4	0	0	0	0	0.0	1	0	1	0	0	2	0	3	0	0	0	0.5	1.000	1B-3
22 yrs.		2030	.293	.416	6754	1977	347	99	95	1.4	990	920	820	598	65	209	48	12435	844	149	1020	6.6	.989	1B-1254, OF-536

WORLD SERIES

Year	Team	Games	BA	SA	AB	H	2B	3B	HR	HR%	R	RBI	BB	SO	SB	AB	H	PO	A	E	DP	TC/G	FA	G by Pos
1935	CHI N	6	.125	.125	24	3	0	0	0	0.0	1	0	0	5	0	0	0	58	3	1	3	10.3	.984	1B-6
1938		4	.462	.538	13	6	1	0	0	0.0	1	0	0	1	0	1	1	4	1	0	0	1.3	1.000	OF-3
1945		7	.423	.615	26	11	2	0	1	3.8	7	5	4	3	0	0	0	71	3	0	0	10.6	1.000	1B-7
3 yrs.		17	.317	.413	63	20	3	0	1	1.6	9	5	4	9	0	1	1	133	7	1	8	8.3	.993	1B-13, OF-3

Ike Caveney

CAVENEY, JAMES CHRISTOPHER
B. Dec. 10, 1894, San Francisco, Calif.   D. July 6, 1949, San Francisco, Calif.
BR TR 5'9" 168 lbs.

Year	Team	Games	BA	SA	AB	H	2B	3B	HR	HR%	R	RBI	BB	SO	SB	AB	H	PO	A	E	DP	TC/G	FA	G by Pos
1922	CIN N	118	.239	.338	394	94	12	9	3	0.8	41	54	29	33	6	0	0	256	404	47	74	6.0	.934	SS-118
1923		138	.277	.381	488	135	21	9	4	0.8	58	63	26	41	5	0	0	313	477	49	86	6.1	.942	SS-138
1924		95	.273	.371	337	92	19	1	4	1.2	36	32	14	21	2	1	0	210	326	44	61	6.1	.924	SS-90, 2B-5
1925		115	.249	.318	358	89	9	5	2	0.6	38	47	28	31	2	4	0	209	349	35	72	5.2	.941	SS-111
4 yrs.		466	.260	.354	1577	410	61	24	13	0.8	173	196	97	126	15	5	0	988	1556	175	293	5.8	.936	SS-457, 2B-5

Cesar Cedeno

CEDENO, CESAR
Born Cesar Cedeno y Encarnacion.
B. Feb. 25, 1951, Santo Domingo, Dominican Republic
BR TR 6'2" 175 lbs.

Year	Team	Games	BA	SA	AB	H	2B	3B	HR	HR%	R	RBI	BB	SO	SB	AB	H	PO	A	E	DP	TC/G	FA	G by Pos
1970	HOU N	90	.310	.451	355	110	21	4	7	2.0	46	42	15	57	17	2	1	211	1	7	0	2.4	.968	OF-90
1971		161	.264	.398	611	161	**40**	6	10	1.6	85	81	25	102	20	4	0	348	6	4	0	2.2	.989	OF-157, 1B-2
1972		139	.320	.537	559	179	**39**	8	22	3.9	103	82	56	62	55	1	0	345	9	7	1	2.6	.981	OF-137
1973		139	.320	.537	525	168	35	2	25	4.8	86	70	41	79	56	4	0	357	10	7	2	2.7	.981	OF-136
1974		160	.269	.461	610	164	29	5	26	4.3	95	102	64	103	57	2	0	446	11	3	4	2.9	.993	OF-157
1975		131	.288	.440	500	144	31	3	13	2.6	93	63	62	52	50	0	0	322	8	6	2	2.6	.982	OF-131
1976		150	.297	.454	575	171	26	5	18	3.1	89	83	55	51	58	4	0	377	11	8	5	2.6	.980	OF-146
1977		141	.279	.457	530	148	36	8	14	2.6	92	71	47	50	61	3	0	335	14	1	2	2.5	.987	OF-137
1978		50	.281	.453	192	54	8	2	7	3.6	31	23	15	24	23	0	0	149	2	2	1	3.1	.987	OF-50
1979		132	.262	.374	470	123	27	4	6	1.3	57	54	64	52	30	11	2	948	35	17	79	7.6	.983	1B-91, OF-40
1980		137	.309	.465	499	154	32	6	10	2.0	71	73	66	72	48	1	0	338	9	8	3	2.6	.977	OF-136
1981		82	.271	.382	306	83	19	0	5	1.6	42	34	24	31	12	2	0	510	28	5	27	6.6	.991	1B-46, OF-34
1982	CIN N	138	.289	.413	492	142	35	1	8	1.6	52	57	41	41	16	7	2	301	5	3	2	2.2	.990	OF-131, 1B-1
1983		98	.232	.361	332	77	16	0	9	2.7	40	39	33	53	13	10	2	258	10	1	8	2.7	.996	OF-73, 1B-17
1984		110	.276	.429	380	105	24	2	10	2.6	59	47	25	54	19	14	2	355	21	0	16	3.5	.982	OF-77, 1B-44
1985	2 teams		CIN	N	(83G	–	.241)		STL	N	(28G	–	.434)											
"	total	111	.291	.443	296	86	16	1	9	3.0	38	49	24	42	14	25	10	351	14	3	27	3.3	.992	1B-57, OF-55
1986	LA N	37	.231	.282	78	18	2	1	0	0.0	7	6	7	13	1	13	3	33	1	2	0	1.0	.944	OF-31
17 yrs.		2006	.285	.443	7310	2087	436	60	199	2.7	1084	976	664	938	550	103	22	5984	195	91	179	3.1	.985	OF-1718, 1B-258

DIVISIONAL PLAYOFF SERIES

Year	Team	Games	BA	SA	AB	H	2B	3B	HR	HR%	R	RBI	BB	SO	SB	AB	H	PO	A	E	DP	TC/G	FA	G by Pos
1981	HOU N	4	.231	.308	13	3	1	0	0	0.0	0	0	2	2	2	0	0	0	0	1	0	0.3	–	1B-4

LEAGUE CHAMPIONSHIP SERIES

Year	Team	Games	BA	SA	AB	H	2B	3B	HR	HR%	R	RBI	BB	SO	SB	AB	H	PO	A	E	DP	TC/G	FA	G by Pos
1980	HOU N	3	.182	.182	11	2	0	0	0	0.0	1	1	0	0	0	0	0	5	0	0	0	1.7	1.000	OF-3

Cesar Cedeno *continued*

Year Team	Games	BA	SA	AB	H	2B	3B	HR	HR%	R	RBI	BB	SO	SB	Pinch Hit AB	Pinch Hit H	PO	A	E	DP	TC/G	FA	G by Pos
1985 STL N	5	.167	.250	12	2	1	0	0	0.0	2	0	2	3	0	2	0	5	0	0	0	1.0	1.000	OF-4
2 yrs.	8	.174	.217	23	4	1	0	0	0.0	3	1	3	3	0	2	0	10	0	0	0	1.3	1.000	OF-7
WORLD SERIES																							
1985 STL N	5	.133	.200	15	2	1	0	0	0.0	1	1	2	2	0	0	0	9	0	0	0	1.8	1.000	OF-5

Orlando Cepeda

CEPEDA, ORLANDO MANUEL (The Baby Bull, Cha-Cha)   BR TR 6'2" 210 lbs.
Born Orlando Manuel Cepeda y Penne.
B. Sept. 17, 1937, Ponce, Puerto Rico

Year Team	Games	BA	SA	AB	H	2B	3B	HR	HR%	R	RBI	BB	SO	SB	Pinch Hit AB	Pinch Hit H	PO	A	E	DP	TC/G	FA	G by Pos
1958 SF N	148	.312	.512	603	188	38	4	25	4.1	88	96	29	84	15	1	0	1322	97	16	131	9.7	.989	1B-147
1959	151	.317	.522	605	192	35	4	27	4.5	92	105	33	100	23	0	0	995	74	22	74	7.2	.980	1B-122, OF-44, 3B-4
1960	151	.297	.497	569	169	36	3	24	4.2	81	96	34	91	15	4	0	681	37	13	40	4.8	.982	OF-91, 1B-63
1961	152	.311	.609	585	182	28	4	46	7.9	105	142	39	91	12	1	0	774	51	5	50	5.5	.994	1B-81, OF-80
1962	162	.306	.518	625	191	26	1	35	5.6	105	114	37	97	10	4	1	1356	88	14	125	9.0	.990	1B-160, OF-2
1963	156	.316	.563	579	183	33	4	34	5.9	100	97	37	70	8	8	2	1262	83	21	91	8.8	.985	1B-150, OF-3
1964	142	.304	.539	529	161	27	2	31	5.9	75	97	43	83	9	2	0	1211	80	18	89	9.2	.986	1B-139, OF-1
1965	33	.176	.294	34	6	1	0	1	2.9	1	5	3	9	0	21	4	28	2	0	1	0.9	1.000	1B-4, OF-2
1966 2 teams		SF N	(19G – .286)		STL N	(123G – .303)																	
" total	142	.301	.473	501	151	26	2	20	4.0	70	73	38	79	9	7	4	1171	63	15	116	8.8	.988	1B-126, OF-8
1967 STL N	151	.325	.524	563	183	37	0	25	4.4	91	111	62	75	11	1	1	1304	90	10	103	9.3	.993	1B-151
1968	157	.248	.378	600	149	26	2	16	2.7	71	73	43	96	8	3	1	1362	90	17	109	9.4	.988	1B-154
1969 ATL N	154	.257	.428	573	147	28	2	22	3.8	74	88	55	76	12	1	0	1318	101	9	91	9.3	.994	1B-153
1970	148	.305	.543	567	173	33	0	34	6.0	87	111	47	75	6	1	1	1288	112	12	100	9.5	.992	1B-148
1971	71	.276	.492	250	69	10	1	14	5.6	31	44	22	29	3	8	1	586	49	5	60	9.0	.992	1B-63
1972 2 teams		ATL N	(28G – .298)		OAK A	(3G – .000)																	
" total	31	.287	.460	87	25	3	0	4	4.6	6	9	7	17	0	8	0	171	13	0	15	5.9	1.000	1B-22
1973 BOS A	142	.289	.444	550	159	25	0	20	3.6	51	86	50	81	0	0	0	0	0	0	0	0.0	–	DH-142
1974 KC A	33	.215	.290	107	23	5	0	1	0.9	3	18	9	16	1	7	2	0	0	0	0	0.0	–	DH-26
17 yrs.	2124	.297	.499	7927	2351	417	27	379	4.8	1131	1365	588	1169	142	77	17	14829	1030	177	1195	7.5	.989	1B-1683, OF-231, DH-168, 3B-4
LEAGUE CHAMPIONSHIP SERIES																							
1969 ATL N	3	.455	.909	11	5	2	0	1	9.1	2	3	1	2	1	0	0	29	1	2	2	10.7	.938	1B-3
WORLD SERIES																							
1962 SF N	5	.158	.211	19	3	1	0	0	0.0	1	2	0	4	0	0	0	39	4	0	6	8.6	1.000	1B-5
1967 STL N	7	.103	.172	29	3	2	0	0	0.0	1	1	0	4	0	0	0	52	4	0	3	8.0	1.000	1B-7
1968	7	.250	.464	28	7	0	0	2	7.1	2	6	2	3	0	0	0	48	4	0	7	7.4	1.000	1B-7
3 yrs.	19	.171	.289	76	13	3	0	2	2.6	4	9	2	11	0	0	0	139	12	0	16	7.9	1.000	1B-19

Ed Cermak

CERMAK, EDWARD HUGO   BR TR 5'11" 170 lbs.
B. Mar. 10, 1882, Cleveland, Ohio   D. Nov. 22, 1911, Cleveland, Ohio

Year Team	Games	BA	SA	AB	H	2B	3B	HR	HR%	R	RBI	BB	SO	SB	Pinch Hit AB	Pinch Hit H	PO	A	E	DP	TC/G	FA	G by Pos
1901 CLE A	1	.000	.000	4	0	0	0	0	0.0	0	0	0		0	0	0	4	1	0	1	5.0	1.000	OF-1

Rick Cerone

CERONE, RICHARD ALDO   BR TR 5'11" 192 lbs.
B. May 19, 1954, Newark, N. J.

Year Team	Games	BA	SA	AB	H	2B	3B	HR	HR%	R	RBI	BB	SO	SB	Pinch Hit AB	Pinch Hit H	PO	A	E	DP	TC/G	FA	G by Pos
1975 CLE A	7	.250	.333	12	3	1	0	0	0.0	0	1	0	1	0	0	0	18	1	0	0	2.7	1.000	C-7
1976	7	.125	.125	16	2	0	0	0	0.0	1	1	0	2	0	1	1	25	1	1	1	3.9	.963	C-6, DH-1
1977 TOR A	31	.200	.270	100	20	4	0	1	1.0	7	10	6	12	0	0	0	146	15	1	1	5.2	.994	C-31
1978	88	.223	.298	282	63	8	2	3	1.1	25	20	23	32	0	4	1	426	44	4	7	5.4	.992	C-84, DH-2
1979	136	.239	.358	469	112	27	4	7	1.5	47	61	37	40	1	2	0	560	68	13	10	4.7	.980	C-136
1980 NY A	147	.277	.432	519	144	30	4	14	2.7	70	85	32	56	1	0	0	800	73	9	9	6.0	.990	C-147
1981	71	.244	.342	234	57	13	2	2	0.9	23	21	12	24	0	2	2	353	26	3	1	5.4	.992	C-69
1982	89	.227	.310	300	68	10	0	5	1.7	29	28	19	27	0	0	0	509	25	6	5	6.1	.989	C-89
1983	80	.220	.272	246	54	7	0	2	0.8	18	22	15	29	0	2	0	412	18	4	2	5.4	.991	C-78, 3B-1
1984	38	.208	.283	120	25	3	0	1	1.7	8	13	9	15	1	1	0	230	9	1	1	6.3	.996	C-38
1985 ATL N	96	.216	.280	282	61	9	0	3	1.1	15	25	29	25	0	7	1	384	48	6	4	4.6	.986	C-91
1986 MIL A	68	.259	.380	216	56	14	0	4	1.9	22	18	15	28	1	0	0	391	44	4	2	6.5	.991	C-68
1987 NY A	113	.243	.335	284	69	12	1	4	1.4	28	23	30	46	0	6	2	542	38	1	6	5.1	.998	C-111, 1B-2, P-2
1988 BOS A	84	.269	.360	264	71	13	1	3	1.1	31	27	20	32	0	4	1	471	28	0	4	5.9	1.000	C-83, DH-1
1989	102	.243	.345	296	72	16	1	4	1.4	28	48	34	40	0	7	3	579	41	10	5	6.2	.984	C-97, DH-1, OF-1
15 yrs.	1157	.241	.340	3640	877	167	15	54	1.5	353	402	282	408	4	35	11	5846	479	63	58	5.5	.990	C-1135, DH-5, 1B-2, P-2, OF-1, 3B-1
DIVISIONAL PLAYOFF SERIES																							
1981 NY A	5	.333	.611	18	6	2	0	1	5.6	1	5	0	2	0	0	0	0	0	0	1	0.2	–	C-5
LEAGUE CHAMPIONSHIP SERIES																							
1980 NY A	3	.333	.583	12	4	0	0	1	8.3	1	1	0	1	0	0	0	14	4	0	0	6.0	1.000	C-3
1981	3	.100	.100	10	1	0	0	0	0.0	1	1	0	0	0	0	0	0	0	0	0	0.0	–	C-3
2 yrs.	6	.227	.364	22	5	0	0	1	4.5	2	2	0	1	0	0	0	14	4	0	0	3.0	1.000	C-6
WORLD SERIES																							
1981 NY A	6	.190	.381	21	4	1	0	1	4.8	2	3	4	2	0	0	0	42	4	0	0	7.7	1.000	C-6

Bob Cerv

CERV, ROBERT HENRY   BR TR 6' 200 lbs.
B. May 5, 1926, Weston, Neb.

Year Team	Games	BA	SA	AB	H	2B	3B	HR	HR%	R	RBI	BB	SO	SB	Pinch Hit AB	Pinch Hit H	PO	A	E	DP	TC/G	FA	G by Pos
1951 NY A	12	.214	.250	28	6	1	0	0	0.0	4	0	4	6	0	3	0	14	0	2	0	1.3	.875	OF-9
1952	36	.241	.356	87	21	3	2	1	1.1	11	8	9	22	0	9	2	52	1	0	0	1.5	1.000	OF-27
1953	8	.000	.000	6	0	0	0	0	0.0	0	0	1	1	0	6	0	0	0	0	0	0.0	–	
1954	56	.260	.470	100	26	6	0	5	5.0	14	13	11	17	0	28	9	25	1	3	0	0.5	.897	OF-24
1955	55	.341	.541	85	29	3	3	3	3.5	17	22	7	16	4	33	11	25	1	0	0	0.5	1.000	OF-20
1956	54	.304	.530	115	35	5	6	3	2.6	16	25	18	13	0	10	0	59	4	1	2	1.2	.984	OF-44

Bob Cerv *continued*

Year	Team	Games	BA	SA	AB	H	2B	3B	HR	HR%	R	RBI	BB	SO	SB	PH AB	PH H	PO	A	E	DP	TC/G	FA	G by Pos
1957	KC A	124	.272	.420	345	94	14	2	11	3.2	35	44	20	57	1	41	9	157	6	6	1	1.4	.964	OF-89
1958		141	.305	.592	515	157	20	7	38	7.4	93	104	50	82	3	6	2	311	13	5	3	2.3	.985	OF-136
1959		125	.285	.479	463	132	22	4	20	4.3	61	87	35	87	3	5	2	231	8	5	2	2.0	.980	OF-119
1960	2 teams	KC A (23G – .256)			NY A (87G – .250)																			
"	total	110	.252	.449	294	74	12	2	14	4.8	46	40	40	53	0	30	8	162	12	4	4	1.6	.978	OF-72, 1B-3
1961	2 teams	LA A (18G – .158)			NY A (57G – .271)																			
"	total	75	.234	.429	175	41	8	1	8	4.6	20	26	13	25	1	22	8	96	5	2	2	1.4	.981	OF-45, 1B-3
1962	2 teams	NY A (14G – .118)			HOU N (19G – .226)																			
"	total	33	.188	.333	48	9	1	0	2	4.2	3	3	4	13	0	20	4	8	1	1	0	0.3	.900	OF-9
12 yrs.		829	.276	.481	2261	624	96	26	105	4.6	320	374	212	392	12	213	55	1140	52	29	14	1.5	.976	OF-594, 1B-6

WORLD SERIES

Year	Team	Games	BA	SA	AB	H	2B	3B	HR	HR%	R	RBI	BB	SO	SB	PH AB	PH H	PO	A	E	DP	TC/G	FA	G by Pos
1955	NY A	5	.125	.313	16	2	0	0	1	6.3	1	1	0	4	0	1	1	10	0	0	0	2.0	1.000	OF-4
1956		1	1.000	1.000	1	1	0	0	0	0.0	0	0	0	0	0	1	1	0	0	0	0	2.0	—	OF-...
1960		4	.357	.357	14	5	0	0	0	0.0	1	0	0	3	0	1	1	8	0	1	0	2.3	.889	OF-3
3 yrs.		10	.258	.355	31	8	0	0	1	3.2	2	1	0	3	0	3	3	18	0	1	0	1.9	.947	OF-7

1st

Ron Cey

CEY, RONALD CHARLES (Penguin)
B. Feb. 15, 1948, Tacoma, Wash.   BR TR 5'10"   185 lbs.

Year	Team	Games	BA	SA	AB	H	2B	3B	HR	HR%	R	RBI	BB	SO	SB	PH AB	PH H	PO	A	E	DP	TC/G	FA	G by Pos
1971	LA N	2	.000	.000	2	0	0	0	0	0.0	0	0	0	2	0	2	0	0	0	0	0	0.0	—	
1972		11	.270	.378	37	10	1	0	1	2.7	3	3	7	10	0	0	0	7	20	3	1	2.7	.900	3B-11
1973		152	.245	.385	507	124	18	4	15	3.0	60	80	74	77	1	7	1	111	328	18	39	3.0	.961	3B-146
1974		159	.262	.397	577	151	20	2	18	3.1	88	97	76	68	1	0	0	155	365	22	25	3.4	.959	3B-158
1975		158	.283	.473	566	160	29	2	25	4.4	72	101	78	74	5	0	0	144	309	19	23	3.0	.960	3B-158
1976		145	.277	.462	502	139	18	3	23	4.6	69	80	89	74	0	1	0	111	334	16	22	3.2	.965	3B-144
1977		153	.241	.450	564	136	22	3	30	5.3	77	110	93	106	3	1	0	138	346	18	29	3.3	.964	3B-153
1978		159	.270	.452	555	150	32	0	23	4.1	84	84	96	96	2	1	0	116	336	16	26	2.9	.966	3B-158
1979		150	.281	.499	487	137	20	1	28	5.7	77	81	86	85	3	0	0	123	265	9	25	2.6	.977	3B-150
1980		157	.254	.452	551	140	25	0	28	5.1	81	77	69	92	2	0	0	127	317	13	24	2.9	.972	3B-157
1981		85	.288	.474	312	90	15	2	13	4.2	42	50	40	55	0	1	1	71	184	16	15	3.2	.941	3B-84
1982		150	.254	.428	556	141	23	1	24	4.3	62	79	57	99	3	1	0	93	320	16	23	2.9	.963	3B-149
1983	CHI N	159	.275	.460	581	160	33	1	24	4.1	73	90	62	85	0	1	0	90	270	17	12	2.4	.955	3B-157
1984		146	.240	.442	505	121	27	0	25	5.0	71	97	61	108	3	2	1	97	230	11	22	2.3	.967	3B-144
1985		145	.232	.408	500	116	18	2	22	4.4	64	63	58	106	1	7	2	75	273	21	21	2.5	.943	3B-140
1986		97	.273	.508	256	70	21	0	13	5.1	42	36	44	66	0	13	3	41	118	8	7	1.7	.952	3B-77
1987	OAK A	45	.221	.394	104	23	6	0	4	3.8	12	11	22	32	0	7	2	56	4	1	4	1.4	.984	DH-30, 1B-7, 3B-3
17 yrs.		2073	.261	.445	7162	1868	328	21	316	4.4	977	1139	1012	1235	24	43	10	1555	4019	224	318	2.8	.961	3B-1989, DH-30, 1B-7

LEAGUE CHAMPIONSHIP SERIES

Year	Team	Games	BA	SA	AB	H	2B	3B	HR	HR%	R	RBI	BB	SO	SB	PH AB	PH H	PO	A	E	DP	TC/G	FA	G by Pos
1974	LA N	4	.313	.688	16	5	3	0	1	6.3	2	2	3	2	0	0	0	2	4	2	1	2.0	.750	3B-4
1977		4	.308	.615	13	4	1	0	1	7.7	4	2	4	1	1	0	0	7	14	1	0	5.5	.955	3B-4
1978		4	.313	.563	16	5	1	0	1	6.3	4	4	2	4	0	0	0	2	13	0	1	3.8	1.000	3B-4
1981		5	.278	.333	18	5	1	0	0	0.0	1	3	3	2	0	0	0	0	13	0	1	2.6	1.000	3B-5
1984	CHI N	5	.158	.368	19	3	1	0	1	5.3	2	3	3	3	0	0	0	1	7	0	0	1.6	1.000	3B-5
5 yrs.		22	.268	.500	82	22	7	0	4	4.9	14	14	13	15	1	0	0	12	38	4	2	2.5	.926	3B-22

WORLD SERIES

Year	Team	Games	BA	SA	AB	H	2B	3B	HR	HR%	R	RBI	BB	SO	SB	PH AB	PH H	PO	A	E	DP	TC/G	FA	G by Pos
1974	LA N	5	.176	.176	17	3	0	0	0	0.0	1	0	3	3	0	0	0	5	9	1	0	3.0	.933	3B-5
1977		6	.190	.381	21	4	1	0	1	4.8	2	3	3	5	0	0	0	5	7	0	0	2.0	1.000	3B-6
1978		6	.286	.429	21	6	0	0	1	4.8	2	4	3	3	0	0	0	2	12	0	1	2.3	1.000	3B-6
1981		6	.350	.500	20	7	0	0	1	5.0	3	6	3	3	0	0	0	4	11	0	1	2.5	1.000	3B-6
4 yrs.		23	.253	.380	79	20	1	0	3	3.8	8	13	12	14	0	0	0	16	39	1	2	2.4	.982	3B-23

Elio Chacon

CHACON, ELIO
Born Elio Chacon y Rodriguez.
B. Oct. 26, 1936, Caracas, Venezuela   BR TR 5'9"   160 lbs.

Year	Team	Games	BA	SA	AB	H	2B	3B	HR	HR%	R	RBI	BB	SO	SB	PH AB	PH H	PO	A	E	DP	TC/G	FA	G by Pos
1960	CIN N	49	.181	.190	116	21	1	0	0	0.0	14	7	14	23	7	3	0	100	95	4	25	4.1	.980	2B-43, OF-2
1961		61	.265	.371	132	35	4	2	2	1.5	26	5	21	22	1	1	0	85	104	2	22	3.1	.990	2B-58, OF-8
1962	NY N	118	.236	.296	368	87	10	3	2	0.5	49	27	76	64	12	3	0	206	333	22	64	4.8	.961	SS-110, 2B-2, 3B-1
3 yrs.		228	.232	.292	616	143	15	5	4	0.6	89	39	111	109	20	7	0	391	532	28	111	4.2	.971	SS-110, 2B-87, OF-10, 3B-1

WORLD SERIES

Year	Team	Games	BA	SA	AB	H	2B	3B	HR	HR%	R	RBI	BB	SO	SB	PH AB	PH H	PO	A	E	DP	TC/G	FA	G by Pos
1961	CIN N	4	.250	.250	12	3	0	0	0	0.0	2	0	1	2	0	1	0	12	9	0	4	5.3	1.000	2B-3

Chet Chadbourne

CHADBOURNE, CHESTER JAMES (Pop)
B. Oct. 26, 1884, Parkman, Me.   D. June 21, 1943, Los Angeles, Calif.   BL TR 5'9"   170 lbs.

Year	Team	Games	BA	SA	AB	H	2B	3B	HR	HR%	R	RBI	BB	SO	SB	PH AB	PH H	PO	A	E	DP	TC/G	FA	G by Pos
1906	BOS A	11	.302	.326	43	13	0	0	0	0.0	7	3	3		1			23	48	6	4	7.0	.922	2B-11, SS-1
1907		10	.289	.289	38	11	0	0	0	0.0	0	1	7		1			16	1	0	0	1.7	1.000	OF-10
1914	KC F	147	.277	.348	581	161	22	8	1	0.2	92	37	69		42	1	0	238	34	10	6	1.9	.965	OF-146
1915		152	.227	.290	587	133	16	9	1	0.2	75	35	62		29	0	0	308	24	7	7	2.2	.976	OF-152
1918	BOS N	27	.260	.298	104	27	2	1	0	0.0	9	6	5	5	5	0	0	60	2	5	1	2.5	.925	OF-27
5 yrs.		347	.255	.316	1353	345	41	18	2	0.1	183	82	146	5	78	1	0	645	109	28	18	2.3	.964	OF-335, 2B-11, SS-1

Dave Chalk

CHALK, DAVID LEE
B. Aug. 30, 1950, Del Rio, Tex.   BR TR 5'10"   175 lbs.

Year	Team	Games	BA	SA	AB	H	2B	3B	HR	HR%	R	RBI	BB	SO	SB	PH AB	PH H	PO	A	E	DP	TC/G	FA	G by Pos
1973	CAL A	24	.232	.261	69	16	2	0	0	0.0	14	6	9	13	0	0	0	36	66	4	20	4.4	.962	SS-22
1974		133	.252	.316	465	117	9	3	5	1.1	44	31	30	57	10	0	0	200	350	34	71	4.4	.942	SS-99, 3B-38
1975		149	.273	.345	513	140	24	2	3	0.6	59	56	66	49	0	0	0	108	333	11	30	3.0	.976	3B-149
1976		142	.217	.253	438	95	14	1	0	0.0	39	33	49	62	0	0	0	176	387	17	54	4.1	.971	SS-102, 3B-49
1977		149	.277	.355	519	144	27	2	3	0.6	58	45	52	69	12	2	0	147	287	25	27	3.1	.946	3B-141, 2B-7, SS-4
1978		135	.253	.285	470	119	12	0	1	0.2	42	34	38	34	5	0	0	216	339	23	62	4.3	.960	SS-97, 2B-29, 3B-22, DH-1

Year Team	Games	BA	SA	AB	H	2B	3B	HR	HR%	R	RBI	BB	SO	SB	Pinch Hit AB	Pinch Hit H	PO	A	E	DP	TC/G	FA	G by Pos

Dave Chalk *continued*

Year Team	Games	BA	SA	AB	H	2B	3B	HR	HR%	R	RBI	BB	SO	SB	AB	H	PO	A	E	DP	TC/G	FA	G by Pos
1979 2 teams	TEX A (9G – .250)			OAK A	(66G – .222)																		
" total	75	.223	.277	220	49	6	0	2	0.9	15	13	29	14	2	8	3	123	154	11	31	3.8	.962	2B-38, SS-19, 3B-16, DH-2
1980 KC A	69	.251	.341	167	42	10	1	1	0.6	19	20	18	27	1	14	2	57	88	6	10	2.2	.960	3B-33, 2B-17, DH-6, SS-1
1981	27	.224	.286	49	11	3	0	0	0.0	2	5	4	2	0	4	2	19	31	1	5	1.9	.980	3B-14, 2B-10, SS-1
9 yrs.	903	.252	.310	2910	733	107	9	15	0.5	292	243	295	327	36	28	7	1082	2035	132	310	3.6	.959	3B-462, SS-345, 2B-101, DH-9

WORLD SERIES

Year Team	Games	BA	SA	AB	H	2B	3B	HR	HR%	R	RBI	BB	SO	SB	AB	H	PO	A	E	DP	TC/G	FA	G by Pos
1980 KC A	1	–	–	0	0	0	0	0	–	1	0	1	0	1	0	0	0	1	0	0	1.0	1.000	3B-1

Joe Chamberlain

CHAMBERLAIN, JOSEPH JEREMIAH
B. May 10, 1910, San Francisco, Calif.   D. Jan. 28, 1983, San Francisco, Calif.
BR TR 6'1"   175 lbs.

Year Team	Games	BA	SA	AB	H	2B	3B	HR	HR%	R	RBI	BB	SO	SB	AB	H	PO	A	E	DP	TC/G	FA	G by Pos
1934 CHI A	43	.241	.333	141	34	5	1	2	1.4	13	17	6	38	1	0	0	42	97	20	12	3.7	.874	SS-26, 3B-14

Al Chambers

CHAMBERS, ALBERT EUGENE
B. Mar. 24, 1961, Harrisburg, Pa.
BL TL 6'4"   210 lbs.

Year Team	Games	BA	SA	AB	H	2B	3B	HR	HR%	R	RBI	BB	SO	SB	AB	H	PO	A	E	DP	TC/G	FA	G by Pos
1983 SEA A	31	.209	.299	67	14	3	0	1	1.5	11	7	18	20	0	7	0	3	0	0	0	0.1	1.000	DH-22, OF-3
1984	22	.224	.306	49	11	1	0	1	2.0	4	4	3	12	2	8	2	18	0	1	0	0.9	.947	OF-13, DH-1
1985	4	.000	.000	4	0	0	0	0	0.0	0	0	0	2	0	4	0	0	0	0	0	0.0	–	
3 yrs.	57	.208	.292	120	25	4	0	2	1.7	15	11	21	34	2	19	2	21	0	1	0	0.4	.955	DH-23, OF-16

Chris Chambliss

CHAMBLISS, CARROLL CHRISTOPHER
B. Dec. 26, 1948, Dayton, Ohio
BL TR 6'1"   195 lbs.

Year Team	Games	BA	SA	AB	H	2B	3B	HR	HR%	R	RBI	BB	SO	SB	AB	H	PO	A	E	DP	TC/G	FA	G by Pos
1971 CLE A	111	.275	.407	415	114	20	4	9	2.2	49	48	40	83	2	2	0	943	55	8	85	9.1	.992	1B-108
1972	121	.292	.397	466	136	27	2	6	1.3	51	44	26	63	3	2	0	1109	56	8	109	9.7	.993	1B-119
1973	155	.273	.390	572	156	30	2	11	1.9	70	53	58	76	4	1	0	1437	114	14	153	10.1	.991	1B-154
1974 2 teams	127	CLE A (17G – .328)		NY A	(110G – .243)																		
" total	127	.255	.349	467	119	20	3	6	1.3	46	50	28	48	0	4	0	1035	84	11	107	8.9	.990	1B-123
1975 NY A	150	.304	.434	562	171	38	4	9	1.6	66	72	29	50	0	3	0	1222	106	12	113	8.9	.991	1B-147
1976	156	.293	.441	641	188	32	6	17	2.7	79	96	27	80	1	0	0	1440	109	9	123	10.0	.994	1B-155, DH-1
1977	157	.287	.445	600	172	32	6	17	2.8	90	90	45	73	4	4	2	1368	98	16	129	9.4	.989	1B-157
1978	162	.274	.382	625	171	26	3	12	1.9	81	90	41	60	2	1	0	1366	111	4	119	9.1	.997	1B-155, DH-7
1979	149	.280	.437	554	155	27	3	18	3.2	61	63	34	53	3	2	1	1299	95	7	135	9.4	.995	1B-134, DH-16
1980 ATL N	158	.282	.440	602	170	37	2	18	3.0	83	72	49	73	7	0	0	1626	101	12	140	11.0	.993	1B-158
1981	107	.272	.403	404	110	25	2	8	2.0	44	51	44	41	4	0	0	1046	94	4	83	10.7	.997	1B-107
1982	157	.270	.436	534	144	25	2	20	3.7	57	86	57	57	7	11	5	1352	138	10	144	9.6	.993	1B-151
1983	131	.280	.481	447	125	24	3	20	4.5	59	78	63	68	2	8	5	1092	89	5	117	9.1	.996	1B-126
1984	133	.257	.362	389	100	14	0	9	2.3	47	44	58	54	1	24	4	996	70	8	84	8.1	.993	1B-109
1985	101	.235	.329	170	40	7	0	3	1.8	16	21	18	22	0	54	11	299	25	1	31	3.2	.997	1B-39
1986	97	.311	.426	122	38	8	0	2	1.6	13	14	15	24	0	68	20	141	6	1	15	1.5	.993	1B-20
1988 NY A	1	.000	.000	1	0	0	0	0	0.0	0	0	0	1	0	1	0	0	0	0	0	0.0	–	
17 yrs.	2173	.279	.415	7571	2109	392	42	185	2.4	912	972	632	926	40	185	48	17771	1351	130	1687	8.9	.993	1B-1962, DH-24

LEAGUE CHAMPIONSHIP SERIES

Year Team	Games	BA	SA	AB	H	2B	3B	HR	HR%	R	RBI	BB	SO	SB	AB	H	PO	A	E	DP	TC/G	FA	G by Pos
1976 NY A	5	.524	.952	21	11	1	1	2	9.5	5	8	0	1	2	0	0	50	3	1	3	10.8	.981	1B-5
1977	5	.059	.059	17	1	0	0	0	0.0	0	0	3	4	0	0	0	35	7	0	2	8.4	1.000	1B-5
1978	4	.400	.400	15	6	0	0	0	0.0	0	2	0	4	0	0	0	28	1	0	1	7.3	1.000	1B-4
1982 ATL N	3	.000	.000	10	0	0	0	0	0.0	1	0	1	0	0	0	0	0	0	0	0	0.0	–	1B-3
4 yrs.	17	.286	.429	63	18	1	1	2	3.2	6	10	4	9	2	0	0	113	11	1	6	7.4	.992	1B-17

WORLD SERIES

Year Team	Games	BA	SA	AB	H	2B	3B	HR	HR%	R	RBI	BB	SO	SB	AB	H	PO	A	E	DP	TC/G	FA	G by Pos
1976 NY A	4	.313	.375	16	5	1	0	0	0.0	1	1	0	2	0	0	0	26	3	1	6	7.5	.967	1B-4
1977	6	.292	.500	24	7	2	0	1	4.2	4	4	0	2	0	0	0	55	5	0	2	10.0	1.000	1B-6
1978	3	.182	.182	11	2	0	0	0	0.0	1	0	1	1	0	0	0	18	0	0	4	6.0	1.000	1B-3
3 yrs.	13	.275	.392	51	14	3	0	1	2.0	6	5	1	5	0	0	0	99	8	1	12	8.3	.991	1B-13

Mike Champion

CHAMPION, ROBERT MICHAEL
B. Feb. 10, 1955, Montgomery, Ala.
BR TR 6'   185 lbs.

Year Team	Games	BA	SA	AB	H	2B	3B	HR	HR%	R	RBI	BB	SO	SB	AB	H	PO	A	E	DP	TC/G	FA	G by Pos
1976 SD N	11	.237	.368	38	9	2	0	1	2.6	4	2	1	3	0	0	0	23	24	3	2	4.5	.940	2B-11
1977	150	.229	.286	507	116	14	6	1	0.2	35	43	27	85	3	1	1	301	348	17	82	4.4	.974	2B-149
1978	32	.226	.302	53	12	0	2	0	0.0	3	4	5	13	0	6	2	24	45	5	12	2.3	.932	2B-20, 3B-4
3 yrs.	193	.229	.293	598	137	16	8	2	0.3	42	49	33	101	3	7	3	348	417	25	96	4.1	.968	2B-180, 3B-4

Bob Chance

CHANCE, ROBERT
B. Sept. 10, 1940, Statesboro, Ga.
BL TR 6'2"   196 lbs.

Year Team	Games	BA	SA	AB	H	2B	3B	HR	HR%	R	RBI	BB	SO	SB	AB	H	PO	A	E	DP	TC/G	FA	G by Pos
1963 CLE A	16	.288	.481	52	15	4	0	2	3.8	5	7	1	10	0	2	0	20	0	2	0	1.4	.909	OF-14
1964	120	.279	.433	390	109	16	1	14	3.6	45	75	40	101	3	19	5	606	24	7	47	5.3	.989	1B-81, OF-31
1965 WAS A	72	.256	.362	199	51	9	0	4	2.0	20	14	18	44	0	19	5	396	25	5	39	5.9	.988	1B-48, OF-3
1966	37	.175	.281	57	10	3	0	1	1.8	1	8	2	23	0	24	4	73	3	2	6	2.1	.974	1B-13
1967	27	.214	.476	42	9	2	0	3	7.1	5	7	7	13	0	13	3	75	5	0	6	3.0	1.000	1B-10
1969 CAL A	5	.143	.143	7	1	0	0	0	0.0	0	1	0	4	0	4	1	10	0	1	0	2.2	.909	1B-1
6 yrs.	277	.261	.406	747	195	34	1	24	3.2	76	112	68	195	3	81	18	1180	57	17	98	4.5	.986	1B-153, OF-48

Frank Chance

CHANCE, FRANK LEROY (Husk, The Peerless Leader)
B. Sept. 9, 1877, Fresno, Calif.   D. Sept. 15, 1924, Los Angeles, Calif.
Manager 1905-14, 1923.
Hall of Fame 1946.
BR TR 6'   190 lbs.

Year Team	Games	BA	SA	AB	H	2B	3B	HR	HR%	R	RBI	BB	SO	SB	AB	H	PO	A	E	DP	TC/G	FA	G by Pos
1898 CHI N	53	.279	.367	147	41	4	3	1	0.7	32	14	7		7	2	1	103	19	13	4	2.5	.904	C-33, OF-17, 1B-3
1899	64	.286	.354	192	55	6	2	1	0.5	37	22	15		10	3	0	168	64	12	6	3.8	.951	C-57, OF-1, 1B-1
1900	56	.295	.396	149	44	9	3	0	0.0	26	13	15		9	4	1	160	66	17	2	4.3	.930	C-51, 1B-1
1901	69	.278	.361	241	67	12	4	0	0.0	38	36	29		30	2	1	143	30	10	3	2.7	.945	OF-50, C-13, 1B-6
1902	75	.284	.369	236	67	9	4	1	0.4	40	31	35		28	4	1	508	47	17	23	7.6	.970	1B-38, C-29, OF-4

Year	Team	Games	BA	SA	AB	H	2B	3B	HR	HR%	R	RBI	BB	SO	SB	Pinch Hit AB	Pinch Hit H	PO	A	E	DP	TC/G	FA	G by Pos

Frank Chance *continued*

Year	Team	Games	BA	SA	AB	H	2B	3B	HR	HR%	R	RBI	BB	SO	SB	PH AB	PH H	PO	A	E	DP	TC/G	FA	G by Pos
1903		125	.327	.440	441	144	24	10	2	0.5	83	81	78		**67**	2	1	1212	68	37	49			
1904		124	.310	.430	451	140	16	10	6	1.3	89	49	36		42	0	0	1213	107	13	48	10.5	.972	1B-121, C-2
1905		118	.316	.434	392	124	16	12	2	0.5	92	70	78		38	3	0	1165	75	13	54	10.8	.990	1B-123, C-1
1906		136	.319	.430	474	151	24	10	3	0.6	**103**	71	70		**57**	0	0	1376	82	16	71	10.6	.990	1B-115
1907		111	.293	.361	382	112	19	2	1	0.3	58	49	51		35	2	1	1129	80	10	64	10.8	.989	1B-136
1908		129	.272	.363	452	123	27	4	2	0.4	65	55	37		27	4	2	1291	86	15	56	11.0	.992	1B-109
1909		93	.272	.346	324	88	16	4	0	0.0	53	46	30		29	0	0	901	40	6	43	10.8	.989	1B-126
1910		88	.298	.393	295	88	12	8	0	0.0	54	36	37	15	16	1	0	773	38	3	48	10.2	.994	1B-92
1911		31	.239	.409	88	21	6	3	1	1.1	23	17	25	13	9	1	0	289	11	3	12	9.3	.996	1B-87
1912		2	.200	.200	5	1	0	0	0	0.0	2	0	3	0	1	0	0	22	0	0	1	9.8	.990	1B-29
1913	NY A	11	.208	.208	24	5	0	0	0	0.0	3	6	8	1	1	3	0	86	5	0	2	11.0	1.000	1B-2
1914		1	–	–	0	0	0	0	0	–	0	0	0	0	0	0	0	1	0	0	0	8.3	1.000	1B-8
17 yrs.		1286	.296	.393	4293	1271	200	79	20	0.5	798	596	554	29	405	31	8	10540	818	185	486	1.0	1.000	1B-1
																						9.0	.984	1B-998, C-186, OF-72

WORLD SERIES

Year	Team	Games	BA	SA	AB	H	2B	3B	HR	HR%	R	RBI	BB	SO	SB	PH AB	PH H	PO	A	E	DP	TC/G	FA	G by Pos
1906	CHI N	6	.238	.286	21	5	0	0	0	0.0	2	1	2		2	0	0	60	2	0	1	10.3	1.000	1B-6
1907		4	.214	.286	14	3	1	0	0	0.0	3	0	3	2	3	0	0	44	1	0	3	11.3	1.000	1B-4
1908		5	.421	.421	19	8	0	0	0	0.0	4	2	3	1	5	0	0	66	0	3	3	13.8	.957	1B-5
1910		5	.353	.529	17	6	1	1	0	0.0	2	4	0	2	0	0	0	51	4	0	2	11.0	1.000	1B-5
4 yrs.		20	.310	.380	71	22	3	1	0	0.0	11	6	8	6	10	0	0	221	7	3	9	11.6	.987	1B-20
															3rd									

Darrel Chaney

CHANEY, DARREL LEE
B. Mar. 9, 1948, Hammond, Ind.

BB TR 6'2" 188 lbs.

Year	Team	Games	BA	SA	AB	H	2B	3B	HR	HR%	R	RBI	BB	SO	SB	PH AB	PH H	PO	A	E	DP	TC/G	FA	G by Pos
1969	CIN N	93	.191	.234	209	40	5	2	0	0.0	21	15	24	75	1	1	1	115	191	17	44	3.5	.947	SS-91
1970		57	.232	.295	95	22	3	0	1	1.1	7	4	3	26	1	9	2	56	90	9	15	2.7	.942	SS-30, 2B-18, 3B-3
1971		10	.125	.125	24	3	0	0	0	0.0	2	1	1	3	0	1	0	16	21	0	1	3.7	1.000	SS-7, 3B-1, 2B-1
1972		83	.250	.337	196	49	7	2	2	1.0	29	19	29	28	1	3	2	100	178	10	30	3.5	.965	SS-64, 3B-12, 2B-10
1973		105	.181	.220	227	41	7	1	0	0.0	27	14	26	50	4	3	2	123	246	14	52	3.6	.963	SS-75, 2B-14, 3B-12
1974		117	.200	.304	135	27	6	1	2	1.5	27	16	26	33	1	0	0	90	135	9	21	2.0	.962	3B-81, 2B-38, SS-12
1975	ATL N	71	.219	.294	160	35	6	0	2	1.3	18	26	14	38	3	5	1	77	164	7	27	3.5	.972	SS-34, 2B-23, 3B-13
1976		153	.252	.331	496	125	20	8	1	0.2	42	50	54	92	5	4	2	243	468	37	88	4.9	.951	SS-151, 3B-1, 2B-1
1977		74	.201	.297	209	42	7	2	3	1.4	22	15	17	44	0	14	3	113	182	8	30	4.1	.974	SS-41, 2B-24
1978		89	.224	.306	245	55	9	1	3	1.2	27	20	25	48	1	15	6	100	199	7	32	3.4	.977	SS-77, 3B-8, 2B-1
1979		63	.162	.205	117	19	5	0	0	0.0	15	10	19	34	1	12	2	45	95	8	16	2.3	.946	SS-39, 2B-5, 3B-4, C-1
11 yrs.		915	.217	.288	2113	458	75	17	14	0.7	237	190	238	471	19	67	21	1078	1969	126	356	3.5	.960	SS-621, 2B-137, 3B-133, C-1

LEAGUE CHAMPIONSHIP SERIES

Year	Team	Games	BA	SA	AB	H	2B	3B	HR	HR%	R	RBI	BB	SO	SB	PH AB	PH H	PO	A	E	DP	TC/G	FA	G by Pos
1972	CIN N	5	.188	.188	16	3	0	0	0	0.0	3	1	1	1	1	0	0	8	16	3	2	5.4	.889	SS-5
1973		5	.000	.000	9	0	0	0	0	0.0	0	0	3	4	0	0	0	2	10	0	3	2.4	1.000	SS-5
2 yrs.		10	.120	.120	25	3	0	0	0	0.0	3	1	4	5	1	0	0	10	26	3	5	3.9	.923	SS-10

WORLD SERIES

Year	Team	Games	BA	SA	AB	H	2B	3B	HR	HR%	R	RBI	BB	SO	SB	PH AB	PH H	PO	A	E	DP	TC/G	FA	G by Pos
1970	CIN N	3	.000	.000	1	0	0	0	0	0.0	0	0	0	1	0	0	0	1	2	0	0	1.0	1.000	SS-3
1972		4	.000	.000	7	0	0	0	0	0.0	0	0	2	2	0	0	0	5	11	0	2	4.0	1.000	SS-3
1975		2	.000	.000	2	0	0	0	0	0.0	0	0	0	1	0	2	0	0	0	0	0	0.0	–	
3 yrs.		9	.000	.000	10	0	0	0	0	0.0	0	0	2	4	0	2	0	6	13	0	2	2.1	1.000	SS-6

Les Channell

CHANNELL, LESTER CLARK (Dude)
B. Mar. 3, 1886, Crestline, Ohio D. May 7, 1954, Denver, Colo.

BL TL 6' 180 lbs.

Year	Team	Games	BA	SA	AB	H	2B	3B	HR	HR%	R	RBI	BB	SO	SB	PH AB	PH H	PO	A	E	DP	TC/G	FA	G by Pos
1910	NY A	6	.316	.316	19	6	0	0	0	0.0	3	3	2		2	0	0	9	0	0	0	1.5	1.000	OF-6
1914		1	1.000	2.000	1	1	1	0	0	0.0	0	0	0		0	1	1	0	0	0	0	0.0	–	
2 yrs.		7	.350	.400	20	7	1	0	0	0.0	3	3	2	0	2	1	1	9	0	0	0	1.3	1.000	OF-6

Charlie Chant

CHANT, CHARLES JOSEPH
B. Aug. 7, 1951, Bell, Calif.

BR TR 6' 190 lbs.

Year	Team	Games	BA	SA	AB	H	2B	3B	HR	HR%	R	RBI	BB	SO	SB	PH AB	PH H	PO	A	E	DP	TC/G	FA	G by Pos
1975	OAK A	5	.000	.000	5	0	0	0	0	0.0	1	0	0	0	0	0	0	1	0	0	0	0.2	1.000	OF-5, DH-1
1976	STL N	15	.143	.143	14	2	0	0	0	0.0	0	0	0	4	0	1	0	15	1	0	0	1.1	1.000	OF-14
2 yrs.		20	.105	.105	19	2	0	0	0	0.0	1	0	0	4	0	1	0	16	1	0	0	0.9	1.000	OF-19, DH-1

Ed Chaplin

CHAPLIN, BERT EDGAR (Chappy)
Born Bert Edgar Chapman.
B. Sept. 25, 1893, Pelzer, S. C. D. Aug. 15, 1978, Sanford, Fla.

BL TR 5'7" 158 lbs.

Year	Team	Games	BA	SA	AB	H	2B	3B	HR	HR%	R	RBI	BB	SO	SB	PH AB	PH H	PO	A	E	DP	TC/G	FA	G by Pos
1920	BOS A	4	.200	.400	5	1	1	0	0	0.0	2	1	4	1	0	1	0	8	1	1	1	2.5	.900	C-2
1921		3	.000	.000	2	0	0	0	0	0.0	0	0	0	1	0	2	0	0	1	0	0	0.3	1.000	C-1
1922		28	.188	.232	69	13	1	1	0	0.0	8	6	9	9	2	6	0	56	16	3	2	2.7	.960	C-21
3 yrs.		35	.184	.237	76	14	2	1	0	0.0	10	7	13	11	2	8	0	64	18	4	3	2.5	.953	C-24

Ben Chapman

CHAPMAN, WILLIAM BENJAMIN
B. Dec. 25, 1908, Nashville, Tenn.
Manager 1945-48.

BR TR 6' 190 lbs.

Year	Team	Games	BA	SA	AB	H	2B	3B	HR	HR%	R	RBI	BB	SO	SB	PH AB	PH H	PO	A	E	DP	TC/G	FA	G by Pos
1930	NY A	138	.316	.474	513	162	31	10	10	1.9	74	81	43	58	14	2	0	232	295	42	47	4.1	.926	3B-91, 2B-45
1931		149	.315	.483	600	189	28	11	17	2.8	120	122	75	77	**61**	1	0	325	47	14	5	2.6	.964	OF-137, 2B-11
1932		150	.299	.473	581	174	41	15	10	1.7	101	107	71	55	**38**	1	0	303	13	17	2	2.2	.949	OF-149
1933		147	.312	.437	565	176	36	4	9	1.6	112	98	72	45	**27**	0	0	288	24	8	4	2.2	.975	OF-147
1934		149	.308	.413	588	181	21	13	5	0.9	82	86	67	68	26	0	0	368	12	13	2	2.6	.967	OF-149
1935		140	.289	.430	553	160	38	8	8	1.4	118	74	61	39	17	2	0	372	25	15	7	2.9	.964	OF-138
1936 2 teams	NY A (36G – .266)				WAS A (97G – .332)																			
" total		133	.315	.472	540	170	50	10	5	0.9	110	81	84	38	20	0	0	377	13	16	4	3.1	.961	OF-133

Year	Team	Games	BA	SA	AB	H	2B	3B	HR	HR%	R	RBI	BB	SO	SB	Pinch Hit AB	Pinch Hit H	PO	A	E	DP	TC/G	FA	G by Pos

Ben Chapman *continued*

Year	Team	Games	BA	SA	AB	H	2B	3B	HR	HR%	R	RBI	BB	SO	SB	AB	H	PO	A	E	DP	TC/G	FA	G by Pos
1937	2 teams	WAS A (35G – .262)			BOS A (113G – .307)																			
"	total	148	.297	.432	553	164	30	12	7	1.3	99	69	83	42	35	2	1	349	11	9	1	2.5	.976	OF-144, SS-1
1938	BOS A	127	.340	.494	480	163	40	8	6	1.3	92	80	65	33	13	1	1	267	16	10	5	2.3	.966	OF-126, 3B-1
1939	CLE A	149	.290	.413	545	158	31	9	6	1.1	101	82	87	30	18	2	1	356	12	11	0	2.5	.971	OF-146
1940		143	.286	.403	548	157	40	6	4	0.7	82	50	78	45	13	3	1	307	10	12	3	2.3	.964	OF-140
1941	2 teams	WAS A (28G – .255)			CHI A (57G – .226)																			
"	total	85	.237	.323	300	71	15	1	3	1.0	35	29	29	20	4	10	2	176	9	1	2	2.2	.995	OF-75
1944	BKN N	20	.368	.474	38	14	4	0	0	0.0	11	11	5	4	1	9	3	3	6	1	0	0.5	.900	P-11
1945	2 teams	BKN N (13G – .136)			PHI N (24G – .314)																			
"	total	37	.260	.288	73	19	2	0	0	0.0	6	7	4	2	0	10	4	17	21	4	3	1.1	.905	P-10, 3B-4
1946	PHI N	1	.000	.000	1	0	0	0	0	0.0	1	0	0	0	0	0	0	0	0	0	0	–	.000	P-1
15 yrs.		1716	.302	.440	6478	1958	407	107	90	1.4	1144	977	824	556	287	43	13	3740	514	173	85	2.6	.961	OF-1494, 3B-96, 2B-56, P-25, SS-1

WORLD SERIES

Year	Team	Games	BA	SA	AB	H	2B	3B	HR	HR%	R	RBI	BB	SO	SB	AB	H	PO	A	E	DP	TC/G	FA	G by Pos
1932	NY A	4	.294	.353	17	5	1	0	0	0.0	1	6	2	4	0	0	0	6	1	0	0	1.8	1.000	OF-4

Calvin Chapman

CHAPMAN, CALVIN LOUIS　　　　　BL TR 5'9"　160 lbs.
B. Dec. 20, 1910, Courtland, Miss.　　　　BB 1935
D. Apr. 1, 1983, Batesville, Miss.

Year	Team	Games	BA	SA	AB	H	2B	3B	HR	HR%	R	RBI	BB	SO	SB	AB	H	PO	A	E	DP	TC/G	FA	G by Pos
1935	CIN N	15	.340	.358	53	18	1	0	0	0.0	6	3	4	5	2	0	0	27	34	4	9	4.3	.938	SS-12, 2B-4
1936		96	.247	.320	219	54	7	3	1	0.5	35	22	16	19	5	40	15	85	49	4	6	1.4	.971	OF-31, 2B-23, 3B-1
2 yrs.		111	.265	.327	272	72	8	3	1	0.4	41	25	20	24	7	40	15	112	83	8	15	1.8	.961	OF-31, 2B-27, SS-12, 3B-1

Fred Chapman

CHAPMAN, WILLIAM FRED (Chappie)　　　　　BR TR 6'1"　185 lbs.
B. July 17, 1916, Liberty, S. C.

Year	Team	Games	BA	SA	AB	H	2B	3B	HR	HR%	R	RBI	BB	SO	SB	AB	H	PO	A	E	DP	TC/G	FA	G by Pos
1939	PHI A	15	.286	.347	49	14	1	1	0	0.0	5	1	1	3	1	0	0	24	38	7	5	4.6	.899	SS-15
1940		26	.159	.174	69	11	1	0	0	0.0	6	4	6	10	1	0	0	40	54	15	12	4.2	.862	SS-25
1941		35	.159	.174	69	11	1	0	0	0.0	1	4	4	15	1	2	1	22	56	8	7	2.5	.907	SS-28, 3B-2, 2B-1
3 yrs.		76	.193	.219	187	36	3	1	0	0.0	12	9	11	28	3	2	1	86	148	30	24	3.5	.886	SS-68, 3B-2, 2B-1

Glenn Chapman

CHAPMAN, GLENN JUSTICE (Pete)　　　　　BR TR 5'11½" 170 lbs.
B. Jan. 21, 1906, Cambridge City, Ind.　D. Nov. 5, 1988, Richmond, Ind.

Year	Team	Games	BA	SA	AB	H	2B	3B	HR	HR%	R	RBI	BB	SO	SB	AB	H	PO	A	E	DP	TC/G	FA	G by Pos
1934	BKN N	67	.280	.387	93	26	5	1	1	1.1	19	10	7	19	1	2	0	66	28	3	4	1.4	.969	OF-40, 2B-14

Harry Chapman

CHAPMAN, HARRY E.　　　　　BR TR 5'11" 160 lbs.
B. Oct. 26, 1887, Severance, Kans. D. Oct. 21, 1918, Nevada, Mo.

Year	Team	Games	BA	SA	AB	H	2B	3B	HR	HR%	R	RBI	BB	SO	SB	AB	H	PO	A	E	DP	TC/G	FA	G by Pos
1912	CHI N	1	.250	.750	4	1	0	1	0	0.0	1	0	0		0	1	0	7	3	0	0	10.0	1.000	C-1
1913	CIN N	2	.500	.500	2	1	0	0	0	0.0	0	0	0	1	0	2	1	0	0	0	0	0.0	–	
1914	STL F	64	.210	.232	181	38	2	1	0	0.0	16	14	13		2	4	1	248	78	9	8	5.2	.973	C-51, OF-1, 2B-1, 1B-1
1915		62	.199	.280	186	37	6	3	1	0.5	19	29	22		4	8	1	293	79	4	6	6.1	.989	C-53
1916	STL A	18	.097	.097	31	3	0	0	0	0.0	2	0	2	5	0	3	0	37	15	1	2	2.9	.981	C-14
5 yrs.		147	.198	.250	404	80	8	5	1	0.2	38	44	37	6	7	17	3	585	175	14	16	5.3	.982	C-119, OF-1, 2B-1, 1B-1

Jack Chapman

CHAPMAN, JOHN CURTIS　　　　　TR 5'11" 170 lbs.
B. May 8, 1843, Brooklyn, N. Y. D. June 10, 1916, Brooklyn, N. Y.
Manager 1876-78, 1882-85, 1889-92.

Year	Team	Games	BA	SA	AB	H	2B	3B	HR	HR%	R	RBI	BB	SO	SB	AB	H	PO	A	E	DP	TC/G	FA	G by Pos
1876	LOU N	17	.239	.254	67	16	1	0	0	0.0	4	5	1	3		0	0	17	2	7	1	1.5	.731	OF-17, 3B-1

John Chapman

CHAPMAN, JOHN JOSEPH　　　　　BR TR 5'10" 180 lbs.
B. Oct. 15, 1899, Centralia, Pa. D. Nov. 3, 1953, Philadelphia, Pa.

Year	Team	Games	BA	SA	AB	H	2B	3B	HR	HR%	R	RBI	BB	SO	SB	AB	H	PO	A	E	DP	TC/G	FA	G by Pos
1924	PHI A	19	.282	.366	71	20	4	1	0	0.0	7	7	4	8	0	0	0	32	37	3	10	3.8	.958	SS-19

Kelvin Chapman

CHAPMAN, KELVIN KEITH　　　　　BR TR 5'11" 173 lbs.
B. June 2, 1956, Willits, Calif.

Year	Team	Games	BA	SA	AB	H	2B	3B	HR	HR%	R	RBI	BB	SO	SB	AB	H	PO	A	E	DP	TC/G	FA	G by Pos
1979	NY N	35	.150	.213	80	12	1	2	0	0.0	7	4	5	15	0	10	2	51	46	2	15	2.8	.980	2B-22, 3B-1
1984		75	.289	.401	197	57	13	0	3	1.5	27	23	19	30	8	14	5	105	133	6	33	3.3	.975	2B-56, 3B-3, SS-1
1985		62	.174	.194	144	25	3	0	0	0.0	16	7	9	15	5	20	6	70	89	5	17	2.6	.970	2B-48, 3B-1
3 yrs.		172	.223	.295	421	94	17	2	3	0.7	50	34	33	60	13	44	13	226	268	13	65	2.9	.974	2B-126, 3B-5, SS-1

Ray Chapman

CHAPMAN, RAYMOND JOHNSON　　　　　BR TR 5'10" 170 lbs.
B. Jan. 15, 1891, Beaver Dam, Ky. D. Aug. 17, 1920, New York, N. Y.

Year	Team	Games	BA	SA	AB	H	2B	3B	HR	HR%	R	RBI	BB	SO	SB	AB	H	PO	A	E	DP	TC/G	FA	G by Pos
1912	CLE A	31	.312	.422	109	34	6	3	0	0.0	29	19	10		10	0	0	72	15	10	5.1	.904		SS-31
1913		140	.258	.341	508	131	19	7	3	0.6	78	39	46	51	29	1	0	299	408	48	59	5.4	.936	SS-138
1914		106	.275	.387	375	103	16	10	2	0.5	59	42	48	48	24	1	0	223	279	42	25	5.1	.923	SS-72, 2B-33
1915		154	.270	.370	570	154	14	17	3	0.5	101	67	70	82	36	0	0	378	469	50	38	5.8	.944	SS-154
1916		109	.231	.289	346	80	10	5	0	0.0	50	27	50	46	21	5	0	207	310	32	35	5.0	.942	SS-52, 3B-36, 2B-16
1917		156	.302	.410	563	170	28	12	3	0.5	98	36	61	65	52	0	0	360	528	59	71	6.1	.938	SS-156
1918		128	.267	.352	446	119	19	8	1	0.2	84	32	84	46	30	0	0	323	398	50	42	6.0	.935	SS-128, OF-1
1919		115	.300	.420	433	130	23	10	3	0.7	75	53	31	38	18	0	0	255	347	36	44	5.5	.944	SS-115
1920		111	.303	.423	435	132	27	8	3	0.7	97	49	52	38	13	0	0	243	371	26	43	5.8	.959	SS-111
9 yrs.		1050	.278	.378	3785	1053	162	80	18	0.5	671	364	452	414	233	7	0	2358	3182	358	367	5.6	.939	SS-957, 2B-49, 3B-36, OF-1

Sam Chapman

CHAPMAN, SAMUEL BLAKE　　　　　BR TR 6' 180 lbs.
B. Apr. 11, 1916, Tiburon, Calif.

Year	Team	Games	BA	SA	AB	H	2B	3B	HR	HR%	R	RBI	BB	SO	SB	AB	H	PO	A	E	DP	TC/G	FA	G by Pos
1938	PHI A	114	.259	.461	406	105	17	7	17	4.2	60	63	55	94	3	3	1	229	8	12	0	2.2	.952	OF-114
1939		140	.269	.432	498	134	24	6	15	3.0	74	64	51	62	11	7	1	497	16	21	8	3.8	.961	OF-117, 1B-19
1940		134	.276	.474	508	140	26	3	23	4.5	88	75	46	96	2	5	2	348	13	14	2	2.8	.963	OF-129
1941		143	.322	.543	552	178	29	9	25	4.5	97	106	47	49	6	2	0	416	21	15	5	3.2	.967	OF-141

Year	Team		Games	BA	SA	AB	H	2B	3B	HR	HR%	R	RBI	BB	SO	SB	Pinch Hit AB	Pinch Hit H	PO	A	E	DP	TC/G	FA	G by Pos

Sam Chapman *continued*

1945			9	.200	.267	30	6	2	0	0	0.0	3	1	2	4	0	0	0	18	0	0	0	2.0	1.000	OF-8
1946			146	.261	.429	545	142	22	5	20	3.7	77	67	54	66	1	1	0	369	13	12	4	2.7	.970	OF-145
1947			149	.252	.379	551	139	18	5	14	2.5	84	83	65	70	1	4	1	428	16	6	2	3.0	.987	OF-146
1948			123	.258	.413	445	115	18	6	13	2.9	58	70	55	50	5	4	0	368	8	7	2	3.1	.982	OF-118
1949			154	.278	.455	589	164	24	6	24	4.1	89	108	80	68	3	0	0	450	11	10	3	3.1	.979	OF-154
1950			144	.251	.434	553	139	20	6	23	4.2	93	95	68	79	3	3	0	428	11	10	4	3.1	.978	OF-140
1951	2 teams	PHI A									(18G – .169)		CLE A			(94G – .228)									
"	total		112	.215	.312	311	67	10	1	6	1.9	31	41	39	44	3	4	0	176	3	4	2	1.6	.978	OF-101, 1B-1
11 yrs.			1368	.266	.438	4988	1329	210	52	180	3.6	754	773	562	682	40	33	5	3727	120	111	32	2.9	.972	OF-1313, 1B-20

Harry Chappas

CHAPPAS, HARRY PERRY
B. Oct. 26, 1957, Mt. Rainier, Md.

BB TR 5'3"   150 lbs.

1978	CHI	A	20	.267	.280	75	20	1	0	0	0.0	11	6	6	11	1	0	0	28	64	0	8	4.6	1.000	SS-20
1979			26	.288	.356	59	17	1	0	1	1.7	9	4	5	5	1	1	1	28	63	7	13	3.8	.929	SS-23
1980			26	.160	.200	50	8	2	0	0	0.0	6	2	4	10	0	3	0	18	36	1	10	2.1	.982	SS-19, DH-2, 2B-1
3 yrs.			72	.245	.283	184	45	4	0	1	0.5	26	12	15	26	2	4	1	74	163	8	31	3.4	.967	SS-62, DH-2, 2B-1

Larry Chappell

CHAPPELL, LaVERNE ASHFORD
B. Feb. 19, 1890, McCluskey, Ill.   D. Nov. 8, 1918, San Francisco, Calif.

BL TL 6'   186 lbs.

1913	CHI	A	60	.231	.279	208	48	8	1	0	0.0	21	15	18	22	7	1	0	114	5	6	1	2.1	.952	OF-59
1914			21	.231	.231	39	9	0	0	0	0.0	3	1	4	11	0	10	1	13	0	1	0	0.7	.929	OF-9
1915			1	.000	.000	1	0	0	0	0	0.0	0	0	0	0	0	1	0	0	0	0	0	0.0	—	
1916	2 teams	CLE A			(3G – .000)		BOS N			(20G – .226)																
"	total		23	.218	.273	55	12	1	1	0	0.0	4	9	3	8	2	8	1	22	0	1	0	1.0	.957	OF-14
1917	BOS	N	4	.000	.000	2	0	0	0	0	0.0	0	0	0	1	0	2	0	0	0	0	0	0.0	—	OF-1
5 yrs.			109	.226	.269	305	69	9	2	0	0.0	28	26	25	42	9	22	3	149	5	8	1	1.5	.951	OF-83

Joe Charboneau

CHARBONEAU, JOSEPH
B. June 17, 1955, Belvedere, Ill.

BR TR 6'2"   205 lbs.

1980	CLE	A	131	.289	.488	453	131	17	2	23	5.1	76	87	49	70	2	8	5	125	6	5	1	1.0	.963	OF-67, DH-57
1981			48	.210	.362	138	29	7	1	4	2.9	14	18	7	22	1	7	2	51	1	2	0	1.1	.963	OF-27, DH-14
1982			22	.214	.393	56	12	2	1	2	3.6	7	9	5	7	0	6	2	21	0	1	0	1.0	.955	OF-18, DH-1
3 yrs.			201	.266	.453	647	172	26	4	29	4.5	97	114	61	99	3	21	9	197	7	8	1	1.1	.962	OF-112, DH-72

Chappy Charles

CHARLES, RAYMOND
Born Charles Shuh Achenbach.
B. Mar. 25, 1881, Phillipsburg, N. J.   D. Aug. 4, 1959, Bethlehem, Pa.

BR TR 5'11"   175 lbs.

1908	STL	N	121	.205	.256	454	93	14	3	1	0.2	39	17	19		15	2	0	215	322	49	25	4.8	.916	2B-65, SS-31, 3B-23
1909	2 teams	STL N			(99G – .236)		CIN N			(13G – .256)																
"	total		112	.238	.277	382	91	9	3	0	0.0	36	34	35		9	0	0	258	312	49	34	5.5	.921	2B-81, SS-31, 3B-2
1910	CIN	N	4	.133	.267	15	2	0	1	0	0.0	1	0	0		0	0	0	8	10	4	2	5.5	.818	SS-4
3 yrs.			237	.219	.266	851	186	23	7	1	0.1	76	51	54		1	24	2	0	481	644	102	61	5.2	.917	2B-146, SS-66, 3B-25

Ed Charles

CHARLES, EDWIN DOUGLAS (The Glider)
B. Apr. 29, 1933, Daytona Beach, Fla.

BR TR 5'10"   170 lbs.

1962	KC	A	147	.288	.454	535	154	24	7	17	3.2	81	74	54	70	20	7	0	148	286	16	28	3.1	.964	3B-140, 2B-2
1963			158	.267	.395	603	161	28	2	15	2.5	82	79	58	79	15	0	0	153	310	25	19	3.1	.949	3B-158
1964			150	.241	.379	557	134	25	2	16	2.9	69	63	64	92	12	5	1	138	259	19	25	2.8	.954	3B-147
1965			134	.269	.388	480	129	19	7	8	1.7	55	56	44	72	13	5	1	151	254	12	29	3.1	.971	3B-128, SS-1, 2B-1
1966	2 teams	KC A			(19G – .246)		NY N			(101G – .238)																
"	total		120	.240	.310	384	92	14	2	3	0.8	37	36	36	71	5	14	6	102	241	19	17	3.0	.948	3B-107
1968	NY	N	117	.276	.434	369	102	11	1	15	4.1	41	53	28	57	5	15	6	79	201	13	19	2.5	.956	3B-106, 1B-2
1969			61	.207	.320	169	35	8	1	3	1.8	21	18	18	31	4	12	4	37	86	7	9	2.1	.946	3B-52
8 yrs.			1005	.263	.397	3482	917	147	30	86	2.5	438	421	332	525	86	68	19	894	1838	122	167	2.8	.957	3B-942, 2B-3, 1B-3, OF-1, SS-1

WORLD SERIES

| 1969 | NY | N | 4 | .133 | .200 | 15 | 2 | 1 | 0 | 0 | 0.0 | 1 | 0 | 0 | 2 | 0 | 0 | 0 | 3 | 9 | 0 | 0 | 3.0 | 1.000 | 3B-4 |

Mike Chartak

CHARTAK, MICHAEL GEORGE (Shotgun)
B. Apr. 28, 1916, Brooklyn, N. Y.   D. July 25, 1967, Cedar Rapids, Iowa

BL TL 6'2"   180 lbs.

1940	NY	A	11	.133	.200	15	2	1	0	0	0.0	2	3	5	5	0	5	1	4	0	0	0	0.4	1.000	OF-3
1942	3 teams	NY A			(5G – .000)		WAS A			(24G – .217)		STL A			(73G – .249)											
"	total		102	.237	.395	334	79	15	4	10	3.0	48	51	54	43	3	12	3	190	12	8	4	2.1	.962	OF-88
1943	STL	A	108	.256	.401	344	88	16	2	10	2.9	38	37	39	55	1	18	3	321	13	9	10	3.2	.974	OF-77, 1B-18
1944			35	.236	.333	72	17	2	1	1	1.4	8	7	6	9	0	17	3	105	5	0	5	3.1	1.000	1B-12, OF-7
4 yrs.			256	.243	.388	765	186	34	7	21	2.7	96	98	104	112	4	52	10	620	30	17	19	2.6	.975	OF-175, 1B-30

WORLD SERIES

| 1944 | STL | A | 2 | .000 | .000 | 2 | 0 | 0 | 0 | 0 | 0.0 | 0 | 0 | 0 | 2 | 0 | 0 | 0 | 0 | 0 | 0 | 0 | 0.0 | — | |

Hal Chase

CHASE, HAROLD HOMER (Prince Hal)
B. Feb. 13, 1883, Los Gatos, Calif.   D. May 18, 1947, Colusa, Calif.
Manager 1910-11.

BR TL 6'   175 lbs.

1905	NY	A	126	.249	.329	465	116	16	6	3	0.6	60	49	15		22	1	1	1175	62	32	63	10.1	.975	1B-122, SS-1, 2B-1
1906			151	.323	.395	597	193	23	10	0	0.0	84	76	13		28	0	0	1506	92	33	54	10.8	.980	1B-150, 2B-1
1907			125	.287	.357	498	143	23	3	2	0.4	72	68	19		32	0	0	1152	79	34	50	10.1	.973	1B-121, OF-4
1908			106	.257	.306	405	104	11	3	1	0.2	50	36	15		27	1	1	1026	65	26	36	10.5	.977	1B-96, 2B-3, 3B-2, P-1
1909			118	.283	.357	474	134	17	3	4	0.8	60	63	20		25	0	0	1202	71	28	53	11.0	.978	1B-118
1910			130	.290	.365	524	152	20	5	3	0.6	67	73	16		40	0	0	1373	65	28	68	11.3	.981	1B-130
1911			133	.315	.419	527	166	32	7	3	0.6	82	62	21		36	0	0	1271	85	37	65	10.5	.973	1B-124, OF-7, 2B-2, SS-1

Year	Team		Games	BA	SA	AB	H	2B	3B	HR	HR%	R	RBI	BB	SO	SB	Pinch Hit AB	Pinch Hit H	PO	A	E	DP	TC/G	FA	G by Pos

Hal Chase *continued*

Year	Team		Games	BA	SA	AB	H	2B	3B	HR	HR%	R	RBI	BB	SO	SB	AB	H	PO	A	E	DP	TC/G	FA	G by Pos
1912			131	.274	.372	522	143	21	9	4	0.8	61	58	17		33	2	0	1173	89	32	50	9.9	.975	1B-121, 2B-8
1913	2 teams	NY A (39G – .212) CHI A (102G – .286)																							
"	total		141	.266	.355	530	141	13	14	2	0.4	64	48	27	54	14	0	0	1340	90	37	69	10.4	.975	1B-131, OF-5, 2B-5
1914	2 teams	CHI A (58G – .267) BUF F (75G – .347)																							
"	total		133	.314	.447	497	156	29	14	3	0.6	70	68	29	19	19	2	1	1322	81	28	60	10.8	.980	1B-131
1915	BUF	F	145	.291	.471	567	165	31	10	17	3.0	85	89	20		23	1	0	1463	83	26	84	10.8	.983	1B-143, OF-1
1916	CIN	N	142	.339	.459	542	184	29	12	4	0.7	66	82	19	48	22	7	2	1023	86	20	73	8.0	.982	1B-98, OF-25, 2B-16
1917			152	.277	.394	602	167	28	15	4	0.7	71	86	15	49	21	0	0	1499	80	28	100	10.6	.983	1B-151
1918			74	.301	.417	259	78	12	6	2	0.8	30	38	13	15	5	5	0	610	38	13	59	8.9	.980	1B-67, OF-2
1919	NY	N	110	.284	.397	408	116	17	7	5	1.2	58	45	17	40	16	2	1	1205	65	21	62	11.7	.984	1B-107
15 yrs.			1917	.291	.391	7417	2158	322	124	57	0.8	980	941	276	225	363	21	6	18340	1131	423	946	10.4	.979	1B-1810, OF-44, 2B-36, SS-2, 3B-2, P-1

Buster Chatham

CHATHAM, CHARLES L. BR TR 5'5" 150 lbs.
B. Dec. 25, 1901, West, Tex. D. Dec. 15, 1975, Waco, Tex.

Year	Team		Games	BA	SA	AB	H	2B	3B	HR	HR%	R	RBI	BB	SO	SB	AB	H	PO	A	E	DP	TC/G	FA	G by Pos
1930	BOS	N	112	.267	.408	404	108	20	11	5	1.2	48	56	37	41	8	4	0	116	200	23	38	3.0	.932	3B-92, SS-17
1931			17	.227	.318	44	10	1	0	1	2.3	4	3	6	6	0	3	0	11	20	5	4	2.1	.861	SS-6, 3B-6
2 yrs.			129	.263	.400	448	118	21	11	6	1.3	52	59	43	47	8	7	0	127	220	28	42	2.9	.925	3B-98, SS-23

Jim Chatterton

CHATTERTON, JAMES M.
B. Oct. 14, 1864, Brooklyn, N.Y. D. Dec. 15, 1944, Tewksbury, Mass.

Year	Team		Games	BA	SA	AB	H	2B	3B	HR	HR%	R	RBI	BB	SO	SB	AB	H	PO	A	E	DP	TC/G	FA	G by Pos
1884	KC	U	4	.133	.200	15	2	1	0	0	0.0	4		2			0	0	25	3	2	2	7.5	.933	OF-2, 1B-2, P-1

Ossie Chavarria

CHAVARRIA, OSVALDO BR TR 5'11" 155 lbs.
Born Osvaldo Chavarria y Quijano.
B. Aug. 5, 1940, Colon, Panama

Year	Team		Games	BA	SA	AB	H	2B	3B	HR	HR%	R	RBI	BB	SO	SB	AB	H	PO	A	E	DP	TC/G	FA	G by Pos
1966	KC	A	86	.241	.325	191	46	10	0	2	1.0	26	10	18	43	3	17	4	105	86	7	23	2.3	.965	OF-26, SS-23, 2B-14, 1B-8, 3B-5
1967			38	.102	.136	59	6	2	0	0	0.0	2	4	7	16	1	8	1	30	38	2	9	1.8	.971	2B-17, 3B-7, OF-3, SS-2
2 yrs.			124	.208	.280	250	52	12	0	2	0.8	28	14	25	59	4	25	5	135	124	9	32	2.2	.966	2B-31, OF-29, SS-25, 3B-12, 1B-8

Harry Cheek

CHEEK, HARRY G. TR
B. Mar. 1, 1879, Sedalia, Mo. D. June 25, 1956, Paramus, N. J.

Year	Team		Games	BA	SA	AB	H	2B	3B	HR	HR%	R	RBI	BB	SO	SB	AB	H	PO	A	E	DP	TC/G	FA	G by Pos
1910	PHI	N	2	.500	.750	4	2	1	0	0	0.0	1	0	0	0	0	0	0	2	0	0	0	1.0	1.000	C-2

Paul Chervinko

CHERVINKO, PAUL BR TR 5'8" 185 lbs.
B. July 23, 1910, Trauger, Pa. D. June 3, 1976, Danville, Ill.

Year	Team		Games	BA	SA	AB	H	2B	3B	HR	HR%	R	RBI	BB	SO	SB	AB	H	PO	A	E	DP	TC/G	FA	G by Pos
1937	BKN	N	30	.146	.188	48	7	0	1	0	0.0	1	2	3	16	0	3	0	56	8	0	0	2.1	1.000	C-26
1938			12	.148	.148	27	4	0	0	0	0.0	0	3	2	0	0	0	0	33	4	1	0	3.2	.974	C-12
2 yrs.			42	.147	.173	75	11	0	1	0	0.0	1	5	5	16	0	3	0	89	12	1	0	2.4	.990	C-38

Cupid Childs

CHILDS, CLARENCE ALGERNON BL TR 5'8" 185 lbs.
B. Aug. 14, 1867, Calvert County, Md. D. Nov. 8, 1912, Baltimore, Md.

Year	Team		Games	BA	SA	AB	H	2B	3B	HR	HR%	R	RBI	BB	SO	SB	AB	H	PO	A	E	DP	TC/G	FA	G by Pos
1888	PHI	N	2	.000	.000	4	0	0	0	0	0.0	0	0	0	0	0	0	0	2	4	1	1	3.5	.857	2B-2
1890	SYR	AA	136	.345	.481	493	170	33	14	2	0.4	109		72		56	0	0	375	369	58	59	5.9	.928	2B-125, SS-1
1891	CLE		141	.281	.374	551	155	21	12	2	0.4	120	83	97	32	39	0	0	371	455	82	54	6.4	.910	2B-141
1892			145	.317	.398	558	177	14	11	3	0.5	136	53	117	20	26	0	0	357	441	53	51	5.9	.938	2B-145
1893			124	.326	.425	485	158	19	10	3	0.6	145	65	120	12	23	0	0	348	424	62	56	6.7	.926	2B-123
1894			118	.353	.459	479	169	21	12	2	0.4	143	52	107	11	17	0	0	313	374	63	51	6.4	.916	2B-118
1895			119	.288	.359	462	133	15	3	4	0.9	96	90	74	24	20	0	0	337	394	63	42	6.7	.921	2B-119
1896			132	.355	.446	498	177	24	9	1	0.2	106	106	100	18	25	0	0	375	487	53	73	6.9	.942	2B-132
1897			114	.338	.419	444	150	15	9	1	0.2	105	61	74		25	0	0	319	384	42	42	6.5	.944	2B-114
1898			110	.288	.337	413	119	9	4	1	0.2	90	31	69		9	0	0	273	370	48	37	6.3	.931	2B-110
1899	STL	N	125	.265	.343	464	123	11	11	1	0.2	73	48	74		11	0	0	323	355	48	45	5.8	.934	2B-125
1900	CHI	N	137	.241	.286	531	128	14	5	0	0.0	67	44	57		15	0	0	323	431	52	57	5.9	.935	2B-137
1901			63	.257	.295	237	61	9	0	0	0.0	24	21	29		3	0	0	146	192	22	34	5.7	.939	2B-62
13 yrs.			1466	.306	.389	5619	1720	205	100	20	0.4	1214	654	990	117	269	0	0	3862	4680	647	602	6.3	.930	2B-1453, SS-1

Pete Childs

CHILDS, GEORGE PETER TR
B. Nov. 15, 1871, Philadelphia, Pa. D. Feb. 15, 1922, Philadelphia, Pa.

Year	Team		Games	BA	SA	AB	H	2B	3B	HR	HR%	R	RBI	BB	SO	SB	AB	H	PO	A	E	DP	TC/G	FA	G by Pos
1901	2 teams	STL N (29G – .266) CHI N (61G – .225)																							
"	total		90	.236	.264	292	69	6	1	0	0.0	35	22	41		4	6	1	169	248	25	23	4.9	.943	2B-80, OF-2, SS-1
1902	PHI	N	123	.194	.206	403	78	5	0	0	0.0	25	25	34		6	0	0	271	349	36	26	5.3	.945	2B-123
2 yrs.			213	.212	.230	695	147	11	1	0	0.0	60	47	75		10	6	1	440	597	61	49	5.2	.944	2B-203, OF-2, SS-1

Pearce Chiles

CHILES, PEARCE NUGET (What's the Use) 5'11" 185 lbs.
B. May 28, 1867, Deepwater, Mo. Deceased.

Year	Team		Games	BA	SA	AB	H	2B	3B	HR	HR%	R	RBI	BB	SO	SB	AB	H	PO	A	E	DP	TC/G	FA	G by Pos
1899	PHI	N	97	.320	.462	338	108	28	7	2	0.6	57	76	16		6	10	2	330	44	25	18	4.1	.937	OF-46, 1B-25, 2B-16
1900			33	.216	.333	111	24	6	2	1	0.9	15	23	6		4	2	0	169	42	6	14	6.6	.972	1B-16, 2B-12, OF-3
2 yrs.			130	.294	.430	449	132	34	9	3	0.7	72	99	22		10	12	2	499	86	31	32	4.7	.950	OF-49, 1B-41, 2B-28

Rich Chiles

CHILES, RICHARD FRANCIS BL TL 5'11" 170 lbs.
B. Nov. 22, 1949, Sacramento, Calif.

Year	Team		Games	BA	SA	AB	H	2B	3B	HR	HR%	R	RBI	BB	SO	SB	AB	H	PO	A	E	DP	TC/G	FA	G by Pos
1971	HOU	N	67	.227	.336	119	27	5	1	2	1.7	12	15	6	20	0	38	11	35	0	0	0	0.5	1.000	OF-27
1972			9	.273	.364	11	3	1	0	0	0.0	0	2	1	1	0	6	1	4	0	0	0	0.4	1.000	OF-2
1973	NY	N	8	.120	.200	25	3	2	0	0	0.0	2	1	0	2	0	0	0	22	1	0	1	2.9	1.000	OF-8
1976	HOU	N	5	.500	.750	4	2	1	0	0	0.0	1	0	0	0	0	4	2	1	0	0	0	0.2	1.000	OF-1
1977	MIN	A	108	.264	.368	261	69	16	1	3	1.1	31	36	23	17	0	29	8	35	0	2	0	0.3	.946	DH-61, OF-22

Year	Team		Games	BA	SA	AB	H	2B	3B	HR	HR%	R	RBI	BB	SO	SB	Pinch Hit AB	H	PO	A	E	DP	TC/G	FA	G by Pos

Rich Chiles *continued*

Year	Team		Games	BA	SA	AB	H	2B	3B	HR	HR%	R	RBI	BB	SO	SB	AB	H	PO	A	E	DP	TC/G	FA	G by Pos
1978			87	.268	.343	198	53	12	0	1	0.5	22	22	20	25	1	21	5	108	3	4	0	1.3	.965	OF-61, DH-8
6 yrs.			284	.254	.350	618	157	37	2	6	1.0	68	76	50	65	1	98	28	205	4	6	1	0.8	.972	OF-121, DH-69

Dino Chiozza

CHIOZZA, DINO JOSEPH (Dynamo)
Brother of Lou Chiozza.
B. June 30, 1912, Memphis, Tenn. D. Apr. 23, 1972, Memphis, Tenn.

BL TR 6' 170 lbs.

Year	Team		Games	BA	SA	AB	H	2B	3B	HR	HR%	R	RBI	BB	SO	SB	AB	H	PO	A	E	DP	TC/G	FA	G by Pos
1935	PHI	N	2	–	–	0	0	0	0	0	–	1	0	0	0	0	0	0	1	0	0	0	0.5	1.000	SS-2

Lou Chiozza

CHIOZZA, LOUIS PEO
Brother of Dino Chiozza.
B. May 17, 1910, Tallulah, La. D. Feb. 28, 1971, Memphis, Tenn.

BL TR 6' 172 lbs.

Year	Team		Games	BA	SA	AB	H	2B	3B	HR	HR%	R	RBI	BB	SO	SB	AB	H	PO	A	E	DP	TC/G	FA	G by Pos
1934	PHI	N	134	.304	.382	484	147	28	5	0	0.0	66	44	34	35	9	9	1	266	298	41	39	4.5	.932	2B-85, 3B-26, OF-17
1935			124	.284	.383	472	134	26	6	3	0.6	71	47	33	44	5	1	0	297	405	39	54	6.0	.947	2B-120, 3B-2
1936			144	.297	.379	572	170	32	6	1	0.2	83	48	37	39	17	2	1	324	144	26	25	3.4	.947	OF-90, 2B-33, 3B-26
1937	NY	N	117	.232	.294	439	102	11	2	4	0.9	49	29	20	30	6	9	2	121	172	17	9	2.6	.945	3B-93, OF-12, 2B-2
1938			57	.235	.346	179	42	7	2	3	1.7	15	17	12	7	5	7	2	80	112	11	9	3.6	.946	2B-34, OF-16, 3B-1
1939			40	.268	.366	142	38	3	1	3	2.1	19	12	9	10	3	0	0	39	76	8	11	3.1	.935	3B-30, SS-8
6 yrs.			616	.277	.361	2288	633	107	22	14	0.6	303	197	145	165	45	28	6	1127	1207	142	147	4.0	.943	2B-274, 3B-178, OF-135, SS-8

WORLD SERIES

Year	Team		Games	BA	SA	AB	H	2B	3B	HR	HR%	R	RBI	BB	SO	SB	AB	H	PO	A	E	DP	TC/G	FA	G by Pos
1937	NY	N	2	.286	.286	7	2	0	0	0	0.0	0	0	1	1	0	0	0	6	0	1	0	3.5	.857	OF-2

Walt Chipple

CHIPPLE, WALTER JOHN
Born Walter John Chlipala.
B. Sept. 26, 1918, Utica, N. Y. D. June 8, 1988, Tonawanda, N. Y.

BR TR 6'½" 168 lbs.

Year	Team		Games	BA	SA	AB	H	2B	3B	HR	HR%	R	RBI	BB	SO	SB	AB	H	PO	A	E	DP	TC/G	FA	G by Pos
1945	WAS	A	18	.136	.136	44	6	0	0	0	0.0	4	5	6	6	0	2	0	42	2	1	1	2.5	.978	OF-13

Tom Chism

CHISM, THOMAS RAYMOND
B. May 9, 1954, Chester, Pa.

BL TL 6'1" 195 lbs.

Year	Team		Games	BA	SA	AB	H	2B	3B	HR	HR%	R	RBI	BB	SO	SB	AB	H	PO	A	E	DP	TC/G	FA	G by Pos
1979	BAL	A	6	.000	.000	3	0	0	0	0	0.0	0	0	0	0	0	0	0	6	0	0	0	1.0	1.000	1B-4

Harry Chiti

CHITI, HARRY
B. Nov. 16, 1932, Kincaid, Ill.

BR TR 6'2½" 221 lbs.

Year	Team		Games	BA	SA	AB	H	2B	3B	HR	HR%	R	RBI	BB	SO	SB	AB	H	PO	A	E	DP	TC/G	FA	G by Pos
1950	CHI	N	3	.333	.333	6	2	0	0	0	0.0	0	0	0	2	0	0	0	1	0	0	0	0.7	1.000	C-1
1951			9	.355	.419	31	11	2	0	0	0.0	1	5	2	2	0	1	0	34	8	4	1	5.1	.913	C-8
1952			32	.274	.451	113	31	5	0	5	4.4	14	13	5	8	0	0	0	170	13	3	6	5.8	.984	C-32
1955			113	.231	.352	338	78	6	1	11	3.3	24	41	25	68	0	1	0	495	69	9	10	5.1	.984	C-113
1956			72	.212	.340	203	43	6	4	4	2.0	17	18	19	35	0	2	0	327	35	7	2	5.1	.981	C-67
1958	KC	A	103	.268	.417	295	79	11	3	9	3.1	32	44	18	48	3	19	3	425	41	6	9	4.6	.987	C-83
1959			55	.272	.444	162	44	11	1	5	3.1	20	25	17	26	0	8	4	228	25	3	5	4.7	.988	C-47
1960	2 teams		KC A	(58G –	.221)	DET	A	(37G –	.163)																
"	total		95	.201	.296	294	59	7	0	7	2.4	25	33	27	45	1	8	2	436	41	8	1	5.1	.984	C-88
1961	DET	A	5	.083	.083	12	1	0	0	0	0.0	0	0	0	2	0	0	0	19	3	0	0	4.4	1.000	C-5
1962	NY	N	15	.195	.220	41	8	1	0	0	0.0	2	0	1	8	0	2	0	62	4	2	1	4.5	.971	C-14
10 yrs.			502	.238	.365	1495	356	49	9	41	2.7	135	179	115	242	4	46	11	2197	240	42	35	4.9	.983	C-458

Felix Chouinard

CHOUINARD, FELIX GEORGE
B. Oct. 5, 1887, Hines, Ill. D. Apr. 28, 1955, Hines, Ill.

BB TR 5'7" 150 lbs.

Year	Team		Games	BA	SA	AB	H	2B	3B	HR	HR%	R	RBI	BB	SO	SB	AB	H	PO	A	E	DP	TC/G	FA	G by Pos
1910	CHI	A	24	.195	.280	82	16	3	2	0	0.0	6	9	8		4	0	0	46	10	2	2	2.4	.966	OF-23, 2B-1
1911			14	.176	.176	17	3	0	0	0	0.0	0				4	0	0	11	4	2	1	1.2	.882	OF-4, 2B-4
1914	3 teams		PIT F	(9G –	.300)	BKN	F	(32G –	.253)	BAL	F	(5G –	.444)												
"	total		46	.280	.356	118	33	2	1	1	0.8	12	12	4		4	11	2	54	16	5	4	1.6	.933	OF-25, 2B-4, SS-1
1915	BKN	F	4	.500	.500	4	2	0	0	0	0.0	0	2	0		0	1	0	1	0	0	0	0.3	1.000	OF-2
4 yrs.			88	.244	.317	221	54	5	4	1	0.5	22	23	12		8	12	2	112	30	9	7	1.7	.940	OF-54, 2B-9, SS-1

Harry Chozen

CHOZEN, HARRY (Choz)
B. Sept. 27, 1915, Winnebago, Minn.

BR TR 5'9" 195 lbs.

Year	Team		Games	BA	SA	AB	H	2B	3B	HR	HR%	R	RBI	BB	SO	SB	AB	H	PO	A	E	DP	TC/G	FA	G by Pos
1937	CIN	N	1	.250	.250	4	1	0	0	0	0.0	0	0	0	0	0	0	0	4	1	1	0	6.0	.833	C-1

Neil Chrisley

CHRISLEY, BARBRA O'NEIL
B. Dec. 16, 1931, Calhoun Falls, S. C.

BL TR 6'3" 187 lbs.

Year	Team		Games	BA	SA	AB	H	2B	3B	HR	HR%	R	RBI	BB	SO	SB	AB	H	PO	A	E	DP	TC/G	FA	G by Pos
1957	WAS	A	26	.157	.235	51	8	2	1	0	0.0	6	3	7	7	0	13	2	16	1	4	0	0.8	.810	OF-11
1958			105	.215	.343	233	50	7	4	5	2.1	19	26	16	18	1	38	10	117	6	1	2	1.2	.992	OF-69, 3B-1
1959	DET	A	65	.132	.330	106	14	3	0	6	5.7	7	11	12	10	0	43	5	28	0	0	0	0.4	1.000	OF-21
1960			96	.255	.395	220	56	10	3	5	2.3	27	24	19	26	2	44	10	109	2	3	0	1.2	.974	OF-47, 1B-2
1961	MIL	N	10	.222	.222	9	2	0	0	0	0.0	1	0	1	1	0	9	2	0	0	0	0		–	
5 yrs.			302	.210	.349	619	130	22	8	16	2.6	60	64	55	62	3	147	29	270	9	8	2	1.0	.972	OF-148, 1B-2, 3B-1

Lloyd Christenbury

CHRISTENBURY, LLOYD REID (Low)
B. Oct. 19, 1893, Mecklenburg County, N. C. D. Dec. 13, 1944, Birmingham, Ala.

BL TR 5'7" 165 lbs.

Year	Team		Games	BA	SA	AB	H	2B	3B	HR	HR%	R	RBI	BB	SO	SB	AB	H	PO	A	E	DP	TC/G	FA	G by Pos
1919	BOS	N	7	.290	.323	31	9	1	0	0	0.0	5	4	2	2	0	0	0	14	2	1	1	2.4	.941	OF-7
1920			65	.208	.264	106	22	2	2	0	0.0	17	14	13	12	0	23	4	41	40	9	7	1.4	.900	OF-14, SS-7, 2B-6, 3B-2
1921			62	.352	.504	125	44	6	2	3	2.4	34	16	21	7	3	17	6	64	80	13	9	2.5	.917	2B-32, OF-12, 3B-2
1922			71	.250	.329	152	38	5	2	1	0.7	22	13	18	11	2	27	9	70	22	6	1	1.4	.939	OF-32, 2B-5, 3B-2
4 yrs.			205	.273	.365	414	113	14	6	4	1.0	78	47	54	32	5	67	19	189	144	29	18	1.8	.920	OF-53, 2B-43, SS-9, 3B-6

Bruce Christensen

CHRISTENSEN, BRUCE RAY
B. Feb. 22, 1948, Madison, Wis.

BL TR 5'11" 160 lbs.

Year	Team		Games	BA	SA	AB	H	2B	3B	HR	HR%	R	RBI	BB	SO	SB	AB	H	PO	A	E	DP	TC/G	FA	G by Pos
1971	CAL	A	29	.270	.286	63	17	1	0	0	0.0	4	3	6	5	0	7	2	25	55	1	13	2.8	.988	SS-24

Year	Team		Games	BA	SA	AB	H	2B	3B	HR	HR%	R	RBI	BB	SO	SB	Pinch Hit AB	H	PO	A	E	DP	TC/G	FA	G by Pos

Cuckoo Christensen

CHRISTENSEN, WALTER NEILS (Seacap)
B. Oct. 24, 1899, San Francisco, Calif. D. Dec. 20, 1984, Menlo Park, Calif.
BL TL 5'6½" 156 lbs.

Year	Team		Games	BA	SA	AB	H	2B	3B	HR	HR%	R	RBI	BB	SO	SB	AB	H	PO	A	E	DP	TC/G	FA	G by Pos
1926	CIN	N	114	.350	.438	329	115	15	7	0	0.0	41	41	40	18	8	18	7	170	6	4	2	1.6	.978	OF-93
1927			57	.254	.286	185	47	6	0	0	0.0	25	16	20	16	4	5	0	106	6	5	3	2.1	.957	OF-50
2 yrs.			171	.315	.383	514	162	21	7	0	0.0	66	57	60	34	12	23	7	276	12	9	5	1.7	.970	OF-143

John Christensen

CHRISTENSEN, JOHN LAWRENCE
B. Sept. 15, 1960, Downey, Calif.
BR TR 6'3" 205 lbs.

Year	Team		Games	BA	SA	AB	H	2B	3B	HR	HR%	R	RBI	BB	SO	SB	AB	H	PO	A	E	DP	TC/G	FA	G by Pos
1984	NY	N	5	.273	.455	11	3	2	0	0	0.0	2	3	1	2	0	1	1	1	0	1	0	0.4	.500	OF-5
1985			51	.186	.319	113	21	4	1	3	2.7	10	13	19	23	1	15	1	41	2	2	0	0.9	.956	OF-38
1987	SEA	A	53	.242	.348	132	32	6	1	2	1.5	19	12	12	28	2	13	2	60	3	0	1	1.2	1.000	OF-43, DH-8
1988	MIN	A	23	.263	.368	38	10	4	0	0	0.0	5	5	3	5	0	6	2	20	0	0	0	0.9	1.000	OF-17
4 yrs.			132	.224	.344	294	66	16	2	5	1.7	36	33	35	58	3	35	6	122	5	3	1	1.0	.977	OF-103, DH-8

Bob Christian

CHRISTIAN, ROBERT CHARLES
B. Oct. 17, 1945, Chicago, Ill. D. Feb. 20, 1974, San Diego, Calif.
BR TR 5'10" 180 lbs.

Year	Team		Games	BA	SA	AB	H	2B	3B	HR	HR%	R	RBI	BB	SO	SB	AB	H	PO	A	E	DP	TC/G	FA	G by Pos
1968	DET	A	3	.333	.667	3	1	1	0	0	0.0	1	1	0	0	0	0	0	3	0	0	0	1.0	1.000	OF-1, 1B-1
1969	CHI	A	39	.217	.318	129	28	4	0	3	2.3	11	16	10	19	3	1	1	66	3	3	0	1.8	.958	OF-38
1970			12	.267	.467	15	4	0	0	1	6.7	3	3	1	4	0	9	3	2	0	0	0	0.2	1.000	OF-4
3 yrs.			54	.224	.340	147	33	5	0	4	2.7	14	19	11	23	3	11	4	71	3	3	0	1.4	.961	OF-43, 1B-1

Mark Christman

CHRISTMAN, MARQUETTE JOSEPH
B. Oct. 21, 1913, Maplewood, Mo. D. Oct. 9, 1976, St. Louis, Mo.
BR TR 5'11" 175 lbs.

Year	Team		Games	BA	SA	AB	H	2B	3B	HR	HR%	R	RBI	BB	SO	SB	AB	H	PO	A	E	DP	TC/G	FA	G by Pos
1938	DET	A	95	.248	.302	318	79	6	4	1	0.3	35	44	27	21	5	0	0	132	212	10	31	3.7	.972	3B-69, SS-21
1939	2 teams		DET A	(6G – .250)		STL A	(79G – .216)																		
"	total		85	.218	.277	238	52	8	3	0	0.0	27	20	20	12	2	11	0	155	214	16	46	4.5	.958	SS-64, 3B-6, 2B-1
1943	STL	A	98	.271	.351	336	91	11	5	2	0.6	31	35	19	19	0	3	0	279	173	3	41	4.6	.993	3B-37, SS-24, 1B-20, 2B-14
1944			148	.271	.353	547	148	25	1	6	1.1	56	83	47	37	5	0	0	205	317	15	36	3.6	.972	3B-145, 1B-3
1945			78	.277	.370	289	80	7	4	4	1.4	32	34	19	19	1	1	0	79	137	6	12	2.8	.973	3B-77
1946			128	.258	.321	458	118	22	2	1	0.2	40	41	22	29	0	6	1	138	308	13	44	3.6	.972	3B-77, SS-47
1947	WAS	A	110	.222	.281	374	83	15	2	1	0.2	27	33	33	16	4	3	1	205	293	11	75	4.6	.978	SS-106, 2B-1
1948			120	.259	.318	409	106	17	2	1	0.2	38	40	25	19	0	8	2	225	277	17	60	4.3	.967	SS-102, 3B-9, 2B-3
1949			49	.214	.313	112	24	2	0	3	2.7	8	18	8	7	0	16	2	69	53	4	10	2.6	.968	3B-23, 1B-6, SS-4, 2B-1
9 yrs.			911	.253	.324	3081	781	113	23	19	0.6	294	348	220	179	17	48	6	1487	1983	95	355	3.9	.973	3B-443, SS-368, 1B-29, 2B-20

WORLD SERIES

Year	Team		Games	BA	SA	AB	H	2B	3B	HR	HR%	R	RBI	BB	SO	SB	AB	H	PO	A	E	DP	TC/G	FA	G by Pos
1944	STL	A	6	.091	.091	22	2	0	0	0	0.0	0	1	0	6	0	0	0	3	9	1	0	2.2	.923	3B-6

Steve Christmas

CHRISTMAS, STEPHEN RANDALL
B. Dec. 9, 1957, Orlando, Fla.
BL TR 6' 190 lbs.

Year	Team		Games	BA	SA	AB	H	2B	3B	HR	HR%	R	RBI	BB	SO	SB	AB	H	PO	A	E	DP	TC/G	FA	G by Pos
1983	CIN	N	9	.059	.059	17	1	0	0	0	0.0	0	1	1	3	0	4	0	28	3	0	0	3.4	1.000	C-7
1984	CHI	A	12	.364	.727	11	4	1	0	1	9.1	1	4	0	2	0	11	4	2	0	0	0	0.2	1.000	C-1
1986	CHI	N	3	.111	.222	9	1	1	0	0	0.0	0	2	0	1	0	1	1	11	2	0	0	4.3	1.000	1B-1, C-1
3 yrs.			24	.162	.297	37	6	2	0	1	2.7	1	7	1	6	0	16	5	41	5	0	0	1.9	1.000	C-9, 1B-1

Joe Christopher

CHRISTOPHER, JOSEPH O'NEAL
B. Dec. 13, 1935, Frederiksted, Virgin Islands
BR TR 5'10" 175 lbs.

Year	Team		Games	BA	SA	AB	H	2B	3B	HR	HR%	R	RBI	BB	SO	SB	AB	H	PO	A	E	DP	TC/G	FA	G by Pos
1959	PIT	N	15	.000	.000	12	0	0	0	0	0.0	6	0	1	4	0	0	0	5	0	0	0	0.3	1.000	OF-9
1960			50	.232	.321	56	13	2	0	1	1.8	21	3	5	8	1	6	0	24	0	0	0	0.5	1.000	OF-17
1961			76	.263	.333	186	49	7	3	0	0.0	25	14	18	24	6	11	3	86	2	2	1	1.2	.978	OF-55
1962	NY	N	119	.244	.362	271	66	10	2	6	2.2	36	32	35	42	11	18	3	133	5	4	4	1.2	.972	OF-94
1963			64	.221	.289	149	33	5	1	1	0.7	19	8	13	21	1	21	3	58	1	1	0	0.9	.983	OF-45
1964			154	.300	.466	543	163	26	8	16	2.9	78	76	48	92	6	9	3	251	10	7	2	1.7	.974	OF-145
1965			148	.249	.339	437	109	18	3	5	1.1	38	40	35	82	4	34	10	180	3	2	0	1.3	.989	OF-112
1966	BOS	A	12	.077	.077	13	1	0	0	0	0.0	1	0	2	4	0	8	0	1	0	0	0	0.1	1.000	OF-2
8 yrs.			638	.260	.374	1667	434	68	17	29	1.7	224	173	157	277	29	107	22	738	21	16	8	1.2	.979	OF-479

WORLD SERIES

Year	Team		Games	BA	SA	AB	H	2B	3B	HR	HR%	R	RBI	BB	SO	SB	AB	H	PO	A	E	DP	TC/G	FA	G by Pos
1960	PIT	N	3	–	–	0	0	0	0	0	–	2	0	0	0	0	0	0	0	0	0	0	0.0	–	

Lloyd Christopher

CHRISTOPHER, LLOYD EUGENE
Brother of Russ Christopher.
B. Dec. 31, 1919, Richmond, Calif.
BR TR 6'2" 190 lbs.

Year	Team		Games	BA	SA	AB	H	2B	3B	HR	HR%	R	RBI	BB	SO	SB	AB	H	PO	A	E	DP	TC/G	FA	G by Pos
1945	2 teams		BOS A	(8G – .286)		CHI N	(1G – .000)																		
"	total		9	.286	.286	14	4	0	0	0	0.0	4	4	3	2	0	1	0	5	0	0	0	0.6	1.000	OF-4
1947	CHI	A	7	.217	.304	23	5	0	1	0	0.0	1	0	2	4	0	0	0	19	1	0	1	2.9	1.000	OF-7
2 yrs.			16	.243	.297	37	9	0	1	0	0.0	5	4	5	6	0	3	0	24	1	0	1	1.6	1.000	OF-11

Hi Church

CHURCH, HIRAM LINCOLN
B. Central Square, N. Y. Deceased.

Year	Team		Games	BA	SA	AB	H	2B	3B	HR	HR%	R	RBI	BB	SO	SB	AB	H	PO	A	E	DP	TC/G	FA	G by Pos
1890	BKN	AA	3	.111	.111	9	1	0	0	0	0.0	1		0			0	0	1	0	0	0	0.3	1.000	OF-3

John Churry

CHURRY, JOHN
B. Nov. 26, 1900, Johnstown, Pa. D. Feb. 8, 1970, Zanesville, Ohio
BR TR 5'9" 172 lbs.

Year	Team		Games	BA	SA	AB	H	2B	3B	HR	HR%	R	RBI	BB	SO	SB	AB	H	PO	A	E	DP	TC/G	FA	G by Pos
1924	CHI	N	6	.143	.286	7	1	1	0	0	0.0	0	0	2	0	0	2	0	7	1	0	0	1.3	1.000	C-3
1925			3	.500	.500	6	3	0	0	0	0.0	1	1	0	0	0	0	0	3	0	0	0	1.3	1.000	C-3
1926			2	.000	.000	4	0	0	0	0	0.0	0	0	1	2	0	1	0	5	0	0	0	2.5	1.000	C-1
1927			1	1.000	1.000	1	1	0	0	0	0.0	0	0	0	0	0	0	0	2	0	0	0	2.0	1.000	C-1
4 yrs.			12	.278	.333	18	5	1	0	0	0.0	1	1	3	2	0	3	0	15	4	0	0	1.6	1.000	C-8

Year	Team		Games	BA	SA	AB	H	2B	3B	HR	HR%	R	RBI	BB	SO	SB	Pinch Hit AB	H	PO	A	E	DP	TC/G	FA	G by Pos

Larry Ciaffone
CIAFFONE, LAWRENCE THOMAS (Symphony)
B. Aug. 17, 1924, Brooklyn, N. Y.
BR TR 5'9½" 185 lbs.

| 1951 | STL | N | 5 | .000 | .000 | 5 | 0 | 0 | 0 | 0 | 0.0 | 0 | 0 | 1 | 2 | 0 | 3 | 0 | 1 | 0 | 0 | 0 | 0.2 | 1.000 | OF-1 |

Darryl Cias
CIAS, DARRYL RICHARD
B. Apr. 23, 1957, New York, N. Y.
BR TR 5'11" 188 lbs.

| 1983 | OAK | A | 19 | .333 | .389 | 18 | 6 | 1 | 0 | 0 | 0.0 | 1 | 1 | 2 | 4 | 1 | 0 | 0 | 27 | 2 | 1 | 1 | 1.6 | .967 | C-19 |

Joe Cicero
CICERO, JOSEPH FRANCIS (Dode)
B. Nov. 18, 1910, Atlantic City, N. J.   D. Mar. 30, 1983, Clearwater, Fla.
BR TR 5'8" 167 lbs.

1929	BOS	A	10	.313	.500	32	10	2	2	0	0.0	6	4	0	3	0			17	0	0	0	1.7	1.000	OF-7
1930			18	.167	.333	30	5	1	2	0	0.0	5	4	1	5	0	11	1	2	0	0	0	0.5	.778	OF-5, 3B-2
1945	PHI	A	12	.158	.158	19	3	0	0	0	0.0	3	0	1	6	0	2	0	7	0	0	0	0.6	1.000	OF-7
3 yrs.			40	.222	.358	81	18	3	4	0	0.0	14	8	2	13	0	16	3	26	5	2	1	0.8	.939	OF-19, 3B-2

Ted Cieslak
CIESLAK, THADDEUS WALTER
B. Nov. 22, 1916, Milwaukee, Wis.
BR TR 5'10" 175 lbs.

| 1944 | PHI | N | 85 | .245 | .318 | 220 | 54 | 10 | 0 | 2 | 0.9 | 18 | 11 | 21 | 17 | 1 | 30 | 5 | 46 | 73 | 15 | 1 | 1.6 | .888 | 3B-48, OF-5 |

Al Cihocki
CIHOCKI, ALBERT JOSEPH
B. May 7, 1924, Nanticoke, Pa.
BR TR 5'11" 185 lbs.

| 1945 | CLE | A | 92 | .212 | .265 | 283 | 60 | 9 | 3 | 0 | 0.0 | 21 | 24 | 11 | 48 | 2 | 0 | 0 | 154 | 208 | 15 | 42 | 4.1 | .960 | SS-41, 3B-29, 2B-23 |

Ed Cihocki
CIHOCKI, EDWARD JOSEPH (Cy)
B. May 9, 1907, Wilmington, Del.   D. Nov. 9, 1987, Newark, Del.
BR TR 5'8" 163 lbs.

1932	PHI	A	1	.000	.000	1	0	0	0	0	0.0	0	0	0	1	0	0	0	0	0	0	0	0.0	–	
1933			33	.144	.227	97	14	2	3	0	0.0	6	9	7	16	0	2	0	45	74	13	17	4.0	.902	SS-28, 3B-1, 2B-1
2 yrs.			34	.143	.224	98	14	2	3	0	0.0	6	9	7	16	0	3	0	45	74	13	17	3.9	.902	SS-28, 3B-1, 2B-1

Gino Cimoli
CIMOLI, GINO NICHOLAS
B. Dec. 18, 1929, San Francisco, Calif.
BR TR 6'1" 180 lbs.

1956	BKN	N	73	.111	.139	36	4	1	0	0	0.0	3	4	1	8	1	4	1	35	0	2	0	0.5	.946	OF-62
1957			142	.293	.410	532	156	22	5	10	1.9	88	57	39	86	3	3	2	265	11	6	2	2.0	.979	OF-138
1958	LA	N	109	.246	.366	325	80	6	3	9	2.8	35	27	18	49	3	8	0	180	10	5	2	1.8	.974	OF-104
1959	STL	N	143	.279	.430	519	145	40	7	8	1.5	61	72	37	73	1	7	1	267	12	6	2	2.0	.979	OF-141
1960	PIT	N	101	.267	.339	307	82	14	4	0	0.0	36	28	32	43	1	10	2	181	5	7	1	1.9	.964	OF-91
1961	2 teams		58	PIT N (21G – .299)		MIL N	(37G – .197)																			
"	total		58	.234	.337	184	43	8	1	3	1.6	16	10	13	28	1	7	1	99	1	2	2	1.8	.980	OF-50
1962	KC	A	152	.275	.420	550	151	20	15	10	1.8	67	71	40	89	2	7	2	231	8	8	2	1.6	.968	OF-147
1963			145	.263	.363	529	139	19	11	4	0.8	56	48	39	72	3	9	4	256	14	4	3	1.9	.985	OF-136
1964	2 teams		42	KC A (4G – .000)		BAL A	(38G – .138)																			
"	total		42	.119	.224	67	8	0	0	2	0.0	7	3	2	14	0	6	1	31	0	3	0	0.8	.912	OF-39
1965	CAL	A	4	.000	.000	5	0	0	0	0	0.0	1	1	0	3	0	2	0	2	0	0	0	0.5	1.000	OF-1
10 yrs.			969	.265	.383	3054	808	133	48	44	1.4	370	321	221	474	21	60	14	1547	61	43	14	1.7	.974	OF-909

WORLD SERIES

1956	BKN	N	1	–	–	0	0	0	0	0	–	0	0	0	0	0	0	0	1	0	0	0	1.0	1.000	OF-1
1960	PIT	N	7	.250	.250	20	5	0	0	0	0.0	4	1	2	4	0	1	1	5	0	0	0	0.7	1.000	OF-6
2 yrs.			8	.250	.250	20	5	0	0	0	0.0	4	1	2	4	0	1	1	6	0	0	0	0.8	1.000	OF-7

Frank Cipriani
CIPRIANI, FRANK DOMINICK
B. Apr. 14, 1941, Buffalo, N. Y.
BR TR 6' 180 lbs.

| 1961 | KC | A | 13 | .250 | .250 | 36 | 9 | 0 | 0 | 0 | 0.0 | 2 | 2 | 2 | 4 | 0 | 2 | 0 | 20 | 0 | 0 | 0 | 1.5 | 1.000 | OF-11 |

George Cisar
CISAR, GEORGE JOSEPH
B. Aug. 25, 1912, Chicago, Ill.
BR TR 6' 175 lbs.

| 1937 | BKN | N | 20 | .207 | .207 | 29 | 6 | 0 | 0 | 0 | 0.0 | 8 | 4 | 2 | 6 | 1 | 3 | 1 | 14 | 0 | 0 | 0 | 0.7 | 1.000 | OF-13 |

Bill Cissell
CISSELL, CHALMER WILLIAM
B. Jan. 3, 1904, Perryville, Mo.   D. Mar. 15, 1949, Chicago, Ill.
BR TR 5'11" 170 lbs.

1928	CHI	A	125	.260	.330	443	115	22	3	1	0.2	66	60	29	41	18	1	1	255	360	41	77	5.2	.938	SS-123
1929			152	.280	.387	618	173	27	12	5	0.8	83	62	28	53	26	0	0	357	459	55	90	5.7	.937	SS-152
1930			141	.270	.363	562	152	28	9	2	0.4	82	48	28	32	16	1	0	290	422	41	69	5.3	.946	2B-106, 3B-24, SS-10
1931			109	.220	.284	409	90	13	5	1	0.2	42	46	16	26	18	0	0	225	302	29	58	5.1	.948	SS-83, 2B-23, 3B-1
1932	2 teams		143	CHI A (12G – .256)		CLE A	(131G – .320)																			
"	total		143	.315	.437	584	184	36	4	7	1.2	85	98	29	25	18	0	0	372	509	36	92	6.4	.961	2B-129, SS-18
1933	CLE	A	112	.230	.340	409	94	21	3	6	1.5	53	33	31	29	6	2	1	238	351	28	47	5.5	.955	2B-62, SS-46, 3B-1
1934	BOS	A	102	.267	.346	416	111	13	4	1	0.2	71	44	28	23	11	2	1	287	292	27	65	5.9	.955	2B-96, SS-7, 3B-2
1937	PHI	A	34	.265	.350	117	31	7	0	1	0.9	15	14	17	10	0	1	0	87	115	8	17	6.2	.962	2B-33
1938	NY	N	38	.268	.349	149	40	6	0	2	1.3	19	18	19	18	1	0	0	90	138	7	20	6.2	.970	2B-33, 3B-6
9 yrs.			956	.267	.360	3707	990	173	43	29	0.8	516	423	212	250	114	7	3	2201	2948	272	535	5.7	.950	2B-482, SS-439, 3B-34

Moose Clabaugh
CLABAUGH, JOHN WILLIAM
B. Nov. 13, 1901, Albany, Mo.   D. July 11, 1984, Tucson, Ariz.
BL TR 6' 185 lbs.

| 1926 | BKN | N | 11 | .071 | .143 | 14 | 1 | 1 | 0 | 0 | 0.0 | 2 | 1 | 0 | 1 | 0 | 9 | 1 | 3 | 0 | 2 | 0 | 0.5 | .600 | OF-2 |

Bobby Clack
CLACK, ROBERT S. (Gentlemanly Bobby)
Born Robert S. Clark.
B. 1851, Brooklyn, N. Y.   D. Oct. 22, 1933, Danvers, Mass.
BR TR 5'9" 153 lbs.

| 1876 | CIN | N | 32 | .161 | .178 | 118 | 19 | 1 | 0 | 0 | 0.0 | 10 | 5 | 5 | 12 | | | 0 | 105 | 33 | 26 | 1 | 5.1 | .841 | OF-17, 2B-8, 1B-5, 3B-3, P-1 |

771

Year	Team		Games	BA	SA	AB	H	2B	3B	HR	HR%	R	RBI	BB	SO	SB	Pinch Hit AB	H	PO	A	E	DP	TC/G	FA	G by Pos

Dave Claire

CLAIRE, DAVID MATTHEW
B. Nov. 17, 1897, Ludington, Mich.   D. Jan. 7, 1956, Las Vegas, Nev.

BR TR 5'8"   164 lbs.

| 1920 | DET | A | 3 | .143 | .143 | 7 | 1 | 0 | 0 | 0 | 0.0 | 1 | 0 | 0 | 0 | 0 | 0 | 0 | 2 | 6 | 2 | 0 | 3.3 | .800 | SS-3 |

Al Clancy

CLANCY, ALBERT HARRISON
B. Aug. 14, 1888, Santa Fe, N. M.   D. Oct. 17, 1951, Las Cruces, N. M.

BR TR 5'10½" 175 lbs.

| 1911 | STL | A | 3 | .000 | .000 | 5 | 0 | 0 | 0 | 0 | 0.0 | 0 | 0 | 0 | | 0 | 1 | 0 | 1 | 3 | 1 | 1 | 1.7 | .800 | 3B-2 |

Bill Clancy

CLANCY, WILLIAM EDWARD
B. Apr. 12, 1879, Redfield, N. Y.   D. Feb. 10, 1948, Oriskany, N. Y.

BR TR 6'2"   180 lbs.

| 1905 | PIT | N | 56 | .229 | .330 | 227 | 52 | 11 | 3 | 2 | 0.9 | 23 | 34 | 4 | | 3 | 0 | 0 | 554 | 27 | 10 | 30 | 10.6 | .983 | 1B-52, OF-4 |

Bud Clancy

CLANCY, JOHN WILLIAM
B. Sept. 15, 1900, Odell, Ill.   D. Sept. 26, 1968, Ottumwa, Iowa

BL TL 6'   170 lbs.

1924	CHI	A	13	.257	.286	35	9	1	0	0	0.0	5	6	3	2	3	4	1	69	3	3	4	5.8	.960	1B-8
1925			4	.000	.000	3	0	0	0	0	0.0	0	0	1	0	0	3	0	0	0	0	0	0.0	—	
1926			12	.342	.500	38	13	2	2	0	0.0	3	7	1	1	0	2	0	104	6	1	11	9.3	.991	1B-10
1927			130	.300	.373	464	139	21	2	3	0.6	46	53	24	24	4	5	1	1184	81	11	76	9.8	.991	1B-123
1928			130	.271	.368	487	132	19	11	2	0.4	64	37	42	25	6	2	0	1175	93	12	104	9.8	.991	1B-128
1929			92	.283	.403	290	82	14	6	3	1.0	36	45	16	19	3	16	4	647	49	6	47	7.6	.991	1B-74
1930			68	.244	.342	234	57	8	3	3	1.3	28	27	12	18	3	7	1	583	24	3	38	9.0	.995	1B-63
1932	BKN	N	53	.306	.342	196	60	4	2	0	0.0	14	16	6	13	0	0	0	524	40	2	55	10.7	.996	1B-53
1934	PHI	N	20	.245	.306	49	12	0	0	1	2.0	8	7	6	4	0	9	2	99	4	0	11	5.2	1.000	1B-10
9 yrs.			522	.281	.368	1796	504	69	26	12	0.7	204	198	111	106	19	48	9	4385	300	38	346	9.0	.992	1B-469

Uke Clanton

CLANTON, EUCAL (Cat)
B. Feb. 19, 1898, Powell, Mo.   D. Feb. 24, 1960, Antlers, Okla.

BL TL 5'8"   165 lbs.

| 1922 | CLE | A | 1 | .000 | .000 | 1 | 0 | 0 | 0 | 0 | 0.0 | 0 | 0 | 0 | | 0 | 1 | 0 | 1 | 0 | 1 | 1 | 2.0 | .500 | 1B-1 |

Aaron Clapp

CLAPP, AARON BRONSON
Brother of John Clapp.
B. July, 1856, Ithaca, N. Y.   D. Jan. 13, 1914, Sayre, Pa.

TR 5'8"   175 lbs.

| 1879 | TRO | N | 36 | .267 | .370 | 146 | 39 | 9 | 3 | 0 | 0.0 | 24 | 18 | 6 | 10 | | 0 | 0 | 279 | 7 | 25 | 10 | 8.6 | .920 | 1B-25, OF-11 |

John Clapp

CLAPP, JOHN EDGAR
Brother of Aaron Clapp.
B. July 17, 1851, Ithaca, N. Y.   D. Dec. 18, 1904, Ithaca, N. Y.
Manager 1878, 1872, 1879-80, 1883.

BR TR 5'7"   194 lbs.

1876	STL	N	64	.305	.332	298	91	4	2	0	0.0	60	29	8	2		0	0	335	56	58	5	7.0	.871	C-61, OF-4, 2B-1
1877			60	.318	.388	255	81	6	6	0	0.0	47	34	8	6		0	0	285	45	42	2	6.2	.887	C-53, OF-10, 1B-1
1878	IND	N	63	.304	.357	263	80	10	2	0	0.0	42	29	13	8		0	0	234	33	21	6	4.6	.927	OF-44, 1B-12, C-9, SS-3, 2B-1
1879	BUF	N	70	.264	.349	292	77	12	5	1	0.3	47	36	11	11		0	0	297	60	40	4	5.7	.899	C-63, OF-7
1880	CIN	N	80	.282	.365	323	91	16	4	1	0.3	33	20	21	10		0	0	436	121	63	5	7.8	.898	C-73, OF-10
1881	CLE	N	68	.253	.314	261	66	12	2	0	0.0	47	25	35	6		0	0	248	79	44	10	5.5	.881	C-48, OF-21
1883	NY	N	20	.178	.178	73	13	0	0	0	0.0	6		5	4		0	0	87	32	15	1	6.7	.888	C-16, OF-5
7 yrs.			425	.283	.344	1765	499	60	21	2	0.1	282	173	101	47		0	0	1922	426	283	33	6.2	.892	C-323, OF-101, 1B-13, SS-3, 2B-2

Doug Clarey

CLAREY, DOUGLAS WILLIAM
B. Apr. 20, 1954, Los Angeles, Calif.

BR TR 6'   180 lbs.

| 1976 | STL | N | 9 | .250 | 1.000 | 4 | 1 | 0 | 0 | 1 | 25.0 | 2 | 2 | 0 | 1 | 0 | 2 | 1 | 3 | 1 | 0 | 0 | 0.4 | 1.000 | 2B-7 |

Allie Clark

CLARK, ALFRED ALOYSIUS
B. June 16, 1923, South Amboy, N. J.

BR TR 6'   195 lbs.

1947	NY	A	24	.373	.493	67	25	5	0	1	1.5	9	14	5	2	0	7	2	36	0	0	0	1.5	1.000	OF-16
1948	CLE	A	81	.310	.443	271	84	5	2	9	3.3	43	38	23	13	0	11	3	115	9	3	3	1.6	.976	OF-65, 3B-5, 1B-1
1949			35	.176	.270	74	13	4	0	1	1.4	8	9	4	7	0	19	2	15	1	0	0	0.5	1.000	OF-17, 1B-1
1950			59	.215	.374	163	35	6	1	6	3.7	19	21	11	10	0	15	2	75	2	1	0	1.3	.987	OF-41
1951 2 teams	CLE	A	(3G – .300)			PHI	A	(56G – .248)																		
" total			59	.251	.421	171	43	12	1	5	2.9	23	25	16	9	1	13	4	72	22	4	4	1.7	.959	OF-35, 3B-10
1952	PHI	A	71	.274	.452	186	51	12	0	7	3.8	23	29	10	19	0	21	7	82	2	1	0	1.2	.988	OF-48, 1B-2
1953 2 teams	PHI	A	(20G – .203)			CHI	A	(9G – .067)																		
" total			29	.180	.326	89	16	4	0	3	3.4	6	13	3	10	0	9	1	39	2	0	2	1.4	1.000	OF-20, 1B-1
7 yrs.			358	.262	.410	1021	267	48	4	32	3.1	131	149	72	70	2	95	21	434	38	9	9	1.3	.981	OF-242, 3B-15, 1B-5

WORLD SERIES

1947	NY	A	3	.500	.500	2	1	0	0	0	0.0	1	1	1	0	0	2	1	2	0	0	0	0.7	1.000	OF-1
1948	CLE	A	1	.000	.000	3	0	0	0	0	0.0	0	0	0	1	0	0	0	2	0	0	0	2.0	1.000	OF-1
2 yrs.			4	.200	.200	5	1	0	0	0	0.0	1	1	1	1	0	2	1	4	0	0	0	1.0	1.000	OF-2

Bill Clark

CLARK, WILLIAM WINFIELD (Win)
B. Apr. 11, 1875, Circleville, Ohio   D. Apr. 15, 1959, Los Angeles, Calif.

BR TR 5'10"   175 lbs.

| 1897 | LOU | N | 7 | .231 | .231 | 26 | 6 | 0 | 0 | 0 | 0.0 | 2 | 2 | 1 | | 1 | 0 | 0 | 12 | 16 | 6 | 1 | 4.9 | .824 | 2B-3, P-3, 3B-1 |

Bob Clark

CLARK, ROBERT H.
B. May 18, 1863, Covington, Ky.   D. Aug. 21, 1919, Covington, Ky.

BR TR 5'10"   175 lbs.

1886	BKN	AA	71	.216	.260	269	58	8	2	0	0.0	37		17		0	0	246	106	64	11	5.9	.846	C-44, OF-17, SS-12
1887			48	.266	.294	177	47	3	1	0	0.0	24		7		15	0	0	201	66	43	7	6.5	.861	C-45, OF-3
1888			45	.240	.333	150	36	5	3	1	0.7	23	20	9		11	0	0	211	62	37	6	6.9	.881	C-36, OF-8, 1B-1
1889			53	.275	.324	182	50	5	2	0	0.0	32	22	26	7	18	0	0	275	86	54	4	7.8	.870	C-53

Year Team	Games	BA	SA	AB	H	2B	3B	HR	HR%	R	RBI	BB	SO	SB	Pinch Hit AB	Pinch Hit H	PO	A	E	DP	TC/G	FA	G by Pos

Bob Clark *continued*

Year Team	Games	BA	SA	AB	H	2B	3B	HR	HR%	R	RBI	BB	SO	SB	PH AB	PH H	PO	A	E	DP	TC/G	FA	G by Pos
1890 BKN N	43	.219	.278	151	33	3	3	0	0.0	24	15	15	8	10	0	0	165	40	40	5	5.7	.837	C-42, OF-1
1891 CIN N	16	.111	.111	54	6	0	0	0	0.0	2	3	6	9	3	0	0	50	16	10	1	4.8	.868	C-16
1893 LOU N	12	.107	.143	28	3	0	0	0	0.0	3	3	5	5	0	0	0	10	11	1	1	1.8	.955	C-16
7 yrs.	288	.230	.280	1011	233	25	11	1	0.1	145	63	85	29	57	0	0	1158	387	249	35	6.2	.861	C-246, OF-30, SS-13, 1B-1

Bobby Clark

CLARK, ROBERT CALE
B. June 13, 1955, Sacramento, Calif. — BR TR 6' 190 lbs.

Year Team	Games	BA	SA	AB	H	2B	3B	HR	HR%	R	RBI	BB	SO	SB	PH AB	PH H	PO	A	E	DP	TC/G	FA	G by Pos
1979 CAL A	19	.296	.463	54	16	2	2	1	1.9	8	5	5	11	1	1	0	41	4	1	0	2.4	.978	OF-19
1980	78	.230	.333	261	60	10	2	5	1.9	26	23	11	42	0	1	0	213	6	4	2	2.9	.982	OF-77
1981	34	.250	.432	88	22	2	1	4	4.5	12	19	7	18	0	7	3	66	5	0	0	2.1	1.000	OF-34
1982	102	.211	.289	90	19	1	0	2	2.2	11	8		29		1	0	88	2	0	0	0.9	1.000	OF-102
1983	76	.231	.354	212	49	9	1	5	2.4	17	21	9	45	0	1	0	122	0	0	0	1.6	1.000	OF-72, DH-2, 3B-1
1984 MIL A	58	.260	.361	169	44	7	2	2	1.2	17	16	16	35	1	5	3	106	0	2	0	1.9	.981	OF-56
1985	29	.226	.258	93	21	3	0	0	0.0	6	8	7	19	1	3	0	72	1	0	0	2.5	1.000	OF-27
7 yrs.	396	.239	.347	967	231	34	7	19	2.0	97	100	55	199	4	20	6	708	18	7	2	1.9	.990	OF-387, DH-2, 3B-1

LEAGUE CHAMPIONSHIP SERIES

Year Team	Games	BA	SA	AB	H	2B	3B	HR	HR%	R	RBI	BB	SO	SB	PH AB	PH H	PO	A	E	DP	TC/G	FA	G by Pos
1979 CAL A	1	.000	.000	3	0	0	0	0	0.0	0	0	0	2	0	0	0	3	0	0	0	3.0	1.000	OF-1
1982	2	–	–	0	0	0	0	0	–	0	0	0	0	0	0	0	0	0	0	0	0.0	–	OF-2
2 yrs.	3	.000	.000	3	0	0	0	0	0.0	0	0	0	2	0	0	0	3	0	0	0	1.0	1.000	OF-3

Cap Clark

CLARK, JOHN CARROLL
B. Sept. 19, 1906, Snow Camp, N. C. D. Feb. 16, 1957, Fayetteville, N. C. — BL TR 5'11" 180 lbs.

Year Team	Games	BA	SA	AB	H	2B	3B	HR	HR%	R	RBI	BB	SO	SB	PH AB	PH H	PO	A	E	DP	TC/G	FA	G by Pos
1938 PHI N	52	.257	.297	74	19	1	1	0	0.0	11	4	9	10	0	20	5	65	8	5	2	1.5	.936	C-29

Danny Clark

CLARK, DANIEL CURREN
B. Jan. 18, 1894, Meridian, Miss. D. May 23, 1937, Meridian, Miss. — BL TR 5'9" 167 lbs.

Year Team	Games	BA	SA	AB	H	2B	3B	HR	HR%	R	RBI	BB	SO	SB	PH AB	PH H	PO	A	E	DP	TC/G	FA	G by Pos
1922 DET A	83	.292	.432	185	54	11	3	3	1.6	31	26	15	11	1	**36**	8	78	100	10	16	2.3	.947	2B-38, OF-5, 3B-1
1924 BOS A	104	.277	.385	325	90	23	3	2	0.6	36	54	50	18	4	10	1	88	173	15	8	2.7	.946	3B-93
1927 STL N	58	.236	.319	72	17	2	2	0	0.0	8	13	8	7	0	40	**12**	25	1	2	1	0.5	.929	OF-9
3 yrs.	245	.277	.392	582	161	36	8	5	0.9	75	93	73	36	5	86	21	191	274	27	25	2.0	.945	3B-94, 2B-38, OF-14

Dave Clark

CLARK, DAVID EARL
B. Sept. 3, 1962, Tupelo, Miss. — BL TR 6'2" 200 lbs.

Year Team	Games	BA	SA	AB	H	2B	3B	HR	HR%	R	RBI	BB	SO	SB	PH AB	PH H	PO	A	E	DP	TC/G	FA	G by Pos
1986 CLE A	18	.276	.448	58	16	1	0	3	5.2	10	9	7	11	1	0	0	26	0	0	0	1.4	1.000	OF-10, DH-7
1987	29	.207	.368	87	18	5	0	3	3.4	11	12	2	24	1	6	0	24	1	0	0	0.9	1.000	OF-13, DH-12
1988	63	.263	.359	156	41	4	1	3	1.9	11	18	17	28	0	19	4	36	0	2	0	0.6	.947	DH-27, OF-23
1989	102	.237	.379	253	60	12	0	8	3.2	21	29	30	63	0	29	7	27	0	1	0	0.3	.964	DH-55, OF-21
4 yrs.	212	.244	.379	554	135	22	1	17	3.1	53	68	56	126	2	54	11	113	1	3	0	0.6	.974	DH-101, OF-67

Earl Clark

CLARK, BAILEY EARL
B. Nov. 6, 1907, Washington, D. C. D. Jan. 16, 1938, Washington, D. C. — BR TR 5'10" 160 lbs.

Year Team	Games	BA	SA	AB	H	2B	3B	HR	HR%	R	RBI	BB	SO	SB	PH AB	PH H	PO	A	E	DP	TC/G	FA	G by Pos
1927 BOS N	13	.273	.295	44	12	1	0	0	0.0	6	3	2	4	0	0	0	30	0	0	0	2.3	1.000	OF-13
1928	27	.304	.402	112	34	9	1	0	0.0	18	10	4	8	0	1	0	77	0	1	0	2.9	.987	OF-27
1929	84	.315	.394	279	88	13	3	1	0.4	43	30	12	30	6	1	0	216	7	5	3	2.7	.978	OF-74
1930	82	.296	.408	233	69	11	3	3	1.3	29	28	7	22	3	17	7	165	3	4	0	2.1	.977	OF-63
1931	16	.220	.260	50	11	2	0	0	0.0	8	4	7	4	1	2	0	30	2	1	0	2.1	.970	OF-14
1932	50	.250	.295	44	11	2	0	0	0.0	11	4	7	7	1	16	5	19	2	0	1	0.4	1.000	OF-16
1933	7	.348	.391	23	8	1	0	0	0.0	3	1	2	1	0	4	0	10	0	0	0	1.4	1.000	OF-7
1934 STL A	13	.171	.220	41	7	2	0	0	0.0	4	1	1	3	0	4	0	22	0	0	0	1.7	1.000	OF-9
8 yrs.	292	.291	.372	826	240	41	7	4	0.5	122	81	37	79	11	44	13	569	14	11	4	2.0	.981	OF-223

Fred Clark

CLARK, ALFRED ROBERT
B. July 16, 1873, San Francisco, Calif. D. July 26, 1956, Ogden, Utah — BL TL 5'11" 170 lbs.

Year Team	Games	BA	SA	AB	H	2B	3B	HR	HR%	R	RBI	BB	SO	SB	PH AB	PH H	PO	A	E	DP	TC/G	FA	G by Pos
1902 CHI N	12	.186	.209	43	8	1	0	0	0.0	1	2	4		1	0	0	115	6	8	9	10.8	.938	1B-12

Glen Clark

CLARK, GLEN ESTER
B. Mar. 7, 1941, Austin, Tex. — BB TR 6'1" 190 lbs.

Year Team	Games	BA	SA	AB	H	2B	3B	HR	HR%	R	RBI	BB	SO	SB	PH AB	PH H	PO	A	E	DP	TC/G	FA	G by Pos
1967 ATL N	4	.000	.000	4	0	0	0	0	0.0	0	0	0	1	0	4	0	0	0	0	0	0.0	–	

Jack Clark

CLARK, JACK ANTHONY (The Ripper)
B. Nov. 10, 1955, New Brighton, Pa. — BR TR 6'2" 205 lbs.

Year Team	Games	BA	SA	AB	H	2B	3B	HR	HR%	R	RBI	BB	SO	SB	PH AB	PH H	PO	A	E	DP	TC/G	FA	G by Pos
1975 SF N	8	.235	.235	17	4	0	0	0	0.0	3	2	1	2	1	3	1	8	1	0	0	1.1	1.000	OF-3, 3B-2
1976	26	.225	.382	102	23	6	2	2	2.0	14	10	8	18	6	0	0	71	3	1	1	2.9	.987	OF-26
1977	136	.252	.407	413	104	17	4	13	3.1	64	51	49	73	12	29	11	226	11	6	2	1.8	.975	OF-114
1978	156	.306	.537	592	181	46	8	25	4.2	90	98	50	72	15	6	2	320	16	6	5	2.2	.982	OF-152
1979	143	.273	.476	527	144	25	2	26	4.9	84	86	63	95	11	2	0	262	13	5	7	2.0	.982	OF-140, 3B-2
1980	127	.284	.517	437	124	20	8	22	5.0	77	82	74	52	2	5	0	229	7	8	1	1.9	.967	OF-120
1981	99	.268	.460	385	103	19	2	17	4.4	60	53	45	45	1	2	0	193	14	4	4	2.1	.981	OF-98
1982	157	.274	.481	563	154	30	3	27	4.8	90	103	90	91	6	4	1	281	10	6	2	1.9	.980	OF-155
1983	135	.268	.441	492	132	25	0	20	4.1	82	66	74	79	5	1	0	262	20	9	5	2.2	.969	OF-133, 1B-2
1984	57	.320	.537	203	65	9	1	11	5.4	33	44	43	29	1	1	0	120	9	2	3	2.3	.985	OF-54, 1B-4
1985 STL N	126	.281	.502	442	124	26	3	22	5.0	71	87	83	88	1	1	0	1128	66	14	102	9.6	.988	1B-121, OF-12
1986	65	.237	.422	232	55	12	2	9	3.9	34	23	45	61	1	1	1	623	35	3	66	10.2	.995	1B-64
1987	131	.286	**.597**	419	120	23	1	35	8.4	93	106	**136**	139	1	1	0	1152	77	14	116	9.5	.989	1B-126, OF-1
1988 NY A	150	.242	.433	496	120	14	0	27	5.4	81	93	113	141	3	12	3	129	8	5	9	0.9	.965	DH-112, OF-19, 1B-10
1989 SD N	142	.242	.459	455	110	19	1	26	5.7	76	94	**132**	145	6	1	1	1157	89	15	99	8.9	.988	1B-131, OF-12
15 yrs.	1658	.271	.480	5775	1563	291	37	282	4.9	952	998	1006	1130	72	72	19	6161	379	98	421	4.0	.985	OF-1039, 1B-458, DH-112, 3B-4

Year	Team		Games	BA	SA	AB	H	2B	3B	HR	HR%	R	RBI	BB	SO	SB	Pinch Hit AB	H	PO	A	E	DP	TC/G	FA	G by Pos

Jack Clark *continued*

LEAGUE CHAMPIONSHIP SERIES

1985	STL	N	6	.381	.524	21	8	0	0	1	4.8	4	4	5	5	0	0	0	55	0	0	3	9.2	1.000	1B-6
1987			1	.000	.000	1	0	0	0	0	0.0	0	0	0	1	0	1	0	0	0	0	0	0.0	—	
2 yrs.			7	.364	.500	22	8	0	0	1	4.5	4	4	5	6	0	1	0	55	0	0	3	7.9	1.000	1B-6

WORLD SERIES

| 1985 | STL | N | 7 | .240 | .320 | 25 | 6 | 2 | 0 | 0 | 0.0 | 1 | 4 | 3 | 9 | 0 | 0 | 0 | 49 | 4 | 0 | 6 | 7.6 | 1.000 | 1B-7 |

Jerald Clark

CLARK, JERALD DWAYNE
B. Aug. 10, 1963, Crockett, Tex.
BR TR 6'4" 189 lbs.

1988	SD	N	6	.200	.267	15	3	0	0	0	0.0	0	3	0	4	0	3	1	10	1	0	0	1.8	1.000	OF-4
1989			17	.195	.317	41	8	2	0	1	2.4	5	7	3	9	0	4	1	16	2	1	0	1.1	.947	OF-14
2 yrs.			23	.196	.304	56	11	3	0	1	1.8	5	10	3	13	0	7	2	26	3	1	0	1.3	.967	OF-18

Jim Clark

CLARK, JAMES
Born James Petrosky.
B. Sept. 21, 1927, Bagley, Pa.
BR TR 5'9" 150 lbs.

| 1948 | WAS | A | 9 | .250 | .250 | 12 | 3 | 0 | 0 | 0 | 0.0 | 1 | 0 | 0 | 2 | 0 | 6 | 2 | 2 | 4 | 0 | 0 | 0.7 | 1.000 | SS-1, 3B-1 |

Jim Clark

CLARK, JAMES EDWARD
B. Apr. 30, 1947, Kansas City, Kans.
BR TR 6'1" 190 lbs.

| 1971 | CLE | A | 13 | .167 | .278 | 18 | 3 | 0 | 1 | 0 | 0.0 | 2 | 0 | 2 | 7 | 0 | 5 | 1 | 13 | 1 | 1 | 2 | 1.2 | .933 | OF-3, 1B-1 |

Jim Clark

CLARK, JAMES FRANCIS
B. Dec. 26, 1887, Brooklyn, N. Y. D. May 20, 1969, Beaumont, Tex.
BR TR 5'11" 175 lbs.

1911	STL	N	14	.167	.278	18	3	0	1	0	0.0	2	3	3	4	2	6	1	6	0	0	0	0.4	1.000	OF-8
1912			2	.000	.000	1	0	0	0	0	0.0	0	0	0	1	0	1	0	0	0	0	0	0.0	—	
2 yrs.			16	.158	.263	19	3	0	1	0	0.0	2	3	3	5	2	7	1	6	0	0	0	0.4	1.000	OF-8

Mel Clark

CLARK, MELVIN EARL
B. July 7, 1926, Letart, W. Va.
BR TR 6' 180 lbs.

1951	PHI	N	10	.323	.452	31	10	1	0	1	3.2	2	3	0	3	0	3	0	13	0	0	0	1.3	1.000	OF-7
1952			47	.335	.445	155	52	6	4	1	0.6	20	15	6	13	2	7	1	81	6	0	1	1.9	1.000	OF-38, 3B-1
1953			60	.298	.389	198	59	10	4	0	0.0	31	19	11	17	1	8	3	104	2	1	0	1.8	.991	OF-51
1954			83	.240	.352	233	56	9	7	1	0.4	26	24	17	21	0	21	2	114	9	5	2	1.5	.961	OF-63
1955			10	.156	.250	32	5	3	0	0	0.0	3	1	3	4	0	2	0	19	3	0	1	2.2	1.000	OF-8
1957	DET	A	5	.000	.000	7	0	0	0	0	0.0	0	1	0	3	0	3	0	4	0	0	0	0.8	1.000	OF-2
6 yrs.			215	.277	.381	656	182	29	15	3	0.5	82	63	37	61	3	44	6	335	20	6	4	1.7	.983	OF-169, 3B-1

Pep Clark

CLARK, HARRY
B. Mar. 20, 1883, Union City, Ohio D. June 8, 1965, Milwaukee, Wis.
BR TR 5'7½" 175 lbs.

| 1903 | CHI | A | 15 | .308 | .431 | 65 | 20 | 4 | 2 | 0 | 0.0 | 7 | 9 | 2 | | 0 | 0 | 0 | 14 | 36 | 7 | 1 | 3.8 | .877 | 3B-15 |

Ron Clark

CLARK, RONALD BRUCE
B. Jan. 14, 1943, Fort Worth, Tex.
BR TR 5'10" 175 lbs.

1966	MIN	A	5	1.000	1.000	1	1	0	0	0	0.0	0	0	0	0	0	0	0	0	0	0	0	0.0	—	3B-1
1967			20	.167	.350	60	10	3	1	2	3.3	7	11	4	9	0	3	0	7	34	5	0	2.3	.891	3B-16
1968			104	.185	.229	227	42	15	1	1	0.4	14	13	16	44	3	12	1	83	173	17	19	2.6	.938	3B-52, SS-43, 2B-10
1969	2 teams			MIN A	(5G – .125)		SEA A	(57G – .196)																	
"	total		62	.193	.222	171	33	5	0	0	0.0	9	12	13	29	1	3	1	79	117	9	17	3.3	.956	SS-38, 3B-17, 2B-5, 1B-1
1971	OAK	A	2	.000	.000	1	0	0	0	0	0.0	0	0	1	0	0	1	0	0	0	0	0	0.0	—	
1972	2 teams			OAK A	(14G – .267)		MIL A	(22G – .185)																	
"	total		36	.203	.362	69	14	3	0	2	2.9	9	6	7	15	0	7	1	39	61	7	16	3.0	.935	2B-22, 3B-13
1975	PHI	N	1	.000	.000	1	0	0	0	0	0.0	0	0	0	1	0	1	0	0	0	0	0	0.0	—	
7 yrs.			230	.189	.258	530	100	16	3	5	0.9	40	43	41	98	4	27	3	208	385	38	52	2.7	.940	3B-99, SS-81, 2B-37, 1B-1

Roy Clark

CLARK, ROY ELLIOT (Pepper)
B. May 11, 1874, New Haven, Conn. D. Nov. 1, 1925, Bridgeport, Conn.
BL TR 5'8½" 170 lbs.

| 1902 | NY | N | 21 | .145 | .158 | 76 | 11 | 1 | 0 | 0 | 0.0 | 4 | 3 | 1 | | 5 | 1 | 0 | 23 | 2 | 1 | 1 | 1.2 | .962 | OF-20 |

Spider Clark

CLARK, OWEN F.
B. Sept. 16, 1867, Brooklyn, N. Y. D. Feb. 8, 1892, Brooklyn, N. Y.
TR 5'10" 150 lbs.

1889	WAS	N	38	.255	.393	145	37	7	2	3	2.1	19	22	6	18	8	0	0	101	75	26	10	5.3	.871	C-14, SS-13, OF-9, 3B-2, 2B-2
1890	BUF	P	69	.265	.327	260	69	11	1	1	0.4	45	25	20	16	8	0	0	168	63	19	14	3.6	.924	OF-34, C-14, 2B-13, 1B-6, 3B-3, SS-1, P-1
2 yrs.			107	.262	.351	405	106	18	3	4	1.0	64	47	26	34	16	0	0	269	138	45	24	4.2	.900	OF-43, C-28, 2B-15, SS-14, 1B-6, 3B-5, P-1

Will Clark

CLARK, WILLIAM NUSCHLER (The Natural, The Thrill)
B. Mar. 13, 1964, New Orleans, La.
BL TL 6'2" 190 lbs.

1986	SF	N	111	.287	.444	408	117	27	2	11	2.7	66	41	34	76	4	9	6	942	72	11	76	9.2	.989	1B-102
1987			150	.308	.580	529	163	29	5	35	6.6	89	91	49	98	5	11	3	1253	103	13	130	9.1	.991	1B-139
1988			162	.282	.508	575	162	31	6	29	5.0	102	109	100	129	9	5	0	1492	104	12	126	9.9	.993	1B-158
1989			159	.333	.546	588	196	38	9	23	3.9	104	111	74	103	8	1	0	1445	111	10	117	9.8	.994	1B-158
4 yrs.			582	.304	.524	2100	638	125	22	98	4.7	361	352	257	406	26	26	9	5132	390	46	449	9.6	.992	1B-557

LEAGUE CHAMPIONSHIP SERIES

| 1987 | SF | N | 7 | .360 | .560 | 25 | 9 | 2 | 0 | 1 | 4.0 | 3 | 3 | 3 | 6 | 1 | 0 | 0 | 63 | 7 | 1 | 10 | 10.1 | .986 | 1B-7 |

Year	Team		Games	BA	SA	AB	H	2B	3B	HR	HR%	R	RBI	BB	SO	SB	Pinch Hit AB	Pinch Hit H	PO	A	E	DP	TC/G	FA	G by Pos

Will Clark *continued*

| 1989 | | | 5 | .650 | 1.200 | 20 | 13 | 3 | 1 | 2 | 10.0 | 8 | 8 | 2 | 2 | 0 | 0 | 0 | 43 | 6 | 0 | 6 | 9.8 | 1.000 | 1B-5 |
| 2 yrs. | | | 12 | .489 | .844 | 45 | 22 | 5 | 1 | 3 | 6.7 | 11 | 11 | 5 | 8 | 1 | 0 | 0 | 106 | 13 | 1 | 16 | 10.0 | .992 | 1B-12 |

WORLD SERIES

| 1989 | SF | N | 4 | .250 | .313 | 16 | 4 | 1 | 0 | 0 | 0.0 | 2 | 0 | 1 | 3 | 0 | 0 | 0 | 40 | 2 | 0 | 2 | 10.5 | 1.000 | 1B-4 |

Willie Clark

CLARK, WILLIAM OTIS (Wee Willie)
B. Aug. 16, 1872, Pittsburgh, Pa. D. Nov. 13, 1932, Pittsburgh, Pa.

1895	NY	N	23	.261	.341	88	23	3	2	0	0.0	9	16	5		6			0	0	0	0	0.0	–	1B-22
1896			72	.291	.372	247	72	12	4	0	0.0	38	33	15	12	8	7	3	634	25	17	40	9.4	.975	1B-65
1897			116	.283	.385	431	122	17	12	1	0.2	63	75	37		18	1	0	1047	67	18	69	9.8	.984	1B-107, OF-7, 3B-1
1898	PIT	N	57	.306	.431	209	64	9	7	1	0.5	29	31	22		0	0	0	601	27	10	29	11.2	.984	1B-57
1899			80	.285	.396	298	85	13	10	0	0.0	49	44	35		11	2	0	837	36	10	37	11.0	.989	1B-78
5 yrs.			348	.288	.390	1273	366	54	35	2	0.2	188	199	114	18	38	10	3	3119	155	55	175	9.6	.983	1B-329, OF-7, 3B-1

Archie Clarke

CLARKE, ARTHUR FRANKLIN
B. May 6, 1865, Providence, R. I. D. Nov. 14, 1949, Brookline, Mass.

BR TR 5'8" 155 lbs.

1890	NY	N	101	.225	.296	395	89	12	8	0	0.0	55	49	32	38	44	0	0	288	138	55	11	4.8	.886	C-36, OF-33, 3B-16, 2B-15, SS-1
1891			48	.190	.224	174	33	2	2	0	0.0	17	21	15	16	5	0	0	195	58	26	7	5.8	.907	C-42, 3B-5, OF-2
2 yrs.			149	.214	.274	569	122	14	10	0	0.0	72	70	47	54	49	0	0	483	196	81	18	5.1	.893	C-78, OF-35, 3B-21, 2B-15, SS-1

Boileryard Clarke

CLARKE, WILLIAM JONES (Old Reliable)
B. Oct. 18, 1868, New York, N. Y. D. July 29, 1959, Princeton, N. J.

BR TR 5'11½" 170 lbs.

1893	BAL	N	49	.175	.230	183	32	1	3	1	0.5	23	24	19	14	2	0	0	232	48	20	8	6.1	.933	C-38, 1B-11
1894			28	.240	.350	100	24	8	0	1	1.0	18	19	16	14	2	0	0	120	22	12	6	5.5	.922	C-23, 1B-5
1895			67	.290	.378	241	70	15	3	0	0.0	38	35	13	18	8	2	0	219	69	17	13	4.6	.944	C-60, 1B-6
1896			80	.297	.410	300	89	14	7	2	0.7	48	71	14	12	7	1	0	319	55	19	16	4.9	.952	C-67, 1B-4
1897			64	.270	.320	241	65	7	1	1	0.4	32	38	9		5	1	0	226	40	15	6	4.4	.947	C-59, 1B-4
1898			82	.242	.274	285	69	5	2	0	0.0	26	27	4		2	3	0	376	71	17	10	5.7	.963	C-70, 1B-10
1899	BOS	N	60	.224	.283	223	50	3	2	2	0.9	25	32	10		2	0	0	213	69	18	4	5.0	.940	C-60
1900			81	.315	.359	270	85	5	2	1	0.4	35	30	9		0	5	2	306	108	27	9	5.4	.939	C-67, 1B-8
1901	WAS	A	110	.280	.360	422	118	15	5	3	0.7	58	54	23		7	0	0	382	122	25	12	4.8	.953	C-107, 1B-3
1902			87	.268	.392	291	78	15	5	7	2.4	31	42	23		1	0	0	288	97	11	8	4.6	.972	C-87
1903			126	.239	.308	465	111	14	6	2	0.4	35	38	15		12	1	0	1039	90	28	45	9.2	.976	1B-88, C-37
1904			85	.211	.247	275	58	8	1	0	0.0	23	17	17		5	5	0	517	86	13	24	7.2	.979	C-52, 1B-29
1905	NY	N	31	.180	.240	50	9	0	1	0	2.0	2	4	1		1	4	1	137	6	4	4	4.7	.973	1B-17, C-12
13 yrs.			950	.256	.327	3346	858	110	32	21	0.6	394	431	176	58	54	22	3	4374	883	226	165	5.8	.959	C-739, 1B-195

Fred Clarke

CLARKE, FRED CLIFFORD (Cap)
Brother of Josh Clarke.
B. Oct. 3, 1872, Winterset, Iowa D. Aug. 14, 1960, Winfield, Kans.
Manager 1897-1915.
Hall of Fame 1945.

BL TR 5'10½" 165 lbs.

1894	LOU	N	76	.268	.416	310	83	11	7	7	2.3	54	48	25	27	25	0	0	162	15	23	2	2.6	.885	OF-76
1895			132	.347	.425	550	191	21	5	4	0.7	96	82	34	24	40	0	0	344	20	49	4	3.1	.881	OF-132
1896			131	.325	.476	517	168	15	18	9	1.7	96	79	43	34	34	0	0	277	18	30	4	2.5	.908	OF-131
1897			128	.390	.533	518	202	30	13	6	1.2	120	67	45		57	1	1	282	18	24	0	2.5	.926	OF-127
1898			149	.307	.401	599	184	23	12	3	0.5	116	47	48		40	0	0	344	19	23	3	2.6	.940	OF-149
1899			148	.342	.435	602	206	23	9	5	0.8	122	70	49		49	1	0	340	29	20	2	2.6	.949	OF-144, SS-3
1900	PIT	N	106	.276	.396	399	110	15	12	3	0.8	85	32	51		21	2	0	263	8	16	2	2.7	.944	OF-104
1901			129	.324	.461	527	171	24	15	6	1.1	118	60	51		23	1	1	283	15	12	1	2.4	.961	OF-127, SS-1, 3B-1
1902			114	.321	.453	461	148	27	14	2	0.4	104	53	51		29	0	0	215	13	10	2	2.1	.958	OF-113
1903			104	.351	.532	427	150	32	15	5	1.2	88	70	41		21	2	1	171	11	7	3	1.8	.963	OF-101, SS-2
1904			72	.306	.410	278	85	7	11	0	0.0	51	25	22		11	2	1	135	4	3	2	2.0	.979	OF-70
1905			141	.299	.402	525	157	18	15	2	0.4	95	51	55		24	3	1	270	16	7	4	2.1	.976	OF-137
1906			118	.309	.412	417	129	14	13	1	0.2	69	39	40		18	7	5	209	15	6	3	1.9	.974	OF-110
1907			148	.289	.389	501	145	18	13	2	0.4	97	59	68		37	4	1	298	15	4	2	2.1	.987	OF-144
1908			151	.265	.363	551	146	18	15	2	0.4	83	53	65		24	0	0	350	15	10	2	2.5	.973	OF-151
1909			152	.287	.373	550	158	16	11	3	0.5	97	68	80		31	0	0	362	17	5	2	2.5	.987	OF-152
1910			123	.263	.373	429	113	23	9	2	0.5	57	63	53	23	12	0	0	284	10	10	4	2.5	.967	OF-118
1911			110	.324	.492	392	127	25	13	5	1.3	73	49	53	27	10	7	3	216	8	7	3	2.1	.974	OF-101
1913			9	.077	.154	13	1	1	0	0	0.0	0	0	0		0	6	1	2	0	0	0	2.1	1.000	OF-2
1914			2	.000	.000	2	0	0	0	0	0.0	0	0	0		0	1	0	0	0	0	0	0.2	–	
1915			1	.500	.500	2	1	0	0	0	0.0	0	0	0		1	0	0	0	0	0	0	0.0	–	OF-1
21 yrs.			2244	.312	.429	8570	2675	361	220 7th	67	0.8	1621	1015	874	135	506	41	16	4807	266	266	43	2.4	.950	OF-2190, SS-6, 3B-1

WORLD SERIES

1903	PIT	N	8	.265	.382	34	9	2	1	0	0.0	3	2	1	5	1	0	0	17	0	1	0	2.3	.944	OF-8
1909			7	.211	.526	19	4	0	0	2	10.5	7	7	5	3	3	0	0	20	0	1	0	3.0	.952	OF-7
2 yrs.			15	.245	.434	53	13	2	1	2	3.8	10	9	6	8	4	0	0	37	0	2	0	2.6	.949	OF-15

Grey Clarke

CLARKE, RICHARD GREY (Noisy)
B. Sept. 26, 1912, Fulton, Ala.

BR TR 5'9" 183 lbs.

| 1944 | CHI | A | 63 | .260 | .331 | 169 | 44 | 10 | 1 | 0 | 0.0 | 14 | 27 | 22 | 6 | 0 | 15 | 1 | 36 | 107 | 9 | 6 | 2.4 | .941 | 3B-45 |

Harry Clarke

CLARKE, HARRY CORSON
B. 1861 D. Mar. 3, 1923, Long Beach, Calif.

| 1889 | WAS | N | 1 | .000 | .000 | 3 | 0 | 0 | 0 | 0 | 0.0 | 0 | 0 | 0 | 1 | 0 | 0 | 0 | 1 | 2 | 0 | 0 | 3.0 | 1.000 | OF-1 |

Year	Team	Games	BA	SA	AB	H	2B	3B	HR	HR%	R	RBI	BB	SO	SB	Pinch Hit AB	Pinch Hit H	PO	A	E	DP	TC/G	FA	G by Pos

Horace Clarke

CLARKE, HORACE MEREDITH
B. June 2, 1940, Frederiksted, Virgin Islands

BB TR 5'9" 170 lbs.

Year	Team	Games	BA	SA	AB	H	2B	3B	HR	HR%	R	RBI	BB	SO	SB	PH AB	PH H	PO	A	E	DP	TC/G	FA	G by Pos
1965	NY A	51	.259	.296	108	28	1	0	1	0.9	13	9	6	6	2	26	9	21	56	5	5	1.6	.939	3B-17, 2B-7, SS-1
1966		96	.266	.381	312	83	10	4	6	1.9	37	28	27	24	5	11	0	146	196	12	48	3.7	.966	SS-63, 2B-16, 3B-4
1967		143	.272	.316	588	160	17	0	3	0.5	74	29	42	64	21	2	2	348	410	8	79	5.4	.990	2B-140
1968		148	.230	.254	579	133	6	1	2	0.3	52	26	23	46	20	6	2	357	444	13	80	5.5	.984	2B-139
1969		156	.285	.367	641	183	26	7	4	0.6	82	48	53	41	33	0	0	373	429	15	112	5.2	.982	2B-156
1970		158	.251	.309	686	172	24	2	4	0.6	81	46	35	35	23	1	0	379	478	18	95	5.5	.979	2B-157
1971		159	.250	.318	625	156	23	7	2	0.3	76	41	64	43	17	4	1	386	455	16	97	5.4	.981	2B-156
1972		147	.241	.302	547	132	20	2	3	0.5	65	37	56	44	18	5	1	347	399	11	104	5.1	.985	2B-143
1973		148	.263	.308	590	155	21	0	2	0.3	60	35	47	48	11	2	1	378	442	18	107	5.7	.979	2B-147
1974	2 teams	NY A	(24G – .234)		SD	N	(42G – .189)																	
"	total	66	.204	.219	137	28	6	1	0	0.0	8	5	12	11	1	34	5	67	74	2	11	2.2	.986	2B-41, DH-1
10 yrs.		1272	.256	.313	4813	1230	150	23	27	0.6	548	304	365	362	151	91	21	2802	3383	118	738	5.0	.981	2B-1102, SS-64, 3B-21, DH-1

Josh Clarke

CLARKE, JOSHUA BALDWIN (Pepper)
Brother of Fred Clarke.
B. Mar. 8, 1879, Winfield, Kans. D. July 2, 1962, Ventura, Calif.

BL TR 5'10" 180 lbs.

Year	Team	Games	BA	SA	AB	H	2B	3B	HR	HR%	R	RBI	BB	SO	SB	PH AB	PH H	PO	A	E	DP	TC/G	FA	G by Pos
1898	LOU N	6	.167	.167	18	3	0	0	0	0.0	0	0	1		0	1	0	11	0	1	0	2.0	.917	OF-5
1905	STL N	50	.257	.353	167	43	3	2	3	1.8	31	18	27		8	4	1	81	56	13	3	3.0	.913	OF-26, 2B-16, SS-4
1908	CLE A	131	.242	.280	492	119	8	4	1	0.2	70	21	76		37	0	0	220	13	9	1	1.8	.963	OF-131
1909		4	.000	.000	12	0	0	0	0	0.0	1	0	2		0	0	0	3	0	2	0	1.3	.600	OF-4
1911	BOS N	32	.233	.367	120	28	7	3	1	0.8	16	4	29	22	6	2	0	68	7	5	1	2.5	.938	OF-30
5 yrs.		223	.239	.302	809	193	18	9	5	0.6	118	43	135	22	51	7	1	383	76	30	5	2.2	.939	OF-196, 2B-16, SS-4

Nig Clarke

CLARKE, JAY JUSTIN
B. Dec. 15, 1882, Amherstburg, Ont., Canada D. June 15, 1949, River Rouge, Mich.

BB TR 5'8" 165 lbs.

Year	Team	Games	BA	SA	AB	H	2B	3B	HR	HR%	R	RBI	BB	SO	SB	PH AB	PH H	PO	A	E	DP	TC/G	FA	G by Pos
1905	3 teams	CLE A	(5G – .111)		DET	A	(3G – .429)		CLE	A	(37G – .202)													
"	total	45	.208	.292	130	27	6	1	1	0.8	12	10	11		0	2	0	187	42	8	3	5.3	.966	C-43
1906	CLE A	57	.358	.486	179	64	12	4	1	0.6	22	21	13		3	0	0	211	58	5	4	4.8	.982	C-54
1907		120	.269	.372	390	105	19	6	3	0.8	44	33	35		3	5	0	470	119	24	9	5.1	.961	C-115
1908		97	.241	.321	290	70	8	6	1	0.3	34	27	30		6	6	0	327	108	14	6	4.6	.969	C-90
1909		55	.274	.323	164	45	4	2	0	0.0	15	14	9		1	10	0	192	65	13	2	4.9	.952	C-44
1910		21	.155	.190	58	9	2	0	0	0.0	4	2	8		0	3	1	82	32	3	0	5.6	.974	C-17
1911	STL A	82	.215	.262	256	55	10	1	0	0.0	22	18	26		2	4	0	288	112	32	17	5.3	.926	C-73, 1B-4
1919	PHI N	26	.242	.290	62	15	3	0	0	0.0	4	2	4	5	1	4	0	63	30	3	1	3.7	.969	C-22
1920	PIT N	3	.000	.000	7	0	0	0	0	0.0	0	0	2		0	1	0	12	4	0	0	5.3	1.000	C-3
9 yrs.		506	.254	.333	1536	390	64	20	6	0.4	157	127	138	9	16	35	1	1832	570	102	42	4.9	.959	C-461, 1B-4

Stu Clarke

CLARKE, WILLIAM STUART
B. Jan. 24, 1906, San Francisco, Calif. D. Aug. 26, 1985, Hayward, Calif.

BR TR 5'8½" 160 lbs.

Year	Team	Games	BA	SA	AB	H	2B	3B	HR	HR%	R	RBI	BB	SO	SB	PH AB	PH H	PO	A	E	DP	TC/G	FA	G by Pos
1929	PIT N	57	.264	.404	178	47	5	7	2	1.1	20	21	19	21	3	0	0	89	151	19	22	4.5	.927	SS-41, 3B-15, 2B-1
1930		4	.444	.667	9	4	0	1	0	0.0	2	2	1	0	0	2	1	6	4	0	0	2.5	1.000	2B-2
2 yrs.		61	.273	.417	187	51	5	8	2	1.1	22	23	20	21	3	2	1	95	155	19	22	4.4	.929	SS-41, 3B-15, 2B-3

Sumpter Clarke

CLARKE, SUMPTER MILLS
Brother of Rufe Clarke.
B. Oct. 18, 1897, Savannah, Ga. D. Mar. 16, 1962, Knoxville, Tenn.

BR TR 5'11" 170 lbs.

Year	Team	Games	BA	SA	AB	H	2B	3B	HR	HR%	R	RBI	BB	SO	SB	PH AB	PH H	PO	A	E	DP	TC/G	FA	G by Pos
1920	CHI N	1	.333	.333	3	1	0	0	0	0.0	0	0	0	1	0	0	0	0	1	0	0	1.0	1.000	3B-1
1923	CLE A	1	.000	.000	3	0	0	0	0	0.0	0	0	0	0	0	0	0	1	0	0	0	1.0	1.000	OF-1
1924		45	.231	.308	104	24	6	1	0	0.0	17	11	6	12	0	2	1	0	0	0	0	0.0		
3 yrs.		47	.227	.300	110	25	6	1	0	0.0	17	11	6	13	0	2	1	1	1	0	0	0.0	1.000	OF-1, 3B-1

Tommy Clarke

CLARKE, THOMAS ALOYSIUS
B. May 9, 1888, New York, N. Y. D. Aug. 14, 1945, Corona, N. Y.

BR TR 5'11" 175 lbs.

Year	Team	Games	BA	SA	AB	H	2B	3B	HR	HR%	R	RBI	BB	SO	SB	PH AB	PH H	PO	A	E	DP	TC/G	FA	G by Pos
1909	CIN N	18	.250	.385	52	13	3	2	0	0.0	8	10	6		3	1	0	85	26	4	1	6.4	.965	C-17
1910		64	.278	.404	151	42	6	5	1	0.7	19	20	19	17	1	7	0	217	52	8	3	4.3	.971	C-56
1911		86	.241	.355	203	49	6	7	1	0.5	20	25	25	22	4	4	0	318	74	13	11	4.7	.968	C-81, 1B-1
1912		72	.281	.356	146	41	7	2	0	0.0	19	22	28	14	9	7	1	239	58	5	7	4.2	.983	C-63
1913		114	.264	.355	330	87	11	8	1	0.3	29	24	39	40	2	13	5	378	131	11	5	4.6	.979	C-100
1914		113	.262	.367	313	82	13	7	2	0.6	30	25	31	30	6	6	1	448	132	16	12	5.3	.973	C-108
1915		96	.288	.336	226	65	7	2	0	0.0	23	21	33	22	7	20	5	294	71	7	7	3.9	.981	C-72
1916		78	.237	.305	177	42	10	1	0	0.0	10	17	24	20	8	25	5	187	58	9	3	3.3	.965	C-51
1917		29	.291	.400	110	32	3	3	1	0.9	11	13	11	12	2	27	9	93	23	1	2	4.0	.991	C-29
1918	CHI N	1	.—	.—	0	—	0	0	0	—	0	0	0	0	0	0	0	0	0	0	0	0.0	.—	C-1
10 yrs.		671	.265	.358	1708	453	66	37	6	0.4	169	191	216	177	42	110	26	2259	625	74	51	4.4	.975	C-578, 1B-1

Buzz Clarkson

CLARKSON, JAMES BUSTER
B. Mar. 13, 1918, Hopkins, S. C. D. Jan. 18, 1989, Jeannette, Pa.

BR TR 5'11" 210 lbs.

Year	Team	Games	BA	SA	AB	H	2B	3B	HR	HR%	R	RBI	BB	SO	SB	PH AB	PH H	PO	A	E	DP	TC/G	FA	G by Pos
1952	BOS N	14	.200	.200	25	5	0	0	0	0.0	3	1	3	3	0	5	1	11	11	2	0	1.7	.917	SS-6, 3B-2

John Clarkson

CLARKSON, JOHN GIBSON
Brother of Dad Clarkson. Brother of Walter Clarkson.
B. July 1, 1861, Cambridge, Mass. D. Feb. 4, 1909, Belmont, Mass.
Hall of Fame 1963.

BR TR 5'10" 155 lbs.

Year	Team	Games	BA	SA	AB	H	2B	3B	HR	HR%	R	RBI	BB	SO	SB	PH AB	PH H	PO	A	E	DP	TC/G	FA	G by Pos
1882	WOR N	3	.364	.545	11	4	2	0	0	0.0	2		0	3		0	0	1	6	1	0	2.7	.875	P-3, 1B-1
1884	CHI N	21	.262	.488	84	22	6	2	3	3.6	16		2	16		0	0	14	45	20	6	3.8	.747	P-14, OF-8, 3B-2, 1B-1
1885		72	.216	.332	283	61	11	5	4	1.4	34	31	3	44		0	0	27	175	20	8	3.1	.910	P-70, OF-3, 3B-1
1886		55	.233	.329	210	49	9	1	3	1.4	21	23	0	38		0	0	20	114	19	3	2.8	.876	P-55, OF-5
1887		63	.242	.395	215	52	5	5	6	2.8	40	25	11	25	6	0	0	39	125	8	5	2.9	.953	P-60, OF-5
1888	BOS N	55	.195	.263	205	40	9	1	1	0.5	20	17	7	48	5	0	0	23	117	21	3	2.9	.870	P-54, OF-1

Year	Team		Games	BA	SA	AB	H	2B	3B	HR	HR%	R	RBI	BB	SO	SB	Pinch Hit AB	Pinch Hit H	PO	A	E	DP	TC/G	FA	G by Pos

John Clarkson *continued*

1889			73	.206	.286	262	54	9	3	2	0.8	36	23	11	59	8	0	0	37	172	27	8	3.2	.886	P-73, OF-2, 3B-1
1890			45	.249	.353	173	43	6	3	2	1.2	18	26	8	31	2	0	0	22	72	17	3	2.5	.847	P-44, OF-1
1891			55	.225	.305	187	42	7	4	0	0.0	28	26	18	51	2	0	0	27	114	13	2	2.8	.916	P-55, OF-1
1892	2 teams	BOS N (16G – .228)				CLE N	(29G – .139)																		
"	total		45	.171	.209	158	27	3	0	1	0.6	15	17	11	39	3	0	0	11	87	15	4	2.5	.867	P-45
1893	CLE	N	37	.206	.305	131	27	6	2	1	0.8	18	17	4	20	2	0	0	15	82	8	1	2.8	.924	P-36, OF-1
1894			22	.200	.255	55	11	0	0	1	1.8	8	7	6	9	1	0	0	3	42	9	2	2.5	.833	P-22
12 yrs.			546	.219	.319	1974	432	73	26	24	1.2	254	214	81	383	29	0	0	239	1151	178	45	2.9	.886	P-531, OF-27, 3B-4, 1B-2

Ellis Clary

CLARY, ELLIS (Cat)
B. Sept. 11, 1916, Valdosta, Ga.   BR TR 5'8"   160 lbs.

1942	WAS	A	76	.275	.313	240	66	9	0	0	0.0	34	16	45	25	2	5	1	163	181	11	37	4.7	.969	2B-69, 3B-2
1943	2 teams	WAS A (73G – .256)				STL A	(23G – .275)																		
"	total		96	.260	.331	323	84	21	1	0	0.0	51	24	55	37	9	4	1	104	156	14	10	2.9	.949	3B-82, 2B-13, SS-1
1944	STL	A	25	.265	.327	49	13	1	0	0	0.0	6	4	12	9	1	9	1	16	28	1	4	1.8	.978	3B-11, 2B-6
1945			26	.211	.316	38	8	1	0	1	2.6	6	2	2	3	0	4	0	16	21	5	3	1.6	.881	3B-16, 2B-3
4 yrs.			223	.263	.323	650	171	32	2	1	0.2	97	46	114	74	12	22	3	299	386	31	54	3.2	.957	3B-111, 2B-81, SS-1

WORLD SERIES

| 1944 | STL | A | 1 | .000 | .000 | 1 | 0 | 0 | 0 | 0 | 0.0 | 0 | 0 | 0 | 0 | 0 | 1 | 0 | 0 | 0 | 0 | 0 | 0.0 | — | |

Bill Clay

CLAY, FREDERICK C.
B. Nov. 23, 1874, Baltimore, Md.   D. Oct. 12, 1917, York, Pa.   TR

| 1902 | PHI | N | 3 | .250 | .250 | 8 | 2 | 0 | 0 | 0 | 0.0 | 1 | 1 | 0 | | 0 | 0 | 0 | 3 | 0 | 1 | 0 | 1.3 | .750 | OF-3 |

Dain Clay

CLAY, DAIN ELMER (Ding-a-Ling)
B. July 10, 1919, Hicksville, Ohio   BR TR 5'10½" 160 lbs.

1943	CIN	N	49	.269	.376	93	25	2	4	0	0.0	19	9	8	14	1	10	3	42	2	3	0	1.0	.936	OF-33
1944			110	.250	.292	356	89	15	0	0	0.0	51	17	17	18	8	5	1	272	4	2	0	2.5	.993	OF-98
1945			153	.280	.335	656	184	29	2	1	0.2	81	50	37	58	19	0	0	446	10	5	3	3.0	.989	OF-152
1946			121	.228	.280	435	99	17	0	2	0.5	52	22	53	40	11	0	0	312	10	4	3	2.7	.988	OF-120
4 yrs.			433	.258	.312	1540	397	63	6	3	0.2	203	98	115	130	39	15	4	1072	26	14	6	2.6	.987	OF-403

Bob Clemens

CLEMENS, ROBERT BAXTER
B. Aug. 9, 1886, Mount Hebron, Mo.   D. Apr. 5, 1964, Marshall, Mo.   BR TR 5'9"   163 lbs.

| 1914 | STL | A | 7 | .231 | .385 | 13 | 3 | 0 | 1 | 0 | 0.0 | 1 | 3 | 2 | 1 | 0 | 2 | 0 | 5 | 1 | 2 | 0 | 1.1 | .750 | OF-5 |

Chet Clemens

CLEMENS, CHESTER SPURGEON
B. May 10, 1917, San Fernando, Calif.   BR TR 6'   175 lbs.

1939	BOS	N	9	.217	.217	23	5	0	0	0	0.0	2	1	1	3	1	1	0	13	0	2	0	1.7	.867	OF-7
1944			19	.176	.353	17	3	1	1	0	0.0	7	2	2	2	0	4	1	6	0	0	0	0.3	1.000	OF-7
2 yrs.			28	.200	.275	40	8	1	1	0	0.0	9	3	3	5	1	5	1	19	0	2	0	0.8	.905	OF-14

Clem Clemens

CLEMENS, CLEMENT LAMBERT
Born Clement Lambert Ulatowski.
B. Nov. 21, 1886, Chicago, Ill.   D. Nov. 2, 1967, St. Petersburg, Fla.   BR TR 5'11" 176 lbs.

1914	CHI	F	13	.148	.148	27	4	0	0	0	0.0	4	2	3		0	5	0	30	8	2	1	3.1	.950	C-8
1915			11	.136	.182	22	3	1	0	0	0.0	3	3	1		0	0	0	29	5	0	1	3.1	.944	C-9, 2B-2
1916	CHI	N	10	.000	.000	15	0	0	0	0	0.0	0	0	1	6	0	1	0	26	6	2	0	3.4	.941	C-9
3 yrs.			34	.109	.125	64	7	1	0	0	0.0	7	5	5	6	0	6	0	85	19	4	2	3.2	.963	C-26, 2B-2

Doug Clemens

CLEMENS, DOUGLAS HORACE
B. June 9, 1939, Leesport, Pa.   BL TR 6'   180 lbs.

1960	STL	N	1	–	–	0	0	0	0	0	–	0	0	0	0	0	0	0	2	0	0	0	2.0	1.000	OF-1
1961			6	.167	.250	12	2	1	0	0	0.0	0	1	0	3	0	3	1	2	0	0	0	0.5	.667	OF-3
1962			48	.237	.301	93	22	1	1	1	1.1	12	12	17	19	0	15	5	38	0	1	0	0.8	.974	OF-34
1963			5	.167	.667	6	1	0	0	1	16.7	1	2	1	2	0	1	0	3	1	0	0	0.8	1.000	OF-3
1964	2 teams	STL N (33G – .205)				CHI N	(54G – .279)																		
"	total		87	.252	.404	218	55	14	5	3	1.4	31	21	24	38	0	19	3	97	7	7	1	1.3	.937	OF-62
1965	CHI	N	128	.221	.288	340	75	11	0	4	1.2	36	26	38	53	5	25	6	145	7	3	0	1.2	.981	OF-105
1966	PHI	N	79	.256	.289	121	31	1	0	1	0.8	10	15	16	25	1	49	12	43	2	0	1	0.6	1.000	OF-28, 1B-1
1967			69	.178	.247	73	13	5	0	0	0.0	2	4	8	15	0	54	11	5	0	0	0	0.1	1.000	OF-10
1968			29	.211	.368	57	12	1	1	2	3.5	6	8	7	13	0	13	3	25	1	0	0	0.9	1.000	OF-17
9 yrs.			452	.229	.321	920	211	34	7	12	1.3	99	88	114	166	6	179	41	360	18	12	2	0.9	.969	OF-263, 1B-1

Wally Clement

CLEMENT, WALLACE OAKES
B. July 21, 1881, Auburn, Me.   D. Nov. 1, 1953, Coral Gables, Fla.   BL TR 5'11" 175 lbs.

1908	PHI	N	16	.222	.306	36	8	3	0	0	0.0	0	0	0		2	8	2	21	1	0	1	1.4	1.000	OF-8
1909	2 teams	PHI N (3G – .000)				BKN N	(92G – .256)																		
"	total		95	.254	.300	343	87	8	4	0	0.0	35	17	18		11	7	1	179	14	7	4	2.1	.965	OF-88
2 yrs.			111	.251	.301	379	95	11	4	0	0.0	35	18	18		13	15	3	200	15	7	5	2.0	.968	OF-96

Roberto Clemente

CLEMENTE, ROBERTO (Bob)
Born Roberto Clemente y Walker.
B. Aug. 18, 1934, Carolina, Puerto Rico   D. Dec. 31, 1972, San Juan, Puerto Rico
Hall of Fame 1973.   BR TR 5'11" 175 lbs.

1955	PIT	N	124	.255	.382	474	121	23	11	5	1.1	48	47	18	60	2	8	2	253	18	6	5	2.2	.978	OF-118
1956			147	.311	.431	543	169	30	7	7	1.3	66	60	13	58	6	11	4	275	20	15	2	2.1	.952	OF-139, 2B-2, 3B-1
1957			111	.253	.348	451	114	17	7	4	0.9	42	30	23	45	0	2	1	272	9	6	1	2.6	.979	OF-109
1958			140	.289	.408	519	150	24	10	6	1.2	69	50	31	41	8	5	1	312	22	6	3	2.4	.982	OF-135
1959			105	.296	.396	432	128	17	7	4	0.9	60	50	15	51	2	0	0	229	10	13	1	2.4	.948	OF-104

Year	Team	Games	BA	SA	AB	H	2B	3B	HR	HR%	R	RBI	BB	SO	SB	Pinch Hit AB	Pinch Hit H	PO	A	E	DP	TC/G	FA	G by Pos

Roberto Clemente *continued*

Year	Team	Games	BA	SA	AB	H	2B	3B	HR	HR%	R	RBI	BB	SO	SB	AB	H	PO	A	E	DP	TC/G	FA	G by Pos
1960		144	.314	.458	570	179	22	6	16	2.8	89	94	39	72	4	3	0	246	19	8	2	1.9	.971	OF-142
1961		146	.351	.559	572	201	30	10	23	4.0	100	89	35	59	4	2	1	256	27	9	5	2.0	.969	OF-144
1962		144	.312	.454	538	168	28	9	10	1.9	95	74	35	73	6	2	0	269	19	8	1	2.1	.973	OF-142
1963		152	.320	.470	600	192	23	8	17	2.8	77	76	31	64	12	3	1	239	11	11	2	1.7	.958	OF-151
1964		155	.339	.484	622	211	40	7	12	1.9	95	87	51	87	5	1	0	289	13	10	2	2.0	.968	OF-154
1965		152	.329	.463	589	194	21	14	10	1.7	91	65	43	78	8	8	2	288	16	10	1	2.1	.968	OF-145
1966		154	.317	.536	638	202	31	11	29	4.5	105	119	46	109	7	1	0	318	17	12	3	2.3	.965	OF-154
1967		147	.357	.554	585	209	26	10	23	3.9	103	110	41	103	9	2	0	273	17	9	4	2.0	.970	OF-145
1968		132	.291	.482	502	146	18	12	18	3.6	74	57	51	77	2	2	0	297	9	5	1	2.4	.984	OF-131
1969		138	.345	.544	507	175	20	12	19	3.7	87	91	56	73	4	3	2	226	14	5	1	1.8	.980	OF-135
1970		108	.352	.556	412	145	22	10	14	3.4	65	60	38	66	3	4	1	189	12	7	2	1.9	.966	OF-104
1971		132	.341	.502	522	178	29	8	13	2.5	82	86	26	65	1	9	3	267	11	2	4	2.1	.993	OF-124
1972		102	.312	.479	378	118	19	7	10	2.6	68	60	29	49	0	7	1	199	5	0	2	2.0	1.000	OF-94
18 yrs.		2433	.317	.475	9454	3000	440	166	240	2.5	1416	1305	621	1230	83	73	19	4697	269	142	42	2.1	.972	OF-2370, 2B-2, 3B-1

LEAGUE CHAMPIONSHIP SERIES

Year	Team	Games	BA	SA	AB	H	2B	3B	HR	HR%	R	RBI	BB	SO	SB	AB	H	PO	A	E	DP	TC/G	FA	G by Pos
1970	PIT N	3	.214	.214	14	3	0	0	0	0.0	1	1	0	4	0	0	0	7	0	0	0	2.3	1.000	OF-3
1971		4	.333	.333	18	6	0	0	0	0.0	2	4	1	6	0	0	0	12	0	0	0	3.0	1.000	OF-4
1972		5	.235	.471	17	4	1	0	1	5.9	1	2	3	5	0	0	0	10	0	0	0	2.0	1.000	OF-5
3 yrs.		12	.265	.347	49	13	1	0	1	2.0	4	7	4	15	0	0	0	29	0	0	0	2.4	1.000	OF-12

WORLD SERIES

Year	Team	Games	BA	SA	AB	H	2B	3B	HR	HR%	R	RBI	BB	SO	SB	AB	H	PO	A	E	DP	TC/G	FA	G by Pos
1960	PIT N	7	.310	.310	29	9	0	0	0	0.0	1	3	0	4	0	0	0	19	0	0	0	2.7	1.000	OF-7
1971		7	.414	.759	29	12	2	1	2	6.9	3	4	2	2	0	0	0	15	0	0	0	2.1	1.000	OF-7
2 yrs.		14	.362 (7th)	.534	58	21	2	1	2	3.4	4	7	2	6	0	0	0	34	0	0	0	2.4	1.000	OF-14

Ed Clements

CLEMENTS, EDWARD
B. Philadelphia, Pa.   Deceased.

Year	Team	Games	BA	SA	AB	H	2B	3B	HR	HR%	R	RBI	BB	SO	SB	AB	H	PO	A	E	DP	TC/G	FA	G by Pos
1890	PIT N	1	.000	.000	1	0	0	0	0	0.0	0	0	0	0	0	0	0	1	1	3	0	5.0	.400	SS-1

Jack Clements

CLEMENTS, JOHN J.
B. June 24, 1864, Philadelphia, Pa.   D. May 23, 1941, Philadelphia, Pa.
Manager 1890.

BL TL 5'8½" 204 lbs.

Year	Team	Games	BA	SA	AB	H	2B	3B	HR	HR%	R	RBI	BB	SO	SB	AB	H	PO	A	E	DP	TC/G	FA	G by Pos
1884	2 teams	PHI U (41G – .282)			PHI N (9G – .233)																			
"	total	50	.275	.401	207	57	13	2	3	1.4	40		13	8		0	0	193	62	45	3	6.0	.850	C-29, OF-22, SS-1
1885	PHI N	52	.191	.298	188	36	11	3	1	0.5	14		2	30		0	0	196	49	32	3	5.3	.884	C-41, OF-11
1886		54	.205	.243	185	38	5	1	0	0.0	15	11	7	34		0	0	334	54	30	3	7.7	.928	C-47, OF-7
1887		66	.280	.402	246	69	13	7	1	0.4	48	47	9	24	7	0	0	338	91	26	10	6.9	.943	C-59, 3B-4, SS-3
1888		86	.245	.304	326	80	8	4	1	0.3	26	32	10	36	3	0	0	496	104	47	6	7.5	.927	C-85, OF-1
1889		78	.284	.384	310	88	17	1	4	1.3	51	35	29	21	3	0	0	380	77	42	7	6.4	.916	C-78
1890		97	.315	.472	381	120	23	8	7	1.8	64	74	45	30	10	0	0	549	95	35	14	7.0	.948	C-91, 1B-5
1891		107	.310	.426	423	131	29	4	4	0.9	58	75	43	19	3	0	0	415	108	41	10	5.3	.927	C-107, 1B-2
1892		109	.264	.415	402	106	25	6	8	2.0	50	76	43	40	7	0	0	557	107	35	12	6.4	.950	C-107, 1B-1
1893		94	.285	.489	376	107	20	3	17	4.5	64	80	39	29	3	2	0	330	76	26	6	4.6	.940	C-92, 1B-1
1894		45	.346	.503	159	55	6	5	3	1.9	26	36	24	7	6	0	0	178	32	12	4	4.9	.946	C-45
1895		88	.394	.612	322	127	27	2	13	4.0	64	75	22	7	3	0	0	280	69	11	7	4.1	.969	C-88
1896		57	.359	.543	184	66	5	7	5	2.7	35	45	17	14	2	3	0	149	51	7	3	3.6	.966	C-53
1897		55	.238	.378	185	44	4	2	6	3.2	18	36	12		3	5	1	163	40	8	3	3.8	.962	C-49
1898	STL N	99	.257	.370	335	86	19	5	3	0.9	39	41	21		1	12	1	287	81	11	8	3.8	.971	C-86
1899	CLE N	4	.250	.250	12	3	0	0	0	0.0	1	0	0		0	0	0	8	7	1	0	4.0	.938	C-4
1900	BOS N	16	.310	.405	42	13	1	0	1	2.4	6	10	3		0	6	0	45	10	3	2	3.6	.948	C-10
17 yrs.		1157	.286	.421	4283	1226	226	60	77	1.8	619	673	339	299	51	28	2	4898	1113	412	101	5.6	.936	C-1073, OF-41, 1B-8, SS-4, 3B-4

Verne Clemons

CLEMONS, VERNE JAMES (Fats)
B. Sept. 8, 1891, Clemons, Iowa   D. May 5, 1959, Bay Pines, Fla.

BR TR 5'9½" 190 lbs.

Year	Team	Games	BA	SA	AB	H	2B	3B	HR	HR%	R	RBI	BB	SO	SB	AB	H	PO	A	E	DP	TC/G	FA	G by Pos
1916	STL A	4	.143	.286	7	1	1	0	0	0.0	0	0	1		0	2	0	5	3	1	0	2.3	.889	C-2
1919	STL N	88	.264	.360	239	63	13	2	2	0.8	14	22	26	13	4	10	5	289	89	7	8	4.4	.982	C-75
1920		112	.281	.355	338	95	10	6	1	0.3	17	36	30	12	1	7	1	408	111	12	11	4.7	.977	C-103
1921		117	.320	.396	341	109	16	2	2	0.6	29	48	33	17	1	8	2	357	101	7	12	4.0	.985	C-109
1922		71	.256	.281	160	41	4	0	0	0.0	9	15	18	5	1	7	1	172	50	1	2	3.1	.996	C-63
1923		57	.285	.369	130	37	9	1	0	0.0	6	13	10	11	0	13	4	124	34	3	1	2.8	.981	C-41
1924		25	.321	.375	56	18	3	0	0	0.0	3	6	2	3	0	7	2	46	11	1	1	2.3	.983	C-17
7 yrs.		474	.286	.360	1271	364	56	11	5	0.4	78	140	119	62	6	54	15	1401	399	32	35	3.9	.983	C-410

Donn Clendenon

CLENDENON, DONN ALVIN
B. July 15, 1935, Neosho, Mo.

BR TR 6'4" 209 lbs.

Year	Team	Games	BA	SA	AB	H	2B	3B	HR	HR%	R	RBI	BB	SO	SB	AB	H	PO	A	E	DP	TC/G	FA	G by Pos
1961	PIT N	9	.314	.400	35	11	1	1	0	0.0	7	2	5	10	0	1	0	15	1	0	0	1.8	1.000	OF-8
1962		80	.302	.477	222	67	8	5	7	3.2	39	28	26	58	16	6	1	414	25	6	44	5.6	.987	1B-52, OF-19
1963		154	.275	.430	563	155	28	7	15	2.7	65	57	39	136	22	5	0	1450	118	15	154	10.3	.991	1B-151
1964		133	.282	.446	457	129	23	8	12	2.6	53	64	26	96	12	15	7	1153	75	14	116	9.3	.989	1B-119
1965		162	.301	.467	612	184	32	14	14	2.3	89	96	48	128	9	3	1	1572	121	28	161	10.6	.984	1B-158, 3B-1
1966		155	.299	.520	571	171	22	10	28	4.9	80	98	52	142	8	4	1	1452	96	24	182	10.1	.985	1B-152
1967		131	.249	.370	478	119	15	2	13	2.7	46	56	34	107	4	4	0	1199	89	15	122	9.9	.988	1B-123
1968		158	.257	.399	584	150	20	6	17	2.9	63	87	47	163	10	2	1	1587	128	17	134	11.0	.990	1B-155
1969	2 teams	MON N (38G – .240)			NY N (72G – .252)																			
"	total	110	.248	.432	331	82	11	1	16	4.8	45	51	25	94	3	24	2	648	47	12	70	6.4	.983	1B-82, OF-12
1970	NY N	121	.288	.515	396	114	18	3	22	5.6	65	97	39	91	4	22	5	722	62	7	72	6.5	.991	1B-100
1971		88	.247	.411	263	65	10	0	11	4.2	29	37	21	78	1	27	2	505	37	8	49	6.3	.985	1B-72

Year	Team	Games	BA	SA	AB	H	2B	3B	HR	HR%	R	RBI	BB	SO	SB	Pinch Hit AB	Pinch Hit H	PO	A	E	DP	TC/G	FA	G by Pos

Donn Clendenon *continued*

Year	Team	Games	BA	SA	AB	H	2B	3B	HR	HR%	R	RBI	BB	SO	SB	PH AB	PH H	PO	A	E	DP	TC/G	FA	G by Pos
1972	STL N	61	.191	.309	136	26	4	0	4	2.9	13	9	17	37	1	20	4	259	26	4	34	4.7	.986	1B-36
12 yrs.		1362	.274	.442	4648	1273	192	57	159	3.4	594	682	379	1140	90	137	25	10976	825	150	1138	8.8	.987	1B-1200, OF-39, 3B-1

WORLD SERIES

Year	Team	Games	BA	SA	AB	H	2B	3B	HR	HR%	R	RBI	BB	SO	SB	PH AB	PH H	PO	A	E	DP	TC/G	FA	G by Pos
1969	NY N	4	.357	1.071	14	5	1	0	3	21.4	4	4	2	6	0	0	0	30	4	0	0	8.5	1.000	1B-4

Elmer Cleveland

CLEVELAND, ELMER ELLSWORTH
B. Sept. 15, 1862, Washington, D. C. D. Oct. 8, 1913, Zimmerman, Pa. BR TR

Year	Team	Games	BA	SA	AB	H	2B	3B	HR	HR%	R	RBI	BB	SO	SB	PH AB	PH H	PO	A	E	DP	TC/G	FA	G by Pos
1884	CIN U	29	.322	.443	115	37	9	1	1	0.9	24		4			0	0	48	54	19	0	4.2	.843	3B-29
1888	2 teams	NY N (9G – .235)			PIT N (30G – .222)																			
"	total	39	.225	.366	142	32	3	4	4	2.8	16	16	8	24	4	0	0	27	52	19	4	2.5	.806	3B-39
1891	COL AA	12	.171	.171	41	7	0	0	0	0.0	12	4	12	9	4	0	0	23	36	11	1	5.8	.843	3B-12
3 yrs.		80	.255	.369	298	76	11	4	5	1.7	52	20	24	33	8	0	0	98	142	49	4	3.6	.830	3B-80

Stan Cliburn

CLIBURN, STANLEY GENE
Brother of Stewart Cliburn.
B. Dec. 19, 1956, Jackson, Miss. BR TR 6' 195 lbs.

Year	Team	Games	BA	SA	AB	H	2B	3B	HR	HR%	R	RBI	BB	SO	SB	PH AB	PH H	PO	A	E	DP	TC/G	FA	G by Pos
1980	CAL A	54	.179	.321	56	10	2	0	2	3.6	7	6	3	9	0	0	0	127	9	4	0	2.6	.971	C-54

Harlond Clift

CLIFT, HARLOND BENTON (Darkie)
B. Aug. 12, 1912, El Reno, Okla. BR TR 5'11" 180 lbs.

Year	Team	Games	BA	SA	AB	H	2B	3B	HR	HR%	R	RBI	BB	SO	SB	PH AB	PH H	PO	A	E	DP	TC/G	FA	G by Pos
1934	STL A	147	.260	.421	572	149	30	10	14	2.4	104	56	84	100	7	5	1	150	245	30	28	2.9	.929	3B-141
1935		137	.295	.436	475	140	26	4	11	2.3	101	69	83	39	0	5	1	144	259	27	14	3.1	.937	3B-127, 2B-6
1936		152	.302	.514	576	174	40	11	20	3.5	145	73	115	68	12	0	0	158	310	24	27	3.2	.951	3B-152
1937		155	.306	.546	571	175	36	7	29	5.1	103	118	98	80	8	0	0	198	405	34	50	4.1	.947	3B-155
1938		149	.290	.554	534	155	25	7	34	6.4	119	118	118	67	10	0	0	176	306	19	31	3.4	.962	3B-149
1939		151	.270	.411	526	142	25	2	15	2.9	90	84	111	55	4	0	0	184	324	25	34	3.5	.953	3B-149
1940		150	.273	.463	523	143	29	5	20	3.8	92	87	104	62	9	2	1	161	329	21	32	3.4	.959	3B-147
1941		154	.255	.430	584	149	33	9	17	2.9	108	84	113	93	6	0	0	195	316	22	27	3.5	.959	3B-154
1942		143	.274	.399	541	148	39	4	7	1.3	108	55	106	48	6	1	0	160	287	28	28	3.3	.941	3B-141, SS-1
1943	2 teams	STL A (105G – .232)			WAS A (8G – .300)																			
"	total	113	.237	.301	409	97	11	3	3	0.7	47	29	59	40	5	0	0	144	264	21	20	3.8	.951	3B-112
1944	WAS A	12	.159	.227	44	7	3	0	0	0.0	4	3	3	3	0	0	0	10	22	6	2	3.2	.842	3B-12
1945		119	.211	.307	375	79	12	0	8	2.1	49	53	76	58	2	8	0	111	214	23	18	2.9	.934	3B-111
12 yrs.		1582	.272	.441	5730	1558	309	62	178	3.1	1070	829	1070	713	69	21	3	1791	3281	280	311	3.4	.948	3B-1550, 2B-6, SS-1

Flea Clifton

CLIFTON, HERMAN EARL
B. Dec. 12, 1909, Cincinnati, Ohio BR TR 5'10" 160 lbs.

Year	Team	Games	BA	SA	AB	H	2B	3B	HR	HR%	R	RBI	BB	SO	SB	PH AB	PH H	PO	A	E	DP	TC/G	FA	G by Pos
1934	DET A	16	.063	.063	16	1	0	0	0	0.0	3	1	1	2	0	8	1	3	7	1	0	0.7	.909	3B-4, 2B-1
1935		43	.255	.300	110	28	5	0	0	0.0	15	9	5	13	2	7	1	34	59	4	9	2.3	.959	3B-21, 2B-5, SS-4
1936		13	.192	.231	26	5	1	0	0	0.0	5	1	4	3	0	1	1	12	16	3	4	2.4	.903	SS-6, 3B-2, 2B-1
1937		15	.116	.140	43	5	1	0	0	0.0	4	2	7	10	3	0	0	21	29	4	4	3.6	.926	3B-7, SS-4, 2B-3
4 yrs.		87	.200	.236	195	39	7	0	0	0.0	27	13	17	28	5	16	3	70	111	12	17	2.2	.938	3B-34, SS-14, 2B-10

WORLD SERIES

Year	Team	Games	BA	SA	AB	H	2B	3B	HR	HR%	R	RBI	BB	SO	SB	PH AB	PH H	PO	A	E	DP	TC/G	FA	G by Pos
1935	DET A	4	.000	.000	16	0	0	0	0	0.0	1	0	2	4	0	0	0	2	9	1	0	3.0	.917	3B-4

Monk Cline

CLINE, JOHN P.
B. Mar. 3, 1858 D. Sept. 23, 1916, Louisville, Ky. BL TL 5'4" 150 lbs.

Year	Team	Games	BA	SA	AB	H	2B	3B	HR	HR%	R	RBI	BB	SO	SB	PH AB	PH H	PO	A	E	DP	TC/G	FA	G by Pos
1882	BAL AA	44	.221	.279	172	38	6	2	0	0.0	18		3			0	0	85	33	28	4	3.3	.808	OF-39, SS-8, 2B-2, 3B-1
1884	LOU AA	94	.290	.381	396	115	16	7	2	0.5	91		27			0	0	146	37	29	1	2.3	.863	OF-90, SS-6
1885		2	.222	.333	9	2	1	0	0	0.0	0		0			0	0	2	1	0	0	1.5	1.000	OF-1, 3B-1
1888	KC AA	73	.235	.294	293	69	13	2	0	0.0	45	19	20		29	0	0	95	27	16	5	1.9	.884	OF-70, 2B-3, 3B-1
1891	LOU AA	21	.303	.368	76	23	3	1	0	0.0	13	12	19	3	2	0	0	27	2	3	0	1.5	.906	OF-21
5 yrs.		234	.261	.334	946	247	39	12	2	0.2	167	31	69	3	31	0	0	355	100	76	10	2.3	.857	OF-221, SS-14, 2B-5, 3B-3

Ty Cline

CLINE, TYRONE ALEXANDER
B. June 15, 1939, Hampton, S. C. BL TL 6'½" 170 lbs.

Year	Team	Games	BA	SA	AB	H	2B	3B	HR	HR%	R	RBI	BB	SO	SB	PH AB	PH H	PO	A	E	DP	TC/G	FA	G by Pos
1960	CLE A	7	.308	.423	26	8	1	1	0	0.0	2	2	0	4	0	1	0	22	0	0	0	3.1	1.000	OF-6
1961		12	.209	.302	43	9	2	1	0	0.0	9	1	6	1	0	1	0	19	0	0	0	1.6	1.000	OF-12
1962		118	.248	.331	375	93	15	5	2	0.5	53	28	28	50	5	10	1	238	3	2	1	2.1	.992	OF-107
1963	MIL N	72	.236	.259	174	41	2	1	0	0.0	17	10	10	31	2	7	3	116	5	1	3	1.7	.992	OF-62
1964		101	.302	.397	116	35	4	2	1	0.9	22	13	8	22	0	40	14	83	5	1	1	0.9	.989	OF-54, 1B-6
1965		123	.191	.241	220	42	5	3	0	0.0	27	10	16	50	2	29	6	142	7	4	2	1.2	.974	OF-86, 1B-5
1966	2 teams	CHI N (7G – .353)			ATL N (42G – .254)																			
"	total	49	.273	.273	88	24	0	0	0	0.0	15	8	3	13	3	22	6	89	2	1	1	1.9	.989	OF-24, 1B-6
1967	2 teams	ATL N (10G – .000)			SF N (64G – .270)																			
"	total	74	.254	.369	130	33	5	5	0	0.0	18	4	9	16	2	24	4	52	0	0	0	0.7	1.000	OF-38
1968	SF N	116	.223	.275	291	65	3	1	0	0.0	37	28	11	26	0	26	5	272	14	4	13	2.5	.986	OF-70, 1B-24
1969	MON N	101	.239	.321	209	50	5	3	2	1.0	26	12	32	22	4	42	9	176	8	2	7	1.8	.989	OF-41, 1B-17
1970	2 teams	MON N (2G – .500)			CIN N (48G – .270)																			
"	total	50	.277	.415	65	18	7	1	0	0.0	13	8	12	11	1	26	7	0	0	0	0	–		OF-20, 1B-2
1971	CIN N	69	.196	.206	97	19	1	0	0	0.0	12	1	18	16	2	39	5	40	0	0	0	0.6	1.000	OF-28, 1B-2
12 yrs.		892	.238	.304	1834	437	53	25	6	0.3	251	125	153	262	22	266	60	1249	44	15	36	1.5	.989	OF-548, 1B-62

LEAGUE CHAMPIONSHIP SERIES

Year	Team	Games	BA	SA	AB	H	2B	3B	HR	HR%	R	RBI	BB	SO	SB	PH AB	PH H	PO	A	E	DP	TC/G	FA	G by Pos
1970	CIN N	2	1.000	3.000	1	1	0	0	0	0.0	2	0	0	0	0	1	1	0	0	0	0	0.0	–	OF-1

WORLD SERIES

Year	Team	Games	BA	SA	AB	H	2B	3B	HR	HR%	R	RBI	BB	SO	SB	PH AB	PH H	PO	A	E	DP	TC/G	FA	G by Pos
1970	CIN N	3	.333	.333	3	1	0	0	0	0.0	0	0	0	0	0	3	1	0	0	0	0	0.0	–	–

Year	Team		Games	BA	SA	AB	H	2B	3B	HR	HR%	R	RBI	BB	SO	SB	Pinch Hit AB	Pinch Hit H	PO	A	E	DP	TC/G	FA	G by Pos

Gene Clines

CLINES, EUGENE ANTHONY
B. Oct. 6, 1946, San Pablo, Calif.
BR TR 5'9" 170 lbs.

Year	Team		Games	BA	SA	AB	H	2B	3B	HR	HR%	R	RBI	BB	SO	SB	AB	H	PO	A	E	DP	TC/G	FA	G by Pos
1970	PIT	N	31	.405	.459	37	15	2	0	0	0.0	4	3	2	5	2	20	8	4	0	0	0	0.1	1.000	OF-7
1971			97	.308	.392	273	84	12	4	1	0.4	52	24	22	36	15	19	7	146	8	3	2	1.6	.981	OF-74
1972			107	.334	.421	311	104	15	6	0	0.0	52	17	16	47	12	19	2	131	7	6	0	1.3	.958	OF-83
1973			110	.263	.329	304	80	11	3	1	0.3	42	23	26	36	8	35	10	145	6	5	0	1.4	.968	OF-77
1974			107	.225	.250	276	62	5	1	0	0.0	29	14	30	40	14	27	6	177	6	2	1	1.7	.989	OF-78
1975	NY	N	82	.227	.286	203	46	6	3	0	0.0	25	10	11	21	4	18	2	98	9	2	2	1.3	.982	OF-60
1976	TEX	A	116	.276	.316	446	123	12	3	0	0.0	52	38	16	52	11	5	2	215	9	3	1	2.0	.987	OF-103, DH-10
1977	CHI	N	101	.293	.397	239	70	12	2	3	1.3	41	25	25	25	1	39	10	68	3	1	0	0.7	.986	OF-63
1978			109	.258	.319	229	59	10	2	0	0.0	31	17	21	28	4	43	10	84	6	2	0	0.8	.978	OF-66
1979			10	.200	.200	10	2	0	0	0	0.0	0	0	0	1	0	10	2	0	0	0	0	0.0	–	
10 yrs.			870	.277	.341	2328	645	85	24	5	0.2	314	187	169	291	71	235	59	1068	54	24	6	1.3	.979	OF-611, DH-10
LEAGUE CHAMPIONSHIP SERIES																									
1971	PIT	N	1	.333	1.333	3	1	0	0	1	33.3	1	1	0	0	0	0	0	1	0	0	0	1.0	1.000	OF-1
1972			2	.000	.000	2	0	0	0	0	0.0	1	0	0	1	0	2	0	0	0	0	0	0.0	–	
1974			2	.000	.000	1	0	0	0	0	0.0	1	0	0	1	0	0	0	0	0	0	0	0.0	–	OF-2
3 yrs.			5	.167	.667	6	1	0	0	1	16.7	3	1	0	2	0	2	0	1	0	0	0	0.2	1.000	OF-3
WORLD SERIES																									
1971	PIT	N	3	.091	.273	11	1	0	1	0	0.0	2	0	1	1	1	0	0	6	0	0	0	2.0	1.000	OF-3

Billy Clingman

CLINGMAN, WILLIAM FREDERICK
B. Nov. 21, 1869, Cincinnati, Ohio D. May 14, 1958, Cincinnati, Ohio
BB TR 5'11" 150 lbs.

Year	Team		Games	BA	SA	AB	H	2B	3B	HR	HR%	R	RBI	BB	SO	SB	AB	H	PO	A	E	DP	TC/G	FA	G by Pos
1890	CIN	N	7	.259	.296	27	7	1	0	0	0.0	2	5	1		0	0	0	8	26	4	4	5.4	.895	SS-6, 2B-1
1891	CIN	AA	1	.200	.400	5	1	1	0	0	0.0	0	0	0		0	0	0	0	2	1	0	3.0	.667	2B-1
1895	PIT	N	106	.259	.322	382	99	16	4	0	0.0	69	45	41	43	19	0	0	137	256	50	16	4.2	.887	3B-106
1896	LOU	N	121	.234	.281	423	99	10	2	2	0.5	57	37	57	51	19	0	0	188	281	38	21	4.2	.925	3B-121
1897			113	.228	.314	395	90	14	7	2	0.5	59	47	37		14	0	0	176	269	25	16	4.2	.947	3B-113
1898			154	.257	.301	538	138	12	6	0	0.0	65	50	51		15	0	0	292	458	70	46	5.3	.915	3B-79, SS-74, OF-1, 2B-1
1899			109	.262	.342	366	96	15	4	2	0.5	67	44	46		13	0	0	195	381	53	43	5.8	.916	SS-109
1900	CHI	N	47	.208	.245	159	33	6	0	0	0.0	15	11	17		6	0	0	81	150	34	19	5.6	.872	SS-47
1901	WAS	A	137	.242	.304	480	116	10	7	2	0.4	66	55	42		10	0	0	290	462	55	56	5.9	.932	SS-137
1903	CLE	A	21	.281	.328	64	18	1	1	0	0.0	10	7	11		2	0	0	39	55	8	7	4.9	.922	2B-11, SS-7, 3B-3
10 yrs.			816	.246	.306	2839	697	86	31	8	0.3	410	301	303	94	98	0	0	1406	2340	338	228	5.0	.917	3B-422, SS-380, 2B-14, OF-1

Jim Clinton

CLINTON, JAMES LAWRENCE (Big Jim)
B. Aug. 10, 1850, New York, N. Y. D. Sept. 3, 1921, Brooklyn, N. Y.
Manager 1872.
BR TR 5'8½" 174 lbs.

Year	Team		Games	BA	SA	AB	H	2B	3B	HR	HR%	R	RBI	BB	SO	SB	AB	H	PO	A	E	DP	TC/G	FA	G by Pos
1876	LOU	N	16	.338	.369	65	22	2	0	0	0.0	8		0	0		0	0	20	7	7	1	2.1	.794	OF-14, 1B-1, P-1
1882	WOR	N	26	.163	.184	98	16	2	0	0	0.0	9	3	7	13		0	0	43	4	17	1	2.5	.734	OF-26
1883	BAL	AA	94	.313	.393	399	125	16	8	0	0.0	69		27			0	0	167	26	39	3	2.5	.832	OF-92, 2B-2
1884			103	.273	.349	433	118	12	6	3	0.7	82		29			0	0	134	20	36	5	1.8	.811	OF-103, 2B-1
1885	CIN	AA	105	.238	.275	408	97	5	5	0	0.0	48		15			0	0	215	14	32	4	2.5	.877	OF-105
1886	BAL	AA	23	.181	.193	83	15	1	0	0	0.0	8		4			0	0	41	1	5	1	2.0	.894	OF-23
6 yrs.			367	.264	.322	1486	393	38	19	3	0.2	224	3	82	13		0	0	620	72	136	15	2.3	.836	OF-363, 2B-3, 1B-1, P-1

Lu Clinton

CLINTON, LUCIEN LOUIS
B. Oct. 13, 1937, Ponca City, Okla.
BR TR 6'1" 185 lbs.

Year	Team		Games	BA	SA	AB	H	2B	3B	HR	HR%	R	RBI	BB	SO	SB	AB	H	PO	A	E	DP	TC/G	FA	G by Pos
1960	BOS	A	96	.228	.379	298	68	17	5	6	2.0	37	37	20	66	4	6	1	165	4	6	2	1.8	.966	OF-89
1961			17	.255	.333	51	13	2	1	0	0.0	4	3	2	10	0	2	0	30	3	0	0	1.9	1.000	OF-13
1962			114	.294	.540	398	117	24	10	18	4.5	63	75	34	79	2	9	2	185	6	4	1	1.7	.979	OF-103
1963			148	.232	.416	560	130	23	7	22	3.9	71	77	49	118	0	2	0	319	7	6	0	2.2	.982	OF-146
1964	2 teams		BOS A (37G – .258)				LA A (91G – .248)																			
"	total		128	.251	.401	426	107	22	3	12	2.8	45	44	40	73	4	7	1	182	18	2	4	1.6	.990	OF-121
1965	3 teams		CAL A (89G – .243)				KC A (1G – .000)					CLE A (12G – .176)														
"	total		102	.233	.331	257	60	13	3	8	3.1	31	10	26	44	1	16	5	122	7	3	1	1.3	.977	OF-83
1966	NY	A	80	.220	.403	159	35	10	2	5	3.1	18	21	16	27	0	14	6	80	2	2	0	1.1	.976	OF-63
1967			6	.500	.750	4	2	1	0	0	0.0	1	2	1	1	0	4	2	0	0	0	0	0.0	–	OF-1
8 yrs.			691	.247	.418	2153	532	112	31	65	3.0	270	269	188	418	12	60	17	1083	47	23	8	1.7	.980	OF-619

Ed Clough

CLOUGH, EDGAR GEORGE (Spec)
B. Oct. 28, 1906, Wiconisco, Pa. D. Jan. 30, 1944, Harrisburg, Pa.
BL TL 6' 188 lbs.

Year	Team		Games	BA	SA	AB	H	2B	3B	HR	HR%	R	RBI	BB	SO	SB	AB	H	PO	A	E	DP	TC/G	FA	G by Pos
1924	STL	N	7	.071	.071	14	1	0	0	0	0.0	0	1	0	3	0	1	0	12	1	0	0	1.9	1.000	OF-6
1925			3	.250	.250	4	1	0	0	0	0.0	0	0	0	0	0	0	0	1	1	0	0	0.7	1.000	P-3
1926			1	.000	.000	1	0	0	0	0	0.0	0	0	0	0	0	0	0	0	0	0	0	0.0	–	P-1
3 yrs.			11	.105	.105	19	2	0	0	0	0.0	0	1	0	3	0	1	0	13	2	0	0	1.4	1.000	OF-6, P-4

Bill Clymer

CLYMER, WILLIAM JOHNSTON (Derby Day)
B. Dec. 18, 1873, Philadelphia, Pa. D. Dec. 26, 1936, Philadelphia, Pa.

Year	Team		Games	BA	SA	AB	H	2B	3B	HR	HR%	R	RBI	BB	SO	SB	AB	H	PO	A	E	DP	TC/G	FA	G by Pos
1891	PHI	AA	3	.000	.000	11	0	0	0	0	0.0	0		0	1	2	1	0	0	8	5	2	0	5.0	.867	SS-3

Otis Clymer

CLYMER, OTIS EDGAR (Gump)
B. Jan. 27, 1876, Pine Grove, Pa. D. Feb. 27, 1926, St. Paul, Minn.
BB TR 5'11" 180 lbs.

Year	Team		Games	BA	SA	AB	H	2B	3B	HR	HR%	R	RBI	BB	SO	SB	AB	H	PO	A	E	DP	TC/G	FA	G by Pos
1905	PIT	N	96	.296	.353	365	108	11	6	0	0.0	74	23	19		23	6	2	138	8	2	5	1.5	.986	OF-89, 1B-1
1906			11	.244	.289	45	11	0	1	0	0.0	7	1	3		1	0	0	17	1	2	0	1.8	.900	OF-11
1907	2 teams		PIT N (22G – .227)				WAS A (57G – .316)																			
"	total		79	.294	.368	272	80	7	5	1	0.4	38	20	23		22	9	3	116	4	13	1	1.7	.902	OF-66, 1B-2
1908	WAS	A	110	.253	.313	368	93	11	4	1	0.3	32	35	20		19	9	3	97	34	10	8	1.3	.929	OF-82, 2B-13, 3B-2
1909			45	.196	.261	138	27	5	2	0	0.0	11	6	17		7	2	0	44	3	4	1	1.1	.922	OF-41

Year	Team	Games	BA	SA	AB	H	2B	3B	HR	HR%	R	RBI	BB	SO	SB	Pinch Hit AB	Pinch Hit H	PO	A	E	DP	TC/G	FA	G by Pos

Otis Clymer *continued*

Year	Team	Games	BA	SA	AB	H	2B	3B	HR	HR%	R	RBI	BB	SO	SB	PH AB	PH H	PO	A	E	DP	TC/G	FA	G by Pos
1913 2 teams	CHI N (30G – .229)				BOS	N	(14G – .324)																	
" total	44	.254	.338	142	36	8	2	0	0.0	20	13	17	21	11	6	2	76	2	7	0	1.9	.918	OF-37
6 yrs.	385	.267	.332	1330	355	42	19	2	0.2	182	98	99	21	83	32	10	488	52	38	15	1.5	.934	OF-326, 2B-13, 1B-3, 3B-2

Gil Coan

COAN, GILBERT FITZGERALD
B. May 18, 1922, Monroe, N. C.
BL TR 6' 180 lbs.

Year	Team	Games	BA	SA	AB	H	2B	3B	HR	HR%	R	RBI	BB	SO	SB	PH AB	PH H	PO	A	E	DP	TC/G	FA	G by Pos
1946 WAS A	59	.209	.328	134	28	3	2	3	2.2	17	9	7	37	2	24	4	62	0	2	0	1.1	.969	OF-29
1947	11	.500	.667	42	21	3	2	0	0.0	5	3	5	6	2	0	0	22	1	0	1	2.1	1.000	OF-11
1948	138	.232	.333	513	119	13	9	7	1.4	56	60	41	78	23	8	1	341	11	11	3	2.6	.970	OF-131
1949	111	.218	.307	358	78	7	8	3	0.8	36	25	29	58	9	11	2	225	8	6	3	2.2	.975	OF-97
1950	104	.303	.429	366	111	17	4	7	1.9	58	50	28	46	10	5	3	220	4	7	1	2.2	.970	OF-98
1951	135	.303	.426	538	163	25	7	9	1.7	85	62	39	62	8	5	0	374	17	14	2	3.0	.965	OF-132
1952	107	.205	.319	332	68	11	6	5	1.5	50	20	32	35	9	16	3	185	4	3	1	1.8	.984	OF-86
1953	68	.196	.286	168	33	1	4	2	1.2	28	17	22	23	7	22	4	105	2	0	1	1.6	1.000	OF-46
1954 BAL A	94	.279	.351	265	74	11	1	2	0.8	29	20	16	17	9	25	2	148	1	5	0	1.6	.968	OF-67
1955 3 teams	BAL A (61G – .238)				CHI	A	(17G – .176)			NY	N	(9G – .154)												
" total	87	.225	.300	160	36	7	1	1	0.6	18	12	13	21	4	29	11	59	5	1	0	0.7	.985	OF-51
1956 NY N	4	.000	.000	1	0	0	0	0	0.0	2	0	0	1	0	1	0	0	0	0	0	0.0	–	
11 yrs.	918	.254	.359	2877	731	98	44	39	1.4	384	278	232	384	83	146	30	1741	53	49	12	2.0	.973	OF-748

Joe Cobb

COBB, JOSEPH STANLEY
Born Joseph Stanley Serafin.
B. Jan. 24, 1895, Hudson, Pa. D. Dec. 24, 1947, Allentown, Pa.
BR TR 5'9" 170 lbs.

Year	Team	Games	BA	SA	AB	H	2B	3B	HR	HR%	R	RBI	BB	SO	SB	PH AB	PH H	PO	A	E	DP	TC/G	FA	G by Pos
1918 DET A	1	–	–	0	0	0	0	0	–	0	0	1	0	0	0	0	0	0	0	0	0.0	–	

Ty Cobb

COBB, TYRUS RAYMOND (The Georgia Peach)
B. Dec. 18, 1886, Narrows, Ga. D. July 17, 1961, Atlanta, Ga.
Manager 1921-26.
Hall of Fame 1936.
BL TR 6'1" 175 lbs.

Year	Team	Games	BA	SA	AB	H	2B	3B	HR	HR%	R	RBI	BB	SO	SB	PH AB	PH H	PO	A	E	DP	TC/G	FA	G by Pos
1905 DET A	41	.240	.300	150	36	6	0	1	0.7	19	15	10		2	0	0	85	6	4	1	2.3	.958	OF-41
1906	98	.320	.406	350	112	13	7	1	0.3	45	41	19		23	1	0	208	14	9	4	2.4	.961	OF-96
1907	150	.350	.473	605	212	29	15	5	0.8	97	116	24		49	0	0	238	30	11	12	1.9	.961	OF-150
1908	150	.324	.475	581	188	36	20	4	0.7	88	108	34		39	0	0	212	23	14	5	1.7	.944	OF-150
1909	156	.377	.517	573	216	33	10	9	1.6	116	107	48		76	0	0	222	24	14	7	1.7	.946	OF-156
1910	140	.385	.554	509	196	36	13	8	1.6	106	91	64		65	3	1	305	18	14	4	2.4	.958	OF-137
1911	146	.420	.621	591	248	47	24	8	1.4	147	144	44		83	0	0	376	24	18	10	2.9	.957	OF-146
1912	140	.410	.586	553	227	30	23	7	1.3	119	90	43		61	0	0	324	21	22	5	2.6	.940	OF-140
1913	122	.390	.535	428	167	18	16	4	0.9	70	67	58	31	52	2	0	262	22	16	8	2.5	.947	OF-118
1914	97	.368	.513	345	127	22	11	2	0.6	69	57	57	22	35	0	0	177	8	10	0	2.0	.949	OF-96
1915	156	.369	.487	563	208	31	13	3	0.5	144	99	118	43	96	0	0	328	22	18	7	2.4	.951	OF-156
1916	145	.371	.493	542	201	31	10	5	0.9	113	68	78	39	68	0	0	335	18	17	9	2.6	.954	OF-143, 1B-1
1917	152	.383	.571	588	225	44	23	7	1.2	107	102	61	34	55	0	0	373	27	11	9	2.7	.973	OF-152
1918	111	.382	.515	421	161	19	14	3	0.7	83	64	41	21	34	3	1	360	29	10	7	3.6	.975	OF-95, 1B-13, P-2, 3B-1, 2B-1
1919	124	.384	.515	497	191	36	13	1	0.2	92	70	38	22	28	0	0	272	19	8	3	2.4	.973	OF-123
1920	112	.334	.451	428	143	28	8	2	0.5	86	63	58	28	14	0	0	246	8	9	2	2.3	.966	OF-112
1921	128	.389	.596	507	197	37	16	12	2.4	124	101	56	19	22	7	1	301	27	10	2	2.6	.970	OF-121
1922	137	.401	.565	526	211	42	16	4	0.8	99	99	55	24	9	2	1	330	14	7	3	2.6	.980	OF-134
1923	145	.340	.469	556	189	40	7	6	1.1	103	88	66	14	9	2	1	362	14	12	2	2.7	.969	OF-141
1924	155	.338	.450	625	211	38	10	4	0.6	115	74	85	18	23	0	0	417	12	6	8	2.8	.986	OF-155
1925	121	.378	.598	415	157	31	12	12	2.9	97	102	65	12	13	12	2	267	10	15	1	2.4	.949	OF-105, P-1
1926	79	.339	.511	233	79	18	5	4	1.7	48	62	26	2	9	18	6	109	4	6	2	1.5	.950	OF-55
1927 PHI A	134	.357	.482	490	175	32	7	5	1.0	104	93	67	12	22	8	2	243	9	8	2	1.9	.969	OF-126
1928	95	.323	.431	353	114	27	4	1	0.3	54	40	34	16	5	10	1	154	7	6	0	1.8	.964	OF-85
24 yrs.	3034	.367	.513	11429	4191	724	297	118	1.0	2245	1961	1249	357	892	69	15	6506	410	275	113	2.4	.962	OF-2933, 1B-14, P-3, 3B-1, 2B-1
	4th		1st		4th	2nd	4th	2nd			1st	4th			2nd									

WORLD SERIES

Year	Team	Games	BA	SA	AB	H	2B	3B	HR	HR%	R	RBI	BB	SO	SB	PH AB	PH H	PO	A	E	DP	TC/G	FA	G by Pos
1907 DET A	5	.200	.300	20	4	0	1	0	0.0	1	1	0	3	0	0	0	9	0	0	0	1.8	1.000	OF-5
1908	5	.368	.421	19	7	1	0	0	0.0	3	4	1	2	2	0	0	3	0	0	0	1.0	.600	OF-5
1909	7	.231	.346	26	6	3	0	0	0.0	3	6	2	2	2	0	0	8	0	1	0	1.3	.889	OF-7
3 yrs.	17	.262	.354	65	17	4	1	0	0.0	7	11	3	7	4	0	0	20	0	3	0	1.4	.870	OF-17

Dave Coble

COBLE, DAVID LAMAR
B. Dec. 24, 1912, Monroe, N. C. D. Oct. 15, 1971, Orlando, Fla.
BR TR 6'1" 183 lbs.

Year	Team	Games	BA	SA	AB	H	2B	3B	HR	HR%	R	RBI	BB	SO	SB	PH AB	PH H	PO	A	E	DP	TC/G	FA	G by Pos
1939 PHI N	15	.280	.320	25	7	1	0	0	0.0	2	0	0	3	0	2	0	27	3	2	0	2.1	.938	C-13

George Cochran

COCHRAN, GEORGE LESLIE
B. Feb. 12, 1889, Rusk, Tex. D. May 21, 1960, Harbor City, Calif.
TR

Year	Team	Games	BA	SA	AB	H	2B	3B	HR	HR%	R	RBI	BB	SO	SB	PH AB	PH H	PO	A	E	DP	TC/G	FA	G by Pos
1918 BOS A	25	.127	.127	63	8	0	0	0	0.0	8	3	11	7	3	1	0	13	39	2	4	2.2	.963	3B-23, SS-1

Dave Cochrane

COCHRANE, DAVID CARTER
B. Jan. 31, 1963, Riverside, Calif.
BB TR 6'2" 180 lbs.

Year	Team	Games	BA	SA	AB	H	2B	3B	HR	HR%	R	RBI	BB	SO	SB	PH AB	PH H	PO	A	E	DP	TC/G	FA	G by Pos
1986 CHI A	19	.194	.274	62	12	2	0	1	1.6	4	2	5	22	0	0	0	10	31	6	1	2.5	.872	3B-18, SS-1
1989 SEA A	54	.235	.382	102	24	4	1	3	2.9	13	7	14	27	0	17	5	78	41	5	14	2.3	.960	SS-30, 3B-9, 1B-9, 2B-4, OF-3, C-2
2 yrs.	73	.220	.341	164	36	6	1	4	2.4	17	9	19	49	0	17	5	88	72	11	15	2.3	.936	SS-31, 3B-27, 1B-9, 2B-4, OF-3, C-2

Year	Team	Games	BA	SA	AB	H	2B	3B	HR	HR%	R	RBI	BB	SO	SB	Pinch Hit AB	Pinch Hit H	PO	A	E	DP	TC/G	FA	G by Pos

Mickey Cochrane

COCHRANE, GORDON STANLEY (Black Mike)   BL TR 5'10½" 180 lbs.
B. Apr. 6, 1903, Bridgewater, Mass.   D. June 28, 1962, Lake Forest, Ill.
Manager 1934-38.
Hall of Fame 1947.

Year	Team	Games	BA	SA	AB	H	2B	3B	HR	HR%	R	RBI	BB	SO	SB	PH AB	PH H	PO	A	E	DP	TC/G	FA	G by Pos
1925	PHI A	134	.331	.448	420	139	21	5	6	1.4	69	55	44	19	7	1	1	419	79	8	9	3.8	.984	C-133
1926		120	.273	.408	370	101	8	9	8	2.2	50	47	56	15	5	1	0	502	90	15	9	5.1	.975	C-115
1927		126	.338	.495	432	146	20	6	12	2.8	80	80	50	7	9	3	1	559	85	9	11	5.2	.986	C-123
1928		131	.293	.464	468	137	26	12	10	2.1	92	57	76	25	7	1	0	645	71	25	8	5.7	.966	C-130
1929		135	.331	.475	514	170	37	8	7	1.4	113	95	69	8	7	0	0	659	77	13	9	5.5	.983	C-135
1930		130	.357	.526	487	174	42	5	10	2.1	110	85	55	18	5	0	0	654	69	5	11	5.6	.993	C-130
1931		122	.349	.553	459	160	31	6	17	3.7	87	89	56	21	2	5	0	560	63	9	9	5.2	.986	C-117
1932		139	.293	.510	518	152	35	4	23	4.4	118	112	100	22	0	2	0	652	94	5	15	5.4	.993	C-137, OF-1
1933		130	.322	.515	429	138	30	4	15	3.5	104	60	106	22	8	2	0	476	67	6	8	4.2	.989	C-128
1934	DET A	129	.320	.412	437	140	32	1	2	0.5	74	76	78	26	8	8	1	517	69	7	7	4.6	.988	C-124
1935		115	.319	.450	411	131	33	3	5	1.2	93	47	96	15	5	3	1	504	50	6	6	4.9	.989	C-110
1936		44	.270	.381	126	34	8	0	2	1.6	24	17	46	15	1	1	0	159	13	3	1	4.0	.983	C-42
1937		27	.306	.490	98	30	10	1	2	2.0	27	12	25	4	0	0	0	103	13	0	1	4.3	1.000	C-27
13 yrs.		1482	.320	.478	5169	1652	333	64	119	2.3	1041	832	857	217	64	27	4	6409	840	111	104	5.0	.985	C-1451, OF-1

WORLD SERIES

Year	Team	Games	BA	SA	AB	H	2B	3B	HR	HR%	R	RBI	BB	SO	SB	PH AB	PH H	PO	A	E	DP	TC/G	FA	G by Pos
1929	PHI A	5	.400	.467	15	6	1	0	0	0.0	5	0	7	0	0	0	0	59	2	0	0	12.2	1.000	C-5
1930		6	.222	.611	18	4	1	0	2	11.1	5	3	5	2	0	0	0	39	1	1	0	6.8	.976	C-6
1931		7	.160	.160	25	4	0	0	0	0.0	2	1	5	2	0	0	0	40	4	1	0	6.4	.978	C-7
1934	DET A	7	.214	.250	28	6	1	0	0	0.0	2	1	4	3	0	0	0	36	5	0	1	5.9	1.000	C-7
1935		6	.292	.333	24	7	1	0	0	0.0	3	1	4	1	0	0	0	32	3	1	1	6.0	.972	C-6
5 yrs.		31	.245	.336	110	27	4	0	2	1.8	17	6	25	8	0	0	0	206	15	3	2	7.2	.987	C-31

6th

Jim Cockman

COCKMAN, JAMES   BR TR 5'6" 145 lbs.
B. Apr. 26, 1873, Guelph, Ont., Canada   D. Sept. 28, 1947, Guelph, Ont., Canada

Year	Team	Games	BA	SA	AB	H	2B	3B	HR	HR%	R	RBI	BB	SO	SB	PH AB	PH H	PO	A	E	DP	TC/G	FA	G by Pos
1905	NY A	13	.105	.105	38	4	0	0	0	0.0	5	2	4		2	0	0	10	18	4	0	2.5	.875	3B-13

Jack Coffey

COFFEY, JOHN FRANCIS   BR TR 5'11" 178 lbs.
B. Jan. 28, 1887, New York, N. Y.   D. Feb. 14, 1966, Bronx, N. Y.

Year	Team	Games	BA	SA	AB	H	2B	3B	HR	HR%	R	RBI	BB	SO	SB	PH AB	PH H	PO	A	E	DP	TC/G	FA	G by Pos
1909	BOS N	73	.187	.233	257	48	4	4	0	0.0	21	20	11		4	0	0	133	213	40	18	5.3	.896	SS-73
1918	2 teams	DET A (22G – .209)			BOS A (15G – .159)																			
"	total	37	.189	.261	111	21	1	2	1	0.9	12	6	11		8	4	0	0	74	106	8	6	5.1	.957	2B-23, 3B-14
2 yrs.		110	.188	.242	368	69	5	6	1	0.3	33	26	22		6	0	0	207	319	48	24	5.2	.916	SS-73, 2B-23, 3B-14

Frank Coggins

COGGINS, FRANKLIN (Swish)   BB TR 6'2" 187 lbs.
B. May 22, 1944, Griffin, Ga.

Year	Team	Games	BA	SA	AB	H	2B	3B	HR	HR%	R	RBI	BB	SO	SB	PH AB	PH H	PO	A	E	DP	TC/G	FA	G by Pos
1967	WAS A	19	.307	.387	75	23	3	0	1	1.3	9	8	2	17	1	0	0	49	59	4	11	5.9	.964	2B-19
1968		62	.175	.222	171	30	6	1	0	0.0	15	7	9	33	1	8	0	122	122	12	33	4.1	.953	2B-52
1972	CHI N	6	.000	.000	1	0	0	0	0	0.0	1	0	1	0	0	1	0	0	0	0	0	0.0	—	
3 yrs.		87	.215	.271	247	53	9	1	1	0.4	25	15	12	50	2	9	0	171	181	16	44	4.2	.957	2B-71

Rich Coggins

COGGINS, RICHARD ALLEN   BL TL 5'8" 170 lbs.
B. Dec. 7, 1950, Indianapolis, Ind.

Year	Team	Games	BA	SA	AB	H	2B	3B	HR	HR%	R	RBI	BB	SO	SB	PH AB	PH H	PO	A	E	DP	TC/G	FA	G by Pos
1972	BAL A	16	.333	.436	39	13	4	0	0	0.0	5	1	1	6	0	2	1	39	1	0	1	2.5	1.000	OF-13
1973		110	.319	.468	389	124	19	9	7	1.8	54	41	28	24	17	7	1	220	6	3	3	2.1	.987	OF-101, DH-1
1974		113	.243	.319	411	100	13	3	4	1.0	53	32	29	31	26	12	1	238	3	4	1	2.2	.984	OF-105
1975	2 teams	MON N (13G – .270)			NY A (51G – .224)																			
"	total	64	.236	.299	144	34	4	1	1	0.7	8	10	8	23	3	5	1	78	2	2	2	1.3	.976	OF-46, DH-9
1976	2 teams	NY A (7G – .250)			CHI A (32G – .156)																			
"	total	39	.160	.180	100	16	2	0	0	0.0	5	6	6	16	4	5	1	48	1	0	0	1.3	1.000	OF-28, DH-1
5 yrs.		342	.265	.361	1083	287	42	13	12	1.1	125	90	72	100	50	31	5	623	13	9	7	1.9	.986	OF-293, DH-11

LEAGUE CHAMPIONSHIP SERIES

Year	Team	Games	BA	SA	AB	H	2B	3B	HR	HR%	R	RBI	BB	SO	SB	PH AB	PH H	PO	A	E	DP	TC/G	FA	G by Pos
1973	BAL A	2	.444	.556	9	4	1	0	0	0.0	1	0	0	0	0	0	0	4	0	0	0	2.0	1.000	OF-2
1974		3	.000	.000	11	0	0	0	0	0.0	0	0	0	3	0	0	0	6	0	0	0	2.0	1.000	OF-3
2 yrs.		5	.200	.250	20	4	1	0	0	0.0	1	0	0	3	0	0	0	10	0	0	0	2.0	1.000	OF-5

Ed Cogswell

COGSWELL, EDWARD   BR TR 5'8" 150 lbs.
B. Feb. 25, 1854, England   D. July 27, 1888, Fitchburg, Mass.

Year	Team	Games	BA	SA	AB	H	2B	3B	HR	HR%	R	RBI	BB	SO	SB	PH AB	PH H	PO	A	E	DP	TC/G	FA	G by Pos
1879	BOS N	49	.322	.377	236	76	8	1	1	0.4	51	18	8	5	0			539	10	19	24	11.6	.967	1B-49
1880	TRO N	47	.301	.364	209	63	7	3	0	0.0	41	13	11	10	0			475	15	20	18	10.9	.961	1B-47
1882	WOR N	13	.137	.157	51	7	1	0	0	0.0	10	1	6	6	0			145	3	10	11	12.2	.937	1B-13
3 yrs.		109	.294	.349	496	146	16	4	1	0.2	102	32	25	21	0			1159	28	49	53	11.3	.960	1B-109

Alta Cohen

COHEN, ALTA ALBERT (Schoolboy)   BL TL 5'10½" 170 lbs.
B. Dec. 25, 1908, New York, N. Y.

Year	Team	Games	BA	SA	AB	H	2B	3B	HR	HR%	R	RBI	BB	SO	SB	PH AB	PH H	PO	A	E	DP	TC/G	FA	G by Pos
1931	BKN N	1	.667	.667	3	2	0	0	0	0.0	1	0	0	0	0	0	0	1	2	0	0	3.0	1.000	OF-1
1932		9	.156	.188	32	5	1	0	0	0.0	1	1	3	7	0	0	0	14	3	3	1	2.2	.850	OF-8
1933	PHI N	19	.188	.219	32	6	1	0	0	0.0	6	1	6	4	0	10	0	17	0	0	0	0.9	1.000	OF-7
3 yrs.		29	.194	.224	67	13	2	0	0	0.0	8	2	9	11	0	10	0	32	5	3	1	1.4	.925	OF-16

Andy Cohen

COHEN, ANDREW HOWARD   BR TR 5'8" 155 lbs.
Brother of Syd Cohen.
B. Oct. 25, 1904, Baltimore, Md.   D. Oct. 29, 1988, El Paso, Tex.
Manager 1960.

Year	Team	Games	BA	SA	AB	H	2B	3B	HR	HR%	R	RBI	BB	SO	SB	PH AB	PH H	PO	A	E	DP	TC/G	FA	G by Pos
1926	NY N	32	.257	.314	35	9	0	0	0	0.0	4	8	1	2	0	7	1	11	29	5	1	1.4	.889	SS-10, 2B-10, 3B-2
1928		129	.274	.403	504	138	24	7	9	1.8	64	59	31	17	3	0	0	310	446	25	91	6.1	.968	2B-126, SS-3, 3B-1

Year	Team	Games	BA	SA	AB	H	2B	3B	HR	HR%	R	RBI	BB	SO	SB	Pinch Hit AB	Pinch Hit H	PO	A	E	DP	TC/G	FA	G by Pos

Andy Cohen *continued*

| 1929 | | 101 | .294 | .383 | 347 | 102 | 12 | 2 | 5 | 1.4 | 40 | 47 | 11 | 15 | 3 | 5 | 0 | 227 | 318 | 20 | 52 | 5.6 | .965 | 2B-94, SS-1, 3B-1 |
| 3 yrs. | | 262 | .281 | .392 | 886 | 249 | 36 | 10 | 14 | 1.6 | 108 | 114 | 43 | 34 | 6 | 12 | 1 | 548 | 793 | 50 | 144 | 5.3 | .964 | 2B-230, SS-14, 3B-4 |

Jimmie Coker

COKER, JAMES GOODWIN
B. Mar. 28, 1936, Holly Hill, S. C.   BR TR 5'11" 195 lbs.

1958	PHI N	2	.167	.167	6	1	0	0	0	0.0	0	0	0	0	0	0	0	11	0	0	0	5.5	1.000	C-2
1960		81	.214	.329	252	54	5	3	6	2.4	18	34	23	45	0	5	1	394	43	8	5	5.5	.982	C-76
1961		11	.400	.560	25	10	1	0	1	4.0	3	4	7	4	1	1	1	59	1	1	0	5.5	.984	C-11
1962		5	.000	.000	3	0	0	0	0	0.0	0	1	1	2	0	3	0	0	0	0	0	0.0	—	
1963	SF N	4	.200	.200	5	1	0	0	0	0.0	0	0	1	2	0	4	1	4	0	0	0	1.0	1.000	C-2
1964	CIN N	11	.313	.469	32	10	2	0	1	3.1	3	4	3	5	0	1	1	63	10	0	0	6.6	1.000	C-11
1965		24	.246	.377	61	15	2	0	2	3.3	3	9	8	16	0	6	1	145	7	1	2	6.4	.993	C-19
1966		50	.252	.387	111	28	3	0	4	3.6	9	14	8	5	0	10	2	205	25	5	2	4.7	.979	C-39, OF-2
1967		45	.186	.289	97	18	2	1	2	2.1	8	4	4	20	0	15	6	146	14	4	4	3.6	.976	C-34
9 yrs.		233	.231	.351	592	137	15	4	16	2.7	44	70	55	99	1	45	13	1027	100	19	13	4.9	.983	C-194, OF-2

Rocky Colavito

COLAVITO, ROCCO DOMENICO
B. Aug. 10, 1933, New York, N. Y.   BR TR 6'3" 190 lbs.

1955	CLE A	5	.444	.667	9	4	2	0	0	0.0	3	0	0	2	0	2	0	7	1	0	1	1.6	1.000	OF-2
1956		101	.276	.531	322	89	11	4	21	6.5	55	65	49	46	0	5	0	177	6	6	0	1.9	.968	OF-98
1957		134	.252	.471	461	116	26	0	25	5.4	66	84	71	80	1	3	1	268	12	11	2	2.2	.962	OF-130
1958		143	.303	**.620**	489	148	26	3	41	8.4	80	113	84	89	0	5	1	327	15	9	11	2.5	.974	OF-129, 1B-11, P-1
1959		154	.257	.512	588	151	24	0	**42**	7.1	90	111	71	86	3	0	0	319	7	5	1	2.1	.985	OF-154
1960	DET A	145	.249	.474	555	138	18	0	35	6.3	67	87	53	80	3	2	0	271	11	7	5	2.0	.976	OF-144
1961		163	.290	.580	583	169	30	2	45	7.7	129	140	113	75	1	2	0	329	16	9	4	2.2	.975	OF-161
1962		161	.273	.514	601	164	30	2	37	6.2	90	112	96	68	2	0	0	359	10	3	1	2.3	.992	OF-161
1963		160	.271	.437	597	162	29	2	22	3.7	91	91	84	78	0	1	0	319	10	4	0	2.1	.988	OF-159
1964	KC A	160	.274	.507	588	161	31	2	34	5.8	89	102	83	56	3	1	1	275	10	8	1	1.8	.973	OF-159
1965	CLE A	162	.287	.468	592	170	25	2	26	4.4	92	**108**	**93**	63	1	0	0	265	9	0	1	1.7	1.000	OF-162
1966		151	.238	.432	533	127	13	0	30	5.6	68	72	76	81	2	5	3	261	10	5	0	1.8	.982	OF-146
1967	2 teams	CLE A (63G – .241)			CHI A (60G – .221)																			
"	total	123	.231	.333	381	88	13	1	8	2.1	30	50	49	41	3	12	3	158	4	5	3	1.4	.970	OF-108
1968	2 teams	LA N (40G – .204)			NY A (39G – .220)																			
"	total	79	.211	.373	204	43	5	2	8	3.9	21	24	29	35	0	17	2	72	3	2	0	1.0	.974	OF-61, P-1
14 yrs.		1841	.266	.489	6503	1730	283	21	374	5.8	971	1159	951	880	19	55	11	3407	124	74	31	2.0	.979	OF-1774, 1B-11, P-2

Mike Colbern

COLBERN, MICHAEL MALLOY
B. Apr. 19, 1955, Santa Monica, Calif.   BR TR 6'3" 205 lbs.

1978	CHI A	48	.270	.362	141	38	5	1	2	1.4	11	20	1	36	0	0	0	203	19	7	4	4.8	.969	C-47, DH-1
1979		32	.241	.325	83	20	5	1	0	0.0	5	8	4	25	0	1	0	121	12	4	4	4.3	.971	C-32
2 yrs.		80	.259	.348	224	58	10	2	2	0.9	16	28	5	61	0	1	0	324	31	11	5	4.6	.970	C-79, DH-1

Nate Colbert

COLBERT, NATHAN
B. Apr. 9, 1946, St. Louis, Mo.   BR TR 6'2" 190 lbs.

1966	HOU N	19	.000	.000	7	0	0	0	0	0.0	3	0	0	4	0	7	0	0	0	0	0	0.0	—	
1968		20	.151	.170	53	8	1	0	0	0.0	5	4	1	23	0	2	0	62	1	2	2	3.3	.969	OF-11, 1B-5
1969	SD N	139	.255	.482	483	123	20	9	24	5.0	64	66	45	123	6	4	0	1217	87	13	96	9.5	.990	1B-134
1970		156	.259	.509	572	148	17	6	38	6.6	84	86	56	150	3	4	0	1406	90	14	126	9.7	.991	1B-153, 3B-1
1971		156	.264	.462	565	149	25	3	27	4.8	81	84	63	119	5	3	1	1372	106	10	125	9.5	.993	1B-153
1972		151	.250	.508	563	141	27	2	38	6.7	87	111	70	127	15	2	0	1290	103	6	119	9.5	.996	1B-150
1973		145	.270	.450	529	143	25	2	22	4.2	73	80	54	146	9	1	0	1300	98	11	124	9.7	.992	1B-144
1974		119	.207	.364	368	76	16	0	14	3.8	53	54	62	108	10	12	4	605	52	9	43	5.6	.986	1B-79, OF-48
1975	2 teams	DET A (45G – .147)			MON N (38G – .173)																			
"	total	83	.156	.316	237	37	8	3	8	3.4	26	29	22	83	0	19	3	558	31	10	49	7.2	.983	1B-66, DH-1
1976	2 teams	MON N (14G – .200)			OAK A (2G – .000)																			
"	total	16	.178	.356	45	8	2	0	2	4.4	5	6	10	19	3	3	1	66	6	2	3	4.6	.973	OF-7, 1B-6, DH-2
10 yrs.		1004	.243	.451	3422	833	141	25	173	5.1	481	520	383	902	52	57	9	7876	574	77	687	8.5	.991	1B-890, OF-66, DH-3, 3B-1

Dick Cole

COLE, RICHARD ROY
B. May 6, 1926, Long Beach, Calif.   BR TR 6'2" 175 lbs.

1951	2 teams	STL N (15G – .194)			PIT N (42G – .236)																			
"	total	57	.225	.282	142	32	5	0	1	0.7	13	14	21	14	0	0	0	118	129	5	30	4.4	.980	2B-48, SS-8
1953	PIT N	97	.272	.336	235	64	13	1	0	0.0	29	23	38	26	2	9	6	156	203	12	42	3.8	.968	SS-77, 2B-7, 1B-1
1954		138	.270	.342	486	131	22	5	1	0.2	40	40	41	48	0	7	1	192	336	28	41	4.0	.950	SS-66, 3B-55, 2B-17
1955		77	.226	.285	239	54	8	3	0	0.0	16	21	18	22	0	11	2	103	158	10	25	3.5	.963	3B-33, 2B-24, SS-12
1956		72	.212	.253	99	21	2	1	0	0.0	7	9	11	9	0	40	7	20	38	2	8	0.8	.967	3B-18, 2B-12, SS-6
1957	MIL N	15	.071	.071	14	1	0	0	0	0.0	1	0	3	5	0	2	0	12	9	1	5	1.5	.955	2B-10, 3B-1, 1B-1
6 yrs.		456	.249	.312	1215	303	50	10	2	0.2	106	107	132	124	2	69	16	601	873	58	151	3.4	.962	SS-169, 2B-118, 3B-107, 1B-2

Willis Cole

COLE, WILLIS RUSSELL
B. Jan. 6, 1882, Milton Junction, Wis. D. Oct. 11, 1965, Madison, Wis.   BR TR 5'8" 170 lbs.

1909	CHI A	46	.236	.315	165	39	7	3	0	0.0	17	16	16		3	0	0	83	5	11	1	2.2	.889	OF-46
1910		22	.175	.225	80	14	2	1	0	0.0	6	2	4		0	0	0	31	6	1	0	1.7	.974	OF-22
2 yrs.		68	.216	.286	245	53	9	4	0	0.0	23	18	20		3	0	0	114	11	12	1	2.0	.912	OF-68

Bob Coleman

COLEMAN, ROBERT HUNTER
B. Sept. 26, 1890, Huntingburg, Ind. D. July 16, 1959, Boston, Mass.
Manager 1943-45.   BR TR 6'2" 190 lbs.

| 1913 | PIT N | 24 | .180 | .220 | 50 | 9 | 2 | 0 | 0 | 0.0 | 5 | 9 | 7 | 8 | 0 | 1 | 0 | 68 | 21 | 2 | 2 | 3.8 | .978 | C-24 |
| 1914 | | 73 | .267 | .327 | 150 | 40 | 4 | 1 | 1 | 0.7 | 11 | 14 | 15 | 32 | 3 | 1 | 0 | 223 | 68 | 7 | 4 | 4.1 | .977 | C-72 |

Bob Coleman *continued*

Year	Team	Games	BA	SA	AB	H	2B	3B	HR	HR%	R	RBI	BB	SO	SB	Pinch Hit AB	H	PO	A	E	DP	TC/G	FA	G by Pos
1916	CLE A	19	.214	.286	28	6	2	0	0	0.0	3	4	7	6	0	5	1	24	11	1	1	1.9	.972	C-12
3 yrs.		116	.241	.298	228	55	8	1	1	0.4	19	27	29	46	3	6	1	315	100	10	7	3.7	.976	C-108

Choo Choo Coleman

COLEMAN, CLARENCE
B. Aug. 25, 1937, Orlando, Fla. BL TR 5'9" 165 lbs.

Year	Team	Games	BA	SA	AB	H	2B	3B	HR	HR%	R	RBI	BB	SO	SB	Pinch Hit AB	H	PO	A	E	DP	TC/G	FA	G by Pos
1961	PHI N	34	.128	.149	47	6	1	0	0	0.0	3	4	2	8	0	20	2	38	4	1	1	1.3	.977	C-14
1962	NY N	55	.250	.441	152	38	7	2	6	3.9	24	17	11	24	2	14	2	187	22	1	2	3.8	.995	C-44
1963		106	.178	.215	247	44	0	0	3	1.2	22	9	24	49	5	11	2	418	54	15	9	4.6	.969	C-91, OF-1
1966		6	.188	.188	16	3	0	0	0	0.0	2	0	0	4	0	0	0	24	2	1	0	4.5	.963	C-5
4 yrs.		201	.197	.281	462	91	8	2	9	1.9	51	30	37	85	7	45	6	667	82	18	12	3.8	.977	C-154, OF-1

Curt Coleman

COLEMAN, CURTIS HANCOCK
B. Feb. 18, 1887, Salem, Ore. D. July 1, 1980, Newport, Ore. BL TR 5'11" 180 lbs.

Year	Team	Games	BA	SA	AB	H	2B	3B	HR	HR%	R	RBI	BB	SO	SB	Pinch Hit AB	H	PO	A	E	DP	TC/G	FA	G by Pos
1912	NY A	12	.243	.351	37	9	4	0	0	0.0	8	4	7	0	2	0		9	23	5	1	3.1	.865	3B-10

Dave Coleman

COLEMAN, DAVID LEE
B. Oct. 26, 1950, Dayton, Ohio BR TR 6'3" 195 lbs.

Year	Team	Games	BA	SA	AB	H	2B	3B	HR	HR%	R	RBI	BB	SO	SB	Pinch Hit AB	H	PO	A	E	DP	TC/G	FA	G by Pos
1977	BOS A	11	.000	.000	12	0	0	0	0	0.0	1	0	1	3	0	4	0	5	0	0	0	0.5	1.000	OF-9

Ed Coleman

COLEMAN, PARKE EDWARD
B. Dec. 1, 1901, Canby, Ore. D. Aug. 5, 1964, Oregon City, Ore. BL TR 6'2" 200 lbs.

Year	Team	Games	BA	SA	AB	H	2B	3B	HR	HR%	R	RBI	BB	SO	SB	Pinch Hit AB	H	PO	A	E	DP	TC/G	FA	G by Pos
1932	PHI A	26	.342	.507	73	25	7	1	1	1.4	13	13	1	6	1	10	2	24	3	0	1	1.0	1.000	OF-16
1933		102	.281	.410	388	109	26	3	6	1.5	48	68	19	51	0	12	2	178	5	10	2	1.9	.948	OF-89
1934		101	.280	.486	329	92	14	6	14	4.3	53	60	29	34	0	15	8	140	8	3	2	1.5	.980	OF-86
1935	2 teams	PHI A (10G – .077)	STL A (108G – .287)																					
"	total	118	.280	.485	410	115	15	9	17	4.1	66	71	53	44	0	14	1	173	11	5	1	1.6	.974	OF-103
1936	STL A	92	.292	.431	137	40	5	4	2	1.5	13	34	15	17	0	62	20	31	0	2	0	0.4	.939	OF-18
5 yrs.		439	.285	.459	1337	381	67	23	40	3.0	193	246	117	152	1	113	33	546	27	20	6	1.4	.966	OF-312

Gordy Coleman

COLEMAN, GORDON CALVIN
B. July 5, 1934, Rockville, Md. BL TR 6'3" 208 lbs.

Year	Team	Games	BA	SA	AB	H	2B	3B	HR	HR%	R	RBI	BB	SO	SB	Pinch Hit AB	H	PO	A	E	DP	TC/G	FA	G by Pos
1959	CLE A	6	.533	.667	15	8	0	1	0	0.0	5	2	1	2	0	2	2	18	3	1	1	3.7	.955	1B-3
1960	CIN N	66	.271	.390	251	68	10	1	6	2.4	26	32	12	32	1	0	0	559	63	1	69	9.4	.998	1B-66
1961		150	.287	.504	520	149	27	4	26	5.0	63	87	45	67	1	6	3	1162	121	11	93	8.6	.991	1B-150
1962		136	.277	.485	476	132	13	1	28	5.9	73	86	36	68	2	15	3	1021	83	12	100	8.2	.989	1B-128
1963		123	.247	.427	365	90	20	2	14	3.8	38	59	29	51	1	19	8	752	65	11	66	6.7	.987	1B-107
1964		89	.242	.369	198	48	6	2	5	2.5	18	27	13	30	2	35	9	352	35	4	28	4.4	.990	1B-49
1965		108	.302	.489	325	98	19	0	14	4.3	39	57	24	38	0	16	6	621	48	6	52	6.3	.991	1B-89
1966		91	.251	.348	227	57	7	0	5	2.2	20	37	16	45	1	25	9	399	29	6	33	4.8	.986	1B-65
1967		4	.000	.000	7	0	0	0	0	0.0	0	0	1	0	0	2	0	9	1	0	0	2.5	1.000	1B-2
9 yrs.		773	.273	.448	2384	650	102	11	98	4.1	282	387	177	333	9	120	40	4893	448	52	442	7.0	.990	1B-659

WORLD SERIES

Year	Team	Games	BA	SA	AB	H	2B	3B	HR	HR%	R	RBI	BB	SO	SB	Pinch Hit AB	H	PO	A	E	DP	TC/G	FA	G by Pos
1961	CIN N	5	.250	.400	20	5	0	1	1	5.0	2	2	0	1	0	0	0	30	4	1	6	7.0	.971	1B-5

Jerry Coleman

COLEMAN, GERALD FRANCIS
B. Sept. 14, 1924, San Jose, Calif.
Manager 1980. BR TR 6' 165 lbs.

Year	Team	Games	BA	SA	AB	H	2B	3B	HR	HR%	R	RBI	BB	SO	SB	Pinch Hit AB	H	PO	A	E	DP	TC/G	FA	G by Pos
1949	NY A	128	.275	.358	447	123	21	5	2	0.4	54	42	63	44	8	1	1	304	331	13	106	5.1	.980	2B-122, SS-4
1950		153	.287	.381	522	150	19	6	6	1.1	69	69	67	38	3	1	0	388	390	19	138	5.2	.976	2B-152, SS-6
1951		121	.249	.315	362	90	11	2	3	0.8	48	43	31	36	6	1	0	272	295	18	92	4.8	.969	2B-120, SS-18
1952		11	.405	.500	42	17	2	1	0	0.0	6	4	5	4	0	0	0	33	34	2	17	6.3	.971	2B-11
1953		8	.200	.200	10	2	0	0	0	0.0	1	0	1	2	0	0	0	11	9	1	4	2.6	.952	2B-7, SS-1
1954		107	.217	.277	300	65	7	1	3	1.0	39	21	26	29	3	0	0	209	252	14	71	4.4	.971	2B-79, SS-30, 3B-1
1955		43	.229	.281	96	22	5	0	0	0.0	11	8	11	11	0	1	0	66	74	4	24	3.3	.972	SS-29, 2B-13, 3B-1
1956		80	.257	.295	183	47	5	1	0	0.0	15	18	12	33	1	2	0	138	152	9	46	3.7	.970	2B-41, SS-24, 3B-18
1957		72	.268	.376	157	42	7	2	2	1.3	23	12	20	21	1	4	1	90	120	9	34	3.0	.959	2B-45, 3B-21, SS-4
9 yrs.		723	.263	.339	2119	558	77	18	16	0.8	267	217	235	218	22	10	2	1511	1657	89	532	4.5	.973	2B-572, SS-116, 3B-41

WORLD SERIES

Year	Team	Games	BA	SA	AB	H	2B	3B	HR	HR%	R	RBI	BB	SO	SB	Pinch Hit AB	H	PO	A	E	DP	TC/G	FA	G by Pos
1949	NY A	5	.250	.400	20	5	3	0	0	0.0	0	4	0	4	0	0	0	10	9	1	3	4.0	.950	2B-5
1950		4	.286	.357	14	4	1	0	0	0.0	2	3	2	0	0	0	0	11	12	0	3	5.8	1.000	2B-4
1951		5	.250	.250	8	2	0	0	0	0.0	2	0	1	2	0	0	0	7	5	0	2	2.4	1.000	2B-5
1955		3	.000	.000	3	0	0	0	0	0.0	0	0	0	1	0	0	0	2	3	0	3	1.7	1.000	SS-3
1956		2	.000	.000	2	0	0	0	0	0.0	0	0	0	0	0	0	0	2	2	0	0	2.0	1.000	2B-2
1957		7	.364	.455	22	8	2	0	0	0.0	2	3	1	0	0	0	0	16	17	0	3	4.7	1.000	2B-7
6 yrs.		26	.275	.362	69	19	6	0	0	0.0	6	9	6	8	0	0	0	48	48	1	14	3.7	.990	2B-23, SS-3

John Coleman

COLEMAN, JOHN FRANCIS
B. Mar. 6, 1863, Saratoga Springs, N.Y.
D. May 31, 1922, Detroit, Mich. BL TR 5'9½" 170 lbs.
BB 1887

Year	Team	Games	BA	SA	AB	H	2B	3B	HR	HR%	R	RBI	BB	SO	SB	Pinch Hit AB	H	PO	A	E	DP	TC/G	FA	G by Pos
1883	PHI N	90	.234	.314	354	83	12	8	0	0.0	33		15	39		0	0	91	132	31	6	2.8	.878	P-65, OF-31, 2B-1
1884	2 teams	PHI N (43G – .246)	PHI AA (28G – .206)																					
"	total	71	.230	.320	278	64	9	5	2	0.7	32		13	20		0	0	106	55	24	3	2.6	.870	OF-51, P-24, 1B-4
1885	PHI AA	96	.299	.412	398	119	15	12	2	0.5	71		25			0	0	130	32	28	5	2.0	.853	OF-93, P-8
1886	2 teams	PHI AA (121G – .246)	PIT AA (11G – .349)																					
"	total	132	.254	.355	535	136	20	17	0	0.0	70		35			0	0	235	32	36	9	2.3	.881	OF-126, 1B-6, P-3, 2B-1
1887	PIT N	115	.293	.396	475	139	21	11	2	0.4	75	54	31	40	25	0	0	226	17	28	3	2.4	.897	OF-115, 1B-2
1888		116	.231	.274	438	101	11	4	0	0.0	49	26	29	52	15	0	0	395	24	20	14	3.8	.954	OF-91, 1B-25
1889	PHI AA	6	.053	.053	19	1	0	0	0	0.0	1	1	1	3	1	0	0	3	10	2	0	2.5	.867	P-5, OF-1

Year	Team		Games	BA	SA	AB	H	2B	3B	HR	HR%	R	RBI	BB	SO	SB	AB	H	PO	A	E	DP	TC/G	FA	G by Pos

John Coleman *continued*

| 1890 | PIT | N | 3 | .182 | .182 | 11 | 2 | 0 | 0 | 0 | 0.0 | 1 | 0 | 3 | 0 | 1 | 0 | 0 | 2 | 1 | 0 | 0 | 1.0 | 1.000 | OF-2, P-2 |
| | 8 yrs. | | 629 | .257 | .345 | 2508 | 645 | 88 | 57 | 6 | 0.2 | 332 | 81 | 152 | 154 | 42 | 0 | 0 | 1188 | 303 | 169 | 40 | 2.6 | .898 | OF-510, P-107, 1B-37, 2B-2 |

Ray Coleman
COLEMAN, RAYMOND LeROY
B. June 4, 1922, Dunsmuir, Calif.
BL TR 5'11" 170 lbs.

1947	STL	A	110	.259	.344	343	89	9	7	2	0.6	34	30	26	32	2	18	3	174	7	3	4	1.7	.984	OF-93
1948	2 teams		STL	A	(17G – .172)		PHI	A	(68G – .243)																
"	total		85	.234	.318	239	56	6	7	0	0.0	34	23	33	22	5	24	2	134	7	4	3	1.7	.972	OF-58
1950	STL	A	117	.271	.430	384	104	25	6	8	2.1	54	55	.32	37	7	17	6	253	7	4	1	2.3	.985	OF-98
1951	2 teams		STL	A	(91G – .282)		CHI	A	(51G – .276)																
"	total		142	.280	.418	522	146	24	12	8	1.5	62	76	39	46	5	6	2	326	12	8	2	2.4	.977	OF-138
1952	2 teams		CHI	A	(85G – .215)		STL	A	(20G – .196)																
"	total		105	.212	.286	241	51	10	1	2	0.8	24	15	18	21	0	16	1	158	5	3	0	1.6	.982	OF-89
	5 yrs.		559	.258	.374	1729	446	74	33	20	1.2	208	199	148	.158	19	81	14	1045	38	22	10	2.0	.980	OF-476

Vince Coleman
COLEMAN, VINCENT MAURICE
B. Sept. 22, 1960, Jacksonville, Fla.
BB TR 6' 170 lbs.

1985	STL	N	151	.267	.335	636	170	20	10	1	0.2	107	40	50	115	110	1	0	305	16	7	1	2.2	.979	OF-150
1986			154	.232	.280	600	139	13	8	0	0.0	94	29	60	98	107	2	1	300	12	9	2	2.1	.972	OF-149
1987			151	.289	.358	623	180	14	10	3	0.5	121	43	70	126	109	1	0	274	16	9	3	2.0	.970	OF-150
1988			153	.260	.339	616	160	20	10	3	0.5	77	38	49	111	81	2	0	290	14	9	1	2.0	.971	OF-150
1989			145	.254	.334	563	143	21	9	2	0.4	94	28	50	90	65	5	2	247	5	10	1	1.8	.962	OF-142
	5 yrs.		754	.261	.329	3038	792	88	47	9	0.3	493	178	279	540	472	11	3	1416	63	44	8	2.0	.971	OF-741

LEAGUE CHAMPIONSHIP SERIES

1985	STL	N	3	.286	.286	14	4	0	0	0	0.0	2	1	0	2	1	0	0	8	0	0	0	2.7	1.000	OF-3
1987			7	.269	.308	26	7	1	0	0	0.0	3	4	4	6	1	0	0	9	1	0	0	1.4	1.000	OF-7
	2 yrs.		10	.275	.300	40	11	1	0	0	0.0	5	4	4	2	0	0	0	17	1	0	0	1.8	1.000	OF-10

WORLD SERIES

| 1987 | STL | N | 7 | .143 | .214 | 28 | 4 | 0 | 0 | 0 | 0.0 | 5 | 2 | 2 | 10 | 6 | 0 | 0 | 10 | 2 | 0 | 0 | 1.7 | 1.000 | OF-7 |

Cad Coles
COLES, CADWALLADER R.
B. Jan. 17, 1889, Rock Hill, S. C. D. June 30, 1942, Miami, Fla.
BL TR 6½" 174 lbs.

| 1914 | KC | F | 78 | .253 | .335 | 194 | 49 | 7 | 3 | 1 | 0.5 | 17 | 25 | 5 | | 6 | 34 | 7 | 83 | 5 | 8 | 2 | 1.2 | .917 | OF-39, 1B-3 |

Chuck Coles
COLES, CHARLES EDWARD
B. June 27, 1931, Fredericktown, Pa.
BL TL 5'9" 180 lbs.

| 1958 | CIN | N | 5 | .182 | .273 | 11 | 2 | 1 | 0 | 0 | 0.0 | 2 | 2 | 6 | 0 | 1 | 0 | 12 | 0 | 0 | 0 | 2.4 | 1.000 | OF-4 |

Darnell Coles
COLES, DARNELL
B. June 2, 1962, San Bernardino, Calif.
BR TR 6'1" 185 lbs.

1983	SEA	A	27	.283	.391	92	26	7	0	1	1.1	9	6	7	12	0	1	0	17	47	4	8	2.5	.941	3B-26
1984			48	.161	.196	143	23	3	1	0	0.0	15	6	17	26	2	0	0	31	63	8	10	2.1	.922	3B-42, DH-6, OF-3
1985	DET	A	27	.237	.356	59	14	4	0	1	1.7	8	5	9	17	0	3	0	25	44	6	10	2.8	.920	SS-15, 3B-7, DH-2, OF-2
1986	DET	A	142	.273	.453	521	142	30	2	20	3.8	67	86	45	84	6	1	0	111	242	23	23	2.6	.939	3B-133, DH-7, OF-2, SS-2
1987	2 teams		DET	A	(53G – .181)		PIT	N	(40G – .227)																
"	total		93	.201	.369	268	54	13	1	10	3.7	34	39	34	43	1	9	2	123	87	20	6	2.5	.913	3B-46, OF-34, 1B-10, DH-3, SS-1
1988	2 teams		PIT	N	(68G – .232)		SEA	A	(55G – .292)																
"	total		123	.261	.438	406	106	23	2	15	3.7	52	70	37	67	4	11	0	166	3	3	0	1.4	.983	OF-102, DH-7, 1B-2, 3B-1
1989	SEA	A	146	.252	.359	535	135	21	3	10	1.9	54	59	27	61	5	8	1	317	76	12	20	2.8	.970	OF-89, 3B-26, 1B-18, DH-12
	7 yrs.		606	.247	.390	2024	500	101	9	57	2.8	239	271	176	310	18	33	3	790	562	76	77	2.4	.947	3B-281, OF-232, DH-34, 1B-30, SS-18

Chris Coletta
COLETTA, CHRISTOPHER MICHAEL
B. Aug. 2, 1944, Brooklyn, N. Y.
BL TL 5'11" 190 lbs.

| 1972 | CAL | A | 14 | .300 | .433 | 30 | 9 | 1 | 0 | 1 | 3.3 | 5 | 7 | 1 | 4 | 0 | 8 | 3 | 3 | 0 | 0 | 0 | 0.2 | 1.000 | OF-7 |

Bill Colgan
COLGAN, WILLIAM H. (Ed)
B. East St. Louis, Ill. D. Aug. 13, 1895, Great Falls, Mont.
180 lbs.

| 1884 | PIT | AA | 48 | .155 | .193 | 161 | 25 | 4 | 1 | 0 | 0.0 | 10 | | 3 | | | 0 | 0 | 234 | 71 | 32 | 5 | 7.0 | .905 | C-44, OF-4 |

Bill Coliver
COLIVER, WILLIAM J.
B. 1867, Detroit, Mich. D. Mar. 24, 1888, Detroit, Mich.

| 1885 | BOS | N | 1 | .000 | .000 | 4 | 0 | 0 | 0 | 0 | 0.0 | 0 | 0 | 1 | 0 | 1 | 0 | 0 | 0 | 0 | 0 | 0 | 0.0 | – | OF-1 |

Bill Collins
COLLINS, WILLIAM J.
B. 1867, Dublin, Ireland D. June 8, 1893, New York, N. Y.
BR

1889	PHI	AA	1	.250	.250	4	1	0	0	0	0.0	0	1	1	0	1	0	0	2	2	1	0	5.0	.800	C-1
1890			1	.000	.000	1	0	0	0	0	0.0	0	0	0	0	0	0	0	1	1	2	0	4.0	.500	SS-1
1891	CLE	N	2	.000	.000	3	0	0	0	0	0.0	0	0	0	0	0	0	0	5	4	1	1	5.0	.900	OF-1, C-1
	3 yrs.		4	.125	.125	8	1	0	0	0	0.0	0	1	1	0	1	0	0	8	7	4	1	4.8	.789	C-2, OF-1, SS-1

Bill Collins
COLLINS, WILLIAM SHIRLEY
B. Mar. 27, 1882, Chesterton, Ind. D. June 26, 1961, San Bernardino, Calif.
BB TR 6' 170 lbs.

| 1910 | BOS | N | 151 | .241 | .291 | 584 | 141 | 6 | 7 | 3 | 0.5 | 67 | 40 | 43 | 48 | 36 | 0 | 0 | 355 | 23 | 9 | 2 | 2.6 | .977 | OF-151 |

Year	Team		Games	BA	SA	AB	H	2B	3B	HR	HR%	R	RBI	BB	SO	SB	Pinch Hit AB	Pinch Hit H	PO	A	E	DP	TC/G	FA	G by Pos

Bill Collins *continued*

1911	**2 teams**	BOS N (17G – .136)			CHI N (7G – .200)																				
"	total		24	.143	.224	49	7	2	1	0	0.0	10	8	2	11	4	1	1	32	1	0	0	1.4	1.000	OF-17, 3B-1
1913	BKN	N	32	.189	.200	95	18	1	0	0	0.0	8	4	8	11	2	4	0	57	1	5	0	2.0	.921	OF-27
1914	BUF	F	21	.149	.277	47	7	2	2	0	0.0	6	2	1		0	4	0	14	5	3	0	1.0	.864	OF-15
4 yrs.			228	.223	.275	775	173	11	10	3	0.4	91	54	54	70	42	9	1	458	30	17	2	2.2	.966	OF-210, 3B-1

Bob Collins

COLLINS, ROBERT JOSEPH
B. Sept. 18, 1909, Pittsburgh, Pa.   D. Apr. 19, 1969, Pittsburgh, Pa.

BR TR 5'11" 176 lbs.

1940	CHI	N	47	.208	.258	120	25	3	0	1	0.8	11	14	14	18	4	4	1	133	23	8	3	3.5	.951	C-42
1944	NY	A	3	.333	.333	3	1	0	0	0	0.0	0	0	1	0	0	0	0	5	1	0	0	2.0	1.000	C-3
2 yrs.			50	.211	.260	123	26	3	0	1	0.8	11	14	15	18	4	4	1	138	24	8	3	3.4	.953	C-45

Chub Collins

COLLINS, CHARLES
B. 1862, Dundas, Ont., Canada   D. May 20, 1914, Dundas, Ont., Canada

1884	**2 teams**	BUF N (45G – .178)			IND AA (38G – .225)																				
"	total		83	.199	.235	307	61	9	1	0	0.0	42		23	36	0	0	0	205	248	53	26	6.1	.895	2B-80, SS-3
1885	DET	N	14	.182	.255	55	10	0	2	0	0.0	8	6	0	11	0	0	0	7	35	11	3	3.8	.792	SS-14
2 yrs.			97	.196	.238	362	71	9	3	0	0.0	50	6	23	47	0	0	0	212	283	64	29	5.8	.886	2B-80, SS-17

Cyril Collins

COLLINS, CYRIL WILSON
B. May 7, 1889, Pulaski, Tenn.   D. Feb. 28, 1941, Knoxville, Tenn.

BR TR 5'9½" 165 lbs.

1913	BOS	N	16	.333	.333	3	1	0	0	0	0.0	3	0	0	1	0	0	0	3	0	0	0	0.2	1.000	OF-9
1914			27	.257	.257	35	9	0	0	0	0.0	5	1	2	8	0	1	0	22	0	2	1	0.9	.917	OF-19
2 yrs.			43	.263	.263	38	10	0	0	0	0.0	8	1	2	9	0	1	0	25	0	2	1	0.6	.926	OF-28

Dan Collins

COLLINS, DANIEL THOMAS
B. July 12, 1854, St. Louis, Mo.   D. Sept. 21, 1883, New Orleans La.,

1876	LOU	N	7	.143	.179	28	4	1	0	0	0.0	3	9	0	2	0	0	0	8	2	1	1	1.6	.909	OF-7

Dave Collins

COLLINS, DAVID SCOTT
B. Oct. 20, 1952, Rapid City, S. D.

BB TL 5'10" 175 lbs.

1975	CAL	A	93	.266	.361	319	85	13	4	3	0.9	41	29	36	55	24	5	4	159	3	2	2	1.8	.988	OF-75, DH-12
1976			99	.263	.334	365	96	12	1	4	1.1	45	28	40	55	32	2	0	160	3	1	0	1.7	.994	OF-71, DH-22
1977	SEA	A	120	.239	.313	402	96	9	3	5	1.2	46	28	33	66	25	7	4	124	6	2	1	1.1	.985	OF-73, DH-40
1978	CIN	N	102	.216	.225	102	22	1	0	0	0.0	13	7	15	18	7	64	14	30	1	1	0	0.3	.969	OF-24
1979			122	.318	.402	396	126	16	4	3	0.8	59	35	27	48	16	28	9	223	3	4	8	1.9	.983	OF-91, 1B-10
1980			144	.303	.370	551	167	20	4	3	0.5	94	35	53	68	79	3	1	337	5	5	1	2.4	.986	OF-141
1981			95	.272	.381	360	98	18	6	3	0.8	63	23	41	41	26	1	0	167	4	4	2	1.8	.977	OF-94
1982	NY	A	111	.253	.330	348	88	12	3	3	0.9	41	25	28	49	13	7	1	498	28	7	30	4.8	.987	OF-60, 1B-52, DH-1
1983	TOR	A	118	.271	.328	402	109	12	4	1	0.2	55	34	43	67	31	18	5	270	9	3	3	2.4	.989	OF-112, 1B-5, DH-4
1984			128	.308	.444	441	136	24	**15**	2	0.5	59	44	33	41	60	14	6	237	11	2	7	2.0	.992	OF-108, 1B-6, DH-4
1985	OAK	A	112	.251	.346	379	95	16	4	4	1.1	52	29	29	37	29	1	0	221	1	5	0	2.0	.978	OF-91
1986	DET	A	124	.270	.329	419	113	18	2	1	0.2	44	27	44	49	27	11	1	211	2	1	1	1.7	.995	OF-94, DH-24
1987	CIN	N	57	.294	.353	85	25	5	0	0	0.0	19	5	11	12	9	35	8	36	0	0	0	0.6	1.000	OF-35, 1B-3
1988			99	.236	.293	174	41	6	2	0	0.0	12	14	11	27	7	58	12	66	2	4	2	0.7	.944	OF-16
1989			78	.236	.274	106	25	4	0	0	0.0	12	7	10	17	3	55	10	41	0	0	0	0.5	1.000	
15 yrs.			1602	.273	.352	4849	1322	186	52	32	0.7	655	370	454	650	388	325	79	2780	78	41	58	1.8	.986	OF-1106, DH-104, 1B-76

LEAGUE CHAMPIONSHIP SERIES

1979	CIN	N	3	.357	.429	14	5	1	0	0	0.0	0	1	0	2	2	0	0	5	0	0	0	1.7	1.000	OF-3

Eddie Collins

COLLINS, EDWARD TROWBRIDGE, SR. (Cocky)
Played as Eddie Sullivan In 1906.   Father of Eddie Collins.
B. May 2, 1887, Millerton, N. Y.   D. Mar. 25, 1951, Boston, Mass.
Manager 1924-26.
Hall of Fame 1939.

BL TR 5'9" 175 lbs.

1906	PHI	A	6	.235	.235	17	4	0	0	0	0.0	1	0	0		1	1	0	9	11	2	0	3.7	.909	SS-3, 3B-1, 2B-1
1907			14	.250	.350	20	5	0	1	0	0.0	2		0	2	0	6	1	11	9	4	1	1.7	.833	SS-6
1908			102	.273	.379	330	90	18	7	1	0.3	39	40	16		8	11	4	184	188	25	12	3.9	.937	2B-47, SS-28, OF-10
1909			153	.346	.449	572	198	30	10	3	0.5	104	56	62		67	0	0	375	410	27	55	5.3	.967	2B-152, SS-1
1910			153	.322	.417	583	188	16	15	3	0.5	81	81	49		**81**	0	0	402	451	25	67	5.7	.972	2B-153
1911			132	.365	.481	493	180	22	13	3	0.6	92	73	62		38	0	0	348	349	24	49	5.5	.967	2B-132
1912			153	.348	.435	543	189	25	11	0	0.0	137	64	101		63	0	0	387	426	38	63	5.6	.955	2B-153
1913			148	.345	.453	534	184	23	13	3	0.6	125	73	85	37	55	0	0	314	449	28	54	5.3	.965	2B-148
1914			152	.344	.452	526	181	23	14	2	0.4	122	85	97	31	58	0	0	354	387	23	55	5.0	.970	2B-152
1915	CHI	A	155	.332	.436	521	173	22	10	4	0.8	118	77	**119**	27	46	0	0	344	487	22	54	5.5	.974	2B-155
1916			155	.308	.396	545	168	14	17	0	0.0	87	52	86	36	40	0	0	346	415	19	75	5.0	.976	2B-155
1917			156	.289	.363	564	163	18	12	0	0.0	91	67	89	16	53	0	0	353	388	24	68	4.9	.969	2B-156
1918			97	.276	.330	330	91	8	2	2	0.6	51	30	73	13	22	1	1	231	285	14	53	5.5	.974	2B-96
1919			140	.319	.405	518	165	19	7	4	0.8	87	80	68	27	**33**	0	0	347	401	20	66	5.5	.974	2B-140
1920			153	.369	.489	601	222	37	13	3	0.5	115	75	69	19	19	0	0	449	471	23	76	6.2	.976	2B-153
1921			139	.337	.424	526	177	20	10	2	0.4	79	58	66	11	12	3	0	376	458	28	84	6.2	.968	2B-136
1922			154	.324	.403	598	194	20	12	1	0.2	92	69	73	16	20	1	0	406	451	21	73	5.7	.976	2B-154
1923			145	.360	.453	505	182	22	5	5	1.0	89	67	84	8	**47**	3	0	347	430	20	77	5.5	.975	2B-142
1924			152	.349	.455	556	194	27	7	6	1.1	108	86	89	16	**42**	2	0	396	446	20	83	5.7	.977	2B-150
1925			118	.346	.442	425	147	26	3	3	0.7	80	80	87	8	19	2	0	290	346	20	74	5.6	.970	2B-116
1926			106	.344	.459	375	129	32	4	1	0.3	66	62	62	8	13	3	0	228	307	15	53	5.2	.973	2B-101
1927	PHI	A	95	.338	.413	225	76	12	1	1	0.4	50	15	60	9	6	34	12	124	150	10	31	3.0	.965	2B-56, SS-1
1928			36	.303	.394	33	10	3	0	0	0.0	3	7	4	4	0	29	8	4	3	0	1	0.0	1.000	2B-2, SS-1
1929			9	.000	.000	7	0	0	0	0	0.0	0	0	2	1	0	7	0	0	0	0	0	0.0		

Year Team	Games	BA	SA	AB	H	2B	3B	HR	HR%	R	RBI	BB	SO	SB	Pinch Hit AB	Pinch Hit H	PO	A	E	DP	TC/G	FA	G by Pos

Eddie Collins *continued*

Year Team	Games	BA	SA	AB	H	2B	3B	HR	HR%	R	RBI	BB	SO	SB	PH AB	PH H	PO	A	E	DP	TC/G	FA	G by Pos
1930	3	.500	.500	2	1	0	0	0	0.0	1	0	0	0	0	2	1	0	0	0	0	0.0	–	
25 yrs.	2826	.333	.428	9949	3311	437	187	47	0.5	1818	1299	1503	286	743	104	27	6621	7716	452	1223	5.2	.969	2B-2650, SS-40, OF-10,
	10th				8th									4th									3B-1

WORLD SERIES

Year Team	Games	BA	SA	AB	H	2B	3B	HR	HR%	R	RBI	BB	SO	SB	PH AB	PH H	PO	A	E	DP	TC/G	FA	G by Pos
1910 PHI A	5	.429	.619	21	9	4	0	0	0.0	5	3	2	0	4	0	0	17	17	1	4	7.0	.971	2B-5
1911	6	.286	.333	21	6	1	0	0	0.0	4	1	2	2	2	0	0	12	22	4	1	6.3	.895	2B-6
1913	5	.421	.632	19	8	0	2	0	0.0	5	3	1	2	3	0	0	16	18	1	5	7.0	.971	2B-5
1914	4	.214	.214	14	3	0	0	0	0.0	0	1	2	1	1	0	0	9	12	0	1	5.3	1.000	2B-4
1917 CHI A	6	.409	.455	22	9	1	0	0	0.0	4	2	2	3	3	0	0	11	23	0	3	5.7	1.000	2B-6
1919	8	.226	.258	31	7	1	0	0	0.0	2	1	1	2	1	0	0	21	31	2	7	6.8	.963	2B-8
6 yrs.	34	.328	.414	128	42	7	2	0	0.0	20	11	10	10	14	0	0	86	123	8	21	6.4	.963	2B-34
					10th	9th								1st									

Eddie Collins

COLLINS, EDWARD TROWBRIDGE, JR.
Son of Eddie Collins.
B. Nov. 23, 1916, Lansdowne, Pa.

BL TR 5'10" 175 lbs.

Year Team	Games	BA	SA	AB	H	2B	3B	HR	HR%	R	RBI	BB	SO	SB	PH AB	PH H	PO	A	E	DP	TC/G	FA	G by Pos
1939 PHI A	32	.238	.286	21	5	1	0	0	0.0	6	0	0	3	1	10	3	11	1	1	0	0.4	.923	OF-6, 2B-1
1941	80	.242	.297	219	53	6	3	0	0.0	29	12	20	24	2	28	6	119	3	4	1	1.6	.968	OF-50
1942	20	.235	.294	34	8	2	0	0	0.0	6	4	4	2	1	5	1	8	0	2	0	0.5	.800	OF-9
3 yrs.	132	.241	.296	274	66	9	3	0	0.0	41	16	24	29	4	43	10	138	4	7	1	1.1	.953	OF-65, 2B-1

Hub Collins

COLLINS, GEORGE HUBBERT
B. Apr. 15, 1864, Louisville, Ky.   D. May 21, 1892, Brooklyn, N. Y.

BR TR 5'8" 160 lbs.

Year Team	Games	BA	SA	AB	H	2B	3B	HR	HR%	R	RBI	BB	SO	SB	PH AB	PH H	PO	A	E	DP	TC/G	FA	G by Pos
1886 LOU AA	27	.287	.356	101	29	3	2	0	0.0	12		5			0	0	49	4	7	0	2.2	.883	OF-24, 3B-2, SS-1, 2B-1, 1B-1
1887	130	.290	.363	559	162	22	8	1	0.2	122		39		71	0	0	305	47	43	6	3.0	.891	OF-109, 2B-10, 1B-8, SS-4, 3B-1
1888 2 teams		LOU	AA (116G – .307)		BKN	AA (12G – .310)																	
" total	128	.307	.423	527	162	31	12	2	0.4	133	53	50		71	0	0	298	134	56	18	3.8	.885	OF-82, 2B-31, SS-15
1889 BKN AA	138	.266	.320	560	149	18	3	2	0.4	139	73	80	41	65	0	0	385	410	61	56	6.2	.929	2B-138
1890 BKN N	129	.278	.386	510	142	32	7	3	0.6	148	69	85	47	85	0	0	298	420	42	56	5.9	.945	2B-129
1891	107	.276	.356	435	120	16	5	3	0.7	82	31	59	63	32	0	0	226	223	48	19	4.6	.903	2B-72, OF-35
1892	21	.299	.379	87	26	5	1	0	0.0	17	17	14	13	4	0	0	37	0	3	0	1.9	.925	OF-21
7 yrs.	680	.284	.369	2779	790	127	38	11	0.4	653	243	332	164	328	0	0	1598	1238	260	155	4.6	.916	2B-381, OF-271, SS-20, 1B-9, 3B-3

Hugh Collins

COLLINS, HUGH
B. Unknown.

150 lbs.

Year Team	Games	BA	SA	AB	H	2B	3B	HR	HR%	R	RBI	BB	SO	SB	PH AB	PH H	PO	A	E	DP	TC/G	FA	G by Pos
1887 NY AA	1	.250	.250	4	1	0	0	0	0.0	0		0		0	0	0	0	0	0	0	0.0	–	C-1

Jimmy Collins

COLLINS, JAMES JOSEPH
B. Jan. 16, 1870, Buffalo, N. Y.   D. Mar. 6, 1943, Buffalo, N. Y.
Manager 1901-06.
Hall of Fame 1945.

BR TR 5'9" 178 lbs.

Year Team	Games	BA	SA	AB	H	2B	3B	HR	HR%	R	RBI	BB	SO	SB	PH AB	PH H	PO	A	E	DP	TC/G	FA	G by Pos
1895 2 teams		BOS	N (11G – .211)		LOU	N (96G – .279)																	
" total	107	.273	.397	411	112	20	5	7	1.7	75	57	37	20	12	0	0	185	200	32	14	3.9	.923	3B-77, OF-28, 2B-2, SS-1
1896 BOS N	84	.296	.398	304	90	10	9	1	0.3	48	46	30	12	10	0	0	141	218	40	18	4.8	.900	3B-80, SS-4
1897	134	.346	.482	529	183	28	13	6	1.1	103	132	41		14	0	0	214	303	47	20	4.2	.917	3B-134
1898	152	.328	.479	597	196	35	5	15	2.5	107	111	40		12	0	0	243	332	42	20	4.1	.932	3B-152
1899	151	.277	.386	599	166	28	11	5	0.8	98	92	40		12	0	0	217	376	36	23	4.2	.943	3B-151
1900	142	.304	.394	586	178	25	5	6	1.0	104	95	34		23	0	0	252	331	40	21	4.4	.936	3B-141, SS-1
1901 BOS A	138	.332	.495	564	187	42	16	6	1.1	109	94	34		19	0	0	203	328	50	24	4.2	.914	3B-138
1902	108	.322	.459	429	138	21	10	6	1.4	71	61	24		18	0	0	143	255	19	14	3.9	.954	3B-107
1903	130	.296	.448	540	160	33	17	5	0.9	87	72	24		23	0	0	178	260	22	19	3.5	.952	3B-130
1904	156	.266	.374	631	168	33	13	3	0.5	85	67	27		19	0	0	191	320	30	15	3.5	.945	3B-156
1905	131	.276	.368	508	140	25	5	4	0.8	66	65	37		18	0	0	164	268	36	12	3.6	.923	3B-131
1906	37	.275	.408	142	39	8	4	1	0.7	17	16	4		1	5	1	43	70	11	2	3.4	.911	3B-32
1907 2 teams		BOS	A (41G – .291)		PHI	A (102G – .274)																	
" total	143	.279	.337	523	146	30	4	0	0.0	51	45	34		8	0	0	143	257	47	13	3.1	.895	3B-141
1908 PHI A	115	.217	.263	433	94	14	3	0	0.0	34	30	20		5	0	0	117	216	26	14	3.1	.928	3B-115
14 yrs.	1728	.294	.408	6796	1997	352	116	65	1.0	1055	983	426	32	194	7	1	2434	3734	478	229	3.8	.928	3B-1685, OF-28, SS-6, 2B-2

WORLD SERIES

Year Team	Games	BA	SA	AB	H	2B	3B	HR	HR%	R	RBI	BB	SO	SB	PH AB	PH H	PO	A	E	DP	TC/G	FA	G by Pos
1903 BOS A	8	.250	.389	36	9	1	2	0	0.0	5	1	1	1	3	0	0	7	22	2	1	3.9	.935	3B-8

Joe Collins

COLLINS, JOSEPH EDWARD
Born Joseph Edward Kollonige.
B. Dec. 3, 1922, Scranton, Pa.   D. Aug. 30, 1989, Union, N. J.

BL TL 6' 185 lbs.

Year Team	Games	BA	SA	AB	H	2B	3B	HR	HR%	R	RBI	BB	SO	SB	PH AB	PH H	PO	A	E	DP	TC/G	FA	G by Pos
1948 NY A	5	.200	.400	5	1	1	0	0	0.0	0	0	0	2	0	5	1	0	0	0	0	0.0	–	
1949	7	.100	.100	10	1	0	0	0	0.0	2	4	6	2	0	0	0	23	0	2	2	3.6	.920	1B-5
1950	108	.234	.420	205	48	8	3	8	3.9	47	28	31	34	5	4	0	481	36	7	62	4.9	.987	1B-99, OF-2
1951	125	.286	.458	262	75	8	5	9	3.4	52	48	34	23	9	5	1	575	57	9	65	5.1	.986	1B-114, OF-15
1952	122	.280	.481	428	120	16	8	18	4.2	69	59	55	47	4	1	0	1047	73	11	123	9.3	.990	1B-119
1953	127	.269	.439	387	104	11	2	17	4.4	72	44	59	36	2	11	0	837	65	11	100	7.2	.988	1B-113, OF-4
1954	130	.271	.446	343	93	20	2	12	3.5	67	46	51	37	2	23	4	759	60	7	105	6.4	.992	1B-117
1955	105	.234	.414	278	65	9	1	13	4.7	40	45	44	32	0	13	5	445	45	2	63	4.7	.996	1B-73, OF-27
1956	100	.225	.347	262	59	5	2	7	2.7	38	43	34	33	3	16	4	346	32	1	37	3.8	.997	1B-51, OF-43
1957	79	.201	.248	149	30	1	0	2	1.3	17	10	24	18	2	32	6	234	15	3	23	3.2	.988	1B-32, OF-15
10 yrs.	908	.256	.421	2329	596	79	24	86	3.7	404	329	338	263	27	110	21	4747	383	53	580	5.7	.990	1B-715, OF-114

Year	Team		Games	BA	SA	AB	H	2B	3B	HR	HR%	R	RBI	BB	SO	SB	Pinch Hit AB	H	PO	A	E	DP	TC/G	FA	G by Pos

Wayne Comer *continued*

Year	Team		Games	BA	SA	AB	H	2B	3B	HR	HR%	R	RBI	BB	SO	SB	AB	H	PO	A	E	DP	TC/G	FA	G by Pos
1970	2 teams	MIL A	(13G – .059)									WAS A	(77G – .233)												
"	total		90	.212	.240	146	31	4	0	0	0.0	22	9	22	19	4	26	3	75	2	4	0	0.9	.951	OF-63, 3B-1
1972	DET A		27	.111	.111	9	1	0	0	0	0.0	1	1	0	1	0	6	1	5	0	0	0	0.2	1.000	OF-17
5 yrs.			316	.229	.336	687	157	22	2	16	2.3	119	67	106	106	22	63	8	389	16	10	6	1.3	.976	OF-247, 3B-2, C-2

WORLD SERIES

Year	Team		Games	BA	SA	AB	H	2B	3B	HR	HR%	R	RBI	BB	SO	SB	AB	H	PO	A	E	DP	TC/G	FA	G by Pos
1968	DET A		1	1.000	1.000	1	1	0	0	0	0.0	0	0	0	0	0	1	1	0	0	0	0	0.0	–	

Charlie Comiskey

COMISKEY, CHARLES ALBERT (Commy, The Old Roman) BR TR 6' 180 lbs.
B. Aug. 15, 1859, Chicago, Ill. D. Oct. 26, 1931, Eagle River, Wis.
Manager 1883-94.
Hall of Fame 1939.

Year	Team		Games	BA	SA	AB	H	2B	3B	HR	HR%	R	RBI	BB	SO	SB	AB	H	PO	A	E	DP	TC/G	FA	G by Pos
1882	STL	AA	78	.243	.310	329	80	9	5	1	0.3	58		4			0	0	861	16	30	25	11.6	.967	1B-77, P-2
1883			96	.294	.397	401	118	17	9	2	0.5	87	11				0	0	1085	20	43	49	12.0	.963	1B-96, OF-1
1884			108	.239	.315	460	110	17	6	2	0.4	76	5				0	0	1193	38	40	56	11.8	.969	1B-108, 2B-1, P-1
1885			83	.256	.359	340	87	15	7	2	0.6	68	14				0	0	879	24	29	34	11.2	.969	1B-83
1886			131	.254	.327	578	147	15	9	3	0.5	95	10				0	0	1186	72	36	71	9.9	.972	1B-122, 2B-9, OF-2
1887			125	.335	.416	538	180	22	5	4	0.7	139		27		117	0	0	1162	75	36	62	10.2	.972	1B-116, 2B-9, OF-3
1888			137	.273	.359	576	157	22	5	6	1.0	102	83	12		72	0	0	1298	50	44	52	10.2	.968	1B-133, OF-5, 2B-3
1889	CHI	P	137	.286	.383	587	168	28	10	3	0.5	105	102	19	19	65	0	0	1227	52	39	71	9.6	.970	1B-134, OF-3, 2B-3, P-1
1890			88	.244	.289	377	92	11	3	0	0.0	53	59	14	17	34	0	0	882	41	33	52	10.9	.965	1B-88
1891	STL	AA	141	.262	.312	580	152	16	2	3	0.5	86	93	33	25	41	0	0	1436	62	31	78	10.8	.980	1B-141, OF-2
1892	CIN	N	141	.227	.290	551	125	14	6	0	0.0	61	71	32	16	30	0	0	1469	73	25	103	11.1	.984	1B-141
1893			64	.220	.274	259	57	12	1	0	0.0	38	26	11	2	9	0	0	675	21	15	57	11.1	.979	1B-64
1894			61	.264	.300	220	58	8	0	0	0.0	26	33	5	5	10	0	0	536	24	16	36	9.4	.972	1B-60, OF-1
13 yrs.			1390	.264	.338	5796	1531	206	68	29	0.5	994	467	197	84	378	0	0	13889	568	417	746	10.7	.972	1B-1363, 2B-25, OF-17, P-4

Jim Command

COMMAND, JAMES DALTON (Igor) BL TR 6'2" 200 lbs.
B. Oct. 15, 1928, Grand Rapids, Mich.

Year	Team		Games	BA	SA	AB	H	2B	3B	HR	HR%	R	RBI	BB	SO	SB	AB	H	PO	A	E	DP	TC/G	FA	G by Pos
1954	PHI	N	9	.222	.444	18	4	1	0	1	5.6	1	6	2	4	0	3	0	5	8	1	0	1.6	.929	3B-6
1955			5	.000	.000	5	0	0	0	0	0.0	0	0	0	0	0	5	0	0	0	0	0	0.0	–	
2 yrs.			14	.174	.348	23	4	1	0	1	4.3	1	6	2	4	0	8	0	5	8	1	0	1.0	.929	3B-6

Adam Comorosky

COMOROSKY, ADAM ANTHONY BR TR 5'10" 167 lbs.
B. Dec. 9, 1905, Swoyersville, Pa. D. Mar. 2, 1951, Swoyersville, Pa.

Year	Team		Games	BA	SA	AB	H	2B	3B	HR	HR%	R	RBI	BB	SO	SB	AB	H	PO	A	E	DP	TC/G	FA	G by Pos
1926	PIT	N	8	.267	.467	15	4	1	0	0	0.0	2	0	1	2	1	0	0	7	0	0	0	0.9	1.000	OF-6
1927			18	.230	.246	61	14	1	0	0	0.0	5	4	3	1	0	1	0	43	1	1	0	2.5	.978	OF-16
1928			51	.295	.398	176	52	6	3	2	1.1	22	34	15	6	1	1	1	118	2	4	1	2.4	.968	OF-49
1929			127	.321	.461	473	152	26	11	6	1.3	86	97	40	22	19	3	0	256	6	10	3	2.1	.963	OF-121
1930			152	.313	.529	597	187	47	23	12	2.0	112	119	51	33	14	0	0	337	12	11	2	2.4	.969	OF-152
1931			99	.243	.291	350	85	12	1	1	0.3	37	48	34	28	11	7	1	214	4	5	2	2.3	.978	OF-90
1932			108	.286	.389	370	106	18	4	4	1.1	54	46	25	20	7	11	3	255	4	5	2	2.4	.981	OF-92
1933			64	.284	.364	162	46	8	1	1	0.6	18	15	4	9	2	32	9	66	1	0	0	1.0	1.000	OF-30
1934	CIN	N	127	.258	.312	446	115	12	6	0	0.0	46	40	34	23	1	4	0	285	5	9	1	2.4	.970	OF-122
1935			59	.248	.328	137	34	3	1	2	1.5	22	14	7	14	1	7	2	79	3	4	0	1.5	.953	OF-40
10 yrs.			813	.285	.400	2787	795	134	51	28	1.0	404	417	214	158	57	67	16	1660	38	49	11	2.1	.972	OF-718

Mike Compton

COMPTON, MICHAEL LYNN BR TR 5'10" 180 lbs.
B. Aug. 15, 1944, Stamford, Conn.

Year	Team		Games	BA	SA	AB	H	2B	3B	HR	HR%	R	RBI	BB	SO	SB	AB	H	PO	A	E	DP	TC/G	FA	G by Pos
1970	PHI	N	47	.164	.209	110	18	0	1	1	0.9	8	7	9	22	0	1	0	265	13	4	1	6.0	.986	C-40

Pete Compton

COMPTON, ANNA SEBASTIAN (Bash) BL TL 5'11" 170 lbs.
B. Sept. 28, 1889, San Marcos, Tex. D. Feb. 3, 1978, Kansas City, Mo.

Year	Team		Games	BA	SA	AB	H	2B	3B	HR	HR%	R	RBI	BB	SO	SB	AB	H	PO	A	E	DP	TC/G	FA	G by Pos
1911	STL	A	28	.271	.308	107	29	4	0	0	0.0	9	5	8		2	0	0	37	7	4	3	1.7	.917	OF-28
1912			100	.280	.354	268	75	6	4	2	0.7	26	30	21		11	27	9	139	9	12	1	1.6	.925	OF-72
1913			61	.180	.330	100	18	5	2	2	2.0	14	17	13	13	2	34	7	23	2	4	1	0.5	.862	OF-21
1915	2 teams	STL F	(2G – .250)			BOS N	(35G – .241)																		
"	total		37	.242	.339	124	30	7	1	1	0.8	10	15	8	11	4	2	1	68	2	2	1	1.9	.972	OF-37
1916	2 teams	BOS N	(34G – .204)			PIT N	(5G – .063)																		
"	total		39	.184	.202	114	21	0	0	0	0.0	14	8	9	7	5	3	0	71	2	5	1	2.0	.936	OF-35
1918	NY	N	21	.217	.250	60	13	0	1	0	0.0	5	5	5	4	2	2	0	30	3	1	0	1.6	.971	OF-19
6 yrs.			286	.241	.312	773	186	24	8	5	0.6	78	80	64	40	26	69	16	368	25	28	7	1.5	.933	OF-212

Clint Conatser

CONATSER, CLINTON ASTOR (Connie) BR TR 5'11" 182 lbs.
B. July 24, 1921, Los Angeles, Calif.

Year	Team		Games	BA	SA	AB	H	2B	3B	HR	HR%	R	RBI	BB	SO	SB	AB	H	PO	A	E	DP	TC/G	FA	G by Pos
1948	BOS	N	90	.277	.384	224	62	9	3	3	1.3	30	23	32	27	0	11	3	146	3	4	1	1.7	.974	OF-76
1949			53	.263	.362	152	40	6	0	3	2.0	10	16	14	19	0	10	3	93	5	5	0	1.9	.951	OF-44
2 yrs.			143	.271	.375	376	102	15	3	6	1.6	40	39	46	46	0	21	4	239	8	9	1	1.8	.965	OF-120

WORLD SERIES

Year	Team		Games	BA	SA	AB	H	2B	3B	HR	HR%	R	RBI	BB	SO	SB	AB	H	PO	A	E	DP	TC/G	FA	G by Pos
1948	BOS	N	2	.000	.000	4	0	0	0	0	0.0	0	1	0	0	0	1	0	1	0	0	0	0.5	1.000	OF-2

Dave Concepcion

CONCEPCION, DAVID ISMAEL BR TR 6'2" 155 lbs.
Born David Ismael Concepcion y Benitez.
B. June 17, 1948, Aragua, Venezuela

Year	Team		Games	BA	SA	AB	H	2B	3B	HR	HR%	R	RBI	BB	SO	SB	AB	H	PO	A	E	DP	TC/G	FA	G by Pos
1970	CIN	N	101	.260	.317	265	69	6	3	1	0.4	38	19	23	45	10	5	1	144	247	22	51	4.1	.947	SS-93, 2B-3
1971			130	.205	.251	327	67	4	4	1	0.3	24	20	18	51	9	1	0	182	310	13	65	3.9	.974	SS-112, 2B-10, 3B-7, OF-5
1972			119	.209	.270	378	79	13	2	2	0.5	40	29	32	65	13	2	0	197	372	19	76	4.9	.968	SS-114, 3B-9, 2B-1
1973			89	.287	.433	328	94	18	3	8	2.4	39	46	21	55	22	2	0	167	292	12	56	5.3	.975	SS-88, OF-2
1974			160	.281	.397	594	167	25	1	14	2.4	70	82	44	79	41	1	0	239	536	30	99	5.0	.963	SS-160

Dave Concepcion *continued*

Year	Team	Games	BA	SA	AB	H	2B	3B	HR	HR%	R	RBI	BB	SO	SB	PH AB	PH H	PO	A	E	DP	TC/G	FA	G by Pos
1975		140	.274	.353	507	139	23	1	5	1.0	62	49	39	51	33	8	2	241	446	16	102	5.0	.977	SS-130, 3B-6
1976		152	.281	.401	576	162	28	7	9	1.6	74	69	49	68	21	3	1	304	506	27	93	5.5	.968	SS-150
1977		156	.271	.369	572	155	26	3	8	1.4	59	64	46	77	29	0	0	280	490	11	101	5.0	.986	SS-156
1978		153	.301	.405	565	170	33	4	6	1.1	75	67	51	83	23	3	1	255	459	23	72	4.8	.969	SS-152
1979		149	.281	.415	590	166	25	3	16	2.7	91	84	64	73	19	1	0	284	495	27	102	5.4	.967	SS-148
1980		156	.260	.360	622	162	31	8	5	0.8	72	77	37	107	12	2	0	265	451	16	98	4.7	.978	SS-155, 2B-1
1981		106	.306	.409	421	129	28	0	5	1.2	57	67	37	61	4	0	0	208	322	22	71	5.2	.960	SS-106
1982		147	.287	.371	572	164	25	4	5	0.9	48	53	45	61	13	3	1	271	459	17	95	5.1	.977	SS-145, 3B-1, 1B-1
1983		143	.233	.280	528	123	22	0	1	0.2	54	47	56	81	14	3	1	227	387	13	67	4.4	.979	SS-139, 3B-6, 1B-1
1984		154	.245	.320	531	130	26	1	4	0.8	46	58	52	72	22	13	1	213	324	17	46	3.6	.969	SS-104, 3B-54, 1B-6
1985		155	.252	.330	560	141	19	2	7	1.3	59	48	50	67	16	6	0	214	405	24	64	4.1	.963	SS-151, 3B-1
1986		90	.260	.344	311	81	13	2	3	1.0	42	30	26	43	13	8	1	153	223	10	53	4.3	.974	SS-60, 1B-12, 3B-10, 2B-10
1987		104	.319	.384	279	89	15	0	1	0.4	32	33	28	24	4	24	8	250	169	5	43	4.1	.988	2B-59, 1B-26, 3B-13, SS-2
1988		84	.198	.244	197	39	9	0	0	0.0	11	8	18	23	3	17	4	151	131	2	36	3.4	.993	2B-46, 1B-16, SS-13, 3B-9, P-1
19 yrs		2488	.267	.357	8723	2326	389	48	101	1.2	993	950	736	1186	321	100	21	4245	7024	326	1390	4.7	.972	SS-2178, 2B-130, 3B-120, 1B-62, OF-7, P-1

LEAGUE CHAMPIONSHIP SERIES

Year	Team	Games	BA	SA	AB	H	2B	3B	HR	HR%	R	RBI	BB	SO	SB	PH AB	PH H	PO	A	E	DP	TC/G	FA	G by Pos
1970	CIN N	3	–	–	0	0	0	0	0	–	0	0	0	0	0	0	0	1	1	0	0	0.7	1.000	SS-3
1972		3	.000	.000	2	0	0	0	0	0.0	0	0	0	0	0	1	0	0	0	0	0	0.0	–	SS-1
1975		3	.455	.727	11	5	0	0	1	9.1	2	1	1	2	2	0	0	6	8	1	2	5.0	.933	SS-3
1976		3	.200	.300	10	2	1	0	0	0.0	4	0	2	1	0	0	0	2	12	0	1	4.7	1.000	SS-3
1979		3	.429	.500	14	6	1	0	0	0.0	1	0	0	3	0	0	0	3	14	0	2	5.7	1.000	SS-3
5 yrs		15	.351	.486	37	13	2	0	1	2.7	7	1	3	6	2	1	0	12	35	1	5	3.2	.979	SS-13

WORLD SERIES

Year	Team	Games	BA	SA	AB	H	2B	3B	HR	HR%	R	RBI	BB	SO	SB	PH AB	PH H	PO	A	E	DP	TC/G	FA	G by Pos
1970	CIN N	3	.333	.556	9	3	0	1	0	0.0	0	3	0	0	0	0	0	2	2	0	0	1.3	1.000	SS-3
1972		6	.308	.462	13	4	0	1	0	0.0	2	2	2	2	1	1	0	4	11	1	1	2.7	.938	SS-5
1975		7	.179	.321	28	5	1	0	1	3.6	3	4	0	1	3	0	0	12	23	1	3	5.1	.972	SS-7
1976		4	.357	.571	14	5	1	0	0	0.0	1	3	1	3	1	0	0	6	11	1	3	4.5	.944	SS-4
4 yrs		20	.266	.438	64	17	2	3	1	1.6	6	12	3	6	5	1	0	24	47	3	7	3.7	.959	SS-19

4th

Onix Concepcion

CONCEPCION, ONIX CARDONA
Born Onix Cardona Concepcion y Cardona.
B. Oct. 5, 1957, Dorado, Puerto Rico

BR TR 5'6" 160 lbs.

Year	Team	Games	BA	SA	AB	H	2B	3B	HR	HR%	R	RBI	BB	SO	SB	PH AB	PH H	PO	A	E	DP	TC/G	FA	G by Pos
1980	KC A	12	.133	.133	15	2	0	0	0	0.0	0	0	0	1	0	2	1	5	10	3	1	1.5	.833	SS-6
1981		2	–	–	0	0	0	0	0	–	0	0	0	0	0	0	0	0	0	0	0	0.0	–	SS-1
1982		74	.234	.288	205	48	9	1	0	0.0	17	15	5	18	2	3	0	92	168	11	28	3.7	.959	SS-46, 2B-24, DH-1
1983		80	.242	.320	219	53	11	3	0	0.0	22	20	12	12	10	3	1	92	175	15	35	3.5	.947	3B-31, 2B-28, SS-21, DH-1
1984		90	.282	.338	287	81	9	2	1	0.3	36	23	14	33	9	1	0	116	295	11	59	4.7	.974	SS-85, 2B-6, 3B-1
1985		131	.204	.245	314	64	5	1	2	0.6	32	20	16	29	4	1	0	127	370	21	63	4.0	.959	SS-128, 2B-2
1987	PIT N	1	1.000	1.000	1	1	0	0	0	0.0	0	0	0	0	0	1	1	0	0	0	0	0.0	–	SS-1
7 yrs		390	.239	.294	1041	249	34	7	3	0.3	108	80	47	93	25	11	3	432	1018	61	186	3.9	.960	SS-288, 2B-60, 3B-32, DH-2

LEAGUE CHAMPIONSHIP SERIES

Year	Team	Games	BA	SA	AB	H	2B	3B	HR	HR%	R	RBI	BB	SO	SB	PH AB	PH H	PO	A	E	DP	TC/G	FA	G by Pos
1984	KC A	3	.000	.000	7	0	0	0	0	0.0	0	0	0	0	0	0	0	0	6	1	0	2.3	.857	SS-3
1985		4	.000	.000	1	0	0	0	0	0.0	0	0	0	0	0	0	0	2	4	0	0	1.5	1.000	SS-4
2 yrs		7	.000	.000	8	0	0	0	0	0.0	0	0	0	0	0	0	0	2	10	1	0	1.9	.923	SS-7

WORLD SERIES

Year	Team	Games	BA	SA	AB	H	2B	3B	HR	HR%	R	RBI	BB	SO	SB	PH AB	PH H	PO	A	E	DP	TC/G	FA	G by Pos
1980	KC A	3	–	–	0	0	0	0	0	–	0	0	0	0	0	0	0	0	0	0	0	0.0	–	SS-2
1985		3	–	–	0	0	0	0	0	–	0	1	0	0	0	0	0	0	2	0	0	0.7	1.000	SS-2
2 yrs		6	–	–	0	0	0	0	0	–	0	1	0	0	0	0	0	0	2	0	0	0.3	1.000	SS-2

Ramon Conde

CONDE, RAMON LUIS (Wito)
Born Ramon Luis Conde y Ramon.
B. Dec. 29, 1934, Juana Diaz, Puerto Rico

BR TR 5'8" 172 lbs.

Year	Team	Games	BA	SA	AB	H	2B	3B	HR	HR%	R	RBI	BB	SO	SB	PH AB	PH H	PO	A	E	DP	TC/G	FA	G by Pos
1962	CHI A	14	.000	.000	16	0	0	0	0	0.0	0	1	3	3	0	5	0	4	4	1	0	0.6	.889	3B-7

Bunk Congalton

CONGALTON, WILLIAM MILLAR
B. Jan. 24, 1875, Guelph, Ont., Canada   D. Aug. 16, 1937, Cleveland, Ohio

BL TL 5'11" 190 lbs.

Year	Team	Games	BA	SA	AB	H	2B	3B	HR	HR%	R	RBI	BB	SO	SB	PH AB	PH H	PO	A	E	DP	TC/G	FA	G by Pos
1902	CHI N	45	.223	.257	179	40	3	0	1	0.6	14	24	7			3	0	71	6	1	1	1.7	.987	OF-45
1905	CLE A	12	.362	.362	47	17	0	0	0	0.0	4	5	2			3	0	10	2	1	0	1.1	.923	OF-12
1906		117	.320	.389	419	134	13	5	2	0.5	51	50	24			12	3	174	6	8	0	1.6	.957	OF-114
1907	2 teams							CLE A (9G – .182)		BOS A (127G – .286)															
"	total	136	.282	.346	518	146	11	8	2	0.4	46	49	24			13	4	179	19	6	4	1.5	.971	OF-132
4 yrs		310	.290	.348	1163	337	27	13	5	0.4	115	128	57			31	7	434	33	16	5	1.6	.967	OF-303

Billy Conigliaro

CONIGLIARO, WILLIAM MICHAEL
Brother of Tony Conigliaro.
B. Aug. 15, 1947, Revere, Mass.

BR TR 6' 180 lbs.

Year	Team	Games	BA	SA	AB	H	2B	3B	HR	HR%	R	RBI	BB	SO	SB	PH AB	PH H	PO	A	E	DP	TC/G	FA	G by Pos
1969	BOS A	32	.288	.563	80	23	6	2	4	5.0	14	7	9	23	1	6	3	25	0	2	0	0.8	.926	OF-24
1970		114	.271	.462	398	108	16	3	18	4.5	59	58	35	73	3	6	1	201	8	7	0	1.9	.968	OF-108
1971		101	.262	.436	351	92	26	1	11	3.1	42	33	25	68	3	4	1	232	5	4	2	2.4	.983	OF-100
1972	MIL A	52	.230	.393	191	44	6	2	7	3.7	22	16	8	54	1	3	1	120	5	1	2	2.4	.992	OF-50
1973	OAK A	48	.200	.255	110	22	2	2	0	0.0	9	14	9	26	1	6	2	70	5	0	0	1.6	1.000	OF-40, 2B-1
5 yrs		347	.256	.429	1130	289	56	10	40	3.5	142	128	86	244	9	25	8	648	23	14	4	2.0	.980	OF-322, 2B-1

LEAGUE CHAMPIONSHIP SERIES

Year	Team	Games	BA	SA	AB	H	2B	3B	HR	HR%	R	RBI	BB	SO	SB	PH AB	PH H	PO	A	E	DP	TC/G	FA	G by Pos
1973	OAK A	1	.000	.000	4	0	0	0	0	0.0	0	0	0	2	0	0	0	5	0	0	0	5.0	1.000	OF-1

Year Team	Games	BA	SA	AB	H	2B	3B	HR	HR%	R	RBI	BB	SO	SB	Pinch Hit AB	H	PO	A	E	DP	TC/G	FA	G by Pos

Billy Conigliaro *continued*

WORLD SERIES

Year Team	Games	BA	SA	AB	H	2B	3B	HR	HR%	R	RBI	BB	SO	SB	AB	H	PO	A	E	DP	TC/G	FA	G by Pos
1973 OAK A	3	.000	.000	3	0	0	0	0	0.0	0	0	0	1	0	3	0	0	0	0	0	0.0	—	

Tony Conigliaro

CONIGLIARO, ANTHONY RICHARD
Brother of Billy Conigliaro.
B. Jan. 7, 1945, Revere, Mass.

BR TR 6'3" 185 lbs.

Year Team	Games	BA	SA	AB	H	2B	3B	HR	HR%	R	RBI	BB	SO	SB	AB	H	PO	A	E	DP	TC/G	FA	G by Pos
1964 BOS A	111	.290	.530	404	117	21	2	24	5.9	69	52	35	78	2	5	1	176	7	5	0	1.7	.973	OF-106
1965	138	.269	.512	521	140	21	5	32	6.1	82	82	51	116	4	0	0	277	11	7	1	2.1	.976	OF-137
1966	150	.265	.487	558	148	26	7	28	5.0	77	93	52	112	0	4	3	244	8	7	1	1.7	.973	OF-146
1967	95	.287	.519	349	100	11	5	20	5.7	59	67	27	58	4	0	0	172	5	3	1	1.9	.983	OF-95
1969	141	.255	.427	506	129	21	3	20	4.0	57	82	48	111	2	4	0	207	4	4	2	1.5	.981	OF-137
1970	146	.266	.498	560	149	20	1	36	6.4	89	116	43	93	4	0	0	252	7	6	1	1.8	.977	OF-146
1971 CAL A	74	.222	.335	266	59	18	0	4	1.5	23	15	23	52	3	2	1	155	6	1	1	2.2	.994	OF-72
1975 BOS A	21	.123	.246	57	7	1	0	2	3.5	8	9	8	9	1	5	0	0	0	0	0	0.0	—	DH-15
8 yrs.	876	.264	.476	3221	849	139	23	166	5.2	464	516	287	629	20	20	5	1483	48	33	7	1.8	.979	OF-839, DH-15

Jocko Conlan

CONLAN, JOHN BERTRAND
B. Dec. 6, 1899, Chicago, Ill. D. Apr. 16, 1989, Scottsdale, Ariz.
Hall of Fame 1974.

BL TL 5'7½" 165 lbs.

Year Team	Games	BA	SA	AB	H	2B	3B	HR	HR%	R	RBI	BB	SO	SB	AB	H	PO	A	E	DP	TC/G	FA	G by Pos
1934 CHI A	63	.249	.324	225	56	11	3	0	0.0	35	16	19	7	2	8	3	122	5	6	1	2.1	.955	OF-54
1935	65	.286	.350	140	40	7	1	0	0.0	20	15	14	6	3	24	5	71	3	3	1	1.2	.961	OF-37
2 yrs.	128	.263	.334	365	96	18	4	0	0.0	55	31	33	13	5	32	8	193	8	9	2	1.6	.957	OF-91

Art Conlon

CONLON, ARTHUR JOSEPH
B. Dec. 10, 1897, Woburn, Mass. D. Aug. 5, 1987, Falmouth, Mass.

BR TR 5'7" 145 lbs.

Year Team	Games	BA	SA	AB	H	2B	3B	HR	HR%	R	RBI	BB	SO	SB	AB	H	PO	A	E	DP	TC/G	FA	G by Pos
1923 BOS N	59	.218	.238	147	32	3	0	0	0.0	23	17	11	11	0	9	3	96	136	12	19	4.1	.951	2B-36, SS-6, 3B-4

Bert Conn

CONN, ALBERT THOMAS
B. Sept. 22, 1879, Philadelphia, Pa. D. Nov. 2, 1944, Philadelphia, Pa.

TR

Year Team	Games	BA	SA	AB	H	2B	3B	HR	HR%	R	RBI	BB	SO	SB	AB	H	PO	A	E	DP	TC/G	FA	G by Pos
1898 PHI N	1	.333	1.000	3	1	0	1	0	0.0	1	1	0		0	0	0	0	1	0	0	1.0	1.000	P-1
1900	6	.333	.444	9	3	1	0	0	0.0	4	1	0	0	0	2	0	3	1	2	0	1.0	.667	P-4
1901	5	.222	.278	18	4	1	0	0	0.0	2	0	0	0	0	0	0	9	13	3	0	5.0	.880	2B-5
3 yrs.	12	.267	.400	30	8	2	1	0	0.0	7	2	0	0	0	2	0	12	15	5	0	2.7	.844	2B-5, P-5

Fritz Connally

CONNALLY, FRITZIE LEE
B. May 19, 1958, Bryan, Tex.

BR TR 6'3" 210 lbs.

Year Team	Games	BA	SA	AB	H	2B	3B	HR	HR%	R	RBI	BB	SO	SB	AB	H	PO	A	E	DP	TC/G	FA	G by Pos
1983 CHI N	8	.100	.100	10	1	0	0	0	0.0	0	5	0	7	1	1	0	3	0	0	0	0.5	1.000	3B-3
1985 BAL A	50	.232	.348	112	26	4	0	3	2.7	16	15	19	21	0	16	5	39	57	2	4	2.0	.980	3B-46, 1B-2, DH-1
2 yrs.	58	.221	.328	122	27	4	0	3	2.5	16	15	19	26	1	23	6	40	60	2	4	1.8	.980	3B-49, 1B-2, DH-1

Red Connally

CONNALLY, JOHN M.
B. 1863, New York, N. Y. D. Mar. 2, 1896, New York, N. Y.

Year Team	Games	BA	SA	AB	H	2B	3B	HR	HR%	R	RBI	BB	SO	SB	AB	H	PO	A	E	DP	TC/G	FA	G by Pos
1886 STL N	2	.000	.000	7	0	0	0	0	0.0	0	0	0	3		0	0	0	0	0	0	0.0	—	OF-2

Bruce Connatser

CONNATSER, BROADUS MILBURN
B. Sept. 19, 1902, Sevierville, Tenn. D. Jan. 27, 1971, Terre Haute, Ind.

BR TR 5'11½" 170 lbs.

Year Team	Games	BA	SA	AB	H	2B	3B	HR	HR%	R	RBI	BB	SO	SB	AB	H	PO	A	E	DP	TC/G	FA	G by Pos
1931 CLE A	12	.286	.347	49	14	3	0	0	0.0	5	4	2	3	0	0	0	116	9	0	4	10.4	1.000	1B-12
1932	23	.233	.317	60	14	3	1	0	0.0	8	4	4	8	1	8	1	109	8	0	7	5.1	1.000	1B-14
2 yrs.	35	.257	.330	109	28	6	1	0	0.0	13	8	6	11	1	8	1	225	17	0	11	6.9	1.000	1B-26

Frank Connaughton

CONNAUGHTON, FRANK H
B. Jan. 1, 1869, Clinton, Mass. D. Dec. 1, 1942, Boston, Mass.

BR TR 5'9" 165 lbs.

Year Team	Games	BA	SA	AB	H	2B	3B	HR	HR%	R	RBI	BB	SO	SB	AB	H	PO	A	E	DP	TC/G	FA	G by Pos
1894 BOS N	46	.345	.456	171	59	9	2	2	1.2	42	33	16	8	3	2	2	87	118	22	11	4.9	.903	SS-33, C-7, OF-4
1896 NY N	88	.260	.302	315	82	3	2	2	0.6	53	43	25	7	22	3	0	133	204	43	20	4.3	.887	SS-54, OF-30
1906 BOS N	12	.205	.205	44	9	0	0	0	0.0	3	1	3		1	0	0	27	30	5	2	5.2	.919	SS-11, 2B-1
3 yrs.	146	.283	.343	530	150	12	4	4	0.8	98	77	44	15	26	5	2	247	352	70	33	4.6	.895	SS-98, OF-34, C-7, 2B-1

Gene Connell

CONNELL, EUGENE JOSEPH
Brother of Joe Connell.
B. May 10, 1906, Hazleton, Pa. D. Aug. 31, 1937, Waverly, N. Y.

BR TR 6'½" 180 lbs.

Year Team	Games	BA	SA	AB	H	2B	3B	HR	HR%	R	RBI	BB	SO	SB	AB	H	PO	A	E	DP	TC/G	FA	G by Pos
1931 PHI N	6	.250	.250	12	3	0	0	0	0.0	1	0	0	3	0	0	0	13	1	0	0	2.3	1.000	C-6

Joe Connell

CONNELL, JOSEPH BERNARD
Brother of Gene Connell.
B. Jan. 16, 1902, Bethlehem, Pa. D. Sept. 21, 1977, Trexlertown, Pa.

BL TL 5'8" 165 lbs.

Year Team	Games	BA	SA	AB	H	2B	3B	HR	HR%	R	RBI	BB	SO	SB	AB	H	PO	A	E	DP	TC/G	FA	G by Pos
1926 NY N	2	.000	.000	1	0	0	0	0	0.0	0	0	0	0	0	0	0	0	0	0	0	0.0	—	

Pete Connell

CONNELL, PETER J.
B. Brooklyn, N. Y. Deceased.

Year Team	Games	BA	SA	AB	H	2B	3B	HR	HR%	R	RBI	BB	SO	SB	AB	H	PO	A	E	DP	TC/G	FA	G by Pos
1886 NY AA	1	.000	.000	5	0	0	0	0	0.0	0		0	0		0	0	1	1	1	0	3.0	.667	3B-1

Tom Connelly

CONNELLY, THOMAS MARTIN
B. Oct. 20, 1897, Chicago, Ill. D. Feb. 18, 1941, Hines, Ill.

BL TR 5'11½" 165 lbs.

Year Team	Games	BA	SA	AB	H	2B	3B	HR	HR%	R	RBI	BB	SO	SB	AB	H	PO	A	E	DP	TC/G	FA	G by Pos
1920 NY A	1	.000	.000	1	0	0	0	0	0.0	0	0	0	0	0	1	0	0	0	0	0	0.0	—	OF-3
1921	4	.200	.200	5	1	0	0	0	0.0	0	1	0	0	0	2	1	7	0	0	0	1.8	1.000	OF-3
2 yrs.	5	.167	.167	6	1	0	0	0	0.0	0	1	0	0	0	2	1	7	0	0	0	1.4	1.000	OF-3

Year Team	Games	BA	SA	AB	H	2B	3B	HR	HR%	R	RBI	BB	SO	SB	Pinch Hit AB	H	PO	A	E	DP	TC/G	FA	G by Pos

Bud Connolly

CONNOLLY, MERVIN THOMAS (Mike)
B. May 25, 1901, San Francisco, Calif. D. June 12, 1964, Berkeley, Calif.
BR TR 5'8" 154 lbs.

Year Team	Games	BA	SA	AB	H	2B	3B	HR	HR%	R	RBI	BB	SO	SB	AB	H	PO	A	E	DP	TC/G	FA	G by Pos
1925 BOS A	43	.262	.346	107	28	7	1	0	0.0	12	21	23	9	0	8	4	61	75	7	14	3.3	.951	SS-34, 3B-2

Ed Connolly

CONNOLLY, EDWARD JOSEPH, SR.
Father of Ed Connolly.
B. July 17, 1908, Brooklyn, N. Y. D. Nov. 12, 1963, Pittsfield, Mass.
BR TR 5'8½" 180 lbs.

Year Team	Games	BA	SA	AB	H	2B	3B	HR	HR%	R	RBI	BB	SO	SB	AB	H	PO	A	E	DP	TC/G	FA	G by Pos
1929 BOS A	5	.000	.000	8	0	0	0	0	0.0	0	0	0	2	0			7	1	1	0	1.8	.889	C-5
1930	27	.188	.229	48	9	2	0	0	0.0	1	7	4	3	0	0	0	39	12	0	1	1.9	1.000	C-26
1931	42	.075	.086	93	7	1	0	0	0.0	3	3	5	18	0	1	0	87	18	2	1	2.5	.981	C-41
1932	75	.225	.297	222	50	8	4	0	0.0	9	21	20	27	0	0	0	233	55	13	0	4.0	.957	C-75
4 yrs.	149	.178	.229	371	66	11	4	0	0.0	13	31	29	50	0	1	0	366	86	16	2	3.1	.966	C-147

Joe Connolly

CONNOLLY, JOSEPH ALOYSIUS
B. Feb. 12, 1888, N. Smithfield, R. I. D. Sept. 1, 1943, Springfield, R. I.
BL TR 5'7½" 165 lbs.

Year Team	Games	BA	SA	AB	H	2B	3B	HR	HR%	R	RBI	BB	SO	SB	AB	H	PO	A	E	DP	TC/G	FA	G by Pos
1913 BOS N	126	.281	.410	427	120	18	11	5	1.2	79	57	66	47	18	1	0	214	16	11	2	1.9	.954	OF-124
1914	120	.306	.494	399	122	28	10	9	2.3	64	65	49	36	12	1	0	168	19	5	1	1.6	.974	OF-118
1915	104	.298	.397	305	91	14	8	0	0.0	48	23	39	35	13	9	1	158	10	5	2	1.7	.971	OF-93
1916	62	.227	.309	110	25	5	2	0	0.0	11	12	14	13	5	25	6	46	4	1	1	0.8	.980	OF-31
4 yrs.	412	.288	.425	1241	358	65	31	14	1.1	202	157	168	131	48	36	7	586	49	22	6	1.6	.967	OF-366
WORLD SERIES																							
1914 BOS N	3	.111	.111	9	1	0	0	0	0.0	1	1	1	1	0	0	0	2	2	1	0	1.7	.800	OF-3

Joe Connolly

CONNOLLY, JOSEPH GEORGE (Coaster Joe)
B. June 4, 1896, San Francisco, Calif. D. Mar. 30, 1960, San Francisco, Calif.
BR TR 6' 170 lbs.

Year Team	Games	BA	SA	AB	H	2B	3B	HR	HR%	R	RBI	BB	SO	SB	AB	H	PO	A	E	DP	TC/G	FA	G by Pos
1921 NY N	2	.000	.000	4	0	0	0	0	0.0	0	0	1	1	0	1	0	2	0	0	0	1.0	1.000	OF-1
1922 CLE A	12	.244	.333	45	11	2	1	0	0.0	6	6	5	8	1	0	0	33	2	1	0	3.0	.972	OF-12
1923	52	.303	.495	109	33	10	1	3	2.8	25	25	13	7	1	9	1	42	2	2	0	0.9	.957	OF-39
1924 BOS A	14	.100	.100	10	1	0	0	0	0.0	1	1	2	2	0	10	1	3	0	0	0	0.2	1.000	OF-3
4 yrs.	80	.268	.417	168	45	12	2	3	1.8	32	32	21	18	2	20	2	80	4	3	0	1.1	.966	OF-55

Tom Connolly

CONNOLLY, THOMAS FRANCIS (Blackie)
B. Dec. 30, 1892, Boston, Mass. D. May 14, 1966, Boston, Mass.
BL TR 5'11" 180 lbs.

Year Team	Games	BA	SA	AB	H	2B	3B	HR	HR%	R	RBI	BB	SO	SB	AB	H	PO	A	E	DP	TC/G	FA	G by Pos
1915 WAS A	50	.184	.234	141	26	3	2	0	0.0	14	7	14	19	5	3	0	57	43	7	4	2.1	.935	3B-24, OF-19, SS-4

Jim Connor

CONNOR, JAMES MATTHEW
Born James Matthew O'Connor.
B. May 11, 1863, Port Jervis, N. Y. D. Sept. 3, 1950, Providence, R. I.
BR TR

Year Team	Games	BA	SA	AB	H	2B	3B	HR	HR%	R	RBI	BB	SO	SB	AB	H	PO	A	E	DP	TC/G	FA	G by Pos
1892 CHI N	9	.059	.059	34	2	0	0	0	0.0	0	0	1	7		0	0	14	19	3	0	4.0	.917	2B-9
1897	77	.291	.393	285	83	10	5	3	1.1	40	38	24		10	2	1	176	293	32	40	6.5	.936	2B-76
1898	138	.226	.279	505	114	9	9	0	0.0	51	67	42		11	0	0	330	437	44	75	5.9	.946	2B-138
1899	69	.205	.244	234	48	7	1	0	0.0	26	24	18		6	0	0	101	211	26	25	4.9	.923	2B-44, 3B-25
4 yrs.	293	.233	.295	1058	247	26	15	3	0.3	117	129	85	7	27	2	1	621	960	105	140	5.8	.938	2B-267, 3B-25

Roger Connor

CONNOR, ROGER
Brother of Joe Connor.
B. July 1, 1857, Waterbury, Conn. D. Jan. 4, 1931, Waterbury, Conn.
Manager 1896.
Hall of Fame 1976.
BL TL 6'3" 220 lbs.

Year Team	Games	BA	SA	AB	H	2B	3B	HR	HR%	R	RBI	BB	SO	SB	AB	H	PO	A	E	DP	TC/G	FA	G by Pos
1880 TRO N	83	.332	.459	340	113	18	8	3	0.9	53	47	13	21		0	0	116	159	60	10	4.0	.821	3B-83
1881	85	.292	.387	367	107	17	6	2	0.5	55	31	15	20		0	0	836	40	46	51	10.8	.950	1B-85
1882	81	.330	.530	349	115	22	18	4	1.1	65	42	13	20		0	0	518	57	44	31	7.6	.929	1B-43, OF-24, 3B-14
1883 NY N	98	.357	.506	409	146	28	15	1	0.2	80		25	16		0	0	958	40	44	37	10.6	.958	1B-98
1884	116	.317	.417	477	151	28	4	4	0.8	98		38	32		0	0	299	234	96	32	5.4	.847	2B-67, OF-37, 3B-12
1885	110	.371	.495	455	169	23	15	1	0.2	102		51	8		0	0	1178	42	31	66	11.4	.975	1B-110
1886	118	.355	.540	485	172	29	20	7	1.4	105	71	41	15		0	0	1164	65	34	55	10.7	.973	1B-118
1887	127	.285	.541	471	134	26	22	17	3.6	113	104	75	50	43	0	0	1325	44	10	67	10.9	.993	1B-127
1888	134	.291	.480	481	140	15	17	14	2.9	98	71	73	44	27	0	0	1346	45	26	59	10.6	.982	1B-133, 2B-1
1889	131	.317	.528	496	157	32	17	13	2.6	117	130	93	46	21	0	0	1266	33	30	68	10.1	.977	1B-131, 3B-1
1890 NY P	123	.349	.541	484	169	24	15	13	2.7	133	103	88	32	22	0	0	1335	80	21	79	11.7	.985	1B-123
1891 NY N	129	.290	.443	479	139	29	13	6	1.3	112	94	83	39	27	0	0	1362	56	25	77	11.2	.983	1B-129
1892 PHI N	155	.294	.463	564	166	37	11	12	2.1	123	73	116	39	22	0	0	1483	59	23	99	10.1	.985	1B-155
1893 NY N	135	.305	.450	511	156	25	8	11	2.2	111	105	91	26	24	0	0	1423	83	40	70	11.5	.974	1B-135, 3B-1
1894 2 teams	NY N (22G – .293)			STL N (99G – .321)																			
" total	121	.316	.552	462	146	35	25	8	1.7	93	93	59	19	19	0	0	1092	83	32	84	10.0	.973	1B-120, OF-1
1895 STL N	104	.329	.508	398	131	29	9	8	2.0	78	77	63	10	9	0	0	953	62	14	60	9.9	.986	1B-103
1896	126	.284	.433	483	137	21	9	11	2.3	71	72	52	14	10	0	0	1217	94	16	48	10.5	.988	1B-126
1897	22	.229	.325	83	19	3	1	1	1.2	13	12	13		3	0	0	237	12	4	6	11.5	.984	1B-22
18 yrs.	1998	.317	.485	7794	2467	441	233	136	1.7	1620	1125	1002	449	227	0	0	18108	1288	596	999	10.0	.970	1B-1758, 3B-111, 2B-68, OF-62
						5th																	

Chuck Connors

CONNORS, KEVIN JOSEPH ALOYSIUS
B. Apr. 10, 1921, Brooklyn, N. Y.
BL TL 6'5" 190 lbs.

Year Team	Games	BA	SA	AB	H	2B	3B	HR	HR%	R	RBI	BB	SO	SB	AB	H	PO	A	E	DP	TC/G	FA	G by Pos
1949 BKN N	1	.000	.000	1	0	0	0	0	0.0	0	0	0	0	0	0	0	0	0	0	0	0.0	–	
1951 CHI N	66	.239	.303	201	48	5	1	2	1.0	16	18	12	25	4	10	1	452	33	8	41	7.5	.984	1B-57
2 yrs.	67	.238	.302	202	48	5	1	2	1.0	16	18	12	25	4	11	1	452	33	8	41	7.4	.984	1B-57

Jerry Connors

CONNORS, JEREMIAH
B. Philadelphia, Pa. Deceased.

Year Team	Games	BA	SA	AB	H	2B	3B	HR	HR%	R	RBI	BB	SO	SB	AB	H	PO	A	E	DP	TC/G	FA	G by Pos
1892 PHI N	1	.000	.000	3	0	0	0	0	0.0	0	0	0	1	0	0	0	0	0	0	0	0.0	–	OF-1

Year	Team		Games	BA	SA	AB	H	2B	3B	HR	HR%	R	RBI	BB	SO	SB	Pinch Hit AB	Pinch Hit H	PO	A	E	DP	TC/G	FA	G by Pos

Joe Connors

CONNORS, JOSEPH P.
B. Paterson, N. J. Deceased.

Year	Team		Games	BA	SA	AB	H	2B	3B	HR	HR%	R	RBI	BB	SO	SB	PH AB	PH H	PO	A	E	DP	TC/G	FA	G by Pos
1884	2 teams	ALT U (3G – .091)					KC	U (3G – .091)																	
"	total		6	.091	.091	22	2	0	0	0	0.0	2		1			0	0	8	7	3	0	3.0	.833	OF-3, P-3, 3B-1

Merv Connors

CONNORS, MERVYN JAMES   BR TR 6'2" 192 lbs.
B. Jan. 23, 1914, Berkeley, Calif.

Year	Team		Games	BA	SA	AB	H	2B	3B	HR	HR%	R	RBI	BB	SO	SB	PH AB	PH H	PO	A	E	DP	TC/G	FA	G by Pos
1937	CHI	A	28	.233	.350	103	24	4	1	2	1.9	12	12	14	19	2	0	0	22	53	6	8	2.9	.926	3B-28
1938			24	.355	.710	62	22	4	0	6	9.7	14	13	9	17	0	7	2	129	11	3	17	6.0	.979	1B-16
	2 yrs.		52	.279	.485	165	46	8	1	8	4.8	26	25	23	36	2	7	2	151	64	9	25	4.3	.960	3B-28, 1B-16

Ben Conroy

CONROY, BERNARD PATRICK   160 lbs.
B. Mar. 14, 1871, Philadelphia, Pa. D. Nov. 25, 1937, Philadelphia, Pa.

Year	Team		Games	BA	SA	AB	H	2B	3B	HR	HR%	R	RBI	BB	SO	SB	PH AB	PH H	PO	A	E	DP	TC/G	FA	G by Pos
1890	PHI	AA	117	.171	.208	404	69	13	1	0	0.0	45		45		17	0	0	221	352	56	39	5.4	.911	SS-74, 2B-42, OF-1

Bill Conroy

CONROY, WILLIAM GORDON   BR TR 6' 185 lbs.
B. Feb. 26, 1915, Bloomington, Ill.

Year	Team		Games	BA	SA	AB	H	2B	3B	HR	HR%	R	RBI	BB	SO	SB	PH AB	PH H	PO	A	E	DP	TC/G	FA	G by Pos
1935	PHI	A	1	.250	.500	4	1	1	0	0	0.0	0	0	1	0	0	0	0	11	0	0	0	11.0	1.000	C-1
1936			1	.500	.500	2	1	0	0	0	0.0	0	0	1	0	0	0	0	3	0	0	0	3.0	1.000	C-1
1937			26	.200	.250	60	12	1	1	0	0.0	4	3	7	9	1	5	1	58	6	0	2	2.5	1.000	C-18, 1B-1
1942	BOS	A	83	.200	.280	250	50	4	2	4	1.6	22	20	40	47	2	0	0	324	40	11	6	4.5	.971	C-83
1943			39	.180	.270	89	16	5	0	1	1.1	13	6	18	19	0	3	1	135	19	5	3	4.1	.969	C-38
1944			19	.213	.255	47	10	2	0	0	0.0	6	4	11	9	0	0	0	60	9	2	2	3.7	.972	C-19
	6 yrs.		169	.199	.274	452	90	13	3	5	1.1	45	33	77	85	3	8	2	591	74	18	13	4.0	.974	C-160, 1B-1

Pep Conroy

CONROY, WILLIAM FREDERICK   BR TR 5'8½" 160 lbs.
B. Jan. 9, 1899, Chicago, Ill. D. Jan. 23, 1970, Chicago, Ill.

Year	Team		Games	BA	SA	AB	H	2B	3B	HR	HR%	R	RBI	BB	SO	SB	PH AB	PH H	PO	A	E	DP	TC/G	FA	G by Pos
1923	WAS	A	18	.133	.233	60	8	2	2	0	0.0	6	2	4	9	0	1	0	56	21	5	7	4.6	.939	3B-10, 1B-6, OF-1

Wid Conroy

CONROY, WILLIAM EDWARD   BR TR 5'9" 158 lbs.
B. Apr. 5, 1877, Camden, N. J. D. Dec. 6, 1959, Mt. Holly, N. J.

Year	Team		Games	BA	SA	AB	H	2B	3B	HR	HR%	R	RBI	BB	SO	SB	PH AB	PH H	PO	A	E	DP	TC/G	FA	G by Pos
1901	MIL	A	131	.256	.350	503	129	20	6	5	1.0	74	64	36		21	0	0	299	427	64	48	6.0	.919	SS-118, 3B-12
1902	PIT	N	99	.244	.312	365	89	10	6	1	0.3	55	47	24		10	0	0	194	327	42	39	5.7	.925	SS-95, OF-3
1903	NY	A	126	.272	.372	503	137	23	12	1	0.2	74	45	32		33	0	0	167	247	36	11	3.6	.920	3B-123, SS-4
1904			140	.243	.335	489	119	18	12	1	0.2	58	52	43		30	0	0	204	295	29	13	3.8	.945	3B-110, SS-27, OF-3
1905			102	.273	.395	385	105	19	11	2	0.5	55	25	32		25	1	0	287	142	24	14	4.4	.947	3B-48, OF-21, SS-18, 1B-9, 2B-3
1906			148	.245	.332	567	139	17	10	4	0.7	67	54	47		32	0	0	295	154	21	15	3.2	.955	OF-97, SS-49, 3B-2
1907			140	.234	.315	530	124	12	11	3	0.6	58	51	30		41	2	0	299	104	24	17	3.1	.944	OF-100, SS-38
1908			141	.237	.296	531	126	22	3	1	0.2	44	39	14		23	0	0	236	285	32	15	3.9	.942	3B-119, 2B-12, OF-10
1909	WAS	A	139	.244	.293	488	119	13	4	1	0.2	44	20	37		24	0	0	170	276	29	18	3.4	.939	3B-120, 2B-13, OF-5, SS-1
1910			105	.254	.311	351	89	11	3	1	0.3	36	27	30		11	6	1	163	99	13	6	2.6	.953	3B-48, OF-46, 2B-5
1911			104	.231	.298	346	80	11	3	2	0.6	40	28	20		12	4	2	118	178	24	11	3.1	.925	3B-85, OF-13, 2B-1
	11 yrs.		1375	.248	.328	5058	1256	176	81	22	0.4	605	452	345		262	14	3	2432	2534	338	207	3.9	.936	3B-667, SS-350, OF-298, 2B-34, 1B-9

Billy Consolo

CONSOLO, WILLIAM ANGELO   BR TR 5'11" 180 lbs.
B. Aug. 18, 1934, Cleveland, Ohio

Year	Team		Games	BA	SA	AB	H	2B	3B	HR	HR%	R	RBI	BB	SO	SB	PH AB	PH H	PO	A	E	DP	TC/G	FA	G by Pos
1953	BOS	A	47	.215	.323	65	14	2	1	1	1.5	9	6	2	23	1	9	1	26	47	6	13	1.7	.924	3B-16, 2B-11
1954			91	.227	.277	242	55	7	1	1	0.4	23	11	33	69	2	4	1	113	184	15	30	3.4	.952	SS-50, 3B-18, 2B-12
1955			8	.222	.222	18	4	0	0	0	0.0	4	0	5	4	0	1	1	11	5	2	1	2.3	.889	2B-4
1956			48	.182	.182	11	2	0	0	0	0.0	13	1	3	5	0	0	0	9	14	2	4	0.5	.920	2B-25
1957			68	.270	.372	196	53	6	1	4	2.0	26	19	23	48	1	0	0	92	189	16	41	4.4	.946	SS-42, 2B-16, 3B-1
1958			46	.125	.181	72	9	2	1	0	0.0	13	5	6	14	0	1	0	37	55	5	16	2.1	.948	2B-13, SS-11, 3B-1
1959	2 teams	BOS A (10G – .214)					WAS	A	(79G – .213)																
"	total		89	.213	.269	216	46	6	3	0	0.0	28	10	38	59	1	8	1	126	242	19	48	4.3	.951	SS-77, 2B-4
1960	WAS	A	100	.207	.305	174	36	4	2	3	1.7	23	15	25	29	1	7	2	97	183	18	39	3.0	.940	SS-82, 2B-12, 3B-2
1961	MIN	A	11	.000	.000	5	0	0	0	0	0.0	0	0	0	1	0	1	0	5	1	0	0	0.5	1.000	SS-3, 2B-3, 3B-1
1962	3 teams	PHI N (13G – .400)					LA	A	(28G – .100)		KC	A	(54G – .240)											
"	total		95	.229	.274	179	41	4	2	0	0.0	18	16	26	45	3	13	4	78	140	13	28	2.4	.944	SS-52, 3B-21, 2B-1
	10 yrs.		603	.221	.289	1178	260	31	11	9	0.8	158	83	161	297	9	44	10	594	1060	96	220	2.9	.945	SS-317, 2B-101, 3B-61

Bill Conway

CONWAY, WILLIAM F.   BR TR 5'8½" 170 lbs.
Brother of Dick Conway.
B. Nov. 28, 1861, Lowell, Mass. D. Dec. 28, 1943, Somerville, Mass.

Year	Team		Games	BA	SA	AB	H	2B	3B	HR	HR%	R	RBI	BB	SO	SB	PH AB	PH H	PO	A	E	DP	TC/G	FA	G by Pos
1884	PHI	N	1	.000	.000	4	0	0	0	0	0.0	0		0	1		0	0	5	2	0	1	7.0	1.000	C-1
1886	BAL	AA	7	.143	.143	14	2	0	0	0	0.0	4		7			0	0	33	4	6	0	6.1	.860	C-7
	2 yrs.		8	.111	.111	18	2	0	0	0	0.0	4		7	1		0	0	38	6	6	1	6.3	.880	C-8

Charlie Conway

CONWAY, CHARLES CONNELL   BR TR 5'11" 155 lbs.
B. Apr. 28, 1886, Youngstown, Ohio D. Sept. 12, 1968, Youngstown, Ohio

Year	Team		Games	BA	SA	AB	H	2B	3B	HR	HR%	R	RBI	BB	SO	SB	PH AB	PH H	PO	A	E	DP	TC/G	FA	G by Pos
1911	WAS	A	2	.333	1.000	3	1	0	1	0	0.0	0	0	0		0	0	0	0	0	1	0	0.5	–	OF-2

Jack Conway

CONWAY, JACK CLEMENTS   BR TR 5'11½" 175 lbs.
B. July 30, 1919, Bryan, Tex.

Year	Team		Games	BA	SA	AB	H	2B	3B	HR	HR%	R	RBI	BB	SO	SB	PH AB	PH H	PO	A	E	DP	TC/G	FA	G by Pos
1941	CLE	A	2	.500	.500	2	1	0	0	0	0.0	0	1	0	0	0	0	0	2	3	0	0	2.5	1.000	SS-2
1946			68	.225	.264	258	58	6	2	0	0.0	24	18	20	36	2	2	0	146	163	17	34	4.8	.948	2B-50, SS-14, 3B-3
1947			34	.180	.220	50	9	2	0	0	0.0	3	5	3	8	0	2	0	22	42	8	10	2.1	.889	SS-24, 2B-5, 3B-1
1948	NY	N	24	.245	.388	49	12	2	1	1	2.0	8	3	5	10	0	2	0	33	45	2	11	3.3	.975	2B-13, SS-6, 3B-3
	4 yrs.		128	.223	.276	359	80	10	3	1	0.3	35	27	28	54	2	6	0	203	253	27	55	3.8	.944	2B-68, SS-46, 3B-7

Year	Team		Games	BA	SA	AB	H	2B	3B	HR	HR%	R	RBI	BB	SO	SB	Pinch Hit AB	Pinch Hit H	PO	A	E	DP	TC/G	FA	G by Pos

Owen Conway

CONWAY, OWEN SYLVESTER
B. Oct. 23, 1890, New York, N. Y.   D. Mar. 12, 1942, Philadelphia, Pa.   TR

| 1915 | PHI | A | 4 | .067 | .067 | 15 | 1 | 0 | 0 | 0 | 0.0 | 2 | 0 | 0 | 3 | 0 | 0 | 0 | 7 | 11 | 6 | 2 | 6.0 | .750 | 3B-4 |

Pete Conway

CONWAY, PETER J.
Brother of Jim Conway.
B. Oct. 30, 1866, Burmont, Pa.   D. Jan. 14, 1903, Media, Pa.   BR TR 5'10½"

1885	BUF	N	29	.111	.200	90	10	5	0	1	1.1	7	7	5	28		0	0	7	54	10	0	2.4	.859	P-27, OF-2, SS-1, 1B-1
1886	2 teams		KC	N	(51G – .242)	DET	N	(12G – .186)																	
"	total		63	.232	.325	237	55	9	2	3	1.3	32	21	6	42		0	0	60	58	22	3	2.2	.843	P-34, OF-32
1887	DET	N	24	.232	.337	95	22	5	1	1	1.1	16	7	2	9	0	0	0	26	37	5	0	2.8	.926	P-17, OF-8
1888			45	.275	.377	167	46	4	2	3	1.8	28	23	8	25	1	0	0	10	96	7	4	2.5	.938	P-45, OF-1
1889	PIT	N	3	.100	.400	10	1	0	0	1	10.0	2	2	1	3	1	0	0	1	6	1	0	2.7	.875	P-3, OF-1
5 yrs.			164	.224	.324	599	134	23	5	9	1.5	85	60	22	107	2	0	0	104	251	45	7	2.4	.888	P-126, OF-44, SS-1, 1B-1

Rip Conway

CONWAY, RICHARD DANIEL
B. Apr. 18, 1896, White Bear, Minn.   D. Dec. 3, 1971, St. Paul, Minn.   BL TR 5'6"   160 lbs.

| 1918 | BOS | N | 14 | .167 | .167 | 24 | 4 | 0 | 0 | 0 | 0.0 | 4 | 2 | 2 | 4 | 1 | 5 | 2 | 10 | 8 | 4 | 0 | 1.6 | .818 | 2B-5, 3B-1 |

Ed Conwell

CONWELL, EDWARD JAMES (Irish)
B. Jan. 29, 1890, Chicago, Ill.   D. May 1, 1926, Norwood Park, Ill.   BR TR 5'11"   155 lbs.

| 1911 | STL | N | 1 | .000 | .000 | 1 | 0 | 0 | 0 | 0 | 0.0 | 0 | 0 | 0 | 1 | 0 | 0 | 0 | 0 | 1 | 0 | 0 | 1.0 | – | 3B-1 |

Herb Conyers

CONYERS, HERBERT LEROY
B. Jan. 8, 1921, Cowgill, Mo.   D. Sept. 16, 1964, Cleveland, Ohio   BL TR 6'5"   210 lbs.

| 1950 | CLE | A | 7 | .333 | .667 | 9 | 3 | 0 | 1 | 1 | 11.1 | 2 | 1 | 1 | 2 | 0 | 1 | 1 | 4 | 2 | 6 | 0 | 0 | 0.9 | 1.000 | 1B-1 |

Dale Coogan

COOGAN, DALE ROGER
B. Aug. 14, 1930, Los Angeles, Calif.   D. Mar. 8, 1989, Mission Viejo, Calif.   BL TL 6'1"   190 lbs.

| 1950 | PIT | N | 53 | .240 | .326 | 129 | 31 | 6 | 1 | 1 | 0.8 | 19 | 13 | 17 | 24 | 0 | 16 | 2 | 263 | 27 | 6 | 28 | 5.6 | .980 | 1B-32 |

Dan Coogan

COOGAN, DANIEL GEORGE
B. Feb. 16, 1875, Philadelphia, Pa.   D. Oct. 28, 1942, Philadelphia, Pa.   128 lbs.

| 1895 | WAS | N | 26 | .221 | .273 | 77 | 17 | 2 | 1 | 0 | 0.0 | 9 | 7 | 13 | 6 | 1 | 1 | 0 | 45 | 53 | 32 | 6 | 5.0 | .754 | SS-18, C-5, OF-2, 3B-1 |

Cliff Cook

COOK, RAYMOND CLIFFORD
B. Aug. 20, 1936, Dallas, Tex.   BR TR 6'   185 lbs.

1959	CIN	N	9	.381	.571	21	8	1	0	0	0.0	5	2	8	1	0	7	13	2	2	2.4	.909	3B-9
1960			54	.208	.315	149	31	7	0	3	2.0	9	13	8	51	0	0	0	50	77	6	8	2.5	.955	3B-47, OF-4
1961			4	.000	.000	5	0	0	0	0	0.0	0	0	0	3	0	0	2	0	0	0.5	1.000	3B-1
1962	2 teams		CIN	N	(6G – .000)	NY	N	(40G – .232)																	
"	total		46	.222	.342	117	26	6	1	2	1.7	12	9	4	36	1	14	4	26	21	6	2	1.2	.887	3B-20, OF-10
1963	NY	N	50	.142	.236	106	15	2	1	2	1.9	9	8	12	37	0	19	4	50	27	4	5	1.6	.951	OF-21, 3B-9, 1B-5
5 yrs.			163	.201	.312	398	80	17	3	7	1.8	33	35	26	136	2	36	8	133	140	18	17	1.8	.938	3B-86, OF-35, 1B-5

Doc Cook

COOK, LUTHER ALMUS
B. June 24, 1886, Witt, Tex.   D. June 30, 1973, Lawrenceburg, Tenn.   BL TR 6'   170 lbs.

1913	NY	A	20	.264	.319	72	19	2	1	0	0.0	9	1	10	4	1	0	0	43	3	3	1	2.5	.939	OF-20
1914			131	.283	.326	470	133	11	3	1	0.2	59	40	44	60	26	5	1	171	15	10	2	1.5	.949	OF-126
1915			132	.271	.338	476	129	16	5	2	0.4	70	33	62	43	29	0	0	188	20	9	4	1.6	.959	OF-131
1916			3	.100	.100	10	1	0	0	0	0.0	0	1	0	2	0	0	0	3	0	0	0	1.0	1.000	OF-3
4 yrs.			286	.274	.329	1028	282	29	9	3	0.3	138	75	116	109	56	5	1	405	38	22	7	1.6	.953	OF-280

Jim Cook

COOK, JAMES FITCHIE
B. Nov. 10, 1879, Dundee, Ill.   D. June 17, 1949, St. Louis, Mo.   BR TR 5'9"   163 lbs.

| 1903 | CHI | N | 8 | .154 | .192 | 26 | 4 | 1 | 0 | 0 | 0.0 | 3 | 2 | 2 | | 1 | 0 | 0 | 17 | 3 | 2 | 0 | 2.8 | .909 | OF-5, 2B-2, 1B-1 |

Paul Cook

COOK, PAUL
B. May 5, 1863, Caledonia, N. Y.   D. May 25, 1905, Rochester, N. Y.   BR TR

1884	PHI	N	3	.083	.083	12	1	0	0	0	0.0	0		0	2		0	0	16	2	4	1	7.3	.818	C-3
1886	LOU	AA	66	.206	.240	262	54	5	2	0	0.0	28		0	10		0	0	532	49	47	22	9.5	.925	1B-43, C-21, OF-2
1887			61	.247	.283	223	55	4	2	0	0.0	34		0	11	15	0	0	270	95	34	5	6.5	.915	C-55, 1B-6
1888			57	.184	.195	185	34	2	0	0	0.0	20	13	5	9	0	0	0	224	81	37	7	6.0	.892	C-53, OF-4, SS-1
1889			81	.227	.269	286	65	10	1	0	0.0	34	15	15	48	11	0	0	323	142	37	8	6.2	.926	C-74, OF-7, SS-1, 1B-1
1890	BKN	P	58	.252	.294	218	55	3	3	0	0.0	32	31	14	18	7	0	0	320	57	30	20	7.0	.926	C-36, 1B-21, OF-1
1891	2 teams		LOU	AA	(45G – .229)	STL	AA	(7G – .200)																	
"	total		52	.225	.253	178	40	3	1	0	0.0	24	24	12	19	4	0	0	259	51	24	6	6.4	.928	C-42, 1B-10
7 yrs.			378	.223	.256	1364	304	27	9	0	0.0	172	83	67	87	46	0	0	1944	477	213	69	7.0	.919	C-284, 1B-81, OF-14, SS-2

Dusty Cooke

COOKE, ALLEN LINDSEY
B. June 23, 1907, Swepsonville, N. C.   D. Nov. 21, 1987, Raleigh, N. C.   BL TR 6'1"   205 lbs.
Manager 1948.

1930	NY	A	92	.255	.421	216	55	12	3	6	2.8	43	29	32	61	4	10	1	133	2	3	1	1.5	.978	OF-73
1931			27	.333	.436	39	13	1	0	1	2.6	10	6	8	11	4	2	0	23	0	0	0	0.9	1.000	OF-11
1932			3	–	–	0	0	0	0	0		1	0	1	0	0	0	0	0	0	0	0		–	
1933	BOS	A	119	.291	.445	454	132	35	10	5	1.1	86	54	67	71	7	2	0	257	6	12	5	2.3	.956	OF-118
1934			74	.244	.369	168	41	8	5	1	0.6	34	26	36	25	7	21	4	79	1	2	0	1.1	.976	OF-44
1935			100	.306	.439	294	90	18	6	3	1.0	51	34	46	24	6	11	2	172	4	5	1	1.8	.972	OF-82
1936			111	.273	.402	341	93	20	3	6	1.8	58	47	72	48	6	13	4	207	3	6	1	1.9	.972	OF-91

Year Team	Games	BA	SA	AB	H	2B	3B	HR	HR%	R	RBI	BB	SO	SB	Pinch Hit AB	Pinch Hit H	PO	A	E	DP	TC/G	FA	G by Pos

Dusty Cooke *continued*

Year Team	Games	BA	SA	AB	H	2B	3B	HR	HR%	R	RBI	BB	SO	SB	PH AB	PH H	PO	A	E	DP	TC/G	FA	G by Pos
1938 CIN N	82	.275	.373	233	64	15	1	2	0.9	41	33	28	36	0	27	5	126	4	5	1	1.6	.963	OF-51
8 yrs.	608	.280	.415	1745	488	109	28	24	1.4	324	229	290	276	32	86	16	997	20	33	10	1.7	.969	OF-470

Fred Cooke

COOKE, FREDERICK B.
B. Oct., 1873, Ill.   Deceased.

Year Team	Games	BA	SA	AB	H	2B	3B	HR	HR%	R	RBI	BB	SO	SB	PH AB	PH H	PO	A	E	DP	TC/G	FA	G by Pos
1897 CLE N	5	.294	.412	17	5	2	0	0	0.0	2	3	3		0	0	0	3	3	1	0	1.4	.857	OF-5

Scott Coolbaugh

COOLBAUGH, SCOTT ROBERT
B. June 13, 1966, Binghamton, N. Y.   BR TR 5'10" 185 lbs.

Year Team	Games	BA	SA	AB	H	2B	3B	HR	HR%	R	RBI	BB	SO	SB	PH AB	PH H	PO	A	E	DP	TC/G	FA	G by Pos
1989 TEX A	25	.275	.412	51	14	1	0	2	3.9	7	7	4	12	0	0	0	7	39	2	3	1.9	.958	3B-23, DH-2

Duff Cooley

COOLEY, DUFF GORDON (Sir Richard)
B. Mar. 14, 1873, Dallas, Tex.   D. Aug. 9, 1937, Dallas, Tex.   BL TR

Year Team	Games	BA	SA	AB	H	2B	3B	HR	HR%	R	RBI	BB	SO	SB	PH AB	PH H	PO	A	E	DP	TC/G	FA	G by Pos
1893 STL N	29	.346	.421	107	37	3	3	0	0.0	20	21	8	9	8	1	0	46	12	4	2	2.1	.935	OF-15, C-10, SS-5
1894	54	.296	.335	206	61	3	1	1	0.5	35	21	12	16	7	1	0	91	22	27	3	2.6	.807	OF-39, 3B-13, SS-1, 1B-1
1895	132	.339	.462	563	191	9	21	6	1.1	106	75	36	29	27	1	0	336	38	29	3	3.1	.928	OF-124, 3B-5, SS-3, C-1
1896 2 teams		STL	N	(40G –	.307)		PHI	N	(64G –	.307)													
" total	104	.307	.375	453	139	11	7	2	0.4	92	35	25	19	30			221	8	19	2	2.4	.923	OF-104
1897 PHI N	133	.329	.420	566	186	14	13	4	0.7	124	40	51		31	0	0	341	16	14	7	2.8	.962	OF-131, 1B-2
1898	149	.312	.407	629	196	24	12	4	0.6	123	55	48		17	0	0	352	15	22	2	2.6	.943	OF-149
1899	94	.276	.360	406	112	15	8	1	0.2	75	31	29		15	1	0	791	34	28	56	9.1	.967	1B-79, OF-14, 2B-1
1900 PIT N	66	.201	.241	249	50	8	1	0	0.0	30	22	14		9	0	0	683	20	8	39	10.8	.989	1B-66
1901 BOS N	63	.258	.338	240	62	13	3	0	0.0	27	27	14		5	0	0	218	9	9	4	3.7	.962	OF-53, 1B-10
1902	135	.296	.372	548	162	26	8	0	0.0	73	58	34		27	1	0	310	13	14	3	2.5	.958	OF-127, 1B-7
1903	138	.289	.378	553	160	26	10	1	0.2	76	70	44		27	0	0	351	14	19	6	2.8	.951	OF-126, 1B-13
1904	122	.272	.373	467	127	18	7	5	1.1	41	70	24		14	0	0	240	3	6	4	2.0	.976	OF-116, 1B-6
1905 DET A	99	.247	.332	377	93	11	9	1	0.3	25	32	26		7	1	1	223	12	10	5	2.5	.959	OF-97
13 yrs.	1318	.294	.380	5364	1576	180	103	25	0.5	847	557	365	73	224	5	1	4203	216	209	136	3.5	.955	OF-1095, 1B-184, 3B-18, C-11, SS-9, 2B-1

Cecil Coombs

COOMBS, CECIL LYSANDER
B. Mar. 18, 1888, Moweaqua, Ill.   D. Nov. 25, 1975, Fort Worth, Tex.   BR TR 5'9" 160 lbs.

Year Team	Games	BA	SA	AB	H	2B	3B	HR	HR%	R	RBI	BB	SO	SB	PH AB	PH H	PO	A	E	DP	TC/G	FA	G by Pos
1914 CHI A	7	.174	.217	23	4	1	0	0	0.0	1	1	1	7	0	0	0	13	2	0	0	2.1	1.000	OF-7

Jack Coombs

COOMBS, JOHN WESLEY (Cy)
B. Nov. 18, 1882, LeGrand, Iowa   D. Apr. 15, 1957, Palestine, Tex.   BB TR 6' 185 lbs.
Manager 1919.

Year Team	Games	BA	SA	AB	H	2B	3B	HR	HR%	R	RBI	BB	SO	SB	PH AB	PH H	PO	A	E	DP	TC/G	FA	G by Pos
1906 PHI A	24	.239	.269	67	16	2	0	0	0.0	9	3	1		2	1	0	16	44	2	4	2.6	.968	P-23
1907	24	.167	.229	48	8	0	0	1	2.1	4	4	0		1	1	0	9	37	1	2	2.0	.979	P-23
1908	78	.255	.355	220	56	9	5	1	0.5	24	23	9		6	5	4	102	48	4	4	2.0	.974	OF-47, P-26
1909	37	.169	.217	83	14	4	0	0	0.0	4	10	4		1	6	1	12	60	2	2	2.0	.973	P-31
1910	46	.220	.242	132	29	3	0	0	0.0	20	9	7		3	1	0	19	77	1	2	2.0	.990	P-45
1911	52	.319	.418	141	45	6	1	2	1.4	31	23	8		5	4	1	24	71	9	3	2.0	.913	P-47
1912	55	.255	.273	110	28	2	0	0	0.0	10	13	14		1	14	4	16	66	0	4	1.5	1.000	P-40
1913	2	.333	.667	3	1	1	0	0	0.0	1	0	0	2	0	0	0	1	0	1	0	1.0	.500	P-2
1914	5	.273	.364	11	3	1	0	0	0.0	0	2	1	1	0	1	0	4	1	0	0	1.0	1.000	OF-2, P-2
1915 BKN N	29	.280	.320	75	21	1	1	0	0.0	8	5	2	17	0	0	0	17	31	1	2	1.7	.980	P-29
1916	27	.180	.213	61	11	2	0	0	0.0	2	3	2	10	0	0	0	7	15	0	1	0.8	1.000	P-27
1917	32	.227	.273	44	10	0	1	0	0.0	2	4	9	9	1	0	0	8	26	1	1	1.1	.971	P-31
1918	46	.168	.230	113	19	3	2	0	0.0	6	3	7	5	1	3	1	20	41	3	0	1.4	.953	P-27, OF-13
1920 DET A	2	.000	.000	2	0	0	0	0	0.0	0	0	0	0	0	0	0	0	0	0	0	0.5	1.000	P-2
14 yrs.	459	.235	.295	1110	261	34	10	4	0.4	123	100	59	44	21	36	11	255	518	25	25	1.7	.969	P-355, OF-62

WORLD SERIES

Year Team	Games	BA	SA	AB	H	2B	3B	HR	HR%	R	RBI	BB	SO	SB	PH AB	PH H	PO	A	E	DP	TC/G	FA	G by Pos
1910 PHI A	3	.385	.462	13	5	1	0	0	0.0	0	3	0	3	0	0	0	1	4	2	0	2.3	.714	P-3
1911	2	.250	.250	8	2	0	0	0	0.0	1	0	0	0	0	0	0	1	2	0	0	1.5	1.000	P-2
1916 BKN N	1	.333	.333	3	1	0	0	0	0.0	0	1	0	0	0	0	0	0	2	0	0	2.0	1.000	P-1
3 yrs.	6	.333	.375	24	8	1	0	0	0.0	1	4	0	3	0	0	0	2	8	2	0	2.0	.833	P-6

William Coon

COON, WILLIAM K.
B. Mar. 21, 1855, Philadelphia, Pa.   D. Aug. 30, 1915, Burlington, N. J.

Year Team	Games	BA	SA	AB	H	2B	3B	HR	HR%	R	RBI	BB	SO	SB	PH AB	PH H	PO	A	E	DP	TC/G	FA	G by Pos
1876 PHI N	54	.227	.259	220	50	5	1	0	0.0	30	22	2	4				106	31	60	2	3.6	.695	OF-29, C-18, 3B-4, 2B-4, P-2

Bill Cooney

COONEY, WILLIAM A.
B. Apr. 4, 1887, Boston, Mass.   D. Nov. 6, 1928, Roxbury, Mass.   TR

Year Team	Games	BA	SA	AB	H	2B	3B	HR	HR%	R	RBI	BB	SO	SB	PH AB	PH H	PO	A	E	DP	TC/G	FA	G by Pos
1909 BOS N	5	.300	.300	10	3	0	0	0	0.0	0	0	0	0	0	0	0	2	6	1	0	1.8	.889	P-3, SS-1, 2B-1
1910	8	.250	.250	12	3	0	0	0	0.0	2	1	2	0	0	5	2	0	0	0	0	0.0	–	OF-2
2 yrs.	13	.273	.273	22	6	0	0	0	0.0	2	1	2	0	0	5	2	2	6	1	0	0.7	.889	P-3, OF-2, SS-1, 2B-1

Jimmy Cooney

COONEY, JAMES EDWARD (Scoops)
Son of Jimmy Cooney.   Brother of Johnny Cooney.   BR TR 5'11" 160 lbs.
B. Aug. 24, 1894, Cranston, R. I.

Year Team	Games	BA	SA	AB	H	2B	3B	HR	HR%	R	RBI	BB	SO	SB	PH AB	PH H	PO	A	E	DP	TC/G	FA	G by Pos
1917 BOS A	11	.222	.250	36	8	1	0	0	0.0	4	3	6	2	0	0	0	30	39	0	7	6.3	1.000	2B-10, SS-1
1919 NY N	5	.214	.214	14	3	0	0	0	0.0	3	1	0	0	0	0	0	7	11	0	2	3.6	1.000	SS-4, 2B-1
1924 STL N	110	.295	.397	383	113	20	8	1	0.3	44	57	20	20	12	0	0	246	331	18	68	5.4	.970	SS-99, 3B-7, 2B-1
1925	54	.273	.353	187	51	11	2	0	0.0	27	18	4	5	1	1	0	97	137	6	31	4.4	.975	SS-37, 2B-15, OF-1
1926 CHI N	141	.251	.312	513	129	18	5	1	0.2	52	47	23	10	11	0	0	344	492	24	107	6.1	.972	SS-141

Year Team	Games	BA	SA	AB	H	2B	3B	HR	HR%	R	RBI	BB	SO	SB	Pinch Hit AB	H	PO	A	E	DP	TC/G	FA	G by Pos

Jimmy Cooney *continued*

Year Team	Games	BA	SA	AB	H	2B	3B	HR	HR%	R	RBI	BB	SO	SB	AB	H	PO	A	E	DP	TC/G	FA	G by Pos
1927 **2 teams**		CHI	N	(33G –	.242)		PHI	N	(76G –	.270)													
" total	109	.261	.302	391	102	14	1	0	0.0	49	21	21	16	5	1	0	230	340	13	64	5.3	.978	SS-107
1928 **BOS** N	18	.137	.137	51	7	0	0	0	0.0	2	3	2	5	1	4	0	27	43	2	11	4.0	.972	SS-11, 2B-4
7 yrs.	448	.262	.327	1575	413	64	16	2	0.1	181	150	76	58	30	6	0	981	1393	63	290	5.4	.974	SS-400, 2B-31, 3B-7, OF-1

Jimmy Cooney

COONEY, JAMES JOSEPH
Father of Jimmy Cooney.   Father of Johnny Cooney.
B. July 9, 1865, Cranston, R. I.   D. July 1, 1903, Cranston, R. I.

BB TR 5'9"   155 lbs.

Year Team	Games	BA	SA	AB	H	2B	3B	HR	HR%	R	RBI	BB	SO	SB	AB	H	PO	A	E	DP	TC/G	FA	G by Pos
1890 CHI N	135	.272	.361	574	156	19	10	4	0.7	114	52	73	23	45	0	0	238	452	47	50	5.5	.936	SS-135, C-1
1891	118	.245	.290	465	114	15	3	0	0.0	84	42	48	17	21	0	0	145	433	52	39	5.3	.9.7	SS-118
1892 **2 teams**	71	CHI	N	(65G –	.172)		WAS	N	(6G –	.160)													
" total	71	.171	.183	263	45	1	1	0	0.0	23	24	27	8	11	0	0	113	224	34	16	5.2	.908	SS-71
3 yrs.	324	.242	.300	1302	315	35	14	4	0.3	221	118	148	48	77	0	0	496	1109	133	105	5.4	.923	SS-324, C-1

Johnny Cooney

COONEY, JOHN WALTER
Son of Jimmy Cooney.   Brother of Jimmy Cooney.
B. Mar. 18, 1901, Cranston, R. I.   D. July 8, 1986, Sarasota, Fla.
Manager 1949.

BR TL 5'10"   165 lbs.

Year Team	Games	BA	SA	AB	H	2B	3B	HR	HR%	R	RBI	BB	SO	SB	AB	H	PO	A	E	DP	TC/G	FA	G by Pos
1921 **BOS** N	8	.200	.200	5	1	0	0	0	0.0	0	0	0	1	0	0	0	2	5	0	0	0.9	1.000	P-8
1922	4	.000	.000	8	0	0	0	0	0.0	0	0	0	1	0	0	0	1	6	0	1	1.8	1.000	P-4
1923	42	.379	.394	66	25	1	0	0	0.0	7	3	4	2	0	1	1	34	17	0	1	1.2	1.000	P-23, OF-11, 1B-1
1924	55	.254	.285	130	33	2	1	0	0.0	10	4	9	5	0	1	1	70	33	5	3	2.0	.954	P-34, OF-14, 1B-1
1925	54	.320	.388	103	33	7	0	0	0.0	17	13	3	6	1	1	0	32	61	5	10	1.8	.949	P-31, 1B-3, OF-1
1926	64	.302	.357	126	38	3	2	0	0.0	17	18	13	7	1	5	3	251	45	3	28	4.7	.990	1B-32, P-19, OF-1
1927	10	.000	.000	1	0	0	0	0	0.0	3	0	0	0	0	1	0	0	0	0	0	0.0	–	P-2
1928	33	.171	.171	41	7	0	0	0	0.0	2	2	4	3	0	3	0	29	32	1	5	1.9	.984	P-24, 1B-3, OF-2
1929	41	.319	.403	72	23	4	1	0	0.0	10	6	3	1	1	5	3	49	16	1	2	1.6	.985	OF-16, P-14
1930	4	.000	.000	3	0	0	0	0	0.0	0	0	0	1	0	1	0	0	4	0	0	1.0	1.000	P-2
1935 **BKN** N	10	.310	.379	29	9	0	1	0	0.0	3	1	3	2	0	0	0	23	0	0	0	2.3	1.000	OF-10
1936	130	.282	.335	507	143	17	5	0	0.0	71	30	24	15	3	0	0	336	11	2	3	2.7	.994	OF-130
1937	120	.293	.358	430	126	18	5	0	0.0	61	37	22	10	5	5	1	281	9	7	2	2.5	.976	OF-111, 1B-2
1938 **BOS** N	120	.271	.352	432	117	25	5	0	0.0	45	17	22	12	2	1	0	296	10	4	9	2.6	.987	OF-110, 1B-2
1939	118	.274	.318	368	101	8	1	2	0.5	39	27	21	8	2	0	0	241	10	2	2	2.1	.992	OF-116, 1B-2
1940	108	.318	.373	365	116	14	3	0	0.0	40	21	25	9	4	1	0	294	9	2	5	2.8	.993	OF-99, 1B-7
1941	123	.319	.385	442	141	25	2	0	0.0	52	29	27	15	3	6	1	315	11	1	7	2.7	.997	OF-111, 1B-4
1942	74	.207	.237	198	41	6	0	0	0.0	23	7	23	5	2	0	0	254	12	2	10	3.6	.993	OF-54, 1B-23
1943 **BKN** N	37	.206	.206	34	7	0	0	0	0.0	7	2	4	3	1	22	4	20	0	0	0	0.5	1.000	1B-3, OF-2
1944 **2 teams**		BKN	N	(7G –	.750)		NY	A	(10G –	.125)													
" total	17	.333	.333	12	4	0	0	0	0.0	1	2	1	0	0	7	3	6	0	0	1	0.4	1.000	OF-4
20 yrs.	1172	.286	.342	3372	965	130	26	2	0.1	408	219	208	107	30	59	17	2534	291	35	90	2.4	.988	OF-792, P-159, 1B-94

Phil Cooney

COONEY, PHILIP CLARENCE
Born Philip Clarence Cohen.
B. Sept. 14, 1882, New York, N. Y.   D. Oct. 6, 1957, New York, N. Y.

BR TR 5'8"   155 lbs.

Year Team	Games	BA	SA	AB	H	2B	3B	HR	HR%	R	RBI	BB	SO	SB	AB	H	PO	A	E	DP	TC/G	FA	G by Pos
1905 NY A	1	.000	.000	3	0	0	0	0	0.0	0	0	0		0	0	0	1	1	0	0	2.0	1.000	3B-1

Cecil Cooper

COOPER, CECIL CELESTER
B. Dec. 20, 1949, Brenham, Tex.

BL TL 6'2"   165 lbs.

Year Team	Games	BA	SA	AB	H	2B	3B	HR	HR%	R	RBI	BB	SO	SB	AB	H	PO	A	E	DP	TC/G	FA	G by Pos
1971 **BOS** A	14	.310	.452	42	13	4	1	0	0.0	9	3	5	4	1	3	2	82	3	1	6	6.1	.988	1B-11
1972	12	.235	.294	17	4	1	0	0	0.0	0	2	2	5	0	9	1	19	0	0	2	1.6	1.000	1B-3
1973	30	.238	.347	101	24	2	0	3	3.0	12	11	7	12	1	1	0	227	17	4	25	8.3	.984	1B-29
1974	121	.275	.396	414	114	24	1	8	1.9	55	43	32	74	2	7	1	637	40	12	66	5.7	.983	1B-74, DH-41
1975	106	.311	.544	305	95	17	6	14	4.6	49	44	19	33	1	18	6	197	20	1	20	2.1	.995	DH-54, 1B-35
1976	123	.282	.457	451	127	22	6	15	3.3	66	78	16	62	7	9	0	600	42	4	49	5.3	.994	1B-66, DH-53
1977 **MIL** A	160	.300	.463	643	193	31	7	20	3.1	86	78	28	110	13	1	0	1386	118	12	134	9.5	.992	1B-148, DH-10
1978	107	.312	.474	407	127	23	2	13	3.2	60	54	32	72	3	4	1	842	66	11	71	8.6	.988	1B-84, DH-19
1979	150	.308	.508	590	182	44	1	24	4.1	83	106	56	77	15	2	1	1323	78	10	119	9.4	.993	1B-135, DH-15
1980	153	.352	.539	622	219	33	4	25	4.0	96	122	39	42	17	1	1	1336	106	5	160	9.5	.997	1B-142, DH-11
1981	106	.320	.495	416	133	35	1	12	2.9	70	60	28	30	5	2	0	987	72	9	111	10.1	.992	1B-101, DH-5
1982	155	.313	.528	654	205	38	3	32	4.9	104	121	32	53	2	0	0	1428	98	5	156	9.9	.997	1B-154, DH-1
1983	160	.307	.508	661	203	37	3	30	4.5	106	126	37	63	2	1	1	1452	87	11	144	9.7	.993	1B-158, DH-2
1984	148	.275	.386	603	166	28	3	11	1.8	63	67	27	59	8	1	0	1061	98	10	106	7.9	.986	1B-122, DH-26
1985	154	.293	.456	631	185	39	8	16	2.5	82	99	30	77	10	1	0	1087	94	17	101	7.8	.986	1B-123, DH-30
1986	134	.258	.373	542	140	24	0	12	2.2	46	75	41	87	1	2	1	697	61	9	78	5.7	.988	1B-90, DH-44
1987	63	.248	.372	250	62	13	0	6	2.4	25	36	17	51	1	0	0	0	0	0	0	0.0	–	DH-62
17 yrs.	1896	.298	.466	7349	2192	415	47	241	3.3	1012	1125	448	911	89	62	15	13361	1000	121	1348	7.6	.992	1B-1475, DH-373

DIVISIONAL PLAYOFF SERIES

Year Team	Games	BA	SA	AB	H	2B	3B	HR	HR%	R	RBI	BB	SO	SB	AB	H	PO	A	E	DP	TC/G	FA	G by Pos
1981 **MIL** A	5	.222	.222	18	4	0	0	0	0.0	1	3	1	3	0	0	0	0	0	1	0	0.2	–	1B-5

LEAGUE CHAMPIONSHIP SERIES

Year Team	Games	BA	SA	AB	H	2B	3B	HR	HR%	R	RBI	BB	SO	SB	AB	H	PO	A	E	DP	TC/G	FA	G by Pos
1975 **BOS** A	3	.400	.600	10	4	2	0	0	0.0	0	1	0	2	0	0	0	24	1	1	3	8.7	.962	1B-3
1982 **MIL** A	5	.150	.250	20	3	2	0	0	0.0	1	4	0	6	0	0	0	0	0	2	0	0.4	–	1B-5
2 yrs.	8	.233	.367	30	7	4	0	0	0.0	1	5	0	8	0	0	0	24	1	3	3	3.5	.893	1B-8

WORLD SERIES

Year Team	Games	BA	SA	AB	H	2B	3B	HR	HR%	R	RBI	BB	SO	SB	AB	H	PO	A	E	DP	TC/G	FA	G by Pos
1975 **BOS** A	5	.053	.105	19	1	1	0	0	0.0	0	0	0	3	0	1	0	40	1	0	1	8.2	1.000	1B-5
1982 **MIL** A	7	.286	.429	28	8	1	0	1	3.6	3	6	1	1	0	0	0	71	10	1	3	11.7	.988	1B-7
2 yrs.	12	.191	.298	47	9	2	0	1	2.1	3	7	1	4	0	1	0	111	11	1	4	10.3	.992	1B-12

Year	Team		Games	BA	SA	AB	H	2B	3B	HR	HR%	R	RBI	BB	SO	SB	Pinch Hit AB	Pinch Hit H	PO	A	E	DP	TC/G	FA	G by Pos

Claude Cooper

COOPER, CLAUDE WILLIAM
B. Apr. 1, 1892, Troupe, Tex.   D. Jan. 21, 1974, Plainview, Tex.

BL TL 5'9"   158 lbs.

Year	Team		Games	BA	SA	AB	H	2B	3B	HR	HR%	R	RBI	BB	SO	SB	PH AB	PH H	PO	A	E	DP	TC/G	FA	G by Pos
1913	NY	N	27	.300	.433	30	9	4	0	0	0.0	11	4	4	6	3	1	0	16	1	2	0	0.7	.895	OF-15
1914	BKN	F	113	.241	.346	399	96	14	11	2	0.5	56	25	26		25	8	3	188	12	16	4	1.9	.926	OF-101
1915			153	.294	.400	527	155	26	12	2	0.4	75	63	77		31	0	0	536	44	19	14	3.9	.968	OF-121, 1B-32
1916	PHI	N	56	.192	.212	104	20	2	0	0	0.0	9	11	7	15	1	22	6	52	2	3	0	1.0	.947	OF-29, 1B-1
1917			24	.103	.138	29	3	1	0	0	0.0	5	1	5	4	0	8	0	12	0	1	0	0.5	.923	OF-12
	5 yrs.		373	.260	.356	1089	283	47	23	4	0.4	156	104	119	25	60	40	9	804	59	41	18	2.4	.955	OF-278, 1B-33
WORLD SERIES																									
1913	NY	N	2	–	–	0	0	0	0	0	–	0	0	0	1	0	1	0	0	0	0	0	0.0	–	

Gary Cooper

COOPER, GARY NATHANIEL
B. Dec. 22, 1956, Savannah, Ga.

BB TR 6'3"   175 lbs.

Year	Team		Games	BA	SA	AB	H	2B	3B	HR	HR%	R	RBI	BB	SO	SB	PH AB	PH H	PO	A	E	DP	TC/G	FA	G by Pos
1980	ATL	N	21	.000	.000	2	0	0	0	0	0.0	3	0	0	1	0	2	1	5	1	0	0	0.3	1.000	OF-13

Pat Cooper

COOPER, ORGE PATTERSON
B. Nov. 26, 1917, Albermarle, N. C.

BR TR 6'3"   180 lbs.

Year	Team		Games	BA	SA	AB	H	2B	3B	HR	HR%	R	RBI	BB	SO	SB	PH AB	PH H	PO	A	E	DP	TC/G	FA	G by Pos
1946	PHI	A	1	–	–	0	0	0	0	0	–	0	0	0	0	0	0	0	0	1	0	0	1.0	1.000	P-1
1947			13	.250	.375	16	4	2	0	0	0.0	0	3	0	5	0	12	3	8	0	0	1	0.6	1.000	1B-1
	2 yrs.		14	.250	.375	16	4	2	0	0	0.0	0	3	0	5	0	12	3	8	1	0	1	0.6	1.000	1B-1, P-1

Walker Cooper

COOPER, WILLIAM WALKER
Brother of Mort Cooper.
B. Jan. 8, 1915, Atherton, Mo.

BR TR 6'3"   210 lbs.

Year	Team		Games	BA	SA	AB	H	2B	3B	HR	HR%	R	RBI	BB	SO	SB	PH AB	PH H	PO	A	E	DP	TC/G	FA	G by Pos
1940	STL	N	6	.316	.368	19	6	1	0	0	0.0	3	2	2	2	1	0	0	19	4	0	0	3.8	1.000	C-6
1941			68	.245	.315	200	49	9	1	1	0.5	19	20	13	14	1	1	5	247	39	10	11	4.4	.966	C-63
1942			125	.281	.434	438	123	32	7	7	1.6	58	65	29	29	4	10	5	519	62	17	6	4.8	.972	C-115
1943			122	.318	.463	449	143	30	4	9	2.0	52	81	19	19	1	10	1	504	49	14	5	4.6	.975	C-112
1944			112	.317	.504	397	126	25	5	13	3.3	56	72	20	19	4	15	5	442	40	10	7	4.4	.980	C-97
1945			4	.389	.389	18	7	0	0	0	0.0	0	3	1	0	0	0	0	27	1	1	0	7.3	.966	C-4
1946	NY	N	87	.268	.396	280	75	10	1	8	2.9	29	46	17	12	0	13	3	277	38	9	3	3.7	.972	C-73
1947			140	.305	.586	515	157	24	8	35	6.8	79	122	24	43	2	6	1	560	51	13	8	4.5	.979	C-132
1948			91	.266	.472	290	77	12	0	16	5.5	40	54	28	29	1	12	2	307	21	7	3	3.7	.979	C-79
1949	2 teams			NY	N	(42G – .211)		CIN	N	(82G – .280)															
"	total		124	.258	.436	454	117	13	4	20	4.4	48	83	28	32	0	5	1	464	61	11	5	4.3	.979	C-117
1950	2 teams			CIN	N	(15G – .191)		BOS	N	(102G – .329)															
"	total		117	.313	.495	384	120	22	3	14	3.6	55	64	30	31	1	12	6	448	54	14	9	4.4	.973	C-101
1951	BOS	N	109	.313	.518	342	107	14	1	18	5.3	42	59	28	18	1	18	2	367	57	8	9	4.0	.981	C-90
1952			102	.235	.361	349	82	12	1	10	2.9	33	55	22	32	1	13	4	417	55	8	8	4.7	.983	C-89
1953	MIL	N	53	.219	.328	137	30	6	0	3	2.2	12	16	12	15	1	17	3	165	6	3	1	3.3	.983	C-35
1954	2 teams			PIT	N	(14G – .200)		CHI	N	(57G – .310)															
"	total		71	.301	.514	173	52	12	2	7	4.0	21	33	23	24	0	23	5	196	31	5	4	3.3	.978	C-50
1955	CHI	N	54	.279	.559	111	31	8	1	7	6.3	11	15	6	19	0	28	6	88	11	4	1	1.9	.961	C-31
1956	STL	N	40	.265	.456	68	18	5	1	2	2.9	5	14	3	8	0	22	3	56	4	1	0	1.5	.984	C-16
1957			48	.269	.474	78	21	5	1	3	3.8	7	10	5	10	0	30	7	62	5	3	0	1.5	.957	C-13
	18 yrs.		1473	.285	.464	4702	1341	240	40	173	3.7	573	812	309	357	18	239	56	5165	589	138	80	4.0	.977	C-1223
WORLD SERIES																									
1942	STL	N	5	.286	.333	21	6	1	0	0	0.0	3	4	0	3	0	0	0	24	2	1	0	5.4	.963	C-5
1943			5	.294	.294	17	5	0	0	0	0.0	1	0	1	1	0	0	0	28	3	2	0	6.6	.939	C-5
1944			6	.318	.500	22	7	2	1	0	0.0	1	2	3	2	0	0	0	54	0	0	0	9.0	1.000	C-6
	3 yrs.		16	.300	.383	60	18	3	1	0	0.0	5	6	3	4	0	0	0	106	5	3	0	7.1	.974	C-16

Joey Cora

CORA, JOSE MANUEL
Born Jose Manuel Cora y Amaro.
B. May 14, 1965, Caguas, Puerto Rico

BR TR 5'7"   150 lbs.

Year	Team		Games	BA	SA	AB	H	2B	3B	HR	HR%	R	RBI	BB	SO	SB	PH AB	PH H	PO	A	E	DP	TC/G	FA	G by Pos
1987	SD	N	77	.237	.282	241	57	7	2	0	0.0	23	13	28	26	15	8	2	123	200	10	32	4.3	.970	2B-66, SS-6
1989			12	.316	.368	19	6	1	0	0	0.0	5	1	1	0	1	0	0	11	15	2	3	2.3	.929	SS-7, 3B-2, 2B-1
	2 yrs.		89	.242	.288	260	63	8	2	0	0.0	28	14	29	26	16	8	2	134	215	12	35	4.1	.967	2B-67, SS-13, 3B-2

Gene Corbett

CORBETT, EUGENE LOUIS
B. Oct. 25, 1913, Winona, Minn.

BL TR 6'1½"   190 lbs.

Year	Team		Games	BA	SA	AB	H	2B	3B	HR	HR%	R	RBI	BB	SO	SB	PH AB	PH H	PO	A	E	DP	TC/G	FA	G by Pos
1936	PHI	N	6	.143	.143	21	3	0	0	0	0.0	1	2	2	3	0	0	0	55	2	0	7	9.5	1.000	1B-6
1937			7	.333	.500	12	4	2	0	0	0.0	4	1	0	0	0	3	1	2	3	1	0	0.9	.833	3B-3, 2B-1
1938			24	.080	.173	75	6	1	0	2	2.7	7	7	6	11	0	1	0	180	11	1	16	8.0	.995	1B-22
	3 yrs.		37	.120	.204	108	13	3	0	2	1.9	12	10	8	14	0	4	1	237	16	2	23	6.9	.992	1B-28, 3B-3, 2B-1

Claude Corbitt

CORBITT, CLAUDE ELLIOTT
B. July 21, 1915, Sunbury, N. C.   D. May 1, 1978, Cincinnati, Ohio

BR TR 5'10"   170 lbs.

Year	Team		Games	BA	SA	AB	H	2B	3B	HR	HR%	R	RBI	BB	SO	SB	PH AB	PH H	PO	A	E	DP	TC/G	FA	G by Pos
1945	BKN	N	2	.500	.500	4	2	0	0	0	0.0	1	0	1	0	0	0	0	3	0	1	2.0	1.000	3B-2
1946	CIN	N	82	.248	.303	274	68	10	1	0	0.4	25	16	23	13	3	2	1	126	229	20	45	4.6	.947	SS-77
1948			87	.256	.298	258	66	11	0	0	0.0	24	18	14	16	4	9	3	138	160	7	24	3.5	.977	2B-52, 3B-16, SS-11
1949			44	.181	.191	94	17	1	0	0	0.0	10	3	9	1	1	3	0	66	55	5	17	2.9	.960	SS-18, 2B-17, 3B-1
	4 yrs.		215	.243	.286	630	153	22	1	1	0.2	60	37	47	30	8	14	4	331	447	32	87	3.8	.960	SS-106, 2B-69, 3B-19

Art Corcoran

CORCORAN, ARTHUR ANDREW (Bunny)
B. Oct. 23, 1894, Roxbury, Mass.   D. July 27, 1958, Chelsea, Mass.

TR

Year	Team		Games	BA	SA	AB	H	2B	3B	HR	HR%	R	RBI	BB	SO	SB	PH AB	PH H	PO	A	E	DP	TC/G	FA	G by Pos
1915	PHI	A	1	.000	.000	4	0	0	0	0	0.0	0	0	0	2	0	0	0	2	1	0	0	3.0	1.000	3B-1

John Corcoran

CORCORAN, JOHN A.
B. 1873, Cincinnati, Ohio   D. Nov. 1, 1901, Cincinnati, Ohio

TL

Year	Team		Games	BA	SA	AB	H	2B	3B	HR	HR%	R	RBI	BB	SO	SB	PH AB	PH H	PO	A	E	DP	TC/G	FA	G by Pos
1895	PIT	N	6	.150	.150	20	3	0	0	0	0.0	1	0	2	0	0	0	0	8	13	2	0	3.8	.913	SS-4, 3B-2

Year	Team		Games	BA	SA	AB	H	2B	3B	HR	HR%	R	RBI	BB	SO	SB	Pinch Hit AB	Pinch Hit H	PO	A	E	DP	TC/G	FA	G by Pos

John Corcoran

CORCORAN, JOHN H.
B. 1860, Lowell, Mass. Deceased.

Year	Team		Games	BA	SA	AB	H	2B	3B	HR	HR%	R	RBI	BB	SO	SB	PH AB	PH H	PO	A	E	DP	TC/G	FA	G by Pos
1884	BKN	AA	52	.211	.265	185	39	4	3	0	0.0	17		8			0	0	205	77	42	5	6.2	.870	C-38, OF-9, 2B-4, SS-2, P-1

Larry Corcoran

CORCORAN, LAWRENCE J.
Brother of Mike Corcoran.
B. Aug. 10, 1859, Brooklyn, N. Y. D. Oct. 14, 1891, Newark, N. J.

BL TR

Year	Team		Games	BA	SA	AB	H	2B	3B	HR	HR%	R	RBI	BB	SO	SB	PH AB	PH H	PO	A	E	DP	TC/G	FA	G by Pos
1880	CHI	N	72	.231	.276	286	66	11	1	0	0.0	41	25	10	33		0	0	42	146	13	4	2.8	.935	P-63, OF-8, SS-8
1881			47	.222	.265	189	42	8	0	0	0.0	25	9	5	22		0	0	31	70	11	0	2.4	.902	P-45, SS-2, OF-1
1882			40	.207	.308	169	35	10	2	1	0.6	23	24	6	18		0	0	22	64	8	1	2.4	.915	P-40, 3B-1
1883			68	.209	.308	263	55	12	7	0	0.0	40		6	62		0	0	56	94	21	4	2.5	.877	P-56, OF-13, SS-3, 2B-1
1884			64	.243	.299	251	61	3	4	1	0.4	43		10	33		0	0	51	142	25	5	3.4	.885	P-60, OF-4, SS-2
1885	2 teams		10	.306	.333	36	11	1	0	0	0.0	9	4	6	2		0	0	6	24	2	2	3.2	.938	P-10, SS-1
"	total	CHI N (7G – .273)				NY N (3G – .357)																			
1886	2 teams		22	.176	.224	85	15	2	1	0	0.0	9	3	7	16		0	0	21	33	22	4	3.5	.711	OF-12, SS-9, P-2
"	total	NY N (1G – .000)				WAS N (21G – .185)																			
1887	IND	N	3	.200	.200	10	2	0	0	0	0.0	2	0	2	1	2	0	0	3	4	0	0	2.3	1.000	OF-2, P-2
8 yrs.			326	.223	.287	1289	287	47	15	2	0.2	192	65	52	187	2	0	0	232	577	102	20	2.8	.888	P-278, OF-40, SS-25, 3B-1, 2B-1

Mickey Corcoran

CORCORAN, MICHAEL JOSEPH
B. Aug. 26, 1882, Buffalo, N. Y. D. Dec. 9, 1950, Buffalo, N. Y.

BR TR 5'8" 165 lbs.

Year	Team		Games	BA	SA	AB	H	2B	3B	HR	HR%	R	RBI	BB	SO	SB	PH AB	PH H	PO	A	E	DP	TC/G	FA	G by Pos
1910	CIN	N	14	.217	.283	46	10	3	0	0	0.0	3	7	5	9	0	0	0	26	46	7	6	5.6	.911	2B-14

Tim Corcoran

CORCORAN, TIMOTHY MICHAEL
B. Mar. 19, 1953, Glendale, Calif.

BL TL 5'11" 175 lbs.

Year	Team		Games	BA	SA	AB	H	2B	3B	HR	HR%	R	RBI	BB	SO	SB	PH AB	PH H	PO	A	E	DP	TC/G	FA	G by Pos
1977	DET	A	55	.282	.398	103	29	3	0	3	2.9	13	15	6	9	0	32	10	38	0	0	0	0.7	1.000	OF-18, DH-3
1978			116	.265	.321	324	86	13	1	1	0.3	37	27	24	27	3	12	2	186	6	3	4	1.7	.985	OF-109, DH-1
1979			18	.227	.273	22	5	1	0	0	0.0	4	6	4	2	1	2	1	45	2	0	2	2.6	1.000	OF-9, 1B-5, DH-2
1980			84	.288	.405	153	44	7	1	3	2.0	20	18	22	10	0	16	3	274	19	5	32	3.5	.983	1B-48, OF-18, DH-5
1981	MIN	A	22	.176	.235	51	9	3	0	0	0.0	4	4	6	7	0	4	0	108	9	0	10	5.3	1.000	1B-16, DH-3
1983	PHI	N	3	.—	.—	0	0	0	0	0	—	0	0	0	0	0	0	0	4	0	0	0	1.3	1.000	1B-3
1984			102	.341	.486	208	71	13	1	5	2.4	30	36	37	27	0	37	10	338	21	1	20	3.5	.997	1B-51, OF-17
1985			103	.214	.258	182	39	6	1	0	0.0	11	22	29	20	0	32	4	389	25	3	27	4.0	.993	1B-59, OF-3
1986	NY	N	6	.000	.000	7	0	0	0	0	0.0	1	0	2	0	0	3	0	8	1	0	1	1.5	1.000	1B-1
9 yrs.			509	.270	.355	1050	283	46	4	12	1.1	120	128	130	102	4	138	30	1390	83	12	96	2.9	.992	1B-183, OF-174, DH-14

Tommy Corcoran

CORCORAN, THOMAS WILLIAM
B. Jan. 4, 1869, New Haven, Conn. D. June 25, 1960, Plainfield, Conn.

BR TR 5'9" 164 lbs.

Year	Team		Games	BA	SA	AB	H	2B	3B	HR	HR%	R	RBI	BB	SO	SB	PH AB	PH H	PO	A	E	DP	TC/G	FA	G by Pos
1890	PIT	P	123	.233	.318	503	117	14	13	1	0.2	80	61	38	45	43	0	0	210	431	84	36	5.9	.884	SS-123
1891	PHI	AA	133	.254	.376	511	130	11	15	7	1.4	84	71	29	56	30	0	0	300	434	72	5	6.1	.911	SS-133
1892	BKN	N	151	.237	.279	613	145	11	6	1	0.2	77	74	34	51	39	0	0	291	495	64	49	5.6	.925	SS-151
1893			115	.275	.355	459	126	11	10	2	0.4	61	58	27	12	14	0	0	218	444	68	44	6.3	.907	SS-115
1894			129	.300	.432	576	173	21	20	5	0.9	123	92	25	17	33	0	0	280	439	76	45	6.2	.904	SS-129
1895			127	.265	.346	535	142	17	10	2	0.4	85	69	23	11	16	0	0	293	488	64	49	6.7	.924	SS-127
1896			132	.289	.361	532	154	15	7	3	0.6	63	73	15	13	16	0	0	323	477	64	69	6.5	.926	SS-132
1897	CIN	N	109	.288	.398	445	128	30	5	3	0.7	76	57	13		15	0	0	286	360	48	51	6.4	.931	SS-63, 2B-47
1898			153	.250	.354	619	155	28	15	2	0.3	80	87	26		19	0	0	353	561	67	76	6.4	.932	SS-153
1899			137	.277	.328	537	149	11	8	0	0.0	91	81	28		32	1	1	302	468	54	55	6.0	.934	SS-123, 2B-14
1900			127	.245	.325	523	128	21	9	1	0.2	64	54	22		27	0	0	273	448	61	59	6.2	.922	SS-124, 2B-5
1901			31	.209	.296	115	24	4	3	0	0.0	14	15	11	6	1	1	69	112	16	20	6.4	.919	SS-30
1902			138	.251	.304	537	135	20	4	0	0.0	54	54	11		20	0	0	294	417	56	49	5.6	.927	SS-137, 2B-1
1903			115	.246	.329	459	113	18	7	2	0.4	61	73	12		12	0	0	263	367	38	42	5.8	.943	SS-115
1904			150	.230	.301	578	133	17	9	2	0.3	55	74	19		19	0	0	353	471	56	54	5.9	.936	SS-150
1905			151	.248	.329	605	150	21	11	2	0.3	70	85	23		28	0	0	344	531	44	67	6.1	.952	SS-151
1906			117	.207	.249	430	89	13	1	1	0.2	29	33	19		8	0	0	263	379	40	51	5.8	.941	SS-117
1907	NY	N	62	.265	.323	226	60	9	2	0	0.0	21	24	7		9	0	0	108	183	19	15	5.0	.939	2B-62
18 yrs.			2200	.256	.336	8803	2251	292	155	34	0.4	1188	1135	382	205	387	2	2	4823	7505	991	836	6.1	.926	SS-2073, 2B-129

Fred Corey

COREY, FREDERICK HARRISON
B. 1857, S. Kingston, R. I. D. Nov. 27, 1912, Providence, R. I.

BR TR

Year	Team		Games	BA	SA	AB	H	2B	3B	HR	HR%	R	RBI	BB	SO	SB	PH AB	PH H	PO	A	E	DP	TC/G	FA	G by Pos
1878	PRO	N	7	.143	.143	21	3	0	0	0	0.0	3	1	0	2		0	0	11	11	1	1	3.3	.957	P-5, 2B-2, 1B-1
1880	WOR	N	41	.174	.246	138	24	8	1	0	0.0	11	6	4	27		0	0	29	24	15	2	1.7	.779	OF-29, P-25, SS-3, 3B-1, 1B-1
1881			51	.222	.300	203	45	8	4	0	0.0	22	10	5	10		0	0	55	71	15	3	2.8	.894	OF-25, P-23, SS-7
1882			64	.247	.369	255	63	7	12	0	0.0	33	29	5	31		0	0	98	117	35	6	3.9	.860	SS-26, P-21, OF-15, 3B-6, 1B-5
1883	PHI	AA	71	.258	.336	298	77	16	2	1	0.3	45		12			0	0	86	150	57	7	4.1	.805	3B-34, P-18, OF-14, 2B-9, SS-1, C-1
1884			104	.276	.421	439	121	17	16	5	1.1	64		17			0	0	121	209	42	10	3.6	.887	3B-104
1885			94	.245	.331	384	94	14	8	1	0.3	61		17			0	0	105	189	43	15	3.6	.872	3B-92, SS-1, P-1
7 yrs.			432	.246	.348	1738	427	70	43	7	0.4	239	46	60	70		0	0	505	771	208	44	3.4	.860	3B-237, P-93, OF-83, SS-38, 2B-11, 1B-7, C-1

Mark Corey

COREY, MARK MUNDELL
B. Nov. 3, 1955, Tucumcari, N. M.

BR TR 6'2" 200 lbs.

Year	Team		Games	BA	SA	AB	H	2B	3B	HR	HR%	R	RBI	BB	SO	SB	PH AB	PH H	PO	A	E	DP	TC/G	FA	G by Pos
1979	BAL	A	13	.154	.154	13	2	0	0	0	0.0	1	1	0	4	1	3	0	10	0	0	0	0.8	1.000	OF-11, DH-1
1980			36	.278	.417	36	10	2	0	1	2.8	7	2	5	7	0	4	1	20	0	0	0	0.6	1.000	OF-34
1981			10	.000	.000	8	0	0	0	0	0.0	2	0	2	2	0	1	0	6	1	0	0	0.7	1.000	OF-9
3 yrs.			59	.211	.298	57	12	2	0	1	1.8	10	3	7	13	1	8	1	36	1	0	0	0.6	1.000	OF-54, DH-1

Year	Team	Games	BA	SA	AB	H	2B	3B	HR	HR%	R	RBI	BB	SO	SB	Pinch Hit AB	H	PO	A	E	DP	TC/G	FA	G by Pos

Chuck Corgan

CORGAN, CHARLES HOWARD   BB TR 5'11"   180 lbs.
B. Dec. 4, 1902, Wagoner, Okla.   D. June 13, 1928, Wagoner, Okla.

Year	Team	Games	BA	SA	AB	H	2B	3B	HR	HR%	R	RBI	BB	SO	SB	AB	H	PO	A	E	DP	TC/G	FA	G by Pos
1925	BKN N	14	.170	.234	47	8	1	1	0	0.0	4	0	3	9	0	0	0	27	52	8	5	6.2	.908	SS-14
1927		19	.263	.281	57	15	1	0	0	0.0	3	1	4	4	0	2	0	24	50	4	5	4.1	.949	2B-13, SS-3
2 yrs.		33	.221	.260	104	23	2	1	0	0.0	7	1	7	13	0	2	0	51	102	12	10	5.0	.927	SS-17, 2B-13

Roy Corhan

CORHAN, ROY GEORGE (Irish)   BR TR 5'9½"   165 lbs.
B. Oct. 21, 1887, Indianapolis, Ind.   D. Nov. 24, 1958, San Francisco, Calif.

Year	Team	Games	BA	SA	AB	H	2B	3B	HR	HR%	R	RBI	BB	SO	SB	AB	H	PO	A	E	DP	TC/G	FA	G by Pos
1911	CHI A	43	.214	.290	131	28	6	2	0	0.0	14	8	15		2	0	0	98	146	20	18	6.1	.924	SS-43
1916	STL N	92	.210	.251	295	62	6	3	0	0.0	30	18	20	31	15	7	3	153	278	39	35	5.1	.917	SS-84
2 yrs.		135	.211	.263	426	90	12	5	0	0.0	44	26	35	31	17	7	3	251	424	59	53	5.4	.920	SS-127

Pop Corkhill

CORKHILL, JOHN STEWART   BL TR 5'10"   180 lbs.
B. Apr. 11, 1858, Parkesburg, Pa.   D. Apr. 4, 1921, Pennsauken, N. J.

Year	Team	Games	BA	SA	AB	H	2B	3B	HR	HR%	R	RBI	BB	SO	SB	AB	H	PO	A	E	DP	TC/G	FA	G by Pos
1883	CIN AA	88	.216	.301	375	81	10	8	2	0.5	53		3			0	0	172	21	14	0	2.4	.932	OF-85, SS-2, 2B-2, 1B-2
1884		110	.274	.378	452	124	13	11	4	0.9	85		6			0	0	253	66	22	9	3.1	.935	OF-92, SS-11, 1B-6, 3B-3, P-1
1885		112	.252	.318	440	111	10	8	1	0.2	64		7			0	0	234	44	17	6	2.6	.942	OF-110, P-8, 1B-3
1886		129	.265	.333	540	143	9	8	4	0.7	81		23			0	0	228	62	29	8	2.5	.909	OF-112, 3B-12, 1B-7, SS-3, P-1
1887		128	.311	.414	541	168	19	11	5	0.9	79		14		30	0	0	310	31	17	7	2.8	.953	OF-128, P-5
1888	2 teams		CIN	AA	(118G – .271)		BKN	AA	(19G – .380)															
"	total	137	.285	.365	561	160	15	12	2	0.4	85	93	19		30	0	0	316	26	13	5	2.6	.963	OF-135, P-2, 2B-1, 1B-1
1889	BKN AA	138	.250	.367	537	134	21	9	8	1.5	91	78	42	24	22	0	0	318	36	19	9	2.7	.949	OF-138, SS-1, 1B-1
1890	BKN N	51	.225	.279	204	46	4	2	1	0.5	23	21	15	11	6	0	0	157	6	3	1	3.3	.982	OF-48, 1B-6
1891	3 teams		PHI	AA	(83G – .209)		CIN	N	(1G – .000)		PIT	N	(41G – .228)											
"	total	125	.213	.279	498	106	8	8	3	0.6	66	51	33	26	19	0	0	266	23	15	6	2.4	.951	OF-125
1892	PIT N	68	.184	.219	256	47	1	4	0	0.0	23	25	12	19	6	0	0	148	13	8	4	2.5	.953	OF-68
10 yrs.		1086	.254	.337	4404	1120	110	81	30	0.7	650	268	174	80	113	0	0	2402	328	157	55	2.7	.946	OF-1041, 1B-26, SS-17, P-17, 3B-15, 2B-3

Pat Corrales

CORRALES, PATRICK (Ike)   BR TR 6'   180 lbs.
B. Mar. 20, 1941, Los Angeles, Calif.
Manager 1978-80, 1982-87.

Year	Team	Games	BA	SA	AB	H	2B	3B	HR	HR%	R	RBI	BB	SO	SB	AB	H	PO	A	E	DP	TC/G	FA	G by Pos
1964	PHI N	2	.000	.000	1	0	0	0	0	0.0	0	0	1	0	0	1	0	0	0	0	0	0.0	–	C-62
1965		63	.224	.316	174	39	8	1	2	1.1	16	15	25	42	0	2	0	358	24	7	2	6.2	.982	C-62
1966	STL N	28	.181	.208	72	13	2	0	0	0.0	5	3	2	17	1	1	0	133	23	4	2	5.7	.975	C-27
1968	CIN N	20	.268	.339	56	15	4	0	0	0.0	3	6	6	16	0	0	0	101	8	1	0	5.5	.991	C-20
1969		29	.264	.375	72	19	5	0	1	1.4	10	5	8	17	0	0	0	133	7	2	3	4.9	.986	C-29
1970		43	.236	.330	106	25	5	1	1	0.9	9	10	8	22	0	3	0	167	11	3	3	4.2	.983	C-42
1971		40	.181	.202	94	17	2	0	0	0.0	6	6	6	17	0	1	0	145	4	3	3	3.8	.980	C-39
1972	2 teams		CIN	N	(2G – .000)		SD	N	(44G – .193)															
"	total	46	.192	.192	120	23	0	0	0	0.0	6	6	13	26	0	1	0	251	23	2	6	6.0	.993	C-45
1973	SD N	29	.208	.264	72	15	2	1	0	0.0	7	3	6	10	0	1	0	130	6	2	1	4.8	.986	C-28
9 yrs.		300	.216	.276	767	166	28	3	4	0.5	63	54	75	167	1	10	0	1418	106	24	17	5.2	.984	C-292

WORLD SERIES

Year	Team	Games	BA	SA	AB	H	2B	3B	HR	HR%	R	RBI	BB	SO	SB	AB	H	PO	A	E	DP	TC/G	FA	G by Pos
1970	CIN N	1	.000	.000	1	0	0	0	0	0.0	0	0	0	0	0	0	0	0	0	0	0	0.0	–	

Vic Correll

CORRELL, VICTOR CROSBY   BR TR 5'10"   185 lbs.
B. Feb. 5, 1946, Washington, D. C.

Year	Team	Games	BA	SA	AB	H	2B	3B	HR	HR%	R	RBI	BB	SO	SB	AB	H	PO	A	E	DP	TC/G	FA	G by Pos
1972	BOS A	1	.500	.500	4	2	0	0	0	0.0	1	1	0	1	0	0	0	9	1	0	0	10.0	1.000	C-1
1974	ATL N	73	.238	.381	202	48	15	1	4	2.0	20	29	21	38	0	14	2	282	40	4	4	4.5	.988	C-59
1975		103	.215	.360	325	70	12	1	11	3.4	37	39	42	66	0	6	2	413	63	13	2	4.7	.973	C-97
1976		69	.225	.350	200	45	6	2	5	2.5	26	16	21	37	0	8	3	319	36	7	1	5.2	.981	C-65
1977		54	.208	.403	144	30	7	0	7	4.9	16	16	22	33	2	4	1	247	38	8	2	5.4	.973	C-49
1978	CIN N	52	.238	.333	105	25	7	0	1	1.0	9	6	8	17	0	2	0	180	18	4	0	3.9	.980	C-52
1979		48	.233	.346	133	31	12	0	1	0.8	14	15	14	26	0	1	1	221	19	2	1	5.0	.992	C-47
1980		10	.421	.474	19	8	1	0	0	0.0	1	3	0	2	0	1	1	33	1	3	0	3.7	.919	C-10
8 yrs.		410	.229	.366	1132	259	60	4	29	2.6	124	125	128	220	2	36	9	1704	216	41	10	4.8	.979	C-380

Phillip Corridan

CORRIDAN, PHILIP
B. Ft. Wayne, Ind.

Year	Team	Games	BA	SA	AB	H	2B	3B	HR	HR%	R	RBI	BB	SO	SB	AB	H	PO	A	E	DP	TC/G	FA	G by Pos
1884	CHI U	2	.143	.143	7	1	0	0	0	0.0	1		0			0	0	4	4	2	0	5.0	.800	2B-2, OF-1

John Corriden

CORRIDEN, JOHN MICHAEL, JR.   BB TR 5'6"   160 lbs.
Son of Red Corriden.
B. Oct. 6, 1918, Logansport, Ind.

Year	Team	Games	BA	SA	AB	H	2B	3B	HR	HR%	R	RBI	BB	SO	SB	AB	H	PO	A	E	DP	TC/G	FA	G by Pos
1946	BKN N	1	–	–	0	0	0	0	0	–	1	0	0	0	0	0	0	0	0	0	0	0.0	–	

Red Corriden

CORRIDEN, JOHN MICHAEL, SR.   BR TR 5'9"   165 lbs.
Father of John Corriden.
B. Sept. 4, 1887, Logansport, Ind.   D. Sept. 28, 1959, Indianapolis, Ind.
Manager 1950.

Year	Team	Games	BA	SA	AB	H	2B	3B	HR	HR%	R	RBI	BB	SO	SB	AB	H	PO	A	E	DP	TC/G	FA	G by Pos
1910	STL A	26	.155	.226	84	13	3	0	1	1.2	19	4	13		5	0	0	61	81	13	3	6.0	.916	SS-14, 3B-12
1912	DET A	38	.203	.246	138	28	6	0	0	0.0	22	5	15		4	3	0	50	81	14	5	3.8	.903	3B-25, 2B-7, SS-3
1913	CHI N	45	.175	.268	97	17	3	0	2	2.1	13	9	9	14	4	4	1	51	83	14	12	3.3	.905	SS-36, 3B-8, 2B-1
1914		107	.230	.318	318	73	9	5	3	0.9	42	29	35	33	13	6	2	179	223	48	30	4.2	.893	SS-96, 3B-8, 2B-3
1915		6	.000	.000	3	0	0	0	0	0.0	1	0	2	1	0	2	0	1	1	1	0	0.5	.667	OF-1, 3B-1
5 yrs.		222	.205	.281	640	131	21	5	6	0.9	97	47	74	48	26	15	3	342	469	90	50	4.1	.900	SS-149, 3B-47, 2B-12, OF-1

Year	Team		Games	BA	SA	AB	H	2B	3B	HR	HR%	R	RBI	BB	SO	SB	Pinch Hit AB	Pinch Hit H	PO	A	E	DP	TC/G	FA	G by Pos

Shine Cortazzo

CORTAZZO, JOHN FRANCIS
B. Sept. 26, 1904, Wilmerding, Pa. D. Mar. 4, 1963, Pittsburgh, Pa.
BR TR 5'3½" 142 lbs.

| 1923 | CHI | A | 1 | .000 | .000 | 1 | 0 | 0 | 0 | 0 | 0.0 | 0 | 0 | 0 | 0 | 0 | 1 | 0 | 0 | 0 | 0 | 0 | 0.0 | – | |

Joe Coscarart

COSCARART, JOSEPH MARVIN
Brother of Pete Coscarart.
B. Nov. 18, 1909, Escondido, Calif.
BR TR 6' 185 lbs.

1935	BOS	N	86	.236	.299	284	67	11	2	1	0.4	30	29	16	28	2	2	0	115	177	14	20	3.6	.954	3B-41, SS-27, 2B-15
1936			104	.245	.302	367	90	11	2	2	0.5	28	44	19	37	0	1	1	103	181	21	18	2.9	.931	3B-97, SS-6, 2B-1
2 yrs.			190	.241	.301	651	157	22	4	3	0.5	58	73	35	65	2	3	1	218	358	35	38	3.2	.943	3B-138, SS-33, 2B-16

Pete Coscarart

COSCARART, PETER JOSEPH
Brother of Joe Coscarart.
B. June 16, 1913, Escondido, Calif.
BR TR 5'11½" 175 lbs.

1938	BKN	N	32	.152	.190	79	12	3	0	0	0.0	10	6	9	18	0	2	0	58	69	6	16	4.2	.955	2B-27
1939			115	.277	.368	419	116	22	2	4	1.0	59	43	46	56	10	0	0	259	348	25	69	5.5	.960	2B-107, 3B-4, SS-2
1940			143	.237	.354	506	120	24	4	9	1.8	55	58	53	59	5	2	1	326	379	31	58	5.1	.958	2B-140
1941			43	.129	.145	62	8	1	0	0	0.0	13	5	7	12	1	15	2	30	45	4	5	1.8	.949	2B-19, SS-1
1942	PIT	N	133	.228	.287	487	111	12	4	3	0.6	57	29	38	56	2	1	1	245	367	32	60	4.8	.950	SS-108, 2B-25
1943			133	.242	.305	491	119	19	6	0	0.0	57	48	46	48	4	1	1	282	415	28	84	5.5	.961	2B-85, SS-47, 3B-1
1944			139	.264	.354	554	146	30	4	4	0.7	89	42	41	57	10	1	0	377	391	26	71	5.7	.967	2B-136, SS-4, OF-1
1945			123	.242	.357	392	95	17	2	8	2.0	59	38	55	55	2	1	0	257	362	14	74	5.1	.978	2B-122, SS-1
1946			3	.500	1.000	2	1	1	0	0	0.0	0	0	0	0	0	2	1	0	0	0	0	0.0	–	SS-1
9 yrs.			864	.243	.329	2992	728	129	22	28	0.9	399	269	295	361	34	25	6	1834	2376	166	437	5.1	.962	2B-661, SS-164, 3B-5, OF-1

WORLD SERIES

| 1941 | BKN | N | 3 | .000 | .000 | 7 | 0 | 0 | 0 | 0 | 0.0 | 1 | 0 | 1 | 2 | 0 | 0 | 0 | 7 | 8 | 0 | 1 | 5.0 | 1.000 | 2B-3 |

Ray Cosey

COSEY, DONALD RAY
B. Feb. 15, 1956, San Rafael, Calif.
BL TL 5'10" 185 lbs.

| 1980 | OAK | A | 9 | .111 | .111 | 9 | 1 | 0 | 0 | 0 | 0.0 | 0 | 0 | 0 | 0 | 0 | 9 | 1 | 0 | 0 | 0 | 0 | 0.0 | – | |

Dan Costello

COSTELLO, DANIEL FRANCIS (Dashing Dan)
B. Sept. 9, 1891, Jessup, Pa. D. Mar. 26, 1936, Pittsburgh, Pa.
BL TR 6'½" 185 lbs.

1913	NY	A	2	.500	.500	2	1	0	0	0	0.0	1	0	0	0	0	0	0	0	0	0	0	0.0	–	
1914	PIT	N	21	.297	.313	64	19	1	0	0	0.0	7	5	8	16	2	1	0	29	3	1	1	1.6	.970	OF-20
1915			71	.216	.264	125	27	4	1	0	0.0	16	11	7	23	7	46	14	27	1	3	0	0.4	.903	OF-17
1916			60	.239	.283	159	38	1	3	0	0.0	11	8	6	23	3	18	5	82	0	2	0	1.4	.976	OF-41
4 yrs.			154	.243	.283	350	85	6	4	0	0.0	35	24	21	62	12	67	20	138	4	6	1	1.0	.959	OF-78

J. A. Costello

Playing record listed under Ken Nash

Henry Cote

COTE, HENRY JOSEPH
B. Dec. 19, 1864, Troy, N. Y. D. Apr. 28, 1940, Troy, N. Y.
TR

1894	LOU	N	10	.290	.484	31	9	2	2	0	0.0	7	3	5	2	2	0	0	40	16	5	3	6.1	.918	C-10
1895			10	.303	.303	33	10	0	0	0	0.0	10	5	3	3	2	0	0	29	5	5	0	3.9	.872	C-10
2 yrs.			20	.297	.391	64	19	2	2	0	0.0	17	8	8	9	4	0	0	69	21	10	3	5.0	.900	C-20

Pete Cote

COTE, WARREN PETER
B. Aug. 30, 1902, Middleton, Mass. D. Oct. 17, 1987, Middleton, Mass.
BR TR 5'6" 148 lbs.

| 1926 | NY | N | 2 | .000 | .000 | 1 | 0 | 0 | 0 | 0 | 0.0 | 0 | 0 | 0 | 0 | 0 | 1 | 0 | 0 | 0 | 0 | 0 | 0.0 | – | |

Dick Cotter

COTTER, RICHARD RAPHAEL
B. Oct. 12, 1889, Manchester, N. H. D. Apr. 4, 1945, Brooklyn, N. Y.
BR TR 5'11" 172 lbs.

1911	PHI	N	20	.283	.283	46	13	0	0	0	0.0	2	5	5	7	1	2	0	56	23	2	2	4.1	.975	C-17
1912	CHI	N	26	.278	.352	54	15	0	2	0	0.0	6	10	6	13	1	1	0	64	19	4	0	3.3	.954	C-24
2 yrs.			46	.280	.320	100	28	0	2	0	0.0	8	15	11	20	2	3	0	120	42	6	2	3.7	.964	C-41

Ed Cotter

COTTER, EDWARD CHRISTOPHER
B. July 4, 1904, Hartford, Conn. D. June 14, 1959, Hartford, Conn.
BR TR 6' 185 lbs.

| 1926 | PHI | N | 17 | .308 | .385 | 26 | 8 | 0 | 1 | 0 | 0.0 | 3 | 1 | 1 | 4 | 1 | 4 | 1 | 7 | 18 | 6 | 0 | 1.8 | .806 | 3B-8, SS-5 |

Harvey Cotter

COTTER, HARVEY LOUIS (Hooks)
B. May 22, 1900, Holden, Mo. D. Aug. 6, 1955, Los Angeles, Calif.
BL TL 5'10" 160 lbs.

1922	CHI	N	1	1.000	2.000	1	1	0	0	0	0.0	0	0	0	0	0	1	1	0	0	0	0	0.0	–	
1924			98	.261	.377	310	81	16	4	4	1.3	39	33	36	31	3	7	2	873	59	10	72	9.6	.989	1B-90
2 yrs.			99	.264	.383	311	82	17	4	4	1.3	39	33	36	31	3	8	3	873	59	10	72	9.5	.989	1B-90

Tom Cotter

COTTER, THOMAS B.
B. Sept. 30, 1866, Waltham, Mass. D. Nov. 22, 1906, Brookline, Mass.
BR TR 5'10½" 149 lbs.

| 1891 | BOS | AA | 6 | .250 | .250 | 12 | 3 | 0 | 0 | 0 | 0.0 | 1 | 4 | 1 | 2 | 1 | 0 | 0 | 11 | 4 | 1 | 0 | 2.7 | .938 | C-5, OF-1 |

Chuck Cottier

COTTIER, CHARLES KEITH
B. Jan. 8, 1936, Delta, Colo.
Manager 1984-86.
BR TR 5'10½" 175 lbs.

| 1959 | MIL | N | 10 | .125 | .167 | 24 | 3 | 1 | 0 | 0 | 0.0 | 1 | 1 | 3 | 7 | 0 | 0 | 0 | 18 | 22 | 1 | 2 | 4.1 | .976 | 2B-10 |
| 1960 | | | 95 | .227 | .301 | 229 | 52 | 8 | 0 | 3 | 1.3 | 29 | 19 | 14 | 21 | 1 | 1 | 1 | 180 | 214 | 13 | 40 | 4.3 | .968 | 2B-92 |

Al Cowens (continued)

Year	Team		Games	BA	SA	AB	H	2B	3B	HR	HR%	R	RBI	BB	SO	SB	PH AB	PH H	PO	A	E	DP	TC/G	FA	G by Pos
1985			122	.265	.451	452	120	32	5	14	3.1	59	69	30	56	0	8	2	198	10	7	2	1.8	.967	OF-110, DH-5
1986			28	.183	.232	82	15	4	0	0	0.0	5	6	3	18	1	7	1	31	2	1	0	1.2	.971	OF-19, DH-1
13 yrs.			1584	.270	.403	5534	1494	276	68	108	2.0	704	717	389	659	120	77	21	2859	123	48	20	1.9	.984	OF-1477, DH-61, 3B-7

LEAGUE CHAMPIONSHIP SERIES

Year	Team		Games	BA	SA	AB	H	2B	3B	HR	HR%	R	RBI	BB	SO	SB	PH AB	PH H	PO	A	E	DP	TC/G	FA	G by Pos
1976	KC	A	5	.190	.286	21	4	0	1	0	0.0	3	0	1	1	2	0	0	15	0	0	0	3.0	1.000	OF-5
1977			5	.263	.421	19	5	0	1	1	5.3	2	5	1	3	0	0	0	14	0	0	0	2.8	1.000	OF-5
1978			4	.133	.133	15	2	0	0	0	0.0	2	1	0	2	0	0	0	5	0	0	0	1.3	1.000	OF-4
3 yrs.			14	.200	.291	55	11	0	1	1	1.8	7	6	2	6	2	0	0	34	0	0	0	2.4	1.000	OF-14

Billy Cox

COX, WILLIAM RICHARD
B. Aug. 29, 1919, Newport, Pa. D. Mar. 30, 1978, Harrisburg, Pa.   BR TR 5'10" 150 lbs.

Year	Team		Games	BA	SA	AB	H	2B	3B	HR	HR%	R	RBI	BB	SO	SB	PH AB	PH H	PO	A	E	DP	TC/G	FA	G by Pos
1941	PIT	N	10	.270	.405	37	10	3	1	0	0.0	4	2	3	2	1	0	0	15	35	3	8	5.3	.943	SS-10
1946			121	.290	.387	411	119	22	6	2	0.5	32	36	26	15	4	3	1	235	323	39	59	4.9	.935	SS-114
1947			132	.274	.442	529	145	30	7	15	2.8	75	54	29	28	5	2	1	220	388	20	63	4.8	.968	SS-129
1948	BKN	N	88	.249	.359	237	59	13	2	3	1.3	36	15	38	19	3	6	1	59	120	8	11	2.1	.957	3B-70, SS-6, 2B-1
1949			100	.233	.351	390	91	18	2	8	2.1	48	40	30	18	5	0	0	104	213	12	28	3.3	.964	3B-100
1950			119	.257	.357	451	116	17	2	8	1.8	62	44	35	24	6	1	0	143	274	16	43	3.6	.963	3B-107, 2B-13, SS-9
1951			142	.279	.411	455	127	25	4	9	2.0	62	51	37	30	5	3	1	141	264	14	26	3.0	.967	3B-139, SS-1
1952			116	.259	.338	455	118	12	3	6	1.3	56	34	25	32	10	4	1	140	188	7	34	2.9	.973	3B-100, SS-10, 2B-9
1953			100	.291	.443	327	95	18	1	10	3.1	44	44	37	21	2	5	1	92	147	7	21	2.5	.972	3B-89, SS-6, 2B-1
1954			77	.235	.319	226	53	9	2	2	0.9	26	17	21	13	0	4	1	93	130	7	15	3.0	.970	3B-58, 2B-11, SS-8
1955	BAL	A	53	.211	.314	194	41	7	2	3	1.5	25	14	17	16	1	3	1	55	104	4	10	3.1	.975	3B-37, 2B-18, SS-6
11 yrs.			1058	.262	.380	3712	974	174	32	66	1.8	470	351	298	218	42	31	8	1297	2186	139	318	3.4	.962	3B-700, SS-299, 2B-53

WORLD SERIES

Year	Team		Games	BA	SA	AB	H	2B	3B	HR	HR%	R	RBI	BB	SO	SB	PH AB	PH H	PO	A	E	DP	TC/G	FA	G by Pos
1949	BKN	N	2	.333	.333	3	1	0	0	0	0.0	0	0	0	1	0	2	1	1	0	0	0	0.5	1.000	3B-1
1952			7	.296	.370	27	8	2	0	0	0.0	4	3	3	4	0	0	0	9	14	1	1	3.4	.958	3B-7
1953			6	.304	.565	23	7	3	0	1	4.3	3	6	1	4	0	0	0	1	10	1	1	2.0	.917	3B-6
3 yrs.			15	.302	.453	53	16	5	0	1	1.9	7	6	4	9	0	2	1	11	24	2	2	2.5	.946	3B-14

Bobby Cox

COX, ROBERT JOE
B. May 21, 1941, Tulsa, Okla.
Manager 1978-85.   BR TR 5'11" 180 lbs.

Year	Team		Games	BA	SA	AB	H	2B	3B	HR	HR%	R	RBI	BB	SO	SB	PH AB	PH H	PO	A	E	DP	TC/G	FA	G by Pos
1968	NY	A	135	.229	.316	437	100	15	1	7	1.6	33	41	41	85	3	3	0	98	279	17	22	2.9	.957	3B-132
1969			85	.215	.293	191	41	7	1	2	1.0	17	17	34	41	0	20	4	50	145	11	17	2.4	.947	3B-56, 2B-6
2 yrs.			220	.225	.309	628	141	22	2	9	1.4	50	58	75	126	3	23	4	148	424	28	39	2.7	.953	3B-188, 2B-6

Dick Cox

COX, ELMER JOSEPH
B. Sept. 30, 1897, Pasadena, Calif. D. June 1, 1966, Morro Bay, Calif.   BR TR 5'7½" 158 lbs.

Year	Team		Games	BA	SA	AB	H	2B	3B	HR	HR%	R	RBI	BB	SO	SB	PH AB	PH H	PO	A	E	DP	TC/G	FA	G by Pos
1925	BKN	N	122	.329	.477	434	143	23	10	7	1.6	68	64	37	29	1	3	1	197	14	7	4	1.8	.968	OF-111
1926			124	.296	.367	398	118	17	4	1	0.3	53	45	46	20	6	6	3	201	12	8	2	1.8	.964	OF-117
2 yrs.			246	.314	.424	832	261	40	14	8	1.0	121	109	83	49	10	14	6	398	26	15	6	1.8	.966	OF-228

Frank Cox

COX, FRANCIS BERNARD (Runt)
B. Aug. 29, 1857, Waltham, Mass. D. June 24, 1928, Hartford, Conn.   5'6"

Year	Team		Games	BA	SA	AB	H	2B	3B	HR	HR%	R	RBI	BB	SO	SB	PH AB	PH H	PO	A	E	DP	TC/G	FA	G by Pos
1884	DET	N	27	.127	.176	102	13	3	1	0	0.0	6		2	36		0	0	28	80	25	7	4.9	.812	SS-27

Jeff Cox

COX, JEFFREY LINDON
B. Nov. 9, 1955, Los Angeles, Calif.   BR TR 5'11" 170 lbs.

Year	Team		Games	BA	SA	AB	H	2B	3B	HR	HR%	R	RBI	BB	SO	SB	PH AB	PH H	PO	A	E	DP	TC/G	FA	G by Pos
1980	OAK	A	59	.213	.231	169	36	3	0	0	0.0	20	9	14	23	8	0	0	107	167	6	28	4.7	.979	2B-58
1981			2	—	—	0	0	0	0	0	—	0	0	0	0	0	0	0	0	1	0	0	0.5	1.000	2B-1
2 yrs.			61	.213	.231	169	36	3	0	0	0.0	20	9	14	23	8	0	0	107	168	6	28	4.6	.979	2B-59

Jim Cox

COX, JAMES CHARLES
B. May 28, 1950, Bloomington, Ill.   BR TR 5'11" 175 lbs.

Year	Team		Games	BA	SA	AB	H	2B	3B	HR	HR%	R	RBI	BB	SO	SB	PH AB	PH H	PO	A	E	DP	TC/G	FA	G by Pos
1973	MON	N	9	.133	.200	15	2	1	0	0	0.0	1	4	0	2	0	2	0	9	10	1	1	2.2	.950	2B-7
1974			77	.220	.292	236	52	9	1	2	0.8	29	26	23	36	2	1	1	148	220	12	45	4.9	.968	2B-72
1975			11	.259	.407	27	7	1	0	1	3.7	1	5	1	2	1	3	0	10	21	0	7	2.8	1.000	2B-8
1976			13	.172	.241	29	5	0	1	0	0.0	2	2	2	2	0	1	0	24	22	2	6	3.8	.958	2B-11
4 yrs.			110	.215	.293	307	66	11	2	3	1.0	33	33	27	44	3	7	1	191	273	15	59	4.4	.969	2B-98

Larry Cox

COX, LARRY EUGENE
B. Sept. 11, 1947, Bluffton, Ohio   BR TR 5'10" 178 lbs.

Year	Team		Games	BA	SA	AB	H	2B	3B	HR	HR%	R	RBI	BB	SO	SB	PH AB	PH H	PO	A	E	DP	TC/G	FA	G by Pos
1973	PHI	N	1	—	—	0	0	0	0	0	—	0	0	0	0	0	0	0	1	0	0	0	1.0	1.000	C-1
1974			30	.170	.208	53	9	2	0	0	0.0	5	4	4	9	0	2	1	90	9	1	0	3.3	.990	C-29
1975			11	.200	.200	5	1	0	0	0	0.0	0	1	1	0	1	1	0	10	0	0	0	0.9	1.000	C-10
1977	SEA	A	35	.247	.376	93	23	6	0	2	2.2	6	6	10	12	1	0	0	138	26	5	2	4.8	.970	C-35
1978	CHI	N	59	.281	.372	121	34	5	0	2	1.7	10	18	12	16	0	0	0	178	26	7	3	3.6	.967	C-58
1979	SEA	A	100	.215	.314	293	63	11	3	4	1.4	32	36	22	39	2	8	0	408	49	9	6	4.7	.981	C-99
1980			105	.202	.292	243	49	6	2	4	1.6	18	20	19	36	1	2	0	412	45	3	5	4.4	.993	C-104
1981	TEX	A	5	.231	.308	13	3	1	0	0	0.0	0	0	0	4	0	0	0	33	2	0	1	7.0	1.000	C-5
1982	CHI	N	2	.000	.000	4	0	0	0	0	0.0	0	1	2	1	0	0	0	5	2	0	1	5.5	1.000	C-2
9 yrs.			348	.221	.314	825	182	31	5	12	1.5	72	85	70	117	5	13	1	1279	159	25	17	4.2	.983	C-343

Ted Cox

COX, WILLIAM TED
B. Jan. 24, 1955, Oklahoma City, Okla.   BR TR 6'3" 195 lbs.

Year	Team		Games	BA	SA	AB	H	2B	3B	HR	HR%	R	RBI	BB	SO	SB	PH AB	PH H	PO	A	E	DP	TC/G	FA	G by Pos
1977	BOS	A	13	.362	.500	58	21	3	1	1	1.7	11	6	3	6	0	0	0	0	0	0	0	0.0	—	DH-13
1978	CLE	A	82	.233	.278	227	53	7	0	1	0.4	14	19	16	30	0	12	1	100	42	4	6	1.8	.973	OF-38, 3B-20, DH-12, 1B-7, SS-1
1979			78	.212	.307	189	40	6	0	4	2.1	17	22	14	27	3	8	2	57	81	6	11	1.8	.958	3B-52, OF-16, 2B-4, DH-1

Year	Team		Games	BA	SA	AB	H	2B	3B	HR	HR%	R	RBI	BB	SO	SB	Pinch Hit AB	Pinch Hit H	PO	A	E	DP	TC/G	FA	G by Pos

Ted Cox *continued*

Year	Team		Games	BA	SA	AB	H	2B	3B	HR	HR%	R	RBI	BB	SO	SB	PH AB	PH H	PO	A	E	DP	TC/G	FA	G by Pos
1980	SEA	A	83	.243	.304	247	60	9	0	2	0.8	17	23	19	25	0	4	3	47	142	11	20	2.4	.945	3B-80
1981	TOR	A	16	.300	.500	50	15	4	0	2	4.0	6	9	5	10	0	0	0	17	19	3	2	2.4	.923	3B-14, DH-1, 1B-1
5 yrs.			272	.245	.324	771	189	29	1	10	1.3	65	79	57	98	3	24	6	221	284	24	39	1.9	.955	3B-166, OF-54, DH-27, 1B-8, 2B-4, SS-1

Toots Coyne

COYNE,
B. Unknown.

TR

Year	Team		Games	BA	SA	AB	H	2B	3B	HR	HR%	R	RBI	BB	SO	SB	PH AB	PH H	PO	A	E	DP	TC/G	FA	G by Pos
1914	PHI	A	1	.000	.000	2	0	0	0	0	0.0	0	0	0	2	0	0	0	0	1	0	0	1.0	1.000	3B-1

Estel Crabtree

CRABTREE, ESTEL CRAYTON (Crabby)
B. Aug. 19, 1903, Crabtree, Ohio   D. Jan. 4, 1967, Logan, Ohio

BL TR 6'   168 lbs.

Year	Team		Games	BA	SA	AB	H	2B	3B	HR	HR%	R	RBI	BB	SO	SB	PH AB	PH H	PO	A	E	DP	TC/G	FA	G by Pos
1929	CIN	N	1	.000	.000	1	0	0	0	0	0.0	0	0	0	1	0	1	0	0	0	0	0	0.0		
1931			117	.269	.377	443	119	12	12	4	0.9	70	37	23	33	3	10	3	265	30	11	9	2.6	.964	OF-101, 3B-4, 1B-2
1932			108	.274	.368	402	110	14	9	2	0.5	38	35	23	26	2	7	3	288	9	3	3	2.8	.990	OF-95
1933	STL	N	23	.265	.353	34	9	3	0	0	0.0	6	3	12	2	1	12	1	18	0	1	0	0.8	.947	OF-7
1941			77	.341	.503	167	57	6	3	5	3.0	27	28	26	24	1	21	7	71	4	0	0	1.0	1.000	OF-50, 3B-1
1942			10	.333	.556	9	3	2	0	0	0.0	1	2	1	3	0	9	3	0	0	0	0	0.0		
1943	CIN	N	95	.276	.346	254	70	12	0	2	0.8	25	26	25	17	1	24	10	135	4	9	2	1.6	.939	OF-64
1944			58	.286	.347	98	28	4	1	0	0.0	7	11	3	3	0	32	9	29	1	0	1	0.5	1.000	OF-19, 1B-2
8 yrs.			489	.281	.382	1408	396	53	25	13	0.9	174	142	113	109	8	116	37	806	48	24	15	1.8	.973	OF-336, 3B-5, 1B-4

Harry Craft

CRAFT, HARRY FRANCIS
B. Apr. 19, 1915, Ellisville, Miss.
Manager 1957-59, 1961-64.

BR TR 6'1"   185 lbs.

Year	Team		Games	BA	SA	AB	H	2B	3B	HR	HR%	R	RBI	BB	SO	SB	PH AB	PH H	PO	A	E	DP	TC/G	FA	G by Pos
1937	CIN	N	10	.310	.405	42	13	2	1	0	0.0	7	4	1	3	0	0	0	22	1	0	0	2.3	1.000	OF-10
1938			151	.270	.418	612	165	28	9	15	2.5	70	83	29	46	3	0	0	436	15	8	3	3.0	.983	OF-151
1939			134	.257	.402	502	129	20	7	13	2.6	58	67	27	54	5	0	0	300	13	6	3	2.4	.981	OF-134
1940			115	.244	.353	422	103	18	5	6	1.4	47	48	17	46	2	3	0	300	8	1	3	2.7	.997	OF-109, 1B-2
1941			119	.249	.368	413	103	15	2	10	2.4	48	59	33	43	4	4	1	280	6	5	1	2.4	.983	OF-115
1942			37	.177	.212	113	20	2	1	0	0.0	7	6	3	11	0	1	0	72	4	1	3	2.1	.987	OF-33
6 yrs.			566	.253	.380	2104	533	85	25	44	2.1	237	267	110	203	14	8	1	1410	47	21	14	2.6	.986	OF-552, 1B-2

WORLD SERIES

Year	Team		Games	BA	SA	AB	H	2B	3B	HR	HR%	R	RBI	BB	SO	SB	PH AB	PH H	PO	A	E	DP	TC/G	FA	G by Pos
1939	CIN	N	4	.091	.091	11	1	0	0	0	0.0	0	0	0	6	0	0	0	7	1	0	0	2.0	1.000	OF-4
1940			1	.000	.000	1	0	0	0	0	0.0	0	0	0	0	0	1	0	0	0	0	0	0.0	—	
2 yrs.			5	.083	.083	12	1	0	0	0	0.0	0	0	0	6	0	1	0	7	1	0	0	1.6	1.000	OF-4

Rodney Craig

CRAIG, RODNEY PAUL
B. Jan. 12, 1958, Los Angeles, Calif.

BB TR 6'1"   195 lbs.

Year	Team		Games	BA	SA	AB	H	2B	3B	HR	HR%	R	RBI	BB	SO	SB	PH AB	PH H	PO	A	E	DP	TC/G	FA	G by Pos
1979	SEA	A	16	.385	.577	52	20	8	1	0	0.0	9	6	1	5	1	1	0	24	0	2	0	1.6	.923	OF-15
1980			70	.238	.346	240	57	15	1	3	1.3	30	20	17	35	3	2	1	155	2	2	1	2.3	.987	OF-63
1982	CLE	A	49	.231	.262	65	15	2	0	0	0.0	7	1	4	6	3	19	2	28	0	1	0	0.6	.966	OF-22, DH-4
1986	CHI	A	10	.200	.200	10	2	0	0	0	0.0	3	0	2	2	0	8	2	0	0	0	0	—		OF-2
4 yrs.			145	.256	.360	367	94	25	2	3	0.8	49	27	24	48	7	30	5	207	2	5	1	1.5	.977	OF-102, DH-4

Dick Cramer

CRAMER, WILLIAM B.
B. Brooklyn, N. Y.   D. Aug. 12, 1885, Camden, N. J.

Year	Team		Games	BA	SA	AB	H	2B	3B	HR	HR%	R	RBI	BB	SO	SB	PH AB	PH H	PO	A	E	DP	TC/G	FA	G by Pos
1883	NY	N	2	.000	.000	6	0	0	0	0	0.0	0		1	5		0	0	0	0	0	0	0.0	—	OF-2

Doc Cramer

CRAMER, ROGER MAXWELL (Flit)
B. July 22, 1905, Beach Haven, N. J.

BL TR 6'2"   185 lbs.

Year	Team		Games	BA	SA	AB	H	2B	3B	HR	HR%	R	RBI	BB	SO	SB	PH AB	PH H	PO	A	E	DP	TC/G	FA	G by Pos
1929	PHI	A	2	.000	.000	6	0	0	0	0	0.0	0	0	0	2	0	1	0	6	0	0	0	3.0	1.000	OF-1
1930			30	.232	.268	82	19	1	1	0	0.0	12	6	2	8	0	8	0	38	2	3	1	1.4	.930	OF-21, SS-1
1931			65	.260	.341	223	58	8	2	2	0.9	37	20	11	15	2	10	3	133	5	3	1	2.2	.979	OF-55
1932			92	.336	.461	384	129	27	6	3	0.8	73	46	17	27	3	4	2	233	7	6	2	2.7	.976	OF-86
1933			152	.295	.396	661	195	27	8	8	1.2	109	75	36	24	5	0	0	387	13	12	2	2.7	.971	OF-152
1934			153	.311	.411	649	202	29	9	6	0.9	99	46	40	35	1	0	0	385	12	6	0	2.6	.985	OF-152
1935			149	.332	.416	644	214	37	4	3	0.5	96	70	37	34	6	0	0	429	6	11	1	3.0	.975	OF-149
1936	BOS	A	154	.292	.362	643	188	31	7	0	0.0	99	41	49	20	4	0	0	443	20	12	6	3.1	.975	OF-154
1937			133	.305	.384	560	171	22	11	0	0.0	90	51	35	14	8	0	0	365	12	12	4	2.9	.969	OF-133
1938			148	.301	.380	658	198	36	8	0	0.0	116	71	51	19	4	0	0	417	16	6	3	3.0	.986	OF-148, P-1
1939			137	.311	.382	589	183	30	6	0	0.0	110	56	36	17	3	2	1	356	12	6	0	2.7	.984	OF-135
1940			150	.303	.384	661	200	27	12	1	0.2	94	51	36	29	3	0	0	333	11	11	2	2.4	.969	OF-149
1941	WAS	A	154	.273	.338	660	180	25	6	2	0.3	93	66	37	15	4	2	0	369	9	6	1	2.5	.984	OF-152
1942	DET	A	151	.263	.317	630	166	26	4	0	0.0	71	43	43	18	4	1	1	352	15	7	6	2.5	.981	OF-150
1943			140	.300	.348	606	182	18	4	1	0.2	79	43	31	13	4	2	1	346	9	4	3	2.6	.989	OF-138
1944			143	.292	.369	578	169	20	9	2	0.3	69	42	37	21	4	0	0	337	13	7	2	2.5	.980	OF-141
1945			141	.275	.379	541	149	22	8	6	1.1	62	58	35	21	2	1	0	314	7	3	4	2.3	.991	OF-140
1946			68	.294	.368	204	60	8	2	1	0.5	26	26	15	8	3	16	4	89	2	0	0	1.3	1.000	OF-50
1947			73	.268	.344	157	42	2	2	2	1.3	21	30	20	5	0	33	9	79	3	3	0	1.2	.965	OF-35
1948			4	.000	.000	4	0	0	0	0	0.0	1	1	3	0	0	2	0	2	0	0	0	0.5	1.000	OF-1
20 yrs.			2239	.296	.375	9140	2705	396	109	37	0.4	1357	842	571	345	62	84	21	5413	174	118	38	2.5	.979	OF-2142, SS-1, P-1

WORLD SERIES

Year	Team		Games	BA	SA	AB	H	2B	3B	HR	HR%	R	RBI	BB	SO	SB	PH AB	PH H	PO	A	E	DP	TC/G	FA	G by Pos
1931	PHI	A	2	.500	.500	2	1	0	0	0	0.0	0	2	0	0	0	2	1	0	0	0	0	0.0	—	
1945	DET	A	7	.379	.379	29	11	0	0	0	0.0	7	4	1	0	1	0	0	21	0	0	0	3.0	1.000	OF-7
2 yrs.			9	.387	.387	31	12	0	0	0	0.0	7	6	1	0	1	2	1	21	0	0	0	2.3	1.000	OF-7

Del Crandall

CRANDALL, DELMAR WESLEY
B. Mar. 5, 1930, Ontario, Calif.
Manager 1972-75, 1983-84.

BR TR 6'1½"   180 lbs.

Del Crandall *continued*

Year	Team	Games	BA	SA	AB	H	2B	3B	HR	HR%	R	RBI	BB	SO	SB	PH AB	PH H	PO	A	E	DP	TC/G	FA	G by Pos
1949	BOS N	67	.263	.368	228	60	10	1	4	1.8	21	34	9	18	2	2	1	287	39	6	5	5.0	.982	C-63
1950		79	.220	.310	255	56	11	0	4	1.6	21	37	13	24	0	1	0	319	41	12	7	4.7	.968	C-75, 1B-1
1953	MIL N	116	.272	.429	382	104	13	1	15	3.9	55	51	33	47	2	8	1	566	62	9	13	5.5	.986	C-108
1954		138	.242	.425	463	112	18	2	21	4.5	60	64	40	56	0	3	1	665	79	8	11	5.4	.989	C-136
1955		133	.236	.457	440	104	15	2	26	5.9	61	62	40	56	2	4	1	611	67	10	8	5.2	.985	C-131
1956		112	.238	.450	311	74	14	2	16	5.1	37	48	35	30	1	5	2	448	44	2	9	4.4	.996	C-109
1957		118	.253	.410	383	97	11	2	15	3.9	45	46	30	38	1	12	4	429	60	7	11	4.2	.986	C-102, OF-9, 1B-1
1958		131	.272	.457	427	116	23	1	18	4.2	50	63	48	38	4	8	3	659	64	7	6	5.6	.990	C-124
1959		150	.257	.423	518	133	19	2	21	4.1	65	72	46	48	4	2	0	783	71	5	15	5.7	.994	C-146
1960		142	.294	.430	537	158	14	1	19	3.5	81	77	34	36	5	4	0	764	70	10	9	5.9	.988	C-141
1961		15	.200	.300	30	6	3	0	0	0.0	0	1	0	0	0	8	0	17	3	0	0	1.3	1.000	C-5
1962		107	.297	.417	350	104	12	3	8	2.3	35	45	27	24	3	14	6	488	55	3	9	5.1	.995	C-90, 1B-5
1963		86	.201	.251	259	52	4	0	3	1.2	18	28	18	22	1	6	0	459	43	4	9	5.9	.992	C-75, 1B-7
1964	SF N	69	.231	.328	195	45	8	1	3	1.5	12	11	22	21	0	6	2	402	30	3	7	6.3	.993	C-65
1965	PIT N	60	.214	.271	140	30	2	0	2	1.4	11	10	14	10	1	0	0	248	23	1	4	4.5	.996	C-60
1966	CLE A	50	.231	.361	108	25	2	0	4	3.7	10	8	14	9	0	2	0	304	15	3	2	6.4	.991	C-49
16 yrs.		1573	.254	.404	5026	1276	179	18	179	3.6	585	657	424	477	26	85	21	7449	766	90	125	5.3	.989	C-1479, 1B-14, OF-9

WORLD SERIES

Year	Team	Games	BA	SA	AB	H	2B	3B	HR	HR%	R	RBI	BB	SO	SB	PH AB	PH H	PO	A	E	DP	TC/G	FA	G by Pos
1957	MIL N	6	.211	.368	19	4	0	0	1	5.3	1	1	1	1	0	0	0	21	4	0	2	4.2	1.000	C-6
1958		7	.240	.360	25	6	0	0	1	4.0	4	3	3	10	0	0	0	43	5	0	2	6.9	1.000	C-7
2 yrs.		13	.227	.364	44	10	0	0	2	4.5	5	4	4	11	0	0	0	64	9	0	4	5.6	1.000	C-13

Doc Crandall

CRANDALL, JAMES OTIS
B. Oct. 8, 1887, Wadena, Ind. D. Aug. 17, 1951, Bell, Calif.
BR TR 5'10½" 180 lbs.

Year	Team	Games	BA	SA	AB	H	2B	3B	HR	HR%	R	RBI	BB	SO	SB	PH AB	PH H	PO	A	E	DP	TC/G	FA	G by Pos
1908	NY N	34	.222	.361	72	16	4	0	2	2.8	8	6	4	0		2	0	15	52	1	2	2.0	.985	P-32, 2B-1
1909		30	.244	.366	41	10	0	1	1	2.4	4	1	1	0	0	0		9	39	3	4	1.7	.941	P-30
1910		45	.342	.521	73	25	2	4	1	1.4	10	13	5	7	1	0	0	12	49	1	3	1.4	.984	P-42, SS-1
1911		61	.239	.372	113	27	1	4	2	1.8	12	21	8	16	2	11	2	17	76	6	3	1.6	.939	P-41, SS-6, 2B-3
1912		50	.313	.438	80	25	6	2	0	0.0	9	19	6	7	0	10	4	4	44	2	0	1.1	.964	P-37, 2B-2, 1B-1
1913	2 teams																							NY N (46G - .319) STL N (2G - .000)
"	total	48	.306	.429	49	15	4	1	0	0.0	7	4	3	10	0	10	2	2	5	0	1	0.1	1.000	P-35, 2B-1
1914	STL F	118	.309	.424	278	86	16	5	2	0.7	40	41	58		3	17	6	106	204	25	12	2.8	.925	2B-63, P-27, OF-1, SS-1
1915		84	.284	.348	141	40	2	2	1	0.7	18	19	27		4	28	5	15	99	5	3	1.4	.958	P-51
1916	STL A	16	.083	.083	12	1	0	0	0	0.0	0	0	2	4	0	12	1	0	1	0		0.1	–	P-2
1918	BOS N	14	.286	.286	28	8	0	0	0	0.0	1	2	4	3	0	5	2	7	10	0	1	1.2	1.000	P-5, OF-3
10 yrs.		500	.285	.398	887	253	35	19	9	1.0	109	126	118	47	9	96	22	192	578	44	29	1.6	.946	P-302, 2B-70, SS-8, OF-4, 1B-1

WORLD SERIES

Year	Team	Games	BA	SA	AB	H	2B	3B	HR	HR%	R	RBI	BB	SO	SB	PH AB	PH H	PO	A	E	DP	TC/G	FA	G by Pos
1911	NY N	3	.500	1.000	2	1	1	0	0	0.0	1	0	2	0	0	0	0	0	2	0	0	0.7	1.000	P-2
1912		1	.000	.000	1	0	0	0	0	0.0	0	0	0	1	0	0	0	0	1	0	0	1.0	1.000	P-2
1913		4	.000	.000	4	0	0	0	0	0.0	0	0	0	2	0	0	0	0	2	0	0	0.5	1.000	P-5
3 yrs.		8	.143	.286	7	1	1	0	0	0.0	1	0	2	1	0	0	0	0	5	0	0	0.6	1.000	

Cannonball Crane

CRANE, EDWARD NICHOLAS
B. May, 1862, Boston, Mass. D. Sept. 19, 1896, Rochester, N.Y.
BR TR 5'10½" 204 lbs.

Year	Team	Games	BA	SA	AB	H	2B	3B	HR	HR%	R	RBI	BB	SO	SB	PH AB	PH H	PO	A	E	DP	TC/G	FA	G by Pos
1884	BOS U	101	.285	.451	428	122	23	6	12	2.8	83		14			0	0	364	102	88	6	5.5	.841	OF-57, C-42, 1B-5, P-4
1885	2 teams																							PRO N (1G - .000) BUF N (13G - .275)
"	total	14	.264	.415	53	14	0	1	2	3.8	5	10	4	9	0	0		20	1	7	0	2.0	.750	OF-14
1886	WAS N	80	.171	.229	292	50	11	3	0	0.0	20	20	13	54	0	0		116	35	20	5	2.1	.883	OF-68, P-10, C-4
1888	NY N	12	.162	.297	37	6	2	0	1	2.7	3	2	3	11	1	0	0	3	23	4	0	2.5	.867	P-12
1889		29	.204	.272	103	21	1	0	2	1.9	16	11	13	21	6	0	0	12	24	11	1	1.6	.766	P-29, 1B-1
1890	NY P	43	.315	.404	146	46	5	4	0	0.0	27	16	10	26	5	0	0	17	71	16	0	2.4	.846	P-43
1891	2 teams																							CIN AA (34G - .155) CIN N (15G - .109)
"	total	49	.141	.160	156	22	0	1	0	0.6	16	9	11	40	7	0	0	13	81	17	2	2.3	.847	P-47, OF-3
1892	NY N	48	.245	.264	163	40	1	1	0	0.0	20	14	11	30	1	0	0	28	69	23	4	2.5	.808	P-47, OF-1
1893	2 teams																							NY N (12G - .462) BKN N (3G - .400)
"	total	15	.452	.516	31	14	2	0	0	0.0	9	3	7	0	0	0	0	3	14	3	0	1.3	.850	P-12, OF-2, 1B-1
9 yrs.		391	.238	.329	1409	335	45	15	18	1.3	199	85	86	191		0	0	576	420	189	18	3.0	.841	P-204, OF-145, C-46, 1B-7

Sam Crane

CRANE, SAMUEL BYREN (Red)
B. Sept. 13, 1894, Harrisburg, Pa. D. Nov. 12, 1955, Philadelphia, Pa.
BR TR 5'11½" 154 lbs.

Year	Team	Games	BA	SA	AB	H	2B	3B	HR	HR%	R	RBI	BB	SO	SB	PH AB	PH H	PO	A	E	DP	TC/G	FA	G by Pos
1914	PHI A	2	.000	.000	6	0	0	0	0	0.0	0	0	2	3	0	0	0	5	8	1	0	7.0	.929	SS-2
1915		8	.087	.174	23	2	2	0	0	0.0	3	1	0	4	0	0	0	16	21	4	2	5.1	.902	SS-6, 2B-1
1916		2	.250	.250	4	1	0	0	0	0.0	0	1	0	2	0	0	0	1	5	0	0	3.0	1.000	SS-2
1917	WAS A	32	.179	.200	95	17	2	0	0	0.0	6	4	4	14	0	0	0	53	75	16	13	4.5	.889	SS-25, 3B-10, 2B-4, OF-3
1920	CIN N	54	.215	.243	144	31	0	0	0	0.0	20	9	7	9	5	0	0	65	91	11	14	3.1	.934	SS-32
1921		73	.233	.298	215	50	10	2	0	0.0	20	16	14	14	2	0	0	130	177	16	32	4.4	.950	SS-63, 3B-2, OF-1
1922	BKN N	3	.250	.375	8	2	1	0	0	0.0	1	0	1	0	0	0	0	8	13	3	2	8.0	.875	SS-3
7 yrs.		174	.208	.255	495	103	19	2	0	0.0	51	30	29	46	7	0	0	278	390	51	63	4.1	.929	SS-133, 3B-12, 2B-5, OF-4

Sam Crane

CRANE, SAMUEL NEWHALL
B. Jan. 2, 1854, Springfield, Mass. D. June 26, 1925, New York, N.Y.
Manager 1880, 1884.
BR TR

Year	Team	Games	BA	SA	AB	H	2B	3B	HR	HR%	R	RBI	BB	SO	SB	PH AB	PH H	PO	A	E	DP	TC/G	FA	G by Pos
1880	BUF N	10	.129	.129	31	4	0	0	0	0.0	4	2	1	8		0	0	31	27	9	5	6.7	.866	2B-10, OF-1
1883	NY AA	96	.235	.287	349	82	8	5	0	0.0	57		13			0	0	283	249	87	26	6.4	.859	2B-96, OF-1
1884	CIN U	80	.233	.291	309	72	9	3	1	0.3	56		11			0	0	224	217	73	27	6.4	.858	2B-80
1885	DET N	68	.192	.273	245	47	4	5	2	0.8	23	20	13	45		0	0	179	197	38	21	6.1	.908	2B-68
1886	2 teams																							DET N (47G - .141) STL N (39G - .172)
"	total	86	.153	.199	301	46	5	3	1	0.3	34	19	21	61		0	0	204	231	48	34	5.6	.901	2B-77, SS-8, OF-4
1887	WAS N	7	.300	.400	30	9	1	0	0	0.0	6	1	0	6	5	0	0	10	22	5	2	5.3	.865	SS-7

Year Team	Games	BA	SA	AB	H	2B	3B	HR	HR%	R	RBI	BB	SO	SB	Pinch Hit AB	Pinch Hit H	PO	A	E	DP	TC/G	FA	G by Pos

Ned Crompton *continued*

Year Team	Games	BA	SA	AB	H	2B	3B	HR	HR%	R	RBI	BB	SO	SB	AB	H	PO	A	E	DP	TC/G	FA	G by Pos
1910 CIN N	1	.000	.000	2	0	0	0	0	0.0	0	0	0	2	0	0	0	0	0	0	0	0.0	–	OF-1
2 yrs.	18	.154	.215	65	10	2	1	0	0.0	7	2	7	2	1	0	0	26	4	3	1	1.8	.909	OF-18

Bill Cronin

CRONIN, WILLIAM PATRICK (Crungy)
B. Dec. 26, 1902, West Newton, Mass. D. Oct. 26, 1966, Newton, Mass.
BR TR 5'8½" 167 lbs.

Year Team	Games	BA	SA	AB	H	2B	3B	HR	HR%	R	RBI	BB	SO	SB	AB	H	PO	A	E	DP	TC/G	FA	G by Pos
1928 BOS N	3	.000	.000	2	0	0	0	0	0.0	1	0	1	0	0	0	0	2	0	0	0	0.7	1.000	C-3
1929	6	.111	.111	9	1	0	0	0	0.0	0	0	0	0	0	0	0	11	2	0	0	2.2	1.000	C-6
1930	66	.253	.315	178	45	9	1	0	0.0	19	17	4	8	0	2	1	203	31	4	5	3.6	.983	C-64
1931	51	.206	.280	107	22	6	1	0	0.0	8	10	7	5	0	1	0	122	21	9	5	3.0	.941	C-50
4 yrs.	126	.230	.294	296	68	15	2	0	0.0	28	27	12	13	0	3	1	338	54	13	10	3.2	.968	C-123

Dan Cronin

CRONIN, DANIEL T.
B. Apr., 1857, Boston, Mass. D. Nov. 30, 1885, Boston, Mass.
5'8" 170 lbs.

Year Team	Games	BA	SA	AB	H	2B	3B	HR	HR%	R	RBI	BB	SO	SB	AB	H	PO	A	E	DP	TC/G	FA	G by Pos
1884 2 teams		CHI U (1G – .250)		STL U (1G – .000)																			
" total	2	.111	.111	9	1	0	0	0	0.0	1		0			0	0	1	0	6	1	3.5	.143	OF-1, 2B-1

Jim Cronin

CRONIN, JAMES JOHN
B. Aug. 7, 1905, Richmond, Calif. D. June 10, 1983, Concord, Calif.
BB TR 5'10½" 150 lbs.

Year Team	Games	BA	SA	AB	H	2B	3B	HR	HR%	R	RBI	BB	SO	SB	AB	H	PO	A	E	DP	TC/G	FA	G by Pos
1929 PHI A	25	.232	.304	56	13	2	1	0	0.0	7	4	5	7	0	0	0	30	56	4	11	3.6	.956	2B-10, SS-9, 3B-4

Joe Cronin

CRONIN, JOSEPH EDWARD
B. Oct. 12, 1906, San Francisco, Calif. D. Sept. 7, 1984, Osterville, Mass.
Manager 1933-47.
Hall of Fame 1956.
BR TR 5'11½" 180 lbs.

Year Team	Games	BA	SA	AB	H	2B	3B	HR	HR%	R	RBI	BB	SO	SB	AB	H	PO	A	E	DP	TC/G	FA	G by Pos
1926 PIT N	38	.265	.337	83	22	2	2	0	0.0	9	11	6	15	0	0	0	55	82	3	19	3.7	.979	2B-27, SS-7
1927	12	.227	.273	22	5	1	0	0	0.0	2	3	2	3	0	2	0	12	10	4	0	2.2	.846	2B-7, SS-4, 1B-1
1928 WAS A	63	.242	.322	227	55	10	4	0	0.0	23	25	22	27	4	0	0	133	190	16	42	5.4	.953	SS-63
1929	145	.281	.421	494	139	29	8	8	1.6	72	61	85	37	5	1	0	286	459	62	92	5.6	.923	SS-143, 2B-1
1930	154	.346	.513	587	203	41	9	13	2.2	127	126	72	36	17	0	0	336	509	35	95	5.7	.960	SS-154
1931	156	.306	.480	611	187	44	13	12	2.0	103	126	81	52	10	0	0	323	488	43	94	5.5	.950	SS-155
1932	143	.318	.492	557	177	43	18	6	1.1	95	116	66	45	7	1	1	306	448	32	95	5.5	.959	SS-141
1933	152	.309	.445	602	186	45	11	5	0.8	89	118	87	49	5	0	0	297	528	34	95	5.7	.960	SS-152
1934	127	.284	.421	504	143	30	9	7	1.4	68	101	53	28	8	0	0	246	486	38	86	6.1	.951	SS-127
1935 BOS A	144	.295	.460	556	164	37	14	9	1.6	70	95	63	40	3	3	0	264	431	37	86	5.1	.949	SS-139
1936	81	.281	.403	295	83	22	4	2	0.7	36	43	32	21	1	1	0	133	229	26	37	4.8	.933	SS-60, 3B-21
1937	148	.307	.486	570	175	40	4	18	3.2	102	110	84	73	5	0	0	300	414	31	89	5.0	.958	SS-148
1938	143	.325	.536	530	172	51	5	17	3.2	98	94	91	60	7	1	0	304	449	36	110	5.5	.954	SS-142
1939	143	.308	.492	520	160	33	3	19	3.7	97	107	87	48	6	0	0	306	437	32	93	5.4	.959	SS-142
1940	149	.285	.502	548	156	35	6	24	4.4	104	111	83	65	7	1	0	253	445	38	89	4.9	.948	SS-146, 3B-2
1941	143	.311	.508	518	161	38	8	16	3.1	98	95	82	55	1	3	1	247	362	27	67	4.4	.958	SS-119, 3B-22, OF-1
1942	45	.304	.494	79	24	3	0	4	5.1	7	24	15	21	0	25	6	47	28	6	7	1.8	.926	3B-11, 1B-5, SS-1
1943	59	.312	.558	77	24	4	0	5	6.5	8	29	11	4	0	42	18	12	18	1	1	0.5	.968	3B-10
1944	76	.241	.356	191	46	7	0	5	2.6	24	28	34	19	1	24	4	428	27	9	39	6.1	.981	1B-49
1945	3	.375	.375	8	3	0	0	0	0.0	1	1	3	2	0	0	0	2	8	0	2	3.3	1.000	3B-3
20 yrs.	2124	.301	.468	7579	2285	515	118	170	2.2	1233	1424	1059	700	87	104	30	4290	6048	510	1238	5.1	.953	SS-1843, 3B-69, 1B-55, 2B-35, OF-1

WORLD SERIES

Year Team	Games	BA	SA	AB	H	2B	3B	HR	HR%	R	RBI	BB	SO	SB	AB	H	PO	A	E	DP	TC/G	FA	G by Pos
1933 WAS A	5	.318	.318	22	7	0	0	0	0.0	1	2	0	2	0	0	0	7	15	1	3	4.6	.957	SS-5

Tom Crooke

CROOKE, THOMAS ALOYSIUS
B. July 26, 1884, Washington, D.C. D. Apr. 5, 1929, Quantico, Va.
BR TR 6' 180 lbs.

Year Team	Games	BA	SA	AB	H	2B	3B	HR	HR%	R	RBI	BB	SO	SB	AB	H	PO	A	E	DP	TC/G	FA	G by Pos
1909 WAS A	3	.286	.429	7	2	1	0	0	0.0	2	2	2		1	0	0	31	0	1	3	10.7	.969	1B-3
1910	8	.190	.238	21	4	1	0	0	0.0	1	1	1		0	2	1	49	2	0	2	6.4	1.000	1B-5
2 yrs.	11	.214	.286	28	6	2	0	0	0.0	3	3	3		1	2	1	80	2	1	5	7.5	.988	1B-8

Jack Crooks

CROOKS, JOHN CHARLES
B. Nov. 9, 1866, St. Paul, Minn. D. Jan. 29, 1918, St. Louis, Mo.
Manager 1892.
BR TR 170 lbs.

Year Team	Games	BA	SA	AB	H	2B	3B	HR	HR%	R	RBI	BB	SO	SB	AB	H	PO	A	E	DP	TC/G	FA	G by Pos
1889 COL AA	12	.326	.512	43	14	2	3	0	0.0	13	7	10	4	10	0	0	31	44	1	4	6.3	.987	2B-12
1890	135	.221	.254	485	107	5	4	1	0.2	86		96		57	0	0	354	350	49	57	5.6	.935	2B-133, 3B-2, OF-1
1891	138	.245	.331	519	127	19	13	0	0.0	110	46	103	47	50	0	0	399	404	36	72	6.1	.957	2B-138
1892 STL N	128	.213	.294	445	95	7	4	7	1.6	82	38	136	52	23	0	0	316	348	55	44	5.6	.924	2B-102, 3B-24, OF-2
1893	128	.237	.306	448	106	10	9	1	0.2	93	48	121	37	31	0	0	223	300	53	21	4.5	.908	3B-123, SS-4, C-1
1895 WAS N	117	.279	.408	409	114	19	8	6	1.5	80	57	68	39	36	0	0	327	364	32	43	6.2	.956	2B-117
1896 2 teams		WAS N (25G – .286)		LOU N (39G – .238)																			
" total	64	.257	.379	206	53	8	1	5	2.4	39	35	36	16	10	1	0	169	170	29	30	5.8	.921	2B-59, 3B-4
1898 STL N	72	.231	.280	225	52	4	2	1	0.4	33	20	40		3	0	0	203	224	19	24	6.2	.957	2B-66, 3B-3, SS-2, OF-1
8 yrs.	794	.240	.321	2780	668	74	44	21	0.8	536	251	610	195	220	1	0	2022	2204	274	295	5.7	.939	2B-627, 3B-156, SS-4, OF-4, C-1

Ed Crosby

CROSBY, EDWARD CARLTON
B. May 26, 1949, Long Beach, Calif.
BL TR 6'2" 175 lbs.

Year Team	Games	BA	SA	AB	H	2B	3B	HR	HR%	R	RBI	BB	SO	SB	AB	H	PO	A	E	DP	TC/G	FA	G by Pos
1970 STL N	38	.253	.316	95	24	4	1	0	0.0	9	6	7	5	0	2	1	44	91	7	17	3.7	.951	SS-35, 3B-3, 2B-2
1972	101	.217	.257	276	60	9	1	0	0.0	27	19	18	27	1	15	4	130	197	10	42	3.3	.970	SS-43, 2B-38, 3B-14
1973 2 teams		STL N (22G – .128)		CIN N (36G – .216)																			
" total	58	.178	.256	90	16	3	1	0	0.0	8	6	11	16	0	13	4	12	28	4	4	0.8	.909	SS-36, 2B-10, 3B-4
1974 CLE A	37	.209	.244	86	18	3	0	0	0.0	11	6	6	12	0	9	3	14	53	5	5	1.9	.931	3B-18, SS-13, 2B-3
1975	61	.234	.258	128	30	3	0	0	0.0	12	7	13	14	0	0	0	69	126	7	18	3.3	.965	SS-30, 2B-19, 3B-13

Year	Team		Games	BA	SA	AB	H	2B	3B	HR	HR%	R	RBI	BB	SO	SB	Pinch Hit AB	Pinch Hit H	PO	A	E	DP	TC/G	FA	G by Pos

Ed Crosby continued

Year	Team		Games	BA	SA	AB	H	2B	3B	HR	HR%	R	RBI	BB	SO	SB	AB	H	PO	A	E	DP	TC/G	FA	G by Pos
1976			2	.500	.500	2	1	0	0	0	0.0	0	0	0	0	0	0	0	0	2	0	0	1.0	1.000	DH-1, 3B-1
6 yrs.			297	.220	.264	677	149	22	4	0	0.0	67	44	55	74	1	39	8	269	497	33	86	2.7	.959	SS-157, 2B-72, 3B-53, DH-1

LEAGUE CHAMPIONSHIP SERIES

Year	Team		Games	BA	SA	AB	H	2B	3B	HR	HR%	R	RBI	BB	SO	SB	AB	H	PO	A	E	DP	TC/G	FA	G by Pos
1973	CIN	N	3	.500	.500	2	1	0	0	0	0.0	0	0	0	1	0	1	0	1	2	0	0	1.0	1.000	SS-2

Frankie Crosetti

CROSETTI, FRANK PETER JOSEPH (The Crow) BR TR 5'10" 165 lbs.
B. Oct. 4, 1910, San Francisco, Calif.

Year	Team		Games	BA	SA	AB	H	2B	3B	HR	HR%	R	RBI	BB	SO	SB	AB	H	PO	A	E	DP	TC/G	FA	G by Pos
1932	NY	A	115	.241	.374	398	96	20	9	5	1.3	47	57	51	51	3	2	0	187	260	29	51	4.1	.939	SS-83, 3B-33, 2B-1
1933			136	.253	.379	451	114	20	5	9	2.0	71	60	55	40	4	2	1	245	384	43	58	4.9	.936	SS-133
1934			138	.265	.401	554	147	22	10	11	2.0	85	67	61	58	5	2	1	263	389	39	79	5.0	.944	SS-119, 3B-23, 2B-1
1935			87	.256	.430	305	78	17	6	8	2.6	49	50	41	27	3	0	0	153	261	16	42	4.9	.963	SS-87
1936			151	.288	.437	632	182	35	7	15	2.4	137	78	90	83	18	0	0	320	463	43	95	5.5	.948	SS-151
1937			149	.234	.352	611	143	29	4	11	1.8	127	49	86	105	13	2	1	313	467	43	86	5.5	.948	SS-147
1938			157	.263	.371	631	166	35	3	9	1.4	113	55	106	99	27	0	0	352	506	47	120	5.8	.948	SS-157
1939			152	.233	.332	656	153	25	5	10	1.5	109	56	65	81	11	0	0	323	460	26	118	5.3	.968	SS-152
1940			145	.194	.273	546	106	23	4	4	0.7	84	31	72	77	14	0	0	246	396	31	73	4.6	.954	SS-145
1941			50	.223	.284	148	33	2	2	1	0.7	13	22	18	14	0	6	1	94	113	12	25	4.4	.945	SS-24
1942			74	.242	.337	285	69	5	5	4	1.4	50	23	31	31	1	1	0	95	139	12	25	3.3	.951	3B-62, SS-8, 2B-2
1943			95	.233	.279	348	81	8	1	2	0.6	36	20	36	47	4	4	1	194	260	26	58	5.1	.946	SS-90
1944			55	.239	.355	197	47	4	2	5	2.5	20	30	11	21	3	1	0	115	150	11	33	5.0	.960	SS-55
1945			130	.238	.293	441	105	12	0	4	0.9	57	48	59	65	7	3	1	264	380	37	86	5.2	.946	SS-126
1946			28	.288	.339	59	17	3	0	0	0.0	4	3	8	2	0	2	0	32	62	6	15	3.6	.940	SS-24
1947			3	.000	.000	1	0	0	0	0	0.0	0	0	0	0	0	1	0	0	0	0	0	0.0	—	SS-1, 2B-1
1948			17	.286	.429	14	4	0	1	0	0.0	4	0	2	0	0	5	1	6	6	0	4	0.7	1.000	2B-6, SS-5
17 yrs.			1682	.245	.354	6277	1541	260	65	98	1.6	1006	649	792	801	113	31	7	3202	4696	421	968	4.9	.949	SS-1515, 3B-131, 2B-11

WORLD SERIES

Year	Team		Games	BA	SA	AB	H	2B	3B	HR	HR%	R	RBI	BB	SO	SB	AB	H	PO	A	E	DP	TC/G	FA	G by Pos
1932	NY	A	4	.133	.200	15	2	1	0	0	0.0	2	0	2	3	0	0	0	9	12	4	0	6.3	.840	SS-4
1936			6	.269	.346	26	7	2	0	0	0.0	5	3	3	5	0	0	0	11	14	2	2	4.5	.926	SS-6
1937			5	.048	.048	21	1	0	0	0	0.0	2	0	2	4	0	0	0	6	17	0	1	4.6	1.000	SS-5
1938			4	.250	.688	16	4	1	0	1	6.3	1	6	2	4	0	0	0	16	10	1	4	6.8	.963	SS-4
1939			4	.063	.063	16	1	0	0	0	0.0	2	0	2	2	0	0	0	6	14	0	4	5.0	1.000	3B-1
1942			1	.000	.000	3	0	0	0	0	0.0	0	0	0	1	0	0	0	1	1	0	0	2.0	1.000	SS-5
1943			5	.278	.278	18	5	0	0	0	0.0	4	1	2	3	1	0	0	9	16	3	3	5.6	.893	SS-5
7 yrs.			29	.174	.261	115	20	5	1	1	0.9	16	11	14	20	1	0	0	58	84	10	13	5.2	.934	SS-28, 3B-1

Amos Cross

CROSS, AMOS C.
Brother of Lave Cross. Brother of Frank Cross.
B. 1861, Austria-Hungary   D. July 16, 1888, Cleveland, Ohio

Year	Team		Games	BA	SA	AB	H	2B	3B	HR	HR%	R	RBI	BB	SO	SB	AB	H	PO	A	E	DP	TC/G	FA	G by Pos
1885	LOU	AA	35	.285	.315	130	37	6	0	0		11		0			0	0	173	48	18	1	6.8	.925	C-35
1886			74	.276	.378	283	78	14	6	1	0.4	51		44			0	0	436	91	46	12	7.7	.920	C-51, 1B-20, SS-2, OF-1
1887			8	.107	.107	28	3	0	0	0	0.0	0		1		0	0	0	23	8	5	2	4.5	.861	C-5, 1B-2, OF-1
3 yrs.			117	.268	.342	441	118	16	7	1	0.2	62		45		0	0	0	632	147	69	15	7.2	.919	C-91, 1B-22, OF-2, SS-2

Clarence Cross

CROSS, CLARENCE (Cleary Daddy)
Born Clarence Crause.
B. Mar. 4, 1856, St. Louis, Mo.   D. June 23, 1931, Seattle, Wash.

Year	Team		Games	BA	SA	AB	H	2B	3B	HR	HR%	R	RBI	BB	SO	SB	AB	H	PO	A	E	DP	TC/G	FA	G by Pos
1884	3 teams	ALT U (2G – .571)				PHI U (2G – .222)				KC U (25G – .215)															
"	total		29	.239	.257	109	26	2	0	0	0.0	14		8			0	0	21	100	37	3	5.4	.766	SS-26, 3B-3
1887	NY	AA	16	.200	.273	55	11	2	1	0	0.0	9		2		0	0	0	14	36	10	2	3.8	.833	SS-13, 3B-4
2 yrs.			45	.226	.262	164	37	4	1	0	0.0	23		10		0	0	0	35	136	47	5	4.8	.784	SS-39, 3B-7

Frank Cross

CROSS, FRANK ATWELL (Mickey) TR
Brother of Amos Cross. Brother of Lave Cross.
B. Jan. 20, 1873, Cleveland, Ohio   D. Nov. 2, 1932, Geauga Lake, Ohio

Year	Team		Games	BA	SA	AB	H	2B	3B	HR	HR%	R	RBI	BB	SO	SB	AB	H	PO	A	E	DP	TC/G	FA	G by Pos
1901	CLE	A	1	.600	.600	5	3	0	0	0	0.0	0	0	0		0	0	0	0	0	0	0	0.0	—	OF-1

Jeff Cross

CROSS, JOFFRE JAMES BR TR 5'11" 160 lbs.
B. Aug. 28, 1918, Tulsa, Okla.

Year	Team		Games	BA	SA	AB	H	2B	3B	HR	HR%	R	RBI	BB	SO	SB	AB	H	PO	A	E	DP	TC/G	FA	G by Pos
1942	STL	N	1	.250	.250	4	1	0	0	0	0.0	0	1	0	1	0	0	0	0	3	0	0	3.0	1.000	SS-1
1946			49	.217	.261	69	15	3	0	0	0.0	17	6	10	8	4	3	0	41	50	4	10	1.9	.958	SS-17, 2B-8, 3B-1
1947			51	.102	.122	49	5	1	0	0	0.0	4	3	10	6	0	1	0	24	47	5	10	1.5	.934	3B-15, SS-14, 2B-2
1948	2 teams	STL N (2G – .000)				CHI N (16G – .100)																				
"	total		18	.100	.100	20	2	0	0	0	0.0	1	0	0	4	0	4	0	3	8	3	0	0.8	.786	SS-9, 2B-1
4 yrs.			119	.162	.190	142	23	4	0	0	0.0	22	10	20	18	4	8	0	68	108	12	20	1.6	.936	SS-41, 3B-16, 2B-11

Lave Cross

CROSS, LAFAYETTE NAPOLEON BR TR 5'8½" 155 lbs.
Brother of Frank Cross. Brother of Amos Cross.
B. May 12, 1866, Milwaukee, Wis.   D. Sept. 6, 1927, Toledo, Ohio
Manager 1899.

Year	Team		Games	BA	SA	AB	H	2B	3B	HR	HR%	R	RBI	BB	SO	SB	AB	H	PO	A	E	DP	TC/G	FA	G by Pos
1887	LOU	AA	54	.266	.335	203	54	8	3	0	0.0	32		15		15	0	0	267	67	34	8	6.8	.908	C-44, OF-10
1888			47	.227	.243	181	41	3	0	0	0.0	20	15	2		10	0	0	219	67	23	4	6.6	.926	C-37, OF-12, SS-2
1889	PHI	AA	55	.221	.281	199	44	8	2	0	0.0	22	23	14	9	11	0	0	278	102	27	7	7.4	.934	C-55
1890	PHI	P	63	.298	.429	245	73	7	8	3	1.2	42	47	12	6	5	0	0	216	70	38	7	5.1	.883	OF-43, C-43, 3B-24, SS-1
1891	PHI	AA	110	.301	.458	402	121	20	14	5	1.2	66	52	38	23	14	0	0	297	103	28	12	3.9	.935	3B-65, C-39, OF-25, 2B-14, SS-5
1892	PHI	N	140	.275	.362	541	149	15	10	4	0.7	84	69	39	16	18	0	0	327	236	35	17	4.3	.941	3B-65, C-39, OF-10, SS-10, 1B-6
1893			96	.299	.398	415	124	17	6	4	1.0	81	78	26	7	18	1	1	291	182	27	27	5.2	.946	C-40, 3B-30, OF-10, SS-10, 1B-6

Year	Team	Games	BA	SA	AB	H	2B	3B	HR	HR%	R	RBI	BB	SO	SB	Pinch Hit AB	H	PO	A	E	DP	TC/G	FA	G by Pos

Lave Cross *continued*

1894		119	.386	.524	529	204	34	9	7	1.3	123	125	29	7	21	0	0	226	259	39	29	4.4	.926	3B-100, C-16, SS-7, 2B-1
1895		125	.271	.364	535	145	26	9	2	0.4	95	101	35	8	21	0	0	191	308	32	23	4.2	.940	3B-125
1896		106	.256	.345	406	104	23	5	1	0.2	63	73	32	14	8	0	0	183	287	29	30	4.7	.942	3B-61, SS-37, 2B-6, OF-2, C-1
1897		88	.259	.363	344	89	17	5	3	0.9	37	51	10		10	0	0	143	217	23	15	4.4	.940	3B-47, 2B-38, OF-2, SS-1
1898	STL N	151	.317	.405	602	191	28	4	3	0.5	71	79	28		14	0	0	218	358	35	22	4.0	.943	3B-149, SS-2
1899	2 teams		CLE N (38G – .286)		STL N (103G – .303)																			3B-149, SS-2
"	total	141	.298	.377	557	166	19	5	5	0.9	76	84	25		13	0	0	223	358	25	32	4.3	.959	3B-141
1900	2 teams		STL N (16G – .295)		BKN N (117G – .293)																			3B-141
"	total	133	.293	.368	522	153	15	6	4	0.8	79	73	26		21	0	0	173	321	29	11	3.9	.945	3B-133
1901	PHI A	100	.331	.469	420	139	28	12	2	0.5	82	73	19		23	0	0	140	236	33	7	4.1	.919	3B-100
1902		137	.342	.440	559	191	39	8	0	0.0	90	108	27		25	0	0	185	306	30	18	3.8	.942	3B-137
1903		137	.292	.356	559	163	22	4	2	0.4	61	90	10		14	0	0	159	228	20	14	3.0	.951	3B-136, 1B-1
1904		155	.290	.379	607	176	31	10	1	0.2	73	71	13		10	0	0	164	247	28	15	2.8	.936	3B-155
1905		147	.266	.333	583	155	29	5	0	0.0	68	77	26		8	0	0	161	249	32	6	3.0	.928	3B-147
1906	WAS A	130	.263	.322	494	130	14	6	1	0.2	55	46	28		19	0	0	157	242	20	9	3.2	.952	3B-130
1907		41	.199	.248	161	32	8	0	0	0.0	13	10	10		3	0	0	38	98	3	2	3.4	.978	3B-41
21 yrs.		2275	.292	.382	9064	2644	411	135	47	0.5	1333	1345	464	90	301	1	1	4256	4541	590	315	4.1	.937	3B-1721, C-324, OF-119, SS-65, 2B-60, 1B-7

WORLD SERIES

| 1905 | PHI A | 5 | .105 | .105 | 19 | 2 | 0 | 0 | 0 | 0.0 | 0 | 0 | 1 | | 1 | 0 | 0 | 6 | 7 | 2 | 0 | 3.0 | .867 | 3B-5 |

Monte Cross

CROSS, MONTFORD MONTGOMERY
B. Aug. 31, 1869, Philadelphia, Pa. D. June 21, 1934, Philadelphia, Pa.   BR TR 6'2'' 180 lbs.

1892	BAL N	15	.160	.160	50	8	0	0	0	0.0	5	2	4		10	2	0	18	39	9	2	4.4	.864	SS-15
1894	PIT N	13	.442	.837	43	19	1	5	2	4.7	14	13	5		4	6	0	34	39	6	7	6.1	.924	SS-13
1895		108	.257	.382	393	101	14	13	3	0.8	67	54	38	38	39	0	0	256	327	77	42	6.1	.883	SS-107, 2B-1
1896	STL N	125	.244	.337	427	104	10	6	6	1.4	66	52	58	48	40	0	0	298	394	84	31	6.2	.892	SS-125
1897		131	.286	.396	462	132	17	11	4	0.9	59	55	62		38	0	0	327	513	73	47	7.0	.920	SS-131
1898	PHI N	149	.257	.330	525	135	25	5	1	0.2	68	50	55		20	0	0	404	506	93	65	6.7	.907	SS-149
1899		154	.257	.339	557	143	25	6	3	0.5	85	65	56		26	0	0	370	529	90	55	6.4	.909	SS-154
1900		131	.202	.258	466	94	11	3	0	0.0	59	62	51		19	0	0	339	459	62	68	6.6	.928	SS-131
1901		139	.197	.236	483	95	14	.1	1	0.2	49	44	52		24	0	0	343	445	65	31	6.1	.924	SS-139
1902	PHI A	137	.231	.302	497	115	22	2	3	0.6	72	59	32		17	0	0	373	466	66	37	6.6	.927	SS-137
1903		137	.247	.319	470	116	21	2	3	0.6	44	45	49		31	0	0	306	396	45	36	5.5	.940	SS-137, 2B-1
1904		153	.189	.256	503	95	23	4	1	0.2	33	38	46		19	0	0	276	424	47	26	4.9	.937	SS-153
1905		78	.270	.355	248	67	17	2	0	0.0	28	24	19		8	0	0	162	198	28	22	5.0	.928	SS-76, 2B-2
1906		134	.200	.272	445	89	23	3	1	0.2	32	40	50		22	0	0	305	411	47	48	5.7	.938	SS-134
1907		77	.206	.282	248	51	9	5	0	0.0	37	18	39		17	1	0	169	226	19	17	5.4	.954	SS-74
15 yrs.		1681	.234	.314	5817	1364	232	68	31	0.5	718	621	616	100	328	1	0	3980	5372	811	534	6.0	.920	SS-1675, 2B-4

WORLD SERIES

| 1905 | PHI A | 5 | .176 | .176 | 17 | 3 | 0 | 0 | 0 | 0.0 | 0 | 0 | 7 | | 0 | 0 | 0 | 12 | 13 | 2 | 0 | 5.4 | .926 | SS-5 |

Frank Crossin

CROSSIN, FRANK PATRICK
B. June 15, 1891, Avondale, Pa. D. Dec. 6, 1965, Kingston, Pa.   BR TR 5'10'' 160 lbs.

1912	STL A	8	.227	.227	22	5	0	0	0	0.0	2	2	1		1	0	0	17	6	2	0	3.1	.920	C-8
1913		4	.250	.250	4	1	0	0	0	0.0	1	0	1	1	0	2	1	5	1	1	0	1.8	.857	C-2
1914		43	.122	.156	90	11	1	1	0	0.0	5	5	10	10	3	2	0	141	42	13	6	4.6	.934	C-41
3 yrs.		55	.147	.172	116	17	1	1	0	0.0	8	7	12	11	4	4	1	163	49	16	6	4.1	.930	C-51

Joe Crotty

CROTTY, JOSEPH P.
B. Dec. 24, 1860, Cincinnati, Ohio D. June 22, 1926, Minneapolis, Minn.   BR TR

1882	2 teams		LOU AA (5G – .100)		STL AA (8G – .143)																			
"	total	13	.125	.146	48	6	1	0	0	0.0	3		3			0	0	59	17	10	4	6.6	.884	C-12, OF-1
1884	CIN U	21	.262	.393	84	22	4	2	1	1.2	11		1			0	0	90	31	14	0	6.4	.896	C-21
1885	LOU AA	39	.155	.171	129	20	2	0	0	0.0	14		3			0	0	199	51	22	3	7.0	.919	C-38, 1B-1
1886	NY AA	14	.170	.213	47	8	0	1	0	0.0	6		4			0	0	60	23	6	1	6.4	.933	C-14
4 yrs.		87	.182	.234	308	56	7	3	1	0.3	34		11			0	0	408	122	52	8	6.7	.911	C-85, OF-1, 1B-1

Jack Crouch

CROUCH, JACK ALBERT (Roxy)
B. June 12, 1903, Salisbury, N.C. D. Aug. 25, 1972, Leesburg, Fla.   BR TR 5'9'' 165 lbs.

1930	STL A	6	.143	.214	14	2	1	0	0	0.0	1	1	3		0	0	0	19	5	0	0	3.7	1.000	C-5
1931		8	.000	.000	12	0	0	0	0	0.0	0	1	1	4	0	1	0	15	2	2	0	2.4	.895	C-7
1933	2 teams		STL A (19G – .167)		CIN N (10G – .125)																			
"	total	29	.152	.217	46	7	0	1	2	2.2	6	6	2	6	1	10	1	32	9	0	1	1.4	1.000	C-15
3 yrs.		43	.125	.181	72	9	1	1	2	1.4	7	8	3	13	1	11	1	66	14	2	1	1.9	.976	C-27

Frank Croucher

CROUCHER, FRANK DONALD (Dingle)
B. July 23, 1914, San Antonio, Tex. D. May 21, 1980, Houston, Tex.   BR TR 5'11'' 165 lbs.

1939	DET A	97	.269	.361	324	87	15	0	5	1.5	38	40	16	42	2	2	0	144	264	29	50	4.5	.934	SS-93, 2B-3
1940		37	.105	.105	57	6	0	0	0	0.0	3	2	4	5	2	5	0	23	30	5	3	1.6	.914	SS-26, 2B-7, 3B-1
1941		136	.254	.325	489	124	21	4	2	0.4	51	39	33	72	0	0	0	270	361	44	85	5.0	.935	SS-136
1942	WAS A	26	.277	.323	65	18	1	1	0	0.0	2	5	3	9	0	7	2	35	60	5	9	3.8	.950	2B-18
4 yrs.		296	.251	.324	935	235	37	5	7	0.7	94	86	56	128	4	14	2	472	715	83	147	4.3	.935	SS-255, 2B-28, 3B-1

WORLD SERIES

| 1940 | DET A | 1 | – | – | 0 | 0 | 0 | 0 | 0 | – | 0 | 0 | 0 | 0 | 0 | 0 | 0 | 0 | 0 | 0 | 0 | 0.0 | – | SS-1 |

Buck Crouse

CROUSE, CLYDE ELSWORTH
B. Jan. 6, 1897, Anderson, Ind. D. Oct. 23, 1983, Muncie, Ind.   BL TR 5'8'' 158 lbs.

Year	Team	Games	BA	SA	AB	H	2B	3B	HR	HR%	R	RBI	BB	SO	SB	Pinch Hit AB	Pinch Hit H	PO	A	E	DP	TC/G	FA	G by Pos

Buck Crouse *continued*

Year	Team	Games	BA	SA	AB	H	2B	3B	HR	HR%	R	RBI	BB	SO	SB	AB	H	PO	A	E	DP	TC/G	FA	G by Pos
1923	CHI A	23	.257	.357	70	18	2	1	1	1.4	6	7	3	4	0	0	0	66	18	4	1	3.8	.955	C-22
1924		94	.259	.308	305	79	10	1	1	0.3	30	44	23	12	3	4	0	298	97	23	9	4.4	.945	C-90
1925		54	.351	.450	131	46	7	0	2	1.5	18	25	12	4	1	6	2	104	36	7	5	2.7	.952	C-48
1926		49	.237	.281	135	32	4	1	0	0.0	10	17	14	7	0	3	0	164	34	3	1	4.1	.985	C-45
1927		85	.239	.288	222	53	11	0	0	0.0	22	20	21	10	4	4	2	202	79	8	10	3.4	.972	C-81
1928		78	.252	.321	218	55	5	2	2	0.9	17	20	19	14	3	2	0	196	61	11	3	3.4	.959	C-76
1929		45	.271	.393	107	29	7	0	2	1.9	11	12	5	7	2	4	0	111	29	3	5	3.2	.979	C-40
1930		42	.254	.339	118	30	8	1	0	0.0	14	15	17	10	1	3	0	155	31	4	4	4.5	.979	C-38
8 yrs.		470	.262	.331	1306	342	54	6	8	0.6	128	160	114	68	14	26	4	1296	385	63	37	3.7	.964	C-440

Don Crow

CROW, DONALD LEROY   BR TR 6'4" 185 lbs.
B. Aug. 18, 1958, Yakima, Wash.

Year	Team	Games	BA	SA	AB	H	2B	3B	HR	HR%	R	RBI	BB	SO	SB	AB	H	PO	A	E	DP	TC/G	FA	G by Pos
1982	LA N	4	.000	.000	4	0	0	0	0	0.0	0	0	0	3	0	0	0	9	1	0	0	2.5	1.000	C-4

George Crowe

CROWE, GEORGE DANIEL   BL TL 6'2" 210 lbs.
B. Mar. 22, 1923, Whiteland, Ind.

Year	Team	Games	BA	SA	AB	H	2B	3B	HR	HR%	R	RBI	BB	SO	SB	AB	H	PO	A	E	DP	TC/G	FA	G by Pos
1952	BOS N	73	.258	.382	217	56	13	1	4	1.8	25	20	18	25	0	17	5	476	42	8	40	7.2	.985	1B-55
1953	MIL N	47	.286	.476	42	12	2	0	2	4.8	6	6	2	7	0	37	9	17	2	0	1	0.4	1.000	1B-9
1955		104	.281	.495	303	85	12	4	15	5.0	41	55	45	44	1	21	5	677	61	8	62	7.2	.989	1B-79
1956	CIN N	77	.250	.486	144	36	2	1	10	6.9	22	23	11	28	0	43	11	225	25	3	15	3.3	.988	1B-32
1957		133	.271	.504	494	134	20	1	31	6.3	71	92	32	62	1	13	5	932	86	11	86	7.7	.989	1B-120
1958		111	.275	.400	345	95	12	5	7	2.0	31	61	41	51	0	20	8	714	53	6	66	7.0	.992	1B-93, 2B-1
1959	STL N	77	.301	.592	103	31	6	0	8	7.8	14	29	5	12	0	**63**	**17**	82	12	0	9	1.2	1.000	1B-14
1960		73	.236	.444	72	17	3	0	4	5.6	5	13	5	16	0	61	15	21	2	0	1	0.3	1.000	1B-5
1961		7	.143	.143	7	1	0	0	0	0.0	0	0	0	1	0	7	1	0	0	0	0	0.0	—	—
9 yrs.		702	.270	.466	1727	467	70	12	81	4.7	215	299	159	246	3	282	76	3144	283	36	280	4.9	.990	1B-407, 2B-1

Bill Crowley

CROWLEY, WILLIAM MICHAEL   BR TR 5'7½" 159 lbs.
B. Apr. 8, 1857, Philadelphia, Pa.   D. July 14, 1891, Gloucester, N. J.

Year	Team	Games	BA	SA	AB	H	2B	3B	HR	HR%	R	RBI	BB	SO	SB	AB	H	PO	A	E	DP	TC/G	FA	G by Pos
1877	LOU N	61	.282	.357	238	67	9	3	1	0.4	30	23	4	13		0	0	123	27	25	2	2.9	.857	OF-58, SS-2, C-2, 3B-1, 2B-1
1879	BUF N	60	.287	.360	261	75	9	5	0	0.0	41	30	6	14		0	0	182	37	33	12	4.2	.869	OF-43, C-10, 1B-7, 2B-3
1880		85	.268	.336	354	95	16	4	0	0.0	57	20	19	23		0	0	204	46	50	3	3.5	.833	OF-74, C-22
1881	BOS N	72	.254	.297	279	71	12	0	0	0.0	33	31	14	15		0	0	130	17	20	5	2.3	.880	OF-72
1883	2 teams			PHI AA (23G – .250)					CLE N	(11G – .293)														
"	total	34	.263	.372	137	36	9	3	0	0.0	19		4	7		0	0	59	3	11	0	2.1	.849	OF-33, 1B-1
1884	BOS N	108	.270	.378	407	110	14	6	6	1.5	50		33	74		0	0	125	22	22	5	1.6	.870	OF-108
1885	BUF N	92	.241	.297	344	83	14	1	1	0.3	29	36	21	32		0	0	152	8	23	1	2.0	.874	OF-92
7 yrs.		512	.266	.341	2020	537	83	22	8	0.4	259	140	101	178		0	0	975	160	184	28	2.6	.861	OF-480, C-34, 1B-8, 2B-4, SS-2, 3B-1

Ed Crowley

CROWLEY, EDGAR JEWEL   BR TR 6'1" 180 lbs.
B. Aug. 6, 1906, Watkinsville, Ga.   D. Apr. 14, 1970, Birmingham, Ala.

Year	Team	Games	BA	SA	AB	H	2B	3B	HR	HR%	R	RBI	BB	SO	SB	AB	H	PO	A	E	DP	TC/G	FA	G by Pos
1928	WAS A	2	.000	.000	1	0	0	0	0	0.0	0	0	0	0	0	0	0	0	0	1	0	0.5	—	3B-1

John Crowley

CROWLEY, JOHN A.   5'10" 164 lbs.
B. Jan. 12, 1862, Lawrence, Mass.   D. Sept. 23, 1896, Lawrence, Mass.

Year	Team	Games	BA	SA	AB	H	2B	3B	HR	HR%	R	RBI	BB	SO	SB	AB	H	PO	A	E	DP	TC/G	FA	G by Pos
1884	PHI N	48	.244	.321	168	41	7	3	0	0.0	26		15	21		0	0	198	49	50	2	6.2	.832	C-48

Terry Crowley

CROWLEY, TERRENCE MICHAEL   BL TL 6' 180 lbs.
B. Feb. 16, 1947, Staten Island, N. Y.

Year	Team	Games	BA	SA	AB	H	2B	3B	HR	HR%	R	RBI	BB	SO	SB	AB	H	PO	A	E	DP	TC/G	FA	G by Pos
1969	BAL A	7	.333	.333	18	6	0	0	0	0.0	2	3	1	4	0	2	0	23	2	0	3	3.6	1.000	1B-3, OF-2
1970		83	.257	.388	152	39	5	0	5	3.3	25	20	35	26	2	31	9	138	6	2	9	1.8	.986	OF-27, 1B-23
1971		18	.174	.174	23	4	0	0	0	0.0	2	1	3	4	0	9	4	7	0	0	0	0.4	1.000	OF-6, 1B-2
1972		97	.231	.405	247	57	10	0	11	4.5	30	29	32	26	0	19	4	170	8	1	7	1.8	.994	OF-68, 1B-15
1973		54	.206	.305	131	27	4	0	3	2.3	16	15	16	14	0	14	3	33	5	3	3	0.8	.927	DH-23, OF-10, 1B-7
1974	CIN N	84	.240	.360	125	30	12	0	1	0.8	11	20	10	16	1	52	10	56	5	2	0	0.8	.968	OF-22, 1B-7
1975		66	.268	.394	71	19	6	0	1	1.4	8	11	7	6	0	49	13	43	4	0	4	0.7	1.000	OF-4, 1B-4
1976	2 teams			ATL N (7G – .000)					BAL A	(33G – .246)														
"	total	40	.224	.239	67	15	1	0	0	0.0	5	6	7	11	0	23	4	13	2	0	1	0.4	1.000	DH-17, 1B-1
1977	BAL A	18	.364	.545	22	8	1	0	1	4.5	3	9	1	3	0	15	7	3	0	0	0	0.2	1.000	DH-7, OF-2, 1B-1
1978		62	.253	.294	95	24	2	0	0	0.0	9	12	8	12	0	38	13	1	1	0	0	0.0	1.000	DH-17, OF-2, 1B-1
1979		61	.317	.476	63	20	5	1	1	1.6	8	8	14	13	0	39	11	5	0	0	1	0.1	1.000	DH-15, 1B-2
1980		92	.288	.476	233	67	8	0	12	5.2	33	50	29	21	0	**37**	**11**	19	5	0	1	0.3	1.000	DH-65, 1B-3
1981		68	.246	.381	134	33	6	0	4	3.0	12	25	29	12	0	21	6	30	2	0	2	0.5	1.000	DH-42, 1B-4
1982		65	.237	.355	93	22	2	0	3	3.2	3	8	21	9	0	35	7	74	6	1	12	1.2	.988	DH-14, 1B-10
1983	MON N	50	.182	.182	44	8	0	0	0	0.0	2	3	9	4	0	35	6	19	0	0	2	0.4	1.000	1B-4
15 yrs.		865	.250	.375	1518	379	62	1	42	2.8	174	229	222	181	3	419 (7th)	108 (8th)	634	46	9	45	0.8	.987	DH-195, OF-141, 1B-87

LEAGUE CHAMPIONSHIP SERIES

Year	Team	Games	BA	SA	AB	H	2B	3B	HR	HR%	R	RBI	BB	SO	SB	AB	H	PO	A	E	DP	TC/G	FA	G by Pos
1973	BAL A	2	.000	.000	2	0	0	0	0	0.0	0	0	0	0	0	2	0	1	0	0	0	0.5	1.000	OF-1
1975	CIN N	1	—	—	0	0	0	0	0	—	0	0	0	0	0	0	0	0	0	0	0	0.0	—	—
1979	BAL A	2	.500	.500	2	1	0	0	0	0.0	0	1	0	0	0	2	1	0	0	0	0	0.0	—	—
3 yrs.		5	.250	.250	4	1	0	0	0	0.0	0	1	0	0	0	4	1	1	0	0	0	0.2	1.000	OF-1

WORLD SERIES

Year	Team	Games	BA	SA	AB	H	2B	3B	HR	HR%	R	RBI	BB	SO	SB	AB	H	PO	A	E	DP	TC/G	FA	G by Pos
1970	BAL A	1	.000	.000	1	0	0	0	0	0.0	0	0	0	1	0	1	0	0	0	0	0	0.0	—	—
1975	CIN N	2	.500	.500	2	1	0	0	0	0.0	0	0	0	0	0	2	1	0	0	0	0	0.0	—	—
1979	BAL A	5	.250	.500	4	1	1	0	0	0.0	0	2	1	0	0	4	1	0	0	0	0	0.0	—	—
3 yrs.		8	.286	.429	7	2	1	0	0	0.0	0	2	1	1 (6th)	0	7	2	0	0	0	0	0.0	—	—

Year	Team	Games	BA	SA	AB	H	2B	3B	HR	HR%	R	RBI	BB	SO	SB	Pinch Hit AB	H	PO	A	E	DP	TC/G	FA	G by Pos

Walt Cruise

CRUISE, WALTON EDWIN
B. May 6, 1890, Childersburg, Ala. D. Jan. 9, 1975, Sylacauga, Ala.
BL TR 6' 175 lbs.

Year	Team	Games	BA	SA	AB	H	2B	3B	HR	HR%	R	RBI	BB	SO	SB	PH AB	PH H	PO	A	E	DP	TC/G	FA	G by Pos
1914	STL N	95	.227	.332	256	58	9	3	4	1.6	20	28	25	42	3	11	3	158	6	4	1	1.8	.976	OF-81
1916		3	.667	.667	3	2	0	0	0	0.0	0	0	0	1	0	1	1	2	0	0	0	0.7	1.000	OF-2
1917		153	.295	.399	529	156	20	10	5	0.9	70	59	38	73	16	1	1	285	15	11	6	2.0	.965	OF-152
1918		70	.271	.400	240	65	5	4	6	2.5	34	39	30	26	2	5	0	103	4	4	0	1.6	.964	OF-65
1919	2 teams		STL N (9G – .095)			BOS N (73G – .216)																		
"	total	82	.206	.248	262	54	8	1	1	0.4	23	21	18	35	8	9	2	135	8	4	1	1.8	.973	OF-71, 1B-2
1920	BOS N	91	.278	.347	288	80	7	5	1	0.3	40	21	31	26	5	6	1	122	10	7	3	1.5	.950	OF-82
1921		108	.346	.503	344	119	16	7	8	2.3	47	55	48	24	10	3	2	252	4	9	3	2.5	.966	OF-102, 1B-2
1922		104	.278	.412	352	98	15	10	4	1.1	51	46	44	20	4	2	0	237	11	12	4	2.5	.954	OF-100, 1B-2
1923		21	.211	.263	38	8	2	0	0	0.0	4	0	3	2	1	9	2	20	0	1	0	1.0	.952	OF-9
1924		9	.444	.889	9	4	1	0	1	11.1	4	3	0	2	0	9	4	0	0	0	0	0.0	–	
	10 yrs.	736	.277	.386	2321	644	83	39	30	1.3	293	272	238	250	49	56	16	1314	58	52	18	1.9	.963	OF-664, 1B-6

Gene Crumling

CRUMLING, EUGENE LEON
B. Apr. 5, 1922, Wrightsville, Pa.
BR TR 6' 180 lbs.

Year	Team	Games	BA	SA	AB	H	2B	3B	HR	HR%	R	RBI	BB	SO	SB	PH AB	PH H	PO	A	E	DP	TC/G	FA	G by Pos
1945	STL N	6	.083	.083	12	1	0	0	0	0.0	0	1	0	1	0	0	0	16	4	0	0	3.3	1.000	C-6

Buddy Crump

CRUMP, ARTHUR ELLIOTT
B. Nov. 29, 1901, Norfolk, Va. D. Sept. 7, 1976, Raleigh, N. C.
BL TL 5'10" 156 lbs.

Year	Team	Games	BA	SA	AB	H	2B	3B	HR	HR%	R	RBI	BB	SO	SB	PH AB	PH H	PO	A	E	DP	TC/G	FA	G by Pos
1924	NY N	1	.000	.000	4	0	0	0	0	0.0	0	1	0	1	0	0	0	2	0	2	0	4.0	.500	OF-1

Press Cruthers

CRUTHERS, CHARLES PRESTON
B. Sept. 8, 1890, Marshallton, Del. D. Dec. 27, 1976, Kenosha, Wis.
BR TR 5'9" 152 lbs.

Year	Team	Games	BA	SA	AB	H	2B	3B	HR	HR%	R	RBI	BB	SO	SB	PH AB	PH H	PO	A	E	DP	TC/G	FA	G by Pos
1913	PHI A	3	.250	.333	12	3	1	0	0	0.0	0	0	0	0	0	0	0	7	5	1	1	4.3	.923	2B-3
1914		4	.200	.333	15	3	0	1	0	0.0	0	1	0	4	0	0	0	13	11	0	1	6.0	1.000	2B-4
	2 yrs.	7	.222	.333	27	6	1	1	0	0.0	0	1	0	4	0	0	0	20	16	1	2	5.3	.973	2B-7

Hector Cruz

CRUZ, HECTOR LOUIS (Heity)
Born Hector Louis Cruz y Dilan. Brother of Jose Cruz.
Brother of Tommy Cruz.
B. Apr. 2, 1953, Arroyo, Puerto Rico
BR TR 5'11" 170 lbs.

Year	Team	Games	BA	SA	AB	H	2B	3B	HR	HR%	R	RBI	BB	SO	SB	PH AB	PH H	PO	A	E	DP	TC/G	FA	G by Pos
1973	STL N	11	.000	.000	11	0	0	0	0	0.0	1	0	1	3	0	4	0	7	0	0	0	0.6	1.000	OF-5
1975		23	.146	.271	48	7	2	2	0	0.0	7	6	2	4	0	6	1	20	4	3	0	1.2	.889	3B-12, OF-6
1976		151	.228	.338	526	120	17	1	13	2.5	54	71	42	119	1	3	0	100	270	26	19	2.6	.934	3B-148
1977		118	.236	.357	339	80	19	2	6	1.8	50	42	46	56	2	15	2	154	10	7	2	1.4	.959	OF-106, 3B-2
1978	2 teams		CHI N (30G – .237)			SF N (79G – .223)																		
"	total	109	.227	.370	273	62	13	1	8	2.9	27	33	24	45	0	30	7	117	32	2	3	1.4	.987	OF-67, 3B-21
1979	2 teams		SF N (16G – .120)			CIN N (74G – .242)																		
"	total	90	.227	.353	207	47	10	2	4	1.9	26	28	34	46	0	16	2	11	2	1	0	0.2	.929	OF-75, 3B-2
1980	CIN N	52	.213	.333	75	16	4	1	1	1.3	5	5	8	16	0	22	1	42	0	2	0	0.8	.955	OF-29
1981	CHI N	53	.229	.468	109	25	5	0	7	6.4	15	15	17	24	2	17	3	33	26	3	0	1.2	.952	3B-18, OF-16
1982		17	.211	.263	19	4	1	0	0	0.0	1	0	2	4	0	15	3	1	0	0	0	0.1	1.000	OF-4
	9 yrs.	624	.225	.353	1607	361	71	9	39	2.4	186	200	176	317	5	128	19	485	344	44	24	1.4	.950	OF-308, 3B-203

LEAGUE CHAMPIONSHIP SERIES

Year	Team	Games	BA	SA	AB	H	2B	3B	HR	HR%	R	RBI	BB	SO	SB	PH AB	PH H	PO	A	E	DP	TC/G	FA	G by Pos
1979	CIN N	2	.200	.400	5	1	0	1	0	0.0	1	0	0	1	0	1	1	3	0	0	0	1.5	1.000	OF-1

Henry Cruz

CRUZ, HENRY ACOSTA
B. Feb. 27, 1952, Christiansted, Virgin Islands
BL TL 6' 175 lbs.

Year	Team	Games	BA	SA	AB	H	2B	3B	HR	HR%	R	RBI	BB	SO	SB	PH AB	PH H	PO	A	E	DP	TC/G	FA	G by Pos
1975	LA N	53	.266	.319	94	25	3	1	0	0.0	8	5	7	6	1	14	2	48	0	2	0	0.9	.960	OF-41
1976		49	.182	.364	88	16	2	1	4	4.5	8	14	9	11	0	20	3	39	1	1	1	0.8	.976	OF-23
1977	CHI A	16	.286	.571	21	6	0	0	2	9.5	3	5	1	3	0	1	0	5	0	1	0	0.4	.833	OF-9
1978		53	.221	.351	77	17	2	1	2	2.6	13	10	8	11	0	11	1	55	4	0	2	1.1	1.000	OF-40, DH-1
	4 yrs.	171	.229	.361	280	64	7	3	8	2.9	32	34	25	31	1	46	6	147	5	4	3	0.9	.974	OF-113, DH-1

Jose Cruz

CRUZ, JOSE (Cheo)
Born Jose Cruz y Dilan. Brother of Tommy Cruz.
Brother of Hector Cruz.
B. Aug. 8, 1947, Arroyo, Puerto Rico
BL TL 6' 170 lbs.

Year	Team	Games	BA	SA	AB	H	2B	3B	HR	HR%	R	RBI	BB	SO	SB	PH AB	PH H	PO	A	E	DP	TC/G	FA	G by Pos
1970	STL N	6	.353	.412	17	6	1	0	0	0.0	2	1	4	0	0	1	1	16	0	0	0	2.7	1.000	OF-4
1971		83	.274	.425	292	80	13	2	9	3.1	46	27	49	35	6	2	1	197	2	5	1	2.5	.975	OF-83
1972		117	.235	.319	332	78	14	4	2	0.6	33	23	36	54	9	13	5	220	9	5	5	2.0	.979	OF-102
1973		132	.227	.379	406	92	22	5	10	2.5	51	57	51	66	10	14	3	276	2	6	1	2.2	.979	OF-118
1974		107	.261	.416	161	42	4	3	5	3.1	24	20	20	27	4	47	11	81	2	2	3	0.8	.976	OF-53, 1B-1
1975	HOU N	120	.257	.403	315	81	15	2	9	2.9	44	49	52	44	6	28	6	187	6	4	0	1.6	.980	OF-94
1976		133	.303	.401	439	133	21	5	4	0.9	49	61	53	46	28	10	3	265	10	8	4	2.1	.972	OF-125
1977		157	.299	.475	579	173	31	10	17	2.9	87	87	69	67	44	4	1	311	11	9	1	2.1	.973	OF-155
1978		153	.315	.460	565	178	34	9	10	1.8	79	83	57	57	37	1	0	328	5	8	1	2.2	.977	OF-152, 1B-2
1979		157	.289	.421	558	161	33	7	9	1.6	73	72	72	66	36	1	0	320	7	14	0	2.2	.959	OF-156
1980		160	.302	.426	612	185	29	7	11	1.8	79	91	60	66	36	2	0	323	16	11	1	2.2	.969	OF-158
1981		107	.267	.425	409	109	16	5	13	3.2	53	55	35	49	5	2	0	237	5	4	2	2.3	.984	OF-105
1982		155	.275	.377	570	157	27	2	9	1.6	62	68	60	67	21	2	1	340	9	13	3	2.3	.964	OF-155
1983		160	.318	.463	594	189	28	8	14	2.4	85	92	65	86	30	2	1	322	9	7	1	2.1	.979	OF-160
1984		160	.312	.462	600	187	28	13	12	2.0	96	95	73	68	22	1	0	310	11	8	1	2.1	.976	OF-160
1985		141	.300	.426	544	163	34	4	9	1.7	69	79	43	74	16	3	0	257	12	8	3	2.0	.971	OF-137
1986		141	.278	.403	479	133	22	4	10	2.1	48	72	55	86	3	8	1	237	5	4	1	1.7	.984	OF-134
1987		126	.241	.400	365	88	17	4	11	3.0	47	38	36	65	4	29	4	178	5	3	0	1.5	.984	OF-97
1988	NY A	38	.200	.263	80	16	2	0	1	1.3	9	7	2	19	3	16	3					0.2	.889	DH-12, OF-8
	19 yrs.	2353	.284	.420	7917	2251	391	94	165	2.1	1036	1077	898	1031	317	189	43	4413	126	120	31	2.0	.974	OF-2156, DH-12, 1B-3

DIVISIONAL PLAYOFF SERIES

Year	Team	Games	BA	SA	AB	H	2B	3B	HR	HR%	R	RBI	BB	SO	SB	PH AB	PH H	PO	A	E	DP	TC/G	FA	G by Pos
1981	HOU N	5	.300	.350	20	6	1	0	0	0.0	0	0	1	3	1	0	0	5	0	1	0	0.2	–	OF-5

Year	Team	Games	BA	SA	AB	H	2B	3B	HR	HR%	R	RBI	BB	SO	SB	Pinch Hit AB	Pinch Hit H	PO	A	E	DP	TC/G	FA	G by Pos

Jose Cruz *continued*

LEAGUE CHAMPIONSHIP SERIES

Year	Team	Games	BA	SA	AB	H	2B	3B	HR	HR%	R	RBI	BB	SO	SB	AB	H	PO	A	E	DP	TC/G	FA	G by Pos
1980	HOU N	5	.400	.600	15	6	1	1	0	0.0	3	4	8	1	0	0	0	19	0	0	0	3.8	1.000	OF-5
1986		6	.192	.192	26	5	0	0	0	0.0	0	2	1	8	0	0	0	11	0	0	0	1.8	1.000	OF-6
2 yrs.		11	.268	.341	41	11	1	1	0	0.0	3	6	9	9	0	0	0	30	0	0	0	2.7	1.000	OF-11

Julio Cruz

CRUZ, JULIO LOUIS
B. Dec. 2, 1954, Brooklyn, N. Y.

BB TR 5'9"   165 lbs.

Year	Team	Games	BA	SA	AB	H	2B	3B	HR	HR%	R	RBI	BB	SO	SB	AB	H	PO	A	E	DP	TC/G	FA	G by Pos
1977	SEA A	60	.256	.296	199	51	3	1	1	0.5	25	7	24	29	15	2	0	114	171	5	29	4.8	.983	2B-54, DH-1
1978		147	.235	.269	550	129	14	1	1	0.2	77	25	69	66	59	0	0	295	482	11	104	5.4	.986	2B-141, SS-5, DH-1
1979		107	.271	.326	414	112	16	2	1	0.2	70	29	62	61	49	0	0	258	361	13	87	5.9	.979	2B-107
1980		119	.209	.258	422	88	9	3	2	0.5	66	16	59	49	45	0	0	269	355	11	85	5.3	.983	2B-115, DH-3
1981		94	.256	.324	352	90	12	3	2	0.6	57	24	39	40	43	1	0	240	297	11	72	5.8	.980	2B-92, SS-1
1982		154	.242	.344	549	133	22	5	8	1.5	83	49	57	71	46	0	0	322	438	10	98	5.0	.987	2B-151, DH-2, SS-2, 3B-1
1983	2 teams		SEA A	(61G – .254)		CHI A	(99G – .251)																	
"	total	160	.252	.326	515	130	19	5	3	0.6	71	52	49	66	57	1	1	141	187	5	43	2.1	.985	2B-157, DH-1
1984	CHI A	143	.222	.311	415	92	14	4	5	1.2	42	43	45	58	14	0	0	273	452	18	92	5.2	.976	2B-141
1985		91	.197	.231	234	46	2	3	0	0.0	28	15	32	40	8	6	3	158	220	7	59	4.2	.982	2B-87, DH-2
1986		81	.215	.225	209	45	2	0	0	0.0	38	19	42	28	7	0	0	132	205	5	45	4.2	.985	2B-78, DH-3
10 yrs.		1156	.237	.299	3859	916	113	27	23	0.6	557	279	478	508	343	10	4	2202	3168	96	714	4.7	.982	2B-1123, DH-13, SS-8, 3B-1

LEAGUE CHAMPIONSHIP SERIES

Year	Team	Games	BA	SA	AB	H	2B	3B	HR	HR%	R	RBI	BB	SO	SB	AB	H	PO	A	E	DP	TC/G	FA	G by Pos
1983	CHI A	4	.333	.333	12	4	0	0	0	0.0	0	3	4	2	0	0	0	10	14	0	2	6.0	1.000	2B-4

Todd Cruz

CRUZ, TODD RUBEN
B. Nov. 23, 1955, Highland Park, Mich.

BR TR 6'   175 lbs.

Year	Team	Games	BA	SA	AB	H	2B	3B	HR	HR%	R	RBI	BB	SO	SB	AB	H	PO	A	E	DP	TC/G	FA	G by Pos
1978	PHI N	3	.500	.500	4	2	0	0	0	0.0	0	2	0	0	0	0	0	1	6	0	0	2.3	1.000	SS-2
1979	KC A	55	.203	.314	118	24	7	0	2	1.7	9	15	3	19	0	0	0	54	118	7	16	3.3	.961	SS-48, 3B-9
1980	2 teams		CAL A	(18G – .275)		CHI A	(90G – .232)																	
"	total	108	.237	.312	333	79	14	1	3	0.9	28	23	14	62	2	2	1	156	323	28	68	4.7	.945	SS-102, 3B-4, OF-1, 2B-1
1982	SEA A	136	.230	.376	492	113	20	2	16	3.3	44	57	12	95	2	0	0	215	439	25	98	5.0	.963	SS-136
1983	2 teams		SEA A	(65G – .190)		BAL A	(81G – .208)																	
"	total	146	.199	.311	437	87	13	3	10	2.3	37	48	22	108	4	5	2	103	235	12	43	2.4	.966	3B-79, SS-63, 2B-2
1984	BAL A	96	.218	.310	142	31	4	0	3	2.1	15	9	8	33	1	14	5	23	104	6	10	1.4	.955	3B-89, DH-1, P-1
6 yrs.		544	.220	.333	1526	336	58	6	34	2.2	133	154	59	317	9	21	8	552	1225	78	235	3.4	.958	SS-351, 3B-181, 2B-3, DH-1, OF-1, P-1

LEAGUE CHAMPIONSHIP SERIES

Year	Team	Games	BA	SA	AB	H	2B	3B	HR	HR%	R	RBI	BB	SO	SB	AB	H	PO	A	E	DP	TC/G	FA	G by Pos
1983	BAL A	4	.133	.133	15	2	0	0	0	0.0	0	1	0	5	0	0	0	6	11	0	1	4.3	1.000	3B-4

WORLD SERIES

Year	Team	Games	BA	SA	AB	H	2B	3B	HR	HR%	R	RBI	BB	SO	SB	AB	H	PO	A	E	DP	TC/G	FA	G by Pos
1983	BAL A	5	.125	.125	16	2	0	0	0	0.0	1	0	0	3	0	0	0	0	17	2	1	3.8	.895	3B-5

Tommy Cruz

CRUZ, CIRILIO
Born Cirilo Cruz y Dilan.   Brother of Jose Cruz.
Brother of Hector Cruz.
B. Feb. 15, 1951, Arroyo, Puerto Rico

BL TL 5'9"   165 lbs.

Year	Team	Games	BA	SA	AB	H	2B	3B	HR	HR%	R	RBI	BB	SO	SB	AB	H	PO	A	E	DP	TC/G	FA	G by Pos
1973	STL N	3	–	–	0	0	0	0	0	–	1	0	0	0	0	0	0	0	0	0	0	0.0	–	OF-1
1977	CHI A	4	.000	.000	2	0	0	0	0	0.0	1	0	0	0	0	1	0	1	0	0	0	0.3	1.000	OF-2
2 yrs.		7	.000	.000	2	0	0	0	0	0.0	2	0	0	0	0	1	0	1	0	0	0	0.1	1.000	OF-3

Mike Cubbage

CUBBAGE, MICHAEL LEE
B. July 21, 1950, Charlottesville, Va.

BL TR 6'   180 lbs.

Year	Team	Games	BA	SA	AB	H	2B	3B	HR	HR%	R	RBI	BB	SO	SB	AB	H	PO	A	E	DP	TC/G	FA	G by Pos
1974	TEX A	9	.000	.000	15	0	0	0	0	0.0	0	0	0	4	0	4	0	7	9	1	4	1.9	.941	3B-3, 2B-2
1975		58	.224	.350	143	32	6	0	4	2.8	12	21	18	14	0	16	1	68	115	8	24	3.3	.958	2B-37, 3B-3, DH-2
1976	2 teams		TEX A	(14G – .219)		MIN A	(104G – .260)																	
"	total	118	.257	.358	374	96	15	1	3	0.8	42	49	49	44	1	8	3	80	218	19	25	2.7	.940	3B-100, DH-8, 2B-7
1977	MIN A	129	.264	.391	417	110	16	5	9	2.2	60	55	37	49	1	13	2	90	266	18	29	2.9	.952	3B-126, DH-1
1978		125	.282	.401	394	111	12	7	7	1.8	40	57	40	44	3	22	8	69	237	9	25	2.5	.971	3B-115, 2B-5
1979		94	.276	.350	243	67	10	1	2	0.8	26	23	39	26	1	17	3	38	94	10	9	1.5	.930	3B-63, DH-21, 2B-1, 1B-1
1980		103	.246	.361	285	70	9	0	8	2.8	29	42	23	37	0	9	1	545	100	4	64	6.3	.994	1B-72, 3B-32, DH-1, 2B-1
1981	NY N	67	.213	.325	80	17	2	2	1	1.3	9	4	9	15	0	44	12	5	21	1	0	0.4	.963	3B-12
8 yrs.		703	.258	.369	1951	503	74	20	34	1.7	218	251	215	233	6	133	33	902	1060	70	180	2.9	.966	3B-454, 1B-73, 2B-53, DH-33

Al Cuccinello

CUCCINELLO, ALFRED EDWARD
Brother of Tony Cuccinello.
B. Nov. 26, 1914, Long Island City, N. Y.

BR TR 5'10"   165 lbs.

Year	Team	Games	BA	SA	AB	H	2B	3B	HR	HR%	R	RBI	BB	SO	SB	AB	H	PO	A	E	DP	TC/G	FA	G by Pos
1935	NY N	54	.248	.376	165	41	7	1	4	2.4	27	20	1	20		3	2	114	140	13	26	4.9	.951	2B-48, 3B-2

Tony Cuccinello

CUCCINELLO, ANTHONY FRANCIS (Chick)
Brother of Al Cuccinello.
B. Nov. 8, 1907, Long Island City, N. Y.

BR TR 5'7"   160 lbs.

Year	Team	Games	BA	SA	AB	H	2B	3B	HR	HR%	R	RBI	BB	SO	SB	AB	H	PO	A	E	DP	TC/G	FA	G by Pos
1930	CIN N	125	.312	.451	443	138	22	5	10	2.3	64	78	47	44	5	3	1	111	211	26	23	2.8	.925	3B-109, 2B-15, SS-4
1931		154	.315	.431	575	181	39	11	2	0.3	69	93	54	28	1	0	0	376	499	28	128	5.9	.969	2B-154
1932	BKN N	154	.281	.415	597	168	32	6	12	2.0	76	77	46	47	5	0	0	385	525	25	113	6.1	.973	2B-154
1933		134	.252	.388	485	122	31	4	9	1.9	58	65	44	40	4	0	0	329	359	17	67	5.3	.976	2B-120, 3B-14
1934		140	.261	.409	528	138	32	2	14	2.7	59	94	49	45	0	1	1	300	417	21	60	5.3	.972	2B-101, 3B-43
1935		102	.292	.431	360	105	20	3	8	2.2	49	53	40	35	3	4	1	192	250	13	57	4.5	.971	2B-64, 3B-36
1936	BOS N	150	.308	.402	565	174	26	3	7	1.2	68	86	58	49	1	0	0	383	559	28	128	6.5	.971	2B-150
1937		152	.271	.405	575	156	36	4	11	1.9	77	80	61	40	2	0	0	330	524	29	92	5.8	.967	2B-151
1938		147	.265	.366	555	147	25	2	6	1.6	62	76	52	32	1	0	0	323	458	21	84	5.5	.974	2B-147

Year	Team	Games	BA	SA	AB	H	2B	3B	HR	HR%	R	RBI	BB	SO	SB	Pinch Hit AB	Pinch Hit H	PO	A	E	DP	TC/G	FA	G by Pos

Tony Cuccinello *continued*

Year	Team	Games	BA	SA	AB	H	2B	3B	HR	HR%	R	RBI	BB	SO	SB	PH AB	PH H	PO	A	E	DP	TC/G	FA	G by Pos
1939		81	.306	.387	310	95	17	1	2	0.6	42	40	26	26	5	1	0	208	246	14	66	5.8	.970	2B-80
1940	2 teams	BOS N (34G – .270)			NY N (88G – .208)																			
"	total	122	.226	.312	433	98	18	2	5	1.2	40	55	24	51	2	6	1	166	268	9	28	3.6	.980	3B-70, 2B-47
1942	BOS N	40	.202	.260	104	21	3	0	1	1.0	8	8	9	11	1	5	2	34	67	4	13	2.6	.962	3B-20, 2B-14
1943	2 teams	BOS N (13G – .000)			CHI A (34G – .272)																			
"	total	47	.230	.320	122	28	5	0	2	1.6	5	13	16	14	3	7	0	40	60	4	7	2.2	.962	3B-34, 2B-2, SS-1
1944	CHI A	38	.262	.285	130	34	3	0	0	0.0	5	17	8	10	2	0	0	42	73	5	7	3.2	.958	3B-30, 2B-6
1945		118	.308	.400	402	124	25	3	2	0.5	50	49	45	19	6	6	1	73	221	20	22	2.7	.936	3B-112
15 yrs.		1704	.280	.394	6184	1729	334	46	94	1.5	730	884	579	497	42	36	7	3292	4737	264	895	4.9	.968	2B-1205, 3B-468, SS-5

Jim Cudworth

CUDWORTH, JAMES ALARIC
B. Aug. 22, 1858, Fairhaven, Mass.   D. Dec. 21, 1943, Middleboro, Mass.   BR TR 6'   165 lbs.

Year	Team	Games	BA	SA	AB	H	2B	3B	HR	HR%	R	RBI	BB	SO	SB	PH AB	PH H	PO	A	E	DP	TC/G	FA	G by Pos
1884	KC U	32	.147	.190	116	17	3	1	0	0.0	7		2			0	0	202	9	8	10	6.8	.963	1B-19, OF-12, P-2

Manuel Cueto

CUETO, MANUEL MELO
Born Manuel Cueto y Melo.
B. Feb. 8, 1892, Guanajay, Cuba   D. June 29, 1942, Regla, Cuba   BR TR 5'5"   157 lbs.

Year	Team	Games	BA	SA	AB	H	2B	3B	HR	HR%	R	RBI	BB	SO	SB	PH AB	PH H	PO	A	E	DP	TC/G	FA	G by Pos
1914	STL F	19	.093	.093	43	4	0	0	0	0.0	2	5			0	0	0	23	22	6	3	2.7	.882	3B-10, SS-5, 2B-2
1917	CIN N	56	.200	.243	140	28	3	0	1	0.7	10	11	16	17	4	5	0	89	26	5	1	2.1	.958	OF-38, 2B-6, C-5
1918		46	.296	.361	108	32	5	1	0	0.0	14	14	19	5	4	2	0	59	43	6	2	2.3	.944	OF-19, 2B-10, SS-9, C-6
1919		29	.250	.273	88	22	2	0	0	0.0	10	4	10	4	5	3	0	49	8	2	3	2.0	.966	OF-25, 3B-1
4 yrs.		150	.227	.266	379	86	10	1	1	0.3	36	31	50	26	13	11	0	220	99	19	9	2.3	.944	OF-82, 2B-18, SS-14, 3B-11, C-11

John Cuff

CUFF, JOHN J.
B. 1864, Jersey City, N. J.   Deceased.

Year	Team	Games	BA	SA	AB	H	2B	3B	HR	HR%	R	RBI	BB	SO	SB	PH AB	PH H	PO	A	E	DP	TC/G	FA	G by Pos
1884	BAL U	3	.091	.182	11	1	1	0	0	0.0	1		1			0	0	12	11	2	1	8.3	.920	C-3

Leon Culberson

CULBERSON, DELBERT LEON
B. Aug. 6, 1919, Hall's Station, Ga.   D. Sept. 17, 1989, Rome, Ga.   BR TR 5'11"   180 lbs.

Year	Team	Games	BA	SA	AB	H	2B	3B	HR	HR%	R	RBI	BB	SO	SB	PH AB	PH H	PO	A	E	DP	TC/G	FA	G by Pos
1943	BOS A	81	.272	.391	312	85	16	6	3	1.0	36	34	31	35	14	1	0	211	10	5	2	2.8	.978	OF-79
1944		75	.238	.333	282	67	11	5	2	0.7	41	21	20	20	6	1	0	182	6	4	2	2.6	.979	OF-72
1945		97	.275	.429	331	91	21	6	6	1.8	26	45	20	37	4	6	1	219	14	8	6	2.5	.967	OF-91
1946		59	.313	.430	179	56	10	1	3	1.7	34	18	16	19	3	4	0	89	10	5	2	1.8	.952	OF-49, 3B-4
1947		47	.238	.250	84	20	1	0	0	0.0	10	11	12	10	1	20	3	36	6	2	1	0.9	.955	OF-25, 3B-4
1948	WAS A	12	.172	.172	29	5	0	0	0	0.0	1	2	8	5	0	1	0	16	1	0	0	1.4	1.000	OF-11
6 yrs.		371	.266	.379	1217	324	59	18	14	1.2	148	131	107	126	28	33	4	753	47	24	13	2.2	.971	OF-327, 3B-8

WORLD SERIES

Year	Team	Games	BA	SA	AB	H	2B	3B	HR	HR%	R	RBI	BB	SO	SB	PH AB	PH H	PO	A	E	DP	TC/G	FA	G by Pos
1946	BOS A	5	.222	.556	9	2	0	0	1	11.1	1	1	1	2	1	2	0	7	0	0	0	1.4	1.000	OF-3

John Cullen

CULLEN, JOHN J.

Year	Team	Games	BA	SA	AB	H	2B	3B	HR	HR%	R	RBI	BB	SO	SB	PH AB	PH H	PO	A	E	DP	TC/G	FA	G by Pos
1884	WIL U	9	.194	.194	31	6	0	0	0	0.0	2		1			0	0	9	8	9	0	2.9	.654	OF-6, SS-3

Tim Cullen

CULLEN, TIMOTHY LEO
B. Feb. 16, 1942, San Francisco, Calif.   BR TR 6'1"   185 lbs.

Year	Team	Games	BA	SA	AB	H	2B	3B	HR	HR%	R	RBI	BB	SO	SB	PH AB	PH H	PO	A	E	DP	TC/G	FA	G by Pos
1966	WAS A	18	.235	.265	34	8	1	0	0	0.0	8	0	2	8	0	6	1	14	19	2	4	1.9	.943	3B-8, 2B-5
1967		124	.236	.269	402	95	7	0	2	0.5	35	31	40	47	4	2	0	219	361	27	67	4.9	.956	SS-69, 2B-46, 3B-15, OF-1
1968	2 teams	CHI A (72G – .200)			WAS A (47G – .272)																			
"	total	119	.230	.320	269	62	11	2	3	1.1	24	29	22	35	0	4	2	173	247	16	51	3.7	.963	2B-87, SS-33, 3B-3
1969	WAS A	119	.209	.249	249	52	7	0	1	0.4	22	15	14	27	1	10	2	173	211	10	47	3.3	.975	2B-105, SS-9, 3B-1
1970		123	.214	.279	262	56	10	2	1	0.4	22	18	31	38	3	12	1	212	265	3	65	3.9	.994	2B-112, SS-6
1971		125	.191	.258	403	77	13	4	2	0.5	34	26	33	47	2	1	0	262	379	11	86	5.2	.983	2B-78, SS-62
1972	OAK A	72	.261	.331	142	37	8	1	0	0.0	10	15	5	17	0	3	1	107	121	11	24	3.3	.954	2B-65, 3B-4, SS-1
7 yrs.		700	.220	.278	1761	387	57	9	9	0.5	155	134	147	219	10	38	7	1160	1603	80	344	4.1	.972	2B-498, SS-180, 3B-31, OF-1

LEAGUE CHAMPIONSHIP SERIES

Year	Team	Games	BA	SA	AB	H	2B	3B	HR	HR%	R	RBI	BB	SO	SB	PH AB	PH H	PO	A	E	DP	TC/G	FA	G by Pos
1972	OAK A	2	.000	.000	1	0	0	0	0	0.0	0	0	0	0	0	0	0	2	0	0	1	1.0	1.000	SS-2

Roy Cullenbine

CULLENBINE, ROY JOSEPH
B. Oct. 18, 1915, Nashville, Tenn.   BB TR 6'1"   195 lbs.
BL 1938,1941

Year	Team	Games	BA	SA	AB	H	2B	3B	HR	HR%	R	RBI	BB	SO	SB	PH AB	PH H	PO	A	E	DP	TC/G	FA	G by Pos
1938	DET A	25	.284	.388	67	19	1	3	0	0.0	12	9	12	9	2	7	2	34	1	0	0	1.4	1.000	OF-17
1939		75	.240	.413	179	43	9	2	6	3.4	31	23	34	29	0	25	4	104	4	9	5	1.6	.923	OF-46, 1B-2
1940	2 teams	BKN N (22G – .180)			STL A (86G – .230)																			
"	total	108	.220	.346	318	70	12	2	8	2.5	49	40	73	45	2	21	3	191	10	3	6	1.9	.985	OF-76, 1B-6
1941	STL A	149	.317	.465	501	159	29	9	9	1.8	82	98	121	43	6	9	3	451	32	14	24	3.3	.972	OF-120, 1B-22
1942	3 teams	STL A (38G – .193)			WAS A (64G – .286)			NY A (21G – .364)																
"	total	123	.276	.400	427	118	33	1	6	1.4	61	62	92	40	1	6	1	226	80	16	10	2.6	.950	OF-77, 3B-28, 1B-6
1943	CLE A	138	.289	.404	488	141	24	4	8	1.6	66	56	96	58	3	5	0	376	23	7	15	2.9	.983	OF-121, 1B-13
1944		154	.284	.445	571	162	34	5	16	2.8	98	80	87	49	4	2	0	275	15	10	6	1.9	.967	OF-151
1945	2 teams	CLE A (8G – .077)			DET A (146G – .277)																			
"	total	154	.272	.444	536	146	28	5	18	3.4	83	93	112	36	2	1	0	329	26	8	3	2.4	.978	OF-150, 3B-3
1946	DET A	113	.335	.537	328	110	21	0	15	4.6	63	56	88	39	2	9	2	293	30	8	15	2.9	.976	OF-81, 1B-21
1947		142	.224	.422	464	104	18	1	24	5.2	82	78	137	51	3	4	0	1184	139	15	111	9.4	.989	1B-138
10 yrs.		1181	.276	.432	3879	1072	209	32	110	2.8	627	599	852	399	26	89	18	3463	360	90	195	3.3	.977	OF-839, 1B-208, 3B-31

WORLD SERIES

Year	Team	Games	BA	SA	AB	H	2B	3B	HR	HR%	R	RBI	BB	SO	SB	PH AB	PH H	PO	A	E	DP	TC/G	FA	G by Pos
1942	NY A	5	.263	.316	19	5	1	0	0	0.0	3	2	1	2	1	0	0	6	0	0	0	1.2	1.000	OF-5
1945	DET A	7	.227	.318	22	5	2	0	0	0.0	5	4	8	2	1	0	0	8	0	0	0	1.1	1.000	OF-7
2 yrs.		12	.244	.317	41	10	3	0	0	0.0	8	6	9	4	2	0	0	14	0	0	0	1.2	1.000	OF-12

Year	Team		Games	BA	SA	AB	H	2B	3B	HR	HR%	R	RBI	BB	SO	SB	Pinch Hit AB	Pinch Hit H	PO	A	E	DP	TC/G	FA	G by Pos

Dick Culler

CULLER, RICHARD BROADUS
B. Jan. 15, 1915, High Point, N. C.   D. June 16, 1964, Chapel Hill, N. C.
BR TR 5'9½" 155 lbs.

1936	PHI	A	9	.237	.237	38	9	0	0	0	0.0	3	1	1	3	0	0	0	20	19	2	4	4.6	.951	2B-7, SS-2
1943	CHI	A	53	.216	.264	148	32	5	1	0	0.0	9	11	16	11	4	0	0	71	121	8	24	3.8	.960	3B-26, 2B-19, SS-3
1944	BOS	N	8	.071	.071	28	2	0	0	0	0.0	2	0	4	2	0	0	0	14	33	5	6	6.5	.904	SS-8
1945			136	.262	.300	527	138	12	1	2	0.4	87	30	50	35	7	1	0	261	400	34	81	5.1	.951	SS-126, 3B-6
1946			134	.255	.299	482	123	15	3	0	0.0	70	33	62	18	7	2	1	279	380	36	68	5.2	.948	SS-132
1947			77	.248	.280	214	53	5	1	0	0.0	20	19	19	15	1	1	1	106	212	11	31	4.3	.967	SS-75
1948	CHI	N	48	.169	.191	89	15	2	0	0	0.0	4	5	13	3	0	1	0	68	115	6	18	3.9	.968	SS-43, 2B-2
1949	NY	N	7	.000	.000	1	0	0	0	0	0.0	0	0	1	0	0	0	0	3	5	1	2	1.3	.889	SS-7
8 yrs.			472	.244	.281	1527	372	39	6	2	0.1	195	99	166	87	19	5	2	822	1285	103	234	4.7	.953	SS-396, 3B-32, 2B-28

Nick Cullop

CULLOP, HENRY NICHOLAS (Tomato Face)
B. Oct. 16, 1900, St. Louis, Mo.   D. Dec. 8, 1978, Gahanna, Ohio
BR TR 6' 200 lbs.

1926	NY	A	2	.500	.500	2	1	0	0	0	0.0	0	0	0	1	0	2	1	0	0	0	0	0.0	–	
1927	2 teams		47	WAS A	(15G – .217)			CLE A	(32G – .235)																
"	total		47	.231	.374	91	21	4	3	1	1.1	11	9	10	25	0	19	5	59	4	1	0	1.4	.984	OF-25, 1B-1, P-1
1929	BKN	N	13	.195	.415	41	8	2	1	2	4.9	7	5	8	7	0	1	0	26	2	0	0	2.2	1.000	OF-11, 1B-1
1930	CIN	N	7	.182	.318	22	4	0	0	1	4.5	2	5	1	9	0	2	0	7	2	0	1	1.3	1.000	OF-5
1931			104	.263	.446	334	88	23	7	8	2.4	29	48	21	86	1	19	3	177	5	6	3	1.7	.968	OF-83
5 yrs.			173	.249	.424	490	122	29	12	11	2.2	49	67	40	128	1	43	9	269	13	7	3	1.7	.976	OF-124, 1B-2, P-1

Wil Culmer

CULMER, WILFRED HILLARD
B. Nov. 11, 1958, Nassau, Bahamas
BR TR 6'4" 210 lbs.

| 1983 | CLE | A | 7 | .105 | .105 | 19 | 2 | 0 | 0 | 0 | 0.0 | 1 | 0 | 4 | 0 | 0 | 0 | 0 | 2 | 0 | 0 | 0 | 0.3 | 1.000 | OF-4, DH-2 |

Benny Culp

CULP, BENJAMIN BALDY
B. Jan. 19, 1914, Philadelphia, Pa.
BR TR 5'9" 175 lbs.

1942	PHI	N	1	–	–	0	0	0	0	0	–	0	0	0	0	0	0	0	1	0	1	0	2.0	.500	C-1
1943			10	.208	.250	24	5	1	0	0	0.0	4	2	3	3	0	0	0	21	2	1	0	2.4	.958	C-10
1944			4	.000	.000	2	0	0	0	0	0.0	1	0	0	0	0	1	0	0	1	0	0	0.3	1.000	C-1
3 yrs.			15	.192	.231	26	5	1	0	0	0.0	5	2	3	3	0	1	0	22	3	2	0	1.8	.926	C-12

Jack Cummings

CUMMINGS, JOHN WILLIAM
B. Apr. 1, 1904, Pittsburgh, Pa.   D. Oct. 5, 1962, West Mifflin, Pa.
BR TR 6' 195 lbs.

1926	NY	N	7	.313	.500	16	5	3	0	0	0.0	3	4	4	2	0	1	1	16	7	1	1	3.4	.958	C-6
1927			43	.363	.538	80	29	6	1	2	2.5	8	14	5	10	0	8	3	64	10	2	1	1.8	.974	C-34
1928			33	.333	.630	27	9	2	0	2	7.4	4	9	3	4	0	25	8	5	0	1	0	0.2	.833	C-4
1929	2 teams		6	NY	N	(3G – .333)		BOS	N	(3G – .167)															
"	total		6	.222	.222	9	2	0	0	0	0.0	0	1	0	2	0	2	1	5	0	2	0	1.2	.714	C-4
4 yrs.			89	.341	.530	132	45	11	1	4	3.0	15	28	12	18	0	36	12	90	17	6	2	1.3	.947	C-48

Bill Cunningham

CUNNINGHAM, WILLIAM ALOYSIUS
B. July 30, 1895, San Francisco, Calif.   D. Sept. 26, 1953, Colusa, Calif.
BR TR 5'8" 155 lbs.

1921	NY	N	40	.276	.368	76	21	2	1	1	1.3	10	12	3	3	0	18	5	35	1	0	0	0.9	1.000	OF-20
1922			85	.328	.437	229	75	15	2	2	0.9	37	33	7	9	4	13	3	155	7	2	3	1.9	.988	OF-70, 3B-1
1923			79	.271	.389	203	55	7	1	5	2.5	22	27	10	9	5	6	0	127	16	1	2	1.8	.993	OF-68, 2B-4
1924	BOS	N	114	.272	.350	437	119	15	8	1	0.2	44	40	32	27	8	5	0	243	16	8	3	2.3	.970	OF-109
4 yrs.			318	.286	.381	945	270	39	12	9	1.0	113	112	52	48	17	42	8	560	40	11	8	1.9	.982	OF-267, 2B-4, 3B-1

WORLD SERIES

1922	NY	N	4	.200	.200	10	2	0	0	0	0.0	0	2	2	1	0	0	0	10	2	0	0	3.0	1.000	OF-4
1923			4	.143	.143	7	1	0	0	0	0.0	0	1	0	0	0	1	0	2	0	1	0	0.8	.667	OF-3
2 yrs.			8	.176	.176	17	3	0	0	0	0.0	0	3	2	1	0	1	0	12	2	1	0	1.9	.933	OF-7

Bill Cunningham

CUNNINGHAM, WILLIAM JAMES
B. June 9, 1888, Schenectady, N. Y.   D. Feb. 21, 1946, Schenectady, N. Y.
BR TR 5'9" 170 lbs.

1910	WAS	A	22	.297	.392	74	22	5	1	0	0.0	3	14	12					36	52	4	7	4.2	.957	2B-22
1911			94	.190	.278	331	63	10	5	3	0.9	34	37	19		10	1	0	168	244	30	18	4.7	.932	2B-93
1912			7	.185	.333	27	5	1	0	1	3.7	5	8	3		2	0	0	8	17	1	1	3.7	.962	2B-7
3 yrs.			123	.208	.301	432	90	16	6	4	0.9	42	59	34		16	1	0	212	313	35	26	4.6	.938	2B-122

George Cunningham

CUNNINGHAM, GEORGE HAROLD
B. July 13, 1894, Sturgeon Lake, Minn.   D. Mar. 10, 1972, Chattanooga, Tenn.
BR TR 5'11" 185 lbs.

1916	DET	A	35	.268	.415	41	11	2	2	0	0.0	7	3	8	12	0	0	0	6	46	2	2	1.5	.963	P-35
1917			44	.176	.265	34	6	0	0	1	2.9	5	3	3	13	0	0	0	4	43	4	3	1.2	.922	P-44
1918			56	.223	.277	112	25	4	1	0	0.0	11	2	16	34	2	8	3	21	35	5	1	1.1	.918	P-27, OF-20
1919			26	.217	.217	23	5	0	0	0	0.0	4	5	9	8	0	6	1	2	16	3	1	0.8	.857	P-17
1921			1	–	–	0	0	0	0	0	0.0	0	0	0	0	0	0	0	1	0	0	0	1.0	1.000	OF-1
5 yrs.			162	.224	.295	210	47	6	3	1	0.5	27	13	36	67	2	14	4	34	140	14	7	1.2	.926	P-123, OF-21

Joe Cunningham

CUNNINGHAM, JOSEPH ROBERT
B. Aug. 27, 1931, Paterson, N. J.
BL TL 6' 180 lbs.

1954	STL	N	85	.284	.445	310	88	11	3	11	3.5	40	50	43	40	1	0	0	814	68	10	96	10.5	.989	1B-85
1956			4	.000	.000	3	0	0	0	0	0.0	1	0	1	1	0	2	0	2	0	0	0	0.5	1.000	1B-1
1957			122	.318	.479	261	83	15	0	9	3.4	50	52	56	29	3	29	11	360	18	3	17	3.1	.992	1B-57, OF-46
1958			131	.312	.496	337	105	20	3	12	3.6	61	57	82	23	4	19	5	418	26	3	21	3.4	.993	1B-67, OF-66
1959			144	.345	.478	458	158	28	6	7	1.5	65	60	88	47	6	8	2	359	14	7	23	2.6	.982	OF-121, 1B-35
1960			139	.280	.386	492	138	28	3	6	1.2	68	39	59	59	1	9	2	298	16	10	8	2.3	.969	OF-116, 1B-15
1961			113	.286	.398	322	92	11	2	7	2.2	40	40	53	32	1	20	5	200	3	5	9	1.8	.976	OF-86, 1B-10
1962	CHI	A	149	.295	.428	526	155	32	7	8	1.5	91	70	101	59	3	3	1	1287	90	8	118	9.3	.994	1B-143, OF-5
1963			67	.286	.367	210	60	12	1	1	0.5	32	31	33	23	1	6	4	535	24	6	39	8.4	.989	1B-58

Year	Team	Games	BA	SA	AB	H	2B	3B	HR	HR%	R	RBI	BB	SO	SB	Pinch Hit AB	Pinch Hit H	PO	A	E	DP	TC/G	FA	G by Pos

Joe Cunningham *continued*

Year	Team	Games	BA	SA	AB	H	2B	3B	HR	HR%	R	RBI	BB	SO	SB	PH AB	PH H	PO	A	E	DP	TC/G	FA	G by Pos
1964	2 teams	CHI A (40G – .250)			WAS A (49G – .214)																			
"	total	89	.231	.278	234	54	11	0	0	0.0	28	17	37	28	0	14	1	580	29	2	53	6.9	.997	1B-74
1965	WAS A	95	.229	.328	201	46	9	1	3	1.5	29	20	46	27	0	27	5	393	24	6	44	4.5	.986	1B-59
1966		3	.125	.125	8	1	0	0	0	0.0	0	0	0	1	0	0	0	10	4	0	1	4.7	1.000	1B-3
12 yrs.		1141	.291	.417	3362	980	177	26	64	1.9	525	436	599	369	16	137	36	5256	316	60	429	4.9	.989	1B-607, OF-440

Ray Cunningham

CUNNINGHAM, RAYMOND LEE
B. Jan. 17, 1908, Mesquite, Tex.   BR TR 5'7½" 150 lbs.

Year	Team	Games	BA	SA	AB	H	2B	3B	HR	HR%	R	RBI	BB	SO	SB	PH AB	PH H	PO	A	E	DP	TC/G	FA	G by Pos
1931	STL N	3	.000	.000	4	0	0	0	0	0.0	0	1	0	0	0	0	0	0	5	0	0	1.7	1.000	3B-3
1932		11	.182	.227	22	4	1	0	0	0.0	4	0	3	4	0	1	0	11	15	0	1	2.4	1.000	3B-8, 2B-2
2 yrs.		14	.154	.192	26	4	1	0	0	0.0	4	1	3	4	0	1	0	11	20	0	1	2.2	1.000	3B-11, 2B-2

Doc Curley

CURLEY, WALTER JAMES
B. Mar. 12, 1874, Upton, Mass.   D. Sept. 23, 1920, Framingham, Mass.   BR TR

Year	Team	Games	BA	SA	AB	H	2B	3B	HR	HR%	R	RBI	BB	SO	SB	PH AB	PH H	PO	A	E	DP	TC/G	FA	G by Pos
1899	CHI N	10	.108	.162	37	4	0	1	0	0.0	7	3			0	0	0	12	27	4	2	4.3	.907	2B-10

Pete Curren

CURREN, PETER
B. Baltimore, Md.   Deceased.

Year	Team	Games	BA	SA	AB	H	2B	3B	HR	HR%	R	RBI	BB	SO	SB	PH AB	PH H	PO	A	E	DP	TC/G	FA	G by Pos
1876	PHI N	3	.333	.417	12	4	1	0	0	0.0	5	2	0	0		0	0	10	2	10	0	7.3	.545	C-2, OF-1

Perry Currin

CURRIN, PERRY GILMORE
B. Sept. 27, 1928, Washington, D. C.   BL TR 6' 175 lbs.

Year	Team	Games	BA	SA	AB	H	2B	3B	HR	HR%	R	RBI	BB	SO	SB	PH AB	PH H	PO	A	E	DP	TC/G	FA	G by Pos
1947	STL A	3	.000	.000	2	0	0	0	0	0.0	0	0	1	0	0	1	0	2	2	0	2	1.3	1.000	SS-1

Jim Curry

CURRY, JAMES E.
B. Mar. 10, 1893, Camden, N. J.   D. Sept. 2, 1938, Lakefield, N. J.   BR TR 5'11" 160 lbs.

Year	Team	Games	BA	SA	AB	H	2B	3B	HR	HR%	R	RBI	BB	SO	SB	PH AB	PH H	PO	A	E	DP	TC/G	FA	G by Pos
1909	PHI A	1	.250	.250	4	1	0	0	0	0.0	1	0		0	0	0	0	0	2	0	0	2.0	1.000	2B-1
1911	NY A	4	.182	.182	11	2	0	0	0	0.0	3	0	1		0	0	0	11	6	5	1	5.5	.773	2B-4
1918	DET A	5	.250	.300	20	5	1	0	0	0.0	1	0	0	0	0	0	0	0	0	0	0			2B-5
3 yrs.		10	.229	.257	35	8	1	0	0	0.0	5	0	1	0	0	0	0	11	8	5	1	2.4	.792	2B-10

Tony Curry

CURRY, GEORGE ANTHONY
B. Dec. 22, 1938, Nassau, Bahamas   BL TL 5'11" 185 lbs.

Year	Team	Games	BA	SA	AB	H	2B	3B	HR	HR%	R	RBI	BB	SO	SB	PH AB	PH H	PO	A	E	DP	TC/G	FA	G by Pos
1960	PHI N	95	.261	.408	245	64	14	2	6	2.4	26	34	16	53	0	31	7	96	2	8	0	1.1	.925	OF-64
1961		15	.194	.250	36	7	2	0	0	0.0	3	3	1	8	0	7	3	8	2	2	0	0.8	.833	OF-8
1966	CLE A	19	.125	.125	16	2	0	0	0	0.0	4	3	3	8	0	16	2	0	0	0	0		–	
3 yrs.		129	.246	.374	297	73	16	2	6	2.0	33	40	20	69	0	54	12	104	4	10	0	0.9	.915	OF-72

Fred Curtis

CURTIS, FREDERICK MARION
B. Oct. 30, 1880, Beaver Lake, Mich.   D. Apr. 5, 1939, Minneapolis, Minn.   BR TR 6'1"

Year	Team	Games	BA	SA	AB	H	2B	3B	HR	HR%	R	RBI	BB	SO	SB	PH AB	PH H	PO	A	E	DP	TC/G	FA	G by Pos
1905	NY A	2	.222	.333	9	2	1	0	0	0.0	0	2	1		1	0	0	17	1	0	0	9.0	1.000	1B-2

Gene Curtis

CURTIS, EUGENE HOLMES (Eude)
B. May 5, 1883, Bethany, W. Va.   D. Jan. 1, 1919, Steubenville, Ohio   BR TR 6'3" 220 lbs.

Year	Team	Games	BA	SA	AB	H	2B	3B	HR	HR%	R	RBI	BB	SO	SB	PH AB	PH H	PO	A	E	DP	TC/G	FA	G by Pos
1903	PIT N	5	.421	.474	19	8	1	0	0	0.0	2	3	1		0	0	0	9	1	2	0	2.4	.833	OF-5

Harry Curtis

CURTIS, HARRY ALBERT
B. Feb. 19, 1883, Portland, Me.   D. Aug. 1, 1951, Evanston, Ill.   TR 5'10½" 170 lbs.

Year	Team	Games	BA	SA	AB	H	2B	3B	HR	HR%	R	RBI	BB	SO	SB	PH AB	PH H	PO	A	E	DP	TC/G	FA	G by Pos
1907	NY N	6	.222	.222	9	2	0	0	0	0.0	2	1	2		2	0	0	16	4	2	1	3.7	.909	C-6

Jim Curtis

CURTIS, JAMES D.
B. Dec. 27, 1861, Coldwater, Mich.   D. Feb. 14, 1945, North Adams, Mass.   BL 5'8½" 157 lbs.

Year	Team	Games	BA	SA	AB	H	2B	3B	HR	HR%	R	RBI	BB	SO	SB	PH AB	PH H	PO	A	E	DP	TC/G	FA	G by Pos
1891	2 teams	CIN N (27G – .269)			WAS AA (29G – .252)																			
"	total	56	.261	.351	211	55	6	5	1	0.5	28	25	22	35	5	0	0	94	13	22	1	2.3	.829	OF-56

Guy Curtright

CURTRIGHT, GUY PAXTON
B. Oct. 18, 1912, Holliday, Mo.   BR TR 5'11" 200 lbs.

Year	Team	Games	BA	SA	AB	H	2B	3B	HR	HR%	R	RBI	BB	SO	SB	PH AB	PH H	PO	A	E	DP	TC/G	FA	G by Pos
1943	CHI A	138	.291	.379	488	142	20	7	3	0.6	67	48	69	60	13	9	2	301	7	9	1	2.3	.972	OF-128
1944		72	.253	.343	198	50	8	2	2	1.0	22	23	23	21	4	22	6	101	8	6	3	1.6	.948	OF-51
1945		98	.281	.407	324	91	15	7	4	1.2	51	32	39	29	3	13	5	196	8	3	0	2.1	.986	OF-84
1946		23	.200	.236	55	11	2	0	0	0.0	7	5	11	14	0	4	2	30	2	0	1	1.4	1.000	OF-15
4 yrs.		331	.276	.374	1065	294	45	16	9	0.8	147	108	142	124	20	48	15	628	25	18	5	2.0	.973	OF-278

Jack Cusick

CUSICK, JOHN PETER
B. June 12, 1928, Weehawken, N. J.   D. Nov. 17, 1989, Edgewood, N. J.   BR TR 6' 170 lbs.

Year	Team	Games	BA	SA	AB	H	2B	3B	HR	HR%	R	RBI	BB	SO	SB	PH AB	PH H	PO	A	E	DP	TC/G	FA	G by Pos
1951	CHI N	65	.177	.256	164	29	3	2	2	1.2	16	16	17	29	2	3	1	78	147	11	25	3.6	.953	SS-56
1952	BOS N	49	.167	.179	78	13	1	0	0	0.0	5	6	6	9	0	9	1	45	52	3	4	2.0	.970	SS-28, 3B-3
2 yrs.		114	.174	.231	242	42	4	2	2	0.8	21	22	23	38	2	12	2	123	199	14	29	2.9	.958	SS-84, 3B-3

Tony Cusick

CUSICK, ANDREW DANIEL
B. 1867, Limerick, Ireland   D. Aug. 6, 1929, Chicago, Ill.   BR TR 5'9½" 190 lbs.

Year	Team	Games	BA	SA	AB	H	2B	3B	HR	HR%	R	RBI	BB	SO	SB	PH AB	PH H	PO	A	E	DP	TC/G	FA	G by Pos
1884	2 teams	WIL U (11G – .147)			PHI N (9G – .138)																			
"	total	20	.143	.143	63	9	0	0	0		2		1		3		0	0	99	40	19	5	7.9	.880	C-15, OF-3, SS-3, 3B-1, 2B-1
1885	PHI N	39	.177	.184	141	25	1	0	0	0.0	12		1	24	0	0		181	60	57	2	7.6	.809	C-38, OF-1
1886		29	.221	.288	104	23	5	1	0	0.0	10	4	3	14	0	0		133	35	19	2	6.4	.898	C-25, OF-3, 1B-1

Year	Team		Games	BA	SA	AB	H	2B	3B	HR	HR%	R	RBI	BB	SO	SB	Pinch Hit AB	H	PO	A	E	DP	TC/G	FA	G by Pos

Tony Cusick *continued*

Year	Team		Games	BA	SA	AB	H	2B	3B	HR	HR%	R	RBI	BB	SO	SB	AB	H	PO	A	E	DP	TC/G	FA	G by Pos
1887			7	.292	.333	24	7	1	0	0	0.0	3	5	3	1	0	0	0	44	8	12	1	9.1	.813	C-4, 1B-3, 2B-1
4 yrs.			95	.193	.220	332	64	7	1	0	0.0	27	9	8	42	0	0	0	457	143	107	10	7.4	.849	C-82, OF-7, 1B-4, SS-3, 2B-2, 3B-1

Ned Cuthbert

CUTHBERT, EDGAR EDWARD BR TR 5'6" 140 lbs.
B. June 20, 1845, Philadelphia, Pa. D. Feb. 6, 1905, St. Louis, Mo.
Manager 1882.

Year	Team		Games	BA	SA	AB	H	2B	3B	HR	HR%	R	RBI	BB	SO	SB	AB	H	PO	A	E	DP	TC/G	FA	G by Pos
1876	STL	N	63	.247	.290	283	70	10	1	0	0.0	46	25	7	4		0	0	95	7	19	2	1.9	.843	OF-63
1877	CIN	N	12	.179	.268	56	10	5	0	0	0.0	6	2	1	2		0	0	34	5	8	2	3.9	.830	OF-12
1882	STL	AA	60	.223	.335	233	52	16	5	0	0.0	28		17			0	0	74	12	10	0	1.6	.896	OF-60
1883			21	.169	.183	71	12	1	0	0	0.0	3		4			0	0	37	5	7	0	2.3	.857	OF-20, 1B-1
1884	BAL	U	44	.202	.232	168	34	5	0	0	0.0	29		10			0	0	41	10	17	0	1.5	.750	OF-44
5 yrs.			200	.219	.280	811	178	37	6	0	0.0	112	27	39	6		0	0	281	39	61	4	1.9	.840	OF-199, 1B-1

George Cutshaw

CUTSHAW, GEORGE WILLIAM (Clancy) BR TR 5'9" 160 lbs.
B. July 27, 1887, Wilmington, Ill. D. Aug. 22, 1973, San Diego, Calif.

Year	Team		Games	BA	SA	AB	H	2B	3B	HR	HR%	R	RBI	BB	SO	SB	AB	H	PO	A	E	DP	TC/G	FA	G by Pos
1912	BKN	N	102	.280	.342	357	100	14	4	0	0.0	41	28	31	16	16	5	1	196	294	22	31	5.0	.957	2B-91, 3B-5, SS-1
1913			147	.267	.385	592	158	23	13	7	1.2	72	80	39	22	39	0	0	402	448	38	79	6.0	.957	2B-147
1914			153	.257	.346	583	150	22	12	2	0.3	69	78	30	32	34	0	0	455	444	38	74	6.1	.959	2B-153
1915			154	.246	.309	566	139	18	9	0	0.0	68	62	34	35	28	0	0	397	473	26	53	5.8	.971	2B-154
1916			154	.260	.320	581	151	21	4	2	0.3	58	63	25	32	27	0	0	361	467	36	51	5.6	.958	2B-154
1917			135	.259	.347	487	126	17	7	4	0.8	42	49	21	26	22	1	0	319	377	27	43	5.4	.963	2B-134
1918	PIT	N	126	.285	.395	463	132	16	10	5	1.1	56	68	27	18	25	0	0	323	366	26	60	5.7	.964	2B-126
1919			139	.242	.320	512	124	15	8	3	0.6	49	51	30	22	36	0	0	344	392	15	56	5.4	.980	2B-139
1920			131	.252	.318	488	123	16	8	0	0.0	56	47	23	10	17	2	0	336	423	25	62	6.0	.968	2B-129
1921			98	.340	.414	350	119	18	4	0	0.0	46	53	11	11	14	14	2	196	253	23	36	4.8	.951	2B-84
1922	DET	A	132	.267	.339	499	133	14	4	2	0.4	57	61	20	13	11	0	0	334	390	21	69	5.6	.972	2B-132
1923			45	.224	.259	143	32	1	2	0	0.0	15	13	9	5	2	0	0	104	151	3	2	5.7	.988	2B-43, 3B-2
12 yrs.			1516	.265	.344	5621	1487	195	89	25	0.4	629	653	300	242	271	22	3	3767	4478	300	616	5.6	.965	2B-1486, 3B-7, SS-1

WORLD SERIES

Year	Team		Games	BA	SA	AB	H	2B	3B	HR	HR%	R	RBI	BB	SO	SB	AB	H	PO	A	E	DP	TC/G	FA	G by Pos
1916	BKN	N	5	.105	.158	19	2	1	0	0	0.0	2	2	1	1	0	0	0	19	13	2	1	6.8	.941	2B-5

Kiki Cuyler

CUYLER, HAZEN SHIRLEY BR TR 5'10½" 180 lbs.
B. Aug. 30, 1899, Harrisville, Mich. D. Feb. 11, 1950, Ann Arbor, Mich.
Hall of Fame 1968.

Year	Team		Games	BA	SA	AB	H	2B	3B	HR	HR%	R	RBI	BB	SO	SB	AB	H	PO	A	E	DP	TC/G	FA	G by Pos
1921	PIT	N	1	.000	.000	3	0	0	0	0	0.0	0	0	0	1	0	0	0	1	0	0	0	1.0	1.000	OF-1
1922			1			0	0	0	0	0	—	0	0	0	0	0	0	0	0	0	0	0	0.0	—	—
1923			11	.250	.325	40	10	1	1	0	0.0	4	2	5	3	2	0	0	26	1	2	0	2.6	.931	OF-11
1924			117	.354	.539	466	165	27	16	9	1.9	94	85	30	62	32	3	1	246	19	16	4	2.4	.943	OF-114
1925			153	.357	.593	617	220	43	26	17	2.8	144	102	58	56	41	0	0	362	21	13	4	2.6	.967	OF-153
1926			157	.321	.459	614	197	31	15	8	1.3	113	92	50	66	35	0	0	405	19	14	4	2.8	.968	OF-157
1927			85	.309	.435	285	88	13	7	3	1.1	60	31	37	36	20	11	2	195	6	4	0	2.4	.980	OF-73
1928	CHI	N	133	.285	.473	499	142	25	9	17	3.4	92	79	51	61	37	5	0	257	18	5	3	2.1	.982	OF-127
1929			139	.360	.532	509	183	29	7	15	2.9	111	102	66	56	43	9	4	288	15	8	6	2.2	.974	OF-129
1930			156	.355	.547	642	228	50	17	13	2.0	155	134	72	49	37	0	0	377	21	8	7	2.6	.980	OF-156
1931			154	.330	.473	613	202	37	12	9	1.5	110	88	72	54	13	1	0	347	11	11	4	2.4	.970	OF-153
1932			110	.291	.442	446	130	19	9	10	2.2	58	77	29	43	9	1	0	239	7	8	1	2.3	.969	OF-109
1933			70	.317	.447	262	83	13	3	5	1.9	37	35	21	29	4	1	0	130	2	3	0	1.9	.978	OF-69
1934			142	.338	.474	559	189	42	8	6	1.1	80	69	31	62	15	0	0	319	15	10	1	2.4	.971	OF-142
1935	2 teams	CHI	N	(45G — .268)		CIN	N	(62G — .251)																	
"	total		107	.258	.361	380	98	13	4	6	1.6	58	40	37	34	8	6	2	221	10	4	3	2.2	.983	OF-99
1936	CIN	N	144	.326	.453	567	185	29	11	7	1.2	96	74	47	67	16	4	2	322	9	9	3	2.4	.974	OF-140
1937			117	.271	.320	406	110	12	4	0	0.0	48	32	36	50	10	10	2	174	8	5	1	1.6	.973	OF-106
1938	BKN	N	82	.273	.399	253	69	10	8	2	0.8	45	23	34	23	6	11	1	125	9	1	1	1.6	.993	OF-68
18 yrs.			1879	.321	.473	7161	2299	394	157	127	1.8	1305	1065	676	752	328	62	14	4034	191	121	42	2.3	.972	OF-1807

WORLD SERIES

Year	Team		Games	BA	SA	AB	H	2B	3B	HR	HR%	R	RBI	BB	SO	SB	AB	H	PO	A	E	DP	TC/G	FA	G by Pos
1925	PIT	N	7	.269	.500	26	7	3	0	1	3.8	3	6	1	4	0	0	0	12	0	1	0	1.9	.923	OF-7
1929	CHI	N	5	.300	.350	20	6	1	0	0	0.0	4	4	1	7	0	0	0	8	0	1	0	1.8	.889	OF-5
1932			4	.278	.611	18	5	1	1	1	5.6	2	2	0	3	1	0	0	5	0	0	0	1.3	1.000	OF-4
3 yrs.			16	.281	.484	64	18	5	1	2	3.1	9	12	2	14	1	0	0	25	0	2	0	1.7	.926	OF-16

Al Cypert

CYPERT, ALFRED BOYD BR TR 5'10½" 150 lbs.
B. Aug. 8, 1889, Little Rock, Ark. D. Jan. 9, 1973, Washington, D. C.

Year	Team		Games	BA	SA	AB	H	2B	3B	HR	HR%	R	RBI	BB	SO	SB	AB	H	PO	A	E	DP	TC/G	FA	G by Pos
1914	CLE	A	1	.000	.000	1	0	0	0	0	0.0	0	0	0	1	0	0	0	0	0	0	0	0.0	—	3B-1

Paul Dade

DADE, LONNIE PAUL BR TR 6'1" 185 lbs.
B. Dec. 7, 1951, Seattle, Wash.

Year	Team		Games	BA	SA	AB	H	2B	3B	HR	HR%	R	RBI	BB	SO	SB	AB	H	PO	A	E	DP	TC/G	FA	G by Pos
1975	CAL	A	11	.200	.333	30	6	4	0	0	0.0	5	1	6	7	0	1	1	8	1	0	0	0.8	1.000	DH-7, OF-3, 3B-1
1976			13	.111	.111	9	1	0	0	0	0.0	2	1	3	3	0	5	1	5	4	1	0	0.8	.900	OF-4, 2B-2, DH-1, 3B-1
1977	CLE	A	134	.291	.356	461	134	15	3	3	0.7	65	45	32	58	16	10	2	192	51	7	3	1.9	.972	OF-99, 3B-26, DH-7, 2B-1
1978			93	.254	.329	307	78	12	1	3	1.0	37	20	34	45	12	8	1	171	6	7	2	2.0	.962	OF-81, DH-9
1979	2 teams	CLE	A	(44G — .282)		SD	N	(76G — .276)																	
"	total		120	.278	.369	453	126	23	4	4	0.9	60	37	26	70	25	6	2	120	167	14	13	2.5	.953	3B-72, OF-41, DH-4
1980	SD	N	68	.189	.189	53	10	0	0	0	0.0	17	3	12	10	4	11	1	14	19	5	1	0.6	.868	3B-21, OF-8, 2B-1
6 yrs.			439	.270	.345	1313	355	54	7	10	0.8	186	107	113	193	57	41	8	510	248	34	19	1.8	.957	OF-236, 3B-121, DH-28, 2B-4

Angie Dagres

DAGRES, ANGELO GEORGE (Junior) BL TL 5'11" 175 lbs.
B. Aug. 22, 1934, Newburyport, Mass.

Year	Team	Games	BA	SA	AB	H	2B	3B	HR	HR%	R	RBI	BB	SO	SB	Pinch Hit AB	Pinch Hit H	PO	A	E	DP	TC/G	FA	G by Pos

Angie Dagres *continued*

Year	Team	Games	BA	SA	AB	H	2B	3B	HR	HR%	R	RBI	BB	SO	SB	PH AB	PH H	PO	A	E	DP	TC/G	FA	G by Pos
1955	BAL A	8	.267	.267	15	4	0	0	0	0.0	5	3	1	2	0	3	1	9	0	2	0	1.4	.818	OF-5

Bill Dahlen

DAHLEN, WILLIAM FREDERICK (Bad Bill)
B. Jan. 5, 1870, Nelliston, N. Y. D. Dec. 5, 1950, Brooklyn, N. Y.
Manager 1910-13.

BR TR 5'9" 180 lbs.

Year	Team	Games	BA	SA	AB	H	2B	3B	HR	HR%	R	RBI	BB	SO	SB	PH AB	PH H	PO	A	E	DP	TC/G	FA	G by Pos
1891	CHI N	135	.260	.390	549	143	18	13	9	1.6	114	76	67	60	21	0	0	217	264	64	21	4.0	.883	3B-84, OF-37, SS-15
1892		143	.291	.422	581	169	23	19	5	0.9	114	58	45	56	60	0	0	297	423	61	43	5.5	.922	SS-72, 3B-68, OF-2, 2B-1
1893		116	.301	.452	485	146	28	15	5	1.0	113	64	58	30	31	0	0	286	337	72	35	6.0	.896	SS-88, OF-17, 2B-10, 3B-3
1894		121	.362	.569	508	184	32	14	15	3.0	150	107	76	33	42	0	0	282	382	75	53	6.1	.899	SS-66, 3B-55
1895		129	.254	.370	516	131	19	10	7	1.4	106	62	61	51	38	0	0	282	527	86	70	6.9	.904	SS-129, OF-1
1896		125	.352	.553	474	167	30	19	9	1.9	137	74	64	36	51	0	0	310	456	71	66	6.7	.915	SS-125
1897		75	.290	.478	276	80	18	8	6	2.2	67	40	43		15	0	0	215	291	38	48	7.3	.930	SS-75
1898		142	.290	.393	521	151	35	8	1	0.2	96	79	58		27	0	0	369	511	76	77	6.7	.921	SS-142
1899	BKN N	121	.283	.395	428	121	22	7	4	0.9	87	76	67		29	0	0	275	418	42	53	6.1	.943	SS-110, 3B-11
1900		133	.259	.344	483	125	16	11	1	0.2	87	69	73		31	0	0	321	517	55	59	6.7	.938	SS-133
1901		131	.261	.357	513	134	17	10	4	0.8	69	82	30		23	0	0	304	457	57	49	6.2	.930	SS-129, 2B-2
1902		138	.264	.351	527	139	26	7	2	0.4	67	74	43		20	0	0	278	440	66	34	5.7	.916	SS-138
1903		138	.262	.342	474	124	17	9	1	0.2	71	64	82		34	0	0	296	477	42	48	5.9	.948	SS-138
1904	NY N	145	.268	.337	523	140	26	2	2	0.4	70	80	44		47	0	0	316	494	61	61	6.0	.930	SS-145
1905		148	.242	.337	520	126	20	4	7	1.3	67	81	62		37	0	0	314	501	45	58	5.8	.948	SS-147, OF-1
1906		143	.240	.297	471	113	18	3	1	0.2	63	49	76		16	0	0	287	454	49	36	5.5	.938	SS-143
1907		143	.207	.254	464	96	20	1	0	0.0	40	34	51		11	0	0	292	426	45	39	5.3	.941	SS-143
1908	BOS N	144	.239	.307	524	125	23	2	3	0.6	50	48	35		10	0	0	291	553	43	58	6.2	.952	SS-144
1909		69	.234	.305	197	46	6	1	2	1.0	22	16	29		4	8	2	119	200	32	21	5.1	.909	SS-49, 2B-6, 3B-2
1910	BKN N	3	.000	.000	2	0	0	0	0	0.0	0	0	0	0	0	2	0	0	0	0	0	0.0	—	SS-3
1911		1	.000	.000	3	0	0	0	0	0.0	0	0	0	3	0	0	0	2	5	0	1	7.0	1.000	SS-1
21 yrs.		2443	.272	.382	9039	2460	414	163	84	0.9	1590	1233	1064	269	547	10	2	5353	8133	80	930	5.6	.994	SS-2132, 3B-223, OF-58, 2B-19

WORLD SERIES

Year	Team	Games	BA	SA	AB	H	2B	3B	HR	HR%	R	RBI	BB	SO	SB	PH AB	PH H	PO	A	E	DP	TC/G	FA	G by Pos
1905	NY N	5	.000	.000	15	0	0	0	0	0.0	1	1	3	2	2	0	0	10	19	0	1	5.8	1.000	SS-5

Babe Dahlgren

DAHLGREN, ELLSWORTH TENNEY
B. June 15, 1912, San Francisco, Calif.

BR TR 6' 190 lbs.

Year	Team	Games	BA	SA	AB	H	2B	3B	HR	HR%	R	RBI	BB	SO	SB	PH AB	PH H	PO	A	E	DP	TC/G	FA	G by Pos
1935	BOS A	149	.263	.392	525	138	27	7	9	1.7	77	63	56	67	6	0	0	1433	69	18	109	10.2	.988	1B-149
1936		16	.281	.421	57	16	3	1	1	1.8	6	7	7	1	2	0	0	136	8	3	10	9.2	.980	1B-16
1937	NY A	1	.000	.000	1	0	0	0	0	0.0	0	0	0	0	0	1	0	0	0	0	0	0.0	—	
1938		29	.186	.209	43	8	1	0	0	0.0	8	1	1	7	0	6	0	37	10	4	2	1.8	.922	3B-8, 1B-6
1939		144	.235	.377	531	125	18	6	15	2.8	71	89	57	54	2	0	0	1303	68	13	140	9.6	.991	1B-144
1940		155	.264	.384	568	150	24	4	12	2.1	51	73	46	54	1	0	0	1488	75	15	143	10.2	.990	1B-155
1941	2 teams		BOS N (44G – .235)			CHI N (99G – .281)																		
"	total	143	.267	.459	525	140	28	2	23	4.4	70	89	59	52	2	1	0	1341	78	13	129	10.0	.991	1B-137, 3B-5
1942	3 teams		CHI N (17G – .214)			STL A (2G – .000)			BKN N (17G – .053)															
"	total	36	.169	.182	77	13	1	0	0	0.0	6	6	8	7	0	8	0	183	14	2	13	5.5	.990	1B-24
1943	PHI N	136	.287	.362	508	146	19	2	5	1.0	55	56	50	39	2	3	2	800	151	24	81	7.2	.975	1B-73, 3B-35, SS-25, C-1
1944	PIT N	158	.289	.419	599	173	28	7	12	2.0	67	101	47	56	2	0	0	1440	128	20	105	10.1	.987	1B-158
1945		144	.250	.354	531	133	24	8	5	0.9	57	75	51	51	1	2	0	1373	93	6	115	10.2	.996	1B-142
1946	STL A	28	.175	.188	80	14	1	0	0	0.0	2	9	8	13	0	4	1	187	18	4	16	7.5	.981	1B-24
12 yrs.		1139	.261	.383	4045	1056	174	37	82	2.0	470	569	390	401	18	25	3	9721	712	122	863	9.3	.988	1B-1028, 3B-48, SS-25, C-1

WORLD SERIES

Year	Team	Games	BA	SA	AB	H	2B	3B	HR	HR%	R	RBI	BB	SO	SB	PH AB	PH H	PO	A	E	DP	TC/G	FA	G by Pos
1939	NY A	4	.214	.571	14	3	2	0	1	7.1	2	2	0	4	0	0	0	41	2	0	4	10.8	1.000	1B-4

Vince Dailey

DAILEY, VINCENT PERRY
B. Dec. 25, 1864, Osceola, Pa. D. Nov. 14, 1919, Hornell, N. Y.

6' 200 lbs.

Year	Team	Games	BA	SA	AB	H	2B	3B	HR	HR%	R	RBI	BB	SO	SB	PH AB	PH H	PO	A	E	DP	TC/G	FA	G by Pos
1890	CLE N	64	.289	.366	246	71	5	7	0	0.0	41	32	33	23	17	0	0	103	13	19	2	2.1	.859	OF-64, P-2

Con Daily

DAILY, CORNELIUS F.
Brother of Ed Daily.
B. Sept. 11, 1864, Blackstone, Mass. D. June 14, 1928, Brooklyn, N. Y.

BL 6' 192 lbs.

Year	Team	Games	BA	SA	AB	H	2B	3B	HR	HR%	R	RBI	BB	SO	SB	PH AB	PH H	PO	A	E	DP	TC/G	FA	G by Pos
1884	PHI U	2	.000	.000	8	0	0	0	0	0.0	0		0			0	0	15	3	3	0	10.5	.857	C-2
1885	PRO N	60	.260	.296	223	58	6	1	0	0.0	20	19	12	20		0	0	296	74	44	14	6.9	.894	C-48, 1B-7, OF-6
1886	BOS N	50	.239	.283	180	43	4	2	0	0.0	25	21	19	29		0	0	264	55	31	5	7.0	.911	C-49
1887		36	.158	.200	120	19	5	0	0	0.0	12	13	9	8	7	0	0	125	44	21	3	5.3	.889	C-36
1888	IND N	57	.218	.257	202	44	6	1	0	0.0	14	14	10	28	15	0	0	279	77	40	10	6.9	.899	C-42, OF-5, 3B-5, 1B-5, 2B-1
1889		62	.251	.297	219	55	6	2	0	0.0	35	26	28	21	14	0	0	294	57	42	9	6.3	.893	C-51, OF-6, 1B-6, 3B-1
1890	BKN P	46	.250	.321	168	42	6	3	0	0.0	20	35	15	14	6	0	0	197	36	25	10	5.6	.903	C-40, 1B-6, OF-1
1891	BKN N	60	.320	.379	206	66	10	1	0	0.0	25	30	15	13	7	0	0	241	68	26	2	5.6	.922	C-55, OF-3, SS-2, 1B-1
1892		80	.234	.277	278	65	10	1	0	0.0	38	28	38	21	18	0	0	356	88	27	9	5.9	.943	C-68, OF-13
1893		61	.265	.316	215	57	4	2	1	0.5	33	32	20	12	13	1	1	226	47	21	2	4.8	.929	C-51, OF-9
1894		67	.256	.376	234	60	14	7	0	0.0	40	32	31	22	8	0	0	271	63	24	12	5.3	.933	C-60, 1B-7
1895		40	.211	.282	142	30	3	2	1	0.7	17	11	10	18	3	0	0	130	25	7	7	4.1	.957	C-39, OF-1
1896	CHI N	9	.074	.074	27	2	0	0	0	0.0	6	7	1			0	0	24	7	1	0	3.6	.969	C-9
13 yrs.		630	.243	.299	2222	541	74	22	2	0.1	280	262	208	208	92	1	1	2718	644	312	83	5.8	.915	C-550, OF-44, 1B-32, 3B-6, SS-2, 2B-1

Ed Daily

DAILY, EDWARD M.
Brother of Con Daily.
B. Sept. 7, 1862, Providence, R. I. D. Oct. 21, 1891, Washington, D. C.

BR TR

Year	Team	Games	BA	SA	AB	H	2B	3B	HR	HR%	R	RBI	BB	SO	SB	PH AB	PH H	PO	A	E	DP	TC/G	FA	G by Pos
1885	PHI N	50	.207	.288	184	38	8	2	1	0.5	22		0	25		0	0	11	87	12	2	2.2	.891	P-50

Year	Team	Games	BA	SA	AB	H	2B	3B	HR	HR%	R	RBI	BB	SO	SB	Pinch Hit AB	Pinch Hit H	PO	A	E	DP	TC/G	FA	G by Pos

Ed Daily *continued*

1886		79	.227	.327	309	70	17	1	4	1.3	40	50	7	34		0	0	98	70	27	3	2.5	.862	OF-56, P-27
1887	2 teams	PHI N (26G – .283)			WAS N	(78G – .251)																		
"	total	104	.259	.374	417	108	17	11	3	0.7	57	53	17	36	34	0	0	144	25	35	1	2.0	.828	OF-99, P-7
1888	WAS N	110	.225	.313	453	102	8	4	8	1.8	56	39	7	42	44	0	0	196	37	22	5	2.3	.914	OF-100, P-9, 1B-1
1889	COL AA	136	.256	.337	578	148	22	8	3	0.5	105	70	38	65	60	0	0	212	27	41	4	2.1	.854	OF-136, P-2
1890	3 teams	BKN AA (91G – .239)			NY N	(4G – .133)			LOU AA	(23G – .250)														
"	total	118	.237	.313	489	116	16	9	1	0.2	93		37	4	62	0	0	147	106	26	6	2.4	.907	OF-78, P-41
1891	2 teams	LOU AA (22G – .250)			WAS AA	(21G – .228)																		
"	total	43	.238	.266	143	34	4	0	0	0.0	23	14	19	16	12	0	0	43	31	17	2	2.1	.813	OF-28, P-15
7 yrs.		640	.239	.326	2573	616	92	35	20	0.8	396	227	125	222	212	0	0	851	383	180	23	2.2	.873	OF-497, P-151, 1B-1

George Daisey

DAISEY, GEORGE K.
B. Altoona, Pa. Deceased.

5'11"   190 lbs.

| 1884 | ALT U | 1 | .000 | .000 | 4 | 0 | 0 | 0 | 0 | 0.0 | 0 | | 0 | | | 0 | 0 | 0 | 0 | 1 | 0 | 1.0 | – | OF-1 |

Pete Dalena

DALENA, PETER MARTIN
B. June 26, 1960, Fresno, Calif.

BL TR 5'11"   200 lbs.

| 1989 | CLE A | 5 | .143 | .286 | 7 | 1 | 1 | 0 | 0 | 0.0 | 0 | 0 | 0 | 3 | 0 | 4 | 1 | 0 | 0 | 0 | 0 | – | DH-1 |

John Daley

DALEY, JOHN FRANCIS (Daley)
B. May 25, 1887, Pittsburgh, Pa.   D. Aug. 31, 1988, Mansfield, Ohio

BR TR 5'7½"   155 lbs.

| 1912 | STL A | 17 | .173 | .231 | 52 | 9 | 0 | 0 | 1 | 1.9 | 7 | 3 | 9 | | 4 | 0 | 0 | 27 | 48 | 15 | 7 | 5.3 | .833 | SS-17 |

Jud Daley

DALEY, JUDSON LAWRENCE
B. Mar. 14, 1884, S. Coventry, Conn.   D. Jan. 26, 1967, Gadsden, Ala.

BL TR 5'8"   172 lbs.

1911	BKN N	19	.231	.292	65	15	2	1	0	0.0	8	7	2	8	2	2	0	37	3	2	0	2.2	.952	OF-16
1912		61	.256	.342	199	51	9	1	2	1.0	22	13	24	17	2	6	3	116	10	7	3	2.2	.947	OF-55
2 yrs.		80	.250	.330	264	66	11	2	2	0.8	30	20	26	25	4	8	3	153	13	9	3	2.2	.949	OF-71

Pete Daley

DALEY, PETER HARVEY
B. Jan. 14, 1930, Grass Valley, Calif.

BR TR 6'   195 lbs.

1955	BOS A	17	.220	.300	50	11	2	1	0	0.0	4	5	3	6	0	4	0	75	4	0	0	4.6	1.000	C-14
1956		59	.267	.439	187	50	11	3	5	2.7	22	29	18	30	1	3	1	228	14	2	1	4.1	.992	C-57
1957		78	.225	.325	191	43	10	0	3	1.6	17	25	16	31	0	1	1	289	20	0	5	4.0	1.000	C-77
1958		27	.321	.500	56	18	2	1	2	3.6	10	8	7	11	0	4	0	88	10	1	1	3.7	.990	C-27
1959		65	.225	.284	169	38	7	0	1	0.6	9	11	13	31	1	9	2	245	28	1	5	4.2	.996	C-58
1960	KC A	73	.263	.390	228	60	10	2	5	2.2	19	25	16	41	0	14	5	263	33	3	3	4.1	.990	C-61, OF-1
1961	WAS A	72	.192	.266	203	39	7	1	2	1.0	12	17	14	37	0	0	0	285	35	4	6	4.5	.988	C-72
7 yrs.		391	.239	.349	1084	259	49	8	18	1.7	93	120	87	187	2	31	9	1473	144	11	21	4.2	.993	C-366, OF-1

Tom Daley

DALEY, THOMAS FRANCIS (Pete)
B. Nov. 13, 1884, DuBois, Pa.   D. Dec. 2, 1934, Los Angeles, Calif.

BL TR 5'5"   168 lbs.

1908	CIN N	14	.109	.109	46	5	0	0	0	0.0	5		3			0	0	17	2	0	1	1.4	1.000	OF-13
1913	PHI A	59	.255	.284	141	36	1	0	0	0.0	13	11	13	28	4	19	2	73	5	3	2	1.4	.963	OF-38
1914	2 teams	PHI A (29G – .256)			NY A	(67G – .251)																		
"	total	96	.253	.329	277	70	7	1	0	0.0	53	16	50	27	12	12	3	74	16	6	2	1.0	.938	OF-81
1915	NY A	10	.250	.250	8	2	0	0	0	0.0	2	2	2	2	1	4	1	2	0	0	1	0.2	1.000	OF-2
4 yrs.		179	.239	.292	472	113	9	8	0	0.0	73	29	68	57	18	35	6	166	23	9	6	1.1	.955	OF-134

Dom Dallessandro

DALLESSANDRO, NICHOLAS DOMINIC (Dim Dom)
B. Oct. 3, 1913, Reading, Pa.   D. Apr. 29, 1988, Indianapolis, Ind.

BL TL 5'6"   168 lbs.

1937	BOS A	68	.231	.293	147	34	7	1	0	0.0	18	11	27	16	2	26	7	54	1	2	0	0.8	.965	OF-35
1940	CHI N	107	.268	.387	287	77	19	6	1	0.3	33	36	34	13	4	29	10	156	1	5	0	1.5	.969	OF-74
1941		140	.272	.391	486	132	36	2	6	1.2	73	85	68	37	3	7	1	292	4	4	0	2.1	.987	OF-131
1942		96	.261	.383	264	69	12	4	4	1.5	30	43	36	18	4	26	9	134	6	2	1	1.5	.986	OF-66
1943		87	.222	.318	176	39	8	3	1	0.6	13	31	40	14	1	32	8	87	2	3	0	1.1	.967	OF-45
1944		117	.304	.438	381	116	19	4	8	2.1	53	74	61	29	1	11	3	212	9	4	2	1.9	.982	OF-106
1946		65	.225	.326	89	20	2	2	1	1.1	4	9	23	12	1	29	6	33	0	1	0	0.5	.971	OF-20
1947		66	.287	.391	115	33	7	1	1	0.9	18	14	21	11	0	32	8	50	1	0	1	0.8	1.000	OF-28
8 yrs.		746	.267	.381	1945	520	110	23	22	1.1	242	303	310	150	16	192	52	1018	24	21	4	1.4	.980	OF-505

Abner Dalrymple

DALRYMPLE, ABNER FRANK
B. Sept. 9, 1857, Warren, Ill.   D. Jan. 25, 1939, Warren, Ill.

BL TR 5'10½"   175 lbs.

1878	MIL N	61	.354	.421	271	96	10	4	0	0.0	52	15	6	29		0	0	128	11	28	3	2.7	.832	OF-61
1879	CHI N	71	.291	.372	333	97	25	1	0	0.0	47	23	4	29		0	0	103	4	40	1	2.1	.728	OF-71
1880		86	.330	.458	382	126	25	12	0	0.0	91	36	3	18		0	0	157	19	29	4	2.4	.859	OF-86
1881		82	.323	.414	362	117	22	4	1	0.3	72	37	15	22		0	0	143	14	31	1	2.3	.835	OF-82
1882		84	.295	.421	397	117	25	11	1	0.3	96	36	14	18		0	0	185	8	27	4	2.6	.877	OF-84
1883		80	.298	.402	363	108	24	4	2	0.6	78		11	29		0	0	149	12	34	3	2.4	.826	OF-80
1884		111	.309	.505	521	161	18	9	22	4.2	111		14	39		0	0	176	18	26	5	2.0	.882	OF-111
1885		113	.274	.445	492	135	27	12	11	2.2	109	58	46	42		0	0	180	16	27	2	2.0	.879	OF-113
1886		82	.233	.353	331	77	7	12	3	0.9	62	26	33	44		0	0	126	15	7	1	1.8	.953	OF-82
1887	PIT N	92	.212	.307	358	76	18	5	2	0.6	45	31	45	43	29	0	0	184	14	22	1	2.4	.900	OF-92
1888		57	.220	.278	227	50	9	2	0	0.0	19	14	6	28	7	0	0	81	9	9	0	1.7	.909	OF-57
1891	MIL AA	32	.311	.459	135	42	7	5	1	0.7	31	22	7	18	6	0	0	44	6	5	1	1.7	.909	OF-32
12 yrs.		951	.288	.410	4172	1202	217	81	43	1.0	813	298	204	359	42	0	0	1656	146	285	26	2.2	.863	OF-951

Bill Dalrymple

DALRYMPLE, WILLIAM DUNN
B. Feb. 7, 1891, Baltimore, Md.   D. July 14, 1967, San Diego, Calif.

TR

Year	Team	Games	BA	SA	AB	H	2B	3B	HR	HR%	R	RBI	BB	SO	SB	Pinch Hit AB	Pinch Hit H	PO	A	E	DP	TC/G	FA	G by Pos

Bill Dalrymple *continued*

Year	Team	Games	BA	SA	AB	H	2B	3B	HR	HR%	R	RBI	BB	SO	SB	AB	H	PO	A	E	DP	TC/G	FA	G by Pos
1915	STL A	2	.000	.000	2	0	0	0	0	0.0	0	0	0	0	0	1	0	0	1	0	0	0.5	1.000	3B-1

Clay Dalrymple

DALRYMPLE, CLAYTON ERROL
B. Dec. 3, 1936, Chico, Calif.   BL TR 6'   190 lbs.

Year	Team	Games	BA	SA	AB	H	2B	3B	HR	HR%	R	RBI	BB	SO	SB	AB	H	PO	A	E	DP	TC/G	FA	G by Pos
1960	PHI N	82	.272	.411	158	43	6	2	4	2.5	11	21	15	21	0	42	12	172	25	7	3	2.5	.966	C-48
1961		129	.220	.294	378	83	11	1	5	1.3	23	42	30	30	0	9	1	551	86	14	10	5.0	.978	C-122
1962		123	.276	.416	370	102	13	3	11	3.0	40	54	70	32	1	9	1	635	61	9	11	5.7	.987	C-119
1963		142	.252	.365	452	114	15	3	10	2.2	40	40	45	55	0	3	1	881	90	19	16	7.0	.981	C-142
1964		127	.238	.343	382	91	16	3	6	1.6	36	46	39	40	0	4	1	737	61	7	11	6.3	.991	C-124
1965		103	.213	.302	301	64	5	5	4	1.3	14	23	34	37	0	5	0	657	70	5	10	7.1	.993	C-102
1966		114	.245	.338	331	81	13	3	4	1.2	30	39	60	57	0	6	0	615	48	5	5	5.9	.993	C-110
1967		101	.172	.239	268	46	7	1	3	1.1	12	21	36	49	1	8	3	558	59	4	7	6.1	.994	C-97
1968		85	.207	.290	241	50	9	1	3	1.2	19	26	22	57	1	6	0	463	34	5	3	5.9	.994	C-80
1969	BAL A	37	.238	.388	80	19	1	1	3	3.8	8	8	13	8	0	8	1	116	17	0	2	3.6	1.000	C-30
1970		13	.219	.344	32	7	1	0	1	3.1	4	3	7	4	0	2	0	78	8	0	0	6.6	1.000	C-11
1971		23	.204	.286	49	10	1	0	1	2.0	6	6	16	13	0	8	0	94	7	3	1	4.5	.971	C-18
12 yrs.		1079	.233	.335	3042	710	98	23	55	1.8	243	327	387	403	3	105	20	5557	566	78	79	5.7	.987	C-1003

WORLD SERIES

Year	Team	Games	BA	SA	AB	H	2B	3B	HR	HR%	R	RBI	BB	SO	SB	AB	H	PO	A	E	DP	TC/G	FA	G by Pos
1969	BAL A	2	1.000	1.000	2	2	0	0	0	0.0	0	0	0	0	0	2	2	0	0	0	0	0.0	–	

Jack Dalton

DALTON, TALBOT PERCY
B. July 3, 1885, Henderson, Tenn.   BR TR 5'10½" 187 lbs.

Year	Team	Games	BA	SA	AB	H	2B	3B	HR	HR%	R	RBI	BB	SO	SB	AB	H	PO	A	E	DP	TC/G	FA	G by Pos
1910	BKN N	77	.227	.300	273	62	9	4	1	0.4	33	21	26	30	5	4	1	129	12	5	3	1.9	.966	OF-72
1914		128	.319	.391	442	141	13	8	1	0.2	65	45	53	39	19	10	4	240	7	9	2	2.0	.965	OF-116
1915	BUF F	132	.293	.359	437	128	17	3	2	0.5	68	46	50		28	12	4	218	11	8	4	1.8	.966	OF-119
1916	DET A	8	.182	.182	11	2	0	0	0	0.0	1	0	0	5	0	2	1	3	0	0	0	0.4	1.000	OF-4
4 yrs.		345	.286	.356	1163	333	39	15	4	0.3	167	112	129	74	52	28	10	590	30	22	9	1.9	.966	OF-311

Bert Daly

DALY, ALBERT JOSEPH
B. Apr. 8, 1881, Bayonne, N. J. D. Sept. 3, 1952, Bayonne, N. J.   BR TR 5'9" 170 lbs.

Year	Team	Games	BA	SA	AB	H	2B	3B	HR	HR%	R	RBI	BB	SO	SB	AB	H	PO	A	E	DP	TC/G	FA	G by Pos
1903	PHI A	10	.190	.381	21	4	0	2	0	0.0	2	4	1		0	2	0	4	8	3	1	1.5	.800	2B-4, 3B-3, SS-1

Joe Daly

DALY, JOSEPH JOHN
Brother of Tom Daly.
B. Sept. 21, 1868, Conshohocken, Pa. D. Mar. 21, 1943, Philadelphia, Pa.   TR 5'8" 157 lbs.

Year	Team	Games	BA	SA	AB	H	2B	3B	HR	HR%	R	RBI	BB	SO	SB	AB	H	PO	A	E	DP	TC/G	FA	G by Pos
1890	PHI AA	21	.280	.360	75	21	4	1	0	0.0	8		3		1	0	0	39	19	13	0	3.4	.817	OF-14, C-9
1891	CLE N	1	.000	.000	3	0	0	0	0	0.0	0		0	2	0	0	0	2	0	0	0	2.0	1.000	OF-1
1892	BOS N	1	–	–	0	0	0	0	0	–	0	0	0	0	0	0	0	2	0	0	0	2.0	1.000	C-1
3 yrs.		23	.269	.346	78	21	4	1	0	0.0	8	0	3	2	1	0	0	43	19	13	0	3.3	.827	OF-15, C-10

Sun Daly

DALY, JAMES J.
B. Jan. 6, 1865, Rutland, Vt. D. Apr. 30, 1938, Albany, N. Y.

Year	Team	Games	BA	SA	AB	H	2B	3B	HR	HR%	R	RBI	BB	SO	SB	AB	H	PO	A	E	DP	TC/G	FA	G by Pos
1892	BAL N	13	.250	.333	48	12	2	0	0	0.0	5	7	1	4	0	0	0	22	2	2	1	2.0	.923	OF-13

Tom Daly

DALY, THOMAS DANIEL
B. Dec. 12, 1891, St. John, N. B., Canada D. Nov. 7, 1946, Bedford, Mass.   BR TR 5'11½" 171 lbs.

Year	Team	Games	BA	SA	AB	H	2B	3B	HR	HR%	R	RBI	BB	SO	SB	AB	H	PO	A	E	DP	TC/G	FA	G by Pos
1913	CHI A	1	.000	.000	3	0	0	0	0	0.0	0	0	0	0	0	1	0	6	1	0	1	7.0	1.000	C-1
1914		61	.233	.248	133	31	2	0	0	0.0	13	8	7	13	3	24	6	60	6	4	3	1.1	.943	OF-23, 3B-5, C-4, 1B-2
1915		29	.191	.213	47	9	1	0	0	0.0	5	3	5	9	0	9	1	61	9	3	0	2.5	.959	C-19, 1B-1
1916	CLE A	31	.219	.260	73	16	1	0	0	0.0	3	8	1	2	0	5	1	86	24	2	3	3.6	.982	C-25, OF-1
1918	CHI N	1	.000	.000	1	0	0	0	0	0.0	0	0	0	0	0	0	0	2	0	1	0	3.0	.667	C-1
1919		25	.220	.260	50	11	0	1	0	0.0	4	1	2	5	0	6	0	55	10	3	2	2.7	.956	C-18
1920		44	.311	.378	90	28	6	0	0	0.0	12	13	2	6	1	14	4	88	18	2	0	2.5	.981	C-29
1921		51	.238	.301	143	34	7	1	0	0.0	12	22	8	8	1	4	1	171	48	6	10	4.4	.973	C-47
8 yrs.		243	.239	.281	540	129	17	3	0	0.0	49	55	25	43	5	62	13	529	116	21	19	2.7	.968	C-144, OF-24, 3B-5, 1B-3

Tom Daly

DALY, THOMAS PETER (Tido)
Brother of Joe Daly.
B. Feb. 7, 1866, Philadelphia, Pa. D. Oct. 29, 1939, Brooklyn, N. Y.   BB TR 5'7" 170 lbs.

Year	Team	Games	BA	SA	AB	H	2B	3B	HR	HR%	R	RBI	BB	SO	SB	AB	H	PO	A	E	DP	TC/G	FA	G by Pos
1887	CHI N	74	.207	.301	256	53	10	4	2	0.8	45	17	20	25	29	0	0	390	161	39	17	8.0	.934	C-64, OF-8, SS-2, 2B-2, 1B-2
1888		65	.192	.256	219	42	2	6	0	0.0	34	29	10	26	10	0	0	411	107	34	10	8.5	.938	C-62, OF-4
1889	WAS N	71	.300	.404	250	75	13	5	1	0.4	39	40	38	28	18	0	0	354	102	43	8	7.0	.914	C-57, 1B-8, 2B-4, OF-3, SS-1
1890	BKN N	82	.243	.353	292	71	9	4	5	1.7	55	43	32	43	20	0	0	491	78	21	14	7.2	.964	C-69, 1B-12, OF-1
1891		58	.250	.385	200	50	11	5	2	1.0	29	27	21	34	7	0	0	289	58	38	8	6.6	.901	C-26, 1B-15, SS-11, OF-7
1892		124	.256	.343	446	114	15	6	4	0.9	76	51	64	61	34	0	0	260	170	33	16	3.7	.929	3B-57, OF-30, C-27, 2B-10
1893		126	.289	.445	470	136	21	14	8	1.7	94	70	65	32	0	0	287	348	77	27	5.7	.892	2B-82, 3B-45
1894		123	.341	.476	492	168	22	10	8	1.6	135	82	77	42	51	0	0	317	354	68	52	6.0	.908	2B-123
1895		120	.281	.367	455	128	17	8	2	0.4	89	68	52	52	28	0	0	318	346	50	42	6.0	.930	2B-120
1896		67	.281	.433	224	63	13	6	3	1.3	43	29	33	25	19	0	0	170	192	37	31	6.0	.907	2B-66, C-1
1898		23	.329	.397	73	24	3	1	0	0.0	11	11	14		6	0	0	56	77	1	12	5.8	.993	2B-23
1899		141	.313	.428	498	156	24	9	5	1.0	95	88	69		43	0	0	377	453	63	69	6.3	.929	2B-141
1900		97	.312	.414	343	107	17	3	4	1.2	70	55	46		27	0	0	261	238	40	41	5.6	.926	2B-93, 1B-3, OF-2
1901		133	.315	.444	520	164	38	10	3	0.6	88	90	42		31	0	0	370	357	37	46	5.8	.944	2B-133
1902	CHI A	137	.225	.288	489	110	23	2	2	0.4	57	54	55		19	0	0	312	370	31	70	5.2	.957	2B-137

Year	Team		Games	BA	SA	AB	H	2B	3B	HR	HR%	R	RBI	BB	SO	SB	Pinch Hit AB	H	PO	A	E	DP	TC/G	FA	G by Pos

Tom Daly *continued*

Year	Team		Games	BA	SA	AB	H	2B	3B	HR	HR%	R	RBI	BB	SO	SB	AB	H	PO	A	E	DP	TC/G	FA	G by Pos
1903	2 teams	CHI A (43G – .207)				CIN N (80G – .293)																			
"	total		123	.265	.365	457	121	25	9	1	0.2	62	57	36		11	1	0	247	324	36	34	4.9	.941	2B-122
16 yrs.			1564	.278	.387	5684	1582	262	103	49	0.9	1022	811	687	401	385	1	0	4910	3735	654	497	5.9	.930	2B-1056, C-306, 3B-102, OF-55, 1B-40, SS-14

Bill Dam

DAM, ELBRIDGE RUST
B. Apr. 4, 1885, Cambridge, Mass.   D. June 22, 1930, Quincy, Mass.

Year	Team		Games	BA	SA	AB	H	2B	3B	HR	HR%	R	RBI	BB	SO	SB	AB	H	PO	A	E	DP	TC/G	FA	G by Pos
1909	BOS	N	1	.500	1.000	2	1	1	0	0	0.0	1	0	1		0	0	0	1	0	0	0	1.0	1.000	OF-1

Jack Damaska

DAMASKA, JACK LLOYD
B. Aug. 21, 1937, Beaver Falls, Pa.   BR TR 5'11" 168 lbs.

Year	Team		Games	BA	SA	AB	H	2B	3B	HR	HR%	R	RBI	BB	SO	SB	AB	H	PO	A	E	DP	TC/G	FA	G by Pos
1963	STL	N	5	.200	.200	5	1	0	0	0	0.0	1	1	0	4	0	4	1	0	0	0	0	0.0	–	OF-1, 2B-1

Harry Damrau

DAMRAU, HARRY ROBERT
B. Sept. 11, 1890, Newburgh, N. Y.   D. Aug. 21, 1957, Staten Island, N. Y.   BR TR 5'10" 178 lbs.

Year	Team		Games	BA	SA	AB	H	2B	3B	HR	HR%	R	RBI	BB	SO	SB	AB	H	PO	A	E	DP	TC/G	FA	G by Pos
1915	PHI	A	16	.196	.214	56	11	1	0	0	0.0	4	3	5	17	1	0	0	16	24	6	1	2.9	.870	3B-16

Jake Daniel

DANIEL, HANDLEY JACOB
B. Apr. 22, 1912, Roanoke, Ala.   BL TL 5'11" 175 lbs.

Year	Team		Games	BA	SA	AB	H	2B	3B	HR	HR%	R	RBI	BB	SO	SB	AB	H	PO	A	E	DP	TC/G	FA	G by Pos
1937	BKN	N	12	.185	.222	27	5	1	0	0	0.0	3	3	3	4	0	2	0	51	3	0	3	4.5	1.000	1B-7

Bert Daniels

DANIELS, BERNARD ELMER
B. Oct. 31, 1882, Danville, Ill.   D. June 6, 1958, Cedar Grove, N. J.   BR TR 5'9½" 180 lbs.

Year	Team		Games	BA	SA	AB	H	2B	3B	HR	HR%	R	RBI	BB	SO	SB	AB	H	PO	A	E	DP	TC/G	FA	G by Pos
1910	NY	A	95	.253	.343	356	90	13	8	1	0.3	68	17	41		41	0	0	208	21	12	4	2.5	.950	OF-85, 3B-6, 1B-4
1911			131	.286	.372	462	132	16	9	2	0.4	74	31	48		40	6	1	256	15	17	6	2.2	.941	OF-120
1912			133	.274	.381	496	136	25	11	2	0.4	72	41	51		37	2	1	277	13	17	1	2.3	.945	OF-131
1913			93	.216	.288	320	69	13	5	0	0.0	52	22	44	36	27	4	1	128	15	5	3	1.6	.966	OF-87
1914	CIN	N	71	.219	.305	269	59	9	7	0	0.0	29	19	19	40	14	0	0	144	7	4	2	2.2	.974	OF-71
5 yrs.			523	.255	.345	1903	486	76	40	5	0.3	295	130	203	76	159	12	3	1013	71	55	16	2.2	.952	OF-494, 3B-6, 1B-4

Fred Daniels

DANIELS, FREDERICK CLINTON (Tony)
B. Dec. 28, 1924, Gastonia, N. C.   BR TR 5'9½" 185 lbs.

Year	Team		Games	BA	SA	AB	H	2B	3B	HR	HR%	R	RBI	BB	SO	SB	AB	H	PO	A	E	DP	TC/G	FA	G by Pos
1945	PHI	N	76	.200	.230	230	46	3	2	0	0.0	15	10	12	22	1	0	0	171	215	20	41	5.3	.951	2B-75, 3B-1

Jack Daniels

DANIELS, HAROLD JACK (Sour Mash)
B. Dec. 21, 1927, Chester, Pa.   BL TL 5'10" 165 lbs.

Year	Team		Games	BA	SA	AB	H	2B	3B	HR	HR%	R	RBI	BB	SO	SB	AB	H	PO	A	E	DP	TC/G	FA	G by Pos
1952	BOS	N	106	.187	.247	219	41	5	1	2	0.9	31	14	28	30	3	17	2	119	6	3	2	1.2	.977	OF-87

Kal Daniels

DANIELS, KALVOSKI
B. Aug. 20, 1963, Vienna, Ga.   BL TR 5'11" 195 lbs.

Year	Team		Games	BA	SA	AB	H	2B	3B	HR	HR%	R	RBI	BB	SO	SB	AB	H	PO	A	E	DP	TC/G	FA	G by Pos
1986	CIN	N	74	.320	.519	181	58	10	4	6	3.3	34	23	22	30	15	23	11	88	0	3	0	1.2	.967	OF-47
1987			108	.334	.617	368	123	24	1	26	7.1	73	64	60	62	26	12	2	178	5	6	0	1.8	.968	OF-94
1988			140	.291	.463	495	144	29	1	18	3.6	95	64	87	94	27	1	0	256	10	5	2	1.9	.982	OF-137
1989	2 teams	CIN N (44G – .218)				LA N (11G – .342)																			
"	total		55	.246	.392	171	42	13	0	4	2.3	33	17	43	33	9	5	0	88	4	0	1	1.7	1.000	OF-49
4 yrs.			377	.302	.508	1215	367	76	6	54	4.4	235	168	212	219	77	41	13	610	19	14	3	1.7	.978	OF-327

Law Daniels

DANIELS, LAWRENCE LONG
B. July 14, 1862, Newton, Mass.   D. Jan. 7, 1929, Waltham, Mass.   BR TR 5'10" 170 lbs.

Year	Team		Games	BA	SA	AB	H	2B	3B	HR	HR%	R	RBI	BB	SO	SB	AB	H	PO	A	E	DP	TC/G	FA	G by Pos
1887	BAL	AA	48	.248	.291	165	41	5	1	0	0.0	23		8		7	0	0	188	44	45	5	5.8	.838	C-26, OF-15, 1B-4, 2B-2, SS-1, 3B-1
1888	KC	AA	61	.202	.225	218	44	2	0	1	0.5	32	28	14		20	0	0	163	71	39	7	4.5	.857	OF-30, C-29, 3B-2, SS-1
2 yrs.			109	.222	.253	383	85	7	1	1	0.3	55	28	22		27	0	0	351	115	84	12	5.0	.847	C-55, OF-45, 1B-4, 3B-3, SS-2, 2B-2

Buck Danner

DANNER, HENRY FREDERICK
B. June 8, 1891, Dedham, Mass.   D. Sept. 21, 1949, Boston, Mass.   BR TR 5'6½" 135 lbs.

Year	Team		Games	BA	SA	AB	H	2B	3B	HR	HR%	R	RBI	BB	SO	SB	AB	H	PO	A	E	DP	TC/G	FA	G by Pos
1915	PHI	A	3	.250	.250	12	3	0	0	0	0.0	1	0	1		0	1	0	5	4	3	0	4.0	.750	SS-3

Harry Danning

DANNING, HARRY (Harry The Horse)
Brother of Ike Danning.
B. Sept. 6, 1911, Los Angeles, Calif.   BR TR 6'1" 190 lbs.

Year	Team		Games	BA	SA	AB	H	2B	3B	HR	HR%	R	RBI	BB	SO	SB	AB	H	PO	A	E	DP	TC/G	FA	G by Pos
1933	NY	N	3	.000	.000	2	0	0	0	0	0.0	0	1	0	0	0	2	0	2	0	0	0	0.7	1.000	C-1
1934			53	.330	.433	97	32	7	0	1	1.0	8	7	1	9	1	16	8	78	13	1	1	1.7	.989	C-37
1935			65	.243	.368	152	37	11	1	2	1.3	16	20	9	15	0	19	2	153	22	4	6	2.8	.978	C-44
1936			32	.159	.246	69	11	2	2	0	0.0	3	4	1	5	0	6	1	70	10	1	2	2.5	.988	C-24
1937			93	.288	.438	292	84	12	4	8	2.7	30	51	18	20	0	11	2	332	57	7	7	4.3	.982	C-86
1938			120	.306	.438	448	137	26	3	9	2.0	59	60	23	40	1	6	2	449	50	8	7	4.2	.984	C-114
1939			135	.313	.479	520	163	28	5	16	3.1	79	74	35	42	4	3	0	550	80	6	13	4.7	.991	C-132
1940			140	.300	.454	524	157	34	4	13	2.5	65	91	35	31	3	9	0	634	91	15	13	5.3	.980	C-131
1941			130	.244	.355	459	112	22	4	7	1.5	58	56	30	25	1	11	3	532	77	4	8	4.7	.993	C-116, 1B-1
1942			119	.279	.350	408	114	20	3	1	0.2	45	34	34	29	3	2	1	459	55	11	7	4.4	.979	C-116
10 yrs.			890	.285	.415	2971	847	162	26	57	1.9	363	397	187	216	13	85	19	3259	455	57	64	4.2	.985	C-801, 1B-1

WORLD SERIES																									
1936	NY	N	2	.000	.000	2	0	0	0	0	0.0	0	0	0	1	0	1	0	3	0	0	0	2.0	.750	C-1
1937			3	.250	.333	12	3	1	0	0	0.0	0	2	0	2	0	0	0	20	1	0	0	7.0	1.000	C-3
2 yrs.			5	.214	.286	14	3	1	0	0	0.0	0	2	0	3	0	1	0	23	1	0	0	5.0	.960	C-4

Year	Team		Games	BA	SA	AB	H	2B	3B	HR	HR%	R	RBI	BB	SO	SB	Pinch Hit AB	Pinch Hit H	PO	A	E	DP	TC/G	FA	G by Pos

Ike Danning

DANNING, IKE
Brother of Harry Danning.
B. Jan. 20, 1905, Los Angeles, Calif. D. Mar. 30, 1983, Santa Monica, Calif.
BR TR 5'10'' 160 lbs.

Year	Team		Games	BA	SA	AB	H	2B	3B	HR	HR%	R	RBI	BB	SO	SB	PH AB	PH H	PO	A	E	DP	TC/G	FA	G by Pos
1928	STL	A	2	.500	.500	6	3	0	0	0	0.0	0	1	1	2	0	0	0	8	3	1	0	6.0	.917	C-2

Fats Dantonio

DANTONIO, JOHN JAMES
B. Dec. 31, 1919, New Orleans, La.
BR TR 5'8'' 165 lbs.

Year	Team		Games	BA	SA	AB	H	2B	3B	HR	HR%	R	RBI	BB	SO	SB	PH AB	PH H	PO	A	E	DP	TC/G	FA	G by Pos
1944	BKN	N	3	.143	.143	7	1	0	0	0	0.0	0	1	0	1	0	0	0	11	0	2	0	4.3	.846	C-3
1945			47	.250	.313	128	32	6	1	0	0.0	12	12	11	6	3	1	1	141	16	12	0	3.6	.929	C-45
2 yrs.			50	.244	.304	135	33	6	1	0	0.0	12	12	11	7	3	1	1	152	16	14	0	3.6	.923	C-48

Babe Danzig

DANZIG, HAROLD P.
B. Apr. 30, 1887, Binghampton, N. Y. D. July 14, 1931, San Francisco, Calif.
BR TR 6'2'' 205 lbs.

Year	Team		Games	BA	SA	AB	H	2B	3B	HR	HR%	R	RBI	BB	SO	SB	PH AB	PH H	PO	A	E	DP	TC/G	FA	G by Pos
1909	BOS	A	6	.154	.154	13	2	0	0	0	0.0	0	0	2		0	2	0	24	0	1	3	4.2	.960	1B-3

Cliff Dapper

DAPPER, CLIFFORD ROLAND
B. Jan. 2, 1920, Los Angeles, Calif.
BR TR 6'2'' 190 lbs.

Year	Team		Games	BA	SA	AB	H	2B	3B	HR	HR%	R	RBI	BB	SO	SB	PH AB	PH H	PO	A	E	DP	TC/G	FA	G by Pos
1942	BKN	N	8	.471	.706	17	8	1	0	1	5.9	2	9	2	2	0	0	0	20	3	0	1	2.9	1.000	C-8

Cliff Daringer

DARINGER, CLIFFORD CLARENCE (Shanty)
Brother of Rolla Daringer.
B. Apr. 10, 1885, Hayden, Ind. D. Dec. 26, 1971, Sacramento, Calif.
BL TR 5'7½'' 155 lbs.

Year	Team		Games	BA	SA	AB	H	2B	3B	HR	HR%	R	RBI	BB	SO	SB	PH AB	PH H	PO	A	E	DP	TC/G	FA	G by Pos
1914	KC	F	64	.263	.288	160	42	2	1	0	0.0	12	16	11		9	4	1	70	142	19	16	3.6	.918	SS-24, 3B-19, 2B-14

Rolla Daringer

DARINGER, ROLLA HARRISON
Brother of Cliff Daringer.
B. Nov. 15, 1888, North Vernon, Ind. D. May 23, 1974, Seymour, Ind.
BL TR 5'10'' 155 lbs.

Year	Team		Games	BA	SA	AB	H	2B	3B	HR	HR%	R	RBI	BB	SO	SB	PH AB	PH H	PO	A	E	DP	TC/G	FA	G by Pos
1914	STL	N	2	.500	.750	4	2	1	0	0	0.0	1	0	1	2	0	1	0	0	2	1	1	1.5	.667	SS-1
1915			10	.087	.087	23	2	0	0	0	0.0	3	0	9	5	0	0	0	13	23	2	5	3.8	.947	SS-10
2 yrs.			12	.148	.185	27	4	1	0	0	0.0	4	0	10	7	0	1	0	13	25	3	6	3.4	.927	SS-11

Alvin Dark

DARK, ALVIN RALPH (Blackie)
B. Jan. 7, 1922, Comanche, Okla.
Manager 1961-64, 1966-71, 1974-75, 1977.
BR TR 5'11'' 185 lbs.

Year	Team		Games	BA	SA	AB	H	2B	3B	HR	HR%	R	RBI	BB	SO	SB	PH AB	PH H	PO	A	E	DP	TC/G	FA	G by Pos
1946	BOS	N	15	.231	.462	13	3	3	0	0	0.0	0	1	0	3	0	0	0	6	14	2	2	1.5	.909	SS-12, OF-1
1948			137	.322	.433	543	175	39	6	3	0.6	85	48	24	36	4	4	3	253	393	25	66	4.9	.963	SS-133
1949			130	.276	.355	529	146	23	5	3	0.6	74	53	31	43	5	0	0	233	395	26	76	5.0	.960	SS-125, 3B-4
1950	NY	N	154	.279	.440	587	164	36	5	16	2.7	79	67	39	60	9	0	0	288	465	30	101	5.1	.962	SS-154
1951			156	.303	.454	646	196	41	7	14	2.2	114	69	42	39	12	0	0	295	465	45	114	5.2	.944	SS-156
1952			151	.301	.431	589	177	29	3	14	2.4	92	73	47	39	6	1	0	324	423	27	116	5.1	.965	SS-150
1953			155	.300	.488	647	194	41	6	23	3.6	126	88	28	34	7	1	0	325	433	24	102	5.0	.969	SS-110, 2B-26, OF-17, 3B-8, P-1
1954			154	.293	.446	644	189	26	6	20	3.1	98	70	27	40	5	0	0	289	487	36	105	5.3	.956	SS-154
1955			115	.282	.394	475	134	20	3	9	1.9	77	45	22	32	2	1	0	213	324	21	70	4.9	.962	SS-115
1956	2 teams		NY N (48G – .252)			STL N (100G – .286)																			
"	total		148	.275	.368	619	170	26	7	6	1.0	73	54	29	46	3	1	0	267	424	29	93	4.9	.960	SS-147
1957	STL	N	140	.290	.381	583	169	25	8	4	0.7	80	64	29	56	3	1	0	276	421	25	105	5.2	.965	SS-139, 3B-1
1958	2 teams		STL N (18G – .297)			CHI N (114G – .295)																			
"	total		132	.295	.364	528	156	16	4	4	0.8	61	48	31	29	1	8	5	121	260	21	30	3.0	.948	3B-119, SS-8
1959	CHI	N	136	.264	.386	477	126	22	9	6	1.3	60	45	55	50	1	1	0	138	260	21	21	3.1	.950	3B-131, 1B-4, SS-1
1960	2 teams		PHI N (55G – .242)			MIL N (50G – .298)																			
"	total		105	.265	.351	339	90	11	3	4	1.2	45	32	26	27	1	17	3	146	90	10	11	2.3	.959	3B-57, OF-25, 1B-11, 2B-3
14 yrs.			1828	.289	.411	7219	2089	358	72	126	1.7	1064	757	430	534	59	35	11	3174	4854	342	1012	4.6	.959	SS-1404, 3B-320, OF-43, 2B-29, 1B-15, P-1

WORLD SERIES

Year	Team		Games	BA	SA	AB	H	2B	3B	HR	HR%	R	RBI	BB	SO	SB	PH AB	PH H	PO	A	E	DP	TC/G	FA	G by Pos
1948	BOS	N	6	.167	.208	24	4	1	0	0	0.0	2	0	0	0	0	0	0	7	12	3	1	3.7	.864	SS-6
1951	NY	N	6	.417	.667	24	10	3	0	1	4.2	5	4	2	3	0	0	0	10	15	0	4	4.2	1.000	SS-6
1954			4	.412	.412	17	7	0	0	0	0.0	2	0	1	1	0	0	0	7	12	1	1	5.0	.950	SS-4
3 yrs.			16	.323	.431	65	21	4	0	1	1.5	9	4	3	6	0	0	0	24	39	4	6	4.2	.940	SS-16

Dell Darling

DARLING, CONRAD
B. Dec. 21, 1861, Erie, Pa. D. Nov. 20, 1904, Erie, Pa.
BR TR 5'8'' 170 lbs.

Year	Team		Games	BA	SA	AB	H	2B	3B	HR	HR%	R	RBI	BB	SO	SB	PH AB	PH H	PO	A	E	DP	TC/G	FA	G by Pos
1883	BUF	N	6	.167	.167	18	3	0	0	0	0.0	1		2	5		0	0	16	5	3	1	4.0	.875	C-6
1887	CHI	N	38	.319	.489	141	45	7	4	3	2.1	28	20	22	18	19	0	0	132	45	23	3	5.3	.885	OF-20, C-20
1888			20	.213	.360	75	16	3	1	2	2.7	12	7	3	12	0	0	0	139	26	12	5	8.9	.932	C-20
1889			36	.192	.217	120	23	1	1	0	0.0	14	7	25	22	5	0	0	172	45	9	2	6.3	.960	C-36
1890	CHI	P	58	.258	.376	221	57	12	4	2	0.9	45	39	29	28	5	0	0	296	72	37	24	7.0	.909	1B-29, SS-15, C-9, OF-7, 2B-3, 3B-2
1891	STL	AA	17	.132	.264	53	7	1	3	0	0.0	9	9	10	11	0	0	0	87	28	15	1	7.6	.885	C-17, 2B-2, SS-1
6 yrs.			175	.240	.354	628	151	24	13	7	1.1	109	82	91	96	29	0	0	842	221	99	36	6.6	.915	C-108, 1B-29, OF-27, SS-16, 2B-5, 3B-2

Jack Darragh

DARRAGH, JAMES S.
B. July 17, 1866, Ebensburg, Pa. D. Aug. 12, 1939, Rochester, N. Y.
BR TR 6'2'' — lbs.

Year	Team		Games	BA	SA	AB	H	2B	3B	HR	HR%	R	RBI	BB	SO	SB	PH AB	PH H	PO	A	E	DP	TC/G	FA	G by Pos
1891	LOU	AA	1	.500	.500	2	1	0	0	0	0.0	0	0	0	0	0	0	0	8	1	0	0	9.0	1.000	1B-1

Bobby Darwin

DARWIN, ARTHUR BOBBY LEE
B. Feb. 16, 1943, Los Angeles, Calif.
BR TR 6'2'' 190 lbs.

Year	Team		Games	BA	SA	AB	H	2B	3B	HR	HR%	R	RBI	BB	SO	SB	PH AB	PH H	PO	A	E	DP	TC/G	FA	G by Pos
1962	LA	A	1	.000	.000	1	0	0	0	0	0.0	0	0	0	1	0	0	0	0	0	1	0	1.0	—	P-1
1969	LA	N	6	—	—	0	0	0	0	0	—	1	0	0	0	0	0	0	0	0	0	0	0.0	—	P-3

Year	Team	Games	BA	SA	AB	H	2B	3B	HR	HR%	R	RBI	BB	SO	SB	Pinch Hit AB	Pinch Hit H	PO	A	E	DP	TC/G	FA	G by Pos

Bobby Darwin *continued*

Year	Team	Games	BA	SA	AB	H	2B	3B	HR	HR%	R	RBI	BB	SO	SB	AB	H	PO	A	E	DP	TC/G	FA	G by Pos
1971		11	.250	.450	20	5	1	0	1	5.0	2	4	2	9	0	7	2	9	0	0	0	0.8	1.000	OF-4
1972	MIN A	145	.267	.442	513	137	20	2	22	4.3	48	80	38	145	2	5	1	289	8	6	1	2.1	.980	OF-142
1973		145	.252	.391	560	141	20	2	18	3.2	69	90	46	137	5	6	0	233	13	5	1	1.7	.980	OF-140, DH-1
1974		152	.264	.442	575	152	13	7	25	4.3	67	94	37	127	1	9	4	254	8	8	1	1.8	.970	OF-142
1975	2 teams		MIN A (48G – .219)			MIL A	(55G – .247)																	
"	total	103	.234	.389	355	83	12	2	13	3.7	45	41	29	98	6	6	2	110	8	3	1	1.2	.975	OF-70, DH-28
1976	2 teams		MIL A (25G – .247)			BOS A	(43G – .179)																	
"	total	68	.207	.352	179	37	8	3	4	2.2	15	18	8	51	1	18	3	68	2	2	0	1.1	.972	OF-38, DH-17
1977	2 teams		BOS A (4G – .222)			CHI N	(11G – .167)																	
"	total	15	.190	.286	21	4	2	0	0	0.0	3	1	0	9	0	10	2	1	0	1	0	0.1	.500	DH-2, OF-2
9 yrs.		646	.251	.412	2224	559	76	16	83	3.7	250	328	160	577	15	61	14	964	39	26	4	1.6	.975	OF-538, DH-48, P-4

Doug Dascenzo

DASCENZO, DOUGLAS CRAIG BB TL 5'7" 150 lbs.
B. June 30, 1964, Cleveland, Ohio

Year	Team	Games	BA	SA	AB	H	2B	3B	HR	HR%	R	RBI	BB	SO	SB	AB	H	PO	A	E	DP	TC/G	FA	G by Pos
1988	CHI N	26	.213	.253	75	16	3	0	0	0.0	9	4	9	4	6	5	0	55	1	0	0	2.2	1.000	OF-20
1989		47	.165	.194	139	23	1	0	1	0.7	20	12	13	13	6	0	0	96	0	0	0	2.0	1.000	OF-45
2 yrs.		73	.182	.215	214	39	4	0	1	0.5	29	16	22	17	12	5	0	151	1	0	0	2.1	1.000	OF-65

Wally Dashiell

DASHIELL, JOHN WALLACE BR TR 5'9½" 170 lbs.
B. May 9, 1902, Jewett, Tex. D. May 20, 1972, Pensacola, Fla.

Year	Team	Games	BA	SA	AB	H	2B	3B	HR	HR%	R	RBI	BB	SO	SB	AB	H	PO	A	E	DP	TC/G	FA	G by Pos
1924	CHI A	1	.000	.000	2	0	0	0	0	0.0	0	0	0	0	0	0	0	1	1	1	0	3.0	.667	SS-1

Jeff Datz

DATZ, JEFFREY WILLIAM BR TR 6'4" 220 lbs.
B. Nov. 28, 1959, Camden, N. J.

Year	Team	Games	BA	SA	AB	H	2B	3B	HR	HR%	R	RBI	BB	SO	SB	AB	H	PO	A	E	DP	TC/G	FA	G by Pos
1989	DET A	7	.200	.200	10	2	0	0	0	0.0	0	1	0	1	0	0	0	17	1	0	0	2.6	1.000	C-6, DH-1

Harry Daubert

DAUBERT, HARRY J. BR TR 6' 165 lbs.
B. June 19, 1892, Columbus, Ohio D. Jan. 8, 1944, Detroit, Mich.

Year	Team	Games	BA	SA	AB	H	2B	3B	HR	HR%	R	RBI	BB	SO	SB	AB	H	PO	A	E	DP	TC/G	FA	G by Pos
1915	PIT N	1	.000	.000	1	0	0	0	0	0.0	0	0	0	1	0	1	0	0	0	0	0	0.0	–	

Jake Daubert

DAUBERT, JACOB ELLSWORTH BL TL 5'10½" 160 lbs.
B. Apr. 17, 1884, Shamokin, Pa. D. Oct. 9, 1924, Cincinnati, Ohio

Year	Team	Games	BA	SA	AB	H	2B	3B	HR	HR%	R	RBI	BB	SO	SB	AB	H	PO	A	E	DP	TC/G	FA	G by Pos
1910	BKN N	144	.264	.389	552	146	15	15	8	1.4	67	50	47	53	23	0	0	1418	72	16	81	10.5	.989	1B-144
1911		149	.307	.391	573	176	17	8	5	0.9	89	45	51	56	32	0	0	1485	88	18	91	10.7	.989	1B-149
1912		145	.308	.415	559	172	19	16	3	0.5	81	66	48	45	29	1	0	1373	76	10	68	10.1	.993	1B-143
1913		139	.350	.423	508	178	17	7	2	0.4	76	52	44	40	25	0	0	1279	80	13	91	9.9	.993	1B-138
1914		126	.329	.432	474	156	17	7	6	1.3	89	45	30	34	25	0	0	1097	48	8	68	9.2	.993	1B-126
1915		150	.301	.381	544	164	21	8	2	0.4	62	47	57	48	11	0	0	1441	102	11	73	10.4	.993	1B-150
1916		127	.316	.397	478	151	16	7	3	0.6	75	33	38	39	21	1	0	1195	66	9	56	10.0	.993	1B-126
1917		125	.261	.299	468	122	4	4	2	0.4	59	30	51	30	11	0	0	1188	82	12	59	10.3	.991	1B-125
1918		108	.308	.429	396	122	12	15	2	0.5	50	47	27	18	10	2	0	1069	63	10	43	10.6	.991	1B-105
1919	CIN N	140	.276	.350	537	148	10	12	2	0.4	79	44	35	23	11	0	0	1437	80	17	75	11.0	.989	1B-140
1920		142	.304	.423	553	168	28	13	4	0.7	97	48	47	29	11	2	0	1358	63	15	90	10.1	.990	1B-140
1921		136	.306	.399	516	158	18	12	2	0.4	69	64	24	16	12	0	0	1290	78	10	98	10.1	.993	1B-136
1922		156	.336	.492	610	205	15	22	12	2.0	114	66	56	21	14	0	0	1652	79	11	127	11.2	.994	1B-156
1923		125	.292	.398	500	146	27	10	2	0.4	63	54	40	20	11	4	1	1224	77	9	95	10.5	.993	1B-121
1924		102	.281	.368	405	114	14	9	1	0.2	47	31	28	17	5	0	0	1128	74	12	84	11.9	.990	1B-102
15 yrs.		2014	.303	.401	7673	2326	250	165	56	0.7	1117	722	623	489	251	11	1	19634	1128	181	1199	10.4	.991	1B-2001

WORLD SERIES

Year	Team	Games	BA	SA	AB	H	2B	3B	HR	HR%	R	RBI	BB	SO	SB	AB	H	PO	A	E	DP	TC/G	FA	G by Pos
1916	BKN N	4	.176	.294	17	3	0	1	0	0.0	1	0	2	3	0	0	0	40	3	0	1	10.8	1.000	1B-4
1919	CIN N	8	.241	.310	29	7	0	1	0	0.0	4	1	1	2	1	0	0	81	5	2	5	11.0	.977	1B-8
2 yrs.		12	.217	.304	46	10	0	2	0	0.0	5	1	3	5	1	0	0	121	8	2	6	10.9	.985	1B-12

Rich Dauer

DAUER, RICHARD FREMONT BR TR 6' 180 lbs.
B. July 27, 1952, San Bernardino, Calif.

Year	Team	Games	BA	SA	AB	H	2B	3B	HR	HR%	R	RBI	BB	SO	SB	AB	H	PO	A	E	DP	TC/G	FA	G by Pos
1976	BAL A	11	.103	.103	39	4	0	0	0	0.0	0	3	1	3	0	1	0	22	22	0	7	4.0	1.000	2B-10
1977		96	.243	.349	304	74	15	1	5	1.6	38	25	20	28	1	12	1	182	233	7	56	4.4	.983	2B-83, 3B-9, DH-2
1978		133	.264	.353	459	121	23	0	6	1.3	57	46	26	22	0	3	1	222	321	7	69	4.1	.987	2B-87, 3B-52, DH-1
1979		142	.257	.355	479	123	20	0	9	1.9	63	61	36	36	0	0	0	234	355	17	72	4.3	.972	2B-103, 3B-44
1980		152	.284	.352	557	158	32	0	2	0.4	71	63	46	19	3	1	0	334	418	8	115	5.0	.989	2B-137, 3B-35
1981		96	.263	.369	369	97	27	0	4	1.1	41	38	27	18	0	1	0	201	256	5	71	4.8	.989	2B-94, 3B-4
1982		158	.280	.373	558	156	24	2	8	1.4	75	57	50	34	0	1	0	289	354	8	75	4.1	.988	2B-123, 3B-61
1983		140	.235	.309	459	108	19	0	5	1.1	49	41	47	29	1	0	0	280	333	11	79	4.4	.987	2B-131, 3B-17
1984		127	.254	.335	397	101	26	0	2	0.5	29	24	24	23	1	2	0	225	329	11	76	4.4	.988	2B-123, 3B-3
1985		85	.202	.264	208	42	7	0	2	1.0	25	14	20	7	0	0	0	126	202	4	44	3.9	.988	2B-73, 3B-17, 1B-1
10 yrs.		1140	.257	.343	3829	984	193	3	43	1.1	448	372	297	219	6	21	2	2115	2823	75	664	4.4	.985	2B-964, 3B-242, DH-3, 1B-1

LEAGUE CHAMPIONSHIP SERIES

Year	Team	Games	BA	SA	AB	H	2B	3B	HR	HR%	R	RBI	BB	SO	SB	AB	H	PO	A	E	DP	TC/G	FA	G by Pos
1979	BAL A	4	.182	.182	11	2	0	0	0	0.0	0	0	0	0	0	0	0	10	12	0	2	5.5	1.000	2B-4
1983		4	.000	.000	14	0	0	0	0	0.0	0	1	0	0	0	0	0	8	12	0	1	5.0	1.000	2B-4
2 yrs.		8	.080	.080	25	2	0	0	0	0.0	0	1	0	0	0	0	0	18	24	0	3	5.3	1.000	2B-8

WORLD SERIES

Year	Team	Games	BA	SA	AB	H	2B	3B	HR	HR%	R	RBI	BB	SO	SB	AB	H	PO	A	E	DP	TC/G	FA	G by Pos
1979	BAL A	6	.294	.529	17	5	1	0	1	5.9	2	1	0	1	0	1	0	10	10	0	1	3.3	1.000	2B-5
1983		5	.211	.263	19	4	1	0	0	0.0	2	3	0	3	0	0	0	13	7	0	4	4.0	1.000	2B-5, 3B-1
2 yrs.		11	.250	.389	36	9	2	0	1	2.8	4	4	0	4	0	1	0	23	17	0	5	3.6	1.000	2B-10, 3B-1

Doc Daugherty

DAUGHERTY, HAROLD RAY BR TR 6' 180 lbs.
B. Oct. 12, 1927, Paris, Pa.

Year	Team	Games	BA	SA	AB	H	2B	3B	HR	HR%	R	RBI	BB	SO	SB	AB	H	PO	A	E	DP	TC/G	FA	G by Pos
1951	DET A	1	.000	.000	1	0	0	0	0	0.0	0	0	0	0	0	1	0	0	0	0	0	0.0	–	

Year	Team	Games	BA	SA	AB	H	2B	3B	HR	HR%	R	RBI	BB	SO	SB	Pinch Hit AB	Pinch Hit H	PO	A	E	DP	TC/G	FA	G by Pos

Jack Daugherty

DAUGHERTY, JOHN MICHAEL
B. July 3, 1960, Hialeah, Fla. BB TL 6' 188 lbs.

Year	Team	Games	BA	SA	AB	H	2B	3B	HR	HR%	R	RBI	BB	SO	SB	PH AB	PH H	PO	A	E	DP	TC/G	FA	G by Pos
1987	MON N	11	.100	.200	10	1	1	0	0	0.0	1	1	0	3	0	9	1	1	1	0	0	0.2	1.000	1B-1
1989	TEX A	52	.302	.406	106	32	4	2	1	0.9	15	10	11	21	2	18	7	132	14	0	12	2.8	1.000	1B-23, DH-8, OF-5
2 yrs.		63	.284	.388	116	33	5	2	1	0.9	16	11	11	24	2	27	8	133	15	0	12	2.3	1.000	1B-24, DH-8, OF-5

Bob Daughters

DAUGHTERS, ROBERT FRANCIS (Red)
B. Aug. 5, 1914, Cincinnati, Ohio   D. Aug. 22, 1988, Southbury, Conn. BR TR 6'2" 185 lbs.

Year	Team	Games	BA	SA	AB	H	2B	3B	HR	HR%	R	RBI	BB	SO	SB	PH AB	PH H	PO	A	E	DP	TC/G	FA	G by Pos
1937	BOS A	1	–	–	0	0	0	0	0	–	1	0	0	0	0	0	0	0	0	0	0	0.0	–	

Darren Daulton

DAULTON, DARREN ARTHUR
B. Jan. 3, 1962, Arkansas City, Kans. BL TR 6' 185 lbs.

Year	Team	Games	BA	SA	AB	H	2B	3B	HR	HR%	R	RBI	BB	SO	SB	PH AB	PH H	PO	A	E	DP	TC/G	FA	G by Pos
1983	PHI N	2	.333	.333	3	1	0	0	0	0.0	1	0	1	1	0	0	0	8	0	0	0	4.0	1.000	C-2
1985		36	.204	.369	103	21	3	1	4	3.9	14	11	16	37	3	5	0	160	15	1	0	4.9	.994	C-28
1986		49	.225	.428	138	31	4	0	8	5.8	18	21	38	41	2	1	0	244	21	4	6	5.5	.985	C-48
1987		53	.194	.310	129	25	6	0	3	2.3	10	13	16	37	0	12	3	210	13	2	6	4.2	.991	C-40, 1B-1
1988		58	.208	.271	144	30	6	0	1	0.7	13	12	17	26	2	15	4	205	15	6	1	3.9	.973	C-44, 1B-1
1989		131	.201	.310	368	74	12	2	8	2.2	29	44	52	58	2	11	2	627	56	11	8	5.3	.984	C-126
6 yrs.		329	.206	.329	885	182	31	3	24	2.7	85	101	140	200	9	44	9	1454	120	24	22	4.9	.985	C-288, 1B-2

Vic Davalillo

DAVALILLO, VICTOR JOSE
Born Victor Jose Davalillo y Romero.   Brother of Yo-Yo Davalillo.
B. July 31, 1936, Cabimas, Venezuela BL TL 5'7" 150 lbs.

Year	Team	Games	BA	SA	AB	H	2B	3B	HR	HR%	R	RBI	BB	SO	SB	PH AB	PH H	PO	A	E	DP	TC/G	FA	G by Pos
1963	CLE A	90	.292	.424	370	108	18	5	7	1.9	44	36	16	41	3	2	2	247	10	3	0	2.9	.988	OF-89
1964		150	.270	.354	577	156	26	2	6	1.0	64	51	34	77	21	5	0	346	11	5	5	2.4	.986	OF-143
1965		142	.301	.372	505	152	19	1	5	1.0	67	40	35	50	26	8	1	320	5	4	0	2.3	.988	OF-134
1966		121	.250	.317	344	86	6	4	3	0.9	42	19	24	37	8	3	1	208	6	3	1	1.8	.986	OF-108
1967		139	.287	.379	359	103	17	5	2	0.6	47	22	10	30	6	20	4	202	5	3	1	1.5	.986	OF-125
1968	2 teams		CLE A	(51G – .239)				CAL A		(93G – .298)														
"	total	144	.277	.355	519	144	17	7	3	0.6	49	31	18	53	25	7	3	296	8	4	3	2.1	.987	OF-135
1969	2 teams		CAL A	(33G – .155)				STL N		(63G – .265)														
"	total	96	.219	.290	169	37	4	1	2	1.2	25	11	13	19	4	43	10	73	1	0	1	0.8	1.000	OF-45, 1B-3, P-2
1970	STL N	111	.311	.437	183	57	14	3	1	0.5	29	33	13	19	4	73	24	67	3	2	1	0.6	.972	OF-54
1971	PIT N	99	.285	.383	295	84	14	6	1	0.3	48	33	11	31	10	27	9	256	15	5	18	2.8	.982	OF-61, 1B-16
1972		117	.318	.413	368	117	19	2	4	1.1	59	28	26	44	14	12	5	200	6	4	2	1.8	.981	OF-97, 1B-8
1973	2 teams		PIT N	(59G – .181)				OAK A		(38G – .188)														
"	total	97	.184	.218	147	27	2	0	1	0.7	14	7	5	11	5	49	10	96	9	3	8	1.1	.972	OF-29, 1B-18, DH-2
1974	OAK A	17	.174	.174	23	4	0	0	0	0.0	0	1	2	2	0	6	1	3	0	0	0	0.2	1.000	OF-6, DH-4
1977	LA N	24	.313	.354	48	15	2	0	0	0.0	3	4	0	6	0	14	4	13	0	0	0	0.5	1.000	OF-12
1978		75	.312	.390	77	24	1	1	1	1.3	15	11	3	7	2	47	12	21	1	0	0	0.3	1.000	OF-25, 1B-2
1979		29	.259	.296	27	7	1	0	0	0.0	2	2	2	2	0	24	6	2	0	0	0	0.1	1.000	OF-3
1980		7	.167	.167	6	1	0	0	0	0.0	1	0	0	1	0	5	1	2	0	0	1	0.3	1.000	1B-1
16 yrs.		1458	.279	.364	4017	1122	160	37	36	0.9	509	329	212	422	125	360	95	2352	80	36	42	1.7	.985	OF-1066, 1B-48, DH-6, P-2

LEAGUE CHAMPIONSHIP SERIES

Year	Team	Games	BA	SA	AB	H	2B	3B	HR	HR%	R	RBI	BB	SO	SB	PH AB	PH H	PO	A	E	DP	TC/G	FA	G by Pos
1971	PIT N	2	.000	.000	2	0	0	0	0	0.0	0	0	0	2	0	2	0	0	0	0	0	0.0		
1972		1	–	–	0	0	0	0	0	–	0	0	0	1	0	0	0	0	0	0	0	0.0		
1973	OAK A	4	.625	1.000	8	5	1	1	0	0.0	2	1	1	0	0	1	1	7	0	1	0	2.0	.875	OF-2, 1B-2
1977	LA N	1	1.000	1.000	1	1	0	0	0	0.0	1	0	0	1	0	0	0	0	0	0	0	0.0	–	
4 yrs.		8	.545	.818	11	6	1	1	0	0.0	3	1	2	1	0	4	2	7	0	1	0	1.0	.875	OF-2, 1B-2

WORLD SERIES

Year	Team	Games	BA	SA	AB	H	2B	3B	HR	HR%	R	RBI	BB	SO	SB	PH AB	PH H	PO	A	E	DP	TC/G	FA	G by Pos
1971	PIT N	3	.333	.333	3	1	0	0	0	0.0	1	0	0	3	0	2	0	0	0	0	0.7	1.000	OF-2	
1973	OAK A	6	.091	.091	11	1	0	0	0	0.0	0	0	2	1	0	2	0	15	0	0	0	2.5	1.000	OF-4, 1B-1
1977	LA N	3	.333	.333	3	1	0	0	0	0.0	0	1	0	1	0	3	1	0	0	0	0	0.0	–	
1978		2	.333	.333	3	1	0	0	0	0.0	0	0	0	0	0	2	1	0	0	0	0	0.0	–	DH-1
4 yrs.		14	.200	.200	20	4	0	0	0	0.0	2	1	2	5	0	9	2	17	0	0	0	1.2	1.000	OF-6, DH-1, 1B-1

2nd

Yo-Yo Davalillo

DAVALILLO, POMPEYO ANTONIO
Born Pompeyo Antonio Davalillo y Romero.   Brother of Vic Davalillo.
B. June 30, 1931, Caracas, Venezuela BR TR 5'3" 140 lbs.

Year	Team	Games	BA	SA	AB	H	2B	3B	HR	HR%	R	RBI	BB	SO	SB	PH AB	PH H	PO	A	E	DP	TC/G	FA	G by Pos
1953	WAS A	19	.293	.310	58	17	1	0	0	0.0	10	2	1	7	1	0	0	39	47	6	10	4.8	.935	SS-17

Jerry DaVanon

DaVANON, FRANK GERALD
B. Aug. 21, 1945, Oceanside, Calif. BR TR 5'11" 175 lbs.

Year	Team	Games	BA	SA	AB	H	2B	3B	HR	HR%	R	RBI	BB	SO	SB	PH AB	PH H	PO	A	E	DP	TC/G	FA	G by Pos
1969	2 teams		SD N	(24G – .136)				STL N		(16G – .300)														
"	total	40	.202	.273	99	20	4	0	1	1.0	11	10	9	20	0	2	0	63	86	8	13	3.9	.949	SS-23, 2B-15
1970	STL N	11	.111	.167	18	2	1	0	0	0.0	2	0	2	5	0	3	0	8	14	0	3	2.0	1.000	3B-5, 2B-3
1971	BAL A	38	.235	.296	81	19	5	0	0	0.0	14	4	12	20	0	0	0	45	59	4	12	2.8	.963	2B-20, SS-11, 3B-3, 1B-1
1973	CAL A	41	.245	.306	49	12	3	0	0	0.0	6	2	3	9	1	0	0	29	45	6	6	2.0	.925	SS-14, 2B-12, 3B-7
1974	STL N	30	.150	.175	40	6	1	0	0	0.0	4	4	4	5	0	1	0	19	35	5	8	2.0	.915	SS-14, 3B-8, 2B-7, OF-1
1975	HOU N	32	.278	.392	97	27	4	2	1	1.0	15	10	16	7	2	3	0	54	94	7	16	4.8	.955	SS-21, 2B-9, 3B-3
1976		61	.290	.402	107	31	3	3	1	0.9	19	20	21	12	0	15	2	53	94	7	16	2.5	.955	SS-17, 2B-17, 3B-9
1977	STL N	9	.000	.000	8	0	0	0	0	0.0	2	0	1	2	0	1	0	4	8	1	0	1.4	.923	2B-5
8 yrs.		262	.234	.315	499	117	21	5	3	0.6	73	50	68	80	3	25	2	275	435	38	74	2.9	.949	SS-100, 2B-88, 3B-35, OF-1, 1B-1

Jim Davenport

DAVENPORT, JAMES HOUSTON
B. Aug. 17, 1933, Siluria, Ala.
Manager 1985. BR TR 5'11" 170 lbs.

Year	Team	Games	BA	SA	AB	H	2B	3B	HR	HR%	R	RBI	BB	SO	SB	PH AB	PH H	PO	A	E	DP	TC/G	FA	G by Pos
1958	SF N	134	.256	.403	434	111	22	3	12	2.8	70	41	33	64	1	1	0	96	232	14	19	2.6	.959	3B-130, SS-5
1959		123	.258	.343	469	121	16	3	6	1.3	65	38	28	65	0	3	0	91	222	7	15	2.6	.978	3B-121, SS-1
1960		112	.251	.358	363	91	15	3	6	1.7	43	38	26	58	0	9	1	83	178	10	14	2.4	.963	3B-103, SS-7

Year	Team	Games	BA	SA	AB	H	2B	3B	HR	HR%	R	RBI	BB	SO	SB	Pinch Hit AB	Pinch Hit H	PO	A	E	DP	TC/G	FA	G by Pos

Jim Davenport *continued*

Year	Team	Games	BA	SA	AB	H	2B	3B	HR	HR%	R	RBI	BB	SO	SB	Pinch Hit AB	Pinch Hit H	PO	A	E	DP	TC/G	FA	G by Pos
1961		137	.278	.443	436	121	28	4	12	2.8	64	65	45	65	4	5	1	119	235	13	25	2.7	.965	3B-132
1962		144	.297	.456	485	144	25	5	14	2.9	83	58	45	76	2	3	1	125	256	19	28	2.8	.953	3B-141
1963		147	.252	.333	460	116	19	3	4	0.9	40	36	32	87	5	13	2	152	230	13	16	2.7	.967	3B-127, 2B-22, SS-1
1964		116	.236	.330	297	70	10	6	2	0.7	24	26	29	46	2	7	0	138	237	11	29	3.3	.972	SS-64, 3B-41, 2B-30
1965		106	.251	.369	271	68	14	3	4	1.5	29	31	21	47	0	14	4	97	147	14	21	2.4	.946	3B-39, SS-37, 2B-26
1966		111	.249	.370	305	76	6	2	9	3.0	42	30	22	40	1	20	5	107	201	14	27	2.9	.957	SS-58, 3B-36, 2B-21, 1B-2
1967		124	.275	.380	295	81	10	3	5	1.7	42	30	39	50	1.	27	10	83	192	4	24	2.3	.986	3B-64, SS-28, 2B-12
1968		113	.224	.246	272	61	1	1	1	0.4	27	17	26	32	0	23	5	58	137	8	17	1.8	.961	3B-82, SS-17, 2B-1
1969		112	.241	.300	303	73	10	1	2	0.7	20	42	29	37	0	14	4	84	159	8	16	2.2	.968	3B-104, OF-1, SS-1, 1B-1
1970		22	.243	.270	37	9	1	0	0	0.0	3	4	7	6	0	11	3	7	7	0	0	0.6	1.000	3B-10
13 yrs.		1501	.258	.367	4427	1142	177	37	77	1.7	552	456	382	673	16	150	36	1240	2433	135	251	2.5	.965	3B-1130, SS-219, 2B-112, 1B-3, OF-1

WORLD SERIES

Year	Team	Games	BA	SA	AB	H	2B	3B	HR	HR%	R	RBI	BB	SO	SB	Pinch Hit AB	Pinch Hit H	PO	A	E	DP	TC/G	FA	G by Pos
1962	SF N	7	.136	.182	22	3	1	0	0	0.0	1	1	4	7	0	0	0	6	12	3	4	3.0	.857	3B-7

Andre David

DAVID, ANDRE ANTER
B. May 18, 1958, Hollywood, Calif.
BL TL 6' 170 lbs.

Year	Team	Games	BA	SA	AB	H	2B	3B	HR	HR%	R	RBI	BB	SO	SB	Pinch Hit AB	Pinch Hit H	PO	A	E	DP	TC/G	FA	G by Pos
1984	MIN A	33	.250	.354	48	12	2	0	1	2.1	5	5	7	11	0	15	2	14	0	0	0	0.4	1.000	OF-14, DH-2
1986		5	.200	.200	5	1	0	0	0	0.0	0	0	0	2	0	4	0	0	0	0	0	0.0	—	
2 yrs.		38	.245	.340	53	13	2	0	1	1.9	5	5	7	13	0	19	2	14	0	0	0	0.4	1.000	OF-14, DH-2

Bill Davidson

DAVIDSON, WILLIAM SIMPSON
B. May 10, 1887, Lafayette, Ind.   D. May 23, 1954, Lincoln, Neb.
BR TR 5'10" 170 lbs.

Year	Team	Games	BA	SA	AB	H	2B	3B	HR	HR%	R	RBI	BB	SO	SB	Pinch Hit AB	Pinch Hit H	PO	A	E	DP	TC/G	FA	G by Pos
1909	CHI N	2	.143	.143	7	1	0	0	0	0.0	2	0	1		1	0	0	3	0	0	0	1.5	1.000	OF-2
1910	BKN N	136	.238	.291	509	121	13	7	0	0.0	48	34	24	54	27	4	0	283	11	12	3	2.3	.961	OF-131
1911		87	.233	.281	292	68	3	4	1	0.3	33	26	16	21	18	8	2	168	4	8	1	2.1	.956	OF-74
3 yrs.		225	.235	.286	808	190	16	11	1	0.1	83	60	41	75	46	12	2	454	15	20	4	2.2	.959	OF-207

Claude Davidson

DAVIDSON, CLAUDE BOUCHER (Davey)
B. Oct. 13, 1896, Boston, Mass.   D. Apr. 18, 1956, Weymouth, Mass.
BL TR 5'11" 155 lbs.

Year	Team	Games	BA	SA	AB	H	2B	3B	HR	HR%	R	RBI	BB	SO	SB	Pinch Hit AB	Pinch Hit H	PO	A	E	DP	TC/G	FA	G by Pos
1918	PHI A	31	.185	.198	81	15	1	0	0	0.0	4	4	5	9	0	7	2	39	39	4	8	2.6	.951	2B-15, OF-8, 3B-1
1919	WAS A	2	.429	.429	7	3	0	0	0	0.0	1	0	1	1	0	0	0	3	4	0	0	3.5	1.000	3B-2
2 yrs.		33	.205	.216	88	18	1	0	0	0.0	5	4	6	10	0	7	2	42	43	4	8	2.7	.955	2B-15, OF-8, 3B-3

Homer Davidson

DAVIDSON, HOMER HURD (Divvy)
B. Oct. 14, 1884, Cleveland, Ohio   D. July 26, 1948, Detroit, Mich.
BR TR 5'10½" 155 lbs.

Year	Team	Games	BA	SA	AB	H	2B	3B	HR	HR%	R	RBI	BB	SO	SB	Pinch Hit AB	Pinch Hit H	PO	A	E	DP	TC/G	FA	G by Pos
1908	CLE A	9	.000	.000	4	0	0	0	0	0.0	0	0	1	0	0	1	0	9	1	0	0	1.1	1.000	C-5, OF-1

Mark Davidson

DAVIDSON, JOHN MARK
B. Feb. 15, 1961, Knoxville, Tenn.
BR TR 6'2" 180 lbs.

Year	Team	Games	BA	SA	AB	H	2B	3B	HR	HR%	R	RBI	BB	SO	SB	Pinch Hit AB	Pinch Hit H	PO	A	E	DP	TC/G	FA	G by Pos
1986	MIN A	36	.118	.162	68	8	3	0	0	0.0	5	2	6	22	2	2	1	48	0	1	0	1.4	.980	OF-31, DH-3
1987		102	.267	.327	150	40	4	1	1	0.7	32	14	13	26	9	6	3	102	3	0	0	1.0	1.000	OF-86, DH-9
1988		100	.217	.311	106	23	7	0	1	0.9	22	10	10	20	3	9	4	103	3	5	1	1.1	.955	OF-91, 3B-1
1989	HOU N	33	.200	.308	65	13	2	1	1	1.5	7	5	7	14	1	12	2	36	0	0	0	1.1	1.000	OF-23
4 yrs.		271	.216	.290	389	84	16	2	3	0.8	66	31	36	82	15	29	10	289	6	6	1	1.1	.980	OF-231, DH-12, 3B-1

LEAGUE CHAMPIONSHIP SERIES

Year	Team	Games	BA	SA	AB	H	2B	3B	HR	HR%	R	RBI	BB	SO	SB	Pinch Hit AB	Pinch Hit H	PO	A	E	DP	TC/G	FA	G by Pos
1987	MIN A	1	—	—	0	0	0	0	0	—	0	0	0	0	0	0	0	0	0	0	0	0.0	—	

WORLD SERIES

Year	Team	Games	BA	SA	AB	H	2B	3B	HR	HR%	R	RBI	BB	SO	SB	Pinch Hit AB	Pinch Hit H	PO	A	E	DP	TC/G	FA	G by Pos
1987	MIN A	2	.000	.000	1	0	0	0	0	0.0	0	0	0	0	0	1	0	0	0	0	0	0.0	—	OF-1

Chick Davies

DAVIES, LLOYD GARRISON
B. Mar. 6, 1892, Peabody, Mass.   D. Sept. 5, 1973, Middletown, Conn.
BL TL 5'8" 145 lbs.

Year	Team	Games	BA	SA	AB	H	2B	3B	HR	HR%	R	RBI	BB	SO	SB	Pinch Hit AB	Pinch Hit H	PO	A	E	DP	TC/G	FA	G by Pos
1914	PHI A	19	.239	.348	46	11	3	1	0	0.0	6	5	5	13	1	6	2	25	3	3	2	1.6	.903	OF-10, P-1
1915		56	.182	.265	132	24	5	3	0	0.0	13	11	14	31	2	16	2	67	14	2	1	1.5	.976	OF-32, P-4
1925	NY N	4	.000	.000	6	0	0	0	0	0.0	1	0	0	1	0	1	0	3	3	0	0	1.5	1.000	P-2, OF-1
1926		38	.222	.222	18	4	0	0	0	0.0	4	1	3	5	0	0	0	4	26	2	2	0.8	.938	P-38
4 yrs.		117	.193	.272	202	39	8	4	0	0.0	24	17	22	50	3	23	4	99	46	7	5	1.3	.954	P-45, OF-43

Alvin Davis

DAVIS, ALVIN GLENN
B. Sept. 9, 1960, Riverside, Calif.
BL TR 6'1" 190 lbs.

Year	Team	Games	BA	SA	AB	H	2B	3B	HR	HR%	R	RBI	BB	SO	SB	Pinch Hit AB	Pinch Hit H	PO	A	E	DP	TC/G	FA	G by Pos
1984	SEA A	152	.284	.497	567	161	34	3	27	4.8	80	116	97	78	5	0	0	1271	94	11	108	9.1	.992	1B-147, DH-7
1985		155	.287	.441	578	166	33	1	18	3.1	78	78	90	71	1	1	1	1438	103	13	131	10.0	.992	1B-154
1986		135	.271	.426	479	130	18	1	18	3.8	66	72	76	68	0	4	0	880	82	14	112	7.2	.986	1B-101, DH-32
1987		157	.295	.516	580	171	37	2	29	5.0	86	100	72	84	0	0	0	1386	96	9	133	9.5	.994	1B-157
1988		140	.295	.462	478	141	24	1	18	3.8	67	69	95	53	1	1	1	980	65	6	111	7.5	.994	1B-115, DH-25
1989		142	.305	.496	498	152	30	1	21	4.2	84	95	101	49	0	3	1	1106	81	10	119	8.4	.992	1B-125, DH-14
6 yrs.		881	.290	.474	3180	921	176	9	131	4.1	461	530	531	403	7	9	3	7061	521	63	714	8.7	.992	1B-799, DH-78

Bill Davis

DAVIS, ARTHUR WILLARD
B. June 6, 1942, Graceville, Minn.
BL TL 6'7" 215 lbs.

Year	Team	Games	BA	SA	AB	H	2B	3B	HR	HR%	R	RBI	BB	SO	SB	Pinch Hit AB	Pinch Hit H	PO	A	E	DP	TC/G	FA	G by Pos
1965	CLE A	10	.300	.400	10	3	1	0	0	0.0	0	0	0	0	0	10	3	0	0	0	0	0.0	—	1B
1966		23	.158	.263	38	6	1	0	1	2.6	2	4	6	9	0	12	3	47	5	1	6	2.3	.981	1B-9
1969	SD N	31	.175	.193	57	10	1	0	0	0.0	1	1	8	18	0	14	2	114	5	1	11	3.9	.992	1B-14
3 yrs.		64	.181	.238	105	19	3	0	1	1.0	3	5	14	28	0	36	8	161	10	2	17	2.7	.988	1B-23

Bob Davis

DAVIS, ROBERT JOHN EUGENE
B. Mar. 1, 1952, Pryor, Okla.
BR TR 6' 180 lbs.

Year	Team	Games	BA	SA	AB	H	2B	3B	HR	HR%	R	RBI	BB	SO	SB	Pinch Hit AB	Pinch Hit H	PO	A	E	DP	TC/G	FA	G by Pos
1973	SD N	5	.091	.091	11	1	0	0	0	0.0	1	0	0	5	0	0	0	32	0	2	1	6.8	.941	C-5

Year Team	Games	BA	SA	AB	H	2B	3B	HR	HR%	R	RBI	BB	SO	SB	Pinch Hit AB	Pinch Hit H	PO	A	E	DP	TC/G	FA	G by Pos

Bob Davis *continued*

Year Team	Games	BA	SA	AB	H	2B	3B	HR	HR%	R	RBI	BB	SO	SB	AB	H	PO	A	E	DP	TC/G	FA	G by Pos
1975	43	.234	.289	128	30	3	2	0	0.0	6	7	11	31	0	2	0	195	18	3	4	5.0	.986	C-43
1976	51	.205	.229	83	17	0	1	0	0.0	7	5	5	13	0	0	0	120	19	5	1	2.8	.965	C-47
1977	48	.181	.234	94	17	2	0	1	1.1	9	10	5	24	0	2	1	136	19	4	2	3.3	.975	C-46
1978	19	.200	.225	40	8	1	0	0	0.0	3	2	1	5	0	3	0	43	5	2	0	2.6	.960	C-16
1979 TOR A	32	.124	.180	89	11	2	0	1	1.1	6	8	6	15	0	0	0	114	11	2	1	4.0	.984	C-32
1980	91	.216	.321	218	47	11	0	4	1.8	18	19	12	25	0	4	1	317	28	6	6	3.9	.983	C-89
1981 CAL A	1	.000	.000	2	0	0	0	0	0.0	0	0	0	0	0	0	0	2	0	0	0	2.0	1.000	C-1
8 yrs.	290	.197	.262	665	131	19	3	6	0.9	50	51	40	118	0	11	2	959	100	24	15	3.7	.978	C-279

Brandy Davis

DAVIS, ROBERT BRANDON
B. Sept. 10, 1928, Newark, Del.

BR TR 6' 170 lbs.

Year Team	Games	BA	SA	AB	H	2B	3B	HR	HR%	R	RBI	BB	SO	SB	AB	H	PO	A	E	DP	TC/G	FA	G by Pos
1952 PIT N	55	.179	.211	95	17	1	1	0	0.0	14	1	11	28	9	11	2	53	2	4	0	1.1	.932	OF-29
1953	12	.205	.256	39	8	2	0	0	0.0	5	2	0	3	0	0	0	21	0	1	0	1.8	.955	OF-9
2 yrs.	67	.187	.224	134	25	3	1	0	0.0	19	3	11	31	9	11	2	74	2	5	0	1.2	.938	OF-38

Brock Davis

DAVIS, BRYSHEAR BENNETT
B. Oct. 19, 1943, Oakland, Calif.

BL TL 5'10" 160 lbs.

Year Team	Games	BA	SA	AB	H	2B	3B	HR	HR%	R	RBI	BB	SO	SB	AB	H	PO	A	E	DP	TC/G	FA	G by Pos
1963 HOU N	34	.200	.291	55	11	2	0	1	1.8	7	2	4	10	0	17	3	18	1	3	0	0.6	.864	OF-14
1964	1	.000	.000	3	0	0	0	0	0.0	0	1	0	1	0	0	0	2	0	0	0	2.0	1.000	OF-1
1966 CHI N	10	.148	.185	27	4	1	0	0	0.0	2	1	5	4	1	3	1	15	0	0	0	1.5	1.000	OF-7
1970	6	.000	.000	3	0	0	0	0	0.0	0	0	1	1	0	3	0	0	0	0	0	0.0	—	OF-1
1971	106	.256	.312	301	77	7	5	0	0.0	22	28	35	34	0	10	1	213	5	4	1	2.1	.982	OF-93
1972 MIL A	85	.318	.331	154	49	2	0	0	0.0	17	12	12	23	6	36	8	63	2	2	0	0.8	.970	OF-43
6 yrs.	242	.260	.306	543	141	12	5	1	0.2	48	43	57	73	7	69	13	311	8	9	1	1.4	.973	OF-159

Butch Davis

DAVIS, WALLACE McARTHUR
B. June 19, 1958, Williamston, N. C.

BR TR 6' 185 lbs.

Year Team	Games	BA	SA	AB	H	2B	3B	HR	HR%	R	RBI	BB	SO	SB	AB	H	PO	A	E	DP	TC/G	FA	G by Pos
1983 KC A	33	.344	.508	122	42	2	6	2	1.6	13	18	4	19	4	0	0	83	1	2	0	2.6	.977	OF-33
1984	41	.147	.224	116	17	3	0	2	1.7	11	12	10	19	4	4	0	69	2	3	1	1.8	.959	OF-35, DH-2
1987 PIT N	7	.143	.286	7	1	1	0	0	0.0	3	0	1	3	0	5	0	3	0	0	0	0.4	1.000	OF-1
1988 BAL A	13	.240	.280	25	6	1	0	0	0.0	2	0	0	8	1	1	0	16	1	0	1	1.3	1.000	OF-10, DH-1
1989	5	.167	.333	6	1	1	0	0	0.0	1	0	0	3	0	1	0	3	0	0	0	0.6	1.000	OF-3, DH-1
5 yrs.	99	.243	.359	276	67	8	6	4	1.4	30	30	15	52	9	11	0	174	4	5	2	1.8	.973	OF-82, DH-4

Chili Davis

DAVIS, CHARLES THEODORE
B. Jan. 17, 1960, Kingston, Jamaica

BB TR 6'3" 195 lbs.

Year Team	Games	BA	SA	AB	H	2B	3B	HR	HR%	R	RBI	BB	SO	SB	AB	H	PO	A	E	DP	TC/G	FA	G by Pos
1981 SF N	8	.133	.133	15	2	0	0	0	0.0	1	0	1	2	3	0	0	7	0	0	0	0.9	1.000	OF-6
1982	154	.261	.410	641	167	27	6	19	3.0	86	76	45	115	24	1	1	404	16	12	4	2.8	.972	OF-153
1983	137	.233	.352	486	113	21	2	11	2.3	54	59	55	108	10	4	1	357	7	9	1	2.7	.976	OF-133
1984	137	.315	.507	499	157	21	6	21	4.2	87	81	42	74	12	15	6	292	9	9	2	2.3	.971	OF-123
1985	136	.270	.412	481	130	25	2	13	2.7	53	56	62	74	15	9	2	279	10	6	2	2.2	.980	OF-126
1986	153	.278	.416	526	146	28	3	13	2.5	71	70	84	96	16	7	1	303	9	9	2	2.1	.972	OF-148
1987	149	.250	.442	500	125	22	1	24	4.8	80	76	72	109	16	20	3	265	6	7	2	1.9	.975	OF-135
1988 CAL A	158	.268	.432	600	161	29	3	21	3.5	81	93	56	118	9	1	0	299	10	19	1	2.1	.942	OF-153, DH-3
1989	154	.271	.436	560	152	24	1	22	3.9	81	90	61	109	3	2	0	270	5	6	0	1.8	.979	OF-147, DH-6
9 yrs.	1186	.268	.425	4308	1153	197	24	144	3.3	594	601	478	805	107	62	15	2476	72	77	14	2.2	.971	OF-1124, DH-9

LEAGUE CHAMPIONSHIP SERIES

Year Team	Games	BA	SA	AB	H	2B	3B	HR	HR%	R	RBI	BB	SO	SB	AB	H	PO	A	E	DP	TC/G	FA	G by Pos
1987 SF N	6	.150	.200	20	3	1	0	0	0.0	2	0	1	4	0	0	0	11	1	1	1	2.2	.923	OF-6

Crash Davis

DAVIS, LAWRENCE COLUMBUS
B. July 14, 1919, Canon, Ga.

BR TR 6' 173 lbs.

Year Team	Games	BA	SA	AB	H	2B	3B	HR	HR%	R	RBI	BB	SO	SB	AB	H	PO	A	E	DP	TC/G	FA	G by Pos
1940 PHI A	23	.269	.313	67	18	1	1	0	0.0	4	9	3	10	1	3	0	53	53	4	11	4.8	.964	2B-19, SS-1
1941	39	.219	.248	105	23	3	0	0	0.0	8	8	11	16	0	7	2	135	68	7	21	5.4	.967	2B-20, 1B-12
1942	86	.224	.283	272	61	8	1	2	0.7	31	26	21	30	1	4	1	179	211	19	31	4.8	.954	2B-57, SS-26, 1B-3
3 yrs.	148	.230	.279	444	102	12	2	2	0.5	43	43	35	56	2	14	3	367	332	30	63	4.9	.959	2B-96, SS-27, 1B-15

Dick Davis

DAVIS, RICHARD EARL
B. Sept. 25, 1953, Long Beach, Calif.

BR TR 6'3" 190 lbs.

Year Team	Games	BA	SA	AB	H	2B	3B	HR	HR%	R	RBI	BB	SO	SB	AB	H	PO	A	E	DP	TC/G	FA	G by Pos
1977 MIL A	22	.275	.314	51	14	2	0	0	0.0	6	1	1	8	0	2	1	13	0	0	0	0.6	1.000	OF-12, DH-6
1978	69	.248	.372	218	54	10	1	5	2.3	28	26	7	23	2	13	3	54	2	0	0	0.8	1.000	DH-34, OF-28
1979	91	.266	.418	335	89	13	1	12	3.6	51	41	16	46	3	6	2	72	1	2	0	0.8	.973	DH-53, OF-35
1980	106	.271	.386	365	99	26	2	4	1.1	50	30	11	43	5	5	2	63	3	2	0	0.6	.971	DH-63, OF-38
1981 PHI N	45	.333	.479	96	32	6	1	2	2.1	12	19	8	13	1	14	5	37	1	1	0	0.9	.974	OF-32
1982 3 teams	PHI N (28G – .279)							TOR A (3G – .286)					PIT N (39G – .182)										
" total	70	.230	.368	152	35	5	2	4	2.6	19	7	19	2	26	6	64	0	1	0	0.9	.985	OF-45, DH-1
6 yrs.	403	.265	.394	1217	323	62	7	27	2.2	160	141	50	152	13	66	18	303	7	6	2	0.8	.981	OF-190, DH-157

DIVISIONAL PLAYOFF SERIES

Year Team	Games	BA	SA	AB	H	2B	3B	HR	HR%	R	RBI	BB	SO	SB	AB	H	PO	A	E	DP	TC/G	FA	G by Pos
1981 PHI N	1	.000	.000	2	0	0	0	0	0.0	0	0	1	0	1	0	0	0	0	0	0	0.0	—	OF-1

Doug Davis

DAVIS, DOUGLAS RAYMOND
B. Sept. 24, 1962, Bloomsburg, Pa.

BR TR 6' 180 lbs.

Year Team	Games	BA	SA	AB	H	2B	3B	HR	HR%	R	RBI	BB	SO	SB	AB	H	PO	A	E	DP	TC/G	FA	G by Pos
1988 CAL A	6	.000	.000	12	0	0	0	0	0.0	1	0	0	3	0	0	0	6	1	1	0	1.3	.875	3B-3, C-3

Eric Davis

DAVIS, ERIC KEITH
B. May 29, 1962, Los Angeles, Calif.

BR TR 6'3" 175 lbs.

Year Team	Games	BA	SA	AB	H	2B	3B	HR	HR%	R	RBI	BB	SO	SB	AB	H	PO	A	E	DP	TC/G	FA	G by Pos
1984 CIN N	57	.224	.466	174	39	10	1	10	5.7	33	30	24	48	10	6	1	125	4	1	2	2.3	.992	OF-51
1985	56	.246	.516	122	30	3	3	8	6.6	26	18	7	39	16	8	1	75	3	1	1	1.4	.987	OF-47
1986	132	.277	.523	415	115	15	3	27	6.5	97	71	68	100	80	4	0	274	2	7	0	2.1	.975	OF-121
1987	129	.293	.593	474	139	23	4	37	7.8	120	100	84	134	50	1	0	380	10	4	4	3.1	.990	OF-128

Year	Team		Games	BA	SA	AB	H	2B	3B	HR	HR%	R	RBI	BB	SO	SB	Pinch Hit AB	Pinch Hit H	PO	A	E	DP	TC/G	FA	G by Pos

Eric Davis *continued*

Year	Team		Games	BA	SA	AB	H	2B	3B	HR	HR%	R	RBI	BB	SO	SB	AB	H	PO	A	E	DP	TC/G	FA	G by Pos
1988			135	.273	.489	472	129	18	3	26	5.5	81	93	65	124	35	3	1	300	2	6	0	2.3	.981	OF-130
1989			131	.281	.541	462	130	14	2	34	7.4	74	101	68	116	21	3	1	298	2	5	1	2.3	.984	OF-125
6 yrs.			640	.275	.530	2119	582	83	16	142	6.7	431	413	316	561	212	25	4	1452	23	24	8	2.3	.984	OF-602

George Davis

DAVIS, GEORGE STACEY   BB TR 5'9"   180 lbs.
B. Aug. 23, 1870, Cohoes, N. Y.   D. Oct. 17, 1940, Philadelphia, Pa.
Manager 1895, 1900-01.

Year	Team		Games	BA	SA	AB	H	2B	3B	HR	HR%	R	RBI	BB	SO	SB	AB	H	PO	A	E	DP	TC/G	FA	G by Pos
1890	CLE	N	136	.264	.375	526	139	22	9	6	1.1	98	73	53	34	22	0	0	288	38	18	10	2.5	.948	OF-133, 2B-2, SS-1
1891			136	.289	.409	570	165	35	12	3	0.5	115	89	53	29	42	0	0	292	76	33	6	2.9	.918	OF-116, 3B-22, P-3
1892			144	.241	.352	597	144	27	12	5	0.8	95	82	58	51	36	0	0	198	241	43	17	3.3	.911	3B-79, OF-44, SS-20, 2B-3
1893	NY	N	133	.355	.554	549	195	22	27	11	2.0	112	119	42	20	37	0	0	181	307	64	27	4.2	.884	3B-133, SS-1
1894			124	.346	.539	492	170	28	20	9	1.8	124	91	66	10	40	0	0	150	247	40	18	3.5	.908	3B-124
1895			110	.340	.500	430	146	36	9	5	1.2	108	101	55	12	48	0	0	296	220	46	27	5.1	.918	3B-81, 1B-14, 2B-10, OF-7
1896			124	.320	.455	494	158	25	12	6	1.2	98	99	50	24	48	0	0	257	314	47	22	5.0	.924	3B-74, SS-45, OF-3, 1B-3
1897			130	.353	.509	519	183	31	10	10	1.9	112	**134**	41		65	0	0	337	434	62	67	6.4	.926	SS-130
1898			121	.307	.381	486	149	20	5	2	0.4	80	86	32		26	0	0	349	421	55	61	6.8	.933	SS-121
1899			108	.337	.418	416	140	21	5	1	0.2	68	57	37		34	0	0	311	412	42	57	7.1	.945	SS-108
1900			114	.319	.406	426	136	20	4	3	0.7	70	61	35		29	0	0	279	450	43	94	6.8	.944	SS-114
1901			130	.309	.428	495	153	26	6	7	1.4	69	65	40		26	0	0	321	443	48	44	6.2	.941	SS-113, 3B-17
1902	CHI	A	132	.299	.402	485	145	27	7	3	0.6	76	93	65		31	1	1	302	428	37	74	5.8	.952	SS-129, 1B-3
1903	NY	N	4	.267	.267	15	4	0	0	0	0.0	2	1	1		0	0	0	11	9	3	0	5.8	.870	SS-4
1904	CHI	A	152	.252	.359	563	142	27	15	1	0.2	75	69	43		32	0	0	347	514	58	62	6.0	.937	SS-152
1905			157	.278	.340	550	153	29	1	1	0.2	74	55	60		31	0	0	330	501	46	56	5.6	.948	SS-157
1906			133	.277	.355	484	134	26	6	0	0.0	63	80	41		27	3	1	266	475	42	45	5.9	.946	SS-129, 2B-1
1907			132	.238	.292	466	111	18	2	0	0.2	59	52	47		15	0	0	223	485	38	53	5.7	.949	SS-131
1908			128	.217	.255	419	91	14	1	0	0.0	41	26	41		22	5	1	291	384	32	31	5.5	.955	2B-95, SS-23, 1B-4
1909			28	.132	.147	68	9	1	0	0	0.0	5	2	10		4	14	1	190	18	5	7	7.6	.977	1B-17, 2B-2
20 yrs.			2376	.295	.406	9050	2667	455	163	74	0.8	1544	1435	870	180	615	23	4	5219	6417	802	778	5.2	.936	SS-1378, 3B-530, OF-303, 2B-113, 1B-41, P-3

WORLD SERIES

Year	Team		Games	BA	SA	AB	H	2B	3B	HR	HR%	R	RBI	BB	SO	SB	AB	H	PO	A	E	DP	TC/G	FA	G by Pos
1906	CHI	A	3	.308	.538	13	4	3	0	0	0.0	4	6	0	1	1	0	0	7	14	2	1	7.7	.913	SS-3

Glenn Davis

DAVIS, GLENN EARLE   BR TR 6'3"   205 lbs.
B. Mar. 28, 1961, Jacksonville, Fla.

Year	Team		Games	BA	SA	AB	H	2B	3B	HR	HR%	R	RBI	BB	SO	SB	AB	H	PO	A	E	DP	TC/G	FA	G by Pos
1984	HOU	N	18	.213	.393	61	13	5	0	2	3.3	6	8	4	12	0	2	0	151	15	2	13	9.3	.988	1B-16
1985			100	.271	.474	350	95	11	0	20	5.7	51	64	27	68	0	4	1	766	57	12	76	8.4	.986	1B-89, OF-9
1986			158	.265	.493	574	152	32	3	31	5.4	91	101	64	72	3	2	0	1253	111	11	90	8.7	.992	1B-156
1987			151	.251	.458	578	145	35	2	27	4.7	70	93	47	84	4	1	0	1283	112	12	89	9.3	.991	1B-151
1988			152	.271	.478	561	152	26	0	30	5.3	78	99	53	77	4	2	0	1355	103	6	104	9.6	.996	1B-151
1989			158	.269	.492	581	156	26	1	34	5.9	87	89	69	123	4	3	1	1347	113	12	101	9.3	.992	1B-156
6 yrs.			737	.264	.478	2705	713	135	6	144	5.3	383	454	264	436	15	14	2	6155	511	55	473	9.1	.992	1B-719, OF-9

LEAGUE CHAMPIONSHIP SERIES

Year	Team		Games	BA	SA	AB	H	2B	3B	HR	HR%	R	RBI	BB	SO	SB	AB	H	PO	A	E	DP	TC/G	FA	G by Pos
1986	HOU	N	6	.269	.423	26	7	1	0	1	3.8	3	3	1	3	0	0	0	62	3	1	2	11.0	.985	1B-6

Harry Davis

DAVIS, HARRY ALBERT (Stinky)   BL TL 5'10½"   175 lbs.
B. May 7, 1908, Shreveport, La.

Year	Team		Games	BA	SA	AB	H	2B	3B	HR	HR%	R	RBI	BB	SO	SB	AB	H	PO	A	E	DP	TC/G	FA	G by Pos
1932	DET	A	140	.269	.388	590	159	32	13	4	0.7	92	74	60	53	12	0	0	1327	75	16	123	10.1	.989	1B-140
1933			66	.214	.283	173	37	8	2	0	0.0	24	14	22	8	2	19	3	433	13	10	33	6.9	.978	1B-44
1937	STL	A	120	.276	.364	450	124	25	3	3	0.7	89	35	71	26	7	7	2	1065	54	10	108	9.4	.991	1B-112, OF-1
3 yrs.			326	.264	.364	1213	320	65	18	7	0.6	205	123	153	87	21	26	5	2825	142	36	264	9.2	.988	1B-296, OF-1

Harry Davis

DAVIS, HARRY H. (Jasper)   BR TR 5'10"   180 lbs.
B. July 19, 1873, Philadelphia, Pa.   D. Aug. 11, 1947, Philadelphia, Pa.
Manager 1912.

Year	Team		Games	BA	SA	AB	H	2B	3B	HR	HR%	R	RBI	BB	SO	SB	AB	H	PO	A	E	DP	TC/G	FA	G by Pos
1895	NY	N	7	.292	.375	24	7	0	1	0	0.0	1	6	2	0	1	0	0	62	4	3	4	9.9	.957	1B-7
1896	2 teams	NY N (64G – .275)				PIT N (44G – .190)																			
"	total		108	.239	.374	401	96	16	16	2	0.5	67	73	44	41	25	1	0	653	37	29	33	6.7	.960	1B-58, OF-50, SS-1
1897	PIT	N	111	.305	.473	429	131	10	**28**	2	0.5	70	63	26		21	2	0	644	85	48	28	7.0	.938	1B-64, 3B-32, OF-14, SS-1
1898	3 teams	PIT N (58G – .293)				LOU N (37G – .217)						WAS N (1G – .000)													
"	total		96	.262	.380	363	95	14	15	2	0.6	49	40	19		13	0	0	913	48	27	53	10.3	.973	1B-88, OF-7, 2B-2
1899	WAS	N	18	.188	.313	64	12	2	3	0	0.0	3	8	8		2	0	0	161	4	2	6	9.3	.988	1B-18
1901	PHI	A	117	.306	.452	496	152	28	10	8	1.6	92	76	23		21	0	0	1265	83	33	67	11.8	.976	1B-117
1902			133	.307	.444	561	172	**43**	8	6	1.1	89	92	30		28	0	0	1255	87	22	58	10.3	.984	1B-128, OF-5
1903			106	.298	.436	420	125	29	7	5	1.2	75	55	24		24	0	0	944	63	30	38	9.8	.971	1B-104, OF-2
1904			102	.309	.490	404	125	21	11	**10**	**2.5**	54	62	23		12	0	0	1011	57	19	33	10.7	.983	1B-102
1905			149	.284	.422	602	171	**47**	6	8	1.3	**92**	**83**	43		36	0	0	1621	91	24	43	11.7	.986	1B-149
1906			145	.292	.459	551	161	42	7	**12**	**2.2**	94	**96**	49		23	0	0	1352	91	37	66	10.2	.975	1B-145
1907			149	.266	.397	582	155	**36**	8	8	1.4	84	87	42		20	0	0	1475	103	38	50	10.8	.976	1B-149
1908			147	.248	.357	513	127	23	9	5	1.0	65	62	61		20	0	0	1410	86	22	44	10.3	.986	1B-147
1909			149	.268	.374	530	142	22	11	4	0.8	73	75	51		22	0	0	1432	74	19	65	10.2	.986	1B-149
1910			139	.248	.309	492	122	19	4	1	0.2	61	41	53		17	0	0	1353	64	20	74	10.3	.986	1B-139
1911			57	.197	.273	183	36	9	1	1	0.5	27	22	24		2	1	0	427	36	11	21	8.3	.977	1B-53
1912	CLE	A	2	.000	.000	5	0	0	0	0	0.0	0	0	0		0	0	0	14	2	1	1	8.5	.941	1B-2
1913	PHI	A	7	.353	.471	17	6	2	0	0	0.0	2	4	1	4	1	1	1	33	4	0	2	5.3	1.000	1B-6
1914			5	.429	.429	7	3	0	0	0	0.0	0	2	1		0	3	1	12	0	0	0	2.4	1.000	1B-1
1915			5	.333	.333	3	1	0	0	0	0.0	4	0	4		0	3	1	0	0	0	0	0.0	–	1B-1
1916			1	–		0	0	0	0	0	0.0	0	0	1		0	0	0	0	0	0	0	0.0	–	
1917			1	.000	.000	1	0	0	0	0	0.0	0	1	0		0	1	0	0	0	0	0	0.0	–	
22 yrs.			1754	.277	.408	6648	1839	363	145	74	1.1	998	951	525	45	285	12	3	16037	1019	385	686	9.9	.978	1B-1627, OF-78, 3B-32, SS-2, 2B-2

Year Team	Games	BA	SA	AB	H	2B	3B	HR	HR%	R	RBI	BB	SO	SB	Pinch Hit AB	H	PO	A	E	DP	TC/G	FA	G by Pos

Harry Davis *continued*

WORLD SERIES

Year Team	Games	BA	SA	AB	H	2B	3B	HR	HR%	R	RBI	BB	SO	SB	AB	H	PO	A	E	DP	TC/G	FA	G by Pos
1905 PHI A	5	.200	.250	20	4	1	0	0	0.0	0	0	0	1	0	0	0	50	1	0	2	10.2	1.000	1B-5
1910	5	.353	.529	17	6	3	0	0	0.0	5	2	3	4	0	0	0	44	1	3	6	9.6	.938	1B-5
1911	6	.208	.250	24	5	1	0	0	0.0	3	5	0	3	0	0	0	54	3	0	1	9.5	1.000	1B-6
3 yrs.	16	.246	.328	61	15	5	0	0	0.0	8	7	3	8	0	0	0	148	5	3	9	9.8	.981	1B-16

Ike Davis

DAVIS, ISAAC MARION
B. June 14, 1895, Pueblo, Colo. D. Apr. 2, 1984, Tucson, Ariz. BR TR 5'7" 155 lbs.

Year Team	Games	BA	SA	AB	H	2B	3B	HR	HR%	R	RBI	BB	SO	SB	AB	H	PO	A	E	DP	TC/G	FA	G by Pos
1919 WAS A	8	.000	.000	14	0	0	0	0	0.0	0	0	0	6	0	0	0	10	2	2	1	1.8	.857	SS-4
1924 CHI A	10	.242	.333	33	8	1	1	0	0.0	5	4	2	5	0	5	0	14	33	3	3	5.0	.940	SS-10
1925	146	.240	.327	562	135	31	9	0	0.0	105	61	71	58	19	2	1	313	472	53	97	5.7	.937	SS-144
3 yrs.	164	.235	.320	609	143	32	10	0	0.0	110	65	73	69	19	7	1	337	507	58	101	5.5	.936	SS-158

Ira Davis

DAVIS, J. IRA (Slats)
B. July 8, 1870, Philadelphia, Pa. D. Dec. 21, 1942, Brooklyn, N. Y.

Year Team	Games	BA	SA	AB	H	2B	3B	HR	HR%	R	RBI	BB	SO	SB	AB	H	PO	A	E	DP	TC/G	FA	G by Pos
1899 NY N	6	.235	.412	17	4	1	1	0	0.0	3	2	0		1	1	0	22	9	5	5	6.0	.861	SS-3, 1B-2

Jacke Davis

DAVIS, JACKE SYLVESTER
B. Mar. 5, 1936, Carthage, Tex. BR TR 5'11" 190 lbs.

Year Team	Games	BA	SA	AB	H	2B	3B	HR	HR%	R	RBI	BB	SO	SB	AB	H	PO	A	E	DP	TC/G	FA	G by Pos
1962 PHI N	48	.213	.280	75	16	0	1	1	1.3	9	6	4	20	1	16	4	25	0	2	0	0.6	.926	OF-26

Jerry Davis

DAVIS, GERALD EDWARD
B. Dec. 25, 1958, Trenton, N. J. BR TR 6' 185 lbs.

Year Team	Games	BA	SA	AB	H	2B	3B	HR	HR%	R	RBI	BB	SO	SB	AB	H	PO	A	E	DP	TC/G	FA	G by Pos
1983 SD N	5	.333	.467	15	5	2	0	0	0.0	3	1	3	4	1	0	0	8	1	0	0	1.8	1.000	OF-5
1985	44	.293	.379	58	17	3	1	0	0.0	10	2	5	7	0	19	4	18	2	1	0	0.5	.952	OF-23
2 yrs.	49	.301	.397	73	22	5	1	0	0.0	13	3	8	11	1	19	4	26	3	1	0	0.6	.967	OF-28

Jody Davis

DAVIS, JODY RICHARD
B. Nov. 12, 1956, Gainesville, Ga. BR TR 6'4" 192 lbs.

Year Team	Games	BA	SA	AB	H	2B	3B	HR	HR%	R	RBI	BB	SO	SB	AB	H	PO	A	E	DP	TC/G	FA	G by Pos
1981 CHI N	56	.256	.361	180	46	5	1	4	2.2	14	21	21	28	0	0	0	274	44	9	4	5.8	.972	C-56
1982	130	.261	.404	418	109	20	2	12	2.9	41	52	36	92	0	1	0	598	89	11	11	5.4	.984	C-129
1983	151	.271	.480	510	138	31	2	24	4.7	56	84	33	93	0	2	0	730	75	13	7	5.4	.984	C-150
1984	150	.256	.419	523	134	24	2	19	3.6	55	94	47	99	5	4	1	811	89	15	9	6.1	.984	C-146
1985	142	.232	.400	482	112	30	0	17	3.5	47	58	48	83	1	11	2	694	84	7	7	5.5	.990	C-138
1986	148	.250	.428	528	132	27	2	21	4.0	61	74	41	110	0	4	0	885	105	8	14	6.7	.992	C-145, 1B-1
1987	125	.248	.418	428	106	12	2	19	4.4	57	51	52	91	1	3	0	749	79	9	11	6.7	.989	C-123
1988 2 teams		CHI N	(88G – .229)		ATL N	(2G – .250)																	
" total	90	.230	.346	257	59	9	0	7	2.7	21	36	29	52	0	13	1	396	34	2	1	4.8	.995	C-76
1989 ATL N	78	.169	.242	231	39	5	0	4	1.7	12	19	23	61	0	8	1	376	40	6	4	5.4	.986	C-72, 1B-2
9 yrs.	1070	.246	.405	3557	875	163	11	127	3.6	364	489	330	709	7	46	5	5513	639	81	68	5.8	.987	C-1035, 1B-3

LEAGUE CHAMPIONSHIP SERIES

Year Team	Games	BA	SA	AB	H	2B	3B	HR	HR%	R	RBI	BB	SO	SB	AB	H	PO	A	E	DP	TC/G	FA	G by Pos
1984 CHI N	5	.389	.833	18	7	2	0	2	11.1	3	6	0	3	0	0	0	23	4	0	0	5.4	1.000	C-5

John Davis

DAVIS, JOHN HUMPHREY (Red)
B. July 15, 1915, Laurel Run, Pa. BR TR 5'11" 172 lbs.

Year Team	Games	BA	SA	AB	H	2B	3B	HR	HR%	R	RBI	BB	SO	SB	AB	H	PO	A	E	DP	TC/G	FA	G by Pos
1941 NY N	21	.214	.257	70	15	3	0	0	0.0	8	5	8	12	0	0	0	19	45	2	4	3.1	.970	3B-21

Jumbo Davis

DAVIS, JAMES J.
B. Sept. 5, 1861, New York, N. Y. D. Feb. 14, 1921, St. Louis, Mo. BL TR 5'11" 190 lbs.

Year Team	Games	BA	SA	AB	H	2B	3B	HR	HR%	R	RBI	BB	SO	SB	AB	H	PO	A	E	DP	TC/G	FA	G by Pos
1884 KC U	7	.207	.207	29	6	0	0	0	0.0	3				0	0	0	5	14	11	0	4.3	.633	3B-7
1886 BAL AA	60	.194	.250	216	42	5	2	0	0.5	23		11		0	0	0	82	114	35	6	3.9	.848	3B-60
1887	130	.309	.485	485	150	23	19	8	1.6	81		28		49	0	0	148	331	98	12	4.4	.830	3B-87, SS-43
1888 KC AA	121	.267	.363	491	131	22	8	3	0.6	70	61	20		42	0	0	167	361	100	27	5.2	.841	3B-113, SS-8
1889 2 teams		KC AA	(62G – .266)		STL AA	(2G – .000)																	
" total	64	.261	.302	245	64	4	3	0	0.0	41	30	18	36	25	0	0	95	140	57	14	4.6	.805	3B-62, OF-1, SS-1
1890 2 teams		STL AA	(21G – .254)		BKN AA	(38G – .303)																	
" total	59	.286	.399	213	61	12	3	2	0.9	41		24		15	0	0	72	140	53	11	4.5	.800	3B-59
1891 WAS AA	12	.318	.477	44	14	3	2	0	0.0	7	9	7	5	8	0	0	19	22	9	2	4.2	.820	3B-12
7 yrs.	453	.272	.379	1723	468	69	37	14	0.8	266	100	108	41	139	0	0	588	1122	363	72	4.6	.825	3B-400, SS-52, OF-1

Kiddo Davis

DAVIS, GEORGE WILLIS
B. Feb. 12, 1902, Bridgeport, Conn. D. Mar. 4, 1983, Bridgeport, Conn. BR TR 5'11" 178 lbs.

Year Team	Games	BA	SA	AB	H	2B	3B	HR	HR%	R	RBI	BB	SO	SB	AB	H	PO	A	E	DP	TC/G	FA	G by Pos
1926 NY A	1	–	–	0	0	0	0	0	0.0	0	0	0	0	0	0	0	0	0	0	0	0.0	–	OF-1
1932 PHI N	137	.309	.424	576	178	39	6	5	0.9	100	57	44	56	16	0	0	411	15	11	6	3.2	.975	OF-133
1933 NY N	126	.258	.371	434	112	20	4	7	1.6	61	37	25	30	10	5	1	248	7	3	3	2.0	.988	OF-120
1934 2 teams		STL N	(16G – .303)		PHI N	(100G – .293)																	
" total	116	.293	.411	426	125	28	5	4	0.9	56	52	30	29	2	5	2	327	14	4	3	3.0	.988	OF-109
1935 NY N	47	.264	.429	91	24	7	1	2	2.2	16	6	10	4	2	21	5	42	1	1	0	0.9	.977	OF-21
1936	47	.239	.254	67	16	1	0	0	0.0	6	5	6	5	0	9	1	40	3	0	0	0.9	1.000	OF-22
1937 2 teams		NY N	(56G – .263)		CIN N	(40G – .257)																	
" total	96	.259	.349	212	55	16	0	1	0.5	39	14	26	13	2	13	4	134	1	7	0	1.5	.951	OF-72
1938 CIN N	5	.278	.333	18	5	1	0	0	0.0	3	0	1	0	0	0	0	8	0	0	0	1.8	1.000	OF-5
8 yrs.	575	.282	.393	1824	515	112	16	19	1.0	281	171	142	141	32	53	13	1210	42	26	12	2.2	.980	OF-483

WORLD SERIES

Year Team	Games	BA	SA	AB	H	2B	3B	HR	HR%	R	RBI	BB	SO	SB	AB	H	PO	A	E	DP	TC/G	FA	G by Pos
1933 NY N	5	.368	.421	19	7	1	0	0	0.0	1	0	0	3	0	0	0	6	0	0	0	1.2	1.000	OF-5
1936	4	.500	.500	2	1	0	0	0	0.0	2	0	0	0	0	2	1	0	0	0	0	0.0	–	
2 yrs.	9	.381	.429	21	8	1	0	0	0.0	3	0	0	3	0	2	1	6	0	0	0	0.7	1.000	OF-5

Year Team	Games	BA	SA	AB	H	2B	3B	HR	HR%	R	RBI	BB	SO	SB	Pinch Hit AB	Pinch Hit H	PO	A	E	DP	TC/G	FA	G by Pos

Lefty Davis

DAVIS, ALFONZO DeFORD   BL TL 5'10"   170 lbs.
B. Feb. 4, 1875, Nashville, Tenn.   D. Feb. 7, 1919, Collins, N. Y.

Year Team	Games	BA	SA	AB	H	2B	3B	HR	HR%	R	RBI	BB	SO	SB	PH AB	PH H	PO	A	E	DP	TC/G	FA	G by Pos
1901 2 teams		BKN N (25G – .209)			PIT N (87G – .313)																		
" total	112	.291	.380	426	124	10	11	2	0.5	98	40	66		26	1	0	180	18	12	7	1.9	.943	OF-110, 2B-1
1902 PIT N	59	.280	.336	232	65	7	3	0	0.0	52	20	35		19	0	0	80	6	5	1	1.5	.945	OF-59
1903 NY A	104	.237	.263	372	88	10	0	0	0.0	54	25	43		11	2	0	176	7	19	1	1.9	.906	OF-102, SS-1
1907 CIN N	73	.229	.297	266	61	5	5	1	0.4	28	25	23		9	2	0	160	11	5	3	2.4	.972	OF-70
4 yrs.	348	.261	.322	1296	338	32	19	3	0.2	232	110	167		65	5	0	596	42	41	12	2.0	.940	OF-341, SS-1, 2B-1

Mike Davis

DAVIS, MICHAEL DWAYNE   BL TL 6'2"   175 lbs.
B. June 11, 1959, San Diego, Calif.

Year Team	Games	BA	SA	AB	H	2B	3B	HR	HR%	R	RBI	BB	SO	SB	PH AB	PH H	PO	A	E	DP	TC/G	FA	G by Pos
1980 OAK A	51	.211	.284	95	20	2	1	1	1.1	11	8	7	14	2	22	4	76	7	1	6	1.6	.988	OF-18, 1B-7, DH-6
1981	17	.050	.100	20	1	1	0	0	0.0	0	0	2	4	0	10	0	3	0	0	0	0.2	1.000	DH-3, OF-2, 1B-1
1982	23	.400	.493	75	30	4	0	1	1.3	12	10	2	8	3	4	1	65	4	5	5	3.2	.932	OF-13, 1B-7
1983	128	.275	.402	443	122	24	4	8	1.8	61	62	27	74	32	6	3	278	16	8	4	2.4	.974	OF-121, DH-3
1984	134	.230	.364	382	88	18	3	9	2.4	47	46	31	66	14	6	2	287	6	12	4	2.3	.961	OF-127, DH-4
1985	154	.287	.484	547	157	34	1	24	4.4	92	82	50	99	24	3	0	370	6	8	1	2.5	.979	OF-151
1986	142	.268	.454	489	131	28	3	19	3.9	77	55	34	91	27	7	2	310	9	9	2	2.3	.973	OF-139
1987	139	.265	.468	494	131	32	1	22	4.5	69	72	42	94	19	11	2	210	3	13	1	1.6	.942	OF-124, DH-14
1988 LA N	108	.196	.270	281	55	11	2	2	0.7	29	17	25	59	7	30	5	121	3	5	2	1.2	.961	OF-76
1989	67	.249	.387	173	43	7	1	5	2.9	21	19	16	28	6	16	3	74	1	1	1	1.1	.987	OF-48
10 yrs.	963	.259	.415	2999	778	161	16	91	3.0	419	371	236	537	134	115	22	1794	55	62	26	2.0	.968	OF-819, DH-30, 1B-15

LEAGUE CHAMPIONSHIP SERIES

Year Team	Games	BA	SA	AB	H	2B	3B	HR	HR%	R	RBI	BB	SO	SB	PH AB	PH H	PO	A	E	DP	TC/G	FA	G by Pos
1981 OAK A	1	1.000	1.000	1	1	0	0	0	0.0	0	0	0	0	0	1	1	0	0	0	0	0.0	–	
1988 LA N	4	.000	.000	2	0	0	0	0	0.0	0	0	1	0	0	2	0	0	0	0	0	0.0	–	
2 yrs.	5	.333	.333	3	1	0	0	0	0.0	0	0	1	0	0	3	1	0	0	0	0	0.0	–	

WORLD SERIES

Year Team	Games	BA	SA	AB	H	2B	3B	HR	HR%	R	RBI	BB	SO	SB	PH AB	PH H	PO	A	E	DP	TC/G	FA	G by Pos
1988 LA N	4	.143	.571	7	1	0	0	1	14.3	3	2	4	0	2	0	0	0	0	0	0	0.0	–	DH-2, OF-1

Odie Davis

DAVIS, ODIE ERNEST   BR TR 6'1"   178 lbs.
B. Aug. 13, 1955, San Antonio, Tex.

Year Team	Games	BA	SA	AB	H	2B	3B	HR	HR%	R	RBI	BB	SO	SB	PH AB	PH H	PO	A	E	DP	TC/G	FA	G by Pos
1980 TEX A	17	.125	.125	8	1	0	0	0	0.0	0	0	1	1	0	2	0	7	15	3	3	1.5	.880	SS-13, 3B-1

Otis Davis

DAVIS, OTIS ALLEN (Scat)   BL TL 6'   160 lbs.
B. Sept. 24, 1920, Charleston, Ark.

Year Team	Games	BA	SA	AB	H	2B	3B	HR	HR%	R	RBI	BB	SO	SB	PH AB	PH H	PO	A	E	DP	TC/G	FA	G by Pos
1946 BKN N	1	–	–	0	0	0	0	0	–	1	0	0	0	0	0	0	0	0	0	0	0.0	–	

Ron Davis

DAVIS, RONALD EVERETTE   BR TR 6'   175 lbs.
B. Oct. 21, 1941, Roanoke Rapids, N. C.

Year Team	Games	BA	SA	AB	H	2B	3B	HR	HR%	R	RBI	BB	SO	SB	PH AB	PH H	PO	A	E	DP	TC/G	FA	G by Pos
1962 HOU N	6	.214	.214	14	3	0	0	0	0.0	1	1	0	7	1	0	0	9	0	0	0	1.5	1.000	OF-5
1966	48	.247	.340	194	48	10	1	2	1.0	21	19	13	26	2	0	0	98	9	2	1	2.3	.982	OF-48
1967	94	.256	.404	285	73	19	1	7	2.5	31	38	17	48	5	15	3	114	7	3	2	1.3	.976	OF-80
1968 2 teams		HOU N (52G – .212)			STL N (33G – .177)																		
" total	85	.203	.280	296	60	14	3	1	0.3	33	17	18	65	1	0	0	175	7	5	1	2.2	.973	OF-77
1969 PIT N	62	.234	.281	64	15	1	1	0	0.0	10	4	7	14	0	8	3	27	1	2	0	0.5	.933	OF-51
5 yrs.	295	.233	.334	853	199	44	6	10	1.2	96	79	56	160	9	23	6	423	24	12	4	1.6	.974	OF-261

WORLD SERIES

Year Team	Games	BA	SA	AB	H	2B	3B	HR	HR%	R	RBI	BB	SO	SB	PH AB	PH H	PO	A	E	DP	TC/G	FA	G by Pos
1968 STL N	2	.000	.000	7	0	0	0	0	0.0	0	0	0	2	0	0	0	5	0	0	0	2.5	1.000	OF-2

Spud Davis

DAVIS, VIRGIL LAWRENCE   BR TR 6'1"   197 lbs.
B. Dec. 20, 1904, Birmingham, Ala.   D. Aug. 14, 1984, Birmingham, Ala.
Manager 1946.

Year Team	Games	BA	SA	AB	H	2B	3B	HR	HR%	R	RBI	BB	SO	SB	PH AB	PH H	PO	A	E	DP	TC/G	FA	G by Pos
1928 2 teams		STL N (2G – .200)			PHI N (67G – .282)																		
" total	69	.280	.345	168	47	2	0	3	1.8	17	19	16	11	0	17	4	155	46	6	7	3.0	.971	C-51
1929 PHI N	98	.342	.490	263	90	18	0	7	2.7	31	48	19	17	1	7	3	198	47	10	7	2.6	.961	C-98
1930	106	.313	.495	329	103	16	1	14	4.3	41	65	17	20	1	9	2	307	50	5	5	3.4	.986	C-96
1931	120	.326	.443	393	128	32	1	4	1.0	30	51	36	28	0	5	0	420	78	3	10	4.2	.994	C-114
1932	125	.336	.522	402	135	23	5	14	3.5	44	70	40	39	1	5	2	408	54	6	15	3.7	.987	C-120
1933	141	.349	.473	495	173	28	3	9	1.8	51	65	32	24	2	6	2	395	69	8	9	3.3	.983	C-132
1934 STL N	107	.300	.464	347	104	22	4	9	2.6	45	65	34	27	0	11	3	459	42	6	7	4.7	.988	C-94
1935	102	.317	.416	315	100	24	2	1	0.3	28	60	33	30	0	13	4	383	34	3	6	4.1	.993	C-81, 1B-5
1936	112	.273	.388	363	99	26	2	4	1.1	24	59	35	34	0	7	2	391	63	7	7	4.1	.985	C-103, 3B-2
1937 CIN N	76	.268	.368	209	56	10	1	3	1.4	19	33	23	15	0	13	5	300	40	7	3	4.6	.980	C-59
1938 2 teams		CIN N (12G – .167)			PHI N (70G – .247)																		
" total	82	.235	.291	251	59	8	0	2	0.8	14	24	19	20	1	8	1	260	34	7	6	3.7	.977	C-74
1939 PHI N	87	.307	.356	202	62	8	1	0	0.0	10	23	24	20	0	2	1	260	40	0	1	3.4	1.000	C-85
1940 PIT N	99	.326	.435	285	93	14	1	5	1.8	23	39	35	20	0	10	3	288	61	12	11	3.6	.967	C-87
1941	57	.252	.308	107	27	4	1	0	0.0	3	6	11	11	0	7	2	97	16	0	3	2.0	1.000	C-49
1944	54	.301	.441	93	28	7	0	2	2.2	6	14	10	8	0	17	8	76	10	3	3	1.6	.966	C-35
1945	23	.242	.303	33	8	2	0	0	0.0	2	6	2	2	0	9	1	26	4	1	1	1.3	.968	C-13
16 yrs.	1458	.308	.430	4255	1312	244	22	77	1.8	388	647	386	326	6	146	45	4423	688	84	100	3.6	.984	C-1291, 1B-5, 3B-2

WORLD SERIES

Year Team	Games	BA	SA	AB	H	2B	3B	HR	HR%	R	RBI	BB	SO	SB	PH AB	PH H	PO	A	E	DP	TC/G	FA	G by Pos
1934 STL N	2	1.000	1.000	2	2	0	0	0	0.0	0	1	0	0	0	2	2	0	0	0	0	0.0	–	

Steve Davis

DAVIS, STEVEN MICHAEL   BR TR 6'1"   200 lbs.
B. Dec. 30, 1953, Oakland, Calif.

Year Team	Games	BA	SA	AB	H	2B	3B	HR	HR%	R	RBI	BB	SO	SB	PH AB	PH H	PO	A	E	DP	TC/G	FA	G by Pos
1979 CHI N	3	.000	.000	4	0	0	0	0	0.0	0	1	0	0	0	0	0	0	3	0	0	1.0	1.000	2B-2, 3B-1

Year	Team	Games	BA	SA	AB	H	2B	3B	HR	HR%	R	RBI	BB	SO	SB	Pinch Hit AB	Pinch Hit H	PO	A	E	DP	TC/G	FA	G by Pos

Tod Davis

DAVIS, THOMAS OSCAR
B. July 24, 1924, Los Angeles, Calif. D. Dec. 31, 1978, West Covina, Calif.

BR TR 6'2" 190 lbs.

Year	Team	Games	BA	SA	AB	H	2B	3B	HR	HR%	R	RBI	BB	SO	SB	Pinch Hit AB	Pinch Hit H	PO	A	E	DP	TC/G	FA	G by Pos
1949	PHI A	31	.267	.333	75	20	0	1	1	1.3	7	6	9	16	0	7	2	31	46	6	15	2.7	.928	SS-14, 3B-12, 2B-1
1951		11	.067	.067	15	1	0	0	0	0.0	0	0	1	3	0	7	1	2	2	0	0	0.4	1.000	2B-2, 3B-1
2 yrs.		42	.233	.289	90	21	0	1	1	1.1	7	6	10	19	0	14	3	33	48	6	15	2.1	.931	SS-14, 3B-13, 2B-3

Tommy Davis

DAVIS, HERMAN THOMAS
B. Mar. 21, 1939, Brooklyn, N. Y.

BR TR 6'2" 195 lbs.

Year	Team	Games	BA	SA	AB	H	2B	3B	HR	HR%	R	RBI	BB	SO	SB	Pinch Hit AB	Pinch Hit H	PO	A	E	DP	TC/G	FA	G by Pos
1959	LA N	1	.000	.000	1	0	0	0	0	0.0	0	0	0	1	0	1	0	0	0	0	0	0.0	—	
1960		110	.276	.426	352	97	18	1	11	3.1	43	44	13	35	6	21	7	153	17	4	2	1.6	.977	OF-87, 3B-5
1961		132	.278	.413	460	128	13	2	15	3.3	60	58	32	53	10	10	3	173	91	17	8	2.1	.940	OF-86, 3B-59
1962		163	.346	.535	665	230	27	9	27	4.1	120	153	33	65	18	2	0	269	60	20	7	2.1	.943	OF-146, 3B-39
1963		146	.326	.457	556	181	19	3	16	2.9	69	88	29	59	15	3	0	204	67	15	10	2.0	.948	OF-129, 3B-40
1964		152	.275	.397	592	163	20	5	14	2.4	70	86	29	68	11	4	2	264	9	5	1	1.8	.982	OF-148
1965		17	.250	.300	60	15	1	1	0	0.0	3	9	2	4	2	1	0	21	1	0	1	1.3	1.000	OF-16
1966		100	.313	.383	313	98	11	1	3	1.0	27	27	16	36	3	22	5	99	9	3	1	1.1	.973	OF-79, 3B-2
1967	NY N	154	.302	.440	577	174	32	0	16	2.8	72	73	31	71	9	4	0	236	7	7	0	1.6	.972	OF-149, 1B-1
1968	CHI A	132	.268	.344	456	122	5	3	8	1.8	30	50	16	48	4	12	4	211	9	8	5	1.7	.965	OF-116, 1B-6
1969	2 teams	SEA A (123G – .271)			HOU N (24G – .241)																			
"	total	147	.266	.370	533	142	32	1	7	1.3	54	89	38	55	20	16	7	210	4	7	0	1.5	.968	OF-133, 1B-1
1970	3 teams	HOU N (57G – .282)			OAK A (66G – .290)					CHI N (11G – .262)														
"	total	134	.284	.387	455	129	23	3	6	1.3	45	65	16	44	10	23	5	196	8	9	10	1.6	.958	OF-108, 1B-8
1971	OAK A	79	.324	.411	219	71	8	1	3	1.4	26	42	15	19	7	28	13	275	37	5	24	4.0	.984	1B-35, OF-16, 2B-3, 3B-2
1972	2 teams	CHI N (15G – .269)			BAL A (26G – .256)																			
"	total	41	.259	.296	108	28	4	0	0	0.0	12	12	8	21	2	15	3	82	5	1	0	2.1	.989	OF-20, 1B-6
1973	BAL A	137	.306	.391	552	169	20	3	7	1.3	53	89	30	56	11	6	4	32	2	1	3	0.3	.971	DH-127, 1B-4
1974		158	.289	.377	626	181	20	1	11	1.8	67	84	34	49	6	4	1	0	0	0	0	0.0	—	DH-155
1975		116	.283	.357	460	130	14	1	6	1.3	43	57	23	52	2	4	1	0	0	0	0	0.0	—	DH-111
1976	2 teams	CAL A (72G – .265)			KC A (8G – .263)																			
"	total	80	.265	.324	238	63	5	0	3	1.3	17	26	16	18	0	21	8	4	0	0	0	0.1	1.000	DH-56, 1B-1
18 yrs.		1999	.294	.405	7223	2121	272	35	153	2.1	811	1052	381	754	136	197	63	2429	326	102	72	1.4	.964	OF-1233, DH-449, 3B-147, 1B-62, 2B-3

LEAGUE CHAMPIONSHIP SERIES

Year	Team	Games	BA	SA	AB	H	2B	3B	HR	HR%	R	RBI	BB	SO	SB	Pinch Hit AB	Pinch Hit H	PO	A	E	DP	TC/G	FA	G by Pos
1971	OAK A	3	.375	.500	8	3	1	0	0	0.0	1	0	0	0	0	1	0	8	0	0	1	2.7	1.000	1B-2
1973	BAL A	5	.286	.333	21	6	1	0	0	0.0	1	2	1	0	0	0	0	0	0	0	0	0.0	—	DH-5
1974		4	.267	.267	15	4	0	0	0	0.0	0	1	0	1	0	0	0	0	0	0	0	0.0	—	DH-4
3 yrs.		12	.295	.341	44	13	2	0	0	0.0	2	3	1	1	0	1	0	8	0	0	1	0.7	1.000	DH-9, 1B-2

WORLD SERIES

Year	Team	Games	BA	SA	AB	H	2B	3B	HR	HR%	R	RBI	BB	SO	SB	Pinch Hit AB	Pinch Hit H	PO	A	E	DP	TC/G	FA	G by Pos
1963	LA N	4	.400	.667	15	6	0	2	0	0.0	0	2	0	1	0	0	0	6	0	0	0	1.5	1.000	OF-4
1966		4	.250	.250	8	2	0	0	0	0.0	0	0	1	1	0	2	2	3	0	0	0	0.8	1.000	OF-3
2 yrs.		8	.348	.522	23	8	0	2	0	0.0	0	2	1	3	0	2	2	9	0	0	0	1.1	1.000	OF-7

Trench Davis

DAVIS, TRENCH NEAL
B. Sept. 12, 1960, Baltimore, Md.

BL TL 6'3" 171 lbs.

Year	Team	Games	BA	SA	AB	H	2B	3B	HR	HR%	R	RBI	BB	SO	SB	Pinch Hit AB	Pinch Hit H	PO	A	E	DP	TC/G	FA	G by Pos
1985	PIT N	2	.143	.143	7	1	0	0	0	0.0	0	0	0	1	0	0	0	2	0	1	0	1.5	.667	OF-2
1986		15	.130	.130	23	3	0	0	0	0.0	2	1	0	4	0	7	1	10	1	1	0	0.8	.917	OF-7
1987	ATL N	6	.000	.000	3	0	0	0	0	0.0	0	0	0	1	0	3	0	0	0	0	0	0.0	—	OF-6
3 yrs.		23	.121	.121	33	4	0	0	0	0.0	3	1	0	5	1	10	1	12	1	2	0	0.7	.867	OF-15

Willie Davis

DAVIS, WILLIAM HENRY
B. Apr. 15, 1940, Mineral Springs, Ark.

BL TL 5'11" 180 lbs.

Year	Team	Games	BA	SA	AB	H	2B	3B	HR	HR%	R	RBI	BB	SO	SB	Pinch Hit AB	Pinch Hit H	PO	A	E	DP	TC/G	FA	G by Pos
1960	LA N	22	.318	.477	88	28	6	1	2	2.3	12	10	4	12	3	0	0	52	1	1	0	2.5	.981	OF-22
1961		128	.254	.451	339	86	19	6	12	3.5	56	45	27	46	12	9	1	224	4	4	1	1.8	.983	OF-114
1962		157	.285	.453	600	171	18	10	21	3.5	103	85	42	72	32	0	0	379	13	15	0	2.6	.963	OF-156
1963		156	.245	.365	515	126	19	8	9	1.7	60	60	25	61	25	4	2	337	16	8	3	2.3	.978	OF-153
1964		157	.294	.413	613	180	23	7	12	2.0	91	77	22	59	42	1	0	400	16	7	2	2.7	.983	OF-155
1965		142	.238	.346	558	133	24	3	10	1.8	52	57	14	81	25	2	1	318	6	11	1	2.4	.967	OF-141
1966		153	.284	.405	624	177	31	6	11	1.8	74	61	15	68	21	0	0	347	9	11	0	2.4	.970	OF-152
1967		143	.257	.367	569	146	27	9	6	1.1	65	41	29	65	20	6	1	300	6	9	2	2.2	.971	OF-138
1968		160	.250	.351	643	161	24	10	7	1.1	86	31	31	88	36	2	0	345	9	10	2	2.3	.973	OF-158
1969		129	.311	.456	498	155	23	8	11	2.2	66	59	33	39	24	4	0	271	8	6	1	2.2	.979	OF-125
1970		146	.305	.438	593	181	23	16	8	1.3	92	93	29	54	38	4	0	342	12	3	4	2.4	.992	OF-143
1971		158	.309	.438	641	198	33	10	10	1.6	84	74	23	47	20	3	1	404	7	8	0	2.7	.981	OF-157
1972		149	.289	.441	615	178	22	7	19	3.1	81	79	27	61	20	2	1	373	10	5	1	2.6	.987	OF-146
1973		152	.285	.444	599	171	29	9	16	2.7	82	77	29	62	17	7	3	344	6	7	1	2.3	.980	OF-146
1974	MON N	153	.295	.427	611	180	27	9	12	2.0	86	89	27	69	25	5	2	369	8	12	1	2.5	.969	OF-151
1975	2 teams	TEX A (42G – .249)			STL N (98G – .291)																			
"	total	140	.277	.424	519	144	27	9	11	2.1	57	67	18	52	23	12	3	287	6	7	3	2.1	.977	OF-131
1976	SD N	141	.268	.375	493	132	18	10	5	1.0	61	46	19	34	14	12	2	349	6	3	2	2.5	.992	OF-128
1979	CAL A	43	.250	.321	56	14	2	1	0	0.0	9	2	4	7	1	24	5	8	0	0	0	0.2	1.000	OF-7, DH-6
18 yrs.		2429	.279	.412	9174	2561	395	138	182	2.0	1217	1053	418	977	398	97	23	5449	143	127	23	2.4	.978	OF-2323, DH-6

LEAGUE CHAMPIONSHIP SERIES

Year	Team	Games	BA	SA	AB	H	2B	3B	HR	HR%	R	RBI	BB	SO	SB	Pinch Hit AB	Pinch Hit H	PO	A	E	DP	TC/G	FA	G by Pos
1979	CAL A	2	.500	1.000	2	1	1	0	0	0.0	1	0	0	0	0	2	1	0	0	0	0	0.0	—	

WORLD SERIES

Year	Team	Games	BA	SA	AB	H	2B	3B	HR	HR%	R	RBI	BB	SO	SB	Pinch Hit AB	Pinch Hit H	PO	A	E	DP	TC/G	FA	G by Pos
1963	LA N	4	.167	.333	12	2	0	0	0	0.0	2	3	0	6	0	0	0	6	0	0	0	1.5	1.000	OF-4
1965		7	.231	.231	26	6	0	0	0	0.0	3	0	3	2	3	0	0	11	0	0	0	1.6	1.000	OF-7
1966		4	.063	.063	16	1	0	0	0	0.0	0	0	0	4	0	0	0	6	0	3	0	2.3	.667	OF-4
3 yrs.		15	.167	.204	54	9	0	0	0	0.0	5	3	3	12	3	0	0	23	0	3	0	1.7	.885	OF-15

Andre Dawson

DAWSON, ANDRE FERNANDO (The Hawk)
B. July 10, 1954, Miami, Fla.

BR TR 6'3" 180 lbs.

Year	Team		Games	BA	SA	AB	H	2B	3B	HR	HR%	R	RBI	BB	SO	SB	Pinch Hit AB	Pinch Hit H	PO	A	E	DP	TC/G	FA	G by Pos

Andre Dawson *continued*

Year	Team		Games	BA	SA	AB	H	2B	3B	HR	HR%	R	RBI	BB	SO	SB	AB	H	PO	A	E	DP	TC/G	FA	G by Pos
1976	MON	N	24	.235	.306	85	20	4	1	0	0.0	9	7	5	13	1	0	0	61	1	2	1	2.7	.969	OF-24
1977			139	.282	.474	525	148	26	9	19	3.6	64	65	34	93	21	5	0	352	9	4	1	2.6	.989	OF-136
1978			157	.253	.442	609	154	24	8	25	4.1	84	72	30	128	28	5	2	411	17	5	2	2.8	.988	OF-153
1979			155	.275	.468	639	176	24	12	25	3.9	90	92	27	115	35	0	0	394	7	5	1	2.8	.988	OF-153
1980			151	.308	.492	577	178	41	7	17	2.9	96	87	44	69	34	3	1	410	14	6	3	2.8	.986	OF-147
1981			103	.302	.553	394	119	21	3	24	6.1	71	64	35	50	26	0	0	327	10	7	1	3.3	.980	OF-103
1982			148	.301	.498	608	183	37	7	23	3.8	107	83	34	96	39	0	0	419	8	8	2	2.9	.982	OF-147
1983			159	.299	.539	633	189	36	10	32	5.1	104	113	38	81	25	1	1	435	6	9	2	2.8	.980	OF-157
1984			138	.248	.409	533	132	23	6	17	3.2	73	86	41	80	13	4	0	297	11	8	2	2.3	.975	OF-134
1985			139	.255	.444	529	135	27	2	23	4.3	65	91	29	92	13	9	3	248	9	7	1	1.9	.973	OF-131
1986			130	.284	.478	496	141	32	2	20	4.0	65	78	37	79	18	3	1	200	11	3	2	1.6	.986	OF-127
1987	CHI	N	153	.287	.568	621	178	24	2	49	7.9	90	137	32	103	11	2	1	271	12	4	0	1.9	.986	OF-152
1988			157	.303	.504	591	179	31	8	24	4.1	78	79	37	73	12	8	2	267	7	3	1	1.8	.989	OF-147
1989			118	.252	.476	416	105	18	6	21	5.0	62	77	35	62	8	5	2	227	4	3	0	2.0	.987	OF-112
14 yrs.			1871	.281	.486	7256	2037	368	83	319	4.4	1058	1131	458	1134	284	45	13	4319	126	74	19	2.4	.984	OF-1823

DIVISIONAL PLAYOFF SERIES

| 1981 | MON | N | 5 | .300 | .400 | 20 | 6 | 0 | 1 | 0 | 0.0 | 1 | 0 | 1 | 6 | 2 | 0 | 0 | 0 | 0 | 1 | 0 | 0.2 | — | OF-5 |

LEAGUE CHAMPIONSHIP SERIES

1981	MON	N	5	.150	.150	20	3	0	0	0	0.0	2	0	0	4	0	0	0	0	0	0	0	0.0	—	OF-5
1989	CHI	N	5	.105	.158	19	2	1	0	0	0.0	0	3	2	6	0	0	0	4	0	0	0	0.8	1.000	OF-5
2 yrs.			10	.128	.154	39	5	1	0	0	0.0	2	3	2	10	0	0	0	4	0	0	0	0.4	1.000	OF-10

Boots Day

DAY, CHARLES FREDERICK
B. Aug. 31, 1947, Ilion, N. Y.

BL TL 5'9'' 160 lbs.

Year	Team		Games	BA	SA	AB	H	2B	3B	HR	HR%	R	RBI	BB	SO	SB	AB	H	PO	A	E	DP	TC/G	FA	G by Pos
1969	STL	N	11	.000	.000	6	0	0	0	0	0.0	1	0	1	1	0	5	0	0	0	0	0	0.0	—	OF-1
1970	2 teams		52			CHI N (11G – .250)			MON N (41G – .269)																	
"	total		52	.267	.302	116	31	4	0	0	0.0	16	5	6	21	3	13	4	81	2	2	0	1.6	.976	OF-42
1971	MON	N	127	.283	.353	371	105	10	2	4	1.1	53	33	33	39	9	15	5	262	10	5	1	2.2	.982	OF-120
1972			128	.233	.272	386	90	7	4	0	0.0	32	30	29	44	3	17	5	225	7	5	3	1.9	.979	OF-117
1973			101	.275	.367	207	57	7	0	4	1.9	36	28	21	28	0	48	13	86	2	0	0	0.9	1.000	OF-51
1974			52	.185	.185	65	12	0	0	0	0.0	8	2	5	8	0	31	3	18	0	0	0	0.3	1.000	OF-16
6 yrs.			471	.256	.312	1151	295	28	6	8	0.7	146	98	95	141	15	129	30	672	21	12	4	1.5	.983	OF-347

Brian Dayett

DAYETT, BRIAN KELLY
B. Jan. 22, 1957, New London, Conn.

BR TR 5'10'' 180 lbs.

Year	Team		Games	BA	SA	AB	H	2B	3B	HR	HR%	R	RBI	BB	SO	SB	AB	H	PO	A	E	DP	TC/G	FA	G by Pos
1983	NY	A	11	.207	.276	29	6	0	0	0	0.0	3	5	2	4	0	3	1	22	1	0	0	2.1	1.000	OF-9
1984			64	.244	.409	127	31	9	0	4	3.1	14	23	9	14	0	7	3	80	3	1	0	1.3	.988	OF-62, DH-1
1985	CHI	N	22	.231	.346	26	6	0	0	1	3.8	1	4	0	6	0	14	4	8	0	0	0	0.4	1.000	OF-10
1986			24	.269	.507	67	18	4	0	4	6.0	7	11	6	10	0	1	0	31	1	0	0	1.3	1.000	OF-24
1987			97	.277	.452	177	49	14	1	5	2.8	20	25	20	37	0	32	7	72	2	0	0	0.8	1.000	OF-78
5 yrs.			218	.258	.430	426	110	27	2	14	3.3	45	68	37	71	0	57	15	213	7	1	0	1.0	.995	OF-183, DH-1

Charlie Deal

DEAL, CHARLES ALBERT
B. Oct. 30, 1891, Wilkinsburg, Pa.   D. Sept. 16, 1979, Covina, Calif.

BR TR 6' 160 lbs.

Year	Team		Games	BA	SA	AB	H	2B	3B	HR	HR%	R	RBI	BB	SO	SB	AB	H	PO	A	E	DP	TC/G	FA	G by Pos
1912	DET	A	41	.225	.282	142	32	4	2	0	0.0	13	11	9			4	0	0	48	113	10	3	4.2	.942	3B-41
1913	2 teams		26			DET A (16G – .220)			BOS N (10G – .306)																	
"	total		26	.256	.314	86	22	1	2	0	0.0	9	6	3	8	3	1	0	25	53	11	4	3.4	.876	3B-15, 2B-10
1914	BOS	N	79	.210	.276	257	54	13	2	0	0.0	17	23	20	23	4	4	0	86	135	13	8	3.0	.944	3B-74, SS-1
1915	STL	F	65	.323	.426	223	72	12	4	1	0.4	21	27	12			10	0	0	76	136	11	9	3.4	.951	3B-65
1916	2 teams		25			STL A (23G – .135)			CHI N (2G – .250)																	
"	total		25	.146	.171	82	12	0	0	0	0.0	9	13	6	8	4	0	0	28	47	2	6	3.1	.974	3B-24, 2B-1
1917	CHI	N	135	.254	.292	449	114	11	3	0	0.0	46	47	19	18	10	5	1	151	254	18	31	3.1	.957	3B-130
1918			119	.239	.290	414	99	9	3	2	0.5	43	34	21	13	11	1	0	144	247	24	21	3.5	.942	3B-118
1919			116	.289	.385	405	117	23	5	2	0.5	37	52	12	12	11	0	0	157	233	11	14	3.5	.973	3B-116
1920			129	.240	.304	450	108	10	5	3	0.7	48	39	20	14	5	1	1	129	268	11	22	3.2	.973	3B-128
1921			115	.289	.393	422	122	19	8	3	0.7	52	66	13	9	3	2	0	122	239	10	19	3.2	.973	3B-113
10 yrs.			850	.257	.327	2930	752	104	34	11	0.4	295	318	135	105	65	14	2	966	1725	121	137	3.3	.957	3B-824, 2B-11, SS-1

WORLD SERIES

1914	BOS	N	4	.125	.250	16	2	2	0	0	0.0	1	0	0			2	0	0	6	11	0	1	4.3	1.000	3B-4
1918	CHI	N	6	.176	.176	17	3	0	0	0	0.0	0	0	0	1	0	0	0	6	9	1	0	2.7	.938	3B-6
2 yrs.			10	.152	.212	33	5	2	0	0	0.0	1	0	0	1	2	0	0	12	20	1	1	3.3	.970	3B-10

Lindsay Deal

DEAL, FRED LINDSAY
B. Sept. 3, 1911, Lenoir, N. C.   D. Apr. 18, 1979, Little Rock, Ark.

BL TR 6' 175 lbs.

Year	Team		Games	BA	SA	AB	H	2B	3B	HR	HR%	R	RBI	BB	SO	SB	AB	H	PO	A	E	DP	TC/G	FA	G by Pos
1939	BKN	N	4	.000	.000	7	0	0	0	0	0.0	0	0	2	0	3	0	0	3	0	0	0	0.8	1.000	OF-1

Snake Deal

DEAL, JOHN WESLEY
B. Jan. 21, 1879, Lancaster, Pa.   D. May 9, 1944, Harrisburg, Pa.

BR TR 6' 164 lbs.

Year	Team		Games	BA	SA	AB	H	2B	3B	HR	HR%	R	RBI	BB	SO	SB	AB	H	PO	A	E	DP	TC/G	FA	G by Pos
1906	CIN	N	65	.208	.251	231	48	4	3	0	0.0	13	21	6			15	0	0	624	46	10	25	10.5	.985	1B-65

Pat Dealey

DEALEY, PATRICK E.
B. Moosup, Conn.   D. Dec. 17, 1924, Buffalo, N. Y.

BR TR

Year	Team		Games	BA	SA	AB	H	2B	3B	HR	HR%	R	RBI	BB	SO	SB	AB	H	PO	A	E	DP	TC/G	FA	G by Pos
1884	STP	U	5	.133	.133	15	2	0	0	0	0.0	2		0			0	0	22	9	4	1	7.0	.886	C-4, OF-1
1885	BOS	N	35	.223	.292	130	29	4	1	1	0.8	18	9	2	14		0	0	168	53	29	11	7.1	.884	C-29, 3B-3, OF-2, SS-2, 1B-1
1886			15	.326	.391	46	15	1	1	0	0.0	9	3	4	4		0	0	76	16	8	1	6.7	.920	C-14, OF-1
1887	WAS	N	58	.272	.321	312	85	8	2	1	0.3	33	18	8	8	36	0	0	171	105	34	9	5.3	.890	C-28, SS-23, OF-5, 3B-5
1890	SYR	AA	18	.182	.197	66	12	1	0	0	0.0	9		5		4	0	0	39	26	12	1	4.3	.844	C-10, 3B-6, OF-2
5 yrs.			131	.251	.301	569	143	14	4	2	0.4	71	30	19	26	40	0	0	476	209	87	23	5.9	.887	C-85, SS-25, 3B-14, OF-11, 1B-1

Year	Team	Games	BA	SA	AB	H	2B	3B	HR	HR%	R	RBI	BB	SO	SB	Pinch Hit AB	Pinch Hit H	PO	A	E	DP	TC/G	FA	G by Pos

Chubby Dean
DEAN, ALFRED LOVELL
B. Aug. 24, 1916, Mt. Airy, N. C.   D. Dec. 21, 1970, Riverside, Calif.
BL TL 5'11"   181 lbs.

Year	Team	Games	BA	SA	AB	H	2B	3B	HR	HR%	R	RBI	BB	SO	SB	PH AB	PH H	PO	A	E	DP	TC/G	FA	G by Pos
1936	PHI A	111	.287	.374	342	98	21	3	1	0.3	41	48	24	24	3	34	13	680	37	8	62	6.5	.989	1B-77
1937		104	.262	.353	309	81	14	4	2	0.6	36	31	42	10	2	23	6	706	40	7	55	7.2	.991	1B-78, P-2
1938		16	.300	.400	20	6	2	0	0	0.0	3	1	1	4	0	9	2	0	8	0	0	0.5	1.000	P-6
1939		80	.351	.403	77	27	4	0	0	0.0	12	19	8	4	0	9	2	0	36	0	0	0.5	.951	P-54
1940		67	.289	.311	90	26	2	0	0	0.0	6	6	16	9	0	28	9	12	36	1	2	0.7	.980	P-30, 1B-1
1941 2 teams	PHI A (27G – .237)				CLE A	(17G – .167)																		
" total		44	.210	.258	62	13	3	0	0	0.0	2	11	7	5	0	14	2	7	28	0	1	0.8	1.000	P-26, 1B-1
1942	CLE A	70	.267	.277	101	27	1	0	0	0.0	4	7	11	7	0	37	5	7	24	2	0	0.5	.939	P-27
1943		41	.196	.196	46	9	0	0	0	0.0	2	5	6	2	0	20	2	2	11	1	1	0.3	.929	P-17
8 yrs.		533	.274	.341	1047	287	47	7	3	0.3	106	128	115	65	5	191	49	1417	220	21	125	3.1	.987	P-162, 1B-157

Tommy Dean
DEAN, TOMMY DOUGLAS
B. Aug. 30, 1945, Iuka, Miss.
BR TR 6'   165 lbs.

Year	Team	Games	BA	SA	AB	H	2B	3B	HR	HR%	R	RBI	BB	SO	SB	PH AB	PH H	PO	A	E	DP	TC/G	FA	G by Pos
1967	LA N	12	.143	.179	28	4	1	0	0	0.0	0	1	2	0	9	0	0	19	33	1	10	4.4	.981	SS-12
1969	SD N	101	.176	.245	273	48	9	2	2	0.7	14	9	27	54	0	0	0	141	255	9	41	4.0	.978	SS-97, 2B-2
1970		61	.222	.304	158	35	5	1	2	1.3	18	13	11	29	2	1	1	84	143	6	30	3.8	.974	SS-55
1971		41	.114	.114	70	8	0	0	0	0.0	2	1	4	13	1	1	1	38	71	5	13	2.8	.956	SS-28, 3B-11, 2B-1
4 yrs.		215	.180	.242	529	95	15	3	4	0.8	35	25	42	105	3	3	2	282	502	21	94	3.7	.974	SS-192, 3B-11, 2B-3

Wayland Dean
DEAN, WAYLAND OGDEN
B. June 20, 1902, Richmond, Va.
D. Apr. 10, 1930, Huntington, W. Va.
BB TR 6'2"   178 lbs.
BL 1926-27

Year	Team	Games	BA	SA	AB	H	2B	3B	HR	HR%	R	RBI	BB	SO	SB	PH AB	PH H	PO	A	E	DP	TC/G	FA	G by Pos
1924	NY N	26	.200	.350	40	8	0	1	2	5.0	5	4	1	9	0	0	0	12	41	3	2	2.2	.946	P-26
1925		33	.235	.373	51	12	2	1	1	2.0	7	7	3	12	0	0	0	10	36	6	1	1.6	.885	P-33
1926	PHI N	63	.265	.392	102	27	4	0	3	2.9	11	19	5	26	0	26	6	6	44	3	3	0.8	.943	P-33
1927 2 teams	PHI N (3G – .667)				CHI N	(2G – .000)																		
" total		5	.667	1.333	3	2	0	0	0	0.0	1	1	0	0	0	1	0	0	2	0	1	0.4	1.000	P-4
4 yrs.		127	.250	.393	196	49	6	2	6	3.1	24	31	9	47	0	27	6	28	123	12	7	1.3	.926	P-96

WORLD SERIES

Year	Team	Games	BA	SA	AB	H	2B	3B	HR	HR%	R	RBI	BB	SO	SB	PH AB	PH H	PO	A	E	DP	TC/G	FA	G by Pos
1924	NY N	1	–	–	0	0	0	0	0	0.0	0	0	0	0	0	0	0	0	0	0	0	0.0	–	P-1

Buddy Dear
DEAR, PAUL STANFORD
B. Dec. 1, 1905, Norfolk, Va.
BR TR 5'8"   143 lbs.

Year	Team	Games	BA	SA	AB	H	2B	3B	HR	HR%	R	RBI	BB	SO	SB	PH AB	PH H	PO	A	E	DP	TC/G	FA	G by Pos
1927	WAS A	2	.000	.000	1	0	0	0	0	0.0	1	0	0	0	0	0	0	0	0	0	0	0.0	–	2B-1

Charlie DeArmond
DeARMOND, CHARLES HOMMER (Hummer)
B. Feb. 13, 1877, Okeana, Ohio   D. Dec. 17, 1933, Morning Sun, Ohio
BR TR 5'10"   165 lbs.

Year	Team	Games	BA	SA	AB	H	2B	3B	HR	HR%	R	RBI	BB	SO	SB	PH AB	PH H	PO	A	E	DP	TC/G	FA	G by Pos
1903	CIN N	11	.282	.385	39	11	2	1	0	0.0	10	7	3		0	0	0	20	16	5	1	3.7	.878	3B-11

John Deasley
DEASLEY, JOHN
Brother of Pat Deasley.
B. Jan., 1861, Philadelphia, Pa.   D. Dec. 25, 1910, Philadelphia, Pa.

Year	Team	Games	BA	SA	AB	H	2B	3B	HR	HR%	R	RBI	BB	SO	SB	PH AB	PH H	PO	A	E	DP	TC/G	FA	G by Pos
1884 2 teams	WAS U (31G – .216)				KC U	(13G – .175)																		
" total		44	.207	.236	174	36	3	1	0	0.0	23		5			0	0	39	118	31	11	4.3	.835	SS-44

Pat Deasley
DEASLEY, THOMAS H.
Brother of John Deasley.
B. Nov. 17, 1857, Philadelphia Pa.,   D. Apr. 1, 1943, Philadelphia, Pa.
BR TR 5'8½"   154 lbs.

Year	Team	Games	BA	SA	AB	H	2B	3B	HR	HR%	R	RBI	BB	SO	SB	PH AB	PH H	PO	A	E	DP	TC/G	FA	G by Pos
1881	BOS N	43	.238	.299	147	35	5	2	0	0.0	13	8	5	10		0	0	159	48	21	6	5.3	.908	C-28, OF-7, SS-7, 1B-2
1882		67	.265	.295	264	70	8	0	0	0.0	36	29	7	22		0	0	372	56	25	1	6.8	.945	C-56, OF-14, SS-1
1883	STL AA	58	.257	.277	206	53	2	1	0	0.0	27		6			0	0	302	59	27	6	6.7	.930	C-56, OF-2
1884		75	.205	.256	254	52	5	4	0	0.0	27		7			0	0	429	120	48	3	8.0	.920	C-75, OF-2, 1B-1
1885	NY N	54	.256	.290	207	53	5	1	0	0.0	22		9	20		0	0	283	81	25	4	7.2	.936	C-54, OF-2, SS-1
1886		41	.266	.322	143	38	6	1	0	0.0	18	17	4	12		0	0	167	42	21	4	5.6	.909	C-30, OF-15
1887		30	.314	.356	118	37	5	0	0	0.0	12	23	9	7	3	0	0	98	37	24	0	5.3	.849	C-24, 3B-7, SS-1
1888	WAS N	34	.157	.165	127	20	1	0	0	0.0	6	4	2	18	2	0	0	180	65	21	3	7.8	.921	C-31, OF-1, SS-1, 2B-1
8 yrs.		402	.244	.282	1466	358	37	9	0	0.0	161	81	49	89	5	0	0	1990	508	212	27	6.7	.922	C-354, OF-43, SS-11, 3B-7, 1B-3, 2B-1

Hank DeBerry
DeBERRY, JOHN HERMAN
B. Dec. 29, 1894, Savannah, Tenn.   D. Sept. 10, 1951, Savannah, Tenn.
BR TR 5'11"   195 lbs.

Year	Team	Games	BA	SA	AB	H	2B	3B	HR	HR%	R	RBI	BB	SO	SB	PH AB	PH H	PO	A	E	DP	TC/G	FA	G by Pos
1916	CLE A	15	.273	.394	33	9	4	0	0	0.0	7	4	6	9	0	1	0	34	13	0	1	3.1	1.000	C-14
1917		25	.273	.333	33	9	2	0	0	0.0	3	1	2	7	0	14	3	22	8	1	1	1.2	.968	C-9
1922	BKN N	85	.301	.382	259	78	10	1	3	1.2	29	35	20	9	4	3	1	309	64	11	5	4.5	.971	C-81
1923		78	.285	.396	235	67	11	6	1	0.4	21	48	20	12	2	13	3	273	65	10	8	4.5	.971	C-60
1924		77	.243	.358	218	53	10	3	3	1.4	20	26	20	21	0	12	2	394	57	3	8	5.9	.993	C-63
1925		67	.259	.342	193	50	8	1	2	1.0	26	24	16	8	2	11	1	309	50	7	4	5.5	.981	C-55
1926		48	.287	.383	115	33	11	0	0	0.0	6	13	8	5	0	10	2	180	22	5	3	4.3	.976	C-37
1927		68	.234	.284	201	47	3	2	1	0.5	15	21	17	7	1	1	1	339	59	5	8	5.9	.988	C-67
1928		82	.252	.298	258	65	8	2	0	0.0	19	23	18	15	3	2	0	377	56	10	5	5.4	.977	C-80
1929		68	.262	.338	210	55	11	1	1	0.5	13	25	17	15	1	1	0	304	36	3	3	5.0	.991	C-68
1930		35	.295	.326	95	28	3	0	0	0.0	11	14	4	10	0	0	0	160	14	4	2	5.1	.978	C-35
11 yrs.		648	.267	.346	1850	494	81	16	11	0.6	170	234	148	119	13	67	13	2701	444	59	48	4.9	.982	C-569

Adam DeBus
DeBUS, ADAM JOSEPH
B. Oct. 7, 1892, Chicago, Ill.   D. May 13, 1977, Chicago, Ill.
BR TR 5'10½"   150 lbs.

Year	Team	Games	BA	SA	AB	H	2B	3B	HR	HR%	R	RBI	BB	SO	SB	PH AB	PH H	PO	A	E	DP	TC/G	FA	G by Pos
1917	PIT N	38	.229	.328	131	30	5	4	0	0.0	9	7	7	14	2	0	0	61	92	19	10	4.5	.890	SS-21, 3B-18

Year	Team	Games	BA	SA	AB	H	2B	3B	HR	HR%	R	RBI	BB	SO	SB	Pinch Hit AB	Pinch Hit H	PO	A	E	DP	TC/G	FA	G by Pos

Doug DeCinces

DeCINCES, DOUGLAS VERNON
B. Aug. 29, 1950, Burbank, Calif. BR TR 6'2" 190 lbs.

Year	Team	Games	BA	SA	AB	H	2B	3B	HR	HR%	R	RBI	BB	SO	SB	PH AB	PH H	PO	A	E	DP	TC/G	FA	G by Pos
1973	BAL A	10	.111	.111	18	2	0	0	0	0.0	2	3	1	5	0	0	0	4	19	2	2	2.5	.920	3B-8, 2B-2, SS-1
1974		1	.000	.000	1	0	0	0	0	0.0	0	0	1	0	0	0	0	0	2	0	0	2.0	1.000	3B-1
1975		61	.251	.395	167	42	6	3	4	2.4	20	23	13	32	0	7	1	92	115	7	20	3.5	.967	3B-34, SS-13, 2B-11, 1B-2
1976		129	.234	.357	440	103	17	2	11	2.5	36	42	29	68	8	2	0	191	257	20	21	3.6	.957	3B-109, 2B-11, 1B-11, SS-2, DH-1
1977		150	.259	.433	522	135	28	3	19	3.6	63	69	64	86	8	1	0	125	331	20	34	3.2	.958	3B-148, DH-1, 2B-1, 1B-1
1978		142	.286	.526	511	146	37	1	28	5.5	72	80	46	81	7	0	0	138	308	14	38	3.2	.970	3B-130, 2B-12
1979		120	.230	.412	422	97	27	1	16	3.8	67	61	54	68	5	0	0	99	247	13	21	3.0	.964	3B-120
1980		145	.249	.403	489	122	23	2	16	3.3	64	64	49	83	11	3	0	122	340	19	41	3.3	.960	3B-142, 1B-1
1981		100	.263	.454	346	91	23	2	13	3.8	49	55	41	32	0	1	0	91	191	17	31	3.0	.943	3B-100, OF-1, 1B-1
1982	CAL A	153	.301	.548	575	173	42	5	30	5.2	94	97	66	80	7	0	0	113	400	22	41	3.5	.959	3B-153, SS-2
1983		95	.281	.495	370	104	19	3	18	4.9	49	65	32	56	2	1	0	79	216	14	26	3.3	.955	3B-84, DH-10
1984		146	.269	.431	547	147	23	3	20	3.7	77	82	53	79	4	1	0	107	266	14	22	2.7	.964	3B-140, DH-5
1985		120	.244	.440	427	104	22	1	20	4.7	50	78	47	71	1	4	1	95	202	13	27	2.6	.958	3B-111, DH-3
1986		140	.256	.459	512	131	20	3	26	5.1	69	96	52	74	2	6	1	119	216	12	19	2.5	.965	3B-132, DH-3, SS-1
1987	2 teams	CAL A (133G – .234)		STL N (4G – .222)																				
"	total	137	.234	.392	462	108	25	0	16	3.5	66	64	70	89	3	10	1	108	234	19	27	2.6	.947	3B-131, 1B-4, SS-1
15 yrs.		1649	.259	.445	5809	1505	312	29	237	4.1	778	879	618	904	58	36	4	1483	3344	206	370	3.1	.959	3B-1543, 2B-43, DH-23, SS-20, 1B-20, OF-1

LEAGUE CHAMPIONSHIP SERIES

Year	Team	Games	BA	SA	AB	H	2B	3B	HR	HR%	R	RBI	BB	SO	SB	PH AB	PH H	PO	A	E	DP	TC/G	FA	G by Pos
1979	BAL A	4	.308	.385	13	4	0	0	0	0.0	4	3	1	1	0	0	0	5	8	0	1	3.3	1.000	3B-4
1982	CAL A	5	.316	.421	19	6	2	0	0	0.0	5	0	1	5	0	0	0	0	3	0	0	0.6	–	3B-5
1986		7	.281	.469	32	9	3	0	1	3.1	2	3	0	2	0	0	0	0	2	0	0	0.3	–	3B-7
3 yrs.		16	.297	.438	64	19	6	0	1	1.6	11	6	2	8	0	0	0	5	8	5	1	1.1	.722	3B-16

WORLD SERIES

Year	Team	Games	BA	SA	AB	H	2B	3B	HR	HR%	R	RBI	BB	SO	SB	PH AB	PH H	PO	A	E	DP	TC/G	FA	G by Pos
1979	BAL A	7	.200	.320	25	5	0	0	1	4.0	2	3	5	5	1	0	0	7	21	3	3	4.4	.903	3B-7

Frank Decker

DECKER, FRANK
B. Feb. 26, 1856, St. Louis, Mo. D. Feb. 5, 1940, St. Louis, Mo. BR TR

Year	Team	Games	BA	SA	AB	H	2B	3B	HR	HR%	R	RBI	BB	SO	SB	PH AB	PH H	PO	A	E	DP	TC/G	FA	G by Pos
1879	SYR N	3	.100	.100	10	1	0	0	0	0.0	0		0	3		0	0	14	0	4	0	6.0	.778	C-2, OF-1, 1B-1
1882	STL AA	2	.250	.250	8	2	0	0	0	0.0	0		0			0	0	6	7	3	1	8.0	.813	2B-2
2 yrs.		5	.167	.167	18	3	0	0	0	0.0	0		0	3		0	0	20	7	7	1	6.8	.794	2B-2, C-2, OF-1, 1B-1

George Decker

DECKER, GEORGE A.
B. June 1, 1869, York, Pa. D. June 9, 1909, Compton, Calif. BL TL 6'1" 180 lbs.

Year	Team	Games	BA	SA	AB	H	2B	3B	HR	HR%	R	RBI	BB	SO	SB	PH AB	PH H	PO	A	E	DP	TC/G	FA	G by Pos
1892	CHI N	78	.227	.306	291	66	6	7	1	0.3	32	28	20	49	9	0	0	95	49	22	6	2.1	.867	OF-62, 2B-16
1893		81	.271	.366	328	89	9	8	2	0.6	57	48	24	49	22	0	0	333	79	33	25	5.5	.926	OF-33, 1B-27, 2B-20, SS-2
1894		91	.313	.451	384	120	17	6	8	2.1	74	92	24	17	23	4	1	497	39	32	32	6.2	.944	1B-48, OF-29, 3B-7, 2B-2, SS-1
1895		73	.276	.374	297	82	9	7	2	0.7	51	41	17	22	11	0	0	212	16	12	10	3.3	.950	OF-57, 1B-11, 3B-3, SS-1, 2B-1
1896		107	.280	.423	421	118	23	11	5	1.2	68	61	23	14	20	0	0	482	29	17	25	4.9	.968	OF-71, 1B-36
1897		111	.290	.386	428	124	12	7	5	1.2	72	63	24		11	1	0	507	35	16	23	5.0	.971	OF-75, 1B-38, 2B-1
1898	2 teams	STL N (76G – .259)		LOU N (42G – .297)																				
"	total	118	.272	.325	434	118	14	3	1	0.2	53	64	29		13	5	2	1055	30	19	49	9.4	.983	1B-107, OF-6
1899	2 teams	LOU N (38G – .267)		WAS N (4G – .000)																				
"	total	42	.250	.326	144	36	8	0	1	0.7	13	18	12		3	1	0	426	16	15	22	10.9	.967	1B-40, OF-1
8 yrs.		701	.276	.376	2727	753	98	49	25	0.9	420	415	173	124	112	11	3	3607	293	166	192	5.8	.959	OF-334, 1B-307, 2B-40, 3B-10, SS-4

Harry Decker

DECKER, EARLE HARRY
B. June, 1865, Lockport, Ill. Deceased. BR TR 5'11" 183 lbs.

Year	Team	Games	BA	SA	AB	H	2B	3B	HR	HR%	R	RBI	BB	SO	SB	PH AB	PH H	PO	A	E	DP	TC/G	FA	G by Pos
1884	2 teams	IND AA (4G – .267)		KC U (23G – .133)																				
"	total	27	.156	.189	90	14	3	0	0	0.0	9		6			0	0	90	21	13	4	4.6	.895	OF-16, C-15
1886	2 teams	DET N (14G – .222)		WAS N (7G – .217)																				
"	total	21	.221	.273	77	17	2	1	0	0.0	2	7	3	14		0	0	118	46	23	1	8.9	.877	C-18, 3B-2, OF-1, SS-1
1889	PHI N	11	.100	.100	30	3	0	0	0	0.0	4	2	2	5	1	0	0	26	20	8	4	4.9	.852	2B-7, C-3, OF-1
1890	2 teams	PHI N (5G – .368)		PIT N (92G – .274)																				
"	total	97	.279	.375	373	104	15	3	5	1.3	57	40	30	37	12	0	0	459	87	49	22	6.1	.918	C-71, 1B-18, OF-6, SS-1, 2B-1
4 yrs.		156	.242	.318	570	138	20	4	5	0.9	72	49	41	56	13	0	0	693	174	93	31	6.2	.903	C-107, OF-24, 1B-18, 2B-8, SS-2, 3B-2

Artie Dede

DEDE, ARTHUR RICHARD
B. July 12, 1895, Brooklyn, N. Y. D. Sept. 6, 1971, Keene, N. H. BR TR 5'9" 155 lbs.

Year	Team	Games	BA	SA	AB	H	2B	3B	HR	HR%	R	RBI	BB	SO	SB	PH AB	PH H	PO	A	E	DP	TC/G	FA	G by Pos
1916	BKN N	1	.000	.000	1	0	0	0	0	0.0	0	0	0	0	0	0	0	1	0	0	0	1.0	1.000	C-1

Raoul Dedeaux

DEDEAUX, RAOUL MARTIAL (Rod)
B. Feb. 17, 1915, New Orleans, La. BR TR 5'11" 160 lbs.

Year	Team	Games	BA	SA	AB	H	2B	3B	HR	HR%	R	RBI	BB	SO	SB	PH AB	PH H	PO	A	E	DP	TC/G	FA	G by Pos
1935	BKN N	2	.250	.250	4	1	0	0	0	0.0	0	1	0	0	0	0	0	2	4	1	1	3.5	.857	SS-2

Jim Dee

DEE, JAMES D.
B. Buffalo, N. Y. Deceased.

Year	Team	Games	BA	SA	AB	H	2B	3B	HR	HR%	R	RBI	BB	SO	SB	PH AB	PH H	PO	A	E	DP	TC/G	FA	G by Pos
1884	PIT AA	12	.125	.125	40	5	0	0	0	0.0	0		1			0	0	13	36	8	6	4.8	.860	SS-12

Shorty Dee

DEE, MAURICE LEO
B. Oct. 4, 1889, Halifax, Nova Scotia, Canada D. Aug. 12, 1971, Jamaica Plains, Mass. BR TR 5'6" 155 lbs.

Year	Team	Games	BA	SA	AB	H	2B	3B	HR	HR%	R	RBI	BB	SO	SB	PH AB	PH H	PO	A	E	DP	TC/G	FA	G by Pos
1915	STL A	1	.000	.000	3	0	0	0	0	0.0	0		1			0	0	1	2	0	0	4.0	.500	SS-1

Year	Team		Games	BA	SA	AB	H	2B	3B	HR	HR%	R	RBI	BB	SO	SB	Pinch Hit AB	H	PO	A	E	DP	TC/G	FA	G by Pos

Rob Deer

DEER, ROBERT GEORGE
B. Sept. 29, 1960, Orange, Calif.
BR TR 6'3" 215 lbs.

Year	Team		Games	BA	SA	AB	H	2B	3B	HR	HR%	R	RBI	BB	SO	SB	AB	H	PO	A	E	DP	TC/G	FA	G by Pos
1984	SF	N	13	.167	.542	24	4	0	0	3	12.5	5	3	7	10	1	3	0	19	0	2	0	1.6	.905	OF-9
1985			78	.185	.377	162	30	5	1	8	4.9	22	20	23	71	0	30	5	127	2	2	4	1.7	.985	OF-37, 1B-10
1986	MIL	A	134	.232	.494	466	108	17	3	33	7.1	75	86	72	179	5	1	1	312	8	8	3	2.4	.976	OF-131, 1B-4
1987			134	.238	.456	474	113	15	2	28	5.9	71	80	86	186	12	2	0	304	16	8	7	2.4	.976	OF-123, 1B-12, DH-4
1988			135	.252	.441	492	124	24	0	23	4.7	71	85	51	153	9	1	0	284	10	3	3	2.2	.990	OF-133, DH-1
1989			130	.210	.425	466	98	18	2	26	5.6	72	65	60	158	4	1	1	267	10	8	1	2.2	.972	OF-125, DH-5
6 yrs.			624	.229	.449	2084	477	79	8	121	5.8	316	339	299	757	31	38	7	1313	46	31	18	2.2	.978	OF-558, 1B-26, DH-10

Charlie Dees

DEES, CHARLES HENRY
B. June 24, 1935, Birmingham, Ala.
BL TL 6'1" 173 lbs.

Year	Team		Games	BA	SA	AB	H	2B	3B	HR	HR%	R	RBI	BB	SO	SB	AB	H	PO	A	E	DP	TC/G	FA	G by Pos
1963	LA	A	60	.307	.416	202	62	11	1	3	1.5	23	27	11	31	3	4	1	474	32	7	41	8.6	.986	1B-56
1964			26	.077	.115	26	2	1	0	0	0.0	3	1	1	4	1	6	1	48	3	1	7	2.0	.981	1B-12
1965	CAL	A	12	.156	.156	32	5	0	0	0	0.0	1	1	1	8	1	4	0	69	2	1	5	6.0	.986	1B-8
3 yrs.			98	.265	.354	260	69	12	1	3	1.2	27	29	13	43	5	14	2	591	37	9	53	6.5	.986	1B-76

Tony DeFate

DeFATE, CLYDE HERBERT
B. Feb. 22, 1895, Kansas City, Mo. D. Sept. 3, 1963, New Orleans, La.
BR TR 5'8½" 158 lbs.

Year	Team		Games	BA	SA	AB	H	2B	3B	HR	HR%	R	RBI	BB	SO	SB	AB	H	PO	A	E	DP	TC/G	FA	G by Pos
1917	2 teams		STL N (14G – .143)								DET A	(3G – .000)													
"	total		17	.125	.125	16	2	0	0	0	0.0	1	1	4	6	0	6	1	1	6	0	1	0.4	1.000	3B-5, 2B-2

Art DeFreitas

DeFREITAS, ARTURO MARCELINO
Born Arturo Marcelino DeFreitas y Simon.
B. Apr. 26, 1953, San Pedro de Macoris, Dominican Republic
BR TR 6'2" 195 lbs.

Year	Team		Games	BA	SA	AB	H	2B	3B	HR	HR%	R	RBI	BB	SO	SB	AB	H	PO	A	E	DP	TC/G	FA	G by Pos
1978	CIN	N	9	.211	.421	19	4	1	0	1	5.3	1	2	1	4	0	2	1	40	3	0	5	4.8	1.000	1B-6
1979			23	.206	.265	34	7	2	0	0	0.0	2	4	0	16	0	17	3	38	0	1	5	1.7	.974	1B-6, OF-1
2 yrs.			32	.208	.321	53	11	3	0	1	1.9	3	6	1	20	0	19	4	78	3	1	10	2.6	.988	1B-12, OF-1

Rube DeGroff

DeGROFF, EDWARD ARTHUR
B. Sept. 2, 1879, Hyde Park, N. Y. D. Dec. 17, 1955, Poughkeepsie, N. Y.
BL 5'11"

Year	Team		Games	BA	SA	AB	H	2B	3B	HR	HR%	R	RBI	BB	SO	SB	AB	H	PO	A	E	DP	TC/G	FA	G by Pos
1905	STL	N	15	.250	.321	56	14	2	1	0	0.0	3	5	5			1	0	27	3	3	1	2.2	.909	OF-15
1906			1	.000	.000	4	0	0	0	0	0.0	1	0	0			0	0	0	0	0	0	0.0	–	OF-1
2 yrs.			16	.233	.300	60	14	2	1	0	0.0	4	5	5			1	0	27	3	3	1	2.1	.909	OF-16

Dutch Dehlman

DEHLMAN, HERMAN J.
B. 1850, Catasauqua, Pa. D. Mar. 13, 1885, Wilkes-Barre, Pa.
Manager 1876.

Year	Team		Games	BA	SA	AB	H	2B	3B	HR	HR%	R	RBI	BB	SO	SB	AB	H	PO	A	E	DP	TC/G	FA	G by Pos
1876	STL	N	64	.184	.208	245	45	6	0	0	0.0	40	9	9	10				750	8	33	21	12.4	.958	1B-64
1877			32	.185	.218	119	22	4	0	0	0.0	24	11	7	21				309	4	23	14	10.5	.932	1B-31, OF-1
2 yrs.			96	.184	.212	364	67	10	0	0	0.0	64	20	16	31				1059	12	56	35	11.7	.950	1B-95, OF-1

Jim Deidel

DEIDEL, JAMES LAWRENCE
B. June 6, 1949, Denver, Colo.
BR TR 6'2" 195 lbs.

Year	Team		Games	BA	SA	AB	H	2B	3B	HR	HR%	R	RBI	BB	SO	SB	AB	H	PO	A	E	DP	TC/G	FA	G by Pos
1974	NY	A	2	.000	.000	2	0	0	0	0	0.0	0	0	0	0	0	0	0	7	1	0	0	4.0	1.000	C-2

Pep Deininger

DEININGER, OTTO CHARLES
B. Oct. 10, 1877, Wasseralfingen, Germany D. Sept. 25, 1950, Boston, Mass.
BL TL 5'8½" 180 lbs.

Year	Team		Games	BA	SA	AB	H	2B	3B	HR	HR%	R	RBI	BB	SO	SB	AB	H	PO	A	E	DP	TC/G	FA	G by Pos
1902	BOS	A	2	.333	.833	6	2	1	1	0	0.0	0	0	0			0	0	0	1	0	1	0.5	1.000	P-2
1908	PHI	N	1	–	–	0	0	0	0	0	0.0	0	0	0			0	0	0	0	0	0	0.0	–	OF-1
1909			55	.260	.314	169	44	9	0	0	0.0	22	16	11			5	6	83	5	2	0	1.6	.978	OF-45, 2B-1
3 yrs.			58	.263	.331	175	46	10	1	0	0.0	22	16	11			5	6	83	6	2	1	1.6	.978	OF-46, P-2, 2B-1

Pat Deisel

DEISEL, EDWARD
B. Apr. 29, 1876, Ripley, Ohio D. Apr. 17, 1948, Cincinnati, Ohio
BR TR 5'5" 145 lbs.

Year	Team		Games	BA	SA	AB	H	2B	3B	HR	HR%	R	RBI	BB	SO	SB	AB	H	PO	A	E	DP	TC/G	FA	G by Pos
1902	BKN	N	1	.667	.667	3	2	0	0	0	0.0	0	1	1			0	0	8	0	0	0	8.0	1.000	C-1
1903	CIN	N	2	–	–	0	0	0	0	0	0.0	0	0	1			0	0	0	0	0	0	0.0	–	C-1
2 yrs.			3	.667	.667	3	2	0	0	0	0.0	0	1	2			0	0	8	0	0	0	2.7	1.000	C-2

Mike Dejan

DEJAN, MICHAEL DAN
B. Jan. 13, 1915, Cleveland, Ohio D. Feb. 2, 1953, West Los Angeles, Calif.
BL TL 6'1" 185 lbs.

Year	Team		Games	BA	SA	AB	H	2B	3B	HR	HR%	R	RBI	BB	SO	SB	AB	H	PO	A	E	DP	TC/G	FA	G by Pos
1940	CIN	N	12	.188	.313	16	3	0	1	0	0.0	1	2	3	3	0	8	1	4	0	0	0	0.3	1.000	OF-2

Ivan DeJesus

DeJESUS, IVAN
Born Ivan DeJesus y Alvarez.
B. Jan. 9, 1953, Santurce, Puerto Rico
BR TR 5'11" 175 lbs.

Year	Team		Games	BA	SA	AB	H	2B	3B	HR	HR%	R	RBI	BB	SO	SB	AB	H	PO	A	E	DP	TC/G	FA	G by Pos
1974	LA	N	3	.333	.333	3	1	0	0	0	0.0	1	0	0	2	0	1	0	1	0	0	0	0.3	1.000	SS-2
1975			63	.184	.230	87	16	2	1	0	0.0	10	2	11	15	1	2	0	45	107	4	18	2.5	.974	SS-63
1976	CHI	N	22	.171	.268	41	7	2	1	0	0.0	4	2	4	9	0	1	0	20	47	3	7	3.2	.957	SS-13, 3B-7
1977			155	.266	.353	624	166	31	7	3	0.5	91	40	56	90	24	1	0	234	595	33	94	5.6	.962	SS-154
1978			160	.278	.354	619	172	24	7	3	0.5	104	35	74	78	41	0	0	232	558	27	96	5.1	.967	SS-160
1979			160	.283	.379	636	180	26	10	5	0.8	92	52	59	82	24	0	0	235	507	32	97	4.8	.959	SS-160
1980			157	.259	.325	618	160	26	3	3	0.5	78	33	60	81	44	0	0	229	529	24	99	5.0	.969	SS-156
1981			106	.194	.233	403	78	8	4	0	0.0	49	13	46	61	21	0	0	221	343	24	81	5.5	.959	SS-106
1982	PHI	N	161	.239	.313	536	128	21	5	3	0.6	53	59	54	70	14	0	0	222	488	21	81	4.5	.971	SS-154, 3B-7
1983			158	.254	.336	497	126	15	7	4	0.8	60	45	53	77	11	0	0	214	438	23	64	4.3	.966	SS-158
1984			144	.257	.306	435	112	15	3	0	0.0	40	35	43	76	12	2	0	166	400	29	57	4.1	.951	SS-141
1985	STL	N	59	.222	.292	72	16	5	0	0	0.0	11	7	4	16	2	24	6	15	40	2	9	1.0	.965	3B-20, SS-13
1986	NY	A	7	.000	.000	4	0	0	0	0	0.0	1	0	1	1	0	0	0	5	4	1	0	1.4	.900	SS-7
1987	SF	N	9	.200	.200	10	2	0	0	0	0.0	1	1	0	1	0	0	1	7	14	4	2	2.8	.840	SS-9

Year	Team		Games	BA	SA	AB	H	2B	3B	HR	HR%	R	RBI	BB	SO	SB	Pinch Hit AB	Pinch Hit H	PO	A	E	DP	TC/G	FA	G by Pos

Ivan DeJesus *continued*

Year	Team		Games	BA	SA	AB	H	2B	3B	HR	HR%	R	RBI	BB	SO	SB	AB	H	PO	A	E	DP	TC/G	FA	G by Pos
1988	DET	A	7	.176	.176	17	3	0	0	0	0.0	1	0	1	4	0	0	0	8	17	3	4	4.0	.893	SS-7
15 yrs.			1371	.254	.326	4602	1167	175	48	21	0.5	595	324	466	664	194	31	6	1854	4087	230	703	4.5	.963	SS-1303, 3B-34

LEAGUE CHAMPIONSHIP SERIES

| 1983 | PHI | N | 4 | .250 | .250 | 12 | 3 | 0 | 0 | 0 | 0.0 | 0 | 1 | 3 | 3 | 0 | 0 | 0 | 4 | 10 | 2 | 0 | 4.0 | .875 | SS-4 |

WORLD SERIES

1983	PHI	N	5	.125	.125	16	2	0	0	0	0.0	0	0	1	2	0	0	0	5	14	1	2	4.0	.950	SS-5
1985	STL	N	1	.000	.000	1	0	0	0	0	0.0	0	0	0	0	0	1	0	0	0	0	0	0.0	—	
2 yrs.			6	.118	.118	17	2	0	0	0	0.0	0	0	1	2	0	1	0	5	14	1	2	3.3	.950	SS-5

Mark DeJohn

DeJOHN, MARK STEPHEN   BB TR 5'11"   170 lbs.
B. Sept. 18, 1953, Middletown, Conn.

| 1982 | DET | A | 24 | .190 | .286 | 21 | 4 | 2 | 0 | 0 | 0.0 | 1 | 1 | 4 | 4 | 1 | 0 | 0 | 20 | 31 | 2 | 10 | 2.2 | .962 | SS-20, 3B-4, 2B-1 |

Bill DeKoning

DeKONING, WILLIAM CALLAHAN, JR.   BR TR 5'11"   185 lbs.
B. Dec. 19, 1918, Brooklyn, N. Y.   D. July 26, 1979, Palm Harbor, Fla.

| 1945 | NY | N | 3 | .000 | .000 | 1 | 0 | 0 | 0 | 0 | 0.0 | 0 | 0 | 1 | 0 | 0 | 1 | 0 | 1 | 0 | 0 | 0 | 0.3 | 1.000 | C-2 |

Ed Delahanty

DELAHANTY, EDWARD JAMES (Big Ed)   BR TR 6'1"   170 lbs.
Brother of Joe Delahanty.   Brother of Frank Delahanty.
Brother of Jim Delahanty.   Brother of Tom Delahanty.
B. Oct. 30, 1867, Cleveland, Ohio   D. July 2, 1903, Niagara Falls, N. Y.
Hall of Fame 1945.

Year	Team		Games	BA	SA	AB	H	2B	3B	HR	HR%	R	RBI	BB	SO	SB	AB	H	PO	A	E	DP	TC/G	FA	G by Pos
1888	PHI	N	74	.228	.293	290	66	12	2	1	0.3	40	31	12	26	38	0	0	157	173	47	20	5.1	.875	2B-56, OF-17
1889			56	.293	.370	246	72	13	3	0	0.0	37	27	14	17	19	0	0	116	61	18	11	3.5	.908	OF-31, 2B-24, SS-1
1890	CLE	P	115	.298	.416	517	154	26	13	3	0.6	107	64	24	30	25	0	0	243	305	94	44	5.6	.854	SS-76, 2B-20, OF-18, 3B-3, 1B-1
1891	PHI	N	128	.243	.333	543	132	19	9	4	0.7	92	86	33	50	25	0	0	466	43	38	20	4.3	.931	OF-99, 1B-27, 2B-3
1892			123	.306	.495	477	146	30	21	6	1.3	79	91	31	32	29	0	0	263	28	18	6	2.5	.942	OF-121, 3B-4
1893			132	.368	.583	595	219	35	18	19	3.2	145	146	47	20	37	0	0	391	78	26	23	3.8	.947	OF-117, 2B-15, 1B-6
1894			114	.400	.561	497	199	36	16	4	0.8	149	131	60	16	21	0	0	325	96	42	19	4.1	.909	OF-88, 1B-12, 3B-9, SS-8, 2B-6
1895			116	.404	.617	480	194	49	10	11	2.3	149	106	86	31	46	0	0	282	55	31	8	3.2	.916	OF-103, SS-9, 2B-6, 3B-1
1896			123	.397	.631	499	198	44	17	13	2.6	131	126	62	22	37	1	1	482	29	21	15	4.3	.961	OF-99, 1B-22, 2B-1
1897			129	.377	.538	530	200	40	15	5	0.9	109	96	60		26	0	0	276	23	9	4	2.4	.971	OF-129, 1B-1
1898			144	.334	.454	548	183	36	9	4	0.7	115	92	77		58	0	0	302	20	12	5	2.3	.964	OF-144
1899			146	.410	.582	581	238	55	9	9	1.5	135	137	55		30	3	2	284	26	10	4	2.2	.969	OF-143
1900			131	.323	.430	539	174	32	10	2	0.4	82	109	41		16	1	0	1299	66	27	86	10.6	.981	1B-130
1901			139	.357	.533	538	192	39	16	8	1.5	106	108	65		29	0	0	732	31	22	22	5.6	.972	OF-84, 1B-58
1902	WAS	A	123	.376	.590	473	178	43	14	10	2.1	103	93	62		16	0	0	379	18	16	5	3.4	.961	OF-111, 1B-13
1903			42	.333	.436	156	52	11	1	1	0.6	22	21	12		3	1	0	74	6	3	1	2.0	.964	OF-40, 1B-1
16 yrs.			1835	.346 5th	.504	7509	2597	520	183	100	1.3	1601	1464	741	244	455	6	3	6071	1058	434	293	4.1	.943	OF-1344, 1B-271, 2B-131, SS-94, 3B-17

Frank Delahanty

DELAHANTY, FRANK GEORGE (Pudgie)   BR TR 5'9"   160 lbs.
Brother of Jim Delahanty.   Brother of Ed Delahanty.
Brother of Tom Delahanty.   Brother of Joe Delahanty.
B. Jan. 29, 1883, Cleveland, Ohio   D. July 22, 1966, Cleveland, Ohio

Year	Team		Games	BA	SA	AB	H	2B	3B	HR	HR%	R	RBI	BB	SO	SB	AB	H	PO	A	E	DP	TC/G	FA	G by Pos
1905	NY	A	9	.222	.259	27	6	1	0	0	0.0	0	2	1		0	1	0	43	2	3	0	5.3	.938	1B-5, OF-3
1906			92	.238	.345	307	73	11	8	2	0.7	37	41	16		11	5	2	180	7	9	1	2.1	.954	OF-92
1907	CLE	A	15	.173	.212	52	9	1	0	0	0.0	3	4	4		2	0	0	19	3	2	0	1.6	.917	OF-15
1908	NY	A	37	.256	.296	125	32	1	2	0	0.0	12	10	10		9	1	0	64	2	3	0	1.9	.957	OF-36
1914	2 teams			BUF	F (79G – .201)		PIT	F (41G – .239)																	
"	total		120	.215	.305	433	93	8	11	3	0.7	54	34	34		28	1	0	179	24	8	2	1.8	.962	OF-114, 2B-4
1915	PIT	F	14	.238	.262	42	10	1	0	0	0.0	3	3	1		0	2	0	20	2	0	0	1.6	1.000	OF-11
6 yrs.			287	.226	.308	986	223	22	22	5	0.5	109	94	66		50	10	2	505	40	25	3	2.0	.956	OF-271, 1B-5, 2B-4

Jim Delahanty

DELAHANTY, JAMES CHRISTOPHER   BR TR 5'10½" 170 lbs.
Brother of Ed Delahanty.   Brother of Frank Delahanty.
Brother of Tom Delahanty.   Brother of Joe Delahanty.
B. June 20, 1879, Cleveland, Ohio   D. Oct. 17, 1953, Cleveland, Ohio

Year	Team		Games	BA	SA	AB	H	2B	3B	HR	HR%	R	RBI	BB	SO	SB	AB	H	PO	A	E	DP	TC/G	FA	G by Pos
1901	CHI	N	17	.190	.222	63	12	2	0	0	0.0	4	4	3		5	0	0	21	29	7	2	3.4	.877	3B-17, 2B-1
1902	NY	N	7	.231	.269	26	6	1	0	0	0.0	3	3	1		0	0	0	11	0	1	0	1.7	.917	OF-7
1904	BOS	N	142	.285	.389	499	142	27	8	3	0.6	56	60	27		16	0	0	214	267	57	13	3.8	.894	3B-113, 2B-18, OF-9, P-1
1905			125	.258	.349	461	119	11	8	5	1.1	50	55	28		12	1	0	186	17	8	1	1.7	.962	OF-124, P-1
1906	CIN	N	115	.280	.364	379	106	21	4	1	0.3	63	39	45		21	3	1	146	179	35	4	3.1	.903	3B-105, SS-5, OF-2
1907	2 teams		STL	A (33G – .221)		WAS	A (109G – .292)																		
"	total		142	.279	.361	499	139	21	7	2	0.4	52	60	41		24	8	0	307	263	41	24	4.3	.933	2B-70, 3B-48, OF-13, 1B-4
1908	WAS	A	83	.317	.394	287	91	11	4	1	0.3	33	30	24		16	2	0	181	232	16	25	5.2	.963	2B-79
1909	2 teams		WAS	A (90G – .222)		DET	A (46G – .253)																		
"	total		136	.232	.316	452	105	23	6	1	0.2	47	41	40		13	5	0	188	227	20	26	3.2	.954	2B-131
1910	DET	A	106	.294	.368	378	111	16	3	2	0.5	67	45	43		15	0	0	246	267	33	36	5.2	.940	2B-106
1911			144	.339	.463	542	184	30	14	3	0.6	83	94	56		15	1	0	917	225	48	41	8.3	.960	1B-72, 2B-59, 3B-12
1912			78	.286	.346	266	76	14	1	0	0.0	34	41	42		9	1	0	148	120	23	19	3.7	.921	2B-44, OF-33
1914	BKN	F	74	.290	.397	214	62	13	5	0	0.0	28	15	25		4	13	2	137	119	12	18	3.6	.955	2B-55, 1B-5
1915			17	.240	.280	25	6	1	0	0	0.0	0	2	3		1	11	1	7	11	3	0	1.2	.857	2B-4
13 yrs.			1186	.283	.373	4091	1159	191	60	18	0.4	520	489	378		151	45	4	2709	1956	304	209	4.2	.939	2B-567, 3B-295, OF-188, 1B-81, SS-5, P-2

WORLD SERIES

| 1909 | DET | A | 7 | .346 | .500 | 26 | 9 | 4 | 0 | 0 | 0.0 | 2 | 4 | 2 | | 5 | 0 | 0 | 11 | 16 | 2 | 0 | 4.1 | .931 | 2B-7 |

Year	Team	Games	BA	SA	AB	H	2B	3B	HR	HR%	R	RBI	BB	SO	SB	Pinch Hit AB	Pinch Hit H	PO	A	E	DP	TC/G	FA	G by Pos

Joe Delahanty

DELAHANTY, JOSEPH NICHOLAS
Brother of Tom Delahanty.   Brother of Jim Delahanty.
Brother of Frank Delahanty.   Brother of Ed Delahanty.
B. Oct. 18, 1875, Cleveland, Ohio   D. Jan. 9, 1936, Cleveland, Ohio

BR TR 5'9"   168 lbs.

1907	STL N	6	.333	.476	21	7	0	0	1	4.8	3	2			3	0	0	14	0	1	0	2.5	.933	OF-6
1908		140	.255	.333	499	127	14	11	1	0.2	37	44	32		11	1	0	243	11	6	1	1.9	.977	OF-138
1909		123	.214	.287	411	88	16	4	2	0.5	28	54	42		10	10	3	203	121	22	11	2.8	.936	OF-63, 2B-48
3 yrs.		269	.238	.316	931	222	30	15	4	0.4	68	100	74		24	11	3	460	132	29	12	2.3	.953	OF-207, 2B-48

Tom Delahanty

DELAHANTY, THOMAS JAMES
Brother of Joe Delahanty.   Brother of Frank Delahanty.
Brother of Jim Delahanty.   Brother of Ed Delahanty.
B. Mar. 9, 1872, Cleveland, Ohio   D. Jan. 10, 1951, Sanford, Fla.

BL TR 5'8"   175 lbs.

1894	PHI N	1	.250	.250	4	1	0	0	0	0.0	0	0	0		1	0	0	5	2	1	0	8.0	.875	2B-1
1896	2 teams		CLE N (16G – .232)			PIT N (1G – .333)																		
"	total	17	.237	.305	59	14	4	0	0	0.0	12	4	8	4	4	0	0	18	36	12	2	3.9	.818	3B-16, SS-1
1897	LOU N	1	.250	.500	4	1	1	0	0	0.0	1	2	0		0	0	0	1	0	2	0	3.0	.333	2B-1
3 yrs.		19	.239	.313	67	16	5	0	0	0.0	13	6	8	5	4	0	0	24	38	15	2	4.1	.805	3B-16, 2B-2, SS-1

Mike de la Hoz

de la HOZ, MIGUEL ANGEL
Born Miguel Angel de la Hoz y Piloto.
B. Oct. 2, 1938, Havana, Cuba

BR TR 5'11"   170 lbs.

1960	CLE A	49	.256	.431	160	41	6	2	6	3.8	20	23	9	12	0	2	1	65	104	10	14	3.7	.944	SS-38, 3B-8
1961		61	.260	.370	173	45	10	0	3	1.7	20	23	7	10	0	16	2	77	116	9	10	3.3	.955	SS-17, 2B-17, 3B-16
1962		12	.083	.083	12	1	0	0	0	0.0	0	0	0	3	0	12	1	0	2	0	0	0.2	1.000	2B-2
1963		67	.267	.433	150	40	10	0	5	3.3	15	25	9	29	0	21	6	69	102	9	20	2.7	.950	2B-34, 3B-6, OF-2, SS-2
1964	MIL N	78	.291	.402	189	55	7	1	4	2.1	25	12	14	22	1	32	11	65	109	10	17	2.4	.946	3B-25, 2B-25, SS-8
1965		81	.256	.330	176	45	3	2	2	1.1	15	11	8	21	0	38	4	61	99	8	20	2.1	.952	SS-41, 3B-22, 2B-10, 1B-1
1966	ATL N	71	.218	.300	110	24	3	0	2	1.8	11	7	5	18	0	37	8	25	35	3	3	0.9	.952	3B-30, 2B-8, SS-1
1967		74	.203	.287	143	29	3	0	3	2.1	10	14	4	14	1	34	8	48	59	2	10	1.5	.982	2B-23, 3B-22, SS-1
1969	CIN N	1	.000	.000	1	0	0	0	0	0.0	0	0	0	1	0	0	0	0	0	0	0			—
9 yrs.		494	.251	.365	1114	280	42	5	25	2.2	116	115	56	130	2	198	36	410	626	51	94	2.2	.953	3B-129, 2B-119, SS-108, OF-2, 1B-1

Bill DeLancey

DeLANCEY, WILLIAM PINKNEY
B. Nov. 28, 1911, Greensboro, N. C.   D. Nov. 28, 1946, Phoenix, Ariz.

BL TR 5'11½"   185 lbs.

1932	STL N	8	.192	.346	26	5	0	2	0	0.0	1	2	1	0	0	0	0	32	8	3	3	5.4	.930	C-8
1934		93	.316	.565	253	80	18	3	13	5.1	41	40	41	37	1	15	3	363	35	8	5	4.4	.980	C-77
1935		103	.279	.419	301	84	14	5	6	2.0	37	41	42	34	0	17	4	372	29	12	6	4.0	.971	C-83
1940		15	.222	.222	18	4	0	0	0	0.0	0	2	1	2	0	1	0	24	2	2	0	1.9	.929	C-12
4 yrs.		219	.289	.472	598	173	32	10	19	3.2	79	85	85	74	1	33	7	791	74	25	14	4.1	.972	C-180

WORLD SERIES

| 1934 | STL N | 7 | .172 | .379 | 29 | 5 | 1 | 0 | 1 | 3.4 | 3 | 4 | 2 | 8 | 0 | 0 | 0 | 50 | 6 | 1 | 1 | 8.1 | .982 | C-7 |

Bill Delaney

DELANEY, WILLIAM L.
B. Mar. 5, 1863, Cincinnati, Ohio   D. Mar. 1, 1942, Canton, Ohio

BR TR

| 1890 | CLE N | 36 | .190 | .241 | 116 | 22 | 1 | 1 | 1 | 0.9 | 16 | 7 | 21 | 19 | 5 | 0 | 0 | 82 | 93 | 14 | 18 | 5.3 | .926 | 2B-36 |

Jesus De La Rosa

De La ROSA, JESUS
B. July 28, 1953, Santo Domingo, Dominican Republic

BR TR 6'1"   185 lbs.

| 1975 | HOU N | 3 | .333 | .667 | 3 | 1 | 1 | 0 | 0 | 0.0 | 1 | 0 | 0 | 1 | 0 | 3 | 1 | 0 | 0 | 0 | 0 | 0.0 | | — |

Luis Delgado

DELGADO, LUIS FELIPE
Born Luis Felipe Delgado y Robles.
B. Feb. 2, 1954, Hatillo, Puerto Rico

BB TL 5'11"   170 lbs.

| 1977 | SEA A | 13 | .182 | .182 | 22 | 4 | 0 | 0 | 0 | 0.0 | 4 | 2 | 1 | 8 | 0 | 0 | 0 | 14 | 1 | 0 | 0 | 1.2 | 1.000 | OF-13 |

Bobby Del Greco

DEL GRECO, ROBERT GEORGE
B. Apr. 7, 1933, Pittsburgh, Pa.

BR TR 5'10½"   185 lbs.

1952	PIT N	99	.217	.279	341	74	14	2	1	0.3	34	20	38	70	6	4	1	246	11	6	3	2.7	.977	OF-93
1956	2 teams		PIT N (14G – .200)			STL N (102G – .215)																		
"	total	116	.214	.355	290	62	16	2	7	2.4	33	21	35	53	1	7	0	228	6	3	0	2.0	.987	OF-107, 3B-3
1957	2 teams		CHI N (20G – .200)			NY A (8G – .429)																		
"	total	28	.234	.277	47	11	2	0	0	0.0	5	3	12	19	2	6	1	32	2	1	0	1.3	.971	OF-22
1958	NY A	12	.200	.200	5	1	0	0	0	0.0	1	0	1	1	0	4	1	5	0	0	0	0.4	1.000	OF-12
1960	PHI N	100	.237	.417	300	71	16	4	10	3.3	48	26	54	64	1	11	3	247	10	8	1	2.7	.970	OF-89
1961	2 teams		PHI N (41G – .259)			KC A (74G – .230)																		
"	total	115	.239	.359	351	84	19	1	7	2.0	48	32	42	48	1	9	1	248	9	3	2	2.2	.988	OF-105, 3B-1, 2B-1
1962	KC A	132	.254	.402	338	86	21	1	9	2.7	61	38	49	62	4	6	1	245	9	4	0	2.0	.984	OF-124
1963		121	.212	.320	306	65	7	1	8	2.6	40	29	40	52	1	8	2	209	5	4	0	1.8	.982	OF-110, 3B-2
1965	PHI N	8	.000	.000	4	0	0	0	0	0.0	1	0	0	3	0	2	0	0	0	0	0	0.0		OF-4
9 yrs.		731	.229	.352	1982	454	95	11	42	2.1	271	169	271	372	16	53	9	1460	52	29	6	2.1	.981	OF-666, 3B-6, 2B-1

Juan Delis

DELIS, JUAN FRANCISCO
B. Feb. 27, 1928, Santiago, Cuba

BR TR 5'11"   170 lbs.

| 1955 | WAS A | 54 | .189 | .227 | 132 | 25 | 3 | 1 | 0 | 0.0 | 12 | 11 | 3 | 15 | 1 | 16 | 2 | 25 | 45 | 6 | 6 | 1.4 | .921 | 3B-24, OF-8, 2B-1 |

Eddie Delker

DELKER, EDWARD ALBERTS
B. Apr. 17, 1907, DeAlto, Pa.

BR TR 5'10½"   170 lbs.

| 1929 | STL N | 22 | .150 | .200 | 40 | 6 | 0 | 1 | 0 | 0.0 | 3 | 5 | 2 | 12 | 0 | 2 | 0 | 16 | 20 | 5 | 2 | 1.9 | .878 | SS-9, 2B-7, 3B-3 |

Year	Team		Games	BA	SA	AB	H	2B	3B	HR	HR%	R	RBI	BB	SO	SB	Pinch Hit AB	Pinch Hit H	PO	A	E	DP	TC/G	FA	G by Pos

Eddie Delker *continued*

Year	Team		Games	BA	SA	AB	H	2B	3B	HR	HR%	R	RBI	BB	SO	SB	AB	H	PO	A	E	DP	TC/G	FA	G by Pos
1931			1	.500	1.000	2	1	1	0	0	0.0	0	2	0	0	0	0	0	1	0	0	0	1.0	1.000	3B-1
1932	2 teams	STL N (20G – .119)				PHI N	(30G – .161)																		
"	total		50	.144	.240	104	15	5	1	1	1.0	8	9	14	21	0	1	0	76	85	10	19	3.4	.942	2B-37, 3B-5, SS-4
1933	PHI	N	25	.171	.293	41	7	3	1	0	0.0	6	1	0	12	0	3	0	26	47	3	5	3.0	.961	2B-17, 3B-4
4 yrs.			98	.155	.251	187	29	9	3	1	0.5	19	15	16	45	0	6	0	119	152	18	26	2.9	.938	2B-61, SS-13, 3B-13

Bert Delmas

DELMAS, ALBERT CHARLES
B. May 20, 1911, San Francisco, Calif. D. Dec. 4, 1979, Huntington Beach, Calif.
BL TR 5'11" 165 lbs.

Year	Team		Games	BA	SA	AB	H	2B	3B	HR	HR%	R	RBI	BB	SO	SB	AB	H	PO	A	E	DP	TC/G	FA	G by Pos
1933	BKN	N	12	.250	.250	28	7	0	0	0	0.0	4	0	1	7	0	1	0	14	17	3	3	2.8	.912	2B-10

Luis De Los Santos

DE LOS SANTOS, LUIS MANUEL
Born Luis Manuel De Los Santos y Martinez.
B. Dec. 29, 1966, San Cristobal, Dominican Republic
BR TR 6'5" 190 lbs.

Year	Team		Games	BA	SA	AB	H	2B	3B	HR	HR%	R	RBI	BB	SO	SB	AB	H	PO	A	E	DP	TC/G	FA	G by Pos
1988	KC	A	11	.091	.227	22	2	1	0	0	0.0	1	1	4	4	0	2	0	31	1	0	3	2.9	1.000	1B-5, DH-3
1989			28	.253	.310	87	22	3	1	0	0.0	6	6	5	14	0	2	0	203	16	3	23	7.9	.986	1B-27
2 yrs.			39	.220	.294	109	24	4	2	0	0.0	7	7	9	18	0	4	0	234	17	3	26	6.5	.988	1B-32, DH-3

Garton Del Savio

DEL SAVIO, GARTON ORVILLE
B. Nov. 26, 1913, New York, N. Y.
BR TR 5'9½" 165 lbs.

Year	Team		Games	BA	SA	AB	H	2B	3B	HR	HR%	R	RBI	BB	SO	SB	AB	H	PO	A	E	DP	TC/G	FA	G by Pos
1943	PHI	N	4	.091	.091	11	1	0	0	0	0.0	0	0	1	0	0	0	0	6	12	3	1	5.3	.857	SS-4

Jim Delsing

DELSING, JAMES HENRY
B. Nov. 13, 1925, Rudolph, Wis.
BL TR 5'10" 175 lbs.

Year	Team		Games	BA	SA	AB	H	2B	3B	HR	HR%	R	RBI	BB	SO	SB	AB	H	PO	A	E	DP	TC/G	FA	G by Pos
1948	CHI	A	20	.190	.190	63	12	0	0	0	0.0	5	5	5	12	0	4	0	36	1	0	0	1.9	1.000	OF-15
1949	NY	A	9	.350	.550	20	7	1	0	1	5.0	5	3	1	2	0	4	2	6	0	0	0	0.7	1.000	OF-5
1950	2 teams	NY A (12G – .400)				STL A	(69G – .263)																		
"	total		81	.269	.311	219	59	5	2	0	0.0	27	17	22	23	1	24	8	150	4	1	3	1.9	.994	OF-53
1951	STL	A	131	.249	.356	449	112	20	2	8	1.8	59	45	56	39	2	4	1	340	15	6	5	2.8	.983	OF-124
1952	2 teams	STL A (93G – .255)				DET A	(33G – .274)																		
"	total		126	.260	.360	411	107	15	7	4	1.0	48	49	36	37	4	11	4	273	5	6	2	2.3	.979	OF-117
1953	DET	A	138	.288	.436	479	138	26	6	11	2.3	77	62	66	39	1	6	1	354	7	3	2	2.6	.992	OF-133
1954			122	.248	.372	371	92	24	2	6	1.6	39	38	49	38	4	13	5	221	5	1	0	1.9	.996	OF-108
1955			114	.239	.374	356	85	14	2	10	2.8	49	60	48	40	2	14	3	178	3	1	1	1.6	.995	OF-101
1956	2 teams	DET A (10G – .000)				CHI A	(55G – .122)																		
"	total		65	.094	.151	53	5	3	0	0	0.0	11	2	13	16	1	21	3	24	1	0	0	0.4	.962	OF-32
1960	KC	A	16	.250	.325	40	10	3	0	0	0.0	2	5	3	6	0	6	0	24	0	0	0	1.5	1.000	OF-10
10 yrs.			822	.255	.366	2461	627	111	21	40	1.6	322	286	299	251	15	107	28	1606	41	19	13	2.0	.989	OF-698

Joe DeMaestri

DeMAESTRI, JOSEPH PAUL (Oats)
B. Dec. 9, 1928, San Francisco, Calif.
BR TR 6' 170 lbs.

Year	Team		Games	BA	SA	AB	H	2B	3B	HR	HR%	R	RBI	BB	SO	SB	AB	H	PO	A	E	DP	TC/G	FA	G by Pos
1951	CHI	A	56	.203	.297	74	15	0	2	1	1.4	8	3	5	11	0	6	1	43	61	5	14	1.9	.954	SS-27, 2B-11, 3B-8
1952	STL	A	81	.226	.301	186	42	9	1	1	0.5	13	18	8	25	0	1	0	106	159	17	31	3.5	.940	SS-77, 2B-3, 2B-1
1953	PHI	A	111	.255	.352	420	107	17	3	6	1.4	53	35	24	39	0	0	0	191	297	18	53	4.6	.964	SS-108
1954			146	.230	.315	539	124	16	3	8	1.5	49	40	20	63	1	3	0	285	408	25	90	4.9	.965	SS-142, 3B-1, 2B-1
1955	KC	A	123	.249	.324	457	114	14	1	6	1.3	42	37	20	47	3	1	1	206	358	21	78	4.8	.964	SS-122
1956			133	.233	.316	434	101	16	1	6	1.4	41	39	25	73	3	1	0	210	407	23	95	4.8	.980	SS-132, 2B-2
1957			135	.245	.360	461	113	14	6	9	2.0	44	33	22	82	6	1	0	248	387	13	87	4.8	.980	SS-134
1958			139	.219	.290	442	97	11	1	6	1.4	32	38	16	84	1	2	1	226	417	13	95	4.7	.980	SS-137
1959			118	.244	.369	352	86	16	5	6	1.7	31	34	28	65	1	2	0	167	320	22	63	4.3	.957	SS-115
1960	NY	A	49	.229	.257	35	8	1	0	0	0.0	8	2	0	9	0	7	1	22	29	1	4	1.1	.981	2B-19, SS-17
1961			30	.146	.146	41	6	0	0	0	0.0	1	2	0	13	0	0	0	24	44	1	11	2.3	.986	SS-18, 2B-5, 3B-4
11 yrs.			1121	.236	.325	3441	813	114	23	49	1.4	322	281	168	511	15	24	4	1728	2887	159	621	4.3	.967	SS-1029, 2B-39, 3B-14

WORLD SERIES

Year	Team		Games	BA	SA	AB	H	2B	3B	HR	HR%	R	RBI	BB	SO	SB	AB	H	PO	A	E	DP	TC/G	FA	G by Pos
1960	NY	A	4	.500	.500	2	1	0	0	0	0.0	1	0	0	1	0	0	0	0	2	0	0	0.5	1.000	SS-3

Frank Demaree

DEMAREE, JOSEPH FRANKLIN
Born Joseph Franklin Dimaria.
B. June 10, 1910, Winters, Calif. D. Aug. 30, 1958, Los Angeles, Calif.
BR TR 5'11½" 185 lbs.

Year	Team		Games	BA	SA	AB	H	2B	3B	HR	HR%	R	RBI	BB	SO	SB	AB	H	PO	A	E	DP	TC/G	FA	G by Pos
1932	CHI	N	23	.250	.304	56	14	3	0	0	0.0	4	6	2	4	0	5	1	31	2	0	1	1.4	1.000	OF-17
1933			134	.272	.377	515	140	24	6	6	1.2	68	51	22	42	4	0	0	321	12	12	1	2.6	.965	OF-133
1935			107	.325	.410	385	125	19	4	2	0.5	60	66	26	23	6	8	2	204	13	6	3	2.1	.973	OF-98
1936			154	.350	.496	605	212	34	8	16	2.6	93	96	49	30	4	0	0	285	16	10	1	2.0	.968	OF-154
1937			154	.324	.485	615	199	36	6	17	2.8	104	115	57	31	6	0	0	283	17	6	6	2.0	.980	OF-154
1938			129	.273	.384	476	130	15	7	8	1.7	63	62	45	34	1	4	1	199	12	6	1	1.7	.972	OF-125
1939	NY	N	150	.304	.418	560	170	27	2	11	2.0	68	79	66	40	2	0	0	329	11	5	2	2.3	.986	OF-150
1940			121	.302	.413	460	139	18	6	7	1.5	68	61	45	39	5	2	1	233	6	5	5	2.0	.980	OF-119
1941	2 teams	NY N (16G – .171)				BOS N	(48G – .230)																		
"	total		64	.216	.318	148	32	5	2	2	1.4	23	16	16	6	2	22	3	60	2	0	0	1.0	1.000	OF-38
1942	BOS	N	64	.225	.299	187	42	5	0	3	1.6	18	24	17	10	2	13	1	114	4	0	1	1.8	1.000	OF-49
1943	STL	N	39	.291	.314	86	25	2	0	0	0.0	5	9	8	4	1	13	1	35	1	1	0	0.9	1.000	OF-23
1944	STL	A	16	.255	.294	51	13	2	0	0	0.0	4	6	3	6	0	2	0	30	1	1	0	2.0	.969	OF-16
12 yrs.			1155	.299	.415	4144	1241	190	36	72	1.7	578	591	359	269	33	67	10	2124	97	51	21	2.0	.978	OF-1076

WORLD SERIES

Year	Team		Games	BA	SA	AB	H	2B	3B	HR	HR%	R	RBI	BB	SO	SB	AB	H	PO	A	E	DP	TC/G	FA	G by Pos
1932	CHI	N	2	.286	.714	7	2	0	0	1	14.3	1	4	0	1	0	0	0	4	0	0	0	2.5	.800	OF-2
1935			6	.250	.542	24	6	1	0	2	8.3	2	2	1	4	0	0	0	8	1	0	0	1.5	1.000	OF-6
1938			3	.100	.100	10	1	0	0	0	0.0	1	0	1	2	0	0	0	6	0	0	0	2.0	1.000	OF-3
1943	STL	N	1	.000	.000	1	0	0	0	0	0.0	0	0	0	0	0	0	0	0	0	0	0	0.0	–	
4 yrs.			12	.214	.452	42	9	1	0	3	7.1	4	6	3	6	0	0	0	18	1	0	0	1.7	.950	OF-11

Billy DeMars

DeMARS, WILLIAM LESTER (Kid)
B. Aug. 26, 1925, Brooklyn, N. Y.

BR TR 5'10" 160 lbs.

Year	Team		Games	BA	SA	AB	H	2B	3B	HR	HR%	R	RBI	BB	SO	SB	Pinch Hit AB	Pinch Hit H	PO	A	E	DP	TC/G	FA	G by Pos
1948	PHI	A	18	.172	.172	29	5	0	0	0	0.0	3	1	5	3	0	2	0	18	25	3	8	2.6	.935	SS-9, 3B-1, 2B-1
1950	STL	A	61	.247	.287	178	44	5	1	0	0.0	25	13	22	13	0	2	0	118	129	19	32	4.4	.929	SS-54, 3B-5
1951			1	.250	.250	4	1	0	0	0	0.0	1	0	1	0	0	0	0	1	4	0	1	5.0	1.000	SS-1
3 yrs.			80	.237	.270	211	50	5	1	0	0.0	29	14	28	16	0	4	0	137	158	22	41	4.0	.931	SS-64, 3B-6, 2B-1

John DeMerit

DeMERIT, JOHN STEPHEN (Thumper)
B. Jan. 8, 1936, West Bend, Wis.

BR TR 6'1½" 195 lbs.

Year	Team		Games	BA	SA	AB	H	2B	3B	HR	HR%	R	RBI	BB	SO	SB	Pinch Hit AB	Pinch Hit H	PO	A	E	DP	TC/G	FA	G by Pos
1957	MIL	N	33	.147	.147	34	5	0	0	0	0.0	8	1	0	8	1	6	1	21	0	0	0	0.6	1.000	OF-13
1958			3	.667	.667	3	2	0	0	0	0.0	1	0	0	0	0	0	0	2	0	0	0	0.7	1.000	OF-2
1959			11	.200	.200	5	1	0	0	0	0.0	4	0	1	2	0	0	0	7	0	0	0	0.6	1.000	OF-4
1961			32	.162	.284	74	12	3	0	2	2.7	5	5	5	19	0	6	1	40	2	0	0	1.3	1.000	OF-21
1962	NY	N	14	.188	.375	16	3	0	0	1	6.3	3	1	2	4	0	1	0	4	0	0	0	0.3	1.000	OF-9
5 yrs.			93	.174	.265	132	23	3	0	3	2.3	21	7	8	33	1	13	2	74	2	0	0	0.8	1.000	OF-49
WORLD SERIES																									
1957	MIL	N	1	–	–	0	0	0	0	0	–	0	0	0	0	0	0	0	0	0	0	0	0.0	–	

Don Demeter

DEMETER, DONALD LEE
B. June 25, 1935, Oklahoma City, Okla.

BR TR 6'4" 190 lbs.

Year	Team		Games	BA	SA	AB	H	2B	3B	HR	HR%	R	RBI	BB	SO	SB	Pinch Hit AB	Pinch Hit H	PO	A	E	DP	TC/G	FA	G by Pos
1956	BKN	N	3	.333	1.333	3	1	0	0	1	33.3	1	1	0	1	0	2	0	1	0	0	0	0.3	1.000	OF-1
1958	LA	N	43	.189	.349	106	20	2	0	5	4.7	11	8	5	32	2	4	0	70	0	0	0	1.6	1.000	OF-39
1959			139	.256	.437	371	95	11	1	18	4.9	55	70	16	87	5	22	3	223	5	4	1	1.7	.983	OF-124
1960			64	.274	.488	168	46	7	1	9	5.4	23	29	8	34	0	8	2	92	2	1	1	1.5	.989	OF-62
1961	2 teams	LA	N (15G – .172)		PHI N (106G – .257)																				
"	total		121	.251	.467	411	103	18	4	21	5.1	57	70	22	80	2	13	2	339	25	4	25	3.0	.989	OF-93, 1B-22
1962	PHI	N	153	.307	.520	550	169	24	3	29	5.3	85	107	41	93	2	6	2	200	177	20	19	2.6	.950	3B-105, OF-63, 1B-1
1963			154	.258	.433	515	133	20	2	22	4.3	63	83	31	93	1	11	2	375	86	14	15	3.1	.971	OF-119, 3B-43, 1B-26
1964	DET	A	134	.256	.460	441	113	22	1	22	5.0	57	80	17	85	4	27	5	366	15	2	13	2.9	.995	OF-88, 1B-23
1965			122	.278	.463	389	108	16	4	16	4.1	50	58	23	65	4	15	6	377	11	4	20	3.2	.990	OF-81, 1B-34
1966	2 teams	DET	A (32G – .212)		BOS A (73G – .292)																				
"	total		105	.268	.458	325	87	18	1	14	4.3	43	41	8	61	2	21	2	203	10	3	4	2.1	.986	OF-84, 1B-6
1967	2 teams	BOS	A (20G – .279)		CLE A (51G – .207)																				
"	total		71	.226	.390	164	37	9	0	6	3.7	22	16	9	27	0	26	7	80	5	1	2	1.2	.988	OF-47, 3B-2
11 yrs.			1109	.265	.459	3443	912	147	17	163	4.7	467	563	180	658	22	155	31	2326	336	53	100	2.4	.980	OF-801, 3B-150, 1B-112
WORLD SERIES																									
1959	LA	N	6	.250	.250	12	3	0	0	0	0.0	2	0	1	3	0	0	0	9	0	0	0	1.5	1.000	OF-6

Steve Demeter

DEMETER, STEPHEN
B. Jan. 27, 1935, Homer City, Pa.

BR TR 5'9½" 185 lbs.

Year	Team		Games	BA	SA	AB	H	2B	3B	HR	HR%	R	RBI	BB	SO	SB	Pinch Hit AB	Pinch Hit H	PO	A	E	DP	TC/G	FA	G by Pos
1959	DET	A	11	.111	.167	18	2	1	0	0	0.0	1	1	0	1	0	9	1	4	6	1	1	1.0	.909	3B-4
1960	CLE	A	4	.000	.000	5	0	0	0	0	0.0	0	0	0	1	0	2	0	3	1	0	1	1.0	1.000	3B-3
2 yrs.			15	.087	.130	23	2	1	0	0	0.0	1	1	0	2	0	11	1	7	7	1	2	1.0	.933	3B-7

Ray Demmitt

DEMMITT, CHARLES RAYMOND
B. Feb. 2, 1884, Illiopolis, Ill. D. Feb. 19, 1956, Glen Ellyn, Ill.

BL TR 5'8½" 170 lbs.

Year	Team		Games	BA	SA	AB	H	2B	3B	HR	HR%	R	RBI	BB	SO	SB	Pinch Hit AB	Pinch Hit H	PO	A	E	DP	TC/G	FA	G by Pos
1909	NY	A	123	.246	.358	427	105	12	12	4	0.9	68	30	55		16	0	0	185	22	21	7	1.9	.908	OF-109
1910	STL	A	10	.174	.217	23	4	1	0	0	0.0	4	2	3		0	2	0	11	2	0	0	1.3	1.000	OF-8
1914	2 teams	DET	A (1G – .000)		CHI A (146G – .258)																				
"	total		147	.258	.342	515	133	13	12	2	0.4	63	46	61	48	12	3	1	217	24	12	3	1.7	.953	OF-142
1915	CHI	A	9	.000	.000	6	0	0	0	0	0.0	0	0	1	2	0	6	0	1	0	0	0	0.1	1.000	OF-3
1917	STL	A	14	.283	.377	53	15	1	2	0	0.0	6	7	0	8	1	0	0	15	0	0	0	1.1	1.000	OF-14
1918			116	.281	.370	405	114	23	5	1	0.2	45	61	38	35	10	1	0	206	25	12	8	2.1	.951	OF-114
1919			79	.238	.327	202	48	11	2	1	0.5	19	19	14	27	3	**27**	6	60	6	10	0	1.0	.868	OF-49
7 yrs.			498	.257	.349	1631	419	61	33	8	0.5	205	165	172	120	42	39	7	695	79	55	18	1.7	.934	OF-439

Gene DeMontreville

DeMONTREVILLE, EUGENE NAPOLEON
Brother of Lee DeMontreville.
B. Mar. 26, 1874, St. Paul, Minn. D. Feb. 18, 1935, Memphis, Tenn.

BR TR 5'8" 165 lbs.

Year	Team		Games	BA	SA	AB	H	2B	3B	HR	HR%	R	RBI	BB	SO	SB	Pinch Hit AB	Pinch Hit H	PO	A	E	DP	TC/G	FA	G by Pos
1894	PIT	N	2	.250	.250	8	2	0	0	0	0.0	0	0	1	4	0	0	0	1	7	1	0	4.5	.889	SS-2
1895	WAS	N	12	.217	.370	46	10	1	3	0	0.0	7	9	3	4	5	0	0	33	45	6	8	7.0	.929	SS-12
1896			133	.343	.452	533	183	24	5	8	1.5	94	77	29	27	28	0	0	305	479	97	53	6.6	.890	SS-133
1897			133	.341	.433	**566**	193	27	8	3	0.5	92	93	21		30	1	1	340	455	91	53	6.7	.897	SS-99, 2B-33
1898	BAL	N	151	.328	.369	567	186	19	2	0	0.0	93	86	52		49	0	0	369	486	60	46	6.1	.934	2B-123, SS-28
1899	2 teams	CHI	N (82G – .281)		BAL N (60G – .279)																				
"	total		142	.280	.345	550	154	19	7	1	0.2	83	76	27		47	0	0	366	503	69	54	6.6	.926	SS-82, 2B-60
1900	BKN	N	69	.244	.286	234	57	8	1	0	0.0	32	28	10		21	1	0	159	176	25	19	5.2	.931	2B-48, SS-12, 3B-7, OF-1, 1B-1
1901	BOS	N	140	.304	.368	570	173	14	4	5	0.9	83	72	17		25	0	0	294	403	43	37	5.3	.942	2B-120, 3B-20
1902			124	.268	.322	481	129	16	5	0	0.0	51	53	12		23	2	0	293	333	43	28	5.4	.936	2B-112, SS-10
1903	WAS	A	12	.273	.318	44	12	2	0	0	0.0	0	3	0		0	0	0	30	26	4	1	5.0	.933	2B-11, SS-1
1904	STL	A	4	.111	.111	9	1	0	0	0	0.0	0	0	2		0	1	0	5	7	0	0	3.0	1.000	2B-3
11 yrs.			922	.305	.374	3608	1100	130	35	17	0.5	535	497	174	35	228	5	1	2195	2920	439	299	6.0	.921	2B-510, SS-379, 3B-27, OF-1, 1B-1

Lee DeMontreville

DeMONTREVILLE, LEON
Brother of Gene DeMontreville.
B. Sept. 23, 1879, St. Paul, Minn. D. Mar. 22, 1962, Pelham Manor, N. Y.

BR TR 5'7" 140 lbs.

Year	Team		Games	BA	SA	AB	H	2B	3B	HR	HR%	R	RBI	BB	SO	SB	Pinch Hit AB	Pinch Hit H	PO	A	E	DP	TC/G	FA	G by Pos
1903	STL	N	26	.243	.314	70	17	3	1	0	0.0	8	7	8		3	5	1	37	52	13	8	3.9	.873	SS-15, 2B-4, OF-1

Rick Dempsey

DEMPSEY, JOHN RIKARD
B. Sept. 13, 1949, Fayetteville, Tenn.

BR TR 6' 180 lbs.

Year	Team		Games	BA	SA	AB	H	2B	3B	HR	HR%	R	RBI	BB	SO	SB	Pinch Hit AB	Pinch Hit H	PO	A	E	DP	TC/G	FA	G by Pos

Rick Dempsey *continued*

Year	Team		Games	BA	SA	AB	H	2B	3B	HR	HR%	R	RBI	BB	SO	SB	PH AB	PH H	PO	A	E	DP	TC/G	FA	G by Pos
1969	MIN	A	5	.500	.667	6	3	1	0	0	0.0	1	0	1	0	0	1	0	5	0	1	0	1.2	.833	C-3
1970			5	.000	.000	7	0	0	0	0	0.0	1	0	1	1	0	1	0	12	0	1	0	2.6	.923	C-3
1971			6	.308	.385	13	4	1	0	0	0.0	2	0	1	1	0	0	0	30	4	2	0	6.0	.944	C-6
1972			25	.200	.225	40	8	1	0	0	0.0	0	0	6	8	0	2	1	67	5	1	0	2.9	.986	C-23
1973	NY	A	6	.182	.182	11	2	0	0	0	0.0	0	0	1	3	0	0	0	9	0	2	0	1.8	.818	C-5
1974			43	.239	.321	109	26	3	0	2	1.8	12	12	8	7	1	12	2	152	22	4	0	4.1	.978	C-31, OF-2, DH-1
1975			71	.262	.338	145	38	8	0	1	0.7	18	11	21	15	0	23	5	92	9	3	1	1.5	.971	C-19, DH-18, OF-8, 3B-1
1976	2 teams		NY A (21G – .119)			BAL A (59G – .213)																			
"	total		80	.194	.204	216	42	2	0	0	0.0	12	12	18	21	1	6	1	308	40	4	8	4.4	.989	C-67, OF-7
1977	BAL	A	91	.226	.315	270	61	7	4	3	1.1	27	34	34	34	2	1	1	416	52	11	10	5.3	.977	C-91
1978			136	.259	.356	441	114	25	0	6	1.4	41	32	48	54	7	4	1	636	79	11	14	5.3	.985	C-135
1979			124	.239	.351	368	88	23	0	6	1.6	48	41	38	37	0	39	11	615	81	7	13	5.7	.990	C-124
1980			119	.262	.425	362	95	26	3	9	2.5	51	40	36	45	3	9	1	544	55	8	10	5.1	.987	C-112, OF-6, 1B-2, DH-1
1981			92	.215	.335	251	54	10	1	6	2.4	24	15	32	36	0	7	0	384	35	1	6	4.6	.998	C-90, DH-1
1982			125	.256	.349	344	88	15	1	5	1.5	35	36	46	37	0	8	3	491	46	5	8	4.3	.991	C-124, DH-1
1983			128	.231	.323	347	80	16	2	4	1.2	33	32	40	54	1	7	0	591	65	2	7	5.1	.997	C-128
1984			109	.230	.364	330	76	11	0	11	3.3	37	34	40	58	1	0	0	453	43	4	5	4.6	.992	C-108
1985			132	.254	.406	362	92	19	0	12	3.3	54	52	50	87	1	0	0	575	49	8	5	4.8	.987	C-131
1986			122	.208	.379	327	68	15	1	13	4.0	42	29	45	78	1	9	1	659	53	7	9	5.9	.990	C-121
1987	CLE	A	60	.177	.270	141	25	10	0	1	0.7	16	9	23	29	0	2	1	293	18	5	3	5.3	.984	C-59
1988	LA	N	77	.251	.455	167	42	13	0	7	4.2	25	30	25	44	1	8	1	333	29	4	4	4.8	.989	C-74
1989			79	.179	.305	151	27	7	0	4	2.6	16	16	30	37	1	24	5	265	35	4	4	3.9	.984	C-62
21 yrs.			1635	.234	.349	4408	1033	213	12	90	2.0	495	435	544	686	19	169	35	6930	720	96	107	4.7	.988	C-1516, OF-23, DH-22, 1B-2, 3B-1

LEAGUE CHAMPIONSHIP SERIES

Year	Team		Games	BA	SA	AB	H	2B	3B	HR	HR%	R	RBI	BB	SO	SB	PH AB	PH H	PO	A	E	DP	TC/G	FA	G by Pos
1979	BAL	A	3	.400	.600	10	4	2	0	0	0.0	3	0	1	0	1	0	0	10	1	0	0	3.7	1.000	C-3
1983			4	.167	.167	12	2	0	0	0	0.0	0	1	1	0	0	0	0	29	5	1	1	8.8	.971	C-4
1988	LA	N	4	.400	.800	5	2	2	0	0	0.0	1	2	1	0	0	1	0	7	0	0	0	1.8	1.000	C-3
3 yrs.			11	.296	.444	27	8	4	0	0	0.0	5	4	3	1	1	1	0	46	6	1	1	4.8	.981	C-10

WORLD SERIES

Year	Team		Games	BA	SA	AB	H	2B	3B	HR	HR%	R	RBI	BB	SO	SB	PH AB	PH H	PO	A	E	DP	TC/G	FA	G by Pos
1979	BAL	A	7	.286	.381	21	6	2	0	0	0.0	3	0	1	3	0	0	0	38	2	0	0	5.7	1.000	C-6
1983			5	.385	.923	13	5	4	0	1	7.7	3	2	2	2	0	0	0	27	4	0	0	6.2	1.000	C-5
1988	LA	N	2	.200	.400	5	1	0	0	0	0.0	0	1	1	2	0	1	0	13	1	0	0	7.0	1.000	C-2
3 yrs.			14	.308	.564	39	12	7	0	1	2.6	6	3	4	7	0	1	0	78	7	0	0	6.1	1.000	C-13

9th

Tod Dennehey

DENNEHEY, THOMAS FRANCIS
B. May 12, 1899, Philadelphia, Pa.   D. Aug. 8, 1977, Philadelphia, Pa.
BL TL 5'10"   180 lbs.

Year	Team		Games	BA	SA	AB	H	2B	3B	HR	HR%	R	RBI	BB	SO	SB	PH AB	PH H	PO	A	E	DP	TC/G	FA	G by Pos
1923	PHI	N	9	.292	.375	24	7	2	0	0	0.0	4	2	1	3	0	0	0	16	0	0	0	1.8	1.000	OF-9

Otto Denning

DENNING, OTTO GEORGE (Dutch)
B. Dec. 28, 1912, Hays, Kans.
BR TR 6'   180 lbs.

Year	Team		Games	BA	SA	AB	H	2B	3B	HR	HR%	R	RBI	BB	SO	SB	PH AB	PH H	PO	A	E	DP	TC/G	FA	G by Pos
1942	CLE	A	92	.210	.290	214	45	14	0	1	0.5	15	19	18	14	0	20	3	217	36	2	6	2.8	.992	C-78, OF-2
1943			37	.240	.287	129	31	6	0	0	0.0	8	13	5	1	3	3	0	326	18	12	39	9.6	.966	1B-34
2 yrs.			129	.222	.289	343	76	20	0	1	0.3	23	32	23	15	3	23	3	543	54	14	45	4.7	.977	C-78, 1B-34, OF-2

Jerry Denny

DENNY, JEREMIAH DENNIS
Born Jeremiah Dennis Eldridge.
B. Mar. 16, 1859, New York, N. Y.   D. Aug. 16, 1927, Houston, Tex.
BR TR 5'11½" 180 lbs.

Year	Team		Games	BA	SA	AB	H	2B	3B	HR	HR%	R	RBI	BB	SO	SB	PH AB	PH H	PO	A	E	DP	TC/G	FA	G by Pos
1881	PRO	N	85	.241	.313	320	77	16	2	1	0.3	38	24	5	44		0	0	144	181	62	12	4.6	.840	3B-85
1882			84	.246	.350	329	81	10	9	2	0.6	54		4	46		0	0	136	206	55	7	4.7	.861	3B-84
1883			98	.275	.443	393	108	26	8	8	2.0	73		9	48		0	0	178	188	52	13	4.3	.876	3B-98
1884			110	.248	.380	439	109	22	9	6	1.4	57		14	58		0	0	237	185	48	11	4.3	.898	3B-99, 1B-9, 2B-3, C-1
1885			83	.223	.321	318	71	14	4	3	0.9	40	25	12	53		0	0	128	157	43	10	4.0	.869	3B-83
1886	STL	N	119	.257	.389	475	122	24	6	9	1.9	58	62	14	68		0	0	186	282	55	24	4.4	.895	3B-117, SS-3
1887	IND	N	122	.324	.502	510	165	34	12	11	2.2	86	97	13	22	29	0	0	219	288	59	24	4.6	.896	3B-116, SS-4, OF-1, 2B-1
1888			126	.261	.408	524	137	27	7	12	2.3	92	63	9	79	32	0	0	236	312	64	23	4.9	.895	3B-96, SS-25, 2B-5, OF-1, P-1
1889			133	.282	.417	578	163	24	0	18	3.1	96	112	27	63	22	0	0	237	309	49	17	4.5	.918	3B-123, 2B-7, SS-5
1890	NY	N	114	.213	.307	437	93	18	7	3	0.7	50	42	28	62	11	0	0	184	237	49	19	4.1	.896	3B-106, SS-7, 2B-1
1891	3 teams		NY N (4G – .250)			CLE N (36G – .225)				PHI N (19G – .288)															
"	total		59	.247	.286	227	56	7	1	0	0.0	22	33	16	32	6	0	0	184	79	23	8	4.8	.920	3B-40, 1B-12, OF-8
1893	LOU	N	44	.246	.337	175	43	5	4	1	0.6	22	22	9	15	4	0	0	97	145	20	16	6.0	.924	SS-42, 3B-2
1894			60	.276	.389	221	61	11	7	0	0.0	26	32	13	12	10	0	0	85	124	30	12	4.0	.874	3B-60
13 yrs.			1237	.260	.384	4946	1286	238	76	74	1.5	714	512	173	602	114	0	0	2251	2693	609	196	4.5	.890	3B-1109, SS-86, 1B-21, 2B-17, OF-10, C-1, P-1

Drew Denson

DENSON, ANDREW
B. Nov. 16, 1965, Cincinnati, Ohio
BB TR 6'5"   210 lbs.

Year	Team		Games	BA	SA	AB	H	2B	3B	HR	HR%	R	RBI	BB	SO	SB	PH AB	PH H	PO	A	E	DP	TC/G	FA	G by Pos
1989	ATL	N	12	.250	.278	36	9	1	0	0	0.0	1	5	3	9	1	0	0	71	11	1	3	6.9	.988	1B-12

Bucky Dent

DENT, RUSSELL EARL
Born Russell Earl O'Dey.
B. Nov. 25, 1951, Savannah, Ga.
Manager 1989.
BR TR 5'9"   170 lbs.

Year	Team		Games	BA	SA	AB	H	2B	3B	HR	HR%	R	RBI	BB	SO	SB	PH AB	PH H	PO	A	E	DP	TC/G	FA	G by Pos
1973	CHI	A	40	.248	.265	117	29	2	0	0	0.0	17	10	10	18	2	1	0	55	134	7	23	4.9	.964	SS-36, 2B-3, 3B-1
1974			154	.274	.347	496	136	15	3	5	1.0	55	45	28	48	3	0	0	251	499	22	108	5.0	.972	SS-154
1975			157	.264	.341	602	159	29	4	3	0.5	52	58	36	48	2	0	0	279	543	16	105	5.3	.981	SS-157
1976			158	.246	.302	562	138	18	4	2	0.4	44	52	43	45	3	1	0	279	468	18	96	4.8	.976	SS-158
1977	NY	A	158	.247	.352	477	118	18	4	8	1.7	54	49	39	28	1	0	0	250	434	18	90	4.4	.974	SS-157

Year	Team	Games	BA	SA	AB	H	2B	3B	HR	HR%	R	RBI	BB	SO	SB	Pinch Hit AB	Pinch Hit H	PO	A	E	DP	TC/G	FA	G by Pos

Bucky Dent *continued*

Year	Team	Games	BA	SA	AB	H	2B	3B	HR	HR%	R	RBI	BB	SO	SB	PH AB	PH H	PO	A	E	DP	TC/G	FA	G by Pos
1978		123	.243	.317	379	92	11	1	5	1.3	40	40	23	24	3	0	0	178	341	10	56	4.3	.981	SS-123
1979		141	.230	.285	431	99	14	2	2	0.5	47	32	37	30	0	0	0	219	512	17	107	5.3	.977	SS-141
1980		141	.262	.354	489	128	26	2	5	1.0	57	52	48	37	0	0	0	224	489	13	77	5.1	.982	SS-141
1981		73	.238	.379	227	54	11	0	7	3.1	20	27	19	17	0	0	0	104	217	10	49	4.5	.970	SS-73
1982	2 teams	NY A	(59G –	.169)		TEX A	(46G –	.219)																
"	total	105	.193	.242	306	59	10	1	1	0.3	27	23	21	21	0	2	0	129	323	14	57	4.4	.970	SS-103
1983	TEX A	131	.237	.297	417	99	15	2	2	0.5	36	34	23	31	3	0	0	150	369	11	71	4.0	.979	SS-129, DH-1
1984	KC A	11	.333	.333	9	3	0	0	0	0.0	2	1	1	2	0	0	0	4	6	0	0	0.9	1.000	SS-9, 3B-2
12 yrs.		1392	.247	.321	4512	1114	169	23	40	0.9	451	423	328	349	17	4	0	2122	4335	156	839	4.8	.976	SS-1381, 3B-3, 2B-3, DH-1

LEAGUE CHAMPIONSHIP SERIES

Year	Team	Games	BA	SA	AB	H	2B	3B	HR	HR%	R	RBI	BB	SO	SB	PH AB	PH H	PO	A	E	DP	TC/G	FA	G by Pos
1977	NY A	5	.214	.286	14	3	1	0	0	0.0	1	2	1	0	0	0	0	10	14	1	0	5.0	.960	SS-5
1978		4	.200	.200	15	3	0	0	0	0.0	0	4	0	0	0	0	0	2	8	1	0	2.8	.909	SS-4
1980		3	.182	.182	11	2	0	0	0	0.0	0	0	0	1	0	0	0	9	12	0	2	7.0	1.000	SS-3
3 yrs.		12	.200	.225	40	8	1	0	0	0.0	1	6	1	1	0	0	0	21	34	2	2	4.8	.965	SS-12

WORLD SERIES

Year	Team	Games	BA	SA	AB	H	2B	3B	HR	HR%	R	RBI	BB	SO	SB	PH AB	PH H	PO	A	E	DP	TC/G	FA	G by Pos
1977	NY A	6	.263	.263	19	5	0	0	0	0.0	0	2	2	1	0	0	0	2	15	1	2	3.0	.944	SS-6
1978		6	.417	.458	24	10	1	0	0	0.0	3	7	1	2	0	0	0	8	16	2	4	4.3	.923	SS-6
2 yrs.		12	.349	.372	43	15	1	0	0	0.0	3	9	3	3	0	0	0	10	31	3	6	3.7	.932	SS-12

Sam Dente

DENTE, SAMUEL JOSEPH (Blackie)
B. Apr. 26, 1922, Harrison, N. J.　　　　BR TR 5'11" 175 lbs.

Year	Team	Games	BA	SA	AB	H	2B	3B	HR	HR%	R	RBI	BB	SO	SB	PH AB	PH H	PO	A	E	DP	TC/G	FA	G by Pos
1947	BOS A	46	.232	.280	168	39	4	2	0	0.0	14	11	19	15	0	0	0	40	83	8	11	2.8	.939	3B-46
1948	STL A	98	.270	.326	267	72	11	2	0	0.0	26	22	22	8	1	17	5	141	216	16	47	3.8	.957	SS-76, 3B-6
1949	WAS A	153	.273	.332	590	161	24	4	1	0.2	48	53	31	24	4	0	0	314	462	35	106	5.3	.957	SS-153
1950		155	.239	.299	603	144	20	5	2	0.3	56	59	39	19	1	0	0	316	497	34	111	5.5	.960	SS-128, 2B-29
1951		88	.238	.275	273	65	8	1	0	0.0	21	29	25	10	3	14	2	161	210	14	52	4.4	.964	SS-65, 2B-10, 3B-5
1952	CHI A	62	.221	.234	145	32	0	1	0	0.0	12	11	5	8	0	12	1	85	95	6	23	3.0	.968	SS-27, 3B-18, OF-6, 2B-6, 1B-2
1953		2	–	–	0	0	0	0	0		0	0	0	0	0	0	0	0	0	0	0	0.0	–	SS-1
1954	CLE A	68	.266	.337	169	45	7	1	1	0.6	18	19	14	4	0	1	1	76	147	8	36	3.4	.965	SS-60, 2B-7
1955		73	.257	.295	105	27	4	0	0	0.0	10	10	12	8	0	3	1	42	105	3	17	2.1	.980	SS-53, 3B-13, 2B-4
9 yrs.		745	.252	.305	2320	585	78	16	4	0.2	205	214	167	96	9	47	10	1175	1815	124	403	4.2	.960	SS-563, 3B-88, 2B-56, OF-6, 1B-2

WORLD SERIES

Year	Team	Games	BA	SA	AB	H	2B	3B	HR	HR%	R	RBI	BB	SO	SB	PH AB	PH H	PO	A	E	DP	TC/G	FA	G by Pos
1954	CLE A	3	.000	.000	3	0	0	0	0	0.0	1	0	1	0	0	0	0	1	1	0	1	0.7	1.000	SS-3

Mike DePangher

DePANGHER, MICHAEL ANTHONY
B. Sept. 11, 1858, Marysville, Calif.　D. July 7, 1915, San Francisco, Calif.　　5'8" 190 lbs.

Year	Team	Games	BA	SA	AB	H	2B	3B	HR	HR%	R	RBI	BB	SO	SB	PH AB	PH H	PO	A	E	DP	TC/G	FA	G by Pos
1884	PHI N	4	.200	.200	10	2	0	0	0	0.0	0		1	3				16	7	2	0	6.3	.920	C-4

Tony DePhillips

DePHILLIPS, ANTHONY ANDREW
B. Sept. 20, 1912, New York, N. Y.　　　　BR TR 6'2" 185 lbs.

Year	Team	Games	BA	SA	AB	H	2B	3B	HR	HR%	R	RBI	BB	SO	SB	PH AB	PH H	PO	A	E	DP	TC/G	FA	G by Pos
1943	CIN N	35	.100	.150	20	2	1	0	0	0.0	0	2	1	5	0	0	0	47	5	1	0	1.5	.981	C-35

Gene Derby

DERBY, EUGENE A.
B. Feb., 1860, New Hampshire　D. Oct. 12, 1928, Buffalo, N. Y.

Year	Team	Games	BA	SA	AB	H	2B	3B	HR	HR%	R	RBI	BB	SO	SB	PH AB	PH H	PO	A	E	DP	TC/G	FA	G by Pos
1885	BAL AA	10	.129	.129	31	4	0	0	0	0.0	4		1					51	9	4	1	6.4	.938	C-9, OF-1

Bob Dernier

DERNIER, ROBERT EUGENE
B. Jan. 5, 1957, Kansas City, Mo.　　　　BR TR 6' 160 lbs.

Year	Team	Games	BA	SA	AB	H	2B	3B	HR	HR%	R	RBI	BB	SO	SB	PH AB	PH H	PO	A	E	DP	TC/G	FA	G by Pos
1980	PHI N	10	.571	.571	7	4	0	0	0	0.0	5	1	1	0	3	0	0	9	0	0	0	0.9	1.000	OF-3
1981		10	.750	.750	4	3	0	0	0	0.0	0	0	0	0	2	0	0	2	0	0	0	0.2	1.000	OF-5
1982		122	.249	.319	370	92	10	2	4	1.1	56	21	36	69	42	1	0	255	5	5	0	2.2	.981	OF-119
1983		122	.231	.290	221	51	10	0	1	0.5	41	15	18	21	35	3	0	164	3	2	1	1.4	.988	OF-107
1984	CHI N	143	.278	.362	536	149	26	5	3	0.6	94	32	63	60	45	2	0	355	5	5	1	2.6	.986	OF-140
1985		121	.254	.316	469	119	20	3	1	0.2	63	21	40	44	31	4	0	310	4	9	1	2.7	.972	OF-116
1986		108	.225	.312	324	73	14	1	4	1.2	32	18	22	41	27	2	2	222	3	3	2	2.1	.987	OF-105
1987		93	.317	.497	199	63	4	4	8	4.0	38	21	19	19	16	31	7	86	2	1	1	1.0	.989	OF-71
1988	PHI N	68	.289	.337	166	48	3	1	1	0.6	19	10	9	19	13	12	5	98	2	2	0	1.5	.980	OF-54
1989		107	.171	.214	187	32	5	0	1	0.5	26	13	14	28	4	41	4	95	1	3	0	0.9	.970	OF-74
10 yrs.		904	.255	.333	2483	634	92	16	23	0.9	374	152	222	301	218	96	18	1596	25	30	6	1.8	.982	OF-794

LEAGUE CHAMPIONSHIP SERIES

Year	Team	Games	BA	SA	AB	H	2B	3B	HR	HR%	R	RBI	BB	SO	SB	PH AB	PH H	PO	A	E	DP	TC/G	FA	G by Pos
1983	PHI N	1	–	–	0	0	0	0	0	–	0	0	0	0	0	0	0	0	0	0	0	0.0	–	OF-1
1984	CHI N	5	.235	.529	17	4	2	0	1	5.9	5	1	5	4	2	0	0	12	1	0	0	2.6	1.000	OF-5
2 yrs.		6	.235	.529	17	4	2	0	1	5.9	5	1	5	4	2	0	0	12	1	0	0	2.2	1.000	OF-6

WORLD SERIES

Year	Team	Games	BA	SA	AB	H	2B	3B	HR	HR%	R	RBI	BB	SO	SB	PH AB	PH H	PO	A	E	DP	TC/G	FA	G by Pos
1983	PHI N	1	–		0	0	0	0	0	–	1	0	0	0	0	0	0	0	0	0	0	0.0	–	

Claud Derrick

DERRICK, CLAUD LESTER (Deek)
B. June 11, 1886, Burton, Ga.　D. July 15, 1974, Clayton, Ga.　　　BR TR 6' 175 lbs.

Year	Team	Games	BA	SA	AB	H	2B	3B	HR	HR%	R	RBI	BB	SO	SB	PH AB	PH H	PO	A	E	DP	TC/G	FA	G by Pos
1910	PHI A	1	.000	.000	1	0	0	0	0	0.0	0	0	0		0	0	0	1	0	1	0	2.0	.500	SS-1
1911		36	.230	.280	100	23	1	2	0	0.0	14	5	7		7	1	0	69	71	4	7	4.0	.972	2B-20, SS-6, 1B-3, 3B-2
1912		21	.241	.276	58	14	0	1	0	0.0	7	7	5		1	3	0	27	57	11	5	4.5	.884	SS-18
1913	NY A	22	.292	.354	65	19	1	0	1	1.5	7	7	5	8	2	2	0	36	59	14	9	5.0	.872	SS-14, 3B-4, 2B-1
1914	2 teams	CIN N	(2G –	.333)		CHI N	(28G –	.219)																
"	total	30	.225	.284	102	23	4	1	0	0.0	7	14	5	13	3	1	0	69	92	19	10	6.0	.894	SS-30
5 yrs.		110	.242	.294	326	79	6	4	1	0.3	35	33	22	21	13	7	0	202	279	49	31	4.8	.908	SS-69, 2B-21, 3B-6, 1B-3

Year	Team	Games	BA	SA	AB	H	2B	3B	HR	HR%	R	RBI	BB	SO	SB	Pinch Hit AB	Pinch Hit H	PO	A	E	DP	TC/G	FA	G by Pos

Jim Derrick
DERRICK, JAMES MICHAEL
B. Sept. 19, 1943, Columbia, S. C.
BL TR 6' 190 lbs.

| 1970 | BOS A | 24 | .212 | .242 | 33 | 7 | 1 | 0 | 0 | 0.0 | 3 | 5 | 0 | 11 | 0 | 21 | 2 | 11 | 0 | 0 | 0 | 0.5 | 1.000 | OF-2, 1B-1 |

Russ Derry
DERRY, ALVA RUSSELL
B. Oct. 7, 1916, Princeton, Mo.
BL TR 6'1" 180 lbs.

1944	NY A	38	.254	.386	114	29	3	0	4	3.5	14	14	20	19	1	7	5	54	2	3	0	1.6	.949	OF-28
1945		78	.225	.419	253	57	6	2	13	5.1	37	45	31	49	1	9	3	170	4	4	2	2.3	.978	OF-68
1946	PHI A	69	.207	.304	184	38	8	5	0	0.0	17	14	27	54	0	16	3	127	3	2	1	1.9	.985	OF-50
1949	STL N	2	.000	.000	2	0	0	0	0	0.0	0	0	0	2	0	2	0	0	0	0	0	0.0	–	
4 yrs.		187	.224	.373	553	124	17	7	17	3.1	68	73	78	124	2	34	11	351	9	9	4	2.0	.976	OF-146

Joe DeSa
DeSA, JOSEPH
B. July 27, 1959, Honolulu, Hawaii   D. Dec. 20, 1986, San Juan, Puerto Rico
BL TL 5'11" 170 lbs.

1980	STL N	7	.273	.273	11	3	0	0	0	0.0	0	0	0	2	0	5	2	3	0	0	0	0.4	1.000	OF-1, 1B-1
1985	CHI A	28	.182	.364	44	8	2	0	2	4.5	5	7	3	6	0	14	2	70	7	0	4	2.8	1.000	1B-9, DH-4, OF-1
2 yrs.		35	.200	.345	55	11	2	0	2	3.6	5	7	3	8	0	19	4	73	7	0	4	2.3	1.000	1B-10, DH-4, OF-2

Gene Desautels
DESAUTELS, EUGENE ABRAHAM (Red)
B. June 13, 1907, Worcester, Mass.
BR TR 5'11" 170 lbs.

1930	DET A	42	.190	.254	126	24	4	2	0	0.0	13	9	7	9	2	0	0	209	23	1	3	5.5	.996	C-42
1931		3	.091	.091	11	1	0	0	0	0.0	1	0	1	1	0	0	0	7	3	0	0	3.3	1.000	C-3
1932		28	.236	.264	72	17	2	0	0	0.0	8	2	13	11	0	3	0	109	13	2	0	4.4	.984	C-24
1933		30	.143	.167	42	6	1	0	0	0.0	5	4	4	6	0	1	0	75	5	2	0	2.7	.976	C-30
1937	BOS A	96	.243	.295	305	74	10	3	0	0.0	33	27	36	26	1	1	1	491	44	4	4	5.6	.993	C-94
1938		108	.291	.369	333	97	16	2	2	0.6	47	48	57	31	1	0	0	423	52	7	7	4.5	.985	C-108
1939		76	.243	.305	226	55	14	0	0	0.0	26	21	33	13	3	2	1	310	48	2	3	4.7	.994	C-73
1940		71	.225	.266	222	50	7	1	0	0.0	19	17	32	13	0	0	0	325	27	3	8	5.0	.992	C-70
1941	CLE A	66	.201	.254	189	38	5	1	1	0.5	20	17	14	12	1	0	0	300	32	1	5	5.0	.997	C-66
1942		62	.247	.278	162	40	5	0	0	0.0	14	9	12	13	1	1	0	180	15	5	0	3.2	.975	C-61
1943		68	.205	.249	185	38	6	1	0	0.0	14	19	11	16	2	2	0	251	28	5	4	4.2	.982	C-66
1945		10	.111	.111	9	1	0	0	0	0.0	1	1	1	1	0	0	0	8	3	0	1	1.1	1.000	C-10
1946	PHI A	52	.215	.254	130	28	3	1	0	0.0	10	13	12	16	1	0	0	151	31	2	1	3.5	.989	C-52
13 yrs.		712	.233	.285	2012	469	73	11	3	0.1	211	186	233	168	12	9	2	2839	325	34	41	4.5	.989	C-699

Orestes Destrade
DESTRADE, ORESTES
Born Orestes Destrade y Cucuas.
B. May 8, 1962, Santiago, Cuba
BB TR 6'4" 210 lbs.

1987	NY A	9	.263	.263	19	5	0	0	0	0.0	5	1	5	5	0	4	0	20	1	0	2	2.3	1.000	1B-3, DH-2
1988	PIT N	36	.149	.234	47	7	1	0	1	2.1	2	3	5	17	0	24	4	61	2	0	3	1.8	1.000	1B-8
2 yrs.		45	.182	.242	66	12	1	0	1	1.5	7	4	10	22	0	28	4	81	3	0	5	1.9	1.000	1B-11, DH-2

Bob Detherage
DETHERAGE, ROBERT WAYNE
B. Sept. 20, 1954, Springfield, Mo.
BR TR 6' 180 lbs.

| 1980 | KC A | 26 | .308 | .500 | 26 | 8 | 2 | 0 | 1 | 3.8 | 2 | 7 | 1 | 4 | 1 | 10 | 1 | 16 | 0 | 0 | 0 | 0.6 | 1.000 | OF-20 |

George Detore
DETORE, GEORGE FRANCIS
B. Nov. 11, 1906, Utica, N. Y.
BR TR 5'8" 170 lbs.

1930	CLE A	3	.167	.250	12	2	1	0	0	0.0	0	2	0	0	0	0	0	1	2	1	1	1.3	.750	3B-3
1931		30	.268	.375	56	15	6	0	0	0.0	3	7	8	0	2	4	0	28	44	8	9	2.7	.900	3B-13, SS-10, 2B-3
2 yrs.		33	.250	.353	68	17	7	0	0	0.0	3	9	8	2	2	4	0	29	46	9	10	2.5	.893	3B-16, SS-10, 2B-3

Ducky Detweiler
DETWEILER, ROBERT STERLING
B. Feb. 15, 1919, Trumbauersville, Pa.
BR TR 5'11" 178 lbs.

1942	BOS N	12	.318	.409	44	14	2	1	0	0.0	3	5	2	7	0	0	0	10	16	2	2	2.3	.929	3B-12
1946		1	.000	.000	1	0	0	0	0	0.0	0	0	0	0	0	1	0	0	0	0	0	0.0	–	
2 yrs.		13	.311	.400	45	14	2	1	0	0.0	3	5	2	7	0	1	0	10	16	2	2	2.2	.929	3B-12

Mike Devereaux
DEVEREAUX, MICHAEL
B. Apr. 10, 1963, Casper, Wyo.
BR TR 6' 195 lbs.

1987	LA N	19	.222	.278	54	12	3	0	0	0.0	7	4	3	10	3	5	0	21	1	0	0	1.2	1.000	OF-18
1988		30	.116	.140	43	5	1	0	0	0.0	4	2	2	10	0	7	1	29	0	0	0	1.0	1.000	OF-26
1989	BAL A	122	.266	.379	391	104	14	3	8	2.0	55	46	36	60	22	14	0	288	1	5	0	2.4	.983	OF-112, DH-5
3 yrs.		171	.248	.346	488	121	18	3	8	1.6	66	52	41	80	25	26	1	338	2	5	0	2.0	.986	OF-156, DH-5

Mickey Devine
DEVINE, WILLIAM PATRICK
B. May 9, 1892, Albany, N. Y.   D. Oct. 1, 1937, Albany, N. Y.
BR TR 5'10" 165 lbs.

1918	PHI N	4	.125	.250	8	1	1	0	0	0.0	0	0	0	1	0	0	0	8	2	1	1	2.8	.909	C-3
1920	BOS A	8	.167	.167	12	2	0	0	0	0.0	1	0	1	2	1	0	0	19	2	1	0	2.8	.955	C-5
1925	NY N	21	.273	.364	33	9	3	0	0	0.0	6	4	2	3	0	4	1	35	7	3	0	2.1	.933	C-11, 3B-1
3 yrs.		33	.226	.302	53	12	4	0	0	0.0	7	4	3	6	1	8	1	62	11	5	1	2.4	.936	C-19, 3B-1

Bernie DeViveiros
DeVIVEIROS, BERNARD JOHN
B. Apr. 19, 1901, Oakland, Calif.
BR TR 5'7" 160 lbs.

1924	CHI A	1	.000	.000	1	0	0	0	0	0.0	0	0	0	0	0	0	0	1	0	2	0	3.0	.333	SS-1
1927	DET A	24	.227	.273	22	5	1	0	0	0.0	4	2	2	8	1	2	0	7	14	2	4	1.0	.913	SS-14, 3B-1
2 yrs.		25	.217	.261	23	5	1	0	0	0.0	4	2	2	8	1	2	0	8	14	4	4	1.0	.846	SS-15, 3B-1

Art Devlin
DEVLIN, ARTHUR McARTHUR
B. Oct. 16, 1879, Washington, D. C.   D. Sept. 18, 1948, Jersey City, N. J.
BR TR 6' 175 lbs.

Year	Team		Games	BA	SA	AB	H	2B	3B	HR	HR%	R	RBI	BB	SO	SB	Pinch Hit AB	Pinch Hit H	PO	A	E	DP	TC/G	FA	G by Pos

Art Devlin *continued*

Year	Team		Games	BA	SA	AB	H	2B	3B	HR	HR%	R	RBI	BB	SO	SB	AB	H	PO	A	E	DP	TC/G	FA	G by Pos
1904	NY	N	130	.281	.354	474	133	16	8	1	0.2	81	66	62		33	0	0	126	285	42	10	3.5	.907	3B-130
1905			153	.246	.310	525	129	14	7	2	0.4	74	61	66		59	0	0	156	299	33	14	3.2	.932	3B-153
1906			148	.299	.390	498	149	23	8	2	0.4	76	65	74		54	0	0	171	355	31	22	3.8	.944	3B-148
1907			143	.277	.324	491	136	16	2	1	0.2	61	54	63		38	0	0	181	292	31	12	3.5	.938	3B-140, SS-3
1908			157	.253	.313	534	135	18	4	2	0.4	59	45	62		19	0	0	203	331	30	19	3.6	.947	3B-157
1909			143	.265	.336	491	130	19	8	0	0.0	61	55	65		24	0	0	191	317	36	21	3.8	.934	3B-142
1910			147	.260	.327	493	128	17	5	2	0.4	71	67	62	32	28	0	0	179	284	33	20	3.4	.933	3B-147
1911			83	.273	.350	260	71	16	2	0	0.0	42	25	42	19	9	0	0	128	154	16	5	3.6	.946	3B-79, SS-6, 2B-6, 1B-6
1912	BOS	N	124	.289	.367	436	126	18	8	0	0.0	59	54	51	37	11	4	1	768	140	15	52	7.4	.984	1B-69, SS-26, 3B-26, OF-1
1913			73	.229	.310	210	48	7	5	0	0.0	19	12	29	17	8	3	2	83	134	6	4	3.1	.973	3B-69
10 yrs.			1301	.269	.338	4412	1185	164	57	10	0.2	603	504	576	105	283	7	3	2186	2591	273	179	3.9	.946	3B-1191, 1B-75, SS-35, 2B-6, OF-1

WORLD SERIES

Year	Team		Games	BA	SA	AB	H	2B	3B	HR	HR%	R	RBI	BB	SO	SB	AB	H	PO	A	E	DP	TC/G	FA	G by Pos
1905	NY	N	5	.250	.313	16	4	1	0	0	0.0	0	1	1	3	3	0	0	7	17	2	0	5.2	.923	3B-5

Jim Devlin

DEVLIN, JAMES RAYMOND
B. Aug. 25, 1922, Plains, Pa.

BL TR 5'11½" 165 lbs.

Year	Team		Games	BA	SA	AB	H	2B	3B	HR	HR%	R	RBI	BB	SO	SB	AB	H	PO	A	E	DP	TC/G	FA	G by Pos
1944	CLE	A	1	.000	.000	1	0	0	0	0	0.0	0	0	0	0	0	0	0	1	1	0	0	2.0	1.000	C-1

Rex DeVogt

DeVOGT, REX EUGENE
B. Jan. 4, 1888, Clare, Mich. D. Nov. 9, 1935, Alma, Mich.

BR TR 5'9" 170 lbs.

Year	Team		Games	BA	SA	AB	H	2B	3B	HR	HR%	R	RBI	BB	SO	SB	AB	H	PO	A	E	DP	TC/G	FA	G by Pos
1913	BOS	N	3	.000	.000	6	0	0	0	0	0.0	0	0	0	3	0	0	0	12	4	1	0	5.7	.941	C-3

Josh Devore

DEVORE, JOSHUA D.
B. Nov. 13, 1887, Murray City, Ohio D. Oct. 6, 1954, Chillicothe, Ohio

BL TL 5'6" 160 lbs.

Year	Team		Games	BA	SA	AB	H	2B	3B	HR	HR%	R	RBI	BB	SO	SB	AB	H	PO	A	E	DP	TC/G	FA	G by Pos
1908	NY	N	5	.167	.167	6	1	0	0	0	0.0	1	2			1	2	0	1	0	0	0	0.2	1.000	OF-2
1909			22	.143	.179	28	4	1	0	0	0.0	6	1	2	3	5	0	0	13	1	3	0	0.8	.824	OF-12
1910			133	.304	.380	490	149	11	10	2	0.4	92	27	46	67	43	1	0	191	18	16	3	1.7	.929	OF-130
1911			149	.280	.365	565	158	19	10	3	0.5	96	50	81	69	61	0	0	241	29	19	5	1.9	.934	OF-149
1912			106	.275	.373	327	90	14	6	2	0.6	66	37	51	43	27	4	0	155	14	15	3	1.7	.918	OF-96
1913 3 teams	NY	N (16G – .190)				CIN	N	(66G – .267)		PHI	N	(23G – .282)													
" total			105	.264	.357	277	73	7	5	3	1.1	43	20	19	32	23	12	3	125	12	12	3	1.4	.919	OF-79
1914 2 teams	PHI	N (30G – .302)				BOS	N	(51G – .227)																	
" total			81	.249	.298	181	45	6	0	1	0.6	27	12	22	19	2	25	11	14	4	1	3	0.2	.947	OF-51
7 yrs.			601	.277	.359	1874	520	58	31	11	0.6	331	149	222	230	160	49	14	740	78	66	17	1.5	.925	OF-519

WORLD SERIES

Year	Team		Games	BA	SA	AB	H	2B	3B	HR	HR%	R	RBI	BB	SO	SB	AB	H	PO	A	E	DP	TC/G	FA	G by Pos
1911	NY	N	6	.167	.208	24	4	1	0	0	0.0	1	3	1	8	1	0	0	16	0	1	0	2.8	.941	OF-6
1912			7	.250	.250	24	6	0	0	0	0.0	4	0	7	5	4	0	0	10	2	2	1	2.0	.857	OF-7
1914	BOS	N	1	.000	.000	1	0	0	0	0	0.0	0	0	0	1	0	1	0	0	0	0	0	0.0	–	
3 yrs.			14	.204	.224	49	10	1	0	0	0.0	5	3	8	14	4	1	0	26	2	3	1	2.2	.903	OF-13

Al DeVormer

DeVORMER, ALBERT E.
B. Aug. 19, 1891, Grand Rapids, Mich. D. Aug. 29, 1966, Grand Rapids, Mich.

BR TR 6'½" 175 lbs.

Year	Team		Games	BA	SA	AB	H	2B	3B	HR	HR%	R	RBI	BB	SO	SB	AB	H	PO	A	E	DP	TC/G	FA	G by Pos
1918	CHI	A	8	.263	.368	19	5	2	0	0	0.0	1					1	0	12	4	0	0	2.0	1.000	C-6, OF-1
1921	NY	A	22	.347	.429	49	17	4	0	0	0.0	6	7	2	4	2	5	1	48	9	3	1	2.7	.950	C-17
1922			24	.203	.305	59	12	4	1	0	0.0	8	11	1	6	0	4	1	66	11	2	0	3.3	.975	C-17, 1B-1
1923	BOS	A	74	.258	.321	209	54	7	3	0	0.0	20	18	6	21	3	12	3	183	48	5	3	3.2	.979	C-55, 1B-2
1927	NY	N	68	.248	.326	141	35	3	1	2	1.4	14	21	11	11	1	8	4	151	29	7	4	2.8	.963	C-54, 1B-3
5 yrs.			196	.258	.333	477	123	20	5	2	0.4	50	57	20	46	7	30	9	460	101	17	8	2.9	.971	C-149, 1B-6, OF-1

WORLD SERIES

Year	Team		Games	BA	SA	AB	H	2B	3B	HR	HR%	R	RBI	BB	SO	SB	AB	H	PO	A	E	DP	TC/G	FA	G by Pos
1921	NY	A	2	.000	.000	1	0	0	0	0	0.0	0	0	0	0	0	0	0	1	0	0	0	0.5	1.000	C-1

Walt Devoy

DEVOY, WALTER JOSEPH
B. Mar. 14, 1885, St. Louis, Mo. D. Dec. 17, 1953, St. Louis, Mo.

5'11" 165 lbs.

Year	Team		Games	BA	SA	AB	H	2B	3B	HR	HR%	R	RBI	BB	SO	SB	AB	H	PO	A	E	DP	TC/G	FA	G by Pos
1909	STL	A	19	.246	.319	69	17	3	1	0	0.0	7	8	3		4	0	0	46		3	0	2.6	.980	OF-16, 1B-3

Jeff DeWillis

DeWILLIS, JEFFREY ALLEN
B. Apr. 13, 1965, Houston, Tex.

BR TR 6'2" 170 lbs.

Year	Team		Games	BA	SA	AB	H	2B	3B	HR	HR%	R	RBI	BB	SO	SB	AB	H	PO	A	E	DP	TC/G	FA	G by Pos
1987	TOR	A	13	.120	.280	25	3	1	0	1	4.0	2	2	2	12	0	0	0	49	5	2	1	4.3	.964	C-13

Charlie Dexter

DEXTER, CHARLES DANA
B. June 15, 1876, Evansville, Ind. D. June 9, 1934, Cedar Rapids, Iowa

BR TR 5'7" 190 lbs.

Year	Team		Games	BA	SA	AB	H	2B	3B	HR	HR%	R	RBI	BB	SO	SB	AB	H	PO	A	E	DP	TC/G	FA	G by Pos
1896	LOU	N	107	.279	.381	402	112	18	7	3	0.7	65	37	17	34	21	5	1	266	71	37	12	3.5	.901	C-55, OF-47
1897			76	.280	.389	257	72	12	5	2	0.8	43	46	21		12	5	0	132	68	27	8	3.0	.881	OF-32, C-23, 3B-14, SS-2
1898			112	.314	.375	421	132	13	5	1	0.2	76	66	26		44	3	1	207	41	12	5	2.3	.954	OF-95, 2B-8, C-7
1899			80	.258	.298	295	76	7	1	1	0.3	47	33	21		21	3	0	137	35	16	3	2.4	.915	OF-71, SS-6
1900	CHI	N	40	.200	.288	125	25	5	0	2	1.6	7	20	1		2	4	1	98	37	6	4	3.5	.957	C-22, OF-13, 2B-1
1901			116	.267	.315	460	123	9	5	1	0.2	46	66	16		22	2	0	618	125	27	32	6.6	.965	1B-54, 3B-25, OF-21, 2B-13, C-3
1902 2 teams	CHI	N (69G – .226)				BOS	N	(48G – .257)																	
" total			117	.238	.292	449	107	15	0	3	0.7	63	44	35		29	0	0	414	184	46	32	5.5	.929	3B-40, SS-22, 1B-22, 2B-19, OF-17
1903	BOS	N	123	.223	.280	457	102	15	1	3	0.7	82	34	61		32	2	0	231	34	21	10	2.3	.927	OF-106, SS-9, C-6
8 yrs.			771	.261	.328	2866	749	94	24	16	0.6	429	346	198	34	183	24	3	2103	595	192	106	3.7	.934	OF-402, C-116, 3B-79, 1B-76, 2B-41, SS-39

Bo Diaz

DIAZ, BAUDILIO JOSE
Born Baudilio Jose Diaz y Seijas.
B. Mar. 23, 1953, Cua, Venezuela.

BR TR 5'11" 185 lbs.

Year	Team		Games	BA	SA	AB	H	2B	3B	HR	HR%	R	RBI	BB	SO	SB	Pinch Hit AB	Pinch Hit H	PO	A	E	DP	TC/G	FA	G by Pos

Bo Diaz *continued*

Year	Team		Games	BA	SA	AB	H	2B	3B	HR	HR%	R	RBI	BB	SO	SB	AB	H	PO	A	E	DP	TC/G	FA	G by Pos
1977	BOS	A	2	.000	.000	1	0	0	0	0	0.0	0	0	0	1	0	1	0	5	0	0	0	2.5	1.000	C-2
1978	CLE	A	44	.236	.315	127	30	4	0	2	1.6	12	11	4	17	0	0	0	183	18	6	4	4.7	.971	C-44
1979			15	.156	.219	32	5	2	0	0	0.0	0	1	2	6	0	0	0	63	6	3	1	4.8	.958	C-15
1980			76	.227	.343	207	47	11	2	3	1.4	15	32	7	27	1	9	2	317	35	4	4	4.7	.989	C-75
1981			63	.313	.533	182	57	19	0	7	3.8	25	38	13	23	2	12	3	247	27	7	0	4.5	.975	C-51, DH-3
1982	PHI	N	144	.288	.450	525	151	29	1	18	3.4	69	85	36	87	3	2	1	850	80	10	7	6.5	.989	C-144
1983			136	.236	.367	471	111	17	0	15	3.2	49	64	38	57	1	4	2	903	97	14	7	7.5	.986	C-134
1984			27	.213	.307	75	16	4	0	1	1.3	5	9	5	13	0	4	0	114	9	1	1	4.6	.992	C-23
1985	2 teams		77	PHI N	(26G – .211)					CIN N		(51G – .261)													
"	total		77	.245	.371	237	58	13	1	5	2.1	21	31	21	25	0	3	0	428	42	8	10	6.2	.983	C-75
1986	CIN	N	134	.272	.380	474	129	21	0	10	2.1	50	56	40	52	1	0	0	732	83	13	10	6.2	.984	C-134
1987			140	.270	.421	496	134	28	1	15	3.0	49	82	19	73	1	2	0	747	70	7	6	5.9	.992	C-137
1988			92	.219	.343	315	69	9	0	10	3.2	26	35	7	41	0	7	0	468	44	5	9	5.6	.990	C-88
1989			43	.205	.265	132	27	5	0	1	0.8	6	8	6	7	0	5	0	237	14	4	1	5.9	.984	C-43
13 yrs.			993	.255	.387	3274	834	162	5	87	2.7	327	452	198	429	9	49	8	5294	525	82	60	5.9	.986	C-965, DH-3

LEAGUE CHAMPIONSHIP SERIES

| 1983 | PHI | N | 4 | .154 | .231 | 13 | 2 | 1 | 0 | 0 | 0.0 | 0 | 0 | 2 | 1 | 0 | 0 | 0 | 32 | 2 | 0 | 0 | 8.5 | 1.000 | C-4 |

WORLD SERIES

| 1983 | PHI | N | 5 | .333 | .400 | 15 | 5 | 0 | 0 | 0 | 0.0 | 1 | 0 | 1 | 2 | 0 | 0 | 0 | 37 | 1 | 1 | 0 | 7.8 | .974 | C-5 |

Edgar Diaz

DIAZ, EDGAR BR TR 6' 165 lbs.
Born Edgar Diaz y Serrano.
B. Feb. 8, 1964, Santurce, Puerto Rico

| 1986 | MIL | A | 5 | .231 | .231 | 13 | 3 | 0 | 0 | 0 | 0.0 | 0 | 0 | 1 | 3 | 0 | 0 | 0 | 6 | 8 | 2 | 2 | 3.2 | .875 | SS-5 |

Mario Diaz

DIAZ, MARIO RAFAEL BR TR 5'10" 145 lbs.
Born Mario Rafael Diaz y Torres.
B. Jan. 10, 1962, Humacao, Puerto Rico

1987	SEA	A	11	.304	.391	23	7	0	1	0	0.0	4	3	0	4	0	1	0	10	25	1	6	3.3	.972	SS-10
1988			28	.306	.375	72	22	5	0	0	0.0	6	9	3	5	0	3	1	31	47	1	11	2.8	.987	SS-21, 2B-4, 3B-1, 1B-1
1989			52	.135	.176	74	10	0	0	1	1.4	9	7	7	7	0	3	1	35	54	5	10	1.8	.947	SS-37, 2B-14, 3B-3
3 yrs.			91	.231	.290	169	39	5	1	1	0.6	19	19	10	16	0	7	2	76	126	7	27	2.3	.967	SS-68, 2B-18, 3B-4, 1B-1

Mike Diaz

DIAZ, MICHAEL ANTHONY BR TR 6'2" 205 lbs.
B. Apr. 15, 1960, San Francisco, Calif.

1983	CHI	N	6	.286	.429	7	2	1	0	0	0.0	0	2	1	0	0	3	1	5	0	0	0	0.8	1.000	C-3
1986	PIT	N	97	.268	.483	209	56	9	0	12	5.7	22	36	19	43	0	33	11	202	8	3	9	2.2	.986	OF-38, 1B-20, 3B-5, C-1
1987			103	.241	.490	241	58	8	2	16	6.6	28	48	31	42	1	32	7	303	23	6	14	3.2	.982	OF-37, 1B-32, C-8
1988	2 teams		87	PIT N	(47G – .230)					CHI A		(40G – .237)													
"	total		87	.235	.314	226	53	9	0	3	1.3	18	17	21	43	0	18	2	415	29	5	35	5.2	.989	1B-45, OF-19, DH-1, C-1
4 yrs.			293	.247	.429	683	169	27	2	31	4.5	70	102	71	128	1	86	21	925	60	14	58	3.4	.986	1B-97, OF-94, C-13, 3B-5, DH-1

Paul Dicken

DICKEN, PAUL FRANKLIN BR TR 6'5" 195 lbs.
B. Oct. 2, 1943, Deland, Fla.

1964	CLE	A	11	.000	.000	11	0	0	0	0	0.0	0	0	0	5	0	11	0	0	0	0	0	0.0	–	
1966			2	.000	.000	2	0	0	0	0	0.0	0	0	0	1	0	2	0	0	0	0	0	0.0	–	
2 yrs.			13	.000	.000	13	0	0	0	0	0.0	0	0	0	6	0	13	0	0	0	0	0	0.0	–	

Buttercup Dickerson

DICKERSON, LOUIS PESSANO BL TR 5'6" 140 lbs.
B. Oct. 11, 1858, Tyaskin, Md. D. July 23, 1920, Baltimore, Md.

1878	CIN	N	29	.309	.366	123	38	5	1	0	0.0	17	9	0	0		0	0	56	1	8	0	2.2	.877	OF-29
1879			81	.291	.440	350	102	18	14	2	0.6	73	57	3	27		0	0	144	9	38	1	2.4	.801	OF-81
1880	2 teams		61	TRO N	(30G – .193)					WOR N		(31G – .293)													
"	total		61	.246	.349	252	62	10	8	0	0.0	37	30	3	5		0	0	126	12	18	5	2.6	.885	OF-61, SS-1
1881	WOR	N	80	.316	.406	367	116	18	6	1	0.3	48	31	8	8		0	0	153	28	22	6	2.5	.892	OF-80
1883	PIT	AA	85	.248	.296	355	88	15	1	0	0.0	62		17			0	0	118	45	46	3	2.5	.780	OF-78, SS-8, 2B-2
1884	3 teams		67	STL U	(46G – .365)					BAL AA		(13G – .214)			LOU AA		(8G – .143)								
"	total		67	.315	.410	295	93	17	4	1	0.3	64		15			0	0	99	21	17	2	2.0	.876	OF-62, 3B-5
1885	BUF	N	5	.048	.095	21	1	1	0	0	0.0	0	1	0	1		4	0	0				1.6	1.000	OF-5
7 yrs.			408	.284	.377	1763	500	84	34	4	0.2	302	127	47	51		0	0	702	118	149	17	2.4	.846	OF-396, SS-9, 3B-5, 2B-2

Bill Dickey

DICKEY, WILLIAM MALCOLM BL TR 6'1½" 185 lbs.
Brother of George Dickey.
B. June 6, 1907, Bastrop, La.
Manager 1946.
Hall of Fame 1954.

1928	NY	A	10	.200	.400	15	3	1	0	0	0.0	1	2	0	2	0	0	0	6	2	0	0	0.8	1.000	C-10
1929			130	.324	.485	447	145	30	6	10	2.2	60	65	14	16	4	3	1	476	95	12	13	4.5	.979	C-127
1930			109	.339	.486	366	124	25	7	5	1.4	55	65	21	14	7	5	3	418	51	11	5	4.4	.977	C-101
1931			130	.327	.442	477	156	17	10	6	1.3	65	78	39	20	2	4	0	670	78	3	6	5.8	.996	C-125
1932			108	.310	.482	423	131	20	4	15	3.5	66	84	34	13	2	0	0	639	53	9	6	6.5	.987	C-108
1933			130	.318	.490	478	152	24	8	14	2.9	58	97	47	14	3	3	0	721	82	6	15	6.2	.993	C-127
1934			104	.322	.494	395	127	24	4	12	3.0	56	72	38	18	0	0	0	527	49	8	13	5.6	.986	C-104
1935			120	.279	.458	448	125	26	6	14	3.1	54	81	35	11	1	1	0	536	62	3	7	5.0	.995	C-118
1936			112	.362	.617	423	153	26	8	22	5.2	99	107	46	16	0	6	2	499	61	14	10	5.1	.976	C-107
1937			140	.332	.570	530	176	35	2	29	5.5	87	133	73	22	3	3	1	692	80	7	11	5.6	.991	C-137
1938			132	.313	.568	454	142	27	4	27	5.9	84	115	75	22	3	6	1	518	94	8	7	4.7	.987	C-126
1939			128	.302	.513	480	145	23	3	24	5.0	98	105	77	37	5	2	0	571	57	7	8	5.0	.989	C-126

Year	Team	Games	BA	SA	AB	H	2B	3B	HR	HR%	R	RBI	BB	SO	SB	Pinch Hit AB	Pinch Hit H	PO	A	E	DP	TC/G	FA	G by Pos

Bill Dickey *continued*

Year	Team	Games	BA	SA	AB	H	2B	3B	HR	HR%	R	RBI	BB	SO	SB	AB	H	PO	A	E	DP	TC/G	FA	G by Pos
1940		106	.247	.355	372	92	11	1	9	2.4	45	54	48	32	0	4	0	425	55	3	9	4.6	.994	C-102
1941		109	.284	.417	348	99	15	5	7	2.0	35	71	45	17	2	6	1	422	45	3	11	4.3	.994	C-104
1942		82	.295	.373	268	79	13	1	2	0.7	28	37	26	11	2	2	0	322	44	9	7	4.6	.976	C-80
1943		85	.351	.492	242	85	18	2	4	1.7	29	33	41	12	2	10	4	322	37	2	5	4.2	.994	C-71
1946		54	.261	.366	134	35	8	0	2	1.5	10	10	19	12	0	11	3	201	29	3	4	4.3	.987	C-39
17 yrs.		1789	.313	.486	6300	1969	343	72	202	3.2	930	1209	678	289	36	67	18	7965	974	108	137	5.1	.988	C-1712

WORLD SERIES

Year	Team	Games	BA	SA	AB	H	2B	3B	HR	HR%	R	RBI	BB	SO	SB	AB	H	PO	A	E	DP	TC/G	FA	G by Pos
1932	NY A	4	.438	.438	16	7	0	0	0	0.0	2	4	2	1	0	0	0	25	1	0	0	6.5	1.000	C-4
1936		6	.120	.240	25	3	0	0	1	4.0	5	5	3	4	0	0	0	38	4	1	0	7.2	.977	C-6
1937		5	.211	.316	19	4	0	1	0	0.0	3	3	2	2	0	0	0	26	1	0	0	5.4	1.000	C-5
1938		4	.400	.600	15	6	0	0	1	6.7	2	2	1	0	1	0	0	31	5	0	0	9.0	1.000	C-4
1939		4	.267	.667	15	4	0	0	2	13.3	2	5	1	2	0	0	0	27	2	0	1	7.3	1.000	C-4
1941		5	.167	.222	18	3	1	0	0	0.0	3	1	3	1	0	0	0	24	2	0	1	5.2	1.000	C-5
1942		5	.263	.263	19	5	0	0	0	0.0	1	0	1	0	0	0	0	25	1	1	0	5.4	.963	C-5
1943		5	.278	.444	18	5	0	0	1	5.6	1	4	2	2	0	0	0	28	3	0	0	6.2	1.000	C-5
8 yrs.		38	.255	.379	145	37	1	1	5	3.4	19	24	15	12	1	0	0	224	19	2	3	6.4	.992	C-38
											8th													

George Dickey

DICKEY, GEORGE WILLARD (Skeets)
Brother of Bill Dickey.
B. July 10, 1915, Kensett, Ark.   D. June 16, 1976, DeWitt, Ark.

BB TR 6'2" 180 lbs.

Year	Team	Games	BA	SA	AB	H	2B	3B	HR	HR%	R	RBI	BB	SO	SB	AB	H	PO	A	E	DP	TC/G	FA	G by Pos
1935	BOS A	5	.000	.000	11	0	0	0	0	0.0	1	1	1	3	0	0	0	7	0	0	0	1.4	1.000	C-4
1936		10	.043	.087	23	1	1	0	0	0.0	2	3	0	0	0	0	0	25	6	3	1	3.4	.912	C-10
1941	CHI A	32	.200	.327	55	11	1	0	2	3.6	6	8	5	7	0	14	3	56	5	0	1	1.9	1.000	C-17
1942		59	.233	.284	116	27	3	0	1	0.9	6	17	9	11	0	31	9	90	11	9	5	1.9	.918	C-29
1946		37	.192	.205	78	15	1	0	0	0.0	8	1	12	13	0	8	3	97	14	0	3	3.0	1.000	C-30
1947		83	.223	.265	211	47	6	0	1	0.5	15	27	34	25	4	4	2	285	35	5	5	3.9	.985	C-80
6 yrs.		226	.204	.253	494	101	12	0	4	0.8	36	54	63	62	4	58	17	560	71	17	15	2.9	.974	C-170

Johnny Dickshot

DICKSHOT, JOHN OSCAR
Born John Oscar Dicksus.
B. Jan. 24, 1910, Waukegan, Ill.

BR TR 6' 195 lbs.

Year	Team	Games	BA	SA	AB	H	2B	3B	HR	HR%	R	RBI	BB	SO	SB	AB	H	PO	A	E	DP	TC/G	FA	G by Pos
1936	PIT N	9	.222	.222	9	2	0	0	0	0.0	2	1	1	2	0	7	1	0	0	0	0	0.0	–	OF-1
1937		82	.254	.348	264	67	8	4	3	1.1	42	33	26	36	0	15	3	109	5	6	2	1.5	.950	OF-64
1938		29	.229	.229	35	8	0	0	0	0.0	3	4	8	5	3	9	3	16	0	0	0	0.6	1.000	OF-10
1939	NY N	10	.235	.235	34	8	0	0	0	0.0	3	5	5	3	0	0	0	13	1	0	1	1.4	1.000	OF-10
1944	CHI A	62	.253	.364	162	41	8	5	0	0.0	18	15	13	10	2	20	5	72	3	2	1	1.2	.974	OF-40
1945		130	.302	.407	486	147	19	10	4	0.8	74	58	48	41	18	5	1	253	13	8	3	2.1	.971	OF-124
6 yrs.		322	.276	.371	990	273	35	19	7	0.7	142	116	101	97	23	56	13	463	22	16	7	1.6	.968	OF-249

Bob Didier

DIDIER, ROBERT DANIEL
B. Feb. 16, 1949, Hattiesburg, Miss.

BB TR 6' 190 lbs.

Year	Team	Games	BA	SA	AB	H	2B	3B	HR	HR%	R	RBI	BB	SO	SB	AB	H	PO	A	E	DP	TC/G	FA	G by Pos
1969	ATL N	114	.256	.307	352	90	16	1	0	0.0	30	32	34	39	1	0	0	633	52	4	3	6.0	.994	C-114
1970		57	.149	.173	168	25	2	1	0	0.0	9	7	12	11	1	0	0	297	25	4	3	5.7	.988	C-57
1971		51	.219	.258	155	34	4	1	0	0.0	9	5	6	17	0	2	1	230	24	0	2	5.0	1.000	C-50
1972		13	.300	.400	40	12	2	1	0	0.0	5	5	2	4	0	2	0	50	11	0	1	4.7	1.000	C-11
1973	DET A	7	.455	.500	22	10	1	0	0	0.0	3	1	3	0	0	0	0	38	5	0	2	6.1	1.000	C-7
1974	BOS A	5	.071	.071	14	1	0	0	0	0.0	0	1	2	1	0	0	0	28	2	1	0	6.2	.968	C-5
6 yrs.		247	.229	.273	751	172	25	4	0	0.0	56	51	59	72	2	4	1	1276	119	9	11	5.7	.994	C-244

LEAGUE CHAMPIONSHIP SERIES

Year	Team	Games	BA	SA	AB	H	2B	3B	HR	HR%	R	RBI	BB	SO	SB	AB	H	PO	A	E	DP	TC/G	FA	G by Pos
1969	ATL N	3	.000	.000	11	0	0	0	0	0.0	0	0	0	2	0	0	0	24	1	0	1	8.3	1.000	C-3

Ernie Diehl

DIEHL, ERNEST GUY
B. Oct. 2, 1877, Cincinnati, Ohio   D. Nov. 6, 1958, Miami, Fla.

BR TR 6'1" 190 lbs.

Year	Team	Games	BA	SA	AB	H	2B	3B	HR	HR%	R	RBI	BB	SO	SB	AB	H	PO	A	E	DP	TC/G	FA	G by Pos
1903	PIT N	1	.333	.333	3	1	0	0	0	0.0	0	0	0		0	0	0	0	0	0	0	0.0	–	OF-1
1904		12	.162	.162	37	6	0	0	0	0.0	6	4	6		3	1	1	15	20	3	1	3.2	.921	OF-7, SS-4
1906	BOS N	3	.455	.636	11	5	0	1	0	0.0	1	0	0		0	0	0	5	1	0	0	2.0	1.000	OF-2, SS-1
1909		1	.500	.750	4	2	1	0	0	0.0	1	0	0		0	0	0	3	1	0	0	5.0	.800	OF-1
4 yrs.		17	.255	.309	55	14	1	1	0	0.0	8	4	6		3	1	1	23	22	3	1	2.9	.918	OF-11, SS-5

Chuck Diering

DIERING, CHARLES EDWARD ALLEN
B. Feb. 5, 1923, St. Louis, Mo.

BR TR 5'10" 165 lbs.

Year	Team	Games	BA	SA	AB	H	2B	3B	HR	HR%	R	RBI	BB	SO	SB	AB	H	PO	A	E	DP	TC/G	FA	G by Pos
1947	STL N	105	.216	.365	74	16	3	1	2	2.7	22	11	19	22	3	8	1	55	3	0	1	0.6	1.000	OF-75
1948		7	.000	.000	7	0	0	0	0	0.0	2	0	2	2	1	0	0	4	1	0	0	0.7	1.000	OF-5
1949		131	.263	.388	369	97	21	8	3	0.8	60	38	35	49	1	1	0	300	7	4	1	2.4	.987	OF-124
1950		89	.250	.353	204	51	12	0	3	1.5	34	18	35	38	1	0	0	178	8	2	2	2.1	.989	OF-81
1951		64	.259	.341	85	22	5	1	0	0.0	9	8	6	15	0	8	3	67	3	0	0	1.1	1.000	OF-44
1952	NY N	41	.174	.304	23	4	1	1	0	0.0	2	2	4	3	0	0	0	25	1	0	0	0.6	1.000	OF-36
1954	BAL A	128	.258	.311	418	108	14	1	2	0.5	35	29	56	57	3	6	2	330	17	6	6	2.8	.983	OF-119
1955		137	.256	.334	371	95	16	2	3	0.8	38	35	57	45	5	4	1	282	74	9	8	2.7	.975	OF-107, 3B-34, SS-12
1956		50	.186	.258	97	18	4	0	1	1.0	15	4	23	19	2	4	0	74	5	2	0	1.6	.975	OF-40, 3B-2
9 yrs.		752	.249	.338	1648	411	76	14	14	0.8	217	141	237	250	16	31	7	1315	119	23	18	1.9	.984	OF-631, 3B-36, SS-12

Bill Dietrick

DIETRICK, WILLIAM ALEXANDER
B. Apr. 20, 1902, Hanover County, Va.   D. May 6, 1946, Bethesda, Md.

BR TR 5'10" 160 lbs.

Year	Team	Games	BA	SA	AB	H	2B	3B	HR	HR%	R	RBI	BB	SO	SB	AB	H	PO	A	E	DP	TC/G	FA	G by Pos
1927	PHI N	5	.167	.167	6	1	0	0	0	0.0	1	0	0	0	0	0	0	4	2	2	2	1.6	.750	SS-5
1928		52	.200	.260	100	20	6	0	0	0.0	13	7	17	10	1	0	0	50	19	2	2	1.4	.972	OF-21, SS-8
2 yrs.		57	.198	.255	106	21	6	0	0	0.0	14	7	17	10	1	15	5	54	21	4	4	1.4	.949	OF-21, SS-13

Year	Team	Games	BA	SA	AB	H	2B	3B	HR	HR%	R	RBI	BB	SO	SB	Pinch Hit AB	Pinch Hit H	PO	A	E	DP	TC/G	FA	G by Pos

Dick Dietz

DIETZ, RICHARD ALLEN
B. Sept. 18, 1941, Crawfordsville, Ind. BR TR 6'1" 195 lbs.

1966 SF N	13	.043	.043	23	1	0	0	0	0.0	1	0	0	9	0	7	0	22	3	0	0	1.9	1.000	C-6
1967	56	.225	.350	120	27	3	0	4	3.3	10	19	25	44	0	15	4	206	19	4	1	4.1	.983	C-43
1968	98	.272	.392	301	82	14	2	6	2.0	21	38	34	68	1	12	6	497	37	13	10	5.6	.976	C-90
1969	79	.230	.406	244	56	8	1	11	4.5	28	35	53	53	0	2	2	432	31	13	5	6.0	.973	C-73
1970	148	.300	.515	493	148	36	2	22	4.5	82	107	109	106	0	9	1	820	58	14	9	6.0	.984	C-139
1971	142	.252	.419	453	114	19	0	19	4.2	58	72	97	86	1	9	4	712	37	14	4	5.4	.982	C-135
1972 LA N	27	.161	.232	56	9	1	0	1	1.8	4	6	14	11	2	7	0	104	12	0	1	4.3	1.000	C-22
1973 ATL	83	.295	.432	139	41	8	1	3	2.2	22	24	49	25	0	18	6	325	29	6	19	4.3	.983	1B-36, C-20
8 yrs.	646	.261	.425	1829	478	89	6	66	3.6	226	301	381	402	4	79	23	3118	226	64	49	5.3	.981	C-528, 1B-36

LEAGUE CHAMPIONSHIP SERIES

| 1971 SF N | 4 | .067 | .067 | 15 | 1 | 0 | 0 | 0 | 0.0 | 0 | 0 | 2 | 5 | 0 | 0 | 0 | 34 | 2 | 0 | 1 | 9.0 | 1.000 | C-4 |

Roy Dietzel

DIETZEL, LEROY LOUIS
B. Jan. 9, 1931, Baltimore, Md. BR TR 6' 190 lbs.

| 1954 WAS A | 9 | .238 | .238 | 21 | 5 | 0 | 0 | 0 | 0.0 | 1 | 1 | 5 | 4 | 0 | 0 | 0 | 10 | 16 | 1 | 4 | 3.0 | .963 | 2B-7, 3B-2 |

Jay Difani

DIFANI, CLARENCE JOSEPH
B. Dec. 21, 1923, Crystal City, Mo. BR TR 6' 170 lbs.

1948 WAS A	2	.000	.000	2	0	0	0	0	0.0	0	0	0	2	0	2	0	0	0	0	0	0.0	–	
1949	2	1.000	2.000	1	1	0	0	0	0.0	0	0	0	0	0	1	1	0	1	0	0	0.5	1.000	2B-1
2 yrs.	4	.333	.667	3	1	0	0	0	0.0	0	0	0	2	0	3	1	0	1	0	0	0.3	1.000	2B-1

Steve Dignan

DIGNAN, STEPHEN E.
B. May 16, 1859, Boston, Mass. D. July 11, 1881, Boston, Mass.

| 1880 2 teams | BOS N (8G – .324) | | | WOR N (3G – .300) | | | | | | | | | | | | | | | | | | | |
| " total | 11 | .318 | .386 | 44 | 14 | 1 | 1 | 0 | 0.0 | 5 | 6 | 0 | 4 | 0 | 0 | 0 | 13 | 3 | 7 | 2 | 2.1 | .696 | OF-11 |

Don Dillard

DILLARD, DAVID DONALD
B. Jan. 8, 1937, Greenville, S. C. BL TR 6'1" 200 lbs.

1959 CLE A	10	.400	.400	10	4	0	0	0	0.0	0	1	0	2	0	10	4	0	0	0	0	0.0	–	
1960	6	.143	.143	7	1	0	0	0	0.0	0	0	1	3	0	5	1	0	0	0	0	0.0	–	OF-1
1961	74	.272	.449	147	40	5	0	7	4.8	27	17	15	28	0	35	15	68	0	0	0	0.9	1.000	OF-39
1962	95	.230	.356	174	40	5	1	5	2.9	22	14	11	25	0	45	11	54	1	2	0	0.6	.965	OF-50
1963 MIL N	67	.235	.378	119	28	6	4	1	0.8	9	12	5	21	0	35	6	34	5	2	0	0.6	.951	OF-30
1965	20	.158	.316	19	3	0	0	1	5.3	1	3	0	6	0	19	3	0	0	0	0	0.0	–	OF-1
6 yrs.	272	.244	.387	476	116	16	5	14	2.9	59	47	32	85	0	149	40	156	6	4	0	0.6	.976	OF-121

Pat Dillard

DILLARD, ROBERT LEE
B. June 12, 1874, Chattanooga, Tenn. D. July 22, 1907, Denver, Colo.

| 1900 STL N | 57 | .230 | .279 | 183 | 42 | 5 | 2 | 0 | 0.0 | 24 | 12 | 13 | | 7 | 8 | 1 | 76 | 51 | 16 | 2 | 2.5 | .888 | OF-26, 3B-21, SS-3 |

Steve Dillard

DILLARD, STEPHEN BRADLEY
B. Feb. 8, 1951, Memphis, Tenn. BR TR 6'1" 171 lbs.

1975 BOS A	1	.400	.400	5	2	0	0	0	0.0	2	0	0	1	0	0	0	5	4	0	1	9.0	1.000	2B-1
1976	57	.275	.377	167	46	14	0	1	0.6	22	15	17	20	6	3	1	58	102	11	21	3.0	.936	3B-18, 2B-17, SS-12, DH-7
1977	66	.241	.312	141	34	7	0	1	0.7	22	13	7	13	4	7	1	90	122	6	23	3.3	.972	2B-45, SS-9, DH-6
1978 DET A	56	.223	.292	130	29	5	2	0	0.0	21	7	6	11	1	1	0	88	118	9	31	3.8	.958	2B-41, DH-4
1979 CHI N	89	.283	.422	166	47	6	1	5	3.0	31	24	17	24	1	17	6	114	138	4	32	2.8	.984	2B-60, 3B-9
1980	100	.225	.316	244	55	8	1	4	1.6	31	27	20	54	2	13	3	92	171	14	19	2.8	.949	3B-51, 2B-38, SS-2
1981	53	.218	.345	119	26	7	1	2	1.7	18	11	8	20	0	11	3	59	96	6	22	3.0	.963	2B-32, 3B-7, SS-2
1982 CHI A	16	.171	.293	41	7	3	1	0	0.0	1	5	1	5	0	0	0	29	42	3	5	4.6	.959	2B-16
8 yrs.	438	.243	.343	1013	246	50	6	13	1.3	148	102	76	147	15	52	14	535	793	53	154	3.2	.962	2B-250, 3B-85, SS-25, DH-17

Pickles Dillhoefer

DILLHOEFER, WILLIAM MARTIN
B. Oct. 13, 1894, Cleveland, Ohio D. Feb. 23, 1922, St. Louis, Mo. BR TR 5'7" 154 lbs.

1917 CHI N	42	.126	.158	95	12	1	1	0	0.0	3	8	2	9	1	4	0	146	49	3	2	4.7	.985	C-37
1918 PHI N	8	.091	.091	11	1	0	0	0	0.0	0	1	1	2	0	1	0	9	3	1	0	1.6	.923	C-6
1919 STL N	45	.213	.278	108	23	3	2	0	0.0	11	12	8	6	5	1	1	122	35	5	6	3.6	.969	C-39
1920	76	.263	.326	224	59	8	3	0	0.0	26	13	13	7	2	2	0	291	72	18	6	5.0	.953	C-73
1921	76	.241	.315	162	39	4	4	0	0.0	19	15	11	7	4	4	0	170	52	11	0	3.1	.953	C-69
5 yrs.	247	.223	.283	600	134	16	10	0	0.0	59	48	35	30	12	13	1	738	211	38	14	4.0	.961	C-224

Bob Dillinger

DILLINGER, ROBERT BERNARD
B. Sept. 17, 1918, Glendale, Calif. BR TR 5'11½" 170 lbs.

1946 STL A	83	.280	.333	225	63	6	3	0	0.0	33	11	19	32	8	18	8	57	103	13	11	2.1	.925	3B-54, SS-1
1947	137	.294	.371	571	168	23	6	3	0.5	70	37	56	38	34	0	0	169	265	19	21	3.3	.958	3B-137
1948	153	.321	.415	644	207	34	10	2	0.3	110	44	65	34	28	1	0	187	242	20	30	2.9	.955	3B-153
1949	137	.324	.417	544	176	22	13	1	0.2	68	51	51	40	20	4	1	166	209	25	22	2.9	.938	3B-133
1950 2 teams	PHI A (84G – .309)			PIT N (58G – .288)																			
" total	142	.301	.410	578	174	29	11	4	0.7	78	50	44	42	9	5	0	152	289	20	31	3.2	.957	3B-135
1951 2 teams	PIT N (12G – .233)			CHI A (89G – .301)																			
" total	101	.292	.342	342	100	9	4	0	0.0	42	20	16	19	5	15	4	81	131	15	10	2.2	.934	3B-80
6 yrs.	753	.306	.391	2904	888	123	47	10	0.3	401	213	251	205	104	43	13	812	1239	112	125	2.9	.948	3B-692, SS-1

Pop Dillon

DILLON, FRANK EDWARD
B. Oct. 17, 1873, Normal, Ill. D. Sept. 12, 1931, Pasadena, Calif. BL TR

| 1899 PIT N | 30 | .256 | .298 | 121 | 31 | 5 | 0 | 0 | 0.0 | 21 | 20 | 5 | | 5 | 0 | 0 | 301 | 17 | 4 | 16 | 10.7 | .988 | 1B-30 |
| 1900 | 5 | .111 | .167 | 18 | 2 | 1 | 0 | 0 | 0.0 | 3 | 1 | 0 | | 0 | 0 | 0 | 47 | 5 | 1 | 2 | 10.6 | .981 | 1B-5 |

Year Team	Games	BA	SA	AB	H	2B	3B	HR	HR%	R	RBI	BB	SO	SB	Pinch Hit AB	Pinch Hit H	PO	A	E	DP	TC/G	FA	G by Pos

Pop Dillon *continued*

Year Team	Games	BA	SA	AB	H	2B	3B	HR	HR%	R	RBI	BB	SO	SB	PH AB	PH H	PO	A	E	DP	TC/G	FA	G by Pos
1901 DET A	74	.288	.391	281	81	14	6	1	0.4	40	42	15		14	0	0	777	44	18	57	11.3	.979	1B-74
1902 2 teams	DET A (66G – .206)			BAL A	(2G – .286)																		
" total	68	.208	.264	250	52	6	4	0	0.0	22	22	18		2	0	0	731	54	20	45	11.8	.975	1B-68
1904 BKN N	135	.258	.317	511	132	18	6	0	0.0	60	31	40		13	0	0	1304	99	25	56	10.6	.982	1B-134
5 yrs.	312	.252	.319	1181	298	44	16	1	0.1	146	116	78		34	0	0	3160	219	68	176	11.0	.980	1B-311

Miguel Dilone

DILONE, MIGUEL ANGEL
Born Miguel Angel Dilone y Reyes.
B. Nov. 1, 1954, Santiago, Dominican Republic

BB TR 6' 160 lbs.

Year Team	Games	BA	SA	AB	H	2B	3B	HR	HR%	R	RBI	BB	SO	SB	PH AB	PH H	PO	A	E	DP	TC/G	FA	G by Pos
1974 PIT N	12	.000	.000	2	0	0	0	0	0.0	3	0	0	1	2	2	0	1	0	0	0	0.1	1.000	OF-2
1975	18	.000	.000	6	0	0	0	0	0.0	8	0	0	1	2	1	0	3	0	0	0	0.2	1.000	OF-2
1976	16	.235	.235	17	4	0	0	0	0.0	7	0	0	5	5	4	0	11	0	0	0	0.7	1.000	OF-3
1977	29	.136	.136	44	6	0	0	0	0.0	5	0	2	3	12	10	1	21	1	0	0	0.8	1.000	OF-17
1978 OAK A	135	.229	.271	258	59	8	0	1	0.4	34	14	23	30	50	1	0	196	4	5	1	1.5	.976	OF-99, 3B-3, DH-1
1979 2 teams	OAK A (30G – .187)			CHI N	(43G – .306)																		
" total	73	.220	.283	127	28	1	2	1	0.8	29	7	8	12	21	2	1	74	0	2	0	1.0	.974	OF-47
1980 CLE A	132	.341	.432	528	180	30	9	0	0.0	82	40	28	45	61	3	0	249	7	7	2	2.0	.973	OF-118, DH-11
1981	72	.290	.346	269	78	5	5	0	0.0	33	19	18	28	29	4	2	126	7	4	1	1.9	.971	OF-56, DH-11
1982	104	.235	.306	379	89	12	3	3	0.8	50	25	25	36	33	12	1	187	3	7	1	1.9	.964	OF-97, DH-1
1983 3 teams	CLE A (32G – .191)			CHI N (4G – .000)				PIT N	(7G – .000)														
" total	43	.183	.254	71	13	3	1	0	0.0	17	7	10	5	8	4	0	47	0	0	0	1.1	1.000	OF-21, DH-2
1984 MON N	88	.278	.367	169	47	8	2	1	0.6	28	10	17	18	27	37	9	76	1	1	0	0.9	.987	OF-41
1985 2 teams	MON N (51G – .190)			SD N	(27G – .217)																		
" total	78	.200	.246	130	26	0	3	0	0.0	18	7	10	19	17	29	4	57	2	3	0	0.8	.952	OF-36
12 yrs.	800	.265	.333	2000	530	67	25	6	0.3	314	129	142	197	267	109	18	1048	25	29	5	1.4	.974	OF-539, DH-26, 3B-3

Dom DiMaggio

DiMAGGIO, DOMINIC PAUL (The Little Professor)
Brother of Vince DiMaggio. Brother of Joe DiMaggio.
B. Feb. 12, 1917, San Francisco, Calif.

BR TR 5'9" 168 lbs.

Year Team	Games	BA	SA	AB	H	2B	3B	HR	HR%	R	RBI	BB	SO	SB	PH AB	PH H	PO	A	E	DP	TC/G	FA	G by Pos
1940 BOS A	108	.301	.464	418	126	32	6	8	1.9	81	46	41	46	7	10	4	239	16	6	5	2.4	.977	OF-94
1941	144	.283	.408	584	165	37	6	8	1.4	117	58	90	57	13	0	0	386	16	15	2	2.9	.964	OF-144
1942	151	.286	.437	622	178	36	8	14	2.3	110	48	70	52	16	0	0	439	19	6	7	3.1	.987	OF-151
1946	142	.316	.427	534	169	24	7	7	1.3	85	73	66	58	10	0	0	390	9	6	2	2.9	.985	OF-142
1947	136	.283	.390	513	145	21	5	8	1.6	75	71	74	62	10	1	0	413	19	10	4	3.3	.977	OF-134
1948	155	.285	.401	648	185	40	4	9	1.4	127	87	101	58	10	0	0	503	13	10	4	3.4	.981	OF-155
1949	145	.307	.420	605	186	34	5	8	1.3	126	60	96	55	9	0	0	420	13	10	1	3.1	.977	OF-144
1950	141	.328	.452	588	193	30	11	7	1.2	131	70	82	68	15	1	1	390	15	7	2	2.9	.983	OF-140
1951	146	.296	.418	639	189	34	4	12	1.9	113	72	73	53	4	0	0	376	15	11	1	2.8	.973	OF-146
1952	128	.294	.377	486	143	20	1	6	1.2	81	33	57	61	6	5	2	303	12	8	4	2.5	.975	OF-123
1953	3	.333	.333	3	1	0	0	0	0.0	0	0	0	1	0	3	1	0	0	0	0	0.0	–	
11 yrs.	1399	.298	.419	5640	1680	308	57	87	1.5	1046	618	750	571	100	21	8	3859	147	89	32	2.9	.978	OF-1373

WORLD SERIES

Year Team	Games	BA	SA	AB	H	2B	3B	HR	HR%	R	RBI	BB	SO	SB	PH AB	PH H	PO	A	E	DP	TC/G	FA	G by Pos
1946 BOS A	7	.259	.370	27	7	3	0	0	0.0	2	3	2	2	0	0	0	19	3	0	1	3.1	1.000	OF-7

Joe DiMaggio

DiMAGGIO, JOSEPH PAUL (Joltin' Joe, The Yankee Clipper)
Brother of Vince DiMaggio. Brother of Dom DiMaggio.
B. Nov. 25, 1914, Martinez, Calif.
Hall of Fame 1955.

BR TR 6'2" 193 lbs.

Year Team	Games	BA	SA	AB	H	2B	3B	HR	HR%	R	RBI	BB	SO	SB	PH AB	PH H	PO	A	E	DP	TC/G	FA	G by Pos
1936 NY A	138	.323	.576	637	206	44	15	29	4.6	132	125	24	39	4	0	0	339	22	8	2	2.7	.978	OF-138
1937	151	.346	.673	621	215	35	15	46	7.4	151	167	64	37	3	1	1	413	21	17	4	3.0	.962	OF-150
1938	145	.324	.581	599	194	32	13	32	5.3	129	140	59	21	6	0	0	366	20	15	4	2.8	.963	OF-145
1939	120	.381	.671	462	176	32	6	30	6.5	108	126	52	20	3	1	1	328	13	5	4	2.9	.986	OF-117
1940	132	.352	.626	508	179	28	9	31	6.1	93	133	61	30	1	2	1	359	5	8	2	2.8	.978	OF-130
1941	139	.357	.643	541	193	43	11	30	5.5	122	125	76	13	4	0	0	385	16	9	5	2.9	.978	OF-139
1942	154	.305	.498	610	186	29	13	21	3.4	123	114	68	36	4	0	0	409	10	8	3	2.8	.981	OF-154
1946	132	.290	.511	503	146	20	8	25	5.0	81	95	59	24	1	1	0	314	15	6	3	2.5	.982	OF-131
1947	141	.315	.522	534	168	31	10	20	3.7	97	97	64	32	3	2	0	316	2	1	0	2.3	.997	OF-139
1948	153	.320	.598	594	190	26	11	39	6.6	110	155	67	30	1	1	1	441	8	13	1	3.0	.972	OF-152
1949	76	.346	.596	272	94	14	6	14	5.1	58	67	55	18	0	0	0	195	1	3	0	2.6	.985	OF-76
1950	139	.301	.585	525	158	33	10	32	6.1	114	122	80	33	0	1	0	376	9	9	1	2.8	.977	OF-137, 1B-1
1951	116	.263	.422	415	109	22	4	12	2.9	72	71	61	36	0	3	2	288	11	3	0	2.6	.990	OF-113
13 yrs.	1736	.325	.579 6th	6821	2214	389	131	361	5.3	1390	1537	790	369	30	12	6	4529	153	105	30	2.8	.978	OF-1721, 1B-1

WORLD SERIES

Year Team	Games	BA	SA	AB	H	2B	3B	HR	HR%	R	RBI	BB	SO	SB	PH AB	PH H	PO	A	E	DP	TC/G	FA	G by Pos
1936 NY A	6	.346	.462	26	9	3	0	0	0.0	3	3	1	3	0	0	0	18	0	1	0	3.2	.947	OF-6
1937	5	.273	.409	22	6	0	0	1	4.5	2	4	0	3	0	0	0	18	0	0	0	3.6	1.000	OF-5
1938	4	.267	.467	15	4	0	0	1	6.7	1	1	0	1	0	0	0	10	0	0	0	2.5	1.000	OF-4
1939	4	.313	.500	16	5	0	0	1	6.3	3	3	1	1	0	0	0	11	0	0	0	2.8	1.000	OF-4
1941	5	.263	.263	19	5	0	0	0	0.0	1	1	2	2	0	0	0	19	0	0	0	3.8	1.000	OF-5
1942	5	.333	.333	21	7	0	0	0	0.0	3	3	0	1	0	0	0	20	0	0	0	4.0	1.000	OF-5
1947	7	.231	.462	26	6	0	0	2	7.7	4	5	6	2	0	0	0	22	0	0	0	3.1	1.000	OF-7
1949	5	.111	.278	18	2	0	0	1	5.6	2	2	3	5	0	0	0	7	0	0	0	1.4	1.000	OF-5
1950	4	.308	.615	13	4	1	0	1	7.7	2	2	3	1	0	0	0	8	0	0	0	2.0	1.000	OF-4
1951	6	.261	.478	23	6	2	0	1	4.3	3	5	2	5	0	0	0	17	0	1	0	2.8	1.000	OF-6
10 yrs.	51 7th	.271	.422	199 3rd	54 4th	6	0	8 7th	4.0	27 5th	30 5th	19 10th	23 10th	0	0	0	150	0	1	0	3.0	.993	OF-51

Vince DiMaggio

DiMAGGIO, VINCENT PAUL
Brother of Dom DiMaggio. Brother of Joe DiMaggio.
B. Sept. 6, 1912, Martinez, Calif. D. Oct. 3, 1986, North Hollywood, Calif.

BR TR 5'11" 183 lbs.

Year	Team		Games	BA	SA	AB	H	2B	3B	HR	HR%	R	RBI	BB	SO	SB	Pinch Hit AB	H	PO	A	E	DP	TC/G	FA	G by Pos

Vince DiMaggio *continued*

Year	Team		Games	BA	SA	AB	H	2B	3B	HR	HR%	R	RBI	BB	SO	SB	AB	H	PO	A	E	DP	TC/G	FA	G by Pos
1937	BOS	N	132	.256	.387	493	126	18	4	13	2.6	56	69	39	111	8	2	0	351	21	7	2	2.9	.982	OF-130
1938			150	.228	.369	540	123	28	3	14	2.6	71	61	65	134	11	0	0	419	19	12	10	3.0	.973	OF-149, 2B-1
1939	CIN	N	8	.071	.143	14	1	1	0	0	0.0	0	2	2	10	0	1	0	11	1	0	1	1.5	1.000	OF-7
1940	2 teams		CIN N (2G – .250)				PIT N (110G – .289)																		
"	total		112	.289	.519	360	104	26	0	19	5.3	61	54	38	83	11	0	0	222	13	5	3	2.1	.979	OF-109
1941	PIT	N	151	.267	.456	528	141	27	5	21	4.0	73	100	68	100	10	0	0	391	11	10	3	2.7	.976	OF-151
1942			143	.238	.385	496	118	22	3	15	3.0	57	75	52	87	10	4	1	383	20	9	5	2.9	.978	OF-138
1943			157	.248	.403	580	144	41	2	15	2.6	64	88	70	126	11	0	0	458	20	8	3	3.1	.984	OF-156, SS-1
1944			109	.240	.401	342	82	20	4	9	2.6	41	50	33	83	6	9	2	235	10	4	4	2.3	.984	OF-101, 3B-1
1945	PHI	N	127	.257	.451	452	116	25	3	19	4.2	64	84	43	91	12	5	1	337	16	2	4	2.8	.994	OF-121
1946	2 teams		PHI N (6G – .211)				NY N (15G – .000)																		
"	total		21	.091	.114	44	4	1	0	0	0.0	3	1	2	12	0	1	0	39	0	1	0	1.9	.975	OF-19
	10 yrs.		1110	.249	.413	3849	959	209	24	125	3.2	491	584	412	837	79	22	4	2846	131	58	35	2.7	.981	OF-1081, SS-1, 3B-1, 2B-1

Mike Dimmel

DIMMEL, MICHAEL WAYNE
B. Oct. 16, 1954, Albert Lea, Minn.   BR TR 6'   180 lbs.

Year	Team		Games	BA	SA	AB	H	2B	3B	HR	HR%	R	RBI	BB	SO	SB	AB	H	PO	A	E	DP	TC/G	FA	G by Pos
1977	BAL	A	25	.000	.000	5	0	0	0	0	0.0	8	0	0	1	1	0	0	14	1	0	0	0.6	1.000	OF-23
1978			8	–		0	0	0	0	0	0.0	2	0	0	0	0	0	0	2	0	1	0	0.4	.667	OF-7
1979	STL	N	6	.333	.333	3	1	0	0	0	0.0	1	0	0	0	0	0	0	3	0	0	0	0.5	1.000	OF-5
	3 yrs.		39	.125	.125	8	1	0	0	0	0.0	11	0	0	1	1	0	0	19	1	1	0	0.5	.952	OF-35

Kerry Dineen

DINEEN, KERRY MICHAEL
B. July 1, 1952, Englewood, N. J.   BL TL 5'11"   165 lbs.

Year	Team		Games	BA	SA	AB	H	2B	3B	HR	HR%	R	RBI	BB	SO	SB	AB	H	PO	A	E	DP	TC/G	FA	G by Pos
1975	NY	A	7	.364	.409	22	8	1	0	0	0.0	3	1	2	1	0	0	0	19	0	0	0	2.7	1.000	OF-7
1976			4	.286	.286	7	2	0	0	0	0.0	0	1	1	2	1	0	0	9	0	1	0	2.5	.900	OF-4
1978	PHI	N	5	.250	.375	8	2	1	0	0	0.0	0	0	1	0	0	3	0	1	0	0	0	0.2	1.000	OF-1
	3 yrs.		16	.324	.378	37	12	2	0	0	0.0	3	2	4	3	1	3	0	29	0	1	0	1.9	.967	OF-12

Vance Dinges

DINGES, VANCE GEORGE (George)
B. May 29, 1915, Elizabeth, N. J.   BL TL 6'2"   175 lbs.

Year	Team		Games	BA	SA	AB	H	2B	3B	HR	HR%	R	RBI	BB	SO	SB	AB	H	PO	A	E	DP	TC/G	FA	G by Pos
1945	PHI	N	109	.287	.353	397	114	15	4	1	0.3	46	36	35	17	5	2	1	527	34	8	41	5.2	.986	OF-65, 1B-42
1946			50	.308	.404	104	32	5	1	1	1.0	7	10	9	12	2	22	3	184	17	3	16	4.1	.985	1B-26, OF-1
	2 yrs.		159	.291	.363	501	146	20	5	2	0.4	53	46	44	29	7	24	4	711	51	11	57	4.9	.986	1B-68, OF-66

Bob DiPietro

DiPIETRO, ROBERT LOUIS PAUL
B. Sept. 1, 1927, San Francisco, Calif.   BR TR 5'11"   185 lbs.

Year	Team		Games	BA	SA	AB	H	2B	3B	HR	HR%	R	RBI	BB	SO	SB	AB	H	PO	A	E	DP	TC/G	FA	G by Pos
1951	BOS	A	4	.091	.091	11	1	0	0	0	0.0	0	0	1	1	0	0	0	4	1	1	1	1.5	.833	OF-3

Gary Disarcina

DISARCINA, GARY THOMAS
B. Nov. 19, 1967, Malden, Mass.   BR TR 6'1"   170 lbs.

Year	Team		Games	BA	SA	AB	H	2B	3B	HR	HR%	R	RBI	BB	SO	SB	AB	H	PO	A	E	DP	TC/G	FA	G by Pos
1989	CAL	A	2	–		0	0	0	0	0	–	0	0	0	0	0	0	0	0	0	0	0	0.0	–	SS-1

Benny Distefano

DISTEFANO, BENITO JAMES
B. Jan. 23, 1962, Brooklyn, N. Y.   BL TL 6'1"   195 lbs.

Year	Team		Games	BA	SA	AB	H	2B	3B	HR	HR%	R	RBI	BB	SO	SB	AB	H	PO	A	E	DP	TC/G	FA	G by Pos
1984	PIT	N	45	.167	.346	78	13	1	2	3	3.8	10	9	5	13	0	14	2	88	9	3	6	2.2	.970	OF-20, 1B-17
1986			31	.179	.282	39	7	1	0	1	2.6	3	5	1	5	0	20	3	13	0	0	0	0.4	1.000	OF-9, 1B-1
1988			16	.345	.621	29	10	3	1	1	3.4	6	6	3	4	0	8	3	41	3	0	1	2.8	1.000	1B-5, OF-2
1989			96	.247	.338	154	38	8	0	2	1.3	12	15	17	30	1	48	13	305	16	6	21	3.4	.982	1B-48, C-3, OF-1
	4 yrs.		188	.227	.360	300	68	13	3	7	2.3	31	35	26	52	1	90	21	447	28	9	28	2.6	.981	1B-71, OF-32, C-3

Dutch Distel

DISTEL, GEORGE ADAM
B. Apr. 15, 1896, Madison, Ind.   D. Feb. 12, 1967, Madison, Ind.   BR TR 5'9"   165 lbs.

Year	Team		Games	BA	SA	AB	H	2B	3B	HR	HR%	R	RBI	BB	SO	SB	AB	H	PO	A	E	DP	TC/G	FA	G by Pos
1918	STL	N	8	.176	.353	17	3	1	1	0	0.0	3	1	2	3	1	0	0	6	14	4	1	3.0	.833	2B-5, SS-2, OF-1

Jack Dittmer

DITTMER, JOHN DOUGLAS
B. Jan. 10, 1928, Elkader, Iowa   BL TR 6'1"   175 lbs.

Year	Team		Games	BA	SA	AB	H	2B	3B	HR	HR%	R	RBI	BB	SO	SB	AB	H	PO	A	E	DP	TC/G	FA	G by Pos
1952	BOS	N	93	.193	.291	326	63	7	2	7	2.1	26	41	26	26	1	3	0	228	267	9	60	5.4	.982	2B-90
1953	MIL	N	138	.266	.367	504	134	22	1	9	1.8	54	63	18	35	1	0	0	290	343	23	95	4.8	.965	2B-138
1954			66	.245	.380	192	47	8	0	6	3.1	22	20	19	17	0	11	2	119	141	6	31	4.0	.977	2B-55
1955			38	.125	.208	72	9	1	1	1	1.4	4	4	4	15	0	11	1	44	42	2	9	2.3	.977	2B-28
1956			44	.245	.314	102	25	4	0	1	1.0	8	6	8	8	0	4	2	64	78	3	15	3.3	.979	2B-42
1957	DET	A	16	.227	.273	22	5	1	0	0	0.0	3	2	2	1	0	12	4	4	4	0	0	0.5	1.000	3B-3, 2B-1
	6 yrs.		395	.232	.333	1218	283	43	4	24	2.0	117	136	77	102	2	41	9	749	875	43	210	4.2	.974	2B-354, 3B-3

Moxie Divis

DIVIS, EDWARD G.
B. 1894, Cleveland, Ohio   D. Dec. 19, 1955, Lakewood, Ohio

Year	Team		Games	BA	SA	AB	H	2B	3B	HR	HR%	R	RBI	BB	SO	SB	AB	H	PO	A	E	DP	TC/G	FA	G by Pos
1916	PHI	A	3	.167	.167	6	1	0	0	0	0.0	0	0	0	2	0	2	0	1	0	0	0	0.3	1.000	OF-1

Leo Dixon

DIXON, LEO MOSES
B. Sept. 4, 1894, Chicago, Ill.   D. Apr. 11, 1984, Chicago, Ill.   BR TR 5'11"   170 lbs.

Year	Team		Games	BA	SA	AB	H	2B	3B	HR	HR%	R	RBI	BB	SO	SB	AB	H	PO	A	E	DP	TC/G	FA	G by Pos
1925	STL	A	76	.224	.302	205	46	11	1	1	0.5	27	19	24	42	3	0	0	233	70	6	8	4.1	.981	C-75
1926			33	.191	.247	89	17	3	1	0	0.0	7	8	11	14	1	0	0	101	29	3	3	4.0	.977	C-33
1927			36	.194	.243	103	20	3	1	0	0.0	6	12	7	6	0	0	0	116	32	10	1	4.4	.937	C-35
1929	CIN	N	14	.167	.233	30	5	2	0	0	0.0	0	2	3	7	0	0	0	42	8	0	0	3.6	1.000	C-14
	4 yrs.		159	.206	.272	427	88	19	3	1	0.2	40	41	45	69	4	0	0	492	139	19	12	4.1	.971	C-157

Dan Dobbek

DOBBEK, DANIEL JOHN
B. Dec. 6, 1934, Ontonagon, Mich.   BL TR 6'   195 lbs.

Year	Team		Games	BA	SA	AB	H	2B	3B	HR	HR%	R	RBI	BB	SO	SB	AB	H	PO	A	E	DP	TC/G	FA	G by Pos
1959	WAS	A	16	.250	.383	60	15	1	2	1	1.7	8	5	5	13	1	0	0	29	1	0	0	1.9	1.000	OF-16

Year	Team		Games	BA	SA	AB	H	2B	3B	HR	HR%	R	RBI	BB	SO	SB	Pinch Hit AB	H	PO	A	E	DP	TC/G	FA	G by Pos

Dan Dobbek *continued*

1960			110	.218	.387	248	54	8	2	10	4.0	32	30	35	41	4	32	5	141	5	4	1	1.4	.973	OF-78
1961	MIN	A	72	.168	.304	125	21	3	1	4	3.2	12	14	13	18	1	23	3	64	1	1	0	0.9	.985	OF-48
3 yrs.			198	.208	.363	433	90	12	5	15	3.5	52	49	53	72	5	55	8	234	7	5	1	1.2	.980	OF-142

John Dobbs

DOBBS, JOHN GORDON   BL TR 5'9½" 170 lbs.
B. June 3, 1876, Chattanooga, Tenn. D. Sept. 9, 1934, Charlotte, N. C.

1901	CIN	N	109	.274	.345	435	119	17	4	2	0.5	71	27	36		19	1	0	196	22	17	5	2.2	.928	OF-100, 3B-8
1902	2 teams		CIN	N	(63G – .297)		CHI	N	(59G – .302)																
"	total		122	.299	.358	491	147	16	5	1	0.2	70	51	37		10	0	0	268	19	9	7	2.4	.970	OF-122
1903	2 teams		CHI	N	(16G – .230)		BKN	N	(111G – .237)																
"	total		127	.236	.316	475	112	16	8	2	0.4	69	63	55		23	1	0	278	12	9	4	2.4	.970	OF-126
1904	BKN	N	101	.248	.303	363	90	16	2	0	0.0	36	30	28		11	3	0	207	19	16	1	2.4	.934	OF-92, SS-2, 2B-2
1905			123	.254	.330	460	117	21	4	2	0.4	59	36	31		15	0	0	246	11	17	1	2.2	.938	OF-123
5 yrs.			582	.263	.332	2224	585	86	23	7	0.3	305	207	187		78	5	1	1195	83	68	18	2.3	.949	OF-563, 3B-8, SS-2, 2B-2

Larry Doby

DOBY, LAWRENCE EUGENE   BL TR 6'1" 180 lbs.
B. Dec. 13, 1924, Camden, S. C.
Manager 1978.

1947	CLE	A	29	.156	.188	32	5	1	0	0	0.0	3	2	1	11	0	21	4	11	4	0	1	0.5	1.000	2B-4, SS-1, 1B-1
1948			121	.301	.490	439	132	23	9	14	3.2	83	66	54	77	9	6	2	287	12	14	3	2.6	.955	OF-114
1949			147	.280	.468	547	153	25	3	24	4.4	106	85	91	90	10	0	0	355	7	9	2	2.5	.976	OF-147
1950			142	.326	.545	503	164	25	5	25	5.0	110	102	98	71	8	2	1	367	2	5	1	2.6	.987	OF-140
1951			134	.295	.512	447	132	27	5	20	4.5	84	69	101	81	4	2	0	321	12	8	3	2.5	.977	OF-132
1952			140	.276	**.541**	519	143	26	8	**32**	6.2	**104**	104	90	**111**	5	3	1	398	11	6	3	3.0	.986	OF-136
1953			149	.263	.487	513	135	18	5	29	5.7	92	102	96	**121**	3	3	1	354	10	6	3	2.5	.984	OF-146
1954			153	.272	.484	577	157	18	4	**32**	5.5	94	**126**	85	94	3	0	0	411	14	2	6	2.8	.995	OF-153
1955			131	.291	.505	491	143	17	5	26	5.3	91	75	61	100	2	2	0	313	6	2	1	2.5	.994	OF-129
1956	CHI	A	140	.268	.466	504	135	22	3	24	4.8	89	102	102	105	0	3	1	371	4	5	2	2.7	.987	OF-137
1957			119	.288	.464	416	120	27	2	14	3.4	57	79	56	79	2	9	1	255	3	4	0	2.2	.985	OF-110
1958	CLE	A	89	.283	.490	247	70	10	1	13	5.3	41	45	26	49	0	18	5	141	5	0	0	1.6	1.000	OF-68
1959	2 teams		DET	A	(18G – .218)		CHI	A	(21G – .241)																
"	total		39	.230	.301	113	26	4	2	0	0.0	6	12	10	22	1	9	2	56	3	3	5	1.6	.952	OF-28, 1B-2
13 yrs.			1533	.283	.490	5348	1515	243	52	253	4.7	960	969	871	1011	47	78	18	3640	93	64	30	2.5	.983	OF-1440, 2B-4, 1B-3, SS-1

WORLD SERIES

1948	CLE	A	6	.318	.500	22	7	1	0	1	4.5	1	2	2	4	0	0	0	11	0	1	0	2.0	.917	OF-6
1954			4	.125	.125	16	2	0	0	0	0.0	0	0	2	4	0	0	0	7	0	0	0	1.8	1.000	OF-4
2 yrs.			10	.237	.342	38	9	1	0	1	2.6	1	2	4	8	0	0	0	18	0	1	0	1.9	.947	OF-10

Ona Dodd

DODD, ORAN A.   BR TR 5'8" 150 lbs.
B. Sept. 14, 1889, Bagwell, Tex. D. Mar. 31, 1929, Newport, Ark.

| 1912 | PIT | N | 5 | .000 | .000 | 9 | 0 | 0 | 0 | 0 | 0.0 | 0 | 1 | 1 | 3 | 0 | 0 | 0 | 1 | 5 | 0 | 1 | 1.2 | 1.000 | 3B-4, 2B-1 |

Tom Dodd

DODD, THOMAS MARION   BR TR 6' 190 lbs.
B. Aug. 15, 1958, Portland, Ore.

| 1986 | BAL | A | 8 | .231 | .462 | 13 | 3 | 0 | 0 | 1 | 7.7 | 2 | 2 | 2 | 2 | 0 | 5 | 1 | 0 | 0 | 0 | 0 | 0.0 | – | DH-6, 3B-1 |

John Dodge

DODGE, JOHN LEWIS   BR TR 5'11½" 165 lbs.
B. Apr. 27, 1889, Bolivar, Tenn. D. June 19, 1916, Mobile, Ala.

1912	PHI	N	30	.120	.130	92	11	1	0	0	0.0	3	3	4	11	2	0	0	48	63	3	5	3.8	.974	3B-23, 2B-5, SS-1
1913	2 teams		PHI	N	(3G – .333)		CIN	N	(94G – .241)																
"	total		97	.242	.353	326	79	8	8	4	1.2	35	45	12	34	11	2	0	98	173	27	10	3.1	.909	3B-91, SS-3
2 yrs.			127	.215	.304	418	90	9	8	4	1.0	38	48	16	45	13	2	0	146	236	30	15	3.2	.927	3B-114, 2B-5, SS-4

Pat Dodson

DODSON, PATRICK NEAL   BL TL 6'4" 210 lbs.
B. Oct. 11, 1959, Santa Monica, Calif.

1986	BOS	A	9	.417	.833	12	5	2	0	1	8.3	3	3	3	3	0	2	1	25	1	0	6	2.9	1.000	1B-7
1987			26	.167	.381	42	7	3	0	2	4.8	4	6	8	13	0	3	1	99	4	0	12	4.0	1.000	1B-21, DH-1
1988			17	.178	.356	45	8	3	1	1	2.2	5	1	6	17	0	2	0	87	12	0	7	5.8	1.000	1B-17
3 yrs.			52	.202	.424	99	20	8	1	4	4.0	12	10	17	33	0	7	2	211	17	0	25	4.4	1.000	1B-45, DH-1

Bobby Doerr

DOERR, ROBERT PERSHING   BR TR 5'11" 175 lbs.
B. Apr. 7, 1918, Los Angeles, Calif.
Hall of Fame 1986.

1937	BOS	A	55	.224	.313	147	33	5	1	2	1.4	22	14	18	25	2	0	0	94	124	6	29	4.1	.973	2B-47
1938			145	.289	.397	509	147	26	7	5	1.0	70	80	59	39	5	0	0	372	420	26	118	5.6	.968	2B-145
1939			127	.318	.448	525	167	28	2	12	2.3	75	73	38	32	1	1	0	336	431	19	95	6.2	.976	2B-126
1940			151	.291	.497	595	173	37	10	22	3.7	87	105	57	53	10	0	0	401	480	21	118	6.0	.977	2B-151
1941			132	.282	.450	500	141	28	4	16	3.2	74	93	43	43	1	0	0	290	389	20	85	5.3	.971	2B-132
1942			144	.290	.455	545	158	35	5	15	2.8	71	102	67	55	4	2	0	376	453	21	105	5.9	.975	2B-142
1943			155	.270	.412	604	163	32	3	16	2.6	78	75	62	59	8	0	0	415	490	9	132	5.9	.990	2B-155
1944			125	.325	**.528**	468	152	30	10	15	3.2	95	81	58	31	5	0	0	341	363	17	96	5.8	.976	2B-125
1946			151	.271	.453	583	158	34	9	18	3.1	95	116	66	67	5	0	0	420	483	13	129	6.1	.986	2B-151
1947			146	.258	.426	561	145	23	10	17	3.0	79	95	59	47	3	0	0	376	466	12	118	5.9	.987	2B-146
1948			140	.285	.505	527	150	23	6	27	5.1	94	111	83	49	3	1	0	366	430	6	119	5.7	.993	2B-138
1949			139	.309	.497	541	167	30	9	18	3.3	91	109	75	33	2	0	0	395	439	17	134	6.1	.980	2B-139
1950			149	.294	.519	586	172	29	11	27	4.6	103	120	67	42	3	0	0	443	431	11	130	5.9	.988	2B-149
1951			106	.289	.448	402	116	21	2	13	3.2	60	73	57	33	2	0	0	303	311	12	99	5.9	.981	2B-106
14 yrs.			1865	.288	.461	7093	2042	381	89	223	3.1	1094	1247	809	608	54	4	0	4928	5710	214	1507	5.8	.980	2B-1852

WORLD SERIES

| 1946 | BOS | A | 6 | .409 | .591 | 22 | 9 | 1 | 0 | 1 | 4.5 | 1 | 3 | 2 | 2 | 0 | 0 | 0 | 18 | 31 | 0 | 3 | 8.2 | 1.000 | 2B-6 |

Year	Team		Games	BA	SA	AB	H	2B	3B	HR	HR%	R	RBI	BB	SO	SB	Pinch Hit AB	Pinch Hit H	PO	A	E	DP	TC/G	FA	G by Pos

John Doherty

DOHERTY, JOHN MICHAEL
B. Aug. 22, 1951, Woburn, Mass.
BL TL 5'11" 185 lbs.

Year	Team		Games	BA	SA	AB	H	2B	3B	HR	HR%	R	RBI	BB	SO	SB	AB	H	PO	A	E	DP	TC/G	FA	G by Pos
1974	CAL	A	74	.256	.368	223	57	14	1	3	1.3	20	15	8	13	2	9	1	538	30	5	55	7.7	.991	1B-70, DH-2
1975			30	.202	.266	94	19	3	0	1	1.1	7	12	8	12	1	2	1	216	14	4	20	7.8	.983	1B-26, DH-1
2 yrs.			104	.240	.338	317	76	17	1	4	1.3	27	27	16	25	3	11	2	754	44	9	75	7.8	.989	1B-96, DH-3

Biddy Dolan

DOLAN, LEON MARK
B. July 9, 1881, Unknown,   D. July 15, 1950, Indianapolis, Ind.
BR TR 6'

Year	Team		Games	BA	SA	AB	H	2B	3B	HR	HR%	R	RBI	BB	SO	SB	AB	H	PO	A	E	DP	TC/G	FA	G by Pos
1914	IND	F	32	.223	.330	103	23	4	2	1	1.0	13	15	12		5	0	0	310	19	7	14	10.5	.979	1B-31

Cozy Dolan

DOLAN, ALBERT J
Born James Alberts.
B. Dec. 23, 1889, Chicago, Ill. D. Dec. 10, 1958, Chicago, Ill.
BR TR 5'10" 160 lbs.

Year	Team		Games	BA	SA	AB	H	2B	3B	HR	HR%	R	RBI	BB	SO	SB	AB	H	PO	A	E	DP	TC/G	FA	G by Pos
1909	CIN	N	3	.167	.167	6	1	0	0	0	0.0	2	0	2		0	0	0	2	4	2	1	2.7	.750	3B-3
1911	NY	A	19	.304	.420	69	21	1	2	1	1.4	19	6	8		12	0	0	21	33	3	4	3.0	.947	3B-19
1912	2 teams			NY	A	(17G – .200)		PHI	N	(11G – .280)															
"	total		28	.236	.355	110	26	3	5	0	0.0	23	18	6	10	8	0	0	28	49	18	2	3.4	.811	3B-28
1913	2 teams			PHI	N	(55G – .262)		PIT	N	(35G – .203)															
"	total		90	.232	.282	259	60	9	2	0	0.0	37	17	16	35	23	13	3	88	111	22	12	2.5	.900	3B-39, OF-12, SS-10, 2B-9, 1B-1
1914	STL	N	126	.240	.321	421	101	16	3	4	1.0	76	32	55	74	42	1	1	205	59	23	3	2.3	.920	OF-97, 3B-29
1915			111	.280	.398	322	90	14	9	2	0.6	53	38	34	37	17	3	1	179	4	14	0	1.8	.929	OF-98
1922	NY	N	1	–	–	0	0	0	0	0		0	0	0	0	0	0	0	0	0	0	0	0.0	–	
7 yrs.			378	.252	.341	1187	299	43	21	7	0.6	210	111	121	156	102	17	5	523	260	82	22	2.3	.905	OF-207, 3B-118, SS-10, 2B-9, 1B-1

Cozy Dolan

DOLAN, PATRICK HENRY
B. Dec. 3, 1872, Cambridge, Mass. D. Mar. 29, 1907, Louisville, Ky.
BL TL 5'10" 160 lbs.

Year	Team		Games	BA	SA	AB	H	2B	3B	HR	HR%	R	RBI	BB	SO	SB	AB	H	PO	A	E	DP	TC/G	FA	G by Pos
1892	WAS	N	5	.231	.231	13	3	0	0	0	0.0	1	1	1		0			6	0	0		1.4	1.000	P-5
1895	BOS	N	26	.241	.313	83	20	4	1	0	0.0	12	7	6	7	3	0	0	14	62	5	2	3.1	.938	P-25, OF-1
1896			6	.143	.143	14	2	0	0	0	0.0	4	0	1		0	0	0	5	8	4	0	2.8	.765	P-6
1900	CHI	N	13	.271	.292	48	13	1	0	0	0.0	5	2	2		2	0	0	18	1	4	0	1.8	.826	OF-13
1901	2 teams			CHI	N	(43G – .263)		BKN	N	(66G – .261)															
"	total		109	.262	.304	424	111	12	3	0	0.0	62	45	24		10	4	1	171	18	14	5	1.9	.931	OF-105
1902	BKN	N	141	.280	.336	592	166	16	7	1	0.2	72	54	33		24	0	0	283	10	20	2	2.2	.936	OF-141
1903	2 teams			CHI	A	(27G – .260)		CIN	N	(93G – .288)															
"	total		120	.282	.350	489	138	25	4	0	0.0	80	65	34		16	0	0	341	27	16	9	3.2	.958	OF-97, 1B-19
1904	CIN	N	129	.284	.383	465	132	8	10	6	1.3	88	51	39		19	3	0	356	29	16	10	3.1	.960	OF-102, 1B-24
1905	2 teams			CIN	N	(22G – .234)		BOS	N	(112G – .275)															
"	total		134	.269	.343	510	137	13	8	0	0.0	51	52	34		23	0	0	325	28	21	9	2.8	.944	OF-120, 1B-15, P-2
1906	BOS	N	152	.248	.299	549	136	20	4	0	0.0	54	39	55		17	0	0	221	43	22	5	1.9	.923	OF-144, 2B-7, P-2, 1B-1
10 yrs.			835	.269	.333	3187	858	99	37	10	0.3	429	316	229	13	114	11	1	1735	232	122	42	2.5	.942	OF-723, 1B-59, P-40, 2B-7

Joe Dolan

DOLAN, JOSEPH
B. Feb. 24, 1873, Baltimore, Md. D. Mar. 24, 1938, Omaha, Neb.
TR 5'10½" 155 lbs.

Year	Team		Games	BA	SA	AB	H	2B	3B	HR	HR%	R	RBI	BB	SO	SB	AB	H	PO	A	E	DP	TC/G	FA	G by Pos
1896	LOU	N	44	.212	.291	165	35	2	1	3	1.8	14	18	9	12	6	0	0	92	159	16	25	6.1	.940	SS-44
1897			36	.211	.256	133	28	2	2	0	0.0	10	7	8		6	0	0	84	113	26	14	6.2	.883	SS-18, 2B-18
1899	PHI	N	61	.257	.324	222	57	6	3	1	0.5	27	30	11		3	0	0	113	190	28	10	5.4	.915	2B-61
1900			74	.198	.261	257	51	7	3	1	0.4	39	27	16		10	0	0	136	198	26	17	4.9	.928	3B-31, 2B-29, SS-12
1901	2 teams			PHI	N	(10G – .081)		PHI	A	(98G – .216)															
"	total		108	.203	.277	375	76	21	2	1	0.3	50	40	28		3	0	0	144	350	57	40	5.1	.897	SS-61, 3B-35, 2B-11, OF-1
5 yrs.			323	.214	.282	1152	247	38	11	6	0.5	140	122	72	12	28	0	0	569	1010	153	106	5.4	.912	SS-135, 2B-119, 3B-66, OF-1

Tom Dolan

DOLAN, THOMAS J.
B. Jan. 10, 1859, New York, N. Y. D. Jan. 16, 1913, St. Louis, Mo.
BR TR

Year	Team		Games	BA	SA	AB	H	2B	3B	HR	HR%	R	RBI	BB	SO	SB	AB	H	PO	A	E	DP	TC/G	FA	G by Pos
1879	CHI	N	1	.000	.000	4	0	0	0	0	0.0	0		0	2		0	0	6	2	0	0	8.0	1.000	C-1
1882	BUF	N	22	.157	.180	89	14	0	1	0	0.0	12		2	11		0	0	72	28	8	1	4.9	.926	C-18, OF-4, 3B-2
1883	STL	AA	81	.214	.268	295	63	9	2	1	0.3	32		9			0	0	269	63	23	6	4.4	.935	OF-82, P-1
1884	2 teams			STL	AA	(35G – .263)		STL	U	(19G – .188)															
"	total		54	.238	.301	206	49	2	2	0	0.0	28		10			0	0	298	81	54	4	8.0	.875	C-48, OF-4, 3B-3
1885	STL	N	3	.222	.222	9	2	0	0	0	0.0	1		0		1	0	0	10	7	4	0	7.0	.810	C-3
1886	2 teams			STL	N	(15G – .250)		BAL	AA	(38G – .152)															
"	total		53	.178	.237	169	30	6	2	0	0.0	21	1	15	9		0	0	267	106	38	2	7.8	.908	C-50, OF-3
1888	STL	AA	11	.194	.222	36	7	1	0	0	0.0	1	1	1		0	0	0	50	14	6	0	6.4	.914	C-11
7 yrs.			225	.204	.256	808	165	25	7	1	0.1	95	2	39	23		0	0	972	301	133	13	6.2	.905	C-131, OF-93, 3B-5, P-1

Frank Doljack

DOLJACK, FRANK JOSEPH
B. Oct. 5, 1907, Cleveland, Ohio D. Jan. 23, 1948, Cleveland, Ohio
BR TR 5'11" 175 lbs.

Year	Team		Games	BA	SA	AB	H	2B	3B	HR	HR%	R	RBI	BB	SO	SB	AB	H	PO	A	E	DP	TC/G	FA	G by Pos
1930	DET	A	20	.257	.473	74	19	5	1	3	4.1	10	17	2	11	0	0	0	38	2	3	1	2.2	.930	OF-20
1931			63	.278	.444	187	52	13	3	4	2.1	20	20	15	17	3	7	0	140	8	12	1	2.5	.925	OF-54
1932			8	.385	.538	26	10	1	0	1	3.8	5	7	2	1	1	0	0	6	0	0	0	0.8	1.000	OF-6
1933			42	.286	.347	147	42	5	2	0	0.0	18	22	14	13	2	5	1	74	6	5	3	2.1	.941	OF-37
1934			56	.233	.333	120	28	7	1	1	0.8	15	19	13	15	2	22	4	67	4	4	0	1.3	.947	OF-30, 1B-3
1943	CLE	A	3	.000	.000	7	0	0	0	0	0.0	0	0	1	2	0	1	0	2	0	0	0	0.7	1.000	OF-3
6 yrs.			192	.269	.398	561	151	31	7	9	1.6	68	85	47	60	8	36	5	327	20	24	5	1.9	.935	OF-150, 1B-3

WORLD SERIES

Year	Team		Games	BA	SA	AB	H	2B	3B	HR	HR%	R	RBI	BB	SO	SB	AB	H	PO	A	E	DP	TC/G	FA	G by Pos
1934	DET	A	2	.000	.000	2	0	0	0	0	0.0	0	0	0	1	0	1	0	1	0	0	0	0.5	1.000	OF-1

Jiggs Donahue

DONAHUE, JOHN AUGUSTUS
Brother of Pat Donahue.
B. July 13, 1879, Springfield, Ohio D. July 19, 1913, Columbus, Ohio
BL TL 6'1" 178 lbs.

Year	Team		Games	BA	SA	AB	H	2B	3B	HR	HR%	R	RBI	BB	SO	SB	AB	H	PO	A	E	DP	TC/G	FA	G by Pos
1900	PIT	N	3	.200	.400	10	2	0	1	0	0.0	1	3	0		1	0	0	8	1	1	0	3.3	.900	C-2, OF-1

Year	Team		Games	BA	SA	AB	H	2B	3B	HR	HR%	R	RBI	BB	SO	SB	Pinch Hit AB	H	PO	A	E	DP	TC/G	FA	G by Pos

Jiggs Donahue *continued*

Year	Team		Games	BA	SA	AB	H	2B	3B	HR	HR%	R	RBI	BB	SO	SB	AB	H	PO	A	E	DP	TC/G	FA	G by Pos
1901	2 teams	PIT N (2G – .000)				MIL A (37G – .306)																			
"	total		39	.306	.426	108	33	5	4	0	0.0	10	16	10		4	5	0	186	30	17	8	6.0	.927	C-20, 1B-13, OF-1
1902	STL	A	30	.236	.303	89	21	1	1	1	1.1	11	7	12		2	2	0	118	29	8	6	5.2	.948	C-23, 1B-5
1904	CHI	A	102	.248	.319	367	91	9	7	1	0.3	46	48	25		18	1	1	1067	85	25	49	11.5	.979	1B-101
1905			149	.287	.349	533	153	22	4	1	0.2	71	76	44		32	0	0	1645	114	21	77	11.9	.988	1B-149
1906			154	.257	.318	556	143	17	7	1	0.2	70	57	48		36	0	0	1697	118	22	62	11.9	.988	1B-154
1907			157	.259	.307	**609**	158	16	5	1	0.2	75	68	28		27	0	0	1846	140	12	78	12.7	.994	1B-157
1908			93	.204	.243	304	62	8	2	0	0.0	22	22	25		14	10	1	968	57	6	30	11.1	.994	1B-83
1909	2 teams	CHI A (2G – .000)				WAS A (84G – .237)																			
"	total		86	.233	.282	287	67	12	1	0	0.0	13	30	23		9	3	2	777	36	13	28	9.6	.984	1B-83
9 yrs.			813	.255	.314	2863	730	90	32	5	0.2	319	327	215		143	21	4	8312	610	125	338	11.1	.986	1B-745, C-45, OF-2

WORLD SERIES

Year	Team		Games	BA	SA	AB	H	2B	3B	HR	HR%	R	RBI	BB	SO	SB	AB	H	PO	A	E	DP	TC/G	FA	G by Pos
1906	CHI	A	6	.333	.556	18	6	2	1	0	0.0	0	4	3	4	0	0	0	79	8	1	3	14.7	.989	1B-6

Jim Donahue

DONAHUE, JAMES AUGUSTUS
B. Jan. 8, 1862, Lockport, Ill.   D. Apr. 19, 1935, Lockport, Ill.
BR TR 6'   175 lbs.

Year	Team		Games	BA	SA	AB	H	2B	3B	HR	HR%	R	RBI	BB	SO	SB	AB	H	PO	A	E	DP	TC/G	FA	G by Pos
1886	NY	AA	49	.199	.199	186	37	0	0	0	0.0	14		10		0	0	0	141	37	22	1	4.1	.890	OF-32, C-19
1887			60	.282	.323	220	62	4	1	1	0.5	33		21		6	0	0	258	95	51	3	6.7	.874	C-51, OF-5, 1B-4, 3B-1, 2B-1
1888	KC	AA	88	.234	.294	337	79	11	3	1	0.3	29	28	21		12	0	0	320	122	51	10	5.6	.897	C-67, OF-18, 3B-5, 2B-1
1889			67	.234	.286	252	59	5	4	0	0.0	30	32	21	20	12	0	0	187	100	46	7	5.0	.862	C-46, OF-14, 3B-10
1891	COL	AA	77	.218	.254	280	61	4	3	0	0.0	27	35	31	18	2	0	0	352	108	28	11	6.3	.943	C-75, OF-1, 1B-1
5 yrs.			341	.234	.275	1275	298	24	11	2	0.2	133	95	104	38	32	0	0	1258	462	198	32	5.6	.897	C-258, OF-70, 3B-16, 1B-5, 2B-2

John Donahue

DONAHUE, JOHN FREDERICK (Jiggs)
B. Apr. 19, 1894, Roxbury, Mass.   D. Oct. 3, 1949, Boston, Mass.
BB TR 5'8"   170 lbs.

Year	Team		Games	BA	SA	AB	H	2B	3B	HR	HR%	R	RBI	BB	SO	SB	AB	H	PO	A	E	DP	TC/G	FA	G by Pos
1923	BOS	A	10	.278	.389	36	10	4	0	0	0.0	5	1	4	5	0	1	1	21	4	0	1	2.5	1.000	OF-9

Pat Donahue

DONAHUE, PATRICK WILLIAM
Brother of Jiggs Donahue.
B. Nov. 3, 1884, Springfield, Ohio   D. Jan. 31, 1966, Springfield, Ohio
BR TR 6'   175 lbs.

Year	Team		Games	BA	SA	AB	H	2B	3B	HR	HR%	R	RBI	BB	SO	SB	AB	H	PO	A	E	DP	TC/G	FA	G by Pos
1908	BOS	A	35	.198	.256	86	17	2	0	1	1.2	8	6	9		0	0	0	143	37	7	2	5.3	.963	C-32, 1B-3
1909			64	.239	.307	176	42	4	1	2	1.1	14	25	17		2	6	2	249	71	6	3	5.1	.982	C-58
1910	3 teams	BOS A (2G – .000)				PHI A (15G – .162)						CLE A (2G – .000)													
"	total		19	.133	.133	45	6	0	0	0	0.0	2	4	3		1	2	0	80	26	0	3	5.6	1.000	C-17
3 yrs.			118	.212	.267	307	65	6	1	3	1.0	24	35	29		3	8	2	472	134	13	8	5.2	.979	C-107, 1B-3

She Donahue

DONAHUE, CHARLES MICHAEL
B. June 29, 1877, Oswego, N. Y.   D. Aug. 28, 1947, New York, N. Y.
BR TR 5'9"

Year	Team		Games	BA	SA	AB	H	2B	3B	HR	HR%	R	RBI	BB	SO	SB	AB	H	PO	A	E	DP	TC/G	FA	G by Pos
1904	2 teams	STL N (4G – .267)				PHI N (58G – .215)																			
"	total		62	.219	.237	215	47	4	0	0	0.0	22	16	3		10	0	0	114	116	38	11	4.3	.858	SS-30, 3B-24, 2B-5, 1B-3

Tim Donahue

DONAHUE, TIMOTHY CORNELIUS
B. June 8, 1870, Raynham, Mass.   D. June 12, 1902, Taunton, Mass.
BL TR 5'11"   180 lbs.

Year	Team		Games	BA	SA	AB	H	2B	3B	HR	HR%	R	RBI	BB	SO	SB	AB	H	PO	A	E	DP	TC/G	FA	G by Pos
1891	BOS	AA	4	.000	.000	7	0	0	0	0	0.0	0	0	0	5	0	0	0	4	1	1	0	1.5	.833	C-4
1895	CHI	N	63	.269	.347	219	59	9	1	2	0.9	29	36	20	25	5	0	0	234	45	26	8	4.8	.915	C-63
1896			57	.218	.282	188	41	10	1	0	0.0	27	20	11	15	11	0	0	235	60	20	7	5.5	.937	C-57
1897			58	.239	.309	188	45	7	3	0	0.0	28	21	9		3	1	1	222	68	17	2	5.3	.945	C-55, SS-2, 1B-1
1898			122	.220	.265	396	87	12	3	0	0.0	52	39	49		17	0	0	450	107	22	16	4.7	.962	C-122
1899			92	.248	.302	278	69	9	3	0	0.0	39	29	34		10	0	0	305	100	21	13	4.6	.951	C-91, 1B-1
1900			67	.236	.292	216	51	10	1	0	0.0	21	17	19		8	0	0	234	64	24	6	4.8	.925	C-66, 2B-1
1902	WAS	A	3	.250	.250	8	2	0	0	0	0.0	0	1	0		0	0	0	8	3	0	0	3.7	1.000	C-3
8 yrs.			466	.236	.294	1500	354	57	12	2	0.1	196	163	142	45	54	1	1	1692	448	131	52	4.9	.942	C-461, SS-2, 1B-2, 2B-1

John Donaldson

DONALDSON, JOHN DAVID
B. May 5, 1943, Charlotte, N. C.
BL TR 5'11"   160 lbs.

Year	Team		Games	BA	SA	AB	H	2B	3B	HR	HR%	R	RBI	BB	SO	SB	AB	H	PO	A	E	DP	TC/G	FA	G by Pos
1966	KC	A	15	.133	.133	30	4	0	0	0	0.0	4	1	3	4	1	5	0	22	12	0	2	2.3	1.000	2B-9
1967			105	.276	.345	377	104	16	5	0	0.0	27	28	37	39	6	4	2	210	230	8	40	4.3	.982	2B-101, SS-1
1968	OAK	A	127	.220	.273	363	80	9	2	2	0.6	37	27	45	44	5	26	6	178	271	13	49	3.6	.972	2B-98, 3B-5, SS-1
1969	2 teams	OAK A (12G – .077)				SEA A (95G – .234)																			
"	total		107	.228	.276	351	80	8	1	1	0.3	23	19	38	40	6	10	0	212	247	13	57	4.4	.972	2B-91, 3B-2, SS-1
1970	OAK	A	41	.247	.326	89	22	2	1	1	1.1	4	11	9	6	1	13	6	31	66	1	9	2.4	.990	2B-21, SS-6, 3B-1
1974			10	.133	.133	15	2	0	0	0	0.0	1	0	0	0	0	1	0	11	14	1	5	2.6	.962	2B-7, 3B-3
6 yrs.			405	.238	.295	1225	292	35	11	4	0.3	96	86	132	133	19	59	14	664	840	36	162	3.8	.977	2B-327, 3B-11, SS-9

Len Dondero

DONDERO, LEONARD PETER (Mike)
B. Sept. 12, 1903, Newark, Calif.
BR TR 5'11"   178 lbs.

Year	Team		Games	BA	SA	AB	H	2B	3B	HR	HR%	R	RBI	BB	SO	SB	AB	H	PO	A	E	DP	TC/G	FA	G by Pos
1929	STL	A	19	.194	.290	31	6	0	0	1	3.2	2	8	0	4	0	4	0	8	10	2	1	1.1	.900	3B-10, 2B-5

Mike Donlin

DONLIN, MICHAEL JOSEPH (Highlonesome)
B. May 30, 1878, Peoria, Ill.   D. Sept. 24, 1933, Hollywood, Calif.
BL TL 5'9"   170 lbs.

Year	Team		Games	BA	SA	AB	H	2B	3B	HR	HR%	R	RBI	BB	SO	SB	AB	H	PO	A	E	DP	TC/G	FA	G by Pos
1899	STL	N	66	.323	.470	266	86	9	6	6	2.3	49	27	17		20	0	0	215	25	29	7	4.1	.892	OF-51, 1B-13, SS-3, P-3
1900			78	.326	.507	276	90	8	6	10	3.6	40	48	14		14	10	**4**	308	11	21	14	4.4	.938	OF-47, 1B-21
1901	BAL	A	121	.347	.481	476	165	23	13	5	1.1	107	67	53		33	1	1	614	36	26	21	5.6	.962	OF-74, 1B-21
1902	CIN	N	34	.294	.392	143	42	4	5	0	0.0	30	9	9		9	1	0	60	6	9	1	2.6	.880	OF-32, SS-1, P-1
1903			126	.351	.516	496	174	25	18	7	1.4	110	67	56		26	2	1	275	20	28	7	2.6	.913	OF-118, 1B-7

Year	Team		Games	BA	SA	AB	H	2B	3B	HR	HR%	R	RBI	BB	SO	SB	Pinch Hit AB	Pinch Hit H	PO	A	E	DP	TC/G	FA	G by Pos

Mike Donlin *continued*

Year	Team		Games	BA	SA	AB	H	2B	3B	HR	HR%	R	RBI	BB	SO	SB	AB	H	PO	A	E	DP	TC/G	FA	G by Pos
1904	2 teams			CIN N	(60G – .356)		NY	N	(42G – .280)																
"	total		102	.329	.457	368	121	18	10	3	0.8	59	52	28		22	6	0	186	12	21	2	2.1	.904	OF-90, 1B-6
1905	NY	N	150	.356	.495	606	216	31	16	7	1.2	**124**	80	56		33	6	0	250	17	19	4	1.9	.934	OF-150
1906			37	.314	.397	121	38	5	1	1	0.8	15	14	11		9	6	0	49	1	3	0	1.4	.943	OF-29, 1B-1
1908			155	.334	.452	593	198	26	13	6	1.0	71	106	23		30	0	0	239	21	6	1	1.7	.977	OF-155
1911	2 teams			NY	N	(12G – .333)		BOS	N	(56G – .315)															
"	total		68	.316	.432	234	74	16	1	3	1.3	36	35	22	18	9	9	2	118	8	12	2	2.0	.913	OF-59
1912	PIT	N	77	.316	.443	244	77	9	8	2	0.8	27	35	20	16	8	13	2	102	8	2	1	1.5	.982	OF-62
1914	NY	N	35	.161	.355	31	5	1	1	1	3.2	1	3	3	5	0	31	5	0	0	0	0	0.0	–	
12 yrs.			1049	.334	.470	3854	1286	175	98	51	1.3	669	543	312	39	213	79	15	2416	165	176	60	2.6	.936	OF-867, 1B-95, SS-4, P-4

WORLD SERIES

Year	Team		Games	BA	SA	AB	H	2B	3B	HR	HR%	R	RBI	BB	SO	SB	AB	H	PO	A	E	DP	TC/G	FA	G by Pos
1905	NY	N	5	.316	.368	19	6	1	0	0	0.0	4	1	2	1	2	0	0	18	1	2	0	4.2	.905	OF-5

Jim Donnelly

DONNELLY, JAMES B. BR TR
B. July 19, 1865, New Haven, Conn. D. Mar. 15, 1915, Meriden, Conn.

Year	Team		Games	BA	SA	AB	H	2B	3B	HR	HR%	R	RBI	BB	SO	SB	AB	H	PO	A	E	DP	TC/G	FA	G by Pos
1884	2 teams			KC	U	(6G – .130)		IND	AA	(40G – .254)															
"	total		46	.236	.280	157	37	18	0	0	0.0	24		6			0	0	46	70	36	2	3.3	.763	3B-29, SS-8, OF-6, 2B-2, C-1
1885	DET	N	56	.232	.294	211	49	4	3	1	0.5	24	22	10	29		0	0	86	103	32	4	3.9	.855	3B-55, 1B-1
1886	KC	N	113	.201	.240	438	88	11	3	0	0.0	51	38	36	57		0	0	153	245	73	13	4.2	.845	3B-113
1887	WAS	N	117	.200	.256	425	85	9	6	1	0.2	51	46	16	26	42	0	0	139	282	64	21	4.1	.868	3B-115, SS-2
1888			122	.201	.241	428	86	9	4	0	0.0	43	23	20	16	44	0	0	133	243	56	16	3.5	.870	3B-117, SS-5
1889			4	.154	.154	13	2	0	0	0	0.0	3	0	2	0	1	0	0	2	6	4	1	3.0	.667	3B-4
1890	STL	AA	11	.333	.333	42	14	0	0	0	0.0	11		8		5	0	0	15	16	8	4	3.5	.795	3B-11
1891	COL	AA	17	.241	.241	54	13	0	0	0	0.0	6	9	13	5	7	0	0	19	46	11	5	4.5	.855	3B-17
1896	BAL	N	106	.328	.414	396	130	14	10	0	0.0	70	71	34	11	38	0	0	140	217	47	15	3.8	.884	3B-106
1897	2 teams			PIT	N	(44G – .193)		NY	N	(23G – .188)															
"	total		67	.191	.220	246	47	7	0	0	0.0	41	25	25		20	0	0	69	122	20	3	3.1	.905	3B-67
1898	STL	N	1	1.000	1.000	1	1	0	0	0	0.0	0	0	0		0	0	0	1	1	0	0	2.0	.500	3B-1
11 yrs.			660	.229	.278	2411	552	57	28	2	0.1	324	234	170	144	157	0	0	802	1351	352	84	3.8	.859	3B-635, SS-15, OF-6, 2B-2, 1B-1, C-1

Joe Donohue

DONOHUE, JOSEPH F.
B. 1869, Syracuse, N. Y. Deceased.

Year	Team		Games	BA	SA	AB	H	2B	3B	HR	HR%	R	RBI	BB	SO	SB	AB	H	PO	A	E	DP	TC/G	FA	G by Pos
1891	PHI	N	6	.318	.364	22	7	1	0	0	0.0	2		3		0	0	0	14	2	2	0	3.0	.889	OF-4, SS-2

Tom Donohue

DONOHUE, THOMAS JAMES BR TR 6' 185 lbs.
B. Nov. 15, 1952, Mineola, N. Y.

Year	Team		Games	BA	SA	AB	H	2B	3B	HR	HR%	R	RBI	BB	SO	SB	AB	H	PO	A	E	DP	TC/G	FA	G by Pos
1979	CAL	A	38	.224	.355	107	24	3	1	3	2.8	13	14	3	29	2	0	0	136	16	3	4	4.1	.981	C-38
1980			84	.188	.243	218	41	4	1	2	0.9	18	14	7	63	5	0	0	330	29	5	5	4.3	.986	C-84
2 yrs.			122	.200	.280	325	65	7	2	5	1.5	31	28	10	92	7	0	0	466	45	8	9	4.3	.985	C-122

Fred Donovan

DONOVAN, FREDERICK MAURICE BR TR
B. Sept. 3, 1876, Lock Haven, Pa. D. Mar. 7, 1916, Springfield, Ill.

Year	Team		Games	BA	SA	AB	H	2B	3B	HR	HR%	R	RBI	BB	SO	SB	AB	H	PO	A	E	DP	TC/G	FA	G by Pos
1895	CLE	N	3	.083	.083	12	1	0	0	0	0.0	1	1	1		2	0	0	13	3	2	1	1	5.3	.938	C-3

Jerry Donovan

DONOVAN, JEREMIAH FRANCIS BR TR
B. Sept. 3, 1876, Lock Haven, Pa. D. June 27, 1938, St. Petersburg, Fla.

Year	Team		Games	BA	SA	AB	H	2B	3B	HR	HR%	R	RBI	BB	SO	SB	AB	H	PO	A	E	DP	TC/G	FA	G by Pos
1906	PHI	N	61	.199	.223	166	33	4	0	0	0.0	11	15	6		2	7	1	222	52	13	4	4.7	.955	C-52, OF-1, SS-1

Mike Donovan

DONOVAN, MICHAEL BERCHMAN BR TR 5'8" 155 lbs.
B. Oct. 18, 1881, Brooklyn, N. Y. D. Feb. 3, 1938, New York, N. Y.

Year	Team		Games	BA	SA	AB	H	2B	3B	HR	HR%	R	RBI	BB	SO	SB	AB	H	PO	A	E	DP	TC/G	FA	G by Pos
1904	CLE	A	2	.000	.000	2	0	0	0	0	0.0	0		0	1	0	0	0	0	0	0	0	0.0	–	SS-1
1908	NY	A	5	.263	.316	19	5	1	0	0	0.0	2	2	0	0	0	1	0	13	9	0	0	4.4	1.000	3B-5
2 yrs.			7	.238	.286	21	5	1	0	0	0.0	2	2	0	1	0	1	0	13	9	0	0	3.1	1.000	3B-5, SS-1

Patsy Donovan

DONOVAN, PATRICK JOSEPH BL TL 5'11½" 175 lbs.
B. Mar. 16, 1865, Queenstown, Ireland D. Dec. 25, 1953, Lawrence, Mass.
Manager 1897, 1899, 1901-04, 1906-08, 1910-11.

Year	Team		Games	BA	SA	AB	H	2B	3B	HR	HR%	R	RBI	BB	SO	SB	AB	H	PO	A	E	DP	TC/G	FA	G by Pos
1890	2 teams			BOS	N	(32G – .257)		BKN	N	(28G – .219)															
"	total		60	.241	.269	245	59	5	1	0	0.0	34	17	13	22	13	0	0	111	7	6	2	2.1	.952	OF-60
1891	2 teams			LOU	AA	(105G – .321)		WAS	AA	(17G – .200)															
"	total		122	.305	.350	509	155	11	3	2	0.4	82	56	34	23	28	0	0	236	17	26	1	2.3	.907	OF-122
1892	2 teams			WAS	N	(40G – .239)		PIT	N	(90G – .294)															
"	total		130	.278	.343	551	153	18	6	2	0.4	106	38	31	29	56	0	0	167	27	31	7	1.7	.862	OF-130
1893	PIT	N	113	.317	.371	499	158	5	8	2	0.4	114	56	42	8	46	1	0	178	16	13	5	1.8	.937	OF-112
1894			132	.302	.394	576	174	21	10	4	0.7	145	76	33	12	41	0	0	267	22	21	5	2.3	.932	OF-132
1895			125	.308	.370	519	160	17	6	1	0.2	114	58	47	19	36	0	0	187	11	8	2	1.6	.961	OF-125
1896			131	.319	.387	573	183	20	5	3	0.5	113	59	35	18	48	0	0	224	24	12	8	2.0	.954	OF-131
1897			120	.322	.384	479	154	16	7	0	0.0	82	57	25		34	0	0	186	17	11	5	1.8	.949	OF-120
1898			147	.302	.357	610	184	16	9	0	0.0	112	37	34		41	0	0	238	21	20	4	1.9	.928	OF-147
1899			121	.294	.347	531	156	11	7	1	0.2	82	55	17		26	0	0	184	9	12	3	1.7	.941	OF-121
1900	STL	N	126	.316	.342	503	159	11	1	0	0.0	78	61	38		**45**	2	1	180	13	10	4	1.6	.951	OF-124
1901			130	.292	.361	527	154	23	5	1	0.2	92	73	27		28	0	0	215	19	5	8	1.8	.979	OF-129
1902			126	.315	.355	502	158	12	4	0	0.0	70	35	28		34	0	0	179	30	9	6	1.7	.959	OF-126
1903			105	.327	.378	410	134	15	3	0	0.0	63	39	25		25	0	0	142	16	8	5	1.6	.952	OF-105
1904	WAS	A	125	.229	.243	436	100	6	0	0	0.0	30	19	24		17	3	0	217	15	9	4	1.9	.963	OF-122
1906	BKN	N	7	.238	.238	21	5	0	0	0	0.0	1	0	1		0	0	0	9	0	0	0	1.3	1.000	OF-6

Year	Team	Games	BA	SA	AB	H	2B	3B	HR	HR%	R	RBI	BB	SO	SB	Pinch Hit AB	Pinch Hit H	PO	A	E	DP	TC/G	FA	G by Pos

Patsy Donovan *continued*

Year	Team	Games	BA	SA	AB	H	2B	3B	HR	HR%	R	RBI	BB	SO	SB	PH AB	PH H	PO	A	E	DP	TC/G	FA	G by Pos
1907		1	.000	.000	1	0	0	0	0	0.0	0	0	0		0	0	0	4	0	0	0	4.0	1.000	OF-1
17 yrs.		1821	.300	.354	7492	2246	207	75	16	0.2	1318	736	453	131	518	7	1	2924	264	201	69	1.9	.941	OF-1813

Tom Donovan

DONOVAN, THOMAS JOSEPH
D. Mar. 25, 1933, Deceased — BR TR 6'2" 168 lbs.

Year	Team	Games	BA	SA	AB	H	2B	3B	HR	HR%	R	RBI	BB	SO	SB	PH AB	PH H	PO	A	E	DP	TC/G	FA	G by Pos
1901	CLE A	18	.254	.324	71	18	3	1	0	0.0	9	5	0		1	0	0	21	6	4	0	1.7	.871	OF-18, P-1

Wild Bill Donovan

DONOVAN, WILLIAM EDWARD
B. Oct. 13, 1876, Lawrence, Mass. D. Dec. 9, 1923, Forsyth, N. Y.
Manager 1915-17, 1921. — BR TR 5'11" 190 lbs.

Year	Team	Games	BA	SA	AB	H	2B	3B	HR	HR%	R	RBI	BB	SO	SB	PH AB	PH H	PO	A	E	DP	TC/G	FA	G by Pos
1898	WAS N	39	.165	.272	103	17	2	3	1	1.0	11	8	4		2	2	1	45	22	8	6	1.9	.893	OF-20, P-17, SS-1, 2B-1
1899	BKN N	5	.231	.308	13	3	1	0	0	0.0	2	0	0		0	0	0	1	5	1	0	1.4	.857	P-5
1900		5	.000	.000	13	0	0	0	0	0.0	0	2	0		0	0	0	0	12	0	0	2.4	1.000	P-5
1901		46	.170	.237	135	23	3	0	2	1.5	16	13	8		1	0	0	14	75	7	5	2.1	.927	P-45
1902		48	.168	.230	161	27	3	2	1	0.6	16	16	9		7	0	0	117	81	7	5	4.3	.966	P-35, 1B-8, OF-4, 2B-1
1903	DET A	40	.242	.298	124	30	3	2	0	0.0	11	12	4		3	2	0	26	71	8	3	2.6	.924	P-35, SS-2, OF-1, 2B-1
1904		46	.271	.321	140	38	2	1	1	0.7	12	6	3		2	2	1	80	89	7	3	3.8	.960	P-34, 1B-8, OF-1
1905		46	.192	.223	130	25	4	0	0	0.0	16	5	12		8	0	0	28	73	7	3	2.3	.935	P-34, OF-8, 2B-2
1906		28	.121	.143	91	11	0	1	0	0.0	5	0	1		6	0	0	17	65	5	1	3.1	.943	P-25, 2B-3, OF-1
1907		37	.266	.367	109	29	7	2	0	0.0	20	19	6		4	4	0	13	56	4	0	2.0	.945	P-32
1908		30	.159	.171	82	13	1	0	0	0.0	5	2	10		2	0	0	16	39	5	0	2.0	.917	P-29
1909		22	.200	.200	45	9	0	0	0	0.0	6	1	2		0	0	0	9	29	1	1	1.8	.974	P-21
1910		26	.145	.159	69	10	1	0	0	0.0	6	2	5		0	0	0	9	33	2	2	1.7	.955	P-26
1911		24	.200	.333	60	12	3	1	1	1.7	11	6	11		1	1	1	4	25	2	0	1.3	.935	P-20
1912		6	.077	.077	13	1	0	0	0	0.0	3	0	1		0	0	0	5	1	1	0	1.2	.857	P-3, OF-2, 1B-2
1915	NY A	10	.083	.083	12	1	0	0	0	0.0	1	0	1	6	0	0	0	1	7	0	0	0.8	1.000	P-9
1916		1	–	–	0	0	0	0	0	–	0	0	0	0	0	0	0	0	0	0	0	0.0	–	P-1
1918	DET A	2	.500	.500	2	1	0	0	0	0.0	0	1	0	0	0	0	0	0	1	0	0	0.5	1.000	P-2
18 yrs.		461	.192	.247	1302	250	30	12	6	0.5	142	93	77	6	36	11	3	385	684	65	29	2.5	.943	P-378, OF-37, 1B-18, 2B-8, SS-3

WORLD SERIES

Year	Team	Games	BA	SA	AB	H	2B	3B	HR	HR%	R	RBI	BB	SO	SB	PH AB	PH H	PO	A	E	DP	TC/G	FA	G by Pos
1907	DET A	2	.000	.000	8	0	0	0	0	0.0	0	0	0	3	0	0	0	3	3	0	0	3.0	1.000	P-2
1908		2	.000	.000	4	0	0	0	0	0.0	0	0	1	1	0	0	0	1	2	1	0	2.0	.750	P-2
1909		2	.000	.000	4	0	0	0	0	0.0	0	0	0	1	0	0	0	0	5	1	0	3.0	.833	P-2
3 yrs.		6	.000	.000	16	0	0	0	0	0.0	0	0	1	5	0	0	0	4	10	2	0	2.7	.875	P-6

Red Dooin

DOOIN, CHARLES SEBASTIAN
B. June 12, 1879, Cincinnati, Ohio D. May 12, 1952, Rochester, N. Y.
Manager 1910-14. — BR TR 5'9½" 165 lbs.

Year	Team	Games	BA	SA	AB	H	2B	3B	HR	HR%	R	RBI	BB	SO	SB	PH AB	PH H	PO	A	E	DP	TC/G	FA	G by Pos
1902	PHI N	94	.231	.270	333	77	7	3	0	0.0	20	35	10		8	4	0	443	117	30	10	6.3	.949	C-84, OF-6
1903		62	.218	.255	188	41	5	1	0	0.0	18	14	8		9	9	3	190	82	17	2	4.7	.941	C-51, OF-1, 1B-1
1904		108	.242	.346	355	86	11	4	6	1.7	41	36	8		15	5	0	447	154	41	12	5.9	.936	C-96, 1B-4, OF-3, 3B-1
1905		113	.250	.311	380	95	13	5	0	0.0	45	36	10		12	5	3	505	152	24	9	6.0	.965	C-107, 3B-1
1906		113	.245	.305	351	86	19	1	0	0.0	25	32	13		15	6	1	475	111	32	9	5.5	.948	C-107
1907		101	.211	.262	313	66	8	4	0	0.0	18	14	15		10	5	1	439	125	24	14	5.8	.959	C-94, OF-1, 2B-1
1908		133	.248	.306	435	108	17	4	0	0.0	28	17	20		1	0	0	554	191	26	17	5.8	.966	C-132
1909		141	.224	.271	468	105	14	1	2	0.4	42	38	21		14	1	0	517	199	40	14	5.4	.947	C-140
1910		103	.242	.305	331	80	13	4	0	0.0	30	30	22	17	10	8	3	473	131	28	14	6.1	.956	C-91, OF-3
1911		74	.328	.409	247	81	15	1	1	0.4	18	16	14	12	6	0	0	436	97	18	5	7.4	.967	C-74
1912		69	.234	.283	184	43	9	0	0	0.0	20	22	5	12	8	8	1	254	69	14	2	4.9	.958	C-58
1913		55	.256	.302	129	33	4	1	0	0.0	6	13	3	9	1	5	2	194	57	10	7	4.7	.962	C-50
1914		53	.178	.220	118	21	2	0	1	0.8	10	8	4	14	4	14	4	151	52	7	4	4.0	.967	C-40
1915	2 teams				CIN N	(10G – .323)			NY N	(46G – .218)														
"	total	56	.239	.277	155	37	2	2	0	0.0	11	9	5	20	1	0	0	227	55	13	4	5.3	.956	C-56
1916	NY N	15	.118	.118	17	2	0	0	0	0.0	1	0	0	3	0	0	0	30	5	1	0	2.4	.972	C-15
15 yrs.		1290	.240	.298	4004	961	139	31	10	0.2	333	344	155	87	133	65	17	5335	1597	325	123	5.6	.955	C-1195, OF-14, 1B-5, 3B-2, 2B-1

Mickey Doolan

DOOLAN, MICHAEL JOSEPH
Born Michael Joseph Doolittle.
B. May 7, 1880, Ashland, Pa. D. Nov. 1, 1951, Orlando, Fla. — BR TR 5'10½" 170 lbs.

Year	Team	Games	BA	SA	AB	H	2B	3B	HR	HR%	R	RBI	BB	SO	SB	PH AB	PH H	PO	A	E	DP	TC/G	FA	G by Pos
1905	PHI N	136	.254	.360	492	125	27	11	1	0.2	53	48	24		17	1	0	299	432	51	45	5.8	.935	SS-135
1906		154	.230	.297	535	123	19	7	1	0.2	41	55	27		16	0	0	395	480	66	51	6.1	.930	SS-154
1907		145	.204	.275	509	104	19	7	1	0.2	33	47	25		18	0	0	327	463	60	59	5.9	.929	SS-145
1908		129	.234	.321	445	104	25	4	2	0.4	29	49	17		5	0	0	269	419	45	32	5.7	.939	SS-129
1909		147	.219	.290	493	108	12	10	1	0.2	39	53	37		10	0	0	352	484	54	58	6.1	.939	SS-147
1910		148	.263	.354	536	141	31	6	2	0.4	58	57	35	56	16	0	0	283	500	43	71	5.6	.948	SS-148
1911		146	.238	.313	512	122	23	6	1	0.2	51	49	44	65	14	1	0	295	474	53	68	5.6	.936	SS-145
1912		146	.258	.335	532	137	26	6	1	0.2	47	62	34	59	6	0	0	289	476	40	49	5.5	.950	SS-146
1913		151	.218	.270	518	113	12	6	1	0.2	32	43	29	68	17	0	0	347	494	52	63	5.9	.942	SS-148, 2B-3
1914	BAL F	145	.245	.323	486	119	23	6	1	0.2	58	53	40		30	0	0	305	476	42	55	5.7	.949	SS-145
1915	2 teams	BAL F	(119G – .186)		CHI F	(24G – .267)																		
"	total	143	.200	.273	490	98	14	8	2	0.4	50	30	26		15	0	0	349	481	52	72	6.2	.941	SS-143
1916	2 teams	CHI N	(28G – .214)		NY N	(18G – .235)																		
"	total	46	.223	.322	121	27	5	2	1	0.8	8	8	10	11	1	3	0	78	123	14	14	4.7	.935	SS-40, 2B-2
1918	BKN N	92	.179	.218	308	55	8	2	0	0.0	14	18	22	24	8	0	0	230	283	17	37	5.8	.968	2B-91
13 yrs.		1728	.230	.306	5977	1376	244	81	15	0.3	513	554	370	283	173	5	0	3818	5585	589	674	5.8	.941	SS-1625, 2B-96

Jack Dooms

DOOMS, HENRY E. (Harry)
B. Jan. 30, 1867, St. Louis, Mo. D. Dec. 14, 1899, St. Louis, Mo.

Year	Team	Games	BA	SA	AB	H	2B	3B	HR	HR%	R	RBI	BB	SO	SB	Pinch Hit AB	H	PO	A	E	DP	TC/G	FA	G by Pos

Jack Dooms *continued*

Year	Team	Games	BA	SA	AB	H	2B	3B	HR	HR%	R	RBI	BB	SO	SB	AB	H	PO	A	E	DP	TC/G	FA	G by Pos
1892	LOU N	1	.000	.000	4	0	0	0	0	0.0	0	0	1	3	0	0	0	0	0	1	0	1.0	–	OF-1

Bill Doran

DORAN, WILLIAM DONALD
B. May 28, 1958, Cincinnati, Ohio   BB TR 5'11" 175 lbs.

Year	Team	Games	BA	SA	AB	H	2B	3B	HR	HR%	R	RBI	BB	SO	SB	AB	H	PO	A	E	DP	TC/G	FA	G by Pos
1982	HOU N	26	.278	.309	97	27	3	0	0	0.0	11	6	4	11	5	0	0	41	78	3	17	4.7	.975	2B-26
1983		154	.271	.364	535	145	12	7	8	1.5	70	39	86	67	12	3	1	347	461	17	109	5.4	.979	2B-153
1984		147	.261	.356	548	143	18	11	4	0.7	92	41	66	69	21	2	0	274	440	12	90	4.9	.983	2B-139, SS-13
1985		148	.287	.434	578	166	31	6	14	2.4	84	59	71	69	23	2	1	345	440	16	108	5.4	.980	2B-147
1986		145	.276	.373	550	152	29	3	6	1.1	92	37	81	57	42	1	0	262	329	16	62	4.2	.974	2B-144
1987		162	.283	.406	625	177	23	3	16	2.6	82	79	82	64	31	0	0	300	432	7	70	4.6	.991	2B-162, SS-3
1988		132	.248	.333	480	119	18	1	7	1.5	66	53	65	60	17	2	1	260	371	8	73	4.8	.987	2B-130
1989		142	.219	.323	507	111	25	2	8	1.6	65	58	59	63	22	8	0	254	345	12	64	4.3	.980	2B-138
8 yrs.		1056	.265	.371	3920	1040	159	33	63	1.6	562	372	514	460	173	18	3	2083	2896	91	593	4.8	.982	2B-1039, SS-16

LEAGUE CHAMPIONSHIP SERIES

Year	Team	Games	BA	SA	AB	H	2B	3B	HR	HR%	R	RBI	BB	SO	SB	AB	H	PO	A	E	DP	TC/G	FA	G by Pos
1986	HOU N	6	.222	.333	27	6	0	0	1	3.7	3	3	2	2	2	0	0	10	17	0	1	4.5	1.000	2B-6

Bill Doran

DORAN, WILLIAM JAMES
B. June 14, 1900, San Francisco, Calif.   D. Mar. 9, 1978, Santa Monica, Calif.   BL TR 5'11½" 175 lbs.

Year	Team	Games	BA	SA	AB	H	2B	3B	HR	HR%	R	RBI	BB	SO	SB	AB	H	PO	A	E	DP	TC/G	FA	G by Pos
1922	CLE A	3	.500	.500	2	1	0	0	0	0.0	0	0	1	0	0	0	0	0	0	0	0	0.0	–	3B-2

Tom Doran

DORAN, THOMAS J.
B. Dec. 2, 1880, Westchester, N. Y.   D. June 22, 1910, New York, N. Y.   BL TR 5'11" 152 lbs.

Year	Team	Games	BA	SA	AB	H	2B	3B	HR	HR%	R	RBI	BB	SO	SB	AB	H	PO	A	E	DP	TC/G	FA	G by Pos
1904	BOS A	12	.125	.188	32	4	0	1	0	0.0	1	0	1		1	1	0	39	5	5	1	4.1	.898	C-11
1905	2 teams				BOS A (2G – .000)				DET A (34G – .160)															
"	total	36	.156	.188	96	15	3	0	0	0.0	8	4	8		2	3	1	125	34	6	0	4.6	.964	C-33
1906	BOS A	2	.000	.000	3	0	0	0	0	0.0	1	0	0		0	0	0	3	1	0	0	2.0	1.000	C-2
3 yrs.		50	.145	.183	131	19	3	1	0	0.0	10	4	12		3	4	1	167	40	11	1	4.4	.950	C-46

Jerry Dorgan

DORGAN, JEREMIAH F.
Brother of Mike Dorgan.
B. 1856, Meriden, Conn.   D. June 10, 1891, New Haven, Conn.   BL TR

Year	Team	Games	BA	SA	AB	H	2B	3B	HR	HR%	R	RBI	BB	SO	SB	AB	H	PO	A	E	DP	TC/G	FA	G by Pos
1880	WOR N	10	.200	.229	35	7	1	0	0	0.0	2	1	0	1		0	0	16	2	4	0	2.2	.818	OF-9, C-1
1882	PHI AA	44	.282	.343	181	51	9	1	0	0.0	25		4			0	0	159	30	30	1	5.0	.863	C-25, OF-22, 3B-1
1884	2 teams				IND AA (34G – .298)				BKN AA (4G – .308)															
"	total	38	.299	.351	154	46	6	0	0	0.0	24		2			0	0	82	23	16	1	3.2	.868	OF-29, C-9
1885	DET N	39	.286	.348	161	46	6	2	0	0.0	23	24	8	10		0	0	55	5	10	2	1.8	.857	OF-39
4 yrs.		131	.282	.339	531	150	22	4	0	0.0	74	25	14	11		0	0	312	60	60	4	3.3	.861	OF-99, C-35, 3B-1

Mike Dorgan

DORGAN, MICHAEL CORNELIUS
Brother of Jerry Dorgan.
B. Oct. 2, 1853, Middletown, Conn.   D. Apr. 26, 1909, Syracuse, N. Y.
Manager 1879-81.   BR TR 5'9" 180 lbs.

Year	Team	Games	BA	SA	AB	H	2B	3B	HR	HR%	R	RBI	BB	SO	SB	AB	H	PO	A	E	DP	TC/G	FA	G by Pos
1877	STL N	60	.308	.395	266	82	9	7	0	0.0	45	23	9	13		0	0	118	21	29	3	2.8	.827	OF-50, C-12, 3B-2, SS-1, 2B-1
1879	SYR N	59	.267	.356	270	72	11	5	1	0.4	38	17	4	13		0	0	275	60	46	10	6.5	.879	1B-21, OF-16, 3B-11, SS-6, C-4, P-2, 2B-1
1880	PRO N	79	.246	.283	321	79	10	1	0	0.0	45	31	10	18		0	0	98	28	24	4	1.9	.840	OF-77, 3B-2, P-1
1881	2 teams				WOR N (51G – .277)				DET N (8G – .235)															
"	total	59	.272	.295	254	69	6	0	0	0.0	41	23	9	4		0	0	367	25	26	13	7.1	.938	OF-28, 1B-27, SS-2, 3B-2
1883	NY N	64	.234	.299	261	61	11	3	0	0.0	32		2	23		0	0	108	11	22	1	2.2	.844	OF-59, C-6, P-1
1884		83	.276	.352	341	94	11	6	1	0.3	61		13	27		0	0	153	52	49	4	3.1	.807	OF-64, P-14, C-6, 2B-3
1885		89	.326	.421	347	113	17	8	0	0.0	60		11	24		0	0	153	11	16	6	2.0	.807	OF-88, 1B-3
1886		118	.292	.369	442	129	19	3	3	0.7	61	79	29	37		0	0	174	14	22	5	1.8	.895	OF-116, 1B-3
1887		71	.258	.293	283	73	10	0	0	0.0	41	34	15	20	22	0	0	140	6	20	1	2.3	.880	OF-69, 1B-2
1890	SYR AA	33	.216	.273	139	30	8	0	0	0.0	19		16		8	0	0	40	5	5	1	1.5	.900	OF-33
10 yrs.		715	.274	.340	2924	802	112	33	5	0.2	443	207	118	179	30	0	0	1626	233	259	48	3.0	.878	OF-600, 1B-54, C-28, P-18, 3B-17, SS-9, 2B-5

Charlie Dorman

DORMAN, CHARLES WILLIAM
B. Apr. 23, 1898, San Francisco, Calif.   D. Nov. 15, 1928, San Francisco, Calif.   BR TR 6'2" 185 lbs.

Year	Team	Games	BA	SA	AB	H	2B	3B	HR	HR%	R	RBI	BB	SO	SB	AB	H	PO	A	E	DP	TC/G	FA	G by Pos
1923	CHI A	1	.500	.500	2	1	0	0	0	0.0	0	0	0	0	0	0	0	1	1	0	0	2.0	1.000	C-1

Red Dorman

DORMAN, DWIGHT DEXTER
B. Oct. 3, 1905, Jacksonville, Ill.   D. July 7, 1974, Anaheim, Calif.   BR TR 5'10½" 180 lbs.

Year	Team	Games	BA	SA	AB	H	2B	3B	HR	HR%	R	RBI	BB	SO	SB	AB	H	PO	A	E	DP	TC/G	FA	G by Pos
1928	CLE A	25	.364	.442	77	28	6	0	0	0.0	12	11	9	6	1	1	1	53	1	5	1	2.4	.915	OF-24

Brian Dorsett

DORSETT, BRIAN RICHARD
B. Apr. 9, 1961, Terre Haute, Ind.   BR TR 6'3" 215 lbs.

Year	Team	Games	BA	SA	AB	H	2B	3B	HR	HR%	R	RBI	BB	SO	SB	AB	H	PO	A	E	DP	TC/G	FA	G by Pos
1987	CLE A	5	.273	.545	11	3	0	0	1	9.1	2	3	0	3	0	2	1	12	0	0	0	2.4	1.000	C-4
1988	CAL A	7	.091	.091	11	1	0	0	0	0.0	0	2	1	5	0	0	0	19	3	0	1	3.1	1.000	C-7
1989	NY A	8	.364	.409	22	8	1	0	0	0.0	3	4	1	3	0	0	0	29	3	0	1	4.0	1.000	C-8
3 yrs.		20	.273	.364	44	12	1	0	1	2.3	5	9	2	11	0	2	1	60	6	0	2	3.3	1.000	C-19

Jerry Dorsey

DORSEY, JEREMIAH
B. 1885, Oakland, Calif.   BL TL 5'11" 175 lbs.

Year	Team	Games	BA	SA	AB	H	2B	3B	HR	HR%	R	RBI	BB	SO	SB	AB	H	PO	A	E	DP	TC/G	FA	G by Pos
1911	PIT N	2	.000	.000	6	0	0	0	0	0.0	0	0	0	1	0	0	0	4	0	0	0	2.0	1.000	OF-1

Herm Doscher

DOSCHER, JOHN HENRY, SR.
Father of Jack Doscher.
B. Dec. 20, 1852, New York, N. Y.   D. Mar. 20, 1934, Buffalo, N. Y.
BR TR 5'10" 182 lbs.

Year	Team	Games	BA	SA	AB	H	2B	3B	HR	HR%	R	RBI	BB	SO	SB	Pinch Hit AB	Pinch Hit H	PO	A	E	DP	TC/G	FA	G by Pos
1879	2 teams	TRO N (47G – .220)			CHI N (3G – .182)																			
"	total	50	.218	.257	202	44	8	0	0	0.0	17	19	2	13				51	101	38	7	3.8	.800	3B-50
1881	CLE N	5	.211	.211	19	4	0	0	0	0.0	2	0	0	2				7	10	2	1	3.8	.895	3B-5
1882		25	.240	.260	104	25	2	0	0	0.0	7	10	0	11				38	45	13	3	3.8	.865	3B-22, OF-2, SS-1
3 yrs.		80	.225	.255	325	73	10	0	0	0.0	26	29	2	26				96	156	53	11	3.8	.826	3B-77, OF-2, SS-1

Dutch Dotterer

DOTTERER, HENRY JOHN
B. Nov. 11, 1931, Syracuse, N. Y.
BR TR 6' 209 lbs.

Year	Team	Games	BA	SA	AB	H	2B	3B	HR	HR%	R	RBI	BB	SO	SB	Pinch Hit AB	Pinch Hit H	PO	A	E	DP	TC/G	FA	G by Pos
1957	CIN N	4	.083	.083	12	1	0	0	0	0.0	0	2	1	2	0	1	0	17	0	0	0	4.3	1.000	C-4
1958		11	.250	.393	28	7	1	0	1	3.6	1	2	2	4	0	3	0	48	4	1	2	4.8	.981	C-8
1959		52	.267	.348	161	43	7	0	2	1.2	21	17	16	23	0	1	0	230	20	2	3	4.8	.992	C-51
1960		33	.228	.367	79	18	5	0	2	2.5	4	11	13	10	0	3	1	122	15	3	1	4.2	.979	C-31
1961	WAS A	7	.263	.368	19	5	2	0	0	0.0	1	1	3	5	0	0	0	26	8	0	0	4.9	1.000	C-7
5 yrs.		107	.247	.348	299	74	15	0	5	1.7	27	33	35	44	0	8	1	443	47	6	6	4.6	.988	C-101

Charlie Dougherty

DOUGHERTY, CHARLES WILLIAM
B. Feb. 7, 1862, Darlington, Wis.   D. Feb. 18, 1925, Milwaukee, Wis.

Year	Team	Games	BA	SA	AB	H	2B	3B	HR	HR%	R	RBI	BB	SO	SB	Pinch Hit AB	Pinch Hit H	PO	A	E	DP	TC/G	FA	G by Pos
1884	ALT U	23	.259	.318	85	22	5	0	0	0.0	6		2			0	0	61	47	17	2	5.4	.864	2B-16, OF-8, SS-1

Patsy Dougherty

DOUGHERTY, PATRICK HENRY
B. Oct. 27, 1876, Andover, N. Y.   D. Apr. 30, 1940, Bolivar, N. Y.
BL TR 6'2" 190 lbs.

Year	Team	Games	BA	SA	AB	H	2B	3B	HR	HR%	R	RBI	BB	SO	SB	Pinch Hit AB	Pinch Hit H	PO	A	E	DP	TC/G	FA	G by Pos
1902	BOS A	108	.342	.397	438	150	19	12	0	0.0	77	34	42		20	3	2	175	9	21	1	1.9	.898	OF-102, 3B-1
1903		139	.331	.424	590	195	19	12	4	0.7	108	59	33		35	0	0	259	16	14	3	2.1	.952	OF-139
1904	2 teams	BOS A (49G – .272)			NY A (106G – .283)																			
"	total	155	.280	.379	647	181	18	14	6	0.9	113	26	44		21	0	0	230	18	20	4	1.7	.925	OF-155
1905	NY A	116	.263	.335	418	110	9	6	3	0.7	56	29	28		17	5	1	173	11	21	2	1.8	.898	OF-108, 3B-1
1906	2 teams	NY A (12G – .192)			CHI A (75G – .233)																			
"	total	87	.226	.298	305	69	11	4	1	0.3	33	31	19		11	0	0	27	3	1	1	0.4	.968	OF-86
1907	CHI A	148	.270	.315	533	144	17	2	1	0.2	69	59	36		33	0	0	209	19	13	4	1.6	.946	OF-148
1908		138	.278	.326	482	134	11	6	0	0.0	68	45	58		47	9	2	173	7	10	1	1.4	.947	OF-138
1909		139	.285	.391	491	140	23	13	1	0.2	71	55	51		36	1	0	184	10	12	0	1.5	.942	OF-138
1910		127	.248	.300	443	110	8	6	1	0.2	45	43	41		22	3	1	158	9	14	2	1.4	.923	OF-121
1911		76	.289	.422	211	61	10	9	0	0.0	39	32	26		19	19	3	78	6	6	1	1.2	.933	OF-56
10 yrs.		1233	.284	.360	4558	1294	138	78	17	0.4	679	413	378		261	40	9	1666	108	132	19	1.5	.931	OF-1191, 3B-2

WORLD SERIES

Year	Team	Games	BA	SA	AB	H	2B	3B	HR	HR%	R	RBI	BB	SO	SB	Pinch Hit AB	Pinch Hit H	PO	A	E	DP	TC/G	FA	G by Pos
1903	BOS A	8	.235	.529	34	8	0	2	2	5.9	3	5	2			0	0	15	3	1	1	2.4	.947	OF-8
1906	CHI A	6	.100	.100	20	2	0	0	0	0.0	1	1	3		2	0	0	4	0	1	0	0.8	.800	OF-6
2 yrs.		14	.185	.370	54	10	0	2	2	3.7	4	6	5		2	0	0	19	3	2	1	1.7	.917	OF-14

John Douglas

DOUGLAS, JOHN FRANKLIN
B. Sept. 14, 1917, Thayer, W. Va.   D. Feb. 11, 1984, Miami, Fla.
BL TL 6'2½" 195 lbs.

Year	Team	Games	BA	SA	AB	H	2B	3B	HR	HR%	R	RBI	BB	SO	SB	Pinch Hit AB	Pinch Hit H	PO	A	E	DP	TC/G	FA	G by Pos
1945	BKN N	5	.000	.000	9	0	0	0	0	0.0	0	0	2	4	0	1	0	33	0	1	1	6.8	.971	1B-4

Astyanax Douglass

DOUGLASS, ASTYANAX SAUNDERS
B. Sept. 19, 1899, Covington, Tex.   D. Jan. 26, 1975, El Paso, Tex.
BL TR 6'1" 190 lbs.

Year	Team	Games	BA	SA	AB	H	2B	3B	HR	HR%	R	RBI	BB	SO	SB	Pinch Hit AB	Pinch Hit H	PO	A	E	DP	TC/G	FA	G by Pos
1921	CIN N	4	.143	.143	7	1	0	0	0	0.0	0	0	0	2		0	0	6	3	0	0	2.3	1.000	C-4
1925		7	.176	.176	17	3	0	0	0	0.0	1	1	1	3		0	0	10	6	2	0	2.6	.889	C-7
2 yrs.		11	.167	.167	24	4	0	0	0	0.0	2	1	1	4		0	0	16	9	2	0	2.5	.926	C-11

Klondike Douglass

DOUGLASS, WILLIAM BINGHAM
B. May 10, 1872, Boston, Pa.   D. Dec. 13, 1953, Bend, Ore.
BL TR 6' 200 lbs.

Year	Team	Games	BA	SA	AB	H	2B	3B	HR	HR%	R	RBI	BB	SO	SB	Pinch Hit AB	Pinch Hit H	PO	A	E	DP	TC/G	FA	G by Pos
1896	STL N	81	.264	.321	296	78	6	4	1	0.3	42	28	35	15	18	1	0	123	22	15	5	2.0	.906	OF-74, C-6, SS-2
1897		125	.329	.405	516	170	15	3	6	1.2	77	50	52		12	1	1	393	80	21	10	4.0	.957	C-61, OF-43, 1B-17, 3B-7, SS-1
1898	PHI N	146	.258	.326	582	150	26	4	0	0.3	105	48	55		18	0	0	1236	73	32	74	9.2	.976	1B-146
1899		77	.255	.320	275	70	6	6	0	0.0	26	27	10		7	1	0	207	83	9	8	3.9	.970	C-66, 3B-4, 1B-4, OF-1
1900		50	.300	.406	160	48	9	4	0	0.0	23	25	13		7	2	1	138	59	14	4	4.2	.934	C-47, 3B-2
1901		51	.324	.370	173	56	6	1	0	0.0	14	23	11		10	3	0	252	30	5	4	5.6	.983	C-41, 1B-6, OF-2
1902		109	.233	.277	408	95	12	3	0	0.0	37	37	23		6	1	0	802	65	19	28	8.1	.979	1B-69, C-29, OF-10
1903		105	.255	.297	377	96	5	4	1	0.3	43	36	28		6	1	0	902	51	19	41	9.2	.979	1B-105
1904		3	.300	.300	10	3	0	0	0	0.0	1	1	0		0	0	0	31	1	1	1	11.0	.970	1B-3
9 yrs.		747	.274	.336	2797	766	85	29	10	0.4	368	275	227	15	84	14	3	4084	464	131	175	6.3	.972	1B-342, C-250, OF-130, 3B-13, SS-3

Taylor Douthit

DOUTHIT, TAYLOR LEE
B. Apr. 22, 1901, Little Rock, Ark.   D. May 28, 1986, Fremont, Calif.
BR TR 5'11½" 175 lbs.

Year	Team	Games	BA	SA	AB	H	2B	3B	HR	HR%	R	RBI	BB	SO	SB	Pinch Hit AB	Pinch Hit H	PO	A	E	DP	TC/G	FA	G by Pos
1923	STL N	9	.185	.333	27	5	0	2	0	0.0	0	0	4		1	2	0	12	1	0	0	1.4	1.000	OF-7
1924		53	.277	.364	173	48	13	1	0	0.0	24	13	16	19	1	2	0	118	5	3	2	2.4	.976	OF-50
1925		30	.274	.384	73	20	3	1	1	1.4	13	8	2	6	4	1	0	50	3	1	1	1.7	.981	OF-21
1926		139	.308	.377	530	163	20	4	3	0.6	96	52	55	46	23	1	0	440	14	20	2	3.4	.958	OF-138
1927		130	.262	.377	488	128	29	6	5	1.0	81	50	52	45	6	4	2	396	8	15	4	3.2	.964	OF-125
1928		154	.295	.372	648	191	35	3	3	0.5	111	43	84	36	11	0	0	547	10	9	4	3.6	.984	OF-154
1929		150	.336	.471	613	206	42	7	9	1.5	128	62	79	49	8	0	0	442	8	12	1	3.1	.974	OF-150
1930		154	.303	.426	664	201	41	10	7	1.1	109	93	60	38	4	0	0	425	8	16	3	2.9	.964	OF-154
1931	2 teams	STL N (36G – .331)			CIN N (95G – .262)																			
"	total	131	.280	.337	507	142	20	3	1	0.2	63	45	53	33	5	0	0	391	6	8	3	3.1	.980	OF-131
1932	CIN N	96	.243	.285	333	81	12	1	1	0.3	28	25	31	29	3	0	0	251	6	4	2	2.7	.985	OF-88

Year	Team		Games	BA	SA	AB	H	2B	3B	HR	HR%	R	RBI	BB	SO	SB	Pinch Hit AB	H	PO	A	E	DP	TC/G	FA	G by Pos

Taylor Douthit *continued*

Year	Team		Games	BA	SA	AB	H	2B	3B	HR	HR%	R	RBI	BB	SO	SB	AB	H	PO	A	E	DP	TC/G	FA	G by Pos
1933	2 teams	CIN N (1G – .000)				CHI N (27G – .225)																			
"	total		28	.225	.296	71	16	5	0	0	0.0	9	5	11	7	2	1	0	37	3	3	0	1.5	.930	OF-18
11 yrs.			1074	.291	.384	4127	1201	220	38	29	0.7	665	396	443	312	67	20	7	3109	70	91	21	3.0	.972	OF-1036

WORLD SERIES

Year	Team		Games	BA	SA	AB	H	2B	3B	HR	HR%	R	RBI	BB	SO	SB	AB	H	PO	A	E	DP	TC/G	FA	G by Pos
1926	STL	N	4	.267	.400	15	4	2	0	0	0.0	3	1	3	1	0	0	0	4	2	0	0	1.5	1.000	OF-4
1928			3	.091	.091	11	1	0	0	0	0.0	1	0	1	1	0	0	0	6	1	0	0	2.3	1.000	OF-3
1930			6	.083	.208	24	2	0	0	1	4.2	1	2	0	2	0	0	0	14	0	0	0	2.3	1.000	OF-6
3 yrs.			13	.140	.240	50	7	2	0	1	2.0	5	3	4	5	0	0	0	24	3	0	0	2.1	1.000	OF-13

Clarence Dow

DOW, CLARENCE G.
B. Oct. 11, 1854, Charlestown, Mass.   D. Mar. 11, 1893, Somerville, Mass.

Year	Team		Games	BA	SA	AB	H	2B	3B	HR	HR%	R	RBI	BB	SO	SB	AB	H	PO	A	E	DP	TC/G	FA	G by Pos
1884	BOS	U	1	.333	.333	6	2	0	0	0	0.0	1		0			0	0	1	2	0	0	3.0	1.000	OF-1

John Dowd

DOWD, JOHN LEO
B. Jan. 3, 1891, S. Weymouth, Mass.   D. Jan. 31, 1981, Fort Lauderdale, Fla.
BR TR 5'8"   170 lbs.

Year	Team		Games	BA	SA	AB	H	2B	3B	HR	HR%	R	RBI	BB	SO	SB	AB	H	PO	A	E	DP	TC/G	FA	G by Pos
1912	NY	A	10	.194	.226	31	6	1	0	0	0.0	1	0	6			0	0	14	28	8	1	5.0	.840	SS-10

Snooks Dowd

DOWD, RAYMOND BERNARD
B. Dec. 20, 1897, Springfield, Mass.   D. Apr. 4, 1962, Northampton, Mass.
BR TR 5'8"   163 lbs.

Year	Team		Games	BA	SA	AB	H	2B	3B	HR	HR%	R	RBI	BB	SO	SB	AB	H	PO	A	E	DP	TC/G	FA	G by Pos
1919	2 teams	DET A (1G – .000)				PHI A (13G – .167)																			
"	total		14	.167	.167	18	3	0	0	0	0.0	4	6	0	5	2	1	0	4	11	2	2	1.2	.882	2B-3, SS-2, OF-1, 3B-1
1926	BKN	N	2	.000	.000	8	0	0	0	0	0.0	0	0	0	0	0	0	0	4	2	0	0	3.0	1.000	2B-2
2 yrs.			16	.115	.115	26	3	0	0	0	0.0	4	6	0	5	2	1	0	8	13	2	2	1.4	.913	2B-5, SS-2, OF-1, 3B-1

Tommy Dowd

DOWD, THOMAS JEFFERSON (Buttermilk Tommy)
B. Apr. 20, 1869, Holyoke, Mass.   D. July 2, 1933, Holyoke, Mass.
Manager 1896-97.
BR TR 5'8"   173 lbs.

Year	Team		Games	BA	SA	AB	H	2B	3B	HR	HR%	R	RBI	BB	SO	SB	AB	H	PO	A	E	DP	TC/G	FA	G by Pos
1891	2 teams	BOS AA (4G – .091)				WAS AA (112G – .259)																			
"	total		116	.255	.322	475	121	9	10	1	0.2	67	44	19	45	39	0	0	240	287	68	38	5.1	.886	2B-107, OF-9
1892	WAS	N	144	.243	.298	584	142	9	10	1	0.2	94	50	34	49	49	0	0	283	315	84	39	4.7	.877	2B-98, OF-23, 3B-18, SS-6
1893	STL	N	132	.282	.343	581	164	18	7	1	0.2	114	54	49	23	59	0	0	225	27	16	9	2.0	.940	OF-132, 2B-1
1894			123	.271	.355	524	142	16	8	4	0.8	92	62	54	33	31	0	0	219	33	20	6	2.2	.926	OF-117, 2B-7, 3B-1
1895			129	.323	.463	505	163	19	17	6	1.2	95	74	30	31	30	2	0	238	40	27	3	2.4	.911	OF-115, 3B-17, 2B-2
1896			126	.265	.369	521	138	17	11	5	1.0	93	46	42	19	40	0	0	293	224	43	24	4.4	.923	2B-78, OF-48
1897	2 teams	STL N (35G – .262)				PHI N (91G – .292)																			
"	total		126	.284	.345	536	152	23	5	0	0.0	93	52	25		41	0	0	237	80	32	8	2.8	.908	OF-103, 2B-24
1898	STL	N	139	.244	.297	586	143	17	7	0	0.0	70	32	30		16	0	0	231	39	25	6	2.1	.915	OF-129, 2B-11
1899	CLE	N	147	.278	.336	605	168	17	6	2	0.3	81	35	48		28	0	0	341	10	17	2	2.5	.954	OF-147
1901	BOS	A	138	.268	.337	594	159	18	7	3	0.5	104	52	38		33	0	0	302	12	20	3	2.4	.940	OF-137, 1B-2, 3B-1
10 yrs.			1320	.271	.345	5511	1492	163	88	23	0.4	903	501	369	200	366	2	0	2609	1067	352	138	3.1	.913	OF-960, 2B-328, 3B-37, SS-6, 1B-2

Ken Dowell

DOWELL, KENNETH ALLEN
B. Jan. 19, 1961, Sacramento, Calif.
BR TR 5'9"   160 lbs.

Year	Team		Games	BA	SA	AB	H	2B	3B	HR	HR%	R	RBI	BB	SO	SB	AB	H	PO	A	E	DP	TC/G	FA	G by Pos
1987	PHI	N	15	.128	.128	39	5	0	0	0	0.0	4	1	2	5	0	0	0	17	36	0	7	3.5	1.000	SS-15

Joe Dowie

DOWIE, JOSEPH E.
B. 1864, New Orleans, La.   D. Unknown.
5'8"   150 lbs.

Year	Team		Games	BA	SA	AB	H	2B	3B	HR	HR%	R	RBI	BB	SO	SB	AB	H	PO	A	E	DP	TC/G	FA	G by Pos
1889	BAL	AA	20	.227	.293	75	17	5	0	0	0.0	12	8	2	10	5	0	0	34	2	2	0	1.9	.947	OF-20

Red Downey

DOWNEY, ALEXANDER CUMMINGS
B. Feb. 6, 1889, Aurora, Ind.   D. July 10, 1949, Detroit, Mich.
BL TL 5'11"   174 lbs.

Year	Team		Games	BA	SA	AB	H	2B	3B	HR	HR%	R	RBI	BB	SO	SB	AB	H	PO	A	E	DP	TC/G	FA	G by Pos
1909	BKN	N	19	.256	.269	78	20	1	0	0	0.0	7	8	2		4	0	0	25	2	0	0	1.4	1.000	OF-19

Tom Downey

DOWNEY, THOMAS EDWARD
B. Jan. 1, 1884, Lewiston, Me.   D. Aug. 3, 1961, Passaic, N. J.
BR TR 6'   170 lbs.

Year	Team		Games	BA	SA	AB	H	2B	3B	HR	HR%	R	RBI	BB	SO	SB	AB	H	PO	A	E	DP	TC/G	FA	G by Pos
1909	CIN	N	119	.231	.288	416	96	9	6	1	0.2	39	32	32		16	0	0	260	363	62	54	5.8	.909	SS-119, C-1
1910			111	.270	.325	378	102	9	3	2	0.5	43	32	34	28	12	0	0	201	281	60	26	4.9	.889	SS-68, 3B-41
1911			111	.261	.344	360	94	16	7	0	0.0	50	36	44	38	10	4	0	218	299	53	28	5.1	.907	SS-93, 2B-6, 3B-5, 1B-2, OF-1
1912	2 teams	PHI N (54G – .292)				CHI N (13G – .182)																			
"	total		67	.280	.378	193	54	6	5	1	0.5	31	27	22	25	3	1	2	78	106	26	5	3.1	.876	3B-49, SS-8, 2B-1
1914	BUF	F	151	.218	.277	541	118	20	3	2	0.4	69	42	40		35	1	0	304	438	29	54	5.1	.962	2B-129, SS-16, 3B-5
1915			92	.199	.248	282	56	9	1	1	0.4	24	19	26		11	5	1	175	200	24	26	4.3	.940	2B-48, 3B-35, SS-2, 1B-1
6 yrs.			651	.240	.304	2170	520	69	25	7	0.3	256	188	198	91	87	17	3	1236	1687	254	193	4.9	.920	SS-306, 2B-184, 3B-135, 1B-3, OF-1, C-1

Brian Downing

DOWNING, BRIAN JAY
B. Oct. 9, 1950, Los Angeles, Calif.
BR TR 5'10"   170 lbs.

Year	Team		Games	BA	SA	AB	H	2B	3B	HR	HR%	R	RBI	BB	SO	SB	AB	H	PO	A	E	DP	TC/G	FA	G by Pos
1973	CHI	A	34	.178	.274	73	13	1	0	2	2.7	5	4	10	17	0	8	2	72	17	5	0	2.8	.947	OF-13, C-11, 3B-8
1974			108	.225	.375	293	66	12	1	10	3.4	41	39	51	72	0	5	0	337	30	2	5	3.4	.995	C-63, OF-39, DH-9
1975			138	.240	.324	420	101	12	1	7	1.7	58	41	76	75	13	0	0	730	84	8	5	6.0	.990	C-137, DH-1
1976			104	.256	.328	317	81	14	0	3	0.9	38	30	40	55	7	3	1	450	38	6	4	4.8	.988	C-93, DH-11
1977			69	.284	.402	169	48	4	2	4	2.4	28	25	34	21	3	3	1	325	28	6	5	5.2	.983	C-61, OF-3, DH-2
1978	CAL	A	133	.255	.342	412	105	15	0	7	1.7	42	46	52	47	3	3	1	681	82	5	6	5.8	.993	C-128, DH-2
1979			148	.326	.462	509	166	27	3	12	2.4	87	75	77	57	3	3	1	669	35	11	5	4.8	.985	C-129, OF-18
1980			30	.290	.419	93	27	6	0	2	2.2	5	25	12	12	0	2	0	69	6	0	0	2.5	1.000	C-16, DH-13
1981			93	.249	.379	317	79	14	0	9	2.8	47	41	46	35	1	2	0	237	18	2	2	2.8	.992	OF-56, C-37, DH-5
1982			158	.281	.482	623	175	37	2	28	4.5	109	84	86	58	2	0	0	321	9	0	0	2.1	1.000	OF-158

Year	Team	Games	BA	SA	AB	H	2B	3B	HR	HR%	R	RBI	BB	SO	SB	Pinch Hit AB	Pinch Hit H	PO	A	E	DP	TC/G	FA	G by Pos

Brian Downing *continued*

Year	Team	Games	BA	SA	AB	H	2B	3B	HR	HR%	R	RBI	BB	SO	SB	PH AB	PH H	PO	A	E	DP	TC/G	FA	G by Pos
1983		113	.246	.429	403	99	15	1	19	4.7	68	53	62	59	1	3	1	160	9	1	0	1.5	.994	OF-84, DH-26
1984		156	.275	.462	539	148	28	2	23	4.3	65	91	70	66	0	3	1	272	5	0	0	1.8	1.000	OF-131, DH-21
1985		150	.263	.427	520	137	23	1	20	3.8	80	85	78	60	5	7	0	244	5	2	0	1.7	.992	OF-121, DH-25
1986		152	.267	.452	513	137	27	4	20	3.9	90	95	90	84	4	8	0	267	5	3	0	1.8	.989	OF-138, DH-10
1987		155	.272	.487	567	154	29	3	29	5.1	110	77	106	85	5	4	0	47	2	0	0	0.3	1.000	DH-118, OF-34
1988		135	.242	.442	484	117	18	2	25	5.2	80	64	81	63	3	3	1	0	0	0	0	0.0	–	DH-132
1989		142	.283	.414	544	154	25	2	14	2.6	59	59	56	87	0	1	0	0	0	0	0	0.0	–	DH-141
17 yrs.		2018	.266	.421	6796	1807	307	24	234	3.4	1012	934	1027	953	48	59	9	4881	373	51	32	2.6	.990	OF-777, C-675, DH-534, 3B-8

LEAGUE CHAMPIONSHIP SERIES

Year	Team		Games	BA	SA	AB	H	2B	3B	HR	HR%	R	RBI	BB	SO	SB	PH AB	PH H	PO	A	E	DP	TC/G	FA	G by Pos
1979	CAL	A	4	.200	.200	15	3	0	0	0	0.0	1	1	1	1	0	0	0	27	0	0	2	6.8	1.000	C-4
1982			5	.158	.211	19	3	1	0	0	0.0	4	0	3	2	0	0	0	0	0	0	0	0.0	–	OF-5
1986			7	.222	.333	27	6	0	0	1	3.7	2	7	4	5	0	0	0	0	0	0	0	0.0	–	OF-7
3 yrs.			16	.197	.262	61	12	1	0	1	1.6	7	8	8	8	0	0	0	27	0	0	2	1.7	1.000	OF-12, C-4

Red Downs

DOWNS, JEROME WILLIS
B. Aug. 22, 1883, Neola, Iowa D. Oct. 19, 1939, Council Bluffs, Iowa   BR TR 5'11" 155 lbs.

Year	Team		Games	BA	SA	AB	H	2B	3B	HR	HR%	R	RBI	BB	SO	SB	PH AB	PH H	PO	A	E	DP	TC/G	FA	G by Pos
1907	DET	A	105	.219	.289	374	82	13	5	1	0.3	28	42	13		3	4	1	188	210	30	11	4.1	.930	2B-80, OF-20, SS-1, 3B-1
1908			84	.221	.287	289	64	10	3	1	0.3	29	35	5		2	1	0	181	266	36	25	5.8	.925	2B-82, 3B-1
1912	2 teams		52	BKN N (9G – .250)		CHI N (43G – .263)																			
"	total		52	.260	.386	127	33	7	3	1	0.8	11	17	10	22	8	11	2	49	96	15	12	3.1	.906	2B-25, SS-9, 3B-5
3 yrs.			241	.227	.304	790	179	30	11	3	0.4	68	94	28	22	13	16	3	418	572	81	48	4.4	.924	2B-187, OF-20, SS-10, 3B-7

WORLD SERIES

Year	Team		Games	BA	SA	AB	H	2B	3B	HR	HR%	R	RBI	BB	SO	SB	PH AB	PH H	PO	A	E	DP	TC/G	FA	G by Pos
1908	DET	A	2	.167	.333	6	1	1	0	0	0.0	1	1	1	2	0	0	0	2	8	1	1	5.5	.909	2B-2

Tom Dowse

DOWSE, THOMAS JOSEPH
B. Aug. 12, 1866, Ireland D. Dec. 14, 1946, Riverside, Calif.   BR TR 5'11" 175 lbs.

Year	Team		Games	BA	SA	AB	H	2B	3B	HR	HR%	R	RBI	BB	SO	SB	PH AB	PH H	PO	A	E	DP	TC/G	FA	G by Pos
1890	CLE	N	40	.208	.233	159	33	2	1	0	0.0	20	9	12	22	3	0	0	151	14	11	10	4.4	.938	OF-26, 1B-10, C-3, P-1
1891	COL	AA	55	.224	.259	201	45	7	0	0	0.0	24	22	13	22	2	0	0	258	52	29	6	6.2	.914	C-51, OF-5
1892	4 teams		65	LOU N (41G – .145)		CIN N (1G – .000)			PHI N (16G – .185)			WAS N (7G – .259)														
"	total		65	.165	.178	230	38	3	0	0	0.0	18	15	4	22	2	1	0	301	68	21	13	6.0	.946	C-48, 1B-11, OF-7, 2B-1
3 yrs.			160	.197	.220	590	116	12	1	0	0.0	62	46	29	66	7	1	0	710	134	61	29	5.7	.933	C-102, OF-38, 1B-21, 2B-1, P-1

Brian Doyle

DOYLE, BRIAN REED
Brother of Denny Doyle.
B. Jan. 26, 1955, Glasgow, Ky.   BL TR 5'10" 160 lbs.

Year	Team		Games	BA	SA	AB	H	2B	3B	HR	HR%	R	RBI	BB	SO	SB	PH AB	PH H	PO	A	E	DP	TC/G	FA	G by Pos
1978	NY	A	39	.192	.192	52	10	0	0	0	0.0	6	0	0	3	0	0	0	39	65	1	14	2.7	.990	2B-29, SS-7, 3B-5
1979			20	.125	.188	32	4	2	0	0	0.0	2	5	3	1	0	0	0	12	27	2	5	2.1	.951	2B-13, 3B-6
1980			34	.173	.227	75	13	1	0	1	1.3	8	5	6	7	1	1	0	40	77	5	14	3.6	.959	2B-20, SS-12, 3B-2
1981	OAK	A	17	.125	.125	40	5	0	0	0	0.0	2	3	1	2	0	0	0	29	39	0	6	4.0	1.000	2B-17
4 yrs.			110	.161	.191	199	32	3	0	1	0.5	18	13	10	13	1	1	0	120	208	8	39	3.1	.976	2B-79, SS-19, 3B-13

LEAGUE CHAMPIONSHIP SERIES

Year	Team		Games	BA	SA	AB	H	2B	3B	HR	HR%	R	RBI	BB	SO	SB	PH AB	PH H	PO	A	E	DP	TC/G	FA	G by Pos
1978	NY	A	3	.286	.286	7	2	0	0	0	0.0	0	1	1	1	0	0	0	3	6	0	0	3.0	1.000	2B-3

WORLD SERIES

Year	Team		Games	BA	SA	AB	H	2B	3B	HR	HR%	R	RBI	BB	SO	SB	PH AB	PH H	PO	A	E	DP	TC/G	FA	G by Pos
1978	NY	A	6	.438	.500	16	7	1	0	0	0.0	4	2	0	0	0	0	0	16	7	0	6	3.8	1.000	2B-6

Conny Doyle

DOYLE, CORNELIUS J.
B. 1858, Holyoke, Mass. D. Jan. 18, 1927, East Orange, N. J.   5'10" 185 lbs.

Year	Team		Games	BA	SA	AB	H	2B	3B	HR	HR%	R	RBI	BB	SO	SB	PH AB	PH H	PO	A	E	DP	TC/G	FA	G by Pos
1883	PHI	N	16	.221	.324	68	15	3	2	0	0.0	3		0	15				23	3	7	0	2.1	.788	OF-16

Danny Doyle

DOYLE, HOWARD JAMES
B. Jan. 24, 1917, McLoud, Okla.   BR TR 6'1" 195 lbs.

Year	Team		Games	BA	SA	AB	H	2B	3B	HR	HR%	R	RBI	BB	SO	SB	PH AB	PH H	PO	A	E	DP	TC/G	FA	G by Pos
1943	BOS	A	13	.209	.233	43	9	1	0	0	0.0	2	6	7	9	0	0	0	46	8	2	0	4.3	.964	C-13

Denny Doyle

DOYLE, ROBERT DENNIS
Brother of Brian Doyle.
B. Jan. 17, 1944, Glasgow, Ky.   BL TR 5'9" 175 lbs.

Year	Team		Games	BA	SA	AB	H	2B	3B	HR	HR%	R	RBI	BB	SO	SB	PH AB	PH H	PO	A	E	DP	TC/G	FA	G by Pos
1970	PHI	N	112	.208	.281	413	86	10	7	2	0.5	43	16	33	64	6	7	0	251	228	11	55	4.4	.978	2B-103
1971			95	.231	.298	342	79	11	1	3	0.9	34	24	19	31	4	3	0	241	264	17	62	5.5	.967	2B-91
1972			123	.249	.296	442	110	14	2	1	0.2	33	26	31	33	6	1	0	265	288	10	66	4.6	.982	2B-119
1973			116	.273	.338	370	101	9	3	1	0.2	45	26	31	32	1	6	1	231	296	14	71	4.7	.974	2B-114
1974	CAL	A	147	.260	.311	511	133	19	2	1	0.2	47	34	25	49	6	1	1	311	405	12	99	5.0	.984	2B-146, SS-2
1975	2 teams		97	CAL A (8G – .067)		BOS A (89G – .310)																				
"	total		97	.298	.412	325	97	21	2	4	1.2	50	36	15	12	5	5	1	17	73	3	4	0.4	.927	2B-90, 3B-7, SS-2
1976	BOS	A	117	.250	.308	432	108	15	5	0	0.0	51	26	22	39	8	8	2	209	311	12	67	4.5	.977	2B-113
1977			137	.240	.308	455	109	13	6	2	0.4	54	49	29	50	2	5	0	230	412	14	90	4.8	.979	2B-137
8 yrs.			944	.250	.316	3290	823	113	28	16	0.5	357	237	205	310	38	36	5	1755	2225	93	514	4.3	.977	2B-913, 3B-7, SS-4

LEAGUE CHAMPIONSHIP SERIES

Year	Team		Games	BA	SA	AB	H	2B	3B	HR	HR%	R	RBI	BB	SO	SB	PH AB	PH H	PO	A	E	DP	TC/G	FA	G by Pos
1975	BOS	A	3	.273	.273	11	3	0	0	0	0.0	3	1	0	1	0	0	0	5	8	1	2	4.7	.929	2B-3

WORLD SERIES

Year	Team		Games	BA	SA	AB	H	2B	3B	HR	HR%	R	RBI	BB	SO	SB	PH AB	PH H	PO	A	E	DP	TC/G	FA	G by Pos
1975	BOS	A	7	.267	.367	30	8	1	1	0	0.0	3	0	2	1	0	0	0	13	23	3	2	5.6	.923	2B-7

Jack Doyle

DOYLE, JOHN JOSEPH (Dirty Jack)
B. Oct. 25, 1869, Killorglin, Ireland D. Dec. 31, 1958, Holyoke, Mass.   BR TR 5'9" 155 lbs.
Manager 1895, 1898.

Year	Team		Games	BA	SA	AB	H	2B	3B	HR	HR%	R	RBI	BB	SO	SB	Pinch Hit AB	Pinch Hit H	PO	A	E	DP	TC/G	FA	G by Pos

Jack Doyle *continued*

Year	Team		Games	BA	SA	AB	H	2B	3B	HR	HR%	R	RBI	BB	SO	SB	PH AB	PH H	PO	A	E	DP	TC/G	FA	G by Pos
1889	COL	AA	11	.278	.361	36	10	1	1	0	0.0	6	3	6	6	9	0	0	34	12	5	1	4.6	.902	C-7, OF-3, 2B-2
1890			77	.268	.393	298	80	17	7	2	0.7	47		13		27	0	0	231	153	54	14	5.7	.877	C-38, SS-25, OF-9, 2B-6, 3B-3
1891	CLE	N	69	.276	.364	250	69	14	4	0	0.0	43	43	26	44	24	0	0	178	73	38	5	4.2	.869	C-29, OF-21, 3B-20, SS-1
1892	2 teams			CLE	N (24G – .295)		NY	N	(90G – .298)																
"	total		114	.297	.403	454	135	26	2	6	1.3	78	69	24	40	47	1	1	297	169	72	16	4.7	.866	C-35, 2B-31, OF-29, 3B-13, SS-8, 1B-1
1893	NY	N	82	.321	.415	318	102	17	5	1	0.3	56	51	27	12	40	0	0	266	89	34	13	4.7	.913	C-48, OF-29, SS-4, 3B-3, 1B-1
1894			105	.369	.499	425	157	30	8	3	0.7	94	100	35	3	42	0	0	1004	66	42	51	10.6	.962	1B-99, C-6
1895			82	.313	.408	319	100	21	3	1	0.3	52	66	24	12	35	2	1	654	96	39	31	9.6	.951	1B-58, 2B-13, 3B-6, C-4
1896	BAL	N	118	.339	.421	487	165	29	4	1	0.2	116	101	42	15	73	0	0	1173	42	33	85	10.6	.974	1B-118, 2B-1
1897			114	.354	.441	460	163	29	4	1	0.2	93	87	29		62	0	0	1105	75	25	72	10.6	.979	1B-114
1898	2 teams			WAS	N (43G – .305)		NY	N	(82G – .283)																
"	total		125	.291	.367	474	138	17	5	3	0.6	68	69	19		23	1	1	642	105	35	40	6.3	.955	1B-62, OF-38, SS-15, 3B-5, 2B-5, C-2
1899	NY	N	118	.299	.384	448	134	15	7	3	0.7	55	76	33		35	1	0	1129	73	30	77	10.4	.976	1B-113, C-5
1900			133	.267	.325	505	135	24	1	1	0.2	69	66	34		34	0	0	1269	96	41	92	10.6	.971	1B-133
1901	CHI	N	75	.232	.277	285	66	9	2	1	0.4	21	39	7		8	0	0	698	60	21	32	10.4	.973	1B-75
1902	2 teams			NY	N (49G – .301)		WAS	A	(78G – .247)																
"	total		127	.267	.341	498	133	27	2	2	0.4	73	39	39		18	0	0	707	235	31	47	7.7	.968	2B-68, 1B-56, OF-4, C-1
1903	BKN	N	139	.313	.387	434	136	19	6	0	0.0	84	91	54		34	0	0	1418	83	29	74	10.6	.981	1B-139
1904	2 teams			BKN	N (8G – .227)		PHI	N	(66G – .220)																
"	total		74	.221	.298	258	57	11	3	1	0.4	22	24	25		5	0	0	668	62	15	28	10.1	.980	1B-73, 2B-1
1905	NY	A	1	.000	.000	3	0	0	0	0	0.0	0		0		0	0	0	10	0	2	0	12.0	.833	1B-1
17 yrs.			1564	.299	.385	6042	1808	314	64	25	0.4	977	924	437	132	516	5	3	11483	1489	546	678	8.6	.960	1B-1043, C-175, OF-133, 2B-127, SS-53, 3B-50

Jeff Doyle

DOYLE, JEFFREY DONALD
B. Oct. 2, 1956, Havre, Mont.

BB TR 5'8" 160 lbs.

1983	STL	N	13	.297	.432	37	11	1	2	0	0.0	4	2	1	3	0	1	0	29	28	2	11	4.5	.966	2B-12

Jim Doyle

DOYLE, JAMES FRANCIS
B. Dec. 25, 1881, Detroit, Mich. D. Feb. 1, 1912, Syracuse, N. Y.

BR TR 5'10" 168 lbs.

1910	CIN	N	7	.154	.308	13	2	2	0	0	0.0	1	1	0	2	0	1	0	5	2	1	0	1.1	.875	3B-3, OF-1
1911	CHI	N	130	.282	.413	472	133	23	12	5	1.1	69	62	40	54	19	3	1	134	278	35	25	3.4	.922	3B-127
2 yrs.			137	.278	.410	485	135	25	12	5	1.0	70	63	40	56	19	4	1	139	280	36	25	3.3	.921	3B-130, OF-1

John Doyle

DOYLE, JOHN ALOYSIUS
B. 1858, Nova Scotia, Canada D. Dec. 24, 1915, Providence, R. I.

1884	PIT	AA	15	.293	.414	58	17	3	2	0	0.0	8		2		0	0	0	17	5	4	0	1.7	.846	OF-14, SS-1

Larry Doyle

DOYLE, LAWRENCE JOSEPH (Laughing Larry)
B. July 31, 1886, Caseyville, Ill. D. Mar. 1, 1974, Saranac Lake, N. Y.

BL TR 5'10" 165 lbs.

1907	NY	N	69	.260	.273	227	59	3	0	0	0.0	16	16	20		3	0	0	128	158	26	7	4.5	.917	2B-69
1908			104	.308	.398	377	116	19	9	0	0.0	65	33	22		17	3	1	180	291	33	28	4.8	.935	2B-102
1909			146	.302	.419	570	172	27	11	6	1.1	86	49	45		30	3	2	292	322	39	51	4.5	.940	2B-143
1910			151	.285	.412	575	164	21	14	8	1.4	97	69	71	26	39	0	0	313	388	53	62	5.0	.930	2B-151
1911			143	.310	.527	526	163	25	25	13	2.5	102	77	71	39	38	2	1	272	340	36	46	4.5	.944	2B-141
1912			143	.330	.471	558	184	33	8	10	1.8	98	90	56	20	36	0	0	313	379	38	68	5.1	.948	2B-143
1913			132	.280	.388	482	135	25	6	5	1.0	67	73	59	29	38	2	1	315	345	31	55	5.2	.955	2B-130
1914			145	.260	.353	539	140	19	5	4	0.7	87	63	58	25	17	0	1	307	379	29	61	4.9	.959	2B-145
1915			150	**.320**	.442	591	**189**	**40**	10	4	0.7	86	70	32	28	22	3	0	313	396	40	66	5.0	.947	2B-150
1916	2 teams			NY	N (113G – .268)		CHI	N	(9G – .395)																
"	total		122	.278	.403	479	133	29	11	3	0.6	61	54	28	24	19	0	0	289	387	27	63	5.8	.962	2B-122
1917	CHI	N	135	.254	.353	476	121	19	5	6	1.3	48	61	48	28	5	7	3	300	348	33	54	5.0	.952	2B-128
1918	NY	N	75	.261	.354	257	67	7	4	3	1.2	38	36	37	10	10	2	2	121	221	11	24	4.7	.969	2B-73
1919			113	.289	.433	381	110	14	10	7	1.8	61	52	31	17	12	11	1	214	311	24	48	4.9	.956	2B-100
1920			137	.285	.363	471	134	21	2	4	0.8	48	50	47	28	11	4	0	278	389	23	61	5.0	.967	2B-133
14 yrs.			1765	.290	.408	6509	1887	299	123	74	1.1	960	793	625	274	297	37	9	3635	4654	443	694	4.9	.949	2B-1730

WORLD SERIES

1911	NY	N	6	.304	.522	23	7	3	1	0	0.0	3	1	2		1	0	0	13	15	1	2	4.8	.966	2B-6
1912			8	.242	.364	33	8	1	0	1	3.0	5	2	3	2	2	0	0	15	26	4	1	5.6	.911	2B-8
1913			5	.150	.150	20	3	0	0	0	0.0	1	2	1		1	0	0	13	19	3	1	7.0	.914	2B-5
3 yrs.			19	.237	.355	76	18	4	1	1	1.3	9	5	4		4	0	0	41	60	8	4	5.7	.927	2B-19

Delos Drake

DRAKE, DELOS DANIEL
B. Dec. 3, 1886, Girard, Ohio D. Oct. 3, 1965, Findlay, Ohio

BL TL 5'11½" 170 lbs.

1911	DET	A	91	.279	.375	315	88	9	9	1	0.3	37	36	17		20	9	3	155	5	11	1	1.9	.936	OF-83, 1B-2
1914	STL	F	138	.251	.335	514	129	18	8	3	0.6	51	42	31		20	7	1	353	21	13	14	2.8	.966	OF-116, 1B-18
1915			102	.265	.364	343	91	23	4	1	0.3	32	41	23		6	1	0	181	10	5	2	1.9	.974	OF-99, 1B-1
3 yrs.			331	.263	.354	1172	308	50	21	5	0.4	120	119	71		43	17	4	689	36	29	17	2.3	.962	OF-298, 1B-21

Larry Drake

DRAKE, LARRY FRANCIS
B. May 4, 1921, McKinney, Tex. D. July 14, 1985, Houston, Tex.

BL TR 6'1½" 195 lbs.

1945	PHI	A	1	.000	.000	2	0	0	0	0	0.0	0	0	2	0	0	2	0	3	0	0	0	2.0	1.000	OF-1
1948	WAS	A	4	.286	.286	7	2	0	0	0	0.0	0	1	3	1	0	3	1	2	0	0	0	0.8	1.000	OF-2
2 yrs.			5	.222	.222	9	2	0	0	0	0.0	0	1	5	1	0	5	1	5	0	0	0	1.0	1.000	OF-3

Lyman Drake

DRAKE, LYMAN C.
B. Ind.

Year Team	Games	BA	SA	AB	H	2B	3B	HR	HR%	R	RBI	BB	SO	SB	Pinch Hit AB	Pinch Hit H	PO	A	E	DP	TC/G	FA	G by Pos

Lyman Drake *continued*

Year Team	Games	BA	SA	AB	H	2B	3B	HR	HR%	R	RBI	BB	SO	SB	AB	H	PO	A	E	DP	TC/G	FA	G by Pos
1884 WAS AA	2	.286	.429	7	2	1	0	0	0.0	0		0			0	0	0	0	1	0	0.5	—	OF-2

Sammy Drake

DRAKE, SAMUEL HARRISON
Brother of Solly Drake.
B. Oct. 7, 1934, Little Rock, Ark.

BB TR 5'11" 175 lbs.

Year Team	Games	BA	SA	AB	H	2B	3B	HR	HR%	R	RBI	BB	SO	SB	AB	H	PO	A	E	DP	TC/G	FA	G by Pos
1960 CHI N	15	.067	.067	15	1	0	0	0	0.0	5	0	1	4	0	4	1	3	3	0	0	0.4	1.000	3B-6, 2B-2
1961	13	.000	.000	5	0	0	0	0	0.0	1	0	1	1	0	2	0	1	0	0	0	0.1	1.000	OF-1
1962 NY N	25	.192	.192	52	10	0	0	0	0.0	2	7	6	12	0	6	3	24	26	2	6	2.1	.962	2B-10, 3B-6
3 yrs.	53	.153	.153	72	11	0	0	0	0.0	8	7	8	17	0	12	4	28	29	2	6	1.1	.966	3B-12, 2B-12, OF-1

Solly Drake

DRAKE, SOLOMON LOUIS
Brother of Sammy Drake.
B. Oct. 23, 1930, Little Rock, Ark.

BB TR 6' 170 lbs.

Year Team	Games	BA	SA	AB	H	2B	3B	HR	HR%	R	RBI	BB	SO	SB	AB	H	PO	A	E	DP	TC/G	FA	G by Pos
1956 CHI N	65	.256	.335	215	55	9	1	2	0.9	29	15	23	35	9	8	3	142	3	1	1	2.2	.993	OF-53
1959 2 teams				LA N (9G – .250)							PHI N (67G – .145)												
" total	76	.157	.171	70	11	1	0	0	0.0	12	3	9	18	6	22	0	37	0	1	0	0.5	.974	OF-41
2 yrs.	141	.232	.295	285	66	10	1	2	0.7	41	18	32	53	15	30	3	179	3	2	1	1.3	.989	OF-94

Jake Drauby

DRAUBY, JACOB C.
B. 1865, Harrisburg, Pa. Deceased.

5'10" 163 lbs.

Year Team	Games	BA	SA	AB	H	2B	3B	HR	HR%	R	RBI	BB	SO	SB	AB	H	PO	A	E	DP	TC/G	FA	G by Pos
1892 WAS N	10	.206	.265	34	7	0	0	0	0.0	3	3	2	12	0	0	0	11	18	9	2	3.8	.763	3B-10

Bill Dreesen

DREESEN, WILLIAM RICHARD
B. July 26, 1904, New York, N. Y. D. Nov. 9, 1971, Mount Vernon, N. Y.

BL TR 5'7½" 160 lbs.

Year Team	Games	BA	SA	AB	H	2B	3B	HR	HR%	R	RBI	BB	SO	SB	AB	H	PO	A	E	DP	TC/G	FA	G by Pos
1931 BOS N	47	.222	.339	180	40	10	4	1	0.6	38	10	23	23	1	1	1	28	83	11	1	2.6	.910	3B-47

Bill Drescher

DRESCHER, WILLIAM CLAYTON (Dutch, Moose)
B. May 23, 1921, Congers, N. Y. D. May 15, 1968, Haverstraw, N. Y.

BL TR 6'2" 190 lbs.

Year Team	Games	BA	SA	AB	H	2B	3B	HR	HR%	R	RBI	BB	SO	SB	AB	H	PO	A	E	DP	TC/G	FA	G by Pos
1944 NY A	4	.143	.143	7	1	0	0	0	0.0	0	0	0	0	0	3	0	7	0	1	0	2.0	.875	C-1
1945	48	.270	.310	126	34	3	1	0	0.0	10	15	8	5	0	14	2	101	13	1	1	2.4	.991	C-33
1946	5	.333	.500	6	2	1	0	0	0.0	0	1	0	0	0	2	0	6	1	0	1	1.4	1.000	C-3
3 yrs.	57	.266	.309	139	37	4	1	0	0.0	10	16	8	5	0	19	2	114	14	2	2	2.3	.985	C-37

Chuck Dressen

DRESSEN, CHARLES WALTER
B. Sept. 20, 1898, Decatur, Ill. D. Aug. 10, 1966, Detroit, Mich.
Manager 1934-37, 1951-53, 1955-57, 1960-61, 1963-66.

BR TR 5'5½" 146 lbs.

Year Team	Games	BA	SA	AB	H	2B	3B	HR	HR%	R	RBI	BB	SO	SB	AB	H	PO	A	E	DP	TC/G	FA	G by Pos
1925 CIN N	76	.274	.372	215	59	8	2	3	1.4	35	19	12	4	5	10	0	54	109	8	9	2.3	.953	3B-47, 2B-5, OF-4
1926	127	.266	.395	474	126	27	11	4	0.8	76	48	49	31	0	0	0	111	284	15	19	3.2	.963	3B-123, OF-1, SS-1
1927	144	.292	.405	548	160	36	10	2	0.4	78	55	71	32	7	1	0	132	319	19	20	3.3	.960	3B-142, SS-2
1928	135	.291	.361	498	145	26	3	1	0.2	72	59	43	22	10	0	0	122	283	27	27	3.2	.938	3B-135
1929	110	.244	.322	401	98	23	3	1	0.2	49	36	41	21	8	5	0	86	191	17	11	2.7	.942	3B-98, 2B-8
1930	33	.211	.211	19	4	0	0	0	0.0	0	1	1	3	0	13	2	3	7	0	0	0.3	1.000	3B-10, 2B-3
1931	15	.067	.067	15	1	0	0	0	0.0	0	0	1	1	0	0	0	4	7	2	1	2.6	.846	3B-4
1933 NY N	16	.222	.311	45	10	4	0	0	0.0	3	3	1	4	0	0	0	14	21	1	2	2.3	.972	3B-16
8 yrs.	646	.272	.369	2215	603	123	29	11	0.5	313	221	219	118	30	29	2	526	1221	89	89	2.8	.952	3B-575, 2B-16, OF-5, SS-3

Lee Dressen

DRESSEN, LEE AUGUST
B. July 23, 1889, Ellinwood, Kans. D. June 30, 1931, Diller, Neb.

BL TL 6' 165 lbs.

Year Team	Games	BA	SA	AB	H	2B	3B	HR	HR%	R	RBI	BB	SO	SB	AB	H	PO	A	E	DP	TC/G	FA	G by Pos
1914 STL N	46	.233	.272	103	24	2	1	0	0.0	16	7	11	20	2	7	1	258	13	5	15	6.0	.982	1B-38
1918 DET A	31	.178	.224	107	19	1	2	0	0.0	10	3	21	10	2	1	0	322	11	4	12	10.9	.988	1B-30
2 yrs.	77	.205	.248	210	43	3	3	0	0.0	26	10	32	30	4	8	1	580	24	9	27	8.0	.985	1B-68

Cameron Drew

DREW, CAMERON STEWARD
B. Feb. 12, 1964, Boston, Mass.

BL TR 6'5" 230 lbs.

Year Team	Games	BA	SA	AB	H	2B	3B	HR	HR%	R	RBI	BB	SO	SB	AB	H	PO	A	E	DP	TC/G	FA	G by Pos
1988 HOU N	7	.188	.313	16	3	0	1	0	0.0	1	1	0	1	0	2	0	10	0	0	0	1.4	1.000	OF-5

Dave Drew

DREW, DAVID
Deceased.

Year Team	Games	BA	SA	AB	H	2B	3B	HR	HR%	R	RBI	BB	SO	SB	AB	H	PO	A	E	DP	TC/G	FA	G by Pos
1884 2 teams				PHI U (2G – .444)							WAS U (13G – .302)												
" total	15	.323	.403	62	20	1	2	0	0.0	9		1			0	0	62	30	12	4	6.9	.885	SS-9, 1B-5, OF-1, 2B-1, P-1

Frank Drews

DREWS, FRANK JOHN
B. May 25, 1916, Buffalo, N. Y. D. Apr. 22, 1972, Buffalo, N. Y.

BR TR 5'10" 175 lbs.

Year Team	Games	BA	SA	AB	H	2B	3B	HR	HR%	R	RBI	BB	SO	SB	AB	H	PO	A	E	DP	TC/G	FA	G by Pos
1944 BOS N	46	.206	.284	141	29	9	1	0	0.0	14	10	25	14	0	0	0	123	132	11	27	5.8	.959	2B-46
1945	49	.204	.245	147	30	4	1	0	0.0	13	19	16	18	0	0	0	98	141	6	27	5.0	.976	2B-48
2 yrs.	95	.205	.264	288	59	13	2	0	0.0	27	29	41	32	0	0	0	221	273	17	54	5.4	.967	2B-94

Dan Driessen

DRIESSEN, DANIEL
B. July 29, 1951, Hilton Head, S. C.

BL TR 5'11" 187 lbs.

Year Team	Games	BA	SA	AB	H	2B	3B	HR	HR%	R	RBI	BB	SO	SB	AB	H	PO	A	E	DP	TC/G	FA	G by Pos
1973 CIN N	102	.301	.385	366	110	15	2	4	1.1	49	47	24	37	8	7	3	160	157	12	30	3.2	.964	3B-87, 1B-35, OF-1
1974	150	.281	.400	470	132	23	6	7	1.5	63	56	48	62	10	14	5	186	206	26	37	2.8	.938	3B-126, 1B-47, OF-3
1975	88	.281	.429	210	59	8	1	7	3.3	38	38	35	30	10	21	6	309	20	5	34	3.8	.985	1B-41, OF-29
1976	98	.247	.402	219	54	11	1	7	3.2	32	44	43	32	14	34	6	314	23	2	33	3.5	.994	1B-40, OF-20
1977	151	.300	.468	536	161	31	4	17	3.2	75	91	64	85	31	6	1	1182	75	7	116	8.4	.994	1B-148
1978	153	.250	.397	524	131	23	3	16	3.1	68	70	75	79	28	5	0	1264	93	6	92	8.9	.996	1B-151
1979	150	.250	.414	515	129	24	3	18	3.5	72	75	62	77	11	7	1	1289	79	9	112	9.2	.993	1B-143
1980	154	.265	.418	524	139	36	3	14	2.7	81	74	93	68	19	1	0	1349	85	7	115	9.4	.995	1B-151

Year Team	Games	BA	SA	AB	H	2B	3B	HR	HR%	R	RBI	BB	SO	SB	Pinch Hit AB	Pinch Hit H	PO	A	E	DP	TC/G	FA	G by Pos

Dan Driessen *continued*

Year Team	Games	BA	SA	AB	H	2B	3B	HR	HR%	R	RBI	BB	SO	SB	PH AB	PH H	PO	A	E	DP	TC/G	FA	G by Pos
1981	82	.236	.386	233	55	14	0	7	3.0	35	33	40	31	2	5	1	558	30	3	54	7.2	.995	1B-74
1982	149	.269	.421	516	139	25	1	17	3.3	64	57	82	62	11	3	0	1239	78	3	123	8.9	.998	1B-144
1983	122	.277	.420	386	107	17	1	12	3.1	57	57	75	51	6	8	2	917	71	4	73	8.1	.996	1B-112
1984 2 teams		CIN N	(81G – .280)		MON N	(51G – .254)																	
" total	132	.269	.455	387	104	24	0	16	4.1	47	60	54	40	2	17	1	870	52	7	69	7.0	.992	1B-115
1985 2 teams		MON N	(91G – .250)		SF N	(54G – .232)																	
" total	145	.243	.351	493	120	26	0	9	1.8	53	47	50	51	2	7	0	1203	91	4	111	9.0	.997	1B-137
1986 2 teams		SF N	(15G – .188)		HOU N	(17G – .292)																	
" total	32	.250	.400	40	10	3	0	1	2.5	7	3	9	6	0	12	3	77	6	0	5	2.6	1.000	1B-16
1987 STL N	24	.233	.317	60	14	2	0	1	1.7	5	11	7	8	0	2	0	141	10	1	13	6.3	.993	1B-21
15 yrs.	1732	.267	.411	5479	1464	282	23	153	2.8	746	763	761	719	154	149	28	11058	1076	96	1017	7.1	.992	1B-1375, 3B-213, OF-53

LEAGUE CHAMPIONSHIP SERIES

Year Team	Games	BA	SA	AB	H	2B	3B	HR	HR%	R	RBI	BB	SO	SB	PH AB	PH H	PO	A	E	DP	TC/G	FA	G by Pos
1973 CIN N	4	.167	.250	12	2	1	0	0	0.0	0	1	0	2	0	0	0	3	2	1	0	1.5	.833	3B-4
1976	1	.000	.000	1	0	0	0	0	0.0	0	0	0	0	0	1	0	0	0	0	0	0.0	–	
1979	3	.083	.083	12	1	0	0	0	0.0	1	0	1	3	0	0	0	32	0	1	2	10.7	1.000	1B-3
1987 STL N	5	.250	.417	12	3	2	0	0	0.0	1	1	1	1	0	2	1	26	3	1	2	6.0	.967	1B-4
4 yrs.	13	.162	.243	37	6	3	0	0	0.0	2	2	2	6	0	3	1	61	5	2	4	5.2	.971	1B-7, 3B-4

WORLD SERIES

Year Team	Games	BA	SA	AB	H	2B	3B	HR	HR%	R	RBI	BB	SO	SB	PH AB	PH H	PO	A	E	DP	TC/G	FA	G by Pos
1975 CIN N	2	.000	.000	2	0	0	0	0	0.0	0	0	0	0	0	2	0	0	0	0	0	0.0	–	
1976	4	.357	.714	14	5	2	0	1	7.1	4	1	2	0	1	0	0	0	0	0	0	0.0	–	DH-4
1987 STL N	4	.231	.385	13	3	2	0	0	0.0	3	1	1	1	0	0	0	27	1	0	0	7.0	1.000	1B-4
3 yrs.	10	.276	.517	29	8	4	0	1	3.4	7	2	3	1	1	2	0	27	1	0	0	2.8	1.000	DH-4, 1B-4

Lew Drill

DRILL, LEWIS L   BR TR 5'6"   186 lbs.
B. May 9, 1877, Browerville, Minn.   D. July 4, 1969, St. Paul, Minn.

Year Team	Games	BA	SA	AB	H	2B	3B	HR	HR%	R	RBI	BB	SO	SB	PH AB	PH H	PO	A	E	DP	TC/G	FA	G by Pos
1902 2 teams		BAL A	(2G – .250)		WAS A	(71G – .262)																	
" total	73	.262	.354	229	60	10	4	1	0.4	35	29	26		5	4	0	204	66	26	5	4.1	.912	C-54, OF-8, 2B-5, 3B-1, 1B-1
1903 WAS A	51	.253	.351	154	39	9	3	0	0.0	11	23	15		4	1	0	226	48	9	9	5.5	.968	C-47, 1B-3
1904 2 teams		WAS A	(46G – .268)		DET A	(51G – .244)																	
" total	97	.255	.328	302	77	13	3	1	0.3	24	24	41		5	2	1	344	84	26	12	4.7	.943	C-78, OF-14, 1B-2
1905 DET A	71	.261	.303	211	55	9	0	0	0.0	17	24	32		7	1	0	345	73	13	10	6.1	.970	C-70
4 yrs.	292	.258	.333	896	231	41	10	2	0.2	87	100	114		21	8	1	1119	271	74	36	5.0	.949	C-249, OF-22, 1B-6, 2B-5, 3B-1

Denny Driscoll

DRISCOLL, JOHN F.   BL TL 5'10½"   160 lbs.
B. Nov. 19, 1855, Lowell, Mass.   D. July 11, 1886, Lowell, Mass.

Year Team	Games	BA	SA	AB	H	2B	3B	HR	HR%	R	RBI	BB	SO	SB	PH AB	PH H	PO	A	E	DP	TC/G	FA	G by Pos
1880 BUF N	18	.154	.169	65	10	1	0	0	0.0	1	4	1	7		0	0	18	10	4	2	1.8	.875	OF-14, P-6
1882 PIT AA	23	.138	.200	80	11	2	0	1	1.3	12		3			0	0	4	50	7	1	2.7	.885	P-23
1883	41	.182	.209	148	27	1	0	0	0.0	19		4			0	0	14	99	14	2	3.1	.890	P-41, OF-4, 3B-1
1884 LOU AA	13	.188	.208	48	9	1	0	0	0.0	5		2			0	0	3	37	9	2	3.8	.816	P-13, OF-2
1885 BUF N	7	.158	.158	19	3	0	0	0	0.0	2	0	2	5		0	0	12	11	9	1	4.6	.719	2B-7
5 yrs.	102	.167	.197	360	60	6	1	1	0.3	39	4	12	12		0	0	51	207	43	8	3.0	.857	P-83, OF-20, 2B-7, 3B-1

Jim Driscoll

DRISCOLL, JAMES BERNARD   BL TR 5'11"   175 lbs.
B. May 14, 1944, Medford, Mass.

Year Team	Games	BA	SA	AB	H	2B	3B	HR	HR%	R	RBI	BB	SO	SB	PH AB	PH H	PO	A	E	DP	TC/G	FA	G by Pos
1970 OAK A	21	.192	.250	52	10	0	0	1	1.9	2	2	2	15	0	5	2	30	29	6	8	3.1	.908	SS-7, 2B-7
1972 TEX A	15	.000	.000	18	0	0	0	0	0.0	0	0	2	3	0	11	0	6	8	1	2	1.0	.933	2B-4, 3B-2
2 yrs.	36	.143	.186	70	10	0	0	1	1.4	2	2	4	18	0	16	2	36	37	7	10	2.2	.913	2B-11, SS-7, 3B-2

Paddy Driscoll

DRISCOLL, JOHN LEO   BR TR 5'8½"   155 lbs.
B. Jan. 11, 1895, Evanston, Ill.   D. June 29, 1968, Chicago, Ill.

Year Team	Games	BA	SA	AB	H	2B	3B	HR	HR%	R	RBI	BB	SO	SB	PH AB	PH H	PO	A	E	DP	TC/G	FA	G by Pos
1917 CHI N	13	.107	.143	28	3	1	0	0	0.0	2	3	2	6	2	0	0	15	24	7	4	3.5	.848	2B-8, 3B-2, SS-1

Mike Drissel

DRISSEL, MICHAEL F.   BR TR 5'11"
B. Dec. 19, 1864, St. Louis, Mo.   D. Feb. 26, 1913, St. Louis, Mo.

Year Team	Games	BA	SA	AB	H	2B	3B	HR	HR%	R	RBI	BB	SO	SB	PH AB	PH H	PO	A	E	DP	TC/G	FA	G by Pos
1885 STL AA	6	.050	.050	20	1	0	0	0	0.0	0		0		0	0	0	23	10	1	1	5.7	.971	C-6

Walt Dropo

DROPO, WALTER (Moose)   BR TR 6'5"   220 lbs.
B. Jan. 30, 1923, Moosup, Conn.

Year Team	Games	BA	SA	AB	H	2B	3B	HR	HR%	R	RBI	BB	SO	SB	PH AB	PH H	PO	A	E	DP	TC/G	FA	G by Pos
1949 BOS A	11	.146	.195	41	6	2	0	0	0.0	3	3	7		0	0	0	103	4	0	13	9.7	1.000	1B-11
1950	136	.322	.583	559	180	28	8	34	6.1	101	**144**	45	75	0	2	0	1142	77	15	147	9.1	.988	1B-134
1951	99	.239	.369	360	86	14	0	11	3.1	37	57	38	52	0	7	2	878	63	12	91	9.6	.987	1B-93
1952 2 teams		BOS A	(37G – .265)		DET A	(115G – .279)																	
" total	152	.276	.477	591	163	24	4	29	4.9	69	97	37	85	2	2	0	1324	99	14	135	9.5	.990	1B-150
1953 DET A	152	.248	.371	606	150	30	3	13	2.1	61	96	29	69	2	2	1	1260	127	14	121	9.2	.990	1B-150
1954	107	.281	.375	320	90	14	0	4	1.3	27	44	24	41	0	18	5	681	54	3	60	6.9	.996	1B-95
1955 CHI A	141	.280	.448	453	127	15	2	19	4.2	55	79	42	71	1	2	1	1101	62	6	104	8.3	.995	1B-140
1956	125	.266	.374	361	96	13	1	8	2.2	42	52	37	51	1	10	2	855	50	6	95	7.3	.993	1B-117
1957	93	.256	.439	223	57	2	0	13	5.8	24	49	16	40	0	31	11	483	39	7	49	5.7	.987	1B-69
1958 2 teams		CHI A	(28G – .192)		CIN N	(63G – .290)																	
" total	91	.266	.449	214	57	8	2	9	4.2	21	39	17	42	0	31	7	398	35	0	39	4.8	1.000	1B-59
1959 2 teams		CIN N	(26G – .103)		BAL A	(62G – .278)																	
" total	88	.242	.405	190	46	10	0	7	3.7	21	23	16	27	0	11	1	489	31	4	54	6.0	.992	1B-77, 3B-2
1960 BAL A	79	.268	.380	179	48	8	0	4	2.2	16	21	20	19	0	14	2	397	27	3	50	5.4	.993	1B-67, 3B-1
1961	14	.259	.370	27	7	0	0	1	3.7	1	2	4	4	0	2	1	62	6	0	11	4.9	1.000	1B-8
13 yrs.	1288	.270	.432	4124	1113	168	22	152	3.7	478	704	328	582	5	132	33	9173	674	84	969	7.7	.992	1B-1174, 3B-3

Keith Drumright

DRUMRIGHT, KEITH ALAN   BL TR 5'10"   170 lbs.
B. Oct. 21, 1954, Springfield, Mo.

Year	Team		Games	BA	SA	AB	H	2B	3B	HR	HR%	R	RBI	BB	SO	SB	Pinch Hit AB	H	PO	A	E	DP	TC/G	FA	G by Pos

Keith Drumright *continued*

Year	Team		Games	BA	SA	AB	H	2B	3B	HR	HR%	R	RBI	BB	SO	SB	PH AB	H	PO	A	E	DP	TC/G	FA	G by Pos
1978	HOU	N	17	.164	.164	55	9	0	0	0	0.0	5	2	3	4	0	0	0	27	41	4	9	4.2	.944	2B-17
1981	OAK	A	31	.291	.326	86	25	1	1	0	0.0	8	11	4	4	0	7	2	38	50	1	7	2.9	.989	2B-19, DH-5
2 yrs.			48	.241	.262	141	34	1	1	0	0.0	13	13	7	8	0	7	2	65	91	5	16	3.4	.969	2B-36, DH-5

DIVISIONAL PLAYOFF SERIES

| 1981 | OAK | A | 1 | .250 | .250 | 4 | 1 | 0 | 0 | 0 | 0.0 | 0 | 0 | 0 | 0 | 0 | 0 | 0 | 0 | 0 | 0 | 0 | 0.0 | — | DH-1 |

LEAGUE CHAMPIONSHIP SERIES

| 1981 | OAK | A | 3 | .000 | .000 | 4 | 0 | 0 | 0 | 0 | 0.0 | 0 | 0 | 1 | 0 | 0 | 0 | 0 | 0 | 0 | 0 | 0 | 0.0 | — | DH-1 |

Jean Dubuc

DUBUC, JEAN JOSEPH OCTAVE (Chauncey)
Born Jean Baptiste Arthur Dubuc.
B. Sept. 15, 1888, St. Johnsbury, Vt.   D. Aug. 28, 1958, Ft. Myers, Fla.

BR TR 5'10½" 185 lbs.

1908	CIN	N	15	.138	.172	29	4	1	0	0	0.0	2	2			0	0	0	6	26	2	0	2.3	.941	P-15
1909			19	.167	.167	18	3	0	0	0	0.0	1	0	2		0	0	0	4	23	5	0	1.7	.844	P-19
1912	DET	A	40	.269	.389	108	29	6	2	1	0.9	16	9	3		0	1	0	12	94	4	5	2.8	.964	P-37, OF-2
1913			68	.267	.393	135	36	5	3	2	1.5	17	11	2	17	1	28	3	16	110	6	7	1.9	.955	P-36, OF-3
1914			70	.226	.331	124	28	8	1	1	0.8	9	11	7	11	1	32	6	14	83	6	3	1.5	.942	P-36
1915			60	.205	.241	112	23	2	1	0	0.0	7	14	8	15	0	17	5	9	86	3	2	1.6	.969	P-39
1916			52	.256	.308	78	20	2	0	0	0.0	3	7	7	12	0	12	2	7	73	4	5	1.6	.952	P-36
1918	BOS	A	5	.167	.167	6	1	0	0	0	0.0	0	0	1	2	0	2	0	0	8	0	0	0.8	1.000	P-2
1919	NY	N	36	.143	.214	42	6	1	1	0	0.0	2	6	0	6	0	1	0	8	46	2	1	1.6	.964	P-36
9 yrs.			365	.230	.314	652	150	23	10	4	0.6	57	56	30	63	2	93	16	78	543	32	23	1.8	.951	P-256, OF-5

WORLD SERIES

| 1918 | BOS | A | 1 | .000 | .000 | 1 | 0 | 0 | 0 | 0 | 0.0 | 0 | 0 | 0 | 1 | 0 | 1 | 0 | 0 | 0 | 0 | 0 | 0.0 | — | — |

Rob Ducey

DUCEY, ROBERT THOMAS
B. May 24, 1965, Toronto, Ontario, Canada

BL TR 6'2" 175 lbs.

1987	TOR	A	34	.188	.271	48	9	1	0	1	2.1	12	6	8	10	2	3	1	31	0	0	0	0.9	1.000	OF-28
1988			27	.315	.426	54	17	4	0	1	1.9	15	6	5	7	1	0	0	35	1	0	0	1.3	1.000	OF-26
1989			41	.211	.263	76	16	4	0	0	0.0	5	7	9	25	2	6	0	56	3	0	2	1.4	1.000	OF-35, DH-1
3 yrs.			102	.236	.315	178	42	9	1	2	0.6	32	19	22	42	5	9	1	122	4	0	2	1.2	1.000	OF-89, DH-1

Dud Dudley

Playing record listed under Dud Lee

John Dudra

DUDRA, JOHN JOSEPH
B. May 27, 1916, Assumption, Ill.   D. Oct. 24, 1965, Pana, Ill.

BR TR 5'11½" 175 lbs.

| 1941 | BOS | N | 14 | .360 | .560 | 25 | 9 | 3 | 1 | 0 | 0.0 | 3 | 3 | 3 | 4 | 0 | 1 | 0 | 20 | 13 | 1 | 5 | 2.4 | .971 | 3B-5, 2B-5, SS-1, 1B-1 |

Pat Duff

DUFF, PATRICK HENRY
B. May 6, 1875, Providence, R. I.   D. Sept. 11, 1925, Providence, R. I.

TR

| 1906 | WAS | A | 1 | .000 | .000 | 1 | 0 | 0 | 0 | 0 | 0.0 | 0 | 0 | 0 | | 0 | 0 | 0 | 0 | 0 | 0 | 0 | 0.0 | — | — |

Charlie Duffee

DUFFEE, CHARLES EDWARD (Home Run)
B. Jan. 27, 1866, Mobile, Ala.   D. Dec. 24, 1894, Mobile, Ala.

BR TR

1889	STL	AA	137	.244	.409	509	124	15	12	15	2.9	93	86	60	81	21	0	0	307	56	31	8	2.9	.921	OF-132, 3B-5, 2B-2
1890			98	.275	.365	378	104	11	7	3	0.8	68		37		20	0	0	163	78	21	11	2.7	.920	OF-66, 3B-33, SS-1
1891	COL	AA	137	.301	.420	552	166	28	4	10	1.8	86	90	42	36	41	0	0	250	53	25	10	2.4	.924	OF-128, 3B-7, SS-2
1892	WAS	N	132	.248	.354	492	122	12	11	6	1.2	64	51	36	33	28	0	0	278	46	30	11	2.7	.915	OF-125, 3B-6, 1B-4
1893	CIN	N	4	.167	.250	12	2	1	0	0	0.0	3	0	5		0	0	0	2	0	3	0	1.3	.400	OF-4
5 yrs.			508	.267	.389	1943	518	67	34	34	1.7	314	227	180	150	110	0	0	1000	233	110	40	2.6	.918	OF-455, 3B-51, 1B-4, SS-3, 2B-2

Frank Duffy

DUFFY, FRANK THOMAS
B. Oct. 14, 1946, Oakland, Calif.

BR TR 6'1" 180 lbs.

1970	CIN	N	6	.182	.364	11	2	2	0	0	0.0	1	0	1	2	1	2	0	4	12	0	4	2.7	1.000	SS-5
1971	2 teams		34	CIN N (13G – .188)		SF N (21G – .179)																			
"	total		34	.182	.205	44	8	1	0	0	0.0	4	3	1	12	1	9	2	24	43	3	10	2.1	.957	SS-16, 3B-1, 2B-1
1972	CLE	A	130	.239	.325	385	92	16	4	3	0.8	23	27	31	54	6	4	1	197	360	13	75	4.4	.977	SS-126
1973			116	.263	.396	361	95	16	4	8	2.2	34	50	25	41	6	0	0	198	377	8	82	5.0	.986	SS-115
1974			158	.233	.310	549	128	18	0	8	1.5	62	48	30	64	7	0	0	242	491	15	83	4.7	.980	SS-158
1975			146	.243	.303	482	117	22	2	1	0.2	44	47	27	60	10	2	0	225	464	16	85	4.8	.977	SS-145
1976			133	.212	.265	392	83	11	2	2	0.5	38	30	29	50	10	1	0	222	344	10	83	4.3	.983	SS-132
1977			122	.201	.287	334	67	13	2	4	1.2	30	31	21	47	8	1	0	145	301	15	62	3.8	.967	SS-121
1978	BOS	A	64	.260	.308	104	27	5	0	0	0.0	12	4	6	11	1	2	1	63	98	8	19	2.6	.953	3B-22, SS-21, 2B-12, DH-6
1979			6	.000	.000	3	0	0	0	0	0.0	0	0	0	1	0	0	0	3	2	0	0	0.8	1.000	2B-3, 1B-1
10 yrs.			915	.232	.311	2665	619	104	14	26	1.0	248	240	171	342	49	21	4	1323	2492	88	503	4.3	.977	SS-839, 3B-23, 2B-16, DH-6, 1B-1

LEAGUE CHAMPIONSHIP SERIES

| 1971 | SF | N | 1 | .000 | .000 | 1 | 0 | 0 | 0 | 0 | 0.0 | 0 | 0 | 0 | 1 | 0 | 1 | 0 | 0 | 0 | 0 | 0 | 0.0 | — | — |

Hugh Duffy

DUFFY, HUGH
B. Nov. 26, 1866, Cranston, R. I.   D. Oct. 19, 1954, Boston, Mass.
Manager 1901, 1904-06, 1910-11, 1921-22.
Hall of Fame 1945.

BR TR 5'7" 168 lbs.

1888	CHI	N	71	.282	.413	298	84	10	4	7	2.3	60	41	9	32	13	0	0	107	30	17	5	2.2	.890	OF-67, SS-3, 3B-1
1889			136	.295	.416	584	172	21	7	12	2.1	144	89	46	30	52	0	0	187	46	32	4	1.9	.879	OF-126, SS-10
1890	CHI	P	137	.320	.470	596	191	36	16	7	1.2	161	82	59	20	78	0	0	255	34	26	5	2.3	.917	OF-137

Year	Team		Games	BA	SA	AB	H	2B	3B	HR	HR%	R	RBI	BB	SO	SB	Pinch Hit AB	H	PO	A	E	DP	TC/G	FA	G by Pos

Hugh Duffy *continued*

Year	Team		Games	BA	SA	AB	H	2B	3B	HR	HR%	R	RBI	BB	SO	SB	AB	H	PO	A	E	DP	TC/G	FA	G by Pos
1891	BOS	AA	127	.336	.448	536	180	20	8	8	1.5	134	108	61	29	85	0	0	176	28	17	3	1.7	.923	OF-124, 3B-3, SS-1
1892	BOS	N	147	.301	.410	612	184	28	12	5	0.8	125	81	60	37	51	0	0	259	19	20	4	2.0	.933	OF-146, 3B-2
1893			131	.363	.461	560	203	23	7	6	1.1	147	118	50	13	44	0	0	313	15	16	6	2.6	.953	OF-131
1894			124	.438[1]	.679	539	236	50	13	18	3.3	160	145	66	15	49	0	0	319	33	31	5	3.1	.919	OF-124, SS-2
1895			131	.352	.482	531	187	30	6	9	1.7	110	100	63	16	42	0	0	322	20	20	7	2.8	.945	OF-130
1896			131	.300	.389	527	158	16	8	5	0.9	93	112	52		45	0	0	267	53	18	5	2.6	.947	OF-126, 2B-9, SS-2
1897			134	.340	.482	550	187	25	10	11	2.0	131	129	52		41	0	0	277	26	8	3	2.3	.974	OF-129, 2B-6, SS-2
1898			152	.298	.373	568	169	13	3	8	1.4	97	108	59		29	0	0	334	18	16	2	2.4	.957	OF-152, 3B-1, 1B-1, C-1
1899			147	.279	.378	588	164	29	7	5	0.9	103	102	39		26	0	0	344	9	11	1	2.5	.970	OF-147
1900			55	.304	.409	181	55	5	4	2	1.1	28	31	16		12	4	1	109	7	5	2	2.2	.959	OF-49, 2B-1
1901	MIL	A	79	.308	.444	286	88	15	9	2	0.7	41	45	16		13	2	0	141	5	5	0	1.9	.967	OF-77
1904	PHI	N	18	.283	.348	46	13	1	1	0	0.0	10	5	13		3	4	1	16	1	3	0	1.1	.850	OF-14
1905			15	.300	.400	40	12	2	1	0	0.0	7	3	1		0	7	3	19	1	2	0	1.5	.909	OF-8
1906			1	.000	.000	0	0	0	0	0	0.0	0	0	0		0	1	0	0	0	0	0	0.0	—	
17 yrs.			1736	.324	.448	7043	2283	324	116	105	1.5	1551	1299	662	211	583	18	5	3445	345	247	52	2.3	.939	OF-1687, SS-20, 2B-16, 3B-7, 1B-1, C-1

Bill Dugan

DUGAN, WILLIAM H.
Brother of Ed Dugan.
B. 1864, Kingston, N. Y.   Deceased.

Year	Team		Games	BA	SA	AB	H	2B	3B	HR	HR%	R	RBI	BB	SO	SB	AB	H	PO	A	E	DP	TC/G	FA	G by Pos
1884	2 teams	RIC	AA (9G – .071)			KC	U	(3G – .000)																	
"	total		12	.059	.088	34	2	1	0	0	0.0	4	0	0		0	0	0	46	12	10	1	5.7	.853	C-9, OF-3

Joe Dugan

DUGAN, JOSEPH ANTHONY (Jumping Joe)
B. May 12, 1897, Mahanoy City, Pa.   D. July 7, 1982, Norwood, Mass.

BR TR 5'11"   160 lbs.

Year	Team		Games	BA	SA	AB	H	2B	3B	HR	HR%	R	RBI	BB	SO	SB	AB	H	PO	A	E	DP	TC/G	FA	G by Pos
1917	PHI	A	43	.194	.254	134	26	8	0	0	0.0	9	16	3	16	0	0	0	61	111	16	13	4.4	.915	SS-39, 2B-2
1918			120	.195	.259	406	79	11	3	3	0.7	25	34	16	55	4	0	0	304	397	48	69	6.2	.936	SS-85, 2B-35
1919			104	.271	.333	387	105	17	2	1	0.3	25	30	11	30	9	0	0	243	319	44	43	5.8	.927	SS-98, 2B-4, 3B-2
1920			123	.322	.442	491	158	40	5	3	0.6	65	60	19	51	5	0	0	225	328	35	48	4.8	.940	3B-59, SS-32, 2B-32
1921			119	.295	.434	461	136	22	6	10	2.2	54	58	28	45	5	0	0	118	208	16	19	2.9	.953	3B-119
1922	2 teams	BOS	A (84G – .287)			NY	A	(60G – .286)																	
"	total		144	.287	.383	593	170	31	4	6	1.0	89	63	22	49	3	1	0	176	306	25	34	3.5	.951	3B-123, SS-20
1923	NY	A	146	.283	.384	644	182	30	7	7	1.1	111	67	25	41	4	0	0	155	300	12	28	3.2	.974	3B-146
1924			148	.302	.390	610	184	31	7	3	0.5	105	56	31	32	1	0	0	178	251	17	22	3.0	.962	3B-148, 2B-2
1925			102	.292	.359	404	118	19	4	0	0.0	50	31	19	20	2	5	1	118	202	10	19	3.2	.970	3B-96
1926			123	.288	.362	434	125	19	5	1	0.2	39	64	25	16	2	1	0	122	221	16	10	2.9	.955	3B-122
1927			112	.269	.362	387	104	24	3	2	0.5	44	43	27	37	1	1	1	93	196	19	15	2.8	.938	3B-111
1928			94	.276	.381	312	86	15	4	6	1.9	33	34	16	15	1	2	0	87	129	11	13	2.4	.952	3B-91
1929	BOS	A	60	.304	.384	125	38	10	0	0	0.0	14	15	8	8	0	26	9	21	43	7	5	1.2	.901	3B-24, SS-5, OF-2, 2B-2
1931	DET	A	8	.235	.235	17	4	0	0	0	0.0	1	0	0	3	0	3	1	4	5	1	0	1.3	.900	3B-5
14 yrs.			1446	.280	.372	5405	1515	277	46	42	0.8	664	571	250	418	37	39	12	1905	3016	277	338	3.6	.947	3B-1046, SS-279, 2B-77, OF-2

WORLD SERIES

Year	Team		Games	BA	SA	AB	H	2B	3B	HR	HR%	R	RBI	BB	SO	SB	AB	H	PO	A	E	DP	TC/G	FA	G by Pos
1922	NY	A	5	.250	.300	20	5	1	0	0	0.0	4	0	0	1	0	0	0	5	8	0	0	2.6	1.000	3B-5
1923			6	.280	.560	25	7	2	1	1	4.0	5	5	3	0	0	0	0	7	13	0	2	3.3	1.000	3B-6
1926			7	.333	.375	24	8	1	0	0	0.0	2	2	1	1	0	0	0	8	14	1	0	3.3	1.000	3B-7
1927			4	.200	.200	15	3	0	0	0	0.0	2	0	0	0	0	0	0	3	6	0	1	2.3	1.000	3B-4
1928			3	.167	.167	6	1	0	0	0	0.0	0	1	0	0	0	0	0	4	0	0	0	1.3	1.000	3B-3
5 yrs.			25	.267	.367	90	24	4	1	1	1.1	13	8	4	2	0	0	0	27	41	1	3	2.8	.986	3B-25

Gus Dugas

DUGAS, AUGUSTIN JOSEPH
B. Mar. 24, 1907, St.-Jean-de-Matha, Que., Canada

BL TL 5'9"   165 lbs.

Year	Team		Games	BA	SA	AB	H	2B	3B	HR	HR%	R	RBI	BB	SO	SB	AB	H	PO	A	E	DP	TC/G	FA	G by Pos
1930	PIT	N	9	.290	.355	31	9	2	0	0	0.0	8	1	7	4	0	0	0	18	1	3	0	2.4	.864	OF-9
1932			55	.237	.423	97	23	3	3	3	3.1	13	12	7	11	0	33	6	40	0	2	0	0.8	.952	OF-20
1933	PHI	N	37	.169	.211	71	12	3	0	0	0.0	4	9	1	9	0	24	5	113	8	2	7	3.3	.984	1B-11, OF-1
1934	WAS	A	24	.053	.105	19	1	1	0	0	0.0	2	1	3	3	0	18	0	3	0	0	0	0.1	1.000	OF-2
4 yrs.			125	.206	.317	218	45	9	3	3	1.4	27	23	18	27	0	75	10	174	9	7	7	1.5	.963	OF-32, 1B-11

Dan Dugdale

DUGDALE, DANIEL EDWARD (Dug)
B. Oct. 28, 1864, Peoria, Ill.   D. Mar. 9, 1934, Seattle, Wash.

Year	Team		Games	BA	SA	AB	H	2B	3B	HR	HR%	R	RBI	BB	SO	SB	AB	H	PO	A	E	DP	TC/G	FA	G by Pos
1886	KC	N	12	.175	.175	40	7	0	0	0	0.0	4	2	2	13		0	0	33	13	8	0	4.5	.852	C-7, OF-6
1894	WAS	N	38	.239	.299	134	32	4	2	0	0.0	19	16	13	14	7	0	0	74	36	18	0	3.4	.859	C-33, 3B-3, OF-2
2 yrs.			50	.224	.270	174	39	4	2	0	0.0	23	18	15	27	7	0	0	107	49	26	0	3.6	.857	C-40, OF-8, 3B-3

Oscar Dugey

DUGEY, OSCAR JOSEPH
B. Oct. 25, 1887, Palestine, Tex.   D. Jan. 1, 1966, Dallas, Tex.

BR TR 5'8"   160 lbs.

Year	Team		Games	BA	SA	AB	H	2B	3B	HR	HR%	R	RBI	BB	SO	SB	AB	H	PO	A	E	DP	TC/G	FA	G by Pos
1913	BOS	N	5	.250	.250	8	2	0	0	0	0.0	0	0	0	0	0	0	0	4	4	2	0	2.0	.800	3B-2, SS-1, 2B-1
1914			58	.193	.239	109	21	2	0	1	0.9	17	10	10	15	10	0	21	4	52	26	8	3	1.5	.907	OF-17, 2B-16, 3B-1
1915	PHI	N	42	.154	.179	39	6	1	0	0	0.0	4	0	7	5	2	16	1	10	22	2	1	0.8	.941	2B-14
1916			41	.220	.280	50	11	3	0	0	0.0	9	1	9	3	9	1	22	36	2	3	1.5	.967	2B-12
1917			44	.194	.278	72	14	4	1	0	0.0	12	9	4	9	3	19	4	32	30	8	3	1.6	.886	2B-15, OF-4
1920	BOS	N	5	—	—	0	0	0	0	0	—	0	0	0	0	0	0	0	0	0	0	0	0.0	—	
6 yrs.			195	.194	.248	278	54	10	1	1	0.4	45	20	31	38	17	66	10	120	118	22	10	1.3	.915	2B-58, OF-21, 3B-3, SS-1

WORLD SERIES

Year	Team		Games	BA	SA	AB	H	2B	3B	HR	HR%	R	RBI	BB	SO	SB	AB	H	PO	A	E	DP	TC/G	FA	G by Pos
1915	PHI	N	2	—	—	0	0	0	0	0	—	0	0	0	1	0	1	0	0	0	0	0	0.0	—	

Jim Duggan

DUGGAN, JAMES ELMER
B. June 3, 1884, Whiteland, Ind.   D. Dec. 5, 1951, Indianapolis, Ind.

BL TL 5'10"   165 lbs.

Year	Team		Games	BA	SA	AB	H	2B	3B	HR	HR%	R	RBI	BB	SO	SB	AB	H	PO	A	E	DP	TC/G	FA	G by Pos
1911	STL	A	1	.000	.000	4	0	0	0	0	0.0	1	1	0	0	0	0	0	11	1	0	2	12.0	1.000	1B-1

Year	Team	Games	BA	SA	AB	H	2B	3B	HR	HR%	R	RBI	BB	SO	SB	Pinch Hit AB	Pinch Hit H	PO	A	E	DP	TC/G	FA	G by Pos

Tommy Dunbar

DUNBAR, THOMAS JEROME
B. Nov. 24, 1959, Graniteville, S. C. BL TL 6'2" 185 lbs.

Year	Team	Games	BA	SA	AB	H	2B	3B	HR	HR%	R	RBI	BB	SO	SB	PH AB	PH H	PO	A	E	DP	TC/G	FA	G by Pos
1983	TEX A	12	.250	.250	24	6	0	0	0	0.0	3	3	5	7	3	0	0	7	0	1	0	0.7	.875	OF-9, DH-1
1984		34	.258	.340	97	25	2	0	2	2.1	9	10	6	16	1	10	2	31	0	2	0	1.0	.939	OF-20, DH-5
1985		45	.202	.269	104	21	4	0	1	1.0	7	5	12	9	0	14	1	14	0	1	0	0.3	.933	DH-18, OF-14
3 yrs.		91	.231	.298	225	52	6	0	3	1.3	19	18	23	32	4	24	3	52	0	4	0	0.6	.929	OF-43, DH-24

Dave Duncan

DUNCAN, DAVID EDWIN
B. Sept. 26, 1945, Dallas, Tex. BR TR 6'2" 190 lbs.

Year	Team	Games	BA	SA	AB	H	2B	3B	HR	HR%	R	RBI	BB	SO	SB	PH AB	PH H	PO	A	E	DP	TC/G	FA	G by Pos
1964	KC A	25	.170	.264	53	9	0	1	1	1.9	2	5	2	20	0	2	1	99	7	2	6	4.3	.981	C-22
1967		34	.188	.376	101	19	4	0	5	5.0	9	11	4	50	0	2	0	176	13	4	2	5.7	.979	C-32
1968	OAK A	82	.191	.293	246	47	4	0	7	2.8	15	28	25	68	1	3	2	474	41	7	5	6.4	.987	C-79
1969		58	.126	.220	127	16	3	0	3	2.4	11	22	19	41	0	4	0	209	15	4	1	3.9	.982	C-56
1970		86	.259	.418	232	60	7	0	10	4.3	21	29	22	38	0	10	4	373	28	9	8	4.8	.978	C-73
1971		103	.253	.419	363	92	13	0	15	4.1	39	40	28	77	1	1	1	678	41	12	3	7.1	.984	C-102
1972		121	.218	.392	403	88	13	0	19	4.7	39	59	34	68	0	8	1	661	43	5	9	5.9	.993	C-113
1973	CLE A	95	.233	.419	344	80	11	1	17	4.9	43	43	35	86	0	3	0	533	41	7	8	6.1	.988	C-86, DH-9
1974		136	.200	.341	425	85	10	1	16	3.8	45	46	42	91	0	1	0	564	48	15	10	4.6	.976	C-134, 1B-3, DH-1
1975	BAL A	96	.205	.345	307	63	7	0	12	3.9	30	41	16	82	0	7	0	397	41	7	8	4.6	.982	C-95
1976		93	.204	.271	284	58	7	0	4	1.4	20	17	25	56	1	0	0	371	35	6	9	4.4	.985	C-93
11 yrs.		929	.214	.357	2885	617	79	4	109	3.8	274	341	252	677	5	39	9	4535	353	79	67	5.3	.984	C-885, DH-10, 1B-3

LEAGUE CHAMPIONSHIP SERIES

Year	Team	Games	BA	SA	AB	H	2B	3B	HR	HR%	R	RBI	BB	SO	SB	PH AB	PH H	PO	A	E	DP	TC/G	FA	G by Pos
1971	OAK A	2	.500	.667	6	3	1	0	0	0.0	0	0	0	2	0	0	0	15	0	0	0	7.5	1.000	C-2
1972		2	.000	.000	2	0	0	0	0	0.0	0	0	1	1	0	1	0	5	1	0	0	3.0	1.000	C-2
2 yrs.		4	.375	.500	8	3	1	0	0	0.0	0	0	1	3	0	1	0	20	1	0	0	5.3	1.000	C-4

WORLD SERIES

Year	Team	Games	BA	SA	AB	H	2B	3B	HR	HR%	R	RBI	BB	SO	SB	PH AB	PH H	PO	A	E	DP	TC/G	FA	G by Pos
1972	OAK A	3	.200	.200	5	1	0	0	0	0.0	0	0	1	3	0	2	1	5	1	0	0	2.0	1.000	C-1

Jim Duncan

DUNCAN, JAMES WILLIAM
B. July 1, 1871, Saltsburg, Pa. D. Oct. 16, 1901, Foxburg, Pa. BR TR 5'8" 140 lbs.

Year	Team	Games	BA	SA	AB	H	2B	3B	HR	HR%	R	RBI	BB	SO	SB	PH AB	PH H	PO	A	E	DP	TC/G	FA	G by Pos
1899 2 teams	WAS N (15G – .234)				CLE N	(31G – .229)																		
" total		46	.230	.336	152	35	4	3	2	1.3	14	14	8		1	2	0	233	41	16	13	6.3	.945	C-28, 1B-17

Mariano Duncan

DUNCAN, MARIANO
Born Mariano Duncan y Nolasco.
B. Mar. 13, 1963, San Pedro de Macoris, Dominican Republic BB TR 6' 165 lbs.

Year	Team	Games	BA	SA	AB	H	2B	3B	HR	HR%	R	RBI	BB	SO	SB	PH AB	PH H	PO	A	E	DP	TC/G	FA	G by Pos
1985	LA N	142	.244	.340	562	137	24	6	6	1.1	74	39	38	113	38	2	1	224	430	30	64	4.8	.956	SS-123, 2B-19
1986		109	.229	.305	407	93	7	0	8	2.0	47	30	30	78	48	2	0	172	317	25	46	4.7	.951	SS-106
1987		76	.215	.322	261	56	8	1	6	2.3	31	18	17	62	11	1	0	101	213	21	40	4.4	.937	SS-67, 2B-7, OF-2
1989 2 teams	LA N (49G – .250)				CIN N	(45G – .247)																		
" total		94	.248	.357	258	64	15	2	3	1.2	32	21	8	51	9	18	7	101	155	14	30	2.9	.948	SS-60, 2B-13, OF-7
4 yrs.		421	.235	.330	1488	350	54	9	23	1.5	184	108	93	304	106	23	8	598	1115	90	180	4.3	.950	SS-356, 2B-39, OF-9

LEAGUE CHAMPIONSHIP SERIES

Year	Team	Games	BA	SA	AB	H	2B	3B	HR	HR%	R	RBI	BB	SO	SB	PH AB	PH H	PO	A	E	DP	TC/G	FA	G by Pos
1985	LA N	5	.222	.444	18	4	2	1	0	0.0	2	1	1	3	1	0	0	7	16	1	3	4.8	.958	SS-5

Pat Duncan

DUNCAN, LOUIS BAIRD
B. Oct. 6, 1893, Coalton, Ohio D. July 17, 1960, Jackson, Ohio BR TR 5'9" 170 lbs.

Year	Team	Games	BA	SA	AB	H	2B	3B	HR	HR%	R	RBI	BB	SO	SB	PH AB	PH H	PO	A	E	DP	TC/G	FA	G by Pos
1915	PIT N	3	.200	.200	5	1	0	0	0	0.0	0	0	0	1	0	2	1	1	0	0	0	0.3	1.000	OF-1
1919	CIN N	31	.244	.411	90	22	3	3	2	2.2	9	17	8	7	2	3	0	51	3	1	1	1.8	.982	OF-27
1920		154	.295	.372	576	170	16	11	2	0.3	75	83	42	42	18	0	0	334	15	13	4	2.4	.964	OF-154
1921		145	.308	.408	532	164	27	10	2	0.4	57	60	44	33	7	0	0	349	19	11	2	2.6	.971	OF-145
1922		151	.328	.479	607	199	44	12	8	1.3	94	94	40	31	12	0	0	316	19	10	4	2.3	.971	OF-151
1923		147	.327	.438	566	185	26	8	7	1.2	92	83	30	27	15	1	0	291	11	2	2	2.1	.993	OF-146
1924		96	.270	.392	319	86	21	6	2	0.6	34	37	20	23	1	13	4	124	3	10	0	1.4	.927	OF-83
7 yrs.		727	.307	.420	2695	827	137	50	23	0.9	361	374	184	164	55	19	5	1466	70	47	13	2.2	.970	OF-707

WORLD SERIES

Year	Team	Games	BA	SA	AB	H	2B	3B	HR	HR%	R	RBI	BB	SO	SB	PH AB	PH H	PO	A	E	DP	TC/G	FA	G by Pos
1919	CIN N	8	.269	.346	26	7	2	0	0	0.0	3	8	2	2	0	0	0	9	1	0	0	1.3	1.000	OF-8

Taylor Duncan

DUNCAN, TAYLOR McDOWELL
B. May 12, 1953, Memphis, Tenn. BR TR 6' 170 lbs.

Year	Team	Games	BA	SA	AB	H	2B	3B	HR	HR%	R	RBI	BB	SO	SB	PH AB	PH H	PO	A	E	DP	TC/G	FA	G by Pos
1977	STL N	8	.333	.583	12	4	0	0	1	8.3	2	2	2	1	0	2	1	0	0	0	0	0.3	1.000	3B-5
1978	OAK A	104	.257	.335	319	82	15	2	2	0.6	25	37	19	38	1	13	1	73	128	9	6	2.0	.957	3B-84, 2B-11, DH-7, SS-1
2 yrs.		112	.260	.344	331	86	15	2	3	0.9	27	39	21	39	1	15	2	73	130	9	6	1.9	.958	3B-89, 2B-11, DH-7, SS-1

Vern Duncan

DUNCAN, VERNON VAN DUKE
B. Jan. 6, 1890, Clayton, N. C. D. June 1, 1954, Daytona Beach, Fla. BL TR 5'9" 155 lbs.

Year	Team	Games	BA	SA	AB	H	2B	3B	HR	HR%	R	RBI	BB	SO	SB	PH AB	PH H	PO	A	E	DP	TC/G	FA	G by Pos
1913	PHI N	8	.417	.500	12	5	1	0	0	0.0	3	1	0	3	0	4	2	1	0	0	0	0.4	1.000	OF-3
1914	BAL F	157	.287	.363	557	160	18	8	2	0.4	99	53	67		13	2	0	266	32	21	8	2.1	.917	OF-148, 3B-8, 2B-1
1915		146	.267	.328	531	142	18	4	2	0.4	68	43	54		19	4	0	285	51	27	12	2.5	.926	OF-124, 3B-21, 2B-1
3 yrs.		311	.279	.347	1100	307	39	12	4	0.4	170	97	121	3	32	10	2	553	84	54	20	2.2	.922	OF-275, 3B-29, 2B-2

Ed Dundon

DUNDON, EDWARD JOSEPH (Dummy)
B. July 10, 1859, Columbus, Ohio D. Aug. 18, 1893, Columbus, Ohio TR

Year	Team	Games	BA	SA	AB	H	2B	3B	HR	HR%	R	RBI	BB	SO	SB	PH AB	PH H	PO	A	E	DP	TC/G	FA	G by Pos
1883	COL AA	26	.161	.172	93	15	1	0	0	0.0	8		3			0	0	24	37	12	3	2.8	.836	P-20, OF-9, 2B-1
1884		26	.140	.209	86	12	2	0	0	0.0	6		5			0	0	60	22	5	3	3.3	.943	OF-16, P-11, 1B-3
2 yrs.		52	.151	.190	179	27	3	0	0	0.0	14		8			0	0	84	59	17	6	3.1	.894	P-31, OF-25, 1B-3, 2B-1

Gus Dundon

DUNDON, AUGUSTUS JOSEPH
B. July 10, 1874, Columbus, Ohio D. Sept. 1, 1940, Pittsburgh, Pa. BR TR 5'10" 165 lbs.

865

Year	Team	Games	BA	SA	AB	H	2B	3B	HR	HR%	R	RBI	BB	SO	SB	Pinch Hit AB	Pinch Hit H	PO	A	E	DP	TC/G	FA	G by Pos

Gus Dundon *continued*

Year	Team		Games	BA	SA	AB	H	2B	3B	HR	HR%	R	RBI	BB	SO	SB	AB	H	PO	A	E	DP	TC/G	FA	G by Pos
1904	CHI	A	108	.228	.268	373	85	9	3	0	0.0	40	36	30		19	0	0	194	289	13	26	4.6	.974	2B-103, 3B-3, SS-2
1905			106	.192	.228	364	70	7	3	0	0.0	30	22	23		14	0	0	223	328	12	25	5.3	.979	2B-104, SS-2
1906			33	.135	.146	96	13	1	0	0	0.0	7	4	11		4	1	0	81	91	14	8	5.6	.925	2B-18, SS-14
3 yrs.			247	.202	.236	833	168	17	6	0	0.0	77	62	64		37	1	0	498	708	39	59	5.0	.969	2B-225, SS-18, 3B-3

Sam Dungan

DUNGAN, SAMUEL MORRISON (Terrible Sammy)
B. Jan. 29, 1866, Ferndale, Calif. D. Mar. 16, 1939, Santa Ana, Calif.
BR 5'11" 180 lbs.

Year	Team		Games	BA	SA	AB	H	2B	3B	HR	HR%	R	RBI	BB	SO	SB	AB	H	PO	A	E	DP	TC/G	FA	G by Pos
1892	CHI	N	113	.284	.360	433	123	19	7	0	0.0	46	53	35	19	15	0	0	183	8	20	2	1.9	.905	OF-113
1893			107	.297	.389	465	138	23	7	2	0.4	86	64	29	8	11	0	0	175	20	17	3	2.0	.920	OF-107
1894	2 teams			CHI N (10G – .231)		LOU	N	(8G – .344)																	
"	total		18	.282	.324	71	20	3	0	0	0.0	11	6	11	2	3	0	0	30	3	1	2	1.9	.971	OF-18
1900	CHI	N	6	.267	.267	15	4	0	0	0	0.0	1	1	1		0	3	1	4	0	1	0	0.8	.800	OF-3
1901	WAS	A	138	.320	.415	559	179	26	12	1	0.2	70	73	40		9	0	0	494	26	16	19	3.9	.970	OF-104, 1B-35
5 yrs.			382	.301	.386	1543	464	71	26	3	0.2	214	197	116	29	38	3	1	886	57	55	26	2.6	.945	OF-345, 1B-35

Lee Dunham

DUNHAM, LELAND HUFFIELD
B. June 9, 1902, Atlanta, Ill. D. May 11, 1961, Atlanta, Ill.
BL TL 5'11" 185 lbs.

Year	Team		Games	BA	SA	AB	H	2B	3B	HR	HR%	R	RBI	BB	SO	SB	AB	H	PO	A	E	DP	TC/G	FA	G by Pos
1926	PHI	N	5	.250	.250	4	1	0	0	0	0.0	0	1	0	1	0	3	0	2	0	0	0	0.4	1.000	1B-2

Bill Dunlap

DUNLAP, WILLIAM JAMES
B. May 1, 1909, Three Rivers, Mass. D. Nov. 29, 1980, Reading, Pa.
BR TR 5'11" 170 lbs.

Year	Team		Games	BA	SA	AB	H	2B	3B	HR	HR%	R	RBI	BB	SO	SB	AB	H	PO	A	E	DP	TC/G	FA	G by Pos
1929	BOS	N	10	.414	.586	29	12	0	1	1	3.4	6	4	4	4	0	1	0	16	0	2	0	1.8	.889	OF-9
1930			16	.069	.103	29	2	1	0	0	0.0	3	0	0	6	0	9	0	15	0	0	0	0.9	1.000	OF-7
2 yrs.			26	.241	.345	58	14	1	1	1	1.7	9	4	4	10	0	10	0	31	0	2	0	1.3	.939	OF-16

Fred Dunlap

DUNLAP, FREDERICK C. (Sure Shot)
B. May 21, 1859, Philadelphia, Pa. D. Dec. 1, 1902, Philadelphia, Pa.
Manager 1882, 1884-85, 1889.
BR TR 5'8" 165 lbs.

Year	Team		Games	BA	SA	AB	H	2B	3B	HR	HR%	R	RBI	BB	SO	SB	AB	H	PO	A	E	DP	TC/G	FA	G by Pos
1880	CLE	N	85	.276	.429	373	103	27	9	4	1.1	61	30	7	32		0	0	252	290	53	44	7.0	.911	2B-85
1881			80	.325	.444	351	114	25	4	3	0.9	60	24	18	24		0	0	258	255	52	41	7.1	.908	2B-79, 3B-1
1882			84	.280	.354	364	102	19	4	0	0.0	68	28	23	26		0	0	268	297	63	62	7.5	.900	2B-84
1883			93	.326	.452	396	129	34	2	4	1.0	81		22	21		0	0	305	290	58	49	7.0	.911	2B-93, OF-1
1884	STL	U	101	**.412**	**.621**	449	185	39	8	13	2.9	160		29			0	0	343	302	51	54	6.9	.927	2B-100, OF-1, P-1
1885	STL	N	106	.270	.333	423	114	11	5	2	0.5	70	25	41	24		0	0	314	374	49	53	7.0	.934	2B-106
1886	2 teams			STL N (71G – .267)		DET	N	(51G – .286)																	
"	total		122	.274	.387	481	132	23	5	7	1.5	85	69	44	51		0	0	333	393	58	64	6.4	.926	2B-122, OF-1
1887	DET	N	65	.265	.441	272	72	13	10	5	1.8	60	45	25	12	15	0	0	212	225	24	44	7.1	.948	2B-65, P-1
1888	PIT	N	82	.262	.333	321	84	12	4	1	0.3	41	36	16	30	24	0	0	240	279	33	44	6.7	.940	2B-82
1889			121	.235	.290	451	106	19	0	2	0.4	59	65	46	33	21	0	0	342	393	39	51	6.4	.950	2B-121
1890	2 teams			PIT N (17G – .172)		NY	P	(1G – .500)																	
"	total		18	.191	.206	68	13	1	1	0	0.0	10	3	7	4	2	0	0	37	54	13	4	5.8	.875	2B-18
1891	WAS	AA	8	.200	.320	25	5	1	1	0	0.0	4	4	5	4	3	0	0	8	19	6	3	4.1	.818	2B-8
12 yrs.			965	.292	.406	3974	1159	224	53	41	1.0	759	329	283	263	65	0	0	2912	3171	499	513	6.8	.924	2B-963, OF-3, P-2, 3B-1

Grant Dunlap

DUNLAP, GRANT LESTER (Snap)
B. Dec. 20, 1923, Stockton, Calif.
BR TR 6'2" 180 lbs.

Year	Team		Games	BA	SA	AB	H	2B	3B	HR	HR%	R	RBI	BB	SO	SB	AB	H	PO	A	E	DP	TC/G	FA	G by Pos
1953	STL	N	16	.353	.647	17	6	0	1	1	5.9	2	3	0	2	0	15	5	0	0	0	0	0.0	–	OF-1

Jack Dunleavy

DUNLEAVY, JOHN FRANCIS
B. Sept. 14, 1879, Harrison, N. J. D. Apr. 12, 1944, South Norwalk, Conn.
TL 5'6" 167 lbs.

Year	Team		Games	BA	SA	AB	H	2B	3B	HR	HR%	R	RBI	BB	SO	SB	AB	H	PO	A	E	DP	TC/G	FA	G by Pos
1903	STL	N	61	.249	.295	193	48	3	3	0	0.0	23	10	13		10	**9**	**4**	58	43	3	5	1.7	.971	OF-38, P-14
1904			51	.233	.326	172	40	7	3	1	0.6	23	14	16		8	0	0	77	20	2	2	1.9	.980	OF-44, P-7
1905			119	.241	.303	435	105	8	8	1	0.2	52	25	55		15	0	0	177	28	8	7	1.8	.962	OF-118, 2B-1
3 yrs.			231	.241	.306	800	193	18	14	2	0.3	98	49	84		33	9	4	312	91	13	14	1.8	.969	OF-200, P-21, 2B-1

George Dunlop

DUNLOP, GEORGE HENRY
B. July 19, 1888, Meriden, Conn. D. Dec. 12, 1972, Meriden, Conn.
BR TR 5'10" 170 lbs.

Year	Team		Games	BA	SA	AB	H	2B	3B	HR	HR%	R	RBI	BB	SO	SB	AB	H	PO	A	E	DP	TC/G	FA	G by Pos
1913	CLE	A	7	.235	.294	17	4	1	0	0	0.0	3	0	5		0	0	0	9	13	1	0	3.3	.957	SS-4, 3B-3
1914			1	.000	.000	3	0	0	0	0	0.0	0	0	1	1	0	0	0	0	1	0	0	1.0	1.000	SS-1
2 yrs.			8	.200	.250	20	4	1	0	0	0.0	3	0	1	6	0	0	0	9	14	1	0	3.0	.958	SS-5, 3B-3

Jack Dunn

DUNN, JOHN JOSEPH (Handyman)
B. Oct. 6, 1872, Meadville, Pa. D. Oct. 22, 1928, Towson, Md.
BR TR 5'9"

Year	Team		Games	BA	SA	AB	H	2B	3B	HR	HR%	R	RBI	BB	SO	SB	AB	H	PO	A	E	DP	TC/G	FA	G by Pos
1897	BKN	N	36	.221	.252	131	29	4	0	0	0.0	20	17	4		2	0	0	31	74	14	3	3.3	.882	P-25, 2B-4, OF-3, 3B-3, SS-1
1898			51	.246	.257	167	41	0	1	0	0.0	21	19	7		3	0	0	42	91	12	6	2.8	.917	P-41, OF-4, SS-4, 3B-2
1899			43	.246	.279	122	30	2	1	0	0.0	21	16	3		3	1	0	21	83	4	1	2.5	.963	P-41, SS-1
1900	2 teams			BKN N (10G – .231)		PHI	N	(10G – .303)																	
"	total		20	.271	.288	59	16	1	0	0	0.0	5	6	1		1	0	0	7	40	3	0	2.5	.940	P-20
1901	2 teams			PHI N (2G – 1.000)		BAL	A	(96G – .249)																	
"	total		98	.251	.298	363	91	9	4	0	0.0	42	36	22		10	0	0	157	207	53	14	4.3	.873	3B-67, SS-19, P-11, OF-1, 2B-1
1902	NY	N	100	.211	.249	342	72	11	1	0	0.0	26	14	20		13	1	0	154	153	23	17	3.3	.930	OF-43, SS-36, 3B-18, P-3, 2B-2
1903			78	.241	.307	257	62	15	0	0	0.0	35	37	15		12	6	1	101	173	26	24	3.8	.913	SS-27, 3B-25, P-19, OF-1
1904			64	.309	.414	181	56	12	1	1	0.6	27	19	11		11	6	1	61	89	15	7	2.6	.909	3B-28, SS-10, 2B-9, OF-7, P-1
8 yrs.			490	.245	.292	1622	397	54	10	1	0.1	197	164	83		55	14	3	574	910	150	72	3.3	.908	3B-143, P-142, SS-98, OF-59, 2B-35

Year	Team		Games	BA	SA	AB	H	2B	3B	HR	HR%	R	RBI	BB	SO	SB	Pinch Hit AB	H	PO	A	E	DP	TC/G	FA	G by Pos

Joe Dunn

DUNN, JOSEPH EDWARD
B. Mar. 11, 1885, Springfield, Ohio   D. Mar. 19, 1944, Springfield, Ohio

BR TR 5'9"   160 lbs.

Year	Team		Games	BA	SA	AB	H	2B	3B	HR	HR%	R	RBI	BB	SO	SB	AB	H	PO	A	E	DP	TC/G	FA	G by Pos
1908	BKN	N	20	.172	.219	64	11	3	0	0	0.0	3	5	0		0	0	0	93	42	6	3	7.1	.957	C-20
1909			10	.160	.200	25	4	1	0	0	0.0	1	2	0		0	3	0	33	7	2	2	4.2	.952	C-7
2 yrs.			30	.169	.213	89	15	4	0	0	0.0	4	7	0		0	3	0	126	49	8	5	6.1	.956	C-27

Ron Dunn

DUNN, RONALD RAY
B. Jan. 24, 1950, Oklahoma City, Okla.

BR TR 5'11"   180 lbs.

Year	Team		Games	BA	SA	AB	H	2B	3B	HR	HR%	R	RBI	BB	SO	SB	AB	H	PO	A	E	DP	TC/G	FA	G by Pos
1974	CHI	N	23	.294	.485	68	20	7	0	2	2.9	6	15	12	8	0	1	0	31	46	7	6	3.7	.917	2B-21, 3B-6
1975			32	.159	.295	44	7	3	0	1	2.3	2	6	6	17	0	17	3	6	17	1	0	0.8	.958	3B-11, OF-2, 2B-1
2 yrs.			55	.241	.411	112	27	10	0	3	2.7	8	21	18	25	0	18	3	37	63	8	6	2.0	.926	2B-22, 3B-17, OF-2

Steve Dunn

DUNN, STEPHEN
B. Dec. 21, 1858, London, Ont., Canada   D. May 5, 1933, London, Ont., Canada

Year	Team		Games	BA	SA	AB	H	2B	3B	HR	HR%	R	RBI	BB	SO	SB	AB	H	PO	A	E	DP	TC/G	FA	G by Pos
1884	STP	U	9	.250	.313	32	8	2	0	0	0.0	2		0			0	0	67	5	4	3	8.4	.947	1B-9, 3B-1

Shawon Dunston

DUNSTON, SHAWON DONNELL (Thunder Pup)
B. Mar. 21, 1963, Brooklyn, N. Y.

BR TR 6'1"   175 lbs.

Year	Team		Games	BA	SA	AB	H	2B	3B	HR	HR%	R	RBI	BB	SO	SB	AB	H	PO	A	E	DP	TC/G	FA	G by Pos
1985	CHI	N	74	.260	.388	250	65	12	4	4	1.6	40	18	19	42	11	0	0	144	248	17	39	5.5	.958	SS-73
1986			150	.250	.410	581	145	36	3	17	2.9	66	68	21	114	13	2	1	320	465	32	96	5.4	.961	SS-149
1987			95	.246	.358	346	85	18	3	5	1.4	40	22	10	68	12	1	0	160	271	14	54	4.7	.969	SS-94
1988			155	.249	.357	575	143	23	6	9	1.6	69	56	16	108	30	3	0	257	455	20	76	4.7	.973	SS-151
1989			138	.278	.403	471	131	20	6	9	1.9	52	60	30	86	19	1	0	213	379	17	76	4.4	.972	SS-138
5 yrs.			612	.256	.384	2223	569	109	22	44	2.0	267	224	96	418	85	7	1	1094	1818	100	341	4.9	.967	SS-605

LEAGUE CHAMPIONSHIP SERIES

Year	Team		Games	BA	SA	AB	H	2B	3B	HR	HR%	R	RBI	BB	SO	SB	AB	H	PO	A	E	DP	TC/G	FA	G by Pos
1989	CHI	N	5	.316	.316	19	6	0	0	0	0.0	2	0	1	1	1	0	0	10	14	1	1	5.0	.960	SS-5

Dan Duran

DURAN, DANIEL JAMES
B. Mar. 16, 1954, Palo Alto, Calif.

BL TL 5'11"   190 lbs.

Year	Team		Games	BA	SA	AB	H	2B	3B	HR	HR%	R	RBI	BB	SO	SB	AB	H	PO	A	E	DP	TC/G	FA	G by Pos
1981	TEX	A	13	.250	.250	16	4	0	0	0	0.0	1	0	1	1	0	5	2	7	1	0	0	0.6	1.000	OF-7, 1B-1

Kid Durbin

DURBIN, BLAINE ALPHONSUS
B. Sept. 10, 1886, Lamar, Kans.   D. Sept. 11, 1943, Kirkwood, Mo.

BL TL 5'8"   155 lbs.

Year	Team		Games	BA	SA	AB	H	2B	3B	HR	HR%	R	RBI	BB	SO	SB	AB	H	PO	A	E	DP	TC/G	FA	G by Pos
1907	CHI	N	11	.333	.333	18	6	0	0	0	0.0	2	0	1			0	0	4	7	0	0	1.0	1.000	OF-5, P-5
1908			14	.250	.286	28	7	1	0	0	0.0	3	0	2			0	2	0	15	0	0	0	1.1	1.000	OF-11
1909	2 teams		CIN	N	(6G –	.200)		PIT	N	(1G –	.000)															
"	total		7	.200	.200	5	1	0	0	0	0.0	1	0	1			0	5	1	0	0	0	0	0.0	—	
3 yrs.			32	.275	.294	51	14	1	0	0	0.0	6	0	4			0	8	1	19	7	0	0	0.8	1.000	OF-16, P-5

Joe Durham

DURHAM, JOSEPH VANN (Pop)
B. July 31, 1931, Newport News, Va.

BR TR 6'1"   186 lbs.

Year	Team		Games	BA	SA	AB	H	2B	3B	HR	HR%	R	RBI	BB	SO	SB	AB	H	PO	A	E	DP	TC/G	FA	G by Pos
1954	BAL	A	10	.225	.300	40	9	0	0	1	2.5	4	3	4	7	0	0	0	22	0	2	0	2.4	.917	OF-10
1957			77	.185	.274	157	29	2	0	4	2.5	19	17	16	42	1	15	1	70	1	0	0	0.9	1.000	OF-59
1959	STL	N	6	.000	.000	5	0	0	0	0	0.0	2	0	0	1	0	2	0	2	0	0	0	0.3	1.000	OF-1
3 yrs.			93	.188	.272	202	38	2	0	5	2.5	25	20	20	50	1	17	1	94	1	2	0	1.0	.979	OF-70

Leon Durham

DURHAM, LEON (Bull)
B. July 31, 1957, Cincinnati, Ohio

BL TL 6'1"   185 lbs.

Year	Team		Games	BA	SA	AB	H	2B	3B	HR	HR%	R	RBI	BB	SO	SB	AB	H	PO	A	E	DP	TC/G	FA	G by Pos
1980	STL	N	96	.271	.426	303	82	15	4	8	2.6	42	42	18	55	8	16	5	180	22	3	8	2.1	.985	OF-78, 1B-8
1981	CHI	N	87	.290	.460	328	95	14	6	10	3.0	42	35	27	53	25	3	1	175	4	5	2	2.1	.973	OF-83, 1B-3
1982			148	.312	.521	539	168	33	7	22	4.1	84	90	66	77	28	5	2	311	12	12	1	2.3	.964	OF-143, 1B-1
1983			100	.258	.466	337	87	18	8	12	3.6	58	55	66	83	12	1	0	203	4	6	2	2.1	.972	OF-95, 1B-6
1984			137	.279	.505	473	132	30	4	23	4.9	86	96	69	86	16	8	2	1162	96	7	96	9.2	.994	1B-130
1985			153	.282	.465	542	153	32	2	21	3.9	58	75	64	99	7	2	0	1421	107	7	121	10.0	.995	1B-151
1986			141	.262	.452	484	127	18	7	20	4.1	66	65	67	98	8	2	0	1231	80	7	101	9.3	.995	1B-141
1987			131	.273	.513	439	120	27	2	27	6.2	70	63	51	92	8	2	2	1049	57	11	90	8.5	.990	1B-123
1988	2 teams		CHI	N	(24G –	.219)		CIN	N	(21G –	.216)															
"	total		45	.218	.403	124	27	9	1	4	3.2	14	8	14	32	0	8	0	296	21	2	24	7.1	.994	1B-37
1989	STL	N	29	.056	.111	18	1	0	0	0	0.0	2	1	2	4	0	11	1	44	5	2	7	1.8	.961	1B-18
10 yrs.			1067	.277	.475	3587	992	192	40	147	4.1	522	530	444	679	106	64	13	6072	408	62	452	6.1	.991	1B-618, OF-399

LEAGUE CHAMPIONSHIP SERIES

Year	Team		Games	BA	SA	AB	H	2B	3B	HR	HR%	R	RBI	BB	SO	SB	AB	H	PO	A	E	DP	TC/G	FA	G by Pos
1984	CHI	N	5	.150	.450	20	3	0	0	2	10.0	2	4	1	4	0	0	0	48	3	1	6	10.4	.981	1B-5

Bobby Durnbaugh

DURNBAUGH, ROBERT EUGENE (Scroggy)
B. Jan. 15, 1933, Dayton, Ohio

BR TR 5'8"   170 lbs.

Year	Team		Games	BA	SA	AB	H	2B	3B	HR	HR%	R	RBI	BB	SO	SB	AB	H	PO	A	E	DP	TC/G	FA	G by Pos
1957	CIN	N	2	.000	.000	1	0	0	0	0	0.0	0	0	0	0	0	0	0	0	1	1	0	1.0	.500	SS-2

George Durning

DURNING, GEORGE DEWEY
B. May 9, 1898, Philadelphia, Pa.   D. Apr. 18, 1986, Tampa, Fla.

BR TR 5'11"   175 lbs.

Year	Team		Games	BA	SA	AB	H	2B	3B	HR	HR%	R	RBI	BB	SO	SB	AB	H	PO	A	E	DP	TC/G	FA	G by Pos
1925	PHI	N	5	.357	.357	14	5	0	0	0	0.0	3	1	2	1	0	1	0	11	2	0	1	2.6	1.000	OF-4

Leo Durocher

DUROCHER, LEO ERNEST (The Lip)
B. July 27, 1905, W. Springfield, Mass.
Manager 1939-46, 1948-55, 1966-73.

BR TR 5'10"   160 lbs.

BB 1929

Year	Team		Games	BA	SA	AB	H	2B	3B	HR	HR%	R	RBI	BB	SO	SB	AB	H	PO	A	E	DP	TC/G	FA	G by Pos
1925	NY	A	2	.000	.000	1	0	0	0	0	0.0	0	0	0	0	0	1	0	0	0	0	0	0.0	—	
1928			102	.270	.338	296	80	8	6	0	0.0	46	31	22	52	1	3	1	158	274	18	42	4.4	.960	2B-66, SS-29
1929			106	.246	.287	341	84	4	5	0	0.0	53	32	34	33	3	1	0	218	318	23	66	5.3	.959	SS-93, 2B-12
1930	CIN	N	119	.243	.328	354	86	15	3	3	0.8	31	32	20	45	0	0	0	240	380	24	82	5.4	.963	SS-103, 2B-13
1931			121	.227	.294	361	82	11	5	1	0.3	26	29	18	32	0	0	0	212	344	20	86	4.8	.965	SS-120

Year	Team		Games	BA	SA	AB	H	2B	3B	HR	HR%	R	RBI	BB	SO	SB	Pinch Hit AB	H	PO	A	E	DP	TC/G	FA	G by Pos

Leo Durocher *continued*

Year	Team		Games	BA	SA	AB	H	2B	3B	HR	HR%	R	RBI	BB	SO	SB	AB	H	PO	A	E	DP	TC/G	FA	G by Pos
1932			143	.217	.293	457	99	22	5	1	0.2	43	33	36	40	3	0	0	283	429	30	76	5.2	.960	SS-142
1933	2 teams	CIN N (16G – .216)					STL N (123G – .258)																		
"	total		139	.253	.334	446	113	19	4	3	0.7	51	44	30	37	3	0	0	275	422	29	74	5.2	.960	SS-139
1934	STL	N	146	.260	.350	500	130	26	5	3	0.6	62	70	33	40	2	0	0	320	407	33	86	5.2	.957	SS-146
1935			143	.265	.376	513	136	23	5	8	1.6	62	78	29	46	4	0	0	313	420	28	81	5.3	.963	SS-142
1936			136	.286	.347	510	146	23	3	1	0.2	57	58	29	47	3	0	0	300	392	21	80	5.2	.971	SS-136
1937			135	.203	.245	477	97	11	3	1	0.2	46	47	38	36	6	0	0	279	381	28	72	5.1	.959	SS-134
1938	BKN	N	141	.219	.284	479	105	18	5	1	0.2	41	56	47	30	3	0	0	287	399	24	90	5.0	.966	SS-141
1939			116	.277	.369	390	108	21	6	1	0.3	42	34	27	24	2	2	0	228	324	25	73	5.0	.957	SS-113, 3B-1
1940			62	.231	.319	160	37	9	1	1	0.6	10	14	12	13	1	1	0	108	138	11	24	4.1	.957	SS-53, 2B-4
1941			18	.286	.310	42	12	1	0	0	0.0	2	6	1	3	0	5	1	17	28	4	3	2.7	.918	SS-12, 2B-1
1943			6	.222	.222	18	4	0	0	0	0.0	1	1	1	2	0	0	0	23	11	0	5	5.7	1.000	SS-6
1945			2	.200	.200	5	1	0	0	0	0.0	1	2	0	0	0	0	0	3	4	0	0	3.5	1.000	2B-2
17 yrs.			1637	.247	.320	5350	1320	210	56	24	0.4	575	567	377	480	31	13	2	3264	4671	318	940	5.0	.961	SS-1509, 2B-98, 3B-1

WORLD SERIES

Year	Team		Games	BA	SA	AB	H	2B	3B	HR	HR%	R	RBI	BB	SO	SB	AB	H	PO	A	E	DP	TC/G	FA	G by Pos
1928	NY	A	4	.000	.000	2	0	0	0	0	0.0	0	0	0	1	0	0	0	1	1	0	1	0.5	1.000	2B-4
1934	STL	N	7	.259	.370	27	7	1	1	0	0.0	4	0	0	0	0	0	0	13	17	0	1	4.3	1.000	SS-7
2 yrs.			11	.241	.345	29	7	1	1	0	0.0	4	0	0	1	0	0	0	14	18	0	2	2.9	1.000	SS-7, 2B-4

Red Durrett

DURRETT, ELMER CHARLES
B. Feb. 3, 1921, Sherman, Tex.

BL TL 5'10"   170 lbs.

Year	Team		Games	BA	SA	AB	H	2B	3B	HR	HR%	R	RBI	BB	SO	SB	AB	H	PO	A	E	DP	TC/G	FA	G by Pos
1944	BKN	N	11	.156	.281	32	5	1	0	1	3.1	3	1	7	10	0	1	0	27	1	2	1	2.7	.933	OF-9
1945			8	.125	.125	16	2	0	0	0	0.0	2	0	3	3	0	2	0	8	0	0	0	1.0	1.000	OF-4
2 yrs.			19	.146	.229	48	7	1	0	1	2.1	5	1	10	13	0	3	0	35	1	2	1	2.0	.947	OF-13

Cedric Durst

DURST, CEDRIC MONTGOMERY
B. Aug. 23, 1896, Austin, Tex.   D. Feb. 16, 1971, San Diego, Calif.

BL TL 5'11"   160 lbs.

Year	Team		Games	BA	SA	AB	H	2B	3B	HR	HR%	R	RBI	BB	SO	SB	AB	H	PO	A	E	DP	TC/G	FA	G by Pos
1922	STL	A	15	.333	.417	12	4	1	0	0	0.0	5	0	0	1	0	3	1	6	0	1	0	0.5	.857	OF-6
1923			45	.212	.412	85	18	2	0	5	5.9	11	11	8	14	0	20	3	84	2	3	6	2.0	.966	OF-10, 1B-8
1926			80	.237	.356	219	52	7	5	3	1.4	32	16	22	19	0	15	3	167	8	4	0	2.2	.978	OF-57, 1B-4
1927	NY	A	65	.248	.326	129	32	4	3	0	0.0	18	25	6	7	0	21	4	48	2	1	0	0.8	.980	OF-36, 1B-2
1928			74	.252	.326	135	34	2	1	2	1.5	18	10	7	9	1	33	3	75	4	1	1	1.1	.988	OF-33, 1B-3
1929			92	.257	.361	202	52	3	3	4	2.0	32	31	15	25	3	16	5	153	5	2	1	1.7	.988	OF-72, 1B-1
1930	2 teams	NY A (8G – .158)					BOS A (102G – .245)																		
"	total		110	.240	.343	321	77	20	5	1	0.3	29	29	17	25	3	25	7	156	4	5	1	1.5	.970	OF-83
7 yrs.			481	.244	.351	1103	269	39	17	15	1.4	145	122	75	100	7	133	26	689	25	17	9	1.5	.977	OF-297, 1B-18

WORLD SERIES

Year	Team		Games	BA	SA	AB	H	2B	3B	HR	HR%	R	RBI	BB	SO	SB	AB	H	PO	A	E	DP	TC/G	FA	G by Pos
1927	NY	A	1	.000	.000	1	0	0	0	0	0.0	0	0	0	0	0	0	0	0	0	0	0	0.0	–	OF-4
1928			4	.375	.750	8	3	0	0	1	12.5	3	2	0	1	0	0	0	3	0	0	0	0.8	1.000	OF-4
2 yrs.			5	.333	.667	9	3	0	0	1	11.1	3	2	0	1	0	0	0	3	0	0	0	0.6	1.000	OF-4

Erv Dusak

DUSAK, ERVIN FRANK (Four Sack)
B. July 29, 1920, Chicago, Ill.

BR TR 6'2"   185 lbs.

Year	Team		Games	BA	SA	AB	H	2B	3B	HR	HR%	R	RBI	BB	SO	SB	AB	H	PO	A	E	DP	TC/G	FA	G by Pos
1941	STL	N	6	.143	.143	14	2	0	0	0	0.0	1	3	2	6	0	0	0	10	0	0	0	1.7	1.000	OF-4
1942			12	.185	.296	27	5	3	0	0	0.0	4	3	3	7	0	1	0	14	5	0	1	1.6	1.000	OF-8, 3B-1
1946			100	.240	.378	275	66	9	1	9	3.3	38	42	33	63	7	7	2	146	32	2	5	1.8	.989	OF-77, 3B-11, 2B-2
1947			111	.284	.378	328	93	7	3	6	1.8	56	28	50	34	1	13	1	181	24	6	3	1.9	.972	OF-89, 3B-7
1948			114	.209	.309	311	65	9	2	6	1.9	60	19	49	55	3	9	3	191	80	5	14	2.4	.982	OF-68, 2B-29, 3B-9, SS-1, P-1
1949			1	–	–	0	0	0	0	0	–	1	0	0	0	0	0	0	0	0	0	0	0.0	–	
1950			23	.083	.167	12	1	1	0	0	0.0	0	0	0	3	0	0	0	6	7	0	1	0.6	1.000	P-14, OF-2
1951	2 teams	STL N (5G – .500)					PIT N (21G – .308)																		
"	total		26	.317	.537	41	13	3	0	2	4.9	7	8	3	12	0	11	4	13	4	1	1	0.7	.944	OF-12, P-8, 3B-2, 2B-2
1952	PIT	N	20	.222	.333	27	6	0	0	1	3.7	1	3	2	8	1	11	2	7	2	2	1	0.6	.818	OF-11
9 yrs.			413	.243	.355	1035	•251	32	6	24	2.3	168	106	142	188	12	44	8	568	154	16	26	1.8	.978	OF-271, 2B-33, 3B-30, P-23, SS-1

WORLD SERIES

Year	Team		Games	BA	SA	AB	H	2B	3B	HR	HR%	R	RBI	BB	SO	SB	AB	H	PO	A	E	DP	TC/G	FA	G by Pos
1946	STL	N	4	.250	.500	4	1	1	0	0	0.0	0	0	2	2	0	1	0	1	0	0	0	0.5	1.000	OF-4

Ward Dwight

DWIGHT, ALBERT WARD
B. Jan. 4, 1856, New York, N. Y.   D. Feb. 20, 1903, San Francisco, Calif.

Year	Team		Games	BA	SA	AB	H	2B	3B	HR	HR%	R	RBI	BB	SO	SB	AB	H	PO	A	E	DP	TC/G	FA	G by Pos
1884	KC	U	12	.233	.279	43	10	2	0	0	0.0	8		0			0	0	48	22	6	2	6.3	.921	C-10, OF-1, 2B-1

Double Joe Dwyer

DWYER, JOSEPH MICHAEL
B. Mar. 27, 1904, Orange, N. J.

BL TL 5'9"   186 lbs.

Year	Team		Games	BA	SA	AB	H	2B	3B	HR	HR%	R	RBI	BB	SO	SB	AB	H	PO	A	E	DP	TC/G	FA	G by Pos
1937	CIN	N	12	.273	.273	11	3	0	0	0	0.0	2	1	1	0	0	11	3	0	0	0	0	0.0	–	

Frank Dwyer

DWYER, JOHN FRANCIS
B. Mar. 25, 1868, Lee, Mass.   D. Feb. 4, 1943, Pittsfield, Mass.
Manager 1902.

BR TR 5'8"   145 lbs.

Year	Team		Games	BA	SA	AB	H	2B	3B	HR	HR%	R	RBI	BB	SO	SB	AB	H	PO	A	E	DP	TC/G	FA	G by Pos
1888	CHI	N	5	.190	.238	21	4	0	0	0	0.0	2	2	0	5	0	0	0	2	10	2	0	2.8	.857	P-5
1889			36	.200	.244	135	27	1	1	1	0.7	14	6	4	8	0	0	0	32	49	8	5	2.5	.910	P-32, OF-3, SS-2
1890	CHI	P	16	.264	.302	53	14	2	0	0	0.0	10	11	0	0	0	0	0	6	24	4	1	2.1	.882	P-12, OF-4
1891	2 teams	CIN AA (37G – .284)					MIL AA (11G – .225)																		
"	total		48	.271	.331	181	49	5	3	0	0.0	25	20	6	16	1	0	0	31	97	11	1	2.9	.921	P-45, OF-4, 2B-2
1892	2 teams	STL N (10G – .080)					CIN N (40G – .163)																		
"	total		50	.149	.175	154	23	0	0	0	0.0	19	6	8	11	2	0	0	23	70	5	3	2.0	.949	P-43, OF-6
1893	CIN	N	38	.200	.267	120	24	0	2	1	0.8	22	17	9	5	2	0	0	47	66	2	7	3.0	.983	P-37, OF-1, 1B-1
1894			54	.267	.378	172	46	9	2	1	0.6	31	16	15	13	0	0	0	26	54	4	6	2.1	.937	P-45, OF-10, SS-2
1895			37	.265	.407	113	30	3	5	1	0.9	14	16	5	5	0	0	0	26	54	4	6	2.3	.952	P-37

Year	Team	Games	BA	SA	AB	H	2B	3B	HR	HR%	R	RBI	BB	SO	SB	Pinch Hit AB	Pinch Hit H	PO	A	E	DP	TC/G	FA	G by Pos

Frank Dwyer *continued*

Year	Team	Games	BA	SA	AB	H	2B	3B	HR	HR%	R	RBI	BB	SO	SB	PH AB	PH H	PO	A	E	DP	TC/G	FA	G by Pos
1896		36	.264	.373	110	29	4	4	0	0.0	17	15	11	15	3	0	0	24	52	6	5	2.3	.927	P-36
1897		37	.266	.298	94	25	1	1	0	0.0	13	10	5		0	0	0	11	42	4	0	1.5	.930	P-37
1898		31	.141	.176	85	12	1	1	0	0.0	11	5	7		1	0	0	11	52	6	3	2.2	.913	P-31
1899		5	.364	.364	11	4	0	0	0	0.0	0	0	0			0	0	1	8	0	1	1.8	1.000	P-5
12 yrs.		393	.230	.298	1249	287	28	21	5	0.4	178	136	70	80	16	2	0	251	591	59	33	2.3	.935	P-365, OF-28, SS-4, 2B-2, 1B-1

Jim Dwyer

DWYER, JAMES EDWARD
B. Jan. 3, 1950, Evergreen Park, Ill.
BL TL 5'10" 165 lbs.

Year	Team	Games	BA	SA	AB	H	2B	3B	HR	HR%	R	RBI	BB	SO	SB	PH AB	PH H	PO	A	E	DP	TC/G	FA	G by Pos
1973	STL N	28	.193	.246	57	11	1	1	0	0.0	7	0	1	5	0	8	1	32	0	0	0	1.1	1.000	OF-20
1974		74	.279	.360	86	24	1	0	2	2.3	13	11	11	16	0	41	10	31	3	0	2	0.5	1.000	OF-25, 1B-3
1975	2 teams	STL N	(21G – .194)		MON N	(60G – .286)																		
"	total	81	.272	.364	206	56	8	1	3	1.5	26	21	27	36	4	21	6	104	8	4	1	1.4	.966	OF-61
1976	2 teams	MON N	(50G – .185)		NY N	(11G – .154)																		
"	total	61	.181	.229	105	19	3	1	0	0.0	9	5	13	11	0	38	6	35	0	1	0	0.6	.972	OF-21
1977	STL N	13	.226	.258	31	7	1	0	0	0.0	4	2	4	5	0	2	1	16	0	0	0	1.2	1.000	OF-12
1978	2 teams	STL N	(34G – .215)		SF N	(73G – .225)																		
"	total	107	.223	.366	238	53	12	2	6	2.5	30	26	37	32	7	24	5	216	15	3	14	2.2	.987	OF-58, 1B-29
1979	BOS A	76	.265	.381	113	30	7	0	2	1.8	19	14	17	9	3	22	7	167	16	4	15	2.5	.979	1B-25, OF-19, DH-4
1980		93	.285	.438	260	74	11	1	9	3.5	41	38	28	23	3	11	2	143	15	4	9	1.7	.975	OF-65, DH-12, 1B-9
1981	BAL A	68	.224	.306	134	30	0	1	3	2.2	16	10	20	19	0	6	0	97	2	2	2	1.5	.980	OF-59, 1B-3, DH-1
1982		71	.304	.493	148	45	4	1	8	4.1	28	15	27	24	2	23	6	87	0	2	0	1.3	.978	OF-49, DH-1, 1B-1
1983		100	.286	.505	196	56	17	1	8	4.1	37	38	31	29	1	33	8	123	2	4	4	1.3	.969	OF-56, 1B-4
1984		76	.255	.360	161	41	9	1	2	1.2	22	21	23	24	1	27	7	83	3	3	1	1.2	.966	OF-52, DH-3
1985		101	.249	.399	233	58	8	3	7	3.0	35	36	37	31	0	26	5	131	4	1	0	1.3	.993	OF-78, DH-3
1986		93	.244	.488	160	39	13	1	8	5.0	18	31	22	31	0	42	9	33	4	0	1	0.4	1.000	DH-24, OF-24, 1B-2
1987		92	.274	.498	241	66	7	1	15	6.2	54	33	37	57	4	24	7	57	1	0	0	0.6	1.000	DH-41, OF-30
1988	2 teams	BAL A	(35G – .226)		MIN A	(20G – .293)																		
"	total	55	.255	.330	94	24	1	0	2	2.1	9	18	25	19	0	24	6	3	0	0	0	0.1	1.000	DH-30, OF-2
1989	2 teams	MIN A	(88G – .316)		MON N	(13G – .300)																		
"	total	101	.315	.404	235	74	12	0	3	1.3	35	25	29	24	2	29	8	0	0	0	0	0.0	–	DH-74, OF-1
17 yrs.		1290	.262	.402	2698	707	115	17	76	2.8	402	344	389	395	26	401	94	1358	73	28	49	1.1	.981	OF-632, DH-193, 1B-75

LEAGUE CHAMPIONSHIP SERIES

| 1983 | BAL A | 2 | .250 | .500 | 4 | 1 | 1 | 0 | 0 | 0.0 | 1 | 0 | 1 | 0 | 0 | 0 | 0 | 4 | 0 | 0 | 0 | 2.0 | 1.000 | OF-1 |

WORLD SERIES

| 1983 | BAL A | 2 | .375 | .875 | 8 | 3 | 1 | 0 | 1 | 12.5 | 3 | 1 | 0 | 0 | 0 | 0 | 0 | 2 | 0 | 0 | 0 | 1.0 | 1.000 | OF-2 |

John Dwyer

DWYER, JOHN E.
B. Lisbon, Ill. Deceased.

| 1882 | CLE N | 1 | .000 | .000 | 3 | 0 | 0 | 0 | 0 | 0.0 | 0 | 1 | 0 | 0 | 0 | 0 | 0 | 1 | 1 | 0 | 0 | 2.0 | 1.000 | OF-1, C-1 |

Jerry Dybzinski

DYBZINSKI, JEROME MATHEW
B. July 7, 1955, Cleveland, Ohio
BR TR 6'2" 180 lbs.

Year	Team	Games	BA	SA	AB	H	2B	3B	HR	HR%	R	RBI	BB	SO	SB	PH AB	PH H	PO	A	E	DP	TC/G	FA	G by Pos
1980	CLE A	114	.230	.294	248	57	11	1	1	0.4	32	23	13	35	4	3	0	146	263	13	47	3.7	.969	SS-73, 2B-29, 3B-4, DH-2
1981		48	.298	.298	57	17	0	0	0	0.0	10	6	5	8	7	1	0	35	70	5	11	2.3	.955	SS-34, 3B-3, 2B-3, DH-1
1982		80	.231	.278	212	49	6	2	0	0.0	19	22	21	25	3	2	0	120	244	17	40	4.8	.955	SS-77, 3B-3
1983	CHI A	127	.230	.289	256	59	10	1	1	0.4	30	32	18	29	11	1	0	141	258	14	40	3.3	.966	SS-118, 3B-9
1984		94	.235	.311	132	31	5	1	1	0.8	17	10	13	12	7	0	0	69	160	7	32	2.5	.970	SS-76, 3B-14, DH-1, 2B-1
1985	PIT N	5	.000	.000	4	0	0	0	0	0.0	0	0	0	0	0	0	0	4	5	1	2	2.0	.900	3B-5
6 yrs.		468	.234	.290	909	213	32	5	3	0.3	108	93	70	109	32	7	0	515	1000	57	177	3.4	.964	SS-378, 3B-38, 2B-33, DH-4

LEAGUE CHAMPIONSHIP SERIES

| 1983 | CHI A | 2 | .250 | .250 | 4 | 1 | 0 | 0 | 0 | 0.0 | 0 | 1 | 0 | 0 | 0 | 0 | 0 | 3 | 9 | 0 | 2 | 6.0 | 1.000 | SS-2 |

Jim Dyck

DYCK, JAMES ROBERT
B. Feb. 3, 1922, Omaha, Neb.
BR TR 6'2" 200 lbs.

Year	Team	Games	BA	SA	AB	H	2B	3B	HR	HR%	R	RBI	BB	SO	SB	PH AB	PH H	PO	A	E	DP	TC/G	FA	G by Pos
1951	STL A	4	.067	.067	15	1	0	0	0	0.0	1	1	0	1	0	0	0	7	6	0	1	3.3	1.000	3B-4
1952		122	.269	.450	402	108	22	3	15	3.7	60	64	50	68	0	9	3	197	154	11	14	3.0	.970	3B-74, OF-48
1953		112	.213	.344	334	71	15	1	9	2.7	38	27	38	40	3	9	0	162	106	15	13	2.5	.947	OF-55, 3B-51
1954	CLE A	2	1.000	1.000	1	1	0	0	0	0.0	0	1	1	0	0	1	1	0	0	0	0	0.0	–	
1955	BAL A	61	.279	.386	197	55	13	1	2	1.0	32	22	28	21	1	9	3	104	37	5	2	2.4	.966	OF-45, 3B-17
1956	2 teams	BAL A	(11G – .217)		CIN N	(18G – .091)																		
"	total	29	.176	.235	34	6	2	0	0	0.0	8	0	13	10	0	9	0	14	3	1	0	0.6	.944	OF-9, 3B-1, 1B-1
6 yrs.		330	.246	.389	983	242	52	5	26	2.6	139	114	131	140	4	37	7	484	306	32	30	2.5	.961	OF-157, 3B-147, 1B-1

Ben Dyer

DYER, BENJAMIN FRANKLIN
B. Feb. 13, 1893, Chicago, Ill. D. Aug. 7, 1959, Kenosha, Wis.
BR TR 5'10" 170 lbs.

Year	Team	Games	BA	SA	AB	H	2B	3B	HR	HR%	R	RBI	BB	SO	SB	PH AB	PH H	PO	A	E	DP	TC/G	FA	G by Pos
1914	NY N	7	.250	.250	4	1	0	0	0	0.0	1	0	0	1	1	0	0	2	5	1	1	1.1	.875	SS-6, 2B-1
1915		7	.211	.316	19	4	0	1	0	0.0	4	0	4	3	1	0	0	9	12	2	0	3.3	.913	3B-6, SS-1
1916	DET A	4	.286	.357	14	4	1	0	0	0.0	4	1	1	1	0	0	0	4	7	0	0	2.8	1.000	SS-4
1917		30	.209	.284	67	14	5	0	0	0.0	5	6	2	17	3	8	0	25	46	10	4	2.7	.877	SS-14, 3B-8
1918		13	.278	.278	18	5	0	0	0	0.0	1	2	0	6	0	6	2	14	5	0	1	1.5	1.000	OF-2, 1B-2, P-2, 2B-1
1919		44	.247	.294	85	21	4	0	0	0.0	11	15	8	19	1	0	8	3	36	62	6	3	2.4	.942	3B-23, SS-11, OF-1
6 yrs.		105	.237	.295	207	49	10	1	0	0.0	27	18	15	47	4	22	5	90	137	19	9	2.3	.923	3B-37, SS-36, OF-3, 2B-2, 1B-2, P-2

Duffy Dyer

DYER, DON ROBERT
B. Aug. 15, 1945, Dayton, Ohio
BR TR 6' 187 lbs.

Year	Team	Games	BA	SA	AB	H	2B	3B	HR	HR%	R	RBI	BB	SO	SB	PH AB	PH H	PO	A	E	DP	TC/G	FA	G by Pos
1968	NY N	1	.333	.333	3	1	0	0	0	0.0	1	1	0	1	0	0	0	8	0	0	0	8.0	1.000	C-1
1969		29	.257	.446	74	19	3	1	3	4.1	5	12	4	22	0	8	3	105	10	1	0	4.0	.991	C-19

Year	Team		Games	BA	SA	AB	H	2B	3B	HR	HR%	R	RBI	BB	SO	SB	Pinch Hit AB	H	PO	A	E	DP	TC/G	FA	G by Pos

Duffy Dyer *continued*

Year	Team		Games	BA	SA	AB	H	2B	3B	HR	HR%	R	RBI	BB	SO	SB	AB	H	PO	A	E	DP	TC/G	FA	G by Pos
1970			59	.209	.257	148	31	1	0	2	1.4	8	12	21	32	1	1	1	294	20	3	6	5.4	.991	C-57
1971			59	.231	.320	169	39	7	1	2	1.2	13	18	14	45	1	9	4	336	21	3	3	6.1	.992	C-53
1972			94	.231	.375	325	75	17	3	8	2.5	33	36	28	71	0	3	2	690	61	6	12	8.1	.992	C-91, OF-1
1973			70	.185	.243	189	35	6	1	1	0.5	9	9	13	40	0	10	2	308	26	2	7	4.8	.994	C-60
1974			63	.211	.232	142	30	1	1	0	0.0	14	10	18	15	0	17	8	196	19	4	4	3.5	.982	C-45
1975	PIT	N	48	.227	.364	132	30	5	2	3	2.3	8	16	6	22	0	11	3	187	14	2	0	4.2	.990	C-36
1976			69	.223	.315	184	41	8	0	3	1.6	12	9	29	35	0	12	5	279	37	2	4	4.6	.994	C-58
1977			94	.241	.322	270	65	11	1	3	1.1	27	19	54	49	6	3	0	502	41	2	10	5.8	.996	C-93
1978			58	.211	.269	175	37	8	1	0	0.0	7	13	18	32	2	1	0	326	23	3	2	6.1	.991	C-55
1979	MON	N	28	.243	.365	74	18	6	0	1	1.4	4	8	9	17	0	1	0	141	10	1	1	5.4	.993	C-27
1980	DET	A	48	.185	.306	108	20	1	0	4	3.7	11	11	13	34	0	3	0	129	10	2	2	2.9	.986	C-37, DH-10
1981			2			0	0	0	0	0	—	0	0	0	0	0	0	0	0	0	0	0	0.0	—	C-2
14 yrs.			722	.221	.315	1993	441	74	11	30	1.5	151	173	228	415	10	81	30	3501	291	31	51	5.3	.992	C-634, DH-10, OF-1

LEAGUE CHAMPIONSHIP SERIES

Year	Team		Games	BA	SA	AB	H	2B	3B	HR	HR%	R	RBI	BB	SO	SB	AB	H	PO	A	E	DP	TC/G	FA	G by Pos
1975	PIT	N	1	—	—	0	0	0	0	0	—	0	1	1	0	0	0	0	0	0	0	0	0.0	—	

WORLD SERIES

Year	Team		Games	BA	SA	AB	H	2B	3B	HR	HR%	R	RBI	BB	SO	SB	AB	H	PO	A	E	DP	TC/G	FA	G by Pos
1969	NY	N	1	.000	.000	1	0	0	0	0	0.0	0	0	0	0	0	1	0	0	0	0	0	0.0	—	

Eddie Dyer

DYER, EDWIN HAWLEY
B. Oct. 11, 1900, Morgan City, La.   D. Apr. 20, 1964, Houston, Tex.
Manager 1946-50.

BL TL 5'11½" 168 lbs.

Year	Team		Games	BA	SA	AB	H	2B	3B	HR	HR%	R	RBI	BB	SO	SB	AB	H	PO	A	E	DP	TC/G	FA	G by Pos
1922	STL	N	6	.333	.667	3	1	1	0	0	0.0	1	0	0	0	0	1	1	3	0	0	0	0.5	1.000	P-2
1923			35	.267	.467	45	12	3	0	2	4.4	17	5	3	5	1	14	3	18	4	0	0	0.6	1.000	OF-8, P-4
1924			50	.237	.342	76	18	2	3	0	0.0	8	8	3	1	1	16	4	10	40	5	1	1.1	.909	P-29, OF-1
1925			31	.097	.129	31	3	1	0	0	0.0	4	0	3	1	1	1	0	0	22	2	1	0.8	.917	P-27
1926			6	.500	.500	2	1	0	0	0	0.0	1	0	0	0	0	0	0	0	3	0	0	0.5	1.000	P-6
1927			1	—	—	0	0	0	0	0	—	0	0	1	0	0	0	0	0	0	0	0	0.0	—	P-1
6 yrs.			129	.223	.344	157	35	7	3	2	1.3	31	13	10	14	3	32	8	31	69	7	2	0.8	.935	P-69, OF-9

Jimmy Dykes

DYKES, JAMES JOSEPH
B. Nov. 10, 1896, Philadelphia, Pa.   D. June 15, 1976, Philadelphia, Pa.
Manager 1934-46, 1951-54, 1958-61.

BR TR 5'9" 185 lbs.

Year	Team		Games	BA	SA	AB	H	2B	3B	HR	HR%	R	RBI	BB	SO	SB	AB	H	PO	A	E	DP	TC/G	FA	G by Pos
1918	PHI	A	59	.188	.237	186	35	3	3	0	0.0	13	13	19	32	3	2	0	139	190	21	33	5.9	.940	2B-56, 3B-1
1919			17	.184	.204	49	9	1	0	0	0.0	4	1	7	11	0	0	0	28	58	5	5	5.4	.945	2B-16
1920			142	.256	.361	546	140	25	4	8	1.5	81	35	52	73	6	0	0	363	457	45	53	6.1	.948	2B-108, 3B-36
1921			155	.274	.452	613	168	32	13	17	2.8	88	77	60	75	6	0	0	434	522	46	88	6.5	.954	2B-155
1922			145	.275	.421	501	138	23	7	12	2.4	66	68	55	98	6	0	0	193	307	30	21	3.7	.943	3B-140, 2B-5
1923			124	.252	.353	416	105	28	1	4	1.0	50	43	35	40	6	0	0	285	366	25	64	5.5	.963	2B-102, SS-20, 3B-2
1924			110	.312	.427	410	128	26	6	3	0.7	68	50	38	59	1	2	1	257	326	26	52	5.5	.957	2B-78, 3B-27, SS-4
1925			122	.323	.471	465	150	32	11	5	1.1	93	55	46	49	3	3	2	225	302	21	45	4.5	.962	3B-64, 2B-58, SS-2
1926			124	.287	.392	429	123	32	5	1	0.2	54	44	49	34	6	1	0	198	322	20	43	4.4	.963	3B-77, 2B-44, SS-1
1927			121	.324	.453	417	135	33	6	3	0.7	61	60	44	23	2	5	3	864	112	16	63	8.2	.984	1B-82, 3B-25, OF-5, SS-5, 2B-5, P-2
1928			85	.277	.384	242	67	11	0	5	2.1	39	30	27	21	2	3	0	166	164	9	21	4.0	.973	2B-32, SS-23, 3B-20, 1B-8, OF-1
1929			119	.327	.539	401	131	34	6	13	3.2	76	79	51	25	8	2	0	203	273	33	41	4.3	.935	SS-60, 3B-48, 2B-13
1930			125	.301	.425	435	131	28	4	6	1.4	69	73	74	53	3	1	0	125	191	13	18	2.6	.960	3B-123, OF-1
1931			101	.273	.389	355	97	28	2	3	0.8	48	46	48	47	1	0	0	136	188	15	27	3.4	.956	3B-87, SS-15
1932			153	.265	.373	558	148	29	5	7	1.3	71	90	77	65	8	1	0	158	282	11	26	2.9	.976	3B-141, SS-10, 2B-1
1933	CHI	A	151	.260	.327	554	144	22	6	1	0.2	49	68	69	37	3	0	0	132	296	21	22	3.0	.953	3B-151
1934			127	.268	.368	456	122	17	4	7	1.5	52	82	64	28	1	1	1	383	252	27	40	5.2	.959	3B-74, 2B-27, 1B-27
1935			117	.288	.387	403	116	24	2	4	1.0	45	61	59	28	4	1	0	290	185	15	29	4.2	.969	3B-98, 1B-16, 2B-3
1936			127	.267	.366	435	116	16	3	7	1.6	42	60	61	36	1	1	0	108	240	18	14	2.9	.951	3B-125
1937			30	.306	.400	85	26	5	0	1	1.2	10	23	9	7	0	4	2	152	27	1	15	6.0	.994	1B-15, 3B-11
1938			26	.303	.461	89	27	4	2	2	2.2	9	13	10	8	0	1	0	75	72	9	13	6.0	.942	2B-23, 3B-1
1939			2	.000	.000	1	0	0	0	0	0.0	0	0	0	0	0	0	0	1	0	0	0	1.5	.667	3B-2
22 yrs.			2282	.280	.400	8046	2256	453	90	109	1.4	1108	1071	954	849	70	28	9	4916	5132	428	733	4.6	.959	3B-1253, 2B-726, 1B-148, SS-140, OF-7, P-2

WORLD SERIES

Year	Team		Games	BA	SA	AB	H	2B	3B	HR	HR%	R	RBI	BB	SO	SB	AB	H	PO	A	E	DP	TC/G	FA	G by Pos
1929	PHI	A	5	.421	.474	19	8	1	0	0	0.0	2	4	1	1	0	0	0	3	4	2	1	1.8	.778	3B-5
1930			6	.222	.556	18	4	3	0	1	5.6	3	5	5	3	0	0	0	8	6	1	1	2.5	.933	3B-6
1931			7	.227	.227	22	5	0	0	0	0.0	1	2	5	1	0	0	0	4	12	0	1	2.3	1.000	3B-7
3 yrs.			18	.288	.407	59	17	4	0	1	1.7	6	11	11	5	0	0	0	15	22	3	3	2.2	.925	3B-18

Len Dykstra

DYKSTRA, LEONARD KYLE (Nails)
B. Feb. 10, 1963, Santa Ana, Calif.

BL TL 5'10" 160 lbs.

Year	Team		Games	BA	SA	AB	H	2B	3B	HR	HR%	R	RBI	BB	SO	SB	AB	H	PO	A	E	DP	TC/G	FA	G by Pos
1985	NY	N	83	.254	.331	236	60	9	3	1	0.4	40	19	30	24	15	9	3	165	6	1	2	2.1	.994	OF-74
1986			147	.295	.445	431	127	27	7	8	1.9	77	45	58	55	31	14	4	283	8	3	2	2.0	.990	OF-139
1987			132	.285	.455	431	123	37	3	10	2.3	86	43	40	67	27	18	5	239	4	3	1	1.9	.988	OF-118
1988			126	.270	.385	429	116	19	3	8	1.9	57	33	30	43	30	12	5	270	3	1	0	2.2	.996	OF-112
1989	2 teams	NY N	(56G – .270)			PHI N	(90G – .222)																			
"	total		146	.237	.356	511	121	32	4	7	1.4	66	32	60	53	30	9	3	332	10	4	0	2.4	.988	OF-139
5 yrs.			634	.268	.399	2038	547	124	20	34	1.7	326	172	218	242	133	62	20	1289	31	12	5	2.1	.991	OF-582

LEAGUE CHAMPIONSHIP SERIES

Year	Team		Games	BA	SA	AB	H	2B	3B	HR	HR%	R	RBI	BB	SO	SB	AB	H	PO	A	E	DP	TC/G	FA	G by Pos
1986	NY	N	6	.304	.565	23	7	1	1	1	4.3	3	3	2	4	1	2	1	10	0	0	0	1.7	1.000	OF-6
1988			7	.429	.857	14	6	3	0	1	7.1	6	3	4	0	0	0	0	9	0	0	0	1.3	1.000	OF-7
2 yrs.			13	.351	.676	37	13	4	1	2	5.4	9	6	6	4	1	2	1	19	0	0	0	1.5	1.000	OF-13

WORLD SERIES

Year	Team		Games	BA	SA	AB	H	2B	3B	HR	HR%	R	RBI	BB	SO	SB	AB	H	PO	A	E	DP	TC/G	FA	G by Pos
1986	NY	N	7	.296	.519	27	8	0	0	2	7.4	4	3	2	7	0	1	1	14	0	0	0	2.0	1.000	OF-7

Year	Team		Games	BA	SA	AB	H	2B	3B	HR	HR%	R	RBI	BB	SO	SB	Pinch Hit AB	Pinch Hit H	PO	A	E	DP	TC/G	FA	G by Pos

John Dyler

DYLER, JOHN F.
B. June, 1852, Louisville, Ky. Deceased.
Manager 1882.

| 1882 | LOU | AA | 1 | .000 | .000 | 4 | 0 | 0 | 0 | 0 | 0.0 | 0 | | 0 | | | 0 | 0 | 0 | 0 | 0 | 0 | 0.0 | – | OF-1 |

Don Eaddy

EADDY, DONALD JOHNSON
B. Feb. 16, 1934, Grand Rapids, Mich. · BR TR 5'11" 165 lbs.

| 1959 | CHI | N | 15 | .000 | .000 | 1 | 0 | 0 | 0 | 0 | 0.0 | 3 | 0 | 0 | 1 | 0 | 0 | 0 | 0 | 1 | 1 | 0 | 0.1 | .500 | 3B-1 |

Bad Bill Eagan

EAGAN, WILLIAM
B. June 1, 1869, Camden, N. J. D. Feb. 14, 1905, Denver, Colo.

1891	STL	AA	83	.215	.318	302	65	11	4	4	1.3	49	43	44	54	21	0	0	177	278	35	29	5.9	.929	2B-83
1893	CHI	N	6	.263	.263	19	5	0	0	0	0.0	3	2	5	5	4	0	0	12	19	3	4	5.7	.912	2B-6
1898	PIT	N	19	.328	.459	61	20	2	3	0	0.0	14	5	8		1	0	0	46	60	10	10	6.1	.914	2B-17
3 yrs.			108	.236	.338	382	90	13	7	4	1.0	66	50	57	59	26	0	0	235	357	48	43	5.9	.925	2B-106

Truck Eagan

EAGAN, CHARLES EUGENE
B. Aug. 10, 1877, San Francisco, Calif. D. Mar. 19, 1949, San Francisco, Calif. · BR TR 5'11" 190 lbs.

| 1901 | 2 teams | | PIT | N | (4G – .083) | | | CLE | A | (5G – .167) | | | | | | | | | | | | | | | |
| " | total | | 9 | .133 | .200 | 30 | 4 | 0 | 1 | 0 | 0.0 | 2 | 4 | 1 | | 1 | 1 | 0 | 7 | 27 | 1 | 0 | 3.9 | .971 | 2B-5, SS-3, 3B-1 |

Bill Eagle

EAGLE, WILLIAM LYCURGUS
B. July 25, 1877, Rockville, Md. D. Apr. 27, 1951, Churchton, Md.

| 1898 | WAS | N | 4 | .308 | .385 | 13 | 4 | 1 | 0 | 0 | 0.0 | 0 | 2 | 0 | | 0 | 0 | 0 | 2 | 1 | 1 | 0 | 1.0 | .750 | OF-4 |

Charlie Eakle

EAKLE, CHARLES EMORY
B. Sept. 27, 1887, Baltimore, Md. D. June 15, 1959, Baltimore, Md.

| 1915 | BAL | F | 2 | .286 | .429 | 7 | 2 | 1 | 0 | 0 | 0.0 | 0 | 0 | 0 | | 1 | 0 | 0 | 1 | 2 | 2 | 0 | 2.5 | .600 | 2B-2 |

Howard Earl

EARL, HOWARD J. (Slim Jim)
B. Feb. 25, 1867, Massachusetts D. Dec. 23, 1916, North Bay, N. Y. · 6'1"

1890	CHI	N	92	.247	.336	384	95	10	3	6	1.6	57	51	18	47	17	0	0	178	158	46	12	4.2	.880	OF-49, 2B-39, SS-4, 1B-3
1891	MIL	AA	31	.248	.341	129	32	5	2	1	0.8	21	17	5	13	3	0	0	61	3	3	1	2.2	.955	OF-30, 1B-2
2 yrs.			123	.248	.337	513	127	15	5	7	1.4	78	68	23	60	20	0	0	239	161	49	13	3.7	.891	OF-79, 2B-39, 1B-5, SS-4

Scott Earl

EARL, WILLIAM SCOTT
B. Sept. 18, 1960, Seymour, Ind. · BR TR 5'11" 165 lbs.

| 1984 | DET | A | 14 | .114 | .171 | 35 | 4 | 0 | 1 | 0 | 0.0 | 3 | 1 | 0 | 9 | 1 | 0 | 0 | 23 | 24 | 2 | 9 | 3.5 | .959 | 2B-14 |

Billy Earle

EARLE, WILLIAM MOFFAT (The Little Globetrotter)
B. Nov. 10, 1867, Philadelphia, Pa. D. May 30, 1946, Omaha, Neb. · BR TR 5'10½" 170 lbs.

1889	CIN	AA	53	.266	.444	169	45	4	7	4	2.4	37	31	30	24	26	0	0	200	34	36	6	5.1	.867	OF-26, C-23, 1B-5
1890	STL	AA	22	.233	.301	73	17	3	1	0	0.0	16		7		6	0	0	124	33	9	1	7.5	.946	C-18, OF-3, SS-1, 3B-1, 2B-1
1892	PIT	N	5	.538	.692	13	7	2	0	0	0.0	5	3	4	1	2	0	0	15	5	2	0	4.4	.909	C-5
1893			27	.253	.442	95	24	4	2	2	2.1	21	15	7	6	1	0	0	99	19	5	2	4.6	.959	C-27
1894	2 teams		LOU	N	(21G – .354)			BKN	N	(14G – .340)															
"	total		35	.348	.409	115	40	7	0	0	0.0	23	13	15	5	6	1	0	94	52	11	1	4.5	.930	C-30, 2B-2, OF-1, 3B-1, 1B-1
5 yrs.			142	.286	.419	465	133	20	6	6	1.3	102	62	63	36	41	1	0	532	143	63	10	5.2	.915	C-103, OF-30, 1B-6, 2B-3, 3B-2, SS-1

Jake Early

EARLY, JACOB WILLARD
B. May 19, 1915, King's Mountain, N. C. D. May 31, 1985, Melbourne, Fla. · BL TR 5'11" 168 lbs.

1939	WAS	A	32	.262	.393	84	22	7	2	0	0.0	8	14	5	14	0	6	2	95	9	4	1	3.4	.963	C-24
1940			80	.257	.408	206	53	8	4	5	2.4	26	14	23	22	0	21	4	276	41	10	5	4.1	.969	C-56
1941			104	.287	.468	355	102	20	7	10	2.8	42	54	24	38	0	6	3	385	52	16	13	4.4	.965	C-100
1942			104	.204	.280	353	72	14	2	3	0.8	31	46	37	37	0	7	0	392	71	9	11	4.5	.981	C-98
1943			126	.258	.362	423	109	23	3	5	1.2	37	60	52	43	5	4	0	443	83	11	10	4.3	.980	C-122
1946			64	.201	.296	189	38	6	0	4	2.1	13	18	23	27	0	0	0	246	45	12	7	4.7	.960	C-64
1947	STL	A	87	.224	.336	214	48	9	3	3	1.4	25	19	54	34	0	1	0	301	43	4	5	4.0	.989	C-85
1948	WAS	A	97	.220	.276	246	54	7	2	1	0.4	22	28	36	33	2	5	2	268	51	3	7	3.3	.991	C-92
1949			53	.246	.297	138	34	4	0	1	0.7	12	11	26	11	0	3	0	160	22	5	6	3.5	.973	C-53
9 yrs.			747	.241	.350	2208	532	98	23	32	1.4	216	264	280	259	7	55	12	2566	417	74	65	4.1	.976	C-694

Mike Easler

EASLER, MICHAEL ANTHONY
B. Nov. 29, 1950, Cleveland, Ohio · BL TR 6' 190 lbs.

1973	HOU	N	6	.000	.000	7	0	0	0	0	0.0	1	0	2	4	0	2	0	1	0	1	0	0.3	.500	OF-2
1974			15	.067	.067	15	1	0	0	0	0.0	0	0	0	5	0	15	1	0	0	1	0	0.0	–	
1975			5	.000	.000	5	0	0	0	0	0.0	0	0	0	1	0	5	0	0	0	0	0	0.0	–	
1976	CAL	A	21	.241	.296	54	13	1	1	0	0.0	6	4	2	11	1	5	1	0	0	0	0	0.0	–	DH-16
1977	PIT	N	10	.444	.722	18	8	2	0	1	5.6	3	5	0	1	0	6	2	7	0	0	0	0.7	1.000	OF-4
1979			55	.278	.444	54	15	1	1	2	3.7	8	11	8	13	0	44	10	0	0	0	0	0.0	–	OF-4
1980			132	.338	.583	393	133	27	3	21	5.3	65	74	43	65	5	12	4	201	6	3	1	1.6	.986	OF-119
1981			95	.286	.431	339	97	18	5	7	2.1	43	42	24	45	4	6	2	188	13	4	2	2.2	.980	OF-90
1982			142	.276	.436	475	131	27	2	15	3.2	52	58	40	85	1	10	4	243	8	7	2	1.8	.973	OF-138
1983			115	.307	.441	381	117	17	2	10	2.6	44	54	22	64	0	17	8	158	6	6	1	1.5	.965	OF-105
1984	BOS	A	156	.313	.516	601	188	31	5	27	4.5	87	91	58	134	1	1	0	256	29	7	21	1.9	.976	DH-126, 1B-29
1985			155	.262	.412	568	149	29	4	16	2.8	71	74	53	129	1	0	5	32	0	3	0	0.2	.914	DH-130, OF-20
1986	NY	A	146	.302	.449	490	148	26	2	14	2.9	64	78	49	87	3	19	4	23	0	1	0	0.2	.958	DH-129, OF-11

Year	Team	Games	BA	SA	AB	H	2B	3B	HR	HR%	R	RBI	BB	SO	SB	Pinch Hit AB	Pinch Hit H	PO	A	E	DP	TC/G	FA	G by Pos

Mike Easler *continued*

1987	2 teams	PHI N (33G – .282)		NY A (65G – .281)																				OF-45, DH-32
"	total	98	.282	.372	277	78	10	0	5	1.8	20	31	20	52	1	22	5	73	5	1	2	0.8	.987	OF-45, DH-32
	14 yrs.	1151	.293	.454	3677	1078	189	25	118	3.2	465	522	321	696	20	169	45	1182	67	33	29	1.1	.974	OF-538, DH-433, 1B-29

LEAGUE CHAMPIONSHIP SERIES

| 1979 | PIT | N | 1 | .000 | .000 | 1 | 0 | 0 | 0 | 0 | 0.0 | 0 | 0 | 0 | 0 | 0 | 1 | 0 | 0 | 0 | 0 | 0 | 0.0 | – | |

WORLD SERIES

| 1979 | PIT | N | 2 | .000 | .000 | 1 | 0 | 0 | 0 | 0 | 0.0 | 0 | 0 | 1 | 0 | 0 | 1 | 0 | 0 | 0 | 0 | 0 | 0.0 | – | |

Carl East

EAST, CARLTON WILLIAM
B. Aug. 27, 1894, Marietta, Ga. D. Jan. 15, 1953, Whitesburg, Ga.
BL TR 6'2" 178 lbs.

1915	STL	A	1	.000	.000	1	0	0	0	0	0.0	0	0	0	0	0	0	0	0	0	0	0	0.0	–	P-1
1924	WAS	A	2	.333	.500	6	2	1	0	0	0.0	1	2	2	1	0	0	0	4	0	1	0	2.5	.800	OF-2
	2 yrs.	3	.286	.429	7	2	1	0	0	0.0	1	2	2	1	0	0	0	4	0	1	0	1.7	.800	OF-2, P-1

Harry East

EAST, HARRY H.
B. Apr., 1863, St. Louis, Mo. Deceased.

| 1882 | BAL | AA | 1 | .000 | .000 | 4 | 0 | 0 | 0 | 0 | 0.0 | | 0 | | | | 0 | 0 | 1 | 2 | 2 | 0 | 5.0 | .600 | 3B-1 |

Luke Easter

EASTER, LUSCIOUS LUKE
B. Aug. 4, 1914, St. Louis, Mo. D. Mar. 29, 1979, Euclid, Ohio
BL TR 6'4½" 240 lbs.

1949	CLE	A	21	.222	.289	45	10	3	0	0	0.0	6	2	8	6	0	6	1	9	0	0	0	0.4	1.000	OF-12
1950			141	.280	.487	540	151	20	4	28	5.2	96	107	70	95	0	1	1	1114	82	11	114	8.6	.991	1B-128, OF-13
1951			128	.270	.481	486	131	12	5	27	5.6	65	103	37	71	0	3	0	1043	84	14	108	8.8	.988	1B-125
1952			127	.263	.513	437	115	10	3	31	7.1	63	97	44	84	1	9	2	940	90	18	87	8.3	.983	1B-118
1953			68	.303	.445	211	64	9	0	7	3.3	26	31	15	35	0	11	4	442	30	9	54	7.1	.981	1B-56
1954			6	.167	.167	6	1	0	0	0	0.0	0	0	0	2	0	6	1	0	0	0	0	0.0	–	
	6 yrs.	491	.274	.481	1725	472	54	12	93	5.4	256	340	174	293	1	36	9	3548	270	52	363	7.9	.987	1B-427, OF-25

Henry Easterday

EASTERDAY, HENRY P.
B. Sept. 16, 1864, Philadelphia, Pa. D. Mar. 30, 1895, Philadelphia, Pa.
BR TR 5'6" 145 lbs.

1884	PHI	U	28	.243	.287	115	28	5	0	0	0.0	12		5			0	0	35	98	19	6	5.4	.875	SS-28
1888	KC	AA	115	.190	.259	401	76	7	6	3	0.7	42	37	31		23	0	0	120	459	73	30	5.7	.888	SS-115
1889	COL	AA	95	.173	.275	324	56	5	8	4	1.2	43	34	41	57	10	0	0	140	340	60	30	5.7	.889	SS-89, 2B-5, 3B-1
1890	3 teams	COL AA (58G – .157)		PHI AA (19G – .147)				LOU AA (7G – .083)																SS-83, 3B-1
"	total	84	.149	.194	289	43	6	2	1	0.3	44		35		10	0	0	122	287	58	28	5.6	.876	SS-83, 3B-1
	4 yrs.	322	.180	.250	1129	203	23	16	8	0.7	141	71	112	57	43	0	0	417	1184	210	94	5.6	.884	SS-315, 2B-5, 3B-2

Paul Easterling

EASTERLING, PAUL
B. Sept. 28, 1905, Reidsville, Ga.
BR TR 5'11" 180 lbs.

1928	DET	A	43	.325	.482	114	37	7	1	3	2.6	17	12	8	24	2	8	3	68	2	6	0	1.8	.921	OF-34
1930			29	.203	.316	79	16	6	0	1	1.3	7	14	6	18	0	2	0	29	3	0	2	1.1	1.000	OF-25
1938	PHI	A	4	.286	.286	7	2	0	0	0	0.0	1	0	1	2	0	3	0	3	0	1	0	1.0	.750	OF-1
	3 yrs.	76	.275	.410	200	55	13	1	4	2.0	25	26	15	44	2	13	3	100	5	7	2	1.5	.938	OF-60

Ted Easterly

EASTERLY, THEODORE HARRISON
B. Apr. 20, 1885, Lincoln, Neb. D. July 6, 1951, Clear Lake, Calif.
BL TR 5'8" 165 lbs.

1909	CLE	A	98	.261	.390	287	75	14	10	1	0.3	32	27	13		8	22	4	335	110	16	9	4.7	.965	C-76
1910			110	.306	.383	363	111	16	6	0	0.0	34	55	21		10	14	4	239	109	15	8	3.3	.959	C-66, OF-30
1911			99	.324	.436	287	93	19	5	1	0.3	34	37	8		6	23	8	168	32	15	3	2.2	.930	OF-54, C-23
1912	2 teams	CLE A (63G – .296)		CHI A (30G – .364)																				C-61, OF-1
"	total	93	.311	.349	241	75	6	0	1	0.4	22	35	9		4	30	13	266	82	15	14	3.9	.959	C-61, OF-1
1913	CHI	A	60	.237	.247	97	23	1	0	0	0.0	3	8	4	9	2	37	8	96	24	3	0	2.1	.976	C-19
1914	KC	F	134	.335	.443	436	146	20	12	1	0.2	58	67	31		10	6	0	570	173	24	16	5.7	.969	C-128
1915			110	.272	.372	309	84	12	5	1	0.3	32	32	21		2	20	8	398	132	17	11	5.0	.969	C-88
	7 yrs.	704	.300	.392	2020	607	88	38	7	0.3	215	261	107	9	42	152	45	2072	662	105	61	4.0	.963	C-461, OF-85

Roy Easterwood

EASTERWOOD, ROY CHARLES (Shag)
B. Jan. 12, 1915, Waxahachie, Tex. D. Aug. 24, 1984, Graham, Tex.
BR TR 6'½" 196 lbs.

| 1944 | CHI | N | 17 | .212 | .364 | 33 | 7 | 2 | 0 | 1 | 3.0 | 1 | 2 | 1 | 11 | 0 | 5 | 1 | 29 | 4 | 0 | 1 | 1.9 | 1.000 | C-12 |

John Easton

EASTON, JOHN DAVID (Goose)
B. Mar. 4, 1933, Trenton, N. J.
BR TR 6'2" 185 lbs.

1955	PHI	N	1	–	–	0	0	0	0	0	–	0	0	0	0	0	0	0	0	0	0	0	0.0	–	
1959			3	.000	.000	3	0	0	0	0	0.0	0	0	0	3	0	3	0	0	0	0	0	0.0		
	2 yrs.	4	.000	.000	3	0	0	0	0	0.0	0	0	0	3	0	3	0	0	0	0	0	0.0		

Eddie Eayrs

EAYRS, EDWIN
B. Nov. 10, 1890, Blackstone, Mass. D. Nov. 30, 1969, Warwick, R. I.
BL TL 5'7" 160 lbs.

1913	PIT	N	4	.167	.167	6	1	0	0	0	0.0		0	2	0	0	2	0	0	2	1	0	0.8	.667	P-2
1920	BOS	N	87	.328	.377	244	80	5	2	1	0.4	31	24	30	18	4	16	5	109	18	6	2	1.5	.955	OF-63, P-7
1921	2 teams	BOS N (15G – .067)		BKN N (8G – .167)																				P-2, OF-1
"	total	23	.095	.095	21	2	0	0	0	0.0	1	2	2	4	0	18	1	0	0	0	0	0.0	–	P-2, OF-1
	3 yrs.	114	.306	.351	271	83	5	2	1	0.4	32	26	32	23	4	36	6	109	20	7	2	1.2	.949	OF-64, P-11

Hi Ebright

EBRIGHT, HIRAM C. (Buck)
B. June 12, 1859, Lancaster County, Pa. D. Oct. 24, 1916, Milwaukee, Wis.
BR TR

| 1889 | WAS | N | 16 | .254 | .407 | 59 | 15 | 2 | 2 | 1 | 1.7 | 7 | 6 | 3 | 8 | 1 | 0 | 0 | 51 | 33 | 11 | 0 | 5.9 | .884 | C-9, OF-4, SS-3 |

Year Team	Games	BA	SA	AB	H	2B	3B	HR	HR%	R	RBI	BB	SO	SB	Pinch Hit AB	Pinch Hit H	PO	A	E	DP	TC/G	FA	G by Pos

Johnny Echols
ECHOLS, JOHN GRESHAM
B. Jan. 9, 1917, Atlanta, Ga. D. Nov. 13, 1972, Atlanta, Ga.
BR TR 5'10½" 175 lbs.

Year Team	Games	BA	SA	AB	H	2B	3B	HR	HR%	R	RBI	BB	SO	SB	PH AB	PH H	PO	A	E	DP	TC/G	FA	G by Pos
1939 STL N	2	–	–	0	0	0	0	0	–	0	0	0	0	0	0	0	0	0	0	0	0.0	–	

Ox Eckhardt
ECKHARDT, OSCAR GEORGE
B. Dec. 23, 1901, Yorktown, Tex. D. Apr. 22, 1951, Yorktown, Tex.
BL TR 6'1" 185 lbs.

Year Team	Games	BA	SA	AB	H	2B	3B	HR	HR%	R	RBI	BB	SO	SB	PH AB	PH H	PO	A	E	DP	TC/G	FA	G by Pos
1932 BOS N	8	.250	.250	8	2	0	0	0	0.0	1	1	0	1	0	8	2	0	0	0	0	0.0		
1936 BKN N	16	.182	.273	44	8	1	0	1	2.3	5	6	5	2	0	3	0	23	1	0	0	1.5	1.000	OF-10
2 yrs.	24	.192	.269	52	10	1	0	1	1.9	6	7	5	3	0	11	2	23	1	0	0	1.0	1.000	OF-10

Charlie Eden
EDEN, CHARLES M.
B. Jan. 18, 1855, Lexington, Ky. D. Sept. 17, 1920, Cincinnati, Ohio
BR TR

Year Team	Games	BA	SA	AB	H	2B	3B	HR	HR%	R	RBI	BB	SO	SB	PH AB	PH H	PO	A	E	DP	TC/G	FA	G by Pos
1877 CHI N	15	.218	.255	55	12	0	1	0	0.0	9	5	3	6				17	2	9	1	1.9	.679	OF-15
1879 CLE N	81	.272	.425	353	96	31	7	3	0.8	40	34	6	20		0	0	114	22	32	3	2.1	.810	OF-80, 1B-3, C-1
1884 PIT AA	32	.270	.418	122	33	7	4	1	0.8	12	7				0	0	40	4	14	0	1.8	.759	OF-31, P-2
1885	98	.254	.328	405	103	18	6	0	0.0	57	17				0	0	113	10	32	2	1.6	.794	OF-96, P-4, 3B-2
4 yrs.	226	.261	.372	935	244	56	18	4	0.4	118	39	33	26		0	0	284	38	87	6	1.8	.787	OF-222, P-6, 1B-3, 3B-2, C-1

Mike Eden
EDEN, EDWARD MICHAEL
B. May 22, 1949, Fort Clayton, Canal Zone
BB TR 5'10" 170 lbs.

Year Team	Games	BA	SA	AB	H	2B	3B	HR	HR%	R	RBI	BB	SO	SB	PH AB	PH H	PO	A	E	DP	TC/G	FA	G by Pos
1976 ATL N	5	.000	.000	8	0	0	0	0	0.0	0	1	0	0	0	2	0	2	5	0	1	1.4	1.000	2B-2
1978 CHI A	10	.118	.118	17	2	0	0	0	0.0	1	0	4	0	0	0	0	14	13	2	5	2.9	.931	SS-5, 2B-4
2 yrs.	15	.080	.080	25	2	0	0	0	0.0	1	1	4	0	0	2	0	16	18	2	6	2.4	.944	2B-6, SS-5

Stump Edington
EDINGTON, JACOB FRANK
B. July 4, 1891, Roleen, Ind. D. Nov. 11, 1969, Bastrop, La.
BL TL 5'8" 170 lbs.

Year Team	Games	BA	SA	AB	H	2B	3B	HR	HR%	R	RBI	BB	SO	SB	PH AB	PH H	PO	A	E	DP	TC/G	FA	G by Pos
1912 PIT N	15	.302	.377	53	16	0	2	0	0.0	4	12	3	1	0	2	0	22	3	0	0	1.7	1.000	OF-14

Dave Edler
EDLER, DAVID DELMAR
B. Aug. 5, 1956, Sioux City, Iowa
BR TR 6' 195 lbs.

Year Team	Games	BA	SA	AB	H	2B	3B	HR	HR%	R	RBI	BB	SO	SB	PH AB	PH H	PO	A	E	DP	TC/G	FA	G by Pos
1980 SEA A	28	.225	.337	89	20	1	0	3	3.4	11	9	8	16	2	0	0	18	64	3	6	3.0	.965	3B-28
1981	29	.141	.179	78	11	3	0	0	0.0	7	5	11	13	3	3	1	18	43	8	4	2.4	.884	3B-26, SS-1
1982	40	.279	.394	104	29	2	2	2	1.9	14	18	11	13	4	5	2	24	53	6	4	2.1	.928	3B-31, DH-2, OF-2
1983	29	.190	.286	63	12	1	1	1	1.6	2	4	5	11	3	4	0	29	22	4	6	1.9	.927	3B-13, DH-6, 1B-5, OF-1
4 yrs.	126	.216	.308	334	72	7	3	6	1.8	34	36	35	53	12	12	3	89	182	21	20	2.3	.928	3B-98, DH-8, 1B-5, OF-3, SS-1

Eddie Edmonson
EDMONSON, EARL EDWARD (Axel)
B. Nov. 20, 1889, Hopewell, Pa. D. May 10, 1971, Leesberg, Fla.
BL TR 6' 175 lbs.

Year Team	Games	BA	SA	AB	H	2B	3B	HR	HR%	R	RBI	BB	SO	SB	PH AB	PH H	PO	A	E	DP	TC/G	FA	G by Pos
1913 CLE A	2	.000	.000	5	0	0	0	0	0.0	0	0	0	0	0	0	0	5	0	1	0	3.0	.833	OF-1, 1B-1

Bob Edmundson
EDMUNDSON, ROBERT E.
B. Apr. 30, 1879, Paris, Ky. D. Aug. 14, 1931, Lawrence, Kans.
BR TR 5'11" 185 lbs.

Year Team	Games	BA	SA	AB	H	2B	3B	HR	HR%	R	RBI	BB	SO	SB	PH AB	PH H	PO	A	E	DP	TC/G	FA	G by Pos
1908 WAS A	26	.188	.263	80	15	4	1	0	0.0	5	2	7		0	2	1	34	2	5	1	1.6	.878	OF-24

Edwards
EDWARDS,
TR

Year Team	Games	BA	SA	AB	H	2B	3B	HR	HR%	R	RBI	BB	SO	SB	PH AB	PH H	PO	A	E	DP	TC/G	FA	G by Pos
1915 PHI A	2	.000	.000	5	0	0	0	0	0.0	0	0	0	3	0	1	0	0	1	0	0	0.5	1.000	2B-1

Bruce Edwards
EDWARDS, CHARLES BRUCE (Bull)
B. July 15, 1923, Quincy, Ill. D. Apr. 25, 1975, Sacramento, Calif.
BR TR 5'8" 180 lbs.

Year Team	Games	BA	SA	AB	H	2B	3B	HR	HR%	R	RBI	BB	SO	SB	PH AB	PH H	PO	A	E	DP	TC/G	FA	G by Pos
1946 BKN N	92	.267	.356	292	78	13	5	1	0.3	24	25	34	20	1	0	0	431	53	9	9	5.4	.982	C-91
1947	130	.295	.418	471	139	15	8	9	1.9	53	80	49	55	2	2	0	592	58	11	11	5.1	.983	C-128
1948	96	.276	.434	286	79	17	2	8	2.8	36	54	26	28	4	9	2	264	43	12	2	3.3	.962	C-48, OF-21, 3B-14, 1B-1
1949	64	.209	.392	148	31	3	0	8	5.4	24	25	25	15	0	17	3	190	13	3	0	3.2	.985	C-41, OF-4, 3B-1
1950	50	.183	.394	142	26	4	1	8	5.6	16	16	13	22	1	8	1	194	19	4	6	4.3	.982	C-38, 1B-2
1951 2 teams																							BKN N (17G – .250) CHI N (51G – .234)
" total	68	.237	.390	177	42	11	2	4	2.3	25	25	17	17	1	22	6	219	25	9	9	3.7	.964	C-42, 1B-9
1952 CHI N	50	.245	.340	94	23	2	2	1	1.1	7	12	8	12	0	24	7	82	8	1	2	1.8	.989	C-22, 2B-1
1954	4	.000	.000	3	0	0	0	0	0.0	0	1	1	2	0	3	0	0	0	0	0	0.0		
1955 WAS A	30	.175	.211	57	10	2	0	0	0.0	5	3	16	6	0	1	0	93	19	3	5	3.8	.974	C-22, 3B-5
1956 CIN N	5	.200	.200	5	1	0	0	0	0.0	0	0	0	2	0	5	1	0	1	1	0	0.3	.500	C-2, 3B-1, 2B-1
10 yrs.	591	.256	.390	1675	429	67	20	39	2.3	191	241	190	179	9	91	22	2065	239	53	44	4.0	.978	C-434, OF-25, 3B-21, 1B-12, 2B-2

WORLD SERIES

Year Team	Games	BA	SA	AB	H	2B	3B	HR	HR%	R	RBI	BB	SO	SB	PH AB	PH H	PO	A	E	DP	TC/G	FA	G by Pos
1947 BKN N	7	.222	.259	27	6	1	0	0	0.0	3	2	2	7	0	0	0	44	4	1	1	7.0	.980	C-7
1949	2	.500	.500	2	1	0	0	0	0.0	0	0	0	1	0	2	1	0	0	0	0	0.0	–	
2 yrs.	9	.241	.276	29	7	1	0	0	0.0	3	2	2	8	0	2	1	44	4	1	1	5.4	.980	C-7

Dave Edwards
EDWARDS, DAVID LEONARD
Brother of Marshall Edwards. Brother of Mike Edwards.
B. Feb. 24, 1954, Los Angeles, Calif.
BR TR 6' 170 lbs.

Year Team	Games	BA	SA	AB	H	2B	3B	HR	HR%	R	RBI	BB	SO	SB	PH AB	PH H	PO	A	E	DP	TC/G	FA	G by Pos
1978 MIN A	15	.250	.386	44	11	3	0	1	2.3	7	9	7	13	1	1	0	35	3	2	1	2.7	.950	OF-15
1979	96	.249	.389	229	57	8	0	8	3.5	42	35	24	45	6	6	0	165	7	3	0	1.8	.983	OF-86, DH-3
1980	81	.250	.335	200	50	9	1	2	1.0	26	20	12	51	2	5	2	144	7	11	1	2.0	.932	OF-72, DH-3
1981 SD N	58	.214	.321	112	24	4	1	2	1.8	13	13	11	24	3	17	4	59	6	2	2	1.2	.970	OF-49
1982	71	.182	.273	55	10	2	0	1	1.8	7	2	1	14	0	20	3	34	0	2	0	0.5	.944	OF-45, 1B-1
5 yrs.	321	.238	.350	640	152	26	2	14	2.2	95	73	55	147	12	49	9	437	23	20	4	1.5	.958	OF-267, DH-6, 1B-1

Year	Team	Games	BA	SA	AB	H	2B	3B	HR	HR%	R	RBI	BB	SO	SB	Pinch Hit AB	H	PO	A	E	DP	TC/G	FA	G by Pos

Doc Edwards

EDWARDS, HOWARD RODNEY
B. Dec. 10, 1936, Red Jacket, W. Va.
Manager 1987-89.　　　　　　　　　　　BR TR 6'2"　215 lbs.

Year	Team	Games	BA	SA	AB	H	2B	3B	HR	HR%	R	RBI	BB	SO	SB	PH AB	PH H	PO	A	E	DP	TC/G	FA	G by Pos
1962	CLE A	53	.273	.378	143	39	6	0	3	2.1	13	9	9	14	0	11	2	223	16	2	2	4.5	.992	C-39
1963	2 teams				CLE A (10G – .258)				KC A (71G – .250)															
"	total	81	.251	.369	271	68	14	0	6	2.2	22	35	13	29	0	11	1	421	33	6	5	5.7	.987	C-73
1964	KC A	97	.224	.310	294	66	10	0	5	1.7	25	28	13	40	0	12	4	522	37	8	7	5.8	.986	C-79, 1B-7
1965	2 teams				KC A (6G – .150)				NY A (45G – .190)															
"	total	51	.183	.233	120	22	3	0	1	0.8	4	9	14	16	1	2	0	230	18	3	6	4.9	.988	C-49
1970	PHI N	35	.269	.269	78	21	0	0	0	0.0	5	6	4	10	0	1	0	177	19	6	6	5.8	.970	C-34
5 yrs.		317	.238	.325	906	216	33	0	15	1.7	69	87	53	109	1	37	7	1573	123	25	26	5.4	.985	C-274, 1B-7

Hank Edwards

EDWARDS, HENRY ALBERT
B. Jan. 29, 1919, Elmwood Place, Ohio　D. June 22, 1988, Santa Ana, Calif.　　　BL TL 6'　190 lbs.

Year	Team	Games	BA	SA	AB	H	2B	3B	HR	HR%	R	RBI	BB	SO	SB	PH AB	PH H	PO	A	E	DP	TC/G	FA	G by Pos
1941	CLE A	16	.221	.309	68	15	1	1	1	1.5	10	6	2	4	0	0	0	23	3	2	0	1.8	.929	OF-16
1942		13	.250	.333	48	12	2	1	0	0.0	6	7	5	8	2	1	0	30	0	1	0	2.4	.968	OF-12
1943		92	.276	.407	297	82	18	6	3	1.0	38	28	30	34	4	15	4	173	4	3	0	2.0	.983	OF-74
1946		124	.301	.509	458	138	33	16	10	2.2	62	54	43	48	1	2	1	226	13	8	1	2.0	.968	OF-123
1947		108	.260	.420	393	102	12	3	15	3.8	54	59	31	55	1	8	3	199	3	2	0	1.9	.990	OF-100
1948		55	.269	.406	160	43	9	2	3	1.9	27	18	18	18	1	12	2	76	1	1	0	1.4	.987	OF-41
1949	2 teams				CLE A (5G – .267)				CHI N (58G – .290)															
"	total	63	.288	.497	191	55	8	4	8	4.2	28	22	20	24	0	6	1	86	4	1	2	1.4	.989	OF-56
1950	CHI N	41	.364	.536	110	40	11	1	2	1.8	13	21	10	13	0	10	0	38	2	1	0	1.0	.976	OF-29
1951	2 teams				BKN N (35G – .226)				CIN N (41G – .315)															
"	total	76	.297	.443	158	47	12	1	3	1.9	15	23	17	26	1	37	8	64	0	1	0	0.9	.985	OF-34
1952	2 teams				CIN N (74G – .283)				CHI A (8G – .333)															
"	total	82	.287	.470	202	58	7	6	6	3.0	26	29	19	24	0	26	4	88	2	1	0	1.1	.989	OF-54
1953	STL N	65	.198	.226	106	21	3	0	0	0.0	6	9	13	10	0	40	12	36	2	0	0	0.6	1.000	OF-21
11 yrs.		735	.280	.440	2191	613	116	41	51	2.3	285	276	208	264	9	157	35	1039	34	21	3	1.5	.981	OF-560

Johnny Edwards

EDWARDS, JOHN ALBAN
B. June 10, 1938, Columbus, Ohio　　　　　　　　　　　　BL TR 6'4"　220 lbs.

Year	Team	Games	BA	SA	AB	H	2B	3B	HR	HR%	R	RBI	BB	SO	SB	PH AB	PH H	PO	A	E	DP	TC/G	FA	G by Pos
1961	CIN N	52	.186	.262	145	27	5	0	2	1.4	14	14	18	28	1	2	0	257	15	5	2	5.3	.982	C-52
1962		133	.254	.392	452	115	28	5	8	1.8	47	50	45	70	1	7	4	807	92	12	11	6.8	.987	C-130
1963		148	.259	.380	495	128	19	4	11	2.2	46	67	45	93	1	2	2	1008	87	6	16	7.4	.995	C-148
1964		126	.281	.390	423	119	23	1	7	1.7	47	55	34	65	1	8	0	890	73	8	17	7.7	.992	C-120
1965		114	.267	.474	371	99	22	2	17	4.6	47	51	50	45	0	11	5	761	61	8	9	7.3	.990	C-110
1966		98	.191	.284	282	54	8	0	6	2.1	24	39	31	42	1	1	0	617	40	5	3	6.8	.992	C-98
1967		80	.206	.263	209	43	6	0	2	1.0	10	20	16	28	1	7	1	454	30	5	4	6.1	.990	C-73
1968	STL N	85	.239	.326	230	55	9	1	3	1.3	14	29	16	20	1	26	7	350	25	3	2	4.4	.992	C-54
1969	HOU N	151	.232	.333	496	115	20	6	6	1.2	52	50	53	69	2	1	0	1135	79	7	9	8.1	.994	C-151
1970		140	.221	.319	458	101	16	4	7	1.5	46	49	51	63	1	2	2	854	74	5	11	6.7	.995	C-139
1971		106	.233	.309	317	74	13	4	1	0.3	18	23	26	38	1	7	2	555	48	3	7	5.7	.995	C-104
1972		108	.268	.373	332	89	16	2	3	0.9	33	40	50	39	2	6	0	645	41	8	8	6.4	.988	C-105
1973		79	.244	.368	250	61	10	2	5	2.0	24	27	19	23	1	7	1	435	22	5	3	5.8	.989	C-76
1974		50	.222	.325	117	26	7	1	1	0.9	8	10	11	12	1	17	5	157	16	2	3	3.5	.989	C-32
14 yrs.		1470	.242	.353	4577	1106	202	32	81	1.8	430	524	465	635	15	104	29	8925	703	82	105	6.6	.992	C-1392

WORLD SERIES

Year	Team	Games	BA	SA	AB	H	2B	3B	HR	HR%	R	RBI	BB	SO	SB	PH AB	PH H	PO	A	E	DP	TC/G	FA	G by Pos
1961	CIN N	3	.364	.545	11	4	2	0	0	0.0	1	2	0	0	0	0	0	17	1	0	0	6.0	1.000	C-3
1968	STL N	1	.000	.000	1	0	0	0	0	0.0	0	0	0	1	0	1	0	0	0	0	0	0.0	–	
2 yrs.		4	.333	.500	12	4	2	0	0	0.0	1	2	0	1	0	1	0	17	1	0	0	4.5	1.000	C-3

Marshall Edwards

EDWARDS, MARSHALL LYNN
Brother of Dave Edwards.　Brother of Mike Edwards.
B. Aug. 27, 1952, Fort Lewis, Wash.　　　　　　　　　BL TL 5'9"　157 lbs.

Year	Team	Games	BA	SA	AB	H	2B	3B	HR	HR%	R	RBI	BB	SO	SB	PH AB	PH H	PO	A	E	DP	TC/G	FA	G by Pos
1981	MIL A	40	.241	.293	58	14	1	1	0	0.0	10	4	0	2	6	0	0	46	1	1	0	1.2	.979	OF-36, DH-1
1982		69	.247	.315	178	44	4	1	2	1.1	24	14	4	8	10	9	3	119	2	2	1	1.8	.984	OF-54, DH-6
1983		51	.297	.338	74	22	1	1	0	0.0	14	5	1	9	5	3	1	57	4	0	1	1.2	1.000	OF-35, DH-4
3 yrs.		160	.258	.316	310	80	6	3	2	0.6	48	23	5	19	21	12	4	222	7	3	2	1.5	.987	OF-125, DH-11

DIVISIONAL PLAYOFF SERIES

Year	Team	Games	BA	SA	AB	H	2B	3B	HR	HR%	R	RBI	BB	SO	SB	PH AB	PH H	PO	A	E	DP	TC/G	FA	G by Pos
1981	MIL A	2	.000	.000	1	0	0	0	0	0.0	0	0	0	0	1	0	0	0	0	0	0	0.0	–	OF-2

LEAGUE CHAMPIONSHIP SERIES

Year	Team	Games	BA	SA	AB	H	2B	3B	HR	HR%	R	RBI	BB	SO	SB	PH AB	PH H	PO	A	E	DP	TC/G	FA	G by Pos
1982	MIL A	3	.000	.000	1	0	0	0	0	0.0	2	0	0	1	0	0	0	0	0	0	0	0.0	–	DH-2, OF-1

WORLD SERIES

Year	Team	Games	BA	SA	AB	H	2B	3B	HR	HR%	R	RBI	BB	SO	SB	PH AB	PH H	PO	A	E	DP	TC/G	FA	G by Pos
1982	MIL A	1	–	–	0	0	0	0	0	0.0	0	0	0	0	0	0	0	0	0	0	0	0.0	–	OF-1

Mike Edwards

EDWARDS, MICHAEL LEWIS
Brother of Dave Edwards.　Brother of Marshall Edwards.
B. Aug. 27, 1952, Fort Lewis, Wash.　　　　　　　　　BR TR 5'10"　154 lbs.

Year	Team	Games	BA	SA	AB	H	2B	3B	HR	HR%	R	RBI	BB	SO	SB	PH AB	PH H	PO	A	E	DP	TC/G	FA	G by Pos
1977	PIT N	7	.000	.000	6	0	0	0	0	0.0	1	0	0	3	0	0	0	7	8	0	2	2.1	1.000	2B-4
1978	OAK A	142	.273	.329	414	113	16	2	1	0.2	48	23	16	32	27	0	0	233	318	22	72	4.0	.962	2B-133, SS-9, DH-4
1979		122	.233	.280	400	93	12	2	1	0.3	35	23	15	37	10	3	1	246	318	22	54	4.8	.962	2B-113, SS-3, DH-2
1980		46	.237	.237	59	14	0	0	0	0.0	10	3	1	5	1	2	1	19	48	2	7	1.5	.971	2B-23, DH-5, OF-1
4 yrs.		317	.250	.298	879	220	28	4	2	0.2	94	49	32	77	38	5	2	505	692	46	135	3.9	.963	2B-273, SS-12, DH-11, OF-1

Ben Egan

EGAN, ARTHUR AUGUSTUS
B. Nov. 20, 1883, Augusta, N. Y.　D. Feb. 18, 1968, Sherrill, N. Y.　　　BR TR 6'　195 lbs.

Year	Team	Games	BA	SA	AB	H	2B	3B	HR	HR%	R	RBI	BB	SO	SB	PH AB	PH H	PO	A	E	DP	TC/G	FA	G by Pos
1908	PHI A	2	.167	.333	6	1	1	0	0	0.0	1	0	1			0	0	11	3	1	0	7.5	.933	C-2
1912		48	.174	.254	138	24	3	4	0	0.0	9	13	6		3	2	1	175	75	11	5	5.4	.958	C-46

Year	Team	Games	BA	SA	AB	H	2B	3B	HR	HR%	R	RBI	BB	SO	SB	Pinch Hit AB	H	PO	A	E	DP	TC/G	FA	G by Pos

Ben Egan *continued*

1914	CLE A	29	.227	.273	88	20	2	1	0	0.0	7	11	3	20	0	2	1	146	48	5	3	6.9	.975	C-27
1915		42	.108	.133	120	13	3	0	0	0.0	4	6	8	14	0	2	0	199	59	8	5	6.3	.970	C-40
4 yrs.		121	.165	.219	352	58	9	5	0	0.0	21	30	18	34	3	6	2	531	185	25	13	6.1	.966	C-115

Dick Egan

EGAN, RICHARD JOSEPH
B. June 23, 1884, Portland, Ore.   D. July 7, 1947, Oakland, Calif.   BR TR 5'11"   162 lbs.

1908	CIN N	18	.206	.279	68	14	3	1	0	0.0	8	5	2		0	7	0	35	47	10	10	5.1	.891	2B-18
1909		127	.275	.329	480	132	14	3	2	0.4	59	53	37		39	1	0	294	402	39	49	5.8	.947	2B-116, SS-10
1910		135	.245	.289	474	116	11	5	0	0.0	70	46	53	38	41	0	0	268	388	27	50	5.1	.960	2B-131, SS-3
1911		153	.249	.292	558	139	11	5	1	0.2	80	56	59	50	37	1	1	341	480	44	67	5.7	.949	2B-152
1912		149	.247	.294	507	125	14	5	0	0.0	69	52	56	26	24	0	0	345	452	22	55	5.5	.973	2B-149
1913		60	.282	.349	195	55	7	3	0	0.0	15	22	15	13	6	4	0	115	151	15	20	4.7	.947	2B-38, SS-17, 3B-2
1914	BKN N	106	.226	.282	337	76	10	3	1	0.3	30	21	22	25	8	6	5	177	256	39	25	4.5	.917	SS-83, 3B-10, OF-3, 2B-2, 1B-1
1915	2 teams		BKN N (3G – .000)					BOS N (83G – .259)																
" total		86	.256	.305	223	57	9	1	0	0.0	20	21	28	18	3	15	3	179	92	16	20	3.3	.944	OF-24, 2B-22, SS-10, 1B-9, 3B-4
1916	BOS N	83	.223	.282	238	53	8	3	0	0.0	23	16	19	21	2	11	5	94	149	16	13	3.1	.938	2B-53, SS-12, 3B-8
9 yrs.		917	.249	.300	3080	767	87	29	4	0.1	374	292	291	191	167	38	14	1848	2417	228	309	4.9	.949	2B-681, SS-135, OF-27, 3B-24, 1B-10

Jim Egan

EGAN, JAMES K. (Troy Terrier)
B. 1858, Derby, Conn.   D. Sept. 26, 1884, New Haven, Conn.   TL

| 1882 | TRO N | 30 | .200 | .261 | 115 | 23 | 3 | 2 | 0 | 0.0 | 15 | 10 | 1 | 21 | | 0 | 0 | 36 | 15 | 20 | 3 | 2.4 | .718 | OF-18, P-12, C-2 |

Tom Egan

EGAN, THOMAS PATRICK
B. June 9, 1946, Los Angeles, Calif.   BR TR 6'4"   218 lbs.

1965	CAL A	18	.263	.316	38	10	0	0	0	0.0	3	3	3	12	0	2	1	61	3	0	0	3.6	1.000	C-16
1966		7	.000	.000	11	0	0	0	0	0.0	0	0	1	5	0	0	0	24	2	0	0	3.7	1.000	C-6
1967		1	.000	.000	1	0	0	0	0	0.0	0	0	0	0	0	0	0	3	0	0	0	3.0	1.000	C-1
1968		16	.116	.209	43	5	1	0	1	2.3	2	4	2	15	0	0	0	72	7	0	2	4.9	1.000	C-14
1969		46	.142	.275	120	17	1	0	5	4.2	7	16	17	41	0	1	0	240	28	4	4	5.9	.985	C-46
1970		79	.238	.324	210	50	6	0	4	1.9	14	20	14	67	0	1	0	367	31	5	4	5.1	.988	C-79
1971	CHI A	85	.239	.410	251	60	11	1	10	4.0	29	34	26	94	1	10	5	445	41	7	3	5.8	.986	C-77, 1B-1
1972		50	.191	.255	141	27	3	0	2	1.4	8	9	4	48	0	11	3	257	19	4	2	5.6	.986	C-46
1974	CAL A	43	.117	.117	94	11	0	0	0	0.0	4	4	4	40	1	2	0	249	21	1	5	6.3	.996	C-41
1975		28	.229	.300	70	16	3	1	0	0.0	7	3	5	14	0	0	0	145	19	4	0	6.1	.965	C-28
10 yrs.		373	.200	.299	979	196	25	3	22	2.2	74	91	80	336	2	30	9	1863	171	27	24	5.5	.987	C-354, 1B-1

Elmer Eggert

EGGERT, ELMER ALBERT (Mose)
B. Jan. 29, 1902, Rochester, N. Y.   D. Apr. 9, 1971, Rochester, N. Y.   BR TR 5'9"   160 lbs.

| 1927 | BOS A | 5 | .000 | .000 | 3 | 0 | 0 | 0 | 0 | 0.0 | 0 | 0 | 1 | 1 | 0 | 2 | 0 | 0 | 0 | 0 | 0 | 0.0 | – | 2B-1 |

Dave Eggler

EGGLER, DAVID DANIEL
B. Apr. 30, 1851, Brooklyn, N. Y.   D. Apr. 5, 1902, Buffalo, N. Y.   BR TR 5'9"   165 lbs.

1876	PHI N	39	.299	.322	174	52	4	0	0	0.0	28	19	2	4				109	6	11	1	3.2	.913	OF-39
1877	CHI N	33	.265	.287	136	36	3	0	0	0.0	20	20	1	5				60	8	11	3	2.4	.861	OF-33
1879	BUF N	78	.208	.268	317	66	5	7	0	0.0	41	27	11	41				114	11	11	2	1.7	.919	OF-78
1883	2 teams	91	BAL AA (53G – .188)					BUF N (38G – .248)																
" total		91	.214	.231	355	76	4	1	0	0.0	28		3	29				175	10	25	2	2.3	.881	OF-91
1884	BUF N	63	.195	.216	241	47	3	1	0	0.0	25		6	54				104	14	15	1	2.1	.887	OF-63
1885		6	.083	.083	24	2	0	0	0	0.0	0		2	4				14	1	1	0	2.7	.938	OF-6
6 yrs.		310	.224	.253	1247	279	19	9	0	0.0	142	66	25	137				576	50	74	9	2.3	.894	OF-310

Red Ehret

EHRET, PHILIP SYDNEY
B. Aug. 31, 1868, Louisville, Ky.   D. July 28, 1940, Cincinnati, Ohio   BR TR 6'   175 lbs.

1888	KC AA	17	.190	.254	63	12	4	0	0	0.0	4	4	1			1	0	24	18	6	0	2.8	.875	OF-10, P-7, 2B-1, 1B-1
1889	LOU AA	67	.252	.333	258	65	6	6	1	0.4	27	31	4	23	4	0	0	43	109	29	4	2.7	.840	P-45, OF-22, SS-1, 3B-1, 2B-1
1890		43	.212	.240	146	31	2	1	0	0.0	11		1		1	0	0	9	64	12	2	2.0	.859	P-43
1891		26	.242	.286	91	22	1	1	0	0.0	5	9	3	15	0	0	0	4	57	9	4	2.7	.871	P-26
1892	PIT N	40	.258	.273	132	34	2	0	0	0.0	12	19	7	22	1	1	0	14	57	12	1	2.1	.855	P-39
1893		40	.176	.221	136	24	3	0	1	0.7	16	17	10	18	1	0	0	12	80	11	0	2.6	.893	P-39
1894		46	.170	.215	135	23	4	1	0	0.0	6	11	8	22	0	0	0	12	61	12	2	1.8	.859	P-46
1895	STL N	37	.219	.292	96	21	2	1	1	1.0	13	9	6	12	1	0	0	11	56	12	1	2.1	.848	P-37
1896	CIN N	34	.196	.245	102	20	2	1	1	1.0	10	20	10	12	2	0	0	15	69	7	3	2.7	.923	P-34, 1B-1
1897		34	.197	.227	66	13	2	0	0	0.0	6	6	4		2	0	0	12	33	2	4	1.4	.957	P-34
1898	LOU N	13	.225	.350	40	9	3	1	0	0.0	3	4	1		0	1	0	3	17	5	0	1.9	.800	P-12
11 yrs.		397	.217	.269	1265	274	32	11	4	0.3	117	130	57	124	15	2	0	159	621	117	20	2.3	.870	P-362, OF-32, 2B-2, 1B-2, SS-1, 3B-1

Hack Eibel

EIBEL, HENRY HACK
B. Dec. 6, 1893, Brooklyn, N. Y.   D. Oct. 16, 1945, Macon, Ga.   BL TL 5'11"   220 lbs.

1912	CLE A	1	.000	.000	3	0	0	0	0	0.0	0	0	0		0	0	0	0	0	0	0	0.0	–	OF-1
1920	BOS A	29	.186	.233	43	8	2	0	0	0.0	4	6	3	6	1	17	3	5	4	1	0	0.3	.900	OF-5, P-3, 1B-1
2 yrs.		30	.174	.217	46	8	2	0	0	0.0	4	6	3	6	1	17	3	5	4	1	0	0.3	.900	OF-6, P-3, 1B-1

Fred Eichrodt

EICHRODT, FREDERICK GEORGE (Ike)
B. Jan. 6, 1903, Chicago, Ill.   D. July 14, 1965, Indianapolis, Ind.   BR TR 5'11½"   167 lbs.

| 1925 | CLE A | 15 | .231 | .327 | 52 | 12 | 3 | 1 | 0 | 0.0 | 4 | 4 | 2 | 7 | 0 | 2 | 0 | 30 | 0 | 2 | 0 | 2.1 | .938 | OF-13 |

Year	Team	Games	BA	SA	AB	H	2B	3B	HR	HR%	R	RBI	BB	SO	SB	Pinch Hit AB	Pinch Hit H	PO	A	E	DP	TC/G	FA	G by Pos

Fred Eichrodt *continued*

Year	Team	Games	BA	SA	AB	H	2B	3B	HR	HR%	R	RBI	BB	SO	SB	AB	H	PO	A	E	DP	TC/G	FA	G by Pos
1926		37	.313	.425	80	25	7	1	0	0.0	14	7	2	11	1	10	2	38	3	1	1	1.1	.976	OF-27
1927		85	.221	.307	267	59	19	2	0	0.0	24	25	16	25	2	4	0	170	13	4	6	2.2	.979	OF-81
1931 CHI	A	34	.214	.274	117	25	5	1	0	0.0	9	15	1	8	0	2	1	70	0	0	0	2.1	1.000	OF-32
4 yrs.		171	.234	.320	516	121	34	5	0	0.0	51	51	21	51	3	18	3	308	16	7	7	1.9	.979	OF-153

Jim Eisenreich

EISENREICH, JAMES MICHAEL   BL TL 5'11" 175 lbs.
B. Apr. 18, 1959, St. Cloud, Minn.

Year	Team	Games	BA	SA	AB	H	2B	3B	HR	HR%	R	RBI	BB	SO	SB	AB	H	PO	A	E	DP	TC/G	FA	G by Pos
1982 MIN	A	34	.303	.424	99	30	6	0	2	2.0	10	9	11	13	0	3	1	72	0	2	0	2.2	.973	OF-30
1983		2	.286	.429	7	2	1	0	0	0.0	1	0	1	1	0	0	0	6	1	0	0	3.5	1.000	OF-2
1984		12	.219	.250	32	7	1	0	0	0.0	1	3	2	4	2	3	1	5	0	0	0	0.4	1.000	DH-6, OF-3
1987 KC	A	44	.238	.467	105	25	8	2	4	3.8	10	21	7	13	1	15	5	0	0	0	0	0.0	-	DH-26
1988		82	.218	.282	202	44	8	1	1	0.5	26	19	6	31	9	9	1	109	0	4	0	1.4	.965	OF-64, DH-13
1989		134	.293	.448	475	139	33	7	9	1.9	64	59	37	44	27	6	2	273	4	3	0	2.1	.989	OF-123, DH-10
6 yrs.		308	.268	.404	920	247	57	10	16	1.7	112	111	64	106	39	36	10	465	5	9	0	1.6	.981	OF-222, DH-55

Kid Elberfeld

ELBERFELD, NORMAN ARTHUR (The Tabasco Kid)   BR TR 5'7" 158 lbs.
B. Apr. 13, 1875, Pomeroy, Ohio   D. Jan. 13, 1944, Chattanooga, Tenn.
Manager 1908.

Year	Team	Games	BA	SA	AB	H	2B	3B	HR	HR%	R	RBI	BB	SO	SB	AB	H	PO	A	E	DP	TC/G	FA	G by Pos
1898 PHI	N	14	.237	.342	38	9	4	0	0	0.0	1	7	5		0	0	0	13	18	8	1	2.8	.795	3B-14
1899 CIN	N	41	.261	.319	138	36	4	2	0	0.0	23	22	15		5	0	0	74	108	25	9	5.0	.879	SS-24, 3B-18
1901 DET	A	122	.310	.429	436	135	21	11	3	0.7	76	76	57		24	0	0	332	411	76	62	6.7	.907	SS-121
1902		130	.260	.326	488	127	17	6	1	0.2	70	64	55		19	0	0	326	459	67	63	6.6	.921	SS-130
1903 2 teams		DET A (35G – .341)						NY	A	(90G – .287)														
" total		125	.301	.383	481	145	23	8	0	0.0	78	64	33		22	0	0	295	410	62	51	6.1	.919	SS-124, 3B-1
1904 NY	A	122	.263	.328	445	117	13	5	2	0.4	55	46	37		18	0	0	237	432	48	44	5.9	.933	SS-122
1905		111	.262	.318	390	102	18	2	0	0.0	48	53	23		18	2	0	244	317	57	35	5.6	.908	SS-108
1906		99	.306	.384	346	106	11	5	2	0.6	59	31	30		19	0	0	200	317	42	18	5.6	.925	SS-98
1907		120	.271	.336	447	121	17	6	0	0.0	61	51	36		22	2	2	295	400	52	31	6.2	.930	SS-118
1908		19	.196	.250	56	11	3	0	0	0.0	11	5	6		1	0	0	36	51	8	2	5.0	.947	SS-17
1909		106	.237	.288	379	90	9	5	0	0.0	47	26	28		23	2	0	196	269	26	30	4.6	.947	SS-61, 3B-43
1910 WAS	A	127	.251	.292	455	114	9	2	2	0.4	53	42	35		19	3	0	166	245	29	17	3.5	.934	3B-113, 2B-10, SS-3
1911		127	.272	.339	404	110	19	4	0	0.0	58	47	65		24	7	1	233	297	31	34	4.4	.945	2B-66, 3B-54
1914 BKN	N	30	.226	.242	62	14	1	0	0	0.0	7	1	2	4	0	6	1	33	35	7	6	2.5	.907	SS-18, 2B-1
14 yrs.		1293	.271	.339	4565	1237	169	56	10	0.2	647	535	427	4	214	24	4	2680	3769	538	403	5.4	.923	SS-944, 3B-243, 2B-77

George Elder

ELDER, GEORGE REZIN   BL TR 5'11" 180 lbs.
B. Mar. 10, 1921, Lebanon, Ky.

Year	Team	Games	BA	SA	AB	H	2B	3B	HR	HR%	R	RBI	BB	SO	SB	AB	H	PO	A	E	DP	TC/G	FA	G by Pos
1949 STL	A	41	.250	.318	44	11	3	0	0	0.0	9	2	4	11	0	17	5	19	0	0	0	0.5	1.000	OF-10

Lee Elia

ELIA, LEE CONSTANTINE   BR TR 5'11" 175 lbs.
B. July 16, 1937, Philadelphia, Pa.
Manager 1982-83, 1987-88.

Year	Team	Games	BA	SA	AB	H	2B	3B	HR	HR%	R	RBI	BB	SO	SB	AB	H	PO	A	E	DP	TC/G	FA	G by Pos
1966 CHI	A	80	.205	.297	195	40	5	2	3	1.5	16	22	15	39	0	1	0	103	186	14	39	3.8	.954	SS-75
1968 CHI	N	15	.176	.176	17	3	0	0	0	0.0	1	3	0	6	0	10	2	3	2	0	0	0.3	1.000	SS-2, 3B-1, 2B-1
2 yrs.		95	.203	.288	212	43	5	2	3	1.4	17	25	15	45	0	11	2	106	188	14	39	3.2	.955	SS-77, 3B-1, 2B-1

Pete Elko

ELKO, PETER (Piccolo Pete)   BR TR 5'11" 185 lbs.
B. June 17, 1918, Wilkes-Barre, Pa.

Year	Team	Games	BA	SA	AB	H	2B	3B	HR	HR%	R	RBI	BB	SO	SB	AB	H	PO	A	E	DP	TC/G	FA	G by Pos
1943 CHI	N	9	.133	.133	30	4	0	0	0	0.0	1	0	4	5	0	0	0	8	15	4	1	3.0	.852	3B-9
1944		7	.227	.273	22	5	1	0	0	0.0	2	0	0	1	0	1	1	6	8	0	1	2.0	1.000	3B-6
2 yrs.		16	.173	.192	52	9	1	0	0	0.0	3	0	4	6	0	1	1	14	23	4	2	2.6	.902	3B-15

Roy Ellam

ELLAM, ROY (Whitey, Slippery)   BR TR 5'10½" 203 lbs.
B. Feb. 8, 1886, Conshohocken, Pa.   D. Oct. 28, 1948, Conshohocken, Pa.

Year	Team	Games	BA	SA	AB	H	2B	3B	HR	HR%	R	RBI	BB	SO	SB	AB	H	PO	A	E	DP	TC/G	FA	G by Pos
1909 CIN	N	10	.190	.429	21	4	0	1	1	4.8	4	4	1		1	0	0	14	20	4	4	3.8	.895	SS-9
1918 PIT	N	26	.130	.169	77	10	1	1	0	0.0	9	2	17	17	2	0	0	42	67	9	6	4.5	.924	SS-26
2 yrs.		36	.143	.224	98	14	1	2	1	1.0	13	6	24	17	3	0	0	56	87	13	10	4.3	.917	SS-35

Frank Ellerbe

ELLERBE, FRANCIS ROGERS (Governor)   BR TR 5'10½" 165 lbs.
B. Dec. 25, 1895, Marion County, S. C.   D. July 8, 1988

Year	Team	Games	BA	SA	AB	H	2B	3B	HR	HR%	R	RBI	BB	SO	SB	AB	H	PO	A	E	DP	TC/G	FA	G by Pos
1919 WAS	A	28	.276	.333	105	29	4	1	0	0.0	13	17	2	15	5	0	0	63	74	8	5	5.2	.945	SS-28
1920		101	.292	.345	336	98	14	2	0	0.0	38	36	19	23	5	6	1	127	210	28	10	3.6	.923	3B-75, SS-19, OF-1
1921 2 teams		WAS A (10G – .200)			STL A	(105G – .288)																		
" total		115	.286	.405	440	126	20	13	2	0.5	66	50	22	44	1	9	2	158	226	19	9	3.5	.953	3B-106
1922 STL	A	91	.246	.319	342	84	16	3	1	0.3	42	33	25	37	1	0	0	137	224	17	20	4.2	.955	3B-91
1923		18	.184	.184	49	9	0	0	0	0.0	6	1	1	5	0	4	0	11	18	1	2	1.7	.967	3B-14
1924 2 teams		STL A (21G – .197)			CLE A	(46G – .258)																		
" total		67	.238	.309	181	43	4	3	1	0.6	14	16	3	12	0	4	0	71	110	7	9	2.8	.963	3B-60, 2B-2
6 yrs.		420	.268	.346	1453	389	58	22	4	0.3	179	153	72	136	12	23	3	567	862	80	55	3.6	.947	3B-346, SS-47, 2B-2, OF-1

Joe Ellick

ELLICK, JOSEPH J.   5'10" 162 lbs.
B. Apr. 3, 1854, Cincinnati, Ohio   D. Apr. 21, 1923, Kansas City, Mo.
Manager 1884.

Year	Team	Games	BA	SA	AB	H	2B	3B	HR	HR%	R	RBI	BB	SO	SB	AB	H	PO	A	E	DP	TC/G	FA	G by Pos
1878 MIL	N	3	.154	.154	13	2	0	0	0	0.0	2	1	0	1		0	0	8	3	3	1	4.7	.786	C-2, 3B-1, P-1
1880 WOR	N	5	.056	.056	18	1	0	0	0	0.0	1	0	1	2		0	0	4	11	2	0	3.4	.882	3B-5
1884 4 teams		CHI U (74G – .255)			PIT U	(18G – .163)		KC	U	(2G – .000)		BAL	U	(7G – .148)										
" total		101	.226	.252	429	97	11	0	0	0.0	73		18			0	0	89	118	30	6	2.3	.873	OF-59, SS-39, 2B-5
3 yrs.		109	.217	.241	460	100	11	0	0	0.0	76	1	19	3		0	0	101	132	35	7	2.5	.869	OF-59, SS-39, 3B-6, 2B-5, C-2, P-1

Year	Team		Games	BA	SA	AB	H	2B	3B	HR	HR%	R	RBI	BB	SO	SB	Pinch Hit AB	Pinch Hit H	PO	A	E	DP	TC/G	FA	G by Pos

Larry Elliot

ELLIOT, LAWRENCE LEE
B. Mar. 5, 1938, San Diego, Calif.

BL TL 6'2" 200 lbs.

Year	Team		Games	BA	SA	AB	H	2B	3B	HR	HR%	R	RBI	BB	SO	SB	PH AB	PH H	PO	A	E	DP	TC/G	FA	G by Pos
1962	PIT	N	8	.300	.600	10	3	0	0	1	10.0	2	2	0	1	0	5	2	3	0	0	0	0.4	1.000	OF-3
1963			4	.000	.000	4	0	0	0	0	0.0	0	0	0	3	0	4	0	0	0	0	0	0.0	–	
1964	NY	N	80	.228	.384	224	51	8	0	9	4.0	27	22	28	55	1	15	3	130	2	2	1	1.7	.985	OF-63
1966			65	.246	.412	199	49	14	2	5	2.5	24	32	17	46	0	10	2	73	10	8	0	1.4	.912	OF-54
4 yrs.			157	.236	.398	437	103	22	2	15	3.4	53	56	45	105	1	34	7	206	12	10	1	1.5	.956	OF-120

Allen Elliott

ELLIOTT, ALLEN CLIFFORD (Ace)
B. Dec. 25, 1897, St. Louis, Mo. D. May 6, 1979, St. Louis, Mo.

BL TR 6' 170 lbs.

Year	Team		Games	BA	SA	AB	H	2B	3B	HR	HR%	R	RBI	BB	SO	SB	PH AB	PH H	PO	A	E	DP	TC/G	FA	G by Pos
1923	CHI	N	53	.250	.357	168	42	8	2	2	1.2	21	29	2	12	3	0	0	450	19	4	36	8.9	.992	1B-52
1924			10	.143	.143	14	2	0	0	0	0.0	0	0	0	1	0	0	0	46	1	0	3	4.7	1.000	1B-10
2 yrs.			63	.242	.341	182	44	8	2	2	1.1	21	29	2	13	3	0	0	496	20	4	39	8.3	.992	1B-62

Bob Elliott

ELLIOTT, ROBERT IRVING
B. Nov. 26, 1916, San Francisco, Calif. D. May 4, 1966, San Diego, Calif.
Manager 1960.

BR TR 6' 185 lbs.

Year	Team		Games	BA	SA	AB	H	2B	3B	HR	HR%	R	RBI	BB	SO	SB	PH AB	PH H	PO	A	E	DP	TC/G	FA	G by Pos
1939	PIT	N	32	.333	.527	129	43	10	3	3	2.3	18	19	9	4	0	2	0	88	1	2	0	2.8	.978	OF-30
1940			148	.292	.421	551	161	34	11	5	0.9	88	64	45	28	13	1	0	302	12	7	0	2.2	.978	OF-147
1941			141	.273	.374	527	144	24	10	3	0.6	74	76	64	52	6	2	0	281	9	9	2	2.1	.970	OF-139
1942			143	.296	.416	560	166	26	7	9	1.6	75	89	52	35	2	1	0	176	286	36	22	3.5	.928	3B-142, OF-1
1943			156	.315	.444	581	183	30	12	7	1.2	82	101	56	24	4	4	0	150	296	25	34	3.0	.947	3B-151, 2B-2, SS-1
1944			143	.297	.465	538	160	28	16	10	1.9	85	108	75	42	9	3	0	169	285	27	22	3.4	.944	3B-140, SS-1
1945			144	.290	.423	541	157	36	6	8	1.5	80	108	64	38	5	3	0	219	185	23	18	3.0	.946	3B-81, OF-61
1946			140	.263	.358	486	128	25	3	5	1.0	50	68	64	44	6	4	2	232	90	7	10	2.4	.979	OF-92, 3B-43
1947	BOS	N	150	.317	.517	555	176	35	5	22	4.0	93	113	87	60	3	2	0	129	302	20	25	3.0	.956	3B-148
1948			151	.283	.474	540	153	24	5	23	4.3	99	100	131	57	6	1	0	146	298	26	18	3.1	.945	3B-150
1949			139	.280	.467	482	135	29	5	17	3.5	77	76	90	38	0	10	5	141	300	17	27	3.3	.963	3B-130
1950			142	.305	.512	531	162	28	5	24	4.5	94	107	68	67	2	5	1	141	256	20	26	2.9	.952	3B-137
1951	NY	N	98	.285	.448	480	137	29	2	15	3.1	73	70	65	56	2	7	1	138	242	24	31	3.0	.941	3B-127
1952			115	.228	.375	272	62	6	2	10	3.7	33	35	36	20	1	18	3	102	31	4	3	1.4	.971	OF-65, 3B-13
1953 2 teams	STL A			(48G – .250)		CHI A		(67G – .260)																	
" total			115	.255	.391	368	94	19	2	9	2.4	43	61	61	39	1	8	2	105	197	14	21	2.7	.956	3B-103, OF-2
15 yrs.			1978	.289	.440	7141	2061	383	94	170	2.4	1064	1195	967	604	60	71	14	2519	2790	261	259	2.8	.953	3B-1365, OF-537, SS-2, 2B-2

WORLD SERIES

Year	Team		Games	BA	SA	AB	H	2B	3B	HR	HR%	R	RBI	BB	SO	SB	PH AB	PH H	PO	A	E	DP	TC/G	FA	G by Pos
1948	BOS	N	6	.333	.619	21	7	0	0	2	9.5	4	5	2	2	0	0	0	11	14	3	1	4.7	.893	3B-6

Carter Elliott

ELLIOTT, CARTER WARD
B. Nov. 29, 1893, Atchison, Kans. D. May 21, 1959, Palm Springs, Calif.

BL TR 5'11" 165 lbs.

Year	Team		Games	BA	SA	AB	H	2B	3B	HR	HR%	R	RBI	BB	SO	SB	PH AB	PH H	PO	A	E	DP	TC/G	FA	G by Pos
1921	CHI	N	12	.250	.321	28	7	2	0	0	0.0	5	0	5	3	0	0	0	24	30	2	4	4.7	.964	SS-10

Gene Elliott

ELLIOTT, EUGENE BIRMINGHOUSE
B. Feb. 8, 1889, Fayette City, Pa. D. Jan. 5, 1976, Huntingdon, Pa.

BL TR 5'7" 150 lbs.

Year	Team		Games	BA	SA	AB	H	2B	3B	HR	HR%	R	RBI	BB	SO	SB	PH AB	PH H	PO	A	E	DP	TC/G	FA	G by Pos
1911	NY	A	5	.077	.154	13	1	1	0	0	0.0	1	1	2		0	2	0	1	1	1	0	0.6	.667	OF-2, 3B-1

Harry Elliott

ELLIOTT, HARRY LEWIS
B. Oct. 30, 1923, San Francisco, Calif.

BR TR 5'9" 175 lbs.

Year	Team		Games	BA	SA	AB	H	2B	3B	HR	HR%	R	RBI	BB	SO	SB	PH AB	PH H	PO	A	E	DP	TC/G	FA	G by Pos
1953	STL	N	24	.254	.441	59	15	6	1	1	1.7	6	6	3	8	0	6	0	34	1	0	0	1.5	1.000	OF-17
1955			68	.256	.316	117	30	4	0	1	0.9	9	12	11	9	0	38	7	44	1	1	0	0.7	.978	OF-28
2 yrs.			92	.256	.358	176	45	10	1	2	1.1	15	18	14	17	0	44	7	78	2	1	0	0.9	.988	OF-45

Randy Elliott

ELLIOTT, RANDY LEE
B. June 5, 1951, Oxnard, Calif.

BR TR 6'2" 190 lbs.

Year	Team		Games	BA	SA	AB	H	2B	3B	HR	HR%	R	RBI	BB	SO	SB	PH AB	PH H	PO	A	E	DP	TC/G	FA	G by Pos
1972	SD	N	14	.204	.306	49	10	3	1	0	0.0	5	6	2	11	0	2	1	29	0	0	0	2.1	1.000	OF-13
1974			13	.212	.333	33	7	1	0	1	3.0	5	2	7	9	0	2	0	10	0	0	0	0.8	1.000	OF-11, 1B-1
1977	SF	N	73	.240	.407	167	40	5	1	7	4.2	17	26	8	24	0	31	11	68	5	2	1	1.0	.973	OF-46
1980	OAK	A	14	.128	.205	39	5	3	0	0	0.0	4	1	1	13	0	4	0	0	0	0	0	0.0	–	DH-11
4 yrs.			114	.215	.354	288	62	12	2	8	2.8	31	35	18	57	0	39	12	107	5	2	1	1.0	.982	OF-70, DH-11, 1B-1

Rowdy Elliott

ELLIOTT, HAROLD B.
B. July 8, 1890, Kokomo, Ind. D. Feb. 12, 1934, San Francisco, Calif.

BR TR 5'9½" 160 lbs.

Year	Team		Games	BA	SA	AB	H	2B	3B	HR	HR%	R	RBI	BB	SO	SB	PH AB	PH H	PO	A	E	DP	TC/G	FA	G by Pos
1910	BOS	N	3	.000	.000	2	0	0	0	0	0.0	0	0	0	0	0	2	0	1	0	0	0	0.3	1.000	C-1
1916	CHI	N	23	.255	.309	55	14	3	0	0	0.0	5	3	3	5	1	4	0	77	17	3	1	4.2	.969	C-18
1917			85	.251	.332	223	56	8	5	0	0.0	18	28	11	11	4	12	4	307	93	13	9	4.9	.969	C-73
1918			5	.000	.000	10	0	0	0	0	0.0	0	0	2	1	0	0	0	15	5	1	0	4.2	.952	C-5
1920	BKN	N	41	.241	.304	112	27	4	0	1	0.9	13	13	3	6	0	2	0	144	44	7	1	4.8	.964	C-39
5 yrs.			157	.241	.311	402	97	15	5	1	0.2	36	44	19	23	5	20	2	544	159	24	11	4.6	.967	C-136

Ben Ellis

ELLIS, BENJAMIN FRANKLIN
B. Pottsville, Pa. Deceased.

Year	Team		Games	BA	SA	AB	H	2B	3B	HR	HR%	R	RBI	BB	SO	SB	PH AB	PH H	PO	A	E	DP	TC/G	FA	G by Pos
1896	PHI	N	4	.063	.063	16	1	0	0	0	0.0	0	0	3	6	0	0	0	5	10	4	1	4.8	.789	SS-2, 3B-2

John Ellis

ELLIS, JOHN CHARLES
B. Aug. 21, 1948, New London, Conn.

BR TR 6'2½" 225 lbs.

Year	Team		Games	BA	SA	AB	H	2B	3B	HR	HR%	R	RBI	BB	SO	SB	PH AB	PH H	PO	A	E	DP	TC/G	FA	G by Pos
1969	NY	A	22	.290	.403	62	18	4	0	1	1.6	9	8	1	11	0	7	2	83	7	2	1	4.2	.978	C-15
1970			78	.248	.403	226	56	12	1	7	3.1	24	29	18	47	0	20	7	461	41	5	35	6.5	.990	1B-53, 3B-5, C-2
1971			83	.244	.340	238	58	12	1	3	1.3	16	34	23	42	0	15	4	625	35	7	66	8.0	.990	1B-65, C-18
1972			52	.294	.456	136	40	5	1	5	3.7	13	25	8	22	0	17	4	190	12	6	5	4.0	.971	C-25, 1B-8
1973	CLE	A	127	.270	.403	437	118	12	1	14	3.2	59	68	46	57	0	5	1	487	31	10	11	4.2	.981	C-72, DH-38, 1B-12

Year	Team		Games	BA	SA	AB	H	2B	3B	HR	HR%	R	RBI	BB	SO	SB	Pinch Hit AB	Pinch Hit H	PO	A	E	DP	TC/G	FA	G by Pos

John Ellis *continued*

1974			128	.285	.421	477	136	23	6	10	2.1	58	64	32	53	1	3	1	823	55	9	61	6.9	.990	1B-69, C-42, DH-21
1975			92	.230	.345	296	68	11	1	7	2.4	22	32	14	33	0	10	5	413	45	13	4	5.1	.972	C-84, DH-3, 1B-2
1976	TEX	A	11	.419	.581	31	13	2	0	1	3.2	4	8	0	4	0	4	1	21	2	0	0	2.1	1.000	C-7, DH-3
1977			49	.235	.395	119	28	7	0	4	3.4	7	15	8	26	0	16	2	89	5	0	1	1.9	1.000	C-16, DH-15, 1B-8
1978			34	.245	.383	94	23	4	0	3	3.2	7	17	6	20	0	5	2	81	10	4	1	2.8	.958	C-22, DH-7
1979			111	.285	.437	316	90	12	0	12	3.8	33	61	15	55	2	26	7	232	12	5	18	2.2	.980	DH-62, 1B-30, C-7
1980			73	.236	.313	182	43	9	1	1	0.5	12	23	14	23	3	15	4	244	12	2	22	3.5	.992	1B-39, DH-20, C-3
1981			23	.138	.241	58	8	3	0	1	1.7	2	7	5	10	0	8	1	140	8	1	16	6.5	.993	1B-18, DH-1
13 yrs.			883	.262	.392	2672	699	116	13	69	2.6	259	391	190	403	6	151	36	3889	275	64	241	4.8	.985	1B-304, C-297, DH-170, 3B-5

Rob Ellis

ELLIS, ROBERT WALTER
B. July 3, 1950, Grand Rapids, Mich.   BR TR 5'11" 180 lbs.

1971	MIL	A	36	.198	.216	111	22	2	0	0	0.0	9	6	12	24	0	4	2	37	23	4	5	1.8	.938	3B-19, OF-15
1974			22	.292	.333	48	14	2	0	0	0.0	4	4	4	11	0	1	0	13	3	0	0	0.7	1.000	OF-11, DH-9, 3B-1
1975			6	.286	.286	7	2	0	0	0	0.0	3	0	0	0	0	0	0	1	0	0	0	0.2	1.000	OF-5, DH-1
3 yrs.			64	.229	.253	166	38	4	0	0	0.0	16	10	16	35	0	5	2	51	26	4	5	1.3	.951	OF-31, 3B-20, DH-10

Rube Ellis

ELLIS, GEORGE WILLIAM
B. Nov. 17, 1885, Dowley, Calif.   D. Mar. 13, 1938, Rivera, Calif.   BL TL 6' 160 lbs.

1909	STL	N	149	.268	.332	575	154	10	9	3	0.5	76	46	54		16	4	1	332	28	17	9	2.5	.955	OF-145
1910			142	.258	.342	550	142	18	8	4	0.7	87	54	62	70	25	0	0	268	25	18	4	2.2	.942	OF-141
1911			155	.250	.339	555	139	20	10	3	0.5	69	66	66	64	9	6	1	297	21	21	3	2.2	.938	OF-148
1912			109	.269	.380	305	82	18	2	4	1.3	47	33	34	36	6	27	8	173	10	14	5	1.8	.929	OF-76
4 yrs.			555	.260	.344	1985	517	66	29	14	0.7	279	199	216	170	56	37	10	1070	84	70	21	2.2	.943	OF-510

Babe Ellison

ELLISON, HERBERT SPENCER
B. Nov. 15, 1895, Rutland, Ark.   D. Aug. 11, 1955, San Francisco, Calif.   BR TR 5'11" 170 lbs.

1916	DET	A	2	.143	.143	7	1	0	0	0	0.0	0	1	0	1	0	0	0	4	1	0	0	2.5	1.000	3B-2
1917			9	.172	.448	29	5	1	2	1	3.4	2	4	6	3	0	0	0	98	1	2	5	11.2	.980	1B-9
1918			7	.261	.304	23	6	1	0	0	0.0	1	2	3	1	1	0	0	8	14	0	1	3.1	1.000	OF-4, 2B-3
1919			56	.216	.246	134	29	4	0	0	0.0	18	11	13	24	4	15	3	59	65	4	7	2.3	.969	2B-25, OF-10, SS-1
1920			61	.219	.290	155	34	7	2	0	0.0	11	21	8	26	4	17	3	365	29	2	14	6.5	.995	1B-38, OF-4, 3B-1
5 yrs.			135	.216	.284	348	75	13	4	1	0.3	32	39	30	55	9	32	6	534	110	8	27	4.8	.988	1B-47, 2B-28, OF-18, 3B-3, SS-1

Verdo Elmore

ELMORE, VERDO WILSON
B. Dec. 10, 1899, Gordo, Ala.   D. Aug. 5, 1969, Birmingham, Ala.   BL TR 5'11" 185 lbs.

| 1924 | STL | A | 7 | .176 | .353 | 17 | 3 | 3 | 0 | 0 | 0.0 | 2 | 0 | 1 | 3 | 0 | 4 | 1 | 0 | 0 | 1 | 0 | 0.1 | — | OF-3 |

Roy Elsh

ELSH, EUGENE ROY (Dory)
B. Mar. 1, 1892, Pennsgrove, N. J.   D. Nov. 12, 1978, Philadelphia, Pa.   BR TR 5'9" 165 lbs.

1923	CHI	A	81	.249	.301	209	52	7	2	0	0.0	28	24	16	23	15	15	4	127	7	6	1	1.7	.957	OF-57
1924			60	.306	.381	147	45	9	1	0	0.0	21	11	10	14	6	16	3	65	3	5	0	1.2	.932	OF-38, 1B-2
1925			32	.188	.208	48	9	1	0	0	0.0	6	4	5	7	2	13	3	25	2	1	2	0.9	.964	OF-16, 1B-3
3 yrs.			173	.262	.319	404	106	17	3	0	0.0	55	39	31	44	23	44	10	217	12	12	3	1.4	.950	OF-111, 1B-5

Kevin Elster

ELSTER, KEVIN DANIEL
B. Aug. 3, 1964, San Pedro, Calif.   BR TR 6'2" 180 lbs.

1986	NY	N	19	.167	.200	30	5	1	0	0	0.0	3	0	3	8	0	0	0	16	35	2	6	2.8	.962	SS-19
1987			5	.400	.600	10	4	2	0	0	0.0	1	1	0	1	0	2	1	4	6	1	0	2.2	.909	SS-3
1988			149	.214	.313	406	87	11	1	9	2.2	41	37	35	47	2	1	0	196	345	13	61	3.7	.977	SS-148
1989			151	.231	.360	458	106	25	2	10	2.2	52	55	34	77	4	0	0	235	374	15	63	4.1	.976	SS-150
4 yrs.			324	.223	.336	904	202	39	3	19	2.1	97	93	72	133	6	3	2	451	760	31	130	3.8	.975	SS-320

LEAGUE CHAMPIONSHIP SERIES

1986	NY	N	4	.000	.000	3	0	0	0	0	0.0	0	0	0	1	0	0	0	2	3	0	1	1.3	1.000	SS-4
1988			5	.250	.375	8	2	1	0	0	0.0	1	1	3	0	0	0	0	7	7	2	2	3.2	.875	SS-5
2 yrs.			9	.182	.273	11	2	1	0	0	0.0	1	1	3	1	0	0	0	9	10	2	2	2.3	.905	SS-9

WORLD SERIES

| 1986 | NY | N | 1 | .000 | .000 | 1 | 0 | 0 | 0 | 0 | 0.0 | 0 | 0 | 0 | 0 | 0 | 0 | 0 | 3 | 3 | 1 | 1 | 7.0 | .857 | SS-1 |

Bones Ely

ELY, FREDERICK WILLIAM
B. June 7, 1863, North Girard, Pa.   D. Jan. 10, 1952, Imola, Calif.   BR TR 6'1" 155 lbs.

1884	BUF	N	1	.000	.000	4	0	0	0	0	0.0	0		0	2		0	0	0	1	1	0	2.0	.500	OF-1, P-1
1886	LOU	AA	10	.156	.156	32	5	0	0	0	0.0	5		2			0	0	9	8	1	0	1.8	.944	P-6, OF-5
1890	SYR	AA	119	.262	.319	496	130	16	6	0	0.0	72		31	44		0	0	298	143	33	20	4.0	.930	OF-78, SS-36, 1B-4, 2B-2, 3B-1, P-1
1891	BKN	N	31	.153	.171	111	17	0	1	0	0.0	9		7	9	4	0	0	58	117	26	9	6.5	.871	SS-28, 3B-2, 2B-1
1893	STL	N	44	.253	.326	178	45	1	6	0	0.0	25	16	17	13	2	0	0	98	139	25	16	6.0	.905	SS-44
1894			127	.306	.463	510	156	20	12	12	2.4	85	89	30	34	23	0	0	276	446	81	51	6.3	.899	SS-126, 2B-1, P-1
1895			117	.259	.308	467	121	16	2	1	0.2	68	46	19	17	28	0	0	247	407	53	52	6.0	.925	SS-117
1896	PIT	N	128	.285	.363	537	153	15	9	3	0.6	85	77	33	33	18	0	0	258	432	62	52	5.9	.918	SS-128
1897			133	.283	.364	516	146	20	8	2	0.4	63	74	25		10	0	0	308	451	60	41	6.2	.927	SS-133
1898			148	.212	.270	519	110	14	5	2	0.4	49	44	24	6		0	0	311	527	51	58	6.0	.943	SS-148
1899			138	.278	.352	522	145	18	6	3	0.6	66	72	22	8		0	0	289	500	59	47	6.1	.930	SS-132, 2B-6
1900			130	.244	.282	475	116	6	6	0	0.0	60	51	17			0	0	242	503	52	62	6.1	.935	SS-130
1901	2 teams		PIT N	(65G – .208)		PHI A	(45G – .216)																		
"	total		110	.212	.265	411	87	12	5	0	0.0	29	44	9		11	0	0	197	372	53	42	5.7	.915	SS-109, 3B-1

Year	Team	Games	BA	SA	AB	H	2B	3B	HR	HR%	R	RBI	BB	SO	SB	Pinch Hit AB	H	PO	A	E	DP	TC/G	FA	G by Pos

Bones Ely *continued*

Year	Team	Games	BA	SA	AB	H	2B	3B	HR	HR%	R	RBI	BB	SO	SB	AB	H	PO	A	E	DP	TC/G	FA	G by Pos
1902	WAS A	105	.262	.310	381	100	11	2	1	0.3	39	62	21		3	0	0	238	350	49	31	6.1	.923	SS-105
14 yrs.		1341	.258	.327	5159	1331	149	68	24	0.5	655	586	257	108	163	1	0	2829	4396	606	481	5.8	.923	SS-1236, OF-84, 2B-10, P-9, 3B-4, 1B-4

Chester Emerson

EMERSON, CHESTER ARTHUR (Chuck)
B. Oct. 27, 1889, Stow, Me. D. July 2, 1971, Augusta, Me.　　　　BL TR 5'8"　165 lbs.

Year	Team	Games	BA	SA	AB	H	2B	3B	HR	HR%	R	RBI	BB	SO	SB	AB	H	PO	A	E	DP	TC/G	FA	G by Pos
1911	PHI A	7	.222	.222	18	4	0	0	0	0.0	2	0	6		1	0	0	17	0	0	0	2.4	1.000	OF-7
1912		1	.000	.000	1	0	0	0	0	0.0	0	0	0		0	1	0	0	0	0	0	0.0		
2 yrs.		8	.211	.211	19	4	0	0	0	0.0	2	0	6		1	1	0	17	0	0	0	2.1	1.000	OF-7

Cal Emery

EMERY, CALVIN WAYNE
B. June 28, 1937, Centre Hall, Pa.　　　　BL TL 6'2"　205 lbs.

Year	Team	Games	BA	SA	AB	H	2B	3B	HR	HR%	R	RBI	BB	SO	SB	AB	H	PO	A	E	DP	TC/G	FA	G by Pos
1963	PHI N	16	.158	.211	19	3	1	0	0	0.0	0	2	0	14	1	0	0	16	0	0	0	1.0	1.000	1B-2

Spoke Emery

EMERY, HERRICK SMITH
B. Dec. 10, 1898, Bay City, Mich. D. June 2, 1975, Cape Canaveral, Fla.　　　　BR TR 5'9"　165 lbs.

Year	Team	Games	BA	SA	AB	H	2B	3B	HR	HR%	R	RBI	BB	SO	SB	AB	H	PO	A	E	DP	TC/G	FA	G by Pos
1924	PHI N	5	.667	.667	3	2	0	0	0	0.0	3	0	0		0	1	0	2	0	0	0	0.4	1.000	OF-1

Frank Emmer

EMMER, FRANK WILLIAM
B. Feb. 17, 1896, Crestline, Ohio D. Oct. 18, 1963, Homestead, Fla.　　　　BR TR 5'8"　150 lbs.

Year	Team	Games	BA	SA	AB	H	2B	3B	HR	HR%	R	RBI	BB	SO	SB	AB	H	PO	A	E	DP	TC/G	FA	G by Pos
1916	CIN N	42	.146	.202	89	13	3	1	0	0.0	8	2	7	27	1	0	0	56	88	17	7	3.8	.894	SS-29, OF-2, 3B-1, 2B-1
1926		80	.196	.281	224	44	7	6	0	0.0	22	18	13	30	1	0	0	141	242	34	40	5.2	.918	SS-79
2 yrs.		122	.182	.259	313	57	10	7	0	0.0	30	20	20	57	2	0	0	197	330	51	47	4.7	.912	SS-108, OF-2, 3B-1, 2B-1

Bob Emmerich

EMMERICH, ROBERT G.
B. Aug. 1, 1897, New York, N. Y. D. Nov. 22, 1948, Bridgeport, Conn.　　　　BR TR 5'3"　155 lbs.

Year	Team	Games	BA	SA	AB	H	2B	3B	HR	HR%	R	RBI	BB	SO	SB	AB	H	PO	A	E	DP	TC/G	FA	G by Pos
1923	BOS N	13	.083	.083	24	2	0	0	0	0.0	3	0	2	3	1	0	0	14	1	0	0	1.2	1.000	OF-8

Bill Endicott

ENDICOTT, WILLIAM FRANKLIN
B. Sept. 4, 1918, Acorn, Mo.　　　　BL TL 5'11½"　175 lbs.

Year	Team	Games	BA	SA	AB	H	2B	3B	HR	HR%	R	RBI	BB	SO	SB	AB	H	PO	A	E	DP	TC/G	FA	G by Pos
1946	STL N	20	.200	.350	20	4	3	0	0	0.0	2	3	4	4	0	14	3	4	0	0	0	0.2	1.000	OF-2

Charlie Engle

ENGLE, CHARLIE AUGUST (Cholly)
B. Aug. 27, 1903, New York, N. Y. D. Oct. 12, 1983, San Antonio, Tex.　　　　BR TR 5'8"　145 lbs.

Year	Team	Games	BA	SA	AB	H	2B	3B	HR	HR%	R	RBI	BB	SO	SB	AB	H	PO	A	E	DP	TC/G	FA	G by Pos
1925	PHI A	1	–	–	0	0	0	0	0		0	0	0	0	0	0	0	0	0	0	0	0.0	–	SS-1
1926		19	.105	.105	19	2	0	0	0	0.0	7	0	10	6	0	0	0	13	27	3	6	2.3	.930	SS-16
1930	PIT N	67	.264	.319	216	57	10	1	0	0.0	34	15	22	20	1	7	2	113	161	15	18	4.3	.948	3B-24, SS-23, 2B-10
3 yrs.		87	.251	.302	235	59	10	1	0	0.0	41	15	32	26	1	7	2	126	188	18	24	3.8	.946	SS-40, 3B-24, 2B-10

Clyde Engle

ENGLE, ARTHUR CLYDE (Hack)
B. Mar. 19, 1884, Dayton, Ohio D. Dec. 26, 1939, Boston, Mass.　　　　BR TR 5'10"　190 lbs.

Year	Team	Games	BA	SA	AB	H	2B	3B	HR	HR%	R	RBI	BB	SO	SB	AB	H	PO	A	E	DP	TC/G	FA	G by Pos
1909	NY A	135	.278	.358	492	137	20	5	3	0.6	66	71	47		18	1	1	299	17	18	5	2.5	.946	OF-134
1910	2 teams	111	NY A (5G – .231)		BOS A (106G – .264)																			
"	total	111	.263	.364	376	99	18	7	2	0.5	59	38	33		13	7	0	135	223	30	17	3.5	.923	3B-51, 2B-27, OF-18, SS-7
1911	BOS A	146	.270	.319	514	139	13	3	2	0.4	58	48	51		24	5	1	636	187	48	34	6.0	.945	1B-65, 3B-51, 2B-13, OF-10
1912		57	.234	.298	171	40	5	3	0	0.0	32	18	28		12	3	0	248	60	13	15	5.6	.960	1B-25, 2B-15, 3B-11, SS-2, OF-1
1913		143	.289	.384	498	144	17	12	2	0.4	75	50	53	41	28	7	0	1241	59	17	56	9.2	.987	1B-133, OF-2
1914	2 teams	87	BOS A (55G – .194)		BUF F (32G – .255)																			
"	total	87	.221	.254	244	54	6	1	0	0.0	26	21	25	11	9	18	4	330	46	14	16	4.5	.964	1B-29, 3B-25, OF-9, 2B-5
1915	BUF F	141	.261	.355	501	131	22	8	3	0.6	56	71	34		24	5	2	261	71	12	11	2.4	.965	OF-100, 2B-21, 3B-17, 1B-1
1916	CLE A	11	.154	.154	26	4	0	0	0	0.0	1	1	0	6	1	0	0	10	12	4	0	2.4	.846	3B-7, 1B-2, OF-1
8 yrs.		831	.265	.341	2822	748	101	39	12	0.4	373	318	271	58	128	47	9	3160	675	156	154	4.8	.961	OF-275, 1B-255, 3B-162, 2B-81, SS-9

WORLD SERIES

Year	Team	Games	BA	SA	AB	H	2B	3B	HR	HR%	R	RBI	BB	SO	SB	AB	H	PO	A	E	DP	TC/G	FA	G by Pos
1912	BOS A	3	.333	.667	3	1	1	0	0	0.0	1	2	0		0	3	1	0	0	0	0	0.0	–	

Dave Engle

ENGLE, RALPH DAVID
B. Nov. 30, 1956, San Diego, Calif.　　　　BR TR 6'3"　210 lbs.

Year	Team	Games	BA	SA	AB	H	2B	3B	HR	HR%	R	RBI	BB	SO	SB	AB	H	PO	A	E	DP	TC/G	FA	G by Pos
1981	MIN A	82	.258	.407	248	64	14	4	5	2.0	29	32	13	37	0	1	0	144	4	3	0	1.8	.980	OF-76, DH-1, 3B-1
1982		58	.226	.349	186	42	7	2	4	2.2	20	16	10	22	0	13	3	63	3	1	1	1.2	.985	OF-34, DH-20
1983		120	.305	.449	374	114	22	4	8	2.1	46	43	28	39	2	20	6	306	26	9	3	2.8	.974	C-73, DH-29, OF-4
1984		109	.266	.353	391	104	20	1	4	1.0	56	38	26	22	0	6	0	376	34	8	3	3.8	.981	C-86, DH-22
1985		70	.256	.448	172	44	8	2	7	4.1	28	25	21	28	2	18	4	66	4	1	1	1.0	.986	DH-38, C-17, OF-3
1986	DET A	35	.256	.337	86	22	7	0	0	0.0	6	4	7	13	0	5	1	185	14	0	20	5.7	1.000	1B-23, DH-5, OF-4, C-3
1987	MON N	59	.226	.310	84	19	4	0	1	1.2	7	14	6	11	1	41	11	33	3	0	0	0.6	1.000	OF-11, C-6, 1B-2, 3B-1
1988		34	.216	.297	37	8	3	0	0	0.0	4	1	5	5	0	23	2	25	1	0	0	0.8	1.000	C-9, OF-4, 3B-1
1989	MIL A	27	.215	.354	65	14	3	0	2	3.1	5	8	4	13	0	6	1	134	12	4	11	5.6	.973	1B-18, DH-3, C-3
9 yrs.		594	.262	.388	1643	431	88	13	31	1.9	201	181	120	190	5	133	28	1332	101	26	39	2.5	.982	C-197, OF-136, DH-118, 1B-43, 3B-3

Charlie English

ENGLISH, CHARLES DEWIE
B. Apr. 8, 1910, Darlington, S. C.　　　　BR TR 5'9½"　160 lbs.

Year	Team	Games	BA	SA	AB	H	2B	3B	HR	HR%	R	RBI	BB	SO	SB	AB	H	PO	A	E	DP	TC/G	FA	G by Pos
1932	CHI A	24	.317	.444	63	20	3	1	1	1.6	7	3	3	7	0	9	2	10	25	8	2	1.8	.814	3B-13, SS-1
1933		3	.444	.667	9	4	2	0	0	0.0	2	1	1	0	0	0	0	6	6	1	2	4.3	.923	2B-3
1936	NY N	6	.000	.000	1	0	0	0	0	.0	0	1	0	0	0	1	0	0	0	0	0	0.0	–	2B-1

Year Team	Games	BA	SA	AB	H	2B	3B	HR	HR%	R	RBI	BB	SO	SB	Pinch Hit AB	Pinch Hit H	PO	A	E	DP	TC/G	FA	G by Pos

Charlie English *continued*

Year Team	Games	BA	SA	AB	H	2B	3B	HR	HR%	R	RBI	BB	SO	SB	AB	H	PO	A	E	DP	TC/G	FA	G by Pos
1937 CIN N	17	.238	.317	63	15	3	1	0	0.0	1	4	0	2	0	0	0	20	34	3	3	3.4	.947	3B-15, 2B-2
4 yrs.	50	.287	.397	136	39	8	2	1	0.7	10	13	4	10	0	10	2	36	65	12	7	2.3	.894	3B-28, 2B-6, SS-1

Gil English

ENGLISH, GILBERT RAYMOND
B. July 2, 1909, Glenola, N. C.   BR TR 5'11" 180 lbs.

Year Team	Games	BA	SA	AB	H	2B	3B	HR	HR%	R	RBI	BB	SO	SB	AB	H	PO	A	E	DP	TC/G	FA	G by Pos
1931 NY N	3	.000	.000	8	0	0	0	0	0.0	0	0	1	3	0	0	0	1	3	0	0	1.3	1.000	3B-3
1932	59	.225	.338	204	46	7	5	2	1.0	22	19	5	20	0	1	0	77	133	14	18	3.8	.938	3B-39, SS-23
1936 DET A	1	.000	.000	1	0	0	0	0	0.0	0	0	0	1	0	0	0	1	1	0	0	2.0	1.000	3B-1
1937 2 teams	DET A (18G – .262)			BOS N	(79G – .290)																		
" total	97	.284	.341	334	95	6	2	3	0.9	31	43	29	31	4	6	4	87	155	10	14	2.6	.960	3B-77, 2B-12
1938 BOS N	53	.248	.321	165	41	6	0	2	1.2	17	21	15	16	1	4	2	39	77	6	3	2.3	.951	SS-46, 3B-2, 2B-2
1944 BKN N	27	.152	.228	79	12	3	0	1	1.3	4	7	6	7	0	1	0	28	51	6	8	3.1	.929	SS-13, 3B-11, 2B-2
6 yrs.	240	.245	.321	791	194	22	7	8	1.0	74	90	56	78	5	12	6	233	420	36	43	2.9	.948	3B-174, SS-38, 2B-16, OF-3

Woody English

ENGLISH, ELWOOD GEORGE
B. Mar. 2, 1907, Fredonia, Ohio   BR TR 5'10" 155 lbs.

Year Team	Games	BA	SA	AB	H	2B	3B	HR	HR%	R	RBI	BB	SO	SB	AB	H	PO	A	E	DP	TC/G	FA	G by Pos
1927 CHI N	87	.290	.365	334	97	14	4	1	0.3	46	28	16	26	1	0	0	179	285	29	47	5.7	.941	SS-84, 3B-1
1928	116	.299	.375	475	142	22	4	2	0.4	68	34	30	28	4	0	0	245	382	36	85	5.7	.946	SS-114, 3B-2
1929	144	.276	.339	608	168	29	3	1	0.2	131	52	68	50	13	0	0	332	497	39	107	6.0	.955	SS-144
1930	156	.335	.511	638	214	36	17	14	2.2	152	59	100	72	3	0	0	256	386	22	76	4.3	.967	3B-83, SS-78
1931	156	.319	.413	634	202	38	8	2	0.3	117	53	68	80	12	0	0	340	482	29	78	5.5	.966	SS-138, 3B-18
1932	127	.272	.360	522	142	23	7	3	0.6	70	47	55	73	5	1	0	162	275	20	30	3.6	.956	3B-93, SS-38
1933	105	.261	.342	398	104	19	2	3	0.8	54	41	53	44	5	0	0	80	174	7	9	2.5	.973	3B-103, SS-1
1934	109	.278	.385	421	117	26	5	3	0.7	65	31	48	65	6	0	0	145	260	14	31	3.8	.967	SS-56, 3B-46, 2B-7
1935	34	.202	.298	84	17	2	0	2	2.4	11	8	20	4	1	4	2	29	54	6	6	2.6	.933	3B-16, SS-12
1936	64	.247	.297	182	45	9	0	0	0.0	33	20	40	28	1	5	0	92	152	5	30	3.9	.980	SS-42, 3B-17, 2B-1
1937 BKN N	129	.238	.299	378	90	16	2	1	0.3	45	42	65	55	4	2	0	239	324	26	64	4.6	.956	SS-116, 3B-11
1938	34	.250	.278	72	18	2	0	0	0.0	9	7	8	11	2	7	1	24	37	2	5	1.9	.968	3B-21, SS-3, 2B-3
12 yrs.	1261	.286	.378	4746	1356	236	52	32	0.7	801	422	571	536	57	19	3	2123	3308	235	568	4.5	.959	SS-826, 3B-400, 2B-22

WORLD SERIES

Year Team	Games	BA	SA	AB	H	2B	3B	HR	HR%	R	RBI	BB	SO	SB	AB	H	PO	A	E	DP	TC/G	FA	G by Pos
1929 CHI N	5	.190	.286	21	4	2	0	0	0.0	1	0	1	6	0	0	0	8	12	4	3	4.8	.833	SS-5
1932	4	.176	.176	17	3	0	0	0	0.0	2	1	2	2	0	0	0	3	4	1	0	2.0	.875	3B-4
2 yrs.	9	.184	.237	38	7	2	0	0	0.0	3	1	3	8	0	0	0	11	16	5	3	3.6	.844	SS-5, 3B-4

Del Ennis

ENNIS, DELMER
B. June 8, 1925, Philadelphia, Pa.   BR TR 6' 195 lbs.

Year Team	Games	BA	SA	AB	H	2B	3B	HR	HR%	R	RBI	BB	SO	SB	AB	H	PO	A	E	DP	TC/G	FA	G by Pos
1946 PHI N	141	.313	.485	540	169	30	6	17	3.1	70	73	39	65	5	3	0	332	16	9	4	2.5	.975	OF-138
1947	139	.275	.410	541	149	25	6	12	2.2	71	81	37	51	9	4	1	320	12	7	2	2.4	.979	OF-135
1948	152	.290	.525	589	171	40	4	30	5.1	86	95	47	58	2	2	1	297	15	14	4	2.1	.957	OF-151
1949	154	.302	.525	610	184	39	11	25	4.1	92	110	59	61	2	0	0	359	16	13	4	2.5	.966	OF-154
1950	153	.311	.551	595	185	34	8	31	5.2	92	**126**	56	59	2	4	0	279	10	9	3	1.9	.970	OF-149
1951	144	.267	.408	532	142	20	5	15	2.8	76	73	68	42	4	8	2	268	14	9	3	2.0	.969	OF-144
1952	151	.289	.475	592	171	30	10	20	3.4	90	107	47	65	6	2	0	277	11	9	1	2.0	.970	OF-149
1953	152	.285	.484	578	165	22	3	29	5.0	79	125	57	53	1	2	0	284	14	6	4	2.0	.980	OF-150
1954	145	.261	.444	556	145	23	2	25	4.5	73	119	50	60	2	1	0	311	9	15	1	2.3	.955	OF-142, 1B-1
1955	146	.296	.518	564	167	24	7	29	5.1	82	120	46	46	4	1	0	298	9	4	2	2.1	.987	OF-145
1956	153	.260	.430	630	164	25	3	26	4.1	80	95	33	62	7	0	0	269	8	11	0	1.9	.962	OF-153
1957 STL N	136	.286	.494	490	140	24	3	24	4.9	61	105	37	50	1	8	3	180	3	11	0	1.4	.943	OF-127
1958	106	.261	.350	329	86	18	1	3	0.9	22	47	15	35	0	22	2	122	11	1	2	1.3	.993	OF-84
1959 2 teams	CIN N (5G – .333)			CHI A	(26G – .219)																		
" total	31	.231	.343	108	25	6	0	2	1.9	11	8	6	12	0	3	1	33	2	0	1	1.2	.921	OF-28
14 yrs.	1903	.284	.472	7254	2063	358	69	288	4.0	985	1284	597	719	45	60	10	3629	150	121	27	2.0	.969	OF-1849, 1B-1

WORLD SERIES

Year Team	Games	BA	SA	AB	H	2B	3B	HR	HR%	R	RBI	BB	SO	SB	AB	H	PO	A	E	DP	TC/G	FA	G by Pos
1950 PHI N	4	.143	.214	14	2	1	0	0	0.0	1	0	0	1	0	0	0	9	0	0	0	2.3	1.000	OF-4

Russ Ennis

ENNIS, RUSSELL ELWOOD (Hack)
B. Mar. 10, 1897, Superior, Wis. D. Jan. 21, 1949, Superior, Wis.   BR TR 5'11½" 160 lbs.

Year Team	Games	BA	SA	AB	H	2B	3B	HR	HR%	R	RBI	BB	SO	SB	AB	H	PO	A	E	DP	TC/G	FA	G by Pos
1926 WAS A	1	–	–	0	0	0	0	0	–	0	0	0	0	0	0	0	0	0	0	0	0.0	–	C-1

George Enright

ENRIGHT, GEORGE ALBERT
B. May 9, 1954, New Britain, Conn.   BR TR 5'11" 175 lbs.

Year Team	Games	BA	SA	AB	H	2B	3B	HR	HR%	R	RBI	BB	SO	SB	AB	H	PO	A	E	DP	TC/G	FA	G by Pos
1976 CHI A	2	.000	.000	1	0	0	0	0	0.0	0	0	0	0	0	0	0	4	0	0	0	2.0	1.000	C-2

Jewel Ens

ENS, JEWEL WINKLEMEYER
Brother of Mutz Ens.
B. Aug. 24, 1889, St. Louis, Mo. D. Jan. 17, 1950, Syracuse, N. Y.   BR TR 5'10½" 165 lbs.
Manager 1929-31.

Year Team	Games	BA	SA	AB	H	2B	3B	HR	HR%	R	RBI	BB	SO	SB	AB	H	PO	A	E	DP	TC/G	FA	G by Pos
1922 PIT N	47	.296	.387	142	42	7	3	0	0.0	18	17	7	9	3	13	3	69	77	7	7	3.3	.954	2B-29, 3B-3, 1B-2, SS-1
1923	12	.276	.379	29	8	1	1	0	0.0	3	5	0	3	2	5	2	39	7	2	5	4.0	.958	1B-4, 3B-2, SS-1
1924	5	.300	.300	10	3	0	0	0	0.0	2	0	0	3	0	0	0	25	1	0	1	5.2	1.000	1B-5
1925	3	.200	.800	5	1	0	0	1	20.0	2	2	0	1	0	0	0	16	0	0	0	5.3	1.000	1B-3
4 yrs.	67	.290	.392	186	54	8	4	1	0.5	25	24	7	16	5	18	5	149	85	9	13	3.6	.963	2B-29, 1B-14, 3B-5, SS-2

Mutz Ens

ENS, ANTON
Brother of Jewel Ens.
B. Nov. 8, 1884, St. Louis, Mo. D. June 28, 1950, St. Louis, Mo.   BL TL 6'1" 180 lbs.

Year Team	Games	BA	SA	AB	H	2B	3B	HR	HR%	R	RBI	BB	SO	SB	AB	H	PO	A	E	DP	TC/G	FA	G by Pos
1912 CHI A	3	.000	.000	6	0	0	0	0	0.0	0	0	0		0	0	0	12	0	2	1	4.7	.857	1B-3

Year	Team		Games	BA	SA	AB	H	2B	3B	HR	HR%	R	RBI	BB	SO	SB	Pinch Hit AB	Pinch Hit H	PO	A	E	DP	TC/G	FA	G by Pos

Charlie Enwright

ENWRIGHT, CHARLES MASSEY
B. Oct. 6, 1887, Sacramento, Calif. D. Jan. 19, 1917, Sacramento, Calif.
BL TR 5'10"

| 1909 | STL | N | 3 | .143 | .143 | 7 | 1 | 0 | 0 | 0 | 0.0 | 1 | 1 | | 0 | 1 | 0 | 2 | 2 | 5 | 0 | 3.0 | .444 | SS-2 |

Jack Enzenroth

ENZENROTH, CLARENCE HERMAN
B. Nov. 4, 1885, Mineral Point, Wis. D. Feb. 21, 1944, Detroit, Mich.
BR TR 5'10" 164 lbs.

1914	2 teams		STL A (3G – .167)			KC	F	(26G – .179)																
"	total		29	.178	.260	73	13	4	1	0	0.0	7	5	7	3	0	2	1	91	31	5	6	4.4	.961	C-27
1915	KC	F	14	.158	.158	19	3	0	0	0	0.0	3	3	6		0	1	1	25	11	1	2	2.6	.973	C-8
2 yrs.			43	.174	.239	92	16	4	1	0	0.0	10	8	13	3	0	3	2	116	42	6	8	3.8	.963	C-35

Jim Eppard

EPPARD, JAMES GERHARD
B. Apr. 27, 1960, South Bend, Ind.
BL TL 6'2" 180 lbs.

1987	CAL	A	8	.333	.333	9	3	0	0	0	0.0	2	0	2	0	0	5	3	1	0	0	0	0.1	1.000	OF-1
1988			56	.283	.327	113	32	3	1	0	0.0	7	14	11	15	0	26	8	63	4	2	2	1.2	.971	OF-17, DH-10, 1B-6
1989			12	.250	.250	12	3	0	0	0	0.0	0	2	1	4	0	9	2	12	0	0	2	1.0	1.000	1B-4
3 yrs.			76	.284	.321	134	38	3	1	0	0.0	9	16	14	19	0	40	13	76	4	2	4	1.1	.976	OF-18, DH-10, 1B-10

Aubrey Epps

EPPS, AUBREY LEE (Yo-Yo)
B. Mar. 3, 1912, Memphis, Tenn. D. Nov. 13, 1984, Ackerman, Miss.
BR TR 5'10" 170 lbs.

| 1935 | PIT | N | 1 | .750 | 1.250 | 4 | 3 | 1 | 0 | 0 | 0.0 | 1 | 3 | 0 | 0 | 0 | 0 | 0 | 6 | 0 | 2 | 0 | 8.0 | .750 | C-1 |

Hal Epps

EPPS, HAROLD FRANKLIN
B. Mar. 26, 1914, Athens, Ga.
BL TL 6' 175 lbs.

1938	STL	N	17	.300	.360	50	15	0	0	1	2.0	8	3	2	4	1	7	0	26	0	1	0	1.6	.963	OF-10
1940			11	.200	.200	15	3	0	0	0	0.0	6	1	0	3	0	2	0	4	0	1	0	0.5	.800	OF-3
1943	STL	A	8	.286	.400	35	10	4	0	0	0.0	2	1	3	4	1	0	0	18	0	0	0	2.3	1.000	OF-8
1944	2 teams		STL A (22G – .177)			PHI	A	(67G – .262)																
"	total		89	.244	.337	291	71	9	9	0	0.0	42	16	32	32	2	10	3	188	7	6	3	2.3	.970	OF-78
4 yrs.			125	.253	.340	391	99	13	9	1	0.3	58	21	37	43	5	19	3	236	7	8	3	2.0	.968	OF-99

Mike Epstein

EPSTEIN, MICHAEL PETER (Superjew)
B. Apr. 4, 1943, Bronx, N. Y.
BL TL 6'3½" 230 lbs.

1966	BAL	A	6	.182	.364	11	2	0	1	0	0.0	1	3	1	3	0	1	0	36	2	0	3	6.3	1.000	1B-4
1967	2 teams		BAL A (9G – .154)			WAS	A	(96G – .229)																
"	total		105	.226	.367	297	67	7	4	9	3.0	32	29	41	79	1	19	3	743	55	10	74	7.7	.988	1B-83
1968	WAS	A	123	.234	.366	385	90	8	2	13	3.4	40	33	48	91	1	13	2	947	70	13	83	8.4	.987	1B-110
1969			131	.278	.551	403	112	18	1	30	7.4	73	85	85	99	2	12	3	1035	69	11	99	8.5	.990	1B-118
1970			140	.256	.444	430	110	15	3	20	4.7	55	56	73	117	2	18	2	1100	70	10	104	8.4	.992	1B-122
1971	2 teams		WAS A (24G – .247)			OAK	A	(104G – .234)																
"	total		128	.237	.413	414	98	14	1	19	4.6	49	60	74	102	1	9	1	228	12	2	32	1.9	.992	1B-120
1972	OAK	A	138	.270	.490	455	123	18	2	26	5.7	63	70	68	68	0	1	0	1111	73	12	101	8.7	.990	1B-137
1973	2 teams		TEX A (27G – .188)			CAL	A	(91G – .215)																
"	total		118	.209	.315	397	83	11	2	9	2.3	39	38	48	73	0	4	1	910	62	7	80	8.3	.993	1B-111
1974	CAL	A	18	.161	.387	62	10	2	0	4	6.5	10	6	10	13	0	0	0	137	12	1	14	8.3	.993	1B-18
9 yrs.			907	.244	.424	2854	695	93	16	130	4.6	362	380	448	645	7	77	12	6247	425	66	590	7.4	.990	1B-823

LEAGUE CHAMPIONSHIP SERIES

1971	OAK	A	2	.200	.200	5	1	0	0	0	0.0	0	0	0	3	0	1	0	4	0	0	2	2.0	1.000	1B-1
1972			5	.188	.375	16	3	0	0	1	6.3	1	1	4	5	0	0	0	55	2	0	5	11.4	1.000	1B-5
2 yrs.			7	.190	.333	21	4	0	0	1	4.8	1	1	4	8	0	1	0	59	2	0	7	8.7	1.000	1B-6

WORLD SERIES

| 1972 | OAK | A | 6 | .000 | .000 | 16 | 0 | 0 | 0 | 0 | 0.0 | 1 | 0 | 5 | 3 | 0 | 0 | 0 | 35 | 2 | 2 | 1 | 6.5 | .949 | 1B-6 |

Joe Erautt

ERAUTT, JOSEPH MICHAEL (Stubby)
Brother of Eddie Erautt.
B. Sept. 1, 1921, Vibank, Sask., Canada D. Oct. 6, 1976, Portland, Ore.
BR TR 5'9" 175 lbs.

1950	CHI	A	16	.222	.222	18	4	0	0	0	0.0	1	1	3	10	2	12	0	12	2	0	0	0.9	1.000	C-5
1951			16	.160	.200	25	4	1	0	0	0.0	3	0	3	2	0	4	1	37	6	1	1	2.8	.977	C-12
2 yrs.			32	.186	.209	43	8	1	0	0	0.0	3	1	4	5	0	14	1	49	8	1	1	1.8	.983	C-17

Hank Erickson

ERICKSON, HENRY NELS (Popeye)
B. Nov. 11, 1907, Chicago, Ill. D. Dec. 13, 1964, Louisville, Ky.
BR TR 6'1" 185 lbs.

| 1935 | CIN | N | 37 | .261 | .375 | 88 | 23 | 3 | 2 | 1 | 1.1 | 9 | 4 | 6 | 4 | 0 | 12 | 2 | 84 | 19 | 3 | 7 | 2.9 | .972 | C-25 |

Cal Ermer

ERMER, CALVIN COOLIDGE
B. Nov. 10, 1923, Baltimore, Md.
Manager 1967-68.
BR TR 6'½" 175 lbs.

| 1947 | WAS | A | 1 | .000 | .000 | 3 | 0 | 0 | 0 | 0 | 0.0 | 0 | 0 | 0 | 0 | 0 | 0 | 0 | 4 | 3 | 0 | 0 | 7.0 | 1.000 | 2B-1 |

Frank Ernaga

ERNAGA, FRANK JOHN
B. Aug. 22, 1930, Susanville, Calif.
BR TR 6'1" 195 lbs.

1957	CHI	N	20	.314	.686	35	11	3	2	2	5.7	9	7	9	14	0	7	1	19	0	1	0	1.0	.950	OF-10
1958			9	.125	.125	8	1	0	0	0	0.0	0	0	0	2	0	8	1	0	0	0	0	0.0	–	
2 yrs.			29	.279	.581	43	12	3	2	2	4.7	9	7	9	16	0	15	2	19	0	1	0	0.7	.950	OF-10

Tex Erwin

ERWIN, ROSS EMIL
B. Dec. 22, 1885, Forney, Tex. D. Apr. 5, 1953, Rochester, N. Y.
BL TR 6' 185 lbs.

1907	DET	A	4	.200	.200	5	1	0	0	0	0.0	0	1	1		0	0	0	7	3	0	0	2.8	.909	C-4
1910	BKN	N	81	.188	.228	202	38	3	1	1	0.5	15	10	24	12	3	12	1	259	114	20	10	4.9	.949	C-68
1911			91	.271	.445	218	59	13	2	7	3.2	30	34	31	23	5	15	4	273	98	11	6	4.2	.971	C-74

Year	Team	Games	BA	SA	AB	H	2B	3B	HR	HR%	R	RBI	BB	SO	SB	Pinch Hit AB	Pinch Hit H	PO	A	E	DP	TC/G	FA	G by Pos

Tex Erwin *continued*

Year	Team	Games	BA	SA	AB	H	2B	3B	HR	HR%	R	RBI	BB	SO	SB	AB	H	PO	A	E	DP	TC/G	FA	G by Pos
1912		59	.211	.278	133	28	3	0	2	1.5	14	14	18	16	1	12	2	176	46	12	3	4.0	.949	C-41
1913		20	.258	.290	31	8	1	0	0	0.0	6	3	4	5	0	7	1	32	6	2	0	2.0	.950	C-13
1914 2 teams	BKN N (9G – .455)				CIN	N	(12G – .314)																	
" total		21	.348	.478	46	16	3	0	1	2.2	5	8	4	4	1	6	3	69	15	3	0	4.1	.966	C-16
6 yrs.		276	.236	.334	635	150	23	3	11	1.7	70	70	82	60	10	52	11	816	282	49	19	4.2	.957	C-216

Nick Esasky

ESASKY, NICHOLAS ANDREW
B. Feb. 24, 1960, Hialeah, Fla.

BR TR 6'3" 190 lbs.

Year	Team	Games	BA	SA	AB	H	2B	3B	HR	HR%	R	RBI	BB	SO	SB	AB	H	PO	A	E	DP	TC/G	FA	G by Pos
1983 CIN N		85	.265	.450	302	80	10	5	12	4.0	41	46	27	99	6	1	0	53	133	13	11	2.3	.935	3B-84
1984		113	.193	.348	322	62	10	5	10	3.1	30	45	52	103	1	12	0	220	137	18	19	3.3	.952	3B-82, 1B-25
1985		125	.262	.465	413	108	21	4	21	5.1	61	66	41	102	3	10	4	169	106	8	16	2.3	.972	3B-62, OF-54, 1B-12
1986		102	.230	.403	330	76	17	2	12	3.6	35	41	47	97	0	5	1	585	33	5	14	6.1	.992	1B-70, OF-42, 3B-1
1987		100	.272	.529	346	94	19	2	22	6.4	48	59	29	76	0	6	1	773	41	6	72	8.2	.993	1B-93, OF-1, 3B-1
1988		122	.243	.412	391	95	17	2	15	3.8	40	62	48	104	7	11	0	982	52	6	70	8.5	.994	1B-116
1989 BOS A		154	.277	.500	564	156	26	5	30	5.3	79	108	66	117	1	4	0	1319	107	6	129	9.3	.996	1B-153, OF-1
7 yrs.		801	.251	.449	2668	671	120	21	122	4.6	334	427	310	698	18	49	6	4101	609	62	331	6.0	.987	1B-469, 3B-230, OF-98

Nino Escalera

ESCALERA, SATURNINO
Born Saturnino Escalera y Cuadrado.
B. Dec. 1, 1929, Santurce, Puerto Rico

BL TL 5'10" 165 lbs.

Year	Team	Games	BA	SA	AB	H	2B	3B	HR	HR%	R	RBI	BB	SO	SB	AB	H	PO	A	E	DP	TC/G	FA	G by Pos
1954 CIN N		73	.159	.203	69	11	1	1	0	0.0	15	3	7	11	1	29	6	44	4	1	1	0.7	.980	OF-14, 1B-8, SS-1

Jim Eschen

ESCHEN, JAMES GODRICH
Father of Larry Eschen.
B. Aug. 21, 1891, Brooklyn, N. Y.   D. Sept. 27, 1960, Sloatsburg, N. Y.

BR TR 5'10½" 160 lbs.

Year	Team	Games	BA	SA	AB	H	2B	3B	HR	HR%	R	RBI	BB	SO	SB	AB	H	PO	A	E	DP	TC/G	FA	G by Pos
1915 CLE A		15	.238	.262	42	10	1	0	0	0.0	11	2	5	9	0	5	2	29	1	1	0	2.1	.968	OF-10

Larry Eschen

ESCHEN, LAWRENCE EDWARD
Son of Jim Eschen.
B. Sept. 22, 1920, Suffern, N. Y.

BR TR 6' 180 lbs.

Year	Team	Games	BA	SA	AB	H	2B	3B	HR	HR%	R	RBI	BB	SO	SB	AB	H	PO	A	E	DP	TC/G	FA	G by Pos
1942 PHI A		12	.000	.000	11	0	0	0	0	0.0	0	4	6	0	0	2	0	11	4	3	0	1.5	.833	SS-7, 2B-1

Angel Escobar

ESCOBAR, ANGEL RUBENQUE
Born Angel Rubenque Escobar y Rivas.
B. May 12, 1965, LaSabana, Venezuela

BB TR 6' 160 lbs.

Year	Team	Games	BA	SA	AB	H	2B	3B	HR	HR%	R	RBI	BB	SO	SB	AB	H	PO	A	E	DP	TC/G	FA	G by Pos
1988 SF N		3	.333	.333	3	1	0	0	0	0.0	1	0	0	0	0	1	0	2	1	0	0	1.0	1.000	SS-1, 3B-1

Jimmy Esmond

ESMOND, JAMES JOSEPH
B. Oct. 8, 1889, Albany, N. Y.   D. June 26, 1948, Troy, N. Y.

BR TR 5'11" 167 lbs.

Year	Team	Games	BA	SA	AB	H	2B	3B	HR	HR%	R	RBI	BB	SO	SB	AB	H	PO	A	E	DP	TC/G	FA	G by Pos
1911 CIN N		73	.273	.369	198	54	4	6	1	0.5	27	11	17	30	7	5	2	138	126	22	21	3.9	.923	SS-44, 3B-14, 2B-2
1912		82	.195	.255	231	45	5	3	1	0.4	24	40	20	31	11	1	0	154	180	25	22	4.4	.930	SS-74
1914 IND F		151	.295	.404	542	160	23	15	2	0.4	74	49	40		25	0	0	317	448	67	54	5.5	.919	SS-151
1915 NWK F		155	.258	.355	569	147	20	10	5	0.9	79	62	59		18	0	0	353	482	54	67	5.7	.939	SS-155
4 yrs.		461	.264	.359	1540	406	52	34	9	0.6	204	162	136	61	61	6	2	962	1236	168	164	5.1	.929	SS-424, 3B-14, 2B-2

Juan Espino

ESPINO, JUAN
Born Juan Espino y Reyes.
B. Mar. 16, 1956, Bonao, Dominican Republic

BR TR 6'1" 190 lbs.

Year	Team	Games	BA	SA	AB	H	2B	3B	HR	HR%	R	RBI	BB	SO	SB	AB	H	PO	A	E	DP	TC/G	FA	G by Pos
1982 NY A		3	.000	.000	2	0	0	0	0	0.0	0	0	0	1	0	0	0	4	0	0	0	1.3	1.000	C-3
1983		10	.261	.391	23	6	0	0	1	4.3	1	3	1	5	0	0	0	38	1	0	0	3.9	1.000	C-10
1985		9	.364	.364	11	4	0	0	0	0.0	0	0	0	0	0	0	0	16	4	0	0	2.2	1.000	C-9
1986		27	.162	.216	37	6	2	0	0	0.0	1	5	2	9	0	1	0	72	6	1	0	2.9	.987	C-27
4 yrs.		49	.219	.288	73	16	2	0	1	1.4	2	8	3	15	0	1	0	130	11	1	0	2.9	.993	C-49

Alvaro Espinoza

ESPINOZA, ALVARO ALBERTO
Born Alvaro Alberto Espinoza y Ramirez.
B. Feb. 19, 1962, Valencia, Venezuela

BR TR 6' 160 lbs.

Year	Team	Games	BA	SA	AB	H	2B	3B	HR	HR%	R	RBI	BB	SO	SB	AB	H	PO	A	E	DP	TC/G	FA	G by Pos
1984 MIN A		1	–	–	0	0	0	0	0	–	0	0	0	0	0	0	0	0	0	0	0	0.0	–	SS-1
1985		32	.263	.298	57	15	2	0	0	0.0	5	9	1	9	0	0	0	25	69	5	15	3.1	.949	SS-31
1986		37	.214	.238	42	9	1	0	0	0.0	4	1	1	10	0	1	0	23	52	4	11	2.1	.949	2B-19, SS-18
1988 NY A		3	.000	.000	3	0	0	0	0	0.0	0	0	0	0	0	0	0	5	2	0	1	2.3	1.000	2B-2, SS-1
1989		146	.282	.332	503	142	23	1	0	0.0	51	41	14	60	3	0	0	237	471	22	114	5.0	.970	SS-146
5 yrs.		219	.274	.321	605	166	26	1	0	0.0	60	51	16	79	3	1	0	290	594	31	141	4.2	.966	SS-197, 2B-21

Sammy Esposito

ESPOSITO, SAMUEL
B. Dec. 15, 1931, Chicago, Ill.

BR TR 5'9" 165 lbs.

Year	Team	Games	BA	SA	AB	H	2B	3B	HR	HR%	R	RBI	BB	SO	SB	AB	H	PO	A	E	DP	TC/G	FA	G by Pos
1952 CHI A		1	.250	.250	4	1	0	0	0	0.0	0	0	0	2	0	0	0	1	2	0	1	4.0	.500	SS-1
1955		3	.000	.000	4	0	0	0	0	0.0	3	0	1	0	0	0	0	1	0	0	0	0.3	1.000	3B-2
1956		81	.228	.342	184	42	8	2	3	1.6	30	25	41	19	1	8	1	52	132	6	19	2.3	.968	3B-61, SS-19, 2B-3
1957		94	.205	.256	176	36	3	0	2	1.1	26	15	38	27	5	11	3	84	168	10	23	2.8	.962	3B-53, SS-22, 2B-2, OF-1
1958		98	.247	.284	81	20	3	0	0	0.0	16	3	12	6	1	7	1	36	78	5	9	1.2	.958	3B-63, SS-22, 2B-2, OF-1
1959		69	.167	.227	66	11	1	0	1	1.5	12	5	11	16	1	0	0	39	57	2	6	1.4	.980	3B-45, SS-14, 2B-2
1960		57	.182	.286	77	14	5	0	1	1.3	14	11	10	20	1	4	1	17	51	5	5	1.3	.932	3B-37, SS-11, 2B-5
1961		63	.170	.255	94	16	5	0	1	1.1	12	8	12	21	1	5	0	51	85	3	11	2.2	.978	3B-28, SS-20, 2B-7
1962		75	.235	.247	81	19	1	0	0	0.0	14	4	17	13	0	3	1	29	72	7	7	1.4	.935	3B-41, SS-20, 2B-7
1963 2 teams	CHI A (1G – .000)				KC	A	(18G – .200)																	
" total		19	.200	.240	25	5	1	0	0	0.0	3	2	3	3	0	1	0	7	15	2	2	1.3	.917	2B-7, SS-4, 3B-3
10 yrs.		560	.207	.277	792	164	27	2	8	1.0	130	73	145	127	7	41	9	317	659	42	82	1.8	.959	3B-333, SS-133, 2B-41, OF-2

Year	Team		Games	BA	SA	AB	H	2B	3B	HR	HR%	R	RBI	BB	SO	SB	Pinch Hit AB	Pinch Hit H	PO	A	E	DP	TC/G	FA	G by Pos

Sammy Esposito *continued*
WORLD SERIES

| 1959 | CHI | A | 2 | .000 | .000 | 2 | 0 | 0 | 0 | 0 | 0.0 | 0 | 0 | 0 | 1 | 0 | 0 | 0 | 1 | 0 | 0 | 0 | 0.5 | 1.000 | 3B-2 |

Cecil Espy
ESPY, CECIL EDWARD
B. Jan. 20, 1963, San Diego, Calif.
BB TR 6'3" 190 lbs.

1983	LA	N	20	.273	.364	11	3	1	0	0	0.0	4	1	1	2	0	2	1	11	0	0	0	0.6	1.000	OF-15
1987	TEX	A	14	.000	.000	8	0	0	0	0	0.0	1	0	1	3	2	1	0	8	1	0	1	0.6	1.000	OF-8
1988			123	.248	.349	347	86	17	6	2	0.6	46	39	20	83	33	13	5	200	11	7	0	1.8	.968	OF-98, DH-12, SS-3, C-2, 2B-1, 1B-1
1989			142	.257	.331	475	122	12	7	3	0.6	65	31	38	99	45	13	6	281	5	3	2	2.0	.990	OF-133, DH-3
4 yrs.			299	.251	.335	841	211	30	13	5	0.6	116	71	60	187	80	29	12	500	17	10	3	1.8	.981	OF-254, DH-15, SS-3, C-2, 2B-1, 1B-1

Chuck Essegian
ESSEGIAN, CHARLES ABRAHAM
B. Aug. 9, 1931, Boston, Mass.
BR TR 5'11" 200 lbs.

1958	PHI	N	39	.246	.456	114	28	5	2	5	4.4	15	16	12	34	0	9	2	59	1	3	0	1.6	.952	OF-30
1959	2 teams		STL N (17G – .179)			LA	N	(24G – .304)																	
"	total		41	.247	.400	85	21	8	1	1	1.2	8	10	8	24	0	22	5	8	1	0	0	0.2	1.000	OF-19
1960	LA	N	52	.215	.367	79	17	3	0	3	3.8	8	8	8	24	0	37	8	29	1	1	0	0.6	.968	OF-18
1961	3 teams		BAL A (1G – .000)			KC	A	(4G – .333)		CLE	A	(60G – .289)													
"	total		65	.289	.555	173	50	8	1	12	6.9	26	36	11	35	0	20	7	89	5	3	1	1.5	.969	OF-50
1962	CLE	A	106	.274	.497	336	92	12	0	21	6.3	59	50	42	68	0	14	2	154	1	1	0	1.5	.994	OF-90
1963	KC	A	101	.225	.329	231	52	9	0	5	2.2	23	27	19	48	0	40	9	95	2	1	0	1.0	.990	OF-53
6 yrs.			404	.255	.446	1018	260	45	4	47	4.6	139	150	97	233	0	142	33	434	11	9	1	1.1	.980	OF-260

WORLD SERIES

| 1959 | LA | N | 4 | .667 | 2.667 | 3 | 2 | 0 | 0 | 2 | 66.7 | 2 | 2 | 1 | 1 | 0 | 4 | 0 | 0 | 0 | 0 | 0 | 0.0 | — | |

Jim Essian
ESSIAN, JAMES SARKIS
B. Jan. 2, 1951, Detroit, Mich.
BR TR 6'2" 195 lbs.

1973	PHI	N	2	.000	.000	3	0	0	0	0	0.0	0	0	0	1	0	2	0	0	0	0	0	0.0	—	C-1
1974			17	.100	.100	20	2	0	0	0	0.0	1	0	2	1	0	1	0	38	4	1	1	2.5	.977	C-15, 3B-1, 1B-1
1975			3	1.000	1.000	1	1	0	0	0	0.0	1	1	1	0	0	1	1	1	1	0	0	1.0	1.000	C-2
1976	CHI	A	78	.246	.281	199	49	7	0	0	0.0	20	21	23	28	2	0	0	320	53	10	10	4.9	.974	C-77, 1B-2, 3B-1
1977			114	.273	.435	322	88	18	2	10	3.1	50	44	52	35	1	0	0	593	62	9	8	5.8	.986	C-111, 3B-2
1978	OAK	A	126	.223	.295	278	62	9	1	3	1.1	21	26	44	22	2	4	0	452	79	10	14	4.3	.982	C-119, DH-3, 1B-3, 2B-1
1979			98	.243	.371	313	76	16	0	8	2.6	34	40	25	29	0	8	2	400	79	9	11	5.0	.982	C-70, 3B-10, OF-4, 1B-4, DH-3
1980			87	.232	.323	285	66	11	0	5	1.8	19	29	30	18	1	8	1	339	46	5	5	4.5	.987	C-68, DH-11, 1B-1
1981	CHI	A	27	.308	.365	52	16	3	0	0	0.0	6	5	4	5	0	2	0	92	9	2	0	3.8	.981	C-25, 3B-1
1982	SEA	A	48	.275	.386	153	42	8	0	3	2.0	14	20	11	7	2	1	1	282	26	2	1	6.5	.994	C-48
1983	CLE	A	48	.204	.312	93	19	4	0	2	2.2	11	11	16	8	0	0	0	170	14	2	3	3.9	.989	C-47, 3B-1
1984	OAK	A	62	.228	.338	136	31	9	0	2	1.5	17	10	23	17	1	3	0	229	30	5	6	4.3	.981	C-59, DH-1, 3B-1
12 yrs.			709	.244	.346	1855	452	85	3	33	1.8	194	207	231	171	9	30	5	2916	403	55	59	4.8	.984	C-642, DH-18, 3B-18, 1B-11, OF-4, 2B-1

Bobby Estalella
ESTALELLA, ROBERTO
Born Roberto Estalella y Ventoza.
B. Apr. 25, 1911, Cardenas, Cuba
BR TR 5'8" 180 lbs.

1935	WAS	A	15	.314	.471	51	16	2	0	2	3.9	9	10	17	7	1	0	0	14	37	6	1	3.8	.895	3B-15
1936			13	.222	.667	9	2	0	2	0	0.0	2	0	4	5	0	9	2	0	0	0	0	0.0	—	
1939			82	.275	.468	280	77	18	6	8	2.9	51	41	40	27	2	8	2	157	3	6	1	2.0	.964	OF-74
1941	STL	A	46	.241	.337	83	20	6	1	0	0.0	7	14	18	13	0	22	6	23	0	0	0	0.5	1.000	OF-17
1942	WAS	A	133	.277	.413	429	119	24	5	8	1.9	68	65	85	42	5	18	4	158	136	15	5	2.3	.951	3B-78, OF-36
1943	PHI	A	117	.259	.409	367	95	14	4	11	3.0	43	63	52	44	1	20	7	225	5	6	1	2.0	.975	OF-97
1944			140	.298	.409	506	151	17	9	7	1.4	54	60	59	60	3	11	4	346	16	4	4	2.6	.989	OF-128, 1B-6
1945			126	.299	.435	451	135	25	6	8	1.8	45	52	74	46	1	9	1	314	10	4	3	2.6	.988	OF-124
1949			8	.250	.250	20	5	0	0	0	0.0	2	3	1	2	0	1	0	9	1	0	1	1.3	1.000	OF-6
9 yrs.			680	.282	.421	2196	620	106	33	44	2.0	279	308	350	246	13	91	26	1246	208	41	17	2.2	.973	OF-482, 3B-93, 1B-6

Dude Esterbrook
ESTERBROOK, THOMAS JOHN
B. June 9, 1857, Staten Island, N. Y.   D. Apr. 30, 1901, Middletown, N. Y.
Manager 1889.
BR TR 5'11" 167 lbs.

1880	BUF	N	64	.241	.296	253	61	12	1	0	0.0	20		35		15		0	0	494	37	45	21	9.0	.922	1B-47, OF-15, 2B-6, SS-1, C-1
1882	CLE	N	45	.246	.302	179	44	4	3	0	0.0	13	19	5	12		0	0	107	15	14	7	3.0	.897	OF-45, 1B-1
1883	NY	AA	97	.253	.310	407	103	9	7	0	0.0	55		15			0	0	110	173	42	8	3.4	.871	3B-97
1884			112	.314	.428	477	150	29	11	1	0.2	110		12			0	0	126	208	43	11	3.4	.886	3B-112
1885	NY	N	88	.256	.340	359	92	14	5	2	0.6	48		4	28		0	0	116	161	36	14	3.6	.885	3B-84, OF-4
1886			123	.264	.351	473	125	20	6	3	0.6	62	43	8	43		0	0	148	219	43	9	3.3	.895	3B-123
1887	NY	AA	26	.168	.178	101	17	1	0	0	0.0	11		6		8	0	0	105	27	22	6	5.9	.857	1B-9, OF-7, SS-5, 2B-5
1888	2 teams		IND N (64G – .220)			LOU	AA	(23G – .226)																	
"	total		87	.221	.263	339	75	14	0	0	0.0	30	24	5	20	16	0	0	851	32	27	40	10.5	.970	1B-84, 3B-3
1889	LOU	AA	11	.318	.386	44	14	3	0	0	0.0	8	9	5	2	4	0	0	79	6	7	3	8.4	.924	1B-8, OF-2, SS-1
1890	NY	N	45	.289	.371	197	57	14	1	0	0.0	29	29	10	8	12	0	0	430	13	7	24	10.0	.984	1B-45
1891	BKN	N	3	.375	.375	8	3	0	0	0	0.0	4					0	0	4	0	1	0	1.7	.800	OF-2, 2B-1
11 yrs.			701	.261	.334	2837	741	120	34	6	0.2	387	159	70	129	42	0	0	2570	891	287	143	5.3	.923	3B-419, 1B-194, OF-75, 2B-12, SS-7, C-1

Francisco Estrada
ESTRADA, FRANCISCO
Born Francisco Estrada y Soto.
B. Feb. 12, 1948, Navojoa, mexico
BR TR 5'8" 182 lbs.

Year	Team	Games	BA	SA	AB	H	2B	3B	HR	HR%	R	RBI	BB	SO	SB	Pinch Hit AB	Pinch Hit H	PO	A	E	DP	TC/G	FA	G by Pos

Francisco Estrada *continued*

Year	Team		Games	BA	SA	AB	H	2B	3B	HR	HR%	R	RBI	BB	SO	SB	AB	H	PO	A	E	DP	TC/G	FA	G by Pos
1971	NY	N	1	.500	.500	2	1	0	0	0	0.0	0	0	0	0	0	0	0	1	0	0	0	1.0	1.000	C-1

Andy Etchebarren

ETCHEBARREN, ANDREW AUGUSTE
B. June 20, 1943, Whittier, Calif.
BR TR 6'1" 190 lbs.

Year	Team		Games	BA	SA	AB	H	2B	3B	HR	HR%	R	RBI	BB	SO	SB	AB	H	PO	A	E	DP	TC/G	FA	G by Pos
1962	BAL	A	2	.333	.333	6	2	0	0	0	0.0	0	1	0	2	0	0	0	7	0	1	0	4.0	.875	C-2
1965			5	.167	.667	6	1	0	0	1	16.7	1	4	0	2	0	0	0	21	2	0	0	4.6	1.000	C-5
1966			121	.221	.364	412	91	14	6	11	2.7	49	50	38	106	0	0	0	799	65	10	7	7.2	.989	C-121
1967			112	.215	.318	330	71	13	0	7	2.1	29	35	38	80	1	6	1	673	57	8	10	6.6	.989	C-110
1968			74	.233	.392	189	44	11	2	5	2.6	20	20	19	46	0	6	2	414	29	1	3	6.0	.998	C-70
1969			73	.249	.350	217	54	9	2	3	1.4	29	26	28	42	1	10	1	380	27	4	1	5.6	.990	C-72
1970			78	.243	.348	230	56	10	1	4	1.7	19	28	21	41	4	8	4	392	29	7	3	5.5	.984	C-76
1971			70	.270	.428	222	60	8	0	9	4.1	21	29	16	40	1	4	1	337	24	5	2	5.2	.986	C-70
1972			71	.202	.287	188	38	6	1	2	1.1	11	21	17	43	0	10	3	334	22	3	2	5.1	.992	C-70
1973			54	.257	.368	152	39	9	1	2	1.3	16	23	12	21	1	4	0	201	14	2	5	4.0	.991	C-51
1974			62	.222	.300	180	40	8	0	2	1.1	13	15	6	26	1	3	1	269	19	7	3	4.8	.976	C-60
1975 2 teams	BAL	A (8G – .200)		CAL	A	(31G – .280)																			
" total			39	.267	.367	120	32	1	1	3	2.5	10	20	14	22	1	1	1	216	17	4	2	6.1	.983	C-38
1976	CAL	A	103	.227	.271	247	56	9	1	0	0.0	15	21	24	37	0	3	1	539	46	12	7	5.8	.980	C-102
1977			80	.254	.289	114	29	2	2	0	0.0	11	14	12	19	3	0	0	289	12	4	0	3.8	.987	C-80
1978	MIL	A	4	.400	.600	5	2	1	0	0	0.0	1	2	1	2	0	0	0	13	2	0	0	3.8	1.000	C-4
15 yrs.			948	.235	.343	2618	615	101	17	49	1.9	245	309	246	529	13	55	15	4884	365	68	45	5.6	.987	C-931

LEAGUE CHAMPIONSHIP SERIES

Year	Team		Games	BA	SA	AB	H	2B	3B	HR	HR%	R	RBI	BB	SO	SB	AB	H	PO	A	E	DP	TC/G	FA	G by Pos
1969	BAL	A	2	.000	.000	4	0	0	0	0	0.0	0	0	0	0	0	0	0	12	0	0	0	6.0	1.000	C-2
1970			2	.111	.111	9	1	0	0	0	0.0	1	0	0	3	0	0	0	12	0	0	0	6.0	1.000	C-2
1971			2	.000	.000	5	0	0	0	0	0.0	0	0	0	1	0	1	0	11	0	0	0	5.5	1.000	C-2
1973			4	.357	.643	14	5	1	0	1	7.1	1	4	0	0	0	0	0	30	2	0	0	8.0	1.000	C-4
1974			2	.333	.333	6	2	0	0	0	0.0	0	0	0	0	0	0	0	7	1	0	0	4.0	1.000	C-2
5 yrs.			12	.211	.316	38	8	1	0	1	2.6	2	4	0	4	0	1	0	72	3	0	0	6.3	1.000	C-12

WORLD SERIES

Year	Team		Games	BA	SA	AB	H	2B	3B	HR	HR%	R	RBI	BB	SO	SB	AB	H	PO	A	E	DP	TC/G	FA	G by Pos
1966	BAL	A	4	.083	.083	12	1	0	0	0	0.0	0	0	2	4	0	0	0	32	1	0	1	8.3	1.000	C-4
1969			2	.000	.000	6	0	0	0	0	0.0	0	0	0	1	0	0	0	16	0	0	0	8.0	1.000	C-2
1970			2	.143	.143	7	1	0	0	0	0.0	1	0	2	3	0	0	0	10	0	1	0	5.5	.909	C-2
1971			1	.000	.000	2	0	0	0	0	0.0	0	0	0	0	0	0	0	6	0	0	0	6.0	1.000	C-1
4 yrs.			9	.074	.074	27	2	0	0	0	0.0	3	0	4	8	0	0	0	64	1	1	1	7.3	.985	C-9

Buck Etchison

ETCHISON, CLARENCE HAMPTON
B. Jan. 27, 1915, Baltimore, Md. D. Jan. 24, 1980, East New Market, Md.
BL TL 6'1" 190 lbs.

Year	Team		Games	BA	SA	AB	H	2B	3B	HR	HR%	R	RBI	BB	SO	SB	AB	H	PO	A	E	DP	TC/G	FA	G by Pos
1943	BOS	N	10	.316	.474	19	6	3	0	0	0.0	2	2	2	2	0	4	2	41	2	2	7	4.5	.956	1B-6
1944			109	.214	.344	308	66	16	0	8	2.6	30	33	33	50	1	21	3	757	48	6	64	7.4	.993	1B-85
2 yrs.			119	.220	.352	327	72	19	0	8	2.4	32	35	35	52	1	25	5	798	50	8	71	7.2	.991	1B-91

Bobby Etheridge

ETHERIDGE, BOBBY LAMAR (Luke)
B. Nov. 25, 1942, Greenville, Miss.
BR TR 5'9" 170 lbs.

Year	Team		Games	BA	SA	AB	H	2B	3B	HR	HR%	R	RBI	BB	SO	SB	AB	H	PO	A	E	DP	TC/G	FA	G by Pos
1967	SF	N	40	.226	.348	115	26	7	2	1	0.9	13	15	7	12	0	4	1	21	53	6	7	2.0	.925	3B-37
1969			56	.260	.351	131	34	9	0	1	0.8	13	10	19	26	0	15	2	23	67	10	5	1.8	.900	3B-39, SS-1
2 yrs.			96	.244	.350	246	60	16	2	2	0.8	26	25	26	38	0	19	3	44	120	16	12	1.9	.911	3B-76, SS-1

Nick Etten

ETTEN, NICHOLAS RAYMOND THOMAS
B. Sept. 19, 1913, Spring Grove, Ill.
BL TL 6'2" 198 lbs.

Year	Team		Games	BA	SA	AB	H	2B	3B	HR	HR%	R	RBI	BB	SO	SB	AB	H	PO	A	E	DP	TC/G	FA	G by Pos
1938	PHI	A	22	.259	.383	81	21	6	2	0	0.0	6	11	9	7	1	0	0	212	10	3	20	10.2	.987	1B-22
1939			43	.252	.406	155	39	11	2	3	1.9	20	29	16	11	0	2	0	376	19	4	29	9.3	.990	1B-41
1941	PHI	N	151	.311	.454	540	168	27	4	14	2.6	78	79	82	33	9	1	0	1286	89	23	124	9.3	.984	1B-150
1942			139	.264	.375	459	121	23	3	8	1.7	37	41	67	26	3	3	2	1152	83	19	99	9.0	.985	1B-135
1943	NY	A	154	.271	.420	583	158	35	5	14	2.4	78	107	76	31	3	0	0	1410	79	17	148	9.8	.989	1B-154
1944			154	.293	.466	573	168	25	4	22	3.8	88	91	97	29	4	0	0	1382	106	16	144	9.8	.989	1B-154
1945			152	.285	.437	565	161	24	4	18	3.2	77	111	90	23	2	0	0	1401	94	17	149	9.9	.989	1B-152
1946			108	.232	.365	323	75	14	1	9	2.8	37	49	38	35	0	22	4	717	55	7	80	7.2	.991	1B-84
1947	PHI	N	14	.244	.415	41	10	4	0	1	2.4	5	8	5	4	0	3	0	94	10	1	4	7.5	.990	1B-11
9 yrs.			937	.277	.423	3320	921	167	25	89	2.7	426	526	480	199	22	31	6	8030	545	107	797	9.3	.988	1B-903

WORLD SERIES

Year	Team		Games	BA	SA	AB	H	2B	3B	HR	HR%	R	RBI	BB	SO	SB	AB	H	PO	A	E	DP	TC/G	FA	G by Pos
1943	NY	A	5	.105	.105	19	2	0	0	0	0.0	0	2	1	2	0	0	0	46	2	1	3	9.8	.980	1B-5

Ferd Eunick

EUNICK, FERNANDES BOWEN
B. Apr. 22, 1892, Baltimore, Md. D. Dec. 9, 1959, Baltimore, Md.
BR TR 5'6" 148 lbs.

Year	Team		Games	BA	SA	AB	H	2B	3B	HR	HR%	R	RBI	BB	SO	SB	AB	H	PO	A	E	DP	TC/G	FA	G by Pos
1917	CLE	A	1	.000	.000	2	0	0	0	0	0.0	0	0	0	0	0	0	0	0	1	0	0	1.0	1.000	3B-1

Frank Eustace

EUSTACE, FRANK JOHN
B. Nov. 7, 1873, New York, N. Y. D. Oct. 20, 1932, Pottsville, Pa.
5'9" 160 lbs.

Year	Team		Games	BA	SA	AB	H	2B	3B	HR	HR%	R	RBI	BB	SO	SB	AB	H	PO	A	E	DP	TC/G	FA	G by Pos
1896	LOU	N	25	.170	.260	100	17	2	2	1	1.0	18	11	6	14	4	0	0	52	77	23	8	6.1	.849	SS-22, 2B-3

Al Evans

EVANS, ALFRED HUBERT
B. Sept. 28, 1916, Kenly, N. C. D. Apr. 6, 1979, Wilson, N. C.
BR TR 5'11" 190 lbs.

Year	Team		Games	BA	SA	AB	H	2B	3B	HR	HR%	R	RBI	BB	SO	SB	AB	H	PO	A	E	DP	TC/G	FA	G by Pos
1939	WAS	A	7	.333	.333	21	7	0	0	0	0.0	2	1	5	2	0	1	0	21	6	1	0	4.0	.964	C-6
1940			14	.320	.400	25	8	2	0	0	0.0	1	7	6	7	1	4	1	34	2	0	0	2.6	1.000	C-9
1941			53	.277	.396	159	44	8	4	1	0.6	16	19	9	18	0	3	0	195	24	7	6	4.3	.969	C-51
1942			74	.229	.256	223	51	4	1	0	0.0	22	10	25	36	3	10	1	254	42	12	5	4.2	.961	C-67
1944			14	.091	.091	22	2	0	0	0	0.0	5	0	2	6	0	1	0	19	4	1	1	1.7	.958	C-8
1945			51	.260	.400	150	39	11	2	2	1.3	19	19	17	22	2	2	0	160	19	5	4	3.6	.973	C-41

Year	Team		Games	BA	SA	AB	H	2B	3B	HR	HR%	R	RBI	BB	SO	SB	Pinch Hit AB	Pinch Hit H	PO	A	E	DP	TC/G	FA	G by Pos

Al Evans *continued*

1946			88	.254	.342	272	69	10	4	2	0.7	30	30	30	28	1	7	0	336	30	13	5	4.3	.966	C-81
1947			99	.241	.304	319	77	8	3	2	0.6	17	23	28	25	2	5	1	389	48	5	14	4.5	.989	C-94
1948			93	.259	.338	228	59	6	3	2	0.9	19	28	38	20	0	11	2	245	38	5	6	3.1	.983	C-85
1949			109	.271	.346	321	87	12	3	2	0.6	32	42	50	19	4	3	1	322	47	3	2	3.4	.992	C-107
1950			90	.235	.304	289	68	8	3	2	0.7	24	30	29	21	0	1	0	289	23	4	8	3.5	.987	C-88
1951	BOS	A	12	.125	.167	24	3	1	0	0	0.0	1	2	4	2	0	1	0	40	1	0	0	3.4	1.000	C-10
12 yrs.			704	.250	.326	2053	514	70	23	13	0.6	188	211	243	206	13	54	6	2304	284	56	51	3.8	.979	C-647

Barry Evans

EVANS, BARRY STEVEN
B. Nov. 30, 1955, Atlanta, Ga.   BR TR 6'1" 185 lbs.

1978	SD	N	24	.267	.300	90	24	1	0	0	0.0	7	4	4	10	0	0	0	13	59	4	4	3.2	.947	3B-24
1979			56	.216	.265	162	35	5	0	1	0.6	9	14	5	16	0	1	1	30	110	7	12	2.6	.952	3B-53, SS-2, 2B-1
1980			73	.232	.312	125	29	3	2	1	0.8	11	14	17	21	1	1	1	52	87	2	13	1.9	.986	3B-43, 2B-19, SS-4, 1B-1
1981			54	.323	.376	93	30	5	0	0	0.0	11	7	9	9	2	16	1	98	33	2	10	2.5	.985	3B-24, 1B-10, 2B-6, SS-2
1982	NY	A	17	.258	.355	31	8	3	0	0	0.0	2	2	6	6	0	1	0	14	26	0	4	1.000		2B-8, 3B-6, SS-4
5 yrs.			224	.251	.309	501	126	17	3	2	0.4	40	41	41	62	3	19	3	207	315	15	42	2.4	.972	3B-150, 2B-34, SS-12, 1B-11

Darrell Evans

EVANS, DARRELL WAYNE
B. May 26, 1947, Pasadena, Calif.   BL TR 6'2" 200 lbs.

1969	ATL	N	12	.231	.231	26	6	0	0	0	0.0	3	1	1	8	0	4	0	4	7	1	0	1.0	.917	3B-6
1970			12	.318	.386	44	14	1	0	0	0.0	4	9	7	5	0	0	0	6	26	2	0	2.8	.941	3B-12
1971			89	.242	.431	260	63	11	1	12	4.6	42	38	39	54	2	10	1	77	138	14	13	2.6	.939	3B-72, OF-3
1972			125	.254	.419	418	106	12	0	19	4.5	67	71	90	58	4	1	0	126	273	25	20	3.4	.941	3B-123
1973			161	.281	.556	595	167	25	8	41	6.9	114	104	**124**	104	6	2	0	266	335	24	44	3.9	.962	3B-146, 1B-20
1974			160	.240	.419	571	137	21	3	25	4.4	99	79	**126**	88	4	0	0	185	367	26	45	3.6	.955	3B-160
1975			156	.243	.406	567	138	22	3	22	3.9	82	73	105	106	12	3	1	164	382	36	41	3.7	.938	3B-156, 1B-3
1976	2 teams						ATL N (44G – .173)				SF N (92G – .222)													
"	total		136	.205	.316	396	81	9	1	11	2.8	53	46	72	71	9	7	0	978	110	10	80	8.1	.991	1B-119, 3B-12
1977	SF	N	144	.254	.416	461	117	18	3	17	3.7	64	72	69	50	9	16	4	324	83	13	15	2.9	.969	OF-81, 1B-41, 3B-35
1978			159	.243	.404	547	133	24	2	20	3.7	82	78	105	64	4	5	1	147	348	25	25	3.3	.952	3B-155
1979			160	.253	.391	562	142	23	2	17	3.0	68	70	91	80	6	2	1	129	369	30	28	3.3	.943	3B-159
1980			154	.264	.414	556	147	23	0	20	3.6	69	78	83	65	17	4	1	232	340	27	35	3.9	.955	3B-140, 1B-14
1981			102	.258	.417	357	92	13	4	12	3.4	51	48	54	33	2	2	0	188	202	14	22	4.0	.965	3B-87, 1B-12
1982			141	.256	.419	465	119	20	4	16	3.4	64	61	77	64	5	12	2	471	233	21	45	5.1	.971	3B-84, 1B-49, SS-13
1983			142	.277	.516	523	145	29	3	30	5.7	94	82	84	81	6	2	1	1001	164	19	67	8.3	.984	1B-113, 3B-32, SS-9
1984	DET	A	131	.232	.384	401	93	11	1	16	4.0	60	63	77	70	2	18	3	331	62	2	34	3.0	.995	DH-62, 1B-47, 3B-19
1985			151	.248	.519	505	125	17	0	**40**	7.9	81	94	85	85	0	10	2	831	125	20	81	6.5	.980	1B-113, DH-33, 3B-7
1986			151	.241	.442	507	122	15	0	29	5.7	78	85	91	105	3	8	3	809	109	2	85	6.1	.998	1B-105, DH-42, 3B-2
1987			150	.257	.501	499	128	20	0	34	6.8	90	99	100	84	6	10	6	815	108	4	86	6.2	.996	1B-105, DH-44, 3B-7
1988			144	.208	.380	437	91	9	0	22	5.0	48	64	84	89	1	23	3	509	58	4	43	4.0	.993	DH-72, 1B-65
1989	ATL	N	107	.207	.355	276	57	6	1	11	4.0	31	39	41	46	0	31	5	371	90	10	37	4.4	.979	1B-50, 3B-28
21 yrs.			2687	.248	.431	8973	2223	329	36	414	4.6	1344	1354	1605 **8th**	1410	98	170	34	7964	3929	329	846	4.5	.973	3B-1442, 1B-856, DH-253, OF-84, SS-22

LEAGUE CHAMPIONSHIP SERIES

1984	DET	A	3	.300	.400	10	3	1	0	0	0.0	1	1	1	0	1	0	0	22	3	0	0	8.3	1.000	1B-3, 3B-1
1987			5	.294	.294	17	5	0	0	0	0.0	0	0	4	2	0	0	0	42	4	3	1	9.8	.939	1B-5, 3B-1
2 yrs.			8	.296	.333	27	8	1	0	0	0.0	1	1	5	2	1	0	0	64	7	3	1	9.3	.959	1B-8, 3B-2

WORLD SERIES

| 1984 | DET | A | 5 | .067 | .067 | 15 | 1 | 0 | 0 | 0 | 0.0 | 1 | 1 | 4 | 4 | 0 | 0 | 0 | 17 | 3 | 0 | 1 | 4.0 | 1.000 | 1B-4, 3B-2 |

Dwight Evans

EVANS, DWIGHT MICHAEL (Dewey)
B. Nov. 3, 1951, Santa Monica, Calif.   BR TR 6'2" 180 lbs.

1972	BOS	A	18	.263	.404	57	15	3	1	1	1.8	2	6	7	13	0	1	0	25	3	0	0	1.6	1.000	OF-17
1973			119	.223	.383	282	63	13	1	10	3.5	46	32	40	52	5	3	0	178	4	1	0	1.5	.995	OF-113
1974			133	.281	.421	463	130	19	8	10	2.2	60	70	38	77	4	12	2	294	8	3	2	2.3	.990	OF-122, DH-7
1975			128	.274	.456	412	113	24	6	13	3.2	61	56	47	60	3	6	0	281	15	4	8	2.3	.987	OF-115, DH-7
1976			146	.242	.431	501	121	34	5	17	3.4	61	62	57	92	6	2	1	324	15	2	4	2.3	.994	OF-145, DH-1
1977			73	.287	.526	230	66	9	2	14	6.1	39	36	28	58	4	7	1	126	2	1	0	1.8	.992	OF-63, DH-17
1978			147	.247	.449	497	123	24	2	24	4.8	75	63	65	119	8	4	1	305	14	6	2	2.2	.982	OF-142, DH-4
1979			152	.274	.456	489	134	24	1	21	4.3	69	58	69	76	6	5	1	307	15	4	5	2.1	.988	OF-149
1980			148	.266	.484	463	123	37	5	18	3.9	72	60	64	98	3	5	0	268	11	5	7	1.9	.982	OF-144, DH-2
1981			108	.296	.522	412	122	19	4	**22**	5.3	84	71	**85**	85	3	0	0	259	12	9	2	2.5	.993	OF-108
1982			162	.292	.534	609	178	37	7	32	5.3	122	98	112	125	3	0	0	346	9	10	3	2.3	.973	OF-161, DH-1
1983			126	.238	.436	470	112	19	4	22	4.7	74	58	70	97	3	5	2	222	6	3	1	1.8	.987	OF-99, DH-21
1984			162	.295	.532	630	186	37	8	32	5.1	**121**	104	96	115	3	0	0	311	7	2	2	2.0	.994	OF-161, DH-1
1985			159	.263	.454	617	162	29	1	29	4.7	110	78	**114**	105	7	0	0	291	9	3	1	1.9	.990	OF-152, DH-7
1986			152	.259	.476	529	137	33	2	26	4.9	86	97	97	117	3	1	0	280	10	5	3	1.9	.983	OF-149, DH-1
1987			154	.305	.569	541	165	37	2	34	6.3	109	123	**106**	98	4	2	0	753	46	13	72	5.3	.984	1B-79, OF-77, DH-4
1988			149	.293	.487	559	164	31	7	21	3.8	96	111	76	99	5	1	0	611	34	9	39	4.4	.986	OF-85, 1B-64, DH-6
1989			146	.285	.463	520	148	27	3	20	3.8	82	100	99	84	3	0	0	153	5	3	1	1.1	.981	OF-77, DH-69
18 yrs.			2382	.273	.477	8281	2262	456	69	366	4.4	1369	1283	1270	1570 **10th**	73	55	10	5334	222	76	151	2.4	.987	OF-2079, DH-148, 1B-143

LEAGUE CHAMPIONSHIP SERIES

1975	BOS	A	3	.100	.200	10	1	1	0	0	0.0	1	1	1	2	0	0	0	7	0	0	0	2.3	1.000	OF-3
1986			7	.214	.357	28	6	1	0	1	3.6	2	4	3	3	0	0	0	11	0	0	0	1.6	1.000	OF-7
1988			4	.167	.250	12	2	1	0	0	0.0	1	1	3	5	0	0	0	11	0	0	0	2.8	1.000	OF-4
3 yrs.			14	.180	.300	50	9	3	0	1	2.0	4	6	7	10	0	0	0	29	0	0	0	2.1	1.000	OF-14

WORLD SERIES

| 1975 | BOS | A | 7 | .292 | .542 | 24 | 7 | 1 | 1 | 1 | 4.2 | 3 | 5 | 3 | 4 | 0 | 0 | 0 | 23 | 1 | 0 | 1 | 3.4 | 1.000 | OF-7 |

Year	Team	Games	BA	SA	AB	H	2B	3B	HR	HR%	R	RBI	BB	SO	SB	Pinch Hit AB	Pinch Hit H	PO	A	E	DP	TC/G	FA	G by Pos

Dwight Evans *continued*

Year	Team	Games	BA	SA	AB	H	2B	3B	HR	HR%	R	RBI	BB	SO	SB	PH AB	PH H	PO	A	E	DP	TC/G	FA	G by Pos
1986		7	.308	.615	26	8	2	0	2	7.7	4	9	4	3	0	0	0	16	1	1	0	2.6	.944	OF-7
2 yrs.		14	.300	.580	50	15	3	1	3	6.0	7	14	7	7	0	0	0	39	2	1	1	3.0	.976	OF-14

Jake Evans

EVANS, JACOB (Bloody Jake)
B. Baltimore, Md. D. Feb. 3, 1907, Baltimore, Md.
TR 5'8" 154 lbs.

Year	Team	Games	BA	SA	AB	H	2B	3B	HR	HR%	R	RBI	BB	SO	SB	PH AB	PH H	PO	A	E	DP	TC/G	FA	G by Pos
1879	TRO N	72	.232	.300	280	65	9	5	0	0.0	30	17	5	18		0	0	153	30	24	4	2.9	.884	OF-72
1880		47	.256	.311	180	46	8	1	0	0.0	31	22	7	15		0	0	69	11	8	4	1.9	.909	OF-47, P-1
1881		83	.241	.308	315	76	11	5	0	0.0	35	28	14	30		0	0	145	31	14	5	2.3	.926	OF-83
1882	WOR N	80	.213	.266	334	71	10	4	0	0.0	33	25	7	22		0	0	142	78	26	8	3.1	.894	OF-68, SS-11, 3B-1, 2B-1, P-1
1883	CLE N	90	.238	.289	332	79	13	2	0	0.0	36		8	38		0	0	133	43	20	2	2.2	.898	OF-86, SS-3, 3B-3, 2B-1, P-1
1884		80	.259	.345	313	81	18	3	1	0.3	32	39	15	49		0	0	150	35	17	6	2.5	.916	OF-76, 2B-4, SS-2
1885	BAL AA	20	.221	.260	77	17	1	1	0	0.0	18		7			0	0	37	5	5	2	2.4	.894	OF-20
7 yrs.		472	.238	.300	1831	435	70	21	1	0.1	215	131	63	172		0	0	829	233	114	31	2.5	.903	OF-452, SS-16, 2B-6, 3B-4, P-3

Joe Evans

EVANS, JOSEPH PATTON (Doc)
B. May 15, 1895, Meridian, Miss. D. Aug. 8, 1953, Gulfport, Miss.
BR TR 5'9" 160 lbs.

Year	Team	Games	BA	SA	AB	H	2B	3B	HR	HR%	R	RBI	BB	SO	SB	PH AB	PH H	PO	A	E	DP	TC/G	FA	G by Pos
1915	CLE A	42	.257	.330	109	28	4	2	0	0.0	17	11	22	18	6	10	3	26	71	13	2	2.6	.882	3B-30, 2B-2
1916		33	.146	.159	82	12	1	0	0	0.0	4	1	7	12	4	3	0	27	59	8	3	2.8	.915	3B-28
1917		132	.190	.242	385	73	4	5	2	0.5	36	33	42	44	12	1	0	138	279	27	20	3.4	.939	3B-127
1918		79	.263	.358	243	64	6	7	1	0.4	38	22	30	29	7	2	1	91	155	18	17	3.3	.932	3B-74
1919		21	.071	.071	14	1	0	0	0	0.0	9	0	2	1	1	0	0	3	9	1	0	0.6	.923	SS-6
1920		55	.349	.506	172	60	9	9	0	0.0	32	23	15	3	6	2	0	93	25	8	0	2.3	.937	OF-43, SS-6
1921		57	.333	.405	153	51	11	0	0	0.0	36	21	19	5	4	1	0	90	8	7	2	1.8	.933	OF-47
1922		75	.269	.338	145	39	6	2	0	0.0	35	22	8	4	11	0	0	92	1	3	0	1.3	.969	OF-49
1923	WAS A	106	.263	.320	372	98	15	3	0	0.0	42	38	27	18	6	6	2	235	48	8	11	2.7	.973	OF-72, 3B-21, 1B-5
1924	STL A	77	.254	.297	209	53	3	3	0	0.0	30	18	23	12	1	24	9	118	3	4	1	1.6	.968	OF-48
1925		55	.314	.390	159	50	12	0	0	0.0	27	20	16	6	6	2	0	96	3	0	2	1.8	1.000	OF-47
11 yrs.		732	.259	.328	2043	529	71	31	3	0.1	306	209	211	152	64	55	17	1009	661	97	58	2.4	.945	OF-306, 3B-280, SS-12, 1B-5, 2B-2

WORLD SERIES

Year	Team	Games	BA	SA	AB	H	2B	3B	HR	HR%	R	RBI	BB	SO	SB	PH AB	PH H	PO	A	E	DP	TC/G	FA	G by Pos
1920	CLE A	4	.308	.308	13	4	0	0	0	0.0	0	0	1	0	0	1	0	7	0	0	0	1.8	1.000	OF-4

Steve Evans

EVANS, LOUIS RICHARD
B. Feb. 17, 1885, Cleveland, Ohio D. Dec. 28, 1943, Cleveland, Ohio
BL TL 5'10½" 175 lbs.

Year	Team	Games	BA	SA	AB	H	2B	3B	HR	HR%	R	RBI	BB	SO	SB	PH AB	PH H	PO	A	E	DP	TC/G	FA	G by Pos
1908	NY N	2	.500	.500	2	1	0	0	0	0.0	0	0	0		0	1	0	0	0	0	0	0.0	—	OF-1
1909	STL N	143	.259	.329	498	129	17	6	2	0.4	67	56	66		14	0	0	235	19	14	11	1.9	.948	OF-141, 1B-2
1910		151	.241	.324	506	122	21	8	2	0.4	73	73	78	63	10	0	0	330	18	11	7	2.4	.969	OF-141, 1B-10
1911		154	.294	.413	547	161	24	13	5	0.9	74	71	46	52	13	3	1	258	17	8	5	1.8	.972	OF-150
1912		135	.283	.403	491	139	23	9	6	1.2	59	72	36	51	11	1	0	219	24	15	2	1.9	.942	OF-134
1913		97	.249	.371	245	61	15	6	1	0.4	18	31	20	28	5	20	4	113	5	4	0	1.3	.967	OF-74, 1B-1
1914	BKN F	145	.348	.556	514	179	41	15	12	2.3	93	96	50		18	7	1	442	35	21	19	3.4	.958	OF-112, 1B-27
1915	2 teams			BKN F (63G – .296)		BAL F (88G – .315)																			
"	total	151	.308	.426	556	171	34	10	4	0.7	94	67	63		15	1	0	206	21	15	6	1.6	.938	OF-149, 1B-5
8 yrs.		978	.287	.407	3359	963	175	67	32	1.0	478	466	359	194	86	33	6	1803	139	88	50	2.1	.957	OF-902, 1B-45

Bill Everett

EVERETT, WILLIAM L. (Bad Bill)
B. Dec. 13, 1868, Fort Wayne, Ind. D. Jan. 19, 1938, Denver, Colo.
BL TR 6'½" 185 lbs.

Year	Team	Games	BA	SA	AB	H	2B	3B	HR	HR%	R	RBI	BB	SO	SB	PH AB	PH H	PO	A	E	DP	TC/G	FA	G by Pos
1895	CHI N	133	.358	.440	550	197	16	10	3	0.5	129	88	33	42	47	0	0	178	272	76	12	4.0	.856	3B-130, 2B-3
1896		132	.320	.403	575	184	16	13	2	0.3	130	46	41	43	46	0	0	213	184	53	10	3.4	.882	3B-97, OF-35
1897		92	.314	.427	379	119	14	7	5	1.3	63	39	36		26	1	0	137	147	43	9	3.6	.869	3B-83, OF-8
1898		149	.319	.364	596	190	15	6	0	0.0	102	69	53		28	0	0	1519	70	42	123	10.9	.974	1B-149
1899		136	.310	.364	536	166	17	5	1	0.2	87	74	31		30	0	0	1491	95	47	103	12.0	.971	1B-136
1900		23	.264	.308	91	24	4	0	0	0.0	10	17	3		2	0	0	264	10	6	14	12.2	.979	1B-23
1901	WAS A	33	.191	.252	115	22	3	2	0	0.0	14	8	15		7	0	0	319	8	11	12	10.2	.967	1B-33
7 yrs.		698	.317	.389	2842	902	85	43	11	0.4	535	341	212	85	186	1	0	4121	786	278	283	7.4	.946	1B-341, 3B-310, OF-43, 2B-3

Hoot Evers

EVERS, WALTER ARTHUR
B. Feb. 8, 1921, St. Louis, Mo.
BR TR 6'2" 180 lbs.

Year	Team	Games	BA	SA	AB	H	2B	3B	HR	HR%	R	RBI	BB	SO	SB	PH AB	PH H	PO	A	E	DP	TC/G	FA	G by Pos
1941	DET A	1	.000	.000	4	0	0	0	0	0.0	0	0	0	2	0	0	0	0	0	0	0	0.0	—	OF-1
1946		81	.266	.359	304	81	8	4	4	1.3	42	33	34	43	7	2	0	196	2	5	0	2.5	.975	OF-76
1947		126	.296	.435	460	136	24	5	10	2.2	67	67	45	49	8	2	1	354	10	8	2	3.0	.978	OF-123
1948		139	.314	.454	538	169	33	6	10	1.9	81	103	51	31	3	1	0	392	8	11	0	3.0	.973	OF-138
1949		132	.303	.434	432	131	21	6	7	1.6	68	72	70	38	6	10	2	319	12	2	2	2.5	.994	OF-123
1950		143	.323	.551	526	170	35	11	21	4.0	100	103	71	40	5	1	1	325	15	1	3	2.4	.997	OF-139
1951		116	.224	.356	393	88	15	2	11	2.8	47	46	40	47	5	8	2	234	9	6	1	2.1	.976	OF-108
1952	2 teams	DET A (1G – 1.000)		BOS A (106G – .262)																				
"	total	107	.264	.430	402	106	17	4	14	3.5	53	59	29	55	5	2	1	219	8	6	3	2.2	.974	OF-105
1953	BOS A	99	.240	.390	300	72	10	4	11	3.7	39	31	23	41	2	7	1	161	3	2	0	1.7	.988	OF-93
1954	3 teams	BOS A (6G – .000)		NY N (12G – .091)		DET A (30G – .183)																		
"	total	48	.152	.241	79	12	4	0	1	1.3	7	8	5	16	1	17	1	38	1	0	0	0.8	1.000	OF-29
1955	2 teams	BAL A (60G – .238)		CLE A (39G – .288)																				
"	total	99	.251	.430	251	63	17	2	8	3.2	31	39	22	40	2	16	6	139	2	1	1	1.4	.993	OF-80
1956	2 teams	CLE A (3G – .000)		BAL A (48G – .241)																				
"	total	51	.241	.295	112	27	3	0	1	0.9	21	4	25	18	1	10	2	63	1	1	1	1.3	.985	OF-36
12 yrs.		1142	.278	.426	3801	1055	187	41	98	2.6	556	565	415	420	45	76	16	2440	71	43	13	2.2	.983	OF-1051

Year	Team		Games	BA	SA	AB	H	2B	3B	HR	HR%	R	RBI	BB	SO	SB	Pinch Hit AB	Pinch Hit H	PO	A	E	DP	TC/G	FA	G by Pos

Joe Evers

EVERS, JOSEPH FRANCIS
Brother of Johnny Evers.
B. Sept. 10, 1891, Troy, N. Y.   D. Jan. 4, 1949, Albany, N. Y.

BR TR 5'9''   135 lbs.

Year	Team		Games	BA	SA	AB	H	2B	3B	HR	HR%	R	RBI	BB	SO	SB	AB	H	PO	A	E	DP	TC/G	FA	G by Pos
1913	NY	N	1	–	–	0	0	0	0	0	0.0	0	0	0	0	0	0	0	0	0	0	0	0.0	–	

Johnny Evers

EVERS, JOHN JOSEPH (The Trojan, The Crab)
Brother of Joe Evers.
B. July 22, 1883, Troy, N. Y.   D. Mar. 28, 1947, Albany, N. Y.
Manager 1913, 1921, 1924.
Hall of Fame 1946.

BL TR 5'9''   125 lbs.

Year	Team		Games	BA	SA	AB	H	2B	3B	HR	HR%	R	RBI	BB	SO	SB	AB	H	PO	A	E	DP	TC/G	FA	G by Pos
1902	CHI	N	26	.225	.225	89	20	0	0	0	0.0	7	2	3			1	0	0	48	87	5	6	5.4	.964	2B-18, SS-8
1903			124	.293	.381	464	136	27	7	0	0.0	70	52	19		25	0	0	268	336	51	40	5.3	.922	2B-110, SS-11, 3B-2
1904			152	.265	.318	532	141	14	7	0	0.0	49	47	28		26	0	0	381	518	54	53	6.3	.943	2B-152
1905			99	.276	.329	340	94	11	2	1	0.3	44	37	27		19	0	0	249	290	36	38	5.8	.937	2B-99
1906			154	.255	.315	533	136	17	6	1	0.2	65	51	36		49	0	0	344	441	44	51	5.4	.947	2B-153, 3B-1
1907			151	.250	.313	508	127	18	4	2	0.4	66	51	38		46	0	0	346	500	32	58	5.8	.964	2B-151
1908			126	.300	.375	416	125	19	6	0	0.0	83	37	66		36	2	1	237	361	25	39	4.9	.960	2B-123
1909			127	.263	.337	463	122	19	6	1	0.2	88	24	73		28	0	0	262	354	38	29	5.1	.942	2B-126
1910			125	.263	.321	433	114	11	7	0	0.0	87	28	108	18	28	0	0	282	347	33	55	5.3	.950	2B-125
1911			46	.226	.290	155	35	4	3	0	0.0	29	7	34	10	6	2	0	79	105	7	19	4.2	.963	2B-33, 3B-11
1912			143	.341	.441	478	163	23	11	1	0.2	73	63	74	18	16	0	0	319	439	32	71	5.5	.959	2B-143
1913			135	.284	.372	444	126	20	5	3	0.7	81	49	50	14	11	0	0	303	426	30	70	5.6	.960	2B-135
1914	BOS	N	139	.279	.338	491	137	20	3	1	0.2	81	40	87	26	12	0	0	301	397	17	73	5.1	.976	2B-139
1915			83	.263	.295	278	73	4	1	1	0.4	38	22	50	16	7	0	0	170	209	16	33	4.8	.959	2B-83
1916			71	.216	.241	241	52	4	1	0	0.0	33	15	40	19	5	0	0	98	175	14	29	4.0	.951	2B-71
1917	2 teams	BOS	N (24G – .193)			PHI	N	(56G – .224)																	
"	total		80	.214	.252	266	57	5	1	1	0.4	25	12	43	21	9	0	0	116	227	12	28	4.4	.966	2B-73, 3B-7
1922	CHI	A	1	.000	.000	3	0	0	0	0	0.0	0	1	2	0	0	0	0	3	0	1	0	6.0	1.000	2B-1
1929	BOS	N	1	–	–	0	0	0	0	0	–	0	0	0	0	0	0	0	0	0	1	0	1.0	–	2B-1
18 yrs.			1783	.270	.334	6134	1658	216	70	12	0.2	919	538	778	142	324	4	1	3806	5215	447	693	5.3	.953	2B-1736, 3B-21, SS-19

WORLD SERIES

Year	Team		Games	BA	SA	AB	H	2B	3B	HR	HR%	R	RBI	BB	SO	SB	AB	H	PO	A	E	DP	TC/G	FA	G by Pos
1906	CHI	N	6	.150	.200	20	3	1	0	0	0.0	2	1	1	3	2	0	0	12	20	1	3	5.5	.970	2B-6
1907			5	.350	.450	20	7	2	0	0	0.0	2	1	0	1	3	0	0	9	12	2	2	4.6	.913	2B-5, SS-1
1908			5	.350	.400	20	7	1	0	0	0.0	5	2	1	2	2	0	0	5	21	1	1	5.4	.963	2B-5
1914	BOS	N	4	.438	.438	16	7	0	0	0	0.0	2	2	2	2	1	0	0	8	16	1	2	6.3	.960	2B-4
4 yrs.			20	.316	.368	76	24	4	0	0	0.0	11	6	4	8	8 [8th]	0	0	34	69	5	8	5.4	.954	2B-20, SS-1

Tom Evers

EVERS, THOMAS FRANCIS
B. Mar. 31, 1852, Troy, N. Y.   D. Mar. 23, 1925, Washington, D. C.

Year	Team		Games	BA	SA	AB	H	2B	3B	HR	HR%	R	RBI	BB	SO	SB	AB	H	PO	A	E	DP	TC/G	FA	G by Pos
1882	BAL	AA	1	.000	.000	4	0	0	0	0	0.0	0				0	0	0	3	0	3	0	6.0	.500	2B-1
1884	WAS	U	109	.232	.251	427	99	6	1	0	0.0	54		7		0	0	0	326	296	94	28	6.6	.869	2B-109
2 yrs.			110	.230	.248	431	99	6	1	0	0.0	54		7		0	0	0	329	296	97	28	6.6	.866	2B-110

Buck Ewing

EWING, WILLIAM
Brother of John Ewing.
B. Oct. 17, 1859, Hoaglands, Ohio   D. Oct. 20, 1906, Cincinnati, Ohio
Manager 1890, 1895-1900.
Hall of Fame 1939.

BR TR 5'10''   188 lbs.

Year	Team		Games	BA	SA	AB	H	2B	3B	HR	HR%	R	RBI	BB	SO	SB	AB	H	PO	A	E	DP	TC/G	FA	G by Pos
1880	TRO	N	13	.178	.200	45	8	1	0	0	0.0	1	5	1	3		0	0	48	7	11	0	5.1	.833	C-10, OF-4
1881			67	.250	.353	272	68	14	7	0	0.0	40	25	7	8		0	0	254	185	43	18	7.2	.911	C-44, SS-22, OF-2, 3B-1
1882			74	.271	.405	328	89	16	11	2	0.6	67	29	10	15		0	0	204	172	47	19	5.7	.889	3B-44, C-25, 2B-4, OF-1, 1B-1, P-1
1883	NY	N	88	.303	.481	376	114	11	13	**10**	2.7	90		20	14		0	0	310	145	50	12	5.7	.901	C-63, OF-14, 2B-11, SS-4, 3B-1
1884			94	.277	.445	382	106	15	**20**	3	0.8	90		28	22		0	0	458	139	46	11	6.8	.928	C-80, OF-12, SS-3, 3B-1, P-1
1885			81	.304	.471	342	104	15	12	6	1.8	81		13	17		0	0	377	119	47	9	6.7	.913	C-63, OF-14, 3B-8, SS-1, 1B-1, P-1
1886			73	.309	.444	275	85	11	7	4	1.5	59	31	16	17		0	0	311	97	36	4	6.1	.919	C-50, OF-23, 1B-2
1887			77	.305	.497	318	97	17	13	6	1.9	83	44	30	33	26	0	0	153	173	48	17	4.9	.872	3B-51, 2B-19, C-8
1888			103	.306	.465	415	127	18	15	6	1.4	83	58	24	28	53	0	0	515	185	53	16	7.3	.930	C-78, 3B-21, SS-4, P-2
1889			99	.327	.477	407	133	23	13	4	1.0	91	87	37	32	34	0	0	525	152	47	10	7.3	.935	C-97, P-3, OF-1
1890	NY	P	83	.338	.545	352	119	19	15	8	2.3	98	72	39	12	36	0	0	374	113	28	8	6.2	.946	C-81, 2B-1, P-1
1891	NY	N	14	.347	.429	49	17	2	1	0	0.0	8	5	5	5	5	0	0	35	33	10	4	5.6	.872	2B-8, C-6
1892			105	.310	.466	393	122	10	15	7	1.8	58	76	38	26	42	0	0	855	97	33	38	9.4	.966	C-30, 2B-2
1893	CLE	N	116	.344	.496	500	172	28	15	6	1.2	117	122	41	18	47	0	0	217	29	21	4	2.3	.921	OF-112, 2B-5, 1B-1, C-1
1894			53	.251	.374	211	53	12	4	2	0.9	32	39	24	9	18	0	0	87	8	10	2	2.0	.905	OF-52, 2B-1
1895	CIN	N	105	.318	.468	434	138	24	13	5	1.2	90	94	30	22	34	0	0	957	79	26	69	10.1	.976	1B-105
1896			69	.278	.373	263	73	14	4	1	0.4	41	38	29	13	41	0	0	669	49	15	41	10.6	.980	1B-69
1897			1	.000	.000	1	0	0	0	0	0.0	0	0	0	0	0	0	0	4	0	1	0	5.0	.800	1B-1
18 yrs.			1315	.303	.455	5363	1625	250	178	70	1.3	1129	738	392	294	336	0	0	6353	1782	572	282	6.6	.934	C-636, 1B-253, OF-235, 3B-127, 2B-51, SS-34, P-9

Reuben Ewing

EWING, REUBEN
Born Reuben Cohen.
B. Nov. 30, 1899, Odessa, Russia   D. Oct. 5, 1970, W. Hartford, Conn.

BR TR 5'4½''   150 lbs.

Year	Team		Games	BA	SA	AB	H	2B	3B	HR	HR%	R	RBI	BB	SO	SB	AB	H	PO	A	E	DP	TC/G	FA	G by Pos
1921	STL	N	3	.000	.000	1	0	0	0	0	0.0	0	0	0	1	0	1	0	1	0	0	0	0.3	1.000	SS-1

Sam Ewing

EWING, SAMUEL JAMES
B. Apr. 9, 1949, Lewisburg, Tenn.

BL TR 6'3''   200 lbs.

Sam Ewing *continued*

Year Team	Games	BA	SA	AB	H	2B	3B	HR	HR%	R	RBI	BB	SO	SB	Pinch AB	Pinch H	PO	A	E	DP	TC/G	FA	G by Pos
1973 CHI A	11	.150	.200	20	3	1	0	0	0.0	1	2	2	6	0	5	1	34	4	0	7	3.5	1.000	1B-4
1976	19	.220	.317	41	9	2	1	0	0.0	3	2	2	8	0	8	3	4	0	0	0	0.2	1.000	DH-12, 1B-1
1977 TOR A	97	.287	.385	244	70	8	2	4	1.6	24	34	19	42	1	27	9	68	1	3	0	0.7	.958	OF-46, DH-27, 1B-2
1978	40	.179	.286	56	10	0	0	2	3.6	3	9	5	9	0	29	5	4	0	0	0	0.1	1.000	DH-9, OF-3
4 yrs.	167	.255	.352	361	92	11	3	6	1.7	31	47	28	65	1	69	18	110	5	3	7	0.7	.975	OF-49, DH-48, 1B-7

Art Ewoldt

EWOLDT, ARTHUR LEE (Sheriff) BR TR 5'10" 165 lbs.
B. Jan. 8, 1894, Paullina, Iowa   D. Dec. 8, 1977, Des Moines, Iowa

Year Team	Games	BA	SA	AB	H	2B	3B	HR	HR%	R	RBI	BB	SO	SB	Pinch AB	Pinch H	PO	A	E	DP	TC/G	FA	G by Pos
1919 PHI A	9	.219	.250	32	7	1	0	0	0.0	2	2	1	5	0	0	0	11	16	0	0	3.0	1.000	3B-9

Homer Ezzell

EZZELL, HOMER ESTELL BR TR 5'10" 158 lbs.
B. Feb. 28, 1896, Victoria, Tex.   D. Aug. 3, 1976, San Antonio, Tex.

Year Team	Games	BA	SA	AB	H	2B	3B	HR	HR%	R	RBI	BB	SO	SB	Pinch AB	Pinch H	PO	A	E	DP	TC/G	FA	G by Pos
1923 STL A	89	.244	.265	279	68	6	0	0	0.0	32	14	15	20	4	2	0	96	175	10	16	3.2	.964	3B-73, 2B-8
1924 BOS A	89	.275	.333	273	75	8	4	0	0.0	33	32	13	20	12	4	0	95	188	14	15	3.3	.953	3B-62, SS-21, C-1
1925	58	.285	.360	186	53	6	4	0	0.0	40	15	19	18	9	0	0	63	97	20	7	3.1	.889	3B-47, 2B-9
3 yrs.	236	.266	.314	738	196	20	8	0	0.0	105	61	47	58	25	6	0	254	460	44	38	3.2	.942	3B-182, SS-21, 2B-17, C-1

Jay Faatz

FAATZ, JAYSON S. BR TR 6'4"
B. Oct. 24, 1860, Weedsport, N. Y.   D. Apr. 10, 1923, Syracuse, N. Y.
Manager 1890.

Year Team	Games	BA	SA	AB	H	2B	3B	HR	HR%	R	RBI	BB	SO	SB	Pinch AB	Pinch H	PO	A	E	DP	TC/G	FA	G by Pos
1884 PIT AA	29	.241	.313	112	27	2	3	0	0.0	18		1				0	283	6	11	16	10.3	.963	1B-29
1888 CLE AA	120	.264	.294	470	124	10	2	0	0.0	73	51	12		64		0	1171	39	13	50	10.2	.989	1B-120
1889 CLE N	117	.231	.294	442	102	12	5	2	0.5	50	38	17	28	27		0	1145	62	24	67	10.5	.981	1B-117
1890 BUF P	32	.189	.252	111	21	0	2	1	0.9	18	16	9	5	2		0	312	7	6	18	10.2	.982	1B-32
4 yrs.	298	.241	.292	1135	274	24	12	3	0.3	159	105	39	33	93		0	2911	114	54	151	10.3	.982	1B-298

Bunny Fabrique

FABRIQUE, ALBERT LaVERNE BB TR 5'8½" 150 lbs.
B. Dec. 23, 1887, Clinton, Mich.   D. Jan. 10, 1960, Ann Arbor, Mich.

Year Team	Games	BA	SA	AB	H	2B	3B	HR	HR%	R	RBI	BB	SO	SB	Pinch AB	Pinch H	PO	A	E	DP	TC/G	FA	G by Pos
1916 BKN N	2	.000	.000	2	0	0	0	0	0.0	0	0	0	1	0	0	0	2	2	0	1	2.0	1.000	SS-2
1917	25	.205	.273	88	18	3	0	1	1.1	8	3	8	9	0	4	0	55	63	17	8	5.4	.874	SS-21
2 yrs.	27	.200	.267	90	18	3	0	1	1.1	8	3	8	10	0	4	0	57	65	17	9	5.1	.878	SS-23

Len Faedo

FAEDO, LEONARDO LAGO, JR. BR TR 6' 170 lbs.
B. May 13, 1960, Tampa, Fla.

Year Team	Games	BA	SA	AB	H	2B	3B	HR	HR%	R	RBI	BB	SO	SB	Pinch AB	Pinch H	PO	A	E	DP	TC/G	FA	G by Pos
1980 MIN A	5	.250	.375	8	2	1	0	0	0.0	1	0	0	0	0	0	0	4	5	2	0	2.2	.818	SS-5
1981	12	.195	.244	41	8	0	1	0	0.0	3	6	1	5	0	0	0	24	42	2	10	5.7	.971	SS-12
1982	90	.243	.310	255	62	8	0	3	1.2	16	22	16	22	1	1	0	129	218	12	52	4.0	.967	SS-88, DH-1
1983	51	.277	.335	173	48	7	0	1	0.6	16	18	4	19	0	0	0	53	133	9	22	3.8	.954	SS-51
1984	16	.250	.327	52	13	1	0	1	1.9	6	6	4	3	0	1	0	22	39	2	4	3.9	.968	SS-15, DH-1
5 yrs.	174	.251	.316	529	133	17	1	5	0.9	42	52	25	49	1	2	0	232	437	27	88	4.0	.961	SS-171, DH-2

Fred Fagin

FAGIN, FREDERICK H.
B. Cincinnati, Ohio Deceased.

Year Team	Games	BA	SA	AB	H	2B	3B	HR	HR%	R	RBI	BB	SO	SB	Pinch AB	Pinch H	PO	A	E	DP	TC/G	FA	G by Pos
1895 STL N	1	.333	.333	3	1	0	0	0	0.0	0	2	0	0	0	0	0	0	3	4	0	11.0	.636	C-1

Bill Fahey

FAHEY, WILLIAM ROGER BL TR 6' 200 lbs.
B. June 14, 1950, Detroit, Mich.

Year Team	Games	BA	SA	AB	H	2B	3B	HR	HR%	R	RBI	BB	SO	SB	Pinch AB	Pinch H	PO	A	E	DP	TC/G	FA	G by Pos
1971 WAS A	2	.000	.000	8	0	0	0	0	0.0	0	0	0	0	0	0	0	8	2	1	0	5.5	.909	C-2
1972 TEX A	39	.168	.210	119	20	2	0	1	0.8	8	10	12	23	4	1	1	236	26	2	4	6.8	.992	C-39
1974	6	.250	.250	16	4	0	0	0	0.0	1	0	0	1	0	0	0	21	0	0	0	3.8	1.000	C-6
1975	21	.297	.378	37	11	1	1	0	0.0	0	3	1	10	0	2	0	54	5	1	1	2.9	.983	C-21
1976	38	.250	.313	80	20	2	0	1	1.3	12	9	11	6	0	1	0	126	19	1	3	3.8	.993	C-38
1977	37	.221	.279	68	15	4	0	0	0.0	3	5	1	8	0	1	0	104	5	0	0	2.9	1.000	C-34
1979 SD N	73	.287	.378	209	60	8	1	3	1.4	14	19	21	17	1	6	1	277	33	2	5	4.3	.994	C-68
1980	93	.257	.378	241	62	4	0	1	0.4	18	22	21	16	2	11	2	309	34	8	6	3.8	.977	C-85
1981 DET A	27	.254	.328	67	17	2	0	1	1.5	5	9	2	4	0	0	0	96	9	2	3	4.0	.981	C-27
1982	28	.149	.179	67	10	0	0	0	0.0	7	4	0	2	0	2	0	85	16	0	2	3.6	1.000	C-28
1983	19	.273	.318	22	6	1	0	0	0.0	4	2	5	3	0	1	0	39	2	0	0	2.2	1.000	C-18
11 yrs.	383	.241	.296	934	225	26	2	7	0.7	75	83	74	93	9	25	4	1355	153	17	24	4.0	.989	C-366

Frank Fahey

FAHEY, FRANCIS RAYMOND BB TR 6'1" 190 lbs.
B. Jan. 22, 1896, Milford, Mass.   D. Mar. 19, 1954, Boston, Mass.

Year Team	Games	BA	SA	AB	H	2B	3B	HR	HR%	R	RBI	BB	SO	SB	Pinch AB	Pinch H	PO	A	E	DP	TC/G	FA	G by Pos
1918 PHI A	10	.176	.235	17	3	1	0	0	0.0	2	1	0	3	0	0	0	4	0	0	0	0.4	1.000	OF-5, P-3

Howard Fahey

FAHEY, HOWARD SIMPSON (Cap, Kid) BR TR 5'7½" 145 lbs.
B. June 24, 1892, Medford, Mass.   D. Oct. 24, 1971, Clearwater, Fla.

Year Team	Games	BA	SA	AB	H	2B	3B	HR	HR%	R	RBI	BB	SO	SB	Pinch AB	Pinch H	PO	A	E	DP	TC/G	FA	G by Pos
1912 PHI A	5	.000	.000	8	0	0	0	0	0.0	0	0	0	0	0	1	0	4	0	1	1	1.0	.800	3B-2, SS-1, 2B-1

Ferris Fain

FAIN, FERRIS ROY (Burrhead) BL TL 5'11" 180 lbs.
B. May 29, 1921, San Antonio, Tex.

Year Team	Games	BA	SA	AB	H	2B	3B	HR	HR%	R	RBI	BB	SO	SB	Pinch AB	Pinch H	PO	A	E	DP	TC/G	FA	G by Pos
1947 PHI A	136	.291	.423	461	134	28	6	7	1.5	70	71	95	34	4	4	0	1141	101	19	118	9.3	.985	1B-132
1948	145	.281	.396	520	146	27	6	7	1.3	81	88	113	37	10	0	0	1284	120	16	148	9.8	.989	1B-145
1949	150	.263	.339	525	138	21	5	3	0.6	81	78	136	51	8	0	0	1275	122	22	194	9.5	.984	1B-150
1950	151	.282	.402	522	147	25	4	10	1.9	83	83	133	26	8	0	0	1286	124	19	192	9.5	.987	1B-151
1951	117	.344	.471	425	146	30	3	6	1.4	63	57	80	20	0	0	0	942	115	14	125	9.2	.987	1B-108, OF-11
1952	145	.327	.429	538	176	43	3	2	0.4	82	59	105	26	3	1	0	1245	150	22	124	9.8	.984	1B-144
1953 CHI A	128	.256	.345	446	114	18	2	6	1.3	73	52	108	28	3	1	1	1108	106	13	98	9.6	.989	1B-127
1954	65	.302	.417	235	71	10	1	5	2.1	30	51	40	14	0	0	0	565	31	8	54	9.3	.987	1B-64

Year	Team	Games	BA	SA	AB	H	2B	3B	HR	HR%	R	RBI	BB	SO	SB	Pinch Hit AB	Pinch Hit H	PO	A	E	DP	TC/G	FA	G by Pos

Ferris Fain *continued*

Year	Team	Games	BA	SA	AB	H	2B	3B	HR	HR%	R	RBI	BB	SO	SB	AB	H	PO	A	E	DP	TC/G	FA	G by Pos
1955	2 teams	DET A (58G – .264)			CLE A (56G – .254)																			
"	total	114	.260	.326	258	67	11	0	2	0.8	32	31	94	25	5	13	4	695	60	8	72	6.7	.990	1B-95
	9 yrs.	1151	.290	.396	3930	1139	213	30	48	1.2	595	570	904	261	46	19	5	9541	929	141	1125	9.2	.987	1B-1116, OF-11

George Fair

FAIR, GEORGE T.
B. Jan. 14, 1856, Boston, Mass. D. Feb. 12, 1939, Roslindale, Mass.　　　5'7½" 140 lbs.

Year	Team	Games	BA	SA	AB	H	2B	3B	HR	HR%	R	RBI	BB	SO	SB	AB	H	PO	A	E	DP	TC/G	FA	G by Pos
1876	NY N	1	.000	.000	4	0	0	0	0	0.0	0	0	0	0		0	0	2	4	2	1	8.0	.750	2B-1

Jim Fairey

FAIREY, JAMES BURKE
B. Sept. 22, 1944, Orangeburg, S. C.　　　BL TL 5'10" 190 lbs.

Year	Team	Games	BA	SA	AB	H	2B	3B	HR	HR%	R	RBI	BB	SO	SB	AB	H	PO	A	E	DP	TC/G	FA	G by Pos
1968	LA N	99	.199	.276	156	31	3	3	1	0.6	17	10	9	32	1	37	8	65	3	4	1	0.7	.944	OF-63
1969	MON N	20	.286	.367	49	14	1	0	1	2.0	6	6	1	7	0	11	2	20	1	2	0	1.2	.913	OF-13
1970		92	.242	.355	211	51	9	3	3	1.4	35	25	14	38	1	37	14	86	1	2	0	1.0	.978	OF-59
1971		92	.245	.310	200	49	8	1	1	0.5	19	19	12	23	3	36	11	85	7	3	1	1.0	.968	OF-58
1972		86	.234	.305	141	33	7	0	1	0.7	9	15	10	21	1	55	10	40	1	3	0	0.5	.932	OF-37
1973	LA N	10	.222	.222	9	2	0	0	0	0.0	0	0	1	1	0	9	2	0	0	0	0	0.0	–	
	6 yrs.	399	.235	.317	766	180	28	7	7	0.9	86	75	47	122	6	185	47	296	13	14	2	0.8	.957	OF-230

Ron Fairly

FAIRLY, RONALD RAY
B. July 12, 1938, Macon, Ga.　　　BL TL 5'10" 175 lbs.

Year	Team	Games	BA	SA	AB	H	2B	3B	HR	HR%	R	RBI	BB	SO	SB	AB	H	PO	A	E	DP	TC/G	FA	G by Pos
1958	LA N	15	.283	.415	53	15	1	0	2	3.8	6	8	6	7	0	0	0	33	0	1	0	2.3	.971	OF-15
1959		118	.238	.344	244	58	12	1	4	1.6	27	23	31	29	0	31	7	97	8	4	1	0.9	.963	OF-88
1960		14	.108	.351	37	4	0	3	1	2.7	6	3	7	12	0	1	0	15	1	0	0	1.1	1.000	OF-13
1961		111	.322	.522	245	79	15	2	10	4.1	42	48	48	22	0	20	6	242	18	3	17	2.4	.989	OF-71, 1B-23
1962		147	.278	.433	460	128	15	7	14	3.0	80	71	75	59	1	7	0	1007	45	11	76	7.2	.990	1B-120, OF-48
1963		152	.271	.388	490	133	21	0	12	2.4	62	77	58	69	5	5	2	946	48	7	74	6.6	.993	1B-119, OF-45
1964		150	.256	.385	454	116	19	5	10	2.2	62	74	65	59	4	9	2	1081	82	15	89	7.9	.987	1B-141
1965		158	.274	.377	555	152	28	1	9	1.6	73	70	76	72	2	3	0	361	13	6	7	2.4	.984	OF-148, 1B-13
1966		117	.288	.464	351	101	20	0	14	4.0	53	61	52	38	3	6	2	264	14	4	20	2.4	.986	OF-98, 1B-25
1967		153	.220	.321	486	107	19	0	10	2.1	45	55	54	51	1	9	1	727	55	11	55	5.2	.986	OF-97, 1B-68
1968		141	.234	.299	441	103	15	1	4	0.9	32	43	41	61	0	12	4	406	26	3	27	3.1	.993	OF-105, 1B-36
1969	2 teams	LA N (30G – .219)			MON N (70G – .289)																			
"	total	100	.274	.476	317	87	16	6	12	3.8	38	47	37	28	1	10	3	543	46	7	58	6.0	.988	1B-64, OF-31
1970	MON N	119	.288	.455	385	111	19	0	15	3.9	54	61	72	64	10	7	2	945	90	5	112	8.7	.995	1B-118, OF-4
1971		146	.257	.396	447	115	23	0	13	2.9	58	71	81	65	1	17	5	1116	104	10	110	8.4	.992	1B-135, OF-10
1972		140	.278	.430	446	124	15	1	17	3.8	51	68	46	45	3	13	4	646	46	6	39	5.0	.991	OF-70, 1B-68
1973		142	.298	.458	413	123	13	1	17	4.1	70	49	86	33	2	25	3	202	5	5	4	1.5	.976	OF-121, 1B-5
1974		101	.245	.411	282	69	9	1	12	4.3	35	43	57	28	2	15	1	603	43	7	41	6.5	.989	1B-67, OF-20
1975	STL N	107	.301	.467	229	69	13	2	7	3.1	32	37	45	22	0	35	12	383	33	8	33	4.0	.981	1B-56, OF-20
1976	2 teams	STL N (73G – .264)			OAK A	(15G – .239)																		
"	total	88	.256	.346	156	40	5	0	3	1.9	22	31	32	24	0	47	11	295	31	1	29	3.7	.997	1B-42
1977	TOR A	132	.279	.465	458	128	24	2	19	4.1	60	64	58	58	0	4	2	375	34	7	28	3.2	.983	DH-58, 1B-40, OF-33
1978	CAL A	91	.217	.366	235	51	5	0	10	4.3	23	40	25	31	0	13	1	482	31	1	47	5.6	.998	1B-78, DH-5
	21 yrs.	2442	.266	.408	7184	1913	307	33	215	3.0	931	1044	1052	877	35	289	68	10769	773	122	867	4.8	.990	1B-1218, OF-1037, DH-63
WORLD SERIES																								
1959	LA N	6	.000	.000	3	0	0	0	0	0.0	0	1	0	0	0	2	0	0	0	0	0	0.0	–	OF-4
1963		4	.000	.000	1	0	0	0	0	0.0	0	0	3	0	0	0	0	3	0	0	0	0.8	1.000	OF-4
1965		7	.379	.690	29	11	3	0	2	6.9	7	6	0	1	0	0	0	8	0	0	0	1.1	1.000	OF-7
1966		3	.143	.143	7	1	0	0	0	0.0	0	0	2	4	0	1	0	3	0	1	0	1.3	.750	OF-2, 1B-1
	4 yrs.	20	.300	.525	40	12	3	0	2	5.0	7	6	5	6	0	3	0	14	0	1	0	0.8	.933	OF-17, 1B-1

Anton Falch

FALCH, ANTON C.
B. Dec. 4, 1860, Milwaukee, Wis. D. Mar. 31, 1936, Wauwatosa, Wis.　　　6'6" 220 lbs.

Year	Team	Games	BA	SA	AB	H	2B	3B	HR	HR%	R	RBI	BB	SO	SB	AB	H	PO	A	E	DP	TC/G	FA	G by Pos
1884	MIL U	5	.111	.111	18	2	0	0	0	0.0	0		0		0	0	0	16	8	3	0	5.4	.889	OF-3, C-2

Bibb Falk

FALK, BIBB AUGUST (Jockey)
Brother of Chet Falk.
B. Jan. 27, 1899, Austin, Tex. D. June 8, 1989, Austin, Tex.
Manager 1933.　　　BL TL 6' 175 lbs.

Year	Team	Games	BA	SA	AB	H	2B	3B	HR	HR%	R	RBI	BB	SO	SB	AB	H	PO	A	E	DP	TC/G	FA	G by Pos
1920	CHI A	7	.294	.471	17	5	1	1	0	0.0	1	2	0	5	0	3	1	5	0	0	0	0.7	1.000	OF-4
1921		152	.285	.402	585	167	31	11	5	0.9	62	82	37	69	4	3	1	288	9	13	5	2.0	.958	OF-149
1922		131	.298	.433	483	144	27	1	12	2.5	58	79	27	55	2	1	0	253	10	10	2	2.1	.963	OF-131
1923		87	.307	.471	274	84	18	6	5	1.8	44	38	25	12	4	7	2	148	6	8	3	1.9	.951	OF-80
1924		138	.352	.487	526	185	37	8	6	1.1	77	99	47	21	6	3	1	292	26	10	4	2.4	.970	OF-134
1925		154	.301	.409	602	181	35	9	8	1.3	80	99	51	25	4	0	0	306	18	14	8	2.2	.959	OF-154
1926		155	.345	.477	566	195	43	4	8	1.4	86	108	66	22	0	0	0	338	16	3	4	2.3	.992	OF-155
1927		145	.327	.465	535	175	35	6	9	1.7	76	83	52	19	5	0	0	372	22	9	9	2.8	.978	OF-145
1928		98	.290	.392	286	83	18	4	1	0.3	42	37	25	16	5	16	3	164	9	5	0	1.8	.972	OF-78
1929	CLE A	126	.309	.502	430	133	30	7	13	3.0	66	94	42	14	4	4	1	219	15	14	4	2.0	.944	OF-121
1930		82	.325	.461	191	62	12	1	4	2.1	34	36	23	8	2	34	13	84	4	3	3	1.1	.967	OF-42
1931		79	.304	.435	161	49	13	1	2	1.2	30	28	17	13	1	43	14	55	1	3	0	0.7	.949	OF-33
	12 yrs.	1354	.314	.448	4656	1463	300	59	69	1.5	656	785	412	279	46	114	36	2524	136	92	38	2.0	.967	OF-1226

Charlie Fallon

FALLON, CHARLES AUGUSTUS
B. Mar. 7, 1881, New York, N. Y. D. June 10, 1960, King's Park, N. Y.　　　BR TR 5'6"

Year	Team	Games	BA	SA	AB	H	2B	3B	HR	HR%	R	RBI	BB	SO	SB	AB	H	PO	A	E	DP	TC/G	FA	G by Pos
1905	NY A	1	–	–	0	0	0	0	0	–	0	0	0	0	0	0	0	0	0	0	0	0.0	–	

George Fallon

FALLON, GEORGE DECATUR (Flash)
B. July 8, 1916, Jersey City, N. J.　　　BR TR 5'9" 155 lbs.

Year	Team		Games	BA	SA	AB	H	2B	3B	HR	HR%	R	RBI	BB	SO	SB	Pinch Hit AB	Pinch Hit H	PO	A	E	DP	TC/G	FA	G by Pos

George Fallon *continued*

Year	Team		Games	BA	SA	AB	H	2B	3B	HR	HR%	R	RBI	BB	SO	SB	AB	H	PO	A	E	DP	TC/G	FA	G by Pos
1937	BKN	N	4	.250	.375	8	2	1	0	0	0.0	0	0	1	0	0	0	0	9	8	2	1	4.8	.895	2B-4
1943	STL	N	36	.231	.244	78	18	1	0	0	0.0	6	5	2	9	0	0	0	65	86	5	18	4.3	.968	2B-36
1944			69	.199	.262	141	28	6	0	1	0.7	16	9	16	11	1	0	0	100	120	6	28	3.3	.973	2B-38, SS-24, 3B-6
1945			24	.236	.309	55	13	2	1	0	0.0	4	7	6	6	1	0	0	39	41	4	8	3.5	.952	SS-20, 2B-4
4 yrs.			133	.216	.270	282	61	10	1	1	0.4	26	21	25	26	2	0	0	213	255	17	55	3.6	.965	2B-82, SS-44, 3B-6

WORLD SERIES

| 1944 | STL | N | 2 | .000 | .000 | 2 | 0 | 0 | 0 | 0 | 0.0 | 0 | 0 | 0 | 1 | 0 | 0 | 0 | 0 | 0 | 0 | 0 | 0.0 | – | 2B-2 |

Pete Falsey

FALSEY, PETER JAMES
B. Apr. 24, 1891, New Haven, Conn.   D. May 23, 1976, Los Angeles, Calif.   BL TL 5'6½" 132 lbs.

| 1914 | PIT | N | 3 | .000 | .000 | 1 | 0 | 0 | 0 | 0 | 0.0 | 0 | 0 | 0 | 1 | 0 | 1 | 0 | 0 | 0 | 0 | 0 | 0.0 | – | |

Jim Fanning

FANNING, WILLIAM JAMES
B. Sept. 14, 1927, Chicago, Ill.
Manager 1981-82, 1984.   BR TR 5'11" 180 lbs.

1954	CHI	N	11	.184	.184	38	7	0	0	0	0.0	2	1	1	7	0	0	0	40	6	0	0	4.2	1.000	C-11
1955			5	.000	.000	10	0	0	0	0	0.0	0	0	1	2	0	0	0	30	2	0	0	6.4	1.000	C-5
1956			1	.250	.250	4	1	0	0	0	0.0	0	0	0	0	0	0	0	5	3	2	1	10.0	.800	C-1
1957			47	.180	.202	89	16	2	0	0	0.0	3	4	4	17	0	12	1	138	14	3	4	3.3	.981	C-35
4 yrs.			64	.170	.184	141	24	2	0	0	0.0	5	5	6	26	0	12	1	213	25	5	5	3.8	.979	C-52

Carmen Fanzone

FANZONE, CARMEN RONALD
B. Aug. 30, 1941, Detroit, Mich.   BR TR 6' 200 lbs.

1970	BOS	A	10	.200	.267	15	3	1	0	0	0.0	0	3	2	2	0	4	0	4	8	4	1	1.6	.750	3B-5
1971	CHI	N	12	.186	.372	43	8	2	0	2	4.7	5	5	2	7	0	2	1	22	9	2	2	2.8	.939	OF-6, 3B-3, 1B-2
1972			86	.225	.383	222	50	11	0	8	3.6	26	42	35	45	2	15	4	243	115	9	21	4.3	.975	3B-36, 1B-21, 2B-13, OF-1, SS-1
1973			64	.273	.440	150	41	7	0	6	4.0	22	22	20	38	1	15	5	193	41	8	13	3.8	.967	3B-25, 1B-24, OF-6
1974			65	.190	.304	158	30	6	0	4	2.5	13	22	15	27	0	15	4	87	82	15	14	2.8	.918	3B-35, 2B-10, 1B-7, OF-1
5 yrs.			237	.224	.372	588	132	27	0	20	3.4	66	94	74	119	3	51	14	549	255	38	51	3.6	.955	3B-104, 1B-54, 2B-23, OF-14, SS-1

Bob Farley

FARLEY, ROBERT JACOB
B. Nov. 15, 1937, Watsontown, Pa.   BL TL 6'2" 200 lbs.

1961	SF	N	13	.100	.100	20	2	0	0	0	0.0	3	1	3	5	0	8	1	7	0	0	1	0.5	1.000	OF-3, 1B-1
1962	2 teams		CHI A (35G – .189)			DET A (36G – .160)																			
"	total		71	.175	.282	103	18	3	1	2	1.9	16	8	27	23	0	33	4	111	7	4	11	1.7	.967	1B-20, OF-6
2 yrs.			84	.163	.252	123	20	3	1	2	1.6	19	9	30	28	0	41	5	118	7	4	12	1.5	.969	1B-21, OF-9

Tom Farley

FARLEY, THOMAS T.
B. Chicago, Ill.   Deceased.

| 1884 | WAS | AA | 14 | .212 | .288 | 52 | 11 | 4 | 0 | 0 | 0.0 | 5 | | 1 | | | 0 | 0 | 24 | 2 | 4 | 1 | 2.1 | .867 | OF-14 |

Alex Farmer

FARMER, ALEXANDER JOHNSON
B. May 9, 1880, New York, N. Y.   D. Mar. 5, 1920, New York, N. Y.   BR TR 6' 175 lbs.

| 1908 | BKN | N | 12 | .167 | .200 | 30 | 5 | 1 | 0 | 0 | 0.0 | 1 | 2 | 1 | | | 0 | 1 | 0 | 50 | 7 | 2 | 2 | 4.9 | .966 | C-11 |

Bill Farmer

FARMER, WILLIAM
B. Dec. 27, 1870, Philadelphia, Pa.   Deceased.   BR TR 5'11½"

| 1888 | 2 teams | | PIT N (2G – .000) | | | PHI AA (3G – .167) | | | | | | | | | | | | | | | | | | | |
| " | total | | 5 | .125 | .125 | 16 | 2 | 0 | 0 | 0 | 0.0 | 0 | 1 | 0 | 1 | 0 | 0 | 0 | 28 | 4 | 3 | 0 | 7.0 | .914 | C-4, OF-1 |

Jack Farmer

FARMER, FLOYD HASKELL
B. July 14, 1892, Granville, Tenn.   D. May 21, 1970, Columbia, La.   BR TR 6' 180 lbs.

1916	PIT	N	55	.271	.355	166	45	6	4	0	0.0	10	14	7	24	1	7	0	81	91	15	7	3.4	.920	2B-31, OF-15, SS-4, 3B-1
1918	CLE	A	7	.222	.222	9	2	0	0	0	0.0	1	1	0	3	2	4	2	6	10	1	0	2.4	.941	3B-5
2 yrs.			62	.269	.349	175	47	6	4	0	0.0	11	15	7	27	3	11	2	87	101	16	7	3.3	.922	2B-31, OF-15, 3B-6, SS-4

Sid Farrar

FARRAR, SIDNEY DOUGLAS
B. Aug. 10, 1859, Paris Hill, Me.   D. May 7, 1935, New York, N. Y.   TR 5'10" 185 lbs.

1883	PHI	N	99	.233	.329	377	88	19	7	1	0.3	41		4	37		0	0	1038	31	39	45	11.2	.965	1B-99
1884			111	.245	.318	428	105	16	6	1	0.2	62		9	25		0	0	1142	42	42	41	11.0	.966	1B-111
1885			111	.245	.329	420	103	20	3	3	0.7	49		28	34		0	0	1153	41	31	50	11.0	.975	1B-111
1886			118	.248	.358	439	109	19	7	5	1.1	55	50	16	47		0	0	1220	45	26	38	10.9	.980	1B-118
1887			116	.282	.395	443	125	20	9	4	0.9	83	72	42	29	24	0	0	1149	46	28	55	10.5	.977	1B-116
1888			131	.244	.325	508	124	24	7	1	0.2	53	53	31	38	21	0	0	1345	53	30	57	10.9	.979	1B-131
1889			130	.268	.342	477	128	22	2	3	0.6	70	58	52	36	28	0	0	1265	42	30	66	10.3	.978	1B-130
1890	PHI	P	127	.254	.341	481	122	17	11	1	0.2	84	69	51	23	9	0	0	1238	58	36	79	10.5	.973	1B-127
8 yrs.			943	.253	.342	3573	904	157	52	19	0.5	497	302	233	269	82	0	0	9550	358	262	431	10.8	.974	1B-943

Bill Farrell

FARRELL, WILLIAM
B. Bridgeport, Conn.   Deceased.

1882	PHI	AA	2	.286	.429	7	2	1	0	0	0.0	2		1			0	0	0	0	0	0	0.0	–	OF-2, C-1
1883	BAL	AA	2	.000	.000	7	0	0	0	0	0.0	0		1			0	0	1	5	2	1	4.0	.750	SS-2
2 yrs.			4	.143	.214	14	2	1	0	0	0.0	2		2			0	0	1	5	2	1	2.0	.750	OF-2, SS-2, C-1

Doc Farrell

FARRELL, EDWARD STEPHEN
B. Dec. 26, 1901, Johnson City, N. Y.   D. Dec. 20, 1966, Livingston, N. J.   BR TR 5'8" 160 lbs.

Year	Team	Games	BA	SA	AB	H	2B	3B	HR	HR%	R	RBI	BB	SO	SB	Pinch Hit AB	Pinch Hit H	PO	A	E	DP	TC/G	FA	G by Pos

Doc Farrell *continued*

Year	Team	Games	BA	SA	AB	H	2B	3B	HR	HR%	R	RBI	BB	SO	SB	PH AB	PH H	PO	A	E	DP	TC/G	FA	G by Pos
1925	NY N	27	.214	.232	56	12	1	0	0	0.0	6	4	4	6	0	3	0	14	46	4	4	2.4	.938	SS-13, 3B-7, 2B-1
1926		67	.287	.392	171	49	10	1	2	1.2	19	23	12	17	0	8	2	111	130	12	23	3.8	.953	SS-53, 2B-3
1927	2 teams	NY N (42G – .387)			BOS N (110G – .292)																			
"	total	152	.316	.389	566	179	23	3	4	0.7	57	92	26	32	4	4	2	331	454	58	67	5.5	.931	SS-93, 2B-40, 3B-20
1928	BOS N	134	.215	.271	483	104	14	2	3	0.6	36	43	26	26	3	1	0	289	419	51	73	5.7	.933	SS-132, 2B-1
1929	2 teams	BOS N (5G – .125)			NY N (63G – .213)																			
"	total	68	.210	.242	186	39	6	0	0	0.0	18	18	9	18	2	8	1	95	131	15	21	3.5	.938	3B-28, 2B-26, SS-5
1930	2 teams	STL N (23G – .213)			CHI N (46G – .292)																			
"	total	69	.264	.333	174	46	7	1	1	0.6	24	22	13	7	1	2	0	114	160	16	32	4.2	.945	SS-53, 2B-7, 1B-1
1932	NY A	26	.175	.222	63	11	1	1	0	0.0	4	4	2	8	0	0	0	39	39	3	9	3.1	.963	2B-16, SS-5, 1B-2, 3B-1
1933		44	.269	.269	93	25	0	1	0	0.0	16	6	16	6	0	0	0	67	77	9	12	3.5	.941	SS-22, 2B-20
1935	BOS A	4	.286	.429	7	2	1	0	0	0.0	1	1	1	0	0	0	0	6	5	1	1	3.0	.917	2B-4
9 yrs.		591	.260	.320	1799	467	63	8	10	0.6	181	213	109	120	14	26	5	1066	1461	169	242	4.6	.937	SS-376, 2B-118, 3B-56, 1B-3

Duke Farrell

FARRELL, CHARLES ANDREW
B. Aug. 31, 1866, Oakdale, Mass.   D. Feb. 15, 1925, Boston, Mass.

BB TR 6'2"   180 lbs.

Year	Team	Games	BA	SA	AB	H	2B	3B	HR	HR%	R	RBI	BB	SO	SB	PH AB	PH H	PO	A	E	DP	TC/G	FA	G by Pos
1888	CHI N	64	.232	.320	241	56	6	3	3	1.2	34	19	4	41	8	0	0	231	53	39	4	5.0	.879	C-33, OF-31, 1B-1
1889		101	.248	.410	407	101	19	7	11	2.7	66	75	41	21	13	0	0	398	123	53	3	5.7	.908	C-76, OF-25
1890	CHI P	117	.290	.404	451	131	21	12	2	0.4	79	84	42	28	8	0	0	587	147	49	21	6.7	.937	C-90, 1B-22, OF-10
1891	BOS AA	122	.302	.474	473	143	19	13	12	2.5	108	110	59	48	21	0	0	305	235	45	15	4.8	.923	3B-66, C-37, OF-23, 1B-4
1892	PIT N	152	.215	.314	605	130	10	13	8	1.3	96	77	46	53	20	0	0	221	291	72	20	3.8	.877	3B-133, OF-20
1893	WAS N	124	.280	.380	511	143	13	13	4	0.8	84	75	47	12	11	0	0	411	232	57	12	5.6	.919	C-81, 3B-41, 1B-3
1894	NY N	114	.284	.424	401	114	20	12	4	1.0	47	66	35	15	9	1	0	510	148	52	14	6.2	.927	C-104, 3B-5, 1B-4
1895		90	.288	.407	312	90	16	9	1	0.3	38	58	38	18	11	2	1	315	115	33	15	5.1	.929	C-62, 3B-24, 1B-2
1896	2 teams	NY N (58G – .283)			WAS N (37G – .300)																			
"	total	95	.290	.389	321	93	14	6	2	0.6	41	67	26	10	4	10	4	219	130	31	14	4.0	.918	C-52, 3B-21, SS-13
1897	WAS N	78	.322	.402	261	84	9	6	0	0.0	41	53	17		8	14	8	226	92	19	11	4.3	.944	C-63, 1B-1
1898		99	.314	.393	338	106	12	1	1	0.3	47	53	34		12	10	5	434	96	27	22	5.6	.952	C-61, 1B-28
1899	2 teams	WAS N (5G – .333)			BKN N (80G – .299)																			
"	total	85	.301	.417	266	80	11	7	2	0.8	42	56	37		7	3	1	260	116	20	9	4.7	.949	C-82
1900	BKN N	76	.275	.352	273	75	11	5	0	0.0	33	39	11		3	2	0	252	88	20	8	4.7	.944	C-74
1901		80	.296	.384	284	84	10	6	1	0.4	38	31	7		7	4	3	443	98	15	16	7.0	.973	C-59, 1B-17
1902		74	.242	.277	264	64	5	2	0	0.0	14	24	12		6	2	0	469	90	12	8	7.7	.979	C-49, 1B-24
1903	BOS A	17	.404	.538	52	21	5	1	0	0.0	5	8	5		1	0	0	71	25	4	1	5.9	.960	C-17
1904		68	.212	.278	198	42	9	2	0	0.0	11	15	15		1	11	1	234	62	13	6	4.5	.958	C-56
1905		7	.286	.333	21	6	1	0	0	0.0	2	2	1		0	0	0	37	10	0	0	6.7	1.000	C-7
18 yrs.		1563	.275	.383	5679	1563	211	123	51	0.9	826	912	477	246	150	59	23	5623	2151	561	199	5.3	.933	C-1003, 3B-290, OF-109, 1B-106, SS-13

WORLD SERIES

Year	Team	Games	BA	SA	AB	H	2B	3B	HR	HR%	R	RBI	BB	SO	SB	PH AB	PH H	PO	A	E	DP	TC/G	FA	G by Pos
1903	BOS A	2	.000	.000	2	0	0	0	0	0.0	0	1	0	0	0	2	0	0	0	0	0	0.0	–	

Jack Farrell

FARRELL, JOHN A. (Moose)
B. July 5, 1857, Newark, N. J.   D. Feb. 10, 1914, Overbrook, N. J.
Manager 1881.

BR TR 5'9"   165 lbs.

Year	Team	Games	BA	SA	AB	H	2B	3B	HR	HR%	R	RBI	BB	SO	SB	PH AB	PH H	PO	A	E	DP	TC/G	FA	G by Pos
1879	2 teams	SYR N (54G – .303)			PRO N (12G – .255)																			
"	total	66	.295	.346	292	86	8	2	1	0.3	45	26	3	13		0	0	204	241	61	24	7.7	.879	2B-66
1880	PRO N	80	.271	.363	339	92	12	5	3	0.9	46	36	10	6		0	0	207	274	61	26	6.8	.887	2B-80
1881		84	.238	.357	345	82	16	5	5	1.4	69	36	29	23		0	0	216	273	68	40	6.6	.878	2B-82, OF-3
1882		84	.254	.361	366	93	21	6	2	0.5	67		16	23		0	0	212	283	71	41	6.7	.875	2B-84
1883		95	.305	.436	420	128	24	11	3	0.7	92		15	21		0	0	258	365	51	51	7.1	.924	2B-95
1884		111	.217	.277	469	102	13	6	1	0.2	70		35	44		0	0	251	353	54	36	5.9	.918	2B-109, 3B-3
1885		68	.206	.253	257	53	7	1	1	0.4	27	19	10	25		0	0	158	194	39	16	5.8	.900	2B-68
1886	2 teams	PHI N (17G – .183)			WAS N (47G – .240)																			
"	total	64	.225	.342	231	52	11	6	2	0.9	31	21	18	23		0	0	121	189	39	14	5.5	.888	2B-64
1887	WAS N	87	.221	.316	339	75	14	9	0	0.0	40	41	20	12	31	0	0	161	287	55	19	5.8	.891	SS-48, 2B-40
1888	BAL AA	103	.204	.299	398	81	19	5	3	0.8	72	36	26	29		0	0	170	354	47	36	5.5	.918	SS-54, 2B-52
1889		42	.210	.248	157	33	3	0	1	0.6	25	26	15	15	14	0	0	65	131	24	13	5.2	.891	SS-42
11 yrs.		884	.243	.332	3613	877	148	55	22	0.6	584	241	197	205	74	0	0	2023	2944	570	316	6.3	.897	2B-740, SS-144, OF-3, 3B-3

Jack Farrell

FARRELL, JOHN J
B. June 16, 1889, Chicago, Ill.   D. Nov. 15, 1916, Hartford, Conn.

BB TR 5'8"   145 lbs.

Year	Team	Games	BA	SA	AB	H	2B	3B	HR	HR%	R	RBI	BB	SO	SB	PH AB	PH H	PO	A	E	DP	TC/G	FA	G by Pos
1914	CHI F	156	.235	.294	524	123	23	4	0	0.0	58	35	52		12	0	0	361	463	40	54	5.5	.954	2B-155, SS-3
1915		70	.216	.270	222	48	10	1	0	0.0	27	14	25		8	0	0	138	182	20	26	4.9	.941	2B-70, SS-1
2 yrs.		226	.229	.287	746	171	33	5	0	0.0	85	49	77		20	0	0	499	645	60	80	5.3	.950	2B-225, SS-4

Joe Farrell

FARRELL, JOSEPH F.
B. 1857, Brooklyn, N. Y.   D. Apr. 18, 1893, Brooklyn, N. Y.

BR   5'6"   160 lbs.

Year	Team	Games	BA	SA	AB	H	2B	3B	HR	HR%	R	RBI	BB	SO	SB	PH AB	PH H	PO	A	E	DP	TC/G	FA	G by Pos
1882	DET N	69	.247	.314	283	70	12	2	1	0.4	34	24	4	20		0	0	129	150	49	11	4.8	.851	3B-42, 2B-18, SS-9
1883		101	.243	.295	444	108	13	5	0	0.0	58		5	29		0	0	111	248	66	13	4.2	.845	3B-101
1884		110	.226	.289	461	104	10	5	3	0.7	59		14	66		0	0	126	198	61	12	3.5	.842	3B-110, OF-1
1886	BAL AA	73	.209	.266	301	63	8	3	1	0.3	36			12		0	0	111	180	46	9	4.6	.864	2B-45, 3B-27, OF-1
4 yrs.		353	.232	.291	1489	345	43	15	5	0.3	187	24	35	115		0	0	477	776	222	45	4.2	.849	3B-280, 2B-63, SS-9, OF-2

John Farrell

FARRELL, JOHN SEBASTIAN (Little Johnny)
B. Dec. 4, 1876, Covington, Ky.   D. May 14, 1921, Kansas City, Mo.

BR TR 5'10"   160 lbs.

Year	Team	Games	BA	SA	AB	H	2B	3B	HR	HR%	R	RBI	BB	SO	SB	PH AB	PH H	PO	A	E	DP	TC/G	FA	G by Pos
1901	WAS A	135	.272	.386	555	151	32	11	2	0.5	100	63	52		25	0	0	332	262	54	46	4.8	.917	2B-72, OF-62, 3B-1
1902	STL N	138	.250	.290	565	141	13	5	0	0.0	68	25	43		9	0	0	337	501	49	76	6.4	.945	2B-118, SS-21
1903		130	.272	.356	519	141	25	8	1	0.2	83	32	48		17	0	0	320	399	54	52	5.9	.930	2B-118, OF-12
1904		131	.255	.312	509	130	23	5	0	0.0	72	20	46		16	1	0	297	450	53	55	6.1	.934	2B-130

Year	Team		Games	BA	SA	AB	H	2B	3B	HR	HR%	R	RBI	BB	SO	SB	Pinch Hit AB	Pinch Hit H	PO	A	E	DP	TC/G	FA	G by Pos

John Farrell *continued*

| 1905 | | | 7 | .167 | .250 | 24 | 4 | 0 | 1 | 0 | 0.0 | 6 | 1 | 4 | | 1 | 0 | 0 | 19 | 14 | 4 | 0 | 5.3 | .892 | 2B-7 |
| 5 yrs. | | | 541 | .261 | .335 | 2172 | 567 | 93 | 28 | 4 | 0.2 | 329 | 141 | 193 | | 68 | 1 | 0 | 1305 | 1626 | 214 | 229 | 5.8 | .932 | 2B-445, OF-74, SS-21, 3B-1 |

Kerby Farrell

FARRELL, MAJOR KERBY
B. Sept. 3, 1913, Leapwood, Tenn. D. Dec. 17, 1975, Nashville, Tenn.
Manager 1957.
BL TL 5'11" 172 lbs.

1943	BOS	N	85	.268	.325	280	75	14	1	0	0.0	11	21	16	15	1	11	2	740	55	4	62	9.4	.995	1B-69, P-5
1945	CHI	A	103	.258	.301	396	102	11	3	0	0.0	44	34	24	18	4	6	3	913	74	11	76	9.7	.989	1B-97
2 yrs.			188	.262	.311	676	177	25	4	0	0.0	55	55	40	33	5	17	5	1653	129	15	138	9.6	.992	1B-166, P-5

John Farrow

FARROW, JOHN JACOB
B. 1852, Verplanck's Point, N. Y. D. Dec. 31, 1914, Perth Amboy, N. J.
BL TR

| 1884 | BKN | AA | 16 | .190 | .224 | 58 | 11 | 2 | 0 | 0 | 0.0 | 7 | | 3 | | | 0 | 0 | 82 | 25 | 10 | 1 | 7.3 | .915 | C-16 |

Buck Fausett

FAUSETT, ROBERT SHAW (Leaky)
B. Apr. 8, 1908, Sheridan, Ark.
BL TR 5'10" 170 lbs.

| 1944 | CIN | N | 13 | .097 | .161 | 31 | 3 | 0 | 1 | 0 | 0.0 | 2 | 1 | 2 | | 0 | 5 | 0 | 6 | 23 | 1 | 1 | 2.3 | .967 | 3B-6, P-2 |

Joe Fautsch

FAUTSCH, JOSEPH ROAMAN
B. Feb. 28, 1887, Minneapolis, Minn. D. Mar. 16, 1971, New Hope, Minn.
BR TR 5'10" 162 lbs.

| 1916 | CHI | A | 1 | .000 | .000 | 1 | 0 | 0 | 0 | 0 | 0.0 | 0 | 0 | 0 | 0 | 0 | 1 | 0 | 0 | 0 | 0 | 0 | 0.0 | — | |

Ernie Fazio

FAZIO, ERNEST JOSEPH
B. Jan. 25, 1942, Oakland, Calif.
BR TR 5'7" 165 lbs.

1962	HOU	N	12	.083	.083	12	1	0	0	0	0.0	2		1	5	0	1	0	5	13	5	1	1.9	.783	SS-10
1963			102	.184	.281	228	42	10	3	2	0.9	31	5	27	70	4	9	2	132	145	8	18	2.8	.972	2B-84, SS-1, 3B-1
1966	KC	A	27	.206	.265	34	7	0	1	0	0.0	3	2	4	10	1	12	1	8	24	0	4	1.2	1.000	2B-10, SS-4
3 yrs.			141	.182	.270	274	50	10	4	2	0.7	37	8	33	85	5	22	3	145	182	13	23	2.4	.962	2B-94, SS-15, 3B-1

Al Federoff

FEDEROFF, ALFRED (Whitey)
B. July 11, 1924, Bairdford, Pa.
BR TR 5'10½" 165 lbs.

1951	DET	A	2	.000	.000	4	0	0	0	0	0.0	0	0	0	0	0	0	0	3	5	1	0	4.5	.889	2B-1
1952			74	.242	.277	231	56	4	2	0	0.0	14	14	16	13	1	0	0	148	203	9	45	4.9	.975	2B-70, SS-7
2 yrs.			76	.238	.272	235	56	4	2	0	0.0	14	14	16	13	1	0	0	151	208	10	45	4.9	.973	2B-71, SS-7

Bill Fehring

FEHRING, WILLIAM PAUL (Dutch)
B. May 31, 1912, Columbus, Ind.
BB TR 6' 195 lbs.

| 1934 | CHI | A | 1 | .000 | .000 | 1 | 0 | 0 | 0 | 0 | 0.0 | 0 | 0 | 0 | 1 | 0 | 0 | 0 | 2 | 0 | 0 | 0 | 2.0 | 1.000 | C-1 |

Eddie Feinberg

FEINBERG, EDWARD ISADORE (Itzy)
B. Sept. 20, 1918, Philadelphia, Pa. D. Apr. 20, 1986, Hollywood, Fla.
BB TR 5'9" 165 lbs.

1938	PHI	N	10	.150	.150	20	3	0	0	0	0.0	1	0	0	1	0	0	0	15	13	1	3	2.9	.966	SS-4, OF-2
1939			6	.222	.278	18	4	1	0	0	0.0	2	0	2	0	0	0	0	4	6	1	2	1.8	.909	2B-4, SS-1
2 yrs.			16	.184	.211	38	7	1	0	0	0.0	2	0	2	1	0	0	0	19	19	2	5	2.5	.950	SS-5, 2B-4, OF-2

Mike Felder

FELDER, MICHAEL OTIS
B. Nov. 18, 1961, Vallejo, Calif.
BB TR 5'8" 160 lbs.

1985	MIL	A	15	.196	.214	56	11	1	0	0	0.0	8	0	5	6	4	1	1	32	1	0	0	2.2	1.000	OF-14
1986			44	.239	.323	155	37	2	4	1	0.6	24	13	13	16	16	0	0	98	0	0	0	2.2	1.000	OF-42, DH-1
1987			108	.266	.353	289	77	5	7	2	0.7	48	31	28	23	34	7	1	190	10	5	3	1.9	.976	OF-99, DH-3, 2B-1
1988			50	.173	.185	81	14	1	0	0	0.0	14	5	0	11	8	2	0	40	1	1	0	0.8	.976	OF-28, DH-16, 2B-1
1989			117	.241	.324	315	76	11	3	3	1.0	50	23	23	38	26	7	3	203	24	4	7	2.0	.983	OF-93, DH-11, 2B-10
5 yrs.			334	.240	.314	896	215	20	14	6	0.7	144	72	69	94	88	17	5	563	36	10	10	1.8	.984	OF-276, DH-31, 2B-12

Marv Felderman

FELDERMAN, MARVIN WILFRED (Coonie)
B. Dec. 20, 1915, Bellevue, Iowa
BR TR 6'1" 187 lbs.

| 1942 | CHI | N | 3 | .167 | .167 | 6 | 1 | 0 | 0 | 0 | 0.0 | 0 | 0 | 1 | 4 | 0 | 0 | 0 | 8 | 2 | 0 | 0 | 3.3 | 1.000 | C-2 |

Gus Felix

FELIX, AUGUST GUENTHER
B. May 24, 1895, Cincinnati, Ohio D. May 12, 1960, Montgomery, Ala.
BR TR 6' 180 lbs.

1923	BOS	N	139	.273	.350	506	138	17	2	6	1.2	64	44	51	65	8	3	1	293	28	17	4	2.4	.950	OF-123, 2B-5, 3B-4
1924			59	.211	.270	204	43	7	1	1	0.5	25	10	18	16	0	3	2	147	6	8	1	2.7	.950	OF-51
1925			121	.307	.405	459	141	25	7	2	0.4	60	66	30	34	5	7	1	328	15	10	3	2.9	.972	OF-114
1926	BKN	N	134	.280	.382	432	121	21	7	3	0.7	64	53	51	32	9	8	1	270	11	13	2	2.2	.956	OF-125
1927			130	.265	.348	445	118	21	8	0	0.0	43	57	39	47	6	11	4	221	13	13	1	1.9	.947	OF-119
5 yrs.			583	.274	.361	2046	561	91	25	12	0.6	256	230	189	194	28	32	9	1259	73	61	11	2.4	.956	OF-532, 2B-5, 3B-4

Junior Felix

FELIX, JUNIOR FRANCISCO
Born Junior Francisco Felix y Sanchez.
B. Oct. 3, 1967, Laguna Sabada, Dominican Republic
BB TR 6' 170 lbs.

| 1989 | TOR | A | 110 | .258 | .395 | 415 | 107 | 14 | 8 | 9 | 2.2 | 62 | 46 | 33 | 101 | 18 | 2 | 0 | 243 | 9 | 9 | 0 | 2.4 | .966 | OF-107, DH-2 |

LEAGUE CHAMPIONSHIP SERIES

| 1989 | TOR | A | 3 | .273 | .364 | 11 | 3 | 1 | 0 | 0 | 0.0 | 0 | 3 | 0 | 2 | 0 | 0 | 0 | 8 | 0 | 0 | 0 | 2.7 | 1.000 | OF-3 |

Jack Feller

FELLER, JACK LELAND
B. Dec. 10, 1936, Adrian, Mich.
BR TR 5'10½" 185 lbs.

Year	Team	Games	BA	SA	AB	H	2B	3B	HR	HR%	R	RBI	BB	SO	SB	Pinch Hit AB	Pinch Hit H	PO	A	E	DP	TC/G	FA	G by Pos

Jack Feller *continued*

| 1958 DET A | | 1 | – | – | 0 | 0 | 0 | 0 | 0 | – | 0 | 0 | 0 | 0 | 0 | 0 | 0 | 1 | 0 | 0 | 0 | 1.0 | 1.000 | C-1 |

Happy Felsch

FELSCH, OSCAR EMIL
B. Aug. 22, 1891, Milwaukee, Wis.   D. Aug. 17, 1964, Milwaukee, Wis.   BR TR 5'11" 175 lbs.

1915 CHI A		121	.248	.363	427	106	18	11	3	0.7	65	53	51	59	16	3	0	247	9	11	1	2.2	.959	OF-118
1916		146	.300	.427	546	164	24	12	7	1.3	73	70	31	67	13	4	2	340	19	7	5	2.5	.981	OF-141
1917		152	.308	.403	575	177	17	10	6	1.0	75	102	33	52	26	0	0	440	24	7	5	3.1	.985	OF-152
1918		53	.252	.325	206	52	2	5	1	0.5	16	20	15	13	6	0	0	149	7	7	5	3.1	.957	OF-53
1919		135	.275	.428	502	138	34	11	7	1.4	68	86	40	35	19	0	0	360	32	13	15	3.0	.968	OF-135
1920		142	.338	.540	556	188	40	15	14	2.5	88	115	37	25	8	0	0	385	25	8	10	2.9	.981	OF-142
6 yrs.		749	.293	.427	2812	825	135	64	38	1.4	385	446	207	251	88	7	2	1921	116	53	41	2.8	.975	OF-741

WORLD SERIES

1917 CHI A		6	.273	.455	22	6	1	0	1	4.5	4	3	1	5	0	0	0	16	2	0	1	3.0	1.000	OF-6
1919		8	.192	.231	26	5	1	0	0	0.0	2	3	1	4	0	0	0	23	1	2	1	3.3	.923	OF-8
2 yrs.		14	.229	.333	48	11	2	0	1	2.1	6	6	2	9	0	0	0	39	3	2	2	3.1	.955	OF-14

John Felske

FELSKE, JOHN FREDERICK
B. May 30, 1942, Chicago, Ill.
Manager 1985-87.   BR TR 6'3" 195 lbs.

1968 CHI N		4	.000	.000	2	0	0	0	0	0.0	0	0	0	1	0	1	0	5	0	1	0	1.5	.833	C-3
1972 MIL A		37	.138	.213	80	11	3	0	1	1.3	6	5	8	23	0	8	2	124	9	3	5	3.7	.978	C-23, 1B-8
1973		13	.136	.227	22	3	0	1	0	0.0	1	4	1	11	0	1	0	41	4	0	1	3.5	1.000	C-7, 1B-6
3 yrs.		54	.135	.212	104	14	3	1	1	1.0	7	9	9	35	0	10	2	170	13	4	6	3.5	.979	C-33, 1B-14

Frank Fennelly

FENNELLY, FRANCIS JOHN
B. Feb. 18, 1860, Fall River, Mass.   D. Aug. 4, 1920, Fall River, Mass.   BR TR 5'8" 168 lbs.

1884 2 teams	WAS AA (62G – .292)				CIN AA (28G – .352)																			
" total		90	.311	.480	379	118	22	15	4	1.1	94		31			0	0	124	310	75	27	5.7	.853	SS-88, 2B-4
1885 CIN AA		112	.273	.445	454	124	14	17	10	2.2	82		38			0	0	151	359	74	46	5.2	.873	SS-112
1886		132	.249	.380	497	124	13	17	6	1.2	113		60			0	0	169	485	117	54	5.8	.848	SS-132
1887		134	.266	.401	526	140	15	16	8	1.5	133		82		74	0	0	161	421	99	31	5.1	.855	SS-134
1888 2 teams	CIN AA (120G – .196)				PHI AA (15G – .234)																			
" total		135	.200	.275	495	99	10	6	3	0.6	77	68	72		48	0	0	184	476	106	41	5.7	.862	SS-127, OF-4, 2B-4
1889 PHI AA		138	.257	.322	513	132	20	5	1	0.2	70	64	65	78	15	0	0	181	453	93	53	5.3	.872	SS-138
1890 BKN AA		45	.247	.360	178	44	8	3	2	1.1	40		30		6	0	0	80	156	38	12	6.1	.861	SS-38, 3B-7
7 yrs.		786	.257	.378	3042	781	102	82	34	1.1	609	132	378	78	143	0	0	1050	2660	602	264	5.5	.860	SS-769, 2B-3, 3B-7, OF-4

Bobby Fenwick

FENWICK, ROBERT RICHARD (Bloop)
B. Dec. 10, 1946, Naha, Okinawa   BR TR 5'9" 165 lbs.

1972 HOU N		36	.180	.240	50	9	3	0	0	0.0	7	4	3	13	0	5	0	22	37	3	12	1.7	.952	2B-17, SS-4, 3B-2
1973 STL N		5	.167	.167	6	1	0	0	0	0.0	0	1	0	2	0	2	0	2	1	1	2	0.8	.750	2B-3
2 yrs.		41	.179	.232	56	10	3	0	0	0.0	7	5	3	15	0	7	0	24	38	4	14	1.6	.939	2B-20, SS-4, 3B-2

Bob Ferguson

FERGUSON, ROBERT V. (Death to Flying Things)
B. Jan. 31, 1845, Brooklyn, N. Y.   D. May 3, 1894, Brooklyn, N. Y.
Manager 1871-84, 1886-87.   BB TR 5'9½" 149 lbs.

1876 HAR N		69	.265	.323	310	82	8	5	0	0.0	48	32	2	11		0	0	124	133	54	5	4.5	.826	3B-69
1877		58	.256	.299	254	65	7	2	0	0.0	40	35	3	10		0	0	113	159	51	6	5.6	.842	3B-56, P-3
1878 CHI N		61	.351	.405	259	91	10	2	0	0.0	44	39	10	12		0	0	91	238	46	17	6.1	.877	SS-57, 2B-4, C-1
1879 TRO N		30	.252	.325	123	31	5	2	0	0.0	18	4	4	3		0	0	53	81	25	9	5.3	.843	3B-24, 2B-6
1880		82	.262	.289	332	87	9	0	0	0.0	55	22	24	24		0	0	294	255	58	38	7.4	.904	2B-82
1881		85	.283	.360	339	96	13	5	1	0.3	56	35	29	12		0	0	263	254	55	47	6.7	.904	2B-85
1882		81	.257	.317	319	82	15	2	0	0.0	44	33	23	21		0	0	248	227	50	38	6.5	.905	2B-79, SS-2
1883 PHI N		86	.258	.298	329	85	9	2	0	0.0	39		18	21		0	0	261	288	88	38	7.4	.862	2B-86, P-1
1884 PIT AA		10	.146	.146	41	6	0	0	0	0.0	2		0			0	0	41	0	6	0	4.7	.872	OF-6, 1B-3, 3B-1
9 yrs.		562	.271	.323	2306	625	76	20	1	0.0	346	200	113	114		0	0	1488	1635	433	198	6.3	.878	2B-342, 3B-150, SS-59, OF-6, P-4, 1B-3, C-1

Charlie Ferguson

FERGUSON, CHARLES J.
B. Apr. 17, 1863, Charlottesville, Va.   D. Apr. 29, 1888, Philadelphia, Pa.   BB TR 6' 165 lbs.

1884 PHI N		52	.246	.305	203	50	6	3	0	0.0	26		19	54		0	0	35	73	13	4	2.3	.893	P-50, OF-5
1885		61	.306	.379	235	72	8	3	1	0.4	42		23	18		0	0	56	89	15	3	2.6	.906	P-48, OF-15
1886		72	.253	.318	261	66	9	1	2	0.8	56	25	37	28		0	0	72	101	14	1	2.6	.925	P-48, OF-27
1887		72	.337	.470	264	89	14	6	3	1.1	67	85	34	19	13	0	0	93	130	22	11	3.4	.910	P-37, 2B-27, OF-6, 3B-5
4 yrs.		257	.288	.372	963	277	37	13	6	0.6	191	110	113	119	13	0	0	256	393	64	19	2.8	.910	P-183, OF-53, 2B-27, 3B-5

Joe Ferguson

FERGUSON, JOSEPH VANCE
B. Sept. 19, 1946, San Francisco, Calif.   BR TR 6'2" 200 lbs.

1970 LA N		5	.250	.250	4	1	0	0	0	0.0	0	2	1	2	0	0	0	9	0	0	0	1.8	1.000	C-3
1971		36	.216	.304	102	22	3	0	2	2.0	13	7	12	15	1	2	1	167	9	3	0	5.0	.983	C-35
1972		8	.292	.542	24	7	3	0	1	4.2	2	5	2	4	0	0	0	42	1	0	1	5.4	1.000	C-7, OF-2
1973		136	.263	.470	487	128	26	0	25	5.1	84	88	87	81	1	1	1	786	57	5	17	6.2	.994	C-122, OF-20
1974		111	.252	.436	349	88	14	0	16	4.6	54	57	75	73	2	6	0	486	40	7	2	4.8	.987	C-82, OF-32
1975		66	.208	.302	202	42	7	0	5	2.5	15	23	35	47	2	8	4	215	20	2	4	3.6	.992	C-35, OF-34
1976 2 teams	LA N (54G – .222)				STL N (71G – .201)																			
" total		125	.211	.353	374	79	14	0	10	2.7	46	39	57	81	6	14	2	409	44	14	8	3.7	.970	C-65, OF-53
1977 HOU N		132	.257	.435	421	108	21	3	16	3.8	59	61	85	79	6	12	2	644	80	11	10	5.6	.985	C-122, 1B-1

Year	Team	Games	BA	SA	AB	H	2B	3B	HR	HR%	R	RBI	BB	SO	SB	Pinch Hit AB	H	PO	A	E	DP	TC/G	FA	G by Pos

Joe Ferguson *continued*

Year	Team	Games	BA	SA	AB	H	2B	3B	HR	HR%	R	RBI	BB	SO	SB	AB	H	PO	A	E	DP	TC/G	FA	G by Pos
1978	2 teams	HOU N (51G – .207)					LA N		(67G – .237)															
"	total	118	.224	.391	348	78	16	0	14	4.0	40	50	71	71	1	5	1	573	52	7	2	5.4	.989	C-113, OF-3
1979	LA N	122	.262	.466	363	95	14	0	20	5.5	54	69	70	68	1	9	1	414	37	9	8	3.8	.980	C-67, OF-52
1980		77	.238	.436	172	41	3	2	9	5.2	20	29	38	46	2	14	2	297	23	7	4	4.2	.979	C-66, OF-1
1981	2 teams	LA N (17G – .143)					CAL A		(12G – .233)															
"	total	29	.205	.318	44	9	2	0	1	2.3	7	6	11	13	0	13	0	41	5	1	1	1.6	.979	C-8, OF-5
1982	CAL A	36	.226	.357	84	19	2	0	3	3.6	10	8	12	19	0	0	0	139	13	1	2	4.3	.993	C-32, OF-2
1983		12	.074	.074	27	2	0	0	0	0.0	3	2	5	8	0	0	0	31	3	1	0	2.9	.971	C-9, OF-3
14 yrs.		1013	.240	.409	3001	719	121	11	122	4.1	407	445	562	607	22	84	14	4253	384	68	59	4.6	.986	C-766, OF-207, 1B-1

LEAGUE CHAMPIONSHIP SERIES

Year	Team	Games	BA	SA	AB	H	2B	3B	HR	HR%	R	RBI	BB	SO	SB	AB	H	PO	A	E	DP	TC/G	FA	G by Pos
1974	LA N	4	.231	.231	13	3	0	0	0	0.0	3	2	5	1	0	0	0	9	0	1	0	2.5	.900	OF-3, C-2
1978		2	.000	.000	2	0	0	0	0	0.0	0	0	0	1	0	2	0	0	0	0	0	0.0	–	
2 yrs.		6	.200	.200	15	3	0	0	0	0.0	3	2	5	2	0	2	0	9	0	1	0	1.7	.900	OF-3, C-2

WORLD SERIES

Year	Team	Games	BA	SA	AB	H	2B	3B	HR	HR%	R	RBI	BB	SO	SB	AB	H	PO	A	E	DP	TC/G	FA	G by Pos
1974	LA N	5	.125	.313	16	2	0	0	1	6.3	2	2	4	6	1	0	0	10	0	2	0	2.4	.833	OF-4, C-2
1978		2	.500	1.000	4	2	2	0	0	0.0	1	0	0	1	0	0	0	11	0	1	0	6.0	.917	C-2
2 yrs.		7	.200	.450	20	4	2	0	1	5.0	3	2	4	7	1	0	0	21	0	3	0	3.4	.875	OF-4, C-4

Felix Fermin

FERMIN, FELIX JOSE
Born Felix Jose Fermin y Minaya.
B. Oct. 9, 1963, Mao Valverde, Dominican Republic

BR TR 5'11" 160 lbs.

Year	Team	Games	BA	SA	AB	H	2B	3B	HR	HR%	R	RBI	BB	SO	SB	AB	H	PO	A	E	DP	TC/G	FA	G by Pos
1987	PIT N	23	.250	.250	68	17	0	0	0	0.0	6	4	4	9	0	0	0	36	62	2	13	4.3	.980	SS-23
1988		43	.276	.322	87	24	0	2	0	0.0	9	2	8	10	3	1	0	51	76	6	14	3.1	.955	SS-43
1989	CLE A	156	.238	.260	484	115	9	1	0	0.0	50	21	41	27	6	0	0	253	517	26	84	5.1	.967	SS-153, 2B-2
3 yrs.		222	.244	.268	639	156	9	3	0	0.0	65	27	53	46	9	1	0	340	655	34	111	4.6	.967	SS-219, 2B-2

Ed Fernandes

FERNANDES, EDWARD PAUL
B. Mar. 11, 1918, Oakland, Calif. D. Nov. 27, 1968, Hayward, Calif.

BB TR 5'9" 185 lbs.

Year	Team	Games	BA	SA	AB	H	2B	3B	HR	HR%	R	RBI	BB	SO	SB	AB	H	PO	A	E	DP	TC/G	FA	G by Pos
1940	PIT N	28	.121	.152	33	4	1	0	0	0.0	1	0	7	6	0	0	0	47	5	1	1	1.9	.981	C-27
1946	CHI A	14	.250	.313	32	8	2	0	0	0.0	4	4	8	7	0	3	0	41	6	4	1	3.6	.922	C-12
2 yrs.		42	.185	.231	65	12	3	0	0	0.0	5	4	15	13	0	3	0	88	11	5	2	2.5	.952	C-39

Chico Fernandez

FERNANDEZ, HUMBERTO
Born Humberto Fernandez y Perez.
B. Mar. 2, 1932, Havana, Cuba

BR TR 6' 165 lbs.

Year	Team	Games	BA	SA	AB	H	2B	3B	HR	HR%	R	RBI	BB	SO	SB	AB	H	PO	A	E	DP	TC/G	FA	G by Pos
1956	BKN N	34	.227	.303	66	15	2	0	1	1.5	11	9	3	10	2	1	0	34	56	2	11	2.7	.978	SS-25
1957	PHI N	149	.262	.336	500	131	14	4	5	1.0	42	51	31	64	18	0	0	241	377	26	69	4.3	.960	SS-149
1958		148	.230	.318	522	120	18	5	6	1.1	38	51	37	48	12	0	0	296	415	18	88	4.9	.975	SS-148
1959		45	.211	.268	123	26	5	1	0	0.0	15	3	10	11	2	0	0	77	86	7	23	3.8	.959	SS-40, 2B-2
1960	DET A	133	.241	.313	435	105	13	3	4	0.9	44	35	39	50	13	2	0	226	381	34	67	4.8	.947	SS-130
1961		133	.248	.322	435	108	15	4	3	0.7	41	40	36	45	8	4	2	217	322	23	59	4.2	.959	SS-121, 3B-8
1962		141	.249	.410	503	125	17	2	20	4.0	64	59	42	69	10	1	0	239	338	24	53	4.3	.960	SS-138, 3B-2, 1B-1
1963	2 teams	DET A (15G – .143)					NY N		(58G – .200)															
"	total	73	.186	.237	194	36	7	0	1	0.5	15	11	15	41	3	15	1	99	131	15	25	3.4	.939	SS-59, 3B-5, 2B-3
8 yrs.		856	.240	.329	2778	666	91	19	40	1.4	270	259	213	338	68	23	3	1429	2106	149	395	4.3	.960	SS-810, 3B-15, 2B-5, 1B-1

Chico Fernandez

FERNANDEZ, LORENZO MARTO
Born Lorenzo Marto Fernandez y Mosquera.
B. Apr. 23, 1939, Havana, Cuba

BR TR 5'10" 160 lbs.

Year	Team	Games	BA	SA	AB	H	2B	3B	HR	HR%	R	RBI	BB	SO	SB	AB	H	PO	A	E	DP	TC/G	FA	G by Pos
1968	BAL A	24	.111	.111	18	2	0	0	0	0.0	1	2	0	9	2	6	9	1	2	0.7	.938	SS-7, 2B-4

Frank Fernandez

FERNANDEZ, FRANK
B. Apr. 16, 1943, Staten Island, N. Y.

BR TR 6' 185 lbs.

Year	Team	Games	BA	SA	AB	H	2B	3B	HR	HR%	R	RBI	BB	SO	SB	AB	H	PO	A	E	DP	TC/G	FA	G by Pos
1967	NY A	9	.214	.393	28	6	2	0	1	3.6	1	4	2	11	1	0	0	43	4	0	0	5.2	1.000	C-7, OF-2
1968		51	.170	.385	135	23	6	1	7	5.2	15	30	35	50	1	1	0	245	28	3	2	5.4	.989	C-45, OF-4
1969		89	.223	.415	229	51	6	1	12	5.2	34	29	65	68	1	11	1	336	30	3	2	4.1	.992	C-65, OF-14
1970	OAK A	94	.214	.413	252	54	5	0	15	6.0	30	44	40	76	1	14	5	407	25	3	6	4.6	.993	C-76, OF-1
1971	3 teams	OAK A (4G – .111)					WAS A		(18G – .100)			CHI N	(17G – .171)											
"	total	39	.138	.313	80	11	2	0	4	5.0	12	9	22	28	0	14	1	114	8	2	0	3.2	.984	C-20, OF-6
1972	CHI N	3	.000	.000	3	0	0	0	0	0.0	0	0	0	2	0	2	0	1	0	0	0	0.3	1.000	C-1
6 yrs.		285	.199	.395	727	145	21	2	39	5.4	92	116	164	231	4	42	7	1146	95	11	10	4.4	.991	C-214, OF-27

Nanny Fernandez

FERNANDEZ, FROILAN
B. Oct. 25, 1918, Wilmington, Calif.

BR TR 5'9" 170 lbs.

Year	Team	Games	BA	SA	AB	H	2B	3B	HR	HR%	R	RBI	BB	SO	SB	AB	H	PO	A	E	DP	TC/G	FA	G by Pos
1942	BOS N	145	.255	.347	577	147	29	3	6	1.0	63	55	38	61	15	3	1	240	210	32	16	3.3	.934	3B-98, OF-44
1946		115	.255	.323	372	95	15	2	4	0.5	37	42	30	44	1	8	1	133	186	21	19	3.0	.938	3B-81, SS-18, OF-14
1947		83	.206	.254	209	43	4	0	2	1.0	16	21	22	20	2	2	0	105	152	18	22	3.3	.935	SS-62, OF-8, 3B-6
1950	PIT N	65	.258	.404	198	51	11	0	6	3.0	23	27	19	17	2	12	6	48	101	12	6	2.5	.925	3B-52
4 yrs.		408	.248	.334	1356	336	59	5	16	1.2	139	145	109	142	20	25	8	526	649	83	63	3.1	.934	3B-237, SS-80, OF-66

Tony Fernandez

FERNANDEZ, OCTAVIO ANTONIO
Born Octavio Antonio Fernandez y Castro.
B. Aug. 6, 1962, San Pedro de Macoris, Dominican Republic

BB TR 6'1" 160 lbs.

Year	Team	Games	BA	SA	AB	H	2B	3B	HR	HR%	R	RBI	BB	SO	SB	AB	H	PO	A	E	DP	TC/G	FA	G by Pos
1983	TOR A	15	.265	.353	34	9	1	1	0	0.0	5	2	2	2	0	2	1	16	17	0	6	2.2	1.000	SS-13, DH-1
1984		88	.270	.356	233	63	5	3	3	1.3	29	19	17	15	5	6	1	119	195	9	41	3.7	.972	SS-73, 3B-10, DH-1
1985		161	.289	.390	564	163	31	10	2	0.4	71	51	43	41	13	3	1	283	478	30	109	4.9	.962	SS-160
1986		163	.310	.428	687	213	33	9	10	1.5	91	65	27	52	25	1	1	294	445	13	103	4.6	.983	SS-163
1987		146	.322	.426	578	186	29	8	5	0.9	90	67	51	48	32	1	0	270	396	14	88	4.7	.979	SS-146
1988		154	.287	.386	648	186	41	4	5	0.8	76	70	45	65	15	0	0	247	470	14	106	4.7	.981	SS-154

Year	Team	Games	BA	SA	AB	H	2B	3B	HR	HR%	R	RBI	BB	SO	SB	Pinch Hit AB	Pinch Hit H	PO	A	E	DP	TC/G	FA	G by Pos

Tony Fernandez *continued*

Year	Team	Games	BA	SA	AB	H	2B	3B	HR	HR%	R	RBI	BB	SO	SB	AB	H	PO	A	E	DP	TC/G	FA	G by Pos
1989		140	.257	.389	573	147	25	9	11	1.9	64	64	29	51	22	0	0	260	475	6	93	5.3	.992	SS-140
7 yrs.		867	.292	.400	3317	967	165	44	36	1.1	426	338	214	274	112	13	4	1489	2476	86	546	4.7	.979	SS-849, 3B-10, DH-2

LEAGUE CHAMPIONSHIP SERIES

1985	TOR A	7	.333	.417	24	8	2	0	0	0.0	2	2	1	2	0	0	0	11	14	2	2	3.9	.926	SS-7
1989		5	.350	.500	20	7	3	0	0	0.0	6	1	1	2	5	0	0	9	15	0	3	4.8	1.000	SS-5
2 yrs.		12	.341	.455	44	15	5	0	0	0.0	8	3	2	4	5	0	0	20	29	2	5	4.3	.961	SS-12

Al Ferrara

FERRARA, ALFRED JOHN (The Bull)
B. Dec. 22, 1939, Brooklyn, N. Y.

BR TR 6'1" 200 lbs.

1963	LA N	21	.159	.227	44	7	0	0	1	2.3	2	1	6	9	0	8	1	18	1	1	0	1.0	.950	OF-11
1965		41	.210	.296	81	17	2	1	1	1.2	5	10	9	20	0	12	3	38	0	3	0	1.0	.927	OF-27
1966		63	.270	.435	115	31	4	0	5	4.3	15	23	9	35	0	31	5	43	0	2	0	0.7	.956	OF-32
1967		122	.277	.467	347	96	16	1	16	4.6	41	50	33	73	0	28	5	135	1	3	0	1.1	.978	OF-94
1968		2	.143	.143	7	1	0	0	0	0.0	0	0	0	2	0	0	0	1	0	1	0	1.0	.500	OF-2
1969	SD N	138	.260	.440	366	95	22	1	14	3.8	39	56	45	69	0	38	7	131	5	6	2	1.0	.958	OF-96
1970		138	.277	.444	372	103	15	4	13	3.5	44	51	46	63	0	36	9	119	2	4	0	0.9	.968	OF-96
1971	2 teams	SD N (17G – .118)		CIN N	(32G – .182)																			
"	total	49	.160	.240	50	8	1	0	1	2.0	2	7	8	15	0	37	6	8	0	0	0	0.2	1.000	OF-7
8 yrs.		574	.259	.423	1382	358	60	7	51	3.7	148	198	156	286	0	190	36	493	9	20	2	0.9	.962	OF-365

WORLD SERIES

| 1966 | LA N | 1 | 1.000 | 1.000 | 1 | 1 | 0 | 0 | 0 | 0.0 | 0 | 0 | 0 | 0 | 0 | 1 | 1 | 0 | 0 | 0 | 0 | 0.0 | – | |

Mike Ferraro

FERRARO, MICHAEL DENNIS
B. Aug. 14, 1944, Kingston, N. Y.
Manager 1983, 1986.

BR TR 5'11" 175 lbs.

1966	NY A	10	.179	.179	28	5	0	0	0	0.0	4	0	3	3	0	0	0	4	21	2	3	2.7	.926	3B-10
1968		23	.161	.184	87	14	0	1	0	0.0	5	1	2	17	0	1	0	16	61	2	3	3.4	.975	3B-22
1969	SEA A	4	.000	.000	4	0	0	0	0	0.0	0	0	1	0	0	4	0	0	0	0	0	0.0	–	
1972	MIL A	124	.255	.323	381	97	18	1	2	0.5	19	29	17	41	0	9	2	94	174	14	16	2.3	.950	3B-115, SS-1
4 yrs.		162	.232	.288	500	116	18	2	2	0.4	28	30	23	61	0	14	2	114	256	18	22	2.4	.954	3B-147, SS-1

Rick Ferrell

FERRELL, RICHARD BENJAMIN
Brother of Wes Ferrell.
B. Oct. 12, 1905, Durham, N. C.
Hall of Fame 1984.

BR TR 5'10" 160 lbs.

1929	STL A	64	.229	.285	144	33	6	1	0	0.0	21	20	32	10	1	16	2	140	35	7	3	2.8	.962	C-45
1930		101	.268	.360	314	84	18	4	1	0.3	43	41	46	10	1	0	0	336	66	7	5	4.0	.983	C-101
1931		117	.306	.427	386	118	30	4	3	0.8	47	57	56	12	2	7	3	412	86	14	11	4.4	.973	C-108
1932		126	.315	.420	438	138	30	5	2	0.5	67	65	66	18	5	6	1	486	78	8	9	4.5	.986	C-120
1933	2 teams	STL A	(22G – .250)		BOS A	(118G – .297)																		
"	total	140	.290	.373	493	143	21	4	4	0.8	58	77	70	23	4	3	1	591	92	7	10	4.9	.990	C-137
1934	BOS A	132	.297	.389	437	130	29	4	1	0.2	50	48	66	20	0	5	1	531	72	6	7	4.6	.990	C-128
1935		133	.301	.413	458	138	34	4	3	0.7	54	61	65	15	4	0	0	520	79	13	12	4.6	.979	C-131
1936		121	.312	.461	410	128	27	5	8	2.0	59	55	65	17	0	1	0	556	55	8	5	5.1	.987	C-121
1937	2 teams	BOS A	(18G – .308)		WAS A	(86G – .229)																		
"	total	104	.244	.285	344	84	8	0	2	0.6	39	36	65	22	1	4	0	434	52	6	6	4.7	.988	C-102
1938	WAS A	135	.292	.382	411	120	24	5	1	0.2	55	58	75	17	1	4	0	512	69	11	15	4.4	.981	C-131
1939		87	.281	.336	274	77	13	1	0	0.0	32	31	41	12	1	4	0	327	46	9	9	4.4	.976	C-83
1940		103	.273	.340	326	89	18	2	0	0.0	35	28	47	15	1	4	0	427	67	10	5	4.9	.980	C-99
1941	2 teams	WAS A	(21G – .273)		STL A	(100G – .252)																		
"	total	121	.256	.336	387	99	19	3	2	0.5	38	36	67	26	3	3	0	425	64	4	12	4.1	.992	C-119
1942	STL A	99	.223	.253	273	61	6	1	0	0.0	20	26	33	13	0	3	0	356	57	6	7	4.2	.986	C-95
1943		74	.239	.273	209	50	7	0	0	0.0	12	20	34	14	0	3	1	327	52	5	7	5.2	.987	C-70
1944	WAS A	99	.277	.316	339	94	11	1	0	0.0	14	25	46	13	2	1	0	403	71	9	8	4.9	.981	C-96
1945		91	.266	.325	286	76	12	1	1	0.3	33	38	43	13	2	8	2	331	64	4	3	4.4	.990	C-83
1947		37	.303	.414	99	30	11	0	0	0.0	10	12	14	7	0	0	0	134	22	1	5	4.2	.994	C-37
18 yrs.		1884	.281	.363	6028	1692	324	45	28	0.5	687	734	931	277	29	73	11	7248	1127	135	139	4.5	.984	C-1806

Wes Ferrell

FERRELL, WESLEY CHEEK
Brother of Rick Ferrell.
B. Feb. 2, 1908, Greensboro, N. C. D. Dec. 9, 1976, Sarasota, Fla.

BR TR 6'2" 195 lbs.

1927	CLE A	1	–	–	0	0	0	0	0	–	0	0	0	0	0	0	0	0	0	0	0	0.0	–	P-1
1928		2	.250	.750	4	1	0	0	0	0.0	0	0	0	0	0	0	0	1	4	0	0	2.5	1.000	P-2
1929		47	.237	.387	93	22	5	3	1	1.1	12	12	6	28	1	4	2	10	63	2	3	1.6	.973	P-43
1930		53	.297	.415	118	35	8	3	0	0.0	19	14	12	15	0	7	3	19	39	2	0	1.1	.967	P-43
1931		48	.319	.621	116	37	6	1	9	7.8	24	30	10	21	0	7	0	19	74	3	2	2.0	.969	P-40
1932		55	.242	.359	128	31	5	2	2	1.6	14	18	6	21	0	17	4	14	59	1	1	1.3	.986	P-38
1933		61	.271	.471	140	38	7	0	7	5.0	26	26	20	22	0	14	2	43	49	0	5	1.5	1.000	P-28, OF-13
1934	BOS A	34	.282	.487	78	22	4	0	4	5.1	12	17	7	15	1	8	3	8	23	1	2	0.9	.969	P-26
1935		75	.347	.533	150	52	5	1	7	4.7	25	32	21	16	0	32	9	9	76	2	1	1.2	.977	P-41
1936		61	.267	.437	135	36	6	1	5	3.7	20	24	14	10	0	19	0	9	42	2	2	0.9	.962	P-39
1937	2 teams	BOS A	(18G – .364)		WAS A	(53G – .255)																		
"	total	71	.281	.353	139	39	7	0	1	0.7	14	25	16	21	0	28	8	11	55	2	4	1.0	.971	P-37
1938	2 teams	WAS A	(26G – .224)		NY A	(5G – .167)																		
"	total	31	.213	.311	61	13	3	0	1	1.6	7	7	16	11	0	2	0	10	41	2	6	1.7	.962	P-28
1939	NY A	3	.125	.250	8	1	1	0	0	0.0	0	1	0	2	0	0	0	4	0	0	1	1.3	1.000	P-3
1940	BKN N	2	.000	.000	2	0	0	0	0	0.0	0	0	0	0	0	1	0	0	3	0	0	1.5	1.000	P-1
1941	BOS N	4	.500	1.250	4	2	0	0	1	25.0	1	2	0	0	0	0	0	1	0	0	0	0.3	1.000	P-4
15 yrs.		548	.280	.446	1176	329	57	12	38	3.2	175	208	129	185	2	139	31	153	533	17	31	1.3	.976	P-374, OF-13

Year	Team		Games	BA	SA	AB	H	2B	3B	HR	HR%	R	RBI	BB	SO	SB	Pinch Hit AB	H	PO	A	E	DP	TC/G	FA	G by Pos

Sergio Ferrer

FERRER, SERGIO
Born Sergio Ferrer y Marrero.
B. Jan. 29, 1951, Santurce, Puerto Rico

BB TR 5'7" 145 lbs.

Year	Team		Games	BA	SA	AB	H	2B	3B	HR	HR%	R	RBI	BB	SO	SB	PH AB	H	PO	A	E	DP	TC/G	FA	G by Pos
1974	MIN	A	24	.281	.351	57	16	0	2	0	0.0	12	0	8	6	3	1	0	18	37	9	7	2.7	.859	SS-20, 2B-1
1975			32	.247	.309	81	20	3	1	0	0.0	14	2	3	11	3	0	0	32	62	6	12	3.1	.940	SS-18, 2B-10, DH-2
1978	NY	N	37	.212	.273	33	7	0	1	0	0.0	8	1	4	7	1	0	0	27	48	2	9	2.1	.974	SS-29, 2B-3, 3B-2
1979			32	.000	.000	7	0	0	0	0	0.0	7	0	2	3	0	0	0	8	10	1	3	0.6	.947	3B-12, SS-5, 2B-4
4 yrs.			125	.242	.303	178	43	3	4	0	0.0	41	3	17	27	7	2	0	85	157	18	31	2.1	.931	SS-72, 2B-18, 3B-14, DH-2

Hobe Ferris

FERRIS, ALBERT SAYLES
B. Dec. 7, 1877, Providence, R. I. D. Mar. 18, 1938, Detroit, Mich.

BR TR 5'8" 162 lbs.

Year	Team		Games	BA	SA	AB	H	2B	3B	HR	HR%	R	RBI	BB	SO	SB	PH AB	H	PO	A	E	DP	TC/G	FA	G by Pos
1901	BOS	A	138	.250	.350	523	131	16	15	2	0.4	68	63	23		13	0	0	359	450	61	68	6.3	.930	2B-138, SS-1
1902			134	.244	.381	499	122	16	14	8	1.6	57	63	21		11	0	0	312	461	39	59	6.1	.952	2B-134
1903			141	.251	.366	525	132	19	7	9	1.7	69	66	25		11	0	0	319	441	40	51	5.7	.950	2B-139, SS-2
1904			156	.213	.306	563	120	23	10	3	0.5	50	63	23		7	0	0	366	460	33	42	5.5	.962	2B-156
1905			141	.220	.361	523	115	24	16	6	1.1	51	59	23		11	0	0	321	425	31	38	5.5	.960	2B-140, OF-1
1906			130	.244	.360	495	121	25	13	2	0.4	47	44	10		8	0	0	323	386	31	42	5.7	.958	2B-126, 3B-4
1907			150	.241	.314	561	135	25	2	4	0.7	41	60	10		11	0	0	424	459	30	43	6.1	.967	2B-150
1908	STL	A	148	.270	.353	555	150	26	7	2	0.4	54	74	14		6	0	0	222	316	27	27	3.8	.952	3B-148
1909			148	.216	.282	556	120	18	5	3	0.5	36	58	12		11	0	0	249	330	36	28	4.2	.941	3B-114, 2B-34
9 yrs.			1286	.239	.340	4800	1146	192	89	39	0.8	473	550	161		89	0	0	2895	3728	328	398	5.4	.953	2B-1017, 3B-266, SS-3, OF-1

WORLD SERIES

Year	Team		Games	BA	SA	AB	H	2B	3B	HR	HR%	R	RBI	BB	SO	SB	PH AB	H	PO	A	E	DP	TC/G	FA	G by Pos
1903	BOS	A	8	.290	.355	31	9	1	0	0	0.0	3	7	0	5	0	0	0	17	19	2	2	4.8	.947	2B-8

Boo Ferriss

FERRISS, DAVID MEADOW
B. Dec. 5, 1921, Shaw, Miss.

BL TR 6'2" 208 lbs.

Year	Team		Games	BA	SA	AB	H	2B	3B	HR	HR%	R	RBI	BB	SO	SB	PH AB	H	PO	A	E	DP	TC/G	FA	G by Pos
1945	BOS	A	61	.267	.367	120	32	7	1	1	0.8	16	19	19	11	0	20	5	22	67	2	10	1.5	.978	P-35
1946			45	.209	.261	115	24	6	0	0	0.0	12	7	7	19	0	4	1	25	43	1	5	1.5	.986	P-40
1947			52	.273	.384	99	27	5	3	0	0.0	11	19	7	10	0	17	4	13	33	2	2	0.9	.958	P-33
1948			31	.243	.270	37	9	1	0	0	0.0	4	6	6	6	0	0	0	10	21	0	1	1.0	1.000	P-31
1949			4	1.000	2.000	1	1	1	0	0	0.0	1	1	0	0	0	0	0	1	0	0	0	0.3	1.000	P-4
1950			1			0	0	0	0	0	–	0	0	0	0	0	0	0	0	0	0	0	0.0		P-1
6 yrs.			194	.250	.333	372	93	20	4	1	0.3	44	52	39	46	0	41	10	71	164	5	18	1.2	.979	P-144

WORLD SERIES

Year	Team		Games	BA	SA	AB	H	2B	3B	HR	HR%	R	RBI	BB	SO	SB	PH AB	H	PO	A	E	DP	TC/G	FA	G by Pos
1946	BOS	A	2	.000	.000	6	0	0	0	0	0.0	0	0	0	1	0	0	0	0	3	0	0	1.5	1.000	P-2

Willy Fetzer

FETZER, WILLIAM McKINNON
B. June 24, 1884, Concord, N. C. D. May 3, 1959, Butner, N. C.

BL TR 5'10½" 180 lbs.

Year	Team		Games	BA	SA	AB	H	2B	3B	HR	HR%	R	RBI	BB	SO	SB	PH AB	H	PO	A	E	DP	TC/G	FA	G by Pos
1906	PHI	A	1	.000	.000	1	0	0	0	0	0.0	0	0	0	0	0	1	0	0	0	0	0	0.0	–	

Chick Fewster

FEWSTER, WILSON LLOYD
B. Nov. 10, 1895, Baltimore, Md. D. Apr. 16, 1945, Baltimore, Md.

BR TR 5'11" 160 lbs.

Year	Team		Games	BA	SA	AB	H	2B	3B	HR	HR%	R	RBI	BB	SO	SB	PH AB	H	PO	A	E	DP	TC/G	FA	G by Pos
1917	NY	A	11	.222	.222	36	8	0	0	0	0.0	2	1	5	5	1	0	0	26	31	5	5	5.6	.919	2B-11
1918			5	.500	.500	2	1	0	0	0	0.0	1	0	0	0	0	1	0	0	0	0	0	0.0	–	2B-2
1919			81	.283	.357	244	69	9	3	1	0.4	38	15	34	36	8	7	3	126	86	18	10	2.8	.922	OF-41, SS-23, 2B-4, 3B-2
1920			21	.286	.333	21	6	1	0	0	0.0	8	1	7	2	4	1	0	9	13	4	1	1.2	.846	SS-5, 2B-2
1921			66	.280	.386	207	58	19	0	1	0.5	44	19	28	43	4	4	0	105	59	12	11	2.7	.932	OF-43, 2B-15
1922	2 teams				NY	A (44G – .242)					BOS			A (23G – .289)											
"	total		67	.260	.330	215	56	8	1	0	0.5	28	18	22	33	10	1	0	100	74	6	6	2.7	.967	OF-38, 3B-23, 2B-2
1923	BOS	A	90	.236	.278	284	67	10	1	0	0.0	32	15	39	35	7	1	0	179	240	33	31	5.0	.927	2B-48, SS-36
1924	CLE	A	101	.267	.317	322	86	12	2	0	0.0	36	36	24	36	12	0	0	200	233	17	36	4.5	.962	2B-94, 3B-5
1925			93	.248	.320	294	73	16	1	1	0.3	39	38	36	25	6	2	1	227	250	30	43	5.5	.941	2B-86, 3B-10, OF-1
1926	BKN	N	105	.243	.326	337	82	16	3	2	0.6	53	24	45	49	9	1	0	225	297	26	38	5.2	.953	2B-103
1927			4	.000	.000	1	0	0	0	0	0.0	1	0	0	0	0	1	0	0	0	0	0	0.0	–	
11 yrs.			644	.258	.326	1963	506	91	12	6	0.3	282	167	240	264	57	22	5	1197	1283	151	181	4.1	.943	2B-367, OF-123, SS-64, 3B-40

WORLD SERIES

Year	Team		Games	BA	SA	AB	H	2B	3B	HR	HR%	R	RBI	BB	SO	SB	PH AB	H	PO	A	E	DP	TC/G	FA	G by Pos
1921	NY	A	4	.200	.500	10	2	1	0	1	10.0	3	2	3	3	0	0	0	7	0	0	0	1.8	1.000	OF-4

Neil Fiala

FIALA, NEIL STEPHEN
B. Aug. 24, 1956, St. Louis, Mo.

BL TR 6'1" 185 lbs.

Year	Team		Games	BA	SA	AB	H	2B	3B	HR	HR%	R	RBI	BB	SO	SB	PH AB	H	PO	A	E	DP	TC/G	FA	G by Pos
1981	2 teams		STL	N (3G – .000)		CIN	N (2G – .500)																		
"	total		5	.200	.200	5	1	0	0	0	0.0	1	1	0	2	0	1	0	0	0	0	0	0.0	–	

Jim Field

FIELD, JAMES C.
B. Apr. 24, 1863, Philadelphia, Pa. D. May 13, 1953, Atlantic City, N. J.

Year	Team		Games	BA	SA	AB	H	2B	3B	HR	HR%	R	RBI	BB	SO	SB	PH AB	H	PO	A	E	DP	TC/G	FA	G by Pos
1883	COL	AA	76	.254	.339	295	75	10	6	1	0.3	31		7			0	0	781	10	52	44	11.1	.938	1B-76
1884			105	.233	.317	417	97	9	7	4	1.0	74		23			0	0	1150	27	52	58	11.7	.958	1B-105
1885	2 teams		PIT	AA (56G – .239)		BAL	AA (38G – .208)																		
"	total		94	.227	.286	353	80	12	3	1	0.3	44		26			0	0	995	28	38	48	11.3	.964	1B-94
1890	ROC	AA	52	.202	.356	188	38	7	5	4	2.1	30		21		8	0	0	486	13	18	24	9.9	.965	1B-51, P-2
1898	WAS	N	5	.095	.095	21	2	0	0	0	0.0	1	0	0		1	0	0	45	2	1	0	9.6	.979	1B-5
5 yrs.			332	.229	.316	1274	292	38	21	10	0.8	180	0	77		9	0	0	3457	80	161	174	11.1	.956	1B-331, P-2

Sam Field

FIELD, SAMUEL JAY
B. Oct. 12, 1848, Philadelphia, Pa. D. Oct. 28, 1904, Sinking Spring, Pa.

BR TR 5'9½" 182 lbs.

Year	Team		Games	BA	SA	AB	H	2B	3B	HR	HR%	R	RBI	BB	SO	SB	PH AB	H	PO	A	E	DP	TC/G	FA	G by Pos
1876	CIN	N	4	.000	.000	14	0	0	0	0	0.0	2	0	1		3	0	0	10	1	5	0	4.0	.688	C-3, 2B-2

Year	Team		Games	BA	SA	AB	H	2B	3B	HR	HR%	R	RBI	BB	SO	SB	Pinch Hit AB	Pinch Hit H	PO	A	E	DP	TC/G	FA	G by Pos

Cecil Fielder

FIELDER, CECIL GRANT
B. Sept. 21, 1963, Los Angeles, Calif.   BR TR 6'3"   230 lbs.

Year	Team		Games	BA	SA	AB	H	2B	3B	HR	HR%	R	RBI	BB	SO	SB	PH AB	PH H	PO	A	E	DP	TC/G	FA	G by Pos
1985	TOR	A	30	.311	.527	74	23	4	0	4	5.4	6	16	6	16	0	4	1	171	17	4	21	6.4	.979	1B-25
1986			34	.157	.325	83	13	2	0	4	4.8	7	13	6	27	0	9	1	37	4	1	3	1.2	.976	DH-22, 1B-7, 3B-2, OF-1
1987			82	.269	.560	175	47	7	1	14	8.0	30	32	20	48	0	19	4	98	6	0	12	1.3	1.000	DH-55, 1B-16, 3B-2
1988			74	.230	.431	174	40	6	1	9	5.2	24	23	14	53	0	21	5	101	12	1	10	1.5	.991	1B-17, 3B-3, 2B-2
4 yrs.			220	.243	.472	506	123	19	2	31	6.1	67	84	46	144	0	53	11	407	39	6	46	2.1	.987	DH-77, 1B-65, 3B-7, 2B-2, OF-1

LEAGUE CHAMPIONSHIP SERIES

| 1985 | TOR | A | 3 | .333 | .667 | 3 | 1 | 1 | 0 | 0 | 0.0 | 0 | 0 | 0 | 1 | 0 | 3 | 1 | 0 | 0 | 0 | 0 | 0.0 | – | |

Bruce Fields

FIELDS, BRUCE ALAN
B. Oct. 6, 1960, Cleveland, Ohio   BL TR 6'   185 lbs.

1986	DET	A	16	.279	.349	43	12	1	1	0	0.0	4	6	1	6	1	2	1	25	0	1	0	1.6	.962	OF-14, DH-1
1988	SEA	A	39	.269	.388	67	18	5	0	1	1.5	8	5	4	11	0	12	3	23	0	0	0	0.6	1.000	OF-23, DH-6
1989			3	.333	.667	3	1	1	0	0	0.0	2	0	0	1	0	2	1	0	0	0	0	0.0	–	OF-1
3 yrs.			58	.274	.381	113	31	7	1	1	0.9	14	11	5	18	1	16	5	48	0	1	0	0.8	.980	OF-38, DH-7

Jocko Fields

FIELDS, JOHN JOSEPH
B. Oct. 20, 1864, Cork, Ireland D. Oct. 14, 1950, Jersey City, N. J.   BR TR 5'10"   160 lbs.

1887	PIT	N	43	.268	.348	164	44	9	2	4			26	17	7	13	7	0	0	141	29	18	2	4.4	.904	OF-27, C-14, 1B-3, 3B-1, P-1
1888			45	.195	.278	169	33	7	2	1	0.6	22	15	8	19	9	0	0	103	25	24	2	3.4	.842	OF-29, C-14, 3B-3
1889			75	.311	.443	289	90	22	5	2	0.7	41	43	29	30	7	0	0	159	30	28	3	2.9	.871	OF-60, C-16
1890	PIT	P	126	.283	.445	526	149	18	20	9	1.7	101	86	57	52	24	0	0	286	107	60	13	3.6	.868	OF-80, 2B-30, C-15, SS-4
1891	2 teams		PIT N (23G – .240)			PHI N (8G – .233)																			
"	total		31	.238	.305	105	25	1	2	0	0.0	14	10	14	15	1	0	0	96	41	24	0	5.2	.851	C-23, SS-8
1892	NY	N	21	.273	.394	66	18	4	2	0	0.0	8	5	9	10	2	0	0	61	19	13	2	4.4	.860	OF-11, C-10
6 yrs.			341	.272	.397	1319	359	65	32	12	0.9	212	176	124	139	50	0	0	846	251	167	22	3.7	.868	OF-207, C-92, 2B-30, SS-12, 3B-4, 1B-3, P-1

Jesus Figueroa

FIGUEROA, JESUS MARIA
Born Jesus Maria Figueroa y Figueroa.
B. Feb. 20, 1957, Santo Domingo, Dominican Republic   BL TL 5'10"   160 lbs.

| 1980 | CHI | N | 115 | .253 | .293 | 198 | 50 | 5 | 0 | 1 | 0.5 | 20 | 11 | 14 | 16 | 2 | 53 | 15 | 89 | 6 | 2 | 2 | 0.8 | .979 | OF-57 |

Sam File

FILE, LAWRENCE SAMUEL
B. May 18, 1922, Chester, Pa.   BR TR 5'11"   160 lbs.

| 1940 | PHI | N | 7 | .077 | .077 | 13 | 1 | 0 | 0 | 0 | 0.0 | 0 | 1 | 0 | 2 | 0 | 0 | 0 | 5 | 14 | 3 | 2 | 3.1 | .864 | SS-6, 3B-1 |

Steve Filipowicz

FILIPOWICZ, STEPHEN CHARLES (Flip)
B. June 28, 1921, Donora, Pa. D. Feb. 21, 1975, Wilkes-Barre, Pa.   BR TR 5'8"   195 lbs.

1944	NY	N	15	.195	.293	41	8	2	1	0	0.0	10	7	3	7	0	1	0	20	0	0	0	1.3	1.000	OF-10, C-1
1945			35	.205	.304	112	23	5	0	2	1.8	14	16	4	13	0	3	0	42	1	3	0	1.3	.935	OF-31
1948	CIN	N	7	.346	.423	26	9	0	1	0	0.0	0	3	2	1	0	0	0	10	1	0	0	1.6	1.000	OF-7
3 yrs.			57	.223	.318	179	40	7	2	2	1.1	24	26	9	21	0	4	0	72	2	3	0	1.4	.961	OF-48, C-1

Jack Fimple

FIMPLE, JOHN JOSEPH
B. Feb. 10, 1959, Darby, Pa.   BR TR 6'2"   185 lbs.

1983	LA	N	54	.250	.358	148	37	8	1	2	1.4	16	22	11	39	1	0	0	336	32	4	2	6.9	.989	C-54
1984			12	.192	.231	26	5	1	0	0	0.0	2	3	1	6	0	0	0	54	4	1	0	4.9	.983	C-12
1986			13	.077	.077	13	1	0	0	0	0.0	2	2	6	6	0	3	0	30	4	0	0	2.6	1.000	C-7, 2B-1, 1B-1
1987	CAL	A	13	.200	.200	10	2	0	0	0	0.0	1	1	1	2	0	0	0	18	3	2	0	1.8	.913	C-13
4 yrs.			92	.228	.315	197	45	9	1	2	1.0	21	28	19	53	1	3	0	438	43	7	2	5.3	.986	C-86, 2B-1, 1B-1

LEAGUE CHAMPIONSHIP SERIES

| 1983 | LA | N | 3 | .143 | .143 | 7 | 1 | 0 | 0 | 0 | 0.0 | 0 | 1 | 0 | 3 | 0 | 0 | 0 | 14 | 0 | 0 | 0 | 5.3 | 1.000 | C-3 |

Jim Finigan

FINIGAN, JAMES LEROY
B. Aug. 19, 1928, Quincy, Ill. D. May 16, 1981, Quincy, Ill.   BR TR 5'11"   175 lbs.

1954	PHI	A	136	.302	.421	487	147	25	6	7	1.4	57	51	64	66	2	1	0	151	305	25	34	3.5	.948	3B-136
1955	KC	A	150	.255	.385	545	139	30	7	9	1.7	72	68	61	49	1	2	1	291	363	20	85	4.5	.970	2B-90, 3B-59
1956			91	.216	.284	250	54	7	2	2	0.8	29	21	30	28	3	9	0	143	175	16	42	3.7	.952	2B-52, 3B-32
1957	DET	A	64	.270	.316	174	47	4	2	0	0.0	20	17	23	18	1	3	0	66	112	9	11	2.9	.952	3B-59, 2B-3
1958	SF	N	23	.200	.280	25	5	2	0	0	0.0	3	1	3	5	0	12	2	4	10	2	2	0.7	.875	2B-8, 3B-4
1959	BAL	A	48	.252	.328	119	30	6	0	1	0.8	14	10	9	10	1	5	2	36	75	4	6	2.4	.965	3B-42, 2B-6, SS-2
6 yrs.			512	.264	.367	1600	422	74	17	19	1.2	195	168	190	176	8	32	5	691	1040	76	180	3.5	.958	3B-332, 2B-159, SS-2

Bill Finley

FINLEY, WILLIAM JAMES
B. Oct. 4, 1863, New York, N. Y. D. Oct. 6, 1912, Asbury Park, N. J.

| 1886 | NY | N | 13 | .182 | .182 | 44 | 8 | 0 | 0 | 0 | 0.0 | 2 | 5 | 1 | 8 | | 0 | 0 | 29 | 10 | 5 | 1 | 3.4 | .886 | OF-8, C-8 |

Bob Finley

FINLEY, ROBERT EDWARD
B. Nov. 25, 1915, Ennis, Tex. D. Jan. 2, 1986, West Covina, Calif.   BR TR 6'1"   200 lbs.

1943	PHI	N	28	.259	.321	81	21	2	0	1	1.2	9	7	4	10	0	4	1	78	23	4	0	3.8	.962	C-24
1944			94	.249	.306	281	70	11	1	1	0.4	18	21	12	25	1	20	4	289	34	11	7	3.6	.967	C-74
2 yrs.			122	.251	.309	362	91	13	1	2	0.6	27	28	16	35	1	24	5	367	57	15	7	3.6	.966	C-98

Steve Finley

FINLEY, STEVEN ALLEN
B. May 12, 1965, Union City, Tenn.   BL TL 6'2"   175 lbs.

| 1989 | BAL | A | 81 | .249 | .318 | 217 | 54 | 5 | 2 | 2 | 0.9 | 35 | 25 | 15 | 30 | 17 | 5 | 1 | 144 | 1 | 2 | 0 | 1.8 | .986 | OF-76, DH-3 |

Year	Team		Games	BA	SA	AB	H	2B	3B	HR	HR%	R	RBI	BB	SO	SB	Pinch Hit AB	Pinch Hit H	PO	A	E	DP	TC/G	FA	G by Pos

Mickey Finn

FINN, CORNELIUS FRANCIS (Neal)
B. Jan. 24, 1904, Brooklyn, N. Y.   D. July 7, 1933, Allentown, Pa.
BR TR 5'11" 168 lbs.

Year	Team		Games	BA	SA	AB	H	2B	3B	HR	HR%	R	RBI	BB	SO	SB	AB	H	PO	A	E	DP	TC/G	FA	G by Pos
1930	BKN	N	87	.278	.359	273	76	13	0	3	1.1	42	30	26	18	3	2	0	182	235	23	63	5.1	.948	2B-81
1931			118	.274	.337	413	113	22	2	0	0.0	46	45	21	42	2	4	1	260	331	15	65	5.1	.975	2B-112
1932			65	.238	.286	189	45	5	2	0	0.0	22	14	11	15	2	3	2	36	96	9	8	2.2	.936	3B-50, 2B-2, SS-1
1933	PHI	N	51	.237	.272	169	40	4	1	0	0.0	15	13	10	14	2	0	0	107	164	10	34	5.5	.964	2B-51
4 yrs.			321	.262	.323	1044	274	44	5	3	0.3	125	102	68	89	9	9	3	585	826	57	170	4.6	.961	2B-246, 3B-50, SS-1

Hal Finney

FINNEY, HAROLD WILSON
Brother of Lou Finney.
B. July 7, 1905, Lafayette, Ala.
BR TR 5'11" 170 lbs.

Year	Team		Games	BA	SA	AB	H	2B	3B	HR	HR%	R	RBI	BB	SO	SB	AB	H	PO	A	E	DP	TC/G	FA	G by Pos
1931	PIT	N	10	.308	.346	26	8	1	0	0	0.0	2	2	0	1	1	4	0	18	3	0	1	2.1	1.000	C-6
1932			31	.212	.303	33	7	3	0	0	0.0	14	4	3	4	0	0	0	30	3	1	0	1.1	.971	C-11
1933			56	.233	.301	133	31	4	1	1	0.8	17	18	3	19	0	7	3	122	12	1	4	2.4	.993	C-47
1934			5	–	–	0	0	0	0	0	–	3	0	0	0	0	0	0	0	0	0	0	0.0	–	C-5
1936			21	.000	.000	35	0	0	0	0	0.0	3	3	0	8	0	0	0	38	5	2	1	2.1	.956	C-14
5 yrs.			123	.203	.260	227	46	8	1	1	0.4	39	27	6	32	1	11	3	208	23	4	6	1.9	.983	C-83

Lou Finney

FINNEY, LOUIS KLOPSCHE
Brother of Hal Finney.
B. Aug. 13, 1910, Buffalo, Ala.   D. Apr. 22, 1966, Lafayette, Ala.
BL TR 6' 180 lbs.

Year	Team		Games	BA	SA	AB	H	2B	3B	HR	HR%	R	RBI	BB	SO	SB	AB	H	PO	A	E	DP	TC/G	FA	G by Pos
1931	PHI	A	9	.375	.458	24	9	0	0	0	0.0	7	3	6	1	0	1	0	19	1	0	1	2.2	1.000	OF-8
1933			74	.267	.371	240	64	12	2	3	1.3	26	32	13	17	1	12	2	136	6	8	1	2.0	.947	OF-63
1934			92	.279	.360	272	76	11	4	1	0.4	32	28	14	17	4	21	4	232	12	9	17	2.8	.964	OF-54, 1B-15
1935			109	.273	.329	410	112	11	6	0	0.0	45	31	18	18	7	14	3	316	15	9	18	3.1	.974	OF-76, 1B-18
1936			151	.302	.377	**653**	197	26	10	1	0.2	100	41	47	22	7	1	0	961	37	13	71	6.7	.987	1B-78, OF-73
1937			92	.251	.343	379	95	14	9	1	0.3	53	20	20	16	2	3	0	519	31	12	39	6.1	.979	1B-50, OF-39, 2B-1
1938			122	.275	.441	454	125	21	12	10	2.2	61	48	39	25	5	14	5	698	28	9	35	6.0	.988	1B-64, OF-46
1939	2 teams		104	.310	.410	271	84	18	3	1	0.4	44	47	26	11	2	**40**	**13**	340	12	6	28	3.4	.983	1B-32, OF-28
"	total	PHI A (9G – .136)				BOS A (95G – .325)																			
1940	BOS	A	130	.320	.463	534	171	31	15	5	0.9	73	73	33	13	5	9	1	652	33	7	41	5.3	.990	OF-69, 1B-51
1941			127	.288	.400	497	143	24	10	4	0.8	83	53	38	17	2	10	5	395	22	14	10	3.4	.968	OF-92, 1B-24
1942			113	.285	.383	397	113	16	7	3	0.8	58	61	29	11	3	15	3	221	8	5	3	2.1	.979	OF-95, 1B-2
1944			68	.287	.347	251	72	11	2	0	0.0	37	32	23	7	1	6	1	528	24	7	53	8.2	.987	1B-59, OF-2
1945	2 teams		59	.274	.377	215	59	8	4	2	0.9	24	22	21	7	0	3	0	234	18	3	14	4.3	.988	OF-36, 1B-22, 3B-1
"	total	BOS A (2G – .000)				STL A (57G – .277)																			
1946	STL	A	16	.300	.300	30	9	0	0	0	0.0	0	3	2	4	0	6	4	14	1	1	0	1.0	.938	OF-7
1947	PHI	N	4	.000	.000	4	0	0	0	0	0.0	0	0	0	0	0	4	0	0	0	0	0	0.0	–	
15 yrs.			1270	.287	.388	4631	1329	203	85	31	0.7	643	494	329	186	39	159	41	5265	248	103	331	4.4	.982	OF-688, 1B-415, 3B-1, 2B-1

Mike Fiore

FIORE, MICHAEL GARY JOSEPH (Lefty)
B. Oct. 11, 1944, Brooklyn, N. Y.
BL TL 6' 175 lbs.

Year	Team		Games	BA	SA	AB	H	2B	3B	HR	HR%	R	RBI	BB	SO	SB	AB	H	PO	A	E	DP	TC/G	FA	G by Pos
1968	BAL	A	6	.059	.059	17	1	0	0	0	0.0	2	0	4	4	0	0	0	31	3	2	7	6.0	.944	1B-5, OF-1
1969	KC	A	107	.274	.428	339	93	14	1	12	3.5	53	35	84	63	4	5	4	709	94	11	54	7.6	.986	1B-91, OF-13
1970	2 teams		66	.164	.180	122	20	2	0	0	0.0	11	8	21	28	1	26	5	191	22	3	14	3.3	.986	1B-37, OF-2
"	total	KC A (25G – .181)				BOS A (41G – .140)																			
1971	BOS	A	51	.177	.258	62	11	2	0	1	1.6	9	6	12	14	0	33	8	74	5	0	8	1.5	1.000	1B-12
1972	2 teams		24	.063	.063	16	1	0	0	0	0.0	0	1	3	6	0	16	1	7	0	0	2	0.3	1.000	1B-6, OF-1
"	total	STL N (17G – .100)				SD N (7G – .000)																			
5 yrs.			254	.227	.333	556	126	18	1	13	2.3	75	50	124	115	5	80	18	1012	124	16	85	4.5	.986	1B-151, OF-17

Dan Firova

FIROVA, DANIEL MICHAEL
B. Oct. 16, 1956, Refugio, Tex.
BR TR 6' 185 lbs.

Year	Team		Games	BA	SA	AB	H	2B	3B	HR	HR%	R	RBI	BB	SO	SB	AB	H	PO	A	E	DP	TC/G	FA	G by Pos
1981	SEA	A	13	.000	.000	2	0	0	0	0	0.0	0	0	0	1	0	0	0	8	0	0	0	0.6	1.000	C-13
1982			3	.000	.000	5	0	0	0	0	0.0	0	0	0	0	0	0	0	8	1	1	0	3.3	.900	C-3
1988	CLE	A	1	–	–	0	0	0	0	0	–	0	0	0	0	0	0	0	0	0	0	0	0.0	–	C-1
3 yrs.			17	.000	.000	7	0	0	0	0	0.0	0	0	0	1	0	0	0	16	1	1	0	1.1	.944	C-17

Bill Fischer

FISCHER, WILLIAM CHARLES
B. Mar. 2, 1891, New York, N. Y.   D. Sept. 4, 1945, Richmond, Va.
BL TR 6' 174 lbs.

Year	Team		Games	BA	SA	AB	H	2B	3B	HR	HR%	R	RBI	BB	SO	SB	AB	H	PO	A	E	DP	TC/G	FA	G by Pos
1913	BKN	N	62	.267	.388	165	44	9	4	1	0.6	16	12	10	5	0	1	0	193	65	7	2	4.3	.974	C-51
1914			43	.257	.305	105	27	1	2	0	0.0	12	8	8	12	1	1	2	136	45	8	6	4.4	.958	C-30
1915	CHI	F	105	.329	.449	292	96	15	4	4	1.4	30	50	24		5	21	7	324	100	12	9	4.2	.972	C-80
1916	2 teams		107	.219	.315	292	64	16	3	2	0.7	26	20	21	11	3	12	0	429	119	15	8	5.3	.973	C-91
"	total	CHI N (65G – .196)				PIT N (42G – .257)																			
1917	PIT	N	95	.286	.376	245	70	9	2	3	1.2	25	25	27	19	11	16	3	279	77	14	8	3.9	.962	C-69, 1B-2
5 yrs.			412	.274	.374	1099	301	50	15	10	0.9	109	115	90	47	20	62	15	1361	406	56	33	4.4	.969	C-321, 1B-2

Mike Fischlin

FISCHLIN, MICHAEL THOMAS
B. Sept. 13, 1955, Sacramento, Calif.
BR TR 6'1" 165 lbs.

Year	Team		Games	BA	SA	AB	H	2B	3B	HR	HR%	R	RBI	BB	SO	SB	AB	H	PO	A	E	DP	TC/G	FA	G by Pos
1977	HOU	N	13	.200	.200	15	3	0	0	0	0.0	0	0	0	0	0	0	0	3	17	0	1	1.5	1.000	SS-12
1978			44	.116	.128	86	10	1	0	0	0.0	3	0	4	9	1	3	0	49	67	9	11	2.8	.928	SS-41
1980			1	.000	.000	1	0	0	0	0	0.0	0	0	0	1	0	0	0	1	0	0	0	1.0	1.000	SS-1
1981	CLE	A	22	.233	.256	43	10	1	0	0	0.0	3	5	3	6	3	0	0	33	39	4	8	3.5	.947	SS-19, 2B-1
1982			112	.268	.319	276	74	12	1	0	0.0	34	21	34	36	9	2	2	142	257	13	43	3.7	.968	SS-101, 3B-8, 2B-6, C-1
1983			95	.209	.276	225	47	5	2	2	0.9	31	23	26	32	9	1	0	169	226	14	59	4.3	.966	2B-71, SS-15, 3B-4, DH-1
1984			85	.226	.308	133	30	4	2	1	0.8	17	14	12	20	2	1	1	104	146	8	30	3.0	.969	2B-58, 3B-17, SS-15
1985			73	.200	.300	60	12	4	1	0	0.0	12	2	5	7	0	0	0	73	89	4	20	2.3	.976	2B-31, SS-22, 1B-6, DH-5, 3B-3
1986	NY	A	71	.206	.225	102	21	2	0	0	0.0	9	3	8	29	0	0	0	63	107	7	18	2.5	.960	SS-42, 2B-27

Year	Team		Games	BA	SA	AB	H	2B	3B	HR	HR%	R	RBI	BB	SO	SB	Pinch Hit AB	Pinch Hit H	PO	A	E	DP	TC/G	FA	G by Pos

Mike Fischlin *continued*

| 1987 | ATL | N | 1 | – | – | 0 | 0 | 0 | 0 | 0 | – | 0 | 0 | 0 | 0 | 0 | 0 | 0 | 0 | 0 | 0 | 0 | 0.0 | – | SS-1 |
| 10 yrs. | | | 517 | .220 | .273 | 941 | 207 | 29 | 6 | 3 | 0.3 | 109 | 68 | 92 | 142 | 24 | 7 | 3 | 637 | 948 | 59 | 190 | 3.2 | .964 | SS-269, 2B-191, 3B-32, DH-6, 1B-6, C-1 |

Sam Fishburn

FISHBURN, SAMUEL E.
B. May 15, 1893, Haverhill, Mass.   D. Apr. 11, 1965, Bethlehem, Pa.   BR TR 5'9'' 157 lbs.

| 1919 | STL | N | 9 | .333 | .500 | 6 | 2 | 1 | 0 | 0 | 0.0 | 0 | 2 | 0 | 0 | 0 | 1 | 1 | 11 | 0 | 0 | 1 | 1.2 | 1.000 | 2B-1, 1B-1 |

John Fishel

FISHEL, JOHN ALAN
B. Nov. 8, 1962, Fullerton, Calif.   BR TR 5'11'' 185 lbs.

| 1988 | HOU | N | 19 | .231 | .346 | 26 | 6 | 0 | 0 | 1 | 3.8 | 1 | 2 | 3 | 6 | 0 | 16 | 3 | 2 | 0 | 0 | 0 | 0.1 | 1.000 | OF-6 |

Fisher

FISHER,
B. Johnstown, Pa.   Deceased.

1884	2 teams		18	.154	.185	65	10	2	0	0	0.0	7		3			0	0	34	19	19	2	4.0	.736	P-8, OF-6, SS-2, 1B-2
"	PHI U (10G – .222)	WIL U (8G – .069)																							
1885	BUF	N	1	.000	.000	4	0	0	0	0	0.0	0	0	0	0	0	0	0	1	3	0	0	4.0	1.000	P-1
2 yrs.			19	.145	.174	69	10	2	0	0	0.0	7	0	3	0		0	0	35	22	19	2	4.0	.750	P-9, OF-6, SS-2, 1B-2

Bob Fisher

FISHER, ROBERT TAYLOR
Brother of Ike Fisher.
B. Nov. 3, 1886, Nashville, Tenn.   D. Aug. 4, 1963, Jacksonville, Fla.   BR TR 5'9½'' 170 lbs.

1912	BKN	N	82	.233	.296	257	60	10	3	0	0.0	27	26	14	32	7	4	0	123	200	30	23	4.3	.915	SS-74, 3B-1, 2B-1
1913			132	.262	.352	474	124	11	10	4	0.8	42	54	10	43	16	11	2	263	364	52	60	5.1	.923	SS-131
1914	CHI	N	15	.300	.420	50	15	2	2	0	0.0	5	5	3	4	2	0	0	20	46	4	3	4.7	.943	SS-15
1915			147	.287	.370	568	163	22	5	5	0.9	70	53	30	51	9	2	0	277	434	51	35	5.2	.933	SS-147
1916	CIN	N	61	.272	.346	136	37	4	3	0	0.0	9	11	8	14	7	25	6	59	84	15	9	2.6	.905	SS-29, 2B-6, OF-1
1918	STL	N	63	.317	.411	246	78	11	3	2	0.8	36	20	15	11	7	0	0	147	232	8	34	6.1	.979	2B-63
1919			3	.273	.364	11	3	1	0	0	0.0	0	1	0	2	0	0	0	9	9	2	2	6.7	.900	2B-3
7 yrs.			503	.276	.359	1742	480	61	26	11	0.6	189	170	80	157	48	42	8	898	1369	162	166	4.8	.933	SS-396, 2B-73, OF-1, 3B-1

Charlie Fisher

FISHER, CHARLES
B. Baltimore, Md.

| 1889 | LOU | AA | 1 | .500 | .500 | 2 | 1 | 0 | 0 | 0 | 0.0 | 0 | 0 | 0 | 0 | 0 | 0 | 0 | 0 | 0 | 0 | 0 | 0.0 | – | OF-1 |

Gus Fisher

FISHER, AUGUST HARRIS
B. Oct. 21, 1885, Pottsborough, Tex.   D. Apr. 8, 1972, Portland, Ore.   BL TR 5'10'' 175 lbs.

1911	CLE	A	70	.261	.320	203	53	6	3	0	0.0	20	12	7		6	10	2	307	96	18	11	6.0	.957	C-58, 1B-1
1912	NY	A	4	.100	.100	10	1	0	0	0	0.0	1	0	0		0	0	0	17	4	0	0	5.3	1.000	C-4
2 yrs.			74	.254	.310	213	54	6	3	0	0.0	21	12	7		6	10	2	324	100	18	11	6.0	.959	C-62, 1B-1

Harry Fisher

FISHER, HARRY C.
B. Philadelphia, Pa.   Deceased.

1884	3 teams		17	.194	.224	67	13	2	0	0	0.0	6		1	3		0	0	26	37	18	2	4.8	.778	3B-10, 2B-6, SS-1, C-1
"	KC U (10G – .200)	CHI U (1G – .667) CLE N (6G – .125)																							
1889	LOU	AA	1	.500	.500	2	1	0	0	0	0.0	0	0	0	0	0	0	0	0	0	0	0	0.0	–	
2 yrs.			18	.203	.232	69	14	2	0	0	0.0	6		1	3		0	0	26	37	18	2	4.5	.778	3B-10, 2B-6, SS-1, C-1

Harry Fisher

FISHER, HARRY DEVERAUX
B. Jan. 3, 1926, Newbury, Ont., Canada   D. Sept. 20, 1981, Waterloo, Ont., Canada   BL TR 6' 180 lbs.

1951	PIT	N	3	.000	.000	3	0	0	0	0	0.0	0	0	0	0	0	3	0	0	0	0	0	0.0	–	P-8
1952			15	.333	.400	15	5	1	0	0	0.0	0	1	0	3	0	7	3	1	1	0	0	0.1	1.000	P-8
2 yrs.			18	.278	.333	18	5	1	0	0	0.0	0	1	0	3	0	10	3	1	1	0	0	0.1	1.000	P-8

Ike Fisher

FISHER, NEWTON
Brother of Bob Fisher.
B. June 28, 1871, Nashville, Tenn.   D. Feb. 28, 1947, Chicago, Ill.   BR TR 5'9½'' 171 lbs.

| 1898 | PHI | N | 9 | .115 | .154 | 26 | 3 | 1 | 0 | 0 | 0.0 | 0 | 0 | 0 | | 1 | 0 | 0 | 24 | 6 | 5 | 1 | 3.9 | .857 | C-8, 3B-1 |

Red Fisher

FISHER, JOHN GUS
B. June 22, 1887, Pittsburgh, Pa.   D. Jan. 31, 1940, Louisville, Ky.   BL TR

| 1910 | STL | A | 23 | .125 | .181 | 72 | 9 | 2 | 1 | 0 | 0.0 | 5 | 3 | 5 | | 3 | 0 | 0 | 27 | 2 | 2 | 0 | 1.3 | .935 | OF-19 |

Showboat Fisher

FISHER, GEORGE ALOYS
B. Jan. 16, 1899, Jennings, Iowa   BL TR 5'10'' 170 lbs.

1923	WAS	A	13	.261	.348	23	6	2	0	0	0.0	4	2	4	3	0	4	1	7	2	3	1	0.9	.750	OF-5
1924			15	.220	.244	41	9	1	0	0	0.0	7	6	6	6	2	4	2	14	0	1	0	1.0	.933	OF-11
1930	STL	N	92	.374	.587	254	95	18	6	8	3.1	49	61	25	21	4	20	8	122	6	5	0	1.4	.962	OF-67
1932	STL	A	18	.182	.182	22	4	0	0	0	0.0	2	2	2	5	0	11	2	6	0	0	0	0.3	1.000	OF-5
4 yrs.			138	.335	.503	340	114	21	6	8	2.4	62	71	37	35	6	39	13	149	8	9	1	1.2	.946	OF-88

WORLD SERIES

| 1930 | STL | N | 2 | .500 | 1.000 | 2 | 1 | 0 | 0 | 0 | 0.0 | 1 | 0 | 2 | 1 | 0 | 2 | 1 | 0 | 0 | 0 | 0 | 0.0 | – | |

Wilbur Fisher

FISHER, WILBUR McCULLOUGH (Levy, hod)
B. July 18, 1894, Greenbottom, W. Va.   D. Oct. 24, 1960, Welch, W. Va.   BL TL 5'11½'' 200 lbs.

| 1916 | PIT | N | 1 | .000 | .000 | 1 | 0 | 0 | 0 | 0 | 0.0 | 0 | 0 | 0 | 0 | 0 | 1 | 0 | 0 | 0 | 0 | 0 | 0.0 | – | |

Year	Team		Games	BA	SA	AB	H	2B	3B	HR	HR%	R	RBI	BB	SO	SB	Pinch Hit AB	Pinch Hit H	PO	A	E	DP	TC/G	FA	G by Pos

Carlton Fisk

FISK, CARLTON ERNEST (Pudge)
B. Dec. 26, 1947, Bellows Falls, Vt. — BR TR 6'3" 200 lbs.

Year	Team		Games	BA	SA	AB	H	2B	3B	HR	HR%	R	RBI	BB	SO	SB	PH AB	PH H	PO	A	E	DP	TC/G	FA	G by Pos
1969	BOS	A	2	.000	.000	5	0	0	0	0	0.0	0	0	0	2	0	1	0	2	0	0	1	1.0	1.000	C-1
1971			14	.313	.521	48	15	2	1	2	4.2	7	6	1	10	0	0	0	72	6	2	1	5.7	.975	C-14
1972			131	.293	.538	457	134	28	9	22	4.8	74	61	52	83	5	0	0	846	72	15	10	7.1	.984	C-131
1973			135	.246	.441	508	125	21	0	26	5.1	65	71	37	99	7	1	1	739	50	14	8	5.9	.983	C-131, DH-3
1974			52	.299	.551	187	56	12	1	11	5.9	36	26	24	23	5	0	0	267	26	6	2	5.8	.980	C-50, DH-2
1975			79	.331	.529	263	87	14	4	10	3.8	47	52	27	32	4	2	0	347	30	8	2	4.9	.979	C-71, DH-6
1976			134	.255	.415	487	124	17	5	17	3.5	76	58	56	71	12	1	0	649	73	12	9	5.5	.984	C-133, DH-1
1977			152	.315	.521	536	169	26	3	26	4.9	106	102	75	85	7	2	0	779	69	11	7	5.7	.987	C-151
1978			157	.284	.475	571	162	39	5	20	3.5	94	88	71	83	7	2	1	734	90	17	13	5.4	.980	C-154, DH-1, OF-1
1979			91	.272	.450	320	87	23	2	10	3.1	49	42	10	38	3	13	3	155	8	3	1	1.8	.982	DH-42, C-39, OF-1
1980			131	.289	.467	478	138	25	3	18	3.8	73	62	36	62	11	0	0	543	56	11	8	4.7	.982	C-115, DH-5, OF-5, 3B-3, 1B-3
1981	CHI	A	96	.263	.361	338	89	12	0	7	2.1	44	45	38	37	3	0	0	479	46	6	14	5.5	.989	C-95, OF-1, 3B-1, 1B-1
1982			135	.267	.403	476	127	17	3	14	2.9	66	65	46	60	17	3	1	648	63	5	8	5.3	.993	C-133, 1B-2
1983			138	.289	.518	488	141	26	4	26	5.3	85	86	46	88	9	6	1	709	46	7	5	5.5	.991	C-133, DH-2
1984			102	.231	.468	359	83	20	1	21	5.8	54	43	26	60	6	11	1	421	38	6	4	4.6	.987	C-90, DH-5
1985			153	.238	.488	543	129	23	1	37	6.8	85	107	52	81	17	1	0	801	60	10	13	5.7	.989	C-130, DH-28
1986			125	.221	.337	457	101	11	0	14	3.1	42	63	22	92	2	8	1	455	44	8	3	4.1	.984	C-71, OF-31, DH-22
1987			135	.256	.460	454	116	22	1	23	5.1	68	71	39	72	1	12	3	597	66	7	22	5.0	.990	C-122, 1B-9, OF-2
1988			76	.277	.542	253	70	8	1	19	7.5	37	50	37	40	0	6	0	338	36	2	7	4.9	.995	C-74
1989			103	.293	.475	375	110	25	2	13	3.5	47	68	36	60	1	3	0	419	37	3	1	4.5	.993	C-90, DH-13
20 yrs.			2141	.271	.465	7603	2063	371	46	336	4.4	1155	1166	731	1178	117	72	12	10000	916	153	139	5.2	.986	C-1928, DH-130, OF-41, 1B-15, 3B-4

LEAGUE CHAMPIONSHIP SERIES

Year	Team		Games	BA	SA	AB	H	2B	3B	HR	HR%	R	RBI	BB	SO	SB	PH AB	PH H	PO	A	E	DP	TC/G	FA	G by Pos
1975	BOS	A	3	.417	.500	12	5	1	0	0	0.0	4	2	0	2	1	0	0	15	0	0	0	5.0	1.000	C-3
1983	CHI	A	4	.176	.235	17	3	1	0	0	0.0	0	0	1	3	0	0	0	27	3	0	0	7.5	1.000	C-4
2 yrs.			7	.276	.345	29	8	2	0	0	0.0	4	2	1	5	1	0	0	42	3	0	0	6.4	1.000	C-7

WORLD SERIES

Year	Team		Games	BA	SA	AB	H	2B	3B	HR	HR%	R	RBI	BB	SO	SB	PH AB	PH H	PO	A	E	DP	TC/G	FA	G by Pos
1975	BOS	A	7	.240	.480	25	6	0	0	2	8.0	5	4	7	7	0	0	0	37	3	2	1	6.0	.952	C-7

Wes Fisler

FISLER, WESTON DICKSON
B. July 5, 1841, Camden, N. J. D. Dec. 25, 1922, Philadelphia, Pa. — 5'6" 137 lbs.

Year	Team		Games	BA	SA	AB	H	2B	3B	HR	HR%	R	RBI	BB	SO	SB	PH AB	PH H	PO	A	E	DP	TC/G	FA	G by Pos
1876	PHI	N	59	.288	.360	278	80	15	1	1	0.4	42	30	2	4		0	0	234	75	30	11	5.7	.912	OF-24, 2B-21, 1B-14, SS-1

Charlie Fitzberger

FITZBERGER, CHARLES CASPAR (Hon)
B. Feb. 13, 1904, Baltimore, Md. D. Jan. 25, 1965, Baltimore, Md. — BL TL 6'1½" 170 lbs.

Year	Team		Games	BA	SA	AB	H	2B	3B	HR	HR%	R	RBI	BB	SO	SB	PH AB	PH H	PO	A	E	DP	TC/G	FA	G by Pos
1928	BOS	N	7	.286	.286	7	2	0	0	0	0.0	0	0	0	3	0	7	2	0	0	0	0	0.0	—	

Dennis Fitzgerald

FITZGERALD, DENNIS S.
B. Mar., 1865, England D. Oct. 16, 1936, New Haven, Conn. — 5'10" 160 lbs.

Year	Team		Games	BA	SA	AB	H	2B	3B	HR	HR%	R	RBI	BB	SO	SB	PH AB	PH H	PO	A	E	DP	TC/G	FA	G by Pos
1890	PHI	AA	2	.250	.250	8	2	0	0	0	0.0	0		0		0	0	0	2	4	3	0	4.5	.667	SS-2

Ed Fitz Gerald

FITZ GERALD, EDWARD RAYMOND
B. May 21, 1924, Santa Ynez, Calif. — BR TR 6' 170 lbs.

Year	Team		Games	BA	SA	AB	H	2B	3B	HR	HR%	R	RBI	BB	SO	SB	PH AB	PH H	PO	A	E	DP	TC/G	FA	G by Pos
1948	PIT	N	102	.267	.336	262	70	9	3	1	0.4	31	35	32	37	3	6	2	338	36	15	4	3.8	.961	C-96
1949			75	.263	.344	160	42	7	0	2	1.3	16	18	8	27	1	16	1	163	22	5	5	2.5	.974	C-56
1950			6	.067	.133	15	1	1	0	0	0.0	1	0	0	3	0	0	0	16	3	1	0	3.3	.950	C-5
1951			55	.227	.289	97	22	6	0	0	0.0	8	13	7	10	1	14	2	98	13	4	2	2.1	.965	C-38
1952			51	.233	.288	73	17	1	0	1	1.4	4	7	7	15	0	29	6	55	5	1	0	1.2	.984	C-18, 3B-2
1953	2 teams			PIT N (6G – .118)			WAS A (88G – .250)																			
"	total		94	.243	.318	305	74	14	0	3	1.0	25	40	19	36	2	6	2	332	36	4	4	4.0	.989	C-90
1954	WAS	A	115	.289	.386	360	104	13	5	4	1.1	33	40	33	22	0	9	2	396	38	12	5	3.9	.973	C-107
1955			74	.237	.309	236	56	3	1	4	1.7	28	19	25	23	0	4	1	304	30	6	5	4.6	.982	C-72
1956			64	.304	.399	148	45	8	0	2	1.4	15	12	20	16	0	16	3	206	19	6	5	3.6	.974	C-50
1957			45	.272	.360	125	34	6	1	1	0.8	14	13	10	9	2	10	4	142	16	6	3	3.6	.963	C-37
1958			58	.263	.289	114	30	3	0	0	0.0	7	11	9	18	0	33	12	125	5	3	5	2.3	.977	C-21, 1B-5
1959	2 teams			WAS A (19G – .194)			CLE A (49G – .271)																			
"	total		68	.246	.319	191	47	4	1	1	0.5	17	9	16	22	0	5	1	260	39	5	5	4.5	.984	C-61
12 yrs.			807	.260	.336	2086	542	82	10	19	0.9	199	217	185	235	9	148	35	2435	262	68	42	3.4	.975	C-651, 1B-5, 3B-2

Howie Fitzgerald

FITZGERALD, HOWARD CHUMNEY (Lefty)
B. May 16, 1902, Eagle Lake, Tex. D. Feb. 27, 1959, Eagle Falls, Tex. — BL TL 5'11½" 163 lbs.

Year	Team		Games	BA	SA	AB	H	2B	3B	HR	HR%	R	RBI	BB	SO	SB	PH AB	PH H	PO	A	E	DP	TC/G	FA	G by Pos
1922	CHI	N	10	.333	.375	24	8	1	0	0	0.0	3	4	3	2	1	3	2	9	0	2	0	1.1	.818	OF-10
1924			7	.158	.158	19	3	0	0	0	0.0	1	2	0	2	0	2	0	4	0	0	0	0.6	1.000	OF-5
1926	BOS	A	31	.258	.278	97	25	2	0	0	0.0	11	8	5	7	1	8	2	28	2	4	0	1.1	.882	OF-23
3 yrs.			48	.257	.279	140	36	3	0	0	0.0	15	14	8	11	2	13	4	41	2	6	0	1.0	.878	OF-38

Matty Fitzgerald

FITZGERALD, MATTHEW WILLIAM
B. Aug. 31, 1880, Albany, N. Y. D. Sept. 22, 1949, Albany, N. Y. — BR TR 6' 185 lbs.

Year	Team		Games	BA	SA	AB	H	2B	3B	HR	HR%	R	RBI	BB	SO	SB	PH AB	PH H	PO	A	E	DP	TC/G	FA	G by Pos
1906	NY	N	4	.667	.667	6	4	0	0	0	0.0	2	2	0		1	1	0	9	0	0	1	2.3	1.000	C-3
1907			7	.133	.200	15	2	1	0	0	0.0	1	1	0		0	1	0	16	4	1	1	3.0	.952	C-6
2 yrs.			11	.286	.333	21	6	1	0	0	0.0	3	3	0		1	2	0	25	4	1	2	2.7	.967	C-9

Mike Fitzgerald

FITZGERALD, JUSTIN HOWARD
B. June 22, 1890, San Mateo, Calif. D. Jan. 17, 1945, San Mateo, Calif. — BL TR 5'8" 160 lbs.

Year	Team		Games	BA	SA	AB	H	2B	3B	HR	HR%	R	RBI	BB	SO	SB	PH AB	PH H	PO	A	E	DP	TC/G	FA	G by Pos
1911	NY	A	16	.270	.297	37	10	1	0	0	0.0	6	6	4		4	7	1	9	1	0	0	0.6	1.000	OF-9

Year	Team	Games	BA	SA	AB	H	2B	3B	HR	HR%	R	RBI	BB	SO	SB	Pinch Hit AB	Pinch Hit H	PO	A	E	DP	TC/G	FA	G by Pos

Mike Fitzgerald *continued*

Year	Team	Games	BA	SA	AB	H	2B	3B	HR	HR%	R	RBI	BB	SO	SB	PH AB	PH H	PO	A	E	DP	TC/G	FA	G by Pos
1918	PHI N	66	.293	.353	133	39	8	0	0	0.0	21	6	13	6	3	30	8	54	2	2	1	0.9	.966	OF-57
2 yrs.		82	.288	.341	170	49	9	0	0	0.0	27	12	17	6	7	37	9	63	3	2	1	0.8	.971	OF-66

Mike Fitzgerald

FITZGERALD, MICHAEL PATRICK
B. Mar. 28, 1964, Savannah, Ga. BR TR 6'1" 200 lbs.

Year	Team	Games	BA	SA	AB	H	2B	3B	HR	HR%	R	RBI	BB	SO	SB	PH AB	PH H	PO	A	E	DP	TC/G	FA	G by Pos
1988	STL N	13	.196	.217	46	9	1	0	0	0.0	4	1	0	9	0	1	0	96	4	1	10	7.8	.990	1B-12

Mike Fitzgerald

FITZGERALD, MICHAEL ROY (Fitz)
B. July 13, 1960, Long Beach, Calif. BR TR 6' 185 lbs.

Year	Team	Games	BA	SA	AB	H	2B	3B	HR	HR%	R	RBI	BB	SO	SB	PH AB	PH H	PO	A	E	DP	TC/G	FA	G by Pos
1983	NY N	8	.100	.250	20	2	0	0	1	5.0	1	2	3	6	0	0	0	37	8	2	2	5.9	.957	C-8
1984		112	.242	.306	360	87	15	1	2	0.6	20	33	24	71	1	7	1	715	47	4	6	6.8	.995	C-107
1985	MON N	108	.207	.288	295	61	7	1	5	1.7	25	34	38	55	5	3	1	542	46	8	7	5.5	.987	C-108
1986		73	.282	.440	209	59	13	1	6	2.9	20	37	27	34	3	3	0	415	35	3	5	6.2	.993	C-71
1987		107	.240	.310	287	69	11	0	3	1.0	32	36	42	54	3	5	2	603	27	12	2	6.0	.981	C-104, 2B-1, 1B-1
1988		63	.271	.419	155	42	6	1	5	3.2	17	23	19	22	2	15	4	262	21	6	2	4.6	.979	C-47, OF-4
1989		100	.238	.386	290	69	18	2	7	2.4	33	42	35	61	3	10	3	465	44	8	5	5.2	.985	C-77, 3B-8, OF-6
7 yrs.		571	.241	.345	1616	389	70	6	29	1.8	148	207	188	303	17	43	11	3039	228	43	29	5.8	.987	C-522, OF-10, 3B-8, 2B-1, 1B-1

Ray Fitzgerald

FITZGERALD, RAYMOND FRANCIS
B. Dec. 5, 1904, Chicopee, Mass. D. Sept. 6, 1977, Westfield, Mass. BR TR 5'9" 168 lbs.

Year	Team	Games	BA	SA	AB	H	2B	3B	HR	HR%	R	RBI	BB	SO	SB	PH AB	PH H	PO	A	E	DP	TC/G	FA	G by Pos
1931	CIN N	1	.000	.000	1	0	0	0	0	0.0	0	0	0	0	0	1	0	0	0	0	0	0.0	—	

Shaun Fitzmaurice

FITZMAURICE, SHAUN EARLE
B. Aug. 25, 1942, Worcester, Mass. BR TR 6' 180 lbs.

Year	Team	Games	BA	SA	AB	H	2B	3B	HR	HR%	R	RBI	BB	SO	SB	PH AB	PH H	PO	A	E	DP	TC/G	FA	G by Pos
1966	NY N	9	.154	.154	13	2	0	0	0	0.0	2	0	2	6	1	1	0	9	1	0	0	1.1	1.000	OF-5

Ed Fitzpatrick

FITZPATRICK, EDWARD HENRY
B. Dec. 9, 1889, Lewiston, Pa. D. Oct. 23, 1965, Bethlehem, Pa. BR TR 5'8" 165 lbs.

Year	Team	Games	BA	SA	AB	H	2B	3B	HR	HR%	R	RBI	BB	SO	SB	PH AB	PH H	PO	A	E	DP	TC/G	FA	G by Pos
1915	BOS N	105	.221	.304	303	67	19	3	0	0.0	54	24	43	36	13	2	0	178	161	10	23	3.3	.971	2B-71, OF-29
1916		83	.213	.264	216	46	8	0	1	0.5	17	18	15	26	5	8	2	114	96	9	14	2.6	.959	2B-46, OF-28
1917		63	.253	.343	178	45	8	4	0	0.0	20	17	12	22	4	3	0	71	67	15	5	2.4	.902	2B-22, OF-19, 3B-15
3 yrs.		251	.227	.301	697	158	35	7	1	0.1	91	59	70	84	22	13	2	363	324	34	42	2.9	.953	2B-139, OF-76, 3B-15

Tom Fitzsimmons

FITZSIMMONS, THOMAS WILLIAM
B. Apr. 6, 1890, Oakland, Calif. D. Dec. 20, 1971, Oakland, Calif. BR TR 6'1" 190 lbs.

Year	Team	Games	BA	SA	AB	H	2B	3B	HR	HR%	R	RBI	BB	SO	SB	PH AB	PH H	PO	A	E	DP	TC/G	FA	G by Pos
1919	BKN N	4	.000	.000	4	0	0	0	0	0.0	1	0	1	2	0	0	0	1	2	0	1.0	.500	3B-4

Max Flack

FLACK, MAX JOHN
B. Feb. 5, 1890, Belleville, Ill. D. July 31, 1975, Belleville, Ill. BL TL 5'7" 148 lbs.

Year	Team	Games	BA	SA	AB	H	2B	3B	HR	HR%	R	RBI	BB	SO	SB	PH AB	PH H	PO	A	E	DP	TC/G	FA	G by Pos
1914	CHI F	134	.247	.301	502	124	15	3	2	0.4	66	39	51		37	1	0	232	18	7	2	1.9	.973	OF-133
1915		141	.314	.423	523	164	20	14	3	0.6	88	45	40		37	3	2	226	24	8	5	1.8	.969	OF-138
1916	CHI N	141	.258	.320	465	120	14	3	3	0.6	65	20	42	43	24	3	0	193	22	2	4	1.5	.991	OF-136
1917		131	.248	.320	447	111	18	7	0	0.0	65	21	51	34	17	10	3	199	14	12	3	1.7	.947	OF-117
1918		123	.257	.360	478	123	17	10	4	0.8	74	41	56	19	17	0	0	199	20	5	5	1.8	.978	OF-121
1919		116	.294	.392	469	138	20	4	6	1.3	71	35	34	13	18	0	0	194	18	3	1	1.9	.986	OF-116
1920		135	.302	.406	520	157	30	6	4	0.8	85	49	52	15	13	2	0	216	16	8	2	1.8	.967	OF-132
1921		133	.301	.400	572	172	31	4	6	1.0	80	37	32	15	17	3	1	244	19	3	2	2.0	.989	OF-130
1922	2 teams		CHI N	(17G – .222)			STL N	(66G – .292)																
"	total	83	.280	.346	321	90	13	1	2	0.6	53	27	33	15	5	1	0	144	5	6	3	1.9	.961	OF-83
1923	STL N	128	.291	.376	505	147	16	9	3	0.6	82	28	41	16	7	6	3	242	8	13	4	2.1	.951	OF-121
1924		67	.263	.373	209	55	11	3	2	1.0	31	21	21	5	3	13	3	90	9	3	0	1.5	.971	OF-52
1925		79	.249	.344	241	60	7	8	0	0.0	23	28	21	9	5	19	3	103	8	1	1	1.4	.991	OF-59
12 yrs.		1411	.278	.366	5252	1461	212	72	35	0.7	783	391	474	184	200	61	15	2282	181	71	32	1.8	.972	OF-1338

WORLD SERIES

Year	Team	Games	BA	SA	AB	H	2B	3B	HR	HR%	R	RBI	BB	SO	SB	PH AB	PH H	PO	A	E	DP	TC/G	FA	G by Pos
1918	CHI N	6	.263	.263	19	5	0	0	0	0.0	2	1	4	1	1	0	0	14	2	1	0	2.8	.941	OF-6

Wally Flager

FLAGER, WALTER LEONARD
B. Nov. 3, 1921, Chicago Heights, Ill. BL TR 5'11" 160 lbs.

Year	Team	Games	BA	SA	AB	H	2B	3B	HR	HR%	R	RBI	BB	SO	SB	PH AB	PH H	PO	A	E	DP	TC/G	FA	G by Pos
1945	2 teams		CIN N	(21G – .212)			PHI N	(49G – .250)																
"	total	70	.241	.300	220	53	5	1	2	0.9	26	21	25	20	1	5	1	121	179	18	29	4.5	.943	SS-63, 2B-1

Ira Flagstead

FLAGSTEAD, IRA JAMES (Pete)
B. Sept. 22, 1893, Montague, Mich. D. Mar. 13, 1940, Olympia, Wash. BR TR 5'9" 165 lbs.

Year	Team	Games	BA	SA	AB	H	2B	3B	HR	HR%	R	RBI	BB	SO	SB	PH AB	PH H	PO	A	E	DP	TC/G	FA	G by Pos
1917	DET A	4	.000	.000	4	0	0	0	0	0.0	0	0	0	1	0	0	0	0	0	0	0	0.0	—	OF-2
1919		97	.331	.481	287	95	22	3	5	1.7	43	41	35	39	6	11	3	140	15	8	4	1.7	.951	OF-83
1920		110	.235	.338	311	73	13	5	3	1.0	40	35	37	27	3	26	6	164	13	6	4	1.7	.967	OF-82
1921		85	.305	.371	259	79	15	1	0	0.0	40	31	21	21	7	7	2	150	165	28	22	4.0	.918	SS-55, OF-12, 2B-8, 3B-1
1922		44	.308	.527	91	28	5	3	3	3.3	21	8	14	16	0	8	2	54	4	2	1	1.4	.967	OF-31
1923	2 teams		DET A	(1G – .000)			BOS A	(109G – .312)																
"	total	110	.311	.454	383	119	23	4	8	2.1	55	53	37	26	8	6	0	218	33	10	8	2.4	.962	OF-102
1924	BOS A	149	.305	.420	560	171	35	7	5	0.9	106	43	75	41	10	5	2	370	9	10	2	2.6	.974	OF-143
1925		148	.280	.385	572	160	38	2	6	1.0	84	61	63	30	5	3	1	429	24	11	6	3.1	.976	OF-144
1926		98	.299	.429	415	124	31	7	3	0.7	65	31	36	22	4	0	0	264	14	5	4	2.9	.982	OF-98
1927		131	.285	.401	466	133	26	8	4	0.9	63	69	57	25	12	2	0	326	19	5	4	2.7	.986	OF-129
1928		140	.290	.392	510	148	41	4	1	0.2	84	39	60	23	12	4	0	346	18	10	4	2.7	.973	OF-135

Year	Team	Games	BA	SA	AB	H	2B	3B	HR	HR%	R	RBI	BB	SO	SB	Pinch Hit AB	H	PO	A	E	DP	TC/G	FA	G by Pos

Ira Flagstead *continued*

Year	Team		Games	BA	SA	AB	H	2B	3B	HR	HR%	R	RBI	BB	SO	SB	AB	H	PO	A	E	DP	TC/G	FA	G by Pos
1929	3 teams	BOS A (14G – .306)		WAS A (18G – .179)		PIT N	(26G – .280)																		
"	total		58	.256	.312	125	32	5	1	0	0.0	22	18	13	8	3	23	9	75	4	2	1	1.4	.975	OF-33
1930	PIT N		44	.250	.385	156	39	7	4	2	1.3	21	21	17	9	1	3	0	70	4	3	1	1.8	.961	OF-40
13 yrs.			1218	.290	.406	4139	1201	261	49	40	1.0	644	450	465	288	71	100	25	2606	322	100	61	2.5	.967	OF-1034, SS-55, 2B-8, 3B-1

Marty Flaherty

FLAHERTY, MARTIN
B. Worcester, Mass.   Deceased.   BL TL

1881	WOR N	1	.000	.000	2	0	0	0	0	0.0	0	0	0	2		0	0	0	0	1	0	1.0	–	OF-1

Pat Flaherty

FLAHERTY, PATRICK HENRY
B. Jan. 31, 1876, St Louis, Mo.   D. Jan. 28, 1946, Chicago, Ill.   5'9"   166 lbs.

1894	LOU N	38	.297	.372	145	43	5	3	0	0.0	15	15	9	6	2	0	0	42	70	19	7	3.4	.855	3B-38

Patsy Flaherty

FLAHERTY, PATRICK JOSEPH
B. June 29, 1876, Mansfield, Pa.   D. Jan. 23, 1968, Alexandria, La.   BL TL 5'8"   165 lbs.

1899	LOU N		7	.208	.333	24	5	1	1	0	0.0	3	6	3			0	0	4	8	5	0	2.4	.706	P-5, OF-2
1900	PIT N		4	.111	.111	9	1	0	0	0	0.0	0		1			0	0	0	10	0	0	2.5	1.000	P-4
1903	CHI A		40	.137	.176	102	14	4	0	0	0.0	7	5	5			4	0	21	107	12	5	3.5	.914	P-40
1904	2 teams	CHI A (5G – .333)		PIT N (36G – .212)																					
"	total		41	.224	.379	116	26	4	2	2	1.7	10	19	12			5	1	34	105	7	3	3.6	.952	P-34, OF-2
1905	PIT N		30	.197	.303	76	15	4	2	0	0.0	7	4	3			0	1	9	70	9	1	2.9	.898	P-27, OF-2
1907	BOS N		41	.191	.304	115	22	3	1	2	1.7	9	11	2			4	1	26	78	9	8	2.8	.920	P-27, OF-8
1908			32	.140	.186	86	12	0	2	0	0.0	8	5	6			2	1	20	79	4	3	3.2	.961	P-31
1910	PHI N		2	.500	.500	2	1	0	0	0	0.0	0	0	0			0	0	1	0	0	0	0.5	1.000	OF-1, P-1
1911	BOS N		38	.287	.426	94	27	3	2	2	2.1	9	20	8	11	2	17	6	26	6	4	0	0.9	.889	OF-19, P-4
9 yrs.			235	.197	.298	624	123	19	13	6	1.0	53	70	40	11	9	28	8	141	463	50	20	2.8	.924	P-173, OF-34

Al Flair

FLAIR, ALBERT DELL (Broadway)
B. July 24, 1916, New Orleans, La.   D. July 25, 1988, New Orleans, La.   BL TL 6'4"   195 lbs.

1941	BOS A	10	.200	.333	30	6	2	1	0	0.0	3	2	1	1	2	0	63	4	0	5	6.7	1.000	1B-8

Charlie Flanagan

FLANAGAN, CHARLES JAMES
B. Dec. 31, 1891, Oakland, Calif.   D. Jan. 8, 1930, San Francisco, Calif.   BR TR 6'   175 lbs.

1913	STL A	4	.000	.000	3	0	0	0	0	0.0	0	0	1	0	1	0	0	0	0	0	0.3	1.000	OF-1, 3B-1

Ed Flanagan

FLANAGAN, EDWARD J.
B. Sept. 15, 1861, Lowell, Mass.   D. Nov. 10, 1926, Lowell, Mass.   6'1"   190 lbs.

1887	PHI AA	19	.250	.350	80	20	5	0	1	1.3	12		3		3	0	0	158	5	9	9	9.1	.948	1B-19
1889	LOU AA	23	.250	.398	88	22	7	3	0	0.0	11	8	7	11	1	0	0	254	10	13	11	12.0	.953	1B-23
2 yrs.		42	.250	.375	168	42	12	3	1	0.6	23	8	10	11	4	0	0	412	15	22	20	10.7	.951	1B-42

Steamer Flanagan

FLANAGAN, JAMES PAUL
B. Apr. 20, 1881, Kingston, Pa.   D. Apr. 21, 1947, Wilkes-Barre, Pa.   BL TL 6'1"   185 lbs.

1905	PIT N	7	.280	.400	25	7	1	1	0	0.0	7	3	1		3	2	0	19	0	0	0	2.7	1.000	OF-5

John Flannery

FLANNERY, JOHN MICHAEL
B. Jan. 25, 1957, Long Beach, Calif.   BR TR 6'3"   173 lbs.

1977	CHI A	7	.000	.000	2	0	0	0	0	0.0	1	0	1	1	0	0	0	1	4	0	1	0.7	1.000	SS-4, DH-1, 3B-1

Tim Flannery

FLANNERY, TIMOTHY EARL
B. Sept. 29, 1957, Tulsa, Okla.   BL TR 5'11"   175 lbs.

1979	SD N	22	.154	.185	65	10	0	1	0	0.0	2	4	4	5	0	0	0	45	60	1	16	4.8	.991	2B-21
1980		95	.240	.281	292	70	12	0	0	0.0	15	25	18	30	2	12	5	140	204	8	34	3.7	.977	2B-53, 3B-41
1981		37	.254	.343	67	17	4	1	0	0.0	4	6	2	4	1	16	6	16	32	2	5	1.4	.960	3B-15, 2B-7
1982		122	.264	.330	379	100	11	7	0	0.0	40	30	30	32	1	16	3	226	278	14	47	4.2	.973	2B-104, 3B-5, SS-2
1983		92	.234	.322	214	50	7	3	1	0.5	24	19	20	23	2	19	4	63	156	4	19	2.4	.982	3B-52, 2B-21, SS-7
1984		86	.273	.391	128	35	3	3	2	1.6	24	10	12	17	4	40	7	36	69	5	12	1.3	.955	2B-22, SS-14, 3B-14
1985		126	.281	.341	384	108	14	3	1	0.3	50	40	58	39	2	13	3	261	287	13	72	4.5	.977	2B-121, 3B-1
1986		134	.280	.345	368	103	11	2	3	0.8	48	28	54	61	3	16	3	226	275	5	56	3.8	.990	2B-108, 3B-23, SS-8
1987		106	.228	.254	276	63	5	1	0	0.0	23	20	42	30	2	23	2	142	226	7	42	3.5	.981	2B-84, 3B-8, SS-2
1988		79	.265	.341	170	45	5	4	0	0.0	16	19	24	32	3	26	8	28	76	3	8	1.4	.972	3B-51, 2B-2, SS-1
1989		73	.231	.308	130	30	5	0	0	0.0	9	8	13	20	2	35	9	14	56	6	3	1.0	.921	3B-33, 2B-1
11 yrs.		972	.255	.317	2473	631	77	25	9	0.4	255	209	277	293	22	216	50	1197	1719	68	314	3.1	.977	2B-544, 3B-243, SS-34

LEAGUE CHAMPIONSHIP SERIES

1984	SD N	3	.500	.500	2	1	0	0	0	0.0	2	0	0	0	0	2	1	0	0	0	0	0.0	–	

WORLD SERIES

1984	SD N	1	1.000	1.000	1	1	0	0	0	0.0	0	0	0	0	0	1	1	1	0	0	0	1.0	1.000	2B-1

Ray Flaskamper

FLASKAMPER, RAYMOND HAROLD (Flash)
B. Oct. 31, 1901, St. Louis, Mo.   D. Feb. 3, 1978, San Antonio, Tex.   BB TR 5'7"   140 lbs.

1927	CHI A	26	.221	.274	95	21	5	0	0	0.0	12	6	13	8	0	1	0	55	70	5	10	5.0	.962	SS-25

Angel Fleitas

FLEITAS, ANGEL FELIX
Born Angel Felix Fleitas y Husta.
B. Nov. 10, 1914, Los Abreus, Cuba   BR TR 5'9"   160 lbs.

1948	WAS A	15	.077	.077	13	1	0	0	0	0.0	1	3	5	0	3	1	7	13	1	0	1.4	.952	SS-7

Year	Team		Games	BA	SA	AB	H	2B	3B	HR	HR%	R	RBI	BB	SO	SB	Pinch Hit AB	Pinch Hit H	PO	A	E	DP	TC/G	FA	G by Pos

Les Fleming

FLEMING, LESLIE HARVEY (Moe)
B. Aug. 7, 1915, Singleton, Tex. D. Mar. 5, 1980, Cleveland, Tex. BL TL 5'10" 185 lbs.

Year	Team		Games	BA	SA	AB	H	2B	3B	HR	HR%	R	RBI	BB	SO	SB	AB	H	PO	A	E	DP	TC/G	FA	G by Pos
1939	DET	A	8	.000	.000	16	0	0	0	0	0.0	0	1	0	4	0	5	0	6	0	0	0	0.8	1.000	OF-3
1941	CLE	A	2	.250	.375	8	2	1	0	0	0.0	0	2	0	0	0	0	0	20	1	0	3	10.5	1.000	1B-2
1942			156	.292	.432	548	160	27	4	14	2.6	71	82	106	57	6	0	0	1503	90	12	152	10.3	.993	1B-156
1945			42	.329	.493	140	46	10	2	3	2.1	18	22	11	5	0	3	1	91	6	5	4	2.4	.951	OF-33, 1B-5
1946			99	.278	.444	306	85	17	5	8	2.6	40	42	50	42	1	17	5	608	62	12	60	6.9	.982	1B-80, OF-1
1947			103	.242	.349	281	68	14	2	4	1.4	39	43	53	42	0	20	6	662	63	8	78	7.1	.989	1B-77
1949	PIT	N	24	.258	.387	31	8	0	2	0	0.0	0	7	6	2	0	16	4	43	0	0	4	1.8	1.000	1B-5
7 yrs.			434	.277	.417	1330	369	69	15	29	2.2	168	199	226	152	7	61	16	2933	222	37	301	7.4	.988	1B-325, OF-37

Tom Fleming

FLEMING, THOMAS VINCENT (Sleuth)
B. Nov. 20, 1873, Philadelphia, Pa. D. Dec. 26, 1957, Boston, Mass. BL TL 5'11" 155 lbs.

Year	Team		Games	BA	SA	AB	H	2B	3B	HR	HR%	R	RBI	BB	SO	SB	AB	H	PO	A	E	DP	TC/G	FA	G by Pos
1899	NY	N	22	.208	.247	77	16	1	1	0	0.0	9	4	1		0	1	0	35	5	4	0	2.0	.909	OF-22
1902	PHI	N	5	.375	.375	16	6	0	0	0	0.0	2	2	1		0	0	0	3	2	0	0	1.0	1.000	OF-5
1904			3	.000	.000	6	0	0	0	0	0.0	0	0	0		0	2	0	0	1	0	0	0.3	1.000	OF-1
3 yrs.			30	.222	.253	99	22	1	1	0	0.0	11	6	2		1	2	0	38	8	4	0	1.7	.920	OF-28

Art Fletcher

FLETCHER, ARTHUR
B. Jan. 5, 1885, Collinsville, Ill. D. Feb. 6, 1950, Los Angeles, Calif.
Manager 1923-26, 1929. BR TR 5'10½" 170 lbs.

Year	Team		Games	BA	SA	AB	H	2B	3B	HR	HR%	R	RBI	BB	SO	SB	AB	H	PO	A	E	DP	TC/G	FA	G by Pos
1909	NY	N	29	.214	.235	98	21	0	1	0	0.0	7	6	1		0	0	0	52	80	17	10	5.1	.886	SS-19, 3B-5, 2B-5
1910			51	.224	.256	125	28	2	1	0	0.0	12	13	4	9	9	4	0	59	67	12	8	2.7	.913	SS-22, 3B-11, 2B-11
1911			112	.319	.429	326	104	17	8	1	0.3	73	37	30	27	20	2	1	153	285	32	27	4.2	.932	SS-74, 3B-21, 2B-13
1912			129	.282	.372	419	118	17	9	1	0.2	64	57	16	29	16	0	0	241	429	53	60	5.6	.927	SS-126, 2B-2, 3B-1
1913			136	.297	.390	538	160	20	9	4	0.7	76	71	24	35	32	0	0	245	435	50	42	5.4	.932	SS-136
1914			135	.286	.379	514	147	26	8	2	0.4	62	79	22	37	15	0	0	299	446	63	0	6.0	.922	SS-135
1915			149	.254	.326	562	143	17	7	3	0.5	59	74	6	36	12	0	0	302	544	58	76	6.1	.936	SS-149
1916			133	.286	.382	500	143	23	8	3	0.6	53	66	13	36	15	0	0	253	497	48	56	6.0	.940	SS-133
1917			151	.260	.343	557	145	24	5	4	0.7	70	56	23	28	12	0	0	276	565	39	71	5.8	.956	SS-151
1918			124	.263	.314	468	123	20	2	0	0.0	51	47	18	26	12	0	0	268	484	32	54	6.3	.959	SS-124
1919			127	.277	.357	488	135	20	5	3	0.6	54	54	9	28	6	0	0	265	521	47	49	6.6	.944	SS-127
1920	2 teams		NY N (41G – .257)			PHI N (102G – .296)																			
"	total		143	.284	.396	550	156	32	9	4	0.7	57	62	16	43	7	1	0	302	522	48	63	6.1	.945	SS-142
1922	PHI	N	110	.280	.409	396	111	20	5	7	1.8	46	53	21	14	3	4	1	202	379	38	63	5.6	.939	SS-106
13 yrs.			1529	.277	.365	5541	1534	238	77	32	0.6	684	675	203	348	159	11	2	2917	5254	537	579	5.7	.938	SS-1444, 3B-38, 2B-31

WORLD SERIES

Year	Team		Games	BA	SA	AB	H	2B	3B	HR	HR%	R	RBI	BB	SO	SB	AB	H	PO	A	E	DP	TC/G	FA	G by Pos
1911	NY	N	6	.130	.174	23	3	1	0	0	0.0	0	1	0	4	0	0	0	11	17	4	1	5.3	.875	SS-6
1912			8	.179	.214	28	5	1	0	0	0.0	1	3	1	4	1	0	0	16	23	4	1	5.4	.907	SS-8
1913			5	.278	.278	18	5	0	0	0	0.0	1	4	1	1	1	0	0	8	10	1	0	3.8	.947	SS-5
1917			6	.200	.240	25	5	1	0	0	0.0	2	0	0	2	0	0	0	9	17	3	1	4.8	.897	SS-6
4 yrs.			25	.191	.223	94	18	3	0	0	0.0	5	8	2	11	2	0	0	44	67	12	3	4.9	.902	SS-25

Darrin Fletcher

FLETCHER, DARRIN GLEN
B. Oct. 3, 1966, Elmhurst, Ill. BL TR 6'2" 195 lbs.

Year	Team		Games	BA	SA	AB	H	2B	3B	HR	HR%	R	RBI	BB	SO	SB	AB	H	PO	A	E	DP	TC/G	FA	G by Pos
1989	LA	N	5	.500	.875	8	4	0	0	1	12.5	1	2	1	0	0	2	1	16	1	0	0	3.4	1.000	C-5

Elbie Fletcher

FLETCHER, ELBURT PRESTON
B. Mar. 18, 1916, Milton, Mass. BL TL 6' 180 lbs.

Year	Team		Games	BA	SA	AB	H	2B	3B	HR	HR%	R	RBI	BB	SO	SB	AB	H	PO	A	E	DP	TC/G	FA	G by Pos
1934	BOS	N	8	.500	.500	4	2	0	0	0	0.0	4	0	0	2	1	0	0	7	0	1	1	1.0	.875	1B-1
1935			39	.236	.318	148	35	7	1	1	0.7	12	9	7	13	1	0	0	353	27	1	22	9.8	.997	1B-39
1937			148	.247	.308	539	133	22	4	1	0.2	56	38	56	64	3	0	0	1587	108	12	117	11.5	.993	1B-148
1938			147	.272	.378	529	144	24	7	6	1.1	71	48	60	40	5	1	0	1424	126	15	108	10.6	.990	1B-146
1939	2 teams		BOS N (35G – .245)			PIT N (102G – .303)																			
"	total		137	.290	.435	476	138	25	6	12	2.5	63	77	67	33	4	4	1	1345	64	13	97	10.4	.991	1B-132
1940	PIT	N	147	.273	.437	510	139	22	7	16	3.1	94	104	119	54	5	0	0	1512	104	11	128	11.1	.993	1B-147
1941			151	.288	.457	521	150	29	13	11	2.1	95	74	118	54	5	0	0	1444	118	14	113	10.4	.991	1B-151
1942			145	.289	.393	506	146	22	5	7	1.4	86	57	105	60	0	1	1	1379	118	12	104	10.4	.992	1B-144
1943			154	.283	.395	544	154	24	5	9	1.7	91	70	95	49	1	0	0	1541	108	6	141	10.7	.996	1B-154
1946			148	.256	.355	532	136	25	8	4	0.8	72	66	111	37	4	0	0	1356	106	8	97	9.9	.995	1B-147
1947			69	.242	.331	157	38	9	1	1	0.6	22	22	29	24	2	18	2	324	25	5	28	5.1	.986	1B-50
1949	BOS	N	122	.262	.402	413	108	19	3	11	2.7	57	51	84	65	1	0	0	965	71	9	96	8.6	.991	1B-121
12 yrs.			1415	.271	.390	4879	1323	228	58	79	1.6	723	616	851	495	32	25	4	13237	975	107	1052	10.1	.993	1B-1380

Frank Fletcher

FLETCHER, OLIVER FRANK (Fletch)
B. Mar. 6, 1891, Hindreth, Ill. D. Oct. 7, 1974, St. Petersburg, Fla. BR TR 5'10" 165 lbs.

Year	Team		Games	BA	SA	AB	H	2B	3B	HR	HR%	R	RBI	BB	SO	SB	AB	H	PO	A	E	DP	TC/G	FA	G by Pos
1914	PHI	N	1	.000	.000	1	0	0	0	0	0.0	0	0	1	0	0	1	0	0	0	0	0	0.0	—	

Scott Fletcher

FLETCHER, SCOTT BRIAN
B. July 30, 1958, Fort Walton Beach, Fla. BR TR 5'11" 168 lbs.

Year	Team		Games	BA	SA	AB	H	2B	3B	HR	HR%	R	RBI	BB	SO	SB	AB	H	PO	A	E	DP	TC/G	FA	G by Pos
1981	CHI	N	19	.217	.304	46	10	4	0	0	0.0	6	1	2	4	0	0	0	34	44	3	10	4.3	.963	2B-13, SS-4, 3B-1
1982			11	.167	.167	24	4	0	0	0	0.0	4	1	4	5	1	0	0	11	23	0	3	3.1	1.000	SS-11
1983	CHI	A	114	.237	.370	262	62	16	5	3	1.1	42	31	29	22	5	0	0	126	308	16	64	3.9	.964	SS-100, 2B-12, 3B-7, DH-1
1984			149	.250	.311	456	114	13	3	3	0.7	46	35	46	46	10	0	0	234	439	19	89	4.6	.973	SS-134, 2B-28, 3B-3
1985			119	.256	.309	301	77	8	1	2	0.7	38	31	35	47	5	12	3	123	208	8	36	2.8	.976	3B-55, 2B-44, 2B-37, DH-2
1986	TEX	A	147	.300	.400	530	159	34	5	3	0.6	82	50	47	59	12	0	0	216	388	16	93	4.2	.974	SS-136, 3B-12, 2B-11, DH-1
1987			156	.287	.374	588	169	28	4	5	0.9	82	63	61	66	13	3	1	249	413	23	98	4.4	.966	SS-155
1988			140	.276	.328	515	142	19	4	0	0.0	59	47	62	34	8	2	0	215	414	11	90	4.6	.983	SS-139

Year	Team		Games	BA	SA	AB	H	2B	3B	HR	HR%	R	RBI	BB	SO	SB	Pinch Hit AB	H	PO	A	E	DP	TC/G	FA	G by Pos

Scott Fletcher *continued*

Year	Team		Games	BA	SA	AB	H	2B	3B	HR	HR%	R	RBI	BB	SO	SB	AB	H	PO	A	E	DP	TC/G	FA	G by Pos
1989	2 teams			TEX	A	(83G – .239)			CHI	A	(59G – .272)														
"	total		142	.253	.311	546	138	25	2	1	0.2	77	43	64	60	2	1	0	241	362	15	88	4.4	.976	SS-89, 2B-53, DH-1
9 yrs.			997	.268	.343	3268	875	147	24	17	0.5	436	302	350	343	56	18	4	1449	2599	111	571	4.2	.973	SS-812, 2B-154, 3B-78, DH-5

LEAGUE CHAMPIONSHIP SERIES

Year	Team		Games	BA	SA	AB	H	2B	3B	HR	HR%	R	RBI	BB	SO	SB	AB	H	PO	A	E	DP	TC/G	FA	G by Pos
1983	CHI	A	3	.000	.000	7	0	0	0	0	0.0	0	0	1	0	0	0	0	3	8	0	1	3.7	1.000	SS-3

Elmer Flick

FLICK, ELMER HARRISON
B. Jan. 11, 1876, Bedford, Ohio   D. Jan. 9, 1971, Bedford, Ohio
Hall of Fame 1963.

BL TR 5'9"   168 lbs.

Year	Team		Games	BA	SA	AB	H	2B	3B	HR	HR%	R	RBI	BB	SO	SB	AB	H	PO	A	E	DP	TC/G	FA	G by Pos
1898	PHI	N	134	.302	.448	453	137	16	13	8	1.8	84	81	86		23	1	0	237	21	19	4	2.1	.931	OF-133
1899			127	.342	.445	485	166	22	11	2	0.4	98	98	42		31	2	1	234	24	19	7	2.2	.931	OF-125
1900			138	.367	.545	545	200	32	16	11	2.0	106	110	56		35	0	0	232	23	24	6	2.0	.914	OF-138
1901			138	.336	.500	542	182	31	17	8	1.5	112	88	52		30	0	0	278	23	12	7	2.3	.962	OF-138
1902	2 teams			PHI	A	(11G – .297)			CLE	A	(110G – .297)														
"	total		121	.297	.410	461	137	22	12	2	0.4	85	64	53		24	0	0	173	14	14	2	1.7	.930	OF-121
1903	CLE	A	142	.299	.414	529	158	23	16	2	0.4	84	51	51		24	0	0	219	15	11	3	1.7	.955	OF-140
1904			150	.306	.453	579	177	31	18	6	1.0	97	56	51		42	0	0	248	42	12	6	2.0	.960	OF-144, 2B-6
1905			131	.306	.466	496	152	29	19	4	0.8	71	64	53		35	0	0	181	20	14	3	1.6	.935	OF-130, 2B-1
1906			157	.311	.439	624	194	33	22	1	0.2	98	62	54		39	0	0	263	38	7	7	2.0	.977	OF-150, 2B-8
1907			147	.302	.412	549	166	15	18	3	0.5	78	58	64		41	0	0	219	22	11	7	1.7	.956	OF-147
1908			9	.229	.257	35	8	1	1	0	0.0	4	2	3		0	0	0	10	1	0	1	1.2	1.000	OF-9
1909			66	.255	.315	235	60	10	2	0	0.0	28	15	22		9	5	2	87	4	4	1	1.4	.958	OF-61
1910			24	.265	.368	68	18	2	1	1	1.5	5	7	10		1	4	0	21	0	1	0	0.9	.955	OF-18
13 yrs.			1484	.313	.446	5601	1755	267	166	48	0.9	950	756	597		334	12	3	2402	247	148	54	1.9	.947	OF-1454, 2B-15

Lew Flick

FLICK, LEWIS MILLER
B. Feb. 18, 1915, Bristol, Tenn.

BL TL 5'9"   155 lbs.

Year	Team		Games	BA	SA	AB	H	2B	3B	HR	HR%	R	RBI	BB	SO	SB	AB	H	PO	A	E	DP	TC/G	FA	G by Pos
1943	PHI	A	1	.600	.600	5	3	0	0	0	0.0	2	0	0	0	0	0	0	3	0	0	0	3.0	1.000	OF-1
1944			19	.114	.114	35	4	0	0	0	0.0	1	2	1	2	1	13	1	9	0	0	0	0.5	1.000	OF-6
2 yrs.			20	.175	.175	40	7	0	0	0	0.0	3	2	1	2	1	13	1	12	0	0	0	0.6	1.000	OF-7

Don Flinn

FLINN, DON RAPHAEL
B. Nov. 17, 1892, Bluffdale, Tex.   D. Mar. 9, 1959, Waco, Tex.

BR TR 6'1"   185 lbs.

Year	Team		Games	BA	SA	AB	H	2B	3B	HR	HR%	R	RBI	BB	SO	SB	AB	H	PO	A	E	DP	TC/G	FA	G by Pos
1917	PIT	N	14	.297	.378	37	11	1	1	0	0.0	1	1	2	1	6	1	2	1	24	0	0	0	1.8	1.000	OF-12

Silver Flint

FLINT, FRANK SYLVESTER
B. Aug. 3, 1855, Philadelphia, Pa.   D. Jan. 14, 1892, Chicago, Ill.
Manager 1879.

BR TR 6'   180 lbs.

Year	Team		Games	BA	SA	AB	H	2B	3B	HR	HR%	R	RBI	BB	SO	SB	AB	H	PO	A	E	DP	TC/G	FA	G by Pos
1878	IND	N	63	.224	.252	254	57	7	0	0	0.0	23	18	2	15		0	0	296	102	44	7	7.0	.900	C-59, OF-9
1879	CHI	N	79	.284	.398	324	92	22	6	1	0.3	46	41	6	44		0	0	343	109	42	6	6.3	.915	C-78, OF-1
1880			74	.162	.225	284	46	10	4	0	0.0	30	17	5	32		0	0	394	119	39	5	7.5	.929	C-67, OF-13
1881			80	.310	.379	306	95	18	0	1	0.3	46	34	6	39		0	0	326	92	27	6	5.6	.939	C-80, OF-8, 1B-1
1882			81	.251	.390	331	83	18	8	4	1.2	48	44	2	50		0	0	446	91	38	3	7.1	.934	C-81, OF-10
1883			85	.265	.358	332	88	23	4	0	0.0	57		3	69		0	0	311	106	61	4	5.6	.872	C-83, OF-23
1884			73	.204	.333	279	57	5	2	9	3.2	35		7	57		0	0	354	110	61	9	7.2	.884	C-73
1885			68	.209	.269	249	52	8	2	1	0.4	27	19	2	52		0	0	356	100	36	2	7.2	.927	C-68, OF-1
1886			54	.202	.277	173	35	6	2	1	0.6	30	13	12	36		0	0	313	94	47	3	8.4	.896	C-54, 1B-3
1887			49	.267	.422	187	50	8	6	3	1.6	22	21	4	28	7	0	0	280	74	34	4	7.9	.912	C-47, 1B-2
1888			22	.182	.221	77	14	3	0	0	0.0	6	3	1	21	1	0	0	96	42	11	7	6.8	.926	C-22
1889			15	.232	.304	56	13	1	0	1	1.8	6	9	3	18	1	0	0	65	19	9	0	6.2	.903	C-15
12 yrs.			743	.239	.330	2852	682	129	34	21	0.7	376	219	53	461	9	0	0	3580	1058	449	56	6.8	.912	C-727, OF-65, 1B-6

Curt Flood

FLOOD, CURTIS CHARLES
B. Jan. 18, 1938, Houston, Tex.

BR TR 5'9"   165 lbs.

Year	Team		Games	BA	SA	AB	H	2B	3B	HR	HR%	R	RBI	BB	SO	SB	AB	H	PO	A	E	DP	TC/G	FA	G by Pos
1956	CIN	N	5	.000	.000	1	0	0	0	0	0.0	0	0	0	1	0	1	0	0	0	0	0	0.0	–	
1957			3	.333	1.333	3	1	0	0	1	33.3	2	1	0	0	0	1	0	1	0	0	0	0.3	1.000	3B-2, 2B-1
1958	STL	N	121	.261	.382	422	110	17	2	10	2.4	50	41	31	56	2	0	0	346	18	8	3	3.1	.978	OF-120, 3B-1
1959			121	.255	.418	208	53	7	3	7	3.4	24	26	16	35	2	10	5	147	1	5	1	1.3	.967	OF-106, 2B-1
1960			140	.237	.354	396	94	20	1	8	2.0	37	38	35	54	0	2	0	291	7	2	0	2.1	.993	OF-134, 3B-1
1961			132	.322	.415	335	108	15	5	2	0.6	53	21	35	33	6	12	4	241	13	4	4	2.0	.984	OF-119
1962			151	.296	.415	635	188	30	5	12	1.9	99	70	42	57	8	0	0	387	12	4	5	2.7	.990	OF-151
1963			158	.302	.403	662	200	34	9	5	0.8	112	63	42	57	17	1	0	401	12	5	2	2.6	.988	OF-158
1964			162	.311	.378	679	211	25	3	5	0.7	97	46	43	53	8	1	0	391	10	5	2	2.5	.988	OF-162
1965			156	.310	.421	617	191	30	3	11	1.8	90	83	51	50	9	5	0	349	7	5	3	2.3	.986	OF-151
1966			160	.267	.364	626	167	21	5	10	1.6	64	78	26	50	14	0	0	391	5	0	1	2.5	1.000	OF-159
1967			134	.335	.414	514	172	24	1	5	1.0	68	50	37	46	2	8	4	314	4	4	1	2.4	.988	OF-126
1968			150	.301	.366	618	186	17	4	5	0.8	71	60	33	58	11	2	0	386	11	7	4	2.7	.983	OF-149
1969			153	.285	.366	606	173	31	3	4	0.7	80	57	48	57	9	2	1	362	14	4	2	2.5	.989	OF-152
1971	WAS	A	13	.200	.200	35	7	0	0	0	0.0	4	2	5	2	0	1	0	16	0	1	0	1.3	.941	OF-10
15 yrs.			1759	.293	.389	6357	1861	271	44	85	1.3	851	636	444	609	88	46	14	4023	114	54	28	2.4	.987	OF-1697, 3B-4, 2B-2

WORLD SERIES

Year	Team		Games	BA	SA	AB	H	2B	3B	HR	HR%	R	RBI	BB	SO	SB	AB	H	PO	A	E	DP	TC/G	FA	G by Pos
1964	STL	N	7	.200	.267	30	6	0	0	0	0.0	5	3	3	1	0	0	0	13	0	0	0	1.9	1.000	OF-7
1967			7	.179	.214	28	5	1	0	0	0.0	2	3	3	3	0	0	0	15	0	0	0	2.1	1.000	OF-7
1968			7	.286	.321	28	8	1	0	0	0.0	4	2	2	2	3	0	0	13	0	0	0	1.9	1.000	OF-7
3 yrs.			21	.221	.267	86	19	2	0	0	0.0	11	8	8	6	3	0	0	41	0	0	0	2.0	1.000	OF-21

Tim Flood

FLOOD, TIMOTHY A.
B. Mar. 13, 1877, Montgomery City, Mo.   D. June 15, 1929, St. Louis, Mo.

BR TR

Year Team	Games	BA	SA	AB	H	2B	3B	HR	HR%	R	RBI	BB	SO	SB	Pinch Hit AB	Pinch Hit H	PO	A	E	DP	TC/G	FA	G by Pos

Tim Flood *continued*

Year Team	Games	BA	SA	AB	H	2B	3B	HR	HR%	R	RBI	BB	SO	SB	Pinch Hit AB	Pinch Hit H	PO	A	E	DP	TC/G	FA	G by Pos
1899 STL N	10	.290	.290	31	9	0	0	0	0.0	0	3	4		1	0	0	15	28	6	3	4.9	.878	2B-10
1902 BKN N	132	.218	.277	476	104	11	4	3	0.6	43	50	23		8	0	0	298	374	41	33	5.4	.942	2B-132, OF-1
1903	89	.249	.311	309	77	15	2	0	0.0	27	32	15		14	2	0	200	227	36	37	5.2	.922	2B-84, SS-2, OF-1
3 yrs.	231	.233	.290	816	190	26	6	3	0.4	70	85	42		23	2	0	513	629	83	73	5.3	.932	2B-226, OF-2, SS-2

Paul Florence

FLORENCE, PAUL ROBERT (Pep)
B. Apr. 22, 1900, Chicago, Ill.   D. May 28, 1986, Gainesville, Fla.   BB TR 6'1"   185 lbs.

Year Team	Games	BA	SA	AB	H	2B	3B	HR	HR%	R	RBI	BB	SO	SB	Pinch Hit AB	Pinch Hit H	PO	A	E	DP	TC/G	FA	G by Pos
1926 NY N	76	.229	.314	188	43	4	3	2	1.1	19	14	23	12	2	0	0	212	41	17	7	3.6	.937	C-76

Gil Flores

FLORES, GILBERTO
Born Gilberto Flores y Garcia.
B. Oct. 27, 1952, Ponce, Puerto Rico   BR TR 6'   185 lbs.

Year Team	Games	BA	SA	AB	H	2B	3B	HR	HR%	R	RBI	BB	SO	SB	Pinch Hit AB	Pinch Hit H	PO	A	E	DP	TC/G	FA	G by Pos
1977 CAL A	104	.278	.365	342	95	19	4	1	0.3	41	26	23	39	12	10	2	177	5	4	2	1.8	.978	OF-85, DH-8
1978 NY N	11	.276	.345	29	8	0	1	0	0.0	8	1	3	5	1	1	0	17	0	1	0	1.6	.944	OF-8
1979	70	.194	.258	93	18	1	1	1	1.1	9	10	8	17	2	39	7	39	1	1	0	0.6	.976	OF-32
3 yrs.	185	.261	.343	464	121	20	6	2	0.4	58	37	34	61	15	50	9	233	6	6	2	1.3	.976	OF-125, DH-8

Jake Flowers

FLOWERS, D'ARCY RAYMOND
B. Mar. 16, 1902, Cambridge, Md.   D. Dec. 27, 1962, Clearwater, Fla.   BR TR 5'11½" 170 lbs.

Year Team	Games	BA	SA	AB	H	2B	3B	HR	HR%	R	RBI	BB	SO	SB	Pinch Hit AB	Pinch Hit H	PO	A	E	DP	TC/G	FA	G by Pos
1923 STL N	13	.094	.125	32	3	1	0	0	0.0	2	0	2	7	1	1	0	15	28	2	1	3.5	.956	SS-7, 3B-2, 2B-2
1926	40	.270	.405	74	20	1	0	3	4.1	13	9	5	9	1	23	6	38	45	3	5	2.2	.965	2B-11, 1B-3, SS-1
1927 BKN N	67	.234	.325	231	54	5	5	2	0.9	26	20	21	25	3	1	0	139	189	19	29	5.2	.945	SS-65, 2B-1
1928	103	.274	.360	339	93	11	6	2	0.6	51	44	47	30	10	3	1	263	273	16	46	5.4	.971	2B-94, SS-6
1929	46	.200	.269	130	26	6	0	1	0.8	16	16	22	6	9	5	2	96	109	8	17	4.6	.962	2B-39
1930	89	.320	.439	253	81	18	3	2	0.8	37	50	21	18	5	16	6	154	200	19	42	4.2	.949	2B-65, OF-1
1931 2 teams				BKN N (22G - .226)						STL N (45G - .248)													
" total	67	.244	.357	168	41	11	1	2	1.2	22	20	16	10	8	12	3	89	135	4	29	3.4	.982	2B-26, SS-23, 3B-1
1932 STL N	67	.255	.332	247	63	11	1	2	0.8	35	18	31	18	7	4	2	75	106	4	14	2.8	.978	SS-7, 2B-2
1933 BKN N	78	.233	.333	210	49	11	2	2	1.0	28	22	24	15	13	7	2	130	158	11	21	3.8	.963	SS-36, 2B-19, 3B-8, OF-1
1934 CIN N	13	.333	.333	9	3	0	0	0	0.0	1	0	1	1	1	9	3	0	0	0	0	0.0	—	
10 yrs.	583	.256	.350	1693	433	75	18	16	0.9	229	201	190	139	58	81	25	999	1243	86	204	4.0	.963	2B-259, SS-145, 3B-65, 1B-3, OF-2

WORLD SERIES

Year Team	Games	BA	SA	AB	H	2B	3B	HR	HR%	R	RBI	BB	SO	SB	Pinch Hit AB	Pinch Hit H	PO	A	E	DP	TC/G	FA	G by Pos
1926 STL N	3	.000	.000	3	0	0	0	0	0.0	0	0	0	1	0	3	0	0	0	0	0	0.0	—	
1931	5	.091	.182	11	1	1	0	0	0.0	1	0	1	0	0	1	0	3	4	1	0	1.6	.875	3B-4
2 yrs.	8	.071	.143	14	1	1	0	0	0.0	1	0	1	1	0	4	0	3	4	1	0	1.0	.875	3B-4

Bobby Floyd

FLOYD, ROBERT NATHAN
B. Oct. 20, 1943, Hawthorne, Calif.   BR TR 6'1"   180 lbs.

Year Team	Games	BA	SA	AB	H	2B	3B	HR	HR%	R	RBI	BB	SO	SB	Pinch Hit AB	Pinch Hit H	PO	A	E	DP	TC/G	FA	G by Pos
1968 BAL A	5	.111	.222	9	1	1	0	0	0.0	1	0	0	3	0	0	0	6	10	0	3	3.2	1.000	SS-4
1969	39	.202	.250	84	17	4	0	0	0.0	7	1	6	17	0	1	0	64	84	6	15	3.9	.961	SS-15, 2B-15, 3B-9
1970 2 teams				BAL A (3G - .000)						KC A (14G - .326)													
" total	17	.311	.400	45	14	4	0	0	0.0	5	9	4	4	0	1	0	27	36	6	5	4.1	.913	SS-10, 3B-6, 2B-1
1971 KC A	31	.152	.197	66	10	3	0	0	0.0	8	2	7	21	0	3	1	34	56	2	14	3.0	.978	SS-15, 2B-8, 3B-1
1972	61	.179	.201	134	24	3	0	0	0.0	9	5	9	29	1	0	0	54	84	5	15	2.3	.965	3B-30, SS-29, 2B-2
1973	51	.333	.397	78	26	3	1	0	0.0	10	8	4	14	1	0	0	52	76	6	14	2.6	.955	2B-25, SS-24
1974	10	.111	.111	9	1	0	0	0	0.0	1	0	2	4	0	0	0	4	13	0	0	1.7	1.000	2B-5, 3B-2, SS-1
7 yrs.	214	.219	.266	425	93	18	1	0	0.0	40	26	28	99	2	4	1	241	359	25	66	2.9	.960	SS-98, 2B-56, 3B-48

Bubba Floyd

FLOYD, LESLIE ROE
B. June 23, 1917, Dallas, Tex.   BR TR 5'11"   160 lbs.

Year Team	Games	BA	SA	AB	H	2B	3B	HR	HR%	R	RBI	BB	SO	SB	Pinch Hit AB	Pinch Hit H	PO	A	E	DP	TC/G	FA	G by Pos
1944 DET A	3	.444	.556	9	4	1	0	0	0.0	1	0	1	0	0	0	0	1	8	0	0	3.0	1.000	SS-3

John Fluhrer

FLUHRER, JOHN L.
Played as William Morris in 1915.
B. Jan. 3, 1894, Adrian, Mich.   D. July 17, 1946, Columbus, Ohio   BR TR 5'9"   165 lbs.

Year Team	Games	BA	SA	AB	H	2B	3B	HR	HR%	R	RBI	BB	SO	SB	Pinch Hit AB	Pinch Hit H	PO	A	E	DP	TC/G	FA	G by Pos
1915 CHI N	6	.333	.333	6	2	0	0	0	0.0	0	0	1	0	1	3	0	1	0	1	0	0.3	.500	OF-2

Doug Flynn

FLYNN, ROBERT DOUGLAS
B. Apr. 18, 1951, Lexington, Ky.   BR TR 5'11"   165 lbs.

Year Team	Games	BA	SA	AB	H	2B	3B	HR	HR%	R	RBI	BB	SO	SB	Pinch Hit AB	Pinch Hit H	PO	A	E	DP	TC/G	FA	G by Pos
1975 CIN N	89	.268	.346	127	34	7	0	1	0.8	17	20	11	13	3	7	1	57	118	2	20	2.0	.989	3B-40, 2B-30, SS-17
1976	93	.283	.338	219	62	5	2	1	0.5	20	20	10	24	2	1	0	107	152	4	33	2.8	.985	2B-55, 3B-23, SS-20
1977 2 teams				CIN N (36G - .250)						NY N (90G - .191)													
" total	126	.197	.232	314	62	7	2	0	0.0	14	19	2	21	1	4	0	171	235	14	42	3.3	.967	SS-69, 2B-38, 3B-27
1978 NY N	156	.237	.289	532	126	12	8	0	0.0	37	36	30	50	3	0	0	332	426	15	91	5.0	.981	2B-128, SS-60
1979	157	.243	.317	555	135	19	5	4	0.7	35	61	17	46	0	1	1	402	421	16	107	5.3	.981	2B-148, SS-20
1980	128	.255	.312	443	113	9	8	0	0.0	46	24	22	20	2	0	0	284	374	6	70	5.2	.991	2B-128, SS-3
1981	105	.222	.292	325	72	12	4	1	0.3	24	20	11	19	1	0	0	229	319	7	61	5.3	.987	2B-100, SS-5
1982 2 teams				TEX A (88G - .211)						MON N (58G - .244)													
" total	146	.225	.268	463	104	12	4	0	0.0	26	39	8	37	6	0	0	296	411	14	88	4.9	.981	2B-113, SS-35
1983 MON N	143	.237	.294	452	107	18	4	0	0.0	44	26	19	38	2	0	0	249	375	11	77	4.4	.983	2B-107, SS-37
1984	124	.243	.281	366	89	12	1	0	0.0	23	17	12	41	0	3	0	189	291	13	66	4.0	.974	2B-88, SS-34
1985 2 teams				MON N (9G - .167)						DET A (32G - .255)													
" total	41	.246	.316	57	14	2	1	0	0.0	2	2	0	3	0	5	1	42	46	1	17	2.2	.989	2B-26, SS-9, 3B-4
11 yrs.	1308	.238	.294	3853	918	115	39	7	0.2	288	284	142	312	20	21	5	2358	3168	103	672	4.3	.982	2B-961, SS-309, 3B-94

LEAGUE CHAMPIONSHIP SERIES

Year Team	Games	BA	SA	AB	H	2B	3B	HR	HR%	R	RBI	BB	SO	SB	Pinch Hit AB	Pinch Hit H	PO	A	E	DP	TC/G	FA	G by Pos
1976 CIN N	1	—	—	0	0	0	0	0	—	0	0	0	0	0	0	0	0	0	0	0	0.0	—	2B-1

Year	Team	Games	BA	SA	AB	H	2B	3B	HR	HR%	R	RBI	BB	SO	SB	Pinch Hit AB	Pinch Hit H	PO	A	E	DP	TC/G	FA	G by Pos

Ed Flynn

FLYNN, EDWARD J.
B. 1864, Chicago, Ill. Deceased.
BL 5'9" 165 lbs.

Year	Team	Games	BA	SA	AB	H	2B	3B	HR	HR%	R	RBI	BB	SO	SB	PH AB	PH H	PO	A	E	DP	TC/G	FA	G by Pos
1887	CLE AA	7	.185	.222	27	5	1	0	0	0.0	0		1		3	0	0	16	9	6	0	4.4	.806	3B-6, OF-1

George Flynn

FLYNN, GEORGE A. (Dibby)
B. May 24, 1871, Chicago, Ill. D, Dec. 28, 1901, Chicago, Ill.

Year	Team	Games	BA	SA	AB	H	2B	3B	HR	HR%	R	RBI	BB	SO	SB	PH AB	PH H	PO	A	E	DP	TC/G	FA	G by Pos
1896	CHI N	29	.255	.302	106	27	1	2	0	0.0	15	4	11	9	12	0	0	66	6	10	3	2.8	.878	OF-29

Jocko Flynn

FLYNN, JOHN A.
B. June 30, 1864, Lawrence, Mass. D. Dec. 30, 1907, Lawrence, Mass.
5'6½" 143 lbs.

Year	Team	Games	BA	SA	AB	H	2B	3B	HR	HR%	R	RBI	BB	SO	SB	PH AB	PH H	PO	A	E	DP	TC/G	FA	G by Pos
1886	CHI N	57	.200	.307	205	41	6	2	4	2.0	40	19	18	45		0	0	34	59	9	2	1.8	.912	P-32, OF-28
1887		1	–	–	0	0	0	0	0	–	0	0	0	0	0	0	0	0	0	1	0	1.0	–	OF-1
2 yrs.		58	.200	.307	205	41	6	2	4	2.0	40	19	18	45		0	0	34	59	10	2	1.8	.903	P-32, OF-29

Joe Flynn

FLYNN, JOSEPH
B. Philadelphia, Pa. Deceased.

Year	Team	Games	BA	SA	AB	H	2B	3B	HR	HR%	R	RBI	BB	SO	SB	PH AB	PH H	PO	A	E	DP	TC/G	FA	G by Pos
1884	2 teams		PHI U (52G – .249)					BOS U (9G – .226)																
"	total	61	.246	.375	240	59	11	4	4	1.7	42		13			0	0	136	40	46	4	3.6	.793	OF-47, C-17, 1B-2, SS-1

John Flynn

FLYNN, JOHN ANTHONY
B. Sept. 7, 1883, Providence, R. I. D. Mar. 23, 1935, Providence, R. I.
BR TR 6'½" 175 lbs.

Year	Team	Games	BA	SA	AB	H	2B	3B	HR	HR%	R	RBI	BB	SO	SB	PH AB	PH H	PO	A	E	DP	TC/G	FA	G by Pos
1910	PIT N	96	.274	.370	332	91	10	2	6	**1.8**	32	52	30	47	6	3	2	869	49	22	54	9.8	.977	1B-93
1911		33	.203	.237	59	12	0	1	0	0.0	5	3	9	8	0	15	3	101	8	1	7	3.3	.991	1B-13, OF-1
1912	WAS A	20	.169	.254	71	12	4	1	0	0.0	9	5	7		2	0	0	176	15	5	9	9.8	.974	1B-20
3 yrs.		149	.249	.335	462	115	14	4	6	1.3	46	60	46	55	8	18	5	1146	72	28	70	8.4	.978	1B-126, OF-1

Mike Flynn

FLYNN, MICHAEL E.
B. Lowell, Mass. Deceased.

Year	Team	Games	BA	SA	AB	H	2B	3B	HR	HR%	R	RBI	BB	SO	SB	PH AB	PH H	PO	A	E	DP	TC/G	FA	G by Pos
1891	BOS AA	1	.000	.000	2	0	0	0	0	0.0	0	0	0	1	0	0	0	4	2	0	0	6.0	1.000	C-1

Jim Fogarty

FOGARTY, JAMES G.
Brother of Joe Fogarty.
B. Feb. 12, 1864, San Francisco, Calif. D. May 20, 1891, San Francisco, Calif.
Manager 1890.
BR TR 5'10½" 180 lbs.

Year	Team	Games	BA	SA	AB	H	2B	3B	HR	HR%	R	RBI	BB	SO	SB	PH AB	PH H	PO	A	E	DP	TC/G	FA	G by Pos
1884	PHI N	97	.212	.283	378	80	12	6	1	0.3	42		20	54		0	0	229	43	34	5	3.2	.889	OF-78, 3B-14, 2B-4, SS-3, P-1
1885		111	.232	.276	427	99	13	3	0	0.0	49		30	37		0	0	273	92	29	12	3.5	.926	OF-88, 2B-10, SS-8, 3B-5
1886		77	.293	.407	280	82	13	5	3	1.1	54	47	42	16		0	0	152	51	22	10	2.9	.902	OF-60, 2B-13, SS-3, 3B-3, P-1
1887		126	.261	.410	495	129	26	12	8	1.6	113	50	**82**	44	102	0	0	274	47	29	10	2.8	.917	OF-123, SS-2, 3B-2, 2B-1, P-1
1888		121	.236	.300	454	107	14	6	1	0.2	72	35	53	66	58	0	0	251	35	25	11	2.6	.920	OF-117, 3B-5, SS-1
1889		128	.259	.375	499	129	15	17	3	0.6	107	54	65	60	**99**	0	0	302	43	15	6	2.8	.958	OF-128, P-4
1890	PHI P	91	.239	.357	347	83	17	6	4	1.2	71	58	59	50	36	0	0	192	17	8	3	2.4	.963	OF-91, 3B-1
7 yrs.		751	.246	.343	2880	709	110	55	20	0.7	508	244	351	327	295	0	0	1673	328	162	57	2.9	.925	OF-685, 3B-30, 2B-28, SS-17, P-7

Joe Fogarty

FOGARTY, JOSEPH J.
Brother of Jim Fogarty.
B. Nov. 8, 1868, San Francisco, Calif. D. Mar. 28, 1918, San Francisco, Calif.

Year	Team	Games	BA	SA	AB	H	2B	3B	HR	HR%	R	RBI	BB	SO	SB	PH AB	PH H	PO	A	E	DP	TC/G	FA	G by Pos
1885	STL N	2	.125	.125	8	1	0	0	0	0.0	1	0	0	1		0	0	2	0	0	0	1.0	1.000	OF-2

Lee Fohl

FOHL, LEO ALEXANDER
B. Nov. 28, 1870, Pittsburgh, Pa. D. Oct. 30, 1965, Cleveland, Ohio
Manager 1915-19, 1921-26.
BL TR 5'10" 175 lbs.

Year	Team	Games	BA	SA	AB	H	2B	3B	HR	HR%	R	RBI	BB	SO	SB	PH AB	PH H	PO	A	E	DP	TC/G	FA	G by Pos
1902	PIT N	1	.000	.000	3	0	0	0	0	0.0	0	1	0		0	0	0	5	2	1	0	8.0	.875	C-1
1903	CIN N	4	.357	.571	14	5	1	1	0	0.0	3	2	0		0	0	0	15	6	1	0	5.5	.955	C-4
2 yrs.		5	.294	.471	17	5	1	1	0	0.0	3	3	0		0	0	0	20	8	2	0	6.0	.933	C-5

Hank Foiles

FOILES, HENRY LEE
B. June 10, 1929, Richmond, Va.
BR TR 6' 195 lbs.

Year	Team	Games	BA	SA	AB	H	2B	3B	HR	HR%	R	RBI	BB	SO	SB	PH AB	PH H	PO	A	E	DP	TC/G	FA	G by Pos
1953	2 teams		CIN N (5G – .154)					CLE A (7G – .143)																
"	total	12	.150	.150	20	3	0	0	0	0.0	3	0	2	3	0	2	0	17	7	2	1	2.2	.923	C-10
1955	CLE A	62	.261	.369	111	29	9	0	1	0.9	13	7	17	18	0	20	6	222	23	3	7	4.0	.988	C-41
1956	2 teams		CLE A (1G – .000)					PIT N (79G – .212)																
"	total	80	.212	.369	222	47	10	2	7	3.2	24	25	17	56	0	5	1	291	30	4	8	4.1	.988	C-74
1957	PIT N	109	.270	.431	281	76	10	4	9	3.2	32	36	37	53	1	4	0	436	32	9	2	4.4	.981	C-109
1958		104	.205	.348	264	54	10	2	8	3.0	31	30	45	53	0	1	0	456	41	5	5	4.8	.990	C-103
1959		53	.225	.375	80	18	3	0	3	3.8	10	4	7	16	0	1	0	153	9	0	3	3.0	1.000	C-51
1960	3 teams		KC A (6G – .571)					CLE A (24G – .279)			DET A (26G – .250)													
"	total	56	.282	.336	131	37	4	0	1	0.8	15	10	11	15	1	6	1	204	23	3	5	4.1	.987	C-46
1961	BAL A	43	.274	.468	124	34	6	0	6	4.8	18	19	12	27	0	4	0	194	17	1	4	4.9	.995	C-38
1962	CIN N	43	.275	.496	131	36	6	1	7	5.3	17	25	13	39	0	5	2	249	14	5	1	6.2	.981	C-41
1963	2 teams		CIN N (1G – .000)					LA A (41G – .214)																
"	total	42	.207	.379	87	18	1	1	4	4.6	8	10	9	13	1	11	2	140	14	4	4	3.8	.975	C-31
1964	LA A	4	.250	.250	4	1	0	0	0	0.0	0	0	0	2	0	4	1	0	0	0	0	0.0	–	
11 yrs.		608	.243	.392	1455	353	59	10	46	3.2	171	166	170	295	3	62	13	2362	209	36	40	4.3	.986	C-544

Curry Foley

FOLEY, CHARLES JOSEPH
B. Jan. 14, 1856, Milltown, Ireland D. Oct. 20, 1898, New York, N. Y.
TL 180 lbs.

Year	Team	Games	BA	SA	AB	H	2B	3B	HR	HR%	R	RBI	BB	SO	SB	PH AB	PH H	PO	A	E	DP	TC/G	FA	G by Pos
1879	BOS N	35	.315	.349	146	46	3	1	0	0.0	16	17	3	4		0	0	29	29	13	0	2.0	.817	P-21, OF-17, 1B-2

Year	Team		Games	BA	SA	AB	H	2B	3B	HR	HR%	R	RBI	BB	SO	SB	Pinch Hit AB	Pinch Hit H	PO	A	E	DP	TC/G	FA	G by Pos

Curry Foley *continued*

Year	Team		Games	BA	SA	AB	H	2B	3B	HR	HR%	R	RBI	BB	SO	SB	PH AB	PH H	PO	A	E	DP	TC/G	FA	G by Pos
1880			80	.292	.361	332	97	13	2	2	0.6	44	31	8	14		0	0	276	63	25	10	4.6	.931	P-36, OF-35, 1B-25
1881	BUF	N	83	.256	.328	375	96	20	2	1	0.3	58	25	7	27		0	0	372	32	38	14	5.3	.914	OF-55, 1B-27, P-10
1882			84	.305	.402	341	104	16	4	3	0.9	51		12	26		0	0	118	22	28	7	2.0	.833	OF-84, P-1
1883			23	.270	.369	111	30	5	3	0	0.0	23		4	12		0	0	44	2	6	0	2.3	.885	OF-23, P-1
5 yrs.			305	.286	.362	1305	373	57	12	6	0.5	192	73	34	83		0	0	839	148	110	31	3.6	.900	OF-214, P-69, 1B-54

Marv Foley

FOLEY, MARVIS EDWIN   BL TR 6'   195 lbs.
B. Aug. 29, 1953, Stanford, Ky.

Year	Team		Games	BA	SA	AB	H	2B	3B	HR	HR%	R	RBI	BB	SO	SB	PH AB	PH H	PO	A	E	DP	TC/G	FA	G by Pos
1978	CHI	A	11	.353	.353	34	12	0	0	0	0.0	3	6	4	6	0	1	0	41	4	3	0	4.4	.938	C-10
1979			34	.247	.340	97	24	3	0	2	2.1	6	10	7	5	0	2	1	128	11	1	1	4.1	.993	C-33
1980			68	.212	.336	137	29	5	0	4	2.9	14	15	9	22	0	8	3	220	17	2	3	3.5	.992	C-64, 1B-3
1982			27	.111	.111	36	4	0	0	0	0.0	1	1	6	4	0	11	1	47	4	1	0	1.9	.981	C-15, 3B-2, DH-1, 1B-1
1984	TEX	A	63	.217	.391	115	25	2	0	6	5.2	13	19	15	24	0	28	7	148	14	2	3	2.6	.988	C-36, DH-4, 3B-1, 1B-1
5 yrs.			203	.224	.334	419	94	10	0	12	2.9	37	51	41	61	0	50	12	584	50	9	7	3.2	.986	C-158, DH-5, 1B-5, 3B-3

Pat Foley

Playing record listed under Willie Greene

Ray Foley

FOLEY, RAYMOND KIRWIN   BL TR 5'11"   173 lbs.
B. June 23, 1906, Naugatuck, Conn.   D. Mar. 22, 1980, Vero Beach, Fla.

Year	Team		Games	BA	SA	AB	H	2B	3B	HR	HR%	R	RBI	BB	SO	SB	PH AB	PH H	PO	A	E	DP	TC/G	FA	G by Pos
1928	NY	N	2	.000	.000	1	0	0	0	0	0.0	1	0	1	1	0	1	0	0	0	0	0	0.0	—	

Tom Foley

FOLEY, THOMAS MICHAEL   BL TR 6'1"   160 lbs.
B. Sept. 9, 1959, Fort Benning, Ga.

Year	Team		Games	BA	SA	AB	H	2B	3B	HR	HR%	R	RBI	BB	SO	SB	PH AB	PH H	PO	A	E	DP	TC/G	FA	G by Pos
1983	CIN	N	68	.204	.265	98	20	4	1	0	0.0	7	9	13	17	1	20	4	54	76	2	16	1.9	.985	SS-37, 2B-5
1984			106	.253	.357	277	70	8	3	5	1.8	26	27	24	36	3	13	5	119	228	11	36	3.4	.969	SS-83, 2B-10, 3B-1
1985	2 teams			CIN N (43G – .196)		PHI N (46G – .266)																			
"	total		89	.240	.336	250	60	13	1	3	1.2	24	23	19	34	2	12	1	127	202	7	47	3.8	.979	SS-60, 2B-18, 3B-1
1986	2 teams			PHI N (39G – .295)		MON N (64G – .257)																			
"	total		103	.266	.357	263	70	15	3	1	0.4	26	23	30	37	10	22	5	117	190	6	29	3.0	.981	SS-53, 2B-26, 3B-1
1987	MON	N	106	.293	.432	280	82	18	3	5	1.8	35	28	11	40	6	24	5	134	190	9	43	3.1	.973	SS-49, 2B-39, 3B-9
1988			127	.265	.377	377	100	21	3	5	1.3	33	43	30	49	2	14	1	204	324	15	61	4.3	.972	2B-89, SS-32, 3B-9
1989			122	.229	.347	375	86	19	2	7	1.9	34	39	45	53	2	12	2	203	317	8	58	4.3	.985	2B-108, 3B-16, SS-14, P-1
7 yrs.			721	.254	.363	1920	488	98	16	26	1.4	185	192	172	266	26	117	23	958	1527	58	290	3.5	.977	SS-328, 2B-295, 3B-52, P-1

Will Foley

FOLEY, WILLIAM BROWN   BR TR 5'9½"   150 lbs.
B. Nov. 15, 1855, Chicago, Ill.   D. Nov. 12, 1916, Chicago, Ill.

Year	Team		Games	BA	SA	AB	H	2B	3B	HR	HR%	R	RBI	BB	SO	SB	PH AB	PH H	PO	A	E	DP	TC/G	FA	G by Pos
1876	CIN	N	58	.226	.258	221	50	3	2	0	0.0	19	9	0	14		0	0	137	111	63	5	5.4	.797	3B-46, C-20
1877			56	.190	.222	216	41	5	1	0	0.0	23	18	4	13		0	0	94	130	44	9	4.8	.836	3B-56
1878	MIL	N	56	.271	.349	229	62	8	5	0	0.0	33	22	7	14		0	0	101	103	39	8	4.3	.840	3B-53, C-7
1879	CIN	N	56	.211	.243	218	46	5	1	0	0.0	22	25	2	16		0	0	90	72	34	8	3.5	.827	3B-29, OF-25, 2B-3
1881	DET	N	5	.133	.133	15	2	0	0	0	0.0	0	1	2	3		0	0	5	5	3	3	2.6	.769	3B-5
1884	CHI	U	19	.282	.324	71	20	1	1	0	0.0	15		5			0	0	18	23	10	2	2.7	.804	3B-19
6 yrs.			250	.228	.271	970	221	22	10	0	0.0	112	75	20	60		0	0	445	444	193	35	4.3	.822	3B-208, C-27, OF-25, 2B-3

Tim Foli

FOLI, TIMOTHY JOHN   BR TR 6'   179 lbs.
B. Dec. 8, 1950, Culver City, Calif.

Year	Team		Games	BA	SA	AB	H	2B	3B	HR	HR%	R	RBI	BB	SO	SB	PH AB	PH H	PO	A	E	DP	TC/G	FA	G by Pos
1970	NY	N	5	.364	.364	11	4	0	0	0	0.0	0	1	0	2	0	1	1	4	10	0	1	2.8	1.000	SS-2, 3B-2
1971			97	.226	.281	288	65	12	2	0	0.0	32	24	18	50	5	2	0	150	199	12	43	3.7	.967	2B-58, 3B-36, SS-12, OF-1
1972	MON	N	149	.241	.281	540	130	12	2	2	0.4	45	35	25	43	11	1	0	281	487	27	94	5.3	.966	SS-148, 2B-1
1973			126	.240	.277	458	110	11	0	2	0.4	37	36	28	40	6	1	0	248	399	27	85	5.3	.960	SS-123, 2B-2, OF-1
1974			121	.254	.290	441	112	10	3	0	0.0	41	39	28	27	8	1	1	220	412	19	85	5.4	.971	SS-120, OF-1
1975			152	.238	.294	572	136	25	2	1	0.2	64	29	36	49	13	3	0	261	497	21	104	5.1	.973	SS-151, 2B-1
1976			149	.264	.366	546	144	36	1	6	1.1	41	54	16	33	6	5	1	249	470	18	102	4.9	.976	SS-146, 3B-1
1977	2 teams			MON N (13G – .175)		SF N (104G – .228)																			
"	total		117	.221	.320	425	94	22	4	4	0.9	32	30	11	20	2	4	2	217	345	13	78	4.9	.977	SS-115, OF-1, 3B-1, 2B-1
1978	NY	N	113	.257	.320	413	106	21	1	1	0.2	37	27	14	30	2	1	0	190	314	15	78	4.6	.966	SS-112
1979	2 teams			NY N (3G – .000)		PIT N (133G – .291)																			
"	total		136	.288	.340	532	153	23	1	1	0.2	70	65	28	14	6	1	0	259	410	15	98	5.0	.978	SS-135
1980	PIT	N	127	.265	.327	495	131	22	0	3	0.6	61	38	19	23	11	1	0	212	402	12	87	4.9	.981	SS-125
1981			86	.247	.297	316	78	12	2	0	0.0	32	20	17	10	7	4	0	140	247	14	52	4.7	.965	SS-81
1982	CAL	A	150	.252	.308	480	121	14	2	3	0.6	46	56	14	22	2	1	0	247	462	12	93	4.8	.983	SS-139, 2B-8, 3B-2
1983			88	.252	.300	330	83	10	0	2	0.6	29	29	5	18	2	0	0	131	298	13	54	5.0	.971	SS-74, 3B-13
1984	NY	A	61	.252	.319	163	41	11	0	0	0.0	8	16	2	16	0	4	0	88	122	6	32	3.5	.972	SS-28, 2B-21, 3B-10, 1B-2
1985	PIT	N	19	.189	.189	37	7	0	0	0	0.0	1	2	4	2	0	6	2	16	34	1	6	2.7	.980	SS-13
16 yrs.			1696	.251	.309	6047	1515	241	20	25	0.4	576	501	265	399	81	35	7	2913	5108	228	1092	4.9	.972	SS-1524, 2B-92, 3B-65, OF-4, 1B-2

LEAGUE CHAMPIONSHIP SERIES

Year	Team		Games	BA	SA	AB	H	2B	3B	HR	HR%	R	RBI	BB	SO	SB	PH AB	PH H	PO	A	E	DP	TC/G	FA	G by Pos
1979	PIT	N	3	.333	.417	12	4	1	0	0	0.0	1	3	0	0	0	0	0	3	9	0	1	4.0	1.000	SS-3
1982	CAL	A	5	.125	.125	16	2	0	0	0	0.0	0	1	0	3	0	0	0	0	0	0	0	0.0	—	SS-5
2 yrs.			8	.214	.250	28	6	1	0	0	0.0	1	4	0	3	0	0	0	3	9	0	1	1.5	1.000	SS-8

WORLD SERIES

Year	Team		Games	BA	SA	AB	H	2B	3B	HR	HR%	R	RBI	BB	SO	SB	PH AB	PH H	PO	A	E	DP	TC/G	FA	G by Pos
1979	PIT	N	7	.333	.433	30	10	1	1	0	0.0	6	3	2	0	0	0	0	8	32	3	7	6.1	.930	SS-7

Dee Fondy

FONDY, DEE VIRGIL   BL TL 6'3"   195 lbs.
B. Oct. 31, 1924, Slaton, Tex.

Year	Team		Games	BA	SA	AB	H	2B	3B	HR	HR%	R	RBI	BB	SO	SB	PH AB	PH H	PO	A	E	DP	TC/G	FA	G by Pos
1951	CHI	N	49	.271	.388	170	46	7	2	3	1.8	23	20	11	20	5	5	1	387	27	10	40	8.7	.976	1B-44
1952			145	.300	.424	554	166	21	9	10	1.8	69	67	28	60	13	2	0	1257	103	14	92	9.5	.990	1B-143
1953			150	.309	.477	595	184	24	11	18	3.0	79	78	44	106	10	1	0	1274	115	18	105	9.4	.987	1B-149
1954			141	.285	.400	568	162	30	4	9	1.6	77	49	35	84	20	2	1	1228	119	9	129	9.6	.993	1B-138

Year	Team	Games	BA	SA	AB	H	2B	3B	HR	HR%	R	RBI	BB	SO	SB	Pinch Hit AB	Pinch Hit H	PO	A	E	DP	TC/G	FA	G by Pos

Dee Fondy *continued*

Year	Team	Games	BA	SA	AB	H	2B	3B	HR	HR%	R	RBI	BB	SO	SB	AB	H	PO	A	E	DP	TC/G	FA	G by Pos
1955		150	.265	.422	574	152	23	8	17	3.0	69	65	35	87	8	0	0	1304	107	13	135	9.5	.991	1B-147
1956		137	.269	.392	543	146	22	9	9	1.7	52	46	20	74	9	4	1	1048	94	17	101	8.5	.985	1B-133
1957	2 teams		CHI	N (11G – .314)		PIT	N (95G – .313)																	
"	total	106	.313	.388	374	117	16	3	2	0.5	45	37	25	68	12	23	6	801	60	15	73	8.3	.983	1B-84
1958	CIN N	89	.218	.266	124	27	1	1	1	0.8	23	11	5	27	7	23	4	160	16	2	15	2.0	.989	1B-36, OF-22
8 yrs.		967	.286	.413	3502	1000	144	47	69	2.0	437	373	203	526	84	60	13	7459	641	98	690	8.5	.988	1B-874, OF-22

Lew Fonseca

FONSECA, LEWIS ALBERT
B. Jan. 21, 1899, Oakland, Calif.   D. Nov. 26, 1989, Ely, Iowa
Manager 1932-34.

BR TR 5'10½" 180 lbs.

Year	Team	Games	BA	SA	AB	H	2B	3B	HR	HR%	R	RBI	BB	SO	SB	AB	H	PO	A	E	DP	TC/G	FA	G by Pos
1921	CIN N	82	.276	.340	297	82	10	3	1	0.3	38	41	8	13	2	2	0	307	155	14	30	5.8	.971	2B-50, OF-16, 1B-16
1922		91	.361	.491	291	105	20	3	4	1.4	55	45	14	18	7	18	8	197	251	14	40	5.1	.970	2B-71
1923		65	.278	.397	237	66	11	4	3	1.3	33	28	9	16	4	6	2	252	176	15	37	6.8	.966	2B-45, 1B-14
1924		20	.228	.298	57	13	2	1	0	0.0	5	9	4	4	1	4	0	62	30	1	4	4.7	.989	2B-10, 1B-6
1925	PHI N	126	.319	.450	467	149	30	5	7	1.5	78	60	21	42	6	5	1	648	245	20	68	7.2	.978	2B-69, 1B-55
1927	CLE A	112	.311	.404	428	133	20	7	2	0.5	60	40	12	17	12	6	1	347	305	16	60	6.0	.976	2B-96, 1B-13
1928		75	.327	.464	263	86	19	4	3	1.1	38	36	13	17	4	0	0	553	78	3	67	8.5	.995	1B-56, 3B-15, SS-4, 2B-1
1929		148	**.369**	.532	566	209	44	15	6	1.1	97	103	50	23	19	1	0	1486	107	8	141	10.8	.995	1B-147
1930		40	.279	.380	129	36	9	2	0	0.0	20	17	7	7	1	5	0	277	29	9	15	7.9	.971	1B-28, 3B-6
1931	2 teams		CLE	A (26G – .370)		CHI	A (121G – .299)																	
"	total	147	.312	.410	573	179	35	6	3	0.5	86	85	40	29	7	4	1	518	68	9	28	4.0	.985	OF-95, 1B-28, 2B-21, 3B-1
1932	CHI A	18	.135	.162	37	5	1	0	0	0.0	6	6	1	7	0	7	3	14	2	0	1	0.9	1.000	OF-8, P-1
1933		23	.203	.339	59	12	2	0	2	3.4	8	15	7	6	1	10	1	138	12	0	15	6.5	1.000	1B-12
12 yrs.		947	.316	.432	3404	1075	203	50	31	0.9	518	485	186	199	64	68	17	4799	1458	109	506	6.7	.983	1B-375, 2B-363, OF-119, 3B-22, SS-4, P-1

Barry Foote

FOOTE, BARRY CLIFTON
B. Feb. 16, 1952, Smithfield, N. C.

BR TR 6'3" 205 lbs.

Year	Team	Games	BA	SA	AB	H	2B	3B	HR	HR%	R	RBI	BB	SO	SB	AB	H	PO	A	E	DP	TC/G	FA	G by Pos
1973	MON N	6	.667	1.000	6	4	0	0	0	0.0	0	1	0	0	0	6	4	0	0	0	0	0.0	–	
1974		125	.262	.414	420	110	23	4	11	2.6	44	60	35	74	2	3	2	640	83	12	12	5.9	.984	C-122
1975		118	.194	.295	387	75	16	1	7	1.8	25	30	17	48	1	0	6	590	50	10	10	5.5	.985	C-115
1976		105	.234	.340	350	82	12	2	7	2.0	32	27	17	32	2	8	2	487	61	6	13	5.3	.989	C-96, 3B-2, 1B-1
1977	2 teams		MON	N (15G – .245)		PHI	N (18G – .219)																	
"	total	33	.235	.420	81	19	4	1	3	3.7	7	11	7	16	0	4	0	121	11	2	2	4.1	.985	C-30
1978	PHI N	39	.158	.211	57	9	0	0	1	1.8	4	4	1	11	0	13	1	78	5	0	0	2.1	1.000	C-31
1979	CHI N	132	.254	.427	429	109	26	0	16	3.7	47	56	34	49	5	5	0	713	63	17	9	6.0	.979	C-129
1980		63	.238	.401	202	48	13	1	6	3.0	16	28	13	18	1	9	2	317	36	3	5	5.7	.992	C-55
1981	2 teams		CHI	N (9G – .000)		NY	A (40G – .208)																	
"	total	49	.177	.327	147	26	4	0	6	4.1	12	11	11	28	0	4	0	30	3	0	2	0.7	1.000	C-42, DH-4, 1B-1
1982	NY A	17	.146	.250	48	7	5	0	0	0.0	4	2	1	11	0	0	0	71	2	2	0	4.4	.973	C-17
10 yrs.		687	.230	.368	2127	489	103	10	57	2.7	191	230	136	287	10	58	14	3047	314	52	53	5.0	.985	C-637, DH-4, 3B-2, 1B-2

DIVISIONAL PLAYOFF SERIES

Year	Team	Games	BA	SA	AB	H	2B	3B	HR	HR%	R	RBI	BB	SO	SB	AB	H	PO	A	E	DP	TC/G	FA	G by Pos
1981	NY A	1	–	–	0	0	0	0	0	0.0	0	0	0	0	0	0	0	0	0	0	0	0.0	–	

LEAGUE CHAMPIONSHIP SERIES

Year	Team	Games	BA	SA	AB	H	2B	3B	HR	HR%	R	RBI	BB	SO	SB	AB	H	PO	A	E	DP	TC/G	FA	G by Pos
1978	PHI N	1	.000	.000	1	0	0	0	0	0.0	0	0	0	0	0	0	0	0	0	0	0	0.0	–	
1981	NY A	2	1.000	1.000	1	1	0	0	0	0.0	0	0	0	0	0	1	1	0	0	0	0	0.0	–	C-1
2 yrs.		3	.500	.500	2	1	0	0	0	0.0	0	0	0	0	0	2	1	0	0	0	0	0.0	–	C-1

WORLD SERIES

Year	Team	Games	BA	SA	AB	H	2B	3B	HR	HR%	R	RBI	BB	SO	SB	AB	H	PO	A	E	DP	TC/G	FA	G by Pos
1981	NY A	1	.000	.000	1	0	0	0	0	0.0	0	0	0	1	0	1	0	0	0	0	0	0.0	–	

Davy Force

FORCE, DAVID W. (Tom Thumb)
B. July 27, 1849, New York, N. Y.   D. June 21, 1918, Englewood, N. J.

BR TR 5'4" 130 lbs.

Year	Team	Games	BA	SA	AB	H	2B	3B	HR	HR%	R	RBI	BB	SO	SB	AB	H	PO	A	E	DP	TC/G	FA	G by Pos
1876	2 teams		PHI	N (60G – .232)		NY	N (1G – .000)																	
"	total	61	.230	.251	287	66	6	0	0	0.0	48	17	5			0	0	112	243	42	11	6.5	.894	SS-61, 3B-2
1877	STL N	58	.262	.311	225	59	5	3	0	0.0	24	22	11	15		0	0	86	175	24	9	4.9	.916	SS-50, 3B-8
1879	BUF N	79	.209	.237	316	66	5	2	0	0.0	36	8	13	37		0	0	75	265	26	26	4.6	.929	SS-78, 3B-1
1880		81	.169	.203	290	49	10	0	0	0.0	22	17	10	35		0	0	222	324	38	37	7.2	.935	2B-53, SS-30
1881		75	.180	.219	278	50	9	1	0	0.0	21	15	11	29		0	0	195	299	32	25	7.0	.939	2B-51, SS-21, OF-3, 3B-1
1882		73	.241	.295	278	67	10	2	1	0.4	39		12	17		0	0	85	230	32	13	4.8	.908	SS-61, 3B-11, 2B-1
1883		96	.217	.262	378	82	11	3	0	0.0	40		12	39		0	0	117	280	53	28	4.7	.882	SS-78, 3B-13, 2B-7
1884		106	.206	.253	403	83	13	3	0	0.0	47		27	41		0	0	113	315	49	21	4.5	.897	SS-105, 2B-1
1885		71	.225	.257	253	57	6	1	0	0.0	20		13	19		0	0	148	213	47	29	5.7	.885	2B-42, SS-24, 3B-6
1886	WAS N	68	.182	.211	242	44	5	1	0	0.0	26	16	17	26		0	0	77	246	34	25	5.3	.905	SS-56, 2B-8, 3B-4
10 yrs.		768	.211	.249	2950	623	80	15	1	0.0	323	112	131	261		0	0	1230	2590	377	224	5.5	.910	SS-564, 2B-163, 3B-46, OF-3

Curt Ford

FORD, CURTIS GLENN
B. Oct. 11, 1960, Jackson, Miss.

BL TR 5'10" 150 lbs.

Year	Team	Games	BA	SA	AB	H	2B	3B	HR	HR%	R	RBI	BB	SO	SB	AB	H	PO	A	E	DP	TC/G	FA	G by Pos
1985	STL N	11	.500	.667	12	6	0	0	0	0.0	2	3	4	1	1	4	2	3	0	1	0	0.4	.750	OF-4
1986		85	.248	.364	214	53	15	2	2	0.9	30	29	23	29	13	25	5	109	7	3	5	1.4	.975	OF-64
1987		89	.285	.408	228	65	9	5	3	1.3	32	26	14	32	11	18	7	157	2	3	0	1.8	.981	OF-75
1988		91	.195	.266	128	25	6	0	1	0.8	11	18	8	26	6	40	9	95	6	2	5	1.1	.981	OF-40, 1B-7
1989	PHI N	108	.218	.289	142	31	5	1	1	0.7	13	13	16	33	5	62	11	46	5	0	0	0.5	1.000	OF-52, 2B-1, 1B-1
5 yrs.		384	.249	.351	724	180	37	8	7	1.0	88	89	65	121	36	149	34	410	20	9	10	1.1	.979	OF-235, 1B-8, 2B-1

LEAGUE CHAMPIONSHIP SERIES

Year	Team	Games	BA	SA	AB	H	2B	3B	HR	HR%	R	RBI	BB	SO	SB	AB	H	PO	A	E	DP	TC/G	FA	G by Pos
1987	STL N	4	.333	.333	9	3	0	0	0	0.0	2	0	1	1	0	1	0	6	0	0	0	1.5	1.000	OF-4

WORLD SERIES

Year	Team	Games	BA	SA	AB	H	2B	3B	HR	HR%	R	RBI	BB	SO	SB	AB	H	PO	A	E	DP	TC/G	FA	G by Pos
1987	STL N	5	.308	.308	13	4	0	0	0	0.0	2	1	1	1	0	1	0	5	0	0	0	1.0	1.000	OF-4

Year	Team		Games	BA	SA	AB	H	2B	3B	HR	HR%	R	RBI	BB	SO	SB	Pinch Hit AB	H	PO	A	E	DP	TC/G	FA	G by Pos

Dan Ford
FORD, DARNELL GLENN (Disco Danny)   BR TR 6'1" 185 lbs.
B. May 19, 1952, Los Angeles, Calif.

Year	Team		Games	BA	SA	AB	H	2B	3B	HR	HR%	R	RBI	BB	SO	SB	PH AB	PH H	PO	A	E	DP	TC/G	FA	G by Pos
1975	MIN	A	130	.280	.434	440	123	21	1	15	3.4	72	59	30	79	6	6	2	246	3	3	2	1.9	.988	OF-120, DH-3
1976			145	.267	.457	514	137	24	7	20	3.9	87	86	36	118	17	6	2	267	6	9	1	1.9	.968	OF-139, DH-3
1977			144	.267	.426	453	121	25	7	11	2.4	66	60	41	79	6	20	7	205	9	8	2	1.5	.964	OF-137, DH-3
1978			151	.274	.424	592	162	36	10	11	1.9	78	82	48	88	7	2	0	376	6	9	2	2.6	.977	OF-149, DH-1
1979	CAL	A	142	.290	.464	569	165	26	5	21	3.7	100	101	40	86	8	1	0	332	10	8	2	2.5	.977	OF-141
1980			65	.279	.420	226	63	11	0	7	3.1	22	26	19	45	0	7	3	75	3	5	0	1.3	.940	OF-45, DH-15
1981			97	.277	.440	375	104	14	1	15	4.0	53	48	23	71	2	0	0	188	3	8	0	2.1	.960	OF-97
1982	BAL	A	123	.235	.371	421	99	21	3	10	2.4	46	43	23	71	5	18	4	263	6	7	2	2.2	.975	OF-119, DH-1
1983			103	.280	.440	407	114	30	4	9	2.2	63	55	29	55	9	2	1	218	2	3	0	2.2	.987	OF-103
1984			25	.231	.308	91	21	4	0	1	1.1	7	5	7	13	1	1	0	36	1	0	0	1.5	1.000	OF-15, DH-8
1985			28	.187	.253	75	14	2	0	1	1.3	4	1	7	17	0	9	1	0	0	0	0	0.0	–	DH-28
11 yrs.			1153	.270	.427	4163	1123	214	38	121	2.9	598	566	303	722	61	72	20	2206	49	60	11	2.0	.974	OF-1065, DH-62

LEAGUE CHAMPIONSHIP SERIES

Year	Team		Games	BA	SA	AB	H	2B	3B	HR	HR%	R	RBI	BB	SO	SB	PH AB	PH H	PO	A	E	DP	TC/G	FA	G by Pos
1979	CAL	A	4	.294	.706	17	5	1	0	2	11.8	2	4	0	0	0	0	0	6	0	1	0	1.8	.857	OF-4
1983	BAL	A	2	.200	.400	5	1	1	0	0	0.0	0	0	0	1	0	1	0	1	0	0	0	0.5	1.000	DH-1, OF-1
2 yrs.			6	.273	.636	22	6	2	0	2	9.1	2	4	0	1	0	1	0	7	0	1	0	1.3	.875	OF-5, DH-1

WORLD SERIES

Year	Team		Games	BA	SA	AB	H	2B	3B	HR	HR%	R	RBI	BB	SO	SB	PH AB	PH H	PO	A	E	DP	TC/G	FA	G by Pos
1983	BAL	A	5	.167	.417	12	2	0	1	1	8.3	1	1	1	5	0	0	0	5	1	0	0	1.2	1.000	OF-4

Ed Ford
FORD, EDWARD L.   5'9½" 160 lbs.
B. 1862, Richmond, Va. Deceased.

Year	Team		Games	BA	SA	AB	H	2B	3B	HR	HR%	R	RBI	BB	SO	SB	PH AB	PH H	PO	A	E	DP	TC/G	FA	G by Pos
1884	RIC	AA	2	.000	.000	5	0	0	0	0	0.0	0		0		0	0	0	13	8	4	0	12.5	.840	SS-1, 1B-1

Hod Ford
FORD, HORACE HILLS   BR TR 5'10" 165 lbs.
B. July 23, 1897, New Haven, Conn. D. Jan. 29, 1977, Winchester, Mass.

Year	Team		Games	BA	SA	AB	H	2B	3B	HR	HR%	R	RBI	BB	SO	SB	PH AB	PH H	PO	A	E	DP	TC/G	FA	G by Pos
1919	BOS	N	10	.214	.286	28	6	0	1	0	0.0	4	3	2	6	0	0	0	13	31	2	3	4.6	.957	SS-8, 3B-2
1920			88	.241	.339	257	62	12	5	1	0.4	16	30	18	25	3	6	0	174	285	19	26	5.4	.960	2B-59, SS-18, 1B-4
1921			152	.279	.360	555	155	29	5	2	0.4	50	61	36	49	2	0	0	393	526	26	64	6.2	.972	2B-119, SS-33
1922			143	.272	.363	515	140	23	9	2	0.4	58	60	30	36	2	0	0	335	481	35	71	6.0	.959	SS-115, 2B-28
1923			111	.271	.366	380	103	16	7	2	0.5	27	50	31	30	1	0	0	252	352	22	67	5.6	.965	2B-95, SS-19
1924	PHI	N	145	.272	.358	530	144	27	5	3	0.6	58	53	27	40	1	0	0	337	543	27	96	6.3	.970	2B-145
1925	BKN	N	66	.273	.338	216	59	11	0	1	0.5	32	15	26	15	0	0	0	126	185	11	33	4.9	.966	SS-66
1926	CIN	N	57	.279	.320	197	55	6	1	0	0.0	14	18	14	12	1	0	0	152	190	13	57	6.2	.963	SS-57
1927			115	.274	.330	409	112	16	2	1	0.2	45	46	33	34	0	0	0	239	354	27	80	5.4	.956	SS-104, 2B-12
1928			149	.241	.291	506	122	17	4	0	0.0	49	54	47	31	1	0	0	355	508	25	128	6.0	.972	SS-149
1929			148	.276	.342	529	146	14	6	3	0.6	68	50	41	25	8	0	0	333	520	35	116	6.0	.961	SS-108, 2B-42
1930			132	.231	.309	424	98	16	7	1	0.2	36	34	24	28	2	1	0	291	415	15	90	5.5	.979	SS-74, 2B-66
1931			84	.229	.286	175	40	8	1	0	0.0	18	13	13	13	0	7	1	111	169	13	43	3.5	.956	SS-73, 2B-3, 3B-1
1932	2 teams		STL	N (1G – .000)		BOS	N	(40G – .274)																	
"	total		41	.268	.361	97	26	5	2	0	0.0	9	6	6	9	0	0	0	59	82	3	17	3.5	.979	2B-20, SS-17, 3B-2
1933	BOS	N	5	.067	.067	15	1	0	0	0	0.0	0	1	3	1	0	0	0	17	23	0	4	8.0	1.000	SS-5
15 yrs.			1446	.263	.337	4833	1269	200	55	16	0.3	484	494	351	354	21	16	1	3187	4664	273	895	5.6	.966	SS-846, 2B-589, 3B-5, 1B-4

Ted Ford
FORD, THEODORE HENRY   BR TR 5'10" 180 lbs.
B. Feb. 7, 1947, Vineland, N. J.

Year	Team		Games	BA	SA	AB	H	2B	3B	HR	HR%	R	RBI	BB	SO	SB	PH AB	PH H	PO	A	E	DP	TC/G	FA	G by Pos
1970	CLE	A	26	.174	.261	46	8	1	0	1	2.2	5	1	3	13	0	12	1	24	1	0	0	1.0	1.000	OF-12
1971			74	.194	.255	196	38	6	0	2	1.0	15	14	9	34	2	19	3	107	4	0	0	1.5	1.000	OF-55
1972	TEX	A	129	.235	.382	429	101	19	1	14	3.3	43	50	37	80	4	10	2	242	11	6	2	2.0	.977	OF-119
1973	CLE	A	11	.225	.275	40	9	0	1	0	0.0	3	3	2	7	1	1	0	6	0	0	0	0.5	1.000	OF-10
4 yrs.			240	.219	.333	711	156	26	2	17	2.4	66	68	51	134	7	42	6	379	16	6	2	1.7	.985	OF-196

Tom Forster
FORSTER, THOMAS W.
B. May 1, 1859, New York, N. Y. D. July 17, 1946, New York, N. Y.

Year	Team		Games	BA	SA	AB	H	2B	3B	HR	HR%	R	RBI	BB	SO	SB	PH AB	PH H	PO	A	E	DP	TC/G	FA	G by Pos
1882	DET	N	21	.092	.092	76	7	0	0	0	0.0	5	2	5	12			0	0	58	54	23	5	6.4	.830	2B-21
1884	PIT	AA	35	.222	.262	126	28	5	0	0	0.0	10		7				0	0	56	116	22	8	5.5	.887	SS-28, 3B-6, 2B-1
1885	NY	AA	57	.221	.272	213	47	7	2	0	0.0	28		17				0	0	135	143	35	21	5.5	.888	2B-52, OF-5
1886			67	.195	.235	251	49	3	2	1	0.4	33		20				0	0	157	202	47	29	6.1	.884	2B-62, OF-4, SS-1
4 yrs.			180	.197	.236	666	131	15	4	1	0.2	76	2	49	12			0	0	406	515	127	63	5.8	.879	2B-136, SS-29, OF-9, 3B-6

Forsythe
FORSYTHE,   TR

Year	Team		Games	BA	SA	AB	H	2B	3B	HR	HR%	R	RBI	BB	SO	SB	PH AB	PH H	PO	A	E	DP	TC/G	FA	G by Pos
1915	BAL	F	1	.000	.000	3	0	0	0	0	0.0	0	0	1		0	0	0	0	2	1	0	3.0	.667	3B-1

George Foss
FOSS, GEORGE DUEWARD (Deeby)   BR TR 5'10½" 170 lbs.
B. June 13, 1897, Register, Ga. D. Nov. 10, 1969, Brandon, Fla.

Year	Team		Games	BA	SA	AB	H	2B	3B	HR	HR%	R	RBI	BB	SO	SB	PH AB	PH H	PO	A	E	DP	TC/G	FA	G by Pos
1921	WAS	A	4	.000	.000	7	0	0	0	0	0.0	0	0	0	1	0	2	0	1	2	1	1	1.0	.750	3B-2

Ray Fosse
FOSSE, RAYMOND EARL   BR TR 6'2" 215 lbs.
B. Apr. 4, 1947, Marion, Ill.

Year	Team		Games	BA	SA	AB	H	2B	3B	HR	HR%	R	RBI	BB	SO	SB	PH AB	PH H	PO	A	E	DP	TC/G	FA	G by Pos
1967	CLE	A	7	.063	.063	16	1	0	0	0	0.0	0	0	0	5	0	0	0	46	7	0	0	7.6	1.000	C-7
1968			1	–	–	0	0	0	0	0	–	0	0	0	0	0	0	0	1	0	0	0	1.0	1.000	C-1
1969			37	.172	.250	116	20	3	0	2	1.7	11	9	8	29	0	0	0	237	18	6	2	7.1	.977	C-37
1970			120	.307	.469	450	138	17	1	18	4.0	62	61	39	55	1	0	0	854	70	10	7	7.8	.989	C-120
1971			133	.276	.397	486	134	21	1	12	2.5	53	62	36	62	4	6	0	767	73	10	22	6.4	.988	C-126, 1B-4
1972			134	.241	.354	457	110	20	1	10	2.2	42	41	45	46	5	8	3	740	71	12	12	6.1	.985	C-124, 1B-3
1973	OAK	A	143	.256	.354	492	126	23	2	7	1.4	37	52	25	62	2	0	0	712	63	10	5	5.5	.987	C-141, DH-2
1974			69	.196	.324	204	40	8	3	4	2.0	20	23	11	31	1	0	0	299	28	9	6	4.9	.973	C-68, DH-1
1975			82	.140	.191	136	19	3	0	0	0.0	14	12	8	19	0	2	0	253	15	5	1	3.3	.982	C-82, 2B-1, 1B-1
1976	CLE	A	90	.301	.362	276	83	9	0	2	0.7	26	30	20	20	1	4	0	493	43	7	10	6.0	.987	C-85, 1B-3, DH-1

Year	Team	Games	BA	SA	AB	H	2B	3B	HR	HR%	R	RBI	BB	SO	SB	Pinch Hit AB	Pinch Hit H	PO	A	E	DP	TC/G	FA	G by Pos

Ray Fosse *continued*

Year	Team	Games	BA	SA	AB	H	2B	3B	HR	HR%	R	RBI	BB	SO	SB	PH AB	PH H	PO	A	E	DP	TC/G	FA	G by Pos
1977	2 teams	CLE A (78G – .265)			SEA A	(11G – .353)																		
"	total	89	.276	.386	272	75	10	1	6	2.2	28	32	9	28	0	1	0	456	49	9	5	5.8	.982	C-85, DH-3, 1B-1
1979	MIL A	19	.231	.327	52	12	3	1	0	0.0	6	2	2	6	0	3	1	41	3	0	1	2.3	1.000	C-13, DH-5, 1B-1
	12 yrs.	924	.256	.367	2957	758	117	13	61	2.1	299	324	203	363	15	25	4	4899	440	78	71	5.9	.986	C-889, 1B-13, DH-12, 2B-1

LEAGUE CHAMPIONSHIP SERIES

Year	Team	Games	BA	SA	AB	H	2B	3B	HR	HR%	R	RBI	BB	SO	SB	PH AB	PH H	PO	A	E	DP	TC/G	FA	G by Pos
1973	OAK A	5	.091	.182	11	1	1	0	0	0.0	2	3	2	2	0	0	0	25	4	0	2	5.8	1.000	C-5
1974		4	.333	.667	12	4	1	0	1	8.3	1	3	1	2	0	0	0	21	3	0	1	6.0	1.000	C-4
1975		1	.000	.000	2	0	0	0	0	0.0	0	0	0	1	0	0	0	3	0	0	1	3.0	1.000	C-1
	3 yrs.	10	.200	.400	25	5	2	0	1	4.0	3	6	3	5	0	0	0	49	7	0	4	5.6	1.000	C-10

WORLD SERIES

Year	Team	Games	BA	SA	AB	H	2B	3B	HR	HR%	R	RBI	BB	SO	SB	PH AB	PH H	PO	A	E	DP	TC/G	FA	G by Pos
1973	OAK A	7	.158	.211	19	3	1	0	0	0.0	0	0	1	4	0	0	0	32	3	0	2	5.0	1.000	C-7
1974		5	.143	.357	14	2	0	0	1	7.1	1	1	1	5	0	0	0	27	1	0	0	5.6	1.000	C-5
	2 yrs.	12	.152	.273	33	5	1	0	1	3.0	1	1	2	9	0	0	0	59	4	0	2	5.3	1.000	C-12

Eddie Foster

FOSTER, EDWARD CUNNINGHAM (Kid)
B. Feb. 13, 1887, Chicago, Ill. D. Jan. 15, 1937, Washington, D. C.   BR TR 5'6½" 145 lbs.

Year	Team	Games	BA	SA	AB	H	2B	3B	HR	HR%	R	RBI	BB	SO	SB	PH AB	PH H	PO	A	E	DP	TC/G	FA	G by Pos
1910	NY A	30	.133	.157	83	11	2	0	0	0.0	5		8		2	7	1	37	63	10	6	3.7	.909	SS-22
1912	WAS A	154	.285	.379	618	176	34	9	2	0.3	98	70	53		27	0	0	168	348	45	22	3.6	.920	3B-154
1913		106	.247	.306	409	101	11	5	1	0.2	56	41	36	31	22	1	0	112	217	36	20	3.4	.901	3B-105
1914		156	.282	.351	616	174	16	10	2	0.3	82	50	60	47	31	0	0	200	247	34	25	3.1	.929	3B-156
1915		154	.275	.348	618	170	25	10	0	0.0	75	52	48	30	20	0	0	253	353	39	45	4.2	.940	3B-79, 2B-75
1916		158	.252	.317	606	153	18	9	1	0.2	75	44	68	26	23	2	0	230	356	33	41	3.9	.947	3B-84, 2B-72
1917		143	.235	.292	554	130	16	8	0	0.0	66	43	46	23	11	0	0	217	331	33	34	4.1	.943	3B-86, 2B-57
1918		129	.283	.320	519	147	13	3	0	0.0	70	29	41	20	12	0	0	159	287	32	31	3.7	.933	3B-127, 2B-2
1919		120	.264	.310	478	126	12	5	0	0.0	57	26	33	21	20	4	1	120	267	22	16	3.4	.946	3B-115
1920	BOS A	117	.259	.334	386	100	17	6	0	0.0	48	41	42	17	10	6	1	127	280	19	29	3.6	.955	3B-88, 2B-21
1921		119	.284	.357	412	117	18	6	0	0.0	51	30	57	15	13	3	2	116	250	21	28	3.3	.946	3B-94, 2B-21
1922	2 teams	BOS A (48G – .211)			STL A	(37G – .306)																		
"	total	85	.265	.292	253	67	7	0	0	0.0	40	15	29	18	4	15	5	64	123	19	14	2.4	.908	3B-65, SS-2, C-2
1923	STL A	27	.180	.200	100	18	2	0	0	0.0	9	4	7	7	0	0	0	42	52	5	8	3.7	.949	2B-20, 3B-7
	13 yrs.	1498	.264	.326	5652	1490	191	71	6	0.1	732	446	528	255	195	38	10	1845	3174	348	319	3.6	.935	3B-1160, 2B-268, SS-24, C-2

Elmer Foster

FOSTER, ELMER ELLSWORTH
B. Aug. 15, 1861, Minneapolis, Minn. D. July 22, 1946, Deep Haven, Minn.   BR TL

Year	Team	Games	BA	SA	AB	H	2B	3B	HR	HR%	R	RBI	BB	SO	SB	PH AB	PH H	PO	A	E	DP	TC/G	FA	G by Pos
1884	2 teams	PHI AA (4G – .182)			PHI U	(1G – .333)																		
"	total	5	.214	.357	14	3	0	1	0	0.0	4		3			0	0	19	9	6	0	6.8	.824	C-5, OF-1
1886	NY AA	35	.184	.200	125	23	0	1	0	0.0	16		7			0	0	77	77	32	4	5.3	.828	2B-21, OF-14
1888	NY N	37	.147	.199	136	20	3	2	0	0.0	15	10	9	20	13	0	0	64	5	14	0	2.2	.831	OF-37, 3B-1
1889		2	.000	.000	4	0	0	0	0	0.0	0	2	0	3	1	2	0	5	0	0	0	2.5	1.000	OF-2
1890	CHI N	27	.248	.467	105	26	4	2	5	4.8	20	23	9	21	18	0	0	69	2	1	0	2.7	.986	OF-27
1891		4	.188	.375	16	3	0	0	1	6.3	3	1	1	2	1	0	0	6	1	1	0	2.0	.875	OF-4
	6 yrs.	110	.188	.280	400	75	7	6	6	1.5	60	34	32	44	34	0	0	240	94	54	4	3.5	.861	OF-85, 2B-21, C-5, 3B-1

George Foster

FOSTER, GEORGE ARTHUR
B. Dec. 1, 1948, Tuscaloosa, Ala.   BR TR 6'1½" 180 lbs.

Year	Team	Games	BA	SA	AB	H	2B	3B	HR	HR%	R	RBI	BB	SO	SB	PH AB	PH H	PO	A	E	DP	TC/G	FA	G by Pos
1969	SF N	9	.400	.400	5	2	0	0	0	0.0	1	0	0	1	0	0	0	3	0	0	0	0.3	1.000	OF-8
1970		9	.316	.632	19	6	1	1	1	5.3	2	4	2	5	0	2	1	10	0	0	0	1.1	1.000	OF-7
1971	2 teams	SF N (36G – .267)			CIN N	(104G – .234)																		
"	total	140	.241	.389	473	114	23	4	13	2.7	50	58	29	120	7	10	2	315	9	5	3	2.4	.985	OF-132
1972	CIN N	59	.200	.283	145	29	4	1	2	1.4	15	12	5	44	2	12	4	71	1	2	1	1.3	.973	OF-47
1973		17	.282	.667	39	11	3	0	4	10.3	6	9	4	7	0	4	0	19	1	0	1	1.2	1.000	OF-13
1974		106	.264	.406	276	73	18	0	7	2.5	31	41	30	52	3	17	3	172	2	2	1	1.7	.989	OF-98
1975		134	.300	.518	463	139	24	4	23	5.0	71	78	40	73	2	9	4	299	11	3	3	2.3	.990	OF-125, 1B-1
1976		144	.306	.530	562	172	21	9	29	5.2	86	121	52	89	17	6	0	322	9	2	3	2.3	.994	OF-142, 1B-1
1977		158	.320	.631	615	197	31	2	52	8.5	124	149	61	107	6	0	0	352	12	3	1	2.3	.992	OF-158
1978		158	.281	.546	604	170	26	7	40	6.6	97	120	70	138	4	1	0	319	10	10	1	2.3	.971	OF-157
1979		121	.302	.561	440	133	18	3	30	6.8	68	98	59	105	0	4	1	214	7	4	1	1.9	.982	OF-116
1980		144	.273	.473	528	144	21	5	25	4.7	79	93	75	99	1	3	0	295	6	1	1	2.1	.997	OF-141
1981		108	.295	.519	414	122	23	2	22	5.3	64	90	51	75	4	0	0	224	8	2	1	2.2	.991	OF-108
1982	NY N	151	.247	.367	550	136	23	2	13	2.4	64	70	50	123	1	11	2	289	12	8	4	2.0	.974	OF-138
1983		157	.241	.419	601	145	19	2	28	4.7	74	90	38	111	1	5	1	314	12	4	3	2.1	.988	OF-153
1984		146	.269	.443	553	149	22	1	24	4.3	67	86	30	122	2	1	0	278	6	7	1	2.0	.976	OF-141
1985		129	.263	.460	452	119	24	1	21	4.6	57	77	46	87	0	6	1	198	7	5	2	1.6	.976	OF-123
1986	2 teams	NY N (72G – .227)			CHI A	(15G – .216)																		
"	total	87	.225	.415	284	64	6	3	14	4.9	30	42	24	61	1	9	0	115	6	4	1	1.4	.968	OF-73, DH-3
	18 yrs.	1977	.274	.480	7023	1925	307	47	348	5.0	986	1239	666	1419	51	104	20	3809	119	62	28	2.0	.984	OF-1880, DH-3, 1B-2

LEAGUE CHAMPIONSHIP SERIES

Year	Team	Games	BA	SA	AB	H	2B	3B	HR	HR%	R	RBI	BB	SO	SB	PH AB	PH H	PO	A	E	DP	TC/G	FA	G by Pos
1972	CIN N	1	–	–	0	0	0	0	0	–	1	0	0	0	0	0	0	0	0	0	0	0.0	–	
1975		3	.364	.364	11	4	0	0	0	0.0	3	0	1	2	1	0	0	7	0	0	0	2.3	1.000	OF-3
1976		3	.167	.667	12	2	0	0	2	16.7	2	4	0	4	0	0	0	7	0	0	0	2.3	1.000	OF-3
1979		3	.200	.500	10	2	0	0	1	10.0	1	2	4	3	0	0	0	6	2	0	0	2.7	1.000	OF-3
	4 yrs.	10	.242	.515	33	8	0	0	3	9.1	7	6	5	9	1	0	0	20	2	0	0	2.2	1.000	OF-9

WORLD SERIES

Year	Team	Games	BA	SA	AB	H	2B	3B	HR	HR%	R	RBI	BB	SO	SB	PH AB	PH H	PO	A	E	DP	TC/G	FA	G by Pos
1972	CIN N	2	–	–	0	0	0	0	0	–	0	0	0	0	0	0	0	0	0	0	0	0.0	–	OF-1
1975		7	.276	.310	29	8	1	0	0	0.0	2	1	1	1	0	0	0	13	1	0	0	2.0	1.000	OF-7
1976		4	.429	.500	14	6	1	0	0	0.0	3	4	2	3	1	0	0	14	0	0	1	3.5	1.000	OF-4
	3 yrs.	13	.326	.372	43	14	2	0	0	0.0	4	6	3	4	1	0	0	27	1	0	1	2.2	1.000	OF-12

Year	Team		Games	BA	SA	AB	H	2B	3B	HR	HR%	R	RBI	BB	SO	SB	Pinch Hit AB	Pinch Hit H	PO	A	E	DP	TC/G	FA	G by Pos

Leo Foster

FOSTER, LEONARD NORRIS — BR TR 5'11" 165 lbs.
B. Feb. 2, 1951, Covington, Ky.

Year	Team		Games	BA	SA	AB	H	2B	3B	HR	HR%	R	RBI	BB	SO	SB	PH AB	PH H	PO	A	E	DP	TC/G	FA	G by Pos
1971	ATL	N	9	.000	.000	10	0	0	0	0	0.0	1	0	0	1	0	2	0	1	8	1	2	1.1	.900	SS-3
1973			3	.167	.333	6	1	0	0	0	0.0	1	0	0	2	0	1	0	5	1	0	1	2.0	1.000	SS-1
1974			72	.196	.241	112	22	2	0	1	0.9	16	5	9	22	1	10	2	49	92	6	14	2.0	.959	SS-43, 2B-10, 3B-3, OF-1
1976	NY	N	24	.203	.288	59	12	2	0	1	1.7	11	15	8	5	3	2	0	18	42	2	2	2.6	.968	3B-9, SS-7, 2B-3
1977			36	.227	.267	75	17	3	0	0	0.0	6	6	5	14	3	5	1	36	47	5	10	2.4	.943	2B-20, SS-8, 3B-2
5 yrs.			144	.198	.252	262	52	8	0	2	0.8	35	26	22	44	7	20	3	109	190	14	29	2.2	.955	SS-62, 2B-33, 3B-14, OF-1

Pop Foster

FOSTER, CLARENCE FRANCIS — BR TR 5'8½"
B. Apr. 8, 1878, New Haven, Conn.   D. Apr. 16, 1944, Princeton, N. J.

Year	Team		Games	BA	SA	AB	H	2B	3B	HR	HR%	R	RBI	BB	SO	SB	PH AB	PH H	PO	A	E	DP	TC/G	FA	G by Pos
1898	NY	N	32	.268	.339	112	30	6	1	0	0.0	10	9	0			0	0	37	25	11	1	2.3	.849	OF-21, 3B-10, SS-2
1899			84	.296	.402	301	89	9	7	3	1.0	48	57	20			7	0	106	9	7	3	1.5	.943	OF-84, SS-1, 3B-1
1900			31	.262	.321	84	22	3	1	0	0.0	19	11	11			0	5	33	47	9	4	2.9	.899	OF-12, SS-7, 2B-5
1901	2 teams			WAS A (103G – .278)			CHI A (12G – .286)																			
"	total		115	.279	.422	427	119	18	11	7	1.6	69	59	45			10	3	1	209	18	18	1	2.1	.927	OF-111, SS-2
4 yrs.			262	.281	.396	924	260	36	20	10	1.1	146	136	76			17	8	1	385	99	45	9	2.0	.915	OF-228, SS-12, 3B-11, 2B-5

Reddy Foster

FOSTER, OSCAR E.
B. 1867, Richmond, Va.   D. Dec. 19, 1908, Richmond, Va.

Year	Team		Games	BA	SA	AB	H	2B	3B	HR	HR%	R	RBI	BB	SO	SB	PH AB	PH H	PO	A	E	DP	TC/G	FA	G by Pos
1896	NY	N	1	.000	.000	1	0	0	0	0	0.0	0		0	1	0	0	0	0	0	0	0	0.0	–	

Roy Foster

FOSTER, ROY — BR TR 6' 185 lbs.
B. July 29, 1945, Bixby, Okla.

Year	Team		Games	BA	SA	AB	H	2B	3B	HR	HR%	R	RBI	BB	SO	SB	PH AB	PH H	PO	A	E	DP	TC/G	FA	G by Pos
1970	CLE	A	139	.268	.468	477	128	26	0	23	4.8	66	60	54	75	3	8	2	188	6	7	0	1.4	.965	OF-131
1971			125	.245	.439	396	97	21	1	18	4.5	51	45	35	48	6	20	5	174	9	6	2	1.5	.968	OF-107
1972			73	.224	.336	143	32	4	0	4	2.8	19	13	21	23	0	26	4	54	2	2	0	0.8	.966	OF-45
3 yrs.			337	.253	.438	1016	257	51	1	45	4.4	136	118	110	146	9	54	11	416	17	15	2	1.3	.967	OF-283

Bob Fothergill

FOTHERGILL, ROBERT ROY (Fat) — BR TR 5'10½" 230 lbs.
B. Aug. 16, 1897, Massillon, Ohio   D. Mar. 20, 1938, Detroit, Mich.

Year	Team		Games	BA	SA	AB	H	2B	3B	HR	HR%	R	RBI	BB	SO	SB	PH AB	PH H	PO	A	E	DP	TC/G	FA	G by Pos
1922	DET	A	42	.322	.454	152	49	12	4	0	0.0	20	29	8	9	1	3	1	50	2	3	1	1.3	.945	OF-39
1923			101	.315	.419	241	76	18	2	1	0.4	34	49	12	19	4	30	9	121	4	3	0	1.3	.977	OF-68
1924			54	.301	.386	166	50	8	3	0	0.0	28	15	5	13	2	9	3	89	2	3	1	1.7	.968	OF-45
1925			71	.353	.451	204	72	14	0	2	1.0	38	28	6	3	2	11	5	120	6	3	2	1.8	.977	OF-59
1926			110	.367	.506	387	142	31	7	3	0.8	63	73	33	23	4	6	4	245	3	10	0	2.3	.961	OF-103
1927			143	.359	.516	527	189	38	9	9	1.7	93	114	47	31	9	5	2	315	3	13	1	2.3	.961	OF-137
1928			111	.317	.481	347	110	28	10	3	0.9	49	63	24	19	8	4	0	179	6	8	0	1.7	.959	OF-90
1929			115	.354	.570	277	98	24	9	6	2.2	42	62	11	11	3	53	19	116	2	4	1	1.1	.967	OF-59
1930	2 teams			DET A (55G – .259)			CHI A (52G – .296)																			
"	total		107	.277	.385	278	77	18	3	2	0.7	24	38	10	18	1	34	6	102	3	10	0	1.1	.913	OF-68
1931	CHI	A	108	.282	.365	312	88	9	4	3	1.0	25	56	17	17	2	31	8	169	2	5	0	1.6	.972	OF-74
1932			116	.295	.431	346	102	24	1	7	2.0	36	50	27	10	4	29	8	136	4	7	0	1.3	.952	OF-86
1933	BOS	N	28	.344	.375	32	11	1	0	0	0.0	1	5	2	4	0	23	7	4	0	0	0	0.1	1.000	OF-4
12 yrs.			1106	.325	.459	3269	1064	225	52	36	1.1	453	582	202	177	40	253	76	1646	37	69	6	1.6	.961	OF-832

Jack Fournier

FOURNIER, JACQUES FRANK — BL TR 6' 195 lbs.
B. Sept. 29, 1892, Au Sable, Mich.   D. Sept. 5, 1973, Tacoma, Wash.

Year	Team		Games	BA	SA	AB	H	2B	3B	HR	HR%	R	RBI	BB	SO	SB	PH AB	PH H	PO	A	E	DP	TC/G	FA	G by Pos
1912	CHI	A	35	.192	.315	73	14	5	2	0	0.0	5	2	4		1	18	5	154	16	2	4	4.9	.988	1B-17
1913			68	.233	.355	172	40	8	5	1	0.6	20	23	21		9	13	1	306	23	5	10	4.9	.985	1B-29, OF-23
1914			109	.311	.443	379	118	14	9	6	1.6	44	44	31	44	10	6	0	1034	79	27	31	10.5	.976	1B-97, OF-6
1915			126	.322	.491	422	136	20	18	5	1.2	86	77	64	37	21	4	2	784	51	17	34	6.8	.980	1B-65, OF-57
1916			105	.240	.367	313	75	13	9	3	1.0	36	44	36	40	19	14	2	857	49	20	47	8.8	.978	1B-85, OF-1
1917			1	.000	.000	1	0	0	0	0	0.0	0	0	0	1	0	1	0	0	0	0	0		–	
1918	NY	A	27	.350	.430	100	35	6	1	0	0.0	9	12	7	7	0	7	0	274	13	7	23	10.9	.976	1B-27
1920	STL	N	141	.306	.438	530	162	33	14	3	0.6	77	61	42	42	26	3	2	1373	88	25	100	10.5	.983	1B-138
1921			149	.343	.505	574	197	27	9	16	2.8	103	86	56	48	20	0	0	1416	73	19	91	10.1	.987	1B-149
1922			128	.295	.470	404	119	23	9	10	2.5	64	61	40	21	6	12	5	902	61	18	63	7.7	.982	1B-109, P-1
1923	BKN	N	133	.351	.588	515	181	30	13	22	4.3	91	102	43	28	11	0	0	1281	82	21	90	10.4	.985	1B-133
1924			154	.334	.536	563	188	25	4	27	4.8	93	116	83	46	7	1	0	1388	99	22	102	9.8	.985	1B-153
1925			145	.350	.569	545	191	21	16	22	4.0	99	130	86	39	4	0	0	1317	82	15	105	9.8	.989	1B-145
1926			87	.284	.473	243	69	9	2	11	4.5	39	48	30	16	0	18	4	548	28	8	19	6.7	.986	1B-64
1927	BOS	N	122	.283	.422	374	106	18	2	10	2.7	55	53	44	16	1	19	8	901	63	11	63	8.0	.989	1B-102
15 yrs.			1530	.313	.483	5208	1631	252	113	136	2.6	821	859	587	408	145	109	29	12535	807	217	782	8.9	.984	1B-1313, OF-87, P-1

Bill Fouser

FOUSER, WILLIAM C.
B. 1855, Philadelphia, Pa.   D. Mar. 1, 1919, Philadelphia, Pa.

Year	Team		Games	BA	SA	AB	H	2B	3B	HR	HR%	R	RBI	BB	SO	SB	PH AB	PH H	PO	A	E	DP	TC/G	FA	G by Pos
1876	PHI	N	21	.135	.157	89	12	0	1	0	0.0	11	2	0	0			0	0	52	56	24	3	6.3	.818	2B-14, OF-7, 1B-1

Dave Foutz

FOUTZ, DAVID LUTHER (Scissors) — BR TR 6'2" 161 lbs.
Brother of Frank Foutz.
B. Sept. 7, 1856, Carroll County, Md.   D. Mar. 5, 1897, Waverly, Md.
Manager 1893-96.

Year	Team		Games	BA	SA	AB	H	2B	3B	HR	HR%	R	RBI	BB	SO	SB	PH AB	PH H	PO	A	E	DP	TC/G	FA	G by Pos
1884	STL	AA	33	.227	.261	119	27	4	6	0	0.0	17		8			0	0	26	45	6	6	2.3	.922	P-25, OF-14
1885			65	.248	.307	238	59	6	4	0	0.0	42		11			0	0	189	109	23	15	4.9	.928	P-47, 1B-15, OF-4
1886			102	.280	.389	414	116	18	9	3	0.7	66		9			0	0	211	86	19	7	3.1	.940	P-59, OF-34, 1B-11
1887			102	.357	.508	423	151	26	13	4	0.9	79		23		22	0	0	282	65	23	11	3.6	.938	OF-50, P-40, 1B-15
1888	BKN	AA	140	.277	.375	563	156	20	13	3	0.5	91	99	28		35	0	0	588	71	28	28	4.9	.959	OF-78, 1B-42, P-23
1889			138	.277	.378	553	153	19	8	7	1.3	118	113	64	23	43	0	0	1376	48	31	66	10.5	.979	1B-134, P-12
1890	BKN	N	129	.303	.432	509	154	25	13	5	1.0	106	98	52	25	42	0	0	1222	44	30	64	10.0	.977	1B-113, OF-13, P-5
1891			130	.257	.349	521	134	26	8	2	0.4	87	73	40	25	48	0	0	1246	60	31	52	10.3	.977	1B-124, P-6, SS-1

Year	Team	Games	BA	SA	AB	H	2B	3B	HR	HR%	R	RBI	BB	SO	SB	Pinch Hit AB	Pinch Hit H	PO	A	E	DP	TC/G	FA	G by Pos

Dave Foutz *continued*

Year	Team	Games	BA	SA	AB	H	2B	3B	HR	HR%	R	RBI	BB	SO	SB	PH AB	PH H	PO	A	E	DP	TC/G	FA	G by Pos
1892		61	.186	.250	220	41	5	3	1	0.5	33	26	14	14	19	1	0	109	62	16	5	3.1	.914	OF-29, P-27, 1B-6
1893		130	.246	.355	557	137	20	10	7	1.3	91	67	32	34	39	0	0	735	36	27	22	6.1	.966	OF-77, 1B-54, P-6
1894		72	.307	.410	293	90	12	9	0	0.0	40	51	14	13	14	0	0	658	33	17	37	9.8	.976	1B-72, P-1
1895		31	.296	.348	115	34	4	1	0	0.0	14	21	4	2	1	3	0	109	3	9	4	3.9	.926	OF-20, 1B-8
1896		2	.250	.375	8	2	1	0	0	0.0	0	0	1	0	0	0	0	7	2	1	0	5.0	.900	OF-1, 1B-1
13 yrs.		1135	.277	.379	4533	1254	186	91	32	0.7	784	548	300	136	263	4	0	6758	664	261	317	6.8	.966	1B-595, OF-320, P-251, SS-1

Frank Foutz

FOUTZ, FRANK HAYES
Brother of Dave Foutz.
B. Apr. 8, 1877, Baltimore, Md. D. Dec. 25, 1961, Lima, Ohio

BR TR

Year	Team	Games	BA	SA	AB	H	2B	3B	HR	HR%	R	RBI	BB	SO	SB	PH AB	PH H	PO	A	E	DP	TC/G	FA	G by Pos
1901	BAL A	20	.236	.403	72	17	4	1	2	2.8	13	14	8		0	0	0	176	11	8	8	9.8	.959	1B-20

Boob Fowler

FOWLER, JOSEPH CHESTER
B. Nov. 11, 1900, Waco, Tex. D. Oct. 8, 1988, Dallas, Tex.

BL TR 5'11½" 180 lbs.

Year	Team	Games	BA	SA	AB	H	2B	3B	HR	HR%	R	RBI	BB	SO	SB	PH AB	PH H	PO	A	E	DP	TC/G	FA	G by Pos
1923	CIN N	11	.333	.485	33	11	0	1	1	3.0	9	6	1	3	1	0	0	22	28	9	6	5.4	.847	SS-10
1924		59	.333	.395	129	43	6	1	0	0.0	20	9	5	15	2	3	0	51	92	10	14	2.6	.935	SS-32, 2B-4, 3B-2
1925		6	.400	.600	5	2	1	0	0	0.0	0	2	0	1	0	5	2	0	0	0	0	0.0	—	
1926	BOS A	2	.125	.125	8	1	0	0	0	0.0	1	1	0	0	0	0	0	2	6	2	0	5.0	.800	3B-2
4 yrs.		78	.326	.406	175	57	7	2	1	0.6	30	18	6	19	3	8	2	75	126	21	20	2.8	.905	SS-42, 3B-4, 2B-4

Bill Fox

FOX, WILLIAM HENRY
B. Jan. 15, 1872, Fiskdale, Mass. D. May 7, 1946, Minneapolis, Minn.

BB TR 5'10" 160 lbs.

Year	Team	Games	BA	SA	AB	H	2B	3B	HR	HR%	R	RBI	BB	SO	SB	PH AB	PH H	PO	A	E	DP	TC/G	FA	G by Pos
1897	WAS N	4	.286	.286	14	4	0	4	0	0.0	4	0	1		0	0	0	12	11	5	3	7.0	.821	SS-2, 2B-2
1901	CIN N	43	.176	.201	159	28	2	1	0	0.0	9	7	4		9	0	0	103	134	11	19	5.8	.956	2B-43
2 yrs.		47	.185	.208	173	32	2	1	0	0.0	13	7	5		9	0	0	115	145	16	22	5.9	.942	2B-45, SS-2

Charlie Fox

FOX, CHARLES FRANCIS (Irish)
B. Oct. 7, 1921, New York, N. Y.
Manager 1970-74, 1976, 1983.

BR TR 5'11" 180 lbs.

Year	Team	Games	BA	SA	AB	H	2B	3B	HR	HR%	R	RBI	BB	SO	SB	PH AB	PH H	PO	A	E	DP	TC/G	FA	G by Pos
1942	NY N	3	.429	.429	7	3	0	0	0	0.0	1	1	1	1	0	0	0	7	0	0	0	2.3	1.000	C-3

Jack Fox

FOX, JOHN PAUL
B. May 21, 1885, Reading, Pa. D. June 28, 1963, Reading, Pa.

BR TR 5'10" 185 lbs.

Year	Team	Games	BA	SA	AB	H	2B	3B	HR	HR%	R	RBI	BB	SO	SB	PH AB	PH H	PO	A	E	DP	TC/G	FA	G by Pos
1908	PHI A	9	.200	.200	30	6	0	0	0	0.0	2	0	0		2	0	0	12	0	1	0	1.4	.923	OF-8

Nellie Fox

FOX, JACOB NELSON
B. Dec. 25, 1927, St. Thomas, Pa. D. Dec. 1, 1975, Baltimore, Md.

BL TR 5'10" 160 lbs.

Year	Team	Games	BA	SA	AB	H	2B	3B	HR	HR%	R	RBI	BB	SO	SB	PH AB	PH H	PO	A	E	DP	TC/G	FA	G by Pos
1947	PHI A	7	.000	.000	3	0	0	0	0	0.0	2	0	1	0	0	2	0	1	0	0	0	0.1	1.000	2B-1
1948		3	.154	.154	13	2	0	0	0	0.0	0	0	1	0	1	0	0	13	6	1	1	6.7	.950	2B-3
1949		88	.255	.296	247	63	6	2	0	0.0	42	21	32	9	2	2	0	191	196	7	68	4.5	.982	2B-77
1950	CHI A	130	.247	.296	457	113	12	7	0	0.0	45	30	35	17	4	8	2	340	344	18	100	5.4	.974	2B-121
1951		147	.313	.425	604	189	32	12	4	0.7	93	55	43	11	9	0	0	413	449	17	112	6.0	.981	2B-147
1952		152	.296	.366	648	192	25	10	0	0.0	76	39	34	14	5	1	0	406	433	13	111	5.6	.985	2B-151
1953		154	.285	.375	624	178	31	8	3	0.5	92	72	49	18	4	0	0	451	426	15	101	5.8	.983	2B-154
1954		155	.319	.391	631	201	24	8	2	0.3	111	47	51	12	16	0	0	400	392	9	103	5.2	.989	2B-155
1955		154	.311	.406	636	198	28	7	6	0.9	100	59	38	15	7	0	0	399	483	24	110	5.9	.974	2B-154
1956		154	.296	.376	649	192	20	10	4	0.6	109	52	44	14	8	0	0	478	396	12	124	5.9	.986	2B-154
1957		155	.317	.415	619	196	27	8	6	1.0	110	61	75	13	5	0	0	453	453	13	141	5.9	.986	2B-155
1958		155	.300	.353	623	187	21	6	0	0.0	82	49	47	11	5	0	0	444	399	13	117	5.5	.985	2B-155
1959		156	.306	.389	624	191	34	6	2	0.3	84	70	71	13	5	0	0	364	453	10	93	5.3	.988	2B-156
1960		150	.289	.372	605	175	24	10	2	0.3	85	59	50	13	2	1	0	412	447	13	126	5.8	.985	2B-149
1961		159	.251	.295	606	152	11	5	2	0.3	67	51	59	12	2	1	0	413	407	15	97	5.3	.982	2B-159
1962		157	.267	.343	621	166	27	7	2	0.3	79	54	38	12	1	3	0	376	428	8	93	5.2	.990	2B-154
1963		137	.260	.306	539	140	19	0	2	0.4	54	42	24	17	0	6	2	305	342	8	71	4.8	.988	2B-134
1964	HOU N	133	.265	.319	442	117	12	6	0	0.0	45	28	27	20	0	13	1	231	317	13	51	4.2	.977	2B-115
1965		21	.268	.317	41	11	2	0	0	0.0	3	1	0	2	0	12	4	12	14	0	2	1.2	1.000	3B-6, 1B-2, 2B-1
19 yrs.		2367	.288	.363	9232	2663	355	112	35	0.4	1279	790	719	216	76	50	10	6102	6385	209	1621	5.4	.984	2B-2295, 3B-6, 1B-2

WORLD SERIES

Year	Team	Games	BA	SA	AB	H	2B	3B	HR	HR%	R	RBI	BB	SO	SB	PH AB	PH H	PO	A	E	DP	TC/G	FA	G by Pos
1959	CHI A	6	.375	.500	24	9	0	0	0	0.0	4	0	4	1	0	0	1	14	23	0	2	6.2	1.000	2B-6

Paddy Fox

FOX, GEORGE B.
B. Dec. 1, 1868, Pottstown, Pa. D. May 8, 1914, Philadelphia, Pa.

Year	Team	Games	BA	SA	AB	H	2B	3B	HR	HR%	R	RBI	BB	SO	SB	PH AB	PH H	PO	A	E	DP	TC/G	FA	G by Pos
1891	LOU AA	6	.105	.211	19	2	0	1	0	0.0	1	2	2	3	0	0	0	0	0	0	0	0.0	—	3B-6
1899	PIT N	13	.244	.366	41	10	0	1	1	2.4	4	3	3		2	1	0	104	10	3	11	9.0	.974	1B-9, C-3
2 yrs.		19	.200	.317	60	12	0	2	1	1.7	5	5	5	3	2	1	0	104	10	3	11	6.2	.974	1B-9, 3B-6, C-3

Pete Fox

FOX, ERVIN
B. Mar. 8, 1909, Evansville, Ind. D. July 5, 1966, Detroit, Mich.

BR TR 5'11" 165 lbs.

Year	Team	Games	BA	SA	AB	H	2B	3B	HR	HR%	R	RBI	BB	SO	SB	PH AB	PH H	PO	A	E	DP	TC/G	FA	G by Pos
1933	DET A	128	.288	.424	535	154	26	13	7	1.3	82	57	23	38	9	3	0	313	5	7	0	2.5	.978	OF-124
1934		128	.285	.364	516	147	31	2	2	0.4	101	45	49	53	25	6	1	245	13	7	4	2.1	.974	OF-121
1935		131	.321	.513	517	166	38	8	15	2.9	116	73	45	52	14	6	3	244	9	3	1	2.0	.988	OF-125
1936		73	.305	.423	220	67	12	1	4	1.8	46	26	34	23	1	15	2	118	3	4	0	1.7	.968	OF-55
1937		148	.331	.476	628	208	39	8	12	1.9	116	82	41	43	12	3	2	321	6	8	0	2.3	.976	OF-143
1938		155	.293	.413	634	186	35	10	7	1.1	91	96	31	39	16	0	0	301	13	2	2	2.0	.994	OF-154
1939		141	.295	.405	519	153	24	6	7	1.3	69	66	35	41	23	14	2	275	12	9	3	2.1	.970	OF-126
1940		93	.289	.403	350	101	17	4	5	1.4	49	48	21	30	7	9	1	169	6	6	0	1.9	.967	OF-85
1941	BOS A	73	.302	.399	268	81	12	7	0	0.0	38	31	21	32	9	7	0	123	5	3	0	1.8	.977	OF-62
1942		77	.262	.395	256	67	15	5	3	1.2	42	42	20	28	8	3	1	111	2	4	0	1.5	.966	OF-71

Year Team	Games	BA	SA	AB	H	2B	3B	HR	HR%	R	RBI	BB	SO	SB	Pinch Hit AB	Pinch Hit H	PO	A	E	DP	TC/G	FA	G by Pos

Pete Fox *continued*

Year Team	Games	BA	SA	AB	H	2B	3B	HR	HR%	R	RBI	BB	SO	SB	PH AB	PH H	PO	A	E	DP	TC/G	FA	G by Pos
1943	127	.288	.366	489	141	24	4	2	0.4	54	44	34	40	22	1	0	261	10	11	2	2.2	.961	OF-125
1944	121	.315	.421	496	156	38	6	1	0.2	70	64	27	34	10	2	0	228	7	3	1	2.0	.987	OF-119
1945	66	.245	.274	208	51	4	1	0	0.0	21	20	11	18	2	5	0	84	5	1	1	1.4	.989	OF-57
13 yrs.	1461	.298	.415	5636	1678	315	75	65	1.2	895	694	392	471	158	74	12	2793	96	68	16	2.0	.977	OF-1367

WORLD SERIES

Year Team	Games	BA	SA	AB	H	2B	3B	HR	HR%	R	RBI	BB	SO	SB	PH AB	PH H	PO	A	E	DP	TC/G	FA	G by Pos
1934 DET A	7	.286	.500	28	8	6	0	0	0.0	1	2	1	4	0	0	0	15	0	0	0	2.1	1.000	OF-7
1935	6	.385	.577	26	10	3	1	0	0.0	1	4	0	1	0	0	0	8	2	1	0	1.8	.909	OF-6
1940	1	.000	.000	1	0	0	0	0	0.0	0	0	0	0	0	1	0	0	0	0	0	0.0	–	
3 yrs.	14	.327	.527	55	18	9	1	0	0.0	2	6	1	5	0	1	0	23	2	1	0	1.9	.962	OF-13
							3rd																

Jimmie Foxx

FOXX, JAMES EMORY (Double X, The Beast)
B. Oct. 22, 1907, Sudlersville, Md.   D. July 21, 1967, Miami, Fla.
Hall of Fame 1951.

BR TR 6'   195 lbs.

Year Team	Games	BA	SA	AB	H	2B	3B	HR	HR%	R	RBI	BB	SO	SB	PH AB	PH H	PO	A	E	DP	TC/G	FA	G by Pos
1925 PHI A	10	.667	.778	9	6	1	0	0	0.0	2	0	0	1	0	9	6	0	0	0	0	0.0	–	C-1
1926	26	.313	.438	32	10	2	1	0	0.0	8	5	1	6	1	8	0	19	5	0	0	0.9	1.000	C-12, OF-3
1927	61	.323	.515	130	42	6	5	3	2.3	23	20	14	11	2	20	7	272	16	7	10	4.8	.976	1B-32, C-5
1928	118	.328	.548	400	131	29	10	13	3.3	85	79	60	43	3	8	2	412	154	17	32	4.9	.971	3B-61, 1B-30, C-20
1929	149	.354	.625	517	183	23	9	33	6.4	123	117	103	70	10	0	0	1233	91	7	100	8.9	.995	1B-142, 3B-7
1930	153	.335	.637	562	188	33	13	37	6.6	127	156	93	66	7	0	0	1362	79	14	101	9.5	.990	1B-153
1931	139	.291	.567	515	150	32	10	30	5.8	93	120	73	84	4	2	1	990	104	15	93	8.0	.986	1B-112, 3B-20, OF-1
1932	154	.364	.749	585	213	33	9	58	9.9	151	169	116	96	3	0	0	1338	97	11	116	9.4	.992	1B-141, 3B-13
1933	149	.356	.703	573	204	37	9	48	8.4	125	163	96	93	2	0	0	1402	94	15	98	10.1	.990	1B-149, SS-1
1934	150	.334	.653	539	180	28	6	44	8.2	120	130	111	75	11	1	0	1388	102	10	134	10.0	.993	1B-140, 3B-9
1935	147	.346	.636	535	185	33	7	36	6.7	118	115	114	99	6	0	0	1226	93	4	108	9.0	.997	1B-121, C-26, 3B-2
1936 BOS A	155	.338	.631	585	198	32	8	41	7.0	130	143	105	119	13	0	0	1254	77	13	108	8.7	.990	1B-139, OF-16, 3B-1
1937	150	.285	.538	569	162	24	6	36	6.3	111	127	99	96	10	0	0	1287	106	8	122	9.3	.994	1B-150, C-1
1938	149	.349	.704	565	197	33	9	50	8.8	139	175	119	76	5	0	0	1282	116	19	153	9.5	.987	1B-149
1939	124	.360	.694	467	168	31	10	35	7.5	130	105	89	72	4	1	0	1101	91	10	104	9.7	.992	1B-123, P-1
1940	144	.297	.581	515	153	30	4	36	7.0	106	119	101	87	4	4	1	1023	100	10	89	7.9	.991	1B-95, C-42, 3B-1
1941	135	.300	.505	487	146	27	8	19	3.9	87	105	93	103	2	4	2	1162	118	14	106	9.6	.989	1B-124, 3B-5, OF-1
1942 2 teams			BOS A (30G – .270)				CHI N	(70G – .205)															
" total	100	.226	.344	305	69	12	0	8	2.6	43	33	40	70	1	18	3	722	58	10	60	7.9	.987	1B-79, C-1
1944 CHI N	15	.050	.100	20	1	0	0	0	0.0	0	2	2	11	0	11	0	9	6	0	0	1.0	1.000	3B-2, C-1
1945 PHI N	89	.268	.420	224	60	11	1	7	3.1	30	38	23	39	0	26	8	304	54	8	19	4.1	.978	1B-40, 3B-14, P-9
20 yrs.	2317	.325	.609	8134	2646	458	125	534	6.6	1751	1921	1452	1311	88	112	30	17786	1561	192	1553	8.4	.990	1B-1919, 3B-135, C-109, OF-21, P-10, SS-1
			4th					9th	7th		6th												

WORLD SERIES

Year Team	Games	BA	SA	AB	H	2B	3B	HR	HR%	R	RBI	BB	SO	SB	PH AB	PH H	PO	A	E	DP	TC/G	FA	G by Pos
1929 PHI A	5	.350	.700	20	7	1	0	2	10.0	5	5	1	1	0	0	0	38	1	0	2	7.8	1.000	1B-5
1930	6	.333	.667	21	7	2	1	1	4.8	3	3	2	4	0	0	0	53	3	0	2	9.3	1.000	1B-6
1931	7	.348	.478	23	8	0	0	1	4.3	3	3	6	5	0	0	0	69	2	1	4	10.3	.986	1B-7
3 yrs.	18	.344	.609	64	22	3	1	4	6.3	11	11	9	10	0	0	0	160	6	1	8	9.3	.994	1B-18
			10th																				

Joe Foy

FOY, JOSEPH ANTHONY
B. Feb. 21, 1943, New York, N. Y.   D. Oct. 12, 1989, Bronx, N. Y.

BR TR 6'   215 lbs.

Year Team	Games	BA	SA	AB	H	2B	3B	HR	HR%	R	RBI	BB	SO	SB	PH AB	PH H	PO	A	E	DP	TC/G	FA	G by Pos
1966 BOS A	151	.262	.413	554	145	23	8	15	2.7	97	63	91	80	2	1	0	169	310	27	35	3.4	.947	3B-139, SS-13
1967	130	.251	.426	446	112	22	4	16	3.6	70	49	46	87	8	13	2	110	204	27	13	2.6	.921	3B-118, OF-1
1968	150	.225	.326	515	116	18	2	10	1.9	65	60	84	91	26	1	0	118	313	30	36	3.1	.935	3B-147, OF-3
1969 KC A	145	.262	.370	519	136	19	2	11	2.1	72	71	74	75	37	1	0	285	230	18	29	3.7	.966	3B-113, OF-16, 1B-16, SS-5, 2B-3
1970 NY N	99	.236	.329	322	76	12	0	6	1.9	39	37	68	58	22	2	0	90	179	18	20	2.9	.937	3B-97
1971 WAS A	41	.234	.297	128	30	8	0	0	0.0	12	11	27	14	4	4	0	44	80	5	12	3.1	.961	3B-37, 2B-3, SS-1
6 yrs.	716	.248	.372	2484	615	102	16	58	2.3	355	291	390	405	99	22	2	816	1316	125	145	3.2	.945	3B-651, OF-20, SS-19, 1B-16, 2B-6

WORLD SERIES

Year Team	Games	BA	SA	AB	H	2B	3B	HR	HR%	R	RBI	BB	SO	SB	PH AB	PH H	PO	A	E	DP	TC/G	FA	G by Pos
1967 BOS A	6	.133	.200	15	2	1	0	0	0.0	2	1	1	5	0	3	0	7	10	1	0	3.0	.944	3B-3

Julio Franco

FRANCO, JULIO CESAR
Born Julio Cesar Robles y Franco.
B. Aug. 23, 1958, Hato Mayor, Dominican Republic

BB TR 6'   160 lbs.

Year Team	Games	BA	SA	AB	H	2B	3B	HR	HR%	R	RBI	BB	SO	SB	PH AB	PH H	PO	A	E	DP	TC/G	FA	G by Pos
1982 PHI N	16	.276	.310	29	8	1	0	0	0.0	3	3	2	4	0	1	0	8	25	0	2	2.1	1.000	SS-11, 3B-2
1983 CLE A	149	.273	.388	560	153	24	8	8	1.4	68	80	27	50	32	0	0	247	438	28	92	4.8	.961	SS-149
1984	160	.286	.348	658	188	22	5	3	0.5	82	79	43	68	19	0	0	280	481	36	116	5.0	.955	SS-159, DH-1
1985	160	.288	.381	636	183	33	4	6	0.9	97	90	54	74	13	2	0	252	437	36	99	4.5	.950	SS-151, 2B-8, DH-1
1986	149	.306	.422	599	183	30	5	10	1.7	80	74	32	66	10	1	0	248	413	19	90	4.6	.972	SS-134, 2B-13, DH-3
1987	128	.319	.428	495	158	24	3	8	1.6	86	52	57	56	32	1	1	175	313	18	56	4.0	.964	SS-111, 2B-9, DH-8
1988	152	.303	.409	613	186	23	6	10	1.6	88	54	56	72	25	0	0	310	434	14	87	5.0	.982	2B-151, DH-1
1989 TEX A	150	.316	.462	548	173	31	5	13	2.4	80	92	66	69	21	1	1	256	386	13	70	4.4	.980	2B-140, DH-10
8 yrs.	1064	.298	.403	4138	1232	188	36	58	1.4	584	524	337	459	152	5	2	1776	2927	164	612	4.6	.966	SS-715, 2B-321, DH-24, 3B-2

Terry Francona

FRANCONA, TERRY JON
Son of Tito Francona.
B. Apr. 22, 1959, Aberdeen, S. D.

BB TL 6'1"   190 lbs.

Year Team	Games	BA	SA	AB	H	2B	3B	HR	HR%	R	RBI	BB	SO	SB	PH AB	PH H	PO	A	E	DP	TC/G	FA	G by Pos
1981 MON N	34	.274	.326	95	26	6	1	1	1.1	11	8	5	6	1	10	5	41	5	0	0	1.4	1.000	OF-26, 1B-1
1982	46	.321	.344	131	42	3	0	0	0.0	14	9	8	11	2	7	2	65	0	3	2	1.5	.956	OF-33, 1B-16
1983	120	.257	.352	230	59	11	1	3	1.3	21	22	6	20	0	38	8	172	10	3	10	1.5	.984	OF-51, 1B-47
1984	58	.346	.467	214	74	19	2	1	0.5	18	18	5	12	0	4	1	431	50	3	43	8.3	.994	1B-50, OF-6
1985	107	.267	.349	281	75	15	1	2	0.7	19	31	12	12	5	31	6	431	40	6	32	4.5	.987	1B-57, OF-28, 3B-1

Year	Team		Games	BA	SA	AB	H	2B	3B	HR	HR%	R	RBI	BB	SO	SB	Pinch Hit AB	Pinch Hit H	PO	A	E	DP	TC/G	FA	G by Pos

Terry Francona *continued*

Year	Team		Games	BA	SA	AB	H	2B	3B	HR	HR%	R	RBI	BB	SO	SB	PH AB	PH H	PO	A	E	DP	TC/G	FA	G by Pos
1986	CHI	N	86	.250	.323	124	31	3	0	2	1.6	13	8	6	6	0	42	8	123	7	0	9	1.5	1.000	OF-30, 1B-23
1987	CIN	N	102	.227	.295	207	47	5	0	3	1.4	16	12	10	12	2	43	11	377	45	2	38	4.2	.995	1B-57, OF-8
1988	CLE	A	62	.311	.363	212	66	8	0	1	0.5	24	12	5	18	0	15	5	47	5	1	3	0.9	.981	DH-38, OF-5, 1B-5
1989	MIL	A	90	.232	.322	233	54	10	1	3	1.3	26	23	8	20	2	8	1	339	26	4	32	4.1	.989	1B-46, DH-23, OF-16, P-1
9 yrs.			705	.274	.352	1727	474	74	6	16	0.9	162	143	65	119	12	197	46	2026	188	22	169	3.2	.990	1B-302, OF-203, DH-61, 3B-1, P-1

DIVISIONAL PLAYOFF SERIES

Year	Team		Games	BA	SA	AB	H	2B	3B	HR	HR%	R	RBI	BB	SO	SB	PH AB	PH H	PO	A	E	DP	TC/G	FA	G by Pos
1981	MON	N	5	.333	.333	12	4	0	0	0	0.0	0	0	2	2	2	0	0	0	0	0	0	0.0	–	OF-5

LEAGUE CHAMPIONSHIP SERIES

Year	Team		Games	BA	SA	AB	H	2B	3B	HR	HR%	R	RBI	BB	SO	SB	PH AB	PH H	PO	A	E	DP	TC/G	FA	G by Pos
1981	MON	N	2	.000	.000	1	0	0	0	0	0.0	0	0	0	1	0	1	0	0	0	0	0	0.0	–	OF-1

Tito Francona

FRANCONA, JOHN PATSY
Father of Terry Francona.
B. Nov. 4, 1933, Aliquippa, Pa.

BL TL 5'11" 190 lbs.

Year	Team		Games	BA	SA	AB	H	2B	3B	HR	HR%	R	RBI	BB	SO	SB	PH AB	PH H	PO	A	E	DP	TC/G	FA	G by Pos
1956	BAL	A	139	.258	.373	445	115	16	4	9	2.0	62	57	51	60	11	18	4	326	13	7	8	2.5	.980	OF-122, 1B-21
1957			97	.233	.358	279	65	8	3	7	2.5	35	38	29	48	7	23	3	130	1	1	2	1.4	.992	OF-73, 1B-4
1958	2 teams		CHI N (41G – .258)			DET A (45G – .246)																			
"	total		86	.254	.330	197	50	8	2	1	0.5	21	20	29	40	2	29	11	73	3	0	1	0.9	1.000	OF-53, 1B-1
1959	CLE	A	122	.363	.566	399	145	17	2	20	5.0	68	79	35	42	2	20	5	432	21	5	21	3.8	.989	OF-64, 1B-35
1960			147	.292	.460	544	159	36	2	17	3.1	84	79	67	67	4	3	0	346	14	4	6	2.5	.989	OF-138, 1B-13
1961			155	.301	.459	592	178	30	8	16	2.7	87	85	56	52	2	7	1	395	11	8	10	2.7	.981	OF-138, 1B-14
1962			158	.272	.401	621	169	28	5	14	2.3	82	70	47	74	3	0	0	1402	127	22	5	9.8	.986	1B-158
1963			142	.228	.346	500	114	29	0	10	2.0	57	41	47	77	9	13	4	292	8	3	3	2.1	.990	OF-122, 1B-11
1964			111	.248	.400	270	67	13	2	8	3.0	35	24	44	46	1	29	6	157	7	2	10	1.5	.988	OF-69, 1B-17
1965	STL	N	81	.259	.402	174	45	6	2	5	2.9	15	19	17	30	1	35	9	137	3	2	8	1.8	.986	1B-34, OF-13
1966			83	.212	.327	156	33	4	1	4	2.6	14	17	7	27	0	41	7	224	18	3	20	3.0	.988	1B-30, OF-9
1967	2 teams		PHI N (27G – .205)			ATL N (82G – .248)																			
"	total		109	.239	.318	327	78	6	1	6	1.8	35	28	27	44	1	27	3	675	48	5	51	6.7	.993	1B-80, OF-7
1968	ATL	N	122	.286	.347	346	99	11	1	2	0.6	32	47	51	45	3	24	5	382	12	4	18	3.3	.990	OF-65, 1B-33
1969	2 teams		ATL N (51G – .295)			OAK A (32G – .341)																			
"	total		83	.318	.457	173	55	7	1	5	2.9	17	42	25	21	0	32	8	222	11	4	15	2.9	.983	1B-26, OF-16
1970	2 teams		OAK A (32G – .242)			MIL A (52G – .231)																			
"	total		84	.235	.296	98	23	3	0	1	1.0	6	10	12	21	1	64	15	123	10	0	13	1.6	1.000	1B-19, OF-1
15 yrs.			1719	.272	.403	5121	1395	224	34	125	2.4	650	656	544	694	46	365	81	5316	305	70	191	3.3	.988	OF-911, 1B-475

Charlie Frank

FRANK, CHARLES
B. May 30, 1870, Mobile, Ala. D. May 24, 1922, Memphis, Tenn.

Year	Team		Games	BA	SA	AB	H	2B	3B	HR	HR%	R	RBI	BB	SO	SB	PH AB	PH H	PO	A	E	DP	TC/G	FA	G by Pos
1893	STL	N	40	.335	.427	164	55	6	3	1	0.6	29	17	18	8	8	0	0	84	9	7	1	2.5	.930	OF-40
1894			80	.279	.398	319	89	12	7	4	1.3	52	42	44	13	14	0	0	191	12	26	4	2.9	.886	OF-77, 1B-3, P-2
2 yrs.			120	.298	.408	483	144	18	10	5	1.0	81	59	62	21	22	0	0	275	21	33	5	2.7	.900	OF-117, 1B-3, P-2

Fred Frank

FRANK, FREDERICK
B. Mar. 11, 1874, Louisa, Ky. D. Mar. 27, 1950, Ashland, Ky.

Year	Team		Games	BA	SA	AB	H	2B	3B	HR	HR%	R	RBI	BB	SO	SB	PH AB	PH H	PO	A	E	DP	TC/G	FA	G by Pos
1898	CLE	N	17	.208	.264	53	11	1	1	0	0.0	3	3	4		1	0	0	40	3	4	2	2.8	.915	OF-17

Franklin

FRANKLIN,
Deceased.

Year	Team		Games	BA	SA	AB	H	2B	3B	HR	HR%	R	RBI	BB	SO	SB	PH AB	PH H	PO	A	E	DP	TC/G	FA	G by Pos
1884	WAS	U	1	.000	.000	3	0	0	0	0	0.0	0		0		0	0	0	2	0	0	0	2.0	1.000	OF-1

Murray Franklin

FRANKLIN, MURRAY ASHER (Moe)
B. Apr. 1, 1914, Chicago, Ill. D. Mar. 16, 1978, Harbor City, Calif.

BR TR 6' 175 lbs.

Year	Team		Games	BA	SA	AB	H	2B	3B	HR	HR%	R	RBI	BB	SO	SB	PH AB	PH H	PO	A	E	DP	TC/G	FA	G by Pos
1941	DET	A	13	.300	.400	10	3	1	0	0	0.0	1	0	2	2	0	7	2	1	2	1	1	0.3	.750	SS-4, 3B-1
1942			48	.260	.344	154	40	7	0	2	1.3	24	16	7	5	0	5	0	82	92	6	17	3.8	.967	SS-32, 2B-7
2 yrs.			61	.262	.348	164	43	8	0	2	1.2	25	16	9	7	0	12	2	83	94	7	18	3.0	.962	SS-36, 2B-7, 3B-1

Herman Franks

FRANKS, HERMAN LOUIS
B. Jan. 4, 1914, Price, Utah
Manager 1965-68, 1977-79.

BL TR 5'10½" 187 lbs.

Year	Team		Games	BA	SA	AB	H	2B	3B	HR	HR%	R	RBI	BB	SO	SB	PH AB	PH H	PO	A	E	DP	TC/G	FA	G by Pos
1939	STL	N	17	.059	.059	17	1	0	0	0	0.0	1		3	3	0	2	0	34	2	1	0	2.2	.973	C-13
1940	BKN	N	65	.183	.237	131	24	4	0	1	0.8	11	14	20	6	2	19	3	183	22	3	3	3.2	.986	C-43
1941			59	.201	.273	139	28	7	0	1	0.7	10	11	14	13	0	2	0	191	21	3	6	3.6	.986	C-54, OF-1
1947	PHI	A	8	.200	.333	15	3	0	1	0	0.0	2	1	4	4	0	2	0	12	1	0	0	1.6	1.000	C-4
1948			40	.224	.347	98	22	7	1	1	1.0	9	14	16	11	0	9	1	113	17	3	2	3.3	.977	C-27
1949	NY	N	1	.667	.667	3	2	0	0	0	0.0	0	1	0	0	0	0	0	4	1	0	0	5.0	1.000	C-1
6 yrs.			190	.199	.275	403	80	18	2	3	0.7	35	43	57	37	2	34	5	537	64	9	11	3.2	.985	C-142, OF-1

WORLD SERIES

Year	Team		Games	BA	SA	AB	H	2B	3B	HR	HR%	R	RBI	BB	SO	SB	PH AB	PH H	PO	A	E	DP	TC/G	FA	G by Pos
1941	BKN	N	1	.000	.000	0	0	0	0	0	0.0	0	0	0	0	0	0	0	1	0	0	0	1.0	1.000	C-1

Joe Frazier

FRAZIER, JOSEPH FILMORE (Cobra Joe)
B. Oct. 6, 1922, Liberty, N. C.
Manager 1976-77.

BL TR 6' 180 lbs.

Year	Team		Games	BA	SA	AB	H	2B	3B	HR	HR%	R	RBI	BB	SO	SB	PH AB	PH H	PO	A	E	DP	TC/G	FA	G by Pos
1947	CLE	A	9	.071	.143	14	1	0	0	0	0.0	1	0	1	1	0	2	0	6	0	1	0	0.8	.857	OF-5
1954	STL	N	81	.295	.500	88	26	5	2	3	3.4	8	18	13	17	0	62	20	16	1	0	0	0.2	.944	OF-11, 1B-1
1955			58	.200	.386	70	14	0	1	4	5.7	12	9	6	12	0	45	4	16	0	0	0	0.3	1.000	OF-14
1956	3 teams		STL N (14G – .211)			CIN N (10G – .235)			BAL A (45G – .257)																	
"	total		69	.245	.400	110	27	8	0	3	2.7	10	18	15	16	0	40	9	35	2	1	0	0.6	.974	OF-26
4 yrs.			217	.241	.415	282	68	15	2	10	3.5	31	45	35	46	0	149	33	73	3	3	0	0.4	.962	OF-56, 1B-1

Year	Team	Games	BA	SA	AB	H	2B	3B	HR	HR%	R	RBI	BB	SO	SB	AB	H	PO	A	E	DP	TC/G	FA	G by Pos

Johnny Frederick

FREDERICK, JOHN HENRY
B. Jan. 26, 1902, Denver, Colo. D. June 18, 1977, Tigard, Ore.
BL TL 5'11" 165 lbs.

Year	Team	Games	BA	SA	AB	H	2B	3B	HR	HR%	R	RBI	BB	SO	SB	AB	H	PO	A	E	DP	TC/G	FA	G by Pos
1929	BKN N	148	.328	.545	628	206	**52**	6	24	3.8	127	75	39	34	6	5	2	410	13	11	1	2.9	.975	OF-143
1930		142	.334	.524	616	206	44	11	17	2.8	120	76	46	34	1	0	0	394	12	4	3	2.9	.990	OF-142
1931		146	.270	.435	611	165	34	8	17	2.8	81	71	31	46	2	1	0	398	10	15	2	2.9	.965	OF-145
1932		118	.299	.508	384	115	28	2	16	4.2	54	56	25	35	1	29	9	201	6	5	2	1.8	.976	OF-88
1933		147	.308	.410	556	171	22	7	7	1.3	65	64	36	14	9	9	2	289	8	9	1	2.1	.971	OF-138
1934		104	.296	.407	307	91	20	1	4	1.3	51	35	33	13	4	18	6	123	13	6	3	1.4	.958	OF-77, 1B-1
6 yrs.		805	.308	.477	3102	954	200	35	85	2.7	498	377	210	176	23	62	19	1815	62	50	12	2.4	.974	OF-733, 1B-1

Ed Freed

FREED, EDWIN CHARLES
B. Aug. 22, 1919, Centre Valley, Pa.
BR TR 5'6" 165 lbs.

Year	Team	Games	BA	SA	AB	H	2B	3B	HR	HR%	R	RBI	BB	SO	SB	AB	H	PO	A	E	DP	TC/G	FA	G by Pos
1942	PHI N	13	.303	.455	33	10	3	1	0	0.0	3	1	4	3	1	2	0	13	2	0	0	1.2	1.000	OF-11

Roger Freed

FREED, ROGER VERNON
B. June 2, 1946, Los Angeles, Calif.
BR TR 6' 190 lbs.

Year	Team	Games	BA	SA	AB	H	2B	3B	HR	HR%	R	RBI	BB	SO	SB	AB	H	PO	A	E	DP	TC/G	FA	G by Pos
1970	BAL A	4	.154	.154	13	2	0	0	0	0.0	0	1	3	4	0	0	0	25	1	0	6	6.5	1.000	1B-3, OF-1
1971	PHI N	118	.221	.313	348	77	12	1	6	1.7	23	37	44	86	0	14	2	185	4	2	1	1.6	.990	OF-106, C-1
1972		73	.225	.395	129	29	4	0	6	4.7	10	18	23	39	0	27	4	64	4	2	2	1.0	.971	OF-46
1974	CIN N	6	.333	.833	6	2	0	0	1	16.7	1	3	1	1	0	6	2	2	0	0	0	0.3	1.000	1B-1
1976	MON N	8	.200	.267	15	3	1	0	0	0.0	0	1	3	5	1	5	1	25	1	0	1	3.3	1.000	1B-3, OF-1
1977	STL N	49	.398	.627	83	33	2	1	5	6.0	10	21	11	9	0	23	9	107	7	1	13	2.3	.991	1B-18, OF-6
1978		52	.239	.370	92	22	6	0	2	2.2	3	20	8	17	1	29	11	113	10	1	13	2.4	.992	1B-15, OF-6
1979		34	.258	.516	31	8	2	0	2	6.5	2	8	5	7	0	27	6	7	1	1	0	0.3	.889	1B-1
8 yrs.		344	.245	.381	717	176	27	2	22	3.1	49	109	95	166	1	131	35	528	28	7	36	1.6	.988	OF-166, 1B-41, C-1

Bill Freehan

FREEHAN, WILLIAM ASHLEY
B. Nov. 29, 1941, Detroit, Mich.
BR TR 6'3" 203 lbs.

Year	Team	Games	BA	SA	AB	H	2B	3B	HR	HR%	R	RBI	BB	SO	SB	AB	H	PO	A	E	DP	TC/G	FA	G by Pos
1961	DET A	4	.400	.400	10	4	0	0	0	0.0	1	4	1	1	0	0	0	14	4	0	0	4.5	1.000	C-3
1963		100	.243	.387	300	73	12	2	9	3.0	37	36	39	56	2	9	3	554	38	3	19	6.0	.995	C-73, 1B-19
1964		144	.300	.462	520	156	14	8	18	3.5	69	80	36	68	5	6	1	930	61	7	7	6.9	.993	C-141, 1B-1
1965		130	.234	.339	431	101	15	0	10	2.3	45	43	39	63	4	3	1	865	57	4	4	7.1	.996	C-129
1966		136	.234	.352	492	115	22	0	12	2.4	47	46	40	72	5	1	1	942	60	4	14	7.4	.996	C-132, 1B-5
1967		155	.282	.447	517	146	23	1	20	3.9	66	74	73	71	1	2	2	1027	68	8	15	7.1	.993	C-147, 1B-11
1968		155	.263	.454	540	142	24	2	25	4.6	73	84	65	64	0	3	1	1133	83	7	26	7.9	.994	C-138, 1B-21, OF-1
1969		143	.262	.405	489	128	16	3	16	3.3	61	49	53	55	1	8	1	959	56	10	14	7.2	.990	C-120, 1B-20
1970		117	.241	.420	395	95	17	3	16	4.1	44	52	52	48	0	3	1	742	42	2	6	6.7	.997	C-114
1971		148	.277	.465	516	143	26	4	21	4.1	57	71	54	48	2	4	1	912	50	4	6	6.5	.996	C-144, OF-1
1972		111	.262	.401	374	98	18	2	10	2.7	51	56	48	51	0	8	3	654	60	8	9	6.5	.989	C-105, 1B-1
1973		110	.234	.313	380	89	10	1	6	1.6	33	29	40	30	0	0	0	638	53	3	5	6.3	.996	C-98, 1B-7
1974		130	.297	.479	445	132	17	5	18	4.0	58	60	42	44	2	1	0	902	81	9	55	7.6	.991	1B-65, C-63, DH-1
1975		120	.246	.398	427	105	17	3	14	3.3	42	47	32	56	2	2	1	635	66	6	12	5.9	.992	C-113, 1B-5
1976		71	.270	.384	237	64	10	1	5	2.1	22	27	12	27	0	6	0	328	34	6	4	5.2	.984	C-61, DH-3, 1B-2
15 yrs.		1774	.262	.412	6073	1591	241	35	200	3.3	706	758	626	753	24	59	16	11235	813	81	196	6.8	.993	C-1581, 1B-157, DH-4, OF-2

LEAGUE CHAMPIONSHIP SERIES

Year	Team	Games	BA	SA	AB	H	2B	3B	HR	HR%	R	RBI	BB	SO	SB	AB	H	PO	A	E	DP	TC/G	FA	G by Pos
1972	DET A	3	.250	.583	12	3	1	0	1	8.3	2	3	0	1	0	0	0	24	3	0	1	9.0	1.000	C-3

WORLD SERIES

Year	Team	Games	BA	SA	AB	H	2B	3B	HR	HR%	R	RBI	BB	SO	SB	AB	H	PO	A	E	DP	TC/G	FA	G by Pos
1968	DET A	7	.083	.125	24	2	1	0	0	0.0	0	2	4	8	0	0	0	45	6	2	1	7.6	.962	C-7

Buck Freeman

FREEMAN, JOHN FRANK
B. Oct. 30, 1871, Catasauqua, Pa. D. June 25, 1949, Wilkes-Barre, Pa.
BL TL 5'9" 169 lbs.

Year	Team	Games	BA	SA	AB	H	2B	3B	HR	HR%	R	RBI	BB	SO	SB	AB	H	PO	A	E	DP	TC/G	FA	G by Pos
1891	WAS AA	5	.222	.278	18	4	1	0	0	0.0	1	1	1		2	0	0	0	10	3	0	2.6	.769	P-5
1898	WAS N	29	.364	.523	107	39	2	3	3	2.8	19	21	7		2	0	0	39	5	1	2	1.6	.978	OF-29
1899		155	.318	.563	588	187	19	25	**25**	4.3	107	122	23		21	0	0	220	17	15	3	1.6	.940	OF-155, P-2
1900	BOS N	117	.301	.452	418	126	19	13	6	1.4	58	65	25		10	8	1	278	16	12	6	2.6	.961	OF-91, 1B-19
1901	BOS A	129	.345	.527	490	169	23	15	12	2.4	86	114	44		17	0	0	1279	55	36	71	10.6	.974	1B-128, OF-1, 2B-1
1902		138	.309	.502	564	174	38	19	11	2.0	75	**121**	32		17	0	0	222	15	14	3	1.8	.944	OF-138
1903		141	.287	.496	567	163	39	20	**13**	2.3	74	104	30		5	0	0	195	13	15	2	1.6	.933	OF-141
1904		157	.280	.412	597	167	20	**19**	7	1.2	64	84	32		7	0	0	216	14	11	4	1.5	.954	OF-157
1905		130	.240	.338	455	109	20	8	3	0.7	59	49	46		8	5	3	649	29	21	20	5.4	.970	1B-72, OF-51, 3B-2
1906		121	.250	.349	392	98	18	9	1	0.3	42	30	28		5	8	3	472	50	9	23	4.4	.983	OF-65, 1B-43, 3B-4
1907		4	.182	.455	11	2	0	1	1	9.1	1	2	3		0	1	0	6	0	0	0	1.5	1.000	OF-3
11 yrs.		1126	.294	.462	4207	1238	199	131	82	1.9	586	713	272	2	92	22	7	3576	224	137	134	3.5	.965	OF-831, 1B-262, P-7, 3B-6, 2B-1

WORLD SERIES

Year	Team	Games	BA	SA	AB	H	2B	3B	HR	HR%	R	RBI	BB	SO	SB	AB	H	PO	A	E	DP	TC/G	FA	G by Pos
1903	BOS A	8	.281	.469	32	9	0	3	0	0.0	6	4	2	2	0	0	0	8	0	0	0	1.0	1.000	OF-8
							4th																	

Jerry Freeman

FREEMAN, FRANK ELLSWORTH (Buck)
B. Dec. 26, 1879, Placerville, Calif. D. Sept. 30, 1952, Los Angeles, Calif.
BL TR 6'2" 220 lbs.

Year	Team	Games	BA	SA	AB	H	2B	3B	HR	HR%	R	RBI	BB	SO	SB	AB	H	PO	A	E	DP	TC/G	FA	G by Pos
1908	WAS A	154	.252	.305	531	134	15	5	1	0.2	45	45	36		6	0	0	1548	66	41	69	10.7	.975	1B-154
1909		19	.167	.208	48	8	0	1	0	0.0	2	3	4		3	4	0	146	7	8	11	8.5	.950	1B-14, OF-1
2 yrs.		173	.245	.297	579	142	15	6	1	0.2	47	48	40		9	4	0	1694	73	49	80	10.5	.973	1B-168, OF-1

John Freeman

FREEMAN, JOHN EDWARD (Buck)
B. Jan. 24, 1901, Boston, Mass. D. Apr. 14, 1958, Washington, D. C.
BR TR 5'8" 160 lbs.

Year	Team	Games	BA	SA	AB	H	2B	3B	HR	HR%	R	RBI	BB	SO	SB	AB	H	PO	A	E	DP	TC/G	FA	G by Pos
1927	BOS A	4	.000	.000	2	0	0	0	0	0.0	0	0	0	0	0	0	0	0	0	0	0	0.0	—	OF-3

915

Year	Team	Games	BA	SA	AB	H	2B	3B	HR	HR%	R	RBI	BB	SO	SB	Pinch Hit AB	H	PO	A	E	DP	TC/G	FA	G by Pos

LaVel Freeman

FREEMAN, LaVEL MAURICE
B. Feb. 18, 1963, Oakland, Calif.
BL TL 5'9" 170 lbs.

Year	Team	Games	BA	SA	AB	H	2B	3B	HR	HR%	R	RBI	BB	SO	SB	PH AB	H	PO	A	E	DP	TC/G	FA	G by Pos
1989	MIL A	2	.000	.000	3	0	0	0	0	0.0	1	0	0	2	0	0	0	0	0	0	0	0.0	–	DH-2

Gene Freese

FREESE, EUGENE LEWIS (Augie)
Brother of George Freese.
B. Jan. 8, 1934, Wheeling, W. Va.
BR TR 5'11" 175 lbs.

Year	Team	Games	BA	SA	AB	H	2B	3B	HR	HR%	R	RBI	BB	SO	SB	PH AB	H	PO	A	E	DP	TC/G	FA	G by Pos
1955	PIT N	134	.253	.426	455	115	21	8	14	3.1	69	44	34	57	5	12	3	183	300	22	57	3.8	.956	3B-65, 2B-57
1956		65	.208	.295	207	43	9	0	3	1.4	17	14	16	45	2	10	0	69	115	4	9	2.9	.979	3B-47, 2B-26
1957		114	.283	.399	346	98	18	2	6	1.7	44	31	17	42	9	30	9	94	149	18	20	2.3	.931	3B-74, OF-10, 2B-10
1958	2 teams	PIT N (17G – .167)					STL N (62G – .257)																	
"	total	79	.249	.411	209	52	11	1	7	3.3	29	18	11	34	1	29	6	82	87	13	14	2.3	.929	SS-28, 2B-14, 3B-4
1959	PHI N	132	.268	.500	400	107	14	5	23	5.8	60	70	43	61	8	20	7	91	160	23	16	2.1	.916	3B-109, 2B-6
1960	CHI A	127	.273	.481	455	124	32	6	17	3.7	60	79	29	65	10	6	1	88	263	20	29	2.9	.946	3B-122
1961	CIN N	152	.277	.466	575	159	27	2	26	4.5	78	87	27	78	8	1	0	125	254	20	23	2.6	.950	3B-151, 2B-1
1962		18	.143	.167	42	6	1	0	0	0.0	2	1	6	8	0	5	0	11	10	0	1	1.2	1.000	3B-10
1963		66	.244	.378	217	53	9	1	6	2.8	20	26	17	42	4	3	0	44	103	11	8	2.4	.930	3B-62, OF-1
1964	PIT N	99	.225	.377	289	65	13	2	9	3.1	33	40	19	45	1	30	5	48	112	14	12	1.8	.920	3B-72
1965	2 teams	PIT N (43G – .263)					CHI A (17G – .281)																	
"	total	60	.268	.348	112	30	4	1	1	0.9	8	12	11	27	0	31	12	16	37	5	2	1.0	.914	3B-27
1966	2 teams	CHI A (48G – .208)					HOU N (21G – .091)																	
"	total	69	.180	.259	139	25	2	0	3	2.2	9	10	13	31	3	29	2	20	79	12	5	1.6	.892	3B-38, 2B-3, OF-1
12 yrs.		1115	.254	.418	3446	877	161	28	115	3.3	429	432	243	535	51	206	45	871	1669	162	196	2.4	.940	3B-781, 2B-117, SS-28, OF-12

WORLD SERIES

Year	Team	Games	BA	SA	AB	H	2B	3B	HR	HR%	R	RBI	BB	SO	SB	PH AB	H	PO	A	E	DP	TC/G	FA	G by Pos
1961	CIN N	5	.063	.125	16	1	1	0	0	0.0	0	0	3	4	0	0	0	6	4	0	1	2.0	1.000	3B-5

George Freese

FREESE, GEORGE WALTER (Bud)
Brother of Gene Freese.
B. Sept. 12, 1926, Wheeling, W. Va.
BR TR 6' 190 lbs.

Year	Team	Games	BA	SA	AB	H	2B	3B	HR	HR%	R	RBI	BB	SO	SB	PH AB	H	PO	A	E	DP	TC/G	FA	G by Pos
1953	DET A	1	.000	.000	1	0	0	0	0	0.0	0	0	0	0	0	1	0	0	0	0	0	0.0	–	
1955	PIT N	51	.257	.374	179	46	8	2	3	1.7	17	22	17	18	1	1	0	50	82	9	3	2.8	.936	3B-50
1961	CHI N	9	.286	.286	7	2	0	0	0	0.0	0	1	1	4	0	7	2	0	0	0	0	0.0	–	
3 yrs.		61	.257	.369	187	48	8	2	3	1.6	17	23	18	22	1	9	2	50	82	9	3	2.3	.936	3B-50

Jim Fregosi

FREGOSI, JAMES LOUIS
B. Apr. 4, 1942, San Francisco, Calif.
Manager 1978-81, 1986-88.
BR TR 6'1" 190 lbs.

Year	Team	Games	BA	SA	AB	H	2B	3B	HR	HR%	R	RBI	BB	SO	SB	PH AB	H	PO	A	E	DP	TC/G	FA	G by Pos
1961	LA A	11	.222	.222	27	6	0	0	0	0.0	7	3	1	4	0	0	0	12	22	2	3	3.3	.944	SS-11
1962		58	.291	.406	175	51	3	4	3	1.7	15	23	18	27	2	0	0	96	150	15	35	4.5	.943	SS-52
1963		154	.287	.422	592	170	29	12	9	1.5	83	50	36	104	2	1	0	271	446	27	90	4.8	.964	SS-151
1964		147	.277	.463	505	140	22	9	18	3.6	86	72	72	87	8	9	3	225	421	23	89	4.6	.966	SS-137
1965	CAL A	161	.277	.407	602	167	19	7	15	2.5	66	64	54	107	13	2	0	312	481	26	93	5.1	.968	SS-160
1966		162	.252	.391	611	154	32	7	13	2.1	78	67	67	89	17	1	0	299	531	35	125	5.3	.960	SS-162, 1B-1
1967		151	.290	.395	590	171	23	6	9	1.5	75	56	49	77	9	0	0	258	435	25	73	4.8	.965	SS-151
1968		159	.244	.365	614	150	21	**13**	9	1.5	77	49	60	101	9	0	0	273	454	29	92	4.8	.962	SS-159
1969		161	.260	.381	580	151	22	6	12	2.1	78	47	93	86	9	1	0	255	465	21	88	4.6	.972	SS-160
1970		158	.278	.459	601	167	33	5	22	3.7	95	82	69	92	6	2	1	313	475	20	103	5.1	.975	SS-150, 1B-6
1971		107	.233	.326	347	81	15	1	5	1.4	31	33	39	61	2	10	3	241	251	22	44	4.8	.957	SS-74, 1B-18, OF-7
1972	NY N	101	.232	.344	340	79	15	4	5	1.5	31	32	38	71	0	7	1	91	162	15	15	2.7	.944	3B-85, SS-6, 1B-3
1973	2 teams	NY N (45G – .234)					TEX A (45G – .268)																	
"	total	90	.253	.374	281	71	10	3	6	2.1	32	27	32	56	1	5	0	145	123	14	23	3.1	.950	3B-34, SS-23, OF-17, 1B-13
1974	TEX A	78	.261	.439	230	60	5	0	12	5.2	31	34	22	41	0	7	2	331	73	5	35	5.2	.988	1B-47, 3B-32
1975		77	.262	.398	191	50	5	0	7	3.7	25	33	20	39	0	20	1	356	35	6	31	5.2	.985	1B-54, DH-13, 3B-4
1976		58	.233	.331	133	31	7	0	2	1.5	17	12	23	33	2	15	3	183	18	2	20	3.5	.990	1B-26, DH-18, 3B-5
1977	2 teams	TEX A (13G – .250)					PIT N (36G – .286)																	
"	total	49	.274	.464	84	23	2	1	4	4.8	14	21	16	14	2	20	3	130	9	2	11	2.9	.986	1B-20, DH-3, 3B-1
1978	PIT N	20	.200	.250	20	4	1	0	0	0.0	3	1	6	8	0	12	4	14	4	2	1	1.0	.900	3B-5, 1B-2
18 yrs.		1902	.265	.398	6523	1726	264	78	151	2.3	844	706	715	1097	76	112	21	3805	4555	291	971	4.5	.966	SS-1396, 1B-190, 3B-166, DH-34, OF-24

Vern Freiburger

FREIBURGER, VERN DONALD
B. Dec. 19, 1923, Detroit, Mich.
BR TL 6'1" 170 lbs.

Year	Team	Games	BA	SA	AB	H	2B	3B	HR	HR%	R	RBI	BB	SO	SB	PH AB	H	PO	A	E	DP	TC/G	FA	G by Pos
1941	CLE A	2	.125	.125	8	1	0	0	0	0.0	0	1	0	2	0	0	0	15	3	1	2	9.5	.947	1B-2

Howard Freigau

FREIGAU, HOWARD EARL (Ty)
B. Aug. 1, 1902, Dayton, Ohio   D. July 18, 1932, Chattanooga, Tenn.
BR TR 5'10½" 160 lbs.

Year	Team	Games	BA	SA	AB	H	2B	3B	HR	HR%	R	RBI	BB	SO	SB	PH AB	H	PO	A	E	DP	TC/G	FA	G by Pos
1922	STL N	3	.000	.000	1	0	0	0	0	0.0	0	0	0	0	0	1	0	2	3	0	1	1.7	1.000	SS-2, 3B-1
1923		113	.263	.327	358	94	18	1	1	0.3	30	35	25	36	5	0	0	273	340	46	57	5.8	.930	SS-87, 2B-16, 1B-9, OF-1, 3B-1
1924		98	.269	.362	376	101	17	6	2	0.5	35	39	19	24	10	0	0	128	172	13	24	3.2	.958	3B-98, SS-2
1925	2 teams	STL N (9G – .154)					CHI N (117G – .307)																	
"	total	126	.299	.430	502	150	22	10	8	1.6	79	71	32	32	10	0	0	195	270	39	42	4.0	.923	3B-96, SS-24, 1B-7, 2B-1
1926	CHI N	140	.270	.368	508	137	27	7	3	0.6	51	51	43	42	6	4	2	136	244	13	22	2.8	.967	3B-135, SS-2, OF-1
1927		30	.233	.291	86	20	5	0	0	0.0	12	10	9	10	0	0	0	22	46	9	3	2.6	.883	3B-30
1928	2 teams	BKN N (17G – .206)					BOS N (52G – .257)																	
"	total	69	.245	.350	143	35	10	1	0	0.7	17	20	10	17	1	26	8	56	69	12	9	2.0	.912	SS-15, 2B-11, 3B-10
7 yrs.		579	.272	.370	1974	537	99	25	15	0.8	224	226	138	161	32	30	10	812	1144	132	158	3.6	.937	3B-371, SS-132, 2B-28, 1B-16, OF-2

Year	Team	Games	BA	SA	AB	H	2B	3B	HR	HR%	R	RBI	BB	SO	SB	Pinch Hit AB	Pinch Hit H	PO	A	E	DP	TC/G	FA	G by Pos

Charlie French

FRENCH, CHARLES CALVIN
B. Oct. 12, 1883, Indianapolis, Ind. D. Mar. 30, 1962, Indianapolis, Ind.
BL TR 5'6" 140 lbs.

Year	Team	Games	BA	SA	AB	H	2B	3B	HR	HR%	R	RBI	BB	SO	SB	PH AB	PH H	PO	A	E	DP	TC/G	FA	G by Pos
1909	BOS A	51	.251	.281	167	42	3	1	0	0.0	13	13	15		8	0	0	86	140	24	14	4.9	.904	2B-28, SS-23
1910	2 teams		BOS A (9G – .200)						CHI A (45G – .165)															
"	total	54	.171	.190	210	36	2	1	0	0.0	21	7	11		5	0	0	82	81	15	9	3.3	.916	2B-36, OF-16
2 yrs.		105	.207	.231	377	78	5	2	0	0.0	34	20	26		13	0	0	168	221	39	23	4.1	.909	2B-64, SS-23, OF-16

Jim French

FRENCH, RICHARD JAMES
B. Aug. 13, 1941, Warren, Ohio
BL TR 5'8" 180 lbs.

Year	Team	Games	BA	SA	AB	H	2B	3B	HR	HR%	R	RBI	BB	SO	SB	PH AB	PH H	PO	A	E	DP	TC/G	FA	G by Pos
1965	WAS A	13	.297	.378	37	11	0	0	1	2.7	4	7	9	5	1	0	0	68	8	2	0	6.0	.974	C-13
1966		10	.208	.250	24	5	1	0	0	0.0	0	3	4	5	0	0	0	45	2	1	0	4.8	.979	C-10
1967		6	.063	.063	16	1	0	0	0	0.0	0	1	3	4	0	0	0	28	2	1	0	5.2	.968	C-6
1968		59	.194	.242	165	32	5	0	1	0.6	9	10	19	19	1	8	1	268	42	5	2	5.3	.984	C-53
1969		63	.184	.297	158	29	6	3	2	1.3	14	13	41	15	1	0	0	316	44	4	8	5.8	.989	C-63
1970		69	.211	.259	166	35	3	1	1	0.6	20	13	38	23	0	7	1	267	23	8	4	4.3	.973	C-62, OF-1
1971		14	.146	.195	41	6	2	0	0	0.0	6	4	7	7	0	0	0	60	7	1	2	4.9	.985	C-14
7 yrs.		234	.196	.262	607	119	17	4	5	0.8	53	51	121	78	3	15	2	1052	128	22	16	5.1	.982	C-221, OF-1

Pat French

FRENCH, FRANK ALEXANDER
B. Sept. 22, 1893, Dover, N.H. D. July 13, 1969, Bath, Me.
BR TR 6'1" 180 lbs.

Year	Team	Games	BA	SA	AB	H	2B	3B	HR	HR%	R	RBI	BB	SO	SB	PH AB	PH H	PO	A	E	DP	TC/G	FA	G by Pos
1917	PHI A	3	.000	.000	2	0	0	0	0	0.0	0	0	0	0	0	0	0	1	0	0	0	0.3	1.000	OF-1

Ray French

FRENCH, RAYMOND EDWARD
B. Jan. 9, 1895, Alameda, Calif. D. Apr. 3, 1978, Alameda, Calif.
BR TR 5'9½" 158 lbs.

Year	Team	Games	BA	SA	AB	H	2B	3B	HR	HR%	R	RBI	BB	SO	SB	PH AB	PH H	PO	A	E	DP	TC/G	FA	G by Pos
1920	NY A	2	.000	.000	2	0	0	0	0	0.0	2	1	0	1	0	0	0	1	0	1	0	1.0	.500	SS-1
1923	BKN N	43	.219	.274	73	16	2	1	0	0.0	14	7	4	7	0	1	0	43	82	18	17	3.3	.874	SS-30
1924	CHI A	37	.179	.214	112	20	4	0	0	0.0	13	11	10	13	3	5	0	38	90	10	9	3.7	.928	SS-28, 2B-3
3 yrs.		82	.193	.235	187	36	6	1	0	0.0	29	19	14	21	3	6	0	82	172	29	26	3.5	.898	SS-59, 2B-3

Walter French

FRENCH, WALTER EDWARD (Fitz)
B. July 12, 1899, Moorestown, N.J. D. May 13, 1984, Mountain Home, Ark.
BL TR 5'7½" 155 lbs.

Year	Team	Games	BA	SA	AB	H	2B	3B	HR	HR%	R	RBI	BB	SO	SB	PH AB	PH H	PO	A	E	DP	TC/G	FA	G by Pos
1923	PHI A	16	.231	.308	39	9	3	0	0	0.0	7	4	2	3	0	3	0	17	1	0	0	1.1	1.000	OF-10
1925		67	.370	.460	100	37	9	0	0	0.0	20	14	1	9	1	37	13	31	3	1	0	0.5	.971	OF-19
1926		112	.305	.393	397	121	18	7	1	0.3	51	36	18	24	2	11	4	186	12	6	7	1.8	.971	OF-99
1927		109	.304	.365	326	99	10	5	0	0.0	48	41	16	14	9	7	0	190	6	9	2	1.9	.956	OF-94
1928		49	.257	.311	74	19	4	0	0	0.0	9	7	2	5	1	27	5	33	1	0	0	0.7	1.000	OF-20
1929		45	.267	.400	45	12	1	1	1	2.2	7	7	5	7	0	28	6	8	0	0	0	0.2	1.000	OF-10
6 yrs.		398	.303	.381	981	297	45	13	2	0.2	142	109	44	62	13	113	28	465	23	16	9	1.3	.968	OF-252

WORLD SERIES

Year	Team	Games	BA	SA	AB	H	2B	3B	HR	HR%	R	RBI	BB	SO	SB	PH AB	PH H	PO	A	E	DP	TC/G	FA	G by Pos
1929	PHI A	1	.000	.000	1	0	0	0	0	0.0	0	0	0	0	0	1	0	1	0	0	0	0.0	–	

Lonny Frey

FREY, LINUS REINHARD (Junior)
B. Aug. 23, 1910, St. Louis, Mo.
BL TR 5'10" 160 lbs.
BB 1933-38

Year	Team	Games	BA	SA	AB	H	2B	3B	HR	HR%	R	RBI	BB	SO	SB	PH AB	PH H	PO	A	E	DP	TC/G	FA	G by Pos
1933	BKN N	34	.319	.400	135	43	5	3	0	0.0	25	12	13	13	4	0	0	66	89	18	11	5.1	.896	SS-34
1934		125	.284	.402	490	139	24	5	8	1.6	77	57	52	54	11	2	0	245	400	40	82	5.5	.942	SS-109, 3B-13
1935		131	.262	.437	515	135	35	11	11	2.1	88	77	66	68	6	0	0	274	401	44	75	5.5	.939	SS-127, 2B-4
1936		148	.279	.372	524	146	29	4	4	0.8	63	60	71	56	7	3	0	303	405	62	64	5.2	.919	SS-117, 2B-30, OF-1
1937	CHI N	78	.278	.369	198	55	9	3	1	0.5	33	22	33	15	6	14	2	90	101	10	18	2.6	.950	SS-30, 2B-13, 3B-9, OF-5
1938	CIN N	124	.265	.365	501	133	26	6	4	0.8	76	36	49	50	4	0	0	281	401	27	81	5.7	.962	2B-121, SS-3
1939		125	.291	.452	484	141	27	9	11	2.3	95	55	72	46	5	1	1	324	412	18	83	6.0	.976	2B-123
1940		150	.266	.371	563	150	23	6	8	1.4	102	54	80	48	22	1	0	366	512	21	111	6.0	.977	2B-150
1941		146	.254	.359	543	138	29	5	6	1.1	78	59	72	37	16	1	1	340	432	24	93	5.5	.970	2B-145
1942		141	.266	.344	523	139	23	6	2	0.4	66	39	87	38	9	1	1	340	424	18	95	5.5	.977	2B-140
1943		144	.263	.334	586	154	20	8	2	0.3	78	43	76	56	7	0	0	399	461	13	112	6.1	.985	2B-144
1946		111	.246	.321	333	82	10	3	3	0.9	46	24	63	31	5	17	4	210	176	15	33	3.6	.963	2B-65, OF-28
1947	2 teams		CHI N (24G – .209)						NY A (24G – .179)															
"	total	48	.197	.225	71	14	2	0	0	0.0	14	5	14	7	3	14	4	17	20	0	4	0.8	1.000	2B-32
1948	2 teams		NY A (1G – .000)						NY N (29G – .255)															
"	total	30	.255	.333	51	13	1	0	1	2.0	7	6	4	6	0	14	2	24	22	4	4	1.7	.920	2B-13
14 yrs.		1535	.269	.374	5517	1482	263	69	61	1.1	848	549	752	525	105	67	14	3279	4256	314	866	5.1	.960	2B-980, SS-420, OF-34, 3B-22

WORLD SERIES

Year	Team	Games	BA	SA	AB	H	2B	3B	HR	HR%	R	RBI	BB	SO	SB	PH AB	PH H	PO	A	E	DP	TC/G	FA	G by Pos
1939	CIN N	4	.000	.000	17	0	0	0	0	0.0	0	0	1	4	0	0	0	8	10	0	4	4.5	1.000	2B-4
1940		3	.000	.000	2	0	0	0	0	0.0	0	0	0	0	0	2	0	0	0	0	0	0.0	–	
1947	NY A	1	.000	.000	1	0	0	0	0	0.0	1	1	0	1	0	0	0	0	0	0	0	0.0	–	
3 yrs.		8	.000	.000	20	0	0	0	0	0.0	1	1	1	5	0	2	0	8	10	0	4	2.3	1.000	2B-4

Pepe Frias

FRIAS, JESUS MARIA
Born Jesus Maria Frias y Andujar.
B. July 14, 1948, San Pedro de Macoris, Dominican Republic
BR TR 5'10" 159 lbs.

Year	Team	Games	BA	SA	AB	H	2B	3B	HR	HR%	R	RBI	BB	SO	SB	PH AB	PH H	PO	A	E	DP	TC/G	FA	G by Pos
1973	MON N	100	.231	.284	225	52	10	1	0	0.0	19	22	10	24	1	2	0	122	215	15	47	3.5	.957	SS-46, 2B-44, 3B-6, OF-1
1974		75	.214	.268	112	24	4	1	0	0.0	12	7	10	14	1	4	1	64	115	5	18	2.5	.973	SS-30, 3B-27, 2B-15, OF-3
1975		51	.125	.156	64	8	2	0	0	0.0	4	7	3	13	1	4	1	55	67	7	16	2.5	.946	SS-29, 3B-11, 2B-7
1976		76	.248	.292	113	28	5	0	0	0.0	7	8	4	14	1	1	1	81	116	11	28	2.7	.947	SS-35, 2B-35, 3B-4
1977		53	.257	.271	70	18	1	0	0	0.0	10	5	0	10	1	13	2	27	50	1	9	1.5	.987	2B-26, SS-14, 3B-1
1978		73	.267	.533	15	4	1	0	0	0.0	5	5	0	3	0	0	0	17	28	0	6	0.6	1.000	2B-61, SS-3
1979	ATL N	140	.259	.320	475	123	21	1	1	0.2	41	44	20	36	3	3	1	229	432	32	79	5.0	.954	SS-137
1980	2 teams		TEX A (116G – .242)						LA N (14G – .222)															
"	total	130	.242	.275	236	57	4	0	0	0.0	28	10	4	23	5	5	1	129	191	18	42	2.6	.947	SS-117, 3B-7, 2B-2

Year	Team		Games	BA	SA	AB	H	2B	3B	HR	HR%	R	RBI	BB	SO	SB	Pinch Hit AB	Pinch Hit H	PO	A	E	DP	TC/G	FA	G by Pos

Pepe Frias *continued*

Year	Team		Games	BA	SA	AB	H	2B	3B	HR	HR%	R	RBI	BB	SO	SB	AB	H	PO	A	E	DP	TC/G	FA	G by Pos
1981	LA	N	25	.250	.278	36	9	1	0	0	0.0	6	3	1	3	0	1	0	15	21	4	3	1.6	.900	SS-15, 2B-6, 3B-1
9 yrs.			723	.240	.290	1346	323	49	8	1	0.1	132	108	49	136	12	35	5	739	1235	93	248	2.9	.955	SS-426, 2B-190, 3B-57, OF-4

Barney Friberg

FRIBERG, GUSTAF BERNHARD
B. Aug. 18, 1899, Manchester, N. H. D. Dec. 8, 1958, Lynn, Mass.

BR TR 5'11" 178 lbs.

Year	Team		Games	BA	SA	AB	H	2B	3B	HR	HR%	R	RBI	BB	SO	SB	AB	H	PO	A	E	DP	TC/G	FA	G by Pos
1919	CHI	N	8	.200	.250	20	4	1	0	0	0.0	0	1	0	2	0	0	0	13	0	0	0	1.6	1.000	OF-7
1920			50	.211	.272	114	24	5	1	0	0.0	11	7	6	20	2	2	0	85	76	6	9	3.3	.964	OF-24, 2B-24
1922			97	.311	.351	296	92	8	2	0	0.0	51	23	37	37	8	12	2	175	21	4	11	2.1	.980	OF-74, 1B-6, 3B-5, 2B-3
1923			146	.318	.473	547	174	27	11	12	2.2	91	88	45	49	13	0	0	168	294	22	33	3.3	.955	3B-146
1924			142	.279	.360	495	138	19	3	5	1.0	67	82	66	53	19	0	0	163	268	21	21	3.2	.954	3B-142
1925	2 teams			CHI	N	(44G –	.257)			PHI	N	(91G –	.270)												
"	total		135	.265	.360	456	121	17	4	6	1.3	53	38	53	57	1	2	0	284	318	25	45	4.6	.960	2B-77, 3B-40, OF-12, 1B-6, SS-2, C-1, P-1
1926	PHI	N	144	.268	.331	478	128	21	3	1	0.2	38	51	57	77	2	0	0	381	512	22	89	6.4	.976	2B-144
1927			111	.233	.278	335	78	8	2	1	0.3	31	28	41	49	3	4	2	134	238	15	24	3.5	.961	3B-103, 2B-5
1928			52	.202	.266	94	19	3	0	1	1.1	11	7	12	16	0	6	1	62	79	11	20	2.9	.928	SS-31, 3B-5, OF-3, 2B-3, 1B-2
1929			128	.301	.437	455	137	21	10	7	1.5	74	55	49	54	1	5	2	252	214	28	35	3.9	.943	SS-73, OF-40, 2B-8, 1B-2
1930			105	.341	.447	331	113	21	1	4	1.2	62	42	47	35	1	7	3	185	175	21	29	3.6	.945	2B-44, OF-35, SS-12, 3B-8
1931			103	.261	.351	353	92	19	5	1	0.3	33	26	33	25	1	3	0	220	268	21	48	4.9	.959	2B-64, 3B-25, 1B-5, SS-3
1932			61	.240	.318	154	37	8	2	0	0.0	17	14	19	23	0	2	0	107	137	11	22	4.2	.957	2B-56
1933	BOS	A	17	.317	.390	41	13	3	0	0	0.0	5	9	6	1	0	3	1	17	32	3	6	3.1	.942	2B-6, 3B-5, SS-2
14 yrs.			1299	.281	.373	4169	1170	181	44	38	0.9	544	471	471	498	51	47	11	2246	2632	210	392	3.9	.959	3B-479, 2B-434, OF-195, SS-123, 1B-21, C-1, P-1

Jim Fridley

FRIDLEY, JAMES RILEY (Big Jim)
B. Sept. 6, 1924, Phillippi, W. Va.

BR TR 6'2" 205 lbs.

Year	Team		Games	BA	SA	AB	H	2B	3B	HR	HR%	R	RBI	BB	SO	SB	AB	H	PO	A	E	DP	TC/G	FA	G by Pos
1952	CLE	A	62	.251	.331	175	44	2	0	4	2.3	23	16	14	40	3	6	1	87	3	2	0	1.5	.978	OF-54
1954	BAL	A	85	.246	.371	240	59	8	5	4	1.7	25	36	21	41	0	18	6	132	1	2	0	1.6	.985	OF-67
1958	CIN	N	5	.222	.444	9	2	2	0	0	0.0	2	1	0	2	0	4	1	1	0	0	0	0.2	1.000	OF-2
3 yrs.			152	.248	.356	424	105	12	5	8	1.9	50	53	35	83	3	28	8	220	4	4	0	1.5	.982	OF-123

Bill Friel

FRIEL, WILLIAM EDWARD
Brother of Pat Friel.
B. Apr. 1, 1876, Renovo, Pa. D. Dec. 24, 1959, St. Louis, Mo.

BL TR 5'10" 215 lbs.

Year	Team		Games	BA	SA	AB	H	2B	3B	HR	HR%	R	RBI	BB	SO	SB	AB	H	PO	A	E	DP	TC/G	FA	G by Pos
1901	MIL	A	106	.266	.370	376	100	13	7	4	1.1	51	35	23		15	3	2	142	183	46	16	3.5	.876	3B-61, OF-28, 2B-9, SS-6
1902	STL	A	80	.240	.311	267	64	9	2	2	0.7	26	20	14		4	5	2	194	94	15	17	3.8	.950	OF-33, 2B-25, 1B-10, 3B-8, SS-3, C-1, P-1
1903			97	.228	.305	351	80	11	8	0	0.0	46	25	23		4	2	1	142	237	39	16	4.3	.907	2B-63, 3B-24, OF-9
3 yrs.			283	.245	.331	994	244	33	17	6	0.6	123	80	60		23	10	5	478	514	100	49	3.9	.908	2B-97, 3B-93, OF-70, 1B-10, SS-9, C-1, P-1

Pat Friel

FRIEL, PATRICK HENRY
Brother of Bill Friel.
B. June 11, 1860, Lewisburg, W. Va. D. Jan. 15, 1924, Providence, R. I.

BB 5'11" 170 lbs.

Year	Team		Games	BA	SA	AB	H	2B	3B	HR	HR%	R	RBI	BB	SO	SB	AB	H	PO	A	E	DP	TC/G	FA	G by Pos
1890	SYR	AA	62	.249	.330	261	65	8	2	3	1.1	51		17		34	0	0	77	7	8	2	1.5	.913	OF-62
1891	PHI	AA	2	.250	.375	8	2	1	0	0	0.0	2	0	0	0	0	0	0	1	0	0	0	0.5	1.000	OF-2
2 yrs.			64	.249	.331	269	67	9	2	3	1.1	53		17		34	0	0	78	7	8	2	1.5	.914	OF-64

Frank Friend

FRIEND, FRANK B.
B. Washington, D. C. D. Sept. 8, 1897, Atlantic City, N. J.

Year	Team		Games	BA	SA	AB	H	2B	3B	HR	HR%	R	RBI	BB	SO	SB	AB	H	PO	A	E	DP	TC/G	FA	G by Pos
1896	LOU	N	2	.200	.200	5	1	0	0	0	0.0	1	0	1	1	0	0	0	3	2	0	0	2.5	1.000	C-2

Owen Friend

FRIEND, OWEN LACEY (Red)
B. Mar. 21, 1927, Granite City, Ill.

BR TR 6'1" 180 lbs.

Year	Team		Games	BA	SA	AB	H	2B	3B	HR	HR%	R	RBI	BB	SO	SB	AB	H	PO	A	E	DP	TC/G	FA	G by Pos
1949	STL	A	2	.375	.375	8	3	0	0	0	0.0	1	0	0	0	0	0	0	4	8	0	1	6.0	1.000	2B-2
1950			119	.237	.352	372	88	15	2	8	2.2	48	50	40	68	2	1	1	271	340	30	68	5.4	.953	2B-93, 3B-24, SS-3
1953	2 teams			DET	A	(31G –	.177)			CLE	A	(34G –	.235)												
"	total		65	.201	.329	164	33	6	0	5	3.0	17	23	11	25	0	2	1	112	126	8	38	3.8	.967	2B-45, SS-8, 3B-1
1955	2 teams			BOS	A	(14G –	.262)			CHI	N	(6G –	.100)												
"	total		20	.231	.288	52	12	3	0	0	0.0	3	2	4	14	0	3	0	23	40	3	5	3.3	.955	SS-15, 3B-2, 2B-1
1956	CHI	N	2	.000	.000	2	0	0	0	0	0.0	0	0	0	2	0	2	0	0	0	0	0	0.0	–	
5 yrs.			208	.227	.339	598	136	24	2	13	2.2	69	76	55	109	2	8	2	410	514	41	112	4.6	.958	2B-141, 3B-27, SS-26

Buck Frierson

FRIERSON, ROBERT LAWRENCE
B. July 29, 1917, Chicota, Tex.

BR TR 6'3" 195 lbs.

Year	Team		Games	BA	SA	AB	H	2B	3B	HR	HR%	R	RBI	BB	SO	SB	AB	H	PO	A	E	DP	TC/G	FA	G by Pos
1941	CLE	A	5	.273	.364	11	3	1	0	0	0.0	2	2	1	1	0	2	1	2	0	0	0	0.4	1.000	OF-3

Fred Frink

FRINK, FRED FERDINAND
B. Aug. 25, 1911, Macon, Ga.

BR TR 6'1" 180 lbs.

Year	Team		Games	BA	SA	AB	H	2B	3B	HR	HR%	R	RBI	BB	SO	SB	AB	H	PO	A	E	DP	TC/G	FA	G by Pos
1934	PHI	N	2	–	–	0	0	0	0	0	–	0	0	0	0	0	0	0	0	0	0	0	0.0	–	OF-1

Charlie Frisbee

FRISBEE, CHARLES AUGUSTUS (Bunt)
B. Feb. 2, 1874, Dows, Iowa D. Nov. 7, 1954, Alden, Iowa

BB TR 5'9" 175 lbs.

Year	Team		Games	BA	SA	AB	H	2B	3B	HR	HR%	R	RBI	BB	SO	SB	AB	H	PO	A	E	DP	TC/G	FA	G by Pos
1899	BOS	N	42	.329	.382	152	50	4	2	0	0.0	22	20	9		10	1	0	68	9	11	1	2.1	.875	OF-40
1900	NY	N	4	.154	.231	13	2	1	0	0	0.0	2	3	2		0	0	0	2	0	3	0	1.3	.400	OF-4
2 yrs.			46	.315	.370	165	52	5	2	0	0.0	24	23	11		10	1	0	70	9	14	1	2.0	.849	OF-44

Year	Team		Games	BA	SA	AB	H	2B	3B	HR	HR%	R	RBI	BB	SO	SB	Pinch Hit AB	H	PO	A	E	DP	TC/G	FA	G by Pos

Frankie Frisch

FRISCH, FRANK FRANCIS (The Fordham Flash)
B. Sept. 9, 1898, Bronx, N. Y. D. Mar. 12, 1973, Wilmington, Del.
Manager 1933-38, 1940-46, 1949-51.
Hall of Fame 1947.
BB TR 5'11" 165 lbs.

Year	Team		Games	BA	SA	AB	H	2B	3B	HR	HR%	R	RBI	BB	SO	SB	AB	H	PO	A	E	DP	TC/G	FA	G by Pos
1919	NY	N	54	.226	.295	190	43	3	2	2	1.1	21	24	4	14	15	3	0	102	134	7	7	4.5	.971	2B-29, 3B-28, SS-1
1920			110	.280	.375	440	123	10	10	4	0.9	57	77	20	18	34	1	0	106	256	12	23	3.4	.968	3B-110, SS-2
1921			153	.341	.485	618	211	31	17	8	1.3	121	100	42	28	49	0	0	226	418	33	52	4.4	.951	3B-93, 2B-61
1922			132	.327	.438	514	168	16	13	5	1.0	101	51	47	13	31	0	0	228	406	22	53	5.0	.966	2B-85, 3B-53, SS-1
1923			151	.348	.485	641	223	32	10	12	1.9	116	111	46	12	29	0	0	327	493	22	83	5.6	.974	2B-135, 3B-17
1924			145	.328	.468	603	198	33	15	7	1.2	121	69	56	24	22	0	0	408	557	27	104	6.8	.973	2B-143, SS-10, 3B-2
1925			120	.331	.472	502	166	26	6	11	2.2	89	48	32	14	21	0	0	215	393	37	45	5.4	.943	3B-46, 2B-42, SS-39
1926			135	.314	.409	545	171	29	4	5	0.9	75	44	33	16	23	1	1	270	486	21	71	5.8	.973	2B-127, 3B-7
1927	STL	N	153	.337	.472	617	208	31	11	10	1.6	112	78	43	10	48	0	0	396	643	22	104	6.9	.979	2B-153, SS-1
1928			141	.300	.441	547	164	29	9	10	1.8	107	86	64	17	29	2	1	383	474	21	80	6.2	.976	2B-139
1929			138	.334	.484	527	176	40	12	5	0.9	93	74	53	12	24	3	2	305	407	22	67	5.3	.970	2B-121, 3B-13, SS-1
1930			133	.346	.520	540	187	46	9	10	1.9	121	114	55	16	15	0	0	315	493	27	96	6.3	.968	2B-123, 3B-10
1931			131	.311	.396	518	161	24	4	4	0.8	96	82	45	13	28	0	0	290	424	19	93	5.6	.974	2B-129
1932			115	.292	.372	486	142	26	2	3	0.6	59	60	25	13	18	0	0	257	319	16	60	5.1	.973	2B-75, 3B-37, SS-4
1933			147	.303	.398	585	177	32	6	4	0.7	74	66	48	16	18	4	2	395	413	18	80	5.6	.978	2B-132, SS-15
1934			140	.305	.398	550	168	30	6	3	0.5	74	75	45	10	11	0	0	325	388	20	80	5.2	.973	2B-115, 3B-25
1935			103	.294	.359	354	104	16	2	1	0.3	52	55	33	16	2	9	1	199	258	10	48	4.5	.979	2B-88, 3B-5
1936			93	.274	.317	303	83	10	0	1	0.3	40	26	36	10	2	8	3	159	194	15	32	4.0	.959	2B-61, 3B-22, SS-1
1937			17	.219	.281	32	7	2	0	0	0.0	3	4	1	0	0	12	2	12	14	0	1	1.5	1.000	2B-17
19 yrs.			2311	.316	.432	9112	2880	466	138	105	1.2	1532	1244	728	272	419	47	12	4918	7170	371	1178	5.4	.970	2B-1775, 3B-468, SS-75

WORLD SERIES

Year	Team		Games	BA	SA	AB	H	2B	3B	HR	HR%	R	RBI	BB	SO	SB	AB	H	PO	A	E	DP	TC/G	FA	G by Pos
1921	NY	N	8	.300	.367	30	9	0	0	0	0.0	5	1	4	3	3	0	0	12	25	2	3	4.9	.949	3B-8
1922			5	.471	.529	17	8	1	0	0	0.0	3	2	1	0	1	0	0	10	20	1	3	6.2	.968	2B-5
1923			6	.400	.480	25	10	0	1	0	0.0	2	1	0	0	0	0	0	17	18	1	7	6.0	.972	2B-6
1924			7	.333	.533	30	10	4	1	0	0.0	1	0	4	1	1	0	0	17	26	0	3	6.1	1.000	2B-7, 3B-1
1928	STL	N	4	.231	.231	13	3	0	0	0	0.0	1	1	2	2	2	0	0	8	13	0	2	5.3	1.000	2B-4
1930			6	.208	.292	24	5	2	0	0	0.0	0	0	1	1	0	1	0	13	14	3	2	5.0	.900	2B-6
1931			7	.259	.333	27	7	2	0	0	0.0	2	1	2	1	0	0	0	23	19	0	5	6.0	1.000	2B-7
1934			7	.194	.226	31	6	1	0	0	0.0	2	4	0	1	0	0	0	16	26	2	1	6.3	.955	2B-7
8 yrs.			50	.294	.376	197	58	10	3	0	0.0	16	10	12	9	9	0	0	116	161	9	26	5.7	.969	2B-42, 3B-9
			8th			4th	3rd	1st	4th							6th									

Emil Frisk

FRISK, JOHN EMIL
B. Oct. 15, 1874, Kalkaska, Mich. D. Jan. 27, 1922, Seattle, Wash.
BL TR 6'1" 190 lbs.

Year	Team		Games	BA	SA	AB	H	2B	3B	HR	HR%	R	RBI	BB	SO	SB	AB	H	PO	A	E	DP	TC/G	FA	G by Pos
1899	CIN	N	9	.280	.320	25	7	1	0	0	0.0	5	2	2		0	0	0	4	15	1	0	2.2	.950	P-9
1901	DET	A	20	.313	.438	48	15	3	0	1	2.1	10	7	3		0	6	2	7	36	8	0	2.6	.843	P-11, OF-2
1905	STL	A	127	.261	.336	429	112	11	6	3	0.7	58	36	42		7	1	1	117	15	11	2	1.1	.923	OF-116
1907			4	.250	.250	4	1	0	0	0	0.0	0	0	1		0	4	1	0	0	0	0	0.0	—	OF-4
4 yrs.			160	.267	.344	506	135	15	6	4	0.8	73	45	48		7	17	4	128	66	20	2	1.3	.907	OF-118, P-20

Harry Fritz

FRITZ, HARRY KOCH (Dutchman)
B. Sept. 30, 1890, Philadelphia, Pa. D. Nov. 4, 1974, Columbus, Ohio
BR TR 5'8" 170 lbs.

Year	Team		Games	BA	SA	AB	H	2B	3B	HR	HR%	R	RBI	BB	SO	SB	AB	H	PO	A	E	DP	TC/G	FA	G by Pos
1913	PHI	A	5	.000	.000	13	0	0	0	0	0.0	1	0	2	4	0	0	0	6	5	2	0	2.6	.846	3B-5
1914	CHI	F	65	.213	.253	174	37	5	1	0	0.0	16	13	18		2	5	1	48	76	10	11	2.1	.925	3B-46, SS-9, 2B-1
1915			79	.250	.356	236	59	8	4	3	1.3	27	26	13		4	3	2	85	109	7	8	2.5	.965	3B-70, 2B-6, SS-1
3 yrs.			149	.227	.303	423	96	13	5	3	0.7	44	39	33	4	6	8	3	139	190	19	19	2.3	.945	3B-121, SS-10, 2B-7

Larry Fritz

FRITZ, LAWRENCE JOSEPH
B. Feb. 14, 1949, East Chicago, Ind.
BL TL 6'2" 225 lbs.

Year	Team		Games	BA	SA	AB	H	2B	3B	HR	HR%	R	RBI	BB	SO	SB	AB	H	PO	A	E	DP	TC/G	FA	G by Pos
1975	PHI	N	1	.000	.000	1	0	0	0	0	0.0	0	0	0	0	0	1	0	0	0	0	0	0.0	—	

Doug Frobel

FROBEL, DOUGLAS STEVEN
B. June 6, 1959, Ottawa, Ontario, Canada
BL TR 6'4" 196 lbs.

Year	Team		Games	BA	SA	AB	H	2B	3B	HR	HR%	R	RBI	BB	SO	SB	AB	H	PO	A	E	DP	TC/G	FA	G by Pos
1982	PIT	N	16	.206	.441	34	7	2	0	2	5.9	5	3	1	11	1	4	1	18	0	0	0	1.1	1.000	OF-12
1983			32	.283	.533	60	17	4	1	3	5.0	10	11	3	17	1	5	1	27	0	1	0	0.9	.964	OF-24
1984			126	.203	.388	276	56	9	3	12	4.3	33	28	24	84	7	17	3	188	9	9	3	1.6	.956	OF-112
1985	2 teams		PIT N (53G – .202)						MON N (12G – .130)																
"	total		65	.189	.258	132	25	6	1	1	0.8	17	11	21	30	4	20	6	58	2	4	1	1.0	.938	OF-42
1987	CLE	A	29	.100	.250	40	4	0	0	2	5.0	5	5	5	13	0	15	2	6	0	0	0	0.2	1.000	OF-12, DH-5
5 yrs.			268	.201	.365	542	109	21	4	20	3.7	70	58	55	155	13	61	13	297	11	14	4	1.2	.957	OF-202, DH-5

Ben Froelich

FROELICH, WILLIAM PALMER
B. Nov. 12, 1887, Pittsburgh, Pa. D. Sept. 1, 1916, Pittsburgh, Pa.
BR TR

Year	Team		Games	BA	SA	AB	H	2B	3B	HR	HR%	R	RBI	BB	SO	SB	AB	H	PO	A	E	DP	TC/G	FA	G by Pos
1909	PHI	N	1	.000	.000	1	0	0	0	0	0.0	0	0	0	0	0	0	0	0	0	0	0	0.0	—	C-1

Jerry Fry

FRY, JERRY RAY
B. Feb. 29, 1956, Salinas, Calif.
BR TR 6' 185 lbs.

Year	Team		Games	BA	SA	AB	H	2B	3B	HR	HR%	R	RBI	BB	SO	SB	AB	H	PO	A	E	DP	TC/G	FA	G by Pos
1978	MON	N	4	.000	.000	9	0	0	0	0	0.0	0	0	1	5	0	0	0	16	1	0	0	4.3	1.000	C-4

Mike Fuentes

FUENTES, MICHAEL JAY
B. July 11, 1958, Miami, Fla.
BR TR 6'3" 190 lbs.

Year	Team		Games	BA	SA	AB	H	2B	3B	HR	HR%	R	RBI	BB	SO	SB	AB	H	PO	A	E	DP	TC/G	FA	G by Pos
1983	MON	N	6	.250	.250	4	1	0	0	0	0.0	1	0	0	2	0	4	1	0	0	0	0	0.0	—	
1984			3	.250	.250	4	1	0	0	0	0.0	0	0	1	2	0	2	1	4	0	0	0	1.3	1.000	OF-1
2 yrs.			9	.250	.250	8	2	0	0	0	0.0	1	0	1	4	0	6	2	4	0	0	0	0.4	1.000	OF-1

Year	Team		Games	BA	SA	AB	H	2B	3B	HR	HR%	R	RBI	BB	SO	SB	Pinch Hit AB	H	PO	A	E	DP	TC/G	FA	G by Pos

Tito Fuentes

FUENTES, RIGOBERTO
Born Rigoberto Fuentes y Peat.
B. Jan. 4, 1944, Havana, Cuba

BR TR 5'11" 175 lbs.
BB 1969

Year	Team		Games	BA	SA	AB	H	2B	3B	HR	HR%	R	RBI	BB	SO	SB	AB	H	PO	A	E	DP	TC/G	FA	G by Pos
1965	SF	N	26	.208	.222	72	15	1	0	0	0.0	12	1	5	14	0	0	0	27	49	5	8	3.1	.938	SS-18, 2B-7, 3B-1
1966			133	.261	.360	541	141	21	3	9	1.7	63	40	9	57	6	1	0	283	403	30	68	5.4	.958	SS-76, 2B-60
1967			133	.209	.294	344	72	12	1	5	1.5	27	29	27	61	4	0	0	276	315	12	79	4.5	.980	2B-130, SS-5
1969			67	.295	.366	183	54	4	3	1	0.5	28	14	15	25	2	1	0	50	117	13	18	2.7	.928	3B-36, SS-30
1970			123	.267	.343	435	116	13	7	2	0.5	49	32	36	52	4	7	0	202	324	19	57	4.4	.965	2B-78, SS-36, 3B-24
1971			152	.273	.356	630	172	28	6	4	0.6	63	52	18	46	12	1	0	373	465	23	109	5.7	.973	2B-152
1972			152	.264	.379	572	151	33	6	7	1.2	64	53	39	56	16	1	0	361	417	29	89	5.3	.964	2B-152
1973			160	.277	.358	656	182	25	5	6	0.9	78	63	45	62	12	0	0	386	479	6	102	5.4	.993	2B-160, 3B-1
1974			108	.249	.297	390	97	15	2	0	0.0	33	22	22	32	7	7	2	238	287	11	70	5.0	.979	2B-103
1975	SD	N	146	.280	.349	565	158	21	3	4	0.7	57	43	25	51	8	2	0	389	448	26	105	5.9	.970	2B-142
1976			135	.263	.310	520	137	18	0	2	0.4	48	36	18	38	5	8	2	339	387	22	91	5.5	.971	2B-127
1977	DET	A	151	.309	.397	615	190	19	10	5	0.8	83	51	38	61	4	1	0	379	459	26	115	5.7	.970	2B-151, DH-1
1978	OAK	A	13	.140	.163	43	6	1	0	0	0.0	5	2	1	6	0	2	0	17	17	2	4	2.8	.944	2B-13
13 yrs.			1499	.268	.347	5566	1491	211	46	45	0.8	610	438	298	561	80	31	4	3320	4167	224	915	5.1	.971	2B-1275, SS-165, 3B-62, DH-1

LEAGUE CHAMPIONSHIP SERIES

| 1971 | SF | N | 4 | .313 | .563 | 16 | 5 | 1 | 0 | 1 | 6.3 | 4 | 2 | 1 | 3 | 0 | 0 | 0 | 9 | 5 | 1 | 1 | 3.8 | .933 | 2B-4 |

Ollie Fuhrman

FUHRMAN, ALFRED GEORGE
B. July 20, 1896, Jordan, Minn. D. Jan. 11, 1969, Peoria, Ill.

BB TR 5'11" 185 lbs.

| 1922 | PHI | A | 6 | .333 | .500 | 6 | 2 | 1 | 0 | 0 | 0.0 | 1 | 0 | 0 | 0 | 0 | 2 | 0 | 5 | 0 | 0 | 0 | 0.8 | 1.000 | C-4 |

Dot Fulghum

FULGHUM, JAMES LAVOISIER
B. July 4, 1900, Valdosta, Ga. D. Nov. 11, 1967, Miami, Fla.

BR TR 5'8½" 165 lbs.

| 1921 | PHI | A | 2 | .000 | .000 | 2 | 0 | 0 | 0 | 0 | 0.0 | 0 | 1 | 1 | 0 | 0 | 0 | 0 | 0 | 0 | 0 | 0 | 0.0 | – | SS-1 |

Frank Fuller

FULLER, FRANK EDWARD (Rabbit)
B. Jan. 1, 1893, Detroit, Mich. D. Oct. 29, 1965, Warren, Mich.

BB TR 5'7" 150 lbs.

1915	DET	A	14	.156	.156	32	5	0	0	0	0.0	6	0	9	7	2	2	1	8	20	2	1	2.1	.933	2B-9, SS-1
1916			20	.100	.100	10	1	0	0	0	0.0	2	1	1	4	3	1	0	4	7	2	2	0.7	.846	2B-8, SS-1
1923	BOS	A	6	.238	.238	21	5	0	0	0	0.0	3	0	1	1	1	0	0	20	20	2	1	7.0	.952	2B-6
3 yrs.			40	.175	.175	63	11	0	0	0	0.0	11	3	11	12	6	3	1	32	47	6	4	2.1	.929	2B-23, SS-2

Harry Fuller

FULLER, HENRY W.
Brother of Shorty Fuller.
B. Dec. 5, 1862, Cincinnati, Ohio D. Dec. 12, 1895, Cincinnati, Ohio

| 1891 | STL | AA | 1 | .000 | .000 | 2 | 0 | 0 | 0 | 0 | 0.0 | 0 | 1 | 0 | 0 | 0 | 0 | 0 | 0 | 2 | 0 | 2.0 | – | 3B-1 |

Jim Fuller

FULLER, JAMES HARDY
B. Nov. 28, 1950, Bethesda, Md.

BR TR 6'3" 215 lbs.

1973	BAL	A	9	.115	.346	26	3	0	0	2	7.7	2	4	1	17	0	3	1	20	2	0	1	2.4	1.000	OF-5, 1B-2, DH-1
1974			64	.222	.392	189	42	11	0	7	3.7	17	28	8	68	1	5	1	131	4	6	2	2.2	.957	OF-59, 1B-4, DH-2
1977	HOU	N	34	.160	.280	100	16	6	0	2	2.0	5	9	10	45	0	5	0	56	5	1	1	1.8	.984	OF-27, 1B-1
3 yrs.			107	.194	.352	315	61	17	0	11	3.5	24	41	19	130	1	13	2	207	11	7	4	2.1	.969	OF-91, 1B-7, DH-3

John Fuller

FULLER, JOHN EDWARD
B. Jan. 29, 1950, Lynwood, Calif.

BL TL 6'2" 180 lbs.

| 1974 | ATL | N | 3 | .333 | .333 | 3 | 1 | 0 | 0 | 0 | 0.0 | 0 | 0 | 0 | 0 | 0 | 2 | 0 | 1 | 0 | 0 | 0 | 0.3 | 1.000 | OF-1 |

Nig Fuller

FULLER, CHARLES F.
B. Mar. 30, 1879, Toledo, Ohio D. Nov. 12, 1947, Toledo, Ohio

BR TR

| 1902 | BKN | N | 3 | .000 | .000 | 9 | 0 | 0 | 0 | 0 | 0.0 | 0 | 1 | 0 | 0 | 0 | 0 | 0 | 11 | 1 | 0 | 0 | 4.0 | 1.000 | C-3 |

Shorty Fuller

FULLER, WILLIAM BENJAMIN
Brother of Harry Fuller.
B. Oct. 10, 1867, Cincinnati, Ohio D. Apr. 11, 1904, Cincinnati, Ohio

BR TR

1888	WAS	N	49	.182	.235	170	31	5	2	0	0.0	11	12	10	14	6	0	0	69	143	38	14	5.1	.848	SS-47, 2B-2
1889	STL	AA	140	.226	.284	517	117	18	6	0	0.0	91	51	52	56	38	0	0	240	459	67	46	5.5	.913	SS-140
1890			130	.278	.335	526	146	9	9	1	0.2	118		73		60	0	0	222	389	91	39	5.4	.873	SS-130
1891			137	.217	.276	586	127	15	7	2	0.3	107	63	67	28	42	0	0	251	422	98	57	5.6	.873	SS-103, 2B-39
1892	NY	N	141	.226	.270	508	115	11	4	1	0.2	74	48	52	22	37	0	0	294	434	92	44	5.8	.888	SS-141
1893			130	.236	.300	474	112	14	8	0	0.0	78	51	60	21	26	0	0	260	464	71	48	6.1	.911	SS-130
1894			93	.283	.359	368	104	14	4	2	0.5	81	46	52	16	32	0	0	213	300	69	40	6.3	.881	SS-89, OF-2, 3B-2, 2B-1
1895			126	.225	.262	458	103	11	3	0	0.0	82	32	64	34	15	0	0	270	499	73	59	6.7	.913	SS-126
1896			18	.167	.167	72	12	0	0	0	0.0	10	7	14	5	4	0	0	42	62	15	8	6.6	.874	SS-18
9 yrs.			964	.236	.290	3679	867	97	43	6	0.2	652	310	444	196	260	0	0	1861	3172	614	355	5.9	.891	SS-924, 2B-42, OF-2, 3B-2

Vern Fuller

FULLER, VERNON GORDON
B. Mar. 1, 1944, Menomonie, Wis.

BR TR 6'1" 170 lbs.

1964	CLE	A	2	.000	.000	1	0	0	0	0	0.0	0	0	0	0	0	1	0	0	0	0	0	0.0	–	
1966			16	.234	.447	47	11	2	1	2	4.3	7	2	7	6	0	0	0	29	27	0	12	3.5	1.000	2B-16
1967			73	.223	.374	206	46	10	0	7	3.4	18	21	19	55	2	6	1	133	144	4	39	3.8	.986	2B-64, SS-2
1968			97	.242	.291	244	59	8	2	0	0.0	14	18	24	49	2	4	0	133	150	7	25	3.0	.976	2B-73, 3B-23, SS-4
1969			108	.236	.335	254	60	11	1	4	1.6	25	22	20	53	2	5	2	222	196	9	55	4.0	.979	2B-102, 3B-7
1970			29	.182	.333	33	6	2	0	1	3.0	3	2	3	9	0	8	1	18	23	3	4	1.5	.932	2B-16, 3B-4, 1B-1
6 yrs.			325	.232	.338	785	182	33	4	14	1.8	67	65	73	172	6	24	4	535	540	23	135	3.4	.979	2B-271, 3B-34, SS-6, 1B-1

Chick Fullis

FULLIS, CHARLES PHILIP
B. Feb. 27, 1904, Girardville, Pa. D. Mar. 28, 1946, Ashland, Pa.
BR TR 5'9" 170 lbs.

Year	Team		Games	BA	SA	AB	H	2B	3B	HR	HR%	R	RBI	BB	SO	SB	PH AB	PH H	PO	A	E	DP	TC/G	FA	G by Pos
1928	NY	N	11	.000	.000	1	0	0	0	0	0.0	5	0	1	0	1	0	0	0	0	0	0	0.0	–	
1929			86	.288	.412	274	79	11	1	7	2.6	67	29	30	26	7	2	0	151	3	6	0	1.9	.963	OF-78
1930			13	.000	.000	6	0	0	0	0	0.0	2	0	0	1	1	5	0	0	0	0	0	0.0	–	OF-2
1931			89	.328	.421	302	99	15	2	3	1.0	61	28	23	13	13	6	3	166	29	4	6	2.2	.980	OF-68, 2B-9
1932			96	.298	.396	235	70	14	3	1	0.4	35	21	11	12	1	32	7	97	2	1	0	1.0	.990	OF-55, 2B-1
1933	PHI	N	151	.309	.380	**647**	200	31	6	1	0.2	91	45	36	34	18	0	0	410	15	10	3	2.9	.977	OF-151, 3B-1
1934	2 teams					PHI N (28G – .225)				STL N (69G – .261)															
"	total		97	.249	.306	301	75	15	1	0	0.0	29	38	24	15	6	15	6	166	3	6	1	1.8	.966	OF-83
1936	STL	N	47	.281	.371	89	25	6	1	0	0.0	15	6	7	11	0	12	2	53	2	0	2	1.2	1.000	OF-26
8 yrs.			590	.295	.380	1855	548	92	14	12	0.6	305	167	132	113	46	73	18	1043	54	27	12	1.9	.976	OF-463, 2B-10, 3B-1
WORLD SERIES																									
1934	STL	N	3	.400	.400	5	2	0	0	0	0.0	0	0	0	0	0	0	0	6	0	1	0	2.3	.857	OF-3

Chick Fulmer

FULMER, CHARLES JOHN
Brother of Washington Fulmer.
B. Feb. 12, 1851, Philadelphia, Pa. D. Feb. 15, 1940, Philadelphia, Pa.
Manager 1876.
BR TR 6' 158 lbs.

Year	Team		Games	BA	SA	AB	H	2B	3B	HR	HR%	R	RBI	BB	SO	SB	PH AB	PH H	PO	A	E	DP	TC/G	FA	G by Pos
1876	LOU	N	66	.273	.356	267	73	9	5	1	0.4	28	29	1		10			83	209	47	12	5.1	.861	SS-66
1879	BUF	N	76	.268	.337	306	82	11	5	0	0.0	30	28	5		34			273	301	60	46	8.3	.905	2B-76
1880			11	.159	.159	44	7	0	0	0	0.0	3	1	2		4			34	33	9	2	6.9	.882	2B-11
1882	CIN	AA	79	.281	.346	324	91	13	4	0	0.0	54		10					130	243	43	14	5.3	.897	SS-79
1883			92	.258	.363	361	93	13	5	5	1.4	52		13					134	243	60	26	4.8	.863	SS-92
1884	2 teams					CIN AA (31G – .175)				STL AA (1G – .000)															
"	total		32	.168	.202	119	20	2	1	0	0.0	13		1					27	73	27	7	4.0	.787	SS-29, OF-2, 3B-1, 2B-1
6 yrs.			356	.258	.332	1421	366	48	20	6	0.4	180	58	32		48	0	0	681	1102	246	107	5.7	.879	SS-266, 2B-88, OF-2, 3B-1

Chris Fulmer

FULMER, CHRISTOPHER
B. July 4, 1858, Tamaqua, Pa. D. Nov. 9, 1931, Tamaqua, Pa.
BR TR 5'8" 165 lbs.

Year	Team		Games	BA	SA	AB	H	2B	3B	HR	HR%	R	RBI	BB	SO	SB	PH AB	PH H	PO	A	E	DP	TC/G	FA	G by Pos
1884	WAS	U	48	.276	.326	181	50	9	0	0	0.0	39		11					267	45	18	4	6.9	.945	C-34, OF-16, 1B-5
1886	BAL	AA	80	.244	.311	270	66	9	3	1	0.4	54		48					480	117	37	5	7.9	.942	C-68, OF-12, P-1
1887			56	.269	.363	201	54	11	4	0	0.0	52		36		35			216	73	31	5	5.7	.903	C-48, OF-8
1888			52	.187	.229	166	31	1	0	0	0.0	20	10	21		10			244	44	32	5	6.2	.900	C-45, OF-7
1889			16	.259	.345	58	15	3	1	0	0.0	11	13	6	12	2			25	2	3	0	1.9	.900	OF-14, C-2
5 yrs.			252	.247	.313	876	216	37	9	1	0.1	176	23	122	12	47	0	0	1232	281	121	19	6.5	.926	C-197, OF-57, 1B-5, P-1

Dave Fultz

FULTZ, DAVID LEWIS (Swarthy Dave)
B. May 29, 1875, Staunton, Va. D. Oct. 29, 1959, Deland, Fla.
BR TR 5'11" 170 lbs.

Year	Team		Games	BA	SA	AB	H	2B	3B	HR	HR%	R	RBI	BB	SO	SB	PH AB	PH H	PO	A	E	DP	TC/G	FA	G by Pos
1898	PHI	N	19	.182	.291	55	10	2	2	0	0.0	7	5	6					35	8	6	1	2.6	.878	OF-14, 2B-3, SS-1
1899	2 teams					PHI N (2G – .400)				BAL N (57G – .295)															
"	total		59	.298	.330	215	64	3	2	0	0.0	31	18	13					104	45	19	3	2.8	.887	OF-31, 2B-3, SS-1
1901	PHI	A	132	.292	.355	561	164	17	9	0	0.0	95	52	32		36	0	0	264	100	33	2	3.0	.917	OF-106, 2B-18, SS-9
1902			129	.302	.368	506	153	20	5	1	0.2	**109**	49	62		44	0	0	263	43	14	6	2.5	.956	OF-114, 2B-16
1903	NY	A	79	.224	.271	295	66	12	1	0	0.0	39	25	25		29	1	0	159	16	15	2	2.4	.921	OF-77, 3B-2
1904			97	.274	.366	339	93	17	4	2	0.6	39	32	24		17	6	2	194	8	5	2	2.1	.976	OF-90
1905			130	.232	.277	422	98	13	3	0	0.0	49	42	39					252	14	9	2	2.1	.967	OF-90
7 yrs.			645	.271	.331	2393	648	84	26	3	0.1	369	223	201		189	15	3	1271	234	101	18	2.5	.937	OF-554, 2B-40, 3B-22, SS-11, 1B-1

Mark Funderburk

FUNDERBURK, MARK CLIFFORD
B. May 16, 1957, Charlotte, N.C.
BR TR 6'4" 226 lbs.

Year	Team		Games	BA	SA	AB	H	2B	3B	HR	HR%	R	RBI	BB	SO	SB	PH AB	PH H	PO	A	E	DP	TC/G	FA	G by Pos
1981	MIN	A	8	.200	.267	15	3	1	0	0	0.0	2	2	2	1	0	2	0	4	0	0	0	0.6	1.000	OF-6, DH-1
1985			23	.314	.529	70	22	7	1	2	2.9	7	13	5	12	0	4	1	15	0	0	0	0.7	1.000	DH-15, OF-5, 1B-1
2 yrs.			31	.294	.482	85	25	8	1	2	2.4	9	15	7	13	0	6	1	19	0	0	0	0.6	1.000	DH-16, OF-11, 1B-1

Liz Funk

FUNK, ELIAS CALVIN
B. Oct. 28, 1904, La Cygne, Kans. D. Jan. 16, 1968, Norman, Okla.
BL TL 5'8½" 160 lbs.

Year	Team		Games	BA	SA	AB	H	2B	3B	HR	HR%	R	RBI	BB	SO	SB	PH AB	PH H	PO	A	E	DP	TC/G	FA	G by Pos
1929	NY	A	1	–	–	0	0	0	0	0	0.0	0	0	0	0	0	0	0	0	0	0	0	0.0	–	
1930	DET	A	140	.275	.389	527	145	26	11	4	0.8	74	65	29	39	12	10	0	354	8	13	4	2.7	.965	OF-129
1932	CHI	A	122	.259	.343	440	114	21	5	2	0.5	59	40	43	19	17	10	1	318	15	7	0	2.8	.979	OF-120
1933			10	.222	.222	9	2	0	0	0	0.0	1	0	1	0	0	8	2	0	0	0	0	0.0	–	OF-2
4 yrs.			273	.267	.367	976	261	47	16	6	0.6	134	105	73	58	29	19	2	672	23	20	8	2.6	.972	OF-251

Carl Furillo

FURILLO, CARL ANTHONY (Skoonj, The Reading Rifle)
B. Mar. 8, 1922, Stony Creek Mills, Pa. D. Jan. 21, 1989, Stony Creek Mills, Pa.
BR TR 6' 190 lbs.

Year	Team		Games	BA	SA	AB	H	2B	3B	HR	HR%	R	RBI	BB	SO	SB	PH AB	PH H	PO	A	E	DP	TC/G	FA	G by Pos
1946	BKN	N	117	.284	.400	335	95	18	6	3	0.9	29	35	31	20	6	4	1	292	9	5	4	2.6	.984	OF-112
1947			124	.295	.437	437	129	24	7	8	1.8	61	88	34	24	7	2	1	287	9	7	3	2.4	.977	OF-121
1948			108	.297	.407	364	108	20	4	4	1.1	55	44	43	32	6	4	0	274	13	5	2	2.7	.983	OF-104
1949			142	.322	.506	549	177	27	10	18	3.3	95	106	37	29	6	0	0	286	13	11	2	2.2	.965	OF-142
1950			153	.305	.460	620	189	30	6	18	2.9	99	106	41	40	8	0	0	246	18	8	2	1.8	.971	OF-153
1951			158	.295	.427	**667**	197	32	4	16	2.4	93	91	43	33	8	1	0	330	24	5	6	2.3	.986	OF-157
1952			134	.247	.351	425	105	18	1	8	1.9	52	59	31	33	1	2	0	225	24	5	6	2.3	.986	OF-157
1953			132	**.344**	.580	479	165	18	6	21	4.4	82	92	32	32	1	2	0	232	11	3	1	1.9	.988	OF-131
1954			150	.294	.444	547	161	23	4	19	3.5	56	96	49	35	2	1	0	306	10	9	3	2.2	.972	OF-149
1955			140	.314	.520	523	164	24	3	26	5.0	83	95	43	43	4	1	0	249	10	5	4	1.9	.981	OF-140
1956			149	.289	.467	523	151	30	0	21	4.0	66	83	57	41	1	3	0	230	10	4	2	1.6	.984	OF-146
1957			119	.306	.461	395	121	17	4	12	3.0	61	66	29	33	1	0	0	153	7	2	1	1.4	.988	OF-107
1958	LA	N	122	.290	.482	411	119	19	3	18	4.4	54	83	35	28	0	5	0	187	5	5	0	1.6	.975	OF-119
1959			50	.290	.333	93	27	4	0	0	0.0	8	13	11	11	0	25		23	0	2	0	0.5	.920	OF-25

Year	Team		Games	BA	SA	AB	H	2B	3B	HR	HR%	R	RBI	BB	SO	SB	Pinch Hit AB	Pinch Hit H	PO	A	E	DP	TC/G	FA	G by Pos

Carl Furillo *continued*

Year	Team		Games	BA	SA	AB	H	2B	3B	HR	HR%	R	RBI	BB	SO	SB	AB	H	PO	A	E	DP	TC/G	FA	G by Pos
1960			8	.200	.400	10	2	0	1	0	0.0	1	1	0	2	0	5	1	2	0	0	0	0.3	1.000	OF-2
15 yrs.			1806	.299	.458	6378	1910	324	56	192	3.0	895	1058	514	436	48	65	14	3322	151	74	34	2.0	.979	OF-1739

WORLD SERIES

Year	Team		Games	BA	SA	AB	H	2B	3B	HR	HR%	R	RBI	BB	SO	SB	AB	H	PO	A	E	DP	TC/G	FA	G by Pos
1947	BKN	N	6	.353	.471	17	6	2	0	0	0.0	2	3	3	0	0	2	2	14	1	1	0	2.7	.938	OF-6
1949			3	.125	.125	8	1	0	0	0	0.0	0	0	1	0	0	1	0	2	0	0	0	0.7	1.000	OF-2
1952			7	.174	.261	23	4	2	0	0	0.0	1	0	3	3	0	0	0	13	0	0	0	1.9	1.000	OF-7
1953			6	.333	.542	24	8	2	0	1	4.2	4	4	1	3	0	0	0	10	0	2	0	2.0	.833	OF-6
1955			7	.296	.444	27	8	1	0	1	3.7	4	3	5	5	0	0	0	7	0	0	0	1.0	1.000	OF-7
1956			7	.240	.320	25	6	2	0	0	0.0	2	1	2	3	0	0	0	7	0	0	0	1.0	1.000	OF-7
1959	LA	N	4	.250	.250	4	1	0	0	0	0.0	0	2	0	1	0	4	1	1	0	0	0	0.0	–	OF-1
7 yrs.			40	.266	.383	128	34	9	0	2	1.6	13	13	13	15	0	7	3	54	1	3	0	1.5	.948	OF-36

3rd — 6th 1st

Ed Fusselbach

FUSSELBACH, EDWARD L.
B. July 4, 1858, Philadelphia, Pa. D. Apr. 14, 1926, Philadelphia, Pa.

5'6" 156 lbs.

Year	Team		Games	BA	SA	AB	H	2B	3B	HR	HR%	R	RBI	BB	SO	SB	AB	H	PO	A	E	DP	TC/G	FA	G by Pos
1882	STL	AA	35	.228	.243	136	31	2	0	0	0.0	13		5			0	0	92	54	25	4	4.9	.854	C-19, OF-15, P-4
1884	BAL	U	68	.284	.366	303	86	16	3	1	0.3	60		3			0	0	395	163	61	6	9.1	.901	C-54, 3B-6, SS-5, OF-4
1885	PHI	AA	5	.316	.368	19	6	1	0	0	0.0	2		0			0	0	30	11	4	0	9.0	.911	C-5
1888	LOU	AA	1	.250	.250	4	1	0	0	0	0.0	0	1	0	0		0	0	0	0	0	0	1.0	1.000	OF-1
4 yrs.			109	.268	.329	462	124	19	3	1	0.2	75	1	8			0	0	517	229	90	10	7.7	.892	C-78, OF-20, 3B-6, SS-5, P-4

Les Fusselman

FUSSELMAN, LESTER LeROY
B. Mar. 7, 1921, Pryor, Okla. D. May 21, 1970, Cleveland, Ohio

BR TR 6'1" 195 lbs.

Year	Team		Games	BA	SA	AB	H	2B	3B	HR	HR%	R	RBI	BB	SO	SB	AB	H	PO	A	E	DP	TC/G	FA	G by Pos
1952	STL	N	32	.159	.254	63	10	3	0	1	1.6	5	3	0	9	0	1	0	97	11	1	1	3.4	.991	C-32
1953			11	.250	.375	8	2	1	0	0	0.0	1	0	0	0	0	0	0	20	2	0	0	2.0	1.000	C-11
2 yrs.			43	.169	.268	71	12	4	0	1	1.4	6	3	0	9	0	1	0	117	13	1	1	3.0	.992	C-43

Bill Gabler

GABLER, WILLIAM LOUIS (Gabe)
B. Aug. 4, 1930, St. Louis, Mo.

BL TR 6'1" 190 lbs.

Year	Team		Games	BA	SA	AB	H	2B	3B	HR	HR%	R	RBI	BB	SO	SB	AB	H	PO	A	E	DP	TC/G	FA	G by Pos
1958	CHI	N	3	.000	.000	3	0	0	0	0	0.0	0	0	0	3	0	3	0	0	0	0	0	0.0	–	

Len Gabrielson

GABRIELSON, LEONARD GARY
Son of Len Gabrielson.
B. Feb. 14, 1940, Oakland, Calif.

BL TR 6'4" 210 lbs.

Year	Team		Games	BA	SA	AB	H	2B	3B	HR	HR%	R	RBI	BB	SO	SB	AB	H	PO	A	E	DP	TC/G	FA	G by Pos
1960	MIL	N	4	.000	.000	3	0	0	0	0	0.0	1	0	1	0	0	3	0	0	0	0	0	0.0	–	OF-1
1963			46	.217	.333	120	26	5	0	3	2.5	14	15	8	23	1	12	4	143	9	4	5	3.4	.974	OF-22, 1B-16, 3B-3
1964	2 teams																								MIL N (24G – .184) CHI N (89G – .246)
"	total		113	.239	.342	310	74	13	2	5	1.6	22	24	20	45	10	25	8	240	12	2	16	2.2	.992	OF-70, 1B-20
1965	2 teams																								CHI N (28G – .250) SF N (88G – .301)
"	total		116	.293	.410	317	93	6	5	7	2.2	40	31	33	64	4	22	4	157	9	3	5	1.5	.982	OF-91, 1B-6
1966	SF	N	94	.217	.296	240	52	7	0	4	1.7	27	16	21	51	0	25	5	116	5	4	5	1.3	.968	OF-67, 1B-6
1967	2 teams																								CAL A (11G – .083) LA N (90G – .261)
"	total		101	.252	.400	250	63	10	3	7	2.8	22	31	17	45	3	34	6	92	7	2	0	1.0	.980	OF-69
1968	LA	N	108	.270	.428	304	82	16	1	10	3.3	38	35	32	47	1	27	7	114	6	3	1	1.1	.976	OF-86
1969			83	.270	.326	178	48	5	1	1	0.6	13	18	12	25	1	36	13	61	1	1	0	0.8	.984	OF-47, 1B-2
1970			43	.190	.238	42	8	2	0	0	0.0	1	6	1	15	0	38	8	3	1	0	1	0.1	1.000	OF-2, 1B-1
9 yrs.			708	.253	.366	1764	446	64	12	37	2.1	178	176	145	315	20	222	55	926	50	19	33	1.4	.981	OF-455, 1B-51, 3B-3

Len Gabrielson

GABRIELSON, LEONARD HILBOURNE
Father of Len Gabrielson.
B. Sept. 8, 1915, Oakland, Calif.

BL TL 6'3" 210 lbs.

Year	Team		Games	BA	SA	AB	H	2B	3B	HR	HR%	R	RBI	BB	SO	SB	AB	H	PO	A	E	DP	TC/G	FA	G by Pos
1939	PHI	N	5	.222	.222	18	4	0	0	0	0.0	3	1	2	3	0	0	0	34	9	1	3	8.8	.977	1B-5

Eddie Gaedel

GAEDEL, EDWARD CARL
B. June 8, 1925, Chicago, Ill. D. June 18, 1961, Chicago, Ill.

BR TL 3'7" 65 lbs.

Year	Team		Games	BA	SA	AB	H	2B	3B	HR	HR%	R	RBI	BB	SO	SB	AB	H	PO	A	E	DP	TC/G	FA	G by Pos
1951	STL	A	1	–	–	0	0	0	0	0	–	0	0	1	0	0	0	0	0	0	0	0	0.0	–	

Gary Gaetti

GAETTI, GARY JOSEPH
B. Aug. 19, 1958, Centralia, Ill.

BR TR 6' 180 lbs.

Year	Team		Games	BA	SA	AB	H	2B	3B	HR	HR%	R	RBI	BB	SO	SB	AB	H	PO	A	E	DP	TC/G	FA	G by Pos
1981	MIN	A	9	.192	.423	26	5	0	0	2	7.7	4	3	0	6	0	1	0	5	17	0	1	2.4	1.000	3B-8, DH-1
1982			145	.230	.443	508	117	25	4	25	4.9	59	84	37	107	0	1	0	106	291	17	36	2.9	.959	3B-142, SS-2
1983			157	.245	.414	584	143	30	3	21	3.6	81	78	54	121	7	2	1	131	361	17	46	3.2	.967	3B-154, SS-3, DH-1
1984			162	.262	.350	588	154	29	4	5	0.9	55	65	44	81	11	0	0	163	335	21	27	3.2	.960	3B-154, OF-8, SS-2
1985			160	.246	.409	560	138	31	0	20	3.6	71	63	37	89	13	1	0	162	316	18	31	3.1	.964	3B-156, OF-4, DH-1, 1B-1
1986			157	.287	.518	596	171	34	1	34	5.7	91	108	52	108	14	1	0	120	335	21	36	3.0	.956	3B-156, SS-2, OF-1, 2B-1
1987			154	.257	.485	584	150	36	2	31	5.3	95	109	37	92	10	3	2	134	261	11	28	2.6	.973	3B-150, DH-2
1988			133	.301	.551	468	141	29	2	28	6.0	66	88	36	85	7	14	4	105	191	7	24	2.3	.977	3B-115, DH-5, 1B-2
1989			130	.251	.404	498	125	11	4	19	3.8	63	75	25	87	6	3	1	115	253	10	24	2.9	.974	3B-125, DH-3, 1B-2
9 yrs.			1207	.259	.445	4412	1144	225	20	185	4.2	585	673	322	776	68	25	8	1041	2360	122	253	2.9	.965	3B-1160, DH-13, OF-13, SS-11, 1B-3, 2B-1

LEAGUE CHAMPIONSHIP SERIES

Year	Team		Games	BA	SA	AB	H	2B	3B	HR	HR%	R	RBI	BB	SO	SB	AB	H	PO	A	E	DP	TC/G	FA	G by Pos
1987	MIN	A	5	.300	.650	20	6	1	0	2	10.0	5	5	1	3	0	0	0	8	7	0	1	3.0	1.000	3B-5

WORLD SERIES

Year	Team		Games	BA	SA	AB	H	2B	3B	HR	HR%	R	RBI	BB	SO	SB	AB	H	PO	A	E	DP	TC/G	FA	G by Pos
1987	MIN	A	7	.259	.519	27	7	2	1	1	3.7	4	4	2	5	2	0	0	6	15	0	2	3.0	1.000	3B-7

Fabian Gaffke

GAFFKE, FABIAN SEBASTIAN
B. Aug. 5, 1913, Milwaukee, Wis.

BR TR 5'10" 185 lbs.

Year	Team	Games	BA	SA	AB	H	2B	3B	HR	HR%	R	RBI	BB	SO	SB	Pinch Hit AB	Pinch Hit H	PO	A	E	DP	TC/G	FA	G by Pos

Fabian Gaffke *continued*

Year	Team	Games	BA	SA	AB	H	2B	3B	HR	HR%	R	RBI	BB	SO	SB	AB	H	PO	A	E	DP	TC/G	FA	G by Pos
1936	BOS A	15	.127	.218	55	7	2	0	1	1.8	5	3	4	5	0	0	0	24	1	0	0	1.7	1.000	OF-15
1937		54	.288	.484	184	53	10	4	6	3.3	32	34	15	25	1	4	1	80	1	0	0	1.6	.965	OF-50
1938		15	.100	.100	10	1	0	0	0	0.0	2	1	3	2	0	8	1	1	1	0	0	0.1	1.000	OF-2, C-1
1939		1	.000	.000	1	0	0	0	0	0.0	0	0	0	1	0	1	0	0	0	0	0	0.0	–	
1941	CLE A	4	.250	.250	4	1	0	0	0	0.0	0	0	2	2	0	2	1	2	0	0	0	0.5	1.000	OF-2
1942		40	.164	.194	67	11	2	0	0	0.0	4	3	6	13	1	24	4	29	0	0	0	0.7	1.000	OF-16
6 yrs.		129	.227	.361	321	73	14	4	7	2.2	43	42	30	47	2	39	7	136	5	0	0	1.1	.979	OF-85, C-1

Phil Gagliano

GAGLIANO, PHILIP JOSEPH
Brother of Ralph Gagliano.
B. Dec. 27, 1941, Memphis, Tenn.

BR TR 6'1" 180 lbs.

Year	Team	Games	BA	SA	AB	H	2B	3B	HR	HR%	R	RBI	BB	SO	SB	AB	H	PO	A	E	DP	TC/G	FA	G by Pos
1963	STL N	10	.400	.400	5	2	0	0	0	0.0	1	1	1	1	0	2	0	5	3	0	0	0.8	1.000	2B-3, 3B-1
1964		40	.259	.379	58	15	4	0	1	1.7	5	9	3	10	0	19	3	26	28	4	6	1.5	.931	2B-12, OF-2, 3B-1, 1B-1
1965		122	.240	.355	363	87	14	2	8	2.2	46	53	40	45	2	26	5	201	169	16	34	3.2	.959	2B-57, OF-25, 3B-19
1966		90	.254	.338	213	54	8	2	2	0.9	23	15	24	29	2	36	4	95	86	2	16	2.0	.989	3B-41, 1B-8, OF-5, 2B-1
1967		73	.221	.281	217	48	7	0	2	0.9	20	21	19	26	0	17	0	115	99	8	16	3.0	.964	2B-27, 3B-25, 1B-4, SS-2
1968		53	.229	.305	105	24	4	2	0	0.0	13	13	7	12	0	17	4	31	52	1	8	1.6	.988	2B-17, 3B-10, OF-5
1969		62	.227	.266	128	29	2	0	1	0.8	7	10	14	12	0	21	2	108	55	2	16	2.7	.988	2B-20, 3B-9, 1B-9, OF-2
1970 2 teams	STL N (18G – .188)				CHI N	(26G – .150)																		
" total		44	.167	.167	72	12	0	0	0	0.0	5	7	6	8	0	16	3	49	33	2	6	1.9	.976	2B-18, 3B-7, 1B-4
1971	BOS A	47	.324	.397	68	22	5	0	0	0.0	11	13	11	5	0	22	8	22	14	0	2	0.8	1.000	OF-11, 2B-7, 3B-4
1972		52	.256	.329	82	21	4	1	0	0.0	9	10	10	13	1	26	9	31	15	2	0	0.9	.958	OF-12, 3B-5, 2B-4, 1B-2
1973	CIN N	63	.290	.319	69	20	2	0	0	0.0	8	7	13	16	0	41	15	9	14	3	1	0.4	.885	2B-4, 3B-2, OF-1, 1B-1
1974		46	.065	.065	31	2	0	0	0	0.0	2	0	15	7	0	29	2	5	2	0	0	0.2	1.000	2B-2, 3B-1, 1B-1
12 yrs.		702	.238	.313	1411	336	50	7	14	1.0	150	159	163	184	5	272	55	697	570	40	105	1.9	.969	2B-172, 3B-125, OF-63, 1B-30, SS-2

LEAGUE CHAMPIONSHIP SERIES

Year	Team	Games	BA	SA	AB	H	2B	3B	HR	HR%	R	RBI	BB	SO	SB	AB	H	PO	A	E	DP	TC/G	FA	G by Pos
1973	CIN N	3	.000	.000	3	0	0	0	0	0.0	0	0	0	2	0	3	0	0	0	0	0	0.0	–	

WORLD SERIES

Year	Team	Games	BA	SA	AB	H	2B	3B	HR	HR%	R	RBI	BB	SO	SB	AB	H	PO	A	E	DP	TC/G	FA	G by Pos
1967	STL N	1	.000	.000	1	0	0	0	0	0.0	0	0	0	0	0	1	0	0	0	0	0	0.0	–	
1968		3	.000	.000	3	0	0	0	0	0.0	0	0	0	3	0	3	0	0	0	0	0	0.0	–	
2 yrs.		4	.000	.000	4	0	0	0	0	0.0	0	0	0	3	0	4	0	0	0	0	0	0.0	–	

Ralph Gagliano

GAGLIANO, RALPH MICHAEL
Brother of Phil Gagliano.
B. Oct. 8, 1946, Memphis, Tenn.

BL TR 5'11" 170 lbs.

Year	Team	Games	BA	SA	AB	H	2B	3B	HR	HR%	R	RBI	BB	SO	SB	AB	H	PO	A	E	DP	TC/G	FA	G by Pos
1965	CLE A	1	–	–	0	0	0	0	0	0.0	0	0	0	0	0	0	0	0	0	0	0	0.0	–	

Greg Gagne

GAGNE, GREGORY CHRISTOPHER
B. Nov. 12, 1961, Fall River, Mass.

BR TR 5'11" 175 lbs.

Year	Team	Games	BA	SA	AB	H	2B	3B	HR	HR%	R	RBI	BB	SO	SB	AB	H	PO	A	E	DP	TC/G	FA	G by Pos
1983	MIN A	10	.111	.148	27	3	1	0	0	0.0	2	3	0	6	0	0	0	10	14	2	2	2.6	.923	SS-10
1984		2	.000	.000	1	0	0	0	0	0.0	2	0	0	0	0	1	0	0	0	0	0	0.0	–	
1985		114	.225	.317	293	66	15	3	2	0.7	37	23	20	57	10	4	1	149	269	14	48	3.8	.968	SS-106, DH-5
1986		156	.250	.398	472	118	22	6	12	2.5	63	54	30	108	12	0	0	228	381	26	96	4.1	.959	SS-155, 2B-4
1987		137	.265	.430	437	116	28	7	10	2.3	68	40	25	84	6	0	0	196	391	18	75	4.4	.970	SS-136, OF-4, 2B-1
1988		149	.236	.397	461	109	20	6	14	3.0	70	48	27	110	15	1	0	202	373	18	79	4.0	.970	SS-146, OF-2, 3B-1, 2B-1
1989		149	.272	.424	460	125	29	7	9	2.0	69	48	17	80	11	5	0	218	389	18	66	4.2	.971	SS-146, OF-1
7 yrs.		717	.250	.396	2151	537	115	29	47	2.2	309	216	119	445	54	11	1	1003	1817	96	366	4.1	.967	SS-699, OF-7, 2B-6, DH-5, 3B-1

LEAGUE CHAMPIONSHIP SERIES

Year	Team	Games	BA	SA	AB	H	2B	3B	HR	HR%	R	RBI	BB	SO	SB	AB	H	PO	A	E	DP	TC/G	FA	G by Pos
1987	MIN A	5	.278	.778	18	5	3	0	2	11.1	5	3	3	4	0	0	0	9	13	2	2	4.8	.917	SS-5

WORLD SERIES

Year	Team	Games	BA	SA	AB	H	2B	3B	HR	HR%	R	RBI	BB	SO	SB	AB	H	PO	A	E	DP	TC/G	FA	G by Pos
1987	MIN A	7	.200	.333	30	6	1	0	1	3.3	5	3	1	6	0	0	0	6	20	2	2	4.0	.929	SS-7

Ed Gagnier

GAGNIER, EDWARD J.
B. Apr. 16, 1883, Paris, France   D. Sept. 13, 1946, Detroit, Mich.

BR TR 5'9" 170 lbs.

Year	Team	Games	BA	SA	AB	H	2B	3B	HR	HR%	R	RBI	BB	SO	SB	AB	H	PO	A	E	DP	TC/G	FA	G by Pos
1914	BKN F	94	.187	.234	337	63	12	2	0	0.0	22	25	13		8	0	0	230	254	35	39	5.5	.933	SS-88, 3B-6
1915 2 teams	BKN F	(20G – .260)			BUF F	(1G – .000)																		
" total		21	.250	.269	52	13	1	0	0	0.0	8	4	10		2	0	0	36	56	6	7	4.7	.939	SS-13, 2B-7
2 yrs.		115	.195	.239	389	76	13	2	0	0.0	30	29	23		10	0	0	266	310	41	46	5.4	.934	SS-101, 2B-7, 3B-6

Chick Gagnon

GAGNON, HAROLD DENNIS
B. Sept. 27, 1897, Millbury, Mass.   D. Apr. 30, 1970, Wilmington, Del.

BR TR 5'7½" 158 lbs.

Year	Team	Games	BA	SA	AB	H	2B	3B	HR	HR%	R	RBI	BB	SO	SB	AB	H	PO	A	E	DP	TC/G	FA	G by Pos
1922	DET A	10	.250	.250	4	1	0	0	0	0.0	2	0	0	2	0	2	1	0	0	0	0	0.1	–	SS-1, 3B-1
1924	WAS A	4	.200	.200	5	1	0	0	0	0.0	1	1	0	0	0	2	1	3	4	0	0	1.8	1.000	SS-2
2 yrs.		14	.222	.222	9	2	0	0	0	0.0	3	1	0	2	0	4	2	3	4	0	0	0.6	.875	SS-3, 3B-1

Del Gainer

GAINER, DELLOS CLINTON (Sheriff)
B. Nov. 10, 1886, Montrose, W. Va.   D. Jan. 29, 1947, Elkins, W. Va.

BR TR 6' 180 lbs.

Year	Team	Games	BA	SA	AB	H	2B	3B	HR	HR%	R	RBI	BB	SO	SB	AB	H	PO	A	E	DP	TC/G	FA	G by Pos
1909	DET A	2	.200	.200	5	1	0	0	0	0.0	0	0	0		0	0	0	12	1	1	0	7.0	.929	1B-2
1911		70	.302	.403	248	75	11	4	2	0.8	32	25	20		10	0	0	671	38	18	36	10.4	.975	1B-69
1912		51	.240	.335	179	43	5	4	0	0.0	28	20	18		14	0	0	547	22	8	25	11.3	.986	1B-50
1913		104	.267	.372	363	97	16	6	2	0.6	47	25	30	45	10	2	1	1118	50	14	55	11.4	.988	1B-102
1914 2 teams	DET A	(1G – .000)			BOS A	(38G – .238)																		
" total		39	.238	.464	84	20	9	2	2	2.4	11	13	8	14	2	8	1	127	33	4	6	4.2	.976	1B-19, 2B-11
1915	BOS A	82	.295	.415	200	59	5	8	1	0.5	30	29	21	31	7	14	4	462	34	6	22	6.1	.988	1B-56, OF-6
1916		56	.254	.359	142	36	6	0	3	2.1	14	18	10	24	5	4	0	362	24	1	18	6.9	.997	1B-48, 2B-2
1917		52	.308	.424	172	53	10	2	2	1.2	28	19	15	21	1	0	0	490	27	6	29	10.1	.989	1B-50
1919		47	.237	.322	118	28	6	2	0	0.0	9	13	13	15	5	0	0	190	12	5	6	4.4	.976	1B-21, OF-18

Year	Team	Games	BA	SA	AB	H	2B	3B	HR	HR%	R	RBI	BB	SO	SB	Pinch Hit AB	Pinch Hit H	PO	A	E	DP	TC/G	FA	G by Pos

Del Gainer *continued*

Year	Team	Games	BA	SA	AB	H	2B	3B	HR	HR%	R	RBI	BB	SO	SB	AB	H	PO	A	E	DP	TC/G	FA	G by Pos
1922	STL N	43	.268	.485	97	26	7	4	2	2.1	19	23	14	6	0	9	1	189	11	5	8	4.8	.976	1B-26, OF-10
10 yrs.		546	.272	.390	1608	438	75	36	14	0.9	218	185	149	156	54	44	8	4168	252	68	205	8.2	.985	1B-443, OF-34, 2B-13

WORLD SERIES

Year	Team	Games	BA	SA	AB	H	2B	3B	HR	HR%	R	RBI	BB	SO	SB	AB	H	PO	A	E	DP	TC/G	FA	G by Pos
1915	BOS A	1	.333	.333	3	1	0	0	0	0.0	1	0	0	0	0	1	0	9	0	0	0	9.0	1.000	1B-1
1916		1	1.000	1.000	1	1	0	0	0	0.0	0	0	0	0	0	1	1	0	0	0	0	0.0	—	
2 yrs.		2	.500	.500	4	2	0	0	0	0.0	1	1	0	0	0	2	1	9	0	0	0	4.5	1.000	1B-1

Joe Gaines

GAINES, ARNESTA JOE   BR TR 6'1" 190 lbs.
B. Nov. 22, 1936, Bryan, Tex.

Year	Team	Games	BA	SA	AB	H	2B	3B	HR	HR%	R	RBI	BB	SO	SB	AB	H	PO	A	E	DP	TC/G	FA	G by Pos
1960	CIN N	11	.200	.200	15	3	0	0	0	0.0	2	1	0	1	0	2	1	6	0	0	0	0.5	1.000	OF-3
1961		5	.000	.000	3	0	0	0	0	0.0	0	2	0	2	1	1	0	1	0	1	0	0.4	.500	OF-3
1962		64	.231	.346	52	12	3	0	1	1.9	12	7	8	16	1	40	12	8	0	0	0	0.1	1.000	OF-13
1963	BAL A	66	.286	.476	126	36	4	1	6	4.8	24	20	20	39	2	25	5	52	0	3	0	0.8	.945	OF-39
1964	2 teams		BAL A	(16G – .154)			HOU N	(89G – .254)																
"	total	105	.246	.387	333	82	9	7	8	2.4	39	36	30	76	8	17	2	141	4	8	1	1.5	.948	OF-86
1965	HOU N	100	.227	.349	229	52	8	1	6	2.6	21	31	18	59	4	32	8	83	1	8	0	0.9	.913	OF-65
1966		11	.077	.154	13	1	0	0	0	0.0	4	0	3	5	0	6	0	1	0	1	0	0.2	.500	OF-3
7 yrs.		362	.241	.379	771	186	25	9	21	2.7	104	95	81	197	14	123	28	292	5	21	1	0.9	.934	OF-212

Ty Gainey

GAINEY, TELMANCH   BL TR 6'1" 190 lbs.
B. Dec. 25, 1960, Cheraw, S. C.

Year	Team	Games	BA	SA	AB	H	2B	3B	HR	HR%	R	RBI	BB	SO	SB	AB	H	PO	A	E	DP	TC/G	FA	G by Pos
1985	HOU N	13	.162	.162	37	6	0	0	0	0.0	5	0	2	9	0	2	0	21	0	2	0	1.8	.913	OF-9
1986		26	.300	.460	50	15	3	1	1	2.0	6	6	6	19	3	6	2	30	0	0	0	1.2	1.000	OF-19
1987		18	.125	.125	24	3	0	0	0	0.0	1	1	2	9	1	11	0	10	0	0	0	0.6	1.000	OF-6
3 yrs.		57	.216	.288	111	24	3	1	1	0.9	12	7	10	37	4	19	2	61	0	2	0	1.1	.968	OF-34

Augie Galan

GALAN, AUGUST JOHN   BB TR 6' 175 lbs.
B. May 25, 1912, Berkeley, Calif.   BL 1945-49

Year	Team	Games	BA	SA	AB	H	2B	3B	HR	HR%	R	RBI	BB	SO	SB	AB	H	PO	A	E	DP	TC/G	FA	G by Pos
1934	CHI N	66	.260	.391	192	50	6	2	5	2.6	31	22	16	15	4	12	5	92	115	8	18	3.3	.963	2B-43, 3B-3, SS-1
1935		154	.314	.467	646	203	41	11	12	1.9	133	79	87	53	22	0	0	351	12	8	4	2.4	.978	OF-154
1936		145	.264	.365	575	152	26	4	8	1.4	74	81	67	50	16	2	0	381	9	5	3	2.7	.987	OF-145
1937		147	.252	.412	611	154	24	10	18	2.9	104	78	79	48	23	0	0	338	44	9	7	2.7	.977	OF-140, 2B-8, SS-2
1938		110	.286	.418	395	113	16	9	6	1.5	52	69	49	17	8	6	0	211	10	3	3	2.0	.987	OF-103
1939		148	.304	.432	549	167	36	8	6	1.1	104	71	75	26	8	3	0	290	6	9	0	2.1	.970	OF-145
1940		68	.230	.359	209	48	14	2	3	1.4	33	22	37	23	9	9	2	119	11	4	2	2.0	.970	OF-54, 2B-2
1941	2 teams		CHI N	(65G – .208)			BKN N	(17G – .259)																
"	total	82	.218	.279	147	32	6	0	1	0.7	21	17	25	11	0	40	7	45	2	2	0	0.6	.959	OF-37
1942	BKN N	69	.263	.340	209	55	16	0	0	0.0	24	22	24	12	2	9	3	136	8	1	2	2.1	.993	OF-55, 1B-4, 2B-3
1943		139	.287	.406	495	142	26	3	9	1.8	83	67	103	39	6	1	0	478	29	7	9	3.7	.986	OF-124, 1B-13
1944		151	.318	.495	547	174	43	9	12	2.2	96	93	101	23	4	4	2	323	10	4	3	2.2	.988	OF-147, 2B-2
1945		152	.307	.441	576	177	36	7	9	1.6	114	92	114	27	13	1	1	693	116	17	59	5.4	.979	1B-66, OF-49, 3B-40
1946		99	.310	.460	274	85	22	5	3	1.1	53	38	68	21	8	7	1	211	44	16	3	2.7	.941	OF-60, 3B-19, 1B-12
1947	CIN N	124	.314	.416	392	123	18	2	6	1.5	60	61	94	19	0	5	2	246	2	3	0	2.0	.988	OF-118
1948		54	.286	.455	77	22	3	2	2	2.6	18	16	26	4	0	26	3	29	0	1	0	0.6	.967	OF-18
1949	2 teams		NY N	(22G – .059)			PHI A	(12G – .308)																
"	total	34	.209	.279	43	9	3	0	0	0.0	4	2	14	5	0	18	2	23	0	0	1	0.7	1.000	OF-10, 1B-3
16 yrs.		1742	.287	.419	5937	1706	336	74	100	1.7	1004	830	979	393	123	143	28	3966	418	97	114	2.6	.978	OF-1359, 1B-98, 3B-62, 2B-58, SS-3

WORLD SERIES

Year	Team	Games	BA	SA	AB	H	2B	3B	HR	HR%	R	RBI	BB	SO	SB	AB	H	PO	A	E	DP	TC/G	FA	G by Pos
1935	CHI N	6	.160	.200	25	4	1	0	0	0.0	2	2	2	2	0	0	0	12	1	1	0	2.3	.929	OF-6
1938		2	.000	.000	2	0	0	0	0	0.0	0	0	0	1	0	2	0	0	0	0	0	0.0	—	
1941	BKN N	2	.000	.000	2	0	0	0	0	0.0	0	0	0	1	0	2	0	0	0	0	0	0.0	—	
3 yrs.		10	.138	.172	29	4	1	0	0	0.0	2	2	2	4	0	4	0	12	1	1	0	1.4	.929	OF-6

Andres Galarraga

GALARRAGA, ANDRES JOSE (Big Cat)   BR TR 6'3" 235 lbs.
Born Andres Jose Padovani y Galarraga.
B. June 18, 1961, Caracas, Venezuela

Year	Team	Games	BA	SA	AB	H	2B	3B	HR	HR%	R	RBI	BB	SO	SB	AB	H	PO	A	E	DP	TC/G	FA	G by Pos
1985	MON N	24	.187	.280	75	14	1	0	2	2.7	9	4	3	18	1	2	1	173	22	1	14	8.2	.995	1B-23
1986		105	.271	.405	321	87	13	0	10	3.1	39	42	30	79	6	7	1	805	40	4	59	8.1	.995	1B-102
1987		147	.305	.459	551	168	40	3	13	2.4	72	90	41	127	7	1	0	1300	103	10	96	9.6	.993	1B-146
1988		157	.302	.540	609	184	42	8	29	4.8	99	92	39	153	13	2	1	1464	103	15	124	10.1	.991	1B-156
1989		152	.257	.434	572	147	30	1	23	4.0	76	85	48	158	12	6	1	1335	91	11	97	9.5	.992	1B-147
5 yrs.		585	.282	.461	2128	600	126	12	77	3.6	295	313	161	535	39	18	4	5077	359	41	390	9.4	.993	1B-574

Milt Galatzer

GALATZER, MILTON   BL TL 5'10" 168 lbs.
B. May 4, 1907, Chicago, Ill. D. Jan. 29, 1976, San Francisco, Calif.

Year	Team	Games	BA	SA	AB	H	2B	3B	HR	HR%	R	RBI	BB	SO	SB	AB	H	PO	A	E	DP	TC/G	FA	G by Pos
1933	CLE A	57	.238	.281	160	38	2	1	1	0.6	19	17	23	21	2	12	2	104	7	2	2	2.0	.982	OF-40, 1B-5
1934		49	.270	.342	196	53	10	2	0	0.0	29	15	21	8	3	0	0	91	7	2	0	2.0	.980	OF-49
1935		93	.301	.359	259	78	9	3	0	0.0	45	19	35	8	4	11	1	134	7	10	0	1.6	.934	OF-81
1936		49	.237	.299	97	23	4	1	0	0.0	12	6	13	8	1	3	0	52	3	2	2	1.2	.965	OF-42, 1B-1, P-1
1939	CIN N	3	.000	.000	5	0	0	0	0	0.0	0	0	0	1	0	0	0	11	0	0	0	3.7	1.000	1B-2
5 yrs.		251	.268	.326	717	192	25	7	1	0.1	105	57	92	46	10	26	3	392	24	16	4	1.7	.963	OF-212, 1B-8, P-1

Archie Galbraith

GALBRAITH, ARCHIBALD VICTOR
B. Sept. 22, 1877, Boxford, Mass. D. Dec. 25, 1971, Northampton, Mass.

Year	Team	Games	BA	SA	AB	H	2B	3B	HR	HR%	R	RBI	BB	SO	SB	AB	H	PO	A	E	DP	TC/G	FA	G by Pos
1902	CHI N	1	—	—	0	0	0	0	0		0	0	0	0	0	0	0	0	0	0	0	0.0	—	3B-1

Al Gallagher

GALLAGHER, ALAN MITCHELL EDWARD GEORGE PATRICK HENRY (Dirty Al)   BR TR 6' 180 lbs.
B. Oct. 19, 1945, San Francisco, Calif.

Year	Team	Games	BA	SA	AB	H	2B	3B	HR	HR%	R	RBI	BB	SO	SB	AB	H	PO	A	E	DP	TC/G	FA	G by Pos
1970	SF N	109	.266	.376	282	75	15	2	4	1.4	31	28	30	37	2	18	7	70	128	6	12	1.9	.971	3B-91

Year	Team	Games	BA	SA	AB	H	2B	3B	HR	HR%	R	RBI	BB	SO	SB	Pinch Hit AB	Pinch Hit H	PO	A	E	DP	TC/G	FA	G by Pos

Al Gallagher *continued*

Year	Team	Games	BA	SA	AB	H	2B	3B	HR	HR%	R	RBI	BB	SO	SB	PH AB	PH H	PO	A	E	DP	TC/G	FA	G by Pos
1971		136	.277	.378	429	119	18	5	5	1.2	47	57	40	57	2	9	3	88	204	15	18	2.3	.951	3B-128
1972		82	.223	.270	233	52	3	1	2	0.9	19	18	33	39	2	12	3	64	120	5	7	2.3	.974	3B-69
1973	2 teams	SF N (5G – .222)			CAL A (110G – .273)																			
"	total	115	.272	.297	320	87	6	1	0	0.0	17	27	35	31	1	9	0	64	187	11	13	2.3	.958	3B-103, SS-1, 2B-1
4 yrs.		442	.263	.337	1264	333	42	9	11	0.9	114	130	138	164	7	48	13	286	639	37	50	2.2	.962	3B-391, SS-1, 2B-1

LEAGUE CHAMPIONSHIP SERIES

Year	Team	Games	BA	SA	AB	H	2B	3B	HR	HR%	R	RBI	BB	SO	SB	PH AB	PH H	PO	A	E	DP	TC/G	FA	G by Pos
1971	SF N	4	.100	.100	10	1	0	0	0	0.0	0	0	0	2	0	0	0	0	4	0	0	1.0	1.000	3B-4

Bill Gallagher

GALLAGHER, WILLIAM H.
B. 1875, Lowell, Mass. Deceased.

Year	Team	Games	BA	SA	AB	H	2B	3B	HR	HR%	R	RBI	BB	SO	SB	PH AB	PH H	PO	A	E	DP	TC/G	FA	G by Pos
1896	PHI N	14	.306	.347	49	15	2	0	0	0.0	9	6	10			0	0	17	42	7	5	4.7	.894	SS-14

Bill Gallagher

GALLAGHER, WILLIAM JOHN
B. Philadelphia, Pa. Deceased.

TL

Year	Team	Games	BA	SA	AB	H	2B	3B	HR	HR%	R	RBI	BB	SO	SB	PH AB	PH H	PO	A	E	DP	TC/G	FA	G by Pos
1883	2 teams	BAL AA (16G – .164)			PHI N (2G – .000)																			
"	total	18	.145	.217	69	10	3	1	0	0.0	10		3	4		0	0	21	13	9	1	2.4	.791	OF-11, P-7, SS-4
1884	PHI U	3	.091	.091	11	1	0	0	0	0.0	1		0			0	0	2	6	2	0	3.3	.800	P-3
2 yrs.		21	.138	.200	80	11	3	1	0	0.0	11		3	4		0	0	23	19	11	1	2.5	.792	OF-11, P-10, SS-4

Bob Gallagher

GALLAGHER, ROBERT COLLINS
B. July 7, 1948, Newton, Mass.

BL TL 6'3" 185 lbs.

Year	Team	Games	BA	SA	AB	H	2B	3B	HR	HR%	R	RBI	BB	SO	SB	PH AB	PH H	PO	A	E	DP	TC/G	FA	G by Pos
1972	BOS A	7	.000	.000	5	0	0	0	0	0.0	0	0	0	3	0	5	0	0	0	0	0	0.0	—	
1973	HOU N	71	.264	.338	148	39	3	1	2	1.4	16	10	3	27	0	29	7	78	1	0	0	1.1	1.000	OF-42, 1B-1
1974		102	.172	.195	87	15	2	0	0	0.0	13	3	12	23	1	40	6	51	1	1	0	0.5	.981	OF-62, 1B-4
1975	NY N	33	.133	.200	15	2	1	0	0	0.0	5	0	1	3	0	10	1	9	0	1	0	0.3	.900	OF-16
4 yrs.		213	.220	.275	255	56	6	1	2	0.8	34	13	16	56	1	84	14	138	2	2	0	0.7	.986	OF-120, 1B-5

Dave Gallagher

GALLAGHER, DAVID THOMAS
B. Sept. 20, 1960, Trenton, N.J.

BR TR 6' 180 lbs.

Year	Team	Games	BA	SA	AB	H	2B	3B	HR	HR%	R	RBI	BB	SO	SB	PH AB	PH H	PO	A	E	DP	TC/G	FA	G by Pos
1987	CLE A	15	.111	.194	36	4	1	1	0	0.0	2	1	2	5	2	0	0	34	1	1	1	2.4	.972	OF-14
1988	CHI A	101	.303	.406	347	105	15	3	5	1.4	59	31	29	40	5	11	2	228	5	0	2	2.3	1.000	OF-95, DH-2
1989		161	.266	.314	601	160	22	1	2	0.2	74	46	46	79	5	2	0	390	8	3	4	2.5	.993	OF-160, DH-1
3 yrs.		277	.273	.342	984	269	38	6	6	0.6	135	78	77	124	12	13	2	652	14	4	7	2.4	.994	OF-269, DH-3

Gil Gallagher

GALLAGHER, LAWRENCE KIRBY
B. Sept. 5, 1896, Washington, D.C. D. Jan. 6, 1957, Washington, D.C.

BB TR 5'8" 155 lbs.

Year	Team	Games	BA	SA	AB	H	2B	3B	HR	HR%	R	RBI	BB	SO	SB	PH AB	PH H	PO	A	E	DP	TC/G	FA	G by Pos
1922	BOS N	7	.045	.091	22	1	1	0	0	0.0	1	2	1	7	0	1	0	4	21	3	0	4.0	.893	SS-6

Jackie Gallagher

GALLAGHER, JOHN LAURENCE
B. Jan. 28, 1902, Providence, R.I. D. Sept. 10, 1984, Gladwyn, Pa.

BL TR 5'10" 175 lbs.

Year	Team	Games	BA	SA	AB	H	2B	3B	HR	HR%	R	RBI	BB	SO	SB	PH AB	PH H	PO	A	E	DP	TC/G	FA	G by Pos
1923	CLE A	1	1.000	1.000	1	1	0	0	0	0.0	0	0	0	0	0	0	0	0	0	0	0	0.0	—	OF-1

Jim Gallagher

GALLAGHER, JAMES E.
B. Findlay, Ohio D. Mar. 29, 1894, Scranton, Pa.

Year	Team	Games	BA	SA	AB	H	2B	3B	HR	HR%	R	RBI	BB	SO	SB	PH AB	PH H	PO	A	E	DP	TC/G	FA	G by Pos
1886	WAS N	1	.200	.200	5	1	0	0	0	0.0	1	0	1	2	0	0	0	1	6	1	0	8.0	.875	SS-1

Joe Gallagher

GALLAGHER, JOSEPH EMMETT (Muscles)
B. Mar. 7, 1914, Buffalo, N.Y.

BR TR 6'2" 210 lbs.

Year	Team	Games	BA	SA	AB	H	2B	3B	HR	HR%	R	RBI	BB	SO	SB	PH AB	PH H	PO	A	E	DP	TC/G	FA	G by Pos
1939	2 teams	NY A (14G – .244)			STL A (71G – .282)																			
"	total	85	.277	.459	307	85	17	3	11	3.6	49	49	20	50	1	5	2	161	9	9	1	2.1	.950	OF-79
1940	2 teams	STL A (23G – .271)			BKN N (57G – .264)																			
"	total	80	.267	.422	180	48	9	2	5	2.8	24	24	6	26	3	42	12	58	2	3	1	0.8	.952	OF-46
2 yrs.		165	.273	.446	487	133	26	5	16	3.3	73	73	26	76	4	47	14	219	11	12	2	1.5	.950	OF-125

John Gallagher

GALLAGHER, JOHN CARROLL
B. Feb. 18, 1892, Pittsburgh, Pa. D. Mar. 30, 1952, Norfolk, Va.

BR TR 5'10½" 156 lbs.

Year	Team	Games	BA	SA	AB	H	2B	3B	HR	HR%	R	RBI	BB	SO	SB	PH AB	PH H	PO	A	E	DP	TC/G	FA	G by Pos
1915	BAL F	40	.198	.230	126	25	4	0	0	0.0	11	4	5		1	0	0	51	100	11	10	4.1	.932	2B-37, SS-5, 3B-1

Shorty Gallagher

GALLAGHER, CHARLES WILLIAM (Charlie)
B. Apr. 30, 1872, Detroit, Mich. D. June 23, 1924, Detroit, Mich.

Year	Team	Games	BA	SA	AB	H	2B	3B	HR	HR%	R	RBI	BB	SO	SB	PH AB	PH H	PO	A	E	DP	TC/G	FA	G by Pos
1901	CLE A	2	.000	.000	4	0	0	0	0	0.0	0	0	0		0	0	0	2	0	1	0	1.5	.667	OF-2

Stan Galle

GALLE, STANLEY JOSEPH
Born Stanley Joseph Galazewski.
B. Feb. 7, 1919, Milwaukee, Wis.

BR TR 5'7" 165 lbs.

Year	Team	Games	BA	SA	AB	H	2B	3B	HR	HR%	R	RBI	BB	SO	SB	PH AB	PH H	PO	A	E	DP	TC/G	FA	G by Pos
1942	WAS A	13	.111	.111	18	2	0	0	0	0.0	3	1	1	0	0	10	2	3	3	1	0	0.5	.857	3B-3

Mike Gallego

GALLEGO, MICHAEL ANTHONY
B. Oct. 31, 1960, Whittier, Calif.

BR TR 5'8" 160 lbs.

Year	Team	Games	BA	SA	AB	H	2B	3B	HR	HR%	R	RBI	BB	SO	SB	PH AB	PH H	PO	A	E	DP	TC/G	FA	G by Pos
1985	OAK A	76	.208	.338	77	16	5	1	1	1.3	13	9	12	14	1	2	0	57	94	1	25	2.0	.993	2B-42, SS-21, 3B-12
1986		20	.270	.324	37	10	2	0	0	0.0	2	4	1	9	0	0	0	24	51	1	6	3.8	.987	2B-19, 3B-2, SS-1
1987		72	.250	.347	124	31	6	0	2	1.6	18	14	12	21	0	4	1	75	122	8	29	2.8	.961	2B-31, 3B-24, SS-17
1988		129	.209	.260	277	58	8	0	2	0.7	38	20	34	53	2	3	0	155	254	8	49	2.8	.981	2B-83, SS-42, 3B-16
1989		133	.252	.328	357	90	14	2	3	0.8	45	30	35	43	7	2	0	211	363	19	86	3.2	.981	SS-94, 2B-41, 3B-3
5 yrs.		430	.235	.310	872	205	35	3	8	0.9	116	77	94	137	10	11	1	522	884	37	195	3.4	.974	2B-216, SS-175, 3B-57, DH-1

LEAGUE CHAMPIONSHIP SERIES

Year	Team	Games	BA	SA	AB	H	2B	3B	HR	HR%	R	RBI	BB	SO	SB	PH AB	PH H	PO	A	E	DP	TC/G	FA	G by Pos
1988	OAK A	4	.083	.083	12	1	0	0	0	0.0	1	0	0	3	0	0	0	7	6	0	4	3.3	1.000	2B-4

Year	Team	Games	BA	SA	AB	H	2B	3B	HR	HR%	R	RBI	BB	SO	SB	Pinch Hit AB	H	PO	A	E	DP	TC/G	FA	G by Pos

Mike Gallego *continued*

| 1989 | | 4 | .273 | .364 | 11 | 3 | 1 | 0 | 0 | 0.0 | 3 | 1 | 0 | 2 | 0 | 0 | 0 | 6 | 14 | 0 | 2 | 5.0 | 1.000 | SS-2, 2B-2 |
| 2 yrs. | | 8 | .174 | .217 | 23 | 4 | 1 | 0 | 0 | 0.0 | 4 | 1 | 0 | 5 | 0 | 0 | 0 | 13 | 20 | 0 | 6 | 4.1 | 1.000 | 2B-6, SS-2 |

WORLD SERIES

1988	OAK A	1	–	–	0	0	0	0	0	–	0	0	0	0	0	0	0	0	0	0	0	0.0	–	2B-1
1989		2	.000	.000	1	0	0	0	0	0.0	0	0	0	0	0	1	0	0	0	0	0	0.0	–	3B-1, 2B-1
2 yrs.		3	.000	.000	1	0	0	0	0	0.0	0	0	0	0	0	1	0	0	0	0	0	0.0	–	2B-2, 3B-1

John Galligan

GALLIGAN, JOHN T.
B. 1868, Easton, Pa.   D. July 17, 1906, New York, N. Y.

5'10''   160 lbs.

| 1889 | LOU AA | 31 | .167 | .200 | 120 | 20 | 0 | 2 | 0 | 0.0 | 6 | 7 | 6 | 17 | 1 | 0 | 0 | 58 | 7 | 6 | 1 | 2.3 | .915 | OF-31 |

Bad News Galloway

GALLOWAY, JAMES CATO
B. Sept. 16, 1887, Iredell, Tex.   D. May 3, 1950, Fort Worth, Tex.

BB TR 6'3''   187 lbs.

| 1912 | STL N | 21 | .185 | .222 | 54 | 10 | 2 | 0 | 0 | 0.0 | 4 | 4 | 5 | 8 | 2 | 3 | 0 | 27 | 46 | 2 | 5 | 3.6 | .973 | 2B-16, SS-1 |

Chick Galloway

GALLOWAY, CLARENCE EDWARD
B. Aug. 4, 1896, Clinton, S. C.   D. Nov. 7, 1969, Clinton, S. C.

BR TR 5'8''   160 lbs.

1919	PHI A	17	.143	.143	63	9	0	0	0	0.0	2	4	1	8	0	0	0	45	49	3	11	5.7	.969	SS-17
1920		98	.201	.252	298	60	9	3	0	0.0	28	18	22	22	2	6	0	200	265	35	29	5.1	.930	SS-84, 2B-4, 3B-3
1921		131	.265	.366	465	123	28	5	3	0.6	42	47	29	43	12	0	0	226	355	48	52	4.8	.924	SS-110, 3B-20, 2B-1
1922		155	.324	.433	571	185	26	9	6	1.1	83	69	39	38	10	0	0	321	493	41	76	5.5	.952	SS-155
1923		134	.278	.361	504	140	18	9	2	0.4	64	62	37	30	12	0	0	285	408	41	73	5.5	.944	SS-134
1924		129	.276	.341	464	128	16	4	2	0.4	41	48	23	23	11	0	0	285	389	34	71	5.5	.952	SS-129
1925		149	.241	.299	481	116	11	4	3	0.6	52	71	59	28	16	1	0	296	431	35	89	5.1	.954	SS-148
1926		133	.240	.301	408	98	13	6	0	0.0	37	49	31	20	8	0	0	274	315	41	49	4.7	.935	SS-133
1927		77	.265	.365	181	48	10	4	0	0.0	15	22	18	9	1	9	6	119	157	15	20	3.8	.948	SS-61, 3B-7
1928	DET A	53	.264	.345	148	39	5	2	1	0.7	17	17	15	3	7	4	2	76	92	11	14	3.4	.939	SS-22, 3B-21, OF-1, 1B-1
10 yrs.		1076	.264	.342	3583	946	136	46	17	0.5	381	407	274	224	79	20	8	2127	2954	304	484	5.0	.944	SS-993, 3B-51, 2B-5, OF-1, 1B-1

Jim Galvin

GALVIN, JAMES JOSEPH
B. Aug. 11, 1907, Somerville, Mass.   D. Sept. 30, 1969, Marietta, Ga.

BR TR 5'11½''   198 lbs.

| 1930 | BOS A | 2 | .000 | .000 | 2 | 0 | 0 | 0 | 0 | 0.0 | 0 | 0 | 0 | 0 | 0 | 2 | 0 | 0 | 0 | 0 | 0 | 0.0 | – | |

Pud Galvin

GALVIN, JAMES FRANCIS (Gentle Jeems, The Little Steam Engine)
B. Dec. 25, 1856, St. Louis, Mo.   D. Mar. 7, 1902, Pittsburgh, Pa.
Manager 1885.
Hall of Fame 1965.

BR TR 5'8''   190 lbs.

1879	BUF N	67	.249	.336	265	66	11	6	0	0.0	34	27	1	**56**		0	0	36	143	27	8	3.1	.869	P-66, SS-1
1880		66	.212	.266	241	51	9	2	0	0.0	25	12	5	**57**		0	0	44	100	21	1	2.5	.873	P-58, OF-19
1881		62	.212	.297	236	50	12	4	0	0.0	19	21	3	**70**		0	0	52	126	22	7	3.2	.890	P-56, OF-14, SS-1
1882		54	.214	.286	206	44	7	4	0	0.0	21		2	49		0	0	22	87	9	1	2.2	.924	P-52, OF-6
1883		80	.220	.276	322	71	11	2	1	0.3	41		3	**79**		0	0	45	130	13	4	2.4	.931	P-76, OF-8
1884		72	.179	.208	274	49	6	1	0	0.0	34		2	80		0	0	32	154	7	3	2.7	.964	P-72, OF-1
1885	2 teams		BUF N (33G – .189)		PIT AA (11G – .105)																			
"	total	44	.169	.238	160	27	4	2	0	0.6	16	10	1	27		0	0	21	98	17	3	3.1	.875	P-44, OF-1
1886	PIT AA	50	.253	.309	194	49	7	2	0	0.0	24		3			0	0	22	101	8	3	2.6	.939	P-50
1887	PIT N	49	.212	.311	193	41	7	3	2	1.0	10	22	1	47	5	0	0	22	123	11	2	3.2	.929	P-49, OF-1
1888		50	.143	.177	175	25	1	1	0	0.6	6	3	1	51	4	0	0	23	113	10	2	2.9	.932	P-50, OF-1
1889		41	.187	.260	150	28	7	2	0	0.0	15	16	3	46	2	0	0	20	72	11	6	2.5	.893	P-41
1890	PIT P	26	.206	.247	97	20	2	1	0	0.0	8	12	6	20	1	0	0	22	71	7	1	3.8	.930	P-26
1891	PIT N	33	.165	.165	109	18	0	0	0	0.0	11	7	3	29	2	0	0	20	52	8	1	2.4	.900	P-33
1892	2 teams		PIT N (12G – .122)		STL N (12G – .051)																			
"	total	24	.088	.100	80	7	1	0	0	0.0	6	5	3	19	0	0	0	7	35	7	1	2.0	.857	P-24
14 yrs.		718	.202	.261	2702	546	85	30	5	0.2	270	135	38	630	12	0	0	388	1405	178	43	2.7	.910	P-697, OF-51, SS-2

John Gamble

GAMBLE, JOHN ROBERT JR.
B. Feb. 10, 1948, Reno, Nev.

BR TR 5'10''   165 lbs.

1972	DET A	6	.000	.000	3	0	0	0	0	0.0	0	0	0	0	0	1	0	3	2	0	0	0.8	1.000	SS-1
1973		7	–	–	0	0	0	0	0	–	1	0	0	0	0	0	0	0	0	0	0	0.0	–	
2 yrs.		13	.000	.000	3	0	0	0	0	0.0	1	0	0	0	0	1	0	3	2	0	0	0.4	1.000	SS-1

Lee Gamble

GAMBLE, LEE JESSE
B. June 28, 1910, Renovo, Pa.

BL TR 6'1''   170 lbs.

1935	CIN N	2	.500	.750	4	2	1	0	0	0.0	2	2	1	0	1	0	0	3	0	0	0	1.5	1.000	OF-2
1938		53	.320	.387	75	24	3	1	0	0.0	13	5	0	6	0	37	11	20	0	0	0	0.4	1.000	OF-9
1939		72	.267	.317	221	59	7	2	0	0.0	24	14	9	14	5	11	1	87	5	1	0	1.3	.989	OF-56
1940		38	.143	.167	42	6	1	0	0	0.0	12	0	1	0	0	9	2	18	1	0	0	0.5	1.000	OF-10
4 yrs.		165	.266	.319	342	91	12	3	0	0.0	51	21	10	21	6	57	14	128	6	1	0	0.8	.993	OF-77

WORLD SERIES

| 1939 | CIN N | 1 | .000 | .000 | 1 | 0 | 0 | 0 | 0 | 0.0 | 0 | 0 | 0 | 1 | 0 | 1 | 0 | 0 | 0 | 0 | 0 | 0.0 | – | |

Oscar Gamble

GAMBLE, OSCAR CHARLES
B. Dec. 20, 1949, Ramer, Ala.

BL TR 5'11''   160 lbs.

1969	CHI N	24	.225	.310	71	16	1	1	1	1.4	6	5	10	12	0	0	0	41	1	4	0	1.9	.913	OF-24
1970	PHI N	88	.262	.345	275	72	12	4	1	0.4	31	19	27	37	5	14	4	148	4	7	0	1.8	.956	OF-74
1971		92	.221	.332	280	62	11	1	6	2.1	24	23	21	35	5	13	4	125	4	4	1	1.4	.970	OF-80
1972		74	.237	.326	135	32	5	2	1	0.7	17	13	19	16	0	30	9	54	2	0	1	0.8	1.000	OF-35, 1B-1

Year	Team	Games	BA	SA	AB	H	2B	3B	HR	HR%	R	RBI	BB	SO	SB	Pinch Hit AB	Pinch Hit H	PO	A	E	DP	TC/G	FA	G by Pos

Oscar Gamble *continued*

Year	Team	Games	BA	SA	AB	H	2B	3B	HR	HR%	R	RBI	BB	SO	SB	Pinch Hit AB	Pinch Hit H	PO	A	E	DP	TC/G	FA	G by Pos
1973	CLE A	113	.267	.464	390	104	11	3	20	5.1	56	44	34	37	3	8	2	67	1	2	0	0.6	.971	DH-70, OF-37
1974		135	.291	.469	454	132	16	4	19	4.2	74	59	48	51	5	7	0	19	1	0	0	0.1	1.000	DH-115, OF-13
1975		121	.261	.454	348	91	16	3	15	4.3	60	45	53	39	11	11	2	146	8	2	2	1.3	.987	OF-82, DH-29
1976	NY A	110	.232	.426	340	79	13	1	17	5.0	43	57	38	38	5	16	6	199	10	4	3	1.9	.981	OF-104, DH-1
1977	CHI A	137	.297	.588	408	121	22	2	31	7.6	75	83	54	54	1	18	8	73	1	1	0	0.5	.987	DH-79, OF-49
1978	SD N	126	.275	.387	375	103	15	3	7	1.9	46	47	51	45	1	13	6	172	12	4	3	1.5	.979	OF-107
1979	2 teams	TEX A (64G – .335)			NY A (36G – .389)																			
"	total	100	.358	.609	274	98	10	1	19	6.9	48	64	50	28	2	18	5	88	5	3	4	1.0	.969	OF-48, DH-43
1980	NY A	78	.278	.567	194	54	10	2	14	7.2	40	50	28	21	2	17	4	65	2	0	1	0.9	1.000	OF-49, DH-20
1981		80	.238	.439	189	45	8	0	10	5.3	24	27	35	23	0	15	5	77	0	0	0	1.0	1.000	OF-43, DH-33
1982		108	.272	.522	316	86	21	2	18	5.7	49	57	58	47	6	18	2	59	6	0	1	0.6	1.000	DH-74, OF-29
1983		74	.261	.456	180	47	10	2	7	3.9	26	26	25	23	0	20	6	64	1	4	1	0.9	.942	OF-32, DH-21
1984		54	.184	.440	125	23	2	0	10	8.0	17	27	25	18	1	13	1	15	1	0	0	0.3	1.000	DH-26, OF-12
1985	CHI A	70	.203	.318	148	30	5	0	4	2.7	20	20	34	22	0	24	3	0	0	0	0	0.0	–	DH-48
17 yrs.		1584	.265	.454	4502	1195	188	31	200	4.4	656	666	610	546	47	255	67	1412	59	35	17	1.0	.977	OF-818, DH-559, 1B-1
DIVISIONAL PLAYOFF SERIES																								
1981	NY A	4	.556	1.333	9	5	1	0	2	22.2	2	3	1	2	0	1	1	0	0	0	0	0.0	–	DH-4
LEAGUE CHAMPIONSHIP SERIES																								
1976	NY A	3	.250	.375	8	2	1	0	0	0.0	1	1	1	1	0	1	1	4	0	2	0	2.0	.667	OF-3
1980		2	.200	.200	5	1	0	0	0	0.0	1	0	1	1	0	1	1	1	0	0	0	0.5	1.000	DH-1, OF-1
1981		3	.167	.167	6	1	0	0	0	0.0	2	1	5	3	0	0	0	0	0	0	0	0.0	–	DH-2, OF-1
3 yrs.		8	.211	.263	19	4	1	0	0	0.0	4	2	7	5	0	2	2	5	0	2	0	0.9	.714	OF-5, DH-3
WORLD SERIES																								
1976	NY A	3	.125	.125	8	1	0	0	0	0.0	0	1	0	0	0	1	0	3	0	0	0	1.0	1.000	OF-2
1981		3	.333	.333	6	2	0	0	0	0.0	1	1	1	0	0	0	0	4	0	0	0	1.3	1.000	OF-2
2 yrs.		6	.214	.214	14	3	0	0	0	0.0	1	2	1	0	0	1	0	7	0	0	0	1.2	1.000	OF-4

Daff Gammons

GAMMONS, JOHN ASHLEY
B. Mar. 17, 1876, New Bedford, Mass. D. Sept. 24, 1963, East Greenwich, R. I.
BR TR 5'11" 170 lbs.

Year	Team	Games	BA	SA	AB	H	2B	3B	HR	HR%	R	RBI	BB	SO	SB	Pinch Hit AB	Pinch Hit H	PO	A	E	DP	TC/G	FA	G by Pos
1901	BOS N	28	.194	.215	93	18	0	1	0	0.0	10	10	3		5	1	0	44	8	11	1	2.3	.825	OF-23, 2B-2, 3B-1

Chick Gandil

GANDIL, CHARLES ARNOLD
B. Jan. 19, 1887, St. Paul, Minn. D. Dec. 13, 1970, Calistoga, Calif.
BR TR 6'1½" 190 lbs.

Year	Team	Games	BA	SA	AB	H	2B	3B	HR	HR%	R	RBI	BB	SO	SB	Pinch Hit AB	Pinch Hit H	PO	A	E	DP	TC/G	FA	G by Pos
1910	CHI A	77	.193	.262	275	53	7	3	2	0.7	21	21	24		12	0	0	857	57	10	34	12.0	.989	1B-74, OF-2
1912	WAS A	117	.305	.431	443	135	20	15	2	0.5	59	81	27		21	0	0	1106	68	12	49	10.1	.990	1B-117
1913		148	.318	.398	550	175	25	8	1	0.2	61	72	36	33	22	3	0	1436	103	15	89	10.5	.990	1B-145
1914		145	.259	.359	526	136	24	10	3	0.6	48	75	44	44	30	0	0	1284	143	13	84	9.9	.991	1B-145
1915		136	.291	.406	485	141	20	15	2	0.4	53	64	29	33	20	2	1	1237	77	19	65	9.8	.986	1B-134
1916	CLE A	146	.259	.341	533	138	26	9	0	0.0	51	72	36	48	13	1	1	1557	105	9	84	11.4	.995	1B-145
1917	CHI A	149	.273	.315	553	151	9	7	0	0.0	53	57	30	36	16	0	0	1405	77	8	84	10.0	.995	1B-149
1918		114	.271	.330	439	119	18	4	0	0.0	49	55	27	19	9	0	0	1123	64	10	70	10.5	.992	1B-114
1919		115	.290	.383	441	128	24	7	1	0.2	54	60	20	20	10	0	0	1116	60	3	71	10.3	.997	1B-115
9 yrs.		1147	.277	.362	4245	1176	173	78	11	0.3	449	557	273	233	153	6	2	11121	754	99	630	10.4	.992	1B-1138, OF-2
WORLD SERIES																								
1917	CHI A	6	.261	.304	23	6	1	0	0	0.0	1	5	0	2	1	0	0	67	4	1	6	12.0	.986	1B-6
1919		8	.233	.300	30	7	0	1	0	0.0	1	5	1	3	1	0	0	79	2	1	6	10.3	.988	1B-8
2 yrs.		14	.245	.302	53	13	1	1	0	0.0	2	10	1	5	2	0	0	146	6	2	12	11.0	.987	1B-14

Bob Gandy

GANDY, ROBERT BRINKLEY (String)
B. Aug. 25, 1893, Jacksonville, Fla. D. June 19, 1945, Jacksonville, Fla.
BL TR 6'3" 180 lbs.

Year	Team	Games	BA	SA	AB	H	2B	3B	HR	HR%	R	RBI	BB	SO	SB	Pinch Hit AB	Pinch Hit H	PO	A	E	DP	TC/G	FA	G by Pos
1916	PHI N	1	.000	.000	2	0	0	0	0	0.0	0	0	0	1	0	0	0	3	0	0	0	3.0	1.000	OF-1

Bob Ganley

GANLEY, ROBERT STEPHEN
B. Apr. 23, 1875, Lowell, Mass. D. Oct. 9, 1945, Lowell, Mass.
BL TL 5'7" 156 lbs.

Year	Team	Games	BA	SA	AB	H	2B	3B	HR	HR%	R	RBI	BB	SO	SB	Pinch Hit AB	Pinch Hit H	PO	A	E	DP	TC/G	FA	G by Pos
1905	PIT N	32	.315	.354	127	40	1	2	0	0.0	12	7	8		3	0	0	46	3	0	0	1.5	1.000	OF-32
1906		137	.258	.295	511	132	7	6	0	0.0	63	31	41		19	3	1	207	16	8	5	1.7	.965	OF-134
1907	WAS A	154	.276	.314	605	167	10	5	1	0.2	73	35	54		40	0	0	276	23	19	5	2.1	.940	OF-154
1908		150	.239	.311	549	131	19	9	1	0.2	61	36	45		30	0	0	280	13	11	1	2.0	.964	OF-150
1909	2 teams	WAS A (19G – .254)			PHI A (80G – .197)																			
"	total	99	.208	.240	337	70	7	2	0	0.0	37	14	29		20	4	0	214	9	4	2	2.3	.982	OF-94
5 yrs.		572	.254	.300	2129	540	44	24	2	0.1	246	123	177		112	7	1	1023	64	42	13	2.0	.963	OF-564

Bill Gannon

GANNON, WILLIAM G.
B. 1876, New Haven, Conn. D. Apr. 26, 1927, Ft. Worth, Tex.

Year	Team	Games	BA	SA	AB	H	2B	3B	HR	HR%	R	RBI	BB	SO	SB	Pinch Hit AB	Pinch Hit H	PO	A	E	DP	TC/G	FA	G by Pos
1898	STL N	1	.000	.000	3	0	0	0	0	0.0	0	0	0		0	0	0	0	2	0	0	2.0	1.000	P-1
1901	CHI N	15	.148	.148	61	9	0	0	0	0.0	2	0	1		5	0	0	16	2	0	0	1.2	1.000	OF-15
2 yrs.		16	.141	.141	64	9	0	0	0	0.0	2	0	1		5	0	0	16	4	0	0	1.3	1.000	OF-15, P-1

Ron Gant

GANT, RONALD EDWIN
B. Mar. 2, 1965, Victoria, Tex.
BR TR 6' 172 lbs.

Year	Team	Games	BA	SA	AB	H	2B	3B	HR	HR%	R	RBI	BB	SO	SB	Pinch Hit AB	Pinch Hit H	PO	A	E	DP	TC/G	FA	G by Pos
1987	ATL N	21	.265	.386	83	22	4	0	2	2.4	9	9	1	11	4	1	0	45	59	3	17	5.1	.972	2B-20
1988		146	.259	.439	563	146	28	8	19	3.4	85	60	46	118	19	2	0	316	417	31	88	5.2	.959	2B-122, 3B-22
1989		75	.177	.335	260	46	8	3	9	3.5	26	25	20	63	9	8	1	70	103	17	8	2.5	.911	3B-53, OF-14
3 yrs.		242	.236	.404	906	214	40	11	30	3.3	120	94	67	192	32	11	1	431	579	51	113	4.4	.952	2B-142, 3B-75, OF-14

Joe Gantenbein

GANTENBEIN, JOSEPH STEPHEN (Sep)
B. Aug. 25, 1916, San Francisco, Calif.
BL TR 5'9" 168 lbs.

Year	Team	Games	BA	SA	AB	H	2B	3B	HR	HR%	R	RBI	BB	SO	SB	Pinch Hit AB	Pinch Hit H	PO	A	E	DP	TC/G	FA	G by Pos
1939	PHI A	111	.290	.388	348	101	14	4	4	1.1	47	36	32	22	1	16	6	178	203	23	30	3.6	.943	2B-76, 3B-14, SS-5

Year	Team	Games	BA	SA	AB	H	2B	3B	HR	HR%	R	RBI	BB	SO	SB	Pinch Hit AB	Pinch Hit H	PO	A	E	DP	TC/G	FA	G by Pos

Joe Gantenbein *continued*

Year	Team	Games	BA	SA	AB	H	2B	3B	HR	HR%	R	RBI	BB	SO	SB	AB	H	PO	A	E	DP	TC/G	FA	G by Pos
1940		75	.239	.350	197	47	6	2	4	2.0	21	23	11	21	1	18	4	57	78	8	11	1.9	.944	3B-45, 1B-6, SS-3, OF-1
2 yrs.		186	.272	.374	545	148	20	6	8	1.5	68	59	43	43	2	34	10	235	281	31	41	2.9	.943	2B-76, 3B-59, SS-8, 1B-6, OF-1

Jim Gantner

GANTNER, JAMES ELMER
B. Jan. 5, 1953, Fond du Lac, Wis.

BL TR 6' 180 lbs.

Year	Team	Games	BA	SA	AB	H	2B	3B	HR	HR%	R	RBI	BB	SO	SB	AB	H	PO	A	E	DP	TC/G	FA	G by Pos
1976	MIL A	26	.246	.261	69	17	1	0	0	0.0	6	7	6	11	1	1	0	17	37	1	3	2.1	.982	3B-24, DH-2
1977		14	.298	.383	47	14	1	0	1	2.1	4	2	2	5	2	1	1	8	29	4	3	2.9	.902	3B-14
1978		43	.216	.258	97	21	1	0	1	1.0	14	8	5	10	2	4	1	46	82	5	13	3.1	.962	2B-21, 3B-15, SS-1, 1B-1
1979		70	.284	.389	208	59	10	3	2	1.0	29	22	16	17	3	0	0	80	161	7	26	3.5	.972	3B-42, 2B-22, SS-3, P-1
1980		132	.282	.376	415	117	21	3	4	1.0	47	40	30	29	11	2	0	159	335	15	70	3.9	.971	3B-69, 2B-66, SS-1
1981		107	.267	.330	352	94	14	1	2	0.6	35	33	29	29	3	3	0	251	352	10	95	5.7	.984	2B-107
1982		132	.295	.369	447	132	17	2	4	0.9	48	43	26	36	6	4	1	307	398	13	104	5.4	.982	2B-131
1983		161	.282	.401	603	170	23	8	11	1.8	85	74	38	46	5	3	0	374	512	14	128	5.6	.984	2B-158
1984		153	.282	.344	613	173	27	1	3	0.5	61	56	30	51	6	2	1	362	469	13	111	5.5	.985	2B-153
1985		143	.254	.327	523	133	15	4	5	1.0	63	44	33	42	11	1	1	278	436	11	94	5.1	.985	2B-124, 3B-24, SS-1
1986		139	.274	.370	497	136	25	1	7	1.4	58	38	26	50	13	2	0	309	353	10	87	4.8	.985	2B-135, 3B-3, DH-1, SS-1
1987		81	.272	.370	265	72	14	1	4	1.5	37	30	19	22	6	3	1	119	193	6	44	3.9	.981	2B-57, 3B-38, DH-1
1988		155	.276	.336	539	149	28	2	0	0.0	67	47	34	50	20	2	1	325	430	11	92	4.9	.986	2B-154, 3B-1
1989		116	.274	.333	409	112	18	3	0	0.0	51	34	21	33	20	1	0	241	362	8	88	5.3	.987	2B-114, DH-2
14 yrs.		1472	.275	.354	5084	1399	215	28	44	0.9	605	478	315	431	109	29	7	2876	4149	128	958	4.9	.982	2B-1242, 3B-230, SS-7, DH-6, 1B-1, P-1

DIVISIONAL PLAYOFF SERIES

Year	Team	Games	BA	SA	AB	H	2B	3B	HR	HR%	R	RBI	BB	SO	SB	AB	H	PO	A	E	DP	TC/G	FA	G by Pos
1981	MIL A	4	.143	.214	14	2	1	0	0	0.0	1	0	0	2	0	0	0	0	2	0	0	0.5	–	2B-4

LEAGUE CHAMPIONSHIP SERIES

Year	Team	Games	BA	SA	AB	H	2B	3B	HR	HR%	R	RBI	BB	SO	SB	AB	H	PO	A	E	DP	TC/G	FA	G by Pos
1982	MIL A	5	.188	.188	16	3	0	0	0	0.0	1	2	1	1	0	0	0	0	0	0	0	0.0	–	2B-5

WORLD SERIES

Year	Team	Games	BA	SA	AB	H	2B	3B	HR	HR%	R	RBI	BB	SO	SB	AB	H	PO	A	E	DP	TC/G	FA	G by Pos
1982	MIL A	7	.333	.583	24	8	4	1	0	0.0	5	4	1	1	0	0	0	9	33	5	2	6.7	.894	2B-7

Babe Ganzel

GANZEL, FOSTER PIRIE
Son of Charlie Ganzel.
B. May 22, 1901, Malden, Mass. D. Feb. 6, 1978, Jacksonville, Fla.

BR TR 5'10½" 172 lbs.

Year	Team	Games	BA	SA	AB	H	2B	3B	HR	HR%	R	RBI	BB	SO	SB	AB	H	PO	A	E	DP	TC/G	FA	G by Pos
1927	WAS A	13	.438	.667	48	21	4	2	1	2.1	7	13	7	3	0	0	0	33	1	2	0	2.8	.944	OF-13
1928		10	.077	.115	26	2	1	0	0	0.0	2	4	1	4	0	3	0	10	1	0	0	1.1	1.000	OF-7
2 yrs.		23	.311	.473	74	23	5	2	1	1.4	9	17	8	7	0	3	0	43	2	2	0	2.0	.957	OF-20

Charlie Ganzel

GANZEL, CHARLES WILLIAM
Father of Babe Ganzel. Brother of John Ganzel.
B. June 18, 1862, Waterford, Wis. D. Apr. 7, 1914, Quincy, Mass.

BR TR 6'1" 188 lbs.

Year	Team	Games	BA	SA	AB	H	2B	3B	HR	HR%	R	RBI	BB	SO	SB	AB	H	PO	A	E	DP	TC/G	FA	G by Pos
1884	STP U	7	.217	.217	23	5	0	0	0	0.0	0					0	0	36	7	2	0	6.4	.956	C-6, OF-1
1885	PHI N	34	.168	.208	125	21	3	1	0	0.0	15		4	13		0	0	176	39	27	3	7.1	.888	C-33, OF-1
1886	2 teams		PHI N (1G – .000)			DET N (57G – .272)																		
"	total	58	.269	.333	216	58	7	2	1	0.5	28	31	7	23		0	0	333	67	39	12	7.6	.911	C-46, OF-7, 1B-5
1887	DET N	57	.260	.330	227	59	6	5	0	0.0	40	20	8	2	3	0	0	301	76	35	8	7.2	.915	C-51, OF-4, 1B-2, 3B-1
1888		95	.249	.316	386	96	13	5	1	0.3	45	46	14	15	12	0	0	288	241	52	24	6.1	.910	2B-49, C-28, 3B-9, OF-5, SS-3, 1B-1
1889	BOS N	73	.265	.324	275	73	3	5	1	0.4	30	43	15	11	13	0	0	292	87	30	19	5.6	.927	C-39, OF-26, 1B-7, SS-6, 3B-1
1890		38	.270	.350	163	44	7	3	0	0.0	21	24	5	6	1	0	0	151	42	8	11	5.3	.960	C-22, OF-15, SS-3, 2B-1
1891		70	.259	.376	263	68	18	5	1	0.4	33	29	12	13	7	0	0	304	61	16	3	5.4	.958	C-59, OF-13
1892		54	.268	.343	198	53	9	3	0	0.0	25	25	18	12	7	0	0	218	50	18	1	5.3	.937	C-51, OF-2, 1B-1
1893		73	.267	.327	281	75	10	2	1	0.4	50	48	22	9	6	1	0	278	49	15	14	4.7	.956	C-40, OF-23, 1B-10
1894		70	.278	.383	266	74	7	6	3	1.1	51	56	19	7	1	1	0	257	58	29	11	4.9	.916	C-59, 1B-7, OF-3, SS-2, 2B-1
1895		80	.264	.318	277	73	2	5	1	0.4	38	52	24	6	1	1	0	358	74	17	10	5.6	.962	C-76, SS-2, 1B-2
1896		47	.263	.291	179	47	2	0	1	0.6	28	18	9	5	2	1	1	170	50	8	6	4.9	.965	C-41, 1B-3, SS-2
1897		30	.267	.362	105	28	4	3	0	0.0	15	14	4		2	2	0	113	27	9	2	5.0	.940	C-27, 1B-2
14 yrs.		786	.259	.330	2984	774	91	45	10	0.3	421	406	161	121	55	6	1	3275	928	305	124	5.7	.932	C-578, OF-100, 2B-51, 1B-40, SS-18, 3B-11

John Ganzel

GANZEL, JOHN HENRY
Brother of Charlie Ganzel.
B. Apr. 7, 1874, Kalamazoo, Mich. D. Jan. 14, 1959, Orlando, Fla.
Manager 1908, 1915.

BR TR 6'½" 195 lbs.

Year	Team	Games	BA	SA	AB	H	2B	3B	HR	HR%	R	RBI	BB	SO	SB	AB	H	PO	A	E	DP	TC/G	FA	G by Pos
1898	PIT N	15	.133	.133	45	6	0	0	0	0.0	5	2	4		0	2	0	102	3	4	5	7.3	.963	1B-12, P-1
1900	CHI N	78	.275	.394	284	78	14	4	4	1.4	29	32	10		5	0	0	817	34	17	40	11.1	.980	1B-78
1901	NY N	138	.215	.262	526	113	13	3	2	0.4	42	66	20		6	0	0	1421	77	21	59	11.0	.986	1B-138
1903	NY A	129	.277	.378	476	132	25	7	3	0.6	62	71	30		9	0	0	1385	94	18	68	11.6	.988	1B-129
1904		130	.260	.376	465	121	16	10	6	1.3	50	48	24		13	4	2	1254	96	18	53	10.5	.987	1B-118, 2B-9, SS-1
1907	CIN N	145	.254	.363	531	135	20	16	2	0.4	61	64	29		9	2	0	1346	84	14	89	10.0	.990	1B-143
1908		112	.250	.351	388	97	16	10	1	0.3	32	53	19		6	5	1	1116	61	12	52	10.6	.990	1B-108
7 yrs.		747	.251	.346	2715	682	104	50	18	0.7	281	336	136		48	13	3	7441	449	104	366	10.7	.987	1B-726, 2B-9, SS-1, P-1

Joe Garagiola

GARAGIOLA, JOSEPH HENRY
B. Feb. 12, 1926, St. Louis, Mo.

BL TR 6' 190 lbs.

Year	Team	Games	BA	SA	AB	H	2B	3B	HR	HR%	R	RBI	BB	SO	SB	AB	H	PO	A	E	DP	TC/G	FA	G by Pos
1946	STL N	74	.237	.308	211	50	4	3	3	1.4	21	22	23	25	0	4	2	260	25	3	6	3.9	.990	C-70
1947		77	.257	.415	183	47	10	2	5	2.7	20	25	40	14	0	4	0	281	23	4	2	4.0	.987	C-74
1948		24	.107	.232	56	6	1	0	2	3.6	9	7	12	9	0	1	0	83	14	1	1	4.1	.990	C-23
1949		81	.261	.357	241	63	14	0	3	1.2	25	26	31	19	0	2	1	332	35	6	1	4.6	.984	C-80

Year	Team	Games	BA	SA	AB	H	2B	3B	HR	HR%	R	RBI	BB	SO	SB	Pinch Hit AB	Pinch Hit H	PO	A	E	DP	TC/G	FA	G by Pos

Joe Garagiola *continued*

Year	Team	Games	BA	SA	AB	H	2B	3B	HR	HR%	R	RBI	BB	SO	SB	AB	H	PO	A	E	DP	TC/G	FA	G by Pos
1950		34	.318	.477	88	28	6	1	2	2.3	8	20	10	7	0	4	0	99	8	0	2	3.1	1.000	C-30
1951	2 teams	STL N	(27G – .194)		PIT N	(72G – .255)																		
"	total	99	.239	.423	284	68	11	4	11	3.9	33	44	41	27	4	12	0	336	36	4	6	3.8	.989	C-84
1952	PIT N	118	.273	.410	344	94	15	4	8	2.3	35	54	50	24	0	12	4	418	63	11	9	4.2	.978	C-105
1953	2 teams	PIT N	(27G – .233)		CHI N	(74G – .272)																		
"	total	101	.262	.365	301	79	14	4	3	1.0	30	35	31	34	1	13	3	378	44	5	2	4.2	.988	C-90
1954	2 teams	CHI N	(63G – .281)		NY N	(5G – .273)																		
"	total	68	.280	.415	164	46	7	0	5	3.0	17	22	29	14	0	11	2	208	23	4	0	3.5	.983	C-58
9 yrs.		676	.257	.385	1872	481	82	16	42	2.2	198	255	267	173	5	63	13	2395	271	38	29	4.0	.986	C-614

WORLD SERIES

| 1946 | STL N | 5 | .316 | .421 | 19 | 6 | 2 | 0 | 0 | 0.0 | 2 | 4 | 0 | 3 | 0 | 0 | 0 | 22 | 2 | 0 | 1 | 4.8 | 1.000 | C-5 |

Bob Garbark

GARBARK, ROBERT MICHAEL
Born Robert Michael Garbach. Brother of Mike Garbark.
B. Nov. 13, 1909, Houston, Tex.

BR TR 5'11" 178 lbs.

1934	CLE A	5	.000	.000	11	0	0	0	0	0.0	1	0	1	3	0	1	0	8	0	0	0	1.6	1.000	C-5
1935		6	.333	.389	18	6	1	0	0	0.0	4	4	5	1	0	0	0	33	3	0	0	6.0	1.000	C-6
1937	CHI N	1	.000	.000	1	0	0	0	0	0.0	0	0	0	0	0	0	0	0	0	0	0	0.0	–	
1938		23	.259	.259	54	14	0	0	0	0.0	2	5	1	0	0	1	0	66	7	0	0	3.2	1.000	C-20, 1B-1
1939		24	.143	.143	21	3	0	0	0	0.0	1	0	3	0	0	2	0	22	3	0	0	1.0	1.000	C-21
1944	PHI A	18	.261	.348	23	6	2	0	0	0.0	2	2	1	0	0	3	0	23	1	0	0	1.3	1.000	C-15
1945	BOS A	68	.261	.291	199	52	6	0	0	0.0	21	17	18	10	0	1	0	249	31	2	9	4.1	.993	C-67
7 yrs.		145	.248	.275	327	81	9	0	0	0.0	31	28	26	17	0	8	0	401	45	2	9	3.1	.996	C-134, 1B-1

Mike Garbark

GARBARK, MICHAEL NATHANIEL
Born Michael Nathanial Garbach. Brother of Bob Garbark.
B. Feb. 2, 1916, Houston, Tex.

BR TR 6' 200 lbs.

1944	NY A	89	.261	.328	299	78	9	4	1	0.3	23	33	25	27	0	4	1	372	47	5	9	4.8	.988	C-85
1945		60	.216	.295	176	38	5	3	1	0.6	23	26	23	12	0	1	0	202	41	7	10	4.2	.972	C-59
2 yrs.		149	.244	.316	475	116	14	7	2	0.4	46	59	48	39	0	5	1	574	88	12	19	4.5	.982	C-144

Barbaro Garbey

GARBEY, BARBARO
Born Barbaro Garbey y Garbey.
B. Dec. 4, 1956, Santiago, Cuba

BR TR 5'10" 170 lbs.

1984	DET A	110	.287	.391	327	94	17	1	5	1.5	45	52	17	35	6	25	8	411	58	12	53	4.4	.975	1B-65, 3B-20, DH-18, OF-10, 2B-3
1985		86	.257	.380	237	61	9	1	6	2.5	27	29	15	37	3	20	3	228	20	3	24	2.9	.988	1B-37, OF-24, DH-21, 3B-1
1988	TEX A	30	.194	.226	62	12	2	0	0	0.0	4	5	4	11	0	10	3	45	8	1	3	1.8	.981	OF-8, 1B-7, 3B-3
3 yrs.		226	.267	.371	626	167	28	2	11	1.8	76	86	36	83	9	55	14	684	86	16	80	3.5	.980	1B-109, OF-42, DH-39, 3B-24, 2B-3

LEAGUE CHAMPIONSHIP SERIES

| 1984 | DET A | 3 | .333 | .333 | 9 | 3 | 0 | 0 | 0 | 0.0 | 1 | 0 | 1 | 0 | 1 | 0 | 0 | 0 | 0 | 0 | 0 | 0.0 | – | DH-2 |

WORLD SERIES

| 1984 | DET A | 4 | .000 | .000 | 12 | 0 | 0 | 0 | 0 | 0.0 | 0 | 0 | 0 | 2 | 0 | 1 | 0 | 0 | 0 | 0 | 0 | 0.0 | – | DH-3 |

Alex Garbowski

GARBOWSKI, ALEXANDER
B. June 25, 1925, Yonkers, N. Y.

BR TR 6'1" 185 lbs.

| 1952 | DET A | 2 | – | – | 0 | 0 | 0 | 0 | 0 | – | 0 | 0 | 0 | 0 | 0 | 0 | 0 | 0 | 0 | 0 | 0 | 0.0 | – | |

Chico Garcia

GARCIA, VINCIO
Born Vincio Garcia y Uzcanga.
B. Dec. 24, 1924, Veracruz, Mexico

BR TR 5'8" 170 lbs.

| 1954 | BAL A | 39 | .113 | .177 | 62 | 7 | 0 | 2 | 0 | 0.0 | 6 | 5 | 8 | 3 | 0 | 5 | 1 | 57 | 44 | 4 | 15 | 2.7 | .962 | 2B-24 |

Damaso Garcia

GARCIA, DAMASO DOMINGO
Born Damaso Domingo Garcia y Sanchez.
B. Feb. 7, 1957, Moca, Dominican Republic

BR TR 6'1" 165 lbs.

1978	NY A	18	.195	.195	41	8	0	0	0	0.0	5	1	2	6	1	0	0	36	35	4	10	4.2	.947	2B-16, SS-3
1979		11	.263	.289	38	10	1	0	0	0.0	3	4	0	2	2	0	0	9	28	4	4	3.7	.902	SS-10, 3B-1
1980	TOR A	140	.278	.381	543	151	30	7	4	0.7	50	46	12	55	13	2	0	316	471	16	112	5.7	.980	2B-138, DH-1
1981		64	.252	.304	250	63	8	1	1	0.4	24	13	9	32	13	1	0	132	181	9	32	5.0	.972	2B-62, DH-1
1982		147	.310	.399	597	185	32	3	5	0.8	89	42	21	44	54	0	0	273	461	15	94	5.1	.980	2B-141, DH-4
1983		131	.307	.390	525	161	23	6	3	0.6	84	38	24	34	31	2	0	266	360	12	75	4.9	.981	2B-130
1984		152	.284	.374	633	180	32	5	5	0.8	79	46	16	46	46	2	2	267	427	14	95	4.7	.980	2B-149, DH-1
1985		146	.282	.377	600	169	25	4	8	1.3	70	65	15	41	28	4	1	302	371	13	88	4.7	.981	2B-143
1986		122	.281	.375	424	119	22	0	6	1.4	57	46	13	32	9	5	3	225	286	8	66	4.3	.985	2B-106, DH-11, 1B-1
1988	ATL N	21	.117	.183	60	7	1	0	1	1.7	3	4	3	10	1	8	1	26	35	1	5	3.0	.984	2B-13
1989	MON N	80	.271	.369	203	55	9	1	3	1.5	26	18	15	20	5	26	4	86	157	7	25	3.1	.972	2B-62, 3B-1
11 yrs.		1032	.283	.371	3914	1108	183	27	36	0.9	490	323	130	322	203	50	11	1938	2812	103	606	4.7	.979	2B-960, DH-18, SS-13, 3B-2, 1B-1

LEAGUE CHAMPIONSHIP SERIES

| 1985 | TOR A | 7 | .233 | .367 | 30 | 7 | 4 | 0 | 0 | 0.0 | 4 | 1 | 3 | 3 | 0 | 0 | 0 | 10 | 10 | 0 | 3 | 2.9 | 1.000 | 2B-7 |

Danny Garcia

GARCIA, DANIEL RAPHAEL
B. Apr. 29, 1954, Brooklyn, N. Y.

BL TL 6'1" 182 lbs.

| 1981 | KC A | 12 | .143 | .143 | 14 | 2 | 0 | 0 | 0 | 0.0 | 4 | 0 | 0 | 2 | 0 | 1 | 0 | 7 | 0 | 0 | 0 | 0.6 | 1.000 | OF-6, 1B-2 |

Year	Team	Games	BA	SA	AB	H	2B	3B	HR	HR%	R	RBI	BB	SO	SB	Pinch Hit AB	Pinch Hit H	PO	A	E	DP	TC/G	FA	G by Pos

Kiko Garcia

GARCIA, ALFONSO RAFAEL
B. Oct. 14, 1953, Martinez, Calif.
BR TR 5'11" 180 lbs.

Year	Team	Games	BA	SA	AB	H	2B	3B	HR	HR%	R	RBI	BB	SO	SB	PH AB	PH H	PO	A	E	DP	TC/G	FA	G by Pos
1976	BAL A	11	.219	.406	32	7	1	1	1	3.1	0	4	0	4	2	0	0	15	27	0	7	3.8	1.000	SS-11
1977		65	.221	.313	131	29	6	0	2	1.5	20	10	6	31	2	0	0	78	152	8	43	3.7	.966	SS-61
1978		79	.263	.339	186	49	6	4	0	0.0	17	13	7	43	7	3	1	87	175	16	35	3.5	.942	SS-74, 2B-3
1979		126	.247	.362	417	103	15	9	5	1.2	54	24	32	87	11	4	0	209	321	27	78	4.4	.952	SS-113, 2B-25, OF-2, 3B-2
1980		111	.199	.235	311	62	8	0	1	0.3	27	27	24	57	8	0	0	177	292	11	65	4.3	.977	SS-96, 2B-27, OF-1
1981	HOU N	48	.272	.331	136	37	6	1	0	0.0	9	15	10	16	2	2	1	58	119	11	14	3.9	.941	SS-28, 3B-13, 2B-9
1982		34	.211	.316	76	16	5	0	1	1.3	5	5	3	15	1	9	1	29	62	5	13	2.8	.948	SS-21, 3B-2, 2B-1
1983	PHI N	84	.288	.415	118	34	7	1	2	1.7	22	9	9	20	1	2	0	94	115	6	18	2.6	.972	SS-30, 3B-23, 2B-1
1984		57	.233	.267	60	14	2	0	0	0.0	6	5	4	11	0	3	0	25	54	2	6	1.4	.975	SS-3, 3B-1
1985		4	.000	.000	3	0	0	0	0	0.0	0	0	0	1	0	0	0	0	2	0	0	0.5	1.000	SS-3, 3B-1
10 yrs.		619	.239	.323	1470	351	56	16	12	0.8	162	112	95	285	34	23	3	772	1319	86	279	3.5	.960	SS-459, 2B-118, 3B-51, OF-3

DIVISIONAL PLAYOFF SERIES

| 1981 | HOU N | 2 | .000 | .000 | 4 | 0 | 0 | 0 | 0 | 0.0 | 0 | 0 | 0 | 1 | 0 | 1 | 0 | 0 | 0 | 0 | 0 | 0.0 | — | SS-1 |

LEAGUE CHAMPIONSHIP SERIES

| 1979 | BAL A | 3 | .273 | .273 | 11 | 3 | 0 | 0 | 0 | 0.0 | 1 | 2 | 2 | 4 | 0 | 0 | 0 | 6 | 16 | 2 | 3 | 8.0 | .917 | SS-3 |

WORLD SERIES

| 1979 | BAL A | 6 | .400 | .600 | 20 | 8 | 2 | 1 | 0 | 0.0 | 4 | 6 | 1 | 3 | 0 | 0 | 0 | 10 | 17 | 1 | 2 | 4.7 | .964 | SS-6 |

Leo Garcia

GARCIA, LEONARDO ANTONIO
Born Leonardo Antonio Garcia y Peralta.
B. Nov. 6, 1962, Santiago, Dominican Republic
BL TL 5'8" 160 lbs.

Year	Team	Games	BA	SA	AB	H	2B	3B	HR	HR%	R	RBI	BB	SO	SB	PH AB	PH H	PO	A	E	DP	TC/G	FA	G by Pos
1987	CIN N	31	.200	.300	30	6	0	1	1	3.3	8	2	4	8	3	9	2	19	0	0	0	0.6	1.000	OF-14
1988		23	.143	.179	28	4	1	0	0	0.0	2	0	4	5	0	12	3	12	0	0	0	0.5	1.000	OF-9
2 yrs.		54	.172	.241	58	10	1	1	1	1.7	10	2	8	13	3	21	5	31	0	0	0	0.6	1.000	OF-23

Pedro Garcia

GARCIA, PEDRO MODESTO
Born Pedro Modesto Garcia y Delfi.
B. Apr. 17, 1950, Guayama, Puerto Rico
BR TR 5'10" 175 lbs.

Year	Team	Games	BA	SA	AB	H	2B	3B	HR	HR%	R	RBI	BB	SO	SB	PH AB	PH H	PO	A	E	DP	TC/G	FA	G by Pos
1973	MIL A	160	.245	.395	580	142	**32**	5	15	2.6	67	54	40	119	11	0	0	405	470	27	111	5.6	.970	2B-160
1974		141	.199	.330	452	90	15	4	12	2.7	46	54	26	67	8	0	0	382	365	23	102	5.5	.970	2B-140
1975		98	.225	.348	302	68	15	2	6	2.0	40	38	18	59	12	1	0	230	293	8	67	5.4	.985	2B-94, DH-1
1976	2 teams	MIL A (41G – .217)			DET A	(77G – .198)																		
"	total	118	.204	.309	333	68	17	3	4	1.2	33	29	13	63	4	3	0	242	314	22	79	4.9	.962	2B-116
1977	TOR A	41	.208	.300	130	27	10	1	0	0.0	10	9	5	21	0	2	0	73	97	5	22	4.3	.971	2B-34, DH-4
5 yrs.		558	.220	.348	1797	395	89	15	37	2.1	196	184	102	329	35	6	0	1332	1539	85	381	5.3	.971	2B-544, DH-5

Al Gardella

GARDELLA, ALFRED STEPHEN
Brother of Danny Gardella.
B. Jan. 11, 1918, New York, N. Y.
BL TL 5'10" 172 lbs.

Year	Team	Games	BA	SA	AB	H	2B	3B	HR	HR%	R	RBI	BB	SO	SB	PH AB	PH H	PO	A	E	DP	TC/G	FA	G by Pos
1945	NY N	16	.077	.077	26	2	0	0	0	0.0	2	1	4	3	0	6	0	70	4	3	2	4.8	.961	1B-8, OF-1

Danny Gardella

GARDELLA, DANIEL LEWIS
Brother of Al Gardella.
B. Feb. 26, 1920, New York, N. Y.
BL TL 5'7½" 160 lbs.

Year	Team	Games	BA	SA	AB	H	2B	3B	HR	HR%	R	RBI	BB	SO	SB	PH AB	PH H	PO	A	E	DP	TC/G	FA	G by Pos
1944	NY N	47	.250	.464	112	28	2	2	6	5.4	20	14	11	13	0	16	4	58	4	6	1	1.4	.912	OF-25
1945		121	.272	.426	430	117	10	1	18	4.2	54	71	46	55	2	11	4	319	22	12	9	2.9	.966	OF-94, 1B-15
1950	STL N	1	.000	.000	1	0	0	0	0	0.0	0	0	0	0	0	1	0	0	0	0	0	0.0	—	
3 yrs.		169	.267	.433	543	145	12	3	24	4.4	74	85	57	68	2	28	8	377	26	18	10	2.5	.957	OF-119, 1B-15

Ron Gardenhire

GARDENHIRE, RONALD CLYDE
B. Oct. 24, 1957, Butzbach, West Germany
BR TR 6' 175 lbs.

Year	Team	Games	BA	SA	AB	H	2B	3B	HR	HR%	R	RBI	BB	SO	SB	PH AB	PH H	PO	A	E	DP	TC/G	FA	G by Pos
1981	NY N	27	.271	.292	48	13	1	0	0	0.0	2	3	5	9	2	0	0	28	50	2	7	3.0	.975	SS-18, 2B-6, 3B-1
1982		141	.240	.313	384	92	17	1	3	0.8	29	33	23	55	5	2	1	235	399	29	68	4.7	.956	SS-135, 3B-1, 2B-1
1983		17	.063	.063	32	2	0	0	0	0.0	1	1	1	4	0	1	0	13	30	0	4	2.5	1.000	SS-15
1984		74	.246	.304	207	51	7	1	1	0.5	20	10	9	43	6	5	2	98	154	12	20	3.6	.955	SS-49, 2B-18, 3B-7
1985		26	.179	.282	39	7	2	1	0	0.0	5	2	8	11	0	6	0	21	32	4	3	2.2	.930	SS-13, 2B-5, 3B-2
5 yrs.		285	.232	.296	710	165	27	3	4	0.6	57	49	46	122	13	14	3	395	665	47	102	3.9	.958	SS-230, 2B-30, 3B-11

Alex Gardner

GARDNER, ALEXANDER
B. Apr. 28, 1861, Toronto, Ont., Canada   D. June 18, 1926, Danvers, Mass.

Year	Team	Games	BA	SA	AB	H	2B	3B	HR	HR%	R	RBI	BB	SO	SB	PH AB	PH H	PO	A	E	DP	TC/G	FA	G by Pos
1884	WAS AA	1	.000	.000	3	0	0	0	0	0.0	0		0		0	0	0	6	3	6	0	15.0	.600	C-1

Art Gardner

GARDNER, ARTHUR JUNIOR
B. Sept. 21, 1952, Madden, Miss.
BL TL 5'11" 175 lbs.

Year	Team	Games	BA	SA	AB	H	2B	3B	HR	HR%	R	RBI	BB	SO	SB	PH AB	PH H	PO	A	E	DP	TC/G	FA	G by Pos
1975	HOU N	13	.194	.194	31	6	0	0	0	0.0	3	2	1	8	1	9	0	14	0	0	0	1.1	1.000	OF-8
1977		66	.154	.154	65	10	0	0	0	0.0	7	3	3	15	0	26	5	31	1	0	1	0.5	1.000	OF-26
1978	SF N	7	.000	.000	3	0	0	0	0	0.0	2	0	0	2	0	3	0	0	0	0	0	0.0	—	
3 yrs.		86	.162	.162	99	16	0	0	0	0.0	12	5	4	25	1	38	5	45	1	0	1	0.5	1.000	OF-34

Billy Gardner

GARDNER, WILLIAM FREDERICK (Shotgun)
B. July 19, 1927, Waterford, Conn.
Manager 1981-85, 1987.
BR TR 6' 170 lbs.

Year	Team	Games	BA	SA	AB	H	2B	3B	HR	HR%	R	RBI	BB	SO	SB	PH AB	PH H	PO	A	E	DP	TC/G	FA	G by Pos
1954	NY N	62	.213	.287	108	23	5	0	1	0.9	10	7	6	19	0	3	1	42	82	2	4	2.0	.984	3B-30, 2B-13, SS-5
1955		59	.203	.316	187	38	10	1	3	1.6	26	17	13	19	0	8	0	76	139	13	29	3.9	.943	SS-38, 3B-10, 2B-4
1956	BAL A	144	.231	.334	515	119	16	2	11	2.1	53	50	29	53	5	1	0	301	386	18	77	4.9	.974	2B-132, SS-25, 3B-6
1957		154	.262	.356	**644**	169	**36**	3	6	0.9	79	55	53	67	10	0	0	406	450	12	103	5.6	.986	2B-148, SS-9

Year	Team	Games	BA	SA	AB	H	2B	3B	HR	HR%	R	RBI	BB	SO	SB	Pinch Hit AB	Pinch Hit H	PO	A	E	DP	TC/G	FA	G by Pos

Billy Gardner *continued*

Year	Team	Games	BA	SA	AB	H	2B	3B	HR	HR%	R	RBI	BB	SO	SB	AB	H	PO	A	E	DP	TC/G	FA	G by Pos
1958		151	.225	.298	560	126	28	2	3	0.5	32	33	34	53	2	0	0	354	356	11	113	4.8	.985	2B-151, SS-13
1959		140	.217	.304	401	87	13	2	6	1.5	34	27	38	61	2	0	0	334	393	18	104	5.3	.976	2B-139, SS-1, 3B-1
1960	WAS A	145	.257	.363	592	152	26	5	9	1.5	71	56	43	76	0	0	0	360	418	21	103	5.5	.974	2B-145, SS-13
1961	2 teams	MIN A (45G – .234)			NY A		(41G – .212)																	
"	total	86	.225	.304	253	57	14	0	2	0.8	24	13	16	32	0	3	1	121	160	11	40	3.4	.962	2B-47, 3B-35
1962	2 teams	NY A (4G – .000)			BOS A		(53G – .271)																	
"	total	57	.270	.335	200	54	9	2	0	0.0	23	12	10	40	0	3	1	81	123	10	23	3.8	.953	2B-39, 3B-8, SS-4
1963	BOS A	36	.190	.238	84	16	2	1	0	0.0	4	1	4	19	0	12	2	37	59	1	13	2.7	.990	2B-21, 3B-2
10 yrs.		1034	.237	.327	3544	841	159	18	41	1.2	356	271	246	439	19	30	5	2112	2566	117	609	4.6	.976	2B-839, SS-108, 3B-92

WORLD SERIES

| 1961 | NY A | 1 | .000 | .000 | 1 | 0 | 0 | 0 | 0 | 0.0 | 0 | 0 | 0 | 0 | 0 | 1 | 0 | 0 | 0 | 0 | 0 | 0.0 | – | |

Earl Gardner

GARDNER, EARLE McCLURKIN
B. Jan. 24, 1884, Sparta, Ill. D. Mar. 2, 1943, Sparta, Ill. BR TR 5'11" 160 lbs.

Year	Team	Games	BA	SA	AB	H	2B	3B	HR	HR%	R	RBI	BB	SO	SB	AB	H	PO	A	E	DP	TC/G	FA	G by Pos
1908	NY A	20	.213	.240	75	16	1	0	0	0.0	7	4	1		0	0	0	49	59	6	13	5.7	.947	2B-20
1909		22	.329	.376	85	28	4	0	0	0.0	12	15	3		4	0	0	35	51	5	3	4.1	.945	2B-22
1910		86	.244	.284	271	66	4	2	1	0.4	36	24	21	9	14	4		169	199	25	36	4.6	.936	2B-70
1911		102	.263	.311	357	94	13	2	0	0.0	36	39	20		14	1	0	181	290	20	44	4.8	.959	2B-101
1912		43	.281	.313	160	45	3	1	0	0.0	14	26	5		11	0	0	93	107	17	11	5.0	.922	2B-43
5 yrs.		273	.263	.304	948	249	26	5	1	0.1	105	108	50		38	15	4	527	706	73	107	4.8	.944	2B-256

Gid Gardner

GARDNER, FRANKLIN WASHINGTON
B. June 9, 1859, Attleborough, Mass. D. Aug. 1, 1914, Cambridge, Mass.

Year	Team	Games	BA	SA	AB	H	2B	3B	HR	HR%	R	RBI	BB	SO	SB	AB	H	PO	A	E	DP	TC/G	FA	G by Pos
1879	TRO N	2	.167	.167	6	1	0	0	0	0.0	1	0	0			0	0	1	2	4	0	3.5	.429	P-2
1880	CLE N	10	.188	.281	32	6	1	1	0	0.0	0	4	2	4		0	0	0	17	3	0	2.0	.850	P-9, OF-1
1883	BAL AA	42	.273	.391	161	44	10	3	1	0.6	28		18			0	0	74	25	22	0	2.9	.818	OF-35, 2B-4, 3B-3, P-2
1884	4 teams	BAL AA (41G – .214)			CHI U		(22G – .247)			PIT U	(16G – .266)			BAL U	(1G – .250)									
"	total	80	.233	.362	326	76	16	10	2	0.6	54		24			0	0	125	34	21	6	2.3	.883	OF-69, 3B-8, 1B-2, SS-1, 2B-1, P-1
1885	BAL AA	44	.218	.294	170	37	5	4	0	0.0	22		12			0	0	129	135	35	17	6.8	.883	2B-39, OF-5, 1B-1, P-1
1887	IND N	18	.175	.238	63	11	1	0	1	1.6	8	8	12	11	7	0	0	26	23	5	1	3.0	.907	OF-11, 3B-7
1888	2 teams	WAS N (2G – .250)			PHI N		(1G – .667)																	
"	total	3	.429	.429	7	3	0	0	0	0.0	0	1	1			0	0	6	5	2	0	4.3	.846	2B-2, SS-1
7 yrs.		199	.233	.339	765	178	33	18	4	0.5	113	13	69	16	7	0	0	361	241	92	24	3.5	.867	OF-121, 2B-53, P-15, 3B-11, 1B-3, SS-2

Larry Gardner

GARDNER, WILLIAM LAWRENCE
B. May 13, 1886, Enosburg Falls, Vt. D. Mar. 11, 1976, St. George, Vt. BL TR 5'8" 165 lbs.

Year	Team	Games	BA	SA	AB	H	2B	3B	HR	HR%	R	RBI	BB	SO	SB	AB	H	PO	A	E	DP	TC/G	FA	G by Pos
1908	BOS A	2	.500	.500	6	3	0	0	0	0.0	0	1	0			0	0	1	0	2	0	1.5	.333	3B-2
1909		19	.297	.432	37	11	1	2	0	0.0	8	5	4		1	5	1	10	16	5	1	1.6	.839	3B-8, SS-5
1910		113	.283	.375	413	117	12	10	2	0.5	55	36	41		8	1	0	222	320	32	28	5.1	.944	2B-113
1911		138	.285	.376	492	140	17	8	4	0.8	80	44	64		27	4	3	244	356	23	34	4.5	.963	3B-72, 2B-62
1912		143	.315	.449	517	163	24	18	3	0.6	88	86	56		25	0	0	167	296	35	16	3.5	.930	3B-143
1913		131	.281	.359	473	133	17	10	0	0.0	64	63	47	34	18	1	0	126	220	21	13	2.8	.943	3B-130
1914		155	.259	.385	553	143	23	19	3	0.5	50	68	35	39	16	2	0	187	312	31	18	3.4	.942	3B-153
1915		127	.258	.326	430	111	14	6	1	0.2	51	55	39	24	11	0	0	134	227	26	16	3.0	.933	3B-127
1916		148	.308	.387	493	152	19	7	2	0.4	47	62	48	27	12	1	0	149	278	21	24	3.0	.953	3B-147
1917		146	.265	.345	501	133	23	7	1	0.2	53	61	54	37	16	0	0	148	315	31	18	3.4	.937	3B-146
1918	PHI A	127	.285	.365	463	132	22	6	1	0.2	50	52	43	22	7	0	0	158	291	17	33	3.7	.964	3B-127
1919	CLE A	139	.300	.393	524	157	29	7	2	0.4	67	79	39	29	7	0	0	143	291	25	23	3.3	.946	3B-139
1920		154	.310	.414	597	185	31	11	3	0.5	72	118	53	25	3	0	0	156	362	13	32	3.4	.976	3B-154
1921		153	.319	.437	586	187	32	14	3	0.5	101	115	65	16	3	1	0	179	335	27	23	3.5	.950	3B-152
1922		137	.285	.377	470	134	31	3	2	0.4	74	68	49	21	9	4	1	133	259	20	24	3.0	.951	3B-128
1923		52	.253	.342	79	20	5	1	0	0.0	4	12	12	7	0	30	9	10	41	2	1	1.0	.962	3B-19
1924		38	.200	.200	50	10	0	0	0	0.0	3	4	5	1	0	22	5	9	18	3	2	0.8	.900	3B-8, 2B-6
17 yrs.		1922	.289	.385	6684	1931	300	129	27	0.4	867	929	654	282	165	75	22	2176	3937	334	307	3.4	.948	3B-1655, 2B-181, SS-5

WORLD SERIES

1912	BOS A	8	.179	.429	28	5	2	1	1	3.6	4	4	2	5	0	0	0	9	12	4	0	3.1	.840	3B-8
1915		5	.235	.353	17	4	0	1	0	0.0	2	0	1	0	0	0	0	5	14	0	0	3.8	1.000	3B-5
1916		5	.176	.529	17	3	0	0	2	11.8	2	6	0	2	0	0	0	7	18	2	1	5.4	.926	3B-5
1920	CLE A	7	.208	.250	24	5	1	0	0	0.0	1	1	1	1	0	0	0	9	15	2	3	3.7	.923	3B-7
4 yrs.		25	.198	.384	86	17	3	2	3	3.5	9	11	4	8	0	0	0	30	59	8	4	3.9	.918	3B-25

Ray Gardner

GARDNER, RAYMOND VINCENT
B. Oct. 25, 1901, Frederick, Md. D. May 3, 1968, Frederick, Md. BR TR 5'8" 145 lbs.

Year	Team	Games	BA	SA	AB	H	2B	3B	HR	HR%	R	RBI	BB	SO	SB	AB	H	PO	A	E	DP	TC/G	FA	G by Pos
1929	CLE A	82	.262	.301	256	67	3	2	0	0.0	28	24	29	16	10	0	0	175	240	21	50	5.3	.952	SS-82
1930		33	.077	.077	13	1	0	0	0	0.0	7	1	0	1	0	1	0	12	19	5	1	1.1	.861	SS-22
2 yrs.		115	.253	.290	269	68	3	2	0	0.0	35	25	29	17	10	1	0	187	259	26	51	4.1	.945	SS-104

Art Garibaldi

GARIBALDI, ARTHUR EDWARD
B. Aug. 20, 1907, San Francisco, Calif. D. Oct. 19, 1967, Sacramento, Calif. BR TR 5'8" 175 lbs.

Year	Team	Games	BA	SA	AB	H	2B	3B	HR	HR%	R	RBI	BB	SO	SB	AB	H	PO	A	E	DP	TC/G	FA	G by Pos
1936	STL N	71	.276	.341	232	64	12	0	1	0.4	30	20	16	30	3	1	0	97	119	11	7	3.2	.952	3B-46, 2B-24

Debs Garms

GARMS, DEBS C.
B. June 26, 1908, Bangs, Tex. D. Dec. 16, 1984, Glen Rose, Tex. BL TR 5'8½" 165 lbs.

Year	Team	Games	BA	SA	AB	H	2B	3B	HR	HR%	R	RBI	BB	SO	SB	AB	H	PO	A	E	DP	TC/G	FA	G by Pos
1932	STL A	34	.284	.373	134	38	7	1	1	0.7	20	8	17	7	1	1	0	79	3	4	1	2.5	.953	OF-33
1933		78	.317	.455	189	60	10	2	4	2.1	35	24	30	21	2	23	5	91	5	4	1	1.3	.960	OF-47
1934		91	.293	.388	232	68	14	4	0	0.0	25	31	27	19	0	27	7	111	4	7	1	1.3	.942	OF-56
1935		10	.267	.267	15	4	0	0	0	0.0	1	0	2	2	0	6	1	4	0	1	0	0.5	.800	OF-2
1937	BOS N	125	.259	.337	478	124	15	8	2	0.4	60	37	37	33	2	10	3	200	69	7	2	2.2	.975	OF-81, 3B-36

Year	Team		Games	BA	SA	AB	H	2B	3B	HR	HR%	R	RBI	BB	SO	SB	Pinch Hit AB	Pinch Hit H	PO	A	E	DP	TC/G	FA	G by Pos

Debs Garms continued

Year	Team		Games	BA	SA	AB	H	2B	3B	HR	HR%	R	RBI	BB	SO	SB	AB	H	PO	A	E	DP	TC/G	FA	G by Pos
1938			117	.315	.364	428	135	19	1	0	0.0	62	47	34	22	4	4	1	174	104	11	8	2.5	.962	OF-63, 3B-54, 2B-1
1939			132	.298	.392	513	153	24	9	2	0.4	68	37	39	20	2	2	0	214	89	12	7	2.4	.962	OF-96, 3B-37
1940	PIT	N	103	.355	.500	358	127	23	7	5	1.4	76	57	23	6	3	18	5	97	126	9	15	2.3	.961	3B-64, OF-19
1941			83	.264	.373	220	58	9	3	3	1.4	25	42	22	12	0	31	10	73	44	9	1	1.5	.929	3B-29, OF-24
1943	STL	N	90	.257	.313	249	64	10	2	0	0.0	26	22	13	8	1	20	6	112	25	9	5	1.6	.938	OF-47, 3B-23, SS-1
1944			73	.201	.221	149	30	3	0	0	0.0	17	5	13	8	0	30	6	48	16	1	1	0.9	.985	OF-23, 3B-21
1945			74	.336	.411	146	49	7	2	0	0.0	23	18	31	3	0	26	10	30	43	3	4	1.0	.961	3B-32, OF-10
12 yrs.			1010	.293	.379	3111	910	141	39	17	0.5	438	328	288	161	18	198	54	1233	526	77	45	1.8	.958	OF-501, 3B-296, SS-1, 2B-1

WORLD SERIES

Year	Team		Games	BA	SA	AB	H	2B	3B	HR	HR%	R	RBI	BB	SO	SB	AB	H	PO	A	E	DP	TC/G	FA	G by Pos
1943	STL	N	2	.000	.000	5	0	0	0	0	0.0	0	0	0	2	0	1	0	1	0	0	0	0.5	1.000	OF-1
1944			2	.000	.000	2	0	0	0	0	0.0	0	0	0	0	0	2	0	0	0	0	0	0.0	–	
2 yrs.			4	.000	.000	7	0	0	0	0	0.0	0	0	0	2	0	3	0	1	0	0	0	0.3	1.000	OF-1

Phil Garner

GARNER, PHILIP MASON (Scrap Iron)
B. Apr. 30, 1948, Jefferson City, Tenn.

BR TR 5'10" 175 lbs.

Year	Team		Games	BA	SA	AB	H	2B	3B	HR	HR%	R	RBI	BB	SO	SB	AB	H	PO	A	E	DP	TC/G	FA	G by Pos
1973	OAK	A	9	.000	.000	5	0	0	0	0	0.0	0	0	0	3	0	0	0	2	3	0	1	0.6	1.000	3B-9
1974			30	.179	.214	28	5	1	0	0	0.0	4	1	1	5	1	0	0	11	24	1	1	1.2	.972	SS-8, 2B-3, DH-2
1975			160	.246	.346	488	120	21	5	6	1.2	46	54	30	65	4	0	0	355	427	26	94	5.1	.968	2B-160, SS-1
1976			159	.261	.400	555	145	29	12	8	1.4	54	74	36	71	35	0	0	378	465	22	91	5.4	.975	2B-159
1977	PIT	N	153	.260	.441	585	152	35	10	17	2.9	99	77	55	65	32	2	0	223	351	17	49	3.9	.971	3B-107, 2B-50, SS-12
1978			154	.261	.400	528	138	25	9	10	1.9	66	66	66	71	27	1	0	258	389	28	63	4.4	.959	2B-83, 3B-81, SS-4
1979			150	.293	.441	549	161	32	8	11	2.0	76	59	55	74	17	0	0	234	396	22	82	4.3	.966	2B-83, 3B-78, SS-14
1980			151	.259	.358	548	142	27	6	5	0.9	62	58	46	53	32	0	0	349	500	21	116	5.8	.976	2B-151, SS-1
1981	2 teams				PIT N (56G – .254)				HOU N (31G – .239)																
"	total		87	.248	.310	294	73	14	1	1	0.3	35	26	36	32	10	3	2	121	148	10	31	3.2	.964	2B-81
1982	HOU	N	155	.274	.423	588	161	33	8	13	2.2	65	83	40	92	24	1	0	285	464	17	94	4.9	.978	2B-136, 3B-18
1983			154	.238	.362	567	135	24	2	14	2.5	76	79	63	84	18	0	0	100	311	24	22	2.8	.945	3B-154
1984			128	.278	.388	374	104	17	6	4	1.1	60	45	43	63	3	24	6	136	251	12	42	3.1	.970	3B-82, 2B-35
1985			135	.268	.400	463	124	23	10	6	1.3	65	51	34	72	14	15	7	101	229	21	24	2.6	.940	3B-123, 2B-15
1986			107	.265	.406	313	83	14	3	9	2.9	43	41	30	45	12	16	3	66	152	23	15	2.3	.905	3B-84, 2B-7
1987	2 teams				HOU N (43G – .223)				LA N (70G – .190)																
"	total		113	.206	.307	238	49	9	0	5	2.1	29	23	28	44	6	24	4	65	144	13	10	2.0	.941	3B-82, 2B-14, SS-2
1988	SF	N	15	.154	.154	13	2	0	0	0	0.0	0	1	1	3	0	13	2	0	0	0	0	0.0	–	3B-2
16 yrs.			1860	.260	.389	6136	1594	299	82	109	1.8	780	738	564	842	225	99	24	2684	4254	257	735	3.9	.964	2B-975, 3B-820, SS-42, DH-2

DIVISIONAL PLAYOFF SERIES

Year	Team		Games	BA	SA	AB	H	2B	3B	HR	HR%	R	RBI	BB	SO	SB	AB	H	PO	A	E	DP	TC/G	FA	G by Pos
1981	HOU	N	5	.111	.111	18	2	0	0	0	0.0	1	0	3	0	0	0	0	0	0	1	0	0.2	–	2B-5

LEAGUE CHAMPIONSHIP SERIES

Year	Team		Games	BA	SA	AB	H	2B	3B	HR	HR%	R	RBI	BB	SO	SB	AB	H	PO	A	E	DP	TC/G	FA	G by Pos
1975	OAK	A	3	.000	.000	5	0	0	0	0	0.0	0	0	0	0	0	0	0	7	4	1	2	4.0	.917	2B-3
1979	PIT	N	3	.417	.833	12	5	0	1	1	8.3	4	1	1	0	0	0	0	8	9	0	2	5.7	1.000	2B-3, SS-1
1986	HOU	N	3	.222	.333	9	2	1	0	0	0.0	1	2	1	2	0	0	0	1	9	0	0	3.3	1.000	3B-3
3 yrs.			9	.269	.500	26	7	1	1	1	3.8	5	3	2	3	0	0	0	16	22	1	4	4.3	.974	2B-6, 3B-3, SS-1

WORLD SERIES

Year	Team		Games	BA	SA	AB	H	2B	3B	HR	HR%	R	RBI	BB	SO	SB	AB	H	PO	A	E	DP	TC/G	FA	G by Pos
1979	PIT	N	7	.500	.667	24	12	4	0	0	0.0	4	5	3	1	0	0	0	21	23	2	10	6.6	.957	2B-7

Ralph Garr

GARR, RALPH ALLEN (Roadrunner)
B. Dec. 12, 1945, Monroe, La.

BL TR 5'11" 185 lbs.

Year	Team		Games	BA	SA	AB	H	2B	3B	HR	HR%	R	RBI	BB	SO	SB	AB	H	PO	A	E	DP	TC/G	FA	G by Pos
1968	ATL	N	11	.286	.286	7	2	0	0	0	0.0	3	0	1	0	1	7	2	0	0	0	0	0.0	–	
1969			22	.222	.259	27	6	1	0	0	0.0	6	2	2	4	1	5	2	6	0	1	0	0.3	.857	OF-7
1970			37	.281	.313	96	27	3	0	0	0.0	18	8	5	12	5	10	1	43	0	0	0	1.2	1.000	OF-21
1971			154	.343	.441	639	219	24	6	9	1.4	101	44	30	68	30	1	1	315	15	11	3	2.2	.968	OF-153
1972			134	.325	.430	554	180	22	0	12	2.2	87	53	25	41	25	3	0	246	8	10	1	2.0	.962	OF-131
1973			148	.299	.415	668	200	32	6	11	1.6	94	55	22	64	35	0	0	293	9	10	2	2.1	.968	OF-148
1974			143	.353	.503	606	214	24	17	11	1.8	87	54	28	52	26	1	1	255	8	9	2	1.9	.967	OF-139
1975			151	.278	.384	625	174	26	11	6	1.0	74	31	44	50	14	3	2	298	12	11	2	2.1	.966	OF-148
1976	CHI	A	136	.300	.387	527	158	22	6	4	0.8	63	36	17	41	14	5	2	254	7	6	2	2.0	.978	OF-125
1977			134	.300	.435	543	163	29	7	10	1.8	78	54	27	44	12	7	1	225	10	3	2	1.8	.987	OF-126, DH-2
1978			118	.275	.377	443	122	18	9	3	0.7	67	29	24	41	7	2	0	205	5	9	2	1.9	.959	OF-109, DH-9
1979	2 teams				CHI A (102G – .280)				CAL A (6G – .125)																
"	total		108	.269	.393	331	89	10	2	9	2.7	34	39	17	22	2	23	6	94	3	5	1	0.9	.951	OF-67, DH-23
1980	CAL	A	21	.190	.214	42	8	1	0	0	0.0	5	3	4	6	0	9	1	3	0	1	0	0.2	.750	DH-8, OF-2
13 yrs.			1317	.306	.416	5108	1562	212	64	75	1.5	717	408	246	445	172	76	19	2237	77	76	17	1.8	.968	OF-1176, DH-42

Adrian Garrett

GARRETT, HENRY ADRIAN
Brother of Wayne Garrett.
B. Jan. 3, 1943, Brooksville, Fla.

BL TR 6'3" 185 lbs.

Year	Team		Games	BA	SA	AB	H	2B	3B	HR	HR%	R	RBI	BB	SO	SB	AB	H	PO	A	E	DP	TC/G	FA	G by Pos
1966	ATL	N	4	.000	.000	3	0	0	0	0	0.0	0	0	0	2	0	3	0	0	0	0	0	0.0	–	OF-1
1970	CHI	N	3	.000	.000	3	0	0	0	0	0.0	0	0	0	3	0	0	0	0	0	0	0	0.0	–	
1971	OAK	A	14	.143	.286	21	3	0	0	1	4.8	1	2	5	7	0	7	0	9	0	0	0	0.6	1.000	OF-5
1972			14	.000	.000	11	0	0	0	0	0.0	0	1	4	4	0	11	0	1	0	0	0	0.1	1.000	OF-2
1973	CHI	N	36	.222	.389	54	12	0	0	3	5.6	7	8	4	18	1	21	6	35	6	2	0	1.2	.953	OF-7, C-6
1974			10	.000	.000	8	0	0	0	0	0.0	0	0	0	6	0	0	0	3	1	0	0	0.4	1.000	C-3, OF-1, 1B-1
1975	2 teams				CHI N (16G – .095)				CAL A (37G – .262)																
"	total		53	.234	.438	128	30	6	0	7	5.5	18	24	15	36	3	9	0	100	12	1	14	2.1	.991	DH-23, 1B-14, OF-2, C-1
1976	CAL	A	29	.125	.188	48	6	3	0	0	0.0	4	3	5	16	0	12	2	43	1	1	2	1.6	.978	C-15, DH-4, 1B-1
8 yrs.			163	.185	.333	276	51	8	0	11	4.0	30	37	31	87	4	72	8	191	20	4	16	1.3	.981	DH-27, C-25, OF-18, 1B-16

Year	Team	Games	BA	SA	AB	H	2B	3B	HR	HR%	R	RBI	BB	SO	SB	Pinch Hit AB	Pinch Hit H	PO	A	E	DP	TC/G	FA	G by Pos

Wayne Garrett

GARRETT, RONALD WAYNE (Red)
Brother of Adrian Garrett.
B. Dec. 3, 1947, Brooksville, Fla.
BL TR 5'11" 175 lbs.

Year	Team	Games	BA	SA	AB	H	2B	3B	HR	HR%	R	RBI	BB	SO	SB	PH AB	PH H	PO	A	E	DP	TC/G	FA	G by Pos
1969	NY N	124	.218	.268	400	87	11	3	1	0.3	38	39	40	75	4	14	1	147	218	11	37	3.0	.971	3B-72, 2B-47, SS-9
1970		114	.254	.421	366	93	17	4	12	3.3	74	45	81	60	5	5	0	152	205	12	34	3.2	.967	3B-70, 2B-45, SS-1
1971		56	.213	.238	202	43	2	0	1	0.5	20	11	28	31	1	2	0	48	100	4	11	2.7	.974	3B-53, 2B-9
1972		111	.232	.315	298	69	13	3	2	0.7	41	29	70	58	3	8	0	114	188	14	19	2.8	.956	3B-82, 2B-22
1973		140	.256	.403	504	129	20	3	16	3.2	76	58	72	74	6	4	4	102	313	26	46	3.2	.941	3B-130, SS-9, 2B-6
1974		151	.224	.337	522	117	14	3	13	2.5	55	53	89	96	4	3	2	123	349	20	33	3.3	.959	3B-144, SS-9
1975		107	.266	.383	274	73	8	3	6	2.2	49	34	50	45	3	12	6	65	161	8	24	2.2	.966	3B-94, SS-3
1976 2 teams	NY N (80G – .223)	MON N (59G – .243)																						
" total		139	.231	.311	428	99	12	2	6	1.4	51	37	82	46	9	17	3	195	314	15	48	3.8	.971	3B-66, 2B-64, SS-1
1977	MON N	68	.270	.358	159	43	6	1	2	1.3	17	22	30	18	2	18	1	34	101	0	2	2.0	1.000	3B-49, 2B-1
1978 2 teams	MON N (49G – .174)	STL N (33G – .333)																						
" total		82	.250	.326	132	33	4	0	2	1.5	17	12	19	26	1	43	9	18	51	4	7	0.9	.945	3B-32
10 yrs.		1092	.239	.341	3285	786	107	22	61	1.9	438	340	561	529	38	126	26	998	2000	114	261	2.8	.963	3B-792, 2B-194, SS-32

LEAGUE CHAMPIONSHIP SERIES

Year	Team	Games	BA	SA	AB	H	2B	3B	HR	HR%	R	RBI	BB	SO	SB	PH AB	PH H	PO	A	E	DP	TC/G	FA	G by Pos
1969	NY N	3	.385	.769	13	5	2	0	1	7.7	3	3	2	1	1	0	0	1	6	0	0	2.3	1.000	3B-3
1973		5	.087	.130	23	2	1	0	0	0.0	1	1	0	5	0	0	0	4	6	1	0	2.3	.909	3B-5
2 yrs.		8	.194	.361	36	7	3	0	1	2.8	4	4	2	7	1	0	0	5	12	1	0	2.3	.944	3B-8

WORLD SERIES

Year	Team	Games	BA	SA	AB	H	2B	3B	HR	HR%	R	RBI	BB	SO	SB	PH AB	PH H	PO	A	E	DP	TC/G	FA	G by Pos
1969	NY N	2	.000	.000	1	0	0	0	0	0.0	0	0	2	1	0	0	0	1	0	1	0	1.0	.500	3B-2
1973		7	.167	.367	30	5	0	0	2	6.7	4	2	5	11	0	0	0	4	19	3	1	3.7	.885	3B-7
2 yrs.		9	.161	.355	31	5	0	0	2	6.5	4	2	7	12	0	0	0	5	19	4	1	3.1	.857	3B-9

Gil Garrido

GARRIDO, GIL GONZALO
B. June 26, 1941, Panama City, Panama
BR TR 5'9" 150 lbs.

Year	Team	Games	BA	SA	AB	H	2B	3B	HR	HR%	R	RBI	BB	SO	SB	PH AB	PH H	PO	A	E	DP	TC/G	FA	G by Pos
1964	SF N	14	.080	.080	25	2	0	0	0	0.0	1	2	2	7	1	0	0	5	26	1	3	2.3	.969	SS-14
1968	ATL N	18	.208	.208	53	11	0	0	0	0.0	5	2	2	2	0	1	0	26	51	1	12	4.3	.987	SS-17
1969		82	.220	.251	227	50	5	1	0	0.0	18	10	16	11	0	0	0	99	192	8	32	3.6	.973	SS-81
1970		101	.264	.308	367	97	5	4	1	0.3	38	19	15	16	0	1	1	162	292	10	46	4.6	.978	SS-80, 2B-26
1971		79	.216	.240	125	27	3	0	0	0.0	8	12	15	12	0	8	3	61	128	6	29	2.5	.969	SS-32, 3B-28, 2B-18
1972		40	.267	.280	75	20	1	0	0	0.0	11	7	11	6	1	3	1	43	62	1	11	2.7	.991	2B-21, SS-10, 3B-3
6 yrs.		334	.237	.268	872	207	14	5	1	0.1	81	51	61	54	2	13	5	396	751	27	133	3.5	.977	SS-234, 2B-65, 3B-31

LEAGUE CHAMPIONSHIP SERIES

Year	Team	Games	BA	SA	AB	H	2B	3B	HR	HR%	R	RBI	BB	SO	SB	PH AB	PH H	PO	A	E	DP	TC/G	FA	G by Pos
1969	ATL N	3	.200	.200	10	2	0	0	0	0.0	0	0	1	1	0	0	0	4	8	0	3	4.0	1.000	SS-3

Rabbit Garriott

GARRIOTT, VIRGIL CECIL
B. Aug. 15, 1916, Harristown, Ill.
BL TR 5'8" 165 lbs.

Year	Team	Games	BA	SA	AB	H	2B	3B	HR	HR%	R	RBI	BB	SO	SB	PH AB	PH H	PO	A	E	DP	TC/G	FA	G by Pos
1946	CHI N	6	.000	.000	5	0	0	0	0	0.0	0	0	0	2	0	5	0	0	0	0	0	0.0	—	

Ford Garrison

GARRISON, ROBERT FORD (Snapper, Rocky)
B. Aug. 29, 1915, Greenville, S. C.
BR TR 5'10½" 180 lbs.

Year	Team	Games	BA	SA	AB	H	2B	3B	HR	HR%	R	RBI	BB	SO	SB	PH AB	PH H	PO	A	E	DP	TC/G	FA	G by Pos
1943	BOS A	36	.279	.357	129	36	5	1	1	0.8	13	11	5	14	0	2	0	77	2	1	0	2.2	.988	OF-32
1944 2 teams	BOS A (13G – .245)	PHI A (121G – .269)																						
" total		134	.267	.331	498	133	16	2	4	0.8	63	39	28	44	10	2	0	320	6	5	0	2.5	.985	OF-131
1945	PHI A	6	.304	.478	23	7	1	0	1	4.3	3	6	4	3	1	1	0	11	1	0	0	2.0	1.000	OF-5
1946		9	.108	.108	37	4	0	0	0	0.0	1	0	0	6	0	1	1	8	0	0	0	0.9	1.000	OF-8
4 yrs.		185	.262	.329	687	180	22	3	6	0.9	80	56	37	67	11	6	1	416	9	6	0	2.3	.986	OF-176

Hank Garrity

GARRITY, FRANCIS JOSEPH
B. Feb. 4, 1908, Boston, Mass. D. Sept. 1, 1962, Boston, Mass.
BR TR 6'1" 185 lbs.

Year	Team	Games	BA	SA	AB	H	2B	3B	HR	HR%	R	RBI	BB	SO	SB	PH AB	PH H	PO	A	E	DP	TC/G	FA	G by Pos
1931	CHI A	8	.214	.286	14	3	1	0	0	0.0	2	1	0	2	0	0	0	11	5	1	1	2.1	.941	C-7

Steve Garvey

GARVEY, STEVEN PATRICK
B. Dec. 22, 1948, Tampa, Fla.
BR TR 5'10" 192 lbs.

Year	Team	Games	BA	SA	AB	H	2B	3B	HR	HR%	R	RBI	BB	SO	SB	PH AB	PH H	PO	A	E	DP	TC/G	FA	G by Pos
1969	LA N	3	.333	.333	3	1	0	0	0	0.0	0	0	0	0	0	3	1	0	0	0	0	0.0	—	
1970		34	.269	.355	93	25	5	0	1	1.1	8	6	6	17	1	10	3	23	59	5	4	2.6	.943	3B-27, 2B-1
1971		81	.227	.382	225	51	12	1	7	3.1	27	26	21	33	1	2	0	53	161	14	11	2.8	.939	3B-79
1972		96	.269	.422	294	79	14	2	9	3.1	36	30	19	36	4	11	3	104	189	28	21	3.3	.913	3B-85, 1B-3
1973		114	.304	.438	349	106	17	3	8	2.3	37	50	11	42	0	30	12	731	27	7	58	6.7	.991	1B-76, OF-10
1974		156	.312	.469	642	200	32	3	21	3.3	95	111	31	66	5	0	0	1536	62	8	108	10.3	.995	1B-156
1975		160	.319	.476	659	210	38	6	18	2.7	85	95	33	66	11	0	0	1500	77	8	96	9.9	.995	1B-160
1976		162	.317	.450	631	200	37	4	13	2.1	85	80	50	69	19	0	0	1583	67	3	138	10.2	.995	1B-160
1977		162	.297	.498	646	192	25	3	33	5.1	91	115	38	90	9	1	0	1606	55	8	137	10.3	.995	1B-160
1978		162	.316	.499	639	202	36	9	21	3.3	89	113	40	70	10	0	0	1546	74	9	121	10.1	.994	1B-162
1979		162	.315	.497	648	204	32	1	28	4.3	92	110	37	59	3	0	0	1402	93	7	101	9.3	.995	1B-162
1980		163	.304	.467	658	200	27	1	26	4.0	78	106	36	67	6	1	0	1502	112	6	122	9.9	.995	1B-162
1981		110	.283	.411	431	122	23	1	10	2.3	63	64	25	49	3	0	0	1019	55	1	84	9.8	.999	1B-110
1982		162	.282	.418	625	176	35	1	16	2.6	66	86	20	86	5	0	0	1539	111	8	132	10.2	.995	1B-158
1983	SD N	100	.294	.459	388	114	22	0	14	3.6	76	59	29	39	1	0	0	888	49	6	69	9.4	.994	1B-100
1984		161	.284	.373	617	175	27	2	8	1.3	72	86	24	64	1	1	1	1232	87	0	117	8.2	1.000	1B-160
1985		162	.281	.430	654	184	34	6	17	2.6	80	81	35	67	0	0	0	1442	92	5	138	9.5	.997	1B-162
1986		155	.255	.408	557	142	22	0	21	3.8	58	81	23	72	1	11	2	1160	53	7	94	7.9	.994	1B-155
1987		27	.211	.276	76	16	2	0	1	1.3	5	9	1	10	0	7	4	138	11	0	10	5.5	1.000	1B-20
19 yrs.		2332	.294	.446	8835	2599	440	43	272	3.1	1143	1308	479	1003	83	82	26	19004	1434	130	1561	8.8	.994	1B-2061, 3B-191, OF-10, 2B-1

DIVISIONAL PLAYOFF SERIES

Year	Team	Games	BA	SA	AB	H	2B	3B	HR	HR%	R	RBI	BB	SO	SB	PH AB	PH H	PO	A	E	DP	TC/G	FA	G by Pos
1981	LA N	5	.368	.789	19	7	0	1	2	10.5	4	4	0	2	0	0	0	0	0	0	0	0.0	—	1B-5

Year Team	Games	BA	SA	AB	H	2B	3B	HR	HR%	R	RBI	BB	SO	SB	Pinch Hit AB	Pinch Hit H	PO	A	E	DP	TC/G	FA	G by Pos

Steve Garvey *continued*

LEAGUE CHAMPIONSHIP SERIES

Year Team	Games	BA	SA	AB	H	2B	3B	HR	HR%	R	RBI	BB	SO	SB	Pinch Hit AB	Pinch Hit H	PO	A	E	DP	TC/G	FA	G by Pos
1974 LA N	4	.389	.778	18	7	1	0	2	11.1	4	5	1	1	0	0	0	40	2	1	6	10.8	.977	1B-4
1977	4	.308	.308	13	4	0	0	0	0.0	2	0	2	1	1	0	0	40	1	0	3	10.3	1.000	1B-4
1978	4	.389	1.222	18	7	1	1	4	22.2	6	7	0	1	0	0	0	44	5	0	4	12.3	1.000	1B-4
1981	5	.286	.429	21	6	0	0	1	4.8	2	2	0	4	0	0	0	0	0	0	0	0.0	–	1B-5
1984 SD N	5	.400	.600	20	8	1	0	1	5.0	1	7	1	2	0	0	0	35	3	0	3	7.6	1.000	1B-5
5 yrs.	22	.356	.678	90	32	3	1	8	8.9	15	21	4	9	1	0	0	159	11	1	16	7.8	.994	1B-22

WORLD SERIES

Year Team	Games	BA	SA	AB	H	2B	3B	HR	HR%	R	RBI	BB	SO	SB	Pinch Hit AB	Pinch Hit H	PO	A	E	DP	TC/G	FA	G by Pos
1974 LA N	5	.381	.381	21	8	0	0	0	0.0	2	1	0	3	0	0	0	34	5	0	4	7.4	1.000	1B-5
1977	6	.375	.625	24	9	1	1	1	4.2	5	3	1	4	0	0	0	59	6	0	4	10.8	1.000	1B-6
1978	6	.208	.250	24	5	1	0	0	0.0	1	0	1	7	1	0	0	58	3	1	4	10.3	.984	1B-6
1981	6	.417	.458	24	10	1	0	0	0.0	3	0	2	5	0	0	0	44	3	0	5	7.8	1.000	1B-6
1984 SD N	5	.200	.300	20	4	2	0	0	0.0	2	2	0	2	0	0	0	34	3	0	4	7.4	1.000	1B-5
5 yrs.	28	.319	.407	113	36	5	1	1	0.9	13	6	4	21	1	0	0	229	18	1	21	8.9	.996	1B-28

Rod Gaspar

GASPAR, RODNEY EARL
B. Apr. 3, 1946, Long Beach, Calif.   BB TL 5'11" 165 lbs.

Year Team	Games	BA	SA	AB	H	2B	3B	HR	HR%	R	RBI	BB	SO	SB	Pinch Hit AB	Pinch Hit H	PO	A	E	DP	TC/G	FA	G by Pos
1969 NY N	118	.228	.279	215	49	6	1	1	0.5	26	14	25	19	7	25	4	104	12	2	6	1.0	.983	OF-91
1970	11	.000	.000	14	0	0	0	0	0.0	4	0	1	4	1	1	0	13	0	0	0	1.2	1.000	OF-8
1971 SD N	16	.118	.118	17	2	0	0	0	0.0	1	2	3	3	0	11	1	4	0	0	0	0.3	1.000	OF-2
1974	33	.214	.214	14	3	0	0	0	0.0	4	1	4	3	0	12	3	6	1	0	0	0.2	1.000	OF-8, 1B-2
4 yrs.	178	.208	.250	260	54	6	1	1	0.4	35	17	33	29	8	49	8	127	13	2	6	0.8	.986	OF-109, 1B-2

LEAGUE CHAMPIONSHIP SERIES

Year Team	Games	BA	SA	AB	H	2B	3B	HR	HR%	R	RBI	BB	SO	SB	Pinch Hit AB	Pinch Hit H	PO	A	E	DP	TC/G	FA	G by Pos
1969 NY N	3	–	–	0	0	0	0	0	–	0	0	0	0	0	0	0	0	0	0	0	0.7	1.000	OF-3

WORLD SERIES

Year Team	Games	BA	SA	AB	H	2B	3B	HR	HR%	R	RBI	BB	SO	SB	Pinch Hit AB	Pinch Hit H	PO	A	E	DP	TC/G	FA	G by Pos
1969 NY N	3	.000	.000	2	0	0	0	0	0.0	1	0	0	0	0	1	0	2	0	0	0	0.7	1.000	OF-1

Tommy Gastall

GASTALL, THOMAS EVERETT
B. June 13, 1932, Fall River, Mass.   D. Sept. 20, 1956, Riviera Beach, Md.   BR TR 6'2" 187 lbs.

Year Team	Games	BA	SA	AB	H	2B	3B	HR	HR%	R	RBI	BB	SO	SB	Pinch Hit AB	Pinch Hit H	PO	A	E	DP	TC/G	FA	G by Pos
1955 BAL A	20	.148	.185	27	4	1	0	0	0.0	4	0	3	5	1	5	1	28	1	1	1	1.5	.967	C-15
1956	32	.196	.232	56	11	2	0	0	0.0	3	4	3	8	0	12	0	67	6	0	1	2.3	1.000	C-20
2 yrs.	52	.181	.217	83	15	3	0	0	0.0	7	4	6	13	1	17	1	95	7	1	2	2.0	.990	C-35

Ed Gastfield

GASTFIELD, EDWARD
B. Aug. 1, 1865, Chicago, Ill.   D. Dec. 1, 1899, Chicago, Ill.

Year Team	Games	BA	SA	AB	H	2B	3B	HR	HR%	R	RBI	BB	SO	SB	Pinch Hit AB	Pinch Hit H	PO	A	E	DP	TC/G	FA	G by Pos
1884 DET N	23	.073	.085	82	6	1	0	0	0.0	6		2	34		0	0	142	53	36	4	10.0	.844	C-19, OF-2, 1B-2
1885 2 teams		DET N (1G – .000)				CHI N (1G – .000)																	
" total	2	.000	.000	6	0	0	0	0	0.0	0		0	3		0	0	14	2	2	1	9.0	.889	C-2
2 yrs.	25	.068	.080	88	6	1	0	0	0.0	6		2	37		0	0	156	55	38	5	10.0	.847	C-21, OF-2, 1B-2

Alex Gaston

GASTON, ALEXANDER NATHANIEL
Brother of Milt Gaston.
B. Mar. 12, 1893, New York, N.Y.   D. Feb. 8, 1976, Santa Monica, Calif.   BR TR 5'9" 170 lbs.

Year Team	Games	BA	SA	AB	H	2B	3B	HR	HR%	R	RBI	BB	SO	SB	Pinch Hit AB	Pinch Hit H	PO	A	E	DP	TC/G	FA	G by Pos
1920 NY N	4	.100	.100	10	1	0	0	0	0.0	0	2	1	2	0	1	0	10	1	1	0	3.0	.917	C-3
1921	20	.227	.364	22	5	1	1	0	0.0	1	3	1	9	0	9	2	19	0	1	0	1.0	.950	C-11
1922	16	.192	.192	26	5	0	0	0	0.0	1	1	0	3	1	3	1	24	3	0	0	1.7	1.000	C-14
1923	22	.205	.333	39	8	2	0	1	2.6	3	5	0	6	0	1	0	34	11	2	0	2.1	.957	C-21
1926 BOS A	98	.223	.259	301	67	5	3	0	0.0	37	21	21	28	3	0	0	284	69	7	5	3.7	.981	C-98
1929	55	.224	.353	116	26	5	2	2	1.7	14	9	6	8	1	4	1	116	25	2	6	2.6	.986	C-49
6 yrs.	215	.218	.284	514	112	13	6	3	0.6	58	40	29	56	5	18	4	487	109	13	11	2.8	.979	C-196

Clarence Gaston

GASTON, CLARENCE EDWIN (Cito)
B. Mar. 17, 1944, San Antonio, Tex.
Manager 1989.   BR TR 6'3" 190 lbs.

Year Team	Games	BA	SA	AB	H	2B	3B	HR	HR%	R	RBI	BB	SO	SB	Pinch Hit AB	Pinch Hit H	PO	A	E	DP	TC/G	FA	G by Pos
1967 ATL N	9	.120	.200	25	3	1	0	0	0.0	1	1	0	5	1	1	0	7	1	2	0	1.1	.800	OF-7
1969 SD N	129	.230	.309	391	90	11	7	2	0.5	20	28	24	117	4	17	1	243	12	11	4	2.1	.959	OF-113
1970	146	.318	.543	584	186	26	9	29	5.0	92	93	41	142	4	4	1	310	7	8	0	2.2	.975	OF-142
1971	141	.228	.386	518	118	13	9	17	3.3	57	61	24	121	1	11	1	271	8	5	1	2.0	.982	OF-133
1972	111	.269	.361	379	102	14	0	7	1.8	30	44	22	76	0	18	4	158	10	4	3	1.5	.977	OF-94
1973	133	.250	.405	476	119	18	4	16	3.4	51	57	20	88	0	13	3	198	16	12	4	1.7	.947	OF-119
1974	106	.213	.322	267	57	11	0	6	2.2	19	33	16	51	0	39	9	119	7	1	1	1.2	.992	OF-63
1975 ATL N	64	.241	.397	141	34	4	0	6	4.3	17	15	17	33	1	25	7	80	2	3	1	1.3	.965	OF-35, 1B-1
1976	69	.291	.410	134	39	4	0	4	3.0	15	25	13	21	1	40	12	58	2	1	2	0.9	.984	OF-28, 1B-2
1977	56	.271	.424	85	23	4	0	3	3.5	6	21	5	19	1	37	12	44	4	1	2	0.9	.980	OF-9, 1B-5
1978 2 teams		ATL N (61G – .229)				PIT N (1G – .500)																	
" total	62	.233	.267	120	28	1	0	1	0.8	6	9	3	20	0	29	9	66	2	3	1	1.1	.958	OF-30, 1B-4
11 yrs.	1026	.256	.397	3120	799	106	30	91	2.9	314	387	185	693	13	234	59	1554	71	51	19	1.6	.970	OF-773, 1B-12

Joe Gates

GATES, JOSEPH DANIEL
B. Oct. 3, 1954, Gary, Ind.   BL TR 5'7" 175 lbs.

Year Team	Games	BA	SA	AB	H	2B	3B	HR	HR%	R	RBI	BB	SO	SB	Pinch Hit AB	Pinch Hit H	PO	A	E	DP	TC/G	FA	G by Pos
1978 CHI A	8	.250	.250	24	6	0	0	0	0.0	6	1	4	6	1	0	0	9	26	1	4	4.5	.972	2B-8
1979	16	.063	.188	16	1	0	1	0	0.0	5	1	2	3	1	3	0	12	17	1	3	1.9	.967	2B-8, DH-1, 3B-1
2 yrs.	24	.175	.225	40	7	0	1	0	0.0	11	2	6	9	2	3	0	21	43	2	7	2.8	.970	2B-16, DH-1, 3B-1

Mike Gates

GATES, MICHAEL GRANT
B. Sept. 20, 1956, Culver City, Calif.   BL TR 6' 165 lbs.

Year Team	Games	BA	SA	AB	H	2B	3B	HR	HR%	R	RBI	BB	SO	SB	Pinch Hit AB	Pinch Hit H	PO	A	E	DP	TC/G	FA	G by Pos
1981 MON N	1	.500	1.500	2	1	0	1	0	0.0	1	0	1	0	0	1	0	0	1	0	0	1.0	1.000	2B-1

Year	Team	Games	BA	SA	AB	H	2B	3B	HR	HR%	R	RBI	BB	SO	SB	Pinch Hit AB	Pinch Hit H	PO	A	E	DP	TC/G	FA	G by Pos

Mike Gates *continued*

Year	Team	Games	BA	SA	AB	H	2B	3B	HR	HR%	R	RBI	BB	SO	SB	PH AB	PH H	PO	A	E	DP	TC/G	FA	G by Pos
1982		36	.231	.298	121	28	2	3	0	0.0	16	8	9	19	0	2	0	53	91	0	18	4.0	1.000	2B-36
2 yrs.		37	.236	.317	123	29	2	4	0	0.0	17	9	9	20	0	3	0	53	92	0	18	3.9	1.000	2B-37

Frank Gatins

GATINS, FRANK ANTHONY
Born Frank Anthony Gestino.
B. Mar. 6, 1871, Johnstown, Pa.   D. Nov. 8, 1911, Johnstown, Pa.

Year	Team	Games	BA	SA	AB	H	2B	3B	HR	HR%	R	RBI	BB	SO	SB	PH AB	PH H	PO	A	E	DP	TC/G	FA	G by Pos
1898	WAS N	17	.224	.259	58	13	2	0	0	0.0	6	5	3		2	0	0	22	42	17	6	4.8	.790	SS-17
1901	BKN N	50	.228	.299	197	45	7	2	1	0.5	21	21	5		6	0	0	73	72	11	7	3.1	.929	3B-46, SS-5
2 yrs.		67	.227	.290	255	58	9	2	1	0.4	27	26	8		8	0	0	95	114	28	13	3.5	.882	3B-46, SS-22

Jim Gaudet

GAUDET, JAMES JENNINGS
B. June 3, 1955, New Orleans, La.   BR TR 6'   185 lbs.

Year	Team	Games	BA	SA	AB	H	2B	3B	HR	HR%	R	RBI	BB	SO	SB	PH AB	PH H	PO	A	E	DP	TC/G	FA	G by Pos
1978	KC A	3	.000	.000	8	0	0	0	0	0.0	0	0	0	3	0	0	0	14	1	1	0	5.3	.938	C-3
1979		3	.167	.167	6	1	0	0	0	0.0	0	0	0	0	0	0	0	13	0	0	0	4.3	1.000	C-3
2 yrs.		6	.071	.071	14	1	0	0	0	0.0	0	0	0	3	0	0	0	27	1	1	0	4.8	.966	C-6

Mike Gaule

GAULE, MICHAEL JOHN
B. Aug. 4, 1869, Baltimore, Md.   D. Jan. 24, 1918, Baltimore, Md.   BL TL 6'2"

Year	Team	Games	BA	SA	AB	H	2B	3B	HR	HR%	R	RBI	BB	SO	SB	PH AB	PH H	PO	A	E	DP	TC/G	FA	G by Pos
1889	LOU AA	1	.000	.000	2	0	0	0	0	0.0	0	0	0	1	0	0	0	0	0	1	0	1.0	—	OF-1

Doc Gautreau

GAUTREAU, WALTER PAUL
B. July 26, 1901, Cambridge, Mass.   D. Aug. 23, 1970, Salt Lake City, Utah   BR TR 5'4"   129 lbs.

Year	Team	Games	BA	SA	AB	H	2B	3B	HR	HR%	R	RBI	BB	SO	SB	PH AB	PH H	PO	A	E	DP	TC/G	FA	G by Pos
1925 2 teams	PHI A (4G – .000)					BOS N	(68G – .262)																	
" total		72	.255	.322	286	73	13	3	0	0.0	45	23	35	16	11	0	0	178	238	11	40	5.9	.974	2B-72
1926	BOS N	79	.267	.331	266	71	9	4	0	0.0	36	8	35	24	17	3	0	170	205	23	42	5.0	.942	2B-74
1927		87	.246	.314	236	58	12	2	0	0.0	38	20	25	20	11	17	0	136	196	12	22	4.0	.965	2B-57
1928		23	.278	.389	18	5	0	1	0	0.0	4	1	4	3	1	15	4	2	2	1	1	0.2	.800	2B-4, SS-1
4 yrs.		261	.257	.324	806	207	34	10	0	0.0	122	52	99	63	40	35	4	486	641	47	105	4.5	.960	2B-207, SS-1

Sid Gautreaux

GAUTREAUX, SIDNEY ALLEN (Pudge)
B. May 4, 1912, Schriever, La.   D. Apr. 19, 1980, Morgan City, La.   BB TR 5'8"   190 lbs.

Year	Team	Games	BA	SA	AB	H	2B	3B	HR	HR%	R	RBI	BB	SO	SB	PH AB	PH H	PO	A	E	DP	TC/G	FA	G by Pos
1936	BKN N	75	.268	.310	71	19	3	0	0	0.0	8	16	9	7	0	55	16	23	3	1	2	0.4	.963	C-15
1937		11	.100	.200	10	1	1	0	0	0.0	0	2	1	1	0	10	1	0	0	0	0		—	
2 yrs.		86	.247	.296	81	20	4	0	0	0.0	8	18	10	8	0	65	17	23	3	1	2	0.3	.963	C-15

Mike Gazella

GAZELLA, MICHAEL
B. Oct. 13, 1896, Olyphant, Pa.   D. Sept. 11, 1978, Odessa, Tex.   BR TR 5'7½"   165 lbs.

Year	Team	Games	BA	SA	AB	H	2B	3B	HR	HR%	R	RBI	BB	SO	SB	PH AB	PH H	PO	A	E	DP	TC/G	FA	G by Pos
1923	NY A	8	.077	.077	13	1	0	0	0	0.0	2	1	2	3	0	0	0	4	9	0	0	1.6	1.000	SS-4, 3B-2, 2B-2
1926		66	.232	.268	168	39	6	0	0	0.0	21	21	25	24	2	9	4	59	103	16	9	2.7	.910	3B-45, SS-11
1927		54	.278	.417	115	32	8	4	0	0.0	17	9	23	16	4	0	0	41	61	5	6	2.0	.953	3B-44, SS-6
1928		32	.232	.232	56	13	0	0	0	0.0	11	2	6	7	2	6	0	10	31	3	1	1.4	.932	3B-14, 2B-4, SS-3
4 yrs.		160	.241	.304	352	85	14	4	0	0.0	51	33	56	50	8	15	4	114	204	24	16	2.1	.930	3B-105, SS-24, 2B-6
WORLD SERIES																								
1926	NY A	1	—	—	0	0	0	0	0	—	0	0	0	0	0	0	0	1	2	0	0	3.0	1.000	3B-1

Dale Gear

GEAR, DALE DUDLEY
B. Feb. 2, 1872, Lone Elm, Kans.   D. Sept. 23, 1951, Topeka, Kans.   BR TR 5'11"   165 lbs.

Year	Team	Games	BA	SA	AB	H	2B	3B	HR	HR%	R	RBI	BB	SO	SB	PH AB	PH H	PO	A	E	DP	TC/G	FA	G by Pos
1896	CLE N	4	.400	.600	15	6	1	0	0	0.0	5	3	1		1	0	0	9	4	2	1	3.8	.867	P-3, 1B-1
1897		7	.167	.208	24	4	1	0	0	0.0	3	2	3		2	0	0	9	3	4	0	2.3	.750	OF-6
1901	WAS A	58	.236	.302	199	47	9	3	0	0.0	17	20	4		2	2	0	56	59	6	3	2.1	.950	OF-34, P-24
3 yrs.		69	.239	.311	238	57	11	3	0	0.0	25	25	8		4	2	0	74	66	12	4	2.2	.921	OF-40, P-27, 1B-1

Lloyd Gearhart

GEARHART, LLOYD WILLIAM (Gary)
B. Aug. 10, 1923, New Lebanon, Ohio   BR TL 5'11"   180 lbs.

Year	Team	Games	BA	SA	AB	H	2B	3B	HR	HR%	R	RBI	BB	SO	SB	PH AB	PH H	PO	A	E	DP	TC/G	FA	G by Pos
1947	NY N	73	.246	.397	179	44	9	0	6	3.4	26	17	17	30	1	20	5	94	4	4	1	1.4	.961	OF-44

Huck Geary

GEARY, EUGENE FRANCIS JOSEPH
B. Jan. 22, 1917, Buffalo, N. Y.   D. Jan. 27, 1981, Cuba, N. Y.   BL TR 5'10½" 170 lbs.

Year	Team	Games	BA	SA	AB	H	2B	3B	HR	HR%	R	RBI	BB	SO	SB	PH AB	PH H	PO	A	E	DP	TC/G	FA	G by Pos
1942	PIT N	9	.227	.227	22	5	0	0	0	0.0	3	2	2	3	0	1	1	17	14	2	5	3.7	.939	SS-8
1943		46	.151	.193	166	25	4	0	1	0.6	17	13	18	6	3	0	0	92	127	10	25	5.0	.956	SS-46
2 yrs.		55	.160	.197	188	30	4	0	1	0.5	20	15	20	9	3	1	1	109	141	12	30	4.8	.954	SS-54

Elmer Gedeon

GEDEON, ELMER JOHN
B. Apr. 15, 1917, Cleveland, Ohio   D. Apr. 20, 1944, St. Pol, France   BR TR 6'4"   196 lbs.

Year	Team	Games	BA	SA	AB	H	2B	3B	HR	HR%	R	RBI	BB	SO	SB	PH AB	PH H	PO	A	E	DP	TC/G	FA	G by Pos
1939	WAS A	5	.200	.200	15	3	0	0	0	0.0	1	1	2	5	0	0	0	17	0	0	0	3.4	1.000	OF-5

Joe Gedeon

GEDEON, ELMER JOSEPH
B. Dec. 5, 1893, Sacramento, Calif.   D. May 19, 1941, San Francisco, Calif.   BR TR 6'   167 lbs.

Year	Team	Games	BA	SA	AB	H	2B	3B	HR	HR%	R	RBI	BB	SO	SB	PH AB	PH H	PO	A	E	DP	TC/G	FA	G by Pos
1913	WAS A	27	.183	.296	71	13	1	2	1	1.4	3	6	4	6	3	2	0	32	16	2	2	1.9	.941	OF-14, 3B-8, 2B-2, SS-1, P-1
1914		3	.000	.000	2	0	0	0	0	0.0	0	1	0	1	0	0	0	2	0	1	0	1.0	.667	OF-3
1916	NY A	122	.211	.262	435	92	14	4	0	0.0	50	27	40	61	14	0	0	235	341	27	55	4.9	.955	2B-122
1917		33	.239	.299	117	28	7	0	0	0.0	15	8	7	13	4	2	0	83	86	3	12	5.2	.983	2B-31
1918	STL A	123	.213	.265	441	94	14	3	1	0.2	39	41	27	29	7	0	0	309	409	17	45	6.0	.977	2B-123
1919		120	.254	.302	437	111	13	4	0	0.0	57	27	50	35	4	1	0	290	345	16	44	5.4	.975	2B-118
1920		153	.292	.366	606	177	33	6	0	0.0	95	61	55	36	1	0	0	365	421	29	75	5.3	.964	2B-153
7 yrs.		581	.244	.304	2109	515	82	19	2	0.1	259	171	180	181	33	5	0	1316	1618	96	233	5.2	.968	2B-549, OF-17, 3B-8, SS-1, P-1

Year	Team		Games	BA	SA	AB	H	2B	3B	HR	HR%	R	RBI	BB	SO	SB	Pinch Hit AB	Pinch Hit H	PO	A	E	DP	TC/G	FA	G by Pos

Rich Gedman

GEDMAN, RICHARD LEO
B. Sept. 26, 1959, Worcester, Mass.
BL TR 6' 210 lbs.

Year	Team		Games	BA	SA	AB	H	2B	3B	HR	HR%	R	RBI	BB	SO	SB	PH AB	PH H	PO	A	E	DP	TC/G	FA	G by Pos
1980	BOS	A	9	.208	.208	24	5	0	0	0	0.0	2	1	0	5	0	5	0	13	0	2	0	1.7	.867	DH-4, C-2
1981			62	.288	.434	205	59	15	0	5	2.4	22	26	9	31	0	3	1	275	30	3	1	5.0	.990	C-59
1982			92	.249	.363	289	72	17	2	4	1.4	30	26	10	37	0	9	2	397	29	10	5	4.7	.977	C-86
1983			81	.294	.412	204	60	16	1	2	1.0	21	18	15	37	0	19	5	274	26	6	5	3.8	.980	C-69
1984			133	.269	.506	449	121	26	4	24	5.3	54	72	29	72	0	15	5	693	58	18	5	5.8	.977	C-125
1985			144	.295	.484	498	147	30	5	18	3.6	66	80	50	79	2	9	4	768	78	15	13	6.0	.983	C-139
1986			135	.258	.424	462	119	29	0	16	3.5	49	65	37	61	1	9	4	866	65	6	10	6.9	.994	C-134
1987			52	.205	.278	151	31	8	0	1	0.7	11	13	10	24	0	4	1	306	14	8	1	6.3	.976	C-51
1988			95	.231	.368	299	69	14	0	9	3.0	33	39	18	49	0	2	0	570	40	5	4	6.5	.992	C-93, DH-1
1989			93	.212	.292	260	55	9	0	4	1.5	24	16	23	47	0	5	1	486	36	10	6	5.7	.981	C-91
10 yrs.			896	.260	.414	2841	738	164	12	83	2.9	312	356	201	442	3	80	23	4648	376	83	50	5.7	.984	C-849, DH-5

LEAGUE CHAMPIONSHIP SERIES

Year	Team		Games	BA	SA	AB	H	2B	3B	HR	HR%	R	RBI	BB	SO	SB	PH AB	PH H	PO	A	E	DP	TC/G	FA	G by Pos
1986	BOS	A	7	.357	.500	28	10	1	0	1	3.6	4	6	0	4	0	0	0	45	4	0	0	7.0	1.000	C-7
1988			4	.357	.571	14	5	0	0	1	7.1	1	1	2	1	0	0	0	34	5	0	1	9.8	1.000	C-4
2 yrs.			11	.357	.524	42	15	1	0	2	4.8	5	7	2	5	0	0	0	79	9	0	1	8.0	1.000	C-11

WORLD SERIES

Year	Team		Games	BA	SA	AB	H	2B	3B	HR	HR%	R	RBI	BB	SO	SB	PH AB	PH H	PO	A	E	DP	TC/G	FA	G by Pos
1986	BOS	A	7	.200	.333	30	6	1	0	1	3.3	1	1	0	10	0	0	0	46	3	2	2	7.3	.961	C-7

Billy Geer

GEER, WILLIAM HENRY HARRISON
Born George Harrison Geer.
B. Aug. 13, 1849, Syracuse, N. Y. D. Jan. 5, 1922, Syracuse, N. Y.
TR 5'8" 160 lbs.

Year	Team		Games	BA	SA	AB	H	2B	3B	HR	HR%	R	RBI	BB	SO	SB	PH AB	PH H	PO	A	E	DP	TC/G	FA	G by Pos
1878	CIN	N	61	.219	.291	237	52	13	2	0	0.0	31	20	10	18		0	0	62	181	38	15	4.6	.865	SS-60, 2B-2
1880	WOR	N	2	.000	.000	6	0	0	0	0	0.0	0	0	0	0		0	0	1	4	1	0	3.0	.833	OF-1, SS-1
1884	2 teams			PHI U (9G – .250)		BKN AA (107G – .210)																				
"	total		116	.213	.290	427	91	17	8	0	0.0	75		42			0	0	187	398	94	35	5.9	.862	SS-115, 2B-2, P-2, 1B-1
1885	LOU	AA	14	.118	.157	51	6	2	0	0	0.0	2		2			0	0	26	49	11	2	6.1	.872	SS-14
4 yrs.			193	.207	.279	721	149	32	10	0	0.0	108	20	54	18		0	0	276	632	144	52	5.5	.863	SS-190, 2B-4, P-2, OF-1, 1B-1

Lou Gehrig

GEHRIG, HENRY LOUIS (The Iron Horse, Columbia Lou)
Born Ludwig Heinrich Gehrig.
B. June 19, 1903, New York, N. Y. D. June 2, 1941, New York, N. Y.
Hall of Fame 1939.
BL TL 6' 200 lbs.

Year	Team		Games	BA	SA	AB	H	2B	3B	HR	HR%	R	RBI	BB	SO	SB	PH AB	PH H	PO	A	E	DP	TC/G	FA	G by Pos
1923	NY	A	13	.423	.769	26	11	4	1	1	3.8	6	9	2	5	0	4	1	53	3	4	4	4.6	.933	1B-9
1924			10	.500	.583	12	6	1	0	0	0.0	2	5	1	3	0	6	2	10	1	0	0	1.1	1.000	1B-2, OF-1
1925			126	.295	.531	437	129	23	10	20	4.6	73	68	46	49	6	6	1	1135	53	15	72	9.5	.988	1B-114, OF-6
1926			155	.313	.549	572	179	47	20	16	2.8	135	107	105	72	6	0	0	1566	73	15	87	10.7	.991	1B-155
1927			155	.373	.765	584	218	52	18	47	8.0	149	175	109	84	10	0	0	1662	88	15	108	11.4	.992	1B-155
1928			154	.374	.648	562	210	47	13	27	4.8	139	142	95	69	4	0	0	1488	79	18	112	10.3	.989	1B-154
1929			154	.300	.582	553	166	33	9	35	6.3	127	126	122	68	4	0	0	1458	82	9	134	10.1	.994	1B-154
1930			154	.379	.721	581	220	42	17	41	7.1	143	174	101	63	12	0	0	1300	89	15	109	9.1	.989	1B-153, OF-1
1931			155	.341	.662	619	211	31	15	46	7.4	163	184	117	56	17	0	0	1355	58	14	120	9.2	.990	1B-154, OF-1
1932			156	.349	.621	596	208	42	9	34	5.7	138	151	108	38	4	0	0	1293	75	18	101	8.9	.987	1B-155
1933			152	.334	.605	593	198	41	12	32	5.4	138	139	92	42	9	0	0	1290	64	9	102	9.0	.993	1B-152
1934			154	.363	.706	579	210	40	6	49	8.5	128	165	109	31	9	0	0	1284	80	8	126	8.9	.994	1B-153, SS-1
1935			149	.329	.583	535	176	26	10	30	5.6	125	119	132	38	8	0	0	1337	82	15	96	9.6	.990	1B-149
1936			155	.354	.696	579	205	37	7	49	8.5	167	152	130	46	3	0	0	1377	82	9	128	9.5	.994	1B-155
1937			157	.351	.643	569	200	37	9	37	6.5	138	159	127	49	4	0	0	1370	74	16	113	9.3	.989	1B-157
1938			157	.295	.523	576	170	32	6	29	5.0	115	114	107	75	6	0	0	1483	100	14	157	10.2	.991	1B-157
1939			8	.143	.143	28	4	0	0	0	0.0	2	1	5	1	0	0	0	64	4	1	8	8.8	.971	1B-8
17 yrs.			2164	.340	.632	8001	2721	535	162	493	6.2	1888	1990	1508	789	102	16	4	19525	1087	196	1574	9.6	.991	1B-2136, OF-9, SS-1
				3rd								7th	3rd												

WORLD SERIES

Year	Team		Games	BA	SA	AB	H	2B	3B	HR	HR%	R	RBI	BB	SO	SB	PH AB	PH H	PO	A	E	DP	TC/G	FA	G by Pos
1926	NY	A	7	.348	.435	23	8	2	0	0	0.0	1	3	5	4	0	0	0	78	1	0	3	11.3	1.000	1B-7
1927			4	.308	.769	13	4	2	2	0	0.0	2	5	3	3	0	0	0	41	3	0	3	11.0	1.000	1B-4
1928			4	.545	1.727	11	6	1	0	4	36.4	5	9	6	0	0	0	0	33	0	0	3	8.3	1.000	1B-4
1932			4	.529	1.118	17	9	1	0	3	17.6	9	8	2	1	0	0	0	37	2	1	1	10.0	.975	1B-4
1936			6	.292	.583	24	7	1	0	2	8.3	5	7	3	2	0	0	0	45	2	0	2	7.8	1.000	1B-6
1937			5	.294	.647	17	5	1	1	1	5.9	4	3	5	4	0	0	0	50	1	0	2	10.2	1.000	1B-5
1938			4	.286	.286	14	4	0	0	0	0.0	4	0	2	3	0	0	0	25	3	0	4	7.0	1.000	1B-4
7 yrs.			34	.361	.731	119	43	8	3	10	8.4	30	35	26	17	0	0	0	309	12	1	18	9.5	.997	1B-34
				8th	3rd		9th	6th	4th	5th	4th	4th	3rd			5th									

Charlie Gehringer

GEHRINGER, CHARLES LEONARD (The Mechanical Man)
B. May 11, 1903, Fowlerville, Mich.
Hall of Fame 1949.
BL TR 5'11" 180 lbs.

Year	Team		Games	BA	SA	AB	H	2B	3B	HR	HR%	R	RBI	BB	SO	SB	PH AB	PH H	PO	A	E	DP	TC/G	FA	G by Pos
1924	DET	A	5	.462	.462	13	6	0	0	0	0.0	2	1	0	1	1	0	0	12	17	1	2	6.0	.967	2B-5
1925			8	.167	.167	18	3	0	0	0	0.0	3	0	2	0	0	2	0	8	20	0	5	3.5	1.000	2B-6
1926			123	.277	.399	459	127	19	17	1	0.2	62	48	30	42	9	6	0	264	340	16	56	5.0	.974	2B-112, 3B-6
1927			133	.317	.441	508	161	29	11	4	0.8	110	61	52	31	17	9	3	304	438	27	84	5.8	.965	2B-121
1928			154	.320	.451	603	193	29	16	6	1.0	108	74	69	22	15	0	0	377	507	35	101	6.0	.962	2B-154
1929			155	.339	.532	634	215	45	19	13	2.1	131	106	64	19	28	1	0	404	501	23	93	6.0	.975	2B-154
1930			154	.330	.534	610	201	47	15	16	2.6	144	98	69	17	19	0	0	399	501	19	97	6.0	.979	2B-154
1931			101	.311	.431	383	119	24	5	4	1.0	67	53	29	15	13	12	1	292	242	11	57	5.4	.980	2B-78, 1B-9
1932			152	.298	.497	618	184	44	11	19	3.1	112	107	68	34	9	0	0	396	495	30	110	6.1	.967	2B-152
1933			155	.325	.468	628	204	42	6	12	1.9	103	105	68	27	5	0	0	358	542	17	111	5.9	.981	2B-155
1934			154	.356	.517	601	214	50	7	11	1.8	134	127	99	25	11	0	0	355	516	17	100	5.8	.981	2B-154
1935			150	.330	.502	610	201	32	8	19	3.1	123	108	79	16	11	2	1	349	489	13	99	5.7	.985	2B-149
1936			154	.354	.555	641	227	60	12	15	2.3	144	116	83	13	4	0	0	397	524	25	116	6.1	.974	2B-154

Year	Team	Games	BA	SA	AB	H	2B	3B	HR	HR%	R	RBI	BB	SO	SB	Pinch Hit AB	Pinch Hit H	PO	A	E	DP	TC/G	FA	G by Pos

Charlie Gehringer *continued*

Year	Team	Games	BA	SA	AB	H	2B	3B	HR	HR%	R	RBI	BB	SO	SB	PH AB	PH H	PO	A	E	DP	TC/G	FA	G by Pos
1937		144	.371	.520	564	209	40	1	14	2.5	133	96	90	25	11	1	0	331	485	12	102	5.8	.986	2B-142
1938		152	.306	.486	568	174	32	5	20	3.5	133	107	112	21	14	0	0	393	455	21	115	5.7	.976	2B-152
1939		118	.325	.544	406	132	29	6	16	3.9	86	86	68	16	4	9	4	245	312	13	67	4.8	.977	2B-107
1940		139	.313	.447	515	161	33	3	10	1.9	108	81	101	17	10	1	0	276	374	19	72	4.8	.972	2B-138
1941		127	.220	.303	436	96	19	4	3	0.7	65	46	95	26	1	10	3	279	324	11	59	4.8	.976	2B-116
1942		45	.267	.333	45	12	0	0	1	2.2	6	7	7	4	0	38	11	7	9	0	1	0.4	1.000	2B-3
19 yrs.		2323	.320	.480	8860	2839	574	146	184	2.1	1774	1427	1185	372	182	91	23	5446	7091	310	1447	5.5	.976	2B-2206, 1B-9, 3B-6
			10th																					

WORLD SERIES

Year	Team	Games	BA	SA	AB	H	2B	3B	HR	HR%	R	RBI	BB	SO	SB	PH AB	PH H	PO	A	E	DP	TC/G	FA	G by Pos
1934	DET A	7	.379	.517	29	11	1	0	1	3.4	5	2	3	0	1	0	0	19	26	3	3	6.9	.938	2B-7
1935		6	.375	.500	24	9	3	0	0	0.0	4	4	2	1	1	0	0	14	25	0	6	6.5	1.000	2B-6
1940		7	.214	.214	28	6	0	0	0	0.0	3	1	2	0	0	0	0	18	20	0	3	5.4	1.000	2B-7
3 yrs.		20	.321	.407	81	26	4	0	1	1.2	12	7	7	1	2	0	0	51	71	3	12	6.3	.976	2B-20

Phil Geier

GEIER, PHILIP LOUIS (Little Phil)
B. Nov. 3, 1876, Washington, D. C. D. Sept. 20, 1967, Spokane, Wash.   BL TR 5'7"   145 lbs.

Year	Team	Games	BA	SA	AB	H	2B	3B	HR	HR%	R	RBI	BB	SO	SB	PH AB	PH H	PO	A	E	DP	TC/G	FA	G by Pos
1896	PHI N	17	.232	.268	56	13	0	0	0	0.0	12	6	9		3	0	0	18	11	4	3	1.9	.879	OF-12, 2B-3, C-2
1897		92	.278	.320	316	88	6	2	1	0.3	51	35	56		19	2	0	174	147	22	8	3.7	.936	OF-45, 2B-37, SS-6, 3B-2
1900	CIN N	30	.257	.336	113	29	1	4	0	0.0	18	10	7		3	1	0	61	7	8	1	2.5	.895	OF-27, 3B-2
1901	2 teams				PHI A	(50G – .232)					MIL A	(11G – .179)												
"	total	61	.224	.272	250	56	6	3	0	0.0	46	24	29		11	0	0	91	15	10	2	1.9	.914	OF-58, 3B-4, SS-2
1904	BOS N	149	.243	.284	580	141	17	2	1	0.2	70	27	56		18	1	0	256	44	28	11	2.2	.915	OF-137, 3B-7, 2B-5, SS-1
5 yrs.		349	.249	.294	1315	327	30	12	2	0.2	197	102	154	7	54	4	0	600	224	72	25	2.6	.920	OF-279, 2B-45, 3B-15, SS-9, C-2

Gary Geiger

GEIGER, GARY MERLE
B. Apr. 4, 1937, Sand Ridge, Ill.   BL TR 6'   168 lbs.

Year	Team	Games	BA	SA	AB	H	2B	3B	HR	HR%	R	RBI	BB	SO	SB	PH AB	PH H	PO	A	E	DP	TC/G	FA	G by Pos
1958	CLE A	91	.231	.272	195	45	3	1	1	0.5	28	6	27	43	2	32	6	133	7	4	1	1.6	.972	OF-53, 3B-2, P-1
1959	BOS A	120	.245	.397	335	82	10	4	11	3.3	45	48	21	55	9	24	9	173	5	2	1	1.5	.989	OF-95
1960		77	.302	.490	245	74	13	3	9	3.7	32	33	23	38	2	12	5	121	9	0	1	1.7	1.000	OF-66
1961		140	.232	.407	499	116	21	6	18	3.6	82	64	87	91	16	5	2	324	12	4	1	2.4	.988	OF-137
1962		131	.249	.408	466	116	18	4	16	3.4	67	54	67	66	18	8	2	287	8	4	1	2.3	.987	OF-129
1963		121	.263	.441	399	105	13	5	16	4.0	67	44	36	63	9	23	3	246	13	5	2	2.2	.981	OF-95, 1B-6
1964		5	.385	.538	13	5	0	1	0	0.0	3	1	2	2	0	1	1	6	0	0	0	1.2	1.000	OF-4
1965		24	.200	.333	45	9	3	0	1	2.2	5	2	13	10	3	7	0	32	0	1	0	1.4	.970	OF-16
1966	ATL N	78	.262	.444	126	33	5	3	4	3.2	23	10	21	29	0	27	4	49	5	1	1	0.7	.982	OF-49
1967		69	.162	.214	117	19	1	1	1	0.9	17	5	20	35	1	24	1	47	2	1	0	0.7	.980	OF-38
1969	HOU N	93	.224	.272	125	28	4	0	0	0.0	19	16	24	34	2	26	7	57	3	2	0	0.7	.968	OF-65
1970		5	.250	.250	4	1	0	0	0	0.0	0	0	0	0	0	2	0	1	0	0	0	0.2	1.000	OF-2
12 yrs.		954	.246	.394	2569	633	91	29	77	3.0	388	283	341	466	62	191	40	1476	64	24	9	1.6	.985	OF-749, 1B-6, 3B-2, P-1

Bill Geiss

GEISS, WILLIAM J
Brother of Emil Geiss.
B. July 15, 1858, Chicago, Ill. D. Sept. 18, 1924, Chicago, Ill.   5'10"   164 lbs.

Year	Team	Games	BA	SA	AB	H	2B	3B	HR	HR%	R	RBI	BB	SO	SB	PH AB	PH H	PO	A	E	DP	TC/G	FA	G by Pos
1884	DET N	75	.177	.265	283	50	11	4	2	0.7	23		6	60				203	218	65	28	6.5	.866	2B-73, OF-1, 1B-1, P-1

Emil Geiss

GEISS, EMIL AUGUST
Brother of Bill Geiss.
B. Mar. 20, 1867, Chicago, Ill. D. Oct. 4, 1911, Chicago, Ill.   BR TR

Year	Team	Games	BA	SA	AB	H	2B	3B	HR	HR%	R	RBI	BB	SO	SB	PH AB	PH H	PO	A	E	DP	TC/G	FA	G by Pos
1887	CHI N	3	.083	.083	12	1	0	0	0	0.0	0	0	0	7	0	0	0	13	4	3	0	6.7	.850	2B-1, 1B-1, P-1

Charley Gelbert

GELBERT, CHARLES MAGNUS
B. Jan. 26, 1906, Scranton, Pa. D. Jan. 13, 1967, Easton, Pa.   BR TR 5'11"   170 lbs.

Year	Team	Games	BA	SA	AB	H	2B	3B	HR	HR%	R	RBI	BB	SO	SB	PH AB	PH H	PO	A	E	DP	TC/G	FA	G by Pos
1929	STL N	146	.262	.367	512	134	29	8	3	0.6	60	65	51	46	8	0	0	338	499	46	95	6.0	.948	SS-146
1930		139	.304	.441	513	156	39	11	3	0.6	92	72	43	41	6	0	0	322	472	44	104	6.0	.947	SS-139
1931		131	.289	.383	447	129	29	5	1	0.2	61	62	54	31	7	0	0	281	435	31	91	5.7	.959	SS-131
1932		122	.268	.376	455	122	28	9	1	0.2	60	45	39	30	8	0	0	246	389	37	69	5.5	.945	SS-122
1935		62	.292	.393	168	49	7	2	2	1.2	24	21	17	18	0	5	1	65	98	5	16	2.7	.970	SS-37, SS-21, 2B-3
1936		93	.229	.329	280	64	15	2	3	1.1	33	27	25	26	2	2	0	107	162	10	31	3.0	.964	3B-60, SS-28, 2B-8
1937	2 teams				CIN N	(43G – .193)					DET A	(20G – .085)												
"	total	63	.161	.217	161	26	4	1	0	0.0	16	14	19	23	1	0	0	110	135	9	27	4.0	.965	SS-53, 2B-9, 3B-1
1939	WAS A	68	.255	.394	188	48	11	5	1	0.6	36	29	30	11	2	16	2	61	123	7	21	2.8	.963	SS-28, 3B-20, 2B-1
1940	2 teams				WAS A	(22G – .370)					BOS A	(30G – .198)												
"	total	52	.262	.338	145	38	9	1	0	0.0	16	15	12	19	0	4	0	47	94	12	8	2.9	.922	3B-29, SS-13, P-2, 2B-1
9 yrs.		876	.267	.374	2869	766	169	43	17	0.6	398	350	290	245	34	33	3	1577	2407	201	462	4.8	.952	SS-681, 3B-147, 2B-22, P-2

WORLD SERIES

Year	Team	Games	BA	SA	AB	H	2B	3B	HR	HR%	R	RBI	BB	SO	SB	PH AB	PH H	PO	A	E	DP	TC/G	FA	G by Pos
1930	STL N	6	.353	.471	17	6	0	1	0	0.0	2	2	5	3	0	0	0	5	23	0	3	4.7	1.000	SS-6
1931		7	.261	.304	23	6	1	0	0	0.0	0	3	2	4	0	0	0	13	29	0	6	6.0	1.000	SS-7
2 yrs.		13	.300	.375	40	12	1	1	0	0.0	2	5	3	7	0	0	0	18	52	0	9	5.4	1.000	SS-13

Frank Genins

GENINS, C. FRANK (Frenchy)
B. Nov. 2, 1866, St. Louis, Mo. D. Sept. 30, 1922, St. Louis, Mo.   TR

Year	Team	Games	BA	SA	AB	H	2B	3B	HR	HR%	R	RBI	BB	SO	SB	PH AB	PH H	PO	A	E	DP	TC/G	FA	G by Pos
1892	2 teams				CIN N	(35G – .182)					STL N	(15G – .196)												
"	total	50	.186	.217	161	30	5	0	0	0.0	17	11	13	23	10	0	0	92	113	31	14	4.7	.869	SS-31, OF-15, 3B-4
1895	PIT N	73	.250	.306	252	63	8	0	2	0.8	43	24	22	14	19	3	0	127	99	29	7	3.5	.886	OF-29, 3B-16, 2B-16, SS-8, 1B-2
1901	CLE A	26	.228	.277	101	23	5	0	0	0.0	15	9	8		3	0	0	60	3	4	1	2.6	.940	OF-26
3 yrs.		149	.226	.272	514	116	18	0	2	0.4	75	44	43	37	32	3	0	279	215	64	22	3.7	.885	OF-70, SS-39, 3B-20, 2B-16, 1B-2

Year	Team		Games	BA	SA	AB	H	2B	3B	HR	HR%	R	RBI	BB	SO	SB	Pinch Hit AB	Pinch Hit H	PO	A	E	DP	TC/G	FA	G by Pos

George Genovese

GENOVESE, GEORGE MICHAEL
B. Feb. 22, 1922, Staten Island, N. Y.

BL TR 5'6½" 160 lbs.

| 1950 | WAS | A | 3 | .000 | .000 | 1 | 0 | 0 | 0 | 0 | 0.0 | 1 | 0 | 1 | 0 | 0 | 1 | 0 | 0 | 0 | 0 | 0 | 0.0 | – | |

Jim Gentile

GENTILE, JAMES EDWARD (Diamond Jim)
B. June 3, 1934, San Francisco, Calif.

BL TL 6'3½" 210 lbs.

1957	BKN	N	4	.167	.667	6	1	0	0	1	16.7	1	1	1	1	0	1	0	14	0	0	3	3.5	1.000	1B-2
1958	LA	N	12	.133	.167	30	4	1	0	0	0.0	0	4	4	6	0	4	1	50	2	1	9	4.4	.981	1B-8
1960	BAL	A	138	.292	.500	384	112	17	0	21	5.5	67	98	68	72	0	28	8	885	52	7	98	6.8	.993	1B-124
1961			148	.302	.646	486	147	25	2	46	9.5	96	141	96	106	1	11	3	1209	100	14	129	8.9	.989	1B-144
1962			152	.251	.475	545	137	21	1	33	6.1	80	87	77	100	1	2	0	1214	121	16	121	8.9	.988	1B-150
1963			145	.248	.429	496	123	16	1	24	4.8	65	72	76	101	1	3	1	1185	110	6	122	9.0	.995	1B-143
1964	KC	A	136	.251	.465	439	110	10	0	28	6.4	71	71	84	122	0	6	1	1018	84	13	92	8.2	.988	1B-128
1965	2 teams		KC A (38G – .246)			HOU N (81G – .242)																			
"	total		119	.243	.443	345	84	16	1	17	4.9	36	53	43	98	0	14	3	783	60	9	65	7.2	.989	1B-103
1966	2 teams		HOU N (49G – .243)			CLE A (33G – .128)																			
"	total		82	.215	.403	191	41	7	1	9	4.7	18	22	26	57	0	30	6	367	35	7	32	5.0	.983	1B-52
9 yrs.			936	.260	.486	2922	759	113	6	179	6.1	434	549	475	663	3	99	23	6725	564	73	671	7.9	.990	1B-854

Sam Gentile

GENTILE, SAMUEL CHRISTOPHER
B. Oct. 12, 1916, Charlestown, Mass.

BL TR 5'11" 180 lbs.

| 1943 | BOS | N | 8 | .250 | .500 | 4 | 1 | 0 | 0 | 0 | 0.0 | 1 | 0 | 1 | 0 | 0 | 4 | 1 | 0 | 0 | 0 | 0 | 0.0 | – | |

Harvey Gentry

GENTRY, HARVEY WILLIAM
B. May 27, 1926, Winston-Salem, N. C.

BL TR 6' 170 lbs.

| 1954 | NY | N | 5 | .250 | .250 | 4 | 1 | 0 | 0 | 0 | 0.0 | 1 | 1 | 0 | 1 | 0 | 4 | 1 | 0 | 0 | 0 | 0 | 0.0 | – | |

Alex George

GEORGE, ALEX THOMAS M.
B. Sept. 27, 1938, Kansas City, Mo.

BL TR 5'11½" 170 lbs.

| 1955 | KC | A | 5 | .100 | .100 | 10 | 1 | 0 | 0 | 0 | 0.0 | 1 | 7 | 0 | 2 | 0 | 6 | 5 | 1 | 1 | 2.4 | .917 | SS-5 | | |

Greek George

GEORGE, CHARLES PETER
B. Dec. 25, 1912, Waycross, Ga.   D. Jan. 30, 1975, St. Louis, Mo.

BR TR 6'2" 200 lbs.

1935	CLE	A	2	–	–	0	0	0	0	0	–	0	0	0	0	0	0	0	2	0	0	0	1.0	1.000	C-1
1936			23	.195	.234	77	15	3	0	0	0.0	3	5	9	16	0	1	0	164	16	1	1	7.9	.994	C-22
1938	BKN	N	7	.200	.300	20	4	0	1	0	0.0	2	0	4	4	0	0	0	23	5	0	1	4.0	1.000	C-7
1941	CHI	N	35	.156	.188	64	10	2	0	0	0.0	4	6	2	10	0	17	0	63	9	2	0	2.1	.973	C-18
1945	PHI	A	51	.174	.217	138	24	4	1	0	0.0	8	11	17	29	0	5	0	161	14	5	3	3.5	.972	C-46
5 yrs.			118	.177	.221	299	53	9	2	0	0.0	15	24	28	59	0	23	0	413	44	8	5	3.9	.983	C-94

Ben Geraghty

GERAGHTY, BENJAMIN RAYMOND
B. July 19, 1912, Jersey City, N. J.   D. June 18, 1963, Jacksonville, Fla.

BR TR 5'11" 175 lbs.

1936	BKN	N	51	.194	.225	129	25	4	0	0	0.0	11	9	8	16	4	0	0	78	89	12	11	3.5	.933	SS-31, 2B-9, 3B-5
1943	BOS	N	8	.000	.000	1	0	0	0	0	0.0	0	0	0	0	0	0	0	2	2	0	0	0.5	1.000	SS-1, 3B-1, 2B-1
1944			11	.250	.250	16	4	0	0	0	0.0	3	0	1	2	0	0	0	10	7	2	0	1.7	.895	2B-4, 3B-3
3 yrs.			70	.199	.226	146	29	4	0	0	0.0	16	9	9	18	4	1	0	90	98	14	11	2.9	.931	SS-32, 2B-14, 3B-9

Craig Gerber

GERBER, CRAIG STUART
B. Jan. 8, 1959, Chicago, Ill.

BL TR 6' 175 lbs.

| 1985 | CAL | A | 65 | .264 | .319 | 91 | 24 | 1 | 2 | 0 | 0.0 | 8 | 6 | 2 | 3 | 0 | 0 | 0 | 56 | 112 | 5 | 7 | 2.7 | .971 | SS-53, 3B-9, DH-1, 2B-1 |

Wally Gerber

GERBER, WALTER (Spooks)
B. Aug. 18, 1891, Columbus, Ohio   D. June 19, 1951, Columbus, Ohio

BR TR 5'10" 152 lbs.

1914	PIT	N	17	.241	.296	54	13	1	1	0	0.0	5	5	2	8	0	0	0	31	62	8	7	5.9	.921	SS-17
1915			56	.194	.208	144	28	2	0	0	0.0	8	7	9	16	6	7	0	83	104	13	11	3.6	.935	SS-23, 3B-23, 2B-2
1917	STL	A	14	.308	.385	39	12	1	1	0	0.0	2	3	3	2	1	0	0	16	38	4	4	4.1	.931	SS-12, 2B-2
1918			56	.240	.263	171	41	4	0	0	0.0	10	10	19	11	2	0	0	109	174	24	20	5.5	.922	SS-56
1919			140	.227	.290	462	105	14	6	1	0.2	43	37	49	36	1	0	0	287	422	45	42	5.4	.940	SS-140
1920			154	.279	.341	584	163	26	2	2	0.3	70	60	58	32	4	0	0	288	513	52	65	5.5	.939	SS-154
1921			114	.278	.360	436	121	12	9	2	0.5	55	48	34	19	3	1	0	269	331	36	60	5.6	.943	SS-113
1922			153	.267	.334	604	161	22	8	1	0.2	81	51	52	34	6	0	0	322	470	47	93	5.5	.944	SS-153
1923			154	.281	.339	605	170	26	3	1	0.2	85	62	54	50	4	0	0	334	461	42	86	5.4	.950	SS-154
1924			148	.272	.329	496	135	20	4	0	0.0	61	55	43	34	4	1	0	317	422	42	77	5.3	.946	SS-146
1925			72	.272	.333	246	67	13	1	0	0.0	29	29	26	15	1	1	0	144	206	19	39	5.1	.949	SS-71
1926			131	.270	.290	411	111	8	0	0	0.0	37	42	40	29	0	1	0	261	358	37	92	5.0	.944	SS-129
1927			142	.224	.295	438	98	13	9	0	0.0	44	45	35	25	2	0	0	290	427	41	91	5.3	.946	SS-141, 3B-1
1928	2 teams		STL A (6G – .278)			BOS A (104G – .213)																			
"	total		110	.217	.245	318	69	7	1	0	0.0	22	28	33	34	6	1	0	207	340	30	54	5.2	.948	SS-109
1929	BOS	N	61	.165	.220	91	15	3	1	0	0.0	6	5	8	12	1	1	0	70	115	10	14	3.2	.949	SS-30, 2B-22
15 yrs.			1522	.257	.313	5099	1309	172	46	7	0.1	558	476	465	357	41	11	0	3028	4443	450	755	5.2	.943	SS-1448, 2B-26, 3B-24

Bob Geren

GEREN, ROBERT PETER
B. Sept. 22, 1961, San Diego, Calif.

BR TR 6'3" 205 lbs.

1988	NY	A	10	.100	.100	10	1	0	0	0	0.0	0	0	2	3	0	0	0	18	3	0	0	2.1	1.000	C-10
1989			65	.288	.454	205	59	5	1	9	4.4	26	27	12	44	0	7	1	308	24	3	4	5.2	.991	C-60, DH-2
2 yrs.			75	.279	.437	215	60	5	1	9	4.2	26	27	14	47	0	7	1	326	27	3	4	4.7	.992	C-70, DH-2

Joe Gerhardt

GERHARDT, JOHN JOSEPH (Move Up Joe)
B. Feb. 14, 1855, Washington, D. C.   D. Mar. 11, 1922, Middletown, N. Y.
Manager 1883-84.

BR TR 6' 160 lbs.

Joe Gerhardt *continued*

Year	Team	Games	BA	SA	AB	H	2B	3B	HR	HR%	R	RBI	BB	SO	SB	Pinch Hit AB	Pinch Hit H	PO	A	E	DP	TC/G	FA	G by Pos
1876	LOU N	65	.260	.336	292	76	10	3	2	0.7	33	18	3		5		0	0	695	44	47	15	12.1	.940	1B-54, 2B-5, SS-3, OF-2, 3B-2
1877		59	.304	.380	250	76	6	5	1	0.4	41	35	5	8		0	0	183	248	52	30	8.2	.892	2B-57, OF-1, SS-1, 1B-1
1878	CIN N	60	.297	.340	259	77	7	2	0	0.0	46	28	7	14		0	0	159	206	38	26	6.7	.906	2B-60
1879		79	.198	.265	313	62	12	3	1	0.3	22	39	3	19		0	0	307	232	55	31	7.5	.907	2B-55, 3B-16, 1B-8, SS-1
1881	DET N	80	.242	.327	297	72	13	6	0	0.0	35	36	7	31		0	0	261	242	51	62	6.9	.908	2B-79, 3B-1
1883	LOU AA	78	.263	.354	319	84	11	9	0	0.0	56			14		0	0	278	263	56	42	7.7	.906	2B-78
1884		106	.220	.277	404	89	7	8	0	0.0	39		13			0	0	341	391	64	64	7.5	.920	2B-105, SS-1
1885	NY N	112	.155	.195	399	62	12	2	0	0.0	43		24	47		0	0	314	352	65	59	6.5	.911	2B-112
1886		123	.190	.249	426	81	11	7	0	0.0	44	40	22	63		0	0	340	355	57	50	6.1	.924	2B-123
1887	2 teams	NY N (1G – .000)		NY AA (85G – .221)																				
"	total	86	.219	.273	311	68	13	2	0	0.0	40		24		15	0	0	289	275	65	48	7.3	.897	2B-84, 3B-2
1890	2 teams	BKN AA (99G – .203)		STL AA (37G – .256)																				
"	total	136	.217	.273	494	107	10	3	4	0.8	49		39		14	0	0	427	440	56	75	6.8	.939	2B-119, 3B-17
1891	LOU AA	2	.000	.000	6	0	0	0	0	0.0	0	0	1	0	0	0	0	4	6	2	0	6.0	.833	2B-2
12 yrs.		986	.227	.289	3770	854	112	50	8	0.2	448	196	162	187	29	0	0	3598	3054	608	502	7.4	.916	2B-879, 1B-63, 3B-38, SS-6, OF-3

Ken Gerhart

GERHART, HAROLD KENNETH
B. May 19, 1961, Charleston, S. C.
BR TR 6' 190 lbs.

Year	Team	Games	BA	SA	AB	H	2B	3B	HR	HR%	R	RBI	BB	SO	SB	PH AB	PH H	PO	A	E	DP	TC/G	FA	G by Pos
1986	BAL A	20	.232	.304	69	16	2	0	1	1.4	4	7	4	18	0	1	0	34	0	1	0	1.8	.971	OF-20
1987		92	.243	.440	284	69	10	2	14	4.9	41	34	17	53	9	3	1	174	3	5	0	2.0	.973	OF-91
1988		103	.195	.344	262	51	10	1	9	3.4	27	23	21	57	7	8	2	192	3	5	1	1.9	.975	OF-93, DH-3
3 yrs.		215	.221	.384	615	136	22	3	24	3.9	72	64	42	128	16	12	3	400	6	11	1	1.9	.974	OF-204, DH-3

George Gerken

GERKEN, GEORGE HERBERT (Pickles)
B. July 28, 1903, Chicago, Ill. D. Oct. 23, 1977, Arcadia, Calif.
BR TR 5'11½" 175 lbs.

Year	Team	Games	BA	SA	AB	H	2B	3B	HR	HR%	R	RBI	BB	SO	SB	PH AB	PH H	PO	A	E	DP	TC/G	FA	G by Pos
1927	CLE A	6	.214	.214	14	3	0	0	0	0.0	1	2	1	3	0	0	0	10	1	1	0	2.0	.917	OF-5
1928		38	.226	.322	115	26	7	2	0	0.0	16	9	12	22	3	0	0	75	3	5	0	2.2	.940	OF-34
2 yrs.		44	.225	.310	129	29	7	2	0	0.0	17	11	13	25	3	0	0	85	4	6	0	2.2	.937	OF-39

Johnny Gerlach

GERLACH, JOHN GLENN
B. May 11, 1917, Shullsburg, Wis.
BR TR 5'9" 165 lbs.

Year	Team	Games	BA	SA	AB	H	2B	3B	HR	HR%	R	RBI	BB	SO	SB	PH AB	PH H	PO	A	E	DP	TC/G	FA	G by Pos
1938	CHI A	9	.280	.280	25	7	0	0	0	0.0	2	1	4	2	0	0	0	17	20	2	9	4.3	.949	SS-8
1939		3	1.000	1.000	2	2	0	0	0	0.0	0				1	1	0	0	1	0	0	0.3	1.000	3B-1
2 yrs.		12	.333	.333	27	9	0	0	0	0.0	2	1	4	2	1	1	0	17	21	2	9	3.3	.950	SS-8, 3B-1

Dick Gernert

GERNERT, RICHARD EDWARD
B. Sept. 28, 1928, Reading, Pa.
BR TR 6'3" 209 lbs.

Year	Team	Games	BA	SA	AB	H	2B	3B	HR	HR%	R	RBI	BB	SO	SB	PH AB	PH H	PO	A	E	DP	TC/G	FA	G by Pos
1952	BOS A	102	.243	.463	367	89	20	2	19	5.2	58	67	35	83	4	4	1	877	67	12	104	9.4	.987	1B-99
1953		139	.253	.415	494	125	15	1	21	4.3	73	71	88	82	0	3	0	1223	84	19	139	9.5	.986	1B-136
1954		14	.261	.348	23	6	2	0	0	0.0	2	1	6	4	0	7	1	47	1	0	5	3.4	1.000	1B-6
1955		7	.200	.300	20	4	2	0	0	0.0	1	1	5	0	0	7	1	35	3	1	2	5.6	.974	1B-5
1956		106	.291	.484	306	89	11	0	16	5.2	53	68	56	57	1	22	4	367	41	4	38	3.9	.990	OF-50, 1B-37
1957		99	.237	.430	316	75	13	3	14	4.4	45	58	39	62	1	18	6	697	50	10	82	7.6	.987	1B-71, OF-16
1958		122	.237	.425	431	102	19	1	20	4.6	59	69	59	78	2	7	3	1101	93	11	118	9.9	.991	1B-114
1959		117	.262	.426	298	78	14	1	11	3.7	41	42	52	49	1	21	4	588	51	4	54	5.5	.994	1B-75, OF-25
1960	2 teams	CHI N (52G – .250)		DET A (21G – .300)																				
"	total	73	.267	.336					1	0.7	14	16	14	24	1	31	8	242	21	3	26	3.6	.989	1B-75, OF-25
1961	2 teams	DET A (6G – .200)		CIN N (40G – .302)																				
"	total	46	.294	.353	68	20	1	0	1	1.5	5	8	8	11	0	25	6	125	17	1	9	3.1	.993	1B-31, OF-11
1962	HOU N	10	.208	.208	24	5	0	0	0	0.0	0	1	5	7	0	1	0	62	2	0	9	6.4	1.000	1B-21
11 yrs.		835	.254	.426	2493	632	104	8	103	4.1	357	402	363	462	10	140	33	5364	430	65	586	7.0	.989	1B-604, OF-102

WORLD SERIES

Year	Team	Games	BA	SA	AB	H	2B	3B	HR	HR%	R	RBI	BB	SO	SB	PH AB	PH H	PO	A	E	DP	TC/G	FA	G by Pos
1961	CIN N	4	.000	.000	4	0	0	0	0	0.0	0	0	0	1	0	4	0	0	0	0	0		–	

Cesar Geronimo

GERONIMO, CESAR FRANCISCO
Born Cesar Francisco Geronimo y Zorrilla.
B. Mar. 11, 1948, El Seibo, Dominican Republic
BL TL 6' 165 lbs.

Year	Team	Games	BA	SA	AB	H	2B	3B	HR	HR%	R	RBI	BB	SO	SB	PH AB	PH H	PO	A	E	DP	TC/G	FA	G by Pos
1969	HOU N	28	.250	.375	8	2	1	0	0	0.0	0	0	0	3	0	5	1	1	0	0	0	0.0	1.000	OF-9
1970		47	.243	.243	37	9	0	0	0	0.0	5	2	2	5	0	11	4	23	0	2	0	0.5	.920	OF-26
1971		94	.220	.329	82	18	2	2	1	1.2	13	6	5	31	2	11	2	42	1	1	0	0.5	.977	OF-64
1972	CIN N	120	.275	.412	255	70	9	7	4	1.6	32	29	24	64	2	12	1	150	10	3	1	1.4	.982	OF-106
1973		139	.210	.309	324	68	14	3	4	1.2	35	33	23	74	5	7	1	243	9	2	2	1.8	.992	OF-130
1974		150	.281	.395	474	133	17	8	7	1.5	73	54	46	96	9	7	0	355	13	5	2	2.5	.987	OF-145
1975		148	.257	.363	501	129	25	5	6	1.2	69	53	48	97	13	3	1	408	12	3	5	2.9	.993	OF-148
1976		149	.307	.414	486	149	24	11	2	0.4	59	49	56	95	22	4	2	386	4	6	2	2.7	.985	OF-146
1977		149	.266	.388	492	131	22	4	10	2.0	54	52	35	89	10	3	1	375	9	3	2	2.6	.992	OF-147
1978		122	.226	.334	296	67	15	1	5	1.7	28	27	43	67	8	11	5	259	3	2	2	2.2	.981	OF-115
1979		123	.239	.343	356	85	17	4	4	1.1	38	38	37	56	1	9	2	291	11	2	2	2.5	.993	OF-118
1980		103	.255	.331	145	37	5	0	2	1.4	16	9	14	24	2	21	5	110	2	0	1	1.1	1.000	OF-86
1981	KC A	59	.246	.331	118	29	0	2	2	1.7	14	13	11	16	6	2	1	96	1	2	0	1.7	.980	OF-57
1982		53	.269	.471	119	32	6	3	4	3.4	14	23	8	16	2	10	2	93	3	0	0	1.8	1.000	OF-44, DH-1
1983		38	.207	.253	87	18	4	0	0	0.0	4	9	2	13	0	6	1	69	2	1	0	1.9	.986	OF-35
15 yrs.		1522	.258	.368	3780	977	161	50	51	1.3	460	392	354	746	82	126	32	2901	81	35	18	2.0	.988	OF-1376, DH-1

DIVISIONAL PLAYOFF SERIES

Year	Team	Games	BA	SA	AB	H	2B	3B	HR	HR%	R	RBI	BB	SO	SB	PH AB	PH H	PO	A	E	DP	TC/G	FA	G by Pos
1981	KC A	1	–	–	0	0	0	0	0	–	0	0	0	0	0	0	0	0	0	0	0	0.0	–	

LEAGUE CHAMPIONSHIP SERIES

Year	Team	Games	BA	SA	AB	H	2B	3B	HR	HR%	R	RBI	BB	SO	SB	PH AB	PH H	PO	A	E	DP	TC/G	FA	G by Pos
1972	CIN N	5	.100	.250	20	2	0	0	1	5.0	2	1	0	2	0	0	0	11	1	0	0	2.4	1.000	OF-5

Year	Team		Games	BA	SA	AB	H	2B	3B	HR	HR%	R	RBI	BB	SO	SB	Pinch Hit AB	Pinch Hit H	PO	A	E	DP	TC/G	FA	G by Pos

Cesar Geronimo *continued*

1973			4	.067	.067	15	1	0	0	0	0.0	0	0	0	7	0	0	0	11	1	0	0	3.0	1.000	OF-4
1975			3	.000	.000	10	0	0	0	0	0.0	0	1	1	7	0	0	0	13	0	0	0	4.3	1.000	OF-3
1976			3	.182	.364	11	2	0	1	0	0.0	0	2	1	3	0	0	0	10	0	0	0	3.3	1.000	OF-3
1979			2	.143	.143	7	1	0	0	0	0.0	0	0	0	5	0	0	0	8	0	1	0	4.5	.889	OF-2
5 yrs.			17	.095	.175	63	6	0	1	1	1.6	2	4	2	24	0	0	0	53	2	1	0	3.3	.982	OF-17

WORLD SERIES

1972	CIN	N	7	.158	.158	19	3	0	0	0	0.0	1	3	1	4	1	0	0	9	0	0	0	1.3	1.000	OF-7
1975			7	.280	.600	25	7	0	1	2	8.0	3	3	3	5	0	0	0	23	1	0	1	3.4	1.000	OF-7
1976			4	.308	.462	13	4	2	0	0	0.0	3	1	2	2	2	0	0	12	0	1	0	3.3	.923	OF-4
3 yrs.			18	.246	.421	57	14	2	1	2	3.5	7	7	6	11	3	0	0	44	1	1	1	2.6	.978	OF-18

Lou Gertenrich

GERTENRICH, LOUIS WILHELM
B. May 4, 1875, Chicago, Ill. D. Oct. 23, 1933, Chicago, Ill.

BR TR 5'8" 175 lbs.

1901	MIL	A	2	.333	.333	3	1	0	0	0	0.0	1	0	0		0	1	0	0	0	0	0	0.0	–	OF-1
1903	PIT	N	1	.000	.000	3	0	0	0	0	0.0	0	0	0		0	0	0	2	0	0	0	2.0	1.000	OF-1
2 yrs.			3	.167	.167	6	1	0	0	0	0.0	1	0	0		0	1	0	2	0	0	0	0.7	1.000	OF-2

Doc Gessler

GESSLER, HARRY HOMER (Brownie)
B. Dec. 23, 1880, Indiana, Pa. D. Dec. 26, 1924, Indiana, Pa.
Manager 1914.

BL TR 5'10" 185 lbs.

1903	2 teams		DET A (29G – .238)			BKN	N	(49G – .247)																	
"	total		78	.243	.347	259	63	13	7	0	0.0	29	30	20		10	4	1	92	5	2	2	1.3	.980	OF-71
1904	BKN	N	104	.290	.384	341	99	18	4	2	0.6	41	28	30		13	12	2	181	17	17	2	2.1	.921	OF-88, 2B-1, 1B-1
1905			126	.290	.369	431	125	17	4	3	0.7	44	46	38		26	7	2	1036	81	36	54	9.2	.969	1B-107, OF-12
1906	2 teams		BKN N (9G – .242)			CHI	N	(34G – .253)																	
"	total		43	.250	.319	116	29	4	2	0	0.0	11	14	15		7	11	2	110	13	5	4	3.0	.961	OF-21, 1B-10
1908	BOS	N	128	.308	.423	435	134	13	4	3	0.7	55	63	51		19	2	0	162	8	9	4	1.4	.950	OF-126
1909	2 teams		BOS A (111G – .298)			WAS	A	(17G – .241)																	
"	total		128	.291	.359	440	128	26	2	0	0.0	66	54	43		20	1	0	176	21	11	2	1.6	.947	OF-127, 1B-2
1910	WAS	A	145	.259	.351	487	126	17	11	2	0.4	58	50	62		18	1	0	161	23	9	3	1.3	.953	OF-144
1911			128	.282	.373	450	127	19	5	4	0.9	65	78	74		29	1	0	135	20	9	2	1.3	.945	OF-126, 1B-1
8 yrs.			880	.281	.371	2959	831	127	49	14	0.5	369	363	333		142	39	9	2053	188	98	73	2.7	.958	OF-715, 1B-121, 2B-1

WORLD SERIES

| 1906 | CHI | N | 2 | .000 | .000 | 1 | 0 | 0 | 0 | 0 | 0.0 | 0 | 0 | 1 | | 0 | 1 | 0 | 0 | 0 | 0 | 0 | 0.0 | – | – |

Charlie Gettig

GETTIG, CHARLES HENRY
B. 1871, Baltimore, Md. D. Apr. 11, 1935, Baltimore, Md.

5'10" 172 lbs.

1896	NY	N	6	.333	.444	9	3	1	0	0	0.0	3	0	0		0	2	0	5	0	0	0.8	1.000	P-4
1897			22	.200	.280	75	15	6	0	0	0.0	8	12	6		3	1	0	19	26	16	1	2.8	.738	3B-7, 2B-6, OF-3, SS-3, P-3
1898			64	.250	.301	196	49	4	0	0	0.0	30	26	15		5	0	0	70	103	21	6	3.0	.892	OF-21, P-17, 2B-12, SS-9, 3B-4, 1B-2, C-1
1899			34	.247	.278	97	24	3	0	0	0.0	7	9	7		4	1	0	27	59	16	0	3.0	.843	P-18, 3B-8, 2B-3, 1B-3, OF-1
4 yrs.			126	.241	.294	377	91	16	2	0	0.0	48	47	28		12	4	0	116	193	53	7	2.9	.854	P-42, OF-25, 2B-21, 3B-19, SS-12, 1B-5, C-1

Tom Gettinger

GETTINGER, THOMAS L.
B. 1869, Md. Deceased.

BL TL 5'10" 180 lbs.

1889	STL	AA	4	.438	.625	16	7	0	0	1	6.3	2	2	2		1	0	0	6	0	2	0	2.0	.750	OF-4
1890			58	.238	.352	227	54	7	5	3	1.3	31	20			8	0	0	62	8	9	1	1.4	.886	OF-58
1895	LOU	N	63	.269	.373	260	70	11	5	2	0.8	28	32	8	15	6	0	0	127	7	14	1	2.3	.905	OF-63, P-2
3 yrs.			125	.260	.372	503	131	18	10	6	1.2	61	34	30	16	14	0	0	195	15	25	2	1.9	.894	OF-125, P-2

Jake Gettman

GETTMAN, JACOB JOHN
B. Oct. 25, 1876, Frank, Russia D. Oct. 4, 1956, Denver, Colo.

BB TL 5'11" 185 lbs.

1897	WAS	N	36	.315	.469	143	45	7	3	3	2.1	28	29	7		8	0	0	49	3	1	0	1.5	.981	OF-36
1898			142	.277	.349	567	157	16	5	5	0.9	75	47	29		32	0	1	261	22	21	7	2.1	.931	OF-139, 1B-2
1899			19	.210	.226	62	13	1	0	0	0.0	5	2	4		4	1	1	50	1	0	0	2.7	1.000	OF-16, 1B-2
3 yrs.			197	.278	.361	772	215	24	8	8	1.0	108	78	40		44	1	1	360	26	22	7	2.1	.946	OF-191, 1B-5

Gus Getz

GETZ, GUSTAVE (Gee-Gee)
B. Aug. 3, 1889, Pittsburgh, Pa. D. May 28, 1969, Keansburg, N. J.

BR TR 5'11" 165 lbs.

1909	BOS	N	40	.223	.236	148	33	0	0	0	0.0	6	9			2	0	0	36	92	10	3	3.5	.928	3B-36, SS-2, 2B-2
1910			54	.194	.208	144	28	0	1	0	0.0	14	7	6	10	2	6	1	57	83	9	6	2.8	.940	3B-22, 2B-13, OF-8, SS-4
1914	BKN	N	55	.248	.295	210	52	8	1	0	0.0	13	20	2	15	9	0	0	69	134	11	12	3.9	.949	3B-55
1915			130	.258	.312	477	123	10	5	2	0.4	39	46	8	14	19	0	0	143	290	24	14	3.5	.947	3B-128, SS-2
1916			40	.219	.271	96	21	1	2	0	0.0	9	8	0	9	7	0	0	53	45	6	4	2.6	.942	3B-20, SS-7, 1B-3
1917	CIN	N	7	.286	.286	14	4	0	0	0	0.0	2	3	3		0	0	0	8	4	2	1	2.0	.857	2B-4, 3B-3
1918	2 teams		CLE A (6G – .133)			PIT	N	(7G – .200)																	
"	total		13	.160	.200	25	4	0	0	0	0.0	2	0	4	2	0	4	0	6	4	5	1	1.2	.667	OF-3, 3B-2
7 yrs.			339	.238	.279	1114	265	22	9	2	0.2	85	93	24	46	41	17	1	372	652	67	41	3.2	.939	3B-266, 2B-19, SS-15, OF-11, 1B-3

WORLD SERIES

| 1916 | BKN | N | 1 | .000 | .000 | 1 | 0 | 0 | 0 | 0 | 0.0 | 0 | 0 | 0 | | 0 | 1 | 0 | 0 | 0 | 0 | 0 | 0.0 | – | – |

Chappie Geygan

GEYGAN, JAMES EDWARD
B. June 3, 1903, Ironton, Ohio D. Mar. 15, 1966, Columbus, Ohio

BR TR 5'11" 170 lbs.

| 1924 | BOS | A | 33 | .256 | .366 | 82 | 21 | 5 | 2 | 0 | 0.0 | 7 | 4 | 4 | 16 | 0 | 1 | 1 | 63 | 76 | 7 | 12 | 4.4 | .952 | SS-32 |

Year	Team	Games	BA	SA	AB	H	2B	3B	HR	HR%	R	RBI	BB	SO	SB	Pinch Hit AB	Pinch Hit H	PO	A	E	DP	TC/G	FA	G by Pos

Chappie Geygan *continued*

Year	Team	Games	BA	SA	AB	H	2B	3B	HR	HR%	R	RBI	BB	SO	SB	AB	H	PO	A	E	DP	TC/G	FA	G by Pos
1925		3	.182	.182	11	2	0	0	0	0.0	0	0	0	2	0	0	0	7	6	3	1	5.3	.813	SS-3
1926		4	.300	.300	10	3	0	0	0	0.0	0	0	1	1	0	1	0	3	5	2	0	2.5	.800	3B-3
3 yrs.		40	.252	.340	103	26	5	2	0	0.0	7	4	5	19	0	2	1	73	87	12	13	4.3	.930	SS-35, 3B-3

Patsy Gharrity

GHARRITY, EDWARD PATRICK
B. Mar. 13, 1892, Parnell, Iowa   D. Oct. 10, 1966, Beloit, Wis.   BR TR 5'10" 170 lbs.

Year	Team	Games	BA	SA	AB	H	2B	3B	HR	HR%	R	RBI	BB	SO	SB	AB	H	PO	A	E	DP	TC/G	FA	G by Pos
1916	WAS A	39	.228	.304	92	21	5	1	0	0.0	8	9	8	18	2	6	0	191	16	3	5	5.4	.986	C-18, 1B-15
1917		76	.284	.313	176	50	5	0	0	0.0	15	18	14	18	7	20	3	374	30	9	19	5.4	.978	1B-46, C-5, OF-1
1918		4	.250	.500	4	1	1	0	0	0.0	0	2	0	1	0	4	1	0	0	0	0	0.0	—	
1919		111	.271	.366	347	94	19	4	2	0.6	35	43	25	39	4	10	1	394	73	17	9	4.4	.965	C-60, OF-33, 1B-7
1920		131	.245	.322	428	105	18	3	3	0.7	51	44	37	52	6	4	0	476	150	23	14	5.0	.965	C-120, 1B-7, OF-1
1921		121	.310	.455	387	120	19	8	7	1.8	62	55	45	44	4	5	2	408	110	12	14	4.4	.977	C-115
1922		96	.256	.414	273	70	16	6	5	1.8	40	45	36	30	3	8	1	282	85	7	9	3.9	.981	C-87
1923		96	.207	.311	251	52	9	4	3	1.2	26	33	22	27	6	20	5	417	47	8	27	4.9	.983	C-35, 1B-33
1929		3	.000	.000	2	0	0	0	0	0.0	0	0	1	2	0	2	0	0	0	0	0	0.0	—	
1930		2	.000	.000	1	0	0	0	0	0.0	0	0	0	0	0	2	0	2	0	0	0	1.0	1.000	1B-1
10 yrs.		679	.262	.366	1961	513	92	26	20	1.0	237	249	188	231	32	80	13	2544	511	79	97	4.6	.975	C-440, 1B-109, OF-35

Joe Giannini

GIANNINI, JOSEPH FRANCIS
B. Sept. 8, 1888, San Francisco, Calif.   D. Sept. 26, 1942, San Francisco, Calif.   BL TR 5'8" 155 lbs.

Year	Team	Games	BA	SA	AB	H	2B	3B	HR	HR%	R	RBI	BB	SO	SB	AB	H	PO	A	E	DP	TC/G	FA	G by Pos
1911	BOS A	1	.500	1.000	2	1	0	0	0	0.0	0	0	0	0	0	0	0	0	2	2	0	4.0	.500	SS-1

John Gibbons

GIBBONS, JOHN MICHAEL
B. June 8, 1962, Great Falls, Mont.   BR TR 5'11" 185 lbs.

Year	Team	Games	BA	SA	AB	H	2B	3B	HR	HR%	R	RBI	BB	SO	SB	AB	H	PO	A	E	DP	TC/G	FA	G by Pos
1984	NY N	10	.065	.065	31	2	0	0	0	0.0	1	3	11		0	1	0	54	5	1	0	6.0	.983	C-9
1986		8	.474	.842	19	9	4	0	1	5.3	4	1	3	5	0	0	0	33	5	0	1	4.8	1.000	C-8
2 yrs.		18	.220	.360	50	11	4	0	1	2.0	5	2	6	16	0	1	0	87	10	1	1	5.4	.990	C-17

Jake Gibbs

GIBBS, JERRY DEAN
B. Nov. 7, 1938, Grenada, Miss.   BL TR 6' 180 lbs.

Year	Team	Games	BA	SA	AB	H	2B	3B	HR	HR%	R	RBI	BB	SO	SB	AB	H	PO	A	E	DP	TC/G	FA	G by Pos
1962	NY A	2	—	—	0	0	0	0	0	—	2	0	0	0	0	0	0	0	0	0	0	0.0	—	3B-1
1963		4	.250	.250	8	2	0	0	0	0.0	1	0	0	1	0	3	2	5	0	0	0	1.3	1.000	C-1
1964		3	.167	.167	6	1	0	0	0	0.0	1	0	0	2	0	1	0	10	0	0	0	3.3	1.000	C-2
1965		37	.221	.324	68	15	1	0	2	2.9	6	7	4	20	0	16	5	106	10	1	1	3.2	.991	C-21
1966		62	.258	.341	182	47	6	0	3	1.6	19	20	19	16	5	5	1	295	27	4	4	5.3	.988	C-54
1967		116	.233	.289	374	87	7	1	4	1.1	33	25	28	57	7	17	3	582	55	16	7	5.6	.975	C-99
1968		124	.213	.277	423	90	12	3	3	0.7	31	29	27	68	9	4	1	642	55	6	7	5.7	.991	C-121
1969		71	.224	.283	219	49	9	0	0	0.0	18	18	23	30	3	2	0	364	31	4	6	5.6	.990	C-66
1970		49	.301	.542	153	46	9	2	8	5.2	23	26	7	14	2	5	1	208	19	3	1	4.7	.987	C-44
1971		70	.218	.335	206	45	9	2	5	2.4	23	21	12	23	2	16	1	229	12	3	1	3.5	.988	C-51
10 yrs.		538	.233	.321	1639	382	53	8	25	1.5	157	146	120	231	28	69	13	2441	209	37	27	5.0	.986	C-459, 3B-1

Charlie Gibson

GIBSON, CHARLES ELLSWORTH
B. Nov. 17, 1879, Sharon, Pa.   D. Nov. 22, 1954, Sharon, Pa.   BR TR 6' 160 lbs.

Year	Team	Games	BA	SA	AB	H	2B	3B	HR	HR%	R	RBI	BB	SO	SB	AB	H	PO	A	E	DP	TC/G	FA	G by Pos
1905	STL A	1	.000	.000	3	0	0	0	0	0.0	0	0	0		0	0	0	2	1	0	0	3.0	1.000	C-1

Charlie Gibson

GIBSON, CHARLES GRIFFIN
B. Nov. 21, 1899, LaGrange, Ga.   BR TR 5'8" 160 lbs.

Year	Team	Games	BA	SA	AB	H	2B	3B	HR	HR%	R	RBI	BB	SO	SB	AB	H	PO	A	E	DP	TC/G	FA	G by Pos
1924	PHI A	12	.133	.133	15	2	0	0	0	0.0	1	1	2	0	0	0	0	14	6	3	0	1.9	.870	C-12

Frank Gibson

GIBSON, FRANK GILBERT
B. Sept. 27, 1890, Omaha, Neb.
D. Apr. 27, 1961, Austin, Tex.   BB TR 6'½" 172 lbs.   BL 1921-22, 1924

Year	Team	Games	BA	SA	AB	H	2B	3B	HR	HR%	R	RBI	BB	SO	SB	AB	H	PO	A	E	DP	TC/G	FA	G by Pos
1913	DET A	20	.140	.158	57	8	1	0	0	0.0	8	2	3	9	2	0	0	57	17	8	1	4.1	.902	C-19, OF-1
1921	BOS N	63	.264	.416	125	33	5	4	2	1.6	14	13	3	17	0	17	4	111	31	3	4	2.3	.979	C-41
1922		66	.299	.421	164	49	7	2	3	1.8	15	20	10	27	4	15	2	245	28	5	14	4.2	.982	C-29, 1B-20
1923		41	.300	.320	50	15	1	0	0	0.0	13	5	7	7	0	15	0	31	5	3	1	1.0	.923	C-20
1924		90	.310	.441	229	71	15	6	1	0.4	25	30	10	23	1	31	0	268	58	11	13	3.7	.967	C-46, 1B-10, 3B-2
1925		104	.278	.402	316	88	23	5	2	0.6	36	50	15	28	3	15	7	276	61	11	7	3.3	.968	C-88, 1B-2
1926		24	.340	.426	47	16	4	0	0	0.0	3	7	4	6	0	12	6	37	12	0	2	2.0	1.000	C-12
1927		60	.222	.251	167	37	1	2	0	0.0	7	19	3	10	2	12	4	130	35	6	3	2.9	.965	C-47
8 yrs.		468	.274	.377	1155	317	57	19	8	0.7	121	146	55	127	12	117	29	1155	247	47	45	3.1	.968	C-302, 1B-32, 3B-2, OF-1

George Gibson

GIBSON, GEORGE C. (Moon)
B. July 22, 1880, London, Ont., Canada   D. Jan. 25, 1967, London, Ont., Canada   BR TR 5'11½" 190 lbs.
Manager 1920-22, 1925, 1932-34.

Year	Team	Games	BA	SA	AB	H	2B	3B	HR	HR%	R	RBI	BB	SO	SB	AB	H	PO	A	E	DP	TC/G	FA	G by Pos
1905	PIT N	46	.178	.267	135	24	2	2	2	1.5	14	14	15		2	1	0	200	54	9	4	5.7	.966	C-44
1906		81	.178	.208	259	46	6	1	0	0.0	8	20	16		1	0	0	336	97	13	10	5.5	.971	C-81
1907		113	.220	.301	382	84	8	7	3	0.8	28	35	18		7	0	0	501	125	18	12	5.7	.972	C-109, 1B-1
1908		143	.228	.296	486	111	19	4	2	0.4	37	45	19		4	3	1	607	136	21	10	5.3	.973	C-140
1909		150	.265	.361	510	135	25	9	2	0.4	42	52	44		9	0	0	655	192	15	9	5.7	.983	C-150
1910		143	.259	.349	482	125	22	6	3	0.6	53	44	47	31	7	0	0	633	203	14	8	5.9	.984	C-143
1911		100	.209	.260	311	65	12	6	0	0.0	32	19	29	16	3	1	1	452	117	12	16	5.8	.979	C-98
1912		95	.240	.327	300	72	14	3	2	0.7	23	35	20	16	0	1	0	484	101	6	11	6.2	.990	C-94
1913		48	.280	.347	118	33	4	2	0	0.0	12	12	10	8	2	2	0	182	34	3	4	4.6	.986	C-48
1914		102	.285	.354	274	78	9	5	0	0.0	19	30	27	27	4	1	0	358	126	13	8	4.9	.974	C-101
1915		120	.251	.336	351	88	15	6	1	0.3	28	30	31	25	5	2	0	551	134	25	14	5.5	.965	C-120
1916		33	.202	.274	84	17	2	4	0	0.0	4	4	3	7	0	2	0	140	39	2	2	5.5	.989	C-29
1917	NY N	35	.171	.207	82	14	3	0	0	0.0	1	5	2	9	0	1	0	116	27	2	4	4.1	.986	C-35

Year	Team		Games	BA	SA	AB	H	2B	3B	HR	HR%	R	RBI	BB	SO	SB	Pinch Hit AB	Pinch Hit H	PO	A	E	DP	TC/G	FA	G by Pos

George Gibson *continued*

Year	Team		Games	BA	SA	AB	H	2B	3B	HR	HR%	R	RBI	BB	SO	SB	AB	H	PO	A	E	DP	TC/G	FA	G by Pos
1918			4	.500	1.000	2	1	1	0	0	0.0	0	0	0	0	0	0	0	1	1	0	0	0.5	1.000	C-4
14 yrs.			1213	.236	.312	3776	893	142	49	15	0.4	295	345	286	132	40	14	4	5216	1386	153	112	5.6	.977	C-1196, 1B-1

WORLD SERIES

| 1909 | PIT | N | 7 | .240 | .320 | 25 | 6 | 2 | 0 | 0 | 0.0 | 2 | 2 | 1 | 1 | 2 | 0 | 0 | 28 | 8 | 0 | 0 | 5.1 | 1.000 | C-7 |

Kirk Gibson

GIBSON, KIRK HAROLD
B. May 28, 1957, Pontiac, Mich.   BL TL 6'3" 215 lbs.

Year	Team		Games	BA	SA	AB	H	2B	3B	HR	HR%	R	RBI	BB	SO	SB	AB	H	PO	A	E	DP	TC/G	FA	G by Pos
1979	DET	A	12	.237	.395	38	9	3	0	1	2.6	3	4	1	3	3	2	0	15	0	0	0	1.3	1.000	OF-10
1980			51	.263	.440	175	46	2	1	9	5.1	23	16	10	45	4	5	1	122	1	1	0	2.4	.992	OF-49, DH-1
1981			83	.328	.479	290	95	11	3	9	3.1	41	40	18	64	17	8	1	142	1	4	0	1.8	.973	OF-67, DH-9
1982			69	.278	.444	266	74	16	2	8	3.0	34	35	25	41	9	1	0	167	4	1	3	2.5	.994	OF-64, DH-4
1983			128	.227	.414	401	91	12	9	15	3.7	60	51	53	96	14	20	5	116	2	3	0	0.9	.975	DH-66, OF-54
1984			149	.282	.516	531	150	23	10	27	5.1	92	91	63	103	29	11	1	245	4	12	2	1.8	.954	OF-139, DH-6
1985			154	.287	.518	581	167	37	5	29	5.0	96	97	71	137	30	3	2	286	4	11	0	1.9	.963	OF-144, DH-8
1986			119	.268	.492	441	118	11	2	28	6.3	84	86	68	107	34	2	1	190	2	2	1	1.6	.990	OF-114, DH-4
1987			128	.277	.489	487	135	25	3	24	4.9	95	79	71	117	26	3	0	253	6	7	0	2.1	.974	OF-148
1988	LA	N	150	.290	.483	542	157	28	1	25	4.6	106	76	73	120	31	3	0	311	6	12	3	2.2	.964	OF-70
1989			71	.213	.368	253	54	8	2	9	3.6	35	28	35	55	12	1	1	146	3	3	2	2.1	.980	OF-70
11 yrs.			1114	.274	.474	4005	1096	176	38	184	4.6	669	603	488	888	209	60	12	1993	30	56	11	1.9	.973	OF-980, DH-102

LEAGUE CHAMPIONSHIP SERIES

1984	DET	A	3	.417	.750	12	5	1	0	1	8.3	2	2	2	1	1	0	0	7	0	0	0	2.3	1.000	OF-3
1987			5	.286	.476	21	6	1	0	1	4.8	4	4	3	8	3	0	0	10	1	0	0	2.2	1.000	OF-5
1988	LA	N	7	.154	.385	26	4	0	0	2	7.7	2	6	3	6	2	0	0	17	1	0	0	2.6	1.000	OF-7
3 yrs.			15	.254	.492	59	15	2	0	4	6.8	8	12	8	15	6	0	0	34	2	0	0	2.4	1.000	OF-15

WORLD SERIES

1984	DET	A	5	.333	.667	18	6	0	0	2	11.1	4	7	4	4	3	0	0	5	0	1	0	1.6	.750	OF-5
1988	LA	N	1	1.000	4.000	1	1	0	0	1	0.0	1	2	0	1	0	1	1	0	0	0	0	0.0	—	
2 yrs.			6	.368	.842	19	7	0	0	3	15.8	5	9	4	4	3	1	1	5	0	1	2	1.3	.750	OF-5

Russ Gibson

GIBSON, JOHN RUSSELL
B. May 6, 1939, Fall River, Mass.   BR TR 6'1" 195 lbs.

Year	Team		Games	BA	SA	AB	H	2B	3B	HR	HR%	R	RBI	BB	SO	SB	AB	H	PO	A	E	DP	TC/G	FA	G by Pos
1967	BOS	A	49	.203	.275	138	28	7	0	1	0.7	8	15	12	31	0	4	0	254	16	0	3	5.5	1.000	C-48
1968			76	.225	.320	231	52	11	1	3	1.3	15	20	8	38	1	3	1	431	36	8	7	6.3	.983	C-74, 1B-1
1969			85	.251	.321	287	72	9	1	3	1.0	21	27	15	25	1	4	1	466	41	11	2	6.1	.979	C-83
1970	SF	N	24	.232	.319	69	16	6	0	1	1.4	3	6	7	12	0	1	0	126	7	4	1	5.7	.971	C-23
1971			25	.193	.298	57	11	1	1	1	1.8	2	7	3	13	0	2	0	79	4	3	0	3.4	.965	C-22
1972			5	.167	.333	12	2	0	1	0	0.0	0	3	0	4	0	1	0	16	1	0	1	3.4	1.000	C-5
6 yrs.			264	.228	.311	794	181	34	4	8	1.0	49	78	44	123	2	15	2	1372	105	26	14	5.7	.983	C-255, 1B-1

WORLD SERIES

| 1967 | BOS | A | 2 | .000 | .000 | 2 | 0 | 0 | 0 | 0 | 0.0 | 0 | 0 | 0 | 2 | 0 | 0 | 0 | 9 | 0 | 0 | 0 | 4.5 | 1.000 | C-2 |

Whitey Gibson

GIBSON, LEIGHTON P.
B. Oct. 6, 1868, Lancaster, Pa. D. Oct. 11, 1907, Talmadge, Pa.   TR 5'9" 178 lbs.

| 1888 | PHI | AA | 1 | .000 | .000 | 3 | 0 | 0 | 0 | 0 | 0.0 | 0 | 0 | 0 | | 0 | 0 | 0 | 2 | 4 | 0 | 0 | 6.0 | 1.000 | C-1 |

Joe Giebel

GIEBEL, JOSEPH HENRY
B. Nov. 30, 1891, Washington, D. C. D. Mar. 17, 1981, Silver Spring, Md.   BR TR 5'10½" 175 lbs.

| 1913 | PHI | A | 1 | .333 | .333 | 3 | 1 | 0 | 0 | 0 | 0.0 | 0 | 0 | 0 | 1 | 0 | 0 | 0 | 5 | 0 | 0 | 0 | 5.0 | 1.000 | C-1 |

Norm Gigon

GIGON, NORMAN PHILLIP
B. May 12, 1938, Teaneck, N. J.   BR TR 6' 195 lbs.

| 1967 | CHI | N | 34 | .171 | .286 | 70 | 12 | 3 | 1 | 1 | 1.4 | 8 | 6 | 4 | 14 | 0 | 15 | 2 | 21 | 36 | 1 | 6 | 1.7 | .983 | 2B-12, OF-4, 3B-1 |

Gus Gil

GIL, TOMAS GUSTAVO
Born Tomas Gustavo Gil y Guillen.
B. Apr. 19, 1939, Caracas, Venezuela   BR TR 5'10" 180 lbs.

1967	CLE	A	51	.115	.156	96	11	4	0	0	0.0	11	5	9	18	0	1	0	79	67	0	13	2.9	1.000	2B-49, 1B-1
1969	SEA	A	92	.222	.253	221	49	7	0	0	0.0	20	17	16	28	2	36	10	65	130	9	16	2.2	.956	3B-38, 2B-18, SS-12
1970	MIL	A	64	.185	.244	119	22	4	0	1	0.8	12	12	21	12	2	11	3	79	74	3	14	2.4	.981	2B-38, 3B-14
1971			14	.156	.188	32	5	1	0	0	0.0	3	3	10	5	1	4	0	20	27	1	3	3.4	.979	2B-8, 3B-6
4 yrs.			221	.186	.226	468	87	16	0	1	0.2	46	37	56	63	5	52	13	243	298	13	46	2.5	.977	2B-113, 3B-58, SS-12, 1B-1

Andy Gilbert

GILBERT, ANDREW
B. July 18, 1914, Latrobe, Pa.   BR TR 6'1" 203 lbs.

1942	BOS	A	6	.091	.091	11	1	0	0	0	0.0	0	1	1	3	0	0	0	6	0	0	0	1.0	1.000	OF-5
1946			2	.000	.000	1	0	0	0	0	0.0	1	0	0	0	0	1	0	0	0	0	0	0.0	—	OF-1
2 yrs.			8	.083	.083	12	1	0	0	0	0.0	1	1	1	3	0	1	0	6	0	0	0	0.8	1.000	OF-6

Billy Gilbert

GILBERT, WILLIAM OLIVER
B. June 21, 1876, Tullytown, Pa. D. Aug. 8, 1927, New York, N. Y.   BR TR 5'4" 153 lbs.

1901	MIL	A	127	.270	.327	492	133	14	7	0	0.0	77	43	31		19	0	0	319	395	49	66	6.0	.936	2B-127
1902	BAL	A	129	.245	.299	445	109	12	3	2	0.4	74	38	45		38	0	0	349	410	78	72	6.5	.907	SS-129
1903	NY	N	128	.252	.281	413	104	9	0	1	0.2	62	40	41		37	0	0	314	366	47	42	5.7	.935	2B-128
1904			146	.253	.299	478	121	13	3	1	0.2	57	54	46		33	0	0	305	466	44	48	5.6	.946	2B-146
1905			115	.247	.293	376	93	11	3	0	0.0	45	24	41		11	0	0	245	367	34	41	5.6	.947	2B-115
1906			104	.231	.267	307	71	6	1	1	0.3	44	27	42		22	4	1	223	324	35	32	5.6	.940	2B-98
1908	STL	N	89	.214	.239	276	59	7	0	0	0.0	12	10	20		6	0	0	222	254	24	23	5.6	.952	2B-89

Billy Gilbert *continued*

Year	Team	Games	BA	SA	AB	H	2B	3B	HR	HR%	R	RBI	BB	SO	SB	PH AB	PH H	PO	A	E	DP	TC/G	FA	G by Pos
1909		12	.172	.172	29	5	0	0	0	0.0	4	1	4		1	0	0	19	28	4	1	4.3	.922	2B-12
8 yrs.		850	.247	.290	2816	695	72	17	5	0.2	375	237	270		167	4	1	1996	2610	315	325	5.8	.936	2B-715, SS-129

WORLD SERIES

Year	Team	Games	BA	SA	AB	H	2B	3B	HR	HR%	R	RBI	BB	SO	SB	PH AB	PH H	PO	A	E	DP	TC/G	FA	G by Pos
1905	NY N	5	.235	.235	17	4	0	0	0	0.0	1	1	0	2	1	0	0	10	16	0	0	5.2	1.000	2B-5

Buddy Gilbert

GILBERT, DREW EDWARD BL TR 6'3" 195 lbs.
B. July 26, 1935, Knoxville, Tenn.

Year	Team	Games	BA	SA	AB	H	2B	3B	HR	HR%	R	RBI	BB	SO	SB	PH AB	PH H	PO	A	E	DP	TC/G	FA	G by Pos
1959	CIN N	7	.150	.450	20	3	0	0	2	10.0	4	2	3	4	0	1	0	15	0	0	0	2.1	1.000	OF-6

Charlie Gilbert

GILBERT, CHARLES MADER BL TL 5'9" 165 lbs.
Son of Larry Gilbert. Brother of Tookie Gilbert.
B. July 8, 1919, New Orleans, La. D. Aug. 13, 1983, New Orleans, La.

Year	Team	Games	BA	SA	AB	H	2B	3B	HR	HR%	R	RBI	BB	SO	SB	PH AB	PH H	PO	A	E	DP	TC/G	FA	G by Pos
1940	BKN N	57	.246	.366	142	35	9	1	2	1.4	23	8	8	13	1	0	8	1	91	4	4	1	1.7	.960	OF-43
1941	CHI N	39	.279	.326	86	24	2	1	0	0.0	11	12	11	6	1	14	2	51	0	0	0	1.3	1.000	OF-22
1942		74	.184	.251	179	33	6	3	0	0.0	18	7	25	24	1	23	2	99	6	2	2	1.4	.981	OF-47
1943		8	.150	.150	20	3	0	0	0	0.0	1	0	3	3	1	2	0	9	1	0	0	1.3	1.000	OF-6
1946 2 teams	CHI N (15G – .077)				PHI N (88G – .242)																			
" total		103	.234	.278	273	64	5	2	1	0.4	36	18	26	22	3	28	0	155	10	0	4	1.6	.976	OF-71
1947	PHI N	83	.237	.336	152	36	5	2	2	1.3	20	10	13	14	1	40	9	70	4	3	2	0.9	.961	OF-37
6 yrs.		364	.229	.299	852	195	27	9	5	0.6	109	55	86	82	7	115	14	475	25	9	9	1.4	.982	OF-226

Harry Gilbert

GILBERT, HARRY H.
Brother of John Gilbert.
B. July 8, 1868, Pottstown, Pa. D. Dec. 23, 1909, Pottstown, Pa.

Year	Team	Games	BA	SA	AB	H	2B	3B	HR	HR%	R	RBI	BB	SO	SB	PH AB	PH H	PO	A	E	DP	TC/G	FA	G by Pos
1890	PIT N	2	.250	.250	8	2	0	0	0	0.0	1	0	0	3	0	0	0	1	5	0	1	3.0	1.000	2B-2

Jack Gilbert

GILBERT, JOHN ROBERT (Jackrabbit)
B. Sept. 7, 1875, Rhinecliff, N. Y. D. July 7, 1941, Albany, N. Y.

Year	Team	Games	BA	SA	AB	H	2B	3B	HR	HR%	R	RBI	BB	SO	SB	PH AB	PH H	PO	A	E	DP	TC/G	FA	G by Pos
1898 2 teams	WAS N (2G – .200)				NY N (1G – .250)																			
" total		3	.222	.222	9	2	0	0	0	0.0	0	1	1		2	0	0	1	1	2	0	1.3	.500	OF-3
1904	PIT N	25	.241	.241	87	21	0	0	0	0.0	13	3	12		3	0	0	30	0	5	0	1.4	.857	OF-25
2 yrs.		28	.240	.240	96	23	0	0	0	0.0	13	4	13		5	0	0	31	1	7	0	1.4	.821	OF-28

John Gilbert

GILBERT, JOHN G.
Brother of Harry Gilbert.
B. Jan. 8, 1864, Pottstown, Pa. D. Nov. 12, 1903, Pottstown, Pa.

Year	Team	Games	BA	SA	AB	H	2B	3B	HR	HR%	R	RBI	BB	SO	SB	PH AB	PH H	PO	A	E	DP	TC/G	FA	G by Pos
1890	PIT N	2	.000	.000	8	0	0	0	0	0.0	0	0	0	2	0	0	0	4	5	0	1	4.5	1.000	SS-2

Larry Gilbert

GILBERT, LAWRENCE WILLIAM BL TL 5'8" 165 lbs.
Father of Charlie Gilbert. Father of Tookie Gilbert.
B. Dec. 3, 1891, New Orleans, La. D. Feb. 17, 1965, New Orleans, La.

Year	Team	Games	BA	SA	AB	H	2B	3B	HR	HR%	R	RBI	BB	SO	SB	PH AB	PH H	PO	A	E	DP	TC/G	FA	G by Pos
1914	BOS N	72	.268	.371	224	60	6	1	5	2.2	32	25	26	34	3	10	1	79	14	2	2	1.3	.979	OF-60
1915		45	.151	.189	106	16	4	0	0	0.0	11	4	11	13	4	14	3	28	4	2	1	0.8	.941	OF-27
2 yrs.		117	.230	.312	330	76	10	1	5	1.5	43	29	37	47	7	24	4	107	18	4	3	1.1	.969	OF-87

WORLD SERIES

Year	Team	Games	BA	SA	AB	H	2B	3B	HR	HR%	R	RBI	BB	SO	SB	PH AB	PH H	PO	A	E	DP	TC/G	FA	G by Pos
1914	BOS N	1	–	–	0	0	0	0	0	–	0	0	1	0	0	0	0	0	0	0	0	0.0	–	–

Mark Gilbert

GILBERT, MARK DAVID BB TR 6' 175 lbs.
B. Aug. 2, 1956, Atlanta, Ga.

Year	Team	Games	BA	SA	AB	H	2B	3B	HR	HR%	R	RBI	BB	SO	SB	PH AB	PH H	PO	A	E	DP	TC/G	FA	G by Pos
1985	CHI A	7	.273	.318	22	6	1	0	0	0.0	3	3	4	5	0	1	0	14	0	0	0	2.0	1.000	OF-7

Pete Gilbert

GILBERT, PETER TR
B. Sept. 6, 1867, Baltic, Conn. D. Jan. 1, 1912, Springfield, Mass.

Year	Team	Games	BA	SA	AB	H	2B	3B	HR	HR%	R	RBI	BB	SO	SB	PH AB	PH H	PO	A	E	DP	TC/G	FA	G by Pos
1890	BAL AA	29	.280	.350	100	28	2	1	1	1.0	25		10		12	0	0	34	55	10	5	3.4	.899	3B-29
1891		139	.230	.304	513	118	15	7	3	0.6	81	72	37	77	31	0	0	201	324	84	34	4.4	.862	3B-139
1892	BAL N	4	.200	.200	15	3	0	0	0	0.0	0	0	1	3	1	0	0	4	12	2	0	4.5	.889	3B-4
1894 2 teams	BKN N (6G – .080)				LOU N (28G – .306)																			
" total		34	.263	.323	133	35	3	1	1	0.8	14	15	6	7	4	0	0	57	69	35	7	4.7	.783	3B-31, 2B-3
4 yrs.		206	.242	.311	761	184	20	9	5	0.7	120	87	54	87	48	0	0	296	460	131	46	4.3	.852	3B-203, 2B-3

Tookie Gilbert

GILBERT, HAROLD JOSEPH BL TR 6'2½" 185 lbs.
Son of Larry Gilbert. Brother of Charlie Gilbert.
B. Apr. 4, 1929, New Orleans, La. D. June 23, 1967, New Orleans, La.

Year	Team	Games	BA	SA	AB	H	2B	3B	HR	HR%	R	RBI	BB	SO	SB	PH AB	PH H	PO	A	E	DP	TC/G	FA	G by Pos
1950	NY N	113	.220	.307	322	71	12	2	4	1.2	40	32	43	36	3	2	0	784	65	10	80	7.6	.988	1B-111
1953		70	.169	.244	160	27	3	0	3	1.9	12	16	22	21	1	23	4	381	26	2	34	5.8	.995	1B-44
2 yrs.		183	.203	.286	482	98	15	2	7	1.5	52	48	65	57	4	25	4	1165	91	12	114	6.9	.991	1B-155

Wally Gilbert

GILBERT, WALTER JOHN BR TR 6' 180 lbs.
B. Dec. 19, 1901, Oscoda, Mich. D. Sept. 7, 1958, Duluth, Minn.

Year	Team	Games	BA	SA	AB	H	2B	3B	HR	HR%	R	RBI	BB	SO	SB	PH AB	PH H	PO	A	E	DP	TC/G	FA	G by Pos
1928	BKN N	39	.203	.229	153	31	4	0	0	0.0	26	3	14	8	2	0	0	30	81	4	7	2.9	.965	3B-39
1929		143	.304	.388	569	173	31	4	3	0.5	88	58	42	29	7	1	0	137	271	19	16	3.0	.956	3B-142
1930		150	.294	.379	623	183	34	5	3	0.5	92	67	47	33	7	0	0	130	312	26	27	3.1	.944	3B-150
1931		145	.266	.333	552	147	25	6	0	0.0	60	46	39	38	3	0	0	125	295	23	14	3.1	.948	3B-145
1932	CIN N	114	.214	.274	420	90	18	2	1	0.2	35	40	20	23	2	2	1	90	198	22	16	2.7	.929	3B-111
5 yrs.		591	.269	.341	2317	624	112	17	7	0.3	301	214	162	131	21	3	1	512	1157	94	80	3.0	.947	3B-587

Year Team	Games	BA	SA	AB	H	2B	3B	HR	HR%	R	RBI	BB	SO	SB	Pinch Hit AB	Pinch Hit H	PO	A	E	DP	TC/G	FA	G by Pos

Rod Gilbreath

GILBREATH, RODNEY JOE
B. Sept. 24, 1952, Laurel, Miss.
BR TR 6'2" 180 lbs.

Year Team	Games	BA	SA	AB	H	2B	3B	HR	HR%	R	RBI	BB	SO	SB	Pinch Hit AB	Pinch Hit H	PO	A	E	DP	TC/G	FA	G by Pos
1972 ATL N	18	.237	.263	38	9	1	0	0	0.0	2	1	2	10	1	4	0	16	26	1	4	2.4	.977	2B-7, 3B-4
1973	29	.284	.338	74	21	2	1	0	0.0	10	2	6	10	2	10	3	16	32	2	4	1.7	.960	3B-22
1974	3	.333	.333	6	2	0	0	0	0.0	2	0	2	0	0	0	0	5	6	0	1	3.7	1.000	2B-2
1975	90	.243	.297	202	49	3	1	2	1.0	24	16	24	26	5	25	10	127	141	6	29	3.1	.978	2B-52, 3B-10, SS-1
1976	116	.251	.329	383	96	11	8	1	0.3	57	32	42	36	7	5	1	245	314	17	77	5.0	.970	2B-104, 3B-7, SS-1
1977	128	.243	.349	407	99	15	2	8	2.0	47	43	45	79	3	5	0	277	308	13	61	4.7	.978	2B-122, 3B-1
1978	116	.245	.331	326	80	13	3	3	0.9	22	31	26	51	7	11	1	108	204	9	22	2.8	.972	3B-62, 2B-39
7 yrs.	500	.248	.329	1436	356	45	15	14	1.0	164	125	147	212	25	60	15	794	1031	48	198	3.7	.974	2B-326, 3B-106, SS-2

Don Gile

GILE, DONALD LOREN (Bear)
B. Apr. 19, 1935, Modesto, Calif.
BR TR 6'6" 220 lbs.

Year Team	Games	BA	SA	AB	H	2B	3B	HR	HR%	R	RBI	BB	SO	SB	Pinch Hit AB	Pinch Hit H	PO	A	E	DP	TC/G	FA	G by Pos
1959 BOS A	3	.200	.300	10	2	1	0	0	0.0	1	1	0	2	0	0	0	17	1	0	0	6.0	1.000	C-3
1960	29	.176	.294	51	9	1	1	1	2.0	6	4	1	13	0	5	0	92	7	1	8	3.4	.990	C-15, 1B-11
1961	8	.278	.444	18	5	0	0	1	5.6	2	1	1	5	0	1	0	45	2	2	3	6.1	.959	1B-6, C-1
1962	18	.049	.122	41	2	0	0	1	2.4	3	3	3	15	0	2	0	90	5	1	11	5.3	.990	1B-14
4 yrs.	58	.150	.258	120	18	2	1	3	2.5	12	9	5	35	0	8	0	244	15	4	22	4.5	.985	1B-31, C-19

Brian Giles

GILES, BRIAN JEFFREY
B. Apr. 27, 1960, Manhattan, Kans.
BR TR 6'1" 165 lbs.

Year Team	Games	BA	SA	AB	H	2B	3B	HR	HR%	R	RBI	BB	SO	SB	Pinch Hit AB	Pinch Hit H	PO	A	E	DP	TC/G	FA	G by Pos
1981 NY N	9	.000	.000	7	0	0	0	0	0.0	0	0	0	3	0	2	0	5	8	0	2	1.4	1.000	SS-2, 2B-2
1982	45	.210	.312	138	29	5	0	3	2.2	14	10	12	29	6	0	0	122	133	2	28	5.7	.992	2B-45, SS-2
1983	145	.245	.298	400	98	15	0	2	0.5	39	27	36	77	17	5	0	309	390	14	90	4.9	.980	2B-140, SS-12
1985 MIL A	34	.172	.241	58	10	1	0	1	1.7	6	1	7	16	2	0	0	48	58	2	10	3.2	.981	SS-20, 2B-13, DH-2
1986 CHI A	9	.273	.273	11	3	0	0	0	0.0	0	1	0	2	0	1	0	15	11	0	6	2.9	1.000	2B-7, SS-1
5 yrs.	242	.228	.292	614	140	21	0	6	1.0	59	39	55	127	25	8	0	499	600	18	136	4.6	.984	2B-207, SS-37, DH-2

George Gilham

GILHAM, GEORGE LOUIS
B. Sept. 8, 1899, Shamokin, Pa. D. Apr. 25, 1937, Lansdowne, Pa.
BR TR 5'11" 164 lbs.

Year Team	Games	BA	SA	AB	H	2B	3B	HR	HR%	R	RBI	BB	SO	SB	Pinch Hit AB	Pinch Hit H	PO	A	E	DP	TC/G	FA	G by Pos
1920 STL N	1	.000	.000	3	0	0	0	0	0.0	0	0	0	1	0	0	0	2	1	1	0	4.0	.750	C-1
1921	1	.000	.000	1	0	0	0	0	0.0	0	0	0	0	0	1	0	0	0	0	0	0.0	—	
2 yrs.	2	.000	.000	4	0	0	0	0	0.0	0	0	0	1	0	1	0	2	1	1	0	2.0	.750	C-1

Frank Gilhooley

GILHOOLEY, FRANK PATRICK (Flash)
B. June 10, 1892, Toledo, Ohio D. July 11, 1959, Toledo, Ohio
BL TR 5'8" 155 lbs.

Year Team	Games	BA	SA	AB	H	2B	3B	HR	HR%	R	RBI	BB	SO	SB	Pinch Hit AB	Pinch Hit H	PO	A	E	DP	TC/G	FA	G by Pos
1911 STL N	1	—	—	0	0	0	0	0		0	0	0	0	0	0	0	0	0	0	0	0.0	—	OF-1
1912	13	.224	.224	49	11	0	0	0	0.0	5	2	3	8	0	1	0	16	1	0	0	1.3	1.000	OF-11
1913 NY A	24	.341	.388	85	29	2	1	0	0.0	10	14	4	9	6	0	0	40	2	1	0	1.8	.977	OF-24
1914	1	.667	.667	3	2	0	0	0	0.0	1	0	0	0	0	0	0	0	0	0	0	0.0	—	OF-1
1915	1	.000	.000	4	0	0	0	0	0.0	0	0	0	1	0	0	0	1	0	0	0	1.0	1.000	OF-1
1916	58	.278	.341	223	62	5	3	1	0.4	40	10	37	17	16	1	1	93	9	3	3	1.8	.971	OF-57
1917	54	.242	.291	165	40	6	1	0	0.0	14	8	30	13	6	2	1	78	5	6	1	1.6	.933	OF-46
1918	112	.276	.337	427	118	13	5	1	0.2	59	23	53	24	7	1	0	206	15	9	8	2.1	.961	OF-111
1919 BOS A	48	.241	.277	112	27	4	0	0	0.0	14	1	12	8	2	10	2	44	3	4	0	1.1	.922	OF-33
9 yrs.	312	.271	.323	1068	289	30	10	2	0.2	142	58	140	80	37	15	4	478	35	23	12	1.7	.957	OF-285

Bob Gilks

GILKS, ROBERT JAMES
B. July 2, 1864, Cincinnati, Ohio D. Aug. 21, 1944, Brunswick, Ga.
BR TR 5'8" 178 lbs.

Year Team	Games	BA	SA	AB	H	2B	3B	HR	HR%	R	RBI	BB	SO	SB	Pinch Hit AB	Pinch Hit H	PO	A	E	DP	TC/G	FA	G by Pos
1887 CLE AA	22	.313	.337	83	26	2	0	0	0.0	12		3		5	0	0	65	33	7	6	4.8	.933	P-13, 1B-6, OF-3, 2B-1
1888	119	.229	.281	484	111	14	4	1	0.2	59	63	7		16	0	0	172	94	38	12	2.6	.875	OF-87, 3B-28, SS-4, P-4, 2B-1
1889 CLE N	53	.238	.281	210	50	5	2	0	0.0	17	18	7	20	6	0	0	172	54	9	9	4.4	.962	OF-29, SS-13, 1B-10, 2B-1
1890	130	.213	.243	544	116	10	3	0	0.0	65	41	32	38	17	0	0	249	39	20	5	2.4	.935	OF-123, P-4, SS-3, 2B-2
1893 BAL N	15	.266	.297	64	17	2	0	0	0.0	10	7	0	3	3	0	0	26	5	1	1	2.1	.969	OF-15
5 yrs.	339	.231	.270	1385	320	33	9	1	0.1	163	129	49	61	47	0	0	684	225	75	33	2.9	.924	OF-257, 3B-28, P-21, SS-20, 1B-16, 2B-5

Jim Gill

GILL, JAMES C.
B. St. Louis, Mo. Deceased.

Year Team	Games	BA	SA	AB	H	2B	3B	HR	HR%	R	RBI	BB	SO	SB	Pinch Hit AB	Pinch Hit H	PO	A	E	DP	TC/G	FA	G by Pos
1889 STL AA	2	.250	.375	8	2	1	0	0	0.0	2	1	1	2	1	0	0	7	1	1	0	4.5	.889	OF-1, 2B-1

Johnny Gill

GILL, JOHN WESLEY (Patcheye)
B. Mar. 27, 1905, Nashville, Tenn. D. Dec. 26, 1984, Nashville, Tenn.
BL TR 6'2" 190 lbs.

Year Team	Games	BA	SA	AB	H	2B	3B	HR	HR%	R	RBI	BB	SO	SB	Pinch Hit AB	Pinch Hit H	PO	A	E	DP	TC/G	FA	G by Pos
1927 CLE A	21	.217	.317	60	13	3	0	1	1.7	8	4	7	13	1	2	2	24	2	0	1	1.2	1.000	OF-17
1928	2	.000	.000	2	0	0	0	0	0.0	0	0	0	1	0	2	0	0	0	0	0	0.0	—	
1931 WAS A	8	.267	.400	30	8	2	1	0	0.0	2	5	1	6	0	0	0	24	2	0	2	3.3	1.000	OF-8
1934	13	.245	.415	53	13	3	0	2	3.8	7	7	2	4	0	0	0	25	0	0	0	1.9	1.000	OF-13
1935 CHI N	3	.333	.667	3	1	1	0	0	0.0	2	1	0	1	0	3	1	0	0	0	0	0.0	—	
1936	71	.253	.420	174	44	8	0	7	4.0	20	28	13	19	0	25	6	72	5	5	1	1.1	.938	OF-41
6 yrs.	118	.245	.398	322	79	17	2	9	3.1	39	45	23	43	1	32	9	145	7	5	4	1.3	.968	OF-79

Warren Gill

GILL, WARREN DARST (Doc)
B. Dec. 21, 1878, Ladoga, Ind. D. Nov. 26, 1952, Laguna Beach, Calif.
BR TR 6'1" 175 lbs.

Year Team	Games	BA	SA	AB	H	2B	3B	HR	HR%	R	RBI	BB	SO	SB	Pinch Hit AB	Pinch Hit H	PO	A	E	DP	TC/G	FA	G by Pos
1908 PIT N	27	.224	.250	76	17	0	1	0	0.0	10	14	11		3	1	1	237	7	0	10	9.0	1.000	1B-25

Sam Gillen

GILLEN, SAMUEL
Born Samuel Gilleland.
B. 1870, Pittsburgh, Pa. D. May 13, 1905, Pittsburgh, Pa.

Year Team	Games	BA	SA	AB	H	2B	3B	HR	HR%	R	RBI	BB	SO	SB	Pinch Hit AB	Pinch Hit H	PO	A	E	DP	TC/G	FA	G by Pos
1893 PIT N	3	.000	.000	6	0	0	0	0	0.0	0	0	0	1	0	0	0	5	2	1		2.7	.750	SS-3

Year	Team	Games	BA	SA	AB	H	2B	3B	HR	HR%	R	RBI	BB	SO	SB	Pinch Hit AB	H	PO	A	E	DP	TC/G	FA	G by Pos

Sam Gillen *continued*

Year	Team	Games	BA	SA	AB	H	2B	3B	HR	HR%	R	RBI	BB	SO	SB	PH AB	PH H	PO	A	E	DP	TC/G	FA	G by Pos
1897	PHI N	75	.259	.319	270	70	10	3	0	0.0	32	27	35			2	0	0	136	203	39	6	5.0	.897	SS-69, 3B-6
2 yrs.		78	.254	.312	276	70	10	3	0	0.0	32	27	35	1		2	0	0	137	208	41	7	4.9	.894	SS-72, 3B-6

Tom Gillen

GILLEN, THOMAS J. B. May 18, 1862, Philadelphia, Pa. D. Jan. 26, 1889, Philadelphia, Pa.   5'8" 160 lbs.

Year	Team	Games	BA	SA	AB	H	2B	3B	HR	HR%	R	RBI	BB	SO	SB	PH AB	PH H	PO	A	E	DP	TC/G	FA	G by Pos
1884	PHI U	29	.155	.172	116	18	2	0	0	0.0	5		1				0	0	154	61	25	1	8.3	.896	C-27, OF-3
1886	DET N	2	.400	.400	10	4	0	0	0	0.0	2	4	0	1			0	0	5	3	1	0	4.5	.889	C-2
2 yrs.		31	.175	.190	126	22	2	0	0	0.0	7	4	1	1			0	0	159	64	26	1	8.0	.896	C-29, OF-3

Carden Gillenwater

GILLENWATER, CARDEN EDISON B. May 13, 1918, Riceville, Tenn.   BR TR 6'1" 175 lbs.

Year	Team	Games	BA	SA	AB	H	2B	3B	HR	HR%	R	RBI	BB	SO	SB	PH AB	PH H	PO	A	E	DP	TC/G	FA	G by Pos
1940	STL N	7	.160	.200	25	4	1	0	0	0.0	1	5	0	2	0	0	0	12	0	0		1.7	1.000	OF-7
1943	BKN N	8	.176	.176	17	3	0	0	0	0.0	1	2	2	3	0	3	0	5	1	0	0	0.8	1.000	OF-5
1945	BOS N	144	.288	.375	517	149	20	2	7	1.4	74	72	73	70	13	3	1	451	24	10	5	3.4	.979	OF-140
1946		99	.228	.295	224	51	10	1	1	0.4	30	14	39	27	3	14	3	180	6	4	2	1.9	.979	OF-78
1948	WAS A	77	.244	.367	221	54	10	4	3	1.4	23	21	39	36	4	11	2	186	4	5	0	2.5	.974	OF-67
5 yrs.		335	.260	.348	1004	261	41	7	11	1.1	129	114	153	138	20	31	3	834	35	19	7	2.7	.979	OF-297

Jim Gillespie

GILLESPIE, JAMES WHEATFIELD B. Buffalo, N. Y. D. Sept. 5, 1921, North Tonawanda, N. Y.   BL TR

Year	Team	Games	BA	SA	AB	H	2B	3B	HR	HR%	R	RBI	BB	SO	SB	PH AB	PH H	PO	A	E	DP	TC/G	FA	G by Pos
1890	BUF P	1	.000	.000	3	0	0	0	0	0.0	0	0	0	2	0	0	0	0	1	3	0	4.0	.250	OF-1

Paul Gillespie

GILLESPIE, PAUL ALLEN B. Sept. 18, 1920, Cartersville, Ga. D. Aug. 11, 1970, Anniston, Ala.   BL TR 6'2" 180 lbs.

Year	Team	Games	BA	SA	AB	H	2B	3B	HR	HR%	R	RBI	BB	SO	SB	PH AB	PH H	PO	A	E	DP	TC/G	FA	G by Pos
1942	CHI N	5	.250	.625	16	4	0	0	2	12.5	3	4	1	2	0	1	0	13	2	0	0	3.0	1.000	C-4
1944		9	.269	.423	26	7	1	0	1	3.8	2	3	2	3	0	2	0	22	6	3	0	3.4	.903	C-7
1945		75	.288	.380	163	47	6	0	3	1.8	12	25	18	9	2	24	7	162	20	2	1	2.5	.989	C-45, OF-1
3 yrs.		89	.283	.405	205	58	7	0	6	2.9	17	31	22	14	2	27	7	197	28	5	1	2.6	.978	C-56, OF-1

WORLD SERIES

Year	Team	Games	BA	SA	AB	H	2B	3B	HR	HR%	R	RBI	BB	SO	SB	PH AB	PH H	PO	A	E	DP	TC/G	FA	G by Pos
1945	CHI N	3	.000	.000	6	0	0	0	0	0.0	0	0	0	2	0	2	0	3	0	0	0	1.0	1.000	C-1

Pete Gillespie

GILLESPIE, PETER PATRICK B. Nov. 30, 1851, Carbondale, Pa. D. May 5, 1910, Carbondale, Pa.   BL TR 6'1½" 178 lbs.

Year	Team	Games	BA	SA	AB	H	2B	3B	HR	HR%	R	RBI	BB	SO	SB	PH AB	PH H	PO	A	E	DP	TC/G	FA	G by Pos
1880	TRO N	82	.243	.347	346	84	20	5	2	0.6	50	24	17	35		0	0	185	14	21	5	2.7	.905	OF-82
1881		84	.276	.333	348	96	14	3	0	0.0	43	41	9	24		0	0	180	16	14	5	2.5	.933	OF-84
1882		74	.275	.339	298	82	5	4	2	0.7	46	32	9	14		0	0	144	9	32	1	2.5	.827	OF-74
1883	NY N	98	.314	.436	411	129	23	12	1	0.2	64	27	19	35		0	0	216	11	26	6	2.6	.897	OF-98
1884		101	.264	.315	413	109	7	4	2	0.5	75		9	35		0	0	159	8	20	1	1.9	.893	OF-101
1885		102	.293	.362	420	123	17	6	0	0.0	67		15	32		0	0	133	12	9	2	1.5	.942	OF-102
1886		97	.273	.346	396	108	13	8	0	0.0	65	58	16	30		0	0	121	6	14	0	1.5	.901	OF-97
1887		76	.264	.346	295	78	9	3	3	1.0	40	37	12	21	37	0	0	91	44	6	1	1.9	.957	OF-76, 3B-1
8 yrs.		714	.276	.354	2927	809	108	45	10	0.3	450	192	106	218	37	0	0	1229	120	142	21	2.1	.905	OF-714, 3B-1

Jim Gilliam

GILLIAM, JAMES WILLIAM (Junior) B. Oct. 17, 1928, Nashville, Tenn. D. Oct. 8, 1978, Inglewood, Calif.   BB TR 5'10½" 175 lbs.

Year	Team	Games	BA	SA	AB	H	2B	3B	HR	HR%	R	RBI	BB	SO	SB	PH AB	PH H	PO	A	E	DP	TC/G	FA	G by Pos
1953	BKN N	151	.278	.415	605	168	31	17	6	1.0	125	63	100	38	21	2	1	332	426	19	102	5.1	.976	2B-149
1954		146	.282	.418	607	171	28	8	13	2.1	107	52	76	30	8	2	0	349	388	17	99	5.2	.977	2B-143, OF-5
1955		147	.249	.355	538	134	20	8	7	1.3	110	40	70	37	15	6	3	309	271	19	64	4.1	.968	2B-99, OF-46
1956		153	.300	.396	594	178	23	8	6	1.0	102	43	95	39	21	1	0	340	332	12	65	4.5	.982	2B-99, OF-56
1957		149	.250	.314	617	154	26	4	2	0.3	89	37	64	31	26	0	0	416	390	11	90	5.5	.987	2B-148, OF-2
1958	LA N	147	.261	.335	555	145	25	5	2	0.4	81	43	78	22	18	5	1	245	176	12	37	2.9	.972	OF-75, 3B-44, 2B-32
1959		145	.282	.345	553	156	18	4	3	0.5	91	34	96	25	23	7	1	143	258	17	20	2.9	.959	3B-132, 2B-8, OF-4
1960		151	.248	.318	557	138	20	2	5	0.9	96	40	96	28	12	2	1	152	331	16	33	3.3	.968	3B-130, 2B-30
1961		144	.244	.344	439	107	26	3	4	0.9	74	32	79	34	8	11	3	195	283	13	54	3.4	.974	3B-74, 2B-71, OF-11
1962		160	.270	.335	588	159	24	1	4	0.7	83	43	93	35	17	2	0	243	283	20	72	4.1	.969	2B-113, 3B-90, OF-1
1963		148	.282	.383	525	148	27	4	6	1.1	77	49	60	28	19	1	0	267	343	13	67	4.2	.979	2B-119, 3B-55
1964		116	.228	.287	334	76	8	3	2	0.6	44	27	42	21	4	13	3	101	171	18	15	2.5	.938	3B-86, 2B-25, OF-2
1965		111	.280	.384	372	104	19	4	4	1.1	54	39	53	31	9	7	1	85	142	10	15	2.1	.958	3B-80, OF-22, 2B-5
1966		88	.217	.268	235	51	9	0	1	0.4	30	16	34	17	2	22	3	43	103	7	8	1.7	.954	3B-70, 2B-2, 1B-2
14 yrs.		1956	.265	.355	7119	1889	304	71	65	0.9	1163	558	1036	416	203	89	18	3220	4002	204	741	3.8	.973	2B-1046, 3B-761, OF-224, 1B-2

WORLD SERIES

Year	Team	Games	BA	SA	AB	H	2B	3B	HR	HR%	R	RBI	BB	SO	SB	PH AB	PH H	PO	A	E	DP	TC/G	FA	G by Pos
1953	BKN N	6	.296	.630	27	8	3	0	2	7.4	4	4	0	0	0	0	0	15	16	1	3	5.3	.969	2B-6
1955		7	.292	.333	24	7	1	0	0	0.0	2	3	8	1	1	0	0	8	13	0	4	3.0	1.000	2B-5, OF-4
1956		7	.083	.083	24	2	0	0	0	0.0	2		7	3	1	0	0	19	17	0	4	5.1	1.000	2B-6, OF-1
1959	LA N	6	.240	.240	25	6	0	0	0	0.0	2	2	2	7	0	0	0	4	10	0	1	2.3	1.000	2B-6
1963		4	.154	.154	13	2	0	0	0	0.0	3	0	3	1	0	0	0	2	2	0	0	1.0	1.000	3B-6
1965		7	.214	.250	28	6	1	0	0	0.0	2	1	2	0	0	0	0	4	7	2	0	1.9	.846	3B-7
1966		2	.000	.000	6	0	0	0	0	0.0	0	1	2	0	0	0	0	3	4	1	1	4.0	.875	3B-2
7 yrs.		39	.211	.286	147	31	5	0	2	1.4	15	12	23 (7th)	9	4	0	0	55	69	4	13	3.3	.969	3B-19, 2B-17, OF-5

Barney Gilligan

GILLIGAN, ANDREW BERNARD B. Jan. 3, 1856, Cambridge, Mass. D. Apr. 1, 1934, Lynn, Mass.   BR TR 5'6½" 130 lbs.

Year	Team	Games	BA	SA	AB	H	2B	3B	HR	HR%	R	RBI	BB	SO	SB	PH AB	PH H	PO	A	E	DP	TC/G	FA	G by Pos
1879	CLE N	52	.171	.220	205	35	6	2	0	0.0	20	11	0	13		0	0	182	54	37	0	5.3	.864	C-27, OF-23, SS-2
1880		30	.172	.303	99	17	4	3	1	1.0	9	13	6	12		0	0	134	48	6	7	6.3	.968	C-23, OF-4, SS-4
1881	PRO N	46	.219	.279	183	40	7	2	0	0.0	19	20	9	24		0	0	194	73	25	9	6.3	.914	C-36, SS-10, OF-1
1882		56	.224	.318	201	45	7	6	0	0.0	32		4	26		0	0	287	87	29	8	7.2	.928	C-54, SS-2
1883		74	.198	.270	263	52	13	2	0	0.0	34		26	32		0	0	379	108	54	10	7.3	.900	C-74

Year	Team	Games	BA	SA	AB	H	2B	3B	HR	HR%	R	RBI	BB	SO	SB	Pinch Hit AB	H	PO	A	E	DP	TC/G	FA	G by Pos

Barney Gilligan *continued*

Year	Team	Games	BA	SA	AB	H	2B	3B	HR	HR%	R	RBI	BB	SO	SB	AB	H	PO	A	E	DP	TC/G	FA	G by Pos
1884		82	.245	.313	294	72	13	2	1	0.3	47		35	41		0	0	613	94	55	7	9.3	.928	C-81, 3B-1, 1B-1
1885		71	.214	.266	252	54	7	3	0	0.0	23	12	23	33		0	0	315	102	63	13	6.8	.869	C-65, SS-5, OF-1, 2B-1
1886	WAS N	81	.190	.238	273	52	9	2	0	0.0	23	17	39	35		0	0	379	108	45	9	6.6	.915	C-71, OF-14, SS-1, 1B-1
1887		28	.200	.256	90	18	2	0	1	1.1	7	6	5	18	2	0	0	99	47	22	4	6.0	.869	C-26, SS-3, OF-1
1888	DET N	1	.200	.200	5	1	0	0	0	0.0	1	0	0	1	0	0	0	5	2	1	1	8.0	.875	C-1
10 yrs.		521	.207	.273	1865	386	68	23	3	0.2	215	79	147	235	2	0	0	2587	723	337	69	7.0	.908	C-458, OF-44, SS-27, 3B-2, 2B-1, 1B-1

Grant Gillis

GILLIS, GRANT
B. Jan. 24, 1901, Grove Hill, Ala.   D. Feb. 4, 1981, Thomasville, Ala.
BR TR 5'10" 165 lbs.

Year	Team	Games	BA	SA	AB	H	2B	3B	HR	HR%	R	RBI	BB	SO	SB	AB	H	PO	A	E	DP	TC/G	FA	G by Pos
1927	WAS A	10	.222	.361	36	8	1	1	0	0.0	8	2	2	0	0	0	0	19	22	0	6	4.1	1.000	SS-10
1928		24	.253	.333	87	22	5	1	0	0.0	13	10	4	5	0	0	0	39	47	8	6	3.9	.915	SS-16, 2B-5, 3B-3
1929	BOS A	28	.247	.301	73	18	4	0	0	0.0	5	11	6	8	0	1	0	40	69	5	11	4.1	.956	2B-25
3 yrs.		62	.245	.327	196	48	12	2	0	0.0	26	23	12	13	0	1	0	98	138	13	23	4.0	.948	2B-30, SS-26, 3B-3

Jim Gilman

GILMAN, JAMES J.
B. Cleveland Ohio,

Year	Team	Games	BA	SA	AB	H	2B	3B	HR	HR%	R	RBI	BB	SO	SB	AB	H	PO	A	E	DP	TC/G	FA	G by Pos
1893	CLE N	2	.286	.286	7	2	0	0	0	0.0	1	1	0	2	0	0	0	1	3	2	0	3.0	.667	2B-2

Pit Gilman

GILMAN, PITKIN CLARK
B. Mar. 14, 1864, Laporte, Ohio   D. Aug. 17, 1950, Elyria, Ohio
BL TL

Year	Team	Games	BA	SA	AB	H	2B	3B	HR	HR%	R	RBI	BB	SO	SB	AB	H	PO	A	E	DP	TC/G	FA	G by Pos
1884	CLE N	2	.100	.100	10	1	0	0	0	0.0	0	0	0	3	0	0	0	5	0	0	0	2.5	1.000	OF-2

Ernie Gilmore

GILMORE, ERNEST GROVER
B. Nov. 1, 1888, Chicago, Ill.   D. Nov. 25, 1919, Sioux City, Iowa
BL TL 5'9½" 170 lbs.

Year	Team	Games	BA	SA	AB	H	2B	3B	HR	HR%	R	RBI	BB	SO	SB	AB	H	PO	A	E	DP	TC/G	FA	G by Pos
1914	KC F	139	.287	.358	530	152	25	5	1	0.2	91	32	37		23	7	2	196	24	6	7	1.6	.973	OF-132
1915		119	.285	.418	411	117	22	15	1	0.2	53	47	26		19	5	4	215	17	5	4	2.0	.979	OF-119
2 yrs.		258	.286	.385	941	269	47	20	2	0.2	144	79	63		42	7	2	411	41	11	11	1.8	.976	OF-251

Tinsley Ginn

GINN, TINSLEY RUCKER
B. Sept. 26, 1891, Royston, Ga.   D. Aug. 30, 1931, Atlanta, Ga.
BL TR 5'9" 180 lbs.

Year	Team	Games	BA	SA	AB	H	2B	3B	HR	HR%	R	RBI	BB	SO	SB	AB	H	PO	A	E	DP	TC/G	FA	G by Pos
1914	CLE A	2	.000	.000	1	0	0	0	0	0.0	0	0	0	0	0	0	0	0	0	0	0	0.0	–	OF-2

Joe Ginsberg

GINSBERG, MYRON NATHAN
B. Oct. 11, 1926, New York, N. Y.
BL TR 5'11" 180 lbs.

Year	Team	Games	BA	SA	AB	H	2B	3B	HR	HR%	R	RBI	BB	SO	SB	AB	H	PO	A	E	DP	TC/G	FA	G by Pos
1948	DET A	11	.361	.361	36	13	0	0	0	0.0	7	1	3	1	0	0	0	46	4	3	3	4.8	.943	C-11
1950		36	.232	.295	95	22	6	0	0	0.0	12	12	11	6	1	4	1	97	8	2	3	3.0	.981	C-31
1951		102	.260	.385	304	79	10	2	8	2.6	44	37	43	21	0	8	2	388	56	10	7	4.5	.978	C-95
1952		113	.221	.336	307	68	13	2	6	2.0	29	36	51	21	1	16	2	442	41	8	7	4.3	.984	C-101
1953	2 teams	DET A (18G – .302)							CLE A (46G – .284)															
"	total	64	.290	.327	162	47	6	0	0	0.0	16	13	24	5	0	12	2	201	22	6	4	3.6	.974	C-54
1954	CLE A	3	.500	1.500	2	1	0	1	0	0.0	0	1	0	0	0	2	1	1	0	0	0	0.3	1.000	C-1
1956	2 teams	KC A (71G – .246)							BAL A (15G – .071)															
"	total	86	.224	.283	223	50	8	1	1	0.4	15	14	25	21	1	18	3	269	31	3	3	3.5	.990	C-65
1957	BAL A	85	.274	.360	175	48	8	2	1	0.6	15	18	18	19	2	18	3	252	20	4	6	3.2	.986	C-66
1958		61	.211	.303	109	23	1	0	3	2.8	4	16	13	14	0	20	4	156	8	1	2	2.7	.994	C-39
1959		65	.181	.211	166	30	2	0	1	0.6	14	14	21	14	1	5	1	241	29	2	4	4.2	.993	C-62
1960	2 teams	BAL A (14G – .267)							CHI A (28G – .253)															
"	total	42	.257	.305	105	27	5	0	0	0.0	11	15	16	9	1	2	0	188	12	5	0	4.9	.976	C-39
1961	2 teams	CHI A (6G – .000)							BOS A (19G – .250)															
"	total	25	.222	.222	27	6	0	0	0	0.0	1	5	1	4	0	16	3	14	1	0	0	0.6	1.000	C-8
1962	NY N	2	.000	.000	5	0	0	0	0	0.0	0	0	0	1	0	0	0	9	2	0	1	5.5	1.000	C-2
13 yrs.		695	.241	.320	1716	414	59	8	20	1.2	168	182	226	125	7	121	22	2304	234	44	40	3.7	.983	C-574

Al Gionfriddo

GIONFRIDDO, ALBERT FRANCIS
B. Mar. 8, 1922, Dysart, Pa.
BL TL 5'6" 165 lbs.

Year	Team	Games	BA	SA	AB	H	2B	3B	HR	HR%	R	RBI	BB	SO	SB	AB	H	PO	A	E	DP	TC/G	FA	G by Pos
1944	PIT N	4	.167	.167	6	1	0	0	0	0.0	0	0	1	1	0	3	1	3	0	0	0	0.8	1.000	OF-1
1945		122	.284	.386	409	116	18	9	2	0.5	74	42	60	22	12	14	2	235	6	9	2	2.0	.964	OF-106
1946		64	.255	.314	102	26	2	2	0	0.0	11	10	14	5	1	24	5	49	2	3	0	0.8	.944	OF-33
1947	2 teams	PIT N (1G – .000)							BKN N (37G – .177)															
"	total	38	.175	.238	63	11	2	1	0	0.0	10	6	16	11	2	13	2	1	0	0	0	0.0	1.000	OF-17
4 yrs.		228	.266	.355	580	154	22	12	2	0.3	95	58	91	39	15	54	10	288	8	12	2	1.4	.961	OF-157

WORLD SERIES

Year	Team	Games	BA	SA	AB	H	2B	3B	HR	HR%	R	RBI	BB	SO	SB	AB	H	PO	A	E	DP	TC/G	FA	G by Pos
1947	BKN N	4	.000	.000	3	0	0	0	0	0.0	2	0	1	0	1	1	0	1	0	0	0	0.3	1.000	OF-1

Tommy Giordano

GIORDANO, THOMAS ARTHUR (T-Bone)
B. Oct. 9, 1925, Newark, N. J.
BR TR 6' 175 lbs.

Year	Team	Games	BA	SA	AB	H	2B	3B	HR	HR%	R	RBI	BB	SO	SB	AB	H	PO	A	E	DP	TC/G	FA	G by Pos
1953	PHI A	11	.175	.375	40	7	2	0	2	5.0	6	5	5	6	0	0	0	31	32	1	11	5.8	.984	2B-11

Joe Girardi

GIRARDI, JOSEPH ELLIOTT
B. Oct. 14, 1964, Peoria, Ill.
BR TR 5'11" 195 lbs.

Year	Team	Games	BA	SA	AB	H	2B	3B	HR	HR%	R	RBI	BB	SO	SB	AB	H	PO	A	E	DP	TC/G	FA	G by Pos
1989	CHI N	59	.248	.331	157	39	10	0	1	0.6	15	14	11	26	2	0	0	332	28	7	1	6.2	.981	C-59

LEAGUE CHAMPIONSHIP SERIES

Year	Team	Games	BA	SA	AB	H	2B	3B	HR	HR%	R	RBI	BB	SO	SB	AB	H	PO	A	E	DP	TC/G	FA	G by Pos
1989	CHI N	4	.100	.100	10	1	0	0	0	0.0	1	0	1	2	0	0	0	20	0	0	0	5.0	1.000	C-4

Tony Giuliani

GIULIANI, ANGELO JOHN
B. Nov. 24, 1912, St. Paul, Minn.
BR TR 5'11" 175 lbs.

Year	Team	Games	BA	SA	AB	H	2B	3B	HR	HR%	R	RBI	BB	SO	SB	AB	H	PO	A	E	DP	TC/G	FA	G by Pos
1936	STL A	71	.217	.232	198	43	3	0	0	0.0	17	13	11	13	0	8	1	226	29	9	7	3.7	.966	C-66
1937		19	.302	.321	53	16	1	0	0	0.0	6	3	3	3	0	0	0	61	10	1	1	3.8	.986	C-19

Year	Team	Games	BA	SA	AB	H	2B	3B	HR	HR%	R	RBI	BB	SO	SB	Pinch Hit AB	Pinch Hit H	PO	A	E	DP	TC/G	FA	G by Pos

Tony Giuliani *continued*

Year	Team	Games	BA	SA	AB	H	2B	3B	HR	HR%	R	RBI	BB	SO	SB	PH AB	PH H	PO	A	E	DP	TC/G	FA	G by Pos
1938	WAS A	46	.217	.252	115	25	4	0	0	0.0	10	15	8	3	1	0	0	138	17	0	4	3.4	1.000	C-46
1939		54	.250	.308	172	43	6	2	0	0.0	20	18	4	7	0	3	1	201	28	5	3	4.3	.979	C-50
1940	BKN N	1	.000	.000	1	0	0	0	0	0.0	0	0	0	0	0	0	0	1	0	0	0	1.0	1.000	C-1
1941		3	.000	.000	2	0	0	0	0	0.0	0	0	0	0	0	0	0	1	0	0	0	1.0	1.000	C-1
1943	WAS A	49	.226	.271	133	30	4	1	0	0.0	5	20	12	14	0	0	0	5	1	0	0	2.0	1.000	C-3
7 yrs.		243	.233	.269	674	157	18	3	0	0.0	58	69	38	40	1	11	2	786	109	22	16	3.8	.976	C-234

Jim Gladd

GLADD, JAMES WALTER
B. Oct. 2, 1922, Fort Gibson, Okla. D. Nov. 8, 1977, Long Beach, Calif.
BR TR 6'2" 190 lbs.

Year	Team	Games	BA	SA	AB	H	2B	3B	HR	HR%	R	RBI	BB	SO	SB	PH AB	PH H	PO	A	E	DP	TC/G	FA	G by Pos
1946	NY N	4	.091	.091	11	1	0	0	0	0.0	0	1	4	0	0	0	0	31	2	0	0	8.3	1.000	C-4

Dan Gladden

GLADDEN, CLINTON DANIEL III
B. July 7, 1957, San Jose, Calif.
BR TR 5'11" 175 lbs.

Year	Team	Games	BA	SA	AB	H	2B	3B	HR	HR%	R	RBI	BB	SO	SB	PH AB	PH H	PO	A	E	DP	TC/G	FA	G by Pos
1983	SF N	18	.222	.302	63	14	2	0	1	1.6	6	9	5	11	4	1	0	53	0	0	0	2.9	1.000	OF-18
1984		86	.351	.447	342	120	17	2	4	1.2	71	31	33	37	31	2	0	232	8	3	1	2.8	.988	OF-85
1985		142	.243	.347	502	122	15	8	7	1.4	64	41	40	78	32	19	8	273	3	7	0	2.0	.975	OF-124
1986		102	.276	.362	351	97	16	1	4	1.1	55	29	39	59	27	9	1	226	7	3	2	2.3	.987	OF-89
1987	MIN A	121	.249	.361	438	109	21	2	8	1.8	69	38	38	72	25	9	2	223	9	3	2	1.9	.987	OF-111, DH-4
1988		141	.269	.403	576	155	32	6	11	1.9	91	62	46	74	28	4	1	319	12	3	5	2.4	.991	OF-141, 3B-1, P-1
1989		121	.295	.410	461	136	23	3	8	1.7	69	46	23	53	23	1	1	245	8	9	3	2.2	.966	OF-117, DH-2, P-1
7 yrs.		731	.276	.385	2733	753	126	22	43	1.6	425	256	224	384	170	45	13	1571	47	28	13	2.3	.983	OF-685, DH-6, P-2, 3B-1

LEAGUE CHAMPIONSHIP SERIES

Year	Team	Games	BA	SA	AB	H	2B	3B	HR	HR%	R	RBI	BB	SO	SB	PH AB	PH H	PO	A	E	DP	TC/G	FA	G by Pos
1987	MIN A	5	.350	.450	20	7	0	0	0	0.0	5	5	2	1	0	0	0	12	0	0	0	2.4	1.000	OF-5

WORLD SERIES

Year	Team	Games	BA	SA	AB	H	2B	3B	HR	HR%	R	RBI	BB	SO	SB	PH AB	PH H	PO	A	E	DP	TC/G	FA	G by Pos
1987	MIN A	7	.290	.516	31	9	1	0	1	3.2	3	7	3	4	2	0	0	12	0	0	0	1.7	1.000	OF-7

Buck Gladman

GLADMAN, JOHN H.
B. 1864, Washington, D. C. Deceased.

Year	Team	Games	BA	SA	AB	H	2B	3B	HR	HR%	R	RBI	BB	SO	SB	PH AB	PH H	PO	A	E	DP	TC/G	FA	G by Pos
1883	PHI N	1	.000	.000	4	0	0	0	0	0.0	1		0		2			0	1	0	0	1.0	1.000	3B-1
1884	WAS AA	56	.156	.219	224	35	5	3	1	0.4	17		3			0	0	70	94	40	6	3.6	.804	3B-53, OF-2, SS-1
1886	WAS N	44	.138	.230	152	21	5	3	1	0.7	17	15	12	30		0	0	53	74	26	8	3.5	.830	3B-44
3 yrs.		101	.147	.221	380	56	10	6	2	0.5	35	15	15	32		0	0	123	169	66	14	3.5	.816	3B-98, OF-2, SS-1

Roland Gladu

GLADU, ROLAND EDOUARD
B. May 10, 1913, Montreal, Que., Canada
BL TR 5'8½" 185 lbs.

Year	Team	Games	BA	SA	AB	H	2B	3B	HR	HR%	R	RBI	BB	SO	SB	PH AB	PH H	PO	A	E	DP	TC/G	FA	G by Pos
1944	BOS N	21	.242	.348	66	16	2	1	1	1.5	5	7	3	8	0	2	0	21	21	5	6	2.2	.894	3B-15, OF-3

Jack Glasscock

GLASSCOCK, JOHN WESLEY (Old Battle Ax)
B. July 22, 1859, Wheeling, W. Va. D. Feb. 24, 1947, Wheeling, W. Va.
Manager 1889, 1892.
BR TR 5'8" 160 lbs.

Year	Team	Games	BA	SA	AB	H	2B	3B	HR	HR%	R	RBI	BB	SO	SB	PH AB	PH H	PO	A	E	DP	TC/G	FA	G by Pos
1879	CLE N	80	.209	.255	325	68	9	3	0	0.0	31	29	6	24			0	0	233	238	43	18	6.4	.916	2B-66, 3B-14
1880		77	.243	.307	296	72	13	3	0	0.0	37	27	2	21			0	0	107	252	44	21	5.2	.891	SS-77
1881		85	.257	.313	335	86	9	5	0	0.0	49	33	15	8			0	0	128	296	46	32	5.5	.902	SS-79, 2B-6
1882		84	.291	.450	358	104	27	9	4	1.1	66	46	13	9			0	0	112	313	47	41	5.6	.900	SS-83, 3B-1
1883		96	.287	.368	383	110	19	6	0	0.0	67		13	23			0	0	145	325	40	31	5.3	.922	SS-93, 2B-3
1884	2 teams		CLE N	(72G – .249)			CIN U	(38G – .419)																
"	total	110	.313	.402	453	142	13	9	3	0.7	93	22	33	16			0	0	182	389	69	24	5.8	.892	SS-105, 2B-5, P-2
1885	STL N	111	.280	.341	446	125	18	3	1	0.2	66	40	29	10			0	0	158	404	50	33	5.5	.918	SS-110, 2B-1
1886		121	.325	.432	486	158	29	7	3	0.6	96	40	38	13			0	0	157	392	57	43	5.0	.906	SS-120, OF-1
1887	IND N	122	.294	.360	483	142	18	7	0	0.0	91	40	41	8	62		0	0	211	493	73	58	6.4	.906	SS-122, P-1
1888		113	.269	.328	442	119	17	3	1	0.2	63	45	14	17	48		0	0	209	347	61	39	5.5	.901	SS-110, 2B-3, P-1
1889		134	.352	.467	582	**205**	40	3	7	1.2	128	85	31	10	57		0	0	249	485	68	61	6.0	.915	SS-132, 2B-2, P-1
1890	NY N	124	**.336**	.439	512	**172**	32	9	1	0.2	91	66	41	8	54		0	0	275	421	69	46	6.2	.910	SS-124
1891		97	.241	.306	369	89	12	6	0	0.0	46	55	36	11	29		0	0	164	274	42	39	4.9	.913	SS-97
1892	STL N	139	.267	.348	566	151	27	5	3	0.5	83	72	44	19	26		0	0	280	472	69	46	5.9	.916	SS-139
1893	2 teams		STL N	(48G – .287)			PIT N	(66G – .341)																
"	total	114	.320	.412	488	156	15	12	2	0.4	81	100	42	7	36		0	0	240	398	53	59	6.1	.923	SS-114
1894	PIT N	86	.280	.361	332	93	10	7	1	0.3	46	63	31	4	18		1	0	189	295	35	46	6.0	.933	SS-85
1895	2 teams		LOU N	(18G – .338)			WAS N	(25G – .230)																
"	total	43	.276	.333	174	48	5	1	1	0.6	29	16	10	4	4		0	0	124	155	29	19	7.2	.906	SS-38, 1B-5
17 yrs.		1736	.290	.374	7030	2040	313	98	27	0.4	1163	779	439	212	334		1	0	3163	5949	895	656	5.8	.911	SS-1628, 2B-86, 3B-15, 1B-5, P-5, OF-1

Tommy Glaviano

GLAVIANO, THOMAS GIATANO (Rabbit)
B. Oct. 26, 1923, Sacramento, Calif.
BR TR 5'9" 175 lbs.

Year	Team	Games	BA	SA	AB	H	2B	3B	HR	HR%	R	RBI	BB	SO	SB	PH AB	PH H	PO	A	E	DP	TC/G	FA	G by Pos
1949	STL N	87	.267	.407	258	69	16	1	6	2.3	32	36	41	35	0	7	3	81	190	20	18	3.3	.931	3B-73, 2B-7
1950		115	.285	.446	410	117	29	2	11	2.7	92	44	90	74	6	4	0	119	269	25	21	3.6	.939	3B-106, 2B-5, SS-1
1951		54	.183	.250	104	19	4	0	1	1.0	20	4	26	18	3	23	4	53	25	2	6	1.5	.975	OF-35, 2B-9
1952		80	.241	.340	162	39	5	1	3	1.9	30	19	27	26	2	10	2	47	95	10	5	1.9	.934	3B-52, 2B-1
1953	PHI N	53	.203	.392	74	15	1	2	3	4.1	17	5	24	20	0	20	2	31	39	6	5	1.4	.921	3B-14, 2B-12, SS-1
5 yrs.		389	.257	.395	1008	259	55	6	24	2.4	191	108	208	173	11	64	11	331	618	63	55	2.6	.938	3B-245, OF-35, 2B-34, SS-2

Bill Gleason

GLEASON, WILLIAM G. (Will)
Brother of Jack Gleason.
B. Nov. 12, 1858, St. Louis, Mo. D. July 21, 1932, St. Louis, Mo.
BR TR 5'8" 170 lbs.

Year	Team	Games	BA	SA	AB	H	2B	3B	HR	HR%	R	RBI	BB	SO	SB	PH AB	PH H	PO	A	E	DP	TC/G	FA	G by Pos
1882	STL AA	79	.288	.363	347	100	11	6	1	0.3	63						0	0	131	294	85	23	6.5	.833	SS-79
1883		98	.287	.393	425	122	21	9	2	0.5	81		6	16			0	0	120	257	56	22	4.4	.871	SS-98
1884		110	.269	.350	472	127	21	7	1	0.2	97		28				0	0	119	316	67	23	4.6	.867	SS-110, 3B-1
1885		112	.252	.311	472	119	9	5	3	0.6	79		29				0	0	115	303	63	18	4.3	.869	SS-112

Year Team	Games	BA	SA	AB	H	2B	3B	HR	HR%	R	RBI	BB	SO	SB	PH AB	PH H	PO	A	E	DP	TC/G	FA	G by Pos

Bill Gleason *continued*

Year Team	Games	BA	SA	AB	H	2B	3B	HR	HR%	R	RBI	BB	SO	SB	PH AB	PH H	PO	A	E	DP	TC/G	FA	G by Pos
1886	125	.269	.323	524	141	18	5	0	0.0	97		43			0	0	128	352	83	37	4.5	.853	SS-125
1887	135	.288	.323	598	172	19	1	0	0.0	135		41	61	23	0	0	169	411	83	27	4.9	.875	SS-135
1888 PHI AA	123	.224	.253	499	112	10	2	0	0.0	55		12		27	0	0	118	371	82	32	4.6	.856	SS-121, 3B-1, 1B-1
1889 LOU AA	16	.241	.253	58	14	2	0	0	0.0	6	5	4	1	1	0	0	26	57	18	4	6.3	.822	SS-16
8 yrs.	798	.267	.327	3395	907	111	35	7	0.2	613	66	179	1	51	0	0	926	2361	537	186	4.8	.860	SS-796, 3B-2, 1B-1

Bill Gleason

GLEASON, WILLIAM PATRICK BR TR 5'6½" 157 lbs.
B. Sept. 6, 1894, Chicago, Ill. D. Jan. 9, 1957, Holyoke, Mass.

Year Team	Games	BA	SA	AB	H	2B	3B	HR	HR%	R	RBI	BB	SO	SB	PH AB	PH H	PO	A	E	DP	TC/G	FA	G by Pos
1916 PIT N	1	.000	.000	2	0	0	0	0	0.0	1		1	0	0	0	0	1	1	0	0	2.0	1.000	2B-1
1917	13	.167	.190	42	7	1	0	0	0.0	3	0	5	5	1	0	0	18	27	1	3	3.5	.978	2B-13
1921 STL A	26	.257	.284	74	19	0	1	0	0.0	6	8	6	6	0	0	0	38	57	4	10	3.8	.960	2B-25
3 yrs.	40	.220	.246	118	26	1	1	0	0.0	9	8	11	11	1	0	0	57	85	5	13	3.7	.966	2B-39

Harry Gleason

GLEASON, HARRY GILBERT BR TR 5'6" 160 lbs.
Brother of Kid Gleason.
B. Mar. 28, 1875, Camden, N. J. D. Oct. 21, 1961, Camden, N. J.

Year Team	Games	BA	SA	AB	H	2B	3B	HR	HR%	R	RBI	BB	SO	SB	PH AB	PH H	PO	A	E	DP	TC/G	FA	G by Pos
1901 BOS A	1	1.000	1.000	1	1	0	0	0	0.0	0		1	0	0	0	0		2	1	1	3.0	.667	3B-1
1902	71	.225	.313	240	54	5	5	2	0.8	30	25	10		6	8	**3**	95	75	15	8	2.6	.919	3B-35, OF-23, 2B-4
1903	6	.154	.231	13	2	1	0	0	0.0	3	2	0			1			3	1		0.7	.750	3B-2
1904 STL	46	.213	.271	155	33	7	1	0	0.0	10	6	4		1	1		66	108	15	11	4.1	.921	SS-20, 3B-20, 2B-5, OF-1
1905	150	.217	.262	535	116	11	5	1	0.2	45	57	34		23			144	292	39	9	3.2	.918	3B-144, 2B-6
5 yrs.	274	.218	.276	944	206	24	11	3	0.3	88	90	48		31	13	3	305	480	71	29	3.1	.917	3B-202, OF-24, SS-20, 2B-15

Jack Gleason

GLEASON, JOHN DAY BR TR 170 lbs.
Brother of Bill Gleason.
B. July 14, 1854, St. Louis, Mo. D. Sept. 4, 1944, St. Louis, Mo.

Year Team	Games	BA	SA	AB	H	2B	3B	HR	HR%	R	RBI	BB	SO	SB	PH AB	PH H	PO	A	E	DP	TC/G	FA	G by Pos
1877 STL N	1	.250	.250	4	1	0	0	0	0.0	0		0	1		0	0	0	0	0	0	0.0	—	OF-1
1882 STL AA	78	.254	.308	331	84	10	1	2	0.6	53		**27**			0	0	112	171	84	11	4.7	.771	3B-73, OF-6, 2B-1
1883 2 teams	STL AA (9G – .235)			LOU AA (84G – .296)																			
" total	93	.290	.355	389	113	11	4	2	0.5	71		29			0	0	92	116	52	6	2.8	.800	3B-92
1884 STL U	92	.324	.433	395	128	30	4	3	0.8	90		23			0	0	95	170	80	11	3.8	.768	3B-84, OF-9, SS-1
1885 STL N	2	.143	.143	7	1	0	0	0	0.0	0		0			0	0	3	3	1		3.5	.857	3B-2
1886 PHI AA	77	.187	.271	299	56	8	7	1	0.3	39		16			0	0	85	150	60	19	3.8	.797	3B-77
6 yrs.	343	.269	.347	1425	383	59	14	8	0.6	253		95	2		0	0	387	610	277	47	3.7	.783	3B-328, OF-16, SS-1, 2B-1

Kid Gleason

GLEASON, WILLIAM J. (Youngster) BB TR 5'7" 158 lbs.
Brother of Harry Gleason.
B. Oct. 26, 1866, Camden, N. J. D. Jan. 2, 1933, Philadelphia, Pa.
Manager 1919-23.

Year Team	Games	BA	SA	AB	H	2B	3B	HR	HR%	R	RBI	BB	SO	SB	PH AB	PH H	PO	A	E	DP	TC/G	FA	G by Pos
1888 PHI N	24	.205	.229	83	17	2	0	0	0.0	4	5	3	16	3	0	0	6	31	7	1	1.8	.841	P-24, OF-1
1889	30	.253	.303	99	25	5	0	0	0.0	11	8	8	12	4	0	0	19	52	10	1	2.7	.877	P-29, 2B-2, OF-1
1890	63	.210	.223	224	47	3	0	0	0.0	22	17	12	21	10	0	0	26	102	11	4	2.2	.921	P-60, 2B-2
1891	65	.248	.290	214	53	5	2	0	0.0	31	17	20	17	6	0	0	47	78	15	3	2.2	.893	P-53, OF-9, SS-4
1892 STL N	66	.215	.288	233	50	5	3	3	1.3	35	25	34	23	7	0	0	0	0	0	0	0.0	—	P-47, OF-11, 2B-10, 1B-1, C-1
1893	59	.256	.327	199	51	6	4	0	0.0	25	20	19	8	2	1	0	53	91	16	3	2.7	.900	P-48, OF-11, SS-1
1894 2 teams	STL N (9G – .250)			BAL N (26G – .349)																			
" total	35	.325	.404	114	37	5	0	0	0.0	25	18	9	3	1	4	**2**	41	38	7	2	2.5	.919	P-29, 1B-2
1895 BAL N	112	.309	.399	421	130	14	12	0	0.0	90	74	33	18	19	3	0	234	277	61	33	5.1	.893	2B-85, 3B-12, P-9, OF-4
1896 NY N	133	.299	.372	541	162	17	5	4	0.7	79	89	42	13	46	0	0	334	404	50	44	5.9	.928	2B-129, SS-3
1897	131	.319	.369	540	172	16	4	1	0.2	85	106	26		43	0	0	383	488	60	58	5.9	.936	2B-144, SS-6
1898	150	.221	.253	570	126	8	5	0	0.0	78	62	39		21	0	0	403	465	50	60	6.3	.946	2B-146
1899	146	.264	.302	576	152	14	4	0	0.0	72	59	24		29	0	0	323	327	51	51	6.3	.927	2B-111, SS-1
1900	111	.248	.295	420	104	11	3	1	0.2	60	29	17		23	0	0	334	457	64	67	6.3	.925	2B-135
1901 DET A	135	.274	.364	547	150	16	12	3	0.5	82	75	41		32	0	0	320	349	42	66	6.0	.941	2B-118
1902	118	.247	.297	441	109	11	4	1	0.2	42	38	25		17	0	0	242	280	23	30	5.1	.958	2B-102, OF-4
1903 PHI N	106	.284	.367	412	117	19	6	1	0.2	65	49	23		12	0	0	380	464	52	44	5.9	.942	2B-152, 3B-1
1904	153	.274	.334	587	161	23	6	0	0.0	61	42	37		17	0	0	365	457	46	49	5.6	.947	2B-155
1905	155	.247	.303	608	150	17	7	1	0.2	95	50	45		16	0	0	215	358	32	39	4.5	.947	2B-135
1906	135	.227	.269	494	112	17	2	0	0.0	47	34	36		17	0	0	112	72	5	11	5.3	.974	2B-26, SS-4, 1B-4, OF-1
1907	36	.143	.167	126	18	3	0	0	0.0	11	6	7		3	1	0	3	1	0	1	2.0	1.000	OF-1, 2B-1
1908	2	.000	.000	1	0	0	0	0	0.0	0		0		0	0	0	1	1	0	0	3.0	.667	2B-1
1912 CHI A	2	.500	.500	2	1	0	0	0	0.0	0		0		0	0	0							2B-1
22 yrs.	1966	.261	.317	7452	1944	216	80	15	0.2	1020	823	500	131	328	10	3	4155	5195	659	604	5.1	.934	2B-1584, P-299, OF-44, SS-19, 3B-16, 1B-7, C-1

Roy Gleason

GLEASON, ROY WILLIAM BB TR 6'5½" 220 lbs.
B. Apr. 9, 1943, Melrose Park, Ill.

Year Team	Games	BA	SA	AB	H	2B	3B	HR	HR%	R	RBI	BB	SO	SB	PH AB	PH H	PO	A	E	DP	TC/G	FA	G by Pos
1963 LA N	8	1.000	2.000	1	1	1	0	0	0.0	3	0	0	0	0	1	1	0	0	0	0	0.0	—	

Jim Gleason

GLEASON, JAMES JOSEPH (Gee Gee) BB TR 6'1" 191 lbs.
B. Mar. 5, 1912, Kansas City, Mo.

Year Team	Games	BA	SA	AB	H	2B	3B	HR	HR%	R	RBI	BB	SO	SB	PH AB	PH H	PO	A	E	DP	TC/G	FA	G by Pos
1936 CLE A	41	.259	.439	139	36	9	2	4	2.9	26	12	18	17	2	7	0	67	1	3	0	1.7	.958	OF-33
1939 CHI N	111	.223	.352	332	74	19	6	4	1.2	43	45	39	46	7	17	4	175	5	8	1	1.7	.957	OF-91
1940	129	.313	.470	485	152	39	11	5	1.0	76	61	54	52	4	5	1	273	14	5	3	2.3	.983	OF-123
1941 CIN N	102	.233	.296	301	70	10	0	3	1.0	47	34	45	30	7	14	3	153	1	3	0	1.5	.981	OF-84
1942	9	.200	.200	20	4	0	0	0	0.0	3	2	2	2	0	3	0	7	1	1	0	1.0	.889	OF-5
5 yrs.	392	.263	.391	1277	336	77	19	16	1.3	195	154	158	147	20	46	8	675	22	20	4	1.8	.972	OF-336

Year	Team	Games	BA	SA	AB	H	2B	3B	HR	HR%	R	RBI	BB	SO	SB	Pinch Hit AB	Pinch Hit H	PO	A	E	DP	TC/G	FA	G by Pos

Frank Gleich

GLEICH, FRANK ELMER (Inch)
B. Mar. 7, 1894, Columbus, Ohio   D. Mar. 27, 1949, Columbus, Ohio   BL TR 5'11" 175 lbs.

Year	Team	Games	BA	SA	AB	H	2B	3B	HR	HR%	R	RBI	BB	SO	SB	PH AB	PH H	PO	A	E	DP	TC/G	FA	G by Pos
1919	NY	A	5	.250	.250	4	1	0	0	0	0.0	0	1	0	0	0	0	0	0	1	0	0.2	–	OF-4
1920		24	.122	.122	41	5	0	0	0	0.0	6	3	6	10	0	9	1	19	0	3	0	0.9	.864	OF-15
2 yrs.		29	.133	.133	45	6	0	0	0	0.0	6	4	7	10	0	9	1	19	0	4	0	0.8	.826	OF-19

Bob Glenalvin

GLENALVIN, ROBERT J.
Born Robert J. Dowling.
B. Jan. 17, 1867, Indianapolis, Ind.   D. Mar. 24, 1944, Detroit, Mich.   TR

Year	Team	Games	BA	SA	AB	H	2B	3B	HR	HR%	R	RBI	BB	SO	SB	PH AB	PH H	PO	A	E	DP	TC/G	FA	G by Pos
1890	CHI	N	66	.268	.380	250	67	10	3	4	1.6	43	26	19	31	30	0	0	128	194	25	20	5.3	.928	2B-66
1893		16	.344	.426	61	21	3	1	0	0.0	11	12	7	3	7	0	0	35	42	6	4	5.2	.928	2B-16
2 yrs.		82	.283	.389	311	88	13	4	4	1.3	54	38	26	34	37	0	0	163	236	31	24	5.2	.928	2B-82

Ed Glenn

GLENN, EDWARD C.
B. Sept. 19, 1860, Richmond, Va.   D. Feb. 10, 1892, Richmond, Va.   BR TR 5'10" 160 lbs.

Year	Team	Games	BA	SA	AB	H	2B	3B	HR	HR%	R	RBI	BB	SO	SB	PH AB	PH H	PO	A	E	DP	TC/G	FA	G by Pos
1884	RIC	AA	43	.246	.320	175	43	2	4	1	0.6	26		5			0	0	85	5	18	2	2.5	.833	OF-43
1886	PIT	AA	71	.191	.249	277	53	6	5	0	0.0	32		17			0	0	124	10	21	2	2.2	.865	OF-71
1888	2 teams		KC	AA	(3G – .000)		BOS	N	(20G – .154)															
"	total	23	.137	.192	73	10	0	2	0	0.0	8	3	2	8	1	0	0	49	2	3	2	2.3	.944	OF-22, 3B-1
3 yrs.		137	.202	.265	525	106	8	11	1	0.2	66	3	24	8	1	0	0	258	17	42	6	2.3	.868	OF-136, 3B-1

Ed Glenn

GLENN, EDWARD D.
B. 1874, Ludlow, Ky.   D. Dec. 6, 1911, Ludlow, Ky.   BR TR

Year	Team	Games	BA	SA	AB	H	2B	3B	HR	HR%	R	RBI	BB	SO	SB	PH AB	PH H	PO	A	E	DP	TC/G	FA	G by Pos
1898	2 teams		WAS	N	(1G – .000)		NY	N	(2G – .250)															
"	total	3	.125	.125	8	1	0	0	0	0.0	1	0	3		1	0	0	2	4	1	0	2.3	.857	SS-3
1902	CHI	N	2	.000	.000	7	0	0	0	0	0.0	0	0	1		0	0	0	0	6	0	0	3.0	1.000	SS-2
2 yrs.		5	.067	.067	15	1	0	0	0	0.0	1	0	4		1	0	0	2	10	1	0	2.6	.923	SS-5

Harry Glenn

GLENN, HARRY MELVILLE
B. June 9, 1890, Shelburn, Ind.   D. Oct. 12, 1918, St. Paul, Minn.   BL TR 6'1" 200 lbs.

Year	Team	Games	BA	SA	AB	H	2B	3B	HR	HR%	R	RBI	BB	SO	SB	PH AB	PH H	PO	A	E	DP	TC/G	FA	G by Pos
1915	STL	N	6	.313	.313	16	5	0	0	0	0.0	1	1	3	0	0	0	0	22	4	2	0	4.7	.929	C-5

Joe Glenn

GLENN, JOSEPH CHARLES (Gabber)
Born Joseph Charles Gurzensky.
B. Nov. 19, 1908, Dickson City, Pa.   D. May 6, 1985, Tunkhannock, Pa.   BR TR 5'11" 175 lbs.

Year	Team	Games	BA	SA	AB	H	2B	3B	HR	HR%	R	RBI	BB	SO	SB	PH AB	PH H	PO	A	E	DP	TC/G	FA	G by Pos
1932	NY	A	6	.125	.125	16	2	0	0	0	0.0	0	0	1	5	0	1	0	17	1	0	0	3.0	1.000	C-5
1933		5	.143	.143	21	3	0	0	0	0.0	1	1	0	3	0	0	0	24	0	0	1	4.8	1.000	C-5
1935		17	.233	.326	43	10	4	0	0	0.0	7	6	4	1	0	1	0	54	7	1	0	3.6	.984	C-16
1936		44	.271	.349	129	35	7	0	1	0.8	21	20	20	10	1	0	1	167	24	6	2	4.5	.970	C-44
1937		25	.283	.396	53	15	2	2	0	0.0	4	9	10	11	0	1	0	79	12	2	1	3.7	.978	C-24
1938		41	.260	.350	123	32	7	2	0	0.0	9	25	10	14	1	1	0	134	15	4	3	3.7	.974	C-40
1939	STL	A	88	.273	.367	286	78	13	1	4	1.4	29	29	31	40	4	4	3	280	48	11	4	3.9	.968	C-82
1940	BOS	A	22	.128	.149	47	6	1	0	0	0.0	3	4	5	7	0	4	1	67	6	3	0	3.5	.961	C-19
8 yrs.		248	.252	.334	718	181	34	5	5	0.7	76	89	81	91	6	12	4	822	113	27	11	3.9	.972	C-235

John Glenn

GLENN, JOHN
B. July 10, 1928, Moultrie, Ga.   BR TR 6'3" 180 lbs.

Year	Team	Games	BA	SA	AB	H	2B	3B	HR	HR%	R	RBI	BB	SO	SB	PH AB	PH H	PO	A	E	DP	TC/G	FA	G by Pos
1960	STL	N	32	.258	.323	31	8	0	1	0	0.0	4	5	0	9	0	3	0	19	0	0	0	0.6	1.000	OF-28

John Glenn

GLENN, JOHN W.
B. 1849, Rochester, N. Y.   D. Nov. 10, 1888, Sandy Hill, N. Y.   BR TR 5'8½" 169 lbs.

Year	Team	Games	BA	SA	AB	H	2B	3B	HR	HR%	R	RBI	BB	SO	SB	PH AB	PH H	PO	A	E	DP	TC/G	FA	G by Pos
1876	CHI	N	66	.304	.351	276	84	9	2	0	0.0	55	32	12	6		0	0	240	5	26	5	4.1	.904	OF-56, 1B-15
1877		50	.228	.267	202	46	6	1	0	0.0	31	20	8	16		0	0	226	11	17	10	5.1	.933	OF-36, 1B-14
2 yrs.		116	.272	.316	478	130	15	3	0	0.0	86	52	20	22		0	0	466	16	43	15	4.5	.918	OF-92, 1B-29

Norm Glockson

GLOCKSON, NORMAN STANLEY
B. June 15, 1894, Blue Island, Ill.   D. Aug. 5, 1955, Maywood, Ill.   BR TR 6'2" 200 lbs.

Year	Team	Games	BA	SA	AB	H	2B	3B	HR	HR%	R	RBI	BB	SO	SB	PH AB	PH H	PO	A	E	DP	TC/G	FA	G by Pos
1914	CIN	N	7	.000	.000	12	0	0	0	0	0.0	0	0	1	6	0	0	0	19	5	2	0	3.7	.923	C-7

Al Glossop

GLOSSOP, ALBAN
B. July 23, 1915, Christopher, Ill.   BB TR 6' 170 lbs.

Year	Team	Games	BA	SA	AB	H	2B	3B	HR	HR%	R	RBI	BB	SO	SB	PH AB	PH H	PO	A	E	DP	TC/G	FA	G by Pos
1939	NY	N	10	.188	.281	32	6	0	0	1	3.1	3	3	4	2	0	0	0	15	34	1	7	5.0	.980	2B-10
1940	2 teams		NY	N	(27G – .209)		BOS	N	(60G – .236)															
"	total	87	.226	.343	239	54	5	1	7	2.9	33	22	27	38	2	25	4	104	188	16	24	3.5	.948	2B-42, 3B-18, SS-10
1942	PHI	N	121	.225	.289	454	102	15	1	4	0.9	33	40	29	35	3	3	1	322	351	27	79	5.8	.961	2B-118, 3B-1
1943	BKN	N	87	.171	.253	217	37	9	0	3	1.4	28	21	28	27	0	11	0	102	161	24	24	3.3	.916	SS-33, 2B-24, 3B-17
1946	CHI	N	4	.000	.000	10	0	0	0	0	0.0	2	0	1	3	0	0	0	9	7	1	0	4.3	.941	SS-2, 2B-2
5 yrs.		309	.209	.291	952	199	29	2	15	1.6	99	86	89	105	5	39	6	552	741	69	134	4.4	.949	2B-196, SS-45, 3B-36

Bill Glynn

GLYNN, WILLIAM VINCENT
B. July 30, 1925, Sussex, N. J.   BL TL 6' 190 lbs.

Year	Team	Games	BA	SA	AB	H	2B	3B	HR	HR%	R	RBI	BB	SO	SB	PH AB	PH H	PO	A	E	DP	TC/G	FA	G by Pos
1949	PHI	N	8	.200	.200	10	2	0	0	0	0.0	0	1	0	3	0	6	2	10	1	0	0	1.4	1.000	1B-1
1952	CLE	A	44	.272	.391	92	25	5	0	2	2.2	15	7	5	16	1	14	3	167	16	5	18	4.3	.973	1B-32
1953		147	.243	.309	411	100	14	2	3	0.7	60	30	44	65	1	10	3	1042	81	8	133	7.7	.993	1B-135, OF-2
1954		111	.251	.380	171	43	3	2	5	2.9	19	18	12	21	1	17	2	424	35	6	38	4.2	.987	1B-96, OF-1
4 yrs.		310	.249	.336	684	170	22	4	10	1.5	94	56	61	105	5	47	10	1643	133	19	189	5.8	.989	1B-264, OF-3

WORLD SERIES

Year	Team	Games	BA	SA	AB	H	2B	3B	HR	HR%	R	RBI	BB	SO	SB	PH AB	PH H	PO	A	E	DP	TC/G	FA	G by Pos
1954	CLE	A	2	.500	1.000	2	1	1	0	0	0.0	0	0	1	0	0	2	1	0	0	0	0	0.0	–	1B-1

Year	Team		Games	BA	SA	AB	H	2B	3B	HR	HR%	R	RBI	BB	SO	SB	Pinch Hit AB	H	PO	A	E	DP	TC/G	FA	G by Pos

John Gochnaur

GOCHNAUR, JOHN PETER
B. Sept. 12, 1875, Altoona, Pa.   D. Sept. 27, 1929, Altoona, Pa.

BR TR 5'9" 160 lbs.

1901	BKN	N	3	.364	.364	11	4	0	0	0	0.0	.	1	2	1		1	0	0	4	9	0	0	4.3	1.000	SS-3
1902	CLE	A	127	.185	.237	459	85	16	4	0	0.0	45	37	38		7	0	0	223	447	48	59	5.7	.933	SS-127
1903			134	.185	.240	438	81	16	4	0	0.0	48	48	48		10	0	0	236	414	98	45	5.6	.869	SS-134
3 yrs.			264	.187	.240	908	170	32	8	0	0.0	94	87	87		18	0	0	463	870	146	104	5.6	.901	SS-264

John Godar

GODAR, JOHN MICHAEL
B. Oct. 25, 1864, Cincinnati, Ohio   D. June 23, 1949, Park Ridge, Ill.

BR TR 5'9" 170 lbs.

1892	BAL	N	5	.214	.214	14	3	0	0	0	0.0	2	1	2	1	1	0	0	4	1	0	0	1.0	1.000	OF-5

Danny Godby

GODBY, DANNY RAY
B. Nov. 4, 1946, Logan, W. Va.

BR TR 6' 185 lbs.

1974	STL	N	13	.154	.154	13	2	0	0	0	0.0	2	1	3	4	0	6	1	8	1	0	0	0.7	1.000	OF-4

Joe Goddard

GODDARD, JOSEPH HAROLD
B. July 23, 1950, Beckley, W. Va.

BR TR 5'11" 181 lbs.

1972	SD	N	12	.200	.257	35	7	2	0	0	0.0	2	5	9	0	0	0	67	5	2	1	6.2	.973	C-12

John Godwin

GODWIN, JOHN HENRY
B. Mar. 10, 1877, East Liverpool, Ohio   D. May 5, 1956, East Liverpool, Ohio

BR TR 6' 190 lbs.

1905	BOS	A	13	.351	.378	37	13	1	0	0	0.0	4	10	3		3	3	0	25	10	4	1	3.0	.897	OF-6, 2B-5
1906			66	.187	.207	193	36	2	1	0	0.0	11	15	6		6	9	2	79	115	26	11	3.3	.882	3B-27, SS-14, OF-10, 2B-3, 1B-1
2 yrs.			79	.213	.235	230	49	3	1	0	0.0	15	25	9		9	12	2	104	125	30	12	3.3	.884	3B-27, OF-16, SS-14, 2B-8, 1B-1

Ed Goebel

GOEBEL, EDWIN
B. Sept. 1, 1899, Brooklyn, N. Y.   D. Aug. 12, 1959, Brooklyn, N. Y.

BR TR 5'11" 170 lbs.

1922	WAS	A	37	.271	.339	59	16	1	0	1	1.7	13	3	8	16	1	13	1	29	1	0	0	0.8	1.000	OF-17

Bill Goeckel

GOECKEL, WILLIAM JOHN
B. Sept. 3, 1871, Wilkes-Barre, Pa.   D. Nov. 1, 1922, Philadelphia, Pa.

BL TL

1899	PHI	N	37	.262	.298	141	37	3	1	0	0.0	17	16	1		6	1	0	384	11	9	12	10.9	.978	1B-36

Chuck Goggin

GOGGIN, CHARLES FRANCIS III
B. July 7, 1945, Pompano Beach, Fla.

BB TR 5'11" 175 lbs.

1972	PIT	N	5	.286	.286	7	2	0	0	0	0.0	0	0	1	1	1	3	0	0	4	0	0	0.8	1.000	2B-1
1973	2 teams		PIT N	(1G – 1.000)		ATL N	(64G – .289)																		
"	total		65	.297	.352	91	27	5	0	0	0.0	19	7	9	19	0	29	8	23	37	5	7	1.0	.923	2B-19, OF-6, SS-5, C-2
1974	BOS	A	2	.000	.000	1	0	0	0	0	0.0	0	0	0	1	0	0	0	0	2	1	2	1.5	.667	2B-2
3 yrs.			72	.293	.343	99	29	5	0	0	0.0	19	7	10	21	1	32	8	23	43	6	9	1.0	.917	2B-22, OF-6, SS-5, C-2

Mike Golden

GOLDEN, MICHAEL HENRY
B. Sept. 11, 1851, Shirley, Mass.   D. Jan. 11, 1929, Rockford, Ill.

BR TR 5'7" 166 lbs.

1878	MIL	N	55	.206	.262	214	44	6	3	0	0.0	16	20	3	35		0	0	75	45	22	2	2.6	.845	OF-39, P-22, 1B-1

Jonah Goldman

GOLDMAN, JONAH JOHN
B. Aug. 29, 1906, New York, N. Y.   D. Aug. 17, 1980, Palm Beach, Fla.

BR TR 5'7" 170 lbs.

1928	CLE	A	7	.238	.286	21	5	1	0	0	0.0	1	2	3	0	0	0	0	13	23	5	2	5.9	.878	SS-7
1930			111	.242	.310	306	74	18	0	1	0.3	32	44	28	25	3	0	0	222	275	27	58	4.7	.948	SS-93, 3B-20
1931			30	.129	.145	62	8	1	0	0	0.0	0	3	4	6	1	0	0	42	82	7	12	4.4	.947	SS-30
3 yrs.			148	.224	.283	389	87	20	0	1	0.3	33	49	35	31	4	0	0	277	380	39	72	4.7	.944	SS-130, 3B-20

Gordon Goldsberry

GOLDSBERRY, GORDON FREDERICK
B. Aug. 30, 1927, Sacramento, Calif.

BL TL 6' 170 lbs.

1949	CHI	A	39	.248	.317	145	36	3	2	1	0.7	25	13	18	9	2	1	0	359	24	4	37	9.9	.990	1B-38
1950			82	.268	.409	127	34	8	2	2	1.6	19	25	26	18	0	39	12	236	29	3	37	3.3	.989	1B-40, OF-3
1951			10	.091	.091	11	1	0	0	0	0.0	4	1	2	2	0	2	0	28	5	0	4	3.3	1.000	1B-8
1952	STL	A	86	.229	.335	227	52	9	3	3	1.3	30	17	34	37	0	10	2	528	40	10	56	6.7	.983	1B-72, OF-2
4 yrs.			217	.241	.343	510	123	20	7	6	1.2	78	56	80	66	2	52	14	1151	98	17	134	5.8	.987	1B-158, OF-5

Walt Goldsby

GOLDSBY, WALTON HUGH
B. Dec. 31, 1861, Louisiana   D. Jan. 11, 1924, Dallas, Tex.

BL

1884	3 teams		STL AA	(5G – .200)		WAS AA	(6G – .375)			RIC AA	(11G – .225)														
"	total		22	.262	.274	84	22	1	0	0	0.0	10		2			0	0	28	4	8	2	1.8	.800	OF-22
1886	WAS	N	6	.222	.278	18	4	1	0	0	0.0	1		2	3		0	0	9	0	2	0	1.8	.818	OF-6
1888	BAL	AA	45	.236	.255	165	39	1	1	0	0.0	13	14	8		17	0	0	53	3	6	0	1.4	.903	OF-45
3 yrs.			73	.243	.262	267	65	3	1	0	0.0	23	15	12		17	0	0	90	7	16	2	1.5	.858	OF-73

Fred Goldsmith

GOLDSMITH, FRED ERNEST
B. May 15, 1852, New Haven, Conn.   D. Mar. 28, 1939, Berkley, Mich.

BR TR 6'1" 195 lbs.

1879	TRO	N	9	.237	.263	38	9	1	0	0	0.0	6	2	1	3		0	0	9	14	5	1	3.1	.821	P-8, OF-2, 1B-1
1880	CHI	N	35	.261	.317	142	37	4	2	0	0.0	24	15	2	15		0	0	55	53	11	0	3.4	.908	P-26, OF-10, 1B-4
1881			42	.241	.310	158	38	3	4	0	0.0	24	16	6	17		0	0	21	97	21	2	3.3	.849	P-39, OF-3
1882			45	.230	.301	183	42	11	0	0	0.0	23	19	4	29		0	0	33	67	7	0	2.4	.935	P-44, 1B-1
1883			60	.221	.311	235	52	12	3	1	0.4	38		4	35		0	0	55	89	24	8	2.8	.857	P-46, OF-16, 1B-2

Year Team	Games	BA	SA	AB	H	2B	3B	HR	HR%	R	RBI	BB	SO	SB	Pinch Hit AB	Pinch Hit H	PO	A	E	DP	TC/G	FA	G by Pos

Fred Goldsmith *continued*

Year Team	Games	BA	SA	AB	H	2B	3B	HR	HR%	R	RBI	BB	SO	SB	AB	H	PO	A	E	DP	TC/G	FA	G by Pos
1884 2 teams	CHI N (22G – .136)			BAL AA (4G – .143)																			
" total	26	.137	.221	95	13	2	0	2	2.1	13		9	26		0	0	17	42	14	0	2.8	.808	P-25, OF-2, 1B-1
6 yrs.	217	.224	.297	851	191	33	10	3	0.4	128	52	26	125		0	0	190	362	82	6	2.9	.871	P-188, OF-33, 1B-9

Lonnie Goldstein

GOLDSTEIN, LESLIE ELMER
B. May 13, 1918, Austin, Tex.
BL TL 6'2½" 190 lbs.

Year Team	Games	BA	SA	AB	H	2B	3B	HR	HR%	R	RBI	BB	SO	SB	AB	H	PO	A	E	DP	TC/G	FA	G by Pos
1943 CIN N	5	.200	.200	5	1	0	0	0	0.0	1	0	2	1	0	3	1	7	0	0	1	1.4	1.000	1B-2
1946	6	.000	.000	5	0	0	0	0	0.0	1	0	1	1	0	5	0	0	0	0	0	0.0		1B-2
2 yrs.	11	.100	.100	10	1	0	0	0	0.0	2	0	3	2	0	8	1	7	0	0	1	0.6	1.000	1B-2

Purnal Goldy

GOLDY, PURNAL WILLIAM
B. Nov. 28, 1937, Camden, N. J.
BR TR 6'5" 200 lbs.

Year Team	Games	BA	SA	AB	H	2B	3B	HR	HR%	R	RBI	BB	SO	SB	AB	H	PO	A	E	DP	TC/G	FA	G by Pos
1962 DET A	20	.229	.400	70	16	1	1	3	4.3	8	12	0	12	0	3	1	26	1	1	0	1.4	.964	OF-15
1963	9	.250	.250	8	2	0	0	0	0.0	1	0	0	4	0	8	2	0	0	0	0	0.0	–	
2 yrs.	29	.231	.385	78	18	1	1	3	3.8	9	12	0	16	0	11	3	26	1	1	0	1.0	.964	OF-15

Stan Goletz

GOLETZ, STANLEY (Stash)
B. May 21, 1918, Crescent, Ohio
BL TL 6'3" 200 lbs.

Year Team	Games	BA	SA	AB	H	2B	3B	HR	HR%	R	RBI	BB	SO	SB	AB	H	PO	A	E	DP	TC/G	FA	G by Pos
1941 CHI A	5	.600	.600	5	3	0	0	0	0.0	0	0	0	5	3	0	0	0	0	0	0	0.0	–	

Mike Goliat

GOLIAT, MIKE MITCHELL
B. Nov. 5, 1925, Yatesboro, Pa.
BR TR 6' 180 lbs.

Year Team	Games	BA	SA	AB	H	2B	3B	HR	HR%	R	RBI	BB	SO	SB	AB	H	PO	A	E	DP	TC/G	FA	G by Pos
1949 PHI N	55	.212	.323	189	40	6	3	3	1.6	24	19	20	32	0	0	0	187	145	9	36	6.2	.974	2B-50, 1B-5
1950	145	.234	.366	483	113	13	6	13	2.7	49	64	53	75	3	5	0	345	393	21	89	5.2	.972	2B-139
1951 2 teams	PHI N (41G – .225)			STL A (5G – .182)																			
" total	46	.221	.329	149	33	2	1	4	2.7	14	16	9	19	0	4	0	97	109	7	26	4.6	.967	2B-39, 3B-2
1952 STL A	3	.000	.000	4	0	0	0	0	0.0	0	0	1	1	0	1	0	4	4	0	3	2.7	1.000	2B-3
4 yrs.	249	.225	.348	825	186	21	10	20	2.4	87	99	83	127	3	10	0	633	651	37	154	5.3	.972	2B-231, 1B-5, 3B-2

WORLD SERIES

Year Team	Games	BA	SA	AB	H	2B	3B	HR	HR%	R	RBI	BB	SO	SB	AB	H	PO	A	E	DP	TC/G	FA	G by Pos
1950 PHI N	4	.214	.214	14	3	0	0	0	0.0	1	1	1	2	0	0	0	13	9	1	0	5.8	.957	2B-4

Walt Golvin

GOLVIN, WALTER GEORGE
B. Feb. 1, 1894, Hershey, Neb. D. June 11, 1973, Gardinia, Calif.
BL TL 6' 165 lbs.

Year Team	Games	BA	SA	AB	H	2B	3B	HR	HR%	R	RBI	BB	SO	SB	AB	H	PO	A	E	DP	TC/G	FA	G by Pos
1922 CHI N	2	.000	.000	2	0	0	0	0	0.0	0	1	0	0	0	0	0	4	0	0	0	2.0	1.000	1B-2

Chile Gomez

GOMEZ, JOSE LUIS
Born Jose Luis Gomez y Rodriguez.
B. Mar. 23, 1909, Villa Union, Mexico
BR TR 5'10" 165 lbs.

Year Team	Games	BA	SA	AB	H	2B	3B	HR	HR%	R	RBI	BB	SO	SB	AB	H	PO	A	E	DP	TC/G	FA	G by Pos
1935 PHI N	67	.230	.243	222	51	3	0	0	0.0	24	16	17	34	2	0	0	150	216	19	36	5.7	.951	SS-36, 2B-32
1936	108	.232	.250	332	77	4	1	0	0.0	24	28	14	32	0	0	0	217	347	37	56	5.6	.938	2B-71, SS-40
1942 WAS A	25	.192	.274	73	14	2	2	0	0.0	8	6	9	7	1	1	0	46	61	3	13	4.4	.973	2B-23, 3B-1
3 yrs.	200	.226	.250	627	142	9	3	0	0.0	56	50	40	73	3	1	0	413	624	59	105	5.5	.946	2B-126, SS-76, 3B-1

Luis Gomez

GOMEZ, LUIS
Born Luis Gomez y Sanchez.
B. Aug. 19, 1951, Guadalajara, Mexico
BR TR 5'9" 150 lbs.

Year Team	Games	BA	SA	AB	H	2B	3B	HR	HR%	R	RBI	BB	SO	SB	AB	H	PO	A	E	DP	TC/G	FA	G by Pos
1974 MIN A	82	.208	.214	168	35	1	0	0	0.0	18	3	12	16	2	0	0	97	194	12	37	3.7	.960	SS-74, 2B-2, DH-1
1975	89	.139	.139	72	10	0	0	0	0.0	7	5	4	12	0	0	0	55	80	3	20	1.6	.978	SS-70, DH-7, 2B-6
1976	38	.193	.211	57	11	1	0	0	0.0	5	3	3	3	1	0	0	36	58	1	17	2.5	.989	SS-24, 2B-8, 3B-4, DH-1, OF-1
1977	32	.246	.369	65	16	4	2	0	0.0	6	11	4	9	0	4	0	46	55	2	15	3.2	.981	2B-19, SS-7, 3B-4, DH-2, OF-1
1978 TOR A	153	.223	.254	413	92	7	3	0	0.0	39	32	34	41	8	0	0	247	400	16	97	4.3	.976	SS-153
1979	59	.239	.282	163	39	7	0	0	0.0	11	11	6	17	1	0	0	70	116	3	25	3.2	.984	3B-22, 2B-20, SS-15
1980 ATL N	121	.191	.212	278	53	6	0	0	0.0	18	24	17	27	0	0	0	135	319	15	55	3.9	.968	SS-119
1981	35	.200	.200	35	7	0	0	0	0.0	4	1	6	4	0	2	0	23	25	4	2	1.5	.923	SS-21, 3B-9, 2B-3, P-1
8 yrs.	609	.210	.239	1251	263	26	5	0	0.0	108	90	86	129	6	6	0	709	1247	56	268	3.3	.972	SS-483, 2B-58, 3B-39, DH-11, OF-2, P-1

Preston Gomez

GOMEZ, PRESTON
Born Pedro Gomez y Martinez.
B. Apr. 20, 1923, Central Preston, Cuba
Manager 1969-72, 1974-75, 1980.
BR TR 5'11" 170 lbs.

Year Team	Games	BA	SA	AB	H	2B	3B	HR	HR%	R	RBI	BB	SO	SB	AB	H	PO	A	E	DP	TC/G	FA	G by Pos
1944 WAS A	8	.286	.429	7	2	1	0	0	0.0	2	2	0	4	0	0	0	4	1	1	0	0.8	.833	SS-2, 2B-2

Randy Gomez

GOMEZ, RANDALL SCOTT
B. Feb. 4, 1957, San Mateo, Calif.
BR TR 5'10" 185 lbs.

Year Team	Games	BA	SA	AB	H	2B	3B	HR	HR%	R	RBI	BB	SO	SB	AB	H	PO	A	E	DP	TC/G	FA	G by Pos
1984 SF N	14	.167	.200	30	5	1	0	0	0.0	0	0	8	3	0	0	0	69	8	4	1	5.8	.951	C-14

Jesse Gonder

GONDER, JESSE LEMAR
B. Jan. 20, 1936, Monticello, Ark.
BL TR 5'10" 180 lbs.

Year Team	Games	BA	SA	AB	H	2B	3B	HR	HR%	R	RBI	BB	SO	SB	AB	H	PO	A	E	DP	TC/G	FA	G by Pos
1960 NY A	7	.286	.714	7	2	0	0	1	14.3	1	3	1	1	0	5	1	7	0	0	0	1.0	1.000	C-1
1961	15	.333	.417	12	4	1	0	0	0.0	2	3	3	1	0	12	4	0	0	0	0	0.0	–	
1962 CIN N	4	.000	.000	4	0	0	0	0	0.0	0	0	0	3	0	4	0	0	0	0	0	0.0	–	
1963 2 teams	CIN N (31G – .313)			NY N (42G – .302)																			
" total	73	.304	.456	158	48	6	0	6	3.8	17	20	7	37	1	34	10	141	18	3	3	2.2	.981	C-38
1964 NY N	131	.270	.370	341	92	11	1	7	2.1	28	35	29	65	0	43	8	397	70	10	7	3.6	.979	C-97

Year	Team	Games	BA	SA	AB	H	2B	3B	HR	HR%	R	RBI	BB	SO	SB	Pinch Hit AB	H	PO	A	E	DP	TC/G	FA	G by Pos

Jesse Gonder *continued*

Year	Team	Games	BA	SA	AB	H	2B	3B	HR	HR%	R	RBI	BB	SO	SB	Pinch Hit AB	H	PO	A	E	DP	TC/G	FA	G by Pos
1965	2 teams	NY	N	(53G – .238)	MIL	N	(31G – .151)																	
"	total	84	.209	.342	158	33	6	0	5	3.2	8	14	15	29	0	52	13	181	28	2	6	2.5	.991	C-44
1966	PIT	N														12	2	238	27	6	4	4.6	.978	C-52
"		59	.225	.388	160	36	3	1	7	4.4	13	16	12	39	0	5	1	56	10	2	0	3.1	.971	C-18
1967	PIT	N																						
"		22	.139	.167	36	5	1	0	0	0.0	4	3	5	9	0									
8 yrs.		395	.251	.377	876	220	28	2	26	3.0	73	94	72	184	1	167	39	1020	153	23	20	3.0	.981	C-250

Rene Gonzales

GONZALES, RENE ADRIAN
B. Sept. 23, 1960, Austin, Tex.

BR TR 6'3" 180 lbs.

Year	Team	Games	BA	SA	AB	H	2B	3B	HR	HR%	R	RBI	BB	SO	SB	Pinch Hit AB	H	PO	A	E	DP	TC/G	FA	G by Pos
1984	MON	N	29	.233	.267	30	7	1	0	0	0.0	5	2	2	5	0	0	0	17	28	2	5	1.6	.957	SS-27
1986		11	.115	.115	26	3	0	0	0	0.0	1	0	2	7	0	0	0	7	19	0	3	2.4	1.000	SS-6, 3B-5
1987	BAL	A	37	.267	.383	60	16	2	1	0	1.7	14	7	3	11	1	0	0	22	43	2	5	1.8	.970	3B-29, 2B-6, SS-1
1988		92	.215	.266	237	51	6	0	2	0.8	13	15	13	32	1	0	0	66	185	8	26	2.8	.969	3B-80, 2B-14, OF-1, 1B-1
1989		71	.217	.259	166	36	4	0	1	0.6	16	11	12	30	5	2	0	103	146	7	37	3.6	.973	2B-54, SS-17, SS-1
5 yrs.		240	.218	.270	519	113	13	1	4	0.8	49	35	32	85	8	2	0	215	421	19	76	2.7	.971	3B-131, 2B-74, SS-37, OF-1, 1B-1

Dan Gonzalez

GONZALEZ, DANIEL DAVID
B. Sept. 30, 1953, Whittier, Calif.

BL TR 6'1" 195 lbs.

Year	Team	Games	BA	SA	AB	H	2B	3B	HR	HR%	R	RBI	BB	SO	SB	Pinch Hit AB	H	PO	A	E	DP	TC/G	FA	G by Pos
1979	DET	A	7	.222	.278	18	4	1	0	0	0.0	1	2	0	2	0	1	3	0	0	0	0.4	1.000	OF-3, DH-1
1980		2	.143	.143	7	1	0	0	0	0.0	1	0	0	1	0	0	1	3	0	1	0	2.0	.750	DH-1, OF-1
2 yrs.		9	.200	.240	25	5	1	0	0	0.0	2	2	0	3	1	4	0	6	0	1	0	0.8	.857	OF-4, DH-2

Denny Gonzalez

GONZALEZ, DENIO MARIANO
Born Denio Mariano Gonzalez y Manzueta.
B. July 22, 1963, Sabana Grande Boya, Dominican Republic

BR TR 5'11" 165 lbs.

Year	Team	Games	BA	SA	AB	H	2B	3B	HR	HR%	R	RBI	BB	SO	SB	Pinch Hit AB	H	PO	A	E	DP	TC/G	FA	G by Pos
1984	PIT	N	26	.183	.244	82	15	3	1	0	0.0	9	4	7	21	1	0	0	26	53	3	10	3.2	.963	3B-11, SS-10, OF-3
1985		35	.226	.355	124	28	4	0	4	3.2	11	12	13	27	2	1	0	44	42	8	5	2.7	.915	3B-21, OF-13, 2B-6
1987		5	.000	.000	7	0	0	0	0	0.0	1	0	1	2	0	4	0	2	1	0	0	0.6	1.000	SS-1
1988		24	.188	.219	32	6	1	0	0	0.0	5	1	6	10	0	10	3	20	22	2	5	1.8	.955	SS-14, 2B-4, 3B-2
1989	CLE	A	8	.294	.353	17	5	1	0	0	0.0	3	1	0	4	0	3	1	0	0	1	0	0.1	–	DH-6, 3B-1
5 yrs.		98	.206	.294	262	54	9	1	4	1.5	29	18	27	64	3	18	4	92	118	14	20	2.3	.938	3B-35, SS-25, OF-16, 2B-10, DH-6

Eusebio Gonzalez

GONZALEZ, EUSEBIO MIGUEL
Born Eusebio Miguel Gonzalez y Lopez.
B. July 13, 1892, Havana, Cuba D. Feb. 14, 1976, Havana, Cuba

BR TR 5'10" 165 lbs.

Year	Team	Games	BA	SA	AB	H	2B	3B	HR	HR%	R	RBI	BB	SO	SB	Pinch Hit AB	H	PO	A	E	DP	TC/G	FA	G by Pos
1918	BOS	A	2	.500	1.500	2	1	0	1	0	0.0	1	0	0	0	0	0	0	1	2	0	0	1.5	1.000	SS-2

Fernando Gonzalez

GONZALEZ, JOSE FERNANDO
Born Jose Fernando Gonzalez y Quinones.
B. June 19, 1950, Arecibo, Puerto Rico

BR TR 5'10" 165 lbs.

Year	Team	Games	BA	SA	AB	H	2B	3B	HR	HR%	R	RBI	BB	SO	SB	Pinch Hit AB	H	PO	A	E	DP	TC/G	FA	G by Pos
1972	PIT	N	3	.000	.000	2	0	0	0	0	0.0	0	0	0	2	0	2	0	0	1	1	0	0.7	.500	3B-1
1973		37	.224	.327	49	11	0	1	1	2.0	5	5	1	11	0	29	8	5	7	1	0	0.4	.923	3B-5
1974	2 teams	KC	A	(9G – .143)	NY	A	(51G – .215)																	
"	total	60	.204	.282	142	29	6	1	1	0.7	12	9	7	11	1	3	0	104	105	5	24	3.6	.977	2B-42, 3B-15, SS-3, DH-1
1977	PIT	N	80	.276	.398	181	50	10	0	4	2.2	17	27	13	21	0	27	10	43	66	2	6	1.4	.982	3B-37, OF-16, 2B-6, SS-2
1978	2 teams	PIT	N	(10G – .190)	SD	N	(100G – .250)																	
"	total	110	.246	.308	341	84	11	2	2	0.6	29	29	19	35	4	9	4	197	262	10	68	4.3	.979	2B-98, 3B-3
1979	SD	N	114	.217	.359	323	70	13	3	9	2.8	22	34	18	34	0	16	4	218	226	11	52	4.0	.976	2B-103, 3B-3
6 yrs.		404	.235	.336	1038	244	40	7	17	1.6	85	104	58	114	8	86	26	567	667	30	150	3.1	.976	2B-249, 3B-64, OF-16, SS-5, DH-1

Jose Gonzalez

Playing record listed under Jose Uribe

Jose Gonzalez

GONZALEZ, JOSE RAFAEL
Born Jose Rafael Gonzalez y Gutierrez.
B. Nov. 23, 1964, Puerto Plata, Dominican Republic

BR TR 6'3" 197 lbs.

Year	Team	Games	BA	SA	AB	H	2B	3B	HR	HR%	R	RBI	BB	SO	SB	Pinch Hit AB	H	PO	A	E	DP	TC/G	FA	G by Pos
1985	LA	N	23	.273	.455	11	3	2	1	0	0.0	6	0	1	0	1	0	0	10	0	0	0	0.4	1.000	OF-18
1986		57	.215	.355	93	20	5	1	2	2.2	15	6	7	29	4	5	1	73	0	6	0	1.4	.924	OF-57
1987		19	.188	.313	16	3	2	0	0	0.0	2	1	2	2	5	2	0	19	1	0	0	1.1	1.000	OF-16
1988		37	.083	.125	24	2	1	0	0	0.0	7	0	2	10	3	9	2	15	0	1	0	0.4	.938	OF-24
1989		95	.268	.360	261	70	11	2	3	1.1	31	18	23	53	9	14	5	171	8	6	2	1.9	.968	OF-87
5 yrs.		231	.242	.346	405	98	21	3	5	1.2	61	25	34	97	22	31	8	288	9	13	2	1.3	.958	OF-202

LEAGUE CHAMPIONSHIP SERIES

Year	Team	Games	BA	SA	AB	H	2B	3B	HR	HR%	R	RBI	BB	SO	SB	Pinch Hit AB	H	PO	A	E	DP	TC/G	FA	G by Pos
1988	LA	N	5	–	–	0	0	0	0	0	–	2	0	0	0	0	1	0	3	0	0	0	0.6	1.000	OF-4

WORLD SERIES

Year	Team	Games	BA	SA	AB	H	2B	3B	HR	HR%	R	RBI	BB	SO	SB	Pinch Hit AB	H	PO	A	E	DP	TC/G	FA	G by Pos
1988	LA	N	4	.000	.000	2	0	0	0	0	0.0	0	0	0	2	0	2	0	2	0	0	0	0.5	1.000	OF-3

Juan Gonzalez

GONZALEZ, JUAN ALBERTO
Born Juan Alberto Gonzalez y Vazquez.
B. Oct. 16, 1969, Vega Baja, Puerto Rico

BR TR 6'3" 175 lbs.

Year	Team	Games	BA	SA	AB	H	2B	3B	HR	HR%	R	RBI	BB	SO	SB	Pinch Hit AB	H	PO	A	E	DP	TC/G	FA	G by Pos
1989	TEX	A	24	.150	.250	60	9	3	0	1	1.7	6	7	6	17	0	1	0	53	0	2	0	2.3	.964	OF-24

Julio Gonzalez

GONZALEZ, JULIO CESAR
Born Julio Cesar Gonzalez y Hernandez.
B. Dec. 25, 1952, Caguas, Puerto Rico

BR TR 5'11" 162 lbs.

Year	Team		Games	BA	SA	AB	H	2B	3B	HR	HR%	R	RBI	BB	SO	SB	Pinch Hit AB	Pinch Hit H	PO	A	E	DP	TC/G	FA	G by Pos

Julio Gonzalez *continued*

Year	Team		Games	BA	SA	AB	H	2B	3B	HR	HR%	R	RBI	BB	SO	SB	PH AB	PH H	PO	A	E	DP	TC/G	FA	G by Pos
1977	HOU	N	110	.245	.316	383	94	18	3	1	0.3	34	27	19	45	3	7	1	154	293	27	56	4.3	.943	SS-63, 2B-45
1978			78	.233	.269	223	52	3	1	1	0.4	24	16	8	31	6	12	1	83	139	7	28	2.9	.969	2B-54, SS-17, 3B-4
1979			68	.249	.298	181	45	5	2	0	0.0	16	10	5	14	2	7	3	92	146	5	27	3.6	.979	2B-32, SS-21, 3B-9
1980			40	.115	.135	52	6	1	0	0	0.0	5	1	1	8	1	10	0	22	31	1	8	1.4	.981	SS-16, 3B-11, 2B-2
1981	STL	N	20	.318	.500	22	7	1	0	1	4.5	2	3	1	3	0	10	2	7	13	1	1	1.1	.952	SS-5, 2B-4, 3B-2
1982			42	.241	.356	87	21	3	2	1	1.1	9	7	1	24	1	12	1	21	44	4	5	1.6	.942	3B-21, 2B-9, SS-1
1983	DET	A	12	.143	.190	21	3	1	0	0	0.0	0	2	1	7	0	0	0	10	26	4	3	3.3	.900	SS-6, 2B-5, 3B-1
7 yrs.			370	.235	.297	969	228	32	8	4	0.4	90	66	36	132	13	58	8	389	692	49	128	3.1	.957	2B-151, SS-129, 3B-48

Mike Gonzalez

GONZALEZ, MIGUEL ANGEL
Born Miguel Angel Gonzalez y Cordero.
B. Sept. 24, 1890, Havana, Cuba   D. Feb. 19, 1977, Havana, Cuba
Manager 1938, 1940.

BR TR 6'1" 200 lbs.

Year	Team		Games	BA	SA	AB	H	2B	3B	HR	HR%	R	RBI	BB	SO	SB	PH AB	PH H	PO	A	E	DP	TC/G	FA	G by Pos
1912	BOS	N	1	.000	.000	2	0	0	0	0	0.0	1	1	0	0	0	0	0	3	4	1	0	8.0	.875	C-1
1914	CIN	N	95	.233	.267	176	41	6	0	0	0.0	19	10	13	16	2	9	2	252	101	17	5	3.9	.954	C-83
1915	STL	N	51	.227	.289	97	22	2	2	0	0.0	12	10	8	9	4	6	1	175	31	2	9	4.1	.990	C-31, 1B-8
1916			118	.239	.308	331	79	15	4	0	0.0	33	29	28	18	5	10	0	483	138	10	15	5.3	.984	C-93, 1B-13
1917			106	.262	.307	290	76	8	1	1	0.3	28	28	22	24	12	17	2	444	110	12	19	5.3	.979	C-68, 1B-18, OF-1
1918			117	.252	.338	349	88	13	4	3	0.9	33	20	39	30	14	8	1	370	124	11	18	4.3	.978	C-100, OF-5, 1B-2
1919	NY	N	58	.190	.228	158	30	6	0	0	0.0	18	8	20	9	3	3	0	205	52	10	5	4.6	.963	C-52, 1B-4
1920			11	.231	.231	13	3	0	0	0	0.0	1	0	3	1	0	2	0	9	4	0	0	1.2	1.000	C-8
1921			13	.375	.417	24	9	1	0	0	0.0	3	0	1	0	0	4	1	55	2	1	5	4.5	.983	1B-6, C-2
1924	STL	N	120	.296	.391	402	119	27	1	3	0.7	34	53	24	22	1	1	1	413	96	7	15	4.3	.986	C-119
1925	2 teams			STL	N	(22G – .310)			CHI	N	(70G – .264)														
"	total		92	.276	.377	268	74	16	1	3	1.1	35	22	19	17	3	9	2	338	53	4	16	4.3	.990	C-72, 1B-9
1926	CHI	N	80	.249	.336	253	63	13	3	1	0.4	24	23	13	17	3	2	0	306	53	4	5	4.5	.989	C-78
1927			39	.241	.324	108	26	4	1	1	0.9	15	15	10	8	1	1	1	136	29	1	6	4.3	.994	C-36
1928			49	.272	.373	158	43	9	2	1	0.6	12	21	12	7	2	4	0	198	35	4	8	4.8	.983	C-45
1929			60	.240	.257	167	40	3	0	0	0.0	15	18	18	14	1	0	0	212	34	2	7	4.1	.992	C-60
1931	STL	N	15	.105	.105	19	2	0	0	0	0.0	1	3	0	3	0	3	0	15	4	0	0	1.3	1.000	C-12
1932			17	.143	.143	14	2	0	0	0	0.0	0	3	0	2	0	10	2	12	1	0	0	0.8	1.000	C-7
17 yrs.			1042	.253	.324	2829	717	123	19	3	0.5	283	263	231	198	52	91	13	3626	871	86	133	4.4	.981	C-867, 1B-60, OF-6

WORLD SERIES

Year	Team		Games	BA	SA	AB	H	2B	3B	HR	HR%	R	RBI	BB	SO	SB	PH AB	PH H	PO	A	E	DP	TC/G	FA	G by Pos
1929	CHI	N	2	.000	.000	1	0	0	0	0	0.0	0	0	0	1	0	1	0	2	0	0	0	1.0	1.000	C-1

Orlando Gonzalez

GONZALEZ, ORLANDO EUGENE
B. Nov. 15, 1951, Havana, Cuba

BR TR 6'2" 180 lbs.

Year	Team		Games	BA	SA	AB	H	2B	3B	HR	HR%	R	RBI	BB	SO	SB	PH AB	PH H	PO	A	E	DP	TC/G	FA	G by Pos
1976	CLE	A	28	.250	.279	68	17	2	0	0	0.0	5	4	5	7	1	6	2	123	8	1	7	4.7	.992	1B-15, OF-7, DH-2
1978	PHI	N	26	.192	.192	26	5	0	0	0	0.0	1	0	1	1	0	14	3	16	0	0	0	0.6	1.000	OF-11, 1B-3
1980	OAK	A	25	.243	.243	70	17	0	0	0	0.0	10	1	9	8	0	4	0	95	8	1	7	4.2	.990	1B-11, DH-8, OF-2
3 yrs.			79	.238	.250	164	39	2	0	0	0.0	16	5	15	16	1	24	5	234	16	2	14	3.2	.992	1B-29, OF-20, DH-10

LEAGUE CHAMPIONSHIP SERIES

Year	Team		Games	BA	SA	AB	H	2B	3B	HR	HR%	R	RBI	BB	SO	SB	PH AB	PH H	PO	A	E	DP	TC/G	FA	G by Pos
1978	PHI	N	1	.000	.000	1	0	0	0	0	0.0	0	0	1	0	0	1	0	0	0	0	0	0.0	—	

Pedro Gonzalez

GONZALEZ, PEDRO
Born Pedro Gonzalez y Olivares.
B. Dec. 12, 1937, San Pedro de Macoris, Dominican Republic

BR TR 6' 176 lbs.

Year	Team		Games	BA	SA	AB	H	2B	3B	HR	HR%	R	RBI	BB	SO	SB	PH AB	PH H	PO	A	E	DP	TC/G	FA	G by Pos
1963	NY	A	14	.192	.231	26	5	1	0	0	0.0	5	0	0	5	1	5	1	17	9	1	2	1.9	.963	2B-7
1964			80	.277	.366	112	31	8	1	0	0.0	18	5	7	22	3	8	1	161	37	3	13	2.5	.985	1B-31, OF-20, 3B-9, 2B-6
1965	2 teams			NY	A	(7G – .400)			CLE	A	(116G – .253)														
"	total		123	.254	.343	405	103	15	3	5	1.2	38	39	18	59	7	8	1	266	287	11	59	4.6	.980	2B-112, OF-3, 3B-2
1966	CLE	A	110	.233	.287	352	82	9	2	2	0.6	21	17	15	54	4	7	3	237	260	8	62	4.6	.984	2B-104, OF-1, 3B-1
1967			80	.228	.275	189	43	6	0	1	0.5	19	8	12	36	4	3	0	124	122	8	29	3.2	.969	2B-64, 3B-4, 1B-4, SS-3
5 yrs.			407	.244	.313	1084	264	39	6	8	0.7	99	70	52	176	22	31	6	805	715	31	165	3.8	.980	2B-293, 1B-35, OF-24, 3B-16, SS-3

WORLD SERIES

Year	Team		Games	BA	SA	AB	H	2B	3B	HR	HR%	R	RBI	BB	SO	SB	PH AB	PH H	PO	A	E	DP	TC/G	FA	G by Pos
1964	NY	A	1	.000	.000	1	0	0	0	0	0.0	0	0	0	0	0	0	0	3	0	0	0	4.0	1.000	3B-1

Tony Gonzalez

GONZALEZ, ANDRES ANTONIO
Born Andres Antonio Gonzalez y Gonzalez.
B. Aug. 28, 1936, Central Cunagua, Cuba

BL TR 5'9" 170 lbs.

Year	Team		Games	BA	SA	AB	H	2B	3B	HR	HR%	R	RBI	BB	SO	SB	PH AB	PH H	PO	A	E	DP	TC/G	FA	G by Pos
1960	2 teams			CIN	N	(39G – .212)			PHI	N	(78G – .299)														
"	total		117	.274	.453	340	93	22	6	9	2.6	37	47	15	74	3	29	6	189	8	5	0	1.7	.975	OF-98
1961	PHI	N	126	.277	.437	426	118	16	8	12	2.8	58	58	49	66	15	16	6	246	7	4	4	2.0	.984	OF-118
1962			118	.302	.494	437	132	16	4	20	4.6	76	63	40	82	17	4	1	268	8	0	4	2.3	1.000	OF-114
1963			155	.306	.436	555	170	36	12	4	0.7	78	66	53	66	9	4	1	263	11	4	2	1.8	.986	OF-151
1964			131	.278	.380	421	117	25	3	4	1.0	55	40	44	74	7	16	3	243	5	1	2	1.9	.996	OF-119
1965			108	.295	.457	370	109	19	1	13	3.5	48	41	31	52	3	11	2	167	3	3	1	1.6	.983	OF-104
1966			132	.286	.406	384	110	20	4	6	1.6	53	40	26	60	2	19	5	206	7	3	1	1.6	.986	OF-121
1967			149	.339	.472	508	172	23	9	9	1.8	74	59	47	58	10	17	7	260	4	1	1	1.8	.996	OF-143
1968			121	.264	.337	416	110	13	4	3	0.7	45	38	40	42	6	8	3	227	4	5	1	1.9	.979	OF-117
1969	2 teams			SD	N	(53G – .225)			ATL	N	(89G – .294)														
"	total		142	.269	.386	502	135	19	2	12	2.4	68	58	46	46	4	13	2	117	3	4	0	0.9	.968	OF-131
1970	2 teams			ATL	N	(123G – .265)			CAL	A	(26G – .304)														
"	total		149	.272	.364	522	142	19	2	8	1.5	66	67	48	56	6	9	2	281	3	5	0	1.9	.983	OF-143
1971	CAL	A	111	.245	.315	314	77	9	2	3	1.0	32	38	28	28	0	29	10	146	4	2	1	1.4	.987	OF-88
12 yrs.			1559	.286	.413	5195	1485	238	57	103	2.0	690	615	467	706	79	178	46	2613	73	38	15	1.7	.986	OF-1447

LEAGUE CHAMPIONSHIP SERIES

Year	Team		Games	BA	SA	AB	H	2B	3B	HR	HR%	R	RBI	BB	SO	SB	PH AB	PH H	PO	A	E	DP	TC/G	FA	G by Pos
1969	ATL	N	3	.357	.643	14	5	1	0	1	7.1	4	2	1	4	0	0	0	3	1	1	0	1.7	.800	OF-3

953

Year	Team	Games	BA	SA	AB	H	2B	3B	HR	HR%	R	RBI	BB	SO	SB	Pinch Hit AB	H	PO	A	E	DP	TC/G	FA	G by Pos

Charlie Gooch

GOOCH, CHARLES FURMAN
B. June 5, 1902, Smyrna, Tenn. D. May 30, 1982, Lanham, Md.
BR TR 5'9" 170 lbs.

Year	Team	Games	BA	SA	AB	H	2B	3B	HR	HR%	R	RBI	BB	SO	SB	PH AB	PH H	PO	A	E	DP	TC/G	FA	G by Pos
1929	WAS A	39	.281	.351	57	16	2	1	0	0.0	6	5	7	8	0	22	7	31	11	2	2	1.1	.955	3B-7, 1B-7, SS-1

Johnny Gooch

GOOCH, JOHN BEVERLEY
B. Nov. 9, 1897, Smyrna, Tenn. D. May 15, 1975, Nashville, Tenn.
BB TR 5'11" 175 lbs.

Year	Team	Games	BA	SA	AB	H	2B	3B	HR	HR%	R	RBI	BB	SO	SB	PH AB	PH H	PO	A	E	DP	TC/G	FA	G by Pos
1921	PIT N	13	.237	.237	38	9	0	0	0	0.0	2	3	3	3	1	0	0	49	15	1	2	5.0	.985	C-13
1922		105	.329	.397	353	116	15	3	1	0.3	45	42	39	15	1	2	1	382	102	15	10	4.8	.970	C-103
1923		66	.277	.361	202	56	10	2	1	0.5	16	20	17	13	2	0	0	217	56	7	7	4.2	.975	C-66
1924		70	.290	.362	224	65	6	5	0	0.0	26	25	16	12	1	1	0	198	47	3	12	3.5	.988	C-69
1925		79	.298	.372	215	64	8	4	0	0.0	24	30	20	16	1	3	0	172	39	7	8	2.8	.968	C-76
1926		86	.271	.362	218	59	15	1	1	0.5	19	42	20	14	1	3	0	202	38	5	6	2.8	.980	C-80
1927		101	.258	.351	291	75	17	2	2	0.7	22	48	19	21	0	9	1	285	57	9	7	3.5	.974	C-91
1928	2 teams		PIT N	(31G – .238)		BKN N	(42G – .317)																	
"	total	73	.282	.331	181	51	3	3	0	0.0	16	17	10	15	0	4	1	204	35	9	6	3.4	.964	C-69
1929	2 teams		BKN N	(1G – .000)		CIN N	(92G – .300)																	
"	total	93	.299	.378	288	86	13	5	0	0.0	22	34	24	10	4	7	1	251	61	8	7	3.4	.975	C-86
1930	CIN N	92	.243	.322	276	67	10	3	2	0.7	29	30	27	15	0	4	0	233	42	13	4	3.1	.955	C-79
1933	BOS A	37	.182	.221	77	14	1	1	0	0.0	6	2	11	7	0	8	1	86	19	1	2	2.9	.991	C-26
11 yrs.		815	.280	.355	2363	662	98	29	7	0.3	227	293	206	141	11	39	5	2279	511	78	71	3.5	.973	C-758

WORLD SERIES

Year	Team	Games	BA	SA	AB	H	2B	3B	HR	HR%	R	RBI	BB	SO	SB	PH AB	PH H	PO	A	E	DP	TC/G	FA	G by Pos
1925	PIT N	3	.000	.000	8	0	0	0	0	0.0	0	0	0	0	0	0	0	9	3	0	0	4.0	1.000	C-3
1927		3	.000	.000	5	0	0	0	0	0.0	0	1	1	1	0	0	0	19	1	0	0	6.7	1.000	C-3
2 yrs.		6	.000	.000	8	0	0	0	0	0.0	0	1	1	1	0	0	0	28	4	0	0	5.3	1.000	C-6

Lee Gooch

GOOCH, LEE CURRIN
B. Feb. 23, 1890, Oxford, N. C. D. May 18, 1966, Raleigh, N. C.
BR TR 6' 190 lbs.

Year	Team	Games	BA	SA	AB	H	2B	3B	HR	HR%	R	RBI	BB	SO	SB	PH AB	PH H	PO	A	E	DP	TC/G	FA	G by Pos
1915	CLE A	2	.500	.500	2	1	0	0	0	0.0	0	0	0	0	0	2	1	0	0	0	0	0.0	–	OF-16
1917	PHI A	17	.288	.373	59	17	2	0	1	1.7	4	8	4	10	0	1	0	24	1	3	0	1.6	.893	OF-16
2 yrs.		19	.295	.377	61	18	2	0	1	1.6	4	8	4	10	0	3	1	24	1	3	0	1.5	.893	OF-16

Gene Good

GOOD, EUGENE J.
B. Dec. 13, 1882, Roxbury, Mass. D. Aug. 6, 1947, Boston, Mass.
BL TL 5'6" 130 lbs.

Year	Team	Games	BA	SA	AB	H	2B	3B	HR	HR%	R	RBI	BB	SO	SB	PH AB	PH H	PO	A	E	DP	TC/G	FA	G by Pos
1906	BOS N	34	.151	.151	119	18	0	0	0	0.0	4	0	13			2	0	50	5	8	1	1.9	.873	OF-34

Wilbur Good

GOOD, WILBUR DAVID (Lefty)
B. Sept. 28, 1885, Punxsutawney, Pa. D. Dec. 30, 1963, Brooksville, Fla.
BL TL 5'6" 165 lbs.

Year	Team	Games	BA	SA	AB	H	2B	3B	HR	HR%	R	RBI	BB	SO	SB	PH AB	PH H	PO	A	E	DP	TC/G	FA	G by Pos
1905	NY A	6	.375	.375	8	3	0	0	0	0.0	0	0	0			0	0	1	7	1	0	1.5	.889	P-5
1908	CLE A	46	.279	.344	154	43	1	3	1	0.6	23	14	13			7	2	62	0	11	0	1.6	.849	OF-42
1909		94	.214	.264	318	68	6	5	0	0.0	33	17	28		13	10	1	110	12	6	2	1.4	.953	OF-80
1910	BOS N	23	.337	.488	86	29	5	4	0	0.0	15	11	6	13	5	0	0	56	7	2	1	2.8	.969	OF-23
1911	2 teams		BOS N	(43G – .267)		CHI N	(58G – .269)																	
"	total	101	.268	.377	310	83	14	7	2	0.6	48	36	23	39	13	12	1	182	16	13	2	2.1	.938	OF-83
1912	CHI N	39	.143	.143	35	5	0	0	0	0.0	7	1	3	7	3	21	3	7	1	0	0	0.2	1.000	OF-10
1913		49	.253	.363	91	23	3	2	1	1.1	11	12	11	16	5	16	4	37	1	1	0	0.8	.974	OF-26
1914		154	.272	.348	580	158	24	7	2	0.3	70	43	53	74	31	0	0	242	25	20	10	1.9	.930	OF-154
1915		128	.253	.337	498	126	18	9	2	0.4	66	27	34	65	19	2	1	192	13	14	4	1.7	.936	OF-125
1916	PHI N	75	.250	.346	136	34	4	3	1	0.7	25	15	8	13	7	22	3	55	4	1	1	0.8	.983	OF-46
1918	CHI A	35	.250	.365	148	37	9	4	0	0.0	24	11	11	16	1	0	0	103	4	2	1	3.1	.982	OF-35
11 yrs.		750	.258	.342	2364	609	84	44	9	0.4	322	187	190	243	104	85	14	1047	90	71	21	1.6	.941	OF-624, P-5

Bill Goodenough

GOODENOUGH, WILLIAM B.
B. 1863, St. Louis, Mo. D. May 24, 1905, St. Louis, Mo.
6'1" 170 lbs.

Year	Team	Games	BA	SA	AB	H	2B	3B	HR	HR%	R	RBI	BB	SO	SB	PH AB	PH H	PO	A	E	DP	TC/G	FA	G by Pos
1893	STL N	10	.161	.194	31	5	1	0	0	0.0	4	2	3	4	2	0	0	21	1	3	0	2.5	.880	OF-10

Mike Goodfellow

GOODFELLOW, MICHAEL J.
B. Oct. 3, 1866, Port Jervis, N. Y. D. Feb. 12, 1920, Newark, N. J.
BR TR 6' 180 lbs.

Year	Team	Games	BA	SA	AB	H	2B	3B	HR	HR%	R	RBI	BB	SO	SB	PH AB	PH H	PO	A	E	DP	TC/G	FA	G by Pos
1887	STL AA	1	.000	.000	4	0	0	0	0	0.0	0		0	0	0	0	0	2	2	1	0	5.0	.800	C-1
1888	CLE AA	68	.245	.271	269	66	7	0	0	0.0	24	29	11		7	0	0	138	12	18	2	2.5	.893	OF-62, C-4, 1B-3, SS-1
2 yrs.		69	.242	.267	273	66	7	0	0	0.0	24	29	11		7	0	0	140	14	19	2	2.5	.890	OF-62, C-5, 1B-3, SS-1

Billy Goodman

GOODMAN, WILLIAM DALE
B. Mar. 22, 1926, Concord, N. C. D. Oct. 1, 1984, Sarasota, Fla.
BL TR 5'11" 165 lbs.

Year	Team	Games	BA	SA	AB	H	2B	3B	HR	HR%	R	RBI	BB	SO	SB	PH AB	PH H	PO	A	E	DP	TC/G	FA	G by Pos
1947	BOS A	12	.182	.182	11	2	0	0	0	0.0	1	1	1	2	0	9	1	2	0	0	0	0.2	1.000	OF-1
1948		127	.310	.387	445	138	27	2	1	0.2	65	66	74	44	5	4	2	1101	73	9	120	9.3	.992	1B-117, 3B-2, 2B-2
1949		122	.298	.363	443	132	23	3	0	0.0	54	56	58	21	2	3	2	1069	79	9	148	9.5	.992	1B-117
1950		110	**.354**	.455	424	150	25	3	4	0.9	91	68	52	25	2	11	2	344	89	9	28	4.0	.980	OF-45, 3B-27, 1B-21, 2B-5, SS-1
1951		141	.297	.374	546	162	34	4	0	0.0	92	50	79	37	7	1	0	742	170	14	96	6.6	.985	1B-62, 2B-44, OF-38, 3B-1
1952		138	.306	.394	513	157	27	3	4	0.8	79	56	48	23	8	6	1	473	367	20	112	6.2	.977	2B-103, 1B-23, 3B-5, OF-4
1953		128	.313	.409	514	161	33	5	2	0.4	73	41	57	11	1	2	2	418	319	21	106	5.9	.972	2B-112, 1B-20
1954		127	.303	.376	489	148	25	4	1	0.2	71	36	51	15	3	10	3	393	248	14	90	5.2	.979	2B-72, OF-13, 3B-12
1955		149	.294	.352	599	176	31	2	0	0.0	100	52	99	44	5	1	0	395	378	24	96	5.3	.970	2B-143, 1B-5, OF-1
1956		105	.293	.404	399	117	22	8	2	0.5	61	38	40	22	0	0	0	215	266	17	69	4.7	.966	2B-95
1957	2 teams		BOS A	(18G – .063)		BAL A	(73G – .308)																	
"	total	91	.294	.387	279	82	11	3	3	1.1	37	33	23	19	0	22	2	134	110	11	20	2.8	.957	3B-54, OF-9, 1B-8, SS-5, 2B-5
1958	CHI A	116	.299	.358	425	127	15	5	0	0.0	41	40	37	21	1	4	2	89	210	14	18	2.7	.955	3B-111, 1B-3, SS-1, 2B-1
1959		104	.250	.321	268	67	14	1	0	0.0	41	28	19	20	3	31	7	61	140	10	11	2.0	.953	3B-74, 2B-3
1960		30	.234	.286	77	18	4	0	0	0.0	5	6	12	8	0	9	0	26	52	1	7	2.6	.987	3B-20, 2B-7
1961		41	.255	.392	51	13	4	0	1	2.0	4	10	7	6	0	27	9	11	14	1	1	0.6	.962	3B-7, 1B-2, 2B-1

Billy Goodman *continued*

Year	Team	Games	BA	SA	AB	H	2B	3B	HR	HR%	R	RBI	BB	SO	SB	Pinch Hit AB	Pinch Hit H	PO	A	E	DP	TC/G	FA	G by Pos
1962	HOU N	82	.255	.292	161	41	4	1	0	0.0	12	10	12	11	0	53	14	36	67	9	8	1.4	.920	2B-31, 3B-17, 1B-1
16 yrs.		1623	.300	.378	5644	1691	299	44	19	0.3	807	591	669	329	37	198	49	5509	2582	183	930	5.1	.978	2B-624, 1B-406, 3B-330, OF-111, SS-7

WORLD SERIES

Year	Team	Games	BA	SA	AB	H	2B	3B	HR	HR%	R	RBI	BB	SO	SB	Pinch Hit AB	Pinch Hit H	PO	A	E	DP	TC/G	FA	G by Pos
1959	CHI A	5	.231	.231	13	3	0	0	0	0.0	1	1	0	5	0	2	0	1	2	0	0	0.6	1.000	3B-5

Ival Goodman

GOODMAN, IVAL RICHARD (Goodie)
B. July 23, 1908, Northview, Mo. D. Nov. 25, 1984, Cincinnati, Ohio

BL TR 5'11" 170 lbs.

Year	Team	Games	BA	SA	AB	H	2B	3B	HR	HR%	R	RBI	BB	SO	SB	Pinch Hit AB	Pinch Hit H	PO	A	E	DP	TC/G	FA	G by Pos
1935	CIN N	148	.269	.429	592	159	23	18	12	2.0	86	72	35	50	14	0	0	322	17	14	4	2.4	.960	OF-146
1936		136	.284	.476	489	139	15	14	17	3.5	81	71	38	53	6	15	5	274	6	8	2	2.1	.972	OF-120
1937		147	.273	.428	549	150	25	12	12	2.2	86	55	55	58	10	3	1	291	13	8	0	2.1	.974	OF-141
1938		145	.292	.533	568	166	27	10	30	5.3	103	92	53	51	3	3	1	306	10	4	1	2.2	.988	OF-142
1939		124	.323	.515	470	152	37	16	7	1.5	85	84	54	32	2	1	1	246	16	5	4	2.2	.981	OF-123
1940		136	.258	.389	519	134	20	6	12	2.3	78	63	60	54	9	0	0	252	6	8	0	2.0	.970	OF-135
1941		42	.268	.349	149	40	5	2	1	0.7	14	12	16	15	1	1	0	84	1	3	0	2.1	.966	OF-40
1942		87	.243	.332	226	55	18	1	0	0.0	21	15	24	32	0	23	6	101	7	1	2	1.3	.991	OF-57
1943	CHI N	80	.320	.449	225	72	10	5	3	1.3	31	15	24	20	4	17	5	120	2	4	1	1.6	.968	OF-61
1944		62	.262	.355	141	37	8	1	1	0.7	24	16	23	15	0	23	6	65	0	0	0	1.0	1.000	OF-35
10 yrs.		1107	.281	.445	3928	1104	188	85	95	2.4	609	525	382	380	49	88	25	2061	78	55	14	2.0	.975	OF-1000

WORLD SERIES

Year	Team	Games	BA	SA	AB	H	2B	3B	HR	HR%	R	RBI	BB	SO	SB	Pinch Hit AB	Pinch Hit H	PO	A	E	DP	TC/G	FA	G by Pos
1939	CIN N	4	.333	.400	15	5	1	0	0	0.0	3	1	1	2	1	0	0	10	1	1	0	3.0	.917	OF-4
1940		7	.276	.345	29	8	2	0	0	0.0	5	5	0	3	0	0	0	10	0	0	0	1.4	1.000	OF-7
2 yrs.		11	.295	.364	44	13	3	0	0	0.0	8	6	1	5	1	0	0	20	1	1	0	2.0	.955	OF-11

Jake Goodman

GOODMAN, JACOB
B. Sept. 14, 1853, Lancaster, Pa. D. Mar. 9, 1890, Reading, Pa.

Year	Team	Games	BA	SA	AB	H	2B	3B	HR	HR%	R	RBI	BB	SO	SB	Pinch Hit AB	Pinch Hit H	PO	A	E	DP	TC/G	FA	G by Pos
1878	MIL N	60	.246	.298	252	62	4	3	1	0.4	28	27	7	33		0	0	693	12	42	15	12.5	.944	1B-60
1882	PIT AA	10	.317	.463	41	13	2	2	0	0.0	5		2			0	0	73	4	3	0	8.0	.963	1B-10
2 yrs.		70	.256	.321	293	75	6	5	1	0.3	33	27	9	33		0	0	766	16	45	15	11.8	.946	1B-70

Ed Goodson

GOODSON, JAMES EDWARD
B. Jan. 25, 1948, Pulaski, Va.

BL TR 6'3" 180 lbs.

Year	Team	Games	BA	SA	AB	H	2B	3B	HR	HR%	R	RBI	BB	SO	SB	Pinch Hit AB	Pinch Hit H	PO	A	E	DP	TC/G	FA	G by Pos
1970	SF N	7	.273	.273	11	3	0	0	0	0.0	1	0	0	2	0	5	2	14	2	1	1	2.4	.941	1B-2
1971		20	.190	.214	42	8	1	0	0	0.0	0	4	1	2	0	7	1	81	7	0	3	4.4	1.000	1B-14
1972		58	.280	.420	150	42	1	1	6	4.0	15	30	8	12	0	15	4	299	27	3	28	5.7	.991	1B-42
1973		102	.302	.453	384	116	20	1	12	3.1	37	53	15	44	0	8	3	64	171	23	13	2.5	.911	3B-93
1974		98	.272	.383	298	81	15	0	6	2.0	25	48	18	22	1	20	6	600	46	2	53	6.6	.997	1B-73, 3B-8
1975	2 teams	SF N	(39G – .207)			ATL N	(47G – .211)																	
"	total	86	.208	.284	197	41	9	0	2	1.0	15	16	9	22	0	40	9	240	52	6	23	3.5	.980	1B-29, 3B-14
1976	LA N	83	.229	.339	118	27	4	0	3	2.5	8	17	8	19	0	56	15	17	27	7	2	0.6	.863	3B-16, 1B-3, OF-2, 2B-1
1977		61	.167	.227	66	11	1	0	1	1.5	3	5	3	10	0	45	8	38	9	0	5	0.8	1.000	1B-13, 3B-4
8 yrs.		515	.260	.374	1266	329	51	2	30	2.4	108	170	63	135	1	196	48	1353	341	42	128	3.4	.976	1B-176, 3B-135, OF-2, 2B-1

LEAGUE CHAMPIONSHIP SERIES

Year	Team	Games	BA	SA	AB	H	2B	3B	HR	HR%	R	RBI	BB	SO	SB	Pinch Hit AB	Pinch Hit H	PO	A	E	DP	TC/G	FA	G by Pos
1977	LA N	1	.000	.000	1	0	0	0	0	0.0	0	0	0	0	0	1	0	0	0	0	0	0.0	–

WORLD SERIES

Year	Team	Games	BA	SA	AB	H	2B	3B	HR	HR%	R	RBI	BB	SO	SB	Pinch Hit AB	Pinch Hit H	PO	A	E	DP	TC/G	FA	G by Pos
1977	LA N	1	.000	.000	1	0	0	0	0	0.0	0	0	0	0	0	1	0	0	0	0	0	0.0	–

Danny Goodwin

GOODWIN, DANNY KAY
B. Sept. 2, 1953, St. Louis, Mo.

BL TR 6'1" 195 lbs.

Year	Team	Games	BA	SA	AB	H	2B	3B	HR	HR%	R	RBI	BB	SO	SB	Pinch Hit AB	Pinch Hit H	PO	A	E	DP	TC/G	FA	G by Pos
1975	CAL A	4	.100	.100	10	1	0	0	0	0.0	0	0	0	5	0	0	0	0	0	0	0	0.0	–	DH-3
1977		35	.209	.330	91	19	6	1	1	1.1	5	8	5	19	0	12	1	0	0	0	0	0.0	–	DH-23
1978		24	.276	.466	58	16	5	0	2	3.4	9	10	10	13	0	8	2	0	0	0	0	0.0	–	DH-15
1979	MIN A	58	.289	.497	159	46	8	5	5	3.1	22	27	11	23	0	11	4	40	2	0	5	0.7	1.000	DH-51, 1B-8
1980		55	.200	.270	115	23	5	0	1	0.9	12	11	17	32	0	22	6	87	6	0	6	1.7	1.000	DH-38, 1B-13
1981		59	.225	.318	151	34	6	1	2	1.3	18	17	16	32	3	10	3	342	20	3	27	6.2	.992	1B-40, DH-5, OF-1
1982	OAK A	17	.212	.404	52	11	2	1	2	3.8	6	8	2	13	0	2	1	0	0	0	0	0.0	–	DH-15
7 yrs.		252	.236	.373	636	150	32	8	13	2.0	72	81	61	137	3	66	17	469	28	3	38	2.0	.994	DH-150, 1B-61, OF-1

Pep Goodwin

GOODWIN, CLAIRE VERNON
B. Dec. 19, 1891, Pocatello, Ida. D. Feb. 15, 1972, Oakland, Calif.

BL TR 5'10½" 160 lbs.

Year	Team	Games	BA	SA	AB	H	2B	3B	HR	HR%	R	RBI	BB	SO	SB	Pinch Hit AB	Pinch Hit H	PO	A	E	DP	TC/G	FA	G by Pos
1914	KC F	112	.235	.316	374	88	15	6	1	0.3	38	32	27		4	6	2	136	275	43	25	4.1	.905	SS-67, 3B-40, 1B-1
1915		81	.236	.266	229	54	5	1	0	0.0	22	16	15		6	14	2	106	180	24	17	3.8	.923	SS-42, 2B-23
2 yrs.		193	.235	.297	603	142	20	7	1	0.2	60	48	42		10	20	4	242	455	67	42	4.0	.912	SS-109, 3B-40, 2B-23, 1B-1

Ray Goolsby

GOOLSBY, RAYMOND DANIEL (Ox)
B. Sept. 5, 1919, Florala, Ala.

BR TR 6'1" 185 lbs.

Year	Team	Games	BA	SA	AB	H	2B	3B	HR	HR%	R	RBI	BB	SO	SB	Pinch Hit AB	Pinch Hit H	PO	A	E	DP	TC/G	FA	G by Pos
1946	WAS A	3	.000	.000	4	0	0	0	0	0.0	0	0	1	1	0	2	0	1	0	0	0	0.3	1.000	OF-1

Greg Goossen

GOOSSEN, GREGORY BRYANT
B. Dec. 14, 1945, Los Angeles, Calif.

BR TR 6'1½" 210 lbs.

Year	Team	Games	BA	SA	AB	H	2B	3B	HR	HR%	R	RBI	BB	SO	SB	Pinch Hit AB	Pinch Hit H	PO	A	E	DP	TC/G	FA	G by Pos
1965	NY N	11	.290	.387	31	9	0	0	1	3.2	2	1	1	7	0	0	0	45	1	1	0	4.3	.979	C-8
1966		13	.188	.344	32	6	0	0	1	3.1	1	5	1	11	0	2	0	29	3	0	0	2.5	1.000	C-11
1967		37	.159	.174	69	11	1	0	0	0.0	2	3	4	26	0	20	4	101	7	3	2	3.0	.973	C-23
1968		38	.208	.274	106	22	4	0	0	0.0	7	9	10	21	0	6	0	237	24	3	18	6.9	.989	1B-30, C-2
1969	SEA A	52	.309	.597	139	43	8	1	10	7.2	19	24	14	29	1	19	2	268	24	2	15	5.7	.993	1B-31, OF-2

Year	Team		Games	BA	SA	AB	H	2B	3B	HR	HR%	R	RBI	BB	SO	SB	Pinch Hit AB	Pinch Hit H	PO	A	E	DP	TC/G	FA	G by Pos

Greg Goossen *continued*

Year	Team		Games	BA	SA	AB	H	2B	3B	HR	HR%	R	RBI	BB	SO	SB	Pinch Hit AB	Pinch Hit H	PO	A	E	DP	TC/G	FA	G by Pos
1970	2 teams	MIL A (21G – .255)				WAS A (21G – .222)																			
"	total		42	.241	.349	83	20	6	0	1	1.2	5	4	12	20	0	19	5	113	8	1	12	2.9	.992	1B-17, OF-5
6 yrs.			193	.241	.383	460	111	24	1	13	2.8	33	44	42	112	1	68	11	793	67	10	47	4.5	.989	1B-78, C-44, OF-7

Glen Gorbous

GORBOUS, GLEN EDWARD
B. July 8, 1930, Drumheller, Alta., Canada

BL TR 6'2" 175 lbs.

Year	Team		Games	BA	SA	AB	H	2B	3B	HR	HR%	R	RBI	BB	SO	SB	Pinch Hit AB	Pinch Hit H	PO	A	E	DP	TC/G	FA	G by Pos
1955	2 teams	CIN N (6G – .333)				PHI N (91G – .237)																			
"	total		97	.244	.351	242	59	12	1	4	1.7	27	27	24	18	0	37	10	125	10	4	2	1.4	.971	OF-62
1956	PHI	N	15	.182	.182	33	6	0	0	0	0.0	1	1	0	1	0	6	0	8	0	0	0	0.5	1.000	OF-8
1957			3	.500	1.000	2	1	0	0	0	0.0	1	1	1	0	0	2	1	0	0	0	0	0.0	—	
3 yrs.			115	.238	.336	277	66	13	1	4	1.4	29	29	25	19	0	45	11	133	10	4	2	1.3	.973	OF-70

Joe Gordon

GORDON, JOSEPH LOWELL (Flash)
B. Feb. 18, 1915, Los Angeles, Calif. D. Apr. 14, 1978, Sacramento, Calif.
Manager 1958-61, 1969.

BR TR 5'10" 180 lbs.

Year	Team		Games	BA	SA	AB	H	2B	3B	HR	HR%	R	RBI	BB	SO	SB	Pinch Hit AB	Pinch Hit H	PO	A	E	DP	TC/G	FA	G by Pos
1938	NY	A	127	.255	.502	458	117	24	7	25	5.5	83	97	56	72	11	1	1	290	450	31	98	6.1	.960	2B-126
1939			151	.284	.506	567	161	32	5	28	4.9	92	111	75	57	11	0	0	370	461	28	116	5.7	.967	2B-151
1940			155	.281	.511	616	173	32	10	30	4.9	112	103	52	57	18	0	0	374	505	23	116	5.8	.975	2B-155
1941			156	.276	.466	588	162	26	7	24	4.1	104	87	72	80	10	0	0	556	414	36	144	6.4	.964	2B-131, 1B-30
1942			147	.322	.491	538	173	29	4	18	3.3	88	103	79	95	12	0	0	354	442	28	121	5.6	.966	2B-147
1943			152	.249	.413	543	135	28	5	17	3.1	82	69	98	75	4	0	0	407	490	29	114	6.1	.969	2B-152
1946			112	.210	.338	376	79	15	0	11	2.9	35	47	49	72	2	4	0	281	346	17	87	5.8	.974	2B-108
1947	CLE	A	155	.272	.496	562	153	27	6	29	5.2	89	93	62	49	7	0	0	341	466	18	110	5.3	.978	2B-155
1948			144	.280	.507	550	154	21	4	32	5.8	96	124	77	68	5	1	0	332	439	23	98	5.5	.971	2B-144, SS-2
1949			148	.251	.407	541	136	18	3	20	3.7	74	84	83	33	5	3	0	297	430	15	123	5.0	.980	2B-145
1950			119	.236	.429	368	87	12	1	19	5.2	59	57	56	44	4	12	1	224	283	16	69	4.4	.969	2B-105
11 yrs.			1566	.268	.466	5707	1530	264	52	253	4.4	914	975	759	702	89	21	2	3826	4726	264	1196	5.6	.970	2B-1519, 1B-30, SS-2

WORLD SERIES

Year	Team		Games	BA	SA	AB	H	2B	3B	HR	HR%	R	RBI	BB	SO	SB	Pinch Hit AB	Pinch Hit H	PO	A	E	DP	TC/G	FA	G by Pos
1938	NY	A	4	.400	.733	15	6	2	0	1	6.7	3	6	1	3	1	0	0	12	12	2	3	6.5	.923	2B-4
1939			4	.143	.143	14	2	0	0	0	0.0	1	1	0	2	0	0	0	7	12	0	4	4.8	1.000	2B-4
1941			5	.500	.929	14	7	1	1	1	7.1	5	7	0	0	0	0	0	6	19	1	5	5.2	.962	2B-5
1942			5	.095	.143	21	2	1	0	0	0.0	1	0	0	7	0	0	0	11	12	0	1	4.6	1.000	2B-5
1943			5	.235	.471	17	4	1	0	1	5.9	2	2	3	3	0	0	0	20	23	0	3	8.6	1.000	2B-5
1948	CLE	A	6	.182	.318	22	4	0	0	1	4.5	3	2	1	2	1	0	0	15	13	1	7	4.8	.966	2B-6
6 yrs.			29	.243	.427	103	25	5	1	4	3.9	12	16	12	17	2	0	0	71	91	4	23	5.7	.976	2B-29

Mike Gordon

GORDON, MICHAEL WILLIAM
B. Sept. 11, 1953, Leominister, Mass.

BB TR 6'3" 215 lbs.

Year	Team		Games	BA	SA	AB	H	2B	3B	HR	HR%	R	RBI	BB	SO	SB	Pinch Hit AB	Pinch Hit H	PO	A	E	DP	TC/G	FA	G by Pos
1977	CHI	N	8	.043	.043	23	1	0	0	0	0.0	2	2	2	8	0	0	0	31	1	1	1	4.1	.970	C-8
1978			4	.200	.200	5	1	0	0	0	0.0	0	0	3	2	0	0	0	14	0	0	0	3.5	1.000	C-4
2 yrs.			12	.071	.071	28	2	0	0	0	0.0	2	2	5	10	0	0	0	45	1	1	1	3.9	.979	C-12

Sid Gordon

GORDON, SIDNEY
B. Aug. 13, 1917, Brooklyn, N. Y. D. June 17, 1975, New York, N. Y.

BR TR 5'10" 185 lbs.

Year	Team		Games	BA	SA	AB	H	2B	3B	HR	HR%	R	RBI	BB	SO	SB	Pinch Hit AB	Pinch Hit H	PO	A	E	DP	TC/G	FA	G by Pos
1941	NY	N	9	.258	.355	31	8	1	1	0	0.0	4	4	6	1	0	0	0	18	0	0	0	2.0	1.000	OF-9
1942			6	.316	.421	19	6	0	1	0	0.0	0	4	2	3	0	0	0	9	12	2	0	3.8	.913	3B-6
1943			131	.251	.373	474	119	9	11	9	1.9	50	63	43	32	2	6	1	551	148	17	59	5.5	.976	3B-53, 1B-41, OF-28, 2B-3
1946			135	.293	.378	450	132	15	4	5	1.1	64	45	60	27	1	5	2	215	62	5	3	2.1	.982	OF-101, 3B-30
1947			130	.272	.442	437	119	19	8	13	3.0	57	57	50	21	2	4	1	254	12	12	0	2.1	.957	OF-124, 3B-2
1948			142	.299	.537	521	156	26	4	30	5.8	100	107	74	39	8	5	0	166	223	19	19	2.9	.953	3B-115, OF-23
1949			141	.284	.505	489	139	26	2	26	5.3	87	90	95	37	1	5	0	151	206	14	18	2.6	.962	3B-123, OF-15, 1B-1
1950	BOS	N	134	.304	.557	481	146	33	4	27	5.6	78	103	78	31	2	1	0	283	32	4	1	2.4	.987	OF-123, 3B-10
1951			150	.287	.500	550	158	28	1	29	5.3	96	109	80	32	2	0	0	300	75	9	9	2.6	.977	OF-122, 3B-34
1952			144	.289	.483	522	151	22	2	25	4.8	69	75	77	49	0	0	0	266	13	1	0	1.9	.996	OF-142, 3B-2
1953	MIL	N	140	.274	.461	464	127	22	4	19	4.1	67	75	71	40	1	3	1	245	10	6	2	1.9	.977	OF-137
1954	PIT	N	131	.306	.438	363	111	12	0	12	3.3	38	49	67	24	0	17	3	149	80	11	6	1.8	.954	OF-73, 3B-40
1955	2 teams	PIT N (16G – .170)				NY N (66G – .243)																			
"	total		82	.225	.382	191	43	7	1	7	3.7	21	26	27	21	0	21	1	69	82	1	10	1.9	.993	3B-39, OF-21
13 yrs.			1475	.283	.466	4992	1415	220	43	202	4.0	735	805	731	356	19	67	9	2676	955	101	127	2.5	.973	OF-918, 3B-454, 1B-42, 2B-3

George Gore

GORE, GEORGE F.
B. May 3, 1857, Saccarappa, Me. D. Sept. 16, 1933, Utica, N. Y.
Manager 1892.

BL TR 5'11" 195 lbs.

Year	Team		Games	BA	SA	AB	H	2B	3B	HR	HR%	R	RBI	BB	SO	SB	Pinch Hit AB	Pinch Hit H	PO	A	E	DP	TC/G	FA	G by Pos
1879	CHI	N	63	.263	.357	266	70	17	4	0	0.0	43	32	8	30		0	0	201	11	20	3	3.7	.914	OF-54, 1B-9
1880			77	.360	.463	322	116	23	2	2	0.6	70	47	21	10		0	0	180	18	23	6	2.9	.896	OF-74, 1B-7
1881			73	.298	.424	309	92	18	9	1	0.3	86	44	27	23		0	0	154	22	25	4	2.8	.876	OF-72, 3B-1, 1B-1
1882			84	.319	.422	367	117	15	7	3	0.8	99	51	29	19		0	0	153	23	33	5	2.5	.842	OF-84
1883			92	.334	.472	392	131	30	9	2	0.5	105		27	13		0	0	195	27	34	4	2.8	.867	OF-92
1884			103	.318	.415	422	134	18	4	5	1.2	104		61	26		0	0	185	25	32	5	2.3	.868	OF-103
1885			109	.313	.454	441	138	21	13	5	1.1	115	51	68	25		0	0	204	17	29	4	2.3	.884	OF-109
1886			118	.304	.444	444	135	20	12	6	1.4	150	63	102	30		0	0	184	20	29	4	2.0	.876	OF-118
1887	NY	N	111	.290	.353	459	133	16	5	1	0.2	95	49	42	18	39	0	0	221	20	30	7	2.4	.889	OF-111
1888			64	.220	.291	254	56	4	4	2	0.8	37	17	30	31	11	0	0	88	4	18	0	1.7	.836	OF-64
1889			120	.305	.420	488	149	21	7	7	1.4	132	54	84	28	28	0	0	239	21	41	5	2.5	.864	OF-120
1890	NY	P	93	.318	.499	399	127	26	8	10	2.5	132	55	77	23	28	0	0	146	11	22	3	1.9	.877	OF-93
1891	NY	N	130	.284	.364	422	120	12	0	2	0.4	103	48	74	34	19	0	0	234	16	25	3	2.1	.909	OF-130
1892	2 teams	NY N (53G – .254)				STL N (20G – .205)																			
"	total		73	.241	.305	266	64	11	3	0	0.0	56	15	67	22	22	0	0	137	11	15	2	2.2	.908	OF-73
14 yrs.			1310	.301	.411	5357	1612	262	94	46	0.9	1327	526	717	332	147	0	0	2521	246	376	53	2.4	.880	OF-1297, 1B-17, 3B-1

Year	Team	Games	BA	SA	AB	H	2B	3B	HR	HR%	R	RBI	BB	SO	SB	Pinch Hit AB	Pinch Hit H	PO	A	E	DP	TC/G	FA	G by Pos

Bob Gorinski

GORINSKI, ROBERT JOHN
B. Jan. 7, 1952, Latrobe, Pa.

BR TR 6'3" 215 lbs.

Year	Team	Games	BA	SA	AB	H	2B	3B	HR	HR%	R	RBI	BB	SO	SB	AB	H	PO	A	E	DP	TC/G	FA	G by Pos
1977	MIN A	54	.195	.322	118	23	4	1	3	2.5	14	22	5	29	1	16	1	44	0	3	0	0.9	.936	OF-37, DH-9

Herb Gorman

GORMAN, HERBERT ALLEN
B. Dec. 18, 1924, San Francisco, Calif.   D. Apr. 5, 1953, San Diego, Calif.

BL TL 5'11" 180 lbs.

Year	Team	Games	BA	SA	AB	H	2B	3B	HR	HR%	R	RBI	BB	SO	SB	AB	H	PO	A	E	DP	TC/G	FA	G by Pos
1952	STL N	1	.000	.000	1	0	0	0	0	0.0	0	0	0	0	0	1	0	0	0	0	0	0.0	—	

Howie Gorman

GORMAN, HOWARD PAUL (Lefty)
B. May 14, 1913, Pittsburgh, Pa.   D. Apr. 29, 1984, Harrisburg, Pa.

BL TL 6'2" 160 lbs.

Year	Team	Games	BA	SA	AB	H	2B	3B	HR	HR%	R	RBI	BB	SO	SB	AB	H	PO	A	E	DP	TC/G	FA	G by Pos
1937	PHI N	13	.211	.263	19	4	1	0	0	0.0	3	1	1	4	0	1	0	0	0	0	0	0.2	.500	OF-7
1938		1	.000	.000	1	0	0	0	0	0.0	0	0	0	1	0	1	0	0	0	0	0	0.0	—	
2 yrs.		14	.200	.250	20	4	1	0	0	0.0	3	1	1	5	0	1	0	0	1	0	0.1	.500	OF-7	

Jack Gorman

GORMAN, JOHN F. (Stooping Jack)
B. 1859, St. Louis, Mo.   D. Sept. 9, 1889, St. Louis, Mo.

Year	Team	Games	BA	SA	AB	H	2B	3B	HR	HR%	R	RBI	BB	SO	SB	AB	H	PO	A	E	DP	TC/G	FA	G by Pos
1883	STL AA	1	.000	.000	4	0	0	0	0	0.0	0		0			0	0	1	1	0	3.0	.667	OF-1	
1884	2 teams	KC U (33G – .277)			PIT AA (8G – .148)																			
"	total	41	.256	.323	164	42	5	3	0	0.0	28		5			0	0	286	15	25	8	8.0	.923	1B-24, OF-8, 3B-6, P-3
2 yrs.		42	.250	.315	168	42	5	3	0	0.0	28		5			0	0	287	16	26	8	7.8	.921	1B-24, OF-9, 3B-6, P-3

John Goryl

GORYL, JOHN ALBERT
B. Oct. 21, 1933, Cumberland, R. I.
Manager 1980-81.

BR TR 5'10" 175 lbs.

Year	Team	Games	BA	SA	AB	H	2B	3B	HR	HR%	R	RBI	BB	SO	SB	AB	H	PO	A	E	DP	TC/G	FA	G by Pos
1957	CHI N	9	.211	.263	38	8	0	0	1	2.6	7	1	5	9	0	0	0	6	14	1	4	2.3	.952	3B-9
1958		83	.242	.365	219	53	9	3	4	1.8	27	14	27	34	0	10	3	91	153	16	26	3.1	.938	3B-44, 2B-35
1959		25	.188	.354	48	9	3	1	1	2.1	1	6	5	3	1	8	1	11	31	1	2	1.7	.977	2B-11, 3B-4
1962	MIN A	37	.192	.500	26	5	0	1	2	7.7	6	2	2	6	0	19	3	2	10	1	1	0.4	.923	2B-4, 3B-1
1963		64	.287	.540	150	43	5	3	9	6.0	29	24	15	29	0	12	2	75	92	7	18	2.7	.960	2B-34, 3B-11, SS-7
1964		58	.140	.175	114	16	0	2	0	0.0	9	1	10	25	1	22	4	73	70	3	9	2.5	.979	2B-28, 3B-13
6 yrs.		276	.225	.371	595	134	19	10	16	2.7	79	48	64	106	2	71	13	258	370	29	60	2.4	.956	2B-112, 3B-81, SS-8

Jim Gosger

GOSGER, JAMES CHARLES
B. Nov. 6, 1942, Port Huron, Mich.

BL TL 5'11" 185 lbs.

Year	Team	Games	BA	SA	AB	H	2B	3B	HR	HR%	R	RBI	BB	SO	SB	AB	H	PO	A	E	DP	TC/G	FA	G by Pos
1963	BOS A	19	.063	.063	16	1	0	0	0	0.0	3	0	3	5	0	6	1	9	0	2	0	0.6	.818	OF-4
1965		81	.256	.410	324	83	15	4	9	2.8	45	35	29	61	3	0	0	195	4	5	2	2.5	.975	OF-81
1966	2 teams	BOS A (40G – .254)			KC A (88G – .224)																			
"	total	128	.234	.359	398	93	18	5	10	2.5	50	44	52	73	5	23	6	224	3	2	0	1.8	.991	OF-109
1967	KC A	134	.242	.351	356	86	14	5	5	1.4	31	36	53	69	5	26	7	201	6	4	1	1.6	.981	OF-113
1968	OAK A	88	.180	.200	150	27	1	1	0	0.0	7	5	17	21	4	18	3	99	5	0	3	1.2	1.000	OF-64
1969	2 teams	SEA A (39G – .109)			NY N (10G – .133)																			
"	total	49	.114	.243	70	8	4	1	1	1.4	4	2	7	17	2	15	1	41	1	0	0	0.9	1.000	OF-31
1970	MON N	91	.263	.372	274	72	11	2	5	1.8	38	37	35	35	5	10	1	252	12	3	15	2.9	.989	OF-71, 1B-19
1971		51	.157	.216	102	16	2	2	0	0.0	7	8	9	17	1	23	3	79	5	2	2	1.7	.977	OF-23, 1B-6
1973	NY N	38	.239	.261	92	22	2	0	0	0.0	9	10	9	16	0	4	0	45	0	0	0	1.2	1.000	OF-35
1974		26	.091	.091	33	3	0	0	0	0.0	3	0	3	2	0	2	0	17	0	0	0	0.7	1.000	OF-24
10 yrs.		705	.226	.331	1815	411	67	16	30	1.7	197	177	217	316	25	127	22	1162	36	18	23	1.7	.985	OF-555, 1B-25

Goose Goslin

GOSLIN, LEON ALLEN
B. Oct. 16, 1900, Salem, N. J.   D. May 15, 1971, Bridgeton, N. J.
Hall of Fame 1968.

BL TR 5'11½" 185 lbs.

Year	Team	Games	BA	SA	AB	H	2B	3B	HR	HR%	R	RBI	BB	SO	SB	AB	H	PO	A	E	DP	TC/G	FA	G by Pos
1921	WAS A	14	.260	.380	50	13	1	1	1	2.0	8	6	6	5	0	0	0	30	1	0	0	2.2	1.000	OF-14
1922		101	.324	.441	358	116	19	7	3	0.8	44	53	25	26	4	5	0	197	8	15	1	2.2	.932	OF-93
1923		150	.300	.453	600	180	29	**18**	9	1.5	86	99	40	53	7	1	1	310	26	15	5	2.3	.957	OF-149
1924		154	.344	.516	579	199	30	17	12	2.1	100	**129**	68	29	16	0	0	369	12	16	4	2.6	.960	OF-154
1925		150	.334	.547	601	201	34	**20**	18	3.0	116	113	53	50	26	0	0	385	24	12	1	2.8	.971	OF-150
1926		147	.354	.543	567	201	26	15	17	3.0	105	108	63	38	8	0	0	373	25	15	8	2.8	.964	OF-147
1927		148	.334	.516	581	194	37	15	13	2.2	96	120	50	28	21	0	0	356	8	17	3	2.6	.955	OF-148
1928		135	**.379**	.614	456	173	36	10	17	3.7	80	102	48	19	16	7	2	266	14	11	4	2.2	.962	OF-125
1929		145	.288	.461	553	159	28	7	18	3.3	82	91	66	33	10	3	3	299	7	10	1	2.2	.968	OF-142
1930	2 teams	WAS A (47G – .271)			STL A (101G – .326)																			
"	total	148	.308	.601	584	180	36	12	37	6.3	115	138	67	54	17	0	0	309	15	12	1	2.3	.964	OF-148
1931	STL A	151	.328	.555	591	194	42	10	24	4.1	114	105	80	41	9	0	0	319	14	14	1	2.3	.960	OF-151
1932		150	.299	.469	572	171	28	9	17	3.0	88	104	92	35	12	0	0	331	19	18	5	2.5	.951	OF-149, 3B-1
1933	WAS A	132	.297	.452	549	163	35	10	10	1.8	97	64	42	32	5	4	2	261	17	10	7	2.2	.965	OF-128
1934	DET A	151	.305	.453	614	187	38	7	13	2.1	106	100	65	38	5	2	0	290	15	15	2	2.1	.953	OF-144
1935		147	.292	.415	590	172	34	6	9	1.5	88	109	56	31	5	3	1	326	6	12	2	2.3	.965	OF-144
1936		147	.315	.526	572	180	33	8	24	4.2	122	125	85	50	14	3	0	266	11	13	1	2.0	.955	OF-144
1937		79	.238	.376	181	43	11	1	4	2.2	30	35	35	18	0	29	9	93	3	5	1	1.3	.950	OF-40, 1B-1
1938	WAS A	38	.158	.316	57	9	3	0	2	3.5	6	8	8	5	0	18	4	25	0	0	0	0.7	1.000	OF-13
18 yrs.		2287	.316	.500	8655	2735	500	173	248	2.9	1483	1609	949	585	175	75	22	4805	225	210	47	2.3	.960	OF-2188, 3B-1, 1B-1

WORLD SERIES

Year	Team	Games	BA	SA	AB	H	2B	3B	HR	HR%	R	RBI	BB	SO	SB	AB	H	PO	A	E	DP	TC/G	FA	G by Pos
1924	WAS A	7	.344	.656	32	11	0	0	3	9.4	4	7	0	7	0	0	0	15	1	0	0	2.3	1.000	OF-7
1925		7	.308	.692	26	8	1	0	3	11.5	6	6	3	3	1	0	0	15	1	0	0	2.3	1.000	OF-7
1933		5	.250	.450	20	5	1	0	1	5.0	2	1	0	1	0	0	0	15	1	0	0	2.1	1.000	OF-5
1934	DET A	7	.241	.276	29	7	1	0	0	0.0	2	1	3	3	0	0	0	8	1	0	0	1.8	1.000	OF-5
1935		6	.273	.318	22	6	1	0	0	0.0	2	3	6	0	0	0	0	20	1	2	0	3.3	.913	OF-7
5 yrs.		32	.287	.488	129	37	5	0	7	5.4	16	18	12	14	1	0	0	70	3	3	0	2.4	.961	OF-32

10th

Howie Goss

GOSS, HOWARD WAYNE
B. Nov. 1, 1934, Wewoka, Okla.

BR TR 6'4" 204 lbs.

Year	Team	Games	BA	SA	AB	H	2B	3B	HR	HR%	R	RBI	BB	SO	SB	Pinch Hit AB	Pinch Hit H	PO	A	E	DP	TC/G	FA	G by Pos

Howie Goss *continued*

Year	Team	Games	BA	SA	AB	H	2B	3B	HR	HR%	R	RBI	BB	SO	SB	PH AB	PH H	PO	A	E	DP	TC/G	FA	G by Pos
1962	PIT N	89	.243	.351	111	27	6	0	2	1.8	19	10	9	36	5	8	2	62	2	1	1	0.7	.985	OF-66
1963	HOU N	133	.209	.328	411	86	18	2	9	2.2	37	44	31	128	4	15	2	276	7	2	2	2.1	.993	OF-123
2 yrs.		222	.216	.333	522	113	24	2	11	2.1	56	54	40	164	9	23	4	338	9	3	3	1.6	.991	OF-189

Dick Gossett

GOSSETT, JOHN STAR
B. Aug. 21, 1891, Dennison, Ohio D. Oct. 6, 1962, Massilon, Ohio
BR TR 5'11" 185 lbs.

Year	Team	Games	BA	SA	AB	H	2B	3B	HR	HR%	R	RBI	BB	SO	SB	PH AB	PH H	PO	A	E	DP	TC/G	FA	G by Pos
1913	NY A	39	.162	.181	105	17	2	0	0	0.0	9	9	10	22	1	1	1	123	50	6	2	4.6	.966	C-38
1914		9	.143	.143	21	3	0	0	0	0.0	3	1	5	5	0	0	0	37	6	1	0	4.9	.977	C-9
2 yrs.		48	.159	.175	126	20	2	0	0	0.0	12	10	15	27	1	1	1	160	56	7	2	4.6	.969	C-47

Julio Gotay

GOTAY, JULIO ENRIQUE
Born Julio Enrique Gotay y Sanchez.
B. June 9, 1939, Fajardo, Puerto Rico
BR TR 6' 180 lbs.

Year	Team	Games	BA	SA	AB	H	2B	3B	HR	HR%	R	RBI	BB	SO	SB	PH AB	PH H	PO	A	E	DP	TC/G	FA	G by Pos
1960	STL N	3	.375	.375	8	3	0	0	0	0.0	1	0	0	2	1	1	1	1	3	1	0	1.7	.800	SS-2, 3B-1
1961		10	.244	.333	45	11	4	0	0	0.0	5	5	3	5	0	0	0	16	25	10	6	5.1	.804	SS-10
1962		127	.255	.309	369	94	12	1	2	0.5	47	27	27	47	7	1	0	190	360	25	70	4.5	.957	SS-120, 2B-8, OF-2, 3B-1
1963	PIT N	4	.500	.500	2	1	0	0	0	0.0	0	0	0	1	0	1	1	2	0	1	0	0.8	.667	2B-1
1964		3	.500	.500	2	1	0	0	0	0.0	1	0	1	0	0	2	1	0	0	0	0	0.0	–	
1965	CAL A	40	.247	.338	77	19	4	0	1	1.3	6	3	4	9	0	8	2	34	63	3	9	2.5	.970	2B-23, 3B-9, SS-1
1966	HOU N	4	.000	.000	5	0	0	0	0	0.0	0	0	0	0	0	3	0	1	1	0	0	0.5	1.000	3B-1
1967		77	.282	.368	234	66	10	2	2	0.9	30	15	15	30	1	19	6	93	143	8	27	3.2	.967	2B-30, SS-20, 3B-3
1968		75	.248	.285	165	41	3	0	1	0.6	9	11	4	21	1	25	8	116	103	4	28	3.0	.982	2B-48, 3B-1
1969		46	.259	.321	81	21	5	0	0	0.0	7	9	7	13	2	30	6	34	41	1	12	1.7	.987	2B-16, 3B-1
10 yrs.		389	.260	.323	988	257	38	6	6	0.6	106	70	61	127	12	90	25	487	739	53	152	3.3	.959	SS-153, 2B-126, 3B-17, OF-2

Charlie Gould

GOULD, CHARLES HARVEY
B. Aug. 21, 1847, Cincinnati, Ohio D. Apr. 10, 1917, Flushing, N. Y.
Manager 1875-76.
BR TR 6' 172 lbs.

Year	Team	Games	BA	SA	AB	H	2B	3B	HR	HR%	R	RBI	BB	SO	SB	PH AB	PH H	PO	A	E	DP	TC/G	FA	G by Pos
1876	CIN N	61	.252	.279	258	65	7	0	0	0.0	27	11	6	11	0			584	14	40	28	10.5	.937	1B-61, P-2
1877		24	.275	.319	91	25	2	1	0	0.0	5	13	5	5	0			231	9	20	13	10.8	.923	1B-24, OF-1
2 yrs.		85	.258	.289	349	90	9	1	0	0.0	32	24	11	16	0			815	23	60	41	10.6	.933	1B-85, P-2, OF-1

Nick Goulish

GOULISH, NICHOLAS EDWARD
B. Nov. 13, 1917, Punxsutawney, Pa. D. May 15, 1984, Youngstown, Ohio
BL TL 6'1" 179 lbs.

Year	Team	Games	BA	SA	AB	H	2B	3B	HR	HR%	R	RBI	BB	SO	SB	PH AB	PH H	PO	A	E	DP	TC/G	FA	G by Pos
1944	PHI N	1	.000	.000	1	0	0	0	0	0.0	0	0	0	0	0	1	0	0	0	0	0	0.0	–	
1945		13	.273	.273	11	3	0	0	0	0.0	4	2	1	3	0	9	2	1	0	0	0	0.1	1.000	OF-2
2 yrs.		14	.250	.250	12	3	0	0	0	0.0	4	2	1	3	0	10	2	1	0	0	0	0.1	1.000	OF-2

Claude Gouzzie

GOUZZIE, CLAUDE
B. 1871, Pa. D. Sept. 21, 1907, Denver, Colo.
BR TR 5'9" 170 lbs.

Year	Team	Games	BA	SA	AB	H	2B	3B	HR	HR%	R	RBI	BB	SO	SB	PH AB	PH H	PO	A	E	DP	TC/G	FA	G by Pos
1903	STL A	1	.000	.000	1	0	0	0	0	0.0	0	0	0	0	0			0	1	0	0	1.0	1.000	2B-1

Hank Gowdy

GOWDY, HENRY MORGAN
B. Aug. 24, 1889, Columbus, Ohio D. Aug. 1, 1966, Columbus, Ohio
Manager 1946.
BR TR 6'2" 182 lbs.

Year	Team	Games	BA	SA	AB	H	2B	3B	HR	HR%	R	RBI	BB	SO	SB	PH AB	PH H	PO	A	E	DP	TC/G	FA	G by Pos
1910	NY N	7	.214	.286	14	3	1	0	0	0.0	1	2	2	3	1	2	0	30	3	2	1	5.0	.943	1B-5
1911 2 teams	NY N (4G – .250)				BOS N (29G – .289)																			
" total		33	.287	.376	101	29	5	2	0	0.0	10	16	6	19	2	3	0	273	15	9	9	9.0	.970	1B-28, C-1
1912	BOS N	44	.271	.448	96	26	6	1	3	3.1	16	10	16	13	3	14	3	138	34	9	7	4.1	.950	C-22, 1B-7
1913		3	.600	.800	5	3	1	0	0	0.0	0	2	3	2	0	0	0	9	0	0	0	3.0	1.000	C-2
1914		128	.243	.347	366	89	17	6	3	0.8	42	46	48	40	14	3	1	534	156	22	16	5.6	.969	C-115, 1B-9
1915		118	.247	.332	316	78	15	3	2	0.6	27	30	41	34	10	1	1	460	148	16	11	5.3	.974	C-118
1916		118	.252	.301	349	88	12	1	1	0.3	32	34	24	33	8	2	0	533	158	14	19	6.0	.980	C-116
1917		49	.214	.260	154	33	7	0	0	0.0	12	14	15	13	2	0	0	204	75	9	3	5.9	.969	C-49
1919		78	.279	.338	219	61	8	1	1	0.5	18	20	19	16	5	2	0	240	105	8	11	4.5	.977	C-74, 1B-1
1920		80	.243	.313	214	52	11	2	0	0.0	14	18	20	15	6	5	2	231	104	7	12	4.3	.980	C-74
1921		64	.299	.402	164	49	7	2	2	1.2	17	17	16	11	2	7	3	162	50	4	3	3.4	.981	C-53
1922		92	.317	.389	221	70	11	1	1	0.5	23	27	24	16	2	17	5	210	63	8	7	3.1	.972	C-72, 1B-1
1923 2 teams	BOS N (23G – .125)				NY N (53G – .328)																			
" total		76	.271	.376	170	46	7	4	1	0.6	18	23	36	14	3	12	3	164	30	3	1	2.6	.985	C-58
1924	NY N	87	.325	.445	191	62	9	1	4	2.1	25	37	26	11	1	9	4	223	51	5	8	3.2	.978	C-78
1925		47	.325	.491	114	37	4	3	3	2.6	14	19	12	7	0	6	3	124	26	0	1	3.2	1.000	C-41
1929	BOS N	10	.438	.438	16	7	0	0	0	0.0	1	3	0	2	0	1	0	11	2	0	1	1.3	1.000	C-9
1930		5	.200	.240	25	5	1	0	0	0.0	3	3	1	0								2.3	.972	C-15
17 yrs.		1050	.270	.357	2735	738	122	27	21	0.8	270	322	311	247	59	85	25	3577	1024	117	110	4.5	.975	C-897, 1B-51

WORLD SERIES

Year	Team	Games	BA	SA	AB	H	2B	3B	HR	HR%	R	RBI	BB	SO	SB	PH AB	PH H	PO	A	E	DP	TC/G	FA	G by Pos
1914	BOS N	4	.545	1.273	11	6	3	1	1	9.1	3	4	5	1	1	0	0	31	4	0	1	8.8	1.000	C-4
1923	NY N	3	.000	.000	4	0	0	0	0	0.0	0	0	1	0	0	1	0	7	0	0	1	2.3	1.000	C-2
1924		7	.259	.259	27	7	0	0	0	0.0	4	1	2	2	0	0	0	37	5	1	0	6.1	.977	C-7
3 yrs.		14	.310	.500	42	13	3	1	1	2.4	7	4	8	3	1	1	0	75	9	1	1	6.1	.988	C-13

Billy Grabarkewitz

GRABARKEWITZ, BILLY CORDELL
B. Jan. 18, 1946, Lockhart, Tex.
BR TR 5'10" 165 lbs.

Year	Team	Games	BA	SA	AB	H	2B	3B	HR	HR%	R	RBI	BB	SO	SB	PH AB	PH H	PO	A	E	DP	TC/G	FA	G by Pos
1969	LA N	34	.092	.138	65	6	1	0	0	0.0	4	4	4	19	1	3	0	20	51	3	4	2.2	.959	SS-18, 3B-6, 2B-3
1970		156	.289	.454	529	153	20	8	17	3.2	92	84	95	149	19	2	1	178	367	21	45	3.6	.963	3B-97, SS-50, 2B-20
1971		44	.225	.296	71	16	5	0	0	0.0	9	6	19	16	1	11	3	33	52	0	10	1.9	1.000	2B-13, 3B-10, SS-1
1972		53	.167	.278	144	24	4	0	4	2.8	17	16	18	53	3	5	1	61	84	11	14	2.9	.929	3B-24, 2B-19, SS-2

Year	Team	Games	BA	SA	AB	H	2B	3B	HR	HR%	R	RBI	BB	SO	SB	Pinch Hit AB	Pinch Hit H	PO	A	E	DP	TC/G	FA	G by Pos

Billy Grabarkewitz *continued*

Year	Team	Games	BA	SA	AB	H	2B	3B	HR	HR%	R	RBI	BB	SO	SB	PH AB	PH H	PO	A	E	DP	TC/G	FA	G by Pos
1973	2 teams		CAL A (61G – .163)				PHI N (25G – .288)																		
"	total	86	.205	.333	195	40	8	1	5	2.6	39	16	40	45	5	16	6	93	110	9	30	2.5	.958	2B-38, 3B-14, OF-2, SS-1
1974	2 teams		PHI N (34G – .133)				CHI N (53G – .248)																		
"	total	87	.226	.310	155	35	3	2	1	1.3	28	14	26	38	4	14	2	83	122	8	10	2.4	.962	2B-45, SS-7, 3B-7, OF-5
1975	OAK A	6	.000	.000	2	0	0	0	0	0.0	0	0	0	1	0	2	0	4	1	1	0	1.0	.833	2B-4, DH-1
7 yrs.		466	.236	.364	1161	274	41	12	28	2.4	189	141	202	321	33	53	13	472	787	53	113	2.8	.960	3B-158, 2B-142, SS-79, OF-7, DH-1

Rod Graber

GRABER, RODNEY BLAINE
B. June 20, 1931, Marshallville, Ohio — BL TL 5'11" 175 lbs.

Year	Team	Games	BA	SA	AB	H	2B	3B	HR	HR%	R	RBI	BB	SO	SB	PH AB	PH H	PO	A	E	DP	TC/G	FA	G by Pos
1958	CLE A	4	.125	.125	8	1	0	0	0	0.0	0	0	1	2	0	2	0	4	0	0	0	1.0	1.000	OF-2

Johnny Grabowski

GRABOWSKI, JOHN PATRICK (Nig)
B. Jan. 7, 1900, Ware, Mass. D. May 23, 1946, Albany, N. Y. — BR TR 5'10" 185 lbs.

Year	Team	Games	BA	SA	AB	H	2B	3B	HR	HR%	R	RBI	BB	SO	SB	PH AB	PH H	PO	A	E	DP	TC/G	FA	G by Pos
1924	CHI A	20	.250	.304	56	14	3	0	0	0.0	10	3	2	4	0	0	0	48	22	2	0	3.6	.972	C-19
1925		21	.304	.435	46	14	4	1	0	0.0	5	10	2	4	0	0	0	48	9	1	0	2.8	.983	C-21
1926		48	.262	.311	122	32	1	1	1	0.8	6	11	4	15	0	8	4	128	22	4	0	3.2	.974	C-38, 1B-1
1927	NY A	70	.277	.328	195	54	2	4	0	0.0	29	25	20	15	0	2	0	197	47	4	3	3.5	.984	C-68
1928		75	.238	.297	202	48	7	1	1	0.5	21	21	10	21	0	0	0	265	32	4	8	4.0	.987	C-75
1929		22	.203	.220	59	12	1	0	0	0.0	4	2	3	6	1	0	0	70	12	5	1	4.0	.943	C-22
1931	DET A	40	.235	.324	136	32	7	1	1	0.7	9	14	6	19	1	1	1	160	28	3	5	4.8	.984	C-39
7 yrs.		296	.252	.314	816	206	25	8	3	0.4	84	86	47	84	1	11	5	916	172	23	17	3.8	.979	C-282, 1B-1

WORLD SERIES

Year	Team	Games	BA	SA	AB	H	2B	3B	HR	HR%	R	RBI	BB	SO	SB	PH AB	PH H	PO	A	E	DP	TC/G	FA	G by Pos
1927	NY A	1	.000	.000	2	0	0	0	0	0.0	0	0	0	0	0	0	0	3	0	0	0	3.0	1.000	C-1

Earl Grace

GRACE, ROBERT EARL
B. Feb. 24, 1907, Barlow, Ky. D. Dec. 22, 1980, Phoenix, Ariz. — BL TR 6' 175 lbs.

Year	Team	Games	BA	SA	AB	H	2B	3B	HR	HR%	R	RBI	BB	SO	SB	PH AB	PH H	PO	A	E	DP	TC/G	FA	G by Pos
1929	CHI N	27	.250	.338	80	20	1	0	2	2.5	7	17	9	7	0	0	0	106	18	0	4	4.6	1.000	C-27
1931	2 teams		CHI N (7G – .111)				PIT N (47G – .280)																		
"	total	54	.270	.340	159	43	6	1	1	0.6	10	21	17	6	0	6	0	137	24	4	5	3.1	.976	C-47
1932	PIT N	115	.274	.397	390	107	17	5	7	1.8	41	55	14	23	0	1	0	364	48	1	10	3.6	.998	C-114
1933		93	.289	.371	291	84	13	1	3	1.0	22	44	26	23	0	4	0	305	37	7	6	3.8	.980	C-88
1934		95	.270	.377	289	78	17	1	4	1.4	27	24	20	19	0	10	5	312	27	6	5	3.6	.983	C-83, 1B-1
1935		77	.263	.348	224	59	8	1	3	1.3	19	29	32	17	1	8	3	269	35	3	9	4.0	.990	C-69
1936	PHI N	86	.249	.353	221	55	11	0	4	1.8	24	32	34	20	0	19	2	217	29	6	3	2.9	.976	C-65
1937		80	.211	.345	223	47	10	1	6	2.7	19	29	33	15	0	13	0	275	30	3	10	3.9	.990	C-64
8 yrs.		627	.263	.365	1877	493	83	10	30	1.6	169	251	185	130	1	61	10	1985	248	30	50	3.6	.987	C-557, 1B-1

Joe Grace

GRACE, JOSEPH LaVERNE
B. Jan. 5, 1914, Gorham, Ill. D. Sept. 18, 1969, Murphysboro, Ill. — BL TR 6'1" 180 lbs.

Year	Team	Games	BA	SA	AB	H	2B	3B	HR	HR%	R	RBI	BB	SO	SB	PH AB	PH H	PO	A	E	DP	TC/G	FA	G by Pos
1938	STL A	12	.340	.362	47	16	1	0	0	0.0	7	4	2	3	0	0	0	13	1	1	0	1.3	.933	OF-12
1939		74	.304	.420	207	63	11	2	3	1.4	35	22	19	24	3	15	5	83	9	3	0	1.3	.968	OF-53
1940		80	.258	.402	229	59	14	2	5	2.2	45	25	26	23	2	17	4	102	7	4	1	1.4	.965	OF-51, C-12
1941		115	.309	.428	362	112	17	4	6	1.7	53	60	57	31	1	15	6	184	15	5	1	1.8	.975	OF-88, C-9
1946	2 teams		STL A (48G – .230)				WAS A (77G – .302)																		
"	total	125	.278	.371	482	134	24	6	3	0.6	60	44	40	39	2	7	2	267	10	11	3	2.3	.962	OF-117
1947	WAS A	78	.248	.359	234	58	9	4	3	1.3	25	17	35	15	1	10	2	162	4	4	0	2.2	.976	OF-67
6 yrs.		484	.283	.393	1561	442	76	18	20	1.3	225	172	179	135	9	64	19	811	46	28	5	1.8	.968	OF-388, C-21

Mark Grace

GRACE, MARK EUGENE
B. June 28, 1964, Winston-Salem, N. C. — BL TL 6'2" 190 lbs.

Year	Team	Games	BA	SA	AB	H	2B	3B	HR	HR%	R	RBI	BB	SO	SB	PH AB	PH H	PO	A	E	DP	TC/G	FA	G by Pos
1988	CHI N	134	.296	.403	486	144	23	4	7	1.4	65	57	60	43	3	7	3	1182	87	17	91	9.6	.987	1B-133
1989		142	.314	.457	510	160	28	3	13	2.5	74	79	80	42	14	1	1	1230	126	6	93	9.6	.996	1B-142
2 yrs.		276	.305	.431	996	304	51	7	20	2.0	139	136	140	85	17	8	4	2412	213	23	184	9.6	.991	1B-275

LEAGUE CHAMPIONSHIP SERIES

Year	Team	Games	BA	SA	AB	H	2B	3B	HR	HR%	R	RBI	BB	SO	SB	PH AB	PH H	PO	A	E	DP	TC/G	FA	G by Pos
1989	CHI N	5	.647	1.118	17	11	3	1	1	5.9	3	8	4	1	0	0	0	44	3	0	1	9.4	1.000	1B-5

Mike Grace

GRACE, MICHAEL LEE
B. June 14, 1956, Pontiac, Mich. — BR TR 6' 175 lbs.

Year	Team	Games	BA	SA	AB	H	2B	3B	HR	HR%	R	RBI	BB	SO	SB	PH AB	PH H	PO	A	E	DP	TC/G	FA	G by Pos
1978	CIN N	5	.000	.000	3	0	0	0	0	0.0	0	0	0	2	0	3	0	2	0	0	0	0.4	1.000	3B-2

John Grady

GRADY, JOHN J.
B. June 18, 1860, Lowell, Mass. D. July 15, 1893, Lowell, Mass. — 5'7" 150 lbs.

Year	Team	Games	BA	SA	AB	H	2B	3B	HR	HR%	R	RBI	BB	SO	SB	PH AB	PH H	PO	A	E	DP	TC/G	FA	G by Pos
1884	ALT U	9	.306	.389	36	11	3	0	0	0.0	5		2			0	0	87	3	10	1	11.1	.900	1B-8, OF-1

Mike Grady

GRADY, MICHAEL WILLIAM (Michaelangelo)
B. Dec. 23, 1869, Kennett Square, Pa. D. Dec. 3, 1943, Kennett Square, Pa. — BR TR 5'11" 190 lbs.

Year	Team	Games	BA	SA	AB	H	2B	3B	HR	HR%	R	RBI	BB	SO	SB	PH AB	PH H	PO	A	E	DP	TC/G	FA	G by Pos
1894	PHI N	60	.363	.516	190	69	13	8	0	0.0	45	40	14	13	3	3	2	175	33	23	11	3.9	.900	C-44, 1B-11, OF-2
1895		46	.325	.390	123	40	3	1	1	0.8	21	23	14	8	5	2	1	109	11	12	2	2.9	.909	C-38, OF-5, 3B-1, 1B-1
1896		72	.318	.471	242	77	20	7	1	0.4	49	44	16	11	10	4	1	173	68	20	12	3.6	.923	C-61, 3B-7
1897	2 teams		PHI N (4G – .154)				STL N (83G – .280)																		
"	total	87	.275	.388	335	92	11	3	7	2.1	49	55	27			7	1	809	52	23	54	10.2	.974	1B-83, C-3, OF-1
1898	NY N	93	.296	.429	287	85	19	5	3	1.0	64	49	38			20	2	321	74	34	7	4.6	.921	C-57, OF-30, 1B-7, SS-3
1899		86	.334	.463	311	104	18	8	2	0.6	47	54	29			20	0	183	140	29	15	4.1	.918	C-43, 3B-35, OF-4, 1B-4
1900		83	.219	.283	251	55	8	4	0	0.0	26	27	34			9	6	247	106	37	18	4.7	.905	C-41, 1B-12, SS-11, 3B-7, OF-5, 2B-2
1901	WAS A	94	.285	.470	347	99	17	10	9	2.6	57	56	27			14	2	688	83	26	38	8.5	.967	1B-59, C-30, OF-3
1904	STL N	101	.313	.474	323	101	15	11	4	1.5	44	43	31			6	7	421	93	20	11	5.3	.963	C-77, 1B-11, 2B-3, 3B-1
1905		100	.286	.434	311	89	20	7	4	1.3	41	41	15			15	9	468	96	26	12	5.9	.956	C-71, 1B-20

Year	Team		Games	BA	SA	AB	H	2B	3B	HR	HR%	R	RBI	BB	SO	SB	Pinch Hit AB	Pinch Hit H	PO	A	E	DP	TC/G	FA	G by Pos

Mike Grady *continued*

1906			97	.250	.343	280	70	11	3	3	1.1	33	27	48		5	5	1	414	85	11	16	5.3	.978	C-60, 1B-38
11 yrs.			919	.294	.425	3000	881	155	67	35	1.2	486	459	311	40	114	42	10	4008	841	261	196	5.6	.949	C-525, 1B-246, 3B-51, OF-50, SS-14, 2B-5

Fred Graff

GRAFF, FREDERICK GOTTLIEB
B. Aug. 25, 1889, Canton, Ohio   D. Oct. 4, 1979, Chattanooga, Tenn.

BR TR 5'10½" 164 lbs.

| 1913 | STL | A | 4 | .400 | .600 | 5 | 2 | 1 | 0 | 0 | 0.0 | 1 | 2 | 3 | 3 | | 0 | 0 | 0 | 4 | 0 | 1 | 1.0 | 1.000 | 3B-4 |

Louis Graff

GRAFF, LOUIS GEORGE (Chappie)
B. July 25, 1866, Philadelphia, Pa.   D. Apr. 16, 1955, Bryn Mawr, Pa.

TR

| 1890 | SYR | AA | 1 | .400 | .600 | 5 | 2 | 1 | 0 | 0 | 0.0 | 0 | | 0 | 0 | | 0 | 0 | 1 | 0 | 2 | 0 | 3.0 | .333 | C-1 |

Milt Graff

GRAFF, MILTON EDWARD
B. Dec. 30, 1930, Jefferson Center, Pa.

BL TR 5'7½" 158 lbs.

1957	KC	A	56	.181	.245	155	28	4	3	0	0.0	16	10	15	10	2	1	1	110	127	3	36	4.3	.988	2B-53
1958			5	.000	.000	1	0	0	0	0	0.0	0	0	0	0	0	1	0	1	0	0	0	0.2	1.000	2B-1
2 yrs.			61	.179	.244	156	28	4	3	0	0.0	16	10	15	10	2	2	1	111	127	3	36	4.0	.988	2B-54

Barney Graham

GRAHAM, BARNEY
B. Philadelphia, Pa.   D. Dec. 31, 1896, Mobile, Ala.

| 1889 | PHI | AA | 4 | .167 | .167 | 18 | 3 | 0 | 0 | 0 | 0.0 | 0 | 0 | 0 | 0 | 0 | 0 | 0 | 2 | 12 | 1 | 1 | 3.8 | .933 | 3B-4 |

Bernie Graham

GRAHAM, BERNARD
B. 1860, Beloit, Wis.   D. Oct. 31, 1886, Mobile, Ala.

| 1884 | 2 teams | | | | CHI | U | (1G – .200) | | | | BAL | U | (41G – .269) | | | | | | | | | | | | |
| " | total | | 42 | .267 | .331 | 172 | 46 | 11 | 0 | 0 | 0.0 | 23 | | 2 | | | 0 | | 75 | 10 | 17 | 3 | 2.4 | .833 | OF-41, 1B-1 |

Bert Graham

GRAHAM, BERT
B. Apr. 3, 1886, Tilton, Ill.   D. June 19, 1971, Cottonwood, Ariz.

BB TR 5'11½" 187 lbs.

| 1910 | STL | A | 8 | .115 | .269 | 26 | 3 | 2 | 1 | 0 | 0.0 | 1 | 5 | 1 | | 0 | 1 | 0 | 51 | 11 | 3 | 3 | 8.1 | .954 | 1B-5, 2B-2 |

Charlie Graham

GRAHAM, CHARLES HENRY
B. Apr. 25, 1878, Santa Clara, Calif.   D. Aug. 29, 1948, San Francisco, Calif.

BR TR 5'11" 180 lbs.

| 1906 | BOS | A | 30 | .233 | .278 | 90 | 21 | 1 | 0 | 1 | 1.1 | 10 | 12 | 10 | | 1 | 3 | 0 | 130 | 54 | 7 | 2 | 6.4 | .963 | C-27 |

Dan Graham

GRAHAM, DANIEL JAY
B. July 19, 1954, Ray, Ariz.

BL TR 6'1" 205 lbs.

1979	MIN	A	2	.000	.000	4	0	0	0	0	0.0	0	0	0	1	0	1	0	0	0	0	0	0.0	–	DH-1
1980	BAL	A	86	.278	.481	266	74	7	1	15	5.6	32	54	14	40	0	1	0	333	42	7	5	4.4	.982	C-73, 3B-9, DH-2
1981			55	.176	.239	142	25	3	0	2	1.4	7	11	13	32	0	8	0	141	24	5	2	3.1	.971	C-40, DH-6, 3B-4
3 yrs.			143	.240	.393	412	99	10	1	17	4.1	39	65	27	72	0	10	0	474	66	12	7	3.9	.978	C-113, 3B-13, DH-9

Jack Graham

GRAHAM, JOHN BERNARD
Son of Peaches Graham.
B. Dec. 24, 1916, Minneapolis, Minn.

BL TL 6'2" 200 lbs.

1946	2 teams				BKN	N	(2G – .200)				NY	N	(100G – .219)												
"	total		102	.218	.422	275	60	6	4	14	5.1	34	47	23	37	1	25	4	181	12	6	0	2.0	.970	OF-62, 1B-9
1949	STL	A	137	.238	.430	500	119	22	1	24	4.8	71	79	61	62	0	1	1	1118	87	19	120	8.9	.984	1B-136
2 yrs.			239	.231	.427	775	179	28	5	38	4.9	105	126	84	99	1	26	5	1299	99	25	120	6.0	.982	1B-145, OF-62

Lee Graham

GRAHAM, LEE WILLARD
B. Sept. 22, 1959, Summerfield, Fla.

BL TL 5'10" 170 lbs.

| 1983 | BOS | A | 5 | .000 | .000 | 6 | 0 | 0 | 0 | 0 | 0.0 | 2 | 1 | 0 | 0 | 0 | 0 | 0 | 6 | 1 | 0 | 0 | 1.4 | 1.000 | OF-3 |

Moonlight Graham

GRAHAM, ARCHIBALD WRIGHT
B. Nov. 9, 1876, Fayetteville, N. C.   D. Aug. 25, 1965, Chisholm, Minn.

BL TR 5'10½" 170 lbs.

| 1905 | NY | N | 1 | – | – | 0 | 0 | 0 | 0 | 0 | 0.0 | 0 | 0 | 0 | 0 | 0 | 0 | 0 | 0 | 0 | 0 | 0 | 0.0 | – | OF-1 |

Peaches Graham

GRAHAM, GEORGE FREDERICK
Father of Jack Graham.
B. Mar. 23, 1877, Aledo, Ill.   D. July 25, 1939, Long Beach, Calif.

BR TR 5'9" 180 lbs.

1902	CLE	A	2	.333	.333	6	2	0	0	0	0.0	0	1	1		0	1	0	2	5	0	0	3.5	1.000	2B-1
1903	CHI	N	1	.000	.000	2	0	0	0	0	0.0	0	0	0		0	0	0	0	3	0	0	3.0	1.000	P-1
1908	BOS	N	75	.274	.298	215	59	5	0	0	0.0	22	22	23		4	8	2	249	86	17	6	4.7	.952	C-62, 2B-5
1909			92	.240	.285	267	64	6	3	0	0.0	27	17	24		7	10	1	200	119	23	15	3.7	.933	C-76, OF-6, SS-1, 3B-1
1910			110	.282	.340	291	82	13	2	0	0.0	31	21	33	15	5	20	7	322	135	17	11	4.3	.964	C-87, 3B-2, OF-1, 1B-1
1911	2 teams				BOS	N	(33G – .273)				CHI	N	(36G – .239)												
"	total		69	.258	.327	159	41	9	1	0	0.0	13	20	25	13	4	13	3	182	56	16	7	3.7	.937	C-54
1912	PHI	N	24	.288	.356	59	17	1	0	1	1.7	6	4	8	5	1	2	2	77	25	6	0	4.5	.944	C-19
7 yrs.			373	.265	.314	999	265	34	6	1	0.1	99	85	114	33	21	54	15	1032	429	79	39	4.1	.949	C-298, OF-7, 2B-6, 3B-3, SS-1, 1B-1, P-1

Roy Graham

GRAHAM, ROY VINCENT
B. Feb. 22, 1895, San Francisco, Calif.   D. Apr. 26, 1933, Manila, Philippines

BR TR 5'10½" 175 lbs.

1922	CHI	A	5	.000	.000	3	0	0	0	0	0.0	0	0	0	0	0	1	0	3	0	0	0	0.6	1.000	C-3
1923			36	.195	.220	82	16	2	0	0	0.0	3	6	9	6	0	2	0	78	15	5	1	2.7	.949	C-33
2 yrs.			41	.188	.212	85	16	2	0	0	0.0	3	6	9	6	0	3	0	81	15	5	1	2.5	.950	C-36

Year	Team	Games	BA	SA	AB	H	2B	3B	HR	HR%	R	RBI	BB	SO	SB	Pinch Hit AB	Pinch Hit H	PO	A	E	DP	TC/G	FA	G by Pos

Skinny Graham

GRAHAM, ARTHUR WILLIAM
B. Aug. 12, 1909, Somerville, Mass. D. July 10, 1967, Cambridge, Mass.
BL TR 5'7" 181 lbs.

Year	Team	Games	BA	SA	AB	H	2B	3B	HR	HR%	R	RBI	BB	SO	SB	PH AB	PH H	PO	A	E	DP	TC/G	FA	G by Pos
1934	BOS A	13	.234	.319	47	11	2	1	0	0.0	7	3	6	13	2	0	0	20	1	0	0	1.6	1.000	OF-13
1935		8	.300	.300	10	3	0	0	0	0.0	1	1	1	3	1	3	1	2	0	0	0	0.3	1.000	OF-2
2 yrs.		21	.246	.316	57	14	2	1	0	0.0	8	4	7	16	3	3	1	22	1	0	0	1.1	1.000	OF-15

Tiny Graham

GRAHAM, DAWSON FRANCIS
B. Sept. 9, 1892, Nashville, Tenn. D. Dec. 29, 1962, Nashville, Tenn.
BR TR 6'2" 185 lbs.

Year	Team	Games	BA	SA	AB	H	2B	3B	HR	HR%	R	RBI	BB	SO	SB	PH AB	PH H	PO	A	E	DP	TC/G	FA	G by Pos
1914	CIN N	25	.230	.246	61	14	1	0	0	0.0	5	3	3	10	1	0	0	187	9	8	14	8.2	.961	1B-25

Wayne Graham

GRAHAM, WAYNE LEON
B. Apr. 6, 1937, Yoakum, Tex.
BR TR 6' 200 lbs.

Year	Team	Games	BA	SA	AB	H	2B	3B	HR	HR%	R	RBI	BB	SO	SB	PH AB	PH H	PO	A	E	DP	TC/G	FA	G by Pos
1963	PHI N	10	.182	.182	22	4	0	0	0	0.0	1	0	1	3	0	3	0	6	0	0	0	0.7	.857	OF-6
1964	NY N	20	.091	.121	33	3	1	0	0	0.0	1	0	0	5	0	12	1	4	7	0	0	0.6	1.000	3B-11
2 yrs.		30	.127	.145	55	7	1	0	0	0.0	2	0	3	6	0	15	1	10	7	1	0	0.6	.944	3B-11, OF-6

Alex Grammas

GRAMMAS, ALEXANDER PETER
B. Apr. 3, 1926, Birmingham, Ala.
Manager 1969, 1976-77.
BR TR 6' 175 lbs.

Year	Team	Games	BA	SA	AB	H	2B	3B	HR	HR%	R	RBI	BB	SO	SB	PH AB	PH H	PO	A	E	DP	TC/G	FA	G by Pos
1954	STL N	142	.264	.342	401	106	17	4	2	0.5	57	29	40	29	6	0	0	253	432	24	100	5.0	.966	SS-142, 3B-1
1955		128	.240	.328	366	88	19	2	3	0.8	32	25	33	36	4	1	0	235	340	19	76	4.6	.968	SS-126
1956 2 teams	STL N (6G – .250)				CIN N (77G – .243)																			
" total		83	.243	.316	152	37	11	0	0	0.0	18	17	17	20	0	2	1	60	105	5	12	2.0	.971	3B-58, SS-17, 2B-5
1957	CIN N	73	.303	.343	99	30	4	0	0	0.0	14	8	10	6	1	2	0	60	75	3	10	1.9	.978	SS-42, 2B-20, 3B-9
1958		105	.218	.255	216	47	8	0	0	0.0	25	12	34	24	2	1	0	126	174	6	32	2.9	.980	SS-61, 3B-38, 2B-14
1959	STL N	131	.269	.342	368	99	14	2	3	0.8	43	30	38	26	3	1	1	216	373	22	80	4.7	.964	SS-130
1960		102	.245	.337	196	48	4	1	4	2.0	20	17	12	15	0	7	2	102	171	9	33	2.8	.968	SS-40, 2B-38, 3B-13
1961		89	.212	.282	170	36	10	1	0	0.0	23	21	19	21	1	5	0	112	182	10	40	3.4	.967	SS-65, 2B-18, 3B-3
1962 2 teams	STL N (21G – .111)				CHI N (23G – .233)																			
" total		44	.205	.244	78	16	3	0	0	0.0	3	4	3	13	1	4	0	34	66	2	14	2.3	.980	SS-29, 2B-5, 3B-1
1963	CHI N	16	.185	.185	27	5	0	0	0	0.0	1	0	0	3	0	3	0	8	13	1	1	1.4	.955	SS-13
10 yrs.		913	.247	.317	2073	512	90	10	12	0.6	236	163	206	193	17	26	5	1206	1931	101	398	3.5	.969	SS-665, 3B-123, 2B-100

Jack Graney

GRANEY, JOHN GLADSTONE
B. June 10, 1886, St. Thomas, Ont., Canada D. Apr. 20, 1978, Louisiana, Mo.
BL TL 5'9" 180 lbs.

Year	Team	Games	BA	SA	AB	H	2B	3B	HR	HR%	R	RBI	BB	SO	SB	PH AB	PH H	PO	A	E	DP	TC/G	FA	G by Pos
1908	CLE A	2	–	–	0	0	0	0	0	0.0	0	0	0		0	0	0	0	0	0	0	0.0	–	P-2
1910		116	.236	.311	454	107	13	9	1	0.2	62	31	37		18	2	1	209	14	12	5	2.0	.949	OF-114
1911		146	.269	.342	527	142	25	5	1	0.2	84	45	66		21	4	2	258	22	22	5	2.1	.927	OF-142
1912		78	.242	.307	264	64	13	2	0	0.0	44	20	50		9	3	0	148	11	7	5	2.1	.958	OF-75
1913		148	.267	.366	517	138	18	12	3	0.6	56	68	48	55	27	3	0	275	16	9	5	2.0	.970	OF-148
1914		130	.265	.352	460	122	17	10	1	0.2	63	39	67	46	20	3	2	274	15	20	0	2.4	.935	OF-127
1915		116	.260	.351	404	105	20	7	1	0.2	42	56	59	29	12	1	0	227	17	7	1	2.2	.972	OF-115
1916		155	.241	.384	589	142	41	14	5	0.8	106	54	102	72	10	1	1	309	22	14	5	2.2	.959	OF-154
1917		146	.228	.325	535	122	29	7	3	0.6	87	35	94	49	16	1	0	288	14	13	6	2.2	.959	OF-145
1918		72	.237	.322	177	42	7	4	0	0.0	27	9	29	13	3	18	7	77	2	2	0	1.1	.975	OF-45
1919		128	.234	.323	461	108	22	8	1	0.2	79	30	105	39	7	1	1	281	13	12	2	2.4	.961	OF-125
1920		62	.296	.382	152	45	11	1	0	0.0	31	13	27	21	4	12	6	76	4	5	0	1.4	.941	OF-47
1921		68	.299	.383	107	32	3	0	2	1.9	19	18	20	9	1	27	5	42	0	3	0	0.7	.933	OF-32
1922		37	.155	.155	58	9	0	0	0	0.0	6	2	9	12	0	19	1	24	1	4	0	0.8	.862	OF-13
14 yrs.		1404	.250	.342	4705	1178	219	79	18	0.4	706	420	713	345	148	92	29	2488	151	130	34	2.0	.953	OF-1282, P-2

WORLD SERIES

Year	Team	Games	BA	SA	AB	H	2B	3B	HR	HR%	R	RBI	BB	SO	SB	PH AB	PH H	PO	A	E	DP	TC/G	FA	G by Pos
1920	CLE A	3	.000	.000	3	0	0	0	0	0.0	0	0	0	2	0	3	0	0	0	0	0	0.0	–	OF-2

Eddie Grant

GRANT, EDWARD LESLIE (Harvard Eddie)
B. May 21, 1883, Franklin, Mass. D. Oct. 5, 1918, Argonne, France
BL TR 5'11½" 168 lbs.

Year	Team	Games	BA	SA	AB	H	2B	3B	HR	HR%	R	RBI	BB	SO	SB	PH AB	PH H	PO	A	E	DP	TC/G	FA	G by Pos
1905	CLE A	2	.375	.375	8	3	0	0	0	0.0	1	0	0		0	0	0	1	4	1	0	3.0	.833	2B-2
1907	PHI N	74	.243	.280	268	65	4	3	0	0.0	26	19	10		10	0	0	106	145	23	6	3.7	.916	3B-74
1908		147	.244	.293	598	146	13	8	0	0.0	69	32	35		27	0	0	228	310	42	24	3.9	.928	3B-134, SS-13
1909		154	.269	.315	631	170	18	4	1	0.2	75	37	35		28	0	0	184	310	22	18	3.4	.957	3B-154
1910		152	.268	.316	579	155	15	5	1	0.2	70	67	39	54	25	0	0	193	256	31	22	3.2	.935	3B-152
1911	CIN N	136	.223	.286	458	102	12	7	0	0.2	49	53	51	47	28	0	0	178	234	27	23	3.2	.938	3B-122, SS-11
1912		96	.239	.294	255	61	6	1	2	0.8	37	20	18	27	11	5	1	119	192	18	22	3.4	.945	SS-56, 3B-15
1913 2 teams	CIN N (27G – .213)				NY N (27G – .200)																			
" total		54	.211	.228	114	24	2	0	0	0.0	20	10	13	12	8	5	1	27	59	6	5	1.7	.935	3B-31, 2B-3, SS-1
1914	NY N	88	.277	.309	282	78	7	1	0	0.0	34	29	23	21	11	2	0	97	191	23	16	3.5	.926	3B-52, SS-21, 2B-16
1915		57	.208	.229	192	40	2	1	0	0.0	18	10	9	20	5	32	7	54	79	4	3	2.4	.971	3B-55, SS-1, 1B-1
10 yrs.		960	.249	.295	3385	844	79	30	5	0.1	399	277	233	181	153	44	9	1187	1780	197	139	3.3	.938	3B-789, SS-103, 2B-30, 1B-1

WORLD SERIES

Year	Team	Games	BA	SA	AB	H	2B	3B	HR	HR%	R	RBI	BB	SO	SB	PH AB	PH H	PO	A	E	DP	TC/G	FA	G by Pos
1913	NY N	2	.000	.000	1	0	0	0	0	0.0	1	0	1	0	0	1	0	0	0	0	0	0.0	–	

Jimmy Grant

GRANT, JAMES CHARLES
B. Oct. 6, 1918, Racine, Wis. D. July 8, 1970, Rochester, Minn.
BL TR 5'8" 166 lbs.

Year	Team	Games	BA	SA	AB	H	2B	3B	HR	HR%	R	RBI	BB	SO	SB	PH AB	PH H	PO	A	E	DP	TC/G	FA	G by Pos
1942	CHI A	12	.167	.250	36	6	1	1	0	0.0	0	1	5	6	0	1	0	15	19	2	3	3.0	.944	3B-10
1943 2 teams	CHI A (58G – .259)				CLE A (15G – .136)																			
" total		73	.247	.370	219	54	11	2	4	1.8	26	23	22	41	4	19	2	46	128	20	11	2.7	.897	3B-56
1944	CLE A	61	.273	.404	99	27	4	3	1	1.0	12	12	11	20	1	32	5	44	51	7	6	1.7	.931	2B-20, 3B-4
3 yrs.		146	.246	.367	354	87	16	6	5	1.4	38	36	38	67	5	52	7	105	198	29	20	2.3	.913	3B-70, 2B-20

Year	Team	Games	BA	SA	AB	H	2B	3B	HR	HR%	R	RBI	BB	SO	SB	Pinch Hit AB	H	PO	A	E	DP	TC/G	FA	G by Pos

Tom Grant

GRANT, THOMAS RAYMOND — BL TR 6'2" 185 lbs.
B. May 28, 1957, Worcester, Mass.

Year	Team	Games	BA	SA	AB	H	2B	3B	HR	HR%	R	RBI	BB	SO	SB	PH AB	PH H	PO	A	E	DP	TC/G	FA	G by Pos
1983	CHI N	16	.150	.200	20	3	1	0	0	0.0	2	2	3	4	0	5	0	6	1	0	0	0.4	1.000	OF-10

George Grantham

GRANTHAM, GEORGE FARLEY (Boots) — BL TR 5'10" 170 lbs.
B. May 20, 1900, Galena, Kans. D. Mar. 16, 1954, Kingman, Ariz.

Year	Team	Games	BA	SA	AB	H	2B	3B	HR	HR%	R	RBI	BB	SO	SB	PH AB	PH H	PO	A	E	DP	TC/G	FA	G by Pos
1922	CHI N	7	.174	.304	23	4	1	1	0	0.0	3	3	1	2	2	1	0	5	4	0	1	1.3	1.000	3B-5
1923		152	.281	.414	570	160	36	8	8	1.4	81	70	71	**92**	43	2	0	374	518	55	90	6.2	.942	2B-150
1924		127	.316	.458	469	148	19	6	12	2.6	85	60	55	**63**	21	2	0	277	442	48	78	6.0	.937	2B-118, 3B-6
1925	PIT N	114	.326	.493	359	117	24	6	8	2.2	74	52	50	29	14	9	1	925	44	11	96	8.6	.989	1B-102
1926		141	.318	.490	449	143	27	13	8	1.8	66	70	60	42	6	6	2	1203	66	13	106	9.1	.990	1B-132
1927		151	.305	.454	531	162	33	11	8	1.5	96	66	74	39	9	0	0	526	375	35	87	6.2	.963	2B-124, 1B-29
1928		124	.323	.486	440	142	24	9	10	2.3	93	85	59	37	9	4	0	1118	73	17	84	9.7	.986	1B-119, 3B-1, 2B-1
1929		110	.307	.533	349	107	23	10	12	3.4	85	90	93	38	10	5	0	301	244	17	60	5.1	.970	2B-76, OF-19, 1B-12
1930		146	.324	.534	552	179	34	14	18	3.3	120	99	81	66	5	1	0	357	492	36	88	6.1	.959	2B-141, 1B-4
1931		127	.305	.452	465	142	26	6	10	2.2	91	46	71	50	5	4	0	856	169	35	101	8.3	.967	1B-78, 2B-51
1932	CIN N	126	.292	.412	493	144	29	6	6	1.2	81	39	56	40	4	0	0	373	352	28	52	6.0	.963	2B-115, 1B-10
1933		87	.204	.327	260	53	14	3	4	1.5	32	28	38	21	4	7	2	274	196	19	42	5.6	.961	2B-72, 1B-17
1934	NY N	32	.241	.414	29	7	2	0	1	3.4	5	4	8	6	0	21	6	22	2	0	1	0.8	1.000	2B-4, 1B-2
13 yrs.		1444	.302	.461	4989	1508	292	93	105	2.1	912	712	717	526	132	62	11	6611	2977	314	886	6.9	.968	2B-848, 1B-507, OF-19, 3B-14

WORLD SERIES

Year	Team	Games	BA	SA	AB	H	2B	3B	HR	HR%	R	RBI	BB	SO	SB	PH AB	PH H	PO	A	E	DP	TC/G	FA	G by Pos
1925	PIT N	5	.133	.133	15	2	0	0	0	0.0	0	0	0	3	1	1	0	42	6	0	3	9.6	1.000	1B-4
1927		3	.364	.455	11	4	1	0	0	0.0	0	0	0	1	0	0	0	6	7	1	1	4.7	.929	2B-3
2 yrs.		8	.231	.269	26	6	1	0	0	0.0	0	0	0	4	1	1	0	48	13	1	4	7.8	.984	1B-4, 2B-3

Mickey Grasso

GRASSO, NEWTON MICHAEL — BR TR 6' 195 lbs.
B. May 10, 1920, Newark, N.J. D. Oct. 15, 1975, Miami, Fla.

Year	Team	Games	BA	SA	AB	H	2B	3B	HR	HR%	R	RBI	BB	SO	SB	PH AB	PH H	PO	A	E	DP	TC/G	FA	G by Pos
1946	NY N	7	.136	.136	22	3	0	0	0	0.0	1	1	0	3	0	0	0	24	5	1	0	4.3	.967	C-7
1950	WAS A	75	.287	.333	195	56	4	1	1	0.5	25	22	25	31	1	6	1	238	38	17	6	3.9	.942	C-69
1951		52	.206	.240	175	36	3	0	1	0.6	16	14	14	17	0	4	0	182	26	7	6	4.1	.967	C-49
1952		115	.216	.241	361	78	9	0	0	0.0	22	27	29	36	1	1	0	485	64	17	4	4.9	.970	C-114
1953		61	.209	.276	196	41	7	0	2	1.0	13	22	9	20	0	2	0	219	24	4	4	4.0	.984	C-59
1954	CLE A	4	.333	.833	6	2	0	0	1	16.7	1	1	1	1	0	0	0	9	1	2	0	3.0	.833	C-4
1955	NY N	8	.000	.000	2	0	0	0	0	0.0	0	0	3	0	0	0	0	9	0	1	0	1.3	.900	C-8
7 yrs.		322	.226	.268	957	216	23	1	5	0.5	78	87	81	108	2	13	1	1166	158	49	20	4.3	.964	C-310

WORLD SERIES

Year	Team	Games	BA	SA	AB	H	2B	3B	HR	HR%	R	RBI	BB	SO	SB	PH AB	PH H	PO	A	E	DP	TC/G	FA	G by Pos
1954	CLE A	1	—	—	0	0	0	0	0	—	0	0	0	0	0	0	0	1	0	0	0	1.0	1.000	C-1

Lew Graulich

GRAULICH, LEWIS
B. Camden, N.J. Deceased.

Year	Team	Games	BA	SA	AB	H	2B	3B	HR	HR%	R	RBI	BB	SO	SB	PH AB	PH H	PO	A	E	DP	TC/G	FA	G by Pos
1891	PHI N	7	.308	.308	26	8	0	0	0	0.0	2	3	1	2	0	0	0	47	3	9	1	8.4	.847	C-4, 1B-3

Frank Graves

GRAVES, FRANK M. — 6' 163 lbs.
B. Nov. 2, 1860, Cincinnati, Ohio Deceased.

Year	Team	Games	BA	SA	AB	H	2B	3B	HR	HR%	R	RBI	BB	SO	SB	PH AB	PH H	PO	A	E	DP	TC/G	FA	G by Pos
1886	STL N	43	.152	.167	138	21	2	0	0	0.0	7	9	7	48		0	0	227	77	41	3	8.0	.881	C-41, OF-3, P-1

Joe Graves

GRAVES, JOSEPH EBENEZER
Brother of Sid Graves. — BL TR 5'10" 160 lbs.
B. Feb. 27, 1906, Marblehead, Mass. D. Dec. 22, 1980, Salem, Mass.

Year	Team	Games	BA	SA	AB	H	2B	3B	HR	HR%	R	RBI	BB	SO	SB	PH AB	PH H	PO	A	E	DP	TC/G	FA	G by Pos
1926	CHI N	2	.000	.000	5	0	0	0	0	0.0	1	0	1	0	0	0	0	0	1	3	1	2.0	.250	3B-2

Sid Graves

GRAVES, SAMUEL SIDNEY (Whitey)
Brother of Joe Graves. — BR TR 6' 170 lbs.
B. Nov. 30, 1901, Marblehead, Mass. D. Dec. 26, 1983, Biddeford, Me.

Year	Team	Games	BA	SA	AB	H	2B	3B	HR	HR%	R	RBI	BB	SO	SB	PH AB	PH H	PO	A	E	DP	TC/G	FA	G by Pos
1927	BOS N	7	.250	.400	20	5	1	0	0	0.0	5	2	1	1	1	1	0	10	2	2	0	2.0	.857	OF-5

Dick Gray

GRAY, RICHARD BENJAMIN — BR TR 5'11" 165 lbs.
B. July 11, 1931, Jefferson, Pa.

Year	Team	Games	BA	SA	AB	H	2B	3B	HR	HR%	R	RBI	BB	SO	SB	PH AB	PH H	PO	A	E	DP	TC/G	FA	G by Pos
1958	LA N	58	.249	.472	197	49	1	6	9	4.6	25	30	19	30	1	4	2	56	139	15	18	3.6	.929	3B-55
1959	2 teams					LA N (21G – .154)				STL N (36G – .314)														
"	total	57	.233	.340	103	24	6	0	3	2.9	17	10	12	20	3	25	5	16	37	3	5	1.0	.946	3B-17, SS-13, 2B-2, OF-1
1960	STL N	9	.000	.000	5	0	0	0	0	0.0	1	0	2	2	0	3	0	2	5	0	2	0.8	1.000	2B-4, 3B-1
3 yrs.		124	.239	.420	305	73	7	6	12	3.9	43	41	33	52	4	32	7	74	181	18	25	2.2	.934	3B-73, SS-13, 2B-6, OF-1

Gary Gray

GRAY, GARY GEORGE — BR TR 6' 187 lbs.
B. Sept. 21, 1952, New Orleans, La.

Year	Team	Games	BA	SA	AB	H	2B	3B	HR	HR%	R	RBI	BB	SO	SB	PH AB	PH H	PO	A	E	DP	TC/G	FA	G by Pos
1977	TEX A	1	.000	.000	2	0	0	0	0	0.0	0	1	0	1	0	0	0	0	0	0	0	0.0	—	OF-1
1978		17	.240	.380	50	12	1	0	2	4.0	4	6	1	12	1	5	1	0	0	0	0	0.0	—	DH-11
1979		16	.238	.238	42	10	0	0	0	0.0	4	1	2	8	1	5	2	0	0	0	0	0.0	—	DH-13
1980	CLE A	28	.148	.278	54	8	1	0	2	3.7	4	4	3	13	0	12	1	16	2	0	1	0.6	1.000	DH-9, OF-6, 1B-6
1981	SEA A	69	.245	.476	208	51	7	1	13	6.3	27	31	4	44	2	19	5	281	16	2	34	4.3	.993	1B-34, DH-15, OF-4
1982		80	.257	.401	269	69	14	2	7	2.6	26	29	24	59	1	7	2	476	31	8	36	6.4	.984	1B-60, DH-14
6 yrs.		211	.240	.402	625	150	23	3	24	3.8	65	71	34	137	5	48	11	773	49	10	71	3.9	.988	1B-100, DH-62, OF-11

Jim Gray

GRAY, JAMES W. — TR
B. Aug. 7, 1862, Pittsburgh, Pa. D. Jan. 31, 1938, Pittsburgh, Pa.

Year	Team	Games	BA	SA	AB	H	2B	3B	HR	HR%	R	RBI	BB	SO	SB	PH AB	PH H	PO	A	E	DP	TC/G	FA	G by Pos
1884	PIT AA	1	.500	.500	2	1	0	0	0	0.0	0		0			0		0	2	2	0	4.0	.500	3B-1

Lorenzo Gray

GRAY, LORENZO
B. Mar. 4, 1958, Mound Bayou, Miss. — BR TR 6'1" 180 lbs.

Year	Team	Games	BA	SA	AB	H	2B	3B	HR	HR%	R	RBI	BB	SO	SB	Pinch Hit AB	Pinch Hit H	PO	A	E	DP	TC/G	FA	G by Pos
1982	CHI A	17	.286	.321	28	8	1	0	0	0.0	4	0	2	4	1	1	0	9	10	3	2	1.3	.864	3B-16
1983		41	.179	.256	78	14	3	0	1	1.3	18	4	8	16	1	3	1	17	46	4	3	1.6	.940	3B-31, DH-7
2 yrs.		58	.208	.274	106	22	4	0	1	0.9	22	4	10	20	2	4	1	26	56	7	5	1.5	.921	3B-47, DH-7

Milt Gray

GRAY, MILTON MARSHALL
B. Feb. 21, 1914, Louisville, Ky. D. June 30, 1969, Quincy, Fla. — BR TR 6'1" 170 lbs.

Year	Team	Games	BA	SA	AB	H	2B	3B	HR	HR%	R	RBI	BB	SO	SB	Pinch Hit AB	Pinch Hit H	PO	A	E	DP	TC/G	FA	G by Pos
1937	WAS A	2	.000	.000	6	0	0	0	0	0.0	0	0	0	1	0	0	0	10	0	0	0	5.0	1.000	C-2

Pete Gray

GRAY, PETER
Born Peter J. Wyshner.
B. Mar. 6, 1915, Nanticoke, Pa. — BL TL 6'1" 169 lbs.

Year	Team	Games	BA	SA	AB	H	2B	3B	HR	HR%	R	RBI	BB	SO	SB	Pinch Hit AB	Pinch Hit H	PO	A	E	DP	TC/G	FA	G by Pos
1945	STL A	77	.218	.261	234	51	6	2	0	0.0	26	13	13	11	5	12	1	162	3	7	1	2.2	.959	OF-61

Reddy Gray

GRAY, JAMES D.
Deceased. — TR

1890 2 teams PIT P (2G — .222) PIT N (1G — .000)

Year	Team	Games	BA	SA	AB	H	2B	3B	HR	HR%	R	RBI	BB	SO	SB	Pinch Hit AB	Pinch Hit H	PO	A	E	DP	TC/G	FA	G by Pos
"	total	3	.167	.417	12	2	0	0	1	8.3	3	3	0	3	0	0	0	10	7	6	1	7.7	.739	2B-2, SS-1
1893	PIT N	2	.444	.556	9	4	1	0	0	0.0	0	2	0	1	0	0	0	3	1	1	0	2.5	.800	SS-2
2 yrs.		5	.286	.476	21	6	1	0	1	4.8	3	5	0	4	0	0	0	13	8	7	1	5.6	.750	SS-3, 2B-2

Stan Gray

GRAY, STANLEY OSCAR (Dolly)
B. Dec. 10, 1888, Ladonia, Tex. D. Oct. 11, 1964, Snyder, Tex. — BR TR 6'1½" 184 lbs.

Year	Team	Games	BA	SA	AB	H	2B	3B	HR	HR%	R	RBI	BB	SO	SB	Pinch Hit AB	Pinch Hit H	PO	A	E	DP	TC/G	FA	G by Pos
1912	PIT N	6	.250	.350	20	5	0	1	0	0.0	4	2	0	3	0	1	0	39	0	0	2	6.5	1.000	1B-4

Danny Green

GREEN, EDWARD
B. Nov. 6, 1876, Burlington, N.J. D. Nov. 9, 1914, Camden, N.J. — BL TR

Year	Team	Games	BA	SA	AB	H	2B	3B	HR	HR%	R	RBI	BB	SO	SB	Pinch Hit AB	Pinch Hit H	PO	A	E	DP	TC/G	FA	G by Pos
1898	CHI N	47	.314	.431	188	59	4	3	4	2.1	26	27	7		12	0	0	87	10	3	5	2.1	.970	OF-47
1899		117	.295	.404	475	140	12	11	6	1.3	90	56	35		18	2	0	175	22	11	11	1.8	.947	OF-115
1900		103	.298	.416	389	116	21	5	5	1.3	63	49	17		28	2	1	218	10	15	2	2.4	.938	OF-101
1901		133	.313	.421	537	168	16	12	6	1.1	82	60	40		31	0	0	312	17	24	7	2.7	.932	OF-133
1902	CHI A	129	.312	.391	481	150	16	11	0	0.0	77	62	53		35	0	0	217	11	14	4	1.9	.942	OF-129
1903		135	.309	.425	499	154	26	7	6	1.2	75	62	47		29	2	1	219	16	17	8	1.9	.933	OF-133
1904		147	.265	.343	536	142	16	10	2	0.4	83	62	63		28	1	0	231	13	9	5	1.7	.964	OF-146
1905		112	.243	.309	379	92	13	6	0	0.0	56	44	53		11	5	0	119	9	12	3	1.3	.914	OF-107
8 yrs.		923	.293	.391	3484	1021	124	65	29	0.8	552	422	315		192	12	2	1578	108	105	45	1.9	.941	OF-911

David Green

GREEN, DAVID ALEJANDRO
Born David Alejandro Green y Casaya.
B. Dec. 4, 1960, Managua, Nicaragua — BR TR 6'3" 170 lbs.

Year	Team	Games	BA	SA	AB	H	2B	3B	HR	HR%	R	RBI	BB	SO	SB	Pinch Hit AB	Pinch Hit H	PO	A	E	DP	TC/G	FA	G by Pos
1981	STL N	21	.147	.176	34	5	1	0	0	0.0	6	2	6	5	0	2	0	31	1	1	0	1.6	.970	OF-18
1982		76	.283	.373	166	47	7	1	2	1.2	21	23	8	29	11	12	4	111	4	1	1	1.5	.991	OF-68
1983		146	.284	.422	422	120	14	10	8	1.9	52	69	26	76	34	20	6	214	10	7	2	1.6	.970	OF-136
1984		126	.268	.416	452	121	14	4	15	3.3	49	65	20	105	17	5	1	1103	70	10	99	9.4	.992	1B-117, OF-14
1985	SF N	106	.248	.347	294	73	10	2	5	1.7	36	20	22	58	6	11	1	645	42	10	54	6.6	.986	1B-78, OF-12
1987	STL N	14	.267	.500	30	8	2	1	1	3.3	4	1	2	5	0	5	0	18	1	2	1	1.5	.905	OF-10, 1B-3
6 yrs.		489	.268	.394	1398	374	48	18	31	2.2	168	180	84	278	68	55	12	2122	128	31	157	4.7	.986	OF-258, 1B-198

LEAGUE CHAMPIONSHIP SERIES

Year	Team	Games	BA	SA	AB	H	2B	3B	HR	HR%	R	RBI	BB	SO	SB	Pinch Hit AB	Pinch Hit H	PO	A	E	DP	TC/G	FA	G by Pos
1982	STL N	2	1.000	1.000	1	1	0	0	0	0.0	1	0	0	0	0	0	0	0	0	0	0	0.0	—	OF-2

WORLD SERIES

Year	Team	Games	BA	SA	AB	H	2B	3B	HR	HR%	R	RBI	BB	SO	SB	Pinch Hit AB	Pinch Hit H	PO	A	E	DP	TC/G	FA	G by Pos
1982	STL N	7	.200	.500	10	2	1	0	0	0.0	3	0	1	3	0	1	0	4	0	0	0	0.6	1.000	OF-4, DH-3

Dick Green

GREEN, RICHARD LARRY
B. Apr. 21, 1941, Sioux City, Iowa — BR TR 5'10" 180 lbs.

Year	Team	Games	BA	SA	AB	H	2B	3B	HR	HR%	R	RBI	BB	SO	SB	Pinch Hit AB	Pinch Hit H	PO	A	E	DP	TC/G	FA	G by Pos
1963	KC A	13	.270	.405	37	10	2	0	1	2.7	5	4	2	10	0	2	0	14	37	3	5	4.2	.944	SS-6, 2B-4
1964		130	.264	.395	435	115	14	5	11	2.5	48	37	27	87	3	2	0	262	361	6	69	4.8	.990	2B-120
1965		133	.232	.363	474	110	15	1	15	3.2	64	55	50	110	0	7	2	252	341	12	73	4.5	.980	2B-126
1966		140	.250	.363	507	127	24	3	9	1.8	58	62	27	101	6	1	0	302	390	16	86	5.1	.977	2B-137, 3B-2
1967		122	.198	.298	349	69	12	4	5	1.4	26	37	30	68	6	14	4	177	198	10	34	3.2	.974	2B-117
1968	OAK A	76	.233	.351	202	47	6	0	6	3.0	19	18	21	41	3	9	3	125	170	8	35	4.0	.974	3B-59, 2B-50, SS-1, 1B-1
1969		136	.275	.427	483	133	25	6	12	2.5	61	64	53	94	2	4	1	302	379	10	93	5.1	.986	2B-131
1970		135	.190	.240	384	73	7	0	4	1.0	34	29	38	73	3	7	2	261	336	13	67	4.5	.979	2B-131
1971		144	.244	.354	475	116	14	1	12	2.5	58	49	51	83	1	1	0	366	384	11	98	5.3	.986	2B-143, SS-1
1972		26	.286	.357	42	12	1	0	0	0.0	1	3	3	5	0	0	0	35	45	3	9	3.2	.964	2B-26
1973		133	.262	.340	332	87	17	0	3	0.9	33	42	21	63	0	0	0	265	298	7	86	4.3	.988	2B-133
1974		100	.213	.275	287	61	8	2	2	0.7	20	22	22	50	0	0	0	233	243	8	67	4.8	.983	2B-100
12 yrs.		1288	.240	.347	4007	960	145	23	80	2.0	427	422	345	785	26	48	14	2594	3182	107	722	4.6	.982	2B-1158, 3B-68, SS-9, C-2, 1B-1

LEAGUE CHAMPIONSHIP SERIES

Year	Team	Games	BA	SA	AB	H	2B	3B	HR	HR%	R	RBI	BB	SO	SB	Pinch Hit AB	Pinch Hit H	PO	A	E	DP	TC/G	FA	G by Pos
1971	OAK A	3	.286	.286	7	2	0	0	0	0.0	0	0	0	0	0	0	0	8	4	0	3	4.0	1.000	2B-3
1972		5	.125	.250	8	1	1	0	0	0.0	0	1	0	0	0	0	0	5	7	0	1	2.4	1.000	2B-5
1973		5	.077	.154	13	1	1	0	0	0.0	0	0	0	4	0	0	0	5	7	0	1	2.4	1.000	2B-5
1974		4	.222	.222	9	2	0	0	0	0.0	0	1	0	4	0	0	0	12	11	2	4	5.0	.920	2B-4
4 yrs.		17	.162	.216	37	6	2	0	0	0.0	0	2	0	8	0	0	0	30	30	4	11	4.1	.942	2B-17

WORLD SERIES

Year	Team	Games	BA	SA	AB	H	2B	3B	HR	HR%	R	RBI	BB	SO	SB	Pinch Hit AB	Pinch Hit H	PO	A	E	DP	TC/G	FA	G by Pos
1972	OAK A	7	.333	.444	18	6	2	0	0	0.0	0	0	0	4	0	0	0	12	13	0	2	3.6	1.000	2B-7
1973		7	.063	.063	16	1	0	0	0	0.0	0	1	0	6	0	0	0	14	11	1	4	3.7	.962	2B-7

Year	Team		Games	BA	SA	AB	H	2B	3B	HR	HR%	R	RBI	BB	SO	SB	Pinch Hit AB	Pinch Hit H	PO	A	E	DP	TC/G	FA	G by Pos

Dick Green *continued*

Year	Team		Games	BA	SA	AB	H	2B	3B	HR	HR%	R	RBI	BB	SO	SB	AB	H	PO	A	E	DP	TC/G	FA	G by Pos
1974			5	.000	.000	13	0	0	0	0	0.0	1	1	1	4	0	0	0	15	14	1	6	6.0	.967	2B-5
3 yrs.			19	.149	.191	47	7	2	0	0	0.0	1	2	2	14	0	0	0	41	38	2	12	4.3	.975	2B-19

Gary Green

GREEN, GARY ALLAN
Son of Freddie Green.
B. Jan. 14, 1962, Pittsburgh, Pa.

BR TR 6'3" 175 lbs.

Year	Team		Games	BA	SA	AB	H	2B	3B	HR	HR%	R	RBI	BB	SO	SB	AB	H	PO	A	E	DP	TC/G	FA	G by Pos
1986	SD	N	13	.212	.242	33	7	1	0	0	0.0	2	2	1	11	0	0	0	16	35	0	9	3.9	1.000	SS-13
1989			15	.259	.370	27	7	3	0	0	0.0	4	0	1	1	0	0	0	6	29	3	7	2.5	.921	SS-11, 3B-1
2 yrs.			28	.233	.300	60	14	4	0	0	0.0	6	2	2	12	0	0	0	22	64	3	16	3.2	.966	SS-24, 3B-1

Gene Green

GREEN, GENE LEROY
B. June 26, 1933, Los Angeles, Calif.   D. May 23, 1981, St. Louis, Mo.

BR TR 6'2½" 200 lbs.

Year	Team		Games	BA	SA	AB	H	2B	3B	HR	HR%	R	RBI	BB	SO	SB	AB	H	PO	A	E	DP	TC/G	FA	G by Pos
1957	STL	N	6	.200	.267	15	3	1	0	0	0.0	0	2	0	3	0	3	0	2	0	0	0	0.3	1.000	OF-3
1958			137	.281	.423	442	124	18	3	13	2.9	47	55	37	48	2	13	1	428	35	9	5	3.4	.981	OF-75, C-48
1959			30	.189	.311	74	14	6	0	1	1.4	8	3	5	18	0	2	0	62	9	2	2	2.4	.973	OF-19, C-11
1960	BAL	A	1	.250	.250	4	1	0	0	0	0.0	0	0	0	0	0	0	0	0	1	0	0	1.0	1.000	OF-1
1961	WAS	A	110	.280	.489	364	102	16	3	18	4.9	52	62	35	65	0	11	2	354	22	5	3	3.5	.987	C-79, OF-21
1962	CLE	A	66	.280	.552	143	40	4	1	11	7.7	16	28	8	21	0	30	10	56	2	2	1	0.9	.967	OF-33, 1B-2
1963	2 teams	CLE A (43G – .205)				CIN N	(15G – .226)																		
"	total		58	.211	.330	109	23	4	0	3	2.8	7	10	4	30	0	31	5	53	5	3	0	1.1	.951	OF-18, C-8
7 yrs.			408	.267	.441	1151	307	49	7	46	4.0	130	160	89	185	2	90	18	955	74	21	11	2.6	.980	OF-170, C-146, 1B-2

Jim Green

GREEN, JAMES R.
B. Cleveland, Ohio   Deceased.

Year	Team		Games	BA	SA	AB	H	2B	3B	HR	HR%	R	RBI	BB	SO	SB	AB	H	PO	A	E	DP	TC/G	FA	G by Pos
1884	WAS	U	10	.139	.167	36	5	1	0	0	0.0	4		0			0	0	5	15	4	0	2.4	.833	3B-9, OF-1

Joe Green

GREEN, JOSEPH HENRY (Tilly)
B. Sept. 17, 1897, Philadelphia, Pa.   D. Feb. 4, 1972, Bryn Mawr, Pa.

BR TR 6'2" 170 lbs.

Year	Team		Games	BA	SA	AB	H	2B	3B	HR	HR%	R	RBI	BB	SO	SB	AB	H	PO	A	E	DP	TC/G	FA	G by Pos
1924	PHI	A	1	.000	.000	1	0	0	0	0	0.0	0	0	0	0	0	1	0	0	0	0	0	0.0	–	

Lenny Green

GREEN, LEONARD CHARLES
B. Jan. 6, 1933, Detroit, Mich.

BL TL 5'11" 170 lbs.

Year	Team		Games	BA	SA	AB	H	2B	3B	HR	HR%	R	RBI	BB	SO	SB	AB	H	PO	A	E	DP	TC/G	FA	G by Pos
1957	BAL	A	19	.182	.364	33	6	1	1	1	3.0	2	5	1	4	0	2	0	19	0	1	0	1.1	.950	OF-15
1958			69	.231	.275	91	21	4	0	0	0.0	10	4	9	18	0	9	1	81	3	0	1	1.2	.965	OF-53
1959	2 teams	BAL A (27G – .292)				WAS A	(88G – .242)																		
"	total		115	.248	.327	214	53	11	3	3	1.4	32	17	21	18	9	35	11	98	6	2	0	0.9	.981	OF-81
1960	WAS	A	127	.294	.430	330	97	16	7	5	1.5	62	33	43	25	21	29	8	219	4	2	0	1.8	.991	OF-100
1961	MIN	A	156	.285	.400	600	171	28	7	9	1.5	92	50	81	50	17	2	1	356	3	8	0	2.4	.978	OF-153
1962			158	.271	.402	619	168	33	3	14	2.3	97	63	88	36	8	3	1	361	8	2	2	2.3	.995	OF-156
1963			145	.239	.325	280	67	10	1	4	1.4	41	27	31	21	3	24	4	165	1	2	0	1.2	.988	OF-119
1964	3 teams	MIN A (26G – .000)				LA A	(39G – .250)				BAL A	(14G – .190)													
"	total		79	.211	.273	128	27	2	0	2	1.6	16	5	21	17	3	33	4	65	1	1	0	0.8	.985	OF-38
1965	BOS	A	119	.276	.429	373	103	24	6	7	1.9	69	24	48	43	8	24	7	198	2	4	1	1.7	.980	OF-95
1966			85	.241	.308	133	32	6	0	1	0.8	18	12	15	19	0	52	14	41	3	1	0	0.5	.978	OF-27
1967	DET	A	58	.278	.364	151	42	8	1	1	0.7	22	13	9	17	1	11	1	57	0	1	0	1.0	.983	OF-44
1968			6	.250	.250	4	1	0	0	0	0.0	0	0	1	0	0	3	1	0	0	0	0	0.0	–	OF-2
12 yrs.			1136	.267	.379	2956	788	138	27	47	1.6	461	253	368	260	78	226	53	1660	29	27	3	1.5	.984	OF-883

Pumpsie Green

GREEN, ELIJAH JERRY
B. Oct. 27, 1933, Oakland, Calif.

BB TR 6' 175 lbs.

Year	Team		Games	BA	SA	AB	H	2B	3B	HR	HR%	R	RBI	BB	SO	SB	AB	H	PO	A	E	DP	TC/G	FA	G by Pos
1959	BOS	A	50	.233	.320	172	40	6	3	1	0.6	30	10	29	22	4	4	0	109	132	7	38	5.0	.972	2B-45, SS-1
1960			133	.242	.338	260	63	10	3	3	1.2	36	21	44	47	3	24	8	151	169	11	33	2.5	.967	2B-69, SS-41
1961			88	.260	.425	219	57	12	3	6	2.7	33	27	42	32	4	25	7	91	172	16	36	3.2	.943	SS-57, 2B-7
1962			56	.231	.341	91	21	2	1	2	2.2	12	11	11	18	1	35	8	22	35	5	8	1.1	.919	2B-18, SS-5
1963	NY	N	17	.278	.426	54	15	1	2	1	1.9	8	5	12	13	0	0	0	12	36	8	2	3.3	.857	3B-16
5 yrs.			344	.246	.364	796	196	31	12	13	1.6	119	74	138	132	12	88	23	385	544	47	117	2.8	.952	2B-139, SS-104, 3B-16

Hank Greenberg

GREENBERG, HENRY BENJAMIN (Hammerin' Hank)
B. Jan. 1, 1911, New York, N.Y.   D. Sept. 4, 1986, Beverly Hills, Calif.
Hall of Fame 1956.

BR TR 6'3½" 210 lbs.

Year	Team		Games	BA	SA	AB	H	2B	3B	HR	HR%	R	RBI	BB	SO	SB	AB	H	PO	A	E	DP	TC/G	FA	G by Pos
1930	DET	A	1	.000	.000	1	0	0	0	0	0.0	0	0	0	0	0	1	0	0	0	0	0	0.0	–	
1933			117	.301	.468	449	135	33	3	12	2.7	59	87	46	78	6	1	0	1133	63	14	111	10.3	.988	1B-117
1934			153	.339	.600	593	201	63	7	26	4.4	118	139	63	93	9	0	0	1454	84	16	124	10.2	.990	1B-153
1935			152	.328	.628	619	203	46	16	36	5.8	121	170	87	91	4	0	0	1437	99	13	142	10.2	.992	1B-152
1936			12	.348	.630	46	16	6	2	1	2.2	10	16	9	6	1	0	0	119	9	1	14	10.8	.992	1B-12
1937			154	.337	.668	594	200	49	14	40	6.7	137	183	102	101	8	0	0	1477	102	13	133	10.3	.992	1B-154
1938			155	.315	.683	556	175	23	4	58	10.4	144	146	119	92	7	0	0	1484	120	14	146	10.4	.991	1B-155
1939			138	.312	.622	500	156	42	7	33	6.6	112	112	91	95	8	1	0	1205	75	9	108	9.3	.993	1B-136
1940			148	.340	.670	573	195	50	8	41	7.2	129	150	93	75	6	0	0	298	14	15	1	2.2	.954	OF-148
1941			19	.269	.463	67	18	5	1	2	3.0	12	12	16	12	1	0	0	32	0	3	0	1.8	.914	OF-19
1945			78	.311	.544	270	84	20	2	13	4.8	47	60	42	40	3	5	2	129	3	0	0	1.7	1.000	OF-72
1946			142	.277	.604	523	145	29	5	44	8.4	91	127	80	88	5	2	0	1272	93	15	110	9.7	.989	1B-140
1947	PIT	N	125	.249	.478	402	100	13	2	25	6.2	71	74	104	73	0	6	1	983	79	9	85	8.6	.992	1B-119
13 yrs.			1394	.313	.605	5193	1628	379	71	331	6.4	1051	1276	852	844	58	16	3	11023	741	122	974	8.5	.990	1B-1138, OF-239
					5th						9th														

WORLD SERIES

Year	Team		Games	BA	SA	AB	H	2B	3B	HR	HR%	R	RBI	BB	SO	SB	AB	H	PO	A	E	DP	TC/G	FA	G by Pos
1934	DET	A	7	.321	.571	28	9	2	1	1	3.6	4	7	4	9	1	0	0	60	4	1	5	9.3	.985	1B-7
1935			2	.167	.667	6	1	0	0	1	16.7	1	2	1	1	0	0	0	17	2	3	2	11.0	.864	1B-2
1940			7	.357	.607	28	10	2	1	1	3.6	5	6	2	5	0	0	0	12	0	0	0	1.7	1.000	OF-7

Hank Greenberg *continued*

Year	Team	Games	BA	SA	AB	H	2B	3B	HR	HR%	R	RBI	BB	SO	SB	PH AB	PH H	PO	A	E	DP	TC/G	FA	G by Pos
1945		7	.304	.696	23	7	3	0	2	8.7	7	7	6	5	0	0	0	8	1	0	0	1.3	1.000	OF-7
4 yrs.		23	.318	.624	85	27	7	2	5	5.9	17	22	13	19	1	0	0	97	7	4	7	4.7	.963	OF-14, 1B-9
				8th	9th																			

Al Greene

GREENE, ALTAR ALPHONSE
B. Nov. 9, 1954, Detroit, Mich. BL TR 5'11" 190 lbs.

Year	Team	Games	BA	SA	AB	H	2B	3B	HR	HR%	R	RBI	BB	SO	SB	PH AB	PH H	PO	A	E	DP	TC/G	FA	G by Pos
1979	DET A	29	.136	.305	59	8	1	0	3	5.1	9	6	10	15	0	6	2	14	0	0	0	0.5	1.000	DH-15, OF-6

June Greene

GREENE, JULIUS FOUST
B. June 25, 1899, Ramseur, N. C. D. Mar. 19, 1974, Glendora, Calif. BL TR 6'2½" 185 lbs.

Year	Team	Games	BA	SA	AB	H	2B	3B	HR	HR%	R	RBI	BB	SO	SB	PH AB	PH H	PO	A	E	DP	TC/G	FA	G by Pos
1928	PHI N	11	.500	.500	6	3	0	0	0	0.0	0	0	3	1	0	6	3	0	2	0	0	0.2	1.000	P-1
1929		21	.211	.263	19	4	1	0	0	0.0	1	0	2	4	0	14	1	0	4	0	0	0.2	1.000	P-5
2 yrs.		32	.280	.320	25	7	1	0	0	0.0	1	0	5	5	0	20	5	1	6	0	0	0.2	1.000	P-6

Willie Greene

GREENE, PATRICK JOSEPH
Played as Pat Foley in 1902.
B. Mar. 20, 1875, Providence, R. I. D. Oct. 20, 1934, Providence, R. I. BR TR 5'8" 150 lbs.

Year	Team	Games	BA	SA	AB	H	2B	3B	HR	HR%	R	RBI	BB	SO	SB	PH AB	PH H	PO	A	E	DP	TC/G	FA	G by Pos
1902	PHI N	19	.169	.185	65	11	1	0	0	0.0	6	1	2		2	0	0	22	40	6	2	3.6	.912	3B-19
1903	2 teams	NY A (4G - .308)				DET A (1G - .000)																		
"	total	5	.250	.313	16	4	1	0	0	0.0	1	0	0		0	1	0	5	11	2	0	3.6	.889	3B-3, SS-1
2 yrs.		24	.185	.210	81	15	2	0	0	0.0	7	1	2		2	1	0	27	51	8	2	3.6	.907	3B-22, SS-1

Jim Greengrass

GREENGRASS, JAMES RAYMOND
B. Oct. 24, 1927, Addison, N. Y. BR TR 6'1" 200 lbs.

Year	Team	Games	BA	SA	AB	H	2B	3B	HR	HR%	R	RBI	BB	SO	SB	PH AB	PH H	PO	A	E	DP	TC/G	FA	G by Pos
1952	CIN N	18	.309	.588	68	21	2	1	5	7.4	10	24	7	12	0	1	0	55	0	2	0	3.2	.965	OF-17
1953		154	.285	.444	606	173	22	7	20	3.3	86	100	47	83	6	1	0	341	11	6	0	2.3	.983	OF-153
1954		139	.280	.494	542	152	27	4	27	5.0	79	95	41	81	0	2	0	298	9	10	0	2.3	.968	OF-137
1955	2 teams	CIN N (13G - .103)				PHI N (94G - .272)																		
"	total	107	.254	.425	362	92	22	2	12	3.3	44	38	42	52	0	8	2	191	15	5	0	1.9	.976	OF-94, 3B-2
1956	PHI N	86	.205	.335	215	44	9	2	5	2.3	24	25	28	43	0	22	6	104	3	1	1	1.3	.991	OF-62
5 yrs.		504	.269	.448	1793	482	82	16	69	3.8	243	282	165	271	6	34	8	989	35	24	1	2.1	.977	OF-463, 3B-2

Mike Greenwell

GREENWELL, MICHAEL LEWIS
B. July 18, 1963, Louisville, Ky. BL TR 6' 170 lbs.

Year	Team	Games	BA	SA	AB	H	2B	3B	HR	HR%	R	RBI	BB	SO	SB	PH AB	PH H	PO	A	E	DP	TC/G	FA	G by Pos
1985	BOS A	17	.323	.742	31	10	1	0	4	12.9	7	8	3	4	1	1	0	14	0	0	0	0.8	1.000	OF-17
1986		31	.314	.371	35	11	2	0	0	0.0	4	4	5	7	0	12	2	18	1	0	1	0.6	1.000	OF-15, DH-3
1987		125	.328	.570	412	135	31	6	19	4.6	71	89	35	40	5	17	5	165	8	6	0	1.4	.966	OF-91, DH-15, C-1
1988		158	.325	.531	590	192	39	8	22	3.7	86	119	87	38	16	0	5	302	6	6	2	2.0	.981	OF-147, DH-11
1989		145	.308	.443	578	178	36	0	14	2.4	87	95	56	44	13	1	1	220	11	8	1	1.6	.967	OF-139, DH-5
5 yrs.		476	.320	.510	1646	526	109	14	59	3.6	255	315	186	133	35	31	8	719	26	20	4	1.6	.974	OF-409, DH-34, C-1

LEAGUE CHAMPIONSHIP SERIES

Year	Team	Games	BA	SA	AB	H	2B	3B	HR	HR%	R	RBI	BB	SO	SB	PH AB	PH H	PO	A	E	DP	TC/G	FA	G by Pos
1986	BOS A	2	.500	.500	2	1	0	0	0	0.0	0	0	0	0	0	2	1	0	0	0	0	0.0	–	
1988		4	.214	.500	14	3	1	0	1	7.1	3	3	3	0	0	0	0	4	0	0	0	1.0	1.000	OF-4
2 yrs.		6	.250	.500	16	4	1	0	1	6.3	3	3	3	0	0	2	1	4	0	0	0	0.7	1.000	OF-4

WORLD SERIES

Year	Team	Games	BA	SA	AB	H	2B	3B	HR	HR%	R	RBI	BB	SO	SB	PH AB	PH H	PO	A	E	DP	TC/G	FA	G by Pos
1986	BOS A	4	.000	.000	3	0	0	0	0	0.0	0	0	1	2	0	3	0	0	0	0	0	0.0	–	

Bill Greenwood

GREENWOOD, WILLIAM F.
B. 1857, Philadelphia, Pa. D. May 2, 1902, Philadelphia, Pa. BB TL 5'7½" 180 lbs.

Year	Team	Games	BA	SA	AB	H	2B	3B	HR	HR%	R	RBI	BB	SO	SB	PH AB	PH H	PO	A	E	DP	TC/G	FA	G by Pos
1882	PHI AA	7	.300	.333	30	9	1	0	0	0.0	8		1		0	0	0	10	2	2	0	2.0	.857	OF-7, 2B-2
1884	BKN AA	92	.216	.275	385	83	8	3	3	0.8	52		10		0	0	0	230	300	59	40	6.4	.900	2B-92, SS-1
1887	BAL AA	118	.263	.319	495	130	16	6	0	0.0	114		54		71	0	0	357	360	56	33	6.6	.928	2B-117, OF-1
1888		115	.191	.227	409	78	13	1	0	0.0	69	29	30		46	0	0	203	299	59	25	4.9	.895	2B-86, SS-28, OF-1
1889	COL AA	118	.225	.312	414	93	7	10	3	0.7	62	49	58	71	37	0	0	313	322	60	50	5.9	.914	2B-118
1890	ROC AA	124	.222	.288	437	97	11	6	2	0.5	76		48		40	0	0	333	346	60	60	6.0	.919	2B-123, SS-1
6 yrs.		574	.226	.287	2170	490	56	26	8	0.4	381	78	201	71	194	0	0	1446	1629	296	208	5.9	.912	2B-538, SS-30, OF-9

Brian Greer

GREER, BRIAN KEITH
B. May 14, 1959, Lynwood, Calif. BR TR 6'3" 210 lbs.

Year	Team	Games	BA	SA	AB	H	2B	3B	HR	HR%	R	RBI	BB	SO	SB	PH AB	PH H	PO	A	E	DP	TC/G	FA	G by Pos
1977	SD N	1	.000	.000	1	0	0	0	0	0.0	0	0	0	1	0	1	0	0	0	0	0	0.0	–	
1979		4	.000	.000	3	0	0	0	0	0.0	0	0	0	1	0	0	0	4	0	0	0	1.0	1.000	OF-4
2 yrs.		5	.000	.000	4	0	0	0	0	0.0	0	0	0	2	0	1	0	4	0	0	0	0.8	1.000	OF-4

Ed Greer

GREER, EDWARD C.
B. 1865, Philadelphia, Pa. D. Feb. 4, 1890, Philadelphia, Pa. BR

Year	Team	Games	BA	SA	AB	H	2B	3B	HR	HR%	R	RBI	BB	SO	SB	PH AB	PH H	PO	A	E	DP	TC/G	FA	G by Pos
1885	BAL AA	56	.199	.232	211	42	7	0	0	0.0	32		8		0	0	0	127	19	16	1	2.9	.901	OF-47, C-12
1886	2 teams	BAL AA (11G - .132)				PHI AA (71G - .193)																		
"	total	82	.185	.235	302	56	6	1	0	0.3	35		10		0	0	0	157	19	17	5	2.4	.912	OF-79, C-3
1887	2 teams	PHI AA (3G - .182)				BKN AA (91G - .254)																		
"	total	94	.251	.320	338	85	13	2	2	0.6	50		25		35	0	0	230	31	22	4	3.0	.922	OF-79, C-16
3 yrs.		232	.215	.268	851	183	26	5	2	0.4	117		43		35	0	0	514	69	55	10	2.8	.914	OF-205, C-31

Tommy Gregg

GREGG, WILLIAM THOMAS
B. July 29, 1963, Boone, N. C. BL TL 6'1" 190 lbs.

Year	Team	Games	BA	SA	AB	H	2B	3B	HR	HR%	R	RBI	BB	SO	SB	PH AB	PH H	PO	A	E	DP	TC/G	FA	G by Pos
1987	PIT N	10	.250	.375	8	2	1	0	0	0.0	3	0	0	2	0	7	2	1	0	0	0	0.1	1.000	OF-4
1988	2 teams	PIT N (14G - .200)				ATL N (11G - .345)																		
"	total	25	.295	.455	44	13	4	0	1	2.3	5	7	3	6	0	12	2	26	0	1	1	1.1	1.000	OF-13

Year	Team	Games	BA	SA	AB	H	2B	3B	HR	HR%	R	RBI	BB	SO	SB	Pinch Hit AB	Pinch Hit H	PO	A	E	DP	TC/G	FA	G by Pos

Tommy Gregg *continued*

Year	Team	Games	BA	SA	AB	H	2B	3B	HR	HR%	R	RBI	BB	SO	SB	PH AB	PH H	PO	A	E	DP	TC/G	FA	G by Pos
1989	ATL N	102	.243	.337	276	67	8	0	6	2.2	24	23	18	45	3	28	6	321	17	2	18	3.3	.994	OF-48, 1B-37
3 yrs.		137	.250	.354	328	82	13	0	7	2.1	32	30	21	53	3	47	10	348	18	2	19	2.7	.995	OF-65, 1B-37

Ed Gremminger

GREMMINGER, LORENZO EDWARD (Battleship)
B. Mar. 30, 1874, Canton, Ohio   D. May 26, 1942, Canton, Ohio   BR TR 6'1" 200 lbs.

Year	Team	Games	BA	SA	AB	H	2B	3B	HR	HR%	R	RBI	BB	SO	SB	PH AB	PH H	PO	A	E	DP	TC/G	FA	G by Pos
1895	CLE N	20	.269	.282	78	21	0	0	0	0.0	10	15	5	13	0			24	38	9	3	3.6	.873	3B-20
1902	BOS N	140	.257	.347	522	134	20	12	1	0.2	55	66	39		7	0	0	222	282	26	15	3.8	.951	3B-140
1903		140	.264	.376	511	135	24	9	5	1.0	57	56	31		12	0	0	217	300	36	20	4.0	.935	3B-140
1904	DET A	83	.214	.285	309	66	13	3	1	0.3	18	28	14		3	0	0	103	123	12	3	2.9	.950	3B-83
4 yrs.		383	.251	.340	1420	356	58	24	7	0.5	140	165	89	13	22	0	0	566	743	83	41	3.6	.940	3B-383

Buddy Gremp

GREMP, LOUIS EDWARD
B. Aug. 5, 1919, Denver, Colo.   BR TR 6'1" 175 lbs.

Year	Team	Games	BA	SA	AB	H	2B	3B	HR	HR%	R	RBI	BB	SO	SB	PH AB	PH H	PO	A	E	DP	TC/G	FA	G by Pos
1940	BOS N	4	.222	.222	9	2	0	0	0	0.0	0	2	0	0	0	1	0	18	1	0	2	4.8	1.000	1B-3
1941		37	.240	.280	75	18	3	0	0	0.0	7	10	5	3	0	8	1	171	10	5	16	5.0	.973	1B-21, 2B-6, C-3
1942		72	.217	.314	207	45	11	0	3	1.4	12	19	13	21	1	8	3	506	35	5	45	7.6	.991	1B-62, 3B-1
3 yrs.		113	.223	.302	291	65	14	0	3	1.0	19	31	18	24	1	17	4	695	46	10	63	6.6	.987	1B-86, 2B-6, C-3, 3B-1

Bill Grey

GREY, WILLIAM TOBIN
B. Apr. 15, 1871, Philadelphia, Pa.   D. Dec. 8, 1932, Philadelphia, Pa.   5'11" 175 lbs.

Year	Team	Games	BA	SA	AB	H	2B	3B	HR	HR%	R	RBI	BB	SO	SB	PH AB	PH H	PO	A	E	DP	TC/G	FA	G by Pos
1890	PHI N	34	.242	.367	128	31	8	4	0	0.0	20	21	6	3	5	0	0	69	42	18	4	3.8	.860	OF-10, 3B-8, 2B-8, C-7, 1B-1
1891		23	.240	.240	75	18	0	0	0	0.0	11	7	3	10	3	0	0	47	13	14	1	3.2	.811	C-11, OF-10, SS-3, 3B-1
1895	CIN N	52	.304	.459	181	55	17	4	1	0.6	24	29	15	8	4	0	0	89	108	24	13	4.3	.891	3B-27, 2B-16, SS-5, C-5, OF-1
1896		46	.207	.240	121	25	2	1	0	0.0	15	17	19	11	6	5	0	81	83	16	9	3.9	.911	2B-12, C-11, SS-8, OF-3, 1B-2, 3B-1
1898	PIT N	137	.229	.280	528	121	17	5	0	0.0	56	67	28		5	0	0	172	258	59	16	3.6	.879	3B-137
5 yrs.		292	.242	.315	1033	250	44	14	1	0.1	126	141	71	32	23	5	0	458	504	131	43	3.7	.880	3B-174, 2B-36, C-34, OF-24, SS-16, 1B-3

Reddy Grey

GREY, ROMER CARL
Born Romer Carl Gray.
B. Jan. 4, 1875, Zanesville, Ohio   D. Nov. 9, 1934, Altadena, Calif.   5'11" 175 lbs.

Year	Team	Games	BA	SA	AB	H	2B	3B	HR	HR%	R	RBI	BB	SO	SB	PH AB	PH H	PO	A	E	DP	TC/G	FA	G by Pos
1903	PIT N	2	.333	.333	6	2	0	0	0	0.0	1	1	1		0	0	0	1	0	0	0	0.5	1.000	OF-2

Bobby Grich

GRICH, ROBERT ANTHONY
B. Jan. 15, 1949, Muskegon, Mich.   BR TR 6'2" 180 lbs.

Year	Team	Games	BA	SA	AB	H	2B	3B	HR	HR%	R	RBI	BB	SO	SB	PH AB	PH H	PO	A	E	DP	TC/G	FA	G by Pos
1970	BAL A	30	.211	.284	95	20	1	3	0	0.0	11	8	9	21	1	1	0	56	79	7	9	4.7	.951	SS-20, 2B-9, 3B-1
1971		7	.300	.400	30	9	0	1	0	3.3	7	6	5	8	1	0	0	11	31	0	4	6.0	1.000	SS-5, 2B-2
1972		133	.278	.415	460	128	21	3	12	2.6	66	50	53	96	13	3	1	299	338	20	81	4.9	.970	2B-45, 1B-16, 3B-8, SS-81
1973		162	.251	.387	581	146	29	7	12	2.1	82	50	107	91	17	0	0	431	509	20	130	5.8	.995	2B-162
1974		160	.263	.431	582	153	29	6	19	3.3	92	82	90	117	17	0	0	484	453	20	132	6.0	.979	2B-160
1975		150	.260	.399	524	136	26	4	13	2.5	81	57	107	88	14	1	0	423	484	21	122	6.2	.977	2B-150
1976		144	.266	.417	518	138	31	4	13	2.5	93	54	86	99	14	3	1	389	400	12	91	5.6	.985	2B-140, 3B-2
1977	CAL A	52	.243	.392	181	44	6	0	7	3.9	24	23	37	40	6	0	0	88	141	4	23	4.6	.983	SS-52
1978		144	.251	.329	487	122	16	2	6	1.2	68	42	75	83	4	0	0	325	419	13	77	5.3	.983	2B-144
1979		153	.294	.537	534	157	30	5	30	5.6	78	101	59	84	1	1	0	340	438	13	111	5.2	.984	2B-153
1980		150	.271	.408	498	135	22	2	14	2.8	60	62	84	108	3	4	2	353	464	9	102	5.5	.989	2B-146, DH-3, 1B-3
1981		100	.304	**.543**	352	107	14	2	**22**	**6.3**	56	61	40	71	2	2	0	230	349	10	85	5.9	.983	2B-100
1982		145	.261	.449	506	132	28	5	19	3.8	74	65	82	109	3	2	1	338	450	11	112	5.5	.986	2B-142, DH-1
1983		120	.292	.460	387	113	17	0	16	4.1	65	62	76	62	2	3	2	271	415	22	94	5.9	.969	2B-118, SS-1
1984		116	.256	.452	363	93	15	1	18	5.0	60	58	57	70	2	2	1	311	282	12	84	5.2	.980	2B-91, 1B-25, 3B-21
1985		144	.242	.372	479	116	17	3	13	2.7	74	53	81	77	3	2	0	331	408	3	115	5.2	.996	2B-116, 1B-16, 3B-15, DH-6
1986		98	.268	.412	313	84	18	0	9	2.9	42	30	39	54	1	14	5	202	231	7	54	4.5	.984	2B-87, 1B-11, 3B-2
17 yrs.		2008	.266	.424	6890	1833	320	47	224	3.3	1033	864	1087	1278	104	39	13	4882	5891	189	1426	5.5	.983	2B-1765, SS-159, 1B-71, 3B-49, DH-10

LEAGUE CHAMPIONSHIP SERIES

Year	Team	Games	BA	SA	AB	H	2B	3B	HR	HR%	R	RBI	BB	SO	SB	PH AB	PH H	PO	A	E	DP	TC/G	FA	G by Pos
1973	BAL A	5	.100	.250	20	2	0	1	1	5.0	1	1	1	5	0	0	0	6	9	0	1	3.0	1.000	2B-5
1974		4	.250	.500	16	4	1	0	1	6.3	2	2	0	1	0	0	0	13	12	1	3	6.5	.962	2B-4
1979	CAL A	4	.154	.231	13	2	1	0	0	0.0	0	2	1	4	0	0	0	4	12	1	4	4.3	.941	2B-4
1982		5	.200	.267	15	3	1	0	0	0.0	1	1	2	2	0	0	0	0	0	0	0	–	–	2B-5
1986		6	.208	.333	24	5	0	0	1	4.2	1	3	1	10	0	0	0	29	9	3	4	6.8	.927	2B-3, 1B-3
5 yrs.		24	.182	.318	88	16	3	1	3	3.4	5	9	5	22	0	0	0	52	42	5	12	4.1	.949	2B-21, 1B-3

Tim Griesenbeck

GRIESENBECK, CARLOS PHILLIPE
B. Dec. 10, 1897, San Antonio, Tex.   D. Mar. 25, 1953, San Antonio, Tex.   BR TR 5'10½" 190 lbs.

Year	Team	Games	BA	SA	AB	H	2B	3B	HR	HR%	R	RBI	BB	SO	SB	PH AB	PH H	PO	A	E	DP	TC/G	FA	G by Pos
1920	STL N	5	.333	.333	3	1	0	0	0	0.0	0	0	0	1	0	1	0	2	0	0	0	0.4	1.000	C-3

Tom Grieve

GRIEVE, THOMAS ALAN
B. Mar. 4, 1948, Pittsfield, Mass.   BR TR 6'2" 190 lbs.

Year	Team	Games	BA	SA	AB	H	2B	3B	HR	HR%	R	RBI	BB	SO	SB	PH AB	PH H	PO	A	E	DP	TC/G	FA	G by Pos
1970	WAS A	47	.198	.336	116	23	5	1	3	2.6	12	10	14	38	0	12	2	46	0	3	0	1.0	.939	OF-39
1972	TEX A	64	.204	.296	142	29	7	1	3	2.1	12	11	11	39	1	17	4	60	4	0	1	1.0	.985	OF-49
1973		66	.309	.528	123	38	6	0	7	5.7	22	21	7	25	1	22	7	68	0	0	0	1.0	1.000	DH-40, OF-38, 1B-1
1974		84	.255	.429	259	66	10	4	9	3.5	30	32	20	48	0	7	2	64	5	0	2	0.8	1.000	OF-63, DH-45
1975		118	.276	.442	369	102	17	1	14	3.8	46	61	22	74	0	14	1	93	3	1	0	0.8	.990	DH-96, OF-52
1976		149	.255	.418	546	139	23	3	20	3.7	57	81	35	119	4	3	1	112	4	2	1	0.8	.983	OF-60, DH-13
1977		79	.225	.352	236	53	7	0	7	3.0	24	20	13	57	1	12	4	77	5	2	1	1.1	.976	OF-26
1978	NY N	54	.208	.297	101	21	3	0	2	2.0	5	8	9	25	0	25	4	43	3	1	0	0.9	.979	OF-26

Year	Team		Games	BA	SA	AB	H	2B	3B	HR	HR%	R	RBI	BB	SO	SB	Pinch Hit AB	Pinch Hit H	PO	A	E	DP	TC/G	FA	G by Pos

Tom Grieve *continued*

Year	Team		Games	BA	SA	AB	H	2B	3B	HR	HR%	R	RBI	BB	SO	SB	AB	H	PO	A	E	DP	TC/G	FA	G by Pos
1979	STL	N	9	.200	.267	15	3	1	0	0	0.0	1	0	4	1	0	1	0	7	0	1	0	0.9	.875	OF-5
9 yrs.			670	.249	.401	1907	474	76	10	65	3.4	209	254	135	424	7	96	18	570	26	11	5	0.9	.982	OF-391, DH-195, 1B-1

Ken Griffey

GRIFFEY, GEORGE KENNETH, SR.
Father of Ken Griffey.
B. Apr. 10, 1950, Donora, Pa.

BL TL 5'11" 190 lbs.

Year	Team		Games	BA	SA	AB	H	2B	3B	HR	HR%	R	RBI	BB	SO	SB	AB	H	PO	A	E	DP	TC/G	FA	G by Pos
1973	CIN	N	25	.384	.570	86	33	5	1	3	3.5	19	14	6	10	4	3	2	25	1	0	0	1.0	1.000	OF-21
1974			88	.251	.361	227	57	9	5	2	0.9	24	19	27	43	9	15	4	115	5	0	1	1.4	1.000	OF-70
1975			132	.305	.402	463	141	15	9	4	0.9	95	46	67	67	16	10	2	202	6	7	0	1.6	.967	OF-119
1976			148	.336	.450	562	189	28	9	6	1.1	111	74	62	65	34	10	3	270	10	6	2	1.9	.979	OF-144
1977			154	.318	.467	585	186	35	8	12	2.1	117	57	69	84	17	4	1	298	10	3	3	2.0	.990	OF-147
1978			158	.288	.417	614	177	33	8	10	1.6	90	63	54	70	23	6	3	296	13	10	2	2.0	.969	OF-154
1979			95	.316	.471	380	120	27	4	8	2.1	62	32	36	39	12	1	1	175	8	3	1	2.0	.984	OF-93
1980			146	.294	.454	544	160	28	10	13	2.4	89	85	62	77	23	7	4	266	5	6	3	1.9	.978	OF-138
1981			101	.311	.409	396	123	21	6	2	0.5	65	34	39	42	12	1	0	268	8	3	1	2.8	.989	OF-99
1982	NY	A	127	.277	.407	484	134	23	2	12	2.5	70	54	39	58	10	7	1	282	8	5	2	2.3	.983	OF-125
1983			118	.306	.437	458	140	21	3	11	2.4	60	46	34	45	6	5	1	870	57	8	82	7.9	.991	1B-101, OF-14, DH-2
1984			120	.273	.381	399	109	20	1	7	1.8	44	56	29	32	2	18	5	422	22	16	23	3.8	.965	OF-82, 1B-27, DH-2
1985			127	.274	.425	438	120	28	4	10	2.3	68	69	41	51	7	18	2	227	8	7	3	1.9	.971	OF-110, DH-7, 1B-1
1986	2 teams			NY A (59G − .303)			ATL N (80G − .308)																		
"	total		139	.306	.492	490	150	22	3	21	4.3	69	58	35	67	14	19	8	232	7	5	4	1.8	.980	OF-128, DH-2, 1B-1
1987	ATL	N	122	.286	.456	399	114	24	1	14	3.5	65	64	46	54	4	18	11	205	8	2	3	1.8	.991	OF-107, 1B-3
1988	2 teams			ATL N (69G − .249)			CIN N (25G − .280)																		
"	total		94	.255	.329	243	62	6	0	4	1.6	26	23	19	31	1	31	5	193	16	4	9	2.3	.981	OF-42, 1B-21
1989	CIN	N	106	.263	.424	236	62	8	3	8	3.4	26	30	29	42	4	42	8	122	2	2	4	1.2	.984	OF-58, 1B-9
17 yrs.			2000	.297	.432	7004	2077	353	77	147	2.1	1100	824	694	877	198	215	61	4468	194	87	141	2.4	.982	OF-1651, 1B-163, DH-13

LEAGUE CHAMPIONSHIP SERIES

Year	Team		Games	BA	SA	AB	H	2B	3B	HR	HR%	R	RBI	BB	SO	SB	AB	H	PO	A	E	DP	TC/G	FA	G by Pos
1973	CIN	N	3	.143	.286	7	1	1	0	0	0.0	0	0	0	1	0	1	0	2	0	0	0	0.7	1.000	OF-2
1975			3	.333	.417	12	4	1	0	0	0.0	4	4	0	3	3	0	0	4	1	0	0	1.7	1.000	OF-3
1976			3	.385	.538	13	5	0	1	0	0.0	2	2	2	1	2	0	0	11	0	0	0	3.7	1.000	OF-3
3 yrs.			9	.313	.438	32	10	2	1	0	0.0	6	6	2	5	5	1	0	17	1	0	0	2.0	1.000	OF-8

WORLD SERIES

Year	Team		Games	BA	SA	AB	H	2B	3B	HR	HR%	R	RBI	BB	SO	SB	AB	H	PO	A	E	DP	TC/G	FA	G by Pos
1975	CIN	N	7	.269	.462	26	7	3	1	0	0.0	4	4	4	2	1	0	0	10	1	0	0	1.6	1.000	OF-7
1976			4	.059	.059	17	1	0	0	0	0.0	2	1	0	1	1	0	0	5	0	0	0	1.3	1.000	OF-4
2 yrs.			11	.186	.302	43	8	3	1	0	0.0	6	5	4	3	2	0	0	15	1	0	0	1.5	1.000	OF-11

Ken Griffey

GRIFFEY, GEORGE KENNETH, JR.
Son of Ken Griffey.
B. Nov. 21, 1969, Donora, Pa.

BL TL 6'3" 195 lbs.

Year	Team		Games	BA	SA	AB	H	2B	3B	HR	HR%	R	RBI	BB	SO	SB	AB	H	PO	A	E	DP	TC/G	FA	G by Pos
1989	SEA	A	127	.264	.420	455	120	23	0	16	3.5	61	61	44	83	16	3	1	302	12	10	6	2.6	.969	OF-127

Alfredo Griffin

GRIFFIN, ALFREDO CLAUDINO
Born Alfredo Claudino Baptist y Griffin.
B. Oct. 6, 1957, Santo Domingo, Dominican Republic

BB TR 5'11" 160 lbs.

Year	Team		Games	BA	SA	AB	H	2B	3B	HR	HR%	R	RBI	BB	SO	SB	AB	H	PO	A	E	DP	TC/G	FA	G by Pos
1976	CLE	A	12	.250	.250	4	1	0	0	0	0.0	0	0	0	2	0	0	0	1	2	1	0	0.3	.750	SS-6, DH-4
1977			14	.146	.171	41	6	1	0	0	0.0	5	3	3	5	2	0	0	17	30	3	6	3.6	.940	SS-13, DH-1
1978			5	.500	.750	4	2	1	0	0	0.0	0	0	2	1	0	0	0	4	7	1	5	2.4	.917	SS-2
1979	TOR	A	153	.287	.364	624	179	22	10	2	0.3	81	31	40	59	21	0	0	272	501	36	124	5.3	.956	SS-153
1980			155	.254	.349	653	166	26	15	2	0.3	63	41	24	58	18	0	0	295	489	37	126	5.3	.955	SS-155
1981			101	.209	.289	388	81	19	6	0	0.0	30	21	17	38	8	1	0	191	279	31	66	5.0	.938	SS-97, 3B-4, 2B-1
1982			162	.241	.314	539	130	20	8	1	0.2	57	48	22	48	10	0	0	319	479	26	92	5.1	.968	SS-162
1983			162	.250	.348	528	132	22	9	4	0.8	62	47	27	44	8	0	0	287	422	25	86	4.5	.966	SS-157, 2B-5, DH-1
1984			140	.241	.298	419	101	8	2	4	1.0	53	30	4	33	11	0	0	230	320	21	72	4.1	.963	SS-115, 2B-21, DH-5
1985	OAK	A	162	.270	.332	614	166	18	7	2	0.3	75	64	20	50	24	0	0	278	440	30	87	4.6	.960	SS-162
1986			162	.285	.364	594	169	23	6	4	0.7	74	51	35	52	33	0	0	282	421	25	85	4.5	.966	SS-162
1987			144	.263	.348	494	130	23	5	3	0.6	69	60	28	41	26	0	0	250	389	24	73	4.6	.964	SS-137, 2B-1
1988	LA	N	95	.199	.253	316	63	8	3	1	0.3	39	27	24	30	7	0	0	145	264	15	44	4.5	.965	SS-93
1989			136	.247	.308	506	125	27	2	0	0.0	49	29	29	57	10	5	1	208	333	14	69	4.1	.975	SS-131
14 yrs.			1603	.253	.329	5724	1451	218	73	23	0.4	658	452	275	518	178	6	1	2779	4376	289	935	4.6	.961	SS-1545, 2B-28, DH-11, 3B-4

LEAGUE CHAMPIONSHIP SERIES

Year	Team		Games	BA	SA	AB	H	2B	3B	HR	HR%	R	RBI	BB	SO	SB	AB	H	PO	A	E	DP	TC/G	FA	G by Pos
1988	LA	N	7	.160	.200	25	4	1	0	0	0.0	1	3	0	5	0	0	0	17	13	0	7	4.3	1.000	SS-7

WORLD SERIES

Year	Team		Games	BA	SA	AB	H	2B	3B	HR	HR%	R	RBI	BB	SO	SB	AB	H	PO	A	E	DP	TC/G	FA	G by Pos
1988	LA	N	5	.188	.188	16	3	0	0	0	0.0	2	0	2	4	0	0	0	7	13	1	2	4.2	.952	SS-5

Doug Griffin

GRIFFIN, DOUGLAS LEE
B. June 4, 1947, South Gate, Calif.

BR TR 6' 160 lbs.

Year	Team		Games	BA	SA	AB	H	2B	3B	HR	HR%	R	RBI	BB	SO	SB	AB	H	PO	A	E	DP	TC/G	FA	G by Pos
1970	CAL	A	18	.127	.145	55	7	1	0	0	0.0	2	4	6	5	0	0	0	24	42	2	9	3.8	.971	2B-11, 3B-8
1971	BOS	A	125	.244	.319	483	118	23	2	3	0.6	51	27	31	45	11	1	0	311	344	9	90	5.3	.986	2B-124
1972			129	.260	.302	470	122	12	1	2	0.4	43	35	45	48	9	0	0	321	331	15	81	5.2	.978	2B-129
1973			113	.255	.323	396	101	14	5	1	0.3	43	33	21	42	7	0	0	294	284	6	77	5.2	.990	2B-113
1974			93	.266	.330	312	83	12	4	0	0.0	35	33	28	21	2	2	1	180	243	9	54	4.6	.979	2B-91, SS-1
1975			100	.240	.272	287	69	6	0	1	0.3	21	29	18	29	2	16	0	195	215	14	45	4.2	.967	2B-99, SS-1
1976			49	.189	.205	127	24	2	0	0	0.0	14	4	9	14	2	2	0	77	98	2	15	3.6	.989	2B-44, DH-2
1977			5	.000	.000	6	0	0	0	0	0.0	0	0	0	0	0	2	0	2	4	0	1	1.2	1.000	2B-3
8 yrs.			632	.245	.299	2136	524	70	12	7	0.3	209	165	158	204	33	24	9	1404	1561	57	372	4.8	.981	2B-614, 3B-8, DH-2, SS-2

WORLD SERIES

Year	Team		Games	BA	SA	AB	H	2B	3B	HR	HR%	R	RBI	BB	SO	SB	AB	H	PO	A	E	DP	TC/G	FA	G by Pos
1975	BOS	A	1	.000	.000	1	0	0	0	0	0.0	0	0	0	0	0	0	0	0	0	0	0	0.0	−	

Year	Team	Games	BA	SA	AB	H	2B	3B	HR	HR%	R	RBI	BB	SO	SB	Pinch Hit AB	Pinch Hit H	PO	A	E	DP	TC/G	FA	G by Pos

Ivy Griffin

GRIFFIN, IVY MOORE
B. Dec. 25, 1896, Thomasville, Ala.   D. Aug. 25, 1957, Gainesville, Fla.
BL TR 5'11"   180 lbs.

Year	Team	Games	BA	SA	AB	H	2B	3B	HR	HR%	R	RBI	BB	SO	SB	PH AB	PH H	PO	A	E	DP	TC/G	FA	G by Pos
1919	PHI A	17	.294	.382	68	20	2	2	0	0.0	5	6	3	10	0	0	0	162	21	2	11	10.9	.989	1B-17
1920		129	.238	.274	467	111	15	1	0	0.0	46	20	15	49	3	1	0	1259	102	15	77	10.7	.989	1B-126, 2B-2
1921		39	.320	.398	103	33	4	2	0	0.0	14	13	5	6	1	10	2	236	13	7	12	6.6	.973	1B-28
3 yrs.		185	.257	.306	638	164	21	5	0	0.0	65	39	23	65	4	11	2	1657	136	24	100	9.8	.987	1B-171, 2B-2

Mike Griffin

GRIFFIN, MICHAEL JOSEPH
B. Mar. 20, 1865, Utica, N. Y.   D. Apr. 10, 1908, Utica, N. Y.
Manager 1898.
BL TR 5'7"   160 lbs.

Year	Team	Games	BA	SA	AB	H	2B	3B	HR	HR%	R	RBI	BB	SO	SB	PH AB	PH H	PO	A	E	DP	TC/G	FA	G by Pos
1887	BAL AA	136	.301	.427	532	160	32	13	3	0.6	142		55		94	0	0	256	13	22	1	2.1	.924	OF-136
1888		137	.256	.336	542	139	21	11	0	0.0	103	46	55		46	0	0	274	27	20	6	2.3	.938	OF-137
1889		137	.279	.394	531	148	21	14	4	0.8	152	48	91	29	39	0	0	298	91	52	12	3.2	.882	OF-109, SS-25, 2B-5
1890	PHI P	115	.286	.407	489	140	29	6	6	1.2	127	54	64	19	30	0	0	278	33	15	10	2.8	.954	OF-115
1891	BKN N	134	.271	.392	521	141	36	9	3	0.6	106	65	57	31	65	0	0	353	31	16	7	3.0	.960	OF-134
1892		129	.277	.383	452	125	17	11	3	0.7	103	66	68	36	49	0	0	268	34	7	8	2.4	.977	OF-127, SS-2
1893		95	.285	.431	362	103	21	7	6	1.7	85	59	59	23	30	0	0	234	25	10	8	2.8	.963	OF-93, 2B-2
1894		107	.365	.499	405	148	29	5	5	1.2	123	75	78	14	39	1	0	297	14	10	5	3.0	.969	OF-106
1895		131	.333	.457	519	173	38	7	4	0.8	140	65	93	29	27	0	0	349	29	14	12	2.8	.964	OF-131, SS-1
1896		122	.308	.424	493	152	27	9	4	0.8	101	51	48	25	23	0	0	316	8	13	1	2.8	.961	OF-122
1897		134	.316	.416	534	169	25	11	2	0.4	136	56	81		16	0	0	353	13	17	6	2.9	.956	OF-134
1898		134	.300	.367	537	161	18	6	2	0.4	88	40	60		15	0	0	314	20	9	7	2.6	.974	OF-134
12 yrs.		1511	.297	.408	5917	1759	314	109	42	0.7	1406	625	809	206	473	1	0	3590	338	205	83	2.7	.950	OF-1478, SS-28, 2B-7

Pug Griffin

GRIFFIN, FRANCIS ARTHUR
B. Apr. 24, 1896, Lincoln, Neb.   D. Oct. 12, 1951, Colorado Springs, Colo.
BR TR 5'11½"   187 lbs.

Year	Team	Games	BA	SA	AB	H	2B	3B	HR	HR%	R	RBI	BB	SO	SB	PH AB	PH H	PO	A	E	DP	TC/G	FA	G by Pos
1917	PHI A	18	.200	.360	25	5	1	0	1	4.0	4	3	1	9	1	13	2	30	3	0	0	1.8	1.000	1B-3
1920	NY N	5	.250	.250	4	1	0	0	0	0.0	0	0	1	2	0	2	0	1	0	0	0	0.2	1.000	OF-2
2 yrs.		23	.207	.345	29	6	1	0	1	3.4	4	3	2	11	1	15	2	31	3	0	1	1.5	1.000	1B-3, OF-2

Sandy Griffin

GRIFFIN, TOBIAS CHARLES
B. July 19, 1858, Fayetteville, N. Y.   D. June 5, 1926, Fayetteville, N. Y.
Manager 1891.
BR TR 5'10"   160 lbs.

Year	Team	Games	BA	SA	AB	H	2B	3B	HR	HR%	R	RBI	BB	SO	SB	PH AB	PH H	PO	A	E	DP	TC/G	FA	G by Pos
1884	NY N	16	.177	.210	62	11	2	0	0	0.0	7		1	19		0	0	14	2	3	1	1.2	.842	OF-16
1890	ROC AA	107	.307	.432	407	125	28	4	5	1.2	85		50		21	0	0	160	8	29	1	1.8	.853	OF-107, 2B-1
1891	WAS AA	20	.275	.391	69	19	4	2	0	0.0	15	10	10	3	2	0	0	30	1	2	1	1.7	.939	OF-20
1893	STL N	23	.196	.228	92	18	1	1	0	0.0	9	9	16	2	2	0	0	46	2	5	0	2.3	.906	OF-23
4 yrs.		166	.275	.376	630	173	35	7	5	0.8	116	19	77	24	25	0	0	250	13	39	3	1.8	.871	OF-166, 2B-1

Tom Griffin

GRIFFIN, THOMAS WILLIAM
B. Jan., 1857, Rockford, Ill.   D. Apr. 17, 1933, Rockford, Ill.
BR TR 5'11"   185 lbs.

Year	Team	Games	BA	SA	AB	H	2B	3B	HR	HR%	R	RBI	BB	SO	SB	PH AB	PH H	PO	A	E	DP	TC/G	FA	G by Pos
1884	MIL U	11	.220	.268	41	9	2	0	0	0.0	5		3			0	0	100	1	9	0	10.0	.918	1B-11

Bart Griffith

GRIFFITH, BARTHOLOMEW JOSEPH
B. Mar. 30, 1896, St. Louis, Mo.   D. May 5, 1973, Bishop, Calif.
BR TR 5'11"   185 lbs.

Year	Team	Games	BA	SA	AB	H	2B	3B	HR	HR%	R	RBI	BB	SO	SB	PH AB	PH H	PO	A	E	DP	TC/G	FA	G by Pos
1922	BKN N	106	.308	.443	325	100	22	8	2	0.6	45	35	5	11	5	23	4	192	11	4	5	2.0	.981	OF-77, 1B-6
1923		79	.294	.383	248	73	8	4	2	0.8	23	37	13	16	1	17	3	111	1	6	0	1.5	.949	OF-62
1924	WAS A	6	.125	.125	8	1	0	0	0	0.0	1	0	0	1	0	4	0	7	0	0	0	1.2	1.000	OF-2
3 yrs.		191	.299	.413	581	174	30	12	4	0.7	69	72	18	28	6	44	7	310	12	10	5	1.7	.970	OF-141, 1B-6

Clark Griffith

GRIFFITH, CLARK CALVIN (Griff, General)
B. Nov. 20, 1869, Clear Creek, Mo.   D. Oct. 27, 1955, Washington, D. C.
Manager 1901-20.
Hall of Fame 1946.
BR TR 5'6½"   156 lbs.

Year	Team	Games	BA	SA	AB	H	2B	3B	HR	HR%	R	RBI	BB	SO	SB	PH AB	PH H	PO	A	E	DP	TC/G	FA	G by Pos
1891	2 teams	STL AA (27G – .156)		BOS AA (10G – .174)																				
"	total	37	.160	.260	100	16	1	2	2	2.0	17	11	14	20	3	1	0	12	51	6	1	1.9	.913	P-34, OF-3
1893	CHI N	4	.182	.182	11	2	0	0	0	0.0	1	2	0	1	0	0	0	2	6	0	0	2.0	1.000	P-4
1894		46	.232	.324	142	33	5	4	0	0.0	27	15	23	9	6	2	1	27	46	10	1	1.8	.880	P-36, OF-7, SS-1
1895		43	.319	.361	144	46	3	0	1	0.7	20	27	16	9	2	0	0	28	81	9	2	2.7	.924	P-42, OF-1
1896		38	.267	.356	135	36	5	2	1	0.7	22	16	9	7	3	2	0	20	79	9	3	2.8	.917	P-36
1897		46	.235	.333	162	38	8	4	0	0.0	27	21	18		2	0	0	31	96	12	4	3.0	.914	P-41, OF-2, SS-2, 3B-1, 1B-1
1898		38	.164	.230	122	20	2	3	0	0.0	15	15	13		1	0	0	18	82	5	2	2.8	.952	P-38
1899		39	.258	.300	120	31	5	0	0	0.0	15	14	14		2	0	0	18	110	11	3	3.6	.921	P-38, SS-1
1900		30	.253	.347	95	24	4	1	1	1.1	16	7	8		2	0	0	9	57	6	0	2.4	.917	P-30
1901	CHI A	35	.303	.427	89	27	3	1	2	2.2	21	14	23		0	0	0	9	78	5	3	2.6	.946	P-35
1902		35	.217	.250	92	20	3	0	0	0.0	11	8	7		0	4	0	13	55	0	1	1.9	1.000	P-28, OF-3
1903	NY A	25	.159	.261	69	11	4	0	1	1.4	5	7	11		0	1	0	8	50	1	1	2.4	.983	P-25
1904		16	.143	.190	42	6	2	0	0	0.0	2	1	4		0	0	0	3	32	2	0	2.3	.946	P-16
1905		26	.219	.313	32	7	1	1	0	0.0	2	5	3		0	0	0	1	23	1	0	1.0	.960	P-25, OF-1
1906		17	.111	.111	18	2	0	0	0	0.0	0	0	3		0	0	0	0	23	1	0	1.4	1.000	P-17
1907		4	.000	.000	2	0	0	0	0	0.0	0	0	0		0	0	0	0	4	1	0	1.3	.800	P-4
1909	CIN N	1	.000	.000	2	0	0	0	0	0.0	0	0	0		0	0	0	1	4	0	0	5.0	1.000	P-1
1910		1	—		0	0	0	0	0	—	0	1	0		0	0	0	0	0	0	0	0.0		
1912	WAS A	1	.000	.000	1	0	0	0	0	0.0	0	0	0		0	0	0	0	2	0	0	2.0	1.000	2B-1, P-1
1913		1	1.000	2.000	1	1	1	0	0	0.0	0	0	0		0	1	1	0	0	0	0	0.0	—	OF-1, P-1
1914		1	1.000	2.000	1	1	1	0	0	0.0	0	1	0		0	0	0	0	0	0	0	0.0		P-1
21 yrs.		484	.233	.310	1380	321	49	17	8	0.6	202	166	166	46	22	9	1	201	879	78	23	2.4	.933	P-453, OF-18, SS-4, 3B-1, 2B-1, 1B-1

Year	Team	Games	BA	SA	AB	H	2B	3B	HR	HR%	R	RBI	BB	SO	SB	Pinch Hit AB	Pinch Hit H	PO	A	E	DP	TC/G	FA	G by Pos

Derrell Griffith

GRIFFITH, ROBERT DERRELL
B. Dec. 12, 1943, Anadarko, Okla.　　BL TR 6'　168 lbs.

Year	Team	Games	BA	SA	AB	H	2B	3B	HR	HR%	R	RBI	BB	SO	SB	AB	H	PO	A	E	DP	TC/G	FA	G by Pos
1963	LA	N	1	.000	.000	2	0	0	0	0	0.0	0	0	0	1	0	1	0	0	0	0	0	0.0	–	2B-1
1964		78	.290	.424	238	69	16	2	4	1.7	27	23	5	21	5	12	1	57	56	23	3	1.7	.831	3B-35, OF-29
1965		22	.171	.244	41	7	0	0	1	2.4	3	2	0	9	0	8	2	17	0	0	0	0.8	1.000	OF-11
1966		23	.067	.067	15	1	0	0	0	0.0	3	2	2	3	0	9	1	5	0	0	0	0.2	1.000	OF-7
4 yrs.		124	.260	.378	296	77	16	2	5	1.7	33	27	7	33	5	30	4	79	56	23	3	1.3	.854	OF-47, 3B-35, 2B-1

Tommy Griffith

GRIFFITH, THOMAS HERMAN
B. Oct. 26, 1889, Prospect, Ohio　D. Apr. 13, 1967, Cincinnati, Ohio　　BL TR 5'10"　175 lbs.

Year	Team	Games	BA	SA	AB	H	2B	3B	HR	HR%	R	RBI	BB	SO	SB	AB	H	PO	A	E	DP	TC/G	FA	G by Pos
1913	BOS	N	37	.252	.323	127	32	4	1	1	0.8	16	12	9	8	1	1	0	55	7	8	1	1.9	.886	OF-35
1914		16	.104	.104	48	5	0	0	0	0.0	3	1	2	6	0	2	2	20	7	2	2	1.8	.931	OF-14
1915	CIN	N	160	.307	.436	583	179	31	16	4	0.7	59	85	41	34	6	0	0	225	11	12	1	1.6	.952	OF-160
1916		155	.266	.346	595	158	28	7	2	0.3	50	61	36	37	16	0	0	238	28	9	5	1.8	.967	OF-155
1917		115	.270	.366	363	98	18	7	1	0.3	45	45	19	23	5	13	4	165	19	5	3	1.6	.974	OF-100
1918		118	.265	.321	427	113	10	4	2	0.5	47	48	39	30	10	0	0	201	18	7	3	1.9	.969	OF-118
1919	BKN	N	125	.281	.372	484	136	18	4	6	1.2	65	57	23	32	8	0	0	210	20	11	3	1.9	.954	OF-125
1920		93	.260	.329	334	87	9	4	2	0.6	41	30	15	18	3	1	1	132	7	4	1	1.5	.972	OF-92
1921		129	.312	.464	455	142	21	6	12	2.6	66	71	36	13	3	4	1	215	27	7	5	1.9	.972	OF-124
1922		99	.316	.453	329	104	17	8	4	1.2	44	49	23	10	7	14	4	167	13	9	4	1.9	.952	OF-82
1923		131	.293	.424	481	141	21	9	8	1.7	70	66	50	19	2	4	0	215	14	18	4	1.7	.927	OF-128
1924		140	.251	.330	482	121	19	5	3	0.6	43	67	34	19	0	0	0	210	9	8	3	1.6	.965	OF-139
1925	2 teams	BKN	N	(7G – .000)	CHI	N	(76G – .285)																	
"	total	83	.280	.427	239	67	12	1	7	2.9	40	27	24	13	3	16	3	111	9	8	1	1.5	.938	OF-62
13 yrs.		1401	.280	.382	4947	1383	208	72	52	1.1	589	619	351	262	70	53	15	2164	189	108	36	1.8	.956	OF-1334

WORLD SERIES

Year	Team	Games	BA	SA	AB	H	2B	3B	HR	HR%	R	RBI	BB	SO	SB	AB	H	PO	A	E	DP	TC/G	FA	G by Pos
1920	BKN	N	7	.190	.286	21	4	2	0	0	0.0	1	3	0	2	0	0	0	9	0	0	0	1.3	1.000	OF-7

Art Griggs

GRIGGS, ART CARLE
B. Dec. 10, 1883, Topeka, Kans.　D. Dec. 19, 1938, Los Angeles, Calif.　　BR TR 5'11"　185 lbs.

Year	Team	Games	BA	SA	AB	H	2B	3B	HR	HR%	R	RBI	BB	SO	SB	AB	H	PO	A	E	DP	TC/G	FA	G by Pos
1909	STL	A	108	.280	.354	364	102	17	5	0	0.0	38	43	24		11	9	1	517	60	22	23	5.5	.963	1B-49, OF-40, 2B-8, SS-1
1910		123	.236	.327	416	98	22	5	2	0.5	28	30	25		11	10	1	322	120	32	29	3.9	.932	OF-49, 2B-41, 1B-17, SS-3, 3B-3
1911	CLE	A	27	.250	.397	68	17	3	2	1	1.5	7	7	5		1	5	1	39	36	3	3	2.9	.962	2B-11, OF-4, 3B-3, 1B-1
1912		89	.304	.414	273	83	16	7	0	0.0	29	39	33		10	18	3	661	43	10	33	8.0	.986	1B-71
1914	BKN	F	40	.286	.384	112	32	6	1	1	0.9	10	15	5		1	12	2	238	8	6	10	6.3	.976	1B-27, OF-1
1915		27	.289	.395	38	11	1	0	1	2.6	4	2	3		0	16	5	56	4	0	3	2.2	1.000	1B-5, OF-1
1918	DET	A	28	.364	.444	99	36	8	0	0	0.0	11	16	10	5	2	2	2	263	9	4	10	9.9	.986	1B-25
7 yrs.		442	.277	.370	1370	379	73	20	5	0.4	127	152	105	5	36	72	15	2096	280	77	111	5.5	.969	1B-195, OF-95, 2B-60, 3B-6, SS-4

Denver Grigsby

GRIGSBY, DENVER CLARENCE
B. Mar. 24, 1901, Jackson, Ky.　D. Nov. 10, 1973, Sapulpa, Okla.　　BL TR 5'9"　155 lbs.

Year	Team	Games	BA	SA	AB	H	2B	3B	HR	HR%	R	RBI	BB	SO	SB	AB	H	PO	A	E	DP	TC/G	FA	G by Pos
1923	CHI	N	24	.292	.417	72	21	5	2	0	0.0	8	5	7	5	1	1	1	41	1	0	0	1.8	1.000	OF-22
1924		124	.299	.375	411	123	18	2	3	0.7	58	48	31	47	10	2	0	244	16	7	4	2.2	.974	OF-121
1925		51	.255	.292	137	35	5	0	0	0.0	20	20	19	12	1	8	0	81	4	3	2	1.7	.966	OF-39
3 yrs.		199	.289	.361	620	179	28	4	3	0.5	86	73	57	64	12	11	1	366	21	10	6	2.0	.975	OF-182

John Grim

GRIM, JOHN HELM
B. Aug. 9, 1867, Lebanon, Ky.　D. July 28, 1961, Indianapolis, Ind.　　BR TR 6'2"　175 lbs.

Year	Team	Games	BA	SA	AB	H	2B	3B	HR	HR%	R	RBI	BB	SO	SB	AB	H	PO	A	E	DP	TC/G	FA	G by Pos
1888	PHI	N	2	.143	.143	7	1	0	0	0	0.0	0		0	0	0	0	0	1	4	2	0	3.5	.714	OF-1, 2B-1
1890	ROC	AA	50	.266	.422	192	51	6	9	2	1.0	30		7		14	0	0	151	99	27	15	5.5	.903	SS-21, C-15, 3B-8, 2B-4, OF-3, 1B-2, P-1
1891	MIL	AA	29	.235	.319	119	28	5	1	1	0.8	14	14	2	5	1	0	0	111	46	15	4	5.9	.913	C-16, 3B-10, 2B-3
1892	LOU	N	97	.243	.316	370	90	16	4	1	0.3	40	36	13	24	18	0	0	405	120	29	17	5.7	.948	C-69, 1B-11, 2B-10, OF-8, SS-1, 3B-1
1893		99	.267	.373	415	111	19	8	3	0.7	68	54	12	10	15	0	0	313	117	23	18	4.6	.949	C-92, 1B-3, 2B-2, OF-1, SS-1
1894		108	.298	.449	410	122	27	7	7	1.7	66	70	16	15	14	1	0	387	177	41	25	5.6	.932	C-77, 2B-24, 1B-7, 3B-1
1895	BKN	N	93	.280	.362	329	92	17	5	0	0.0	54	44	13	9	9	0	0	261	103	20	10	4.1	.948	C-91, OF-1, 1B-1
1896		81	.267	.342	281	75	13	1	2	0.7	32	35	12	14	7	0	0	277	82	22	8	4.7	.942	C-77, 1B-5
1897		80	.248	.290	290	72	10	1	0	0.0	26	25	1		3	3	0	241	98	19	6	4.5	.947	C-77
1898		52	.281	.320	178	50	5	1	0	0.0	17	11	8		1	0	0	155	56	11	6	4.3	.950	C-52
1899		15	.277	.298	47	13	1	0	0	0.0	3	7	1		0	3	0	39	17	2	3	3.9	.966	C-12
11 yrs.		706	.267	.359	2638	705	119	37	16	0.6	350	296	85	77	82	7	0	2341	919	211	114	4.9	.939	C-578, 2B-44, 1B-29, SS-23, 3B-20, OF-14, P-1

Ed Grimes

GRIMES, EDWARD ADELBERT
B. Sept. 8, 1905, Chicago, Ill.　D. Oct. 5, 1974, Chicago, Ill.　　BR TR 5'10"　178 lbs.

Year	Team	Games	BA	SA	AB	H	2B	3B	HR	HR%	R	RBI	BB	SO	SB	AB	H	PO	A	E	DP	TC/G	FA	G by Pos
1931	STL	A	43	.263	.351	57	15	1	0	0	0.0	9	5	9	3	1	5	0	17	24	4	0	1.0	.911	3B-22, 2B-4, SS-3
1932		31	.235	.265	68	16	0	1	0	0.0	7	13	6	12	0	3	0	17	38	6	5	2.0	.902	3B-18, 2B-2, SS-1
2 yrs.		74	.248	.304	125	31	1	1	3	0	0.0	16	18	15	15	1	8	0	34	62	10	5	1.4	.906	3B-40, 2B-6, SS-4

Oscar Grimes

GRIMES, OSCAR RAY, JR.
Son of Ray Grimes.
B. Apr. 13, 1915, Minerva, Ohio　　BR TR 5'11"　178 lbs.

Year	Team	Games	BA	SA	AB	H	2B	3B	HR	HR%	R	RBI	BB	SO	SB	AB	H	PO	A	E	DP	TC/G	FA	G by Pos
1938	CLE	A	4	.200	.400	10	2	0	1	0	0.0	2	0	2	0	0	1	0	10	2	0	2	3.0	1.000	2B-2, 1B-1
1939		119	.269	.385	364	98	20	5	4	1.1	51	56	56	61	8	3	0	501	192	22	75	6.0	.969	2B-48, 1B-43, SS-37
1940		11	.000	.000	13	0	0	0	0	0.0	3	0	0	5	0	1	0	21	6	1	2	2.5	.964	1B-4, 3B-1
1941		77	.238	.348	244	58	9	4	4	1.6	28	24	39	47	4	1	0	572	62	5	60	8.3	.992	1B-62, 2B-13, 3B-1
1942		51	.179	.202	84	15	2	0	0	0.0	10	2	13	17	3	9	1	55	52	8	12	2.3	.930	2B-24, 3B-8, SS-1, 1B-1
1943	NY	A	9	.150	.150	20	3	0	0	0	0.0	4	1	3	7	0	4	0	10	8	0	6	2.0	1.000	SS-3, 1B-1

Year	Team		Games	BA	SA	AB	H	2B	3B	HR	HR%	R	RBI	BB	SO	SB	Pinch Hit AB	Pinch Hit H	PO	A	E	DP	TC/G	FA	G by Pos

Oscar Grimes *continued*

Year	Team		Games	BA	SA	AB	H	2B	3B	HR	HR%	R	RBI	BB	SO	SB	AB	H	PO	A	E	DP	TC/G	FA	G by Pos
1944			116	.279	.403	387	108	17	8	5	1.3	44	46	59	57	6	1	0	140	246	24	24	3.5	.941	3B-97, SS-20
1945			142	.265	.358	480	127	19	7	4	0.8	64	45	97	73	7	1	0	166	297	31	35	3.5	.937	3B-141, 1B-1
1946	2 teams	NY A (14G – .205)			PHI A	(59G – .262)																			
"	total		73	.252	.291	230	58	6	0	1	0.4	29	24	28	36	2	7	2	142	155	20	36	4.3	.937	2B-48, SS-11, 3B-6
9 yrs.			602	.256	.352	1832	469	73	24	18	1.0	235	200	297	303	30	28	3	1617	1020	111	252	4.6	.960	3B-254, 2B-135, 1B-113, SS-72

Ray Grimes

GRIMES, OSCAR RAY, SR.
Father of Oscar Grimes.   Brother of Roy Grimes.
B. Sept. 11, 1893, Bergholz, Ohio   D. May 25, 1953, Minerva, Ohio

BR TR 5'11" 168 lbs.

Year	Team		Games	BA	SA	AB	H	2B	3B	HR	HR%	R	RBI	BB	SO	SB	AB	H	PO	A	E	DP	TC/G	FA	G by Pos
1920	BOS	A	1	.250	.250	4	1	0	0	0	0.0	1	0	1	0	0	0	0	13	0	0	2	13.0	1.000	1B-1
1921	CHI	N	147	.321	.449	530	170	38	6	6	1.1	91	79	70	55	5	0	0	1544	68	12	93	11.0	.993	1B-147
1922			138	.354	.572	509	180	45	12	14	2.8	99	99	75	33	7	0	0	1378	68	19	106	10.6	.987	1B-138
1923			64	.329	.407	216	71	7	2	2	0.9	32	36	24	17	5	2	0	629	30	6	46	10.4	.991	1B-62
1924			51	.299	.475	177	53	6	5	5	2.8	33	34	28	15	4	1	0	530	12	10	40	10.8	.982	1B-50
1926	PHI	N	32	.297	.347	101	30	5	0	0	0.0	13	15	6	13	0	3	0	241	16	5	28	8.2	.981	1B-28
6 yrs.			433	.329	.480	1537	505	101	25	27	1.8	269	263	204	133	21	6	0	4335	194	52	315	10.6	.989	1B-426

Roy Grimes

GRIMES, AUSTIN ROY
Brother of Ray Grimes.
B. Sept. 11, 1893, Bergholz, Ohio   D. Sept. 13, 1954, Gilford Lake, Ohio

BR TR 6'1" 185 lbs.

Year	Team		Games	BA	SA	AB	H	2B	3B	HR	HR%	R	RBI	BB	SO	SB	AB	H	PO	A	E	DP	TC/G	FA	G by Pos
1920	NY	N	26	.158	.175	57	9	1	0	0	0.0	5	3	3	8	1	5	1	24	49	4	3	3.0	.948	2B-21

Charlie Grimm

GRIMM, CHARLES JOHN (Jolly Cholly)
B. Aug. 25, 1896, St. Louis, Mo.   D. Nov. 15, 1983, Scottsdale, Ariz.
Manager 1932-38, 1944-49, 1952-56, 1960.

BL TL 5'11½" 173 lbs.

Year	Team		Games	BA	SA	AB	H	2B	3B	HR	HR%	R	RBI	BB	SO	SB	AB	H	PO	A	E	DP	TC/G	FA	G by Pos
1916	PHI	A	12	.091	.091	22	2	0	0	0	0.0	2	4	0	4	0	4	0	7	0	1	0	0.7	.875	OF-7
1918	STL	N	50	.220	.270	141	31	7	0	0	0.0	11	12	6	15	2	5	0	389	17	12	24	8.4	.971	1B-42, OF-2, 3B-1
1919	PIT	N	12	.318	.477	44	14	1	3	0	0.0	6	6	2	4	1	0	0	118	2	4	1	10.3	.968	1B-11
1920			148	.227	.289	533	121	13	7	2	0.4	38	54	30	40	7	0	0	1496	95	8	95	10.8	.995	1B-148
1921			151	.274	.409	562	154	21	17	7	1.2	62	71	31	38	6	1	0	1517	67	9	93	10.5	.994	1B-150
1922			154	.292	.383	593	173	28	13	0	0.0	64	76	43	15	6	0	0	1478	68	10	104	10.1	.994	1B-154
1923			152	.345	.480	563	194	29	13	7	1.2	78	99	41	43	6	0	0	1453	81	8	130	10.1	.995	1B-152
1924			151	.288	.389	542	156	29	12	2	0.4	53	63	37	22	3	0	0	1596	72	8	139	11.1	.995	1B-151
1925	CHI	N	141	.306	.439	519	159	29	5	10	1.9	73	76	38	25	4	2	0	1317	73	15	125	10.0	.989	1B-139
1926			147	.277	.403	524	145	30	6	8	1.5	58	82	49	25	3	0	0	1416	68	18	139	10.2	.988	1B-147
1927			147	.311	.398	543	169	29	6	2	0.4	74	45	21	3	0	0		1437	99	15	117	10.6	.990	1B-147
1928			147	.294	.386	547	161	25	5	5	0.9	67	62	39	20	7	0	0	1458	70	10	147	10.5	.993	1B-147
1929			120	.298	.436	463	138	28	3	10	2.2	66	91	42	25	3	0	0	1228	74	10	114	10.9	.992	1B-120
1930			114	.289	.403	429	124	27	2	6	1.4	58	66	41	26	1	1	0	1040	68	6	103	9.8	.995	1B-113
1931			146	.331	.458	531	176	33	11	4	0.8	65	66	53	29	1	1	0	1357	79	10	107	9.9	.993	1B-144
1932			149	.307	.425	570	175	42	2	7	1.2	66	80	35	22	2	0	0	1429	123	11	127	10.5	.993	1B-149
1933			107	.247	.320	384	95	15	2	3	0.8	38	37	23	15	1	2	0	979	84	4	94	10.0	.996	1B-104
1934			75	.296	.390	267	79	8	1	5	1.9	24	47	16	12	1	1	0	683	43	4	39	9.7	.995	1B-74
1935			2	.000	.000	8	0	0	0	0	0.0	0	0	0	1	0	0	0	27	1	0	4	14.0	1.000	1B-2
1936			39	.250	.303	132	33	4	0	1	0.8	13	16	5	8	0	4	1	297	33	0	31	8.5	1.000	1B-35
20 yrs.			2164	.290	.397	7917	2299	394	108	79	1.0	908	1078	578	410	57	21	1	20722	1217	163	1733	10.2	.993	1B-2129, OF-9, 3B-1

WORLD SERIES

Year	Team		Games	BA	SA	AB	H	2B	3B	HR	HR%	R	RBI	BB	SO	SB	AB	H	PO	A	E	DP	TC/G	FA	G by Pos
1929	CHI	N	5	.389	.556	18	7	0	0	1	5.6	2	4	1	2	0	0	0	40	1	0	4	8.2	1.000	1B-5
1932			4	.333	.467	15	5	2	0	0	0.0	2	1	2	2	0	0	0	28	3	0	5	7.8	1.000	1B-4
2 yrs.			9	.364	.515	33	12	2	0	1	3.0	4	5	3	4	0	0	0	68	4	0	9	8.0	1.000	1B-9

Moose Grimshaw

GRIMSHAW, MYRON FREDERICK
B. Nov. 30, 1875, St. Johnsville, N. Y.   D. Dec. 11, 1936, Canajoharie, N. Y.

BB TR 6'1" 173 lbs.

Year	Team		Games	BA	SA	AB	H	2B	3B	HR	HR%	R	RBI	BB	SO	SB	AB	H	PO	A	E	DP	TC/G	FA	G by Pos
1905	BOS	A	85	.239	.323	285	68	2	4	4	1.4	39	35	21			4	11	3	768	35	16	35	9.6	.980	1B-74
1906			110	.290	.383	428	124	16	12	0	0.0	46	48	23			5	0	0	1165	64	16	39	11.3	.987	1B-110
1907			64	.204	.265	181	37	7	2	0	0.0	19	33	16			6	14	2	168	11	6	10	2.9	.968	OF-23, 1B-15, SS-2
3 yrs.			259	.256	.340	894	229	31	16	4	0.4	104	116	60			15	25	5	2101	110	38	84	8.7	.983	1B-199, OF-23, SS-2

Marquis Grissom

GRISSOM, MARQUIS DEON
B. Apr. 17, 1967, Atlanta, Ga.

BR TR 5'11" 190 lbs.

Year	Team		Games	BA	SA	AB	H	2B	3B	HR	HR%	R	RBI	BB	SO	SB	AB	H	PO	A	E	DP	TC/G	FA	G by Pos
1989	MON	N	26	.257	.324	74	19	2	0	1	1.4	16	2	12	21	1	3	0	32	1	2	0	1.3	.943	OF-23

Dick Groat

GROAT, RICHARD MORROW
B. Nov. 4, 1930, Wilkinsburg, Pa.

BR TR 5'11½" 180 lbs.

Year	Team		Games	BA	SA	AB	H	2B	3B	HR	HR%	R	RBI	BB	SO	SB	AB	H	PO	A	E	DP	TC/G	FA	G by Pos
1952	PIT	N	95	.284	.313	384	109	6	1	1	0.3	38	29	19	27	2	1	0	229	272	25	61	5.5	.952	SS-94
1955			151	.267	.351	521	139	28	2	4	0.8	45	51	38	26	0	1	0	330	450	32	107	5.4	.961	SS-149
1956			142	.273	.321	520	142	19	3	0	0.0	40	37	35	25	0	0	0	288	424	34	75	5.3	.954	SS-141, 3B-2
1957			125	.315	.437	501	158	30	5	7	1.4	58	54	27	28	0	0	0	226	385	21	74	5.1	.967	SS-123, 3B-2
1958			151	.300	.408	584	175	36	9	3	0.5	67	66	23	32	2	1	0	307	461	20	127	5.2	.975	SS-149
1959			147	.275	.361	593	163	22	7	5	0.8	74	51	32	35	0	2	0	301	473	29	97	5.5	.964	SS-145
1960			138	**.325**	.394	573	186	26	4	2	0.3	85	50	39	35	0	1	0	237	443	24	92	5.1	.966	SS-136
1961			148	.275	.367	596	164	25	6	6	1.0	71	55	40	44	2	1	0	237	474	32	117	5.0	.957	SS-144, 3B-1
1962			161	.294	.361	678	199	34	3	2	0.3	76	61	31	61	2	0	0	314	521	38	126	5.4	.956	SS-161
1963	STL	N	158	.319	.450	631	201	**43**	11	6	1.0	85	73	56	58	3	1	0	257	448	26	91	4.6	.964	SS-158
1964			161	.292	.371	636	186	35	6	1	0.2	70	70	44	42	1	1	0	249	499	40	91	4.9	.949	SS-160
1965			153	.254	.315	587	149	26	5	0	0.0	55	52	56	50	1	6	3	242	455	27	87	4.7	.963	SS-148, 3B-2
1966	PHI	N	155	.260	.320	584	152	21	4	2	0.3	58	53	40	38	2	1	0	278	491	20	81	5.1	.975	SS-139, 3B-20, 1B-1

Year	Team		Games	BA	SA	AB	H	2B	3B	HR	HR%	R	RBI	BB	SO	SB	Pinch Hit AB	H	PO	A	E	DP	TC/G	FA	G by Pos

Dick Groat *continued*

1967	**2 teams**	PHI N (10G – .115)				SF	N	(34G	–	.171)																
"	total		44	.156	.188	96	15	1	1	0	0.0	7	5	10	11	0	14	1	31	68	8	15	2.4	.925	SS-30, 2B-1
14 yrs.			1929	.286	.366	7484	2138	352	67	39	0.5	829	707	490	512	14	32	5	3526	5864	376	1241	5.1	.961	SS-1877, 3B-27, 2B-1, 1B-1

WORLD SERIES

1960	PIT	N	7	.214	.286	28	6	2	0	0	0.0	3	2	0	1	0	0	0	12	12	2	2	3.7	.923	SS-7
1964	STL	N	7	.192	.308	26	5	1	1	0	0.0	3	1	4	3	0	0	0	11	16	2	6	4.1	.931	SS-7
2 yrs.			14	.204	.296	54	11	3	1	0	0.0	6	3	4	4	0	0	0	23	28	4	8	3.9	.927	SS-14

Heinie Groh

GROH, HENRY KNIGHT
Brother of Lew Groh.
B. Sept. 18, 1889, Rochester, N. Y.   D. Aug. 22, 1968, Cincinnati, Ohio
Manager 1918.

BR TR 5'8"   158 lbs.

1912	NY	N	27	.271	.354	48	13	2	1	0	0.0	8	3	8	7	6	0	0	34	41	8	4	3.1	.904	2B-12, SS-7, 3B-6
1913	**2 teams**	NY N (4G – .000)				CIN	N	(117G	–	.282)																
"	total		121	.281	.376	399	112	19	5	3	0.8	51	48	38	37	24	0	0	256	366	24	44	5.3	.963	2B-113, SS-5, 3B-2
1914	CIN	N	139	.288	.358	455	131	18	4	2	0.4	59	32	64	28	24	2	0	257	399	45	57	5.0	.936	2B-134, SS-2
1915			160	.290	.390	587	170	32	9	3	0.5	72	50	50	33	12	0	0	216	360	18	46	3.7	.970	3B-131, 2B-29
1916			149	.269	.374	553	149	24	14	2	0.4	85	28	**84**	34	13	1	0	226	369	23	43	4.1	.963	3B-110, 2B-33, SS-5
1917			156	.304	.411	599	**182**	**39**	11	1	0.2	91	53	71	30	15	1	0	186	340	18	30	3.5	.967	3B-154, 2B-2
1918			126	.320	.396	493	158	**28**	3	1	0.2	**88**	37	54	24	11	0	0	180	253	14	37	3.5	.969	3B-126
1919			122	.310	.431	448	139	17	11	5	1.1	79	63	56	26	21	0	0	171	226	12	22	3.4	.971	3B-121
1920			145	.298	.393	550	164	28	12	0	0.0	86	49	60	29	16	1	0	180	255	14	30	3.1	.969	3B-144, SS-1
1921			97	.331	.417	357	118	19	6	0	0.0	54	48	36	17	22	0	0	97	188	15	27	3.1	.950	3B-97
1922	NY	N	115	.265	.350	426	113	21	3	3	0.7	63	51	53	21	5	5	1	100	207	11	25	2.8	.965	3B-110
1923			123	.290	.385	465	135	22	5	4	0.9	91	48	60	22	3	5	1	117	233	9	18	2.9	.975	3B-118
1924			145	.281	.360	559	157	32	3	2	0.4	82	46	52	29	8	0	0	121	286	7	13	2.9	.983	3B-145
1925			25	.231	.292	65	15	4	0	0	0.0	7	4	6	3	0	4	1	16	18	3	1	1.5	.919	3B-16, 2B-2
1926			12	.229	.286	35	8	2	0	0	0.0	2	3	2	2	0	4	1	6	13	1	1	1.7	.950	3B-7
1927	PIT	N	14	.286	.314	35	10	1	0	0	0.0	2	3	2	2	0	2	1	9	14	1	0	1.7	.958	3B-12
16 yrs.			1676	.292	.384	6074	1774	308	87	26	0.4	920	566	696	345	180	26	5	2172	3568	223	398	3.6	.963	3B-1299, 2B-325, SS-20

WORLD SERIES

1919	CIN	N	8	.172	.241	29	5	2	0	0	0.0	6	6	6	4	0	0	0	8	19	2	2	3.6	.931	3B-8
1922	NY	N	5	.474	.579	19	9	0	1	0	0.0	4	0	2	1	0	0	0	6	14	0	0	4.0	1.000	3B-5
1923			6	.182	.273	22	4	0	1	0	0.0	3	2	3	1	0	0	0	4	15	0	1	3.2	1.000	3B-6
1924			1	1.000	1.000	1	1	0	0	0	0.0	0	0	0	0	0	1	1	0	0	0	0	0.0	–	
1927	PIT	N	1	.000	.000	1	0	0	0	0	0.0	0	0	0	0	0	1	0	0	0	0	0	0.0	–	
5 yrs.			21	.264	.347	72	19	2	2	0	0.0	13	4	11	6	0	2	1	18	48	2	3	3.2	.971	3B-19

Lew Groh

GROH, LEWIS CARL (Silver)
Brother of Heinie Groh.
B. Oct. 16, 1883, Rochester, N. Y.   D. Oct. 20, 1960, Rochester, N. Y.

BR TR

| 1919 | PHI | A | 2 | .000 | .000 | 4 | 0 | 0 | 0 | 0 | 0.0 | 0 | 0 | 0 | 2 | 0 | 1 | 0 | 0 | 1 | 0 | 0 | 0.5 | 1.000 | 3B-1 |

George Grosart

GROSART, GEORGE ALBERT
B. 1879, Meadville, Pa.   D. Apr. 18, 1902, Homestead, Pa.

| 1901 | BOS | N | 7 | .115 | .115 | 26 | 3 | 0 | 0 | 0 | 0.0 | 4 | 1 | 0 | | | 0 | 0 | 18 | 0 | 0 | 0 | 2.6 | 1.000 | OF-7 |

Emil Gross

GROSS, EMIL MICHAEL
B. Mar. 4, 1858, Chicago, Ill.   D. Aug. 24, 1921, Eagle River, Wis.

BR TR 6'   190 lbs.

1879	PRO	N	30	.348	.492	132	46	9	5	0	0.0	31	24	4	8		0	0	152	39	22	1	7.1	.897	C-30
1880			87	.259	.337	347	90	18	3	1	0.3	43	34	16	15		0	0	429	126	86	5	7.4	.866	C-87
1881			51	.275	.385	182	50	9	4	1	0.5	15	24	13	11		0	0	241	70	38	6	6.8	.891	C-50, OF-1
1883	PHI	N	57	.307	.489	231	71	25	7	1	0.4	39		12	18		0	0	210	70	77	1	6.3	.784	C-55, OF-2
1884	CHI	U	23	.358	.589	95	34	6	2	4	4.2	13		6			0	0	103	44	28	1	7.6	.840	C-15, OF-9
5 yrs.			248	.295	.427	987	291	67	21	7	0.7	141	82	51	52		0	0	1135	349	251	13	7.0	.855	C-237, OF-12

Greg Gross

GROSS, GREGORY EUGENE
B. Aug. 1, 1952, York, Pa.

BL TL 5'10"   160 lbs.

1973	HOU	N	14	.231	.333	39	9	2	1	0	0.0	5	1	4	4	2	4	0	13	2	0	0	1.1	1.000	OF-9
1974			156	.314	.377	589	185	21	8	0	0.0	78	36	76	39	12	5	2	296	15	2	4	2.0	.994	OF-151
1975			132	.294	.364	483	142	14	10	0	0.0	67	41	63	37	2	8	1	216	14	10	2	1.8	.958	OF-121
1976			128	.286	.329	426	122	13	3	0	0.0	52	27	64	39	2	13	1	208	13	5	4	1.8	.978	OF-115
1977	CHI	N	115	.322	.460	239	77	10	4	5	2.1	43	32	33	19	0	39	10	109	3	1	0	1.0	.991	OF-71
1978			124	.265	.349	347	92	12	7	1	0.3	34	39	33	19	3	20	5	182	6	4	1	1.5	.979	OF-111
1979	PHI	N	111	.333	.402	174	58	6	3	0	0.0	21	15	29	5	5	51	14	82	5	2	2	0.8	.978	OF-73
1980			127	.240	.312	154	37	7	2	0	0.0	19	12	24	7	1	39	10	69	5	2	0	0.6	.974	OF-91, 1B-1
1981			83	.225	.304	102	23	6	1	0	0.0	14	7	15	5	2	39	6	48	7	1	2	0.7	.982	OF-55
1982			119	.299	.328	134	40	4	0	0	0.0	14	10	19	8	4	53	**19**	55	3	1	0	0.5	.983	OF-71
1983			136	.302	.376	245	74	12	3	0	0.0	25	29	34	16	3	33	7	105	1	1	0	0.8	.991	OF-110, 1B-1
1984			112	.322	.376	202	65	9	1	0	0.0	19	16	24	11	1	46	13	195	13	2	9	1.9	.990	OF-48, 1B-28
1985			93	.260	.314	169	44	5	2	0	0.0	21	14	32	9	1	41	7	66	8	0	1	0.8	1.000	OF-52, 1B-8
1986			87	.248	.297	101	25	5	0	0	0.0	11	8	21	11	1	52	13	40	6	0	1	0.5	1.000	OF-27, 1B-5, P-1
1987			114	.286	.353	133	38	4	1	1	0.8	14	12	25	12	0	55	15	53	2	0	1	0.5	1.000	OF-50, 1B-11
1988			98	.203	.211	133	27	1	0	0	0.0	10	5	16	3	0	52	13	108	7	1	13	1.2	.991	OF-37, 1B-14
1989	HOU	N	60	.200	.200	75	15	0	0	0	0.0	2	4	11	6	1	37	1	37	1	1	2	0.7	.974	OF-12, 1B-6, P-2
17 yrs.			1809	.287	.351	3745	1073	130	46	7	0.2	449	308	523	250	39	588	143	1882	108	33	43	1.1	.984	OF-1204, 1B-74, P-2
																	1st	3rd							

DIVISIONAL PLAYOFF SERIES

| 1981 | PHI | N | 4 | .000 | .000 | 4 | 0 | 0 | 0 | 0 | 0.0 | 0 | 0 | 0 | 0 | 0 | 3 | 0 | 0 | 0 | 0 | 0 | 0.0 | – | OF-2 |

Year	Team		Games	BA	SA	AB	H	2B	3B	HR	HR%	R	RBI	BB	SO	SB	Pinch Hit AB	H	PO	A	E	DP	TC/G	FA	G by Pos

Greg Gross *continued*

LEAGUE CHAMPIONSHIP SERIES

Year	Team		Games	BA	SA	AB	H	2B	3B	HR	HR%	R	RBI	BB	SO	SB	AB	H	PO	A	E	DP	TC/G	FA	G by Pos
1980	PHI	N	4	.750	.750	4	3	0	0	0	0.0	2	1	0	0	0	2	2	1	0	0	0	0.3	1.000	OF-1
1983			4	.000	.000	5	0	0	0	0	0.0	1	0	2	2	0	0	0	4	0	0	0	1.0	1.000	OF-3
2 yrs.			8	.333	.333	9	3	0	0	0	0.0	3	1	2	2	0	2	2	5	0	0	0	0.6	1.000	OF-4

WORLD SERIES

Year	Team		Games	BA	SA	AB	H	2B	3B	HR	HR%	R	RBI	BB	SO	SB	AB	H	PO	A	E	DP	TC/G	FA	G by Pos
1980	PHI	N	4	.000	.000	2	0	0	0	0	0.0	0	0	0	1	0	1	0	1	0	0	0	0.3	1.000	OF-3
1983			2	.000	.000	6	0	0	0	0	0.0	0	0	0	0	0	0	0	8	0	0	0	4.0	1.000	OF-2
2 yrs.			6	.000	.000	8	0	0	0	0	0.0	0	0	0	1	0	1	0	9	0	0	0	1.5	1.000	OF-5

Turkey Gross

GROSS, EWELL
B. Feb. 21, 1896, Mesquite, Tex.   D. Jan. 11, 1936, Dallas, Tex.   BR TR 6'   165 lbs.

Year	Team		Games	BA	SA	AB	H	2B	3B	HR	HR%	R	RBI	BB	SO	SB	AB	H	PO	A	E	DP	TC/G	FA	G by Pos
1925	BOS	A	9	.094	.156	32	3	0	1	0	0.0	2	2	2	2	0	0	0	12	29	1	4	4.7	.976	SS-9

Wayne Gross

GROSS, WAYNE DALE
B. Jan. 14, 1952, Riverside, Calif.   BL TR 6'2"   210 lbs.

Year	Team		Games	BA	SA	AB	H	2B	3B	HR	HR%	R	RBI	BB	SO	SB	AB	H	PO	A	E	DP	TC/G	FA	G by Pos
1976	OAK	A	10	.222	.222	18	4	0	0	0	0.0	0	1	2	5	0	5	2	30	1	1	2	3.2	.969	DH-3, 1B-3, OF-2
1977			146	.233	.416	485	113	21	1	22	4.5	66	63	86	84	5	0	0	127	242	27	26	2.7	.932	3B-145, 1B-1
1978			118	.200	.323	285	57	10	2	7	2.5	18	23	40	63	0	12	2	120	150	22	25	2.5	.925	3B-106, 1B-15
1979			138	.224	.367	442	99	19	1	14	3.2	54	50	72	62	4	5	2	252	225	21	27	3.6	.958	3B-120, 1B-18, OF-2
1980			113	.281	.467	366	103	20	3	14	3.8	45	61	44	39	5	13	3	125	136	11	16	2.4	.960	3B-99, 1B-10, DH-1
1981			82	.206	.366	243	50	7	1	10	4.1	29	31	34	28	2	9	1	68	127	12	7	2.5	.942	3B-73, 1B-2, DH-1
1982			129	.251	.358	386	97	14	0	9	2.3	41	41	53	50	3	20	6	203	189	11	31	3.1	.973	3B-108, 1B-16, DH-1
1983			137	.233	.392	339	79	18	0	12	3.5	34	44	36	52	3	8	3	473	113	9	51	4.3	.985	1B-74, 3B-67, DH-1, P-1
1984	BAL	A	127	.216	.442	342	74	9	1	22	6.4	53	64	68	69	1	13	4	69	205	18	13	2.3	.938	3B-117, 1B-3, DH-1
1985			103	.235	.424	217	51	8	0	11	5.1	31	18	46	48	1	29	7	81	102	10	15	1.9	.948	3B-67, DH-10, 1B-9
1986	OAK	A	3	.000	.000	2	0	0	0	0	0.0	0	0	0	1	0	2	0	0	0	1	0	0.3	—	3B-1
11 yrs.			1106	.233	.395	3125	727	126	9	121	3.9	373	396	482	496	24	116	30	1548	1490	143	213	2.9	.955	3B-903, 1B-151, DH-18, OF-4, P-1

DIVISIONAL PLAYOFF SERIES

Year	Team		Games	BA	SA	AB	H	2B	3B	HR	HR%	R	RBI	BB	SO	SB	AB	H	PO	A	E	DP	TC/G	FA	G by Pos
1981	OAK	A	2	.400	1.000	5	2	0	0	1	20.0	1	3	0	0	0	1	0	0	0	0	0	0.0	—	3B-1

LEAGUE CHAMPIONSHIP SERIES

Year	Team		Games	BA	SA	AB	H	2B	3B	HR	HR%	R	RBI	BB	SO	SB	AB	H	PO	A	E	DP	TC/G	FA	G by Pos
1981	OAK	A	3	.000	.000	5	0	0	0	0	0.0	0	0	0	3	0	3	0	0	0	0	0	0.0	—	3B-3

Howdie Grossklos

GROSSKLOS, HOWARD HOFFMAN
B. Apr. 9, 1907, Pittsburgh, Pa.   BR TR 5'9"   176 lbs.

Year	Team		Games	BA	SA	AB	H	2B	3B	HR	HR%	R	RBI	BB	SO	SB	AB	H	PO	A	E	DP	TC/G	FA	G by Pos
1930	PIT	N	2	.333	.333	3	1	0	0	0	0.0	0	0	0	0	0	1	0	0	1	0	0	0.5	—	SS-1
1931			53	.280	.348	161	45	7	2	0	0.0	13	20	11	16	1	12	4	93	117	5	36	4.1	.977	2B-39, SS-3
1932			17	.100	.100	20	2	0	0	0	0.0	1	1	0	3	0	16	2	2	1	2	0	0.3	.800	SS-1
3 yrs.			72	.261	.321	184	48	7	2	0	0.0	14	21	11	19	1	29	6	95	119	7	36	3.1	.968	2B-39, SS-5

Jerry Grote

GROTE, GERALD WAYNE
B. Oct. 6, 1942, San Antonio, Tex.   BR TR 5'10"   185 lbs.

Year	Team		Games	BA	SA	AB	H	2B	3B	HR	HR%	R	RBI	BB	SO	SB	AB	H	PO	A	E	DP	TC/G	FA	G by Pos
1963	HOU	N	3	.200	.200	5	1	0	0	0	0.0	0	1	1	3	0	0	0	10	0	0	0	3.3	1.000	C-3
1964			100	.181	.262	298	54	9	3	3	1.0	26	24	20	75	0	2	0	522	52	9	5	5.8	.985	C-98
1966	NY	N	120	.237	.315	317	75	12	2	3	0.9	26	31	40	81	4	5	1	519	55	11	8	4.9	.981	C-115, 3B-2
1967			120	.195	.253	344	67	8	0	4	1.2	25	23	14	65	2	2	0	609	62	7	8	5.7	.990	C-119
1968			124	.282	.349	404	114	18	0	3	0.7	29	31	44	81	1	8	2	754	60	5	8	6.6	.994	C-115
1969			113	.252	.351	365	92	12	3	6	1.6	38	40	32	59	2	4	1	718	63	7	11	7.0	.991	C-112
1970			126	.255	.308	415	106	14	1	2	0.5	38	34	36	39	2	0	0	855	46	8	12	7.2	.991	C-125
1971			125	.270	.347	403	109	25	0	2	0.5	35	35	40	47	1	4	0	892	41	9	4	7.5	.990	C-122
1972			64	.210	.288	205	43	5	1	3	1.5	15	21	26	27	1	4	0	407	43	1	5	7.0	.998	C-59, 3B-3, OF-1
1973			84	.256	.316	285	73	10	2	1	0.4	17	32	13	23	0	1	0	546	37	4	1	7.0	.993	C-81, 3B-2
1974			97	.257	.335	319	82	8	1	5	1.6	25	36	33	33	0	3	0	549	36	7	1	6.1	.988	C-94
1975			119	.295	.373	386	114	14	5	2	0.5	28	39	38	23	0	8	2	706	55	4	8	6.4	.995	C-111
1976			101	.272	.365	323	88	14	2	4	1.2	30	28	38	19	1	10	4	622	49	5	6	6.7	.993	C-95, OF-2
1977 2 teams		NY N (42G – .270)				LA N	(18G – .259)																		
" total			60	.268	.303	142	38	3	1	0	0.0	11	11	11	17	0	11	3	131	29	2	2	2.7	.988	C-44, 3B-13
1978	LA	N	41	.271	.343	70	19	5	0	0	0.0	5	9	10	5	0	2	1	125	21	3	0	3.6	.980	C-32, 3B-7
1981 2 teams		KC A (22G – .304)				LA N	(2G – .000)																		
" total			24	.293	.431	58	17	3	1	1	1.7	4	9	3	3	1	0	0	89	6	0	0	4.0	1.000	C-23
16 yrs.			1421	.252	.326	4339	1092	160	22	39	0.9	352	404	399	600	15	62	14	8054	655	82	79	6.2	.991	C-1348, 3B-27, OF-3

LEAGUE CHAMPIONSHIP SERIES

Year	Team		Games	BA	SA	AB	H	2B	3B	HR	HR%	R	RBI	BB	SO	SB	AB	H	PO	A	E	DP	TC/G	FA	G by Pos
1969	NY	N	3	.167	.250	12	2	1	0	0	0.0	3	1	1	1	0	0	0	22	1	0	0	7.7	1.000	C-3
1973			5	.211	.211	19	4	0	0	0	0.0	2	2	1	3	0	0	0	42	1	1	0	8.8	.977	C-5
1977	LA	N	2	—	—	0	0	0	0	0	—	0	0	1	0	0	0	0	0	0	0	0	0.0	—	C-1
1978			1	—	—	0	0	0	0	0	—	0	0	0	0	0	0	0	2	0	0	0	2.0	1.000	C-1
4 yrs.			11	.194	.226	31	6	1	0	0	0.0	5	3	3	7	0	0	0	66	2	1	0	6.3	.986	C-10

WORLD SERIES

Year	Team		Games	BA	SA	AB	H	2B	3B	HR	HR%	R	RBI	BB	SO	SB	AB	H	PO	A	E	DP	TC/G	FA	G by Pos
1969	NY	N	5	.211	.316	19	4	0	0	0	0.0	1	1	1	3	0	0	0	29	2	0	0	6.2	1.000	C-5
1973			7	.267	.267	30	8	0	0	0	0.0	2	0	0	1	0	0	0	67	5	0	1	10.3	1.000	C-7
1977	LA	N	1	.000	.000	1	0	0	0	0	0.0	0	0	0	0	0	0	0	3	3	0	0	6.0	1.000	C-1
1978			2	—	—	0	0	0	0	0	—	0	0	0	0	0	0	0	3	0	0	0	1.5	1.000	C-2
4 yrs.			15	.240	.280	50	12	0	0	0	0.0	3	1	1	4	0	0	0	102	10	0	1	7.5	1.000	C-15

Johnny Groth

GROTH, JOHN THOMAS
B. July 23, 1926, Chicago, Ill.   BR TR 6'   182 lbs.

Year	Team		Games	BA	SA	AB	H	2B	3B	HR	HR%	R	RBI	BB	SO	SB	AB	H	PO	A	E	DP	TC/G	FA	G by Pos
1946	DET	A	4	.000	.000	9	0	0	0	0	0.0	1	0	1	3	0	1	0	6	0	0	0	1.5	1.000	OF-4
1947			2	.250	.250	4	1	0	0	0	0.0	0	2	1	0	0	1	0	5	0	0	0	2.5	1.000	OF-1

Year	Team		Games	BA	SA	AB	H	2B	3B	HR	HR%	R	RBI	BB	SO	SB	Pinch Hit AB	Pinch Hit H	PO	A	E	DP	TC/G	FA	G by Pos

Johnny Groth *continued*

Year	Team		Games	BA	SA	AB	H	2B	3B	HR	HR%	R	RBI	BB	SO	SB	AB	H	PO	A	E	DP	TC/G	FA	G by Pos
1948			6	.471	.824	17	8	3	0	1	5.9	3	5	1	1	0	1	0	8	1	1	1	1.7	.900	OF-4
1949			103	.293	.471	348	102	19	5	11	3.2	60	73	65	27	3	3	0	247	8	9	3	2.6	.966	OF-99
1950			157	.306	.451	566	173	30	8	12	2.1	95	85	95	27	1	0	0	374	9	6	0	2.5	.985	OF-157
1951			118	.299	.393	428	128	29	1	3	0.7	41	49	31	32	1	6	2	266	12	3	3	2.4	.993	OF-112
1952			141	.284	.357	524	149	22	2	4	0.8	56	51	51	39	2	3	0	329	14	5	3	2.5	.986	OF-139
1953	STL	A	141	.253	.370	557	141	27	4	10	1.8	65	57	42	53	5	0	0	425	18	4	5	3.2	.991	OF-141
1954	CHI	A	125	.275	.372	422	116	20	0	7	1.7	41	60	42	37	3	1	0	314	7	4	3	2.6	.988	OF-125
1955	2 teams		CHI A	(32G – .338)			WAS A	(63G – .219)																	
"	total		95	.254	.381	260	66	11	5	4	1.5	35	28	24	31	3	14	5	183	3	2	1	2.0	.989	OF-74
1956	KC	A	95	.258	.398	244	63	13	3	5	2.0	22	37	30	31	1	13	4	140	8	0	3	1.6	1.000	OF-84
1957	2 teams		KC A	(55G – .254)			DET A	(38G – .291)																	
"	total		93	.278	.340	162	45	10	0	0	0.0	21	18	13	13	0	4	0	110	0	1	0	1.2	.991	OF-86
1958	DET	A	88	.281	.384	146	41	5	2	2	1.4	24	11	13	19	0	16	6	95	2	1	1	1.1	.990	OF-80
1959			55	.235	.353	102	24	7	1	1	1.0	12	10	7	14	0	13	4	58	0	1	0	1.1	.983	OF-41
1960			25	.368	.421	19	7	1	0	0	0.0	3	2	3	1	0	8	3	6	0	0	0	0.2	1.000	OF-8
15 yrs.			1248	.279	.395	3808	1064	197	31	60	1.6	480	486	419	329	19	83	24	2566	82	36	23	2.2	.987	OF-1155

Roy Grover

GROVER, ROY ARTHUR
B. Jan. 17, 1892, Snohomish, Wash.   D. Feb. 7, 1978, Milwaukie, Ore.   BR TR 5'8''   150 lbs.

Year	Team		Games	BA	SA	AB	H	2B	3B	HR	HR%	R	RBI	BB	SO	SB	AB	H	PO	A	E	DP	TC/G	FA	G by Pos
1916	PHI	A	20	.273	.338	77	21	1	2	0	0.0	8	7	6	10	5	0	1	40	40	4	7	4.2	.952	2B-20
1917			141	.224	.284	482	108	15	7	0	0.0	45	34	43	53	12	1	0	279	425	29	51	5.2	.960	2B-139
1919	2 teams		PHI A	(22G – .232)			WAS A	(24G – .187)																	
"	total		46	.206	.214	131	27	1	0	0	0.0	14	9	11	16	2	5	0	88	81	14	9	4.0	.923	2B-36, 3B-3
3 yrs.			207	.226	.277	690	156	17	9	0	0.0	67	50	60	79	19	6	0	407	546	47	67	4.8	.953	2B-195, 3B-3

Harvey Grubb

GRUBB, HARVEY HARRISON
B. Sept. 18, 1890, Lexington, N. C.   D. Jan. 25, 1970, Corpus Christi, Tex.   BR TR 6'   165 lbs.

Year	Team		Games	BA	SA	AB	H	2B	3B	HR	HR%	R	RBI	BB	SO	SB	AB	H	PO	A	E	DP	TC/G	FA	G by Pos
1912	CLE	A	1	–	–	0	0	0	0	0	–	0	0	0	0	0	0	0	1	0	0	0	1.0	1.000	OF-1

Johnny Grubb

GRUBB, JOHN RAYMOND, JR.
B. Aug. 4, 1948, Richmond, Va.   BL TR 6'3''   175 lbs.

Year	Team		Games	BA	SA	AB	H	2B	3B	HR	HR%	R	RBI	BB	SO	SB	AB	H	PO	A	E	DP	TC/G	FA	G by Pos
1972	SD	N	7	.333	.476	21	7	1	0	0	0.0	4	1	1	3	0	1	0	16	0	0	0	2.3	1.000	OF-6
1973			113	.311	.445	389	121	23	3	8	2.1	52	37	37	50	9	12	7	229	11	3	1	2.2	.988	OF-102, 3B-2
1974			140	.286	.403	444	127	20	4	8	1.8	53	42	46	47	4	17	3	321	8	8	1	2.4	.976	OF-122, 3B-2
1975			144	.269	.363	553	149	36	2	4	0.7	72	38	59	59	2	6	0	334	3	3	0	2.4	.991	OF-139
1976			109	.284	.385	384	109	22	1	5	1.3	54	27	65	53	1	5	0	248	7	6	7	2.4	.977	OF-98, 1B-9, 3B-3
1977	CLE	A	34	.301	.462	93	28	3	3	2	2.2	8	14	19	18	0	1	0	47	2	0	0	1.4	1.000	OF-28, DH-4
1978	2 teams		CLE A	(113G – .265)			TEX A	(21G – .394)																	
"	total		134	.275	.460	411	113	19	6	15	3.6	62	67	70	65	6	11	5	213	16	6	5	1.8	.974	OF-123, DH-3
1979	TEX	A	102	.273	.426	289	79	14	0	10	3.5	42	37	34	44	2	24	6	135	8	2	4	1.4	.986	OF-82, DH-6
1980			110	.277	.427	274	76	12	1	9	3.3	40	32	42	35	2	28	7	112	6	1	0	1.1	.952	OF-77, DH-8
1981			67	.231	.332	199	46	9	1	3	1.5	26	26	23	25	0	9	2	95	2	1	0	1.5	.990	OF-58
1982			103	.279	.370	308	86	13	3	3	1.0	35	26	39	37	0	14	4	135	4	5	1	1.4	.965	OF-77, DH-18
1983	DET	A	57	.254	.410	134	34	5	2	4	3.0	20	22	28	17	0	10	4	34	1	0	0	0.6	1.000	OF-26, DH-18
1984			86	.267	.432	176	47	5	0	8	4.5	25	17	36	36	1	22	8	47	0	0	0	0.5	1.000	OF-36, DH-33
1985			78	.245	.400	155	38	7	1	5	3.2	19	25	24	25	0	24	4	23	0	0	0	0.3	1.000	DH-33, OF-18
1986			81	.333	.590	210	70	13	1	13	6.2	32	51	28	28	0	19	5	26	1	0	0	0.3	1.000	DH-52, OF-19
1987			59	.202	.307	114	23	6	0	2	1.8	9	13	15	16	0	21	4	42	1	0	0	0.7	1.000	OF-31, DH-16, 3B-1
16 yrs.			1424	.278	.413	4154	1153	207	29	99	2.4	553	475	566	558	27	224	59	2057	70	40	20	1.5	.982	OF-1042, DH-191, 1B-9, 3B-8

LEAGUE CHAMPIONSHIP SERIES

Year	Team		Games	BA	SA	AB	H	2B	3B	HR	HR%	R	RBI	BB	SO	SB	AB	H	PO	A	E	DP	TC/G	FA	G by Pos
1984	DET	A	1	.250	.500	4	1	1	0	0	0.0	0	2	0	0	0	0	0	0	0	0	0	0.0	–	
1987			4	.571	.571	7	4	0	0	0	0.0	0	0	0	3	2	0	0	0	0	0	0	0.0	–	DH-1
2 yrs.			5	.455	.545	11	5	1	0	0	0.0	0	2	0	3	2	0	0	0	0	0	0	0.0	–	DH-1

WORLD SERIES

Year	Team		Games	BA	SA	AB	H	2B	3B	HR	HR%	R	RBI	BB	SO	SB	AB	H	PO	A	E	DP	TC/G	FA	G by Pos
1984	DET	A	4	.333	.333	3	1	0	0	0	0.0	0	0	0	0	0	0	0	0	0	0	0	0.0	–	DH-2

Frank Grube

GRUBE, FRANKLIN THOMAS (Hans)
B. Jan. 7, 1905, Easton, Pa.   D. July 2, 1945, New York, N. Y.   BR TR 5'9''   190 lbs.

Year	Team		Games	BA	SA	AB	H	2B	3B	HR	HR%	R	RBI	BB	SO	SB	AB	H	PO	A	E	DP	TC/G	FA	G by Pos
1931	CHI	A	88	.219	.294	265	58	13	2	1	0.4	29	24	22	22	2	6	1	248	50	7	3	3.5	.977	C-81
1932			93	.282	.354	277	78	16	2	0	0.0	36	31	33	13	6	1	0	303	55	16	5	4.0	.957	C-92
1933			85	.230	.281	256	59	13	0	0	0.0	23	23	38	20	1	1	0	266	44	5	5	3.7	.984	C-83
1934	STL	A	65	.288	.347	170	49	10	0	0	0.0	22	11	24	11	2	0	0	186	21	8	4	3.3	.963	C-55
1935	2 teams		STL A	(3G – .333)			CHI A	(9G – .368)																	
"	total		12	.360	.480	25	9	3	0	0	0.0	4	6	3	3	0	0	0	36	6	2	0	3.7	.955	C-12
1936	CHI	A	33	.161	.204	93	15	2	1	0	0.0	9	6	11	15	1	2	0	89	19	1	2	3.3	.991	C-32
1941	STL	A	18	.154	.205	39	6	2	0	0	0.0	1	1	2	4	0	0	0	45	13	3	1	3.4	.951	C-18
7 yrs.			394	.244	.308	1125	274	59	5	1	0.1	121	107	131	88	12	19	1	1173	208	42	20	3.6	.970	C-373

Kelly Gruber

GRUBER, KELLY WAYNE
B. Feb. 26, 1962, Houston, Tex.   BR TR 6'   175 lbs.

Year	Team		Games	BA	SA	AB	H	2B	3B	HR	HR%	R	RBI	BB	SO	SB	AB	H	PO	A	E	DP	TC/G	FA	G by Pos
1984	TOR	A	15	.063	.250	16	1	0	0	1	6.3	1	2	0	5	0	4	1	6	12	2	0	1.3	.900	3B-12, OF-2, SS-1
1985			5	.231	.231	13	3	0	0	0	0.0	0	1	0	3	0	1	1	2	6	0	0	1.6	1.000	3B-5, 2B-1
1986			87	.196	.343	143	28	4	1	5	3.5	20	15	5	27	2	9	2	43	77	7	8	1.5	.945	3B-42, DH-14, 2B-14, OF-9, SS-5
1987			138	.235	.399	341	80	14	3	12	3.5	50	36	17	70	12	16	2	76	200	13	19	2.1	.955	3B-119, SS-21, 2B-7, OF-2
1988			158	.278	.438	569	158	33	5	16	2.8	75	81	38	92	23	1	0	121	365	16	35	3.2	.968	3B-156, 2B-7, OF-2, SS-1
1989			135	.290	.448	545	158	24	4	18	3.3	83	73	30	60	10	1	0	121	295	22	16	3.2	.950	3B-119, OF-16, DH-1, SS-1
6 yrs.			538	.263	.421	1627	428	75	13	52	3.2	229	208	90	257	47	34	7	369	955	60	78	2.6	.957	3B-453, OF-31, SS-29, 2B-29, DH-15

Year	Team		Games	BA	SA	AB	H	2B	3B	HR	HR%	R	RBI	BB	SO	SB	Pinch Hit AB	Pinch Hit H	PO	A	E	DP	TC/G	FA	G by Pos

Kelly Gruber *continued*

LEAGUE CHAMPIONSHIP SERIES

| 1989 | TOR | A | 5 | .294 | .353 | 17 | 5 | 1 | 0 | 0 | 0.0 | 2 | 1 | 3 | 2 | 1 | 0 | 0 | 4 | 8 | 0 | 1 | 2.4 | 1.000 | 3B-5 |

Sig Gryska

GRYSKA, SIGMUND STANLEY
B. Nov. 4, 1915, Chicago, Ill.

BR TR 5'11½" 173 lbs.

1938	STL	A	7	.476	.667	21	10	2	1	0	0.0	3	4	3	3	0	0	0	14	17	3	5	4.9	.912	SS-7
1939			18	.265	.306	49	13	2	0	0	0.0	4	8	6	10	3	3	1	20	35	8	4	3.5	.873	SS-14
2 yrs.			25	.329	.414	70	23	4	1	0	0.0	7	12	9	13	3	3	1	34	52	11	9	3.9	.887	SS-21

Marv Gudat

GUDAT, MARVIN JOHN
B. Aug. 27, 1905, Goliad, Tex.   D. Mar. 1, 1954, Los Angeles, Calif.

BL TL 5'11"   162 lbs.

1929	CIN	N	9	.200	.200	10	2	0	0	0	0.0	0	0	0	0	0	0	0	0	4	1	0	0.6	.800	P-7
1932	CHI	N	60	.255	.351	94	24	4	1	1	1.1	15	15	16	10	0	30	10	77	4	2	4	1.4	.976	OF-14, 1B-8, P-1
2 yrs.			69	.250	.337	104	26	4	1	1	1.0	15	15	16	10	0	32	10	77	8	3	4	1.3	.966	OF-14, 1B-8, P-8

WORLD SERIES

| 1932 | CHI | N | 2 | .000 | .000 | 2 | 0 | 0 | 0 | 0 | 0.0 | 0 | 0 | 0 | 1 | 0 | 2 | 0 | 0 | 0 | 0 | 0 | 0.0 | — | |

Mike Guerra

GUERRA, FERMIN
Born Fermin Guerra y Romero.
B. Oct. 11, 1912, Havana, Cuba

BR TR 5'10"   155 lbs.

1937	WAS	A	1	.000	.000	3	0	0	0	0	0.0	0	0	0	2	0	0	0	3	0	1	0	4.0	.750	C-1
1944			75	.281	.348	210	59	7	2	1	0.5	29	29	13	14	8	6	3	211	32	10	8	3.4	.960	C-58, OF-1
1945			56	.210	.254	138	29	1	1	1	0.7	11	15	10	12	4	12	3	163	28	2	3	3.4	.990	C-38
1946			41	.253	.301	83	21	2	1	0	0.0	3	4	5	6	1	10	1	75	16	6	4	2.4	.938	C-27
1947	PHI	A	72	.215	.244	209	45	2	2	0	0.0	20	18	10	15	1	7	1	203	36	9	5	3.4	.964	C-62
1948			53	.211	.289	142	30	4	2	1	0.7	18	23	18	13	2	2	0	163	20	5	1	3.5	.973	C-47
1949			98	.265	.349	298	79	14	1	3	1.0	41	31	37	26	3	1	0	328	48	7	3	3.9	.982	C-95
1950			87	.282	.377	252	71	10	4	2	0.8	25	26	16	12	1	9	1	253	33	3	8	3.3	.990	C-78
1951	2 teams		BOS A (10G – .156)		WAS A (72G – .201)																				
"	total		82	.195	.224	246	48	2	1	1	0.4	21	22	22	23	4	4	1	238	29	5	1	3.3	.982	C-76
9 yrs.			565	.242	.303	1581	382	42	14	9	0.6	168	168	131	123	24	51	10	1637	242	48	33	3.4	.975	C-482, OF-1

Mario Guerrero

GUERRERO, MARIO MIGUEL
Born Mario Miguel Guerrero y Abud.
B. Sept. 28, 1949, Santo Domingo, Dominican Republic

BR TR 5'10"   155 lbs.

1973	BOS	A	66	.233	.274	219	51	5	2	0	0.0	19	11	10	21	2	0	0	106	183	8	49	4.5	.973	SS-46, 2B-24
1974			93	.246	.282	284	70	6	2	0	0.0	18	23	13	22	3	0	0	136	266	13	50	4.5	.969	SS-93
1975	STL	N	64	.239	.288	184	44	9	0	0	0.0	17	11	10	7	0	0	0	76	198	13	29	4.5	.955	SS-64
1976	CAL	A	83	.284	.340	268	76	12	0	1	0.4	24	18	7	12	0	1	0	129	172	14	32	3.8	.956	SS-41, 2B-41, DH-7
1977			86	.283	.344	244	69	8	2	1	0.4	17	28	4	16	0	27	4	61	105	2	18	2.0	.988	SS-31, DH-19, 2B-12
1978	OAK	A	143	.275	.345	505	139	18	4	3	0.6	27	38	15	35	0	2	0	258	330	26	67	4.3	.958	SS-142
1979			46	.229	.259	166	38	5	0	0	0.0	12	18	6	7	0	3	0	68	129	10	33	4.5	.952	SS-43
1980			116	.239	.307	381	91	16	2	2	0.5	32	23	19	32	3	0	0	184	276	18	50	4.1	.962	SS-116
8 yrs.			697	.257	.312	2251	578	79	12	7	0.3	166	170	84	152	8	33	4	1018	1659	104	328	4.0	.963	SS-576, 2B-77, DH-26

Pedro Guerrero

GUERRERO, PEDRO (Pete)
B. June 29, 1956, San Pedro de Macoris, Dominican Republic

BR TR 5'11"   176 lbs.

1978	LA	N	5	.625	.875	8	5	0	1	0	0.0	3	1	0	0	0	1	1	25	0	0	0	5.2	1.000	1B-4
1979			25	.242	.371	62	15	2	0	2	3.2	7	9	1	14	2	7	3	53	4	1	1	2.3	.983	OF-12, 1B-8, 3B-3
1980			75	.322	.497	183	59	9	1	7	3.8	27	31	12	31	2	17	11	103	37	3	5	1.9	.979	OF-40, 2B-12, 3B-3, 1B-2
1981			98	.300	.464	347	104	17	2	12	3.5	46	48	34	57	5	4	1	165	55	11	5	2.4	.952	OF-75, 3B-21, 1B-1
1982			150	.304	.536	575	175	27	5	32	5.6	87	100	65	89	22	0	0	282	53	12	9	2.3	.965	OF-137, 3B-24
1983			160	.298	.531	584	174	28	6	32	5.5	87	103	72	110	23	1	1	130	308	31	22	2.9	.934	3B-157, 1B-2
1984			144	.303	.462	535	162	29	4	16	3.0	85	72	49	105	9	7	1	271	151	22	24	3.1	.950	3B-76, OF-58, 1B-16
1985			137	.320	**.577**	487	156	22	2	33	6.8	99	87	83	68	12	3	0	251	123	13	18	2.8	.966	OF-81, 3B-44, 1B-12
1986			31	.246	.541	61	15	3	0	5	8.2	7	10	2	19	0	17	3	39	1	0	4	1.3	1.000	OF-10, 1B-4
1987			152	.338	.539	545	184	25	2	27	5.0	89	89	74	85	9	4	0	482	44	17	30	3.5	.978	OF-109, 1B-40
1988	2 teams		LA N (59G – .298)		STL N (44G – .268)																				
"	total		103	.286	.418	364	104	14	2	10	2.7	40	65	46	59	4	1	0	466	99	12	26	5.6	.979	1B-52, 3B-45, OF-9
1989	STL	N	162	.311	.477	570	177	42	1	17	3.0	60	117	79	84	2	1	1	1445	72	15	99	9.5	.990	1B-160
12 yrs.			1242	.308	.504	4321	1330	218	26	193	4.5	637	732	517	721	90	63	22	3712	948	132	243	3.9	.972	OF-531, 3B-373, 1B-301, 2B-12

DIVISIONAL PLAYOFF SERIES

| 1981 | LA | N | 5 | .176 | .412 | 17 | 3 | 1 | 0 | 1 | 5.9 | 1 | 1 | 2 | 4 | 1 | 0 | 0 | 0 | 0 | 1 | 0 | 0.2 | — | 3B-5 |

LEAGUE CHAMPIONSHIP SERIES

1981	LA	N	5	.105	.263	19	2	0	1	1	5.3	1	2	1	4	0	0	0	0	0	0	0	—	OF-5
1983			4	.250	.500	12	3	1	1	0	0.0	1	2	3	3	0	0	0	0	9	0	1	2.3	1.000	3B-4
1985			6	.250	.300	20	5	1	0	0	0.0	2	4	5	2	0	0	0	11	0	0	0	1.8	1.000	OF-6
3 yrs.			15	.196	.333	51	10	2	1	1	2.0	4	8	9	9	0	0	0	11	9	0	1	1.3	1.000	OF-11, 3B-4

WORLD SERIES

| 1981 | LA | N | 6 | .333 | .762 | 21 | 7 | 1 | 1 | 2 | 9.5 | 2 | 7 | 2 | 6 | 0 | 0 | 0 | 17 | 1 | 0 | 0 | 3.0 | 1.000 | OF-6 |

Ozzie Guillen

GUILLEN, OSWALDO JOSE
Born Oswaldo Jose Guillen y Barrios.
B. Jan. 20, 1964, Ocumare del Tuy, Venezuela

BL TR 5'11"   160 lbs.

1985	CHI	A	150	.273	.358	491	134	21	9	1	0.2	71	33	12	36	7	13	6	220	382	12	80	4.1	.980	SS-150
1986			159	.250	.311	547	137	19	4	2	0.4	58	47	12	52	8	2	0	261	459	22	93	4.7	.970	SS-157, DH-1
1987			149	.279	.354	560	156	22	7	2	0.4	64	51	22	52	25	2	1	266	475	19	105	5.1	.975	SS-149

Year	Team	Games	BA	SA	AB	H	2B	3B	HR	HR%	R	RBI	BB	SO	SB	Pinch Hit AB	H	PO	A	E	DP	TC/G	FA	G by Pos

Ozzie Guillen *continued*

Year	Team	Games	BA	SA	AB	H	2B	3B	HR	HR%	R	RBI	BB	SO	SB	PH AB	PH H	PO	A	E	DP	TC/G	FA	G by Pos
1988		156	.261	.314	566	148	16	7	0	0.0	58	39	25	40	25	0	0	273	570	20	115	5.5	.977	SS-156
1989		155	.253	.318	597	151	20	8	1	0.2	63	54	15	48	36	0	0	272	512	22	106	5.2	.973	SS-155
5 yrs.		769	.263	.330	2761	726	98	35	6	0.2	314	224	86	228	101	17	2	1292	2398	95	499	4.9	.975	SS-767, DH-1

Bob Guindon

GUINDON, ROBERT JOSEPH
B. Sept. 4, 1943, Brookline, Mass.
BL TL 6'2" 185 lbs.

Year	Team	Games	BA	SA	AB	H	2B	3B	HR	HR%	R	RBI	BB	SO	SB	PH AB	PH H	PO	A	E	DP	TC/G	FA	G by Pos
1964	BOS A	5	.125	.250	8	1	1	0	0	0.0	0	0	1	4	0	0	0	8	0	0	0	1.6	1.000	OF-1, 1B-1

Ben Guiney

GUINEY, BENJAMIN FRANKLIN
B. Nov. 16, 1858, Detroit, Mich.   D. Dec. 5, 1930, Detroit, Mich.
BB TR 6'   170 lbs.

Year	Team	Games	BA	SA	AB	H	2B	3B	HR	HR%	R	RBI	BB	SO	SB	PH AB	PH H	PO	A	E	DP	TC/G	FA	G by Pos
1883	DET N	1	.200	.200	5	1	0	0	0	0.0	1		0	1		0	0	0	0	1	0	1.0	—	OF-1
1884		2	.000	.000	7	0	0	0	0	0.0	0		0	3		0	0	3	3	2	0	4.0	.750	C-2
2 yrs.		3	.083	.083	12	1	0	0	0	0.0	1		0	4		0	0	3	3	3	0	3.0	.667	C-2, OF-1

Ben Guintini

GUINTINI, BENJAMIN JOHN
B. Jan. 13, 1920, Los Banos, Calif.
BR TR 6'1½" 190 lbs.

Year	Team	Games	BA	SA	AB	H	2B	3B	HR	HR%	R	RBI	BB	SO	SB	PH AB	PH H	PO	A	E	DP	TC/G	FA	G by Pos
1946	PIT N	2	.000	.000	3	0	0	0	0	0.0	0	0	0	1	0	1	0	1	0	0	0	0.5	1.000	OF-1
1950	PHI A	3	.000	.000	4	0	0	0	0	0.0	0	0	0	2	0	2	0	0	1	0	0	0.3	1.000	OF-1
2 yrs.		5	.000	.000	7	0	0	0	0	0.0	0	0	0	3	0	3	0	1	1	0	0	0.4	1.000	OF-2

Lou Guisto

GUISTO, LOUIS JOSEPH
B. Jan. 16, 1895, Napa, Calif.   D. Oct. 15, 1989, Napa, Calif.
BR TR 5'11" 193 lbs.

Year	Team	Games	BA	SA	AB	H	2B	3B	HR	HR%	R	RBI	BB	SO	SB	PH AB	PH H	PO	A	E	DP	TC/G	FA	G by Pos
1916	CLE A	6	.158	.158	19	3	0	0	0	0.0	2		4	3	1	0	0	66	3	0	3	11.5	1.000	1B-6
1917		73	.185	.225	200	37	4	2	0	0.0	9	29	25	18	3	11	2	611	33	7	45	8.9	.989	1B-59
1921		2	.500	.500	2	1	0	0	0	0.0	0	1	0	1	0	1	1	5	1	0	0	3.0	1.000	1B-1
1922		35	.250	.393	84	21	10	1	0	0.0	7	9	2	7	0	10	3	202	14	1	15	6.2	.995	1B-24
1923		40	.181	.215	144	26	5	0	0	0.0	17	18	15	15	1	0	0	389	28	5	30	10.6	.988	1B-40
5 yrs.		156	.196	.252	449	88	19	3	0	0.0	35	59	46	44	5	22	6	1273	79	13	93	8.8	.990	1B-130

Brad Gulden

GULDEN, BRADLEY LEE
B. June 10, 1956, New Ulm, Minn.
BL TR 5'10" 175 lbs.

Year	Team	Games	BA	SA	AB	H	2B	3B	HR	HR%	R	RBI	BB	SO	SB	PH AB	PH H	PO	A	E	DP	TC/G	FA	G by Pos
1978	LA N	3	.000	.000	4	0	0	0	0	0.0	0	0	0	2	0	0	0	8	1	0	1	3.0	1.000	C-3
1979	NY A	40	.163	.207	92	15	4	0	0	0.0	10	6	9	16	0	0	0	178	24	1	4	5.1	.995	C-40
1980		2	.333	1.333	3	1	0	0	1	33.3	1	2	0	0	0	0	0	3	0	0	0	1.5	1.000	C-2
1981	SEA A	8	.188	.313	16	3	2	0	0	0.0	0	1	0	2	0	4	0	24	3	0	0	3.4	1.000	C-6, DH-2
1982	MON N	5	.000	.000	6	0	0	0	0	0.0	1	0	1	1	0	3	0	6	2	0	0	1.6	1.000	C-2
1984	CIN N	107	.226	.308	292	66	8	2	4	1.4	31	33	33	35	2	20	3	485	53	14	8	5.2	.975	C-100
1986	SF N	17	.091	.091	22	2	0	0	0	0.0	2	1	2	5	0	9	0	26	1	0	0	1.6	1.000	C-10
7 yrs.		182	.200	.276	435	87	14	2	5	1.1	45	43	45	61	2	36	3	730	84	15	13	4.6	.982	C-163, DH-2

Tom Gulley

GULLEY, THOMAS JEFFERSON
B. Dec. 25, 1899, Garner, N. C.   D. Nov. 24, 1966, St. Charles, Ark.
BL TR 5'11" 178 lbs.

Year	Team	Games	BA	SA	AB	H	2B	3B	HR	HR%	R	RBI	BB	SO	SB	PH AB	PH H	PO	A	E	DP	TC/G	FA	G by Pos
1923	CLE A	2	.333	.667	3	1	1	0	0	0.0	1	0	0	0	0	1	0	1	0	0	0	0.5	1.000	OF-1
1924		8	.150	.250	20	3	1	0	0	0.0	4	1	3	0	0	3	0	14	0	1	0	1.9	.933	OF-5
1926	CHI A	16	.229	.371	35	8	3	1	0	0.0	5	8	5	2	0	4	1	19	0	0	0	1.2	1.000	OF-12
3 yrs.		26	.207	.345	58	12	4	2	0	0.0	10	9	8	4	0	8	1	34	0	1	0	1.3	.971	OF-18

Ted Gullic

GULLIC, THEODORE JASPER
B. Jan. 2, 1907, Koshkonong, Mo.
BR TR 6'2" 175 lbs.

Year	Team	Games	BA	SA	AB	H	2B	3B	HR	HR%	R	RBI	BB	SO	SB	PH AB	PH H	PO	A	E	DP	TC/G	FA	G by Pos
1930	STL A	92	.250	.344	308	77	7	5	4	1.3	39	44	27	43	4	6	0	165	17	5	3	2.0	.973	OF-82, 1B-3
1933		104	.243	.372	304	74	18	3	5	1.6	34	35	15	38	3	24	4	229	74	5	8	3.0	.984	OF-36, 3B-33, 1B-14
2 yrs.		196	.247	.358	612	151	25	8	9	1.5	73	79	42	81	7	30	4	394	91	10	11	2.5	.980	OF-118, 3B-33, 1B-17

Glenn Gulliver

GULLIVER, GLENN JAMES
B. Oct. 15, 1954, Detroit, Mich.
BL TR 5'11" 175 lbs.

Year	Team	Games	BA	SA	AB	H	2B	3B	HR	HR%	R	RBI	BB	SO	SB	PH AB	PH H	PO	A	E	DP	TC/G	FA	G by Pos
1982	BAL A	50	.200	.269	145	29	7	0	1	0.7	24	5	37	18	0	1	0	34	97	6	4	2.7	.970	3B-50
1983		23	.213	.277	47	10	3	0	0	0.0	5	2	9	5	0	4	0	14	31	0	3	2.0	1.000	3B-21
2 yrs.		73	.203	.271	192	39	10	0	1	0.5	29	7	46	23	0	5	0	48	128	4	9	2.5	.978	3B-71

Ad Gumbert

GUMBERT, ADDISON COURTNEY
Brother of Billy Gumbert.
B. Oct. 10, 1868, Pittsburgh, Pa.   D. Apr. 23, 1925, Pittsburgh, Pa.
BR TR 5'10" 200 lbs.

Year	Team	Games	BA	SA	AB	H	2B	3B	HR	HR%	R	RBI	BB	SO	SB	PH AB	PH H	PO	A	E	DP	TC/G	FA	G by Pos
1888	CHI N	7	.333	.417	24	8	0	1	0	0.0	3	2	0	2	0	0	0	4	8	1	0	1.9	.923	P-6, OF-2
1889		41	.288	.471	153	44	3	2	7	4.6	30	29	11	36	2	0	0	48	44	15	1	2.6	.860	P-31, OF-13
1890	BOS P	44	.241	.366	145	35	7	1	3	2.1	23	20	18	26	5	0	0	24	83	14	0	2.8	.884	P-39, OF-7
1891	CHI N	34	.305	.448	105	32	7	4	0	0.0	18	16	13	14	4	0	0	19	56	8	4	2.4	.904	P-32, OF-1, 1B-1
1892		52	.236	.281	178	42	1	2	0	0.6	18	8	14	24	1	0	0	20	97	11	2	2.5	.914	P-46, OF-7
1893	PIT N	29	.221	.316	95	21	3	3	0	0.0	17	10	10	16	0	0	0	19	24	1	3	1.5	.977	P-22, OF-7
1894		38	.292	.442	113	33	4	5	1	0.9	18	19	6	20	1	1	0	18	49	4	3	1.9	.944	P-37
1895	BKN N	34	.361	.485	97	35	6	0	2	2.1	21	13	7	10	0	0	0	15	48	5	0	2.0	.926	P-33, OF-1
1896	2 teams		BKN N (5G – .182)		PHI N (11G – .265)																			
"	total	16	.244	.400	45	11	2	1	1	2.2	7	7	1	5	1	0	0	5	28	2	1	2.2	.943	P-16
9 yrs.		295	.273	.395	955	261	33	19	15	1.6	155	124	80	153	18	1	0	172	437	61	13	2.3	.909	P-262, OF-38, 1B-1

Fred Gunkle

GUNKLE, FREDERICK W.
B. Dubuque, Iowa   Deceased.

Year	Team	Games	BA	SA	AB	H	2B	3B	HR	HR%	R	RBI	BB	SO	SB	PH AB	PH H	PO	A	E	DP	TC/G	FA	G by Pos
1879	CLE N	1	.000	.000	3	0	0	0	0	0.0	1	0	0	1	0	0	0	2	0	3	0	5.0	.400	OF-1, C-1

Year	Team		Games	BA	SA	AB	H	2B	3B	HR	HR%	R	RBI	BB	SO	SB	Pinch Hit AB	Pinch Hit H	PO	A	E	DP	TC/G	FA	G by Pos

Hy Gunning

GUNNING, HYLAND
B. Aug. 6, 1888, Maplewood, N. J. D. Mar. 28, 1975, Togus, Me.
BL TR 6'1½" 189 lbs.

Year	Team		Games	BA	SA	AB	H	2B	3B	HR	HR%	R	RBI	BB	SO	SB	PH AB	PH H	PO	A	E	DP	TC/G	FA	G by Pos
1911	BOS	A	4	.111	.111	9	1	0	0	0	0.0	0	2	2		0	0	0	25	0	0	0	6.3	1.000	1B-4

Tom Gunning

GUNNING, THOMAS FRANCIS
B. Mar. 4, 1862, Newmarket, N. H. D. Mar. 17, 1931, Fall River, Mass.
BR TR 5'10" 160 lbs.

Year	Team		Games	BA	SA	AB	H	2B	3B	HR	HR%	R	RBI	BB	SO	SB	PH AB	PH H	PO	A	E	DP	TC/G	FA	G by Pos
1884	BOS	N	12	.111	.178	45	5	1	1	0	0.0		1	1	12		0	0	60	14	7	1	6.8	.914	C-12
1885			48	.184	.201	174	32	3	0	0	0.0	17	15	5	29		0	0	252	68	45	4	7.6	.877	C-48
1886			27	.224	.265	98	22	2	1	0	0.0	15	7	3	19		0	0	162	27	23	4	7.9	.892	C-27
1887	PHI	N	28	.260	.365	104	27	6	1	1	1.0	22	16	5	6	18	0	0	133	55	22	6	7.5	.895	C-28
1888	PHI	AA	23	.196	.196	92	18	0	0	0	0.0	18	5	2		14	0	0	130	38	20	4	8.2	.894	C-23
1889			8	.250	.458	24	6	0	1	1	4.2	3	1	0	4	3	0	0	24	7	6	2	4.6	.838	C-8
6 yrs.			146	.205	.253	537	110	12	4	2	0.4	79	44	16	70	35	0	0	761	209	123	21	7.5	.887	C-146

Joe Gunson

GUNSON, JOSEPH BROOK
B. Mar. 23, 1863, Philadelphia, Pa. D. Nov. 15, 1942, Philadelphia, Pa.
BR TR 5'6" 160 lbs.

Year	Team		Games	BA	SA	AB	H	2B	3B	HR	HR%	R	RBI	BB	SO	SB	PH AB	PH H	PO	A	E	DP	TC/G	FA	G by Pos
1884	WAS	U	45	.139	.151	166	23	2	0	0	0.0	15		3			0	0	237	59	33	0	7.3	.900	C-33, OF-18
1889	KC	AA	34	.197	.238	122	24	3	1	0	0.0	15	12	3	17	2	0	0	118	44	27	2	5.6	.857	C-32, OF-1, 3B-1
1892	BAL	N	89	.213	.277	314	67	10	5	0	0.0	35	32	16	17	2	0	0	324	98	37	6	5.2	.919	C-67, OF-20, 1B-2, 2B-1
1893	2 teams		STL N (40G – .272)			CLE N (21G – .260)																			
"	total		61	.268	.295	224	60	6	0	0	0.0	31	24	12	6	0	2	1	198	58	18	6	4.5	.934	C-55, OF-5
4 yrs.			229	.211	.251	826	174	21	6	0	0.0	96	68	34	40	4	2	1	877	259	115	14	5.5	.908	C-187, OF-44, 1B-2, 3B-1, 2B-1

Ernie Gust

GUST, ERNEST HERMAN FRANK (Red)
B. Jan. 24, 1888, Bay City, Mich. D. Oct. 26, 1945, Maupin, Ore.
BR TR 6' 170 lbs.

Year	Team		Games	BA	SA	AB	H	2B	3B	HR	HR%	R	RBI	BB	SO	SB	PH AB	PH H	PO	A	E	DP	TC/G	FA	G by Pos
1911	STL	A	3	.000	.000	12	0	0	0	0	0.0	0	0	0	0		0	0	35	2	1	2	12.7	.974	1B-3

Frankie Gustine

GUSTINE, FRANK WILLIAM
B. Feb. 20, 1920, Hoopeston, Ill.
BR TR 6' 175 lbs.

Year	Team		Games	BA	SA	AB	H	2B	3B	HR	HR%	R	RBI	BB	SO	SB	PH AB	PH H	PO	A	E	DP	TC/G	FA	G by Pos
1939	PIT	N	22	.186	.229	70	13	3	0	0	0.0	5	3	9	4	0	0	0	17	52	8	3	3.5	.896	3B-22
1940			133	.281	.374	524	147	32	7	1	0.2	59	55	35	39	7	3	1	288	402	43	92	5.5	.941	2B-130
1941			121	.270	.359	463	125	24	7	1	0.2	46	46	28	38	5	2	0	293	353	36	47	5.6	.947	2B-104, 3B-15
1942			115	.229	.294	388	89	11	4	2	0.5	34	35	29	27	5	3	0	233	316	27	54	5.0	.953	2B-108, SS-2, 3B-2, C-1
1943			112	.290	.355	414	120	21	3	0	0.0	40	43	32	36	12	5	1	213	345	33	65	5.3	.944	SS-68, 2B-40, 1B-1
1944			127	.230	.304	405	93	18	3	2	0.5	42	42	33	41	8	1	0	206	351	36	55	4.7	.939	SS-116, 2B-11, 3B-1
1945			128	.280	.370	478	134	27	5	2	0.4	67	66	37	33	8	1	0	248	366	41	63	5.1	.937	SS-104, 2B-29, C-1
1946			131	.259	.378	495	128	23	6	8	1.6	60	52	40	52	2	1	0	319	387	24	70	5.6	.967	2B-113, SS-13, 3B-7
1947			156	.297	.409	616	183	30	6	9	1.5	102	67	63	65	5	0	0	198	330	31	35	3.6	.945	3B-156
1948			131	.267	.379	449	120	19	2	9	2.0	68	42	42	62	5	10	2	119	256	21	21	3.0	.947	3B-119
1949	CHI	N	76	.226	.352	261	59	13	4	4	1.5	29	27	18	22	3	5	0	104	157	16	28	3.6	.942	3B-55, 2B-16
1950	STL	A	9	.158	.211	19	3	1	0	0	0.0	1	2	3	8	0	1	0	10	8	3	3	2.3	.857	3B-6
12 yrs.			1261	.265	.359	4582	1214	222	47	38	0.8	553	480	369	427	60	32	4	2248	3323	319	536	4.7	.946	2B-551, 3B-383, SS-303, C-2, 1B-1

Bucky Guth

GUTH, CHARLES HENRY
B. Aug. 18, 1947, Baltimore, Md.
BR TR 6'1" 180 lbs.

Year	Team		Games	BA	SA	AB	H	2B	3B	HR	HR%	R	RBI	BB	SO	SB	PH AB	PH H	PO	A	E	DP	TC/G	FA	G by Pos
1972	MIN	A	3	.000	.000	3	0	0	0	0	0.0	1	0	0	0	0	0	0	0	4	0	0	1.3	1.000	SS-1

Cesar Gutierrez

GUTIERREZ, CESAR DARIO (Coca)
B. Jan. 26, 1943, Coro, Venezuela
BR TR 5'9" 155 lbs.

Year	Team		Games	BA	SA	AB	H	2B	3B	HR	HR%	R	RBI	BB	SO	SB	PH AB	PH H	PO	A	E	DP	TC/G	FA	G by Pos
1967	SF	N	18	.143	.143	21	3	0	0	0	0.0	4	0	1	4	1	1	1	17	20	3	4	2.2	.949	SS-15, 2B-1
1969	2 teams		SF N (15G – .217)			DET A (17G – .245)																			
"	total		32	.236	.264	72	17	2	0	0	0.0	9	0	11	5	2	2	1	28	61	7	6	3.0	.927	SS-20, 3B-7
1970	DET	A	135	.243	.299	415	101	11	6	0	0.0	40	22	18	39	4	0	0	183	326	23	60	3.9	.957	SS-135
1971			38	.189	.189	37	7	0	0	0	0.0	8	4	0	3	0	9	3	14	26	1	4	1.1	.976	SS-14, 3B-5, 2B-2
4 yrs.			223	.235	.281	545	128	13	6	0	0.0	61	26	30	51	7	12	5	242	433	33	74	3.2	.953	SS-184, 3B-12, 2B-3

Jackie Gutierrez

GUTIERREZ, JOAQUIN FERNANDO
Born Joaquin Fernando Gutierrez y Hernandez.
B. June 27, 1960, Cartagena, Colombia
BR TR 5'11" 168 lbs.

Year	Team		Games	BA	SA	AB	H	2B	3B	HR	HR%	R	RBI	BB	SO	SB	PH AB	PH H	PO	A	E	DP	TC/G	FA	G by Pos
1983	BOS	A	5	.300	.300	10	3	0	0	0	0.0	2	0	1	1	0	0	0	9	6	1	1	3.2	.938	SS-4
1984			151	.263	.316	449	118	12	3	2	0.4	55	29	15	49	12	0	0	228	347	31	60	4.0	.949	SS-150
1985			103	.218	.273	275	60	5	2	2	0.7	33	21	12	37	10	1	0	143	238	23	47	3.9	.943	SS-99
1986	BAL	A	61	.186	.207	145	27	3	0	0	0.0	8	4	3	27	3	0	0	96	108	4	29	3.4	.981	2B-53, 3B-6, DH-1
1987			3	.000	.000	1	0	0	0	0	0.0	0	0	0	0	0	0	0	0	0	0	0	0.0	—	3B-1, 2B-1
1988	PHI	N	33	.247	.299	77	19	4	0	0	0.0	8	9	2	9	0	1	0	28	59	8	7	2.9	.916	SS-22, 3B-13
6 yrs.			356	.237	.285	957	227	24	5	4	0.4	106	63	33	123	25	2	0	504	758	67	144	3.7	.950	SS-275, 2B-54, 3B-20, DH-1

Don Gutteridge

GUTTERIDGE, DONALD JOSEPH
B. June 19, 1912, Pittsburg, Kans.
Manager 1969-70.
BR TR 5'10½" 165 lbs.

Year	Team		Games	BA	SA	AB	H	2B	3B	HR	HR%	R	RBI	BB	SO	SB	PH AB	PH H	PO	A	E	DP	TC/G	FA	G by Pos
1936	STL	N	23	.319	.538	91	29	8	4	3	3.3	13	16	1	14	3	0	0	25	34	2	3	2.7	.967	3B-23
1937			119	.271	.421	447	121	26	10	7	1.6	66	61	25	66	12	8	1	145	192	9	20	2.9	.974	3B-105, SS-8
1938			142	.255	.397	552	141	21	15	9	1.6	61	64	29	49	14	2	0	244	344	45	56	4.5	.929	3B-73, SS-68
1939			148	.269	.376	524	141	27	4	7	1.3	71	54	27	70	5	2	0	136	204	24	24	2.5	.934	3B-143, SS-2
1940			69	.269	.398	108	29	5	0	3	2.8	19	14	5	15	3	20	2	24	33	8	3	0.9	.877	3B-39
1942	STL	A	147	.255	.339	616	157	27	11	1	0.2	90	50	59	54	16	1	1	377	455	23	94	5.8	.973	2B-145, 3B-2
1943			132	.273	.366	538	147	35	6	1	0.2	77	36	50	46	10	1	0	328	331	29	64	5.2	.958	2B-132
1944			148	.245	.342	603	148	27	11	3	0.5	89	36	51	63	20	1	0	368	407	35	95	5.5	.957	2B-146

Year	Team		Games	BA	SA	AB	H	2B	3B	HR	HR%	R	RBI	BB	SO	SB	Pinch Hit AB	H	PO	A	E	DP	TC/G	FA	G by Pos

Don Gutteridge *continued*

Year	Team		Games	BA	SA	AB	H	2B	3B	HR	HR%	R	RBI	BB	SO	SB	AB	H	PO	A	E	DP	TC/G	FA	G by Pos
1945			143	.238	.304	543	129	24	3	2	0.4	72	49	43	46	9	1	0	357	334	22	66	5.0	.969	2B-128, OF-14
1946	BOS	A	22	.234	.362	47	11	3	0	1	2.1	8	6	2	7	0	1	0	15	25	4	3	2.0	.909	2B-9, 3B-8
1947			54	.168	.229	131	22	2	0	2	1.5	20	5	17	13	3	5	1	56	73	8	11	2.5	.942	2B-20, 3B-19
1948	PIT	N	4	.000	.000	2	0	0	0	0	0.0	0	0	0	1	0	2	0	0	0	0	0	0.0	—	
12 yrs.			1151	.256	.362	4202	1075	200	64	39	0.9	586	391	309	444	95	44	5	2075	2432	209	439	4.1	.956	2B-580, 3B-412, SS-78, OF-14

WORLD SERIES

Year	Team		Games	BA	SA	AB	H	2B	3B	HR	HR%	R	RBI	BB	SO	SB	AB	H	PO	A	E	DP	TC/G	FA	G by Pos
1944	STL	A	6	.143	.190	21	3	1	0	0	0.0	1	0	3	5	0	0	0	15	11	3	3	4.8	.897	2B-6
1946	BOS	A	3	.400	.400	5	2	0	0	0	0.0	1	1	0	0	0	0	0	0	2	0	0	0.7	1.000	2B-2
2 yrs.			9	.192	.231	26	5	1	0	0	0.0	2	1	3	5	0	0	0	15	13	3	3	3.4	.903	2B-8

Doug Gwosdz

GWOSDZ, DOUGLAS WAYNE (Eyechart)
B. June 20, 1960, Houston, Tex.

BR TR 5'11" 180 lbs.

Year	Team		Games	BA	SA	AB	H	2B	3B	HR	HR%	R	RBI	BB	SO	SB	AB	H	PO	A	E	DP	TC/G	FA	G by Pos
1981	SD	N	16	.167	.250	24	4	2	0	0	0.0	1	3	3	6	0	4	0	40	5	0	3	2.8	1.000	C-13
1982			7	.176	.176	17	3	0	0	0	0.0	1	0	2	7	0	1	0	34	2	0	0	5.1	1.000	C-7
1983			39	.109	.182	55	6	1	0	1	1.8	7	4	7	19	0	5	1	95	5	3	0	2.6	.971	C-32
1984			7	.250	.250	8	2	0	0	0	0.0	0	1	2	5	0	0	0	25	1	1	0	3.9	.963	C-6
4 yrs.			69	.144	.202	104	15	3	0	1	1.0	9	8	14	37	0	10	1	194	13	4	3	3.1	.981	C-58

Chris Gwynn

GWYNN, CHRISTOPHER KARLTON
Brother of Tony Gwynn.
B. Oct. 13, 1964, Los Angeles, Calif.

BL TL 6' 200 lbs.

Year	Team		Games	BA	SA	AB	H	2B	3B	HR	HR%	R	RBI	BB	SO	SB	AB	H	PO	A	E	DP	TC/G	FA	G by Pos
1987	LA	N	17	.219	.250	32	7	1	0	0	0.0	2	2	1	7	0	6	0	12	0	0	0	0.7	1.000	OF-10
1988			12	.182	.182	11	2	0	0	0	0.0	1	0	1	2	0	9	2	0	0	0	0	—		OF-4
1989			32	.235	.324	68	16	4	1	0	0.0	8	7	2	9	1	14	3	26	1	0	1	0.8	1.000	OF-19
3 yrs.			61	.225	.288	111	25	5	1	0	0.0	11	9	4	18	1	29	5	38	1	0	1	0.6	1.000	OF-33

Tony Gwynn

GWYNN, ANTHONY KEITH
Brother of Chris Gwynn.
B. May 9, 1960, Los Angeles, Calif.

BL TL 5'11" 185 lbs.

Year	Team		Games	BA	SA	AB	H	2B	3B	HR	HR%	R	RBI	BB	SO	SB	AB	H	PO	A	E	DP	TC/G	FA	G by Pos
1982	SD	N	54	.289	.389	190	55	12	2	1	0.5	33	17	14	16	8	4	1	110	1	1	0	2.1	.991	OF-52
1983			86	.309	.372	304	94	12	2	1	0.3	34	37	23	21	7	6	1	163	9	1	1	2.0	.994	OF-81
1984			158	.351	.444	606	213	21	10	5	0.8	88	71	59	23	33	2	1	345	11	4	2	2.3	.989	OF-156
1985			154	.317	.408	622	197	29	5	6	1.0	90	46	45	33	14	2	0	337	14	4	2	2.3	.989	OF-152
1986			160	.329	.467	642	211	33	7	14	2.2	107	59	52	35	37	1	0	337	19	4	3	2.3	.989	OF-160
1987			157	.370	.511	589	218	36	13	7	1.2	119	54	82	35	56	0	0	298	13	6	1	2.0	.981	OF-156
1988			133	.313	.415	521	163	22	5	7	1.3	64	70	51	40	26	0	0	264	8	5	1	2.1	.982	OF-133
1989			158	.336	.424	604	203	27	7	4	0.7	82	62	56	30	40	0	0	353	13	6	1	2.4	.984	OF-157
8 yrs.			1060	.332	.437	4078	1354	192	51	45	1.1	617	416	382	233	221	17	4	2207	88	31	13	2.2	.987	OF-1047

LEAGUE CHAMPIONSHIP SERIES

Year	Team		Games	BA	SA	AB	H	2B	3B	HR	HR%	R	RBI	BB	SO	SB	AB	H	PO	A	E	DP	TC/G	FA	G by Pos
1984	SD	N	5	.368	.526	19	7	3	0	0	0.0	6	3	1	2	0	0	0	9	0	0	0	1.8	1.000	OF-5

WORLD SERIES

Year	Team		Games	BA	SA	AB	H	2B	3B	HR	HR%	R	RBI	BB	SO	SB	AB	H	PO	A	E	DP	TC/G	FA	G by Pos
1984	SD	N	5	.263	.263	19	5	0	0	0	0.0	1	0	3	2	1	0	0	12	1	1	1	2.8	.929	OF-5

Dick Gyselman

GYSELMAN, RICHARD RONALD
B. Apr. 6, 1908, San Francisco, Calif.

BR TR 6'2" 170 lbs.

Year	Team		Games	BA	SA	AB	H	2B	3B	HR	HR%	R	RBI	BB	SO	SB	AB	H	PO	A	E	DP	TC/G	FA	G by Pos
1933	BOS	N	58	.239	.303	155	37	6	2	0	0.0	10	12	7	21	0	3	1	47	97	11	5	2.7	.929	3B-42, 2B-5, SS-1
1934			24	.167	.250	36	6	1	1	0	0.0	7	4	2	11	0	4	1	10	13	7	2	1.3	.767	3B-15, 2B-2
2 yrs.			82	.225	.293	191	43	7	3	0	0.0	17	16	9	32	0	7	2	57	110	18	7	2.3	.903	3B-57, 2B-7, SS-1

Bert Haas

HAAS, BERTHOLD JOHN
B. Feb. 8, 1914, Naperville, Ill.

BR TR 5'11" 178 lbs.

Year	Team		Games	BA	SA	AB	H	2B	3B	HR	HR%	R	RBI	BB	SO	SB	AB	H	PO	A	E	DP	TC/G	FA	G by Pos
1937	BKN	N	16	.400	.520	25	10	3	0	0	0.0	2	2	1	1	0	9	4	18	0	0	1	1.1	1.000	OF-4, 1B-3
1938			1	—	—	0	0	0	0	0	0.0	0	0	0	0	0	0	0	0	0	0	0	0.0	—	
1942	CIN	N	154	.239	.326	585	140	21	6	6	1.0	59	54	59	54	6	0	0	235	276	36	38	3.6	.934	3B-146, 1B-6, OF-2
1943			101	.262	.386	332	87	17	6	4	1.2	39	44	22	26	6	16	4	432	97	9	52	5.3	.983	1B-44, 3B-23, OF-18
1946			140	.264	.351	535	141	24	7	3	0.6	57	50	33	42	6	0	1	1355	105	9	142	10.5	.994	1B-131, 3B-6
1947			135	.286	.369	482	138	17	7	3	0.6	58	67	42	27	9	11	2	680	25	16	49	5.3	.978	OF-69, 1B-53
1948	PHI	N	95	.282	.357	333	94	9	2	4	1.2	35	34	36	25	8	9	2	366	107	24	26	5.2	.952	3B-54, 1B-35
1949	2 teams		PHI	N	(2G –	.000)	NY	N	(54G –	.260)																
"	total		56	.257	.362	105	27	3	1	1	1.0	12	10	6	9	0	19	4	166	19	6	14	3.4	.969	1B-23, 3B-11
1951	CHI	A	25	.163	.279	43	7	0	1	1	2.3	1	2	5	4	0	11	3	44	5	0	4	2.0	1.000	1B-7, OF-4, 3B-1
9 yrs.			723	.264	.355	2440	644	93	32	22	0.9	263	263	204	188	51	77	20	3296	634	100	326	5.6	.975	1B-302, 3B-241, OF-97

Bruno Haas

HAAS, BRUNO PHILIP (Boon)
B. May 5, 1891, Worcester, Mass. D. June 5, 1952, Sarasota, Fla.

BB TL 5'10" 180 lbs.

Year	Team		Games	BA	SA	AB	H	2B	3B	HR	HR%	R	RBI	BB	SO	SB	AB	H	PO	A	E	DP	TC/G	FA	G by Pos
1915	PHI	A	12	.056	.056	18	1	0	0	0	0.0	1	0	1	7	0	1	0	9	6	1	0	1.3	.938	P-6, OF-3

Eddie Haas

HAAS, GEORGE EDWIN
B. May 26, 1935, Paducah, Ky.
Manager 1985.

BL TR 5'11" 178 lbs.

Year	Team		Games	BA	SA	AB	H	2B	3B	HR	HR%	R	RBI	BB	SO	SB	AB	H	PO	A	E	DP	TC/G	FA	G by Pos
1957	CHI	N	14	.208	.250	24	5	1	0	0	0.0	1	4	1	5	0	8	1	4	0	0	0	0.3	1.000	OF-4
1958	MIL	N	9	.357	.357	14	5	0	0	0	0.0	2	1	2	1	0	4	3	5	0	0	0	0.6	1.000	OF-3
1960			32	.219	.375	32	7	2	0	1	3.1	4	5	5	14	0	25	6	2	0	0	0	0.1	1.000	OF-2
3 yrs.			55	.243	.329	70	17	3	0	1	1.4	7	10	8	20	0	37	11	11	0	0	0	0.2	1.000	OF-9

Mule Haas

HAAS, GEORGE WILLIAM
B. Oct. 15, 1903, Montclair, N. J. D. June 30, 1974, New Orleans, La.

BL TR 6'1" 175 lbs.

Year	Team		Games	BA	SA	AB	H	2B	3B	HR	HR%	R	RBI	BB	SO	SB	Pinch Hit AB	Pinch Hit H	PO	A	E	DP	TC/G	FA	G by Pos

Mule Haas *continued*

Year	Team		Games	BA	SA	AB	H	2B	3B	HR	HR%	R	RBI	BB	SO	SB	AB	H	PO	A	E	DP	TC/G	FA	G by Pos
1925	PIT	N	4	.000	.000	3	0	0	0	0	0.0	1	0	0	1	0	1	0	2	0	0	0	0.5	1.000	OF-2
1928	PHI	A	91	.280	.422	332	93	21	4	6	1.8	41	39	23	20	2	8	0	175	9	5	1	2.1	.974	OF-82
1929			139	.313	.498	578	181	41	9	16	2.8	115	82	34	38	0	0	0	373	10	7	2	2.8	.982	OF-139
1930			132	.299	.398	532	159	33	4	2	0.4	91	68	43	33	2	1	0	360	11	9	5	2.9	.976	OF-131
1931			102	.323	.475	440	142	29	4	8	1.8	82	56	30	29	0	0	0	272	6	3	4	2.8	.989	OF-102
1932			143	.305	.405	558	170	28	5	6	1.1	91	65	62	49	1	6	3	372	6	5	2	2.7	.987	OF-137
1933	CHI	A	146	.287	.362	585	168	33	4	1	0.2	97	51	65	41	0	0	0	347	9	6	2	2.5	.983	OF-146
1934			106	.268	.348	351	94	16	3	2	0.6	54	22	47	22	1	13	4	204	5	2	1	2.0	.991	OF-89
1935			92	.291	.382	327	95	22	1	2	0.6	44	40	37	17	4	7	2	183	4	2	1	2.1	.989	OF-84
1936			119	.284	.358	408	116	26	2	0	0.0	75	46	64	29	1	15	3	253	11	5	8	2.3	.981	OF-96, 1B-7
1937			54	.207	.288	111	23	3	3	0	0.0	8	15	16	10	1	16	2	254	19	8	22	5.2	.972	1B-32, OF-2
1938	PHI	A	40	.205	.231	78	16	2	0	0	0.0	7	12	12	10	0	20	1	67	2	0	3	1.7	1.000	OF-12, 1B-6
12 yrs.			1168	.292	.402	4303	1257	254	45	43	1.0	706	496	433	299	12	87	15	2862	92	52	51	2.6	.983	OF-1022, 1B-45

WORLD SERIES

Year	Team		Games	BA	SA	AB	H	2B	3B	HR	HR%	R	RBI	BB	SO	SB	AB	H	PO	A	E	DP	TC/G	FA	G by Pos
1929	PHI	A	5	.238	.524	21	5	0	0	2	9.5	3	6	1	3	0	0	0	5	0	0	0	1.0	1.000	OF-5
1930			6	.111	.222	18	2	0	0	0	0.0	1	1	1	3	0	0	0	14	0	0	0	2.3	1.000	OF-6
1931			7	.130	.174	23	3	1	0	0	0.0	1	2	3	5	0	0	0	17	0	0	0	2.4	1.000	OF-7
3 yrs.			18	.161	.306	62	10	1	0	2	3.2	5	9	5	11	0	0	0	36	0	0	0	2.0	1.000	OF-18

Emil Haberer — HABERER, EMIL KARL BR TR 6'1" 204 lbs.
B. Feb. 2, 1878, Cincinnati, Ohio D. Oct. 19, 1951, Louisville, Ky.

Year	Team		Games	BA	SA	AB	H	2B	3B	HR	HR%	R	RBI	BB	SO	SB	AB	H	PO	A	E	DP	TC/G	FA	G by Pos
1901	CIN	N	6	.167	.278	18	3	0	0	0	0.0	2	1	3		0	1	0	21	6	5	3	5.3	.844	3B-3, 1B-2
1903			5	.077	.077	13	1	0	0	0	0.0	1	0	2		0	1	1	11	3	1	0	3.0	.933	C-4
1909			5	.188	.250	16	3	1	0	0	0.0	1	2	0		0	1	0	15	2	2	1	3.8	.895	C-4
3 yrs.			16	.149	.213	47	7	1	0	0	0.0	4	3	5		0	3	1	47	11	8	4	4.1	.879	C-8, 3B-3, 1B-2

Irv Hach — HACH, IRVIN WILLIAM (Major) BR TR
B. June 6, 1873, Louisville, Ky. D. Aug. 13, 1936, Louisville, Ky.

Year	Team		Games	BA	SA	AB	H	2B	3B	HR	HR%	R	RBI	BB	SO	SB	AB	H	PO	A	E	DP	TC/G	FA	G by Pos
1897	LOU	N	16	.216	.255	51	11	2	0	0	0.0	5	3	5		1	0	0	24	38	9	4	4.4	.873	2B-9, 3B-7

Stan Hack — HACK, STANLEY CAMFIELD (Smiling Stan) BL TR 6' 170 lbs.
B. Dec. 6, 1909, Sacramento, Calif. D. Dec. 15, 1979, Dixon, Ill.
Manager 1954-56, 1958.

Year	Team		Games	BA	SA	AB	H	2B	3B	HR	HR%	R	RBI	BB	SO	SB	AB	H	PO	A	E	DP	TC/G	FA	G by Pos
1932	CHI	N	72	.236	.365	178	42	5	6	2	1.1	32	19	17	16	5	14	2	36	90	12	5	1.9	.913	3B-51
1933			20	.350	.483	60	21	3	1	1	1.7	10	2	8	3	1	2	0	19	40	1	8	3.0	.983	3B-17
1934			111	.289	.366	402	116	16	6	1	0.2	54	21	45	42	11	2	0	102	198	16	10	2.8	.949	3B-109
1935			124	.311	.436	427	133	23	9	4	0.9	75	64	65	17	14	5	2	153	244	21	26	3.4	.950	3B-111, 1B-7
1936			149	.298	.392	561	167	27	4	6	1.1	102	78	89	39	17	0	0	225	210	17	28	3.0	.962	3B-140, 1B-11
1937			154	.297	.375	582	173	27	6	2	0.3	106	63	83	42	16	1	0	172	251	14	30	2.8	.968	3B-152
1938			152	.320	.432	609	195	34	11	4	0.7	109	67	94	39	16	0	0	178	300	23	26	3.3	.956	3B-156
1939			156	.298	.398	641	191	28	6	8	1.2	112	56	65	35	17	0	0	177	278	21	15	3.1	.956	3B-156
1940			149	.317	.439	603	191	38	6	8	1.3	101	40	75	24	21	0	0	182	304	23	27	3.4	.955	3B-150, 1B-1
1941			151	.317	.427	586	186	33	5	7	1.2	111	45	99	40	10	0	0	139	295	21	22	3.0	.954	3B-150, 1B-1
1942			140	.300	.409	553	166	36	3	6	1.1	91	39	94	40	9	5	0	154	261	15	21	3.1	.965	3B-139
1943			144	.289	.366	533	154	24	4	3	0.6	78	35	82	27	6	7	0	149	264	17	11	3.0	.960	3B-136
1944			98	.282	.352	383	108	16	1	3	0.8	65	32	53	21	5	4	1	226	174	19	23	4.3	.955	3B-75, 1B-18
1945			150	.323	.405	597	193	29	7	2	0.3	110	43	99	30	12	0	0	233	314	14	29	3.7	.975	3B-146, 1B-5
1946			92	.285	.350	323	92	13	4	0	0.0	55	26	83	32	3	2	0	102	168	9	6	3.0	.968	3B-90
1947			76	.271	.333	240	65	11	2	0	0.0	28	12	41	19	0	10	2	64	136	8	11	2.7	.962	3B-66
16 yrs.			1938	.301	.397	7278	2193	363	81	57	0.8	1239	642	1092	466	165	45	7	2311	3527	251	298	3.1	.959	3B-1836, 1B-47

WORLD SERIES

Year	Team		Games	BA	SA	AB	H	2B	3B	HR	HR%	R	RBI	BB	SO	SB	AB	H	PO	A	E	DP	TC/G	FA	G by Pos
1932	CHI	N	1	–	–	0	0	0	0	0	–	0	0	0	0	0	0	0	0	0	0	0	0.0	–	3B-6, SS-1
1935			6	.227	.364	22	5	1	1	0	0.0	2	0	2	2	1	0	0	5	11	0	0	2.7	1.000	3B-6, SS-1
1938			4	.471	.529	17	8	1	0	0	0.0	3	1	1	2	0	0	0	4	4	0	0	2.0	1.000	3B-4
1945			7	.367	.467	30	11	3	0	0	0.0	1	4	4	2	0	0	0	12	13	3	0	4.0	.893	3B-7
4 yrs.			18	.348	.449	69	24	5	1	0	0.0	6	5	7	6	1	0	0	21	28	3	0	2.9	.942	3B-17, SS-1

Rich Hacker — HACKER, RICHARD WARREN BB TR 6' 160 lbs.
B. Oct. 6, 1947, Belleville, Ill.

Year	Team		Games	BA	SA	AB	H	2B	3B	HR	HR%	R	RBI	BB	SO	SB	AB	H	PO	A	E	DP	TC/G	FA	G by Pos
1971	MON	N	16	.121	.152	33	4	1	0	0	0.0	2	2	3	12	0	0	0	17	44	1	9	3.9	.984	SS-16

Jim Hackett — HACKETT, JAMES JOSEPH (Sunny Jim) BR TR 6'2" 185 lbs.
B. Oct. 1, 1877, Jacksonville, Ill. D. Mar. 28, 1961, Douglas, Mich.

Year	Team		Games	BA	SA	AB	H	2B	3B	HR	HR%	R	RBI	BB	SO	SB	AB	H	PO	A	E	DP	TC/G	FA	G by Pos
1902	STL	N	6	.286	.333	21	6	1	0	0	0.0	2	4	2		1	0	0	6	7	3	0	2.7	.813	P-4, OF-2
1903			99	.228	.311	351	80	13	8	0	0.0	24	36	19		2	3	0	949	53	29	63	10.4	.972	1B-89, P-7
2 yrs.			105	.231	.312	372	86	14	8	0	0.0	26	40	21		3	3	0	955	60	32	63	10.0	.969	1B-89, P-11, OF-2

Mert Hackett — HACKETT, MORTIMER MARTIN TR 5'10½" 175 lbs.
Brother of Walter Hackett.
B. Nov. 11, 1859, Cambridge, Mass. D. Feb. 22, 1938, Cambridge, Mass.

Year	Team		Games	BA	SA	AB	H	2B	3B	HR	HR%	R	RBI	BB	SO	SB	AB	H	PO	A	E	DP	TC/G	FA	G by Pos
1883	BOS	N	46	.235	.380	179	42	8	6	1	1.1	20	24	1	48		0	0	255	58	34	2	7.5	.902	C-44, OF-4
1884			72	.205	.280	268	55	13	2	1	0.4	28		2	66		0	0	513	108	50	2	9.3	.925	C-71, 3B-1
1885			34	.183	.261	115	21	7	1	0	0.0	9	4	2	28		0	0	194	53	27	6	8.1	.901	C-34
1886	KC	N	62	.217	.317	230	50	8	3	3	1.3	18	25	4	59		0	0	262	63	28	6	5.7	.921	C-52, OF-13
1887	IND	N	42	.238	.361	147	35	6	3	2	1.4	12	10	7	24	4	0	0	130	52	13	4	4.6	.933	C-40, OF-2, 1B-1
5 yrs.			256	.216	.318	939	203	42	15	8	0.9	87	63	16	225	4	0	0	1354	334	152	20	7.2	.917	C-241, OF-19, 3B-1, 1B-1

Walter Hackett — HACKETT, WALTER HENRY
Brother of Mert Hackett.
B. Aug. 15, 1857, Cambridge, Mass. D. Oct. 2, 1920, Cambridge, Mass.

Year	Team		Games	BA	SA	AB	H	2B	3B	HR	HR%	R	RBI	BB	SO	SB	Pinch Hit AB	Pinch Hit H	PO	A	E	DP	TC/G	FA	G by Pos

Walter Hackett *continued*

Year	Team		Games	BA	SA	AB	H	2B	3B	HR	HR%	R	RBI	BB	SO	SB	AB	H	PO	A	E	DP	TC/G	FA	G by Pos
1884	BOS	U	103	.243	.296	415	101	19	0	1	0.2	71		7				0	0	126	294	71	12	4.8	.855	SS-103
1885	BOS	N	35	.184	.208	125	23	3	0	0	0.0	8	9	3	22		0	0	59	86	22	9	4.8	.868	2B-20, SS-15
2 yrs.			138	.230	.276	540	124	22	0	1	0.2	79	9	10	22		0	0	185	380	93	21	4.8	.859	SS-118, 2B-20

Harvey Haddix

HADDIX, HARVEY (The Kitten)
B. Sept. 18, 1925, Medway, Ohio

BL TL 5'9½" 170 lbs.

Year	Team		Games	BA	SA	AB	H	2B	3B	HR	HR%	R	RBI	BB	SO	SB	AB	H	PO	A	E	DP	TC/G	FA	G by Pos
1952	STL	N	9	.214	.214	14	3	0	0	0	0.0	3		1	5		0	0	0	5	1	0	0.7	.833	P-7, OF-1
1953			48	.289	.412	97	28	3	3	1	1.0	21	11	5	19		0	2	15	43	2	5	1.3	.967	P-36
1954			61	.194	.280	93	18	4	2	0	0.0	16	4	5	11	2	0	0	14	39	3	3	0.9	.946	P-43
1955			37	.164	.288	73	12	2	2	1	1.4	10	7	4	15		0	0	14	38	4	2	1.5	.929	P-37
1956	2 teams			STL	N	(5G – .222)				PHI	N	(46G – .237)														
"	total		51	.235	.284	102	24	5	0	0	0.0	7	11	7	13	0	15	4	10	31	1	1	0.8	.976	P-35
1957	PHI	N	41	.309	.382	68	21	3	1	0	0.0	6	6	3	12	1	7	1	10	15	2	0	0.7	.926	P-27
1958	CIN	N	42	.180	.295	61	11	4	0	1	1.6	11	1	8	18	0	2	0	10	26	1	1	0.9	.973	P-29
1959	PIT	N	31	.145	.193	83	12	4	0	0	0.0	3	5	3	17	0	0	0	8	35	0	3	1.4	1.000	P-31
1960			29	.254	.313	67	17	4	0	0	0.0	7	7	3	15	0	0	0	9	46	1	2	1.9	.982	P-29
1961			31	.143	.196	56	8	3	0	0	0.0	2	3	6	14	0	0	0	5	29	2	4	1.2	.944	P-29
1962			28	.250	.404	52	13	3	1	1	1.9	9	5	1	11	0	0	0	10	19	2	2	1.1	.935	P-28
1963	BAL	A	50	.182	.364	11	2	0	0	0	0.0	0	2	0	1	0	1	0	5	10	1	0	0.3	.938	P-49
1964			49	.000	.000	19	0	0	0	0	0.0	0	0	0	10	0	1	0	4	16	0	1	0.4	1.000	P-49
1965			24	.000	.000	2	0	0	0	0	0.0	0	0	0	1	0	0	0	1	6	1	0	0.3	.875	P-24
14 yrs.			531	.212	.296	798	169	37	9	4	0.5	95	64	46	162	4	28	7	115	358	21	24	0.9	.957	P-453, OF-1

WORLD SERIES

Year	Team		Games	BA	SA	AB	H	2B	3B	HR	HR%	R	RBI	BB	SO	SB	AB	H	PO	A	E	DP	TC/G	FA	G by Pos
1960	PIT	N	2	.333	.333	3	1	0	0	0	0.0	0	0	0	1	0	0	0	1	1	0	0	1.0	1.000	P-2

George Haddock

HADDOCK, GEORGE SILAS (Gentleman George)
B. Dec. 25, 1866, Portsmouth, N. H.   D. Apr. 18, 1926, Boston, Mass.

BR TR 5'11" 155 lbs.

Year	Team		Games	BA	SA	AB	H	2B	3B	HR	HR%	R	RBI	BB	SO	SB	AB	H	PO	A	E	DP	TC/G	FA	G by Pos
1888	WAS	N	2	.200	.200	5	1	0	0	0	0.0	0	0	0					2	8	1	0	5.5	.909	P-2
1889			34	.223	.304	112	25	3	0	2	1.8	13	14	19	27	3	0	0	14	55	9	3	2.3	.885	P-33, OF-3
1890	BUF	P	42	.247	.322	146	36	11	0	0	0.0	21	24	24	32	3	0	0	26	88	9	2	2.9	.927	P-35, OF-7
1891	BOS	AA	58	.243	.324	185	45	4	1	3	1.6	30	23	21	46	3	0	0	27	116	14	2	2.7	.911	P-51, OF-8
1892	BKN	N	47	.177	.228	158	28	6	1	0	0.0	23	11	12	31	2	0	0	23	81	12	5	2.5	.897	P-46, OF-1
1893			29	.282	.376	85	24	1	2	1	1.2	21	7	8	15	2	0	0	13	19	10	1	1.4	.762	P-23, OF-7
1894	2 teams			PHI	N	(10G – .172)				WAS	N	(5G – .188)														
"	total		15	.178	.311	45	8	2	2	0	0.0	6	4	4	4	1	0	0	6	20	1	0	1.8	.963	P-14, OF-1
7 yrs.			227	.227	.304	736	167	27	6	6	0.8	114	83	89	157	14	0	0	111	387	56	12	2.4	.899	P-204, OF-27

Kent Hadley

HADLEY, KENT WILLIAM
B. Dec. 17, 1934, Pocatello, Ida.

BL TL 6'3" 190 lbs.

Year	Team		Games	BA	SA	AB	H	2B	3B	HR	HR%	R	RBI	BB	SO	SB	AB	H	PO	A	E	DP	TC/G	FA	G by Pos
1958	KC	A	3	.182	.182	11	2	0	0	0	0.0	1	0	0	4	0	1	0	21	0	0	1	7.0	1.000	1B-2
1959			113	.253	.403	288	73	11	1	10	3.5	40	39	24	74	0	16	2	656	42	8	66	6.2	.989	1B-95
1960	NY	A	55	.203	.422	64	13	2	0	4	6.3	8	11	6	19	0	29	6	99	6	1	10	1.9	.991	1B-24
3 yrs.			171	.242	.399	363	88	13	1	14	3.9	49	50	30	97	1	46	8	776	48	9	77	4.9	.989	1B-121

Bill Haeffner

HAEFFNER, WILLIAM BERNARD
B. July 8, 1894, Philadelphia, Pa.   D. Jan. 27, 1982, Delaware County, Pa.

BR TR 5'9" 165 lbs.

Year	Team		Games	BA	SA	AB	H	2B	3B	HR	HR%	R	RBI	BB	SO	SB	AB	H	PO	A	E	DP	TC/G	FA	G by Pos
1915	PHI	A	3	.250	.250	4	1	0	0	0	0.0	0	0	0	1	0	0	0	0	1	0	0	0.3	1.000	C-3
1920	PIT	N	54	.194	.229	175	34	4	1	0	0.0	8	14	8	14	1	0	0	192	48	7	1	4.6	.972	C-52
1928	NY	N	2	.000	.000	1	0	0	0	0	0.0	0	0	0	0	0	0	0	3	0	1	0	2.0	.750	C-2
3 yrs.			59	.194	.228	180	35	4	1	0	0.0	8	14	8	15	1	0	0	195	49	8	1	4.3	.968	C-57

Bud Hafey

HAFEY, DANIEL ALBERT
Brother of Tom Hafey.
B. Aug. 6, 1912, Berkeley, Calif.   D. July 27, 1986, Sacramento, Calif.

BR TR 6' 185 lbs.

Year	Team		Games	BA	SA	AB	H	2B	3B	HR	HR%	R	RBI	BB	SO	SB	AB	H	PO	A	E	DP	TC/G	FA	G by Pos
1935	2 teams			CHI	A	(2G – .000)				PIT	N	(58G – .228)														
"	total		60	.228	.408	184	42	11	6	6	3.3	30	16	16	48	0	5	1	125	5	4	3	2.2	.970	OF-47
1936	PIT	N	39	.212	.381	118	25	6	1	4	3.4	19	13	10	27	0	9	0	66	3	5	0	1.9	.932	OF-29
1939	2 teams			CIN	N	(6G – .154)				PHI	N	(18G – .176)														
"	total		24	.172	.203	64	11	2	0	0	0.0	4	4	4	16	2	5	1	37	2	0	0	1.6	1.000	OF-17, P-2
3 yrs.			123	.213	.363	366	78	19	3	10	2.7	53	33	30	91	2	19	2	228	10	9	3	2.0	.964	OF-93, P-2

Chick Hafey

HAFEY, CHARLES JAMES
B. Feb. 12, 1903, Berkeley, Calif.   D. July 2, 1973, Calistoga, Calif.
Hall of Fame 1971.

BR TR 6' 185 lbs.

Year	Team		Games	BA	SA	AB	H	2B	3B	HR	HR%	R	RBI	BB	SO	SB	AB	H	PO	A	E	DP	TC/G	FA	G by Pos
1924	STL	N	24	.253	.418	91	23	5	2	2	2.2	10	22	4	8	1	0	0	48	3	4	1	2.3	.927	OF-24
1925			93	.302	.425	358	108	25	2	5	1.4	36	57	10	29	3	5	1	180	9	9	2	2.1	.955	OF-88
1926			78	.271	.427	225	61	19	2	4	1.8	30	38	11	36	2	22	7	106	6	3	1	1.5	.974	OF-54
1927			103	.329	.590	346	114	26	5	18	5.2	62	63	36	41	12	9	5	179	19	4	7	2.0	.980	OF-94
1928			138	.337	.604	520	175	46	6	27	5.2	101	111	40	53	8	4	0	287	13	11	3	2.3	.965	OF-133
1929			134	.338	.632	517	175	47	9	29	5.6	101	125	45	42	7	3	0	278	8	10	1	2.2	.966	OF-130
1930			120	.336	.652	446	150	39	12	26	5.8	108	107	46	51	12	1	0	189	11	5	0	1.7	.976	OF-116
1931			122	.349	.569	450	157	35	8	16	3.6	94	95	39	43	11	4	1	226	4	4	1	1.9	.983	OF-118
1932	CIN	N	83	.344	.466	253	87	19	3	2	0.8	34	36	22	20	4	18	5	131	5	5	5	1.7	.965	OF-83
1933			144	.303	.421	568	172	34	6	7	1.2	77	62	40	44	3	0	0	364	16	5	5	2.7	.987	OF-144
1934			140	.293	.471	535	157	29	6	18	3.4	75	67	52	63	4	0	0	380	7	13	1	2.9	.968	OF-140
1935			15	.339	.525	59	20	6	1	1	1.7	10	9	4	6	1	0	0	31	0	3	0	2.3	.912	OF-15
1937			89	.261	.447	257	67	11	5	9	3.5	39	41	23	42	2	23	3	128	5	4	0	1.5	.971	OF-64
13 yrs.			1283	.317	.526	4625	1466	341	67	164	3.5	777	833	372	477	70	88	22	2527	106	80	22	2.1	.971	OF-1203

WORLD SERIES

Year	Team		Games	BA	SA	AB	H	2B	3B	HR	HR%	R	RBI	BB	SO	SB	AB	H	PO	A	E	DP	TC/G	FA	G by Pos
1926	STL	N	7	.185	.259	27	5	0	0	0	0.0	2	0	2	0	0	0	0	21	1	0	0	3.1	1.000	OF-7

Year	Team		Games	BA	SA	AB	H	2B	3B	HR	HR%	R	RBI	BB	SO	SB	Pinch Hit AB	H	PO	A	E	DP	TC/G	FA	G by Pos

Chick Hafey *continued*

Year	Team		Games	BA	SA	AB	H	2B	3B	HR	HR%	R	RBI	BB	SO	SB	AB	H	PO	A	E	DP	TC/G	FA	G by Pos
1928			4	.200	.200	15	3	0	0	0	0.0	0	0	1	4	0	0	0	8	0	1	0	2.3	.889	OF-4
1930			6	.273	.500	22	6	5	0	0	0.0	2	2	1	3	0	0	0	9	0	0	0	1.5	1.000	OF-6
1931			6	.167	.167	24	4	0	0	0	0.0	1	0	0	5	1	0	0	8	1	1	0	1.5	.889	OF-6
4 yrs.			23	.205	.284	88	18	7	0	0	0.0	5	2	2	19	1	0	0	46	1	2	0	2.1	.959	OF-23
						9th																			

Tom Hafey

HAFEY, THOMAS FRANCIS (The Arm)
Brother of Bud Hafey.
B. July 12, 1913, Berkeley, Calif.   BR TR 6'1" 180 lbs.

Year	Team		Games	BA	SA	AB	H	2B	3B	HR	HR%	R	RBI	BB	SO	SB	AB	H	PO	A	E	DP	TC/G	FA	G by Pos
1939	NY	N	70	.242	.359	256	62	10	1	6	2.3	37	26	10	44	1	0	0	61	130	8	10	2.8	.960	3B-70
1944	STL	A	8	.357	.500	14	5	2	0	0	0.0	1	2	1	4	0	3	1	9	1	0	0	1.3	1.000	OF-4, 1B-1
2 yrs.			78	.248	.367	270	67	12	1	6	2.2	38	28	11	48	1	3	1	70	131	8	10	2.7	.962	3B-70, OF-4, 1B-1

Bill Hague

HAGUE, WILLIAM L.
Born William L. Haug.
B. 1852, Philadelphia, Pa.   Deceased.   BR TR 5'9" 164 lbs.

Year	Team		Games	BA	SA	AB	H	2B	3B	HR	HR%	R	RBI	BB	SO	SB	AB	H	PO	A	E	DP	TC/G	FA	G by Pos
1876	LOU	N	67	.265	.303	294	78	8	0	1	0.3	31	22	2	10		0	0	67	90	52	5	3.1	.751	3B-67, SS-1
1877			59	.266	.312	263	70	7	1	1	0.4	38	24	7	18		0	0	78	78	29	4	3.1	.843	3B-59
1878	PRO	N	62	.204	.216	250	51	3	0	0	0.0	21	25	5	34		0	0	81	177	21	5	4.5	.925	3B-62
1879			51	.225	.249	209	47	3	1	0	0.0	20	21	3	19		0	0	54	122	38	2	4.2	.822	3B-51
4 yrs.			239	.242	.273	1016	246	21	2	2	0.2	110	92	17	81		0	0	280	467	140	16	3.7	.842	3B-239, SS-1

Joe Hague

HAGUE, JOE CLARENCE
B. Apr. 25, 1944, Huntington, W. Va.   BL TL 6' 195 lbs.

Year	Team		Games	BA	SA	AB	H	2B	3B	HR	HR%	R	RBI	BB	SO	SB	AB	H	PO	A	E	DP	TC/G	FA	G by Pos
1968	STL	N	7	.235	.412	17	4	0	0	1	5.9	2	1	2	2	0	1	0	19	1	1	1	3.0	.952	OF-3, 1B-2
1969			40	.170	.270	100	17	2	1	2	2.0	8	8	12	23	0	14	1	104	5	2	3	2.8	.982	OF-17, 1B-9
1970			139	.271	.417	451	122	16	4	14	3.1	58	68	63	87	2	17	7	749	51	5	66	5.8	.994	1B-82, OF-52
1971			129	.226	.392	380	86	9	3	16	4.2	46	54	58	69	0	17	2	676	50	5	63	5.7	.993	1B-91, OF-36
1972	2 teams		STL N (27G – .237)			CIN N (69G – .246)																			
"	total		96	.243	.416	214	52	12	2	7	3.3	25	31	37	36	1	32	11	190	11	0	16	2.1	1.000	1B-44, OF-22
1973	CIN	N	19	.152	.212	33	5	2	0	0	0.0	2	1	5	5	1	8	3	26	2	0	3	1.5	1.000	OF-5, 1B-4
6 yrs.			430	.239	.391	1195	286	41	10	40	3.3	141	163	177	222	4	89	24	1764	120	13	152	4.4	.993	1B-232, OF-135

LEAGUE CHAMPIONSHIP SERIES

Year	Team		Games	BA	SA	AB	H	2B	3B	HR	HR%	R	RBI	BB	SO	SB	AB	H	PO	A	E	DP	TC/G	FA	G by Pos
1972	CIN	N	3	.000	.000	1	0	0	0	0	0.0	0	0	2	1	0	1	0	0	0	0	0	0.0	–	

WORLD SERIES

Year	Team		Games	BA	SA	AB	H	2B	3B	HR	HR%	R	RBI	BB	SO	SB	AB	H	PO	A	E	DP	TC/G	FA	G by Pos
1972	CIN	N	3	.000	.000	3	0	0	0	0	0.0	0	0	0	3	0	3	0	0	0	0	0			OF-1

Dick Hahn

HAHN, RICHARD FREDERICK
B. July 24, 1916, Canton, Ohio   BR TR 5'11" 176 lbs.

Year	Team		Games	BA	SA	AB	H	2B	3B	HR	HR%	R	RBI	BB	SO	SB	AB	H	PO	A	E	DP	TC/G	FA	G by Pos
1940	WAS	A	1	.000	.000	3	0	0	0	0	0.0	0	0	0	0	0	0	0	1	1	2	0	4.0	.500	C-1

Don Hahn

HAHN, DONALD ANTONE
B. Nov. 16, 1948, San Francisco, Calif.   BR TR 6'1" 180 lbs.

Year	Team		Games	BA	SA	AB	H	2B	3B	HR	HR%	R	RBI	BB	SO	SB	AB	H	PO	A	E	DP	TC/G	FA	G by Pos
1969	MON	N	4	.111	.111	9	1	0	0	0	0.0	0	2	0	5	0	0	0	3	1	0	0	1.0	1.000	OF-3
1970			82	.255	.309	149	38	8	0	0	0.0	22	8	27	27	4	18	5	65	5	1	1	0.9	.986	OF-61
1971	NY	N	98	.236	.292	178	42	5	1	1	0.6	16	11	21	32	2	8	2	140	2	4	1	1.5	.973	OF-80
1972			17	.162	.162	37	6	0	0	0	0.0	0	1	4	12	0	6	0	8	0	0	0	0.5	1.000	OF-10
1973			93	.229	.290	262	60	10	0	2	0.8	22	21	22	43	1	9	2	176	2	2	0	1.9	.989	OF-87
1974			110	.251	.337	323	81	14	1	4	1.2	34	28	37	34	2	8	3	217	8	3	0	2.1	.987	OF-106
1975	3 teams		PHI N (9G – .000)			STL N (7G – .125)			SD N (34G – .231)																
"	total		50	.179	.308	39	7	1	2	0	0.0	10	3	11	5	1	5	0	32	2	0	0	0.7	1.000	OF-37
7 yrs.			454	.236	.303	997	235	38	4	7	0.7	104	74	122	158	11	54	12	641	20	10	2	1.5	.985	OF-384

LEAGUE CHAMPIONSHIP SERIES

Year	Team		Games	BA	SA	AB	H	2B	3B	HR	HR%	R	RBI	BB	SO	SB	AB	H	PO	A	E	DP	TC/G	FA	G by Pos
1973	NY	N	5	.235	.235	17	4	0	0	0	0.0	2	1	2	4	0	0	0	12	0	0	0	2.4	1.000	OF-5

WORLD SERIES

Year	Team		Games	BA	SA	AB	H	2B	3B	HR	HR%	R	RBI	BB	SO	SB	AB	H	PO	A	E	DP	TC/G	FA	G by Pos
1973	NY	N	7	.241	.345	29	7	1	1	0	0.0	2	2	1	6	0	0	0	13	1	1	0	2.1	.933	OF-7

Ed Hahn

HAHN, WILLIAM EDGAR
B. Aug. 27, 1875, Nevada, Ohio   D. Nov. 29, 1941, Des Moines, Iowa   BL TR 160 lbs.

Year	Team		Games	BA	SA	AB	H	2B	3B	HR	HR%	R	RBI	BB	SO	SB	AB	H	PO	A	E	DP	TC/G	FA	G by Pos
1905	NY	A	43	.319	.350	160	51	5	0	0	0.0	32	11	25		1	0	0	83	5	4	1	2.1	.957	OF-43
1906	2 teams		NY A (11G – .091)			CHI A (130G – .227)																			
"	total		141	.221	.257	506	112	8	5	0	0.0	82	28	72		21	1	0	16	0	0	0	0.1	1.000	OF-137
1907	CHI	A	156	.255	.294	592	151	9	7	0	0.0	87	45	84		17	0	0	182	24	2	6	1.3	.990	OF-156
1908			122	.251	.313	447	112	12	8	0	0.0	58	21	39		11	3	1	160	4	6	2	1.4	.965	OF-118
1909			76	.181	.213	287	52	6	0	1	0.3	30	16	31		9	0	0	93	3	1	1	1.3	.990	OF-76
1910			15	.113	.151	53	6	2	0	0	0.0	2	1	7		0	0	0	14	0	1	0	1.0	.933	OF-15
6 yrs.			553	.237	.278	2045	484	42	20	1	0.0	291	122	258		59	4	1	548	36	14	10	1.1	.977	OF-545

WORLD SERIES

Year	Team		Games	BA	SA	AB	H	2B	3B	HR	HR%	R	RBI	BB	SO	SB	AB	H	PO	A	E	DP	TC/G	FA	G by Pos
1906	CHI	A	6	.273	.273	22	6	0	0	0	0.0	4	0	1		1	0	0	3	0	0	0	0.5	1.000	OF-6

Ed Haigh

HAIGH, EDWARD E.
B. Feb. 7, 1867, Philadelphia, Pa.   D. Feb. 13, 1953, Atlantic City, N. J.

Year	Team		Games	BA	SA	AB	H	2B	3B	HR	HR%	R	RBI	BB	SO	SB	AB	H	PO	A	E	DP	TC/G	FA	G by Pos
1892	STL	N	1	.250	.250	4	1	0	0	0	0.0	0	0	0	2	0	0	0	0	0	0	0	0.0	–	OF-1

Hinkey Haines

HAINES, HENRY LUTHER
B. Dec. 23, 1898, Red Lion, Pa.   D. Jan. 9, 1979, Sharon Hills, Pa.   BR TR 5'10" 170 lbs.

Year	Team		Games	BA	SA	AB	H	2B	3B	HR	HR%	R	RBI	BB	SO	SB	AB	H	PO	A	E	DP	TC/G	FA	G by Pos
1923	NY	A	28	.160	.240	25	4	2	0	0	0.0	9	3	4	5	3	3	0	17	1	0	0	0.6	1.000	OF-14

Year	Team		Games	BA	SA	AB	H	2B	3B	HR	HR%	R	RBI	BB	SO	SB	Pinch Hit AB	Pinch Hit H	PO	A	E	DP	TC/G	FA	G by Pos

Hinkey Haines *continued*

WORLD SERIES

| 1923 | NY | A | 2 | .000 | .000 | 1 | 0 | 0 | 0 | 0 | 0.0 | 1 | 0 | 0 | 0 | 0 | 0 | 0 | 0 | 0 | 0 | 0 | 0.0 | – | OF-2 |

Jerry Hairston

HAIRSTON, JERRY WAYNE
Brother of John Hairston. Son of Sam Hairston.
B. Feb. 16, 1952, Birmingham, Ala.

BB TR 5'10" 170 lbs.

1973	CHI	A	60	.271	.333	210	57	11	1	0	0.0	25	23	33	30	0	2	0	194	13	5	11	3.5	.976	OF-33, 1B-19, DH-8
1974			45	.229	.294	109	25	7	0	0	0.0	8	8	13	18	0	12	2	24	1	2	0	0.6	.926	OF-22, DH-10
1975			69	.283	.320	219	62	8	0	0	0.0	26	23	46	23	1	3	0	111	6	6	1	1.8	.951	OF-59, DH-8
1976			44	.227	.277	119	27	2	2	0	0.0	20	10	24	19	1	4	1	71	1	2	0	1.7	.973	OF-40
1977	2 teams	CHI A (13G – .308)				PIT	N	(51G – .192)																	
"	total		64	.231	.359	78	18	4	0	2	2.6	8	10	11	17	0	34	7	28	1	1	0	0.5	.967	OF-25, 2B-1
1981	CHI	A	9	.280	.440	25	7	1	0	1	4.0	5	6	2	4	0	2	1	14	0	1	0	1.7	.933	OF-7
1982			85	.233	.456	90	21	5	0	5	5.6	11	18	9	15	0	47	11	34	2	0	1	0.4	1.000	OF-36, DH-2
1983			101	.294	.500	126	37	9	1	5	4.0	17	22	23	16	0	62	17	29	1	1	0	0.3	.968	OF-32, DH-4
1984			115	.260	.401	227	59	13	2	5	2.2	41	19	41	29	2	59	18	57	2	2	0	0.5	.967	OF-37, DH-20
1985			95	.243	.343	140	34	8	0	2	1.4	9	20	29	18	0	53	14	5	0	0	0	0.1	1.000	DH-29, OF-5
1986			101	.271	.404	225	61	15	0	5	2.2	32	26	26	26	0	46	14	132	9	0	11	1.4	1.000	DH-29, 1B-19, OF-11
1987			66	.230	.413	126	29	8	0	5	4.0	14	20	25	25	0	32	8	82	5	1	7	1.3	.989	DH-13, OF-13, 1B-7
1988			2	.000	.000	2	0	0	0	0	0.0	0	0	0	0	0	2	0	0	0	0	0	0.0	–	
1989			3	.333	.333	3	1	0	0	0	0.0	0	0	0	0	0	3	1	0	0	0	0	0.0	–	DH-2
14 yrs.			859	.258	.371	1699	438	91	6	30	1.8	216	205	282	240	4	361	94	781	41	21	31	1.0	.975	OF-320, DH-125, 1B-45, 2B-1

LEAGUE CHAMPIONSHIP SERIES

| 1983 | CHI | A | 2 | .000 | .000 | 3 | 0 | 0 | 0 | 0 | 0.0 | 0 | 0 | 1 | 1 | 0 | 2 | 0 | 1 | 0 | 1 | 0 | 1.0 | .500 | OF-2 |

John Hairston

HAIRSTON, JOHN LOUIS
Son of Sam Hairston. Brother of Jerry Hairston.
B. Aug. 29, 1945, Birmingham, Ala.

BR TR 6'2" 200 lbs.

| 1969 | CHI | N | 3 | .250 | .250 | 4 | 1 | 0 | 0 | 0 | 0.0 | 0 | 0 | 0 | 2 | 0 | 1 | 1 | 3 | 1 | 0 | 0 | 1.3 | 1.000 | OF-1, C-1 |

Sam Hairston

HAIRSTON, SAMUEL
Father of Jerry Hairston. Father of John Hairston.
B. Jan. 28, 1920, Crawford, Miss.

BR TR 5'10½" 187 lbs.

| 1951 | CHI | A | 4 | .400 | .600 | 5 | 2 | 1 | 0 | 0 | 0.0 | 1 | 1 | 2 | 0 | 0 | 1 | 0 | 3 | 0 | 0 | 0 | 0.8 | 1.000 | C-2 |

Chet Hajduk

HAJDUK, CHESTER
B. July 21, 1918, Chicago, Ill.

BR TR 6' 195 lbs.

| 1941 | CHI | A | 1 | .000 | .000 | 1 | 0 | 0 | 0 | 0 | 0.0 | 0 | 0 | 0 | 0 | 0 | 1 | 0 | 0 | 0 | 0 | 0 | 0.0 | – | |

George Halas

HALAS, GEORGE STANLEY
B. Feb. 2, 1895, Chicago, Ill. D. Oct. 31, 1983, Chicago, Ill.

BB TR 6' 164 lbs.

| 1919 | NY | A | 12 | .091 | .091 | 22 | 2 | 0 | 0 | 0 | 0.0 | 0 | 0 | 0 | 8 | 0 | 4 | 0 | 8 | 0 | 0 | 0 | 0.7 | 1.000 | OF-6 |

John Haldeman

HALDEMAN, JOHN AVERY
B. Dec. 2, 1855, Pewee Valley, Ky. D. Sept. 17, 1899, Louisville, Ky.

BL TR 5'10" 175 lbs.

| 1877 | LOU | N | 1 | .000 | .000 | 4 | 0 | 0 | 0 | 0 | 0.0 | 0 | 0 | 0 | 0 | | | | 0 | 4 | 3 | 0 | 7.0 | .571 | 2B-1 |

Bob Hale

HALE, ROBERT HOUSTON
B. Nov. 7, 1933, Sarasota, Fla.

BL TL 5'10" 195 lbs.

1955	BAL	A	67	.357	.407	182	65	7	1	0	0.0	13	29	5	19	0	26	10	300	33	9	25	5.1	.974	1B-44
1956			85	.237	.309	207	49	10	1	1	0.5	18	24	11	10	0	36	6	366	29	10	33	4.8	.975	1B-51
1957			42	.250	.250	44	11	0	0	0	0.0	2	3	2	2	0	35	9	22	1	0	1	0.5	1.000	1B-5
1958			19	.350	.450	20	7	2	0	0	0.0	2	3	2	1	0	15	5	11	3	0	3	0.7	1.000	1B-2
1959			40	.185	.241	54	10	3	0	0	0.0	2	7	2	6	0	30	7	48	2	0	5	1.3	1.000	1B-8
1960	CLE	A	70	.300	.400	70	21	7	0	0	0.0	2	12	3	6	0	63	19	14	3	1	1	0.3	.944	1B-5
1961	2 teams	CLE A (42G – .167)				NY	A	(11G – .154)																	
"	total		53	.163	.224	49	8	0	0	1	2.0	2	7	1	7	0	44	6	15	1	0	1	0.3	1.000	1B-5
7 yrs.			376	.273	.335	626	171	29	2	2	0.3	41	89	26	51	0	249	62	776	72	20	69	2.3	.977	1B-120

Chip Hale

HALE, WALTER WILLIAM
B. Dec. 2, 1964, Santa Clara, Calif.

BL TR 5'11" 180 lbs.

| 1989 | MIN | A | 28 | .209 | .254 | 67 | 14 | 3 | 0 | 0 | 0.0 | 6 | 4 | 1 | 6 | 0 | 8 | 0 | 15 | 40 | 1 | 8 | 2.0 | .982 | 2B-16, 3B-9, DH-2 |

George Hale

HALE, GEORGE WAGNER (Ducky)
B. Aug. 3, 1894, Dexter, Kans. D. Nov. 1, 1945, Wichita, Kans.

BR TR 5'10" 160 lbs.

1914	STL	A	6	.182	.182	11	2	0	0	0	0.0	1	0	0	3	0	0	0	9	8	2	0	3.2	.895	C-6
1916			4	.000	.000	1	0	0	0	0	0.0	0	0	0	1	0	0	0	3	0	0	0	0.8	1.000	C-3
1917			38	.197	.262	61	12	2	1	0	0.0	4	8	10	12	0	7	2	75	26	8	3	2.9	.927	C-28
1918			12	.133	.167	30	4	1	0	0	0.0	1	1	1	5	0	1	0	41	11	1	1	4.4	.981	C-11
4 yrs.			60	.175	.223	103	18	3	1	0	0.0	5	9	11	21	0	9	2	128	45	11	4	3.1	.940	C-48

John Hale

HALE, JOHN STEVEN
B. Aug. 5, 1953, Fresno, Calif.

BL TR 6'2" 195 lbs.

1974	LA	N	4	1.000	1.250	4	4	1	0	0	0.0	2	2	0	1	0	1	1	0	0	0	0	0.0	–	OF-3
1975			71	.211	.333	204	43	7	0	6	2.9	20	22	26	51	1	7	2	128	2	3	0	1.9	.977	OF-68
1976			44	.154	.198	91	14	2	1	0	0.0	4	8	16	14	4	6	0	55	3	1	0	1.3	.983	OF-37
1977			79	.241	.352	108	26	4	1	2	1.9	10	11	15	28	2	5	1	68	1	0	0	0.9	.986	OF-73

Year	Team	Games	BA	SA	AB	H	2B	3B	HR	HR%	R	RBI	BB	SO	SB	Pinch Hit AB	H	PO	A	E	DP	TC/G	FA	G by Pos

John Hale *continued*

Year	Team	Games	BA	SA	AB	H	2B	3B	HR	HR%	R	RBI	BB	SO	SB	AB	H	PO	A	E	DP	TC/G	FA	G by Pos
1978	SEA A	107	.171	.265	211	36	8	0	4	1.9	24	22	34	64	3	6	1	160	1	2	0	1.5	.988	OF-98, DH-3
1979		54	.222	.365	63	14	3	0	2	3.2	6	7	12	26	0	8	0	34	0	0	0	0.6	1.000	OF-42, DH-2
6 yrs.		359	.201	.305	681	137	25	2	14	2.1	66	72	103	183	10	33	5	445	7	7	0	1.3	.985	OF-321, DH-5

Odell Hale

HALE, ARVEL ODELL (Bad News)
B. Aug. 10, 1908, Hosston, La.   D. June 9, 1980, El Dorado, Ark.

BR TR 5'10"   175 lbs.

Year	Team	Games	BA	SA	AB	H	2B	3B	HR	HR%	R	RBI	BB	SO	SB	AB	H	PO	A	E	DP	TC/G	FA	G by Pos
1931	CLE A	25	.283	.424	92	26	2	4	1	1.1	14	5	8	8	2	0	0	34	51	12	4	3.9	.876	3B-15, 2B-10, SS-1
1933		98	.276	.462	351	97	19	8	10	2.8	49	64	30	37	2	3	1	237	287	29	47	5.6	.948	2B-73, 3B-21
1934		143	.302	.471	563	170	44	6	13	2.3	82	101	48	50	8	3	1	412	488	41	108	6.6	.956	2B-137, 3B-5
1935		150	.304	.486	589	179	37	11	16	2.7	80	101	52	55	15	1	0	160	313	31	17	3.4	.938	3B-149, 2B-1
1936		153	.316	.506	620	196	50	13	14	2.3	126	87	64	43	8	2	0	172	338	28	28	3.5	.948	3B-148, 2B-3
1937		154	.267	.371	561	150	32	4	6	1.1	74	82	56	41	9	1	1	276	406	22	61	4.6	.969	3B-90, 2B-64
1938		130	.278	.399	496	138	32	2	8	1.6	69	69	44	39	8	3	1	304	343	25	72	5.2	.963	2B-127
1939		108	.312	.439	253	79	16	2	4	1.6	36	48	25	18	4	35	10	142	147	11	31	2.8	.963	2B-73, 3B-2
1940		48	.220	.320	50	11	3	1	0	0.0	3	6	5	7	0	40	8	2	5	3	0	0.2	.700	3B-3
1941	2 teams																							
	BOS A (12G – .208)				NY N (41G – .196)																			
"	total	53	.198	.262	126	25	5	0	1	0.8	18	10	21	17	1	12	1	99	76	9	16	3.5	.951	2B-30, 3B-6
10 yrs.		1062	.289	.441	3701	1071	240	51	73	2.0	551	573	353	315	57	100	23	1838	2454	211	384	4.2	.953	2B-518, 3B-439, SS-1

Sammy Hale

HALE, SAMUEL DOUGLAS
B. Sept. 10, 1896, Glen Rose, Tex.   D. Sept. 6, 1974, Wheeler, Tex.

BR TR 5'8½"   160 lbs.

Year	Team	Games	BA	SA	AB	H	2B	3B	HR	HR%	R	RBI	BB	SO	SB	AB	H	PO	A	E	DP	TC/G	FA	G by Pos
1920	DET A	76	.293	.397	116	34	3	3	1	0.9	13	14	5	15	2	52	17	14	32	5	2	0.7	.902	3B-16, OF-4, 2B-1
1921		9	.000	.000	2	0	0	0	0	0.0	2	0	0	1	0	0	0	0	0	0	0	0.0	–	
1923	PHI A	115	.288	.396	434	125	22	8	3	0.7	68	51	17	31	8	5	2	85	222	28	17	2.9	.916	3B-107
1924		80	.318	.410	261	83	14	2	2	0.8	41	17	17	19	3	14	2	42	111	9	10	2.2	.944	3B-55, OF-5, SS-1, C-1
1925		110	.345	.540	391	135	30	11	8	2.0	62	63	17	27	7	12	4	98	174	24	19	2.7	.919	3B-96, 2B-1
1926		111	.281	.440	327	92	22	9	4	1.2	49	43	13	36	1	28	6	82	152	13	16	2.2	.947	3B-77, OF-1
1927		131	.313	.423	501	157	24	8	5	1.0	77	81	32	32	11	1	0	152	247	16	46	3.2	.961	3B-128
1928		88	.309	.468	314	97	20	9	4	1.3	38	58	9	21	2	8	3	86	189	20	17	3.4	.932	3B-79
1929		101	.277	.338	379	105	14	3	1	0.3	51	40	12	18	6	0	0	94	172	12	14	2.8	.947	3B-99, 2B-1
1930	STL A	62	.274	.358	190	52	8	1	2	1.1	21	25	8	12	2	12	2	46	80	7	5	2.1	.947	3B-47
10 yrs.		883	.302	.424	2915	880	157	54	30	1.0	422	392	130	218	41	134	36	699	1379	134	146	2.5	.939	3B-704, OF-10, 2B-3, SS-1, C-1

Fred Haley

HALEY, FRED
B. Wheeling, W. Va.   Deceased.

TR

Year	Team	Games	BA	SA	AB	H	2B	3B	HR	HR%	R	RBI	BB	SO	SB	AB	H	PO	A	E	DP	TC/G	FA	G by Pos
1880	TRO N	2	.000	.000	7	0	0	0	0	0.0	0	0	1	2		0	0	11	4	5	0	10.0	.750	C-2

Ray Haley

HALEY, RICHARD TIMOTHY
B. Jan. 23, 1891, Danbury, Iowa   D. Oct. 8, 1973, Bradenton, Fla.

BR TR 5'11"   180 lbs.

Year	Team	Games	BA	SA	AB	H	2B	3B	HR	HR%	R	RBI	BB	SO	SB	AB	H	PO	A	E	DP	TC/G	FA	G by Pos
1915	BOS A	5	.143	.286	7	1	1	0	0	0.0	2	0	0	0	0	0	0	10	4	0	0	2.8	1.000	C-4
1916	2 teams																							
	BOS A (1G – .000)				PHI A (34G – .231)																			
"	total	35	.229	.275	109	25	5	0	0	0.0	8	4	6	20	0	0	0	154	65	4	7	6.4	.982	C-33
1917	PHI A	41	.276	.316	98	27	2	1	0	0.0	7	11	4	12	2	7	0	99	27	7	3	3.2	.947	C-34
3 yrs.		81	.248	.294	214	53	8	1	0	0.0	17	15	11	32	2	9	0	263	96	11	10	4.6	.970	C-71

Al Hall

HALL, ARCHIBALD W.
B. Worcester, Mass.   D. Feb. 10, 1885, Warren, Pa.

Year	Team	Games	BA	SA	AB	H	2B	3B	HR	HR%	R	RBI	BB	SO	SB	AB	H	PO	A	E	DP	TC/G	FA	G by Pos
1879	TRO N	67	.258	.301	306	79	7	3	0	0.0	30	14	3	13		0	0	126	18	27	3	2.6	.842	OF-67
1880	CLE N	3	.125	.125	8	1	0	0	0	0.0	1	0	0	0		0	0	1	0	0	0	0.3	1.000	OF-3
2 yrs.		70	.255	.296	314	80	7	3	0	0.0	31	14	3	13		0	0	127	18	27	3	2.5	.843	OF-70

Albert Hall

HALL, ALBERT
B. Mar. 7, 1958, Birmingham, Ala.

BB TR 5'11"   155 lbs.

Year	Team	Games	BA	SA	AB	H	2B	3B	HR	HR%	R	RBI	BB	SO	SB	AB	H	PO	A	E	DP	TC/G	FA	G by Pos
1981	ATL N	6	.000	.000	2	0	0	0	0	0.0	1	0	1	1	0	0	0	0	0	0	0	0.0	–	OF-2
1982		5	–	–	0	0	0	0	0	–	1	0	0	0	0	0	0	0	0	0	0	0.0	–	
1983		10	.000	.000	8	0	0	0	0	0.0	2	0	2	2	1	1	0	3	0	1	0	0.4	.750	OF-4
1984		87	.261	.338	142	37	6	1	1	0.7	25	9	10	18	6	13	5	64	4	5	1	0.8	.932	OF-66
1985		54	.149	.191	47	7	0	1	0	0.0	5	3	9	12	1	32	5	7	2	1	0	0.2	.900	OF-13
1986		16	.240	.280	50	12	0	1	0	0.0	6	1	5	6	8	1	0	26	1	3	0	1.9	.900	OF-14
1987		92	.284	.411	292	83	20	4	3	1.0	54	24	38	36	33	5	1	148	5	3	1	1.7	.981	OF-69
1988		85	.247	.299	231	57	7	1	0	0.4	27	15	21	35	15	16	2	137	7	4	1	1.7	.973	OF-63
1989	PIT N	20	.182	.303	33	6	1	0	0	0.0	4	1	3	5	3	7	2	10	0	1	0	0.6	.909	OF-12
9 yrs.		375	.251	.335	805	202	37	8	5	0.6	125	53	89	115	67	96	21	395	19	18	3	1.2	.958	OF-243

Bill Hall

HALL, WILLIAM LEMUEL
B. July 30, 1928, Moultrie, Ga.   D. Jan. 1, 1986, Moultrie, Ga.

BL TR 5'11"   165 lbs.

Year	Team	Games	BA	SA	AB	H	2B	3B	HR	HR%	R	RBI	BB	SO	SB	AB	H	PO	A	E	DP	TC/G	FA	G by Pos
1954	PIT N	5	.000	.000	7	0	0	0	0	0.0	0	0	0	0	0	3	0	4	0	0	0	0.8	1.000	C-1
1956		1	.000	.000	3	0	0	0	0	0.0	0	0	0	1	0	0	0	7	1	0	1	8.0	1.000	C-1
1958		51	.284	.362	116	33	6	0	1	0.9	15	15	15	13	0	1	0	195	24	4	4	4.4	.982	C-51
3 yrs.		57	.262	.333	126	33	6	0	1	0.8	15	15	15	14	0	4	0	206	25	4	5	4.1	.983	C-53

Bob Hall

HALL, ROBERT PRILL
B. Dec. 20, 1878, Baltimore, Md.   D. Dec. 1, 1950, Wellesley, Mass.

TR 5'10"   158 lbs.

Year	Team	Games	BA	SA	AB	H	2B	3B	HR	HR%	R	RBI	BB	SO	SB	AB	H	PO	A	E	DP	TC/G	FA	G by Pos
1904	PHI N	46	.160	.184	163	26	4	0	0	0.0	11	17	14		5	0	0	149	80	31	13	5.7	.881	3B-20, SS-15, 1B-11
1905	2 teams																							
	NY N (1G – .333)				BKN N (56G – .236)																			
"	total	57	.238	.296	206	49	4	1	2	1.0	22	15	11		8	4	0	147	37	19	4	3.6	.906	OF-43, 2B-7, 1B-3
2 yrs.		103	.203	.247	369	75	8	1	2	0.5	33	32	25		13	4	0	296	117	50	17	4.5	.892	OF-43, 3B-20, SS-15, 1B-14, 2B-7

Year	Team		Games	BA	SA	AB	H	2B	3B	HR	HR%	R	RBI	BB	SO	SB	Pinch Hit AB	H	PO	A	E	DP	TC/G	FA	G by Pos

Charley Hall

HALL, CHARLES LOUIS (Sea Lion)
Born Carlos Clolo.
B. July 27, 1885, Ventura, Calif.   D. Dec. 6, 1943, Ventura, Calif.

BL TR 6'1"   187 lbs.

Year	Team		Games	BA	SA	AB	H	2B	3B	HR	HR%	R	RBI	BB	SO	SB	AB	H	PO	A	E	DP	TC/G	FA	G by Pos
1906	CIN	N	17	.128	.170	47	6	2	0	0	0.0	7	2	2			0	1	17	29	4	3	2.9	.920	P-14, 1B-2
1907			12	.269	.346	26	7	0	1	0	0.0	1	1	0			0	1	3	14	1	0	1.5	.944	P-11
1909	BOS	A	11	.158	.158	19	3	0	0	0	0.0	0	4	0			0	0	5	16	1	2	2.0	.955	P-11
1910			47	.207	.329	82	17	2	4	0	0.0	6	8	6			1	8	9	62	4	0	1.6	.947	P-35, OF-3
1911			39	.141	.234	64	9	1	1	1	1.6	6	8	4			0	7	4	30	2	0	0.9	.944	P-32
1912			34	.267	.413	75	20	4	2	1	1.3	10	14	4			0	1	9	59	3	0	2.1	.958	P-34
1913			43	.214	.286	42	9	1	1	0	0.0	2	2	1	10		0	7	6	27	2	1	0.8	.943	P-35, 3B-1
1916	STL	N	10	.143	.143	14	2	0	0	0	0.0	0	1	0	6		0	0	6	13	2	2	1.6	.875	P-10
1918	DET		6	.000	.000	2	0	0	0	0	0.0	0	0	0	0		0	0	1	1	1	1	0.5	.667	P-6
9 yrs.			219	.197	.288	371	73	10	9	2	0.5	32	40	17	16	1	24	2	55	251	20	9	1.5	.939	P-188, OF-3, 1B-2, 3B-1

WORLD SERIES

Year	Team		Games	BA	SA	AB	H	2B	3B	HR	HR%	R	RBI	BB	SO	SB	AB	H	PO	A	E	DP	TC/G	FA	G by Pos
1912	BOS	A	2	.750	1.000	4	3	1	0	0	0.0	0	0	1	0	0	0	0	0	5	1	0	3.0	.833	P-2

Charlie Hall

HALL, CHARLES WALTER (Doc)
B. Aug. 24, 1863, Toulon, Ill.   D. June 24, 1921, Tacoma, Wash.

Year	Team		Games	BA	SA	AB	H	2B	3B	HR	HR%	R	RBI	BB	SO	SB	AB	H	PO	A	E	DP	TC/G	FA	G by Pos
1887	NY	AA	3	.083	.083	12	1	0	0	0	0.0	1		2		1	0	0	9	0	0	0	3.0	1.000	OF-3

Dick Hall

HALL, RICHARD WALLACE
B. Sept. 27, 1930, St. Louis, Mo.

BR TR 6'6"   200 lbs.

Year	Team		Games	BA	SA	AB	H	2B	3B	HR	HR%	R	RBI	BB	SO	SB	AB	H	PO	A	E	DP	TC/G	FA	G by Pos
1952	PIT	N	26	.138	.150	80	11	1	0	0	0.0	6	2	2	17	0	5	1	44	11	1	0	2.2	.982	OF-14, 3B-5
1953			7	.167	.167	24	4	0	0	0	0.0	2	1	1	3	1	1	0	21	23	1	6	6.4	.978	2B-7
1954			112	.239	.310	310	74	8	4	2	0.6	38	27	33	46	3	12	1	235	5	11	1	2.2	.956	OF-102
1955			21	.175	.275	40	7	1	0	1	2.5	3	3	6	5	0	3	1	9	6	0	0	0.7	1.000	P-15, OF-3
1956			33	.345	.345	29	10	0	0	0	0.0	5	1	5	7	0	12	6	6	7	0	0	0.4	1.000	P-19, 1B-1
1957			10	.000	.000	1	0	0	0	0	0.0	0	0	0	1	0	0	0	0	0	0	0	0.0	—	P-8
1959			2	.000	.000	2	0	0	0	0	0.0	0	0	0	1	0	0	0	0	0	0	0	0.0	—	P-2
1960	KC	A	32	.107	.107	56	6	0	0	0	0.0	5	4	4	15	1	0	0	9	28	3	1	1.3	.925	P-29
1961	BAL	A	30	.139	.139	36	5	0	0	0	0.0	4	1	3	13	0	0	0	9	23	1	1	1.1	.970	P-29
1962			44	.167	.208	24	4	1	0	0	0.0	3	1	4	9	0	0	0	9	17	0	1	0.6	1.000	P-43
1963			48	.464	.607	28	13	1	0	1	3.6	7	4	0	8	0	0	0	7	21	0	1	0.6	1.000	P-47
1964			45	.125	.125	16	2	0	0	0	0.0	1	3	1	3	0	1	0	7	12	0	1	0.4	1.000	P-45
1965			49	.333	.467	15	5	2	0	0	0.0	1	4	1	4	0	0	0	4	8	1	2	0.3	.923	P-48
1966			32	.167	.167	12	2	0	0	0	0.0	0	2	0	5	0	2	0	4	10	0	0	0.4	1.000	P-32
1967	PHI	N	48	.071	.071	14	1	0	0	0	0.0	0	0	0	5	0	0	0	2	21	0	1	0.5	1.000	P-48
1968			32	.333	.333	3	1	0	0	0	0.0	0	0	0	1	0	0	0	2	6	0	0	0.3	1.000	P-32
1969	BAL	A	39	.286	.286	7	2	0	0	0	0.0	1	2	1	1	0	0	0	4	6	0	2	0.3	1.000	P-39
1970			32	.083	.083	12	1	0	0	0	0.0	2	1	0	3	0	0	0	3	3	0	0	0.2	1.000	P-32
1971			27	.400	.600	5	2	1	0	0	0.0	0	0	0	0	0	0	0	1	3	1	0	0.2	.800	P-27
19 yrs.			669	.210	.259	714	150	15	4	4	0.6	79	56	61	147	6	35	9	376	211	19	17	0.9	.969	P-495, OF-119, 2B-7, 3B-5, 1B-1

LEAGUE CHAMPIONSHIP SERIES

Year	Team		Games	BA	SA	AB	H	2B	3B	HR	HR%	R	RBI	BB	SO	SB	AB	H	PO	A	E	DP	TC/G	FA	G by Pos
1969	BAL	A	1	—	—	0	0	0	0	0	—	0	0	0	0	0	0	0	0	0	0	0	0.0	—	P-1
1970			1	.500	.500	2	1	0	0	0	0.0	0	0	0	1	0	0	0	0	0	0	0	0.0	—	P-1
2 yrs.			2	.500	.500	2	1	0	0	0	0.0	0	0	0	1	0	0	0	0	0	0	0	0.0	—	P-2

WORLD SERIES

Year	Team		Games	BA	SA	AB	H	2B	3B	HR	HR%	R	RBI	BB	SO	SB	AB	H	PO	A	E	DP	TC/G	FA	G by Pos
1969	BAL	A	1	—	—	0	0	0	0	0	—	0	0	0	0	0	0	0	0	0	0	0	0.0	—	P-1
1970			1	.000	.000	1	0	0	0	0	0.0	0	0	0	1	0	0	0	0	0	0	0	0.0	—	P-1
1971			1	—	—	0	0	0	0	0	—	0	0	0	0	0	0	0	1	0	0	0	1.0	1.000	P-1
3 yrs.			3	.000	.000	1	0	0	0	0	0.0	0	0	0	1	0	0	0	1	0	0	0	0.3	1.000	P-3

George Hall

HALL, GEORGE WILLIAM
B. Mar. 29, 1849, Stepney, England   D. June 11, 1923, Ridgewood N. Y.,

BL   5'7"   142 lbs.

Year	Team		Games	BA	SA	AB	H	2B	3B	HR	HR%	R	RBI	BB	SO	SB	AB	H	PO	A	E	DP	TC/G	FA	G by Pos
1876	PHI	N	60	.366	.545	268	98	7	13	5	1.9	51	45	8	4			0	150	7	39	3	3.3	.801	OF-60
1877	LOU	N	61	.323	.439	269	87	15	8	0	0.0	53	26	12	19			0	92	7	11	1	1.8	.900	OF-61
2 yrs.			121	.345	.492	537	185	22	21	5	0.9	104	71	20	23			0	242	14	50	4	2.5	.837	OF-121

Irv Hall

HALL, IRVIN GLADSTONE
B. Oct. 7, 1918, Alberton, Md.

BR TR 5'10½"   160 lbs.

Year	Team		Games	BA	SA	AB	H	2B	3B	HR	HR%	R	RBI	BB	SO	SB	AB	H	PO	A	E	DP	TC/G	FA	G by Pos
1943	PHI	A	151	.256	.298	544	139	15	4	0	0.0	37	54	22	42	10	1	1	300	440	41	93	5.2	.948	SS-148, 3B-1, 2B-1
1944			143	.268	.333	559	150	20	8	0	0.0	60	45	31	46	2	2	0	366	419	26	71	5.7	.968	2B-97, SS-40, 1B-4
1945			151	.261	.305	616	161	17	5	0	0.0	62	50	35	42	3	0	0	422	498	21	108	6.2	.978	2B-151
1946			63	.249	.303	185	46	6	2	0	0.0	19	19	9	18	1	13	2	115	122	7	23	3.9	.971	2B-40, SS-7
4 yrs.			508	.261	.311	1904	496	58	19	0	0.0	178	168	97	148	16	16	3	1203	1479	95	295	5.5	.966	2B-289, SS-195, 1B-4, 3B-1

Jimmie Hall

HALL, JIMMIE RANDOLPH
B. Mar. 17, 1938, Mt. Holly, N. C.

BL TR 6'   175 lbs.

Year	Team		Games	BA	SA	AB	H	2B	3B	HR	HR%	R	RBI	BB	SO	SB	AB	H	PO	A	E	DP	TC/G	FA	G by Pos
1963	MIN	A	156	.260	.521	497	129	21	5	33	6.6	88	80	63	101	3	13	5	306	13	6	5	2.1	.982	OF-143
1964			149	.282	.480	510	144	20	3	25	4.9	61	75	44	112	5	10	3	323	13	5	0	2.3	.985	OF-137
1965			148	.285	.464	522	149	25	4	20	3.8	81	86	51	79	14	10	2	282	7	7	2	2.0	.976	OF-141
1966			120	.239	.449	356	85	7	4	20	5.6	52	47	33	66	1	21	4	175	6	4	1	1.5	.978	OF-103
1967	CAL	A	129	.249	.404	401	100	8	3	16	4.0	54	55	42	65	4	14	8	197	6	2	1	1.6	.990	OF-120
1968	2 teams					CAL A (46G – .214)						CLE A	(58G – .198)												
"	total		104	.207	.262	237	49	7	0	2	0.8	19	16	26	38	2	35	6	109	1	2	1	1.1	.982	OF-68
1969	3 teams					CLE A (4G – .000)			NY A	(80G – .236)			CHI N	(11G – .208)										
"	total		95	.224	.337	246	55	9	5	3	1.2	23	27	22	42	9	22	5	144	6	5	4	1.6	.968	OF-58, 1B-7

Year	Team	Games	BA	SA	AB	H	2B	3B	HR	HR%	R	RBI	BB	SO	SB	Pinch Hit AB	Pinch Hit H	PO	A	E	DP	TC/G	FA	G by Pos

Jimmie Hall *continued*

Year	Team	Games	BA	SA	AB	H	2B	3B	HR	HR%	R	RBI	BB	SO	SB	PH AB	PH H	PO	A	E	DP	TC/G	FA	G by Pos
1970	2 teams	CHI N (28G – .094)			ATL N (39G – .213)																			OF-36
"	total	67	.165	.278	79	13	3	0	2	2.5	9	5	6	26	0	29	4	27	1	0	0	0.4	1.000	OF-36
8 yrs.		968	.254	.434	2848	724	100	24	121	4.2	387	391	287	529	38	154	37	1563	53	31	14	1.7	.981	OF-806, 1B-7

WORLD SERIES

Year	Team	Games	BA	SA	AB	H	2B	3B	HR	HR%	R	RBI	BB	SO	SB	PH AB	PH H	PO	A	E	DP	TC/G	FA	G by Pos
1965	MIN A	2	.143	.143	7	1	0	0	0	0.0	0	0	1	5	0	0	0	2	0	0	0	1.0	1.000	OF-2

Mel Hall

HALL, MELVIN, JR.
B. Sept. 16, 1960, Lyons, N. Y.

BL TL 6' 185 lbs.

Year	Team	Games	BA	SA	AB	H	2B	3B	HR	HR%	R	RBI	BB	SO	SB	PH AB	PH H	PO	A	E	DP	TC/G	FA	G by Pos
1981	CHI N	10	.091	.364	11	1	0	0	1	9.1	1	4	0	7	1	0	0	0	0	0	0	0.0	–	OF-3
1982		24	.263	.350	80	21	3	2	0	0.0	6	4	5	17	0	1	0	42	4	3	1	2.0	.939	OF-22
1983		112	.283	.488	410	116	23	5	17	4.1	60	56	42	101	6	2	1	239	8	3	2	2.2	.988	OF-112
1984	2 teams	CHI N (48G – .280)			CLE A (83G – .257)																			OF-115, DH-9
"	total	131	.265	.425	407	108	24	6	11	2.7	68	52	47	78	3	14	3	212	8	4	2	1.7	.982	OF-115, DH-9
1985	CLE A	23	.318	.409	66	21	6	0	0	0.0	7	12	8	12	0	6	2	18	0	0	0	0.8	1.000	OF-15, DH-5
1986		140	.296	.493	442	131	29	2	18	4.1	68	77	33	65	6	19	6	233	7	7	1	1.9	.972	OF-126, DH-7
1987		142	.280	.439	485	136	21	1	18	3.7	57	76	20	68	5	17	2	264	3	3	2	1.9	.989	OF-122, DH-14
1988		150	.280	.392	515	144	32	4	6	1.2	69	71	28	50	7	11	4	288	3	10	1	2.0	.967	OF-141, DH-6
1989	NY A	113	.260	.427	361	94	9	0	17	4.7	54	58	21	37	0	16	4	141	3	1	2	1.3	.993	OF-75, DH-34
9 yrs.		845	.278	.439	2777	772	147	18	88	3.2	390	408	205	432	27	93	23	1437	36	31	11	1.8	.979	OF-731, DH-75

Russ Hall

HALL, ROBERT RUSSELL
B. Sept. 29, 1871, Shelbyville, Ky. D. July 1, 1937, Los Angeles, Calif.

TL

Year	Team	Games	BA	SA	AB	H	2B	3B	HR	HR%	R	RBI	BB	SO	SB	PH AB	PH H	PO	A	E	DP	TC/G	FA	G by Pos
1898	STL N	39	.245	.273	143	35	2	1	0	0.0	13	10	7		1	0	0	53	114	32	14	5.1	.839	SS-35, 3B-3, OF-1
1901	CLE A	1	.500	.500	4	2	0	0	0	0.0	2	0	0		0	0	0	1	2	3	0	6.0	.500	SS-1
2 yrs.		40	.252	.279	147	37	2	1	0	0.0	15	10	7		1	0	0	54	116	35	14	5.1	.829	SS-36, 3B-3, OF-1

Tom Haller

HALLER, THOMAS FRANK
B. June 23, 1937, Lockport, Ill.

BL TR 6'4'' 195 lbs.

Year	Team	Games	BA	SA	AB	H	2B	3B	HR	HR%	R	RBI	BB	SO	SB	PH AB	PH H	PO	A	E	DP	TC/G	FA	G by Pos
1961	SF N	30	.145	.258	62	9	1	0	2	3.2	5	8	9	23	0	4	0	117	7	0	4	4.1	1.000	C-25
1962		99	.261	.515	272	71	13	1	18	6.6	53	55	51	59	1	9	0	472	38	4	6	5.2	.992	C-91
1963		98	.255	.430	298	76	8	1	14	4.7	32	44	34	45	4	8	2	506	39	4	7	5.6	.993	C-85, OF-7
1964		117	.253	.428	388	98	14	3	16	4.1	43	48	55	51	4	7	1	739	50	9	12	6.8	.989	C-113, OF-3
1965		134	.251	.389	422	106	4	3	16	3.8	40	49	47	67	0	3	1	864	50	12	9	6.9	.987	C-133
1966		142	.240	.461	471	113	19	2	27	5.7	74	67	53	74	1	10	1	830	59	8	8	6.3	.991	C-136, 1B-4
1967		141	.251	.415	455	114	23	5	14	3.1	54	49	62	61	0	12	5	797	64	3	5	6.1	.997	C-136, OF-1
1968	LA N	144	.285	.388	474	135	27	5	4	0.8	37	53	46	76	1	12	1	863	81	6	23	6.6	.994	C-139
1969		134	.263	.357	445	117	18	3	6	1.3	46	39	48	58	0	7	3	800	48	7	4	6.4	.992	C-132
1970		112	.286	.465	325	93	16	6	10	3.1	47	47	32	35	3	12	5	524	26	4	7	4.9	.993	C-106
1971		84	.267	.366	202	54	5	0	5	2.5	23	32	25	30	0	17	6	320	34	8	3	4.3	.978	C-67
1972	DET A	59	.207	.331	121	25	5	2	2	1.7	7	13	15	14	0	20	2	220	15	0	1	4.0	1.000	C-36
12 yrs.		1294	.257	.414	3935	1011	153	31	134	3.4	461	504	477	593	14	121	27	7052	511	65	89	5.9	.991	C-1199, OF-11, 1B-4

LEAGUE CHAMPIONSHIP SERIES

Year	Team	Games	BA	SA	AB	H	2B	3B	HR	HR%	R	RBI	BB	SO	SB	PH AB	PH H	PO	A	E	DP	TC/G	FA	G by Pos
1972	DET A	1	.000	.000	1	0	0	0	0	0.0	0	0	0	0	0	1	0	0	0	0	0	0.0	–	

WORLD SERIES

Year	Team	Games	BA	SA	AB	H	2B	3B	HR	HR%	R	RBI	BB	SO	SB	PH AB	PH H	PO	A	E	DP	TC/G	FA	G by Pos
1962	SF N	4	.286	.571	14	4	1	0	1	7.1	1	3	0	2	0	0	0	29	2	0	1	7.8	1.000	C-4

Newt Halliday

HALLIDAY, NEWTON REESE
B. June 18, 1896, Chicago, Ill. D. Apr. 6, 1918, Great Lakes, Ill.

BR TR 6'1'' 175 lbs.

Year	Team	Games	BA	SA	AB	H	2B	3B	HR	HR%	R	RBI	BB	SO	SB	PH AB	PH H	PO	A	E	DP	TC/G	FA	G by Pos
1916	PIT N	1	.000	.000	1	0	0	0	0	0.0	0	0	0	1	0	0	0	3	1	0	0	4.0	1.000	1B-1

Jocko Halligan

HALLIGAN, WILLIAM E.
B. Dec. 8, 1868, Avon, N. Y. D. Feb. 13, 1945, Buffalo, N. Y.

5'9'' 166 lbs.

Year	Team	Games	BA	SA	AB	H	2B	3B	HR	HR%	R	RBI	BB	SO	SB	PH AB	PH H	PO	A	E	DP	TC/G	FA	G by Pos
1890	BUF P	57	.251	.355	211	53	9	2	3	1.4	28	33	20	19	7	0	0	104	27	36	3	2.9	.784	OF-43, C-16
1891	CIN N	61	.312	.449	247	77	13	6	3	1.2	43	44	24	25	5	0	0	89	6	16	1	1.8	.856	OF-61
1892	2 teams	CIN N (26G – .287)			BAL N (46G – .270)																			OF-48, 1B-19, C-5
"	total	72	.276	.398	279	77	8	7	4	1.4	52	55	42	33	11	1	0	258	17	25	11	4.2	.917	OF-48, 1B-19, C-5
3 yrs.		190	.281	.403	737	207	30	15	10	1.4	123	132	86	77	23	1	0	451	50	77	15	3.0	.867	OF-152, C-21, 1B-19

Ed Hallinan

HALLINAN, EDWARD S.
B. Aug. 23, 1888, San Francisco, Calif. D. Aug. 24, 1940, San Francisco, Calif.

BR TR 5'9'' 168 lbs.

Year	Team	Games	BA	SA	AB	H	2B	3B	HR	HR%	R	RBI	BB	SO	SB	PH AB	PH H	PO	A	E	DP	TC/G	FA	G by Pos
1911	STL A	52	.207	.237	169	35	3	1	0	0.0	13	14	14		4	0	0	120	136	25	24	5.4	.911	SS-34, 2B-15, 3B-3
1912		28	.221	.244	86	19	2	0	0	0.0	11	1	5		3	1	0	48	62	17	13	4.5	.866	SS-26
2 yrs.		80	.212	.239	255	54	5	1	0	0.0	24	15	19		7	1	0	168	198	42	37	5.1	.897	SS-60, 2B-15, 3B-3

Jimmy Hallinan

HALLINAN, JAMES H.
B. May 27, 1849, Ireland D. Oct. 28, 1879, Chicago, Ill.

BL TL 5'9'' 172 lbs.

Year	Team	Games	BA	SA	AB	H	2B	3B	HR	HR%	R	RBI	BB	SO	SB	PH AB	PH H	PO	A	E	DP	TC/G	FA	G by Pos
1876	NY N	54	.279	.383	240	67	7	6	2	0.8	45	36	2	4		0	0	49	178	73	7	5.6	.757	SS-50, 2B-4, OF-2
1877	2 teams	CIN N (16G – .370)			CHI N (19G – .281)																			OF-19, 2B-16
"	total	35	.321	.377	162	52	5	2	0	0.0	35	18	5	13		0	0	79	37	22	9	3.9	.841	OF-19, 2B-16
1878	2 teams	CHI N (16G – .284)			IND N (3G – .250)																			OF-14, 2B-5
"	total	19	.278	.342	79	22	5	0	0	0.0	14	3	5	8		0	0	30	14	14	1	3.1	.759	OF-14, 2B-5
3 yrs.		108	.293	.374	481	141	17	8	2	0.4	94	57	12	15		0	0	158	229	109	17	4.6	.780	SS-50, OF-35, 2B-25

Bill Hallman

HALLMAN, WILLIAM HARRY
B. Mar. 15, 1876, Philadelphia, Pa. D. Apr. 23, 1950, Philadelphia, Pa.

BL TL

Year	Team	Games	BA	SA	AB	H	2B	3B	HR	HR%	R	RBI	BB	SO	SB	PH AB	PH H	PO	A	E	DP	TC/G	FA	G by Pos
1901	MIL A	139	.246	.328	549	135	27	6	2	0.4	70	47	41		12	0	0	226	22	26	6	2.0	.905	OF-139
1903	CHI A	63	.208	.280	207	43	7	4	0	0.0	29	18	31		11	6	0	114	7	6	0	2.0	.953	OF-57
1906	PIT N	23	.270	.360	89	24	3	1	1	1.1	12	6	15		3	0	0	40	3	3	0	2.0	.935	OF-23

Year	Team		Games	BA	SA	AB	H	2B	3B	HR	HR%	R	RBI	BB	SO	SB	Pinch Hit AB	H	PO	A	E	DP	TC/G	FA	G by Pos

Bill Hallman *continued*

Year	Team		Games	BA	SA	AB	H	2B	3B	HR	HR%	R	RBI	BB	SO	SB	AB	H	PO	A	E	DP	TC/G	FA	G by Pos
1907			94	.222	.255	302	67	6	2	0	0.0	39	15	33		21	9	2	134	9	5	1	1.6	.966	OF-84
4 yrs.			319	.235	.303	1147	269	43	13	3	0.3	150	86	120		47	15	2	514	41	40	7	1.9	.933	OF-303

Bill Hallman

HALLMAN, WILLIAM WILSON
B. Mar. 31, 1867, Pittsburgh, Pa. D. Sept. 11, 1920, Philadelphia, Pa.
Manager 1897.

BR TR 5'8"

Year	Team		Games	BA	SA	AB	H	2B	3B	HR	HR%	R	RBI	BB	SO	SB	AB	H	PO	A	E	DP	TC/G	FA	G by Pos
1888	PHI	N	18	.206	.302	63	13	4	1	0	0.0	5	6	1	12	1	0	0	54	24	12	2	5.0	.867	C-10, 2B-4, OF-3, SS-1, 3B-1
1889			119	.253	.346	462	117	21	8	2	0.4	67	60	36	54	20	0	0	278	370	79	46	6.1	.891	SS-106, 2B-13, C-1
1890	PHI	P	84	.267	.360	356	95	16	7	1	0.3	59	37	33	24	6	0	0	194	103	36	15	4.0	.892	OF-34, C-26, 2B-14, 3B-10, SS-2
1891	PHI	AA	141	.283	.394	587	166	21	13	6	1.0	112	69	38	56	18	0	0	327	399	55	53	5.5	.930	2B-141
1892	PHI	N	138	.292	.382	586	171	27	10	2	0.3	106	84	32	52	19	0	0	335	379	49	60	5.5	.936	2B-138
1893			132	.307	.398	596	183	28	7	4	0.7	119	76	51	27	22	0	0	388	375	36	61	6.1	.955	2B-120, 1B-12
1894			119	.309	.374	505	156	19	7	0	0.0	107	66	36	15	36	0	0	318	320	48	62	5.8	.930	2B-119
1895			124	.314	.386	539	169	26	5	1	0.2	94	91	34	20	16	0	0	300	401	45	57	6.0	.940	2B-122, SS-3
1896			120	.320	.390	469	150	21	3	2	0.4	82	83	45	23	16	0	0	304	368	39	62	5.9	.945	2B-120, P-1
1897	2 teams		PHI	N	(31G – .262)		STL	N	(79G – .221)																
"	total		110	.233	.264	424	99	9	2	0	0.0	47	41	32		13	0	0	289	327	36	45	5.9	.945	2B-108, 1B-3
1898	BKN	N	134	.244	.303	509	124	10	7	2	0.4	57	63	29		9	0	0	273	432	45	47	5.6	.940	2B-124, 3B-10
1901	2 teams		CLE	A	(5G – .211)		PHI	N	(123G – .184)																
"	total		128	.185	.235	464	86	13	5	0	0.0	48	41	28		13	0	0	221	333	22	23	4.5	.962	2B-90, 3B-33, SS-5
1902	PHI	N	73	.248	.311	254	63	8	4	0	0.0	15	35	14		9	1	1	71	147	16	3	3.2	.932	3B-72
1903			63	.212	.288	198	42	11	2	0	0.0	20	17	16		2	6	0	148	101	16	6	4.2	.940	2B-22, 3B-19, 1B-9, OF-4, SS-3
14 yrs.			1503	.272	.348	6012	1634	234	81	20	0.3	938	769	425	283	200	7	1	3500	4079	534	542	5.4	.934	2B-1135, 3B-145, SS-120, OF-41, C-37, 1B-24, P-1

Jim Halpin

HALPIN, JAMES NATHANIEL
B. Oct. 4, 1863, England D. Jan. 4, 1893, Boston, Mass.

Year	Team		Games	BA	SA	AB	H	2B	3B	HR	HR%	R	RBI	BB	SO	SB	AB	H	PO	A	E	DP	TC/G	FA	G by Pos
1882	WOR	N	2	.000	.000	8	0	0	0	0	0.0	0		0		0	0	0	3	2	3	0	4.0	.625	3B-2
1884	WAS	U	46	.185	.202	168	31	3	0	0	0.0	24		2		0	0	0	44	97	36	4	3.8	.797	SS-39, 3B-7
1885	DET	N	15	.130	.167	54	7	2	0	0	0.0	3	1	1	12	0	0	0	12	54	12	3	5.2	.846	SS-15
3 yrs.			63	.165	.187	230	38	5	0	0	0.0	27	1	3	12	0	0	0	59	153	51	7	4.2	.806	SS-54, 3B-9

Al Halt

HALT, ALVA WILLIAM
B. Nov. 23, 1890, Sandusky, Ohio D. Jan. 22, 1973, Sandusky, Ohio

BR TR 6' 180 lbs.

Year	Team		Games	BA	SA	AB	H	2B	3B	HR	HR%	R	RBI	BB	SO	SB	AB	H	PO	A	E	DP	TC/G	FA	G by Pos
1914	BKN	F	80	.234	.307	261	61	6	2	3	1.1	26	25	13		11	4	0	168	186	43	30	5.0	.892	SS-71, 2B-3, OF-1
1915			151	.250	.336	524	131	22	7	3	0.6	41	64	39		20	0	0	240	349	48	33	4.2	.925	3B-111, SS-40
1918	CLE	A	26	.174	.203	69	12	2	0	0	0.0	9	1	9	12	4	1	0	33	43	2	4	3.0	.974	3B-14, SS-4, 2B-4, 1B-2
3 yrs.			257	.239	.316	854	204	30	9	6	0.7	76	90	61	12	35	5	0	441	578	93	67	4.3	.916	3B-125, SS-115, 2B-7, 1B-2, OF-1

Charlie Hamburg

HAMBURG, CHARLES H.
Also known as Charles H. Hambrick.
B. Nov. 22, 1863, Louisville, Ky. D. May 18, 1931, Union, N. J.

6' 175 lbs.

Year	Team		Games	BA	SA	AB	H	2B	3B	HR	HR%	R	RBI	BB	SO	SB	AB	H	PO	A	E	DP	TC/G	FA	G by Pos
1890	LOU	AA	133	.272	.344	485	132	22	2	3	0.6	93		69		46	0	0	229	16	14	3	1.9	.946	OF-133

Sam Hamby

HAMBY, JAMES SANFORD (Cracker)
B. July 29, 1897, Wilkesboro, N. C.

BR TR 6' 170 lbs.

Year	Team		Games	BA	SA	AB	H	2B	3B	HR	HR%	R	RBI	BB	SO	SB	AB	H	PO	A	E	DP	TC/G	FA	G by Pos
1926	NY	N	1	.000	.000	3	0	0	0	0	0.0	0	0	0	0	0	0	0	3	0	0	0	5.0	.600	C-1
1927			21	.192	.231	52	10	0	1	0	0.0	6	5	7	7	1	1	0	49	17	7	1	3.5	.904	C-19
2 yrs.			22	.182	.218	55	10	0	1	0	0.0	6	5	7	7	1	1	0	52	17	7	1	3.5	.885	C-20

Billy Hamilton

HAMILTON, WILLIAM ROBERT (Sliding Billy)
B. Feb. 16, 1866, Newark, N. J. D. Dec. 16, 1940, Worcester, Mass.
Hall of Fame 1961.

BR TL 5'6" 165 lbs.

Year	Team		Games	BA	SA	AB	H	2B	3B	HR	HR%	R	RBI	BB	SO	SB	AB	H	PO	A	E	DP	TC/G	FA	G by Pos
1888	KC	AA	35	.264	.357	129	34	4	4	0	0.0	21	11	4		19	0	0	45	4	2	0	1.5	.961	OF-35
1889			137	.301	.395	534	161	17	12	3	0.6	144	77	87	41	117	0	0	202	20	37	6	1.9	.857	OF-137
1890	PHI	N	123	.325	.399	496	161	13	9	2	0.4	133	49	83	37	102	0	0	232	23	34	4	2.3	.882	OF-123
1891			133	**.340**	.421	527	**179**	23	7	2	0.4	**141**	60	**102**	28	**111**	0	0	287	17	31	7	2.5	.907	OF-133
1892			139	.330	.410	554	183	21	7	3	0.5	132	53	81	29	57	0	0	291	26	28	7	2.5	.919	OF-139
1893			82	.380	.524	355	135	22	7	5	1.4	110	44	63	7	43	0	0	228	8	16	6	3.1	.937	OF-82
1894			131	.399	.519	559	223	25	15	4	0.7	**196**[1]	87	**126**	17	99	0	0	361	15	14	4	3.0	.964	OF-129
1895			123	.389	.495	517	201	22	6	7	1.4	**166**	74	96	30	97	0	0	313	11	31	5	2.9	.913	OF-123
1896	BOS	N	131	.365	.463	523	191	24	9	3	0.6	152	52	**110**	29	**83**	0	0	276	8	20	2	2.3	.934	OF-131
1897			127	.343	.414	507	174	17	5	3	0.6	**152**	61	105		66	0	0	296	10	12	0	2.5	.962	OF-126
1898			110	.369	.453	417	154	16	5	3	0.7	110	50	87		**54**	0	0	189	8	21	2	2.0	.904	OF-110
1899			84	.310	.350	297	92	7	1	1	0.3	63	33	72		19	2	0	166	11	9	2	2.0	.952	OF-81
1900			136	.333	.396	520	161	13	9	1	0.2	102	47	107		29	0	0	326	14	19	6	2.6	.947	OF-136
1901			102	.292	.361	349	102	11	2	3	0.9	70	38	64		19	3	2	232	14	14	4	2.5	.945	OF-99
14 yrs.			1593	.344 (8th)	.432	6284	2163	242	94	40	0.6	1692	736	1187	218	915	5	2	3444	182	288	55	2.5	.926	OF-1584

Darryl Hamilton

HAMILTON, DARRYL QUINN
B. Dec. 3, 1963, Baton Rouge, La.

BL TR 6'1" 180 lbs.

Year	Team		Games	BA	SA	AB	H	2B	3B	HR	HR%	R	RBI	BB	SO	SB	AB	H	PO	A	E	DP	TC/G	FA	G by Pos
1988	MIL	A	44	.184	.252	103	19	4	0	1	1.0	14	11	12	9	7	3	1	75	1	0	0	1.7	1.000	OF-37, DH-3

Jeff Hamilton

HAMILTON, JEFFREY ROBERT
B. Mar. 19, 1964, Flint, Mich.

BR TR 6'3" 190 lbs.

Jeff Hamilton *continued*

Year	Team		Games	BA	SA	AB	H	2B	3B	HR	HR%	R	RBI	BB	SO	SB	PH AB	PH H	PO	A	E	DP	TC/G	FA	G by Pos
1986	LA	N	71	.224	.361	147	33	5	0	5	3.4	22	19	2	43	0	6	0	40	87	4	6	1.8	.969	3B-66, SS-2
1987			35	.217	.253	83	18	3	0	0	0.0	5	1	7	22	0	6	0	27	60	6	5	2.7	.935	3B-31, SS-1
1988			111	.236	.353	309	73	14	2	6	1.9	34	33	10	51	0	9	3	67	160	14	9	2.2	.942	3B-105, SS-2, 2B-1, P-1
1989			151	.245	.378	548	134	35	1	12	2.2	45	56	20	71	0	5	1	139	234	19	29	2.6	.952	3B-147, SS-1, 2B-1, P-1
4 yrs.			368	.237	.359	1087	258	57	3	23	2.1	106	109	39	187	0	26	6	273	541	43	49	2.3	.950	3B-349, SS-6, 2B-1, 1B-1, P-1

LEAGUE CHAMPIONSHIP SERIES

Year	Team		Games	BA	SA	AB	H	2B	3B	HR	HR%	R	RBI	BB	SO	SB	PH AB	PH H	PO	A	E	DP	TC/G	FA	G by Pos
1988	LA	N	7	.217	.217	23	5	0	0	0	0.0	2	1	3	4	0			9	10	2	0	3.0	.905	3B-7

WORLD SERIES

Year	Team		Games	BA	SA	AB	H	2B	3B	HR	HR%	R	RBI	BB	SO	SB	PH AB	PH H	PO	A	E	DP	TC/G	FA	G by Pos
1988	LA	N	5	.105	.105	19	2	0	0	0	0.0	1	0	1	4	0			2	5	1	0	1.6	.875	3B-5

Tom Hamilton

HAMILTON, THOMAS BAIL (Ham)
B. Sept. 29, 1925, Altoona, Kans. D. Nov. 29, 1973, Tyler, Tex.

BL TR 6'4" 213 lbs.

Year	Team		Games	BA	SA	AB	H	2B	3B	HR	HR%	R	RBI	BB	SO	SB	PH AB	PH H	PO	A	E	DP	TC/G	FA	G by Pos
1952	PHI	A	9	.200	.300	10	2	1	0	0	0.0	0	0	1	1	0	4	1	11	0	0	1	1.2	1.000	1B-5
1953			58	.196	.232	56	11	2	0	0	0.0	8	5	7	11	0	43	8	22	2	0	0	0.4	1.000	1B-7, OF-2
2 yrs.			67	.197	.242	66	13	3	0	0	0.0	8	5	8	12	0	47	9	33	2	0	1	0.5	1.000	1B-12, OF-2

Ken Hamlin

HAMLIN, KENNETH LEE
B. May 18, 1935, Detroit, Mich.

BR TR 5'10" 170 lbs.

Year	Team		Games	BA	SA	AB	H	2B	3B	HR	HR%	R	RBI	BB	SO	SB	PH AB	PH H	PO	A	E	DP	TC/G	FA	G by Pos
1957	PIT	N	2	.000	.000	1	0	0	0	0	0.0	0	0	0			2	0	2	0	0	0	1.0	1.000	SS-1
1959			3	.125	.125	8	1	0	0	0	0.0	0	2	1			2	1	4	6	0	2	3.3	1.000	SS-3
1960	KC	A	140	.224	.271	428	96	10	2	2	0.5	51	24	44	48	1	1	1	195	341	25	61	4.0	.955	SS-139
1961	LA	A	42	.209	.275	91	19	3	0	1	1.1	4	5	11	9	0	2	1	63	93	6	25	3.9	.963	SS-39
1962	WAS	A	98	.253	.325	292	74	12	0	3	1.0	29	22	22	22	7	6	2	126	210	13	47	3.6	.963	SS-87, 2B-2
1965			117	.273	.370	362	99	21	4	4	1.1	45	22	33	45	8	9	2	185	210	12	45	3.5	.971	2B-77, SS-47, 3B-1
1966			66	.215	.291	158	34	7	1	1	0.6	13	16	13	21	1	18	1	91	120	8	28	3.3	.963	2B-50, 3B-1
7 yrs.			468	.241	.311	1340	323	53	4	11	0.8	143	89	125	146	17	36	7	666	980	64	208	3.7	.963	SS-316, 2B-129, 3B-2

Jack Hammond

HAMMOND, WALTER CHARLES (Wobby)
B. Feb. 26, 1891, Amsterdam, N.Y. D. Mar. 4, 1942, Kenosha, Wis.

BR TR 5'11" 170 lbs.

Year	Team		Games	BA	SA	AB	H	2B	3B	HR	HR%	R	RBI	BB	SO	SB	PH AB	PH H	PO	A	E	DP	TC/G	FA	G by Pos
1915	CLE	A	35	.214	.262	84	18	2	1	0	0.0	9	4	1	19	0	9	1	24	42	3	5	2.0	.957	2B-19
1922 2 teams	CLE A	(1G – .250)			PIT N	(9G – .273)																			
" total			10	.267	.267	15	4	0	0	0	0.0	4	0	1	0	0	0	0	9	8	2	2	1.9	.895	2B-5
2 yrs.			45	.222	.263	99	22	2	1	0	0.0	13	4	2	19	0	9	1	33	50	5	7	2.0	.943	2B-24

Steve Hammond

HAMMOND, STEVEN BENJAMIN
B. May 9, 1957, Atlanta, Ga.

BL TR 6'2" 190 lbs.

Year	Team		Games	BA	SA	AB	H	2B	3B	HR	HR%	R	RBI	BB	SO	SB	PH AB	PH H	PO	A	E	DP	TC/G	FA	G by Pos
1982	KC	A	46	.230	.310	126	29	5	1	1	0.8	14	11	4	18	0	11	2	81	3	0	1	1.8	1.000	OF-37, DH-1

Garvin Hamner

HAMNER, WESLEY GARVIN (Wes)
Brother of Granny Hamner.
B. Mar. 18, 1924, Richmond, Va.

BR TR 5'11" 172 lbs.

Year	Team		Games	BA	SA	AB	H	2B	3B	HR	HR%	R	RBI	BB	SO	SB	PH AB	PH H	PO	A	E	DP	TC/G	FA	G by Pos
1945	PHI	N	32	.198	.228	101	20	3	0	0	0.0	12	5	7	9	2	0	0	66	81	15	13	5.1	.907	2B-21, SS-9, 3B-1

Granny Hamner

HAMNER, GRANVILLE WILBUR
Brother of Garvin Hamner.
B. Apr. 26, 1927, Richmond, Va.

BR TR 5'10" 163 lbs.

Year	Team		Games	BA	SA	AB	H	2B	3B	HR	HR%	R	RBI	BB	SO	SB	PH AB	PH H	PO	A	E	DP	TC/G	FA	G by Pos
1944	PHI	N	21	.247	.260	77	19	1	0	0	0.0	6	5	3	7	0	0	0	27	98	9	17	6.4	.933	SS-21
1945			14	.171	.220	41	7	1	0	0	0.0	3	6	1	3	0	0	0	31	37	11	7	5.6	.857	SS-13
1946			2	.143	.143	7	1	0	0	0	0.0	0	0	0	3	0	0	0	1	5	1	1	5.5	1.000	SS-2
1947			2	.286	.286	7	2	0	0	0	0.0	1	0	1	0	0	0	0	5	6	0	1	5.5	1.000	SS-2
1948			129	.260	.350	446	116	21	5	3	0.7	42	48	22	39	2	4	1	280	506	32	101	5.3	.961	SS-154
1949			154	.263	.353	**662**	174	32	5	6	0.9	83	53	25	47	6	0	0	293	513	48	100	5.4	.944	SS-157
1950			157	.270	.380	637	172	27	5	11	1.7	78	82	39	35	2	0	0	255	458	31	93	5.0	.958	SS-150
1951			150	.255	.363	589	150	23	7	9	1.5	61	71	29	32	10	0	0	267	470	38	102	5.1	.951	SS-151
1952			151	.275	.428	596	164	30	5	17	2.9	74	87	27	51	7	1	0	285	459	37	105	5.1	.953	2B-93, SS-71
1953			154	.276	.455	609	168	30	8	21	3.4	90	92	32	28	2	1	0	362	416	18	98	5.2	.977	2B-152, SS-1
1954			152	.299	.466	596	178	39	11	13	2.2	83	89	53	44	1	0	0	201	261	21	51	4.6	.957	2B-82, SS-32
1955			104	.257	.343	405	104	12	4	5	1.2	57	43	41	30	0	0	0	183	307	32	70	4.3	.939	SS-110, 2B-11, P-3
1956			122	.224	.329	401	90	24	3	4	1.0	42	42	30	42	2	5	1	264	291	21	55	4.3	.964	2B-125, SS-5, P-1
1957			133	.227	.345	502	114	19	5	10	2.0	59	62	34	42	3	8	0	44	79	3	11	3.6	.976	3B-22, 2B-11, SS-3
1958			35	.301	.444	133	40	7	3	2	1.5	18	16	8	16	0	0	0							
1959 2 teams	PHI N	(21G – .297)			CLE A	(27G – .164)																			
" total			48	.229	.351	131	30	5	1	3	2.3	14	9	6	13	0	17	2	43	79	5	10	2.6	.961	SS-25, 2B-7, 3B-6
1962	KC	A	3	—	—	0	0	0	0	0	—	0	0	0	0	0	0	0					0.3	1.000	P-3
17 yrs.			1531	.262	.383	5839	1529	272	62	104	1.8	711	708	351	432	35	37	4	2811	4304	334	888	4.9	.955	SS-934, 2B-568, 3B-31, P-7

WORLD SERIES

Year	Team		Games	BA	SA	AB	H	2B	3B	HR	HR%	R	RBI	BB	SO	SB	PH AB	PH H	PO	A	E	DP	TC/G	FA	G by Pos
1950	PHI	N	4	.429	.714	14	6	2	1	0	0.0	1	0	1	0	2	1	0	6	7	1	1	3.5	.929	SS-4

Ike Hampton

HAMPTON, ISAAC BERNARD
B. Aug. 22, 1951, Camden, S.C.

BB TR 6'1" 185 lbs.

Year	Team		Games	BA	SA	AB	H	2B	3B	HR	HR%	R	RBI	BB	SO	SB	PH AB	PH H	PO	A	E	DP	TC/G	FA	G by Pos
1974	NY	N	4	.000	.000	4	0	0	0	0	0.0	0	1	0	3	0	3	0	2	0	0	0	0.5	1.000	C-1
1975	CAL	A	31	.152	.197	66	10	3	0	0	0.0	8	4	7	19	0	3	1	113	15	8	1	4.4	.941	C-28, SS-2, 3B-1
1976			3	.000	.000	2	0	0	0	0	0.0	0	0	0	2	0	2	0	87	5	3	0	1.8	.968	C-47
1977			52	.295	.523	44	13	1	0	3	6.8	5	9	2	10	0	9	2	20	1	2	0	1.2	.913	C-13, DH-4, 1B-3
1978			19	.214	.571	14	3	0	1	1	7.1	2	2	2	5	0									

Year	Team	Games	BA	SA	AB	H	2B	3B	HR	HR%	R	RBI	BB	SO	SB	Pinch Hit AB	Pinch Hit H	PO	A	E	DP	TC/G	FA	G by Pos

Ike Hampton *continued*

Year	Team	Games	BA	SA	AB	H	2B	3B	HR	HR%	R	RBI	BB	SO	SB	PH AB	PH H	PO	A	E	DP	TC/G	FA	G by Pos
1979		4	.400	.400	5	2	0	0	0	0.0	0	0	0	1	0	1	0	10	2	0	0	3.0	1.000	1B-2
6 yrs.		113	.207	.341	135	28	4	1	4	3.0	15	18	11	38	1	10	3	234	25	13	2	2.4	.952	C-91, DH-5, SS-3, 1B-3, 3B-1

Bert Hamric

HAMRIC, ODBERT HERMAN
B. Mar. 1, 1928, Clarksburg, W. Va. D. Aug. 4, 1984, Springboro, Ohio
BL TR 6' 165 lbs.

Year	Team	Games	BA	SA	AB	H	2B	3B	HR	HR%	R	RBI	BB	SO	SB	PH AB	PH H	PO	A	E	DP	TC/G	FA	G by Pos
1955	BKN N	2	.000	.000	1	0	0	0	0	0.0	0	0	0	1	0	1	0	0	0	0	0	0.0	–	
1958	BAL A	8	.125	.125	8	1	0	0	0	0.0	0	0	0	6	0	8	1	0	0	0	0	0.0	–	
2 yrs.		10	.111	.111	9	1	0	0	0	0.0	0	0	0	7	0	9	1	0	0	0	0	0.0	–	

Ray Hamrick

HAMRICK, RAYMOND BERNARD
B. Aug. 1, 1921, Nashville, Tenn.
BR TR 5'11½" 160 lbs.

Year	Team	Games	BA	SA	AB	H	2B	3B	HR	HR%	R	RBI	BB	SO	SB	PH AB	PH H	PO	A	E	DP	TC/G	FA	G by Pos
1943	PHI N	44	.200	.231	160	32	3	1	0	0.0	12	9	8	28	0	0	0	86	114	10	12	4.8	.952	2B-31, SS-12
1944		74	.205	.257	292	60	10	1	1	0.3	22	23	23	34	1	0	0	160	293	25	55	6.5	.948	SS-74
2 yrs.		118	.204	.248	452	92	13	2	1	0.2	34	32	31	62	1	0	0	246	407	35	67	5.8	.949	SS-86, 2B-31

Buddy Hancken

HANCKEN, MORRIS MEDLOCK
B. Aug. 30, 1914, Birmingham, Ala.
BR TR 6'1" 175 lbs.

Year	Team	Games	BA	SA	AB	H	2B	3B	HR	HR%	R	RBI	BB	SO	SB	PH AB	PH H	PO	A	E	DP	TC/G	FA	G by Pos
1940	PHI A	1	–	–	0	0	0	0	0	–	0	0	0	0	0	0	0	1	0	0	0	1.0	1.000	C-1

Fred Hancock

HANCOCK, FRED JAMES
B. Mar. 28, 1920, Allenport, Pa. D. Mar. 12, 1986, Clearwater, Fla.
BR TR 5'8" 170 lbs.

Year	Team	Games	BA	SA	AB	H	2B	3B	HR	HR%	R	RBI	BB	SO	SB	PH AB	PH H	PO	A	E	DP	TC/G	FA	G by Pos
1949	CHI A	39	.135	.212	52	7	2	1	0	0.0	7	8	9	9	0	5	1	22	28	2	10	1.3	.962	SS-27, 3B-3, OF-1

Garry Hancock

HANCOCK, RONALD GARRY
B. Jan. 23, 1954, Tampa, Fla.
BL TL 6' 175 lbs.

Year	Team	Games	BA	SA	AB	H	2B	3B	HR	HR%	R	RBI	BB	SO	SB	PH AB	PH H	PO	A	E	DP	TC/G	FA	G by Pos
1978	BOS A	38	.225	.263	80	18	3	0	0	0.0	10	4	1	12	0	8	3	29	3	0	1	0.8	1.000	OF-19, DH-13
1980		46	.287	.443	115	33	6	0	4	3.5	9	19	3	11	0	12	2	49	3	2	0	1.2	.963	OF-27, DH-12
1981		26	.156	.222	45	7	3	0	0	0.0	4	3	2	4	0	12	1	11	2	0	0	0.5	1.000	OF-8, DH-4
1982		11	.000	.000	14	0	0	0	0	0.0	3	0	1	1	0	4	0	4	0	0	0	0.4	1.000	OF-7
1983	OAK A	101	.273	.418	256	70	7	3	8	3.1	29	30	5	13	2	14	7	249	10	4	17	2.6	.985	OF-67, 1B-27, DH-9
1984		51	.217	.250	60	13	2	0	0	0.0	2	8	0	1	0	33	6	24	0	0	1	0.5	1.000	OF-18, DH-5, 1B-4, P-1
6 yrs.		273	.247	.358	570	141	21	3	12	2.1	57	64	12	42	2	83	19	366	18	6	19	1.4	.985	OF-146, DH-43, 1B-31, P-1

Mike Handiboe

HANDIBOE, ALOYSIUS JAMES (Coalyard Mike)
B. July 21, 1887, Washington, D. C. D. Jan. 31, 1953, Savannah, Ga.
BL TL 5'10" 155 lbs.

Year	Team	Games	BA	SA	AB	H	2B	3B	HR	HR%	R	RBI	BB	SO	SB	PH AB	PH H	PO	A	E	DP	TC/G	FA	G by Pos
1911	NY A	5	.067	.067	15	1	0	0	0	0.0	0	0	0	2		0	0	7	0	0	0	1.4	1.000	OF-4

Gene Handley

HANDLEY, EUGENE LOUIS
Brother of Lee Handley.
B. Nov. 25, 1914, Kennett, Mo.
BR TR 5'10½" 165 lbs.

Year	Team	Games	BA	SA	AB	H	2B	3B	HR	HR%	R	RBI	BB	SO	SB	PH AB	PH H	PO	A	E	DP	TC/G	FA	G by Pos
1946	PHI A	89	.251	.323	251	63	8	5	0	0.0	31	21	22	25	8	8	3	163	152	17	33	3.7	.949	2B-68, 3B-4, SS-1
1947		36	.256	.300	90	23	2	1	0	0.0	10	8	10	2	1	3	0	43	58	7	11	3.0	.935	2B-17, 3B-10, SS-1
2 yrs.		125	.252	.317	341	86	10	6	0	0.0	41	29	32	27	9	11	3	206	210	24	44	3.5	.945	2B-85, 3B-14, SS-2

Lee Handley

HANDLEY, LEE ELMER (Jeep)
Brother of Gene Handley.
B. July 13, 1913, Clarion, Iowa D. Apr. 8, 1970, Pittsburgh, Pa.
BR TR 5'7" 160 lbs.

Year	Team	Games	BA	SA	AB	H	2B	3B	HR	HR%	R	RBI	BB	SO	SB	PH AB	PH H	PO	A	E	DP	TC/G	FA	G by Pos
1936	CIN N	24	.308	.397	78	24	1	0	2	2.6	10	8	7	16	3	1	0	49	58	8	8	4.8	.930	2B-16, 3B-7
1937	PIT N	127	.250	.363	480	120	21	12	3	0.6	59	37	37	40	5	0	0	296	375	35	67	5.6	.950	2B-126, 3B-1
1938		139	.268	.372	570	153	25	8	6	1.1	91	51	53	31	7	0	0	119	304	23	26	3.2	.948	3B-136
1939		101	.285	.356	376	107	14	5	1	0.3	43	42	32	20	17	1	0	83	180	18	14	2.8	.936	3B-100
1940		98	.281	.341	302	85	7	4	1	0.3	50	17	27	16	7	4	1	89	143	19	15	2.6	.924	3B-80, 2B-7
1941		124	.288	.344	459	132	18	4	0	0.0	59	33	35	22	16	6	1	125	247	21	19	3.2	.947	3B-114
1944		40	.221	.244	86	19	2	0	0	0.0	7	5	3	5	1	4	1	51	56	4	10	2.8	.964	2B-19, 3B-11, SS-3
1945		98	.298	.372	312	93	16	2	1	0.3	39	32	20	16	7	11	5	85	183	15	13	2.9	.947	3B-79
1946		116	.238	.298	416	99	8	7	1	0.2	43	28	29	20	4	5	0	116	239	17	13	3.2	.954	3B-102, 2B-3
1947	PHI N	101	.253	.310	277	70	10	3	0	0.0	17	42	24	18	1	7	2	93	149	9	8	2.5	.964	3B-83, 2B-3, SS-1
10 yrs.		968	.269	.345	3356	902	122	45	15	0.4	418	297	267	204	68	39	10	1106	1934	169	193	3.3	.947	3B-713, 2B-174, SS-4

Harry Hanebrink

HANEBRINK, HARRY ALOYSIUS
B. Nov. 12, 1927, St. Louis, Mo.
BL TR 6' 165 lbs.

Year	Team	Games	BA	SA	AB	H	2B	3B	HR	HR%	R	RBI	BB	SO	SB	PH AB	PH H	PO	A	E	DP	TC/G	FA	G by Pos
1953	MIL N	51	.238	.313	80	19	1	1	1	1.3	8	8	6	8	1	25	2	39	55	2	18	1.9	.979	2B-21, 3B-1
1957		6	.286	.286	7	2	0	0	0	0.0	0	0	1	2	0	4	1	0	4	0	0	0.7	1.000	3B-2
1958		63	.188	.301	133	25	3	0	4	3.0	14	10	13	9	0	19	5	58	10	1	1	1.1	.986	OF-33, 3B-7
1959	PHI N	57	.258	.340	97	25	3	1	1	1.0	10	7	2	12	0	41	11	17	28	5	6	0.9	.900	2B-15, 3B-9, OF-1
4 yrs.		177	.224	.315	317	71	7	2	6	1.9	32	25	22	31	1	89	19	114	97	8	25	1.2	.963	2B-36, OF-34, 3B-19

WORLD SERIES

Year	Team	Games	BA	SA	AB	H	2B	3B	HR	HR%	R	RBI	BB	SO	SB	PH AB	PH H	PO	A	E	DP	TC/G	FA	G by Pos
1958	MIL N	2	.000	.000	2	0	0	0	0	0.0	0	0	0	0	0	2	0	0	0	0	0	0.0	–	

Fred Haney

HANEY, FRED GIRARD (Pudge)
B. Apr. 25, 1898, Albuquerque, N. M. D. Nov. 9, 1977, Beverly Hills, Calif.
Manager 1939-41, 1953-59.
BR TR 5'6" 170 lbs.

Year	Team	Games	BA	SA	AB	H	2B	3B	HR	HR%	R	RBI	BB	SO	SB	PH AB	PH H	PO	A	E	DP	TC/G	FA	G by Pos
1922	DET A	81	.352	.423	213	75	7	4	0	0.0	41	25	32	14	3	9	3	158	112	12	17	3.5	.957	3B-42, 1B-11, SS-2
1923		142	.282	.348	503	142	13	4	4	0.8	85	67	45	23	12	0	0	261	351	28	47	4.5	.956	3B-126, SS-16
1924		86	.309	.371	256	79	11	1	1	0.4	54	30	39	13	7	13	4	57	163	18	10	2.8	.924	3B-59, SS-4, 2B-3
1925		114	.279	.332	398	111	15	3	0	0.0	84	40	66	29	11	5	1	115	207	16	22	3.0	.953	3B-107
1926	BOS A	138	.221	.284	462	102	15	7	0	0.0	47	52	74	28	13	1	0	149	322	21	30	3.6	.957	3B-137

Year	Team		Games	BA	SA	AB	H	2B	3B	HR	HR%	R	RBI	BB	SO	SB	Pinch Hit AB	H	PO	A	E	DP	TC/G	FA	G by Pos

Fred Haney *continued*

Year	Team		Games	BA	SA	AB	H	2B	3B	HR	HR%	R	RBI	BB	SO	SB	AB	H	PO	A	E	DP	TC/G	FA	G by Pos
1927	2 teams			BOS A (47G – .276)		CHI N (4G – .000)																			
"	total		51	.269	.395	119	32	4	1	3	2.5	23	12	25	14	4	14	4	61	56	8	5	2.5	.936	3B-34, OF-1
1929	STL	N	10	.115	.231	26	3	1	1	0	0.0	4	2	1	2	0	2	1	8	15	1	2	2.4	.958	3B-6
7 yrs.			622	.275	.342	1977	544	66	21	8	0.4	338	228	282	123	50	44	13	809	1226	104	133	3.4	.951	3B-440, 2B-72, SS-22, 1B-11, OF-1

Larry Haney

HANEY, WALLACE LARRY
B. Nov. 19, 1942, Charlottesville, Va.   BR TR 6'2" 195 lbs.

Year	Team		Games	BA	SA	AB	H	2B	3B	HR	HR%	R	RBI	BB	SO	SB	AB	H	PO	A	E	DP	TC/G	FA	G by Pos
1966	BAL	A	20	.161	.232	56	9	1	0	1	1.8	3	3	1	15	0	1	0	123	6	2	1	6.6	.985	C-20
1967			58	.268	.390	164	44	11	0	3	1.8	13	20	6	28	1	1	0	311	31	3	3	5.9	.991	C-57
1968			38	.236	.326	89	21	3	1	1	1.1	5	5	0	19	0	6	1	149	18	1	3	4.4	.994	C-32
1969	2 teams		75	SEA A (22G – .254)		OAK A (53G – .151)																			
"	total		75	.193	.324	145	28	7	0	4	2.8	11	19	13	31	1	2	1	255	24	6	5	3.8	.979	C-73
1970	OAK	A	2	.000	.000	2	0	0	0	0	0.0	0	0	0	1	0	1	0	6	0	0	0	3.0	1.000	C-1
1972			5	.000	.000	4	0	0	0	0	0.0	0	0	0	1	0	1	0	4	0	1	0	1.0	.800	C-4, 2B-1
1973	2 teams		4	OAK A (2G – .500)		STL N (2G – .000)																			
"	total		4	.333	.333	3	1	0	0	0	0.0	0	0	0	1	0	0	0	4	0	0	0	1.0	1.000	C-4
1974	OAK	A	76	.165	.248	121	20	4	0	2	1.7	12	3	3	18	1	1	0	219	21	3	2	3.2	.988	C-73, 3B-3, 1B-2
1975			47	.192	.308	26	5	0	0	1	3.8	3	2	1	4	0	0	0	70	4	0	1	1.6	1.000	C-43, 3B-4
1976			88	.226	.237	177	40	2	0	0	0.0	12	10	13	26	0	1	0	290	45	9	2	3.9	.974	C-87
1977	MIL	A	63	.228	.244	127	29	2	0	0	0.0	7	10	5	30	0	0	0	223	32	4	3	4.1	.985	C-63
1978			4	.200	.200	5	1	0	0	0	0.0	0	1	0	0	0	0	0	6	0	0	0	1.5	1.000	C-4
12 yrs.			480	.215	.289	919	198	30	1	12	1.3	68	73	44	175	3	14	3	1660	181	29	20	3.9	.984	C-461, 3B-7, 1B-2, 2B-1

WORLD SERIES

Year	Team		Games	BA	SA	AB	H	2B	3B	HR	HR%	R	RBI	BB	SO	SB	AB	H	PO	A	E	DP	TC/G	FA	G by Pos
1974	OAK	A	2	–	–	0	0	0	0	0	–	0	0	0	0	0	0	0	6	0	0	0	3.0	1.000	C-2

Charlie Hanford

HANFORD, CHARLES JOSEPH
B. June 3, 1881, Tunstall, England   D. July 19, 1963, Trenton, N. J.   BR TR 5'6½" 145 lbs.

Year	Team		Games	BA	SA	AB	H	2B	3B	HR	HR%	R	RBI	BB	SO	SB	AB	H	PO	A	E	DP	TC/G	FA	G by Pos
1914	BUF	F	155	.291	.447	597	174	28	13	13	2.2	83	90	32		37	0	0	331	24	10	5	2.4	.973	OF-155
1915	CHI	F	77	.240	.318	179	43	4	5	0	0.0	27	22	12		10	26	7	66	2	2	0	0.9	.971	OF-43
2 yrs.			232	.280	.418	776	217	32	18	13	1.7	110	112	44		47	26	7	397	26	12	5	1.9	.972	OF-198

Pat Hanifin

HANIFIN, PATRICK JAMES
B. 1868, Nova Scotia, Canada   D. Nov. 5, 1908, Springfield, Mass.

Year	Team		Games	BA	SA	AB	H	2B	3B	HR	HR%	R	RBI	BB	SO	SB	AB	H	PO	A	E	DP	TC/G	FA	G by Pos
1897	BKN	N	10	.250	.250	20	5	0	0	0	0.0	4	2	1		4	3	1	16	3	3	1	2.2	.864	OF-3, 2B-2

Jay Hankins

HANKINS, JAY NELSON
B. Nov. 7, 1935, St. Louis County, Mo.   BL TR 5'7" 170 lbs.

Year	Team		Games	BA	SA	AB	H	2B	3B	HR	HR%	R	RBI	BB	SO	SB	AB	H	PO	A	E	DP	TC/G	FA	G by Pos
1961	KC	A	76	.185	.272	173	32	0	3	3	1.7	23	6	8	17	2	3	1	97	1	3	0	1.3	.970	OF-65
1963			10	.176	.324	34	6	0	1	1	2.9	2	4	0	3	0	1	1	19	1	1	1	2.1	.952	OF-9
2 yrs.			86	.184	.280	207	38	0	4	4	1.9	25	10	8	20	2	4	2	116	2	4	1	1.4	.967	OF-74

Frank Hankinson

HANKINSON, FRANK EDWARD
B. Apr. 29, 1856, New York, N. Y.   D. Apr. 5, 1911, Palisades Park, N. J.   BR TR 5'11" 168 lbs.

Year	Team		Games	BA	SA	AB	H	2B	3B	HR	HR%	R	RBI	BB	SO	SB	AB	H	PO	A	E	DP	TC/G	FA	G by Pos
1878	CHI	N	58	.267	.338	240	64	8	3	1	0.4	38	27	5	36				95	138	33	9	4.6	.876	3B-57, P-1
1879			44	.181	.205	171	31	4	0	0	0.0	14	8	2	14				42	87	14	1	3.3	.902	P-26, OF-14, 3B-5
1880	CLE	N	69	.209	.278	263	55	7	4	1	0.4	32	19	1	23				79	101	29	7	3.0	.861	3B-56, OF-12, P-4
1881	TRO	N	85	.193	.249	321	62	15	0	1	0.3	34	19	10	41				152	170	34	22	4.2	.904	3B-84, SS-1
1883	NY	N	94	.220	.312	337	74	13	6	2	0.6	40		19	38				123	166	44	9	3.5	.868	3B-93, OF-1
1884			105	.231	.324	389	90	16	7	2	0.5	44		23	59				135	182	47	8	3.5	.871	3B-105, OF-1
1885	NY	AA	105	.224	.285	362	81	12	2	2	0.6	43		12					106	212	33	9	3.7	.906	3B-94, P-1
1886			136	.241	.299	522	126	14	5	2	0.4	66		49					181	316	72	26	4.2	.873	3B-136
1887			127	.268	.373	512	137	29	11	1	0.2	79		38		19			161	276	69	26	4.0	.864	3B-127
1888	KC	AA	37	.174	.232	155	27	4	1	1	0.6	20	20	11	2				72	84	18	12	4.7	.897	2B-13, SS-9, OF-7, 3B-7, 1B-2
10 yrs.			849	.228	.301	3272	747	122	39	13	0.4	410	93	170	211	21	0	0	1146	1732	393	129	3.9	.880	3B-764, OF-35, P-32, 2B-13, SS-10, 1B-2

Bill Hanlon

HANLON, WILLIAM HENRY (Big Bill)
B. Mar. 16, 1865, Sacramento, Calif.   D. Mar. 18, 1951, Sacramento, Calif.   6'

Year	Team		Games	BA	SA	AB	H	2B	3B	HR	HR%	R	RBI	BB	SO	SB	AB	H	PO	A	E	DP	TC/G	FA	G by Pos
1903	CHI	N	8	.095	.095	21	2	0	0	0	0.0	4	2	6		1	0	0	92	4	2	2	12.3	.980	1B-8

Ned Hanlon

HANLON, EDWARD HUGH
B. Aug. 22, 1857, Montville, Conn.   D. Apr. 14, 1937, Baltimore, Md.   BL TR 5'9½" 170 lbs.
Manager 1889-1907.

Year	Team		Games	BA	SA	AB	H	2B	3B	HR	HR%	R	RBI	BB	SO	SB	AB	H	PO	A	E	DP	TC/G	FA	G by Pos
1880	CLE	N	73	.246	.304	280	69	10	3	0	0.0	30	32	11	30				140	18	35	5	2.6	.819	OF-69, SS-4
1881	DET	N	76	.279	.397	305	85	14	8	2	0.7	63	28	22	11				143	20	24	4	2.5	.872	OF-74, SS-2
1882			82	.231	.360	347	80	18	6	5	1.4	68	38	26	25				197	20	27	8	3.0	.889	OF-82, 2B-1
1883			100	.242	.360	413	100	13	2	1	0.2	65		34	44				247	41	44	10	3.3	.867	OF-90, 2B-11
1884			114	.264	.364	450	119	18	6	5	1.1	86		40	52				241	30	39	5	2.7	.874	OF-114
1885			105	.302	.389	424	128	18	8	1	0.2	93	29	47	18				220	19	38	2	2.6	.863	OF-105
1886			126	.235	.296	494	116	8	6	4	0.8	105	60	57	39				205	18	17	4	1.9	.929	OF-126, 2B-1
1887			118	.274	.357	471	129	13	7	4	0.8	79	69	30	24	69			264	18	30	4	2.6	.904	OF-118
1888			109	.266	.346	459	122	6	8	5	1.1	64	39	15	32	38			230	7	21	3	2.4	.919	OF-109
1889	PIT	N	116	.239	.325	461	110	14	10	2	0.4	81	37	58	25	53			277	18	26	2	2.8	.919	OF-116
1890	PIT	P	118	.278	.343	472	131	16	6	1	0.2	106	44	80	24	65			291	15	30	4	2.8	.911	OF-118
1891	PIT	N	119	.266	.327	455	121	12	8	0	0.0	87	60	48	30	54			219	25	33	1	2.3	.881	OF-119, SS-1
1892	BAL	N	11	.163	.233	43	7	1	1	0	0.0	3	2	3	3	0			20	2	6	0	2.5	.786	OF-11
13 yrs.			1267	.260	.340	5074	1317	159	79	30	0.6	930	438	471	357	279	0	0	2694	251	370	52	2.6	.888	OF-1251, 2B-13, SS-7

Year	Team	Games	BA	SA	AB	H	2B	3B	HR	HR%	R	RBI	BB	SO	SB	Pinch Hit AB	Pinch Hit H	PO	A	E	DP	TC/G	FA	G by Pos

John Hanna

HANNA, JOHN
B. Nov. 3, 1863, Philadelphia, Pa.   D. Nov. 7, 1930, Philadelphia, Pa.

| 1884 | 2 teams | WAS AA (23G – .066) | | | RIC AA (22G – .194) | | | | | | | | | | | | | | | | | | | |
| " | total | 45 | .126 | .154 | 143 | 18 | 2 | 1 | 0 | 0.0 | 14 | | 6 | | | 0 | 0 | 210 | 77 | 35 | 5 | 7.2 | .891 | C-39, OF-6, SS-1 |

Truck Hannah

HANNAH, JAMES HARRISON
B. June 5, 1889, Larimore, N. D.   D. Apr. 27, 1982, Fountain Valley, Calif.   BR TR 6'1"   190 lbs.

1918	NY A	90	.220	.268	250	55	6	0	2	0.8	24	21	51	25	5	2	0	343	111	12	16	5.2	.974	C-88
1919		75	.238	.313	227	54	8	3	1	0.4	14	21	22	19	0	1	1	299	66	7	12	5.0	.981	C-73, 1B-1
1920		79	.247	.320	259	64	11	1	2	0.8	24	25	24	35	2	1	0	308	64	15	1	4.9	.961	C-78
3 yrs.		244	.235	.300	736	173	25	4	5	0.7	62	67	97	79	7	4	1	950	241	34	29	5.0	.972	C-239, 1B-1

Jack Hannifin

HANNIFIN, JOHN JOSEPH
B. Feb. 25, 1883, Holyoke, Mass.   D. Oct. 27, 1945, Northampton, Mass.   BR TR 5'11"   167 lbs.

1906	2 teams	PHI A (1G – 1.000)			NY N (10G – .200)																			
"	total	11	.226	.290	31	7	0	1	0	0.0	4	3	2			1	0	12	22	5	2	3.5	.872	SS-6, 3B-3, 2B-1
1907	NY N	56	.228	.336	149	34	7	3	1	0.7	16	15	15			6	7	1	271	36	4	9	5.6	.987	1B-29, 3B-10, SS-9, OF-2
1908	2 teams	NY N (1G – .000)			BOS N (74G – .206)																			
"	total	75	.205	.266	259	53	6	2	2	0.8	30	22	28			7	11	2	152	179	19	15	4.7	.946	3B-35, 2B-22, SS-15, OF-8
3 yrs.		142	.214	.292	439	94	13	6	3	0.7	50	40	45			14	18	3	435	237	28	26	4.9	.960	3B-48, SS-30, 1B-29, 2B-23, OF-10

Bob Hansen

HANSEN, ROBERT JOSEPH
B. May 26, 1948, Boston, Mass.   BL TL 6'   195 lbs.

1974	MIL A	58	.295	.432	88	26	4	1	2	2.3	8	9	3	16	2	34	14	11	0	0	0	0.2	1.000	DH-18, 1B-3
1976		24	.164	.180	61	10	1	0	0	0.0	4	4	6	8	0	7	1	0	0	0	0	0.0	–	DH-14, 1B-1
2 yrs.		82	.242	.329	149	36	5	1	2	1.3	12	13	9	24	2	41	15	11	0	0	0	0.1	1.000	DH-32, 1B-4

Doug Hansen

HANSEN, DOUGLAS WILLIAM
B. Dec. 16, 1928, Los Angeles, Calif.   BR TR 6'   180 lbs.

| 1951 | CLE A | 3 | – | – | 0 | 0 | 0 | 0 | 0 | – | 2 | 0 | 0 | 0 | 0 | 0 | 0 | 0 | 0 | 0 | 0 | 0.0 | – | |

Ron Hansen

HANSEN, RONALD LAVERN
B. Apr. 5, 1938, Oxford, Neb.   BR TR 6'3"   190 lbs.

1958	BAL A	12	.000	.000	19	0	0	0	0	0.0	1	1	1	7	0	0	0	10	23	2	4	2.9	.943	SS-12
1959		2	.000	.000	4	0	0	0	0	0.0	0	0	1	1	0	0	0	2	6	1	1	4.5	.889	SS-2
1960		153	.255	.440	530	135	22	5	22	4.2	72	86	69	94	3	1	0	325	456	29	110	5.3	.964	SS-153
1961		155	.248	.347	533	132	13	2	12	2.3	51	51	60	96	1	0	0	272	460	31	118	4.9	.959	SS-149, 2B-7
1962		71	.173	.255	196	34	7	0	3	1.5	12	17	30	36	0	2	0	114	159	10	37	4.0	.965	SS-64
1963	CHI A	144	.226	.351	482	109	17	2	13	2.7	55	67	78	74	1	0	0	247	483	13	95	5.2	.983	SS-144
1964		158	.261	.419	575	150	25	3	20	3.5	85	68	73	73	1	0	0	292	514	21	105	5.2	.975	SS-158
1965		162	.235	.344	587	138	23	4	11	1.9	61	66	60	73	1	0	0	287	527	26	97	5.2	.969	SS-161, 2B-1
1966		23	.176	.189	74	13	1	0	0	0.0	3	4	15	10	0	1	0	49	73	7	17	5.6	.946	SS-23
1967		157	.233	.321	498	116	20	0	8	1.6	35	51	64	51	0	0	0	243	482	27	91	4.8	.964	SS-157
1968	2 teams	WAS A (86G – .185)			CHI A (40G – .230)																			
"	total	126	.196	.312	362	71	15	0	9	2.5	35	32	46	61	0	6	2	170	336	21	54	4.2	.960	SS-88, 3B-34, 2B-2
1969	CHI A	85	.259	.335	185	48	6	1	2	1.1	15	22	18	25	2	25	6	216	83	8	28	3.6	.974	2B-26, 1B-21, SS-8, 3B-7
1970	NY A	59	.297	.473	91	27	4	0	4	4.4	13	14	19	9	0	28	4	25	57	1	7	1.4	.988	SS-15, 3B-11, 2B-1
1971		61	.207	.269	145	30	3	0	2	1.4	6	20	9	27	0	22	4	52	72	8	16	2.2	.939	3B-30, 2B-9, SS-3
1972	KC A	16	.133	.133	30	4	0	0	0	0.0	2	2	3	6	0	7	1	5	28	1	3	2.1	.971	SS-6, 3B-4, 2B-1
15 yrs.		1384	.234	.351	4311	1007	156	17	106	2.5	446	501	551	643	9	95	19	2309	3759	206	783	4.5	.967	SS-1143, 3B-86, 2B-47, 1B-21

Don Hanski

HANSKI, DONALD THOMAS
Born Donald Thomas Hanyzewski.
B. Feb. 27, 1916, LaPorte, Ind.   D. Sept. 2, 1957, Worth, Ill.   BL TL 5'11"   180 lbs.

1943	CHI A	9	.238	.286	21	5	1	0	0	0.0	1	2	0	5	0	3	0	37	3	2	5	4.7	.952	1B-5, P-1
1944		2	.000	.000	1	0	0	0	0	0.0	0	0	0	0	0	0	0	0	0	0	0	0.0	–	P-2
2 yrs.		11	.227	.273	22	5	1	0	0	0.0	1	2	0	5	0	3	0	37	3	2	5	3.8	.952	1B-5, P-3

Joe Hanson

HANSON, JOSEPH
B. St. Louis, Mo.   TR

| 1913 | NY A | 1 | .000 | .000 | 2 | 0 | 0 | 0 | 0 | 0.0 | 0 | 0 | 0 | 0 | 0 | 0 | 0 | 1 | 1 | 0 | 0 | 2.0 | 1.000 | C-1 |

John Happenny

HAPPENNY, JOHN CLIFFORD (Cliff)
B. May 18, 1901, Waltham, Mass.   D. Dec. 29, 1988, Coral Springs, Fla.   BR TR 5'11"   165 lbs.

| 1923 | CHI A | 32 | .221 | .279 | 86 | 19 | 5 | 0 | 0 | 0.0 | 7 | 10 | 3 | 13 | 1 | 0 | 1 | 0 | 39 | 64 | 7 | 13 | 3.4 | .936 | 2B-20, SS-8 |

Bill Harbidge

HARBIDGE, WILLIAM ARTHUR
B. Mar. 29, 1855, Philadelphia, Pa.   D. Mar. 17, 1924, Philadelphia, Pa.   BL TL   162 lbs.

1876	HAR N	30	.217	.255	106	23	2	1	0	0.0	11	6	3	2		0	0	111	31	36	1	5.9	.798	C-24, OF-6, 1B-2
1877		41	.222	.275	167	37	5	2	0	0.0	18	8	3	6		0	0	163	41	33	2	5.8	.861	C-32, OF-5, 2B-4, 3B-1
1878	CHI N	54	.296	.346	240	71	12	0	0	0.0	32	37	6	13		0	0	265	67	46	1	7.0	.878	C-50, OF-8
1879		4	.111	.111	18	2	0	0	0	0.0	3		0	5		0	0	3	1	3	0	1.8	.571	OF-4
1880	TRO N	9	.370	.444	27	10	0	1	0	0.0	3	2	0	3		0	0	38	10	7	2	6.1	.873	C-9, OF-1
1882		32	.187	.211	123	23	1	0	0	0.0	11	13	10	17		0	0	107	5	17	4	4.0	.868	OF-23, 1B-6, C-3
1883	PHI N	73	.221	.286	280	62	21	0	0	0.0	32		24	20		0	0	138	79	62	3	3.8	.778	OF-44, SS-11, 2B-9, C-7, 3B-5
1884	CIN U	82	.279	.361	341	95	12	5	2	0.6	59		25			0	0	121	31	17	3	2.1	.899	OF-80, SS-3, 1B-2
8 yrs.		325	.248	.306	1302	323	44	13	2	0.2	168	67	71	66		0	0	946	265	221	16	4.4	.846	OF-171, C-125, SS-14, 2B-13, 1B-10, 3B-6

989

Year	Team		Games	BA	SA	AB	H	2B	3B	HR	HR%	R	RBI	BB	SO	SB	Pinch Hit AB	Pinch Hit H	PO	A	E	DP	TC/G	FA	G by Pos

Scott Hardesty

HARDESTY, SCOTT DURBIN
B. Jan. 26, 1870, Bellville, Ohio. D. Oct. 29, 1944, Fostoria, Ohio.

Year	Team		Games	BA	SA	AB	H	2B	3B	HR	HR%	R	RBI	BB	SO	SB	AB	H	PO	A	E	DP	TC/G	FA	G by Pos
1899	NY	N	22	.222	.222	72	16	0	0	0	0.0	4	4	1		2	0	0	48	68	12	10	5.8	.906	SS-20, 1B-2

Pat Hardgrove

HARDGROVE, WILLIAM HENRY BR TR 5'10" 158 lbs.
B. May 10, 1895, Palmyra, Kans. D. Jan. 26, 1973, Jackson, Miss.

| 1918 | CHI | A | 2 | .000 | .000 | 2 | 0 | 0 | 0 | 0 | 0.0 | 0 | 0 | 0 | 0 | 0 | 0 | 2 | 0 | 0 | 0 | 0 | 0.0 | — | |

Lew Hardie

HARDIE, LOUIS W. 5'11" 180 lbs.
B. Aug. 24, 1864, New York, N. Y. D. Mar. 5, 1929, Oakland, Calif.

1884	PHI	N	3	.375	.625	8	3	2	0	0	0.0	0	2			0	0	5	1	1	0	2.3	.857	C-3
1886	CHI	N	16	.176	.176	51	9	0	0	0	0.0	4	3	4	10		0	0	68	16	3	1	5.4	.966	C-13, OF-2, 3B-1
1890	BOS	N	47	.227	.319	185	42	8	0	3	1.6	17	17	18	36	4	0	0	171	49	28	5	5.3	.887	C-25, OF-15, 3B-7, SS-1, 1B-1
1891	BAL	AA	15	.232	.339	56	13	0	3	0	0.0	7	1	8	10	3	0	0	34	1	0	0	2.3	1.000	OF-15
4 yrs.			81	.223	.307	300	67	10	3	3	1.0	28	21	30	56	7	0	0	278	67	32	6	4.7	.915	C-41, OF-32, 3B-8, SS-1, 1B-1

Bud Hardin

HARDIN, WILLIAM EDGAR BR TR 5'10" 165 lbs.
B. June 14, 1922, Shelby, N. C.

| 1952 | CHI | N | 3 | .143 | .143 | 7 | 1 | 0 | 0 | 0 | 0.0 | 1 | 0 | 0 | 0 | 0 | 1 | 0 | 6 | 4 | 0 | 1 | 3.3 | 1.000 | SS-2, 2B-1 |

Lou Harding

HARDING, LOUIS EDWARD (Jumbo) 5'9½" 213 lbs.
B. San Francisco, Calif. Deceased.

| 1886 | STL | AA | 1 | .333 | .667 | 3 | 1 | 1 | 0 | 0 | 0.0 | 0 | | 0 | | | 0 | 0 | 4 | 4 | 1 | 0 | 9.0 | .889 | C-1 |

Carroll Hardy

HARDY, CARROLL WILLIAM BR TR 6' 185 lbs.
B. May 18, 1933, Sturgis, S. D.

1958	CLE	A	27	.204	.327	49	10	3	0	1	2.0	10	6	6	14	1	6	1	35	2	0	0	1.4	1.000	OF-17
1959			32	.208	.226	53	11	1	0	0	0.0	12	2	3	7	1	12	1	41	0	0	0	1.3	1.000	OF-15
1960	2 teams		CLE A (29G – .111)			BOS A (73G – .234)																			
"	total		102	.221	.319	163	36	6	2	2	1.2	33	16	19	42	3	7	2	105	3	3	1	1.1	.973	OF-76
1961	BOS	A	85	.263	.381	281	74	20	2	3	1.1	46	36	26	53	4	14	3	142	7	6	3	1.8	.961	OF-76
1962			115	.215	.345	362	78	13	5	8	2.2	52	36	54	68	3	7	0	205	7	2	1	1.9	.991	OF-105
1963	HOU	N	15	.227	.295	44	10	3	0	0	0.0	5	3	3	7	1	4	0	17	1	1	0	1.3	.947	OF-10
1964			46	.185	.242	157	29	1	1	2	1.3	13	12	8	30	0	5	1	100	3	1	0	2.3	.990	OF-41
1967	MIN	A	11	.375	.750	8	3	0	0	1	12.5	1	2	1	1	0	7	3	0	0	0	0	0.0	—	OF-4
8 yrs.			433	.225	.330	1117	251	47	10	17	1.5	172	113	120	222	13	62	11	645	23	13	5	1.6	.981	OF-344

Jack Hardy

HARDY, JOHN D. (Do-Little) BR TR 6' 185 lbs.
B. June 23, 1877, Cleveland, Ohio. D. Oct. 20, 1921, Cleveland, Ohio.

1903	CLE	A	5	.158	.211	19	3	1	0	0	0.0	1	1	1		0	0	0	5	0	0	0	1.0	1.000	OF-5
1907	CHI	N	1	.250	.250	4	1	0	0	0	0.0	0	0	0		0	0	0	9	1	1	0	11.0	.909	C-1
1909	WAS	A	10	.167	.167	24	4	0	0	0	0.0	3	4	1		0	0	0	35	7	1	1	4.3	.977	C-9, 2B-1
1910			7	.250	.250	8	2	0	0	0	0.0	1	0	0		0	2	0	11	3	2	2	2.3	.875	C-4, OF-1
4 yrs.			23	.182	.200	55	10	1	0	0	0.0	5	5	2		1	2	0	60	11	4	3	3.3	.947	C-14, OF-6, 2B-1

Gary Hargis

HARGIS, GARY LYNN BR TR 5'11" 165 lbs.
B. Nov. 2, 1956, Minneapolis, Minn.

| 1979 | PIT | N | 1 | — | — | 0 | 0 | 0 | 0 | 0 | | 0 | 0 | 0 | 0 | 0 | 0 | 0 | 0 | 0 | 0 | 0 | 0.0 | — | |

Bubbles Hargrave

HARGRAVE, EUGENE FRANKLIN BR TR 5'10½" 174 lbs.
Brother of Pinky Hargrave.
B. July 15, 1892, New Haven, Ind. D. Feb. 23, 1969, Cincinnati, Ohio.

1913	CHI	N	3	.333	.333	3	1	0	0	0	0.0	0	1	0	0	0	1	0	3	1	0	0	1.3	1.000	C-2
1914			23	.222	.278	36	8	2	0	0	0.0	3	2	0	4	2	7	1	34	6	3	0	1.9	.930	C-16
1915			15	.158	.263	19	3	0	1	0	0.0	2	2	1	5	0	6	1	13	7	0	0	1.3	1.000	C-9
1921	CIN	N	93	.289	.426	263	76	17	8	1	0.4	28	38	12	15	4	19	3	270	50	9	2	3.5	.973	C-73
1922			98	.316	.513	320	101	22	10	7	2.2	49	57	26	18	7	10	0	261	60	6	5	3.3	.982	C-87
1923			118	.333	.521	378	126	23	9	10	2.6	54	78	44	22	4	7	1	404	90	6	12	4.2	.988	C-109
1924			98	.301	.455	312	94	19	10	3	1.0	42	33	30	20	2	6	2	322	80	7	7	4.2	.983	C-91
1925			87	.300	.414	273	82	13	6	2	0.7	28	33	25	23	4	3	0	283	42	7	1	3.8	.979	C-84
1926			105	**.353**	.525	326	115	22	8	6	1.8	42	62	25	17	2	11	3	276	50	4	7	3.1	.988	C-93
1927			102	.308	.387	305	94	18	3	0	0.0	36	35	31	18	0	9	1	261	57	4	10	3.2	.988	C-92
1928			65	.295	.389	190	56	10	0	3	1.6	19	23	13	14	4	6	2	181	37	2	2	3.4	.991	C-57
1930	NY	A	45	.278	.343	108	30	7	0	0	0.0	11	12	10	9	0	11	0	112	13	1	0	2.8	.992	C-34
12 yrs.			852	.310	.452	2533	786	155	58	29	1.1	314	376	217	165	29	96	14	2420	493	49	46	3.5	.983	C-747

Pinky Hargrave

HARGRAVE, WILLIAM McKINLEY BB TR 5'8½" 180 lbs. BR 1923-26, BL 1933
Brother of Bubbles Hargrave.
B. Jan. 31, 1896, New Haven, Ind. D. Oct. 3, 1942, Fort Wayne, Ind.

1923	WAS	A	33	.288	.322	59	17	2	0	0	0.0	4	8	2	6	0	18	7	19	9	2	2	0.9	.933	3B-8, C-5, OF-1
1924			24	.152	.242	33	5	1	0	0	0.0	3	5	1	4	0	14	1	17	2	0	0	0.8	1.000	C-8
1925	2 teams		WAS A (5G – .500)			STL A (67G – .284)																			
"	total		72	.290	.476	231	67	15	2	8	3.5	34	43	14	15	2	9	5	217	45	5	4	3.7	.981	C-63
1926	STL	A	92	.281	.464	235	66	16	3	7	3.0	20	37	10	38	1	33	9	165	50	7	5	2.4	.977	C-59
1928	DET	A	121	.274	.439	321	88	13	5	10	3.1	38	63	32	28	4	25	9	301	35	8	5	2.8	.977	C-88
1929			76	.330	.443	185	61	12	0	3	1.6	26	26	20	24	2	26	5	175	38	6	7	2.9	.973	C-48

Year	Team	Games	BA	SA	AB	H	2B	3B	HR	HR%	R	RBI	BB	SO	SB	Pinch Hit AB	Pinch Hit H	PO	A	E	DP	TC/G	FA	G by Pos

Pinky Hargrave *continued*

Year	Team	Games	BA	SA	AB	H	2B	3B	HR	HR%	R	RBI	BB	SO	SB	PH AB	PH H	PO	A	E	DP	TC/G	FA	G by Pos
1930	2 teams	DET A (55G – .285)		WAS A	(10G – .194)																		
"	total	65	.268	.458	168	45	10	2	6	3.6	21	25	23	13	3	15	2	214	18	3	6	3.6	.987	C-49
1931	WAS A	40	.325	.463	80	26	8	0	1	1.3	6	19	9	12	1	15	4	79	8	2	1	2.2	.978	C-25
1932	BOS N	82	.263	.410	217	57	14	3	4	1.8	20	33	24	18	1	7	2	206	39	8	4	3.1	.968	C-73
1933		45	.178	.178	73	13	0	0	0	0.0	5	6	5	7	1	18	1	59	7	3	3	1.5	.957	C-25
10 yrs.		650	.278	.428	1602	445	91	16	39	2.4	177	265	140	165	17	180	45	1452	251	42	39	2.7	.976	C-443, 3B-8, OF-1

Charlie Hargreaves

HARGREAVES, CHARLES RUSSELL
B. Dec. 14, 1896, Trenton, N. J. D. May 9, 1979, Neptune, N. J.   BR TR 6'   170 lbs.

Year	Team	Games	BA	SA	AB	H	2B	3B	HR	HR%	R	RBI	BB	SO	SB	PH AB	PH H	PO	A	E	DP	TC/G	FA	G by Pos
1923	BKN N	20	.281	.281	57	16	0	0	0	0.0	5	4	1	1	0	5	1	48	10	5	0	3.2	.921	C-15
1924		15	.407	.481	27	11	2	0	0	0.0	4	5	1	1	0	5	1	24	4	0	1	1.9	1.000	C-9
1925		45	.277	.337	83	23	3	1	0	0.0	9	13	6	1	1	22	5	69	21	2	2	2.0	.978	C-18, 1B-2
1926		85	.250	.361	208	52	13	2	2	1.0	14	23	19	10	1	13	2	224	65	4	6	3.4	.986	C-70
1927		44	.286	.323	133	38	3	1	0	0.0	9	11	14	7	1	2	0	160	32	3	6	4.4	.985	C-44
1928	2 teams	BKN N (20G – .197)		PIT N	(79G – .285)																		
"	total	99	.268	.321	321	86	10	2	1	0.3	18	37	18	15	2	2	0	311	60	13	8	3.9	.966	C-97
1929	PIT N	102	.268	.345	328	88	12	5	1	0.3	33	44	16	12	1	1	0	308	56	7	7	3.6	.981	C-102
1930		11	.226	.258	31	7	1	0	0	0.0	4	2	2	1	0	0	0	50	9	0	1	5.4	1.000	C-11
8 yrs.		421	.270	.336	1188	321	44	11	4	0.3	96	139	77	49	6	50	9	1194	257	34	30	3.5	.977	C-366, 1B-2

Mike Hargrove

HARGROVE, DUDLEY MICHAEL
B. Oct. 26, 1949, Perryton, Tex.   BL TL 6'   195 lbs.

Year	Team	Games	BA	SA	AB	H	2B	3B	HR	HR%	R	RBI	BB	SO	SB	PH AB	PH H	PO	A	E	DP	TC/G	FA	G by Pos
1974	TEX A	131	.323	.424	415	134	18	6	4	1.0	57	66	49	42	0	10	3	638	72	9	57	5.5	.987	1B-91, DH-32, OF-6
1975		145	.303	.416	519	157	22	2	11	2.1	82	62	79	66	4	8	4	513	45	13	24	3.9	.977	OF-96, 1B-48, DH-12
1976		151	.287	.384	541	155	30	1	7	1.3	80	58	97	64	2	4	0	1222	110	21	103	9.0	.984	1B-141, DH-5
1977		153	.305	.476	525	160	28	4	18	3.4	98	69	103	59	2	2	0	1393	100	11	134	9.8	.993	1B-152
1978		146	.251	.346	494	124	24	1	7	1.4	63	40	107	47	2	2	0	1221	116	17	90	9.3	.987	1B-140, DH-4
1979	2 teams	SD N (52G – .192)		CLE A	(100G – .325)																		
"	total	152	.289	.428	463	134	26	2	10	2.2	75	64	88	55	2	16	3	679	33	7	47	4.7	.990	OF-65, 1B-65, DH-7
1980	CLE A	160	.304	.404	589	179	22	2	11	1.9	86	85	111	36	4	0	0	1391	88	10	128	9.3	.993	1B-160
1981		94	.317	.401	322	102	21	0	2	0.6	43	49	60	16	5	2	2	766	76	9	67	9.1	.989	1B-88, DH-4
1982		160	.271	.338	591	160	26	1	4	0.7	67	65	101	58	2	0	0	1293	123	5	110	8.9	.996	1B-153, DH-5
1983		134	.286	.367	469	134	21	4	3	0.6	57	57	78	57	2	0	0	1098	115	7	131	9.1	.994	1B-131, DH-1
1984		133	.267	.335	352	94	14	2	2	0.6	44	44	53	38	0	12	1	790	83	8	86	6.6	.991	1B-124
1985		107	.285	.352	284	81	14	1	1	0.4	31	27	39	29	1	20	3	599	66	6	66	6.3	.991	1B-84, DH-2, OF-1
12 yrs.		1666	.290	.391	5564	1614	266	28	80	1.4	783	686	965	550	24	80	18	11603	1027	123	1043	7.7	.990	1B-1377, OF-168, DH-72

John Harkins

HARKINS, JOHN JOSEPH (Pa)
B. Apr. 12, 1859, New Brunswick, N. J. D. Nov. 18, 1940, New Brunswick, N. J.   BR TR 6'1"   205 lbs.

Year	Team	Games	BA	SA	AB	H	2B	3B	HR	HR%	R	RBI	BB	SO	SB	PH AB	PH H	PO	A	E	DP	TC/G	FA	G by Pos
1884	CLE N	61	.205	.240	229	47	4	2	0	0.0	24	20	7	45		0	0	43	85	25	3	2.5	.837	P-46, OF-17, SS-1, 3B-1
1885	BKN AA	43	.264	.333	159	42	4	2	1	0.6	20		9			0	0	45	63	21	0	3.0	.837	P-34, OF-9, 3B-1
1886		41	.225	.303	142	32	4	2	1	0.7	18		17			0	0	29	61	11	2	2.5	.891	P-34, OF-8
1887		27	.235	.286	98	23	5	0	0	0.0	10		7			0	0	13	37	6	2	2.1	.893	P-24, OF-4, 2B-1
1888	BAL AA	1	.000	.000	3	0	0	0	0	0.0	1	0	1		4	0	0	0	4	0	0	4.0	1.000	P-1
5 yrs.		173	.228	.284	631	144	17	6	2	0.3	73	20	41	45	4	0	0	130	250	63	7	2.6	.858	P-139, OF-38, 3B-2, SS-1, 2B-1

Tim Harkness

HARKNESS, THOMAS WILLIAM
B. Dec. 23, 1937, Lachine, Que., Canada   BL TL 6'2"   182 lbs.

Year	Team	Games	BA	SA	AB	H	2B	3B	HR	HR%	R	RBI	BB	SO	SB	PH AB	PH H	PO	A	E	DP	TC/G	FA	G by Pos
1961	LA N	5	.500	.750	8	4	2	0	0	0.0	4	0	3	1	0	1	1	11	1	0	2	2.4	1.000	1B-2
1962		92	.258	.387	62	16	2	0	2	3.2	9	7	10	20	1	30	8	116	8	0	14	1.3	1.000	1B-59
1963	NY N	123	.211	.339	375	79	12	3	10	2.7	35	41	36	79	4	16	1	898	112	14	73	8.3	.986	1B-106
1964		39	.282	.368	117	33	2	1	2	1.7	11	13	9	18	1	9	0	251	28	2	32	7.2	.993	1B-32
4 yrs.		259	.235	.356	562	132	18	4	14	2.5	59	61	58	118	7	57	10	1276	149	16	121	5.6	.989	1B-199

Dick Harley

HARLEY, RICHARD JOSEPH
B. Sept. 25, 1872, Philadelphia, Pa. D. Apr. 3, 1952, Philadelphia, Pa.   BL TR 5'10½" 150 lbs.

Year	Team	Games	BA	SA	AB	H	2B	3B	HR	HR%	R	RBI	BB	SO	SB	PH AB	PH H	PO	A	E	DP	TC/G	FA	G by Pos
1897	STL N	89	.291	.361	330	96	4	3	3	0.9	43	35	36		23	0	0	186	19	23	3	2.6	.899	OF-89
1898		142	.246	.275	549	135	6	5	0	0.0	74	42	34		13	1	1	311	26	27	3	2.6	.926	OF-141
1899	CLE N	142	.250	.307	567	142	15	7	1	0.2	70	50	40		15	0	0	299	27	27	7	2.5	.924	OF-142
1900	CIN N	5	.429	.476	21	9	1	0	0	0.0	2	5	1		4	0	0	6	0	0	1	1.2	1.000	OF-5
1901		133	.273	.327	535	146	13	2	4	0.7	69	27	31		37	0	0	245	20	30	2	2.2	.898	OF-133
1902	DET A	125	.281	.344	491	138	9	8	2	0.4	59	44	36		20	0	0	238	15	19	1	2.2	.930	OF-125
1903	CHI N	104	.231	.259	386	89	9	1	0	0.0	72	33	45		27	2	2	162	18	15	2	1.9	.923	OF-103
7 yrs.		740	.262	.312	2879	755	59	27	10	0.3	389	236	223		139	3	3	1447	125	141	18	2.3	.918	OF-738

Larry Harlow

HARLOW, LARRY DUANE
B. Nov. 13, 1951, Colorado Springs, Colo.   BL TL 6'2"   185 lbs.

Year	Team	Games	BA	SA	AB	H	2B	3B	HR	HR%	R	RBI	BB	SO	SB	PH AB	PH H	PO	A	E	DP	TC/G	FA	G by Pos
1975	BAL A	4	.333	.333	3	1	0	0	0	0.0	1	0	0	0	0	0	0	2	0	0	0	0.5	1.000	OF-4
1977		46	.208	.250	48	10	0	1	0	0.0	4	0	5	8	6	3	0	47	0	6	0	1.2	.887	OF-38
1978		147	.243	.354	460	112	25	1	8	1.7	67	26	55	72	14	9	0	313	7	7	2	2.2	.979	OF-138, P-1
1979	2 teams	BAL A (38G – .268)		CAL A	(62G – .233)																		
"	total	100	.240	.305	200	48	9	2	0	0.0	27	15	32	38	2	8	2	147	4	4	1	1.6	.974	OF-89, DH-1
1980	CAL A	109	.276	.385	301	83	13	4	4	1.3	47	27	48	61	3	12	4	235	11	6	5	2.3	.976	OF-94, DH-1, 1B-1
1981		43	.207	.220	82	17	1	0	0	0.0	13	4	16	25	1	7	0	52	1	0	0	1.3	.981	OF-39
6 yrs.		449	.248	.339	1094	271	48	8	12	1.1	159	72	156	205	26	39	6	796	23	24	8	1.9	.972	OF-402, DH-2, 1B-1, P-1

LEAGUE CHAMPIONSHIP SERIES

Year	Team	Games	BA	SA	AB	H	2B	3B	HR	HR%	R	RBI	BB	SO	SB	PH AB	PH H	PO	A	E	DP	TC/G	FA	G by Pos
1979	CAL A	3	.125	.250	8	1	1	0	0	0.0	0	1	1	2	0	0	0	6	0	0	0	2.0	1.000	OF-2

Bill Harman

HARMAN, WILLIAM BELL
B. Jan. 2, 1919, Bridgewater, Va.   BR TR 6'4"   200 lbs.

Year	Team		Games	BA	SA	AB	H	2B	3B	HR	HR%	R	RBI	BB	SO	SB	Pinch Hit AB	Pinch Hit H	PO	A	E	DP	TC/G	FA	G by Pos

Bill Harman *continued*

| 1941 | PHI | N | 15 | .071 | .071 | 14 | 1 | 0 | 0 | 0 | 0.0 | 1 | 0 | 0 | 3 | 0 | 5 | 0 | 4 | 4 | 0 | 0 | 0.5 | 1.000 | C-5, P-5 |

Chuck Harmon

HARMON, CHARLES BYRON
B. Apr. 23, 1926, Washington, Ind.   BR TR 6'2'' 175 lbs.

1954	CIN	N	94	.238	.304	286	68	7	3	2	0.7	39	25	17	27	7	23	3	86	132	8	22	2.4	.965	3B-67, 1B-3
1955			96	.253	.389	198	50	6	3	5	2.5	31	28	26	24	9	15	4	126	50	6	6	1.9	.967	3B-39, OF-32, 1B-4
1956	2 teams		CIN N (13G – .000)			STL N (20G – .000)																			
"	total		33	.000	.000	19	0	0	0	0	0.0	4	0	2	2	1	3	0	16	0	0	1	0.5	1.000	OF-17, 1B-4, 3B-1
1957	2 teams		STL N (9G – .333)			PHI N (57G – .256)																			
"	total		66	.258	.326	89	23	2	2	0	0.0	16	6	1	4	8	10	3	54	8	1	4	1.0	.984	OF-33, 3B-5, 1B-2
	4 yrs.		289	.238	.326	592	141	15	8	7	1.2	90	59	46	57	25	51	10	282	190	15	33	1.7	.969	3B-112, OF-82, 1B-13

Terry Harmon

HARMON, TERRY WALTER
B. Apr. 12, 1944, Toledo, Ohio   BR TR 6'2'' 180 lbs.

1967	PHI	N	2	–	–	0	0	0	0	0	0.0	0	0	0	0	0	0	0	0	0	0	0	0.0	–	
1969			87	.239	.289	201	48	8	1	0	0.0	25	16	22	31	1	18	4	94	169	7	42	3.1	.974	SS-38, 2B-19, 3B-2
1970			71	.248	.326	129	32	2	4	0	0.0	16	7	12	22	6	9	2	64	81	2	16	2.1	.986	SS-37, 2B-14, 3B-2
1971			79	.204	.240	221	45	4	2	0	0.0	27	12	20	45	3	10	0	144	191	7	44	4.3	.980	2B-58, SS-9, 3B-3, 1B-2
1972			73	.284	.367	218	62	8	2	2	0.9	35	13	29	28	3	8	1	116	164	5	32	3.9	.982	2B-50, SS-15, 3B-5
1973			72	.209	.230	148	31	3	0	0	0.0	17	8	13	14	1	15	2	100	103	3	26	2.9	.985	2B-43, SS-19, 3B-1
1974			27	.133	.133	15	2	0	0	0	0.0	5	0	3	3	0	9	2	9	6	0	1	0.6	1.000	SS-7, 2B-5
1975			48	.181	.250	72	13	1	2	0	0.0	14	5	9	13	3	0	0	32	65	1	9	2.0	.990	SS-25, 2B-7, 3B-1
1976			42	.295	.393	61	18	4	1	0	0.0	12	6	3	10	3	7	2	28	49	3	7	1.9	.963	SS-19, 2B-13, 3B-5
1977			46	.183	.300	60	11	1	0	2	3.3	13	5	6	9	0	3	0	37	65	8	14	2.4	.927	2B-28, SS-16, 3B-3
	10 yrs.		547	.233	.292	1125	262	31	12	4	0.4	164	72	117	175	17	69	13	624	893	36	191	2.8	.977	2B-237, SS-185, 3B-22, 1B-2

LEAGUE CHAMPIONSHIP SERIES

| 1976 | PHI | N | 1 | – | – | 0 | 0 | 0 | 0 | 0 | – | 1 | 0 | 0 | 0 | 0 | 0 | 0 | 0 | 0 | 0 | 0 | 0.0 | – | |

Brian Harper

HARPER, BRIAN DAVID
B. Oct. 16, 1959, Los Angeles, Calif.   BR TR 6'2'' 195 lbs.

1979	CAL	A	1	.000	.000	2	0	0	0	0	0.0	0	0	0	1	0	1	0	0	0	0	0	0.0	–	DH-1
1981			4	.273	.273	11	3	0	0	0	0.0	1	1	0	1	0	1	0	5	0	1	0	1.5	.833	OF-2, DH-1
1982	PIT	N	20	.276	.517	29	8	1	0	2	6.9	4	4	1	4	0	12	5	10	0	0	0	0.5	1.000	OF-8
1983			61	.221	.427	131	29	4	1	7	5.3	16	20	2	15	0	27	6	40	0	0	0	0.7	1.000	OF-35, 1B-1
1984			48	.259	.348	112	29	4	0	2	1.8	4	11	5	11	0	11	2	57	3	1	0	1.3	.984	OF-37, C-2
1985	STL	N	43	.250	.327	52	13	4	0	0	0.0	5	8	2	3	0	26	7	15	5	0	0	0.5	1.000	OF-13, 3B-6, C-2, 1B-1
1986	DET	A	19	.139	.167	36	5	1	0	0	0.0	2	3	3	4	0	4	2	25	2	1	2	1.5	.964	OF-11, DH-6, 1B-2, C-2
1987	OAK	A	11	.235	.294	17	4	1	0	0	0.0	1	3	0	4	0	4	1	0	0	0	0	0.0	–	DH-7, OF-1
1988	MIN	A	60	.295	.428	166	49	11	1	3	1.8	15	20	10	12	0	7	1	208	15	2	0	3.8	.991	C-48, DH-5, 3B-2
1989			126	.325	.449	385	125	24	0	8	2.1	43	57	13	16	2	7	1	462	36	11	7	4.0	.978	C-101, DH-19, OF-3, 3B-2, 1B-2
	10 yrs.		393	.282	.409	941	265	50	2	22	2.3	91	127	36	69	3	100	25	822	61	16	9	2.3	.982	C-155, OF-110, DH-39, 3B-10, 1B-6

LEAGUE CHAMPIONSHIP SERIES

| 1985 | STL | N | 1 | .000 | .000 | 1 | 0 | 0 | 0 | 0 | 0.0 | 0 | 0 | 0 | 0 | 0 | 1 | 0 | 0 | 0 | 0 | 0 | 0.0 | – | |

WORLD SERIES

| 1985 | STL | N | 4 | .250 | .250 | 4 | 1 | 0 | 0 | 0 | 0.0 | 0 | 1 | 0 | 1 | 0 | 4 | 1 | 0 | 0 | 0 | 0 | 0.0 | – | |

George Harper

HARPER, GEORGE WASHINGTON
B. June 24, 1892, Arlington, Ky.   D. Aug. 18, 1978, Magnolia, Ark.   BL TR 5'8'' 167 lbs.

1916	DET	A	44	.161	.179	56	9	1	0	0	0.0	4	3	5	8	0	24	4	15	3	2	1	0.5	.900	OF-14
1917			47	.205	.231	117	24	3	0	0	0.0	12	11	15	2	16	4	48	2	1	0	1.1	.980	OF-31
1918			69	.242	.282	227	55	5	2	0	0.0	19	16	18	14	3	3	0	125	5	6	2	2.0	.956	OF-64
1922	CIN	N	128	.340	.442	430	146	22	8	2	0.5	67	68	35	22	11	14	3	220	15	11	2	1.9	.955	OF-109
1923			61	.256	.392	125	32	4	2	3	2.4	14	16	11	9	0	28	7	56	3	2	1	1.0	.967	OF-29
1924	2 teams		CIN N (28G – .270)			PHI N (109G – .294)																			
"	total		137	.291	.474	485	141	29	6	16	3.3	75	58	51	28	11	2	270	16	4	4	2.1	.986	OF-131
1925	PHI	N	132	.349	.558	495	173	35	7	18	3.6	86	97	28	32	10	6	3	319	16	10	5	2.6	.971	OF-126
1926			56	.314	.505	194	61	6	5	7	3.6	32	38	16	7	6	1	1	111	2	7	1	2.1	.942	OF-55
1927	NY	N	145	.331	.495	483	160	19	6	16	3.3	85	87	84	27	7	3	1	299	13	8	5	2.2	.975	OF-142
1928	2 teams		NY N (19G – .228)			STL N (99G – .305)																			
"	total		118	.292	.505	329	96	9	2	19	5.8	52	65	61	19	3	13	4	196	17	4	3	1.8	.982	OF-103
1929	BOS	N	136	.291	.433	457	133	25	5	10	2.2	65	68	69	27	5	5	0	266	7	8	2	2.1	.972	OF-130
	11 yrs.		1073	.303	.455	3398	1030	158	43	91	2.7	505	528	389	208	58	115	27	1925	99	63	26	1.9	.970	OF-934

WORLD SERIES

| 1928 | STL | N | 3 | .111 | .111 | 9 | 1 | 0 | 0 | 0 | 0.0 | 1 | 0 | 2 | 2 | 0 | 0 | 0 | 5 | 0 | 0 | 0 | 1.7 | 1.000 | OF-3 |

Terry Harper

HARPER, TERRY JOE
B. Aug. 19, 1955, Douglasville, Ga.   BR TR 6'1'' 195 lbs.

1980	ATL	N	21	.185	.259	54	10	2	1	0	0.0	3	3	6	5	2	3	0	30	0	1	0	1.5	.968	OF-18
1981			40	.260	.356	73	19	1	0	2	2.7	9	8	11	17	5	15	3	38	2	1	1	1.0	.976	OF-27
1982			48	.287	.347	150	43	3	0	2	1.3	16	16	14	28	7	8	1	74	4	1	1	1.6	.987	OF-41
1983			80	.264	.383	201	53	13	0	3	1.5	19	26	20	42	6	18	3	95	5	5	0	1.3	.952	OF-60
1984			40	.157	.206	102	16	3	1	0	0.0	4	8	4	21	1	12	2	60	3	0	0	1.6	1.000	OF-29
1985			138	.264	.407	492	130	15	2	17	3.5	58	72	44	76	9	12	3	215	10	5	0	1.7	.978	OF-131
1986			106	.257	.392	265	68	12	0	8	3.0	26	30	29	39	3	32	6	92	5	3	0	0.9	.970	OF-83

Year	Team		Games	BA	SA	AB	H	2B	3B	HR	HR%	R	RBI	BB	SO	SB	Pinch Hit AB	Pinch Hit H	PO	A	E	DP	TC/G	FA	G by Pos

Terry Harper *continued*

Year	Team		Games	BA	SA	AB	H	2B	3B	HR	HR%	R	RBI	BB	SO	SB	PH AB	PH H	PO	A	E	DP	TC/G	FA	G by Pos
1987	2 teams	DET A (31G – .203)				PIT N (36G – .288)																			
"	total		67	.246	.385	130	32	6	0	4	3.1	12	17	16	19	1	23	2	45	0	1	0	0.7	.978	OF-34, DH-15
	8 yrs.		540	.253	.371	1467	371	55	5	36	2.5	147	180	144	248	37	123	20	649	29	17	2	1.3	.976	OF-423, DH-15

LEAGUE CHAMPIONSHIP SERIES

Year	Team		Games	BA	SA	AB	H	2B	3B	HR	HR%	R	RBI	BB	SO	SB	PH AB	PH H	PO	A	E	DP	TC/G	FA	G by Pos
1982	ATL	N	1	.000	.000	1	0	0	0	0	0.0	1	0	0	0	0	0	0	0	0	0	0	0.0	–	OF-1

Tommy Harper

HARPER, TOMMY
B. Oct. 14, 1940, Oak Grove, La.

BR TR 5'9" 165 lbs.

Year	Team		Games	BA	SA	AB	H	2B	3B	HR	HR%	R	RBI	BB	SO	SB	PH AB	PH H	PO	A	E	DP	TC/G	FA	G by Pos
1962	CIN	N	6	.174	.174	23	4	0	0	0	0.0	2	1	1	6	1	0	0	6	7	1	1	2.3	.929	3B-6
1963			129	.260	.377	408	106	12	3	10	2.5	67	37	44	72	12	6	2	224	7	1	1	1.8	.983	OF-118, 3B-1
1964			102	.243	.309	317	77	5	2	4	1.3	42	22	39	56	24	10	3	149	6	1	2	1.5	.994	OF-92, 3B-2
1965			159	.257	.393	646	166	28	3	18	2.8	126	64	78	127	35	0	0	279	10	5	0	1.8	.983	OF-159, 3B-2, 2B-1
1966			149	.278	.363	553	154	22	5	5	0.9	85	31	57	85	29	3	1	257	5	1	2	1.8	.996	OF-147
1967			103	.225	.345	365	82	17	3	7	1.9	55	22	43	51	23	1	0	208	6	1	0	2.1	.995	OF-100
1968	CLE	A	130	.217	.374	235	51	15	2	6	2.6	26	26	26	56	11	14	2	121	1	2	0	1.0	.984	OF-115, 2B-2
1969	SEA	A	148	.235	.311	537	126	10	2	9	1.7	78	41	95	90	73	5	1	232	268	22	42	3.5	.958	3B-59, 2B-59, OF-26
1970	MIL	A	154	.296	.522	604	179	35	4	31	5.1	104	82	77	107	38	2	1	192	330	28	33	3.6	.949	3B-128, 2B-22, OF-13
1971			152	.258	.385	585	151	26	3	14	2.4	79	52	65	92	25	4	1	227	118	18	11	2.4	.950	OF-90, 3B-70, 2B-1
1972	BOS	A	144	.254	.388	556	141	29	2	14	2.5	92	49	67	104	25	0	0	321	4	5	4	2.3	.985	OF-144
1973			147	.281	.422	566	159	23	3	17	3.0	92	71	61	93	54	0	0	251	4	5	4	2.3	.985	OF-143, DH-1
1974			118	.237	.318	443	105	15	3	5	1.1	66	24	46	65	28	5	4	105	2	2	0	0.9	.982	OF-61, DH-51
1975	2 teams	CAL A (89G – .239)				OAK N (34G – .319)																			
"	total		123	.254	.342	354	90	14	1	5	1.4	51	38	43	60	26	7	3	246	10	6	22	2.1	.977	DH-60, 1B-35, OF-18, 3B-2
1976	BAL	A	46	.234	.338	77	18	5	0	1	1.3	8	7	10	16	4	10	4	2	0	0	0	0.0	1.000	DH-27, OF-1, 1B-1
	15 yrs.		1810	.257	.379	6269	1609	256	36	146	2.3	972	567	753	1080	408	67	22	2820	787	100	120	2.0	.973	OF-1227, 3B-270, DH-139, 2B-85, 1B-36

LEAGUE CHAMPIONSHIP SERIES

Year	Team		Games	BA	SA	AB	H	2B	3B	HR	HR%	R	RBI	BB	SO	SB	PH AB	PH H	PO	A	E	DP	TC/G	FA	G by Pos
1975	OAK	A	1	–	–	0	0	0	0	0	–	0	0	1	0	0	0	0	0	0	0	0	0.0	–	

Toby Harrah

HARRAH, COLBERT DALE
B. Oct. 26, 1948, Sissonville, W. Va.

BR TR 6' 175 lbs.

Year	Team		Games	BA	SA	AB	H	2B	3B	HR	HR%	R	RBI	BB	SO	SB	PH AB	PH H	PO	A	E	DP	TC/G	FA	G by Pos
1969	WAS	A	8	.000	.000	1	0	0	0	0	0.0	4	0	0	0	0	0	0	0	0	0	0	–	–	SS-1
1971			127	.230	.290	383	88	11	3	2	0.5	45	22	40	48	10	4	1	187	321	24	70	4.2	.955	SS-116, 3B-7
1972	TEX	A	116	.259	.321	374	97	14	3	1	0.3	47	31	34	31	16	3	2	166	308	20	64	4.3	.960	SS-106
1973			118	.260	.364	461	120	16	1	10	2.2	64	50	46	49	10	1	0	155	332	27	45	4.4	.947	SS-76, 3B-52
1974			161	.260	.417	573	149	23	2	21	3.7	79	74	50	65	15	0	0	283	474	29	98	4.9	.963	SS-158, 3B-3
1975			151	.293	.458	522	153	24	1	20	3.8	81	93	98	71	23	0	0	253	481	29	82	5.1	.962	SS-118, 3B-28, 2B-21
1976			155	.260	.377	584	152	21	1	15	2.6	64	67	91	59	8	1	1	294	481	37	82	5.2	.954	SS-146, 3B-5, DH-4
1977			159	.263	.479	539	142	25	5	27	5.0	90	87	109	73	27	0	0	108	278	15	20	2.5	.963	3B-159, SS-1
1978			139	.229	.360	450	103	17	3	12	2.7	56	59	83	66	31	2	2	129	330	11	40	3.4	.977	3B-91, SS-49
1979	CLE	A	149	.279	.444	527	147	25	1	20	3.8	99	77	89	60	20	1	0	113	215	19	30	2.3	.945	3B-127, SS-33, DH-9
1980			160	.267	.380	561	150	22	4	11	2.0	100	72	98	60	17	1	0	121	319	13	28	2.8	.971	3B-156, DH-3, SS-2
1981			103	.291	.388	361	105	12	4	5	1.4	64	44	57	44	12	1	1	64	180	13	12	2.5	.949	3B-101, SS-3, DH-1
1982			162	.304	.490	602	183	29	4	25	4.2	100	78	84	52	17	1	0	126	279	12	25	2.6	.971	3B-159, 2B-3, SS-2
1983			138	.266	.365	526	140	23	1	9	1.7	81	53	75	49	16	0	0	101	273	11	32	2.8	.971	3B-137, DH-1, 2B-1
1984	NY	A	88	.217	.296	253	55	9	4	1	0.4	40	27	42	28	3	11	2	52	132	6	17	2.2	.968	3B-74, 2B-4, OF-1
1985	TEX	A	126	.270	.389	396	107	18	1	9	2.3	65	44	113	60	11	4	3	212	351	6	71	4.5	.989	2B-122, SS-2, DH-1
1986			95	.218	.367	289	63	18	2	7	2.4	36	41	44	53	2	4	0	166	211	7	49	4.0	.982	2B-93
	17 yrs.		2155	.264	.395	7402	1954	307	40	195	2.6	1115	919	1153	868	238	35	12	2530	4965	279	765	3.6	.964	3B-1099, SS-813, 2B-244, DH-19, OF-1

Billy Harrell

HARRELL, WILLIAM
B. July 18, 1928, Norristown, Pa.

BR TR 6'1½" 180 lbs.

Year	Team		Games	BA	SA	AB	H	2B	3B	HR	HR%	R	RBI	BB	SO	SB	PH AB	PH H	PO	A	E	DP	TC/G	FA	G by Pos
1955	CLE	A	13	.421	.421	19	8	0	0	0	0.0	2	1	3	3	1	1	0	7	18	2	1	2.1	.926	SS-11
1957			22	.263	.368	57	15	1	1	1	1.8	5	4	7	7	3	3	1	21	40	6	6	3.0	.910	SS-14, 3B-6, 2B-1
1958			101	.218	.328	229	50	4	0	7	3.1	36	19	15	36	12	9	1	81	159	9	32	2.5	.964	3B-46, SS-45, 2B-7, OF-1
1961	BOS	A	37	.162	.216	37	6	2	0	0	0.0	10	1	1	8	1	6	0	26	23	2	6	1.4	.961	3B-10, SS-7, 1B-2
	4 yrs.		173	.231	.327	342	79	7	1	8	2.3	54	26	23	54	17	19	2	135	240	19	45	2.3	.952	SS-77, 3B-62, 2B-8, 1B-2, OF-1

John Harrell

HARRELL, JOHN ROBERT
B. Nov. 27, 1947, Long Beach, Calif.

BR TR 6'2" 190 lbs.

Year	Team		Games	BA	SA	AB	H	2B	3B	HR	HR%	R	RBI	BB	SO	SB	PH AB	PH H	PO	A	E	DP	TC/G	FA	G by Pos
1969	SF	N	2	.500	.500	6	3	0	0	0	0.0	0	2	2	1	0	0	0	10	1	0	1	5.5	1.000	C-2

Bud Harrelson

HARRELSON, DERREL McKINLEY
B. June 6, 1944, Niles, Calif.

BB TR 5'11" 160 lbs.
BR 1965

Year	Team		Games	BA	SA	AB	H	2B	3B	HR	HR%	R	RBI	BB	SO	SB	PH AB	PH H	PO	A	E	DP	TC/G	FA	G by Pos
1965	NY	N	19	.108	.189	37	4	1	1	0	0.0	3	0	2	11	0	0	0	28	36	3	6	3.5	.955	SS-18
1966			33	.222	.323	99	22	2	2	0	0.0	20	4	13	23	7	2	1	52	91	1	26	4.4	.993	SS-29
1967			151	.254	.304	540	137	16	4	1	0.2	59	28	48	64	12	0	0	254	467	32	88	5.0	.958	SS-149
1968			111	.219	.251	402	88	7	3	0	0.0	38	14	29	68	4	6	0	199	317	15	58	4.8	.972	SS-106
1969			123	.248	.306	395	98	11	6	0	0.0	42	24	54	54	1	0	0	243	347	19	70	5.0	.969	SS-119
1970			157	.243	.309	564	137	18	8	1	0.2	72	42	95	74	23	2	0	305	401	21	84	4.6	.971	SS-156
1971			142	.252	.303	547	138	16	6	0	0.0	55	32	53	59	28	0	0	257	441	16	86	5.0	.978	SS-140
1972			115	.215	.266	418	90	10	4	0	0.0	54	24	58	57	12	0	0	191	334	16	51	4.7	.970	SS-115
1973			106	.258	.309	356	92	12	3	0	0.0	35	20	48	49	5	0	0	153	315	10	49	4.5	.979	SS-103
1974			106	.227	.266	331	75	10	0	1	0.3	48	13	71	39	9	2	0	196	325	17	65	5.1	.968	SS-97
1975			34	.219	.247	73	16	2	0	0	0.0	5	3	12	13	0	2	1	44	67	7	18	3.5	.941	SS-34
1976			118	.234	.298	359	84	12	4	1	0.3	34	26	63	56	9	1	0	183	330	20	44	4.5	.962	SS-117
1977			107	.178	.227	269	48	6	2	1	0.4	25	12	27	28	5	1	0	141	239	6	41	3.6	.984	SS-98

Year	Team	Games	BA	SA	AB	H	2B	3B	HR	HR%	R	RBI	BB	SO	SB	Pinch Hit AB	H	PO	A	E	DP	TC/G	FA	G by Pos

Bud Harrelson *continued*

Year	Team	Games	BA	SA	AB	H	2B	3B	HR	HR%	R	RBI	BB	SO	SB	AB	H	PO	A	E	DP	TC/G	FA	G by Pos
1978	PHI N	71	.214	.223	103	22	1	0	0	0.0	16	9	18	21	5	7	0	72	109	4	31	2.6	.978	2B-43, SS-15
1979		53	.282	.366	71	20	6	0	0	0.0	7	7	13	14	3	0	0	63	71	4	13	2.6	.971	2B-25, SS-17, 3B-9, OF-1
1980	TEX A	87	.272	.322	180	49	6	0	1	0.6	26	9	29	23	4	0	0	121	222	18	58	4.1	.950	SS-87, 2B-2
16 yrs.		1533	.236	.288	4744	1120	136	45	7	0.1	539	267	633	653	127	22	2	2502	4112	209	788	4.5	.969	SS-1400, 2B-70, 3B-9, OF-1

LEAGUE CHAMPIONSHIP SERIES

Year	Team	Games	BA	SA	AB	H	2B	3B	HR	HR%	R	RBI	BB	SO	SB	AB	H	PO	A	E	DP	TC/G	FA	G by Pos
1969	NY N	3	.182	.455	11	2	1	1	0	0.0	2	3	1	2	0	0	0	6	6	1	2	4.3	.923	SS-3
1973		5	.167	.167	18	3	0	0	0	0.0	1	2	1	1	0	0	0	12	14	0	3	5.2	1.000	SS-5
2 yrs.		8	.172	.276	29	5	1	1	0	0.0	3	5	2	3	0	0	0	18	20	1	5	4.9	.974	SS-8

WORLD SERIES

Year	Team	Games	BA	SA	AB	H	2B	3B	HR	HR%	R	RBI	BB	SO	SB	AB	H	PO	A	E	DP	TC/G	FA	G by Pos
1969	NY N	5	.176	.176	17	3	0	0	0	0.0	1	0	3	4	0	0	0	12	17	0	0	5.8	1.000	SS-5
1973		7	.250	.292	24	6	1	0	0	0.0	2	1	5	3	0	0	0	11	24	0	1	5.0	1.000	SS-7
2 yrs.		12	.220	.244	41	9	1	0	0	0.0	3	1	8	7	0	0	0	23	41	0	1	5.3	1.000	SS-12

Ken Harrelson

HARRELSON, KENNETH SMITH (Hawk)
B. Sept. 4, 1941, Woodruff, S. C.   BR TR 6'2" 190 lbs.

Year	Team	Games	BA	SA	AB	H	2B	3B	HR	HR%	R	RBI	BB	SO	SB	AB	H	PO	A	E	DP	TC/G	FA	G by Pos
1963	KC A	79	.230	.363	226	52	10	1	6	2.7	16	23	23	58	1	17	5	326	17	7	24	4.4	.980	1B-34, OF-28
1964		49	.194	.381	139	27	5	0	7	5.0	15	12	13	34	0	12	4	145	15	1	14	3.3	.994	OF-24, 1B-15
1965		150	.238	.429	483	115	17	3	23	4.8	61	66	66	112	9	21	5	1049	71	10	93	7.5	.991	1B-125, OF-4
1966 2 teams	KC A (63G – .224)				WAS A	(71G – .248)																		
" total		134	.237	.348	460	109	13	1	12	2.6	49	50	53	112	13	4	1	1129	86	14	95	9.2	.989	1B-128, OF-3
1967 3 teams	WAS A (26G – .203)				KC A	(61G – .305)			BOS A	(23G – .200)														
" total		110	.255	.414	333	85	15	1	12	3.6	42	54	29	44	10	24	5	553	41	4	38	5.4	.993	1B-69, OF-23
1968	BOS A	150	.275	.518	535	147	17	4	35	6.5	79	109	69	90	2	2	1	376	17	3	10	2.6	.992	OF-132, 1B-19
1969 2 teams	BOS A (10G – .217)				CLE A	(149G – .222)																		
" total		159	.221	.419	565	125	14	4	30	5.3	89	92	99	102	17	2	0	402	22	5	23	2.7	.988	OF-144, 1B-26
1970	CLE A	17	.282	.385	39	11	1	0	1	2.6	3	1	6	4	0	4	1	80	7	0	5	5.1	1.000	1B-13
1971		52	.199	.304	161	32	2	0	5	3.1	20	14	24	21	1	5	2	320	23	4	29	6.7	.988	1B-40, OF-7
9 yrs.		900	.239	.414	2941	703	94	14	131	4.5	374	421	382	577	53	91	24	4380	299	48	341	5.3	.990	1B-469, OF-365

WORLD SERIES

Year	Team	Games	BA	SA	AB	H	2B	3B	HR	HR%	R	RBI	BB	SO	SB	AB	H	PO	A	E	DP	TC/G	FA	G by Pos
1967	BOS A	4	.077	.077	13	1	0	0	0	0.0	0	1	1	3	0	0	0	5	0	0	0	1.3	1.000	OF-4

Andy Harrington

HARRINGTON, ANDREW MATTHEW
B. Feb. 12, 1903, Mountain View, Calif. D. Jan. 29, 1979, Boise, Ida.   BR TR 5'11" 170 lbs.

Year	Team	Games	BA	SA	AB	H	2B	3B	HR	HR%	R	RBI	BB	SO	SB	AB	H	PO	A	E	DP	TC/G	FA	G by Pos
1925	DET A	1	.000	.000	1	0	0	0	0	0.0	0	0	0	1	0	1	0	0	0	0	0	0.0	–	

Jerry Harrington

HARRINGTON, JEREMIAH PETER
B. Aug. 12, 1869, Keokuk, Iowa D. Apr. 16, 1913, Keokuk, Iowa   BR TR 5'11" 220 lbs.

Year	Team	Games	BA	SA	AB	H	2B	3B	HR	HR%	R	RBI	BB	SO	SB	AB	H	PO	A	E	DP	TC/G	FA	G by Pos
1890	CIN N	65	.246	.297	236	58	7	1	1	0.4	25	23	15	29	4	0	0	345	73	19	3	6.7	.957	C-65
1891		92	.228	.306	333	76	10	5	2	0.6	25	41	19	34	4	0	0	388	106	50	6	5.9	.908	C-92, 3B-1
1892		22	.213	.230	61	13	1	0	0	0.0	6	3	6	1	0	0	0	76	22	2	0	4.5	.980	C-22, 1B-1
1893	LOU N	10	.111	.139	36	4	1	0	0	0.0	4	6	3	9	0	0	0	23	6	5	1	3.4	.853	C-10
4 yrs.		189	.227	.287	666	151	19	6	3	0.5	60	73	43	73	8	0	0	832	207	76	10	5.9	.932	C-189, 3B-1, 1B-1

Joe Harrington

HARRINGTON, JOSEPH C.
B. Dec. 21, 1869, Fall River, Mass. D. Sept. 13, 1933, Fall River, Mass.   5'8½" 162 lbs.

Year	Team	Games	BA	SA	AB	H	2B	3B	HR	HR%	R	RBI	BB	SO	SB	AB	H	PO	A	E	DP	TC/G	FA	G by Pos
1895	BOS N	18	.277	.431	65	18	0	2	2	3.1	21	13	7	5	3	0	0	47	57	10	7	6.3	.912	2B-18
1896		54	.197	.268	198	39	5	3	1	0.5	25	25	19	17	2	0	0	62	110	42	8	4.0	.804	3B-49, SS-4, 2B-1
2 yrs.		72	.217	.308	263	57	5	5	3	1.1	46	38	26	22	5	0	0	109	167	52	15	4.6	.841	3B-49, 2B-19, SS-4

Mike Harrington

HARRINGTON, CHARLES MICHAEL
B. Oct. 8, 1934, Hattiesburg, Miss.   BR TR 6'4" 205 lbs.

Year	Team	Games	BA	SA	AB	H	2B	3B	HR	HR%	R	RBI	BB	SO	SB	AB	H	PO	A	E	DP	TC/G	FA	G by Pos
1963	PHI N	1	–	–	0	0	0	0	0	–	0	0	0	0	0	0	0	0	0	0	0	0.0	–	

Alonzo Harris

HARRIS, ALONZO (Candy)
B. Sept. 17, 1947, Selma, Ala.   BB TR 6' 160 lbs.

Year	Team	Games	BA	SA	AB	H	2B	3B	HR	HR%	R	RBI	BB	SO	SB	AB	H	PO	A	E	DP	TC/G	FA	G by Pos
1967	HOU N	6	.000	.000	1	0	0	0	0	0.0	0	0	0	1	0	0	0	0	0	0	0	0.0	–	

Billy Harris

HARRIS, JAMES WILLIAM
B. Nov. 24, 1943, Hamlet, N. C.   BL TR 6' 175 lbs.

Year	Team	Games	BA	SA	AB	H	2B	3B	HR	HR%	R	RBI	BB	SO	SB	AB	H	PO	A	E	DP	TC/G	FA	G by Pos
1968	CLE A	38	.213	.287	94	20	5	1	0	0.0	10	3	8	22	2	5	1	40	71	4	11	3.0	.965	2B-27, 3B-10, SS-1
1969	KC A	5	.286	.429	7	2	1	0	0	0.0	1	0	0	1	0	4	1	1	2	0	0	0.6	1.000	2B-1
2 yrs.		43	.218	.297	101	22	6	1	0	0.0	11	3	8	23	2	9	2	41	73	4	11	2.7	.966	2B-28, 3B-10, SS-1

Bob Harris

HARRIS, ROBERT NED
B. July 9, 1916, Ames, Iowa D. Dec. 18, 1976, West Palm Beach, Fla.   BL TL 5'11" 175 lbs.

Year	Team	Games	BA	SA	AB	H	2B	3B	HR	HR%	R	RBI	BB	SO	SB	AB	H	PO	A	E	DP	TC/G	FA	G by Pos
1941	DET A	26	.213	.344	61	13	3	1	1	1.6	11	4	6	13	1	11	1	16	0	0	0	0.6	1.000	OF-12
1942		121	.271	.430	398	108	16	10	9	2.3	53	45	49	35	5	15	6	164	5	10	2	1.5	.944	OF-104
1943		114	.254	.362	354	90	14	3	6	1.7	43	32	47	29	6	18	5	192	6	8	2	1.8	.961	OF-96
1946		1	.000	.000	1	0	0	0	0	0.0	0	0	0	0	0	1	0	0	0	0	0	0.0	–	
4 yrs.		262	.259	.393	814	211	33	14	16	2.0	107	81	102	77	12	45	12	372	11	18	4	1.5	.955	OF-212

Bucky Harris

HARRIS, STANLEY RAYMOND
B. Nov. 8, 1896, Port Jervis, N. Y. D. Nov. 8, 1977, Bethesda, Md.
Manager 1924-43, 1947-48, 1950-56.
Hall of Fame 1975.   BR TR 5'9½" 156 lbs.

Year	Team	Games	BA	SA	AB	H	2B	3B	HR	HR%	R	RBI	BB	SO	SB	AB	H	PO	A	E	DP	TC/G	FA	G by Pos
1919	WAS A	8	.214	.286	28	6	2	0	0	0.0	0	4	1	3	0	0	0	21	28	4	4	6.6	.925	2B-8
1920		137	.300	.381	506	152	26	6	1	0.2	76	68	41	36	16	1	1	345	401	33	59	5.7	.958	2B-135

Year	Team	Games	BA	SA	AB	H	2B	3B	HR	HR%	R	RBI	BB	SO	SB	Pinch Hit AB	Pinch Hit H	PO	A	E	DP	TC/G	FA	G by Pos

Bucky Harris *continued*

Year	Team	Games	BA	SA	AB	H	2B	3B	HR	HR%	R	RBI	BB	SO	SB	PH AB	PH H	PO	A	E	DP	TC/G	FA	G by Pos
1921		154	.289	.354	584	169	22	8	0	0.0	82	54	54	39	29	0	0	407	481	38	91	6.0	.959	2B-154
1922		154	.269	.346	602	162	24	8	2	0.3	95	40	52	38	25	0	0	479	483	30	116	6.4	.970	2B-154
1923		145	.282	.382	532	150	21	13	2	0.4	60	70	50	29	23	0	0	418	451	36	120	6.2	.960	2B-144, SS-1
1924		143	.268	.358	544	146	28	9	1	0.2	88	58	56	41	19	0	0	393	386	26	100	5.6	.968	2B-143
1925		144	.287	.358	551	158	30	3	1	0.2	91	66	64	21	14	0	0	402	429	26	107	6.0	.970	2B-144
1926		141	.283	.395	537	152	39	9	1	0.2	94	63	58	41	16	0	0	356	427	30	74	5.8	.963	2B-141
1927		128	.267	.328	475	127	20	3	1	0.2	98	55	66	33	18	0	0	316	413	21	68	5.9	.972	2B-128
1928		99	.204	.263	358	73	11	5	0	0.0	34	28	27	26	5	0	0	254	326	18	61	6.0	.970	2B-96, OF-1, 3B-1
1929	DET A	7	.091	.091	11	1	0	0	0	0.0	3	0	2	2	1	0	0	5	13	2	0	2.9	.900	2B-4, SS-1
1931		4	.125	.250	8	1	1	0	0	0.0	1	0	1	1	0	0	0	5	6	0	1	2.8	1.000	2B-3
12 yrs.		1264	.274	.354	4736	1297	224	64	9	0.2	722	506	472	310	166	1	1	3401	3844	264	801	5.9	.965	2B-1254, SS-2, OF-1, 3B-1

WORLD SERIES

Year	Team	Games	BA	SA	AB	H	2B	3B	HR	HR%	R	RBI	BB	SO	SB	PH AB	PH H	PO	A	E	DP	TC/G	FA	G by Pos
1924	WAS A	7	.333	.515	33	11	0	0	2	6.1	5	7	1	4	0	0	0	26	28	2	8	8.0	.964	2B-7
1925		7	.087	.087	23	2	0	0	0	0.0	2	0	1	3	0	0	0	24	18	0	5	6.0	1.000	2B-7
2 yrs.		14	.232	.339	56	13	0	0	2	3.6	7	7	2	7	0	0	0	50	46	2	13	7.0	.980	2B-14

Charlie Harris

HARRIS, CHARLES JENKINS
B. Oct. 21, 1877, Macon, Ga. D. Mar. 14, 1963, Gainesville, Fla.

BR TR 5'8" 200 lbs.

Year	Team	Games	BA	SA	AB	H	2B	3B	HR	HR%	R	RBI	BB	SO	SB	PH AB	PH H	PO	A	E	DP	TC/G	FA	G by Pos
1899	BAL N	30	.279	.324	68	19	3	0	0	0.0	16		3			4	1	20	31	6	2	1.9	.895	3B-21, OF-3, 2B-2, SS-1

Dave Harris

HARRIS, DAVID STANLEY (Sheriff)
B. July 14, 1900, Summerfield, N. C. D. Sept. 18, 1973, Atlanta, Ga.

BR TR 5'11" 195 lbs.

Year	Team	Games	BA	SA	AB	H	2B	3B	HR	HR%	R	RBI	BB	SO	SB	PH AB	PH H	PO	A	E	DP	TC/G	FA	G by Pos
1925	BOS N	92	.265	.374	340	90	8	7	5	1.5	49	36	27	44	6	1	0	217	12	9	3	2.6	.962	OF-90
1928		7	.118	.176	17	2	1	0	0	0.0	2	0	2	6	0	1	0	10	0	2	0	1.7	.833	OF-6
1930	2 teams	CHI A	(33G – .244)		WAS A	(73G – .317)																		
"	total	106	.296	.522	291	86	21	9	9	3.1	56	57	35	57	6	21	9	152	9	2	3	1.5	.988	OF-82, 2B-1
1931	WAS A	77	.312	.506	231	72	14	8	5	2.2	49	50	49	38	7	13	5	111	9	4	1	1.6	.950	OF-60
1932		81	.327	.538	156	51	7	4	6	3.8	26	29	19	34	4	43	14	66	3	5	0	0.9	.932	OF-34
1933		82	.260	.418	177	46	9	2	5	2.8	33	38	25	26	3	24	8	101	5	3	1	1.3	.972	OF-45, 1B-6, 3B-2
1934		97	.251	.362	235	59	14	3	2	0.9	28	37	39	40	2	26	4	111	16	4	2	1.4	.969	OF-64, 3B-5
7 yrs.		542	.281	.444	1447	406	74	33	32	2.2	243	247	196	245	28	129	40	768	46	31	10	1.6	.963	OF-381, 3B-7, 1B-6, 2B-1

WORLD SERIES

Year	Team	Games	BA	SA	AB	H	2B	3B	HR	HR%	R	RBI	BB	SO	SB	PH AB	PH H	PO	A	E	DP	TC/G	FA	G by Pos
1933	WAS A	3	.000	.000	2	0	0	0	0	0.0	0	0	2	0	0	1	0	2	0	0	0	0.7	1.000	OF-1

Frank Harris

HARRIS, FRANK WALTER
B. Nov. 2, 1858, Pittsburgh, Pa. D. Nov. 26, 1939, East Moline, Ill.

BR TR

Year	Team	Games	BA	SA	AB	H	2B	3B	HR	HR%	R	RBI	BB	SO	SB	PH AB	PH H	PO	A	E	DP	TC/G	FA	G by Pos
1884	ALT U	24	.263	.305	95	25	2	1	0	0.0	10		3			0	0	179	8	11	1	8.3	.944	1B-17, OF-8

Gail Harris

HARRIS, BOYD GAIL
B. Oct. 15, 1931, Abingdon, Va.

BL TL 6' 195 lbs.

Year	Team	Games	BA	SA	AB	H	2B	3B	HR	HR%	R	RBI	BB	SO	SB	PH AB	PH H	PO	A	E	DP	TC/G	FA	G by Pos
1955	NY N	79	.232	.403	263	61	9	0	12	4.6	27	36	20	46	0	4	2	617	50	12	65	8.6	.982	1B-75
1956		12	.132	.263	38	5	0	1	2	2.6	2	3	3	10	0	1	0	108	9	3	12	10.0	.975	1B-11
1957		90	.240	.418	225	54	7	3	9	4.0	28	31	16	28	1	25	2	502	37	8	53	6.1	.985	1B-61
1958	DET A	134	.273	.481	451	123	18	8	20	4.4	63	83	36	60	1	14	5	942	79	15	90	7.7	.986	1B-122
1959		114	.221	.327	349	77	4	3	9	2.6	39	39	29	49	0	22	4	728	57	6	59	6.9	.992	1B-93
1960		8	.000	.000	5	0	0	0	0	0.0	0	0	2	1	0	3	0	8	1	0	1	1.1	1.000	1B-5
6 yrs.		437	.240	.406	1331	320	38	15	51	3.8	159	190	106	194	2	69	13	2905	233	44	280	7.3	.986	1B-367

Joe Harris

HARRIS, JOSEPH (Moon)
B. May 20, 1891, Coulters, Pa. D. Dec. 10, 1959, Renton, Pa.

BR TR 5'9" 170 lbs.

Year	Team	Games	BA	SA	AB	H	2B	3B	HR	HR%	R	RBI	BB	SO	SB	PH AB	PH H	PO	A	E	DP	TC/G	FA	G by Pos
1914	NY A	2	.000	.000	1	0	0	0	0	0.0	0	0	3	1	0	0	0	11	0	0	0	5.5	1.000	OF-1, 1B-1
1917	CLE A	112	.304	.385	369	112	22	4	0	0.0	40	45	55	32	11	8	0	1029	89	18	58	10.1	.984	1B-95, OF-5, 3B-1
1919		62	.375	.489	184	69	16	1	1	0.5	30	46	33	21	2	12	4	458	44	6	23	8.2	.988	1B-46, OF-5
1922	BOS A	119	.316	.478	408	129	30	9	6	1.5	53	54	30	15	2	15	4	359	29	13	14	3.4	.968	OF-83, 1B-21
1923		142	.335	.520	483	162	28	11	13	2.7	82	76	52	27	7	4	1	357	16	12	5	2.7	.969	OF-132, 1B-9
1924		134	.301	.430	491	148	36	4	3	0.6	82	77	81	25	6	10	0	1275	101	10	100	10.3	.993	1B-127, OF-3
1925	2 teams	BOS A	(8G – .158)		WAS A	(100G – .323)																		
"	total	108	.313	.564	319	100	21	10	13	4.1	64	61	56	33	5	10	1	506	42	6	42	5.1	.989	1B-63, OF-41
1926	WAS A	92	.307	.486	257	79	13	9	5	1.9	43	55	37	9	2	18	4	354	20	3	20	4.1	.992	1B-36, OF-35
1927	PIT N	129	.326	.472	411	134	27	9	5	1.2	57	73	48	19	0	10	2	1057	78	11	84	8.9	.990	1B-116, OF-3
1928	2 teams	PIT N	(16G – .391)		BKN N	(55G – .236)																		
"	total	71	.268	.402	112	30	8	2	1	0.9	10	10	18	6	0	42	9	57	7	1	8	0.9	.985	OF-16, 1B-6
10 yrs.		971	.317	.472	3035	963	201	64	47	1.5	461	517	413	188	35	121	25	5463	426	80	354	6.1	.987	1B-520, OF-319, SS-4, 3B-1

WORLD SERIES

Year	Team	Games	BA	SA	AB	H	2B	3B	HR	HR%	R	RBI	BB	SO	SB	PH AB	PH H	PO	A	E	DP	TC/G	FA	G by Pos
1925	WAS A	7	.440	.880	25	11	2	0	3	12.0	5	6	3	4	0	0	0	9	1	0	0	1.4	1.000	OF-7
1927	PIT N	4	.200	.200	15	3	0	0	0	0.0	0	1	0	0	0	0	0	35	2	0	2	9.3	1.000	1B-4
2 yrs.		11	.350	.625	40	14	2	0	3	7.5	5	7	3	4	0	0	0	44	3	0	2	4.3	1.000	OF-7, 1B-4

John Harris

HARRIS, JOHN THOMAS, JR.
B. Sept. 13, 1954, Portland, Ore.

BL TL 6'3" 205 lbs.

Year	Team	Games	BA	SA	AB	H	2B	3B	HR	HR%	R	RBI	BB	SO	SB	PH AB	PH H	PO	A	E	DP	TC/G	FA	G by Pos
1979	CAL A	1	.000	.000	2	0	0	0	0	0.0	0	0	0	0	0	0	0	6	0	0	0	6.0	1.000	1B-1
1980		19	.293	.561	41	12	5	0	2	4.9	8	7	7	4	0	7	1	63	3	0	4	3.5	1.000	1B-10, OF-3
1981		36	.247	.403	77	19	3	0	3	3.9	5	9	3	11	0	19	3	85	5	2	9	2.6	.978	1B-11, OF-10, DH-1
3 yrs.		56	.258	.450	120	31	8	0	5	4.2	13	16	10	15	0	26	4	154	8	2	13	2.9	.988	1B-22, OF-13, DH-1

Lenny Harris

HARRIS, LEONARD ANTHONY
B. Oct. 28, 1964, Miami, Fla.

BL TR 5'10" 195 lbs.

Year	Team	Games	BA	SA	AB	H	2B	3B	HR	HR%	R	RBI	BB	SO	SB	PH AB	PH H	PO	A	E	DP	TC/G	FA	G by Pos
1988	CIN N	16	.372	.395	43	16	1	0	0	0.0	7	8	5	4	4	0	0	14	33	1	2	3.0	.979	3B-10, 2B-6

Year	Team	Games	BA	SA	AB	H	2B	3B	HR	HR%	R	RBI	BB	SO	SB	Pinch Hit AB	H	PO	A	E	DP	TC/G	FA	G by Pos

Lenny Harris *continued*

Year	Team	Games	BA	SA	AB	H	2B	3B	HR	HR%	R	RBI	BB	SO	SB	AB	H	PO	A	E	DP	TC/G	FA	G by Pos
1989	2 teams	CIN	N	(61G – .223)		LA	N	(54G – .252)																
"	total	115	.236	.299	335	79	10	1	3	0.9	36	26	20	33	14	20	8	147	168	15	32	2.9	.955	2B-46, 3B-24, OF-21, SS-18
	2 yrs.	131	.251	.310	378	95	11	1	3	0.8	43	34	25	37	18	20	8	161	201	16	34	2.9	.958	2B-52, 3B-34, OF-21, SS-18

Spence Harris

HARRIS, ANTHONY SPENCER BL TL 5'9" 145 lbs.
B. Aug. 12, 1900, Duluth, Minn. D. July 3, 1982, Minneapolis, Minn.

Year	Team	Games	BA	SA	AB	H	2B	3B	HR	HR%	R	RBI	BB	SO	SB	AB	H	PO	A	E	DP	TC/G	FA	G by Pos
1925	CHI A	56	.283	.337	92	26	2	0	1	1.1	12	13	14	13	1	24	7	42	3	2	0	0.8	.957	OF-27
1926		80	.252	.356	222	56	11	3	2	0.9	36	27	20	15	8	14	2	106	6	6	2	1.5	.949	OF-63
1929	WAS A	6	.214	.286	14	3	1	0	0	0.0	1	1	0	3	1	0	0	7	0	0	0	1.2	1.000	OF-4
1930	PHI A	22	.184	.204	49	9	1	0	0	0.0	4	5	5	2	0	7	1	21	2	1	1	1.1	.958	OF-13
	4 yrs.	164	.249	.329	377	94	15	3	3	0.8	53	46	39	33	10	45	10	176	11	9	3	1.2	.954	OF-107

Vic Harris

HARRIS, VICTOR LANIER BB TR 5'11" 165 lbs.
B. Mar. 27, 1950, Los Angeles, Calif.

Year	Team	Games	BA	SA	AB	H	2B	3B	HR	HR%	R	RBI	BB	SO	SB	AB	H	PO	A	E	DP	TC/G	FA	G by Pos
1972	TEX A	61	.140	.177	186	26	5	1	0	0.0	8	10	12	39	7	4	0	113	135	10	30	4.2	.961	2B-58, SS-1
1973		152	.249	.342	555	138	14	7	8	1.4	71	44	55	81	13	1	0	354	79	21	16	3.0	.954	OF-113, 3B-25, 2B-18
1974	CHI N	62	.195	.255	200	39	6	3	0	0.0	18	11	29	26	9	4	0	122	144	16	20	4.5	.943	2B-56
1975		51	.179	.179	56	10	0	0	0	0.0	6	5	6	7	0	24	4	15	14	2	2	0.6	.935	OF-11, 3B-7, 2B-5
1976	STL N	97	.228	.309	259	59	12	3	1	0.4	21	19	16	55	1	23	4	173	103	14	21	3.0	.954	2B-37, OF-35, 3B-12, SS-1
1977	SF N	69	.261	.370	165	43	12	0	2	1.2	28	14	19	36	2	25	3	69	96	8	21	2.5	.954	2B-27, SS-11, 3B-9, OF-3
1978		53	.150	.220	100	15	4	0	1	1.0	8	11	11	24	0	16	1	40	58	5	8	1.9	.951	SS-22, 2B-10, OF-6
1980	MIL A	34	.213	.315	89	19	4	1	1	1.1	8	7	12	13	4	1	0	59	4	2	1	1.9	.969	OF-31, 3B-2, 2B-1
	8 yrs.	579	.217	.295	1610	349	57	15	13	0.8	168	121	160	281	36	98	12	945	633	78	119	2.9	.953	2B-212, OF-199, 3B-55, SS-35

Ben Harrison

HARRISON, LEO J. BR
B. Unknown. Deceased.

Year	Team	Games	BA	SA	AB	H	2B	3B	HR	HR%	R	RBI	BB	SO	SB	AB	H	PO	A	E	DP	TC/G	FA	G by Pos
1901	WAS A	1	.000	.000	2	0	0	0	0	0.0	0	0	1		0	0	0	0	0	0	0	0.0	–	OF-1

Chuck Harrison

HARRISON, CHARLES WILLIAM BR TR 5'10" 185 lbs.
B. Apr. 25, 1941, Abilene, Tex.

Year	Team	Games	BA	SA	AB	H	2B	3B	HR	HR%	R	RBI	BB	SO	SB	AB	H	PO	A	E	DP	TC/G	FA	G by Pos
1965	HOU N	15	.200	.356	45	9	4	0	1	2.2	9	8	9	9	0	2	0	107	8	2	9	7.8	.983	1B-12
1966		119	.256	.380	434	111	23	2	9	2.1	52	52	37	69	2	5	0	974	78	8	68	8.9	.992	1B-114
1967		70	.243	.350	177	43	7	3	2	1.1	13	26	13	30	0	11	4	438	27	6	24	6.7	.987	1B-59
1969	KC A	75	.221	.296	213	47	5	1	3	1.4	18	18	16	20	1	20	4	415	36	3	27	6.1	.993	1B-55
1971		49	.217	.287	143	31	4	0	2	1.4	9	21	11	19	0	11	1	335	24	3	31	7.4	.992	1B-39
	5 yrs.	328	.238	.343	1012	241	43	6	17	1.7	94	126	85	147	3	49	9	2269	173	22	159	7.5	.991	1B-279

Tom Harrison

HARRISON, THOMAS JAMES BR TR 6'3" 200 lbs.
B. Jan. 18, 1945, Trail, B. C., Canada

Year	Team	Games	BA	SA	AB	H	2B	3B	HR	HR%	R	RBI	BB	SO	SB	AB	H	PO	A	E	DP	TC/G	FA	G by Pos
1965	KC A	2	–	–	0	0	0	0	0	0	0	0	0	0	0	0	0	0	0	0	0	0.0	–	P-1

Sam Harshaney

HARSHANEY, SAMUEL BR TR 6' 180 lbs.
B. May 1, 1910, Madison, Ill.

Year	Team	Games	BA	SA	AB	H	2B	3B	HR	HR%	R	RBI	BB	SO	SB	AB	H	PO	A	E	DP	TC/G	FA	G by Pos
1937	STL A	5	.091	.182	11	1	1	0	0	0.0	0	3	0	0	0	0	0	15	4	2	0	4.2	.905	C-4
1938		11	.292	.292	24	7	0	0	0	0.0	2	0	3	2	0	1	1	35	4	1	0	3.6	.975	C-10
1939		42	.241	.255	145	35	2	0	0	0.0	15	15	9	8	0	6	3	153	23	1	3	4.2	.994	C-36
1940		3	.000	.000	1	0	0	0	0	0.0	0	0	1	0	0	1	0	0	0	0	0	0.0	–	C-2
	4 yrs.	61	.238	.254	181	43	3	0	0	0.0	17	15	16	10	0	8	4	203	31	4	3	3.9	.983	C-52

Jack Harshman

HARSHMAN, JOHN ELVIN BL TL 6'2" 178 lbs.
B. July 12, 1927, San Diego, Calif.

Year	Team	Games	BA	SA	AB	H	2B	3B	HR	HR%	R	RBI	BB	SO	SB	AB	H	PO	A	E	DP	TC/G	FA	G by Pos
1948	NY N	5	.250	.250	8	2	0	0	0	0.0	1	1	1	3	0	2	0	17	1	0	2	3.6	1.000	1B-3
1950		9	.125	.313	32	4	0	0	2	6.3	3	4	3	6	0	0	0	83	7	1	7	10.1	.989	1B-9
1952		3	.000	.000	2	0	0	0	0	0.0	0	0	0	0	0	1	0	0	2	0	0	0.7	1.000	P-2
1954	CHI A	36	.143	.268	56	8	1	0	2	3.6	6	5	12	21	0	1	0	5	27	1	1	0.9	.970	P-35, 1B-1
1955		32	.183	.300	60	11	1	0	2	3.3	6	8	9	17	0	0	0	3	29	1	1	1.0	.970	P-32
1956		36	.169	.437	71	12	1	0	6	8.5	8	19	11	21	0	1	0	2	29	4	3	1.0	.886	P-34
1957		30	.222	.400	45	10	2	0	2	4.4	5	5	10	17	0	0	0	3	15	1	1	0.6	.947	P-30
1958	BAL A	47	.195	.427	82	16	1	0	6	7.3	11	14	17	22	0	9	2	5	43	1	1	1.0	.980	P-34, OF-1
1959	3 teams	BAL	A	(15G – .200)		BOS	A	(9G – .143)			CLE	A	(21G – .206)											
"	total	45	.196	.275	51	10	1	0	2	2.0	7	8	9	8	0	9	1	8	25	0	0	0.7	1.000	P-35
1960	CLE A	15	.176	.235	17	3	1	0	0	0.0	0	1	0	4	0	0	0	2	5	0	1	0.5	1.000	P-15
	10 yrs.	258	.179	.347	424	76	8	0	21	5.0	46	65	72	119	0	22	3	128	183	9	19	1.2	.972	P-217, 1B-13, OF-1

Bill Hart

HART, WILLIAM FRANKLIN (Uncle Billy) TR 5'10" 163 lbs.
B. July 19, 1865, Louisville, Ky. D. Sept. 19, 1936, Cincinnati, Ohio

Year	Team	Games	BA	SA	AB	H	2B	3B	HR	HR%	R	RBI	BB	SO	SB	AB	H	PO	A	E	DP	TC/G	FA	G by Pos
1886	PHI AA	22	.137	.178	73	10	1	0	0	0.0	3		3			0	0	7	40	5	1	2.4	.904	P-22
1887		3	.077	.077	13	1	0	0	0	0.0	0	0	0			0	0	0	8	5	0	4.3	.615	P-3
1892	BKN N	37	.192	.328	125	24	3	4	2	1.6	14	17	7	22	4	0	0	31	59	9	1	2.7	.909	P-28, OF-12
1895	PIT N	36	.236	.321	106	25	5	2	0	0.0	8	11	1	12	1	0	0	12	84	5	4	2.8	.950	P-36
1896	STL N	49	.186	.273	161	30	4	5	0	0.0	9	15	3	15	7	0	0	38	106	8	3	3.1	.947	P-42, OF-8
1897		46	.250	.321	156	39	1	2	2	1.3	14	14	1		4	0	0	31	76	10	4	2.5	.915	P-39, OF-6, 1B-1
1898	PIT N	16	.240	.280	50	12	0	1	0	0.0	4	3	1		1	0	0	3	34	6	3	2.7	.860	P-16
1901	CLE A	20	.219	.219	64	14	0	0	0	0.0	7	6	1		0	0	0	5	55	3	2	3.2	.952	P-20
	8 yrs.	229	.207	.282	748	155	14	15	4	0.5	59	66	17	49	17	0	0	127	462	51	18	2.8	.920	P-206, OF-26, 1B-1

Year	Team		Games	BA	SA	AB	H	2B	3B	HR	HR%	R	RBI	BB	SO	SB	Pinch Hit AB	Pinch Hit H	PO	A	E	DP	TC/G	FA	G by Pos

Bill Hart

HART, WILLIAM WOODROW
B. Mar. 4, 1913, Wiconisco, Pa.   D. July 29, 1968, Lykins, Pa.
BR TR 6'   175 lbs.

Year	Team	Games	BA	SA	AB	H	2B	3B	HR	HR%	R	RBI	BB	SO	SB	PH AB	PH H	PO	A	E	DP	TC/G	FA	G by Pos
1943	BKN N	8	.158	.158	19	3	0	0	0	0.0	0	1	1	2	0	1	0	7	17	0	4	3.0	1.000	3B-6, SS-1
1944		29	.178	.267	90	16	4	2	0	0.0	8	4	9	7	1	2	1	37	74	7	7	4.1	.941	SS-25, 3B-2
1945		58	.230	.348	161	37	6	2	3	1.9	27	27	14	21	7	8	1	56	72	11	8	2.4	.921	3B-39, SS-8
3 yrs.		95	.207	.307	270	56	10	4	3	1.1	35	32	24	30	8	11	2	100	163	18	19	3.0	.936	3B-47, SS-34

Burt Hart

HART, JAMES BURTON
B. June 28, 1870, Lone Tree Lake, Minn.   D. Jan. 29, 1921, Sacramento, Calif.
BB 6'3"   200 lbs.

Year	Team	Games	BA	SA	AB	H	2B	3B	HR	HR%	R	RBI	BB	SO	SB	PH AB	PH H	PO	A	E	DP	TC/G	FA	G by Pos
1901	BAL A	58	.311	.374	206	64	3	5	0	0.0	33	23	20		7	0	0	561	9	14	28	10.1	.976	1B-58

Hub Hart

HART, JAMES HENRY
B. Feb. 2, 1878, Everett, Mass.   D. Oct. 10, 1960, Fort Wayne, Ind.
BL TR 5'11"   170 lbs.

Year	Team	Games	BA	SA	AB	H	2B	3B	HR	HR%	R	RBI	BB	SO	SB	PH AB	PH H	PO	A	E	DP	TC/G	FA	G by Pos
1905	CHI A	10	.118	.118	17	2	0	0	0	0.0	2		4		0	4	0	21	2	0	0	2.3	1.000	C-6
1906		17	.162	.162	37	6	0	0	0	0.0	1	0	2		0	2	0	36	7	3	1	2.7	.935	C-15
1907		29	.271	.286	70	19	1	0	0	0.0	6	7	5		1	4	0	85	23	5	2	3.9	.956	C-25
3 yrs.		56	.218	.226	124	27	1	0	0	0.0	9	11	10		1	10	0	142	32	8	3	3.3	.956	C-46

Jim Ray Hart

HART, JAMES RAY
B. Oct. 30, 1941, Hookerton, N. C.
BR TR 5'11"   185 lbs.

Year	Team	Games	BA	SA	AB	H	2B	3B	HR	HR%	R	RBI	BB	SO	SB	PH AB	PH H	PO	A	E	DP	TC/G	FA	G by Pos
1963	SF N	7	.200	.250	20	4	1	0	0	0.0	1	2	3	6	0	0	0	10	9	0	1	2.7	1.000	3B-7
1964		153	.286	.498	566	162	15	6	31	5.5	71	81	47	94	5	2	0	143	278	28	25	2.9	.938	3B-149, OF-6
1965		160	.299	.487	591	177	30	6	23	3.9	91	96	47	75	6	3	2	151	231	34	16	2.6	.918	3B-144, OF-15
1966		156	.285	.510	578	165	23	4	33	5.7	88	93	48	75	2	1	0	131	283	26	24	2.8	.941	3B-139, OF-17
1967		158	.289	.509	578	167	26	7	29	5.0	98	99	77	100	1	1	0	141	180	18	11	2.1	.947	3B-89, OF-72
1968		136	.258	.444	480	124	14	3	23	4.8	67	78	46	74	3	3	1	165	112	19	12	2.2	.936	3B-72, OF-65
1969		95	.254	.331	236	60	9	0	3	1.3	27	26	28	49	0	23	7	80	7	6	1	1.0	.935	OF-68, 3B-3
1970		76	.282	.431	255	72	12	1	8	3.1	30	37	30	29	0	4	1	60	71	12	2	1.9	.916	3B-56, OF-18
1971		31	.256	.410	39	10	0	0	2	5.1	5	5	6	8	0	23	6	7	3	1	2	0.4	.909	OF-3, 3B-3
1972		24	.304	.557	79	24	5	0	5	6.3	10	8	6	10	0	3	0	17	22	5	2	1.8	.886	3B-20
1973	2 teams		SF N	(5G – .000)		NY	A	(114G – .254)																	
"	total	119	.251	.415	342	86	13	2	13	3.8	29	53	39	46	0	9	1	0	3	2	0	0.0	.600	DH-106, 1B-1
1974	NY A	10	.053	.053	19	1	0	0	0	0.0	1	0	3	7	0	5	0	0	0	0	0	0.0	–	DH-4
12 yrs.		1125	.278	.467	3783	1052	148	29	170	4.5	518	578	380	573	17	80	19	905	1199	151	96	2.0	.933	3B-682, OF-264, DH-110, 1B-1

LEAGUE CHAMPIONSHIP SERIES

Year	Team	Games	BA	SA	AB	H	2B	3B	HR	HR%	R	RBI	BB	SO	SB	PH AB	PH H	PO	A	E	DP	TC/G	FA	G by Pos
1971	SF N	3	.000	.000	5	0	0	0	0	0.0	0	0	0	2	0	1	0	0	2	0	0	0.7	1.000	3B-1

Mike Hart

HART, JAMES MICHAEL
B. Dec. 20, 1951, Kalamazoo, Mich.
BB TR 6'3"   185 lbs.

Year	Team	Games	BA	SA	AB	H	2B	3B	HR	HR%	R	RBI	BB	SO	SB	PH AB	PH H	PO	A	E	DP	TC/G	FA	G by Pos
1980	TEX A	5	.250	.250	4	1	0	0	0	0.0	1	0	1	1	0	1	0	0	0	0	0	0.2	1.000	OF-2

Mike Hart

HART, MICHAEL LAWRENCE
B. Feb. 17, 1958, Milwaukee, Wis.
BL TL 5'11"   185 lbs.

Year	Team	Games	BA	SA	AB	H	2B	3B	HR	HR%	R	RBI	BB	SO	SB	PH AB	PH H	PO	A	E	DP	TC/G	FA	G by Pos
1984	MIN A	13	.172	.172	29	5	0	0	0	0.0	0	5	1	2	0	3	0	24	1	0	0	1.9	1.000	OF-11
1987	BAL A	34	.158	.342	76	12	2	0	4	5.3	7	12	6	19	1	2	0	74	0	0	0	2.2	1.000	OF-32
2 yrs.		47	.162	.295	105	17	2	0	4	3.8	7	17	7	21	1	5	0	98	1	0	0	2.1	1.000	OF-43

Tom Hart

HART, THOMAS HENRY
B. June 15, 1869, Canaan, N. Y.   D. Sept. 17, 1939, Gardner, Mass.

Year	Team	Games	BA	SA	AB	H	2B	3B	HR	HR%	R	RBI	BB	SO	SB	PH AB	PH H	PO	A	E	DP	TC/G	FA	G by Pos
1891	WAS AA	8	.125	.125	24	3	0	0	0	0.0	1		2	2	1	1	0	19	8	0	0	3.4	1.000	C-5, OF-3

Bruce Hartford

HARTFORD, BRUCE DANIEL
B. May 14, 1892, Chicago, Ill.   D. May 25, 1975, Los Angeles, Calif.
BR TR 6½"   190 lbs.

Year	Team	Games	BA	SA	AB	H	2B	3B	HR	HR%	R	RBI	BB	SO	SB	PH AB	PH H	PO	A	E	DP	TC/G	FA	G by Pos
1914	CLE A	8	.182	.227	22	4	1	0	0	0.0	5	0	4		0	0	0	5	16	2	0	2.9	.913	SS-8

Chris Hartje

HARTJE, CHRISTIAN HENRY
B. Mar. 25, 1915, San Francisco, Calif.   D. June 26, 1946, Seattle, Wash.
BR TR 5'10½"   165 lbs.

Year	Team	Games	BA	SA	AB	H	2B	3B	HR	HR%	R	RBI	BB	SO	SB	PH AB	PH H	PO	A	E	DP	TC/G	FA	G by Pos
1939	BKN N	9	.313	.375	16	5	1	0	0	0.0	2	5	1	0	1	1	1	9	1	1	0	1.2	.909	C-8

Chick Hartley

HARTLEY, WALTER SCOTT
B. Aug. 22, 1880, Philadelphia, Pa.   D. July 18, 1948, Philadelphia, Pa.
BR TR 5'8"   180 lbs.

Year	Team	Games	BA	SA	AB	H	2B	3B	HR	HR%	R	RBI	BB	SO	SB	PH AB	PH H	PO	A	E	DP	TC/G	FA	G by Pos
1902	NY N	1	.000	.000	4	0	0	0	0	0.0	0	0	0		0	0	0	2	0	0	0	2.0	1.000	OF-1

Grover Hartley

HARTLEY, GROVER ALLEN (Slick)
B. July 2, 1888, Osgood, Ind.   D. Oct. 19, 1964, Daytona Beach, Fla.
BR TR 5'11"   175 lbs.

Year	Team	Games	BA	SA	AB	H	2B	3B	HR	HR%	R	RBI	BB	SO	SB	PH AB	PH H	PO	A	E	DP	TC/G	FA	G by Pos
1911	NY N	11	.222	.333	18	4	2	0	0	0.0	1	1	1		1	1	0	44	7	2	0	4.8	.962	C-10
1912		25	.235	.353	34	8	2	1	0	0.0	3	7	8	4	2	2	0	63	9	3	1	3.0	.960	C-25
1913		23	.316	.316	19	6	0	0	0	0.0	4	0	1		2	4	1	41	7	1	0	2.1	.980	C-21, 1B-1
1914	STL F	86	.288	.382	212	61	13	2	1	0.5	24	25	12		1	24	8	249	79	11	12	3.9	.968	C-32, 2B-13, 1B-9, 3B-3, OF-2
1915		120	.274	.365	394	108	21	6	1	0.3	47	50	42		10	6	0	565	151	21	11	6.1	.972	C-113, 1B-1
1916	STL A	89	.225	.261	222	50	8	0	0	0.0	19	12	30	24	4	9	2	263	98	12	10	4.2	.968	C-75
1917		19	.231	.231	13	3	0	0	0	0.0	2		2	1	0	11	2	6	4	1	0	0.6	.909	C-4, SS-1, 3B-1
1924	NY N	4	.286	.429	7	2	1	0	0	0.0	1	1	0	1	0	1	0	6	2	0	0	2.0	1.000	C-3
1925		46	.316	.347	95	30	1	0	0	0.0	9	8	8	3	1	7	2	137	27	4	14	3.7	.976	C-37, 1B-8
1926		13	.048	.048	21	1	0	0	0	0.0	0	0	5		0	0	0	31	4	0	1	2.7	1.000	C-13
1927	BOS A	103	.275	.332	244	67	11	0	1	0.4	23	31	22	14	1	15	2	214	51	9	5	2.7	.967	C-86
1929	CLE A	24	.273	.333	33	9	0	1	0	0.0	2	8	1	2	0	8	1	16	0	0	0	0.7	1.000	C-13
1930		1	.750	.750	4	3	0	0	0	0.0	0	1	0		0	0	0	3	1	0	0	4.0	.750	C-1

Year Team	Games	BA	SA	AB	H	2B	3B	HR	HR%	R	RBI	BB	SO	SB	Pinch Hit AB	H	PO	A	E	DP	TC/G	FA	G by Pos

Grover Hartley *continued*

Year Team	Games	BA	SA	AB	H	2B	3B	HR	HR%	R	RBI	BB	SO	SB	PH AB	PH H	PO	A	E	DP	TC/G	FA	G by Pos
1934 STL A	5	.333	.667	3	1	1	0	0	0.0	0	0	1	0	0	2	1	3	0	0	0	0.6	1.000	C-2
14 yrs.	569	.268	.337	1319	353	60	11	3	0.2	135	144	135	50	29	80	19	1640	440	65	54	3.8	.970	C-435, 1B-19, 2B-13, 3B-4, OF-2, SS-1

Fred Hartman

HARTMAN, FREDERICK ORRIN (Dutch) BR TR
B. Apr. 25, 1868, Allegheny, Pa. D. Nov. 11, 1938, McKeesport, Pa.

Year Team	Games	BA	SA	AB	H	2B	3B	HR	HR%	R	RBI	BB	SO	SB	PH AB	PH H	PO	A	E	DP	TC/G	FA	G by Pos
1894 PIT N	49	.319	.451	182	58	4	7	2	1.1	41	20	16	11	12			65	97	23	6	3.8	.876	3B-49
1897 STL N	124	.306	.390	516	158	21	8	2	0.4	67	67	26		18	0	0	159	253	63	14	3.8	.867	3B-124
1898 NY N	123	.272	.364	475	129	16	11	2	0.4	57	88	25		11	0	0	146	280	57	16	3.9	.882	3B-123
1899	50	.236	.328	174	41	3	5	1	0.6	25	16	12		2	0	0	56	100	20	11	3.5	.886	3B-50
1901 CHI A	120	.309	.431	473	146	23	13	3	0.6	77	89	25		31	1	1	151	263	49	15	3.9	.894	3B-119
1902 STL N	114	.216	.255	416	90	10	3	0	0.0	30	52	14		14	2	1	168	241	42	11	4.0	.907	3B-105, SS-4, 1B-3
6 yrs.	580	.278	.368	2236	622	77	47	10	0.4	297	332	118	11	88	3	2	745	1234	254	73	3.9	.886	3B-570, SS-4, 1B-3

J. C. Hartman

HARTMAN, J. C. BR TR 6' 175 lbs.
B. Apr. 15, 1934, Cottonton, Ala.

Year Team	Games	BA	SA	AB	H	2B	3B	HR	HR%	R	RBI	BB	SO	SB	PH AB	PH H	PO	A	E	DP	TC/G	FA	G by Pos
1962 HOU N	51	.223	.257	148	33	6	0	0	0.0	11	5	4	16	1	2	0	87	121	6	31	4.2	.972	SS-48
1963	39	.122	.133	90	11	0	0	0	0.0	2	3	2	13	1	7	2	45	69	6	14	3.1	.950	SS-32
2 yrs.	90	.185	.210	238	44	6	0	0	0.0	13	8	6	29	2	9	2	132	190	12	45	3.7	.964	SS-80

Gabby Hartnett

HARTNETT, CHARLES LEO BR TR 6'1" 195 lbs.
B. Dec. 20, 1900, Woonsocket, R. I. D. Dec. 20, 1972, Park Ridge, Ill.
Manager 1938-40.
Hall of Fame 1955.

Year Team	Games	BA	SA	AB	H	2B	3B	HR	HR%	R	RBI	BB	SO	SB	PH AB	PH H	PO	A	E	DP	TC/G	FA	G by Pos
1922 CHI N	31	.194	.236	72	14	1	1	0	0.0	4	4	6	8	1	4	1	79	29	2	0	3.5	.982	C-27
1923	85	.268	.442	231	62	12	2	8	3.5	28	39	25	22	4	15	2	413	39	5	25	5.4	.989	C-39, 1B-31
1924	111	.299	.523	354	106	17	7	16	4.5	56	67	39	37	10	4	0	369	97	18	12	4.4	.963	C-105
1925	117	.289	.555	398	115	28	3	24	6.0	61	67	36	77	1	6	2	409	114	23	15	4.7	.958	C-110
1926	93	.275	.468	284	78	25	3	8	2.8	35	41	32	37	0	3	1	307	86	9	6	4.3	.978	C-88
1927	127	.294	.454	449	132	32	5	10	2.2	56	80	44	42	2	2	1	479	99	16	21	4.7	.973	C-125
1928	120	.302	.523	388	117	26	9	14	3.6	61	57	65	32	3	2	0	455	103	6	14	4.7	.989	C-118
1929	25	.273	.591	22	6	2	1	1	4.5	2	9	5	5	1	20	6	4	0	0	0	0.2	1.000	C-1
1930	141	.339	.630	508	172	31	3	37	7.3	84	122	55	62	0	3	2	646	68	8	11	5.1	.989	C-136
1931	116	.282	.434	380	107	32	1	8	2.1	53	70	52	48	3	10	0	444	68	10	16	4.5	.981	C-105
1932	121	.271	.436	406	110	25	3	12	3.0	52	52	51	59	0	2	1	498	75	10	10	4.8	.983	C-117, 1B-1
1933	140	.276	.433	490	135	21	4	16	3.3	55	88	37	51	1	0	0	550	77	7	17	4.5	.989	C-140
1934	130	.299	.502	438	131	21	1	22	5.0	58	90	37	46	0	1	0	605	86	3	11	5.3	.996	C-129
1935	116	.344	.545	413	142	32	6	13	3.1	67	91	41	46	1	6	1	477	77	9	11	4.9	.984	C-110
1936	121	.307	.443	424	130	25	6	7	1.7	49	64	30	36	0	7	0	504	75	5	8	4.8	.991	C-114
1937	110	.354	.548	356	126	21	6	12	3.4	47	82	43	19	0	8	2	436	65	2	7	4.6	.996	C-101
1938	88	.274	.445	299	82	19	1	10	3.3	40	59	48	17	1	4	2	358	40	2	8	4.5	.995	C-83
1939	97	.278	.467	306	85	18	2	12	3.9	36	59	37	32	0	8	3	336	47	3	3	4.0	.992	C-86
1940	37	.266	.359	64	17	3	0	1	1.6	3	12	8	7	0	13	5	70	10	4	2	2.3	.952	C-22, 1B-1
1941 NY N	64	.300	.433	150	45	5	0	5	3.3	20	26	12	14	0	26	8	138	15	1	1	2.4	.994	C-34
20 yrs.	1990	.297	.489	6432	1912	396	64	236	3.7	867	1179	703	697	28	144	37	7577	1270	143	198	4.5	.984	C-1790, 1B-33

WORLD SERIES

Year Team	Games	BA	SA	AB	H	2B	3B	HR	HR%	R	RBI	BB	SO	SB	PH AB	PH H	PO	A	E	DP	TC/G	FA	G by Pos
1929 CHI N	3	.000	.000	3	0	0	0	0	0.0	0	0	0	3	0	3	0	0	0	0	0	0.0	–	
1932	4	.313	.625	16	5	2	0	1	6.3	2	1	1	3	0	0	0	31	5	1	2	9.3	.973	C-4
1935	6	.292	.417	24	7	0	0	1	4.2	1	2	0	3	0	0	0	33	6	0	0	6.5	1.000	C-6
1938	3	.091	.273	11	1	0	1	0	0.0	0	0	0	2	0	0	0	14	3	0	0	5.7	1.000	C-3
4 yrs.	16	.241	.426	54	13	2	1	2	3.7	3	3	1	11	0	3	0	78	14	1	2	5.8	.989	C-13

Pat Hartnett

HARTNETT, PATRICK J. (Happy) 6'1" 175 lbs.
B. Oct. 20, 1863, Boston, Mass. D. Apr. 10, 1935, Boston, Mass.

Year Team	Games	BA	SA	AB	H	2B	3B	HR	HR%	R	RBI	BB	SO	SB	PH AB	PH H	PO	A	E	DP	TC/G	FA	G by Pos
1890 STL AA	14	.189	.264	53	10	2	1	0	0.0	6		6		1	0	0	140	5	7	2	10.9	.954	1B-14

Greg Harts

HARTS, GREGORY RUDOLPH BL TL 6' 168 lbs.
B. Apr. 21, 1950, Atlanta, Ga.

Year Team	Games	BA	SA	AB	H	2B	3B	HR	HR%	R	RBI	BB	SO	SB	PH AB	PH H	PO	A	E	DP	TC/G	FA	G by Pos
1973 NY N	3	.500	.500	2	1	0	0	0	0.0	0	0	0	0	0	2	1	0	0	0	0	0.0	–	

Topsy Hartsel

HARTSEL, TULLY FREDERICK BL TL 5'5" 155 lbs.
B. June 26, 1874, Polk, Ohio D. Oct. 14, 1944, Toledo, Ohio

Year Team	Games	BA	SA	AB	H	2B	3B	HR	HR%	R	RBI	BB	SO	SB	PH AB	PH H	PO	A	E	DP	TC/G	FA	G by Pos
1898 LOU N	22	.324	.324	71	23	0	0	0	0.0	11	9	11		2	0	0	25	2	2	1	1.3	.931	OF-21
1899	30	.240	.347	75	18	1	1	1	1.3	8	7	11		1	6	2	36	2	3	1	1.4	.927	OF-22
1900 CIN N	18	.328	.484	64	21	2	1	2	3.1	10	5	8		7	0	0	22	0	1	0	1.3	.957	OF-18
1901 CHI N	140	.335	.475	558	187	25	16	7	1.3	111	54	74		41	0	0	273	16	15	3	2.2	.951	OF-140
1902 PHI A	137	.283	.391	545	154	20	12	5	0.9	109	58	87		47	0	0	238	18	12	2	2.0	.955	OF-137
1903	98	.311	.477	373	116	19	14	5	1.3	65	26	49		13	1	0	144	6	5	0	1.6	.968	OF-96
1904	147	.253	.341	534	135	17	12	2	0.4	79	25	75		19	0	0	216	15	10	2	1.6	.959	OF-147
1905	148	.276	.347	533	147	22	8	0	0.0	88	28	121		36	1	0	253	6	17	1	1.9	.938	OF-147
1906	144	.255	.364	533	136	21	9	1	0.2	96	30	88		31	0	0	238	15	8	5	1.8	.969	OF-144
1907	143	.280	.367	507	142	23	6	3	0.6	93	29	106		20	0	0	191	11	7	2	1.5	.967	OF-143
1908	129	.243	.330	460	112	16	6	4	0.9	73	29	93		15	0	0	211	6	9	2	1.8	.960	OF-129
1909	83	.270	.322	267	72	8	2	0	0.0	30	18	48		3	4	2	140	5	7	0	1.7	.966	OF-74
1910	90	.221	.277	285	63	10	3	0	0.0	45	22	58		11	4	0	113	8	7	2	1.4	.945	OF-83
1911	25	.237	.289	38	9	2	0	0	0.0	8	1	8		0	11	2	13	3	1	0	0.7	.941	OF-10
14 yrs.	1354	.276	.370	4843	1335	182	93	30	0.6	826	341	837		246	31	6	2113	108	102	21	1.7	.956	OF-1311

WORLD SERIES

Year Team	Games	BA	SA	AB	H	2B	3B	HR	HR%	R	RBI	BB	SO	SB	PH AB	PH H	PO	A	E	DP	TC/G	FA	G by Pos
1905 PHI A	5	.294	.353	17	5	1	0	0	0.0	1	0	2		2	0	0	9	1	1	0	2.2	.909	OF-5

Year	Team	Games	BA	SA	AB	H	2B	3B	HR	HR%	R	RBI	BB	SO	SB	Pinch Hit AB	Pinch Hit H	PO	A	E	DP	TC/G	FA	G by Pos

Topsy Hartsel *continued*

Year	Team	Games	BA	SA	AB	H	2B	3B	HR	HR%	R	RBI	BB	SO	SB	AB	H	PO	A	E	DP	TC/G	FA	G by Pos
1910		1	.200	.200	5	1	0	0	0	0.0	2	0	0	1	2	0	0	2	0	0	0	2.0	1.000	OF-1
2 yrs.		6	.273	.318	22	6	1	0	0	0.0	3	0	2	2	4	0	0	11	1	1	0	2.2	.923	OF-6

Roy Hartsfield

HARTSFIELD, ROY THOMAS
B. Oct. 25, 1925, Chattahoochee, Ga.
Manager 1977-79.   BR TR 5'9" 165 lbs.

Year	Team	Games	BA	SA	AB	H	2B	3B	HR	HR%	R	RBI	BB	SO	SB	AB	H	PO	A	E	DP	TC/G	FA	G by Pos
1950	BOS N	107	.277	.372	419	116	15	2	7	1.7	62	24	27	61	7	8	3	236	247	26	53	4.8	.949	2B-96
1951		120	.271	.344	450	122	11	2	6	1.3	63	31	41	73	7	6	0	336	293	20	87	5.4	.969	2B-114
1952		38	.262	.355	107	28	4	3	0	0.0	13	4	5	12	0	1	0	61	73	7	10	3.7	.950	2B-29
3 yrs.		265	.273	.358	976	266	30	7	13	1.3	138	59	73	146	14	15	3	633	613	53	150	4.9	.959	2B-239

Clint Hartung

HARTUNG, CLINTON CLARENCE (Floppy, The Hondo Hurricane)
B. Aug. 10, 1922, Hondo, Tex.   BR TR 6'5" 210 lbs.

Year	Team	Games	BA	SA	AB	H	2B	3B	HR	HR%	R	RBI	BB	SO	SB	AB	H	PO	A	E	DP	TC/G	FA	G by Pos
1947	NY N	34	.309	.543	94	29	4	3	4	4.3	13	13	3	21	0	4	1	15	22	2	0	1.1	.949	P-23, OF-7
1948		43	.179	.232	56	10	1	1	0	0.0	5	3	7	24	0	4	2	6	29	0	1	0.8	1.000	P-36
1949		38	.190	.381	63	12	0	0	4	6.3	7	7	4	21	0	4	0	9	36	2	1	1.2	.957	P-33
1950		32	.302	.605	43	13	2	1	3	7.0	7	10	1	13	0	9	3	14	23	2	0	1.2	.949	P-20, OF-2, 1B-1
1951		21	.205	.227	44	9	1	0	0	0.0	4	2	1	9	0	7	3	11	1	0	0	0.6	1.000	OF-12
1952		28	.218	.385	78	17	2	1	3	3.8	6	8	9	24	0	3	1	38	3	3	1	1.6	.932	OF-24
6 yrs.		196	.238	.407	378	90	10	6	14	3.7	42	43	25	112	0	31	10	93	114	9	3	1.1	.958	P-112, OF-45, 1B-1

WORLD SERIES

Year	Team	Games	BA	SA	AB	H	2B	3B	HR	HR%	R	RBI	BB	SO	SB	AB	H	PO	A	E	DP	TC/G	FA	G by Pos
1951	NY N	2	.000	.000	4	0	0	0	0	0.0	0	0	0	0	0	0	0	1	1	1	0	1.5	.667	OF-2

Roy Hartzell

HARTZELL, ROY ALLEN
B. July 6, 1881, Golden, Colo. D. Nov. 6, 1961, Golden, Colo.   BL TR 5'8½" 155 lbs.

Year	Team	Games	BA	SA	AB	H	2B	3B	HR	HR%	R	RBI	BB	SO	SB	AB	H	PO	A	E	DP	TC/G	FA	G by Pos
1906	STL A	113	.213	.230	404	86	7	0	0	0.0	43	24	19		21	1	0	125	227	44	13	3.5	.889	3B-103, SS-6, 2B-2
1907		60	.236	.295	220	52	3	5	0	0.0	20	13	11		7	3	0	88	120	16	6	3.7	.929	3B-38, 2B-15, OF-2, SS-2
1908		115	.265	.320	422	112	5	6	2	0.5	41	32	19		24	2	0	161	88	24	11	2.4	.912	OF-82, SS-18, 3B-7, 2B-4
1909		152	.271	.308	595	161	12	5	0	0.0	64	32	29		14	1	0	257	219	34	20	3.4	.933	OF-85, SS-65, 2B-1
1910		151	.218	.271	542	118	13	5	2	0.4	52	30	49		18	0	0	233	316	42	34	3.9	.929	3B-89, SS-38, OF-23
1911	NY A	144	.296	.387	527	156	17	11	3	0.6	67	91	63		22	1	0	195	253	29	20	3.3	.939	3B-124, SS-12, OF-8
1912		123	.272	.356	416	113	10	11	1	0.2	50	38	64		20	1	0	220	141	35	6	3.2	.912	3B-56, OF-55, SS-10, 2B-2
1913		141	.259	.300	490	127	18	1	1	0.2	60	38	67	40	26	3	2	286	270	32	36	4.2	.946	2B-81, OF-30, 3B-21, SS-4
1914		137	.233	.308	481	112	15	9	1	0.2	55	32	68	38	22	4	0	249	26	9	2	2.1	.968	OF-128, 2B-5
1915		119	.251	.313	387	97	11	2	3	0.8	39	60	57	37	7	5	3	208	21	9	2	2.0	.962	OF-107, 2B-5, 3B-2
1916		33	.188	.203	64	12	1	0	0	0.0	12	7	9	3	1	5	1	27	1	0	0	0.8	1.000	OF-28
11 yrs.		1288	.252	.309	4548	1146	112	55	12	0.3	503	397	455	118	182	26	6	2049	1682	274	152	3.1	.932	OF-548, 3B-440, SS-155, 2B-115

Luther Harvel

HARVEL, LUTHER RAYMOND (Red)
B. Sept. 30, 1905, Cambria, Ill. D. Apr. 10, 1986, Kansas City, Mo.   BR TR 5'11" 180 lbs.

Year	Team	Games	BA	SA	AB	H	2B	3B	HR	HR%	R	RBI	BB	SO	SB	AB	H	PO	A	E	DP	TC/G	FA	G by Pos
1928	CLE A	40	.221	.279	136	30	6	1	0	0.0	12	12	4	17	1	1	0	86	6	5	0	2.4	.948	OF-39

Ervin Harvey

HARVEY, ERVIN KING (Zaza)
B. Jan. 5, 1879, Saratoga, Calif. D. June 3, 1954, Santa Monica, Calif.   BL TL

Year	Team	Games	BA	SA	AB	H	2B	3B	HR	HR%	R	RBI	BB	SO	SB	AB	H	PO	A	E	DP	TC/G	FA	G by Pos
1900	CHI N	2	.000	.000	3	0	0	0	0	0.0	0		0	1	0	1	0	1	0	0	0	0.5	1.000	P-1
1901	2 teams		CHI A	(17G – .250)		CLE A	(45G – .353)																		
"	total	62	.333	.443	210	70	8	6	1	0.5	32	27	11		16	1	0	87	42	14	6	2.3	.902	OF-45, P-16
1902	CLE A	12	.348	.391	46	16	2	0	0	0.0	5	5	3		1	0	0	16	2	0	1	1.5	1.000	OF-12
3 yrs.		76	.332	.429	259	86	10	6	1	0.4	37	32	14		17	2	0	104	44	14	7	2.1	.914	OF-57, P-17

Ziggy Hasbrook

HASBROOK, ROBERT LYNDON
B. Nov. 21, 1893, Grundy Center, Iowa D. Feb. 9, 1976, Garland, Tex.   BR TR 6'1" 180 lbs.

Year	Team	Games	BA	SA	AB	H	2B	3B	HR	HR%	R	RBI	BB	SO	SB	AB	H	PO	A	E	DP	TC/G	FA	G by Pos
1916	CHI A	9	.125	.125	8	1	0	0	0	0.0	1	0	1		2	0	0	24	3	0	1	3.0	1.000	1B-7
1917		2	.000	.000	1	0	0	0	0	0.0	1	0	0		0	0	0	0	2	0	1	1.0	1.000	2B-1
2 yrs.		11	.111	.111	9	1	0	0	0	0.0	2	0	1		2	0	0	24	5	0	2	2.6	1.000	1B-7, 2B-1

Don Hasenmayer

HASENMAYER, DONALD IRVIN
B. Apr. 4, 1927, Roslyn, Pa.   BR TR 5'10½" 180 lbs.

Year	Team	Games	BA	SA	AB	H	2B	3B	HR	HR%	R	RBI	BB	SO	SB	AB	H	PO	A	E	DP	TC/G	FA	G by Pos
1945	PHI N	5	.111	.111	18	2	0	0	0	0.0	1	1	2	1	0	0	0	10	20	2	1	6.4	.938	2B-4, 3B-1
1946		6	.083	.167	12	1	1	0	0	0.0	0	0	0	2	0	1	0	4	7	0	2	1.8	1.000	3B-3
2 yrs.		11	.100	.133	30	3	1	0	0	0.0	1	1	2	3	0	1	0	14	27	2	3	3.9	.953	3B-4, 2B-4

Mickey Haslin

HASLIN, MICHAEL JOSEPH
B. Oct. 31, 1910, Wilkes-Barre, Pa.   BR TR 5'8" 165 lbs.

Year	Team	Games	BA	SA	AB	H	2B	3B	HR	HR%	R	RBI	BB	SO	SB	AB	H	PO	A	E	DP	TC/G	FA	G by Pos
1933	PHI N	26	.236	.258	89	21	2	0	0	0.0	9	3	5	1	1	0	0	52	79	6	12	5.3	.956	2B-26
1934		72	.265	.355	166	44	8	2	1	0.6	28	11	16	13	1	16	5	67	98	11	11	2.4	.938	3B-26, 2B-21, SS-4
1935		110	.265	.344	407	108	17	3	3	0.7	53	52	19	25	1	5	3	247	299	39	54	5.3	.933	SS-87, 3B-11, 2B-9
1936	2 teams		PHI N	(16G – .344)		BOS N	(36G – .279)																		
"	total	52	.304	.387	168	51	2	3	2	1.2	20	17	8	14	0	10	2	57	86	11	18	3.0	.929	3B-22, 2B-19
1937	NY N	27	.190	.214	42	8	1	0	0	0.0	8	5	9	3	1	2	0	13	47	4	6	2.4	.938	SS-9, 3B-4, 2B-4
1938		31	.324	.441	102	33	3	0	3	2.9	13	15	4	4	0	1	0	35	66	8	8	3.5	.927	3B-15, 2B-13
6 yrs.		318	.272	.350	974	265	33	8	9	0.9	125	109	59	64	8	32	8	471	675	79	109	3.9	.936	SS-100, 2B-92, 3B-78

Pete Hasney

HASNEY, PETER JAMES
B. May 26, 1865, England D. May 24, 1908, Philadelphia, Pa.

Year	Team	Games	BA	SA	AB	H	2B	3B	HR	HR%	R	RBI	BB	SO	SB	AB	H	PO	A	E	DP	TC/G	FA	G by Pos
1890	PHI AA	2	.143	.143	7	1	0	0	0	0.0	1		1		0	0	0	0	0	2	0	1.0	–	OF-2

Year	Team		Games	BA	SA		AB	H	2B	3B		HR	HR%		R	RBI		BB	SO	SB	Pinch Hit AB	H		PO	A	E	DP	TC/G	FA		G by Pos

Bill Hassamaer

HASSAMAER, WILLIAM LOUIS (Roaring Bill)
B. July 26, 1864, St. Louis, Mo. D. May 29, 1910, St. Louis, Mo.
6' 180 lbs.

1894	WAS N	118	.322	.482	494	159	33	17	4	0.8	106	90	41	20	16	1	0	225	135	45	14	3.4	.889	OF-68, 3B-31, 2B-14, SS-4
1895	2 teams		WAS N (85G – .279)			LOU N (23G – .208)																			
"	total	108	.264	.341	454	120	20	6	1	0.2	49	74	29	17	8	0	0	370	40	16	22	3.9	.962	OF-75, 1B-30, SS-2, 3B-1, 2B-1
1896	LOU N	30	.245	.349	106	26	5	0	2	1.9	8	14	14	7	1	1	0	292	31	8	24	11.0	.976	1B-29
3 yrs.		256	.289	.408	1054	305	58	23	7	0.7	163	178	84	44	25	2	0	887	206	69	60	4.5	.941	OF-143, 1B-59, 3B-32, 2B-15, SS-6

Buddy Hassett

HASSETT, JOHN ALOYSIUS
B. Sept. 5, 1911, New York, N. Y.
BL TL 5'11" 180 lbs.

1936	BKN N	156	.310	.405	635	197	29	11	3	0.5	79	82	35	17	5	0	0	1401	121	26	89	9.9	.983	1B-156
1937		137	.304	.387	556	169	31	6	1	0.2	71	53	20	19	13	0	0	1140	116	21	96	9.3	.984	1B-131, OF-7
1938		115	.293	.361	335	98	11	6	0	0.0	49	40	32	19	3	32	12	215	18	11	6	2.1	.954	1B-71, 1B-8
1939	BOS N	147	.308	.354	590	182	15	3	2	0.3	72	60	29	14	13	2	1	1184	114	20	127	9.0	.985	1B-127, OF-23
1940		124	.234	.293	458	107	19	4	0	0.0	59	27	25	16	4	12	0	899	91	21	102	8.2	.979	1B-98, OF-13
1941		118	.296	.346	405	120	9	4	1	0.2	59	33	36	15	10	16	5	895	78	9	92	8.3	.991	1B-99
1942	NY A	132	.284	.364	538	153	16	6	5	0.9	80	48	32	16	5	0	0	1128	118	11	130	9.5	.991	1B-132
7 yrs.		929	.292	.362	3517	1026	130	40	12	0.3	469	343	209	116	53	62	18	6862	651	119	642	8.2	.984	1B-751, OF-114

WORLD SERIES

| 1942 | NY A | 3 | .333 | .444 | 9 | 3 | 1 | 0 | 0 | 0.0 | 0 | 2 | 0 | 1 | 0 | 0 | 0 | 15 | 1 | 1 | 0 | 5.7 | .941 | 1B-3 |

Ron Hassey

HASSEY, RONALD WILLIAM
B. Feb. 27, 1953, Tucson, Ariz.
BL TR 6'2" 200 lbs.

1978	CLE A	25	.203	.284	74	15	0	0	2	2.7	5	9	5	7	2	1	0	130	15	1	1	5.8	.993	C-24
1979		75	.287	.404	223	64	14	0	4	1.8	20	32	19	19	1	7	2	368	29	3	5	5.3	.993	C-68, 1B-2, DH-1
1980		130	.318	.446	390	124	18	4	8	2.1	43	65	49	51	0	18	6	564	52	4	9	4.8	.994	C-113, DH-7, 1B-3
1981		61	.232	.268	190	44	4	0	1	0.5	8	25	17	11	0	4	2	327	44	3	7	6.1	.992	C-56, 1B-5, DH-1
1982		113	.251	.353	323	81	18	0	5	1.5	33	34	53	32	3	10	3	566	38	4	6	5.4	.993	C-105, DH-2, 1B-2
1983		117	.270	.384	341	92	21	0	6	1.8	48	42	38	35	2	9	3	514	43	3	4	4.8	.995	C-113, DH-1
1984	2 teams		CLE A (48G – .255)			CHI A (19G – .333)																			
"	total	67	.269	.341	182	49	5	1	2	1.1	16	24	19	32	1	9	2	263	18	2	3	4.2	.993	C-50, 1B-5, DH-1
1985	NY A	92	.296	.509	267	79	16	1	13	4.9	31	42	28	21	0	20	5	420	20	7	4	4.9	.984	C-69, DH-22, 1B-2
1986	2 teams		NY A (64G – .298)			CHI A (49G – .353)																			
"	total	113	.323	.481	341	110	25	0	9	2.6	45	49	46	27	1	18	10	318	14	4	4	3.0	.988	C-62, DH-37
1987	CHI A	49	.214	.338	145	31	9	0	3	2.1	15	12	17	11	0	6	0	114	12	2	4	2.6	1.000	C-24, DH-18
1988	OAK A	107	.257	.368	323	83	15	0	7	2.2	32	45	30	42	2	14	2	465	31	3	7	4.7	.994	C-91, DH-9
1989		97	.228	.328	268	61	12	0	5	1.9	29	23	24	45	1	16	3	425	25	4	4	4.7	.991	C-78, DH-2, 1B-1
12 yrs.		1046	.272	.391	3067	833	157	7	65	2.1	325	402	345	333	13	132	38	4474	341	38	58	4.6	.992	C-853, DH-81, 1B-20

LEAGUE CHAMPIONSHIP SERIES

1988	OAK A	4	.500	1.000	8	4	1	0	1	12.5	2	3	1	1	0	0	0	13	0	0	0	3.3	1.000	C-4
1989		2	.167	.167	6	1	0	0	0	0.0	0	1	1	2	0	0	0	10	0	0	0	5.0	1.000	C-2
2 yrs.		6	.357	.643	14	5	1	0	1	7.1	2	4	2	3	0	0	0	23	0	0	0	3.8	1.000	C-6

WORLD SERIES

| 1988 | OAK A | 5 | .250 | .250 | 8 | 2 | 0 | 0 | 0 | 0.0 | 0 | 1 | 3 | 1 | 0 | 1 | 1 | 28 | 1 | 0 | 0 | 5.8 | 1.000 | C-4 |

Joe Hassler

HASSLER, JOSEPH FREDERICK
B. Apr. 7, 1905, Fort Smith, Ark. D. Sept. 4, 1971, Duncan, Okla.
BR TR 6' 165 lbs.

1928	PHI A	28	.265	.324	34	9	2	0	0	0.0	5	3	2	4	0	2	0	26	32	8	5	2.4	.879	SS-28
1929		4	.000	.000	4	0	0	0	0	0.0	1	0	0	2	0	0	0	1	2	2	0	1.3	.600	SS-2
1930	STL A	5	.250	.250	8	2	0	0	0	0.0	3	1	0	1	0	0	0	3	6	0	3	1.8	1.000	SS-3
3 yrs.		37	.239	.283	46	11	2	0	0	0.0	9	4	2	7	0	2	0	30	40	10	8	2.2	.875	SS-33

Gene Hasson

HASSON, CHARLES EUGENE
B. July 20, 1915, Connellsville, Pa.
BL TL 6' 197 lbs.

1937	PHI A	28	.306	.520	98	30	6	3	3	3.1	12	14	13	14	0	0	0	290	8	0	31	10.6	1.000	1B-28
1938		19	.275	.464	69	19	6	2	1	1.4	10	12	12	7	0	0	0	154	6	7	17	8.8	.958	1B-19
2 yrs.		47	.293	.497	167	49	12	5	4	2.4	22	26	25	21	0	0	0	444	14	7	48	9.9	.985	1B-47

Scott Hastings

HASTINGS, WINFIELD SCOTT
B. Aug. 10, 1846, Hillsboro, Ohio D. Aug. 14, 1907, Sawtelle, Calif.
Manager 1871-72.
BR TR 5'8" 161 lbs.

1876	LOU N	67	.258	.286	283	73	1	0	0	0.0	36	21	5	11	0	0	0	122	17	27	4	2.5	.837	OF-65, C-5
1877	CIN N	20	.141	.155	71	10	1	0	0	0.0	7	3	3	6	0	0	0	63	24	23	1	5.5	.791	C-20, OF-1
2 yrs.		87	.234	.260	354	83	7	1	0	0.0	43	24	8	17	0	0	0	185	41	50	5	3.2	.819	OF-66, C-25

Billy Hatcher

HATCHER, WILLIAM AUGUSTUS
B. Oct. 4, 1960, Williams, Ariz.
BR TR 5'9" 175 lbs.

1984	CHI N	8	.111	.111	9	1	0	0	0	0.0	1	0	1	0	2	3	0	2	0	0	0	0.4	1.000	OF-4
1985		53	.245	.368	163	40	12	1	2	1.2	24	10	8	12	2	9	1	77	2	1	0	1.5	.988	OF-44
1986	HOU N	127	.258	.356	419	108	15	4	6	1.4	55	36	22	52	38	4	0	226	7	4	0	1.9	.983	OF-121
1987		141	.296	.415	564	167	28	3	11	2.0	96	63	42	70	53	1	1	276	16	4	6	2.1	.986	OF-140
1988		145	.268	.370	530	142	25	4	7	1.3	79	52	37	56	32	5	1	280	7	5	2	2.0	.983	OF-142
1989	2 teams		HOU N (108G – .228)			PIT N (27G – .244)																			
"	total	135	.231	.308	481	111	19	3	4	0.8	59	51	30	62	24	15	5	250	3	2	1	1.9	.992	OF-124
6 yrs.		609	.263	.364	2166	569	99	15	30	1.4	314	212	140	252	151	37	8	1111	34	16	9	1.9	.986	OF-575

LEAGUE CHAMPIONSHIP SERIES

| 1986 | HOU N | 6 | .280 | .400 | 25 | 7 | 0 | 0 | 1 | 4.0 | 4 | 2 | 3 | 2 | 3 | 2 | 1 | 11 | 0 | 1 | 0 | 2.0 | .917 | OF-6 |

Year	Team		Games	BA	SA	AB	H	2B	3B	HR	HR%	R	RBI	BB	SO	SB	Pinch Hit AB	Pinch Hit H	PO	A	E	DP	TC/G	FA	G by Pos

Mickey Hatcher

HATCHER, MICHAEL VAUGHN, JR.
B. Mar. 15, 1955, Cleveland, Ohio
BR TR 6'2" 200 lbs.

Year	Team		Games	BA	SA	AB	H	2B	3B	HR	HR%	R	RBI	BB	SO	SB	PH AB	PH H	PO	A	E	DP	TC/G	FA	G by Pos
1979	LA	N	33	.269	.366	93	25	4	1	1	1.1	9	5	7	12	1	6	1	47	24	5	0	2.3	.934	OF-19, 3B-17
1980			57	.226	.286	84	19	2	0	1	1.2	4	5	2	12	0	21	4	31	23	3	2	1.0	.947	OF-25, 3B-18
1981	MIN	A	99	.255	.350	377	96	23	2	3	0.8	36	37	15	29	3	2	1	296	11	3	5	3.1	.990	OF-91, 1B-7, 3B-2, DH-1
1982			84	.249	.343	277	69	13	2	3	1.1	23	26	8	27	0	9	3	81	17	1	1	1.2	.990	OF-47, DH-29, 3B-5
1983			105	.317	.445	375	119	15	3	9	2.4	50	47	14	19	2	15	6	199	11	3	9	2.0	.986	OF-56, DH-39, 1B-7, 3B-1
1984			152	.302	.406	576	174	35	5	5	0.9	61	69	37	34	0	2	0	364	20	9	10	2.6	.977	OF-100, DH-37, 1B-17, 3B-1
1985			116	.282	.365	444	125	28	0	3	0.7	46	49	16	23	0	6	2	246	7	3	4	2.2	.988	OF-97, DH-11, 1B-4
1986			115	.278	.366	317	88	13	3	3	0.9	40	32	19	26	2	38	6	220	16	4	16	2.1	.983	OF-46, DH-28, 1B-22, 3B-3
1987	LA	N	101	.282	.429	287	81	19	1	7	2.4	27	42	20	19	2	16	1	277	105	11	36	3.9	.972	3B-49, 1B-37, OF-7
1988			88	.293	.361	191	56	8	0	1	0.5	22	25	7	7	0	38	12	189	19	3	7	2.4	.986	OF-29, 1B-25, 3B-3
1989			94	.295	.379	224	66	9	2	2	0.9	18	25	13	16	1	34	6	89	21	4	7	1.2	.965	OF-48, 3B-16, 1B-5, P-1
11 yrs.			1044	.283	.382	3245	918	169	19	38	1.2	336	362	158	224	11	187	42	2039	274	49	97	2.3	.979	OF-565, DH-145, 1B-124, 3B-115, P-1

LEAGUE CHAMPIONSHIP SERIES

| 1988 | LA | N | 6 | .238 | .333 | 21 | 5 | 2 | 0 | 0 | 0.0 | 4 | 3 | 3 | 0 | 0 | 0 | 0 | 34 | 1 | 2 | 6 | 6.2 | .946 | 1B-6, OF-1 |

WORLD SERIES

| 1988 | LA | N | 5 | .368 | .737 | 19 | 7 | 1 | 0 | 2 | 10.5 | 5 | 5 | 1 | 3 | 0 | 0 | 0 | 8 | 0 | 0 | 0 | 1.6 | 1.000 | OF-5 |

Fred Hatfield

HATFIELD, FRED JAMES
B. Mar. 18, 1925, Lanett, Ala.
BL TR 6'1" 171 lbs.

Year	Team		Games	BA	SA	AB	H	2B	3B	HR	HR%	R	RBI	BB	SO	SB	PH AB	PH H	PO	A	E	DP	TC/G	FA	G by Pos
1950	BOS	A	10	.250	.250	12	3	0	0	0	0.0	3	2	3	1	0	1	0	4	9	0	2	1.3	1.000	3B-3
1951			80	.172	.258	163	28	4	2	2	1.2	23	14	22	27	1	14	2	40	124	7	15	2.1	.959	3B-49
1952	2 teams	BOS A (19G – .320)		DET A (112G – .236)																					
"	total		131	.240	.300	466	112	13	3	3	0.6	48	28	39	54	2	0	0	132	289	14	35	3.3	.968	3B-124, SS-9
1953	DET	A	109	.254	.325	311	79	11	1	3	1.0	41	19	40	34	3	19	7	120	208	9	34	3.1	.973	3B-54, 2B-28, SS-1
1954			81	.294	.376	218	64	12	0	2	0.9	31	25	28	24	4	17	5	129	152	11	33	3.6	.962	2B-54, 3B-15
1955			122	.232	.341	413	96	15	3	8	1.9	51	33	61	49	3	3	0	252	324	21	80	4.9	.965	2B-92, 3B-16, SS-14
1956	2 teams	DET A (8G – .250)		CHI A (106G – .262)																					
"	total		114	.261	.357	333	87	9	1	7	2.1	48	35	39	37	1	12	2	91	197	11	22	2.6	.963	3B-100, 2B-4, SS-3
1957	CHI	A	69	.202	.228	114	23	3	0	0	0.0	14	8	15	20	1	23	4	23	74	5	10	1.5	.951	3B-44
1958	2 teams	CLE A (3G – .125)		CIN N (3G – .000)																					
"	total		6	.111	.111	9	1	0	0	0	0.0	1	1	0	2	0	1	0	6	6	0	0	1.2	1.000	3B-2
9 yrs.			722	.242	.321	2039	493	67	10	25	1.2	259	165	248	247	15	91	20	792	1383	78	231	3.1	.965	3B-407, 2B-178, SS-27

Gil Hatfield

HATFIELD, GILBERT
Brother of John Hatfield.
B. Jan. 27, 1855, Hoboken, N. J.   D. May 27, 1921, Hoboken, N. J.
TR 5'9" 168 lbs.

Year	Team		Games	BA	SA	AB	H	2B	3B	HR	HR%	R	RBI	BB	SO	SB	PH AB	PH H	PO	A	E	DP	TC/G	FA	G by Pos
1885	BUF	N	11	.133	.200	30	4	0	1	0	0.0	1	0	0	11		0	0	10	23	6	0	3.5	.846	3B-8, 2B-3
1887	NY	N	2	.429	.571	7	3	1	0	0	0.0	2	3	0	1		0	0	5	3	0	0	4.0	1.000	3B-2
1888			28	.181	.190	105	19	1	0	0	0.0	7	9	2	18	8	0	0	30	63	24	5	4.2	.795	3B-14, SS-13, OF-1, 2B-1
1889			32	.184	.224	125	23	2	0	1	0.8	21	12	9	15	9	0	0	55	85	22	7	5.1	.864	SS-24, P-6, 3B-2
1890	NY	P	71	.279	.376	287	80	13	6	1	0.3	32	37	17	19	12	0	0	81	156	55	13	4.1	.812	3B-42, SS-27, P-3, OF-1
1891	WAS	AA	134	.256	.316	500	128	11	8	1	0.2	83	48	50	49	43	0	0	268	396	98	43	5.7	.871	SS-105, 3B-27, P-4, OF-3
1893	BKN	N	34	.292	.417	120	35	3	3	2	1.7	24	19	17	5	9	0	0	47	65	16	2	3.8	.875	3B-34
1895	LOU	N	5	.188	.188	16	3	0	0	0	0.0	3	1	1	1	0	0	0	3	6	1	0	2.0	.900	3B-3, SS-2
8 yrs.			317	.248	.317	1190	295	31	18	5	0.4	173	129	96	109	81	0	0	499	797	222	70	4.8	.854	SS-171, 3B-132, P-13, OF-5, 2B-4

John Hatfield

HATFIELD, JOHN VAN BUSKIRK
Brother of Gil Hatfield.
B. July 20, 1847, N. J.   D. Feb. 20, 1909, Long Island City, N. Y.
Manager 1873.
5'10" 165 lbs.

Year	Team		Games	BA	SA	AB	H	2B	3B	HR	HR%	R	RBI	BB	SO	SB	PH AB	PH H	PO	A	E	DP	TC/G	FA	G by Pos
1876	NY	N	1	.250	.250	4	1	0	0	0	0.0	0	1	0		0	0		0	4	1	0	6.0	.833	2B-1

Grady Hatton

HATTON, GRADY EDGEBERT
B. Oct. 7, 1922, Beaumont, Tex.
Manager 1966-68.
BL TR 5'8½" 170 lbs.

Year	Team		Games	BA	SA	AB	H	2B	3B	HR	HR%	R	RBI	BB	SO	SB	PH AB	PH H	PO	A	E	DP	TC/G	FA	G by Pos
1946	CIN	N	116	.271	.422	436	118	18	3	14	3.2	56	69	66	53	6	0	0	110	194	20	14	2.8	.938	3B-116, OF-2
1947			146	.281	.448	524	147	24	8	16	3.1	91	77	81	50	7	7	2	143	248	26	18	2.9	.938	3B-136
1948			133	.240	.345	458	110	17	2	9	2.0	58	44	72	50	7	3	1	145	248	28	22	3.2	.933	3B-123, 2B-3, SS-2, OF-1
1949			137	.263	.413	537	141	38	5	11	2.0	71	69	62	48	4	1	0	143	290	11	29	3.2	.975	3B-136
1950			130	.260	.379	438	114	17	1	11	2.5	67	54	70	39	6	4	1	146	230	18	19	3.0	.954	3B-126, SS-1, 2B-1
1951			96	.254	.335	331	84	9	3	4	1.2	41	37	33	32	4	7	2	104	178	8	24	3.0	.972	3B-87, OF-2
1952			128	.212	.312	433	92	14	1	9	2.1	48	57	66	60	5	7	1	316	289	6	68	4.8	.990	2B-120
1953			83	.233	.396	159	37	3	1	7	4.4	22	22	29	24	0	38	7	133	56	1	30	2.3	.995	2B-35, 1B-10, 3B-5
1954	3 teams	CIN N (1G – .000)		CHI A (13G – .167)		BOS A (99G – .281)																			
"	total		113	.270	.372	333	90	13	3	5	1.5	43	43	63	28	0	2	0	96	222	10	22	2.9	.970	3B-103, 1B-4, SS-1
1955	BOS	A	126	.245	.326	380	93	11	4	4	1.1	48	49	76	28	0	12	1	97	225	8	22	2.6	.976	3B-111, 2B-1
1956	3 teams	BOS A (5G – .400)		STL N (44G – .247)		BAL A (27G – .148)																			
"	total		76	.209	.273	139	29	2	2	1	0.7	14	12	26	13	1	35	9	48	75	4	11	1.7	.969	3B-28, 2B-13
1960	CHI	N	28	.342	.342	38	13	0	0	0	0.0	3	7	2	5	0	16	3	11	16	2	2	1.0	.931	2B-8
12 yrs.			1312	.254	.374	4206	1068	166	33	91	2.2	562	533	646	430	42	138	27	1492	2271	142	281	3.0	.964	3B-956, 2B-196, 1B-14, OF-5, SS-4

Art Haugher

HAUGHER, JOHN ARTHUR
B. Nov. 18, 1893, Delhi, Ohio   D. Aug. 2, 1944, Redwood City, Calif.
BL TR 5'11" 168 lbs.

Year	Team		Games	BA	SA	AB	H	2B	3B	HR	HR%	R	RBI	BB	SO	SB	PH AB	PH H	PO	A	E	DP	TC/G	FA	G by Pos
1912	CLE	A	15	.056	.056	18	1	0	0	0	0.0	0	0	1		0	10	1	4	0	0	0	0.3	1.000	OF-5

Year	Team		Games	BA	SA	AB	H	2B	3B	HR	HR%	R	RBI	BB	SO	SB	Pinch Hit AB	Pinch Hit H	PO	A	E	DP	TC/G	FA	G by Pos

Arnold Hauser

HAUSER, ARNOLD GEORGE (Pee Wee)
B. Sept. 25, 1888, Chicago, Ill. D. May 22, 1966, Aurora, Ill. BR TR 5'6" 145 lbs.

Year	Team		Games	BA	SA	AB	H	2B	3B	HR	HR%	R	RBI	BB	SO	SB	PH AB	PH H	PO	A	E	DP	TC/G	FA	G by Pos
1910	STL	N	119	.205	.251	375	77	7	2	2	0.5	37	36	49	39	15	1	0	212	346	41	31	5.0	.932	SS-117, 3B-1
1911			136	.241	.311	515	124	11	8	3	0.6	61	46	26	67	24	0	0	225	402	56	52	5.0	.918	SS-134, 3B-2
1912			133	.259	.324	479	124	14	7	1	0.2	73	42	39	69	26	1	1	262	446	50	54	5.7	.934	SS-132
1913			22	.289	.422	45	13	0	3	0	0.0	3	9	2	1	1	8	4	18	25	5	4	2.2	.896	SS-8, 2B-4
1915	CHI	F	23	.204	.222	54	11	1	0	0	0.0	6	4	5	1	2	0	0	28	43	11	7	3.6	.866	SS-16, 3B-6
5 yrs.			433	.238	.300	1468	349	33	20	6	0.4	180	137	121	177	68	10	5	745	1262	163	148	5.0	.925	SS-407, 3B-9, 2B-4

Joe Hauser

HAUSER, JOSEPH JOHN (Unser Choe)
B. Jan. 12, 1899, Milwaukee, Wis. BL TL 5'10½" 175 lbs.

Year	Team		Games	BA	SA	AB	H	2B	3B	HR	HR%	R	RBI	BB	SO	SB	PH AB	PH H	PO	A	E	DP	TC/G	FA	G by Pos
1922	PHI	A	111	.323	.481	368	119	21	5	9	2.4	61	43	30	37	1	16	6	936	55	14	61	9.1	.986	1B-94
1923			146	.307	.473	537	165	21	10	16	3.0	93	94	69	52	6	0	0	1475	86	15	109	10.8	.990	1B-146
1924			149	.288	.516	562	162	31	8	27	4.8	97	115	56	52	7	1	0	1513	94	12	131	10.9	.993	1B-146
1926			91	.192	.341	229	44	10	0	8	3.5	31	36	39	34	1	22	5	630	35	3	39	7.3	.996	1B-65
1928			95	.260	.517	300	78	19	5	16	5.3	61	59	52	45	4	7	0	811	41	12	51	9.1	.986	1B-88
1929	CLE	A	37	.250	.500	48	12	1	1	3	6.3	8	9	4	8	0	25	5	65	5	1	2	1.9	.986	1B-8
6 yrs.			629	.284	.478	2044	580	103	29	79	3.9	351	356	250	228	19	71	16	5430	316	57	393	9.2	.990	1B-547

George Hausmann

HAUSMANN, GEORGE JOHN
B. Feb. 11, 1916, St. Louis, Mo. BR TR 5'5" 145 lbs.

Year	Team		Games	BA	SA	AB	H	2B	3B	HR	HR%	R	RBI	BB	SO	SB	PH AB	PH H	PO	A	E	DP	TC/G	FA	G by Pos
1944	NY	N	131	.266	.333	466	124	20	4	1	0.2	70	30	40	25	3	1	0	301	350	27	66	5.2	.960	2B-122
1945			154	.279	.339	623	174	15	8	2	0.3	98	45	73	46	7	0	0	376	489	29	65	5.8	.968	2B-154
1949			16	.128	.170	47	6	0	1	0	0.0	5	3	7	6	0	1	0	25	37	1	8	3.9	.984	2B-13
3 yrs.			301	.268	.329	1136	304	35	13	3	0.3	173	78	120	77	10	2	0	702	876	57	139	5.4	.965	2B-289

Charlie Hautz

HAUTZ, CHARLES A.
B. Feb. 5, 1852, St. Louis, Mo. D. Jan. 24, 1929, St. Louis, Mo. 5'7" 150 lbs.

Year	Team		Games	BA	SA	AB	H	2B	3B	HR	HR%	R	RBI	BB	SO	SB	PH AB	PH H	PO	A	E	DP	TC/G	FA	G by Pos
1884	PIT	AA	7	.208	.208	24	5	0	0	0	0.0	0		3			0	0	50	2	1	3	7.6	.981	1B-5, OF-2

Bill Hawes

HAWES, WILLIAM HILDRETH
B. Nov. 17, 1853, Nashua, N. H. D. June 16, 1940, Lowell, Mass. BR TR 5'10" 155 lbs.

Year	Team		Games	BA	SA	AB	H	2B	3B	HR	HR%	R	RBI	BB	SO	SB	PH AB	PH H	PO	A	E	DP	TC/G	FA	G by Pos
1879	BOS	N	38	.200	.258	155	31	3	3	0	0.0	19	9	2	13		0	0	60	15	14	2	2.3	.843	OF-34, C-5
1884	CIN	U	79	.278	.355	349	97	7	4	4	1.1	80		5			0	0	274	10	27	4	3.9	.913	OF-58, 1B-21
2 yrs.			117	.254	.325	504	128	10	7	4	0.8	99	9	7	13		0	0	334	25	41	6	3.4	.898	OF-92, 1B-21, C-5

Roy Hawes

HAWES, ROY LEE
B. July 5, 1926, Shiloh, Ill. BL TL 6'2" 190 lbs.

Year	Team		Games	BA	SA	AB	H	2B	3B	HR	HR%	R	RBI	BB	SO	SB	PH AB	PH H	PO	A	E	DP	TC/G	FA	G by Pos
1951	WAS	A	3	.167	.167	6	1	0	0	0	0.0	0	0	0	1	0	2	1	13	0	0	0	4.3	1.000	1B-1

Thorny Hawkes

HAWKES, THORNDIKE PROCTOR
B. Oct. 15, 1852, Danvers, Mass. D. Feb. 3, 1929, Danvers, Mass. BR TR 5'8" 135 lbs.

Year	Team		Games	BA	SA	AB	H	2B	3B	HR	HR%	R	RBI	BB	SO	SB	PH AB	PH H	PO	A	E	DP	TC/G	FA	G by Pos
1879	TRO	N	64	.208	.240	250	52	6	1	0	0.0	24		4	14		0	0	220	264	56	26	8.4	.896	2B-64
1884	WAS	AA	38	.278	.331	151	42	4	2	0	0.0	16		4			0	0	128	107	22	10	6.8	.914	2B-38, OF-2
2 yrs.			102	.234	.274	401	94	10	3	0	0.0	40	20	8	14		0	0	348	371	78	36	7.8	.902	2B-102, OF-2

Chicken Hawks

HAWKS, NELSON LOUIS
B. Feb. 3, 1896, San Francisco, Calif. D. May 26, 1973, San Rafael, Calif. BL TL 5'11" 167 lbs.

Year	Team		Games	BA	SA	AB	H	2B	3B	HR	HR%	R	RBI	BB	SO	SB	PH AB	PH H	PO	A	E	DP	TC/G	FA	G by Pos
1921	NY	A	41	.288	.479	73	21	3	2	2	2.7	16	15	5	12	0	23	8	32	0	1	0	0.8	.970	OF-15
1925	PHI	N	105	.322	.447	320	103	15	5	5	1.6	52	45	32	33	3	13	5	775	45	12	64	7.9	.986	1B-90
2 yrs.			146	.316	.453	393	124	17	7	7	1.8	68	60	37	45	3	36	13	807	45	13	64	5.9	.985	1B-90, OF-15

Howie Haworth

HAWORTH, HOMER HOWARD (Cully)
B. Aug. 27, 1893, Newburg, Ore. D. Jan. 28, 1953, Troutdale, Ore. BL TR 5'10½" 165 lbs.

Year	Team		Games	BA	SA	AB	H	2B	3B	HR	HR%	R	RBI	BB	SO	SB	PH AB	PH H	PO	A	E	DP	TC/G	FA	G by Pos
1915	CLE	A	7	.143	.143	7	1	0	0	0	0.0	0	2	2	0	1	0	0	10	1	1	0	1.7	.917	C-5

Jack Hayden

HAYDEN, JOHN FRANCIS
B. Oct. 21, 1880, Bryn Mawr, Pa. D. Aug. 3, 1942, Haverford, Pa. BR TL 5'9"

Year	Team		Games	BA	SA	AB	H	2B	3B	HR	HR%	R	RBI	BB	SO	SB	PH AB	PH H	PO	A	E	DP	TC/G	FA	G by Pos
1901	PHI	A	51	.265	.332	211	56	6	4	0	0.0	35	17	18		4	1	0	63	11	14	0	1.7	.841	OF-50
1906	BOS	A	85	.280	.332	322	90	6	4	1	0.3	22	13	17		6	0	0	136	7	4	1	1.7	.973	OF-85
1908	CHI	N	11	.200	.244	45	9	2	0	0	0.0	3	2	1		1	0	0	19	0	0	0	1.7	1.000	OF-11
3 yrs.			147	.268	.325	578	155	14	8	1	0.2	60	32	36		11	1	0	218	18	18	1	1.7	.929	OF-146

Bill Hayes

HAYES, WILLIAM ERNEST
B. Oct. 24, 1957, Cheverly, Md. BR TR 6' 195 lbs.

Year	Team		Games	BA	SA	AB	H	2B	3B	HR	HR%	R	RBI	BB	SO	SB	PH AB	PH H	PO	A	E	DP	TC/G	FA	G by Pos
1980	CHI	N	4	.222	.333	9	2	1	0	0	0.0	0	0	0	3	0	1	0	9	2	0	0	2.8	1.000	C-3
1981			1	—	—	0	0	0	0	0	—	0	0	0	0	0	0	0	0	0	0	0	0.0	—	C-1
2 yrs.			5	.222	.333	9	2	1	0	0	0.0	0	0	0	3	0	1	0	9	2	0	0	2.2	1.000	C-4

Charlie Hayes

HAYES, CHARLES DEWAYNE
B. May 29, 1965, Hattiesburg, Miss. BR TR 6' 190 lbs.

Year	Team		Games	BA	SA	AB	H	2B	3B	HR	HR%	R	RBI	BB	SO	SB	PH AB	PH H	PO	A	E	DP	TC/G	FA	G by Pos
1988	SF	N	7	.091	.091	11	1	0	0	0	0.0	0	0	0	3	0	2	0	5	0	0	0	0.7	1.000	OF-4, 3B-3
1989	2 teams	SF N (3G – .200)		PHI N (84G – .258)																					
"	total		87	.257	.391	304	78	15	1	8	2.6	26	43	11	50	3	5	2	51	174	22	15	2.8	.911	3B-85
2 yrs.			94	.251	.381	315	79	15	1	8	2.5	26	43	11	53	3	7	2	56	174	22	15	2.7	.913	3B-88, OF-4

Frankie Hayes

HAYES, FRANK WHITMAN (Blimp)
B. Oct. 13, 1914, Jamesburg, N. J. D. June 22, 1955, Point Pleasant, N. J. BR TR 6' 185 lbs.

Year	Team		Games	BA	SA	AB	H	2B	3B	HR	HR%	R	RBI	BB	SO	SB	PH AB	PH H	PO	A	E	DP	TC/G	FA	G by Pos
1933	PHI	A	3	.000	.000	5	0	0	0	0	0.0	0	0	0	0	0	0	0	7	1	1	0	3.0	.889	C-3
1934			92	.226	.339	248	56	10	0	6	2.4	24	30	20	44	2	4	3	279	36	15	4	3.6	.955	C-89

Frankie Hayes *continued*

Year	Team	Games	BA	SA	AB	H	2B	3B	HR	HR%	R	RBI	BB	SO	SB	Pinch Hit AB	Pinch Hit H	PO	A	E	DP	TC/G	FA	G by Pos
1936		144	.271	.388	505	137	25	2	10	2.0	59	67	46	58	3	1	0	489	69	16	8	4.0	.972	C-143
1937		60	.261	.489	188	49	11	1	10	5.3	24	38	29	34	0	4	1	208	23	7	4	4.0	.971	C-56
1938		99	.291	.475	316	92	19	3	11	3.5	56	55	54	51	2	7	3	319	38	9	2	3.7	.975	C-90
1939		124	.283	.510	431	122	28	5	20	4.6	66	83	40	55	4	10	5	380	60	10	12	3.6	.978	C-114
1940		136	.308	.477	465	143	23	4	16	3.4	73	70	61	59	9	2	1	531	63	18	9	4.5	.971	C-134, 1B-2
1941		126	.280	.442	439	123	27	4	12	2.7	66	63	62	56	2	3	0	403	65	8	11	3.8	.983	C-123
1942	2 teams	PHI	A	(21G — .238)	STL	A	(56G — .252)																	
"	total	77	.248	.320	222	55	10	2	2	0.9	22	22	37	47	1	6	2	241	36	6	2	3.7	.979	C-71
1943	STL A	88	.188	.276	250	47	7	0	5	2.0	16	30	37	36	1	9	3	301	41	6	8	4.0	.983	C-76, 1B-1
1944	PHI A	155	.248	.367	581	144	18	6	13	2.2	62	78	57	59	2	0	0	637	89	13	11	4.8	.982	C-155, 1B-1
1945	2 teams	PHI	A	(32G — .227)	CLE	A	(119G — .236)																	
"	total	151	.234	.352	495	116	17	7	9	1.8	51	57	71	66	2	0	0	639	91	8	29	4.9	.989	C-151
1946	2 teams	CLE	A	(51G — .256)	CHI	A	(53G — .212)																	
"	total	104	.233	.331	335	78	18	0	5	1.5	26	34	50	59	2	2	1	501	48	11	6	5.4	.980	C-100
1947	BOS A	5	.154	.154	13	2	0	0	0	0.0	0	1	0	1	0	1	0	20	2	2	1	4.8	.917	C-4
14 yrs.		1364	.259	.400	4493	1164	213	32	119	2.6	545	628	564	627	30	49	19	4955	662	130	107	4.2	.977	C-1309, 1B-4

Jack Hayes

HAYES, JOHN J.
B. June 27, 1861, Brooklyn, N. Y. Deceased.   TR

Year	Team	Games	BA	SA	AB	H	2B	3B	HR	HR%	R	RBI	BB	SO	SB	Pinch Hit AB	Pinch Hit H	PO	A	E	DP	TC/G	FA	G by Pos
1882	WOR N	78	.270	.399	326	88	22	4	4	1.2	27	54	6	26		0	0	162	40	41	4	3.1	.831	OF-58, C-15, 3B-5, SS-1
1883	PIT AA	85	.262	.382	351	92	23	5	3	0.9	41		15			0	0	354	85	49	2	5.7	.900	C-62, OF-18, SS-5, 1B-5, 2B-1
1884	2 teams	PIT	AA	(33G — .226)	BKN	AA	(16G — .235)																	
"	total	49	.229	.291	175	40	9	1	0	0.0	15		7			0	0	274	59	27	7	7.3	.925	C-38, OF-5, 1B-5, 2B-1
1885	BKN AA	42	.131	.153	137	18	3	0	0	0.0	10		5			0	0	209	53	29	4	6.9	.900	C-42
1886	WAS N	26	.191	.326	89	17	3	0	3	3.4	8	9	4	23		0	0	85	23	8	2	4.5	.931	C-14, OF-12, 2B-1
1887	BAL AA	8	.143	.250	28	4	3	0	0	0.0	2		0			0	0	7	5	6	0	2.3	.667	OF-4, 3B-3, C-1
1890	BKN P	12	.190	.190	42	8	0	0	0	0.0	3	5	2	4	0	0	0	23	4	11	1	2.8	.818	OF-6, SS-3, C-2, 2B-1
7 yrs.		300	.233	.331	1148	267	63	10	10	0.9	106	68	39	53	0	0	0	1114	269	166	20	5.2	.893	C-174, OF-103, 1B-10, SS-9, 3B-8, 2B-4

Jackie Hayes

HAYES, MINTER CARNEY
B. July 19, 1906, Clanton, Ala. D. Feb. 9, 1983, Birmingham, Ala.   BR TR 5'10½" 165 lbs.

Year	Team	Games	BA	SA	AB	H	2B	3B	HR	HR%	R	RBI	BB	SO	SB	Pinch Hit AB	Pinch Hit H	PO	A	E	DP	TC/G	FA	G by Pos
1927	WAS A	10	.241	.241	29	7	0	0	0	0.0	2	2	1	2	0	2	0	12	22	1	2	3.5	.971	SS-8, 3B-1
1928		60	.257	.319	210	54	7	3	0	0.0	30	22	5	10	3	2	1	134	177	10	36	5.4	.969	2B-41, SS-15, 3B-2
1929		123	.276	.351	424	117	20	3	2	0.5	52	57	24	29	4	2	0	181	312	18	57	4.2	.965	3B-63, 2B-56, SS-2
1930		51	.283	.367	166	47	7	2	1	0.6	25	20	7	8	2	5	1	149	110	5	33	5.2	.981	2B-29, 3B-9, 1B-8
1931		38	.222	.259	108	24	2	1	0	0.0	11	8	6	4	2	7	1	58	62	4	8	3.3	.968	2B-19, 3B-8, SS-3
1932	CHI A	117	.257	.333	475	122	20	5	2	0.4	53	54	30	28	7	0	0	274	386	30	83	5.9	.957	2B-97, SS-10, 3B-10
1933		138	.258	.331	535	138	23	5	2	0.4	65	47	55	36	2	0	0	344	497	16	89	6.2	.981	2B-138
1934		62	.257	.319	226	58	9	1	1	0.4	19	31	23	20	3	0	0	147	188	7	35	5.5	.980	2B-61
1935		89	.267	.347	329	88	14	0	4	1.2	45	45	29	15	3	5	0	202	275	17	48	5.6	.966	2B-85
1936		108	.312	.444	417	130	34	3	5	1.2	53	84	35	25	4	0	0	253	380	15	82	6.0	.977	2B-89, SS-13, 3B-2
1937		143	.229	.300	573	131	27	4	2	0.3	63	79	41	37	1	0	0	353	490	14	115	6.0	.984	2B-143
1938		62	.328	.445	238	78	21	2	1	0.4	40	20	24	6	3	1	0	146	183	8	51	5.4	.976	2B-61
1939		72	.249	.316	269	67	12	3	0	0.0	34	23	27	10	0	2	0	172	201	10	51	5.3	.974	2B-69
1940		18	.195	.244	41	8	0	1	0	0.0	2	1	2	11	0	2	0	21	32	1	8	3.0	.981	2B-15
14 yrs.		1091	.265	.344	4040	1069	196	33	20	0.5	494	493	309	241	34	29	3	2446	3315	156	698	5.4	.974	2B-903, 3B-95, SS-51, 1B-8

Mike Hayes

HAYES, MICHAEL
B. 1853, Cleveland, Ohio Deceased.   5'7½" 170 lbs.

Year	Team	Games	BA	SA	AB	H	2B	3B	HR	HR%	R	RBI	BB	SO	SB	Pinch Hit AB	Pinch Hit H	PO	A	E	DP	TC/G	FA	G by Pos
1876	NY N	5	.143	.333	21	3	0	2	0	0.0	1	2	0	0		0	0	15	0	2	0	3.4	.882	OF-5

Von Hayes

HAYES, VON FRANCIS
B. Aug. 31, 1958, Stockton, Calif.   BL TR 6'5" 185 lbs.

Year	Team	Games	BA	SA	AB	H	2B	3B	HR	HR%	R	RBI	BB	SO	SB	Pinch Hit AB	Pinch Hit H	PO	A	E	DP	TC/G	FA	G by Pos
1981	CLE A	43	.257	.394	109	28	8	2	1	0.9	21	17	14	10	8	9	4	30	4	3	1	0.9	.919	DH-21, OF-13, 3B-5
1982		150	.250	.389	527	132	25	3	14	2.7	65	82	42	63	32	11	2	323	17	6	6	2.3	.983	OF-139, 3B-5, 1B-4
1983	PHI N	124	.265	.370	351	93	9	5	6	1.7	45	32	36	55	20	21	5	165	7	5	0	1.4	.972	OF-103
1984		152	.292	.447	561	164	27	6	16	2.9	85	67	59	84	48	12	5	341	2	4	1	2.3	.988	OF-148
1985		152	.263	.398	570	150	30	4	13	2.3	76	70	61	99	21	6	4	368	9	6	1	2.5	.984	OF-146
1986		158	.305	.480	610	186	46	2	19	3.1	107	98	74	77	24	2	0	1247	100	13	106	8.6	.990	1B-134, OF-31
1987		158	.277	.473	556	154	36	5	21	3.8	84	84	121	77	16	4	0	1216	80	13	100	8.3	.990	1B-144, OF-32
1988		104	.272	.409	367	100	28	2	6	1.6	43	45	49	59	20	5	1	756	58	9	66	7.9	.989	1B-85, OF-16, 3B-3
1989		154	.259	.461	540	140	27	2	26	4.8	93	78	101	103	28	4	0	426	47	9	24	3.1	.981	OF-128, 1B-30, 3B-10
9 yrs.		1195	.274	.432	4191	1147	236	31	122	2.9	619	573	557	627	217	74	18	4872	324	68	305	4.4	.987	OF-756, 1B-397, 3B-23, DH-21

LEAGUE CHAMPIONSHIP SERIES

Year	Team	Games	BA	SA	AB	H	2B	3B	HR	HR%	R	RBI	BB	SO	SB	Pinch Hit AB	Pinch Hit H	PO	A	E	DP	TC/G	FA	G by Pos
1983	PHI N	2	.000	.000	2	0	0	0	0	0.0	0	0	0	1	0	1	0	0	0	0	0	0.0	—	OF-1

WORLD SERIES

Year	Team	Games	BA	SA	AB	H	2B	3B	HR	HR%	R	RBI	BB	SO	SB	Pinch Hit AB	Pinch Hit H	PO	A	E	DP	TC/G	FA	G by Pos
1983	PHI N	4	.000	.000	3	0	0	0	0	0.0	0	0	0	1	0	0	0	1	0	0	0	0.3	1.000	OF-1

Ray Hayworth

HAYWORTH, RAYMOND HALL
Brother of Red Hayworth.
B. Jan. 29, 1904, High Point, N. C.   BR TR 6' 180 lbs.

Year	Team	Games	BA	SA	AB	H	2B	3B	HR	HR%	R	RBI	BB	SO	SB	Pinch Hit AB	Pinch Hit H	PO	A	E	DP	TC/G	FA	G by Pos
1926	DET A	12	.273	.273	11	3	0	0	0	0.0	1	5	1	1		0	0	9	0	0	0	0.8	1.000	C-8
1929		14	.256	.256	43	11	0	0	0	0.0	5	4	3	8		0	0	46	12	3	1	4.4	.951	C-14
1930		77	.278	.379	227	63	15	4	0	0.0	24	22	20	19	0	0	0	277	27	7	4	4.0	.977	C-76
1931		88	.256	.315	273	70	10	3	0	0.0	28	25	19	27	0	0	0	334	61	11	5	4.6	.973	C-88
1932		108	.293	.382	338	99	20	2	2	0.6	41	44	31	22	1	3	1	399	59	4	8	4.3	.991	C-105
1933		134	.245	.299	425	104	14	3	1	0.2	37	45	35	28	0	1	0	546	79	4	14	4.7	.994	C-133

Year	Team		Games	BA	SA	AB	H	2B	3B	HR	HR%	R	RBI	BB	SO	SB	Pinch Hit AB	Pinch Hit H	PO	A	E	DP	TC/G	FA	G by Pos

Ray Hayworth *continued*

Year	Team		Games	BA	SA	AB	H	2B	3B	HR	HR%	R	RBI	BB	SO	SB	AB	H	PO	A	E	DP	TC/G	FA	G by Pos
1934			54	.293	.347	167	49	5	2	0	0.0	20	27	16	22	0	1	0	226	23	4	3	4.7	.984	C-54
1935			51	.309	.411	175	54	14	2	0	0.0	22	22	9	14	0	3	1	211	35	1	4	4.8	.996	C-48
1936			81	.240	.292	250	60	10	0	1	0.4	31	30	39	18	0	1	0	305	28	4	5	4.2	.988	C-81
1937			30	.269	.333	78	21	2	0	1	1.3	9	8	14	15	0	1	0	118	14	1	2	4.4	.992	C-28
1938	2 teams	DET A (8G – .211)				BKN	N	(5G – .000)																	
"	total		13	.174	.174	23	4	0	0	0	0.0	1	5	4	5	1	2	1	36	1	1	0	2.9	.974	C-10
1939	2 teams	BKN N (21G – .154)				NY	N	(5G – .231)																	
"	total		26	.179	.231	39	7	2	0	0	0.0	1	1	4	8	0	1	0	51	7	0	0	2.2	1.000	C-23
1942	STL	A	1	1.000	1.000	1	1	0	0	0	0.0	0	0	0	0	0	1	1	0	0	0	0	0.0	–	C-6
1944	BKN	N	7	.000	.000	10	0	0	0	0	0.0	0	0	2	1	0	0	0	18	2	0	0	2.9	1.000	C-2
1945			2	.000	.000	2	0	0	0	0	0.0	0	0	1	0	0	0	0	5	0	0	0	2.5	1.000	
	15 yrs.		698	.265	.332	2062	546	92	16	5	0.2	221	238	198	188	2	19	4	2581	348	40	46	4.3	.987	C-676

WORLD SERIES

| 1934 | DET | A | 1 | – | – | 0 | 0 | 0 | 0 | 0 | – | 0 | 0 | 0 | 0 | 0 | 0 | 0 | 1 | 0 | 0 | 0 | 1.0 | 1.000 | C-1 |

Red Hayworth

HAYWORTH, MYRON CLAUDE
Brother of Ray Hayworth.
B. May 14, 1915, High Point, N. C.

BR TR 6'1½" 200 lbs.

1944	STL	A	89	.223	.283	269	60	11	1	1	0.4	20	25	10	13	0	4	1	336	39	13	4	4.4	.966	C-86
1945			56	.194	.219	160	31	4	0	0	0.0	7	17	7	6	0	2	0	216	23	2	5	4.3	.992	C-55
	2 yrs.		145	.212	.259	429	91	15	1	1	0.2	27	42	17	19	0	6	1	552	62	15	9	4.3	.976	C-141

WORLD SERIES

| 1944 | STL | A | 6 | .118 | .176 | 17 | 2 | 1 | 0 | 0 | 0.0 | 1 | 1 | 3 | 1 | 0 | 0 | 0 | 45 | 2 | 1 | 0 | 8.0 | .979 | C-6 |

Drungo Hazewood

HAZEWOOD, DRUNGO LaRUE
B. Sept. 2, 1959, Mobile, Ala.

BR TR 6'3" 210 lbs.

| 1980 | BAL | A | 6 | .000 | .000 | 5 | 0 | 0 | 0 | 0 | 0.0 | 1 | 0 | 0 | 4 | 0 | 0 | 0 | 1 | 0 | 0 | 0 | 0.2 | 1.000 | OF-3 |

Bob Hazle

HAZLE, ROBERT SIDNEY (Hurricane)
B. Dec. 9, 1930, Laurens, S. C.

BL TR 6' 190 lbs.

1955	CIN	N	6	.231	.231	13	3	0	0	0	0.0	0	0	0	3	1	0	0	12	1	0	0	2.2	1.000	OF-4
1957	MIL	N	41	.403	.649	134	54	12	0	7	5.2	26	27	18	15	1	1	1	57	1	6	0	1.6	.906	OF-40
1958	2 teams	MIL N (20G – .179)				DET	A	(43G – .241)																	
"	total		63	.211	.281	114	24	2	0	2	1.8	11	10	14	17	0	29	6	45	0	0	0	0.7	1.000	OF-32
	3 yrs.		110	.310	.467	261	81	14	0	9	3.4	37	37	32	35	1	33	8	114	2	6	0	1.1	.951	OF-76

WORLD SERIES

| 1957 | MIL | N | 4 | .154 | .154 | 13 | 2 | 0 | 0 | 0 | 0.0 | 2 | 0 | 0 | 2 | 0 | 0 | 0 | 6 | 0 | 0 | 0 | 1.5 | 1.000 | OF-4 |

Doc Hazleton

HAZLETON, WILLARD CARPENTER
B. Aug. 28, 1876, Strafford, Vt. D. Mar. 17, 1941, Burlington, Vt.

| 1902 | STL | N | 7 | .130 | .130 | 23 | 3 | 0 | 0 | 0 | 0.0 | 0 | 0 | 0 | | 0 | 2 | 0 | 67 | 4 | 2 | 8 | 10.4 | .973 | 1B-7 |

Fran Healy

HEALY, FRANCIS XAVIER
B. Sept. 6, 1946, Holyoke, Mass.

BR TR 6'5" 220 lbs.

1969	KC	A	6	.400	.500	10	4	1	0	0	0.0	0	0	0	2	1	0	0	16	1	0	0	2.8	1.000	C-5
1971	SF	N	47	.280	.376	93	26	3	0	2	2.2	10	11	15	24	1	22	5	104	8	4	1	2.5	.966	C-22
1972			45	.152	.222	99	15	4	0	1	1.0	12	8	13	24	0	1	0	174	21	1	3	4.4	.995	C-43
1973	KC	A	95	.276	.409	279	77	15	2	6	2.2	25	34	31	56	3	1	0	429	43	10	4	5.1	.979	C-92, DH-1
1974			139	.252	.375	445	112	24	2	9	2.0	59	53	62	73	16	5	0	620	64	16	4	5.0	.977	C-138
1975			56	.255	.335	188	48	5	2	2	1.1	16	18	14	19	4	2	2	258	17	5	2	5.0	.982	C-51, DH-4
1976	2 teams	KC A (8G – .125)				NY	A	(46G – .267)																	
"	total		54	.243	.264	144	35	3	0	0	0.0	12	10	13	27	5	7	0	134	20	2	0	2.9	.987	C-37, DH-2
1977	NY	A	27	.224	.299	67	15	5	0	0	0.0	10	7	6	13	1	1	0	98	3	3	0	3.9	.971	C-26
1978			1	.000	.000	1	0	0	0	0	0.0	0	0	0	1	0	0	0	0	0	0	0	0.0	–	C-1
	9 yrs.		470	.250	.350	1326	332	60	8	20	1.5	144	141	154	242	30	41	11	1833	177	41	14	4.4	.980	C-415, DH-7

Francis Healy

HEALY, FRANCIS XAVIER PAUL
B. July 29, 1910, Holyoke, Mass.

BR TR 5'9½" 175 lbs.

1930	NY	N	7	.000	.000	2	0	0	0	0	0.0	0	0	0	2	0	0	0	0	0	0	0	0.0	–	C-1
1931			6	.143	.143	7	1	0	0	0	0.0	1	0	0	0	0	0	0	10	0	0	2	1.7	1.000	C-6
1932			14	.250	.313	32	8	2	0	0	0.0	5	4	2	8	0	2	0	43	5	2	0	3.6	.960	C-11
1934	STL	N	15	.308	.385	13	4	1	0	0	0.0	3	1	0	0	0	8	3	4	1	0	1	0.3	1.000	C-2, OF-1, 3B-1
	4 yrs.		42	.241	.296	54	13	3	0	0	0.0	9	5	2	10	0	12	3	57	6	2	3	1.5	.969	C-20, OF-1, 3B-1

Tom Healy

HEALY, THOMAS FITZGERALD
B. Oct. 30, 1895, Altoona, Pa. D. Jan. 10, 1977, Cleveland, Ohio

BR TR 6' 172 lbs.

1915	PHI	A	23	.221	.234	77	17	1	0	0	0.0	11	5	6	4	0	1	0	29	44	5	4	3.4	.936	3B-17, SS-1
1916			6	.261	.391	23	6	1	0	0	0.0	4	2	1	2	1	0	0	6	12	1	1	3.2	.947	3B-6
	2 yrs.		29	.230	.270	100	23	2	0	0	0.0	15	7	7	6	1	1	0	35	56	6	5	3.3	.938	3B-23, SS-1

Charlie Heard

HEARD, CHARLES
B. Jan. 30, 1872, Philadelphia, Pa. D. Feb. 20, 1945, Philadelphia, Pa.

BR TR 6'2" 190 lbs.

| 1890 | PIT | N | 12 | .186 | .233 | 43 | 8 | 2 | 0 | 0 | 0.0 | 2 | 0 | 1 | 15 | 0 | 0 | 0 | 7 | 6 | 6 | 1 | 1.6 | .684 | OF-6, P-6 |

Ed Hearn

HEARN, EDMUND
B. Sept. 17, 1888, Ventura, Calif. D. Sept. 8, 1952, Sawtelle, Calif.

BR TR 5'9" 160 lbs.

| 1910 | BOS | A | 2 | .000 | .000 | 2 | 0 | 0 | 0 | 0 | 0.0 | 0 | 0 | 0 | | 0 | 0 | 0 | 3 | 4 | 1 | 0 | 4.0 | .875 | SS-2 |

Year Team	Games	BA	SA	AB	H	2B	3B	HR	HR%	R	RBI	BB	SO	SB	Pinch Hit AB	Pinch Hit H	PO	A	E	DP	TC/G	FA	G by Pos

Ed Hearn
HEARN, EDWARD JOHN
B. Aug. 23, 1960, Stuart, Fla.　　　　BR TR 6'3" 215 lbs.

Year Team	Games	BA	SA	AB	H	2B	3B	HR	HR%	R	RBI	BB	SO	SB	PH AB	PH H	PO	A	E	DP	TC/G	FA	G by Pos
1986 NY N	49	.265	.390	136	36	5	0	4	2.9	16	10	12	19	0	6	2	223	11	3	1	4.8	.987	C-45
1987 KC A	6	.294	.412	17	5	2	0	0	0.0	2	3	4	2	0	1	0	25	0	0	0	4.2	1.000	C-5
1988	7	.222	.333	18	4	2	0	0	0.0	1	1	0	1	0	2	1	12	1	0	0	1.9	1.000	C-4, DH-2
3 yrs.	62	.263	.386	171	45	9	0	4	2.3	19	14	16	22	0	9	3	260	12	3	1	4.4	.989	C-54, DH-2

Hugh Hearne
HEARNE, HUGH JOSEPH
B. Apr. 18, 1873, Troy, N. Y.　 D. Sept. 22, 1932, Troy, N. Y.　　BR TR 5'8" 182 lbs.

Year Team	Games	BA	SA	AB	H	2B	3B	HR	HR%	R	RBI	BB	SO	SB	PH AB	PH H	PO	A	E	DP	TC/G	FA	G by Pos
1901 BKN N	2	.400	.400	5	2	0	0	0	0.0	1	3	0			0	0	4	3	0	0	3.5	1.000	C-2
1902	66	.281	.325	231	65	10	0	0	0.0	22	28	16			3	1	298	67	13	7	5.7	.966	C-65
1903	26	.281	.404	57	16	3	2	0	0.0	8	4	3			2	6	73	27	4	1	4.0	.962	C-17, 1B-2
3 yrs.	94	.283	.341	293	83	13	2	0	0.0	31	35	19			5	7	375	97	17	8	5.2	.965	C-84, 1B-2

Jeff Hearron
HEARRON, JEFFREY VERNON
B. Nov. 19, 1961, Long Beach, Calif.　　　　BR TR 6'1" 195 lbs.

Year Team	Games	BA	SA	AB	H	2B	3B	HR	HR%	R	RBI	BB	SO	SB	PH AB	PH H	PO	A	E	DP	TC/G	FA	G by Pos
1985 TOR A	4	.143	.143	7	1	0	0	0	0.0	0	0	0	2	0	0	0	16	1	0	0	4.3	1.000	C-4
1986	12	.217	.261	23	5	1	0	0	0.0	2	4	3	7	0	0	0	47	3	1	0	4.3	.980	C-12
2 yrs.	16	.200	.233	30	6	1	0	0	0.0	2	4	3	9	0	0	0	63	4	1	0	4.3	.985	C-16

LEAGUE CHAMPIONSHIP SERIES

Year Team	Games	BA	SA	AB	H	2B	3B	HR	HR%	R	RBI	BB	SO	SB	PH AB	PH H	PO	A	E	DP	TC/G	FA	G by Pos
1985 TOR A	2	—	—	0	0	0	0	0	0.0	0	0	0	0	0	0	0	2	0	0	0	1.0	1.000	C-2

Bill Heath
HEATH, WILLIAM CHRIS
B. Mar. 10, 1939, Yuba City, Calif.　　　　BL TR 5'8" 175 lbs.

Year Team	Games	BA	SA	AB	H	2B	3B	HR	HR%	R	RBI	BB	SO	SB	PH AB	PH H	PO	A	E	DP	TC/G	FA	G by Pos
1965 CHI A	1	.000	.000	1	0	0	0	0	0.0	0	0	0	0	0	0	0					0.0	—	
1966 HOU N	55	.301	.350	123	37	6	0	0	0.0	12	8	9	11	1	16	4	167	20	1	1	3.4	.995	C-37
1967 2 teams		HOU N (9G – .091)				DET A (20G – .125)																	
" total	29	.116	.116	43	5	0	0	0	0.0	0	4	5	7	0	19	2	58	6	0	2	2.2	1.000	C-12
1969 CHI N	27	.156	.219	32	5	0	1	0	0.0	1	1	12	4	0	12	2	44	3	1	1	1.8	.979	C-9
4 yrs.	112	.236	.276	199	47	6	1	0	0.0	13	13	26	22	1	48	8	269	29	2	4	2.7	.993	C-58

Jeff Heath
HEATH, JOHN GEOFFREY
B. Apr. 1, 1915, Ft. William, Ont., Canada　 D. Dec. 9, 1975, Seattle, Wash.　　BL TR 5'11½" 200 lbs.

Year Team	Games	BA	SA	AB	H	2B	3B	HR	HR%	R	RBI	BB	SO	SB	PH AB	PH H	PO	A	E	DP	TC/G	FA	G by Pos
1936 CLE A	12	.341	.634	41	14	3	1	1	2.4	6	6	3	4	1			10	0	0	0	0.9	1.000	OF-12
1937	20	.230	.377	61	14	1	4	0	0.0	8	8	9	6	1			27	0	0	0	1.4	1.000	OF-14
1938	126	.343	.602	502	172	31	18	21	4.2	104	112	33	55	3	3	1	254	5	7	2	2.1	.974	OF-122
1939	121	.292	.494	431	126	31	7	14	3.2	64	69	41	64	8	13	3	263	7	10	2	2.3	.964	OF-108
1940	100	.219	.399	356	78	16	3	14	3.9	55	50	40	62	5	10	1	197	6	6	1	2.1	.971	OF-90
1941	151	.340	.586	585	199	32	20	24	4.1	89	123	50	69	18	0	0	259	20	15	1	1.9	.949	OF-151
1942	147	.278	.442	568	158	37	13	10	1.8	82	76	62	66	9	0	0	326	12	7	3	2.3	.980	OF-146
1943	118	.274	.481	424	116	22	6	18	4.2	58	79	63	58	5	7	1	264	4	9	1	2.3	.968	OF-111
1944	60	.331	.490	151	50	5	2	5	3.3	20	33	18	12	0	22	9	76	4	4	1	1.4	.952	OF-37
1945	102	.305	.508	370	113	16	7	15	4.1	60	61	56	39	3	1	0	214	3	6	1	2.2	.973	OF-101
1946 2 teams		WAS A (48G – .283)				STL A (86G – .275)																	
" total	134	.278	.473	482	134	32	6	16	3.3	69	84	73	73	0	4	1	239	3	6	2	1.9	.965	OF-130
1947 STL A	141	.251	.485	491	123	20	7	27	5.5	81	85	88	87	2	1	0	297	7	4	4	2.2	.987	OF-140
1948 BOS N	115	.319	.582	364	116	26	5	20	5.5	64	76	51	46	2	9	0	223	6	2	2	2.0	.991	OF-106
1949	36	.306	.613	111	34	7	0	9	8.1	17	23	15	26	0	6	3	56	2	1	0	1.6	.983	OF-31
14 yrs.	1383	.293	.509	4937	1447	279	102	194	3.9	777	887	593	670	56	82	20	2705	85	80	21	2.1	.972	OF-1299

Kelly Heath
HEATH, KELLY MARK
B. Sept. 4, 1957, Plattsburg, N. Y.　　　　BR TR 5'7" 155 lbs.

Year Team	Games	BA	SA	AB	H	2B	3B	HR	HR%	R	RBI	BB	SO	SB	PH AB	PH H	PO	A	E	DP	TC/G	FA	G by Pos
1982 KC A	1	.000	.000	1	0	0	0	0	0.0	0	0	0	0	0	0	0	1	2	0	1	3.0	1.000	2B-1

Mickey Heath
HEATH, MINOR WILSON
B. Oct. 30, 1903, Toledo, Ohio　 D. July 30, 1986, Dallas, Tex.　　BL TL 6' 175 lbs.

Year Team	Games	BA	SA	AB	H	2B	3B	HR	HR%	R	RBI	BB	SO	SB	PH AB	PH H	PO	A	E	DP	TC/G	FA	G by Pos
1931 CIN N	7	.269	.269	26	7	0	0	0	0.0	2	3	2	5	0	0	0	57	3	0	7	8.6	1.000	1B-7
1932	39	.201	.254	134	27	1	3	0	0.0	14	15	20	23	0	0	0	399	31	4	28	11.1	.991	1B-39
2 yrs.	46	.213	.256	160	34	1	3	0	0.0	16	18	22	28	0	0	0	456	34	4	35	10.7	.992	1B-46

Mike Heath
HEATH, MICHAEL THOMAS
B. Feb. 5, 1955, Tampa, Fla.　　　　BR TR 5'11" 180 lbs.

Year Team	Games	BA	SA	AB	H	2B	3B	HR	HR%	R	RBI	BB	SO	SB	PH AB	PH H	PO	A	E	DP	TC/G	FA	G by Pos
1978 NY A	33	.228	.283	92	21	3	1	0	0.0	6	8	4	9	0	0	0	151	11	5	1	5.1	.970	C-33
1979 OAK A	74	.256	.322	258	66	8	0	3	1.2	19	27	17	18	1	5	3	167	32	5	2	2.8	.975	OF-46, C-22, 3B-7, DH-3
1980	92	.243	.298	305	74	10	2	1	0.3	27	33	16	28	3	1	0	292	20	4	5	3.4	.987	C-47, DH-31, OF-8
1981	84	.236	.346	301	71	7	1	8	2.7	26	30	13	36	3	6	1	399	45	10	6	5.4	.978	C-78, OF-6
1982	101	.242	.352	318	77	18	4	3	0.9	43	39	27	36	3	2	0	368	54	12	8	4.3	.972	C-90, OF-10, 3B-5
1983	96	.281	.383	345	97	17	0	6	1.7	45	33	18	59	3	1	0	362	47	11	6	4.4	.974	C-80, OF-24, DH-2, 3B-2
1984	139	.248	.396	475	118	21	5	13	2.7	49	64	26	72	7	10	1	495	56	8	6	4.0	.986	C-108, OF-45, 3B-2, SS-1
1985	138	.250	.408	436	109	18	6	13	3.0	71	55	41	63	7	6	3	539	67	12	10	4.5	.981	C-112, OF-35, 3B-13
1986 2 teams		STL N (65G – .205)				DET A (30G – .265)																	
" total	95	.226	.354	288	65	11	1	8	2.8	30	36	27	53	6	4	0	405	39	13	5	4.8	.972	C-92, OF-2, 3B-1
1987 DET A	93	.281	.430	270	76	16	0	8	3.0	34	33	21	42	1	12	3	384	43	5	8	4.6	.988	C-67, OF-24, 3B-4, 1B-4, SS-3, DH-1, 2B-1
1988	86	.247	.365	219	54	7	2	5	2.3	24	18	18	32	1	6	0	361	24	6	3	4.5	.985	C-75, OF-9
1989	122	.263	.389	396	104	16	2	10	2.5	38	43	24	71	7	11	3	584	68	10	10	5.4	.985	C-117, 3B-4, OF-3, DH-1
12 yrs.	1153	.252	.369	3703	932	152	24	78	2.1	412	419	252	519	47	69	18	4507	506	101	72	4.4	.980	C-921, OF-212, DH-38, 3B-38, 1B-4, SS-3, 2B-1

DIVISIONAL PLAYOFF SERIES

Year Team	Games	BA	SA	AB	H	2B	3B	HR	HR%	R	RBI	BB	SO	SB	PH AB	PH H	PO	A	E	DP	TC/G	FA	G by Pos
1981 OAK A	2	.000	.000	8	0	0	0	0	0.0	0	0	0	1	0	0	0	0	0	0	0	0.0	—	C-2

Year	Team		Games	BA	SA	AB	H	2B	3B	HR	HR%	R	RBI	BB	SO	SB	Pinch Hit AB	H	PO	A	E	DP	TC/G	FA	G by Pos

Mike Heath *continued*

LEAGUE CHAMPIONSHIP SERIES

Year	Team		Games	BA	SA	AB	H	2B	3B	HR	HR%	R	RBI	BB	SO	SB	Pinch Hit AB	H	PO	A	E	DP	TC/G	FA	G by Pos
1981	OAK	A	3	.333	.333	6	2	0	0	0	0.0	1	0	0	1	0	0	0	0	0	0	0	0.0	–	C-2, OF-1
1987	DET	A	3	.286	.714	7	2	0	0	1	14.3	1	2	0	0	0	0	0	14	0	0	0	4.7	1.000	C-3
2 yrs.			6	.308	.538	13	4	0	0	1	7.7	2	2	0	1	0	0	0	14	0	0	0	2.3	1.000	C-5, OF-1

WORLD SERIES

| 1978 | NY | A | 1 | – | – | 0 | 0 | 0 | 0 | 0 | – | 0 | 0 | 0 | 0 | 0 | 0 | 0 | 0 | 0 | 0 | 0 | 0.0 | – | C-1 |

Tommy Heath

HEATH, THOMAS GEORGE
B. Aug. 18, 1913, Akron, Colo. D. Feb. 26, 1967, Los Gatos, Calif.

BR TR 5'10½" 185 lbs.

1935	STL	A	47	.237	.269	93	22	3	0	0	0.0	10	9	20	13	0	10	3	97	10	2	3	2.3	.982	C-37
1937			17	.233	.395	43	10	0	2	1	2.3	4	3	10	3	0	2	1	55	6	0	1	3.6	1.000	C-14
1938			70	.227	.325	194	44	13	0	2	1.0	22	22	35	24	0	3	1	315	42	5	5	5.2	.986	C-65
3 yrs.			134	.230	.318	330	76	16	2	3	0.9	36	34	65	40	0	15	5	467	58	7	9	4.0	.987	C-116

Cliff Heathcote

HEATHCOTE, CLIFTON EARL
B. Jan. 24, 1898, Glen Rock, Pa. D. Jan. 19, 1939, York, Pa.

BL TL 5'10½" 160 lbs.

1918	STL	N	88	.259	.345	348	90	12	3	4	1.1	37	32	20	40	12	0	0	222	6	16	0	2.8	.934	OF-88
1919			114	.279	.339	401	112	13	4	1	0.2	53	29	20	41	26	9	3	249	10	8	3	2.3	.970	OF-101, 1B-2
1920			133	.284	.372	489	139	18	8	3	0.6	55	56	25	31	21	3	0	296	26	12	3	2.5	.964	OF-129
1921			62	.244	.308	156	38	6	2	0	0.0	18	9	10	7	7	1	1	83	5	7	0	1.5	.926	OF-51
1922	2 teams					STL	N (34G – .245)			CHI	N (76G – .280)														
"	total		110	.270	.370	341	92	13	9	1	0.3	48	48	27	19	5	12	3	224	7	7	2	2.2	.971	OF-92
1923	CHI	N	117	.249	.308	393	98	14	3	1	0.3	48	27	25	22	32	2	0	231	14	5	1	2.1	.980	OF-112
1924			113	.309	.393	392	121	19	7	0	0.0	66	30	28	28	26	1	0	228	7	5	3	2.1	.979	OF-111
1925			109	.263	.366	380	100	14	5	5	1.3	57	39	39	26	15	10	1	241	21	8	8	2.5	.970	OF-99
1926			139	.276	.412	510	141	33	6	10	2.0	98	53	58	30	18	3	1	306	22	5	8	2.4	.985	OF-133
1927			83	.294	.408	228	67	12	4	2	0.9	28	25	20	16	6	17	0	136	13	2	7	1.8	.987	OF-57
1928			67	.285	.409	137	39	8	0	3	2.2	26	18	17	12	6	21	5	67	5	2	0	1.1	.973	OF-39
1929			82	.313	.415	224	70	17	0	2	0.9	45	31	25	17	9	22	7	131	4	2	1	1.7	.985	OF-52
1930			70	.260	.520	150	39	10	1	9	6.0	30	18	18	15	4	31	5	66	4	1	0	1.0	.986	OF-35
1931	CIN	N	90	.258	.365	252	65	15	6	0	0.0	24	28	32	16	3	25	6	164	13	2	4	2.0	.989	OF-59
1932	2 teams					CIN	N (8G – .000)			PHI	N (30G – .282)														
"	total		38	.262	.381	42	11	2	0	1	2.4	10	5	3	3	0	20	4	47	3	2	7	1.4	.962	1B-7
15 yrs.			1415	.275	.375	4443	1222	206	55	42	0.9	643	448	367	325	190	183	36	2691	160	84	48	2.1	.971	OF-1158, 1B-9

WORLD SERIES

| 1929 | CHI | N | 2 | .000 | .000 | 1 | 0 | 0 | 0 | 0 | 0.0 | 0 | 0 | 0 | 0 | 0 | 1 | 0 | 0 | 0 | 0 | 0 | 0.0 | – | |

Richie Hebner

HEBNER, RICHARD JOSEPH
B. Nov. 26, 1947, Boston, Mass.

BL TR 6'1" 195 lbs.

1968	PIT	N	2	.000	.000	1	0	0	0	0	0.0	0	0	0	0	0	0	0	0	0	0	0	0.0	–	
1969			129	.301	.420	459	138	23	4	8	1.7	72	47	53	53	4	4	1	81	240	19	32	2.6	.944	3B-124, 1B-1
1970			120	.290	.464	420	122	24	8	11	2.6	60	46	42	48	2	6	2	64	235	19	24	2.7	.940	3B-117
1971			112	.271	.487	388	105	17	8	17	4.4	50	67	32	68	2	7	2	89	172	14	21	2.5	.949	3B-108
1972			124	.300	.508	427	128	24	4	19	4.4	63	72	52	54	0	5	1	76	210	9	17	2.4	.969	3B-121
1973			144	.271	.477	509	138	28	1	25	4.9	73	74	56	60	0	7	1	92	260	23	19	2.6	.939	3B-139
1974			146	.291	.449	550	160	21	6	18	3.3	97	68	60	53	0	7	1	115	304	28	34	3.1	.937	3B-141
1975			128	.246	.392	472	116	16	4	15	3.2	65	57	43	48	0	3	1	86	244	19	27	2.7	.946	3B-126
1976			132	.249	.366	434	108	21	3	8	1.8	60	51	47	39	1	7	0	87	236	16	16	2.6	.953	3B-126
1977	PHI	N	118	.285	.484	397	113	17	4	18	4.5	67	62	61	46	7	10	3	933	85	11	93	8.9	.989	1B-103, 3B-13, 2B-1
1978			137	.283	.464	435	123	22	3	17	3.9	61	71	53	58	4	9	5	994	94	8	90	8.0	.993	1B-117, 3B-19, 2B-1
1979	NY	N	136	.268	.393	473	127	25	2	10	2.1	54	79	59	59	3	4	1	125	248	23	27	2.9	.942	3B-134, 1B-6
1980	DET	A	104	.290	.466	341	99	10	7	12	3.5	48	82	38	45	0	11	6	485	84	4	45	5.5	.993	1B-61, 3B-32, DH-5
1981			78	.226	.345	226	51	8	1	5	2.2	19	28	27	28	1	11	1	531	29	3	36	7.2	.995	1B-61, DH-11
1982	2 teams					DET	A (68G – .274)			PIT	N (25G – .300)														
"	total		93	.281	.434	249	70	8	0	10	4.0	31	30	30	24	5	17	3	338	28	4	16	4.0	.989	1B-44, OF-21, DH-20, 3B-1
1983	PIT	N	78	.265	.395	162	43	4	1	5	3.1	23	26	17	28	1	27	8	63	45	2	4	1.4	.982	3B-40, OF-7, 1B-7
1984	CHI	N	44	.333	.444	81	27	3	0	2	2.5	12	8	10	15	1	26	8	39	26	1	6	1.5	.985	3B-14, OF-3, 1B-3
1985			83	.217	.308	120	26	2	0	3	2.5	10	22	7	15	0	59	12	110	24	4	15	1.7	.971	1B-12, 3B-7, OF-1
18 yrs.			1908	.276	.438	6144	1694	273	57	203	3.3	865	890	687	741	38	221	55	4308	2564	207	512	3.7	.971	3B-1262, 1B-415, DH-36, OF-32, 2B-2

LEAGUE CHAMPIONSHIP SERIES

1970	PIT	N	2	.667	1.000	6	4	2	0	0	0.0	0	0	2	1	0	0	0	0	4	0	0	2.0	1.000	3B-2
1971			4	.294	.706	17	5	1	0	2	11.8	4	4	0	4	0	0	0	4	3	1	0	2.0	.875	3B-4
1972			5	.188	.250	16	3	1	0	0	0.0	2	1	1	4	0	0	0	5	11	0	1	3.2	1.000	3B-5
1974			4	.231	.462	13	3	0	0	1	7.7	1	4	1	4	0	0	0	5	7	0	1	3.0	1.000	3B-4
1975			4	.333	.417	12	4	1	0	0	0.0	1	1	0	1	0	0	0	0	8	0	1	2.0	1.000	3B-4
1977	PHI	N	4	.357	.500	14	5	2	0	0	0.0	2	0	1	1	0	0	0	32	0	0	1	8.0	1.000	1B-4
1978			3	.111	.111	9	1	0	0	0	0.0	0	0	1	0	0	1	0	21	0	0	0	7.0	1.000	1B-3
1984	CHI	N	1	.000	.000	1	0	0	0	0	0.0	0	0	0	0	0	0	0	0	0	0	0	0.0	–	
8 yrs.			26	.284	.466	88	25	7	0	3	3.4	10	12	5	14	0	4	0	67	27	1	7	3.7	.989	3B-18, 1B-5

WORLD SERIES

| 1971 | PIT | N | 3 | .167 | .417 | 12 | 2 | 0 | 0 | 1 | 8.3 | 2 | 3 | 3 | 3 | 0 | 0 | 0 | 1 | 3 | 1 | 1 | 1.7 | .800 | 3B-3 |

Mike Hechinger

HECHINGER, MICHAEL VINCENT
B. Feb. 14, 1890, Chicago, Ill. D. Aug. 13, 1967, Chicago, Ill.

BR TR 6' 175 lbs.

| 1912 | CHI | N | 2 | .000 | .000 | 3 | 0 | 0 | 0 | 0 | 0.0 | 0 | 0 | 2 | 0 | 0 | 0 | 0 | 7 | 2 | 0 | 0 | 4.5 | 1.000 | C-2 |

Year	Team		Games	BA	SA	AB	H	2B	3B	HR	HR%	R	RBI	BB	SO	SB	Pinch Hit AB	Pinch Hit H	PO	A	E	DP	TC/G	FA	G by Pos

Mike Hechinger *continued*

1913	2 teams	CHI N (2G – .000)				BKN	N	(9G – .182)																		
"	total		11	.154	.231	13	2	1	0	0	0.0	1	0	0	2	0	7	1	4	1	0	0	0.5	1.000	C-4
	2 yrs.		13	.125	.188	16	2	1	0	0	0.0	1	0	2	2	0	7	1	11	3	0	0	1.1	1.000	C-6

Guy Hecker

HECKER, GUY JACKSON (Blond Guy)
B. Apr. 3, 1856, Youngville, Pa.   D. Dec. 3, 1938, Wooster, Ohio
Manager 1890.

BR TR 6'   190 lbs.

1882	LOU	AA	78	.276	.368	340	94	14	4	3	0.9	62		5			0	0	699	68	31	43	10.2	.961	1B-66, P-13, OF-2
1883			79	.273	.339	322	88	6	6	1	0.3	56		10			0	0	144	100	24	7	3.4	.910	P-55, OF-23, 1B-10
1884			78	.297	.430	316	94	14	8	4	1.3	53		10			0	0	55	145	12	3	2.7	.943	P-76, OF-5
1885			72	.273	.337	297	81	9	2	2	0.7	48		5			0	0	174	106	15	16	4.1	.949	P-54, 1B-17, OF-3
1886			84	**.341**	.446	343	117	14	5	4	1.2	76		32			0	0	260	102	35	16	4.7	.912	P-52, 1B-22, OF-17
1887			91	.319	.441	370	118	21	4	4	1.1	89		31		48	0	0	429	82	29	27	5.9	.946	1B-43, P-33, OF-16
1888			56	.227	.289	211	48	9	2	0	0.0	32	29	11		20	0	0	305	57	25	12	6.9	.935	OF-30, 1B-30, P-28
1889			82	.284	.376	327	93	17	5	1	0.3	42	36	18	27	17	0	0	616	55	23	45	8.5	.967	1B-65, P-17, OF-1
1890	PIT	N	86	.226	.318	340	77	13	9	0	0.0	43	38	19	17	13	0	0	627	53	28	26	8.2	.960	1B-69, P-14, OF-7
	9 yrs.		706	.283	.376	2866	810	117	47	19	0.7	501	103	141	44	98	0	0	3309	768	222	195	6.1	.948	P-342, 1B-322, OF-104

Danny Heep

HEEP, DANIEL WILLIAM
B. July 3, 1957, San Antonio, Tex.

BL TL 5'11"   185 lbs.

1979	HOU	N	14	.143	.143	14	2	0	0	0	0.0	1	4	0	10	0	7	0	0	0	0.5	1.000	OF-2
1980			33	.276	.368	87	24	8	0	0	0.0	6	6	8	9	0	8	2	188	8	2	8	6.0	.990	1B-22
1981			33	.250	.281	96	24	3	0	0	0.0	6	11	10	11	0	9	4	198	9	2	12	6.3	.990	1B-22, OF-1
1982			85	.237	.379	198	47	14	1	4	2.0	16	22	21	31	0	23	6	192	6	1	10	2.3	.995	OF-39, 1B-16
1983	NY	N	115	.253	.395	253	64	12	0	8	3.2	30	21	29	40	3	40	11	159	11	0	12	1.5	1.000	OF-61, 1B-14
1984			99	.231	.312	199	46	9	2	1	0.5	36	12	27	22	3	38	8	137	7	4	4	1.5	.973	OF-48, 1B-10
1985			95	.280	.421	271	76	17	0	7	2.6	26	42	27	27	1	13	1	154	5	4	3	1.7	.975	OF-78, 1B-4
1986			86	.282	.421	195	55	8	2	5	2.6	24	33	30	31	1	30	9	83	2	1	1	1.0	.988	OF-56
1987	LA	N	60	.163	.204	98	16	4	0	0	0.0	7	9	8	10	1	35	5	52	6	1	3	1.0	.983	OF-22, 1B-6
1988			95	.242	.255	149	36	2	0	0	0.0	14	11	22	13	2	44	4	129	10	3	5	1.5	.979	OF-32, 1B-12, P-1
1989	BOS	A	113	.300	.400	320	96	17	0	5	1.6	36	49	29	26	0	20	4	216	14	3	18	2.1	.987	OF-75, 1B-19, DH-9
	11 yrs.		828	.259	.362	1880	486	94	5	30	1.6	201	218	212	224	12	270	55	1515	78	21	76	1.9	.987	OF-414, 1B-125, DH-9, P-1

LEAGUE CHAMPIONSHIP SERIES

1980	HOU	N	1	.000	.000	1	0	0	0	0	0.0	0	0	0	0	0	0	0	0	0	0	0	0.0	–	
1986	NY	N	5	.250	.250	4	1	0	0	0	0.0	0	1	0	2	0	3	1	0	0	0	0	0.0	–	OF-1
1988	LA	N	3	.000	.000	1	0	0	0	0	0.0	0	0	1	1	0	1	0	0	0	0	0	0.0	–	
	3 yrs.		9	.167	.167	6	1	0	0	0	0.0	0	1	1	3	0	5	1	0	0	0	0	0.0	–	OF-1

WORLD SERIES

1986	NY	N	5	.091	.091	11	1	0	0	0	0.0	1	2	1	1	0	2	0	1	0	0	0	0.2	1.000	DH-2, OF-1
1988	LA	N	3	.250	.375	8	2	1	0	0	0.0	0	0	0	2	0	2	0	0	0	0	0	0.0	–	DH-1, OF-1
	2 yrs.		8	.158	.211	19	3	1	0	0	0.0	1	2	1	3	0	4	0	1	0	0	0	0.1	1.000	DH-3, OF-2

Don Heffner

HEFFNER, DONALD HENRY (Jeep)
B. Feb. 8, 1911, Rouzerville, Pa.   D. Aug. 1, 1989, Pasadena, Calif.
Manager 1966.

BR TR 5'10"   155 lbs.

1934	NY	A	72	.261	.320	241	63	8	3	0	0.0	29	25	25	18	1	2	2	158	179	10	46	4.8	.971	2B-68
1935			10	.306	.444	36	11	3	1	0	0.0	3	8	4	1	0	0	0	20	29	1	5	5.0	.980	2B-10
1936			19	.229	.313	48	11	2	1	0	0.0	7	6	6	5	0	2	1	19	38	2	7	3.1	.966	3B-8, 2B-5, SS-3
1937			60	.249	.328	201	50	6	5	0	0.0	23	21	19	19	1	4	1	127	132	6	30	4.4	.977	2B-38, SS-13, 3B-3, OF-1, 1B-1
1938	STL	A	141	.245	.319	473	116	23	3	2	0.4	47	69	65	53	1	0	0	365	363	22	103	5.3	.971	2B-141
1939			110	.267	.312	375	100	12	2	1	0.3	45	35	48	39	1	4	2	222	315	29	54	5.1	.949	SS-73, 2B-32
1940			126	.236	.310	487	115	23	2	3	0.6	52	53	50	37	1	1	0	311	426	17	102	6.0	.977	2B-125
1941			110	.233	.278	399	93	14	2	0	0.0	48	17	38	27	5	6	1	224	307	14	52	5.0	.974	2B-105
1942			26	.167	.222	36	6	2	0	0	0.0	2	3	1	4	1	7	2	34	19	3	5	2.9	.946	2B-6, 1B-4
1943	2 teams	STL A (18G – .121)				PHI	A	(52G – .208)																		
"	total		70	.194	.227	211	41	7	0	0	0.0	19	10	20	14	3	6	1	126	145	6	31	4.0	.978	2B-60, 1B-2
1944	DET	A	6	.211	.263	19	4	1	0	0	0.0	0	5	1	0	0	1	0	12	13	1	4	4.3	.962	2B-5
	11 yrs.		743	.241	.303	2526	610	99	19	6	0.2	275	248	270	218	18	33	10	1618	1966	111	439	5.0	.970	2B-595, SS-89, 3B-11, 1B-7, OF-1

Jim Hegan

HEGAN, JAMES EDWARD
Father of Mike Hegan.
B. Aug. 3, 1920, Lynn, Mass.   D. June 17, 1984, Swampscott, Mass.

BR TR 6'2"   195 lbs.

1941	CLE	A	16	.319	.426	47	15	2	0	1	2.1	4	5	4	7	0	0	0	63	10	2	2	4.7	.973	C-16
1942			68	.194	.224	170	33	5	0	0	0.0	10	11	11	31	1	2	1	227	32	6	7	3.9	.977	C-66
1946			88	.236	.314	271	64	11	5	0	0.0	29	17	17	44	1	0	0	486	47	5	11	6.1	.991	C-87
1947			135	.249	.344	378	94	14	5	4	1.1	38	42	41	49	3	1	0	566	54	7	14	4.6	.989	C-133
1948			144	.248	.407	472	117	21	6	14	3.0	60	61	48	74	6	3	0	637	76	7	17	5.0	.990	C-142
1949			152	.224	.338	468	105	19	5	8	1.7	54	55	49	89	1	0	0	651	73	7	16	4.8	.990	C-152
1950			131	.219	.383	415	91	16	5	14	3.4	53	58	42	52	1	0	0	656	64	5	14	5.5	.993	C-129
1951			133	.238	.346	416	99	17	5	6	1.4	60	43	38	72	0	2	0	597	66	6	9	5.0	.991	C-129
1952			112	.225	.324	333	75	17	2	4	1.2	39	41	29	47	0	1	0	498	53	7	7	5.0	.987	C-107
1953			112	.217	.348	299	65	10	1	9	3.0	37	37	25	41	1	0	0	399	42	11	3	4.0	.976	C-106
1954			139	.234	.374	423	99	12	7	11	2.6	56	40	34	48	0	1	0	661	49	4	9	5.1	.994	C-137
1955			116	.220	.339	304	67	5	2	9	3.0	30	40	34	33	0	1	0	583	34	2	12	5.3	.997	C-111
1956			122	.222	.340	315	70	15	2	6	1.9	42	34	49	54	1	3	1	648	28	10	2	5.6	.985	C-118
1957			58	.216	.345	148	32	7	0	4	2.7	14	15	16	23	0	1	0	287	14	0	4	5.2	1.000	C-58

Year	Team	Games	BA	SA	AB	H	2B	3B	HR	HR%	R	RBI	BB	SO	SB	Pinch Hit AB	Pinch Hit H	PO	A	E	DP	TC/G	FA	G by Pos

Jim Hegan *continued*

Year	Team	Games	BA	SA	AB	H	2B	3B	HR	HR%	R	RBI	BB	SO	SB	PH AB	PH H	PO	A	E	DP	TC/G	FA	G by Pos
1958	2 teams	DET A (45G – .192)		PHI N (25G – .220)																				
"	total	70	.201	.280	189	38	12	0	1	0.5	19	13	14	48	0	0	0	315	27	2	5	4.9	.994	C-70
1959	2 teams	PHI N (25G – .196)		SF N (21G – .133)																				
"	total	46	.173	.198	81	14	2	0	0	0.0	1	8	9	20	0	0	0	156	17	3	3	3.8	.983	C-46
1960	CHI N	24	.209	.372	43	9	2	1	1	2.3	4	5	1	10	0	2	0	76	9	2	2	3.6	.977	C-22
17 yrs.		1666	.228	.344	4772	1087	187	46	92	1.9	550	525	456	742	15	20	2	7506	695	86	136	5.0	.990	C-1629

WORLD SERIES

Year	Team	Games	BA	SA	AB	H	2B	3B	HR	HR%	R	RBI	BB	SO	SB	PH AB	PH H	PO	A	E	DP	TC/G	FA	G by Pos
1948	CLE A	6	.211	.368	19	4	0	0	1	5.3	2	5	1	4	0	0	0	25	5	0	1	5.0	1.000	C-6
1954		4	.154	.231	13	2	1	0	0	0.0	1	0	1	1	0	0	0	27	3	0	0	7.5	1.000	C-4
2 yrs.		10	.188	.313	32	6	1	0	1	3.1	3	5	2	5	0	0	0	52	8	0	1	6.0	1.000	C-10

Mike Hegan

HEGAN, JAMES MICHAEL
Son of Jim Hegan.
B. July 21, 1942, Cleveland, Ohio

BL TL 6'1" 188 lbs.

Year	Team	Games	BA	SA	AB	H	2B	3B	HR	HR%	R	RBI	BB	SO	SB	PH AB	PH H	PO	A	E	DP	TC/G	FA	G by Pos
1964	NY A	5	.000	.000	5	0	0	0	0	0.0	0	1	2	0	1	0	17	4	0	2	4.2	1.000	1B-2
1966		13	.205	.256	39	8	0	0	1	0.0	7	2	7	11	1	0	0	103	8	1	6	8.6	.991	1B-13
1967		68	.136	.212	118	16	4	1	1	0.8	12	3	20	40	7	5	2	326	20	0	29	5.1	1.000	1B-54, OF-10
1969	SEA A	95	.292	.461	267	78	9	6	8	3.0	54	37	62	61	6	8	2	236	20	6	15	2.8	.977	OF-64, 1B-19
1970	MIL A	148	.244	.366	476	116	21	2	11	2.3	70	52	67	116	9	14	5	1104	113	7	104	8.3	.994	1B-139, OF-8
1971	2 teams	MIL A (46G – .221)		OAK A (65G – .236)																				
"	total	111	.226	.345	177	40	7	1	4	2.3	24	14	31	32	2	22	8	435	45	1	34	4.3	.998	1B-92, OF-2
1972	OAK A	98	.329	.430	79	26	3	1	1	1.3	13	5	7	20	1	31	7	170	11	0	22	1.8	1.000	1B-64, OF-3
1973	2 teams	OAK A (75G – .183)		NY A (37G – .275)																				
"	total	112	.243	.391	202	49	5	2	7	3.5	20	19	12	51	0	20	2	512	31	0	38	4.9	.991	1B-93, DH-3, OF-3
1974	2 teams	NY A (18G – .226)		MIL A (89G – .237)																				
"	total	107	.235	.391	243	57	9	1	9	3.7	24	41	38	43	1	18	4	273	13	1	21	2.7	.997	DH-37, 1B-34, OF-17
1975	MIL A	93	.251	.379	203	51	11	0	5	2.5	19	22	31	42	1	18	4	241	21	2	19	2.8	.992	OF-42, 1B-27, DH-5
1976		80	.248	.362	218	54	4	3	5	2.3	30	31	25	54	0	10	1	88	6	2	3	1.2	.979	DH-40, OF-20, 1B-10
1977		35	.170	.283	53	9	0	0	2	3.8	8	3	10	17	0	16	1	48	4	1	3	1.5	.981	OF-8, DH-7, 1B-6
12 yrs.		965	.242	.371	2080	504	73	18	53	2.5	281	229	311	489	28	163	36	3553	296	26	301	4.0	.993	1B-553, OF-177, DH-92

LEAGUE CHAMPIONSHIP SERIES

Year	Team	Games	BA	SA	AB	H	2B	3B	HR	HR%	R	RBI	BB	SO	SB	PH AB	PH H	PO	A	E	DP	TC/G	FA	G by Pos
1971	OAK A	1	.000	.000	1	0	0	0	0	0.0	0	0	0	0	0	1	0	0	0	0	0	0.0	–	1B-1
1972		3	.000	.000	1	0	0	0	0	0.0	1	0	0	1	0	1	0	1	0	0	0	0.3	1.000	1B-1
2 yrs.		4	.000	.000	2	0	0	0	0	0.0	1	0	0	1	0	2	0	1	0	0	0	0.3	1.000	1B-1

WORLD SERIES

Year	Team	Games	BA	SA	AB	H	2B	3B	HR	HR%	R	RBI	BB	SO	SB	PH AB	PH H	PO	A	E	DP	TC/G	FA	G by Pos
1964	NY A	3	.000	.000	1	0	0	0	0	0.0	1	0	1	0	0	1	0	11	1	0	1	2.0	1.000	1B-5
1972	OAK A	6	.200	.200	5	1	0	0	0	0.0	0	0	1	3	0	2	0	11	1	0	1	1.3	1.000	1B-5
2 yrs.		9	.167	.167	6	1	0	0	0	0.0	1	0	2	3	0	3	0	11	1	0	1	1.3	1.000	1B-5

Bob Hegman

HEGMAN, ROBERT HILMER
B. Feb. 26, 1958, Springfield, Minn.

BR TR 6'1" 180 lbs.

Year	Team	Games	BA	SA	AB	H	2B	3B	HR	HR%	R	RBI	BB	SO	SB	PH AB	PH H	PO	A	E	DP	TC/G	FA	G by Pos
1985	KC A	1	–	–	0	0	0	0	0	0	0	0	0	0	0	0	0	0	0	0	0	0.0	–	2B-1

Jack Heidemann

HEIDEMANN, JACK SEALE
B. July 11, 1949, Brenham, Tex.

BR TR 6' 175 lbs.

Year	Team	Games	BA	SA	AB	H	2B	3B	HR	HR%	R	RBI	BB	SO	SB	PH AB	PH H	PO	A	E	DP	TC/G	FA	G by Pos
1969	CLE A	3	.000	.000	3	0	0	0	0	0.0	0	0	0	2	0	0	0	1	5	0	0	2.0	1.000	SS-3
1970		133	.211	.292	445	94	14	2	6	1.3	44	37	34	88	2	1	0	216	354	23	79	4.5	.961	SS-132
1971		81	.208	.238	240	50	7	0	0	0.0	16	9	12	46	1	0	0	113	188	7	34	3.8	.977	SS-81
1972		10	.150	.150	20	3	0	0	0	0.0	0	2	0	3	0	0	0	10	17	1	2	2.8	.964	SS-10
1974	2 teams	CLE A (12G – .091)		STL N (47G – .271)																				
"	total	59	.247	.259	81	20	1	0	0	0.0	10	3	5	12	0	0	0	47	52	3	9	1.7	.971	SS-49, 3B-7, 2B-1, 1B-1
1975	NY N	61	.214	.290	145	31	4	2	1	0.7	12	16	17	28	1	18	1	72	89	10	14	2.8	.942	SS-44, 3B-4, 2B-1
1976	2 teams	NY N (5G – .083)		MIL A (69G – .219)																				
"	total	74	.209	.253	158	33	1	0	2	1.3	11	10	7	24	1	6	0	79	96	3	22	2.4	.983	3B-40, 2B-25, SS-3, DH-1
1977	MIL A	5	.000	.000	1	0	0	0	0	0.0	0	1	0	0	1	0	0	2	1	0	1	0.6	1.000	DH-3, 2B-1
8 yrs.		426	.211	.268	1093	231	27	4	9	0.8	94	75	78	203	5	31	1	540	802	47	162	3.3	.966	SS-322, 3B-51, 2B-28, DH-4, 1B-1

Emmett Heidrick

HEIDRICK, JOHN EMMETT (Snags)
B. July 29, 1876, Queenstown, Pa. D. Jan. 20, 1916, Clarion, Pa.

BL TR 6' 185 lbs.

Year	Team	Games	BA	SA	AB	H	2B	3B	HR	HR%	R	RBI	BB	SO	SB	PH AB	PH H	PO	A	E	DP	TC/G	FA	G by Pos
1898	CLE N	19	.303	.382	76	23	2	2	0	0.0	10	8	3			3	0	29	5	6	1	2.1	.850	OF-19
1899	STL N	146	.328	.421	591	194	21	14	2	0.3	109	82	34			55	1	211	34	20	6	1.8	.925	OF-145
1900		85	.301	.383	339	102	6	8	2	0.6	51	45	18			22	2	215	21	10	4	2.9	.959	OF-83
1901		118	.339	.470	502	170	24	12	6	1.2	94	67	21			32	0	258	15	16	2	2.4	.945	OF-118
1902	STL A	110	.289	.396	447	129	19	10	3	0.7	75	56	34			17	0	268	16	21	4	2.8	.931	OF-109, SS-1, 3B-1, P-1
1903		120	.280	.395	461	129	20	15	1	0.2	55	42	19			19	1	252	17	13	5	2.4	.954	OF-119, C-1
1904		133	.273	.342	538	147	14	10	1	0.2	66	36	16			35	3	291	22	12	6	2.4	.963	OF-130
1908		26	.215	.312	93	20	2	2	1	1.1	8	6	1			3	0	42	3	2	1	1.8	.957	OF-25
8 yrs.		757	.300	.399	3047	914	108	73	16	0.5	468	342	146			186	8	1	1566	133	100	29	2.4	.944	OF-748, SS-1, 3B-1, C-1, P-1

Chink Heileman

HEILEMAN, JOHN GEORGE
B. Aug. 10, 1872, Cincinnati, Ohio D. July 19, 1940, Cincinnati, Ohio

BR TR 5'8" 155 lbs.

Year	Team	Games	BA	SA	AB	H	2B	3B	HR	HR%	R	RBI	BB	SO	SB	PH AB	PH H	PO	A	E	DP	TC/G	FA	G by Pos
1901	CIN N	5	.133	.200	15	2	1	0	0	0.0	1	1	0			0	0	0	4	5	4	2	2.6	.692	3B-4, 2B-1

Harry Heilmann

HEILMANN, HARRY EDWIN (Slug)
B. Aug. 3, 1894, San Francisco, Calif. D. July 9, 1951, Southfield, Mich.
Hall of Fame 1952.

BR TR 6'1" 195 lbs.

Year	Team	Games	BA	SA	AB	H	2B	3B	HR	HR%	R	RBI	BB	SO	SB	PH AB	PH H	PO	A	E	DP	TC/G	FA	G by Pos
1914	DET A	67	.225	.313	182	41	8	1	2	1.1	25	22	22	29	1	11	3	209	31	11	11	3.7	.956	OF-29, 1B-16, 2B-6
1916		136	.282	.410	451	127	30	11	2	0.4	57	76	42	40	9	16	5	433	47	13	16	3.6	.974	OF-77, 1B-30, 2B-9

Year	Team		Games	BA	SA	AB	H	2B	3B	HR	HR%	R	RBI	BB	SO	SB	Pinch Hit AB	Pinch Hit H	PO	A	E	DP	TC/G	FA	G by Pos

Harry Heilmann *continued*

Year	Team		Games	BA	SA	AB	H	2B	3B	HR	HR%	R	RBI	BB	SO	SB	PH AB	PH H	PO	A	E	DP	TC/G	FA	G by Pos
1917			150	.281	.387	556	156	22	11	5	0.9	57	86	41	54	11	0	0	466	40	13	13	3.5	.975	OF-123, 1B-27
1918			79	.276	.406	286	79	10	6	5	1.7	34	44	35	10	13	1	1	427	28	8	13	5.9	.983	OF-40, 1B-37, 2B-2
1919			140	.320	.477	537	172	30	15	8	1.5	74	95	37	41	7	0	0	1402	78	31	61	10.8	.979	1B-140
1920			145	.309	.429	543	168	28	5	9	1.7	66	89	39	32	3	1	0	1234	86	19	52	9.2	.986	1B-122, OF-21
1921			149	**.394**	.606	602	**237**	43	14	19	3.2	114	139	53	37	2	1	1	257	13	11	2	1.9	.961	OF-143, 1B-4
1922			118	.356	.598	455	162	27	10	21	4.6	92	92	58	28	8	0	0	200	11	10	3	1.9	.955	OF-115, 1B-5
1923			144	**.403**	.632	524	211	44	11	18	3.4	121	115	74	40	8	1	1	373	21	13	7	2.8	.968	OF-130, 1B-12
1924			153	.346	.533	570	197	**45**	16	10	1.8	107	113	78	41	13	2	0	317	35	10	10	2.4	.972	OF-147, 1B-4
1925			150	**.393**	.569	573	225	40	11	13	2.3	97	133	67	27	6	2	1	278	9	9	1	2.0	.970	OF-148
1926			141	.367	.534	502	184	41	8	9	1.8	90	103	67	19	6	6	1	228	18	7	4	1.8	.972	OF-134
1927			141	**.398**	.616	505	201	50	9	14	2.8	106	120	72	16	11	5	1	218	11	8	5	1.7	.966	OF-135
1928			151	.328	.507	558	183	38	10	14	2.5	83	107	57	45	7	1	0	449	34	9	22	3.3	.982	OF-126, 1B-25
1929			125	.344	.565	453	156	41	7	15	3.3	86	120	50	39	5	7	1	193	8	7	3	1.7	.966	OF-113, 1B-1
1930	CIN	N	142	.333	.577	459	153	43	6	19	4.1	79	91	64	50	2	12	5	457	30	19	22	3.6	.962	OF-106, 1B-19
1932			15	.258	.323	31	8	2	0	0	0.0	3	6	0	2	0	9	3	49	3	1	2	3.5	.981	1B-6
17 yrs.			2146	.342	.520	7787	2660	542	151	183	2.4	1291	1551	856	550	112	75	23	7190	503	199	247	3.7	.975	OF-1587, 1B-448, 2B-17

Val Heim

HEIM, VAL RAYMOND
B. Nov. 4, 1920, Plymouth, Wis.
BL TR 5'11" 170 lbs.

Year	Team		Games	BA	SA	AB	H	2B	3B	HR	HR%	R	RBI	BB	SO	SB	PH AB	PH H	PO	A	E	DP	TC/G	FA	G by Pos
1942	CHI	A	13	.200	.267	45	9	1	1	0	0.0	6	7	5	3	1	1	0	23	0	1	0	1.8	.958	OF-12

Fred Heimach

HEIMACH, FREDERICK AMOS (Lefty)
B. Jan. 27, 1901, Camden, N. J. D. June 1, 1973, Fort Myers, Fla.
BL TL 6' 175 lbs.

Year	Team		Games	BA	SA	AB	H	2B	3B	HR	HR%	R	RBI	BB	SO	SB	PH AB	PH H	PO	A	E	DP	TC/G	FA	G by Pos
1920	PHI	A	1	.000	.000	1	0	0	0	0	0.0	0	0	0	0	0	0	0	1	5	0	0	6.0	1.000	P-1
1921			1	.250	.250	4	1	0	0	0	0.0	0	1	0	1	0	0	0	1	5	0	0	6.0	1.000	P-1
1922			37	.250	.333	60	15	3	1	0	0.0	6	7	5	12	1	0	0	7	46	3	4	1.5	.946	P-37
1923			63	.254	.331	118	30	4	1	1	0.8	14	11	4	18	0	12	4	69	56	6	3	2.1	.954	P-40, 1B-6
1924			58	.322	.400	90	29	3	2	0	0.0	14	12	3	8	1	16	7	11	57	2	1	1.2	.971	P-40
1925			15	.167	.167	6	1	0	0	0	0.0	3	0	0	2	0	1	0	1	6	0	1	0.5	1.000	P-10
1926 2 teams	PHI	A	(14G – .100)			BOS	A	(26G – .295)																	
" total			40	.259	.278	54	14	1	0	0	0.0	2	4	3	13	0	6	4	8	58	4	3	1.8	.943	P-33
1928	NY	A	18	.167	.167	30	5	0	0	0	0.0	2	2	2	6	0	5	1	16	0	2	0	0.9	1.000	P-13
1929			36	.184	.286	49	9	2	0	1	2.0	5	2	3	12	0	4	0	6	37	0	1	1.2	1.000	P-35
1930	BKN	N	13	.250	.250	4	1	0	0	0	0.0	0	0	0	1	0	4	1	0	3	0	1	0.2	1.000	P-9
1931			39	.197	.230	61	12	0	1	0	0.0	3	5	4	7	0	7	3	8	44	0	3	1.3	1.000	P-31
1932			37	.164	.255	55	9	2	0	1	1.8	9	4	1	18	0	1	0	10	41	0	1	1.4	1.000	P-36
1933			10	.200	.200	10	2	0	0	0	0.0	0	1	0	0	0	0	0	0	6	0	1	0.6	1.000	P-10
13 yrs.			368	.236	.299	542	128	15	5	3	0.6	58	49	28	98	2	52	20	122	380	15	21	1.4	.971	P-296, 1B-6

Bud Heine

HEINE, WILLIAM HENRY
B. Sept. 22, 1900, Elmira, N. Y. D. Sept. 2, 1976, Ft. Lauderdale, Fla.
BL TR 5'8" 145 lbs.

Year	Team		Games	BA	SA	AB	H	2B	3B	HR	HR%	R	RBI	BB	SO	SB	PH AB	PH H	PO	A	E	DP	TC/G	FA	G by Pos
1921	NY	N	1	.000	.000	2	0	0	0	0	0.0	0	0	0	0	0	0	0	1	2	0	0	3.0	1.000	2B-1

Tom Heintzelman

HEINTZELMAN, THOMAS KENNETH
Son of Ken Heintzelman.
B. Nov. 3, 1946, St. Charles, Mo.
BR TR 6'1" 180 lbs.

Year	Team		Games	BA	SA	AB	H	2B	3B	HR	HR%	R	RBI	BB	SO	SB	PH AB	PH H	PO	A	E	DP	TC/G	FA	G by Pos
1973	STL	N	23	.310	.310	29	9	0	0	0	0.0	5	0	3	3	0	15	4	8	13	0	3	0.9	1.000	2B-6
1974			38	.230	.324	74	17	4	0	1	1.4	10	6	9	14	0	7	1	41	56	2	12	2.6	.980	2B-28, 3B-2, SS-1
1977	SF	N	2	.000	.000	2	0	0	0	0	0.0	0	0	0	0	0	2	0	0	0	0	0	–		
1978			27	.229	.429	35	8	1	0	2	5.7	2	6	2	5	0	19	4	5	19	0	1	0.9	1.000	2B-5, 3B-3, 1B-2
4 yrs.			90	.243	.343	140	34	5	0	3	2.1	17	12	14	22	0	43	9	54	88	2	16	1.6	.986	2B-39, 3B-5, 1B-2, SS-1

John Heinzman

HEINZMAN, JOHN PETER
B. Sept. 27, 1863, New Albany, Ind. D. Nov. 10, 1914, Louisville, Ky.
BR TR

Year	Team		Games	BA	SA	AB	H	2B	3B	HR	HR%	R	RBI	BB	SO	SB	PH AB	PH H	PO	A	E	DP	TC/G	FA	G by Pos
1886	LOU	AA	1	.000	.000	5	0	0	0	0	0.0	1		0			0	0	7	0	0	0	7.0	1.000	1B-1

Bob Heise

HEISE, ROBERT LOWELL
B. May 12, 1947, San Antonio, Tex.
BR TR 6' 175 lbs.

Year	Team		Games	BA	SA	AB	H	2B	3B	HR	HR%	R	RBI	BB	SO	SB	PH AB	PH H	PO	A	E	DP	TC/G	FA	G by Pos
1967	NY	N	16	.323	.387	62	20	4	0	0	0.0	7	3	3	1	0	0	0	46	43	3	6	5.8	.967	2B-12, SS-3, 3B-2
1968			6	.217	.217	23	5	0	0	0	0.0	3	1	1	1	0	0	0	6	8	1	5	2.5	.933	2B-6, 2B-1
1969			4	.300	.400	10	3	1	0	0	0.0	1	0	3	2	0	1	1	4	5	0	0	2.3	1.000	SS-3
1970	SF	N	67	.234	.299	154	36	5	1	1	0.6	15	22	5	13	0	7	2	78	124	13	24	3.2	.940	SS-33, 2B-28, 3B-2
1971 2 teams	SF	N	(13G – .000)			MIL	A	(68G – .254)																	
" total			81	.240	.275	200	48	7	0	0	0.0	12	7	7	16	1	10	1	100	163	11	40	3.4	.960	SS-54, 3B-13, 2B-4, OF-1
1972	MIL	A	95	.266	.310	271	72	10	1	0	0.0	23	12	12	14	1	18	5	125	170	6	31	3.2	.980	2B-49, 3B-24, SS-9
1973			49	.204	.224	98	20	2	0	0	0.0	8	4	4	4	1	0	0	50	79	5	9	2.7	.963	2B-24, 3B-9, 2B-4, 1B-4
1974 2 teams	STL	N	(3G – .143)			CAL	A	(29G – .267)																	
" total			32	.256	.341	82	21	7	0	0	0.0	7	6	5	10	0	2	0	44	63	0	15	3.3	1.000	2B-20, 3B-6, SS-3
1975	BOS	A	63	.214	.238	126	27	3	0	0	0.0	12	21	4	6	0	2	0	52	106	10	12	2.7	.940	3B-45, 2B-14, SS-4, 1B-1
1976			32	.268	.304	56	15	2	0	0	0.0	5	5	1	2	0	1	0	27	43	5	7	2.3	.933	3B-22, SS-9, 2B-1
1977	KC	A	54	.258	.323	62	16	2	1	0	0.0	11	5	2	8	0	1	0	42	67	6	19	2.1	.948	SS-21, 2B-21, 3B-12, 1B-1
11 yrs.			499	.247	.293	1144	283	43	3	1	0.1	104	86	47	77	2	41	9	574	871	60	168	3.0	.960	SS-174, 2B-154, 3B-135, 1B-6, OF-1

Al Heist

HEIST, ALFRED MICHAEL
B. Oct. 5, 1927, Brooklyn, N. Y.
BR TR 6'2" 185 lbs.

Year	Team		Games	BA	SA	AB	H	2B	3B	HR	HR%	R	RBI	BB	SO	SB	PH AB	PH H	PO	A	E	DP	TC/G	FA	G by Pos
1960	CHI	N	41	.275	.412	102	28	5	3	1	1.0	11	6	10	12	3	10	2	65	2	1	0	1.7	.985	OF-33
1961			109	.255	.383	321	82	14	3	7	2.2	48	37	39	51	3	8	1	211	9	5	0	2.1	.978	OF-99
1962	HOU	N	27	.222	.236	72	16	1	0	0	0.0	4	3	3	9	0	4	0	36	1	1	0	1.4	.974	OF-23
3 yrs.			177	.255	.368	495	126	20	6	8	1.6	63	46	52	72	6	22	3	312	12	7	0	1.9	.979	OF-155

Year	Team		Games	BA	SA	AB	H	2B	3B	HR	HR%	R	RBI	BB	SO	SB	Pinch Hit AB	Pinch Hit H	PO	A	E	DP	TC/G	FA	G by Pos

Heinie Heitmuller

HEITMULLER, WILLIAM FREDERICK
B. 1883, San Francisco, Calif. D. Oct. 8, 1912, Los Angeles, Calif.
BR TR 6'2" 215 lbs.

Year	Team		Games	BA	SA	AB	H	2B	3B	HR	HR%	R	RBI	BB	SO	SB	PH AB	PH H	PO	A	E	DP	TC/G	FA	G by Pos
1909	PHI	A	64	.286	.405	210	60	9	8	0	0.0	36	15	18		7	4	2	111	4	9	2	1.9	.927	OF-60
1910			31	.243	.297	111	27	2	2	0	0.0	11	7	7		6	3	1	49	2	1	2	1.7	.981	OF-28
2 yrs.			95	.271	.368	321	87	11	10	0	0.0	47	22	25		13	7	3	160	6	10	4	1.9	.943	OF-88

Woodie Held

HELD, WOODSON GEORGE
B. Mar. 25, 1932, Sacramento, Calif.
BR TR 5'10½" 167 lbs.

Year	Team		Games	BA	SA	AB	H	2B	3B	HR	HR%	R	RBI	BB	SO	SB	PH AB	PH H	PO	A	E	DP	TC/G	FA	G by Pos
1954	NY	A	4	.000	.000	3	0	0	0	0	0.0	2	0	2	1	0	0	0	2	3	0	1	1.3	1.000	SS-4, 3B-1
1957	2 teams			NY A (1G – .000)		KC A (92G – .239)																			
"	total		93	.239	.483	327	78	14	3	20	6.1	48	50	37	81	4	1	0	266	12	1	2	3.0	.996	OF-92
1958	2 teams			KC A (47G – .214)		CLE A (67G – .194)																			
"	total		114	.204	.309	275	56	6	1	7	2.5	25	33	25	64	1	11	1	178	55	7	7	2.1	.971	OF-84, SS-15, 3B-8
1959	CLE	A	143	.251	.465	525	132	19	3	29	5.5	82	71	47	118	1	1	0	217	365	20	51	4.2	.967	SS-103, 3B-40, OF-6, 2B-3
1960			109	.258	.471	376	97	15	1	21	5.6	45	67	44	73	0	1	0	208	345	19	87	5.2	.969	SS-109
1961			146	.267	.468	509	136	23	5	23	4.5	67	78	69	111	0	2	1	258	393	27	90	4.6	.960	SS-144
1962			139	.249	.406	466	116	12	2	19	4.1	55	58	73	107	5	3	1	227	377	27	102	4.5	.957	SS-133, 3B-5, OF-1
1963			133	.248	.435	416	103	19	4	17	4.1	61	61	61	96	2	9	2	243	260	13	53	3.9	.975	2B-96, OF-35, SS-5, 3B-3
1964			118	.236	.420	364	86	13	0	18	4.9	50	49	43	88	1	8	0	183	182	14	40	3.2	.963	2B-52, OF-41, 3B-30
1965	WAS	A	122	.247	.452	332	82	16	2	16	4.8	46	54	49	74	0	15	2	183	15	8	5	1.7	.961	OF-106, 3B-5, 2B-4, SS-2
1966	BAL	A	56	.207	.305	82	17	3	1	1	1.2	6	7	14	30	0	34	6	23	18	2	1	0.8	.953	OF-10, 2B-5, SS-3, 3B-3
1967	2 teams			BAL A (26G – .146)		CAL A (58G – .220)																			
"	total		84	.203	.319	182	37	6	0	5	2.7	19	23	24	53	0	22	1	66	92	4	17	1.9	.975	3B-24, OF-19, SS-13, 2B-12
1968	2 teams			CAL A (33G – .111)		CHI A (40G – .167)																			
"	total		73	.141	.162	99	14	2	0	0	0.0	9	2	10	29	0	22	3	46	24	2	3	1.0	.972	OF-36, 3B-10, 2B-6, SS-5
1969	CHI	N	56	.143	.317	63	9	2	0	3	4.8	9	6	13	19	0	19	2	23	15	0	1	0.7	1.000	OF-18, SS-3, 3B-3, 2B-1
14 yrs.			1390	.240	.421	4019	963	150	22	179	4.5	524	559	509	944	14	147	19	2123	2156	144	460	3.2	.967	SS-539, OF-448, 2B-179, 3B-132

Hank Helf

HELF, HENRY HARTZ
B. Aug. 26, 1913, Austin, Tex. D. Oct. 27, 1984, Austin, Tex.
BR TR 6'1" 196 lbs.

Year	Team		Games	BA	SA	AB	H	2B	3B	HR	HR%	R	RBI	BB	SO	SB	PH AB	PH H	PO	A	E	DP	TC/G	FA	G by Pos
1938	CLE	A	6	.077	.077	13	1	0	0	0	0.0	1	1	1	1	0	1	0	13	5	1	1	3.2	.947	C-5
1940			1	.000	.000	1	0	0	0	0	0.0	0	0	0	0	0	0	0	1	0	0	0	1.0	1.000	C-1
1946	STL	A	71	.192	.352	182	35	11	0	6	3.3	17	21	9	40	0	1	0	251	51	11	7	4.4	.965	C-69
3 yrs.			78	.184	.332	196	36	11	0	6	3.1	18	22	10	41	0	2	0	265	56	12	8	4.3	.964	C-75

Ty Helfrich

HELFRICH, EMORY WILBUR
B. Oct. 9, 1890, Pleasantville, N. J. D. Mar. 18, 1955, Pleasantville, N. J.
BR TR 5'10" 178 lbs.

Year	Team		Games	BA	SA	AB	H	2B	3B	HR	HR%	R	RBI	BB	SO	SB	PH AB	PH H	PO	A	E	DP	TC/G	FA	G by Pos
1915	BKN	F	43	.240	.298	104	25	6	0	0	0.0	12	5	15		2	5	0	45	81	12	4	3.2	.913	2B-34, OF-1

Tony Hellman

HELLMAN, ANTHONY JOSEPH
B. May 29, 1861, Cincinnati, Ohio D. Mar. 29, 1898, Cincinnati, Ohio

Year	Team		Games	BA	SA	AB	H	2B	3B	HR	HR%	R	RBI	BB	SO	SB	PH AB	PH H	PO	A	E	DP	TC/G	FA	G by Pos
1886	BAL	AA	1	.000	.000	3	0	0	0	0	0.0	0		0		0	0	0	10	2	0	0	12.0	1.000	C-1

Tommy Helms

HELMS, TOMMY VANN
B. May 5, 1941, Charlotte, N. C.
Manager 1988-89.
BR TR 5'10" 165 lbs.

Year	Team		Games	BA	SA	AB	H	2B	3B	HR	HR%	R	RBI	BB	SO	SB	PH AB	PH H	PO	A	E	DP	TC/G	FA	G by Pos
1964	CIN	N	2	.000	.000	1	0	0	0	0	0.0	0	0	0	0	0	0	0	0	0	0	0	0.0	—	
1965			21	.381	.524	42	16	2	2	0	0.0	4	6	3	7	1	10	3	17	22	1	6	1.9	.975	SS-8, 3B-2, 2B-1
1966			138	.284	.380	542	154	23	1	9	1.7	72	49	24	31	3	5	3	155	258	13	25	3.1	.969	3B-113, 2B-20
1967			137	.274	.356	497	136	27	4	2	0.4	40	35	24	41	5	3	1	264	347	21	75	4.6	.967	2B-88, SS-46
1968			127	.288	.363	507	146	28	2	2	0.4	35	47	12	27	5	0	0	322	372	15	82	5.6	.979	2B-127, SS-2, 3B-1
1969			126	.269	.317	480	129	18	1	1	0.2	38	40	18	33	4	1	0	325	347	17	89	5.5	.975	2B-125, SS-4
1970			150	.237	.282	575	136	21	1	1	0.2	42	45	21	33	2	2	0	353	412	13	107	5.2	.983	2B-148, SS-12
1971			150	.258	.325	547	141	26	1	3	0.5	40	52	26	33	1	0	0	395	468	9	130	5.8	.990	2B-149
1972	HOU	N	139	.259	.346	518	134	20	5	5	1.0	45	60	24	27	4	0	0	353	441	17	115	5.8	.979	2B-139
1973			146	.287	.368	543	156	28	2	4	0.7	46	61	32	21	1	0	0	325	438	9	104	5.3	.988	2B-146
1974			137	.279	.363	452	126	21	1	5	1.1	32	50	23	27	5	6	1	308	360	10	99	4.9	.985	2B-133
1975			64	.207	.222	135	28	2	0	0	0.0	7	14	10	8	0	27	9	58	109	2	19	2.6	.988	2B-42, 3B-3, SS-1
1976	PIT	N	62	.276	.391	87	24	5	1	1	1.1	10	13	5	5	0	23	8	30	46	3	8	1.3	.962	3B-22, 2B-11, SS-1
1977	2 teams			PIT N (15G – .000)		BOS A (21G – .271)																			
"	total		36	.225	.296	71	16	2	0	1	1.4	5	5	4	7	0	15	2	4	4	0	0	0.2	1.000	DH-13, 3B-2, 2B-1
14 yrs.			1435	.269	.342	4997	1342	223	21	34	0.7	414	477	231	301	33	93	27	2909	3624	130	859	4.6	.980	2B-1129, 3B-143, SS-74, DH-13

LEAGUE CHAMPIONSHIP SERIES

Year	Team		Games	BA	SA	AB	H	2B	3B	HR	HR%	R	RBI	BB	SO	SB	PH AB	PH H	PO	A	E	DP	TC/G	FA	G by Pos
1970	CIN	N	3	.273	.273	11	3	0	0	0	0.0	0	0	0	1	0	0	0	11	12	0	1	7.7	1.000	2B-3

WORLD SERIES

Year	Team		Games	BA	SA	AB	H	2B	3B	HR	HR%	R	RBI	BB	SO	SB	PH AB	PH H	PO	A	E	DP	TC/G	FA	G by Pos
1970	CIN	N	5	.222	.222	18	4	0	0	0	0.0	1	0	1	1	0	0	0	10	13	0	2	4.6	1.000	2B-5

Heinie Heltzel

HELTZEL, WILLIAM WADE
B. Dec. 21, 1913, York, Pa.
BR TR 5'10" 150 lbs.

Year	Team		Games	BA	SA	AB	H	2B	3B	HR	HR%	R	RBI	BB	SO	SB	PH AB	PH H	PO	A	E	DP	TC/G	FA	G by Pos
1943	BOS	N	29	.151	.186	86	13	3	0	0	0.0	6	5	7	13	0	0	0	18	48	9	3	2.6	.880	3B-29
1944	PHI	N	11	.182	.227	22	4	1	0	0	0.0	1	0	2	3	0	0	0	17	17	3	1	3.4	.919	SS-10
2 yrs.			40	.157	.194	108	17	4	0	0	0.0	7	5	9	16	0	0	0	35	65	12	4	2.8	.893	3B-29, SS-10

Ed Hemingway

HEMINGWAY, EDSON MARSHALL
B. May 8, 1893, Sheridan, Mich. D. July 5, 1969, Grand Rapids, Mich.
BB TR 5'11½" 165 lbs.

Year	Team		Games	BA	SA	AB	H	2B	3B	HR	HR%	R	RBI	BB	SO	SB	PH AB	PH H	PO	A	E	DP	TC/G	FA	G by Pos
1914	STL	A	3	.000	.000	5	0	0	0	0	0.0	0	0	1	1	1	0	0	4	2	0	0	2.0	1.000	3B-3
1917	NY	N	7	.320	.440	25	8	1	0	0	0.0	3	1	2	1	0	0	0	8	15	1	2	3.4	.958	3B-7

Year	Team		Games	BA	SA	AB	H	2B	3B	HR	HR%	R	RBI	BB	SO	SB	Pinch Hit AB	Pinch Hit H	PO	A	E	DP	TC/G	FA	G by Pos

Ed Hemingway *continued*

Year	Team		Games	BA	SA	AB	H	2B	3B	HR	HR%	R	RBI	BB	SO	SB	AB	H	PO	A	E	DP	TC/G	FA	G by Pos
1918	PHI	N	33	.213	.269	108	23	4	1	0	0.0	7	12	7	9	4	0	0	69	95	8	9	5.2	.953	2B-25, 3B-3, 1B-1
3 yrs.			43	.225	.290	138	31	5	2	0	0.0	10	13	10	11	7	0	0	81	112	9	11	4.7	.955	2B-25, 3B-13, 1B-1

Scott Hemond

HEMOND, SCOTT MATHEW
B. Nov. 18, 1965, Taunton, Mass.   BR TR 6'   205 lbs.

Year	Team		Games	BA	SA	AB	H	2B	3B	HR	HR%	R	RBI	BB	SO	SB	AB	H	PO	A	E	DP	TC/G	FA	G by Pos
1989	OAK	A	4	–	–	0	0	0	0	0	–	2	0	0	0	0	0	0	0	0	0	0	0.0	–	DH-3

Ducky Hemp

HEMP, WILLIAM H.
B. Dec. 27, 1867, St. Louis, Mo.   D. Mar. 6, 1923, St. Louis, Mo.

Year	Team		Games	BA	SA	AB	H	2B	3B	HR	HR%	R	RBI	BB	SO	SB	AB	H	PO	A	E	DP	TC/G	FA	G by Pos
1887	LOU	AA	1	.333	.667	3	1	0	0	0	0.0	1		1		0	0	0	0	1	0	1.0	–	OF-1
1890	2 teams			PIT	N	(21G – .235)		SYR	AA	(9G – .152)															
"	total		30	.211	.254	114	24	1	2	0	0.0	10	4	8	12	4	0	0	48	9	7	5	2.1	.891	OF-30
2 yrs.			31	.214	.265	117	25	2	2	0	0.0	11	4	9	12	4	0	0	48	9	8	5	2.1	.877	OF-31

Charlie Hemphill

HEMPHILL, CHARLES JUDSON (Eagle Eye)
Brother of Frank Hemphill.
B. Apr. 20, 1876, Greenville, Mich.   D. June 22, 1953, Detroit, Mich.   BL TL 5'9"   160 lbs.

Year	Team		Games	BA	SA	AB	H	2B	3B	HR	HR%	R	RBI	BB	SO	SB	AB	H	PO	A	E	DP	TC/G	FA	G by Pos
1899	2 teams			STL	N	(11G – .243)		CLE	N	(55G – .277)															
"	total		66	.272	.364	239	65	3	5	3	1.3	27	26	12		3	1	1	74	8	16	2	1.5	.837	OF-64
1901	BOS	A	136	.261	.332	545	142	10	10	3	0.6	71	62	39		11	0	0	188	22	17	4	1.7	.925	OF-136
1902	2 teams			CLE	A	(25G – .266)		STL	A	(103G – .317)															
"	total		128	.308	.418	510	157	16	11	6	1.2	81	69	49		27	6	2	200	23	16	7	1.9	.933	OF-120, 2B-2
1903	STL	A	105	.245	.300	383	94	6	3	3	0.8	36	29	23		16	1	0	155	17	7	4	1.7	.961	OF-104
1904			114	.256	.308	438	112	13	2	2	0.5	47	45	35		23	4	1	179	14	15	5	1.8	.928	OF-108, 2B-1
1906			154	.289	.383	585	169	19	12	4	0.7	90	62	43		33	0	0	304	17	13	1	2.2	.961	OF-154
1907			153	.259	.322	603	156	20	9	0	0.0	66	38	51		14	0	0	320	12	15	2	2.3	.957	OF-153
1908	NY	A	142	.297	.356	505	150	12	9	0	0.0	62	44	59		42	0	0	285	13	20	2	2.2	.937	OF-142
1909			73	.243	.282	181	44	5	1	0	0.0	23	10	32		10	24	6	75	6	2	1	1.1	.976	OF-45
1910			102	.239	.288	351	84	9	4	0	0.0	45	20	55		19	4	1	159	10	5	2	1.7	.971	OF-94
1911			69	.284	.338	201	57	4	2	1	0.5	32	15	37		9	9	0	95	4	5	0	1.5	.952	OF-56
11 yrs.			1242	.271	.341	4541	1230	117	68	22	0.5	580	421	435		207	49	11	2034	146	131	30	1.9	.943	OF-1176, 2B-3

Frank Hemphill

HEMPHILL, FRANK VERNON
Brother of Charlie Hemphill.
B. May 13, 1878, Greenville, Mich.   D. Nov. 16, 1950, Chicago, Ill.   BR TR 5'11"   165 lbs.

Year	Team		Games	BA	SA	AB	H	2B	3B	HR	HR%	R	RBI	BB	SO	SB	AB	H	PO	A	E	DP	TC/G	FA	G by Pos
1906	CHI	A	13	.075	.075	40	3	0	0	0	0.0	0	2	9		1	0	0	31	1	1	0	2.5	.970	OF-13
1909	WAS	A	1	.000	.000	3	0	0	0	0	0.0	0				0	0	0	2	0	0	0	2.0	1.000	OF-1
2 yrs.			14	.070	.070	43	3	0	0	0	0.0	0	2	9		1	0	0	33	1	1	0	2.5	.971	OF-14

Rollie Hemsley

HEMSLEY, RALSTON BURDETT
B. June 24, 1907, Syracuse, Ohio   D. July 31, 1972, Washington, D. C.   BR TR 5'10"   170 lbs.

Year	Team		Games	BA	SA	AB	H	2B	3B	HR	HR%	R	RBI	BB	SO	SB	AB	H	PO	A	E	DP	TC/G	FA	G by Pos
1928	PIT	N	50	.271	.331	133	36	2	3	0	0.0	14	18	4	10	1	1	0	127	24	6	4	3.1	.962	C-49
1929			88	.289	.404	235	68	13	7	0	0.0	31	37	11	22	1	6	0	240	48	14	7	3.4	.954	C-80
1930			104	.253	.367	324	82	19	6	2	0.6	45	45	22	21	3	5	1	325	50	8	11	3.7	.979	C-98
1931	2 teams		76		PIT	N	(10G – .171)		CHI	N	(66G – .309)														
"	total		76	.289	.444	239	69	20	4	3	1.3	31	32	20	33	4	9	3	271	45	7	7	4.3	.978	C-75
1932	CHI	N	60	.238	.424	151	36	10	4	4	2.6	27	20	10	16	2	8	3	174	18	5	3	3.3	.975	C-47, OF-1
1933	2 teams		81		CIN	N	(49G – .190)		STL	A	(32G – .242)														
"	total		81	.213	.284	211	45	10	1	1	0.5	16	22	17	20	0	7	1	207	35	8	3	3.1	.968	C-68
1934	STL	A	123	.309	.427	431	133	31	7	2	0.5	47	52	29	37	6	5	2	499	92	16	15	4.9	.974	C-114, OF-6
1935			144	.290	.381	504	146	32	7	0	0.0	57	48	44	41	3	6	1	510	105	13	10	4.4	.979	C-141
1936			116	.263	.353	377	99	24	2	2	0.5	43	39	46	30	2	8	2	340	68	13	16	3.6	.969	C-114
1937			100	.222	.302	334	74	12	3	3	0.9	30	28	25	29	0	4	0	338	71	13	13	4.2	.969	C-94, 1B-2
1938	CLE	A	66	.296	.409	203	60	11	3	2	1.0	27	28	23	14	1	6	0	358	38	8	5	6.1	.980	C-58
1939			107	.263	.342	395	104	17	4	2	0.5	58	36	26	26	2	0	0	499	58	9	7	5.3	.984	C-106
1940			119	.267	.368	416	111	20	5	4	1.0	46	42	22	25	1	2	0	591	65	4	8	5.5	.994	C-117
1941			98	.240	.330	288	69	10	5	2	0.7	29	24	18	18	2	2	0	401	42	9	4	4.6	.980	C-96
1942	2 teams		67		CIN	N	(36G – .113)		NY	A	(31G – .294)														
"	total		67	.190	.240	200	38	4	3	0	0.0	19	22	9	20	1	4	0	302	26	5	6	5.0	.985	C-63
1943	NY	A	62	.239	.339	180	43	6	3	2	1.1	12	24	13	9	0	10	1	234	31	5	3	4.4	.981	C-52
1944			81	.268	.366	284	76	12	5	2	0.7	23	26	9	13	0	6	0	298	41	6	7	4.3	.983	C-76
1946	PHI	N	49	.223	.266	139	31	4	1	0	0.0	7	11	9	10	1	6	0	170	42	5	10	4.4	.977	C-45
1947			2	.333	.333	3	1	0	0	0	0.0	0	1	0	0	0	3	1	3	0	0	0	1.5	1.000	C-2
19 yrs.			1593	.262	.360	5047	1321	257	72	31	0.6	562	555	357	395	29	89	18	5887	899	154	143	4.4	.978	C-1495, OF-7, 1B-2

WORLD SERIES

Year	Team		Games	BA	SA	AB	H	2B	3B	HR	HR%	R	RBI	BB	SO	SB	AB	H	PO	A	E	DP	TC/G	FA	G by Pos
1932	CHI	N	3	.000	.000	3	0	0	0	0	0.0	0	0	0	3	0	3	0	0	0	0	0	0.0	–	C-1

Solly Hemus

HEMUS, SOLOMON JOSEPH
B. Apr. 17, 1923, Phoenix, Ariz.
Manager 1959-61.   BL TR 5'9"   165 lbs.

Year	Team		Games	BA	SA	AB	H	2B	3B	HR	HR%	R	RBI	BB	SO	SB	AB	H	PO	A	E	DP	TC/G	FA	G by Pos
1949	STL	N	20	.333	.364	33	11	1	0	0	0.0	8	2	7	3	0	2	0	29	24	1	4	2.7	.981	2B-16
1950			11	.133	.200	15	2	1	0	0	0.0	1	0	2	4	0	5	0	2	8	0	1	0.9	1.000	3B-5
1951			128	.281	.381	420	118	18	9	2	0.5	68	32	75	31	7	4	0	221	376	21	86	4.8	.966	SS-105, 2B-12
1952			151	.268	.425	570	153	28	8	15	2.6	105	52	96	55	1	1	0	256	459	30	104	4.9	.960	SS-148, 2B-3
1953			154	.279	.443	585	163	32	11	14	2.4	110	61	86	40	2	2	1	257	477	27	90	4.9	.965	SS-150, 2B-3
1954			124	.304	.430	214	65	15	3	2	0.9	43	27	55	27	5	38	10	85	151	10	29	2.0	.959	SS-66, 3B-27, 2B-12
1955			96	.243	.383	206	50	10	2	5	2.4	36	21	27	22	1	37	4	56	91	5	10	1.6	.967	3B-43, 2B-40, SS-2
1956	2 teams		86		STL	N	(8G – .200)		PHI	N	(78G – .289)														
"	total		86	.286	.458	192	55	10	4	5	2.6	25	26	29	21	1	33	9	95	95	5	18	2.3	.974	2B-49, 3B-1
1957	PHI	N	70	.185	.259	108	20	0	0	5	2.6	25	20	20	8	1	33	6	51	45	2	10	1.4	.980	2B-24
1958			105	.284	.416	334	95	14	3	8	2.4	53	36	51	34	3	20	3	188	220	13	52	4.0	.969	2B-84, 3B-1

Year	Team		Games	BA	SA	AB	H	2B	3B	HR	HR%	R	RBI	BB	SO	SB	Pinch Hit AB	Pinch Hit H	PO	A	E	DP	TC/G	FA	G by Pos

Solly Hemus *continued*

| 1959 | STL | N | 24 | .235 | .353 | 17 | 4 | 2 | 0 | 0 | 0.0 | 2 | 1 | 8 | 2 | 0 | 14 | 2 | 0 | 5 | 0 | 0 | 0.2 | 1.000 | 3B-1, 2B-1 |
| 11 yrs. | | | 969 | .273 | .411 | 2694 | 736 | 137 | 41 | 51 | 1.9 | 459 | 263 | 456 | 247 | 21 | 189 | 31 | 1240 | 1951 | 114 | 404 | 3.4 | .966 | SS-471, 2B-241, 3B-80 |

Dave Henderson

HENDERSON, DAVID LEE (Hendu)
B. July 21, 1958, Merced, Calif.

BR TR 6'2" 210 lbs.

1981	SEA	A	59	.167	.333	126	21	3	0	6	4.8	17	13	16	24	2	6	1	105	4	0	1	1.8	1.000	OF-58
1982			104	.253	.441	324	82	17	1	14	4.3	47	48	36	67	2	4	0	249	11	4	4	2.5	.985	OF-101
1983			137	.269	.444	484	130	24	5	17	3.5	50	55	28	93	9	4	1	304	17	6	4	2.4	.982	OF-133, DH-3
1984			112	.280	.466	350	98	23	0	14	4.0	42	43	19	56	5	5	1	242	11	3	5	2.3	.988	OF-97, DH-10
1985			139	.241	.388	502	121	28	2	14	2.8	70	68	48	104	6	2	1	335	8	5	3	2.6	.986	OF-138
1986	2 teams		SEA A (103G – .276)			BOS A (36G – .196)																			
"	total		139	.265	.459	388	103	22	4	15	3.9	59	47	39	110	2	8	2	193	9	4	1	1.5	.981	OF-112, DH-22
1987	2 teams		BOS A (75G – .234)			SF N (15G – .238)																			
"	total		90	.234	.410	205	48	12	0	8	3.9	32	26	30	53	3	15	3	124	1	5	0	1.4	.962	OF-73
1988	OAK	A	146	.304	.525	507	154	38	1	24	4.7	100	94	47	92	2	6	3	382	5	7	2	2.7	.982	OF-143
1989			152	.250	.380	579	145	24	3	15	2.6	77	80	54	131	8	4	0	385	5	9	1	2.6	.977	OF-149, DH-2
9 yrs.			1078	.260	.435	3465	902	191	16	127	3.7	494	474	317	730	39	54	12	2319	71	43	21	2.3	.982	OF-1004, DH-37

LEAGUE CHAMPIONSHIP SERIES

1986	BOS	A	5	.111	.444	9	1	0	0	1	11.1	3	4	2	2	0	0	0	11	0	0	0	2.2	1.000	OF-5
1988	OAK	A	4	.375	.625	16	6	1	0	1	6.3	2	4	1	7	0	0	0	11	0	2	0	3.3	.846	OF-4
1989			5	.263	.579	19	5	3	0	1	5.3	4	1	2	5	0	0	0	22	0	0	0	4.4	1.000	OF-5
3 yrs.			14	.273	.568	44	12	4	0	3	6.8	9	9	5	14	0	0	0	44	0	2	0	3.3	.957	OF-14

WORLD SERIES

1986	BOS	A	7	.400	.760	25	10	1	1	2	8.0	6	5	2	6	0	0	0	22	0	0	0	3.1	1.000	OF-7
1988	OAK	A	5	.300	.400	20	6	2	0	0	0.0	1	1	2	7	0	0	0	12	0	0	0	2.4	1.000	OF-5
1989			4	.308	.923	13	4	2	0	2	15.4	6	4	4	3	0	0	0	13	0	0	0	3.3	1.000	OF-4
3 yrs.			16	.345	.672	58	20	5	1	4	6.9	13	10	8	16	0	0	0	47	0	2	0	2.9	1.000	OF-16
			4th																						

Ken Henderson

HENDERSON, KENNETH JOSEPH
B. June 15, 1946, Carroll, Iowa

BB TR 6'2" 180 lbs.
BL 1967

1965	SF	N	63	.192	.233	73	14	1	1	0	0.0	10	7	9	19	1	7	0	47	2	1	2	0.8	.980	OF-48
1966			11	.310	.517	29	9	1	1	1	3.4	4	1	2	3	0	1	0	11	0	1	0	1.1	.917	OF-10
1967			65	.190	.274	179	34	3	0	4	2.2	15	14	19	52	0	11	3	86	3	5	1	1.4	.947	OF-52
1968			3	.333	.333	3	1	0	0	0	0.0	1	0	2	1	0	0	0	2	0	0	0	0.7	1.000	OF-2
1969			113	.225	.332	374	84	14	4	6	1.6	42	44	42	64	6	1	0	175	12	6	2	1.7	.969	OF-111, 3B-3
1970			148	.294	.460	554	163	35	3	17	3.1	104	88	87	78	20	4	1	272	15	10	2	2.0	.966	OF-140
1971			141	.264	.429	504	133	26	6	15	3.0	80	65	84	76	18	2	0	277	3	10	1	2.1	.966	OF-138, 1B-1
1972			130	.257	.437	439	113	21	2	18	4.1	60	51	38	66	14	7	1	247	14	7	3	2.1	.974	OF-123
1973	CHI	A	73	.260	.378	262	68	13	0	6	2.3	32	32	27	49	3	1	1	102	1	3	0	1.5	.972	OF-44, DH-26
1974			162	.292	.467	602	176	35	5	20	3.3	76	95	66	112	12	0	0	462	7	6	3	2.9	.987	OF-162
1975			140	.251	.355	513	129	20	3	9	1.8	65	53	74	65	5	3	1	394	7	4	0	2.9	.990	OF-137, DH-1
1976	ATL	N	138	.262	.395	435	114	19	0	13	3.0	52	61	62	68	5	10	2	219	3	3	0	1.7	.987	OF-122
1977	TEX	A	75	.258	.377	244	63	14	0	5	2.0	23	23	18	37	2	9	2	113	0	2	0	1.5	.983	OF-65, DH-3
1978	2 teams		NY N (7G – .227)			CIN N (64G – .167)																			
"	total		71	.175	.307	166	29	8	1	4	2.4	12	23	27	36	0	28	6	93	0	0	0	1.3	1.000	OF-45
1979	2 teams		CIN N (10G – .231)			CHI N (62G – .235)																			
"	total		72	.234	.330	94	22	3	0	2	2.1	12	10	15	18	0	50	9	21	0	1	0	0.3	.955	OF-25
1980	CHI	N	44	.195	.305	82	16	3	0	2	2.4	7	9	17	19	0	19	3	31	3	2	1	0.8	.944	OF-22
16 yrs.			1444	.257	.396	4553	1168	216	26	122	2.7	595	576	589	763	86	153	29	2552	70	61	15	1.9	.977	OF-1246, DH-30, 3B-3, 1B-1

LEAGUE CHAMPIONSHIP SERIES

| 1971 | SF | N | 4 | .313 | .375 | 16 | 5 | 1 | 0 | 0 | 0.0 | 3 | 2 | 2 | 1 | 1 | 0 | 0 | 4 | 0 | 0 | 0 | 1.0 | 1.000 | OF-4 |

Rickey Henderson

HENDERSON, RICKEY HENLEY
B. Dec. 25, 1957, Chicago, Ill.

BR TL 5'10" 180 lbs.

1979	OAK	A	89	.274	.336	351	96	13	3	1	0.3	49	26	34	39	33	0	0	215	5	6	0	2.5	.973	OF-88
1980			158	.303	.399	591	179	22	4	9	1.5	111	53	117	54	100	0	0	407	15	7	1	2.7	.984	OF-157, DH-1
1981			108	.319	.437	423	135	18	7	6	1.4	89	35	64	68	56	1	0	327	7	7	0	3.2	.979	OF-107
1982			149	.267	.382	536	143	24	4	10	1.9	119	51	116	94	130	6	1	379	2	9	0	2.6	.977	OF-144, DH-4
1983			145	.292	.421	513	150	25	7	9	1.8	105	48	103	80	108	6	1	349	9	3	1	2.5	.992	OF-142, DH-1
1984			142	.293	.458	502	147	27	4	16	3.2	113	58	86	81	66	2	0	341	7	11	1	2.5	.969	OF-140
1985	NY	A	143	.314	.516	547	172	28	5	24	4.4	146	72	99	65	80	1	0	439	7	9	3	3.2	.980	OF-141, DH-1
1986			153	.263	.469	608	160	31	5	28	4.6	130	74	89	81	87	3	0	426	4	6	0	2.8	.986	OF-146, DH-5
1987			95	.291	.497	358	104	17	3	17	4.7	78	37	80	52	41	2	0	189	3	4	1	2.1	.980	OF-66, DH-24
1988			140	.305	.399	554	169	30	2	6	1.1	118	50	82	54	93	0	0	320	7	12	5	2.4	.965	OF-136, DH-3
1989	2 teams		NY A (65G – .247)			OAK A (85G – .294)																			
"	total		150	.274	.399	541	148	26	3	12	2.2	113	57	126	68	77	2	2	335	6	4	1	2.3	.988	OF-147, DH-3
11 yrs.			1472	.290	.429	5524	1603	261	47	138	2.5	1171	561	996	736	871	17	3	3727	72	78	13	2.6	.980	OF-1417, DH-42
																3rd									

DIVISIONAL PLAYOFF SERIES

| 1981 | OAK | A | 3 | .182 | .182 | 11 | 2 | 0 | 0 | 0 | 0.0 | 3 | 0 | 2 | 2 | 2 | 0 | 0 | 0 | 0 | 0 | 0 | 0.0 | – | OF-3 |

LEAGUE CHAMPIONSHIP SERIES

1981	OAK	A	3	.364	.727	11	4	1	0	1	9.1	2	1	1	2	0	0	0	1	0	0	0	0.3	–	OF-3
1989			5	.400	1.000	15	6	1	1	2	13.3	8	5	7	0	8	0	0	13	0	1	0	2.8	.929	OF-5
2 yrs.			8	.385	.885	26	10	3	2	2	7.7	8	6	8	2	10	0	0	13	0	2	0	1.9	.867	OF-8

WORLD SERIES

| 1989 | OAK | A | 4 | .474 | .895 | 19 | 9 | 1 | 2 | 1 | 5.3 | 4 | 3 | 2 | 2 | 3 | 0 | 0 | 9 | 0 | 0 | 0 | 2.3 | 1.000 | OF-4 |

Steve Henderson

HENDERSON, STEPHEN CURTIS (Hendu)
B. Nov. 18, 1952, Houston, Tex.
BR TR 6'2" 190 lbs.

Year	Team	Games	BA	SA	AB	H	2B	3B	HR	HR%	R	RBI	BB	SO	SB	PH AB	PH H	PO	A	E	DP	TC/G	FA	G by Pos
1977	NY N	99	.297	.480	350	104	16	6	12	3.4	67	65	43	79	6	2	0	189	4	4	1	2.0	.980	OF-97
1978		157	.266	.399	587	156	30	9	10	1.7	83	65	60	109	13	4	4	315	18	11	3	2.2	.968	OF-155
1979		98	.306	.440	350	107	16	8	5	1.4	42	39	38	58	13	3	2	201	6	2	3	2.1	.990	OF-94
1980		143	.290	.402	513	149	17	8	8	1.6	75	58	62	90	23	8	1	299	7	6	1	2.2	.981	OF-136
1981	CHI N	82	.293	.411	287	84	9	5	5	1.7	32	35	42	61	5	4	0	152	4	8	2	2.0	.951	OF-77
1982		92	.233	.335	257	60	12	4	2	0.8	23	29	22	64	6	25	6	126	5	6	0	1.5	.956	OF-70
1983	SEA A	121	.294	.450	436	128	32	3	10	2.3	50	54	44	82	10	6	1	182	5	6	2	1.7	.970	OF-112, DH-6
1984		109	.262	.409	325	85	13	3	10	3.1	42	35	38	62	2	15	4	84	4	6	0	0.9	.936	OF-53, DH-51
1985	OAK A	85	.301	.420	193	58	8	3	3	1.6	25	31	18	34	0	27	8	79	3	4	0	1.0	.953	OF-58, DH-1
1986		11	.077	.115	26	2	1	0	0	0.0	2	3	5	7	0	2	0	8	0	2	0	0.9	.800	OF-7, DH-1
1987		46	.289	.430	114	33	7	0	3	2.6	14	9	12	19	0	11	1	33	0	2	0	0.8	.943	OF-31, DH-9
1988	HOU N	42	.217	.261	46	10	2	0	0	0.0	7	14	1	30	6	14	1	0	0	0.4	1.000	OF-8, 1B-1
12 yrs.		1085	.280	.413	3484	976	162	49	68	2.0	459	428	386	677	79	137	33	1682	67	57	12	1.7	.968	OF-898, DH-68, 1B-1

George Hendrick

HENDRICK, GEORGE ANDREW
B. Oct. 18, 1949, Los Angeles, Calif.
BR TR 6'3" 195 lbs.

Year	Team	Games	BA	SA	AB	H	2B	3B	HR	HR%	R	RBI	BB	SO	SB	PH AB	PH H	PO	A	E	DP	TC/G	FA	G by Pos
1971	OAK A	42	.237	.289	114	27	4	1	0	0.0	8	8	3	20	0	5	2	52	1	1	0	1.3	.981	OF-36
1972		58	.182	.306	121	22	1	1	4	3.3	10	15	3	22	3	19	5	68	0	0	0	1.2	1.000	OF-41
1973	CLE A	113	.268	.452	440	118	18	0	21	4.8	64	61	25	71	7	3	1	242	7	3	1	2.2	.988	OF-110
1974		139	.279	.444	495	138	23	1	19	3.8	65	67	33	73	6	5	0	355	9	4	2	2.6	.989	OF-133, DH-1
1975		145	.258	.431	561	145	21	2	24	4.3	82	86	40	78	6	2	1	338	4	6	1	2.4	.983	OF-143
1976		149	.265	.448	551	146	20	3	25	4.5	72	81	51	82	4	1	1	288	13	4	6	2.0	.987	OF-146
1977	SD N	152	.311	.492	541	168	25	2	23	4.3	75	81	61	74	11	9	2	386	11	7	2	2.7	.983	OF-142
1978 2 teams	SD N (36G – .243)				STL N (102G – .288)																			
" total		138	.278	.467	493	137	31	1	20	4.1	64	75	40	60	2	5	3	313	6	2	3	2.3	.994	OF-134
1979	STL N	140	.300	.456	493	148	27	1	16	3.2	67	75	49	62	2	7	2	254	20	2	7	2.0	.993	OF-138
1980		150	.302	.498	572	173	33	2	25	4.4	75	109	32	67	6	3	0	322	10	2	2	2.2	.994	OF-149
1981		101	.284	.485	394	112	19	3	18	4.6	67	61	41	44	4	0	0	227	6	4	0	2.3	.983	OF-101
1982		136	.282	.450	515	145	20	5	19	3.7	65	104	37	80	3	2	1	238	6	5	1	1.8	.980	OF-134
1983		144	.318	.493	529	168	33	2	18	3.4	73	97	51	76	3	5	1	904	79	8	72	6.9	.992	1B-92, OF-51
1984		120	.277	.406	441	122	28	1	9	2.0	57	69	32	75	0	4	0	189	9	2	1	1.7	.990	OF-116, 1B-1
1985 2 teams	PIT N (69G – .230)				CAL A (16G – .122)																			
" total		85	.215	.310	297	64	16	0	4	1.3	28	31	22	50	1	6	2	151	3	4	0	1.9	.975	OF-77, DH-1
1986	CAL A	102	.272	.473	283	77	13	1	14	4.9	45	47	26	41	1	3	0	188	9	5	5	2.0	.975	OF-93, 1B-7, DH-4
1987		65	.241	.395	162	39	10	0	5	3.1	14	25	14	18	0	15	6	114	5	3	7	1.9	.975	OF-45, 1B-9, DH-5
1988		69	.244	.323	127	31	1	0	3	2.4	12	19	7	20	0	29	8	129	9	3	10	2.0	.979	OF-45, 1B-9, DH-5
18 yrs.		2048	.278	.446	7129	1980	343	27	267	3.7	941	1111	567	1013	59	131	38	4758	207	65	117	2.5	.987	OF-1813, 1B-121, DH-14

LEAGUE CHAMPIONSHIP SERIES

Year	Team	Games	BA	SA	AB	H	2B	3B	HR	HR%	R	RBI	BB	SO	SB	PH AB	PH H	PO	A	E	DP	TC/G	FA	G by Pos
1972	OAK A	5	.143	.143	7	1	0	0	0	0.0	2	0	0	1	0	4	0	1	0	0	0	0.2	1.000	OF-1
1982	STL N	3	.308	.308	13	4	0	0	0	0.0	2	2	1	2	0	0	0	0	0	0	0	0.0	–	OF-3
1986	CAL A	3	.083	.083	12	1	0	0	0	0.0	0	0	0	2	0	0	0	14	2	0	0	5.3	1.000	OF-2, 1B-1
3 yrs.		11	.188	.188	32	6	0	0	0	0.0	4	2	1	5	0	4	1	15	2	0	0	1.5	1.000	OF-6, 1B-1

WORLD SERIES

Year	Team	Games	BA	SA	AB	H	2B	3B	HR	HR%	R	RBI	BB	SO	SB	PH AB	PH H	PO	A	E	DP	TC/G	FA	G by Pos
1972	OAK A	5	.133	.133	15	2	0	0	0	0.0	3	0	1	0	0	0	0	12	0	0	0	2.4	1.000	OF-5
1982	STL N	7	.321	.321	28	9	0	0	0	0.0	5	5	2	1	0	0	0	10	1	0	0	1.6	1.000	OF-7
2 yrs.		12	.256	.256	43	11	0	0	0	0.0	8	5	3	1	0	0	0	22	1	0	0	1.9	1.000	OF-12

Harvey Hendrick

HENDRICK, HARVEY (Gink)
B. Nov. 9, 1897, Mason, Tenn. D. Oct. 29, 1941, Covington, Tenn.
BL TR 6'2" 190 lbs.

Year	Team	Games	BA	SA	AB	H	2B	3B	HR	HR%	R	RBI	BB	SO	SB	PH AB	PH H	PO	A	E	DP	TC/G	FA	G by Pos
1923	NY A	37	.273	.485	66	18	3	1	3	4.5	9	12	2	8	3	24	6	16	2	1	0	0.5	.947	OF-12
1924		40	.263	.303	76	20	0	0	1	1.3	7	11	2	7	1	21	4	38	1	1	0	1.0	.975	OF-17
1925	CLE A	25	.286	.464	28	8	1	2	0	0.0	2	9	3	5	0	16	6	26	2	0	1	1.1	1.000	1B-3
1927	BKN N	128	.310	.424	458	142	18	11	4	0.9	55	50	24	40	29	10	3	560	40	11	38	4.8	.982	OF-64, 1B-53, 2B-1
1928		126	.318	.478	135	15	10	11	2.6	83	59	54	34	16	13	5	110	202	26	20	2.7	.923	3B-91, OF-17
1929		110	.354	.560	384	136	25	6	14	3.6	69	82	31	20	14	13	7	467	62	16	29	5.0	.971	OF-42, 1B-39, 3B-7, SS-4
1930		68	.257	.419	167	43	10	1	5	3.0	29	28	20	19	2	16	4	92	5	4	6	1.5	.960	OF-42, 1B-7
1931 2 teams	BKN N (1G – .000)				CIN N (137G – .315)																			
" total		138	.315	.414	531	167	32	9	1	0.2	74	75	53	40	3	1	0	1348	67	18	147	10.4	.987	1B-137
1932 2 teams	STL N (28G – .250)				CIN N (94G – .302)																			
" total		122	.294	.406	470	138	32	3	5	1.1	64	45	28	38	3	9	3	936	78	18	75	8.5	.983	1B-94, 3B-12, OF-5
1933	CHI N	69	.291	.455	189	55	13	3	4	2.1	30	23	13	17	4	19	6	344	25	8	39	5.5	.979	1B-38, OF-8, 3B-1
1934	PHI N	59	.293	.362	116	34	8	0	0	0.0	12	19	9	15	0	31	7	69	4	4	4	1.4	.951	OF-3, 3B-7, 1B-7
11 yrs.		922	.308	.443	2910	896	157	46	48	1.6	434	413	239	243	75	173	51	4006	493	107	359	5.0	.977	1B-378, OF-219, 3B-118, SS-4, 2B-1

WORLD SERIES

Year	Team	Games	BA	SA	AB	H	2B	3B	HR	HR%	R	RBI	BB	SO	SB	PH AB	PH H	PO	A	E	DP	TC/G	FA	G by Pos
1923	NY A	1	.000	.000	1	0	0	0	0	0.0	0	0	0	0	0	1	0	0	0	0	0	0.0	–	

Ellie Hendricks

HENDRICKS, ELROD JEROME
B. Dec. 22, 1940, Charlotte Amalie, Virgin Islands
BL TR 6'1" 175 lbs.

Year	Team	Games	BA	SA	AB	H	2B	3B	HR	HR%	R	RBI	BB	SO	SB	PH AB	PH H	PO	A	E	DP	TC/G	FA	G by Pos
1968	BAL A	79	.202	.372	183	37	8	1	7	3.8	19	23	19	51	0	27	4	303	21	3	3	4.1	.991	C-53
1969		105	.244	.383	295	72	5	0	12	4.1	36	38	39	44	0	16	5	488	41	1	2	5.0	.998	C-87, 1B-4
1970		106	.242	.382	322	78	9	0	12	3.7	32	41	33	44	0	16	3	509	35	8	6	5.2	.986	C-95
1971		101	.250	.386	316	79	14	1	9	2.8	33	42	39	38	0	11	3	453	34	7	8	4.9	.986	C-90, 1B-3
1972 2 teams	BAL A (33G – .155)				CHI N (17G – .116)																			
" total		50	.142	.228	127	18	2	0	2	1.6	13	10	25	27	0	4	0	213	22	4	4	4.8	.983	C-44
1973	BAL A	41	.178	.337	101	18	5	1	3	3.0	9	15	10	22	0	2	0	148	9	1	3	3.9	.994	C-38
1974		66	.208	.340	159	33	8	1	3	1.9	18	16	17	25	0	14	5	194	13	0	4	3.1	1.000	C-54, DH-1, 1B-1
1975		85	.215	.377	223	48	14	0	8	3.6	32	38	34	40	0	8	1	332	36	2	3	4.4	.995	C-83

Year	Team		Games	BA	SA	AB	H	2B	3B	HR	HR%	R	RBI	BB	SO	SB	Pinch Hit AB	Pinch Hit H	PO	A	E	DP	TC/G	FA	G by Pos

Ellie Hendricks *continued*

Year	Team		Games	BA	SA	AB	H	2B	3B	HR	HR%	R	RBI	BB	SO	SB	AB	H	PO	A	E	DP	TC/G	FA	G by Pos
1976	2 teams	BAL A (28G – .139)				NY A (26G – .226)																			
"	total		54	.174	.280	132	23	2	0	4	3.0	8	9	10	23	0	12	2	147	17	3	2	3.1	.982	C-45
1977	NY	A	10	.273	.636	11	3	1	0	1	9.1	1	5	0	2	0	3	1	11	0	0	0	1.1	1.000	C-6
1978	BAL	A	13	.333	.556	18	6	1	0	1	5.6	4	1	3	3	0	6	1	19	2	1	0	1.7	.955	C-6, DH-1, P-1
1979			1	.000	.000	1	0	0	0	0	0.0	0	0	0	0	0	1	0	1	0	1	0	2.0	.500	C-1
	12 yrs.		711	.220	.361	1888	415	66	7	62	3.3	205	230	229	319	1	119	25	2818	230	31	33	4.3	.990	C-602, 1B-8, DH-2, P-1

LEAGUE CHAMPIONSHIP SERIES

Year	Team		Games	BA	SA	AB	H	2B	3B	HR	HR%	R	RBI	BB	SO	SB	AB	H	PO	A	E	DP	TC/G	FA	G by Pos
1969	BAL	A	3	.250	.500	8	2	2	0	0	0.0	2	3	1	1	0	0	0	18	0	0	0	6.0	1.000	C-3
1970			1	.400	.400	5	2	0	0	0	0.0	2	0	0	0	0	0	0	5	0	0	0	5.0	1.000	C-1
1971			2	.500	1.250	4	2	0	0	1	25.0	1	2	1	1	0	0	0	6	0	0	0	3.0	1.000	C-2
1974			3	.167	.167	6	1	0	0	0	0.0	1	0	1	3	0	0	0	11	1	0	0	4.0	1.000	C-3
1976	NY	A	1	1.000	1.000	1	1	0	0	0	0.0	0	0	0	0	0	1	1	0	0	0	0	0.0	—	
	5 yrs.		10	.333	.542	24	8	2	0	1	4.2	6	5	3	5	0	2	1	40	1	0	0	4.1	1.000	C-9

WORLD SERIES

Year	Team		Games	BA	SA	AB	H	2B	3B	HR	HR%	R	RBI	BB	SO	SB	AB	H	PO	A	E	DP	TC/G	FA	G by Pos
1969	BAL	A	3	.100	.100	10	1	0	0	0	0.0	1	0	1	0	0	0	0	21	1	0	1	7.3	1.000	C-3
1970			3	.364	.727	11	4	1	0	1	9.1	1	4	1	2	0	0	0	17	2	1	0	6.7	.950	C-3
1971			6	.263	.316	19	5	1	0	0	0.0	3	1	3	3	0	0	0	40	4	1	0	7.5	.978	C-6
1976	NY	A	2	.000	.000	2	0	0	0	0	0.0	0	0	0	0	0	2	0	0	0	0	0	—		
	4 yrs.		14	.238	.357	42	10	2	0	1	2.4	5	5	5	5	0	2	0	78	7	2	1	6.2	.977	C-12

Jack Hendricks

HENDRICKS, JOHN CHARLES
B. Apr. 9, 1875, Joliet, Ill. D. May 13, 1943, Chicago, Ill.
Manager 1918, 1924-29.

BL TL 5'11½" 160 lbs.

Year	Team		Games	BA	SA	AB	H	2B	3B	HR	HR%	R	RBI	BB	SO	SB	AB	H	PO	A	E	DP	TC/G	FA	G by Pos
1902	2 teams	NY N (8G – .231)				CHI N (2G – .571)																			
"	total		10	.303	.424	33	10	2	1	0	0.0	1	0	2		2	1	0	18	1	1	0	2.0	.950	OF-9
1903	WAS	A	32	.179	.241	112	20	1	3	0	0.0	10	4	13		3	0	0	40	1	5	1	1.4	.891	OF-32
	2 yrs.		42	.207	.283	145	30	3	4	0	0.0	11	4	15		5	1	0	58	2	6	1	1.6	.909	OF-41

Claude Hendrix

HENDRIX, CLAUDE RAYMOND
B. Apr. 13, 1889, Olathe, Kans. D. Mar. 22, 1944, Allentown, Pa.

BR TR 6' 195 lbs.

Year	Team		Games	BA	SA	AB	H	2B	3B	HR	HR%	R	RBI	BB	SO	SB	AB	H	PO	A	E	DP	TC/G	FA	G by Pos
1911	PIT	N	22	.098	.171	41	4	1	1	0	0.0	2	2	1	15	0	0	0	12	45	1	2	2.6	.983	P-22
1912			39	.322	.529	121	39	10	6	1	0.8	25	15	3	18	1	5	2	7	91	3	2	2.6	.970	P-39
1913			53	.273	.434	99	27	5	4	1	1.0	13	8	3	16	0	8	0	6	67	4	6	1.5	.948	P-42
1914	CHI	F	52	.231	.300	130	30	3	0	2	1.5	15	13	7		3	2	1	10	137	5	5	2.9	.967	P-49
1915			50	.265	.469	113	30	7	2	4	3.5	22	18	5		1	9	2	11	69	3	2	1.7	.964	P-40
1916	CHI	N	45	.200	.275	80	16	3	0	1	1.3	4	5	6	24	1	7	1	10	65	4	2	1.8	.949	P-36
1917			48	.256	.314	86	22	3	1	0	0.0	7	7	5	20	1	5	1	6	52	4	1	1.3	.935	P-40, OF-2
1918			35	.264	.462	91	24	3	3	3	3.3	14	17	4	11	1	3	1	6	75	2	1	2.4	.976	P-32
1919			36	.192	.244	78	15	1	0	1	1.3	6	6	2	19	0	3	1	5	67	1	0	2.0	.986	P-33
1920			34	.181	.217	83	15	0	0	0	0.0	10	6	3	11	2	7	1	4	56	5	1	1.9	.923	P-27
	10 yrs.		414	.241	.362	922	222	39	17	13	1.4	118	97	39	134	9	49	10	77	724	32	22	2.0	.962	P-360, OF-2

WORLD SERIES

Year	Team		Games	BA	SA	AB	H	2B	3B	HR	HR%	R	RBI	BB	SO	SB	AB	H	PO	A	E	DP	TC/G	FA	G by Pos
1918	CHI	N	2	1.000	1.000	1	1	0	0	0	0.0	0	0	0	0	0	1	1	0	0	0	0	0.0	—	P-1

Tim Hendryx

HENDRYX, TIMOTHY GREEN
B. Jan. 31, 1891, LeRoy, Ill. D. Aug. 14, 1957, Corpus Christi, Tex.

BR TR 5'9" 170 lbs.

Year	Team		Games	BA	SA	AB	H	2B	3B	HR	HR%	R	RBI	BB	SO	SB	AB	H	PO	A	E	DP	TC/G	FA	G by Pos
1911	CLE	A	2	.250	.250	4	1	0	0	0	0.0	0	0	0		0	0	0	3	0	0	0	2.5	1.000	3B-2
1912			23	.243	.429	70	17	2	4	1	1.4	9	14	8		3	1	0	44	1	0	0	2.0	1.000	OF-22
1915	NY	A	13	.200	.250	40	8	2	0	0	0.0	4	1	4		2	1	0	28	2	1	0	2.4	.968	OF-12
1916			15	.290	.435	62	18	7	1	0	0.0	10	5	8		4	0	0	18	1	0	0	1.3	1.000	OF-15
1917			125	.249	.359	393	98	14	7	5	1.3	43	44	62	45	6	16	4	215	17	11	1	1.9	.955	OF-107
1918	STL	A	88	.279	.370	219	61	14	3	0	0.0	22	33	37	35	4	18	0	108	4	2	2	1.3	.982	OF-65
1920	BOS	A	99	.328	.413	363	119	21	5	0	0.0	54	73	42	27	7	1	0	208	6	8	1	2.2	.964	OF-98
1921			49	.241	.328	137	33	8	2	0	0.0	10	21	24	13	1	6	1	66	2	3	0	1.4	.958	OF-41
	8 yrs.		414	.276	.377	1288	355	68	22	6	0.5	152	191	185	128	26	43	5	689	36	25	4	1.8	.967	OF-360, 3B-2

Dave Hengel

HENGEL, DAVID LEE
B. Dec. 18, 1961, Oakland, Calif.

BR TR 6' 185 lbs.

Year	Team		Games	BA	SA	AB	H	2B	3B	HR	HR%	R	RBI	BB	SO	SB	AB	H	PO	A	E	DP	TC/G	FA	G by Pos
1986	SEA	A	21	.190	.254	63	12	1	0	1	1.6	3	6	1	13	0	4	1	9	1	0	0	0.5	1.000	DH-11, OF-8
1987			10	.316	.474	19	6	0	0	1	5.3	2	4	1	4	0	4	2	7	0	1	0	0.8	.875	OF-7, DH-1
1988			26	.167	.283	60	10	1	0	2	3.3	3	7	1	15	0	8	1	20	0	1	0	0.8	.952	DH-12, OF-12
1989	CLE	A	12	.120	.160	25	3	1	0	0	0.0	2	1	2	4	0	3	0	12	1	0	0	1.1	1.000	OF-9, DH-3
	4 yrs.		69	.186	.275	167	31	3	0	4	2.4	10	18	4	36	0	19	4	48	2	2	0	0.8	.962	OF-36, DH-27

Moxie Hengle

HENGLE, EMERY J.
Brother of Ed Hengle.
B. Oct. 7, 1857, Chicago, Ill. D. Dec. 11, 1924, River Forest, Ill.

5'8" 144 lbs.

Year	Team		Games	BA	SA	AB	H	2B	3B	HR	HR%	R	RBI	BB	SO	SB	AB	H	PO	A	E	DP	TC/G	FA	G by Pos
1884	2 teams	CHI U (19G – .203)				STP U (9G – .152)																			
"	total		28	.187	.252	107	20	3	2	0	0.0	11		3			0	0	65	62	19	5	5.2	.870	2B-28
1885	BUF	N	7	.154	.154	26	4	0	0	0	0.0	2	0	1			0	0	14	8	5	1	3.9	.815	2B-5, OF-3
	2 yrs.		35	.180	.233	133	24	3	2	0	0.0	13	0	4	2		0	0	79	70	24	6	4.9	.861	2B-33, OF-3

Gail Henley

HENLEY, GAIL CURTICE
B. Oct. 15, 1928, Wichita, Kans.

BL TR 5'9" 180 lbs.

Year	Team		Games	BA	SA	AB	H	2B	3B	HR	HR%	R	RBI	BB	SO	SB	AB	H	PO	A	E	DP	TC/G	FA	G by Pos
1954	PIT	N	14	.300	.433	30	9	1	0	1	3.3	7	2	4	4	0	5	1	13	1	0	0	1.0	1.000	OF-9

Butch Henline

HENLINE, WALTER JOHN
B. Dec. 20, 1894, Fort Wayne, Ind. D. Oct. 9, 1957, Sarasota, Fla.

BR TR 5'10" 175 lbs.

Year	Team	Games	BA	SA	AB	H	2B	3B	HR	HR%	R	RBI	BB	SO	SB	Pinch Hit AB	Pinch Hit H	PO	A	E	DP	TC/G	FA	G by Pos

Butch Henline *continued*

Year	Team	Games	BA	SA	AB	H	2B	3B	HR	HR%	R	RBI	BB	SO	SB	AB	H	PO	A	E	DP	TC/G	FA	G by Pos
1921	2 teams		NY	N	(1G – .000)			PHI	N	(33G – .306)														
"	total	34	.304	.321	112	34	2	0	0	0.0	8	8	2	7	1	2	0	113	44	2	5	4.7	.987	C-32
1922	PHI N	125	.316	.479	430	136	20	4	14	3.3	57	64	36	33	2	4	2	400	113	9	13	4.2	.983	C-119
1923		111	.324	.448	330	107	14	3	7	2.1	45	46	37	33	7	12	3	291	71	8	8	3.3	.978	C-96, OF-1
1924		115	.284	.426	289	82	18	4	5	1.7	41	35	27	15	1	28	7	249	76	9	12	2.9	.973	C-83, OF-1
1925		93	.304	.479	263	80	12	5	8	3.0	43	48	24	16	3	18	2	211	53	12	9	3.0	.957	C-68, OF-1
1926		99	.283	.360	283	80	14	1	2	0.7	32	30	21	18	1	17	4	244	48	9	12	3.0	.970	C-77, 1B-4, OF-2
1927	BKN N	67	.266	.373	177	47	10	3	1	0.6	12	18	17	10	1	7	1	216	50	15	6	4.2	.947	C-60
1928		55	.212	.295	132	28	3	1	2	1.5	12	8	17	8	2	8	2	141	22	4	1	3.0	.976	C-45
1929		27	.242	.323	62	15	2	0	1	1.6	5	7	9	9	0	5	0	72	15	3	2	3.3	.967	C-21
1930	CHI A	3	.125	.125	8	1	0	0	0	0.0	1	2	3	0	0	0	0	10	2	0	0	4.0	1.000	C-3
1931		11	.067	.133	15	1	1	0	0	0.0	2	2	2	4	0	5	1	14	2	2	0	1.6	.889	C-4
11 yrs.		740	.291	.414	2101	611	96	21	40	1.9	258	268	192	156	18	106	22	1961	496	73	68	3.4	.971	C-608, OF-6, 1B-4

Les Hennessy

HENNESSY, LESTER BAKER
B. Dec. 12, 1893, Lynn, Mass. D. Nov. 20, 1976, New York, N. Y. BR TR 6' 190 lbs.

Year	Team	Games	BA	SA	AB	H	2B	3B	HR	HR%	R	RBI	BB	SO	SB	AB	H	PO	A	E	DP	TC/G	FA	G by Pos
1913	DET A	12	.136	.136	22	3	0	0	0	0.0	2	0	3	6	2	2	0	8	14	3	0	2.1	.880	2B-9

Bobby Henrich

HENRICH, ROBERT EDWARD
B. Dec. 24, 1938, Lawrence, Kans. BR TR 6'1" 185 lbs.

Year	Team	Games	BA	SA	AB	H	2B	3B	HR	HR%	R	RBI	BB	SO	SB	AB	H	PO	A	E	DP	TC/G	FA	G by Pos
1957	CIN N	29	.200	.200	10	2	0	0	0	0.0	8	1	1	4	0	4	1	3	7	1	1	0.4	.909	SS-7, OF-6, 3B-2, 2B-1
1958		5	.000	.000	3	0	0	0	0	0.0	2	0	0	2	0	0	0	2	0	0	0	0.8	1.000	SS-2
1959		14	.000	.000	3	0	0	0	0	0.0	3	0	0	1	0	1	0	2	0	0	0	0.1	1.000	SS-5, 3B-1
3 yrs.		48	.125	.125	16	2	0	0	0	0.0	13	1	1	7	0	5	1	7	9	1	1	0.4	.941	SS-14, OF-6, 3B-3, 2B-1

Fritz Henrich

HENRICH, FRANK WILDE
B. May 8, 1899, Cincinnati, Ohio D. May 1, 1959, Philadelphia, Pa. BL TL 5'10" 160 lbs.

Year	Team	Games	BA	SA	AB	H	2B	3B	HR	HR%	R	RBI	BB	SO	SB	AB	H	PO	A	E	DP	TC/G	FA	G by Pos
1924	PHI N	36	.211	.256	90	19	4	0	0	0.0	4	4	2	12	0	4	0	42	2	1	0	1.3	.978	OF-32

Tommy Henrich

HENRICH, THOMAS DAVID (Old Reliable)
B. Feb. 20, 1913, Massillon, Ohio BL TL 6' 180 lbs.

Year	Team	Games	BA	SA	AB	H	2B	3B	HR	HR%	R	RBI	BB	SO	SB	AB	H	PO	A	E	DP	TC/G	FA	G by Pos
1937	NY A	67	.320	.553	206	66	14	5	8	3.9	39	42	35	17	4	7	1	90	6	3	1	1.5	.970	OF-59
1938		131	.270	.490	471	127	24	7	22	4.7	109	91	92	32	6	1	0	239	14	4	1	2.0	.984	OF-130
1939		99	.277	.429	347	96	18	4	9	2.6	64	57	51	23	7	11	4	207	7	2	1	2.2	.991	OF-88, 1B-1
1940		90	.307	.539	293	90	28	5	10	3.4	57	53	48	30	1	12	4	152	10	5	2	1.9	.970	OF-76, 1B-2
1941		144	.277	.519	538	149	27	5	31	5.8	106	85	81	40	3	4	1	280	13	6	4	2.1	.980	OF-139
1942		127	.267	.431	483	129	30	5	13	2.7	77	67	58	42	4	3	1	278	13	3	14	2.3	.990	OF-119, 1B-7
1946		150	.251	.411	565	142	25	4	19	3.4	92	83	87	63	5	0	0	588	32	7	40	4.2	.989	OF-111, 1B-41
1947		142	.287	.485	550	158	35	13	16	2.9	109	98	71	54	3	5	1	337	14	5	8	2.5	.986	OF-132, 1B-6
1948		146	.308	.554	588	181	42	14	25	4.3	138	100	76	42	2	1	0	568	29	11	45	4.2	.982	OF-102, 1B-46
1949		115	.287	.526	411	118	20	3	24	5.8	90	85	86	34	2	2	0	555	33	7	66	5.2	.988	OF-61, 1B-52
1950		73	.272	.536	151	41	6	8	6	4.0	20	34	27	6	0	33	7	224	7	3	23	3.2	.987	1B-34
11 yrs.		1284	.282	.491	4603	1297	269	73	183	4.0	901	795	712	383	37	79	19	3518	178	56	205	2.9	.985	OF-1017, 1B-189

WORLD SERIES

Year	Team	Games	BA	SA	AB	H	2B	3B	HR	HR%	R	RBI	BB	SO	SB	AB	H	PO	A	E	DP	TC/G	FA	G by Pos
1938	NY A	4	.250	.500	16	4	1	0	1	6.3	3	1	0	1	0	0	0	6	0	1	0	1.8	.857	OF-4
1941		5	.167	.389	18	3	1	0	1	5.6	4	1	3	3	0	0	0	6	0	0	0	1.2	1.000	OF-5
1947		7	.323	.484	31	10	2	0	1	3.2	2	5	2	0	0	0	0	12	0	0	0	1.7	1.000	OF-7
1949		5	.263	.421	19	5	0	0	1	5.3	4	1	3	0	0	0	0	48	1	0	4	9.8	1.000	1B-5
4 yrs.		21	.262	.452	84	22	4	0	4	4.8	13	8	8	7	0	0	0	72	1	1	4	3.5	.986	OF-16, 1B-5

Olaf Henriksen

HENRIKSEN, OLAF (Swede)
B. Apr. 26, 1888, Kirkerup, Denmark D. Oct. 17, 1962, Norwood, Mass. BL TL 5'7½" 158 lbs.

Year	Team	Games	BA	SA	AB	H	2B	3B	HR	HR%	R	RBI	BB	SO	SB	AB	H	PO	A	E	DP	TC/G	FA	G by Pos
1911	BOS A	27	.366	.409	93	34	2	1	0	0.0	17	8	14		4	2	0	38	3	2	1	1.6	.953	OF-25
1912		37	.321	.411	56	18	3	1	0	0.0	20	8	14		4	25	6	10	0	1	0	0.3	.909	OF-10
1913		30	.375	.400	40	15	1	0	0	0.0	8	2	7	5	3	17	6	9	0	0	0	0.3	1.000	OF-7
1914		61	.263	.337	95	25	2	1	1	1.1	16	5	22	12	5	26	5	35	1	2	0	0.6	.947	OF-27
1915		73	.196	.261	92	18	2	2	0	0.0	9	13	18	7	1	31	7	27	2	1	2	0.4	.967	OF-25
1916		68	.202	.263	99	20	2	2	0	0.0	13	11	19	15	2	21	4	43	2	0	0	0.7	1.000	OF-31
1917		15	.083	.083	12	1	0	0	0	0.0	1	1	3	4	0	12	1	0	0	0	0	0.0	–	
7 yrs.		311	.269	.329	487	131	12	7	1	0.2	84	48	97	15	134	29	162	8	6	3	0.6	.966	OF-125

WORLD SERIES

Year	Team	Games	BA	SA	AB	H	2B	3B	HR	HR%	R	RBI	BB	SO	SB	AB	H	PO	A	E	DP	TC/G	FA	G by Pos
1912	BOS A	2	1.000	2.000	1	1	1	0	0	0.0	0	1	0	0	0	1	1	0	0	0	0	0.0		
1915		2	.000	.000	2	0	0	0	0	0.0	0	0	0	2	0	2	0	0	0	0	0	0.0		
1916		1	–	–	0	0	0	0	0	–	1	0	1	1	0	0	0	0	0	0	0	0.0	–	
3 yrs.		5	.333	.667	3	1	1	0	0	0.0	1	1	1	3	0	3	1	0	0	0	0	0.0	–	

George Henry

HENRY, GEORGE WASHINGTON
B. Aug. 10, 1863, Philadelphia, Pa. D. Dec. 30, 1934, Lynn, Mass. BR TR 5'9" 180 lbs.

Year	Team	Games	BA	SA	AB	H	2B	3B	HR	HR%	R	RBI	BB	SO	SB	AB	H	PO	A	E	DP	TC/G	FA	G by Pos
1893	CIN N	21	.277	.313	83	23	3	0	0	0.0	11	13	11	12	2	0	0	49	6	2	1	2.7	.965	OF-21

John Henry

HENRY, JOHN MICHAEL
B. Sept. 2, 1863, Springfield, Mass. D. June 11, 1939, Hartford, Conn. TL

Year	Team	Games	BA	SA	AB	H	2B	3B	HR	HR%	R	RBI	BB	SO	SB	AB	H	PO	A	E	DP	TC/G	FA	G by Pos
1884	CLE N	9	.154	.154	26	4	0	0	0	0.0	2	0	0	12		0	0	7	12	1	0	2.2	.950	P-5, OF-4
1885	BAL AA	10	.265	.353	34	9	3	0	0	0.0	4		1			0	0	10	18	2	1	3.0	.933	P-9, OF-1
1886	WAS N	4	.357	.357	14	5	0	0	0	0.0	3	0	0	3		0	0	2	3	1	0	1.5	.833	P-4
1890	NY N	37	.243	.285	144	35	6	0	0	0.0	19	16	7	12	12	0	0	56	4	9	1	1.9	.870	OF-37
4 yrs.		60	.243	.284	218	53	9	0	0	0.0	28	16	8	27	12	0	0	75	37	13	2	2.1	.896	OF-42, P-18

Year	Team	Games	BA	SA	AB	H	2B	3B	HR	HR%	R	RBI	BB	SO	SB	Pinch Hit AB	Pinch Hit H	PO	A	E	DP	TC/G	FA	G by Pos

John Henry

HENRY, JOHN PARK (Bull)
B. Dec. 26, 1889, Amherst, Mass.   D. Nov. 24, 1941, Fort Huachuca, Ariz.   BR TR 6'   190 lbs.

Year	Team	Games	BA	SA	AB	H	2B	3B	HR	HR%	R	RBI	BB	SO	SB	AB	H	PO	A	E	DP	TC/G	FA	G by Pos
1910	WAS A	28	.149	.184	87	13	1	1	0	0.0	2	5	2		2	0	0	165	35	1	10	7.2	.995	C-18, 1B-10
1911		85	.203	.222	261	53	5	0	0	0.0	24	21	25		8	3	0	549	123	21	15	8.2	.970	C-51, 1B-30
1912		63	.194	.225	191	37	4	1	0	0.0	23	9	31		10	0	0	347	113	11	7	7.5	.977	C-63
1913		96	.223	.293	273	61	8	4	1	0.4	26	26	30	43	5	0	0	476	127	11	9	6.4	.982	C-96
1914		91	.169	.226	261	44	7	4	0	0.0	22	20	37	47	7	0	0	513	124	13	9	7.1	.980	C-91
1915		95	.220	.278	277	61	9	2	1	0.4	20	22	36	28	10	1	0	478	122	17	4	6.5	.972	C-94
1916		117	.249	.308	305	76	12	3	0	0.0	28	46	49	40	12	1	0	538	124	13	17	5.8	.981	C-116
1917		65	.190	.227	163	31	6	0	0	0.0	10	18	24	16	1	4	0	274	54	4	5	5.1	.988	C-59
1918	BOS N	43	.206	.225	102	21	2	0	0	0.0	6	4	10	15	0	3	1	121	38	6	5	3.8	.964	C-38
9 yrs.		683	.207	.254	1920	397	54	15	2	0.1	161	171	244	189	55	12	1	3461	860	97	82	6.5	.978	C-626, 1B-40

Ron Henry

HENRY, RONALD BAXTER
B. Aug. 7, 1936, Chester, Pa.   BR TR 6'1"   180 lbs.

Year	Team	Games	BA	SA	AB	H	2B	3B	HR	HR%	R	RBI	BB	SO	SB	AB	H	PO	A	E	DP	TC/G	FA	G by Pos
1961	MIN A	20	.143	.143	28	4	0	0	0	0.0	1	3	2	7	0	14	3	22	2	0	0	1.2	1.000	C-5, 1B-1
1964		22	.122	.341	41	5	1	0	2	4.9	4	5	2	17	0	11	1	54	6	1	2	2.8	.984	C-13
2 yrs.		42	.130	.261	69	9	1	0	2	2.9	5	8	4	24	0	25	4	76	8	1	2	2.0	.988	C-18, 1B-1

Snake Henry

HENRY, FREDERICK MARSHALL
B. July 19, 1895, Waynesville, N. C.   D. Oct. 12, 1987, Wendell, N. C.   BL TL 6'   170 lbs.

Year	Team	Games	BA	SA	AB	H	2B	3B	HR	HR%	R	RBI	BB	SO	SB	AB	H	PO	A	E	DP	TC/G	FA	G by Pos
1922	BOS N	18	.197	.288	66	13	4	1	0	0.0	5	5	2	2	0	0	0	170	12	1	7	10.2	.995	1B-18
1923		11	.111	.111	9	1	0	0	0	0.0	1	2	1	7	1	9	1	0	0	0	0	—		
2 yrs.		29	.187	.267	75	14	4	1	0	0.0	6	7	3	9	1	9	1	170	12	1	7	6.3	.995	1B-18

Babe Herman

HERMAN, FLOYD CAVES
B. June 26, 1903, Buffalo, N. Y.   D. Nov. 27, 1987, Glendale, Calif.   BL TL 6'4"   190 lbs.

Year	Team	Games	BA	SA	AB	H	2B	3B	HR	HR%	R	RBI	BB	SO	SB	AB	H	PO	A	E	DP	TC/G	FA	G by Pos
1926	BKN N	137	.319	.500	496	158	35	11	11	2.2	64	81	44	53	8	6	2	974	64	17	55	7.7	.984	1B-101, OF-35
1927		130	.272	.481	412	112	26	9	14	3.4	65	73	39	41	4	20	7	969	68	21	64	8.1	.980	1B-105, OF-1
1928		134	.340	.514	486	165	37	6	12	2.5	64	91	38	36	1	6	1	225	12	16	2	1.9	.937	OF-127
1929		146	.381	.612	569	217	42	13	21	3.7	105	113	55	45	21	3	2	260	11	17	3	2.0	.941	OF-141, 1B-2
1930		153	.393	.678	614	241	48	11	35	5.7	143	130	66	56	18	0	0	260	10	6	1	1.8	.978	OF-153
1931		151	.313	.525	610	191	43	16	18	3.0	93	97	50	65	17	0	0	287	24	13	7	2.1	.960	OF-150
1932	CIN N	148	.326	.541	577	188	38	19	16	2.8	87	87	60	45	7	2	1	392	18	13	6	2.9	.969	OF-146
1933	CHI N	137	.289	.502	508	147	36	12	16	3.1	77	93	50	57	6	5	4	252	12	11	1	2.0	.957	OF-131
1934		125	.304	.488	467	142	34	5	14	3.0	65	84	35	71	1	6	2	251	10	7	7	2.1	.974	OF-113, 1B-7
1935	2 teams	PIT N	(26G – .235)		CIN N	(92G – .335)																		
"	total	118	.316	.486	430	136	31	6	10	2.3	52	65	38	35	5	10	0	319	15	9	12	2.9	.974	OF-91, 1B-17
1936	CIN N	119	.279	.458	380	106	25	2	13	3.4	59	71	39	36	4	19	4	184	4	6	1	1.6	.969	OF-92, 1B-4
1937	DET A	17	.300	.450	20	6	3	0	0	0.0	2	3	1	6	2	14	3	3	0	0	0	0.2	1.000	OF-2
1945	BKN N	37	.265	.382	34	9	1	0	1	2.9	6	9	5	7	0	29	6	0	0	0	0	0.0	—	
13 yrs.		1552	.324	.532	5603	1818	399	110	181	3.2	882	997	520	553	94	120	32	4376	248	137	159	3.1	.971	OF-1185, 1B-236

Billy Herman

HERMAN, WILLIAM JENNINGS BRYAN
B. July 7, 1909, New Albany, Ind.
Manager 1947, 1964-66.
Hall of Fame 1975.   BR TR 5'11"   180 lbs.

Year	Team	Games	BA	SA	AB	H	2B	3B	HR	HR%	R	RBI	BB	SO	SB	AB	H	PO	A	E	DP	TC/G	FA	G by Pos
1931	CHI N	25	.327	.398	98	32	7	0	0	0.0	14	16	13	6	2	0	0	76	79	10	17	6.6	.939	2B-25
1932		154	.314	.404	656	206	42	7	1	0.2	102	51	40	33	14	0	0	401	527	38	102	6.3	.961	2B-154
1933		153	.279	.342	619	173	35	2	0	0.0	82	44	45	34	5	0	0	466	512	45	114	6.7	.956	2B-153
1934		113	.303	.395	456	138	21	6	3	0.7	79	42	34	31	6	1	0	278	385	17	64	6.0	.975	2B-111
1935		154	.341	.476	666	**227**	**57**	6	7	1.1	113	83	42	29	6	0	0	416	520	35	109	6.3	.964	2B-154
1936		153	.334	.470	632	211	57	7	5	0.8	101	93	59	30	5	0	0	457	492	24	110	6.4	.975	2B-153
1937		138	.335	.479	564	189	35	11	8	1.4	106	65	56	21	2	1	0	384	468	41	97	6.5	.954	2B-137
1938		152	.277	.359	624	173	34	7	1	0.2	86	56	59	31	3	1	0	404	517	18	111	6.2	.981	2B-151
1939		156	.307	.453	623	191	34	18	7	1.1	111	70	66	31	9	0	0	377	485	29	95	5.7	.967	2B-156
1940		135	.292	.452	558	163	24	7	5	0.9	77	57	47	30	1	0	0	366	448	22	94	6.2	.974	2B-135
1941	2 teams	CHI N	(11G – .194)		BKN N	(133G – .291)																		
"	total	144	.285	.371	572	163	30	5	3	0.5	81	41	67	43	1	0	0	37	33	6	7	0.5	.921	2B-144
1942	BKN N	155	.256	.331	571	146	34	2	2	0.4	76	65	72	52	6	0	0	412	404	23	99	5.4	.973	2B-153, 1B-3
1943		153	.330	.417	585	193	41	2	2	0.3	76	100	66	26	4	0	0	345	390	21	71	4.9	.972	2B-117, 3B-37
1946	2 teams	BKN N	(47G – .288)		BOS N	(75G – .306)																		
"	total	122	.298	.413	436	130	31	5	3	0.7	56	50	69	23	3	4	1	352	207	16	61	4.7	.972	2B-76, 3B-63, 1B-22
1947	PIT N	15	.213	.298	47	10	4	0	0	0.0	3	6	2	7	0	1	0	20	15	0	2	2.3	1.000	2B-10, 1B-2
15 yrs.		1922	.304	.407	7707	2345	486	82	47	0.6	1163	839	737	428	67	8	1	4791	5482	345	1153	5.5	.968	2B-1829, 3B-100, 1B-27

WORLD SERIES

Year	Team	Games	BA	SA	AB	H	2B	3B	HR	HR%	R	RBI	BB	SO	SB	AB	H	PO	A	E	DP	TC/G	FA	G by Pos
1932	CHI N	4	.222	.278	18	4	1	0	0	0.0	5	1	0	2	0	0	0	5	12	1	6	4.5	.944	2B-4
1935		6	.333	.625	24	8	2	1	1	4.2	3	6	0	4	0	0	0	15	19	1	6	5.8	.971	2B-6
1938		4	.188	.188	16	3	0	0	0	0.0	1	0	1	4	0	0	0	5	14	2	2	5.3	.905	2B-4
1941	BKN N	4	.125	.125	8	1	0	0	0	0.0	0	0	2	0	0	0	0	4	13	0	2	4.3	1.000	2B-4
4 yrs.		18	.242	.364	66	16	3	1	1	1.5	9	7	4	9	0	0	0	29	58	4	14	5.1	.956	2B-18

Al Hermann

HERMANN, ALBERT BARTEL
B. Mar. 28, 1899, Milltown, N. J.   D. Aug. 20, 1980, Lewes, Del.   BR TR 6'   180 lbs.

Year	Team	Games	BA	SA	AB	H	2B	3B	HR	HR%	R	RBI	BB	SO	SB	AB	H	PO	A	E	DP	TC/G	FA	G by Pos
1923	BOS N	31	.237	.280	93	22	4	0	0	0.0	2	11	0	7	3	7	0	62	52	6	5	3.9	.950	2B-15, 3B-5, 1B-4
1924		1	.000	.000	1	0	0	0	0	0.0	0	0	0	0	0	0	0	0	0	0	0	—		
2 yrs.		32	.234	.277	94	22	4	0	0	0.0	2	11	0	7	3	8	0	62	52	6	5	3.8	.950	2B-15, 3B-5, 1B-4

Gene Hermanski

HERMANSKI, EUGENE VICTOR
B. May 11, 1920, Pittsfield, Mass.   BL TR 5'11½"   185 lbs.

Year	Team	Games	BA	SA	AB	H	2B	3B	HR	HR%	R	RBI	BB	SO	SB	AB	H	PO	A	E	DP	TC/G	FA	G by Pos
1943	BKN N	18	.300	.367	60	18	4	0	0	0.0	6	12	11	7	1	0	0	36	4	1	1	2.3	.976	OF-18
1946		64	.200	.255	110	22	2	2	0	0.0	15	8	17	10	2	24	2	45	0	3	0	0.8	.938	OF-34

Year Team	Games	BA	SA	AB	H	2B	3B	HR	HR%	R	RBI	BB	SO	SB	Pinch Hit AB	Pinch Hit H	PO	A	E	DP	TC/G	FA	G by Pos

Gene Hermanski *continued*

Year Team	Games	BA	SA	AB	H	2B	3B	HR	HR%	R	RBI	BB	SO	SB	Pinch Hit AB	Pinch Hit H	PO	A	E	DP	TC/G	FA	G by Pos
1947	79	.275	.434	189	52	7	1	7	3.7	36	39	28	7	5	12	4	105	5	2	0	1.4	.982	OF-66
1948	133	.290	.493	400	116	22	7	15	3.8	63	60	64	46	15	12	3	225	13	7	1	1.8	.971	OF-119
1949	87	.299	.487	224	67	12	3	8	3.6	48	42	47	21	12	13	5	140	7	3	1	1.7	.980	OF-77
1950	94	.298	.450	289	86	17	3	7	2.4	36	34	36	26	2	12	3	172	5	2	0	1.9	.989	OF-78
1951 2 teams	BKN	N	(31G – .250)		CHI	N	(75G – .281)																
" total	106	.273	.370	311	85	16	1	4	1.3	36	25	45	42	3	20	7	175	11	6	2	1.8	.969	OF-94
1952 CHI N	99	.255	.320	275	70	6	0	4	1.5	28	34	29	32	2	21	10	146	7	3	3	1.6	.981	OF-76
1953 2 teams	CHI	N	(18G – .150)		PIT	N	(41G – .177)																
" total	59	.167	.206	102	17	1	0	1	1.0	8	5	12	21	1	29	4	44	0	0	0	0.7	1.000	OF-26
9 yrs.	739	.272	.404	1960	533	85	18	46	2.3	276	259	289	212	43	143	38	1088	52	27	8	1.6	.977	OF-588
WORLD SERIES																							
1947 BKN N	7	.158	.263	19	3	0	1	0	0.0	4	1	3	3	0	0	0	15	0	0	0	2.1	1.000	OF-7
1949	4	.308	.462	13	4	0	1	0	0.0	1	2	3	3	0	0	0	7	0	0	0	1.8	1.000	OF-4
2 yrs.	11	.219	.344	32	7	0	2	0	0.0	5	3	6	6	0	0	0	22	0	0	0	2.0	1.000	OF-11

Angel Hermoso

HERMOSO, ANGEL REMIGIO (Remy)
B. Oct. 1, 1947, Carabobo, Venezuela

BR TR 5'8" 155 lbs.

Year Team	Games	BA	SA	AB	H	2B	3B	HR	HR%	R	RBI	BB	SO	SB	Pinch Hit AB	Pinch Hit H	PO	A	E	DP	TC/G	FA	G by Pos
1967 ATL N	11	.308	.308	26	8	0	0	0	0.0	3	0	2	4	1	0	0	16	24	2	4	3.8	.952	SS-9, 2B-2
1969 MON N	28	.162	.162	74	12	0	0	0	0.0	6	3	5	10	3	3	0	35	60	4	18	3.5	.960	2B-18, SS-6
1970	1	.000	.000	1	0	0	0	0	0.0	0	0	0	0	0	0	0	1	1	0	0	0.5	1.000	3B-1, 2B-1
1974 CLE A	48	.221	.262	122	27	3	1	0	0.0	15	5	7	7	2	1	0	86	121	7	27	4.5	.967	2B-45
4 yrs.	91	.211	.233	223	47	3	1	0	0.0	25	8	14	21	6	5	0	138	206	13	49	3.9	.964	2B-66, SS-15, 3B-1

Enzo Hernandez

HERNANDEZ, ENZO OCTAVIO
B. Feb. 12, 1949, Valle de Guanape, Puerto Rico

BR TR 5'8" 155 lbs.

Year Team	Games	BA	SA	AB	H	2B	3B	HR	HR%	R	RBI	BB	SO	SB	Pinch Hit AB	Pinch Hit H	PO	A	E	DP	TC/G	FA	G by Pos
1971 SD N	143	.222	.250	549	122	9	3	0	0.0	58	12	54	34	21	0	0	260	445	33	82	5.2	.955	SS-143
1972	114	.195	.249	329	64	11	2	1	0.3	33	15	22	25	24	1	0	169	319	19	59	4.4	.963	SS-107, OF-3
1973	70	.223	.239	247	55	2	1	0	0.0	26	9	17	14	15	2	0	106	190	7	42	4.3	.977	SS-67
1974	147	.232	.277	512	119	19	2	0	0.0	55	34	38	36	37	1	1	229	449	24	64	4.8	.966	SS-145
1975	116	.218	.265	344	75	12	2	0	0.0	37	19	26	25	20	0	0	168	327	18	70	4.4	.965	SS-111
1976	113	.256	.321	340	87	13	3	1	0.3	31	24	32	16	12	3	2	132	344	18	64	4.4	.964	SS-101
1977	7	.000	.000	3	0	0	0	0	0.0	1	0	0	0	0	0	0	4	6	0	0	1.4	1.000	SS-7
1978 LA N	4	.000	.000	3	0	0	0	0	0.0	0	0	0	1	0	0	0	0	0	0	0	0.0	–	SS-2
8 yrs.	714	.224	.266	2327	522	66	13	2	0.1	241	113	189	151	129	7	3	1068	2080	119	381	4.6	.964	SS-683, OF-3

Jackie Hernandez

HERNANDEZ, JACINTO
Born Jacinto Hernandez y Zulueta.
B. Sept. 11, 1940, Central Tinguaro, Cuba

BR TR 5'11" 165 lbs.

Year Team	Games	BA	SA	AB	H	2B	3B	HR	HR%	R	RBI	BB	SO	SB	Pinch Hit AB	Pinch Hit H	PO	A	E	DP	TC/G	FA	G by Pos
1965 CAL A	6	.333	.500	6	2	1	0	0	0.0	1	0	0	1	0	0	0	1	3	2	0	1.0	.667	SS-2, 3B-1
1966	58	.043	.043	23	1	0	0	0	0.0	19	2	1	4	1	2	0	22	24	4	7	0.9	.920	3B-11, SS-8, 2B-8, OF-3
1967 MIN A	29	.143	.143	28	4	0	0	0	0.0	3	0	1	6	0	2	0	27	24	2	4	1.8	.962	SS-15, 3B-13
1968	83	.176	.221	199	35	3	0	2	1.0	13	17	9	52	5	0	0	122	197	25	44	4.1	.927	SS-79, 1B-1
1969 KC A	145	.222	.282	504	112	14	2	4	0.8	54	40	38	111	17	0	0	306	375	33	60	4.9	.954	SS-144
1970	83	.231	.282	238	55	4	1	2	0.8	14	10	15	50	1	3	1	142	187	17	38	4.2	.951	SS-77
1971 PIT N	88	.206	.300	233	48	7	3	3	1.3	30	26	17	45	1	1	0	109	252	18	42	4.3	.953	SS-75, 3B-9
1972	72	.188	.256	176	33	7	1	1	0.6	12	14	9	43	0	0	0	110	182	22	34	4.4	.930	SS-68, 3B-4
1973	54	.247	.315	73	18	1	2	0	0.0	8	12	8	12	0	2	1	45	81	8	19	2.5	.940	SS-49
9 yrs.	618	.208	.270	1480	308	37	9	12	0.8	153	121	93	324	25	10	2	884	1325	131	248	3.8	.944	SS-517, 3B-38, 2B-8, OF-3, 1B-1
LEAGUE CHAMPIONSHIP SERIES																							
1971 PIT N	4	.231	.231	13	3	0	0	0	0.0	2	1	0	4	0	0	0	7	9	1	2	4.3	.941	SS-4
WORLD SERIES																							
1971 PIT N	7	.222	.222	18	4	0	0	0	0.0	2	1	2	5	1	0	0	9	16	0	3	3.6	1.000	SS-7

Keith Hernandez

HERNANDEZ, KEITH (Mex)
B. Oct. 20, 1953, San Francisco, Calif.

BL TL 6' 180 lbs.

Year Team	Games	BA	SA	AB	H	2B	3B	HR	HR%	R	RBI	BB	SO	SB	Pinch Hit AB	Pinch Hit H	PO	A	E	DP	TC/G	FA	G by Pos
1974 STL N	14	.294	.441	34	10	1	2	0	0.0	3	2	7	8	0	3	1	70	1	2	8	5.2	.973	1B-9
1975	64	.250	.362	188	47	8	2	3	1.6	20	20	17	26	0	9	3	469	36	2	34	7.9	.996	1B-56
1976	129	.289	.428	374	108	21	5	7	1.9	54	46	49	53	4	17	4	862	107	10	87	7.6	.990	1B-110
1977	161	.291	.459	560	163	41	4	15	2.7	90	91	79	88	7	6	1	1453	106	12	146	9.8	.992	1B-158
1978	159	.255	.389	542	138	32	4	11	2.0	90	64	82	68	13	5	1	1436	96	10	124	9.7	.994	1B-158
1979	161	.344	.513	610	210	48	11	11	1.8	116	105	80	78	11	2	2	1489	146	8	145	10.2	.995	1B-160
1980	159	.321	.494	595	191	39	8	16	2.7	111	99	86	73	14	2	0	1572	115	9	146	10.7	.995	1B-157
1981	103	.306	.463	376	115	27	4	8	2.1	65	48	61	45	12	2	0	1056	86	3	99	11.1	.997	1B-98, OF-3
1982	160	.299	.413	579	173	33	6	7	1.2	79	94	100	67	19	1	1	1591	135	11	140	10.9	.994	1B-158, OF-4
1983 2 teams	STL	N	(55G – .284)		NY	N	(95G – .306)																
" total	150	.297	.433	538	160	23	7	12	2.2	77	63	88	72	9	5	1	1418	147	13	147	10.5	.992	1B-144
1984 NY N	154	.311	.449	550	171	31	0	15	2.7	83	94	97	89	2	1	0	1214	142	8	127	8.9	.994	1B-153
1985	158	.309	.430	593	183	34	4	10	1.7	87	91	77	59	3	1	0	1310	139	4	113	9.2	.997	1B-157
1986	149	.310	.446	551	171	34	1	13	2.4	94	83	94	69	2	0	0	1199	149	5	115	9.1	.996	1B-149
1987	154	.290	.436	587	170	28	2	18	3.1	87	89	81	104	0	1	0	1298	149	10	110	9.5	.993	1B-154
1988	95	.276	.417	348	96	16	0	11	3.2	43	55	31	57	2	1	0	734	77	2	63	8.6	.998	1B-93
1989	75	.233	.326	215	50	8	0	4	1.9	18	19	27	39	0	17	2	405	31	4	22	5.9	.991	1B-58
16 yrs.	2045	.298	.440	7240	2156	424	60	161	2.2	1117	1063	1056	995	98	75	17	17576	1662	113	1626	9.5	.994	1B-1972, OF-7
LEAGUE CHAMPIONSHIP SERIES																							
1982 STL N	3	.333	.333	12	4	0	0	0	0.0	3	1	2	3	0	0	0	0	0	0	0	0.0	–	1B-3
1986 NY N	6	.269	.385	26	7	1	1	0	0.0	3	3	3	6	0	0	0	66	11	0	5	12.8	1.000	1B-6

Year	Team		Games	BA	SA	AB	H	2B	3B	HR	HR%	R	RBI	BB	SO	SB	Pinch Hit AB	H	PO	A	E	DP	TC/G	FA	G by Pos

Keith Hernandez *continued*

| 1988 | | | 7 | .269 | .385 | 26 | 7 | 0 | 0 | 1 | 3.8 | 2 | 5 | 6 | 7 | 1 | 0 | 0 | 57 | 4 | 1 | 2 | 8.9 | .984 | 1B-7 |
| 3 yrs. | | | 16 | .281 | .375 | 64 | 18 | 1 | 1 | 1 | 1.6 | 8 | 9 | 11 | 16 | 1 | 0 | 0 | 123 | 15 | 1 | 7 | 8.7 | .993 | 1B-16 |

WORLD SERIES

1982	STL	N	7	.259	.444	27	7	2	0	1	3.7	4	8	4	2	0	0	0	62	7	2	10	10.1	.972	1B-7
1986	NY	N	7	.231	.231	26	6	0	0	0	0.0	1	4	5	1	0	0	0	48	4	1	4	7.6	.981	1B-7
2 yrs.			14	.245	.340	53	13	2	0	1	1.9	5	12	9	3	0	0	0	110	11	3	14	8.9	.976	1B-14

Leo Hernandez

HERNANDEZ, LEONARDO JESUS
Born Leonardo Jesus Antiah y Hernandez.
B. Nov. 6, 1959, Santa Lucia, Venezuela

BR TR 5'11" 170 lbs.

1982	BAL	A	2	.000	.000	2	0	0	0	0	0.0	0	0	0	2	0	2	0	0	0	0	0	0.0	–	3B-64
1983			64	.246	.374	203	50	6	1	6	3.0	21	26	12	19	1	0	0	44	109	13	3	2.6	.922	3B-64
1985			12	.045	.045	22	1	0	0	0	0.0	0	0	0	4	0	6	0	2	0	0	0	0.2	1.000	DH-8, OF-1, 1B-1
1986	NY	A	7	.227	.455	22	5	2	0	1	4.5	2	4	1	8	0	0	0	5	10	0	0	2.1	1.000	3B-7, SS-1, 2B-1
4 yrs.			85	.225	.349	249	56	8	1	7	2.8	23	30	13	33	1	8	0	51	119	13	3	2.2	.929	3B-71, DH-8, OF-1, SS-1, 2B-1, 1B-1

Pedro Hernandez

HERNANDEZ, PEDRO JULIO
Born Pedro Julio Montas y Hernandez.
B. Apr. 4, 1959, La Romana, Dominican Republic

BR TR 6'1" 160 lbs.

1979	TOR	A	3	–	–	0	0	0	0	0	–	1	0	0	0	0	0	0	0	0	0	0	0.0	–	DH-2
1982			8	.000	.000	9	0	0	0	0	0.0	1	0	0	3	0	3	0	0	0	0	0	0.0	–	DH-3, 3B-2, OF-1
2 yrs.			11	.000	.000	9	0	0	0	0	0.0	2	0	0	3	0	3	0	0	0	0	0	0.0	–	DH-5, 3B-2, OF-1

Rudy Hernandez

HERNANDEZ, RODOLFO
Born Rodolfo Hernandez y Acosta.
B. Oct. 18, 1951, Empalme, Mexico

BR TR 5'9" 150 lbs.

| 1972 | CHI | A | 8 | .190 | .190 | 21 | 4 | 0 | 0 | 0 | 0.0 | 1 | 0 | 0 | 3 | 0 | 2 | 1 | 10 | 16 | 0 | 3 | 3.3 | 1.000 | SS-6 |

Sal Hernandez

HERNANDEZ, SALVADOR JOSE (Chico)
Born Salvador Jose Hernandez y Ramos.
B. Jan. 3, 1916, Havana, Cuba   D. Jan. 3, 1986, Havana, Cuba

BR TR 6'1" 195 lbs.

1942	CHI	N	47	.229	.271	118	27	5	0	0	0.0	6	7	11	13	0	3	1	140	17	4	0	3.4	.975	C-43
1943			43	.270	.302	126	34	4	0	0	0.0	10	9	9	9	0	2	0	132	21	3	1	3.6	.981	C-41
2 yrs.			90	.250	.287	244	61	9	0	0	0.0	16	16	20	22	0	5	1	272	38	7	1	3.5	.978	C-84

Toby Hernandez

HERNANDEZ, RAFAEL TOBIAS
Born Rafael Tobias Hernandez y Alvarado.
B. Nov. 30, 1958, Calabozo, Venezuela

BR TR 6'1" 160 lbs.

| 1984 | TOR | A | 3 | .500 | .500 | 2 | 1 | 0 | 0 | 0 | 0.0 | 1 | 0 | 0 | 0 | 0 | 0 | 0 | 1 | 0 | 0 | 0 | 0.3 | 1.000 | C-3 |

Larry Herndon

HERNDON, LARRY DARNELL
B. Nov. 3, 1953, Sunflower, Tex.

BR TR 6'3" 190 lbs.

1974	STL	N	12	1.000	1.000	1	1	0	0	0	0.0	3	0	0	0	0	0	0	1	0	0	0	0.1	1.000	OF-1
1976	SF	N	115	.288	.356	337	97	11	3	2	0.6	42	23	23	45	12	6	2	226	8	8	4	2.1	.967	OF-110
1977			49	.239	.358	109	26	4	3	1	0.9	13	5	5	20	4	5	1	87	2	4	0	1.9	.957	OF-44
1978			151	.259	.335	471	122	15	9	1	0.2	52	32	35	71	13	4	2	369	3	10	0	2.5	.974	OF-149
1979			132	.257	.384	354	91	14	5	7	2.0	35	36	29	70	8	19	7	196	10	8	2	1.6	.963	OF-122
1980			139	.258	.385	493	127	17	11	8	1.6	54	49	19	91	8	21	6	247	8	11	1	1.9	.959	OF-122
1981			96	.288	.415	364	105	15	8	5	1.4	48	41	20	55	15	4	0	207	8	5	1	2.3	.977	OF-93
1982	DET	A	157	.292	.480	614	179	21	13	23	3.7	92	88	38	92	12	3	0	328	11	6	3	2.2	.983	OF-155, DH-3
1983			153	.302	.478	603	182	28	9	20	3.3	88	92	46	95	9	5	1	283	6	15	1	2.0	.951	OF-133, DH-19
1984			125	.280	.400	407	114	18	5	7	1.7	52	43	32	63	6	24	7	199	7	3	0	1.7	.986	OF-117, DH-4
1985			137	.244	.384	443	108	12	7	12	2.7	45	37	33	79	2	5	3	273	7	7	4	2.1	.976	OF-136
1986			106	.247	.385	283	70	13	1	8	2.8	33	37	27	40	2	26	6	156	2	2	1	1.5	.988	OF-83, DH-18
1987			89	.324	.520	225	73	13	2	9	4.0	32	47	23	35	1	21	8	82	4	1	1	1.0	.989	OF-57, DH-23
1988			76	.224	.322	174	39	5	0	4	2.3	16	20	23	37	0	17	4	21	0	0	0	0.3	1.000	DH-53, OF-15
14 yrs.			1537	.273	.409	4878	1334	186	76	107	2.2	605	550	353	793	92	160	47	2675	76	80	17	1.8	.972	OF-1337, DH-120

LEAGUE CHAMPIONSHIP SERIES

1984	DET	A	2	.200	.800	5	1	0	0	1	20.0	1	1	1	2	0	0	0	6	0	0	0	3.0	1.000	OF-2
1987			3	.333	.444	9	3	1	0	0	0.0	1	2	1	1	0	1	1	2	0	1	0	1.0	.667	OF-2, DH-1
2 yrs.			5	.286	.571	14	4	1	0	1	7.1	2	3	2	3	0	1	1	8	0	1	0	1.8	.889	OF-4, DH-1

WORLD SERIES

| 1984 | DET | A | 5 | .333 | .533 | 15 | 5 | 0 | 0 | 1 | 6.7 | 3 | 3 | 2 | 2 | 0 | 0 | 0 | 6 | 0 | 0 | 0 | 1.2 | 1.000 | OF-5 |

Tom Hernon

HERNON, THOMAS H.
B. Nov. 4, 1866, E. Bridgewater, Mass.   D. Feb. 4, 1902, New Bedford, Mass.

BR TR

| 1897 | CHI | N | 4 | .063 | .063 | 16 | 1 | 0 | 0 | 0 | 0.0 | 2 | 2 | 0 | | 1 | 0 | 0 | 10 | 0 | 0 | 0 | 2.5 | 1.000 | OF-4 |

Ed Herr

HERR, EDWARD JOSEPH
B. May 18, 1862, St. Louis, Mo.   D. July 18, 1943, St. Louis, Mo.

BR TR 5'9½" 179 lbs.

1887	CLE	AA	11	.273	.318	44	12	2	0	0	0.0	6		6		6			18	17	13	1	4.4	.729	3B-11
1888	STL	AA	43	.267	.372	172	46	7	1	3	1.7	21	43	11		9	0	0	66	77	20	4	3.8	.877	SS-28, OF-11, 3B-4
1890			12	.220	.317	41	9	2	1	0	0.0	5		5		2	0	0	19	12	7	1	3.2	.816	2B-7, OF-4, 3B-1
3 yrs.			66	.261	.354	257	67	11	2	3	1.2	32	43	22		13	0	0	103	106	40	6	3.8	.839	SS-28, 3B-16, OF-15, 2B-7

Year	Team		Games	BA	SA	AB	H	2B	3B	HR	HR%	R	RBI	BB	SO	SB	Pinch Hit AB	Pinch Hit H	PO	A	E	DP	TC/G	FA	G by Pos

Tommy Herr

HERR, THOMAS MITCHELL
B. Apr. 4, 1956, Lancaster, Pa.   BB TR 6' 175 lbs.

Year	Team		Games	BA	SA	AB	H	2B	3B	HR	HR%	R	RBI	BB	SO	SB	PH AB	PH H	PO	A	E	DP	TC/G	FA	G by Pos
1979	STL	N	14	.200	.200	10	2	0	0	0	0.0	4	1	2	2	1	1	0	12	11	0	3	1.6	1.000	2B-6
1980			76	.248	.347	222	55	12	5	0	0.0	29	15	16	21	9	9	2	124	184	7	47	4.1	.978	2B-58, SS-14
1981			103	.268	.345	411	110	14	9	0	0.0	50	46	39	30	23	0	0	211	374	5	74	5.7	.992	2B-103
1982			135	.266	.320	493	131	19	4	0	0.0	83	36	57	56	25	5	2	263	427	9	97	5.2	.987	2B-128
1983			89	.323	.412	313	101	14	4	2	0.6	43	31	43	27	6	5	2	178	245	6	60	4.8	.986	2B-86
1984			145	.276	.346	558	154	23	2	4	0.7	67	49	49	56	13	1	1	328	452	6	106	5.4	.992	2B-144
1985			159	.302	.416	596	180	38	3	8	1.3	97	110	80	55	31	1	1	337	448	12	120	5.0	.985	2B-158
1986			152	.252	.331	559	141	30	4	2	0.4	48	61	73	75	22	0	0	352	414	9	121	5.1	.988	2B-152
1987			141	.263	.331	510	134	29	0	2	0.4	73	83	68	62	19	2	1	306	350	7	103	4.7	.989	2B-137
1988	2 teams		STL N	(15G – .260)		MIN A	(86G – .263)																		
"	total		101	.263	.325	354	93	16	0	2	0.6	46	24	51	51	13	10	3	168	230	5	63	4.0	.988	2B-88, DH-3, SS-2
1989	PHI	N	151	.287	.364	561	161	25	6	2	0.4	65	37	54	63	10	8	3	281	415	7	80	4.7	.990	2B-144
11 yrs.			1266	.275	.354	4587	1262	220	37	22	0.5	605	493	532	498	172	42	15	2560	3550	73	874	4.9	.988	2B-1204, SS-16, DH-3

LEAGUE CHAMPIONSHIP SERIES

Year	Team		Games	BA	SA	AB	H	2B	3B	HR	HR%	R	RBI	BB	SO	SB	PH AB	PH H	PO	A	E	DP	TC/G	FA	G by Pos
1982	STL	N	3	.231	.308	13	3	1	0	0	0.0	1	0	1	2	0	0	0	0	0	0	0	0.0	–	2B-3
1985			6	.333	.667	21	7	4	0	1	4.8	2	6	5	2	1	0	0	13	10	0	3	3.8	1.000	2B-6
1987			7	.222	.222	27	6	0	0	0	0.0	0	3	0	1	1	0	0	12	11	1	3	3.4	.958	2B-7
3 yrs.			16	.262	.393	61	16	5	0	1	1.6	3	9	6	5	2	0	0	25	21	1	6	2.9	.979	2B-16

WORLD SERIES

Year	Team		Games	BA	SA	AB	H	2B	3B	HR	HR%	R	RBI	BB	SO	SB	PH AB	PH H	PO	A	E	DP	TC/G	FA	G by Pos
1982	STL	N	7	.160	.240	25	4	2	0	0	0.0	3	5	3	3	0	0	0	11	19	1	6	4.4	.968	2B-7
1985			7	.154	.231	26	4	2	0	0	0.0	2	0	2	2	0	0	0	11	13	0	8	3.4	1.000	2B-7
1987			7	.250	.357	28	7	0	0	1	3.6	2	1	2	2	0	0	0	23	17	0	1	5.7	1.000	2B-7
3 yrs.			21	.190	.278	79	15	4	0	1	1.3	6	6	7	7	0	0	0	45	49	1	15	4.5	.989	2B-21

Jose Herrera

HERRERA, JOSE CONCEPCION (Loco)
Born Jose Concepcion Herrera y Ontiveros.
B. Apr. 8, 1942, San Lorenzo, Venezuela   BR TR 5'8" 165 lbs.

Year	Team		Games	BA	SA	AB	H	2B	3B	HR	HR%	R	RBI	BB	SO	SB	PH AB	PH H	PO	A	E	DP	TC/G	FA	G by Pos
1967	HOU	N	5	.250	.250	4	1	0	0	0	0.0	1	0	1	0	1	4	1	0	0	0	0	0.0	–	
1968			27	.240	.290	100	24	5	0	0	0.0	9	7	4	12	0	4	1	37	20	4	4	2.3	.934	OF-17, 2B-7
1969	MON	N	47	.286	.373	126	36	5	0	2	1.6	7	12	3	14	1	13	3	48	2	1	0	1.1	.980	OF-31, 2B-9, 3B-1
1970			1	.000	.000	1	0	0	0	0	0.0	0	1	0	1	0	1	0	0	0	0	0	0.0	–	
4 yrs.			80	.264	.333	231	61	10	0	2	0.9	16	20	7	28	1	22	5	85	22	5	4	1.4	.955	OF-48, 2B-9, 3B-1

Mike Herrera

HERRERA, RAMON
B. Dec. 19, 1897, Havana, Cuba   D. Feb. 3, 1978, Havana, Cuba   BR TR 5'6" 147 lbs.

Year	Team		Games	BA	SA	AB	H	2B	3B	HR	HR%	R	RBI	BB	SO	SB	PH AB	PH H	PO	A	E	DP	TC/G	FA	G by Pos
1925	BOS	A	10	.385	.385	39	15	0	0	0	0.0	2	8	2	2	1	0	0	25	43	3	3	7.1	.958	2B-10
1926			74	.257	.325	237	61	14	1	0	0.0	20	19	15	13	0	4	0	135	212	14	34	4.9	.961	2B-48, 3B-16, SS-4
2 yrs.			84	.275	.333	276	76	14	1	0	0.0	22	27	17	15	1	4	0	160	255	17	37	5.1	.961	2B-58, 3B-16, SS-4

Pancho Herrera

HERRERA, JUAN FRANCISCO
Born Juan Francisco Herrera y Willavicencio.
B. June 16, 1934, Santiago, Cuba   BR TR 6'3" 220 lbs.

Year	Team		Games	BA	SA	AB	H	2B	3B	HR	HR%	R	RBI	BB	SO	SB	PH AB	PH H	PO	A	E	DP	TC/G	FA	G by Pos
1958	PHI	N	29	.270	.365	63	17	3	0	1	1.6	5	6	7	15	1	2	0	52	31	1	6	2.9	.988	3B-16, 1B-11
1960			145	.281	.455	512	144	26	6	17	3.3	61	71	51	**136**	2	3	1	1053	155	15	99	8.4	.988	1B-134, 2B-17
1961			126	.258	.408	400	103	17	2	13	3.3	56	51	55	120	5	10	3	1003	96	8	104	8.8	.993	1B-115
3 yrs.			300	.271	.430	975	264	46	8	31	3.2	122	128	113	271	8	15	4	2108	282	24	209	8.0	.990	1B-260, 2B-17, 3B-16

Lefty Herring

HERRING, SILAS CLARKE
B. Mar. 4, 1880, Philadelphia, Pa.   D. Feb. 11, 1965, Massapequa, N. Y.   BL TL 5'11" 160 lbs.

Year	Team		Games	BA	SA	AB	H	2B	3B	HR	HR%	R	RBI	BB	SO	SB	PH AB	PH H	PO	A	E	DP	TC/G	FA	G by Pos
1899	WAS	N	2	1.000	1.000	1	1	0	0	0	0.0	1	0	1		0	0	0	1	0	0	0.5	1.000	P-2
1904	WAS	A	15	.174	.196	46	8	1	0	0	0.0	3	2	7		0	0	0	105	10	2	6	7.8	.983	1B-10, OF-5
2 yrs.			17	.191	.213	47	9	1	0	0	0.0	4	2	8		0	0	0	105	11	2	6	6.9	.983	1B-10, OF-5, P-2

Ed Herrmann

HERRMANN, EDWARD MARTIN
B. Aug. 27, 1946, San Diego, Calif.   BL TR 6'1" 195 lbs.

Year	Team		Games	BA	SA	AB	H	2B	3B	HR	HR%	R	RBI	BB	SO	SB	PH AB	PH H	PO	A	E	DP	TC/G	FA	G by Pos
1967	CHI	A	2	.667	1.000	3	2	1	0	0	0.0	1	1	0	0	0	0	0	12	0	0	0	6.5	1.000	C-2
1969			102	.231	.341	290	67	8	0	8	2.8	31	31	30	35	0	11	1	420	41	8	7	4.6	.983	C-92
1970			96	.283	.505	297	84	9	0	19	6.4	42	52	31	41	0	7	1	433	51	6	8	5.1	.988	C-88
1971			101	.214	.347	294	63	6	0	11	3.7	32	35	44	48	2	7	0	556	56	3	5	6.1	.995	C-97
1972			116	.249	.359	354	88	9	0	10	2.8	23	40	43	37	0	5	2	641	69	8	10	6.2	.989	C-112
1973			119	.224	.354	379	85	17	1	10	2.6	42	39	31	55	2	2	0	617	70	11	11	5.9	.984	C-114, DH-2
1974			107	.259	.381	367	95	13	1	10	2.7	32	39	16	49	1	0	0	561	55	8	8	5.8	.987	C-107
1975	NY	A	80	.255	.410	200	51	9	2	6	3.0	16	30	16	23	0	19	3	121	18	3	5	1.8	.979	DH-35, C-24
1976	2 teams		CAL A	(29G – .174)		HOU N	(79G – .204)																		
"	total		108	.199	.283	311	62	11	0	5	1.6	19	33	29	48	0	11	2	486	46	10	6	5.0	.982	C-106
1977	HOU	N	56	.291	.354	158	46	7	0	1	0.6	7	17	15	18	1	7	2	280	29	3	2	5.6	.990	C-49
1978	2 teams		HOU N	(16G – .111)		MON N	(19G – .175)																		
"	total		35	.145	.171	76	11	2	0	0	0.0	2	3	4	7	0	10	3	104	11	1	1	3.2	.991	C-26
11 yrs.			922	.240	.364	2729	654	92	4	80	2.9	247	320	260	361	6	72	12	4231	442	61	65	5.1	.987	C-817, DH-37

John Herrnstein

HERRNSTEIN, JOHN ELLETT
B. Mar. 31, 1938, Hampton, Va.   BL TL 6'3" 215 lbs.

Year	Team		Games	BA	SA	AB	H	2B	3B	HR	HR%	R	RBI	BB	SO	SB	PH AB	PH H	PO	A	E	DP	TC/G	FA	G by Pos
1962	PHI	N	6	.200	.200	5	1	0	0	0	0.0	1	1	1	3	0	5	1	0	0	0	0	0.0	–	OF-1
1963			15	.167	.417	12	2	0	0	1	8.3	1	1	1	5	0	10	1	7	0	0	0	0.5	1.000	OF-2, 1B-1
1964			125	.234	.360	303	71	12	4	6	2.0	38	25	22	67	1	21	7	531	22	6	33	4.5	.989	OF-69, 1B-68
1965			63	.200	.259	85	17	2	0	1	1.2	8	5	2	18	0	30	5	123	9	2	13	2.1	.985	1B-18, OF-14
1966	3 teams		PHI N	(4G – .100)		CHI N	(9G – .176)		ATL N	(17G – .222)															
"	total		30	.178	.178	45	8	0	0	0	0.0	5	2	3	22	0	20	4	46	0	1	3	1.6	.979	OF-8, 1B-4
5 yrs.			239	.220	.322	450	99	14	4	8	1.8	52	34	29	115	1	86	18	707	31	9	49	3.1	.988	OF-94, 1B-91

Year	Team	Games	BA	SA	AB	H	2B	3B	HR	HR%	R	RBI	BB	SO	SB	PH AB	PH H	PO	A	E	DP	TC/G	FA	G by Pos

Rick Herrscher
HERRSCHER, RICHARD FRANKLIN
B. Nov. 3, 1936, St. Louis, Mo.   BR TR 6'2½" 187 lbs.

Year	Team	Games	BA	SA	AB	H	2B	3B	HR	HR%	R	RBI	BB	SO	SB	PH AB	PH H	PO	A	E	DP	TC/G	FA	G by Pos
1962	NY N	35	.220	.340	50	11	3	0	1	2.0	5	6	5	11	0	8	2	83	19	2	11	3.0	.981	1B-10, 3B-6, OF-4, SS-3

Earl Hersh
HERSH, EARL WALTER
B. May 21, 1932, Ebbvale, Md.   BL TL 6' 205 lbs.

Year	Team	Games	BA	SA	AB	H	2B	3B	HR	HR%	R	RBI	BB	SO	SB	PH AB	PH H	PO	A	E	DP	TC/G	FA	G by Pos
1956	MIL N	7	.231	.462	13	3	3	0	0	0.0	0	0	0	5	0	5	0	0	0	0	1	0.1	-	OF-2

Mike Hershberger
HERSHBERGER, NORMAN MICHAEL
B. Oct. 9, 1939, Massillon, Ohio   BR TR 5'10" 175 lbs.

Year	Team	Games	BA	SA	AB	H	2B	3B	HR	HR%	R	RBI	BB	SO	SB	PH AB	PH H	PO	A	E	DP	TC/G	FA	G by Pos
1961	CHI A	15	.309	.364	55	17	3	0	0	0.0	9	5	2	2	1	1	0	29	2	0	0	2.1	1.000	OF-13
1962		148	.262	.333	427	112	14	2	4	0.9	54	46	37	36	10	13	3	236	7	4	0	1.7	.984	OF-135
1963		135	.279	.361	476	133	26	2	3	0.6	64	45	39	39	9	14	2	230	13	6	3	1.8	.976	OF-119
1964		141	.230	.290	452	104	15	3	2	0.4	55	31	48	47	8	10	1	231	10	4	2	1.7	.984	OF-134
1965	KC A	150	.231	.312	494	114	15	5	5	1.0	43	48	37	42	7	9	5	238	14	3	7	1.7	.988	OF-144
1966		146	.253	.340	538	136	27	7	2	0.4	55	57	47	37	13	5	0	285	14	7	3	2.1	.977	OF-143
1967		142	.254	.317	480	122	25	1	1	0.2	55	49	38	40	10	12	5	206	17	4	2	1.6	.982	OF-130
1968	OAK A	99	.272	.386	246	67	9	2	5	2.0	23	32	21	22	8	12	5	128	5	3	0	1.4	.978	OF-90
1969		51	.202	.240	129	26	2	0	1	0.8	11	10	10	15	1	15	3	50	0	1	0	1.0	.980	OF-35
1970	MIL A	49	.235	.316	98	23	5	0	1	1.0	7	6	10	8	1	16	3	34	1	2	0	0.8	.946	OF-35
1971	CHI A	74	.260	.345	177	46	9	0	2	1.1	22	15	30	23	6	20	5	96	1	4	0	1.4	.960	OF-59
11 yrs.		1150	.252	.328	3572	900	150	22	26	0.7	398	344	319	311	74	127	32	1763	84	38	17	1.6	.980	OF-1037

Willard Hershberger
HERSHBERGER, WILLARD McKEE
B. May 28, 1910, Lemon Cove, Calif.   D. Aug. 3, 1940, Boston, Mass.   BR TR 5'10½" 167 lbs.

Year	Team	Games	BA	SA	AB	H	2B	3B	HR	HR%	R	RBI	BB	SO	SB	PH AB	PH H	PO	A	E	DP	TC/G	FA	G by Pos
1938	CIN N	49	.276	.324	105	29	3	1	0	0.0	12	12	5	5	1	7	1	108	13	6	2	2.6	.953	C-39, 2B-1
1939		63	.345	.420	174	60	9	2	0	0.0	23	32	9	4	1	3	0	204	21	3	2	3.6	.987	C-60
1940		48	.309	.374	123	38	4	2	0	0.0	6	26	6	6	0	9	4	121	11	2	0	2.8	.985	C-37
3 yrs.		160	.316	.381	402	127	16	5	0	0.0	41	70	20	16	2	19	5	433	45	11	4	3.1	.978	C-136, 2B-1

WORLD SERIES

Year	Team	Games	BA	SA	AB	H	2B	3B	HR	HR%	R	RBI	BB	SO	SB	PH AB	PH H	PO	A	E	DP	TC/G	FA	G by Pos
1939	CIN N	3	.500	.500	2	1	0	0	0	0.0	0	1	0	0	0	1	1	1	0	0	0	0.3	1.000	C-2

Neal Hertweck
HERTWECK, NEAL CHARLES
B. Nov. 22, 1931, St. Louis, Mo.   BL TL 6'1½" 175 lbs.

Year	Team	Games	BA	SA	AB	H	2B	3B	HR	HR%	R	RBI	BB	SO	SB	PH AB	PH H	PO	A	E	DP	TC/G	FA	G by Pos
1952	STL N	2	.000	.000	6	0	0	0	0	0.0	0	0	1	1	0	0	0	20	1	0	4	10.5	1.000	1B-2

Steve Hertz
HERTZ, STEPHEN ALLAN
B. Feb. 26, 1945, Fairfield, Ohio   BR TR 6'1" 195 lbs.

Year	Team	Games	BA	SA	AB	H	2B	3B	HR	HR%	R	RBI	BB	SO	SB	PH AB	PH H	PO	A	E	DP	TC/G	FA	G by Pos
1964	HOU N	5	.000	.000	4	0	0	0	0	0.0	0	0	0	3	0	2	0	1	0	0	0	0.2	1.000	3B-2

Buck Herzog
HERZOG, CHARLES LINCOLN
B. July 9, 1885, Baltimore, Md.   D. Sept. 4, 1953, Baltimore, Md.
Manager 1914-16.   BR TR 5'11" 160 lbs.

Year	Team	Games	BA	SA	AB	H	2B	3B	HR	HR%	R	RBI	BB	SO	SB	PH AB	PH H	PO	A	E	DP	TC/G	FA	G by Pos
1908	NY N	64	.300	.363	160	48	6	2	0	0.0	38	11	36		16	3	0	83	159	22	21	4.1	.917	2B-42, SS-11, 3B-3, OF-1
1909		42	.185	.200	130	24	2	0	0	0.0	16	8	13		2	1	0	53	9	6	3	1.6	.912	OF-29, 3B-4, 2B-4, SS-1
1910	BOS N	106	.250	.342	380	95	20	3	3	0.8	51	32	30	34	13	1	0	110	223	31	17	3.4	.915	3B-105
1911 2 teams	BOS N (79G - .310)		NY N (69G - .267)																					
" total		148	.290	.418	541	157	33	9	6	1.1	90	67	47	40	48	1	0	249	404	46	40	4.7	.934	SS-75, 3B-69, 2B-3
1912	NY N	140	.263	.355	482	127	20	9	2	0.4	72	47	57	34	37	0	0	159	308	29	21	3.5	.942	3B-140
1913		96	.286	.390	290	83	15	3	3	1.0	46	31	22	12	23	2	1	97	142	13	18	2.6	.948	3B-84, 2B-2
1914	CIN N	138	.281	.347	498	140	14	8	1	0.2	54	40	42	27	46	0	0	344	475	53	60	6.3	.939	SS-137, 1B-2
1915		155	.264	.328	579	153	14	10	1	0.2	61	42	34	21	35	0	0	400	515	53	90	6.2	.945	SS-153, 1B-2
1916 2 teams	CIN N (79G - .267)		NY N (77G - .261)																					
" total		156	.264	.333	561	148	24	6	1	0.2	70	49	36	34		1	1	317	462	44	59	5.3	.947	SS-74, 2B-44, 3B-39, OF-1
1917	NY N	114	.235	.312	417	98	18	2	0	0.5	69	31	31	36	12	0	0	251	327	32	60	5.4	.948	2B-113
1918	BOS N	118	.228	.279	473	108	12	6	0	0.0	57	26	29	28	10	0	0	374	342	30	50	6.3	.960	2B-99, 1B-12, SS-7
1919 2 teams	BOS N (73G - .280)		CHI N (52G - .275)																					
" total		125	.278	.348	468	130	12	9	1	0.2	42	42	23	18	28	2	1	213	342	19	37	4.6	.967	2B-122, 1B-1
1920	CHI N	91	.193	.236	305	59	9	2	0	0.0	39	19	20	21	8	2	0	154	241	29	32	4.7	.932	2B-59, 3B-28, 1B-1
13 yrs.		1493	.259	.335	5284	1370	191	75	20	0.4	705	445	427	307	312	13	3	2804	3949	407	508	4.8	.943	2B-488, 3B-472, SS-458, OF-31, 1B-18

WORLD SERIES

Year	Team	Games	BA	SA	AB	H	2B	3B	HR	HR%	R	RBI	BB	SO	SB	PH AB	PH H	PO	A	E	DP	TC/G	FA	G by Pos
1911	NY N	6	.190	.286	21	4	2	0	0	0.0	3	0	2	3	2	0	0	7	14	3	0	4.0	.875	3B-6
1912		8	.400	.600	30	12	4	1	0	0.0	6	4	1	2	2	0	0	11	16	1	0	3.4	1.000	3B-8
1913		5	.053	.053	19	1	0	0	0	0.0	2	0	0	1	0	0	0	6	8	0	0	2.8	1.000	3B-5
1917		6	.250	.333	24	6	0	1	0	0.0	1	2	0	4	0	0	0	12	12	2	3	4.3	.923	2B-6
4 yrs.		25	.245	.351	94	23	6	2	0	0.0	11	6	3	11	4	0	0	36	50	5	4	3.6	.945	3B-19, 2B-6

Whitey Herzog
HERZOG, DORREL NORMAN ELVERT (The White Rat)
B. Nov. 9, 1931, New Athens, Ill.
Manager 1973-89.   BL TL 5'11" 182 lbs.

Year	Team	Games	BA	SA	AB	H	2B	3B	HR	HR%	R	RBI	BB	SO	SB	PH AB	PH H	PO	A	E	DP	TC/G	FA	G by Pos
1956	WAS A	117	.245	.337	421	103	13	7	4	1.0	49	35	35	74	8	11	5	274	10	7	3	2.5	.976	OF-103, 1B-5
1957		36	.167	.205	78	13	3	0	0	0.0	7	4	13	12	1	10	0	53	0	1	0	1.5	.981	OF-28
1958 2 teams	WAS A (8G - .000)		KC A (88G - .240)																					
" total		96	.228	.277	101	23	1	2	0	0.0	11	9	17	26	0	32	7	146	6	3	9	1.6	.981	OF-44, 1B-22
1959	KC A	38	.293	.390	123	36	7	1	0	0.0	25	9	34	23	1	2	1	87	2	3	1	2.4	.967	OF-34, 1B-1
1960		83	.266	.417	252	67	10	2	8	3.2	43	38	40	32	0	12	5	137	6	4	3	1.8	.973	OF-69, 1B-2
1961	BAL A	113	.291	.409	323	94	11	6	5	1.5	39	35	50	41	1	18	6	143	2	0	0	1.3	1.000	OF-98
1962		99	.266	.403	263	70	13	1	7	2.7	34	35	41	36	2	26	5	132	4	3	0	1.4	.978	OF-70

Year	Team		Games	BA	SA	AB	H	2B	3B	HR	HR%	R	RBI	BB	SO	SB	Pinch Hit AB	Pinch Hit H	PO	A	E	DP	TC/G	FA	G by Pos

Whitey Herzog *continued*

| 1963 | DET | A | 52 | .151 | .226 | 53 | 8 | 2 | 1 | 0 | 0.0 | 5 | 7 | 11 | 17 | 0 | 35 | 4 | 44 | 1 | 1 | 2 | 0.9 | .978 | 1B-7, OF-4 |
| | 8 yrs. | | 634 | .257 | .365 | 1614 | 414 | 60 | 20 | 25 | 1.5 | 213 | 172 | 241 | 261 | 13 | 146 | 33 | 1016 | 31 | 22 | 18 | 1.7 | .979 | OF-450, 1B-37 |

Otto Hess

HESS, OTTO C.
B. Nov. 13, 1878, Berne, Switzerland D. Feb. 24, 1926, Tucson, Ariz.   BL TL 6'1" 170 lbs.

1902	CLE	A	7	.071	.071	14	1	0	0	0	0.0	2	1	2		0	0	0	4	16	3	0	3.3	.870	P-7
1904			34	.120	.160	100	12	2	1	0	0.0	4	5	3		0	1	0	25	49	5	0	2.3	.937	P-21, OF-12
1905			54	.251	.343	175	44	8	1	2	1.1	15	13	7		2	0	0	74	67	9	2	2.8	.940	OF-27, P-26
1906			53	.201	.260	154	31	5	2	0	0.0	13	11	2		1	5	0	29	87	6	4	2.3	.951	P-43, OF-5
1907			19	.133	.133	30	4	0	0	0	0.0	4	0	4		1	1	0	6	26	2	0	1.8	.941	P-17, OF-2
1908			8	.000	.000	14	0	0	0	0	0.0	0	0	1		0	0	0	4	3	0	0	0.9	1.000	OF-4, P-4
1912	BOS	N	33	.245	.372	94	23	4	4	0	0.0	10	10	0	26	0	0	0	11	47	3	3	1.8	.951	P-33
1913			35	.313	.410	83	26	0	1	2	2.4	9	11	7	15	0	5	0	11	58	4	2	2.1	.945	P-29
1914			31	.234	.319	47	11	1	0	1	2.1	5	6	1	11	0	12	2	22	33	2	3	1.8	.965	P-14, 1B-5
1915			5	.400	.600	5	2	1	0	0	0.0	1	1	0	2	0	0	0	1	4	0	1	1.2	.833	P-4, 1B-1
	10 yrs.		279	.215	.291	716	154	21	9	5	0.7	63	58	27	54	4	24	2	187	390	35	14	2.2	.943	P-198, OF-50, 1B-6

Tom Hess

HESS, THOMAS
Born Thomas Heslin.
B. Aug. 15, 1875, Brooklyn, N. Y. D. Dec. 15, 1945, Albany, N. Y.

| 1892 | BAL | N | 1 | .000 | .000 | 2 | 0 | 0 | 0 | 0 | 0.0 | 0 | 0 | 0 | 0 | 0 | 0 | 0 | 0 | 0 | 0 | 0 | 0.0 | – | C-1 |

Gus Hetling

HETLING, AUGUST JULIUS
B. Nov. 21, 1885, St. Louis, Mo. D. Oct. 13, 1962, Wichita, Kans.   BR TR 5'10" 165 lbs.

| 1906 | DET | A | 2 | .143 | .143 | 7 | 1 | 0 | 0 | 0 | 0.0 | 0 | 0 | 0 | | 0 | 0 | 0 | 3 | 2 | 0 | 0 | 2.5 | 1.000 | 3B-2 |

George Heubel

HEUBEL, GEORGE A.
B. 1849, Paterson, N. J. D. Jan. 22, 1896, Philadelphia, Pa.   5'11½" 178 lbs.

| 1876 | NY | N | 1 | .000 | .000 | 4 | 0 | 0 | 0 | 0 | 0.0 | 0 | 0 | 0 | | 0 | 0 | 0 | 6 | 0 | 2 | 0 | 8.0 | .750 | 1B-1 |

Johnnie Heving

HEVING, JOHN ALOYSIUS
Brother of Joe Heving.
B. Apr. 29, 1896, Covington, Ky. D. Dec. 24, 1968, Salisbury, N. C.   BR TR 6' 175 lbs.

1920	STL	A	1	.000	.000	1	0	0	0	0	0.0	0	0	0	0	0	0	0	0	0	0	0	0.0	–	
1924	BOS	A	44	.287	.352	108	31	5	1	0	0.0	15	10	10	7	0	15	3	93	33	4	1	3.0	.969	C-29
1925			45	.168	.227	119	20	7	0	0	0.0	14	6	12	7	0	10	3	103	35	6	1	3.2	.958	C-34
1928			82	.259	.329	158	41	7	2	0	0.0	11	11	11	10	1	18	7	153	25	6	2	2.2	.967	C-62
1929			76	.319	.372	188	60	4	3	0	0.0	26	23	8	7	1	19	4	207	40	3	4	3.3	.988	C-55
1930			75	.277	.327	220	61	5	3	0	0.0	15	17	11	14	2	3	1	195	37	3	7	3.1	.987	C-71
1931	PHI	A	42	.239	.327	113	27	3	2	1	0.9	8	12	6	8	0	2	1	139	11	1	0	3.6	.993	C-40
1932			33	.273	.377	77	21	6	1	0	0.0	14	10	7	6	0	5	1	85	5	0	2	2.7	1.000	C-28
	8 yrs.		398	.265	.330	984	261	37	12	1	0.1	103	89	65	59	4	73	20	975	186	23	17	3.0	.981	C-319
WORLD SERIES																									
1931	PHI	A	1	.000	.000	1	0	0	0	0	0.0	0	0	0	0	0	1	0	0	0	0	0	0.0	–	

Mike Heydon

HEYDON, MICHAEL EDWARD
B. July 15, 1874, Missouri D. Oct. 13, 1913, Indianapolis, Ind.   BL TR 6'

1898	BAL	N	3	.111	.111	9	1	0	0	0	0.0	2	1	2		0	0	0	8	3	1	0	4.0	.917	C-3
1899	WAS	N	3	.000	.000	3	0	0	0	0	0.0	0	0	2		0	1	0	3	2	1	0	2.0	.833	C-2
1901	STL	N	16	.209	.349	43	9	1	1	1	2.3	2	6	5		2	1	0	54	10	4	2	4.3	.941	C-13, OF-1
1904	CHI	A	4	.100	.200	10	1	1	0	0	0.0	2	0	1		0	0	0	16	5	0	1	5.3	1.000	C-4
1905	WAS	A	77	.192	.265	245	47	7	4	1	0.4	20	26	21		5	0	0	368	125	23	7	6.7	.955	C-77
1906			49	.159	.221	145	23	7	1	0	0.0	14	10	14		2	0	0	200	68	18	4	5.8	.937	C-49
1907			62	.183	.201	164	30	3	0	0	0.0	14	9	25		3	4	0	247	52	12	4	5.0	.961	C-57
	7 yrs.		214	.179	.239	619	111	19	6	2	0.3	52	53	70		12	6	0	896	265	59	19	5.7	.952	C-205, OF-1

Jack Hiatt

HIATT, JACK E.
B. July 27, 1942, Bakersfield, Calif.   BR TR 6'2" 190 lbs.

1964	LA	A	9	.375	.375	16	6	0	0	0	0.0	2	2	2	3	0	4	3	17	2	1	2	2.2	.950	C-3, 1B-2
1965	SF	N	40	.284	.388	67	19	4	0	1	1.5	5	7	12	14	0	16	6	119	10	3	4	3.3	.977	C-21, 1B-7
1966			18	.304	.391	23	7	2	0	0	0.0	2	1	4	5	0	9	3	49	6	1	4	3.1	.982	1B-7
1967			73	.275	.431	153	42	6	0	6	3.9	24	26	27	37	0	31	8	303	18	4	25	4.5	.988	1B-36, C-3, OF-2
1968			90	.232	.348	224	52	10	2	4	1.8	14	34	41	61	0	21	6	387	37	2	6	4.7	.995	C-58, 1B-10
1969			69	.196	.325	194	38	4	0	7	3.6	18	34	48	58	0	2	0	359	30	3	10	5.7	.992	C-60, 1B-3
1970	2 teams			MON N (17G – .326)		CHI N (66G – .242)																			
"	total		83	.258	.357	221	57	14	1	2	0.9	23	29	45	62	0	7	0	466	24	7	1	6.0	.986	C-75, 1B-4
1971	HOU	N	69	.276	.351	174	48	8	1	1	0.6	16	16	35	39	0	4	2	329	20	3	6	5.1	.991	C-65, 1B-1
1972	2 teams			HOU N (10G – .200)		CAL A (22G – .289)																			
"	total		32	.257	.371	70	18	3	1	1	1.4	6	5	10	16	0	7	2	84	8	0	1	2.9	1.000	C-27
	9 yrs.		483	.251	.363	1142	287	51	5	22	1.9	110	154	224	295	0	101	30	2113	155	24	59	4.7	.990	C-312, 1B-70, OF-2

Jim Hibbs

HIBBS, JAMES KERR
B. Sept. 10, 1944, Klamath Falls, Ore.   BR TR 6' 190 lbs.

| 1967 | CAL | A | 3 | .000 | .000 | 3 | 0 | 0 | 0 | 0 | 0.0 | 0 | 0 | 0 | 2 | 0 | 3 | 0 | 0 | 0 | 0 | 0 | 0.0 | – | |

Ed Hickey

HICKEY, EDWARD A.
B. Aug. 18, 1872, Cleveland, Ohio D. Mar. 25, 1941, Tacoma, Wash.

| 1901 | CHI | N | 10 | .162 | .162 | 37 | 6 | 0 | 0 | 0 | 0.0 | 4 | 3 | 2 | | 0 | 0 | 0 | 8 | 18 | 9 | 2 | 3.5 | .743 | 3B-10 |

Year	Team		Games	BA	SA	AB	H	2B	3B	HR	HR%	R	RBI	BB	SO	SB	Pinch Hit AB	H	PO	A	E	DP	TC/G	FA	G by Pos

Mike Hickey

HICKEY, MICHAEL FRANCIS
B. Dec. 25, 1871, Chicopee, Mass. D. June 11, 1918, Springfield, Mass.
BR TR 5'10½" 150 lbs.

Year	Team		Games	BA	SA	AB	H	2B	3B	HR	HR%	R	RBI	BB	SO	SB	AB	H	PO	A	E	DP	TC/G	FA	G by Pos
1899	BOS	N	1	.333	.333	3	1	0	0	0	0.0	0	0	0			0	0	3	5	1	0	9.0	.889	2B-1

Jim Hickman

HICKMAN, DAVID JAMES
B. May 19, 1894, Union City, Tenn. D. Dec. 30, 1965, Brooklyn, N. Y.
BR TR 5'7½" 170 lbs.

Year	Team		Games	BA	SA	AB	H	2B	3B	HR	HR%	R	RBI	BB	SO	SB	AB	H	PO	A	E	DP	TC/G	FA	G by Pos
1915	BAL	F	20	.210	.321	81	17	4	1	1	1.2	7	7	4		5	0	0	45	7	2	2	2.7	.963	OF-20
1916	BKN	N	9	.200	.200	5	1	0	0	0	0.0	3	0	2	0	1	0	0	2	0	0	0	0.2	1.000	OF-3
1917			114	.219	.330	370	81	15	4	6	1.6	46	36	17	66	14	8	1	222	22	15	6	2.3	.942	OF-101
1918			53	.234	.359	167	39	4	7	1	0.6	16	16	8	31	5	3	0	76	9	8	1	1.8	.914	OF-46
1919			57	.192	.240	104	20	3	1	0	0.0	14	11	6	17	2	8	1	47	3	2	1	0.9	.962	OF-29
5 yrs.			253	.217	.322	727	158	26	13	8	1.1	84	70	37	114	27	19	2	392	41	27	10	1.8	.941	OF-199

Jim Hickman

HICKMAN, JAMES LUCIUS
B. May 10, 1937, Henning, Tenn.
BR TR 6'3" 192 lbs.

Year	Team		Games	BA	SA	AB	H	2B	3B	HR	HR%	R	RBI	BB	SO	SB	AB	H	PO	A	E	DP	TC/G	FA	G by Pos
1962	NY	N	140	.245	.401	392	96	18	2	13	3.3	54	46	47	96	4	13	3	265	7	8	0	2.0	.971	OF-124
1963			146	.229	.399	494	113	21	6	17	3.4	53	51	44	120	0	11	1	194	109	20	16	2.2	.938	OF-82, 3B-59
1964			139	.257	.377	409	105	14	1	11	2.7	48	57	36	90	0	31	8	237	8	6	1	1.8	.976	OF-113, 3B-1
1965			141	.236	.407	369	87	18	0	15	4.1	32	40	27	76	3	29	5	386	29	9	22	3.0	.979	OF-91, 1B-30, 3B-14
1966			58	.238	.356	160	38	7	0	4	2.5	15	16	13	34	2	11	1	183	17	2	16	3.5	.990	OF-45, 1B-17
1967	LA	N	65	.163	.245	98	16	6	1	0	0.0	7	10	14	28	1	25	3	54	3	0	1	0.9	1.000	OF-37, 3B-2, 1B-2, P-1
1968	CHI	N	75	.223	.367	188	42	6	3	5	2.7	22	23	18	38	1	12	2	115	4	3	0	1.6	.975	OF-66
1969			134	.237	.467	338	80	11	2	21	6.2	38	54	47	74	2	18	5	153	6	3	0	1.2	.981	OF-125
1970			149	.315	.582	514	162	33	4	32	6.2	102	115	93	99	0	2	0	706	67	10	47	5.3	.987	OF-79, 1B-74
1971			117	.256	.449	383	98	13	2	19	5.0	50	60	50	61	0	12	2	470	34	3	28	4.3	.994	OF-69, 1B-44
1972			115	.272	.462	368	100	15	2	17	4.6	65	64	52	64	1	13	3	708	70	6	61	6.8	.992	1B-77, OF-27
1973			92	.244	.313	201	49	1	2	3	1.5	27	20	42	42	1	34	6	411	31	5	37	4.9	.989	1B-51, OF-13
1974	STL	N	50	.267	.367	60	16	0	1	2	3.3	5	4	8	10	0	30	6	65	7	1	14	1.5	.986	1B-14, 3B-1
13 yrs.			1421	.252	.426	3974	1002	163	25	159	4.0	518	560	491	832	17	241	45	3947	392	76	243	3.1	.983	OF-871, 1B-309, 3B-77, P-1

Piano Legs Hickman

HICKMAN, CHARLES TAYLOR
B. Mar. 4, 1876, Taylortown, Pa. D. Apr. 19, 1934, Morgantown, W. Va.
BR TR 5'11½" 215 lbs.

Year	Team		Games	BA	SA	AB	H	2B	3B	HR	HR%	R	RBI	BB	SO	SB	AB	H	PO	A	E	DP	TC/G	FA	G by Pos
1897	BOS	N	2	.667	1.667	3	2	0	0	1	33.3	1	2	0			0	0	1	1	0	1	1.0	1.000	P-2
1898			19	.259	.293	58	15	2	0	0	0.0	4	7	1			0	0	79	5	4	8	4.6	.955	OF-7, 1B-6, P-6
1899			19	.397	.651	63	25	2	7	0	0.0	15	15	2			1	0	27	12	6	3	2.4	.867	P-11, OF-7, 1B-1
1900	NY	N	127	.313	.482	473	148	19	17	9	1.9	66	91	17			10	0	194	277	87	19	4.4	.844	3B-120, OF-7
1901			112	.282	.392	401	113	20	6	4	1.0	44	62	15			5	8	1	154	154	35	10	3.1	.898	OF-50, SS-23, 3B-15, P-9, 2B-7, 1B-2
1902	2 teams		BOS	A	(28G – .296)		CLE	A	(102G – .380)																
"	total		130	.363	.541	534	194	36	13	11	2.1	74	110	15			9	1	0	1140	55	45	63	9.5	.964	1B-98, OF-27, 2B-3, P-1
1903	CLE	A	130	.330	.502	518	171	31	11	12	2.3	67	97	17			14	0	0	1323	88	45	69	11.2	.969	1B-125, 2B-7
1904	2 teams		CLE	A	(86G – .288)		DET	A	(42G – .243)																
"	total		128	.274	.437	481	132	28	16	6	1.2	52	67	24			12	1	1	874	192	42	42	8.7	.962	1B-79, 2B-45, OF-1
1905	2 teams		DET	A	(59G – .221)		WAS	A	(88G – .311)																
"	total		147	.277	.405	573	159	37	12	4	0.7	69	66	21			6	0	0	378	298	49	27	4.9	.932	2B-85, OF-47, 1B-15
1906	WAS	A	120	.284	.421	451	128	25	5	9	2.0	53	57	14			9	1	0	305	39	13	10	3.0	.964	OF-95, 1B-18, 3B-5, 2B-1
1907	2 teams		WAS	A	(60G – .285)		CHI	A	(21G – .261)																
"	total		81	.282	.389	216	61	12	4	1	0.5	23	24	18			22	4	312	30	18	13	4.4	.950	1B-30, OF-21, 2B-3, P-1
1908	CLE	A	65	.234	.305	197	46	6	1	2	1.0	16	16	9			2	16	4	248	23	13	7	4.4	.954	OF-28, 1B-20, 2B-1
12 yrs.			1080	.301	.447	3968	1194	218	92	59	1.5	484	614	153			72	49	10	5035	1174	357	272	6.1	.946	1B-394, OF-290, 2B-152, 3B-140, P-30, SS-23

Buddy Hicks

HICKS, CLARENCE WALTER
B. Feb. 15, 1927, Belvedere, Calif.
BB TR 5'10" 170 lbs.

Year	Team		Games	BA	SA	AB	H	2B	3B	HR	HR%	R	RBI	BB	SO	SB	AB	H	PO	A	E	DP	TC/G	FA	G by Pos
1956	DET	A	26	.213	.255	47	10	2	0	0	0.0	5	5	3	2	0	2	0	21	31	0	5	2.0	1.000	SS-16, 2B-6, 3B-1

Jim Hicks

HICKS, JAMES EDWARD
B. May 18, 1940, East Chicago, Ind.
BR TR 6'3" 205 lbs.

Year	Team		Games	BA	SA	AB	H	2B	3B	HR	HR%	R	RBI	BB	SO	SB	AB	H	PO	A	E	DP	TC/G	FA	G by Pos
1964	CHI	A	2	–	–	0	0	0	0	0	0.0	0	0	0	0	0	0	0	0	0	0	0	0.0	–	
1965			13	.263	.474	19	5	1	0	1	5.3	2	2	0	9	0	8	2	3	0	1	0	0.3	.750	OF-5
1966			18	.192	.269	26	5	0	0	1	0.0	3	1	1	5	0	2	0	26	0	1	0	1.5	.963	OF-10, 1B-2
1969	2 teams		STL	N	(19G – .182)		CAL	A	(37G – .083)																
"	total		56	.130	.304	92	12	0	2	4	4.3	11	11	17	32	1	17	0	97	3	1	7	1.8	.990	OF-25, 1B-8
1970	CAL	A	4	.250	.250	4	1	0	0	0	0.0	0	0	0	2	0	4	1	0	0	0	0	0.0	–	
5 yrs.			93	.163	.319	141	23	1	2	6	3.5	16	14	18	48	1	31	3	126	3	3	7	1.4	.977	OF-40, 1B-10

Joe Hicks

HICKS, WILLIAM JOSEPH
B. Apr. 7, 1933, Ivy, Va.
BL TR 6' 180 lbs.

Year	Team		Games	BA	SA	AB	H	2B	3B	HR	HR%	R	RBI	BB	SO	SB	AB	H	PO	A	E	DP	TC/G	FA	G by Pos
1959	CHI	A	6	.429	.429	7	3	0	0	0	0.0	1	0	1	0	0	2	1	3	0	0	0	0.7	1.000	OF-4
1960			36	.191	.213	47	9	1	0	0	0.0	3	2	6	9	0	17	4	14	0	0	0	0.4	1.000	OF-14
1961	WAS	A	12	.172	.276	29	5	0	1	1	3.4	2	1	0	4	0	6	2	14	1	0	0	1.3	1.000	OF-7
1962			102	.224	.374	174	39	4	2	6	3.4	20	14	15	34	3	61	9	74	1	3	0	0.8	.962	OF-42
1963	NY	N	56	.226	.371	159	36	6	1	5	3.1	16	22	7	31	0	16	3	83	1	3	1	1.6	.966	OF-41
5 yrs.			212	.221	.349	416	92	11	3	12	2.9	41	39	29	73	3	102	20	188	4	6	1	0.9	.970	OF-108

Nat Hicks

HICKS, NATHANIEL WOODHULL
B. Apr. 19, 1845, Hempstead, N. Y. D. Apr. 21, 1907, Hoboken, N. J.
Manager 1875.
BR TR 6'1" 186 lbs.

Year	Team		Games	BA	SA	AB	H	2B	3B	HR	HR%	R	RBI	BB	SO	SB	AB	H	PO	A	E	DP	TC/G	FA	G by Pos
1876	NY	N	45	.234	.266	188	44	4	1	0	0.0	20	15	3	4			0	0	222	47	94	3	8.1	.741	C-45
1877	CIN	N	8	.188	.188	32	6	0	0	0	0.0	3	3	1	2			0	0	32	15	7	3	6.8	.870	C-8
2 yrs.			53	.227	.255	220	50	4	1	0	0.0	23	18	4	6			0	0	254	62	101	6	7.9	.758	C-53

Year	Team		Games	BA	SA	AB	H	2B	3B	HR	HR%	R	RBI	BB	SO	SB	Pinch Hit AB	Pinch Hit H	PO	A	E	DP	TC/G	FA	G by Pos

Mahlon Higbee

HIGBEE, MAHLON JESSE
B. Aug. 16, 1901, Louisville, Ky. D. Apr. 7, 1968, DePauw, Ind.
BR TR 5'11" 165 lbs.

| 1922 | NY | N | 3 | .400 | .700 | 10 | 4 | 0 | 0 | 1 | 10.0 | 2 | 5 | 0 | 2 | 0 | 0 | 0 | 2 | 0 | 0 | 0 | 0.7 | 1.000 | OF-3 |

Bill Higdon

HIGDON, WILLIAM TRAVIS
B. Apr. 27, 1924, Camp Hill, Ala. D. Aug. 30, 1986, Pascagoula, Miss.
BL TR 6'1" 193 lbs.

| 1949 | CHI | A | 11 | .304 | .435 | 23 | 7 | 3 | 0 | 0 | 0.0 | 3 | 1 | 6 | 3 | 1 | 4 | 1 | 9 | 1 | 0 | 0 | 0.9 | 1.000 | OF-6 |

Bill Higgins

HIGGINS, WILLIAM EDWARD
B. Sept. 8, 1861, Wilmington, Del. D. Apr. 25, 1919, Wilmington, Del.
TR

1888	BOS	N	14	.185	.204	54	10	1	0	0	0.0	5	4	1	3	1	0	0	44	52	10	12	7.6	.906	2B-14
1890	2 teams		STL	AA	(67G – .252)		SYR	AA	(1G – .250)																
"	total		68	.252	.294	262	66	7	2	0	0.0	40		24		7	0	0	172	208	19	35	5.9	.952	2B-68
2 yrs.			82	.241	.278	316	76	8	2	0	0.0	45	4	25	3	8	0	0	216	260	29	47	6.2	.943	2B-82

Bob Higgins

HIGGINS, ROBERT STONE
B. Sept. 23, 1886, Fayetteville, Tenn. D. May 25, 1941, Chattanooga, Tenn.
BR TR 5'8" 176 lbs.

1909	CLE	A	8	.087	.087	23	2	0	0	0	0.0	0	0	0		0	0	0	38	10	0	1	6.0	1.000	C-8
1911	BKN	N	4	.300	.300	10	3	0	0	0	0.0	1	2	1	0	1	1	1	11	3	1	0	3.8	.933	C-2, 3B-1
1912			1	.000	.000	2	0	0	0	0	0.0	0	0	0	1	0	0	0	3	0	1	0	4.0	.750	C-1
3 yrs.			13	.143	.143	35	5	0	0	0	0.0	1	2	1	1	1	1	1	52	13	2	1	5.2	.970	C-11, 3B-1

Mark Higgins

HIGGINS, MARK DOUGLAS
B. July 9, 1963, Miami, Fla.
BR TR 6'2" 210 lbs.

| 1989 | CLE | A | 6 | .100 | .100 | 10 | 1 | 0 | 0 | 0 | 0.0 | 1 | 0 | 1 | 6 | 0 | 1 | 0 | 18 | 3 | 0 | 1 | 3.5 | 1.000 | 1B-5 |

Pinky Higgins

HIGGINS, MICHAEL FRANKLIN
B. May 27, 1909, Red Oak, Tex. D. Mar. 21, 1969, Dallas, Tex.
Manager 1955-62.
BR TR 6'1" 185 lbs.

1930	PHI	A	14	.250	.333	24	6	0	0	0	0.0	1	0	4	5	0	4	0	4	7	0	0	0.8	1.000	3B-5, 2B-2, SS-1
1933			152	.314	.487	567	178	34	11	14	2.5	85	99	61	53	2	0	0	159	270	24	23	3.0	.947	3B-152
1934			144	.330	.508	543	179	37	6	16	2.9	89	90	56	70	9	0	0	147	247	37	34	3.0	.914	3B-144
1935			133	.296	.504	524	155	32	4	23	4.4	69	94	42	62	6	1	1	162	214	21	15	3.0	.947	3B-131
1936			146	.289	.420	550	159	32	2	12	2.2	89	80	67	61	7	1	0	151	266	26	24	3.0	.941	3B-145
1937	BOS	A	153	.302	.425	570	172	33	5	9	1.6	88	106	76	51	2	1	1	161	258	29	29	2.9	.935	3B-152
1938			139	.303	.406	524	159	29	5	5	1.0	77	106	71	55	10	1	0	140	272	39	28	3.2	.914	3B-138
1939	DET	A	132	.276	.380	489	135	23	2	8	1.6	57	76	56	41	7	2	1	140	241	36	22	3.2	.914	3B-130
1940			131	.271	.415	480	130	24	3	13	2.7	70	76	61	31	4	1	0	133	239	29	16	3.1	.928	3B-129
1941			147	.298	.422	540	161	28	3	11	2.0	79	73	67	45	5	2	0	153	304	26	14	3.3	.946	3B-145
1942			143	.267	.409	499	133	34	2	11	2.2	65	79	72	21	3	5	0	134	243	30	24	2.8	.926	3B-137
1943			138	.277	.377	523	145	20	1	10	1.9	62	84	57	31	2	0	0	156	253	26	22	3.2	.940	3B-138
1944			148	.297	.409	543	161	32	4	7	1.3	79	76	81	34	4	2	1	146	311	22	21	3.2	.954	3B-146
1946	2 teams		DET	A	(18G – .217)		BOS	A	(64G – .275)																
"	total		82	.262	.354	260	68	14	2	2	0.8	20	36	29	30	0	5	1	18	31	4	2	0.6	.925	3B-76
14 yrs.			1802	.292	.428	6636	1941	374	50	141	2.1	930	1075	800	590	61	25	5	1804	3156	349	274	2.9	.934	3B-1768, 2B-2, SS-1

WORLD SERIES

1940	DET	A	7	.333	.667	24	8	3	1	1	4.2	2	6	3	6	0	0	0	4	30	2	1	5.1	.944	3B-7
1946	BOS	A	7	.208	.250	24	5	1	0	0	0.0	1	2	2	0	0	0	0	6	6	2	0	2.0	.857	3B-7
2 yrs.			14	.271	.458	48	13	4	1	1	2.1	3	8	5	3	0	0	0	10	36	4	1	3.6	.920	3B-14

Andy High

HIGH, ANDREW AIRD (Handy Andy)
Brother of Charlie High. Brother of Hugh High.
B. Nov. 21, 1897, Ava, Ill. D. Feb. 22, 1981, Toledo, Ohio
BL TR 5'6" 155 lbs.

1922	BKN	N	153	.283	.396	579	164	27	10	6	1.0	82	65	59	26	3	0	0	167	316	23	28	3.3	.955	3B-130, SS-22, 2B-1
1923			123	.270	.387	426	115	23	9	3	0.7	51	37	47	13	4	0	0	194	276	23	38	4.0	.953	3B-80, SS-45, 2B-5
1924			144	.328	.448	582	191	26	13	6	1.0	98	61	57	16	3	0	0	328	478	29	56	5.8	.965	2B-133, 3B-17, SS-1
1925	2 teams		BKN	N	(44G – .200)		BOS	N	(60G – .288)																
"	total		104	.257	.350	334	86	15	2	4	1.2	42	34	38	7	3	17	5	80	143	10	15	2.2	.957	3B-71, 2B-12, SS-3
1926	BOS	N	130	.296	.387	476	141	17	10	2	0.4	55	66	39	9	4	4	2	200	287	27	36	4.0	.947	3B-81, 2B-49
1927			113	.302	.419	384	116	15	9	4	1.0	59	46	26	11	4	13	6	113	147	20	15	2.5	.929	3B-73, 2B-19
1928	STL	N	111	.285	.389	368	105	14	3	6	1.6	58	37	37	10	2	17	4	91	164	14	20	2.4	.948	3B-73, 2B-19
1929			146	.295	.411	603	178	32	4	10	1.7	95	63	38	18	7	1	1	150	265	13	33	2.9	.970	3B-123, 2B-22
1930			72	.279	.381	215	60	12	2	2	0.9	34	29	23	6	1	17	5	37	71	1	5	1.5	.991	3B-48, 2B-3
1931			63	.267	.328	131	35	6	1	0	0.0	20	19	24	4	0	19	5	32	64	1	9	1.5	.990	3B-23, 2B-19
1932	CIN	N	84	.188	.230	191	36	4	2	0	0.0	16	12	23	7	1	23	7	43	77	7	7	1.5	.945	3B-46, 2B-12
1933			24	.209	.326	43	9	2	0	1	2.3	4	6	5	1	0	10	2	8	21	1	1	1.3	.967	3B-11, 2B-2
1934	PHI	N	47	.206	.235	68	14	2	0	0	0.0	4	7	9	3	1	23	5	14	17	3	3	0.7	.912	3B-14, 2B-2
13 yrs.			1314	.284	.388	4400	1250	195	65	44	1.0	618	482	425	130	33	144	42	1457	2326	172	266	3.0	.957	3B-790, 2B-287, SS-89

WORLD SERIES

1928	STL	N	4	.294	.412	17	5	2	0	0	0.0	1	1	1	3	0	0	0	2	5	0	1	1.8	1.000	3B-4
1930			1	.500	.500	2	1	0	0	0	0.0	1	0	0	0	0	0	0	0	0	0	0	0.0	–	3B-1
1931			4	.267	.267	15	4	0	0	0	0.0	3	0	0	2	0	0	0	3	9	0	0	3.0	1.000	3B-4
3 yrs.			9	.294	.353	34	10	2	0	0	0.0	5	1	1	5	0	0	0	5	14	0	1	2.1	1.000	3B-9

Charlie High

HIGH, CHARLES EDWIN
Brother of Andy High. Brother of Hugh High.
B. Dec. 1, 1898, Ava, Ill. D. Sept. 11, 1960, Oak Grove, Ore.
BL TR 5'9" 170 lbs.

| 1919 | PHI | A | 11 | .069 | .069 | 29 | 2 | 0 | 0 | 0 | 0.0 | 2 | 3 | 4 | 2 | 2 | 0 | 0 | 16 | 1 | 1 | 0 | 1.6 | .944 | OF-9 |

Year	Team	Games	BA	SA	AB	H	2B	3B	HR	HR%	R	RBI	BB	SO	SB	Pinch Hit AB	Pinch Hit H	PO	A	E	DP	TC/G	FA	G by Pos

Charlie High *continued*

Year	Team	Games	BA	SA	AB	H	2B	3B	HR	HR%	R	RBI	BB	SO	SB	PH AB	PH H	PO	A	E	DP	TC/G	FA	G by Pos
1920		17	.308	.415	65	20	2	1	1	1.5	7	6	3	6	0	0	0	27	3	4	0	2.0	.882	OF-17
2 yrs		28	.234	.309	94	22	2	1	1	1.1	9	7	6	10	2	2	0	43	4	5	0	1.9	.904	OF-26

Hugh High

HIGH, HUGH JENKIN (Bunny, Lefty)
Brother of Andy High. Brother of Charlie High.
B. Oct. 24, 1887, Pottstown, Pa. D. Nov. 16, 1962, St. Louis, Mo.

BL TL 5'7½" 155 lbs.

Year	Team	Games	BA	SA	AB	H	2B	3B	HR	HR%	R	RBI	BB	SO	SB	PH AB	PH H	PO	A	E	DP	TC/G	FA	G by Pos
1913	DET A	80	.230	.273	183	42	6	1	0	0.0	18	16	28	24	6	19	5	104	8	2	0	1.4	.982	OF-50
1914		80	.266	.326	184	49	5	3	0	0.0	25	17	26	21	7	19	3	92	2	4	1	1.2	.959	OF-53
1915	NY A	119	.258	.342	427	110	19	7	1	0.2	51	43	62	47	22	1	1	254	10	5	1	2.3	.981	OF-117
1916		115	.263	.326	377	99	13	4	1	0.3	44	28	47	44	13	5	1	216	14	12	2	2.1	.950	OF-109
1917		103	.236	.307	365	86	11	6	1	0.3	37	19	48	31	8	2	0	188	16	3	3	2.0	.986	OF-100
1918		7	.000	.000	10	0	0	0	0	0.0	0	1	0	1	0	3	0	6	1	0	1	1.0	1.000	OF-4
6 yrs		504	.250	.318	1546	386	54	21	3	0.2	176	123	212	168	56	49	10	860	51	26	8	1.9	.972	OF-433

Dick Higham

HIGHAM, RICHARD
B. July, 1851, England D. Mar. 18, 1905, Chicago, Ill.
Manager 1874.

BL TR

Year	Team	Games	BA	SA	AB	H	2B	3B	HR	HR%	R	RBI	BB	SO	SB	PH AB	PH H	PO	A	E	DP	TC/G	FA	G by Pos
1876	HAR N	67	.327	.407	312	102	21	2	0	0.0	59	35	2	7	0	0	0	99	35	26	1	2.4	.838	OF-59, C-13, SS-1, 2B-1
1878	PRO N	62	.320	.416	281	90	22	1	1	0.4	60	29	5	16	0	0	0	77	28	25	4	2.1	.808	OF-62, C-1
1880	TRO N	1	.200	.200	5	1	0	0	0	0.0	1	0	0	0	0	0	0	1	0	0	0	1.0	1.000	OF-1, C-1
3 yrs		130	.323	.410	598	193	43	3	1	0.2	120	64	7	23	0	0	0	177	63	51	5	2.2	.825	OF-122, C-15, SS-1, 2B-1

John Hiland

HILAND, JOHN WILLIAM
B. 1861, Philadelphia, Pa. D. Apr. 10, 1901, Philadelphia, Pa.

TL

Year	Team	Games	BA	SA	AB	H	2B	3B	HR	HR%	R	RBI	BB	SO	SB	PH AB	PH H	PO	A	E	DP	TC/G	FA	G by Pos
1885	PHI N	3	.000	.000	9	0	0	0	0	0.0	0		0	4		0	0	6	4	2	0	4.0	.833	2B-3

George Hildebrand

HILDEBRAND, GEORGE ALBERT
B. Sept. 6, 1878, San Francisco, Calif. D. May 30, 1960, Woodland Hills, Calif.

BR TR 5'8" 170 lbs.

Year	Team	Games	BA	SA	AB	H	2B	3B	HR	HR%	R	RBI	BB	SO	SB	PH AB	PH H	PO	A	E	DP	TC/G	FA	G by Pos
1902	BKN N	11	.220	.244	41	9	1	0	0	0.0	3	5	3		0		0	27	2	0	0	2.6	1.000	OF-11

Palmer Hildebrand

HILDEBRAND, PALMER MARION (Pete)
B. Dec. 23, 1884, Schauck, Ohio D. Jan. 25, 1960, North Canton, Ohio

BR TR 5'11" 170 lbs.

Year	Team	Games	BA	SA	AB	H	2B	3B	HR	HR%	R	RBI	BB	SO	SB	PH AB	PH H	PO	A	E	DP	TC/G	FA	G by Pos
1913	STL N	26	.164	.200	55	9	2	0	0	0.0	3	1	1	10	1	2	0	71	21	3	5	3.7	.968	C-22, OF-1

R. E. Hildebrand

HILDEBRAND, R. E.
B. Unknown. Deceased.

Year	Team	Games	BA	SA	AB	H	2B	3B	HR	HR%	R	RBI	BB	SO	SB	PH AB	PH H	PO	A	E	DP	TC/G	FA	G by Pos
1902	CHI N	1	.000	.000	4	0	0	0	0	0.0	0		0	0		0	0	0	0	0	0	1.0	1.000	OF-1

Belden Hill

HILL, BELDEN L.
B. Aug. 24, 1864, Kewanee, Ill. D. Oct. 22, 1934, Cedar Rapids, Iowa

BL TR 6'

Year	Team	Games	BA	SA	AB	H	2B	3B	HR	HR%	R	RBI	BB	SO	SB	PH AB	PH H	PO	A	E	DP	TC/G	FA	G by Pos
1890	BAL AA	9	.167	.233	30	5	2	0	0	0.0	3		3		6	0	0	24	18	7	2	5.4	.857	3B-9

Donnie Hill

HILL, DONALD EARL
B. Nov. 12, 1960, Pomona, Calif.

BB TR 5'10" 165 lbs.

Year	Team	Games	BA	SA	AB	H	2B	3B	HR	HR%	R	RBI	BB	SO	SB	PH AB	PH H	PO	A	E	DP	TC/G	FA	G by Pos
1983	OAK A	53	.266	.348	158	42	7	0	2	1.3	20	15	4	21	1	1	0	87	136	9	24	4.4	.961	SS-53
1984		73	.230	.299	174	40	6	0	2	1.1	21	16	5	12	1	5	0	102	128	12	28	3.3	.950	SS-66, 2B-4, DH-2, 3B-2
1985		123	.285	.351	393	112	13	2	3	0.8	45	48	23	33	8	2	0	228	320	15	56	4.6	.973	2B-122
1986		108	.283	.378	339	96	16	2	4	1.2	37	29	23	38	5	15	4	104	213	9	31	3.0	.972	2B-68, 3B-33, DH-3, SS-2
1987	CHI A	111	.239	.368	410	98	14	6	9	2.2	57	46	30	35	1	3	1	167	278	14	55	4.1	.969	2B-84, 3B-32, DH-1
1988		83	.217	.281	221	48	6	1	2	0.9	17	20	26	32	3	12	3	118	152	8	38	3.3	.971	2B-59, 3B-12, DH-5
6 yrs		551	.257	.346	1695	436	62	11	22	1.3	197	174	111	171	19	38	8	806	1227	67	232	3.8	.968	2B-337, SS-121, 3B-79, DH-11

Glenallen Hill

HILL, GLENALLEN
B. Mar. 22, 1965, Santa Cruz, Calif.

BR TR 6'3" 210 lbs.

Year	Team	Games	BA	SA	AB	H	2B	3B	HR	HR%	R	RBI	BB	SO	SB	PH AB	PH H	PO	A	E	DP	TC/G	FA	G by Pos
1989	TOR A	19	.288	.346	52	15	0	0	1	1.9	4	7	3	12	2	0	0	27	0	1	0	1.5	.964	OF-16, DH-3

Herman Hill

HILL, HERMAN ALEXANDER
B. Oct. 12, 1945, Tuskegee, Ala. D. Dec. 14, 1970, Valencia, Venezuela

BL TR 6'2" 190 lbs.

Year	Team	Games	BA	SA	AB	H	2B	3B	HR	HR%	R	RBI	BB	SO	SB	PH AB	PH H	PO	A	E	DP	TC/G	FA	G by Pos
1969	MIN A	16	.000	.000	2	0	0	0	0	0.0	4	0	0	1	1	1	0	0	0	0	0	0.0	—	OF-2
1970		27	.091	.091	22	2	0	0	0	0.0	8	0	0	6	0	4	0	15	1	0	0	0.6	1.000	OF-14
2 yrs		43	.083	.083	24	2	0	0	0	0.0	12	0	0	7	1	5	0	15	1	0	0	0.4	1.000	OF-16

Hugh Hill

HILL, HUGH ELLIS
Brother of Still Bill Hill.
B. July 21, 1879, Ringgold, Ga. D. Sept. 6, 1958, Cincinnati, Ohio

BL TR 5'11½" 168 lbs.

Year	Team	Games	BA	SA	AB	H	2B	3B	HR	HR%	R	RBI	BB	SO	SB	PH AB	PH H	PO	A	E	DP	TC/G	FA	G by Pos
1903	CLE A	1	.000	.000	1	0	0	0	0	0.0	0	0	0		0	0	0	0	0	0	0	0.0	—	
1904	STL N	23	.226	.366	93	21	2	1	3	3.2	13	4	2		3	0	0	41	2	0	1	1.9	1.000	OF-23
2 yrs		24	.223	.362	94	21	2	1	3	3.2	13	4	2		3	1	0	41	2	0	1	1.8	1.000	OF-23

Hunter Hill

HILL, HUNTER BENJAMIN
B. June 21, 1879, Austin, Tex. D. Feb. 22, 1959, Austin, Tex.

BR TR

Year	Team	Games	BA	SA	AB	H	2B	3B	HR	HR%	R	RBI	BB	SO	SB	PH AB	PH H	PO	A	E	DP	TC/G	FA	G by Pos
1903	STL A	86	.243	.297	317	77	11	3	0	0.0	30	25	8		2	0	0	110	165	23	10	3.5	.923	3B-86
1904	2 teams		STL A	(58G – .215)		WAS A	(77G – .197)																	
"	total	135	.204	.226	509	104	9	1	0	0.0	37	31	17		14	2	0	170	205	59	7	3.2	.864	3B-127, OF-6
1905	WAS A	104	.209	.254	374	78	12	1	1	0.3	37	24	32		10	1	1	130	206	34	10	3.6	.908	3B-103
3 yrs		325	.216	.253	1200	259	32	5	1	0.1	104	80	57		26	3	1	410	576	116	27	3.4	.895	3B-316, OF-6

Year	Team		Games	BA	SA	AB	H	2B	3B	HR	HR%	R	RBI	BB	SO	SB	Pinch Hit AB	Pinch Hit H	PO	A	E	DP	TC/G	FA	G by Pos

Jesse Hill

HILL, JESSE TERRILL
B. Jan. 20, 1907, Yates, Mo.   BR TR 5'9"   165 lbs.

Year	Team		Games	BA	SA	AB	H	2B	3B	HR	HR%	R	RBI	BB	SO	SB	PH AB	PH H	PO	A	E	DP	TC/G	FA	G by Pos
1935	NY	A	107	.293	.390	392	115	20	3	4	1.0	69	33	42	32	14	7	2	203	9	11	1	2.1	.951	OF-94
1936	WAS	A	85	.305	.429	233	71	19	5	0	0.0	50	34	29	23	11	16	5	83	5	3	1	1.1	.967	OF-60
1937	2 teams	WAS A (33G – .217)				PHI A	(70G – .293)																		
"	total		103	.272	.356	334	91	14	4	2	0.6	56	41	44	36	18	7	0	236	4	9	0	2.4	.964	OF-89
3 yrs.			295	.289	.388	959	277	53	12	6	0.6	175	108	115	91	43	30	5	522	18	23	2	1.9	.959	OF-243

John Hill

HILL, OLIVER CLINTON
B. Oct. 16, 1912, Powder Springs, Ga.   D. Sept. 20, 1970, Decatur, Ga.   BL TR 5'11"   178 lbs.

Year	Team		Games	BA	SA	AB	H	2B	3B	HR	HR%	R	RBI	BB	SO	SB	PH AB	PH H	PO	A	E	DP	TC/G	FA	G by Pos
1939	BOS	N	2	.500	1.000	2	1	1	0	0	0.0	1	0	0	0	0	2	1	0	0	0	0	0.0	–	

Marc Hill

HILL, MARC KEVIN
B. Feb. 18, 1952, Elsberry, Mo.   BR TR 6'3"   205 lbs.

Year	Team		Games	BA	SA	AB	H	2B	3B	HR	HR%	R	RBI	BB	SO	SB	PH AB	PH H	PO	A	E	DP	TC/G	FA	G by Pos
1973	STL	N	1	.000	.000	3	0	0	0	0	0.0	0	0	0	1	0	0	0	5	0	0	0	5.0	1.000	C-1
1974			10	.238	.286	21	5	1	0	0	0.0	2	2	4	5	0	1	0	41	5	0	0	4.6	1.000	C-9
1975	SF	N	72	.214	.319	182	39	4	0	5	2.7	14	23	25	27	0	16	3	282	27	2	7	4.3	.994	C-60, 3B-1
1976			54	.183	.290	131	24	5	0	3	2.3	11	15	10	19	0	4	1	186	24	1	3	3.9	.995	C-49, 1B-1
1977			108	.250	.366	320	80	10	0	9	2.8	28	50	34	34	0	7	2	505	57	6	4	5.3	.989	C-102
1978			117	.243	.316	358	87	15	1	3	0.8	20	36	45	39	1	5	3	592	56	9	3	5.6	.986	C-116, 1B-2
1979			63	.207	.278	169	35	3	0	3	1.8	20	15	26	25	0	6	1	285	31	3	5	5.1	.991	C-58, 1B-1
1980	2 teams	SF N (17G – .171)				SEA A	(29G – .229)																		
"	total		46	.207	.315	111	23	4	1	2	1.8	9	9	9	17	0	3	0	162	18	3	2	4.0	.984	C-43
1981	CHI	A	16	.000	.000	6	0	0	0	0	0.0	0	0	0	1	0	3	0	11	1	0	0	0.8	1.000	C-14, 3B-1, 1B-1
1982			53	.261	.386	88	23	2	0	3	3.4	9	13	6	13	0	2	1	136	16	1	2	2.9	.993	C-49, 3B-1, 1B-1
1983			58	.226	.293	133	30	6	0	1	0.8	11	11	9	24	0	4	2	215	12	2	1	3.9	.991	C-55, DH-2, 1B-1
1984			77	.233	.373	193	45	10	1	5	2.6	15	20	9	26	0	5	0	315	17	3	6	4.4	.991	C-72, 1B-2
1985			40	.133	.160	75	10	2	0	0	0.0	5	4	12	9	0	0	0	185	13	3	1	5.0	.985	C-37, 3B-1
1986			22	.158	.158	19	3	0	0	0	0.0	2	0	1	3	0	0	0	59	7	0	0	3.0	1.000	C-22
14 yrs.			737	.223	.317	1809	404	62	3	34	1.9	146	198	185	243	1	58	13	2979	284	33	34	4.5	.990	C-687, 1B-9, 3B-4, DH-2

Homer Hillebrand

HILLEBRAND, HOMER HILLER HENRY
B. Oct. 10, 1879, Freeport, Ill.   D. Jan. 20, 1974, Elsinore, Calif.   BR TL 5'8"   165 lbs.

Year	Team		Games	BA	SA	AB	H	2B	3B	HR	HR%	R	RBI	BB	SO	SB	PH AB	PH H	PO	A	E	DP	TC/G	FA	G by Pos
1905	PIT	N	39	.236	.300	110	26	3	2	0	0.0	9	7	6		1	1	0	190	20	7	8	5.6	.968	1B-16, P-10, OF-7, C-3
1906			7	.238	.286	21	5	1	0	0	0.0	1	3	1		0	0	0	4	19	0	2	3.3	1.000	P-7
1908			1	–	–	0	0	0	0	0	0.0	0	0	0		0	0	0	0	0	0	0	0.0	–	P-1
3 yrs.			47	.237	.298	131	31	4	2	0	0.0	10	10	7		1	1	0	194	39	7	10	5.1	.971	P-18, 1B-16, OF-7, C-3

Chuck Hiller

HILLER, CHARLES JOSEPH (Iron Hands)
B. Oct. 1, 1934, Johnsburg, Ill.   BL TR 5'11"   170 lbs.

Year	Team		Games	BA	SA	AB	H	2B	3B	HR	HR%	R	RBI	BB	SO	SB	PH AB	PH H	PO	A	E	DP	TC/G	FA	G by Pos
1961	SF	N	70	.238	.321	240	57	12	1	2	0.8	38	12	32	30	4	2	0	133	158	8	34	4.3	.973	2B-67
1962			161	.276	.334	602	166	22	2	3	0.5	94	48	55	49	5	0	0	367	417	29	105	5.0	.964	2B-161
1963			111	.223	.300	417	93	10	2	6	1.4	44	33	20	23	3	5	0	224	277	19	48	4.7	.963	2B-109
1964			80	.180	.244	205	37	8	1	1	0.5	21	17	17	23	1	22	5	113	145	7	29	3.3	.974	2B-60, 3B-1
1965	2 teams	SF N (7G – .143)				NY N	(100G – .238)																		
"	total		107	.235	.341	293	69	11	1	6	2.0	25	22	14	25	1	33	7	151	183	14	39	3.3	.960	2B-82, OF-4, 3B-2
1966	NY	N	108	.280	.350	254	71	8	2	2	0.8	25	14	15	22	0	45	15	110	153	5	32	2.5	.981	2B-45, 3B-14, OF-9
1967	2 teams	NY N (25G – .093)				PHI N	(31G – .302)																		
"	total		56	.186	.227	97	18	4	0	0	0.0	4	5	4	15	0	38	7	33	46	3	10	1.5	.963	2B-20
1968	PIT	N	11	.385	.462	13	5	1	0	0	0.0	2	1	0	0	0	9	4	4	2	1	0	0.6	.857	2B-2
8 yrs.			704	.243	.316	2121	516	76	9	20	0.9	253	152	157	187	14	154	38	1135	1381	86	297	3.7	.967	2B-546, 3B-17, OF-13

WORLD SERIES

Year	Team		Games	BA	SA	AB	H	2B	3B	HR	HR%	R	RBI	BB	SO	SB	PH AB	PH H	PO	A	E	DP	TC/G	FA	G by Pos
1962	SF	N	7	.269	.500	26	7	3	0	1	3.8	4	5	3	4	0	0	0	16	22	1	7	5.6	.974	2B-7

Hob Hiller

HILLER, HARVEY MAX
B. May 12, 1893, East Mauch Chunk, Pa.   D. Dec. 27, 1956, Lehighton, Pa.   BR TR 5'8"   162 lbs.

Year	Team		Games	BA	SA	AB	H	2B	3B	HR	HR%	R	RBI	BB	SO	SB	PH AB	PH H	PO	A	E	DP	TC/G	FA	G by Pos
1920	BOS	A	17	.172	.276	29	5	1	1	0	0.0	4	2	2	5	0	1	0	8	20	2	1	1.8	.933	3B-6, SS-5, 2B-2, OF-1
1921			1	.000	.000	1	0	0	0	0	0.0	0	0	0	0	0	1	0	0	0	0	0	0.0	–	
2 yrs.			18	.167	.267	30	5	1	1	0	0.0	4	2	2	5	0	2	0	8	20	2	1	1.7	.933	3B-6, SS-5, 2B-2, OF-1

Ed Hilley

HILLEY, EDWARD GARFIELD (Whitey)
B. June 17, 1879, Cleveland, Ohio   D. Nov. 14, 1956, Cleveland, Ohio   BR TR 5'10½"   170 lbs.

Year	Team		Games	BA	SA	AB	H	2B	3B	HR	HR%	R	RBI	BB	SO	SB	PH AB	PH H	PO	A	E	DP	TC/G	FA	G by Pos
1903	PHI	A	1	.333	.333	3	1	0	0	0	0.0	1	0	1		0	0	0	3	1	1	1	5.0	.800	3B-1

Mack Hillis

HILLIS, MALCOLM DAVID
B. July 23, 1901, Cambridge, Mass.   D. June 16, 1961, Cambridge, Mass.   BR TR 5'10"   165 lbs.

Year	Team		Games	BA	SA	AB	H	2B	3B	HR	HR%	R	RBI	BB	SO	SB	PH AB	PH H	PO	A	E	DP	TC/G	FA	G by Pos
1924	NY	A	1	.000	.000	1	0	0	0	0	0.0	1	0	0	0	0	0	0	0	0	0	0	0.0	–	2B-1
1928	PIT	N	11	.250	.556	36	9	2	3	1	2.8	6	7	0	6	1	2	0	14	25	2	2	3.7	.951	2B-8, 3B-1
2 yrs.			12	.243	.541	37	9	2	3	1	2.7	7	7	0	6	1	2	0	14	25	2	2	3.4	.951	2B-9, 3B-1

Pat Hilly

HILLY, WILLIAM EDWARD
Born William Edward Hilgerink.
B. Feb. 24, 1887, Fostoria, Ohio   D. July 25, 1953, Eureka, Mo.   BR TR 5'11"   180 lbs.

Year	Team		Games	BA	SA	AB	H	2B	3B	HR	HR%	R	RBI	BB	SO	SB	PH AB	PH H	PO	A	E	DP	TC/G	FA	G by Pos
1914	PHI	N	8	.300	.300	10	3	0	0	0	0.0	2	1	1	5	0	1	1	6	0	0	0	0.8	1.000	OF-4

Dave Hilton

HILTON, JOHN DAVID
B. Sept. 15, 1950, Uvalde, Tex.   BR TR 5'11"   191 lbs.

Year	Team		Games	BA	SA	AB	H	2B	3B	HR	HR%	R	RBI	BB	SO	SB	PH AB	PH H	PO	A	E	DP	TC/G	FA	G by Pos
1972	SD	N	13	.213	.298	47	10	2	1	0	0.0	2	5	3	6	1	0	0	12	19	2	1	2.5	.939	3B-13
1973			70	.197	.299	234	46	9	0	5	2.1	21	16	19	35	2	0	0	79	141	6	19	3.2	.973	3B-47, 2B-23
1974			74	.240	.309	217	52	8	2	1	0.5	17	12	13	28	3	10	1	70	113	12	17	2.6	.938	3B-55, 2B-15

Year	Team		Games	BA	SA	AB	H	2B	3B	HR	HR%	R	RBI	BB	SO	SB	Pinch Hit AB	Pinch Hit H	PO	A	E	DP	TC/G	FA	G by Pos

Dave Hilton *continued*

Year	Team		Games	BA	SA	AB	H	2B	3B	HR	HR%	R	RBI	BB	SO	SB	AB	H	PO	A	E	DP	TC/G	FA	G by Pos
1975			4	.000	.000	8	0	0	0	0	0.0	0	0	0	0	0	0	0	2	7	1	0	2.5	.900	3B-4
4 yrs.			161	.213	.298	506	108	19	3	6	1.2	40	33	35	69	6	10	1	163	280	21	37	2.9	.955	3B-119, 2B-38

Jack Himes

HIMES, JOHN HERB
B. Sept. 22, 1878, Bryan, Ohio. D. Dec. 16, 1949, Joliet, Ill.

BL TR 6'2" 180 lbs.

Year	Team		Games	BA	SA	AB	H	2B	3B	HR	HR%	R	RBI	BB	SO	SB	AB	H	PO	A	E	DP	TC/G	FA	G by Pos
1905	STL	N	12	.146	.146	41	6	0	0	0	0.0	3	0	1		0	1	0	17	1	0	0	1.5	1.000	OF-11
1906			40	.271	.329	155	42	5	2	0	0.0	10	14	7		4	0	0	76	10	2	2	2.2	.977	OF-40
2 yrs.			52	.245	.291	196	48	5	2	0	0.0	13	14	8		4	1	0	93	11	2	2	2.0	.981	OF-51

Bill Hinchman

HINCHMAN, WILLIAM WHITE
Brother of Harry Hinchman.
B. Apr. 4, 1883, Philadelphia, Pa. D. Feb. 21, 1963, Columbus, Ohio

BR TR 5'11" 190 lbs.

Year	Team		Games	BA	SA	AB	H	2B	3B	HR	HR%	R	RBI	BB	SO	SB	AB	H	PO	A	E	DP	TC/G	FA	G by Pos
1905	CIN	N	17	.255	.373	51	13	4	1	0	0.0	10	10	13		4	0	0	31	6	5	1	2.5	.881	OF-12, 3B-4, 1B-1
1906			18	.204	.259	54	11	1	1	0	0.0	7	1	8		2	1	1	23	3	1	2	1.5	.963	OF-16
1907	CLE	A	152	.228	.305	514	117	19	9	1	0.2	62	50	47		15	0	0	278	22	11	6	2.0	.965	OF-150, 1B-4, 2B-1
1908			137	.231	.353	464	107	23	8	6	1.3	55	59	38		9	3	0	236	201	36	27	3.5	.924	OF-75, SS-51, 1B-4
1909			139	.258	.372	457	118	20	13	2	0.4	57	53	41		22	2	1	241	18	24	4	2.0	.915	OF-131, SS-6
1915	PIT	N	156	.307	.438	577	177	33	14	5	0.9	72	77	48	75	17	0	0	261	17	9	5	1.8	.969	OF-156
1916			152	.315	.427	555	175	18	16	4	0.7	64	76	54	61	10	1	0	496	20	16	12	3.5	.970	OF-124, 1B-31
1917			69	.189	.275	244	46	5	5	2	0.8	27	29	33	27	5	0	0	275	18	11	10	4.4	.964	OF-48, 1B-20
1918			50	.234	.315	111	26	5	2	0	0.0	10	13	15	8	1	19	6	51	10	3	0	1.3	.953	OF-40, 1B-3
1920			18	.188	.188	16	3	0	0	0	0.0	0	1	1	3	0	16	3	0	0	0	0	0.0	–	
10 yrs.			908	.261	.368	3043	793	128	69	20	0.7	364	369	298	174	85	42	11	1892	315	116	67	2.6	.950	OF-752, 1B-63, SS-57, 3B-4, 2B-1

Harry Hinchman

HINCHMAN, HARRY SIBLEY
Brother of Bill Hinchman.
B. Aug. 4, 1878, Philadelphia, Pa. D. Jan. 19, 1933, Toledo, Ohio

BB TR 5'11" 165 lbs.

Year	Team		Games	BA	SA	AB	H	2B	3B	HR	HR%	R	RBI	BB	SO	SB	AB	H	PO	A	E	DP	TC/G	FA	G by Pos
1907	CLE	A	15	.216	.314	51	11	3	1	0	0.0	3	9	5		2	0	0	25	60	9	5	6.3	.904	2B-15

Hunkey Hines

HINES, HENRY FRED
B. Sept. 29, 1867, Elgin, Ill. D. Jan. 2, 1928, Rockford, Ill.

BR TR 5'7" 165 lbs.

Year	Team		Games	BA	SA	AB	H	2B	3B	HR	HR%	R	RBI	BB	SO	SB	AB	H	PO	A	E	DP	TC/G	FA	G by Pos
1895	BKN	N	2	.250	.250	8	2	0	0	0	0.0	3	1	2		0	0	0	5	0	0	0	2.5	1.000	OF-2

Mike Hines

HINES, MICHAEL P.
B. 1864, Ireland D. Mar. 14, 1910, New Bedford, Mass.

BR TL 5'10" 176 lbs.

Year	Team		Games	BA	SA	AB	H	2B	3B	HR	HR%	R	RBI	BB	SO	SB	AB	H	PO	A	E	DP	TC/G	FA	G by Pos
1883	BOS	N	63	.225	.290	231	52	13	1	0	0.0	38	16	7	36	0	0	0	388	104	62	5	8.8	.888	C-59, OF-7
1884			35	.174	.197	132	23	3	0	0	0.0	16		3	24	0	0	0	255	64	28	7	9.9	.919	C-35
1885	3 teams		18	.194	.278	72	14	4	1	0	0.0	12	4	4	7	0	0	0	28	9	9	0	2.6	.804	OF-14, C-4
"	total	BOS N (14G – .232)			BKN AA (3G – .077)		PRO N	(1G – .000)																	
1888	BOS	N	4	.125	.250	16	2	0	1	0	0.0	3	2	2	0	0	0	0	16	1	3	0	5.0	.850	OF-3, C-1
4 yrs.			120	.202	.259	451	91	20	3	0	0.0	69	22	16	67	0	0	0	687	178	102	12	8.1	.895	C-99, OF-24

Paul Hines

HINES, PAUL A.
B. Mar. 1, 1852, Washington, D. C. D. July 10, 1935, Hyattsville, Md.

BR TR 5'9½" 173 lbs.

Year	Team		Games	BA	SA	AB	H	2B	3B	HR	HR%	R	RBI	BB	SO	SB	AB	H	PO	A	E	DP	TC/G	FA	G by Pos
1876	CHI	N	64	.331	.439	305	101	21	3	2	0.7	62	59	1	3		0	0	159	8	14	4	2.8	.923	OF-64, 2B-1
1877			60	.280	.375	261	73	11	7	0	0.0	44	23	1	8		0	0	102	40	36	5	3.0	.798	OF-49, 2B-11
1878	PRO	N	62	.358	.486	257	92	13	4	4	1.6	42	50	2	10		0	0	109	20	24	4	2.5	.843	OF-61, SS-1
1879			85	.357	.482	409	146	25	10	2	0.5	81	52	8	16		0	0	146	24	26	3	2.3	.867	OF-85
1880			85	.307	.396	374	115	20	2	3	0.8	64	35	13	17		0	0	197	37	15	11	2.9	.940	OF-75, 2B-6, 1B-4
1881			80	.285	.404	361	103	27	5	2	0.6	65	31	13	12		0	0	193	23	28	4	3.1	.885	OF-78, 2B-4, 1B-1
1882			84	.309	.467	379	117	28	10	4	1.1	73		10	14		0	0	175	16	29	7	2.6	.868	OF-82, 1B-2
1883			97	.299	.416	442	132	32	4	4	0.9	94		18	23		0	0	268	27	24	10	3.3	.925	OF-89, 1B-9
1884			114	.302	.435	490	148	36	10	3	0.6	94		44	28		0	0	266	20	29	9	2.8	.908	OF-108, 1B-7, P-1
1885			98	.270	.345	411	111	20	4	1	0.2	63	35	19	18		0	0	245	25	37	4	3.1	.879	OF-92, 1B-4, SS-1, 3B-1, 2B-1
1886	WAS	N	121	.312	.462	487	152	30	8	9	1.8	80	56	35	21		0	0	311	66	47	6	3.5	.889	OF-92, 3B-15, 1B-10, SS-3, 2B-3
1887			123	.308	.458	478	147	32	5	10	2.1	83	72	48	24	46	0	0	270	39	35	7	2.8	.898	OF-109, 1B-7, 2B-5, SS-4
1888	IND	N	133	.281	.366	513	144	26	3	4	0.8	84	58	41	45	31	0	0	312	18	30	9	2.7	.917	OF-125, 1B-6, SS-2
1889			121	.305	.401	486	148	27	1	6	1.2	77	72	49	22	34	0	0	1121	61	43	66	10.1	.965	1B-109, OF-12
1890	2 teams	PIT N (31G – .182)			BOS N	(69G – .264)																			
"	total		100	.239	.302	394	94	13	3	2	0.5	52	57	43	27	15	0	0	318	19	27	11	3.6	.926	OF-83, 1B-18
1891	WAS	AA	54	.282	.364	206	58	7	5	0	0.0	25	31	21	16	6	0	0	144	9	17	7	3.1	.900	OF-47, 1B-8
16 yrs.			1481	.301	.413	6253	1881	368	84	56	0.9	1083	631	366	304	132	0	0	4336	452	461	167	3.5	.912	OF-1251, 1B-185, 2B-31, 3B-16, SS-13, P-1

Gordie Hinkle

HINKLE, DANIEL GORDON
B. Apr. 3, 1905, Toronto, Ohio D. Mar. 19, 1972, Houston, Tex.

BR TR 6' 185 lbs.

Year	Team		Games	BA	SA	AB	H	2B	3B	HR	HR%	R	RBI	BB	SO	SB	AB	H	PO	A	E	DP	TC/G	FA	G by Pos
1934	BOS	A	27	.173	.280	75	13	6	1	0	0.0	7	9	7	23	0	0	0	107	11	1	2	4.4	.992	C-26

George Hinshaw

HINSHAW, GEORGE ADDISON
B. Oct. 23, 1959, Los Angeles, Calif.

BR TR 6' 185 lbs.

Year	Team		Games	BA	SA	AB	H	2B	3B	HR	HR%	R	RBI	BB	SO	SB	AB	H	PO	A	E	DP	TC/G	FA	G by Pos
1982	SD	N	6	.267	.267	15	4	0	0	0	0.0	1	3	5		0	1	0	9	1	0	0	1.7	1.000	OF-6
1983			7	.438	.500	16	7	1	0	0	0.0	1	2	4		0	1	0	6	5	0	0	1.6	1.000	3B-5, 2B-1
2 yrs.			13	.355	.387	31	11	1	0	0	0.0	2	5	9		0	1	0	15	6	0	0	1.6	1.000	OF-6, 3B-5, 2B-1

Paul Hinson

HINSON, JAMES PAUL
B. May 9, 1904, Van Leer, Tenn. D. Sept. 23, 1960, Muskogee, Okla.

BR TR 5'10" 150 lbs.

Year	Team		Games	BA	SA	AB	H	2B	3B	HR	HR%	R	RBI	BB	SO	SB	AB	H	PO	A	E	DP	TC/G	FA	G by Pos
1928	BOS	A	3	–	–	0	0	0	0	0	–	1	0	0	0	0	0	0	0	0	0	0	0.0	–	

Year	Team	Games	BA	SA	AB	H	2B	3B	HR	HR%	R	RBI	BB	SO	SB	Pinch Hit AB	Pinch Hit H	PO	A	E	DP	TC/G	FA	G by Pos

Chuck Hinton

HINTON, CHARLES EDWARD
B. May 3, 1934, Rocky Mount, N. C.   BR TR 6'1" 180 lbs.

Year	Team	Games	BA	SA	AB	H	2B	3B	HR	HR%	R	RBI	BB	SO	SB	PH AB	PH H	PO	A	E	DP	TC/G	FA	G by Pos
1961	WAS A	106	.260	.381	339	88	13	5	6	1.8	51	34	40	81	22	11	4	175	6	7	4	1.8	.963	OF-92
1962		151	.310	.472	542	168	25	6	17	3.1	73	75	47	66	28	2	0	259	36	4	16	2.0	.987	OF-136, 2B-12, SS-1
1963		150	.269	.426	566	152	20	12	15	2.7	80	55	64	79	25	0	0	345	43	10	9	2.7	.975	OF-125, 3B-19, 1B-6, SS-2
1964		138	.274	.414	514	141	25	7	11	2.1	71	53	57	77	17	5	1	258	7	4	3	1.9	.985	OF-131, 3B-2
1965	CLE A	133	.255	.448	431	110	17	6	18	4.2	59	54	53	65	17	16	2	408	71	13	30	3.7	.974	OF-72, 1B-40, 2B-23, 3B-1
1966		123	.256	.402	348	89	9	3	12	3.4	46	50	35	66	10	17	4	203	6	5	3	1.7	.977	OF-104, 1B-6, 2B-2
1967		147	.245	.355	498	122	19	3	10	2.0	55	37	43	100	6	12	4	243	9	6	2	1.8	.977	OF-136, 2B-5
1968	CAL A	116	.195	.333	267	52	10	3	7	2.6	28	23	24	61	3	32	4	390	60	7	32	3.9	.985	1B-48, OF-37, 3B-13, 2B-9
1969	CLE A	94	.256	.388	121	31	3	2	3	2.5	18	19	8	22	2	40	10	37	15	3	1	0.6	.945	OF-40, 3B-14
1970		107	.318	.477	195	62	4	0	9	4.6	24	29	25	34	0	37	11	229	15	2	14	2.3	.992	1B-40, OF-35, C-4, 2B-3, 3B-2
1971		88	.224	.374	147	33	7	0	5	3.4	13	14	20	34	0	43	5	123	5	0	16	1.5	1.000	OF-20, 1B-20, C-5
11 yrs.		1353	.264	.412	3968	1048	152	47	113	2.8	518	443	416	685	130	215	45	2670	273	61	130	2.2	.980	OF-928, 1B-160, 2B-54, 3B-51, C-9, SS-3

John Hinton

HINTON, JOHN ROBERT (Red)
B. June 28, 1876, Pittsburgh, Pa.   D. Aug. 8, 1920, Braddock, Pa.   BR TR 6' 200 lbs.

Year	Team	Games	BA	SA	AB	H	2B	3B	HR	HR%	R	RBI	BB	SO	SB	PH AB	PH H	PO	A	E	DP	TC/G	FA	G by Pos
1901	BOS N	4	.077	.077	13	1	0	0	0	0.0	0	0	2		0	0	0	4	5	3	0	3.0	.750	3B-4

Tommy Hinzo

HINZO, THOMAS LEE
B. June 18, 1964, San Diego, Calif.   BB TR 5'10" 170 lbs.

Year	Team	Games	BA	SA	AB	H	2B	3B	HR	HR%	R	RBI	BB	SO	SB	PH AB	PH H	PO	A	E	DP	TC/G	FA	G by Pos
1987	CLE A	67	.265	.358	257	68	9	3	3	1.2	31	21	10	47	9	1	0	115	204	9	44	4.9	.973	2B-67
1989		18	.000	.000	17	0	0	0	0	0.0	4	0	2	6	1	1	0	9	7	3	1	1.1	.842	2B-6, DH-1, SS-1
2 yrs.		85	.248	.336	274	68	9	3	3	1.1	35	21	12	53	10	2	0	124	211	12	45	4.1	.965	2B-73, DH-1, SS-1

Gene Hiser

HISER, GENE TAYLOR
B. Dec. 11, 1948, Baltimore, Md.   BL TL 5'11" 175 lbs.

Year	Team	Games	BA	SA	AB	H	2B	3B	HR	HR%	R	RBI	BB	SO	SB	PH AB	PH H	PO	A	E	DP	TC/G	FA	G by Pos
1971	CHI N	17	.207	.207	29	6	0	0	0	0.0	4	1	4	8	1	5	1	19	0	0	0	1.1	1.000	OF-9
1972		32	.196	.196	46	9	0	0	0	0.0	2	4	6	8	1	11	1	21	2	0	1	0.7	1.000	OF-15
1973		100	.174	.229	109	19	3	0	1	0.9	15	6	11	17	4	37	6	48	0	1	0	0.5	.980	OF-64
1974		12	.235	.294	17	4	1	0	0	0.0	2	1	0	3	0	5	1	8	0	0	0	0.7	1.000	OF-8
1975		45	.242	.290	62	15	3	0	0	0.0	11	6	11	7	0	24	8	28	0	0	1	0.6	1.000	OF-18, 1B-1
5 yrs.		206	.202	.240	263	53	7	0	1	0.4	34	18	32	43	6	82	17	124	2	1	2	0.6	.992	OF-114, 1B-1

Larry Hisle

HISLE, LARRY EUGENE
B. May 5, 1947, Portsmouth, Ohio   BR TR 6'2" 193 lbs.

Year	Team	Games	BA	SA	AB	H	2B	3B	HR	HR%	R	RBI	BB	SO	SB	PH AB	PH H	PO	A	E	DP	TC/G	FA	G by Pos
1968	PHI N	7	.364	.455	11	4	1	0	0	0.0	1	1	1	4	0	1	0	8	0	0	0	1.1	1.000	OF-6
1969		145	.266	.459	482	128	23	5	20	4.1	75	56	48	152	18	2	0	324	11	8	2	2.4	.977	OF-140
1970		126	.205	.353	405	83	22	4	10	2.5	52	44	53	139	5	3	0	262	5	6	0	2.2	.978	OF-121
1971		36	.197	.237	76	15	3	0	0	0.0	7	3	6	22	1	5	1	48	2	2	0	1.4	.962	OF-27
1973	MIN A	143	.272	.422	545	148	25	6	15	2.8	88	64	64	128	11	1	1	337	11	9	0	2.5	.975	OF-143
1974		143	.286	.465	510	146	20	7	19	3.7	68	79	48	112	12	9	1	279	4	6	1	2.0	.979	OF-137
1975		80	.314	.494	255	80	9	2	11	4.3	37	51	27	39	17	5	3	118	2	3	0	1.5	.976	OF-58, DH-14
1976		155	.272	.394	581	158	19	5	14	2.4	81	96	56	93	31	1	0	361	16	6	1	2.5	.984	OF-154
1977		141	.302	.533	546	165	36	3	28	5.1	95	119	56	106	21	2	1	287	11	8	2	2.2	.974	OF-134, DH-6
1978	MIL A	142	.290	.533	520	151	24	0	34	6.5	96	115	67	90	10	4	1	172	6	4	2	1.3	.978	OF-87, DH-51
1979		26	.281	.448	96	27	7	0	3	3.1	18	14	11	19	1	1	1	17	0	0	0	0.7	1.000	DH-15, OF-10
1980		17	.283	.583	60	17	0	0	6	10.0	16	16	14	7	1	0	0	0	0	0	0	0.0	—	DH-17
1981		27	.230	.414	87	20	4	0	4	4.6	11	11	6	17	0	4	0	0	0	0	0	0.0	—	DH-24
1982		9	.129	.323	31	4	0	0	2	6.5	7	5	5	13	0	1	1	0	0	0	0	0.0	—	DH-8
14 yrs.		1197	.273	.452	4205	1146	193	32	166	3.9	652	674	462	941	128	39	10	2213	70	52	8	2.0	.978	OF-1017, DH-135

Billy Hitchcock

HITCHCOCK, WILLIAM CLYDE
Brother of Jim Hitchcock.
B. July 31, 1916, Inverness, Ala.
Manager 1960, 1962-63, 1966-67.   BR TR 6'1½" 185 lbs.

Year	Team	Games	BA	SA	AB	H	2B	3B	HR	HR%	R	RBI	BB	SO	SB	PH AB	PH H	PO	A	E	DP	TC/G	FA	G by Pos
1942	DET A	85	.211	.246	280	59	8	1	0	0.0	27	29	26	21	2	0	0	157	199	21	39	4.4	.944	SS-80, 3B-1
1946	2 teams	DET A (3G – .000)			WAS A (98G – .212)																			
"	total	101	.210	.249	357	75	8	3	0	0.0	27	25	27	52	2	1	0	166	231	21	34	4.1	.950	SS-53, 3B-46, 2B-1
1947	STL A	80	.222	.255	275	61	2	2	1	0.4	25	28	21	34	3	5	0	209	190	14	45	5.2	.966	2B-46, 3B-17, SS-7, 1B-5
1948	BOS A	49	.298	.379	124	37	3	2	1	0.8	15	20	7	9	0	12	3	54	82	4	15	2.9	.971	3B-15, 2B-15
1949		55	.204	.259	147	30	6	1	0	0.0	22	9	17	11	2	16	0	277	30	3	33	5.6	.990	1B-29, 2B-8
1950	PHI A	115	.273	.361	399	109	22	5	1	0.3	35	54	103	32	3	8	3	299	319	22	105	5.6	.966	2B-107, SS-1
1951		77	.306	.401	222	68	10	4	1	0.5	27	36	21	23	2	11	3	100	150	14	31	3.4	.947	3B-45, 2B-23, 1B-1
1952		119	.246	.292	407	100	8	4	1	0.2	45	45	39	45	1	4	0	202	235	22	34	3.9	.952	3B-104, 1B-13
1953	DET A	22	.211	.211	38	8	0	0	0	0.0	8	0	3	3	0	6	1	10	18	2	2	1.4	.933	3B-12, SS-1, 2B-1
9 yrs.		703	.243	.299	2249	547	67	22	5	0.2	231	257	264	230	15	63	10	1474	1454	123	338	4.3	.960	3B-240, 2B-201, SS-142, 1B-48

Jim Hitchcock

HITCHCOCK, JAMES FRANKLIN
Brother of Billy Hitchcock.
B. June 28, 1911, Inverness, Ala.   D. June 23, 1959, Montgomery, Ala.   BR TR 5'11" 175 lbs.

Year	Team	Games	BA	SA	AB	H	2B	3B	HR	HR%	R	RBI	BB	SO	SB	PH AB	PH H	PO	A	E	DP	TC/G	FA	G by Pos
1938	BOS N	28	.171	.171	76	13	0	0	0	0.0	2	7	2	11	1	0	0	48	61	15	13	4.4	.879	SS-24, 3B-2

Myril Hoag

HOAG, MYRIL OLIVER
B. Mar. 9, 1908, Davis, Calif.   D. July 28, 1971, High Springs, Fla.   BR TR 5'11" 180 lbs.

Year	Team	Games	BA	SA	AB	H	2B	3B	HR	HR%	R	RBI	BB	SO	SB	PH AB	PH H	PO	A	E	DP	TC/G	FA	G by Pos
1931	NY A	44	.143	.214	28	4	2	0	0	0.0	6	3	1	9	0	10	1	12	2	0	0	0.3	1.000	OF-23, 3B-1
1932		46	.370	.519	54	20	5	0	1	1.9	18	7	7	13	1	3	1	26	3	1	0	0.7	.967	OF-35, 1B-1
1934		97	.267	.351	251	67	8	2	3	1.2	45	34	21	21	1	7	0	142	7	4	2	1.6	.974	OF-86
1935		48	.255	.336	110	28	4	1	1	0.9	13	13	12	19	4	5	0	66	2	1	0	1.4	.986	OF-37

Year	Team		Games	BA	SA	AB	H	2B	3B	HR	HR%	R	RBI	BB	SO	SB	Pinch Hit AB	Pinch Hit H	PO	A	E	DP	TC/G	FA	G by Pos

Myril Hoag *continued*

Year	Team		Games	BA	SA	AB	H	2B	3B	HR	HR%	R	RBI	BB	SO	SB	PH AB	PH H	PO	A	E	DP	TC/G	FA	G by Pos
1936			45	.301	.468	156	47	9	4	3	1.9	23	34	7	16	3	3	1	82	2	4	1	2.0	.955	OF-39
1937			106	.301	.423	362	109	19	8	3	0.8	48	46	33	33	4	7	2	181	8	9	2	1.9	.955	OF-99
1938			85	.277	.352	267	74	14	3	0	0.0	28	48	25	31	4	15	3	132	5	5	3	1.7	.965	OF-70
1939	STL	A	129	.295	.421	482	142	23	4	10	2.1	58	75	24	35	9	12	4	218	13	7	2	1.8	.971	OF-117, P-1
1940			76	.262	.366	191	50	11	0	3	1.6	20	26	13	30	2	28	5	64	4	2	0	0.9	.971	OF-46
1941	2 teams	STL A (1G – .000)														CHI A (106G – .255)									
"	total		107	.255	.312	381	97	13	3	1	0.3	30	44	27	29	6	6	2	215	6	10	1	2.2	.957	OF-99
1942	CHI	A	113	.240	.308	412	99	18	2	2	0.5	47	37	36	21	17	1	1	266	12	8	4	2.5	.972	OF-112
1944	2 teams	CHI A (17G – .229)														CLE A (67G – .285)									
"	total		84	.277	.335	325	90	10	3	1	0.3	38	31	35	24	7	4	0	200	11	11	4	2.6	.950	OF-80
1945	CLE	A	40	.211	.297	128	27	5	3	0	0.0	10	3	11	18	1	1	0	73	5	1	1	2.0	.987	OF-33, P-2
13 yrs.			1020	.271	.364	3147	854	141	33	28	0.9	384	401	252	298	59	102	20	1677	80	63	20	1.8	.965	OF-876, P-3, 3B-1, 1B-1

WORLD SERIES

Year	Team		Games	BA	SA	AB	H	2B	3B	HR	HR%	R	RBI	BB	SO	SB	PH AB	PH H	PO	A	E	DP	TC/G	FA	G by Pos
1932	NY	A	1	–	–	0	0	0	0	0	–	1	0	0	0	0	0	0	0	0	0	0	0.0	–	
1937			5	.300	.500	20	6	1	0	1	5.0	4	2	0	1	0	0	0	11	0	0	0	2.2	1.000	OF-5
1938			2	.400	.600	5	2	1	0	0	0.0	3	1	0	1	0	1	0	1	0	0	0	0.5	1.000	OF-1
3 yrs.			8	.320	.520	25	8	2	0	1	4.0	8	3	0	2	0	1	0	12	0	0	0	1.5	1.000	OF-6

Don Hoak

HOAK, DONALD ALBERT (Tiger)
B. Feb. 5, 1928, Roulette, Pa. D. Oct. 9, 1969, Pittsburgh, Pa.

BR TR 6'1" 170 lbs.

Year	Team		Games	BA	SA	AB	H	2B	3B	HR	HR%	R	RBI	BB	SO	SB	PH AB	PH H	PO	A	E	DP	TC/G	FA	G by Pos
1954	BKN	N	88	.245	.398	261	64	9	5	7	2.7	41	26	25	39	8	11	2	71	139	11	12	2.5	.950	3B-75
1955			94	.240	.362	279	67	13	5	5	1.8	50	19	46	50	4	9	4	82	183	11	15	2.9	.960	3B-78
1956	CHI	N	121	.215	.311	424	91	18	4	5	1.2	51	37	41	46	8	5	1	122	158	15	16	2.4	.949	3B-110
1957	CIN	N	149	.293	.482	529	155	39	2	19	3.6	78	89	74	54	8	0	0	194	270	14	29	3.2	.971	3B-149, 2B-1
1958			114	.261	.376	417	109	30	0	6	1.4	51	50	43	54	6	1	0	133	244	14	29	3.4	.964	3B-112, SS-1
1959	PIT	N	155	.294	.399	564	166	29	3	8	1.4	60	65	71	75	9	0	0	169	322	20	31	3.3	.961	3B-155
1960			155	.282	.445	553	156	24	3	16	2.9	97	79	74	74	3	0	0	132	324	25	34	3.1	.948	3B-155
1961			145	.298	.451	503	150	27	7	12	2.4	72	61	73	52	4	2	2	137	267	20	29	2.9	.953	3B-143
1962	PHI	N	121	.241	.350	411	99	14	8	5	1.2	63	48	49	49	4	3	1	93	220	10	19	2.7	.969	3B-116
1963			115	.231	.324	377	87	11	3	6	1.6	35	24	27	52	5	9	2	88	205	13	13	2.7	.958	3B-106
1964			6	.000	.000	4	0	0	0	0	0.0	0	0	0	2	0	4	0	0	0	0	0	0.0	–	
11 yrs.			1263	.265	.396	4322	1144	214	44	89	2.1	598	498	523	530	64	39	9	1221	2332	153	227	2.9	.959	3B-1199, SS-1, 2B-1

WORLD SERIES

Year	Team		Games	BA	SA	AB	H	2B	3B	HR	HR%	R	RBI	BB	SO	SB	PH AB	PH H	PO	A	E	DP	TC/G	FA	G by Pos
1955	BKN	N	3	.333	.333	3	1	0	0	0	0.0	0	0	2	0	0	0	0	1	1	0	0	0.7	1.000	3B-1
1960	PIT	N	7	.217	.304	23	5	2	0	0	0.0	3	3	4	1	0	0	0	8	10	1	2	2.7	.947	3B-7
2 yrs.			10	.231	.308	26	6	2	0	0	0.0	3	3	6	1	0	0	0	9	11	1	2	2.1	.952	3B-8

Bill Hobbs

HOBBS, WILLIAM LEE
B. May 7, 1893, Grant's Lick, Ky. D. Jan. 5, 1945, Hamilton, Ohio

BR TR 5'9½" 155 lbs.

Year	Team		Games	BA	SA	AB	H	2B	3B	HR	HR%	R	RBI	BB	SO	SB	PH AB	PH H	PO	A	E	DP	TC/G	FA	G by Pos
1913	CIN	N	4	.000	.000	4	0	0	0	0	0.0	0	0	0	2	0	0	0	0	3	0	0	0.8	1.000	3B-1, 2B-1
1916			6	.182	.273	11	2	1	0	0	0.0	1	1	2	0	1	0	0	9	27	2	3	6.3	.947	SS-6
2 yrs.			10	.133	.200	15	2	1	0	0	0.0	1	1	2	3	1	1	0	9	30	2	3	4.1	.951	SS-6, 3B-1, 2B-1

Dick Hoblitzell

HOBLITZELL, RICHARD CARLETON
B. Oct. 26, 1888, Waverly, W. Va. D. Nov. 14, 1962, Parkersburg, W. Va.

BL TL 6' 172 lbs.

Year	Team		Games	BA	SA	AB	H	2B	3B	HR	HR%	R	RBI	BB	SO	SB	PH AB	PH H	PO	A	E	DP	TC/G	FA	G by Pos
1908	CIN	N	32	.254	.316	114	29	3	2	0	0.0	8	8	7		2	0	0	313	24	5	11	10.7	.985	1B-32
1909			142	.308	.418	517	159	23	11	4	0.8	59	67	44		17	0	0	1444	74	28	80	10.9	.982	1B-142
1910			155	.278	.380	611	170	24	13	4	0.7	85	70	47	32	28	0	0	1461	83	24	66	10.1	.985	1B-148, 2B-7
1911			158	.289	.415	622	180	19	13	11	1.8	81	97	42	44	32	0	0	1442	91	16	81	9.8	.990	1B-158
1912			148	.294	.405	558	164	32	12	2	0.4	73	85	48	28	23	0	0	1326	87	21	73	9.7	.985	1B-147
1913			137	.285	.376	502	143	23	7	3	0.6	59	68	35	26	18	3	2	1373	60	17	76	10.6	.988	1B-134
1914	2 teams	CIN N (78G – .210)														BOS A (68G – .319)									
"	total		146	.262	.342	477	125	18	10	0	0.0	62	62	45	47	19	1	0	1429	61	24	65	10.4	.984	1B-143
1915	BOS	A	124	.283	.396	399	113	15	12	2	0.5	54	61	38	26	9	4	1	1095	63	15	51	9.5	.987	1B-117
1916			130	.259	.305	417	108	17	1	0	0.0	57	50	47	28	10	3	0	1225	67	15	64	10.1	.989	1B-126
1917			120	.257	.343	420	108	19	7	1	0.2	49	47	46	22	12	2	2	1274	52	14	58	11.2	.990	1B-118
1918			25	.159	.174	69	11	1	0	0	0.0	4	4	8	3	5	3	3	209	15	1	18	9.0	.996	1B-19
11 yrs.			1317	.278	.374	4706	1310	194	88	27	0.6	591	619	407	256	173	18	5	12591	677	180	643	10.2	.987	1B-1284, 2B-7

WORLD SERIES

Year	Team		Games	BA	SA	AB	H	2B	3B	HR	HR%	R	RBI	BB	SO	SB	PH AB	PH H	PO	A	E	DP	TC/G	FA	G by Pos
1915	BOS	A	5	.313	.313	16	5	0	1	0	0.0	1	1	0	1	0	0	0	35	5	1	2	8.2	.976	1B-5
1916			5	.235	.412	17	4	1	1	0	0.0	3	2	6	0	1	0	0	69	4	0	4	14.6	1.000	1B-5
2 yrs.			10	.273	.364	33	9	1	1	0	0.0	4	3	6	1	1	0	0	104	9	1	6	11.4	.991	1B-10

Butch Hobson

HOBSON, CLELL LAVERN, JR.
B. Aug. 17, 1951, Tuscaloosa, Ala.

BR TR 6'1" 193 lbs.

Year	Team		Games	BA	SA	AB	H	2B	3B	HR	HR%	R	RBI	BB	SO	SB	PH AB	PH H	PO	A	E	DP	TC/G	FA	G by Pos
1975	BOS	A	2	.250	.250	4	1	0	0	0	0.0	0	0	0	2	0	0	0	1	3	0	0	2.0	1.000	3B-1
1976			76	.234	.387	269	63	7	5	8	3.0	34	34	15	62	0	0	0	60	146	14	11	2.9	.936	3B-76
1977			159	.265	.489	593	157	33	5	30	5.1	77	112	27	**162**	5	0	0	128	272	23	27	2.7	.946	3B-159
1978			147	.250	.408	512	128	26	2	17	3.3	65	80	50	122	1	0	0	122	261	43	25	2.9	.899	3B-133, DH-14
1979			146	.261	.496	528	138	26	7	28	5.3	74	93	30	78	3	1	0	110	251	25	17	2.6	.935	3B-142, 2B-1
1980			93	.228	.349	324	74	6	0	11	3.4	35	39	25	69	1	1	0	52	109	16	5	1.9	.910	3B-57, DH-36
1981	CAL	A	85	.235	.336	268	63	7	4	4	1.5	27	36	35	60	1	1	0	85	139	17	13	2.8	.929	3B-83, DH-2
1982	NY	A	30	.172	.207	58	10	2	0	0	0.0	2	3	1	14	0	12	3	37	2	2	3	1.4	.951	DH-15, 1B-11
8 yrs.			738	.248	.423	2556	634	107	23	98	3.8	314	397	183	569	11	17	4	595	1183	140	101	2.6	.927	3B-651, DH-67, 1B-11, 2B-1

Ed Hock

HOCK, EDWARD FRANCIS
B. Mar. 27, 1899, Franklin Furnace, Ohio D. Nov. 21, 1963, Portsmouth, Ohio

BL TR 5'10½" 165 lbs.

Year	Team		Games	BA	SA	AB	H	2B	3B	HR	HR%	R	RBI	BB	SO	SB	PH AB	PH H	PO	A	E	DP	TC/G	FA	G by Pos
1920	STL	N	1	–	–	0	0	0	0	0	–	0	0	0	0	0	0	0	0	0	0	0	0.0	–	OF-1
1923	CIN	N	2	–	–	0	0	0	0	0	–	0	0	0	0	0	0	0	0	0	0	0	0.0	–	

Year	Team		Games	BA	SA	AB	H	2B	3B	HR	HR%	R	RBI	BB	SO	SB	Pinch Hit AB	Pinch Hit H	PO	A	E	DP	TC/G	FA	G by Pos

Ed Hock *continued*

Year	Team		Games	BA	SA	AB	H	2B	3B	HR	HR%	R	RBI	BB	SO	SB	AB	H	PO	A	E	DP	TC/G	FA	G by Pos
1924			16	.100	.100	10	1	0	0	0	0.0	7	0	0	2	0	4	1	6	0	0	0	0.4	1.000	OF-2
3 yrs.			19	.100	.100	10	1	0	0	0	0.0	7	0	0	2	0	4	1	6	0	0	0	0.3	1.000	OF-3

Oris Hockett

HOCKETT, ORIS LEON
B. Sept. 29, 1909, Amboy, Ind.   D. Mar. 23, 1969, Torrance, Calif.

BL TR 5'9"   182 lbs.

Year	Team		Games	BA	SA	AB	H	2B	3B	HR	HR%	R	RBI	BB	SO	SB	AB	H	PO	A	E	DP	TC/G	FA	G by Pos
1938	BKN	N	21	.329	.471	70	23	5	1	1	1.4	8	8	4	9	0	4	2	24	1	3	0	1.3	.893	OF-17
1939			9	.231	.231	13	3	0	0	0	0.0	3	1	1	1	0	7	2	1	1	0	0	0.2	1.000	OF-1
1941	CLE	A	2	.333	.333	6	2	0	0	0	0.0	0	1	2	0	0	0	0	2	0	0	0	1.0	1.000	OF-2
1942			148	.250	.344	601	150	22	7	7	1.2	85	48	45	45	12	1	0	284	12	6	3	2.0	.980	OF-145
1943			141	.276	.354	601	166	33	4	2	0.3	70	51	45	45	13	2	0	347	13	15	3	2.7	.960	OF-139
1944			124	.289	.381	457	132	29	5	1	0.2	47	50	35	27	8	14	2	275	6	5	1	2.3	.983	OF-110
1945	CHI		106	.293	.381	417	122	23	4	2	0.5	46	55	27	30	10	0	0	273	5	5	3	2.7	.982	OF-106
7 yrs.			551	.276	.365	2165	598	112	21	13	0.6	259	214	159	157	43	28	6	1206	40	34	10	2.3	.973	OF-520

Johnny Hodapp

HODAPP, URBAN JOHN
B. Sept. 26, 1905, Cincinnati, Ohio   D. June 14, 1980, Cincinnati, Ohio

BR TR 6'   185 lbs.

Year	Team		Games	BA	SA	AB	H	2B	3B	HR	HR%	R	RBI	BB	SO	SB	AB	H	PO	A	E	DP	TC/G	FA	G by Pos
1925	CLE	A	37	.238	.292	130	31	5	1	0	0.0	12	14	11	7	2	0	0	42	79	5	7	3.4	.960	3B-37
1926			3	.200	.200	5	1	0	0	0	0.0	0	1	0	1	0	0	0	1	2	1	0	1.3	.750	3B-3
1927			75	.304	.454	240	73	15	3	5	2.1	25	40	14	23	2	7	3	111	133	16	19	3.5	.938	3B-67, 1B-4
1928			116	.323	.432	449	145	31	6	2	0.4	51	73	20	20	2	3	2	233	224	20	34	4.1	.958	3B-101, 1B-13
1929			90	.327	.456	294	96	12	7	4	1.4	30	51	15	14	3	16	4	162	271	10	32	4.9	.977	2B-72
1930			154	.354	.502	635	**225**	**51**	8	9	1.4	111	121	32	29	6	0	0	403	557	30	103	6.4	.970	2B-154
1931			122	.295	.365	468	138	19	4	2	0.4	71	56	27	23	1	1	0	274	413	22	73	5.8	.969	2B-121
1932	2 teams			CLE	A	(7G –	.125)					CHI	A	(68G –	.227)										
"	total		75	.219	.313	192	42	9	0	3	1.6	23	20	11	5	1	23	2	82	31	8	5	1.6	.934	OF-31, 2B-12, 3B-4
1933	BOS	A	115	.312	.424	413	129	27	5	3	0.7	55	54	33	14	1	6	3	344	335	26	68	6.1	.963	2B-101, 1B-10
9 yrs.			787	.311	.425	2826	880	169	34	28	1.0	378	429	163	136	18	56	14	1652	2045	138	341	4.9	.964	2B-460, 3B-212, OF-31, 1B-27

Mel Hoderlein

HODERLEIN, MELVIN ANTHONY
B. June 24, 1923, Mt. Carmel, Ohio

BB TR 5'10"   185 lbs.

Year	Team		Games	BA	SA	AB	H	2B	3B	HR	HR%	R	RBI	BB	SO	SB	AB	H	PO	A	E	DP	TC/G	FA	G by Pos
1951	BOS	A	9	.357	.571	14	5	1	1	0	0.0	4	1	6	2	1	0	0	12	10	2	4	2.7	.917	3B-3, 2B-3
1952	WAS	A	72	.269	.327	208	56	8	2	0	0.0	16	17	18	22	2	13	2	138	168	7	43	4.3	.978	2B-58
1953			23	.191	.191	47	9	0	0	0	0.0	5	5	6	9	0	10	2	18	28	2	6	2.1	.958	2B-11, SS-2
1954			14	.160	.200	25	4	1	0	0	0.0	1	1	1	4	0	3	0	13	22	3	5	2.7	.921	SS-6, 2B-5
4 yrs.			118	.252	.306	294	74	10	3	0	0.0	22	24	31	37	2	27	4	181	228	14	58	3.6	.967	2B-77, SS-8, 3B-3

Bert Hodge

HODGE, EDWARD BURTON
B. May 25, 1917, Knoxville, Tenn.

BL TR 5'11"   170 lbs.

Year	Team		Games	BA	SA	AB	H	2B	3B	HR	HR%	R	RBI	BB	SO	SB	AB	H	PO	A	E	DP	TC/G	FA	G by Pos
1942	PHI	N	8	.182	.182	11	2	0	0	0	0.0	0	0	1	0	0	6	2	1	2	0	0	0.4	1.000	3B-2

Gomer Hodge

HODGE, HAROLD MORRIS
B. Apr. 3, 1944, Rutherfordton, N. C.

BB TR 6'2"   185 lbs.

Year	Team		Games	BA	SA	AB	H	2B	3B	HR	HR%	R	RBI	BB	SO	SB	AB	H	PO	A	E	DP	TC/G	FA	G by Pos
1971	CLE	A	80	.205	.277	83	17	3	0	1	1.2	3	9	4	19	0	**68**	**16**	20	3	0	4	0.3	1.000	3B-3, 1B-3, 2B-2

Gil Hodges

HODGES, GILBERT RAYMOND
Born Gilbert Ray Hodge.
B. Apr. 4, 1924, Princeton, Ind.   D. Apr. 2, 1972, West Palm Beach, Fla.
Manager 1963-71.

BR TR 6'1½"   200 lbs.

Year	Team		Games	BA	SA	AB	H	2B	3B	HR	HR%	R	RBI	BB	SO	SB	AB	H	PO	A	E	DP	TC/G	FA	G by Pos
1943	BKN	N	1	.000	.000	2	0	0	0	0	0.0	0	0	1	2	1	0	0	1	2	2	1	5.0	.600	3B-1
1947			28	.156	.260	77	12	3	1	1	1.3	9	7	14	19	0	4	1	79	12	4	2	3.4	.958	C-24
1948			134	.249	.376	481	120	18	5	11	2.3	48	70	43	61	7	2	0	990	72	17	90	8.1	.984	1B-96, C-38
1949			156	.285	.453	596	170	23	4	23	3.9	94	115	66	64	10	0	0	1336	80	7	142	9.1	.995	1B-156
1950			153	.283	.508	561	159	26	2	32	5.7	98	113	73	73	6	0	0	1273	100	8	159	9.0	.994	1B-153
1951			158	.268	.527	582	156	25	3	40	6.9	118	103	93	**99**	9	0	0	1365	126	12	171	9.5	.992	1B-158
1952			153	.254	.500	508	129	27	1	32	6.3	87	102	107	90	2	0	0	1322	116	11	152	9.5	.992	1B-153
1953			141	.302	.550	520	157	22	7	31	6.0	101	122	75	84	1	1	1	1062	101	9	106	8.3	.992	1B-127, OF-24
1954			154	.304	.579	579	176	23	5	42	7.3	106	130	74	84	3	0	0	1381	132	7	129	9.9	.995	1B-154
1955			150	.289	.500	546	158	24	5	27	4.9	75	102	80	91	2	0	0	1291	106	14	126	9.4	.990	1B-139, OF-16
1956			153	.265	.507	550	146	29	4	32	5.8	86	87	76	91	3	0	0	1234	103	12	105	8.8	.991	1B-138, OF-30, C-1
1957			150	.299	.511	579	173	28	7	27	4.7	94	98	63	91	5	0	0	1319	117	14	116	9.7	.990	1B-150, 3B-2, 2B-1
1958	LA	N	141	.259	.434	475	123	15	1	22	4.6	68	64	52	87	8	9	1	932	103	9	137	7.4	.991	1B-122, 3B-15, OF-9, C-1
1959			124	.276	.513	413	114	19	2	25	6.1	57	80	58	92	3	7	1	896	74	8	80	7.9	.992	1B-113, 3B-4
1960			101	.198	.371	197	39	8	1	8	4.1	22	30	26	37	0	15	0	411	44	5	42	4.6	.989	1B-92, 3B-10
1961			109	.242	.372	215	52	4	0	8	3.7	25	31	24	43	3	28	7	454	37	1	44	4.5	.998	1B-100
1962	NY	N	54	.252	.472	127	32	1	0	9	7.1	15	17	15	27	0	9	2	315	32	5	23	6.5	.986	1B-47
1963			11	.227	.227	22	5	0	0	0	0.0	2	3	3	2	0	0	0	61	8	0	7	6.3	1.000	1B-10
18 yrs.			2071	.273	.487	7030	1921	295	48	370	5.3	1105	1274	943	1137	63	77	13	15722	1365	145	1632	8.3	.992	1B-1908, OF-79, C-64, 3B-32, 2B-1

WORLD SERIES

Year	Team		Games	BA	SA	AB	H	2B	3B	HR	HR%	R	RBI	BB	SO	SB	AB	H	PO	A	E	DP	TC/G	FA	G by Pos
1947	BKN	N	1	.000	.000	1	0	0	0	0	0.0	0	0	0	0	1	0	0	0	0	0	0	0.0	–	
1949			5	.235	.412	17	4	0	0	1	5.9	2	4	1	4	0	0	0	38	3	0	0	8.2	1.000	1B-5
1952			7	.000	.000	21	0	0	0	0	0.0	1	1	5	6	0	0	0	60	5	1	4	9.4	.985	1B-7
1953			6	.364	.500	22	8	0	0	1	4.5	3	1	3	3	1	0	0	47	4	1	2	8.7	.981	1B-6
1955			7	.292	.417	24	7	0	0	1	4.2	2	5	3	2	0	0	0	74	4	0	11	11.1	1.000	1B-7
1956			7	.304	.522	23	7	2	0	1	4.3	4	8	5	4	0	0	0	54	5	1	8	8.4	1.000	1B-7
1959	LA	N	6	.391	.609	23	9	0	1	1	4.3	2	2	1	2	0	0	0	53	3	0	6	9.3	1.000	1B-6
7 yrs.			39	.267	.412	131	35	2	1	5	3.8	15	21	17	22	1	1	0	326	24	2	31	9.0	.994	1B-38

Year Team	Games	BA	SA	AB	H	2B	3B	HR	HR%	R	RBI	BB	SO	SB	Pinch Hit AB	Pinch Hit H	PO	A	E	DP	TC/G	FA	G by Pos

Ron Hodges

HODGES, RONALD WRAY
B. June 22, 1949, Rocky Mount, Va.

BL TR 6'1" 185 lbs.

Year Team	Games	BA	SA	AB	H	2B	3B	HR	HR%	R	RBI	BB	SO	SB	PH AB	PH H	PO	A	E	DP	TC/G	FA	G by Pos
1973 NY N	45	.260	.299	127	33	2	0	1	0.8	5	18	11	19	0	5	2	241	13	2	0	5.7	.992	C-40
1974	59	.221	.338	136	30	4	0	4	2.9	16	14	19	11	0	13	2	227	14	12	1	4.3	.953	C-44
1975	9	.206	.412	34	7	1	0	2	5.9	3	4	1	6	0	0	0	69	1	0	0	7.8	1.000	C-9
1976	56	.226	.342	155	35	6	0	4	2.6	21	24	27	16	2	7	2	262	18	7	0	5.1	.976	C-52
1977	66	.265	.325	117	31	4	0	1	0.9	6	5	9	17	0	39	9	112	19	1	3	2.0	.992	C-27
1978	47	.255	.314	102	26	4	1	0	0.0	4	7	10	11	1	16	4	145	20	3	5	3.6	.982	C-30
1979	59	.163	.209	86	14	4	0	0	0.0	4	5	19	16	0	29	3	82	16	2	1	1.7	.980	C-22
1980	36	.238	.286	42	10	2	0	0	0.0	4	5	10	13	1	22	4	47	9	1	0	1.6	.982	C-9
1981	35	.302	.419	43	13	2	0	1	2.3	5	6	5	8	1	25	6	23	1	0	0	0.7	1.000	C-7
1982	80	.246	.373	228	56	12	1	5	2.2	26	27	41	40	4	12	4	362	35	8	4	5.1	.980	C-74
1983	110	.260	.308	250	65	12	0	0	0.0	20	21	49	42	0	14	6	360	45	12	4	3.8	.971	C-96
1984	64	.208	.264	106	22	3	0	1	0.9	5	11	23	18	1	24	6	165	20	4	2	3.0	.979	C-35
12 yrs.	666	.240	.322	1426	342	56	2	19	1.3	119	147	224	217	10	206	48	2095	211	52	20	3.5	.978	C-445

WORLD SERIES

Year Team	Games	BA	SA	AB	H	2B	3B	HR	HR%	R	RBI	BB	SO	SB	PH AB	PH H	PO	A	E	DP	TC/G	FA	G by Pos
1973 NY N	1	–	–	0	0	0	0	0	–	0	0	1	0	0	0	0	0	0	0	0	0.0	–	

Ralph Hodgin

HODGIN, ELMER RALPH
B. Feb. 10, 1916, Greensboro, N. C.

BL TR 5'10" 167 lbs.

Year Team	Games	BA	SA	AB	H	2B	3B	HR	HR%	R	RBI	BB	SO	SB	PH AB	PH H	PO	A	E	DP	TC/G	FA	G by Pos
1939 BOS N	32	.208	.229	48	10	1	0	0	0.0	4	4	3	4	1	20	4	15	0	0	0	0.5	1.000	OF-9
1943 CHI A	117	.314	.415	407	128	22	8	1	0.2	52	50	20	24	3	20	8	121	122	9	7	2.2	.964	3B-56, OF-42
1944	121	.295	.385	465	137	25	7	1	0.2	56	51	21	14	3	6	2	170	216	18	22	3.3	.955	3B-82, OF-33
1946	87	.252	.298	258	65	10	1	0	0.0	32	25	19	6	0	29	9	114	3	2	0	1.4	.983	OF-57
1947	59	.294	.400	180	53	10	3	1	0.6	26	24	13	4	1	16	1	99	2	1	0	1.7	.990	OF-41
1948	114	.266	.338	331	88	11	5	1	0.3	28	34	21	11	0	33	7	184	9	6	0	1.7	.970	OF-79
6 yrs.	530	.285	.367	1689	481	79	24	4	0.2	198	188	97	63	8	124	31	703	352	36	29	2.1	.967	OF-261, 3B-138

Paul Hodgson

HODGSON, PAUL JOSEPH DENIS
B. Apr. 14, 1960, Montreal, Que., Canada

BR TR 6'2" 190 lbs.

Year Team	Games	BA	SA	AB	H	2B	3B	HR	HR%	R	RBI	BB	SO	SB	PH AB	PH H	PO	A	E	DP	TC/G	FA	G by Pos
1980 TOR A	20	.220	.341	41	9	0	1	1	2.4	5	5	3	12	0	0	0	19	1	0	0	1.0	1.000	OF-11, DH-3

Art Hoelskoetter

HOELSKOETTER, ARTHUR H.
B. Sept. 30, 1882, St. Louis, Mo. D. Aug. 3, 1954, St. Louis, Mo.

BR TR 6'2"

Year Team	Games	BA	SA	AB	H	2B	3B	HR	HR%	R	RBI	BB	SO	SB	PH AB	PH H	PO	A	E	DP	TC/G	FA	G by Pos
1905 STL N	24	.241	.289	83	20	2	1	0	0.0	7	5	3		1	0	0	40	46	4	4	3.8	.956	3B-20, 2B-3, P-1
1906	94	.224	.262	317	71	6	3	0	0.0	21	14	4		2	0	0	109	173	19	10	3.2	.937	3B-53, SS-16, OF-12, P-12, 2B-1
1907	119	.247	.293	396	98	6	3	2	0.5	21	28	27		5	2	0	450	267	42	40	6.4	.945	2B-73, 1B-27, OF-8, C-8, 3B-2, P-2
1908	62	.232	.290	155	36	7	1	0	0.0	10	6	6		1	16	3	187	65	16	7	4.3	.940	C-41, 3B-2, 2B-1, 1B-1
4 yrs.	299	.237	.282	951	225	21	8	2	0.2	59	53	40		9	18	3	786	551	81	61	4.7	.943	2B-78, 3B-77, C-49, 1B-28, OF-20, SS-16, P-15

John Hoey

HOEY, JOHN BERNARD
B. Nov. 10, 1881, Watertown, Mass. D. Nov. 14, 1947, Waterbury, Conn.

BL TL 5'9" 185 lbs.

Year Team	Games	BA	SA	AB	H	2B	3B	HR	HR%	R	RBI	BB	SO	SB	PH AB	PH H	PO	A	E	DP	TC/G	FA	G by Pos
1906 BOS A	94	.244	.288	361	88	4	1	0	0.0	27	24	14		10	0	0	155	7	15	0	1.9	.915	OF-94
1907	39	.219	.260	96	21	2	1	0	0.0	7	8	1		2	18	8	24	0	4	0	0.7	.857	OF-21
1908	13	.163	.163	43	7	0	0	0	0.0	5	3	0		1	2	1	11	2	0	0	1.0	1.000	OF-11
3 yrs.	146	.232	.272	500	116	10	5	0	0.0	39	35	15		13	20	9	190	9	19	0	1.5	.913	OF-126

Stew Hofferth

HOFFERTH, STEWART EDWARD
B. Jan. 27, 1913, Logansport, Ind.

BR TR 6'2" 195 lbs.

Year Team	Games	BA	SA	AB	H	2B	3B	HR	HR%	R	RBI	BB	SO	SB	PH AB	PH H	PO	A	E	DP	TC/G	FA	G by Pos
1944 BOS N	66	.200	.261	180	36	8	1	1	0.6	14	26	11	5	0	16	1	158	22	3	3	2.8	.984	C-47
1945	50	.235	.300	170	40	2	0	3	1.8	13	15	14	11	1	5	1	168	31	4	7	4.1	.980	C-45
1946	20	.207	.259	58	12	1	0	0	0.0	3	10	3	6	0	5	0	66	3	0	0	3.5	1.000	C-15
3 yrs.	136	.216	.277	408	88	11	1	4	1.0	30	51	28	22	1	26	2	392	56	7	10	3.3	.985	C-107

Danny Hoffman

HOFFMAN, DANIEL JOHN
B. Mar. 12, 1880, Canaan, Conn. D. Mar. 14, 1922, Manchester, Conn.

BL TL 5'9" 175 lbs.

Year Team	Games	BA	SA	AB	H	2B	3B	HR	HR%	R	RBI	BB	SO	SB	PH AB	PH H	PO	A	E	DP	TC/G	FA	G by Pos
1903 PHI A	74	.246	.347	248	61	5	7	2	0.8	29	22	6		7	11	5	111	4	6	0	1.6	.950	OF-62, P-1
1904	53	.299	.426	204	61	7	5	3	1.5	31	24	5		9	2	0	83	5	6	1	1.8	.936	OF-51
1905	119	.262	.335	454	119	10	10	1	0.2	64	35	33		46	1	0	214	12	14	4	2.0	.942	OF-119
1906 2 teams			PHI A (7G – .227)		NY A (100G – .256)																		
" total	107	.254	.319	342	87	10	6	0	0.0	38	23	30		33	2	0	188	9	12	1	2.0	.943	OF-105
1907 NY A	136	.253	.308	517	131	10	3	4	0.8	81	46	42		30	1	0	286	20	15	4	2.4	.953	OF-135
1908 STL A	99	.251	.322	363	91	9	7	1	0.3	41	25	23		17	0	0	185	19	8	8	2.1	.962	OF-99
1909	110	.269	.336	387	104	6	7	0	0.0	44	26	41		24	0	0	230	10	8	6	2.3	.968	OF-109
1910	106	.237	.292	380	90	11	5	0	0.0	20	27	34		3	0	0	202	14	9	5	2.1	.960	OF-106
1911	24	.210	.296	81	17	3	2	0	0.0	11	7	12		3	0	0	63	6	7	1	3.2	.908	OF-23
9 yrs.	828	.256	.328	2976	761	71	52	13	0.4	359	235	226		185	17	5	1562	99	85	30	2.1	.951	OF-809, P-1

WORLD SERIES

Year Team	Games	BA	SA	AB	H	2B	3B	HR	HR%	R	RBI	BB	SO	SB	PH AB	PH H	PO	A	E	DP	TC/G	FA	G by Pos
1905 PHI A	1	.000	.000	1	0	0	0	0	0.0	0	0	1		0	1	0	0	0	0	0	0.0	–	

Dutch Hoffman

HOFFMAN, CLARENCE CASPER
B. Jan. 28, 1904, Freeburg, Ill. D. Dec. 6, 1962, Belleville, Ill.

BR TR 6' 175 lbs.

Year Team	Games	BA	SA	AB	H	2B	3B	HR	HR%	R	RBI	BB	SO	SB	PH AB	PH H	PO	A	E	DP	TC/G	FA	G by Pos
1929 CHI A	103	.258	.362	337	87	16	5	3	0.9	27	37	24	28	6	19	6	237	4	4	2	2.4	.984	OF-89

Glenn Hoffman

HOFFMAN, GLENN EDWARD
B. July 7, 1958, Orange, Calif.

BR TR 6'1" 175 lbs.

Year Team	Games	BA	SA	AB	H	2B	3B	HR	HR%	R	RBI	BB	SO	SB	PH AB	PH H	PO	A	E	DP	TC/G	FA	G by Pos
1980 BOS A	114	.285	.397	312	89	15	4	4	1.3	37	42	19	41	2	2	1	78	202	17	19	2.6	.943	3B-110, SS-5, 2B-2

Year	Team	Games	BA	SA	AB	H	2B	3B	HR	HR%	R	RBI	BB	SO	SB	Pinch Hit AB	H	PO	A	E	DP	TC/G	FA	G by Pos

Glenn Hoffman *continued*

Year	Team		Games	BA	SA	AB	H	2B	3B	HR	HR%	R	RBI	BB	SO	SB	AB	H	PO	A	E	DP	TC/G	FA	G by Pos
1981			78	.231	.285	242	56	10	0	1	0.4	28	20	12	25	0	0	0	132	234	15	62	4.9	.961	SS-78, 3B-1
1982			150	.209	.311	469	98	23	2	7	1.5	53	49	30	69	0	0	0	246	439	20	93	4.7	.972	SS-150
1983			143	.260	.340	473	123	24	1	4	0.8	56	41	30	76	1	0	0	240	417	26	82	4.8	.962	SS-143
1984			64	.189	.243	74	14	4	0	0	0.0	8	4	5	10	0	3	2	43	74	5	18	1.9	.959	SS-56, 3B-4, 2B-2
1985			96	.276	.416	279	77	17	2	6	2.2	40	34	25	40	2	0	0	157	232	11	61	4.2	.973	SS-93, 3B-3, 2B-3
1986			12	.217	.304	23	5	2	0	0	0.0	0	1	2	3	0	0	0	15	11	2	3	2.3	.929	SS-11, 3B-7
1987	2 teams	BOS A (21G – .200)				LA N (40G – .220)																			
"	total		61	.214	.257	187	40	8	0	0	0.0	15	16	10	32	0	2	0	85	152	7	28	4.0	.971	SS-56, 3B-3, 2B-2
1989	CAL A		48	.212	.269	104	22	3	0	1	1.0	9	3	3	13	0	1	0	45	75	3	12	2.6	.976	SS-23, 3B-18, 2B-4, DH-1, 1B-1
9 yrs.			766	.242	.331	2163	524	106	9	23	1.1	247	210	136	309	5	8	3	1041	1836	106	378	3.9	.964	SS-615, 3B-146, 2B-13, DH-1, 1B-1

Hickey Hoffman

HOFFMAN, OTTO CHARLES
B. Oct. 27, 1856, Cleveland, Ohio   D. Oct. 27, 1915, Peoria, Ill.

Year	Team	Games	BA	SA	AB	H	2B	3B	HR	HR%	R	RBI	BB	SO	SB	AB	H	PO	A	E	DP	TC/G	FA	G by Pos
1879	CLE N	2	.000	.000	6	0	0	0	0	0.0	0	0	0	3		0	0	9	4	2	1	7.5	.867	C-2, OF-1

Izzy Hoffman

HOFFMAN, HARRY C.
B. Jan. 5, 1875, Bridgeport, N. J.   D. Nov. 13, 1942, Philadelphia, Pa.   BL TL

Year	Team	Games	BA	SA	AB	H	2B	3B	HR	HR%	R	RBI	BB	SO	SB	AB	H	PO	A	E	DP	TC/G	FA	G by Pos
1904	WAS A	10	.100	.133	30	3	1	0	0	0.0	1	2		0	1	0	0	19	1	0	1	2.0	1.000	OF-9
1907	BOS N	19	.279	.337	86	24	3	1	0	0.0	17	3	6		2	0	0	22	4	3	1	1.5	.897	OF-19
2 yrs.		29	.233	.284	116	27	4	1	0	0.0	18	4	8		2	1	0	41	5	3	2	1.7	.939	OF-28

John Hoffman

HOFFMAN, JOHN EDWARD (Pork Chop)
B. Oct. 31, 1943, Aberdeen, S. D.   BL TR 6'   190 lbs.

Year	Team	Games	BA	SA	AB	H	2B	3B	HR	HR%	R	RBI	BB	SO	SB	AB	H	PO	A	E	DP	TC/G	FA	G by Pos
1964	HOU N	6	.067	.067	15	1	0	0	0	0.0	0	1	0	7	0	1	0	18	1	0	0	3.2	1.000	C-5
1965		2	.333	.333	6	2	0	0	0	0.0	0	1	0	3	0	0	0	8	0	0	0	4.0	1.000	C-2
2 yrs.		8	.143	.143	21	3	0	0	0	0.0	0	2	1	10	0	1	0	26	1	0	0	3.4	1.000	C-7

Larry Hoffman

HOFFMAN, LAWRENCE CHARLES
B. July 18, 1882, Chicago, Ill.   D. Dec. 29, 1948, Chicago, Ill.   BR TR

Year	Team	Games	BA	SA	AB	H	2B	3B	HR	HR%	R	RBI	BB	SO	SB	AB	H	PO	A	E	DP	TC/G	FA	G by Pos
1901	CHI N	6	.318	.364	22	7	1	0	0	0.0	2	6	0		1	0	0	6	8	3	0	2.8	.824	3B-5, 2B-1

Ray Hoffman

HOFFMAN, RAYMOND LAMONT
B. June 4, 1917, Detroit, Mich.   BL TR 6'½"   175 lbs.

Year	Team	Games	BA	SA	AB	H	2B	3B	HR	HR%	R	RBI	BB	SO	SB	AB	H	PO	A	E	DP	TC/G	FA	G by Pos
1942	WAS A	7	.053	.053	19	1	0	0	0	0.0	2	2	1	1	0	0	0	6	16	5	0	3.9	.815	3B-6

Tex Hoffman

HOFFMAN, EDWARD ADOLPH
B. Nov. 30, 1893, San Antonio, Tex.   D. May 19, 1947, New Orleans, La.   BL TR 6'1"   200 lbs.

Year	Team	Games	BA	SA	AB	H	2B	3B	HR	HR%	R	RBI	BB	SO	SB	AB	H	PO	A	E	DP	TC/G	FA	G by Pos
1915	CLE A	9	.154	.154	13	2	0	0	0	0.0	1	2	1	5	1	0	5	1	2	1	0	0.4	.750	3B-3

Jesse Hoffmeister

HOFFMEISTER, JESSE H.
B. Toledo, Ohio   Deceased.

Year	Team	Games	BA	SA	AB	H	2B	3B	HR	HR%	R	RBI	BB	SO	SB	AB	H	PO	A	E	DP	TC/G	FA	G by Pos
1897	PIT N	48	.309	.484	188	58	6	9	3	1.6	33	36	8		6	0	0	48	70	31	7	3.1	.792	3B-48

Bobby Hofman

HOFMAN, ROBERT GEORGE
B. Oct. 5, 1925, St. Louis, Mo.   BR TR 5'10"   160 lbs.

Year	Team	Games	BA	SA	AB	H	2B	3B	HR	HR%	R	RBI	BB	SO	SB	AB	H	PO	A	E	DP	TC/G	FA	G by Pos
1949	NY N	19	.208	.208	48	10	0	0	0	0.0	4	3	5	6	0	2	0	23	39	4	8	3.5	.939	2B-16
1952		32	.286	.476	63	18	2	2	3	3.2	11	4	8	10	0	7	1	41	46	5	9	2.9	.946	2B-21, 3B-2, 1B-1
1953		74	.266	.544	169	45	7	2	12	7.1	21	34	12	23	1	34	13	55	83	7	18	2.0	.952	3B-23, 2B-17
1954		71	.224	.456	125	28	5	0	8	6.4	12	30	17	15	0	36	10	192	32	4	25	3.2	.982	1B-21, 2B-10, 3B-8
1955		96	.266	.464	207	55	7	2	10	4.8	32	28	22	31	0	40	9	259	59	1	30	3.3	.997	1B-24, 2B-19, C-19, 3B-5
1956		47	.179	.196	56	10	1	0	0	0.0	1	2	6	8	0	26	5	44	12	2	1	1.2	.966	3B-7, C-7, 1B-3, 2B-2
1957		2	.000	.000	2	0	0	0	0	0.0	0	0	0	1	0	2	0	0	0	0	0	0.0	—	
7 yrs.		341	.248	.442	670	166	22	6	32	4.8	81	101	70	94	1	147	38	614	271	23	91	2.7	.975	2B-85, 1B-49, 3B-45, C-26

Solly Hofman

HOFMAN, ARTHUR FREDERICK (Circus Solly)
B. Oct. 29, 1882, St. Louis, Mo.   D. Mar. 10, 1956, St. Louis, Mo.   BR TR 6'   160 lbs.

Year	Team		Games	BA	SA	AB	H	2B	3B	HR	HR%	R	RBI	BB	SO	SB	AB	H	PO	A	E	DP	TC/G	FA	G by Pos
1903	PIT N		3	.000	.000	2	0	0	0	0	0.0	1	0	0		0	1	0	0	0	0	0	0.0	—	OF-2
1904	CHI N		7	.269	.385	26	7	0	0	1	3.8	7	4	1		2	0	0	8	4	1	1	1.9	.923	OF-6, SS-1
1905			86	.237	.324	287	68	14	4	1	0.3	43	38	20		15	1	1	248	212	23	18	5.6	.952	2B-59, SS-9, 1B-9, OF-3, 3B-3
1906			64	.256	.328	195	50	2	3	2	1.0	30	20	20		13	3	0	253	52	7	18	4.9	.978	OF-23, 1B-21, SS-9, 3B-4, 2B-4
1907			134	.268	.311	470	126	11	3	1	0.2	67	36	41		29	0	0	433	144	31	36	4.5	.949	OF-68, SS-42, 1B-18, 3B-4, 2B-3
1908			120	.243	.319	411	100	15	5	2	0.5	55	42	33		15	4	2	532	97	23	16	5.4	.965	OF-50, 1B-37, 2B-22, 3B-9
1909			153	.285	.351	527	150	21	4	2	0.4	60	58	53		20	0	0	347	16	13	5	2.5	.965	OF-153
1910			136	.325	.461	468	155	17	6	3	0.6	83	86	65	34	29	0	0	461	28	12	14	3.7	.976	OF-110, 1B-24, 3B-1
1911			143	.252	.305	512	129	17	2	2	0.4	66	70	66	40	30	0	0	583	28	14	22	4.4	.978	OF-107, 1B-36
1912	2 teams	CHI N (36G – .272)				PIT N (17G – .283)																			
"	total		53	.275	.371	178	49	15	1	0	0.0	35	20	27	19	5	2	0	183	12	3	11	3.7	.985	OF-42, 1B-9
1913	PIT N		28	.229	.337	83	19	5	2	0	0.0	11	7	8	6	3	2	1	50	3	2	1	2.0	.964	OF-24
1914	BKN F		147	.287	.412	515	148	25	12	5	1.0	65	83	54		34	0	0	443	312	32	54	5.4	.959	2B-108, 1B-22, OF-21, SS-1
1915	BUF F		109	.234	.298	346	81	10	6	0	0.0	29	27	30		12	13	5	231	29	8	7	2.5	.970	OF-82, 1B-11, 3B-4, 2B-2, SS-1

Year Team	Games	BA	SA	AB	H	2B	3B	HR	HR%	R	RBI	BB	SO	SB	Pinch Hit AB	Pinch Hit H	PO	A	E	DP	TC/G	FA	G by Pos

Solly Hofman *continued*

Year Team	Games	BA	SA	AB	H	2B	3B	HR	HR%	R	RBI	BB	SO	SB	PH AB	PH H	PO	A	E	DP	TC/G	FA	G by Pos
1916 **2 teams**		NY A (6G – .296)			CHI N (5G – .313)																		
" total	11	.302	.465	43	13	3	2	0	0.0	2	4	3	3	1	1	0	24	3	0	0	2.5	1.000	OF-10
14 yrs.	1194	.269	.352	4072	1095	162	60	19	0.5	554	495	421	102	208	29	9	3796	940	169	203	4.1	.966	OF-701, 2B-198, 1B-187, SS-63, 3B-25

WORLD SERIES

Year Team	Games	BA	SA	AB	H	2B	3B	HR	HR%	R	RBI	BB	SO	SB	PH AB	PH H	PO	A	E	DP	TC/G	FA	G by Pos
1906 CHI N	6	.304	.348	23	7	1	0	0	0.0	3	2	3	4	1	0	0	10	1	0	0	1.8	1.000	OF-6
1908	5	.316	.421	19	6	0	1	0	0.0	2	4	1	4	2	1	0	10	1	0	1	2.2	1.000	OF-5
1910	5	.267	.267	15	4	0	0	0	0.0	2	2	4	3	0	0	0	7	0	1	0	1.6	.875	OF-5
3 yrs.	16	.298	.351	57	17	1	1	0	0.0	7	8	8	11	3	1	0	27	2	1	1	1.9	.967	OF-16

Fred Hofmann

HOFMANN, FRED (Bootnose)
B. June 10, 1894, St. Louis, Mo. D. Nov. 19, 1964, St. Helena, Calif.

BR TR 5'11½" 175 lbs.

Year Team	Games	BA	SA	AB	H	2B	3B	HR	HR%	R	RBI	BB	SO	SB	PH AB	PH H	PO	A	E	DP	TC/G	FA	G by Pos
1919 NY A	1	.000	.000	1	0	0	0	0	0.0	0	0	0	0	0	1	0	1	0	0	0	2.0	1.000	C-1
1920	15	.292	.292	24	7	0	0	0	0.0	3	1	1	2	0	1	0	17	2	2	0	1.4	.905	C-14
1921	23	.177	.274	62	11	1	1	1	1.6	7	5	5	13	0	3	1	76	11	4	1	4.0	.956	C-18, 1B-1
1922	37	.297	.484	91	27	5	3	2	2.2	13	10	9	12	0	6	0	91	11	4	0	2.9	.962	C-29
1923	72	.290	.403	238	69	10	4	3	1.3	24	26	18	27	2	2	2	292	34	7	7	4.6	.979	C-70
1924	62	.175	.241	166	29	6	1	1	0.6	17	11	12	15	2	6	1	179	45	2	2	3.6	.991	C-54
1925	3	.000	.000	2	0	0	0	0	0.0	0	0	0	0	0	2	0	1	0	0	0	0.3	1.000	C-1
1927 BOS A	87	.272	.369	217	59	19	1	0	0.0	20	24	21	26	2	5	1	241	59	18	4	3.7	.943	C-81
1928	78	.226	.276	199	45	8	1	0	0.0	14	16	11	25	0	7	0	223	44	5	7	3.5	.982	C-71
9 yrs.	378	.247	.339	1000	247	49	11	7	0.7	98	93	77	120	6	32	5	1120	208	42	21	3.6	.969	C-339, 1B-1

WORLD SERIES

Year Team	Games	BA	SA	AB	H	2B	3B	HR	HR%	R	RBI	BB	SO	SB	PH AB	PH H	PO	A	E	DP	TC/G	FA	G by Pos
1923 NY A	2	.000	.000	1	0	0	0	0	0.0	0	0	1	0	0	1	0	0	0	0	0	0.0	–	

Eddie Hogan

HOGAN, ROBERT EDWARD
B. Apr., 1860, St. Louis, Mo. Deceased.

BR 5'7" 153 lbs.

Year Team	Games	BA	SA	AB	H	2B	3B	HR	HR%	R	RBI	BB	SO	SB	PH AB	PH H	PO	A	E	DP	TC/G	FA	G by Pos
1882 STL AA	1	.333	.333	3	1	0	0	0	0.0	1		0			0	0	0	1	2	0	3.0	.333	P-1
1884 MIL U	11	.081	.108	37	3	1	0	0	0.0	6		7			0	0	16	9	6	1	2.8	.806	OF-11
1887 NY AA	32	.200	.267	120	24	6	1	0	0.0	22		30		12	0	0	40	13	20	1	2.3	.726	OF-29, SS-4, 3B-1
1888 CLE AA	78	.227	.331	269	61	16	6	0	0.0	60	24	50		30	0	0	104	8	13	1	1.6	.896	OF-78
4 yrs.	122	.207	.294	429	89	23	7	0	0.0	89	24	87		42	0	0	160	31	41	3	1.9	.823	OF-118, SS-4, 3B-1, P-1

Happy Hogan

HOGAN, WILLIAM HENRY
Brother of George Hogan.
B. Sept. 14, 1884, North San Juan, Calif. D. Sept. 28, 1974, San Jose, Calif.

BR TR 5'10" 175 lbs.

Year Team	Games	BA	SA	AB	H	2B	3B	HR	HR%	R	RBI	BB	SO	SB	PH AB	PH H	PO	A	E	DP	TC/G	FA	G by Pos
1911 **2 teams**		PHI A (7G – .105)			STL A (123G – .260)																		
" total	130	.253	.340	462	117	18	8	2	0.4	54	64	43		18	1	0	315	30	25	6	2.8	.932	OF-123, 1B-5
1912 STL A	107	.214	.261	360	77	10	2	1	0.3	32	36	34		17	8	1	229	14	7	6	2.3	.972	OF-99
2 yrs.	237	.236	.305	822	194	28	10	3	0.4	86	100	77		35	9	1	544	44	32	12	2.6	.948	OF-222, 1B-5

Harry Hogan

HOGAN, HARRY S.
B. Nov. 1, 1875, Syracuse, N. Y. D. Jan. 24, 1934, Syracuse, N. Y.

Year Team	Games	BA	SA	AB	H	2B	3B	HR	HR%	R	RBI	BB	SO	SB	PH AB	PH H	PO	A	E	DP	TC/G	FA	G by Pos
1901 CLE A	1	.000	.000	4	0	0	0	0	0.0	0	0	0		0	0	0	0	0	0	0	0.0	–	OF-1

Ken Hogan

HOGAN, KENNETH TIMOTHY
B. Oct. 9, 1902, Cleveland, Ohio D. Jan. 2, 1980, Cleveland, Ohio

BL TR 5'9" 145 lbs.

Year Team	Games	BA	SA	AB	H	2B	3B	HR	HR%	R	RBI	BB	SO	SB	PH AB	PH H	PO	A	E	DP	TC/G	FA	G by Pos
1921 CIN N	1	.000	.000	2	0	0	0	0	0.0	0	0	0	0	0	0	0	0	0	0	0	0.0	–	OF-1
1923 CLE A	1	–	–	0	0	0	0	–		0	0	0	0	0	0	0	0	0	0	0	0.0	–	
1924	2	.000	.000	1	0	0	0	0	0.0	0	0	0	1	0	1	0	0	0	0	0	0.0	–	
3 yrs.	4	.000	.000	3	0	0	0	0	0.0	0	0	0	1	0	1	0	0	0	0	0	0.0	–	OF-1

Marty Hogan

HOGAN, MARTIN F.
B. Oct. 25, 1871, Wensbury, England D. Aug. 16, 1923, Youngstown, Ohio

5'8" 145 lbs.

Year Team	Games	BA	SA	AB	H	2B	3B	HR	HR%	R	RBI	BB	SO	SB	PH AB	PH H	PO	A	E	DP	TC/G	FA	G by Pos
1894 **2 teams**		CIN N (6G – .130)			STL N (29G – .280)																		
" total	35	.252	.341	123	31	3	4	0	0.0	15	16	4	17	9	0	0	52	6	8	5	1.9	.879	OF-35
1895 STL N	5	.167	.222	18	3	1	0	0	0.0	2	2	3	0	2	0	0	13	2	3	0	3.6	.833	OF-5
2 yrs.	40	.241	.326	141	34	4	4	0	0.0	17	18	7	17	11	0	0	65	8	11	5	2.1	.869	OF-40

Shanty Hogan

HOGAN, JAMES FRANCIS
B. Mar. 21, 1906, Somerville, Mass. D. Apr. 7, 1967, Boston, Mass.

BR TR 6'1" 240 lbs.

Year Team	Games	BA	SA	AB	H	2B	3B	HR	HR%	R	RBI	BB	SO	SB	PH AB	PH H	PO	A	E	DP	TC/G	FA	G by Pos
1925 BOS N	9	.286	.429	21	6	1	1	0	0.0	2	3	1	3	0	4	0	8	0	0	0	0.9	1.000	OF-5
1926	4	.286	.500	14	4	1	1	0	0.0	1	5	0	0	0	0	0	18	5	4	0	6.8	.852	C-4
1927	71	.288	.410	229	66	17	1	3	1.3	24	32	9	23	2	9	1	215	54	4	3	3.8	.985	C-61
1928 NY N	131	.333	.477	411	137	25	2	10	2.4	48	71	42	25	0	6	1	389	57	10	11	3.5	.978	C-124
1929	102	.300	.388	317	95	13	0	5	1.6	19	45	25	22	1	9	2	286	47	7	5	3.3	.979	C-93
1930	122	.339	.517	389	132	26	2	13	3.3	60	75	21	24	2	24	8	386	46	8	5	3.6	.982	C-96
1931	123	.301	.439	396	119	17	1	12	3.0	42	65	29	29	1	10	0	469	54	2	10	4.3	.996	C-113
1932	140	.287	.378	502	144	18	2	8	1.6	36	77	26	22	0	4	2	522	71	10	11	4.3	.983	C-136
1933 BOS N	96	.253	.302	328	83	7	0	3	0.9	15	30	13	9	0	1	0	280	56	1	11	3.5	.997	C-90
1934	92	.262	.337	279	73	5	2	4	1.4	20	34	16	13	0	2	0	291	53	5	8	3.8	.986	C-90
1935	59	.301	.387	163	49	8	0	2	1.2	9	25	21	8	0	3	1	175	25	2	2	3.4	.990	C-56
1936 WAS A	19	.323	.431	65	21	4	0	1	1.5	8	7	11	2	1	0	0	83	8	1	5	4.8	.989	C-19
1937	21	.152	.152	66	10	4	0	0	0.0	4	5	6	4	0	0	0	76	17	2	2	4.5	.979	C-21
13 yrs.	989	.295	.406	3180	939	146	12	61	1.9	288	474	220	188	6	72	15	3198	493	56	73	3.8	.985	C-908, OF-5

Bert Hogg

HOGG, WILBERT GEORGE (Sonny)
B. Apr. 21, 1913, Detroit, Mich. D. Nov. 5, 1973, Detroit, Mich.

BR TR 5'11½" 162 lbs.

Year Team	Games	BA	SA	AB	H	2B	3B	HR	HR%	R	RBI	BB	SO	SB	PH AB	PH H	PO	A	E	DP	TC/G	FA	G by Pos
1934 BKN N	2	.000	.000	1	0	0	0	0	0.0	0	0	0	0	0	0	0	0	0	0	0	0.0	–	3B-1

Year	Team		Games	BA	SA	AB	H	2B	3B	HR	HR%	R	RBI	BB	SO	SB	Pinch Hit AB	H	PO	A	E	DP	TC/G	FA	G by Pos

George Hogriever

HOGRIEVER, GEORGE C.
B. Mar. 17, 1869, Cincinnati, Ohio   D. Jan. 26, 1961, Appleton, Wis.
BR TR 5'8" 160 lbs.

Year	Team		Games	BA	SA	AB	H	2B	3B	HR	HR%	R	RBI	BB	SO	SB	PH AB	H	PO	A	E	DP	TC/G	FA	G by Pos
1895	CIN	N	69	.272	.389	239	65	8	7	2	0.8	61	34	36	17	41	0	0	184	12	19	3	3.1	.912	OF-66, 2B-3
1901	MIL	A	54	.235	.299	221	52	10	2	0	0.0	25	16	30		7	0	0	134	3	15	1	2.8	.901	OF-54
2 yrs.			123	.254	.346	460	117	18	9	2	0.4	86	50	66	17	48	0	0	318	15	34	4	3.0	.907	OF-120, 2B-3

Bill Hohman

HOHMAN, WILLIAM HENRY
B. Nov. 27, 1903, Brooklyn, Md.   D. Oct. 29, 1968, Baltimore, Md.
BR TR 6' 178 lbs.

Year	Team		Games	BA	SA	AB	H	2B	3B	HR	HR%	R	RBI	BB	SO	SB	PH AB	H	PO	A	E	DP	TC/G	FA	G by Pos
1927	PHI	N	7	.278	.278	18	5	0	0	0	0.0	1	0	2	3	0	0	0	10	1	1	0	1.7	.917	OF-6

Eddie Hohnhorst

HOHNHORST, EDWARD HICKS
B. Jan. 31, 1885, Ky.   D. Mar. 28, 1916, Covington, Ky.
BL TL 6'1" 175 lbs.

Year	Team		Games	BA	SA	AB	H	2B	3B	HR	HR%	R	RBI	BB	SO	SB	PH AB	H	PO	A	E	DP	TC/G	FA	G by Pos
1910	CLE	A	17	.323	.403	62	20	3	1	0	0.0	8	6	4		3	0	0	165	7	5	9	10.4	.972	1B-17
1912			14	.204	.222	54	11	1	0	0	0.0	5	2	2		5	0	0	148	8	6	9	11.6	.963	1B-14
2 yrs.			31	.267	.319	116	31	4	1	0	0.0	13	8	6		8	0	0	313	15	11	18	10.9	.968	1B-31

Chris Hoiles

HOILES, CHRISTPHER ALLEN
B. Mar. 20, 1965, Bowling Green, Ohio
BR TR 6' 195 lbs.

Year	Team		Games	BA	SA	AB	H	2B	3B	HR	HR%	R	RBI	BB	SO	SB	PH AB	H	PO	A	E	DP	TC/G	FA	G by Pos
1989	BAL	A	6	.111	.222	9	1	1	0	0	0.0	0	1	1	3	0	2	0	11	0	0	0	1.8	1.000	DH-3, C-3

Bill Holbert

HOLBERT, WILLIAM H.
B. Mar. 14, 1855, Baltimore, Md.   D. Mar. 1, 1935, Laurel, Md.
Manager 1879.
BR TR

Year	Team		Games	BA	SA	AB	H	2B	3B	HR	HR%	R	RBI	BB	SO	SB	PH AB	H	PO	A	E	DP	TC/G	FA	G by Pos
1876	LOU	N	12	.256	.256	43	11	0	0	0	0.0	3	5	0	3			0	0	62	24	16	3	8.5	.843	C-12
1878	MIL	N	45	.185	.197	173	32	2	0	0	0.0	10	12	3	14			0	0	107	47	26	2	4.0	.856	OF-30, C-21
1879	2 teams		SYR	N	(59G – .201)		TRO	N	(4G – .267)																
"	total		63	.205	.205	244	50	0	0	0	0.0	12	23	1	21			0	0	296	73	42	5	6.5	.898	C-60, OF-4
1880	TRO	N	60	.189	.222	212	40	5	1	0	0.0	18	8	9	18			0	0	268	107	37	6	6.9	.910	C-58, OF-3
1881			46	.272	.289	180	49	3	0	0	0.0	16	14	3	13			0	0	206	70	26	10	6.6	.914	C-43, OF-3
1882			71	.183	.203	251	46	5	0	0	0.0	24	23	11	22			0	0	269	152	59	14	6.8	.877	C-58, 3B-12, OF-3
1883	NY	AA	73	.237	.274	299	71	9	0	0	0.0	26		1				0	0	530	139	60	8	10.0	.918	C-68, OF-5, 2B-1
1884			65	.208	.227	255	53	5	0	0	0.0	28		7				0	0	383	147	55	7	9.0	.906	C-59, OF-5, SS-1
1885			56	.173	.188	202	35	3	0	0	0.0	13		8				0	0	256	96	44	7	7.1	.889	C-39, OF-13, 3B-5
1886			48	.205	.251	171	35	4	2	0	0.0	8		6				0	0	270	106	33	8	8.5	.919	C-45, OF-3, SS-1
1887			69	.227	.267	255	58	4	0	0	0.0	20		7		12		0	0	311	114	46	14	6.8	.902	C-60, 1B-8, SS-2, 2B-1
1888	BKN	AA	15	.120	.140	50	6	1	0	0	0.0	4	1	2		0		0	0	74	26	8	2	7.2	.926	C-15
12 yrs.			623	.208	.232	2335	486	41	7	0	0.0	182	86	58	91	12		0	0	3032	1101	452	86	7.4	.901	C-538, OF-69, 3B-17, 1B-8, SS-4, 2B-2

Sammy Holbrook

HOLBROOK, JAMES MARBURY
B. July 17, 1910, Meridian, Miss.
BR TR 5'11" 189 lbs.

Year	Team		Games	BA	SA	AB	H	2B	3B	HR	HR%	R	RBI	BB	SO	SB	PH AB	H	PO	A	E	DP	TC/G	FA	G by Pos
1935	WAS	A	52	.259	.348	135	35	2	2	2	1.5	20	25	30	16	0	6	1	145	12	8	0	3.2	.952	C-47

Bill Holden

HOLDEN, WILLIAM PAUL
B. Sept. 7, 1889, Birmingham, Ala.   D. Sept. 14, 1971, Pensacola, Fla.
BR TR 6' 170 lbs.

Year	Team		Games	BA	SA	AB	H	2B	3B	HR	HR%	R	RBI	BB	SO	SB	PH AB	H	PO	A	E	DP	TC/G	FA	G by Pos
1913	NY	A	18	.302	.396	53	16	3	1	0	0.0	6	8	8	5	0	2	1	37	5	1	0	2.4	.977	OF-16
1914	2 teams		NY	A	(50G – .182)		CIN	N	(11G – .214)																
"	total		61	.187	.223	193	36	3	2	0	0.0	14	13	19	31	2	5	0	110	4	2	0	1.9	.983	OF-55
2 yrs.			79	.211	.260	246	52	6	3	0	0.0	20	21	27	36	2	7	1	147	9	3	0	2.0	.981	OF-71

Joe Holden

HOLDEN, JOSEPH FRANCIS (Socks)
B. June 4, 1913, St. Clair, Pa.
BL TR 5'8" 175 lbs.

Year	Team		Games	BA	SA	AB	H	2B	3B	HR	HR%	R	RBI	BB	SO	SB	PH AB	H	PO	A	E	DP	TC/G	FA	G by Pos
1934	PHI	N	10	.071	.071	14	1	0	0	0	0.0	1	0	0	2	0	4	0	15	4	0	0	1.9	1.000	C-6
1935			6	.111	.111	9	1	0	0	0	0.0	0	0	0	3	1	2	0	6	0	0	0	1.0	1.000	C-4
1936			1	.000	.000	1	0	0	0	0	0.0	0	0	0	0	0	1	0	0	0	0	0	0.0	–	
3 yrs.			17	.083	.083	24	2	0	0	0	0.0	1	0	0	5	1	7	0	21	4	0	0	1.5	1.000	C-10

Jim Holdsworth

HOLDSWORTH, JAMES (Long Jim)
B. July 14, 1850, New York, N. Y.   D. Mar. 22, 1918, New York, N. Y.
BR TR

Year	Team		Games	BA	SA	AB	H	2B	3B	HR	HR%	R	RBI	BB	SO	SB	PH AB	H	PO	A	E	DP	TC/G	FA	G by Pos
1876	NY	N	52	.266	.295	241	64	3	2	0	0.0	23	19	1	2			0	0	119	14	15	2	2.8	.899	OF-49, 2B-3
1877	HAR	N	55	.254	.288	260	66	5	2	0	0.0	26	20	2	8			0	0	79	11	18	1	2.0	.833	OF-55
1882	TRO	N	1	.000	.000	3	0	0	0	0	0.0	0	0	0	1			0	0	1	0	0	0	2.0	1.000	OF-1
1884	IND	AA	5	.111	.111	18	2	0	0	0	0.0	1		2				0	0	12	1	1	1	2.8	.929	OF-5
4 yrs.			113	.253	.284	522	132	8	4	0	0.0	50	39	5	11			0	0	211	27	34	4	2.4	.875	OF-110, 2B-3

Walter Holke

HOLKE, WALTER HENRY (Union Man)
B. Dec. 25, 1892, St. Louis, Mo.   D. Oct. 12, 1954, St. Louis, Mo.
BB TL 6'1½" 185 lbs.

Year	Team		Games	BA	SA	AB	H	2B	3B	HR	HR%	R	RBI	BB	SO	SB	PH AB	H	PO	A	E	DP	TC/G	FA	G by Pos
1914	NY	N	2	.333	.333	6	2	0	0	0	0.0	0	0	0	0	0	0	0	17	2	1	1	10.0	.950	1B-2
1916			34	.351	.423	111	39	4	2	0	0.0	16	13	6	16	10	0	0	331	13	1	15	10.1	.997	1B-34
1917			153	.277	.338	527	146	12	7	2	0.4	55	55	34	54	13	0	0	1635	70	19	104	11.3	.989	1B-153
1918			88	.252	.337	326	82	17	4	0	0.3	38	27	10	26	10	0	0	938	68	10	50	11.5	.990	1B-88
1919	BOS	N	137	.292	.342	518	151	14	6	0	0.0	48	48	21	25	19	1	0	1474	95	11	86	11.5	.993	1B-136
1920			144	.294	.377	551	162	15	11	3	0.5	53	64	28	31	4	1	1	1528	81	14	97	11.3	.991	1B-143
1921			150	.261	.337	579	151	15	10	3	0.5	60	63	17	41	6	0	0	1471	86	4	100	10.4	.997	1B-150
1922			105	.291	.334	395	115	4	4	0	0.0	35	46	14	23	6	0	0	1017	44	8	65	11.3	.993	1B-105
1923	PHI	N	147	.311	.418	562	175	31	4	7	1.2	64	70	16	37	7	1	1	1425	69	13	136	10.3	.991	1B-146, P-1
1924			148	.300	.394	563	169	23	6	6	1.1	60	64	25	33	3	0	0	1516	90	12	134	10.9	.993	1B-148
1925	2 teams		PHI	N	(39G – .244)		CIN	N	(65G – .280)																
"	total		104	.270	.355	318	86	13	4	2	0.6	35	37	20	18	1	15	4	806	47	3	76	8.2	.996	1B-88
11 yrs.			1212	.287	.363	4456	1278	153	58	24	0.5	464	487	191	304	81	18	6	12158	665	96	864	10.7	.993	1B-1193, P-1

Year Team	Games	BA	SA	AB	H	2B	3B	HR	HR%	R	RBI	BB	SO	SB	Pinch Hit AB	Pinch Hit H	PO	A	E	DP	TC/G	FA	G by Pos

Walter Holke *continued*

WORLD SERIES

| 1917 NY N | 6 | .286 | .381 | 21 | 6 | 2 | 0 | 0 | 0.0 | 2 | 1 | 0 | 6 | 0 | 0 | 0 | 66 | 0 | 1 | 1 | 11.2 | .985 | 1B-6 |

Bill Hollahan

HOLLAHAN, WILLIAM JAMES (Happy)
B. Nov. 22, 1896, New York, N. Y. D. Nov. 27, 1965, New York, N. Y.   BR TR 5'9" 165 lbs.

| 1920 WAS A | 3 | .250 | .250 | 4 | 1 | 0 | 0 | 0 | 0.0 | 0 | 1 | 1 | 2 | 1 | 0 | 0 | 5 | 2 | 0 | 0 | 2.3 | 1.000 | 3B-3 |

Dutch Holland

HOLLAND, ROBERT CLYDE
B. Oct. 12, 1903, Middlesex, N. C. D. June 16, 1967, Lumberton, N. C.   BR TR 6'1" 190 lbs.

1932 BOS N	39	.295	.397	156	46	11	1	1	0.6	15	18	12	20	0	0	0	94	3	1	0	2.5	.990	OF-39
1933	13	.258	.355	31	8	3	0	0	0.0	3	3	3	8	1	6	1	13	0	2	0	1.2	.867	OF-7
1934 CLE A	50	.250	.406	128	32	12	1	2	1.6	19	13	13	11	0	16	2	44	1	2	0	0.9	.957	OF-31
3 yrs.	102	.273	.397	315	86	26	2	3	1.0	37	34	28	39	1	22	3	151	4	5	0	1.6	.969	OF-77

Will Holland

HOLLAND, WILLARD A.
B. Fort Wayne, Ind.   5'10" 180 lbs.

| 1889 BAL AA | 40 | .189 | .224 | 143 | 27 | 1 | 2 | 0 | 0.0 | 13 | 16 | 9 | 28 | 4 | 0 | 0 | 38 | 102 | 24 | 9 | 4.1 | .854 | SS-39, OF-1 |

Gary Holle

HOLLE, GARY CHARLES
B. Aug. 11, 1954, Albany, N. Y.   BR TL 6'6" 210 lbs.

| 1979 TEX A | 5 | .167 | .333 | 6 | 1 | 0 | 0 | 0 | 0.0 | 0 | 1 | 0 | 0 | 0 | 4 | 1 | 11 | 0 | 0 | 1 | 2.2 | 1.000 | 1B-1 |

Bug Holliday

HOLLIDAY, JAMES WEAR
B. Feb. 8, 1867, St. Louis, Mo. D. Feb. 15, 1910, Cincinnati, Ohio   BR TR 5'11" 151 lbs.

1889 CIN AA	135	.343	.519	563	193	28	7	19	3.4	107	104	43	59	46	0	0	234	29	22	6	2.1	.923	OF-135
1890 CIN N	131	.270	.382	518	140	18	14	4	0.8	93	75	49	36	50	0	0	253	20	15	5	2.2	.948	OF-131
1891	111	.319	.473	442	141	21	10	9	2.0	74	84	37	28	30	0	0	186	13	13	3	1.9	.939	OF-111
1892	152	.292	.449	602	176	23	16	13	2.2	114	91	57	39	43	0	0	271	21	21	6	2.1	.933	OF-152, P-1
1893	126	.310	.428	500	155	24	10	5	1.0	108	89	73	22	32	0	0	285	14	17	5	2.5	.946	OF-125, 1B-1
1894	122	.383	.536	519	199	24	8	13	2.5	125	119	40	20	29	1	0	251	22	26	5	2.5	.913	OF-119, 1B-1
1895	32	.299	.402	127	38	9	2	0	0.0	25	20	10	3	6	0	0	60	3	4	1	2.1	.940	OF-32
1896	29	.321	.369	84	27	4	0	0	0.0	17	8	9	4	1	6	3	64	6	6	2	2.6	.921	OF-16, 1B-5, SS-1, P-1
1897	61	.313	.431	195	61	9	4	2	1.0	50	20	27		6	8	3	108	22	9	2	2.3	.935	OF-42, SS-4, 2B-3, 1B-3
1898	30	.236	.274	106	25	2	1	0	0.0	21	7	14		5	1	0	61	1	2	1	2.1	.969	OF-28
10 yrs.	929	.316	.453	3656	1155	162	72	65	1.8	734	617	359	211	248	16	6	1773	151	135	36	2.2	.934	OF-891, 1B-10, SS-5, 2B-3, P-2

Stan Hollmig

HOLLMIG, STANLEY ERNEST (Hondo)
B. Jan. 2, 1926, Fredericksburg, Tex. D. Dec. 4, 1981, San Antonio, Tex.   BR TR 6'2½" 190 lbs.

1949 PHI N	81	.255	.371	251	64	11	6	2	0.8	28	26	20	43	1	14	3	108	5	5	1	1.5	.958	OF-66
1950	11	.250	.417	12	3	1	0	0	0.0	1	1	0	3	0	8	2	3	0	0	0	0.3	1.000	OF-3
1951	2	.000	.000	2	0	0	0	0	0.0	0	0	0	0	0	2	0	0	0	0	0	0.0	—	
3 yrs.	94	.253	.370	265	67	13	6	2	0.8	29	27	20	46	1	24	5	111	5	5	1	1.3	.959	OF-69

Charlie Hollocher

HOLLOCHER, CHARLES JACOB
B. June 11, 1896, St. Louis, Mo. D. Aug. 14, 1940, Frontenac, Mo.   BL TR 5'7½" 158 lbs.

1918 CHI N	131	.316	.397	509	161	23	6	2	0.4	72	38	47	30	26	0	0	278	418	53	39	5.7	.929	SS-131
1919	115	.270	.347	430	116	14	5	3	0.7	51	26	44	19	16	0	0	219	418	40	49	5.9	.941	SS-115
1920	80	.319	.389	301	96	17	2	0	0.0	53	22	41	15	20	0	0	196	280	23	34	6.2	.954	SS-80
1921	140	.289	.384	558	161	28	8	3	0.5	71	37	43	13	5	3	1	282	491	30	72	5.7	.963	SS-137
1922	152	.340	.444	592	201	37	8	3	0.5	90	69	58	5	19	0	0	332	502	30	89	5.7	.965	SS-152
1923	66	.342	.423	260	89	14	2	1	0.4	46	28	26	5	9	1	0	124	212	13	35	5.3	.963	SS-65
1924	76	.245	.336	286	70	12	4	2	0.7	28	21	18	7	4	5	1	156	248	13	42	5.5	.969	SS-71
7 yrs.	760	.304	.392	2936	894	145	35	14	0.5	411	241	277	94	99	9	2	1587	2569	202	360	5.7	.954	SS-751

WORLD SERIES

| 1918 CHI N | 6 | .190 | .286 | 21 | 4 | 0 | 1 | 0 | 0.0 | 2 | 0 | 1 | 1 | 2 | 0 | 0 | 12 | 17 | 1 | 6 | 5.0 | .967 | SS-6 |

Ed Holly

HOLLY, EDWARD WILLIAM
Born Edward William Ruthlavy.
B. July 6, 1879, Chicago, Ill. D. Nov. 27, 1973, Williamsport, Pa.   BR TR 5'10" 165 lbs.

1906 STL N	10	.059	.059	34	2	0	0	0	0.0	1	7	5		0	0	0	24	22	3	7	4.9	.939	SS-10
1907	149	.230	.279	544	125	18	3	1	0.2	55	40	36		16	0	0	326	480	64	45	5.8	.926	SS-147, 2B-3
1914 PIT F	100	.246	.294	350	86	9	4	0	0.0	28	26	17		14	3	2	241	267	31	31	5.4	.942	SS-94, OF-2, 2B-1
1915	16	.262	.310	42	11	2	0	0	0.0	8	5	5		3	1	1	24	26	7	4	3.6	.877	SS-11, 3B-3
4 yrs.	275	.231	.278	970	224	29	7	1	0.1	92	78	63		33	4	3	615	795	105	87	5.5	.931	SS-262, 2B-4, 3B-3, OF-2

Billy Holm

HOLM, WILLIAM FREDERICK
B. July 21, 1912, Chicago, Ill. D. July 27, 1977, East Chicago, Ind.   BR TR 5'10½" 168 lbs.

1943 CHI N	7	.067	.067	15	1	0	0	0	0.0	0	0	2	4	0	0	0	21	4	0	0	3.6	1.000	C-7
1944	54	.136	.152	132	18	2	0	0	0.0	10	6	16	19	1	3	0	166	18	4	2	3.5	.979	C-50
1945 BOS A	58	.185	.215	135	25	2	1	0	0.0	12	9	23	17	1	1	0	170	30	4	3	3.5	.980	C-57
3 yrs.	119	.156	.177	282	44	4	1	0	0.0	22	15	41	40	2	4	0	357	52	8	5	3.5	.981	C-114

Wattie Holm

HOLM, ROSCOE ALBERT
B. Dec. 28, 1901, Peterson, Iowa D. May 19, 1950, Everly, Iowa   BR TR 5'9½" 160 lbs.

1924 STL N	81	.294	.355	293	86	10	4	0	0.0	40	23	8	16	1	5	1	178	12	4	2	2.4	.979	OF-64, C-9, 3B-4
1925	13	.207	.259	58	12	1	0	0	0.0	10	2	3	1	1	0	0	40	1	1	1	3.2	.976	OF-13
1926	55	.285	.333	144	41	5	1	0	0.0	18	21	18	14	3	15	5	75	1	3	1	1.4	.962	OF-39

Year	Team	Games	BA	SA	AB	H	2B	3B	HR	HR%	R	RBI	BB	SO	SB	Pinch Hit AB	Pinch Hit H	PO	A	E	DP	TC/G	FA	G by Pos

Wattie Holm *continued*

Year	Team	Games	BA	SA	AB	H	2B	3B	HR	HR%	R	RBI	BB	SO	SB	PH AB	PH H	PO	A	E	DP	TC/G	FA	G by Pos
1927		110	.286	.411	419	120	27	8	3	0.7	55	66	24	29	4	4	2	205	25	7	2	2.2	.970	OF-97, 3B-9
1928		102	.277	.394	386	107	24	6	3	0.8	61	47	32	17	1	9	4	118	145	22	9	2.8	.923	3B-83, OF-7
1929		64	.233	.330	176	41	5	6	0	0.0	21	14	12	8	1	17	3	116	4	7	2	2.0	.945	OF-44, 3B-1
1932		11	.176	.235	17	3	1	0	0	0.0	2	1	3	1	0	5	1	9	0	0	0	0.8	1.000	OF-4
7 yrs.		436	.275	.370	1493	410	73	26	6	0.4	207	174	100	86	11	55	16	741	188	44	17	2.2	.955	OF-268, 3B-97, C-9

WORLD SERIES

Year	Team	Games	BA	SA	AB	H	2B	3B	HR	HR%	R	RBI	BB	SO	SB	PH AB	PH H	PO	A	E	DP	TC/G	FA	G by Pos
1926	STL N	5	.125	.125	16	2	0	0	0	0.0	1	1	1	2	0	1	0	7	0	0	0	1.4	1.000	OF-4
1928		3	.167	.167	6	1	0	0	0	0.0	0	1	0	1	0	2	0	4	0	0	0	1.3	1.000	OF-1
2 yrs.		8	.136	.136	22	3	0	0	0	0.0	1	2	1	3	0	3	0	11	0	0	0	1.4	1.000	OF-5

Gary Holman

HOLMAN, GARY RICHARD
B. Jan. 25, 1944, Long Beach, Calif.   BL TL 6'1"   200 lbs.

Year	Team	Games	BA	SA	AB	H	2B	3B	HR	HR%	R	RBI	BB	SO	SB	PH AB	PH H	PO	A	E	DP	TC/G	FA	G by Pos
1968	WAS A	75	.294	.376	85	25	5	1	0	0.0	10	7	13	15	0	32	11	75	9	1	3	1.1	.988	1B-33, OF-10
1969		41	.161	.194	31	5	1	0	0	0.0	1	2	4	7	0	26	5	15	0	0	1	0.4	1.000	1B-11, OF-3
2 yrs.		116	.259	.328	116	30	6	1	0	0.0	11	9	17	22	0	58	16	90	9	1	4	0.9	.990	1B-44, OF-13

Ducky Holmes

HOLMES, HOWARD ELBERT
B. July 8, 1883, Dayton, Ohio   D. Sept. 18, 1945, Dayton, Ohio   BR TR 5'10"   160 lbs.

Year	Team	Games	BA	SA	AB	H	2B	3B	HR	HR%	R	RBI	BB	SO	SB	PH AB	PH H	PO	A	E	DP	TC/G	FA	G by Pos
1906	STL N	9	.185	.185	27	5	0	0	0	0.0	2	2	2		0	0	0	37	9	1	2	5.2	.979	C-9

Ducky Holmes

HOLMES, JAMES WILLIAM
B. Jan. 28, 1869, Des Moines, Iowa   D. Aug. 6, 1932, Truro, Iowa   BL TR 5'6"   170 lbs.

Year	Team	Games	BA	SA	AB	H	2B	3B	HR	HR%	R	RBI	BB	SO	SB	PH AB	PH H	PO	A	E	DP	TC/G	FA	G by Pos
1895	LOU N	40	.373	.516	161	60	10	2	3	1.9	33	20	12	9	9	0	0	49	32	21	2	2.6	.794	OF-29, SS-8, 3B-4, P-2
1896		47	.270	.319	141	38	3	2	0	0.0	22	18	13	5	8	**10**	3	44	14	19	3	1.6	.753	OF-33, P-2, SS-1, 2B-1
1897	2 teams				LOU N (2G – .000)				NY N (79G – .268)															
"	total	81	.265	.339	310	82	8	6	1	0.3	51	44	19		30	2	0	117	19	16	4	1.9	.895	OF-77, SS-2
1898	2 teams				STL N (23G – .238)				BAL N (113G – .285)															
"	total	136	.276	.339	510	141	11	10	1	0.2	63	64	25		29	1	1	286	19	23	7	2.4	.930	OF-135
1899	BAL N	138	.320	.423	553	177	31	7	4	0.7	80	66	39	·50	0	0	321	24	27	5	2.7	.927	OF-138
1901	DET A	131	.294	.406	537	158	28	10	4	0.7	90	62	37		35	0	0	217	18	24	5	2.0	.907	OF-131
1902		92	.257	.337	362	93	15	4	2	0.6	50	33	28		16	0	0	155	16	9	5	2.0	.950	OF-92
1903	2 teams				WAS A (21G – .225)				CHI A (86G – .279)															
"	total	107	.270	.330	415	112	10	6	1	0.2	66	26	30		35	3	0	188	34	14	0	2.2	.941	OF-96, 3B-7, 2B-2
1904	CHI A	68	.311	.438	251	78	11	9	1	0.4	42	19	14		13	5	**2**	111	8	3	3	1.8	.975	OF-63
1905		92	.201	.259	328	66	15	2	0	0.0	42	22	19		11	3	**2**	150	11	11	1	1.9	.936	OF-89
10 yrs.		932	.282	.367	3601	1014	142	58	17	0.5	539	374	236	14	236	24	8	1638	195	167	35	2.1	.917	OF-883, SS-11, 3B-11, P-4, 2B-3

Fred Holmes

HOLMES, FREDERICK C.
B. July 1, 1878, Chicago, Ill.   D. Feb. 13, 1956, Norwood Park, Ill.   BR TR

Year	Team	Games	BA	SA	AB	H	2B	3B	HR	HR%	R	RBI	BB	SO	SB	PH AB	PH H	PO	A	E	DP	TC/G	FA	G by Pos
1903	NY A	1	–	–	0	0	0	0	0		0	0	1	0	0	0	0	5	0	1	0	6.0	.833	1B-1
1904	CHI N	1	.333	.667	3	1	1	0	0	0.0	1	0	0	0	0	0	0	4	1	0	0	5.0	1.000	C-1
2 yrs.		2	.333	.667	3	1	1	0	0	0.0	1	0	1	0	0	0	0	9	1	1	0	5.5	.909	1B-1, C-1

Tommy Holmes

HOLMES, THOMAS FRANCIS (Kelly)
B. Mar. 29, 1917, Brooklyn, N. Y.   BL TL 5'10"   180 lbs.
Manager 1951-52.

Year	Team	Games	BA	SA	AB	H	2B	3B	HR	HR%	R	RBI	BB	SO	SB	PH AB	PH H	PO	A	E	DP	TC/G	FA	G by Pos
1942	BOS N	141	.278	.357	558	155	24	4	4	0.7	56	41	64	10	2	0	0	373	16	4	4	2.8	.990	OF-140
1943		152	.270	.378	**629**	170	33	10	5	0.8	75	41	58	20	7	0	0	408	18	3	3	2.8	.993	OF-152
1944		155	.309	.456	631	195	42	6	13	2.1	93	73	61	11	4	0	0	426	14	4	7	2.9	.991	OF-155
1945		154	.352	**.577**	636	**224**	**47**	6	**28**	4.4	125	117	70	9	15	0	0	334	13	6	4	2.3	.983	OF-154
1946		149	.310	.424	568	176	35	6	6	1.1	80	79	58	14	7	2	1	294	17	4	7	2.1	.987	OF-146
1947		150	.309	.416	618	**191**	33	3	9	1.5	90	53	44	16	3	1	0	336	12	4	4	2.3	.989	OF-147
1948		139	.325	.439	585	190	35	7	6	1.0	85	61	46	20	1	2	1	283	8	3	3	2.1	.983	OF-137
1949		117	.266	.403	380	101	20	4	8	2.1	47	59	39	6	1	12	4	210	10	3	4	1.9	.987	OF-103
1950		105	.298	.450	322	96	20	1	9	2.8	44	51	33	6	0	15	4	151	6	0	0	1.5	1.000	OF-88
1951		27	.172	.241	29	5	2	0	0	0.0	4	5	4	4	0	22	3	2	0	0	0	0.1	1.000	OF-3
1952	BKN N	31	.111	.139	36	4	1	0	0	0.0	2	1	4	4	0	23	0	6	1	0	0	0.2	1.000	OF-6
11 yrs.		1320	.302	.432	4992	1507	292	47	88	1.8	698	581	480	122	40	77	15	2823	115	33	37	2.3	.989	OF-1231

WORLD SERIES

Year	Team	Games	BA	SA	AB	H	2B	3B	HR	HR%	R	RBI	BB	SO	SB	PH AB	PH H	PO	A	E	DP	TC/G	FA	G by Pos
1948	BOS N	6	.192	.192	26	5	0	0	0	0.0	3	1	0	0	0	0	0	10	2	0	1	2.0	1.000	OF-6
1952	BKN N	3	.000	.000	1	0	0	0	0	0.0	0	0	0	0	0	0	0	2	0	0	0	0.7	1.000	OF-3
2 yrs.		9	.185	.185	27	5	0	0	0	0.0	3	1	0	0	0	0	0	12	2	0	1	1.6	1.000	OF-9

Jim Holt

HOLT, JAMES WILLIAM
B. May 27, 1944, Graham, N. C.   BL TR 6'   180 lbs.

Year	Team	Games	BA	SA	AB	H	2B	3B	HR	HR%	R	RBI	BB	SO	SB	PH AB	PH H	PO	A	E	DP	TC/G	FA	G by Pos
1968	MIN A	70	.208	.245	106	22	4	0	0	0.0	9	8	4	20	0	26	4	35	2	1	1	0.5	.974	OF-38, 1B-1
1969		12	.357	.571	14	5	0	0	1	7.1	3	2	0	4	0	7	4	4	0	0	1	0.3	1.000	OF-5, 1B-1
1970		142	.266	.342	319	85	9	3	3	0.9	37	40	17	32	3	14	3	208	7	1	4	1.5	.995	OF-130, 1B-2
1971		126	.259	.318	340	88	11	3	1	0.3	35	29	16	28	5	13	4	219	4	3	3	1.8	.987	OF-106, 1B-3
1972		10	.444	.593	27	12	1	0	1	3.7	6	6	0	4	0	4	1	16	2	1	0	1.9	.947	OF-7, 1B-1
1973		132	.297	.442	441	131	26	3	11	2.5	52	58	29	43	0	11	5	415	26	2	15	3.4	.995	OF-102, 1B-33
1974	2 teams				MIN A (79G – .254)				OAK A (30G – .143)															
"	total	109	.234	.280	239	56	11	0	0	0.0	25	16	15	25	0	24	0	504	49	2	62	5.1	.996	1B-84, OF-5, DH-3
1975	OAK A	102	.220	.293	123	27	3	0	2	1.6	7	16	11	11	0	**43**	**10**	192	18	2	19	2.1	.991	1B-52, DH-4, OF-2, C-1
1976		4	.286	.571	7	2	2	0	0	0.0	0	2	1	2	0	0	0	0	0	0	0	0.0		DH-2
9 yrs.		707	.265	.352	1616	428	64	10	19	1.2	174	177	93	166	8	144	32	1593	103	12	101	2.4	.993	OF-395, 1B-177, DH-9, C-1

LEAGUE CHAMPIONSHIP SERIES

Year	Team	Games	BA	SA	AB	H	2B	3B	HR	HR%	R	RBI	BB	SO	SB	PH AB	PH H	PO	A	E	DP	TC/G	FA	G by Pos
1970	MIN A	3	.000	.000	5	0	0	0	0	0.0	0	0	0	2	0	1	0	3	0	1	0	1.3	.750	OF-3
1974	OAK A	2	–	–	0	0	0	0	0		0	0	0	0	0	0	0	1	0	0	0	0.5	1.000	1B-1

Year	Team		Games	BA	SA	AB	H	2B	3B	HR	HR%	R	RBI	BB	SO	SB	Pinch Hit AB	H	PO	A	E	DP	TC/G	FA	G by Pos

Jim Holt *continued*

Year	Team		Games	BA	SA	AB	H	2B	3B	HR	HR%	R	RBI	BB	SO	SB	AB	H	PO	A	E	DP	TC/G	FA	G by Pos
1975			3	.333	.667	3	1	1	0	0	0.0	0	0	0	0	0	2	1	1	2	0	0	1.0	1.000	1B-1
3 yrs.			8	.125	.250	8	1	1	0	0	0.0	0	0	1	2	0	3	1	5	2	1	0	1.0	.875	OF-3, 1B-2

WORLD SERIES

| 1974 | OAK | A | 4 | .667 | .667 | 3 | 2 | 0 | 0 | 0 | 0.0 | 0 | 2 | 0 | 0 | 0 | 3 | 2 | 1 | 0 | 0 | 1 | 0.3 | 1.000 | 1B-1 |

Red Holt

HOLT, JAMES EMMETT MADISON
B. July 25, 1894, Dayton, Tenn. D. Feb. 2, 1961, Birmingham, Ala. BB TL 5'11" 175 lbs.

| 1925 | PHI | A | 27 | .273 | .386 | 88 | 24 | 7 | 0 | 1 | 1.1 | 13 | 8 | 12 | 9 | 0 | 1 | 0 | 268 | 17 | 4 | 21 | 10.7 | .986 | 1B-25 |

Roger Holt

HOLT, ROGER BOYD
B. Apr. 8, 1956, Daytona Beach, Fla. BB TR 5'11" 165 lbs.

| 1980 | NY | A | 2 | .167 | .167 | 6 | 1 | 0 | 0 | 0 | 0.0 | 0 | 1 | 1 | 2 | 0 | 0 | 0 | 3 | 9 | 0 | 0 | 6.0 | 1.000 | 2B-2 |

Marty Honan

HONAN, MARTIN WELDON
B. 1870, Chicago, Ill. D. Aug. 20, 1908, Chicago, Ill.

1890	CHI	N	1	.000	.000	3	0	0	0	0	0.0	0	1	0	0	0	0	0	6	0	1	0	7.0	.857	C-1
1891			5	.167	.333	12	2	0	1	0	0.0	1	3	1	5	0	0	0	18	8	1	0	5.4	.963	C-5
2 yrs.			6	.133	.267	15	2	0	1	0	0.0	1	4	1	5	0	0	0	24	8	2	0	5.7	.941	C-6

Abie Hood

HOOD, ALBIE LARRISON
B. Jan. 31, 1903, Sanford, N. C. D. Oct. 14, 1989, Chesapeake, Va. BL TR 5'7" 152 lbs.

| 1925 | BOS | N | 5 | .286 | .524 | 21 | 6 | 2 | 0 | 1 | 4.8 | 2 | 2 | 1 | 0 | 0 | 0 | 0 | 12 | 11 | 2 | 0 | 5.0 | .920 | 2B-5 |

Wally Hood

HOOD, WALLACE JAMES, SR.
Father of Wally Hood.
B. Feb. 9, 1895, Whittier, Calif. D. May 2, 1965, Hollywood, Calif. BR TR 5'11½" 160 lbs.

1920	2 teams		BKN N (7G – .143)			PIT N (2G – .000)																			
"	total		9	.133	.200	15	2	1	0	0	0.0	5	1	5	4	3	1	0	16	1	1	0	2.0	.944	OF-5
1921	BKN	N	56	.262	.385	65	17	1	2	1	1.5	16	4	9	14	2	20	4	22	0	1	0	0.4	.957	OF-20
1922			2	–	–	0	0	0	0	0	0.0	0	0	0	2	0	0	0	0	0	0	0	0.0		
3 yrs.			67	.238	.350	80	19	2	2	1	1.3	23	5	14	18	5	21	4	38	1	2	0	0.6	.951	OF-25

Alex Hooks

HOOKS, ALEXANDER MARCUS
B. Aug. 29, 1906, Edgewood, Tex. BL TL 6'1" 183 lbs.

| 1935 | PHI | A | 15 | .227 | .295 | 44 | 10 | 3 | 0 | 0 | 0.0 | 4 | 4 | 3 | 10 | 0 | 4 | 1 | 85 | 5 | 0 | 11 | 6.0 | 1.000 | 1B-10 |

Harry Hooper

HOOPER, HARRY BARTHOLOMEW
B. Aug. 24, 1887, Bell Station, Calif. D. Dec. 18, 1974, Santa Cruz, Calif. BL TR 5'10" 168 lbs.
Hall of Fame 1971.

1909	BOS	A	81	.282	.325	255	72	3	4	0	0.0	29	12	16		15	4	2	124	14	7	3	1.8	.952	OF-74
1910			155	.267	.329	584	156	9	10	2	0.3	81	27	62		40	0	0	241	30	18	7	1.9	.938	OF-155
1911			130	.311	.395	524	163	20	6	4	0.8	93	45	73		38	0	0	181	27	10	1	1.7	.954	OF-130
1912			147	.242	.327	590	143	20	12	2	0.3	98	53	66		29	0	0	220	22	9	6	1.7	.964	OF-147
1913			148	.288	.399	586	169	29	12	4	0.7	100	40	60	51	26	1	0	248	25	9	7	1.9	.968	OF-147, P-1
1914			141	.258	.364	530	137	23	15	1	0.2	85	41	58	47	19	1	0	231	23	7	5	1.9	.973	OF-140
1915			149	.235	.327	566	133	20	13	2	0.4	90	51	89	36	22	0	0	255	23	8	7	1.9	.972	OF-147
1916			151	.271	.350	575	156	20	11	1	0.2	75	37	80	35	27	0	0	266	19	10	5	2.0	.966	OF-151
1917			151	.256	.349	559	143	21	11	3	0.5	89	45	80	40	21	0	0	245	20	8	3	1.8	.971	OF-151
1918			126	.289	.405	474	137	26	13	1	0.2	81	44	75	25	24	0	0	221	16	9	8	2.0	.963	OF-126
1919			128	.267	.360	491	131	25	6	3	0.6	76	49	79	28	23	0	0	262	19	6	2	2.2	.979	OF-128
1920			139	.312	.470	536	167	30	17	7	1.3	91	53	88	27	16	0	0	263	22	11	2	2.1	.963	OF-139
1921	CHI	A	108	.327	.470	419	137	26	5	8	1.9	74	58	55	21	13	0	0	182	12	5	3	1.8	.975	OF-108
1922			152	.304	.444	602	183	35	8	11	1.8	111	80	68	33	16	3	0	288	19	12	7	2.1	.962	OF-149
1923			145	.288	.410	576	166	32	4	10	1.7	87	65	68	22	18	2	1	272	15	13	3	2.1	.960	OF-143
1924			130	.328	.481	476	156	27	8	10	2.1	107	62	65	26	16	5	2	251	22	4	8	2.1	.986	OF-123
1925			127	.265	.380	442	117	23	5	6	1.4	62	55	54	21	12	2	0	231	16	6	4	2.0	.976	OF-124
17 yrs.			2308	.281	.387	8785	2466	389	160	75	0.9	1429	817	1136	412	375	18	5	3981	344	151	81	1.9	.966	OF-2282, P-1

WORLD SERIES

1912	BOS	A	8	.290	.419	31	9	2	1	0	0.0	3	2	4	4	2	0	0	16	3	0	1	2.4	1.000	OF-8
1915			5	.350	.650	20	7	0	0	2	10.0	4	3	2	4	0	0	0	8	0	1	0	1.8	.889	OF-5
1916			5	.333	.476	21	7	1	1	0	0.0	6	1	3	1	1	0	0	8	2	0	1	2.0	1.000	OF-5
1918			6	.200	.200	20	4	0	0	0	0.0	0	0	2	2	0	0	0	11	0	0	0	1.8	1.000	OF-6
4 yrs.			24	.293	.435	92	27	3	2	2	2.2	13	6	11	11	3	0	0	43	5	1	2	2.0	.980	OF-24

Buster Hoover

HOOVER, WILLIAM J.
B. 1863, Philadelphia, Pa. Deceased. BR TR 6'1" 178 lbs.

1884	2 teams		PHI U (63G – .364)			PHI N (10G – .190)																			
"	total		73	.341	.467	317	108	21	8	1	0.3	82		16	9		0	0	147	77	50	11	3.8	.818	OF-47, SS-15, 2B-6, 1B-6, 3B-1
1886	BAL	AA	40	.217	.306	157	34	2	6	0	0.0	25		16			0	0	70	3	14	0	2.2	.839	OF-40
1892	CIN	N	14	.176	.176	51	9	0	0	0	0.0	7	2	5	4	1	0	0	25	3	1	2	2.1	.966	OF-14
3 yrs.			127	.288	.390	525	151	23	14	1	0.2	114	2	37	13	1	0	0	242	83	65	13	3.1	.833	OF-101, SS-15, 2B-6, 1B-6, 3B-1

Charlie Hoover

HOOVER, CHARLES E.
B. Sept. 9, 1865, Mound City, Ill. Deceased. TR

| 1888 | KC | AA | 3 | .300 | .300 | 10 | 3 | 0 | 0 | 0 | 0.0 | 0 | 1 | 0 | | | 0 | 0 | 13 | 5 | 3 | 0 | 7.0 | .857 | C-3 |

Year	Team	Games	BA	SA	AB	H	2B	3B	HR	HR%	R	RBI	BB	SO	SB	Pinch Hit AB	Pinch Hit H	PO	A	E	DP	TC/G	FA	G by Pos

Charlie Hoover *continued*

Year	Team	Games	BA	SA	AB	H	2B	3B	HR	HR%	R	RBI	BB	SO	SB	PH AB	PH H	PO	A	E	DP	TC/G	FA	G by Pos
1889		71	.248	.306	258	64	2	5	1	0.4	44	25	29	38	9	0	0	272	108	40	8	5.9	.905	C-66, 3B-4, OF-3
2 yrs.		74	.250	.306	268	67	2	5	1	0.4	44	26	29	38	9	0	0	285	113	43	8	6.0	.902	C-69, 3B-4, OF-3

Joe Hoover

HOOVER, ROBERT JOSEPH
B. Apr. 15, 1915, Brawley, Calif. D. Sept. 2, 1965, Los Angeles, Calif.   BR TR 5'11" 175 lbs.

Year	Team	Games	BA	SA	AB	H	2B	3B	HR	HR%	R	RBI	BB	SO	SB	PH AB	PH H	PO	A	E	DP	TC/G	FA	G by Pos
1943	DET A	144	.243	.318	575	140	15	8	4	0.7	78	38	36	101	6	0	0	301	393	41	84	5.1	.944	SS-144
1944		120	.236	.290	441	104	20	2	0	0.0	67	29	35	66	7	0	0	258	406	48	103	5.9	.933	SS-119, 2B-1
1945		74	.257	.360	222	57	10	5	1	0.5	33	17	21	35	6	0	0	126	163	17	35	4.1	.944	SS-68
3 yrs.		338	.243	.316	1238	301	45	15	5	0.4	178	84	92	202	19	0	0	685	962	106	222	5.2	.940	SS-331, 2B-1

WORLD SERIES

Year	Team	Games	BA	SA	AB	H	2B	3B	HR	HR%	R	RBI	BB	SO	SB	PH AB	PH H	PO	A	E	DP	TC/G	FA	G by Pos
1945	DET A	1	.333	.333	3	1	0	0	0	0.0	1	1	0	0	0	0	0	1	1	0	1	2.0	1.000	SS-1

Don Hopkins

HOPKINS, DONALD
B. Jan. 9, 1952, West Point, Miss.   BL TR 6'1" 175 lbs.

Year	Team	Games	BA	SA	AB	H	2B	3B	HR	HR%	R	RBI	BB	SO	SB	PH AB	PH H	PO	A	E	DP	TC/G	FA	G by Pos
1975	OAK A	82	.167	.167	6	1	0	0	0	0.0	25	0	2	0	21	3	0	3	0	0	0	0.0	1.000	DH-20, OF-5
1976		3	–	–	0	0	0	0	0	–	0	0	0	0	0	0	0	0	0	0	0	0.0		DH-2
2 yrs.		85	.167	.167	6	1	0	0	0	0.0	25	0	2	0	21	3	0	3	0	0	0	0.0	1.000	DH-22, OF-5

LEAGUE CHAMPIONSHIP SERIES

Year	Team	Games	BA	SA	AB	H	2B	3B	HR	HR%	R	RBI	BB	SO	SB	PH AB	PH H	PO	A	E	DP	TC/G	FA	G by Pos
1975	OAK A	1	–	–	0	0	0	0	0	–	0	0	0	0	0	0	0	0	0	0	0	0.0	–	DH-1

Gail Hopkins

HOPKINS, GAIL EASON
B. Feb. 19, 1943, Tulsa, Okla.   BL TR 5'10" 198 lbs.

Year	Team	Games	BA	SA	AB	H	2B	3B	HR	HR%	R	RBI	BB	SO	SB	PH AB	PH H	PO	A	E	DP	TC/G	FA	G by Pos
1968	CHI A	29	.216	.270	37	8	2	0	0	0.0	4	2	6	3	0	20	4	45	1	0	3	1.6	1.000	1B-7
1969		124	.265	.381	373	99	13	3	8	2.1	52	46	50	28	2	21	6	903	51	6	81	7.7	.994	1B-101
1970		116	.286	.383	287	82	8	1	6	2.1	32	29	28	19	0	36	10	645	42	9	67	6.0	.987	1B-77, C-8
1971	KC A	103	.278	.431	295	82	16	1	9	3.1	35	47	37	13	3	17	5	669	57	7	76	7.1	.990	1B-83
1972		53	.211	.239	71	15	2	0	0	0.0	1	5	7	4	0	34	6	98	2	1	7	1.9	.990	1B-13, 3B-1
1973		74	.246	.348	138	34	6	1	2	1.4	17	16	29	15	1	19	7	32	3	0	3	0.5	1.000	DH-36, 1B-10
1974	LA N	15	.222	.222	18	4	0	0	0	0.0	1	0	3	1	0	11	4	20	3	0	0	1.5	1.000	1B-2, C-2
7 yrs.		514	.266	.376	1219	324	47	6	25	2.1	142	145	160	83	6	158	42	2412	159	23	237	5.0	.991	1B-293, DH-36, C-10, 3B-1

Marty Hopkins

HOPKINS, MEREDITH HILLIARD
B. Feb. 22, 1907, Wolfe City, Tex.   D. Nov. 20, 1963, Dallas, Tex.   BR TR 5'11" 175 lbs.

Year	Team	Games	BA	SA	AB	H	2B	3B	HR	HR%	R	RBI	BB	SO	SB	PH AB	PH H	PO	A	E	DP	TC/G	FA	G by Pos
1934	2 teams		PHI N	(10G – .120)			CHI A		(67G – .214)															
"	total	77	.204	.268	235	48	9	0	2	0.9	28	31	49	31	0	1	0	69	149	9	6	2.9	.960	3B-72
1935	CHI A	59	.222	.285	144	32	3	0	2	1.4	20	17	36	23	1	1	0	35	82	8	7	2.1	.936	3B-49, 2B-5
2 yrs.		136	.211	.274	379	80	12	0	4	1.1	48	48	85	54	1	2	0	104	231	17	13	2.6	.952	3B-121, 2B-5

Mike Hopkins

HOPKINS, MICHAEL JOSEPH
B. Nov. 1, 1872, Glasgow, Scotland   D. Feb. 5, 1952, Pittsburgh, Pa.   BR TR 5'8" 160 lbs.

Year	Team	Games	BA	SA	AB	H	2B	3B	HR	HR%	R	RBI	BB	SO	SB	PH AB	PH H	PO	A	E	DP	TC/G	FA	G by Pos
1902	PIT N	1	1.000	1.500	2	2	0	0	0	0.0	0	0	0		0	0	0	3	1	0	0	4.0	1.000	C-1

Sis Hopkins

HOPKINS, JOHN WINTON (Buck)
B. Jan. 3, 1883, Grafton, Va.   D. Oct. 2, 1929, Phoebus, Va.   BR TR 5'10" 165 lbs.

Year	Team	Games	BA	SA	AB	H	2B	3B	HR	HR%	R	RBI	BB	SO	SB	PH AB	PH H	PO	A	E	DP	TC/G	FA	G by Pos
1907	STL N	15	.136	.205	44	6	3	0	0	0.0	7	3	10		2	0	0	21	0	3	0	1.6	.875	OF-15

Johnny Hopp

HOPP, JOHN LEONARD (Hippity)
B. July 18, 1916, Hastings, Neb.   BL TL 5'10" 170 lbs.

Year	Team	Games	BA	SA	AB	H	2B	3B	HR	HR%	R	RBI	BB	SO	SB	PH AB	PH H	PO	A	E	DP	TC/G	FA	G by Pos
1939	STL N	6	.500	.750	4	2	1	0	0	0.0	1	2	1	1	0	3	2	6	1	0	1	1.2	1.000	1B-1
1940		80	.270	.388	152	41	7	4	1	0.7	24	14	9	21	3	23	4	129	4	4	4	1.7	.971	OF-39, 1B-10
1941		134	.303	.436	445	135	25	11	4	0.9	83	50	50	63	15	6	1	542	21	8	24	4.3	.986	OF-91, 1B-39
1942		95	.258	.382	314	81	16	7	3	1.0	41	37	36	40	14	3	1	746	44	14	68	8.5	.983	1B-88
1943		91	.224	.307	241	54	10	2	2	0.8	33	25	24	22	8	4	0	286	17	12	23	3.5	.962	OF-52, 1B-27
1944		139	.336	.499	527	177	35	9	11	2.1	106	72	58	47	15	2	0	352	4	1	1	2.6	.997	OF-131, 1B-6
1945		124	.289	.395	446	129	22	8	3	0.7	67	44	49	24	14	6	1	375	16	7	13	3.2	.982	OF-104, 1B-15
1946	BOS N	129	.333	.440	445	148	23	8	3	0.7	71	48	34	34	21	8	3	670	45	11	45	5.6	.985	1B-68, OF-58
1947		134	.288	.358	430	124	20	2	2	0.5	74	32	58	30	13	7	0	296	2	6	0	2.3	.980	OF-125
1948	PIT N	120	.278	.385	392	109	15	12	3	0.3	64	31	40	25	14	5	2	403	21	4	22	3.5	.998	1B-80, OF-25
1949	2 teams		PIT N	(105G – .318)			BKN N		(8G – .000)															
"	total	113	.306	.408	385	118	14	5	1	0.3	55	39	37	32	9	13	5	682	47	8	69	6.5	.989	1B-79, OF-20
1950	2 teams		PIT N	(106G – .340)			NY A		(19G – .333)															
"	total	125	.339	.528	345	117	26	6	9	2.6	60	55	51	18	7	28	8	554	34	6	63	4.8	.990	1B-82, OF-13
1951	NY A	46	.206	.317	63	13	1	0	2	3.2	10	4	9	11	2	19	4	121	5	1	10	2.8	.992	1B-25
1952	2 teams		NY A	(15G – .160)			DET A		(42G – .217)															
"	total	57	.197	.211	71	14	1	0	0	0.0	9	5	8	10	2	33	8	59	5	0	8	1.1	1.000	1B-13, OF-4
14 yrs.		1393	.296	.414	4260	1262	216	74	46	1.1	698	458	464	378	128	169	44	5221	266	79	351	4.0	.986	OF-717, 1B-478

WORLD SERIES

Year	Team	Games	BA	SA	AB	H	2B	3B	HR	HR%	R	RBI	BB	SO	SB	PH AB	PH H	PO	A	E	DP	TC/G	FA	G by Pos
1942	STL N	5	.176	.176	17	3	0	0	0	0.0	3	0	1	1	0	0	0	46	3	1	2	10.0	.980	1B-5
1943		1	.000	.000	4	0	0	0	0	0.0	0	0	0	0	0	0	0	1	0	0	0	1.0	1.000	OF-1
1944		6	.185	.185	27	5	0	0	0	0.0	2	0	0	0	0	0	0	14	0	0	0	2.3	1.000	OF-6
1950	NY A	3	.000	.000	2	0	0	0	0	0.0	0	0	1	0	0	0	0	7	1	0	2	2.7	1.000	1B-3
1951		1	–	–	0	0	0	0	0	–	0	0	0	0	0	1	0	0	0	0	0	0.0	–	
5 yrs.		16	.160	.160	50	8	0	0	0	0.0	5	0	2	1	0	0	0	68	4	1	4	4.6	.986	1B-8, OF-7

Shags Horan

HORAN, JOSEPH PATRICK
B. Sept. 6, 1895, St. Louis, Mo.   D. Feb. 13, 1969, Torrance, Calif.   BR TR 5'10" 170 lbs.

Year	Team	Games	BA	SA	AB	H	2B	3B	HR	HR%	R	RBI	BB	SO	SB	PH AB	PH H	PO	A	E	DP	TC/G	FA	G by Pos
1924	NY A	22	.290	.323	31	9	1	0	0	0.0	4	7	1	5	0	7	2	9	1	0	0	0.5	1.000	OF-13

Year Team	Games	BA	SA	AB	H	2B	3B	HR	HR%	R	RBI	BB	SO	SB	Pinch Hit AB	H	PO	A	E	DP	TC/G	FA	G by Pos

Sam Horn

HORN, SAMUEL LEE
B. Nov. 2, 1963, Dallas, Tex. BL TL 6'5" 215 lbs.

Year Team	Games	BA	SA	AB	H	2B	3B	HR	HR%	R	RBI	BB	SO	SB	AB	H	PO	A	E	DP	TC/G	FA	G by Pos
1987 BOS A	46	.278	.589	158	44	7	0	14	8.9	31	34	17	55	0	6	1	0	0	0	0	0.0	–	DH-40
1988	24	.148	.246	61	9	0	0	2	3.3	4	8	11	20	0	4	0	0	0	0	0	0.0	–	DH-16
1989	33	.148	.185	54	8	2	0	0	0.0	1	4	8	16	0	17	4	5	0	0	0	0.2	1.000	DH-14, 1B-2
3 yrs.	103	.223	.432	273	61	9	0	16	5.9	36	46	36	91	0	27	5	5	0	0	0	0.0	1.000	DH-70, 1B-2

Bob Horner

HORNER, JAMES ROBERT
B. Aug. 6, 1957, Junction City, Kans. BR TR 6'1" 195 lbs.

Year Team	Games	BA	SA	AB	H	2B	3B	HR	HR%	R	RBI	BB	SO	SB	AB	H	PO	A	E	DP	TC/G	FA	G by Pos
1978 ATL N	89	.266	.539	323	86	17	1	23	7.1	50	63	24	42	0	0	0	81	199	13	17	3.3	.956	3B-89
1979	121	.314	.552	487	153	15	1	33	6.8	66	98	22	74	0	1	0	470	167	22	43	5.4	.967	3B-82, 1B-45
1980	124	.268	.529	463	124	14	1	35	7.6	81	89	27	50	3	3	1	80	253	23	20	2.9	.935	3B-121, 1B-1
1981	79	.277	.460	300	83	10	0	15	5.0	42	42	32	39	2	0	0	51	129	12	6	2.4	.938	3B-79
1982	140	.261	.501	499	130	24	0	32	6.4	85	97	66	75	3	3	0	102	217	10	20	2.4	.970	3B-137
1983	104	.303	.528	386	117	25	1	20	5.2	75	68	50	63	4	0	0	78	153	10	18	2.3	.959	3B-104, 1B-1
1984	32	.274	.425	113	31	8	0	3	2.7	15	19	14	17	0	0	0	21	61	3	6	2.7	.965	3B-32
1985	130	.267	.499	483	129	25	3	27	5.6	61	89	50	57	1	4	1	917	119	11	111	8.1	.989	1B-87, 3B-40
1986	141	.273	.472	517	141	22	0	27	5.2	70	87	52	72	1	2	2	1378	102	8	138	10.6	.995	1B-139
1988 STL N	60	.257	.354	206	53	9	1	3	1.5	15	33	32	23	0	3	2	463	40	5	39	8.5	.990	1B-57
10 yrs.	1020	.277	.499	3777	1047	169	8	218	5.8	560	685	369	512	14	16	6	3641	1440	117	418	5.1	.977	3B-684, 1B-330

LEAGUE CHAMPIONSHIP SERIES

Year Team	Games	BA	SA	AB	H	2B	3B	HR	HR%	R	RBI	BB	SO	SB	AB	H	PO	A	E	DP	TC/G	FA	G by Pos
1982 ATL N	3	.091	.091	11	1	0	0	0	0.0	0	0	0	2	0	0	0	0	0	0	0	0.0	–	3B-3

Rogers Hornsby

HORNSBY, ROGERS (Rajah)
B. Apr. 27, 1896, Winters, Tex. D. Jan. 5, 1963, Chicago, Ill.
Manager 1925-28, 1930-37, 1952-53.
Hall of Fame 1942. BR TR 5'11" 175 lbs.

Year Team	Games	BA	SA	AB	H	2B	3B	HR	HR%	R	RBI	BB	SO	SB	AB	H	PO	A	E	DP	TC/G	FA	G by Pos
1915 STL N	18	.246	.281	57	14	2	0	0	0.0	5	4	2	6	0	0	0	48	46	8	12	5.7	.922	SS-18
1916	139	.313	.444	495	155	17	15	6	1.2	63	65	40	63	17	1	1	325	315	45	35	4.9	.934	3B-83, SS-45, 1B-15, 2B-1
1917	145	.327	.484	523	171	24	17	8	1.5	86	66	45	34	17	1	0	268	527	52	82	5.8	.939	SS-144
1918	115	.281	.416	416	117	19	11	5	1.2	51	60	40	43	8	4	2	211	434	46	55	6.0	.933	SS-109, OF-2
1919	138	.318	.430	512	163	15	9	8	1.6	68	71	48	41	17	0	0	233	367	34	39	4.6	.946	3B-72, SS-37, 2B-25, 1B-5
1920	149	.370	.559	589	218	44	20	9	1.5	96	94	60	50	12	0	0	343	524	34	76	6.0	.962	2B-149
1921	154	.397	.639	592	235	44	18	21	3.5	131	126	60	48	13	0	0	340	487	27	63	5.5	.968	2B-142, OF-6, SS-3, 3B-3, 1B-1
1922	154	.401	.722	623	250	46	14	42	6.7	141	152	65	50	17	0	0	398	473	30	81	5.9	.967	2B-154
1923	107	.384	.627	424	163	32	10	17	4.0	89	83	55	29	3	1	0	323	299	21	61	6.0	.967	2B-96, 1B-10
1924	143	.424	.696	536	227	43	14	25	4.7	121	94	89	32	5	0	0	301	517	30	102	5.9	.965	2B-143
1925	138	.403	.756	504	203	41	10	39	7.7	133	143	83	39	5	0	0	287	416	34	95	5.3	.954	2B-136
1926	134	.317	.463	527	167	34	5	11	2.1	96	93	61	39	3	0	0	245	433	27	73	5.3	.962	2B-134
1927 NY N	155	.361	.586	568	205	32	9	26	4.6	133	125	86	38	9	0	0	299	582	25	98	5.8	.972	2B-155
1928 BOS N	140	.387	.632	486	188	42	7	21	4.3	99	94	107	41	5	0	0	295	450	21	85	5.5	.973	2B-140
1929 CHI N	156	.380	.679	602	229	47	8	39	6.5	156	149	87	65	2	0	0	286	547	23	106	5.5	.973	2B-156
1930	42	.308	.433	104	32	5	1	2	1.9	15	18	12	12	0	15	4	44	76	11	16	3.1	.916	2B-25
1931	100	.331	.574	357	118	37	1	16	4.5	64	90	56	23	1	4	2	128	255	22	30	4.1	.946	2B-69, 3B-26
1932	19	.224	.310	58	13	2	0	1	1.7	10	7	10	4	0	3	1	17	10	4	0	1.6	.871	OF-10, 3B-6
1933 2 teams	STL N	(46G – .325)		STL A	(11G – .333)																		
" total	57	.326	.500	92	30	7	0	3	3.3	11	23	14	7	1	35	11	24	35	2	7	1.1	.967	2B-17
1934 STL A	24	.304	.522	23	7	2	0	1	4.3	2	11	7	4	0	15	5	2	3	0	1	0.2	1.000	OF-1, 3B-1
1935	10	.208	.333	24	5	3	0	0	0.0	1	3	3	6	0	3	1	38	5	0	1	4.3	1.000	1B-3, 2B-2, 3B-1
1936	2	.400	.400	5	2	0	0	0	0.0	1	2	1	0	0	0	0	10	0	0	0	5.0	1.000	1B-1
1937	20	.321	.429	56	18	3	0	1	1.8	7	11	7	5	0	3	0	30	41	4	10	3.8	.947	2B-17
23 yrs.	2259	.358	.577	8173	2930	541	169	301	3.7	1579	1584	1038	679	135	86	26	4495	6842	500	1128	5.2	.958	2B-1561, SS-356, 3B-192, 1B-35, OF-19
		2nd	7th																				

WORLD SERIES

Year Team	Games	BA	SA	AB	H	2B	3B	HR	HR%	R	RBI	BB	SO	SB	AB	H	PO	A	E	DP	TC/G	FA	G by Pos
1926 STL N	7	.250	.286	28	7	1	0	0	0.0	2	4	2	2	1	0	0	15	21	0	4	5.1	1.000	2B-7
1929 CHI N	5	.238	.381	21	5	1	1	0	0.0	4	1	1	8	0	0	0	9	11	1	4	4.2	.952	2B-5
2 yrs.	12	.245	.327	49	12	1	1	0	0.0	6	5	3	10	1	0	0	24	32	1	8	4.8	.982	2B-12

Joe Hornung

HORNUNG, MICHAEL JOSEPH (Ubbo Ubbo)
B. June 12, 1857, Carthage, N. Y. D. Oct. 30, 1931, New York, N. Y. BR TR 5'8½" 164 lbs.

Year Team	Games	BA	SA	AB	H	2B	3B	HR	HR%	R	RBI	BB	SO	SB	AB	H	PO	A	E	DP	TC/G	FA	G by Pos
1879 BUF N	78	.266	.367	319	85	18	7	0	0.0	46	38	2	27		0	0	135	12	26	2	2.2	.850	OF-77, 1B-1
1880	85	.266	.363	342	91	8	11	1	0.3	47	42	8	29		0	0	311	36	36	7	4.5	.906	OF-67, 1B-18, 2B-5, P-1
1881 BOS N	83	.241	.346	324	78	12	6	2	0.6	40	25	5	25		0	0	198	19	12	5	2.8	.948	OF-83
1882	85	.302	.440	388	117	14	11	1	0.3	67	50	2	25		0	0	196	15	15	4	2.7	.934	OF-84, 1B-1
1883	98	.278	.446	446	124	25	13	8	1.8	107	66	8	54		0	0	175	15	13	3	2.1	.936	OF-98, 3B-1
1884	115	.268	.400	518	139	27	10	7	1.4	119		17	80		0	0	233	14	21	3	2.3	.922	OF-110, 1B-6
1885	25	.202	.284	109	22	4	1	1	0.9	14	7	1	20		0	0	33	1	3	0	1.5	.919	OF-25
1886	94	.257	.356	424	109	12	2	2	0.5	67	40	10	62		0	0	187	12	11	1	2.2	.948	OF-94
1887	98	.270	.355	437	118	10	6	5	1.1	85	49	17	28	41	0	0	192	23	15	3	2.3	.935	OF-98
1888	107	.239	.318	431	103	11	7	3	0.7	61	53	16	39	29	0	0	151	10	9	4	1.6	.947	OF-107
1889 BAL AA	135	.229	.293	533	122	13	9	1	0.2	73	78	22	72	34	0	0	251	32	27	10	2.3	.913	OF-134, 3B-1
1890 NY N	120	.238	.292	513	122	18	5	0	0.0	62	65	12	37	39	0	0	488	36	24	28	4.6	.956	OF-77, 1B-36, 3B-5, SS-2
12 yrs.	1123	.257	.350	4784	1230	172	90	31	0.6	788	513	120	498	143	0	0	2550	225	212	66	2.7	.929	OF-1054, 1B-62, 3B-7, 2B-5, SS-2, P-1

Tony Horton

HORTON, ANTHONY DARRIN
B. Dec. 6, 1944, Santa Monica, Calif. BR TR 6'3" 210 lbs.

Year Team	Games	BA	SA	AB	H	2B	3B	HR	HR%	R	RBI	BB	SO	SB	AB	H	PO	A	E	DP	TC/G	FA	G by Pos
1964 BOS A	36	.222	.286	126	28	5	0	1	0.8	9	8	3	20	0	6	0	94	5	2	3	2.8	.980	OF-24, 1B-8
1965	60	.294	.485	163	48	8	1	7	4.3	23	23	18	36	0	14	3	311	24	7	30	5.7	.980	1B-44
1966	6	.136	.136	22	3	0	0	0	0.0	0	2	0	2	0	0	0	43	5	0	7	8.0	1.000	1B-6

Year	Team	Games	BA	SA	AB	H	2B	3B	HR	HR%	R	RBI	BB	SO	SB	Pinch Hit AB	Pinch Hit H	PO	A	E	DP	TC/G	FA	G by Pos

Tony Horton *continued*

Year	Team	Games	BA	SA	AB	H	2B	3B	HR	HR%	R	RBI	BB	SO	SB	PH AB	PH H	PO	A	E	DP	TC/G	FA	G by Pos
1967	2 teams	BOS A (21G – .308)				CLE A (106G – .281)																		
"	total	127	.284	.418	402	114	16	4	10	2.5	37	53	18	57	3	31	10	811	50	11	66	6.9	.987	1B-100
1968	CLE A	133	.249	.411	477	119	29	3	14	2.9	57	59	34	56	3	9	2	972	63	8	80	7.8	.992	1B-128
1969		159	.278	.461	625	174	25	4	27	4.3	77	93	37	91	3	2	0	1179	100	14	130	8.1	.989	1B-157
1970		115	.269	.453	413	111	19	3	17	4.1	48	59	30	54	3	8	3	898	73	6	106	8.5	.994	1B-112
7 yrs.		636	.268	.430	2228	597	102	15	76	3.4	251	297	140	319	12	72	18	4308	320	48	422	7.4	.990	1B-555, OF-24

Willie Horton

HORTON, WILLIE WATTERSON
B. Oct. 18, 1942, Arno, Va.   BR TR 5'11" 209 lbs.

Year	Team	Games	BA	SA	AB	H	2B	3B	HR	HR%	R	RBI	BB	SO	SB	PH AB	PH H	PO	A	E	DP	TC/G	FA	G by Pos
1963	DET A	15	.326	.488	43	14	2	1	1	2.3	6	4	0	8	2	5	3	13	0	0	0	0.9	1.000	OF-9
1964		25	.163	.288	80	13	1	3	1	1.3	6	10	11	20	0	3	1	33	0	2	0	1.4	.943	OF-23
1965		143	.273	.490	512	140	20	2	29	5.7	69	104	48	101	5	3	0	249	9	3	1	1.8	.989	OF-141, 3B-1
1966		146	.262	.481	526	138	22	6	27	5.1	72	100	44	103	1	9	2	233	4	5	1	1.7	.979	OF-137
1967		122	.274	.481	401	110	20	3	19	4.7	47	67	36	80	0	11	3	165	5	5	2	1.4	.971	OF-110
1968		143	.285	.543	512	146	20	2	36	7.0	68	85	49	110	0	5	1	212	6	6	2	1.6	.973	OF-139
1969		141	.262	.465	508	133	17	1	28	5.5	66	91	52	93	3	5	1	272	8	8	0	2.0	.972	OF-136
1970		96	.305	.501	371	113	18	2	17	4.6	53	69	28	43	0	0	0	154	10	3	1	1.7	.982	OF-96
1971		119	.289	.496	450	130	25	1	22	4.9	64	72	37	75	1	2	0	176	8	7	1	1.6	.963	OF-118
1972		108	.231	.387	333	77	9	5	11	3.3	44	36	27	47	0	12	1	131	6	0	1	1.3	1.000	OF-98
1973		111	.316	.501	411	130	19	3	17	4.1	42	53	23	57	1	3	1	160	2	10	0	1.5	.942	OF-107, DH-1
1974		72	.298	.529	238	71	8	1	15	6.3	32	47	21	36	0	6	3	106	2	6	0	1.6	.947	OF-64, DH-1
1975		159	.275	.421	615	169	13	1	25	4.1	62	92	44	109	1	0	0	0	0	0	0	0.0	–	DH-159
1976		114	.262	.409	401	105	17	0	14	3.5	40	56	49	63	0	6	1	0	0	0	0	0.0	–	DH-105
1977	2 teams	DET A (1G – .250)				TEX A (139G – .289)																		
"	total	140	.289	.430	523	151	23	3	15	2.9	55	75	42	117	2	6	2	16	0	1	0	0.1	.941	DH-128, OF-11
1978	3 teams	CLE A (50G – .249)				OAK A (32G – .314)				TOR A (33G – .205)														
"	total	115	.252	.389	393	99	21	0	11	2.8	38	60	28	69	1	9	3	1	0	2	0	0.0	.333	DH-105, OF-1
1979	SEA A	162	.279	.458	646	180	19	5	29	4.5	77	106	42	112	1	0	0	0	0	0	0	0.0	–	DH-162
1980		97	.221	.328	335	74	10	1	8	2.4	32	36	39	70	0	5	0	0	0	0	0	0.0	–	DH-92
18 yrs.		2028	.273	.457	7298	1993	284	40	325	4.5	873	1163	620	1313	20	90	24	1921	60	58	8	1.0	.972	OF-1190, DH-753, 3B-1

LEAGUE CHAMPIONSHIP SERIES

| 1972 | DET A | 5 | .100 | .100 | 10 | 1 | 0 | 0 | 0 | 0.0 | 0 | 0 | 1 | 3 | 0 | 0 | 0 | 6 | 0 | 0 | 0 | 1.2 | 1.000 | OF-3 |

WORLD SERIES

| 1968 | DET A | 7 | .304 | .565 | 23 | 7 | 1 | 1 | 1 | 4.3 | 6 | 3 | 5 | 6 | 0 | 0 | 0 | 5 | 1 | 1 | 0 | 1.0 | .857 | OF-7 |

Tim Hosley

HOSLEY, TIMOTHY KENNETH
B. May 10, 1947, Spartanburg, S. C.   BR TR 5'11" 185 lbs.

Year	Team	Games	BA	SA	AB	H	2B	3B	HR	HR%	R	RBI	BB	SO	SB	PH AB	PH H	PO	A	E	DP	TC/G	FA	G by Pos
1970	DET A	7	.167	.417	12	2	0	0	1	8.3	1	2	0	6	0	4	1	22	0	0	0	3.6	1.000	C-4
1971		7	.188	.563	16	3	0	0	2	12.5	2	6	0	1	0	4	0	26	0	0	0	3.7	1.000	C-4, 1B-1
1973	OAK A	13	.214	.214	14	3	0	0	0	0.0	3	2	2	3	0	4	1	19	1	1	0	1.6	.952	C-12
1974		11	.286	.286	7	2	0	0	0	0.0	3	1	1	2	0	4	1	13	1	0	0	1.3	1.000	C-8, 1B-1
1975	CHI N	62	.255	.433	141	36	7	0	6	4.3	22	20	27	25	1	10	2	254	16	9	3	4.5	.968	C-53
1976	2 teams	CHI N (1G – .000)				OAK A (37G – .164)																		
"	total	38	.161	.250	56	9	2	0	1	1.8	4	4	8	12	0	12	2	79	13	3	0	2.5	.968	C-37
1977	OAK A	39	.192	.231	78	15	0	0	1	1.3	5	10	16	13	0	5	1	81	13	5	0	2.5	.949	C-19, DH-12, 1B-3
1978		13	.304	.391	23	7	2	0	0	0.0	1	3	1	6	0	7	2	22	3	1	0	2.0	.962	C-2, DH-1
1981		18	.095	.238	21	2	0	0	1	4.8	2	5	2	5	0	14	1	3	0	1	0	0.2	.750	DH-4, 1B-1
9 yrs.		208	.215	.342	368	79	11	0	12	3.3	43	53	57	73	1	64	11	519	50	20	3	2.8	.966	C-139, DH-17, 1B-6

Chuck Hostetler

HOSTETLER, CHARLES CLOYD
B. Sept. 22, 1903, McClellandtown, Pa.   D. Feb. 18, 1971, Fort Collins, Colo.   BL TR 6' 175 lbs.

Year	Team	Games	BA	SA	AB	H	2B	3B	HR	HR%	R	RBI	BB	SO	SB	PH AB	PH H	PO	A	E	DP	TC/G	FA	G by Pos
1944	DET A	90	.298	.347	265	79	9	2	0	0.0	42	20	21	31	4	19	4	129	5	2	1	1.5	.985	OF-65
1945		42	.159	.227	44	7	3	0	0	0.0	3	2	7	8	0	30	6	8	0	1	0	0.2	.889	OF-8
2 yrs.		132	.278	.330	309	86	12	2	0	0.0	45	22	28	39	4	49	10	137	5	3	1	1.1	.979	OF-73

WORLD SERIES

| 1945 | DET A | 3 | .000 | .000 | 3 | 0 | 0 | 0 | 0 | 0.0 | 0 | 0 | 0 | 0 | 0 | 3 | 0 | 0 | 0 | 0 | 0 | 0.0 | – | |

Dave Hostetler

HOSTETLER, DAVID ALAN
B. Mar. 27, 1956, Pasadena, Calif.   BR TR 6'4" 215 lbs.

Year	Team	Games	BA	SA	AB	H	2B	3B	HR	HR%	R	RBI	BB	SO	SB	PH AB	PH H	PO	A	E	DP	TC/G	FA	G by Pos
1981	MON N	5	.500	1.000	6	3	0	0	1	16.7	1	1	0	2	0	3	0	4	0	0	2	0.8	1.000	1B-2
1982	TEX A	113	.232	.433	418	97	12	3	22	5.3	53	67	42	113	2	1	0	1099	48	12	102	10.3	.990	1B-109, DH-3
1983		94	.220	.372	304	67	9	2	11	3.6	31	46	42	103	0	8	1	11	0	0	0	0.1	1.000	DH-88, 1B-2
1984		37	.220	.378	82	18	2	1	3	3.7	7	10	13	27	0	9	2	90	8	0	9	2.6	1.000	1B-14, DH-13
1988	PIT N	6	.250	.250	8	2	0	0	0	0.0	0	0	0	3	0	4	1	15	2	1	0	3.0	.944	1B-4, C-1
5 yrs.		255	.229	.407	818	187	23	6	37	4.5	92	124	97	248	2	25	4	1219	58	13	113	5.1	.990	1B-131, DH-104, C-1

Pete Hotaling

HOTALING, PETER JAMES (Monkey)
B. Dec. 16, 1856, Mohawk, N. Y.   D. July 3, 1928, Cleveland, Ohio   BR TR 5'8" 166 lbs.

Year	Team	Games	BA	SA	AB	H	2B	3B	HR	HR%	R	RBI	BB	SO	SB	PH AB	PH H	PO	A	E	DP	TC/G	FA	G by Pos
1879	CIN N	81	.279	.390	369	103	20	9	1	0.3	64	27	12	17		0	0	158	52	37	8	3.0	.850	OF-69, C-8, 2B-6, 3B-3
1880	CLE N	78	.240	.342	325	78	17	8	0	0.0	40	41	10	30		0	0	120	15	16	5	1.9	.894	OF-78, C-2
1881	WOR N	77	.309	.385	317	98	15	3	1	0.3	51	35	18	12		0	0	153	28	31	2	2.8	.854	OF-74, C-3
1882	BOS N	84	.259	.328	378	98	16	5	0	0.0	64	28	16	21		0	0	150	16	26	5	2.3	.865	OF-84
1883	CLE N	100	.259	.345	417	108	20	8	0	0.0	54		12	31		0	0	181	23	42	5	2.5	.829	OF-100
1884		102	.243	.333	408	99	16	6	3	0.7	69	27	28	50		0	0	174	23	35	5	2.3	.849	OF-102, 2B-1
1885	BKN AA	94	.257	.316	370	95	9	5	1	0.3	73		49			0	0	159	17	21	3	2.1	.893	OF-94
1887	CLE AA	126	.299	.424	505	151	28	13	3	0.6	108	53			43	0	0	267	23	31	5	2.5	.903	OF-126
1888		98	.251	.298	403	101	7	6	0	0.0	67	55	26		35	0	0	170	10	25	7	2.1	.878	OF-98
9 yrs.		840	.267	.353	3492	931	148	63	9	0.3	590	213	224	161	78	0	0	1532	207	264	45	2.4	.868	OF-825, C-13, 2B-7, 3B-3

Year	Team		Games	BA	SA	AB	H	2B	3B	HR	HR%	R	RBI	BB	SO	SB	Pinch Hit AB	Pinch Hit H	PO	A	E	DP	TC/G	FA	G by Pos

Ken Hottman

HOTTMAN, KENNETH ROGER
B. May 7, 1948, Stockton, Calif.
BR TR 5'11" 190 lbs.

| 1971 | CHI | A | 6 | .125 | .125 | 16 | 2 | 0 | 0 | 0 | 0.0 | 1 | 0 | 1 | 2 | 0 | 1 | 0 | 5 | 0 | 0 | 0 | 0.8 | 1.000 | OF-5 |

Sadie Houck

HOUCK, SARGENT PERRY
B. 1856, Washington, D. C.   D. May 26, 1919, Washington, D. C.
BR TR 5'7" 151 lbs.

1879	BOS	N	80	.267	.402	356	95	24	9	2	0.6	69	49	4	11		0	0	109	103	46	11	3.2	.822	OF-47, SS-33
1880	2 teams		BOS	N	(12G – .149)		PRO	N	(49G – .201)																
"	total		61	.190	.294	231	44	7	7	1	0.4	29	24	3	12		0	0	107	11	20	0	2.3	.855	OF-61
1881	DET	N	75	.279	.380	308	86	16	6	1	0.3	43	36	6	6		0	0	88	241	50	40	5.1	.868	SS-75
1883			101	.252	.353	416	105	18	12	0	0.0	52		9	18		0	0	162	328	85	36	5.7	.852	SS-101
1884	PHI	AA	108	.297	.396	472	140	19	14	0	0.0	93		7			0	0	122	379	60	30	5.2	.893	SS-108, 2B-1
1885			93	.255	.327	388	99	10	9	0	0.0	74		10			0	0	121	362	77	34	6.0	.863	SS-93
1886	2 teams		BAL	AA	(61G – .192)		WAS	N	(52G – .215)																
"	total		113	.202	.231	455	92	11	1	0	0.0	43	14	6	28		0	0	150	331	83	16	5.0	.853	SS-106, 2B-6, OF-1
1887	NY	AA	10	.152	.182	33	5	1	0	0	0.0	3		3		2	0	0	10	42	11	4	6.3	.825	SS-10, 2B-1
8 yrs.			641	.250	.338	2659	666	106	58	4	0.2	406	123	48	75	2	0	0	869	1797	432	171	4.8	.861	SS-526, OF-109, 2B-8

Ralph Houk

HOUK, RALPH GEORGE (Major)
B. Aug. 9, 1919, Lawrence, Kans.
Manager 1961-63, 1966-78, 1981-84.
BR TR 5'11" 193 lbs.

1947	NY	A	41	.272	.326	92	25	3	1	0	0.0	7	12	11	5	0	0	0	138	13	2	0	3.7	.987	C-41
1948			14	.276	.345	29	8	2	0	0	0.0	3	3	0	0	0	0	0	41	5	0	1	3.3	1.000	C-14
1949			5	.571	.571	7	4	0	0	0	0.0	0	1	0	1	0	0	0	8	0	1	0	1.8	.889	C-5
1950			10	.111	.222	9	1	1	0	0	0.0	0	1	0	2	0	1	1	12	1	1	0	1.4	.929	C-9
1951			3	.200	.200	5	1	0	0	0	0.0	0	2	0	1	0	0	0	2	1	0	0	1.0	1.000	C-3
1952			9	.333	.333	6	2	0	0	0	0.0	0	0	1	0	0	0	0	10	1	1	1	1.3	.917	C-9
1953			8	.222	.222	9	2	0	0	0	0.0	2	1	0	1	0	0	0	10	0	0	0	1.3	1.000	C-8
1954			1	.000	.000	1	0	0	0	0	0.0	0	0	0	0	0	1	0	0	0	0	0	0.0		
8 yrs.			91	.272	.323	158	43	6	1	0	0.0	12	20	12	10	0	2	1	221	21	5	2	2.7	.980	C-89

WORLD SERIES

1947	NY	A	1	1.000	1.000	1	1	0	0	0	0.0	0	0	0	0	0	1	1	0	0	0	0	0.0		—
1952			1	.000	.000	1	0	0	0	0	0.0	0	0	0	0	0	1	0	0	0	0	0	0.0		—
2 yrs.			2	.500	.500	2	1	0	0	0	0.0	0	0	0	0	0	2	1	0	0	0	0	0.0		—

Frank House

HOUSE, HENRY FRANKLIN (Pig)
B. Feb. 18, 1930, Bessemer, Ala.
BL TR 6'1½" 190 lbs.

1950	DET	A	5	.400	.600	5	2	1	0	0	0.0	0	1	0	0	0	0	0	4	1	0	0	1.0	1.000	C-5
1951			18	.220	.341	41	9	2	0	1	2.4	3	4	6	2	1	0	0	56	11	3	1	3.9	.957	C-18
1954			114	.250	.366	352	88	12	1	9	2.6	35	38	31	34	2	9	1	434	56	4	7	4.3	.992	C-107
1955			102	.259	.436	328	85	11	1	15	4.6	37	53	22	25	0	12	3	423	35	6	5	4.5	.987	C-93
1956			94	.240	.364	321	77	6	2	10	3.1	44	44	21	19	1	9	3	450	33	7	8	5.2	.986	C-88
1957			106	.259	.345	348	90	9	0	7	2.0	31	36	35	26	1	7	2	535	54	2	5	5.6	.997	C-97
1958	KC	A	76	.252	.371	202	51	6	3	6	3.0	16	24	12	13	1	19	7	236	22	2	4	3.4	.992	C-55
1959			98	.236	.303	347	82	14	3	1	0.3	32	30	20	23	0	4	1	447	43	9	7	5.1	.982	C-95
1960	CIN	N	23	.179	.250	28	5	2	0	0	0.0	0	3	0	2	0	17	3	21	2	0	1	1.0	1.000	C-8
1961	DET	A	17	.227	.364	22	5	1	1	0	0.0	3	3	4	2	0	3	0	36	1	1	0	2.2	.974	C-14
10 yrs.			653	.248	.362	1994	494	64	11	47	2.4	202	235	151	147	6	81	20	2642	258	34	38	4.5	.988	C-580

Charlie Householder

HOUSEHOLDER, CHARLES F.
B. 1856, Harrisburg, Pa.   Deceased.
BR TR 5'7" 150 lbs.

| 1884 | 2 teams | | CHI | U | (66G – .234) | | PIT | U | (17G – .258) | | | | | | | | | | | | | | | | |
| " | total | | 83 | .239 | .319 | 310 | 74 | 12 | 5 | 1 | 0.3 | 32 | | 12 | | | 0 | 0 | 99 | 66 | 37 | 7 | 2.4 | .817 | 3B-41, OF-40, SS-3, P-2 |

Charlie Householder

HOUSEHOLDER, CHARLES W.
B. 1856, Harrisburg, Pa.   D. Dec. 26, 1908, Harrisburg, Pa.
BL TL 5'11" 158 lbs.

1882	BAL	AA	74	.254	.342	307	78	10	7	1	0.3	42		4			0	0	762	20	23	30	10.9	.971	1B-74, C-3
1884	BKN	AA	76	.242	.352	273	66	15	3	3	1.1	28		12			0	0	580	63	43	23	9.0	.937	1B-40, C-31, OF-6, 2B-1
2 yrs.			150	.248	.347	580	144	25	10	4	0.7	70		16			0	0	1342	83	66	53	9.9	.956	1B-114, C-34, OF-6, 2B-1

Ed Householder

HOUSEHOLDER, EDWARD H.
B. Oct. 12, 1869, Pittsburgh, Pa.   D. July 3, 1924, Los Angeles, Calif.

| 1903 | BKN | N | 12 | .209 | .209 | 43 | 9 | 0 | 0 | 0 | 0.0 | 5 | 9 | 2 | | 3 | 0 | 0 | 28 | 1 | 1 | 1 | 2.5 | .967 | OF-12 |

Paul Householder

HOUSEHOLDER, PAUL WESLEY
B. Sept. 4, 1958, Columbus, Ohio
BB TR 6' 180 lbs.

1980	CIN	N	20	.244	.311	45	11	1	0	0	0.0	3	7	1	13	1	7	2	16	2	0	0	0.9	1.000	OF-14
1981			23	.275	.420	69	19	4	0	2	2.9	12	9	10	16	3	4	1	32	1	0	0	1.4	1.000	OF-19
1982			138	.211	.326	417	88	11	5	9	2.2	40	34	30	77	17	10	1	220	14	2	4	1.7	.992	OF-131
1983			123	.255	.387	380	97	24	4	6	1.6	40	43	44	60	12	17	3	221	5	2	0	1.9	.991	OF-112
1984	2 teams		CIN	N	(14G – .083)		STL	N	(13G – .143)																
"	total		27	.115	.154	26	3	1	0	0	0.0	4	0	3	6	1	11	1	9	0	0	0	0.4	1.000	OF-18
1985	MIL	A	95	.258	.418	299	77	15	0	11	3.7	41	34	27	60	1	4	1	202	5	3	0	2.2	.986	OF-91, DH-3
1986			26	.218	.321	78	17	3	1	1	1.3	4	16	7	16	1	2	0	35	1	0	0	1.4	1.000	OF-22, DH-3
1987	HOU	N	14	.083	.167	12	1	1	0	0	0.0	2	1	4	2	0	7	1	3	0	0	0	0.2	1.000	OF-7
8 yrs.			466	.236	.363	1326	313	60	11	29	2.2	146	144	126	250	36	61	10	738	29	7	5	1.7	.991	OF-414, DH-6

John Houseman

HOUSEMAN, JOHN FRANKLIN
B. Jan. 10, 1870, Holland   D. Nov. 4, 1922, Chicago, Ill.
160 lbs.

| 1894 | CHI | N | 4 | .400 | .733 | 15 | 6 | 3 | 1 | 0 | 0.0 | 5 | 4 | 5 | 3 | 2 | 0 | 0 | 8 | 16 | 2 | 4 | 6.5 | .923 | SS-3, 2B-1 |

Year	Team	Games	BA	SA	AB	H	2B	3B	HR	HR%	R	RBI	BB	SO	SB	Pinch Hit AB	Pinch Hit H	PO	A	E	DP	TC/G	FA	G by Pos

John Houseman *continued*

Year	Team	Games	BA	SA	AB	H	2B	3B	HR	HR%	R	RBI	BB	SO	SB	AB	H	PO	A	E	DP	TC/G	FA	G by Pos
1897 STL N		80	.245	.309	278	68	6	6	0	0.0	34	21	28		16	2	1	174	149	27	10	4.4	.923	2B-41, OF-33, SS-5, 3B-3
2 yrs.		84	.253	.331	293	74	9	7	0	0.0	39	25	33	3	18	2	1	182	165	29	14	4.5	.923	2B-42, OF-33, SS-8, 3B-3

Ben Houser

HOUSER, BENJAMIN FRANKLIN
B. Nov. 30, 1883, Shenandoah, Pa.   D. Jan. 15, 1952, Augusta, Me.

BL TL 6'1"   185 lbs.

Year	Team	Games	BA	SA	AB	H	2B	3B	HR	HR%	R	RBI	BB	SO	SB	AB	H	PO	A	E	DP	TC/G	FA	G by Pos
1910 PHI A		34	.188	.290	69	13	3	2	0	0.0	9	7	7		0	8	2	160	7	0	10	4.9	1.000	1B-26
1911 BOS N		20	.254	.310	71	18	1	0	1	1.4	11	9	8	6	2	0	0	160	11	2	13	8.7	.988	1B-20
1912		83	.286	.428	332	95	17	3	8	2.4	38	52	22	29	1	24	9	759	37	11	48	9.7	.986	1B-83
3 yrs.		137	.267	.390	472	126	21	5	9	1.9	58	68	37	35	3	32	11	1079	55	13	71	8.4	.989	1B-129

Fred Houtz

HOUTZ, FRED FRITZ (Lefty)
B. Sept. 4, 1875, Connersville, Ind.   D. Feb. 15, 1959, Wapakoneta, Ohio

BL TL 5'10"   170 lbs.

Year	Team	Games	BA	SA	AB	H	2B	3B	HR	HR%	R	RBI	BB	SO	SB	AB	H	PO	A	E	DP	TC/G	FA	G by Pos
1899 CIN N		5	.235	.353	17	4	0	1	0	0.0	1	0	4		1	0	0	17	4	0	2	4.2	1.000	OF-5

Steve Hovley

HOVLEY, STEPHEN EUGENE
B. Dec. 18, 1944, Ventura, Calif.

BL TL 5'10"   188 lbs.

Year	Team	Games	BA	SA	AB	H	2B	3B	HR	HR%	R	RBI	BB	SO	SB	AB	H	PO	A	E	DP	TC/G	FA	G by Pos
1969 SEA A		91	.277	.365	329	91	14	3	3	0.9	41	20	30	34	10	7	0	175	8	2	3	2.0	.989	OF-84
1970 2 teams	MIL A (40G – .281)				OAK A	(72G – .190)																		
" total		112	.243	.285	235	57	10	0	0	0.0	25	17	22	22	8	31	8	126	2	3	1	1.2	.977	OF-80
1971 OAK A		24	.111	.185	27	3	2	0	0	0.0	3	3	7	9	2	10	2	15	1	0	0	0.7	1.000	OF-11
1972 KC A		105	.270	.352	196	53	5	1	3	1.5	24	24	24	29	3	37	9	103	6	2	0	1.1	.982	OF-68
1973		104	.254	.323	232	59	8	1	2	0.9	29	24	33	34	6	13	2	114	4	3	1	1.2	.975	OF-79, DH-15
5 yrs.		436	.258	.330	1019	263	39	5	8	0.8	122	88	116	128	29	98	21	533	21	10	5	1.3	.982	OF-322, DH-15

Dave Howard

HOWARD, DAVID AUSTIN (Del)
B. May 1, 1889, Washington, D. C.   D. Jan. 26, 1956, Dallas, Tex.

BR TR 5'11"   165 lbs.

Year	Team	Games	BA	SA	AB	H	2B	3B	HR	HR%	R	RBI	BB	SO	SB	AB	H	PO	A	E	DP	TC/G	FA	G by Pos
1912 WAS A		1	–	–	0	0	0	0	0	–	1	0	0	0	0	0	0	0	0	0	0	0.0	–	
1915 BKN F		24	.222	.250	36	8	1	0	0	0.0	5	1	1		0	1	1	20	31	4	0	2.3	.927	2B-12, OF-2, SS-1, 3B-1
2 yrs.		25	.222	.250	36	8	1	0	0	0.0	6	1	1		0	1	1	20	31	4	0	2.2	.927	2B-12, OF-2, SS-1, 3B-1

Del Howard

HOWARD, GEORGE ELMER
Brother of Ivon Howard.
B. Dec. 24, 1877, Kenney, Ill.   D. Dec. 24, 1956, Seattle, Wash.

BL TR 6'   180 lbs.

Year	Team	Games	BA	SA	AB	H	2B	3B	HR	HR%	R	RBI	BB	SO	SB	AB	H	PO	A	E	DP	TC/G	FA	G by Pos
1905 PIT N		123	.292	.370	435	127	18	5	2	0.5	56	63	27		19	3	0	947	53	23	58	8.3	.978	1B-90, OF-28, P-1
1906 BOS N		147	.261	.330	545	142	19	8	1	0.2	46	54	26		17	0	0	280	172	41	16	3.4	.917	OF-87, 2B-45, SS-14, 1B-2
1907 2 teams	BOS N (50G – .273)				CHI N	(51G – .230)																		
" total		101	.254	.304	335	85	6	4	1	0.3	30	26	17		14	11	3	373	35	13	22	4.2	.969	OF-53, 1B-33, 2B-3
1908 CHI N		96	.279	.330	315	88	7	3	1	0.3	42	26	23		11	6	2	155	12	6	1	1.8	.965	OF-81, 1B-5
1909		69	.197	.251	203	40	4	2	1	0.5	25	24	18		6	8	0	593	32	13	29	9.2	.980	1B-57
5 yrs.		536	.263	.326	1833	482	54	22	6	0.3	199	193	111		67	28	5	2348	304	96	126	5.1	.965	OF-249, 1B-187, 2B-48, SS-14, P-1

WORLD SERIES

Year	Team	Games	BA	SA	AB	H	2B	3B	HR	HR%	R	RBI	BB	SO	SB	AB	H	PO	A	E	DP	TC/G	FA	G by Pos
1907 CHI N		2	.200	.200	5	1	0	0	0	0.0	0	0	0	2	1	1	0	10	1	0	0	5.5	1.000	1B-1
1908		1	.000	.000	1	0	0	0	0	0.0	0	0	0	0	0	1	0	0	0	0	0	0.0	–	
2 yrs.		3	.167	.167	6	1	0	0	0	0.0	0	0	0	2	1	2	0	10	1	0	0	3.7	1.000	1B-1

Doug Howard

HOWARD, DOUGLAS LYNN
B. Feb. 6, 1948, Salt Lake City, Utah

BR TR 6'3"   185 lbs.

Year	Team	Games	BA	SA	AB	H	2B	3B	HR	HR%	R	RBI	BB	SO	SB	AB	H	PO	A	E	DP	TC/G	FA	G by Pos
1972 CAL A		11	.263	.289	38	10	1	0	0	0.0	4	2	1	3	0	1	0	18	3	1	3	2.0	.955	OF-8, 3B-1, 1B-1
1973		8	.095	.095	21	2	0	0	0	0.0	2	1	1	6	0	2	0	9	1	0	0	1.3	1.000	OF-6, 3B-1, 1B-1
1974		22	.231	.282	39	9	0	1	0	0.0	5	5	2	1	1	9	3	29	3	0	1	1.5	1.000	OF-8, 1B-5, DH-3
1975 STL N		17	.207	.310	29	6	0	0	1	3.4	1	1	0	7	0	10	3	60	6	0	5	3.9	1.000	1B-7
1976 CLE A		39	.211	.256	90	19	4	0	0	0.0	7	13	3	13	1	4	1	211	20	2	20	6.0	.991	1B-32, DH-4, OF-2
5 yrs.		97	.212	.258	217	46	5	1	1	0.5	19	22	7	30	2	26	7	327	33	3	29	3.7	.992	1B-46, OF-24, DH-7, 3B-2

Elston Howard

HOWARD, ELSTON GENE (Ellie)
B. Feb. 23, 1929, St. Louis, Mo.   D. Dec. 14, 1980, New York, N. Y.

BR TR 6'2"   196 lbs.

Year	Team	Games	BA	SA	AB	H	2B	3B	HR	HR%	R	RBI	BB	SO	SB	AB	H	PO	A	E	DP	TC/G	FA	G by Pos
1955 NY A		97	.290	.477	279	81	8	7	10	3.6	33	43	20	36	0	21	4	147	13	3	5	1.7	.982	OF-75, C-9
1956		98	.262	.362	290	76	8	3	5	1.7	35	34	21	30	0	12	5	205	16	1	5	2.3	.995	OF-65, C-26
1957		110	.253	.379	356	90	13	4	8	2.2	33	44	16	43	0	2	3	266	19	6	5	2.6	.979	OF-71, C-32, 1B-2
1958		103	.314	.479	376	118	19	5	11	2.9	45	66	22	60	1	9	5	447	29	2	13	4.6	.996	C-67, OF-24, 1B-5
1959		125	.273	.476	443	121	24	6	18	4.1	59	73	20	57	0	11	3	712	49	10	41	6.2	.987	1B-50, C-43, OF-28
1960		107	.245	.353	323	79	11	3	6	1.9	29	39	28	43	3	14	5	410	40	6	9	4.3	.987	C-91, OF-1
1961		129	.348	.549	446	155	17	5	21	4.7	64	77	28	65	0	14	4	725	47	6	16	6.0	.992	C-111, 1B-9
1962		136	.279	.474	494	138	23	5	21	4.3	63	91	31	76	1	7	1	713	44	4	12	5.6	.995	C-129
1963		135	.287	.528	487	140	21	6	28	5.7	75	85	35	68	0	5	1	786	51	5	8	6.2	.994	C-132
1964		150	.313	.455	550	172	27	3	15	2.7	63	84	48	73	1	6	1	939	67	2	9	6.7	.998	C-146
1965		110	.233	.345	391	91	15	1	9	2.3	38	45	24	65	0	12	6	644	44	6	8	6.3	.991	C-95, 1B-5, OF-1
1966		126	.256	.356	410	105	19	2	6	1.5	38	35	35	65	0	12	5	665	52	9	17	5.8	.988	C-100, 1B-13
1967 2 teams	NY A (66G – .196)				BOS A	(42G – .147)																		
" total		108	.178	.244	315	56	9	0	4	1.3	22	28	21	60	0	19	2	313	27	5	6	3.2	.986	C-89, 1B-1
1968 BOS A		71	.241	.335	203	49	4	0	5	2.5	22	18	22	45	1	3	0	377	30	2	3	5.8	.995	C-68
14 yrs.		1605	.274	.427	5363	1471	218	50	167	3.1	619	762	373	786	9	154	38	7349	528	67	156	4.9	.992	C-1138, OF-265, 1B-85

WORLD SERIES

Year	Team	Games	BA	SA	AB	H	2B	3B	HR	HR%	R	RBI	BB	SO	SB	AB	H	PO	A	E	DP	TC/G	FA	G by Pos
1955 NY A		7	.192	.308	26	5	0	0	1	3.8	3	3	1	8	0	0	0	11	1	0	0	1.7	1.000	OF-7
1956		1	.400	1.200	5	2	1	0	1	20.0	1	1	1	0	0	0	0	2	0	0	0	2.0	1.000	OF-1
1957		6	.273	.545	11	3	0	0	1	9.1	1	2	3	1	0	3	1	22	1	1	0	4.0	.958	1B-3
1958		6	.222	.222	18	4	0	0	0	0.0	4	2	1	4	1	1	0	14	2	0	2	2.7	1.000	OF-6
1960		5	.462	.923	13	6	1	1	1	7.7	4	4	1	0	0	1	0	11	0	0	0	2.2	1.000	C-4
1961		5	.250	.550	20	5	1	0	1	5.0	1	4	1	5	0	0	0	31	0	0	0	6.2	1.000	C-5

Year	Team		Games	BA	SA	AB	H	2B	3B	HR	HR%	R	RBI	BB	SO	SB	Pinch Hit AB	Pinch Hit H	PO	A	E	DP	TC/G	FA	G by Pos

Elston Howard *continued*

Year	Team		Games	BA	SA	AB	H	2B	3B	HR	HR%	R	RBI	BB	SO	SB	PH AB	PH H	PO	A	E	DP	TC/G	FA	G by Pos
1962			6	.143	.190	21	3	1	0	0	0.0	1	1	1	4	0	0	0	37	1	0	1	6.3	1.000	C-6
1963			4	.333	.333	15	5	0	0	0	0.0	0	1	0	3	0	0	0	30	2	0	1	8.0	1.000	C-4
1964			7	.292	.333	24	7	1	0	0	0.0	5	4	6	0	0	0	40	2	1	0	6.1	.977	C-7
1967	BOS	A	7	.111	.111	18	2	0	0	0	0.0	0	1	1	2	0	0	0	23	1	0	0	3.4	1.000	C-7
10 yrs.			54	.246	.386	171	42	7	1	5	2.9	25	19	12	37	1	5	2	221	10	2	5	4.3	.991	C-33, OF-14, 1B-3
			3rd			8th	10th	9th				7th			2nd										

Frank Howard

HOWARD, FRANK OLIVER (The Capital Punisher, Hondo)
B. Aug. 8, 1936, Columbus, Ohio
Manager 1981, 1983.

BR TR 6'7" 255 lbs.

Year	Team		Games	BA	SA	AB	H	2B	3B	HR	HR%	R	RBI	BB	SO	SB	PH AB	PH H	PO	A	E	DP	TC/G	FA	G by Pos
1958	LA	N	8	.241	.379	29	7	1	0	1	3.4	3	2	1	11	0	0	0	12	1	0	0	1.6	1.000	OF-8
1959			9	.143	.381	21	3	0	0	1	4.8	2	6	2	9	0	4	1	10	0	0	0	1.1	1.000	OF-6
1960			117	.268	.464	448	120	15	2	23	5.1	55	77	32	108	0	2	0	196	11	4	3	1.8	.981	OF-115, 1B-4
1961			99	.296	.517	267	79	10	2	15	5.6	36	45	21	50	0	19	7	122	10	8	2	1.4	.943	OF-65, 1B-7
1962			141	.296	.560	493	146	25	6	31	6.3	80	119	39	108	1	11	2	187	19	6	4	1.5	.972	OF-131
1963			123	.273	.518	417	114	16	1	28	6.7	58	64	33	116	0	15	3	190	4	8	0	1.6	.960	OF-111
1964			134	.226	.432	433	98	13	2	24	5.5	60	69	51	113	1	10	0	183	2	4	0	1.4	.979	OF-122
1965	WAS	A	149	.289	.477	516	149	22	6	21	4.1	53	84	55	112	0	10	1	204	5	4	0	1.4	.981	OF-138
1966			146	.278	.442	493	137	19	4	18	3.7	52	71	53	104	1	9	1	216	5	4	1	1.6	.982	OF-135
1967			149	.256	.511	519	133	20	2	36	6.9	71	89	60	155	0	5	0	225	6	3	1	1.6	.987	OF-141, 1B-4
1968			158	.274	**.552**	598	164	28	3	44	7.4	79	106	54	141	0	1	1	576	52	19	39	4.1	.971	OF-107, 1B-55
1969			161	.296	.574	592	175	17	2	48	8.1	111	111	102	96	1	1	0	602	34	14	38	4.0	.978	OF-114, 1B-70
1970			161	.283	.546	566	160	15	1	44	7.8	90	126	132	125	1	0	0	601	31	11	41	4.0	.983	OF-120, 1B-48
1971			153	.279	.474	549	153	25	2	26	4.7	60	83	77	121	1	5	0	555	65	4	40	4.1	.992	OF-100, 1B-68
1972	2 teams		109	TEX A (95G – .244)								DET A (14G – .242)													
"	total		109	.244	.369	320	78	10	0	10	3.1	29	38	46	63	1	17	3	521	32	13	44	5.2	.977	1B-76, OF-22
1973	DET	A	85	.256	.463	227	58	9	1	12	5.3	26	29	24	28	0	7	1	12	0	1	0	0.2	.923	DH-76, 1B-2
16 yrs.			1902	.273	.499	6488	1774	245	35	382	5.9	865	1119	782	1460	8	116	20	4412	277	104	213	2.5	.978	OF-1435, 1B-334, DH-76

WORLD SERIES

| 1963 | LA | N | 3 | .300 | .700 | 10 | 3 | 1 | 0 | 1 | 10.0 | 2 | 1 | 0 | 2 | 0 | 0 | 0 | 4 | 0 | 0 | 0 | 1.3 | 1.000 | OF-3 |

Ivon Howard

HOWARD, IVON CHESTER
Brother of Del Howard.
B. Oct. 12, 1882, Kenney, Ill. D. Mar. 30, 1967, Medford, Ore.

BB TR 5'10" 170 lbs.

Year	Team		Games	BA	SA	AB	H	2B	3B	HR	HR%	R	RBI	BB	SO	SB	PH AB	PH H	PO	A	E	DP	TC/G	FA	G by Pos
1914	STL	A	81	.244	.292	209	51	6	2	0	0.0	21	20	28	42	14	11	3	256	64	10	5	4.1	.970	3B-33, 1B-28, OF-2, SS-1
1915			113	.278	.361	324	90	10	7	1	0.3	43	43	43	48	29	17	3	488	90	12	33	5.2	.980	1B-48, 3B-23, OF-17, SS-2, 2B-1
1916	CLE	A	81	.187	.272	246	46	11	5	0	0.0	20	23	30	34	9	6	0	167	228	11	20	5.0	.973	2B-65, 1B-7
1917			27	.103	.103	39	4	0	0	0	0.0	7	0	3	5	1	6	0	18	17	2	1	1.4	.946	3B-6, OF-4, 2B-4
4 yrs.			302	.233	.304	818	191	27	14	1	0.1	91	86	104	129	53	40	6	929	399	35	59	4.5	.974	1B-83, 2B-70, 3B-62, OF-23, SS-3

Larry Howard

HOWARD, LAWRENCE RAYFORD
B. June 6, 1945, Columbus, Ohio

BR TR 6'3" 200 lbs.

Year	Team		Games	BA	SA	AB	H	2B	3B	HR	HR%	R	RBI	BB	SO	SB	PH AB	PH H	PO	A	E	DP	TC/G	FA	G by Pos
1970	HOU	N	31	.307	.443	88	27	6	0	2	2.3	11	16	10	23	0	4	2	130	12	1	0	4.6	.993	C-26, 1B-2, OF-1
1971			24	.234	.375	64	15	3	0	2	3.1	6	14	3	17	0	5	1	106	12	1	2	5.0	.992	C-22
1972			54	.223	.306	157	35	7	0	2	1.3	16	13	17	30	0	2	0	323	15	7	2	6.4	.980	C-53, OF-1
1973	2 teams		24	HOU N (20G – .167)								ATL N (4G – .125)													
"	total		24	.161	.214	56	9	3	0	0	0.0	3	4	7	15	0	2	0	87	8	1	0	4.0	.990	C-22
4 yrs.			133	.236	.337	365	86	19	0	6	1.6	36	47	37	85	0	13	3	646	47	10	4	5.3	.986	C-123, OF-2, 1B-2

Mike Howard

HOWARD, MICHAEL FREDERIC
B. Apr. 2, 1958, Seattle, Wash.

BB TR 6'2" 185 lbs.

Year	Team		Games	BA	SA	AB	H	2B	3B	HR	HR%	R	RBI	BB	SO	SB	PH AB	PH H	PO	A	E	DP	TC/G	FA	G by Pos
1981	NY	N	14	.167	.208	24	4	1	0	0	0.0	4	3	4	6	2	0	0	18	1	0	1	1.5	.952	OF-14
1982			33	.179	.256	39	7	0	0	1	2.6	5	3	6	7	2	5	2	32	6	0	1	1.2	1.000	OF-22, 2B-3
1983			1	.333	.333	3	1	0	0	0	0.0	0	1	0	1	0	0	0	0	0	0	0	0.0	–	OF-1
3 yrs.			48	.182	.242	66	12	1	0	1	1.5	9	7	10	14	4	5	2	50	8	1	1	1.2	.983	OF-37, 2B-3

Paul Howard

HOWARD, PAUL JOSEPH (Del)
B. May 20, 1884, Boston, Mass. D. Aug. 29, 1968, Miami, Fla.

BR TR 5'8" 170 lbs.

Year	Team		Games	BA	SA	AB	H	2B	3B	HR	HR%	R	RBI	BB	SO	SB	PH AB	PH H	PO	A	E	DP	TC/G	FA	G by Pos
1909	BOS	A	6	.200	.267	15	3	1	0	0	0.0	2	2	3			0	0	2	1	0	0	0.5	1.000	OF-6

Wilbur Howard

HOWARD, WILBUR LEON
B. Jan. 8, 1949, Lowell, N. C.

BR TR 6'2" 170 lbs.

Year	Team		Games	BA	SA	AB	H	2B	3B	HR	HR%	R	RBI	BB	SO	SB	PH AB	PH H	PO	A	E	DP	TC/G	FA	G by Pos
1973	MIL	A	16	.205	.205	39	8	0	0	0	0.0	3	1	2	10	0	0	0	29	2	1	0	2.0	.969	OF-12, DH-1
1974	HOU	N	64	.216	.306	111	24	4	0	2	1.8	19	5	5	18	4	9	2	65	3	0	1	1.1	1.000	OF-50
1975			121	.283	.365	392	111	16	8	0	0.0	62	21	21	67	32	23	6	194	7	1	0	1.7	.995	OF-95
1976			94	.220	.293	191	42	7	2	1	0.5	26	18	7	28	7	24	6	98	8	5	2	1.2	.955	OF-63, 2B-2
1977			87	.257	.321	187	48	6	1	2	1.1	22	13	5	30	11	24	7	105	5	1	1	1.3	.991	OF-62, 2B-4
1978			84	.230	.291	148	34	4	1	1	0.7	17	13	5	22	6	51	12	43	3	0	0	0.5	1.000	OF-16, C-3, 2B-1
6 yrs.			466	.250	.322	1068	267	37	11	6	0.6	149	71	45	175	60	131	33	534	28	8	4	1.2	.986	OF-298, 2B-7, C-3, DH-1

Jim Howarth

HOWARTH, JAMES EUGENE JR.
B. Mar. 7, 1947, Biloxi, Miss.

BL TL 5'11" 175 lbs.

Year	Team		Games	BA	SA	AB	H	2B	3B	HR	HR%	R	RBI	BB	SO	SB	PH AB	PH H	PO	A	E	DP	TC/G	FA	G by Pos
1971	SF	N	7	.231	.308	13	3	1	0	0	0.0	3	2	3	3	0	1	0	9	0	0	0	1.3	1.000	OF-6
1972			74	.235	.294	119	28	4	0	1	0.8	16	7	16	18	3	39	13	70	1	1	0	1.0	.986	OF-25, 1B-4
1973			65	.200	.233	90	18	1	0	0	0.0	8	7	7	8	0	26	6	46	1	0	1	0.7	1.000	OF-33, 1B-1
1974			6	.000	.000	4	0	0	0	0	0.0	0	0	0	0	0	4	0	0	0	0	0	0.0	–	OF-1
4 yrs.			152	.217	.265	226	49	6	1	1	0.4	27	16	26	29	3	70	19	125	2	1	1	0.8	.992	OF-65, 1B-5

Year Team	Games	BA	SA	AB	H	2B	3B	HR	HR%	R	RBI	BB	SO	SB	Pinch Hit AB	Pinch Hit H	PO	A	E	DP	TC/G	FA	G by Pos

Art Howe

HOWE, ARTHUR HENRY JR.
B. Dec. 15, 1946, Pittsburgh, Pa.
Manager 1989.
BR TR 6'2" 190 lbs.

Year Team	Games	BA	SA	AB	H	2B	3B	HR	HR%	R	RBI	BB	SO	SB	PH AB	PH H	PO	A	E	DP	TC/G	FA	G by Pos
1974 PIT N	29	.243	.365	74	18	4	1	1	1.4	10	5	9	13	0	8	4	11	49	4	8	2.2	.938	3B-20, SS-2
1975	63	.171	.253	146	25	9	0	1	0.7	13	10	15	15	1	18	4	19	89	7	4	1.8	.939	3B-42, SS-3
1976 HOU N	21	.138	.172	29	4	1	0	0	0.0	0	0	6	6	0	7	1	7	16	1	3	1.1	.958	3B-8, 2B-2
1977	125	.264	.412	413	109	23	7	8	1.9	44	58	41	60	0	6	3	213	333	8	52	4.4	.986	2B-96, 3B-19, SS-11
1978	119	.293	.436	420	123	33	3	7	1.7	46	55	34	41	2	3	1	240	302	13	51	4.7	.977	2B-107, 3B-11, 1B-1
1979	118	.248	.352	355	88	15	2	6	1.7	32	33	36	37	3	11	1	188	261	7	42	3.9	.985	2B-68, 3B-59, 1B-3
1980	110	.283	.445	321	91	12	5	10	3.1	34	46	34	29	1	18	2	598	86	10	52	6.3	.986	1B-77, 3B-25, SS-5, 2B-3
1981	103	.296	.404	361	107	22	4	3	0.8	43	36	41	23	1	3	1	67	206	9	19	2.7	.968	3B-98, 1B-2
1982	110	.238	.326	365	87	15	1	5	1.4	29	38	41	45	2	3	0	344	174	7	47	4.8	.987	3B-72, 1B-35
1984 STL N	89	.216	.295	139	30	5	0	2	1.4	17	12	18	18	0	21	6	71	80	3	14	1.7	.981	3B-45, 1B-11, 2B-8, SS-5
1985	4	.000	.000	3	0	0	0	0	0.0	0	0	0	3	0	3	0	5	1	0	1	1.5	1.000	3B-1, 1B-1
11 yrs	891	.260	.379	2626	682	139	23	43	1.6	268	293	275	287	10	101	23	1763	1597	69	293	3.8	.980	3B-400, 2B-284, 1B-130, SS-26

DIVISIONAL PLAYOFF SERIES

Year Team	Games	BA	SA	AB	H	2B	3B	HR	HR%	R	RBI	BB	SO	SB	PH AB	PH H	PO	A	E	DP	TC/G	FA	G by Pos
1981 HOU N	5	.235	.412	17	4	0	0	1	5.9	1	1	2	1	0	0	0	0	0	0	0	0.0	–	3B-5

LEAGUE CHAMPIONSHIP SERIES

Year Team	Games	BA	SA	AB	H	2B	3B	HR	HR%	R	RBI	BB	SO	SB	PH AB	PH H	PO	A	E	DP	TC/G	FA	G by Pos
1974 PIT N	1	.000	.000	1	0	0	0	0	0.0	0	0	0	0	0	0	0	0	0	0	0	0.0	–	
1980 HOU N	5	.200	.400	15	3	1	1	0	0.0	0	2	2	2	0	0	0	29	3	0	3	6.4	1.000	1B-4
2 yrs	6	.188	.375	16	3	1	1	0	0.0	0	2	2	2	0	1	0	29	3	0	3	5.3	1.000	1B-4

Shorty Howe

HOWE, JOHN
B. New York, N. Y. Deceased.

Year Team	Games	BA	SA	AB	H	2B	3B	HR	HR%	R	RBI	BB	SO	SB	PH AB	PH H	PO	A	E	DP	TC/G	FA	G by Pos
1890 NY N	19	.172	.172	64	11	0	0	0	0.0	4	4	3	2	1	0	0	36	58	12	3	5.6	.887	2B-18, 3B-1
1893	1	.600	.600	5	3	0	0	0	0.0	1	2	0	0	1	0	0	0	2	3	0	5.0	.400	3B-1
2 yrs	20	.203	.203	69	14	0	0	0	0.0	5	6	3	2	4	0	0	36	60	15	3	5.6	.865	2B-18, 3B-2

Dixie Howell

HOWELL, HOMER ELLIOTT
B. Apr. 24, 1919, Louisville, Ky.
BR TR 5'11½" 190 lbs.
BB 1947

Year Team	Games	BA	SA	AB	H	2B	3B	HR	HR%	R	RBI	BB	SO	SB	PH AB	PH H	PO	A	E	DP	TC/G	FA	G by Pos
1947 PIT N	76	.276	.383	214	59	11	0	4	1.9	23	25	27	34	1	1	0	272	30	8	2	4.1	.974	C-74
1949 CIN N	64	.244	.326	172	42	6	1	2	1.2	17	18	8	21	0	8	4	191	35	3	2	3.6	.987	C-56
1950	82	.223	.299	224	50	9	1	2	0.9	30	22	32	31	0	1	0	338	26	5	4	4.5	.986	C-81
1951	77	.251	.319	207	52	6	1	2	1.0	22	18	15	34	0	4	2	275	24	4	5	3.9	.987	C-73
1952	17	.189	.432	37	7	1	1	2	5.4	4	4	3	9	0	5	0	43	9	1	0	3.1	.981	C-12
1953 BKN N	1	.000	.000	1	0	0	0	0	0.0	0	0	0	1	0	1	0	0	0	0	0	0.0	–	
1955	16	.262	.357	42	11	4	0	0	0.0	2	5	1	7	0	4	1	49	4	1	0	3.4	.981	C-13
1956	7	.231	.385	13	3	2	0	0	0.0	0	1	1	3	0	2	0	21	1	0	0	3.1	1.000	C-6
8 yrs	340	.246	.337	910	224	39	4	12	1.3	98	93	87	140	1	26	7	1189	129	22	13	3.9	.984	C-315

Harry Howell

HOWELL, HENRY HARRY (Handsome Harry)
B. Nov. 14, 1876, New Jersey D. May 22, 1956, Spokane, Wash.
BR TR 5'9"

Year Team	Games	BA	SA	AB	H	2B	3B	HR	HR%	R	RBI	BB	SO	SB	PH AB	PH H	PO	A	E	DP	TC/G	FA	G by Pos
1898 BKN N	2	.250	.250	8	2	0	0	0	0.0	1	1			0	0	0	1	5	0	1	3.0	1.000	P-2
1899 BAL N	28	.146	.220	82	12	2	2	0	0.0	4	3	3		0	0	0	10	53	4	1	2.4	.940	P-28
1900 BKN N	22	.286	.405	42	12	2	0	1	2.4	6	6	6		1	0	0	6	31	2	1	1.8	.949	P-21
1901 BAL A	53	.218	.356	188	41	10	5	2	1.1	26	26	5		6	0	0	59	93	16	6	3.2	.905	P-37, OF-9, SS-6, 1B-2, 2B-1
1902	96	.268	.395	347	93	16	11	2	0.6	42	42	18		7	1	0	152	208	26	10	4.0	.933	2B-26, P-26, OF-18, 3B-15, SS-11, 1B-1
1903 NY A	40	.217	.311	106	23	3	2	1	0.9	14	12	5		1	4	0	38	81	7	3	3.2	.944	P-25, 3B-7, SS-5, 2B-1, 1B-1
1904 STL A	36	.221	.327	113	25	5	2	1	0.9	9	6	4		0	2	1	26	143	5	1	4.8	.971	P-34
1905	41	.193	.289	135	26	6	2	1	0.7	9	10	3		0	0	0	26	179	8	3	5.2	.962	P-38, OF-3
1906	35	.125	.173	104	13	3	1	0	0.0	5	6	6		2	0	0	31	111	10	2	4.3	.934	P-35
1907	44	.237	.333	114	27	5	0	2	1.8	12	7	7		2	0	0	42	125	3	4	3.9	.982	P-42, OF-2
1908	41	.183	.267	120	22	7	0	1	0.8	10	9	4		0	0	0	21	101	5	3	3.1	.961	P-41
1909	18	.176	.206	34	6	1	0	0	0.0	5	3	2		0	0	0	15	25	4	2	2.4	.909	P-10, 3B-7, OF-1
1910	1	.000	.000	0	0	0	0	0	0.0	0	0	0		0	0	0	0	1	0	0	1.0	1.000	P-1
13 yrs	457	.216	.319	1395	302	60	25	11	0.8	143	131	64		19	7	1	427	1156	90	37	3.7	.946	P-340, OF-33, 3B-29, 2B-28, SS-22, 1B-4

Jack Howell

HOWELL, JACK ROBERT
B. Aug. 18, 1961, Tucson, Ariz.
BL TR 6' 185 lbs.

Year Team	Games	BA	SA	AB	H	2B	3B	HR	HR%	R	RBI	BB	SO	SB	PH AB	PH H	PO	A	E	DP	TC/G	FA	G by Pos
1985 CAL A	43	.197	.336	137	27	4	0	5	3.6	19	18	16	33	1	2	1	33	75	8	10	2.7	.931	3B-42
1986	63	.272	.470	151	41	14	2	4	2.6	26	21	19	28	2	16	4	38	57	2	5	1.5	.979	3B-39, OF-8, DH-2
1987	138	.245	.461	449	110	18	5	23	5.1	64	64	57	118	4	18	6	185	95	7	15	2.1	.976	OF-89, 3B-48, 2B-13
1988	154	.254	.422	500	127	32	4	16	3.2	59	63	46	130	2	4	1	97	249	17	19	2.4	.953	3B-152, OF-2
1989	144	.228	.411	474	108	19	4	20	4.2	56	52	52	125	2	3	1	97	322	11	27	3.0	.974	3B-142, OF-4
5 yrs	542	.241	.427	1711	413	87	13	68	4.0	224	218	190	434	9	43	13	450	798	45	76	2.4	.965	3B-423, OF-103, 2B-13, DH-2

LEAGUE CHAMPIONSHIP SERIES

Year Team	Games	BA	SA	AB	H	2B	3B	HR	HR%	R	RBI	BB	SO	SB	PH AB	PH H	PO	A	E	DP	TC/G	FA	G by Pos
1986 CAL A	2	.000	.000	1	0	0	0	0	0.0	0	0	1	1	0	1	0	0	0	0	0	0.0	–	

Red Howell

HOWELL, MURRAY DONALD (Porky)
B. Jan. 29, 1909, Atlanta, Ga. D. Oct. 1, 1950, Travelers Rest, S. C.
BR TR 6' 215 lbs.

Year Team	Games	BA	SA	AB	H	2B	3B	HR	HR%	R	RBI	BB	SO	SB	PH AB	PH H	PO	A	E	DP	TC/G	FA	G by Pos
1941 CLE A	11	.286	.286	7	2	0	0	0	0.0	2	4	0	2	0	7	2	0	0	0	0	0.0	–	

Roy Howell

HOWELL, ROY LEE
B. Dec. 18, 1953, Lompoc, Calif.
BL TR 6'1" 190 lbs.

Roy Howell *continued*

Year Team	Games	BA	SA	AB	H	2B	3B	HR	HR%	R	RBI	BB	SO	SB	PH AB	PH H	PO	A	E	DP	TC/G	FA	G by Pos
1974 TEX A	13	.250	.341	44	11	1	0	1	2.3	2	3	2	10	0	1	0	5	24	3	1	2.5	.906	3B-12
1975	125	.251	.379	383	96	15	2	10	2.6	43	51	39	79	2	12	4	80	214	21	32	2.5	.933	3B-115, DH-5
1976	140	.253	.367	491	124	28	2	8	1.6	55	53	30	106	1	8	1	103	245	28	20	2.7	.926	3B-130, DH-8
1977 2 teams	TEX A (7G – .000)			TOR A (96G – .316)																			
" total	103	.302	.430	381	115	17	1	10	2.6	41	44	44	80	4	19	1	94	165	13	13	2.6	.952	3B-88, DH-10, OF-2, 1B-1
1978 TOR A	140	.270	.376	551	149	28	3	8	1.5	67	61	44	78	0	2	0	116	306	22	27	3.2	.950	3B-131, OF-5, DH-1
1979	138	.247	.405	511	126	28	4	15	2.9	60	72	42	91	1	2	0	108	290	20	28	3.0	.952	3B-133, DH-4
1980	142	.269	.413	528	142	28	9	10	1.9	51	57	50	92	0	0	0	105	257	16	24	2.7	.958	3B-138, DH-2
1981 MIL A	76	.238	.373	244	58	13	1	6	2.5	37	33	23	39	0	8	0	58	100	6	10	2.2	.963	3B-53, DH-13, 1B-3, OF-1
1982	98	.260	.350	300	78	11	2	4	1.3	31	38	21	39	0	12	2	28	2	2	1	0.3	.938	DH-84, 1B-4, OF-2
1983	69	.278	.448	194	54	9	6	4	2.1	23	25	15	29	1	16	4	20	4	1	4	0.4	.960	DH-54, 1B-2
1984	68	.232	.348	164	38	5	1	4	2.4	12	17	8	31	0	16	2	40	69	9	11	1.7	.924	3B-46, DH-8, 1B-4
11 yrs.	1112	.261	.389	3791	991	183	31	80	2.1	422	454	318	674	9	96	14	757	1676	141	171	2.3	.945	3B-846, DH-189, 1B-14, OF-10

DIVISIONAL PLAYOFF SERIES

Year Team	Games	BA	SA	AB	H	2B	3B	HR	HR%	R	RBI	BB	SO	SB	PH AB	PH H	PO	A	E	DP	TC/G	FA	G by Pos
1981 MIL A	4	.400	.400	5	2	0	0	0	0.0	0	0	2	2	0	1	1	0	0	0	0	0.0	—	DH-3

LEAGUE CHAMPIONSHIP SERIES

Year Team	Games	BA	SA	AB	H	2B	3B	HR	HR%	R	RBI	BB	SO	SB	PH AB	PH H	PO	A	E	DP	TC/G	FA	G by Pos
1982 MIL A	1	.000	.000	3	0	0	0	0	0.0	0	0	0	1	0	0	0	0	0	0	0	0.0	—	DH-1

WORLD SERIES

Year Team	Games	BA	SA	AB	H	2B	3B	HR	HR%	R	RBI	BB	SO	SB	PH AB	PH H	PO	A	E	DP	TC/G	FA	G by Pos
1982 MIL A	4	.000	.000	11	0	0	0	0	0.0	1	0	0	3	0	0	0	0	0	0	0	0.0	—	DH-4

Bill Howerton

HOWERTON, WILLIAM RAY (Hopalong)
B. Dec. 12, 1921, Lompoc, Calif. BL TR 5'11" 185 lbs.

Year Team	Games	BA	SA	AB	H	2B	3B	HR	HR%	R	RBI	BB	SO	SB	PH AB	PH H	PO	A	E	DP	TC/G	FA	G by Pos
1949 STL N	9	.308	.385	13	4	1	0	0	0.0	1	1	0	2	0	3	1	9	0	1	0	1.1	.900	OF-6
1950	110	.281	.492	313	88	20	8	10	3.2	50	59	47	60	0	17	5	183	2	6	0	1.7	.969	OF-94
1951 2 teams	STL N (24G – .262)			PIT N (80G – .274)																			
" total	104	.271	.475	284	77	16	3	12	4.2	39	41	36	56	1	29	4	130	10	8	2	1.4	.946	OF-70, 3B-4
1952 2 teams	PIT N (13G – .320)			NY N (11G – .067)																			
" total	24	.225	.325	40	9	2	1	0	0.0	5	5	9	7	0	13	1	15	1	3	0	0.8	.842	OF-8, 3B-1
4 yrs.	247	.274	.472	650	178	39	12	22	3.4	95	106	92	125	1	62	12	337	13	18	2	1.5	.951	OF-178, 3B-5

Dann Howitt

HOWITT, DANN PAUL JOHN
B. Feb. 13, 1964, Battle Creek, Mich. BL TR 6'5" 205 lbs.

Year Team	Games	BA	SA	AB	H	2B	3B	HR	HR%	R	RBI	BB	SO	SB	PH AB	PH H	PO	A	E	DP	TC/G	FA	G by Pos
1989 OAK A	3	.000	.000	3	0	0	0	0	0.0	0	0	0	2	0	1	0	2	0	0	0	0.7	1.000	OF-1, 1B-1

Dan Howley

HOWLEY, DANIEL PHILIP (Dapper Dan)
B. Oct. 16, 1885, E. Weymouth, Mass. D. Mar. 10, 1944, E. Weymouth, Mass.
Manager 1927-32. BR TR 6' 187 lbs.

Year Team	Games	BA	SA	AB	H	2B	3B	HR	HR%	R	RBI	BB	SO	SB	PH AB	PH H	PO	A	E	DP	TC/G	FA	G by Pos
1913 PHI N	26	.125	.188	32	4	2	0	0	0.0	5	2	4	4	3	0	0	48	14	3	2	2.5	.954	C-22

Dick Howser

HOWSER, RICHARD DALTON
B. May 14, 1936, Miami, Fla. D. June 17, 1987, Kansas City, Mo.
Manager 1978, 1980-86. BR TR 5'8" 155 lbs.

Year Team	Games	BA	SA	AB	H	2B	3B	HR	HR%	R	RBI	BB	SO	SB	PH AB	PH H	PO	A	E	DP	TC/G	FA	G by Pos
1961 KC A	158	.280	.362	611	171	29	6	3	0.5	108	45	92	38	37	1	0	299	427	38	85	4.8	.950	SS-157
1962	83	.238	.350	286	68	8	3	6	2.1	53	34	38	8	19	0	0	138	191	13	37	4.1	.962	SS-72
1963 2 teams	KC A (15G – .195)			CLE A (49G – .247)																			
" total	64	.236	.276	203	48	5	0	1	0.5	29	11	29	21	9	1	1	101	113	11	21	3.5	.951	SS-54
1964 CLE A	162	.256	.319	637	163	23	4	3	0.5	101	52	76	39	20	0	0	291	463	20	100	4.8	.974	SS-162
1965	107	.235	.283	307	72	8	2	1	0.3	47	6	57	25	17	12	3	144	211	7	41	3.4	.981	SS-73, 2B-17
1966	67	.229	.350	140	32	9	1	2	1.4	18	4	15	23	2	8	0	53	95	5	16	2.3	.967	SS-26, 2B-26
1967 NY A	63	.268	.309	149	40	6	0	0	0.0	18	10	25	15	1	17	4	64	76	3	18	2.3	.979	2B-22, 3B-12, SS-3
1968	85	.153	.180	150	23	2	1	0	0.0	24	8	35	17	0	40	8	61	106	3	19	2.0	.982	2B-29, 3B-2, SS-1
8 yrs.	789	.248	.318	2483	617	90	17	16	0.6	398	165	367	186	105	85	16	1151	1682	100	337	3.7	.966	SS-548, 2B-94, 3B-14

Dummy Hoy

HOY, WILLIAM ELLSWORTH
B. May 23, 1862, Houckstown, Ohio D. Dec. 15, 1961, Cincinnati, Ohio BL TR 5'4" 148 lbs.

Year Team	Games	BA	SA	AB	H	2B	3B	HR	HR%	R	RBI	BB	SO	SB	PH AB	PH H	PO	A	E	DP	TC/G	FA	G by Pos
1888 WAS N	136	.274	.338	503	138	10	8	2	0.4	77	29	69	48	82	0	0	296	26	37	7	2.6	.897	OF-136
1889	127	.274	.320	507	139	11	6	0	0.0	98	39	75	30	35	0	0	255	29	35	4	2.5	.890	OF-127
1890 BUF P	122	.298	.371	493	147	17	8	1	0.2	107	53	94	36	39	0	0	290	25	30	10	2.8	.913	OF-122, 2B-1
1891 STL AA	141	.291	.360	567	165	14	5	5	0.9	136	66	119	25	59	0	0	255	26	28	3	2.2	.909	OF-141
1892 WAS N	152	.280	.354	593	166	19	8	3	0.5	108	75	86	23	60	0	0	275	16	38	3	2.2	.884	OF-152
1893	130	.245	.287	564	138	12	6	0	0.0	106	45	66	9	48	0	0	281	26	37	8	2.2	.892	OF-130
1894 CIN N	128	.312	.437	506	158	22	12	5	0.9	114	70	87	18	30	0	0	314	29	40	3	3.0	.896	OF-128
1895	107	.277	.403	429	119	21	12	3	0.7	93	55	52	8	50	0	0	235	14	33	6	2.6	.883	OF-107
1896	121	.298	.409	443	132	23	7	4	0.9	120	57	65	13	50	1	1	303	14	18	3	2.8	.946	OF-120
1897	128	.292	.376	497	145	24	6	2	0.4	87	42	54		37	0	0	359	10	26	5	3.1	.934	OF-128
1898 LOU N	148	.304	.416	582	177	15	16	6	1.0	104	66	49		37	0	0	348	19	21	6	2.6	.946	OF-148
1899	154	.306	.398	633	194	17	13	5	0.8	116	49	61		32	0	0	321	21	27	8	2.4	.927	OF-154
1901 CHI A	132	.294	.400	527	155	28	11	2	0.4	112	60	86		27	0	0	278	16	13	6	2.3	.958	OF-132
1902 CIN N	72	.290	.384	279	81	16	2	2	0.7	48	20	41		11	0	0	149	4	11	1	2.3	.933	OF-72
14 yrs.	1798	.288	.374	7123	2054	249	121	40	0.6	1426	726	1004	210	597	1	1	3959	275	394	73	2.6	.915	OF-1797, 2B-1

Kent Hrbek

HRBEK, KENT ALLEN (Herbie)
B. May 21, 1960, Minneapolis, Minn. BL TR 6'4" 200 lbs.

Year Team	Games	BA	SA	AB	H	2B	3B	HR	HR%	R	RBI	BB	SO	SB	PH AB	PH H	PO	A	E	DP	TC/G	FA	G by Pos
1981 MIN A	24	.239	.358	67	16	5	0	1	1.5	5	7	5	9	0	5	2	124	4	0	14	5.3	1.000	1B-13, DH-8
1982	140	.301	.485	532	160	21	4	23	4.3	82	92	54	80	3	1	0	1174	88	9	125	9.1	.993	1B-138, DH-2
1983	141	.297	.489	515	153	41	5	16	3.1	75	84	57	71	4	3	0	1151	89	13	125	8.9	.990	1B-137, DH-2
1984	149	.311	.522	559	174	31	3	27	4.8	80	107	65	87	1	1	0	1320	99	14	113	9.6	.990	1B-148, DH-1
1985	158	.278	.444	593	165	31	2	21	3.5	78	93	67	87	1	5	2	1339	114	8	114	9.2	.995	1B-156, DH-2

Year Team	Games	BA	SA	AB	H	2B	3B	HR	HR%	R	RBI	BB	SO	SB	Pinch Hit AB	Pinch Hit H	PO	A	E	DP	TC/G	FA	G by Pos

Kent Hrbek *continued*

1986	149	.267	.478	550	147	27	1	29	5.3	85	91	71	81	2	3	0	1218	104	10	137	8.9	.992	1B-147, DH-1
1987	143	.285	.545	477	136	20	1	34	7.1	85	90	84	60	5	5	1	1179	68	5	112	8.8	.996	1B-137, DH-1
1988	143	.312	.520	510	159	31	0	25	4.9	75	76	67	54	0	2	1	842	57	3	92	6.3	.997	1B-105, DH-37
1989	109	.272	.517	375	102	17	0	25	6.7	59	84	53	35	3	4	1	723	60	4	66	7.2	.995	1B-89, DH-18
9 yrs.	1156	.290	.496	4178	1212	224	16	201	4.8	624	724	523	564	19	29	8	9070	683	66	898	8.5	.993	1B-1070, DH-72

LEAGUE CHAMPIONSHIP SERIES

| 1987 MIN A | 5 | .150 | .300 | 20 | 3 | 0 | 0 | 1 | 5.0 | 4 | 1 | 3 | 0 | 0 | 0 | 0 | 40 | 3 | 0 | 3 | 8.6 | 1.000 | 1B-5 |

WORLD SERIES

| 1987 MIN A | 7 | .208 | .333 | 24 | 5 | 0 | 0 | 1 | 4.2 | 4 | 6 | 5 | 3 | 0 | 0 | 0 | 68 | 2 | 0 | 3 | 10.0 | 1.000 | 1B-7 |

Walt Hriniak

HRINIAK, WALTER JOHN
B. May 22, 1943, Natick, Mass. BL TR 5'11" 180 lbs.

1968 ATL N	9	.346	.346	26	9	0	0	0	0.0	0	3	0	3	0	0	0	57	1	2	0	6.7	.967	C-9
1969 2 teams			ATL N (7G – .143)					SD N (31G – .227)															
" total	38	.219	.219	73	16	0	0	0	0.0	4	1	10	12	0	15	2	105	7	2	1	3.0	.982	C-25
2 yrs.	47	.253	.253	99	25	0	0	0	0.0	4	4	10	15	0	15	2	162	8	4	1	3.7	.977	C-34

Al Hubbard

HUBBARD, ALLEN
B. Dec. 9, 1860, Westfield, Mass. D. Dec. 14, 1930, Newton, Mass.

| 1883 PHI AA | 2 | .333 | .333 | 6 | 2 | 0 | 0 | 0 | 0.0 | 2 | | 1 | | 0 | 0 | 0 | 7 | 4 | 4 | 0 | 7.5 | .733 | SS-1, C-1 |

Glenn Hubbard

HUBBARD, GLENN DEE
B. Sept. 25, 1957, Hahn, West Germany BR TR 5'9" 150 lbs.

1978 ATL N	44	.258	.319	163	42	4	0	2	1.2	15	13	10	20	2	0	0	102	130	5	30	5.4	.979	2B-44
1979	97	.231	.295	325	75	12	0	3	0.9	34	29	27	43	0	6	1	193	268	15	57	4.9	.968	2B-91
1980	117	.248	.374	431	107	21	3	9	2.1	55	43	49	69	7	0	0	268	405	15	91	5.9	.978	2B-117
1981	99	.235	.349	361	85	13	5	6	1.7	39	33	33	59	4	0	0	188	344	5	50	5.4	.991	2B-98
1982	145	.248	.350	532	132	25	1	9	1.7	75	59	59	62	4	0	0	312	505	14	111	5.7	.983	2B-144
1983	148	.263	.402	517	136	24	6	12	2.3	65	70	55	71	3	1	0	313	484	12	103	5.5	.985	2B-148
1984	120	.234	.380	397	93	27	2	9	2.3	53	43	55	61	4	4	2	237	405	8	78	5.4	.988	2B-117
1985	142	.232	.314	439	102	21	0	5	1.1	51	39	56	54	4	4	1	339	539	10	127	6.3	.989	2B-140
1986	143	.230	.304	408	94	16	1	4	1.0	42	36	66	74	3	0	0	282	487	19	120	5.5	.976	2B-142
1987	141	.264	.381	443	117	33	2	5	1.1	69	38	77	57	1	2	0	284	478	11	114	5.5	.986	2B-139
1988 OAK A	105	.255	.340	294	75	12	2	3	1.0	35	33	33	50	1	1	0	195	267	6	60	4.5	.987	2B-104, DH-1
1989	53	.198	.313	131	26	6	0	3	2.3	12	12	19	20	2	4	0	82	132	7	34	4.2	.968	2B-48, DH-3
12 yrs.	1354	.244	.349	4441	1084	214	22	70	1.6	545	448	539	640	35	23	4	2795	4444	127	975	5.4	.983	2B-1332, DH-4

LEAGUE CHAMPIONSHIP SERIES

| 1982 ATL N | 3 | .222 | .222 | 9 | 2 | 0 | 0 | 0 | 0.0 | 1 | 1 | 0 | 3 | 0 | 0 | 0 | 0 | 0 | 0 | 0 | 0.0 | – | 2B-3 |

WORLD SERIES

| 1988 OAK A | 4 | .250 | .250 | 12 | 3 | 0 | 0 | 0 | 0.0 | 2 | 0 | 1 | 2 | 1 | 0 | 0 | 5 | 7 | 1 | 0 | 3.3 | .923 | 2B-4 |

Ken Hubbs

HUBBS, KENNETH DOUGLASS
B. Dec. 23, 1941, Riverside, Calif. D. Feb. 15, 1964, Provo, Utah BR TR 6'2" 175 lbs.

1961 CHI N	10	.179	.393	28	5	1	1	1	3.6	4	2	0	8	0	1	0	13	15	0	2	2.8	1.000	2B-8
1962	160	.260	.346	661	172	24	9	5	0.8	90	49	35	129	3	1	0	363	489	15	103	5.4	.983	2B-159
1963	154	.235	.322	566	133	19	3	8	1.4	54	47	39	93	8	2	1	338	493	22	96	5.5	.974	2B-152
3 yrs.	324	.247	.336	1255	310	44	13	14	1.1	148	98	74	230	11	5	1	714	997	37	201	5.4	.979	2B-319

Clarence Huber

HUBER, CLARENCE BILL (Gilly)
B. Oct. 27, 1896, Tyler, Tex. D. Feb. 22, 1965, Laredo, Tex. BR TR 5'10" 165 lbs.

1920 DET A	11	.214	.310	42	9	2	1	0	0.0	4	5	0	5	0	0	0	21	28	5	0	4.9	.907	3B-11
1921	1	–	–	0	0	0	0	0	–	0	0	0	0	0	0	0	1	0	0	0	1.0	1.000	3B-1
1925 PHI N	124	.284	.406	436	124	28	5	5	1.1	46	54	17	33	3	4	2	107	199	17	16	2.6	.947	3B-120
1926	118	.245	.335	376	92	17	7	1	0.3	45	34	42	29	9	2	2	110	214	15	22	2.9	.956	3B-115
4 yrs.	254	.263	.370	854	225	47	13	6	0.7	95	93	59	67	12	6	4	239	441	37	38	2.8	.948	3B-247

Otto Huber

HUBER, OTTO
B. Mar. 12, 1914, Garfield, N. J. D. Apr. 9, 1989, Passaic, N. J. BR TR 5'10" 165 lbs.

| 1939 BOS N | 11 | .273 | .318 | 22 | 6 | 1 | 0 | 0 | 0.0 | 2 | 3 | 0 | 1 | 0 | 2 | 1 | 8 | 12 | 1 | 1 | 1.9 | .952 | 3B-4, 2B-4 |

Dave Hudgens

HUDGENS, DAVID MARK
B. Dec. 5, 1956, Oroville, Calif. BL TL 6'2" 200 lbs.

| 1983 OAK A | 6 | .143 | .143 | 7 | 1 | 0 | 0 | 0 | 0.0 | 0 | 0 | 3 | 0 | 0 | 3 | 0 | 4 | 0 | 0 | 0 | 0.7 | 1.000 | 1B-3, DH-1 |

Jimmy Hudgens

HUDGENS, JAMES PRICE
B. Aug. 24, 1902, Newburg, Mo. D. Aug. 26, 1955, St. Louis, Mo. BL TL 6' 180 lbs.

1923 STL N	6	.250	.333	12	3	1	0	0	0.0	2	0	1	3	0	2	0	37	3	1	1	6.8	.976	1B-3, 2B-1
1925 CIN N	3	.429	.857	7	3	1	1	0	0.0	0	0	1	0	0	0	0	34	1	0	2	11.7	1.000	1B-3
1926	17	.250	.300	20	5	1	0	0	0.0	2	1	1	0	0	10	3	33	2	0	1	2.1	1.000	1B-6
3 yrs.	26	.282	.410	39	11	3	1	0	0.0	4	1	5	4	0	12	3	104	6	1	4	4.3	.991	1B-12, 2B-1

Rex Hudler

HUDLER, REX ALLEN
B. Sept. 2, 1960, Tempe, Ariz. BR TR 6'1" 180 lbs.

1984 NY A	9	.143	.286	7	1	1	0	0	0.0	1	0	1	2	0	0	0	4	7	0	1	1.2	1.000	2B-9
1985	20	.157	.196	51	8	0	1	0	0.0	4	1	1	9	0	0	0	42	51	2	14	4.8	.979	2B-16, SS-1, 1B-1
1986 BAL A	14	.000	.000	1	0	0	0	0	0.0	1	0	0	1	0	0	0	2	3	1	0	0.4	.833	2B-13, 3B-1
1988 MON N	77	.273	.412	216	59	14	2	4	1.9	38	14	10	34	29	3	0	116	168	10	30	3.8	.966	2B-41, SS-27, OF-4

Year	Team	Games	BA	SA	AB	H	2B	3B	HR	HR%	R	RBI	BB	SO	SB	Pinch Hit AB	Pinch Hit H	PO	A	E	DP	TC/G	FA	G by Pos

Rex Hudler continued

Year	Team	Games	BA	SA	AB	H	2B	3B	HR	HR%	R	RBI	BB	SO	SB	PH AB	PH H	PO	A	E	DP	TC/G	FA	G by Pos
1989		92	.245	.406	155	38	7	0	6	3.9	21	13	6	23	15	27	4	59	59	7	13	1.4	.944	2B-38, OF-23, SS-18
5 yrs.		212	.247	.381	430	106	22	3	10	2.3	66	28	18	71	45	30	4	223	288	20	58	2.5	.962	2B-117, SS-46, OF-27, 3B-1, 1B-1

Johnny Hudson

HUDSON, JOHN WILSON
B. June 30, 1912, Bryan, Tex.   D. Nov. 7, 1970, Bryan, Tex.   BR TR 5'10'' 160 lbs.

Year	Team	Games	BA	SA	AB	H	2B	3B	HR	HR%	R	RBI	BB	SO	SB	PH AB	PH H	PO	A	E	DP	TC/G	FA	G by Pos
1936	BKN N	6	.167	.167	12	2	0	0	0	0.0	1	0	2	1	0	0	0	10	8	3	1	3.5	.857	SS-4, 2B-1
1937		13	.185	.333	27	5	4	0	0	0.0	3	2	3	9	0	0	0	9	19	4	2	2.5	.875	SS-11, 2B-1
1938		135	.261	.335	498	130	21	5	2	0.4	59	37	39	76	7	1	0	304	398	27	79	5.4	.963	2B-132, SS-3
1939		109	.254	.338	343	87	17	3	2	0.6	46	32	30	36	5	12	3	175	260	18	56	4.2	.960	SS-50, 2B-45, 3B-1
1940		85	.218	.274	179	39	4	3	0	0.0	13	19	9	26	2	4	2	94	146	15	20	3.0	.941	SS-38, 2B-27, 3B-1
1941	CHI N	50	.202	.242	99	20	4	0	0	0.0	8	6	3	15	3	11	0	41	68	9	9	2.4	.924	SS-17, 2B-13, 3B-10
1945	NY N	28	.000	.000	11	0	0	0	0	0.0	8	0	1	1	0	4	0	5	4	1	0	0.4	.900	3B-5, 2B-2
7 yrs.		426	.242	.314	1169	283	50	11	4	0.3	138	96	87	164	17	33	5	638	903	77	167	3.8	.952	2B-221, SS-123, 3B-17

Nat Hudson

HUDSON, NATHANIEL P.
B. Jan. 12, 1869, Chicago, Ill.   D. Mar. 14, 1928, Chicago, Ill.   TR

Year	Team	Games	BA	SA	AB	H	2B	3B	HR	HR%	R	RBI	BB	SO	SB	PH AB	PH H	PO	A	E	DP	TC/G	FA	G by Pos
1886	STL AA	43	.233	.273	150	35	4	1	0	0.0	16		11		0	0	0	53	38	6	2	2.3	.938	P-29, OF-12, 1B-3
1887		13	.250	.333	48	12	2	1	0	0.0	7		4		0	0	0	9	7	3	0	1.5	.842	P-9, OF-6
1888		56	.255	.321	196	50	7	0	2	1.0	27	28	18		9	0	0	89	55	9	4	2.7	.941	P-39, OF-16, 1B-3, SS-1
1889		13	.250	.365	52	13	1	1	1	1.9	6	10	2	11	1	0	0	20	12	3	0	2.7	.914	P-9, OF-6, 1B-3
4 yrs.		125	.247	.312	446	110	14	3	3	0.7	56	38	35	11	10	0	0	171	112	21	6	2.4	.931	P-86, OF-40, 1B-9, SS-1

Frank Huelsman

HUELSMAN, FRANK ELMER
B. June 5, 1874, St. Louis, Mo.   D. June 9, 1959, Affton, Mo.   BR TR 6'2'' 210 lbs.

Year	Team	Games	BA	SA	AB	H	2B	3B	HR	HR%	R	RBI	BB	SO	SB	PH AB	PH H	PO	A	E	DP	TC/G	FA	G by Pos
1897	STL N	2	.286	.429	7	2	1	0	0	0.0	0	0	0		0	0	0	0	0	1	0	0.5	—	OF-2
1904	4 teams		CHI A (4G – .143)		DET A (4G – .333)		STL A (20G – .221)		WAS A (84G – .248)															
"	total	112	.245	.343	396	97	23	5	2	0.5	28	35	31		7	4	0	162	7	7	2	1.6	.960	OF-107
1905	WAS A	126	.271	.397	421	114	28	8	3	0.7	48	62	31		14	1	0	189	7	15	2	1.7	.929	OF-123
3 yrs.		240	.258	.371	824	213	52	13	5	0.6	76	97	62		18	8	1	351	14	23	4	1.6	.941	OF-232

Mike Huff

HUFF, MICHAEL KALE
B. Aug. 11, 1963, Honolulu, Hawaii   BR TR 6'1'' 180 lbs.

Year	Team	Games	BA	SA	AB	H	2B	3B	HR	HR%	R	RBI	BB	SO	SB	PH AB	PH H	PO	A	E	DP	TC/G	FA	G by Pos
1989	LA N	12	.200	.360	25	5	1	0	1	4.0	2	3	6	0	3	1	18	0	0	0	1.5	1.000	OF-9

Ben Huffman

HUFFMAN, BENJAMIN FRANKLIN
B. June 26, 1914, Rileyville, Va.   BB TR 5'11½'' 175 lbs.

Year	Team	Games	BA	SA	AB	H	2B	3B	HR	HR%	R	RBI	BB	SO	SB	PH AB	PH H	PO	A	E	DP	TC/G	FA	G by Pos
1937	STL A	76	.273	.341	176	48	9	1	0	0.6	18	24	10	7	1	32	7	140	20	5	4	2.2	.970	C-42

Ed Hug

HUG, EDWARD AMBROSE
B. July 14, 1880, Fayetteville, Ohio   D. May 11, 1953, Cincinnati, Ohio   BR TR

Year	Team	Games	BA	SA	AB	H	2B	3B	HR	HR%	R	RBI	BB	SO	SB	PH AB	PH H	PO	A	E	DP	TC/G	FA	G by Pos
1903	BKN N	1	—	—	0	0	0	0	0	–	0	0	1		0	0	0	0	0	0	0	0.0	—	C-1

Miller Huggins

HUGGINS, MILLER JAMES (Hug, The Mighty Mite)
B. Mar. 27, 1879, Cincinnati, Ohio   D. Sept. 25, 1929, New York, N. Y.   BB TR 5'6½'' 140 lbs.
Manager 1913-29.
Hall of Fame 1964.

Year	Team	Games	BA	SA	AB	H	2B	3B	HR	HR%	R	RBI	BB	SO	SB	PH AB	PH H	PO	A	E	DP	TC/G	FA	G by Pos
1904	CIN N	140	.263	.328	491	129	12	7	2	0.4	96	30	88		13	0	0	337	448	46	32	5.9	.945	2B-140
1905		149	.273	.326	564	154	11	8	1	0.2	117	38	103		27	0	0	346	525	51	55	6.2	.945	2B-149
1906		146	.292	.338	545	159	11	7	0	0.0	81	26	71		41	0	0	341	458	44	62	5.8	.948	2B-146
1907		156	.248	.289	561	139	12	4	1	0.2	64	31	83		28	0	0	353	443	32	73	5.3	.961	2B-156
1908		135	.239	.287	498	119	14	5	0	0.0	65	23	58		30	4	1	302	406	30	45	5.5	.959	2B-135
1909		57	.214	.245	159	34	3	1	0	0.0	18	6	28		11	10	1	95	125	16	14	4.1	.932	2B-31, 3B-15
1910	STL N	151	.265	.320	547	145	15	6	1	0.2	101	36	116	46	34	0	0	325	452	30	58	5.3	.963	2B-151
1911		138	.261	.312	509	133	19	2	1	0.2	106	24	96	52	37	1	1	281	439	29	62	5.4	.961	2B-136
1912		120	.304	.357	431	131	15	4	0	0.0	82	29	87	31	35	5	0	272	337	37	50	5.4	.943	2B-114
1913		120	.286	.318	381	109	12	0	0	0.0	73	27	91	49	23	5	1	266	339	14	44	5.2	.977	2B-112
1914		148	.263	.318	509	134	17	4	1	0.2	85	24	105	63	32	1	0	328	428	28	58	5.3	.964	2B-147
1915		107	.241	.283	353	85	5	2	1	0.3	57	24	74	68	13	0	0	194	315	23	44	5.0	.957	2B-107
1916		18	.333	.333	9	3	0	0	0	0.0	2	0	2	3	3	0	0	10	10	0	0	1.1	1.000	2B-7
13 yrs.		1585	.265	.314	5557	1474	146	50	9	0.2	947	318	1002	312	324	30	6	3450	4725	380	597	5.4	.956	2B-1531, 3B-15

Bill Hughes

HUGHES, WILLIAM R.
B. Nov. 25, 1866, Bladensville, Ill.   D. Aug. 25, 1943, Santa Ana, Calif.   BL TL

Year	Team	Games	BA	SA	AB	H	2B	3B	HR	HR%	R	RBI	BB	SO	SB	PH AB	PH H	PO	A	E	DP	TC/G	FA	G by Pos
1884	WAS U	14	.122	.122	49	6	0	0	0	0.0	5		2		0	0	0	92	3	7	2	7.3	.931	1B-9, OF-6
1885	PHI AA	4	.188	.375	16	3	1	1	0	0.0	3		1		0	0	0	4	2	1	0	1.8	.857	OF-2, P-2
2 yrs.		18	.138	.185	65	9	1	1	0	0.0	8		3		0	0	0	96	5	8	2	6.1	.927	1B-9, OF-8, P-2

Joe Hughes

HUGHES, JOSEPH THOMPSON
B. Feb. 21, 1880, Pardo, Pa.   D. Mar. 13, 1951, Cleveland, Ohio   BR TR 5'10'' 165 lbs.

Year	Team	Games	BA	SA	AB	H	2B	3B	HR	HR%	R	RBI	BB	SO	SB	PH AB	PH H	PO	A	E	DP	TC/G	FA	G by Pos
1902	CHI N	1	.000	.000	3	0	0	0	0	0.0	0	0	0		0	0	0	0	0	0	0	0.0	—	OF-1

Keith Hughes

HUGHES, KEITH WILLS
B. Sept. 12, 1963, Bryn Mawr, Pa.   BL TL 6'3'' 210 lbs.

Year	Team	Games	BA	SA	AB	H	2B	3B	HR	HR%	R	RBI	BB	SO	SB	PH AB	PH H	PO	A	E	DP	TC/G	FA	G by Pos
1987	2 teams		NY A (4G – .000)		PHI N (37G – .263)																			
"	total	41	.250	.375	80	20	2	0	2	2.5	8	10	7	13	0	23	8	26	0	1	0	0.7	.963	OF-23
1988	BAL A	41	.194	.324	108	21	4	2	2	1.9	10	14	16	27	1	8	0	59	4	2	2	1.6	.969	OF-31
2 yrs.		82	.218	.303	188	41	6	2	4	2.1	18	24	23	40	1	31	8	85	4	3	2	1.1	.967	OF-54

Year	Team		Games	BA	SA	AB	H	2B	3B	HR	HR%	R	RBI	BB	SO	SB	Pinch Hit AB	Pinch Hit H	PO	A	E	DP	TC/G	FA	G by Pos

Roy Hughes

HUGHES, ROY JOHN (Sage, Jeep)
B. Jan. 11, 1911, Cincinnati, Ohio

BR TR 5'10½" 167 lbs.

Year	Team		Games	BA	SA	AB	H	2B	3B	HR	HR%	R	RBI	BB	SO	SB	PH AB	PH H	PO	A	E	DP	TC/G	FA	G by Pos
1935	CLE	A	82	.293	.372	266	78	15	3	0	0.0	18	14	13	6	0			152	216	17	44	4.7	.956	2B-40, SS-29, 3B-1
1936			152	.295	.378	638	188	35	9	0	0.0	112	63	57	40	20	0	0	421	466	25	98	6.0	.973	2B-152
1937			104	.277	.355	346	96	12	6	1	0.3	57	40	40	22	11	11	4	157	233	13	32	3.9	.968	3B-58, 2B-32
1938	STL	A	58	.281	.375	96	27	3	0	2	2.1	16	13	12	11	3	30	6	45	60	4	16	1.9	.963	2B-21, 3B-5, SS-2
1939	2 teams		STL A	(17G – .087)		PHI	N	(65G – .228)																	
"	total		82	.215	.254	260	56	5	1	1	0.4	28	17	25	22	4	5	1	194	198	6	34	4.9	.985	2B-71, SS-1
1944	CHI	N	126	.287	.351	478	137	16	6	1	0.2	86	28	35	30	16	7	4	220	303	20	54	4.3	.963	3B-66, SS-52
1945			69	.261	.306	222	58	8	1	0	0.0	34	8	16	18	6	5	1	120	157	13	28	4.2	.955	SS-36, 2B-21, 3B-9, 1B-2
1946	PHI	N	89	.236	.283	276	65	11	1	0	0.0	23	22	19	15	7	12	3	123	144	11	27	3.1	.960	SS-34, 3B-31, 2B-7, 1B-1
8 yrs.			762	.273	.340	2582	705	105	27	5	0.2	396	205	222	175	80	76	19	1432	1777	109	333	4.4	.967	2B-344, 3B-170, SS-154, 1B-3

WORLD SERIES

Year	Team		Games	BA	SA	AB	H	2B	3B	HR	HR%	R	RBI	BB	SO	SB	PH AB	PH H	PO	A	E	DP	TC/G	FA	G by Pos
1945	CHI	N	6	.294	.353	17	5	1	0	0	0.0	1	3	4	5	0	0	0	13	17	0	2	5.0	1.000	SS-6

Terry Hughes

HUGHES, TERRY WAYNE
B. May 13, 1949, Spartanburg, S. C.

BR TR 6'1" 185 lbs.

Year	Team		Games	BA	SA	AB	H	2B	3B	HR	HR%	R	RBI	BB	SO	SB	PH AB	PH H	PO	A	E	DP	TC/G	FA	G by Pos
1970	CHI	N	2	.333	.333	3	1	0	0	0	0.0	0	0	0	0	0	1	1	0	0	0	0	0.0	–	OF-1, 3B-1
1973	STL	N	11	.214	.286	14	3	1	0	0	0.0	1	1	1	4	0	4	1	9	4	0	1	1.2	1.000	3B-5, 1B-1
1974	BOS	A	41	.203	.275	69	14	2	0	1	1.4	5	6	6	18	0	1	0	25	44	3	5	1.8	.958	3B-36, DH-1
3 yrs.			54	.209	.279	86	18	3	0	1	1.2	6	7	7	22	0	6	2	34	48	3	6	1.6	.965	3B-42, DH-1, OF-1, 1B-1

Tom Hughes

HUGHES, THOMAS FRANKLIN
B. Aug. 6, 1907, Emmet, Ark.

BL TR 6'1" 190 lbs.

Year	Team		Games	BA	SA	AB	H	2B	3B	HR	HR%	R	RBI	BB	SO	SB	PH AB	PH H	PO	A	E	DP	TC/G	FA	G by Pos
1930	DET	A	17	.373	.508	59	22	2	3	0	0.0	8	5	4	8	0	0	0	26	0	3	0	1.7	.897	OF-16

Emil Huhn

HUHN, EMIL HUGO (Hap)
B. Mar. 10, 1892, North Vernon, Ind.   D. Sept. 5, 1925, Camden, S. C.

BR TR 6' 180 lbs.

Year	Team		Games	BA	SA	AB	H	2B	3B	HR	HR%	R	RBI	BB	SO	SB	PH AB	PH H	PO	A	E	DP	TC/G	FA	G by Pos
1915	NWK	F	124	.227	.282	415	94	18	1	1	0.2	34	41	28		13	8	1	1071	71	18	70	9.4	.984	1B-101, C-16
1916	CIN	N	37	.255	.330	94	24	3	2	0	0.0	4	3	2	11	0	3	1	172	25	1	7	5.4	.995	C-18, 1B-14, OF-1
1917			23	.196	.294	51	10	1	2	0	0.0	2	3	2	5	1	7	1	50	15	2	0	2.9	.970	C-15
3 yrs.			184	.229	.291	560	128	22	5	1	0.2	40	47	32	16	14	18	3	1293	111	21	77	7.7	.985	1B-115, C-49, OF-1

Billy Hulen

HULEN, WILLIAM FRANKLIN
B. Mar. 12, 1870, Dixon, Calif.   D. Oct. 2, 1947, Santa Rosa, Calif.

BL TL 5'8" 148 lbs.

Year	Team		Games	BA	SA	AB	H	2B	3B	HR	HR%	R	RBI	BB	SO	SB	PH AB	PH H	PO	A	E	DP	TC/G	FA	G by Pos
1896	PHI	N	88	.265	.360	339	90	18	7	0	0.0	87	38	55	20	23	1	1	182	208	56	33	5.1	.874	SS-73, OF-12, 2B-2
1899	WAS	N	19	.147	.162	68	10	1	0	0	0.0	10	3	10		5	0	0	25	67	10	2	5.4	.902	SS-19
2 yrs.			107	.246	.327	407	100	19	7	0	0.0	97	41	65	20	28	1	1	207	275	66	35	5.1	.880	SS-92, OF-12, 2B-2

Tim Hulett

HULETT, TIMOTHY CRAIG
B. Jan. 20, 1960, Springfield, Ill.

BR TR 6' 185 lbs.

Year	Team		Games	BA	SA	AB	H	2B	3B	HR	HR%	R	RBI	BB	SO	SB	PH AB	PH H	PO	A	E	DP	TC/G	FA	G by Pos
1983	CHI	A	6	.200	.200	5	1	0	0	0	0.0	0	0	0	0	1	0	0	8	6	2	1	2.7	.875	2B-6
1984			8	.000	.000	7	0	0	0	0	0.0	1	0	1	4	1	1	0	4	15	0	2	2.4	1.000	3B-4, 2B-3
1985			141	.268	.375	395	106	19	4	5	1.3	52	36	30	81	6	2	1	117	256	24	41	2.8	.940	3B-115, 2B-28, OF-1
1986			150	.231	.379	520	120	16	5	17	3.3	53	44	21	91	4	5	1	179	331	15	54	3.5	.971	3B-89, 2B-66
1987			68	.217	.346	240	52	10	0	7	2.9	20	28	10	41	0	0	0	55	142	9	19	3.0	.956	3B-61, 2B-8
1989	BAL	A	33	.278	.423	97	27	5	0	3	3.1	12	18	10	17	0	1	0	70	71	4	13	4.4	.972	2B-23, 3B-11
6 yrs.			406	.242	.372	1264	306	50	9	32	2.5	138	126	72	234	12	9	2	433	821	54	130	3.2	.959	3B-280, 2B-134, OF-1

Rudy Hulswitt

HULSWITT, RUDOLPH EDWARD
B. Feb. 23, 1877, Newport, Ky.   D. Jan. 16, 1950, Louisville, Ky.

BR TR 5'8½" 165 lbs.

Year	Team		Games	BA	SA	AB	H	2B	3B	HR	HR%	R	RBI	BB	SO	SB	PH AB	PH H	PO	A	E	DP	TC/G	FA	G by Pos
1899	LOU	N	1	–	–	0	0	0	0	0	–	0	0	0		0	0	0	1	1	4	0	6.0	.333	SS-1
1902	PHI	N	128	.272	.322	497	135	11	7	0	0.0	59	38	30		12	0	0	320	405	67	38	6.2	.915	SS-125, 3B-3
1903			138	.247	.329	519	128	22	9	1	0.2	56	58	28		10	0	0	354	430	81	43	6.3	.906	SS-138
1904			113	.244	.298	406	99	11	4	1	0.2	36	36	16		8	0	0	273	310	56	42	5.7	.912	SS-113
1908	CIN	N	119	.228	.285	386	88	5	7	1	0.3	27	28	30		7	0	0	245	370	42	37	5.5	.936	SS-118, 2B-1
1909	STL	N	82	.280	.329	289	81	8	3	0	0.0	21	29	19		7	4	1	166	228	30	20	5.2	.929	SS-65, 2B-12
1910			63	.248	.331	133	33	7	2	0	0.0	9	14	13	10	5	31	6	40	80	21	4	2.2	.851	SS-30, 2B-2
7 yrs.			644	.253	.314	2230	564	64	32	3	0.1	208	203	136	10	49	35	7	1399	1824	301	184	5.5	.915	SS-590, 2B-15, 3B-3

John Hummel

HUMMEL, JOHN EDWIN (Silent John)
B. Apr. 4, 1883, Bloomsburg, Pa.   D. May 18, 1959, Springfield, Mass.

BR TR 5'11" 160 lbs.

Year	Team		Games	BA	SA	AB	H	2B	3B	HR	HR%	R	RBI	BB	SO	SB	PH AB	PH H	PO	A	E	DP	TC/G	FA	G by Pos
1905	BKN	N	30	.266	.367	109	29	3	4	0	0.0	19	7	9		6	0	0	62	90	6	13	5.3	.962	2B-30
1906			97	.199	.259	286	57	6	4	1	0.3	20	21	36		10	8	2	310	156	18	25	5.0	.963	2B-50, OF-21, 1B-15
1907			107	.234	.313	342	80	12	3	3	0.9	41	31	26		8	10	2	321	162	16	23	4.7	.968	2B-44, OF-33, 1B-12, SS-8
1908			154	.241	.320	594	143	11	12	4	0.7	51	41	34		20	0	0	367	182	18	25	3.7	.968	OF-95, 2B-43, SS-9, 1B-8
1909			146	.280	.363	542	152	15	9	4	0.7	54	52	22		16	2	0	728	207	35	38	6.6	.964	1B-54, 2B-38, SS-36, OF-17
1910			153	.244	.351	578	141	21	13	5	0.9	67	74	57	81	21	0	0	344	424	28	67	5.2	.965	2B-153
1911			137	.270	.392	477	129	21	11	5	1.0	54	58	67	66	16	3	0	337	362	21	61	5.3	.971	2B-127, 1B-4, SS-2
1912			122	.282	.404	411	116	21	7	5	1.2	55	54	49	55	7	9	0	297	168	11	22	3.9	.977	2B-58, OF-44, 1B-11
1913			67	.242	.379	198	48	7	7	2	1.0	20	24	13	23	4	15	3	126	66	8	24	3.0	.960	2B-28, SS-17, 1B-6, 3B-3
1914			73	.264	.389	208	55	8	9	0	0.0	25	20	16	25	5	17	2	339	21	6	13	5.0	.984	1B-36, OF-19, SS-1, 2B-1
1915			53	.230	.310	100	23	2	3	0	0.0	6	8	6	11	1	17	2	95	4	0	5	1.9	1.000	OF-20, 1B-11, SS-1
1918	NY	A	22	.295	.377	61	18	1	2	0	0.0	9	4	11	8	3	4	1	58	3	2	3	2.9	.968	OF-15, 1B-3, 2B-1
12 yrs.			1161	.254	.352	3906	991	128	84	29	0.7	421	394	346	269	117	85	12	3384	1845	169	319	4.6	.969	2B-548, OF-292, 1B-160, SS-74

Al Humphrey

HUMPHREY, ALBERT
B. Feb. 28, 1886, Ashtabula, Ohio   D. May 13, 1961, Ashtabula, Ohio

BL TR 5'11" 180 lbs.

Year	Team	Games	BA	SA	AB	H	2B	3B	HR	HR%	R	RBI	BB	SO	SB	Pinch Hit AB	Pinch Hit H	PO	A	E	DP	TC/G	FA	G by Pos

Steve Huntz *continued*

| 1975 | SD | N | 22 | .151 | .226 | 53 | 8 | 4 | 0 | 0 | 0.0 | 3 | 4 | 7 | 8 | 0 | 6 | 0 | 15 | 33 | 3 | 6 | 2.3 | .941 | 3B-16, 2B-2 |
| 5 yrs. | | 237 | .206 | .314 | 636 | 131 | 19 | 1 | 16 | 2.5 | 81 | 60 | 108 | 122 | 1 | 31 | 2 | 244 | 467 | 32 | 77 | 3.1 | .957 | SS-116, 3B-79, 2B-30 |

Dave Huppert

HUPPERT, DAVID BLAIN
B. Apr. 1, 1957, Southgate, Calif.
BR TR 6'1" 190 lbs.

1983	BAL	A	2	–	–	0	0	0	0	0	–	0	0	0	0	0	0	0	3	0	0	0	1.5	1.000	C-2
1985	MIL	A	15	.048	.048	21	1	0	0	0	0.0	1	0	2	7	0	0	0	45	3	2	2	3.3	.960	C-15
2 yrs.		17	.048	.048	21	1	0	0	0	0.0	1	0	2	7	0	0	0	48	3	2	2	3.1	.962	C-17

Clint Hurdle

HURDLE, CLINTON MERRICK
B. July 30, 1957, Big Rapids, Mich.
BL TR 6'3" 195 lbs.

1977	KC	A	9	.308	.538	26	8	0	0	2	7.7	5	7	2	7	0	0	0	17	0	0	0	1.9	1.000	OF-9
1978		133	.264	.398	417	110	25	5	7	1.7	48	56	56	84	1	8	5	544	30	12	48	4.4	.980	OF-78, 1B-52, DH-1, 3B-1
1979		59	.240	.386	171	41	10	3	3	1.8	16	30	28	24	0	7	1	89	2	3	0	1.6	.968	OF-50, DH-4, 3B-1
1980		130	.294	.458	395	116	31	2	10	2.5	50	60	34	61	0	9	3	233	8	10	1	1.9	.960	OF-126
1981		28	.329	.553	76	25	3	1	4	5.3	12	15	13	10	0	2	1	59	1	0	0	2.1	1.000	OF-28
1982	CIN	N	19	.206	.235	34	7	1	0	0	0.0	2	1	2	6	0	3	1	17	2	1	0	1.1	.950	OF-17
1983	NY	N	13	.182	.242	33	6	2	0	0	0.0	3	2	2	10	0	4	0	1	15	4	2	1.5	.800	3B-9, OF-1
1985		43	.195	.354	82	16	4	0	3	3.7	7	7	13	20	0	16	0	89	7	1	0	2.3	.990	C-17, OF-10
1986	STL	N	78	.195	.299	154	30	5	1	3	1.9	18	15	26	38	0	22	6	334	31	3	31	4.7	.992	1B-39, OF-10, C-5, 3B-4
1987	NY	N	3	.333	.333	3	1	0	0	0	0.0	1	0	0	1	0	2	0	1	0	0	0	0.3	1.000	1B-1
10 yrs.		515	.259	.403	1391	360	81	12	32	2.3	162	193	176	261	1	73	17	1384	96	34	82	2.9	.978	OF-329, 1B-92, C-22, 3B-15, DH-5

DIVISIONAL PLAYOFF SERIES

| 1981 | KC | A | 3 | .273 | .273 | 11 | 3 | 0 | 0 | 0 | 0.0 | 0 | 0 | 1 | 0 | 0 | 0 | 0 | 0 | 0 | 0 | 0 | 0.0 | – | OF-3 |

LEAGUE CHAMPIONSHIP SERIES

1978	KC	A	4	.375	.625	8	3	1	0	0	0.0	1	2	3	0	1	0	6	1	0	1	1.8	1.000	OF-2
1980		3	.000	.000	2	0	0	0	0	0.0	0	0	1	1	0	0	0	1	0	0	0	0.3	1.000	OF-2
2 yrs.		7	.300	.500	10	3	1	0	0	0.0	1	1	2	4	0	1	0	7	1	0	1	1.1	1.000	OF-4

WORLD SERIES

| 1980 | KC | A | 4 | .417 | .500 | 12 | 5 | 1 | 0 | 0 | 0.0 | 1 | 0 | 2 | 1 | 1 | 0 | 0 | 8 | 0 | 0 | 0 | 2.0 | 1.000 | OF-4 |

Jerry Hurley

HURLEY, JEREMIAH JOSEPH
B. June 15, 1863, Boston, Mass. D. Sept. 17, 1950, Boston, Mass.
BR TR 6' 190 lbs.

1889	BOS	N	1	.000	.000	4	0	0	0	0	0.0	0	0	0	0	0	0	0	2	2	1	0	5.0	.800	OF-1, C-1
1890	PIT	P	8	.273	.318	22	6	1	0	0	0.0	2	2	5	0	0	0	0	27	3	3	0	4.1	.909	C-7, OF-1
1891	CIN	AA	24	.212	.318	66	14	3	2	0	0.0	10	6	12	13	2	0	0	89	11	15	2	4.8	.870	C-24, OF-1, 1B-1
3 yrs.		33	.217	.304	92	20	4	2	0	0.0	15	8	14	18	2	0	0	118	16	19	2	4.6	.876	C-32, OF-3, 1B-1

Pat Hurley

HURLEY, JEREMIAH
B. Apr., 1875, New York, N. Y. D. Dec. 27, 1919, New York, N. Y.
BR TR

1901	CIN	N	9	.048	.048	21	1	0	0	0	0.0	1	0	1	0	0	1	0	2	0	39	6	3	0	5.3	.938	C-7
1907	BKN	N	1	.000	.000	2	0	0	0	0	0.0	0	0	1	0	0	0	0	4	1	0	0	5.0	1.000	C-1
2 yrs.		10	.043	.043	23	1	0	0	0	0.0	1	0	2	1	0	2	0	43	7	3	0	5.3	.943	C-8

Don Hurst

HURST, FRANK O'DONNELL
B. Aug. 12, 1905, Maysville, Ky. D. Dec. 6, 1952, Los Angeles, Calif.
BL TL 6' 215 lbs.

1928	PHI	N	107	.285	.508	396	113	23	4	19	4.8	73	64	68	40	3	3	0	964	68	12	92	9.8	.989	1B-104
1929		154	.304	.525	589	179	29	4	31	5.3	100	125	80	36	10	0	0	1509	112	24	125	10.7	.985	1B-154
1930		119	.327	.522	391	128	19	3	17	4.3	78	78	46	22	6	13	3	857	59	17	92	7.8	.982	1B-96, OF-7
1931		137	.305	.468	489	149	37	5	11	2.2	63	91	64	28	8	2	0	1206	104	18	117	9.7	.986	1B-135
1932		150	.339	.547	579	196	41	4	24	4.1	109	143	65	27	10	0	0	1341	94	10	105	9.6	.993	1B-150
1933		147	.267	.389	550	147	27	8	8	1.5	58	76	48	32	3	5	1	1355	114	23	132	10.1	.985	1B-142
1934	2 teams	PHI N (40G – .262)		CHI N (51G – .199)																				
"	total	91	.228	.331	281	64	14	0	5	1.8	29	33	20	25	1	9	2	730	35	8	69	8.5	.990	1B-87
7 yrs.		905	.298	.478	3275	976	190	28	115	3.5	510	610	391	210	41	32	6	7962	586	112	732	9.6	.987	1B-868, OF-7

Jeff Huson

HUSON, JEFFREY KENT (Huey)
B. Aug. 15, 1964, Scottsdale, Ariz.
BL TR 6'3" 180 lbs.

1988	MON	N	20	.310	.357	42	13	2	0	0	0.0	7	3	4	3	2	2	0	18	41	4	5	3.2	.937	SS-15, 2B-2, OF-1, 3B-1
1989		32	.162	.230	74	12	5	0	0	0.0	1	2	6	6	3	4	1	40	65	8	11	3.5	.929	SS-20, 2B-9, 3B-1
2 yrs.		52	.216	.276	116	25	7	0	0	0.0	8	5	10	9	5	6	1	58	106	12	16	3.4	.932	SS-35, 2B-11, 3B-2, OF-1

Carl Husta

HUSTA, CARL LAWRENCE (Sox)
B. Apr. 8, 1902, Egg Harbor, N. J. D. Nov. 6, 1951, Kingston, N. Y.
BR TR 5'11" 176 lbs.

| 1925 | PHI | A | 6 | .136 | .136 | 22 | 3 | 0 | 0 | 0 | 0.0 | 2 | 2 | 2 | 3 | 0 | 0 | 0 | 18 | 22 | 1 | 4 | 6.8 | .976 | SS-6 |

Harry Huston

HUSTON, HARRY EMANUEL KRESS
B. Oct. 14, 1883, Bellefontaine, Ohio D. Oct. 13, 1969, Blackwell, Okla.
BR TR 5'9" 168 lbs.

| 1906 | PHI | N | 2 | .000 | .000 | 4 | 0 | 0 | 0 | 0 | 0.0 | 0 | 0 | 0 | 0 | 0 | 0 | 0 | 5 | 2 | 0 | 0 | 3.5 | 1.000 | C-2 |

Warren Huston

HUSTON, WARREN LLEWELLYN
B. Oct. 31, 1913, Newtonville, Mass.
BR TR 6' 170 lbs.

1937	PHI	A	38	.130	.185	54	7	3	0	0	0.0	3	2	9	5	3	0	0	40	58	9	17	2.8	.916	2B-16, SS-15, 3B-2
1944	BOS	N	33	.200	.218	55	11	1	0	0	0.0	7	1	8	5	0	0	0	26	44	3	2	2.2	.959	3B-20, 2B-5, SS-4
2 yrs.		71	.165	.202	109	18	4	0	0	0.0	12	4	10	14	0	3	0	66	102	12	19	2.5	.933	3B-22, 2B-21, SS-19

Year Team	Games	BA	SA	AB	H	2B	3B	HR	HR%	R	RBI	BB	SO	SB	Pinch Hit AB	Pinch Hit H	PO	A	E	DP	TC/G	FA	G by Pos

Joe Hutcheson

HUTCHESON, JOSEPH JOHNSON (Poodles)
B. Feb. 5, 1905, Springtown, Tex.
BL TR 6'2" 200 lbs.

Year Team	Games	BA	SA	AB	H	2B	3B	HR	HR%	R	RBI	BB	SO	SB	PH AB	PH H	PO	A	E	DP	TC/G	FA	G by Pos
1933 BKN N	55	.234	.364	184	43	4	1	6	3.3	19	21	15	13	1	10	1	84	8	1	2	1.7	.989	OF-45

Ed Hutchinson

HUTCHINSON, EDWIN FORREST
B. May 19, 1867, Pittsburgh, Pa. D. July 19, 1934, Colfax, Calif.
BL TR 5'11" 175 lbs.

Year Team	Games	BA	SA	AB	H	2B	3B	HR	HR%	R	RBI	BB	SO	SB	PH AB	PH H	PO	A	E	DP	TC/G	FA	G by Pos
1890 CHI N	4	.059	.118	17	1	1	0	0	0.0	0	0	0	0	0	0	0	6	12	0	1	4.5	1.000	2B-4

Fred Hutchinson

HUTCHINSON, FREDERICK CHARLES
B. Aug. 12, 1919, Seattle, Wash. D. Nov. 12, 1964, Bradenton, Fla.
Manager 1952-54, 1956-64.
BL TR 6'2" 190 lbs.

Year Team	Games	BA	SA	AB	H	2B	3B	HR	HR%	R	RBI	BB	SO	SB	PH AB	PH H	PO	A	E	DP	TC/G	FA	G by Pos
1939 DET A	13	.382	.412	34	13	1	0	0	0.0	5	6	2	0	0	0	0	6	13	0	1	1.5	1.000	P-13
1940	17	.267	.300	30	8	1	0	0	0.0	1	2	0	0	0	0	0	2	16	2	1	1.2	.900	P-17
1941	2	.000	.000	2	0	0	0	0	0.0	0	0	0	2	0	0	0	0	0	0	0	0.0	–	
1946	40	.315	.360	89	28	4	0	0	0.0	11	13	6	1	0	9	2	11	47	1	3	1.5	.983	P-28
1947	56	.302	.443	106	32	5	2	2	1.9	8	15	6	6	2	22	6	15	40	1	1	1.0	.982	P-33
1948	76	.205	.241	112	23	1	0	1	0.9	11	12	23	9	3	32	7	19	45	0	5	0.8	1.000	P-33
1949	38	.247	.301	73	18	2	1	0	0.0	12	7	8	5	1	4	1	18	39	1	5	1.5	.983	P-33
1950	44	.326	.400	95	31	7	0	0	0.0	15	20	12	3	0	4	1	17	50	4	6	1.6	.944	P-39
1951	47	.188	.212	85	16	2	0	0	0.0	7	7	7	4	0	13	2	17	45	4	1	1.4	.939	P-31
1952	17	.056	.056	18	1	0	0	0	0.0	0	0	3	0	0	5	1	1	15	0	1	0.9	1.000	P-12
1953	4	.167	.667	6	1	0	0	1	16.7	1	1	0	0	0	0	0	1	6	0	0	1.5	1.000	P-3, 1B-1
11 yrs.	354	.263	.326	650	171	23	3	4	0.6	71	83	67	30	6	91	20	112	310	13	24	1.2	.970	P-242, 1B-1

WORLD SERIES

Year Team	Games	BA	SA	AB	H	2B	3B	HR	HR%	R	RBI	BB	SO	SB	PH AB	PH H	PO	A	E	DP	TC/G	FA	G by Pos
1940 DET A	1	–	–	0	0	0	0	0	–	0	0	0	0	0	0	0	0	0	0	0	0.0	–	P-1

Roy Hutson

HUTSON, ROY LEE
B. Feb. 27, 1902, Luray, Mo. D. May 20, 1957, La Mesa, Calif.
BL TR 5'9" 165 lbs.

Year Team	Games	BA	SA	AB	H	2B	3B	HR	HR%	R	RBI	BB	SO	SB	PH AB	PH H	PO	A	E	DP	TC/G	FA	G by Pos
1925 BKN N	7	.500	.500	8	4	0	0	0	0.0	1	1	1	1	0	0	0	4	0	0	0	0.6	1.000	OF-4

Jim Hutto

HUTTO, JAMES NEAMON JR
B. Oct. 17, 1947, Norfolk, Va.
BR TR 5'11" 195 lbs.

Year Team	Games	BA	SA	AB	H	2B	3B	HR	HR%	R	RBI	BB	SO	SB	PH AB	PH H	PO	A	E	DP	TC/G	FA	G by Pos
1970 PHI N	57	.185	.304	92	17	2	0	3	3.3	7	12	5	20	0	26	6	71	4	0	4	1.3	1.000	OF-22, 1B-12, C-5, 3B-1
1975 BAL A	4	.000	.000	5	0	0	0	0	0.0	0	0	0	2	0	1	0	6	0	0	0	1.5	1.000	C-3
2 yrs.	61	.175	.289	97	17	2	0	3	3.1	7	12	5	22	0	27	6	77	4	0	4	1.3	1.000	OF-22, 1B-12, C-8, 3B-1

Tom Hutton

HUTTON, THOMAS GEORGE
B. Apr. 20, 1946, Los Angeles, Calif.
BL TL 5'11" 180 lbs.

Year Team	Games	BA	SA	AB	H	2B	3B	HR	HR%	R	RBI	BB	SO	SB	PH AB	PH H	PO	A	E	DP	TC/G	FA	G by Pos
1966 LA N	3	.000	.000	2	0	0	0	0	0.0	0	0	0	0	0	2	0	2	0	0	0	0.7	1.000	1B-3
1969	16	.271	.271	48	13	0	0	0	0.0	2	4	5	7	0	0	0	130	19	1	9	9.4	.993	1B-16
1972 PHI N	134	.260	.344	381	99	16	2	4	1.0	40	38	56	24	5	19	8	648	38	6	47	5.2	.991	1B-87, OF-48
1973	106	.263	.368	247	65	11	0	5	2.0	31	29	32	31	3	37	10	527	43	1	61	5.4	.998	1B-71
1974	96	.240	.356	208	50	6	3	4	1.9	32	33	30	13	2	22	8	285	15	2	25	3.1	.993	1B-39, OF-33
1975	113	.248	.339	165	41	6	0	3	1.8	24	24	27	10	2	36	11	316	33	3	38	3.1	.991	1B-71, OF-12
1976	95	.202	.282	124	25	5	1	1	0.8	15	13	27	11	1	19	5	294	28	0	25	3.4	1.000	1B-72, OF-1
1977	107	.309	.420	81	25	3	0	2	2.5	12	11	12	10	1	34	10	143	15	1	11	1.5	.994	1B-73, OF-9
1978 2 teams	TOR A (64G – .254)			MON N (39G – .203)																			
" total	103	.241	.319	232	56	12	0	2	0.9	23	14	29	16	1	24	4	225	7	1	10	2.3	.996	OF-60, 1B-26
1979 MON N	86	.253	.337	83	21	2	1	1	1.2	14	13	10	7	0	43	11	89	11	0	4	1.2	1.000	1B-25, OF-9
1980	62	.218	.255	55	12	2	0	0	0.0	2	5	4	10	0	43	10	20	1	0	3	0.3	1.000	1B-7, OF-4, P-1
1981	31	.103	.103	29	3	0	0	0	0.0	1	2	2	1	0	17	2	23	2	0	2	0.8	1.000	1B-9, OF-2
12 yrs.	952	.248	.334	1655	410	63	7	22	1.3	196	186	234	140	15	294	79	2702	212	15	235	3.1	.995	1B-499, OF-178, P-1

LEAGUE CHAMPIONSHIP SERIES

Year Team	Games	BA	SA	AB	H	2B	3B	HR	HR%	R	RBI	BB	SO	SB	PH AB	PH H	PO	A	E	DP	TC/G	FA	G by Pos
1976 PHI N	1	.000	.000	1	0	0	0	0	0.0	0	0	0	1	0	1	0	0	0	0	0	0.0	–	
1977	3	.000	.000	3	0	0	0	0	0.0	0	0	0	0	0	2	0	5	0	0	0	1.7	1.000	1B-1
2 yrs.	4	.000	.000	4	0	0	0	0	0.0	0	0	0	1	0	3	0	5	0	0	0	1.3	1.000	1B-1

Ham Hyatt

HYATT, ROBERT HAMILTON
B. Nov. 1, 1884, Buncombe County, N.C. D. Sept. 11, 1963, Liberty Lake, Wash.
BL TR 6'1" 185 lbs.

Year Team	Games	BA	SA	AB	H	2B	3B	HR	HR%	R	RBI	BB	SO	SB	PH AB	PH H	PO	A	E	DP	TC/G	FA	G by Pos
1909 PIT N	48	.299	.463	67	20	3	4	0	0.0	9	7	3		1	**37**	**9**	28	6	1	3	0.7	.971	OF-6, 1B-2
1910	74	.263	.377	175	46	5	6	1	0.6	19	30	8	14	3	31	6	327	19	5	19	4.7	.986	1B-38, OF-4
1912	46	.289	.340	97	28	3	1	0	0.0	13	22	6	8	2	27	6	26	2	2	2	0.7	.933	OF-15, 1B-3
1913	63	.333	.605	81	27	6	2	4	4.9	8	16	6	8	0	52	15	41	2	2	1	0.7	.956	OF-5, 1B-5
1914	74	.215	.316	79	17	3	1	1	1.3	2	15	7	14	1	**58**	**14**	51	0	1	1	0.7	.981	1B-7, C-1
1915 STL N	106	.268	.376	295	79	8	9	2	0.7	23	46	28	24	5	14	3	656	23	9	32	6.5	.987	1B-81, OF-25
1918 NY A	53	.229	.336	131	30	8	0	2	1.5	11	10	8	8	1	21	4	84	6	0	6	1.7	1.000	OF-25, 1B-5
7 yrs.	464	.267	.388	925	247	36	23	10	1.1	85	146	63	76	11	240	57	1213	58	20	66	2.8	.985	1B-141, OF-80, C-1

WORLD SERIES

Year Team	Games	BA	SA	AB	H	2B	3B	HR	HR%	R	RBI	BB	SO	SB	PH AB	PH H	PO	A	E	DP	TC/G	FA	G by Pos
1909 PIT N	2	.000	.000	4	0	0	0	0	–	0	1	1		0	3	0	0	0	0	0	0.0	–	OF-1

Pat Hynes

HYNES, PATRICK J.
B. Mar. 12, 1884, St. Louis, Mo. D. Mar. 12, 1907, St. Louis, Mo.
TL

Year Team	Games	BA	SA	AB	H	2B	3B	HR	HR%	R	RBI	BB	SO	SB	PH AB	PH H	PO	A	E	DP	TC/G	FA	G by Pos
1903 STL N	1	.000	.000	3	0	0	0	0	0.0	0	0	0			0		1	0	1	0	2.0	.500	P-1
1904 STL A	66	.236	.287	254	60	7	3	0	0.0	23	15	3		3	0	0	73	5	8	0	1.3	.907	OF-63, P-5
2 yrs.	67	.233	.284	257	60	7	3	0	0.0	23	15	3		3	0	0	74	5	9	0	1.3	.898	OF-63, P-6

Pete Incaviglia

INCAVIGLIA, PETER JOSEPH (Inky)
B. Apr. 2, 1964, Pebble Beach, Calif.
BR TR 6'1" 225 lbs.

Year Team	Games	BA	SA	AB	H	2B	3B	HR	HR%	R	RBI	BB	SO	SB	PH AB	PH H	PO	A	E	DP	TC/G	FA	G by Pos
1986 TEX A	153	.250	.463	540	135	21	2	30	5.6	82	88	55	**185**	3	4	0	157	6	14	1	1.2	.921	OF-114, DH-36

Year	Team		Games	BA	SA	AB	H	2B	3B	HR	HR%	R	RBI	BB	SO	SB	Pinch Hit AB	Pinch Hit H	PO	A	E	DP	TC/G	FA	G by Pos

Pete Incaviglia *continued*

1987			139	.271	.497	509	138	26	4	27	5.3	85	80	48	168	9	3	0	216	8	13	0	1.7	.945	OF-132, DH-6
1988			116	.249	.467	418	104	19	3	22	5.3	59	54	39	153	6	0	0	172	12	2	1	1.6	.989	OF-93, DH-21
1989			133	.236	.453	453	107	27	4	21	4.6	48	81	32	136	5	5	2	213	7	6	2	1.7	.973	OF-125, DH-5
4 yrs.			541	.252	.470	1920	484	93	13	100	5.2	274	303	174	642	23	12	2	758	33	35	4	1.5	.958	OF-464, DH-68

Alexis Infante

INFANTE, FERMIN ALEXIS
Born Fermin Alexis Infante y Carpio.
B. Dec. 4, 1961, Barquisimeto, Venezuela

BR TR 5'10" 175 lbs.

1987	TOR	A	1	–	–	0	0	0	0	0	–	0	0	0	0	0	0	0	0	0	0	0	0.0	–	SS-1
1988			19	.200	.200	15	3	0	0	0	0.0	7	0	2	4	0	0	0	4	6	1	0	0.6	.909	3B-9, SS-2
1989			20	.167	.167	12	2	0	0	0	0.0	1	0	0	1	1	0	0	6	13	0	3	1.0	1.000	SS-9, DH-4, 3B-4, 2B-1
3 yrs.			40	.185	.185	27	5	0	0	0	0.0	8	0	2	5	1	0	0	10	19	1	3	0.8	.967	SS-13, 3B-12, DH-4, 2B-1

Scotty Ingerton

INGERTON, WILLIAM JOHN
B. Apr. 19, 1886, Peninsula, Ohio D. June 15, 1956, Cleveland, Ohio

BR TR 6'1" 172 lbs.

| 1911 | BOS | N | 136 | .250 | .340 | 521 | 130 | 24 | 4 | 5 | 1.0 | 63 | 61 | 39 | 68 | 6 | 3 | 0 | 367 | 192 | 29 | 24 | 4.3 | .951 | 3B-58, OF-43, 1B-17, 2B-11, SS-4 |

Charlie Ingraham

INGRAHAM, CHARLES
B. Apr., 1860, Youngstown, Ohio Deceased.

5'11" 170 lbs.

| 1883 | BAL | AA | 1 | .250 | .250 | 4 | 1 | 0 | 0 | 0 | 0.0 | 0 | | 0 | | 0 | 0 | 0 | 4 | 1 | 1 | 0 | 6.0 | .833 | C-1 |

Mel Ingram

INGRAM, MELVIN DAVID
B. July 4, 1904, Asheville, N. C. D. Oct. 28, 1979, Medford, Ore.

BR TR 5'11½" 175 lbs.

| 1929 | PIT | N | 3 | – | – | 0 | 0 | 0 | 0 | 0 | – | 1 | 0 | 0 | 0 | 0 | 0 | 0 | 0 | 0 | 0 | 0 | 0.0 | – | |

Dane Iorg

IORG, DANE CHARLES
Brother of Garth Iorg.
B. May 11, 1950, Eureka, Calif.

BL TR 6' 180 lbs.

1977	2 teams		PHI N	(12G – .167)		STL N	(30G – .313)																		
"	total		42	.242	.274	62	15	2	0	0	0.0	5	6	6	7	0	21	6	71	4	2	6	1.8	.974	1B-9, OF-7
1978	STL	N	35	.271	.341	85	23	4	1	0	0.0	6	4	4	10	0	11	2	33	5	0	0	1.1	1.000	OF-25
1979			79	.291	.380	179	52	11	1	1	0.6	12	21	12	28	1	39	11	121	7	2	1	1.6	.985	OF-39, 1B-10
1980			105	.303	.438	251	76	23	1	3	1.2	33	36	20	34	1	38	10	134	2	1	2	1.3	.993	OF-63, 1B-5, 3B-1
1981			75	.327	.424	217	71	11	2	2	0.9	23	39	7	9	2	14	4	125	7	3	1	1.8	.978	OF-57, 1B-8, 3B-2
1982			102	.294	.361	238	70	14	1	0	0.0	17	34	23	23	0	27	7	177	10	3	6	1.9	.984	OF-63, 1B-10, 3B-2
1983			58	.267	.362	116	31	9	1	0	0.0	6	11	10	11	1	20	6	127	5	3	11	2.3	.978	OF-22, 1B-11
1984	2 teams		STL N	(15G – .143)		KC A	(78G – .255)																		
"	total		93	.243	.384	263	64	18	2	5	1.9	30	33	15	21	0	20	6	35	2	0	4	0.4	1.000	1B-49, OF-27, 3B-1
1985	KC	A	64	.223	.331	130	29	9	1	1	0.8	7	21	8	16	0	27	4	55	4	0	2	0.9	1.000	OF-32, DH-2, 1B-2, 3B-1
1986	SD	N	90	.226	.321	106	24	2	1	2	1.9	10	11	2	21	0	70	13	43	2	0	3	0.5	1.000	1B-10, 3B-6, OF-3, P-2
10 yrs.			743	.276	.378	1647	455	103	11	14	0.9	149	216	107	180	5	287	69	921	48	14	37	1.3	.986	OF-338, 1B-114, 3B-13, DH-2, P-2

LEAGUE CHAMPIONSHIP SERIES

1984	KC	A	2	.500	.500	2	1	0	0	0	0.0	0	1	0	0	0	2	1	0	0	0	0	0.0	–	
1985			4	.500	1.000	2	1	1	0	0	0.0	0	0	2	0	0	2	1	0	0	0	0	0.0	–	
2 yrs.			6	.500	.750	4	2	1	0	0	0.0	0	1	2	0	0	4	2	0	0	0	0	0.0	–	

WORLD SERIES

1982	STL	N	5	.529	.882	17	9	4	1	0	0.0	4	1	0	0	0	0	0	0	0	0	0	0.0	–	DH-5
1985	KC	A	2	.500	.500	2	1	0	0	0	0.0	0	2	0	0	0	2	1	0	0	0	0	0.0	–	
2 yrs.			7	.526	.842	19	10	4	1	0	0.0	4	3	0	0	0	2	1	0	0	0	0	0.0	–	DH-5

Garth Iorg

IORG, GARTH RAY
Brother of Dane Iorg.
B. Oct. 12, 1954, Arcata, Calif.

BR TR 5'11" 170 lbs.

1978	TOR	A	19	.163	.163	49	8	0	0	0	0.0	3	3	3	4	0	0	0	34	51	3	14	4.6	.966	2B-18
1980			80	.248	.329	222	55	10	1	2	0.9	24	14	12	39	2	7	2	122	155	3	45	3.5	.989	2B-32, 3B-20, OF-14, 1B-11, DH-2, SS-1
1981			70	.242	.293	215	52	11	0	0	0.0	17	10	7	31	2	7	1	98	178	12	33	4.1	.958	2B-46, 3B-17, 1B-1
1982			129	.285	.365	417	119	20	5	1	0.2	45	36	12	38	3	22	4	114	236	14	30	2.8	.962	3B-100, 2B-30, DH-1
1983			122	.275	.376	375	103	22	5	2	0.5	40	39	13	45	7	16	5	106	223	9	31	2.8	.973	3B-85, 2B-39, SS-1
1984			121	.227	.304	247	56	10	3	1	0.4	24	25	5	16	1	25	4	66	117	10	18	1.6	.948	3B-112, 2B-7, DH-1
1985			131	.313	.469	288	90	11	2	7	2.4	33	37	21	26	2	27	7	71	192	9	24	2.1	.967	3B-104, 2B-23
1986			137	.260	.352	327	85	19	1	3	0.9	30	44	20	47	3	28	10	92	185	12	16	2.1	.958	3B-90, 2B-52, SS-2
1987			122	.210	.284	310	65	11	0	4	1.3	35	30	21	52	2	15	3	149	221	7	36	3.1	.981	2B-91, 3B-28, DH-5
9 yrs.			931	.258	.347	2450	633	125	16	20	0.8	251	238	114	298	22	147	41	852	1558	79	247	2.7	.968	3B-556, 2B-338, OF-14, 1B-12, DH-9, SS-6

LEAGUE CHAMPIONSHIP SERIES

| 1985 | TOR | A | 7 | .133 | .133 | 15 | 2 | 0 | 0 | 0 | 0.0 | 1 | 0 | 1 | 3 | 0 | 2 | 0 | 5 | 10 | 0 | 4 | 2.1 | 1.000 | 3B-6 |

Happy Iott

IOTT, FREDERICK (Dimples)
Born Frederick Hoyot.
B. July 7, 1876, Houlton, Me. D. Feb. 17, 1941, Island Falls, Me.

BR TR 5'10" 175 lbs.

| 1903 | CLE | A | 3 | .200 | .200 | 10 | 2 | 0 | 0 | 0 | 0.0 | 1 | 0 | 2 | | 1 | 0 | 0 | 7 | 0 | 1 | 0 | 2.7 | .875 | OF-3 |

Hal Irelan

IRELAN, HAROLD (Grump)
B. Aug. 5, 1890, Burnettsville, Ind. D. July 16, 1944, Carmel, Ind.

BB TR 5'7" 165 lbs.

| 1914 | PHI | N | 67 | .236 | .303 | 165 | 39 | 8 | 0 | 1 | 0.6 | 16 | 16 | 21 | 22 | 3 | 12 | 6 | 118 | 147 | 26 | 13 | 4.3 | .911 | 2B-44, SS-3, 3B-2, 1B-2 |

Year	Team		Games	BA	SA	AB	H	2B	3B	HR	HR%	R	RBI	BB	SO	SB	Pinch Hit AB	H	PO	A	E	DP	TC/G	FA	G by Pos

Tim Ireland

IRELAND, TIMOTHY NEAL CHRISTOPHER
B. Mar. 14, 1953, Oakland, Calif. BB TR 6' 180 lbs.

Year	Team		Games	BA	SA	AB	H	2B	3B	HR	HR%	R	RBI	BB	SO	SB	AB	H	PO	A	E	DP	TC/G	FA	G by Pos
1981	KC	A	4	–	–	0	0	0	0	0	–	1	0	0	0	0	0	0	3	0	0	0	0.8	1.000	1B-4
1982			7	.143	.143	7	1	0	0	0	0.0	2	0	1	1	0	0	0	4	5	1	1	1.4	.900	2B-4, OF-2, 3B-1
2 yrs.			11	.143	.143	7	1	0	0	0	0.0	3	0	1	1	0	0	0	7	5	1	1	1.2	.923	2B-4, 1B-4, OF-2, 3B-1

Ed Irvin

IRVIN, WILLIAM EDWARD
B. 1882, Philadelphia, Pa. D. Feb. 18, 1916, Philadelphia, Pa. TR

Year	Team		Games	BA	SA	AB	H	2B	3B	HR	HR%	R	RBI	BB	SO	SB	AB	H	PO	A	E	DP	TC/G	FA	G by Pos
1912	DET	A	1	.667	2.000	3	2	0	2	0	0.0	0	0	0		0	0	0	0	1	1	0	2.0	.500	3B-1

Monte Irvin

IRVIN, MONFORD MERRILL
B. Feb. 25, 1919, Columbus, Ala. BR TR 6'1" 195 lbs.
Hall of Fame 1973.

Year	Team		Games	BA	SA	AB	H	2B	3B	HR	HR%	R	RBI	BB	SO	SB	AB	H	PO	A	E	DP	TC/G	FA	G by Pos
1949	NY	N	36	.224	.316	76	17	3	2	0	0.0	7	7	17	11	0	13	0	56	17	1	6	2.1	.986	OF-10, 3B-5, 1B-5
1950			110	.299	.497	374	112	19	5	15	4.0	61	66	52	41	3	4	1	569	51	12	62	5.7	.981	1B-59, OF-49, 3B-1
1951			151	.312	.514	558	174	19	11	24	4.3	94	121	89	44	12	1	1	585	60	9	48	4.3	.986	OF-112, 1B-39
1952			46	.310	.437	126	39	2	1	4	3.2	10	21	10	11	0	14	2	44	3	0	1	1.0	1.000	OF-32
1953			124	.329	.541	444	146	21	5	21	4.7	72	97	55	34	2	8	2	244	10	7	4	2.1	.973	OF-113
1954			135	.262	.438	432	113	13	3	19	4.4	62	64	70	23	7	9	3	276	7	8	0	2.2	.973	OF-128, 3B-1, 1B-1
1955			51	.253	.333	150	38	7	1	1	0.7	16	17	17	15	3	6	1	94	4	4	0	2.0	.961	OF-45
1956	CHI	N	111	.271	.460	339	92	13	3	15	4.4	44	50	41	41	1	18	7	216	6	2	0	2.0	.991	OF-96
8 yrs.			764	.293	.475	2499	731	97	31	99	4.0	366	443	351	220	28	73	17	2084	158	43	121	3.0	.981	OF-585, 1B-104, 3B-7

WORLD SERIES

Year	Team		Games	BA	SA	AB	H	2B	3B	HR	HR%	R	RBI	BB	SO	SB	AB	H	PO	A	E	DP	TC/G	FA	G by Pos
1951	NY	N	6	.458	.542	24	11	0	0	0	0.0	4	2	2	1	2	0	0	17	0	1	0	3.0	.944	OF-6
1954			4	.222	.333	9	2	1	0	0	0.0	1	2	0	3	0	0	0	8	0	1	0	2.3	.889	OF-4
2 yrs.			10	.394	.485	33	13	1	0	0	0.0	5	4	2	4	2	0	0	25	0	2	0	2.7	.926	OF-10

Arthur Irwin

IRWIN, ARTHUR ALBERT
Brother of John Irwin. BL TR 5'8½" 158 lbs.
B. Feb. 14, 1858, Toronto, Ont., Canada D. July 16, 1921, Atlantic Ocean
Manager 1889, 1891-92, 1894-96, 1898-99.

Year	Team		Games	BA	SA	AB	H	2B	3B	HR	HR%	R	RBI	BB	SO	SB	AB	H	PO	A	E	DP	TC/G	FA	G by Pos
1880	WOR	N	85	.259	.344	352	91	19	4	1	0.3	53	27	11	27		0	0	98	345	53	27	5.8	.893	SS-82, 3B-3, C-1
1881			50	.267	.325	206	55	8	2	0	0.0	27	24	7	4		0	0	50	155	36	11	4.8	.851	SS-50
1882			84	.219	.279	333	73	12	4	0	0.0	30	30	14	34		0	0	125	270	78	24	5.6	.835	SS-84
1883	PRO	N	98	.286	.374	406	116	22	7	0	0.0	67		12	38		0	0	100	301	66	29	4.8	.859	SS-94, 2B-4
1884			102	.240	.304	404	97	14	3	2	0.5	73		28	52		0	0	99	308	55	20	4.5	.881	SS-102, P-1
1885			59	.179	.197	218	39	2	1	0	0.0	16	14	14	29		0	0	70	212	43	17	5.5	.868	SS-58, 3B-1, 2B-1
1886	PHI	N	101	.233	.282	373	87	6	6	0	0.0	51	34	35	39		0	0	137	323	58	21	5.1	.888	SS-100, 3B-1
1887			100	.254	.350	374	95	14	8	2	0.5	65	56	48	26	19	0	0	178	301	58	30	5.4	.892	SS-100
1888			125	.219	.263	448	98	12	4	0	0.0	51	28	33	56	19	0	0	209	383	64	33	5.2	.902	SS-122, 2B-3
1889	2 teams		PHI N (18G – .219)			WAS N	(85G – .233)																			
" total			103	.231	.295	386	89	15	5	0	0.0	58	42	48	43	15	0	0	192	325	65	42	5.7	.888	SS-103, 2B-1, P-1
1890	BOS	P	96	.260	.314	354	92	17	1	0	0.0	60	45	57	29	16	0	0	137	331	65	44	5.6	.878	SS-96
1891	BOS	AA	6	.118	.118	17	2	0	0	0	0.0	1	0	2	1	0	0	0	7	14	6	5	4.5	.778	SS-6
1894	PHI	N	1	–	–	0	0	0	0	0	–	0	0	0	0	0	0	0	0	0	0	0	0.0	–	SS-1
13 yrs.			1010	.241	.305	3871	934	141	45	5	0.1	552	308	309	378	69	0	0	1402	3268	647	303	5.3	.878	SS-947, 3B-56, 2B-9, P-2, C-1

Charlie Irwin

IRWIN, CHARLES EDWIN
B. Feb. 15, 1869, Clinton, Ill. D. Sept. 21, 1925, Chicago, Ill. BL TR 5'10" 160 lbs.

Year	Team		Games	BA	SA	AB	H	2B	3B	HR	HR%	R	RBI	BB	SO	SB	AB	H	PO	A	E	DP	TC/G	FA	G by Pos
1893	CHI	N	21	.305	.427	82	25	6	2	0	0.0	14	13	10	1	4	0	0	55	66	12	10	6.3	.910	SS-21
1894			128	.289	.422	498	144	24	9	8	1.6	84	95	63	23	35	0	0	207	341	89	35	5.0	.860	3B-67, SS-61
1895			3	.200	.200	10	2	0	0	0	0.0	4	0	2	1	0	0	0	3	6	1	1	3.3	.900	SS-3
1896	CIN	N	127	.296	.361	476	141	16	6	1	0.2	77	67	26	17	31	0	0	200	262	34	28	3.9	.931	3B-127
1897			134	.289	.364	505	146	26	6	0	0.0	89	74	47		27	0	0	186	236	27	19	3.4	.940	3B-134
1898			136	.240	.305	501	120	14	5	3	0.6	77	55	31		18	0	0	223	305	34	20	4.1	.940	3B-136
1899			90	.232	.306	314	73	4	3	1	0.3	42	52	26		26	2	1	124	165	27	9	3.5	.915	3B-78, SS-6, 2B-3, 1B-1
1900			87	.273	.363	333	91	15	6	1	0.3	59	44	14		9	2	0	125	191	25	14	3.9	.927	3B-61, SS-16, OF-6, 2B-3
1901	2 teams		CIN N (67G – .238)			BKN N	(65G – .215)																			
" total			132	.227	.293	502	114	25	4	0	0.0	50	45	28		17	0	0	175	245	36	15	3.5	.921	3B-132
1902	BKN	N	131	.273	.317	458	125	14	0	2	0.4	59	43	39		13	0	0	174	247	34	21	3.5	.925	3B-130, SS-1
10 yrs.			989	.267	.344	3679	981	144	46	16	0.4	555	488	286	42	180	4	0	1472	2064	319	172	3.9	.917	3B-865, SS-108, OF-6, 2B-6, 1B-1

John Irwin

IRWIN, JOHN
Brother of Arthur Irwin. BL TR 5'10" 168 lbs.
B. July 21, 1861, Toronto, Ont., Canada D. Feb. 28, 1934, Boston, Mass.

Year	Team		Games	BA	SA	AB	H	2B	3B	HR	HR%	R	RBI	BB	SO	SB	AB	H	PO	A	E	DP	TC/G	FA	G by Pos
1882	WOR	N	1	.000	.000	4	0	0	0	0	0.0	0		0	2		0	0	7	0	4	1	11.0	.636	1B-1
1884	BOS	U	105	.234	.319	432	101	22	6	1	0.2	81		15			0	0	117	191	87	7	3.8	.780	3B-105
1886	PHI	AA	3	.231	.308	13	3	1	0	0	0.0	4		0			0	0	2	7	2	0	3.7	.818	SS-2, 3B-1
1887	WAS	N	8	.355	.613	31	11	2	0	2	6.5	3	6	3	6	6	0	0	13	19	5	1	4.6	.865	SS-5, 3B-4
1888			37	.222	.294	126	28	5	2	0	0.0	14	8	5	18	15	0	0	66	97	30	6	5.2	.845	SS-27, 3B-10
1889			58	.289	.373	228	66	11	4	0	0.0	42	25	25	14	10	0	0	82	129	32	14	4.2	.868	3B-58
1890	BUF	P	77	.234	.295	308	72	11	4	0	0.0	62	34	43	19	18	0	0	184	155	32	27	4.8	.914	3B-64, 1B-12, 2B-1
1891	2 teams		BOS AA (19G – .222)			LOU AA	(14G – .273)																			
" total			33	.244	.315	127	31	3	4	0	0.0	13	22	11	15	7	0	0	43	33	17	1	2.8	.817	OF-17, 3B-16, SS-1
8 yrs.			322	.246	.326	1269	312	55	19	3	0.2	222	92	102	74	56	0	0	514	631	209	57	4.2	.846	3B-258, SS-35, OF-17, 1B-13, 2B-1

Tommy Irwin

IRWIN, THOMAS ANDREW
B. Dec. 20, 1912, Altoona, Pa. BR TR 5'11" 165 lbs.

Year	Team		Games	BA	SA	AB	H	2B	3B	HR	HR%	R	RBI	BB	SO	SB	Pinch Hit AB	Pinch Hit H	PO	A	E	DP	TC/G	FA	G by Pos

Tommy Irwin *continued*

| 1938 | CLE | A | 3 | .111 | .111 | 9 | 1 | 0 | 0 | 0 | 0.0 | 1 | 0 | 3 | 1 | 0 | 0 | 0 | 3 | 8 | 0 | 2 | 3.7 | 1.000 | SS-3 |

Walt Irwin

IRWIN, WALTER KINGSLEY (Lightning)   BR TR 5'10½" 170 lbs.
B. Sept. 23, 1897, Henrietta, Pa.   D. Aug. 18, 1976, Spring Lake, Mich.

| 1921 | STL | N | 4 | .000 | .000 | 1 | 0 | 0 | 0 | 0 | 0.0 | 1 | 0 | 0 | 1 | 0 | 1 | 0 | 0 | 0 | 0 | 0 | 0.0 | — | |

Orlando Isales

ISALES, ORLANDO   BR TR 5'9" 175 lbs.
Born Orlando Isales y Pizarro.
B. Dec. 22, 1959, Santurce, Puerto Rico

| 1980 | PHI | N | 3 | .400 | .800 | 5 | 2 | 0 | 1 | 0 | 0.0 | 1 | 3 | 1 | 0 | 0 | 0 | 0 | 3 | 0 | 0 | 0 | 1.0 | 1.000 | OF-2 |

Frank Isbell

ISBELL, WILLIAM FRANK (Bald Eagle)   BL TR 5'11" 190 lbs.
B. Aug. 21, 1875, Delevan, N. Y.   D. July 15, 1941, Wichita, Kans.

1898	CHI	N	45	.233	.258	159	37	4	0	0	0.0	17	8	3		3	0	0	54	43	19	5	2.6	.836	OF-28, P-13, 3B-3, 2B-3, SS-2
1901	CHI	A	137	.257	.329	556	143	15	8	3	0.5	93	70	36		52	0	0	1389	107	32	79	11.2	.979	1B-137, 2B-2, SS-1, 3B-1, P-1
1902			137	.252	.318	515	130	14	4	4	0.8	62	59	14		38	0	0	1405	105	22	100	11.2	.986	1B-133, SS-4, C-1, P-1
1903			138	.242	.332	546	132	25	9	2	0.4	52	59	12		26	0	0	1225	136	35	58	10.1	.975	1B-117, 3B-19, 2B-2, OF-1, SS-1
1904			96	.210	.271	314	66	10	3	1	0.3	27	34	16		19	3	0	663	145	25	29	8.7	.970	1B-57, 2B-27, OF-5, SS-4
1905			94	.296	.440	341	101	21	11	2	0.6	55	45	15		15	0	0	219	136	13	18	3.9	.965	2B-42, OF-40, 1B-9, SS-2
1906			143	.279	.352	549	153	18	11	0	0.0	71	57	30		37	0	0	313	363	36	36	5.0	.949	2B-132, OF-14, C-1, P-1
1907			125	.243	.311	486	118	19	7	0	0.0	60	41	22		22	1	0	285	386	30	42	5.6	.957	2B-119, OF-5, SS-1, P-1
1908			84	.247	.322	320	79	15	3	1	0.3	31	49	19		18	1	0	864	104	18	30	11.7	.982	1B-65, 2B-18
1909			120	.224	.291	433	97	17	6	0	0.0	33	33	23		23	5	2	1226	80	12	51	11.0	.991	1B-101, OF-9, 2B-5
10 yrs.			1119	.250	.326	4219	1056	158	62	13	0.3	501	455	190		253	10	2	7643	1605	242	448	8.5	.974	1B-619, 2B-350, OF-102, 3B-23, P-17, SS-15, C-2

WORLD SERIES

| 1906 | CHI | A | 6 | .308 | .462 | 26 | 8 | 4 | 0 | 0 | 0.0 | 4 | 4 | 0 | 6 | 1 | 0 | 0 | 11 | 16 | 5 | 1 | 5.3 | .844 | 2B-6 |

Mike Ivie

IVIE, MICHAEL WILSON   BR TR 6'3" 205 lbs.
B. Aug. 8, 1952, Atlanta, Ga.

1971	SD	N	6	.471	.471	17	8	0	0	0	0.0	0	3	1		1	1	0	22	2	0	4.0	1.000	C-6
1974			12	.088	.176	34	3	0	0	1	2.9	1	3	2	8	0	1	0	67	5	1	9	6.1	.986	1B-11
1975			111	.249	.366	377	94	16	2	8	2.1	36	46	20	63	4	9	3	540	138	23	54	6.3	.967	1B-78, 3B-61, C-1
1976			140	.291	.415	405	118	19	5	7	1.7	51	70	30	41	6	4	0	1032	71	7	90	7.9	.994	1B-135, 3B-2, C-2
1977			134	.272	.395	489	133	29	2	9	1.8	66	66	39	57	3	15	2	886	93	11	79	7.4	.989	1B-105, 3B-25
1978	SF	N	117	.308	.475	318	98	14	3	11	3.5	34	55	27	45	3	31	12	579	18	5	33	5.1	.992	1B-76, OF-22
1979			133	.286	.547	402	115	18	3	27	6.7	58	89	47	80	5	23	9	752	47	4	51	6.0	.995	1B-98, OF-24, 3B-4, 2B-1
1980			79	.241	.346	286	69	16	1	4	1.4	21	25	19	40	1	6	1	669	32	5	46	8.9	.993	1B-72
1981	2 teams						SF	N	(7G – .294)			HOU	N	(19G – .238)											
"	total		26	.254	.339	59	15	5	0	0	0.0	3	9	2	12	0	13	4	113	15	1	7	5.0	.992	1B-15
1982	2 teams						HOU	N	(7G – .333)			DET	A	(80G – .232)											
"	total		87	.234	.445	265	62	12	1	14	5.3	35	38	25	51	0	17	4	0	0	0	0	0.0	—	DH-79
1983	DET	A	12	.214	.310	42	9	4	0	0	0.0	4	7	2	4	0	0	0	86	6	0	6	7.7	1.000	1B-12
11 yrs.			857	.269	.421	2694	724	133	17	81	3.0	309	411	214	402	22	120	35	4746	427	57	375	6.1	.989	1B-602, 3B-92, DH-79, OF-46, C-9, 2B-1

Hank Izquierdo

IZQUIERDO, ENRIQUE ROBERTO   BR TR 5'11" 175 lbs.
Born Enrique Roberto Izquierdo y Valdez.
B. Mar. 20, 1931, Matanzas, Cuba

| 1967 | MIN | A | 16 | .269 | .346 | 26 | 7 | 2 | 0 | 0 | 0.0 | 4 | 2 | 1 | 2 | 0 | 1 | 0 | 65 | 7 | 1 | 1 | 4.6 | .986 | C-16 |

Ray Jablonski

JABLONSKI, RAYMOND LEO (Jabbo)   BR TR 5'10" 175 lbs.
B. Dec. 17, 1926, Chicago, Ill.   D. Nov. 25, 1985, Chicago, Ill.

1953	STL	N	157	.268	.427	604	162	23	5	21	3.5	64	112	34	61	2	0	0	94	278	27	27	2.5	.932	3B-157
1954			152	.296	.419	611	181	33	3	12	2.0	80	104	49	42	9	2	2	127	299	34	25	3.0	.926	3B-149, 1B-1
1955	CIN	N	74	.240	.403	221	53	9	0	9	4.1	28	28	13	35	0	17	4	69	46	11	3	1.7	.913	OF-28, 3B-28
1956			130	.256	.432	407	104	25	1	15	3.7	42	66	37	57	2	14	5	117	172	9	11	2.3	.970	3B-127, 2B-1
1957	NY	N	107	.289	.433	305	88	15	1	9	3.0	37	57	31	47	0	28	6	99	136	12	20	2.3	.951	3B-70, 1B-6, OF-1
1958	SF	N	82	.230	.461	230	53	15	1	12	5.2	28	46	17	50	2	31	9	49	91	8	2	1.8	.946	3B-57
1959	2 teams						STL	N	(60G – .253)			KC	A	(25G – .262)											
"	total		85	.257	.388	152	39	6	0	5	3.3	15	22	11	30	1	53	8	20	43	5	5	0.8	.926	3B-36, SS-1
1960	KC	A	21	.219	.250	32	7	1	0	0	0.0	3	3	4	8	0	13	3	4	13	1	0	0.9	.944	3B-6
8 yrs.			808	.268	.423	2562	687	126	11	83	3.2	297	438	196	330	16	158	37	579	1078	107	93	2.2	.939	3B-630, OF-29, 1B-7, SS-1, 2B-1

Fred Jacklitsch

JACKLITSCH, FREDERICK LAWRENCE   BR TR 5'9" 180 lbs.
B. May 24, 1876, Brooklyn, N. Y.   D. July 18, 1937, Brooklyn, N. Y.

1900	PHI	N	5	.182	.273	11	2	1	0	0	0.0	0	3	0		0	2	0	2	1	0	1	0.6	1.000	C-3
1901			33	.250	.333	120	30	4	3	0	0.0	14	24	12		2	1	0	126	40	5	3	5.2	.971	C-30, 3B-1
1902			38	.202	.237	114	23	4	0	0	0.0	8	8	9		2	1	0	123	31	13	0	4.4	.922	C-29, OF-1
1903	BKN	N	60	.267	.364	176	47	8	3	1	0.6	31	21	33		4	6	2	203	72	9	7	4.7	.968	C-53, OF-1, 2B-1
1904			26	.234	.299	77	18	3	1	0	0.0	8	8	7		7	2	0	130	32	14	6	6.8	.920	1B-11, 2B-8, C-5
1905	NY	A	3	.000	.000	3	0	0	0	0	0.0	1	1	1		0	0	0	6	1	0	0	7.0	1.000	C-1
1907	PHI	N	73	.213	.248	202	43	7	0	0	0.0	19	17	27		7	8	0	314	99	8	18	5.8	.981	C-58, 1B-6, OF-1
1908			37	.221	.256	86	19	3	0	0	0.0	6	7	14		3	5	1	126	38	4	1	4.5	.976	C-30
1909			20	.313	.406	32	10	1	0	0	0.0	6	2	10		1	5	2	45	10	3	0	2.9	.948	C-11, 1B-1
1910			25	.196	.255	51	10	3	0	0	0.0	7	5	9	9	0	7	2	80	24	2	0	4.2	.981	C-13, 1B-2, 3B-1, 2B-1

Year	Team		Games	BA	SA	AB	H	2B	3B	HR	HR%	R	RBI	BB	SO	SB	Pinch Hit AB	H	PO	A	E	DP	TC/G	FA	G by Pos

Fred Jacklitsch *continued*

1914	BAL	F	122	.276	.380	337	93	21	4	2	0.6	40	48	52		7	4	1	580	167	9	13	6.2	.988	C-118
1915			49	.237	.348	135	32	9	0	2	1.5	20	13	31		2	2	0	206	51	2	8	5.3	.992	C-45, SS-1
1917	BOS	N	1	–	–	0	0	0	0	0	–	0	0	0		0	0	0	0	0	0	0	1.0	1.000	C-1
13 yrs.			490	.243	.320	1344	327	64	12	5	0.4	160	153	201	9	35	52	8	1942	566	69	57	5.3	.973	C-397, 1B-19, 2B-11, OF-3, 3B-2, SS-1

Bill Jackson JACKSON, WILLIAM RILEY   BL TL 5'11½" 160 lbs.
B. Apr. 4, 1881, Pittsburgh, Pa. D. Sept. 24, 1958, Peoria, Ill.

1914	CHI	F	26	.040	.040	25	1	0	0	0	0.0	2	1	3		0	8	0	24	1	1	2	1.0	.962	OF-6, 1B-4
1915			50	.163	.204	98	16	1	0	1	1.0	15	12	14		3	8	1	276	17	5	10	6.0	.983	1B-36, OF-1
2 yrs.			76	.138	.171	123	17	1	0	1	0.8	17	13	17		3	16	1	300	18	6	12	4.3	.981	1B-40, OF-7

Bo Jackson JACKSON, VINCENT EDWARD   BR TR 6'1" 222 lbs.
B. Nov. 30, 1962, Bessemer, Ala.

1986	KC	A	25	.207	.329	82	17	2	1	2	2.4	9	9	7	34	3	0	0	29	2	4	0	1.4	.886	OF-23, DH-1
1987			116	.235	.455	396	93	17	2	22	5.6	46	53	30	158	10	2	0	180	9	9	1	1.7	.955	OF-113, DH-1
1988			124	.246	.472	439	108	16	4	25	5.7	63	68	25	146	27	1	0	246	11	7	2	2.1	.973	OF-121, DH-2
1989			135	.256	.495	515	132	15	6	32	6.2	86	105	39	172	26	1	0	224	11	8	2	1.8	.967	OF-110, DH-24
4 yrs.			400	.244	.467	1432	350	50	13	81	5.7	204	235	101	510	66	4	0	679	33	28	5	1.9	.962	OF-367, DH-28

Charlie Jackson JACKSON, CHARLES HERBERT (Lefty)   BL TL 5'9" 150 lbs.
B. Feb. 7, 1894, Granite City, Ill. D. May 27, 1968, Radford, Va.

1915	CHI	A	1	.000	.000	1	0	0	0	0	0.0	0	0	0	1	0	1	0	0	0	0	0	0.0	–	
1917	PIT	N	41	.240	.298	121	29	3	2	0	0.0	7	1	10	22	4	2	0	65	5	1	0	1.7	.986	OF-36
2 yrs.			42	.238	.295	122	29	3	2	0	0.0	7	1	10	23	4	3	0	65	5	1	0	1.7	.986	OF-36

Chuck Jackson JACKSON, CHARLES LEO   BR TR 6' 185 lbs.
B. Mar. 19, 1963, Seattle, Wash.

1987	HOU	N	35	.211	.296	71	15	3	0	1	1.4	3	6	7	19	1	5	1	12	39	2	4	1.5	.962	3B-16, OF-13, SS-1
1988			46	.229	.349	83	19	5	1	1	1.2	7	8	7	16	1	9	2	12	51	7	6	1.5	.900	3B-32, OF-3, SS-3
2 yrs.			81	.221	.325	154	34	8	1	2	1.3	10	14	14	35	2	14	3	24	90	9	10	1.5	.927	3B-48, OF-16, SS-4

Darrin Jackson JACKSON, DARRIN JAY   BR TR 6' 185 lbs.
B. Aug. 22, 1963, Los Angeles, Calif.

1985	CHI	N	5	.091	.091	11	1	0	0	0	0.0	0	0	0	3	0	1	0	7	0	0	0	1.4	1.000	OF-4
1987			7	.800	1.000	5	4	1	0	0	0.0	2	0	0	0	0	4	3	1	0	0	0	0.1	1.000	OF-5
1988			100	.266	.452	188	50	11	3	6	3.2	29	20	5	28	4	21	5	116	1	2	0	1.2	.983	OF-74
1989	2 teams					CHI	N	(45G – .229)					SD	N	(25G – .207)										
"	total		70	.218	.329	170	37	7	0	4	2.4	17	20	13	34	1	14	1	121	5	5	4	1.9	.962	OF-63
4 yrs.			182	.246	.393	374	92	19	3	10	2.7	48	40	18	65	5	40	9	245	6	7	4	1.4	.973	OF-146

George Jackson JACKSON, GEORGE CHRISTOPHER (Hickory)   BR TR 6'½" 180 lbs.
B. Oct. 14, 1882, Springfield, Mo. D. Nov. 25, 1972, Cleburne, Tex.

1911	BOS	N	39	.347	.449	147	51	11	2	0	0.0	28	25	12	21	12	0	0	74	4	6	1	2.2	.929	OF-39
1912			110	.262	.350	397	104	13	5	4	1.0	55	48	38	72	22	2	0	230	20	15	3	2.4	.943	OF-107
1913			3	.300	.300	10	3	0	0	0	0.0	2	0	0	2	0	0	0	6	1	1	0	2.7	.875	OF-3
3 yrs.			152	.285	.375	554	158	24	7	4	0.7	85	73	50	95	34	2	0	310	25	22	4	2.3	.938	OF-149

Henry Jackson JACKSON, HENRY EVERETT   BR TR 6'2" 185 lbs.
B. June 23, 1861, Union City, Ind. D. Sept. 14, 1932, Chicago, Ill.

| 1887 | IND | N | 10 | .263 | .289 | 38 | 10 | 1 | 0 | 0 | 0.0 | 1 | 3 | 0 | 12 | 2 | 0 | 0 | 108 | 3 | 8 | 7 | 11.9 | .933 | 1B-10 |

Jim Jackson JACKSON, JAMES BENNER   BR TR
B. Nov. 28, 1877, Philadelphia, Pa. D. Oct. 9, 1955, Philadelphia, Pa.

1901	BAL	A	99	.250	.330	364	91	17	3	2	0.5	42	50	20		11	3	0	234	4	7	1	2.5	.971	OF-96
1902	NY	N	35	.182	.245	110	20	5	1	0	0.0	14	13	15		6	1	0	57	4	7	0	1.9	.897	OF-34
1905	CLE	A	108	.257	.318	421	108	12	4	2	0.5	58	31	34		15	0	0	196	21	13	3	2.1	.943	OF-105, 3B-3
1906			105	.214	.270	374	80	13	4	0	0.0	44	38	38		25	1	0	189	5	5	2	1.9	.975	OF-105
4 yrs.			347	.236	.301	1269	299	47	12	4	0.3	158	132	107		57	5	0	676	34	32	6	2.1	.957	OF-340, 3B-3

Joe Jackson JACKSON, JOSEPH JEFFERSON (Shoeless Joe)   BL TR 6'1" 200 lbs.
B. July 16, 1889, Pickens County, S. C. D. Dec. 5, 1951, Greenville, S. C.

1908	PHI	A	5	.130	.130	23	3	0	0	0	0.0	0	3	0		0	0	0	6	1	1	0	1.6	.875	OF-5
1909			5	.294	.294	17	5	0	0	0	0.0	3	3	1		0	1	0	10	0	2	0	2.4	.833	OF-4
1910	CLE	A	20	.387	.587	75	29	2	5	1	1.3	15	11	8		4	0	0	40	2	1	1	2.2	.977	OF-20
1911			147	.408	.590	571	233	45	19	7	1.2	126	83	56		41	0	0	242	32	12	8	1.9	.958	OF-147
1912			152	.395	.579	572	226	44	26	3	0.5	121	90	54		35	2	1	273	30	16	2	2.1	.950	OF-150
1913			148	.373	.551	528	197	39	17	7	1.3	109	71	80	26	26	0	0	211	28	18	5	1.7	.930	OF-148
1914			122	.338	.464	453	153	22	13	3	0.7	61	53	41	34	22	2	1	195	13	7	4	1.8	.967	OF-119
1915	2 teams					CLE	A	(82G – .331)					CHI	A	(46G – .265)										
"	total		128	.308	.445	461	142	20	14	5	1.1	63	81	52	23	16	4	2	436	27	15	13	3.7	.969	OF-95, 1B-27
1916	CHI	A	155	.341	.495	592	202	40	21	3	0.5	91	78	46	25	24	0	0	290	17	8	5	2.0	.975	OF-155
1917			146	.301	.429	538	162	20	17	5	0.9	91	75	57	25	13	1	0	341	18	6	4	2.5	.984	OF-145
1918			17	.354	.492	65	23	2	2	1	1.5	9	20	8	1	3	0	0	36	1	0	0	2.2	1.000	OF-17
1919			139	.351	.506	516	181	31	14	7	1.4	79	96	60	10	9	0	0	252	15	9	4	2.0	.967	OF-139
1920			146	.382	.589	570	218	42	20	12	2.1	105	121	56	14	9	0	0	314	14	12	2	2.3	.965	OF-145
13 yrs.			1330	.356 3rd	.518	4981	1774	307	168	54	1.1	873	785	519	158	202	11	4	2646	198	107	48	2.2	.964	OF-1289, 1B-27

WORLD SERIES

| 1917 | CHI | A | 6 | .304 | .304 | 23 | 7 | 0 | 0 | 0 | 0.0 | 4 | 2 | 1 | 0 | 1 | 0 | 0 | 9 | 1 | 0 | 0 | 1.7 | 1.000 | OF-6 |

Year	Team		Games	BA	SA	AB	H	2B	3B	HR	HR%	R	RBI	BB	SO	SB	Pinch Hit AB	Pinch Hit H	PO	A	E	DP	TC/G	FA	G by Pos

Joe Jackson *continued*

Year	Team		Games	BA	SA	AB	H	2B	3B	HR	HR%	R	RBI	BB	SO	SB	PH AB	PH H	PO	A	E	DP	TC/G	FA	G by Pos
1919			8	.375	.563	32	12	3	0	1	3.1	5	6	1	2	0	0	0	16	1	0	1	2.1	1.000	OF-8
2 yrs.			14	.345	.455	55	19	3	0	1	1.8	9	8	2	2	1	0	0	25	2	0	1	1.9	1.000	OF-14

Ken Jackson

JACKSON, KENNETH BERNARD
B. Aug. 21, 1963, Shreveport, La.
BR TR 6'1" 190 lbs.

| 1987 | PHI | N | 8 | .250 | .375 | 16 | 4 | 2 | 0 | 0 | 0.0 | 1 | 2 | 1 | 4 | 0 | 0 | 0 | 6 | 15 | 1 | 1 | 2.8 | .955 | SS-8 |

Lou Jackson

JACKSON, LOUIS CLARENCE
B. July 26, 1935, Riverton, La.   D. May 27, 1969, Tokyo, Japan
BL TR 5'10" 168 lbs.

1958	CHI	N	24	.171	.371	35	6	2	1	1	2.9	5	6	1	9	0	11	1	9	0	0	0	0.4	1.000	OF-12
1959			6	.250	.250	4	1	0	0	0	0.0	2	1	0	2	0	4	1	0	0	0	0	0.0	–	
1964	BAL	A	4	.375	.375	8	3	0	0	0	0.0	0	0	0	2	0	3	0	4	0	0	0	1.0	1.000	OF-1
3 yrs.			34	.213	.362	47	10	2	1	1	2.1	7	7	1	13	0	18	2	13	0	0	0	0.4	1.000	OF-13

Randy Jackson

JACKSON, RANSOM JOSEPH (Handsome Ransom)
B. Feb. 10, 1926, Little Rock, Ark.
BR TR 6'1½" 180 lbs.

1950	CHI	N	34	.225	.396	111	25	4	3	3	2.7	13	6	7	25	4	7	0	26	56	8	3	2.6	.911	3B-27
1951			145	.275	.425	557	153	24	6	16	2.9	78	76	47	44	14	2	1	198	323	24	32	3.8	.956	3B-143
1952			116	.232	.351	379	88	8	5	9	2.4	44	34	27	42	6	10	2	93	203	13	13	2.7	.958	3B-104, OF-1
1953			139	.285	.476	498	142	22	8	19	3.8	61	66	42	61	8	7	0	141	265	22	24	3.1	.949	3B-133
1954			126	.273	.450	484	132	17	6	19	3.9	77	67	44	55	2	2	0	118	266	18	21	3.2	.955	3B-124
1955			138	.265	.445	499	132	13	7	21	4.2	73	70	58	58	0	3	1	125	247	20	26	2.8	.949	3B-134
1956	BKN	N	101	.274	.446	307	84	15	7	8	2.6	37	53	28	38	2	21	5	84	184	2	19	2.7	.993	3B-80
1957			48	.198	.252	131	26	1	0	2	1.5	7	16	9	20	0	4	2	27	53	2	7	1.7	.976	3B-34
1958	2 teams	LA N (35G – .185)			CLE A (29G – .242)																				
"	total		64	.218	.365	156	34	6	1	5	3.2	15	17	8	28	0	21	4	38	98	11	10	2.3	.925	3B-41
1959	2 teams	CLE A (3G – .143)			CHI N (41G – .243)																				
"	total		44	.235	.358	81	19	5	1	1	1.2	7	10	11	11	0	16	1	20	30	3	2	1.2	.943	3B-24, OF-1
10 yrs.			955	.261	.421	3203	835	115	44	103	3.2	412	415	281	382	36	93	16	870	1725	123	157	2.8	.955	3B-844, OF-2

WORLD SERIES

| 1956 | BKN | N | 3 | .000 | .000 | 3 | 0 | 0 | 0 | 0 | 0.0 | 0 | 0 | 0 | 2 | 0 | 3 | 0 | 0 | 0 | 0 | 0 | 0.0 | – | |

Reggie Jackson

JACKSON, REGINALD MARTINEZ (Mr. October)
B. May 18, 1946, Wyncote, Pa.
BL TL 6' 195 lbs.

1967	KC	A	35	.178	.305	118	21	4	4	1	0.8	13	6	10	46	1	2	0	55	1	4	0	1.7	.933	OF-34
1968	OAK	A	154	.250	.452	553	138	13	6	29	5.2	82	74	50	171	14	1	0	269	14	12	5	1.9	.959	OF-151
1969			152	.275	.608	549	151	36	3	47	8.6	123	118	114	142	13	2	1	278	14	11	2	2.0	.964	OF-150
1970			149	.237	.458	426	101	21	2	23	5.4	57	66	75	135	26	7	2	251	8	12	0	1.8	.956	OF-142
1971			150	.277	.508	567	157	29	3	32	5.6	87	80	63	161	16	5	1	285	15	7	3	2.0	.977	OF-145
1972			135	.265	.473	499	132	25	2	25	5.0	72	75	59	125	9	0	0	301	5	9	5	2.3	.971	OF-135
1973			151	.293	.531	539	158	28	2	32	5.9	99	117	76	111	22	4	0	302	4	9	0	2.1	.971	OF-145, DH-3
1974			148	.289	.514	506	146	25	1	29	5.7	90	93	86	105	25	3	0	296	8	10	2	2.1	.968	OF-127, DH-19
1975			157	.253	.511	593	150	39	3	36	6.1	91	104	67	133	17	1	0	315	13	12	5	2.2	.965	OF-147, DH-9
1976	BAL	A	134	.277	.502	498	138	27	2	27	5.4	84	91	54	108	28	2	1	284	8	11	3	2.3	.964	OF-121, DH-11
1977	NY	A	146	.286	.550	525	150	39	2	32	6.1	93	110	74	129	17	3	0	236	7	13	0	1.8	.947	OF-127, DH-18
1978			139	.274	.477	511	140	13	5	27	5.3	82	97	58	133	14	1	1	212	6	3	1	1.6	.986	OF-104, DH-35
1979			131	.297	.544	465	138	24	2	29	6.2	78	89	65	107	9	3	1	274	7	4	2	2.2	.986	OF-125, DH-11
1980			143	.300	.597	514	154	22	4	41	8.0	94	111	83	122	1	3	1	174	3	7	0	1.3	.962	OF-94, DH-46
1981			94	.237	.428	334	79	17	1	15	4.5	33	54	46	82	0	1	1	111	3	3	0	1.4	.974	OF-61, DH-33
1982	CAL	A	153	.275	.532	530	146	17	1	39	7.4	92	101	85	156	4	11	3	200	6	6	1	1.4	.972	OF-139, DH-5
1983			116	.194	.340	397	77	14	1	14	3.5	43	49	52	140	0	10	2	66	4	1	0	0.6	.986	DH-62, OF-47
1984			143	.223	.406	525	117	17	2	25	4.8	67	81	55	141	8	7	1	7	0	0	0	0.0	1.000	DH-134, OF-3
1985			143	.252	.487	460	116	27	0	27	5.9	64	85	78	138	1	12	1	112	6	7	1	0.9	.944	OF-81, DH-52
1986			132	.241	.408	419	101	12	2	18	4.3	65	58	92	115	1	14	4	4	1	1	0	0.0	.833	DH-121, OF-4
1987	OAK	A	115	.220	.402	336	74	14	1	15	4.5	42	43	33	97	2	29	7	30	0	0	0	0.3	1.000	DH-79, OF-20
21 yrs.			2820	.262	.490	9864	2584	463	49	563 6th	5.7	1551	1702	1375	2597 1st	228	121	31	4062	133	142	31	1.5	.967	OF-2102, DH-638

DIVISIONAL PLAYOFF SERIES

| 1981 | NY | A | 5 | .300 | .600 | 20 | 6 | 0 | 0 | 2 | 10.0 | 4 | 4 | 1 | 5 | 0 | 0 | 0 | 0 | 0 | 0 | 0 | – | | OF-5 |

LEAGUE CHAMPIONSHIP SERIES

1971	OAK	A	3	.333	.917	12	4	1	0	2	16.7	2	2	0	1	0	0	0	9	0	0	0	3.3	1.000	OF-3
1972			5	.278	.333	18	5	1	0	0	0.0	1	2	1	6	2	0	0	14	0	1	0	3.0	.933	OF-5
1973			5	.143	.143	21	3	0	0	0	0.0	0	0	0	6	0	0	0	19	0	0	0	3.8	1.000	OF-5
1974			4	.167	.250	12	2	1	0	0	0.0	1	1	3	2	0	0	0	0	0	0	0	0.0	–	DH-3, OF-1
1975			3	.417	.667	12	5	0	0	1	8.3	1	3	0	2	0	0	0	5	1	0	1	2.0	1.000	OF-3
1977	NY	A	5	.125	.125	16	2	0	0	0	0.0	1	2	2	1	1	1	1	10	1	0	0	2.2	1.000	OF-4, DH-1
1978			4	.462	1.000	13	6	1	0	2	15.4	5	6	3	4	0	0	0	4	0	0	0	1.0	1.000	DH-3, OF-1
1980			3	.273	.364	11	3	1	0	0	0.0	0	1	0	5	0	0	0	5	0	0	0	1.7	1.000	OF-3
1981			2	.000	.000	4	0	0	0	0	0.0	1	0	1	1	0	0	0	0	0	0	0	0.0	–	OF-2
1982	CAL	A	5	.111	.278	18	2	0	0	1	5.6	1	2	1	7	0	0	0	0	0	0	0	0.0	–	OF-5
1986			6	.192	.269	26	5	2	0	0	0.0	2	2	7	7	0	0	0	0	0	0	0	0.0	–	DH-6
11 yrs.			45	.227	.380	163	37	7	0	6	3.7	16	20	17	41	4	1	1	66	3	1	1	1.6	.986	OF-32, DH-13

WORLD SERIES

1973	OAK	A	7	.310	.586	29	9	3	1	1	3.4	3	6	2	7	0	0	0	17	0	0	0	2.4	1.000	OF-7
1974			5	.286	.571	14	4	1	0	1	7.1	3	1	5	3	1	0	0	6	1	1	0	1.6	.875	OF-5
1977	NY	A	6	.450	1.250	20	9	1	0	5	25.0	10	8	3	4	0	0	0	9	0	0	0	1.5	1.000	OF-6
1978			6	.391	.696	23	9	1	0	2	8.7	2	8	3	7	0	0	0	0	0	0	0	0.0	–	DH-6

Year Team	Games	BA	SA	AB	H	2B	3B	HR	HR%	R	RBI	BB	SO	SB	Pinch Hit AB	Pinch Hit H	PO	A	E	DP	TC/G	FA	G by Pos

Reggie Jackson *continued*

Year Team	Games	BA	SA	AB	H	2B	3B	HR	HR%	R	RBI	BB	SO	SB	PH AB	PH H	PO	A	E	DP	TC/G	FA	G by Pos
1981	3	.333	.667	12	4	1	0	1	8.3	3	1	2	3	0	0	0	5	0	1	0	2.0	.833	OF-3
5 yrs.	27	.357	.755	98	35	7	1	10	10.2	21	24	15	24	1	0	0	37	1	2	0	1.5	.950	OF-21, DH-6
		9th	1st				9th		5th	2nd	10th	8th									8th		

Ron Jackson

JACKSON, RONALD HARRIS
B. Oct. 22, 1933, Kalamazoo, Mich.　　　　BR TR 6'7'' 225 lbs.

Year Team	Games	BA	SA	AB	H	2B	3B	HR	HR%	R	RBI	BB	SO	SB	PH AB	PH H	PO	A	E	DP	TC/G	FA	G by Pos
1954 CHI A	40	.280	.452	93	26	4	0	4	4.3	10	20	6	20	2	7	1	244	9	3	15	6.4	.988	1B-35
1955	40	.203	.324	74	15	1	0	2	2.7	10	7	8	22	1	7	4	162	9	2	14	4.3	.988	1B-29
1956	22	.214	.321	56	12	3	0	1	1.8	7	4	10	13	1	3	0	138	11	0	16	6.8	1.000	1B-19
1957	13	.317	.467	60	19	3	0	2	3.3	4	8	1	12	0	0	0	125	5	1	10	10.1	.992	1B-13
1958	61	.233	.404	146	34	4	0	7	4.8	19	21	18	46	2	22	4	289	16	1	29	5.0	.997	1B-38
1959	10	.214	.500	14	3	1	0	1	7.1	3	2	1	0	0	5	1	30	1	0	3	3.1	1.000	1B-5
1960 BOS A	10	.226	.290	31	7	2	0	0	0.0	1	0	1	6	0	1	0	66	5	2	10	7.3	.973	1B-9
7 yrs.	196	.245	.395	474	116	18	1	17	3.6	54	52	45	119	6	45	10	1054	56	9	97	5.7	.992	1B-148

Ron Jackson

JACKSON, RONNIE DAMIEN
B. May 9, 1953, Birmingham, Ala.　　　　BR TR 6' 200 lbs.

Year Team	Games	BA	SA	AB	H	2B	3B	HR	HR%	R	RBI	BB	SO	SB	PH AB	PH H	PO	A	E	DP	TC/G	FA	G by Pos
1975 CAL A	13	.231	.282	39	9	2	0	0	0.0	2	2	2	10	1	1	0	19	4	2	0	1.9	.920	OF-9, 3B-3, DH-1
1976	127	.227	.344	410	93	18	3	8	2.0	44	40	30	58	5	5	1	91	225	16	20	2.6	.952	3B-114, 2B-7, DH-6, OF-4
1977	106	.243	.390	292	71	15	2	8	2.7	38	28	24	42	3	20	8	314	75	6	33	3.7	.985	1B-43, 3B-30, DH-20, OF-3, SS-1
1978	105	.297	.421	387	115	18	6	6	1.6	49	57	16	31	2	5	1	606	88	8	56	6.7	.989	1B-75, 3B-31, DH-1, OF-1
1979 MIN A	159	.271	.429	583	158	40	5	14	2.4	85	68	51	59	3	4	0	1448	140	9	175	10.0	.994	1B-157, OF-1, SS-1, 3B-1
1980	131	.265	.391	396	105	29	3	5	1.3	48	42	28	41	1	21	4	1000	74	10	105	8.3	.991	1B-119, OF-15, 3B-2, DH-1
1981 2 teams		MIN A	(54G – .263)		DET A	(31G – .284)																	
" total	85	.270	.396	270	73	17	1	5	1.9	29	40	18	26	6	10	1	547	45	5	46	7.0	.992	1B-65, OF-7, DH-6, 3B-3
1982 CAL A	53	.331	.415	142	47	6	0	2	1.4	15	19	10	12	0	8	4	317	31	2	37	6.6	.994	1B-37, 3B-9
1983	102	.230	.351	348	80	16	1	8	2.3	41	39	27	33	2	12	2	402	114	13	43	5.2	.975	3B-38, 1B-35, DH-16, OF-15
1984 2 teams		CAL A	(33G – .165)		BAL A	(12G – .286)																	
" total	45	.193	.244	119	23	4	1	0	0.0	5	7	7	17	0	8	1	208	35	4	22	5.5	.984	1B-21, 3B-19, OF-1
10 yrs.	926	.259	.385	2986	774	165	22	56	1.9	356	342	213	329	23	94	22	4952	831	75	537	6.3	.987	1B-552, 3B-250, OF-56, DH-51, 2B-7, SS-2

LEAGUE CHAMPIONSHIP SERIES

Year Team	Games	BA	SA	AB	H	2B	3B	HR	HR%	R	RBI	BB	SO	SB	PH AB	PH H	PO	A	E	DP	TC/G	FA	G by Pos
1982 CAL A	1	1.000	1.000	1	1	0	0	0	0.0	0	0	0	0	0	1	1	0	0	0	0	0.0	–	

Sonny Jackson

JACKSON, ROLAND THOMAS
B. July 9, 1944, Washington, D. C.　　　　BL TR 5'9'' 150 lbs.

Year Team	Games	BA	SA	AB	H	2B	3B	HR	HR%	R	RBI	BB	SO	SB	PH AB	PH H	PO	A	E	DP	TC/G	FA	G by Pos
1963 HOU N	1	.000	.000	3	0	0	0	0	0.0	0	0	0	1	0	0	0	0	5	1	0	6.0	.833	SS-1
1964	9	.348	.391	23	8	1	0	0	0.0	3	1	2	3	1	1	0	8	12	3	1	2.6	.870	SS-7
1965	10	.130	.130	23	3	0	0	0	0.0	1	0	1	1	1	1	0	16	15	1	3	3.2	.969	SS-8, 3B-1
1966	150	.292	.334	596	174	6	5	3	0.5	80	25	42	53	49	0	0	270	449	37	73	5.0	.951	SS-150
1967	129	.237	.283	520	123	18	3	0	0.0	67	25	36	45	22	2	0	204	379	35	63	4.8	.943	SS-128
1968 ATL N	105	.226	.268	358	81	8	2	1	0.3	37	19	25	35	16	2	1	132	307	22	35	4.4	.952	SS-99
1969	98	.239	.289	318	76	3	5	1	0.3	41	27	35	33	12	2	0	161	254	17	48	4.4	.961	SS-97
1970	103	.259	.320	328	85	14	3	0	0.0	60	20	45	27	11	8	1	123	240	26	40	3.8	.933	SS-87
1971	149	.258	.324	547	141	20	5	2	0.4	58	25	35	45	7	2	0	336	8	7	0	2.4	.980	OF-145
1972	60	.238	.333	126	30	6	3	0	0.0	20	8	7	9	1	23	8	47	62	3	9	1.9	.973	SS-17, OF-10, 3B-6
1973	117	.209	.252	206	43	5	2	0	0.0	29	12	22	13	6	27	8	93	89	6	10	1.6	.968	OF-56, SS-36
1974	5	.429	.429	7	3	0	0	0	0.0	0	0	0	0	0	4	2	2	0	0	0	0.4	1.000	OF-1
12 yrs.	936	.251	.303	3055	767	81	28	7	0.2	396	162	250	265	126	72	20	1392	1820	158	282	3.6	.953	SS-630, OF-212, 3B-7

LEAGUE CHAMPIONSHIP SERIES

Year Team	Games	BA	SA	AB	H	2B	3B	HR	HR%	R	RBI	BB	SO	SB	PH AB	PH H	PO	A	E	DP	TC/G	FA	G by Pos
1969 ATL N	1	–	–	0	0	0	0	0	–	0	0	0	0	0	0	0	0	0	0	0	0.0	–	SS-1

Travis Jackson

JACKSON, TRAVIS CALVIN (Stonewall)
B. Nov. 2, 1903, Waldo, Ark.　D. July 27, 1987, Waldo, Ark.　　　BR TR 5'10½'' 160 lbs.
Hall of Fame 1982.

Year Team	Games	BA	SA	AB	H	2B	3B	HR	HR%	R	RBI	BB	SO	SB	PH AB	PH H	PO	A	E	DP	TC/G	FA	G by Pos
1922 NY N	3	.000	.000	8	0	0	0	0	0.0	1	0	0	2	0	0	0	3	7	1	1	3.7	.909	SS-3
1923	96	.275	.391	327	90	12	7	4	1.2	45	37	22	40	3	4	2	107	265	23	31	4.1	.942	SS-60, 3B-31, 2B-1
1924	151	.302	.428	596	180	26	8	11	1.8	81	76	21	56	6	0	0	332	534	58	101	6.1	.937	SS-151
1925	112	.285	.397	411	117	15	2	9	2.2	51	59	24	43	8	2	0	277	366	40	64	6.1	.941	SS-110
1926	111	.327	.494	385	126	24	8	8	2.1	64	51	20	26	2	2	1	259	352	24	72	5.7	.962	SS-108, OF-1
1927	127	.318	.486	469	149	29	4	14	3.0	67	98	32	30	8	1	0	292	449	37	85	6.1	.952	SS-124, 3B-2
1928	150	.270	.436	537	145	35	6	14	2.6	73	77	56	46	8	1	0	354	547	45	112	6.3	.952	SS-149
1929	149	.294	.490	551	162	21	12	21	3.8	92	94	64	56	10	0	0	329	552	28	110	6.1	.969	SS-149
1930	116	.339	.529	431	146	27	8	13	3.0	70	82	32	25	6	1	0	218	441	30	72	5.9	.956	SS-115
1931	145	.310	.420	555	172	26	10	5	0.9	65	71	36	23	13	0	0	303	496	25	79	5.7	.970	SS-145
1932	52	.256	.415	195	50	17	1	4	2.1	23	38	13	16	1	1	0	106	166	22	31	5.7	.925	SS-52
1933	53	.246	.287	122	30	5	0	0	0.0	11	12	8	11	2	9	1	52	87	11	16	2.8	.927	SS-21, 3B-21
1934	137	.268	.436	523	140	26	7	16	3.1	75	101	37	71	1	0	0	292	477	43	61	5.9	.947	SS-130, 3B-9
1935	128	.301	.440	511	154	20	12	9	1.8	74	80	29	64	3	0	0	139	220	20	13	3.0	.947	3B-128
1936	126	.230	.297	465	107	8	1	7	1.5	41	53	18	56	1	0	0	110	218	16	10	2.7	.953	3B-116, SS-9
15 yrs.	1656	.291	.433	6086	1768	291	86	135	2.2	833	929	412	565	71	23	5	3173	5177	423	858	5.3	.952	SS-1326, 3B-307, OF-1, 2B-1

WORLD SERIES

Year Team	Games	BA	SA	AB	H	2B	3B	HR	HR%	R	RBI	BB	SO	SB	PH AB	PH H	PO	A	E	DP	TC/G	FA	G by Pos
1923 NY N	1	.000	.000	1	0	0	0	0	0.0	0	0	0	1	0	1	0	0	0	0	0	0.0	–	
1924	7	.074	.074	27	2	0	0	0	0.0	3	1	1	4	1	0	0	8	20	3	3	4.4	.903	SS-7
1933	5	.222	.278	18	4	1	0	0	0.0	3	2	1	3	0	0	0	3	16	1	2	4.0	.950	3B-5

Year	Team		Games	BA	SA	AB	H	2B	3B	HR	HR%	R	RBI	BB	SO	SB	Pinch Hit AB	Pinch Hit H	PO	A	E	DP	TC/G	FA	G by Pos

Travis Jackson *continued*

| 1936 | | | 6 | .190 | .190 | 21 | 4 | 0 | 0 | 0 | 0.0 | 1 | 1 | 1 | 3 | 0 | 0 | 0 | 2 | 8 | 3 | 1 | 2.2 | .769 | 3B-6 |
| 4 yrs. | | | 19 | .149 | .164 | 67 | 10 | 1 | 0 | 0 | 0.0 | 7 | 4 | 3 | 10 | 1 | 1 | 0 | 13 | 44 | 7 | 6 | 3.4 | .891 | 3B-11, SS-7 |

Lamar Jacobs

JACOBS, LAMAR GARY (Jake) BR TR 6' 175 lbs.
B. June 9, 1937, Youngstown, Ohio

1960	WAS	A	6	.000	.000	2	0	0	0	0	0.0	0	0	0	0	0	2	0	0	0	0	0	0.0	–	
1961	MIN	A	4	.250	.250	8	2	0	0	0	0.0	0	0	0	2	0	1	0	2	0	0	0	0.5	1.000	OF-3
2 yrs.			10	.200	.200	10	2	0	0	0	0.0	0	0	0	2	0	3	0	2	0	0	0	0.2	1.000	OF-3

Mike Jacobs

JACOBS, MORRIS ELMORE
B. 1877 D. Mar. 21, 1949, Louisville, Ky.

| 1902 | CHI | N | 5 | .211 | .211 | 19 | 4 | 0 | 0 | 0 | 0.0 | 2 | | 0 | | | 0 | 0 | 0 | 9 | 13 | 3 | 1 | 5.0 | .880 | SS-5 |

Otto Jacobs

JACOBS, OTTO ALBERT BR TR 5'9" 180 lbs.
B. Apr. 19, 1889, Chicago, Ill. D. Nov. 19, 1955, Chicago, Ill.

| 1918 | CHI | A | 29 | .205 | .274 | 73 | 15 | 3 | 1 | 0 | 0.0 | 4 | 3 | 5 | 8 | 0 | 7 | 1 | 64 | 21 | 4 | 3 | 3.1 | .955 | C-21 |

Ray Jacobs

JACOBS, RAYMOND F. BR TR 6' 160 lbs.
B. Jan. 2, 1902, Salt Lake City, Utah D. Apr. 4, 1952, Los Angeles, Calif.

| 1928 | CHI | N | 2 | .000 | .000 | 2 | 0 | 0 | 0 | 0 | 0.0 | 0 | 0 | 0 | 1 | 0 | 2 | 0 | 0 | 0 | 0 | 0 | 0.0 | – | |

Spook Jacobs

JACOBS, FORREST VANDERGRIFT BR TR 5'8½" 155 lbs.
B. Nov. 4, 1925, Cheswold, Del.

1954	PHI	A	132	.258	.283	508	131	11	1	0	0.0	63	26	60	22	17	0		347	300	17	98	5.0	.974	2B-131
1955	KC	A	13	.261	.261	23	6	0	0	0	0.0	7	1	3	0	1	0		9	9	0	4	1.4	1.000	2B-7
1956 2 teams	KC	A (32G – .216)	PIT	N (11G – .162)																					
" total			43	.201	.239	134	27	5	0	0	0.0	17	6	17	10	4	0		104	95	9	31	4.8	.957	2B-42
3 yrs.			188	.247	.274	665	164	16	1	0	0.0	87	33	80	32	22	0		460	404	26	133	4.7	.971	2B-180

Baby Doll Jacobson

JACOBSON, WILLIAM CHESTER BR TR 6'3" 215 lbs.
B. Aug. 16, 1890, Cable, Ill. D. Jan. 16, 1977, Orion, Ill.

1915 2 teams	DET	A (37G – .215)	STL	A (34G – .209)																					
" total			71	.211	.344	180	38	12	3	2	1.1	18	13	15	40	3	22	5	172	7	3	6	2.6	.984	OF-39, 1B-10
1917	STL	A	148	.248	.340	529	131	23	7	4	0.8	53	55	31	67	10	6	1	411	25	15	10	3.0	.967	OF-131, 1B-11
1919			120	.323	.453	455	147	31	8	4	0.9	70	51	24	47	9	5	2	345	11	16	4	3.1	.957	OF-105, 1B-8
1920			154	.355	.501	609	216	34	14	9	1.5	97	122	46	37	11	0	0	394	18	9	5	2.7	.979	OF-154, 1B-1
1921			151	.352	.487	599	211	38	14	5	0.8	90	90	42	30	8	0	0	469	19	7	11	3.3	.986	OF-141, 1B-11
1922			145	.317	.463	555	176	22	16	9	1.6	88	102	46	36	19	1	0	431	11	16	12	3.2	.965	OF-137, 1B-7
1923			147	.309	.419	592	183	29	6	8	1.4	76	81	29	27	6	1	0	409	10	11	4	2.9	.974	OF-146
1924			152	.318	.528	579	184	41	12	19	3.3	103	97	35	45	6	0	0	484	7	7	4	3.3	.986	OF-151
1925			142	.341	.513	540	184	30	9	15	2.8	103	76	45	26	8	2	1	383	18	13	9	2.9	.969	OF-139
1926 2 teams	STL	A (50G – .286)	BOS	A (98G – .305)																					
" total			148	.299	.436	576	172	51	2	8	1.4	62	90	31	36	5	0	0	298	9	8	1	2.1	.975	OF-148
1927 3 teams	BOS	A (45G – .245)	CLE	A (32G – .252)	PHI	A (17G – .229)																			
" total			94	.246	.334	293	72	17	3	0	0.0	27	42	11	19	1	9	0	181	5	8	0	2.1	.959	OF-84
11 yrs.			1472	.311	.451	5507	1714	328	94	84	1.5	787	819	355	410	86	46	9	3977	140	113	66	2.9	.973	OF-1375, 1B-48

Merwin Jacobson

JACOBSON, MERWIN JOHN WILLIAM (Jake) BL TL 5'11½" 165 lbs.
B. Mar. 7, 1894, New Britain, Conn. D. Jan. 13, 1978, Baltimore, Md.

1915	NY	N	8	.083	.083	24	2	0	0	0	0.0	0		1	5		2	0	9	1	1	0	1.4	.909	OF-5
1916	CHI	N	4	.231	.231	13	3	0	0	0	0.0	2	0	1	4	2	0	0	8	0	0	0	2.0	1.000	OF-4
1926	BKN	N	110	.247	.292	288	71	9	2	0	0.0	41	23	36	24	5	17	5	191	5	5	2	1.8	.975	OF-86
1927			11	.000	.000	6	0	0	0	0	0.0	4	1	0	1	0	5	0	1	0	0	0	0.1	1.000	OF-3
4 yrs.			133	.230	.269	331	76	9	2	0	0.0	47	24	38	34	7	24	5	209	6	6	2	1.7	.973	OF-98

Brook Jacoby

JACOBY, BROOK WALLACE BR TR 5'11" 175 lbs.
B. Nov. 23, 1959, Philadelphia, Pa.

1981	ATL	N	11	.200	.200	10	2	0	0	0	0.0	0	1	0	3	0	8	2	3	4	0	1	0.6	1.000	3B-3
1983			4	.000	.000	0	0	0	0	0	0.0	0	0	0	1	0	2	0	0	2	0	0	0.5	1.000	3B-2
1984	CLE	A	126	.264	.369	439	116	19	3	7	1.6	64	40	32	73	3	0	0	86	188	14	17	2.3	.951	3B-126, SS-1
1985			161	.274	.426	606	166	26	3	20	3.3	72	87	48	120	2	1	0	114	319	19	26	2.8	.958	3B-161, 2B-1
1986			158	.288	.441	583	168	30	4	17	2.9	83	80	56	137	2	0	0	109	292	25	24	2.7	.941	3B-158
1987			155	.300	.541	540	162	26	4	32	5.9	73	69	75	73	2	1	1	192	261	22	24	3.1	.954	3B-144, DH-4
1988			152	.241	.335	552	133	25	0	9	1.6	59	49	48	101	2	1	0	99	298	10	23	2.7	.975	3B-151
1989			147	.272	.416	519	141	26	5	13	2.5	49	64	62	90	2	0	0	92	268	17	15	2.6	.955	3B-144, DH-3
8 yrs.			914	.273	.421	3257	888	152	19	98	3.0	400	390	321	598	13	14	3	695	1632	107	130	2.7	.956	3B-889, DH-7, 1B-7, SS-1, 2B-1

Harry Jacoby

JACOBY, HARRY
B. Philadelphia, Pa. Deceased.

1882	BAL	AA	31	.174	.223	121	21	1	1	1	0.8	17		7			0	0	46	59	26	3	4.2	.802	3B-19, OF-13
1885			11	.140	.186	43	6	2	0	0	0.0	4		2			0	0	21	22	5	2	4.4	.896	2B-11
2 yrs.			42	.165	.213	164	27	3	1	1	0.6	21		9			0	0	67	81	31	5	4.3	.827	3B-19, OF-13, 2B-11

Art Jahn

JAHN, ARTHUR CHARLES BR TR 6' 180 lbs.
B. Dec. 2, 1895, Struble, Iowa D. Jan. 9, 1948, Little Rock, Ark.

| 1925 | CHI | N | 58 | .301 | .416 | 226 | 68 | 10 | 8 | 0 | 0.0 | 30 | 37 | 11 | 20 | 2 | 0 | 0 | 124 | 5 | 2 | 3 | 2.3 | .985 | OF-58 |

Year	Team	Games	BA	SA	AB	H	2B	3B	HR	HR%	R	RBI	BB	SO	SB	Pinch Hit AB	Pinch Hit H	PO	A	E	DP	TC/G	FA	G by Pos

Art Jahn *continued*

Year	Team	Games	BA	SA	AB	H	2B	3B	HR	HR%	R	RBI	BB	SO	SB	PH AB	PH H	PO	A	E	DP	TC/G	FA	G by Pos
1928	2 teams	NY	N (10G – .276)		PHI	N (36G – .223)																		
"	total	46	.236	.301	123	29	5	0	1	0.8	15	18	6	16	0	8	1	63	2	1	1	1.4	.985	OF-39
2 yrs.		104	.278	.375	349	97	15	8	1	0.3	45	55	17	36	2	8	1	187	7	3	4	1.9	.985	OF-97

Art James

JAMES, ARTHUR, JR.
B. Aug. 2, 1952, Detroit, Mich.   BL TL 6'   170 lbs.

Year	Team	Games	BA	SA	AB	H	2B	3B	HR	HR%	R	RBI	BB	SO	SB	PH AB	PH H	PO	A	E	DP	TC/G	FA	G by Pos
1975	DET A	11	.225	.275	40	9	2	0	0	0.0	2	1	1	3	1	0	0	33	0	0	0	3.0	1.000	OF-11

Bernie James

JAMES, ROBERT EUGENE
B. Sept. 2, 1905, Angleton, Tex.   BB TR 5'9½" 150 lbs.
BR 1929,
BL 1930

Year	Team	Games	BA	SA	AB	H	2B	3B	HR	HR%	R	RBI	BB	SO	SB	PH AB	PH H	PO	A	E	DP	TC/G	FA	G by Pos
1929	BOS N	46	.307	.376	101	31	3	2	0	0.0	12	9	9	13	3	7	1	70	56	8	11	2.9	.940	2B-32, OF-1
1930		8	.182	.273	11	2	1	0	0	0.0	1	1	0	1	0	1	0	5	11	1	1	2.1	.941	2B-7
1933	NY N	60	.224	.280	125	28	2	1	1	0.8	22	10	8	12	5	5	2	76	94	10	20	3.0	.944	2B-26, SS-6, 3B-5
3 yrs.		114	.257	.321	237	61	6	3	1	0.4	35	20	17	26	8	13	3	151	161	19	32	2.9	.943	2B-65, SS-6, 3B-5, OF-1

Bert James

JAMES, BERTON HULDON (Jesse)
B. July 7, 1886, Coopertown, Tenn. D. Jan. 2, 1959, Adairville, Ky.   BL TR 5'11" 185 lbs.

Year	Team	Games	BA	SA	AB	H	2B	3B	HR	HR%	R	RBI	BB	SO	SB	PH AB	PH H	PO	A	E	DP	TC/G	FA	G by Pos
1909	STL N	6	.286	.286	21	6	0	0	0	0.0	1	0	4		1	0	0	9	1	1	1	1.8	.909	OF-6

Charlie James

JAMES, CHARLES WESLEY
B. Dec. 22, 1937, St. Louis, Mo.   BR TR 6'1" 195 lbs.

Year	Team	Games	BA	SA	AB	H	2B	3B	HR	HR%	R	RBI	BB	SO	SB	PH AB	PH H	PO	A	E	DP	TC/G	FA	G by Pos
1960	STL N	43	.180	.320	50	9	1	0	2	4.0	5	5	1	12	0	9	1	21	1	2	1	0.6	.917	OF-37
1961		108	.255	.355	349	89	19	2	4	1.1	43	44	15	59	2	19	3	151	3	6	1	1.5	.963	OF-90
1962		129	.276	.392	388	107	13	4	8	2.1	50	59	10	58	3	12	4	156	7	2	1	1.3	.988	OF-116
1963		116	.268	.406	347	93	14	2	10	2.9	34	45	10	64	2	18	10	169	4	1	1	1.5	.994	OF-101
1964		88	.223	.335	233	52	9	1	5	2.1	24	17	11	58	0	31	8	76	3	3	0	0.9	.963	OF-60
1965	CIN N	26	.205	.205	39	8	0	0	0	0.0	2	2	1	9	0	19	4	10	0	1	0	0.4	.909	OF-7
6 yrs.		510	.255	.369	1406	358	56	9	29	2.1	158	172	48	260	7	108	30	583	18	15	4	1.2	.976	OF-411

WORLD SERIES

Year	Team	Games	BA	SA	AB	H	2B	3B	HR	HR%	R	RBI	BB	SO	SB	PH AB	PH H	PO	A	E	DP	TC/G	FA	G by Pos
1964	STL N	3	.000	.000	3	0	0	0	0	0.0	0	0	0	1	0	3	0	0	0	0	0	0.0	–	

Chris James

JAMES, DONALD CHRIS
B. Oct. 4, 1962, Rusk, Tex.   BR TR 6'1" 190 lbs.

Year	Team	Games	BA	SA	AB	H	2B	3B	HR	HR%	R	RBI	BB	SO	SB	PH AB	PH H	PO	A	E	DP	TC/G	FA	G by Pos
1986	PHI N	16	.283	.413	46	13	0	1	1	2.2	5	5	1	13	0	6	2	19	0	0	0	1.2	1.000	OF-11
1987		115	.293	.525	358	105	20	6	17	4.7	48	54	27	67	3	9	5	198	5	2	1	1.8	.990	OF-108
1988		150	.242	.389	566	137	24	1	19	3.4	57	66	31	73	7	4	1	282	51	9	6	2.3	.974	OF-116, 3B-31
1989	2 teams	PHI	N (45G – .207)		SD	N (87G – .264)																		
"	total	132	.243	.367	482	117	17	2	13	2.7	55	65	26	68	5	8	2	215	27	7	4	1.9	.972	OF-116, 3B-17
4 yrs.		413	.256	.416	1452	372	64	9	50	3.4	165	190	85	221	15	27	10	714	83	18	11	2.0	.978	OF-351, 3B-48

Cleo James

JAMES, CLEO JOEL
B. Aug. 31, 1940, Clarksdale, Miss.   BR TR 5'10" 176 lbs.

Year	Team	Games	BA	SA	AB	H	2B	3B	HR	HR%	R	RBI	BB	SO	SB	PH AB	PH H	PO	A	E	DP	TC/G	FA	G by Pos
1968	LA N	10	.200	.300	10	2	1	0	0	0.0	2	0	0	6	0	6	1	2	0	0	0	0.2	1.000	OF-2
1970	CHI N	100	.210	.324	176	37	7	2	3	1.7	33	14	17	24	5	6	0	115	5	0	1	1.2	1.000	OF-90
1971		54	.287	.373	150	43	7	0	2	1.3	25	13	10	16	6	3	1	90	5	2	2	1.8	.979	OF-48, 3B-2
1973		44	.111	.111	45	5	0	0	0	0.0	9	0	1	6	5	10	1	23	1	1	0	0.6	.960	OF-22
4 yrs.		208	.228	.318	381	87	15	2	5	1.3	69	27	28	52	16	25	3	230	11	3	3	1.2	.988	OF-162, 3B-2

Dion James

JAMES, DION
B. Nov. 9, 1962, Philadelphia, Pa.   BL TL 6'1" 170 lbs.

Year	Team	Games	BA	SA	AB	H	2B	3B	HR	HR%	R	RBI	BB	SO	SB	PH AB	PH H	PO	A	E	DP	TC/G	FA	G by Pos
1983	MIL A	11	.100	.100	20	2	0	0	0	0.0	1	1	2	2	1	0	0	12	1	0	0	1.2	1.000	OF-9, DH-2
1984		128	.295	.377	387	114	19	5	1	0.3	52	30	32	41	10	17	3	252	7	3	1	2.0	.989	OF-118
1985		18	.224	.245	49	11	1	0	0	0.0	5	3	6	6	0	4	0	20	0	0	0	1.1	1.000	OF-11, DH-3
1987	ATL N	134	.312	.472	494	154	37	6	10	2.0	80	61	70	63	10	11	1	262	4	1	1	2.0	.996	OF-126
1988		132	.256	.350	386	99	17	5	3	0.8	46	30	58	59	9	15	3	222	5	3	0	1.7	.987	OF-120
1989	2 teams	ATL	N (63G – .259)		CLE	A (71G – .306)																		
"	total	134	.287	.366	415	119	18	0	5	1.2	41	40	49	49	2	28	5	211	8	3	5	1.7	.986	OF-83, DH-27, 1B-10
6 yrs.		557	.285	.388	1751	499	92	16	19	1.1	225	165	217	220	32	75	12	979	25	10	7	1.8	.990	OF-467, DH-32, 1B-10

Skip James

JAMES, PHILIP ROBERT
B. Oct. 21, 1949, Elmhurst, Ill.   BL TL 6' 185 lbs.

Year	Team	Games	BA	SA	AB	H	2B	3B	HR	HR%	R	RBI	BB	SO	SB	PH AB	PH H	PO	A	E	DP	TC/G	FA	G by Pos
1977	SF N	10	.267	.333	15	4	1	0	0	0.0	3	3	2	3	0	2	0	46	4	0	2	5.0	1.000	1B-9
1978		41	.095	.143	21	2	1	0	0	0.0	5	3	4	5	1	10	1	58	6	0	5	1.6	1.000	1B-27
2 yrs.		51	.167	.222	36	6	2	0	0	0.0	8	6	6	8	1	12	1	104	10	0	7	2.2	1.000	1B-36

Charlie Jamieson

JAMIESON, CHARLES DEVINE
B. Feb. 7, 1893, Paterson, N. J. D. Oct. 27, 1969, Paterson, N. J.   BL TL 5'8½" 165 lbs.

Year	Team	Games	BA	SA	AB	H	2B	3B	HR	HR%	R	RBI	BB	SO	SB	PH AB	PH H	PO	A	E	DP	TC/G	FA	G by Pos
1915	WAS A	17	.279	.382	68	19	3	2	0	0.0	9	7	6	9	0	0	0	36	5	0	0	2.4	1.000	OF-17
1916		64	.248	.276	145	36	4	0	0	0.0	16	13	18	18	5	13	4	90	7	8	4	1.6	.924	OF-41, 1B-4, P-1
1917	2 teams	WAS	A (20G – .171)		PHI	A (85G – .265)																		
"	total	105	.257	.288	382	98	8	2	0	0.0	45	29	43	41	8	12	5	135	12	11	4	1.5	.930	OF-92, P-1
1918	PHI A	110	.202	.238	416	84	11	2	0	0.0	50	11	54	30	11	4	1	184	21	10	4	2.0	.953	OF-102, P-5
1919	CLE A	26	.353	.588	17	6	2	1	0	0.0	3	2	0	2	2	9	3	5	2	1	0	0.3	.875	P-4, OF-3
1920		108	.319	.411	370	118	17	7	1	0.3	69	40	41	26	6	14	3	194	15	8	0	2.0	.963	OF-98, 1B-4
1921		140	.310	.414	536	166	33	10	1	0.2	94	45	67	27	8	2	2	277	17	8	3	2.2	.974	OF-137
1922		145	.323	.429	567	183	29	11	3	0.5	87	57	54	22	15	1	1	289	18	7	5	2.2	.978	OF-144, P-2
1923		152	.345	.447	644	222	36	12	2	0.3	130	51	80	37	19	0	0	360	18	10	1	2.6	.974	OF-152
1924		143	.359	.458	594	213	34	8	2	0.3	98	53	47	15	21	1	0	330	11	9	6	2.4	.974	OF-139
1925		138	.296	.379	557	165	24	7	4	0.7	109	42	72	26	14	3	1	324	16	16	4	2.6	.955	OF-135

Year Team	Games	BA	SA	AB	H	2B	3B	HR	HR%	R	RBI	BB	SO	SB	Pinch Hit AB	Pinch Hit H	PO	A	E	DP	TC/G	FA	G by Pos

Charlie Jamieson *continued*

Year Team	Games	BA	SA	AB	H	2B	3B	HR	HR%	R	RBI	BB	SO	SB	AB	H	PO	A	E	DP	TC/G	FA	G by Pos
1926	143	.299	.395	555	166	33	7	2	0.4	89	45	53	22	9	0	0	293	15	13	5	2.2	.960	OF-143
1927	127	.309	.380	489	151	23	6	0	0.0	73	36	64	14	7	0	0	300	13	10	2	2.5	.969	OF-127
1928	112	.307	.374	433	133	18	4	1	0.2	63	37	56	20	3	0	0	282	22	5	1	2.8	.984	OF-111
1929	102	.291	.357	364	106	22	1	0	0.0	56	26	50	12	2	4	2	192	8	4	1	2.0	.980	OF-93
1930	103	.301	.374	366	110	22	1	1	0.3	64	52	36	20	5	6	1	162	7	8	0	1.7	.955	OF-95
1931	28	.302	.395	43	13	2	1	0	0.0	7	4	5	1	1	19	6	11	0	2	0	0.5	.846	OF-7
1932	16	.063	.125	16	1	1	0	0	0.0	0	0	2	3	0	11	0	3	1	0	0	0.3	1.000	OF-2
18 yrs.	1779	.303	.385	6562	1990	322	80	18	0.3	1062	550	748	345	132	87	25	3467	208	130	40	2.1	.966	OF-1638, P-13, 1B-8

WORLD SERIES

Year Team	Games	BA	SA	AB	H	2B	3B	HR	HR%	R	RBI	BB	SO	SB	AB	H	PO	A	E	DP	TC/G	FA	G by Pos
1920 CLE A	6	.333	.400	15	5	1	0	0	0.0	2	1	1	0	1	1	0	8	1	0	1	1.5	1.000	OF-5

Vic Janowicz

JANOWICZ, VICTOR FELIX
B. Feb. 26, 1930, Elyria, Ohio

BR TR 5'9" 185 lbs.

Year Team	Games	BA	SA	AB	H	2B	3B	HR	HR%	R	RBI	BB	SO	SB	AB	H	PO	A	E	DP	TC/G	FA	G by Pos
1953 PIT N	42	.252	.341	123	31	1	2	2	1.6	10	8	5	31	0	5	1	104	15	8	2	3.0	.937	C-35
1954	41	.151	.192	73	11	3	0	0	0.0	10	2	7	24	0	11	2	16	32	5	3	1.3	.906	3B-18, OF-1
2 yrs.	83	.214	.286	196	42	6	1	2	1.0	20	10	12	55	0	16	3	120	47	13	5	2.2	.928	C-35, 3B-18, OF-1

Ray Jansen

JANSEN, RAYMOND WILLIAM
B. Jan. 16, 1889, St. Louis, Mo.   D. Mar. 19, 1934, St. Louis, Mo.

BR TR 5'11" 155 lbs.

Year Team	Games	BA	SA	AB	H	2B	3B	HR	HR%	R	RBI	BB	SO	SB	AB	H	PO	A	E	DP	TC/G	FA	G by Pos
1910 STL A	1	.800	.800	5	4	0	0	0	0.0	0	0	0	0	0	0	0	2	5	3	0	10.0	.700	3B-1

Heinie Jantzen

JANTZEN, WALTER C.
B. Apr. 9, 1890, Chicago, Ill.   D. Apr. 1, 1948, Hines, Ill.

BR TR 5'11½" 170 lbs.

Year Team	Games	BA	SA	AB	H	2B	3B	HR	HR%	R	RBI	BB	SO	SB	AB	H	PO	A	E	DP	TC/G	FA	G by Pos
1912 STL A	31	.185	.227	119	22	0	1	1	0.8	10	8	4		3	0	0	53	6	0	3	1.9	1.000	OF-31

Hal Janvrin

JANVRIN, HAROLD CHANDLER (Childe Harold)
B. Aug. 27, 1892, Haverhill, Mass.   D. Mar. 1, 1962, Boston, Mass.

BR TR 5'11½" 168 lbs.

Year Team	Games	BA	SA	AB	H	2B	3B	HR	HR%	R	RBI	BB	SO	SB	AB	H	PO	A	E	DP	TC/G	FA	G by Pos
1911 BOS A	9	.148	.185	27	4	1	0	0	0.0	2	1	3		0	0	0	43	7	6	1	6.2	.893	3B-5, 1B-4
1913	86	.207	.264	276	57	5	1	3	1.1	18	25	23	27	17	5	0	172	177	26	17	4.4	.931	SS-48, 3B-19, 2B-8, 1B-6
1914	143	.238	.305	492	117	18	6	1	0.2	65	51	38	50	29	0	0	669	237	43	50	6.6	.955	2B-57, 1B-56, SS-20, 3B-6
1915	99	.269	.304	316	85	9	1	0	0.0	41	37	14	27	8	3	1	135	204	32	18	3.7	.914	SS-64, 3B-20, 2B-8
1916	117	.223	.284	310	69	11	4	0	0.0	32	26	32	32	6	7	1	203	233	28	37	4.0	.940	SS-59, 2B-39, 1B-4, 3B-3
1917	55	.197	.220	127	25	3	0	0	0.0	21	8	11	13	2	4	1	63	108	11	17	3.3	.940	2B-38, SS-10, 1B-1
1919 2 teams	WAS A	(61G – .178)		STL N	(7G – .214)																		
" total	68	.180	.225	222	40	5	1	1	0.5	18	14	21	19	8	3	1	122	128	24	14	4.0	.912	2B-58, SS-3, 3B-1
1920 STL N	87	.274	.344	270	74	8	4	1	0.4	33	28	17	19	5	4	1	307	93	13	33	4.7	.969	SS-27, 1B-25, OF-20, 2B-6
1921 2 teams	STL N	(18G – .281)		BKN N	(44G – .196)																		
" total	62	.218	.258	124	27	5	0	0	0.0	13	19	8	6	4	8	1	98	59	12	7	2.7	.929	SS-17, 2B-11, 1B-8, 3B-5, OF-1
1922 BKN N	30	.298	.386	57	17	3	1	0	0.0	7	1	4	4	0	5	2	22	38	9	4	2.3	.870	2B-15, SS-4, 3B-2, OF-1, 1B-1
10 yrs.	756	.232	.287	2221	515	68	18	6	0.3	250	210	171	197	79	39	8	1834	1284	204	198	4.4	.939	SS-252, 2B-240, 1B-105, 3B-61, OF-22

WORLD SERIES

Year Team	Games	BA	SA	AB	H	2B	3B	HR	HR%	R	RBI	BB	SO	SB	AB	H	PO	A	E	DP	TC/G	FA	G by Pos
1915 BOS A	1	.000	.000	1	0	0	0	0	0.0	0	0	0	0	0	0	0	1	0	0	0	1.0	1.000	SS-1
1916	5	.217	.348	23	5	3	0	0	0.0	2	1	0	6	0	0	0	8	16	2	4	5.2	.923	2B-5
2 yrs.	6	.208	.333	24	5	3	0	0	0.0	2	1	0	6	0	0	0	9	16	2	4	4.5	.926	2B-5, SS-1

Roy Jarvis

JARVIS, LeROY GILBERT
B. June 27, 1926, Shawnee, Okla.

BR TR 5'9" 160 lbs.

Year Team	Games	BA	SA	AB	H	2B	3B	HR	HR%	R	RBI	BB	SO	SB	AB	H	PO	A	E	DP	TC/G	FA	G by Pos
1944 BKN N	1	.000	.000	1	0	0	0	0	0.0	0	0	0	0	0	0	0	1	0	0	0	1.0	1.000	C-1
1946 PIT N	2	.250	.250	4	1	0	0	0	0.0	0	0	1	1	0	1	0	4	0	1	0	2.5	.800	C-1
1947	18	.156	.244	45	7	1	0	1	2.2	4	4	6	5	0	2	0	50	8	2	1	3.3	.967	C-15
3 yrs.	21	.160	.240	50	8	1	0	1	2.0	4	4	7	7	0	3	0	55	8	3	1	3.1	.955	C-17

Paul Jata

JATA, PAUL
B. Sept. 4, 1949, Astoria, N. Y.

BR TR 6'1" 190 lbs.

Year Team	Games	BA	SA	AB	H	2B	3B	HR	HR%	R	RBI	BB	SO	SB	AB	H	PO	A	E	DP	TC/G	FA	G by Pos
1972 DET A	32	.230	.257	74	17	2	0	0	0.0	8	3	7	14	0	12	4	116	6	0	6	3.8	.992	1B-12, OF-10, C-1

Alfredo Javier

JAVIER, IGNACIO ALFREDO
Born Ignacio Alfredo Wilkes y Javier.
B. Feb. 4, 1954, San Pedro de Macoris, Dominican Republic

BR TR 5'11" 170 lbs.

Year Team	Games	BA	SA	AB	H	2B	3B	HR	HR%	R	RBI	BB	SO	SB	AB	H	PO	A	E	DP	TC/G	FA	G by Pos
1976 HOU N	8	.208	.208	24	5	0	0	0	0.0	1	0	2	5	0	1	0	7	0	0	0	0.9	1.000	OF-7

Julian Javier

JAVIER, MANUEL JULIAN (Hoolie, The Phantom)
Born Manuel Julian Javier y Liranzo.   Father of Stan Javier.
B. Aug. 9, 1936, San Francisco De Macoris, Dominican Republic

BR TR 6'1" 175 lbs.

Year Team	Games	BA	SA	AB	H	2B	3B	HR	HR%	R	RBI	BB	SO	SB	AB	H	PO	A	E	DP	TC/G	FA	G by Pos
1960 STL N	119	.237	.341	451	107	19	8	4	0.9	55	21	21	72	19	0	0	272	338	24	71	5.3	.962	2B-119
1961	113	.279	.337	445	124	14	3	2	0.4	58	41	30	51	11	0	0	239	332	20	82	5.2	.966	2B-113
1962	155	.263	.356	598	157	25	5	7	1.2	97	39	47	73	26	0	0	344	416	19	96	5.0	.976	2B-151, SS-4
1963	161	.263	.381	609	160	27	9	9	1.5	82	46	24	86	18	0	0	377	415	25	93	5.1	.969	2B-161
1964	155	.241	.363	535	129	19	5	12	2.2	66	65	30	82	9	0	0	360	401	27	97	5.1	.966	2B-154
1965	77	.227	.314	229	52	6	4	2	0.9	34	23	8	44	5	0	0	128	179	8	40	4.1	.975	2B-69
1966	147	.228	.324	460	105	13	5	7	1.5	52	31	26	63	11	0	0	306	364	13	89	4.6	.981	2B-145
1967	140	.281	.404	520	146	16	3	14	2.7	68	64	25	92	6	2	0	311	352	24	72	4.9	.965	2B-138
1968	139	.260	.347	519	135	25	4	4	0.8	54	52	24	61	10	0	0	304	339	16	68	4.7	.976	2B-139
1969	143	.282	.408	493	139	28	2	10	2.0	59	42	40	74	8	4	1	244	374	21	70	4.5	.967	2B-141
1970	139	.251	.306	513	129	16	3	2	0.4	62	42	24	70	6	3	2	329	413	15	84	5.4	.980	2B-137

Year	Team		Games	BA	SA	AB	H	2B	3B	HR	HR%	R	RBI	BB	SO	SB	Pinch Hit AB	Pinch Hit H	PO	A	E	DP	TC/G	FA	G by Pos

Julian Javier *continued*

Year	Team		Games	BA	SA	AB	H	2B	3B	HR	HR%	R	RBI	BB	SO	SB	PH AB	PH H	PO	A	E	DP	TC/G	FA	G by Pos
1971			90	.259	.347	259	67	6	4	3	1.2	32	28	9	33	5	9	2	164	188	8	45	4.0	.978	2B-80, 3B-1
1972	CIN	N	44	.209	.297	91	19	2	0	2	2.2	3	12	6	11	1	20	4	15	38	5	4	1.3	.914	3B-19, 2B-5, 1B-1
13 yrs.			1622	.257	.355	5722	1469	216	55	78	1.4	722	506	314	812	135	38	9	3393	4149	225	911	4.8	.971	2B-1552, 3B-20, SS-4, 1B-1

WORLD SERIES

Year	Team		Games	BA	SA	AB	H	2B	3B	HR	HR%	R	RBI	BB	SO	SB	PH AB	PH H	PO	A	E	DP	TC/G	FA	G by Pos
1964	STL	N	1	-	-	0	0	0	0	0	-	1	0	0	0	0	0	0	0	1	0	0	1.0	1.000	2B-1
1967			7	.360	.600	25	9	3	0	1	4.0	2	4	0	6	0	0	0	12	20	1	4	4.7	.970	2B-7
1968			7	.333	.370	27	9	1	0	0	0.0	1	3	3	4	1	0	0	14	14	0	3	4.0	1.000	2B-7
1972	CIN	N	4	.000	.000	2	0	0	0	0	0.0	0	0	0	0	0	2	0	0	0	0	0	0.0	-	2B-7
4 yrs.			19	.333	.463	54	18	4	0	1	1.9	4	7	3	10	1	2	0	26	35	1	7	3.3	.984	2B-15

Stan Javier

JAVIER, STANLEY JULIAN
Born Stanley Julian Javier y DeJavier. Son of Julian Javier.
B. Sept. 1, 1965, San Francisco De Macoris, Dominican Republic
BB TR 6' 180 lbs.

Year	Team		Games	BA	SA	AB	H	2B	3B	HR	HR%	R	RBI	BB	SO	SB	PH AB	PH H	PO	A	E	DP	TC/G	FA	G by Pos
1984	NY	A	7	.143	.143	7	1	0	0	0	0.0	1	0	0	1	0	0	0	3	0	0	0	0.4	1.000	OF-5
1986	OAK	A	59	.202	.272	114	23	8	0	0	0.0	13	8	16	27	8	0	0	118	1	0	1	2.0	1.000	OF-51, DH-2
1987			81	.185	.258	151	28	3	1	2	1.3	22	9	19	33	3	7	0	149	5	3	4	1.9	.981	OF-71, 1B-6, DH-1
1988			125	.257	.320	397	102	13	3	2	0.5	49	35	32	63	20	9	2	274	7	5	5	2.3	.983	OF-115, 1B-4, DH-2
1989			112	.248	.316	310	77	12	3	1	0.3	42	28	31	45	12	7	0	221	8	2	5	2.1	.991	OF-107, 2B-1, 1B-1
5 yrs.			384	.236	.302	979	231	36	7	5	0.5	127	80	98	169	43	23	2	765	21	10	12	2.1	.987	OF-349, 1B-11, DH-5, 2B-1

LEAGUE CHAMPIONSHIP SERIES

Year	Team		Games	BA	SA	AB	H	2B	3B	HR	HR%	R	RBI	BB	SO	SB	PH AB	PH H	PO	A	E	DP	TC/G	FA	G by Pos
1988	OAK	A	2	.500	.500	4	2	0	0	0	0.0	0	1	1	1	0	0	0	5	0	0	0	2.5	1.000	OF-2
1989			1	.000	.000	2	0	0	0	0	0.0	0	0	0	1	0	0	0	1	0	0	0	1.0	1.000	OF-1
2 yrs.			3	.333	.333	6	2	0	0	0	0.0	0	1	1	2	0	0	0	6	0	0	0	2.0	1.000	OF-3

WORLD SERIES

Year	Team		Games	BA	SA	AB	H	2B	3B	HR	HR%	R	RBI	BB	SO	SB	PH AB	PH H	PO	A	E	DP	TC/G	FA	G by Pos
1988	OAK	A	3	.500	.500	4	2	0	0	0	0.0	0	2	0	0	0	0	0	1	0	0	0	0.3	1.000	OF-2
1989			1	-	-	0	0	0	0	0	-	0	0	0	0	0	0	0	0	0	0	0	0.0	-	OF-1
2 yrs.			4	.500	.500	4	2	0	0	0	0.0	0	2	0	0	0	0	0	1	0	0	0	0.3	1.000	OF-3

Tex Jeanes

JEANES, ERNEST LEE
B. Dec. 19, 1900, Maypearl, Tex. D. Apr. 5, 1973, Longview, Tex.
BR TR 6' 176 lbs.

Year	Team		Games	BA	SA	AB	H	2B	3B	HR	HR%	R	RBI	BB	SO	SB	PH AB	PH H	PO	A	E	DP	TC/G	FA	G by Pos
1921	CLE	A	4	.500	.500	2	1	0	0	0	0.0	0	2	1	0	0	0	0	1	1	0	0	0.5	1.000	OF-4
1922			1	.000	.000	1	0	0	0	0	0.0	0	0	1	0	0	0	0	0	0	0	0	0.0	-	OF-1, P-1
1925	WAS	A	15	.263	.474	19	5	1	0	1	5.3	2	4	3	2	1	2	1	9	0	0	0	0.6	1.000	OF-13
1926			21	.233	.300	30	7	2	0	0	0.0	6	3	0	3	0	7	2	21	0	0	0	1.0	1.000	OF-14
1927	NY	N	11	.300	.300	20	6	0	0	0	0.0	5	0	2	2	0	3	1	15	1	0	0	1.5	1.000	OF-6, P-1
5 yrs.			52	.264	.347	72	19	3	0	1	1.4	15	9	7	7	1	12	4	46	2	0	0	0.9	1.000	OF-38, P-2

Hal Jeffcoat

JEFFCOAT, HAROLD BENTLEY
Brother of George Jeffcoat.
B. Sept. 6, 1924, West Columbia, S. C.
BR TR 5'10½" 185 lbs.

Year	Team		Games	BA	SA	AB	H	2B	3B	HR	HR%	R	RBI	BB	SO	SB	PH AB	PH H	PO	A	E	DP	TC/G	FA	G by Pos
1948	CHI	N	134	.279	.355	473	132	16	4	4	0.8	53	42	24	68	8	14	6	307	12	8	3	2.4	.976	OF-119
1949			108	.245	.344	363	89	18	6	2	0.6	43	26	20	48	12	5	2	250	12	10	2	2.5	.963	OF-101
1950			66	.235	.352	179	42	13	1	2	1.1	21	18	6	23	7	8	1	83	6	3	0	1.4	.967	OF-53
1951			113	.273	.403	278	76	20	2	4	1.4	44	27	16	23	8	9	3	166	11	2	5	1.6	.989	OF-87
1952			102	.219	.330	297	65	17	2	4	1.3	29	30	15	40	7	1	0	218	16	1	2	2.3	.996	OF-95
1953			106	.235	.328	183	43	3	1	4	2.2	22	22	21	26	5	2	0	175	6	5	2	1.8	.973	OF-100
1954			56	.258	.484	31	8	2	1	1	3.2	13	6	1	7	2	0	0	13	20	4	1	0.7	.892	P-43, OF-3
1955			52	.174	.304	23	4	0	0	1	4.3	3	1	2	9	0	0	0	4	24	3	1	0.6	.903	P-50
1956	CIN	N	49	.148	.185	54	8	2	0	0	0.0	5	5	3	20	0	0	0	21	42	2	4	1.3	.969	P-38
1957			53	.203	.449	69	14	3	1	4	5.8	13	11	5	20	0	0	0	16	30	2	5	0.9	.958	P-37
1958			50	.556	.556	9	5	0	0	0	0.0	0	1	0	2	0	0	0	9	19	0	2	0.6	1.000	P-49, OF-1
1959	2 teams			CIN N (17G – 1.000)		STL N (12G – .000)																				
" total			29	.250	.500	4	1	1	0	0	0.0	4	0	0	3	0	0	0	5	5	0	1	0.3	1.000	P-28
12 yrs.			918	.248	.355	1963	487	95	18	26	1.3	249	188	114	289	49	39	12	1267	203	40	28	1.6	.974	OF-559, P-245

Gregg Jefferies

JEFFERIES, GREGORY SCOTT
B. Aug. 1, 1967, Burlingame, Calif.
BB TR 5'11" 175 lbs.

Year	Team		Games	BA	SA	AB	H	2B	3B	HR	HR%	R	RBI	BB	SO	SB	PH AB	PH H	PO	A	E	DP	TC/G	FA	G by Pos
1987	NY	N	6	.500	.667	6	3	1	0	0	0.0	0	2	0	0	0	6	3	0	0	0	0	0.0	-	
1988			29	.321	.596	109	35	8	2	6	5.5	19	17	8	10	5	1	0	33	46	2	9	2.8	.975	3B-20, 2B-10
1989			141	.258	.392	508	131	28	2	12	2.4	72	56	39	46	21	7	1	242	280	14	44	3.8	.974	2B-123, 3B-20
3 yrs.			176	.271	.430	623	169	37	4	18	2.9	91	75	47	56	26	14	4	275	326	16	53	3.5	.974	2B-133, 3B-40

LEAGUE CHAMPIONSHIP SERIES

Year	Team		Games	BA	SA	AB	H	2B	3B	HR	HR%	R	RBI	BB	SO	SB	PH AB	PH H	PO	A	E	DP	TC/G	FA	G by Pos
1988	NY	N	7	.333	.407	27	9	0	0	0	0.0	2	1	4	0	0	0	0	5	8	1	0	2.0	.929	3B-7

Stan Jefferson

JEFFERSON, STANLEY
B. Dec. 4, 1962, New York, N. Y.
BB TR 5'11" 175 lbs.

Year	Team		Games	BA	SA	AB	H	2B	3B	HR	HR%	R	RBI	BB	SO	SB	PH AB	PH H	PO	A	E	DP	TC/G	FA	G by Pos
1986	NY	N	14	.208	.375	24	5	1	0	1	4.2	6	3	2	8	0	5	0	13	0	0	0	0.9	1.000	OF-7
1987	SD	N	116	.230	.339	422	97	8	7	8	1.9	59	29	39	92	34	9	0	232	3	3	1	2.1	.987	OF-107
1988			49	.144	.216	111	16	1	2	1	0.9	16	4	9	22	5	3	0	62	0	0	0	1.3	1.000	OF-38
1989	2 teams			NY A (10G – .083)		BAL A (35G – .260)																				
" total			45	.245	.381	139	34	7	0	4	2.9	20	21	4	26	10	6	1	82	3	1	1	1.9	.988	OF-39, DH-3
4 yrs.			224	.218	.329	696	152	17	9	14	2.0	101	57	54	148	49	23	1	389	6	4	2	1.8	.990	OF-191, DH-3

Irv Jeffries

JEFFRIES, IRVINE FRANKLIN
B. Sept. 10, 1905, Louisville, Ky. D. June 8, 1982, Louisville, Ky.
BR TR 5'10" 175 lbs.

Year	Team		Games	BA	SA	AB	H	2B	3B	HR	HR%	R	RBI	BB	SO	SB	PH AB	PH H	PO	A	E	DP	TC/G	FA	G by Pos
1930	CHI	A	40	.237	.330	97	23	3	0	2	2.1	14	11	4	13	2	1	0	31	56	6	6	2.3	.935	SS-13, 3B-10
1931			79	.224	.296	223	50	10	0	2	0.9	29	16	14	9	1	3	0	83	130	14	9	2.9	.938	3B-61, 2B-6, SS-5

Year	Team		Games	BA	SA	AB	H	2B	3B	HR	HR%	R	RBI	BB	SO	SB	Pinch Hit AB	Pinch Hit H	PO	A	E	DP	TC/G	FA	G by Pos

Irv Jeffries *continued*

Year	Team		Games	BA	SA	AB	H	2B	3B	HR	HR%	R	RBI	BB	SO	SB	AB	H	PO	A	E	DP	TC/G	FA	G by Pos
1934	PHI	N	56	.246	.349	175	43	6	0	4	2.3	28	19	15	10	2	2	0	123	157	11	42	5.2	.962	2B-52, 3B-1
3 yrs.			175	.234	.321	495	116	19	0	8	1.6	71	46	32	21	6	8	0	237	343	31	57	3.5	.949	3B-72, 2B-58, SS-18

Frank Jelincich

JELINCICH, FRANK ANTHONY (Jelly)
B. Sept. 3, 1919, San Jose, Calif.   BR TR 6'2" 198 lbs.

| 1941 | CHI | N | 4 | .125 | .125 | 8 | 1 | 0 | 0 | 0 | 0.0 | 0 | 2 | 1 | 2 | 0 | 2 | 0 | 1 | 0 | 0 | 0 | 0.3 | 1.000 | OF-2 |

Greg Jelks

JELKS, GREGORY DION
B. Aug. 16, 1961, Cherokee, Ala.   BR TR 6'2" 190 lbs.

| 1987 | PHI | N | 10 | .091 | .182 | 11 | 1 | 1 | 0 | 0 | 0.0 | 2 | 0 | 3 | 4 | 0 | 1 | 0 | 19 | 2 | 1 | 0 | 2.2 | .955 | 3B-4, 1B-2, OF-1 |

Steve Jeltz

JELTZ, LARRY STEVEN
B. May 28, 1959, Paris, France   BB TR 5'11" 180 lbs.

1983	PHI	N	13	.125	.375	8	1	0	1	0	0.0	0	1	1	2	0	3	0	4	5	0	1	0.7	1.000	2B-4, SS-2, 3B-2
1984			28	.206	.279	68	14	0	1	1	1.5	7	7	7	11	2	0	0	37	93	1	8	4.7	.992	SS-27, 3B-1
1985			89	.189	.219	196	37	4	1	0	0.0	17	12	26	55	1	0	0	106	215	14	38	3.8	.958	SS-86
1986			145	.219	.262	439	96	11	4	0	0.0	44	36	65	97	6	5	2	229	406	22	81	4.5	.967	SS-141
1987			114	.232	.304	293	68	9	6	0	0.0	37	12	39	54	1	1	1	192	271	14	55	4.2	.971	SS-114, OF-1
1988			148	.187	.237	379	71	11	4	0	0.0	39	27	59	58	3	3	0	195	368	14	73	3.9	.976	SS-148
1989			116	.243	.338	263	64	7	3	4	1.5	28	25	45	44	4	13	2	111	205	6	33	2.8	.981	SS-63, 3B-30, 2B-23, OF-1
7 yrs.			653	.213	.272	1646	351	42	20	5	0.3	172	120	242	321	17	25	5	874	1563	71	289	3.8	.972	SS-581, 3B-33, 2B-27, OF-2

Joe Jenkins

JENKINS, JOSEPH DANIEL
B. Oct. 12, 1890, Shelbyville, Tenn.   D. June 21, 1974, Fresno, Calif.   BR TR 5'11" 170 lbs.

1914	STL	A	19	.125	.219	32	4	1	0	0	0.0	0	1	2	9	1	0		24	3	2	0	1.5	.931	C-9
1917	CHI	A	10	.111	.111	9	1	0	0	0	0.0	0	2	0	5	0	9	1	0	0	0	0	0.0	–	
1919			11	.158	.211	19	3	1	0	0	0.0	0	0	1	1	1	7	1	10	4	3	0	1.5	.824	C-4
3 yrs.			40	.133	.200	60	8	2	1	0	0.0	0	3	2	17	3	25	3	34	7	5	0	1.2	.891	C-13

John Jenkins

JENKINS, JOHN ROBERT
B. July 7, 1896, Bosworth, Mo.   D. Aug. 3, 1968, Columbia, Mo.   BR TR 5'8" 160 lbs.

| 1922 | CHI | A | 5 | .000 | .000 | 3 | 0 | 0 | 0 | 0 | 0.0 | 0 | 1 | 0 | 2 | 0 | 1 | 0 | 1 | 1 | 1 | 0 | 0.6 | .667 | SS-1, 2B-1 |

Tom Jenkins

JENKINS, THOMAS GRIFFITH (Tut)
B. Apr. 10, 1898, Camden, Ala.   D. May 3, 1979, Weymouth, Mass.   BL TR 6'1½" 174 lbs.

1925	BOS	A	15	.297	.359	64	19	1	0	0	0.0	9	5	3	4	0	1	0	30	0	2	0	2.1	.938	OF-15
1926 2 teams	BOS	A (21G – .180)			PHI	A	(6G – .174)																		
" total			27	.178	.247	73	13	3	1	0	0.0	6	6	3	9	0	8	2	39	0	0	0	1.4	1.000	OF-19
1929	STL	A	21	.182	.273	22	4	0	1	0	0.0	1	0	4	8	0	15	2	2	0	0	0	0.1	1.000	OF-3
1930			2	.250	.625	8	2	1	1	0	0.0	1	3	0	1	0	0	0	4	0	0	0	2.0	1.000	OF-2
1931			81	.265	.352	230	61	7	2	3	1.3	20	25	17	25	1	23	7	93	6	5	1	1.3	.952	OF-58
1932			25	.323	.339	62	20	1	0	0	0.0	5	5	1	6	0	13	5	29	2	2	0	1.3	.939	OF-12
6 yrs.			171	.259	.336	459	119	14	6	3	0.7	42	44	28	53	1	59	16	197	8	9	1	1.3	.958	OF-109

Alamazoo Jennings

JENNINGS, ALFRED GORDEN
B. Nov. 30, 1850, Newport, Ky.   D. Nov. 2, 1894, Cincinnati, Ohio

| 1878 | MIL | N | 1 | .000 | .000 | 2 | 0 | 0 | 0 | 0 | 0.0 | 0 | 0 | 1 | 0 | | 0 | 0 | 2 | 1 | 4 | 0 | 7.0 | .429 | C-1 |

Bill Jennings

JENNINGS, WILLIAM LEE
B. Sept. 28, 1925, St. Louis, Mo.   BR TR 6'2" 175 lbs.

| 1951 | STL | A | 64 | .179 | .251 | 195 | 35 | 10 | 2 | 0 | 0.0 | 20 | 13 | 26 | 42 | 1 | 0 | | 141 | 165 | 15 | 39 | 5.0 | .953 | SS-64 |

Doug Jennings

JENNINGS, JAMES DOUGLAS
B. Sept. 30, 1964, Atlanta, Ga.   BL TL 5'10" 175 lbs.

1988	OAK	A	71	.208	.297	101	21	6	0	1	1.0	9	15	21	28	0	27	5	85	5	1	8	1.3	.989	OF-23, 1B-14, DH-2
1989			4	.000	.000	4	0	0	0	0	0.0	0	0	0	2	0	1	0	2	0	0	0	0.5	1.000	OF-3
2 yrs.			75	.200	.286	105	21	6	0	1	1.0	9	15	21	30	0	28	5	87	5	1	8	1.2	.989	OF-26, 1B-14, DH-2

Hughie Jennings

JENNINGS, HUGH AMBROSE (Hustling Hughie)
B. Apr. 2, 1869, Pittston, Pa.   D. Feb. 1, 1928, Scranton, Pa.   BR TR 5'8½" 165 lbs.
Manager 1907-20, 1924.
Hall of Fame 1945.

1891	LOU	AA	90	.292	.372	360	105	10	8	1	0.3	53	58	17	36	12	0	0	364	236	57	38	7.3	.913	SS-70, 1B-17, 3B-3
1892	LOU	N	152	.222	.273	594	132	16	4	2	0.3	65	61	30	30	28	0	0	343	537	90	59	6.4	.907	SS-152
1893 2 teams	LOU	N (23G – .136)			BAL	N	(16G – .255)																		
" total			39	.182	.224	143	26	3	0	1	0.7	12	15	7	6	0	0	0	86	126	25	15	6.1	.895	SS-38, OF-1
1894	BAL	N	128	.335	.479	501	168	28	16	4	0.8	134	109	37	17	37	0	0	307	499	63	69	6.8	.928	SS-128
1895			131	.386	.512	529	204	41	7	4	0.8	159	125	24	17	53	0	0	425	457	56	71	7.2	.940	SS-131
1896			130	.401	.488	521	209	27	9	0	0.0	125	121	19	11	70	0	0	377	476	66	70	7.1	.928	SS-130
1897			117	.355	.469	439	156	26	9	2	0.5	133	79	42		60	1	0	335	425	55	54	7.0	.933	SS-116
1898			143	.328	.421	534	175	25	11	1	0.2	135	87	78		28	0	0	365	440	62	51	6.1	.928	SS-115, 2B-27, OF-1
1899 2 teams	BAL	N (2G – .375)			BKN	N	(67G – .296)																		
" total			69	.299	.420	224	67	3	12	0	0.0	44	42	22		18	1	1	480	56	19	28	8.0	.966	1B-50, SS-12, 2B-3
1900	BKN	N	115	.272	.347	441	120	18	6	1	0.2	61	69	31		31	1	1	1053	84	23	71	10.1	.980	1B-112, 2B-3
1901	PHI	N	82	.275	.368	302	83	21	2	1	0.3	38	39	25		13	0	0	750	46	18	21	9.9	.978	1B-80, SS-1, 2B-1
1902			78	.277	.363	289	80	16	3	1	0.3	31	32	14		8	0	0	677	63	15	33	9.7	.980	1B-69, SS-5, 2B-4
1903	BKN	N	6	.235	.235	17	4	0	0	0	0.0	2	1	1		1	2	0	7	0	0	0	1.2	1.000	OF-4
1907	DET	A		.250	.500	4	1	1	0	0	0.0	0	0	0		0	0	0	2	3	3	0	8.0	.625	SS-1, 2B-1

Year	Team	Games	BA	SA	AB	H	2B	3B	HR	HR%	R	RBI	BB	SO	SB	Pinch Hit AB	Pinch Hit H	PO	A	E	DP	TC/G	FA	G by Pos

Hughie Jennings *continued*

Year	Team	Games	BA	SA	AB	H	2B	3B	HR	HR%	R	RBI	BB	SO	SB	PH AB	PH H	PO	A	E	DP	TC/G	FA	G by Pos
1909		2	.500	.500	4	2	0	0	0	0.0	1	2	0		0	0	0	9	1	0	2	5.0	1.000	1B-2
1912		1	.000	.000	1	0	0	0	0	0.0	0	0	0		0	1	0	0	0	0	0	0.0	—	
1918		1	—	—	0	0	0	0	0	—	0	0	0	0	0	0	0	2	0	0	0	2.0	1.000	1B-1
17 yrs.		1285	.312	.407	4903	1532	235	87	18	0.4	993	840	347	117	359	6	2	5582	3449	552	582	7.5	.942	SS-899, 1B-331, 2B-38, OF-6, 3B-3

Jackie Jensen

JENSEN, JACK EUGENE
B. Mar. 9, 1927, San Francisco, Calif. D. July 14, 1982, Charlottesville, Va.
BR TR 5'11" 190 lbs.

Year	Team	Games	BA	SA	AB	H	2B	3B	HR	HR%	R	RBI	BB	SO	SB	PH AB	PH H	PO	A	E	DP	TC/G	FA	G by Pos
1950	NY A	45	.171	.300	70	12	2	2	1	1.4	13	5	7	8	4	6	1	36	0	2	0	0.8	.947	OF-23
1951		56	.298	.500	168	50	8	1	8	4.8	30	25	18	18	8	6	1	106	6	3	1	2.1	.974	OF-48
1952	2 teams		NY A (7G – .105)		WAS A	(144G – .286)																		
"	total	151	.280	.402	589	165	30	6	10	1.7	83	82	67	44	18	3	1	291	17	7	1	2.1	.978	OF-148
1953	WAS A	147	.266	.408	552	147	32	8	10	1.8	87	84	73	51	18	1	0	274	9	5	0	2.0	.983	OF-146
1954	BOS A	152	.276	.472	580	160	25	7	25	4.3	92	117	79	52	22	1	0	331	12	5	0	2.3	.986	OF-151
1955		152	.275	.479	574	158	27	6	26	4.5	95	**116**	89	63	16	0	0	281	11	7	3	2.0	.977	OF-150
1956		151	.315	.497	578	182	23	11	20	3.5	80	97	89	43	11	0	0	291	13	12	2	2.1	.962	OF-151
1957		145	.281	.469	544	153	29	2	23	4.2	82	103	75	66	8	1	1	251	16	11	4	1.9	.960	OF-144
1958		154	.286	.535	548	157	31	0	35	6.4	83	122	99	65	9	1	0	293	14	6	3	2.0	.981	OF-153
1959		148	.277	.492	535	148	31	0	28	5.2	101	112	88	67	20	2	0	311	12	6	4	2.2	.982	OF-146
1961		137	.263	.392	498	131	21	2	13	2.6	64	66	66	69	9	6	0	274	14	4	2	2.1	.986	OF-131
11 yrs.		1438	.279	.460	5236	1463	259	45	199	3.8	810	929	750	546	143	27	4	2739	124	68	20	2.0	.977	OF-1391

WORLD SERIES

Year	Team	Games	BA	SA	AB	H	2B	3B	HR	HR%	R	RBI	BB	SO	SB	PH AB	PH H	PO	A	E	DP	TC/G	FA	G by Pos
1950	NY A	1	—	—	0	0	0	0	0	—	0	0	0	0	0	0	0	0	0	0	0	0.0	—	

Woody Jensen

JENSEN, FORREST DOCENUS
B. Aug. 11, 1907, Bremerton, Wash.
BL TL 5'10½" 160 lbs.

Year	Team	Games	BA	SA	AB	H	2B	3B	HR	HR%	R	RBI	BB	SO	SB	PH AB	PH H	PO	A	E	DP	TC/G	FA	G by Pos
1931	PIT N	73	.243	.326	267	65	5	4	3	1.1	43	17	10	18	4	3	1	182	2	5	1	2.6	.974	OF-67
1932		7	.000	.000	5	0	0	0	0	0.0	2	0	0	2	0	5	0	0	0	0	0	0.0	—	OF-1
1933		70	.296	.362	196	58	7	3	0	0.0	29	15	8	2	1	23	6	95	1	2	0	1.4	.980	OF-40
1934		88	.290	.364	283	82	13	4	0	0.0	34	27	4	13	2	21	6	143	1	1	0	1.6	.993	OF-66
1935		143	.324	.429	627	203	28	7	8	1.3	97	62	15	14	9	3	2	290	6	7	1	2.1	.977	OF-143
1936		153	.283	.404	**696**	197	34	10	10	1.4	98	58	16	19	2	0	0	338	6	9	1	2.3	.975	OF-153
1937		124	.279	.389	509	142	29	5	5	1.0	77	45	15	29	2	3	1	256	5	10	1	2.2	.963	OF-120
1938		68	.200	.232	125	25	4	0	0	0.0	12	10	1	3	0	23	4	45	0	5	0	0.7	.900	OF-38
1939		12	.167	.167	12	2	0	0	0	0.0	0	1	0	0	0	6	1	0	1	0	0	0.1	1.000	OF-3
9 yrs.		738	.285	.382	2720	774	114	37	26	1.0	392	235	69	100	20	87	21	1349	22	39	4	1.9	.972	OF-631

Dan Jessee

JESSEE, DANIEL EDWARD
B. Feb. 22, 1901, Olive Hill, Ky. D. Apr. 30, 1970, Venice, Fla.
BL TR 5'10" 165 lbs.

Year	Team	Games	BA	SA	AB	H	2B	3B	HR	HR%	R	RBI	BB	SO	SB	PH AB	PH H	PO	A	E	DP	TC/G	FA	G by Pos
1929	CLE A	1	—	—	0	0	0	0	0	—	0	0	0	0	0	0	0	0	0	0	0	0.0	—	

Garry Jestadt

JESTADT, GARRY ARTHUR
B. Mar. 19, 1947, Chicago, Ill.
BR TR 6'2" 188 lbs.

Year	Team	Games	BA	SA	AB	H	2B	3B	HR	HR%	R	RBI	BB	SO	SB	PH AB	PH H	PO	A	E	DP	TC/G	FA	G by Pos
1969	MON N	6	.000	.000	6	0	0	0	0	0.0	1	1	0	1	0	4	0	2	0	1	0	0.5	.667	SS-1
1971	2 teams		CHI N (3G – .000)		SD N	(75G – .291)																		
"	total	78	.286	.354	192	55	13	0	0	0.0	17	13	11	24	1	4	1	66	142	13	11	2.8	.941	3B-50, 2B-23, SS-1
1972	SD N	92	.246	.344	256	63	5	1	6	2.3	15	22	13	21	0	23	5	106	134	13	27	2.8	.949	2B-48, 3B-25, SS-3
3 yrs.		176	.260	.344	454	118	18	1	6	1.3	33	36	24	45	1	31	6	174	276	27	38	2.7	.943	3B-75, 2B-71, SS-5

John Jeter

JETER, JOHN
B. Oct. 24, 1944, Shreveport, La.
BR TR 6'1" 180 lbs.

Year	Team	Games	BA	SA	AB	H	2B	3B	HR	HR%	R	RBI	BB	SO	SB	PH AB	PH H	PO	A	E	DP	TC/G	FA	G by Pos
1969	PIT N	28	.310	.517	29	9	1	1	1	3.4	7	6	3	15	1	3	1	12	1	0	0	0.5	1.000	OF-20
1970		85	.238	.341	126	30	3	2	2	1.6	27	12	13	34	9	17	5	53	2	0	0	0.6	1.000	OF-56
1971	SD N	18	.320	.413	75	24	4	0	1	1.3	8	3	2	16	2	1	0	57	1	2	1	3.3	.967	OF-17
1972		110	.221	.316	326	72	4	3	7	2.1	25	21	18	92	11	20	5	222	1	3	0	2.1	.987	OF-91
1973	CHI A	89	.240	.383	300	72	14	4	7	2.3	38	26	9	74	4	8	1	144	3	7	0	1.7	.955	OF-72, DH-3
1974	CLE A	6	.353	.412	17	6	1	0	0	0.0	3	1	1	6	1	1	0	5	0	1	0	1.0	.833	OF-6
6 yrs.		336	.244	.360	873	213	27	10	18	2.1	108	69	46	237	28	50	12	493	8	13	1	1.5	.975	OF-262, DH-3

LEAGUE CHAMPIONSHIP SERIES

Year	Team	Games	BA	SA	AB	H	2B	3B	HR	HR%	R	RBI	BB	SO	SB	PH AB	PH H	PO	A	E	DP	TC/G	FA	G by Pos
1970	PIT N	3	.000	.000	2	0	0	0	0	0.0	0	0	0	2	0	1	0	2	0	0	0	0.7	1.000	OF-1

Sam Jethroe

JETHROE, SAMUEL (Jet)
B. Jan. 20, 1922, East St. Louis, Ill.
BB TR 6'1" 178 lbs.

Year	Team	Games	BA	SA	AB	H	2B	3B	HR	HR%	R	RBI	BB	SO	SB	PH AB	PH H	PO	A	E	DP	TC/G	FA	G by Pos
1950	BOS N	141	.273	.442	582	159	28	8	18	3.1	100	58	52	93	**35**	0	0	355	17	12	6	2.7	.969	OF-141
1951		148	.280	.460	572	160	29	10	18	3.1	101	65	57	88	**35**	5	2	356	18	10	5	2.6	.974	OF-140
1952		151	.232	.357	608	141	23	7	13	2.1	79	58	68	112	28	0	0	413	10	13	3	2.9	.970	OF-151
1954	PIT N	2	.000	.000	1	0	0	0	0	0.0	0	0	0	0	0	1	0	1	0	0	0	0.5	1.000	OF-1
4 yrs.		442	.261	.418	1763	460	80	25	49	2.8	280	181	177	293	98	6	2	1125	45	35	14	2.7	.971	OF-433

Elvio Jimenez

JIMENEZ, FELIX ELVIO
Born Felix Elvio Jimenez y Rivera. Brother of Manny Jimenez.
B. Jan. 6, 1940, San Pedro de Macoris, Dominican Republic
BR TR 5'9" 170 lbs.

Year	Team	Games	BA	SA	AB	H	2B	3B	HR	HR%	R	RBI	BB	SO	SB	PH AB	PH H	PO	A	E	DP	TC/G	FA	G by Pos
1964	NY A	1	.333	.333	6	2	0	0	0	0.0	0	0	0	0	0	0	0	4	0	0	0	4.0	1.000	OF-1

Houston Jimenez

JIMENEZ, ALFONSO
Born Alfonso Jimenez y Gonzalez.
B. Oct. 30, 1957, Navojoa, Mexico
BR TR 5'8" 144 lbs.

Year	Team	Games	BA	SA	AB	H	2B	3B	HR	HR%	R	RBI	BB	SO	SB	PH AB	PH H	PO	A	E	DP	TC/G	FA	G by Pos
1983	MIN A	36	.174	.256	86	15	5	1	0	0.0	5	9	4	11	0	0	0	43	83	4	20	3.6	.969	SS-36
1984		108	.201	.245	298	60	11	0	0	0.0	28	19	15	34	0	0	0	145	273	18	59	4.0	.959	SS-107

Houston Jimenez *continued*

Year Team	Games	BA	SA	AB	H	2B	3B	HR	HR%	R	RBI	BB	SO	SB	PH AB	PH H	PO	A	E	DP	TC/G	FA	G by Pos
1987 PIT N	5	.000	.000	6	0	0	0	0	0.0	0	0	1	2	0	1	0	3	8	0	1	2.2	1.000	SS-2, 2B-2
1988 CLE A	9	.048	.048	21	1	0	0	0	0.0	1	1	0	2	0	0	0	13	28	1	5	4.7	.976	2B-7, SS-2
4 yrs.	158	.185	.234	411	76	16	2	0	0.0	34	29	20	49	0	1	0	204	392	23	85	3.9	.963	SS-147, 2B-9

Manny Jimenez

JIMENEZ, MANUEL EMILIO
Born Manuel Emilio Jimenez y Rivera. Brother of Elvio Jimenez.
B. Nov. 19, 1938, San Pedro de Macoris, Dominican Republic
BL TR 6'1" 185 lbs.

Year Team	Games	BA	SA	AB	H	2B	3B	HR	HR%	R	RBI	BB	SO	SB	PH AB	PH H	PO	A	E	DP	TC/G	FA	G by Pos
1962 KC A	139	.301	.428	479	144	24	2	11	2.3	48	69	31	34	0	17	7	185	7	3	0	1.4	.985	OF-122
1963	60	.280	.338	157	44	9	0	0	0.0	12	15	16	14	0	15	2	66	6	3	0	1.3	.960	OF-40
1964	95	.225	.436	204	46	7	0	12	5.9	19	38	15	24	0	41	9	59	3	4	1	0.7	.939	OF-49
1966	13	.114	.171	35	4	0	1	0	0.0	1	1	6	4	0	2	0	9	1	1	0	0.8	.909	OF-12
1967 PIT N	50	.250	.393	56	14	2	0	2	3.6	3	10	1	4	0	42	12	4	0	0	0	0.1	1.000	OF-6
1968	66	.303	.394	66	20	1	1	1	1.5	7	11	6	15	0	53	10	6	0	1	0	0.1	.857	OF-5
1969 CHI N	6	.167	.167	6	1	0	0	0	0.0	0	0	0	2	0	6	1	0	0	0	0	0.0	–	
7 yrs.	429	.272	.401	1003	273	43	4	26	2.6	90	144	75	97	0	176	41	329	17	12	1	0.8	.966	OF-234

Pete Johns

JOHNS, WILLIAM R.
B. Jan. 17, 1889, Cleveland, Ohio   D. Aug. 9, 1964, Cleveland, Ohio
BR TR 5'10" 165 lbs.

Year Team	Games	BA	SA	AB	H	2B	3B	HR	HR%	R	RBI	BB	SO	SB	PH AB	PH H	PO	A	E	DP	TC/G	FA	G by Pos
1915 CHI A	28	.210	.250	100	21	2	1	0	0.0	7	11	8	11	2	0	0	37	62	6	5	3.8	.943	3B-28
1918 STL A	46	.180	.213	89	16	1	1	0	0.0	5	11	4	6	0	20	2	105	22	5	5	2.9	.962	1B-10, OF-4, SS-4, 3B-4, 2B-2
2 yrs.	74	.196	.233	189	37	3	2	0	0.0	12	22	12	17	2	20	2	142	84	11	10	3.2	.954	3B-32, 1B-10, OF-4, SS-4, 2B-2

Abbie Johnson

JOHNSON, ALBERT J.
B. July 26, 1872, Sweden   D. May 2, 1924, Oak Forest, Ill.

Year Team	Games	BA	SA	AB	H	2B	3B	HR	HR%	R	RBI	BB	SO	SB	PH AB	PH H	PO	A	E	DP	TC/G	FA	G by Pos
1896 LOU N	25	.230	.276	87	20	2	1	0	0.0	10	14	4	6	0	0	0	57	61	8	9	5.0	.937	2B-25
1897	48	.242	.292	161	39	6	1	0	0.0	16	23	13		2	2	0	96	119	27	15	5.0	.888	2B-33, SS-12
2 yrs.	73	.238	.286	248	59	8	2	0	0.0	26	37	17	6	2	2	0	153	180	35	24	5.0	.905	2B-58, SS-12

Alex Johnson

JOHNSON, ALEXANDER
B. Dec. 7, 1942, Helena, Ark.
BR TR 6' 205 lbs.

Year Team	Games	BA	SA	AB	H	2B	3B	HR	HR%	R	RBI	BB	SO	SB	PH AB	PH H	PO	A	E	DP	TC/G	FA	G by Pos
1964 PHI N	43	.303	.495	109	33	7	1	4	3.7	18	18	6	26	1	7	2	47	1	1	0	1.1	.980	OF-35
1965	97	.294	.443	262	77	9	3	8	3.1	27	28	15	60	4	27	8	109	3	4	0	1.2	.966	OF-82
1966 STL N	25	.186	.279	86	16	0	1	2	2.3	7	6	5	18	1	2	0	23	2	1	0	1.0	.962	OF-22
1967	81	.223	.314	175	39	9	2	1	0.6	20	12	9	26	6	20	5	91	7	3	2	1.0	.970	OF-57
1968 CIN N	149	.312	.395	603	188	32	6	2	0.3	79	58	26	71	16	9	1	243	8	14	2	1.8	.947	OF-140
1969	139	.315	.463	523	165	18	4	17	3.3	86	88	25	69	11	9	3	222	5	18	1	1.8	.932	OF-132
1970 CAL A	156	**.329**	.459	614	202	26	6	14	2.3	85	86	35	68	17	0	0	269	11	12	0	1.9	.959	OF-156
1971	65	.260	.318	242	63	8	0	2	0.8	19	21	15	34	5	5	0	84	3	7	0	1.4	.926	OF-61
1972 CLE A	108	.239	.340	356	85	10	1	8	2.2	31	37	22	40	6	10	0	145	4	7	1	1.4	.955	OF-95
1973 TEX A	158	.287	.377	624	179	26	3	8	1.3	62	68	32	82	10	1	1	72	4	1	0	0.5	.987	DH-116, OF-47
1974 2 teams	TEX A (114G – .291) NY A (10G – .214)																						
" total	124	.287	.362	481	138	15	3	5	1.0	60	43	28	62	20	6	8	168	6	8	2	1.5	.956	OF-82, DH-36
1975 NY A	52	.261	.345	119	31	5	1	1	0.8	15	15	7	21	2	14	5	9	0	0	0	0.2	1.000	DH-28, OF-7
1976 DET A	125	.268	.354	429	115	15	2	6	1.4	41	45	19	49	14	16	5	159	7	8	1	1.4	.954	OF-90, DH-19
13 yrs.	1322	.288	.392	4623	1331	180	33	78	1.7	550	525	244	626	113	126	30	1641	61	84	9	1.4	.953	OF-1006, DH-199

Bill Johnson

JOHNSON, WILLIAM LAWRENCE
B. Oct. 18, 1892, Chicago, Ill.   D. Nov. 3, 1950, Los Angeles, Calif.
BL TR 5'11" 170 lbs.

Year Team	Games	BA	SA	AB	H	2B	3B	HR	HR%	R	RBI	BB	SO	SB	PH AB	PH H	PO	A	E	DP	TC/G	FA	G by Pos
1916 PHI A	4	.267	.333	15	4	1	0	0	0.0	0	1	0	4	0	0	0	4	0	0	0	1.0	1.000	OF-4
1917	48	.174	.257	109	19	2	2	1	0.9	7	8	8	14	4	16	2	31	5	4	2	0.8	.900	OF-30
2 yrs.	52	.185	.266	124	23	3	2	1	0.8	8	9	8	18	4	16	2	35	5	4	2	0.8	.909	OF-34

Bill Johnson

JOHNSON, WILLIAM T. (Sleepy Bill)
B. Chester, Pa.   D. 1921
BL TL

Year Team	Games	BA	SA	AB	H	2B	3B	HR	HR%	R	RBI	BB	SO	SB	PH AB	PH H	PO	A	E	DP	TC/G	FA	G by Pos
1884 PHI U	1	.000	.000	4	0	0	0	0	0.0	0		0			0	0	0	0	0	0	0.0	–	OF-1
1887 IND N	11	.190	.190	42	8	0	0	0	0.0	3	3	0	6	5	0	0	11	2	4	0	1.5	.765	OF-11
1890 BAL AA	24	.295	.379	95	28	2	3	0	0.0	15		7		8	0	0	39	6	7	3	2.2	.865	OF-24
1891	129	.271	.369	480	130	13	14	2	0.4	101	79	89	55	32	0	0	235	28	37	5	2.3	.877	OF-129
1892 BAL N	4	.133	.133	15	2	0	0	0	0.0	2		2		0	0	0	4	0	2	0	1.5	.667	OF-4
5 yrs.	169	.264	.351	636	168	15	17	2	0.3	121	84	98	61	45	0	0	289	36	50	8	2.2	.867	OF-169

Billy Johnson

JOHNSON, WILLIAM RUSSELL (Bull)
B. Aug. 30, 1918, Montclair, N. J.
BR TR 5'10" 180 lbs.

Year Team	Games	BA	SA	AB	H	2B	3B	HR	HR%	R	RBI	BB	SO	SB	PH AB	PH H	PO	A	E	DP	TC/G	FA	G by Pos
1943 NY A	155	.280	.367	592	166	24	6	5	0.8	70	94	53	30	3	0	0	183	326	18	32	3.4	.966	3B-155
1946	85	.260	.382	296	77	14	5	4	1.4	51	35	31	42	1	10	1	71	163	11	15	2.9	.955	3B-74
1947	132	.285	.417	494	141	19	8	10	2.0	67	95	44	43	1	0	0	136	204	17	12	2.7	.952	3B-132
1948	127	.294	.446	446	131	20	6	12	2.7	59	64	41	30	1	8	2	147	213	20	25	3.0	.947	3B-118
1949	113	.249	.374	329	82	11	3	8	2.4	48	56	48	44	1	13	6	207	146	13	26	3.3	.964	3B-81, 1B-21, 2B-1
1950	108	.260	.376	327	85	16	2	6	1.8	44	40	42	30	1	4	1	96	169	12	21	2.6	.957	3B-100, 1B-5
1951 2 teams	NY A (15G – .300) STL N (124G – .262)																						
" total	139	.266	.411	482	128	26	1	14	2.9	57	68	53	49	5	1	0	107	332	11	32	3.2	.976	3B-137
1952 STL N	94	.252	.323	282	71	10	2	2	0.7	23	34	34	21	1	5	0	56	177	12	10	2.6	.951	3B-89
1953	11	.200	.400	5	1	0	0	0	0.0	1	0	0	0	0	4	1	0	0	0	0	0.8	1.000	3B-11
9 yrs.	964	.271	.391	3253	882	141	33	61	1.9	419	487	347	290	13	41	10	1004	1738	114	174	3.0	.960	3B-897, 1B-26, 2B-1

WORLD SERIES

Year Team	Games	BA	SA	AB	H	2B	3B	HR	HR%	R	RBI	BB	SO	SB	PH AB	PH H	PO	A	E	DP	TC/G	FA	G by Pos
1943 NY A	5	.300	.450	20	6	0	0	0	0.0	3	3	0	3	0	0	0	2	9	1	0	2.4	.917	3B-5
1947	7	.269	.500	26	7	0	0	3	0.0	8	2	3	4	0	0	0	11	14	0	1	3.6	1.000	3B-7
1949	2	.143	.143	7	1	0	0	0	0.0	0	0	0	2	0	0	0	2	5	0	0	3.5	1.000	3B-2

Year	Team		Games	BA	SA	AB	H	2B	3B	HR	HR%	R	RBI	BB	SO	SB	Pinch Hit AB	Pinch Hit H	PO	A	E	DP	TC/G	FA	G by Pos

Randy Johnson *continued*

| 1982 | MIN | A | 89 | .248 | .419 | 234 | 58 | 10 | 0 | 10 | 4.3 | 26 | 33 | 30 | 46 | 0 | 22 | 2 | 2 | 0 | 0 | 0 | 0.0 | 1.000 | DH-67, OF-2 |
| 2 yrs. | | | 101 | .244 | .402 | 254 | 62 | 10 | 0 | 10 | 3.9 | 26 | 36 | 32 | 50 | 0 | 27 | 4 | 4 | 0 | 0 | 0 | 0.0 | 1.000 | DH-71, OF-3, 1B-1 |

Randy Johnson

JOHNSON, RONDIN ALLEN
B. Dec. 16, 1958, Bremerton, Wash. BB TR 5'10" 160 lbs.

| 1986 | KC | A | 11 | .258 | .323 | 31 | 8 | 0 | 1 | 0 | 0.0 | 1 | 2 | 0 | 3 | 0 | 0 | 0 | 14 | 32 | 0 | 5 | 4.2 | 1.000 | 2B-11 |

Ron Johnson

JOHNSON, RONALD DAVID
B. Mar. 23, 1956, Long Beach, Calif. BR TR 6'2" 223 lbs.

1982	KC	A	8	.286	.429	14	4	2	0	0	0.0	2	0	4	3	0	0	0	39	2	1	3	5.3	.976	1B-7
1983			9	.259	.259	27	7	0	0	0	0.0	2	1	3	1	0	0	0	66	3	2	9	7.9	.972	1B-7, C-2
1984	MON	N	5	.200	.200	5	1	0	0	0	0.0	0	1	0	2	0	2	0	5	0	0	0	1.0	1.000	1B-2, OF-1
3 yrs.			22	.261	.304	46	12	2	0	0	0.0	4	2	7	6	0	2	0	110	5	3	12	5.4	.975	1B-16, C-2, OF-1

Roy Johnson

JOHNSON, ROY CLEVELAND
Brother of Bob Johnson.
B. Feb. 23, 1903, Pryor, Okla. D. Sept. 10, 1973, Tacoma, Wash.
Manager 1944. BL TR 5'9" 175 lbs.

1929	DET	A	146	.314	.475	640	201	45	14	10	1.6	128	69	67	60	20	2	0	377	25	31	5	3.0	.928	OF-146
1930			125	.275	.409	462	127	30	13	2	0.4	84	35	40	46	17	6	2	218	15	16	4	2.0	.936	OF-118
1931			151	.279	.438	621	173	37	19	8	1.3	107	55	72	51	33	1	1	332	25	15	8	2.5	.960	OF-150
1932 2 teams	DET A (49G – .251)					BOS A			(94G – .299)																
" total			143	.282	.451	543	153	38	6	14	2.6	103	69	64	67	20	9	4	269	9	21	0	2.1	.930	OF-133
1933	BOS	A	133	.313	.466	483	151	30	7	10	2.1	88	95	55	36	13	7	1	280	14	25	3	2.4	.922	OF-125
1934			143	.320	.467	569	182	43	10	7	1.2	85	119	54	36	11	5	1	260	12	15	1	2.0	.948	OF-137
1935			145	.315	.423	553	174	33	9	3	0.5	70	66	74	34	11	3	2	267	21	17	1	2.1	.944	OF-142
1936	NY	A	63	.265	.367	147	39	8	2	1	0.7	21	19	21	14	3	20	3	66	2	4	0	1.1	.944	OF-33
1937 2 teams	NY A (12G – .294)					BOS N			(85G – .277)																
" total			97	.280	.363	311	87	11	3	3	1.0	29	28	41	31	6	20	4	152	5	10	0	1.7	.940	OF-75, 3B-1
1938	BOS	N	7	.172	.172	29	5	0	0	0	0.0	2	1	1	5	1	0	0	10	0	3	0	1.9	.769	OF-7
10 yrs.			1153	.296	.438	4358	1292	275	83	58	1.3	717	556	489	380	135	73	18	2231	128	157	22	2.2	.938	OF-1066, 3B-1

WORLD SERIES

| 1936 | NY | A | 2 | .000 | .000 | 1 | 0 | 0 | 0 | 0 | 0.0 | 0 | 0 | 0 | 1 | 0 | 1 | 0 | 0 | 0 | 0 | 0 | 0.0 | – | |

Roy Johnson

JOHNSON, ROY EDWARD
B. June 27, 1959, Parkin, Ark. BL TL 6'5" 205 lbs.

1982	MON	N	17	.219	.281	32	7	2	0	0	0.0	2	2	1	6	0	5	1	18	0	0	0	1.1	1.000	OF-11
1984			16	.152	.303	33	5	2	0	1	3.0	2	2	7	10	1	6	2	15	0	1	0	1.0	.938	OF-10
1985			3	.000	.000	5	0	0	0	0	0.0	0	0	0	3	0	0	0	0	0	0	0	0.0	–	OF-3
3 yrs.			36	.171	.271	70	12	4	0	1	1.4	4	4	8	19	1	11	3	33	0	1	0	0.9	.971	OF-24

Spud Johnson

JOHNSON, JOHN RALPH
B. 1860, Canada Deceased. BL TL 5'9" 175 lbs.

1889	COL	AA	116	.283	.370	459	130	14	10	2	0.4	91	79	39	47	34	0	0	156	87	41	10	2.4	.856	OF-69, 3B-44, 1B-2, SS-1
1890			135	.346	.461	538	186	23	18	1	0.2	106		48		43	0	0	164	12	14	1	1.4	.926	OF-135
1891	CLE	N	80	.257	.309	327	84	8	3	1	0.3	49	46	22	23	16	0	0	110	10	17	1	1.7	.876	OF-79, 1B-1
3 yrs.			331	.302	.392	1324	400	45	31	4	0.3	246	125	109	70	93	0	0	430	109	72	12	1.8	.882	OF-283, 3B-44, 1B-3, SS-1

Stan Johnson

JOHNSON, STANLEY LUCIUS
B. Feb. 12, 1937, Dallas, Tex. BL TL 5'10" 180 lbs.

1960	CHI	A	5	.167	.667	6	1	0	0	1	16.7	1	1	0	1	0	5	1	1	0	0	0	0.2	1.000	OF-2
1961	KC	A	3	.000	.000	3	0	0	0	0	0.0	1	0	2	1	0	1	0	0	0	0	0	0.0	–	OF-2
2 yrs.			8	.111	.444	9	1	0	0	1	11.1	2	1	2	2	0	6	1	1	0	0	0	0.1	1.000	OF-4

Tim Johnson

JOHNSON, TIMOTHY EVALD
B. July 22, 1949, Grand Forks, N. D. BL TR 6'1" 170 lbs.

1973	MIL	A	136	.213	.243	465	99	10	2	0	0.0	39	32	29	93	6	2	0	253	381	25	88	4.8	.962	SS-135
1974			93	.245	.331	245	60	7	7	0	0.0	25	25	11	48	4	4	1	139	230	9	51	4.1	.976	SS-64, 2B-26, DH-1, OF-1, 3B-1
1975			38	.141	.153	85	12	1	0	0	0.0	6	2	6	17	3	5	2	38	63	5	8	2.8	.953	3B-11, 2B-11, SS-10, DH-3, 1B-2
1976			105	.275	.311	273	75	4	3	0	0.0	25	14	19	32	4	1	0	167	238	8	42	3.9	.981	2B-100, 3B-17, SS-1, 1B-1
1977			30	.061	.091	33	2	1	0	0	0.0	5	2	5	10	1	10	1	17	19	2	5	1.3	.947	2B-10, SS-6, DH-4, 3B-4, OF-1
1978 2 teams	MIL A (3G – .000)					TOR A			(68G – .241)																
" total			71	.232	.256	82	19	2	0	0	0.0	10	3	10	16	1	0	4	38	92	2	17	1.9	.985	SS-51, 2B-13
1979	TOR	A	43	.186	.233	86	16	2	1	0	0.0	6	6	8	15	1	0	1	91	70	7	24	3.9	.958	2B-25, SS-9, 1B-7
7 yrs.			516	.223	.265	1269	283	27	13	0	0.0	116	84	88	231	18	27	4	743	1093	58	235	3.7	.969	SS-267, 2B-185, 3B-42, 1B-10, DH-8, OF-2

Tony Johnson

JOHNSON, ANTHONY CLAIR
B. June 23, 1956, Memphis, Tenn. BR TR 6'3" 195 lbs.

1981	MON	N	2	.000	.000	1	0	0	0	0	0.0	0	0	0	0	0	0	0	0	0	0	0	0.0	–	OF-1
1982	TOR	A	70	.235	.367	98	23	2	1	3	3.1	17	14	11	26	3	10	3	45	2	1	0	0.7	.979	DH-28, OF-28
2 yrs.			72	.232	.364	99	23	2	1	3	3.0	17	14	11	26	3	10	3	45	2	1	0	0.7	.979	OF-29, DH-28

Wallace Johnson

JOHNSON, WALLACE DARNELL
B. Dec. 25, 1956, Gary, Ind. BB TR 6' 173 lbs.

| 1981 | MON | N | 11 | .222 | .444 | 9 | 2 | 0 | 1 | 0 | 0.0 | 1 | 3 | 1 | 1 | 1 | 7 | 2 | 1 | 2 | 0 | 1 | 0.3 | 1.000 | 2B-1 |
| 1982 | | | 36 | .193 | .263 | 57 | 11 | 0 | 2 | 0 | 0.0 | 5 | 2 | 5 | 5 | 4 | 21 | 4 | 22 | 18 | 2 | 4 | 1.2 | .952 | 2B-13 |

Year Team	Games	BA	SA	AB	H	2B	3B	HR	HR%	R	RBI	BB	SO	SB	Pinch Hit AB	Pinch Hit H	PO	A	E	DP	TC/G	FA	G by Pos

Wallace Johnson *continued*

Year Team	Games	BA	SA	AB	H	2B	3B	HR	HR%	R	RBI	BB	SO	SB	PH AB	PH H	PO	A	E	DP	TC/G	FA	G by Pos
1983 2 teams		MON	N	(3G – .500)				SF	N	(7G – .125)													
" total	10	.200	.200	10	2	0	0	0	0.0	1	1	1	0	1	7	1	3	2	0	1	0.5	1.000	2B-1
1984 MON N	17	.208	.208	24	5	0	0	0	0.0	3	4	5	4	0	10	3	27	3	1	3	1.8	.968	1B-4
1986	61	.283	.346	127	36	3	1	1	0.8	13	10	7	9	6	37	11	204	17	2	15	3.7	.991	1B-27
1987	75	.247	.341	85	21	5	0	1	1.2	7	14	7	6	5	61	17	68	2	2	4	1.0	.972	1B-9
1988	86	.309	.383	94	29	5	1	0	0.0	7	3	12	15	0	64	22	80	9	1	3	1.0	.989	1B-13, 2B-1
1989	85	.272	.368	114	31	3	1	2	1.8	9	17	7	12	1	59	14	130	7	4	8	1.7	.972	1B-18
8 yrs.	381	.263	.340	520	137	16	6	4	0.8	46	54	45	52	18	266	74	535	60	12	39	1.6	.980	1B-71, 2B-16

DIVISIONAL PLAYOFF SERIES

Year Team	Games	BA	SA	AB	H	2B	3B	HR	HR%	R	RBI	BB	SO	SB	PH AB	PH H	PO	A	E	DP	TC/G	FA	G by Pos
1981 MON N	2	.500	.500	2	1	0	0	0	0.0	0	1	0	0	0	2	1	0	0	0	0	0.0	–	

Walter Johnson

JOHNSON, WALTER PERRY (The Big Train, Barney) BR TR 6'1" 200 lbs.
B. Nov. 6, 1887, Humboldt, Kans. D. Dec. 10, 1946, Washington, D. C.
Manager 1929-35.
Hall of Fame 1936.

Year Team	Games	BA	SA	AB	H	2B	3B	HR	HR%	R	RBI	BB	SO	SB	PH AB	PH H	PO	A	E	DP	TC/G	FA	G by Pos
1907 WAS A	14	.111	.167	36	4	0	1	0	0.0	3	1	1		0	0	0	5	20	3	1	2.0	.893	P-14
1908	36	.165	.253	79	13	3	2	0	0.0	7	5	6		0	0	0	4	56	4	3	1.8	.938	P-36
1909	40	.129	.188	101	13	3	0	1	1.0	6	6	1		0	0	0	15	73	7	2	2.4	.926	P-40
1910	45	.175	.277	137	24	6	1	2	1.5	14	12	4		2	0	0	23	90	6	3	2.6	.950	P-45
1911	42	.234	.344	128	30	5	3	1	0.8	18	15	0		1	2	1	14	95	4	8	2.7	.965	P-40
1912	55	.264	.403	144	38	6	4	2	1.4	16	20	7		2	5	0	15	93	4	4	2.0	.964	P-50
1913	54	.261	.433	134	35	5	6	2	1.5	12	14	5	14	2	5	2	22	82	0	7	1.9	1.000	P-47, OF-1
1914	55	.221	.331	136	30	4	1	3	2.2	23	16	10	27	2	3	0	30	102	5	6	2.5	.964	P-51, OF-1
1915	64	.231	.374	147	34	7	4	2	1.4	14	17	8	34	0	12	2	23	95	6	7	1.9	.952	P-47, OF-4
1916	58	.232	.324	142	33	2	4	1	0.7	14	7	11	28	0	9	2	17	72	6	2	1.6	.937	P-48
1917	57	.254	.362	130	33	12	1	0	0.0	15	15	9	30	1	9	1	16	82	0	2	1.7	1.000	P-47
1918	65	.267	.367	150	40	4	4	1	0.7	10	18	9	18	2	20	5	22	71	2	4	1.5	.979	P-39, OF-4
1919	56	.192	.272	125	24	1	3	1	0.8	13	8	12	17	1	14	3	23	69	1	5	1.7	.989	P-39, OF-3
1920	35	.261	.406	69	18	1	3	1	1.4	7	8	6	12	0	11	2	7	28	3	0	1.1	.921	P-21, OF-2
1921	38	.270	.333	111	30	7	0	0	0.0	10	10	6	14	0	2	0	4	51	1	1	1.5	.982	P-35
1922	43	.204	.259	108	22	3	0	1	0.9	8	15	2	12	0	2	0	11	66	0	2	1.8	1.000	P-41
1923	43	.194	.290	93	18	3	3	1	1.1	11	13	4	15	0	0	0	13	51	2	7	1.5	.970	P-43
1924	39	.283	.389	113	32	9	0	1	0.9	18	14	3	11	0	1	0	9	53	0	2	1.6	1.000	P-38
1925	36	.433	.577	97	42	6	1	2	2.1	12	20	3	6	0	6	2	5	37	0	2	1.2	1.000	P-30
1926	35	.194	.272	103	20	5	1	1	1.0	6	10	3	11	0	2	0	11	38	1	1	1.4	.980	P-33
1927	26	.348	.522	46	16	2	0	2	4.3	6	10	3	4	0	7	1	5	25	0	3	1.2	1.000	P-18
21 yrs.	936	.236	.342	2329	549	94	41	24	1.0	243	256	113	253	13	110	21	294	1349	55	72	1.8	.968	P-802, OF-15

WORLD SERIES

Year Team	Games	BA	SA	AB	H	2B	3B	HR	HR%	R	RBI	BB	SO	SB	PH AB	PH H	PO	A	E	DP	TC/G	FA	G by Pos
1924 WAS A	3	.111	.111	9	1	0	0	0	0.0	0	0	0	0	0	0	0	1	4	1	2	2.0	.833	P-3
1925	3	.091	.091	11	1	0	0	0	0.0	0	0	0	3	0	0	0	0	4	0	0	1.3	1.000	P-3
2 yrs.	6	.100	.100	20	2	0	0	0	0.0	0	0	0	3	0	0	0	1	8	1	2	1.7	.900	P-6

Dick Johnston

JOHNSTON, RICHARD FREDERICK BR TR 5'8" 155 lbs.
B. Apr. 6, 1863, Kingston, N. Y. D. Apr. 4, 1934, Detroit, Mich.

Year Team	Games	BA	SA	AB	H	2B	3B	HR	HR%	R	RBI	BB	SO	SB	PH AB	PH H	PO	A	E	DP	TC/G	FA	G by Pos
1884 RIC AA	39	.281	.425	146	41	5	5	2	1.4	23		2			0	0	87	13	17	3	3.0	.855	OF-37, SS-2
1885 BOS N	26	.234	.369	111	26	6	3	1	0.9	17	23	0	15		0	0	40	8	9	2	2.2	.842	OF-26
1886	109	.240	.334	413	99	18	9	1	0.2	48	57	3	70		0	0	243	29	33	4	2.8	.892	OF-109
1887	127	.258	.393	507	131	13	20	5	1.0	87	77	16	35	52	0	0	339	34	27	9	3.1	.933	OF-127
1888	135	.296	.472	585	173	31	18	12	2.1	102	68	15	33	35	0	0	286	30	36	3	2.6	.898	OF-135
1889	132	.228	.301	539	123	16	4	5	0.9	80	67	41	60	34	0	0	267	22	26	6	2.4	.917	OF-132
1890 2 teams		BOS	P	(2G – .111)				NY	P	(77G – .242)													
" total	79	.238	.321	315	75	9	7	1	0.3	37	43	18	26	7	0	0	169	19	22	3	2.7	.895	OF-78, SS-2
1891 CIN AA	99	.221	.309	376	83	11	2	6	1.6	59	51	38	44	12	0	0	193	20	25	4	2.4	.895	OF-99
8 yrs.	746	.251	.366	2992	751	109	68	33	1.1	453	386	133	283	140	0	0	1624	175	195	34	2.7	.902	OF-743, SS-4

Doc Johnston

JOHNSTON, WHEELER ROGER BL TL 6' 170 lbs.
Brother of Jimmy Johnston.
B. Sept. 9, 1887, Cleveland, Tenn. D. Feb. 17, 1961, Chattanooga, Tenn.

Year Team	Games	BA	SA	AB	H	2B	3B	HR	HR%	R	RBI	BB	SO	SB	PH AB	PH H	PO	A	E	DP	TC/G	FA	G by Pos
1909 CIN N	3	.000	.000	10	0	0	0	0	0.0	1	1	0			0	0	25	2	0	0	9.0	1.000	1B-3
1912 CLE A	43	.280	.390	164	46	7	4	0	0.6	22	11	11		8	2	0	330	17	3	27	8.1	.991	1B-41
1913	133	.255	.347	530	135	19	12	2	0.4	74	39	35	65	19	0	0	1319	76	15	76	10.6	.989	1B-133
1914	103	.244	.294	340	83	15	1	0	0.0	43	23	28	46	14	7	2	853	36	12	43	8.7	.987	1B-89, OF-2
1915 PIT N	147	.265	.372	543	144	19	12	5	0.9	71	64	38	40	26	0	0	1453	48	13	65	10.3	.991	1B-147
1916	114	.213	.287	404	86	10	10	0	0.0	33	39	20	42	17	3	0	1042	47	14	44	9.7	.987	1B-110
1918 CLE A	74	.227	.286	273	62	12	2	0	0.0	30	25	26	19	12	1	0	738	40	9	25	10.6	.989	1B-73
1919	102	.305	.384	331	101	17	3	1	0.3	42	33	25	18	21	4	1	957	57	16	57	10.1	.984	1B-98
1920	147	.292	.385	535	156	24	10	2	0.4	68	71	28	32	13	0	0	1427	91	12	83	10.4	.992	1B-147
1921	118	.297	.401	384	114	20	7	2	0.5	53	44	29	15	3	3	1	960	62	12	72	8.8	.988	1B-116
1922 PHI N	71	.250	.358	260	65	10	7	1	0.4	41	29	24	15	7	6	0	641	31	7	34	9.6	.990	1B-65
11 yrs.	1055	.263	.351	3774	992	154	68	14	0.4	478	379	264	292	139	26	4	9745	507	113	526	9.8	.989	1B-1022, OF-2

WORLD SERIES

Year Team	Games	BA	SA	AB	H	2B	3B	HR	HR%	R	RBI	BB	SO	SB	PH AB	PH H	PO	A	E	DP	TC/G	FA	G by Pos
1920 CLE A	5	.273	.273	11	3	0	0	0	0.0	1	0	1	1	1	1	0	27	6	0	3	6.6	1.000	1B-5

Fred Johnston

JOHNSTON, WILFRED IVY (Red Top) BR TR 5'10½" 160 lbs.
B. July 9, 1900, Pineville, N. C. D. July 14, 1959, Tyler, Tex.

Year Team	Games	BA	SA	AB	H	2B	3B	HR	HR%	R	RBI	BB	SO	SB	PH AB	PH H	PO	A	E	DP	TC/G	FA	G by Pos
1924 BKN N	4	.250	.250	4	1	0	0	0	0.0	1	0	0	1	0	0	0	1	2	1	0	1.0	.750	3B-1, 2B-1

Greg Johnston

JOHNSTON, GREGORY BERNARD BL TL 6' 175 lbs.
B. Feb. 12, 1955, Los Angeles, Calif.

Year	Team		Games	BA	SA	AB	H	2B	3B	HR	HR%	R	RBI	BB	SO	SB	Pinch Hit AB	Pinch Hit H	PO	A	E	DP	TC/G	FA	G by Pos

Greg Johnston *continued*

Year	Team		Games	BA	SA	AB	H	2B	3B	HR	HR%	R	RBI	BB	SO	SB	AB	H	PO	A	E	DP	TC/G	FA	G by Pos
1979	SF	N	42	.203	.270	74	15	2	0	1	1.4	5	7	2	17	0	27	6	27	1	1	0	0.7	.966	OF-18
1980	MIN	A	14	.185	.296	27	5	3	0	0	0.0	3	1	2	4	0	3	1	25	0	0	0	1.8	1.000	OF-14
1981			7	.125	.125	16	2	0	0	0	0.0	2	0	2	5	0	0	0	11	1	0	1	1.7	1.000	OF-6
3 yrs.			63	.188	.256	117	22	5	0	1	0.9	10	8	6	26	0	30	7	63	2	1	1	1.0	.985	OF-38

Jimmy Johnston

JOHNSTON, JAMES HARLE
Brother of Doc Johnston.
B. Dec. 10, 1889, Cleveland, Tenn. D. Feb. 14, 1967, Chattanooga, Tenn.

BR TR 5'10" 160 lbs.

Year	Team		Games	BA	SA	AB	H	2B	3B	HR	HR%	R	RBI	BB	SO	SB	AB	H	PO	A	E	DP	TC/G	FA	G by Pos
1911	CHI	A	1	.000	.000	2	0	0	0	0	0.0	0	2	0	0	0	0	0	1	0	0	0	1.0	1.000	OF-1
1914	CHI	N	50	.228	.327	101	23	3	2	1	1.0	9	8	4	9	3	11	2	69	16	8	3	1.9	.914	OF-28, 2B-4
1916	BKN	N	118	.252	.327	425	107	13	8	1	0.2	58	26	35	38	22	1	1	224	16	9	3	2.1	.964	OF-106
1917			103	.270	.324	330	89	10	4	0	0.0	33	25	23	28	16	8	1	269	37	17	5	3.1	.947	OF-92, 1B-14, SS-4, 3B-3, 2B-3
1918			123	.281	.347	484	136	16	8	0	0.0	54	27	33	31	22	1	0	382	48	13	13	3.6	.971	OF-96, 1B-21, 3B-4, 2B-1
1919			117	.281	.336	405	114	11	4	1	0.2	56	23	29	26	11	9	1	201	302	20	32	4.5	.962	2B-87, OF-14, 1B-2, SS-1
1920			155	.291	.361	635	185	17	12	1	0.2	87	52	43	23	19	0	0	171	289	32	22	3.2	.935	3B-146, OF-7, SS-3
1921			152	.325	.460	624	203	41	14	5	0.8	104	56	45	26	28	0	0	168	321	35	37	3.4	.933	3B-150, SS-3
1922			138	.319	.400	567	181	20	7	4	0.7	110	49	38	17	18	0	0	300	434	42	71	5.6	.946	2B-62, SS-50, 3B-26
1923			151	.325	.426	625	203	29	11	4	0.6	111	60	53	15	16	1	0	369	532	51	63	6.3	.946	2B-84, SS-52, 3B-14
1924			86	.298	.365	315	94	11	2	2	0.6	51	29	27	10	5	7	4	171	219	24	32	4.8	.942	SS-63, 3B-10, 1B-4, OF-1
1925			123	.297	.355	431	128	13	3	2	0.5	63	43	45	15	7	12	4	189	119	34	15	2.8	.901	3B-81, OF-20, 1B-8, SS-2
1926	2 teams	BOS	N (23G – .246)			NY	N	(37G – .232)																	
"	total		60	.238	.270	126	30	1	0	1	0.8	18	10	16	8	2	25	5	25	24	5	3	0.9	.907	OF-15, 3B-14, 2B-2
13 yrs.			1377	.294	.374	5070	1493	185	75	22	0.4	754	410	391	246	169	75	18	2539	2357	290	299	3.8	.944	3B-448, OF-380, 2B-243, SS-178, 1B-49

WORLD SERIES

Year	Team		Games	BA	SA	AB	H	2B	3B	HR	HR%	R	RBI	BB	SO	SB	AB	H	PO	A	E	DP	TC/G	FA	G by Pos
1916	BKN	N	3	.300	.500	10	3	0	1	0	0.0	1	0	1	0	0	1	1	1	0	1	0	0.7	.500	OF-2
1920			4	.214	.214	14	3	0	0	0	0.0	2	0	0	2	1	0	0	2	8	0	1	2.5	1.000	3B-4
2 yrs.			7	.250	.333	24	6	0	1	0	0.0	3	0	1	2	1	1	1	3	8	1	1	1.7	.917	3B-4, OF-2

Johnny Johnston

JOHNSTON, JOHN THOMAS
B. Mar. 28, 1890, Longview, Tex. D. Mar. 7, 1940, San Diego, Calif.

BL TR 5'11" 172 lbs.

Year	Team		Games	BA	SA	AB	H	2B	3B	HR	HR%	R	RBI	BB	SO	SB	AB	H	PO	A	E	DP	TC/G	FA	G by Pos
1913	STL	A	109	.224	.297	380	85	14	4	2	0.5	37	27	42	51	11	3	0	222	23	9	3	2.3	.965	OF-106

Rex Johnston

JOHNSTON, REX DAVID
B. Nov. 8, 1937, Colton, Calif.

BR TR 6'1½" 202 lbs.

Year	Team		Games	BA	SA	AB	H	2B	3B	HR	HR%	R	RBI	BB	SO	SB	AB	H	PO	A	E	DP	TC/G	FA	G by Pos
1964	PIT	N	14	.000	.000	7	0	0	0	0	0.0	1	0	3	0	0	3	0	2	0	0	0	0.1	1.000	OF-8

Jay Johnstone

JOHNSTONE, JOHN WILLIAM
B. Nov. 20, 1945, Manchester, Conn.

BL TR 6'1" 175 lbs.
BB 1966

Year	Team		Games	BA	SA	AB	H	2B	3B	HR	HR%	R	RBI	BB	SO	SB	AB	H	PO	A	E	DP	TC/G	FA	G by Pos
1966	CAL	A	61	.264	.378	254	67	12	4	3	1.2	35	17	11	36	3	0	0	114	2	3	1	2.0	.975	OF-61
1967			79	.209	.274	230	48	7	1	2	0.9	18	10	5	37	3	21	5	141	3	4	0	1.9	.973	OF-63
1968			41	.261	.313	115	30	4	1	0	0.0	11	3	7	15	2	8	0	58	4	1	1	1.5	.984	OF-29
1969			148	.270	.381	540	146	20	5	10	1.9	64	59	38	75	3	4	1	331	12	6	4	2.4	.983	OF-144
1970			119	.238	.403	320	76	10	5	11	3.4	34	39	24	53	1	23	5	200	7	4	3	1.8	.981	OF-100
1971	CHI	A	124	.260	.425	388	101	14	1	16	4.1	53	40	38	50	10	11	3	232	9	8	1	2.0	.968	OF-119
1972			113	.188	.268	261	49	9	4	4	1.5	27	17	25	42	2	19	6	154	5	2	1	1.4	.988	OF-97
1973	OAK	A	23	.107	.143	28	3	1	0	0	0.0	1	3	2	4	0	11	0	7	0	0	0	0.3	1.000	OF-7, DH-4, 2B-2
1974	PHI	N	64	.295	.475	200	59	10	4	6	3.0	30	30	24	28	5	6	4	88	4	3	1	1.5	.968	OF-59
1975			122	.329	.454	350	115	19	2	7	2.0	50	54	42	39	7	25	10	152	10	4	3	1.4	.976	OF-101
1976			129	.318	.457	440	140	38	4	5	1.1	62	53	41	39	5	12	2	293	10	8	2	2.4	.974	OF-122, 1B-6
1977			112	.284	.479	363	103	18	4	15	4.1	64	59	38	38	3	14	5	294	15	1	17	2.8	.997	OF-91, 1B-19
1978	2 teams	PHI	N (35G – .179)			NY	A	(36G – .262)																	
"	total		71	.223	.264	121				1	0.8	9	10	10	19	0	28	2	78	7	1	9	1.2	.988	OF-29, 1B-8, DH-5
1979	2 teams	NY	A (23G – .208)			SD	N	(75G – .294)																	
"	total		98	.277	.341	249	69	9	2	1	0.4	17	39	20	28	2	25	6	217	18	4	10	2.4	.983	OF-64, 1B-22, DH-3
1980	LA	N	109	.307	.406	251	77	15	2	2	0.8	31	20	24	29	3	41	11	100	9	4	0	1.0	.965	OF-61
1981			61	.205	.349	83	17	3	0	3	3.6	8	6	7	13	0	38	11	33	4	1	2	0.6	.974	OF-16, 1B-2
1982	2 teams	LA	N (21G – .077)			CHI	N	(98G – .249)																	
"	total		119	.241	.404	282	68	14	1	10	3.5	40	45	45	43	0	26	3	154	8	3	0	1.4	.982	OF-86
1983	CHI	N	86	.257	.436	140	36	7	0	6	4.3	16	22	20	24	1	38	6	55	3	4	1	0.7	.935	OF-44
1984			52	.288	.370	73	21	2	0	0	0.0	8	7	3	18	0	39	10	12	0	0	0	0.2	1.000	OF-15
1985	LA	N	17	.133	.200	15	2	1	0	0	0.0	0	2	1	2	0	15	2	0	0	0	0	0.0	–	
20 yrs.			1748	.267	.394	4703	1254	215	38	102	2.2	578	531	429	632	50	404 10th	92	2713	130	61	56	1.7	.979	OF-1308, 1B-57, DH-12, 2B-2

DIVISIONAL PLAYOFF SERIES

Year	Team		Games	BA	SA	AB	H	2B	3B	HR	HR%	R	RBI	BB	SO	SB	AB	H	PO	A	E	DP	TC/G	FA	G by Pos
1981	LA	N	1	.000	.000	1	0	0	0	0	0.0	0	0	0	0	0	1	0	0	0	0	0	0.0	–	

LEAGUE CHAMPIONSHIP SERIES

Year	Team		Games	BA	SA	AB	H	2B	3B	HR	HR%	R	RBI	BB	SO	SB	AB	H	PO	A	E	DP	TC/G	FA	G by Pos
1976	PHI	N	3	.778	1.111	9	7	1	1	0	0.0	1	2	1	0	0	1	1	3	0	0	0	1.0	1.000	OF-2
1977			2	.200	.200	5	1	0	0	0	0.0	0	0	1	0	0	1	0	4	0	0	0	2.0	1.000	OF-2
1981	LA	N	2	.000	.000	2	0	0	0	0	0.0	0	0	0	3	0	2	0	0	0	0	0	0.0	–	
1985			1	.000	.000	1	0	0	0	0	0.0	0	0	0	1	0	1	0	0	0	0	0	0.0	–	
4 yrs.			8	.471	.647	17	8	1	1	0	0.0	1	2	1	4	0	5	1	7	0	0	0	0.9	1.000	OF-4

WORLD SERIES

Year	Team		Games	BA	SA	AB	H	2B	3B	HR	HR%	R	RBI	BB	SO	SB	AB	H	PO	A	E	DP	TC/G	FA	G by Pos
1978	NY	A	2	–	–	0	0	0	0	0	0.0	0	0	0	0	0	0	0	1	0	0	0	0.5	1.000	OF-2
1981	LA	N	3	.667	1.667	3	2	0	0	1	33.3	1	3	0	3	0	2	1	0	0	0	0	0.0	–	
2 yrs.			5	.667	1.667	3	2	0	0	1	33.3	1	3	0	3	0	2	1	1	0	0	0	0.2	1.000	OF-2

Stan Jok

JOK, STANLEY EDWARD (Tucker)
B. May 3, 1926, Buffalo, N. Y.   D. Mar. 6, 1972, Buffalo, N. Y.   BR TR 6'   190 lbs.

Year	Team	Games	BA	SA	AB	H	2B	3B	HR	HR%	R	RBI	BB	SO	SB	PH AB	PH H	PO	A	E	DP	TC/G	FA	G by Pos
1954	2 teams	PHI N (3G – .000)				CHI A (3G – .167)																		
"	total	6	.133	.133	15	2	0	0	0	0.0	1	2	1	4	0	3	0	3	7	0	1	1.7	1.000	3B-3
1955	CHI A	6	.250	1.000	4	1	0	0	1	25.0	3	2	1	1	0	0	0	2	4	1	0	1.2	.857	3B-3, OF-1
2 yrs.		12	.158	.316	19	3	0	0	1	5.3	4	4	2	5	0	3	0	5	11	1	1	1.4	.941	3B-6, OF-1

Smead Jolley

JOLLEY, SMEAD POWELL (Smudge)
B. Jan. 14, 1902, Wesson, Ark.   BL TR 6'3½"   210 lbs.

Year	Team	Games	BA	SA	AB	H	2B	3B	HR	HR%	R	RBI	BB	SO	SB	PH AB	PH H	PO	A	E	DP	TC/G	FA	G by Pos
1930	CHI A	152	.313	.492	616	193	38	12	16	2.6	76	114	28	52	3	1	1	249	17	14	4	1.8	.950	OF-151
1931		54	.300	.482	110	33	11	0	3	2.7	5	28	7	4	0	30	14	29	1	5	1	0.6	.857	OF-23
1932	2 teams	CHI A (12G – .357)				BOS A (137G – .309)																		
"	total	149	.312	.476	573	179	30	5	18	3.1	60	106	30	29	1	6	1	266	15	16	3	2.0	.946	OF-137, C-5
1933	BOS A	118	.282	.445	411	116	32	4	9	2.2	47	65	24	20	1	15	4	178	12	9	3	1.7	.955	OF-102
4 yrs.		473	.305	.475	1710	521	111	21	46	2.7	188	313	89	105	5	52	20	722	45	44	11	1.7	.946	OF-413, C-5

Jones

JONES,
B. Johnstown, Pa.

Year	Team	Games	BA	SA	AB	H	2B	3B	HR	HR%	R	RBI	BB	SO	SB	PH AB	PH H	PO	A	E	DP	TC/G	FA	G by Pos
1884	WAS AA	4	.294	.294	17	5	0	0	0	0.0	2		1		0	0	0	6	0	0	0	1.5	1.000	OF-4

Bill Jones

JONES, WILLIAM
B. Syracuse, N. Y.

Year	Team	Games	BA	SA	AB	H	2B	3B	HR	HR%	R	RBI	BB	SO	SB	PH AB	PH H	PO	A	E	DP	TC/G	FA	G by Pos
1882	BAL AA	4	.067	.067	15	1	0	0	0	0.0	1		0			0	0	9	5	2	0	4.0	.875	OF-2, C-2
1884	PHI U	4	.143	.143	14	2	0	0	0	0.0	2		1			0	0	23	4	7	1	8.5	.794	C-4, OF-1
2 yrs.		8	.103	.103	29	3	0	0	0	0.0	3		1			0	0	32	9	9	1	6.3	.820	C-6, OF-3

Bill Jones

JONES, WILLIAM DENNIS (Midget)
B. Apr. 8, 1887, Hartland, N. B., Canada   D. Oct. 10, 1946, Boston, Mass.   BL TR 5'6½"   157 lbs.

Year	Team	Games	BA	SA	AB	H	2B	3B	HR	HR%	R	RBI	BB	SO	SB	PH AB	PH H	PO	A	E	DP	TC/G	FA	G by Pos
1911	BOS N	24	.216	.294	51	11	2	1	0	0.0	6	3	15	7	1	3	1	36	3	6	0	1.9	.867	OF-18
1912		3	.500	.500	2	1	0	0	0	0.0	0	2	0	1	0	2	1	0	0	0	0	0.0		
2 yrs.		27	.226	.302	53	12	2	1	0	0.0	6	5	15	8	1	5	2	36	3	6	0	1.7	.867	OF-18

Binky Jones

JONES, JOHN JOSEPH
B. July 11, 1899, St. Louis, Mo.   D. May 13, 1961, St. Louis, Mo.   BR TR 5'9"   154 lbs.

Year	Team	Games	BA	SA	AB	H	2B	3B	HR	HR%	R	RBI	BB	SO	SB	PH AB	PH H	PO	A	E	DP	TC/G	FA	G by Pos
1924	BKN N	10	.108	.135	37	4	1	0	0	0.0	0	2	0	3	0	0	0	17	27	5	6	4.9	.898	SS-10

Bob Jones

JONES, ROBERT WALTER (Ducky)
B. Dec. 2, 1889, Clayton, Calif.   D. Aug. 30, 1964, San Diego, Calif.   BL TR 6'   170 lbs.

Year	Team	Games	BA	SA	AB	H	2B	3B	HR	HR%	R	RBI	BB	SO	SB	PH AB	PH H	PO	A	E	DP	TC/G	FA	G by Pos
1917	DET A	46	.156	.221	77	12	1	2	0	0.0	16	2	4	8	3	10	2	26	57	6	2	1.9	.933	2B-18, 3B-8
1918		74	.275	.352	287	79	14	4	0	0.0	43	21	17	16	7	3	1	143	83	11	8	3.2	.954	3B-63, 1B-6
1919		127	.260	.335	439	114	18	6	1	0.2	37	57	34	39	11	0	0	134	219	21	14	2.9	.943	3B-127
1920		81	.249	.306	265	66	6	3	1	0.4	35	18	22	22	3	5	0	90	158	15	9	3.2	.943	3B-67, 2B-5, SS-1
1921		141	.303	.383	554	168	23	9	1	0.2	82	72	37	24	8	0	0	194	324	27	12	3.9	.950	3B-141
1922		124	.257	.325	455	117	10	6	3	0.7	65	44	36	18	8	3	0	161	267	17	22	3.6	.962	3B-119
1923		100	.250	.320	372	93	15	4	1	0.3	51	40	29	13	7	0	0	109	224	16	17	3.5	.954	3B-97
1924		110	.272	.361	393	107	27	4	0	0.0	52	47	20	20	1	3	1	108	196	14	12	2.9	.956	3B-106
1925		50	.236	.277	148	35	6	0	0	0.0	18	15	9	5	1	3	1	43	91	2	5	2.7	.985	3B-46
9 yrs.		853	.265	.337	2990	791	120	38	7	0.2	399	316	208	156	49	27	5	1008	1619	129	101	3.2	.953	3B-774, 2B-23, 1B-6, SS-1

Bobby Jones

JONES, ROBERT OLIVER
B. Oct. 11, 1949, Elkton, Md.   BL TL 6'2"   195 lbs.

Year	Team	Games	BA	SA	AB	H	2B	3B	HR	HR%	R	RBI	BB	SO	SB	PH AB	PH H	PO	A	E	DP	TC/G	FA	G by Pos
1974	TEX A	2	.000	.000	5	0	0	0	0	0.0	0	0	0	1	0	0	0	5	0	0	0	2.5	1.000	OF-2
1975		9	.091	.091	11	1	0	0	0	0.0	2	0	3	3	0	0	0	6	0	0	0	0.7	1.000	OF-5, DH-2
1976	CAL A	78	.211	.355	166	35	6	0	6	3.6	22	17	14	30	3	17	2	98	6	1	0	1.3	.990	OF-62, DH-2
1977		14	.176	.353	17	3	0	0	1	5.9	3	3	4	5	0	6	1	0	0	0	0	0.0		DH-6
1981	TEX A	10	.265	.559	34	9	1	0	3	8.8	4	7	1	7	0	0	0	20	4	0	0	2.4	1.000	OF-10
1983		41	.222	.319	72	16	4	0	1	1.4	5	11	5	17	0	23	4	24	0	0	0	0.6	1.000	DH-11, OF-11, 1B-1
1984		64	.259	.371	143	37	4	0	4	2.8	14	22	10	19	1	24	5	139	7	1	8	2.3	.993	OF-22, 1B-15, DH-4
1985		83	.224	.351	134	30	2	0	5	3.7	14	23	11	30	1	42	10	44	0	1	1	0.5	1.000	OF-30, DH-10, 1B-4
1986		13	.095	.095	21	2	0	0	0	0.0	1	3	2	5	0	2	1	29	1	1	2	2.4	.968	OF-9, 1B-2
9 yrs.		314	.221	.348	603	133	17	0	20	3.3	65	86	50	117	5	115	23	365	18	3	11	1.2	.992	OF-151, DH-34, 1B-22

Charley Jones

JONES, CHARLES WESLEY (Long Charley)
Born Benjamin Wesley Rippay.
B. Apr. 3, 1850, County, N. C.   Deceased.   BR TR 5'11½"   202 lbs.

Year	Team	Games	BA	SA	AB	H	2B	3B	HR	HR%	R	RBI	BB	SO	SB	PH AB	PH H	PO	A	E	DP	TC/G	FA	G by Pos
1876	CIN N	64	.286	.420	276	79	17	4	4	1.4	40	38	7	17		0	0	151	11	27	2	3.0	.857	OF-64
1877	3 teams	CIN N (17G – .304)				CHI N (2G – .375)				CIN N (38G – .313)														
"	total	57	.313	.471	240	75	12	10	2	0.8	53	38	15	25		0	0	238	15	37	6	5.1	.872	OF-48, 1B-10
1878	CIN N	61	.310	.441	261	81	11	7	3	1.1	50	39	4	17		0	0	120	9	15	1	2.4	.896	OF-61
1879	BOS N	83	.315	.510	355	112	22	10	9	2.5	85	62	29	38		0	0	162	20	13	1	2.3	.933	OF-83
1880		66	.300	.429	280	84	15	3	4	1.4	46	38	11	27		0	0	108	11	25	3	2.2	.826	OF-66
1883	CIN AA	90	.294	.473	391	115	15	11	11	2.8	84		20			0	0	172	12	26	1	2.3	.876	OF-90
1884		113	.314	.470	472	148	19	17	7	1.5	117		37			0	0	207	12	28	2	2.2	.887	OF-113
1885		112	.322	.456	487	157	19	17	4	0.8	108		21			0	0	214	24	29	6	2.4	.891	OF-112
1886		127	.270	.388	500	135	22	11	5	1.0	87		61			0	0	217	23	33	1	2.1	.879	OF-127
1887	2 teams	CIN AA (41G – .314)				NY AA (62G – .255)																		
"	total	103	.278	.411	400	111	18	7	5	1.3	58		31		15	0	0	188	25	23	8	2.3	.903	OF-103, P-2, 1B-1
1888	KC AA	6	.160	.240	25	4	0	1	0	0.0	2	5	1		0	0	0	8	1	3	0	2.0	.750	OF-6
11 yrs.		882	.299	.443	3687	1101	170	98	55	1.5	728	220	237	124	16	0	0	1785	161	259	29	2.5	.883	OF-873, 1B-11, P-2

Year	Team		Games	BA	SA	AB	H	2B	3B	HR	HR%	R	RBI	BB	SO	SB	Pinch Hit AB	Pinch Hit H	PO	A	E	DP	TC/G	FA	G by Pos

Charlie Jones

JONES, CHARLES C. (Casey)
B. June 2, 1876, Butler, Pa.   D. Apr. 2, 1947, Lusten, Minn.   BR TR 6'1"

Year	Team		Games	BA	SA	AB	H	2B	3B	HR	HR%	R	RBI	BB	SO	SB	PH AB	PH H	PO	A	E	DP	TC/G	FA	G by Pos
1901	BOS	A	10	.146	.195	41	6	2	0	0	0.0	6	6	1		2	0	0	13	0	1	0	1.4	.929	OF-10
1905	WAS	A	142	.208	.267	544	113	18	4	2	0.4	68	41	31		24	0	0	240	24	11	6	1.9	.960	OF-142
1906			131	.241	.326	497	120	11	11	3	0.6	56	42	24		34	2	0	282	20	12	7	2.4	.962	OF-128, 2B-1
1907			121	.265	.343	437	116	14	10	0	0.0	48	37	22		26	2	0	267	14	8	4	2.4	.972	OF-111, 2B-5, 1B-4, SS-2
1908	STL	A	74	.232	.289	263	61	11	2	0	0.0	37	17	14		14	2	0	116	13	5	2	1.8	.963	OF-72
5 yrs.			478	.233	.304	1782	416	56	27	5	0.3	215	143	92		100	6	0	918	71	37	19	2.1	.964	OF-463, 2B-6, 1B-4, SS-2

Charlie Jones

JONES, CHARLES F.
B. New York, N. Y.   Deceased.

Year	Team		Games	BA	SA	AB	H	2B	3B	HR	HR%	R	RBI	BB	SO	SB	PH AB	PH H	PO	A	E	DP	TC/G	FA	G by Pos
1884	BKN	AA	25	.178	.189	90	16	1	0	0	0.0	10		5			0	0	38	49	13	5	4.0	.870	2B-13, 3B-11, OF-2
1885	NY	AA	1	.250	.250	4	1	0	0	0	0.0	0		0			0	0	2	4	0	0	6.0	1.000	3B-1
2 yrs.			26	.181	.191	94	17	1	0	0	0.0	10		5			0	0	40	53	13	5	4.1	.877	2B-13, 3B-12, OF-2

Chris Jones

JONES, CHRISTOPHER DALE
B. July 13, 1957, Los Angeles, Calif.   BL TL 6'   183 lbs.

Year	Team		Games	BA	SA	AB	H	2B	3B	HR	HR%	R	RBI	BB	SO	SB	PH AB	PH H	PO	A	E	DP	TC/G	FA	G by Pos
1985	HOU	N	31	.200	.200	25	5	0	0	0	0.0	0	1	3	7	0	14	3	15	0	0	0	0.5	1.000	OF-15
1986	SF	N	3	.000	.000	1	0	0	0	0	0.0	0	0	0	1	1	1	0	0	0	0	0	0.0	—	
2 yrs.			34	.192	.192	26	5	0	0	0	0.0	0	1	3	7	1	15	3	15	0	0	0	0.4	1.000	OF-15

Clarence Jones

JONES, CLARENCE WOODROW
B. Nov. 7, 1941, Zanesville, Ohio   BL TL 6'2"   185 lbs.

Year	Team		Games	BA	SA	AB	H	2B	3B	HR	HR%	R	RBI	BB	SO	SB	PH AB	PH H	PO	A	E	DP	TC/G	FA	G by Pos
1967	CHI	N	53	.252	.348	135	34	7	0	2	1.5	13	16	14	33	0	9	3	133	5	3	7	2.7	.979	OF-31, 1B-13
1968			5	.000	.000	2	0	0	0	0	0.0	0	0	2	1	0	2	0	2	0	0	0	0.4	1.000	1B-1
2 yrs.			58	.248	.343	137	34	7	0	2	1.5	13	16	16	34	0	11	3	135	5	3	7	2.5	.979	OF-31, 1B-14

Cleon Jones

JONES, CLEON JOSEPH
B. Aug. 4, 1942, Plateau, Ala.   BR TL 6'   185 lbs.

Year	Team		Games	BA	SA	AB	H	2B	3B	HR	HR%	R	RBI	BB	SO	SB	PH AB	PH H	PO	A	E	DP	TC/G	FA	G by Pos
1963	NY	N	6	.133	.133	15	2	0	0	0	0.0	1	1	0	4	0	2	0	6	0	0	0	1.0	1.000	OF-5
1965			30	.149	.203	74	11	1	0	1	1.4	2	9	2	23	1	9	2	36	2	0	0	1.3	1.000	OF-23
1966			139	.275	.372	495	136	16	4	8	1.6	74	57	30	62	16	11	0	275	10	6	2	2.1	.979	OF-129
1967			129	.246	.331	411	101	10	5	5	1.2	46	30	19	57	12	13	2	210	5	5	3	1.7	.977	OF-115
1968			147	.297	.452	509	151	29	4	14	2.8	63	55	31	98	23	10	1	226	7	9	0	1.6	.963	OF-139
1969			137	.340	.482	483	164	25	4	12	2.5	92	75	64	60	16	4	2	322	11	2	3	2.4	.994	OF-122, 1B-15
1970			134	.277	.417	506	140	25	8	10	2.0	71	63	57	87	12	5	0	243	10	5	3	1.9	.981	OF-130
1971			136	.319	.473	505	161	24	6	14	2.8	63	69	53	87	6	5	1	248	4	5	1	1.9	.981	OF-132
1972			106	.245	.331	375	92	15	1	5	1.3	39	52	30	83	1	3	0	310	20	6	10	3.2	.982	OF-84, 1B-20
1973			92	.260	.395	339	88	13	0	11	3.2	48	48	28	51	1	4	3	168	6	6	0	2.0	.967	OF-92
1974			124	.282	.421	461	130	23	1	13	2.8	62	60	38	79	3	6	1	220	8	7	0	1.9	.970	OF-120
1975			21	.240	.260	50	12	1	0	0	0.0	2	2	3	6	0	9	3	9	0	0	0	0.4	1.000	OF-12
1976	CHI	A	12	.200	.225	40	8	1	0	0	0.0	2	3	5	5	0	1	0	7	0	0	0	0.6	1.000	OF-8, DH-3
13 yrs.			1213	.281	.404	4263	1196	183	33	93	2.2	565	524	360	702	91	82	15	2280	83	51	22	2.0	.979	OF-1111, 1B-35, DH-3

LEAGUE CHAMPIONSHIP SERIES

Year	Team		Games	BA	SA	AB	H	2B	3B	HR	HR%	R	RBI	BB	SO	SB	PH AB	PH H	PO	A	E	DP	TC/G	FA	G by Pos
1969	NY	N	3	.429	.786	14	6	2	0	1	7.1	4	4	1	2	2	0	0	11	0	0	0	3.7	1.000	OF-3
1973			5	.300	.400	20	6	2	0	0	0.0	3	3	2	4	0	0	0	10	0	1	0	2.2	.909	OF-5
2 yrs.			8	.353	.559	34	12	4	0	1	2.9	7	7	3	6	2	0	0	21	0	1	0	2.8	.955	OF-8

WORLD SERIES

Year	Team		Games	BA	SA	AB	H	2B	3B	HR	HR%	R	RBI	BB	SO	SB	PH AB	PH H	PO	A	E	DP	TC/G	FA	G by Pos
1969	NY	N	5	.158	.211	19	3	1	0	0	0.0	2	0	0	1	0	0	0	7	0	0	0	1.4	1.000	OF-5
1973			7	.286	.464	28	8	2	0	1	3.6	5	1	4	2	0	0	0	11	1	1	0	1.9	.923	OF-7
2 yrs.			12	.234	.362	47	11	3	0	1	2.1	7	1	4	3	0	0	0	18	1	1	0	1.7	.950	OF-12

Cobe Jones

JONES, COBURN DYAS
B. Aug. 21, 1907, Denver, Colo.   D. June 3, 1969, Denver, Colo.   BB TR 5'7"   155 lbs.

Year	Team		Games	BA	SA	AB	H	2B	3B	HR	HR%	R	RBI	BB	SO	SB	PH AB	PH H	PO	A	E	DP	TC/G	FA	G by Pos
1928	PIT	N	2	.500	.500	2	1	0	0	0	0.0	0	0	0	0	0	0	0	0	1	0	0	0.5	1.000	SS-2
1929			25	.254	.365	63	16	5	1	0	0.0	6	4	1	5	1	9	2	28	29	5	6	2.5	.919	SS-15
2 yrs.			27	.262	.369	65	17	5	1	0	0.0	6	4	1	5	1	9	2	28	30	5	6	2.3	.921	SS-17

Dalton Jones

JONES, JAMES DALTON
B. Dec. 10, 1943, McComb, Miss.   BL TR 6'1"   180 lbs.

Year	Team		Games	BA	SA	AB	H	2B	3B	HR	HR%	R	RBI	BB	SO	SB	PH AB	PH H	PO	A	E	DP	TC/G	FA	G by Pos
1964	BOS	A	118	.230	.342	374	86	16	4	6	1.6	37	39	22	38	6	35	11	182	196	17	41	3.3	.957	2B-85, SS-1, 3B-1
1965			112	.270	.373	367	99	13	5	5	1.4	41	37	28	45	8	28	4	80	177	17	18	2.4	.938	3B-81, 2B-8
1966			115	.234	.365	252	59	11	5	4	1.6	26	23	22	27	1	48	13	133	126	12	26	2.4	.956	2B-70, 3B-3
1967			89	.289	.409	159	46	6	2	3	1.9	18	25	11	23	0	47	13	23	61	6	6	1.0	.933	3B-30, 2B-19, 1B-1
1968			111	.234	.314	354	83	13	0	4	1.4	38	29	17	53	1	28	11	491	80	7	55	5.2	.988	1B-56, 2B-26, 3B-8
1969			111	.220	.318	336	74	18	3	4	1.2	50	33	39	36	1	18	3	702	64	7	61	7.0	.991	1B-81, 3B-9, 2B-1
1970	DET	A	89	.220	.351	191	42	7	0	6	3.1	29	21	33	33	1	29	11	111	99	4	26	2.4	.981	2B-35, 3B-18, 1B-10
1971			83	.254	.399	138	35	5	0	5	3.6	15	11	9	21	1	45	13	25	17	2	3	0.5	.955	OF-16, 3B-13, 1B-3, 2B-1
1972 2 teams	DET A (7G – .000)					TEX A (72G – .159)																			
" total			79	.152	.241	158	24	2	0	4	2.5	14	19	10	33	1	32	2	58	63	3	11	1.6	.976	3B-23, 2B-17, 1B-7, OF-2
9 yrs.			907	.235	.343	2329	548	91	19	41	1.8	268	237	191	309	20	310	81	1805	883	75	247	3.0	.973	2B-262, 3B-186, 1B-158, OF-18, SS-1

WORLD SERIES

Year	Team		Games	BA	SA	AB	H	2B	3B	HR	HR%	R	RBI	BB	SO	SB	PH AB	PH H	PO	A	E	DP	TC/G	FA	G by Pos
1967	BOS	A	6	.389	.389	18	7	0	0	0	0.0	2	1	1	3	0	1	1	4	8	0	2	2.0	1.000	3B-4

Darryl Jones

JONES, DARRYL LEE
Brother of Lynn Jones.
B. June 5, 1951, Meadville, Pa.   BR TR 5'10"   175 lbs.

Year	Team		Games	BA	SA	AB	H	2B	3B	HR	HR%	R	RBI	BB	SO	SB	PH AB	PH H	PO	A	E	DP	TC/G	FA	G by Pos
1979	NY	A	18	.255	.404	47	12	5	1	0	0.0	6	6	2	7	0	2	2	1	0	0	0	0.1	1.000	DH-15, OF-2

Year	Team		Games	BA	SA	AB	H	2B	3B	HR	HR%	R	RBI	BB	SO	SB	Pinch Hit AB	Pinch Hit H	PO	A	E	DP	TC/G	FA	G by Pos

Ricky Jones

JONES, RICKY MIRON
B. June 4, 1958, Tupelo, Miss.
BR TR 6'3" 186 lbs.

Year	Team		Games	BA	SA	AB	H	2B	3B	HR	HR%	R	RBI	BB	SO	SB	PH AB	PH H	PO	A	E	DP	TC/G	FA	G by Pos
1986	BAL	A	16	.182	.242	33	6	2	0	0	0.0	2	4	7	8	0	0	0	19	38	0	9	3.6	1.000	2B-11, 3B-6

Ron Jones

JONES, RONALD GLEN
B. June 11, 1964, Sequin, Tex.
BL TR 5'10" 195 lbs.

Year	Team		Games	BA	SA	AB	H	2B	3B	HR	HR%	R	RBI	BB	SO	SB	PH AB	PH H	PO	A	E	DP	TC/G	FA	G by Pos
1988	PHI	N	33	.290	.548	124	36	6	1	8	6.5	15	26	2	14	0	1	0	70	1	0	0	2.2	1.000	OF-32
1989			12	.290	.484	31	9	0	0	2	6.5	7	4	9	1	1	0	0	27	1	0	1	2.3	1.000	OF-12
2 yrs.			45	.290	.535	155	45	6	1	10	6.5	22	30	11	15	1	1	0	97	2	0	1	2.2	1.000	OF-44

Ross Jones

JONES, ROSS A.
B. Jan. 14, 1960, Miami, Fla.
BR TR 6'2" 185 lbs.

Year	Team		Games	BA	SA	AB	H	2B	3B	HR	HR%	R	RBI	BB	SO	SB	PH AB	PH H	PO	A	E	DP	TC/G	FA	G by Pos
1984	NY	N	17	.100	.200	10	1	1	0	0	0.0	2	3	4	0	3	0	0	0	·7	1	2	0.5	.875	SS-7, 2B-1
1986	SEA	A	11	.095	.095	21	2	0	0	0	0.0	0	0	0	4	0	0	0	9	11	0	2	1.8	1.000	SS-4, 2B-3, 3B-2, DH-1
1987	KC	A	39	.254	.325	114	29	4	2	0	0.0	10	10	5	15	1	0	0	46	111	4	15	4.1	.975	SS-36, 2B-3
3 yrs.			67	.221	.283	145	32	5	2	0	0.0	12	11	8	23	1	3	0	55	129	5	19	2.8	.974	SS-47, 2B-7, 3B-2, DH-1

Ruppert Jones

JONES, RUPPERT SANDERSON
B. Mar. 12, 1955, Dallas, Tex.
BL TL 5'10" 170 lbs.

Year	Team		Games	BA	SA	AB	H	2B	3B	HR	HR%	R	RBI	BB	SO	SB	PH AB	PH H	PO	A	E	DP	TC/G	FA	G by Pos
1976	KC	A	28	.216	.333	51	11	1	1	1	2.0	9	7	3	16	0	9	1	21	0	0	0	0.8	1.000	OF-17, DH-3
1977	SEA	A	160	.263	.454	597	157	26	8	24	4.0	85	76	55	120	13	1	0	465	11	9	3	3.0	.981	OF-155, DH-4
1978			129	.235	.337	472	111	24	3	6	1.3	48	46	55	85	22	1	0	393	10	6	2	3.2	.985	OF-128
1979			162	.267	.444	622	166	29	9	21	3.4	109	78	85	78	33	1	0	453	13	5	4	2.9	.989	OF-161
1980	NY	A	83	.223	.357	328	73	11	3	9	2.7	38	42	34	50	18	0	0	246	4	3	1	3.0	.988	OF-82
1981	SD	N	105	.249	.370	397	99	34	1	4	1.0	53	39	43	66	7	0	0	295	9	2	3	2.9	.993	OF-104
1982			116	.283	.425	424	120	20	2	12	2.8	69	61	62	90	18	2	0	314	3	5	1	2.8	.984	OF-114
1983			133	.233	.394	335	78	12	3	12	3.6	42	49	35	58	11	18	3	268	6	6	3	2.1	.979	OF-111, 1B-5
1984	DET	A	79	.284	.516	215	61	12	1	12	5.6	26	37	21	47	2	15	6	150	4	0	1	1.9	1.000	OF-73, DH-2
1985	CAL	A	125	.231	.447	389	90	17	2	21	5.4	66	67	57	82	7	13	0	179	12	1	5	1.5	.995	OF-73, DH-43
1986			126	.229	.427	393	90	21	3	17	4.3	73	49	64	87	10	12	3	205	5	4	0	1.7	.981	OF-66, DH-3
1987			85	.245	.432	192	47	8	2	8	4.2	25	28	20	38	2	27	6	81	1	3	0	1.0	.965	OF-66, DH-3
12 yrs.			1331	.250	.416	4415	1103	215	38	147	3.3	643	579	534	817	143	99	19	3070	78	44	23	2.4	.986	OF-1205, DH-55, 1B-5

LEAGUE CHAMPIONSHIP SERIES

Year	Team		Games	BA	SA	AB	H	2B	3B	HR	HR%	R	RBI	BB	SO	SB	PH AB	PH H	PO	A	E	DP	TC/G	FA	G by Pos
1984	DET	A	2	.000	.000	5	0	0	0	0	0.0	1	0	1	1	0	1	0	5	0	0	0	2.5	1.000	OF-2
1986	CAL	A	6	.176	.235	17	3	1	0	0	0.0	4	2	5	2	0	0	0	6	0	0	0	1.0	1.000	OF-5
2 yrs.			8	.136	.182	22	3	1	0	0	0.0	5	2	6	3	0	1	0	11	0	0	0	1.4	1.000	OF-7

WORLD SERIES

Year	Team		Games	BA	SA	AB	H	2B	3B	HR	HR%	R	RBI	BB	SO	SB	PH AB	PH H	PO	A	E	DP	TC/G	FA	G by Pos
1984	DET	A	2	.000	.000	3	0	0	0	0	0.0	0	0	0	1	0	0	0	3	0	0	0	1.5	1.000	OF-2

Tex Jones

JONES, WILLIAM RODERICK
B. Aug. 4, 1885, Marion, Kans. D. Feb. 26, 1938, Wichita, Kans.
BR TR 6' 192 lbs.

Year	Team		Games	BA	SA	AB	H	2B	3B	HR	HR%	R	RBI	BB	SO	SB	PH AB	PH H	PO	A	E	DP	TC/G	FA	G by Pos
1911	CHI	A	9	.194	.226	31	6	1	0	0	0.0	4	4	3		1	0	0	96	12	0	6	12.0	1.000	1B-9

Tim Jones

JONES, WILLIAM TIMOTHY
B. Dec. 1, 1962, Sumter, S. C.
BL TR 5'10" 172 lbs.

Year	Team		Games	BA	SA	AB	H	2B	3B	HR	HR%	R	RBI	BB	SO	SB	PH AB	PH H	PO	A	E	DP	TC/G	FA	G by Pos
1988	STL	N	31	.269	.269	52	14	0	0	0	0.0	2	3	4	10	4	9	1	26	40	1	7	2.2	.985	SS-9, 2B-8, 3B-1
1989			42	.293	.373	75	22	6	0	0	0.0	11	7	7	8	1	10	2	33	48	2	4	2.0	.976	SS-12, 2B-12, 3B-5, OF-1, C-1
2 yrs.			73	.283	.331	127	36	6	0	0	0.0	13	10	11	18	5	19	3	59	88	3	11	2.1	.980	SS-21, 2B-20, 3B-6, OF-1, C-1

Tom Jones

JONES, THOMAS
B. Jan. 22, 1877, Honesdale, Pa. D. June 21, 1923, Danville, Pa.
BR TR 6'1" 195 lbs.

Year	Team		Games	BA	SA	AB	H	2B	3B	HR	HR%	R	RBI	BB	SO	SB	PH AB	PH H	PO	A	E	DP	TC/G	FA	G by Pos
1902	BAL	A	37	.283	.384	159	45	8	4	0	0.0	22	14	2		1	0	0	341	22	17	23	10.3	.955	1B-37, 2B-1
1904	STL	A	156	.243	.309	625	152	15	10	2	0.3	53	68	15		16	0	0	1485	149	21	54	10.6	.987	1B-134, 2B-23, OF-4
1905			135	.242	.282	504	122	16	2	0	0.0	45	48	30		5	0	0	1502	105	25	52	12.1	.985	1B-135
1906			144	.252	.315	539	136	22	6	0	0.0	51	30	24		27	1	0	1476	116	25	55	11.2	.985	1B-143
1907			155	.250	.291	549	137	17	3	0	0.0	53	34	34		24	0	0	1687	103	31	69	11.7	.983	1B-155
1908			155	.246	.284	549	135	14	2	1	0.2	43	50	30		18	0	0	1616	90	24	79	11.2	.986	1B-155
1909	2 teams					STL A (97G – .249)					DET A (44G – .281)														
"	total		141	.259	.308	490	127	18	3	0	0.0	43	47	23		22	0	0	1027	76	12	58	7.9	.989	1B-139, 3B-2
1910	DET	A	135	.255	.303	432	110	13	4	0	0.0	32	45	35		22	0	0	1405	67	23	50	11.1	.985	1B-135
8 yrs.			1058	.251	.303	3847	964	123	34	3	0.1	342	336	193		135	1	0	10539	728	178	440	10.8	.984	1B-1033, 2B-24, OF-4, 3B-2

WORLD SERIES

Year	Team		Games	BA	SA	AB	H	2B	3B	HR	HR%	R	RBI	BB	SO	SB	PH AB	PH H	PO	A	E	DP	TC/G	FA	G by Pos
1909	DET	A	7	.250	.292	24	6	1	0	0	0.0	3	2	2		1	0	0	71	1	1	1	10.4	.986	1B-7

Tracy Jones

JONES, TRACY DONALD
B. Mar. 31, 1961, Hawthorne, Calif.
BR TR 6'3" 180 lbs.

Year	Team		Games	BA	SA	AB	H	2B	3B	HR	HR%	R	RBI	BB	SO	SB	PH AB	PH H	PO	A	E	DP	TC/G	FA	G by Pos
1986	CIN	N	46	.349	.453	86	30	3	0	2	2.3	16	10	9	5	7	12	2	46	1	0	0	1.0	1.000	OF-24, 1B-2
1987			117	.290	.437	359	104	17	3	10	2.8	53	44	23	40	31	25	6	189	2	2	0	1.6	.990	OF-95
1988	2 teams					CIN N (37G – .229)					MON N (53G – .333)														
"	total		90	.295	.371	224	66	6	1	3	1.3	29	24	20	18	18	23	6	96	2	2	0	1.1	.980	OF-68
1989	2 teams					SF N (40G – .186)					DET A (46G – .259)														
"	total		86	.231	.322	255	59	14	0	3	1.2	22	38	21	30	3	16	3	107	0	0	0	1.3	.991	OF-66, DH-8
4 yrs.			339	.280	.391	924	259	40	4	18	1.9	120	116	73	93	59	76	17	438	5	5	0	1.3	.989	OF-253, DH-8, 1B-2

Willie Jones

JONES, WILLIE EDWARD (Puddin' Head)
B. Aug. 16, 1925, Dillon, S. C. D. Oct. 18, 1983, Cincinnati, Ohio
BR TR 6'2" 205 lbs.

Willie Jones *continued*

Year	Team	Games	BA	SA	AB	H	2B	3B	HR	HR%	R	RBI	BB	SO	SB	Pinch Hit AB	Pinch Hit H	PO	A	E	DP	TC/G	FA	G by Pos
1947	PHI N	18	.226	.258	62	14	0	1	0	0.0	5	10	7	0	2	1	0	19	41	6	3	3.7	.909	3B-17
1948		17	.333	.467	60	20	2	0	2	3.3	9	9	3	5	0	0	0	30	33	5	1	4.0	.926	3B-17
1949		149	.244	.421	532	130	35	1	19	3.6	71	77	65	66	3	3	0	181	308	27	19	3.5	.948	3B-145
1950		157	.267	.456	610	163	28	1	25	4.1	100	88	61	40	5	0	0	190	323	25	30	3.4	.954	3B-157
1951		148	.285	.470	564	161	28	5	22	3.9	79	81	60	47	6	0	0	190	286	17	33	3.3	.947	3B-147
1952		147	.250	.383	541	135	12	3	18	3.3	60	72	53	36	5	0	0	216	281	16	31	3.5	.969	3B-147
1953		149	.225	.385	481	108	16	2	19	4.0	61	70	85	45	1	1	1	176	253	11	36	3.0	.975	3B-147
1954		142	.271	.402	535	145	28	3	12	2.2	64	56	61	54	4	1	1	184	277	15	23	3.4	.968	3B-141
1955		146	.258	.401	516	133	20	3	16	3.1	65	81	77	51	6	0	0	202	235	18	22	3.1	.960	3B-146
1956		149	.277	.429	520	144	20	4	17	3.3	88	78	92	49	5	0	0	202	264	13	23	3.2	.973	3B-149
1957		133	.218	.332	440	96	19	2	9	2.0	58	47	61	41	1	7	2	140	197	12	18	2.6	.966	3B-126
1958		118	.271	.420	398	108	15	1	14	3.5	52	60	49	45	1	5	2	141	186	11	13	2.9	.967	3B-110, 1B-1
1959	3 teams					PHI N (47G – .269)			CLE A (11G – .222)			CIN N (72G – .249)												
"	total	130	.255	.421	411	105	22	2	14	3.4	57	56	48	43	0	11	2	135	191	11	16	2.6	.967	3B-118
1960	CIN N	79	.268	.376	149	40	7	0	3	2.0	16	27	31	16	1	27	10	44	59	4	5	1.4	.963	3B-46, 2B-1
1961		9	.000	.000	7	0	0	0	0	0.0	1	0	2	3	0	6	0	0	0	1	0	0.1	–	3B-1
15 yrs.		1691	.258	.410	5826	1502	252	33	190	3.3	786	812	755	541	40	62	18	2050	2934	192	273	3.1	.963	3B-1614, 2B-1, 1B-1

WORLD SERIES

Year	Team	Games	BA	SA	AB	H	2B	3B	HR	HR%	R	RBI	BB	SO	SB	Pinch Hit AB	Pinch Hit H	PO	A	E	DP	TC/G	FA	G by Pos
1950	PHI N	4	.286	.357	14	4	1	0	0	0.0	1	0	0	3	0	0	0	8	9	1	0	4.5	.944	3B-4

Bubber Jonnard

JONNARD, CLARENCE JAMES
Brother of Claude Jonnard.
B. Nov. 23, 1897, Nashville, Tenn.   D. Aug. 23, 1977, New York, N. Y.   BR TR 6'1" 185 lbs.

Year	Team	Games	BA	SA	AB	H	2B	3B	HR	HR%	R	RBI	BB	SO	SB	Pinch Hit AB	Pinch Hit H	PO	A	E	DP	TC/G	FA	G by Pos
1920	CHI A	2	.000	.000	5	0	0	0	0	0.0	0	0	0	1	0	1	0	4	2	1	1	3.5	.857	C-1
1922	PIT N	10	.238	.333	21	5	0	1	0	0.0	4	2	2	4	0	0	0	30	7	1	0	3.8	.974	C-10
1926	PHI N	19	.118	.147	34	4	1	0	0	0.0	3	2	3	4	0	4	0	30	7	2	1	2.1	.949	C-15
1927		53	.294	.336	143	42	6	0	0	0.0	18	14	7	7	0	7	5	93	24	4	3	2.3	.967	C-41
1929	STL N	18	.097	.097	31	3	0	0	0	0.0	1	2	0	6	0	0	0	39	5	2	1	2.6	.957	C-18
1935	PHI N	1	.000	.000	1	0	0	0	0	0.0	0	0	0	0	0	0	0	1	0	0	0	1.0	1.000	C-1
6 yrs.		103	.230	.268	235	54	7	0	0	0.0	26	20	12	23	0	12	5	197	45	10	6	2.4	.960	C-86

Eddie Joost

JOOST, EDWIN DAVID
B. June 5, 1916, San Francisco, Calif.
Manager 1954.   BR TR 6' 175 lbs.

Year	Team	Games	BA	SA	AB	H	2B	3B	HR	HR%	R	RBI	BB	SO	SB	Pinch Hit AB	Pinch Hit H	PO	A	E	DP	TC/G	FA	G by Pos
1936	CIN N	13	.154	.192	26	4	0	0	0	0.0	1	1	2	5	0	0	0	15	22	1	4	2.9	.974	SS-7, 2B-5
1937		6	.083	.083	12	1	0	0	0	0.0	0	0	0	0	0	0	0	8	13	3	2	4.0	.875	2B-6
1939		42	.252	.336	143	36	6	3	0	0.0	23	14	12	15	1	4	0	94	101	12	23	4.9	.942	2B-32, SS-6
1940		88	.216	.266	278	60	7	2	1	0.4	24	24	32	40	4	0	0	161	270	16	51	5.1	.964	SS-78, 2B-7, 3B-4
1941		152	.253	.337	537	136	25	4	4	0.7	67	40	69	59	9	0	0	326	429	46	88	5.3	.943	SS-147, 2B-4, 1B-2, 3B-1
1942		142	.224	.320	562	126	30	3	6	1.1	65	41	62	57	9	0	0	299	434	50	93	5.5	.936	SS-130, 2B-15
1943	BOS N	124	.185	.252	421	78	16	3	2	0.5	34	20	68	80	5	0	0	247	341	33	53	5.0	.947	3B-67, 2B-60, SS-1
1945		35	.248	.312	141	35	7	1	0	0.0	16	9	13	7	0	0	0	64	76	12	13	4.3	.921	2B-19, 3B-16
1947	PHI A	151	.206	.330	540	111	22	3	13	2.4	76	64	114	110	6	0	0	370	452	38	100	5.7	.956	SS-151
1948		135	.250	.395	509	127	22	2	16	3.1	99	55	119	87	2	0	0	325	409	20	115	5.6	.973	SS-135
1949		144	.263	.453	525	138	25	3	23	4.4	128	81	149	80	2	0	0	352	442	25	126	5.7	.969	SS-144
1950		131	.233	.384	476	111	12	3	18	3.8	79	58	101	68	5	0	0	241	389	29	117	5.0	.956	SS-131
1951		140	.289	.461	553	160	28	5	19	3.4	107	78	106	70	10	0	0	325	422	20	115	5.0	.974	SS-140
1952		146	.244	.415	540	132	26	3	20	3.7	94	75	122	94	5	0	0	278	431	28	81	5.0	.962	SS-146
1953		51	.249	.384	177	44	6	0	6	3.4	39	15	45	24	3	0	0	102	147	11	33	5.1	.958	SS-51
1954		19	.362	.489	47	17	3	0	1	2.1	7	9	10	10	0	2	0	14	32	1	5	2.5	.979	SS-9, 3B-5, 2B-1
1955	BOS A	55	.193	.336	119	23	2	0	5	4.2	15	17	17	21	0	17	5	55	92	12	23	2.9	.925	SS-20, 2B-17, 3B-2
17 yrs.		1574	.239	.366	5606	1339	238	35	134	2.4	874	601	1041	827	61	23	5	3276	4502	357	1042	5.2	.956	SS-1296, 2B-166, 3B-95, 1B-2

WORLD SERIES

Year	Team	Games	BA	SA	AB	H	2B	3B	HR	HR%	R	RBI	BB	SO	SB	Pinch Hit AB	Pinch Hit H	PO	A	E	DP	TC/G	FA	G by Pos
1940	CIN N	7	.200	.200	25	5	0	0	0	0.0	0	2	1	2	0	0	0	14	12	0	6	3.7	1.000	2B-7

Buck Jordan

JORDAN, BAXTER BYERLY
B. Jan. 16, 1907, Cooleemee, N. C.   BL TR 6' 170 lbs.

Year	Team	Games	BA	SA	AB	H	2B	3B	HR	HR%	R	RBI	BB	SO	SB	Pinch Hit AB	Pinch Hit H	PO	A	E	DP	TC/G	FA	G by Pos
1927	NY N	5	.200	.200	5	1	0	0	0	0.0	0	0	0	3	0	5	1	0	0	0	0	0.0	–	
1929		2	.500	1.000	2	1	1	0	0	0.0	0	0	0	0	0	1	0	0	0	0	1	0.5	1.000	
1931	WAS A	9	.222	.333	18	4	2	0	0	0.0	1	0	0	3	0	1	0	45	0	1	3	5.1	.978	1B-7
1932	BOS N	49	.321	.434	212	68	12	3	2	0.9	27	29	4	5	1	0	0	514	31	5	48	11.2	.991	1B-49
1933		152	.286	.386	588	168	29	9	4	0.7	77	46	34	22	4	2	0	1513	88	14	117	10.6	.991	1B-150
1934		124	.311	.413	489	152	26	9	2	0.4	68	58	35	19	3	7	6	1165	66	14	85	10.0	.989	1B-117
1935		130	.279	.383	470	131	24	5	5	1.1	62	35	19	17	3	19	5	876	79	17	59	7.5	.983	1B-95, 3B-8, OF-2
1936		138	.323	.405	555	179	27	5	3	0.5	81	66	45	22	2	2	0	1307	96	10	137	10.2	.993	1B-136
1937	2 teams					BOS N (8G – .250)			CIN N (98G – .282)															
"	total	106	.281	.352	324	91	14	3	1	0.3	46	28	25	14	6	28	7	669	46	8	55	6.8	.989	1B-76
1938	2 teams					CIN N (9G – .286)			PHI N (87G – .300)															
"	total	96	.300	.363	317	95	18	1	0	0.0	31	18	19	4	1	19	6	176	115	4	24	3.1	.986	3B-58, 1B-17
10 yrs.		811	.299	.391	2980	890	153	35	17	0.6	396	281	182	109	20	84	25	6266	521	73	529	8.5	.989	1B-648, 3B-66, OF-2

Dutch Jordan

JORDAN, ADOLPH OTTO
B. Jan. 5, 1880, Pittsburgh, Pa.   D. Dec. 23, 1972, West Allegheny, Pa.   BR TR 5'10" 185 lbs.

Year	Team	Games	BA	SA	AB	H	2B	3B	HR	HR%	R	RBI	BB	SO	SB	Pinch Hit AB	Pinch Hit H	PO	A	E	DP	TC/G	FA	G by Pos
1903	BKN N	78	.236	.285	267	63	11	1	0	0.0	27	21	19		9	1	0	145	161	27	15	4.3	.919	2B-54, 3B-18, OF-4, 1B-1
1904		87	.179	.234	252	45	10	2	0	0.0	21	19	13		7	2	1	167	196	17	17	4.4	.955	2B-70, 3B-11, 1B-4
2 yrs.		165	.208	.260	519	108	21	3	0	0.0	48	40	32		16	3	1	312	357	44	32	4.3	.938	2B-124, 3B-29, 1B-5, OF-4

Year Team	Games	BA	SA	AB	H	2B	3B	HR	HR%	R	RBI	BB	SO	SB	Pinch Hit AB	H	PO	A	E	DP	TC/G	FA	G by Pos

Jimmy Jordan

JORDAN, JAMES WILLIAM (Lord)
B. Jan. 13, 1908, Tucapau, S. C. D. Dec. 4, 1957, Gastonia, N. C. BR TR 5'9" 157 lbs.

Year Team	Games	BA	SA	AB	H	2B	3B	HR	HR%	R	RBI	BB	SO	SB	AB	H	PO	A	E	DP	TC/G	FA	G by Pos
1933 BKN N	70	.256	.322	211	54	12	1	0	0.0	16	17	4	6	3	2	1	122	203	12	27	4.8	.964	SS-51, 2B-11
1934	97	.266	.322	369	98	17	2	0	0.0	34	43	9	32	1	1	0	171	256	21	50	4.6	.953	SS-51, 2B-41, 3B-9
1935	94	.278	.302	295	82	7	0	0	0.0	26	30	9	17	3	14	5	177	279	14	39	5.0	.970	2B-46, SS-28, 3B-5
1936	115	.234	.291	398	93	15	1	2	0.5	26	28	15	21	1	4	1	235	275	15	44	4.6	.971	2B-98, 3B-6, SS-1
4 yrs.	376	.257	.308	1273	327	51	4	2	0.2	102	118	37	76	8	21	7	705	1013	62	160	4.7	.965	2B-196, SS-131, 3B-20

Mike Jordan

JORDAN, MICHAEL HENRY
B. Feb. 7, 1863, Lawrence, Mass. D. Sept. 25, 1940, Lawrence, Mass.

Year Team	Games	BA	SA	AB	H	2B	3B	HR	HR%	R	RBI	BB	SO	SB	AB	H	PO	A	E	DP	TC/G	FA	G by Pos
1890 PIT N	37	.096	.104	125	12	1	0	0	0.0	8	6	15	19	5	0	0	62	9	4	0	2.0	.947	OF-37

Ricky Jordan

JORDAN, PAUL SCOTT
B. May 26, 1965, Richmond, Calif. BR TR 6'5" 210 lbs.

Year Team	Games	BA	SA	AB	H	2B	3B	HR	HR%	R	RBI	BB	SO	SB	AB	H	PO	A	E	DP	TC/G	FA	G by Pos
1988 PHI N	69	.308	.491	273	84	15	1	11	4.0	41	43	7	39	1	0	0	579	35	5	41	9.0	.992	1B-69
1989	144	.285	.407	523	149	22	3	12	2.3	63	75	23	62	4	10	4	1271	61	9	99	9.3	.993	1B-140
2 yrs.	213	.293	.436	796	233	37	4	23	2.9	104	118	30	101	5	10	4	1850	96	14	140	9.2	.993	1B-209

Scott Jordan

JORDAN, SCOTT ALLAN
B. May 27, 1963, Waco, Tex. BR TR 6' 175 lbs.

Year Team	Games	BA	SA	AB	H	2B	3B	HR	HR%	R	RBI	BB	SO	SB	AB	H	PO	A	E	DP	TC/G	FA	G by Pos
1988 CLE A	7	.111	.111	9	1	0	0	0	0.0	0	1	0	3	0	0	0	10	0	0	0	1.4	1.000	OF-6

Slats Jordan

JORDAN, CLARENCE VEASEY
B. Sept. 26, 1879, Baltimore, Md. D. Dec. 7, 1953, Catonsville, Md. BL TL 6'1" 190 lbs.

Year Team	Games	BA	SA	AB	H	2B	3B	HR	HR%	R	RBI	BB	SO	SB	AB	H	PO	A	E	DP	TC/G	FA	G by Pos
1901 BAL A	1	.000	.000	3	0	0	0	0	0.0	0	0	0	0	0	0	0	13	0	2	0	15.0	.867	1B-1
1902	1	.000	.000	4	0	0	0	0	0.0	0	0	0	0	0	0	0	0	0	0	0	0.0	—	OF-1
2 yrs.	2	.000	.000	7	0	0	0	0	0.0	0	0	0	0	0	0	0	13	0	2	0	7.5	.867	OF-1, 1B-1

Tim Jordan

JORDAN, TIMOTHY JOSEPH (Hoboken)
B. Feb. 14, 1879, New York, N. Y. D. Sept. 13, 1949, Bronx, N. Y. BL TL 6'1" 170 lbs.

Year Team	Games	BA	SA	AB	H	2B	3B	HR	HR%	R	RBI	BB	SO	SB	AB	H	PO	A	E	DP	TC/G	FA	G by Pos
1901 WAS A	6	.200	.250	20	4	1	0	0	0.0	2	2	3		0	0	0	62	2	4	2	11.3	.941	1B-6
1903 NY A	2	.125	.125	8	1	0	0	0	0.0	2	0			0	0	0	16	0	2	3	9.0	.889	1B-2
1906 BKN N	129	.262	.422	450	118	20	8	12	2.7	67	78	59		16	3	0	1240	64	30	44	10.3	.978	1B-126
1907	147	.274	.363	485	133	15	8	4	0.8	43	53	74		10	3	0	1417	78	31	71	10.4	.980	1B-143
1908	148	.247	.371	515	127	18	5	12	2.3	58	60	59		9	1	0	1462	55	28	52	10.4	.982	1B-146
1909	103	.273	.379	330	90	20	3	3	0.9	47	36	59		13	7	1	937	29	17	36	9.5	.983	1B-95
1910	5	.200	.800	5	1	0	0	1	20.0	1	3	1		0	5	1	0	0	0	0	0.0	—	
7 yrs.	540	.261	.382	1813	474	74	24	32	1.8	220	232	254	2	48	19	2	5134	228	112	208	10.1	.980	1B-518

Tom Jordan

JORDAN, THOMAS JEFFERSON
B. Sept. 5, 1919, Lawton, Okla. BR TR 6'1½" 195 lbs.

Year Team	Games	BA	SA	AB	H	2B	3B	HR	HR%	R	RBI	BB	SO	SB	AB	H	PO	A	E	DP	TC/G	FA	G by Pos
1944 CHI A	14	.267	.333	45	12	1	0	0	0.0	2	3	1	0	0	0	0	48	6	3	0	4.1	.947	C-14
1946 2 teams	CHI A (10G – .267)				CLE A (14G – .200)																		
" total	24	.220	.380	50	11	3	1	1	2.0	3	3	3	2	1	10	1	43	6	1	1	2.1	.980	C-15
1948 STL A	1	.000	.000	1	0	0	0	0	0.0	0	0	0	1	0	0	0	0	0	0	0	0.0	—	
3 yrs.	39	.240	.354	96	23	4	2	1	1.0	5	6	4	2	1	11	1	91	12	4	1	2.7	.963	C-29

Arndt Jorgens

JORGENS, ARNDT LUDWIG
Brother of Orville Jorgens.
B. May 18, 1905, Modum, Norway D. Mar. 1, 1980, Wilmette, Ill. BR TR 5'9" 160 lbs.

Year Team	Games	BA	SA	AB	H	2B	3B	HR	HR%	R	RBI	BB	SO	SB	AB	H	PO	A	E	DP	TC/G	FA	G by Pos
1929 NY A	18	.324	.412	34	11	3	0	0	0.0	6	4	7		0	2	0	41	6	1	1	2.7	.979	C-15
1930	16	.367	.467	30	11	3	0	0	0.0	7	1	2	4	0	0	0	43	5	2	1	3.1	.960	C-16
1931	46	.270	.320	100	27	1	2	0	0.0	12	14	9	3	0	4	0	144	10	6	0	3.5	.963	C-40
1932	55	.219	.318	151	33	7	1	2	1.3	13	19	14	11	0	0	0	240	20	9	3	4.9	.967	C-55
1933	21	.220	.400	50	11	3	0	2	4.0	9	13	12	3	1	3	0	108	8	2	2	5.3	.982	C-19
1934	58	.208	.251	183	38	6	1	0	0.0	14	20	23	24	2	1	0	288	20	5	7	5.4	.984	C-56
1935	36	.238	.262	84	20	2	0	0	0.0	6	8	12	10	0	3	0	130	12	0	5	3.9	1.000	C-33
1936	31	.273	.348	66	18	3	1	0	0.0	5	5	2	3	0	3	1	87	9	1	0	3.1	.990	C-30
1937	13	.130	.174	23	3	1	0	0	0.0	3	3	2	5	0	1	0	27	2	0	1	2.2	1.000	C-11
1938	9	.235	.353	17	4	2	0	0	0.0	3	2	3	3	0	1	0	18	6	2	0	2.9	.923	C-8
1939	3	—		0	0	0	0	0	—	1	0	0	0	0	0	0	2	0	0	0	0.7	1.000	C-2
11 yrs.	306	.238	.310	738	176	31	5	4	0.5	79	89	85	73	3	17	2	1128	92	28	19	4.1	.978	C-285

Mike Jorgensen

JORGENSEN, MICHAEL
B. Aug. 16, 1948, Passaic, N. J. BL TL 6' 195 lbs.

Year Team	Games	BA	SA	AB	H	2B	3B	HR	HR%	R	RBI	BB	SO	SB	AB	H	PO	A	E	DP	TC/G	FA	G by Pos
1968 NY N	8	.143	.214	14	2	1	0	0	0.0	0	0	0	4	0	4	0	32	1	0	3	4.1	1.000	1B-4
1970	76	.195	.356	87	17	3	1	3	3.4	15	4	10	23	2	15	2	145	12	3	9	2.1	.981	1B-50, OF-10
1971	45	.220	.373	118	26	1	1	5	4.2	16	11	11	24	1	13	2	64	2	3	1	1.5	.957	OF-31, 1B-1
1972 MON N	113	.231	.384	372	86	12	3	13	3.5	48	47	53	75	12	10	2	801	57	6	66	7.6	.993	1B-76, OF-28
1973	138	.230	.344	413	95	16	2	9	2.2	49	47	64	49	16	13	4	1002	80	5	88	7.9	.995	1B-123, OF-11
1974	131	.310	.488	287	89	16	1	11	3.8	45	59	70	39	3	26	8	653	54	0	47	5.4	.999	1B-91, OF-29
1975	144	.261	.422	445	116	18	0	18	4.0	58	67	79	75	3	17	4	1153	91	7	123	8.7	.994	1B-133, OF-6
1976	125	.254	.382	343	87	13	0	6	1.7	36	23	52	48	7	14	0	651	58	8	59	5.7	.989	1B-81, OF-41
1977 2 teams	MON N (19G – .200)				OAK A (66G – .246)																		
" total	85	.242	.381	223	54	14	1	8	3.6	21	32	28	48	3	18	1	388	36	4	27	5.0	.991	1B-53, OF-20, DH-2
1978 TEX A	96	.196	.258	97	19	3	0	1	1.0	9	18	10	13	3	3	0	317	31	2	23	3.6	.994	1B-78, OF-9, DH-1
1979	90	.223	.382	157	35	7	0	6	3.8	21	16	14	29	0	19	2	320	31	4	28	3.9	.989	1B-60, OF-20, DH-2
1980 NY N	119	.255	.355	321	82	11	0	7	2.2	43	43	46	55	0	19	2	562	37	4	33	5.1	.993	1B-72, OF-31
1981	86	.205	.352	122	25	2	1	5	4.1	8	15	12	24	1	29	5	143	9	1	8	1.8	.993	1B-40, OF-19
1982	120	.254	.360	114	29	6	0	2	1.8	16	14	21	24	1	48	15	131	5	2	14	1.2	.986	1B-56, OF-16

Year	Team		Games	BA	SA	AB	H	2B	3B	HR	HR%	R	RBI	BB	SO	SB	Pinch Hit AB	Pinch Hit H	PO	A	E	DP	TC/G	FA	G by Pos

Mike Jorgensen *continued*

Year	Team		Games	BA	SA	AB	H	2B	3B	HR	HR%	R	RBI	BB	SO	SB	AB	H	PO	A	E	DP	TC/G	FA	G by Pos
1983	2 teams	NY N (38G – .250)				ATL	N	(57G – .250)																	
"	total		95	.250	.389	72	18	4	0	2	2.8	10	11	10	12	0	45	12	81	6	0	11	0.9	1.000	1B-38, OF-6
1984	2 teams	ATL N (31G – .269)				STL	N	(59G – .245)																	
"	total		90	.250	.347	124	31	5	2	1	0.8	9	17	13	23	0	38	10	222	19	2	30	2.7	.992	1B-47, OF-4
1985	STL	N	72	.196	.250	112	22	6	0	0	0.0	14	11	31	27	2	22	3	318	17	2	32	4.7	.994	1B-49, OF-2
17 yrs.			1633	.243	.373	3421	833	132	13	95	2.8	429	426	532	589	58	353	72	6983	546	54	602	4.6	.993	1B-1052, OF-283, DH-5

LEAGUE CHAMPIONSHIP SERIES

| 1985 | STL | N | 2 | .000 | .000 | 2 | 0 | 0 | 0 | 0 | 0.0 | 0 | 0 | 0 | 1 | 0 | 2 | 0 | 0 | 0 | 0 | 0 | 0.0 | – | |

WORLD SERIES

| 1985 | STL | N | 2 | .000 | .000 | 3 | 0 | 0 | 0 | 0 | 0.0 | 0 | 0 | 0 | 0 | 0 | 2 | 0 | 1 | 0 | 0 | 0 | 0.5 | 1.000 | OF-1 |

Pinky Jorgensen

JORGENSEN, CARL
B. Nov. 21, 1914, Laton, Calif.

BR TR 6'1" 195 lbs.

| 1937 | CIN | N | 6 | .286 | .286 | 14 | 4 | 0 | 0 | 0 | 0.0 | 1 | 1 | 1 | 2 | 0 | 1 | 0 | 6 | 1 | 1 | 0 | 1.3 | .875 | OF-4 |

Spider Jorgensen

JORGENSEN, JOHN DONALD
B. Nov. 3, 1919, Folsom, Calif.

BL TR 5'9" 155 lbs.

1947	BKN	N	129	.274	.410	441	121	29	8	5	1.1	57	67	58	45	4	1	1	116	235	19	26	2.9	.949	3B-128
1948			31	.300	.444	90	27	6	1	1	1.1	15	13	16	13	1	5	3	22	33	7	3	2.0	.887	3B-24
1949			53	.269	.343	134	36	5	1	1	0.7	15	14	23	13	0	13	2	28	59	5	5	1.7	.946	3B-36
1950	2 teams	BKN N (2G – .000)				NY	N	(24G – .135)																	
"	total		26	.128	.128	39	5	0	0	0	0.0	5	5	6	2	0	17	2	7	15	2	1	0.9	.917	3B-6
1951	NY	N	28	.235	.353	51	12	0	0	2	3.9	5	8	3	2	0	16	3	14	1	0	0	0.5	1.000	OF-11, 3B-1
5 yrs.			267	.266	.384	755	201	40	11	9	1.2	97	107	106	75	5	52	11	187	343	33	35	2.1	.941	3B-195, OF-11

WORLD SERIES

1947	BKN	N	7	.200	.300	20	4	2	0	0	0.0	1	3	2	4	0	0	0	8	12	2	1	3.1	.909	3B-7
1949			4	.182	.364	11	2	2	0	0	0.0	1	0	2	0	0	1	0	1	6	0	0	1.8	1.000	3B-3
2 yrs.			11	.194	.323	31	6	4	0	0	0.0	2	3	4	4	0	1	0	9	18	2	1	2.6	.931	3B-10

Terry Jorgensen

JORGENSEN, TERRY ALLEN
B. Sept. 2, 1966, Kewaunee, Wis.

BR TR 6'4" 208 lbs.

| 1989 | MIN | A | 10 | .174 | .217 | 23 | 4 | 1 | 0 | 0 | 0.0 | 1 | 2 | 4 | 5 | 0 | 0 | 0 | 4 | 19 | 1 | 3 | 2.4 | .958 | 3B-9 |

Felix Jose

JOSE, DOMINGO FELIX
B. May 8, 1965, Santo Domingo, Dominican Republic

BB TR 6'1" 190 lbs.

1988	OAK	A	8	.333	.500	6	2	1	0	0	0.0	2	1	0	1	1	2	0	8	0	0	0	1.0	1.000	OF-6
1989			20	.193	.228	57	11	2	0	0	0.0	3	5	4	13	0	3	1	35	2	1	0	1.9	.974	OF-19
2 yrs.			28	.206	.254	63	13	3	0	0	0.0	5	6	4	14	1	5	1	43	2	1	0	1.6	.978	OF-25

Rick Joseph

JOSEPH, RICARDO EMELINDO
B. Aug. 24, 1939, San Pedro de Macoris, Dominican Republic
D. Sept. 8, 1979, Santo Domingo, Dominican Republic

BR TR 6'1" 192 lbs.

1964	KC	A	17	.222	.259	54	12	2	0	0	0.0	3	3	1	11	0	4	0	102	12	5	14	7.0	.958	1B-12, 3B-3
1967	PHI	N	17	.220	.341	41	9	2	0	1	2.4	4	5	4	10	0	5	1	94	9	0	7	6.1	1.000	1B-13
1968			66	.219	.310	155	34	5	0	3	1.9	20	12	16	35	0	24	7	256	38	5	24	4.5	.983	1B-30, 3B-14, OF-1
1969			99	.273	.398	264	72	15	0	6	2.3	35	37	22	57	2	25	3	162	112	11	21	2.9	.961	3B-58, 1B-17, 2B-1
1970			71	.227	.336	119	27	2	1	3	2.5	7	10	6	28	0	37	11	68	8	5	5	1.1	.938	OF-12, 1B-10, 3B-9
5 yrs.			270	.243	.349	633	154	26	1	13	2.1	69	65	51	141	2	95	22	682	179	26	71	3.3	.971	3B-84, 1B-82, OF-13, 2B-1

Duane Josephson

JOSEPHSON, DUANE CHARLES
B. June 3, 1942, New Hampton, Iowa

BR TR 6' 190 lbs.

1965	CHI	A	4	.111	.111	9	1	0	0	0	0.0	2	0	2	4	0	0	0	21	1	0	0	5.5	1.000	C-4
1966			11	.237	.263	38	9	1	0	0	0.0	3	3	3	3	0	0	0	66	8	2	1	6.9	.974	C-11
1967			62	.238	.291	189	45	5	1	1	0.5	11	9	6	24	0	5	0	292	24	0	3	5.1	1.000	C-59
1968			128	.247	.353	434	107	16	6	4	0.9	35	45	18	52	2	11	3	641	86	7	15	5.7	.990	C-122
1969			52	.241	.321	162	39	6	2	1	0.6	19	20	13	17	0	7	3	227	27	4	1	5.0	.984	C-47
1970			96	.316	.407	285	90	12	1	4	1.4	28	41	24	28	1	14	5	353	38	6	7	4.1	.985	C-84
1971	BOS	A	91	.245	.395	306	75	14	1	10	3.3	38	39	22	35	2	5	1	491	32	6	5	5.8	.989	C-87
1972			26	.268	.378	82	22	4	1	1	1.2	11	7	4	11	0	4	1	155	9	3	8	6.4	.982	1B-16, C-6
8 yrs.			470	.258	.358	1505	388	58	12	23	1.5	147	164	92	174	5	46	13	2246	225	28	40	5.3	.989	C-420, 1B-16

Von Joshua

JOSHUA, VON EVERETT
B. May 1, 1948, Oakland, Calif.

BL TL 5'10" 170 lbs.

1969	LA	N	14	.250	.250	8	2	0	0	0	0.0	0	2	1	1	0	1	0	4	0	1	0	0.4	.800	OF-8
1970			72	.266	.358	109	29	1	3	1	0.9	23	8	6	24	2	21	5	47	1	3	1	0.7	.941	OF-41
1971			11	.000	.000	7	0	0	0	0	0.0	2	0	1	0	0	5	0	7	0	0	0	0.6	1.000	OF-5
1973			75	.252	.327	159	40	4	1	2	1.3	19	17	8	29	7	25	8	61	2	1	0	0.9	.984	OF-46
1974			81	.234	.315	124	29	5	1	1	0.8	11	16	7	17	3	45	8	33	0	2	0	0.4	.943	OF-35
1975	SF	N	129	.318	.448	507	161	25	10	7	1.4	75	43	32	75	20	11	4	279	10	2	3	2.3	.993	OF-117
1976	2 teams	SF N (42G – .263)				MIL	A	(107G – .267)																	
"	total		149	.266	.347	579	154	18	7	5	0.9	57	30	22	78	9	10	3	338	13	9	5	2.4	.975	OF-140, DH-1
1977	MIL	A	144	.261	.384	536	140	25	7	9	1.7	58	49	21	74	12	12	1	311	8	10	4	2.3	.970	OF-140
1979	LA	N	94	.282	.408	142	40	7	1	3	2.1	22	14	7	23	1	48	9	56	2	2	0	0.6	.967	OF-46
1980	SD	N	53	.238	.397	63	15	2	1	2	3.2	8	7	5	15	0	39	9	26	1	0	1	0.5	1.000	OF-12, 1B-2
10 yrs.			822	.273	.380	2234	610	87	31	30	1.3	277	184	108	338	55	217	47	1162	37	30	10	1.5	.976	OF-590, 1B-2, DH-1

LEAGUE CHAMPIONSHIP SERIES

| 1974 | LA | N | 1 | – | – | 0 | 0 | 0 | 0 | 0 | – | 0 | 0 | 0 | 0 | 0 | 0 | 0 | 0 | 0 | 0 | 0 | 0.0 | – | |

Year	Team		Games	BA	SA	AB	H	2B	3B	HR	HR%	R	RBI	BB	SO	SB	Pinch Hit AB	H	PO	A	E	DP	TC/G	FA	G by Pos

Von Joshua *continued*
WORLD SERIES

| 1974 | LA | N | 4 | .000 | .000 | 4 | 0 | 0 | 0 | 0 | 0.0 | 0 | 0 | 0 | 0 | 0 | 4 | 0 | 0 | 0 | 0 | 0 | 0.0 | – | |

Ted Jourdan

JOURDAN, THEODORE CHARLES
B. Sept. 5, 1895, New Orleans, La. D. Sept. 23, 1961, New Orleans, La.   BL TL 6'   175 lbs.

1916	CHI	A	3	.000	.000	2	0	0	0	0	0.0	0	0	1	1	2	1	0	0	0	0	0	0.0	–	
1917			17	.147	.206	34	5	0	1	0	0.0	2	2	1	3	0	3	0	68	5	2	2	4.4	.973	1B-14
1918			7	.100	.100	10	1	0	0	0	0.0	1	1	0	0	0	5	1	12	0	0	0	1.7	1.000	1B-2
1920			48	.240	.293	150	36	6	1	0	0.0	16	8	17	17	3	8	1	369	18	7	35	8.2	.982	1B-40
4 yrs.			75	.214	.265	196	42	6	2	0	0.0	19	11	19	21	5	18	2	449	23	9	37	6.4	.981	1B-56

Pop Joy

JOY, ALOYSIUS C.
B. June 11, 1860, Washington, D. C. D. June 28, 1937, Washington, D. C.

| 1884 | WAS | U | 36 | .215 | .215 | 130 | 28 | 0 | 0 | 0 | 0.0 | 12 | | 2 | | | 0 | 0 | 331 | 7 | 12 | 14 | 9.7 | .966 | 1B-36 |

Joyce

JOYCE,
Deceased.

| 1886 | WAS | N | 1 | – | – | 0 | 0 | 0 | 0 | 0 | – | 0 | 0 | 0 | 0 | | 0 | 0 | 0 | 0 | 0 | 0 | 0.0 | – | OF-1 |

Bill Joyce

JOYCE, WILLIAM MICHAEL (Scrappy Bill)
B. Sept. 21, 1865, St. Louis, Mo. D. May 8, 1941, St. Louis, Mo.   BL TR 5'11"   185 lbs.
Manager 1896-98.

1890	BKN	P	133	.252	.368	489	123	18	18	1	0.2	121	78	123	77	43	0	0	176	284	107	22	4.3	.811	3B-133
1891	BOS	AA	65	.309	.506	243	75	9	15	3	1.2	76	51	63	27	36	0	0	90	149	41	12	4.3	.854	3B-64, 1B-1
1892	BKN	N	97	.245	.398	372	91	15	12	6	1.6	89	45	82	55	23	0	0	148	164	50	8	3.7	.862	3B-94, OF-3
1894	WAS	N	99	.355	.648	355	126	25	14	17	4.8	103	89	87	33	21	0	0	152	183	52	20	3.9	.866	3B-99
1895			126	.312	.527	474	148	25	13	17	3.6	110	95	96	54	29	0	0	186	232	77	16	3.9	.844	3B-126
1896	2 teams		WAS	N	(81G – .313)		NY	N	(49G – .370)																
"	total		130	.333	.524	475	158	25	12	14	2.9	121	94	101	34	45	0	0	205	296	62	22	4.3	.890	3B-97, 2B-33
1897	NY	N	109	.304	.433	388	118	15	13	3	0.8	109	64	78		33	0	0	187	199	66	19	4.1	.854	3B-106, 1B-2
1898			145	.258	.392	508	131	20	9	10	2.0	91	91	88		34	0	0	1271	121	54	73	10.0	.963	1B-130, 3B-14, 2B-2
8 yrs.			904	.294	.468	3304	970	152	106	71	2.1	820	607	718	280	264	0	0	2415	1628	509	192	5.0	.888	3B-733, 1B-133, 2B-35, OF-3

Mike Joyce

Playing record listed under Mike O'Neill

Wally Joyner

JOYNER, WALLACE KEITH (Wally World)
B. June 16, 1962, Atlanta, Ga.   BL TL 6'2"   185 lbs.

1986	CAL	A	154	.290	.457	593	172	27	3	22	3.7	82	100	57	58	5	4	1	1222	139	15	128	8.9	.989	1B-152
1987			149	.285	.528	564	161	33	1	34	6.0	100	117	72	64	8	2	0	1276	92	10	133	9.2	.993	1B-149
1988			158	.295	.419	597	176	31	2	13	2.2	81	85	55	51	8	4	2	1369	143	8	148	9.6	.995	1B-156
1989			159	.282	.420	593	167	30	2	16	2.7	78	79	46	58	3	2	1	1487	99	4	146	10.0	.997	1B-159
4 yrs.			620	.288	.455	2347	676	121	8	85	3.6	341	381	230	231	24	12	4	5354	473	37	555	9.5	.994	1B-616

LEAGUE CHAMPIONSHIP SERIES

| 1986 | CAL | A | 3 | .455 | .909 | 11 | 5 | 2 | 0 | 1 | 9.1 | 3 | 2 | 2 | 0 | 0 | 0 | 0 | 26 | 1 | 0 | 2 | 9.0 | 1.000 | 1B-3 |

Oscar Judd

JUDD, THOMAS WILLIAM OSCAR (Ossie)
B. Feb. 14, 1908, London, Ontario, Canada   BL TL 6'½"   180 lbs.

1941	BOS	A	10	.500	.750	4	2	1	0	0	0.0	2	2	3	0	0	1	0	0	4	1	0	0.5	.800	P-7
1942			36	.269	.418	67	18	2	1	2	3.0	10	4	3	7	0	5	1	6	29	1	1	1.0	.972	P-31
1943			27	.259	.315	54	14	1	1	0	0.0	2	0	5	4	0	2	0	9	41	3	4	2.0	.943	P-23
1944			10	.182	.182	11	2	0	0	0	0.0	4	1	3	0	0	1	0	1	4	0	0	0.5	1.000	P-9
1945	2 teams		BOS	A	(2G – .500)		PHI	N	(27G – .267)																
"	total		29	.281	.344	32	9	2	0	0	0.0	4	2	4	4	0	3	0	4	23	0	0	0.9	1.000	P-25
1946	PHI	N	46	.316	.405	79	25	2	1	1	1.3	7	8	4	4	0	14	2	10	50	0	0	1.3	1.000	P-30
1947			44	.188	.281	64	12	2	0	0	0.0	6	2	4	16	0	10	2	7	33	1	3	0.9	.976	P-32
1948			4	.167	.333	6	1	0	0	0	0.0	1	0	1	2	0	0	0	1	2	1	0	1.0	.750	P-4
8 yrs.			206	.262	.356	317	83	11	5	3	0.9	36	19	27	37	0	36	5	38	186	7	8	1.1	.970	P-161

Frank Jude

JUDE, FRANK
B. 1884, Libby, Minn. D. May 4, 1961, Brownsville, Tex.   BR TR 5'7"   150 lbs.

| 1906 | CIN | N | 80 | .208 | .263 | 308 | 64 | 6 | 4 | 1 | 0.3 | 31 | 31 | 16 | | 7 | 0 | 0 | 95 | 14 | 4 | 1 | 1.4 | .965 | OF-80 |

Joe Judge

JUDGE, JOSEPH IGNATIUS
B. May 25, 1894, Brooklyn, N. Y. D. Mar. 11, 1963, Washington, D. C.   BL TL 5'8½"   155 lbs.

1915	WAS	A	12	.415	.463	41	17	2	0	0	0.0	7	9	4	6	2	0	0	97	5	1	7	8.6	.990	1B-10, OF-2
1916			103	.220	.298	336	74	10	8	0	0.0	42	31	54	44	18	0	0	935	69	14	53	9.9	.986	1B-103
1917			102	.285	.415	393	112	15	15	2	0.5	62	50	40	40	17	0	0	906	60	12	59	9.6	.988	1B-100
1918			130	.261	.341	502	131	23	7	1	0.2	56	46	49	32	20	0	0	1304	92	21	71	10.9	.985	1B-130
1919			135	.288	.409	521	150	33	12	2	0.4	83	31	81	35	23	2	0	1177	78	15	66	9.4	.988	1B-133
1920			126	.333	.462	493	164	19	15	5	1.0	103	51	65	34	12	0	0	1194	62	10	67	10.0	.992	1B-124
1921			153	.301	.412	622	187	26	11	7	1.1	87	72	68	35	21	0	0	1417	89	6	109	9.9	.996	1B-152
1922			148	.294	.450	591	174	32	15	10	1.7	84	81	50	20	5	1	1	1413	101	6	131	10.3	.996	1B-148
1923			113	.314	.417	405	127	24	6	2	0.5	56	63	58	20	11	1	0	1070	88	8	113	10.3	.993	1B-112
1924			140	.324	.450	516	167	38	9	8	1.6	71	79	53	21	13	0	0	1276	86	8	108	9.8	.994	1B-140
1925			112	.314	.487	376	118	31	5	8	2.1	65	66	55	21	7	2	0	901	71	7	92	8.7	.993	1B-109
1926			134	.291	.442	453	132	25	11	7	1.5	70	92	53	25	6	3	0	1145	95	8	90	9.3	.994	1B-128
1927			137	.308	.418	522	161	29	11	2	0.4	68	71	45	22	10	1	0	1309	71	6	79	10.1	.996	1B-136

Year	Team	Games	BA	SA	AB	H	2B	3B	HR	HR%	R	RBI	BB	SO	SB	Pinch Hit AB	Pinch Hit H	PO	A	E	DP	TC/G	FA	G by Pos

Joe Judge *continued*

Year	Team	Games	BA	SA	AB	H	2B	3B	HR	HR%	R	RBI	BB	SO	SB	PH AB	PH H	PO	A	E	DP	TC/G	FA	G by Pos
1928		153	.306	.417	542	166	31	10	3	0.6	78	93	80	19	16	3	1	1412	92	6	118	9.9	.996	1B-149
1929		143	.315	.442	543	171	35	8	6	1.1	83	71	73	33	12	1	0	1323	88	6	116	9.9	.996	1B-142
1930		126	.326	.509	442	144	29	11	10	2.3	83	80	60	29	13	9	3	1050	67	2	95	8.9	.996	1B-117
1931		35	.284	.324	74	21	3	0	0	0.0	11	9	8	8	0	18	4	155	10	1	9	4.7	.994	1B-15
1932		82	.258	.364	291	75	16	3	3	1.0	45	29	37	19	3	4	0	668	46	2	71	8.7	.997	1B-78
1933 2 teams	BKN	N (42G – .214)		BOS	A	(35G – .296)																		
" total		77	.255	.318	220	56	10	2	0	0.0	27	31	20	14	3	18	4	502	29	3	45	6.9	.994	1B-56
1934 BOS	A	10	.333	.467	15	5	2	0	0	0.0	3	2	2	1	0	8	2	24	1	0	1	2.5	1.000	1B-2
20 yrs.		2171	.298	.420	7898	2352	433	159	71	0.9	1184	1037	965	478	213	75	18	19278	1300	142	1500	9.5	.993	1B-2084, OF-2

WORLD SERIES

Year	Team	Games	BA	SA	AB	H	2B	3B	HR	HR%	R	RBI	BB	SO	SB	PH AB	PH H	PO	A	E	DP	TC/G	FA	G by Pos
1924 WAS	A	7	.385	.423	26	10	1	0	0	0.0	4	0	5	2	0	0	0	62	4	1	8	9.6	.985	1B-7
1925		7	.174	.348	23	4	1	0	1	4.3	2	4	3	2	0	0	0	59	2	0	8	8.7	1.000	1B-7
2 yrs.		14	.286	.388	49	14	2	0	1	2.0	6	4	8	4	0	0	0	121	6	1	16	9.1	.992	1B-14

Walt Judnich

JUDNICH, WALTER FRANKLIN
B. Jan. 24, 1917, San Francisco, Calif.　D. July 12, 1971, Glendale, Calif.　　BL TL 6'1" 205 lbs.

Year	Team	Games	BA	SA	AB	H	2B	3B	HR	HR%	R	RBI	BB	SO	SB	PH AB	PH H	PO	A	E	DP	TC/G	FA	G by Pos
1940 STL	A	137	.303	.520	519	157	27	7	24	4.6	97	89	54	57	8	4	1	356	7	4	4	2.7	.989	OF-133
1941		146	.284	.456	546	155	40	4	14	2.6	90	83	80	45	5	6	3	383	11	8	3	2.8	.980	OF-140
1942		132	.313	.499	457	143	22	6	17	3.7	78	82	74	41	3	9	4	330	4	3	0	2.6	.991	OF-122
1946		142	.262	.411	511	134	23	4	15	2.9	60	72	60	54	0	3	0	409	6	2	2	2.9	.995	OF-137
1947		144	.258	.426	500	129	24	3	18	3.6	58	64	60	62	2	1	1	1105	77	13	118	8.3	.989	1B-129, OF-15
1948 CLE	A	79	.257	.372	218	56	13	3	2	0.9	36	29	56	23	2	10	2	240	11	4	19	3.2	.984	OF-49, 1B-20
1949 PIT	N	10	.229	.257	35	8	1	0	0	0.0	5	1	1	2	0	2	0	27	0	0	0	2.7	1.000	OF-8
7 yrs.		790	.281	.452	2786	782	150	29	90	3.2	424	420	385	298	20	36	11	2850	116	34	146	3.8	.989	OF-604, 1B-149

WORLD SERIES

Year	Team	Games	BA	SA	AB	H	2B	3B	HR	HR%	R	RBI	BB	SO	SB	PH AB	PH H	PO	A	E	DP	TC/G	FA	G by Pos
1948 CLE	A	4	.077	.077	13	1	0	0	0	0.0	1	1	1	4	0	0	0	7	0	0	0	1.8	1.000	OF-4

Lyle Judy

JUDY, LYLE LeROY (Punch)
B. Nov. 15, 1913, Lawrenceville, Ill.　　BR TR 5'10" 150 lbs.

Year	Team	Games	BA	SA	AB	H	2B	3B	HR	HR%	R	RBI	BB	SO	SB	PH AB	PH H	PO	A	E	DP	TC/G	FA	G by Pos
1935 STL	N	8	.000	.000	11	0	0	0	0	0.0	2	0	2	2	2	0	0	9	7	0	2	2.0	1.000	2B-5

Red Juelich

JUELICH, JOHN SAMUEL
B. Sept. 20, 1916, St. Louis, Mo.　D. Dec. 25, 1970, St. Louis, Mo.　　BR TR 5'11½" 168 lbs.

Year	Team	Games	BA	SA	AB	H	2B	3B	HR	HR%	R	RBI	BB	SO	SB	PH AB	PH H	PO	A	E	DP	TC/G	FA	G by Pos
1939 PIT	N	17	.239	.326	46	11	2	0	0	0.0	5	4	2	4	0	3	0	21	24	3	5	2.8	.938	2B-10, 3B-2

George Jumonville

JUMONVILLE, GEORGE BENEDICT
B. May 16, 1917, Mobile, Ala.　　BR TR 6' 175 lbs.

Year	Team	Games	BA	SA	AB	H	2B	3B	HR	HR%	R	RBI	BB	SO	SB	PH AB	PH H	PO	A	E	DP	TC/G	FA	G by Pos
1940 PHI	N	11	.088	.088	34	3	0	0	0	0.0	0	0	1	6	0	0	0	20	21	2	3	3.9	.953	SS-10, 3B-1
1941		6	.429	.857	7	3	0	0	1	14.3	1	2	0	0	0	3	2	1	4	0	0	0.8	1.000	SS-1, 2B-1
2 yrs.		17	.146	.220	41	6	0	0	1	2.4	1	2	1	6	0	3	2	21	25	2	3	2.8	.958	SS-11, 3B-1, 2B-1

Ed Jurak

JURAK, EDWARD JAMES (Lizard)
B. Oct. 24, 1957, Hollywood, Calif.　　BR TR 6'2" 185 lbs.

Year	Team	Games	BA	SA	AB	H	2B	3B	HR	HR%	R	RBI	BB	SO	SB	PH AB	PH H	PO	A	E	DP	TC/G	FA	G by Pos
1982 BOS	A	12	.333	.333	21	7	0	0	0	0.0	3	7	2	4	0	0	0	7	17	2	1	2.2	.923	3B-11, OF-1
1983		75	.277	.377	159	44	8	4	0	0.0	19	18	18	25	1	4	2	197	117	11	34	4.3	.966	SS-38, 1B-19, 3B-12, DH-5, 2B-1
1984		47	.242	.364	66	16	3	1	1	1.5	6	7	12	12	0	3	1	92	40	3	20	2.9	.978	1B-19, 2B-14, 3B-9, SS-2
1985		26	.231	.231	13	3	0	0	0	0.0	4	0	1	3	0	3	0	5	10	2	0	0.7	.882	3B-7, SS-3, DH-2, OF-1, 1B-1
1988 OAK	A	3	.000	.000	1	0	0	0	0	0.0	1	0	0	0	0	1	0	0	0	0	0	0.0	–	3B-1
1989 SF	N	30	.238	.238	42	10	0	0	0	0.0	2	1	5	5	0	18	4	20	17	5	2	1.4	.881	SS-6, 3B-5, 2B-4, OF-2, 1B-1
6 yrs.		193	.265	.344	302	80	11	5	1	0.3	35	33	38	49	1	29	7	321	201	23	57	2.8	.958	SS-49, 3B-45, 1B-40, 2B-19, DH-7, OF-4

Bill Jurges

JURGES, WILLIAM FREDERICK
B. May 9, 1908, Bronx, N. Y.
Manager 1959-60.　　BR TR 5'11" 175 lbs.

Year	Team	Games	BA	SA	AB	H	2B	3B	HR	HR%	R	RBI	BB	SO	SB	PH AB	PH H	PO	A	E	DP	TC/G	FA	G by Pos
1931 CHI	N	88	.201	.287	293	59	15	5	0	0.0	34	23	25	41	2	1	0	113	202	11	32	3.7	.966	3B-54, 2B-33, SS-3
1932		115	.253	.348	396	100	24	4	2	0.5	40	52	19	26	1	1	0	227	401	23	70	5.7	.965	SS-103, 3B-5
1933		143	.269	.359	487	131	17	6	5	1.0	49	50	26	39	3	0	0	298	476	34	95	5.7	.958	SS-143
1934		100	.246	.366	358	88	15	2	8	2.2	43	33	19	34	1	0	0	205	334	19	63	5.6	.966	SS-98
1935		146	.241	.314	519	125	33	1	1	0.2	69	59	42	39	3	0	0	348	484	31	99	5.9	.964	SS-146
1936		118	.280	.350	429	120	25	-1	1	0.2	51	42	23	25	4	0	0	249	379	26	80	5.5	.960	SS-116
1937		129	.298	.389	450	134	18	10	1	0.2	53	65	42	41	2	0	0	258	370	16	74	5.0	.975	SS-128
1938		137	.245	.303	465	114	18	3	1	0.2	53	47	58	53	3	0	0	277	417	34	82	5.3	.953	SS-136
1939 NY	N	138	.285	.398	543	155	21	11	6	1.1	84	63	47	34	3	0	0	295	482	28	95	5.8	.965	SS-137
1940		63	.252	.322	214	54	3	3	2	0.9	23	36	25	14	2	0	0	123	196	11	36	5.2	.967	SS-63
1941		134	.293	.386	471	138	25	2	5	1.1	50	61	47	36	1	1	0	230	432	30	82	5.2	.957	SS-134
1942		127	.256	.289	464	119	7	1	2	0.4	45	30	43	42	1	3	1	251	401	15	67	5.3	.978	SS-124
1943		136	.229	.279	481	110	8	2	4	0.8	46	29	53	38	2	0	0	236	359	25	54	4.6	.960	SS-99, 3B-28
1944		85	.211	.240	246	52	2	1	1	0.4	28	23	23	20	1	14	2	64	149	8	13	2.6	.964	SS-61, SS-10, 2B-1
1945		61	.324	.403	176	57	3	1	3	1.7	22	24	24	11	1	7	2	55	116	10	4	3.0	.945	3B-44, SS-8
1946 CHI	N	82	.222	.281	221	49	9	2	0	0.0	26	17	43	28	1	0	0	127	212	8	26	4.2	.977	SS-73, 3B-7, 2B-2
1947		14	.200	.325	40	8	2	0	1	2.5	9	9	9	9	0	1	0	13	36	4	10	3.8	.925	SS-14
17 yrs.		1816	.258	.335	6253	1613	245	55	43	0.7	721	656	568	530	36	36	9	3369	5446	333	982	5.0	.964	SS-1535, 3B-199, 2B-36

WORLD SERIES

Year	Team	Games	BA	SA	AB	H	2B	3B	HR	HR%	R	RBI	BB	SO	SB	PH AB	PH H	PO	A	E	DP	TC/G	FA	G by Pos
1932 CHI	N	3	.364	.455	11	4	1	0	0	0.0	1	1	0	1	0	0	0	12	8	2	5	7.3	.909	SS-3
1935		6	.250	.250	16	4	0	0	0	0.0	3	1	4	4	0	0	0	16	15	1	4	5.3	.969	SS-6

Year	Team		Games	BA	SA	AB	H	2B	3B	HR	HR%	R	RBI	BB	SO	SB	Pinch Hit AB	H	PO	A	E	DP	TC/G	FA	G by Pos

Bill Jurges *continued*

Year	Team		Games	BA	SA	AB	H	2B	3B	HR	HR%	R	RBI	BB	SO	SB	AB	H	PO	A	E	DP	TC/G	FA	G by Pos
1938			4	.231	.308	13	3	1	0	0	0.0	0	0	1	3	0	0	0	11	7	1	2	4.8	.947	SS-4
3 yrs.			13	.275	.325	40	11	2	0	0	0.0	4	2	5	8	1	0	0	39	30	4	11	5.6	.945	SS-13

Joe Just   JUST, JOSEPH ERWIN   BR TR 5'11" 185 lbs.
Born Joseph Erwin Juszczak.
B. Jan. 8, 1916, Milwaukee, Wis.

Year	Team		Games	BA	SA	AB	H	2B	3B	HR	HR%	R	RBI	BB	SO	SB	AB	H	PO	A	E	DP	TC/G	FA	G by Pos
1944	CIN	N	11	.182	.182	11	2	0	0	0	0.0	0	0	0	2	0	1	0	12	0	1	0	1.2	.923	C-10
1945			14	.147	.147	34	5	0	0	0	0.0	2	2	4	7	0	0	0	31	5	2	0	2.7	.947	C-14
2 yrs.			25	.156	.156	45	7	0	0	0	0.0	2	2	4	9	0	1	0	43	5	3	0	2.0	.941	C-24

Dave Justice   JUSTICE, DAVID CHRISTOPHER   BL TL 6'3" 195 lbs.
B. Apr. 14, 1966, Cincinnati, Ohio

Year	Team		Games	BA	SA	AB	H	2B	3B	HR	HR%	R	RBI	BB	SO	SB	AB	H	PO	A	E	DP	TC/G	FA	G by Pos
1989	ATL	N	16	.235	.353	51	12	3	0	1	2.0	7	3	9	2	2	0	0	24	0	0	0	1.5	1.000	OF-16

Skip Jutze   JUTZE, ALFRED HENRY   BR TR 5'11" 190 lbs.
B. May 28, 1946, Queens, N. Y.

Year	Team		Games	BA	SA	AB	H	2B	3B	HR	HR%	R	RBI	BB	SO	SB	AB	H	PO	A	E	DP	TC/G	FA	G by Pos
1972	STL	N	21	.239	.268	71	17	2	0	0	0.0	5	1	16		0	4	0	93	15	4	1	5.3	.964	C-17
1973	HOU	N	90	.223	.245	278	62	6	0	0	0.0	18	18	19	37	0	3	0	450	31	8	4	5.4	.984	C-86
1974			8	.231	.231	13	3	0	0	0	0.0	0	1	1	1	0	0	0	16	2	0	0	2.3	1.000	C-7
1975			51	.226	.247	93	21	2	0	0	0.0	9	6	2	4	1	2	0	147	15	2	3	3.2	.988	C-47
1976			42	.152	.239	92	14	2	3	0	0.0	7	6	4	16	0	2	1	125	21	2	5	3.5	.986	C-42
1977	SEA	A	42	.220	.321	109	24	2	0	3	2.8	10	15	7	12	0	3	0	170	15	3	3	4.5	.984	C-40
6 yrs.			254	.215	.259	656	141	14	3	3	0.5	45	51	34	86	1	14	1	1001	99	19	16	4.4	.983	C-239

Jack Kading   KADING, JOHN FREDERICK   BR TR 6'3" 190 lbs.
B. Nov. 27, 1884, Waukesha, Wis.   D. June 2, 1964, Chicago, Ill.

Year	Team		Games	BA	SA	AB	H	2B	3B	HR	HR%	R	RBI	BB	SO	SB	AB	H	PO	A	E	DP	TC/G	FA	G by Pos
1910	PIT	N	8	.304	.478	23	7	2	1	0	0.0	5	4	4	5	0	0	0	70	7	0	5	9.6	1.000	1B-8
1914	CHI	F	3	.000	.000	3	0	0	0	0	0.0	0	0	0	0	0	3	0	0	0	0	0	—		1B-8
2 yrs.			11	.269	.423	26	7	2	1	0	0.0	5	4	4	5	0	3	0	70	7	0	5	7.0	1.000	1B-8

Jake Kafora   KAFORA, FRANK JACOB (Tomatoes)   BR TR 6' 180 lbs.
B. Oct. 16, 1888, Chicago, Ill.   D. Mar. 23, 1928, Chicago, Ill.

Year	Team		Games	BA	SA	AB	H	2B	3B	HR	HR%	R	RBI	BB	SO	SB	AB	H	PO	A	E	DP	TC/G	FA	G by Pos
1913	PIT	N	1	.000	.000	1	0	0	0	0	0.0	1	0	1		0	0	0	1	0	0	0	1.0	1.000	C-1
1914			21	.130	.130	23	3	0	0	0	0.0	2	0	5	7	0	3	0	27	5	0	0	1.5	1.000	C-17
2 yrs.			22	.125	.125	24	3	0	0	0	0.0	3	0	6	7	0	3	0	28	5	0	0	1.5	1.000	C-18

Ike Kahdot   KAHDOT, ISAAC LEONARD (Chief)   BR TR 5'5½" 145 lbs.
B. Oct. 22, 1901, Georgetown, Okla.

Year	Team		Games	BA	SA	AB	H	2B	3B	HR	HR%	R	RBI	BB	SO	SB	AB	H	PO	A	E	DP	TC/G	FA	G by Pos
1922	CLE	A	4	.000	.000	2	0	0	0	0	0.0	0	0	1	0	0	0	0	1	2	0	1	0.8	1.000	3B-2

Nick Kahl   KAHL, NICHOLAS ALEXANDER   BR TR 5'9" 185 lbs.
B. Apr. 10, 1879, Coulterville, Ill.   D. July 13, 1959, Sparta, Ill.

Year	Team		Games	BA	SA	AB	H	2B	3B	HR	HR%	R	RBI	BB	SO	SB	AB	H	PO	A	E	DP	TC/G	FA	G by Pos
1905	CLE	A	39	.221	.267	131	29	4	1	0	0.0	16	21	4		1	6	1	62	95	10	3	4.3	.940	2B-31, OF-1, SS-1

Bob Kahle   KAHLE, ROBERT WAYNE   BR TR 6' 170 lbs.
B. Nov. 23, 1915, Newcastle, Ind.   D. Dec. 16, 1988, Inglewood, Calif.

Year	Team		Games	BA	SA	AB	H	2B	3B	HR	HR%	R	RBI	BB	SO	SB	AB	H	PO	A	E	DP	TC/G	FA	G by Pos
1938	BOS	N	8	.333	.333	3	1	0	0	0	0.0	2	0	0	0	0	3	1	0	0	0	0	0.0	—	

Owen Kahn   KAHN, OWEN EARLE (Jack)   BR TR 5'11" 160 lbs.
B. June 5, 1905, Richmond, Va.   D. Jan. 17, 1981, Richmond, Va.

Year	Team		Games	BA	SA	AB	H	2B	3B	HR	HR%	R	RBI	BB	SO	SB	AB	H	PO	A	E	DP	TC/G	FA	G by Pos
1930	BOS	N	1	.—	.—	0	0	0	0	0	—	1	0	0	0	0	0	0	0	0	0	0	0.0	—	

Mike Kahoe   KAHOE, MICHAEL JOSEPH   BR TR 6' 185 lbs.
B. Sept. 3, 1873, Yellow Springs, Ohio   D. May 14, 1949, Akron, Ohio

Year	Team		Games	BA	SA	AB	H	2B	3B	HR	HR%	R	RBI	BB	SO	SB	AB	H	PO	A	E	DP	TC/G	FA	G by Pos
1895	CIN	N	3	.000	.000	4	0	0	0	0	0.0	0	0	0		0	0	0	2	0	0	0	0.7	1.000	C-3
1899			14	.167	.238	42	7	1	1	0	0.0	2	4	0		1	1	0	48	18	3	3	4.9	.957	C-13
1900			52	.189	.257	175	33	3	3	1	0.6	18	9	4		3	0	0	207	80	15	6	5.8	.950	C-51, SS-1
1901	2 teams		CIN	N	(4G – .308)			CHI	N	(67G – .224)															
"	total		71	.228	.304	250	57	12	2	1	0.4	21	21	9		5	0	0	418	81	17	11	7.3	.967	C-67, 1B-6
1902	2 teams		CHI	N	(7G – .222)			STL	A	(55G – .244)															
"	total		62	.242	.335	215	52	10	2	2	0.9	21	30	6		4	2	1	231	59	13	5	4.9	.957	C-57, 3B-2, SS-1
1903	STL	A	77	.189	.258	244	46	7	5	0	0.0	26	23	11		1	4	0	333	64	12	8	5.3	.971	C-71, OF-2
1904			72	.216	.250	236	51	6	1	0	0.0	9	12	8		4	2	0	307	91	13	9	5.7	.968	C-72
1905	PHI	N	16	.255	.294	51	13	2	0	0	0.0	2	4	1		1	0	0	58	20	2	2	5.0	.975	C-15
1907	2 teams		CHI	N	(5G – .400)			WAS	A	(17G – .191)															
"	total		22	.228	.246	57	13	1	0	0	0.0	3	2	0		0	3	1	70	20	2	2	4.2	.978	C-18, 1B-1
1908	WAS	A	17	.185	.222	27	5	1	0	0	0.0	1	0	0		0	6	1	51	7	1	1	3.5	.983	C-11
1909			4	.125	.125	8	1	0	0	0	0.0	0	0	0		0	2	1	9	4	2	0	3.8	.867	C-3
11 yrs.			410	.212	.276	1309	278	43	14	4	0.3	103	105	39		21	20	3	1734	444	80	41	5.5	.965	C-378, 1B-7, OF-2, SS-2, 3B-2

Al Kaiser   KAISER, ALFRED EDWARD (Deerfoot)   BR TR 5'9" 165 lbs.
B. Aug. 3, 1886, Cincinnati, Ohio   D. Apr. 11, 1969, Cincinnati, Ohio

Year	Team		Games	BA	SA	AB	H	2B	3B	HR	HR%	R	RBI	BB	SO	SB	AB	H	PO	A	E	DP	TC/G	FA	G by Pos
1911	2 teams		CHI	N	(27G – .250)			BOS	N	(65G – .203)															
"	total		92	.217	.306	281	61	5	7	2	0.7	36	22	17	38	10	10	2	136	9	13	3	1.7	.918	OF-81
1912	BOS	N	4	.000	.000	13	0	0	0	0	0.0	0	0	0	3	0	0	0	8	1	1	0	2.5	.900	OF-4
1914	IND	F	59	.230	.299	187	43	10	0	1	0.5	22	16	17		6	7	2	107	4	13	0	2.1	.895	OF-50, 1B-1
3 yrs.			155	.216	.295	481	104	15	7	3	0.6	58	38	34	41	16	17	4	251	14	27	3	1.9	.908	OF-135, 1B-1

Year	Team	Games	BA	SA	AB	H	2B	3B	HR	HR%	R	RBI	BB	SO	SB	Pinch Hit AB	Pinch Hit H	PO	A	E	DP	TC/G	FA	G by Pos

John Kalahan

KALAHAN, JOHN JOSEPH
B. Sept. 30, 1878, Philadelphia, Pa.   D. June 20, 1952, Philadelphia, Pa.
BR TR 6' 165 lbs.

Year	Team	Games	BA	SA	AB	H	2B	3B	HR	HR%	R	RBI	BB	SO	SB	PH AB	PH H	PO	A	E	DP	TC/G	FA	G by Pos
1903	PHI A	1	.000	.000	5	0	0	0	0	0.0	0	0	0		0	0	0	5	1	0	0	6.0	1.000	C-1

Charlie Kalbfus

KALBFUS, CHARLES HENRY
B. Dec. 28, 1864, Washington, D.C.   D. Nov. 18, 1941, Washington, D. C.
BR TR 5'11" 145 lbs.

Year	Team	Games	BA	SA	AB	H	2B	3B	HR	HR%	R	RBI	BB	SO	SB	PH AB	PH H	PO	A	E	DP	TC/G	FA	G by Pos
1884	WAS U	1	.200	.200	5	1	0	0	0	0.0	1		0		0	0	0	0	0	0	0	0.0	–	OF-1

Frank Kalin

KALIN, FRANK BRUNO (Fats)
Born Frank Bruno Kalinkiewicz.
B. Oct. 3, 1917, Steubenville, Ohio   D. Jan. 12, 1975, Weirtown, W. Va.
BR TR 6' 200 lbs.

Year	Team	Games	BA	SA	AB	H	2B	3B	HR	HR%	R	RBI	BB	SO	SB	PH AB	PH H	PO	A	E	DP	TC/G	FA	G by Pos
1940	PIT N	3	.000	.000	3	0	0	0	0	0.0	0	1	2	1	0	1	0	2	0	1	0	1.0	.667	OF-2
1943	CHI A	4	.000	.000	4	0	0	0	0	0.0	0	0	0	4	0	4	0	0	0	0	0	0.0	–	
2 yrs.		7	.000	.000	7	0	0	0	0	0.0	0	1	2	0	0	5	0	2	0	1	0	0.4	.667	OF-2

Al Kaline

KALINE, ALBERT WILLIAM
B. Dec. 19, 1934, Baltimore, Md.
Hall of Fame 1980.
BR TR 6'1½" 175 lbs.

Year	Team	Games	BA	SA	AB	H	2B	3B	HR	HR%	R	RBI	BB	SO	SB	PH AB	PH H	PO	A	E	DP	TC/G	FA	G by Pos
1953	DET A	30	.250	.357	28	7	0	0	1	3.6	9	2	1	5	1	1	0	11	1	0	0	0.4	1.000	OF-20
1954		138	.276	.347	504	139	18	3	4	0.8	42	43	22	45	9	3	1	283	16	9	0	2.2	.971	OF-135
1955		152	**.340**	.546	588	**200**	24	8	27	4.6	121	102	82	57	6	0	0	306	14	7	4	2.2	.979	OF-152
1956		153	.314	.530	617	194	32	10	27	4.4	96	128	70	55	7	0	0	343	18	6	4	2.4	.984	OF-153
1957		149	.295	.478	577	170	29	4	23	4.0	83	90	43	38	11	5	1	319	13	5	2	2.3	.985	OF-145
1958		146	.313	.490	543	170	34	7	16	2.9	84	85	54	47	7	2	0	316	23	2	4	2.3	.994	OF-145
1959		136	.327	**.530**	511	167	19	2	27	5.3	86	94	72	42	10	0	0	364	4	4	0	2.7	.989	OF-136
1960		147	.278	.426	551	153	29	4	15	2.7	77	68	65	47	19	4	2	367	5	5	1	2.6	.987	OF-142
1961		153	.324	.515	586	190	**41**	7	19	3.2	116	82	66	42	14	5	3	379	10	4	3	2.6	.990	OF-147, 3B-1
1962		100	.304	.593	398	121	16	6	29	7.3	78	94	47	39	4	0	0	225	8	4	1	2.4	.983	OF-100
1963		145	.312	.514	551	172	24	3	27	4.9	89	101	54	48	6	5	3	257	5	2	0	1.8	.992	OF-140
1964		146	.293	.469	525	154	31	5	17	3.2	77	68	75	51	4	9	2	278	6	3	2	2.0	.990	OF-136
1965		125	.281	.471	399	112	18	2	18	4.5	72	72	72	49	6	11	4	195	3	3	0	1.6	.985	OF-112, 3B-1
1966		142	.288	.534	479	138	29	1	29	6.1	85	88	81	66	5	3	1	279	7	2	1	2.0	.993	OF-136
1967		131	.308	.541	458	141	28	2	25	5.5	94	78	83	47	8	1	0	217	14	4	2	1.8	.983	OF-130
1968		102	.287	.428	327	94	14	1	10	3.1	49	53	55	39	6	10	5	283	14	7	15	3.0	.977	OF-74, 1B-22
1969		131	.272	.447	456	124	17	0	21	4.6	74	69	54	61	1	7	2	257	11	7	7	2.1	.975	OF-118, 1B-9
1970		131	.278	.450	467	130	24	4	16	3.4	64	71	77	49	2	3	0	530	34	6	40	4.4	.989	OF-91, 1B-52
1971		133	.294	.462	405	119	19	2	15	3.7	69	54	82	57	4	12	3	234	7	0	3	1.8	1.000	OF-129, 1B-5
1972		106	.313	.475	278	87	11	2	10	3.6	46	32	28	33	1	24	**10**	148	9	1	5	1.5	.994	OF-84, 1B-11
1973		91	.255	.394	310	79	13	0	10	3.2	40	45	29	28	4	9	0	347	13	1	32	4.0	.997	OF-63, 1B-36
1974		147	.262	.389	558	146	28	2	13	2.3	71	64	65	75	2	1	0	0	0	0	0	0.0	–	DH-146
22 yrs.		2834 9th	.297	.480	10116	3007	498	75	399	3.9	1622	1583	1277	1020	137	115	37	5938	235	82	126	2.2	.987	OF-2488, DH-146, 1B-135, 3B-2

LEAGUE CHAMPIONSHIP SERIES

Year	Team	Games	BA	SA	AB	H	2B	3B	HR	HR%	R	RBI	BB	SO	SB	PH AB	PH H	PO	A	E	DP	TC/G	FA	G by Pos
1972	DET A	5	.263	.421	19	5	0	0	1	5.3	3	1	2	2	0	0	0	12	0	1	0	2.6	.923	OF-5

WORLD SERIES

Year	Team	Games	BA	SA	AB	H	2B	3B	HR	HR%	R	RBI	BB	SO	SB	PH AB	PH H	PO	A	E	DP	TC/G	FA	G by Pos
1968	DET A	7	.379	.655	29	11	2	0	2	6.9	6	8	0	7	0	0	0	18	0	0	0	2.6	1.000	OF-7

Willie Kamm

KAMM, WILLIAM EDWARD
B. Feb. 2, 1900, San Francisco, Calif.   D. Dec. 21, 1988, Belmont, Calif.
BR TR 5'10½" 170 lbs.

Year	Team	Games	BA	SA	AB	H	2B	3B	HR	HR%	R	RBI	BB	SO	SB	PH AB	PH H	PO	A	E	DP	TC/G	FA	G by Pos
1923	CHI A	149	.292	.430	544	159	39	6	6	1.1	57	87	62	82	17	0	0	173	352	22	29	3.7	.960	3B-149
1924		147	.254	.364	528	134	28	6	6	1.1	58	93	64	59	9	0	0	190	312	15	31	3.5	.971	3B-145
1925		152	.279	.393	509	142	32	4	6	1.2	82	83	**90**	36	11	0	0	182	310	22	32	3.4	.957	3B-152
1926		143	.294	.385	480	141	24	10	0	0.0	63	62	77	24	14	1	0	177	323	11	16	3.6	.978	3B-142
1927		148	.270	.378	540	146	32	13	0	0.0	85	59	70	18	7	2	0	236	279	15	21	3.6	.972	3B-146
1928		155	.308	.411	552	170	30	12	1	0.2	70	84	73	22	17	0	0	243	278	12	33	3.4	.977	3B-155
1929		147	.268	.369	523	140	32	6	3	0.6	72	63	75	23	12	2	1	221	270	11	27	3.4	.978	3B-145
1930		112	.269	.396	331	89	21	6	3	0.9	49	47	51	20	5	5	0	142	209	23	17	3.3	.939	3B-105
1931	2 teams	CHI A (18G – .254)			CLE A (114G – .295)																			
"	total	132	.290	.386	469	136	35	5	0	0.0	77	75	71	19	14	0	0	158	240	23	33	3.2	.945	3B-132
1932	CLE A	148	.286	.403	524	150	34	9	3	0.6	76	83	75	36	6	0	0	164	299	16	20	3.2	.967	3B-148
1933		133	.282	.336	447	126	17	2	1	0.2	59	47	54	27	7	2	0	153	221	6	16	2.9	.984	3B-131
1934		121	.269	.345	386	104	23	3	0	0.0	52	42	62	38	7	4	2	109	248	8	24	3.0	.978	3B-118
1935		6	.333	.333	18	6	0	0	0	0.0	2	1	0	1	0	2	0	3	4	1	0	1.3	.875	3B-4
13 yrs.		1693	.281	.384	5851	1643	347	85	29	0.5	802	826	824	405	126	18	3	2151	3345	185	299	3.4	.967	3B-1672

Alex Kampouris

KAMPOURIS, ALEXIS WILLIAM
B. Nov. 13, 1912, Sacramento, Calif.
BR TR 5'8" 155 lbs.

Year	Team	Games	BA	SA	AB	H	2B	3B	HR	HR%	R	RBI	BB	SO	SB	PH AB	PH H	PO	A	E	DP	TC/G	FA	G by Pos
1934	CIN N	19	.197	.212	66	13	0	0	0	0.0	6	3	3	18	2	2	0	35	53	5	7	4.9	.946	2B-16
1935		148	.246	.361	499	123	26	5	7	1.4	46	62	32	84	8	2	0	381	426	41	88	5.7	.952	2B-141, SS-6
1936		122	.239	.332	355	85	10	4	5	1.4	43	46	24	46	3	1	0	271	376	21	71	5.5	.969	2B-119, OF-1
1937		146	.249	.424	458	114	21	4	17	3.7	62	71	60	65	2	1	0	367	439	33	87	5.7	.961	2B-146
1938	2 teams	CIN N (21G – .257)			NY N (82G – .246)																			
"	total	103	.249	.345	342	85	10	1	7	2.0	48	44	37	63	0	3	0	241	321	16	63	5.6	.972	2B-100
1939	NY N	74	.249	.403	201	50	10	1	5	2.5	23	29	30	41	0	1	0	154	193	11	35	4.8	.969	2B-62, 3B-11
1941	BKN N	16	.314	.588	51	16	4	2	2	3.9	8	9	11	8	0	1	0	31	45	1	7	4.8	.987	2B-15
1942		9	.238	.429	21	5	2	1	0	0.0	3	3	4	0	4	0	0	16	16	1	5	3.3	.970	2B-9
1943	2 teams	BKN N (19G – .227)			WAS A (51G – .207)																			
"	total	70	.212	.296	189	40	8	1	2	1.1	33	17	47	31	7	6	2	109	127	14	21	3.6	.944	3B-33, 2B-28, OF-1
9 yrs.		708	.243	.367	2182	531	94	20	45	2.1	272	284	244	360	22	17	2	1605	1996	143	384	5.3	.962	2B-636, 3B-44, SS-6, OF-2

Year	Team		Games	BA	SA	AB	H	2B	3B	HR	HR%	R	RBI	BB	SO	SB	Pinch Hit AB	H	PO	A	E	DP	TC/G	FA	G by Pos

Frank Kane

KANE, FRANCIS THOMAS (Sugar)
Played as Frank Kiley in 1915. Born Francis Thomas Kiley.
B. Mar. 9, 1895, Whitman, Mass. D. Dec. 2, 1962, Brockton, Mass.

BL TR 5'11½" 175 lbs.

1915	BKN	F	3	.200	.400	10	2	0	1	0	0.0	2	2	0		0	0		0	5	1	0	0	2.0	1.000	OF-2
1919	NY	A	1	.000	.000	1	0	0	0	0	0.0	0	0	0		0	1		0	0	0	0	0	0.0	–	
2 yrs.			4	.182	.364	11	2	0	1	0	0.0	2	2	0		0	2		0	5	1	0	0	1.5	1.000	OF-2

Jerry Kane

KANE, WILLIAM JEREMIAH
B. 1867, Collinsville, Ill. Deceased.

BR TR 6' 175 lbs.

| 1890 | STL | AA | 8 | .200 | .200 | 25 | 5 | 0 | 0 | 0 | 0.0 | 3 | | 2 | | 0 | 0 | 0 | 46 | 5 | 4 | 1 | 6.9 | .927 | 1B-5, C-4 |

Jim Kane

KANE, JAMES JOSEPH (Shamus)
B. Nov. 27, 1881, Scranton, Pa. D. Oct. 2, 1947, Omaha, Neb.

BL TL 6'2" 225 lbs.

| 1908 | PIT | N | 55 | .241 | .303 | 145 | 35 | 3 | 3 | 0 | 0.0 | 16 | 22 | 12 | | 5 | 14 | 1 | 378 | 24 | 14 | 19 | 7.6 | .966 | 1B-40 |

John Kane

KANE, JOHN FRANCIS
B. Sept. 24, 1882, Chicago, Ill. D. Jan. 28, 1934, St. Anthony, Ida.

BR TR 5'6" 138 lbs.

1907	CIN	N	79	.248	.347	262	65	9	4	3	1.1	40	19	22		20	2	1	120	80	19	2	2.8	.913	OF-42, 3B-25, SS-6, 2B-2
1908			130	.213	.288	455	97	11	7	3	0.7	61	23	43		30	1	0	298	17	6	2	2.5	.981	OF-127, 2B-1
1909	CHI	N	20	.089	.111	45	4	1	0	0	0.0	6	5	2		1	2	0	26	24	3	3	2.7	.943	OF-8, SS-3, 3B-3, 2B-2
1910			32	.242	.290	62	15	0	0	1	1.6	11	12	9		2	0	0	31	14	3	1	1.5	.938	OF-18, 2B-6, 3B-4, SS-2
4 yrs.			261	.220	.297	824	181	21	11	7	0.8	118	59	76		53	5	1	475	135	31	8	2.5	.952	OF-195, 3B-32, SS-11, 2B-11

WORLD SERIES

| 1910 | CHI | N | 1 | – | – | 0 | 0 | 0 | 0 | 0 | – | 0 | | 0 | | 0 | 0 | 0 | 0 | 0 | 0 | 0 | 0.0 | – | |

Johnny Kane

KANE, JOHN FRANCIS
B. Feb. 19, 1900, Chicago, Ill. D. June 25, 1956, Chicago, Ill.

BB TR 5'10½" 162 lbs.

| 1925 | CHI | A | 14 | .179 | .196 | 56 | 10 | 1 | 0 | 0 | 0.0 | 6 | 3 | 0 | | 3 | 0 | 0 | 22 | 49 | 3 | 6 | 5.3 | .959 | SS-8, 2B-6 |

Tom Kane

KANE, THOMAS JOSEPH (Sugar)
B. Dec. 15, 1906, Chicago, Ill. D. Nov. 26, 1973, Chicago, Ill.

BR TR 5'10½" 160 lbs.

| 1938 | BOS | N | 2 | .000 | .000 | 2 | 0 | 0 | 0 | 0 | 0.0 | 0 | 0 | 2 | | 0 | 0 | 0 | 2 | 2 | 0 | 0 | 2.0 | 1.000 | 2B-2 |

Rod Kanehl

KANEHL, RODERICK EDWIN (Hot Rod)
B. Apr. 1, 1934, Wichita, Kans.

BR TR 6'1" 180 lbs.

1962	NY	N	133	.248	.322	351	87	10	2	4	1.1	52	27	23	36	8	11	3	235	230	32	57	3.7	.936	2B-62, 3B-30, OF-20, 1B-3, SS-2
1963			109	.241	.288	191	46	6	0	1	0.5	26	9	5	26	6	21	5	128	35	12	7	1.6	.931	OF-58, 3B-13, 2B-12, 1B-3
1964			98	.232	.280	254	59	7	1	1	0.4	25	11	7	18	3	15	3	161	125	6	26	3.0	.979	2B-34, OF-25, 3B-19, 1B-2
3 yrs.			340	.241	.300	796	192	23	3	6	0.8	103	47	35	80	17	47	11	524	390	50	90	2.8	.948	2B-108, OF-103, 3B-62, 1B-8, SS-2

Heinie Kappel

KAPPEL, HENRY
Brother of Joe Kappel.
B. 1862, Philadelphia, Pa. D. Aug. 27, 1905, Philadelphia, Pa.

BR TR 5'8" 160 lbs.

1887	CIN	AA	23	.282	.372	78	22	3	2	0	0.0	11		2		3	0	0	35	42	14	3	4.0	.846	3B-9, OF-7, 2B-6, SS-1
1888			36	.259	.364	143	37	4	4	1	0.7	18	15	2		20	0	0	50	91	39	11	5.0	.783	SS-25, 2B-10, 3B-1
1889	COL	AA	46	.272	.422	173	47	7	5	3	1.7	25	21	21	28	10	0	0	69	128	40	7	5.2	.831	SS-23, 3B-23
3 yrs.			105	.269	.391	394	106	14	11	4	1.0	54	36	25	28	33	0	0	154	261	93	21	4.8	.817	SS-49, 3B-33, 2B-16, OF-7

Joe Kappel

KAPPEL, JOSEPH
Brother of Heinie Kappel.
B. Apr. 27, 1857, Philadelphia, Pa. D. July 8, 1929, Philadelphia, Pa.

BR 5'10" 165 lbs.

1884	PHI	N	4	.067	.067	15	1	0	0	0	0.0	1		0	2		0	0	16	8	9	0	8.3	.727	C-4
1890	PHI	AA	56	.240	.303	208	50	8	1	1	0.5	29		20		12	0	0	75	92	31	8	3.5	.843	OF-23, SS-18, 3B-11, C-3, 2B-2
2 yrs.			60	.229	.287	223	51	8	1	1	0.4	30		20	2		12	0	0	91	100	40	8	3.9	.827	OF-23, SS-18, 3B-11, C-7, 2B-2

Ron Karkovice

KARKOVICE, RONALD JOSEPH
B. Aug. 8, 1963, Union, N. J.

BR TR 6'1" 210 lbs.

1986	CHI	A	37	.247	.443	97	24	7	0	4	4.1	13	13	9	37	1	0	0	227	19	1	4	6.7	.996	C-37
1987			39	.071	.141	85	6	0	0	2	2.4	7	7	7	40	3	0	0	147	20	3	3	4.4	.982	C-37
1988			46	.174	.287	115	20	4	0	3	2.6	10	9	7	30	4	0	0	190	24	1	4	4.7	.995	C-46
1989			71	.264	.385	182	48	9	2	3	1.6	21	24	10	56	0	0	0	299	47	5	6	4.9	.986	C-68, DH-2
4 yrs.			193	.205	.330	479	98	20	2	12	2.5	51	53	33	163	8	0	0	863	110	10	17	5.1	.990	C-188, DH-2

Bill Karlon

KARLON, WILLIAM JOHN (Hank)
B. Jan. 21, 1909, Palmer, Mass. D. Dec. 7, 1964, Ware, Mass.

BR TR 6'1" 190 lbs.

| 1930 | NY | A | 2 | .000 | .000 | 5 | 0 | 0 | 0 | 0 | 0.0 | 0 | | 0 | 1 | | 0 | 1 | 0 | 1 | 0 | 0 | 0 | 0.5 | 1.000 | OF-1 |

Marty Karow

KAROW, MARTIN GREGORY
Born Martin Gregory Karowsky.
B. July 18, 1904, Braddock, Pa. D. Apr. 27, 1986, Bryan, Tex.

BR TR 5'10½" 170 lbs.

| 1927 | BOS | A | 6 | .200 | .300 | 10 | 2 | 1 | 0 | 0 | 0.0 | 0 | 0 | 0 | 2 | 0 | 1 | 1 | 2 | 6 | 0 | 3 | 1.3 | 1.000 | SS-3, 3B-2 |

Benn Karr

KARR, BENJAMIN JOYCE (Baldy)
B. Nov. 28, 1893, Mt. Pleasant, Miss. D. Dec. 8, 1968, Memphis, Tenn.

BL TR 6' 175 lbs.

Year	Team	Games	BA	SA	AB	H	2B	3B	HR	HR%	R	RBI	BB	SO	SB	Pinch Hit AB	Pinch Hit H	PO	A	E	DP	TC/G	FA	G by Pos

Benn Karr continued

Year	Team	Games	BA	SA	AB	H	2B	3B	HR	HR%	R	RBI	BB	SO	SB	PH AB	PH H	PO	A	E	DP	TC/G	FA	G by Pos
1920	BOS A	57	.280	.387	75	21	5	0	1	1.3	8	15	6	18	0	29	9	5	18	2	0	0.4	.920	P-26
1921		43	.258	.290	62	16	2	0	0	0.0	7	9	4	16	1	14	1	2	30	2	0	0.8	.941	P-26
1922		66	.214	.235	98	21	2	0	0	0.0	7	4	4	7	1	22	2	9	44	5	3	0.9	.914	P-41
1925	CLE A	46	.261	.348	92	24	5	0	1	1.1	11	17	7	8	0	13	3	14	57	4	5	1.6	.947	P-32
1926		31	.222	.333	45	10	5	0	0	0.0	8	4	3	4	0	1	0	6	35	2	0	1.4	.953	P-30
1927		22	.200	.250	20	4	1	0	0	0.0	2	0	4	6	1	0	0	4	29	2	0	1.6	.943	P-22
6 yrs.		265	.245	.311	392	96	20	0	2	0.5	43	49	27	59	3	79	15	40	213	17	8	1.0	.937	P-177

John Karst

KARST, JOHN GOTTLIEB (King)
B. Oct. 15, 1893, Philadelphia, Pa. D. May 21, 1976, Cape May, N. J. BL TR 5'11½" 175 lbs.

Year	Team	Games	BA	SA	AB	H	2B	3B	HR	HR%	R	RBI	BB	SO	SB	PH AB	PH H	PO	A	E	DP	TC/G	FA	G by Pos
1915	BKN N	1	–	–	0	0	0	0	0	–	0	0	0	0	0	0	0	0	0	1	0	1.0	1.000	3B-1

Eddie Kasko

KASKO, EDWARD MICHAEL
B. June 27, 1932, Linden, N. J. BR TR 6' 180 lbs.
Manager 1970-73.

Year	Team	Games	BA	SA	AB	H	2B	3B	HR	HR%	R	RBI	BB	SO	SB	PH AB	PH H	PO	A	E	DP	TC/G	FA	G by Pos
1957	STL N	134	.273	.334	479	131	16	5	1	0.2	59	35	33	53	6	5	1	118	248	15	26	2.8	.961	3B-120, SS-13, 2B-1
1958		104	.220	.282	259	57	8	1	2	0.8	20	22	21	25	1	10	3	136	218	13	54	3.5	.965	SS-77, 2B-12, 3B-1
1959	CIN N	118	.283	.350	329	93	14	1	2	0.6	39	31	14	38	2	2	0	192	295	13	63	4.2	.974	SS-84, 3B-31, 2B-2
1960		126	.292	.378	479	140	21	1	6	1.3	56	51	46	37	9	7	2	194	287	15	47	3.9	.970	3B-86, 2B-33, SS-15
1961		126	.271	.335	469	127	22	1	2	0.4	64	27	32	37	4	7	2	214	301	18	60	4.2	.966	SS-112, 3B-12, 2B-6
1962		134	.278	.356	533	148	26	2	4	0.8	74	41	35	44	3	4	1	120	253	23	31	3.0	.942	3B-114, SS-21
1963		76	.241	.332	199	48	9	2	3	1.5	25	10	21	29	0	14	3	57	108	7	13	2.3	.959	3B-48, SS-15, 2B-1
1964	HOU N	133	.243	.283	448	109	16	1	0	0.0	45	22	37	52	4	4	2	229	388	15	72	4.8	.976	SS-128, 3B-2
1965		68	.247	.302	215	53	7	1	1	0.5	18	10	11	20	1	8	2	98	155	6	27	3.8	.977	SS-59, 3B-2
1966	BOS A	58	.213	.287	136	29	7	0	1	0.7	11	12	15	19	1	20	3	55	96	4	16	2.7	.974	SS-20, 3B-10, 2B-8
10 yrs.		1077	.264	.331	3546	935	146	13	22	0.6	411	261	265	353	31	81	19	1413	2349	129	409	3.6	.967	SS-544, 3B-426, 2B-63

WORLD SERIES

Year	Team	Games	BA	SA	AB	H	2B	3B	HR	HR%	R	RBI	BB	SO	SB	PH AB	PH H	PO	A	E	DP	TC/G	FA	G by Pos
1961	CIN N	5	.318	.318	22	7	0	0	0	0.0	1	1	0	2	0	0	0	13	13	1	5	5.4	.963	SS-5

Ray Katt

KATT, RAYMOND FREDERICK
B. May 9, 1927, New Braunfels, Tex. BR TR 6'2" 190 lbs.

Year	Team	Games	BA	SA	AB	H	2B	3B	HR	HR%	R	RBI	BB	SO	SB	PH AB	PH H	PO	A	E	DP	TC/G	FA	G by Pos
1952	NY N	9	.222	.222	27	6	0	0	0	0.0	4	1	1	5	0	0	0	39	4	0	0	4.8	1.000	C-8
1953		8	.172	.207	29	5	1	0	0	0.0	2	1	3	0	0	0	0	33	6	1	0	5.0	.975	C-8
1954		86	.255	.435	200	51	7	1	9	4.5	26	33	19	29	1	5	0	265	23	8	4	3.4	.973	C-82
1955		124	.215	.313	326	70	7	2	7	2.1	27	28	22	38	1	3	2	482	45	7	7	4.3	.987	C-122
1956	2 teams			NY N	(37G – .228)		STL N	(47G – .259)																	
"	total	84	.247	.429	259	64	4	1	13	5.0	21	34	12	40	0	0	0	395	34	8	1	5.2	.982	C-84
1957	NY N	72	.230	.297	165	38	3	1	2	1.2	11	17	15	35	1	7	2	238	25	5	4	3.7	.981	C-68
1958	STL N	19	.171	.268	41	7	1	0	1	2.4	1	4	4	6	0	5	0	63	4	2	2	3.6	.971	C-14
1959		15	.292	.375	24	7	2	0	0	0.0	0	2	0	8	0	0	0	38	2	1	0	2.7	.976	C-14
8 yrs.		417	.232	.356	1071	248	29	4	32	3.0	92	120	74	164	2	21	4	1553	143	32	18	4.1	.981	C-400

Benny Kauff

KAUFF, BENJAMIN MICHAEL
B. Jan. 5, 1890, Pomeroy, Ohio D. Nov. 17, 1961, Columbus, Ohio BL TL 5'8" 157 lbs.

Year	Team	Games	BA	SA	AB	H	2B	3B	HR	HR%	R	RBI	BB	SO	SB	PH AB	PH H	PO	A	E	DP	TC/G	FA	G by Pos
1912	NY A	5	.273	.273	11	3	0	0	0	0.0	4	2	3		1	0	0	4	0	0	0	0.8	1.000	OF-4
1914	IND F	154	.370	.534	571	211	44	13	8	1.4	120	95	72		75	0	0	310	31	17	5	2.3	.953	OF-154
1915	BKN F	136	.342	.509	483	165	23	11	12	2.5	92	83	85		55	0	0	317	32	15	7	2.7	.959	OF-136
1916	NY N	154	.264	.408	552	146	22	15	9	1.6	71	74	68	65	40	0	0	329	22	14	6	2.4	.962	OF-154
1917		153	.308	.388	559	172	22	4	5	0.9	89	68	59	54	30	0	0	357	12	9	4	2.5	.976	OF-153
1918		67	.315	.437	270	85	19	4	2	0.7	41	39	16	30	9	0	0	147	11	8	4	2.5	.952	OF-67
1919		135	.277	.422	491	136	27	7	10	2.0	73	67	39	45	21	1	1	306	18	17	3	2.5	.950	OF-134
1920		55	.274	.446	157	43	12	3	3	1.9	31	26	25	14	3	1	1	111	10	5	0	2.3	.960	OF-51
8 yrs.		859	.311	.450	3094	961	169	57	49	1.6	521	454	367	208	234	4	2	1881	136	85	29	2.4	.960	OF-853

WORLD SERIES

Year	Team	Games	BA	SA	AB	H	2B	3B	HR	HR%	R	RBI	BB	SO	SB	PH AB	PH H	PO	A	E	DP	TC/G	FA	G by Pos
1917	NY N	6	.160	.440	25	4	1	0	2	8.0	2	5	0	2	1	0	0	7	0	1	0	1.3	.875	OF-6

Dick Kauffman

KAUFFMAN, HOWARD RICHARD
B. June 22, 1888, East Lewisburg, Pa. D. Apr. 16, 1948, Mifflinburg, Pa. BB TR 6'3" 190 lbs.

Year	Team	Games	BA	SA	AB	H	2B	3B	HR	HR%	R	RBI	BB	SO	SB	PH AB	PH H	PO	A	E	DP	TC/G	FA	G by Pos
1914	STL A	7	.267	.333	15	4	1	0	0	0.0	1	2	3	3	0	0	0	29	0	1	0	4.3	.967	1B-6
1915		37	.258	.355	124	32	8	2	0	0.0	9	14	5	27	0	4	1	293	16	5	22	8.5	.984	1B-32, OF-1
2 yrs.		44	.259	.353	139	36	9	2	0	0.0	10	16	5	30	0	5	1	322	16	6	22	7.8	.983	1B-38, OF-1

Charlie Kavanagh

KAVANAGH, CHARLES HUGH (Silk)
B. June 9, 1893, Chicago, Ill. D. Sept. 6, 1973, Reedsburg, Wis. BR TR 5'9" 165 lbs.

Year	Team	Games	BA	SA	AB	H	2B	3B	HR	HR%	R	RBI	BB	SO	SB	PH AB	PH H	PO	A	E	DP	TC/G	FA	G by Pos
1914	CHI A	5	.200	.200	5	1	0	0	0	0.0	2	0	2	0	0	5	1	0	0	0	0	0.0	–	

Leo Kavanagh

KAVANAGH, LEO DANIEL
B. Aug. 9, 1894, Chicago, Ill. D. Aug. 10, 1950, Chicago, Ill. BR TR 5'9" 180 lbs.

Year	Team	Games	BA	SA	AB	H	2B	3B	HR	HR%	R	RBI	BB	SO	SB	PH AB	PH H	PO	A	E	DP	TC/G	FA	G by Pos
1914	CHI F	5	.273	.273	11	3	0	0	0	0.0	1		1	1	0	0	0	7	6	0	1	2.6	1.000	SS-5

Marty Kavanagh

KAVANAGH, MARTIN JOSEPH
B. June 13, 1891, Harrison, N. J. D. July 28, 1960, Eloise, Mich. BR TR 6' 187 lbs.

Year	Team	Games	BA	SA	AB	H	2B	3B	HR	HR%	R	RBI	BB	SO	SB	PH AB	PH H	PO	A	E	DP	TC/G	FA	G by Pos
1914	DET A	127	.248	.351	439	109	21	6	4	0.9	60	35	41	42	16	8	1	264	334	45	30	5.1	.930	2B-115, 1B-4
1915		113	.295	.452	332	98	14	13	4	1.2	55	49	42	44	8	20	10	563	121	19	24	6.2	.973	1B-44, 2B-42, OF-2, SS-2
1916	2 teams			DET A	(58G – .141)		CLE A	(19G – .250)																	
"	total	77	.180	.270	122	22	6	1	1	0.8	10	15	11	20	0	46	7	34	35	7	3	1.0	.908	OF-11, 2B-11, 3B-3, 1B-1
1917	CLE A	14	.000	.000	14	0	0	0	0	0.0	1	0	3	2	0	9	0	2	1	0	1	0.2	1.000	OF-2

Year	Team	Games	BA	SA	AB	H	2B	3B	HR	HR%	R	RBI	BB	SO	SB	Pinch Hit AB	Pinch Hit H	PO	A	E	DP	TC/G	FA	G by Pos

Marty Kavanagh *continued*

Year	Team	Games	BA	SA	AB	H	2B	3B	HR	HR%	R	RBI	BB	SO	SB	AB	H	PO	A	E	DP	TC/G	FA	G by Pos
1918	3 teams		CLE A (13G – .211)		STL N (12G – .182)			DET A (13G – .273)																
"	total	38	.222	.294	126	28	6	0	1	0.8	12	23	21	14	2	2	0	267	23	11	13	7.9	.963	1B-24, OF-8, 2B-4
5 yrs.		369	.249	.362	1033	257	47	20	10	1.0	138	122	118	122	26	85	18	1130	514	82	71	4.7	.952	2B-172, 1B-73, OF-23, 3B-3, SS-2

Bill Kay

KAY, WALTER BROCTON (King Bill)
B. Feb. 14, 1878, New Castle, Va.   D. Dec. 3, 1945, Roanoke, Va.

BL TR 6'2"   180 lbs.

Year	Team	Games	BA	SA	AB	H	2B	3B	HR	HR%	R	RBI	BB	SO	SB	AB	H	PO	A	E	DP	TC/G	FA	G by Pos
1907	WAS A	25	.333	.383	60	20	1	1	0	0.0	8	7	0		0	11	3	19	1	0	0	0.8	1.000	OF-12

Eddie Kazak

KAZAK, EDWARD TERRANCE
Born Edward Terrance Tkaczuk.
B. July 18, 1920, Steubenville, Ohio

BR TR 6'   175 lbs.

Year	Team	Games	BA	SA	AB	H	2B	3B	HR	HR%	R	RBI	BB	SO	SB	AB	H	PO	A	E	DP	TC/G	FA	G by Pos
1948	STL N	6	.273	.409	22	6	3	0	0	0.0	1	2	0		0	0	0	7	11	2	2	3.3	.900	3B-6
1949		92	.304	.423	326	99	15	3	6	1.8	43	42	29	17	0	7	2	74	187	23	22	3.1	.919	3B-80, 2B-5
1950		93	.256	.357	207	53	2	2	5	2.4	21	23	18	19	0	42	10	36	95	9	7	1.5	.936	3B-48
1951		11	.182	.242	33	6	2	0	0	0.0	2	4	5	5	0	1	0	11	17	2	1	2.7	.933	3B-10
1952	2 teams	STL N (3G – .000)			CIN N (13G – .067)																			
"	total	16	.059	.176	17	1	0	0	0	0.0	2	0	0	2	0	9	1	5	2	1	0	0.5	.875	3B-4, 1B-1
5 yrs.		218	.273	.383	605	165	22	6	11	1.8	69	71	52	45	0	59	13	133	312	37	32	2.2	.923	3B-148, 2B-5, 1B-1

Ted Kazanski

KAZANSKI, THEODORE STANLEY
B. Jan. 25, 1934, Hamtramck, Mich.

BR TR 6'1"   175 lbs.

Year	Team	Games	BA	SA	AB	H	2B	3B	HR	HR%	R	RBI	BB	SO	SB	AB	H	PO	A	E	DP	TC/G	FA	G by Pos
1953	PHI N	95	.217	.308	360	78	17	5	2	0.6	39	27	26	53	1	0	0	185	239	23	53	4.7	.949	SS-95
1954		39	.135	.183	104	14	2	0	1	1.0	7	8	4	14	0	1	0	43	77	7	18	3.3	.945	SS-38
1955		9	.083	.333	12	1	0	0	1	8.3	1	1	1	1	0	1	0	5	9	0	1	1.6	1.000	SS-4, 3B-4
1956		117	.211	.277	379	80	11	1	4	1.1	35	34	20	41	0	0	0	246	261	11	68	4.4	.979	2B-116, SS-1
1957		62	.265	.362	185	49	7	1	3	1.6	15	11	17	20	1	5	1	64	95	5	21	2.6	.970	3B-36, 2B-22, SS-3
1958		95	.228	.315	289	66	12	2	3	1.0	21	35	22	34	2	5	1	140	175	8	41	3.4	.975	2B-59, SS-22, 3B-16
6 yrs.		417	.217	.299	1329	288	49	9	14	1.1	118	116	90	163	4	13	2	683	856	54	202	3.8	.966	2B-197, SS-163, 3B-56

Bob Kearney

KEARNEY, ROBERT HENRY
B. Oct. 3, 1956, San Antonio, Tex.

BR TR 6'   190 lbs.

Year	Team	Games	BA	SA	AB	H	2B	3B	HR	HR%	R	RBI	BB	SO	SB	AB	H	PO	A	E	DP	TC/G	FA	G by Pos
1979	SF N	2	–	–	0	0	0	0	0	–	0	0	1	0	0	0	0	0	0	0	0	0.0	–	C-1
1981	OAK A	1	–	–	0	0	0	0	0	–	0	0	0	0	0	0	0	0	0	0	0	0.0	–	C-1
1982		22	.169	.211	71	12	3	0	0	0.0	7	5	3	10	0	0	0	114	14	4	1	6.0	.970	C-22
1983		108	.255	.372	298	76	11	0	8	2.7	33	32	21	50	1	8	0	437	41	9	5	4.5	.982	C-101, DH-3
1984	SEA A	133	.225	.334	431	97	24	1	7	1.6	39	43	18	72	7	0	0	823	63	11	9	6.7	.988	C-133
1985		108	.243	.354	305	74	14	1	6	2.0	24	27	11	59	1	0	0	529	50	3	7	5.4	.995	C-108
1986		81	.240	.377	204	49	10	0	6	2.9	23	25	12	35	0	4	0	419	46	5	3	5.8	.989	C-79
1987		24	.170	.298	47	8	1	0	1	0.0	5	1	1	9	0	0	0	94	10	2	0	4.4	.981	C-24
8 yrs.		479	.233	.346	1356	316	66	3	27	2.0	131	133	67	235	9	12	0	2416	224	34	25	5.6	.987	C-469, DH-3

Ted Kearns

KEARNS, EDWARD JOSEPH
B. Jan. 1, 1900, Trenton, N. J.   D. Dec. 21, 1949, Trenton, N. J.

BR TR 5'11"   185 lbs.

Year	Team	Games	BA	SA	AB	H	2B	3B	HR	HR%	R	RBI	BB	SO	SB	AB	H	PO	A	E	DP	TC/G	FA	G by Pos
1924	CHI N	4	.250	.375	16	4	0	1	0	0.0	1	1	0	1	0	0	0	29	2	0	3	7.8	1.000	1B-4
1925		3	.500	.500	2	1	0	0	0	0.0	0	0	0	0	0	0	0	3	0	0	1	1.0	1.000	1B-3
2 yrs.		7	.278	.389	18	5	0	1	0	0.0	1	1	0	1	0	0	0	32	2	0	4	4.9	1.000	1B-7

Tom Kearns

KEARNS, THOMAS J. (Dasher)
B. Nov. 9, 1860, Rochester, N. Y.   D. Dec. 7, 1938, Buffalo, N. Y.

TR 5'7"   160 lbs.

Year	Team	Games	BA	SA	AB	H	2B	3B	HR	HR%	R	RBI	BB	SO	SB	AB	H	PO	A	E	DP	TC/G	FA	G by Pos
1880	BUF N	2	.000	.000	7	0	0	0	0	0.0	0		0			0	0	10	2	6	0	9.0	.667	C-2
1882	DET N	4	.308	.462	13	4	2	0	0	0.0	2		1	0	4	0	0	3	8	4	0	3.8	.733	2B-4
1884		21	.203	.228	79	16	0	1	0	0.0	9		0	2	10	0	0	48	50	23	5	5.8	.810	2B-21
3 yrs.		27	.202	.242	99	20	2	1	0	0.0	11		1	2	14	0	0	61	60	33	5	5.7	.786	2B-25, C-2

Eddie Kearse

KEARSE, EDWARD PAUL (Truck)
B. Feb. 23, 1916, San Francisco, Calif.   D. July 15, 1968, Eureka, Calif.

BR TR 6'1"   195 lbs.

Year	Team	Games	BA	SA	AB	H	2B	3B	HR	HR%	R	RBI	BB	SO	SB	AB	H	PO	A	E	DP	TC/G	FA	G by Pos
1942	NY A	11	.192	.192	26	5	0	0	0	0.0	2	2	3	1	1	0	0	42	7	0	0	4.5	1.000	C-11

Chick Keating

KEATING, WALTER FRANCIS
B. Aug. 8, 1891, Philadelphia, Pa.   D. July 13, 1959, Philadelphia, Pa.

BR TR 5'9½"   155 lbs.

Year	Team	Games	BA	SA	AB	H	2B	3B	HR	HR%	R	RBI	BB	SO	SB	AB	H	PO	A	E	DP	TC/G	FA	G by Pos
1913	CHI N	2	.200	.400	5	1	1	0	0	0.0	0	1	0	0	0	0	0	6	1	0	0	3.5	1.000	SS-2
1914		20	.100	.167	30	3	0	1	0	0.0	3	0	6	9	0	0	0	15	24	2	2	2.1	.951	SS-16
1915		4	.000	.000	8	0	0	0	0	0.0	1	0	0	3	1	1	0	4	5	3	0	3.0	.750	SS-2
1926	PHI N	4	.000	.000	2	0	0	0	0	0.0	1	0	0	1	0	0	0	1	2	1	0	1.0	.750	SS-2, 2B-2, 3B-1
4 yrs.		30	.089	.156	45	4	1	1	0	0.0	5	1	6	13	1	1	0	26	32	6	2	2.1	.906	SS-22, 2B-2, 3B-1

Greg Keatley

KEATLEY, GREGORY STEVEN
B. Sept. 12, 1953, Princeton, W. Va.

BR TR 6'2"   200 lbs.

Year	Team	Games	BA	SA	AB	H	2B	3B	HR	HR%	R	RBI	BB	SO	SB	AB	H	PO	A	E	DP	TC/G	FA	G by Pos
1981	KC A	2	–	–	0	0	0	0	0	–	0	0	0	0	0	0	0	1	0	0	0	0.5	1.000	C-2

Pat Keedy

KEEDY, CHARLES PATRICK
B. Jan. 10, 1958, Birmingham, Ala.

BR TR 6'4"   205 lbs.

Year	Team	Games	BA	SA	AB	H	2B	3B	HR	HR%	R	RBI	BB	SO	SB	AB	H	PO	A	E	DP	TC/G	FA	G by Pos
1985	CAL A	3	.500	1.500	4	2	1	0	1	25.0	1	1	0	1	0	0	0	1	0	0	0	0.3	1.000	3B-2, OF-1
1987	CHI A	17	.171	.341	41	7	1	0	2	4.9	7	2	2	14	1	0	0	17	32	2	5	3.0	.961	3B-11, 1B-2, OF-1, SS-1, 2B-1
1989	CLE A	9	.214	.357	14	3	2	0	0	0.0	3	1	2	5	0	2	0	4	7	1	1	1.3	.917	OF-3, 3B-2, DH-1, SS-1, 1B-1
3 yrs.		29	.203	.424	59	12	4	0	3	5.1	10	4	4	19	1	2	0	22	39	3	6	2.2	.953	3B-15, OF-5, 1B-3, SS-2, DH-1, 2B-1

Year	Team		Games	BA	SA	AB	H	2B	3B	HR	HR%	R	RBI	BB	SO	SB	Pinch Hit AB	Pinch Hit H	PO	A	E	DP	TC/G	FA	G by Pos

Willie Keeler

KEELER, WILLIAM HENRY (Wee Willie)
B. Mar. 3, 1872, Brooklyn, N. Y.   D. Jan. 1, 1923, Brooklyn, N. Y.
Hall of Fame 1939.

BL TL 5'4½" 140 lbs.

Year	Team		Games	BA	SA	AB	H	2B	3B	HR	HR%	R	RBI	BB	SO	SB	AB	H	PO	A	E	DP	TC/G	FA	G by Pos
1892	NY	N	14	.321	.377	53	17	3	0	0	0.0	7	6	3	3	5	0	0	15	21	5	1	2.9	.878	3B-14
1893	2 teams			NY	N	(7G – .333)			BKN	N	(20G – .313)													
"	total		27	.317	.442	104	33	3	2	2	1.9	19	16	9	5	5	0	0	34	39	16	2	3.3	.820	3B-12, OF-11, SS-2, 2B-2
1894	BAL	N	129	.361	.507	590	213	27	22	5	0.8	165	94	40	6	32	0	0	217	26	16	4	2.0	.938	OF-128, 2B-1
1895			131	.391	.508	565	221	24	15	4	0.7	162	78	37	12	47	0	0	244	21	10	5	2.1	.964	OF-131
1896			127	.386	.496	544	210	22	13	4	0.7	153	82	37	9	67	0	0	227	20	8	6	2.0	.969	OF-126
1897			129	.424	.544	564	239	27	19	1	0.2	153	74	35		64	0	0	217	12	7	2	1.8	.970	OF-129
1898			128	.385	.410	561	216	7	2	1	0.2	126	44	31		28	1	0	211	14	9	2	1.8	.962	OF-128, 3B-1
1899	BKN	N	141	.379	.451	570	216	12	13	1	0.2	140	61	37		45	0	0	208	21	5	4	1.7	.979	OF-141
1900			136	.362	.449	563	204	13	12	4	0.7	106	68	30		41	0	0	227	23	16	4	1.8	.940	OF-136, 2B-1
1901			136	.355	.443	589	209	16	15	2	0.3	123	43	21		23	0	0	194	36	9	6	1.8	.962	OF-125, 3B-10, 2B-3
1902			132	.338	.396	556	188	18	7	0	0.0	86	38	21		19	0	0	208	14	5	4	1.7	.978	OF-132
1903	NY	A	132	.318	.373	515	164	14	7	0	0.0	95	32	32		24	0	0	183	15	15	4	1.6	.930	OF-128, 3B-4
1904			143	.343	.409	543	186	14	8	2	0.4	78	40	35		21	1	1	186	16	14	7	1.5	.935	OF-142
1905			149	.302	.363	560	169	14	4	4	0.7	81	38	43		19	0	0	207	38	11	2	1.7	.957	OF-139, 2B-12, 3B-3
1906			152	.304	.338	592	180	8	3	2	0.3	96	33	40		23	0	0	213	16	3	3	1.5	.987	OF-152
1907			107	.234	.255	423	99	5	2	0	0.0	50	17	15		7	0	0	144	13	5	1	1.5	.969	OF-107
1908			91	.263	.288	323	85	3	1	1	0.3	38	14	31		14	3	0	123	9	9	2	1.5	.936	OF-88
1909			99	.264	.319	360	95	7	5	1	0.3	44	32	24		10	3	0	111	9	4	2	1.3	.968	OF-95
1910	NY	N	19	.300	.300	10	3	0	0	0	0.0	5	0	3	1	1	9	2	1	0	0	0	0.1	1.000	OF-2
19 yrs.			2122	.343 9th	.418	8585	2947	237	150	34	0.4	1727	810	524	36	495	17	3	3170	363	167	65	1.7	.955	OF-2040, 3B-44, 2B-19, SS-2

Bob Keely

KEELY, ROBERT WILLIAM
B. Aug. 22, 1909, St. Louis, Mo.

BR TR 6' 175 lbs.

Year	Team		Games	BA	SA	AB	H	2B	3B	HR	HR%	R	RBI	BB	SO	SB	AB	H	PO	A	E	DP	TC/G	FA	G by Pos
1944	STL	N	1	–	–	0	0	0	0	0	0.0	0	0	0	0	0	0	0	1	0	0	0	1.0	1.000	C-1
1945			1	.000	.000	1	0	0	0	0	0.0	0	0	0	0	0	0	0	1	0	0	0	1.0	1.000	C-1
2 yrs.			2	.000	.000	1	0	0	0	0	0.0	0	0	0	0	0	0	0	2	0	0	0	1.0	1.000	C-2

Bill Keen

KEEN, WILLIAM BROWN (Buster)
B. Aug. 16, 1892, Oglethorpe, Ga.   D. July 16, 1947, South Point, Ohio

BR TR 6' 181 lbs.

Year	Team		Games	BA	SA	AB	H	2B	3B	HR	HR%	R	RBI	BB	SO	SB	AB	H	PO	A	E	DP	TC/G	FA	G by Pos
1911	PIT	N	6	.000	.000	7	0	0	0	0	0.0	1	4	0	5	0	0	6	0	0	0	1.0	1.000	1B-1

Jim Keenan

KEENAN, JAMES WILLIAM
B. Feb. 10, 1858, New Haven, Conn.   D. Sept. 21, 1926, Cincinnati, Ohio

BR TR 5'10" 186 lbs.

Year	Team		Games	BA	SA	AB	H	2B	3B	HR	HR%	R	RBI	BB	SO	SB	AB	H	PO	A	E	DP	TC/G	FA	G by Pos
1880	BUF	N	2	.143	.143	7	1	0	0	0	0.0	1	0	1	1		0	0	11	7	1	0	9.5	.947	C-2
1882	PIT	AA	25	.219	.323	96	21	7	0	1	1.0	10		1			0	0	145	22	19	3	7.4	.898	C-22, OF-3, SS-1
1884	IND	AA	68	.293	.418	249	73	14	4	3	1.2	36		16			0	0	462	80	45	6	8.6	.923	C-59, 1B-6, OF-2, SS-1, P-1
1885	CIN	AA	36	.265	.333	132	35	2	2	1	0.8	16		8			0	0	191	38	19	2	6.9	.923	C-33, 1B-4, P-1
1886			44	.270	.399	148	40	4	3	3	2.0	31		18			0	0	220	54	24	6	6.8	.919	C-30, OF-7, 3B-5, 1B-4, P-2
1887			47	.253	.287	174	44	4	1	0	0.0	19		11			7	0	252	68	21	15	7.3	.938	C-38, 1B-11
1888			85	.233	.323	313	73	9	8	1	0.3	38	40	22			9	0	506	120	30	13	7.7	.954	C-69, 1B-16
1889			87	.287	.453	300	86	10	11	6	2.0	52	60	48	35	18	0	0	503	99	22	25	7.2	.965	C-66, 1B-21, 3B-1
1890	CIN	N	54	.139	.223	202	28	4	2	3	1.5	21	19	19	36	5	0	0	271	64	16	6	6.5	.954	C-50, 1B-2, 3B-1
1891			75	.202	.317	252	51	7	5	4	1.6	30	33	33	39	2	0	0	590	53	31	22	9.0	.954	1B-41, C-34, 3B-1
10 yrs.			523	.241	.348	1873	452	61	36	22	1.2	254	152	177	111	41	0	0	3151	605	228	98	7.6	.943	C-403, 1B-105, OF-13, 3B-8, P-4, SS-2

Jim Keesey

KEESEY, JAMES WARD
B. Oct. 27, 1902, Perryville, Mo.   D. Sept. 5, 1951, Boise, Ida.

BR TR 6'½" 170 lbs.

Year	Team		Games	BA	SA	AB	H	2B	3B	HR	HR%	R	RBI	BB	SO	SB	AB	H	PO	A	E	DP	TC/G	FA	G by Pos
1925	PHI	A	5	.400	.400	5	2	0	0	0	0.0	1	1	0	2	0	3	2	2	0	0	0	0.4	1.000	1B-2
1930			11	.250	.333	12	3	1	0	0	0.0	2	2	1	2	0	8	2	10	0	1	2	1.0	.909	1B-3
2 yrs.			16	.294	.353	17	5	1	0	0	0.0	3	3	1	4	0	11	4	12	0	1	2	0.8	.923	1B-5

Bill Keinzil

KEINZIL, WILLIAM
B. Philadelphia, Pa.   Deceased.

BL TL

Year	Team		Games	BA	SA	AB	H	2B	3B	HR	HR%	R	RBI	BB	SO	SB	AB	H	PO	A	E	DP	TC/G	FA	G by Pos
1882	PHI	AA	9	.333	.545	33	11	3	2	0	0.0	8		5			0	0	15	1	3	0	2.1	.842	OF-9
1884	PHI	U	67	.254	.351	299	76	13	8	0	0.0	76		21			0	0	87	18	31	2	2.0	.772	OF-67
2 yrs.			76	.262	.370	332	87	16	10	0	0.0	84		26			0	0	102	19	34	2	2.0	.781	OF-76

Bill Keister

KEISTER, WILLIAM HOFFMAN (Wagon Tongue)
B. Aug. 17, 1874, Baltimore, Md.   D. Aug. 19, 1924, Baltimore, Md.

BL TR 5'5½" 168 lbs.

Year	Team		Games	BA	SA	AB	H	2B	3B	HR	HR%	R	RBI	BB	SO	SB	AB	H	PO	A	E	DP	TC/G	FA	G by Pos
1896	BAL	N	15	.241	.293	58	14	3	0	0	0.0	8	5	3	5	4	1	0	16	27	8	2	3.4	.843	2B-8, 3B-6
1898	BOS	N	10	.167	.233	30	5	2	0	0	0.0	5	4	0		1	0	1	10	16	0	2	2.6	1.000	SS-4, 2B-4, OF-1
1899	BAL	N	136	.329	.449	523	172	22	16	3	0.6	96	73	16		33	0	0	265	401	66	36	5.4	.910	SS-90, 2B-46, OF-1
1900	STL	N	126	.300	.398	497	149	26	10	1	0.2	78	72	25		32	1	1	224	345	50	27	4.9	.919	2B-116, SS-7, 3B-3
1901	BAL	A	115	.328	.482	442	145	20	21	2	0.5	78	93	18		24	2	0	231	322	97	30	5.7	.851	SS-112
1902	WAS	A	119	.300	.462	483	145	33	9	9	1.9	82	90	14		27	1	0	229	166	34	14	3.6	.921	OF-65, 2B-40, 3B-14, SS-2
1903	PHI	N	100	.320	.445	400	128	27	7	3	0.8	53	63	14		11	1	0	133	22	10	1	1.7	.939	OF-100
7 yrs.			621	.312	.440	2433	758	133	63	18	0.7	400	400	90	5	131	6	1	1108	1299	265	112	4.3	.901	SS-215, 2B-214, OF-167, 3B-23

Mickey Keliher

KELIHER, MAURICE MICHAEL
B. Jan. 11, 1890, Washington, D. C.   D. Sept. 7, 1930, Washington, D. C.

BL TL 6' 175 lbs.

Year	Team		Games	BA	SA	AB	H	2B	3B	HR	HR%	R	RBI	BB	SO	SB	AB	H	PO	A	E	DP	TC/G	FA	G by Pos
1911	PIT	N	2	.000	.000	7	0	0	0	0	0.0	0	0	0	5	0	1	0	6	1	1	1	4.0	.875	1B-2

Year	Team		Games	BA	SA	AB	H	2B	3B	HR	HR%	R	RBI	BB	SO	SB	Pinch Hit AB	H	PO	A	E	DP	TC/G	FA	G by Pos

Nat Kellogg

KELLOGG, NATHANIEL MONROE
B. Sept. 28, 1858, Dorchester, Iowa D. 1915

5'9" 175 lbs.

Year	Team		Games	BA	SA	AB	H	2B	3B	HR	HR%	R	RBI	BB	SO	SB	AB	H	PO	A	E	DP	TC/G	FA	G by Pos
1885	DET	N	5	.118	.176	17	2	1	0	0	0.0	4	0	1	5		0	0	6	12	5	1	4.6	.783	SS-5

Bill Kelly

KELLY, WILLIAM HENRY (Big Bill)
B. Dec. 28, 1899, Syracuse, N. Y.

BR TR 6' 190 lbs.

Year	Team		Games	BA	SA	AB	H	2B	3B	HR	HR%	R	RBI	BB	SO	SB	AB	H	PO	A	E	DP	TC/G	FA	G by Pos
1920	PHI	A	9	.231	.308	13	3	1	0	0	0.0	0	0	0	2	0	7	2	11	1	0	0	1.3	1.000	1B-2
1928	PHI	N	23	.169	.211	71	12	1	1	0	0.0	6	5	7	20	0	0	0	216	14	2	19	10.1	.991	1B-23
2 yrs.			32	.179	.226	84	15	2	1	0	0.0	6	5	7	22	0	7	2	227	15	2	19	7.6	.992	1B-25

Bill Kelly

KELLY, WILLIAM JOSEPH
B. May 1, 1886, Baltimore, Md. D. June 3, 1940, Detroit, Mich.

BR TR 6'½" 183 lbs.

Year	Team		Games	BA	SA	AB	H	2B	3B	HR	HR%	R	RBI	BB	SO	SB	AB	H	PO	A	E	DP	TC/G	FA	G by Pos
1910	STL	N	2	.000	.000	2	0	0	0	0	0.0	1	0	1	0	0	0	0	0	0	0	0	0.0	–	C-1
1911	PIT	N	6	.125	.125	8	1	0	0	0	0.0	0	0	0	2	0	5	1	11	0	0	0	1.8	1.000	C-1
1912			48	.318	.394	132	42	3	2	1	0.8	20	11	2	16	8	3	0	174	29	2	1	4.3	.990	C-39
1913			48	.268	.341	82	22	2	2	0	0.0	11	9	2	12	1	5	2	135	31	7	3	3.6	.960	C-40
4 yrs.			104	.290	.362	224	65	5	4	1	0.4	32	20	5	30	9	14	3	320	60	9	4	3.7	.977	C-81

Bob Kelly

KELLY, JAMES ROBERT
Also known as Robert John Taggert.
B. Feb. 1, 1884, Bloomfield, N. J. D. Apr. 10, 1961, Kingsport, Tenn.

BL TR 5'11" 180 lbs.

Year	Team		Games	BA	SA	AB	H	2B	3B	HR	HR%	R	RBI	BB	SO	SB	AB	H	PO	A	E	DP	TC/G	FA	G by Pos
1914	PIT	N	32	.227	.318	44	10	2	1	0	0.0	4	3	2	3	0	22	7	12	1	0	0	0.4	1.000	OF-7
1915	PIT	F	148	.294	.405	524	154	12	17	4	0.8	68	50	35		38	0	0	292	27	16	5	2.3	.952	OF-148
1918	BOS	N	35	.329	.390	146	48	1	4	0	0.0	19	4	9	9	4	0	0	82	2	4	0	2.5	.955	OF-35
3 yrs.			215	.297	.396	714	212	15	22	4	0.6	91	57	46	12	42	22	7	386	30	20	5	2.0	.954	OF-190

Bob Kelly

KELLY, ROBERT BROWN (Speed)
B. Aug. 12, 1884, Bryan, Ohio D. May 6, 1949, Goshen, Ind.

BR TR 6'2" 185 lbs.

Year	Team		Games	BA	SA	AB	H	2B	3B	HR	HR%	R	RBI	BB	SO	SB	AB	H	PO	A	E	DP	TC/G	FA	G by Pos
1909	WAS	A	17	.143	.238	42	6	2	1	0	0.0	3	1	3		1	2	0	10	27	9	2	2.7	.804	3B-10, 2B-3, OF-1

Charlie Kelly

KELLY, CHARLES H.
Deceased.

Year	Team		Games	BA	SA	AB	H	2B	3B	HR	HR%	R	RBI	BB	SO	SB	AB	H	PO	A	E	DP	TC/G	FA	G by Pos
1883	PHI	N	2	.143	.429	7	1	0	1	0	0.0	1		0	3		0	0	3	4	3	1	5.0	.700	3B-2
1886	PHI	AA	1	.000	.000	3	0	0	0	0	0.0	0		0			0	0	0	2	4	0	6.0	.333	SS-1
2 yrs.			3	.100	.300	10	1	0	1	0	0.0	1		0	3		0	0	3	6	7	1	5.3	.563	3B-2, SS-1

Dale Kelly

KELLY, DALE PATRICK
B. Aug. 27, 1955, Santa Maria, Calif.

BR TR 6'3" 210 lbs.

Year	Team		Games	BA	SA	AB	H	2B	3B	HR	HR%	R	RBI	BB	SO	SB	AB	H	PO	A	E	DP	TC/G	FA	G by Pos
1980	TOR	A	3	.286	.286	7	2	0	0	0	0.0	0	0	0	4	0	0	0	17	0	0	0	5.7	1.000	C-3

George Kelly

KELLY, GEORGE LANGE (Highpockets)
Brother of Ren Kelly.
B. Sept. 10, 1895, San Francisco, Calif. D. Oct. 13, 1984, Burlingame, Calif.
Hall of Fame 1973.

BR TR 6'4" 190 lbs.

Year	Team		Games	BA	SA	AB	H	2B	3B	HR	HR%	R	RBI	BB	SO	SB	AB	H	PO	A	E	DP	TC/G	FA	G by Pos
1915	NY	N	17	.158	.237	38	6	0	0	1	2.6	2	4	1	9	0	2	0	62	4	2	1	4.0	.971	1B-9, OF-4
1916			49	.158	.211	76	12	2	1	0	0.0	4	3	6	24	1	23	5	107	2	2	5	2.3	.982	1B-13, OF-12, 3B-1
1917	2 teams			NY N (11G – .000)		PIT N (8G – .087)																			
"	total		19	.067	.133	30	2	1	0	0	0.0	2	0	1	12	0	3	0	70	4	0	4	4.0	.974	1B-9, OF-3, 2B-1, P-1
1919	NY	N	32	.290	.411	107	31	6	2	1	0.9	12	14	3	15	1	0	0	341	11	2	17	11.1	.994	1B-32
1920			155	.266	.397	590	157	22	11	11	1.9	69	94	41	92	6	0	0	1759	103	11	115	12.1	.994	1B-155
1921			149	.308	.528	587	181	42	9	23	3.9	95	122	40	73	4	0	0	1552	115	17	132	11.3	.990	1B-149
1922			151	.328	.497	592	194	33	8	17	2.9	96	107	30	65	12	0	0	1642	103	13	123	11.6	.993	1B-151
1923			145	.307	.452	560	172	23	5	16	2.9	82	103	47	64	14	0	0	1568	60	12	111	11.3	.993	1B-145
1924			144	.324	.531	571	185	37	9	21	3.7	91	136	38	52	7	2	0	1357	79	13	107	10.1	.991	1B-125, OF-14, 2B-5, 3B-1
1925			147	.309	.471	586	181	29	3	20	3.4	87	99	35	54	5	0	0	567	411	18	81	6.8	.982	2B-108, 1B-25, OF-17
1926			136	.303	.445	499	151	24	4	13	2.6	70	80	36	52	4	5	0	1233	144	15	101	10.2	.989	1B-114, 2B-18
1927	CIN	N	61	.270	.446	222	60	16	4	5	2.3	27	21	11	23	1	1	0	476	64	8	49	9.0	.985	1B-49, 2B-13, OF-2
1928			116	.296	.435	402	119	33	7	3	0.9	46	58	28	35	2	2	0	927	70	11	100	8.7	.989	1B-99, OF-13
1929			147	.293	.428	577	169	45	9	5	0.9	73	103	33	61	7	0	0	1537	103	11	127	11.2	.993	1B-147
1930	2 teams			CIN N (51G – .287)		CHI N (39G – .331)																			
"	total		90	.308	.432	354	109	16	2	8	2.3	40	54	14	36	1	1	0	917	67	0	75	11.0	.995	1B-89
1932	BKN	N	64	.243	.356	202	49	9	1	4	2.0	23	22	22	27	0	1	0	576	36	10	48	9.7	.984	1B-62, OF-1
16 yrs.			1622	.297	.452	5993	1778	337	76	148	2.5	819	1020	386	694	65	40	5	14691	1376	152	1196	10.0	.991	1B-1373, 2B-145, OF-66, 3B-2, P-1
WORLD SERIES																									
1921	NY	N	8	.233	.267	30	7	1	0	0	0.0	3	3	3	10	0	0	0	86	7	0	3	11.6	1.000	1B-8
1922			5	.278	.278	18	5	0	0	0	0.0	0	2	0	3	0	0	0	61	1	0	2	12.4	1.000	1B-5
1923			6	.182	.182	22	4	0	0	0	0.0	1	1	1	2	0	0	0	63	4	1	5	11.3	.985	1B-6
1924			7	.290	.419	31	9	1	0	1	3.2	7	4	1	8	0	0	0	52	5	1	2	8.3	.983	OF-4, 1B-4, 2B-1
4 yrs.			26	.248	.297	101	25	2	0	1	1.0	11	10	5 10th	23	0	0	0	262	17	2	12	10.8	.993	1B-23, OF-4, 2B-1

Honest John Kelly

KELLY, JOHN O.
B. Oct. 31, 1856, New York, N. Y. D. Mar. 27, 1926, Malba, N. Y.
Manager 1887-88.

6'½" 185 lbs.

Year	Team		Games	BA	SA	AB	H	2B	3B	HR	HR%	R	RBI	BB	SO	SB	AB	H	PO	A	E	DP	TC/G	FA	G by Pos
1879	2 teams			SYR N (10G – .111)		TRO N (6G – .227)																			
"	total		16	.155	.172	58	9	1	0	0	0.0	5	2	0	7		0	0	57	17	18	1	5.8	.804	C-11, OF-2, 1B-2, 3B-1

Joe Kelly

KELLY, JOSEPH HENRY
B. Sept. 23, 1886, Weir City, Kans. D. Aug. 16, 1977, St. Joseph, Mo.

BR TR 5'9" 172 lbs.

Year	Team	Games	BA	SA	AB	H	2B	3B	HR	HR%	R	RBI	BB	SO	SB	Pinch Hit AB	H	PO	A	E	DP	TC/G	FA	G by Pos

Joe Kelly *continued*

Year	Team	Games	BA	SA	AB	H	2B	3B	HR	HR%	R	RBI	BB	SO	SB	AB	H	PO	A	E	DP	TC/G	FA	G by Pos
1914	PIT N	141	.222	.301	508	113	19	9	1	0.2	47	48	39	59	21	2	0	319	15	19	3	2.5	.946	OF-138
1916	CHI N	54	.254	.343	169	43	7	1	2	1.2	18	15	10	8	1	8	1	98	4	5	0	2.0	.953	OF-46
1917	BOS N	116	.222	.299	445	99	9	8	3	0.7	41	36	26	45	21	0	0	284	16	17	8	2.7	.946	OF-116
1918		47	.232	.297	155	36	2	4	0	0.0	20	15	6	12	12	2	1	93	4	7	0	2.2	.933	OF-45
1919		18	.141	.156	64	9	1	0	0	0.0	3	3	3	11	2	2	1	30	3	2	0	1.9	.943	OF-16
5 yrs.		376	.224	.298	1341	300	38	22	6	0.4	129	117	80	143	66	14	3	824	42	50	11	2.4	.945	OF-361

Joe Kelly

KELLY, JOSEPH JAMES
B. Apr. 23, 1900, New York, N. Y.   D. Nov. 24, 1967, Lynbrook, N. Y.

BL TL 6'   180 lbs.

Year	Team	Games	BA	SA	AB	H	2B	3B	HR	HR%	R	RBI	BB	SO	SB	AB	H	PO	A	E	DP	TC/G	FA	G by Pos
1926	CHI N	65	.335	.455	176	59	15	3	0	0.0	16	32	7	11	0	24	9	58	3	3	0	1.0	.953	OF-39
1928		32	.212	.288	52	11	1	0	1	1.9	3	7	1	3	0	21	3	105	6	3	8	3.6	.974	1B-10
2 yrs.		97	.307	.417	228	70	16	3	1	0.4	19	39	8	14	0	45	12	163	9	6	8	1.8	.966	OF-39, 1B-10

John Kelly

KELLY, JOHN B.
B. Mar. 13, 1879, Clifton Heights, Pa.   D. Mar. 19, 1944, Baltimore, Md.

5'9"   165 lbs.

Year	Team	Games	BA	SA	AB	H	2B	3B	HR	HR%	R	RBI	BB	SO	SB	AB	H	PO	A	E	DP	TC/G	FA	G by Pos
1907	STL N	53	.188	.213	197	37	5	0	0	0.0	12	6	13		7	1	0	85	7	3	4	1.8	.968	OF-52

Kick Kelly

KELLY, JOHN FRANCIS (Father)
B. 1859, Patterson, N. J.   D. Apr. 13, 1908, Patterson, N. J.

BR TR 6'   185 lbs.

Year	Team	Games	BA	SA	AB	H	2B	3B	HR	HR%	R	RBI	BB	SO	SB	AB	H	PO	A	E	DP	TC/G	FA	G by Pos
1882	CLE N	30	.135	.154	104	14	2	0	0	0.0	6	5	1	24		0	0	113	35	37	2	6.2	.800	C-30
1883	2 teams	BAL AA (48G – .228)				PHI N (1G – .000)																		
"	total	49	.224	.288	205	46	9	2	0	0.0	18		3	2		0	0	189	39	58	3	5.8	.797	C-38, OF-14
1884	2 teams	CIN U (38G – .282)				WAS U (4G – .357)																		
"	total	42	.288	.359	156	45	6	1	1	0.6	24		6			0	0	239	67	44	3	8.3	.874	C-40, OF-3
3 yrs.		121	.226	.282	465	105	17	3	1	0.2	48	5	10	26		0	0	541	141	139	8	6.8	.831	C-108, OF-17

King Kelly

KELLY, MICHAEL JOSEPH
B. Dec. 31, 1857, Troy, N. Y.   D. Nov. 8, 1894, Boston, Mass.
Manager 1887, 1890-91.
Hall of Fame 1945.

BR TR 5'10"   170 lbs.

Year	Team	Games	BA	SA	AB	H	2B	3B	HR	HR%	R	RBI	BB	SO	SB	AB	H	PO	A	E	DP	TC/G	FA	G by Pos
1878	CIN N	60	.283	.321	237	67	7	1	0	0.0	29	27	7	7		0	0	150	65	43	5	4.3	.833	OF-47, C-17, 3B-2
1879		77	.348	.493	345	120	20	12	2	0.6	78	47	8	14		0	0	164	139	58	4	4.7	.839	3B-33, OF-29, C-21, 2B-1
1880	CHI N	84	.291	.401	344	100	17	9	1	0.3	72	60	12	22		0	0	111	68	42	3	2.6	.810	OF-64, C-17, 3B-14, SS-1, 2B-1, P-1
1881		82	.323	.433	353	114	**27**	3	2	0.6	84	55	16	14		0	0	121	52	33	3	2.5	.840	OF-72, C-11, 3B-8
1882		84	.305	.432	377	115	**37**	4	1	0.3	81	55	10	27		0	0	133	149	59	12	4.1	.827	SS-42, OF-38, C-12, 3B-3, 1B-1
1883		98	.255	.388	428	109	28	10	3	0.7	92		16	35		0	0	183	91	63	7	3.4	.813	OF-82, C-38, 2B-3, 3B-2, P-1
1884		108	**.354**	.524	452	160	28	5	13	2.9	120		46	24		0	0	201	141	86	10	4.0	.799	OF-63, C-28, SS-12, 3B-10, 1B-2, P-2
1885		107	.288	.436	438	126	24	9	9	2.1	124	74	46	24		0	0	259	112	58	5	4.0	.865	OF-69, C-37, 2B-6, 3B-2, 1B-2
1886		118	**.388**	.534	451	175	32	11	4	0.9	155	79	83	33		0	0	387	141	59	11	5.0	.899	OF-56, C-53, 1B-9, 3B-8, 2B-6, SS-5
1887	BOS N	116	.322	.488	484	156	34	11	8	1.7	120	63	55	40	84	0	0	252	163	72	24	4.2	.852	OF-61, 2B-30, C-24, P-3, SS-2, 3B-2
1888		107	.318	.480	440	140	22	11	9	2.0	85	71	31	39	56	0	0	395	150	66	10	5.7	.892	C-76, P-34
1889		125	.294	.448	507	149	**41**	5	9	1.8	120	78	65	40	68	0	0	211	53	44	6	2.5	.857	OF-113, C-23
1890	BOS P	89	.326	.450	340	111	18	6	4	1.2	83	66	52	22	51	0	0	274	145	55	12	5.3	.884	C-56, SS-27, OF-6, 1B-4, 3B-2, P-1
1891	3 teams	CIN AA (82G – .297)				BOS AA (4G – .267)				BOS N (16G – .231)														
"	total	102	.286	.389	350	100	16	7	2	0.6	65	62	57	40	29	0	0	351	159	59	19	5.6	.896	C-81, OF-21, 3B-8, 2B-6, 1B-5, P-3, SS-1
1892	BOS N	78	.189	.235	281	53	7	4	2	0.7	40	41	39	31	24	0	0	340	101	47	13	6.3	.904	C-72, OF-2, 3B-2, 1B-2, P-1
1893	NY N	20	.269	.284	67	18	1	0	0	0.0	9	15	6	5	3	2	0	55	22	10	1	4.4	.885	C-17, OF-1
16 yrs.		1455	.308	.438	5894	1813	359	102	69	1.2	1357	793	549	417	315	2	0	3587	1751	854	145	4.3	.862	OF-758, C-583, 3B-96, SS-90, 2B-53, 1B-25, P-12

Pat Kelly

KELLY, HAROLD PATRICK
B. July 30, 1944, Philadelphia, Pa.

BL TL 6'1"   185 lbs.

Year	Team	Games	BA	SA	AB	H	2B	3B	HR	HR%	R	RBI	BB	SO	SB	AB	H	PO	A	E	DP	TC/G	FA	G by Pos
1967	MIN A	8	.000	.000	1	0	0	0	0	0.0	1	0	0	1	0	1	0	0	0	0	0	0.0		
1968		12	.114	.257	35	4	2	0	1	2.9	2	2	3	10	0	2	0	20	0	1	0	1.8	.955	OF-10
1969	KC A	112	.264	.388	417	110	20	4	8	1.9	61	32	49	70	40	3	0	237	12	5	3	2.3	.980	OF-107
1970		136	.235	.314	452	106	16	1	6	1.3	56	38	76	105	34	17	1	254	8	10	2	2.0	.963	OF-118
1971	CHI A	67	.291	.390	213	62	6	3	3	1.4	32	22	36	29	14	7	4	100	7	1	0	1.6	.991	OF-61
1972		119	.261	.368	402	105	14	4	5	1.2	57	24	55	69	32	17	3	173	8	6	3	1.6	.968	OF-109
1973		144	.280	.347	550	154	24	5	1	0.2	77	44	65	91	22	7	2	254	9	6	2	1.9	.978	OF-141, DH-1
1974		122	.281	.361	424	119	16	3	4	0.9	60	21	46	48	18	3	0	79	2	2	0	0.7	.976	DH-67, OF-53
1975		133	.274	.406	471	129	21	7	9	1.9	73	45	58	69	18	5	1	222	4	2	1	1.7	.991	OF-115, DH-14
1976		107	.254	.386	311	79	20	3	5	1.6	42	34	45	45	15	20	7	37	1	0	0	0.4	.950	DH-63, OF-26
1977	BAL A	120	.256	.375	360	92	13	4	10	2.8	50	49	53	75	25	21	6	181	2	3	1	1.6	.984	OF-109, DH-1
1978		100	.274	.445	274	75	12	1	11	4.0	38	40	34	58	10	18	6	123	4	3	1	1.3	.969	OF-80, DH-2
1979		68	.288	.536	153	44	11	0	9	5.9	25	25	20	25	4	23	11	36	0	0	0	0.5	1.000	OF-24, DH-18
1980		89	.260	.365	200	52	10	1	3	1.5	38	26	34	54	10	29	8	48	4	0	1	0.6	1.000	OF-36, DH-8
1981	CLE A	48	.213	.307	75	16	4	0	1	1.3	8	16	14	9	2	24	3	6	0	0	0	0.1	1.000	DH-18, OF-8
15 yrs.		1385	.264	.377	4338	1147	189	35	76	1.8	620	418	588	768	250	187	51	1770	61	42	15	1.4	.978	OF-997, DH-214

LEAGUE CHAMPIONSHIP SERIES

Year	Team	Games	BA	SA	AB	H	2B	3B	HR	HR%	R	RBI	BB	SO	SB	AB	H	PO	A	E	DP	TC/G	FA	G by Pos
1979	BAL A	3	.364	.636	11	4	0	0	1	9.1	3	4	1	3	2	0	0	3	0	0	0	1.0	1.000	OF-2, DH-1

WORLD SERIES

Year	Team	Games	BA	SA	AB	H	2B	3B	HR	HR%	R	RBI	BB	SO	SB	AB	H	PO	A	E	DP	TC/G	FA	G by Pos
1979	BAL A	5	.250	.250	4	1	0	0	0	0.0	0	1	1	0	0	4	1	0	0	0	0	0.0	–	

Year	Team		Games	BA	SA	AB	H	2B	3B	HR	HR%	R	RBI	BB	SO	SB	Pinch Hit AB	H	PO	A	E	DP	TC/G	FA	G by Pos

Red Kelly
KELLY, ALBERT MICHAEL
B. Nov. 15, 1884, Union, Ill.   D. Feb. 4, 1961, Zephyrhills, Fla.
BR TR 5'11½" 165 lbs.

Year	Team		Games	BA	SA	AB	H	2B	3B	HR	HR%	R	RBI	BB	SO	SB	AB	H	PO	A	E	DP	TC/G	FA	G by Pos
1910	CHI	A	14	.156	.200	45	7	0	1	0	0.0	6	1	7		0	0	0	18	1	0	0	1.4	1.000	OF-14

Roberto Kelly
KELLY, ROBERTO CONRADO
Born Roberto Conrado Kelly y Gray.
B. Oct. 1, 1964, Panama City, Panama
BR TR 6'2" 180 lbs.

Year	Team		Games	BA	SA	AB	H	2B	3B	HR	HR%	R	RBI	BB	SO	SB	AB	H	PO	A	E	DP	TC/G	FA	G by Pos
1987	NY	A	23	.269	.385	52	14	3	0	1	1.9	12	7	5	15	9	0	0	42	0	2	0	1.9	.955	OF-17
1988			38	.247	.364	77	19	4	1	1	1.3	9	7	3	15	5	1	1	70	1	1	0	1.9	.986	OF-30
1989			137	.302	.417	441	133	18	3	9	2.0	65	48	41	89	35	2	2	353	9	6	2	2.7	.984	OF-137
3 yrs.			198	.291	.407	570	166	25	4	11	1.9	86	62	49	119	49	3	3	465	10	9	2	2.4	.981	OF-184

Tom Kelly
KELLY, JAY THOMAS
B. Aug. 15, 1950, Graceville, Minn.
Manager 1986-89.
BL TL 5'11" 188 lbs.

Year	Team		Games	BA	SA	AB	H	2B	3B	HR	HR%	R	RBI	BB	SO	SB	AB	H	PO	A	E	DP	TC/G	FA	G by Pos
1975	MIN	A	49	.181	.244	127	23	5	0	1	0.8	11	11	15	22	0	5	1	360	28	6	27	8.0	.985	1B-43, OF-2

Van Kelly
KELLY, VAN HOWARD
B. Mar. 18, 1946, Charlotte, N. C.
BL TR 5'11" 180 lbs.

Year	Team		Games	BA	SA	AB	H	2B	3B	HR	HR%	R	RBI	BB	SO	SB	AB	H	PO	A	E	DP	TC/G	FA	G by Pos
1969	SD	N	73	.244	.330	209	51	7	1	3	1.4	16	15	12	24	0	16	4	47	104	6	10	2.2	.962	3B-49, 2B-10
1970			38	.169	.236	89	15	3	0	1	1.1	9	9	15	21	0	11	1	23	46	2	3	1.9	.972	3B-27, 2B-1
2 yrs.			111	.221	.302	298	66	10	1	4	1.3	25	24	27	45	0	27	5	70	150	8	13	2.1	.965	3B-76, 2B-11

Billy Kelsey
KELSEY, GEORGE WILLIAM
B. Aug. 24, 1881, Covington, Ohio   D. Apr. 25, 1968, Springfield, Ohio
BR TR 5'10" 150 lbs.

Year	Team		Games	BA	SA	AB	H	2B	3B	HR	HR%	R	RBI	BB	SO	SB	AB	H	PO	A	E	DP	TC/G	FA	G by Pos
1907	PIT	N	2	.400	.400	5	2	0	0	0	0.0	1	0	0		0	0	0	5	2	0	0	3.5	1.000	C-2

Ken Keltner
KELTNER, KENNETH FREDERICK
B. Oct. 31, 1916, Milwaukee, Wis.
BR TR 6' 190 lbs.

Year	Team		Games	BA	SA	AB	H	2B	3B	HR	HR%	R	RBI	BB	SO	SB	AB	H	PO	A	E	DP	TC/G	FA	G by Pos
1937	CLE	A	1	.000	.000	1	0	0	0	0	0.0	0	1	0	0	0	0	0	0	1	0	0	1.0	1.000	3B-1
1938			149	.276	.497	576	159	31	9	26	4.5	86	113	33	75	4	0	0	141	271	19	19	2.9	.956	3B-149
1939			154	.325	.489	587	191	35	11	13	2.2	84	97	51	41	6	0	0	187	297	13	40	3.2	.974	3B-154
1940			149	.254	.418	543	138	24	10	15	2.8	67	77	51	56	10	1	0	170	277	22	27	3.1	.953	3B-148
1941			149	.269	.485	581	156	31	13	23	4.0	83	84	51	56	2	0	0	181	346	16	36	3.6	.971	3B-149
1942			152	.287	.383	624	179	34	4	6	1.0	72	78	20	36	4	1	0	166	353	30	38	3.6	.945	3B-151
1943			110	.260	.375	427	111	31	3	4	0.9	47	39	36	20	2	3	1	113	228	11	24	3.2	.969	3B-107
1944			149	.295	.466	573	169	41	9	13	2.3	74	91	53	29	4	0	0	168	369	18	37	3.7	.968	3B-149
1946			116	.241	.387	398	96	17	1	13	3.3	47	45	30	38	0	4	1	112	195	11	18	2.7	.965	3B-112
1947			151	.257	.383	541	139	29	3	11	2.0	49	76	59	45	5	1	0	156	266	12	29	2.9	.972	3B-150
1948			153	.297	.522	558	166	24	4	31	5.6	91	119	89	52	2	0	0	123	312	14	27	2.9	.969	3B-153
1949			80	.232	.382	246	57	9	2	8	3.3	35	30	38	26	0	10	2	51	145	4	11	2.5	.980	3B-69
1950	BOS	A	13	.321	.393	28	9	2	0	0	0.0	2	2	3	6	0	4	1	9	10	1	1	1.5	.950	3B-8, 1B-1
13 yrs.			1526	.276	.441	5683	1570	308	69	163	2.9	737	852	514	480	39	24	5	1577	3070	171	307	3.2	.965	3B-1500, 1B-1

WORLD SERIES

Year	Team		Games	BA	SA	AB	H	2B	3B	HR	HR%	R	RBI	BB	SO	SB	AB	H	PO	A	E	DP	TC/G	FA	G by Pos
1948	CLE	A	6	.095	.095	21	2	0	0	0	0.0	3	0	2	3	0	0	0	3	11	1	1	2.5	.933	3B-6

John Kelty
KELTY, JOHN JAMES (Chief)
B. 1867, Jersey City, N. J.   Deceased.
5'10" 175 lbs.

Year	Team		Games	BA	SA	AB	H	2B	3B	HR	HR%	R	RBI	BB	SO	SB	AB	H	PO	A	E	DP	TC/G	FA	G by Pos
1890	PIT	N	59	.237	.319	207	49	10	2	1	0.5	24	27	22	42	10	0	0	100	6	12	1	2.0	.898	OF-59

Billie Kemmer
KEMMER, WILLIAM E.
Deceased.
BR TR 6'2"

Year	Team		Games	BA	SA	AB	H	2B	3B	HR	HR%	R	RBI	BB	SO	SB	AB	H	PO	A	E	DP	TC/G	FA	G by Pos
1895	LOU	N	11	.184	.263	38	7	0	0	1	2.6	5	3	2	4	0	0	0	34	23	10	4	6.1	.851	3B-9, 1B-2

Rudy Kemmler
KEMMLER, RUDOLPH
Born Rudolph Kemler.
B. 1860, Chicago, Ill.   D. June 20, 1909, Chicago, Ill.
BR TR

Year	Team		Games	BA	SA	AB	H	2B	3B	HR	HR%	R	RBI	BB	SO	SB	AB	H	PO	A	E	DP	TC/G	FA	G by Pos
1879	PRO	N	2	.143	.143	7	1	0	0	0	0.0	0		0	0		0	0	13	7	4	0	12.0	.833	C-2
1881	CLE	N	1	.000	.000	3	0	0	0	0	0.0	0		0	1		0	0	5	2	0	1	7.0	1.000	C-1
1882	2 teams			CIN	AA	(3G – .091)				PIT	AA	(24G – .253)													
"	total		27	.236	.282	110	26	5	0	0	0.0	7		1			0	0	131	39	15	1	6.9	.919	C-26, OF-2
1883	COL	AA	84	.208	.239	318	66	6	2	0	0.0	27		13			0	0	390	99	73	11	6.7	.870	C-82, OF-2
1884			61	.199	.242	211	42	3	3	0	0.0	28		15			0	0	293	77	37	4	6.7	.909	C-58, 1B-2, OF-1
1885	PIT	AA	18	.203	.266	64	13	2	1	0	0.0	2		2			0	0	86	28	17	0	7.3	.870	C-18
1886	STL	AA	35	.138	.154	123	17	2	0	0	0.0	13		8			0	0	182	65	23	4	7.7	.915	C-32, 1B-3
1889	COL	AA	8	.115	.115	26	3	0	0	0	0.0	2		3			0	0	35	18	4	1	7.1	.930	C-8
8 yrs.			236	.195	.230	862	168	18	6	0	0.0	79		42	5		0	0	1135	335	173	22	7.0	.895	C-227, OF-5, 1B-5

Steve Kemp
KEMP, STEVEN F.
B. Aug. 7, 1954, San Angelo, Tex.
BL TL 6' 195 lbs.

Year	Team		Games	BA	SA	AB	H	2B	3B	HR	HR%	R	RBI	BB	SO	SB	AB	H	PO	A	E	DP	TC/G	FA	G by Pos
1977	DET	A	151	.257	.422	552	142	29	4	18	3.3	75	88	71	93	3	3	0	252	10	5	1	1.8	.981	OF-148
1978			159	.277	.399	582	161	18	4	15	2.6	75	79	97	87	2	2	1	325	11	8	2	2.2	.977	OF-157
1979			134	.318	.543	490	156	26	4	26	5.3	88	105	68	70	5	4	1	229	12	6	2	1.8	.976	OF-120, DH-11
1980			135	.293	.474	508	149	23	4	21	4.1	88	101	69	64	5	6	2	197	4	1	3	1.5	.995	OF-85, DH-46
1981			105	.277	.419	372	103	18	0	9	2.4	52	49	70	48	9	3	1	207	4	3	0	2.0	.986	OF-92, DH-12
1982	CHI	A	160	.286	.428	580	166	23	1	19	3.3	91	98	89	83	7	3	1	280	6	7	1	1.8	.976	OF-154, DH-2
1983	NY	A	109	.241	.399	373	90	17	3	12	3.2	53	49	41	37	1	9	2	215	5	3	3	2.0	.987	OF-101, DH-12
1984			94	.291	.403	313	91	12	1	7	2.2	37	41	40	54	4	9	2	138	2	4	0	1.5	.972	OF-75, DH-12
1985	PIT	N	92	.250	.347	236	59	13	2	2	0.8	19	21	25	54	1	27	9	105	1	0	0	1.2	1.000	OF-63
1986			13	.188	.375	16	3	0	0	1	6.3	1	1	4	6	1	5	0	9	0	0	0	0.7	1.000	OF-4

Year	Team	Games	BA	SA	AB	H	2B	3B	HR	HR%	R	RBI	BB	SO	SB	Pinch Hit AB	Pinch Hit H	PO	A	E	DP	TC/G	FA	G by Pos

Steve Kemp *continued*

Year	Team	Games	BA	SA	AB	H	2B	3B	HR	HR%	R	RBI	BB	SO	SB	PH AB	PH H	PO	A	E	DP	TC/G	FA	G by Pos
1988	TEX A	16	.222	.222	36	8	0	0	0	0.0	2	2	2	9	1	5	1	6	0	0	0	0.4	1.000	DH-7, OF-5, 1B-1
11 yrs.		1168	.278	.431	4058	1128	179	25	130	3.2	581	634	576	605	39	76	20	1963	55	37	12	1.8	.982	OF-1004, DH-92, 1B-1

Fred Kendall

KENDALL, FRED LYN
B. Jan. 31, 1949, Torrance, Calif.
BR TR 6'1" 185 lbs.

Year	Team	Games	BA	SA	AB	H	2B	3B	HR	HR%	R	RBI	BB	SO	SB	PH AB	PH H	PO	A	E	DP	TC/G	FA	G by Pos
1969	SD N	10	.154	.154	26	4	0	0	0	0.0	2	0	2	5	0	1	0	37	5	0	0	4.2	1.000	C-9
1970		4	.000	.000	9	0	0	0	0	0.0	0	1	0	1	0	1	0	7	1	0	0	2.0	1.000	C-2, OF-1, 1B-1
1971		49	.171	.207	111	19	1	0	1	0.9	2	7	7	16	1	7	1	184	14	0	1	4.0	1.000	C-39, 3B-1, 1B-1
1972		91	.216	.322	273	59	3	4	6	2.2	18	18	11	42	0	8	1	506	41	3	11	6.0	.995	C-82, 1B-1
1973		145	.282	.396	507	143	23	3	10	2.0	39	59	30	35	3	5	1	749	64	13	7	5.7	.984	C-138
1974		141	.231	.333	424	98	15	2	8	1.9	32	45	49	33	0	21	6	631	64	12	12	5.0	.983	C-133
1975		103	.199	.248	286	57	12	1	0	0.0	16	24	26	28	0	18	4	337	38	9	6	3.7	.977	C-85
1976		146	.246	.296	456	112	17	0	2	0.4	30	39	36	42	1	1	0	582	54	4	6	4.4	.994	C-146
1977	CLE A	103	.249	.325	317	79	13	1	3	0.9	18	39	16	27	0	1	0	506	35	5	5	5.3	.991	C-102, DH-1
1978	BOS A	20	.195	.220	41	8	1	0	0	0.0	3	4	1	2	0	2	0	107	11	2	7	6.0	.983	1B-13, C-5
1979	SD N	46	.167	.216	102	17	2	0	1	1.0	8	6	11	7	0	8	4	162	19	4	3	4.0	.978	C-40, 1B-2
1980		19	.292	.292	24	7	0	0	0	0.0	2	2	0	3	0	5	2	31	1	2	0	1.8	.941	C-14, 1B-1
12 yrs.		877	.234	.312	2576	603	86	11	31	1.2	170	244	189	240	5	78	19	3839	347	54	58	4.8	.987	C-795, 1B-19, DH-1, OF-1, 3B-1

Al Kenders

KENDERS, ALBERT DANIEL GEORGE
B. Apr. 4, 1937, Barrington, N. J.
BR TR 6' 185 lbs.

Year	Team	Games	BA	SA	AB	H	2B	3B	HR	HR%	R	RBI	BB	SO	SB	PH AB	PH H	PO	A	E	DP	TC/G	FA	G by Pos
1961	PHI N	10	.174	.217	23	4	1	0	0	0.0	0	1	0	7	0	0	0	27	3	0	1	3.0	1.000	C-10

Ed Kenna

KENNA, EDWARD ALOYISIUS (Scrap Iron)
B. Sept. 30, 1897, San Francisco, Calif. D. Aug. 21, 1972, San Francisco, Calif.
BR TR 5'7½" 150 lbs.

Year	Team	Games	BA	SA	AB	H	2B	3B	HR	HR%	R	RBI	BB	SO	SB	PH AB	PH H	PO	A	E	DP	TC/G	FA	G by Pos
1928	WAS A	41	.297	.390	118	35	4	2	1	0.8	14	20	14	8	1	7	2	104	26	8	3	3.4	.942	C-34

Bob Kennedy

KENNEDY, ROBERT DANIEL
Father of Terry Kennedy.
B. Aug. 18, 1920, Chicago, Ill.
Manager 1963-65, 1968.
BR TR 6'2" 193 lbs.

Year	Team	Games	BA	SA	AB	H	2B	3B	HR	HR%	R	RBI	BB	SO	SB	PH AB	PH H	PO	A	E	DP	TC/G	FA	G by Pos
1939	CHI A	3	.250	.250	8	2	0	0	0	0.0	0	1	0	0	0	1	0	0	3	1	0	1.3	.750	3B-2
1940		154	.252	.315	606	153	23	3	3	0.5	74	52	42	58	3	0	0	178	322	33	25	3.5	.938	3B-154
1941		76	.206	.276	257	53	9	3	1	0.4	16	29	17	23	5	0	0	88	153	17	12	3.4	.934	3B-71
1942		113	.231	.299	412	95	18	5	0	0.0	37	38	22	41	11	1	0	130	209	15	17	3.1	.958	3B-96, OF-16
1946		113	.258	.350	411	106	13	5	5	1.2	43	34	24	42	6	5	2	176	87	16	7	2.5	.943	OF-75, 3B-29
1947		115	.262	.362	428	112	19	3	6	1.4	47	48	18	38	3	4	0	205	10	7	3	1.9	.968	OF-106, 3B-1
1948	2 teams				CHI A (30G – .248)				CLE A (66G – .301)															
"	total	96	.269	.360	186	50	11	3	0	0.0	14	19	8	23	0	12	6	103	10	2	3	1.2	.983	OF-80, 2B-2, 1B-1
1949	CLE A	121	.276	.417	464	117	23	5	9	1.9	49	57	37	40	5	2	0	203	56	3	8	2.2	.989	OF-98, 3B-21
1950		146	.291	.409	540	157	27	5	9	1.7	79	54	53	31	3	0	0	294	13	4	3	2.1	.987	OF-144
1951		108	.246	.383	321	79	15	4	7	2.2	30	29	34	33	4	4	0	174	9	6	2	1.8	.968	OF-106
1952		22	.300	.425	40	12	3	1	0	0.0	6	12	9	1	1	5	0	25	12	0	1	1.7	1.000	OF-13, 3B-3
1953		100	.236	.323	161	38	5	0	3	1.9	22	22	19	11	0	6	2	91	0	0	1	0.9	1.000	OF-89
1954	2 teams				CLE A (1G – .000)				BAL A (106G – .251)															
"	total	107	.251	.359	323	81	13	2	6	1.9	37	45	28	43	2	17	4	121	131	15	10	2.5	.944	3B-71, OF-22
1955	2 teams				BAL A (26G – .143)				CHI A (83G – .304)															
"	total	109	.264	.412	284	75	11	2	9	3.2	38	48	26	26	0	23	4	129	77	7	17	2.0	.967	3B-56, OF-34, 1B-9
1956	2 teams				CHI A (8G – .077)				DET A (69G – .232)															
"	total	77	.221	.311	190	42	5	0	4	2.1	17	22	26	23	2	19	2	91	43	12	5	1.9	.918	3B-33, OF-29
1957	2 teams				CHI A (4G – .000)				BKN N (19G – .129)															
"	total	23	.121	.242	33	4	1	0	1	3.0	5	4	1	6	0	7	1	8	2	0	0	0.4	1.000	OF-9, 3B-3
16 yrs.		1483	.254	.355	4624	1176	196	41	63	1.4	514	514	364	443	45	108	21	2016	1139	138	113	2.2	.958	OF-821, 3B-540, 1B-10, 2B-2

WORLD SERIES

Year	Team	Games	BA	SA	AB	H	2B	3B	HR	HR%	R	RBI	BB	SO	SB	PH AB	PH H	PO	A	E	DP	TC/G	FA	G by Pos
1948	CLE A	3	.500	.500	2	1	0	0	0	0.0	0	1	0	1	0	0	0	2	0	0	0	0.7	1.000	OF-3

Doc Kennedy

KENNEDY, MICHAEL JOSEPH
B. Aug. 11, 1853, Brooklyn, N. Y. D. May 25, 1920, Grove, N. Y.
BR TR

Year	Team	Games	BA	SA	AB	H	2B	3B	HR	HR%	R	RBI	BB	SO	SB	PH AB	PH H	PO	A	E	DP	TC/G	FA	G by Pos
1879	CLE N	49	.290	.368	193	56	8	2	1	0.5	19	18	2	10		0	0	318	52	42	4	8.4	.898	C-46, 1B-4
1880		66	.200	.248	250	50	10	1	0	0.0	26	18	5	12		0	0	398	68	52	9	7.8	.900	C-65, OF-2
1881		39	.313	.373	150	47	7	1	0	0.0	19	15	5	13		0	0	215	38	23	4	7.1	.917	C-35, OF-3, 3B-1
1882		1	.333	.333	3	1	0	0	0	0.0	0	0	0	0		0	0	9	3	3	0	21.0	.857	C-1
1883	BUF N	5	.316	.316	19	6	0	0	0	0.0	3		3	2		0	0	21	6	5	2	5.2	.808	OF-4, 1B-1
5 yrs.		160	.260	.319	615	160	25	4	1	0.2	67	51	15	37		0	0	961	167	125	19	7.8	.900	C-147, OF-9, 1B-5, 3B-1

Ed Kennedy

KENNEDY, EDWARD
B. Apr. 1, 1856, Carbondale, Pa. D. May 20, 1905, New York, N. Y.

Year	Team	Games	BA	SA	AB	H	2B	3B	HR	HR%	R	RBI	BB	SO	SB	PH AB	PH H	PO	A	E	DP	TC/G	FA	G by Pos
1883	NY AA	94	.219	.292	356	78	6	7	2	0.6	57		17			0	0	112	10	16	0	1.5	.884	OF-94
1884		103	.190	.225	378	72	6	2	1	0.3	49		16			0	0	142	18	14	5	1.7	.920	OF-100, SS-1, 2B-1, C-1
1885		96	.203	.266	349	71	8	4	2	0.6	35		12			0	0	154	15	32	1	2.1	.841	OF-96
1886	BKN AA	6	.182	.182	22	4	0	0	0	0.0	1		2			0	0	10	0	1	0	1.8	.909	OF-6
4 yrs.		299	.204	.259	1105	225	20	13	5	0.5	142		47			0	0	418	43	63	6	1.8	.880	OF-296, SS-1, 2B-1, C-1

Ed Kennedy

KENNEDY, WILLIAM EDWARD
B. Apr. 5, 1861, Bellevue, Ky. D. Dec. 22, 1912, Cheyenne, Wyo.
BR TR 5'7" 160 lbs.

Year	Team	Games	BA	SA	AB	H	2B	3B	HR	HR%	R	RBI	BB	SO	SB	PH AB	PH H	PO	A	E	DP	TC/G	FA	G by Pos
1884	CIN U	13	.208	.271	48	10	1	1	0	0.0	6		1			0	0	14	24	5	1	3.3	.884	3B-8, SS-4, OF-1

Year	Team	Games	BA	SA	AB	H	2B	3B	HR	HR%	R	RBI	BB	SO	SB	Pinch Hit AB	Pinch Hit H	PO	A	E	DP	TC/G	FA	G by Pos

Jim Kennedy
KENNEDY, JAMES EARL
Brother of Junior Kennedy.
B. Nov. 1, 1946, Tulsa, Okla.
BL TR 5'9" 160 lbs.

Year	Team	Games	BA	SA	AB	H	2B	3B	HR	HR%	R	RBI	BB	SO	SB	PH AB	PH H	PO	A	E	DP	TC/G	FA	G by Pos
1970	STL N	12	.125	.125	24	3	0	0	0	0.0	1	0	0	0	0	1	0	19	20	4	5	3.6	.907	SS-7, 2B-5

John Kennedy
KENNEDY, JOHN EDWARD
B. May 29, 1941, Chicago, Ill.
BR TR 6' 185 lbs.

Year	Team	Games	BA	SA	AB	H	2B	3B	HR	HR%	R	RBI	BB	SO	SB	PH AB	PH H	PO	A	E	DP	TC/G	FA	G by Pos
1962	WAS A	14	.262	.381	42	11	0	1	1	2.4	6	2	2	7	0	3	2	15	30	3	4	3.4	.938	SS-9, 3B-2
1963		36	.177	.226	62	11	1	1	0	0.0	3	4	6	22	2	3	0	19	49	4	5	2.0	.944	3B-26, SS-2
1964		148	.230	.324	482	111	16	4	7	1.5	55	35	29	119	3	3	0	168	322	25	42	3.5	.951	3B-106, SS-49, 2B-2
1965	LA N	104	.171	.229	105	18	3	0	1	1.0	12	5	8	33	1	3	0	40	74	4	6	1.1	.966	3B-95, SS-5
1966		125	.201	.281	274	55	9	2	3	1.1	15	24	10	64	1	1	0	102	210	8	32	2.6	.975	3B-87, SS-28, 2B-15
1967	NY A	78	.196	.235	179	35	4	0	1	0.6	22	17	17	35	2	5	2	83	152	16	21	3.2	.936	SS-36, 3B-34, 2B-2
1969	SEA A	61	.234	.367	128	30	3	1	4	3.1	18	14	14	25	4	5	0	63	82	10	13	2.5	.935	SS-33, 3B-23
1970	2 teams		MIL A	(25G – .255)			BOS A	(43G – .256)																
"	total	68	.255	.413	184	47	9	1	6	3.3	23	23	11	23	0	8	1	71	112	9	14	2.8	.953	3B-38, 2B-18, SS-4, 1B-1
1971	BOS A	74	.276	.412	272	75	12	5	5	1.8	41	22	14	42	1	2	1	114	163	13	35	3.9	.955	2B-37, SS-33, 3B-5
1972		71	.245	.335	212	52	11	1	2	0.9	22	22	18	40	0	5	0	110	141	13	34	3.7	.951	2B-32, SS-27, 3B-11
1973		67	.181	.271	155	28	9	1	1	0.6	17	16	12	45	0	1	0	92	108	6	30	3.1	.971	2B-31, 3B-24, DH-9
1974		10	.133	.333	15	2	0	0	1	6.7	3	1	1	6	0	0	0	8	11	4	3	2.3	.826	2B-6, 3B-4
12 yrs.		856	.225	.323	2110	475	77	17	32	1.5	237	185	142	461	14	39	6	885	1454	115	239	2.9	.953	3B-455, SS-226, 2B-143, DH-9, 1B-1

WORLD SERIES

Year	Team	Games	BA	SA	AB	H	2B	3B	HR	HR%	R	RBI	BB	SO	SB	PH AB	PH H	PO	A	E	DP	TC/G	FA	G by Pos
1965	LA N	4	.000	.000	1	0	0	0	0	0.0	0	0	0	0	0	0	0	0	2	1	0	0.8	.667	3B-4
1966		2	.200	.200	5	1	0	0	0	0.0	0	0	0	0	0	0	0	0	3	0	0	1.5	1.000	3B-2
2 yrs.		6	.167	.167	6	1	0	0	0	0.0	0	0	0	0	0	0	0	0	5	1	0	1.0	.833	3B-6

John Kennedy
KENNEDY, JOHN IRVIN
B. Nov. 23, 1934, Sumter, S. C.
BR TR 5'10" 175 lbs.

Year	Team	Games	BA	SA	AB	H	2B	3B	HR	HR%	R	RBI	BB	SO	SB	PH AB	PH H	PO	A	E	DP	TC/G	FA	G by Pos
1957	PHI N	5	.000	.000	2	0	0	0	0	0.0	0	0	1	0	0	0	0	0	1	1	1	0.4	.500	3B-2

Junior Kennedy
KENNEDY, JUNIOR RAYMOND
Brother of Jim Kennedy.
B. Aug. 9, 1950, Fort Gibson, Okla.
BR TR 5'11" 175 lbs.

Year	Team	Games	BA	SA	AB	H	2B	3B	HR	HR%	R	RBI	BB	SO	SB	PH AB	PH H	PO	A	E	DP	TC/G	FA	G by Pos
1974	CIN N	22	.158	.158	19	3	0	0	0	0.0	2	0	6	4	0	2	0	15	13	2	1	1.4	.933	2B-17, 3B-5
1978		89	.255	.293	157	40	2	2	0	0.0	22	11	31	28	4	13	2	94	142	5	28	2.7	.979	2B-71, SS-5, 3B-4
1979		83	.273	.318	220	60	7	0	1	0.5	29	17	28	31	4	17	4	105	162	5	30	3.3	.982	2B-59, SS-5, 3B-4
1980		104	.261	.335	337	88	16	3	1	0.3	31	34	36	34	3	1	0	200	303	6	53	4.9	.988	2B-103
1981		27	.250	.273	44	11	1	0	0	0.0	5	5	1	5	0	4	1	22	32	1	8	2.0	.982	2B-16, 3B-5
1982	CHI N	105	.219	.264	242	53	3	1	2	0.8	22	25	21	34	1	4	0	138	228	12	35	3.6	.968	2B-71, SS-28, 3B-7
1983		17	.136	.136	22	3	0	0	0	0.0	3	3	1	6	0	4	0	12	17	0	3	1.7	1.000	2B-7, 3B-4, SS-1
7 yrs.		447	.248	.299	1041	258	29	6	4	0.4	114	95	124	142	12	45	7	586	897	31	158	3.4	.980	2B-344, SS-34, 3B-29

Ray Kennedy
KENNEDY, RAYMOND LINCOLN
B. May 19, 1895, Pittsburgh, Pa.   D. Jan. 18, 1969, Casselberry, Fla.
BR TR 5'9" 165 lbs.

Year	Team	Games	BA	SA	AB	H	2B	3B	HR	HR%	R	RBI	BB	SO	SB	PH AB	PH H	PO	A	E	DP	TC/G	FA	G by Pos
1916	STL A	1	.000	.000	1	0	0	0	0	0.0	0	0	0	0	0	1	0	0	0	0	0	0.0	–	

Snapper Kennedy
KENNEDY, SHERMAN MONTGOMERY
B. Nov. 1, 1878, Conneaut, Ohio   D. Aug. 15, 1945, Pasadena, Tex.
BB TR 5'10" 165 lbs.

Year	Team	Games	BA	SA	AB	H	2B	3B	HR	HR%	R	RBI	BB	SO	SB	PH AB	PH H	PO	A	E	DP	TC/G	FA	G by Pos
1902	CHI N	1	.000	.000	5	0	0	0	0	0.0	0	0	0	0	0	0	0	5	0	0	0	5.0	1.000	OF-1

Terry Kennedy
KENNEDY, TERRENCE EDWARD
Son of Bob Kennedy.
B. June 4, 1956, Euclid, Ohio
BL TR 6'3" 220 lbs.

Year	Team	Games	BA	SA	AB	H	2B	3B	HR	HR%	R	RBI	BB	SO	SB	PH AB	PH H	PO	A	E	DP	TC/G	FA	G by Pos
1978	STL N	10	.172	.172	29	5	0	0	0	0.0	0	2	4	3	0	1	0	46	4	1	1	5.1	.980	C-10
1979		33	.284	.404	109	31	7	0	2	1.8	11	17	6	20	0	5	1	135	7	1	1	4.3	.993	C-32
1980		84	.254	.375	248	63	12	3	4	1.6	28	34	28	34	0	12	2	231	22	7	3	3.1	.973	C-41, OF-28
1981	SD N	101	.301	.385	382	115	24	1	2	0.5	32	41	22	53	0	3	0	465	63	20	12	5.4	.964	C-100
1982		153	.295	.486	562	166	42	1	21	3.7	75	97	26	91	1	5	2	777	66	9	18	5.6	.989	C-139, 1B-12
1983		149	.284	.434	549	156	27	2	17	3.1	47	98	51	89	1	4	2	807	82	12	12	6.0	.987	C-143, 1B-4
1984		148	.240	.353	530	127	16	1	14	2.6	54	57	33	99	1	5	0	708	54	14	6	5.2	.982	C-140, 1B-5
1985		143	.261	.372	532	139	27	1	10	1.9	54	74	31	102	0	5	2	662	68	10	12	5.2	.986	C-123
1986		141	.264	.403	432	114	22	1	12	2.8	46	57	37	74	0	23	11	692	70	8	13	5.5	.990	C-142
1987	BAL A	143	.250	.385	512	128	13	1	18	3.5	51	62	35	112	1	5	0	750	58	6	11	5.7	.993	C-142
1988		85	.226	.298	265	60	10	0	3	1.1	20	16	15	53	0	8	1	332	23	2	3	4.2	.994	C-79
1989	SF N	125	.239	.324	355	85	15	0	5	1.4	19	34	35	56	1	11	3	519	47	8	6	4.6	.986	C-121, 1B-2
12 yrs.		1315	.264	.388	4505	1189	215	11	108	2.4	437	589	323	786	5	87	24	6124	564	98	98	5.2	.986	C-1217, OF-28, 1B-23

LEAGUE CHAMPIONSHIP SERIES

Year	Team	Games	BA	SA	AB	H	2B	3B	HR	HR%	R	RBI	BB	SO	SB	PH AB	PH H	PO	A	E	DP	TC/G	FA	G by Pos
1984	SD N	5	.222	.222	18	4	0	0	0	0.0	2	1	1	3	0	0	0	28	4	0	1	6.4	1.000	C-5
1989	SF N	5	.188	.250	16	3	1	0	0	0.0	0	1	1	4	0	0	0	26	1	0	2	5.4	1.000	C-5
2 yrs.		10	.206	.235	34	7	1	0	0	0.0	2	2	2	7	0	0	0	54	5	0	3	5.9	1.000	C-10

WORLD SERIES

Year	Team	Games	BA	SA	AB	H	2B	3B	HR	HR%	R	RBI	BB	SO	SB	PH AB	PH H	PO	A	E	DP	TC/G	FA	G by Pos
1984	SD N	5	.211	.421	19	4	1	0	1	5.3	2	3	1	1	0	0	0	30	2	0	1	6.4	1.000	C-5
1989	SF N	4	.167	.167	12	2	0	0	0	0.0	1	2	1	3	0	0	0	23	1	1	1	6.3	.960	C-4
2 yrs.		9	.194	.323	31	6	1	0	1	3.2	3	5	2	4	0	0	0	53	3	1	2	6.3	.982	C-9

Jerry Kenney
KENNEY, GERALD TENNYSON, JR.
B. June 30, 1945, St. Louis, Mo.
BL TR 6'1" 170 lbs.

Year	Team	Games	BA	SA	AB	H	2B	3B	HR	HR%	R	RBI	BB	SO	SB	PH AB	PH H	PO	A	E	DP	TC/G	FA	G by Pos
1967	NY A	20	.310	.397	58	18	2	0	1	1.7	4	5	10	8	2	2	0	29	50	4	5	4.2	.952	SS-18

Year	Team	Games	BA	SA	AB	H	2B	3B	HR	HR%	R	RBI	BB	SO	SB	Pinch Hit AB	Pinch Hit H	PO	A	E	DP	TC/G	FA	G by Pos

Jerry Kenney *continued*

Year	Team	Games	BA	SA	AB	H	2B	3B	HR	HR%	R	RBI	BB	SO	SB	AB	H	PO	A	E	DP	TC/G	FA	G by Pos
1969		130	.257	.311	447	115	14	2	2	0.4	49	34	48	36	25	11	4	146	236	7	29	3.0	.982	3B-83, OF-31, SS-10
1970		140	.193	.282	404	78	10	7	4	1.0	46	35	52	44	20	1	0	114	307	17	19	3.1	.961	3B-135, 2B-2
1971		120	.262	.311	325	85	10	3	0	0.0	50	20	56	38	9	4	0	74	249	15	24	2.8	.956	3B-109, SS-5, 1B-1
1972		50	.210	.227	119	25	2	0	0	0.0	16	7	16	13	3	4	1	57	132	6	30	3.9	.969	SS-45, 3B-1
1973	CLE A	5	.250	.375	16	4	0	1	0	0.0	2	2	2	0	0	0	0	9	12	0	1	4.2	1.000	2B-5
6 yrs.		465	.237	.299	1369	325	38	13	7	0.5	165	103	184	139	59	22	5	429	986	49	108	3.1	.967	3B-328, SS-78, OF-31, 2B-7, 1B-1

Dick Kenworthy

KENWORTHY, RICHARD LEE
B. Apr. 1, 1941, Red Oak, Iowa

BR TR 5'9" 170 lbs.

Year	Team	Games	BA	SA	AB	H	2B	3B	HR	HR%	R	RBI	BB	SO	SB	AB	H	PO	A	E	DP	TC/G	FA	G by Pos
1962	CHI A	3	.000	.000	4	0	0	0	0	0.0	0	0	0	3	0	1	0	1	4	0	2	1.7	1.000	2B-2
1964		2	.000	.000	2	0	0	0	0	0.0	0	0	0	1	0	2	0	0	0	0	0	0.0	—	
1965		3	.200	.200	1	0	0	0	0	0.0	0	0	0	0	0	1	0	0	0	0	0	0.0	—	
1966		9	.200	.200	25	5	0	0	0	0.0	1	0	0	0	0	3	1	0	7	1	0	0.9	.875	3B-6
1967		50	.227	.412	97	22	4	1	4	4.1	9	11	4	17	0	15	0	16	51	2	1	1.4	.971	3B-35
1968		58	.221	.238	122	27	2	0	0	0.0	2	2	5	21	0	19	5	21	70	6	3	1.7	.938	3B-38
6 yrs.		125	.215	.295	251	54	6	1	4	1.6	12	13	10	42	0	41	6	38	132	9	6	1.4	.950	3B-79, 2B-2

Duke Kenworthy

KENWORTHY, WILLIAM JENNINGS (Iron Duke)
B. July 4, 1886, Cambridge, Ohio D. Sept. 21, 1950, Eureka, Calif.

BB TR 5'7" 165 lbs.

Year	Team	Games	BA	SA	AB	H	2B	3B	HR	HR%	R	RBI	BB	SO	SB	AB	H	PO	A	E	DP	TC/G	FA	G by Pos
1912	WAS A	12	.237	.263	38	9	1	0	0	0.0	6	2	2		3	2	0	14	3	0	0	1.4	1.000	OF-10
1914	KC F	146	.317	.525	545	173	40	14	15	2.8	93	91	36		37	1	0	437	407	43	79	6.1	.952	2B-145
1915		122	.298	.432	396	118	30	7	3	0.8	59	52	28		20	6	1	237	285	35	35	4.7	.937	2B-108, OF-7
1917	STL A	5	.100	.100	10	1	0	0	0	0.0	1	1	1		1	1	0	6	10	2	3	3.6	.889	2B-4
4 yrs.		285	.304	.473	989	301	71	21	18	1.8	159	146	67	1	61	10	1	694	705	80	117	5.2	.946	2B-257, OF-17

Joe Keough

KEOUGH, JOSEPH WILLIAM
Brother of Marty Keough.
B. Jan. 7, 1946, Pomona, Calif.

BL TL 6' 185 lbs.

Year	Team	Games	BA	SA	AB	H	2B	3B	HR	HR%	R	RBI	BB	SO	SB	AB	H	PO	A	E	DP	TC/G	FA	G by Pos
1968	OAK A	34	.214	.316	98	21	2	1	2	2.0	7	18	8	11	1	1	0	51	0	2	0	1.6	.964	OF-29, 1B-1
1969	KC A	70	.187	.199	166	31	2	0	0	0.0	17	7	13	13	5	20	3	83	2	0	1	1.2	1.000	OF-49, 1B-1
1970		57	.322	.443	183	59	6	2	4	2.2	28	21	23	18	1	4	2	176	13	4	13	3.4	.979	OF-34, 1B-18
1971		110	.248	.325	351	87	14	2	3	0.9	34	30	35	26	0	11	4	164	4	1	1	1.6	.982	OF-16
1972		56	.219	.250	64	14	2	0	0	0.0	8	5	8	7	2	31	8	12	1	0	1	0.2	1.000	OF-16
1973	CHI A	5	.000	.000	1	0	0	0	0	0.0	1	0	0	0	0	1	0	0	0	0	0	0.0	—	
6 yrs.		332	.246	.319	863	212	26	5	9	1.0	95	81	87	75	9	74	18	486	22	9	16	1.6	.983	OF-228, 1B-20

Marty Keough

KEOUGH, RICHARD MARTIN
Father of Matt Keough. Brother of Joe Keough.
B. Apr. 14, 1935, Oakland, Calif.

BL TL 6' 180 lbs.

Year	Team	Games	BA	SA	AB	H	2B	3B	HR	HR%	R	RBI	BB	SO	SB	AB	H	PO	A	E	DP	TC/G	FA	G by Pos
1956	BOS A	3	.000	.000	2	0	0	0	0	0.0	1	1	1	0	0	2	0	0	0	0	0	0.0	—	
1957		9	.059	.059	17	1	0	0	0	0.0	1	1	0	4	0	3	0	16	0	0	0	1.8	1.000	OF-7
1958		68	.220	.322	118	26	3	3	1	0.8	21	9	7	29	1	34	5	54	0	2	1	0.8	.964	OF-25, 1B-2
1959		96	.243	.418	251	61	13	5	7	2.8	40	27	26	40	3	27	7	164	5	1	2	1.8	.994	OF-69, 1B-3
1960	2 teams				BOS A	(38G – .248)				CLE A	(65G – .248)													
"	total	103	.248	.346	254	63	11	1	4	1.6	34	20	17	31	4	32	5	125	5	1	0	1.3	.992	OF-71
1961	WAS A	135	.249	.410	390	97	18	9	9	2.3	57	34	32	60	12	17	4	308	13	6	10	2.4	.982	OF-100, 1B-10
1962	CIN N	111	.278	.422	230	64	8	2	7	3.0	34	27	21	31	3	20	4	236	22	5	12	2.4	.981	OF-71, 1B-29
1963		95	.227	.401	172	39	8	2	6	3.5	21	21	25	37	1	24	4	250	24	2	25	2.9	.993	1B-46, OF-28
1964		109	.257	.395	276	71	9	1	9	3.3	29	28	22	58	1	34	9	119	5	1	4	1.1	.992	OF-81, 1B-4
1965		62	.116	.116	43	5	0	0	0	0.0	14	3	3	14	0	21	4	75	5	1	4	1.3	.988	1B-32, OF-4
1966	2 teams				ATL N	(17G – .059)				CHI N	(33G – .231)													
"	total	50	.163	.186	43	7	1	0	0	0.0	4	6	6	15	1	31	5	29	0	1	0	0.6	.967	OF-8, 1B-4
11 yrs.		841	.242	.379	1796	434	71	23	43	2.4	256	176	164	318	26	243	47	1376	79	20	58	1.8	.986	OF-464, 1B-130

John Kerins

KERINS, JOHN NELSON
B. July 15, 1858, Indianapolis, Ind. D. Sept. 8, 1919, Louisville, Ky.
Manager 1888.

BR TR 5'10" 177 lbs.

Year	Team	Games	BA	SA	AB	H	2B	3B	HR	HR%	R	RBI	BB	SO	SB	AB	H	PO	A	E	DP	TC/G	FA	G by Pos
1884	IND AA	93	.216	.310	361	78	10	3	6	1.7	58		6			0	0	896	43	31	20	10.4	.968	1B-87, C-5, OF-4, 3B-1
1885	LOU AA	112	.243	.353	456	111	9	16	3	0.7	65		20			0	0	1071	74	65	52	10.8	.946	1B-96, C-19, OF-3, 3B-1
1886		120	.269	.370	487	131	19	9	4	0.8	113		66			0	0	991	183	67	37	10.3	.946	C-65, 1B-47, OF-7, SS-1
1887		112	.294	.443	476	140	18	19	5	1.1	101		38	49		0	0	964	111	55	33	10.1	.951	1B-74, C-35, OF-5
1888		83	.235	.313	319	75	11	4	2	0.6	38	41	25	16		0	0	344	70	55	6	5.7	.883	OF-47, C-33, 1B-4, 3B-2, 2B-1
1889	2 teams				LOU AA	(2G – .333)				BAL AA	(16G – .283)													
"	total	18	.290	.339	62	18	3	0	0	0.0	9	15	2	5		0	0	74	11	6	1	5.1	.934	1B-9, C-5, OF-4, SS-1
1890	STL AA	18	.127	.159	63	8	2	0	0	0.0	8		8		2	0	0	172	10	6	12	10.4	.968	1B-17, C-1
7 yrs.		556	.252	.357	2224	561	72	51	20	0.9	392	56	165	69		0	0	4512	502	285	161	9.5	.946	1B-334, C-163, OF-70, 3B-4, SS-2, 2B-1

Orie Kerlin

KERLIN, ORIE MILTON (Cy)
B. Jan. 23, 1891, Summerfield, La. D. Oct. 29, 1974, Shreveport, La.

BL TR 5'7" 149 lbs.

Year	Team	Games	BA	SA	AB	H	2B	3B	HR	HR%	R	RBI	BB	SO	SB	AB	H	PO	A	E	DP	TC/G	FA	G by Pos
1915	PIT F	3	.000	.000	1	0	0	0	0	0.0	0	0	0		0	0	0	0	0	0	0	0.0	—	C-3

Bill Kern

KERN, WILLIAM GEORGE
B. Feb. 28, 1933, Coplay, Pa.

BR TR 6'2" 184 lbs.

Year	Team	Games	BA	SA	AB	H	2B	3B	HR	HR%	R	RBI	BB	SO	SB	AB	H	PO	A	E	DP	TC/G	FA	G by Pos
1962	KC A	8	.250	.438	16	4	0	0	1	6.3	1	1	0	3	0	5	2	3	2	0	0	0.6	1.000	OF-3

George Kernek

KERNEK, GEORGE BOYD
B. Jan. 12, 1940, Holdenville, Okla.

BL TL 6'3" 170 lbs.

Year	Team	Games	BA	SA	AB	H	2B	3B	HR	HR%	R	RBI	BB	SO	SB	AB	H	PO	A	E	DP	TC/G	FA	G by Pos
1965	STL N	10	.290	.452	31	9	3	1	0	0.0	6	3	2	4	0	3	0	65	5	2	9	7.2	.972	1B-7

Year	Team		Games	BA	SA	AB	H	2B	3B	HR	HR%	R	RBI	BB	SO	SB	Pinch Hit AB	H	PO	A	E	DP	TC/G	FA	G by Pos

George Kernek *continued*

Year			Games	BA	SA	AB	H	2B	3B	HR	HR%	R	RBI	BB	SO	SB	AB	H	PO	A	E	DP	TC/G	FA	G by Pos
1966			20	.240	.280	50	12	0	1	0	0.0	5	3	4	9	1	4	1	114	8	2	14	6.2	.984	1B-16
2 yrs.			30	.259	.346	81	21	3	2	0	0.0	11	6	6	13	1	7	1	179	13	4	23	6.5	.980	1B-23

Dan Kerns

KERNS, DANIEL P.
B. Philadelphia, Pa.

Year	Team		Games	BA	SA	AB	H	2B	3B	HR	HR%	R	RBI	BB	SO	SB	AB	H	PO	A	E	DP	TC/G	FA	G by Pos
1920	PHI	A	1	.000	.000	1	0	0	0	0	0.0	0	0	0	0	0	1	0	0	0	0	0	0.0	—	

Russ Kerns

KERNS, RUSSELL ELDON
B. Nov. 10, 1920, Fremont, Ohio

BL TR 6' 188 lbs.

Year	Team		Games	BA	SA	AB	H	2B	3B	HR	HR%	R	RBI	BB	SO	SB	AB	H	PO	A	E	DP	TC/G	FA	G by Pos
1945	DET	A	1	.000	.000	1	0	0	0	0	0.0	0	0	0	0	0	1	0	0	0	0	0	0.0	—	

Buddy Kerr

KERR, JOHN JOSEPH
B. Nov. 6, 1922, Astoria, N. Y.

BR TR 6'2" 175 lbs.

Year	Team		Games	BA	SA	AB	H	2B	3B	HR	HR%	R	RBI	BB	SO	SB	AB	H	PO	A	E	DP	TC/G	FA	G by Pos
1943	NY	N	27	.286	.378	98	28	3	0	2	2.0	14	12	8	5	1	0	0	60	90	7	10	5.8	.955	SS-27
1944			150	.266	.387	548	146	31	4	9	1.6	68	63	37	32	14	0	0	328	507	40	81	5.8	.954	SS-149
1945			149	.249	.319	546	136	20	3	4	0.7	53	40	41	34	5	1	0	333	515	32	81	5.9	.964	SS-148
1946			145	.249	.338	497	124	20	3	6	1.2	50	40	53	31	7	1	1	264	428	14	68	4.9	.980	SS-126, 3B-18
1947			138	.287	.386	547	157	23	5	7	1.3	73	49	36	49	2	0	0	270	460	17	77	5.4	.977	SS-138
1948			144	.240	.288	496	119	16	4	0	0.0	41	46	56	36	9	1	1	269	456	25	72	5.2	.967	SS-143
1949			90	.209	.227	220	46	4	0	0	0.0	16	19	21	23	0	0	0	125	224	15	33	4.0	.959	SS-89
1950	BOS	N	155	.227	.310	507	115	24	6	2	0.4	45	46	50	50	0	0	0	310	471	28	97	5.2	.965	SS-155
1951			69	.186	.227	172	32	4	0	1	0.6	18	18	22	20	0	1	0	115	177	9	37	4.4	.970	SS-63, 2B-5
9 yrs.			1067	.249	.328	3631	903	145	25	31	0.9	378	333	324	280	38	3	2	2074	3328	187	556	5.2	.967	SS-1038, 3B-18, 2B-5

Doc Kerr

KERR, JOHN JONAS
B. Jan. 17, 1882, Del Roy, Ohio   D. June 9, 1937, Baltimore, Md.

BB TR 5'10½" 190 lbs.

Year	Team		Games	BA	SA	AB	H	2B	3B	HR	HR%	R	RBI	BB	SO	SB	AB	H	PO	A	E	DP	TC/G	FA	G by Pos
1914	2 teams	PIT F (42G – .239)				BAL F	(14G – .265)																		
"	total		56	.248	.381	105	26	5	3	1	1.0	7	8	11		1	20	4	147	43	5	2	3.5	.974	C-31, 1B-1
1915	BAL	F	3	.333	.333	6	2	0	0	0	0.0	1	0	1		0	0	0	9	1	0	0	3.3	1.000	C-2, 1B-1
2 yrs.			59	.252	.378	111	28	5	3	1	0.9	8	8	12		1	20	4	156	44	5	2	3.5	.976	C-33, 1B-2

John Kerr

KERR, JOHN FRANCIS
B. Nov. 26, 1898, San Francisco, Calif.

BR TR 5'8" 158 lbs.
BB 1923-24

Year	Team		Games	BA	SA	AB	H	2B	3B	HR	HR%	R	RBI	BB	SO	SB	AB	H	PO	A	E	DP	TC/G	FA	G by Pos
1923	DET	A	19	.214	.238	42	9	1	0	0	0.0	4	1	4	5	0	1	0	19	45	9	5	3.8	.877	SS-15
1924			17	.273	.273	11	3	0	0	0	0.0	4	1	0	0	0	7	2	1	0	0	0	0.1	1.000	3B-3, OF-2
1929	CHI	A	127	.258	.332	419	108	20	4	1	0.2	50	39	31	24	9	1	1	307	459	23	84	6.2	.971	2B-122
1930			70	.289	.410	266	77	11	6	3	1.1	37	27	21	23	4	0	0	172	218	9	40	5.7	.977	2B-51, SS-19
1931			128	.268	.329	444	119	17	2	2	0.5	51	50	35	22	9	4	1	307	383	25	79	5.6	.965	2B-117, 3B-7, SS-1
1932	WAS	A	51	.273	.333	132	36	6	1	0	0.0	14	15	13	3	3	10	1	73	97	9	17	3.5	.950	2B-17, SS-14, 3B-8
1933			28	.200	.200	40	8	0	0	0	0.0	5	0	3	2	0	5	1	25	31	2	4	2.1	.966	2B-16, 3B-1
1934			31	.272	.311	103	28	4	0	0	0.0	8	12	8	13	1	1	1	63	76	4	10	4.6	.972	3B-17, 2B-13
8 yrs.			471	.266	.337	1457	388	59	13	6	0.4	172	145	115	92	26	29	7	967	1309	81	239	5.0	.966	2B-336, SS-49, 3B-36, OF-2

WORLD SERIES

Year	Team		Games	BA	SA	AB	H	2B	3B	HR	HR%	R	RBI	BB	SO	SB	AB	H	PO	A	E	DP	TC/G	FA	G by Pos
1933	WAS	A	1	—	—	0	0	0	0	0	—	0	0	0	0	0	0	0	0	0	0	0	0.0	—	

Mel Kerr

KERR, JOHN MELVILLE
B. May 22, 1903, Souris, Man., Canada   D. Aug. 9, 1980, Vero Beach, Fla.

BL TL 5'11½" 155 lbs.

Year	Team		Games	BA	SA	AB	H	2B	3B	HR	HR%	R	RBI	BB	SO	SB	AB	H	PO	A	E	DP	TC/G	FA	G by Pos
1925	CHI	N	1	—	—	0	0	0	0	0	—	1	0	0	0	0	0	0	0	0	0	0	0.0	—	

Dan Kerwin

KERWIN, DANIEL PATRICK
B. July 9, 1879, Philadelphia, Pa.   D. July 13, 1960, Philadelphia, Pa.

BL TL 5'9" 164 lbs.

Year	Team		Games	BA	SA	AB	H	2B	3B	HR	HR%	R	RBI	BB	SO	SB	AB	H	PO	A	E	DP	TC/G	FA	G by Pos
1903	CIN	N	2	.667	.833	6	4	1	0	0	0.0	1	1	2		0	0	0	1	0	1	0	1.0	.500	OF-2

Don Kessinger

KESSINGER, DONALD EULON
B. July 17, 1942, Forrest City, Ark.
Manager 1979.

BB TR 6'1" 170 lbs.
BR 1964-65

Year	Team		Games	BA	SA	AB	H	2B	3B	HR	HR%	R	RBI	BB	SO	SB	AB	H	PO	A	E	DP	TC/G	FA	G by Pos
1964	CHI	N	4	.167	.167	12	2	0	0	0	0.0	1	0	0	1	0	2	0	3	7	0	1	2.5	1.000	SS-4
1965			106	.201	.233	309	62	4	3	0	0.0	19	14	20	44	1	0	0	176	338	28	69	5.1	.948	SS-105
1966			150	.274	.302	533	146	8	2	1	0.2	50	43	26	46	13	0	0	202	474	35	68	4.7	.951	SS-148
1967			145	.231	.272	580	134	10	7	0	0.0	61	42	33	80	6	0	0	215	457	19	77	4.8	.973	SS-143
1968			160	.240	.287	655	157	14	7	1	0.2	63	32	38	86	9	1	0	263	573	33	97	5.4	.962	SS-159
1969			158	.273	.366	664	181	38	6	4	0.6	109	53	61	70	11	1	0	266	542	20	101	5.2	.976	SS-157
1970			154	.266	.349	631	168	21	14	1	0.2	100	39	66	59	12	0	0	257	501	22	86	5.1	.972	SS-154
1971			155	.258	.316	617	159	18	6	2	0.3	77	38	52	54	15	2	0	263	512	27	97	5.2	.966	SS-154
1972			149	.274	.334	577	158	20	6	1	0.2	77	39	67	44	8	3	0	259	504	28	90	5.3	.965	SS-146
1973			160	.262	.310	577	151	22	3	0	0.0	52	43	57	44	6	2	0	274	526	30	109	5.2	.964	SS-158
1974			153	.259	.321	599	155	20	7	1	0.2	83	42	62	54	7	3	0	259	476	32	87	5.0	.958	SS-150
1975			154	.243	.319	601	146	26	10	0	0.0	77	46	68	47	4	2	0	210	464	24	103	4.5	.966	SS-140, 3B-13
1976	STL	N	145	.239	.313	502	120	22	6	1	0.2	55	40	61	51	3	1	0	266	435	24	105	5.0	.967	SS-113, 2B-31, 3B-2
1977	2 teams	STL N (59G – .239)				CHI A	(39G – .235)																		
"	total		98	.237	.281	253	60	14	1	0	0.0	26	18	27	33	2	15	0	135	200	13	46	3.6	.963	SS-47, 2B-37, 3B-13
1978	CHI	A	131	.255	.309	431	110	18	1	1	0.2	35	31	36	34	2	1	0	183	335	13	62	4.1	.976	SS-123, 2B-9
1979			56	.200	.282	110	22	6	0	1	0.9	14	7	10	12	1	1	0	61	109	2	17	3.1	.988	SS-54, 2B-1, 1B-1
16 yrs.			2078	.252	.312	7651	1931	254	80	14	0.2	899	527	684	759	100	33	0	3292	6453	350	1215	4.9	.965	SS-1955, 2B-78, 3B-28, 1B-1

Year	Team	Games	BA	SA	AB	H	2B	3B	HR	HR%	R	RBI	BB	SO	SB	Pinch Hit AB	Pinch Hit H	PO	A	E	DP	TC/G	FA	G by Pos

Henry Kessler

KESSLER, HENRY (Lucky)
B. 1847, Brooklyn, N. Y.   D. Jan. 9, 1900, Franklin, Pa.

BR TR 5'10''   144 lbs.

Year	Team	Games	BA	SA	AB	H	2B	3B	HR	HR%	R	RBI	BB	SO	SB	PH AB	PH H	PO	A	E	DP	TC/G	FA	G by Pos
1876	CIN N	59	.258	.278	248	64	5	0	0	0.0	26	11	7	10	○		0	0	77	125	52	13	4.3	.795	SS-46, OF-16
1877		6	.100	.100	20	2	0	0	0	0.0	0	0	2	1			0	0	13	8	15	2	6.0	.583	C-5, 1B-1
2 yrs.		65	.246	.265	268	66	5	0	0	0.0	26	11	9	11			0	0	90	133	67	15	4.5	.769	SS-46, OF-16, C-5, 1B-1

Fred Ketcham

KETCHAM, FREDERICK L.
B. July 27, 1875, Elmira, N. Y.   D. Mar. 12, 1908, Cortland, N. Y.

BL TR

Year	Team	Games	BA	SA	AB	H	2B	3B	HR	HR%	R	RBI	BB	SO	SB	PH AB	PH H	PO	A	E	DP	TC/G	FA	G by Pos
1899	LOU N	15	.295	.311	61	18	1	0	0	0.0	13	5	0		2	0	0	17	0	0	0	1.1	1.000	OF-15
1901	PHI A	5	.227	.227	22	5	0	0	0	0.0	5	2	0		0	0	0	7	0	1	0	1.6	.875	OF-5
2 yrs.		20	.277	.289	83	23	1	0	0	0.0	18	7	0		2	0	0	24	0	1	0	1.3	.960	OF-20

Phil Ketter

KETTER, PHILIP
B. Hutchinson, Kans.

TR

Year	Team	Games	BA	SA	AB	H	2B	3B	HR	HR%	R	RBI	BB	SO	SB	PH AB	PH H	PO	A	E	DP	TC/G	FA	G by Pos
1912	STL A	2	.333	.333	6	2	0	0	0	0.0	1	0	0		0	0	0	3	3	0	0	3.0	1.000	C-2

Sam Khalifa

KHALIFA, SAM
B. Dec. 5, 1963, Fontana, Calif.

BR TR 5'10''   160 lbs.

Year	Team	Games	BA	SA	AB	H	2B	3B	HR	HR%	R	RBI	BB	SO	SB	PH AB	PH H	PO	A	E	DP	TC/G	FA	G by Pos
1985	PIT N	95	.238	.319	320	76	14	3	2	0.6	30	31	34	56	5	0	0	156	316	16	45	5.1	.967	SS-95
1986		64	.185	.225	151	28	6	0	0	0.0	8	4	19	28	0	1	0	94	168	10	25	4.3	.963	SS-60, 2B-6
1987		5	.176	.176	17	3	0	0	0	0.0	1	2	0	2	0	0	0	5	6	1	1	2.4	.917	SS-5
3 yrs.		164	.219	.285	488	107	20	3	2	0.4	39	37	53	86	5	1	0	255	490	27	71	4.7	.965	SS-160, 2B-6

Hod Kibbie

KIBBIE, HORACE KENT
B. July 18, 1903, Fort Worth, Tex.   D. Oct. 19, 1975, Fort Worth, Tex.

BR TR 5'10''   150 lbs.

Year	Team	Games	BA	SA	AB	H	2B	3B	HR	HR%	R	RBI	BB	SO	SB	PH AB	PH H	PO	A	E	DP	TC/G	FA	G by Pos
1925	BOS N	11	.268	.317	41	11	2	0	0	0.0	5	2	5	6	0	0	0	23	40	5	5	6.2	.926	2B-8, SS-3

Jack Kibble

KIBBLE, JOHN WESTLY (Happy)
B. Jan. 2, 1892, Seatonville, Ill.   D. Dec. 13, 1969, Roundup, Mont.

BB TR 5'9½''   154 lbs.

Year	Team	Games	BA	SA	AB	H	2B	3B	HR	HR%	R	RBI	BB	SO	SB	PH AB	PH H	PO	A	E	DP	TC/G	FA	G by Pos
1912	CLE A	5	.000	.000	8	0	0	0	0	0.0	1	0	0		0	0	0	5	11	0	3	3.2	1.000	3B-4, 2B-1

Steve Kiefer

KIEFER, STEVEN GEORGE
B. Oct. 18, 1960, Chicago, Ill.

BR TR 6'1''   175 lbs.

Year	Team	Games	BA	SA	AB	H	2B	3B	HR	HR%	R	RBI	BB	SO	SB	PH AB	PH H	PO	A	E	DP	TC/G	FA	G by Pos
1984	OAK A	23	.175	.300	40	7	1	2	0	0.0	7	2	2	10	2	1	1	15	35	5	5	2.4	.909	SS-17, DH-3, 3B-2
1985		40	.197	.288	66	13	1	1	1	1.5	8	10	1	18	0	1	0	15	37	7	5	1.5	.881	3B-34, DH-2
1986	MIL A	2	.000	.000	6	0	0	0	0	0.0	0	0	0	4	0	0	0	7	8	0	2	7.5	1.000	SS-2
1987		28	.202	.394	99	20	4	0	5	5.1	17	17	7	28	0	2	1	16	50	2	4	2.4	.971	3B-26, 2B-4
1988		7	.300	.700	10	3	1	0	1	10.0	2	1	2	3	0	1	0	4	8	1	2	1.9	.923	3B-4, 2B-4
1989	NY A	5	.125	.125	8	1	0	0	0	0.0	0	0	0	5	0	0	0	1	1	0	0	0.4	1.000	3B-5
6 yrs.		105	.192	.341	229	44	7	3	7	3.1	34	30	12	68	2	5	2	58	139	15	18	2.0	.929	3B-71, SS-19, 2B-8, DH-5

Pete Kilduff

KILDUFF, PETER JOHN
B. Apr. 4, 1893, Weir City, Kans.   D. Feb. 14, 1930, Pittsburg, Kans.

BR TR 5'7''   155 lbs.

Year	Team	Games	BA	SA	AB	H	2B	3B	HR	HR%	R	RBI	BB	SO	SB	PH AB	PH H	PO	A	E	DP	TC/G	FA	G by Pos
1917	2 teams		NY N (31G – .205)				CHI N (56G – .277)																	
"	total	87	.257	.346	280	72	12	5	1	0.4	35	27	16	30	13	0	0	141	203	25	33	4.2	.932	SS-56, 2B-26, 3B-1
1918	CHI N	30	.204	.269	93	19	2	2	0	0.0	7	13	7	7	1	0	0	72	72	10	18	5.1	.935	2B-30
1919	2 teams		CHI N (31G – .273)				BKN N (32G – .301)																	
"	total	63	.286	.366	161	46	7	3	0	0.0	14	16	22	16	6	2	1	51	103	17	11	2.7	.901	3B-40, 2B-9, SS-7
1920	BKN N	141	.272	.360	478	130	26	8	0	0.0	62	58	58	43	2	1	0	322	463	28	71	5.8	.966	2B-134, 3B-5
1921		107	.288	.406	372	107	15	10	3	0.8	45	45	31	36	6	1	0	243	383	24	58	6.1	.963	2B-105, 3B-1
5 yrs.		428	.270	.364	1384	374	62	28	4	0.3	163	159	134	132	28	5	2	829	1224	104	191	5.0	.952	2B-304, SS-63, 3B-47

WORLD SERIES

Year	Team	Games	BA	SA	AB	H	2B	3B	HR	HR%	R	RBI	BB	SO	SB	PH AB	PH H	PO	A	E	DP	TC/G	FA	G by Pos
1920	BKN N	7	.095	.095	21	2	0	0	0	0.0	0	1	4		0	0	0	15	28	0	4	6.1	1.000	2B-7

Frank Kiley

Playing record listed under Frank Kane

John Kiley

KILEY, JOHN FREDERICK
B. July 1, 1859, South Dedham, Mass.   D. Dec. 18, 1940, Norwood, Mass.

BL TL

Year	Team	Games	BA	SA	AB	H	2B	3B	HR	HR%	R	RBI	BB	SO	SB	PH AB	PH H	PO	A	E	DP	TC/G	FA	G by Pos
1884	WAS AA	14	.214	.321	56	12	2	2	0	0.0	9		3			0	0	15	1	12	0	2.0	.571	OF-14
1891	BOS N	1	.000	.000	2	0	0	0	0	0.0	0	1			0	0	0	0	2	0	0	2.0	1.000	P-1
2 yrs.		15	.207	.310	58	12	2	2	0	0.0	9	0	4	1	0	0	0	15	3	12	0	2.0	.600	OF-14, P-1

Pat Kilhullen

KILHULLEN, JOSEPH ISADORE
B. Aug. 10, 1890, Carbondale, Pa.   D. Nov. 2, 1922, Oakland, Calif.

BR TR 5'9''   175 lbs.

Year	Team	Games	BA	SA	AB	H	2B	3B	HR	HR%	R	RBI	BB	SO	SB	PH AB	PH H	PO	A	E	DP	TC/G	FA	G by Pos
1914	PIT N	1	.000	.000	1	0	0	0	0	0.0	0	0	0		0	0	0	0	0	0	0	0.0	–	C-1

Harmon Killebrew

KILLEBREW, HARMON CLAYTON (Killer)
B. June 29, 1936, Payette, Ida.
Hall of Fame 1984.

BR TR 6'   195 lbs.

Year	Team	Games	BA	SA	AB	H	2B	3B	HR	HR%	R	RBI	BB	SO	SB	PH AB	PH H	PO	A	E	DP	TC/G	FA	G by Pos
1954	WAS A	9	.308	.385	13	4	0	0	0	0.0	1	3	2	3	0	2	0	5	2	0	0	0.8	1.000	2B-3
1955		38	.200	.363	80	16	1	0	4	5.0	12	7	9	31	0	13	1	24	49	5	3	2.1	.936	3B-23, 2B-3
1956		44	.222	.394	99	22	0	0	5	5.1	10	13	10	39	0	21	2	24	44	4	4	1.6	.944	3B-20, 2B-4
1957		9	.290	.548	31	9	2	0	2	6.5	4	5	2	8	0	2	1	2	16	1	2	2.1	.947	3B-7, 2B-1
1958		13	.194	.194	31	6	0	0	0	0.0	2	2	0	12	0	4	1	8	13	0	1	1.6	1.000	3B-9
1959		153	.242	.516	546	132	20	2	42	7.7	98	105	90	116	3	0	0	135	325	30	18	3.2	.939	3B-150, OF-4
1960		124	.276	.534	442	122	19	1	31	7.0	84	80	71	106	1	4	2	629	135	17	76	6.3	.978	1B-71, 3B-65
1961	MIN A	150	.288	.606	541	156	20	7	46	8.5	94	122	107	109	1	1	0	1003	143	23	101	7.8	.980	1B-119, 3B-45, OF-2
1962		155	.243	.545	552	134	21	1	48	8.7	85	126	106	142	1	1	1	241	5	9	4	1.6	.965	OF-151, 1B-4

Year	Team		Games	BA	SA	AB	H	2B	3B	HR	HR%	R	RBI	BB	SO	SB	Pinch Hit AB	Pinch Hit H	PO	A	E	DP	TC/G	FA	G by Pos

Harmon Killebrew *continued*

Year	Team		Games	BA	SA	AB	H	2B	3B	HR	HR%	R	RBI	BB	SO	SB	AB	H	PO	A	E	DP	TC/G	FA	G by Pos
1963			142	.258	**.555**	515	133	18	0	**45**	8.7	88	96	72	105	0	3	1	219	7	3	0	1.6	.987	OF-137
1964			158	.270	.548	577	156	11	1	**49**	8.5	95	111	93	135	0	1	0	232	1	7	0	1.5	.971	OF-157
1965			113	.269	.501	401	108	16	1	25	6.2	78	75	72	69	0	2	1	743	113	12	67	7.7	.986	1B-72, 3B-44, OF-1
1966			162	.281	.538	569	160	27	1	39	6.9	89	110	**103**	98	0	1	0	435	205	18	41	4.1	.973	3B-108, 1B-42, OF-18
1967			163	.269	.558	547	147	24	1	**44**	8.0	105	113	**131**	111	1	0	0	1285	89	12	100	8.5	.991	1B-160, 3B-3
1968			100	.210	.420	295	62	7	2	17	5.8	40	40	70	70	0	9	1	601	71	7	51	6.8	.990	1B-77, 3B-11
1969			162	.276	.584	555	153	20	2	**49**	8.8	106	**140**	**145**	84	8	0	0	639	219	22	67	5.4	.975	3B-105, 1B-80
1970			157	.271	.546	527	143	20	1	41	7.8	96	113	128	84	0	2	0	312	212	20	28	3.5	.963	3B-138, 1B-28
1971			147	.254	.464	500	127	19	1	28	5.6	61	**119**	114	96	3	4	1	700	149	13	55	5.9	.985	1B-90, 3B-64
1972			139	.231	.450	433	100	13	2	26	6.0	53	74	94	91	0	8	0	995	99	9	82	7.9	.992	1B-130
1973			69	.242	.347	248	60	9	1	5	2.0	29	32	41	59	0	2	0	431	45	1	42	6.9	.998	1B-57, DH-9
1974			122	.222	.360	333	74	7	0	13	3.9	28	54	45	61	0	30	11	218	21	2	21	2.0	.992	DH-57, 1B-33
1975	KC	A	106	.199	.375	312	62	13	0	14	4.5	25	44	54	70	1	9	1	28	0	0	4	0.3	1.000	DH-92, 1B-6
22 yrs.			2435	.256	.509	8147	2086	290	24	573 5th	7.0 3rd	1283	1584	1559	1699 9th	19	118	24	8909	1963	215	767	4.6	.981	1B-969, 3B-792, OF-470, DH-158, 2B-11

LEAGUE CHAMPIONSHIP SERIES

Year	Team		Games	BA	SA	AB	H	2B	3B	HR	HR%	R	RBI	BB	SO	SB	AB	H	PO	A	E	DP	TC/G	FA	G by Pos
1969	MIN	A	3	.125	.250	8	1	1	0	0	0.0	2	0	6	2	0	0	0	6	3	0	0	3.0	1.000	3B-3
1970			3	.273	.818	11	3	0	0	2	18.2	2	4	2	4	0	0	0	7	0	0	1	2.3	1.000	3B-2, 1B-1
2 yrs.			6	.211	.579	19	4	1	0	2	10.5	4	4	8	6	0	0	0	13	3	0	1	2.7	1.000	3B-5, 1B-1

WORLD SERIES

Year	Team		Games	BA	SA	AB	H	2B	3B	HR	HR%	R	RBI	BB	SO	SB	AB	H	PO	A	E	DP	TC/G	FA	G by Pos
1965	MIN	A	7	.286	.429	21	6	0	0	1	4.8	2	2	6	4	0	0	0	11	7	1	0	2.7	.947	3B-7

Bill Killefer

KILLEFER, WILLIAM LAVIER (Reindeer Bill)
Brother of Red Killefer.
B. Oct. 10, 1887, Bloomingdale, Mich. D. July 3, 1960, Elsmere, Del.
Manager 1921-25, 1930-33.
BR TR 5'10½" 200 lbs.

Year	Team		Games	BA	SA	AB	H	2B	3B	HR	HR%	R	RBI	BB	SO	SB	AB	H	PO	A	E	DP	TC/G	FA	G by Pos
1909	STL	A	11	.138	.138	29	4	0	0	0	0.0	0	1	0		0	2	0	36	21	6	2	5.7	.905	C-11
1910			74	.124	.155	193	24	2	2	0	0.0	14	7	12		0	1	0	311	124	29	16	6.3	.938	C-73
1911	PHI	N	6	.188	.188	16	3	0	0	0	0.0	3	2	0	2	0	0	0	29	10	1	1	6.7	.975	C-6
1912			85	.224	.280	268	60	6	3	1	0.4	18	21	4	14	6	0	0	407	134	15	17	6.5	.973	C-85
1913			120	.244	.300	360	88	14	3	0	0.0	25	24	4	17	2	1	0	570	166	9	16	6.5	.988	C-118, 1B-1
1914			98	.234	.274	299	70	10	1	0	0.0	27	27	8	17	3	8	3	464	154	14	11	6.4	.978	C-90
1915			105	.238	.278	320	76	9	2	0	0.0	26	24	18	14	5	1	0	539	126	19	6	6.5	.972	C-105
1916			97	.217	.294	286	62	5	4	3	1.0	22	27	8	14	2	4	0	443	89	8	15	5.6	.985	C-91
1917			125	.274	.303	409	112	12	0	0	0.0	28	31	15	21	4	4	0	617	138	12	14	6.1	.984	C-120
1918	CHI	N	104	.233	.281	331	77	10	3	0	0.0	30	22	17	10	5	0	0	487	110	11	12	5.8	.982	C-104
1919			103	.286	.330	315	90	10	1	0	0.0	17	22	15	8	5	3	0	478	124	8	7	5.9	.987	C-100
1920			62	.220	.267	191	42	7	1	0	0.0	16	16	8	5	2	1	0	304	80	9	6	6.3	.977	C-61
1921			45	.323	.331	133	43	1	0	0	0.0	11	16	4	3	3	1	1	147	43	7	6	4.4	.964	C-42
13 yrs.			1035	.238	.283	3150	751	86	21	4	0.1	237	240	113	126	39	26	4	4832	1319	148	129	6.1	.977	C-1006, 1B-1

WORLD SERIES

Year	Team		Games	BA	SA	AB	H	2B	3B	HR	HR%	R	RBI	BB	SO	SB	AB	H	PO	A	E	DP	TC/G	FA	G by Pos
1915	PHI	N	1	.000	.000	1	0	0	0	0	0.0	0	0	0		0	1	0	0	0	0	0	0.0	–	
1918	CHI	N	6	.118	.176	17	2	1	0	0	0.0	2	2	2		0	0	0	26	6	0	1	5.3	1.000	C-6
2 yrs.			7	.111	.167	18	2	1	0	0	0.0	2	2	2		0	1	0	26	6	0	1	4.6	1.000	C-6

Red Killefer

KILLEFER, WADE HAMPTON (Lollypop)
Brother of Bill Killefer.
B. Apr. 13, 1884, Bloomingdale, Mich. D. Sept. 4, 1958, Los Angeles, Calif.
BR TR 5'9½" 175 lbs.

Year	Team		Games	BA	SA	AB	H	2B	3B	HR	HR%	R	RBI	BB	SO	SB	AB	H	PO	A	E	DP	TC/G	FA	G by Pos
1907	DET	A	1	.000	.000	4	0	0	0	0	0.0	0	0	0		0	0	0	2	0	0	0	2.0	1.000	OF-1
1908			28	.213	.227	75	16	1	0	0	0.0	9	11	3		4	0	0	48	54	12	9	4.1	.895	2B-16, SS-7, 3B-4
1909	2 teams			DET	A	(23G – .279)		WAS	A	(40G – .174)															
"	total		63	.209	.264	182	38	3	2	1	0.5	17	9	16		6	7	3	103	77	20	9	3.2	.900	OF-25, 2B-20, 3B-6, C-3, SS-1
1910	WAS	A	106	.229	.284	345	79	17	1	0	0.0	35	24	29		17	4	1	190	234	29	27	4.3	.936	2B-88, OF-12
1914	CIN	N	42	.277	.333	141	39	6	1	0	0.0	16	12	20	18	11	1	0	60	12	4	0	1.8	.947	OF-37, 2B-5, 3B-1
1915			155	.272	.333	555	151	25	11	1	0.2	75	41	38	33	12	2	0	339	17	11	6	2.4	.970	OF-153, 1B-2
1916	2 teams			CIN	N	(70G – .244)		NY	N	(2G – 1.000)															
"	total		72	.247	.306	235	58	9	1	1	0.4	29	19	22	8	7	3	2	138	6	5	2	2.1	.966	OF-68
7 yrs.			467	.248	.314	1537	381	61	16	3	0.2	181	116	128	59	57	17	6	880	400	81	53	2.9	.940	OF-296, 2B-129, 3B-11, SS-8, C-3, 1B-2

Matt Kilroy

KILROY, MATTHEW ALOYSIUS (Matches)
Brother of Mike Kilroy.
B. June 21, 1866, Philadelphia, Pa. D. Mar. 2, 1940, Philadelphia, Pa.
BL TL 5'9" 175 lbs.

Year	Team		Games	BA	SA	AB	H	2B	3B	HR	HR%	R	RBI	BB	SO	SB	AB	H	PO	A	E	DP	TC/G	FA	G by Pos
1886	BAL	AA	68	.174	.197	218	38	3	1	0	0.0	33		21			0	0	32	116	28	1	2.6	.841	P-68, OF-2
1887			72	.247	.318	239	59	5	6	0	0.0	46		31		12	0	0	39	167	22	2	3.2	.904	P-69, OF-4, SS-1
1888			43	.179	.241	145	26	5	2	0	0.0	13	19	11		10	0	0	21	61	6	2	2.0	.932	P-40, OF-7
1889			65	.274	.361	208	57	3	6	1	0.5	32	26	23	26	13	0	0	30	142	18	4	2.9	.905	P-59, OF-8
1890	BOS	P	31	.215	.247	93	20	1	1	0	0.0	11	8	12	9	11	0	0	28	60	10	2	3.2	.898	P-30, OF-2, SS-1, 3B-1
1891	CIN	AA	8	.150	.150	20	3	0	0	0	0.0	2	0	4	2	0	0	0	3	14	2	0	2.4	.895	P-7, OF-1
1892	WAS	N	4	.200	.200	10	2	0	0	0	0.0	0	0	1	0	0	0	0	3	14	2	0	4.8	.895	P-4
1893	LOU	N	5	.438	.625	16	7	3	0	0	0.0	4	3	1	3	0	0	0	1	12	1	0	2.8	.929	P-5
1894			8	.118	.118	17	2	0	0	0	0.0	2	0	1	0	0	0	0	6	13	4	0	2.9	.826	P-8
1898	CHI	N	26	.229	.292	96	22	4	1	0	0.0	20	10	13		0	0	0	21	31	4	2	2.2	.929	P-13, OF-12
10 yrs.			330	.222	.280	1062	236	24	17	1	0.1	163	67	118	46	47	1	0	184	630	97	13	2.8	.894	P-303, OF-36, SS-2, 3B-1

Dick Kimble

KIMBLE, RICHARD LEWIS
B. July 27, 1915, Buchtel, Ohio
BL TR 5'9" 160 lbs.

Year	Team		Games	BA	SA	AB	H	2B	3B	HR	HR%	R	RBI	BB	SO	SB	AB	H	PO	A	E	DP	TC/G	FA	G by Pos
1945	WAS	A	20	.245	.306	49	12	1	1	0	0.0	5	1	5	2	0	4	0	19	38	3	5	3.0	.950	SS-15

Year	Team		Games	BA	SA	AB	H	2B	3B	HR	HR%	R	RBI	BB	SO	SB	Pinch Hit AB	Pinch Hit H	PO	A	E	DP	TC/G	FA	G by Pos

Bruce Kimm

KIMM, BRUCE EDWARD B. June 29, 1951, Cedar Rapids, Iowa BR TR 5'11" 175 lbs.

Year	Team		Games	BA	SA	AB	H	2B	3B	HR	HR%	R	RBI	BB	SO	SB	AB	H	PO	A	E	DP	TC/G	FA	G by Pos
1976	DET	A	63	.263	.336	152	40	8	0	1	0.7	13	6	15	20	4	0	0	256	33	9	5	4.7	.970	C-61, DH-2
1977			14	.080	.120	25	2	1	0	0	0.0	2	1	0	4	0	0	0	43	3	2	0	3.4	.958	C-12, DH-2
1979	CHI	N	9	.091	.091	11	1	0	0	0	0.0	0	0	0	0	0	0	0	30	1	1	0	3.6	.969	C-9
1980	CHI	A	100	.243	.291	251	61	10	1	0	0.0	20	19	17	26	1	3	0	375	26	6	2	4.1	.985	C-98
4 yrs.			186	.237	.292	439	104	19	1	1	0.2	35	26	32	50	5	3	0	704	63	18	7	4.2	.977	C-180, DH-4

Wally Kimmick

KIMMICK, WALTER LYONS B. May 30, 1897, Turtle Creek, Pa. BR TR 5'11" 174 lbs.

Year	Team		Games	BA	SA	AB	H	2B	3B	HR	HR%	R	RBI	BB	SO	SB	AB	H	PO	A	E	DP	TC/G	FA	G by Pos
1919	STL	N	2	.000	.000	1	0	0	0	0	0.0	1	0	1	0	1	1	0	0	1	0	0	0.5	1.000	SS-1
1921	CIN	N	3	.167	.167	6	1	0	0	0	0.0	0	1	0	1	0	1	0	1	3	2	1	2.0	.667	3B-2
1922			39	.247	.292	89	22	2	1	0	0.0	11	12	3	12	0	3	0	44	87	4	11	3.5	.970	SS-30, 2B-3, 3B-1
1923			29	.225	.275	80	18	2	1	0	0.0	11	6	5	15	3	2	0	41	78	3	10	4.2	.975	2B-17, 3B-4, SS-1
1925	PHI	N	70	.305	.376	141	43	3	2	1	0.7	16	10	22	26	0	11	4	62	95	9	9	2.4	.946	SS-28, 3B-21, 2B-13
1926			20	.214	.357	28	6	2	1	0	0.0	0	2	3	7	0	6	1	25	8	4	1	1.9	.892	1B-5, SS-4, 3B-4, 2B-1
6 yrs.			163	.261	.325	345	90	9	6	1	0.3	39	31	34	61	4	24	5	173	272	22	32	2.9	.953	SS-64, 2B-34, 3B-32, 1B-5

Chad Kimsey

KIMSEY, CLYDE ELIAS B. Aug. 6, 1906, Copperhill, Tenn. D. Dec. 3, 1942, Pryor, Okla. BL TR 6'3½" 200 lbs.

Year	Team		Games	BA	SA	AB	H	2B	3B	HR	HR%	R	RBI	BB	SO	SB	AB	H	PO	A	E	DP	TC/G	FA	G by Pos
1929	STL	A	29	.267	.533	30	8	2	0	2	6.7	6	4	1	8	0	5	1	7	25	1	2	1.1	.970	P-24
1930			60	.343	.514	70	24	4	1	2	2.9	14	14	5	16	1	16	2	2	32	2	0	0.6	.944	P-42
1931			47	.270	.459	37	10	1	0	2	5.4	5	5	8	11	1	4	0	6	31	3	1	0.9	.925	P-42
1932	2 teams			STL A (34G – .333)		CHI A (7G – .000)																				
"	total		41	.300	.350	20	6	1	1	0	0.0	1	1	1	4	1	1	0	4	30	2	2	0.9	.944	P-40
1933	CHI	A	28	.152	.152	33	5	0	0	0	0.0	1	1	0	9	0	1	0	2	28	0	2	1.1	1.000	P-28
1936	DET	A	22	.313	.500	16	5	1	1	0	0.0	3	1	1	5	0	0	0	3	18	1	0	1.0	.955	P-22
6 yrs.			227	.282	.432	206	58	9	2	6	2.9	30	26	16	53	2	27	3	24	164	9	7	0.9	.954	P-198

Jerry Kindall

KINDALL, GERALD DONALD (Slim) B. May 27, 1935, St. Paul, Minn. BR TR 6'2½" 175 lbs. BB 1960

Year	Team		Games	BA	SA	AB	H	2B	3B	HR	HR%	R	RBI	BB	SO	SB	AB	H	PO	A	E	DP	TC/G	FA	G by Pos
1956	CHI	N	32	.164	.218	55	9	1	1	0	0.0	7	0	6	17	1	0	0	33	53	4	12	2.8	.956	SS-18
1957			72	.160	.276	181	29	3	0	6	3.3	18	12	8	48	1	10	2	73	109	15	10	2.7	.924	2B-28, 3B-19, SS-9
1958			3	.167	.333	6	1	0	0	0	0.0	0	0	0	3	0	0	0	6	5	0	2	3.7	1.000	2B-3
1960			89	.240	.346	246	59	16	2	2	0.8	17	23	5	52	4	3	0	147	222	13	45	4.3	.966	2B-82, SS-2
1961			96	.242	.419	310	75	23	3	9	2.9	37	44	18	89	2	7	1	206	233	26	61	4.8	.944	2B-50, SS-47
1962	CLE	A	154	.232	.349	530	123	21	1	13	2.5	51	55	45	107	4	0	0	358	494	19	114	5.7	.978	2B-154
1963			86	.205	.295	234	48	4	1	5	2.1	27	20	18	71	3	3	1	134	183	9	31	3.8	.972	SS-46, 2B-37, 1B-4
1964	2 teams			CLE A (23G – .360)		MIN A (62G – .148)																				
"	total		85	.183	.261	153	28	3	0	3	2.0	13	8	9	51	0	0	0	161	116	7	28	3.3	.975	2B-51, 1B-24, SS-7
1965	MIN	A	125	.196	.289	342	67	12	1	6	1.8	41	36	36	97	2	2	1	246	266	23	63	4.3	.957	2B-106, 3B-10, SS-7
9 yrs.			742	.213	.327	2057	439	83	9	44	2.1	211	198	145	535	17	25	5	1364	1681	116	366	4.3	.963	2B-511, SS-136, 3B-29, 1B-28

Ralph Kiner

KINER, RALPH McPHERRAN B. Oct. 27, 1922, Santa Rita, N. M. Hall of Fame 1975. BR TR 6'2" 195 lbs.

Year	Team		Games	BA	SA	AB	H	2B	3B	HR	HR%	R	RBI	BB	SO	SB	AB	H	PO	A	E	DP	TC/G	FA	G by Pos
1946	PIT	N	144	.247	.430	502	124	17	3	23	4.6	63	81	74	109	3	3	0	339	6	11	0	2.5	.969	OF-140
1947			152	.313	.639	565	177	23	4	51	9.0	118	127	98	81	1	0	0	390	8	7	1	2.7	.983	OF-152
1948			156	.265	.533	555	147	19	5	40	7.2	104	123	112	61	1	1	1	382	6	10	1	2.6	.975	OF-154
1949			152	.310	.658	549	170	19	5	54	9.8	116	127	117	61	6	0	0	311	12	7	3	2.2	.979	OF-152
1950			150	.272	.590	547	149	21	6	47	8.6	112	118	122	79	2	0	0	287	13	11	2	2.1	.965	OF-150
1951			151	.309	.627	531	164	31	6	42	7.9	124	109	137	57	2	0	0	751	36	18	60	5.3	.978	OF-94, 1B-58
1952			149	.244	.500	516	126	17	2	37	7.2	90	87	110	77	3	0	0	250	9	8	0	1.8	.970	OF-149
1953	2 teams			PIT N (41G – .270)		CHI N (117G – .283)																				
"	total		158	.279	.512	562	157	20	3	35	6.2	100	116	100	88	2	1	0	282	11	8	3	1.9	.973	OF-157
1954	CHI	N	147	.285	.487	557	159	36	5	22	3.9	88	73	76	90	2	0	0	298	6	9	1	2.1	.971	OF-147
1955	CLE	A	113	.243	.452	321	78	13	0	18	5.6	56	54	65	46	0	28	11	141	2	2	0	1.3	.986	OF-87
10 yrs.			1472	.279	.548	5205	1451	216	39	369	7.1	971	1015	1011	749	22	33	12	3431	109	91	71	2.5	.975	OF-1382, 1B-58
											2nd														

Charlie King

KING, CHARLES GILBERT (Chick) B. Nov. 10, 1930, Paris, Tenn. BR TR 6'2" 190 lbs.

Year	Team		Games	BA	SA	AB	H	2B	3B	HR	HR%	R	RBI	BB	SO	SB	AB	H	PO	A	E	DP	TC/G	FA	G by Pos
1954	DET	A	11	.214	.286	28	6	0	1	0	0.0	4	3	3	8	0	4	0	22	1	1	1	2.2	.958	OF-7
1955			7	.238	.238	21	5	0	0	0	0.0	2	1	0	2	0	0	0	12	0	1	0	1.9	.923	OF-6
1956			7	.222	.222	9	2	0	0	0	0.0	0	0	1	4	0	2	0	4	0	1	0	0.7	.800	OF-4
1958	CHI	N	8	.250	.250	8	2	0	0	0	0.0	1	1	3	1	0	1	0	6	0	0	0	0.8	1.000	OF-7
1959	2 teams			CHI N (7G – .000)		STL N (5G – .429)																				
"	total		12	.300	.300	10	3	0	0	0	0.0	3	0	0	3	0	0	0	9	0	0	0	0.8	1.000	OF-5
5 yrs.			45	.237	.263	76	18	0	1	0	0.0	11	5	8	18	0	7	0	53	1	3	1	1.3	.947	OF-29

Fred King

Playing record listed under John Butler

Hal King

KING, HAROLD B. Feb. 1, 1944, Oviedo, Fla. BL TR 6'1" 200 lbs.

Year	Team		Games	BA	SA	AB	H	2B	3B	HR	HR%	R	RBI	BB	SO	SB	AB	H	PO	A	E	DP	TC/G	FA	G by Pos
1967	HOU	N	15	.250	.364	44	11	1	2	0	0.0	6	2	6	4	0	4	1	62	8	0	0	4.7	1.000	C-11
1968			27	.145	.218	55	8	2	1	0	0.0	4	2	7	16	0	11	1	83	8	3	0	3.5	.968	C-19
1970	ATL	N	89	.260	.461	204	53	8	0	11	5.4	29	30	32	41	0	26	6	316	14	5	1	3.8	.985	C-62
1971			86	.207	.328	198	41	9	0	5	2.5	14	19	29	43	0	26	6	274	23	5	0	3.5	.983	C-60
1972	TEX	A	50	.180	.320	122	22	5	0	4	3.3	12	12	25	35	0	12	0	181	16	6	3	4.1	.970	C-38
1973	CIN	N	35	.186	.465	43	8	0	0	4	9.3	5	10	6	10	0	26	1	26	1	0	1	0.8	1.000	C-9

Year	Team		Games	BA	SA	AB	H	2B	3B	HR	HR%	R	RBI	BB	SO	SB	Pinch Hit AB	H	PO	A	E	DP	TC/G	FA	G by Pos

Hal King *continued*

| 1974 | | | 20 | .176 | .235 | 17 | 3 | 1 | 0 | 0 | 0.0 | 1 | 3 | 3 | 4 | 0 | 14 | 3 | 6 | 1 | 0 | 0 | 0.4 | 1.000 | C-5 |
| 7 yrs. | | | 322 | .214 | .366 | 683 | 146 | 26 | 3 | 24 | 3.5 | 67 | 82 | 104 | 158 | 1 | 119 | 22 | 948 | 71 | 19 | 6 | 3.2 | .982 | C-204 |

LEAGUE CHAMPIONSHIP SERIES

| 1973 | CIN | N | 3 | .500 | .500 | 2 | 1 | 0 | 0 | 0 | 0.0 | 0 | 0 | 1 | 1 | 0 | 2 | 1 | 0 | 0 | 0 | 0 | 0.0 | — | — |

Jeff King

KING, JEFFREY WAYNE
B. Dec. 26, 1964, Marion, Ind.　　BR　TR　6'1"　175 lbs.

| 1989 | PIT | N | 75 | .195 | .353 | 215 | 42 | 13 | 3 | 5 | 2.3 | 31 | 19 | 20 | 34 | 4 | 15 | 3 | 403 | 59 | 4 | 36 | 6.2 | .991 | 1B-46, 3B-13, 2B-7, SS-1 |

Jim King

KING, JAMES HUBERT
B. Aug. 27, 1932, Elkins, Ark.　　BL　TR　6'　185 lbs.

1955	CHI	N	113	.256	.425	301	77	12	3	11	3.7	43	45	24	39	2	18	4	184	10	2	2	1.7	.990	OF-93
1956			118	.249	.445	317	79	13	2	15	4.7	32	54	30	40	1	34	6	187	10	2	2	1.7	.990	OF-82
1957	STL	N	22	.314	.314	35	11	0	0	0	0.0	1	2	4	2	0	16	4	7	0	0	0	0.3	1.000	OF-8
1958	SF	N	34	.214	.393	56	12	2	1	2	3.6	8	8	10	8	0	14	3	18	0	0	0	0.5	1.000	OF-15
1961	WAS	A	110	.270	.449	263	71	12	1	11	4.2	43	46	38	45	4	17	1	139	7	3	2	1.4	.980	OF-91, C-1
1962			132	.243	.387	333	81	15	0	11	3.3	39	35	55	37	4	31	8	178	9	4	4	1.4	.979	OF-101
1963			136	.231	.444	459	106	16	5	24	5.2	61	62	45	43	3	22	4	213	13	3	2	1.7	.987	OF-123
1964			134	.241	.412	415	100	15	1	18	4.3	44	56	55	65	3	22	7	240	10	7	0	1.9	.973	OF-121
1965			120	.213	.430	258	55	10	2	14	5.4	46	49	44	50	1	37	8	127	7	1	1	1.1	.993	OF-88
1966			117	.248	.403	310	77	14	2	10	3.2	41	30	38	41	4	34	7	147	4	2	0	1.3	.987	OF-85
1967	3 teams			WAS A (47G – .210)		CHI A (23G – .120)		CLE A (19G – .143)																	
"	total		89	.175	.234	171	30	3	2	1	0.6	14	14	20	31	1	42	11	66	0	2	0	0.8	.971	OF-44, C-1
11 yrs.			1125	.240	.411	2918	699	112	19	117	4.0	374	401	363	401	23	287	63	1506	70	26	13	1.4	.984	OF-851, C-2

Lee King

KING, EDWARD LEE
B. Dec. 26, 1892, Hundred, W. Va.　D. Sept. 16, 1967, Shinston, W. Va.　　BR　TR　5'8"　160 lbs.

1916	PIT	N	8	.111	.111	18	2	0	0	0	0.0	0	0	0	7	0	2	0	2	0	0	0	0.9	.714	OF-8
1917			111	.249	.320	381	95	14	5	1	0.3	32	35	15	58	8	9	3	198	16	7	6	2.0	.968	OF-102
1918			36	.232	.321	112	26	3	2	1	0.9	9	11	11	15	3	0	0	50	0	5	0	1.5	.909	OF-36
1919	NY	N	21	.100	.150	20	2	1	0	0	0.0	5	1	1	6	0	9	1	2	0	1	0	0.1	.667	OF-7
1920			93	.276	.429	261	72	11	4	7	2.7	32	42	21	38	3	12	2	167	8	9	1	2.0	.951	OF-84
1921	2 teams			NY N (39G – .223)		PHI N (64G – .269)																			
"	total		103	.255	.406	310	79	23	6	1	1.3	42	39	21	43	1	7	2	167	15	17	0	1.9	.915	OF-92, 1B-1
1922	2 teams			PHI N (19G – .226)		NY N (20G – .176)																			
"	total		39	.207	.391	87	18	8	1	2	2.3	14	15	13	8	1	7	1	34	1	2	1	0.9	.946	OF-20, 1B-5
7 yrs.			411	.247	.366	1189	294	60	18	15	1.3	134	144	82	175	16	46	9	622	41	43	8	1.7	.939	OF-349, 1B-6

WORLD SERIES

| 1922 | NY | N | 2 | 1.000 | 1.000 | 1 | 1 | 0 | 0 | 0 | 0.0 | 0 | 1 | 0 | 0 | 0 | 0 | 0 | 0 | 0 | 0 | 0 | 0.0 | — | OF-2 |

Lee King

KING, EDWARD LEE
B. Mar. 28, 1894, Waltham, Mass.　D. Sept. 7, 1938, Newton Centre, Mass.　　BR　TR　5'10"　150 lbs.

1916	PHI	A	42	.188	.222	144	27	1	2	0	0.0	13	8	7	15	4	2	0	53	44	13	5	2.6	.882	OF-22, SS-11, 3B-5, 2B-2
1919	BOS	N	2	.000	.000	1	0	0	0	0	0.0	0	0	0	0	0	1	0	0	0	0	0	0.0	—	—
2 yrs.			44	.186	.221	145	27	1	2	0	0.0	13	8	7	15	4	3	0	53	44	13	5	2.5	.882	OF-22, SS-11, 3B-5, 2B-2

Lynn King

KING, LYNN PAUL (Dig)
B. Nov. 28, 1907, Villisca, Iowa　D. May 11, 1972, Atlantic, Iowa　　BL　TR　5'9"　165 lbs.

1935	STL	N	8	.182	.182	22	4	0	0	0	0.0	6	0	4	1	2	0	0	26	0	0	0	3.3	1.000	OF-6
1936			78	.190	.230	100	19	2	1	0	0.0	12	10	9	14	2	25	5	59	1	1	1	0.8	.984	OF-34
1939			89	.235	.259	85	20	2	0	0	0.0	10	11	15	3	2	35	10	53	1	1	0	0.6	.982	OF-44
3 yrs.			175	.208	.237	207	43	4	1	0	0.0	28	21	28	18	6	61	15	138	2	2	1	0.8	.986	OF-84

Sam King

KING, SAMUEL WARREN
B. May 17, 1852, Peabody, Mass.　D. Aug. 11, 1922, Peabody, Mass.　　BL　6'

| 1884 | WAS | AA | 12 | .178 | .222 | 45 | 8 | 2 | 0 | 0 | 0.0 | 3 | | 1 | | | 0 | 0 | 121 | 4 | 12 | 6 | 11.4 | .912 | 1B-12 |

Silver King

KING, CHARLES FREDERICK
Born Charles Frederick Koenig.
B. Jan. 11, 1868, St. Louis, Mo.　D. May 21, 1938, St. Louis, Mo.　　BR　TR　6'　170 lbs.

1886	KC	N	7	.045	.045	22	1	0	0	0	0.0	0	1	2	12		0	0	13	3	0	0	2.3	.813	P-5, OF-2
1887	STL	AA	62	.207	.243	222	46	6	1	0	0.0	28		24		10	0	0	35	70	16	1	2.0	.868	P-46, OF-17
1888			66	.208	.300	207	43	4	6	1	0.5	25	14	40		6	0	0	33	119	12	4	2.5	.927	P-66, OF-2
1889			56	.228	.296	189	43	7	3	0	0.0	37	30	22	40	3	0	0	19	91	5	2	2.1	.957	P-56, 1B-2, OF-1
1890	CHI	P	58	.168	.249	185	31	2	5	1	0.5	24	16	13	22	3	0	0	22	139	6	5	2.9	.964	P-56, OF-1, 1B-1
1891	PIT	N	49	.169	.223	148	25	2	3	0	0.0	12	9	14	31	0	0	0	19	67	10	5	2.0	.896	P-48, 3B-1
1892	NY	N	52	.210	.311	167	35	2	4	2	1.2	27	23	16	26	1	0	0	22	81	11	4	2.2	.904	P-52
1893	2 teams			NY N (7G – .176)		CIN N (17G – .162)																			
"	total		24	.167	.222	54	9	0	0	0	0.0	13	4	15	16	0	0	0	8	32	3	1	1.8	.930	P-24
1896	WAS	N	22	.276	.379	58	16	6	0	0	0.0	9	12	8		1	0	0	6	19	1	0	1.2	.962	P-22
1897			24	.193	.228	57	11	2	0	0	0.0	8	7	12		0	0	0	2	40	2	1	1.8	.955	P-23
10 yrs.			420	.199	.268	1309	260	33	23	4	0.3	183	116	166	162	24	0	0	166	671	69	23	2.2	.924	P-398, OF-23, 1B-3, 3B-1

Wes Kingdon

KINGDON, WESCOTT WILLIAM
B. July 4, 1900, Los Angeles, Calif.　D. Apr. 19, 1975, Capistrano, Calif.　　BR　TR　5'8"　148 lbs.

| 1932 | WAS | A | 18 | .324 | .471 | 34 | 11 | 3 | 1 | 0 | 0.0 | 10 | 3 | 5 | 2 | 0 | 5 | 1 | 8 | 15 | 1 | 2 | 1.3 | .958 | 3B-8, SS-4 |

Year	Team		Games	BA	SA	AB	H	2B	3B	HR	HR%	R	RBI	BB	SO	SB	Pinch Hit AB	H	PO	A	E	DP	TC/G	FA	G by Pos

Mike Kingery

KINGERY, MICHAEL SCOTT
B. Mar. 29, 1961, St. James, Minn.

BL TL 6' 180 lbs.

Year	Team		Games	BA	SA	AB	H	2B	3B	HR	HR%	R	RBI	BB	SO	SB	AB	H	PO	A	E	DP	TC/G	FA	G by Pos
1986	KC	A	62	.258	.388	209	54	8	5	3	1.4	25	14	12	30	7	5	2	102	6	3	2	1.8	.973	OF-59
1987	SEA	A	120	.280	.449	354	99	25	4	9	2.5	38	52	27	43	7	9	3	226	15	2	3	2.0	.992	OF-114, DH-4
1988			57	.203	.276	123	25	6	0	1	0.8	21	9	19	23	3	5	0	102	6	2	1	1.9	.982	OF-44, 1B-10
1989			31	.224	.342	76	17	3	0	2	2.6	14	6	7	14	1	6	0	70	0	0	0	2.3	1.000	OF-23
4 yrs.			270	.256	.394	762	195	42	9	15	2.0	98	81	65	110	18	25	5	500	27	7	6	2.0	.987	OF-240, 1B-10, DH-4

Dave Kingman

KINGMAN, DAVID ARTHUR (Kong)
B. Dec. 21, 1948, Pendleton, Ore.

BR TR 6'6" 210 lbs.

Year	Team		Games	BA	SA	AB	H	2B	3B	HR	HR%	R	RBI	BB	SO	SB	AB	H	PO	A	E	DP	TC/G	FA	G by Pos
1971	SF	N	41	.278	.557	115	32	10	2	6	5.2	17	24	9	35	5	7	1	168	9	4	9	4.4	.978	1B-20, OF-14
1972			135	.225	.462	472	106	17	4	29	6.1	65	83	51	140	16	5	0	496	159	22	49	5.0	.968	3B-59, 1B-56, OF-22
1973			112	.203	.479	305	62	10	1	24	7.9	54	55	41	122	8	7	1	313	146	22	30	4.3	.954	3B-60, 1B-46, P-2
1974			121	.223	.440	350	78	18	2	18	5.1	41	55	37	125	8	11	3	696	98	25	69	6.8	.969	1B-91, 3B-21, OF-2
1975	NY	N	134	.231	.494	502	116	22	1	36	7.2	65	88	34	153	7	5	0	526	69	14	37	4.5	.977	OF-71, 1B-58, 3B-12
1976			123	.238	.506	474	113	14	1	37	7.8	70	86	28	135	7	1	0	293	18	9	11	2.6	.972	OF-111, 1B-16
1977	4 teams																								
"	total	NY N (58G − .209)	132	.221	.444	439	97	20	0	26	5.9	47	78	28	143	5	23	4	406	29	9	16	3.4	.980	OF-75, 1B-38, DH-6, 3B-2
1978	CHI	N	119	.266	.542	395	105	17	4	28	7.1	65	79	39	111	3	8	1	226	10	6	6	2.0	.975	OF-100, 1B-6
1979			145	.288	**.613**	532	153	19	5	48	9.0	97	115	45	131	4	5	3	240	11	12	3	1.8	.954	OF-139
1980			81	.278	.522	255	71	8	0	18	7.1	31	57	21	44	2	16	6	119	10	8	0	1.7	.942	OF-61, 1B-2
1981	NY	N	100	.221	.456	353	78	11	3	22	6.2	40	59	55	105	6	1	0	548	34	20	39	6.0	.967	1B-56, OF-48
1982			149	.204	.432	535	109	9	1	37	6.9	80	99	59	156	4	5	0	1232	69	18	88	8.9	.986	1B-143
1983			100	.198	.383	248	49	7	0	13	5.2	25	29	22	57	2	39	7	450	28	3	43	4.8	.994	1B-50, OF-5
1984	OAK	A	147	.268	.505	549	147	23	1	35	6.4	68	118	44	119	2	0	0	55	2	0	3	0.4	1.000	DH-139, 1B-9
1985			158	.238	.417	592	141	16	0	30	5.1	66	91	62	114	3	2	1	50	1	0	3	0.3	1.000	DH-149, 1B-9
1986			144	.210	.431	561	118	19	0	35	6.2	70	94	33	126	3	2	0	17	0	2	2	0.1	.895	DH-140, 1B-3
16 yrs.			1941	.236	.478	6677	1575	240	25	442	6.6 5th	901	1210	608	1816 5th	85	137	27	5835	693	174	408	3.5	.974	OF-648, 1B-603, DH-434, 3B-154, P-2

LEAGUE CHAMPIONSHIP SERIES

Year	Team		Games	BA	SA	AB	H	2B	3B	HR	HR%	R	RBI	BB	SO	SB	AB	H	PO	A	E	DP	TC/G	FA	G by Pos
1971	SF	N	4	.111	.111	9	1	0	0	0	0.0	0	0	1	3	0	1	0	5	0	0	0	1.3	1.000	OF-2

Henry Kingman

KINGMAN, HENRY LEES
B. Apr. 3, 1892, Tientsin, China D. Dec. 27, 1982, Oakland, Calif.

BL TL 6'1½" 165 lbs.

Year	Team		Games	BA	SA	AB	H	2B	3B	HR	HR%	R	RBI	BB	SO	SB	AB	H	PO	A	E	DP	TC/G	FA	G by Pos
1914	NY	A	4	.000	.000	3	0	0	0	0	0.0	1	0	2	0	0	3	0	1	0	0	0	0.3	1.000	1B-1

Walt Kinlock

KINLOCK, WALTER
B. 1878, St. Joseph, Mo. Deceased.

Year	Team		Games	BA	SA	AB	H	2B	3B	HR	HR%	R	RBI	BB	SO	SB	AB	H	PO	A	E	DP	TC/G	FA	G by Pos
1895	STL	N	1	.333	.333	3	1	0	0	0	0.0	0	0	0	2	0	0	0	4	1	0	1	5.0	1.000	3B-1

Bob Kinsella

KINSELLA, ROBERT FRANCIS (Red)
B. Jan. 5, 1899, Springfield, Ill. D. Dec. 30, 1951, Los Angeles, Calif.

BL TR 5'9½" 165 lbs.

Year	Team		Games	BA	SA	AB	H	2B	3B	HR	HR%	R	RBI	BB	SO	SB	AB	H	PO	A	E	DP	TC/G	FA	G by Pos
1919	NY	N	3	.222	.222	9	2	0	0	0	0.0	1	0	0	3	1	0	0	1	0	1	0	0.7	.500	OF-3
1920			1	.333	.333	3	1	0	0	0	0.0	0	1	0	2	0	0	0	1	0	1	0	2.0	.500	OF-1
2 yrs.			4	.250	.250	12	3	0	0	0	0.0	1	1	0	5	1	0	0	2	0	2	0	1.0	.500	OF-4

Kinsler

KINSLER,
B. Staten Island, N. Y. Deceased.

Year	Team		Games	BA	SA	AB	H	2B	3B	HR	HR%	R	RBI	BB	SO	SB	AB	H	PO	A	E	DP	TC/G	FA	G by Pos
1893	NY	N	1	.000	.000	3	0	0	0	0	0.0	1	0	1	1	0	0	0	1	0	0	0	1.0	1.000	OF-1

Tom Kinslow

KINSLOW, THOMAS F.
B. Jan. 12, 1866, Washington, D. C. D. Feb. 22, 1901, Washington, D. C.

BR TR 5'10" 160 lbs.

Year	Team		Games	BA	SA	AB	H	2B	3B	HR	HR%	R	RBI	BB	SO	SB	AB	H	PO	A	E	DP	TC/G	FA	G by Pos
1886	WAS	N	3	.250	.250	8	2	0	0	0	0.0	1	1	0			0	0	11	4	0	0	5.0	1.000	C-3
1887	NY	AA	2	.000	.000	6	0	0	0	0	0.0	0		0			0	0	6	3	0	0	4.5	1.000	C-2
1890	BKN	P	64	.264	.409	242	64	11	6	4	1.7	30	46	10	22	2	0	0	298	72	37	7	6.4	.909	C-64
1891	BKN	N	61	.237	.263	228	54	6	0	0	0.0	22	33	9	23	3	0	0	252	54	26	6	5.4	.922	C-61
1892			66	.305	.443	246	75	6	11	2	0.8	37	40	13	16	4	0	0	355	89	32	6	7.2	.933	C-66
1893			78	.244	.333	312	76	8	4	4	1.3	38	45	11	13	4	0	0	291	80	27	11	5.1	.932	C-76, OF-2
1894			62	.305	.408	223	68	5	6	2	0.9	39	41	20	11	4	0	0	219	47	24	4	4.7	.908	C-61, 1B-1
1895	PIT	N	19	.226	.258	62	14	2	0	0	0.0	10	5	2	2	1	0	0	67	10	3	1	4.2	.963	C-18
1896	LOU	N	8	.280	.360	25	7	0	1	0	0.0	4	7	1	5	0	2	0	23	4	4	2	3.9	.871	C-5, 1B-1
1898	2 teams	WAS N (3G − .111)				STL N (14G − .283)																			
"	total		17	.258	.323	62	16	2	1	0	0.0	5	4	1			0	0	49	21	7	4	4.5	.909	C-17, 1B-1
10 yrs.			380	.266	.361	1414	376	40	29	12	0.8	186	222	67	92	18	3	0	1571	384	163	41	5.6	.923	C-373, 1B-3, OF-2

Walt Kinzie

KINZIE, WALTER HARRIS
B. Mar. 16, 1857, Ky. D. Nov. 5, 1909, Chicago, Ill.

5'10½" 161 lbs.

Year	Team		Games	BA	SA	AB	H	2B	3B	HR	HR%	R	RBI	BB	SO	SB	AB	H	PO	A	E	DP	TC/G	FA	G by Pos
1882	DET	N	13	.094	.132	53	5	0	1	0	0.0	5	2	0	8		0	0	8	38	8	1	4.2	.852	SS-13
1884	2 teams	CHI N (19G − .159)				STL AA (2G − .111)																			
"	total		21	.154	.253	91	14	3	0	2	2.2	4		0	13		0	0	26	55	17	4	4.7	.827	SS-17, 3B-2, 2B-2
2 yrs.			34	.132	.208	144	19	3	1	2	1.4	9	2	0	21		0	0	34	93	25	5	4.5	.836	SS-30, 3B-2, 2B-2

Ed Kippert

KIPPERT, EDWARD AUGUST
B. Jan. 3, 1880, Detroit, Mich. D. June 3, 1960, Detroit, Mich.

BR TR 5'10½" 180 lbs.

Year	Team		Games	BA	SA	AB	H	2B	3B	HR	HR%	R	RBI	BB	SO	SB	AB	H	PO	A	E	DP	TC/G	FA	G by Pos
1914	CIN	N	2	.000	.000	2	0	0	0	0	0.0	0	0	0	0	0	0	0	1	0	0	0	0.5	1.000	OF-2

Jim Kirby

KIRBY, JAMES HERSCHEL
B. May 5, 1923, Nashville, Tenn.

BR TR 5'11" 175 lbs.

Year	Team		Games	BA	SA	AB	H	2B	3B	HR	HR%	R	RBI	BB	SO	SB	AB	H	PO	A	E	DP	TC/G	FA	G by Pos
1949	CHI	N	3	.500	.500	2	1	0	0	0	0.0	0	0	0	0	0	2	1	0	0	0	0	0.0	−	

Year	Team		Games	BA	SA	AB	H	2B	3B	HR	HR%	R	RBI	BB	SO	SB	Pinch Hit AB	Pinch Hit H	PO	A	E	DP	TC/G	FA	G by Pos

LaRue Kirby

KIRBY, LaRUE
B. Dec. 30, 1889, Eureka, Mich. D. June 10, 1961, Lansing, Mich.
BB TR 6' 185 lbs.

Year	Team		Games	BA	SA	AB	H	2B	3B	HR	HR%	R	RBI	BB	SO	SB	PH AB	PH H	PO	A	E	DP	TC/G	FA	G by Pos
1912	NY	N	3	.200	.400	5	1	1	0	0	0.0	1	0	0	0	0	0	0	2	3	0	0	1.7	1.000	P-3
1914	STL	F	52	.246	.338	195	48	6	3	2	1.0	21	18	14		5	0	0	100	7	3	2	2.1	.973	OF-50
1915			61	.213	.275	178	38	7	2	0	0.0	15	16	17		3	5	1	88	8	4	2	1.6	.960	OF-52, P-1
3 yrs.			116	.230	.310	378	87	14	5	2	0.5	37	34	31		8	5	1	190	18	7	4	1.9	.967	OF-102, P-4

Tom Kirk

KIRK, THOMAS DANIEL
B. Sept. 27, 1927, Philadelphia, Pa. D. Aug. 1, 1974, Philadelphia, Pa.
BL TL 5'10½" 182 lbs.

Year	Team		Games	BA	SA	AB	H	2B	3B	HR	HR%	R	RBI	BB	SO	SB	PH AB	PH H	PO	A	E	DP	TC/G	FA	G by Pos
1947	PHI	A	1	.000	.000	1	0	0	0	0	0.0	0	0	0	0	0	1	0	0	0	0	0	0.0	–	

Jay Kirke

KIRKE, JUDSON FABIAN
B. June 16, 1888, Fleichmans, N.Y. D. Aug. 31, 1968, New Orleans, La.
BL TR 6' 195 lbs.

Year	Team		Games	BA	SA	AB	H	2B	3B	HR	HR%	R	RBI	BB	SO	SB	PH AB	PH H	PO	A	E	DP	TC/G	FA	G by Pos
1910	DET	A	8	.200	.240	25	5	1	0	0	0.0	3	3	1		0	1	0	16	17	3	1	4.5	.917	2B-7, OF-1
1911	BOS	N	20	.360	.528	89	32	5	5	0	0.0	9	12	2	6	3	0	0	68	11	4	2	4.2	.952	OF-14, 1B-3, SS-1, 3B-1, 2B-1
1912			103	.320	.407	359	115	11	4	4	1.1	53	62	9	46	7	17	4	108	45	23	6	1.7	.869	OF-71, 3B-32, 1B-1
1913			18	.237	.289	38	9	2	0	0	0.0	3	3	1	6	0	5	1	19	5	2	0	1.4	.923	OF-13
1914	CLE	A	67	.273	.343	242	66	10	2	1	0.4	18	25	7	30	5	7	3	235	15	4	10	3.8	.984	OF-42, 1B-18
1915			87	.310	.395	339	105	19	2	2	0.6	35	40	14	21	5	0	0	886	52	13	37	10.9	.986	1B-87
1918	NY	N	17	.250	.268	56	14	1	0	0	0.0	1	3	1	3	0	1	0	165	12	4	7	10.6	.978	1B-16
7 yrs.			320	.301	.385	1148	346	49	13	7	0.6	122	148	35	112	21	30	8	1497	157	53	63	5.3	.969	OF-141, 1B-125, 3B-33, 2B-8, SS-1

Willie Kirkland

KIRKLAND, WILLIE CHARLES
B. Feb. 17, 1934, Siluria, Ala.
BL TR 6'1" 206 lbs.

Year	Team		Games	BA	SA	AB	H	2B	3B	HR	HR%	R	RBI	BB	SO	SB	PH AB	PH H	PO	A	E	DP	TC/G	FA	G by Pos
1958	SF	N	122	.258	.447	418	108	25	6	14	3.3	48	56	43	69	3	9	3	187	12	8	4	1.7	.961	OF-115
1959			126	.272	.475	463	126	22	3	22	4.8	64	68	42	84	5	8	2	212	8	7	0	1.8	.969	OF-117
1960			146	.252	.454	515	130	21	10	21	4.1	59	65	44	86	12	5	0	252	16	6	5	1.9	.978	OF-143
1961	CLE	A	146	.259	.474	525	136	22	5	27	5.1	84	95	48	77	7	13	2	290	12	8	5	2.1	.974	OF-138
1962			137	.200	.377	419	84	9	1	21	5.0	56	72	43	62	9	13	1	233	11	7	0	1.8	.972	OF-125
1963			127	.230	.375	427	98	13	2	15	3.5	51	47	45	99	8	21	8	234	11	4	2	2.0	.984	OF-112
1964	2 teams					BAL A (66G – .200)							WAS A (32G – .216)												
"	total		98	.206	.345	252	52	11	0	8	3.2	22	35	23	56	3	13	2	125	7	5	3	1.4	.964	OF-85
1965	WAS	A	123	.231	.401	312	72	9	1	14	4.5	38	54	19	65	3	35	6	151	3	2	0	1.3	.987	OF-92
1966			124	.190	.325	163	31	2	1	6	3.7	21	17	16	50	2	51	12	56	3	1	0	0.5	.983	OF-68
9 yrs.			1149	.240	.422	3494	837	134	29	148	4.2	443	509	323	648	52	168	36	1740	83	48	19	1.6	.974	OF-995

Ed Kirkpatrick

KIRKPATRICK, EDGAR LEON
B. Oct. 8, 1944, Spokane, Wash.
BL TR 5'11½" 195 lbs.

Year	Team		Games	BA	SA	AB	H	2B	3B	HR	HR%	R	RBI	BB	SO	SB	PH AB	PH H	PO	A	E	DP	TC/G	FA	G by Pos
1962	LA	A	3	.000	.000	6	0	0	0	0	0.0	0	0	0	2	0	0	0	10	0	0	0	3.3	1.000	C-1
1963			34	.195	.338	77	15	5	0	2	2.6	4	7	6	19	1	14	1	82	5	1	1	2.6	.989	C-14, OF-10
1964			75	.242	.356	219	53	13	3	2	0.9	20	22	23	30	2	13	4	90	3	3	0	1.3	.969	OF-63
1965	CAL	A	19	.260	.452	73	19	5	0	3	4.1	8	8	3	9	1	0	0	28	3	1	0	1.7	.969	OF-19
1966			117	.192	.327	312	60	7	4	9	2.9	31	44	51	67	7	17	5	169	5	1	1	1.5	.994	OF-102, 1B-3
1967			3	.000	.000	8	0	0	0	0	0.0	0	0	0	2	0	1	0	4	0	0	0	1.3	1.000	C-2, OF-1
1968			89	.230	.273	161	37	4	0	1	0.6	23	15	25	32	1	43	14	62	5	3	1	0.8	.957	OF-45, C-4, 1B-2
1969	KC	A	120	.257	.451	315	81	11	4	14	4.4	40	49	43	42	3	34	5	204	13	1	1	1.8	.995	OF-82, C-8, 3B-2, 1B-2, 2B-1
1970			134	.229	.406	424	97	17	2	18	4.2	59	62	55	65	4	21	4	626	70	12	25	5.3	.983	C-89, OF-19, 1B-16
1971			120	.219	.332	365	80	12	1	9	2.5	46	46	48	60	3	9	5	412	30	8	6	3.8	.982	OF-61, C-59
1972			113	.275	.396	364	100	15	1	9	2.5	43	43	51	50	3	5	2	590	49	6	5	5.7	.991	C-108, 1B-1
1973			126	.263	.375	429	113	24	3	6	1.4	61	45	46	48	3	2	0	264	11	4	0	2.2	.986	OF-108, C-14, DH-8
1974	PIT	N	116	.247	.347	271	67	9	0	6	2.2	32	38	51	30	1	33	5	561	32	6	55	5.2	.990	1B-59, OF-14, C-6
1975			89	.236	.375	144	34	5	0	5	3.5	15	16	18	22	1	42	13	167	9	0	10	2.0	1.000	1B-28, OF-14
1976			83	.233	.295	163	34	9	0	1	0.6	14	16	14	40	1	40	6	205	14	4	15	2.7	.982	1B-25, OF-9, 3B-1
1977	3 teams					PIT N (21G – .143)							TEX A (20G – .188)						MIL A (29G – .273)						
"	total		70	.222	.288	153	34	7	0	1	0.7	15	13	22	25	1	18	7	145	7	4	8	2.2	.974	OF-30, 1B-13, DH-8, 3B-2, C-1
16 yrs.			1311	.238	.363	3467	824	143	18	85	2.5	411	424	456	518	34	294	71	3619	259	54	128	3.0	.986	OF-577, C-306, 1B-149, DH-16, 3B-5, 2B-1

LEAGUE CHAMPIONSHIP SERIES

Year	Team		Games	BA	SA	AB	H	2B	3B	HR	HR%	R	RBI	BB	SO	SB	PH AB	PH H	PO	A	E	DP	TC/G	FA	G by Pos
1974	PIT	N	3	.000	.000	9	0	0	0	0	0.0	0	0	2	0	0	0	0	22	0	0	2	7.3	1.000	1B-3
1975			2	.000	.000	2	0	0	0	0	0.0	0	0	0	0	0	2	0	0	0	0	0	0.0	–	
2 yrs.			5	.000	.000	11	0	0	0	0	0.0	0	0	2	0	0	2	0	22	0	0	2	4.4	1.000	1B-3

Enos Kirkpatrick

KIRKPATRICK, ENOS CLAIRE
B. Dec. 8, 1885, Pittsburgh, Pa. D. Apr. 14, 1964, Pittsburgh, Pa.
BR TR 5'10" 175 lbs.

Year	Team		Games	BA	SA	AB	H	2B	3B	HR	HR%	R	RBI	BB	SO	SB	PH AB	PH H	PO	A	E	DP	TC/G	FA	G by Pos
1912	BKN	N	32	.191	.223	94	18	1	1	0	0.0	13	6	9	15	5	1	0	29	67	4	3	3.1	.960	3B-29, SS-3
1913			48	.247	.348	89	22	4	1	1	1.1	13	5	3	18	5	13	2	110	36	7	6	3.2	.954	SS-10, 1B-8, 2B-6, 3B-4
1914	BAL	F	55	.253	.351	174	44	7	2	2	1.1	22	16	18		10	2	1	47	88	11	3	2.7	.925	3B-36, SS-11, OF-3, 1B-1
1915			68	.240	.310	171	41	8	2	0	0.0	22	19	24		12	5	1	101	108	20	11	3.4	.913	3B-28, 2B-21, SS-5, 1B-5
4 yrs.			203	.237	.314	528	125	20	6	3	0.6	70	46	54	33	32	21	4	287	299	42	23	3.1	.933	3B-97, SS-29, 2B-27, 1B-14, OF-3

Joe Kirrene

KIRRENE, JOSEPH JOHN
B. Oct. 4, 1931, San Francisco, Calif.
BR TR 6'2" 195 lbs.

Year	Team		Games	BA	SA	AB	H	2B	3B	HR	HR%	R	RBI	BB	SO	SB	PH AB	PH H	PO	A	E	DP	TC/G	FA	G by Pos
1950	CHI	A	1	.250	.250	4	1	0	0	0	0.0	0	0	0	1	0	0	0	1	1	0	0	2.0	1.000	3B-1
1954			9	.304	.348	23	7	1	0	0	0.0	4	4	5	2	1	0	0	7	11	1	2	2.1	.947	3B-9
2 yrs.			10	.296	.333	27	8	1	0	0	0.0	4	4	5	3	1	0	0	8	12	1	2	2.1	.952	3B-10

Year	Team		Games	BA	SA	AB	H	2B	3B	HR	HR%	R	RBI	BB	SO	SB	Pinch Hit AB	Pinch Hit H	PO	A	E	DP	TC/G	FA	G by Pos

Ernie Kish

KISH, ERNEST ALEXANDER
B. Feb. 6, 1918, Washington, D. C.   BL TR 5'9½" 170 lbs.

| 1945 | PHI | A | 43 | .245 | .309 | 110 | 27 | 5 | 1 | 0 | 0.0 | 10 | 10 | 9 | 9 | 0 | 9 | 2 | 52 | 3 | 4 | 0 | 1.4 | .932 | OF-30 |

Frank Kitson

KITSON, FRANK L.
B. Apr. 11, 1872, Hopkins, Mich.   D. Apr. 14, 1930, Allegan, Mich.   BL TR 5'11" 165 lbs.

1898	BAL	N	31	.314	.395	86	27	1	3	0	0.0	13	16	5		2	3	2	16	33	6	0	1.8	.891	P-17, OF-11
1899			45	.201	.269	134	27	7	1	0	0.0	13	8	6		7	4	0	12	69	2	1	1.8	.976	P-40
1900	BKN	N	43	.294	.358	109	32	5	1	0	0.0	20	16	6		2	2	0	13	39	5	0	1.3	.912	P-40, OF-1
1901			47	.263	.353	133	35	5	2	1	0.8	22	16	4		0	6	2	19	56	4	2	1.7	.949	P-38, OF-2, 1B-1
1902			39	.265	.389	113	30	3	4	1	0.9	9	11	3		0	7	3	7	69	3	1	2.0	.962	P-31
1903	DET	A	36	.181	.216	116	21	0	2	0	0.0	12	4	2		2	0	0	15	69	3	0	2.4	.966	P-31, OF-5
1904			27	.208	.250	72	15	0	0	1	1.4	9	4	1		0	1	0	6	68	4	2	2.9	.949	P-26
1905			33	.184	.207	87	16	2	0	0	0.0	8	4	3		0	0	0	5	65	7	0	2.3	.909	P-33
1906	WAS	A	31	.244	.411	90	22	4	4	1	1.1	9	12	8		1	1	0	5	62	3	1	2.3	.957	P-30
1907	2 teams		WAS	A	(5G – .125)		NY	A	(12G – .261)																
"	total		17	.226	.226	31	7	0	0	0	0.0	4	4	1		0	0	0	4	21	3	0	1.6	.893	P-17
	10 yrs.		349	.239	.314	971	232	27	17	4	0.4	119	95	39		14	24	7	102	551	40	7	2.0	.942	P-303, OF-19, 1B-1

Chris Kitsos

KITSOS, CHRISTOPHER ANESTOS
B. Feb. 11, 1928, New York, N. Y.   BB TR 5'9" 165 lbs.

| 1954 | CHI | N | 1 | – | – | 0 | 0 | 0 | 0 | 0 | – | 0 | 0 | 0 | 0 | 0 | 0 | 0 | 0 | 2 | 0 | 0 | 2.0 | 1.000 | SS-1 |

Ron Kittle

KITTLE, RONALD DALE (Kitty)
B. Jan. 5, 1958, Gary, Ind.   BR TR 6'4" 200 lbs.

1982	CHI	A	20	.241	.414	29	7	2	0	1	3.4	3	7	3	12	0	13	6	3	0	0	0	0.2	1.000	OF-5, DH-3
1983			145	.254	.504	520	132	19	3	35	6.7	75	100	39	150	8	6	0	234	7	9	0	1.7	.964	OF-139, DH-2
1984			139	.215	.453	466	100	15	0	32	6.9	67	74	49	137	3	13	4	226	14	7	2	1.8	.972	OF-124, DH-7
1985			116	.230	.467	379	87	12	0	26	6.9	51	58	31	92	1	9	0	88	2	1	1	0.8	.989	DH-57, OF-57
1986	2 teams		CHI	A	(86G – .213)		NY	A	(30G – .238)																
"	total		116	.218	.420	376	82	13	0	21	5.6	42	60	35	110	4	12	2	39	3	0	0	0.4	1.000	DH-86, OF-21
1987	NY	A	59	.277	.535	159	44	5	0	12	7.5	21	28	10	36	0	13	1	4	1	0	0	0.1	1.000	DH-49, OF-2
1988	CLE	A	75	.258	.533	225	58	8	0	18	8.0	31	43	16	65	0	13	5	0	0	0	0	0.0	–	DH-63
1989	CHI	A	51	.302	.556	169	51	10	0	11	6.5	26	37	22	42	0	3	1	216	12	4	28	4.5	.983	1B-27, DH-17, OF-5
	8 yrs.		721	.241	.482	2323	561	84	3	156	6.7	316	407	205	644	16	82	15	810	39	31	31	1.2	.976	OF-353, DH-284, 1B-27

LEAGUE CHAMPIONSHIP SERIES

| 1983 | CHI | A | 3 | .286 | .429 | 7 | 2 | 1 | 0 | 0 | 0.0 | 1 | 0 | 1 | 2 | 0 | 0 | 0 | 0 | 0 | 0 | 0 | 0.0 | – | OF-3 |

Mal Kittridge

KITTRIDGE, MALACHI JEDDIDAH
B. Oct. 12, 1869, Clinton, Mass.   D. June 23, 1928, Gary, Ind.   BR TR 5'7" 170 lbs.
Manager 1904.

1890	CHI	N	96	.201	.270	333	67	8	5	3	0.9	46	35	39	53	7	0	0	458	113	34	9	6.3	.944	C-96
1891			79	.209	.291	296	62	8	5	2	0.7	26	27	17	28	4	0	0	384	87	30	5	6.3	.940	C-79
1892			69	.179	.201	229	41	5	0	0	0.0	19	10	11	27	4	0	0	359	81	26	5	6.8	.945	C-69
1893			70	.231	.329	255	59	9	5	2	0.8	32	30	17	15	3	0	0	260	81	22	4	5.2	.939	C-70
1894			51	.315	.387	168	53	8	2	0	0.0	36	23	26	20	2	0	0	209	36	20	4	5.2	.925	C-51
1895			60	.226	.325	212	48	6	3	3	1.4	30	29	16	9	6	0	0	197	48	6	4	4.2	.976	C-59
1896			65	.223	.265	215	48	4	1	1	0.5	17	19	14	14	6	0	0	251	56	12	12	4.9	.962	C-64, P-1
1897			79	.202	.271	262	53	5	5	1	0.4	25	30	22		9	0	0	324	75	20	6	5.3	.952	C-79
1898	LOU	N	86	.244	.317	287	70	8	5	1	0.3	27	31	15		9	0	0	258	80	21	10	4.2	.944	C-86
1899	2 teams		LOU	N	(45G – .202)		WAS	N	(44G – .150)																
"	total		89	.176	.202	262	46	5	1	0	0.0	25	23	36		5	3	1	280	117	16	9	4.6	.961	C-86
1901	BOS	N	114	.252	.304	381	96	14	0	2	0.5	24	40	32		5	0	0	581	136	12	7	6.4	.984	C-113
1902			80	.235	.286	255	60	7	0	2	0.8	18	30	24		4	7	1	363	99	9	5	5.9	.981	C-72
1903	2 teams		BOS	N	(32G – .212)		WAS	A	(60G – .214)																
"	total		92	.213	.241	291	62	6	1	0	0.0	18	22	21		2	0	0	398	118	11	7	5.7	.979	C-90
1904	WAS	A	81	.242	.268	265	64	7	0	0	0.0	11	24	8		2	2	0	346	99	8	4	5.6	.982	C-79
1905			76	.164	.197	238	39	8	0	0	0.0	13	14	15		1	0	0	323	113	10	8	5.9	.978	C-75
1906	2 teams		WAS	A	(27G – .179)		CLE	A	(1G – .000)																
"	total		28	.173	.173	81	14	0	0	0	0.0	5	3	1		0	0	0	124	18	7	1	5.3	.953	C-28
	16 yrs.		1215	.219	.274	4030	882	108	31	17	0.4	372	390	314	166	64	14	2	5115	1363	263	100	5.5	.961	C-1196, P-1

Billy Klaus

KLAUS, WILLIAM JOSEPH
Brother of Bobby Klaus.
B. Dec. 9, 1928, Fox Lake, Ill.   BL TR 5'9" 160 lbs.

1952	BOS	N	7	.000	.000	4	0	0	0	0	0.0	3	1	1		0	3	0	1	0	1	0	0.3	.500	SS-4
1953	MIL	N	2	.000	.000	2	0	0	0	0	0.0	1	1	0		0	0	0	0	0	0	0	0.0	–	
1955	BOS	A	135	.283	.377	541	153	26	2	7	1.3	83	60	60	44	6	2	0	214	411	31	55	4.9	.953	SS-126, 3B-8
1956			135	.271	.387	520	141	29	5	7	1.3	91	59	90	43	1	5	1	155	306	27	26	3.6	.945	3B-106, SS-26
1957			127	.252	.369	477	120	18	4	10	2.1	76	42	55	53	2	8	2	204	417	25	93	5.1	.961	SS-118
1958			61	.159	.239	88	14	4	0	1	1.1	5	7	5	16	0	39	6	18	35	7	2	1.0	.883	SS-27
1959	BAL	A	104	.249	.312	321	80	11	0	3	0.9	33	25	51	38	2	4	0	120	231	13	28	3.5	.964	SS-59, 3B-49, 2B-1
1960			46	.209	.326	43	9	2	0	1	2.3	8	6	9	9	0	3	0	29	52	2	14	1.8	.976	2B-30, SS-12, 3B-2
1961	WAS	A	91	.227	.359	251	57	8	2	7	2.8	26	30	30	34	2	18	3	64	155	8	11	2.5	.965	3B-51, SS-18, OF-1, 2B-1
1962	PHI	N	102	.206	.302	248	51	8	2	4	1.6	30	20	29	43	1	28	5	93	142	9	21	2.4	.963	3B-53, SS-30, 2B-11
1963			11	.056	.056	18	1	0	0	0	0.0	1	0	1	4	0	8	1	7	9	1	0	0.7	1.000	SS-5, 3B-3
	11 yrs.		821	.249	.351	2513	626	106	15	40	1.6	357	250	331	285	14	120	18	899	1756	123	251	3.4	.956	SS-425, 3B-272, 2B-43, OF-1

Bobby Klaus

KLAUS, ROBERT FRANCIS
Brother of Billy Klaus.
B. Dec. 27, 1937, Spring Grove, Ill.   BR TR 5'10" 170 lbs.

Bobby Klaus *continued*

Year	Team	Games	BA	SA	AB	H	2B	3B	HR	HR%	R	RBI	BB	SO	SB	Pinch Hit AB	Pinch Hit H	PO	A	E	DP	TC/G	FA	G by Pos
1964	2 teams CIN N (40G – .183) NY N (56G – .244)																							
"	total	96	.225	.334	302	68	13	4	4	1.3	35	17	29	43	4	7	0	127	186	10	22	3.4	.969	2B-43, 3B-39, SS-8
1965	NY N	119	.191	.253	288	55	12	0	2	0.7	30	12	45	49	1	4	1	179	254	11	54	3.7	.975	2B-72, SS-28, 3B-25
2 yrs.		215	.208	.295	590	123	25	4	6	1.0	65	29	74	92	5	11	1	306	440	21	76	3.6	.973	2B-115, 3B-64, SS-36

Ollie Klee

KLEE, OLLIE CHESTER (Babe)
B. May 20, 1900, Piqua, Ohio D. Feb. 9, 1977, Toledo, Ohio

BL TL 5'9½" 160 lbs.

Year	Team	Games	BA	SA	AB	H	2B	3B	HR	HR%	R	RBI	BB	SO	SB	Pinch Hit AB	Pinch Hit H	PO	A	E	DP	TC/G	FA	G by Pos
1925	CIN N	3	.000	.000	1	0	0	0	0	0.0	0	0	0	1	0	0	0	0	0	0	0	0.0	–	OF-1

Chuck Klein

KLEIN, CHARLES HERBERT
B. Oct. 7, 1904, Indianapolis, Ind. D. Mar. 28, 1958, Indianapolis, Ind.
Hall of Fame 1980.

BL TR 6' 185 lbs.

Year	Team	Games	BA	SA	AB	H	2B	3B	HR	HR%	R	RBI	BB	SO	SB	Pinch Hit AB	Pinch Hit H	PO	A	E	DP	TC/G	FA	G by Pos
1928	PHI N	64	.360	.577	253	91	14	4	11	4.3	41	34	14	22	0	1	0	128	7	3	0	2.2	.978	OF-63
1929		149	.356	.657	616	219	45	6	43	7.0	126	145	54	61	5	0	0	321	18	12	3	2.4	.966	OF-149
1930		156	.386	.687	648	250	59	8	40	6.2	158	170	54	50	4	0	0	362	44	17	10	2.7	.960	OF-156
1931		148	.337	.584	594	200	34	10	31	5.2	121	121	59	49	7	0	0	292	13	9	0	2.1	.971	OF-148
1932		154	.348	.646	650	226	50	15	38	5.8	152	137	60	49	20	0	0	331	29	15	3	2.4	.960	OF-154
1933		152	.368	.602	606	223	44	2	28	4.6	101	120	56	36	15	0	0	339	21	5	5	2.4	.986	OF-152
1934	CHI N	115	.301	.510	435	131	27	2	20	4.6	78	80	47	38	3	5	2	222	6	9	2	2.1	.962	OF-110
1935		119	.293	.488	434	127	14	4	21	4.8	71	73	41	42	4	6	1	215	11	10	7	2.0	.958	OF-111
1936	2 teams CHI N (29G – .294) PHI N (117G – .309)																							
"	total	146	.306	.512	601	184	35	7	25	4.2	102	105	49	59	6	0	0	276	16	23	2	2.2	.927	OF-146
1937	PHI N	115	.325	.512	406	132	20	2	15	3.7	74	57	39	21	3	13	3	175	11	10	3	1.7	.949	OF-102
1938		129	.247	.356	458	113	22	2	8	1.7	53	61	38	30	7	10	1	229	8	10	1	1.9	.960	OF-119
1939	2 teams PHI N (25G – .191) PIT N (85G – .300)																							
"	total	110	.284	.486	317	90	18	5	12	3.8	45	56	36	21	2	26	11	153	5	7	1	1.5	.958	OF-77, 1B-1
1940	PHI N	116	.218	.333	354	77	16	2	7	2.0	39	37	44	30	2	18	2	180	4	3	2	1.6	.984	OF-116
1941		50	.123	.164	73	9	0	0	1	1.4	6	3	10	6	0	31	5	22	1	1	0	0.5	.958	OF-14
1942		14	.071	.071	14	1	0	0	0	0.0	0	0	4	2	0	14	1	0	0	0	0	0.0	–	OF-1
1943		12	.100	.100	20	2	0	0	0	0.0	0	3	0	3	0	10	1	0	0	0	0	0.1	–	OF-2
1944		4	.143	.143	7	1	0	0	0	0.0	0	0	0	0	0	5	0	1	0	0	0	1.3	1.000	OF-1
17 yrs.		1753	.320	.543	6486	2076	398	74	300	4.6	1168	1202	601	521	79	137	28	3250	194	135	39	2.0	.962	OF-1620, 1B-1

WORLD SERIES

Year	Team	Games	BA	SA	AB	H	2B	3B	HR	HR%	R	RBI	BB	SO	SB	Pinch Hit AB	Pinch Hit H	PO	A	E	DP	TC/G	FA	G by Pos
1935	CHI N	5	.333	.583	12	4	0	0	1	8.3	2	2	0	2	0	3	1	4	0	0	0	0.8	1.000	OF-3

Lou Klein

KLEIN, LOUIS FRANK
B. Oct. 22, 1918, New Orleans, La. D. June 20, 1976, Metairie, La.
Manager 1961-62, 1965.

BR TR 5'11" 167 lbs.

Year	Team	Games	BA	SA	AB	H	2B	3B	HR	HR%	R	RBI	BB	SO	SB	Pinch Hit AB	Pinch Hit H	PO	A	E	DP	TC/G	FA	G by Pos
1943	STL N	154	.287	.410	627	180	28	14	7	1.1	91	62	50	70	9	0	0	356	444	27	118	5.4	.967	2B-126, SS-51
1945		19	.228	.386	57	13	4	1	1	1.8	12	6	14	9	0	0	0	38	23	3	4	3.4	.953	OF-7, SS-7, 3B-4, 2B-2
1946		23	.194	.258	93	18	3	0	1	1.1	12	4	9	7	1	0	0	58	60	3	18	5.3	.975	2B-23
1949		58	.219	.325	114	25	6	0	2	1.8	25	12	22	20	0	18	3	33	85	11	10	2.2	.915	SS-21, 2B-9, 3B-7
1951	2 teams CLE A (2G – .000) PHI A (49G – .229)																							
"	total	51	.226	.377	146	33	7	0	5	3.4	22	17	10	13	0	9	0	85	107	5	32	3.9	.975	2B-42
5 yrs.		305	.259	.381	1037	269	48	15	16	1.5	162	101	105	119	10	27	3	570	719	49	182	4.4	.963	2B-202, SS-79, 3B-11, OF-7

WORLD SERIES

Year	Team	Games	BA	SA	AB	H	2B	3B	HR	HR%	R	RBI	BB	SO	SB	Pinch Hit AB	Pinch Hit H	PO	A	E	DP	TC/G	FA	G by Pos
1943	STL N	5	.136	.136	22	3	0	0	0	0.0	0	0	1	2	0	0	0	10	13	2	4	5.0	.920	2B-5

Red Kleinow

KLEINOW, JOHN PETER
B. July 20, 1879, Milwaukee, Wis. D. Oct. 9, 1929, New York, N.Y.

BR TR 5'10" 165 lbs.

Year	Team	Games	BA	SA	AB	H	2B	3B	HR	HR%	R	RBI	BB	SO	SB	Pinch Hit AB	Pinch Hit H	PO	A	E	DP	TC/G	FA	G by Pos
1904	NY A	68	.206	.282	209	43	8	4	0	0.0	12	16	15	4	2	0		278	71	12	5	5.3	.967	C-62, 3B-2, OF-1
1905		88	.221	.281	253	56	6	3	1	0.4	23	24	20	7	2	0		389	85	11	4	5.5	.977	C-83, 1B-3
1906		96	.220	.276	268	59	9	3	0	0.0	30	31	24	8	0	0		382	102	14	8	5.2	.972	C-95, 1B-1
1907		90	.264	.316	269	71	6	4	0	0.0	16	26	24	5	3	0		326	97	14	5	4.9	.968	C-86, 1B-1
1908		96	.168	.204	279	47	3	2	1	0.4	16	13	22	5	5	0		283	118	15	5	4.3	.964	C-89, 2B-2
1909		78	.228	.320	206	47	11	4	0	0.0	24	15	25	7	1	0		343	83	15	6	5.7	.966	C-77
1910	2 teams NY A (6G – .417) BOS A (50G – .150)																							
"	total	56	.170	.195	159	27	1	0	0	0.6	11	10	21	5	3	0		285	69	11	12	6.5	.970	C-54
1911	2 teams BOS A (8G – .214) PHI N (4G – .125)																							
"	total	12	.182	.227	22	4	1	0	0	0.0	0	0	2	1	1	0		32	11	0	0	3.6	1.000	C-12
8 yrs.		584	.213	.269	1665	354	45	22	3	0.2	146	135	153	1	42	16	2	2318	636	92	45	5.2	.970	C-558, 1B-5, 3B-2, 2B-2, OF-1

Jay Kleven

KLEVEN, JAY ALLEN
B. Dec. 2, 1949, Oakland, Calif.

BR TR 6'2" 190 lbs.

Year	Team	Games	BA	SA	AB	H	2B	3B	HR	HR%	R	RBI	BB	SO	SB	Pinch Hit AB	Pinch Hit H	PO	A	E	DP	TC/G	FA	G by Pos
1976	NY N	2	.200	.200	5	1	0	0	0	0.0	0	0	0	2	0	1	0	10	0	0	0	5.0	1.000	C-2

Lou Klimchock

KLIMCHOCK, LOUIS STEPHEN
B. Oct. 15, 1939, Hostetter, Pa.

BL TR 5'11" 180 lbs.

Year	Team	Games	BA	SA	AB	H	2B	3B	HR	HR%	R	RBI	BB	SO	SB	Pinch Hit AB	Pinch Hit H	PO	A	E	DP	TC/G	FA	G by Pos
1958	KC A	2	.200	.500	10	2	0	0	1	10.0	2	1	0	1	0	0	0	2	6	0	1	4.0	1.000	2B-2
1959		17	.273	.470	66	18	1	0	4	6.1	10	13	1	6	0	1	0	34	41	4	11	4.6	.949	2B-16
1960		10	.300	.300	10	3	0	0	0	0.0	0	0	0	0	0	9	2	0	0	0	0	0.0	–	2B-1
1961		57	.215	.289	121	26	4	1	1	0.8	8	16	5	13	0	32	6	92	11	6	4	1.9	.945	1B-11, OF-7, 3B-6, 2B-1
1962	MIL N	8	.000	.000	8	0	0	0	0	0.0	0	0	0	2	0	8	0	0	0	0	0	0.0	–	2B-1
1963	2 teams WAS A (9G – .143) MIL N (24G – .196)																							
"	total	33	.183	.200	60	11	0	0	0	0.0	7	3	0	13	0	20	3	79	15	1	12	2.9	.989	1B-12, 2B-3
1964	MIL N	10	.333	.429	21	7	2	0	0	0.0	3	2	1	2	0	3	0	3	4	0	0	0.7	1.000	3B-4, 2B-2
1965		34	.077	.077	39	3	0	0	0	0.0	3	3	2	8	0	29	2	20	4	2	0	0.8	.923	1B-4
1966	NY N	5	.000	.000	5	0	0	0	0	0.0	0	0	0	5	0	5	0	0	0	0	0	0.0	–	

Year	Team	Games	BA	SA	AB	H	2B	3B	HR	HR%	R	RBI	BB	SO	SB	Pinch Hit AB	Pinch Hit H	PO	A	E	DP	TC/G	FA	G by Pos

Lou Klimchock *continued*

Year	Team	Games	BA	SA	AB	H	2B	3B	HR	HR%	R	RBI	BB	SO	SB	PH AB	PH H	PO	A	E	DP	TC/G	FA	G by Pos
1968	CLE A	11	.133	.133	15	2	0	0	0	0.0	0	3	1	0	0	7	0	1	2	2	0	0.5	.600	3B-4, 2B-1, 1B-1
1969		90	.287	.422	258	74	13	2	6	2.3	26	26	18	14	0	15	2	83	116	10	15	2.3	.952	3B-56, 2B-21, C-1
1970		41	.161	.214	56	9	0	0	1	1.8	5	2	3	9	0	30	4	39	9	0	6	1.2	1.000	2B-5, 1B-5
12 yrs.		318	.232	.330	669	155	21	3	13	1.9	64	69	31	71	0	161	21	353	208	25	49	1.8	.957	3B-70, 2B-52, 1B-33, OF-7, C-1

Bobby Kline

KLINE, JOHN ROBERT
B. Jan. 27, 1929, St. Petersburg, Fla.

BR TR 6' 179 lbs.

Year	Team	Games	BA	SA	AB	H	2B	3B	HR	HR%	R	RBI	BB	SO	SB	PH AB	PH H	PO	A	E	DP	TC/G	FA	G by Pos
1955	WAS A	77	.221	.257	140	31	5	0	0	0.0	12	9	11	27	0	0	0	107	164	16	38	3.7	.944	SS-69, 2B-4, 3B-3, P-1

Johnny Kling

KLING, JOHN (Noisy)
Brother of Bill Kling.
B. Feb. 25, 1875, Kansas City, Mo.   D. Jan. 31, 1947, Kansas City, Mo.
Manager 1912.

BR TR 5'9½" 160 lbs.

Year	Team	Games	BA	SA	AB	H	2B	3B	HR	HR%	R	RBI	BB	SO	SB	PH AB	PH H	PO	A	E	DP	TC/G	FA	G by Pos
1900	CHI N	15	.294	.392	51	15	3	1	0	0.0	8	7	2		0	0	0	49	15	7	2	4.7	.901	C-15
1901		74	.277	.324	253	70	6	3	0	0.0	26	21	9		7	4	1	328	75	21	7	5.7	.950	C-69, OF-1, 1B-1
1902		114	.286	.343	434	124	19	3	0	0.0	50	57	29		23	1	0	472	160	19	17	5.7	.971	C-112, SS-1
1903		132	.297	.428	491	146	29	13	3	0.6	67	68	22		23	0	0	565	189	24	13	5.9	.969	C-132
1904		123	.243	.296	452	110	18	0	2	0.4	41	46	16		7	2	0	560	135	20	8	5.8	.972	C-104, OF-10, 1B-6
1905		111	.218	.279	380	83	8	6	1	0.3	26	52	28		13	1	0	549	137	24	12	6.4	.966	C-106, OF-4, 1B-1
1906		107	.312	.420	343	107	15	8	2	0.6	45	46	23		14	7	2	520	127	12	7	6.2	.982	C-96, OF-3
1907		104	.284	.386	334	95	15	8	1	0.3	44	43	27		9	3	0	509	111	8	12	6.0	.987	C-98, 1B-2
1908		126	.276	.382	424	117	23	5	4	0.9	51	59	21		16	2	0	607	153	17	12	6.2	.978	C-117, OF-6, 1B-2
1910		91	.269	.360	297	80	17	2	2	0.7	31	32	37	27	3	4	0	407	118	11	10	5.9	.979	C-86
1911 2 teams	CHI N (27G – .175)				BOS N	(75G – .224)																		
" total		102	.212	.293	321	68	11	3	3	0.9	40	29	38	43	1	4	1	424	140	26	8	5.8	.956	C-96, 3B-1
1912	BOS N	81	.317	.405	252	80	10	3	2	0.8	26	30	15	30	3	7	2	322	108	19	20	5.5	.958	C-74
1913	CIN N	80	.273	.364	209	57	7	6	0	0.0	20	23	14	14	2	15	3	259	94	9	3	4.5	.975	C-63
13 yrs.		1260	.272	.357	4241	1152	181	61	20	0.5	475	513	281	114	121	50	9	5571	1562	217	131	5.8	.970	C-1168, OF-24, 1B-12, SS-1, 3B-1

WORLD SERIES

Year	Team	Games	BA	SA	AB	H	2B	3B	HR	HR%	R	RBI	BB	SO	SB	PH AB	PH H	PO	A	E	DP	TC/G	FA	G by Pos
1906	CHI N	6	.176	.235	17	3	1	0	0	0.0	2	0	4	3	0	0	0	46	10	1	3	9.5	.982	C-6
1907		5	.211	.211	19	4	0	0	0	0.0	2	1	1	4	0	0	0	25	9	1	0	7.0	.971	C-5
1908		5	.250	.313	16	4	1	0	0	0.0	2	1	2	2	0	0	0	32	6	0	1	7.6	1.000	C-5
1910		5	.077	.077	13	1	0	0	0	0.0	0	1	1	2	0	0	0	11	7	0	0	3.6	1.000	C-3
4 yrs.		21	.185	.215	65	12	2	0	0	0.0	6	3	8	11	0	0	0	114	32	2	4	7.0	.986	C-19

Rudy Kling

KLING, RUDOLPH A.
B. Mar. 23, 1870, St. Louis, Mo.   D. Mar. 14, 1937, St. Louis, Mo.

BR TR 5'10" 178 lbs.

Year	Team	Games	BA	SA	AB	H	2B	3B	HR	HR%	R	RBI	BB	SO	SB	PH AB	PH H	PO	A	E	DP	TC/G	FA	G by Pos
1902	STL N	4	.200	.200	10	2	0	0	0	0.0	1	4			1	0	0	9	7	3	2	4.8	.842	SS-4

Joe Klinger

KLINGER, JOSEPH JOHN
B. Aug. 2, 1902, Canonsburg, Pa.   D. July 31, 1960, Little Rock, Ark.

BR TR 6' 190 lbs.

Year	Team	Games	BA	SA	AB	H	2B	3B	HR	HR%	R	RBI	BB	SO	SB	PH AB	PH H	PO	A	E	DP	TC/G	FA	G by Pos
1927	NY N	3	.400	.400	5	2	0	0	0	0.0	0	0	0	2	0	0	0	3	0	0	0	1.0	1.000	OF-1
1930	CHI A	4	.375	.375	8	3	0	0	0	0.0	0	1	0	0	0	0	0	14	0	0	2	3.5	1.000	1B-2, C-2
2 yrs.		7	.385	.385	13	5	0	0	0	0.0	0	1	0	2	0	0	0	17	0	0	2	2.4	1.000	1B-2, C-2, OF-1

Nap Kloza

KLOZA, JOHN CLARENCE
B. Sept. 7, 1903, Poland   D. June 11, 1962, Milwaukee, Wis.

BR TR 5'11" 180 lbs.

Year	Team	Games	BA	SA	AB	H	2B	3B	HR	HR%	R	RBI	BB	SO	SB	PH AB	PH H	PO	A	E	DP	TC/G	FA	G by Pos
1931	STL A	3	.143	.143	7	1	0	0	0	0.0	1	0	1	4	0	1	0	1	1	0	0	0.7	1.000	OF-3
1932		19	.154	.308	13	2	0	1	0	0.0	4	2	4	4	0	10	1	2	0	0	0	0.1	1.000	OF-3
2 yrs.		22	.150	.250	20	3	0	1	0	0.0	5	2	5	8	0	11	1	3	1	0	0	0.2	1.000	OF-6

Joe Klugmann

KLUGMANN, JOE
B. Mar. 26, 1895, St. Louis, Mo.   D. July 18, 1951, Moberly, Mo.

BR TR 5'11" 175 lbs.

Year	Team	Games	BA	SA	AB	H	2B	3B	HR	HR%	R	RBI	BB	SO	SB	PH AB	PH H	PO	A	E	DP	TC/G	FA	G by Pos
1921	CHI N	6	.286	.286	21	6	0	0	0	0.0	3	2	1	2	0	1	1	15	16	1	1	5.3	.969	2B-5
1922		2	.000	.000	2	0	0	0	0	0.0	0	0	0	0	0	0	0	2	3	0	1	2.5	1.000	2B-2
1924	BKN N	31	.165	.215	79	13	2	1	0	0.0	7	3	2	9	0	1	0	52	65	9	14	4.1	.929	2B-28, SS-1
1925	CLE A	38	.329	.482	85	28	9	2	0	0.0	12	12	8	4	3	3	1	64	67	7	10	3.6	.949	2B-29, 1B-4, 3B-2
4 yrs.		77	.251	.342	187	47	11	3	0	0.0	22	17	11	15	3	5	2	133	151	17	26	3.9	.944	2B-64, 1B-4, 3B-2, SS-1

Elmer Klumpp

KLUMPP, ELMER EDWARD
B. Aug. 26, 1906, St. Louis, Mo.

BR TR 6' 184 lbs.

Year	Team	Games	BA	SA	AB	H	2B	3B	HR	HR%	R	RBI	BB	SO	SB	PH AB	PH H	PO	A	E	DP	TC/G	FA	G by Pos
1934	WAS A	12	.133	.133	15	2	0	0	0	0.0	2	0	0	1	0	0	0	15	1	2	0	1.5	.889	C-11
1937	BKN N	5	.091	.091	11	1	0	0	0	0.0	0	2	1	4	0	1	0	16	1	0	0	3.4	1.000	C-3
2 yrs.		17	.115	.115	26	3	0	0	0	0.0	2	2	1	5	0	1	0	31	2	2	0	2.1	.943	C-14

Billy Klusman

KLUSMAN, WILLIAM F.
B. Mar. 24, 1865, Cincinnati, Ohio   D. June 24, 1907, Cincinnati, Ohio

BR TR 5'10½" 185 lbs.

Year	Team	Games	BA	SA	AB	H	2B	3B	HR	HR%	R	RBI	BB	SO	SB	PH AB	PH H	PO	A	E	DP	TC/G	FA	G by Pos
1888	BOS N	28	.168	.262	107	18	4	0	2	1.9	9	11	5	13	3	0	0	63	75	13	6	5.4	.914	2B-28
1890	STL AA	15	.277	.415	65	18	4	1	1	1.5	9		1		1	0	0	16	44	7	3	4.5	.896	2B-15
2 yrs.		43	.209	.320	172	36	8	1	3	1.7	18	11	6	13	4	0	0	79	119	20	9	5.1	.908	2B-43

Ted Kluszewski

KLUSZEWSKI, THEODORE BERNARD (Klu)
B. Sept. 10, 1924, Argo, Ill.   D. Mar. 29, 1988, Cincinnati, Ohio

BL TL 6'2" 225 lbs.

Year	Team	Games	BA	SA	AB	H	2B	3B	HR	HR%	R	RBI	BB	SO	SB	PH AB	PH H	PO	A	E	DP	TC/G	FA	G by Pos
1947	CIN N	9	.100	.100	10	1	0	0	0	0.0	1	2	1	2	0	5	0	10	0	0	1	1.1	1.000	1B-2
1948		113	.274	.451	379	104	23	4	12	3.2	49	57	18	32	1	15	5	833	65	9	60	8.0	.990	1B-98
1949		136	.309	.411	531	164	26	2	8	1.5	63	68	19	24	3	2	1	1140	65	14	109	9.0	.989	1B-134
1950		134	.307	.515	538	165	37	0	25	4.6	76	111	33	28	3	2	0	1123	61	15	101	8.9	.987	1B-131

Year	Team	Games	BA	SA	AB	H	2B	3B	HR	HR%	R	RBI	BB	SO	SB	Pinch Hit AB	Pinch Hit H	PO	A	E	DP	TC/G	FA	G by Pos

Ted Kluszewski *continued*

Year	Team	Games	BA	SA	AB	H	2B	3B	HR	HR%	R	RBI	BB	SO	SB	AB	H	PO	A	E	DP	TC/G	FA	G by Pos
1951		154	.259	.387	607	157	35	2	13	2.1	74	77	35	33	6	1	0	1381	88	5	115	9.6	.997	1B-154
1952		135	.320	.509	497	159	24	11	16	3.2	62	86	47	28	3	3	1	1121	66	8	116	8.9	.993	1B-133
1953		149	.316	.570	570	180	25	0	40	7.0	97	108	55	34	2	1	0	1285	58	7	149	9.1	.995	1B-147
1954		149	.326	.642	573	187	28	3	**49**	**8.6**	104	**141**	78	35	0	0	0	1237	101	5	166	9.0	.996	1B-149
1955		153	.314	.585	612	**192**	25	0	47	7.7	116	113	66	40	1	0	0	1388	86	8	153	9.7	.995	1B-153
1956		138	.302	.536	517	156	14	1	35	6.8	91	102	49	31	1	7	1	1166	89	13	110	9.2	.990	1B-131
1957		69	.268	.465	127	34	7	0	6	4.7	12	21	5	5	0	47	12	161	15	2	11	2.6	.989	1B-23
1958	PIT N	100	.292	.402	301	88	13	4	4	1.3	29	37	26	16	0	24	9	591	36	4	62	6.3	.994	1B-72
1959	2 teams		PIT N	(60G – .262)		CHI A	(31G – .297)																	
"	total	91	.278	.404	223	62	12	2	4	1.8	22	27	14	24	0	39	7	210	15	0	16	2.5	1.000	1B-49
1960	CHI A	81	.293	.425	181	53	9	0	5	2.8	20	39	22	10	0	34	8	325	19	1	38	4.3	.997	1B-39
1961	LA A	107	.243	.460	263	64	12	0	15	5.7	32	39	24	23	0	43	9	520	28	6	51	5.2	.989	1B-66
15 yrs.		1718	.298	.498	5929	1766	290	29	279	4.7	848	1028	492	365	20	223	53	12491	792	97	1258	7.8	.993	1B-1481

WORLD SERIES

Year	Team	Games	BA	SA	AB	H	2B	3B	HR	HR%	R	RBI	BB	SO	SB	AB	H	PO	A	E	DP	TC/G	FA	G by Pos
1959	CHI A	6	.391	.826	23	9	1	0	3	13.0	5	10	2	0	0	0	0	59	3	0	2	10.3	1.000	1B-6

Mickey Klutts

KLUTTS, GENE ELLIS
B. Sept. 20, 1954, Montebello, Calif.   BR TR 5'11" 170 lbs.

Year	Team	Games	BA	SA	AB	H	2B	3B	HR	HR%	R	RBI	BB	SO	SB	AB	H	PO	A	E	DP	TC/G	FA	G by Pos
1976	NY A	2	.000	.000	3	0	0	0	0	0.0	0	0	0	1	0	0	0	4	3	1	0	4.0	.875	SS-2
1977		5	.267	.533	15	4	1	0	1	6.7	3	4	2	1	0	0	0	5	15	0	1	4.0	1.000	3B-4, SS-1
1978		1	1.000	1.500	2	2	1	0	0	0.0	1	0	0	0	0	0	0	1	2	1	1	4.0	.750	3B-1
1979	OAK A	24	.192	.288	73	14	2	1	1	1.4	3	4	7	20	0	0	0	35	50	7	6	3.8	.924	SS-10, 2B-8, 3B-6, DH-2
1980		75	.269	.401	197	53	14	0	4	2.0	20	21	13	41	1	5	3	63	104	9	8	2.3	.949	3B-62, SS-8, 2B-7, DH-1
1981		15	.370	.696	46	17	0	0	5	10.9	9	11	2	4	0	1	1	7	15	1	1	1.5	.957	3B-14
1982		55	.178	.229	157	28	8	0	0	0.0	10	14	9	18	0	9	2	41	82	7	6	2.4	.946	3B-49
1983	TOR A	22	.256	.465	43	11	0	0	3	7.0	3	5	1	11	0	7	3	4	11	0	2	0.7	1.000	3B-17, DH-2
8 yrs.		199	.241	.371	536	129	26	1	14	2.6	49	59	34	101	1	22	9	160	282	26	25	2.4	.944	3B-153, SS-21, 2B-15, DH-5

DIVISIONAL PLAYOFF SERIES

Year	Team	Games	BA	SA	AB	H	2B	3B	HR	HR%	R	RBI	BB	SO	SB	AB	H	PO	A	E	DP	TC/G	FA	G by Pos
1981	OAK A	2	.143	.143	7	1	0	0	0	0.0	0	0	0	1	0	0	0	0	0	0	0	0.0	–	3B-2

LEAGUE CHAMPIONSHIP SERIES

Year	Team	Games	BA	SA	AB	H	2B	3B	HR	HR%	R	RBI	BB	SO	SB	AB	H	PO	A	E	DP	TC/G	FA	G by Pos
1981	OAK A	3	.429	.429	7	3	0	0	0	0.0	1	0	0	1	0	0	0	0	0	1	0	0.3	–	3B-3

Clyde Kluttz

KLUTTZ, CLYDE FRANKLIN
B. Dec. 12, 1917, Rockwell, N. C. D. May 12, 1979, Salisbury, N. C.   BR TR 6' 193 lbs.

Year	Team	Games	BA	SA	AB	H	2B	3B	HR	HR%	R	RBI	BB	SO	SB	AB	H	PO	A	E	DP	TC/G	FA	G by Pos
1942	BOS N	72	.267	.338	210	56	10	1	1	0.5	21	31	7	13	0	15	6	200	29	5	5	3.3	.979	C-57
1943		66	.246	.280	207	51	7	0	0	0.0	13	20	15	9	0	9	1	176	43	6	5	3.4	.973	C-55
1944		81	.279	.376	229	64	12	2	2	0.9	20	19	13	14	0	23	4	199	40	5	5	3.0	.980	C-58
1945	2 teams		BOS N	(25G – .296)		NY N	(73G – .279)																	
"	total	98	.284	.389	303	86	18	1	4	1.3	34	31	17	16	1	20	3	259	43	6	6	3.1	.981	C-76
1946	2 teams		NY N	(5G – .375)		STL N	(52G – .265)																	
"	total	57	.271	.319	144	39	7	0	0	0.0	8	15	10	11	0	5	3	183	24	5	4	3.7	.976	C-51
1947	PIT N	73	.302	.466	232	70	9	2	6	2.6	26	42	17	18	1	4	1	247	55	4	7	4.2	.987	C-69
1948		94	.221	.325	271	60	12	2	4	1.5	26	20	20	19	3	3	1	298	54	8	8	3.8	.978	C-91
1951	2 teams		STL A	(4G – .500)		WAS A	(53G – .308)																	
"	total	57	.313	.393	163	51	10	0	1	0.6	17	23	21	8	0	9	2	168	16	6	2	3.3	.968	C-47
1952	WAS A	58	.229	.285	144	33	5	0	1	0.7	7	11	12	11	0	6	1	163	27	4	4	3.3	.979	C-52
9 yrs.		656	.268	.354	1903	510	90	8	19	1.0	172	212	132	119	5	94	22	1893	331	49	46	3.5	.978	C-556

Otto Knabe

KNABE, FRANZ OTTO (Dutch)
B. June 12, 1884, Carrick, Pa. D. May 17, 1961, Philadelphia, Pa.   BR TR 5'8" 175 lbs.
Manager 1914-15.

Year	Team	Games	BA	SA	AB	H	2B	3B	HR	HR%	R	RBI	BB	SO	SB	AB	H	PO	A	E	DP	TC/G	FA	G by Pos
1905	PIT N	3	.300	.400	10	3	1	0	0	0.0	0	2	3			0	0	2	9	3	1	4.7	.786	3B-3
1907	PHI N	129	.255	.338	444	113	16	9	1	0.2	67	34	52		18	2	0	301	338	26	54	5.2	.961	2B-121, OF-5
1908		151	.218	.294	555	121	26	8	0	0.0	63	27	49		27	0	0	344	470	26	42	5.6	.969	2B-151
1909		114	.234	.281	402	94	13	3	0	0.0	40	33	35		9	2	0	237	312	36	38	5.1	.938	2B-109, OF-1
1910		137	.261	.325	510	133	18	6	1	0.2	73	44	47	42	15	1	0	383	381	37	72	5.8	.954	2B-136
1911		142	.237	.294	528	125	15	6	1	0.2	99	42	94	35	23	1	0	310	412	38	54	5.4	.950	2B-142
1912		126	.282	.326	426	120	11	4	0	0.0	56	46	55	20	16	3	1	258	342	30	45	5.0	.952	2B-123
1913		148	.263	.342	571	150	25	7	2	0.4	70	53	45	26	14	0	0	311	466	33	58	5.5	.959	2B-148
1914	BAL F	147	.226	.303	469	106	26	2	2	0.4	45	42	53		10	3	1	287	389	31	49	4.8	.956	2B-144
1915		103	.253	.325	320	81	16	2	1	0.3	38	25	37		7	8	2	203	264	12	52	4.7	.975	2B-94, OF-1
1916	2 teams		PIT N	(28G – .191)		CHI N	(57G – .276)																	
"	total	85	.244	.299	234	57	11	1	0	0.0	21	16	15	24	4	5	2	117	212	18	20	4.1	.948	2B-70, OF-1, SS-1, 3B-1
11 yrs.		1285	.247	.313	4469	1103	178	48	8	0.2	572	364	485	147	143	24	6	2753	3595	290	485	5.2	.956	2B-1238, OF-8, 3B-4, SS-1

Cotton Knaupp

KNAUPP, HENRY ANTONE
B. Aug. 13, 1889, San Antonio, Tex. D. July 6, 1967, New Orleans, La.   BR TR 5'9" 165 lbs.

Year	Team	Games	BA	SA	AB	H	2B	3B	HR	HR%	R	RBI	BB	SO	SB	AB	H	PO	A	E	DP	TC/G	FA	G by Pos
1910	CLE A	18	.237	.322	59	14	3	1	0	0.0	3	11	8		1	0	0	27	57	11	6	5.3	.884	SS-18
1911		13	.103	.128	39	4	1	0	0	0.0	2	0			3	0	0	17	36	2	2	4.2	.964	SS-13
2 yrs.		31	.184	.245	98	18	4	1	0	0.0	5	11	8		4	0	0	44	93	13	8	4.8	.913	SS-31

Alan Knicely

KNICELY, ALAN LEE
B. May 19, 1955, Harrisonburg, Va.   BR TR 6' 190 lbs.

Year	Team	Games	BA	SA	AB	H	2B	3B	HR	HR%	R	RBI	BB	SO	SB	AB	H	PO	A	E	DP	TC/G	FA	G by Pos
1979	HOU N	7	.000	.000	6	0	0	0	0	0.0	0	0	2	2	0	1	0	2	0	0	0	0.3	1.000	C-3
1980		1	.000	.000	1	0	0	0	0	0.0	0	0	0	1	0	1	0	0	0	0	0	0.0	–	
1981		3	.571	1.429	7	4	0	0	2	28.6	2	2	0	1	0	1	1	11	2	0	0	4.3	1.000	C-2, OF-1
1982		59	.188	.248	133	25	2	0	2	1.5	10	12	14	30	0	17	1	128	15	4	2	2.5	.973	C-23, OF-16, 3B-1
1983	CIN N	59	.224	.316	98	22	3	0	2	2.0	11	10	16	28	0	19	4	124	13	0	3	2.3	1.000	C-31, OF-8, 1B-2
1984		10	.138	.138	29	4	0	0	0	0.0	0	5	3	6	0	1	0	60	5	1	5	6.6	.985	1B-8, C-1

Alan Knicely *continued*

Year	Team	Games	BA	SA	AB	H	2B	3B	HR	HR%	R	RBI	BB	SO	SB	Pinch Hit AB	H	PO	A	E	DP	TC/G	FA	G by Pos
1985	2 teams	CIN N (48G – .253)			PHI N (7G – .000)																			
"	total	55	.242	.388	165	40	9	0	5	3.0	17	26	16	38	0	8	0	235	13	8	2	4.7	.969	C-46, 1B-1
1986	STL N	34	.195	.268	82	16	3	0	1	1.2	8	6	17	21	1	5	1	187	16	1	20	6.0	.995	1B-29, C-2
	8 yrs.	228	.213	.315	521	111	17	0	12	2.3	48	61	68	128	1	54	7	747	64	14	32	3.6	.983	C-108, 1B-40, OF-25, 3B-1

Austin Knickerbocker   KNICKERBOCKER, AUSTIN JAY
B. Oct. 15, 1918, Bangall, N. Y.   BR TR 5'11" 185 lbs.

Year	Team	Games	BA	SA	AB	H	2B	3B	HR	HR%	R	RBI	BB	SO	SB	Pinch Hit AB	H	PO	A	E	DP	TC/G	FA	G by Pos
1947	PHI A	21	.250	.396	48	12	3	2	0	0.0	8	2	3	4	0	2	2	32	1	2	0	1.7	.943	OF-14

Bill Knickerbocker   KNICKERBOCKER, WILLIAM HART
B. Dec. 29, 1911, Los Angeles, Calif.   D. Sept. 8, 1963, Sebastopol, Calif.   BR TR 5'11" 170 lbs.

Year	Team	Games	BA	SA	AB	H	2B	3B	HR	HR%	R	RBI	BB	SO	SB	Pinch Hit AB	H	PO	A	E	DP	TC/G	FA	G by Pos
1933	CLE A	80	.226	.326	279	63	16	3	2	0.7	20	32	11	30	1	1	0	151	233	25	37	5.1	.939	SS-80
1934		146	.317	.408	593	188	32	5	4	0.7	82	67	25	40	6	0	0	262	451	28	106	5.1	.962	SS-146
1935		132	.298	.380	540	161	34	5	0	0.0	77	55	27	31	2	3	0	247	453	32	82	5.5	.956	SS-128
1936		155	.294	.400	618	182	35	3	8	1.3	81	73	56	30	5	0	0	313	486	40	97	5.4	.952	SS-155
1937	STL A	121	.261	.365	491	128	29	5	4	0.8	53	61	30	32	3	0	0	220	379	26	64	5.2	.958	SS-115, 2B-6
1938	NY A	46	.250	.383	128	32	8	3	1	0.8	15	21	11	10	0	9	1	82	89	3	25	3.8	.983	2B-34, SS-3
1939		6	.154	.231	13	2	1	0	0	0.0	2	1	0	2	0	2	0	6	12	0	1	3.0	1.000	SS-2, 2B-2
1940		45	.242	.347	124	30	8	1	1	0.8	17	10	14	8	1	7	2	33	77	6	18	2.6	.948	SS-19, 3B-17
1941	CHI A	89	.245	.385	343	84	23	2	7	2.0	51	29	41	27	6	1	0	204	221	13	58	4.9	.970	2B-88
1942	PHI A	87	.253	.304	289	73	12	0	1	0.3	25	19	29	30	1	6	0	178	220	16	45	4.8	.961	2B-81, SS-1
	10 yrs.	907	.276	.374	3418	943	198	27	28	0.8	423	368	244	238	25	29	3	1696	2621	189	533	5.0	.958	SS-649, 2B-211, 3B-17

Joe Knight   KNIGHT, JOSEPH WILLIAM (Quiet Joe)
B. Sept. 28, 1859, Port Stanley, Ont., Canada   D. Oct. 18, 1938, St. Thomas, Ont., Canada   BL TL 5'11" 185 lbs.

Year	Team	Games	BA	SA	AB	H	2B	3B	HR	HR%	R	RBI	BB	SO	SB	Pinch Hit AB	H	PO	A	E	DP	TC/G	FA	G by Pos
1884	PHI N	6	.250	.375	24	6	3	0	0	0.0	2		0	2		0	0	3	12	4	0	3.2	.789	P-6
1890	CIN N	127	.312	.424	481	150	26	8	4	0.8	67	67	38	31	17	0	0	224	11	19	0	2.0	.925	OF-127
	2 yrs.	133	.309	.422	505	156	29	8	4	0.8	69	67	38	33	17	0	0	227	23	23	0	2.1	.916	OF-127, P-6

John Knight   KNIGHT, JOHN WESLEY (Schoolboy)
B. Oct. 6, 1885, Philadelphia, Pa.   D. Dec. 19, 1965, Walnut Creek, Calif.   BR TR 6'2½" 180 lbs.

Year	Team	Games	BA	SA	AB	H	2B	3B	HR	HR%	R	RBI	BB	SO	SB	Pinch Hit AB	H	PO	A	E	DP	TC/G	FA	G by Pos
1905	PHI A	88	.203	.274	325	66	12	1	3	0.9	28	29	9			4	5	0	145	189	40	9	4.3	.893	SS-81, 3B-2
1906		74	.194	.273	253	49	7	2	3	1.2	29	20	19			6	0	0	82	149	19	6	3.4	.924	3B-67, 2B-7
1907	2 teams	PHI A (38G – .222)			BOS A (100G – .212)																			
"	total	138	.214	.275	499	107	16	4	2	0.4	37	41	29			9	2	0	189	304	53	23	4.0	.903	3B-134, SS-4
1909	NY A	116	.236	.286	360	85	8	5	0	0.0	46	40	37			15	1	0	369	269	48	34	5.9	.930	1B-19, 2B-18
1910		117	.312	.413	414	129	25	4	3	0.7	58	45	34			23	2	1	439	281	37	48	6.5	.951	SS-79, 1B-23, 2B-7, 3B-4, OF-1
1911		132	.268	.351	470	126	16	7	3	0.6	69	62	42			18	1	0	491	354	68	53	6.9	.926	SS-82, 1B-27, 2B-21, 3B-1
1912	WAS A	32	.161	.204	93	15	2	1	0	0.0	10	9	16			4	0	0	95	49	8	10	4.8	.947	2B-27, 1B-5
1913	NY A	70	.236	.276	250	59	10	0	0	0.0	24	24	25	27	7	0	0	544	115	17	32	9.7	.975	1B-50, 2B-21
	8 yrs.	767	.239	.309	2664	636	96	24	14	0.5	301	270	211	27	86	11	1	2354	1710	290	215	5.7	.933	SS-324, 3B-208, 1B-124, 2B-101, OF-1

Lon Knight   KNIGHT, ALONZO P.
B. June 16, 1853, Philadelphia, Pa.   D. Apr. 23, 1932, Philadelphia, Pa.   Manager 1885.   BR TR 5'11½" 165 lbs.

Year	Team	Games	BA	SA	AB	H	2B	3B	HR	HR%	R	RBI	BB	SO	SB	Pinch Hit AB	H	PO	A	E	DP	TC/G	FA	G by Pos
1876	PHI N	55	.250	.313	240	60	9	3	0	0.0	32	24	2	2		0	0	156	48	40	10	4.4	.836	P-34, 1B-13, OF-9, 2B-6
1880	WOR N	49	.239	.323	201	48	11	3	0	0.0	31	24	5	8		0	0	47	22	11	1	1.6	.863	OF-49
1881	DET N	83	.271	.344	340	92	16	3	1	0.3	67	52	23	21		0	0	119	24	18	6	1.9	.888	OF-82, 2B-1, 1B-1
1882		86	.207	.277	347	72	12	6	0	0.0	39	24	16	21		0	0	129	25	24	2	2.1	.865	OF-84, 1B-2
1883	PHI AA	97	.252	.354	429	108	23	9	1	0.2	98		21			0	0	129	37	28	5	2.0	.856	OF-93, 3B-3, 2B-2
1884		108	.271	.364	484	131	18	12	1	0.2	94		10			0	0	165	39	19	6	2.1	.915	OF-108, P-2, 1B-1
1885	2 teams	PHI AA (29G – .210)			PRO N (25G – .160)																			
"	total	54	.190	.210	200	38	2	1	0	0.0	25	8	20	17		0	0	88	17	7	5	2.1	.938	OF-54, P-2
	7 yrs.	532	.245	.323	2241	549	91	37	3	0.1	386	129	97	69		0	0	833	212	147	35	2.2	.877	OF-479, P-38, 1B-17, 2B-9, 3B-3

Ray Knight   KNIGHT, CHARLES RAY
B. Dec. 28, 1952, Albany, Ga.   BR TR 6'1" 185 lbs.

Year	Team	Games	BA	SA	AB	H	2B	3B	HR	HR%	R	RBI	BB	SO	SB	Pinch Hit AB	H	PO	A	E	DP	TC/G	FA	G by Pos
1974	CIN N	14	.182	.273	11	2	1	0	0	0.0	1	2	0	2	0	0	0	2	8	0	0	0.7	1.000	3B-14
1977		80	.261	.370	92	24	5	1	1	1.1	8	13	9	16	1	26	6	45	46	4	8	1.2	.958	3B-37, 2B-17, OF-5, SS-3
1978		83	.200	.292	65	13	3	0	1	1.5	7	4	3	13	0	16	2	13	41	7	1	0.7	.885	3B-60, 2B-4, OF-3, SS-1, 1B-1
1979		150	.318	.454	551	175	37	4	10	1.8	64	79	38	57	4	1	0	120	262	15	26	2.6	.962	3B-149
1980		162	.264	.417	618	163	39	7	14	2.3	71	78	36	62	1	1	0	120	291	13	19	2.6	.969	3B-162
1981		106	.259	.370	386	100	23	1	6	1.6	43	34	33	51	2	1	0	69	176	11	18	2.4	.957	3B-105
1982	HOU N	158	.294	.402	609	179	36	6	6	1.0	72	70	48	58	2	0	0	1002	186	17	94	7.6	.986	1B-96, 3B-67
1983		145	.304	.444	507	154	36	4	9	1.8	43	70	42	62	2	4	0	1285	73	9	131	9.4	.993	1B-143
1984	2 teams	HOU N (88G – .223)			NY N (27G – .280)																			
"	total	115	.237	.299	371	88	14	0	3	0.8	28	35	21	43	1	10	4	256	132	9	27	3.5	.977	3B-81, 1B-27
1985	NY N	90	.218	.328	271	59	12	0	6	2.2	22	36	13	32	1	16	1	56	113	7	5	2.0	.960	3B-73, 2B-2, 1B-1
1986		137	.298	.424	486	145	24	2	11	2.3	51	76	40	63	2	0	0	94	204	16	17	2.3	.949	3B-132, 1B-3
1987	BAL A	150	.256	.373	563	144	24	0	14	2.5	46	65	39	90	1	1	1	169	284	19	35	3.1	.960	3B-130, DH-14, 1B-6
1988	DET A	105	.217	.301	299	65	12	2	3	1.0	34	33	20	30	1	23	2	438	42	4	40	4.6	.992	1B-64, 3B-11, OF-2
	13 yrs.	1495	.271	.390	4829	1311	266	27	84	1.7	490	595	343	579	14	105	18	3669	1858	131	421	3.8	.977	3B-1021, 1B-339, 2B-23, DH-14, OF-10, SS-4

LEAGUE CHAMPIONSHIP SERIES

Year	Team	Games	BA	SA	AB	H	2B	3B	HR	HR%	R	RBI	BB	SO	SB	Pinch Hit AB	H	PO	A	E	DP	TC/G	FA	G by Pos
1979	CIN N	3	.286	.357	14	4	1	0	0	0.0	0	2	1	0	0	0	0	5	0	0	0	1.7	1.000	3B-3

Year	Team	Games	BA	SA	AB	H	2B	3B	HR	HR%	R	RBI	BB	SO	SB	Pinch Hit AB	Pinch Hit H	PO	A	E	DP	TC/G	FA	G by Pos

Ray Knight *continued*

| 1986 | NY | N | 6 | .167 | .167 | 24 | 4 | 0 | 0 | 0 | 0.0 | 1 | 2 | 1 | 5 | 0 | 0 | 0 | 5 | 19 | 1 | 0 | 4.2 | .960 | 3B-6 |
| 2 yrs. | | | 9 | .211 | .237 | 38 | 8 | 1 | 0 | 0 | 0.0 | 1 | 2 | 1 | 7 | 1 | 0 | 0 | 5 | 24 | 1 | 0 | 3.3 | .967 | 3B-9 |

WORLD SERIES

| 1986 | NY | N | 6 | .391 | .565 | 23 | 9 | 1 | 0 | 1 | 4.3 | 4 | 5 | 2 | 2 | 0 | 0 | 0 | 5 | 6 | 1 | 0 | 2.0 | .917 | 3B-6 |

Pete Knisely

KNISELY, PETER COLE   BR TR 5'9" 185 lbs.
B. Aug. 11, 1887, Waynesburg, Pa.   D. July 1, 1948, Brownsville, Pa.

1912	CIN	N	21	.328	.522	67	22	7	3	0	0.0	10	7	4	5	3	3	0	32	10	3	2	2.1	.933	OF-13, 2B-3, SS-1
1913	CHI	N	2	.000	.000	2	0	0	0	0	0.0	0	0	0	1	0	2	0	0	0	0	0	0.0	—	
1914			37	.130	.159	69	9	0	1	0	0.0	5	5	5	6	0	19	4	36	3	1	2	1.1	.975	OF-16
1915			64	.246	.313	134	33	9	0	0	0.0	12	17	15	18	1	17	4	59	16	8	4	1.3	.904	OF-34, 2B-9
4 yrs.			124	.235	.324	272	64	16	4	0	0.0	27	29	24	30	4	41	8	127	29	12	8	1.4	.929	OF-63, 2B-12, SS-1

Mike Knode

KNODE, KENNETH THOMSON   BL TR 5'10" 160 lbs.
Brother of Ray Knode.
B. Nov. 8, 1895, Westminster, Md.   D. Dec. 20, 1980, South Bend, Ind.

| 1920 | STL | N | 42 | .231 | .277 | 65 | 15 | 1 | 1 | 0 | 0.0 | 11 | 9 | 5 | 6 | 1 | 18 | 4 | 22 | 17 | 5 | 0 | 1.0 | .886 | OF-9, 2B-4, SS-2, 3B-2 |

Ray Knode

KNODE, ROBERT TROXELL (Bob)   BL TL 5'10" 160 lbs.
Brother of Mike Knode.
B. Jan. 28, 1901, Westminster, Md.   D. Apr. 13, 1982, Battle Creek, Mich.

1923	CLE	A	22	.289	.447	38	11	0	0	2	5.3	7	4	2	4	1	0	0	112	7	1	8	5.5	.992	1B-21
1924			11	.243	.270	37	9	1	0	0	0.0	6	4	3	0	2	0	0	110	9	1	11	10.9	.992	1B-10
1925			45	.250	.296	108	27	5	0	0	0.0	13	11	10	4	3	3	0	270	19	3	27	6.5	.990	1B-34
1926			31	.333	.458	24	8	1	1	0	0.0	6	2	2	3	0	5	2	57	4	1	3	2.0	.984	1B-11
4 yrs.			109	.266	.338	207	55	7	1	2	1.0	32	21	17	11	6	8	2	549	39	6	49	5.4	.990	1B-76

Punch Knoll

KNOLL, CHARLES ELMER   BR TR 5'7½" 170 lbs.
B. Oct. 7, 1881, Evansville, Ind.   D. Feb. 8, 1960, Evansville, Ind.

| 1905 | WAS | A | 85 | .213 | .295 | 244 | 52 | 10 | 5 | 0 | 0.0 | 24 | 29 | 9 | | 3 | 8 | 3 | 135 | 9 | 8 | 1 | 1.8 | .947 | OF-70, C-5, 1B-2 |

Bobby Knoop

KNOOP, ROBERT FRANK   BR TR 6'1" 170 lbs.
B. Oct. 18, 1938, Sioux City, Iowa

1964	LA	A	162	.216	.280	486	105	8	1	7	1.4	42	38	46	109	3	1	0	357	522	20	123	5.5	.978	2B-161
1965	CAL	A	142	.269	.383	465	125	24	4	7	1.5	47	43	31	101	3	0	0	331	402	22	89	5.3	.971	2B-142
1966			161	.232	.386	590	137	18	11	17	2.9	54	72	43	144	1	0	0	381	488	17	135	5.5	.981	2B-161
1967			159	.245	.352	511	125	18	5	9	1.8	51	38	44	136	2	0	0	376	392	11	91	4.9	.986	2B-159
1968			152	.249	.324	494	123	20	4	3	0.6	48	39	35	122	3	1	1	350	425	15	94	5.2	.981	2B-151
1969	2 teams		CAL A	(27G – .197)	CHI A	(104G – .229)																			
"	total		131	.224	.315	416	93	15	1	7	1.7	39	47	48	84	3	1	0	335	386	12	90	5.6	.984	2B-131
1970	CHI	A	130	.229	.308	402	92	13	2	5	1.2	34	36	34	79	0	3	1	276	403	11	102	5.3	.984	2B-126
1971	KC	A	72	.205	.286	161	33	8	1	1	0.6	14	11	15	36	1	16	3	89	120	7	31	3.0	.968	2B-52, 3B-1
1972			44	.237	.289	97	23	5	0	0	0.0	8	7	9	16	2	9	2	61	80	4	24	3.3	.972	2B-33, 3B-4
9 yrs.			1153	.236	.334	3622	856	129	29	56	1.5	337	331	305	833	16	31	7	2556	3218	119	779	5.1	.980	2B-1116, 3B-5

Fritz Knothe

KNOTHE, WILFRED EDGAR   BR TR 5'10½" 180 lbs.
Brother of George Knothe.
B. May 1, 1903, Passaic, N. J.   D. Mar. 27, 1963, Passaic, N. J.

1932	BOS	N	89	.238	.308	344	82	19	1	1	0.3	45	36	39	37	5	1	1	81	168	14	7	3.0	.947	3B-87
1933	2 teams		BOS N	(44G – .228)	PHI N	(41G – .150)																			
"	total		85	.196	.247	271	53	7	2	1	0.4	25	17	19	44	3	5	0	98	165	11	18	3.2	.960	3B-65, SS-9, 2B-4
2 yrs.			174	.220	.281	615	135	26	3	2	0.3	70	53	58	81	8	6	1	179	333	25	25	3.1	.953	3B-152, SS-9, 2B-4

George Knothe

KNOTHE, GEORGE BERTRAM   BR TR 5'10" 165 lbs.
Brother of Fritz Knothe.
B. Jan. 12, 1898, Bayonne, N. J.   D. July 3, 1981, Dover, N. J.

| 1932 | PHI | N | 6 | .083 | .167 | 12 | 1 | 1 | 0 | 0 | 0.0 | 2 | 0 | 0 | 0 | 0 | 0 | 0 | 4 | 8 | 1 | 2 | 2.2 | .923 | 2B-5 |

Joe Knotts

KNOTTS, JOSEPH STEVEN   BR TR
B. Mar. 3, 1884, Greensboro, Pa.   D. Sept. 15, 1950, Philadelphia, Pa.

| 1907 | BOS | N | 3 | .000 | .000 | 8 | 0 | 0 | 0 | 0 | 0.0 | 0 | 1 | 0 | | 0 | 0 | 0 | 10 | 4 | 0 | 0 | 4.7 | 1.000 | C-3 |

Jake Knowdell

KNOWDELL, JACOB AUGUSTUS   5'7½" 148 lbs.
B. July 27, 1840, Brooklyn, N. Y.   Deceased.

| 1878 | MIL | N | 4 | .214 | .286 | 14 | 3 | 1 | 0 | 0 | 0.0 | 2 | | 2 | | 0 | 3 | | 0 | 13 | 5 | 4 | 0 | 5.5 | .818 | C-2, OF-1, SS-1 |

Jimmy Knowles

KNOWLES, JAMES   5'9" 160 lbs.
B. 1859, Toronto, Ont., Canada   Deceased.

1884	2 teams		PIT AA	(46G – .231)	BKN AA	(41G – .235)																			
"	total		87	.233	.319	335	78	10	8	1	0.3	38		8			0	0	818	51	45	38	10.5	.951	1B-75, 3B-11, SS-1
1886	WAS	N	115	.212	.318	443	94	16	11	3	0.7	43	35	15	73		0	0	264	346	81	41	6.0	.883	2B-62, 3B-53
1887	NY	AA	16	.250	.300	60	15	1	1	0	0.0	12	1	1		6	0	0	49	37	7	4	5.8	.925	2B-16, 3B-1
1890	ROC	AA	123	.281	.369	491	138	12	8	5	1.0	83		59		55	0	0	162	303	63	19	4.3	.881	3B-123
1892	NY	N	16	.153	.169	59	9	1	0	0	0.0	9	7	6	8	2	0	0	14	26	10	2	3.1	.800	3B-15, SS-1
5 yrs.			357	.241	.329	1388	334	40	28	9	0.6	185	42	89	81	63	0	0	1307	763	206	104	6.4	.909	3B-203, 2B-78, 1B-75, SS-2

Andy Knox

KNOX, ANDREW JACKSON (Dasher)   BR TR
B. Jan. 5, 1864, Philadelphia, Pa.   D. Sept. 14, 1940, Philadelphia, Pa.

Year	Team		Games	BA	SA	AB	H	2B	3B	HR	HR%	R	RBI	BB	SO	SB	Pinch Hit AB	H	PO	A	E	DP	TC/G	FA	G by Pos

Andy Knox *continued*

| 1890 | PHI | AA | 21 | .253 | .293 | 75 | 19 | 3 | 0 | 0 | 0.0 | 6 | | 9 | | 5 | 0 | 0 | 205 | 5 | 8 | 8 | 10.4 | .963 | 1B-21 |

Cliff Knox

KNOX, CLIFFORD HIRAM (Bud)
B. Jan. 7, 1902, Coalville, Iowa   D. Sept. 24, 1965, Oskaloosa, Iowa   BB TR 5'11½" 178 lbs.

| 1924 | PIT | N | 6 | .222 | .222 | 18 | 4 | 0 | 0 | 0 | 0.0 | 1 | 2 | 0 | 0 | 0 | 0 | 0 | 23 | 10 | 3 | 2 | 6.0 | .917 | C-6 |

John Knox

KNOX, JOHN CLINTON
B. July 26, 1948, Newark, N. J.   BL TR 6'   170 lbs.

1972	DET	A	14	.077	.154	13	1	1	0	0	0.0	1	2	0	9	0	3	10	0	3	0.9	1.000	2B-4
1973			12	.281	.313	32	9	1	0	0	0.0	1	3	3	3	1	0	17	17	0	3	2.8	1.000	2B-9
1974			55	.307	.341	88	27	1	1	0	0.0	11	6	6	13	5	4	1	55	54	5	20	2.1	.956	2B-33, DH-1, 3B-1
1975			43	.267	.279	86	23	1	0	0	0.0	8	2	10	9	1	5	2	38	62	5	10	2.4	.952	2B-23, DH-3, 3B-3
4 yrs.			124	.274	.301	219	60	4	1	0	0.0	21	11	20	27	7	18	4	113	143	10	36	2.1	.962	2B-69, DH-4, 3B-4

LEAGUE CHAMPIONSHIP SERIES

| 1972 | DET | A | 1 | – | – | 0 | 0 | 0 | 0 | 0 | 0.0 | 0 | 0 | 0 | 0 | 0 | 0 | 0 | 0 | 0 | 0 | 0 | 0.0 | – | |

Nick Koback

KOBACK, NICHOLAS NICHOLIE
B. July 19, 1935, Hartford, Conn.   BR TR 6'   187 lbs.

1953	PIT	N	7	.125	.250	16	2	0	1	0	0.0	1	0	1	4	0	1	1	8	2	0	0	1.4	1.000	C-6
1954			4	.000	.000	10	0	0	0	0	0.0	0	0	0	8	0	0	0	14	0	0	0	3.5	1.000	C-4
1955			5	.286	.286	7	2	0	0	0	0.0	0	0	0	1	0	3	1	4	1	0	0	1.0	1.000	C-2
3 yrs.			16	.121	.182	33	4	0	1	0	0.0	1	0	1	13	0	4	2	26	3	0	0	1.8	1.000	C-12

Barney Koch

KOCH, BARNETT
B. Mar. 23, 1923, Campbell, Neb.   D. June 6, 1987, Tacoma, Wash.   BR TR 5'8" 140 lbs.

| 1944 | BKN | N | 33 | .219 | .240 | 96 | 21 | 2 | 0 | 0 | 0.0 | 11 | 1 | 3 | 9 | 0 | 1 | 1 | 65 | 65 | 6 | 10 | 4.1 | .956 | 2B-29, SS-1 |

Brad Kocher

KOCHER, BRADLEY WILSON
B. Jan. 16, 1888, White Haven, Pa.   D. Jan. 13, 1965, White Haven, Pa.   BR TR 5'11" 188 lbs.

1912	DET	A	24	.206	.286	63	13	3	1	0	0.0	5	9	2		0	1	0	68	26	10	3	4.3	.904	C-23
1915	NY	N	4	.455	.636	11	5	0	1	0	0.0	3	2	0	1	0	1	0	12	4	0	0	4.0	1.000	C-3
1916			34	.108	.138	65	7	2	0	0	0.0	1	1	2	10	0	4	1	75	15	2	1	2.7	.978	C-30
3 yrs.			62	.180	.245	139	25	5	2	0	0.0	9	12	4	11	0	6	1	155	45	12	4	3.4	.943	C-56

Pete Koegel

KOEGEL, PETER JOHN
B. July 31, 1947, Mineola, N. Y.   BR TR 6'6½" 230 lbs.

1970	MIL	A	7	.250	.625	8	2	0	0	1	12.5	2	1	1	3	0	6	2	1	0	0	0	0.1	1.000	OF-1
1971	2 teams			MIL	A	(2G – .000)		PHI	N	(12G – .231)															
"	total		14	.207	.241	29	6	0	0	0	0.0	1	3	4	9	0	4	1	28	3	0	2	2.2	1.000	C-7, OF-1, 1B-1
1972	PHI	N	41	.143	.184	49	7	2	0	0	0.0	3	1	6	16	0	21	2	43	5	1	3	1.2	.980	1B-8, C-5, 3B-4, OF-2
3 yrs.			62	.174	.244	86	15	3	0	1	1.2	5	11	28	0	31	5	72	8	1	5	1.3	.988	C-12, 1B-9, OF-4, 3B-4

Ben Koehler

KOEHLER, BERNARD JAMES
B. Jan. 26, 1877, Schoerndorn, Germany   D. May 21, 1961, South Bend, Ind.   BR TR 5'10½" 175 lbs.

1905	STL	A	142	.237	.297	536	127	14	6	2	0.4	55	47	32		22	0	0	347	41	10	18	2.8	.975	OF-127, 1B-12, 2B-6
1906			66	.220	.237	186	41	1	1	0	0.0	27	15	24		9	5	1	95	26	8	7	2.0	.938	OF-52, 2B-7, SS-1, 3B-1
2 yrs.			208	.233	.281	722	168	15	7	2	0.3	82	62	56		31	5	1	442	67	18	25	2.5	.966	OF-179, 2B-13, 1B-12, SS-1, 3B-1

Pip Koehler

KOEHLER, HORACE LEVERING
B. Jan. 16, 1902, Gilbert, Pa.   D. Dec. 8, 1986, Tacoma, Wash.   BR TR 5'10" 165 lbs.

| 1925 | NY | N | 12 | .000 | .000 | 2 | 0 | 0 | 0 | 0 | 0.0 | 1 | 0 | 1 | 0 | 1 | 0 | 0 | 3 | 0 | 0 | 0 | 0.3 | 1.000 | OF-3 |

Len Koenecke

KOENECKE, LEONARD GEORGE
B. Jan. 18, 1904, Baraboo, Wis.   D. Sept. 17, 1935, Toronto, Ont., Canada   BL TR 5'11½" 192 lbs.

1932	NY	N	42	.255	.380	137	35	5	0	4	2.9	33	14	11	13	3	1	0	61	0	5	0	1.6	.924	OF-35
1934	BKN	N	123	.320	.509	460	147	31	7	14	3.0	79	73	70	38	8	2	0	310	6	2	0	2.6	.994	OF-121
1935			100	.283	.372	325	92	13	2	4	1.2	43	27	43	45	0	8	0	222	3	8	0	2.3	.966	OF-91
3 yrs.			265	.297	.441	922	274	49	9	22	2.4	155	114	124	96	11	11	0	593	9	15	0	2.3	.976	OF-247

Mark Koenig

KOENIG, MARK ANTHONY
B. July 19, 1902, San Francisco, Calif.   BB TR 6'   180 lbs.
BL 1928

1925	NY	A	28	.209	.282	110	23	6	1	0	0.0	14	4	5	4	0	0	0	53	81	8	16	5.1	.944	SS-28
1926			147	.271	.363	617	167	26	8	5	0.8	93	62	43	37	4	6	1	281	422	52	66	5.1	.931	SS-141
1927			123	.285	.382	526	150	20	11	3	0.6	99	62	25	21	3	1	0	262	423	47	76	6.0	.936	SS-122
1928			132	.319	.415	533	170	19	10	4	0.8	89	63	32	19	3	3	3	260	328	49	69	4.8	.923	SS-125
1929			116	.292	.416	373	109	27	5	3	0.8	44	41	23	17	1	16	1	137	216	32	34	3.3	.917	SS-61, 3B-37, 2B-1
1930	2 teams			NY	A	(21G – .230)		DET	A	(76G – .240)															
"	total		97	.238	.299	341	81	14	2	1	0.3	46	25	26	20	2	4	0	153	244	35	54	4.5	.919	SS-89, 3B-2, P-2, OF-1
1931	DET	A	106	.253	.349	364	92	24	4	1	0.3	33	39	14	12	8	15	4	191	238	28	41	4.5	.939	2B-55, SS-35, P-3
1932	CHI	N	33	.353	.510	102	36	5	1	3	2.9	15	11	3	5	0	2	0	58	106	12	21	5.3	.932	SS-33
1933			80	.284	.390	218	62	12	1	3	1.4	32	25	15	9	5	4	0	72	134	14	25	2.8	.936	3B-37, 2B-28
1934	CIN	N	151	.272	.336	633	172	26	6	1	0.2	60	67	15	24	5	2	0	321	405	48	59	5.1	.938	3B-64, SS-58, 2B-26, 1B-4
1935	NY	N	107	.283	.336	396	112	10	4	1	0.3	40	37	13	18	0	9	1	178	294	18	39	4.6	.963	2B-64, SS-21, 3B-15
1936			42	.276	.397	58	16	4	0	1	1.7	6	3	0	4	0	17	4	21	38	7	14	1.6	.894	SS-10, 2B-8, 3B-3
12 yrs.			1162	.279	.367	4271	1190	195	49	28	0.7	572	443	222	190	31	94	18	1987	2929	350	514	4.5	.934	SS-749, 3B-158, 2B-156, P-5, 1B-4, OF-1

WORLD SERIES

| 1926 | NY | A | 7 | .125 | .156 | 32 | 4 | 1 | 0 | 0 | 0.0 | 2 | 2 | 0 | 6 | 0 | 0 | 0 | 12 | 24 | 4 | 3 | 5.7 | .900 | SS-7 |

Year	Team	Games	BA	SA	AB	H	2B	3B	HR	HR%	R	RBI	BB	SO	SB	Pinch Hit AB	Pinch Hit H	PO	A	E	DP	TC/G	FA	G by Pos

Mark Koenig *continued*

Year	Team	Games	BA	SA	AB	H	2B	3B	HR	HR%	R	RBI	BB	SO	SB	PH AB	PH H	PO	A	E	DP	TC/G	FA	G by Pos
1927		4	.500	.611	18	9	2	0	0	0.0	5	2	0	2	0	0	0	6	8	0	1	3.5	1.000	SS-4
1928		4	.158	.158	19	3	0	0	0	0.0	1	0	0	1	0	0	0	8	11	2	3	5.3	.905	SS-4
1932	CHI N	2	.250	.750	4	1	0	1	0	0.0	1	1	1	0	0	0	0	4	3	0	1	3.5	1.000	SS-1
1936	NY N	3	.333	.333	3	1	0	0	0	0.0	0	0	0	1	0	3	1	1	0	0	0	0.3	1.000	2B-1
5 yrs.		20	.237	.303	76	18	3	1	0	0.0	9	5	1	10	0	3	1	31	46	6	8	4.2	.928	SS-16, 2B-1

Dick Kokos

KOKOS, RICHARD JEROME   BL TL 5'8½" 170 lbs.
Born Richard Jerome Kokoszka.
B. Feb. 28, 1928, Chicago, Ill. D. Apr. 9, 1986, Chicago, Ill.

Year	Team	Games	BA	SA	AB	H	2B	3B	HR	HR%	R	RBI	BB	SO	SB	PH AB	PH H	PO	A	E	DP	TC/G	FA	G by Pos
1948	STL A	71	.298	.426	258	77	15	3	4	1.6	40	40	28	32	4	1	0	126	8	5	2	2.0	.964	OF-71
1949		143	.261	.459	501	131	28	1	23	4.6	80	77	66	91	3	6	2	290	16	6	5	2.2	.981	OF-138
1950		143	.261	.447	490	128	27	5	18	3.7	77	67	88	73	8	14	2	342	8	11	2	2.5	.970	OF-127
1953		107	.241	.411	299	72	12	0	13	4.3	41	38	56	53	0	25	6	152	5	6	1	1.5	.963	OF-83
1954	BAL A	11	.200	.500	10	2	0	0	1	10.0	1	1	4	3	0	8	2	3	0	0	0	0.3	1.000	OF-1
5 yrs.		475	.263	.441	1558	410	82	9	59	3.8	239	223	242	252	15	54	12	913	37	28	10	2.1	.971	OF-420

Gary Kolb

KOLB, GARY ALAN   BL TR 6' 194 lbs.
B. Mar. 13, 1940, Rock Falls, Ill.

Year	Team	Games	BA	SA	AB	H	2B	3B	HR	HR%	R	RBI	BB	SO	SB	PH AB	PH H	PO	A	E	DP	TC/G	FA	G by Pos
1960	STL N	9	.000	.000	3	0	0	0	0	0.0	0	0	0	0	0	0	0	4	0	0	0	0.4	1.000	OF-2
1962		6	.357	.357	14	5	0	0	0	0.0	1	0	1	3	0	0	0	9	0	0	0	1.5	1.000	OF-6
1963		75	.271	.479	96	26	1	5	3	3.1	23	10	22	26	2	6	0	52	1	1	1	0.7	.981	OF-58, 3B-1, C-1
1964	MIL N	36	.188	.203	64	12	1	0	0	0.0	7	2	6	10	3	5	0	26	17	4	2	1.3	.915	OF-14, 3B-7, 2B-6, C-2
1965	2 teams		MIL N	(24G – .259)			NY N		(40G – .167)															
"	total	64	.188	.231	117	22	2	0	1	0.9	11	8	4	34	3	20	5	51	5	2	2	0.9	.966	OF-42, 3B-1, 1B-1
1968	PIT N	74	.218	.319	119	26	4	1	2	1.7	16	6	11	17	2	31	6	56	11	5	3	1.0	.931	OF-25, C-10, 3B-4, 2B-1
1969		29	.081	.108	37	3	1	0	0	0.0	4	3	2	14	0	20	1	29	4	0	0	1.1	1.000	C-7
7 yrs.		293	.209	.296	450	94	9	6	6	1.3	63	29	46	104	10	82	12	227	38	12	8	0.9	.957	OF-147, C-20, 3B-13, 2B-7, 1B-1

Don Kolloway

KOLLOWAY, DONALD MARTIN (Butch, Cab)   BR TR 6'3" 200 lbs.
B. Aug. 4, 1918, Posen, Ill.

Year	Team	Games	BA	SA	AB	H	2B	3B	HR	HR%	R	RBI	BB	SO	SB	PH AB	PH H	PO	A	E	DP	TC/G	FA	G by Pos
1940	CHI A	10	.225	.250	40	9	1	0	0	0.0	5	3	0	3	1	0	0	19	28	4	7	5.1	.922	2B-10
1941		71	.271	.354	280	76	8	3	3	1.1	33	24	6	12	11	3	1	152	185	18	29	5.0	.949	2B-62, 1B-4
1942		147	.273	.368	601	164	40	4	3	0.5	72	60	30	39	16	0	0	636	360	28	108	7.0	.973	2B-116, 1B-33
1943		85	.216	.287	348	75	14	4	1	0.3	29	33	9	30	11	0	0	246	240	16	71	5.9	.968	2B-85
1946		123	.280	.363	482	135	23	4	3	0.6	45	53	9	29	14	1	0	267	353	24	82	5.2	.963	2B-90, 3B-31
1947		124	.278	.359	485	135	25	4	2	0.4	49	35	17	34	11	7	2	378	331	27	86	5.9	.963	2B-99, 1B-11, 3B-8
1948		119	.273	.369	417	114	14	4	6	1.4	60	38	18	18	2	12	3	264	303	22	63	4.9	.963	2B-83, 3B-18
1949	2 teams		CHI A	(4G – .000)			DET A		(126G – .294)															
"	total	130	.292	.355	487	142	19	3	2	0.4	71	47	49	26	7	12	2	613	196	18	94	6.4	.978	2B-62, 1B-57, 3B-9
1950	DET A	125	.289	.388	467	135	20	4	6	1.3	55	62	29	28	1	5	1	1088	88	13	133	9.5	.989	1B-118, 2B-1
1951		78	.255	.302	212	54	7	0	1	0.5	28	17	15	12	2	17	4	452	49	4	53	6.5	.992	1B-59
1952		65	.243	.329	173	42	9	0	2	1.2	19	21	7	19	0	25	5	266	44	7	19	4.9	.978	1B-32, 2B-8
1953	PHI A	2	.000	.000	1	0	0	0	0	0.0	0	0	0	0	0	1	0	0	0	0	0	0.0	–	3B-1
12 yrs.		1079	.271	.353	3993	1081	180	30	29	0.7	466	393	189	251	76	83	18	4381	2177	181	745	6.2	.973	2B-616, 1B-314, 3B-67

Karl Kolseth

KOLSETH, KARL DICKEY   BL TR 6' 182 lbs.
B. Dec. 25, 1892, Somerville, Mass. D. May 3, 1956, Cumberland, Md.

Year	Team	Games	BA	SA	AB	H	2B	3B	HR	HR%	R	RBI	BB	SO	SB	PH AB	PH H	PO	A	E	DP	TC/G	FA	G by Pos
1915	BAL F	6	.261	.391	23	6	1	1	0	0.0	1	1	1		0	0	0	63	2	6	5	11.8	.915	1B-6

Fred Kommers

KOMMERS, FREDERICK RAYMOND (Bugs)   BL TR 6' 175 lbs.
B. Mar. 31, 1886, Chicago, Ill. D. June 14, 1943, Chicago, Ill.

Year	Team	Games	BA	SA	AB	H	2B	3B	HR	HR%	R	RBI	BB	SO	SB	PH AB	PH H	PO	A	E	DP	TC/G	FA	G by Pos
1913	PIT N	40	.232	.316	155	36	5	4	0	0.0	14	22	10	29	1	0	0	94	1	2	0	2.4	.979	OF-40
1914	2 teams		STL F	(76G – .307)			BAL F		(16G – .214)															
"	total	92	.294	.427	286	84	10	8	4	1.4	38	42	31		7	10	4	122	11	13	1	1.6	.911	OF-79
2 yrs.		132	.272	.388	441	120	15	12	4	0.9	52	64	41	29	8	10	4	216	12	15	1	1.8	.938	OF-119

Brad Komminsk

KOMMINSK, BRAD LYNN   BR TR 6'2" 202 lbs.
B. Apr. 4, 1961, Lima, Ohio

Year	Team	Games	BA	SA	AB	H	2B	3B	HR	HR%	R	RBI	BB	SO	SB	PH AB	PH H	PO	A	E	DP	TC/G	FA	G by Pos
1983	ATL N	19	.222	.278	36	8	2	0	0	0.0	2	4	5	7	0	7	2	16	1	1	0	0.9	.944	OF-13
1984		90	.203	.316	301	61	10	0	8	2.7	37	36	29	77	18	10	4	135	2	1	0	1.5	.993	OF-80
1985		106	.227	.360	300	68	12	3	4	1.3	52	21	38	71	10	15	0	161	2	7	0	1.6	.959	OF-92
1986		5	.400	.400	5	2	0	0	0	0.0	1	1	0	1	0	4	1	1	2	0	0	0.6	1.000	OF-2, 3B-2
1987	MIL A	7	.067	.067	15	1	0	0	0	0.0	0	0	1	7	1	1	0	10	0	0	0	1.4	1.000	OF-5, DH-1
1989	CLE A	71	.237	.389	198	47	8	2	8	4.0	27	33	24	55	8	5	1	181	3	1	1	2.6	.995	OF-68
6 yrs.		298	.219	.338	855	187	32	5	20	2.3	119	95	97	218	37	39	7	504	10	10	1	1.8	.981	OF-260, 3B-2, DH-1

Ed Konetchy

KONETCHY, EDWARD JOSEPH (Big Ed)   BR TR 6'2½" 195 lbs.
B. Sept. 3, 1885, LaCrosse, Wis. D. May 27, 1947, Fort Worth, Tex.

Year	Team	Games	BA	SA	AB	H	2B	3B	HR	HR%	R	RBI	BB	SO	SB	PH AB	PH H	PO	A	E	DP	TC/G	FA	G by Pos
1907	STL N	90	.252	.361	330	83	11	8	3	0.9	34	30	26		13	0	0	922	71	25	46	11.3	.975	1B-90
1908		154	.248	.354	545	135	19	12	5	0.9	46	50	38		16	0	0	1610	122	24	61	11.4	.986	1B-154
1909		152	.286	.396	576	165	23	14	4	0.7	88	80	65		25	0	0	1584	97	26	71	11.2	.985	1B-152
1910		144	.302	.425	520	157	23	16	3	0.6	87	78	78	59	18	0	0	1499	98	15	81	11.2	.991	1B-144, P-1
1911		158	.289	.433	571	165	38	13	6	1.1	90	88	81	63	27	0	0	1652	71	16	85	11.0	.991	1B-158
1912		143	.314	.455	538	169	26	13	8	1.5	81	82	62	66	25	0	0	1396	91	13	77	10.5	.991	1B-142, OF-1
1913		139	.273	.418	502	137	18	17	7	1.4	74	68	53	41	27	0	0	1432	91	7	71	11.0	.995	1B-139, P-1
1914	PIT N	154	.249	.343	563	140	23	9	4	0.7	56	51	32	48	20	0	0	1576	93	9	70	10.9	.995	1B-154
1915	PIT F	152	.314	.483	576	181	31	18	10	1.7	79	93	41		27	0	0	1536	81	10	83	10.7	.994	1B-152
1916	BOS N	158	.260	.373	566	147	29	13	3	0.5	76	70	43	46	13	0	0	1626	96	18	96	11.0	.990	1B-158
1917		130	.272	.380	474	129	19	13	2	0.4	56	54	36	40	16	0	0	1351	70	8	65	11.0	.994	1B-129
1918		119	.236	.307	437	103	15	5	2	0.5	33	56	32	35	5	0	0	1239	65	11	70	11.1	.992	1B-112, OF-6, P-1

Year	Team		Games	BA	SA	AB	H	2B	3B	HR	HR%	R	RBI	BB	SO	SB	Pinch Hit AB	Pinch Hit H	PO	A	E	DP	TC/G	FA	G by Pos

Ed Konetchy *continued*

Year	Team		Games	BA	SA	AB	H	2B	3B	HR	HR%	R	RBI	BB	SO	SB	AB	H	PO	A	E	DP	TC/G	FA	G by Pos
1919	BKN	N	132	.298	.391	486	145	24	9	1	0.2	46	47	29	39	14	0	0	1288	89	9	62	10.5	.994	1B-132
1920			131	.308	.431	497	153	22	12	5	1.0	62	63	33	18	3	1	0	1332	79	14	70	10.9	.990	1B-130
1921	2 teams	BKN N (55G – .269)											PHI N (72G – .321)												
"	total		127	.299	.458	465	139	23	9	11	2.4	63	82	40	38	6	2	0	1335	83	20	79	11.3	.986	1B-125
15 yrs.			2083	.281	.402	7646	2148	344	181	74	1.0	971	992	689	493	255	4	0	21378	1297	224	1087	11.0	.990	1B-2071, OF-7, P-3

WORLD SERIES

| 1920 | BKN | N | 7 | .174 | .261 | 23 | 4 | 0 | 1 | 0 | 0.0 | 0 | 2 | 3 | 2 | 0 | 0 | 0 | 70 | 8 | 1 | 4 | 11.3 | .987 | 1B-7 |

Mike Konnick

KONNICK, MICHAEL ALOYSIUS
B. Jan. 13, 1889, Glen Lyon, Pa.   D. July 9, 1971, Wilkes-Barre, Pa.
BR TR 5'9"   180 lbs.

1909	CIN	N	2	.400	.600	5	2	1	0	0	0.0	0	1	0		0	0	0	6	1	0	0	3.5	1.000	C-2
1910			1	.000	.000	3	0	0	0	0	0.0	0	0	1	0	0	0	0	2	2	0	0	4.0	1.000	SS-1
2 yrs.			3	.250	.375	8	2	1	0	0	0.0	0	1	1	0	0	0	0	8	3	0	0	3.7	1.000	C-2, SS-1

Bruce Konopka

KONOPKA, BRUNO BRUCE
B. Sept. 16, 1919, Hammond, Ind.
BL TL 6'2"   190 lbs.

1942	PHI	A	5	.300	.300	10	3	0	0	0	0.0	2	1	1	2	0	2	1	17	1	0	2	3.6	1.000	1B-3
1943			2	.000	.000	2	0	0	0	0	0.0	0	0	0	1	0	2	0	0	0	0	0	0.0	–	
1946			38	.237	.301	93	22	4	1	0	0.0	7	9	4	8	0	17	5	148	17	1	13	4.4	.994	1B-20, OF-1
3 yrs.			45	.238	.295	105	25	4	1	0	0.0	9	10	5	10	0	21	6	165	18	1	15	4.1	.995	1B-23, OF-1

Jarry Koons

KOONS, HENRY M.
B. 1863, Philadelphia, Pa.   Deceased.
BR TR 5'8"   174 lbs.

| 1884 | 2 teams | ALT U (21G – .231) | | | | | | | | | | | | CHI U (1G – .000) | | | | | | | | | | | |
| " | total | | 22 | .222 | .272 | 81 | 18 | 2 | 1 | 0 | 0.0 | 8 | | 2 | | | 0 | 0 | 45 | 45 | 14 | 1 | 4.7 | .865 | 3B-22, C-1 |

George Kopacz

KOPACZ, GEORGE FELIX (Sonny)
B. Feb. 26, 1941, Chicago, Ill.
BL TL 6'1"   195 lbs.

1966	ATL	N	6	.000	.000	9	0	0	0	0	0.0	0	1	0	5	0	4	0	10	0	1	0	1.8	.909	1B-2
1970	PIT	N	10	.188	.188	16	3	0	0	0	0.0	1	0	0	5	0	7	1	17	0	0	2	1.7	1.000	1B-3
2 yrs.			16	.120	.120	25	3	0	0	0	0.0	2	0	1	10	0	11	1	27	0	1	2	1.8	.964	1B-5

Larry Kopf

KOPF, WILLIAM LORENZ
Played as Fred Brady 1913.   Brother of Wally Kopf.
B. Nov. 3, 1890, Bristol, Conn.   D. Oct. 15, 1986, Hamilton County, Ohio
BB TR 5'9"   160 lbs.

1913	CLE	A	5	.222	.222	9	2	0	0	0	0.0	1	1	0	0	0	0	0	5	10	1	1	3.2	.938	2B-3, 3B-1
1914	PHI	A	35	.188	.275	69	13	2	2	0	0.0	8	12	8	14	6	5	1	52	51	13	3	3.3	.888	SS-13, 3B-8, 2B-5
1915			118	.225	.269	386	87	10	2	1	0.3	39	33	41	45	5	0	0	205	279	48	30	4.5	.910	SS-74, 3B-42, 2B-2
1916	CIN	N	11	.275	.325	40	11	2	0	0	0.0	2	5	1	8	1	0	0	16	33	3	4	4.7	.942	SS-11
1917			148	.255	.326	573	146	19	8	2	0.3	81	26	28	48	17	2	1	276	470	68	59	5.5	.916	SS-145
1919			135	.270	.326	503	136	18	5	0	0.0	51	58	28	27	18	0	0	273	407	41	39	5.3	.943	SS-135
1920			126	.245	.303	458	112	15	6	0	0.0	56	59	35	24	14	1	1	251	371	47	39	5.3	.930	SS-123, 3B-2, 2B-2, OF-1
1921			107	.218	.264	367	80	8	3	1	0.3	36	25	43	20	3	1	0	207	322	31	39	5.2	.945	SS-93, 2B-4, 3B-3, OF-1
1922	BOS	N	126	.266	.298	466	124	6	3	1	0.2	59	37	45	22	8	1	1	259	382	45	58	5.4	.934	SS-123, 3B-13
1923			39	.275	.312	138	38	3	1	0	0.0	15	10	13	6	0	0	0	86	133	23	26	6.2	.905	SS-37, 2B-4
10 yrs.			850	.249	.301	3009	749	83	30	5	0.2	348	266	242	214	72	15	5	1630	2458	320	259	5.2	.927	SS-664, 2B-98, 3B-69, OF-2

WORLD SERIES

| 1919 | CIN | N | 8 | .222 | .370 | 27 | 6 | 0 | 2 | 0 | 0.0 | 3 | 2 | 3 | 2 | 0 | 0 | 0 | 10 | 29 | 1 | 4 | 5.0 | .975 | SS-8 |

Wally Kopf

KOPF, WALTER HENRY
Brother of Larry Kopf.
B. July 10, 1899, Stonington, Conn.   D. Apr. 30, 1979, Cincinnati, Ohio
BL TR 5'11"   168 lbs.

| 1921 | NY | N | 2 | .333 | .333 | 3 | 1 | 0 | 0 | 0 | 0.0 | 0 | 0 | 1 | 1 | 0 | 0 | 0 | 0 | 6 | 0 | 1 | 3.0 | 1.000 | 3B-2 |

Merlin Kopp

KOPP, MERLIN HENRY (Manny)
B. Jan. 2, 1892, Toledo, Ohio   D. May 6, 1960, Sacramento, Calif.
BB TR 5'8"   158 lbs.

1915	WAS	A	16	.250	.250	32	8	0	0	0	0.0	2	0	5		6	2		14	0	1	0	0.9	.933	OF-9
1918	PHI	A	96	.234	.292	363	85	7	7	0	0.0	60	18	42	55	22	0	0	221	20	7	6	2.6	.972	OF-96
1919			75	.226	.281	235	53	2	4	1	0.4	34	12	42	43	16	4	0	127	7	11	0	1.9	.924	OF-65
3 yrs.			187	.232	.286	630	146	9	11	1	0.2	96	30	89	105	39	10	2	362	27	19	6	2.2	.953	OF-170

Joe Koppe

KOPPE, JOSEPH
Born Joseph Kopchia.
B. Oct. 19, 1930, Detroit, Mich.
BR TR 5'10"   165 lbs.

1958	MIL	N	16	.444	.444	9	4	0	0	0	0.0	3	0	1	1	0	0	0	5	10	3	3	1.1	.833	SS-3
1959	PHI	N	126	.261	.386	422	110	18	7	7	1.7	68	28	41	80	7	0	0	225	362	27	67	4.9	.956	SS-113, 2B-11
1960			58	.171	.235	170	29	6	1	1	0.6	13	13	23	47	3	1	0	107	136	13	24	4.4	.949	SS-55, 3B-2
1961	2 teams	PHI N (6G – .000)												LA A (91G – .251)											
"	total		97	.249	.340	341	85	12	2	5	1.5	47	40	45	77	3	0	0	137	258	22	52	4.3	.947	SS-93, 2B-3, 3B-1
1962	LA	A	128	.227	.301	375	85	16	0	4	1.1	47	40	73	84	2	2	0	203	369	27	66	4.7	.955	SS-118, 2B-5, 3B-4
1963			76	.210	.272	143	30	4	1	1	0.7	11	12	9	30	0	20	4	69	94	6	17	2.2	.964	SS-19, 3B-18, 2B-14, OF-3
1964			54	.257	.310	113	29	4	0	1	0.0	10	6	14	16	0	3	1	61	118	12	24	3.5	.937	SS-31, 2B-13, 3B-3
1965	CAL	A	23	.212	.333	33	7	1	0	1	3.0	3	2	3	10	1	3	1	23	40	1	6	2.8	.984	2B-10, SS-4, 3B-4
8 yrs.			578	.236	.324	1606	379	61	12	19	1.2	202	141	209	345	16	29	6	830	1387	111	257	4.0	.952	SS-436, 2B-56, 3B-32, OF-3

George Kopshaw

KOPSHAW, GEORGE KARL
B. July 5, 1895, Passaic, N. J.   D. Dec. 26, 1934, Lynchburg, Va.
BR TR 5'11½"   176 lbs.

Year	Team	Games	BA	SA	AB	H	2B	3B	HR	HR%	R	RBI	BB	SO	SB	Pinch Hit AB	H	PO	A	E	DP	TC/G	FA	G by Pos

George Kopshaw *continued*

| 1923 | STL N | 2 | .200 | .400 | 5 | 1 | 0 | 0 | 0 | 0.0 | 1 | 0 | 0 | 1 | 0 | 0 | 0 | 2 | 0 | 0 | 0 | 1.0 | 1.000 | C-1 |

Steve Korcheck

KORCHECK, STEPHEN JOSEPH (Hoss)
B. Aug. 11, 1932, McClellandtown, Pa.   BR TR 6'1" 205 lbs.

1954	WAS A	2	.143	.143	7	1	0	0	0	0.0	0	0	0	2	0	0	0	5	1	1	0	3.5	.857	C-2
1955		13	.278	.333	36	10	2	0	0	0.0	3	2	0	5	0	3	1	46	7	0	2	4.1	1.000	C-12
1958		21	.078	.157	51	4	2	1	0	0.0	6	1	1	16	0	1	0	68	9	2	2	3.8	.975	C-20
1959		22	.157	.196	51	8	2	0	0	0.0	3	4	5	13	0	0	0	103	8	3	3	5.2	.974	C-22
4 yrs.		58	.159	.214	145	23	6	1	0	0.0	12	7	6	36	0	4	1	222	25	6	7	4.4	.976	C-56

Art Kores

KORES, ARTHUR EMIL (Dutch)
B. July 22, 1886, Milwaukee, Wis.   D. Mar. 26, 1974, Milwaukee, Wis.   BR TR 5'9" 167 lbs.

| 1915 | STL F | 60 | .234 | .313 | 201 | 47 | 9 | 2 | 1 | 0.5 | 18 | 22 | 21 | | 6 | 0 | 0 | 80 | 161 | 10 | 12 | 4.2 | .960 | 3B-60 |

Andy Kosco

KOSCO, ANDREW JOHN
B. Oct. 5, 1941, Youngstown, Ohio   BR TR 6'3" 205 lbs.

1965	MIN A	23	.236	.364	55	13	4	0	1	1.8	3	6	1	15	0	8	3	35	3	0	1	1.7	1.000	OF-14, 1B-2
1966		57	.222	.291	158	35	5	0	2	1.3	11	13	7	31	0	14	6	99	2	2	3	1.8	.981	OF-40, 1B-5
1967		9	.143	.179	28	4	1	0	0	0.0	4	4	2	4	0	3	1	12	0	1	0	1.4	.923	OF-7
1968	NY A	131	.240	.382	466	112	19	1	15	3.2	47	59	16	71	2	11	4	403	24	9	18	3.3	.979	OF-95, 1B-28
1969	LA N	120	.248	.422	424	105	13	2	19	4.5	51	74	21	66	0	13	5	161	5	3	3	1.4	.982	OF-109, 1B-3
1970		74	.228	.388	224	51	12	0	8	3.6	21	27	1	40	1	16	2	102	2	2	0	1.4	.981	OF-58, 1B-1
1971	MIL A	98	.227	.379	264	60	6	2	10	3.8	27	39	24	57	1	28	8	264	25	3	23	3.0	.990	OF-45, 1B-29, 3B-12
1972	2 teams				CAL A (49G – .239)						BOS A			(17G – .213)										
"	total	66	.233	.439	189	44	6	3	9	4.8	20	19	7	32	1	17	3	81	3	1	0	1.3	.988	OF-48
1973	CIN N	47	.280	.568	118	33	7	0	9	7.6	17	21	13	26	0	13	3	59	1	0	0	1.3	1.000	OF-36, 1B-1
1974		33	.189	.243	37	7	2	0	0	0.0	3	5	7	8	0	20	4	7	2	0	0	0.4	.846	3B-8, OF-1
10 yrs.		658	.236	.394	1963	464	75	8	73	3.7	204	267	99	350	5	143	39	1220	73	23	48	2.0	.983	OF-453, 1B-69, 3B-20

LEAGUE CHAMPIONSHIP SERIES

| 1973 | CIN N | 3 | .300 | .300 | 10 | 3 | 0 | 0 | 0 | 0.0 | 0 | 0 | 2 | 3 | 0 | 0 | 0 | 12 | 0 | 1 | 0 | 4.3 | .923 | OF-3 |

Clem Koshorek

KOSHOREK, CLEMENT JOHN (Scooter)
B. June 20, 1926, Royal Oak, Mich.   BR TR 5'6" 165 lbs.

1952	PIT N	98	.261	.314	322	84	17	0	0	0.0	27	15	26	39	4	8	1	149	232	18	47	4.1	.955	SS-33, 2B-27, 3B-26
1953		1	.000	.000	1	0	0	0	0	0.0	0	0	0	1	0	1	0	0	0	0	0	0.0		
2 yrs.		99	.260	.313	323	84	17	0	0	0.0	27	15	26	40	4	9	1	149	232	18	47	4.0	.955	SS-33, 2B-27, 3B-26

Mike Kosman

KOSMAN, MICHAEL THOMAS
B. Dec. 10, 1917, Hamtramck, Mich.   BR TR 5'9" 160 lbs.

| 1944 | CIN N | 1 | – | – | 0 | 0 | 0 | 0 | 0 | | 0 | 0 | 0 | 0 | 0 | 0 | 0 | 0 | 0 | 0 | 0 | 0.0 | | |

Fred Koster

KOSTER, FREDERICK CHARLES (Fritz)
B. Dec. 21, 1905, Louisville, Ky.   D. Apr. 24, 1979, St. Matthews, Ky.   BL TL 5'10½" 165 lbs.

| 1931 | PHI N | 76 | .225 | .265 | 151 | 34 | 2 | 2 | 0 | 0.0 | 21 | 8 | 14 | 21 | 4 | 19 | 3 | 80 | 4 | 7 | 1 | 1.2 | .923 | OF-41 |

Frank Kostro

KOSTRO, FRANK JERRY
B. Aug. 4, 1937, Windber, Pa.   BR TR 6'2" 190 lbs.

1962	DET A	16	.268	.341	41	11	3	0	0	0.0	5	3	1	6	0	4	1	9	20	1	2	1.9	.967	3B-11
1963	2 teams				DET A (31G – .231)						LA A			(43G – .222)										
"	total	74	.225	.298	151	34	4	0	2	1.3	10	10	15	30	0	36	7	85	44	4	8	1.8	.970	3B-25, 1B-8, OF-6
1964	MIN A	59	.272	.340	103	28	5	0	3	2.9	10	12	4	21	0	35	10	17	33	4	2	0.9	.926	3B-12, 2B-7, OF-2, 1B-1
1965		20	.161	.226	31	5	2	0	0	0.0	2	1	4	5	0	6	0	10	18	5	6	1.7	.848	2B-7, 3B-6, OF-2
1967		32	.323	.323	31	10	0	0	0	0.0	4	2	3	2	0	23	9	1	0	0	0	0.0	1.000	OF-3, 3B-1
1968		63	.241	.296	108	26	4	1	0	0.0	9	9	6	20	0	36	7	54	2	0	1	0.9	1.000	OF-24, 1B-5
1969		2	.000	.000	2	0	0	0	0	0.0	0	0	0	1	0	2	0	0	0	0	0	0.0	–	
7 yrs.		266	.244	.321	467	114	17	2	5	1.1	40	37	33	85	0	142	34	176	117	14	19	1.2	.954	3B-55, OF-37, 2B-14, 1B-14

Ernie Koy

KOY, ERNEST ANYZ (Chief)
B. Sept. 17, 1909, Sealy, Tex.   BR TR 6' 200 lbs.

1938	BKN N	142	.299	.468	521	156	29	13	11	2.1	78	76	38	76	15	3	1	306	7	5	4	2.2	.984	OF-135, 3B-1
1939		123	.278	.445	425	118	37	5	8	1.9	57	67	39	64	11	9	1	252	4	10	1	2.2	.962	OF-114
1940	2 teams				BKN N (24G – .229)						STL N			(93G – .310)										
"	total	117	.301	.452	396	119	21	6	9	2.3	53	60	31	62	13	7	0	217	2	6	0	1.9	.973	OF-110
1941	2 teams				STL N (13G – .200)						CIN N			(67G – .250)										
"	total	80	.242	.357	244	59	12	2	4	1.6	29	31	15	30	1	13	3	110	3	1	1	1.4	.991	OF-61
1942	2 teams				CIN N (3G – .000)						PHI N			(91G – .244)										
"	total	94	.242	.346	260	63	9	3	4	1.5	21	26	14	52	0	9	2	149	4	3	1	1.7	.981	OF-78
5 yrs.		556	.279	.427	1846	515	108	29	36	2.0	238	260	137	284	40	41	7	1034	20	25	7	1.9	.977	OF-498, 3B-1

Al Kozar

KOZAR, ALBERT KENNETH
B. July 5, 1922, McKees Rocks, Pa.   BR TR 5'9½" 173 lbs.

1948	WAS A	150	.250	.326	577	144	25	8	1	0.2	61	58	66	52	4	0	0	348	444	27	89	5.5	.967	2B-149
1949		105	.269	.357	350	94	15	2	4	1.1	46	31	25	23	2	4	0	232	235	11	57	4.6	.977	2B-102
1950	2 teams				WAS A (20G – .200)						CHI A			(10G – .300)										
"	total	30	.215	.277	65	14	1	0	1	1.5	11	5	5	11	0	6	0	39	51	3	11	3.1	.968	2B-19, 3B-1
3 yrs.		285	.254	.334	992	252	41	10	6	0.6	118	94	96	86	6	10	0	619	730	41	157	4.9	.971	2B-270, 3B-1

Year Team	Games	BA	SA	AB	H	2B	3B	HR	HR%	R	RBI	BB	SO	SB	Pinch Hit AB	Pinch Hit H	PO	A	E	DP	TC/G	FA	G by Pos

Joe Kracher

KRACHER, JOSEPH PETER (Jug)
B. Nov. 4, 1915, Philadelphia, Pa. D. Dec. 24, 1981, San Angelo, Tex.
BR TR 5'11" 185 lbs.

Year Team	Games	BA	SA	AB	H	2B	3B	HR	HR%	R	RBI	BB	SO	SB	PH AB	PH H	PO	A	E	DP	TC/G	FA	G by Pos
1939 PHI N	5	.200	.200	5	1	0	0	0	0.0	1	0	2	1	0	2	1	1	0	0	0	0.2	1.000	C-2

Clarence Kraft

KRAFT, CLARENCE OTTO (Big Boy)
B. June 9, 1887, Evansville, Ind. D. Mar. 26, 1958, Fort Worth, Tex.
BR TR 6' 190 lbs.

Year Team	Games	BA	SA	AB	H	2B	3B	HR	HR%	R	RBI	BB	SO	SB	PH AB	PH H	PO	A	E	DP	TC/G	FA	G by Pos
1914 BOS N	3	.333	.333	3	1	0	0	0	0.0	0	0	0	1	0	2	0	4	0	0	0	1.3	1.000	1B-1

Ed Kranepool

KRANEPOOL, EDWARD EMIL (The Krane)
B. Nov. 8, 1944, New York, N. Y.
BL TL 6'3" 205 lbs.

Year Team	Games	BA	SA	AB	H	2B	3B	HR	HR%	R	RBI	BB	SO	SB	PH AB	PH H	PO	A	E	DP	TC/G	FA	G by Pos
1962 NY N	3	.167	.333	6	1	1	0	0	0.0	0	0	0	1	0	0	0	9	3	0	0	4.0	1.000	1B-3
1963	86	.209	.289	273	57	12	2	2	0.7	22	14	18	50	4	13	3	228	18	4	17	2.9	.984	OF-55, 1B-20
1964	119	.257	.393	420	108	19	4	10	2.4	47	45	32	50	0	10	2	983	80	10	78	9.0	.991	1B-104, OF-6
1965	153	.253	.371	525	133	24	4	10	1.9	44	53	39	71	1	11	4	1375	93	12	116	9.7	.992	1B-147
1966	146	.254	.399	464	118	15	2	16	3.4	51	57	41	66	1	7	1	1180	86	12	100	8.8	.991	1B-132, OF-11
1967	141	.269	.373	469	126	17	1	10	2.1	37	54	37	51	0	9	1	1137	87	10	103	8.8	.992	1B-139
1968	127	.231	.295	373	86	13	1	3	0.8	29	20	19	39	0	16	3	924	75	6	76	7.9	.994	1B-113, OF-2
1969	112	.238	.368	353	84	9	2	11	3.1	36	49	37	32	3	7	1	812	64	6	76	7.9	.993	1B-106, OF-2
1970	43	.170	.170	47	8	0	0	0	0.0	2	3	5	2	0	31	4	47	3	0	5	1.2	1.000	1B-8
1971	122	.280	.447	421	118	20	4	14	3.3	61	58	38	33	1	8	2	795	61	2	67	7.0	.998	1B-108, OF-11
1972	122	.269	.394	327	88	15	1	8	2.4	28	34	34	35	1	16	4	705	48	3	65	6.2	.996	1B-108, OF-1
1973	100	.239	.306	284	68	12	2	1	0.4	28	35	30	28	1	16	2	448	28	2	39	4.8	.996	1B-51, OF-32
1974	94	.300	.415	217	65	11	1	4	1.8	20	24	18	14	1	35	17	207	9	5	18	2.4	.977	OF-33, 1B-24
1975	106	.323	.409	325	105	16	0	4	1.2	42	43	27	21	1	20	8	671	46	2	51	6.8	.997	1B-82, OF-4
1976	123	.292	.410	415	121	17	1	10	2.4	47	49	35	38	1	10	4	721	35	3	48	6.2	.996	1B-86, OF-31
1977	108	.281	.448	281	79	17	0	10	3.6	40	40	23	20	1	29	13	347	30	4	21	3.5	.990	OF-42, 1B-41
1978	66	.210	.346	81	17	2	0	3	3.7	7	19	8	12	0	50	15	36	4	0	3	0.6	1.000	OF-12, 1B-3
1979	82	.232	.303	155	36	5	0	2	1.3	7	17	13	18	0	37	6	215	19	0	18	2.9	1.000	1B-29, OF-8
18 yrs.	1853	.261	.377	5436	1418	225	25	118	2.2	536	614	454	581	15	325	90	10840	789	81	901	6.3	.993	1B-1304, OF-250

LEAGUE CHAMPIONSHIP SERIES

Year Team	Games	BA	SA	AB	H	2B	3B	HR	HR%	R	RBI	BB	SO	SB	PH AB	PH H	PO	A	E	DP	TC/G	FA	G by Pos
1969 NY N	3	.250	.333	12	3	1	0	0	0.0	2	1	1	1	0	0	0	20	3	0	2	7.7	1.000	1B-3
1973	1	.500	.500	2	1	0	0	0	0.0	0	2	0	0	0	0	0	2	0	0	0	2.0	1.000	OF-1
2 yrs.	4	.286	.357	14	4	1	0	0	0.0	2	3	1	2	0	0	0	22	3	0	2	6.3	1.000	1B-3, OF-1

WORLD SERIES

Year Team	Games	BA	SA	AB	H	2B	3B	HR	HR%	R	RBI	BB	SO	SB	PH AB	PH H	PO	A	E	DP	TC/G	FA	G by Pos
1969 NY N	1	.250	1.000	4	1	0	0	1	25.0	1	1	0	0	0	0	0	7	0	0	0	7.0	1.000	1B-1
1973	4	.000	.000	3	0	0	0	0	0.0	0	0	0	3	0	3	0	0	0	0	0	—		1B-1
2 yrs.	5	.143	.571	7	1	0	0	1	14.3	1	1	0	3	0	3	0	7	0	0	0	1.4	1.000	1B-1

Charlie Krause

KRAUSE, CHARLES
Also appeared in box score as Krouse
B. Oct. 2, 1873, Detroit, Mich. D. Mar. 30, 1948, Eloise, Mich.
TR

Year Team	Games	BA	SA	AB	H	2B	3B	HR	HR%	R	RBI	BB	SO	SB	PH AB	PH H	PO	A	E	DP	TC/G	FA	G by Pos
1901 CIN N	1	.250	.250	4	1	0	0	0	0.0	0	0	0		0	0	0	1	2	2	0	5.0	.600	2B-1

Danny Kravitz

KRAVITZ, DANIEL (Dusty, Beak)
B. Dec. 21, 1930, Lopez, Pa.
BL TR 5'11" 195 lbs.

Year Team	Games	BA	SA	AB	H	2B	3B	HR	HR%	R	RBI	BB	SO	SB	PH AB	PH H	PO	A	E	DP	TC/G	FA	G by Pos
1956 PIT N	32	.265	.441	68	18	2	2	2	2.9	6	10	5	9	1	12	0	93	10	6	2	3.4	.945	C-26, 3B-2
1957	19	.146	.171	41	6	1	0	0	0.0	2	4	2	10	0	9	1	45	9	0	1	2.8	1.000	C-15
1958	45	.240	.340	100	24	3	2	1	1.0	9	5	11	10	0	8	1	103	16	4	3	2.7	.967	C-37
1959	52	.253	.377	162	41	9	1	3	1.9	18	21	5	14	0	8	3	198	19	3	3	4.2	.986	C-45
1960 2 teams						PIT N	(8G – .000)			KC A	(59G – .234)												
" total	67	.227	.354	181	41	7	2	4	2.2	17	14	12	21	0	18	4	217	16	7	3	3.6	.971	C-48
5 yrs.	215	.236	.355	552	130	22	7	10	1.8	52	54	35	64	1	55	8	656	70	20	12	3.5	.973	C-171, 3B-2

Mike Kreevich

KREEVICH, MICHAEL ANDREAS
B. June 10, 1908, Mount Olive, Ill.
BR TR 5'7½" 168 lbs.

Year Team	Games	BA	SA	AB	H	2B	3B	HR	HR%	R	RBI	BB	SO	SB	PH AB	PH H	PO	A	E	DP	TC/G	FA	G by Pos
1931 CHI N	5	.167	.167	12	2	0	0	0	0.0	0	0	0	6	1	1	0	5	1	0	0	1.2	1.000	OF-4
1935 CHI A	6	.435	.522	23	10	2	0	0	0.0	3	2	1	0	1	0	0	8	4	0	0	2.0	1.000	3B-6
1936	137	.307	.433	550	169	32	11	5	0.9	99	69	61	46	10	3	2	300	17	12	5	2.4	.964	OF-133
1937	144	.302	.468	583	176	29	16	12	2.1	94	73	43	45	10	3	1	401	13	5	4	2.9	.988	OF-138
1938	129	.297	.436	489	145	26	12	6	1.2	73	73	55	23	13	3	0	379	7	10	2	3.1	.975	OF-127
1939	145	.323	.436	541	175	30	8	5	0.9	85	77	59	40	23	3	0	425	26	12	4	3.2	.974	OF-139, 3B-4
1940	144	.265	.387	582	154	27	10	8	1.4	86	55	34	49	0	3	0	428	12	8	3	3.1	.982	OF-144
1941	121	.232	.305	436	101	16	8	0	0.0	44	37	35	26	17	7	4	302	7	2	2	2.6	.994	OF-113
1942 PHI A	116	.255	.309	444	113	19	1	0	0.2	57	30	47	31	7	6	2	314	4	6	0	2.8	.981	OF-107
1943 STL A	60	.255	.292	161	41	6	0	0	0.0	24	10	26	13	4	7	1	146	5	1	1	2.5	.993	OF-51
1944	105	.301	.405	402	121	15	6	5	1.2	55	44	27	24	3	5	0	282	4	4	0	2.8	.986	OF-100
1945 2 teams				STL A	(81G – .237)			WAS A	(45G – .278)														
" total	126	.252	.327	453	114	19	3	3	0.7	56	44	58	38	11	7	2	328	6	5	0	2.7	.985	OF-118
12 yrs.	1238	.283	.391	4676	1321	221	75	45	1.0	676	514	446	341	115	45	12	3318	106	65	21	2.8	.981	OF-1174, 3B-10

WORLD SERIES

Year Team	Games	BA	SA	AB	H	2B	3B	HR	HR%	R	RBI	BB	SO	SB	PH AB	PH H	PO	A	E	DP	TC/G	FA	G by Pos
1944 STL A	6	.231	.346	26	6	3	0	0	0.0	0	0	0	5	0	0	0	20	2	0	0	3.7	1.000	OF-6

Charlie Krehmeyer

KREHMEYER, CHARLES L.
B. July 5, 1863, St. Louis, Mo. D. Feb. 10, 1926, St. Louis, Mo.
BL TL

Year Team	Games	BA	SA	AB	H	2B	3B	HR	HR%	R	RBI	BB	SO	SB	PH AB	PH H	PO	A	E	DP	TC/G	FA	G by Pos
1884 STL AA	21	.229	.257	70	16	0	1	0	0.0	3		2			0	0	56	7	12	1	3.6	.840	OF-15, C-7, 1B-1
1885 2 teams				LOU AA	(7G – .226)			STL N	(1G – .000)														
" total	8	.206	.294	34	7	1	1	0	0.0	4		1	2		0	0	32	8	11	0	6.4	.784	C-5, OF-2, 1B-1
2 yrs.	29	.221	.269	104	23	1	2	0	0.0	7		3	2		0	0	88	15	23	1	4.3	.817	OF-17, C-12, 1B-2

Year	Team	Games	BA	SA	AB	H	2B	3B	HR	HR%	R	RBI	BB	SO	SB	Pinch Hit AB	H	PO	A	E	DP	TC/G	FA	G by Pos

Ralph Kreitz

KREITZ, RALPH WESLEY (Red)
B. Nov. 13, 1885, Plum Creek, Neb.   D. July 20, 1941, Portland, Ore.   BR TR 5'9½" 175 lbs.

Year	Team	Games	BA	SA	AB	H	2B	3B	HR	HR%	R	RBI	BB	SO	SB	PH AB	PH H	PO	A	E	DP	TC/G	FA	G by Pos
1911	CHI A	7	.235	.294	17	4	1	0	0	0.0	0	0	2		0	0	0	24	4	0	1	4.0	1.000	C-7

Wayne Krenchicki

KRENCHICKI, WAYNE RICHARD
B. Sept. 17, 1954, Trenton, N. J.   BL TR 6'1" 180 lbs.

Year	Team	Games	BA	SA	AB	H	2B	3B	HR	HR%	R	RBI	BB	SO	SB	PH AB	PH H	PO	A	E	DP	TC/G	FA	G by Pos
1979	BAL A	16	.190	.238	21	4	1	0	0	0.0	1	0	0	0	0	0	0	12	12	2	1	1.6	.923	SS-7, 2B-6
1980		9	.143	.143	14	2	0	0	0	0.0	1	0	1	3	0	1	0	9	9	0	2	2.0	1.000	SS-6, DH-1, 2B-1
1981		33	.214	.286	56	12	4	0	0	0.0	7	6	4	9	0	1	0	23	56	3	12	2.5	.963	SS-16, 2B-7, 3B-6, DH-1
1982	CIN N	94	.283	.358	187	53	6	1	2	1.1	19	21	13	23	5	28	7	40	103	6	10	1.6	.960	3B-70, 2B-9
1983	2 teams	CIN	N (51G – .273)		DET	A	(59G – .278)																	
"	total	110	.276	.333	210	58	9	0	1	0.5	24	27	19	31	0	18	2	50	116	9	14	1.6	.949	3B-87, 2B-7, SS-6, 1B-3
1984	CIN N	97	.298	.470	181	54	9	2	6	3.3	18	22	19	23	0	36	7	35	92	5	6	1.4	.962	3B-62, 2B-3, 1B-3
1985		90	.272	.393	173	47	9	0	4	2.3	16	25	28	20	0	32	5	35	87	4	9	1.4	.968	3B-52, 2B-3
1986	MON N	101	.240	.312	221	53	6	2	2	0.9	21	23	22	32	2	31	7	325	59	6	26	3.9	.985	1B-41, 3B-24, OF-1, 2B-1
8 yrs.		550	.266	.359	1063	283	44	5	15	1.4	107	124	106	141	7	147	28	529	534	35	80	2.0	.968	3B-301, 1B-47, 2B-37, SS-35, DH-2, OF-1

Charlie Kress

KRESS, CHARLES STEVEN (Chuck)
B. Dec. 9, 1921, Philadelphia, Pa.   BL TL 6' 190 lbs.

Year	Team	Games	BA	SA	AB	H	2B	3B	HR	HR%	R	RBI	BB	SO	SB	PH AB	PH H	PO	A	E	DP	TC/G	FA	G by Pos
1947	CIN N	11	.148	.148	27	4	0	0	0	0.0	4	0	6	4	0	2	1	52	5	1	5	5.5	.983	1B-8
1949	2 teams	CIN	N (27G – .207)		CHI	A	(97G – .278)																	
"	total	124	.272	.364	382	104	20	6	1	0.3	48	47	42	49	6	11	3	979	70	8	109	8.5	.992	1B-111
1950	CHI A	3	.000	.000	8	0	0	0	0	0.0	0	0	1	3	0	1	0	19	1	0	2	6.7	1.000	1B-2
1954	2 teams	DET	A (24G – .189)		BKN	N	(13G – .083)																	
"	total	37	.163	.204	49	8	0	1	0	0.0	5	5	1	4	0	27	4	64	5	3	5	1.9	.958	1B-8, OF-1
4 yrs.		175	.249	.328	466	116	20	7	1	0.2	57	52	49	59	6	41	7	1114	83	12	121	6.9	.990	1B-129, OF-1

Red Kress

KRESS, RALPH
B. Jan. 2, 1907, Columbia, Calif.   D. Nov. 29, 1962, Los Angeles, Calif.   BR TR 5'11½" 165 lbs.

Year	Team	Games	BA	SA	AB	H	2B	3B	HR	HR%	R	RBI	BB	SO	SB	PH AB	PH H	PO	A	E	DP	TC/G	FA	G by Pos
1927	STL A	7	.304	.609	23	7	2	1	1	4.3	3	3	3	3	0	0	0	12	25	1	4	5.4	.974	SS-7
1928		150	.273	.371	560	153	26	10	3	0.5	78	81	48	70	5	0	0	318	400	55	99	5.2	.929	SS-150
1929		147	.305	.436	557	170	38	4	9	1.6	82	107	52	54	5	1	0	312	441	43	94	5.4	.946	SS-146
1930		154	.313	.487	614	192	43	8	16	2.6	94	112	50	56	3	0	0	306	406	51	87	5.0	.933	SS-123, 3B-31
1931		150	.311	.493	605	188	46	8	16	2.6	87	114	46	48	3	1	0	305	206	31	28	3.6	.943	3B-84, OF-40, SS-38, 1B-10
1932	2 teams	STL	A (14G – .173)		CHI	A	(135G – .285)																	
"	total	149	.275	.425	567	156	42	5	11	1.9	85	66	51	42	7	0	0	304	228	37	46	3.8	.935	OF-64, SS-53, 3B-33
1933	CHI A	129	.248	.377	467	116	20	5	10	2.1	47	78	37	40	4	12	6	1185	60	29	83	9.9	.977	1B-111, OF-8
1934	2 teams	CHI	A (8G – .286)		WAS	A	(56G – .228)																	
"	total	64	.232	.351	185	43	4	3	4	2.2	21	25	20	22	3	9	2	333	35	2	21	5.8	.995	1B-30, OF-10, 2B-9, SS-1, 3B-1
1935	WAS A	84	.298	.405	252	75	13	4	2	0.8	32	42	25	16	3	18	4	157	211	14	61	4.5	.963	SS-53, 1B-5, P-3, OF-2, 2B-1
1936		109	.284	.427	391	111	20	6	8	2.0	51	51	39	25	6	5	0	266	315	30	75	5.6	.951	SS-64, 2B-33, 1B-5
1938	STL A	150	.302	.408	566	171	33	3	7	1.2	74	79	69	47	5	1	1	321	388	26	100	4.9	.965	SS-150
1939	2 teams	STL	A (13G – .279)		DET	A	(51G – .242)																	
"	total	64	.250	.305	200	50	8	0	1	0.5	24	24	23	18	3	6	4	111	152	16	39	4.4	.943	SS-38, 2B-16, 3B-4
1940	DET A	33	.222	.303	99	22	3	1	1	1.0	13	11	10	12	0	5	3	45	74	8	6	3.8	.937	3B-17, SS-12
1946	NY N	1	.000	.000	1	0	0	0	0	0.0	0	0	0	0	0	0	0	3	0	0	0	5.0	1.000	P-1
14 yrs.		1391	.286	.420	5087	1454	298	58	89	1.7	691	799	474	453	47	58	20	3977	2944	343	743	5.2	.953	SS-835, 3B-170, 1B-161, OF-124, 2B-59, P-4

Chad Kreuter

KREUTER, CHAD MICHAEL
B. Aug. 26, 1964, Greenbrae, Calif.   BB TR 6'2" 190 lbs.

Year	Team	Games	BA	SA	AB	H	2B	3B	HR	HR%	R	RBI	BB	SO	SB	PH AB	PH H	PO	A	E	DP	TC/G	FA	G by Pos
1988	TEX A	16	.275	.412	51	14	2	1	1	2.0	3	5	7	13	0	0	0	93	8	1	0	6.4	.990	C-16
1989		87	.152	.266	158	24	3	0	5	3.2	16	9	27	40	0	1	0	453	26	4	4	5.6	.992	C-85
2 yrs.		103	.182	.301	209	38	5	1	6	2.9	19	14	34	53	0	1	0	546	34	5	4	5.7	.991	C-101

Paul Krichell

KRICHELL, PAUL BERNARD
B. Dec. 19, 1882, New York, N. Y.   D. June 4, 1957, New York, N. Y.   BR TR 5'7" 150 lbs.

Year	Team	Games	BA	SA	AB	H	2B	3B	HR	HR%	R	RBI	BB	SO	SB	PH AB	PH H	PO	A	E	DP	TC/G	FA	G by Pos
1911	STL A	28	.232	.268	82	19	3	0	0	0.0	6	8	4		2	3	0	80	36	7	2	4.4	.943	C-25
1912		57	.217	.255	161	35	6	0	0	0.0	19	8	19		2	0	0	255	72	14	9	6.0	.959	C-57
2 yrs.		85	.222	.259	243	54	9	0	0	0.0	25	16	23		4	3	0	335	108	21	11	5.5	.955	C-82

Bill Krieg

KRIEG, WILLIAM FREDERICK
B. Jan. 29, 1859, Petersburg, Ill.   D. Mar. 25, 1930, Chillicothe, Ill.   BR TR 5'8" 180 lbs.

Year	Team	Games	BA	SA	AB	H	2B	3B	HR	HR%	R	RBI	BB	SO	SB	PH AB	PH H	PO	A	E	DP	TC/G	FA	G by Pos
1884	2 teams	CHI	U (61G – .229)		PIT	U	(10G – .359)																	
"	total	71	.247	.330	279	69	15	4	0	0.0	35		11			0	0	471	117	57	4	9.1	.912	C-52, OF-20, SS-1, 1B-1
1885	2 teams	CHI	N (1G – .000)		BKN	AA	(17G – .150)																	
"	total	18	.143	.254	63	9	4	0	1	1.6	7		2	2		0	0	100	18	12	3	7.2	.908	C-12, 1B-5, OF-1
1886	WAS N	27	.255	.408	98	25	6	3	1	1.0	13	15	3	12		0	0	227	5	6	7	8.8	.975	1B-27
1887		25	.253	.379	95	24	4	1	2	2.1	9	17	7	5	2	0	0	148	5	5	5	6.3	.968	1B-16, OF-9
4 yrs.		141	.237	.344	535	127	29	8	4	0.7	62	32	23	19	2	0	0	946	145	80	19	8.3	.932	C-64, 1B-49, OF-30, SS-1

Mickey Krietner

KRIETNER, ALBERT JOSEPH
B. Oct. 10, 1922, Nashville, Tenn.   BR TR 6'3" 190 lbs.

Year	Team	Games	BA	SA	AB	H	2B	3B	HR	HR%	R	RBI	BB	SO	SB	PH AB	PH H	PO	A	E	DP	TC/G	FA	G by Pos
1943	CHI N	3	.375	.375	8	3	0	0	0	0.0	0	2	1	2	0	0	0	8	1	0	0	3.0	1.000	C-3
1944		39	.153	.176	85	13	2	0	0	0.0	3	3	8	16	0	0	0	104	13	1	3	3.0	.992	C-39
2 yrs.		42	.172	.194	93	16	2	0	0	0.0	3	5	9	18	0	0	0	112	14	1	3	3.0	.992	C-42

John Kroner

KRONER, JOHN HAROLD
B. Nov. 13, 1908, St. Louis, Mo.   D. Apr. 26, 1968, St. Louis, Mo.   BR TR 6' 165 lbs.

Year	Team		Games	BA	SA	AB	H	2B	3B	HR	HR%	R	RBI	BB	SO	SB	Pinch Hit AB	H	PO	A	E	DP	TC/G	FA	G by Pos

John Kroner *continued*

Year	Team		Games	BA	SA	AB	H	2B	3B	HR	HR%	R	RBI	BB	SO	SB	AB	H	PO	A	E	DP	TC/G	FA	G by Pos
1935	BOS	A	2	.250	.250	4	1	0	0	0	0.0	4	0	1	1	0	0	0	0	1	0	0	0.5	1.000	3B-2
1936			84	.292	.443	298	87	17	8	4	1.3	40	62	26	24	2	1	0	146	211	18	36	4.5	.952	2B-38, 3B-28, SS-18, OF-1
1937	CLE	A	86	.237	.314	283	67	14	1	2	0.7	29	26	22	25	1	9	2	157	203	14	46	4.3	.963	2B-64, 3B-11
1938			51	.248	.410	117	29	16	0	1	0.9	13	17	19	6	0	7	1	107	91	7	25	4.0	.966	2B-31, 1B-7, 3B-3, SS-1
4 yrs.			223	.262	.385	702	184	47	9	7	1.0	83	105	68	56	3	17	3	410	506	39	107	4.3	.959	2B-133, 3B-44, SS-19, 1B-7, OF-1

Mike Krsnich

KRSNICH, MICHAEL
Brother of Rocky Krsnich.
B. Sept. 24, 1931, West Allis, Wis.

BR TR 6'1" 190 lbs.

Year	Team		Games	BA	SA	AB	H	2B	3B	HR	HR%	R	RBI	BB	SO	SB	AB	H	PO	A	E	DP	TC/G	FA	G by Pos
1960	MIL	N	4	.333	.444	9	3	1	0	0	0.0	0	0	0	0	0	2	1	5	0	0	0	1.3	1.000	OF-3
1962			11	.083	.167	12	1	1	0	0	0.0	0	2	0	4	0	6	1	2	1	0	1	0.3	1.000	OF-3, 3B-1, 1B-1
2 yrs.			15	.190	.286	21	4	2	0	0	0.0	0	4	0	4	0	8	2	7	1	0	1	0.5	1.000	OF-6, 3B-1, 1B-1

Rocky Krsnich

KRSNICH, ROCCO PETER
Brother of Mike Krsnich.
B. Aug. 5, 1927, West Allis, Wis.

BR TR 6'1" 174 lbs.

Year	Team		Games	BA	SA	AB	H	2B	3B	HR	HR%	R	RBI	BB	SO	SB	AB	H	PO	A	E	DP	TC/G	FA	G by Pos
1949	CHI	A	16	.218	.364	55	12	3	1	1	1.8	7	9	6	4	0	0	0	18	40	4	4	3.9	.935	2B-16
1952			40	.231	.385	91	21	7	2	1	1.1	11	15	12	9	0	2	0	45	72	5	6	3.1	.959	3B-37
1953			64	.202	.287	129	26	8	0	1	0.8	9	14	12	11	0	6	1	31	100	10	7	2.2	.929	3B-57
3 yrs.			120	.215	.335	275	59	18	3	3	1.1	27	38	30	24	0	8	1	94	212	19	17	2.7	.942	3B-94, 2B-16

Ernie Krueger

KRUEGER, ERNEST GEORGE
B. Dec. 27, 1890, Chicago, Ill. D. Apr. 22, 1976, Waukegan, Ill.

BR TR 5'10½" 185 lbs.

Year	Team		Games	BA	SA	AB	H	2B	3B	HR	HR%	R	RBI	BB	SO	SB	AB	H	PO	A	E	DP	TC/G	FA	G by Pos
1913	CLE	A	5	.000	.000	6	0	0	0	0	0.0	0	0	0	2	0	1	0	4	3	0	0	1.4	1.000	C-4
1915	NY	A	10	.172	.207	29	5	1	0	0	0.0	3	0	0	5	0	2	0	30	8	4	1	4.2	.905	C-8
1917	2 teams			NY	N (8G – .000)		BKN	N	(31G – .272)																
"	total		39	.242	.341	91	22	2	2	1	1.1	10	6	5	6	1	9	1	121	25	4	4	3.8	.973	C-29
1918	BKN	N	30	.287	.379	87	25	4	2	0	0.0	4	7	4	9	2	7	2	104	38	2	3	4.8	.986	C-23
1919			80	.248	.381	226	56	7	4	5	2.2	24	36	19	25	4	10	2	305	88	15	4	5.1	.963	C-66
1920			52	.288	.363	146	42	4	2	1	0.7	21	17	16	13	2	5	1	165	46	9	4	4.2	.959	C-46
1921			65	.264	.436	163	43	11	4	3	1.8	18	20	14	12	2	14	3	179	39	7	4	3.5	.969	C-52
1925	CIN	N	37	.307	.386	88	27	4	0	1	1.1	7	7	6	8	1	6	0	75	12	5	3	2.5	.946	C-30
8 yrs.			318	.263	.376	836	220	33	14	11	1.3	87	93	64	85	12	54	9	983	259	46	21	4.1	.964	C-258

WORLD SERIES

Year	Team		Games	BA	SA	AB	H	2B	3B	HR	HR%	R	RBI	BB	SO	SB	AB	H	PO	A	E	DP	TC/G	FA	G by Pos
1920	BKN	N	4	.167	.167	6	1	0	0	0	0.0	0	0	0	0	0	1	0	10	2	0	1	3.0	1.000	C-3

Otto Krueger

KRUEGER, ARTHUR WILLIAM (Oom Paul)
B. Sept. 17, 1876, Chicago, Ill. D. Feb. 20, 1961, St. Louis, Mo.

BR TR 5'7" 165 lbs.

Year	Team		Games	BA	SA	AB	H	2B	3B	HR	HR%	R	RBI	BB	SO	SB	AB	H	PO	A	E	DP	TC/G	FA	G by Pos
1899	CLE	N	13	.227	.250	44	10	1	0	0	0.0	4	2	8		1	0	0	22	27	10	4	4.5	.831	3B-9, SS-2, 2B-2
1900	STL	N	12	.400	.686	35	14	3	2	1	2.9	8	3	10		0	0	0	20	26	8	2	4.5	.852	2B-12
1901			142	.275	.363	520	143	16	12	2	0.4	77	79	50		19	0	0	171	275	60	11	3.6	.881	3B-142
1902			128	.266	.315	467	124	7	8	0	0.0	55	46	29		14	3	0	206	426	75	48	5.4	.894	SS-107, 3B-18
1903	PIT	N	80	.246	.344	256	63	6	6	1	0.4	42	28	21		5	4	1	109	113	20	17	3.0	.917	SS-29, OF-28, 3B-13, 2B-3
1904			86	.194	.243	268	52	6	1	1	0.4	34	26	29		8	8	1	115	117	23	10	3.0	.910	OF-33, SS-32, 3B-10
1905	PHI	N	46	.184	.211	114	21	1	1	0	0.0	10	12	13		1	16	3	44	66	8	10	2.6	.932	SS-23, OF-6, 3B-1
7 yrs.			507	.251	.322	1704	427	40	33	4	0.3	230	196	160		48	31	5	687	1050	204	102	3.8	.895	SS-193, 3B-193, OF-67, 2B-17

Chris Krug

KRUG, EVERETT BEN
B. Dec. 25, 1939, Los Angeles, Calif.

BR TR 6'4" 200 lbs.

Year	Team		Games	BA	SA	AB	H	2B	3B	HR	HR%	R	RBI	BB	SO	SB	AB	H	PO	A	E	DP	TC/G	FA	G by Pos
1965	CHI	N	60	.201	.320	169	34	5	0	5	3.0	16	24	13	52	0	3	0	273	27	6	5	5.1	.980	C-58
1966			11	.214	.250	28	6	1	0	0	0.0	1	1	1	8	0	1	0	55	5	0	2	5.5	1.000	C-10
1969	SD	N	8	.059	.059	17	1	0	0	0	0.0	0	0	1	6	0	1	0	28	2	2	0	4.0	.938	C-7
3 yrs.			79	.192	.290	214	41	6	0	5	2.3	17	25	15	66	0	5	0	356	34	8	7	5.0	.980	C-75

Gary Krug

KRUG, GARY EUGENE
B. Feb. 12, 1955, Garden City, Kans.

BL TL 6'4" 225 lbs.

Year	Team		Games	BA	SA	AB	H	2B	3B	HR	HR%	R	RBI	BB	SO	SB	AB	H	PO	A	E	DP	TC/G	FA	G by Pos
1981	CHI	N	7	.400	.400	5	2	0	0	0	0.0	1	1	0	5	2	0	0	0	0	0	0.0	–	P-7

Henry Krug

KRUG, HENRY CHARLES
B. Dec. 4, 1876, San Francisco, Calif. D. Jan. 14, 1908, San Francisco, Calif.

BR TR

Year	Team		Games	BA	SA	AB	H	2B	3B	HR	HR%	R	RBI	BB	SO	SB	AB	H	PO	A	E	DP	TC/G	FA	G by Pos
1902	PHI	N	53	.227	.273	198	45	3	3	0	0.0	20	14	7		2	0	0	116	62	12	10	3.6	.937	OF-28, 2B-13, SS-9, 3B-6

Marty Krug

KRUG, MARTIN JOHN
B. Sept. 10, 1888, Koblenz, Germany D. June 27, 1966, Glendale, Calif.

BR TR 5'9" 165 lbs.

Year	Team		Games	BA	SA	AB	H	2B	3B	HR	HR%	R	RBI	BB	SO	SB	AB	H	PO	A	E	DP	TC/G	FA	G by Pos
1912	BOS	A	16	.308	.410	39	12	2	1	0	0.0	6	7	5		2	2	0	19	26	5	4	3.1	.900	SS-9, 2B-4
1922	CHI	N	127	.276	.371	450	124	23	4	4	0.9	67	60	43	43	7	0	0	174	255	32	30	3.6	.931	3B-104, 2B-23, SS-1
2 yrs.			143	.278	.374	489	136	25	5	4	0.8	73	67	48	43	9	2	0	193	281	37	34	3.6	.928	3B-104, 2B-27, SS-10

Art Kruger

KRUGER, ARTHUR T.
B. Mar. 16, 1881, San Antonio, Tex. D. Nov. 28, 1949, Hondo, Calif.

BR TR 6' 185 lbs.

Year	Team		Games	BA	SA	AB	H	2B	3B	HR	HR%	R	RBI	BB	SO	SB	AB	H	PO	A	E	DP	TC/G	FA	G by Pos
1907	CIN	N	100	.233	.322	317	74	10	9	0	0.0	25	28	18		10	4	0	199	11	6	3	2.2	.972	OF-96
1910	2 teams			CLE	A	(62G – .170)		BOS	N	(1G – .000)															
"	total		63	.170	.223	224	38	6	3	0	0.0	19	14	20		12	5	0	116	10	6	3	2.1	.955	OF-62
1914	KC	F	122	.259	.372	441	114	24	7	4	0.9	45	47	23		11	2	0	249	14	10	1	2.2	.963	OF-120
1915			80	.238	.317	240	57	9	2	2	0.8	24	26	12		5	14	4	116	8	2	2	1.6	.984	OF-66
4 yrs.			365	.232	.321	1222	283	49	21	6	0.5	113	115	73		38	21	4	680	43	24	9	2.0	.968	OF-344

Year	Team	Games	BA	SA	AB	H	2B	3B	HR	HR%	R	RBI	BB	SO	SB	Pinch Hit AB	Pinch Hit H	PO	A	E	DP	TC/G	FA	G by Pos

John Kruk

KRUK, JOHN MARTIN
B. Feb. 9, 1961, Charleston, W. Va.   BL TL 5'10''   170 lbs.

Year	Team	Games	BA	SA	AB	H	2B	3B	HR	HR%	R	RBI	BB	SO	SB	PH AB	PH H	PO	A	E	DP	TC/G	FA	G by Pos
1986	SD N	122	.309	.424	278	86	16	2	4	1.4	33	38	45	58	2	32	8	139	6	3	3	1.2	.980	OF-74, 1B-9
1987		138	.313	.488	447	140	14	2	20	4.5	72	91	73	93	18	12	6	911	78	5	74	7.2	.995	1B-101, OF-29
1988		120	.241	.362	378	91	17	1	9	2.4	54	44	80	68	5	7	2	634	37	3	45	5.6	.996	1B-63, OF-55
1989	2 teams		SD N (31G – .184)		PHI N (81G – .331)																			
"	total	112	.300	.437	357	107	13	6	8	2.2	53	44	44	53	3	8	1	212	9	4	4	2.0	.982	OF-99, 1B-7
4 yrs.		492	.290	.431	1460	424	60	11	41	2.8	212	217	242	272	28	59	17	1896	130	15	126	4.1	.993	OF-257, 1B-180

Dick Kryhoski

KRYHOSKI, RICHARD DAVID
B. Mar. 24, 1925, Leonia, N. J.   BL TL 6'2''   182 lbs.

Year	Team	Games	BA	SA	AB	H	2B	3B	HR	HR%	R	RBI	BB	SO	SB	PH AB	PH H	PO	A	E	DP	TC/G	FA	G by Pos
1949	NY A	54	.294	.401	177	52	10	3	1	0.6	18	27	9	17	2	2	0	363	31	7	39	7.4	.983	1B-51
1950	DET A	53	.219	.349	169	37	10	0	4	2.4	20	19	8	11	0	5	2	409	27	4	44	8.3	.991	1B-47
1951		119	.287	.437	421	121	19	4	12	2.9	58	57	28	29	1	10	4	964	81	9	95	8.9	.991	1B-112
1952	STL A	111	.243	.383	342	83	13	1	11	3.2	38	42	23	42	2	25	4	680	49	8	80	6.6	.989	1B-86
1953		104	.278	.497	338	94	18	4	16	4.7	35	50	26	33	0	19	4	685	66	6	7	7.3	.992	1B-88
1954	BAL A	100	.260	.327	300	78	13	2	1	0.3	32	34	19	24	0	23	3	591	52	5	52	6.5	.992	1B-69
1955	KC A	28	.213	.255	47	10	2	0	0	0.0	2	2	6	7	0	13	1	76	6	1	7	3.0	.988	1B-14
7 yrs.		569	.265	.403	1794	475	85	14	45	2.5	203	231	119	163	5	97	24	3768	312	40	324	7.2	.990	1B-467

Tony Kubek

KUBEK, ANTHONY CHRISTOPHER
B. Oct. 12, 1936, Milwaukee, Wis.   BL TR 6'3''   190 lbs.

Year	Team	Games	BA	SA	AB	H	2B	3B	HR	HR%	R	RBI	BB	SO	SB	PH AB	PH H	PO	A	E	DP	TC/G	FA	G by Pos
1957	NY A	127	.297	.381	431	128	21	3	3	0.7	56	39	24	48	6	8	1	189	183	20	33	3.1	.949	OF-50, SS-41, 3B-38, 2B-1
1958		138	.265	.317	559	148	21	1	2	0.4	66	48	25	57	5	1	0	249	453	28	98	5.3	.962	SS-134, OF-3, 2B-1, 1B-1
1959		132	.279	.391	512	143	25	7	6	1.2	67	51	24	46	3	4	1	219	256	15	49	3.7	.969	SS-67, OF-53, 3B-17, 2B-1
1960		147	.273	.401	568	155	25	3	14	2.5	77	62	31	42	3	6	2	251	444	22	84	4.9	.969	SS-136, OF-29
1961		153	.276	.395	617	170	38	6	8	1.3	84	46	27	60	1	8	2	261	449	30	107	4.8	.959	SS-145
1962		45	.314	.432	169	53	6	1	4	2.4	28	17	12	17	2	2	1	88	117	9	27	4.8	.958	SS-35, OF-6
1963		135	.257	.343	557	143	21	3	7	1.3	72	44	28	68	4	1	1	227	403	13	80	4.8	.980	SS-132, OF-1
1964		106	.229	.340	415	95	16	3	8	1.9	46	31	26	55	4	2	0	186	307	11	52	4.8	.978	SS-99
1965		109	.218	.295	339	74	5	3	5	1.5	26	35	20	48	1	12	4	138	190	14	53	3.6	.964	SS-93, OF-3, 1B-1
9 yrs.		1092	.266	.364	4167	1109	178	30	57	1.4	522	373	217	441	29	44	12	1808	2850	162	583	4.4	.966	SS-882, OF-145, 3B-55, 2B-3, 1B-2

WORLD SERIES

Year	Team	Games	BA	SA	AB	H	2B	3B	HR	HR%	R	RBI	BB	SO	SB	PH AB	PH H	PO	A	E	DP	TC/G	FA	G by Pos
1957	NY A	7	.286	.500	28	8	0	0	2	7.1	4	4	0	4	0	0	0	17	5	2	0	3.4	.917	OF-5, 3B-2
1958		7	.048	.048	21	1	0	0	0	0.0	0	1	1	7	0	0	0	9	15	2	2	3.7	.923	SS-7
1960		7	.333	.367	30	10	1	0	0	0.0	6	3	2	2	0	0	0	10	21	3	4	4.9	.912	SS-7, OF-2
1961		5	.227	.227	22	5	0	0	0	0.0	3	1	1	4	0	0	0	5	11	0	1	3.2	1.000	SS-5
1962		7	.276	.310	29	8	1	0	0	0.0	2	1	1	3	0	0	0	12	17	1	3	4.3	.967	SS-7
1963		4	.188	.188	16	3	0	0	0	0.0	1	0	0	3	0	0	0	5	13	0	5	4.5	1.000	SS-4
6 yrs.		37	.240	.295	146	35	2	0	2	1.4	16	10	5	23	0	0	0	58	82	8	15	4.0	.946	SS-30, OF-7, 3B-2

10th

Ted Kubiak

KUBIAK, THEODORE RODGER
B. May 12, 1942, New Brunswick, N. J.   BL TR 6'   175 lbs.
BB 1968

Year	Team	Games	BA	SA	AB	H	2B	3B	HR	HR%	R	RBI	BB	SO	SB	PH AB	PH H	PO	A	E	DP	TC/G	FA	G by Pos
1967	KC A	53	.157	.196	102	16	2	1	0	0.0	6	5	12	20	0	15	2	37	58	3	7	1.8	.969	SS-20, 2B-10, 3B-5
1968	OAK A	48	.250	.325	120	30	5	2	0	0.0	10	8	8	18	1	13	2	60	78	11	13	3.1	.926	2B-24, SS-12
1969		92	.249	.305	305	76	9	1	2	0.7	38	27	25	35	2	14	3	153	215	10	41	4.1	.974	SS-42, 2B-33
1970	MIL A	158	.252	.313	540	136	9	6	4	0.7	63	41	72	51	4	0	0	361	412	19	98	5.0	.976	2B-91, SS-73
1971	2 teams		MIL A (89G – .227)		STL N (32G – .250)																			
"	total	121	.232	.337	332	77	9	7	4	1.2	34	27	52	43	1	12	2	220	278	18	52	4.3	.965	2B-62, SS-56
1972	2 teams		TEX A (46G – .224)		OAK A (51G – .181)																			
"	total	97	.205	.248	210	43	7	1	0	0.0	19	15	21	23	0	9	1	76	77	2	17	1.6	.987	2B-74, SS-15, 3B-2
1973	OAK A	106	.220	.313	182	40	6	1	3	1.6	15	17	12	19	1	4	1	117	186	8	41	2.9	.974	2B-83, SS-26, 3B-2
1974		99	.209	.223	220	46	3	0	0	0.0	22	18	18	15	1	4	0	129	175	6	38	3.1	.981	2B-71, SS-19, 3B-14, DH-2
1975	2 teams		OAK A (20G – .250)		SD N (87G – .224)																			
"	total	107	.228	.254	224	51	6	0	0	0.0	15	18	26	20	3	13	2	63	157	7	17	2.1	.969	3B-71, 2B-17, SS-7, 1B-1
1976	SD N	96	.236	.278	212	50	5	2	0	0.0	16	26	25	28	0	39	2	77	110	4	21	2.0	.979	3B-27, 2B-25, SS-6, 1B-1
10 yrs.		977	.231	.289	2447	565	61	21	13	0.5	238	202	271	272	13	123	15	1293	1746	88	345	3.2	.972	2B-490, SS-276, 3B-121, DH-2, 1B-2

LEAGUE CHAMPIONSHIP SERIES

Year	Team	Games	BA	SA	AB	H	2B	3B	HR	HR%	R	RBI	BB	SO	SB	PH AB	PH H	PO	A	E	DP	TC/G	FA	G by Pos
1972	OAK A	4	.500	.500	4	2	0	0	0	0.0	0	1	0	0	0	0	0	0	0	0	0	0.0	–	2B-3, SS-1
1973		3	.000	.000	2	0	0	0	0	0.0	0	0	0	0	0	0	0	1	0	0	1	0.3	1.000	2B-3
2 yrs.		7	.333	.333	6	2	0	0	0	0.0	0	1	0	0	0	0	0	1	0	0	1	0.1	1.000	2B-6, SS-1

WORLD SERIES

Year	Team	Games	BA	SA	AB	H	2B	3B	HR	HR%	R	RBI	BB	SO	SB	PH AB	PH H	PO	A	E	DP	TC/G	FA	G by Pos
1972	OAK A	4	.333	.333	3	1	0	0	0	0.0	0	0	0	0	0	0	0	4	3	0	1	1.8	1.000	2B-4
1973		4	.000	.000	3	0	0	0	0	0.0	1	1	0	1	0	0	0	5	7	0	1	3.0	1.000	2B-4
2 yrs.		8	.167	.167	6	1	0	0	0	0.0	1	1	0	1	0	0	0	9	10	0	1	2.4	1.000	2B-8

Jack Kubiszyn

KUBISZYN, JOHN HENRY
B. Dec. 19, 1936, Buffalo, N. Y.   BR TR 5'11''   170 lbs.

Year	Team	Games	BA	SA	AB	H	2B	3B	HR	HR%	R	RBI	BB	SO	SB	PH AB	PH H	PO	A	E	DP	TC/G	FA	G by Pos
1961	CLE A	25	.214	.214	42	9	0	0	0	0.0	4	0	2	5	0	6	0	15	28	0	3	1.7	1.000	3B-8, SS-7, 2B-2
1962		25	.169	.254	59	10	2	0	1	1.7	3	2	5	7	0	5	1	32	48	3	14	3.3	.964	SS-18, 3B-1
2 yrs.		50	.188	.238	101	19	2	0	1	1.0	7	2	7	12	0	11	1	47	76	3	17	2.5	.976	SS-25, 3B-9, 2B-2

Gil Kubski

KUBSKI, GILBERT THOMAS
B. Oct. 12, 1954, Longview, Tex.   BL TR 6'3''   185 lbs.

Year	Team	Games	BA	SA	AB	H	2B	3B	HR	HR%	R	RBI	BB	SO	SB	PH AB	PH H	PO	A	E	DP	TC/G	FA	G by Pos
1980	CAL A	22	.254	.302	63	16	3	0	0	0.0	11	6	6	10	1	1	0	36	2	0	0	1.7	1.000	OF-20

Steve Kuczek

KUCZEK, STANISLAW LEO
B. Dec. 28, 1924, Amsterdam, N. Y.   BR TR 6'   160 lbs.

Year	Team	Games	BA	SA	AB	H	2B	3B	HR	HR%	R	RBI	BB	SO	SB	Pinch Hit AB	Pinch Hit H	PO	A	E	DP	TC/G	FA	G by Pos

Steve Kuczek *continued*

Year	Team	Games	BA	SA	AB	H	2B	3B	HR	HR%	R	RBI	BB	SO	SB	AB	H	PO	A	E	DP	TC/G	FA	G by Pos
1949	BOS N	1	1.000	2.000	1	1	1	0	0	0.0	0	0	0	0	0	1	1	0	0	0	0	0.0	—	

Willie Kuehne

KUEHNE, WILLIAM J.
B. Oct. 24, 1858, Leipzig, Germany D. Oct. 27, 1921, Sulphur Springs, Ohio   TR   185 lbs.

Year	Team	Games	BA	SA	AB	H	2B	3B	HR	HR%	R	RBI	BB	SO	SB	AB	H	PO	A	E	DP	TC/G	FA	G by Pos
1883	COL AA	95	.227	.332	374	85	8	14	1	0.3	38		2			0	0	132	212	72	21	4.4	.827	3B-69, 2B-18, SS-7, OF-3
1884		110	.236	.381	415	98	13	16	5	1.2	48		9			0	0	120	219	46	13	3.5	.881	3B-109, OF-1
1885	PIT AA	104	.226	.341	411	93	9	19	0	0.0	54		15			0	0	109	214	51	16	3.6	.864	3B-97, SS-7
1886		117	.204	.314	481	98	16	17	1	0.2	73		19			0	0	303	99	29	11	3.7	.933	OF-54, 3B-47, 1B-18
1887	PIT N	102	.299	.425	402	120	18	15	1	0.2	68	41	14	39	17	0	0	166	321	62	31	5.4	.887	SS-91, 3B-4, 1B-4, OF-3
1888		138	.235	.336	524	123	22	11	3	0.6	60	62	9	68	34	0	0	208	327	51	29	4.2	.913	3B-75, SS-63
1889		97	.246	.362	390	96	20	5	5	1.3	43	57	9	36	15	0	0	147	187	34	17	3.8	.908	3B-75, OF-13, 2B-5, SS-2, 1B-2
1890	PIT P	126	.239	.352	528	126	21	12	5	0.9	66	73	28	37	21	0	0	159	304	82	18	4.3	.850	3B-126
1891	2 teams		COL AA (68G – .215)		LOU AA (41G – .277)																			
"	total	109	.238	.293	420	100	12	1	3	0.7	60	40		35	31	0	0	141	241	46	23	3.9	.893	3B-109
1892	3 teams		LOU N (76G – .167)		STL N (7G – .143)				CIN N (6G – .208)															
"	total	89	.168	.224	339	57	6	5	1	0.3	26	40	14	45	7	0	0	128	195	46	23	4.1	.875	3B-86, 2B-2, SS-1
10 yrs.		1087	.232	.338	4284	996	145	115	25	0.6	536	313	137	260	125	0	0	1613	2319	519	202	4.1	.883	3B-797, SS-171, OF-74, 2B-25, 1B-24

Harvey Kuenn

KUENN, HARVEY EDWARD
B. Dec. 4, 1930, West Allis, Wis. D. Feb. 28, 1988, Peoria, Ariz.   BR TR 6'2"   187 lbs.
Manager 1975, 1982-83.

Year	Team	Games	BA	SA	AB	H	2B	3B	HR	HR%	R	RBI	BB	SO	SB	AB	H	PO	A	E	DP	TC/G	FA	G by Pos
1952	DET A	19	.325	.400	80	26	2	2	0	0.0	2	8	2	1	2	0	0	44	57	4	12	5.5	.962	SS-19
1953		155	.308	.386	679	209	33	7	2	0.3	94	48	50	31	6	0	0	308	441	21	78	5.0	.973	SS-155
1954		155	.306	.390	656	201	28	6	5	0.8	81	48	29	13	9	0	0	294	496	28	85	5.3	.966	SS-155
1955		145	.306	.423	620	190	38	5	8	1.3	101	62	40	27	8	4	1	253	378	29	83	4.6	.956	SS-141
1956		146	.332	.470	591	196	32	7	12	2.0	96	88	55	34	9	6	1	219	388	20	86	4.3	.968	SS-141, OF-1
1957		151	.277	.388	624	173	30	6	9	1.4	74	44	47	28	5	1	0	251	387	30	91	4.4	.955	SS-136, 3B-17, 1B-1
1958		139	.319	.442	561	179	39	3	8	1.4	73	54	51	34	5	1	1	358	9	6	1	2.7	.984	OF-138
1959		139	.353	.501	561	198	42	7	9	1.6	99	71	48	37	7	1	0	247	6	3	0	1.8	.988	OF-137
1960	CLE A	126	.308	.416	474	146	24	0	9	1.9	65	54	55	25	3	4	1	222	13	9	3	1.9	.963	OF-119, 3B-5
1961	SF N	131	.265	.361	471	125	22	4	5	1.1	60	46	47	34	5	10	4	190	43	10	5	1.9	.959	OF-93, 3B-32, SS-1
1962		130	.304	.433	487	148	23	5	10	2.1	73	68	49	37	3	9	2	180	47	8	5	1.8	.966	OF-105, 3B-30
1963		120	.290	.374	417	121	13	2	6	1.4	61	31	44	38	2	15	2	115	60	13	3	1.6	.931	OF-64, 3B-53
1964		111	.262	.353	351	92	16	2	4	1.1	42	22	35	32	0	17	5	136	9	6	4	1.4	.960	OF-88, 1B-11, 3B-2
1965	2 teams		SF N (23G – .237)		CHI N (54G – .217)																			
"	total	77	.223	.251	179	40	5	0	0	0.0	15	12	32	16	4	25	7	81	8	3	1	1.2	.967	OF-49, 1B-8
1966	2 teams		CHI N (3G – .333)		PHI N (86G – .296)																			
"	total	89	.296	.352	162	48	9	0	0	0.0	15	15	10	17	0	48	11	130	3	1	11	1.5	.993	OF-32, 1B-13, 3B-1
15 yrs.		1833	.303	.408	6913	2092	356	56	87	1.3	951	671	594	404	68	141	35	3028	2345	191	468	3.0	.966	OF-826, SS-748, 3B-140, 1B-33

WORLD SERIES

Year	Team	Games	BA	SA	AB	H	2B	3B	HR	HR%	R	RBI	BB	SO	SB	AB	H	PO	A	E	DP	TC/G	FA	G by Pos
1962	SF N	4	.083	.083	12	1	0	0	0	0.0	1	0	1	1	0	0	0	11	0	0	0	2.8	1.000	OF-4

Joe Kuhel

KUHEL, JOSEPH ANTHONY
B. June 25, 1906, Cleveland, Ohio D. Feb. 26, 1984, Kansas City, Kans.   BL TL 6'   180 lbs.
Manager 1948-49.

Year	Team	Games	BA	SA	AB	H	2B	3B	HR	HR%	R	RBI	BB	SO	SB	AB	H	PO	A	E	DP	TC/G	FA	G by Pos
1930	WAS A	18	.286	.429	63	18	3	3	0	0.0	9	17	5	6	1	1	0	149	8	3	10	8.9	.981	1B-16
1931		139	.269	.410	524	141	34	8	8	1.5	70	85	47	45	7	0	0	1255	57	12	119	9.5	.991	1B-139
1932		101	.291	.415	347	101	21	5	4	1.2	52	52	32	19	5	9	1	761	45	5	64	8.0	.994	1B-85
1933		153	.322	.467	602	194	34	10	11	1.8	89	107	59	48	17	0	0	1498	61	7	126	10.2	.996	1B-153
1934		63	.289	.392	263	76	12	3	3	1.1	49	25	30	14	2	0	0	618	23	4	62	10.2	.994	1B-63
1935		151	.261	.338	633	165	25	9	2	0.3	99	74	78	44	9	0	0	1425	87	14	150	10.1	.991	1B-151
1936		149	.321	.502	588	189	42	9	16	2.7	107	118	64	30	15	0	0	1452	75	11	138	10.3	.993	1B-149, 3B-1
1937		136	.283	.400	547	155	24	11	6	1.1	73	61	63	39	6	0	0	1242	85	9	141	9.8	.993	1B-136
1938	CHI A	117	.267	.410	412	110	27	4	8	1.9	67	51	72	35	9	6	0	1136	59	14	97	10.3	.988	1B-111
1939		139	.300	.460	546	164	24	4	15	2.7	107	56	64	51	18	0	0	1256	72	11	113	9.6	.992	1B-136
1940		155	.280	.488	603	169	28	4	27	4.5	111	94	87	59	12	0	0	1395	91	18	112	9.7	.988	1B-155
1941		155	.250	.392	600	150	39	5	12	2.0	99	63	70	55	20	1	0	1444	108	11	113	10.2	.994	1B-151
1942		115	.249	.332	413	103	14	4	4	1.0	60	52	60	22	22	3	0	1085	70	11	94	10.1	.991	1B-112
1943	WAS A	153	.213	.284	531	113	21	1	5	0.9	55	46	76	45	14	0	0	1471	106	8	143	10.4	.995	1B-153
1944		139	.278	.378	518	144	26	7	4	0.8	90	51	68	40	11	1	1	1251	83	17	119	9.7	.987	1B-138
1945		142	.285	.400	533	152	29	13	2	0.4	79	75	79	31	10	1	0	1323	94	16	101	10.1	.989	1B-141
1946	2 teams		WAS A (14G – .150)		CHI A (64G – .273)																			
"	total	78	.264	.368	258	68	9	3	4	1.6	26	22	26	26	4	8	2	625	41	4	67	8.6	.994	1B-68
1947	CHI A	3	.000	.000	4	0	0	0	0	0.0	0	0	0	1	0	3	0	0	0	0	0	0.0	—	
18 yrs.		2104	.277	.406	7984	2212	412	111	131	1.6	1236	1049	980	612	178	36	4	19386	1165	174	1769	9.9	.992	1B-2057, 3B-1

WORLD SERIES

Year	Team	Games	BA	SA	AB	H	2B	3B	HR	HR%	R	RBI	BB	SO	SB	AB	H	PO	A	E	DP	TC/G	FA	G by Pos
1933	WAS A	5	.150	.150	20	3	0	0	0	0.0	1	1	1	4	0	0	0	59	3	0	4	12.4	1.000	1B-5

Kenny Kuhn

KUHN, KENNETH HAROLD
B. Mar. 20, 1937, Louisville, Ky.   BL TR 5'10½" 175 lbs.

Year	Team	Games	BA	SA	AB	H	2B	3B	HR	HR%	R	RBI	BB	SO	SB	AB	H	PO	A	E	DP	TC/G	FA	G by Pos
1955	CLE A	4	.333	.333	6	2	0	0	0	0.0	0	0	1	0	0	0	0	1	3	0	0	1.0	1.000	SS-4
1956		27	.273	.318	22	6	1	0	0	0.0	7	2	0	4	0	1	0	13	14	1	4	1.0	.964	SS-17, 2B-5
1957		40	.170	.170	53	9	0	0	0	0.0	5	5	4	9	1	0	0	26	15	2	2	1.1	.953	2B-14, 3B-2, SS-1
3 yrs.		71	.210	.222	81	17	1	0	0	0.0	12	7	5	13	1	1	0	40	32	3	6	1.1	.960	SS-22, 2B-19, 3B-2

Year Team	Games	BA	SA	AB	H	2B	3B	HR	HR%	R	RBI	BB	SO	SB	Pinch Hit AB	H	PO	A	E	DP	TC/G	FA	G by Pos

Walt Kuhn

KUHN, WALTER CHARLES (Red)
B. Feb. 2, 1884, Fresno, Calif. D. June 14, 1935, Fresno, Calif.

BR TR 5'7" 162 lbs.

Year Team	Games	BA	SA	AB	H	2B	3B	HR	HR%	R	RBI	BB	SO	SB	AB	H	PO	A	E	DP	TC/G	FA	G by Pos
1912 CHI A	75	.202	.242	178	36	7	0	0	0.0	16	10	20		5	0	0	318	104	15	8	5.8	.966	C-75
1913	26	.160	.180	50	8	1	0	0	0.0	5	5	13	8	1	2	0	75	22	2	1	3.8	.980	C-24
1914	17	.275	.300	40	11	1	0	0	0.0	4	0	8	11	2	0	0	60	17	1	3	4.6	.987	C-16
3 yrs.	118	.205	.239	268	55	9	0	0	0.0	25	15	41	19	8	2	0	453	143	18	12	5.2	.971	C-115

Charlie Kuhns

KUHNS, CHARLES B.
B. Oct. 27, 1877, Freeport, Pa. D. July 15, 1922, Pittsburgh, Pa.

5'9" 160 lbs.

Year Team	Games	BA	SA	AB	H	2B	3B	HR	HR%	R	RBI	BB	SO	SB	AB	H	PO	A	E	DP	TC/G	FA	G by Pos
1897 PIT N	1	.000	.000	3	0	0	0	0	0.0	0	0	1		0	0	0	1	3	2	0	6.0	.667	3B-1
1899 BOS N	7	.278	.278	18	5	0	0	0	0.0	2	3	2		0	0	0	6	14	5	2	3.6	.800	SS-3, 3B-3
2 yrs.	8	.238	.238	21	5	0	0	0	0.0	2	3	3		0	0	0	7	17	7	2	3.9	.774	3B-4, SS-3

Duane Kuiper

KUIPER, DUANE EUGENE
B. June 19, 1950, Racine, Wis.

BL TR 6' 175 lbs.

Year Team	Games	BA	SA	AB	H	2B	3B	HR	HR%	R	RBI	BB	SO	SB	AB	H	PO	A	E	DP	TC/G	FA	G by Pos
1974 CLE A	10	.500	.591	22	11	1	1	0	0.0	7	4	2	2	1	1	1	16	19	0	3	3.5	1.000	2B-8
1975	90	.292	.329	346	101	11	1	0	0.0	42	25	30	19	19	0	0	192	230	12	65	4.8	.972	2B-87, DH-1
1976	135	.263	.312	506	133	13	6	0	0.0	47	37	30	42	10	4	0	321	367	11	95	5.2	.984	2B-128, 1B-5, DH-2
1977	148	.277	.333	610	169	15	8	1	0.2	62	50	37	55	11	0	0	334	449	12	104	5.4	.985	2B-148
1978	149	.283	.338	547	155	18	6	0	0.0	52	43	19	35	4	0	0	341	408	16	91	5.1	.979	2B-149
1979	140	.255	.294	479	122	9	5	0	0.0	46	39	37	27	4	0	0	345	380	9	89	5.2	.988	2B-140
1980	42	.282	.315	149	42	5	0	0	0.0	10	9	13	8	0	0	0	87	111	1	28	4.7	.995	2B-42
1981	72	.257	.286	206	53	6	0	0	0.0	15	14	8	13	1	4	2	118	174	5	24	4.1	.983	2B-72
1982 SF N	107	.280	.330	218	61	9	1	0	0.0	26	17	32	24	2	44	14	101	124	5	24	2.1	.978	2B-51
1983	72	.250	.284	176	44	2	2	0	0.0	14	14	27	13	0	10	2	107	140	3	17	3.5	.988	2B-64
1984	83	.200	.209	115	23	1	0	0	0.0	8	11	12	10	0	47	9	62	66	4	14	1.6	.970	2B-31, 1B-1
1985	9	.600	.600	5	3	0	0	0	0.0					0	5	3	0	0	0	0	0.0	—	
12 yrs.	1057	.271	.316	3379	917	91	29	1	0.0	329	263	248	255	52	115	31	2024	2468	78	554	4.3	.983	2B-920, 1B-6, DH-3

Jeff Kunkel

KUNKEL, JEFFREY WILLIAM
Son of Bill Kunkel.
B. Mar. 25, 1962, West Palm Beach, Fla.

BR TR 6'2" 175 lbs.

Year Team	Games	BA	SA	AB	H	2B	3B	HR	HR%	R	RBI	BB	SO	SB	AB	H	PO	A	E	DP	TC/G	FA	G by Pos
1984 TEX A	50	.204	.324	142	29	3	3	3	2.1	13	7	2	35	4	0	0	81	120	17	22	4.4	.922	SS-48, DH-1
1985	2	.250	.250	4	1	0	0	0	0.0	1	0	0	3	0	0	0	2	5	0	1	3.5	1.000	SS-2
1986	8	.231	.462	13	3	0	0	1	7.7	3	2	0	3	0	1	0	4	6	3	0	1.6	.769	SS-5, DH-1
1987	15	.219	.313	32	7	0	0	1	3.1	1	2	0	10	0	1	0	19	27	3	8	3.3	.939	2B-10, OF-3, 3B-3, DH-1, SS-1, 1B-1
1988	55	.227	.357	154	35	8	3	2	1.3	14	15	4	35	0	3	0	78	119	8	23	3.7	.961	2B-28, SS-19, 3B-10, OF-6, DH-3, P-1
1989	108	.270	.437	293	79	21	2	8	2.7	39	29	20	75	3	6	1	143	168	22	27	3.1	.934	SS-59, OF-30, 2B-8, DH-5, 3B-4, P-1
6 yrs.	238	.241	.386	638	154	31	8	15	2.4	71	55	26	160	7	11	1	327	445	53	81	3.5	.936	SS-134, 2B-46, OF-39, 3B-17, DH-11, P-2, 1B-1

Rusty Kuntz

KUNTZ, RUSSELL JAY
B. Feb. 4, 1955, Orange, Calif.

BR TR 6'3" 190 lbs.

Year Team	Games	BA	SA	AB	H	2B	3B	HR	HR%	R	RBI	BB	SO	SB	AB	H	PO	A	E	DP	TC/G	FA	G by Pos
1979 CHI A	5	.091	.091	11	1	0	0	0	0.0	0	0	2	6	0	0	0	12	1	0	1	2.6	1.000	OF-5
1980	36	.226	.290	62	14	4	0	0	0.0	5	3	5	13	1	3	2	45	2	1	1	1.3	.979	OF-34
1981	67	.255	.291	55	14	2	0	0	0.0	15	4	6	8	1	3	0	54	0	0	0	0.8	1.000	OF-51, DH-5
1982	21	.192	.231	26	5	1	0	0	0.0	4	3	2	8	0	0	0	21	0	0	0	1.0	1.000	OF-21
1983 2 teams CHI A (28G – .262)				MIN A	(31G – .190)																		
" total	59	.211	.303	142	30	6	3	2.1		19	6	18	41	1	4	1	106	3	2	1	1.9	.982	OF-57, DH-1
1984 DET A	84	.286	.414	140	40	12	0	2	1.4	32	22	25	28	2	12	5	74	2	1	1	0.9	.987	OF-67, DH-10
1985	5	.000	.000	5	0	0	0	0	0.0	0	0	2	2	0	4	0	0	0	1	0	0.2	—	DH-3, 1B-1
7 yrs.	277	.236	.322	441	104	23	0	5	1.1	75	38	60	106	5	26	8	312	8	5	4	1.2	.985	OF-235, DH-19, 1B-1

LEAGUE CHAMPIONSHIP SERIES

Year Team	Games	BA	SA	AB	H	2B	3B	HR	HR%	R	RBI	BB	SO	SB	AB	H	PO	A	E	DP	TC/G	FA	G by Pos
1984 DET A	1	.000	.000	1	0	0	0	0	0.0	0	0	0	0	0	0	0	0	0	0	0	0.0	—	OF-1

WORLD SERIES

Year Team	Games	BA	SA	AB	H	2B	3B	HR	HR%	R	RBI	BB	SO	SB	AB	H	PO	A	E	DP	TC/G	FA	G by Pos
1984 DET A	2	.000	.000	1	0	0	0	0	0.0	1	0	1	0	1	0	0	0	0	0	0	0.0	—	

Whitey Kurowski

KUROWSKI, GEORGE JOHN
B. Apr. 19, 1918, Reading, Pa.

BR TR 5'11" 193 lbs.

Year Team	Games	BA	SA	AB	H	2B	3B	HR	HR%	R	RBI	BB	SO	SB	AB	H	PO	A	E	DP	TC/G	FA	G by Pos
1941 STL N	5	.333	.556	9	3	2	0	0	0.0	1	2	0	1	0	1	0	2	3	0	0	1.0	1.000	3B-4
1942	115	.254	.391	366	93	17	3	9	2.5	51	42	33	60	7	9	0	124	194	19	19	2.9	.944	3B-104, OF-1, SS-1
1943	139	.287	.439	522	150	24	8	13	2.5	69	70	31	54	3	1	0	167	257	21	29	3.2	.953	3B-137, SS-2
1944	149	.270	.449	555	150	25	7	20	3.6	95	87	58	40	2	2	0	192	290	17	21	3.3	.966	3B-146, 2B-9, SS-1
1945	133	.323	.511	511	165	27	3	21	4.1	84	102	45	45	1	1	0	174	238	16	28	3.2	.963	3B-131, SS-6
1946	142	.301	.462	519	156	32	5	14	2.7	76	89	72	47	2	3	1	175	249	15	17	3.1	.966	3B-138
1947	146	.310	.544	513	159	27	6	27	5.3	108	104	87	56	4	4	1	140	250	19	17	2.8	.954	3B-141
1948	77	.214	.277	220	47	8	0	2	0.9	34	20	42	28	0	9	1	55	100	10	7	2.1	.939	3B-65
1949	10	.143	.143	14	2	0	0	0	0.0	0	0	1	0	0	8	2	3	2	0	0	0.5	1.000	3B-2
9 yrs.	916	.286	.455	3229	925	162	32	106	3.3	518	529	369	332	19	38	5	1032	1583	117	138	3.0	.957	3B-868, SS-10, 2B-9, OF-1

WORLD SERIES

Year Team	Games	BA	SA	AB	H	2B	3B	HR	HR%	R	RBI	BB	SO	SB	AB	H	PO	A	E	DP	TC/G	FA	G by Pos
1942 STL N	5	.267	.600	15	4	0	1	1	6.7	3	5	2	3	0	0	0	7	4	1	0	2.4	.917	3B-5
1943	5	.222	.278	18	4	1	0	0	0.0	2	1	0	3	0	0	0	8	8	2	0	3.6	.889	3B-5
1944	6	.217	.261	23	5	1	0	0	0.0	2	1	1	4	0	0	0	4	15	0	1	3.2	1.000	3B-6
1946	7	.296	.407	27	8	3	0	0	0.0	5	2	3	3	0	0	0	13	9	1	2	3.3	.957	3B-7
4 yrs.	23	.253	.373	83	21	5	1	1	1.2	12	9	3	13	0	0	0	32	36	4	3	3.1	.944	3B-23

Craig Kusick

KUSICK, CRAIG ROBERT
B. Sept. 30, 1948, Milwaukee, Wis.

BR TR 6'3" 210 lbs.

Year	Team	Games	BA	SA	AB	H	2B	3B	HR	HR%	R	RBI	BB	SO	SB	Pinch Hit AB	Pinch Hit H	PO	A	E	DP	TC/G	FA	G by Pos

Craig Kusick *continued*

Year	Team	Games	BA	SA	AB	H	2B	3B	HR	HR%	R	RBI	BB	SO	SB	AB	H	PO	A	E	DP	TC/G	FA	G by Pos
1973	MIN A	15	.250	.292	48	12	2	0	0	0.0	4	4	7	9	0	1	0	89	5	1	7	6.3	.989	1B-11, DH-2, OF-2
1974		76	.239	.403	201	48	7	1	8	4.0	36	26	35	36	0	7	2	479	42	2	45	6.9	.996	1B-75
1975		57	.237	.404	156	37	8	0	6	3.8	14	27	21	23	0	9	3	372	31	4	45	7.1	.990	1B-51
1976		109	.259	.432	266	69	13	0	11	4.1	33	36	35	44	5	35	3	109	17	3	16	1.2	.977	DH-79, 1B-23
1977		115	.254	.433	268	68	12	0	12	4.5	34	45	49	60	3	**38**	**10**	133	7	4	9	1.3	.972	DH-85, 1B-23
1978		77	.173	.272	191	33	3	2	4	2.1	23	20	37	38	0	24	4	228	22	4	14	3.3	.984	DH-35, 1B-27, OF-9
1979 2 teams	MIN A (24G – .241)			TOR A	(24G – .204)																			
" total		48	.222	.407	108	24	5	0	5	4.6	11	13	10	18	0	10	1	209	18	4	20	4.8	.983	1B-28, DH-13, P-1
7 yrs.		497	.235	.392	1238	291	50	3	46	3.7	155	171	194	228	11	124	23	1619	142	22	156	3.6	.988	1B-238, DH-214, OF-11, P-1

Art Kusnyer

KUSNYER, ARTHUR WILLIAM
B. Dec. 19, 1945, Akron, Ohio
BR TR 6'2" 197 lbs.

Year	Team	Games	BA	SA	AB	H	2B	3B	HR	HR%	R	RBI	BB	SO	SB	AB	H	PO	A	E	DP	TC/G	FA	G by Pos
1970	CHI A	4	.100	.100	10	1	0	0	0	0.0	0	0	0	4	0	1	0	12	4	1	0	4.3	.941	C-3
1971	CAL A	6	.154	.154	13	2	0	0	0	0.0	0	0	0	3	0	0	0	19	4	1	0	4.0	.958	C-6
1972		64	.207	.263	179	37	2	1	2	1.1	13	13	16	33	0	2	0	362	33	10	3	6.3	.975	C-63
1973		41	.125	.156	64	8	2	0	0	0.0	5	3	2	12	0	0	0	130	13	3	2	3.6	.979	C-41
1976	MIL A	15	.118	.147	34	4	1	0	0	0.0	2	3	1	5	1	0	0	41	4	3	2	3.2	.938	C-14
1978	KC A	9	.231	.538	13	3	1	0	1	7.7	1	2	2	4	0	0	0	32	3	2	0	4.1	.946	C-9
6 yrs.		139	.176	.230	313	55	6	1	3	1.0	21	21	21	61	1	3	0	596	61	20	7	4.9	.970	C-136

Joe Kustus

KUSTUS, JOSEPH JULIUS
B. Sept. 5, 1882, Detroit, Mich. D. Apr. 27, 1916, Eloise, Mich.
BR TR 5'10"

Year	Team	Games	BA	SA	AB	H	2B	3B	HR	HR%	R	RBI	BB	SO	SB	AB	H	PO	A	E	DP	TC/G	FA	G by Pos
1909	BKN N	53	.145	.191	173	25	5	0	1	0.6	12	11	11		9	3	0	92	6	5	1	1.9	.951	OF-50

Randy Kutcher

KUTCHER, RANDY SCOTT
B. Apr. 30, 1960, Anchorage, Alaska
BR TR 5'11" 170 lbs.

Year	Team	Games	BA	SA	AB	H	2B	3B	HR	HR%	R	RBI	BB	SO	SB	AB	H	PO	A	E	DP	TC/G	FA	G by Pos
1986	SF N	71	.237	.409	186	44	9	1	7	3.8	28	16	11	41	6	13	1	111	11	1	3	1.7	.992	OF-51, SS-13, 3B-4, 2B-3
1987		14	.188	.375	16	3	1	1	0	0.0	7	1	1	5	1	2	0	14	5	0	1	1.4	1.000	OF-6, 3B-2, 2B-2, SS-1
1988	BOS A	19	.167	.250	12	2	1	0	0	0.0	2	0	0	2	0	0	0	6	5	1	0	0.6	1.000	OF-7, 3B-2
1989		77	.225	.363	160	36	10	3	2	1.3	28	18	11	46	3	5	2	112	8	3	0	1.6	.976	OF-57, DH-6, 3B-6, C-1
4 yrs.		181	.227	.382	374	85	21	5	9	2.4	65	35	23	94	10	20	3	243	29	5	4	1.5	.982	OF-121, SS-14, 3B-14, DH-6, 2B-5, C-1

Joe Kutina

KUTINA, JOSEPH PETER
B. Jan. 16, 1885, Chicago, Ill. D. Apr. 13, 1945, Chicago, Ill.
BR TR 6'2" 205 lbs.

Year	Team	Games	BA	SA	AB	H	2B	3B	HR	HR%	R	RBI	BB	SO	SB	AB	H	PO	A	E	DP	TC/G	FA	G by Pos
1911	STL A	26	.257	.446	101	26	6	2	3	3.0	12	15	2		2	0	0	250	15	5	16	10.4	.981	1B-26
1912		67	.205	.293	205	42	9	3	1	0.5	18	18	13		0	15	2	491	24	8	28	7.8	.985	1B-51, OF-1
2 yrs.		93	.222	.343	306	68	15	5	4	1.3	30	33	15		2	15	2	741	39	13	44	8.5	.984	1B-77, OF-1

Al Kvasnak

KVASNAK, ALEXANDER
B. Jan. 11, 1921, Sagamore, Pa.
BR TR 6'1" 170 lbs.

Year	Team	Games	BA	SA	AB	H	2B	3B	HR	HR%	R	RBI	BB	SO	SB	AB	H	PO	A	E	DP	TC/G	FA	G by Pos
1942	WAS A	5	.182	.182	11	2	0	0	0	0.0	3	0	2	1	0	2	1	5	0	0	0	1.0	1.000	OF-3

Andy Kyle

KYLE, ANDREW EWING
B. Oct. 29, 1889, Toronto, Ont., Canada D. Sept. 6, 1971, Toronto, Ont., Canada
BL TL 5'8" 160 lbs.

Year	Team	Games	BA	SA	AB	H	2B	3B	HR	HR%	R	RBI	BB	SO	SB	AB	H	PO	A	E	DP	TC/G	FA	G by Pos
1912	CIN N	9	.333	.381	21	7	1	0	0	0.0	3	4	4	2	0	2	0	15	1	0	0	1.8	1.000	OF-7

Chet Laabs

LAABS, CHESTER PETER
B. Apr. 30, 1912, Milwaukee, Wis. D. Jan. 26, 1983, Warren, Mich.
BR TR 5'8" 175 lbs.

Year	Team	Games	BA	SA	AB	H	2B	3B	HR	HR%	R	RBI	BB	SO	SB	AB	H	PO	A	E	DP	TC/G	FA	G by Pos
1937	DET A	72	.240	.434	242	58	13	5	8	3.3	31	37	24	66	6	9	2	133	2	4	0	1.9	.971	OF-62
1938		64	.237	.398	211	50	7	3	7	3.3	26	37	15	52	3	11	3	128	4	4	1	2.1	.971	OF-53
1939 2 teams	DET A (5G – .313)			STL A	(95G – .300)																			
" total		100	.300	.489	333	100	21	6	10	3.0	53	64	35	62	4	16	2	212	8	7	0	2.3	.969	OF-84
1940	STL A	105	.271	.505	218	59	11	5	10	4.6	32	40	34	59	3	35	**14**	124	3	4	1	1.2	.969	OF-63
1941		118	.278	.482	392	109	23	6	15	3.8	64	59	51	59	5	16	5	217	6	4	2	1.9	.982	OF-100
1942		144	.275	.498	520	143	21	7	27	5.2	90	99	88	88	0	3	1	276	13	9	3	2.1	.970	OF-139
1943		151	.250	.409	580	145	27	7	17	2.9	83	85	73	**105**	5	1	0	346	16	9	4	2.5	.976	OF-150
1944		66	.234	.378	201	47	10	2	5	2.5	28	23	29	33	3	11	0	108	3	0	0	1.7	1.000	OF-55
1945		35	.239	.358	109	26	4	3	1	0.9	15	8	16	17	0	4	0	68	1	1	0	2.0	.986	OF-35
1946		80	.261	.492	264	69	13	0	16	6.1	40	52	20	50	0	6	0	151	5	2	2	2.0	.987	OF-72
1947	PHI A	15	.219	.344	32	7	1	0	1	3.1	5	5	4	7	1	1	0	17	1	0	0	1.2	1.000	OF-7
11 yrs.		950	.262	.452	3102	813	151	44	117	3.8	467	509	389	595	32	115	30	1780	62	44	15	2.0	.977	OF-820

WORLD SERIES

Year	Team	Games	BA	SA	AB	H	2B	3B	HR	HR%	R	RBI	BB	SO	SB	AB	H	PO	A	E	DP	TC/G	FA	G by Pos
1944	STL A	5	.200	.400	15	3	1	1	0	0.0	1	0	2	6	0	1	0	5	1	0	0	1.2	1.000	OF-4

Coco Laboy

LABOY, JOSE ALBERTO
B. July 3, 1940, Ponce, Puerto Rico
BR TR 5'10" 165 lbs.

Year	Team	Games	BA	SA	AB	H	2B	3B	HR	HR%	R	RBI	BB	SO	SB	AB	H	PO	A	E	DP	TC/G	FA	G by Pos
1969	MON N	157	.258	.409	562	145	29	1	18	3.2	53	83	40	96	0	1	0	115	307	25	28	2.8	.944	3B-156
1970		137	.199	.299	432	86	26	1	5	1.2	37	53	31	81	0	7	0	107	200	17	20	2.4	.948	3B-132, 2B-3
1971		76	.252	.298	151	38	4	0	1	0.7	10	14	11	19	0	15	5	40	68	7	4	1.5	.939	3B-65, 2B-2
1972		28	.261	.420	69	18	2	1	3	4.3	6	14	9	16	0	2	0	18	34	1	2	1.9	.981	3B-24, OF-1, 2B-1
1973		22	.121	.242	33	4	1	0	1	3.0	2	2	5	8	0	3	0	13	19	4	2	1.6	.889	3B-20, OF-1, 2B-1
5 yrs.		420	.233	.354	1247	291	62	3	28	2.2	108	166	97	220	0	28	5	293	628	54	56	2.3	.945	3B-397, 2B-9, SS-2, OF-1

Candy LaChance

LaCHANCE, GEORGE JOSEPH
B. Feb. 15, 1870, Waterbury, Conn. D. Aug. 18, 1932, Waterville, Conn.
BB TR 6'1" 183 lbs.

Year	Team	Games	BA	SA	AB	H	2B	3B	HR	HR%	R	RBI	BB	SO	SB	AB	H	PO	A	E	DP	TC/G	FA	G by Pos
1893	BKN N	11	.171	.200	35	6	1	0	0	0.0	6		2	12	0	0	0	18	4	10	0	2.9	.688	C-6, OF-5
1894		68	.323	.494	257	83	13	8	5	1.9	48	52	16	32	20	0	0	525	19	15	26	8.2	.973	1B-56, C-10, OF-3

Year	Team	Games	BA	SA	AB	H	2B	3B	HR	HR%	R	RBI	BB	SO	SB	Pinch Hit AB	Pinch Hit H	PO	A	E	DP	TC/G	FA	G by Pos

Candy LaChance *continued*

1895		127	.312	.427	536	167	22	8	8	1.5	99	108	29	48	37	0	0	1290	53	24	68	10.8	.982	1B-125, OF-3
1896		89	.284	.448	348	99	10	13	7	2.0	60	58	23	32	17	0	0	956	37	14	62	11.3	.986	1B-89
1897		126	.308	.446	520	160	28	16	4	0.8	86	90	15		26	0	0	1289	64	30	76	11.0	.978	1B-126
1898		136	.247	.346	526	130	23	7	5	1.0	62	65	31		23	1	0	934	163	49	73	8.4	.957	1B-74, SS-48, OF-13
1899	BAL	125	.307	.405	472	145	23	10	1	0.2	65	75	21		31	0	0	1272	40	21	72	10.7	.984	1B-125
1901	CLE A	133	.303	.381	548	166	22	9	1	0.2	81	75	7		11	0	0	1342	58	30	73	10.8	.979	1B-133
1902	BOS A	138	.279	.351	541	151	13	4	6	1.1	60	56	18		8	0	0	1544	46	27	80	11.7	.983	1B-138
1903		141	.257	.328	522	134	22	6	1	0.2	60	53	28		12	0	0	1471	57	25	68	11.0	.984	1B-141
1904		157	.227	.283	573	130	19	5	1	0.2	55	47	23		7	0	0	1691	59	14	65	11.2	.992	1B-157
1905		12	.146	.171	41	6	1	0	0	0.0	1	5	6		0	0	0	154	7	2	6	13.6	.988	1B-12
12 yrs.		1263	.280	.379	4919	1377	197	86	39	0.8	678	690	219	124	192	1	0	12486	607	261	669	10.6	.980	1B-1176, SS-48, OF-24, C-16

WORLD SERIES

| 1903 | BOS A | 8 | .222 | .370 | 27 | 6 | 2 | 1 | 0 | 0.0 | 5 | 4 | 3 | 2 | 0 | 0 | 0 | 79 | 3 | 3 | 3 | 10.6 | .965 | 1B-8 |

Rene Lachemann

LACHEMANN, RENE GEORGE
Brother of Marcel Lachemann.
B. May 4, 1945, Los Angeles, Calif.
Manager 1981-84.

BR TR 6' 198 lbs.

1965	KC A	92	.227	.394	216	49	7	1	9	4.2	20	29	12	57	0	23	4	361	27	8	3	4.3	.980	C-75
1966		7	.200	.400	5	1	0	0	0	0.0	0	0	0	1	0	1	0	10	1	0	1	1.6	1.000	C-6
1968	OAK A	19	.150	.167	60	9	1	0	0	0.0	3	4	1	11	0	4	0	82	5	3	0	4.7	.967	C-16
3 yrs.		118	.210	.345	281	59	9	1	9	3.2	23	33	13	69	0	28	4	453	33	11	4	4.2	.978	C-97

Pete LaCock

LaCOCK, RALPH PIERRE II
B. Jan. 17, 1952, Burbank, Calif.

BL TL 6'2" 200 lbs.

1972	CHI N	5	.500	.500	6	3	0	0	0	0.0	3	4	0	1	1	1	1	2	0	0	0	0.4	1.000	OF-3
1973		11	.250	.313	16	4	1	0	0	0.0	0	1	2	2	0	7	3	5	1	0	0	0.5	1.000	OF-5
1974		35	.182	.264	110	20	4	1	1	0.9	9	8	12	16	0	4	1	134	12	2	5	4.2	.986	OF-22, 1B-11
1975		106	.229	.341	249	57	8	1	6	2.4	30	30	37	27	0	26	9	479	45	6	39	5.0	.989	1B-53, OF-26
1976		106	.221	.373	244	54	9	2	8	3.3	34	28	42	37	1	39	7	454	33	13	47	4.7	.974	1B-54, OF-19
1977	KC A	88	.303	.408	218	66	12	1	3	1.4	25	29	15	25	2	22	8	203	19	2	16	2.5	.991	1B-29, DH-26, OF-12
1978		118	.295	.419	322	95	21	2	5	1.6	44	48	21	27	1	23	3	700	39	5	67	6.3	.993	1B-106
1979		132	.277	.380	408	113	25	4	3	0.7	54	56	37	26	2	18	3	829	68	3	79	6.8	.997	1B-108, DH-16
1980		114	.205	.263	156	32	6	0	1	0.6	14	18	17	10	1	12	5	311	22	2	28	2.9	.994	1B-86, OF-29
9 yrs.		715	.257	.366	1729	444	86	11	27	1.6	214	224	182	171	8	152	40	3117	239	33	281	4.7	.990	1B-447, OF-116, DH-42

LEAGUE CHAMPIONSHIP SERIES

1977	KC A	1	.000	.000	1	0	0	0	0	0.0	0	0	1	1	0	1	0	4	0	0	0	4.0	1.000	1B-1
1978		4	.364	.727	11	4	2	1	0	0.0	1	1	3	1	1	1	0	25	1	0	3	6.5	1.000	1B-3
1980		1	—	—	0	0	0	0	0	—	0	0	0	0	0	0	0	0	0	0	0	0.0	—	1B-1
3 yrs.		6	.333	.667	12	4	2	1	0	0.0	1	1	4	2	1	2	0	29	1	0	3	5.0	1.000	1B-5

WORLD SERIES

| 1980 | KC A | 1 | — | — | 0 | 0 | 0 | 0 | 0 | 0.0 | 0 | 0 | 0 | 0 | 0 | 0 | 0 | 2 | 0 | 0 | 1 | 2.0 | 1.000 | 1B-1 |

Guy Lacy

LACY, OSCEOLA GUY
B. June 12, 1897, Cleveland, Tenn. D. Nov. 19, 1953, Cleveland, Tenn.

BL TR 5'11½" 170 lbs.

| 1926 | CLE A | 13 | .167 | .292 | 24 | 4 | 0 | 0 | 1 | 4.2 | 2 | 2 | 2 | 2 | 0 | 0 | 0 | 18 | 24 | 2 | 3 | 3.4 | .955 | 2B-11, 3B-2 |

Lee Lacy

LACY, LEONDAUS
B. Apr. 10, 1948, Longview, Tex.

BR TR 6'1" 175 lbs.

1972	LA N	60	.259	.313	243	63	7	3	0	0.0	34	12	19	37	5	2	1	125	161	8	38	4.9	.973	2B-58
1973		57	.207	.222	135	28	2	0	0	0.0	14	8	15	34	2	13	1	80	85	6	22	3.0	.965	2B-41
1974		48	.282	.359	78	22	6	0	0	0.0	13	8	2	14	2	11	3	38	53	3	8	2.0	.968	2B-34, 3B-1
1975		101	.314	.451	306	96	11	5	7	2.3	44	40	22	29	5	21	4	152	75	13	11	2.4	.946	OF-43, 2B-33, SS-1
1976	2 teams	103			338	91	11	3	3	0.9	42	34	22	25	3	17	5	193	111	9	28	3.0	.971	2B-46, OF-42, 3B-4
"	total		.269	.346																				
1977	LA N	75	.266	.414	169	45	7	0	6	3.6	28	21	10	21	4	24	6	56	69	4	11	1.7	.969	OF-32, 2B-22, 3B-12
1978		103	.261	.518	245	64	16	4	13	5.3	29	40	27	30	7	34	13	114	64	9	7	1.8	.952	OF-44, 2B-24, 3B-9, SS-1
1979	PIT N	84	.247	.412	182	45	9	3	5	2.7	17	15	22	36	6	33	7	77	8	3	1	1.0	.966	OF-41, 2B-5
1980		109	.335	.511	278	93	20	4	7	2.5	45	33	28	33	18	16	5	175	11	3	1	1.7	.984	OF-88, 3B-3
1981		78	.268	.385	213	57	11	4	2	0.9	31	10	11	29	24	13	3	121	8	3	1	1.7	.977	OF-63, 3B-1
1982		121	.312	.415	359	112	16	3	5	1.4	66	31	32	57	40	13	3	186	9	7	1	1.7	.965	OF-113, 3B-2
1983		108	.302	.406	288	87	12	3	4	1.4	40	13	22	36	31	20	6	167	2	0	0	1.6	1.000	OF-98
1984		138	.321	.464	474	152	26	3	12	2.5	66	70	32	61	21	8	0	272	18	2	4	2.1	.993	OF-127, 2B-2
1985	BAL A	121	.293	.409	492	144	22	4	9	1.8	69	48	39	95	10	4	2	231	9	4	0	2.0	.984	OF-115, DH-5
1986		130	.287	.391	491	141	18	0	11	2.2	77	47	37	71	4	11	3	239	8	2	4	1.9	.993	OF-120, DH-3
1987		87	.244	.399	258	63	13	3	7	2.7	35	28	32	49	3	12	4	135	11	4	2	1.7	.973	OF-80, DH-4
16 yrs.		1523	.286	.410	4549	1303	207	42	91	2.0	650	458	372	657	185	252	65	2361	702	80	139	2.1	.975	OF-1006, 2B-275, 3B-32, DH-12, SS-2

1976 2 teams ATL N (50G – .272) LA N (53G – .266)

LEAGUE CHAMPIONSHIP SERIES

1974	LA N	1	—	—	0	0	0	0	0	—	0	0	0	0	0	0	0	0	0	0	0	0.0	—	
1977		1	1.000	1.000	1	1	0	0	0	0.0	1	0	0	0	0	1	1	0	0	0	0	0.0	—	
1978		2	.000	.000	2	0	0	0	0	0.0	0	0	0	0	0	1	0	0	0	0	0	0.0	—	
3 yrs.		4	.333	.333	3	1	0	0	0	0.0	1	0	0	0	0	3	1	0	0	0	0	0.0	—	

WORLD SERIES

1974	LA N	1	.000	.000	1	0	0	0	0	0.0	0	0	0	1	0	1	0	0	0	0	0	0.0	—	
1977		4	.429	.429	7	3	0	0	0	0.0	1	2	1	1	0	2	1	2	0	0	0	0.5	1.000	OF-2
1978		4	.143	.143	14	2	0	0	0	0.0	3	0	0	3	0	0	0	5	0	0	0	0.0	—	DH-4

Year	Team		Games	BA	SA	AB	H	2B	3B	HR	HR%	R	RBI	BB	SO	SB	Pinch Hit AB	H	PO	A	E	DP	TC/G	FA	G by Pos

Lee Lacy *continued*

Year	Team		Games	BA	SA	AB	H	2B	3B	HR	HR%	R	RBI	BB	SO	SB	AB	H	PO	A	E	DP	TC/G	FA	G by Pos
1979	PIT	N	4	.250	.250	4	1	0	0	0	0.0	0	0	0	1	0	4	1	0	0	0	0	0.0	–	DH-4, OF-2
4 yrs.			13	.231	.231	26	6	0	0	0	0.0	1	3	2	6	0	7	2	2	0	0	0	0.2	1.000	
													6th												

Hi Ladd

LADD, ARTHUR CLIFFORD (Uncle Hiram)
B. Feb. 9, 1870, Willimantic, Conn.   D. May 7, 1948, Cranston, R. I.   BL TR 6'4"   180 lbs.

Year	Team		Games	BA	SA	AB	H	2B	3B	HR	HR%	R	RBI	BB	SO	SB	AB	H	PO	A	E	DP	TC/G	FA	G by Pos
1898	2 teams			PIT N (1G – .000)		BOS N (1G – .250)																			
"	total		2	.200	.200	5	1	0	0	0	0.0	1	0	0	0	0	1	0	2	0	0	0	1.0	1.000	OF-1

Steve Ladew

LADEW, STEPHEN
B. St. Louis, Mo.   Deceased.

Year	Team		Games	BA	SA	AB	H	2B	3B	HR	HR%	R	RBI	BB	SO	SB	AB	H	PO	A	E	DP	TC/G	FA	G by Pos
1889	KC	AA	2	.000	.000	4	0	0	0	0	0.0	0	0	0	3	0	0	0	1	0	1	0	1.0	1.000	OF-1, P-1

Joe Lafata

LAFATA, JOSEPH JOSEPH
B. Aug. 3, 1921, Detroit, Mich.   BL TL 6'   163 lbs.

Year	Team		Games	BA	SA	AB	H	2B	3B	HR	HR%	R	RBI	BB	SO	SB	AB	H	PO	A	E	DP	TC/G	FA	G by Pos
1947	NY	N	62	.221	.295	95	21	1	0	2	2.1	13	18	15	18	1	31	6	46	3	1	2	0.8	.980	OF-19, 1B-2
1948			1	.000	.000	1	0	0	0	0	0.0	0	0	0	1	0	1	0	0	0	0	0	0.0	–	
1949			64	.236	.343	140	33	2	2	3	2.1	18	16	9	23	1	14	6	296	10	5	25	4.9	.984	1B-47
3 yrs.			127	.229	.322	236	54	3	2	5	2.1	31	34	24	42	1	46	12	342	13	6	27	2.8	.983	1B-49, OF-19

Flip Lafferty

LAFFERTY, FRANK BERNARD
B. May 4, 1854, Scranton, Pa.   D. Feb. 8, 1910, Wilmington, Del.   TR

Year	Team		Games	BA	SA	AB	H	2B	3B	HR	HR%	R	RBI	BB	SO	SB	AB	H	PO	A	E	DP	TC/G	FA	G by Pos
1876	PHI	N	1	.000	.000	3	0	0	0	0	0.0	0	0	0	0		0	0	1	2	1	1	4.0	.750	P-1
1877	LOU	N	4	.059	.118	17	1	1	0	0	0.0	2	0	0	4		0	0	3	0	1	0	1.0	.750	OF-4
2 yrs.			5	.050	.100	20	1	1	0	0	0.0	2	0	0	4		0	0	4	2	2	1	1.6	.750	OF-4, P-1

Ty LaForest

LaFOREST, BYRON JOSEPH
B. Apr. 18, 1917, Edmondston, N. B., Canada   D. May 5, 1947, Arlington, Mass.   BR TR 5'8"   160 lbs.

Year	Team		Games	BA	SA	AB	H	2B	3B	HR	HR%	R	RBI	BB	SO	SB	AB	H	PO	A	E	DP	TC/G	FA	G by Pos
1945	BOS	A	52	.250	.353	204	51	7	4	2	1.0	25	16	10	35	4	0	0	51	97	5	11	2.9	.967	3B-45, OF-5

Roger LaFrancois

LaFRANCOIS, ROGER VICTOR
B. Aug. 2, 1954, Norwich, Conn.   BL TR 6'2"   202 lbs.

Year	Team		Games	BA	SA	AB	H	2B	3B	HR	HR%	R	RBI	BB	SO	SB	AB	H	PO	A	E	DP	TC/G	FA	G by Pos
1982	BOS	A	8	.400	.500	10	4	1	0	0	0.0	1	1	0	0	0	2	1	15	0	0	0	1.9	1.000	C-8

Mike Laga

LAGA, MICHAEL RUSSELL
B. June 14, 1960, Ridgewood, N. J.   BL TL 6'2"   210 lbs.

Year	Team		Games	BA	SA	AB	H	2B	3B	HR	HR%	R	RBI	BB	SO	SB	AB	H	PO	A	E	DP	TC/G	FA	G by Pos
1982	DET	A	27	.261	.466	88	23	9	0	3	3.4	6	11	4	23	1	4	1	163	4	1	18	6.2	.994	1B-19, DH-8
1983			12	.190	.190	21	4	0	0	0	0.0	2	2	1	9	0	3	1	9	1	0	2	0.8	1.000	DH-6, 1B-5
1984			9	.545	.545	11	6	0	0	0	0.0	1	3	1	1	0	3	3	12	1	0	1	1.4	1.000	DH-4, 1B-4
1985			9	.167	.361	36	6	1	0	2	5.6	3	6	0	9	0	0	0	33	5	1	4	4.3	.974	DH-5, 1B-4
1986	2 teams			DET A (15G – .200)		STL N (18G – .217)																			
"	total		33	.209	.462	91	19	5	0	6	6.6	13	16	10	31	0	5	1	207	21	0	19	6.9	1.000	1B-28, DH-3
1987	STL	N	17	.138	.276	29	4	1	0	1	3.4	4	4	2	7	0	5	1	66	7	2	10	4.4	.973	1B-12
1988			41	.130	.160	100	13	0	0	1	1.0	5	4	2	21	0	5	2	293	17	0	26	7.6	1.000	1B-37
1989	SF	N	17	.200	.400	20	4	1	0	1	5.0	1	7	1	6	0	11	2	16	1	0	0	1.0	1.000	1B-4
8 yrs.			165	.199	.348	396	79	17	0	14	3.5	35	51	21	108	1	36	8	799	57	4	80	5.2	.995	1B-113, DH-26

Joe Lahoud

LAHOUD, JOSEPH MICHAEL (Duck)
B. Apr. 14, 1947, Danbury, Conn.   BL TL 6'1"   198 lbs.

Year	Team		Games	BA	SA	AB	H	2B	3B	HR	HR%	R	RBI	BB	SO	SB	AB	H	PO	A	E	DP	TC/G	FA	G by Pos
1968	BOS	A	29	.192	.244	78	15	1	0	1	1.3	5	6	16	16	0	6	2	23	2	2	0	0.9	.926	OF-25
1969			101	.188	.335	218	41	5	0	9	4.1	32	21	40	43	2	25	2	91	3	2	0	1.0	.979	OF-66, 1B-1
1970			17	.245	.388	49	12	1	0	2	4.1	6	5	7	6	0	4	2	23	1	1	0	1.6	.963	OF-13
1971			107	.215	.438	256	55	9	3	14	5.5	39	32	40	45	2	29	8	139	4	1	3	1.3	.993	OF-69
1972	MIL	A	111	.237	.399	316	75	9	3	12	3.8	35	34	45	54	3	11	4	189	2	5	0	1.8	.974	OF-97
1973			96	.204	.311	225	46	9	0	5	2.2	29	26	27	36	5	15	4	85	2	0	1	0.9	1.000	DH-41, OF-40
1974	CAL	A	127	.271	.458	325	88	16	3	13	4.0	46	44	47	57	4	14	4	156	6	4	2	1.3	.976	OF-106, DH-10
1975			76	.214	.359	192	41	6	2	6	3.1	21	33	48	33	2	9	2	41	1	0	0	0.6	1.000	DH-35, OF-29
1976	2 teams			CAL A (42G – .177)		TEX A (38G – .225)																			
"	total		80	.200	.265	185	37	1	0	1	0.5	18	9	28	32	1	21	3	54	0	2	0	0.7	.964	DH-50, OF-31
1977	KC	A	34	.262	.431	65	17	5	0	2	3.1	8	8	11	16	1	12	3	18	2	1	0	0.6	.952	OF-15, DH-4
1978			13	.125	.125	16	2	0	0	0	0.0	0	0	0	11	0	12	2	0	0	0	0	0.0	–	DH-1, OF-1
11 yrs.			791	.223	.372	1925	429	68	12	65	3.4	239	218	309	339	20	158	36	819	25	18	6	1.1	.979	OF-492, DH-141, 1B-1

LEAGUE CHAMPIONSHIP SERIES

Year	Team		Games	BA	SA	AB	H	2B	3B	HR	HR%	R	RBI	BB	SO	SB	AB	H	PO	A	E	DP	TC/G	FA	G by Pos
1977	KC	A	1	.000	.000	1	0	0	0	0	0.0	2	0	2	0	0	0	0	0	0	0	0	0.0	–	DH-1

Dick Lajeskie

LAJESKIE, RICHARD EDWARD
B. Jan. 8, 1926, Passaic, N. J.   D. Aug. 15, 1976, Ramsey, N. J.   BR TR 5'11"   175 lbs.

Year	Team		Games	BA	SA	AB	H	2B	3B	HR	HR%	R	RBI	BB	SO	SB	AB	H	PO	A	E	DP	TC/G	FA	G by Pos
1946	NY	N	6	.200	.200	10	2	0	0	0	0.0	3	0	3	2	0	0	0	7	20	1	1	4.7	.964	2B-4

Nap Lajoie

LAJOIE, NAPOLEON (Larry)
B. Sept. 5, 1874, Woonsocket, R. I.   D. Feb. 7, 1959, Daytona Beach, Fla.   BR TR 6'1"   195 lbs.
Manager 1905-09.
Hall of Fame 1937.

Year	Team		Games	BA	SA	AB	H	2B	3B	HR	HR%	R	RBI	BB	SO	SB	AB	H	PO	A	E	DP	TC/G	FA	G by Pos
1896	PHI	N	39	.326	.543	175	57	12	7	4	2.3	36	42	1		11	7	0	363	11	2	27	9.6	.995	1B-39
1897			126	.361	.569	545	197	40	23	9	1.7	107	127	15		20	0	0	1117	45	20	45	9.4	.983	1B-108, OF-19, 3B-2
1898			147	.324	.461	608	197	43	11	6	1.0	113	127	21		25	0	0	449	407	46	60	6.1	.949	2B-146, 1B-1
1899			76	.378	.554	312	118	19	9	6	1.9	70	70	12		13	4	2	236	232	22	39	6.4	.955	2B-67, OF-5
1900			102	.337	.510	451	152	33	12	7	1.6	95	92	10		22	0	0	287	341	30	66	6.5	.954	2B-102, 3B-1
1901	PHI	A	131	.422	.635	543	229	48	13	14	2.6	145	125	24		27	0	0	430	424	34	63	6.8	.962	2B-119, SS-12

Year	Team	Games	BA	SA	AB	H	2B	3B	HR	HR%	R	RBI	BB	SO	SB	Pinch Hit AB	Pinch Hit H	PO	A	E	DP	TC/G	FA	G by Pos

Nap Lajoie *continued*

Year	Team	Games	BA	SA	AB	H	2B	3B	HR	HR%	R	RBI	BB	SO	SB	AB	H	PO	A	E	DP	TC/G	FA	G by Pos
1902	2 teams	PHI A	(1G – .250)		CLE A	(86G – .368)																		
"	total	87	.366	.551	352	129	34	5	7	2.0	81	65	19		19	0	0	272	286	15	49	6.6	.974	2B-87
1903	CLE A	126	.355	.533	488	173	40	13	7	1.4	90	93	24		22	1	0	378	407	36	61	6.5	.956	2B-123, 3B-1, 1B-1
1904		140	.381	.554	554	211	50	14	6	1.1	92	102	27		31	1	0	378	386	38	52	5.7	.953	2B-95, SS-44, 1B-2
1905		65	.329	.422	249	82	13	2	2	0.8	29	41	17		11	1	0	198	179	3	27	5.8	.992	2B-59, 1B-5
1906		152	.355	.460	602	214	49	7	0	0.0	88	91	30		20	0	0	389	479	28	81	5.9	.969	2B-130, 3B-15, SS-7
1907		137	.299	.393	509	152	30	6	2	0.4	53	63	30		24	0	0	409	472	26	66	6.6	.971	2B-128, 1B-9
1908		157	.289	.375	581	168	32	6	2	0.3	77	74	47		15	0	0	460	543	37	78	6.6	.964	2B-156, 1B-1
1909		128	.324	.431	469	152	33	7	1	0.2	56	47	35		13	0	0	282	373	28	60	5.3	.959	2B-120, 1B-8
1910		159	.384	.514	591	227	51	7	4	0.7	92	76	60		26	0	0	512	438	31	63	6.2	.968	2B-149, 1B-10, SS-4
1911		90	.365	.454	315	115	20	1	2	0.6	36	60	26		13	9	4	479	109	14	33	6.7	.977	1B-41, 2B-37
1912		117	.368	.462	448	165	34	4	0	0.0	66	90	28		18	0	0	412	261	24	62	6.0	.966	2B-97, 1B-20
1913		137	.335	.404	465	156	25	2	1	0.2	67	68	33	17	17	9	2	279	363	20	59	4.8	.970	2B-126
1914		121	.258	.305	419	108	14	3	0	0.0	37	50	32	15	14	9	1	487	233	22	67	6.1	.970	2B-80, 1B-31
1915	PHI A	129	.280	.355	490	137	24	5	1	0.2	40	61	11	16	10	1	0	318	373	26	67	5.6	.964	2B-110, SS-10, 1B-5, 3B-2
1916		113	.246	.312	426	105	14	4	2	0.5	33	35	14	26	15	1	0	307	332	17	62	5.8	.974	2B-105, 1B-5, OF-2
	21 yrs.	2479	.338	.466	9592	3244	658	161	83	0.9	1503	1599	516	85	382	35	9	8442	6694	519	1211	6.3	.967	2B-2036, 1B-286, SS-77, OF-26, 3B-21
						10th	5th																	

Eddie Lake

LAKE, EDWARD ERVING
B. Mar. 18, 1916, Antioch, Calif.   BR TR 5'7" 159 lbs.

Year	Team	Games	BA	SA	AB	H	2B	3B	HR	HR%	R	RBI	BB	SO	SB	AB	H	PO	A	E	DP	TC/G	FA	G by Pos
1939	STL N	2	.250	.250	4	1	0	0	0	0.0	1	0	0	0	0	0	0	3	3	1	1	3.5	.857	SS-2
1940		32	.212	.348	66	14	3	0	2	3.0	12	7	12	17	1	5	0	35	39	3	4	2.4	.961	2B-17, SS-6
1941		45	.105	.132	76	8	2	0	0	0.0	9	0	15	22	3	6	1	40	56	9	11	2.3	.914	SS-15, 3B-15, 2B-5
1943	BOS A	75	.199	.287	216	43	10	0	3	1.4	26	16	47	35	3	2	0	128	195	13	43	4.5	.961	SS-63
1944		57	.206	.246	126	26	5	0	0	0.0	21	8	23	22	5	1	0	54	117	13	29	3.2	.929	SS-41, P-6, 3B-3, 3B-1
1945		133	.279	.410	473	132	27	1	11	2.3	81	51	106	37	9	1	0	265	459	40	112	5.7	.948	SS-130, 2B-1
1946	DET A	155	.254	.339	587	149	24	1	8	1.4	105	31	103	69	15	0	0	232	391	35	85	4.2	.947	SS-155
1947		158	.211	.322	602	127	19	6	12	2.0	96	46	120	54	11	0	0	268	441	43	94	4.8	.943	SS-158
1948		64	.263	.323	198	52	6	0	2	1.0	51	18	57	20	3	0	0	122	147	8	31	4.3	.971	2B-45, 3B-17
1949		94	.196	.254	240	47	9	1	1	0.4	38	15	61	33	2	12	2	113	167	10	37	3.1	.966	SS-38, 2B-19, 3B-18
1950		20	.000	.000	7	0	0	0	0	0.0	3	1	1	3	0	7	0					0.0	–	SS-1, 3B-1
	11 yrs.	835	.231	.323	2595	599	105	4	39	1.5	442	193	546	312	52	34	3	1260	2015	175	447	4.1	.949	SS-609, 2B-90, 3B-52, P-6

Fred Lake

LAKE, FREDERICK LOVETT
B. Oct. 16, 1866, Nova Scotia, Canada   D. Nov. 24, 1931, Boston, Mass.   BR TR
Manager 1908-10.

Year	Team	Games	BA	SA	AB	H	2B	3B	HR	HR%	R	RBI	BB	SO	SB	AB	H	PO	A	E	DP	TC/G	FA	G by Pos
1891	BOS N	5	.143	.143	7	1	0	0	0	0.0	1	0	2	4	0	0	0	3	2	0	0	1.0	1.000	C-4, OF-1
1894	LOU N	16	.286	.405	42	12	3	0	1	2.4	8	10	11	6	2	0	0	36	21	11	5	4.3	.838	2B-6, SS-5, C-5
1897	BOS N	19	.242	.306	62	15	4	0	0	0.0	2	5	1		2	1	0	49	15	2	0	3.5	.970	C-18
1898	PIT N	5	.077	.077	13	1	0	0	0	0.0	1	1	2		0	1	0	33	1	0	3	6.8	1.000	1B-3
1910	BOS N	3	.000	.000	1	0	0	0	0	0.0	0	0	1		0	1	0						–	
	5 yrs.	48	.232	.304	125	29	6	0	1	0.8	12	16	17	10	4	3	0	121	39	13	8	3.6	.925	C-27, 2B-6, SS-5, 1B-3, OF-1

Steve Lake

LAKE, STEVEN MICHAEL
B. Mar. 14, 1957, Inglewood, Calif.   BR TR 6'1" 180 lbs.

Year	Team	Games	BA	SA	AB	H	2B	3B	HR	HR%	R	RBI	BB	SO	SB	AB	H	PO	A	E	DP	TC/G	FA	G by Pos
1983	CHI N	38	.259	.365	85	22	4	1	1	1.2	9	7	2	6	0	6	0	115	22	0	3	3.6	1.000	C-32
1984		25	.222	.407	54	12	4	0	2	3.7	4	7	0	7	0	1	0	72	13	4	0	3.6	.955	C-24
1985		58	.151	.193	119	18	2	0	1	0.8	5	11	3	21	1	4	1	182	25	1	1	3.6	.995	C-55
1986	2 teams	CHI N	(10G – .421)		STL N	(26G – .245)																		
"	total	36	.294	.412	68	20	2	0	2	2.9	8	14	3	7	0	0	0	105	9	2	3	3.2	.983	C-36
1987	STL N	74	.251	.346	179	45	7	2	2	1.1	19	19	10	18	0	14	4	253	21	1	2	3.7	.983	C-59
1988		36	.278	.389	54	15	3	0	1	1.9	5	4	3	9	0	17	5	51	8	1	1	1.7	.983	C-19
1989	PHI N	58	.252	.335	155	39	5	1	2	1.3	9	14	12	20	0	7	3	262	33	3	3	5.1	.990	C-55
	7 yrs.	325	.239	.335	714	171	27	4	11	1.5	59	76	33	94	1	48	13	1040	131	12	13	3.6	.990	C-280

LEAGUE CHAMPIONSHIP SERIES

1984	CHI N	1	1.000	2.000	1	1	1	0	0	0.0	0	0	0	0	0	0	0	0	0	0	0	0.0	–	C-1

WORLD SERIES

1987	STL N	3	.333	.333	3	1	0	0	0	0.0	0	1	0	0	0	0	0	8	1	0	0	3.0	1.000	C-3

Al Lakeman

LAKEMAN, ALBERT WESLEY (Moose)
B. Dec. 31, 1918, Cincinnati, Ohio   D. May 25, 1976, Spartanburg, S. C.   BR TR 6'2" 195 lbs.

Year	Team	Games	BA	SA	AB	H	2B	3B	HR	HR%	R	RBI	BB	SO	SB	AB	H	PO	A	E	DP	TC/G	FA	G by Pos
1942	CIN N	20	.158	.184	38	6	1	0	0	0.0	0	2	3	10	0	2	0	57	7	2	2	3.3	.970	C-17
1943		22	.255	.327	55	14	2	0	1	0.0	5	6	3	11	0	1	0	55	8	0	2	2.9	1.000	C-21
1944		1	.000	.000	1	0	0	0	0	0.0	0	0	0	1	0	0	0	0	0	0	0	0.0	–	
1945		76	.256	.415	258	66	9	4	8	3.1	22	31	17	45	0	2	0	226	31	10	4	3.5	.963	C-74
1946		23	.133	.133	30	4	0	0	0	0.0	0	2	7	0	16	0	12	2	0	0	0.6	1.000	C-6
1947	2 teams	CIN N	(2G – .000)		PHI N	(55G – .159)																		
"	total	57	.158	.272	184	29	3	0	6	3.3	11	19	5	40	0	5	0	286	18	4	16	5.4	.987	1B-29, C-23
1948	PHI N	32	.162	.235	68	11	2	0	1	1.5	2	4	5	22	0	9	1	73	4	0	0	2.4	1.000	C-22, P-1
1949	BOS N	3	.167	.167	6	1	0	0	0	0.0	1	0	1	0	0	1	0	19	2	0	2	7.0	1.000	1B-2
1954	DET A	5	.000	.000	6	0	0	0	0	0.0	0	0	0	4	0	0	0	10	0	0	0	2.0	1.000	C-4
	9 yrs.	239	.203	.314	646	131	17	5	15	2.3	40	66	36	137	0	38	1	738	72	16	26	3.5	.981	C-167, 1B-31, P-1

Bud Lally

LALLY, DANIEL J.
B. Aug. 12, 1867, Jersey City, N. J.   D. Apr. 14, 1936, Milwaukee, Wis.   BL TR 5'11½" 210 lbs.

Year	Team	Games	BA	SA	AB	H	2B	3B	HR	HR%	R	RBI	BB	SO	SB	AB	H	PO	A	E	DP	TC/G	FA	G by Pos
1891	PIT N	41	.224	.315	143	32	6	2	1	0.7	24	17	16	20	0	0	0	45	2	9	0	1.4	.839	OF-41
1897	STL N	87	.279	.366	355	99	15	5	2	0.6	56	42	9		12	0	0	223	12	25	3	3.0	.904	OF-84, 1B-3
	2 yrs.	128	.263	.351	498	131	21	7	3	0.6	80	59	25	20	12	0	0	268	14	34	3	2.5	.892	OF-125, 1B-3

Year	Team	Games	BA	SA	AB	H	2B	3B	HR	HR%	R	RBI	BB	SO	SB	Pinch Hit AB	Pinch Hit H	PO	A	E	DP	TC/G	FA	G by Pos

Ray Lamanno

LAMANNO, RAYMOND SIMOND
B. Nov. 17, 1919, Oakland, Calif.
BR TR 6' 185 lbs.

Year	Team	Games	BA	SA	AB	H	2B	3B	HR	HR%	R	RBI	BB	SO	SB	PH AB	PH H	PO	A	E	DP	TC/G	FA	G by Pos
1941	CIN N	1	–	–	0	0	0	0	0	–	0	0	0	0	0	0	0	1	0	0	0	1.0	1.000	C-1
1942		111	.264	.404	371	98	12	2	12	3.2	40	43	31	54	0	7	1	421	59	11	7	4.4	.978	C-104
1946		85	.243	.305	239	58	12	2	1	0.4	18	30	11	26	0	21	4	222	37	7	6	3.1	.974	C-61
1947		118	.257	.358	413	106	21	3	5	1.2	33	50	28	39	0	9	2	556	62	9	6	5.3	.986	C-109
1948		127	.242	.273	385	93	12	0	0	0	31	27	48	32	2	3	0	537	49	13	11	4.7	.978	C-125
5 yrs.		442	.252	.338	1408	355	57	5	18	1.3	122	150	118	151	2	40	7	1737	207	40	30	4.5	.980	C-400

Bill Lamar

LAMAR, WILLIAM HARMONG (Good Time Bill)
B. Mar. 21, 1897, Rockville, Md.
D. May 24, 1970, Rockport, Mass.
BL TR 6'1" 185 lbs.
BB 1927

Year	Team	Games	BA	SA	AB	H	2B	3B	HR	HR%	R	RBI	BB	SO	SB	PH AB	PH H	PO	A	E	DP	TC/G	FA	G by Pos
1917	NY A	11	.244	.244	41	10	0	0	0	0.0	2	3	0	2	1	0	0	26	1	0	0	2.5	1.000	OF-11
1918		28	.227	.255	110	25	3	0	0	0.0	12	2	6	2	2	1	1	58	3	8	2	2.5	.884	OF-27
1919	2 teams		NY A (11G – .188)		BOS A	(48G – .291)																		
"	total	59	.280	.329	164	46	8	1	0	0.0	19	14	7	10	4	19	3	69	7	6	1	1.4	.927	OF-39, 1B-1
1920	BKN N	24	.273	.364	44	12	4	0	0	0.0	5	4	0	1	0	10	3	12	1	0	0	0.5	1.000	OF-12
1921		3	.333	.333	3	1	0	0	0	0.0	2	0	0	0	0	2	1	0	0	0	0	0.0	–	OF-1
1924	PHI A	87	.330	.474	367	121	22	5	7	1.9	68	48	18	21	8	0	0	184	13	6	4	2.3	.970	OF-87
1925		138	.356	.468	568	202	39	8	3	0.5	85	77	21	17	2	6	1	283	18	15	4	2.3	.953	OF-131
1926		116	.284	.389	419	119	17	6	5	1.2	62	50	18	15	4	8	3	199	10	10	2	1.9	.954	OF-105
1927		84	.299	.426	324	97	23	3	4	1.2	48	47	16	10	4	5	1	148	9	8	1	2.0	.952	OF-79
9 yrs.		550	.310	.417	2040	633	114	23	19	0.9	303	245	86	78	25	51	13	979	62	53	14	2.0	.952	OF-492, 1B-1

WORLD SERIES

Year	Team	Games	BA	SA	AB	H	2B	3B	HR	HR%	R	RBI	BB	SO	SB	PH AB	PH H	PO	A	E	DP	TC/G	FA	G by Pos
1920	BKN N	3	.000	.000	3	0	0	0	0	0.0	0	0	0	0	0	3	0	0	0	0	0	0.0	–	

Lyman Lamb

LAMB, LAYMON RAYMOND
B. Mar. 17, 1895, Lincoln, Neb.   D. Oct. 5, 1955, Fayetteville, Ark.
BR TR 5'7" 150 lbs.

Year	Team	Games	BA	SA	AB	H	2B	3B	HR	HR%	R	RBI	BB	SO	SB	PH AB	PH H	PO	A	E	DP	TC/G	FA	G by Pos
1920	STL A	9	.375	.458	24	9	2	0	0	0.0	4	4	0	7	2	2	1	10	0	0	0	1.1	1.000	OF-7
1921		45	.254	.373	134	34	9	2	1	0.7	18	17	4	12	0	5	1	38	62	6	3	2.4	.943	3B-23, 2B-7, OF-6
2 yrs.		54	.272	.386	158	43	11	2	1	0.6	22	21	4	19	2	7	2	48	62	6	3	2.1	.948	3B-23, OF-13, 2B-7

Pete Lamer

LAMER, PIERRE
Born Pierre Lamere.
B. 1874, Hoboken, N. J.   D. Oct. 24, 1931, Brooklyn, N. Y.
TR

Year	Team	Games	BA	SA	AB	H	2B	3B	HR	HR%	R	RBI	BB	SO	SB	PH AB	PH H	PO	A	E	DP	TC/G	FA	G by Pos
1902	CHI N	2	.222	.222	9	2	0	0	0	0.0	2		0	0	0	0	0	9	3	2	1	7.0	.857	C-2
1907	CIN N	1	.000	.000	2	0	0	0	0	0.0	0		0	0	0	0	0	0	1	0	0	1.0	1.000	C-1
2 yrs.		3	.182	.182	11	2	0	0	0	0.0	2		0	0	0	0	0	9	4	2	1	5.0	.867	C-3

Gene Lamont

LAMONT, GENE WILLIAM
B. Dec. 25, 1946, Rockford, Ill.
BL TR 6'1" 195 lbs.

Year	Team	Games	BA	SA	AB	H	2B	3B	HR	HR%	R	RBI	BB	SO	SB	PH AB	PH H	PO	A	E	DP	TC/G	FA	G by Pos
1970	DET A	15	.295	.477	44	13	3	1	2	2.3	3	4	2	9	0	0	0	87	8	0	0	6.3	1.000	C-15
1971		7	.067	.067	15	1	0	0	0	0.0	2	1	0	5	0	0	0	38	2	2	0	6.0	.952	C-7
1972		1	–	–	0	0	0	0	0	–	0	0	0	0	0	0	0	1	0	0	0	1.0	1.000	C-1
1974		60	.217	.359	92	20	4	0	3	3.3	9	8	7	19	0	0	0	204	21	6	0	3.9	.974	C-60
1975		4	.375	.500	8	3	1	0	0	0.0	1	1	0	2	1	0	0	14	3	1	0	4.5	.944	C-4
5 yrs.		87	.233	.371	159	37	8	1	4	2.5	15	14	9	35	1	0	0	344	34	9	0	4.4	.977	C-87

Bobby LaMotte

LaMOTTE, ROBERT EUGENE
B. Feb. 15, 1898, Savannah, Ga.   D. Nov. 2, 1970, Chatham, Ga.
BR TR 5'11" 160 lbs.

Year	Team	Games	BA	SA	AB	H	2B	3B	HR	HR%	R	RBI	BB	SO	SB	PH AB	PH H	PO	A	E	DP	TC/G	FA	G by Pos
1920	WAS A	4	.000	.000	3	0	0	0	0	0.0	0	0	1	0	0	0	0	0	4	1	0	1.3	.800	SS-1, 3B-1
1921		16	.195	.195	41	8	0	0	0	0.0	5	2	5	0	0	0	0	20	43	4	0	4.2	.940	SS-12
1922		68	.252	.332	214	54	10	2	1	0.5	22	23	15	21	6	0	0	101	147	11	17	3.8	.958	3B-62, SS-6
1925	STL A	97	.272	.368	356	97	20	4	2	0.6	61	51	34	22	5	2	0	223	275	39	57	5.5	.927	SS-93, 3B-3
1926		36	.203	.329	79	16	4	3	0	0.0	11	9	11	6	0	4	0	47	66	10	15	3.4	.919	SS-30, 3B-1
5 yrs.		221	.253	.341	693	175	34	9	3	0.4	99	85	66	50	11	6	0	391	535	65	89	4.5	.934	SS-142, 3B-67

Keith Lampard

LAMPARD, CHRISTOPHER KEITH
B. Dec. 20, 1945, Warrington, England
BL TR 6'2" 197 lbs.

Year	Team	Games	BA	SA	AB	H	2B	3B	HR	HR%	R	RBI	BB	SO	SB	PH AB	PH H	PO	A	E	DP	TC/G	FA	G by Pos
1969	HOU N	9	.250	.500	12	3	0	0	1	8.3	2	2	0	3	0	7	3	3	1	0	0	0.4	1.000	OF-1
1970		53	.236	.375	72	17	8	1	0	0.0	8	5	5	24	0	38	9	25	2	0	0	0.5	1.000	OF-16, 1B-2
2 yrs.		62	.238	.393	84	20	8	1	1	1.2	10	7	5	27	0	45	12	28	3	0	0	0.5	1.000	OF-17, 1B-2

Tom Lampkin

LAMPKIN, THOMAS MICHAEL
B. Mar. 4, 1964, Cincinnati, Ohio
BL TR 5'11" 180 lbs.

Year	Team	Games	BA	SA	AB	H	2B	3B	HR	HR%	R	RBI	BB	SO	SB	PH AB	PH H	PO	A	E	DP	TC/G	FA	G by Pos
1988	CLE A	4	.000	.000	4	0	0	0	0	0.0	1	0	0	1	0	1	0	3	0	0	0	0.8	1.000	C-3

Rick Lancellotti

LANCELLOTTI, RICHARD ANTHONY
B. July 5, 1956, Providence, R. I.
BL TL 6'3" 195 lbs.

Year	Team	Games	BA	SA	AB	H	2B	3B	HR	HR%	R	RBI	BB	SO	SB	PH AB	PH H	PO	A	E	DP	TC/G	FA	G by Pos
1982	SD N	17	.179	.231	39	7	2	0	0	0.0	2	4	2	8	0	8	1	63	2	1	7	3.9	.985	1B-7, OF-3
1986	SF N	15	.222	.556	18	4	0	0	2	11.1	2	6	0	7	0	13	4	7	0	0	0	0.5	1.000	OF-1, 1B-1
2 yrs.		32	.193	.333	57	11	2	0	2	3.5	4	10	2	15	0	21	5	70	2	1	7	2.3	.986	1B-8, OF-4

Doc Land

LAND, WILLIAM GILBERT
Born Doc Burrell Land.
B. May 14, 1903, Bennsville, Miss.   D. Apr. 14, 1986, Livingston, Ala.
BL TL 5'11" 165 lbs.

Year	Team	Games	BA	SA	AB	H	2B	3B	HR	HR%	R	RBI	BB	SO	SB	PH AB	PH H	PO	A	E	DP	TC/G	FA	G by Pos
1929	WAS A	1	.000	.000	3	0	0	0	0	0.0	0	0	0	1	0	0	0	1	0	0	0	1.0	1.000	OF-1

Grover Land

LAND, GROVER CLEVELAND
B. Sept. 22, 1884, Frankfort, Ky.   D. July 22, 1958, Phoenix, Ariz.
BR TR 6' 190 lbs.

Year	Team		Games	BA	SA	AB	H	2B	3B	HR	HR%	R	RBI	BB	SO	SB	Pinch Hit AB	Pinch Hit H	PO	A	E	DP	TC/G	FA	G by Pos

Grover Land *continued*

1908	CLE	A	8	.188	.188	16	3	0	0	0	0.0	1	2	0		0	0	0	18	3	1	0	2.8	.955	C-8
1910			34	.207	.207	111	23	0	0	0	0.0	4	7	2		1	0	0	169	47	4	3	6.5	.982	C-33
1911			35	.140	.187	107	15	1	2	0	0.0	5	10	3		2	0	0	148	50	8	5	5.9	.961	C-34, 1B-1
1913			17	.234	.255	47	11	1	0	0	0.0	3	9	4	1	1	1	1	83	26	9	3	6.9	.924	C-17
1914	BKN	F	102	.275	.304	335	92	6	2	0	0.0	24	29	12		7	5	1	490	147	20	11	6.4	.970	C-97
1915			96	.259	.317	290	75	13	2	0	0.0	25	22	6		3	14	3	314	114	18	13	4.6	.960	C-81
6 yrs.			292	.242	.278	906	219	21	6	0	0.0	62	79	27	1	14	20	5	1222	387	60	35	5.7	.964	C-270, 1B-1

Ken Landenberger

LANDENBERGER, KENNETH HENRY (Red)
B. July 29, 1928, Lyndhurst, Ohio   D. July 28, 1960, Cleveland, Ohio

BL TL 6'3"   200 lbs.

| 1952 | CHI | A | 2 | .200 | .200 | 5 | 1 | 0 | 0 | 0 | 0.0 | 0 | 0 | 0 | 2 | 0 | 1 | 0 | 8 | 1 | 0 | 0 | 4.5 | 1.000 | 1B-1 |

Rafael Landestoy

LANDESTOY, RAFAEL SILVALDO
Born Rafael Silvaldo Landestoy y Santana.
B. May 28, 1953, Bani, Dominican Republic

BB TR 5'10"   165 lbs.

1977	LA	N	15	.278	.278	18	5	0	0	0	0.0	6	3	2	2	0	0	8	18	0	2	1.7	1.000	2B-8, SS-3
1978	HOU	N	59	.266	.298	218	58	5	1	0	0.0	18	9	8	23	7	9	1	66	132	4	19	3.4	.980	SS-50, 2B-2
1979			129	.270	.344	282	76	9	6	0	0.0	33	30	29	24	13	14	2	168	237	12	54	3.2	.971	2B-114, SS-3
1980			149	.247	.328	393	97	13	8	1	0.3	42	27	31	37	23	26	3	185	295	9	67	3.3	.982	2B-94, SS-65, 3B-3
1981	2 teams			HOU N (35G – .149)		CIN N (12G – .182)																				
"	total		47	.153	.188	85	13	1	1	0	0.0	8	5	17	9	5	10	1	55	64	4	11	2.6	.967	2B-34
1982	CIN	N	73	.189	.243	111	21	3	0	1	0.9	11	9	8	14	2	35	11	41	54	0	11	1.3	1.000	3B-21, 2B-16, OF-3, SS-2
1983	2 teams			CIN N (7G – .000)		LA N (64G – .172)																				
"	total		71	.159	.246	69	11	1	1	1	1.4	6	1	3	33	4	34	7	28	3	7	0.9	.954	2B-14, OF-11, 3B-11, 1B-2, SS-1
1984	LA	N	53	.185	.241	54	10	0	0	1	1.9	10	2	1	18	3	22	24	6	5	1.0	.885	2B-14, 3B-11, OF-5
8 yrs.			596	.237	.300	1230	291	32	17	4	0.3	134	83	100	123	54	145	25	579	852	38	176	2.5	.974	2B-296, SS-124, 3B-46, OF-19, 1B-2

LEAGUE CHAMPIONSHIP SERIES

1980	HOU	N	5	.222	.222	9	2	0	0	0	0.0	3	2	1	0	1	0	0	3	4	0	0	1.4	1.000	2B-3, SS-1
1983	LA	N	2	.000	.000	2	0	0	0	0	0.0	0	0	0	2	0	2	0	0	0	0	0	0.0	–	
2 yrs.			7	.182	.182	11	2	0	0	0	0.0	3	2	1	1	1	2	0	3	4	0	0	1.0	1.000	2B-3, SS-1

WORLD SERIES

| 1977 | LA | N | 1 | – | – | 0 | 0 | 0 | 0 | 0 | – | 0 | 0 | 0 | 0 | 0 | 0 | 0 | 0 | 0 | 0 | 0 | 0.0 | – | |

Jim Landis

LANDIS, JAMES HENRY
B. Mar. 9, 1934, Fresno, Calif.

BR TR 6'1"   180 lbs.

1957	CHI	A	96	.212	.296	274	58	11	3	2	0.7	38	16	45	61	14	4	1	192	8	3	4	2.1	.985	OF-90
1958			142	.277	.434	523	145	23	7	15	2.9	72	64	52	80	19	1	0	331	9	5	1	2.4	.986	OF-142
1959			149	.272	.379	515	140	26	7	5	1.0	78	60	78	68	20	0	0	420	10	3	2	2.9	.993	OF-148
1960			148	.253	.389	494	125	25	6	10	2.0	89	49	80	84	23	0	0	372	10	6	3	2.6	.985	OF-147
1961			140	.283	.470	534	151	18	8	22	4.1	87	85	65	71	19	2	0	389	9	5	3	2.9	.988	OF-139
1962			149	.228	.375	534	122	21	6	15	2.8	82	61	80	105	19	4	1	360	2	2	1	2.4	.995	OF-144
1963			133	.225	.369	396	89	6	6	13	3.3	56	45	47	75	8	11	3	264	6	2	0	2.0	.993	OF-124
1964			106	.208	.272	298	62	8	4	1	0.3	30	18	36	64	5	7	1	183	7	1	2	1.8	.995	OF-101
1965	KC	A	118	.239	.310	364	87	15	1	3	0.8	46	36	57	84	8	13	3	258	0	4	0	2.2	.985	OF-108
1966	CLE	A	85	.222	.323	158	35	7	0	3	1.9	23	14	20	25	2	22	4	86	0	0	0	1.0	1.000	OF-61
1967	3 teams			HOU N (50G – .252)		DET A (25G – .208)		BOS A (5G – .143)																		
"	total		80	.237	.364	198	47	11	1	4	2.0	24	19	28	50	2	16	1	72	8	1	1	1.0	.988	OF-61
11 yrs.			1346	.247	.375	4288	1061	169	50	93	2.2	625	467	588	767	139	80	14	2927	69	32	17	2.2	.989	OF-1265

WORLD SERIES

| 1959 | CHI | A | 6 | .292 | .292 | 24 | 7 | 0 | 0 | 0 | 0.0 | 6 | 1 | 7 | 1 | 0 | 0 | 0 | 9 | 0 | 1 | 0 | 1.7 | .900 | OF-6 |

Ken Landreaux

LANDREAUX, KENNETH FRANCIS
B. Dec. 22, 1954, Los Angeles, Calif.

BL TR 5'10"   165 lbs.

1977	CAL	A	23	.250	.342	76	19	5	1	0	0.0	6	5	5	15	1	0	0	59	5	2	2	2.9	.970	OF-22
1978			93	.223	.346	260	58	7	5	5	1.9	37	23	20	20	7	7	2	138	6	2	0	1.6	.986	OF-83, DH-1
1979	MIN	A	151	.305	.450	564	172	27	5	15	2.7	81	83	37	57	10	7	1	292	10	6	1	2.0	.981	OF-147
1980			129	.281	.417	484	136	23	11	7	1.4	56	62	39	42	8	3	2	231	8	6	0	1.9	.976	OF-120, DH-6
1981	LA	N	99	.251	.367	390	98	16	4	7	1.8	48	41	25	42	18	4	1	210	4	0	0	2.2	1.000	OF-95
1982			129	.284	.410	461	131	23	7	7	1.5	71	50	39	54	31	11	1	281	3	4	1	2.2	.986	OF-117
1983			141	.281	.451	481	135	25	3	17	3.5	63	66	34	52	30	4	1	299	4	3	1	2.2	.990	OF-137
1984			134	.251	.374	438	110	11	5	11	2.5	39	47	29	35	10	16	3	212	3	3	2	1.6	.986	OF-129
1985			147	.268	.405	482	129	26	4	12	2.5	70	50	33	37	15	22	4	267	4	7	1	1.9	.975	OF-140
1986			103	.261	.364	283	74	13	2	4	1.4	34	29	22	39	10	31	6	145	5	3	0	1.5	.955	OF-85
1987			115	.203	.324	182	37	4	0	6	3.3	17	23	16	28	1	50	10	72	5	4	3	0.7	.951	OF-63
11 yrs.			1264	.268	.400	4101	1099	180	45	91	2.2	522	479	299	421	145	155	31	2206	57	44	11	1.8	.981	OF-1138, DH-7

DIVISIONAL PLAYOFF SERIES

| 1981 | LA | N | 5 | .200 | .250 | 20 | 4 | 1 | 0 | 0 | 0.0 | 1 | 1 | 0 | 1 | 0 | 0 | 0 | 0 | 0 | 0 | 0 | 0.0 | – | OF-5 |

LEAGUE CHAMPIONSHIP SERIES

1981	LA	N	5	.100	.200	10	1	1	0	0	0.0	0	0	3	3	0	0	0	0	0	0	0	0.0	–	OF-5
1983			4	.143	.143	14	2	0	0	0	0.0	0	1	1	3	0	0	0	12	0	0	0	3.0	1.000	OF-4
1985			5	.389	.556	18	7	3	0	0	0.0	4	2	1	1	0	1	0	7	0	0	0	1.4	1.000	OF-4
3 yrs.			14	.238	.333	42	10	4	0	0	0.0	4	3	5	6	0	1	0	19	0	0	0	1.4	1.000	OF-13

WORLD SERIES

| 1981 | LA | N | 5 | .167 | .333 | 6 | 1 | 1 | 0 | 0 | 0.0 | 1 | 0 | 0 | 2 | 1 | 2 | 1 | 6 | 0 | 0 | 0 | 1.2 | 1.000 | OF-3 |

Year	Team		Games	BA	SA	AB	H	2B	3B	HR	HR%	R	RBI	BB	SO	SB	Pinch Hit AB	Pinch Hit H	PO	A	E	DP	TC/G	FA	G by Pos

Hobie Landrith

LANDRITH, HOBERT NEAL
B. Mar. 16, 1930, Decatur, Ill.
BL TR 5'10" 170 lbs.

Year	Team		Games	BA	SA	AB	H	2B	3B	HR	HR%	R	RBI	BB	SO	SB	PH AB	PH H	PO	A	E	DP	TC/G	FA	G by Pos
1950	CIN	N	4	.214	.214	14	3	0	0	0	0.0	1	1	2	1	0	0	0	15	2	0	0	4.3	1.000	C-4
1951			4	.385	.462	13	5	1	0	0	0.0	3	0	1	1	0	0	0	23	2	0	0	6.3	1.000	C-4
1952			15	.260	.340	50	13	4	0	0	0.0	1	4	0	4	0	1	1	56	7	0	0	4.2	1.000	C-14
1953			52	.240	.331	154	37	3	1	3	1.9	15	16	12	8	2	4	2	179	13	3	4	3.8	.985	C-47
1954			48	.198	.383	81	16	0	0	5	6.2	12	14	18	9	1	5	2	123	15	2	1	2.9	.986	C-42
1955			43	.253	.425	87	22	3	0	4	4.6	9	7	10	14	0	16	3	86	14	0	3	2.3	1.000	C-27
1956	CHI	N	111	.221	.311	312	69	10	3	4	1.3	22	32	39	38	0	15	4	483	55	14	9	5.0	.975	C-99
1957	STL	N	75	.243	.313	214	52	6	0	3	1.4	18	26	25	27	1	10	1	339	29	5	3	5.0	.987	C-67
1958			70	.215	.306	144	31	4	0	3	2.1	9	13	26	21	0	24	5	227	16	2	3	3.5	.992	C-45
1959	SF	N	109	.251	.332	283	71	14	0	3	1.1	30	29	43	23	0	2	1	576	45	5	5	5.7	.992	C-109
1960			71	.242	.311	190	46	10	0	1	0.5	18	20	23	11	1	2	0	346	23	13	5	5.4	.966	C-70
1961			43	.239	.380	71	17	4	0	2	2.8	11	10	12	7	0	13	2	126	9	2	2	3.2	.985	C-30
1962	2 teams			NY	N	(23G –	.289)			BAL	A	(60G –	.222)												
"	total		83	.236	.349	212	50	7	1	5	2.4	24	24	27	12	0	2	0	376	37	9	5	5.1	.979	C-81
1963	2 teams			BAL	A	(2G –	.000)			WAS	A	(42G –	.175)												
"	total		44	.173	.231	104	18	3	0	1	1.0	6	7	15	12	0	7	0	161	17	4	3	4.1	.978	C-38
14 yrs.			772	.233	.327	1929	450	69	5	34	1.8	179	203	253	188	5	101	21	3116	284	59	43	4.5	.983	C-677

Don Landrum

LANDRUM, DONALD LeROY
B. Feb. 16, 1936, Santa Rosa, Calif.
BL TR 6' 180 lbs.

Year	Team		Games	BA	SA	AB	H	2B	3B	HR	HR%	R	RBI	BB	SO	SB	PH AB	PH H	PO	A	E	DP	TC/G	FA	G by Pos
1957	PHI	N	2	.143	.286	7	1	1	0	0	0.0	2	1	0	2	0	0	0	9	0	0	0	4.5	1.000	OF-2
1960	STL	N	13	.245	.408	49	12	0	1	2	4.1	7	3	4	6	3	0	0	34	1	0	0	2.7	1.000	OF-13
1961			28	.167	.242	66	11	2	0	1	1.5	5	3	5	14	1	1	0	42	3	0	1	1.6	1.000	OF-25, 2B-1
1962	2 teams			STL	N	(32G –	.314)			CHI	N	(83G –	.282)												
"	total		115	.286	.330	273	78	5	2	1	0.4	40	18	34	33	11	20	2	141	3	4	3	1.3	.973	OF-85
1963	CHI	N	84	.242	.282	227	55	4	1	1	0.4	27	10	13	42	6	24	3	100	3	3	0	1.3	.972	OF-57
1964			11	.000	.000	11	0	0	0	0	0.0	2	0	1	2	0	8	0	1	1	0	0	0.2	1.000	OF-1
1965			131	.226	.334	425	96	20	4	6	1.4	60	34	36	84	14	15	2	241	3	3	0	1.9	.988	OF-115
1966	SF	N	72	.186	.255	102	19	4	0	1	1.0	9	7	9	18	1	18	2	55	6	2	0	0.9	.968	OF-54
8 yrs.			456	.234	.310	1160	272	36	8	12	1.0	151	75	104	200	36	86	9	623	20	12	4	1.4	.982	OF-352, 2B-1

Jesse Landrum

LANDRUM, JESSE GLENN
B. July 31, 1912, Crockett, Tex. D. June 27, 1983, Beaumont, Tex.
BR TR 5'11½" 175 lbs.

Year	Team		Games	BA	SA	AB	H	2B	3B	HR	HR%	R	RBI	BB	SO	SB	PH AB	PH H	PO	A	E	DP	TC/G	FA	G by Pos
1938	CHI	A	4	.000	.000	6	0	0	0	0	0.0	0	1	2	1	0	1	0	3	0	1	0.8	1.000	2B-3

Tito Landrum

LANDRUM, TERRY LEE
B. Oct. 25, 1954, Joplin, Mo.
BR TR 5'11" 175 lbs.

Year	Team		Games	BA	SA	AB	H	2B	3B	HR	HR%	R	RBI	BB	SO	SB	PH AB	PH H	PO	A	E	DP	TC/G	FA	G by Pos
1980	STL	N	35	.247	.325	77	19	2	2	0	0.0	6	7	6	17	3	5	1	40	1	1	0	1.2	.976	OF-29
1981			81	.261	.370	119	31	5	4	0	0.0	13	10	6	14	4	11	3	72	6	0	1	1.0	1.000	OF-67
1982			79	.278	.403	72	20	3	0	2	2.8	12	14	8	18	0	18	4	50	2	0	1	0.7	1.000	OF-56
1983	2 teams			STL	N	(6G –	.200)			BAL	A	(26G –	.310)												
"	total		32	.298	.447	47	14	1	1	1	2.1	8	4	2	13	1	9	2	6	0	0	0	0.2	1.000	OF-31
1984	STL	N	105	.272	.387	173	47	9	1	3	1.7	21	26	10	27	3	23	9	93	1	2	0	0.9	.979	OF-88
1985			85	.280	.429	161	45	8	2	4	2.5	21	21	19	30	1	24	8	91	2	0	1	1.1	1.000	OF-73
1986			96	.210	.283	205	43	7	1	2	1.0	24	17	20	41	3	28	5	131	6	1	1	1.4	.993	OF-78
1987	2 teams			STL	N	(30G –	.200)			LA	N	(51G –	.239)												
"	total		81	.222	.282	117	26	4	0	1	0.9	13	10	10	30	2	35	8	77	2	1	0	1.0	.988	OF-54, 1B-1
1988	BAL	A	13	.125	.208	24	3	0	1	0	0.0	2	1	2	4	0	1	0	15	0	0	0	1.2	1.000	OF-12, DH-1
9 yrs.			607	.249	.353	995	248	40	12	13	1.3	120	111	85	196	17	154	40	575	20	5	4	1.0	.992	OF-488, DH-1, 1B-1

LEAGUE CHAMPIONSHIP SERIES

Year	Team		Games	BA	SA	AB	H	2B	3B	HR	HR%	R	RBI	BB	SO	SB	PH AB	PH H	PO	A	E	DP	TC/G	FA	G by Pos
1983	BAL	A	4	.200	.500	10	2	0	0	1	10.0	2	1	0	1	0	0	0	5	0	0	0	1.3	1.000	OF-3
1985	STL	N	6	.429	.429	14	6	0	0	0	0.0	2	4	1	1	1	1	1	6	0	0	0	1.0	1.000	OF-5
2 yrs.			10	.333	.458	24	8	0	0	1	4.2	4	5	1	3	1	1	1	11	0	0	0	1.1	1.000	OF-8

WORLD SERIES

Year	Team		Games	BA	SA	AB	H	2B	3B	HR	HR%	R	RBI	BB	SO	SB	PH AB	PH H	PO	A	E	DP	TC/G	FA	G by Pos
1983	BAL	A	3	–	–	0	0	0	0	0	0.0	0	0	0	0	0	0	0	1	0	0	0	0.3	1.000	OF-3
1985	STL	N	7	.360	.560	25	9	2	0	1	4.0	3	1	0	2	0	0	0	12	1	0	1	1.9	1.000	OF-7
2 yrs.			10	.360	.560	25	9	2	0	1	4.0	3	1	0	2	1	0	0	13	1	0	1	1.4	1.000	OF-10

Chappy Lane

LANE, GEORGE M.
B. Pittsburgh, Pa. D. Mar. 8, 1896, Pittsburgh, Pa.

Year	Team		Games	BA	SA	AB	H	2B	3B	HR	HR%	R	RBI	BB	SO	SB	PH AB	PH H	PO	A	E	DP	TC/G	FA	G by Pos
1882	PIT	AA	57	.178	.276	214	38	8	2	3	1.4	26		5			0	0	516	22	18	21	9.8	.968	1B-43, OF-13, C-2
1884	TOL	AA	57	.228	.330	215	49	9	5	1	0.5	26		2			0	0	493	32	34	18	9.8	.939	1B-46, OF-9, 3B-2, C-1
2 yrs.			114	.203	.303	429	87	17	7	4	0.9	52		7			0	0	1009	54	52	39	9.8	.953	1B-89, OF-22, C-3, 3B-2

Dick Lane

LANE, RICHARD HARRISON
B. June 28, 1927, Highland Park, Mich.
BR TR 5'11" 178 lbs.

Year	Team		Games	BA	SA	AB	H	2B	3B	HR	HR%	R	RBI	BB	SO	SB	PH AB	PH H	PO	A	E	DP	TC/G	FA	G by Pos
1949	CHI	A	12	.119	.119	42	5	0	0	0	0.0	4	4	5	3	0	1	0	25	2	0	0	2.3	1.000	OF-11

Hunter Lane

LANE, JAMES HUNTER (Dodo)
B. July 20, 1900, Pulaski, Tenn.
BR TR 5'11" 165 lbs.

Year	Team		Games	BA	SA	AB	H	2B	3B	HR	HR%	R	RBI	BB	SO	SB	PH AB	PH H	PO	A	E	DP	TC/G	FA	G by Pos
1924	BOS	N	7	.067	.067	15	1	0	0	0	0.0	0	0	1	1	0	2	0	7	4	1	0	1.7	.917	3B-4, 2B-1

Marv Lane

LANE, MARVIN
B. Jan. 18, 1950, Sandersville, Ga.
BR TR 5'11" 180 lbs.

Year	Team		Games	BA	SA	AB	H	2B	3B	HR	HR%	R	RBI	BB	SO	SB	PH AB	PH H	PO	A	E	DP	TC/G	FA	G by Pos
1971	DET	A	8	.143	.143	14	2	0	0	0	0.0	1	1	1	3	0	2	0	6	0	0	0	0.8	1.000	OF-6
1972			8	.000	.000	6	0	0	0	0	0.0	2	0	0	2	0	1	0	3	0	0	0	0.4	1.000	OF-3
1973			6	.250	.625	8	2	0	0	1	12.5	2	2	1	2	0	1	0	7	0	0	0	1.2	1.000	OF-4
1974			50	.233	.350	103	24	4	1	2	1.9	16	9	19	24	2	5	3	70	3	1	0	1.5	.986	OF-46, DH-1

Year	Team	Games	BA	SA	AB	H	2B	3B	HR	HR%	R	RBI	BB	SO	SB	Pinch Hit AB	Pinch Hit H	PO	A	E	DP	TC/G	FA	G by Pos

Marv Lane *continued*

Year	Team	Games	BA	SA	AB	H	2B	3B	HR	HR%	R	RBI	BB	SO	SB	AB	H	PO	A	E	DP	TC/G	FA	G by Pos
1976		18	.188	.208	48	9	1	0	0	0.0	3	5	6	11	0	3	0	23	1	1	0	1.4	.960	OF-15
5 yrs.		90	.207	.296	179	37	5	1	3	1.7	23	17	28	42	2	11	3	109	4	2	0	1.3	.983	OF-74, DH-1

Don Lang

LANG, DONALD CHARLES
B. Mar. 15, 1915, Selma, Calif.

BR TR 6' 175 lbs.

Year	Team	Games	BA	SA	AB	H	2B	3B	HR	HR%	R	RBI	BB	SO	SB	AB	H	PO	A	E	DP	TC/G	FA	G by Pos
1938	CIN N	21	.260	.420	50	13	3	1	1	2.0	5	11	2	7	0	2	2	17	26	2	3	2.1	.956	3B-15, SS-1, 2B-1
1948	STL N	117	.269	.356	323	87	14	1	4	1.2	30	31	47	38	2	16	1	86	191	11	15	2.5	.962	3B-95, 2B-2
2 yrs.		138	.268	.365	373	100	17	2	5	1.3	35	42	49	45	2	18	3	103	217	13	18	2.4	.961	3B-110, 2B-3, SS-1

Bill Lange

LANGE, WILLIAM ALEXANDER (Little Eva)
B. June 6, 1871, San Francisco, Calif. D. July 23, 1950, San Francisco, Calif.

BR TR 6'1½" 190 lbs.

Year	Team	Games	BA	SA	AB	H	2B	3B	HR	HR%	R	RBI	BB	SO	SB	AB	H	PO	A	E	DP	TC/G	FA	G by Pos
1893	CHI N	117	.281	.380	469	132	8	7	8	1.7	92	88	52	20	47	0	0	303	250	60	28	5.2	.902	2B-57, OF-40, 3B-8, SS-7, C-7
1894		111	.328	.446	442	145	16	9	6	1.4	84	90	56	18	65	0	0	270	29	36	10	3.0	.893	OF-109, SS-2, 3B-1
1895		123	.389	.575	478	186	27	16	10	2.1	120	98	55	24	67	0	0	298	28	27	6	2.9	.924	OF-123
1896		122	.326	.465	469	153	21	16	4	0.9	114	92	65	24	84	0	0	314	18	24	3	2.9	.933	OF-121, C-1
1897		118	.340	.480	479	163	24	14	5	1.0	119	83	48		73	0	0	264	17	16	4	2.5	.946	OF-118
1898		113	.319	.441	442	141	16	10	6	1.4	79	69	36		22	0	0	286	19	9	5	2.8	.971	OF-111, 1B-2
1899		107	.325	.416	416	135	21	7	1	0.2	81	58	38		41	0	0	373	26	11	20	3.8	.973	OF-94, 1B-14
7 yrs.		811	.330	.459	3195	1055	133	79	40	1.3	689	578	350	86	399	0	0	2108	387	183	76	3.3	.932	OF-716, 2B-57, 1B-16, SS-9, 3B-9, C-8

Frank Lange

LANGE, FRANK HERMAN (Seagan)
B. Oct. 28, 1883, Columbus, Wis. D. Dec. 26, 1945, Madison, Wis.

BR TR 5'11" 180 lbs.

Year	Team	Games	BA	SA	AB	H	2B	3B	HR	HR%	R	RBI	BB	SO	SB	AB	H	PO	A	E	DP	TC/G	FA	G by Pos
1910	CHI A	23	.255	.333	51	13	4	0	0	0.0	3	8	2			0	0	5	29	5	1	1.7	.872	P-23
1911		54	.289	.421	76	22	6	2	0	0.0	7	16	7		19	8	0	7	41	9	2	1.1	.842	P-29
1912		40	.215	.308	65	14	4	1	0	0.0	4	7	4		9	2	0	6	42	5	1	1.3	.906	P-31
1913		17	.167	.222	18	3	1	0	0	0.0	1	1	3	5	5	1	1	1	17	0	3	1.1	1.000	P-12
4 yrs.		134	.248	.348	210	52	15	3	0	0.0	15	32	16	5	33	11	1	19	129	19	7	1.2	.886	P-95

Sam Langford

LANGFORD, ELTON J.
B. May 21, 1900, Briggs, Tex.

BL TR 6' 180 lbs.

Year	Team	Games	BA	SA	AB	H	2B	3B	HR	HR%	R	RBI	BB	SO	SB	AB	H	PO	A	E	DP	TC/G	FA	G by Pos
1926	BOS A	1	.000	.000	1	0	0	0	0	0.0	0	0	0	1	0	1	0	0	0	0	0	0.0	–	
1927	CLE A	20	.269	.388	67	18	5	0	1	1.5	10	7	5	7	0	0	0	39	1	0	0	2.0	1.000	OF-20
1928		110	.276	.382	427	118	17	8	4	0.9	50	50	21	35	3	3	1	239	5	7	2	2.3	.972	OF-107
3 yrs.		131	.275	.382	495	136	22	8	5	1.0	61	57	26	43	3	4	1	278	6	7	2	2.2	.976	OF-127

Bob Langsford

LANGSFORD, ROBERT WILLIAM
Born Robert Hugo Lankswert.
B. Aug. 5, 1865, Louisville, Ky. D. Jan. 10, 1907, Louisville, Ky.

BR TR

Year	Team	Games	BA	SA	AB	H	2B	3B	HR	HR%	R	RBI	BB	SO	SB	AB	H	PO	A	E	DP	TC/G	FA	G by Pos
1899	LOU N	1	.000	.000	4	0	0	0	0	0.0	0	0	0	0	0	0	0	3	2	0	0	5.0	1.000	SS-1

Hal Lanier

LANIER, HAROLD CLIFTON
Son of Max Lanier.
B. July 4, 1942, Denton, N. C.
Manager 1986-88.

BR TR 6'2" 180 lbs.
BB 1967

Year	Team	Games	BA	SA	AB	H	2B	3B	HR	HR%	R	RBI	BB	SO	SB	AB	H	PO	A	E	DP	TC/G	FA	G by Pos
1964	SF N	98	.274	.347	383	105	16	3	2	0.5	40	28	5	44	2	2	0	226	298	11	48	5.5	.979	2B-98, SS-3
1965		159	.226	.289	522	118	15	9	0	0.0	41	39	21	67	2	1	0	294	445	18	75	4.8	.976	2B-158, SS-1
1966		149	.231	.290	459	106	14	2	3	0.7	37	37	16	49	1	1	0	303	423	13	80	5.0	.982	2B-112, SS-41
1967		151	.213	.255	525	112	16	3	0	0.0	37	42	16	61	2	0	0	253	519	20	92	5.2	.975	SS-137, 2B-34
1968		151	.206	.239	486	100	14	1	0	0.0	37	27	12	57	2	1	0	282	496	17	72	5.3	.979	SS-150
1969		150	.228	.251	495	113	9	1	0	0.0	37	35	25	68	0	0	0	252	530	25	98	5.4	.969	SS-150
1970		134	.231	.279	438	101	13	1	2	0.5	33	41	21	41	1	0	0	263	399	22	85	5.1	.968	SS-130, 2B-4, 1B-2
1971		109	.233	.286	206	48	8	0	1	0.5	21	13	15	26	0	3	0	91	130	6	19	2.1	.974	3B-83, 2B-13, SS-8, 1B-3
1972	NY A	60	.214	.243	103	22	3	0	0	0.0	5	6	2	13	1	3	2	32	87	4	13	2.1	.967	3B-47, SS-9, 2B-3
1973		35	.209	.244	86	18	3	0	0	0.0	9	5	3	10	0	0	0	45	81	4	16	3.7	.969	SS-26, 2B-8, 3B-1
10 yrs.		1196	.228	.275	3703	843	111	20	8	0.2	297	273	136	436	11	11	2	2041	3408	140	598	4.7	.975	SS-655, 2B-430, 3B-131, 1B-5

LEAGUE CHAMPIONSHIP SERIES

Year	Team	Games	BA	SA	AB	H	2B	3B	HR	HR%	R	RBI	BB	SO	SB	AB	H	PO	A	E	DP	TC/G	FA	G by Pos
1971	SF N	1	.000	.000	1	0	0	0	0	0.0	0	0	0	0	0	0	0	1	0	0	0	1.0	1.000	3B-1

Rimp Lanier

LANIER, LORENZO
B. Oct. 19, 1948, Tuskegee, Ala.

BL TR 5'8" 150 lbs.

Year	Team	Games	BA	SA	AB	H	2B	3B	HR	HR%	R	RBI	BB	SO	SB	AB	H	PO	A	E	DP	TC/G	FA	G by Pos
1971	PIT N	6	.000	.000	4	0	0	0	0	0.0	0	0	0	1	0	4	0	0	0	0	0	0.0	–	

Les Lanning

LANNING, LESTER ALFRED (Red)
B. May 13, 1895, Harvard, Ill. D. June 13, 1962, Bristol, Conn.

BL TL 5'9" 165 lbs.

Year	Team	Games	BA	SA	AB	H	2B	3B	HR	HR%	R	RBI	BB	SO	SB	AB	H	PO	A	E	DP	TC/G	FA	G by Pos
1916	PHI A	19	.182	.242	33	6	2	0	0	0.0	5	1	10	9	0	3	0	10	8	1	0	1.0	.947	OF-9, P-6

Carney Lansford

LANSFORD, CARNEY RAY
Brother of Joe Lansford.
B. Feb. 7, 1957, San Jose, Calif.

BR TR 6'2" 195 lbs.

Year	Team	Games	BA	SA	AB	H	2B	3B	HR	HR%	R	RBI	BB	SO	SB	AB	H	PO	A	E	DP	TC/G	FA	G by Pos
1978	CAL A	121	.294	.406	453	133	23	2	8	1.8	63	52	31	67	20	2	0	94	186	18	18	2.5	.940	3B-117, SS-2, DH-1
1979		157	.287	.436	654	188	30	5	19	2.9	114	79	39	115	20	0	0	135	263	7	29	2.6	.983	3B-157
1980		151	.261	.390	602	157	27	3	15	2.5	87	80	50	93	14	1	1	151	250	19	29	2.8	.955	3B-150
1981	BOS A	102	.336	.439	399	134	23	3	4	1.0	61	52	34	28	15	1	0	70	180	13	17	2.6	.951	3B-86, DH-16
1982		128	.301	.444	482	145	28	4	11	2.3	65	63	46	48	9	1	0	83	216	10	19	2.4	.968	3B-114, DH-13
1983	OAK A	80	.308	.475	299	92	16	2	10	3.3	43	45	22	33	3	3	1	60	163	10	19	2.9	.957	3B-78, SS-1
1984		151	.300	.439	597	179	31	5	14	2.3	70	74	40	62	9	0	0	137	268	18	27	2.8	.957	3B-151

Carney Lansford *continued*

Year	Team	Games	BA	SA	AB	H	2B	3B	HR	HR%	R	RBI	BB	SO	SB	PH AB	PH H	PO	A	E	DP	TC/G	FA	G by Pos
1985		98	.277	.429	401	111	18	2	13	3.2	51	46	18	27	2	1	0	85	119	5	11	2.1	.976	3B-97
1986		151	.284	.421	591	168	16	4	19	3.2	80	72	39	51	16	1	0	480	170	6	37	4.3	.991	3B-100, 1B-60, DH-2, 2B-1
1987		151	.289	.455	554	160	27	4	19	3.4	89	76	60	44	27	2	1	156	258	7	20	2.8	.983	3B-142, 1B-17, DH-4
1988		150	.279	.360	556	155	20	2	7	1.3	80	57	35	35	29	4	0	125	221	7	18	2.4	.980	3B-143, 1B-9, 2B-1
1989		148	.336	.405	551	185	28	2	2	0.4	81	52	51	25	37	0	0	195	188	13	20	2.7	.967	3B-136, 1B-15, DH-3
12 yrs.		1588	.294	.422	6139	1807	287	38	141	2.3	884	748	465	628	201	16	3	1771	2482	133	264	2.8	.970	3B-1471, 1B-101, DH-39, SS-3, 2B-2

LEAGUE CHAMPIONSHIP SERIES

Year	Team	Games	BA	SA	AB	H	2B	3B	HR	HR%	R	RBI	BB	SO	SB	PH AB	PH H	PO	A	E	DP	TC/G	FA	G by Pos
1979	CAL A	4	.294	.294	17	5	0	0	0	0.0	2	3	1	2	1	0	0	4	8	0	3	3.0	1.000	3B-4
1988	OAK A	4	.294	.529	17	5	1	0	1	5.9	4	2	0	2	0	0	0	7	8	0	2	3.8	1.000	3B-4
1989		3	.455	.455	11	5	0	0	0	0.0	2	4	2	1	2	0	0	1	2	0	0	1.0	1.000	3B-3
3 yrs.		11	.333	.422	45	15	1	0	1	2.2	8	9	3	5	3	0	0	12	18	0	5	2.7	1.000	3B-11

WORLD SERIES

Year	Team	Games	BA	SA	AB	H	2B	3B	HR	HR%	R	RBI	BB	SO	SB	PH AB	PH H	PO	A	E	DP	TC/G	FA	G by Pos
1988	OAK A	5	.167	.167	18	3	0	0	0	0.0	2	1	2	2	0	0	0	8	7	0	1	3.0	1.000	3B-5
1989		4	.438	.688	16	7	1	0	1	6.3	5	4	3	1	0	0	0	5	5	0	0	2.5	1.000	3B-4
2 yrs.		9	.294	.412	34	10	1	0	1	2.9	7	5	5	3	0	0	0	13	12	0	1	2.8	1.000	3B-9

Joe Lansford

LANSFORD, JOSEPH DALE
Brother of Carney Lansford.
B. Jan. 15, 1961, Santa Clara, Calif.
BR TR 6'5" 225 lbs.

Year	Team	Games	BA	SA	AB	H	2B	3B	HR	HR%	R	RBI	BB	SO	SB	PH AB	PH H	PO	A	E	DP	TC/G	FA	G by Pos
1982	SD N	13	.182	.182	22	4	0	0	0	0.0	6	3	6	4	0	3	0	69	3	1	9	5.6	.986	1B-9
1983		12	.250	.625	8	2	0	0	1	12.5	1	2	0	3	0	1	0	11	1	0	1	1.0	1.000	1B-8
2 yrs.		25	.200	.300	30	6	0	0	1	3.3	7	5	6	7	0	9	1	80	4	1	10	3.4	.988	1B-17

Pete Lapan

LAPAN, PETER NELSON
B. June 25, 1891, Easthampton, Mass. D. Jan. 5, 1953, Norwalk, Calif.
BR TR 5'7" 165 lbs.

Year	Team	Games	BA	SA	AB	H	2B	3B	HR	HR%	R	RBI	BB	SO	SB	PH AB	PH H	PO	A	E	DP	TC/G	FA	G by Pos
1922	WAS A	11	.324	.441	34	11	1	0	1	2.9	7	6	3	4	1	0	0	36	10	2	0	4.4	.958	C-11
1923		2	.000	.000	2	0	0	0	0	0.0	0	0	0	0	0	2	0	0	0	0	0	0.0	—	
2 yrs.		13	.306	.417	36	11	1	0	1	2.8	7	6	3	4	1	2	0	36	10	2	0	3.7	.958	C-11

Ralph LaPointe

LaPOINTE, RALPH ROBERT
B. Jan. 8, 1922, Winooski, Vt. D. Sept. 13, 1967, Burlington, Vt.
BR TR 5'11" 185 lbs.

Year	Team	Games	BA	SA	AB	H	2B	3B	HR	HR%	R	RBI	BB	SO	SB	PH AB	PH H	PO	A	E	DP	TC/G	FA	G by Pos
1947	PHI N	56	.308	.355	211	65	7	0	1	0.5	33	15	17	15	8	2	1	82	158	11	25	4.5	.956	SS-54
1948	STL N	87	.225	.239	222	50	3	0	0	0.0	27	15	18	19	1	2	0	143	158	12	36	3.6	.962	2B-44, SS-25, 3B-1
2 yrs.		143	.266	.296	433	115	10	0	1	0.2	60	30	35	34	9	4	1	225	316	23	61	3.9	.959	SS-79, 2B-44, 3B-1

Frank LaPorte

LaPORTE, FRANK BREYFOGLE (Pot)
B. Feb. 6, 1880, Uhrichsville, Ohio D. Sept. 25, 1939, Newcomerstown, Ohio
BR TR 5'8" 175 lbs.

Year	Team	Games	BA	SA	AB	H	2B	3B	HR	HR%	R	RBI	BB	SO	SB	PH AB	PH H	PO	A	E	DP	TC/G	FA	G by Pos
1905	NY A	11	.400	.500	40	16	1	0	1	2.5	4	12	1		1	1	0	19	26	4	4	4.5	.918	2B-11
1906		123	.264	.368	454	120	23	9	2	0.4	60	54	22		10	3	1	133	229	35	16	3.2	.912	3B-114, 2B-5, OF-1
1907		130	.270	.360	470	127	20	11	0	0.0	56	48	27		10	2	0	157	125	30	6	2.4	.904	3B-64, OF-63, 1B-1
1908	2 teams				BOS A (62G – .237)		NY A (39G – .262)																		
"	total	101	.249	.316	301	75	4	8	0	0.0	21	30	20		6	19	5	130	192	19	17	3.4	.944	2B-53, OF-16, 3B-12
1909	NY A	89	.298	.379	309	92	19	3	0	0.0	35	31	18		5	5	2	142	208	23	30	4.2	.938	2B-83
1910		124	.264	.338	432	114	14	6	2	0.5	43	67	33		16	6	1	175	246	21	21	3.6	.952	2B-79, OF-24, 3B-15
1911	STL A	136	.314	.446	507	159	37	12	2	0.4	71	82	34		4	0	0	289	409	36	59	5.4	.951	2B-133, 3B-3
1912	2 teams				STL A (80G – .312)		WAS A (39G – .309)																		
"	total	119	.311	.393	402	125	20	5	1	0.2	45	55	32		10	10	0	183	215	27	34	3.6	.936	2B-76, OF-32
1913	WAS A	79	.252	.306	242	61	5	4	0	0.0	25	18	17	16	10	8	1	83	114	9	13	2.6	.956	3B-46, 2B-13, OF-12
1914	IND F	133	.311	.436	505	157	27	12	4	0.8	86	107	36		15	1	0	300	373	31	61	5.3	.956	2B-132
1915	NWK F	148	.253	.351	550	139	28	10	2	0.4	55	56	48		14	2	0	330	431	32	69	5.4	.960	2B-146
11 yrs.		1193	.281	.376	4212	1185	198	80	14	0.3	501	560	288	16	101	57	10	1941	2568	267	330	4.0	.944	2B-731, 3B-254, OF-148, 1B-1

Jack Lapp

LAPP, JOHN WALKER
B. Sept. 10, 1884, Frazer, Pa. D. Feb. 6, 1920, Philadelphia, Pa.
BL TR 5'8"

Year	Team	Games	BA	SA	AB	H	2B	3B	HR	HR%	R	RBI	BB	SO	SB	PH AB	PH H	PO	A	E	DP	TC/G	FA	G by Pos
1908	PHI A	13	.143	.200	35	5	0	1	0	0.0	4	1	5		0	0	0	55	16	4	0	5.8	.947	C-13
1909		21	.339	.429	56	19	3	1	0	0.0	8	10	3		1	2	0	95	26	8	2	6.1	.938	C-19
1910		71	.234	.286	192	45	4	3	0	0.0	18	17	20		0	7	3	361	88	9	6	6.5	.980	C-63
1911		68	.353	.467	167	59	10	3	1	0.6	35	26	24		4	6	3	296	51	9	8	5.2	.975	C-57, 1B-4
1912		90	.292	.399	281	82	15	6	1	0.4	26	35	19		3	8	4	354	105	20	10	5.3	.958	C-82
1913		81	.227	.290	238	54	4	4	1	0.4	23	20	37	26	1	2	0	315	110	14	5	5.4	.968	C-77, 1B-1
1914		69	.231	.286	199	46	7	2	0	0.0	22	19	31	14	1	3	1	330	88	10	4	6.2	.977	C-67
1915		112	.272	.375	312	85	16	5	1	0.3	26	30	29		5	10	4	470	118	19	23	5.4	.969	C-89, 1B-12
1916	CHI A	40	.208	.228	101	21	0	1	0	0.0	6	7	8	10	1	4	0	131	41	2	2	4.4	.989	C-34
9 yrs.		565	.263	.343	1581	416	59	26	5	0.3	168	166	177	79	16	42	15	2407	643	95	60	5.6	.970	C-501, 1B-17

WORLD SERIES

Year	Team	Games	BA	SA	AB	H	2B	3B	HR	HR%	R	RBI	BB	SO	SB	PH AB	PH H	PO	A	E	DP	TC/G	FA	G by Pos
1910	PHI A	1	.250	.250	4	1	0	0	0	0.0	1	0	0		0	0	0	4	2	0	0	6.0	1.000	C-1
1911		2	.250	.250	8	2	0	0	0	0.0	1	0	1		0	0	0	18	8	0	0	13.0	1.000	C-2
1913		1	.250	.250	4	1	0	0	0	0.0	0	0	0	1	0	0	0	7	1	0	0	8.0	1.000	C-1
1914		1	.000	.000	1	0	0	0	0	0.0	0	1	0	1	0	0	0	2	1	0	0	3.0	1.000	C-1
4 yrs.		5	.235	.235	17	4	0	0	0	0.0	1	1	1	4	0	0	0	31	12	0	0	8.6	1.000	C-5

Norm Larker

LARKER, NORMAN HOWARD JOHN
B. Dec. 27, 1930, Beaver Meadows, Pa.
BL TL 6' 185 lbs.

Year	Team	Games	BA	SA	AB	H	2B	3B	HR	HR%	R	RBI	BB	SO	SB	PH AB	PH H	PO	A	E	DP	TC/G	FA	G by Pos
1958	LA N	99	.277	.427	253	70	16	4	4	1.6	32	29	29	21	1	29	7	239	17	5	18	2.6	.981	OF-43, 1B-25
1959		108	.289	.418	311	90	14	1	8	2.6	37	49	26	25	0	24	7	491	48	5	53	5.0	.991	1B-55, OF-30
1960		133	.323	.430	440	142	26	3	5	1.1	55	78	36	24	1	15	6	917	80	7	81	7.5	.993	1B-119, OF-2
1961		97	.270	.387	282	76	16	1	5	1.8	29	38	24	42	0	10	2	589	52	3	68	6.6	.995	1B-86, OF-1
1962	HOU N	147	.263	.374	506	133	19	5	9	1.8	58	63	70	47	1	10	6	1153	103	11	103	8.6	.991	1B-135, OF-6

Year	Team		Games	BA	SA	AB	H	2B	3B	HR	HR%	R	RBI	BB	SO	SB	Pinch Hit AB	Pinch Hit H	PO	A	E	DP	TC/G	FA	G by Pos

Norm Larker *continued*

1963	2 teams	MIL N (64G – .177)				SF N (19G – .071)																			
"	total		83	.168	.224	161	27	6	0	1	0.6	15	14	26	26	0	30	4	344	35	5	26	4.6	.987	1B-53
6 yrs.			667	.275	.390	1953	538	97	15	32	1.6	226	271	211	165	3	118	32	3733	335	36	349	6.2	.991	1B-473, OF-82

WORLD SERIES

| 1959 | LA | N | 6 | .188 | .188 | 16 | 3 | 0 | 0 | 0 | 0.0 | 2 | 0 | 2 | 3 | 0 | 0 | 0 | 12 | 1 | 0 | 0 | 2.2 | 1.000 | OF-6 |

Barry Larkin

LARKIN, BARRY LOUIS   BR TR 6'   185 lbs.
B. Apr. 28, 1964, Cincinnati, Ohio

1986	CIN	N	41	.283	.403	159	45	4	3	3	1.9	27	19	9	21	8	4	0	51	125	4	22	4.4	.978	SS-36, 2B-3
1987			125	.244	.371	439	107	16	2	12	2.7	64	43	36	52	21	4	1	168	358	19	72	4.4	.965	SS-119
1988			151	.296	.429	588	174	32	5	12	2.0	91	56	41	24	40	2	0	231	470	29	67	4.8	.960	SS-148
1989			97	.342	.446	325	111	14	4	4	1.2	47	36	20	23	10	10	4	142	267	10	31	4.3	.976	SS-82
4 yrs.			414	.289	.413	1511	437	66	14	31	2.1	229	154	106	120	79	20	5	592	1220	62	192	4.5	.967	SS-385, 2B-3

Ed Larkin

LARKIN, EDWARD FRANCIS   BR TR 5'8"
B. July 1, 1885, Wyalusing, Pa.   D. Mar. 28, 1934, Wyalusing, Pa.

| 1909 | PHI | A | 2 | .167 | .167 | 6 | 1 | 0 | 0 | 0 | 0.0 | 0 | 1 | 1 | | | 0 | 0 | 9 | 1 | 3 | 0 | 6.5 | .769 | C-2 |

Gene Larkin

LARKIN, EUGENE THOMAS   BB TR 6'3"   195 lbs.
B. Oct. 24, 1962, Flushing, N. Y.

1987	MIN	A	85	.266	.382	233	62	11	2	4	1.7	23	28	25	31	1	17	5	165	10	2	12	2.1	.989	DH-40, 1B-26
1988			149	.267	.382	505	135	30	2	8	1.6	56	70	68	55	3	4	0	466	28	3	46	3.3	.994	DH-86, 1B-60
1989			136	.267	.368	446	119	25	1	6	1.3	61	46	54	57	5	11	3	524	28	4	45	4.1	.993	1B-67, DH-41, OF-32
3 yrs.			370	.267	.377	1184	316	66	5	18	1.5	140	144	147	143	9	32	8	1155	66	9	103	3.3	.993	DH-167, 1B-153, OF-32

LEAGUE CHAMPIONSHIP SERIES

| 1987 | MIN | A | 1 | 1.000 | 2.000 | 1 | 1 | 1 | 0 | 0 | 0.0 | 0 | 1 | 0 | 0 | 0 | 1 | 1 | 0 | 0 | 0 | 0 | 0.0 | – | |

WORLD SERIES

| 1987 | MIN | A | 5 | .000 | .000 | 3 | 0 | 0 | 0 | 0 | 0.0 | 1 | 0 | 1 | 0 | 0 | 3 | 0 | 1 | 0 | 0 | 0 | 0.2 | 1.000 | DH-1, 1B-1 |

Henry Larkin

LARKIN, HENRY E. (Ted)   BR TR 5'10"   170 lbs.
B. Jan. 12, 1860, Reading, Pa.   D. Jan. 31, 1942, Reading, Pa.
Manager 1890.

1884	PHI	AA	85	.276	.423	326	90	21	9	3	0.9	59		15			0	0	107	11	20	1	1.6	.855	OF-85, 2B-2
1885			108	.329	.525	453	149	37	14	8	1.8	114		26			0	0	208	23	31	9	2.4	.882	OF-108
1886			139	.319	.450	565	180	36	11	2	0.4	133		59			0	0	264	21	44	2	2.4	.866	OF-139
1887			126	.310	.421	497	154	22	12	3	0.6	105		48		37	0	0	416	47	36	23	4.0	.928	OF-93, 1B-23, 2B-10
1888			135	.269	.403	546	147	28	12	7	1.3	92	101	33		20	0	0	1263	69	56	51	10.3	.960	1B-122, 2B-14
1889			133	.318	.426	516	164	23	12	3	0.6	105	74	83	41	11	0	0	1234	38	38	89	9.8	.971	1B-131, 3B-1, OF-1
1890	CLE	P	125	.332	.484	506	168	32	15	5	1.0	93	112	65	18	5	0	0	1268	40	30	63	10.7	.978	1B-125, OF-1
1891	PHI	AA	133	.279	.441	526	147	27	14	10	1.9	94	93	66	56	2	0	0	1029	34	31	56	8.2	.972	1B-111, OF-23
1892	WAS	N	119	.280	.390	464	130	13	7	8	1.7	76	96	39	21	21	0	0	1122	69	39	77	10.3	.968	1B-117, OF-2
1893			81	.317	.436	319	101	20	3	4	1.3	54	73	50	5	1	0	0	781	29	31	48	10.4	.963	1B-81
10 yrs.			1184	.303	.440	4718	1430	259	114	53	1.1	925	549	484	141	97	0	0	7692	381	356	419	7.1	.958	1B-710, OF-451, 2B-27, 3B-1

Terry Larkin

LARKIN, FRANK S.   BR TR
B. 1856, Brooklyn, N. Y.   D. Sept. 16, 1894, Brooklyn N. Y.,

1876	NY	N	1	.000	.000	4	0	0	0	0	0.0	0	0	0	0		0	0	0	2	2	0	4.0	.500	P-1
1877	HAR	N	58	.228	.311	228	52	6	5	1	0.4	28	18	5	23		0	0	31	99	20	1	2.6	.867	P-56, 3B-2, 2B-1
1878	CHI	N	58	.288	.363	226	65	9	4	0	0.0	33	32	17	17		0	0	20	95	21	0	2.3	.846	P-56, OF-1, 3B-1
1879			60	.219	.289	228	50	12	2	0	0.0	26	18	8	24		0	0	10	80	9	1	1.7	.909	P-58, OF-3
1880	TRO	N	6	.150	.200	20	3	1	0	0	0.0	1	1	3	4		0	0	5	11	1	2	2.8	.941	P-5, OF-2, SS-1
1884	2 teams	WAS U (17G – .243)				RIC AA (40G – .201)																			
"	total		57	.215	.258	209	45	1	4	0	0.0	28		13			0	0	123	145	40	16	5.4	.870	2B-40, 3B-17
6 yrs.			240	.235	.303	915	215	29	15	1	0.1	116	69	46	68		0	0	189	432	93	20	3.0	.870	P-176, 2B-41, 3B-20, OF-6, SS-1

Bob Larmore

LARMORE, ROBERT McKAHAN (Red)   BR TR 5'10½" 185 lbs.
B. Dec. 6, 1896, Anderson, Ind.   D. Jan. 15, 1964, St. Louis, Mo.

| 1918 | STL | N | 4 | .286 | .286 | 7 | 2 | 0 | 0 | 0 | 0.0 | 0 | 1 | 0 | 2 | 2 | 0 | 0 | 3 | 4 | 2 | 0 | 2.3 | .778 | SS-2 |

Sam LaRoque

LaROQUE, SAMUEL H J   5'11"   190 lbs.
B. Feb. 26, 1864, St. Mathias, Que., Canada   Deceased.

1888	DET	N	2	.444	.444	9	4	0	0	0	0.0	1	1	0	0	0	0	0	7	8	4	3	9.5	.789	2B-2
1890	PIT	N	111	.242	.313	434	105	20	4	1	0.2	59	40	35	29	27	0	0	292	321	76	35	6.2	.890	2B-78, SS-31, 1B-2, OF-1
1891	2 teams	PIT N (1G – .000)				LOU AA (10G – .314)																			
"	total		11	.282	.462	39	11	2	1	1	2.6	6	8	5	9	1	0	0	31	25	9	4	5.9	.862	2B-10, 3B-1, 1B-1
3 yrs.			124	.249	.328	482	120	22	5	2	0.4	66	50	41	39	28	0	0	330	354	89	42	6.2	.885	2B-90, SS-31, 1B-3, OF-1, 3B-1

Vic LaRose

LaROSE, VICTOR RAYMOND   BR TR 5'11"   180 lbs.
B. Dec. 23, 1944, Los Angeles, Calif.

| 1968 | CHI | N | 4 | .000 | .000 | 2 | 0 | 0 | 0 | 0 | 0.0 | 0 | 0 | 0 | 1 | 0 | 0 | 0 | 1 | 5 | 1 | 0 | 1.8 | .857 | SS-2, 2B-2 |

Harry LaRoss

LaROSS, HARRY RAYMOND (Spike)   BR TR 5'11½" 170 lbs.
B. Jan. 12, 1888, Easton, Pa.   D. May 22, 1954, Chicago, Ill.

| 1914 | CIN | N | 22 | .229 | .250 | 48 | 11 | 1 | 0 | 0 | 0.0 | 7 | 5 | 2 | 10 | 4 | 0 | 0 | 15 | 2 | 6 | 0 | 1.0 | .739 | OF-20 |

Year	Team		Games	BA	SA	AB	H	2B	3B	HR	HR%	R	RBI	BB	SO	SB	Pinch Hit AB	Pinch Hit H	PO	A	E	DP	TC/G	FA	G by Pos

Don Larsen

LARSEN, DON JAMES
B. Aug. 7, 1929, Michigan City, Ind.
BR TR 6'4" 215 lbs.

Year	Team		Games	BA	SA	AB	H	2B	3B	HR	HR%	R	RBI	BB	SO	SB	PH AB	PH H	PO	A	E	DP	TC/G	FA	G by Pos
1953	STL	A	50	.284	.457	81	23	3	1	3	3.7	11	10	4	14	0	10	1	8	29	2	1	0.8	.949	P-38, OF-1
1954	BAL	A	44	.250	.409	88	22	5	3	1	1.1	6	4	5	15	0	15	0	14	34	1	3	1.1	.980	P-29
1955	NY	A	21	.146	.317	41	6	1	0	2	4.9	4	7	4	13	0	3	1	5	13	1	3	0.9	.947	P-19
1956			45	.241	.380	79	19	5	0	2	2.5	10	12	6	17	0	7	2	13	23	3	3	0.9	.923	P-38
1957			31	.250	.339	56	14	5	0	0	0.0	6	5	6	11	0	1	0	10	20	2	2	1.0	.938	P-27
1958			28	.306	.571	49	15	1	0	4	8.2	9	13	5	9	0	7	2	5	14	2	2	0.8	.905	P-19
1959			29	.255	.298	47	12	2	0	0	0.0	8	8	7	15	0	3	1	5	22	2	1	1.0	.931	P-25
1960	KC	A	23	.207	.241	29	6	1	0	0	0.0	3	3	0	11	0	1	0	4	8	1	1	0.6	.923	P-22
1961	2 teams			KC	A	(18G – .300)			CHI	A	(25G – .320)														
"	total		43	.311	.444	45	14	0	0	2	4.4	4	8	1	10	0	12	5	8	17	0	0	0.6	1.000	P-33, OF-1
1962	SF	N	52	.200	.280	25	5	0	1	0	0.0	3	1	0	7	0	4	0	4	15	0	3	0.4	1.000	P-49
1963			46	.182	.182	11	2	0	0	0	0.0	0	0	0	4	0	0	0	4	12	1	0	0.4	.941	P-46
1964	2 teams			SF	N	(6G – .000)			HOU	N	(31G – .097)														
"	total		37	.094	.125	32	3	1	0	0	0.0	0	0	0	4	0	3	0	9	19	1	1	0.8	.966	P-36
1965	2 teams			HOU	N	(1G – .000)			BAL	A	(27G – .273)														
"	total		28	.231	.308	13	3	1	0	0	0.0	1	0	0	5	0	0	0	6	16	1	1	0.8	.957	P-28
1967	CHI	N	3	–	–	0	0	0	0	0	–	0	0	0	0	0	0	0	0	2	0	1	0.7	1.000	P-3
14 yrs.			480	.242	.371	596	144	25	5	14	2.3	65	72	43	138	0	66	12	95	244	17	22	0.7	.952	P-412, OF-2

WORLD SERIES

Year	Team		Games	BA	SA	AB	H	2B	3B	HR	HR%	R	RBI	BB	SO	SB	PH AB	PH H	PO	A	E	DP	TC/G	FA	G by Pos
1955	NY	A	1	.000	.000	2	0	0	0	0	0.0	0	0	0	0	0	0	0	0	1	0	0	1.0	1.000	P-1
1956			2	.333	.333	3	1	0	0	0	0.0	1	0	0	1	0	0	0	0	1	0	0	0.5	1.000	P-1
1957			2	.000	.000	2	0	0	0	0	0.0	1	0	2	1	0	0	0	0	1	0	1	0.5	1.000	P-2
1958			2	.000	.000	2	0	0	0	0	0.0	0	0	1	0	0	0	0	0	1	0	0	0.5	1.000	P-2
1962	SF	N	3	–	–	0	0	0	0	0	–	0	0	0	0	0	0	0	1	0	0	0	0.3	1.000	P-3
5 yrs.			10	.111	.111	9	1	0	0	0	0.0	2	0	3	2	0	0	0	2	3	0	1	0.5	1.000	P-10

Swede Larsen

LARSEN, ERLING ADELL
B. Nov. 15, 1913, Jersey City, N. J.
BR TR 5'11" 175 lbs.

Year	Team		Games	BA	SA	AB	H	2B	3B	HR	HR%	R	RBI	BB	SO	SB	PH AB	PH H	PO	A	E	DP	TC/G	FA	G by Pos
1936	BOS	N	3	.000	.000	1	0	0	0	0	0.0	0	0	0	0	0	0	0	1	0	0	0	0.3	1.000	2B-2

Tony LaRussa

LaRUSSA, ANTHONY
B. Oct. 4, 1944, Tampa, Fla.
Manager 1979-89.
BR TR 6' 175 lbs.

Year	Team		Games	BA	SA	AB	H	2B	3B	HR	HR%	R	RBI	BB	SO	SB	PH AB	PH H	PO	A	E	DP	TC/G	FA	G by Pos
1963	KC	A	34	.250	.318	44	11	1	1	0	0.0	4	1	7	12	0	1	1	29	25	2	8	1.6	.964	SS-14, 2B-3
1968	OAK	A	5	.333	.333	3	1	0	1	0	0.0	0	0	0	0	0	3	1	0	0	0	0	0.0	–	
1969			8	.000	.000	8	0	0	0	0	0.0	0	1	0	1	0	8	0	0	0	0	0	0.0	–	
1970			52	.198	.255	106	21	4	1	0	0.0	6	6	15	19	0	11	2	67	89	5	21	3.1	.969	2B-44
1971	2 teams			OAK	A	(23G – .000)			ATL	N	(9G – .286)														
"	total		32	.133	.133	15	2	0	0	0	0.0	4	0	1	5	0	6	0	16	13	3	5	1.0	.906	2B-16, SS-4, 3B-2
1973	CHI	N	1	–	–	0	0	0	0	0	–	1	0	0	0	0	0	0	0	0	0	0	0.0	–	
6 yrs.			132	.199	.250	176	35	5	2	0	0.0	15	7	23	37	0	29	4	112	127	10	34	1.9	.960	2B-63, SS-18, 3B-2

Lyn Lary

LARY, LYNFORD HOBART
B. Jan. 28, 1906, Armona, Calif. D. Jan. 9, 1973, Downey, Calif.
BR TR 6' 165 lbs.

Year	Team		Games	BA	SA	AB	H	2B	3B	HR	HR%	R	RBI	BB	SO	SB	PH AB	PH H	PO	A	E	DP	TC/G	FA	G by Pos
1929	NY	A	80	.309	.428	236	73	9	2	5	2.1	48	26	24	15	4	7	0	67	147	11	19	2.8	.951	3B-55, SS-14, 2B-2
1930			117	.289	.386	464	134	20	8	3	0.6	93	52	45	40	14	3	0	224	324	35	58	5.0	.940	SS-113
1931			155	.280	.416	610	171	35	9	10	1.6	100	107	88	54	13	0	0	321	484	46	85	5.5	.946	SS-155
1932			91	.232	.343	280	65	14	4	3	1.1	56	39	52	28	9	1	0	180	223	25	42	4.7	.942	SS-80, 1B-5, 3B-2, 2B-2, OF-1
1933			52	.220	.291	127	28	3	3	0	0.0	25	13	28	17	2	4	0	55	72	7	10	2.6	.948	3B-28, SS-16, 1B-3, OF-1
1934	2 teams			NY	A	(1G – .000)			BOS	A	(129G – .241)														
"	total		130	.241	.322	419	101	20	4	2	0.5	58	54	67	51	12	0	0	264	396	25	67	5.3	.964	SS-129, 1B-1
1935	2 teams			WAS	A	(39G – .194)			STL	A	(93G – .288)														
"	total		132	.268	.371	474	127	29	7	2	0.4	86	42	76	53	28	3	1	321	384	29	79	5.6	.960	SS-123
1936	STL	A	155	.289	.366	620	179	30	6	2	0.3	112	52	117	54	37	0	0	339	495	38	88	5.6	.956	SS-155
1937	CLE	A	156	.290	.421	644	187	46	7	8	1.2	110	77	88	64	18	0	0	325	489	31	95	5.4	.963	SS-156
1938			141	.268	.361	568	152	36	4	3	0.5	94	51	88	65	23	0	0	296	399	26	88	5.1	.964	SS-141
1939	3 teams			CLE	A	(3G – .000)			BKN	N	(29G – .161)	STL	N	(34G – .187)											
"	total		66	.176	.231	108	19	4	1	0	0.0	18	10	28	22	2	3	0	77	95	10	14	2.8	.945	SS-44, 3B-10
1940	STL	A	27	.056	.111	54	3	1	1	0	0.0	5	3	4	7	0	6	0	29	33	3	7	2.4	.954	SS-12, 2B-1
12 yrs.			1302	.269	.372	4604	1239	247	56	38	0.8	805	526	705	470	162	27	1	2498	3541	286	652	4.9	.955	SS-1138, 3B-95, 1B-9, 2B-5, OF-2

Don Lassetter

LASSETTER, DONALD O'NEAL
B. Mar. 27, 1933, Newnan, Ga.
BR TR 6'3" 200 lbs.

Year	Team		Games	BA	SA	AB	H	2B	3B	HR	HR%	R	RBI	BB	SO	SB	PH AB	PH H	PO	A	E	DP	TC/G	FA	G by Pos
1957	STL	N	4	.154	.308	13	2	1	0	0	0.0	2	0	1	3	0	1	0	9	0	0	0	2.3	1.000	OF-3

Arlie Latham

LATHAM, WALTER ARLINGTON (The Freshest Man on Earth)
B. Mar. 15, 1860, W. Lebanon, N. H. D. Nov. 29, 1952, Garden City, N. Y.
Manager 1896.
BR TR 5'8" 150 lbs.

Year	Team		Games	BA	SA	AB	H	2B	3B	HR	HR%	R	RBI	BB	SO	SB	PH AB	PH H	PO	A	E	DP	TC/G	FA	G by Pos
1880	BUF	N	22	.127	.190	79	10	3	1	0	0.0	9	3		1	8		0	0	31	36	7	1	3.4	.905	SS-12, OF-10, C-1
1883	STL	AA	98	.236	.300	406	96	12	7	0	0.0	86		18				0	0	120	256	58	14	4.4	.866	3B-98, C-1
1884			110	.274	.367	474	130	17	12	1	0.2	115		19				0	0	142	302	70	16	4.7	.864	3B-110, C-1
1885			110	.206	.256	485	100	15	3	1	0.2	84		18				0	0	116	224	49	16	3.5	.874	3B-109, C-2
1886			134	.301	.374	578	174	23	8	1	0.2	152		55				0	0	139	290	88	22	3.9	.830	3B-133, 2B-1
1887			136	.316	.413	627	198	35	10	2	0.3	163		45		129		0	0	169	305	66	19	4.0	.878	3B-132, 2B-5, C-2
1888			133	.265	.326	570	151	19	5	2	0.4	119	31	43		109		0	0	178	287	62	19	4.0	.882	3B-133, SS-1
1889			118	.246	.307	512	126	13	3	4	0.8	110	49	42	30	69		0	0	204	256	59	23	4.4	.886	3B-116, 2B-3

Year	Team		Games	BA	SA	AB	H	2B	3B	HR	HR%	R	RBI	BB	SO	SB	Pinch Hit AB	H	PO	A	E	DP	TC/G	FA	G by Pos

Arlie Latham *continued*

Year	Team		Games	BA	SA	AB	H	2B	3B	HR	HR%	R	RBI	BB	SO	SB	AB	H	PO	A	E	DP	TC/G	FA	G by Pos
1890	2 teams	CHI P (52G – .229)																							CIN N (41G – .250)
"	total		93	.238	.302	378	90	13	4	1	0.3	82	35	45	40	52	0	0	119	222	52	19	4.2	.868	3B-93, OF-1
1891	CIN N		135	.272	.386	533	145	20	10	7	1.3	119	53	74	35	87	0	0	177	370	75	24	4.6	.879	3B-135, C-1
1892			152	.238	.283	622	148	20	4	0	0.0	111	44	60	54	66	0	0	192	354	71	29	4.1	.885	3B-142, 2B-9, OF-1
1893			127	.282	.350	531	150	18	6	2	0.4	101	49	62	20	57	0	0	172	281	55	23	4.0	.892	3B-127
1894			129	.313	.403	524	164	23	6	4	0.8	129	60	60	24	59	0	0	163	255	67	23	3.8	.862	3B-127, 2B-2
1895			112	.311	.380	460	143	14	6	2	0.4	93	69	42	25	48	0	0	141	200	55	16	3.5	.861	3B-108, 1B-3, 2B-1
1896	STL N		8	.200	.200	35	7	0	0	0	0.0	3	5	4	3	2	0	0	14	15	10	2	4.9	.744	3B-8
1899	WAS N		6	.167	.167	6	1	0	0	0	0.0	1	0	1		0	2	1	2	0	1	0	0.5	1.000	2B-2
1909	NY N		4	.000	.000	2	0	0	0	0	0.0	1	0	0		1	0	0	0	2	0	0	0.5	1.000	
	17 yrs.		1627	.269	.341	6822	1833	245	85	27	0.4	1478	398	589	239	679	3	1	2079	3655	844	267	4.0	.872	3B-1571, 2B-24, OF-13, SS-13, C-8, 1B-3

Juice Latham

LATHAM, GEORGE WARREN (Jumbo)
B. Sept. 6, 1852, Utica, N. Y.   D. May 26, 1914, Utica, N. Y.
Manager 1875, 1882.

BR TR   240 lbs.

Year	Team		Games	BA	SA	AB	H	2B	3B	HR	HR%	R	RBI	BB	SO	SB	AB	H	PO	A	E	DP	TC/G	FA	G by Pos
1877	LOU N		59	.291	.371	278	81	10	6	0	0.0	42	22	5		6	0	0	659	24	36	28	12.2	.950	1B-59
1882	PHI AA		74	.285	.328	323	92	10	2	0	0.0	47		10			0	0	792	12	23	28	11.2	.972	1B-74
1883	LOU AA		88	.250	.302	368	92	7	6	0	0.0	60		12			0	0	676	82	55	49	9.2	.932	1B-67, 2B-14, SS-9
1884			77	.169	.198	308	52	3	3	0	0.0	31		8			0	0	790	32	33	48	11.1	.961	1B-76, 3B-1
	4 yrs.		298	.248	.298	1277	317	30	17	0	0.0	180	22	35		6	0	0	2917	150	147	153	10.8	.954	1B-276, 2B-14, SS-9, 3B-1

Chick Lathers

LATHERS, CHARLES TEN EYCK
B. Oct. 22, 1888, Detroit, Mich.   D. July 26, 1971, Petoskey, Mich.

BL TR 6'   180 lbs.

Year	Team		Games	BA	SA	AB	H	2B	3B	HR	HR%	R	RBI	BB	SO	SB	AB	H	PO	A	E	DP	TC/G	FA	G by Pos
1910	DET A		41	.232	.256	82	19	2	0	0	0.0	4	3	8		0	14	3	30	60	10	5	2.4	.900	3B-13, 2B-7, SS-4
1911			29	.222	.244	45	10	1	0	0	0.0	5	4	5		0	4	2	21	33	5	2	2.0	.915	2B-9, 3B-8, SS-4, 1B-3
	2 yrs.		70	.228	.252	127	29	3	0	0	0.0	9	7	13		0	18	5	51	93	15	7	2.3	.906	3B-21, 2B-16, SS-8, 1B-3

Tacks Latimer

LATIMER, CLIFFORD WESLEY
B. Nov. 30, 1877, Loveland, Ohio   D. Apr. 24, 1936, Loveland, Ohio

TR 6'   160 lbs.

Year	Team		Games	BA	SA	AB	H	2B	3B	HR	HR%	R	RBI	BB	SO	SB	AB	H	PO	A	E	DP	TC/G	FA	G by Pos
1898	NY N		5	.294	.353	17	5	1	0	0	0.0	1		0		0	0	0	16	8	4	1	5.6	.857	C-4, OF-2
1899	LOU N		9	.276	.310	29	8	1	0	0	0.0	3	4	2		0	1	0	38	10	3	0	5.7	.941	C-8, 1B-1
1900	PIT N		4	.333	.417	12	4	1	0	0	0.0	1	2	0		0	0	0	14	4	1	0	4.8	.947	C-4
1901	BAL A		1	.250	.250	4	1	0	0	0	0.0	0	0	0		0	0	0	4	0	0	0	4.0	1.000	C-1
1902	BKN N		8	.042	.042	24	1	0	0	0	0.0	0	0	0		1	0	0	26	10	2	0	4.8	.947	C-8
	5 yrs.		27	.221	.256	86	19	3	0	0	0.0	5	7	2		1	0	0	98	32	10	1	5.2	.929	C-25, OF-2, 1B-1

Charlie Lau

LAU, CHARLES RICHARD
B. Apr. 12, 1933, Romulus, Mich.   D. Mar. 18, 1984, Key Colony Beach, Fla.

BL TR 6'   190 lbs.

Year	Team		Games	BA	SA	AB	H	2B	3B	HR	HR%	R	RBI	BB	SO	SB	AB	H	PO	A	E	DP	TC/G	FA	G by Pos
1956	DET A		3	.222	.222	9	2	0	0	0	0.0	1	0	0	1	0	0	0	17	0	0	0	5.7	1.000	C-3
1958			30	.147	.221	68	10	1	2	0	0.0	8	6	12	15	0	4	1	120	10	2	3	4.4	.985	C-27
1959			2	.167	.167	6	1	0	0	0	0.0	0	0	0	2	0	1	0	11	1	0	1	6.0	1.000	C-2
1960	MIL N		21	.189	.226	53	10	2	0	0	0.0	4	2	6	10	0	7	0	94	11	0	2	5.0	1.000	C-16
1961	2 teams	MIL N (28G – .207)																							BAL A (17G – .170)
"	total		45	.194	.256	129	25	5	0	1	0.8	6	9	15	14	1	2	0	204	13	5	4	4.9	.977	C-42
1962	BAL A		81	.294	.462	197	58	11	2	6	3.0	21	37	7	11	1	30	11	269	15	1	1	3.5	.996	C-56
1963	2 teams	BAL A (29G – .188)																							KC A (62G – .294)
"	total		91	.272	.366	235	64	13	0	3	1.3	19	32	15	22	1	29	4	306	20	7	3	3.7	.979	C-58
1964	2 teams	KC A (43G – .271)																							BAL A (62G – .259)
"	total		105	.264	.391	276	73	22	2	3	1.1	27	23	27	45	0	28	7	422	25	4	2	4.3	.991	C-82
1965	BAL A		68	.295	.409	132	39	5	2	2	1.5	15	18	17	18	0	29	8	165	9	2	1	2.6	.989	C-35
1966			18	.500	.833	12	6	2	1	0	0.0	1	5	4	1	0	12	6	0	0	0	0	0.0	—	
1967	2 teams	BAL A (11G – .125)																							ATL N (52G – .200)
"	total		63	.189	.283	53	10	2	0	1	1.9	3	8	6	11	0	53	10	0	0	0	0	0.0	—	
	11 yrs.		527	.255	.365	1170	298	63	9	16	1.4	105	140	109	150	3	195	47	1608	104	21	17	3.3	.988	C-321

Billy Lauder

LAUDER, WILLIAM
B. Feb. 23, 1874, New York, N. Y.   D. May 20, 1933, Norwalk, Conn.

BR TR 5'10"   160 lbs.

Year	Team		Games	BA	SA	AB	H	2B	3B	HR	HR%	R	RBI	BB	SO	SB	AB	H	PO	A	E	DP	TC/G	FA	G by Pos
1898	PHI N		97	.263	.357	361	95	14	7	2	0.6	42	67	19		6	0	0	132	171	47	6	3.6	.866	3B-97
1899			151	.268	.333	583	156	17	6	3	0.5	74	90	34		15	0	0	210	307	62	22	3.8	.893	3B-151
1901	PHI A		2	.125	.125	8	1	0	0	0	0.0	1	0	0		0	0	0	4	6	2	0	6.0	.833	3B-2
1902	NY N		125	.237	.288	482	114	20	1	1	0.2	41	44	10		19	0	0	195	252	45	17	3.9	.909	3B-121, OF-4
1903			108	.281	.314	395	111	13	0	0	0.0	52	53	14		19	0	0	140	194	34	10	3.4	.908	3B-108
	5 yrs.		483	.261	.321	1829	477	64	14	6	0.3	210	254	77		59	0	0	681	930	190	55	3.7	.895	3B-479, OF-4

Tim Laudner

LAUDNER, TIMOTHY JON
B. June 7, 1958, Mason City, Iowa

BR TR 6'3"   212 lbs.

Year	Team		Games	BA	SA	AB	H	2B	3B	HR	HR%	R	RBI	BB	SO	SB	AB	H	PO	A	E	DP	TC/G	FA	G by Pos
1981	MIN A		14	.163	.349	43	7	2	0	2	4.7	4	5	3	17	0	0	0	49	5	0	0	3.9	1.000	C-12, DH-2
1982			93	.255	.392	306	78	19	1	7	2.3	37	33	34	74	0	0	0	454	41	12	5	5.5	.976	C-93
1983			62	.185	.345	168	31	9	0	6	3.6	20	18	15	49	0	4	2	259	22	4	5	4.6	.986	C-57, DH-4
1984			87	.206	.389	262	54	16	1	10	3.8	31	35	18	78	0	8	2	362	38	9	2	4.7	.978	C-81, DH-2
1985			72	.238	.396	164	39	5	0	7	4.3	16	19	12	45	0	6	0	236	19	8	3	3.7	.970	C-68, 1B-1
1986			76	.244	.451	193	47	10	0	10	5.2	21	29	24	56	1	15	2	299	13	5	4	4.2	.984	C-68
1987			113	.191	.389	288	55	7	1	16	5.6	30	43	23	80	1	9	1	547	29	7	5	5.2	.992	C-101, 1B-7, DH-2
1988			117	.251	.408	375	94	18	1	13	3.5	38	54	36	89	0	4	0	624	35	5	9	5.7	.992	C-109, DH-4, 1B-3
1989			100	.222	.351	239	53	11	1	6	2.5	24	27	25	65	1	11	5	347	16	3	3	3.7	.992	C-68, DH-19, 1B-11
	9 yrs.		734	.225	.391	2038	458	97	5	77	3.8	221	263	190	553	3	55	12	3177	218	53	36	4.7	.985	C-657, DH-33, 1B-22

LEAGUE CHAMPIONSHIP SERIES

Year	Team		Games	BA	SA	AB	H	2B	3B	HR	HR%	R	RBI	BB	SO	SB	AB	H	PO	A	E	DP	TC/G	FA	G by Pos
1987	MIN A		5	.071	.143	14	1	1	0	0	0.0	1	2	2	5	0	0	0	31	2	0	0	6.6	1.000	C-5

WORLD SERIES

Year	Team		Games	BA	SA	AB	H	2B	3B	HR	HR%	R	RBI	BB	SO	SB	AB	H	PO	A	E	DP	TC/G	FA	G by Pos
1987	MIN A		7	.318	.500	22	7	1	0	1	4.5	4	4	5	4	0	0	0	46	2	0	1	6.9	1.000	C-7

Year	Team		Games	BA	SA	AB	H	2B	3B	HR	HR%	R	RBI	BB	SO	SB	Pinch Hit AB	Pinch Hit H	PO	A	E	DP	TC/G	FA	G by Pos

Chuck Lauer

LAUER, JOHN CHARLES
B. 1865, Pittsburgh, Pa. Deceased.   TR

Year	Team		Games	BA	SA	AB	H	2B	3B	HR	HR%	R	RBI	BB	SO	SB	PH AB	PH H	PO	A	E	DP	TC/G	FA	G by Pos
1884	PIT	AA	13	.114	.114	44	5	0	0	0	0.0	5		0			0	0	16	3	3	0	1.7	.864	OF-10, P-3, 1B-1
1889	PIT	N	4	.188	.188	16	3	0	0	0	0.0	2	1	0	5	0	0	0	16	8	5	0	7.3	.828	C-3, OF-1
1890	CHI	N	2	.250	.375	8	2	1	0	0	0.0	1	2	0	0	0	0	0	12	3	3	0	9.0	.833	C-2
3 yrs.			19	.147	.162	68	10	1	0	0	0.0	8	3	0	5	0	0	0	44	14	11	0	3.6	.841	OF-11, C-5, P-3, 1B-1

Bill Lauterborn

LAUTERBORN, WILLIAM BERNARD
B. June 9, 1879, Hornell, N. Y.   D. Apr. 19, 1965, Andover, N. Y.   BR TR 5'6"   140 lbs.

Year	Team		Games	BA	SA	AB	H	2B	3B	HR	HR%	R	RBI	BB	SO	SB	PH AB	PH H	PO	A	E	DP	TC/G	FA	G by Pos
1904	BOS	N	20	.275	.304	69	19	2	0	0	0.0	7	2	1		1	1	0	39	60	6	2	5.3	.943	2B-20
1905			67	.185	.200	200	37	1	1	0	0.0	11	9	12		1	9	2	89	132	32	3	3.8	.874	3B-29, 2B-23, SS-3, OF-2
2 yrs.			87	.208	.227	269	56	3	1	0	0.0	18	11	13		2	9	2	128	192	38	5	4.1	.894	2B-43, 3B-29, SS-3, OF-2

Cookie Lavagetto

LAVAGETTO, HARRY ARTHUR
B. Dec. 1, 1912, Oakland, Calif.
Manager 1957-61.   BR TR 6'   170 lbs.

Year	Team		Games	BA	SA	AB	H	2B	3B	HR	HR%	R	RBI	BB	SO	SB	PH AB	PH H	PO	A	E	DP	TC/G	FA	G by Pos
1934	PIT	N	87	.220	.322	304	67	16	3	3	1.0	41	46	32	39	6	2	1	214	234	18	39	5.4	.961	2B-83
1935			78	.290	.364	231	67	9	4	0	0.0	27	19	18	15	1	16	3	100	143	15	10	3.3	.942	2B-42, 3B-15
1936			60	.244	.371	197	48	15	2	2	1.0	21	26	15	13	0	9	0	100	132	16	25	4.1	.935	2B-37, 3B-13, SS-1
1937	BKN	N	149	.282	.406	503	142	26	6	8	1.6	64	70	74	41	13	4	0	281	368	34	64	4.6	.950	2B-100, 3B-45
1938			137	.273	.405	487	133	34	6	6	1.2	68	79	68	31	15	3	0	142	240	28	28	3.0	.932	3B-132, 2B-4
1939			153	.300	.416	587	176	28	5	10	1.7	93	87	78	30	14	4	2	163	278	24	28	3.0	.948	3B-149
1940			118	.257	.344	448	115	21	3	4	0.9	56	43	70	32	4	1	0	137	191	24	12	3.0	.932	3B-116
1941			132	.277	.370	441	122	24	7	1	0.2	75	78	80	21	7	10	0	117	215	22	17	2.7	.938	3B-120
1946			88	.236	.318	242	57	9	1	3	1.2	36	27	38	17	3	11	2	70	108	14	11	2.2	.927	3B-67
1947			41	.261	.406	69	18	1	0	3	4.3	6	11	12	5	0	17	4	40	31	2	3	1.8	.973	3B-18, 1B-3
10 yrs.			1043	.269	.377	3509	945	183	37	40	1.1	487	486	485	244	63	77	12	1364	1940	197	237	3.4	.944	3B-675, 2B-266, 1B-3, SS-1

WORLD SERIES

Year	Team		Games	BA	SA	AB	H	2B	3B	HR	HR%	R	RBI	BB	SO	SB	PH AB	PH H	PO	A	E	DP	TC/G	FA	G by Pos
1941	BKN	N	3	.100	.100	10	1	0	0	0	0.0	1		2		0	0	0	2	1	0	0	1.0	1.000	3B-3
1947			5	.143	.286	7	1	1	0	0	0.0	0	3	0	2	0	5	1	0	1	0	0	0.2	1.000	3B-3
2 yrs.			8	.118	.176	17	2	1	0	0	0.0	1	3	2	2	0	5	1	2	2	0	0	0.5	1.000	3B-6

Mike LaValliere

LaVALLIERE, MICHAEL EUGENE (Spanky)
B. Aug. 18, 1960, Charlotte, N. C.   BL TR 5'10"   180 lbs.

Year	Team		Games	BA	SA	AB	H	2B	3B	HR	HR%	R	RBI	BB	SO	SB	PH AB	PH H	PO	A	E	DP	TC/G	FA	G by Pos
1984	PHI	N	6	.000	.000	7	0	0	0	0	0.0	0	0	0	2	0	0	0	20	2	0	0	3.7	1.000	C-6
1985	STL	N	12	.147	.176	34	5	1	0	0	0.0	2	6	7	3	0	0	0	48	5	0	3	4.4	1.000	C-12
1986			110	.234	.310	303	71	10	2	3	1.0	18	30	36	37	0	4	0	468	47	6	8	4.7	.988	C-108
1987	PIT	N	121	.300	.365	340	102	19	0	1	0.3	33	36	43	32	0	14	5	584	70	5	11	5.4	.992	C-112
1988			120	.261	.330	352	92	18	0	2	0.6	24	47	50	34	3	10	1	565	55	8	6	5.2	.987	C-114
1989			68	.316	.400	190	60	10	0	2	1.1	15	23	29	24	0	3	0	306	24	3	3	4.9	.991	C-65
6 yrs.			437	.269	.339	1226	330	58	2	8	0.7	92	142	167	132	3	31	6	1991	203	22	31	5.1	.990	C-417

Doc Lavan

LAVAN, JOHN LEONARD
B. Oct. 28, 1890, Grand Rapids, Mich.   D. May 29, 1952, Detroit, Mich.   BR TR 5'8½"   151 lbs.

Year	Team		Games	BA	SA	AB	H	2B	3B	HR	HR%	R	RBI	BB	SO	SB	PH AB	PH H	PO	A	E	DP	TC/G	FA	G by Pos
1913	2 teams	STL A	(46G – .141)			PHI A	(5G – .071)																		
"	total		51	.135	.172	163	22	2	0	0	0.0	9	5	10	46	3	0	0	88	153	25	24	5.2	.906	SS-51
1914	STL	A	74	.264	.339	239	63	7	4	1	0.4	21	21	17	39	6	0	0	178	193	34	17	5.5	.916	SS-73
1915			157	.218	.284	514	112	17	7	1	0.2	44	48	42	83	13	0	0	313	475	75	81	5.5	.913	SS-157
1916			110	.236	.280	343	81	13	1	0	0.0	32	19	32	38	7	3	1	217	386	32	52	5.8	.950	SS-106
1917			118	.239	.290	355	85	8	5	0	0.0	19	30	19	34	5	1	0	244	354	50	70	5.5	.923	SS-110, 2B-7
1918	WAS	A	117	.278	.323	464	129	17	2	0	0.0	44	45	14	21	12	0	0	275	354	57	43	5.9	.917	SS-117, OF-1
1919	STL	N	100	.242	.295	356	86	12	2	1	0.3	25	25	11	30	4	1	0	207	352	43	49	6.0	.929	SS-99
1920			142	.289	.374	516	149	21	10	1	0.2	52	63	19	38	11	4	1	327	489	50	77	6.1	.942	SS-138
1921			150	.259	.350	560	145	23	11	2	0.4	58	82	23	30	7	0	0	382	540	49	88	6.5	.950	SS-150
1922			89	.227	.265	264	60	8	1	0	0.0	24	27	13	10	3	1	0	172	258	30	40	5.2	.935	SS-82, 3B-5
1923			50	.198	.279	111	22	6	0	1	0.9	10	12	9	7	0	2	1	83	104	14	14	4.0	.930	SS-40, 3B-4, 1B-3, 2B-1
1924			5	.000	.000	6	0	0	0	0	0.0	0	0	0	0	0	0	0	3	10	2	2	3.8	.867	SS-2, 2B-2
12 yrs.			1162	.245	.308	3891	954	134	45	7	0.2	338	377	209	376	71	12	3	2489	3668	461	543	5.7	.930	SS-1125, 2B-10, 3B-9, 1B-3, OF-1

Art LaVigne

LaVIGNE, ARTHUR DAVID
B. Jan. 26, 1885, Worcester, Mass.   D. July 18, 1950, Worcester, Mass.   BR TR 5'10"   162 lbs.

Year	Team		Games	BA	SA	AB	H	2B	3B	HR	HR%	R	RBI	BB	SO	SB	PH AB	PH H	PO	A	E	DP	TC/G	FA	G by Pos
1914	BUF	F	51	.156	.178	90	14	2	0	0	0.0	10	4	7		0	1	0	151	45	6	4	4.0	.970	C-34, 1B-3

Johnny Lavin

LAVIN, JOHN
B. Bay City, Mich. Deceased.   5'11"   175 lbs.

Year	Team		Games	BA	SA	AB	H	2B	3B	HR	HR%	R	RBI	BB	SO	SB	PH AB	PH H	PO	A	E	DP	TC/G	FA	G by Pos
1884	STL	AA	16	.212	.250	52	11	2	0	0	0.0	9		3			0	0	17	1	6	0	1.5	.750	OF-16

Rudy Law

LAW, RUDY KARL
B. Oct. 7, 1956, Waco, Tex.   BL TL 6'1"   165 lbs.

Year	Team		Games	BA	SA	AB	H	2B	3B	HR	HR%	R	RBI	BB	SO	SB	PH AB	PH H	PO	A	E	DP	TC/G	FA	G by Pos
1978	LA	N	11	.250	.250	12	3	0	0	0	0.0	2	1	2	3	1	0	0	3	0	0	0	0.3	1.000	OF-6
1980			128	.260	.302	388	101	5	4	1	0.3	55	23	23	27	40	16	4	233	6	3	0	1.9	.988	OF-106
1982	CHI	A	121	.318	.438	336	107	15	8	3	0.9	55	32	23	41	36	17	3	215	2	6	0	1.8	.973	OF-94, DH-3
1983			141	.283	.369	501	142	20	7	3	0.6	95	34	42	34	77	13	4	302	5	2	2	2.2	.994	OF-132, DH-3
1984			136	.251	.345	487	122	14	7	6	1.2	68	37	39	42	29	11	5	322	5	5	2	2.4	.985	OF-130
1985			125	.259	.374	390	101	21	6	4	1.0	62	35	27	40	29	17	6	226	7	3	3	1.9	.987	OF-120, DH-3
1986	KC	A	87	.261	.388	307	80	26	5	3	1.0	42	36	29	22	14	8	1	145	2	2	0	1.7	.987	OF-77, DH-2
7 yrs.			749	.271	.366	2421	656	101	37	18	0.7	379	198	184	210	228	83	23	1446	27	21	10	2.0	.986	OF-665, DH-11

LEAGUE CHAMPIONSHIP SERIES

Year	Team		Games	BA	SA	AB	H	2B	3B	HR	HR%	R	RBI	BB	SO	SB	PH AB	PH H	PO	A	E	DP	TC/G	FA	G by Pos
1983	CHI	A	4	.389	.444	18	7	1	0	0	0.0	1	0	0	1	2	0	0	10	0	0	0	2.5	1.000	OF-4

Year	Team		Games	BA	SA	AB	H	2B	3B	HR	HR%	R	RBI	BB	SO	SB	Pinch Hit AB	H	PO	A	E	DP	TC/G	FA	G by Pos

Vance Law

LAW, VANCE AARON
Son of Vern Law.
B. Oct. 1, 1956, Boise, Ida.

BR TR 6'2" 185 lbs.

Year	Team		Games	BA	SA	AB	H	2B	3B	HR	HR%	R	RBI	BB	SO	SB	AB	H	PO	A	E	DP	TC/G	FA	G by Pos
1980	PIT	N	25	.230	.311	74	17	2	2	0	0.0	11	3	3	7	2	3	1	31	54	3	8	3.5	.966	2B-11, SS-8, 3B-1
1981			30	.134	.164	67	9	0	1	0	0.0	1	3	2	15	1	2	0	50	58	0	10	3.6	1.000	2B-19, SS-7, 3B-2
1982	CHI	A	114	.281	.384	359	101	20	1	5	1.4	40	54	26	46	4	1	1	156	313	26	52	4.3	.947	SS-85, 3B-39, 2B-10, OF-1
1983			145	.243	.348	408	99	21	5	4	1.0	55	42	51	56	3	0	0	94	311	14	28	2.9	.967	3B-139, 2B-3, SS-2, DH-1, OF-1
1984			151	.252	.403	481	121	18	2	17	3.5	60	59	41	75	4	4	2	119	246	16	32	2.5	.958	3B-137, 2B-22, OF-5, SS-4
1985	MON	N	147	.266	.405	519	138	30	6	10	1.9	75	52	86	96	6	5	0	420	402	12	98	5.7	.986	2B-126, 1B-20, 3B-11, OF-1
1986			112	.225	.325	360	81	17	2	5	1.4	37	44	37	66		6	1	273	299	4	59	5.1	.993	2B-94, 1B-20, 3B-13, P-3, OF-1
1987			133	.273	.422	436	119	27	1	12	2.8	52	56	51	62	8	5	1	258	308	11	54	4.3	.981	2B-106, 3B-22, 1B-17, P-3
1988	CHI	N	151	.293	.412	556	163	29	2	11	2.0	73	78	55	79	1	1	0	112	272	19	22	2.7	.953	3B-150, OF-1
1989			130	.235	.355	408	96	22	3	7	1.7	38	42	38	73	2	10	0	76	168	13	13	2.0	.949	3B-119, OF-1
10 yrs.			1138	.257	.380	3668	944	186	25	71	1.9	442	433	390	575	34	37	6	1589	2431	118	376	3.6	.971	3B-633, 2B-391, SS-106, 1B-57, OF-11, P-6, DH-1

LEAGUE CHAMPIONSHIP SERIES

Year	Team		Games	BA	SA	AB	H	2B	3B	HR	HR%	R	RBI	BB	SO	SB	AB	H	PO	A	E	DP	TC/G	FA	G by Pos
1983	CHI	A	4	.182	.182	11	2	0	0	0	0.0	0	1	1	3	0	0	0	2	9	1	1	3.0	.917	3B-4
1989	CHI	N	2	.000	.000	3	0	0	0	0	0.0	0	0	1	3	0	1	0	0	0	0	0	0.0	–	3B-1
2 yrs.			6	.143	.143	14	2	0	0	0	0.0	0	1	1	6	0	1	0	2	9	1	1	2.0	.917	3B-5

Garland Lawing

LAWING, GARLAND FREDERICK (Knobby)
B. Aug. 26, 1919, Gastonia, N. C.

BR TR 6'1" 180 lbs.

Year	Team		Games	BA	SA	AB	H	2B	3B	HR	HR%	R	RBI	BB	SO	SB	AB	H	PO	A	E	DP	TC/G	FA	G by Pos
1946	2 teams			CIN	N	(2G – .000)							NY	N	(8G – .167)										
"	total		10	.133	.133	15	2	0	0	0	0.0	2	0	0	5	0	3	1	6	0	0	0	0.6	1.000	OF-5

Tom Lawless

LAWLESS, THOMAS JAMES
B. Dec. 19, 1956, Erie, Pa.

BR TR 5'11" 170 lbs.

Year	Team		Games	BA	SA	AB	H	2B	3B	HR	HR%	R	RBI	BB	SO	SB	AB	H	PO	A	E	DP	TC/G	FA	G by Pos
1982	CIN	N	49	.212	.248	165	35	6	0	0	0.0	19	4	9	30	16	1	0	87	136	5	35	4.7	.978	2B-47
1984	2 teams		54	CIN	N	(43G – .250)							MON	N	(11G – .176)										
"	total		54	.237	.299	97	23	3	0	1	1.0	11	2	8	16	7	5	1	50	52	1	8	1.9	.990	2B-32, 3B-6
1985	STL	N	47	.207	.293	58	12	3	1	0	0.0	8	8	5	4	2	9	2	19	44	1	4	1.4	.984	3B-13, 2B-11
1986			46	.282	.308	39	11	1	0	0	0.0	5	3	2	8	12	2	0	11	15	2	1	0.6	.929	3B-12, 2B-7, OF-1
1987			19	.080	.120	25	2	1	0	0	0.0	5	0	3	5	2	5	0	5	15	0	3	1.1	1.000	2B-7, 3B-3, OF-1
1988			54	.154	.262	65	10	2	1	1	1.5	9	3	7	9	6	10	1	23	29	0	3	1.0	1.000	3B-24, OF-6, 2B-5, 1B-1
1989	TOR	A	59	.229	.243	70	16	1	0	0	0.0	20	3	7	12	12	7	3	39	26	3	6	1.2	.956	OF-16, DH-12, 3B-12, 2B-7, C-1
7 yrs.			328	.210	.262	519	109	17	2	2	0.4	77	23	41	84	53	49	9	234	317	12	60	1.7	.979	2B-116, 3B-70, OF-24, DH-12, 1B-1, C-1

LEAGUE CHAMPIONSHIP SERIES

Year	Team		Games	BA	SA	AB	H	2B	3B	HR	HR%	R	RBI	BB	SO	SB	AB	H	PO	A	E	DP	TC/G	FA	G by Pos
1987	STL	N	3	.333	.333	6	2	0	0	0	0.0	0	0	1	1	0	2	1	1	4	0	0	1.7	1.000	3B-2, OF-1

WORLD SERIES

Year	Team		Games	BA	SA	AB	H	2B	3B	HR	HR%	R	RBI	BB	SO	SB	AB	H	PO	A	E	DP	TC/G	FA	G by Pos
1985	STL	N	1	–	–	0	0	0	0	0	0.0	0	0	0	0	0	0	0	0	0	0	0	0.0	–	
1987			3	.100	.400	10	1	0	0	1	10.0	1	3	0	4	0	0	0	3	6	1	1	3.3	.900	3B-3
2 yrs.			4	.100	.400	10	1	0	0	1	10.0	1	3	0	4	0	0	0	3	6	1	1	2.5	.900	3B-3

Mike Lawlor

LAWLOR, MICHAEL H.
B. Mar. 11, 1854, Troy, N. Y. D. Aug. 3, 1918, Troy, N. Y.

TR 6' 180 lbs.

Year	Team		Games	BA	SA	AB	H	2B	3B	HR	HR%	R	RBI	BB	SO	SB	AB	H	PO	A	E	DP	TC/G	FA	G by Pos
1880	TRO	N	4	.111	.111	9	1	0	0	0	0.0	1		0	1			0	0	18	8	4	0	7.5	.867	C-4
1884	WAS	U	2	.000	.000	7	0	0	0	0	0.0	0			0			0	0	15	5	0	0	10.0	1.000	C-2
2 yrs.			6	.063	.063	16	1	0	0	0	0.0	1		1	1			0	0	33	13	4	0	8.3	.920	C-6

Bill Lawrence

LAWRENCE, WILLIAM HENRY
B. Mar. 11, 1906, San Mateo, Calif.

BR TR 6'4" 194 lbs.

Year	Team		Games	BA	SA	AB	H	2B	3B	HR	HR%	R	RBI	BB	SO	SB	AB	H	PO	A	E	DP	TC/G	FA	G by Pos
1932	DET	A	25	.217	.239	46	10	1	0	0	0.0	3	5	5	0	2	0	39	2	0	1	1.6	1.000	OF-15

Jim Lawrence

LAWRENCE, JAMES ROSS
B. Feb. 12, 1939, Hamilton, Ont., Canada

BL TR 6'1" 185 lbs.

Year	Team		Games	BA	SA	AB	H	2B	3B	HR	HR%	R	RBI	BB	SO	SB	AB	H	PO	A	E	DP	TC/G	FA	G by Pos
1963	CLE	A	2	–	–	0	0	0	0	0	0.0	0	0	0	0	0	0	0	3	0	1	0	2.0	.750	C-2

Otis Lawry

LAWRY, OTIS CARROLL (Rabbit)
B. Nov. 1, 1893, Fairfield, Me. D. Oct. 23, 1965, China, Me.

BL TR 5'8" 133 lbs.

Year	Team		Games	BA	SA	AB	H	2B	3B	HR	HR%	R	RBI	BB	SO	SB	AB	H	PO	A	E	DP	TC/G	FA	G by Pos
1916	PHI	A	41	.203	.203	123	25	0	0	0	0.0	10	4	9	21	4	5	0	39	71	11	8	3.0	.909	2B-29, OF-5
1917			30	.164	.182	55	9	1	0	0	0.0	7	1	2	9	1	4	1	24	35	5	2	2.1	.922	2B-17, OF-1
2 yrs.			71	.191	.197	178	34	1	0	0	0.0	17	5	11	30	5	9	1	63	106	16	10	2.6	.914	2B-46, OF-6

Marcus Lawton

LAWTON, MARCUS DWAYNE
B. Aug. 18, 1965, Gulfport, Miss.

BB TR 6'1" 160 lbs.

Year	Team		Games	BA	SA	AB	H	2B	3B	HR	HR%	R	RBI	BB	SO	SB	AB	H	PO	A	E	DP	TC/G	FA	G by Pos
1989	NY	A	10	.214	.214	14	3	0	0	0	0.0	1	0	0	3	1	2	0	9	0	2	0	1.1	.818	OF-8, DH-1

Gene Layden

LAYDEN, EUGENE FRANCIS
B. Mar. 14, 1894, Pittsburgh, Pa. D. Dec. 12, 1984, Pittsburgh, Pa.

BL TL 5'10" 160 lbs.

Year	Team		Games	BA	SA	AB	H	2B	3B	HR	HR%	R	RBI	BB	SO	SB	AB	H	PO	A	E	DP	TC/G	FA	G by Pos
1915	NY	A	3	.286	.286	7	2	0	0	0	0.0	2	0	0	1	0	0	0	3	0	1	0	1.3	.750	OF-2

Pete Layden

LAYDEN, PETER JOHN
B. Dec. 30, 1919, Dallas, Tex. D. July 18, 1982, Edna, Tex.

BR TR 5'11" 185 lbs.

Year	Team		Games	BA	SA	AB	H	2B	3B	HR	HR%	R	RBI	BB	SO	SB	AB	H	PO	A	E	DP	TC/G	FA	G by Pos
1948	STL	A	41	.250	.288	104	26	2	1	0	0.0	11	4	6	10	4	8	2	69	3	2	0	1.8	.973	OF-30

Year	Team		Games	BA	SA	AB	H	2B	3B	HR	HR%	R	RBI	BB	SO	SB	Pinch Hit AB	Pinch Hit H	PO	A	E	DP	TC/G	FA	G by Pos

Herman Layne

LAYNE, HERMAN
B. Feb. 13, 1901, New Haven, W. Va. D. Aug. 27, 1973, Gallipolis, Ohio
BR TR 5'11" 165 lbs.

Year	Team		Games	BA	SA	AB	H	2B	3B	HR	HR%	R	RBI	BB	SO	SB	AB	H	PO	A	E	DP	TC/G	FA	G by Pos
1927	PIT	N	11	.000	.000	6	0	0	0	0	0.0	3	0	1	0	0	1	0	0	0	1	0	0.1	–	OF-2

Hilly Layne

LAYNE, IVORIA HILLIS (Tony)
B. Feb. 23, 1918, Whitewell, Tenn.
BL TR 6' 170 lbs.

Year	Team		Games	BA	SA	AB	H	2B	3B	HR	HR%	R	RBI	BB	SO	SB	AB	H	PO	A	E	DP	TC/G	FA	G by Pos
1941	WAS	A	13	.280	.320	50	14	2	0	0	0.0	8	6	4	5	1	0	0	12	29	2	1	3.3	.953	3B-13
1944			33	.195	.218	87	17	2	0	0	0.0	6	8	6	10	2	13	2	27	49	3	5	2.4	.962	3B-18, 2B-3
1945			61	.299	.408	147	44	5	4	1	0.7	23	14	10	7	0	23	4	34	53	4	3	1.5	.956	3B-33
3 yrs.			107	.264	.335	284	75	9	4	1	0.4	37	28	20	22	3	36	6	73	131	9	9	2.0	.958	3B-64, 2B-3

Les Layton

LAYTON, LESTER LEE
B. Nov. 18, 1921, Nardin, Okla.
BR TR 6' 165 lbs.

Year	Team		Games	BA	SA	AB	H	2B	3B	HR	HR%	R	RBI	BB	SO	SB	AB	H	PO	A	E	DP	TC/G	FA	G by Pos
1948	NY	N	63	.231	.429	91	21	4	4	2	2.2	14	12	6	21	1	32	8	38	1	2	0	0.7	.951	OF-20

Johnny Lazor

LAZOR, JOHN PAUL
B. Sept. 9, 1912, Taylor, Wash.
BL TR 5'9½" 180 lbs.

Year	Team		Games	BA	SA	AB	H	2B	3B	HR	HR%	R	RBI	BB	SO	SB	AB	H	PO	A	E	DP	TC/G	FA	G by Pos
1943	BOS	A	83	.226	.293	208	47	10	2	0	0.0	21	13	21	25	5	17	2	135	7	3	0	1.7	.979	OF-63
1944			16	.083	.125	24	2	1	0	0	0.0	0	0	1	0	0	8	1	8	2	0	0	0.6	1.000	OF-6, C-1
1945			101	.310	.424	335	104	19	2	5	1.5	35	45	18	17	3	17	5	141	6	6	0	1.5	.961	OF-81
1946			23	.138	.241	29	4	0	0	1	3.4	1	4	0	11	0	16	1	6	0	0	0	0.3	1.000	OF-7
4 yrs.			223	.263	.357	596	157	30	4	6	1.0	57	62	40	53	8	58	9	290	15	9	0	1.4	.971	OF-157, C-1

Tony Lazzeri

LAZZERI, ANTHONY MICHAEL (Poosh 'Em Up)
B. Dec. 6, 1903, San Francisco, Calif. D. Aug. 6, 1946, San Francisco, Calif.
BR TR 5'11½" 170 lbs.

Year	Team		Games	BA	SA	AB	H	2B	3B	HR	HR%	R	RBI	BB	SO	SB	AB	H	PO	A	E	DP	TC/G	FA	G by Pos
1926	NY	A	155	.275	.462	589	162	28	14	18	3.1	79	114	54	96	16	0	0	309	478	35	74	5.3	.957	2B-149, SS-5, 3B-1
1927			153	.309	.482	570	176	29	8	18	3.2	92	102	69	82	22	0	0	281	525	29	75	5.5	.954	2B-113, SS-38, 3B-9
1928			116	.332	.535	404	134	30	11	10	2.5	62	82	43	50	15	4	1	236	331	26	56	5.1	.956	2B-116
1929			147	.354	.561	545	193	37	11	18	3.3	101	106	69	45	9	0	0	475	627	53	131	7.9	.954	2B-147, SS-61
1930			143	.303	.462	571	173	34	15	9	1.6	109	121	60	62	4	1	0	294	382	26	59	4.9	.963	2B-77, 3B-60, SS-8, OF-1, 1B-1
1931			135	.267	.401	484	129	27	7	8	1.7	67	83	79	80	18	7	5	255	341	26	56	4.6	.958	2B-90, 3B-39
1932			141	.300	.506	510	153	28	16	15	2.9	79	113	82	64	11	3	1	364	412	17	70	5.6	.979	2B-133, 3B-5
1933			139	.294	.486	523	154	22	12	18	3.4	94	104	73	62	15	1	0	338	407	25	71	5.5	.968	2B-138
1934			123	.267	.445	438	117	24	6	14	3.2	59	67	71	64	11	1	1	254	316	18	59	4.8	.969	2B-92, 3B-30
1935			130	.273	.417	477	130	18	6	13	2.7	72	83	63	75	11	5	3	303	354	22	76	5.2	.968	2B-118, SS-9
1936			150	.287	.441	537	154	29	6	14	2.6	82	109	97	65	8	0	0	348	418	25	88	5.3	.968	2B-148, SS-2
1937			126	.244	.399	446	109	21	3	14	3.1	56	70	71	76	7	1	0	251	382	22	64	5.2	.966	2B-125
1938	CHI	N	54	.267	.433	120	32	5	0	5	4.2	21	23	22	30	0	14	2	49	75	7	12	2.4	.947	SS-25, 3B-7, 2B-4, OF-1
1939	2 teams			BKN N (14G – .282)		NY N (13G – .295)																			
"	total		27	.289	.458	83	24	2	0	4	4.8	13	14	17	13	1	1	0	40	59	10	10	4.0	.908	3B-15, 2B-11
14 yrs.			1739	.292	.467	6297	1840	334	115	178	2.8	986	1191	870	864	148	38	13	3797	5107	341	901	5.3	.963	2B-1461, 3B-166, SS-148, OF-2, 1B-1

WORLD SERIES

Year	Team		Games	BA	SA	AB	H	2B	3B	HR	HR%	R	RBI	BB	SO	SB	AB	H	PO	A	E	DP	TC/G	FA	G by Pos
1926	NY	A	7	.192	.231	26	5	1	0	0	0.0	2	3	1	6	1	0	0	14	19	1	2	4.9	.971	2B-7
1927			4	.267	.333	15	4	1	0	0	0.0	1	2	1	4	0	0	0	10	18	1	4	7.3	.966	2B-4
1928			4	.250	.333	12	3	1	0	0	0.0	2	0	1	0	0	0	0	2	7	2	1	2.8	.818	2B-4
1932			4	.294	.647	17	5	0	0	2	11.8	4	5	2	1	0	2	0	8	11	1	1	5.0	.950	2B-4
1936			6	.250	.400	20	5	0	1	1	5.0	4	7	4	4	0	0	0	13	17	0	1	5.0	1.000	2B-6
1937			5	.400	.733	15	6	0	1	1	6.7	3	2	3	3	0	0	0	11	16	0	1	5.4	1.000	2B-5
1938	CHI	N	2	.000	.000	2	0	0	0	0	0.0	0	0	0	1	0	2	0	0	0	0	0	0.0	–	
7 yrs.			32	.262	.421	107	28	3	1	4	3.7	16	19	12	19	2	2	0	58	88	5	10	4.7	.967	2B-30

Freddy Leach

LEACH, FREDERICK
B. Nov. 23, 1897, Springfield, Mo. D. Dec. 10, 1981, Hagerman, Ida.
BL TR 5'11" 183 lbs.

Year	Team		Games	BA	SA	AB	H	2B	3B	HR	HR%	R	RBI	BB	SO	SB	AB	H	PO	A	E	DP	TC/G	FA	G by Pos
1923	PHI	N	52	.260	.327	104	27	4	0	1	1.0	9	16	3	14	1	23	4	38	0	2	0	0.8	.950	OF-26
1924			8	.464	.821	28	13	2	1	2	7.1	6	7	2	1	0	0	0	8	1	0	0	1.1	1.000	OF-7
1925			65	.312	.442	292	91	15	4	5	1.7	47	28	5	21	1	0	0	178	2	9	1	2.9	.952	OF-65
1926			129	.329	.484	492	162	29	7	11	2.2	73	71	16	33	6	5	1	313	15	7	2	2.6	.979	OF-123
1927			140	.306	.444	536	164	30	4	12	2.2	69	83	21	32	2	1	0	385	26	8	10	3.0	.981	OF-139
1928			145	.304	.469	588	179	36	11	13	2.2	83	96	30	30	4	0	0	545	29	8	33	4.0	.986	OF-120, 1B-25
1929	NY	N	113	.290	.431	411	119	22	6	8	1.9	74	47	17	14	10	17	5	149	2	4	0	1.4	.974	OF-95
1930			126	.327	.482	544	178	19	13	13	2.4	90	71	22	25	3	2	0	208	11	5	4	1.8	.978	OF-125
1931			129	.309	.421	515	159	30	5	6	1.2	75	61	29	9	4	2	0	239	6	6	1	1.9	.976	OF-125
1932	BOS	N	84	.247	.318	223	55	9	2	1	0.4	21	29	18	10	1	30	8	126	2	3	0	1.6	.977	OF-50
10 yrs.			991	.307	.446	3733	1147	196	53	72	1.9	543	509	163	189	32	80	18	2189	94	52	51	2.4	.978	OF-874, 1B-25

Rick Leach

LEACH, RICHARD MAX
B. May 4, 1957, Ann Arbor, Mich.
BL TL 6'1" 180 lbs.

Year	Team		Games	BA	SA	AB	H	2B	3B	HR	HR%	R	RBI	BB	SO	SB	AB	H	PO	A	E	DP	TC/G	FA	G by Pos
1981	DET	A	54	.193	.289	83	16	3	1	1	1.2	9	11	16	15	1	10	2	149	14	0	15	3.0	1.000	1B-32, OF-15, DH-2
1982			82	.239	.330	218	52	7	2	3	1.4	23	12	21	29	4	14	2	430	29	2	36	5.6	.996	1B-56, OF-14, DH-4
1983			99	.248	.355	242	60	17	0	3	1.2	22	26	19	21	2	18	4	465	45	4	37	5.2	.992	1B-73, OF-13, DH-3
1984	TOR	A	65	.261	.375	88	23	6	2	0	0.0	11	7	8	14	0	22	8	92	14	0	9	1.6	1.000	OF-23, 1B-15, DH-6, P-1
1985			16	.200	.257	35	7	0	1	0	0.0	2	1	3	9	0	4	1	78	6	1	8	5.3	.988	1B-10, OF-4
1986			110	.309	.435	246	76	14	1	5	2.0	35	39	13	24	0	31	10	107	5	3	11	1.0	.974	DH-42, OF-39, 1B-7
1987			98	.282	.405	195	55	11	1	3	1.5	26	25	25	25	0	28	7	57	1	1	0	0.6	.983	OF-43, DH-42, 1B-5
1988			87	.276	.352	199	55	13	1	0	0.0	21	23	18	27	0	19	1	93	5	1	0	1.1	1.000	OF-45, DH-25, 1B-4
1989	TEX	A	110	.272	.351	239	65	14	1	1	0.4	32	23	32	33	2	30	6	74	5	3	2	0.7	.962	DH-44, OF-41, 1B-4
9 yrs.			721	.265	.365	1545	409	87	10	16	1.0	181	167	155	197	8	176	41	1545	121	14	119	2.3	.992	OF-241, 1B-206, DH-168, P-1

Year	Team		Games	BA	SA	AB	H	2B	3B	HR	HR%	R	RBI	BB	SO	SB	Pinch Hit AB	Pinch Hit H	PO	A	E	DP	TC/G	FA	G by Pos

Tommy Leach

LEACH, THOMAS WILLIAM
B. Nov. 4, 1877, French Creek, N. Y.   D. Sept. 29, 1969, Haines City, Fla.
BR TR 5'6½" 150 lbs.

Year	Team		Games	BA	SA	AB	H	2B	3B	HR	HR%	R	RBI	BB	SO	SB	AB	H	PO	A	E	DP	TC/G	FA	G by Pos
1898	LOU	N	3	.300	.300	10	3	0	0	0	0.0	0	0	0		0	0	0	2	7	3	0	4.0	.750	3B-3, 2B-1
1899			106	.288	.379	406	117	10	6	5	1.2	75	57	37		19	0	0	194	278	61	17	5.0	.886	3B-80, SS-25, 2B-2
1900	PIT	N	51	.213	.263	160	34	1	2	1	0.6	20	16	21		8	1	0	74	117	24	9	4.2	.888	3B-31, SS-8, 2B-7, OF-4
1901			98	.305	.414	374	114	12	13	1	0.3	64	44	20		16	2	1	130	208	35	11	3.8	.906	3B-92, SS-4
1902			135	.280	.442	514	144	21	22	6	1.2	97	85	45		25	1	0	170	316	39	10	3.9	.926	3B-134
1903			127	.298	.438	507	151	16	17	7	1.4	97	87	40		22	0	0	178	292	65	16	4.2	.879	3B-127
1904			146	.257	.335	579	149	15	12	2	0.3	92	56	45		23	0	0	212	371	60	18	4.4	.907	3B-146
1905			131	.257	.345	499	128	10	14	2	0.4	71	53	37		17	0	0	245	141	16	15	3.1	.960	OF-71, 3B-58, SS-2, 2B-2
1906			133	.286	.342	476	136	10	7	1	0.2	66	39	33		21	6	3	209	143	20	4	2.8	.946	3B-65, OF-60, SS-1
1907			149	.303	.404	547	166	19	12	4	0.7	102	43	40		43	0	0	332	95	24	12	3.0	.947	OF-111, 3B-33, SS-6, 2B-1
1908			152	.259	.381	583	151	24	16	5	0.9	93	41	54		24	0	0	205	295	33	19	3.5	.938	3B-150, OF-2
1909			151	.261	.368	587	153	29	8	6	1.0	126	43	66		27	0	0	355	38	13	5	2.7	.968	OF-138, 3B-13
1910			135	.270	.357	529	143	24	5	4	0.8	83	52	38	62	18	1	0	358	17	14	5	2.9	.964	OF-131, SS-2, 2B-1
1911			108	.238	.324	386	92	12	6	3	0.8	60	43	46	50	19	4	0	226	42	7	6	2.5	.975	OF-89, SS-13, 3B-1
1912	2 teams					PIT N (28G – .299)				CHI N (82G – .242)															
"	total		110	.257	.340	362	93	14	5	2	0.6	74	51	67	29	20	4	2	255	22	7	7	2.6	.975	OF-97, 3B-4
1913	CHI	N	130	.289	.423	454	131	23	10	6	1.3	99	32	77	44	21	7	3	276	17	6	5	2.3	.980	OF-119, 3B-2
1914			153	.263	.373	577	152	24	9	7	1.2	80	46	79	50	16	1	0	346	42	18	5	2.7	.956	OF-137, 3B-16
1915	CIN	N	107	.224	.275	335	75	7	5	0	0.0	42	17	56	38	20	9	1	200	9	9	2	2.0	.959	OF-96
1918	PIT	N	30	.194	.306	72	14	2	3	0	0.0	14	5	19	5	2	2	0	40	10	5	2	1.8	.909	OF-23, SS-3
19 yrs.			2155	.270	.371	7957	2146	273	172	62	0.8	1355	810	820	278	361	38	10	4007	2460	459	168	3.2	.934	OF-1078, 3B-955, SS-64, 2B-14

WORLD SERIES

Year	Team		Games	BA	SA	AB	H	2B	3B	HR	HR%	R	RBI	BB	SO	SB	AB	H	PO	A	E	DP	TC/G	FA	G by Pos
1903	PIT	N	8	.273	.515	33	9	0	4	0	0.0	3	7	1		2	0	0	5	16	4	0	3.1	.840	3B-8
1909			7	.320	.480	25	8	4	0	0	0.0	8	2	2	1	1	0	0	20	3	0	0	3.3	1.000	OF-6, 3B-1
2 yrs.			15	.293	.500	58	17	4	4	0	0.0	11	9	3	1	3	0	0	25	19	4	0	3.2	.917	3B-9, OF-6

1st

Dan Leahy

LEAHY, DANIEL C.
B. Aug. 8, 1870, Nashville, Tenn.   D. Dec. 25, 1915, Nashville, Tenn.

Year	Team		Games	BA	SA	AB	H	2B	3B	HR	HR%	R	RBI	BB	SO	SB	AB	H	PO	A	E	DP	TC/G	FA	G by Pos
1896	PHI	N	2	.333	.500	6	2	1	0	0	0.0	0	1	1		2	0	0	4	8	2	0	7.0	.857	SS-2

Tom Leahy

LEAHY, THOMAS JOSEPH
B. June 2, 1869, New Haven, Conn.   D. June 11, 1951, New Haven, Conn.
TR

Year	Team		Games	BA	SA	AB	H	2B	3B	HR	HR%	R	RBI	BB	SO	SB	AB	H	PO	A	E	DP	TC/G	FA	G by Pos
1897	2 teams					PIT N (24G – .261)				WAS N (19G – .385)															
"	total		43	.306	.396	144	44	5	4	0	0.0	22	19	16		9	0	0	63	37	16	2	2.7	.862	OF-23, 3B-11, C-7, 2B-3
1898	WAS	N	15	.182	.218	55	10	2	0	0	0.0	10	5	8		6	0	0	26	34	4	3	4.3	.938	3B-12, 2B-3
1901	2 teams					MIL A (33G – .242)				PHI A (5G – .333)															
"	total		38	.254	.351	114	29	7	2	0	0.0	19	11	12		3	3	2	102	41	9	5	4.0	.941	C-29, OF-4, SS-1, 2B-1
1905	STL	N	35	.227	.299	97	22	1	3	0	0.0	3	7	8		0	6	1	91	31	7	1	3.7	.946	C-29
4 yrs.			131	.256	.337	410	105	15	9	0	0.0	54	42	44		18	9	3	282	143	36	11	3.5	.922	C-65, OF-27, 3B-23, 2B-7, SS-1

Fred Lear

LEAR, FREDERICK FRANCIS (King)
B. Apr. 7, 1894, New York, N. Y.   D. Oct. 13, 1955, East Orange, N. J.
BR TR 6'½" 180 lbs.

Year	Team		Games	BA	SA	AB	H	2B	3B	HR	HR%	R	RBI	BB	SO	SB	AB	H	PO	A	E	DP	TC/G	FA	G by Pos
1915	PHI	A	2	.000	.000	2	0	0	0	0	0.0	0	0	0	2	0	0	0	3	0	0	0	2.5	.600	3B-2
1918	CHI	N	2	.000	.000	1	0	0	0	0	0.0	0	0	0	1	0	0	0	0	0	0	0	0.0		
1919			40	.224	.329	76	17	3	1	1	1.3	8	11	8	11	2	14	2	121	27	5	6	3.8	.967	2B-9, 1B-9, SS-3
1920	NY	N	31	.253	.310	87	22	0	1	1	1.1	12	7	8	15	0	4	1	20	39	5	5	2.0	.952	3B-24, 2B-1
4 yrs.			75	.235	.313	166	39	3	2	2	1.2	20	18	17	28	2	19	3	144	66	10	11	2.9	.955	3B-26, 2B-10, 1B-9, SS-3

Bill Leard

LEARD, WILLIAM WALLACE (Wild Bill)
B. Oct. 14, 1885, Oneida, N. Y.   D. Jan. 15, 1970, San Francisco, Calif.
BR TR 5'10" 155 lbs.

Year	Team		Games	BA	SA	AB	H	2B	3B	HR	HR%	R	RBI	BB	SO	SB	AB	H	PO	A	E	DP	TC/G	FA	G by Pos
1917	BKN	N	3	.000	.000	3	0	0	0	0	0.0	0	0	0	1	0	1	0	0	0	0	0	0.0	–	2B-1

Jack Leary

LEARY, JOHN J.
B. 1858, New Haven, Conn.   Deceased.
TL 5'11" 186 lbs.

Year	Team		Games	BA	SA	AB	H	2B	3B	HR	HR%	R	RBI	BB	SO	SB	AB	H	PO	A	E	DP	TC/G	FA	G by Pos
1880	BOS	N	1	.000	.000	3	0	0	0	0	0.0	1		1		0	0	0	0	2	0	0	2.0	1.000	OF-1, P-1
1881	DET	N	3	.273	.545	11	3	1	1	0	0.0	2		1		0	0	0	5	2	2	0	3.0	.778	OF-2, P-2
1882	2 teams					PIT AA (60G – .292)				BAL AA (4G – .222)															
"	total		64	.287	.360	275	79	8	3	2	0.7	35		5		0	0	0	78	81	49	2	3.3	.764	3B-33, OF-28, P-6, 2B-1, 1B-1
1883	2 teams					LOU AA (40G – .188)				BAL AA (3G – .182)															
"	total		43	.188	.301	176	33	1	5	3	1.7	17		2		0	0	0	72	112	44	14	5.3	.807	SS-40, 2B-3
1884	2 teams					ALT U (8G – .091)				CHI U (10G – .175)															
"	total		18	.137	.151	73	10	1	0	0	0.0	1		0		0	0	0	36	20	20	0	4.2	.737	OF-9, P-5, 3B-4, 2B-4
5 yrs.			129	.232	.314	538	125	11	9	5	0.9	56	4	10	1	0	0	0	191	217	115	16	4.1	.780	OF-40, SS-40, 3B-37, P-14, 2B-8, 1B-1

John Leary

LEARY, JOHN LOUIS (Jack)
B. May 2, 1891, Waltham, Mass.   D. Aug. 18, 1961, Waltham, Mass.
BR TR 5'11½" 180 lbs.

Year	Team		Games	BA	SA	AB	H	2B	3B	HR	HR%	R	RBI	BB	SO	SB	AB	H	PO	A	E	DP	TC/G	FA	G by Pos
1914	STL	A	144	.265	.343	533	141	28	7	0	0.0	35	45	10	71	9	2	1	1323	91	20	68	10.0	.986	1B-130, C-15
1915			75	.242	.286	227	55	10	0	0	0.0	19	15	5	36	2	11	4	469	41	13	42	7.0	.975	1B-53, C-11
2 yrs.			219	.258	.326	760	196	38	7	0	0.0	54	60	15	107	11	13	5	1792	132	33	110	8.9	.983	1B-183, C-26

Hal Leathers

LEATHERS, HAROLD LANGFORD (Chuck)
B. Dec. 2, 1898, Selma, Calif.   D. Apr. 12, 1977, Modesto, Calif.
BL TR 5'8" 152 lbs.

Year	Team		Games	BA	SA	AB	H	2B	3B	HR	HR%	R	RBI	BB	SO	SB	AB	H	PO	A	E	DP	TC/G	FA	G by Pos
1920	CHI	N	9	.304	.478	23	7	1	0	1	4.3	3	3	1	1	1	1	0	15	21	7	0	4.8	.837	SS-6, 2B-3

Year	Team		Games	BA	SA	AB	H	2B	3B	HR	HR%	R	RBI	BB	SO	SB	Pinch Hit AB	Pinch Hit H	PO	A	E	DP	TC/G	FA	G by Pos

Emil Leber

LEBER, EMIL BOHMIEL
B. May 15, 1881, Cleveland, Ohio D. Nov. 6, 1924, Cleveland, Ohio

BR TR 5'11" 170 lbs.

Year	Team		Games	BA	SA	AB	H	2B	3B	HR	HR%	R	RBI	BB	SO	SB	PH AB	PH H	PO	A	E	DP	TC/G	FA	G by Pos
1905	CLE	A	2	.000	.000	6	0	0	0	0	0.0	1	0	1		0	0	0	0	4	0	0	2.0	1.000	3B-2

Bevo LeBourveau

LeBOURVEAU, DeWITT WILEY
B. Aug. 24, 1894, Dana, Calif. D. Dec. 9, 1947, Nevada City, Calif.

BL TR 5'11" 175 lbs.

Year	Team		Games	BA	SA	AB	H	2B	3B	HR	HR%	R	RBI	BB	SO	SB	PH AB	PH H	PO	A	E	DP	TC/G	FA	G by Pos
1919	PHI	N	17	.270	.270	63	17	0	0	0	0.0	4	0	10	8	2	0	0	27	6	0	0	1.9	1.000	OF-17
1920			84	.257	.333	261	67	7	2	3	1.1	29	12	11	36	9	8	1	133	16	8	1	1.9	.949	OF-72
1921			93	.295	.438	281	83	12	5	6	2.1	42	35	29	51	4	16	9	126	7	13	2	1.6	.911	OF-76
1922			74	.269	.389	167	45	8	3	2	1.2	24	20	24	29	0	25	4	77	4	7	1	1.2	.920	OF-42
1929	PHI	A	12	.313	.438	16	5	0	1	0	0.0	1	2	5	1	0	9	1	8	0	0	0	0.7	1.000	OF-3
5 yrs.			280	.275	.379	788	217	27	11	11	1.4	100	69	79	125	15	58	15	371	33	28	4	1.5	.935	OF-210

Bill Lee

LEE, WILLIAM JOSEPH
B. Jan. 9, 1892, Bayonne, N. J. D. Jan. 6, 1984, West Hazleton, Pa.

BR TR 5'9" 165 lbs.

Year	Team		Games	BA	SA	AB	H	2B	3B	HR	HR%	R	RBI	BB	SO	SB	PH AB	PH H	PO	A	E	DP	TC/G	FA	G by Pos
1915	STL	A	18	.186	.203	59	11	1	0	0	0.0	2	4	6	5	1	2	1	40	5	1	1	2.6	.978	OF-15, 3B-1
1916			7	.182	.182	11	2	0	0	0	0.0	1	0	1	0	0	3	2	5	0	0	0	0.7	1.000	OF-3
2 yrs.			25	.186	.200	70	13	1	0	0	0.0	3	4	7	6	1	5	3	45	5	1	1	2.0	.980	OF-18, 3B-1

Cliff Lee

LEE, CLIFFORD WALKER
B. Aug. 4, 1896, Lexington, Neb. D. Aug. 25, 1980, Denver, Colo.

BR TR 6'1" 175 lbs.

Year	Team		Games	BA	SA	AB	H	2B	3B	HR	HR%	R	RBI	BB	SO	SB	PH AB	PH H	PO	A	E	DP	TC/G	FA	G by Pos
1919	PIT	N	42	.196	.286	112	22	4	2	0	0.0	5	5	6	8	2	8	1	96	17	5	0	2.8	.958	C-28, OF-6
1920			37	.237	.316	76	18	2	2	0	0.0	9	8	4	14	0	16	3	55	24	2	3	2.2	.975	C-19, OF-2
1921	PHI	N	88	.308	.427	286	88	14	4	4	1.4	31	29	13	34	5	10	6	546	25	10	35	6.6	.983	1B-48, OF-27, C-2
1922			122	.322	.540	422	136	29	6	17	4.0	65	77	32	43	2	13	3	340	17	10	19	3.0	.973	OF-89, 1B-18, 3B-1
1923			107	.321	.493	355	114	20	4	11	3.1	54	47	20	39	3	12	1	267	13	8	11	2.7	.972	OF-83, 1B-16
1924	2 teams		PHI	N	(21G – .250)	CIN	N	(6G – .333)																	
"	total		27	.258	.435	62	16	4	2	1	1.6	5	5	2	7	0	7	2	64	3	0	4	2.5	1.000	OF-14, 1B-4
1925	CLE	A	77	.322	.491	230	74	15	6	4	1.7	43	42	21	33	2	7	2	129	7	7	2	1.9	.951	OF-70
1926			21	.175	.275	40	7	1	0	1	2.5	4	2	6	8	0	8	1	25	0	0	0	1.2	1.000	OF-9, C-3
8 yrs.			521	.300	.462	1583	475	87	28	38	2.4	216	216	104	186	14	81	19	1522	106	42	74	3.2	.975	OF-300, 1B-86, C-52, 3B-1

Dud Lee

LEE, ERNEST DUDLEY
Played as Dud Dudley in 1920-21.
B. Aug. 22, 1899, Denver, Colo. D. Jan. 7, 1971, Denver, Colo.

BL TR 5'9" 150 lbs.

Year	Team		Games	BA	SA	AB	H	2B	3B	HR	HR%	R	RBI	BB	SO	SB	PH AB	PH H	PO	A	E	DP	TC/G	FA	G by Pos
1920	STL	A	1	1.000	1.000	2	2	0	0	0	0.0	2	1	0	0	0	0	0	0	1	2	0	3.0	.333	SS-1
1921			72	.167	.211	180	30	4	2	0	0.0	18	11	14	34	1	0	0	138	152	19	30	4.3	.939	SS-31, 2B-30, 3B-3
1924	BOS	A	94	.253	.313	288	73	9	4	0	0.0	36	29	40	17	8	3	0	198	246	30	43	5.0	.937	SS-90
1925			84	.224	.275	255	57	7	3	0	0.0	22	19	34	19	2	0	0	188	260	37	64	5.8	.924	SS-84
1926			2	.143	.143	7	1	0	0	0	0.0	2	0	0	0	0	0	0	4	3	0	1	3.5	1.000	SS-2
5 yrs.			253	.223	.275	732	163	20	9	0	0.0	80	60	88	70	12	3	0	528	662	88	138	5.1	.931	SS-208, 2B-30, 3B-3

Hal Lee

LEE, HAROLD BURNHAM (Sheriff)
B. Feb. 15, 1905, Ludlow, Miss. D. Sept. 4, 1989, Pascagoula, Miss.

BR TR 5'11" 180 lbs.

Year	Team		Games	BA	SA	AB	H	2B	3B	HR	HR%	R	RBI	BB	SO	SB	PH AB	PH H	PO	A	E	DP	TC/G	FA	G by Pos
1930	BKN	N	22	.162	.243	37	6	0	0	1	2.7	5	4	4	5	0	7	1	17	0	0	0	0.8	1.000	OF-12
1931	PHI	N	44	.221	.344	131	29	10	0	2	1.5	13	12	10	18	0	5	1	86	1	3	1	2.0	.967	OF-38
1932			149	.303	.497	595	180	42	10	18	3.0	76	85	36	45	6	0	0	380	11	14	3	2.7	.965	OF-148
1933	2 teams		PHI	N	(46G – .287)	BOS	N	(88G – .221)																	
"	total		134	.244	.353	479	117	27	11	1	0.2	57	40	36	39	2	1	0	304	11	7	2	2.4	.978	OF-132
1934	BOS	N	139	.292	.405	521	152	23	6	8	1.5	70	79	47	43	3	7	1	327	14	10	5	2.5	.972	OF-128, 2B-4
1935			112	.303	.374	422	128	16	0	0	0.0	49	39	18	25	0	2	0	273	7	11	0	2.6	.962	OF-110
1936			152	.253	.336	565	143	24	7	3	0.5	46	64	52	50	4	1	0	319	5	9	1	2.2	.973	OF-150
7 yrs.			752	.275	.392	2750	755	144	40	33	1.2	316	323	203	225	15	23	3	1706	49	54	12	2.4	.970	OF-718, 2B-4

Leonidas Lee

LEE, LEONIDAS PYRRHUS
Born Leonidas Pyrrhus Funkhouser.
B. Dec. 13, 1860, St. Louis, Mo. D. June 11, 1912, Hendersonville, N. C.

Year	Team		Games	BA	SA	AB	H	2B	3B	HR	HR%	R	RBI	BB	SO	SB	PH AB	PH H	PO	A	E	DP	TC/G	FA	G by Pos
1877	STL	N	4	.278	.333	18	5	1	0	0	0.0	0	0	0	1		0	0	6	1	4	0	2.8	.636	OF-4, SS-1

Leron Lee

LEE, LERON
B. Mar. 4, 1948, Bakersfield, Calif.

BL TR 6' 196 lbs.

Year	Team		Games	BA	SA	AB	H	2B	3B	HR	HR%	R	RBI	BB	SO	SB	PH AB	PH H	PO	A	E	DP	TC/G	FA	G by Pos
1969	STL	N	7	.217	.261	23	5	1	0	0	0.0	3	0	3	8	0	0	0	7	1	0	0	1.1	1.000	OF-7
1970			121	.227	.352	264	60	13	1	6	2.3	28	23	24	66	5	38	9	120	3	4	0	1.0	.969	OF-77
1971	2 teams		STL	N	(25G – .179)	SD	N	(79G – .273)																	
"	total		104	.264	.405	284	75	21	2	5	1.8	32	23	22	57	4	26	3	90	6	9	1	1.0	.914	OF-76
1972	SD	N	101	.300	.497	370	111	23	7	12	3.2	50	47	29	58	2	4	2	186	6	5	2	2.0	.975	OF-96
1973			118	.237	.297	333	79	7	2	3	0.9	36	30	33	61	4	30	7	154	7	5	0	1.4	.970	OF-84
1974	CLE	A	79	.233	.353	232	54	13	0	5	2.2	18	25	15	42	3	17	2	131	5	6	1	1.8	.958	OF-62, DH-2
1975	2 teams		CLE	A	(13G – .130)	LA	N	(48G – .256)																	
"	total		61	.212	.288	66	14	5	0	0	0.0	5	2	5	14	1	46	10	8	0	0	0	0.1	1.000	OF-9, DH-3
1976	LA	N	23	.133	.178	45	6	1	0	0	0.0	1	2	2	9	0	14	3	12	0	0	0	0.5	1.000	OF-10
8 yrs.			614	.250	.375	1617	404	83	13	31	1.9	173	152	133	315	19	175	36	708	28	29	4	1.2	.962	OF-421, DH-5

Manny Lee

LEE, MANUEL
Born Manuel Lora y Lee.
B. June 17, 1965, San Pedro de Macoris, Dominican Republic

BB TR 5'9" 150 lbs.

Year	Team		Games	BA	SA	AB	H	2B	3B	HR	HR%	R	RBI	BB	SO	SB	PH AB	PH H	PO	A	E	DP	TC/G	FA	G by Pos
1985	TOR	A	64	.200	.200	40	8	0	0	0	0.0	9	0	2	9	1	3	1	34	56	3	11	1.5	.968	2B-38, DH-8, SS-8, 3B-5
1986			35	.205	.269	78	16	0	1	1	1.3	8	7	4	10	0	0	0	36	76	2	11	3.3	.982	2B-29, SS-5, 3B-2
1987			56	.256	.347	121	31	2	3	1	0.8	14	11	6	13	2	3	2	77	110	5	26	3.4	.974	2B-40, SS-26
1988			116	.291	.365	381	111	16	3	2	0.5	38	38	26	64	3	2	0	250	308	12	71	4.9	.979	2B-98, SS-23, 3B-8
1989			99	.260	.333	300	78	9	2	3	1.0	27	34	20	60	4	13	1	152	201	11	51	3.7	.970	2B-40, SS-28, 3B-17, DH-13, OF-1
5 yrs.			370	.265	.337	920	244	27	9	7	0.8	96	90	58	156	10	21	4	549	751	33	170	3.6	.975	2B-232, SS-90, 3B-32, DH-21, OF-1

Year	Team		Games	BA	SA	AB	H	2B	3B	HR	HR%	R	RBI	BB	SO	SB	Pinch Hit AB	Pinch Hit H	PO	A	E	DP	TC/G	FA	G by Pos

Manny Lee *continued*
LEAGUE CHAMPIONSHIP SERIES

1985	TOR	A	1	–	–	0	0	0	0	0	–	0	0	0	0	0	0	0	0	0	0	0	0.0	–	2B-1
1989			2	.250	.250	8	2	0	0	0	0.0	2	0	0	1	0	0	0	4	1	0	1	2.5	1.000	2B-2
2 yrs.			3	.250	.250	8	2	0	0	0	0.0	2	0	0	1	0	0	0	4	1	0	1	1.7	1.000	2B-3

Watty Lee
LEE, WYATT ARNOLD (Indian)
B. Aug. 12, 1879, Lynch's Station, Va. D. Mar. 6, 1936, Washington, D. C.
BL TL 5'10½" 171 lbs.

1901	WAS	A	43	.256	.349	129	33	6	3	0	0.0	15	12	7			0	2	16	82	7	3	2.4	.933	P-36, OF-7
1902			109	.256	.366	391	100	21	5	4	1.0	61	45	33			8	3	176	46	19	1	2.2	.921	OF-95, P-13
1903			75	.208	.277	231	48	8	4	0	0.0	17	13	18			5	5	113	64	9	5	2.5	.952	OF-47, P-22
1904	PIT	N	8	.333	.500	12	4	0	1	0	0.0	1	0	0			0	3	1	7	1	0	1.1	.889	P-5
4 yrs.			235	.242	.338	763	185	35	13	4	0.5	94	70	58			13	13	3	306	199	36	9	2.3	.933	OF-149, P-76

Gene Leek
LEEK, EUGENE HAROLD
B. July 15, 1936, San Diego, Calif.
BR TR 6' 185 lbs.

1959	CLE	A	13	.222	.389	36	8	3	0	1	2.8	7	5	2	7	0	0	0	8	19	2	0	2.2	.931	3B-13, SS-1
1961	LA	A	57	.226	.357	199	45	9	1	5	2.5	16	20	7	54	0	0	0	71	146	12	17	4.0	.948	3B-49, SS-7, OF-1
1962			7	.143	.143	14	2	0	0	0	0.0	0	0	0	6	0	2	1	5	4	0	1	1.3	1.000	3B-4
3 yrs.			77	.221	.349	249	55	12	1	6	2.4	23	25	9	67	0	2	1	84	169	14	18	3.5	.948	3B-66, SS-8, OF-1

Dave Leeper
LEEPER, DAVID DALE
B. Oct. 30, 1959, Santa Ana, Calif.
BL TL 5'11" 170 lbs.

1984	KC	A	4	.000	.000	6	0	0	0	0	0.0	1	0	0	1	0	1	0	4	0	1	0	1.0	1.000	OF-2, DH-1
1985			15	.088	.088	34	3	0	0	0	0.0	1	4	1	3	0	8	1	13	0	1	0	0.9	.929	OF-8
2 yrs.			19	.075	.075	40	3	0	0	0	0.0	2	4	1	4	0	9	1	17	0	1	0	0.9	.944	OF-10, DH-1

George Lees
LEES, GEORGE EDWARD
B. Feb. 2, 1895, Bethlehem, Pa. D. Jan. 2, 1980, Mechanicsburg, Pa.
BR TR 5'9" 150 lbs.

| 1921 | CHI | A | 20 | .214 | .262 | 42 | 9 | 2 | 0 | 0 | 0.0 | 3 | 4 | 3 | 0 | | 4 | 0 | 32 | 7 | 2 | 1 | 2.1 | .951 | C-16 |

Bill LeFebvre
LeFEBVRE, WILFRID HENRY (Lefty)
B. Nov. 11, 1915, Natick, R. I.
BL TL 5'11½" 180 lbs.

1938	BOS	A	1	1.000	4.000	1	1	0	0	1	0.0	1	1	0	0	0	0	0	0	0	0	0	0.0	–	P-1
1939			7	.300	.300	10	3	0	0	0	0.0	3	1	2	2	0	2	1	1	2	0	0	0.4	1.000	P-5
1943	WAS	A	7	.286	.500	14	4	3	0	0	0.0	0	1	1	0	0	1	1	1	6	0	1	1.0	1.000	P-6
1944			60	.258	.355	62	16	2	2	0	0.0	4	8	12	9	0	29	10	17	14	1	3	0.5	.969	P-24, 1B-2
4 yrs.			75	.276	.414	87	24	5	2	1	1.1	8	11	15	11	0	32	12	19	22	1	4	0.6	.976	P-36, 1B-2

Jim Lefebvre
LEFEBVRE, JAMES KENNETH (Frenchy)
B. Jan. 7, 1942, Inglewood, Calif.
Manager 1989.
BB TR 6' 180 lbs.

1965	LA	N	157	.250	.369	544	136	21	4	12	2.2	57	69	71	92	3	2	1	349	429	24	91	5.1	.970	2B-156
1966			152	.274	.460	544	149	23	3	24	4.4	69	74	48	72	1	3	1	268	389	16	63	4.4	.976	2B-119, 3B-40
1967			136	.261	.366	494	129	18	5	8	1.6	51	50	44	64	1	7	0	173	321	18	39	3.8	.965	3B-92, 2B-34, 1B-5
1968			84	.241	.343	286	69	12	1	4	1.7	23	31	26	55	0	5	1	179	161	8	33	4.1	.977	2B-62, 3B-16, OF-5, 1B-3
1969			95	.236	.349	275	65	15	2	4	1.5	29	44	48	37	2	11	4	154	185	6	26	3.6	.983	3B-44, 2B-37, 1B-6
1970			109	.252	.344	314	79	15	1	4	1.3	33	44	29	42	1	17	3	168	212	6	41	3.5	.984	2B-70, 3B-20, 1B-1
1971			119	.245	.384	388	95	14	2	12	3.1	40	68	39	55	0	15	4	247	274	9	71	4.5	.983	2B-102, 3B-7
1972			70	.201	.337	169	34	8	0	5	3.0	11	24	17	30	0	25	6	70	99	4	24	2.5	.977	2B-33, 3B-11
8 yrs.			922	.251	.378	3014	756	126	18	74	2.5	313	404	322	447	8	85	20	1608	2070	91	388	4.1	.976	2B-613, 3B-230, 1B-15, OF-5

WORLD SERIES

1965	LA	N	3	.400	.400	10	4	0	0	0	0.0	2	0	0	0	0	0	0	3	7	1	0	3.7	.909	2B-3
1966			4	.167	.417	12	2	0	0	1	8.3	1	1	3	4	0	0	0	10	10	0	3	5.0	1.000	2B-4
2 yrs.			7	.273	.409	22	6	0	0	1	4.5	3	1	3	4	0	0	0	13	17	1	3	4.4	.968	2B-7

Joe Lefebvre
LEFEBVRE, JOSEPH HENRY
B. Feb. 22, 1956, Concord, N. H.
BL TR 5'10" 170 lbs.

1980	NY	A	74	.227	.407	150	34	1	4	8	5.3	26	21	27	30	1	5	2	75	3	2	1	1.1	.975	OF-71
1981	SD	N	86	.256	.439	246	63	13	4	8	3.3	31	31	35	33	6	5	2	167	6	1	2	2.0	.994	OF-84
1982			102	.238	.326	239	57	9	1	4	1.7	25	21	18	50	0	34	8	72	74	3	6	1.5	.980	3B-39, OF-36, C-3
1983	**2 teams**		SD N (18G – .250)			PHI N (101G – .310)																			
"	total		119	.306	.522	278	85	20	8	8	2.9	35	39	33	49	5	40	11	7	5	0	1	1.0	1.000	OF-80, 3B-13, C-5
1984	PHI	N	52	.250	.363	160	40	9	0	3	1.9	22	18	23	37	0	8	4	83	4	3	1	1.7	.967	OF-47, 3B-1
1986			14	.111	.111	18	2	0	0	0	0.0	0	0	0	3	0	5	0	4	0	0	0	0.3	1.000	OF-3
6 yrs.			447	.258	.414	1091	281	52	13	31	2.8	139	130	139	204	11	100	28	408	92	9	11	1.1	.982	OF-321, 3B-53, C-8

LEAGUE CHAMPIONSHIP SERIES

1980	NY	A	1	–	–	0	0	0	0	0	0.0	0	0	0	0	0	0	0	0	0	0	0	1.0	1.000	OF-1
1983	PHI	N	2	.000	.000	2	0	0	0	0	0.0	0	0	1	0	0	1	0	2	0	0	0	0.7	1.000	OF-2
2 yrs.			3	.000	.000	2	0	0	0	0	0.0	0	0	1	0	0	1	0	2	0	0	0	0.7	1.000	OF-3

WORLD SERIES

| 1983 | PHI | N | 3 | .200 | .400 | 5 | 1 | 1 | 0 | 0 | 0.0 | 0 | 0 | 2 | 0 | 0 | 0 | 0 | 3 | 0 | 0 | 0 | 1.0 | 1.000 | OF-2 |

Al LeFevre
LeFEVRE, ALFREDO MODESTO
B. Sept. 16, 1898, New York, N. Y. D. Jan. 21, 1982, Glen Cove, N. Y.
BR TR 5'10½" 160 lbs.

| 1920 | NY | N | 17 | .148 | .222 | 27 | 4 | 0 | 1 | 0 | 0.0 | 5 | 0 | 13 | 0 | 1 | 0 | 0 | 12 | 29 | 0 | 4 | 2.4 | 1.000 | SS-9, 2B-6, 3B-1 |

Year	Team	Games	BA	SA	AB	H	2B	3B	HR	HR%	R	RBI	BB	SO	SB	Pinch Hit AB	Pinch Hit H	PO	A	E	DP	TC/G	FA	G by Pos

Wade Lefler

LEFLER, WADE HAMPTON
B. June 5, 1896, Cooleemee, N. C. D. Mar. 6, 1981, Hickory, N. C.
BL TR 5'11" 162 lbs.

Year	Team	Games	BA	SA	AB	H	2B	3B	HR	HR%	R	RBI	BB	SO	SB	PH AB	PH H	PO	A	E	DP	TC/G	FA	G by Pos
1924	2 teams				BOS N (1G – .000)								WAS A (5G – .625)											
"	total	6	.556	.889	9	5	3	0	0	0.0	0	4	0	1	0	5	3	2	0	0	0	0.3	1.000	OF-1

Ron LeFlore

LeFLORE, RONALD
B. June 16, 1948, Detroit, Mich.
BR TR 6' 200 lbs.

Year	Team	Games	BA	SA	AB	H	2B	3B	HR	HR%	R	RBI	BB	SO	SB	PH AB	PH H	PO	A	E	DP	TC/G	FA	G by Pos
1974	DET A	59	.260	.323	254	66	8	1	2	0.8	37	13	13	58	23	0	0	151	8	11	3	2.9	.935	OF-59
1975		136	.258	.347	550	142	13	6	8	1.5	66	37	33	139	28	0	0	317	13	9	3	2.5	.973	OF-134
1976		135	.316	.410	544	172	23	8	4	0.7	93	39	51	111	58	1	0	381	14	11	1	3.0	.973	OF-132, DH-1
1977		154	.325	.475	652	212	30	10	16	2.5	100	57	37	121	39	3	2	365	12	11	0	2.5	.972	OF-154
1978		155	.297	.405	666	198	30	3	12	1.8	**126**	62	65	104	**68**	0	0	440	9	11	4	3.0	.976	OF-155
1979		148	.300	.415	600	180	22	10	9	1.5	110	57	52	95	78	1	1	293	6	3	3	2.0	.990	OF-113, DH-34
1980	MON N	139	.257	.363	521	134	21	11	4	0.8	95	39	62	99	**97**	1	1	233	14	11	1	1.9	.957	OF-130
1981	CHI A	82	.246	.300	337	83	10	4	0	0.0	46	24	28	70	36	0	0	162	6	7	2	2.1	.960	OF-82
1982		91	.287	.392	334	96	15	4	4	1.2	58	25	22	91	28	5	1	179	7	12	1	2.2	.939	OF-83, DH-2
9 yrs.		1099	.288	.392	4458	1283	172	57	59	1.3	731	353	363	888	455	11	5	2521	89	86	18	2.5	.968	OF-1042, DH-37

Lou Legett

LEGETT, LOUIS ALFRED (Doc)
B. June 1, 1901, New Orleans, La. D. Mar. 6, 1988, New Orleans, La.
BR TR 5'10" 166 lbs.

Year	Team	Games	BA	SA	AB	H	2B	3B	HR	HR%	R	RBI	BB	SO	SB	PH AB	PH H	PO	A	E	DP	TC/G	FA	G by Pos
1929	BOS N	39	.160	.185	81	13	2	0	0	0.0	7	6	3	18	2	9	2	58	16	7	1	2.1	.914	C-28
1933	BOS A	8	.200	.400	5	1	1	0	0	0.0	1	1	0	0	0	2	0	4	0	0	0	0.5	1.000	C-2
1934		19	.289	.289	38	11	0	0	0	0.0	4	1	2	4	0	1	1	36	7	1	0	2.3	.977	C-17
1935		2	–	–	0	0	0	0	0	–	1	0	0	0	0	0	0	0	0	0	0	0.0	–	–
4 yrs.		68	.202	.226	124	25	3	0	0	0.0	13	8	5	22	2	12	3	98	23	8	1	1.9	.938	C-47

Greg Legg

LEGG, GREGORY LYNN
B. Apr. 21, 1960, San Jose, Calif.
BR TR 6'1" 185 lbs.

Year	Team	Games	BA	SA	AB	H	2B	3B	HR	HR%	R	RBI	BB	SO	SB	PH AB	PH H	PO	A	E	DP	TC/G	FA	G by Pos
1986	PHI N	11	.450	.500	20	9	1	0	0	0.0	2	1	0	3	0	6	2	4	16	1	1	1.9	.952	2B-4, SS-1
1987		3	.000	.000	2	0	0	0	0	0.0	1	0	0	0	0	0	0	3	1	0	1	1.3	1.000	SS-1, 3B-1, 2B-1
2 yrs.		14	.409	.455	22	9	1	0	0	0.0	3	1	0	3	0	6	2	7	17	1	2	1.8	.960	2B-5, SS-2, 3B-1

Mickey Lehane

LEHANE, MICHAEL PATRICK
B. R. I. Deceased.
BR 6'1½" 180 lbs.

Year	Team	Games	BA	SA	AB	H	2B	3B	HR	HR%	R	RBI	BB	SO	SB	PH AB	PH H	PO	A	E	DP	TC/G	FA	G by Pos
1884	WAS U	3	.333	.500	12	4	2	0	0	0.0	1		0			0	0	1	10	5	0	5.3	.688	SS-3, OF-1, 3B-1
1890	COL AA	140	.211	.268	512	108	19	5	0	0.0	54		43		13	0	0	1430	73	27	80	10.9	.982	1B-140
1891		137	.215	.272	511	110	12	7	1	0.2	59	52	34	77	16	0	0	1362	71	28	98	10.7	.981	1B-137
3 yrs.		280	.214	.272	1035	222	33	12	1	0.1	114	52	77	77	29	0	0	2793	154	60	178	10.7	.980	1B-277, SS-3, OF-1, 3B-1

Paul Lehner

LEHNER, PAUL EUGENE (Gulliver)
B. July 1, 1920, Dolomite, Ala. D. Dec. 27, 1967, Birmingham, Ala.
BL TL 5'9" 160 lbs.

Year	Team	Games	BA	SA	AB	H	2B	3B	HR	HR%	R	RBI	BB	SO	SB	PH AB	PH H	PO	A	E	DP	TC/G	FA	G by Pos
1946	STL A	16	.222	.333	45	10	1	2	0	0.0	6	5	1	5	0	4	1	15	1	1	0	1.1	.941	OF-12
1947		135	.248	.381	483	120	25	9	7	1.4	59	48	28	29	5	6	2	344	1	7	0	2.6	.980	OF-127
1948		103	.276	.363	333	92	15	4	2	0.6	23	46	30	19	0	13	6	235	5	6	3	2.4	.976	OF-89, 1B-2
1949		104	.229	.303	297	68	13	0	3	1.0	25	37	16	20	0	26	7	314	14	4	13	3.2	.988	OF-55, 1B-18
1950	PHI A	114	.309	.436	427	132	17	5	9	2.1	48	52	32	33	1	8	3	247	10	5	1	2.3	.981	OF-101
1951	4 teams				PHI A (9G – .143)								CHI A (23G – .208)					STL A (21G – .134)			CLE A (12G – .231)			
"	total	65	.172	.250	180	31	9	1	1	0.6	14	7	18	19	4	19	4	108	5	1	0	1.8	.991	OF-45
1952	BOS A	3	.667	.667	3	2	0	0	0	0.0	0	2	0	1	0	1	1	3	0	0	0	1.0	1.000	OF-2
7 yrs.		540	.257	.364	1768	455	80	21	22	1.2	175	197	127	118	6	77	24	1266	36	24	17	2.5	.982	OF-431, 1B-20

Clarence Lehr

LEHR, CLARENCE EMANUEL (King)
B. May 16, 1886, Escanaba, Mich. D. Jan. 31, 1948, Detroit, Mich.
BR TR 5'11" 165 lbs.

Year	Team	Games	BA	SA	AB	H	2B	3B	HR	HR%	R	RBI	BB	SO	SB	PH AB	PH H	PO	A	E	DP	TC/G	FA	G by Pos
1911	PHI N	23	.148	.148	27	4	0	0	0	0.0	2	2	0	7	0	6	1	10	8	1	4	0.8	.947	OF-5, SS-4, 2B-4

Hank Leiber

LEIBER, HENRY EDWARD
B. Jan. 17, 1911, Phoenix, Ariz.
BR TR 6'1½" 205 lbs.

Year	Team	Games	BA	SA	AB	H	2B	3B	HR	HR%	R	RBI	BB	SO	SB	PH AB	PH H	PO	A	E	DP	TC/G	FA	G by Pos
1933	NY N	6	.200	.200	10	2	0	0	0	0.0	0	0	0	2	0	5	0	3	1	0	0	0.7	1.000	OF-1
1934		63	.241	.332	187	45	5	3	2	1.1	17	25	4	13	1	12	2	99	3	3	1	1.7	.971	OF-51
1935		154	.331	.512	613	203	37	4	22	3.6	110	107	48	29	0	0	0	357	5	13	2	2.4	.965	OF-154
1936		101	.279	.457	337	94	19	7	9	2.7	44	67	37	41	1	12	1	165	9	7	3	1.8	.961	OF-86, 1B-1
1937		51	.293	.429	184	54	7	4	4	2.2	24	32	15	27	1	5	1	78	1	1	0	1.6	.988	OF-46
1938		98	.269	.442	360	97	18	4	12	3.3	50	65	31	45	0	8	3	181	6	5	3	2.0	.974	OF-89
1939	CHI N	112	.310	.556	365	113	16	1	24	6.6	65	88	59	42	1	8	1	249	5	6	0	2.3	.977	OF-98
1940		117	.302	.482	440	133	24	2	17	3.9	68	86	45	68	1	3	0	302	19	5	10	2.8	.985	OF-103, 1B-12
1941		53	.216	.377	162	35	5	0	7	4.3	20	25	16	25	0	9	0	192	8	5	13	3.9	.976	OF-29, 1B-15
1942	NY N	58	.218	.340	147	32	6	0	4	2.7	11	23	19	27	0	14	4	93	6	2	1	1.7	.980	OF-41, P-1
10 yrs.		813	.288	.462	2805	808	137	24	101	3.6	410	518	274	319	5	76	12	1719	63	47	33	2.2	.974	OF-698, 1B-28, P-1

WORLD SERIES

Year	Team	Games	BA	SA	AB	H	2B	3B	HR	HR%	R	RBI	BB	SO	SB	PH AB	PH H	PO	A	E	DP	TC/G	FA	G by Pos
1936	NY N	2	.000	.000	6	0	0	0	0	0.0	0	2	0	2	0	0	0	13	1	0	1	7.0	1.000	OF-2
1937		3	.364	.364	11	4	0	0	0	0.0	2	1	3	1	0	0	0	7	0	0	0	2.3	1.000	OF-3
2 yrs.		5	.235	.235	17	4	0	0	0	0.0	2	3	3	3	0	0	0	20	1	0	1	4.2	1.000	OF-5

Nemo Leibold

LEIBOLD, HARRY LORAN
B. Feb. 17, 1892, Butler, Ind. D. Feb. 4, 1977, Detroit, Mich.
BL TR 5'6½" 157 lbs.

Year	Team	Games	BA	SA	AB	H	2B	3B	HR	HR%	R	RBI	BB	SO	SB	PH AB	PH H	PO	A	E	DP	TC/G	FA	G by Pos
1913	CLE A	84	.259	.339	286	74	11	6	0	0.0	37	12	21	43	16	10	1	142	12	9	1	1.9	.945	OF-72
1914		114	.264	.311	402	106	13	3	0	0.0	46	32	54	56	12	6	1	221	22	18	4	2.3	.931	OF-107
1915	2 teams				CLE A (57G – .256)								CHI A (36G – .230)											
"	total	93	.249	.299	281	70	6	4	0	0.0	38	15	39	27	6	14	5	204	15	5	0	2.4	.978	OF-75
1916	CHI A	45	.244	.305	82	20	1	2	0	0.0	5	13	7	7	0	20	4	31	1	0	2	0.7	1.000	OF-24
1917		125	.236	.292	428	101	12	6	0	0.0	59	29	74	34	27	3	0	204	18	9	3	1.8	.961	OF-122

Year	Team	Games	BA	SA	AB	H	2B	3B	HR	HR%	R	RBI	BB	SO	SB	Pinch Hit AB	Pinch Hit H	PO	A	E	DP	TC/G	FA	G by Pos

Nemo Leibold *continued*

Year	Team	Games	BA	SA	AB	H	2B	3B	HR	HR%	R	RBI	BB	SO	SB	PH AB	PH H	PO	A	E	DP	TC/G	FA	G by Pos
1918		116	.250	.316	440	110	14	6	1	0.2	57	31	63	32	13	1	0	259	16	6	5	2.4	.979	OF-114
1919		122	.302	.353	434	131	18	2	0	0.0	81	26	72	30	17	0	0	218	26	19	4	2.2	.928	OF-122
1920		108	.220	.281	413	91	16	3	1	0.2	61	28	55	30	7	3	1	190	18	5	5	2.0	.977	OF-108
1921	BOS A	123	.306	.388	467	143	26	6	1	0.2	88	30	41	27	13	5	0	283	15	16	9	2.6	.949	OF-117
1922		81	.258	.306	271	70	8	1	1	0.4	42	18	41	14	1	9	3	190	10	7	3	2.6	.966	OF-71
1923	2 teams		BOS A	(12G – .111)			WAS A	(95G – .305)																
"	total	107	.294	.366	333	98	13	4		0.3	69	22	54	18	7	9	2	195	14	5	3	2.0	.977	OF-94
1924	WAS A	84	.293	.350	246	72	6	4	0	0.0	41	20	42	10	6	11	1	148	7	1	0	1.9	.994	OF-70
1925		56	.274	.310	84	23	1	1	0	0.0	14	7	8	7	1	19	3	34	3	1	1	0.7	.974	OF-26, 3B-1
	13 yrs.	1258	.266	.327	4167	1109	145	48	4	0.1	638	283	571	335	133	110	21	2319	177	101	40	2.1	.961	OF-1122, 3B-1

WORLD SERIES

Year	Team	Games	BA	SA	AB	H	2B	3B	HR	HR%	R	RBI	BB	SO	SB	PH AB	PH H	PO	A	E	DP	TC/G	FA	G by Pos
1917	CHI A	2	.400	.400	5	2	0	0	0	0.0	1	2	1	1	0	2	0	1	0	0	0	0.5	1.000	OF-2
1919		5	.056	.056	18	1	0	0	0	0.0	0	0	2	3	1	0	0	5	2	0	0	1.4	1.000	OF-5
1924	WAS A	3	.167	.333	6	1	1	0	0	0.0	1	0	1	0	0	2	1	2	0	0	0	0.7	1.000	OF-1
1925		3	.500	1.000	2	1	1	0	0	0.0	1	0	1	0	0	2	1	0	0	0	0	0.0	–	
	4 yrs.	13	.161	.226	31	5	2	0	0	0.0	3	2	5	4	1	7	2	8	2	0	0	0.8	1.000	OF-8
																	6th							

Elmer Leifer

LEIFER, ELMER EDWIN
B. May 23, 1893, Clarington, Ohio   D. Sept. 26, 1948, Everett, Wash.
BL TR 5'9½" 170 lbs.

Year	Team	Games	BA	SA	AB	H	2B	3B	HR	HR%	R	RBI	BB	SO	SB	PH AB	PH H	PO	A	E	DP	TC/G	FA	G by Pos
1921	CHI A	9	.300	.300	10	3	0	0	0	0.0	0	1	0	4	0	1	1	1	0	0	0.2	1.000	OF-1, 3B-1

John Leighton

LEIGHTON, JOHN ATKINSON
B. Oct. 4, 1861, Peabody, Mass.   D. Oct. 31, 1956, Lynn, Mass.
5'11" 170 lbs.

Year	Team	Games	BA	SA	AB	H	2B	3B	HR	HR%	R	RBI	BB	SO	SB	PH AB	PH H	PO	A	E	DP	TC/G	FA	G by Pos
1890	SYR AA	7	.296	.370	27	8	2	0	0	0.0	6		3		2	0		15	0	1	0	2.3	.938	OF-7

Bill Leinhauser

LEINHAUSER, WILLIAM CHARLES
B. Nov. 4, 1893, Philadelphia, Pa.   D. Apr. 14, 1978, Elkins Park, Pa.
BR TR 5'10" 150 lbs.

Year	Team	Games	BA	SA	AB	H	2B	3B	HR	HR%	R	RBI	BB	SO	SB	PH AB	PH H	PO	A	E	DP	TC/G	FA	G by Pos
1912	DET A	1	.000	.000	4	0	0	0	0	0.0	0	0	0	0	0	0	0	0	1	0	0	1.0	1.000	OF-1

Ed Leip

LEIP, EDGAR ELLSWORTH
B. Nov. 29, 1910, Trenton, N. J.   D. Nov. 24, 1983, Zephyrhills, Fla.
BR TR 5'9" 160 lbs.

Year	Team	Games	BA	SA	AB	H	2B	3B	HR	HR%	R	RBI	BB	SO	SB	PH AB	PH H	PO	A	E	DP	TC/G	FA	G by Pos
1939	WAS A	9	.344	.375	32	11	1	0	0	0.0	4	2	2	4	0	1	0	15	24	2	5	4.6	.951	2B-8
1940	PIT N	3	.200	.200	5	1	0	0	0	0.0	2	0	0	0	0	1	0	2	2	0	1	1.3	1.000	2B-2
1941		15	.200	.360	25	5	0	2	0	0.0	1	3	1	2	1	3	0	10	19	4	2	2.2	.879	2B-7, 3B-1
1942		3	–	–	0	0	0	0	0	–	0	0	0	0	0	0	0	0	0	0	0	0.0	–	
	4 yrs.	30	.274	.355	62	17	1	2	0	0.0	7	5	3	6	1	4	0	27	45	6	8	2.6	.923	2B-17, 3B-1

Frank Leja

LEJA, FRANK JOHN
B. Feb. 7, 1936, Holyoke, Mass.
BL TL 6'4" 205 lbs.

Year	Team	Games	BA	SA	AB	H	2B	3B	HR	HR%	R	RBI	BB	SO	SB	PH AB	PH H	PO	A	E	DP	TC/G	FA	G by Pos
1954	NY A	12	.200	.200	5	1	0	0	0	0.0	0	1	0	3	0	3	0	3	0	0	0	0.3	1.000	1B-6
1955		7	.000	.000	2	0	0	0	0	0.0	1	0	0	1	0	1	0	2	0	0	1	0.3	1.000	1B-2
1962	LA A	7	.000	.000	16	0	0	0	0	0.0	2	0	1	6	0	2	0	38	3	2	4	6.1	.953	1B-4
	3 yrs.	26	.043	.043	23	1	0	0	0	0.0	3	1	1	8	0	6	0	43	3	2	5	1.8	.958	1B-12

Larry LeJeune

LeJEUNE, SHELDON ALDENBERT
B. July 22, 1885, Chicago, Ill.   D. Apr. 21, 1952, Eloise, Mich.
BR TR 6' 180 lbs.

Year	Team	Games	BA	SA	AB	H	2B	3B	HR	HR%	R	RBI	BB	SO	SB	PH AB	PH H	PO	A	E	DP	TC/G	FA	G by Pos
1911	BKN N	6	.158	.158	19	3	0	0	0	0.0	2	2	8	2	0	9	0	2	0	1.8	.818	OF-6
1915	PIT N	18	.169	.200	65	11	0	1	0	0.0	4	2	2	7	4	0	43	4	3	1	2.8	.940	OF-18
	2 yrs.	24	.167	.190	84	14	0	1	0	0.0	6	4	4	15	6	0	52	4	5	1	2.5	.918	OF-24

Don LeJohn

LeJOHN, DONALD EVERETT
B. May 13, 1934, Daisytown, Pa.
BR TR 5'10" 175 lbs.

Year	Team	Games	BA	SA	AB	H	2B	3B	HR	HR%	R	RBI	BB	SO	SB	PH AB	PH H	PO	A	E	DP	TC/G	FA	G by Pos
1965	LA N	34	.256	.282	78	20	2	0	0	0.0	2	7	5	13	1	10	2	9	38	2	2	1.4	.959	3B-26

WORLD SERIES

Year	Team	Games	BA	SA	AB	H	2B	3B	HR	HR%	R	RBI	BB	SO	SB	PH AB	PH H	PO	A	E	DP	TC/G	FA	G by Pos
1965	LA N	1	.000	.000	1	0	0	0	0	0.0	0	0	0	1	0	1	0	0	0	0	0	0.0	–	

Jack Lelivelt

LELIVELT, JOHN FRANK
Brother of Bill Lelivelt.
B. Nov. 14, 1885, Chicago, Ill.   D. Jan. 20, 1941, Seattle, Wash.
BL TL 5'11" 175 lbs.

Year	Team	Games	BA	SA	AB	H	2B	3B	HR	HR%	R	RBI	BB	SO	SB	PH AB	PH H	PO	A	E	DP	TC/G	FA	G by Pos
1909	WAS A	91	.292	.355	318	93	8	6	0	0.0	25	24	19		8	0	0	179	14	6	3	2.2	.970	OF-91
1910		110	.265	.311	347	92	10	3	0	0.0	40	33	40		20	13	2	217	17	10	7	2.2	.959	OF-89, 1B-7
1911		72	.320	.409	225	72	12	4	0	0.0	29	22	22		7	16	6	142	18	9	2	2.3	.947	OF-49, 1B-7
1912	NY A	36	.362	.537	149	54	6	7	2	1.3	12	23	4		7	0	0	75	4	3	2	2.3	.963	OF-36
1913	2 teams		NY A	(17G – .214)			CLE A	(23G – .391)																
"	total	40	.294	.373	51	15	2	1	0	0.0	2	11	2	5	2	35	12	12	1	0	0	0.3	1.000	OF-5
1914	CLE A	32	.328	.438	64	21	5	1	0	0.0	6	13	2	10	2	19	5	15	0	1	0	0.5	.938	OF-12, 1B-1
	6 yrs.	381	.301	.381	1154	347	43	22	2	0.2	114	126	89	15	46	83	25	640	54	29	14	1.9	.960	OF-282, 1B-15

Johnnie LeMaster

LeMASTER, JOHNNIE LEE
B. June 19, 1954, Portsmouth, Ohio
BR TR 6'2" 165 lbs.

Year	Team	Games	BA	SA	AB	H	2B	3B	HR	HR%	R	RBI	BB	SO	SB	PH AB	PH H	PO	A	E	DP	TC/G	FA	G by Pos
1975	SF N	22	.189	.324	74	14	4	0	2	2.7	4	9	4	15	2	0	0	26	62	3	12	4.1	.967	SS-22
1976		33	.210	.280	100	21	3	2	0	0.0	9	9	2	21	2	2	0	54	109	11	17	5.3	.937	SS-31
1977		68	.149	.201	134	20	5	1	0	0.0	13	8	13	27	2	2	0	66	134	14	16	3.1	.935	SS-54, 3B-2
1978		101	.235	.335	272	64	18	3	1	0.4	23	14	21	45	6	2	0	135	261	14	40	4.1	.966	SS-96, 2B-2
1979		108	.254	.324	343	87	11	2	3	0.9	42	29	23	55	9	2	0	160	303	20	32	4.5	.959	SS-106
1980		135	.215	.306	405	87	16	6	3	0.7	33	31	25	57	0	0	0	200	372	26	54	4.4	.957	SS-134
1981		104	.253	.287	324	82	9	1	0	0.0	27	28	24	46	3	0	0	166	294	17	57	4.6	.964	SS-103
1982		130	.216	.266	436	94	14	1	2	0.5	34	30	31	78	13	0	0	223	382	23	63	4.8	.963	SS-130

Year	Team	Games	BA	SA	AB	H	2B	3B	HR	HR%	R	RBI	BB	SO	SB	Pinch Hit AB	Pinch Hit H	PO	A	E	DP	TC/G	FA	G by Pos

Johnnie LeMaster *continued*

Year	Team	Games	BA	SA	AB	H	2B	3B	HR	HR%	R	RBI	BB	SO	SB	PH AB	PH H	PO	A	E	DP	TC/G	FA	G by Pos
1983		141	.240	.307	534	128	16	1	6	1.1	81	30	60	96	39	1	0	215	402	23	58	4.5	.964	SS-139
1984		132	.217	.282	451	98	13	2	4	0.9	46	32	31	97	17	1	1	222	391	23	70	4.8	.964	SS-129
1985 3 teams		SF N (12G – .000)			CLE A (11G – .150)				PIT N		(22G – .155)													
" total		45	.128	.160	94	12	0	0	1	1.1	5	8	6	23	1	1	0	74	98	5	20	3.9	.972	SS-41
1987	OAK A	20	.083	.083	24	2	0	0	0	0.0	3	1	1	4	0	0	0	14	24	1	5	2.0	.974	3B-8, SS-7, 2B-5
12 yrs.		1039	.222	.289	3191	709	109	19	22	0.7	320	229	241	564	94	9	1	1555	2832	180	444	4.4	.961	SS-992, 3B-10, 2B-7

Steve Lembo

LEMBO, STEPHEN NEAL
B. Nov. 13, 1926, Brooklyn, N. Y.   D. Dec. 4, 1989, Flushing, N. Y.

BR TR 6'1"   185 lbs.

Year	Team	Games	BA	SA	AB	H	2B	3B	HR	HR%	R	RBI	BB	SO	SB	PH AB	PH H	PO	A	E	DP	TC/G	FA	G by Pos
1950	BKN N	5	.167	.167	6	1	0	0	0	0.0	1	0	0	1	0	0	0	16	3	0	1	3.8	1.000	C-5
1952		2	.200	.200	5	1	0	0	0	0.0	0	1	0	1	0	0	0	9	0	0	0	4.5	1.000	C-2
2 yrs.		7	.182	.182	11	2	0	0	0	0.0	1	1	1	1	0	0	0	25	3	0	1	4.0	1.000	C-7

Mark Lemke

LEMKE, MARK ALAN
B. Aug. 13, 1965, Utica, N. Y.

BB TR 5'10"   167 lbs.

Year	Team	Games	BA	SA	AB	H	2B	3B	HR	HR%	R	RBI	BB	SO	SB	PH AB	PH H	PO	A	E	DP	TC/G	FA	G by Pos
1988	ATL N	16	.224	.293	58	13	4	0	0	0.0	8	2	4	5	0	0	0	47	51	3	11	6.3	.970	2B-16
1989		14	.182	.364	55	10	2	1	2	3.6	4	10	5	7	0	1	1	25	40	0	7	4.6	1.000	2B-14
2 yrs.		30	.204	.327	113	23	6	1	2	1.8	12	12	9	12	0	1	1	72	91	3	18	5.5	.982	2B-30

Bob Lemon

LEMON, ROBERT GRANVILLE
B. Sept. 22, 1920, San Bernardino, Calif.
Manager 1970-72, 1977-79, 1981-82.
Hall of Fame 1976.

BL TR 6'   180 lbs.

Year	Team	Games	BA	SA	AB	H	2B	3B	HR	HR%	R	RBI	BB	SO	SB	PH AB	PH H	PO	A	E	DP	TC/G	FA	G by Pos
1941	CLE A	5	.250	.250	4	1	0	0	0	0.0	0	0	0	1	0	3	1	1	1	0	0	0.4	1.000	3B-1
1942		5	.000	.000	5	0	0	0	0	0.0	0	0	0	3	0	3	0	0	1	1	0	0.4	.500	3B-1
1946		55	.180	.247	89	16	3	0	1	1.1	9	4	7	18	0	7	1	46	30	2	7	1.4	.974	P-32, OF-12
1947		47	.321	.607	56	18	4	3	2	3.6	11	5	6	9	0	3	1	13	46	1	4	1.3	.983	P-37, OF-2
1948		52	.286	.487	119	34	9	0	5	4.2	20	21	8	23	0	4	1	23	86	4	8	2.2	.965	P-43
1949		46	.269	.556	108	29	6	2	7	6.5	17	19	10	20	0	8	4	34	71	4	5	2.4	.963	P-37
1950		72	.272	.485	136	37	9	1	6	4.4	21	26	13	25	0	26	6	22	66	4	6	1.3	.957	P-44
1951		56	.206	.353	102	21	4	1	3	2.9	11	13	9	22	0	14	4	21	60	2	5	1.5	.976	P-42
1952		54	.226	.315	124	28	5	0	2	1.6	14	9	4	21	0	8	1	32	79	2	7	2.1	.982	P-42
1953		51	.232	.384	112	26	9	1	2	1.8	12	17	7	20	2	6	1	31	74	3	15	2.1	.972	P-41
1954		40	.214	.337	98	21	4	1	2	2.0	11	10	6	24	0	3	1	22	57	3	8	2.1	.963	P-36
1955		49	.244	.282	78	19	0	1	1	1.3	11	9	13	16	0	9	4	16	43	1	3	1.2	.983	P-35
1956		43	.194	.355	93	18	0	0	5	5.4	8	12	9	21	0	5	3	24	61	6	6	2.1	.934	P-39
1957		25	.065	.152	46	3	1	0	1	2.2	2	1	0	14	0	4	0	12	31	0	5	1.7	1.000	P-21
1958		15	.231	.231	13	3	0	0	0	0.0	1	1	1	4	0	6	3	1	7	0	1	0.5	1.000	P-11
15 yrs.		615	.232	.386	1183	274	54	9	37	3.1	148	147	93	241	2	109	31	298	713	33	80	1.7	.968	P-460, OF-14, 3B-2

WORLD SERIES

Year	Team	Games	BA	SA	AB	H	2B	3B	HR	HR%	R	RBI	BB	SO	SB	PH AB	PH H	PO	A	E	DP	TC/G	FA	G by Pos
1948	CLE A	2	.000	.000	7	0	0	0	0	0.0	0	0	0	0	0	0	0	3	9	0	1	6.0	1.000	P-2
1954		3	.000	.000	6	0	0	0	0	0.0	0	0	1	1	0	1	0	2	2	0	0	1.3	1.000	P-2
2 yrs.		5	.000	.000	13	0	0	0	0	0.0	0	0	1	1	0	1	0	5	11	0	1	3.2	1.000	P-4

Chet Lemon

LEMON, CHESTER EARL
B. Feb. 12, 1955, Jackson, Miss.

BR TR 6'   185 lbs.

Year	Team	Games	BA	SA	AB	H	2B	3B	HR	HR%	R	RBI	BB	SO	SB	PH AB	PH H	PO	A	E	DP	TC/G	FA	G by Pos
1975	CHI A	9	.257	.314	35	9	2	0	0	0.0	2	1	2	6	1	1	0	5	7	1	0	1.4	.923	3B-6, DH-2, OF-1
1976		132	.246	.328	451	111	15	5	4	0.9	46	38	28	65	13	1	0	353	12	3	1	2.8	.992	OF-131
1977		150	.273	.459	553	151	38	4	19	3.4	99	67	52	88	8	0	0	512	12	12	2	3.6	.978	OF-149
1978		105	.300	.510	357	107	24	6	13	3.6	51	55	39	46	5	1	0	284	8	5	2	2.8	.983	OF-95, DH-10
1979		148	.318	.496	556	177	44	2	17	3.1	79	86	56	68	7	0	0	411	10	10	2	2.9	.977	OF-147, DH-1
1980		147	.292	.442	514	150	32	6	11	2.1	76	51	71	56	6	1	0	347	11	7	2	2.5	.981	OF-139, DH-6, 2B-1
1981		94	.302	.491	328	99	23	6	9	2.7	50	50	33	48	5	0	0	240	2	4	1	2.6	.984	OF-93
1982	DET A	125	.266	.447	436	116	20	1	19	4.4	75	52	56	69	1	2	1	242	11	4	2	2.1	.984	OF-121, DH-1
1983		145	.255	.464	491	125	21	5	24	4.9	78	69	54	70	0	2	1	406	6	5	3	2.9	.988	OF-145
1984		141	.287	.495	509	146	34	6	20	3.9	77	76	51	83	5	3	1	427	6	2	1	3.1	.995	OF-140, DH-1
1985		145	.265	.439	517	137	28	4	18	3.5	69	68	45	93	0	1	0	411	6	4	3	2.9	.990	OF-144
1986		126	.251	.407	403	101	21	3	12	3.0	45	53	39	59	2	8	2	316	6	5	1	2.6	.985	OF-124
1987		146	.277	.481	470	130	30	3	20	4.3	75	75	70	82	0	11	5	350	4	3	1	2.4	.992	OF-145
1988		144	.264	.436	512	135	29	4	17	3.3	67	64	59	65	1	2	0	296	8	8	3	2.2	.974	OF-144
1989		127	.237	.343	414	98	19	2	7	1.7	45	47	46	71	1	13	4	189	16	3	0	1.6	.985	OF-111, DH-13
15 yrs.		1884	.274	.445	6546	1792	380	57	210	3.2	934	852	701	963	55	46	14	4789	115	76	24	2.6	.985	OF-1829, DH-34, 3B-6, 2B-1

LEAGUE CHAMPIONSHIP SERIES

Year	Team	Games	BA	SA	AB	H	2B	3B	HR	HR%	R	RBI	BB	SO	SB	PH AB	PH H	PO	A	E	DP	TC/G	FA	G by Pos
1984	DET A	3	.000	.000	13	0	0	0	0	0.0	1	0	0	0	0	0	0	9	0	0	0	3.0	1.000	OF-3
1987		5	.278	.611	18	5	0	0	2	11.1	4	4	1	4	0	0	0	13	0	0	0	2.6	1.000	OF-5
2 yrs.		8	.161	.355	31	5	0	0	2	6.5	5	4	1	5	0	0	0	22	0	0	0	2.8	1.000	OF-8

WORLD SERIES

Year	Team	Games	BA	SA	AB	H	2B	3B	HR	HR%	R	RBI	BB	SO	SB	PH AB	PH H	PO	A	E	DP	TC/G	FA	G by Pos
1984	DET A	5	.294	.294	17	5	0	0	0	0.0	1	1	2	2	2	0	0	15	0	0	0	3.0	1.000	OF-5

Jim Lemon

LEMON, JAMES ROBERT
B. Mar. 23, 1928, Covington, Va.
Manager 1968.

BR TR 6'4"   200 lbs.

Year	Team	Games	BA	SA	AB	H	2B	3B	HR	HR%	R	RBI	BB	SO	SB	PH AB	PH H	PO	A	E	DP	TC/G	FA	G by Pos
1950	CLE A	12	.176	.294	34	6	1	0	1	2.9	4	1	3	12	0	3	1	13	1	3	1	1.4	.824	OF-10
1953		16	.174	.261	46	8	1	0	1	2.2	5	5	3	15	0	3	0	26	1	4	0	1.9	.871	OF-11, 1B-2
1954	WAS A	37	.234	.344	128	30	2	3	2	1.6	12	13	9	34	0	4	1	58	0	3	0	1.6	.951	OF-33
1955		10	.200	.400	25	5	2	0	1	4.0	3	4	3	3	0	4	1	12	0	1	0	1.3	.923	OF-6
1956		146	.271	.502	538	146	21	11	27	5.0	77	96	65	138	2	1	0	301	11	12	6	2.2	.963	OF-141
1957		137	.284	.448	518	147	22	6	17	3.3	58	64	49	94	1	4	1	253	8	10	2	2.0	.963	OF-131, 1B-3

Year	Team	Games	BA	SA	AB	H	2B	3B	HR	HR%	R	RBI	BB	SO	SB	Pinch Hit AB	Pinch Hit H	PO	A	E	DP	TC/G	FA	G by Pos

Jim Lemon *continued*

Year	Team	Games	BA	SA	AB	H	2B	3B	HR	HR%	R	RBI	BB	SO	SB	AB	H	PO	A	E	DP	TC/G	FA	G by Pos
1958		142	.246	.467	501	123	15	9	26	5.2	65	75	50	120	2	8	3	255	8	6	2	1.9	.978	OF-137
1959		147	.279	.510	531	148	18	3	33	6.2	73	100	46	99	5	5	1	281	4	9	0	2.0	.969	OF-142
1960		148	.269	.508	528	142	10	1	38	7.2	81	100	67	114	0	5	1	251	11	11	1	1.8	.960	OF-145
1961	MIN A	129	.258	.423	423	109	26	1	14	3.3	57	52	44	98	1	10	2	182	7	12	0	1.6	.940	OF-120
1962		12	.176	.353	17	3	0	0	1	5.9	1	5	3	4	0	8	1	1	0	0	0	0.1	1.000	OF-3
1963	3 teams		MIN A (7G – .118)		PHI N (31G – .271)				CHI A (36G – .200)															
"	total	74	.218	.301	156	34	8	0	3	1.9	10	15	21	55	0	26	6	166	7	5	18	2.4	.972	1B-25, OF-22
12 yrs.		1010	.262	.460	3445	901	120	35	164	4.8	446	529	363	787	13	83	22	1799	58	76	30	1.9	.961	OF-901, 1B-30

Don Lenhardt

LENHARDT, DONALD EUGENE (Footsie)   BR TR 6'3''   190 lbs.
B. Oct. 4, 1922, Alton, Ill.

Year	Team	Games	BA	SA	AB	H	2B	3B	HR	HR%	R	RBI	BB	SO	SB	AB	H	PO	A	E	DP	TC/G	FA	G by Pos
1950	STL A	139	.273	.481	480	131	22	6	22	4.6	75	81	90	94	3	10	3	709	58	11	79	5.6	.986	1B-86, OF-39, 3B-10
1951	2 teams		STL A (31G – .262)		CHI A (64G – .266)																			
"	total	95	.265	.460	302	80	12	1	15	5.0	32	63	30	38	2	13	3	179	2	3	0	1.9	.984	OF-80, 1B-3
1952	3 teams		BOS A (30G – .295)		DET A (45G – .188)				STL A (18G – .271)															
"	total	93	.239	.397	297	71	10	2	11	3.7	41	42	47	44	0	10	2	177	7	2	6	2.0	.989	OF-81, 1B-2
1953	STL A	97	.317	.465	303	96	15	0	10	3.3	37	35	41	41	1	17	4	153	16	6	1	1.8	.966	OF-77, 3B-6
1954	2 teams		BAL A (13G – .152)		BOS A (44G – .273)																			
"	total	57	.232	.374	99	23	5	0	3	3.0	7	18	6	18	0	35	6	37	6	0	0	0.8	1.000	OF-20, 1B-2, 3B-1
5 yrs.		481	.271	.450	1481	401	64	9	61	4.1	192	239	214	235	6	85	18	1255	89	22	86	2.8	.984	OF-297, 1B-93, 3B-17

Bob Lennon

LENNON, ROBERT ALBERT (Arch)   BL TL 6'   200 lbs.
B. Sept. 15, 1928, Brooklyn, N. Y.

Year	Team	Games	BA	SA	AB	H	2B	3B	HR	HR%	R	RBI	BB	SO	SB	AB	H	PO	A	E	DP	TC/G	FA	G by Pos
1954	NY N	3	.000	.000	3	0	0	0	0	0.0	0	0	0	0	0	3	0	0	0	0	0	0.0	–	OF-21
1956		26	.182	.200	55	10	1	0	0	0.0	3	1	4	17	0	3	0	21	2	3	2	1.0	.885	OF-21
1957	CHI N	9	.143	.333	21	3	1	0	1	4.8	2	3	1	9	0	5	0	4	0	0	0	0.4	1.000	OF-4
3 yrs.		38	.165	.228	79	13	2	0	1	1.3	5	4	5	26	0	11	0	25	2	3	2	0.8	.900	OF-25

Ed Lennox

LENNOX, JAMES EDGAR (Eggie)   BR TR 5'10''   174 lbs.
B. Nov. 3, 1885, Camden, N. J. D. Oct. 26, 1939, Camden, N. J.

Year	Team	Games	BA	SA	AB	H	2B	3B	HR	HR%	R	RBI	BB	SO	SB	AB	H	PO	A	E	DP	TC/G	FA	G by Pos
1906	PHI A	6	.059	.118	17	1	1	0	0	0.0	1	0	1		0	0	0	9	21	3	0	5.5	.909	3B-6
1909	BKN N	126	.262	.359	435	114	18	9	2	0.5	33	44	47		11	5	1	167	210	16	18	3.1	.959	3B-121
1910		110	.259	.357	367	95	19	4	3	0.8	19	32	36	39	7	10	1	135	149	15	14	2.7	.950	3B-100
1912	CHI N	27	.235	.346	81	19	4	1	1	1.2	13	16	12	10	1	2	1	25	32	4	1	2.3	.934	3B-24
1914	PIT F	124	.312	.493	430	134	25	10	11	2.6	71	84	71		1	10	0	136	193	16	12	2.8	.954	3B-123
1915		55	.302	.453	53	16	3	1	1	1.9	1	9	7		0	45	14	5	10	0	0	0.3	1.000	3B-3
6 yrs.		448	.274	.400	1383	379	70	25	18	1.3	138	185	174	49	38	63	17	477	615	54	45	2.6	.953	3B-377

Jim Lentine

LENTINE, JAMES MATTHEW   BR TR 6'   175 lbs.
B. July 16, 1954, Los Angeles, Calif.

Year	Team	Games	BA	SA	AB	H	2B	3B	HR	HR%	R	RBI	BB	SO	SB	AB	H	PO	A	E	DP	TC/G	FA	G by Pos
1978	STL N	8	.182	.182	11	2	0	0	0	0.0	1	1	0	1	1	1	0	4	0	0	0	0.5	1.000	OF-3
1979		11	.391	.435	23	9	1	0	0	0.0	2	1	3	6	0	3	2	12	1	0	1	1.2	1.000	OF-8
1980	2 teams		STL N (9G – .100)		DET A (67G – .261)																			
"	total	76	.251	.327	171	43	8	1	1	0.6	20	18	28	32	2	10	2	102	5	4	0	1.5	.964	OF-61, DH-9
3 yrs.		95	.263	.332	205	54	9	1	1	0.5	23	20	31	38	3	14	4	118	6	4	1	1.3	.969	OF-72, DH-9

Eddie Leon

LEON, EDUARDO ANTONIO   BR TR 6'   170 lbs.
B. Aug. 11, 1946, Tucson, Ariz.

Year	Team	Games	BA	SA	AB	H	2B	3B	HR	HR%	R	RBI	BB	SO	SB	AB	H	PO	A	E	DP	TC/G	FA	G by Pos
1968	CLE A	6	.000	.000	1	0	0	0	0	0.0	0	0	0	0	0	0	0	3	5	0	3	1.3	1.000	SS-6
1969		64	.239	.310	213	51	6	0	3	1.4	20	19	19	37	2	0	0	114	185	15	43	4.9	.952	SS-64
1970		152	.248	.353	549	136	20	4	10	1.8	58	56	47	89	1	0	0	368	419	18	112	5.3	.978	2B-141, SS-23, 3B-1
1971		131	.261	.326	429	112	12	2	4	0.9	35	35	34	69	3	4	1	271	325	12	84	4.6	.980	2B-107, SS-24
1972		89	.200	.271	225	45	2	1	4	1.8	14	16	20	42	0	23	5	103	179	6	39	3.2	.979	2B-36, SS-35
1973	CHI A	127	.228	.291	399	91	10	3	3	0.8	37	30	34	103	1	2	0	202	392	17	80	4.8	.972	SS-122, 2B-3
1974		31	.109	.130	46	5	1	0	0	0.0	1	3	2	12	0	0	0	37	49	3	18	2.9	.966	SS-21, 2B-7, 3B-2, DH-1
1975	NY A	1			0	0	0	0	0	–	0	0	0	0	0	0	0	0	0	0	0	0.0	–	SS-1
8 yrs.		601	.236	.313	1862	440	51	10	24	1.3	165	159	156	358	7	29	6	1098	1554	71	379	4.5	.974	SS-296, 2B-294, 3B-3, DH-1

Andy Leonard

LEONARD, ANDREW JACKSON   BR TR 5'7''   168 lbs.
B. June 1, 1846, County Cavan, Ireland D. Aug. 22, 1903, Roxbury, Mass.

Year	Team	Games	BA	SA	AB	H	2B	3B	HR	HR%	R	RBI	BB	SO	SB	AB	H	PO	A	E	DP	TC/G	FA	G by Pos
1876	BOS N	64	.281	.327	303	85	10	2	0	0.0	53	27	4	6		0	0	157	87	35	12	4.4	.875	OF-35, 2B-30
1877		58	.287	.305	272	78	5	0	0	0.0	46	27	5	5		0	0	107	53	24	5	3.2	.870	OF-37, SS-21
1878		60	.260	.328	262	68	8	5	0	0.0	41	16	3	19		0	0	65	8	21	1	1.6	.777	OF-60
1880	CIN N	33	.211	.256	133	28	3	0	1	0.8	15	17	8	11		0	0	29	75	21	4	3.8	.832	SS-23, 3B-10
4 yrs.		215	.267	.311	970	259	26	7	1	0.1	155	87	20	41		0	0	358	223	101	22	3.2	.852	OF-132, SS-44, 2B-30, 3B-10

Jeffrey Leonard

LEONARD, JEFFREY (Hac-Man)   BR TR 6'2''   200 lbs.
B. Sept. 22, 1955, Philadelphia, Pa.

Year	Team	Games	BA	SA	AB	H	2B	3B	HR	HR%	R	RBI	BB	SO	SB	AB	H	PO	A	E	DP	TC/G	FA	G by Pos
1977	LA N	11	.300	.500	10	3	0	1	0	0.0	1	2	1	4	0	3	0	7	0	0	0	0.6	1.000	OF-10
1978	HOU N	8	.385	.462	26	10	2	0	0	0.0	2	4	1	2	0	1	0	16	1	0	1	2.1	1.000	OF-8
1979		134	.290	.350	411	119	15	5	0	0.0	47	47	46	68	23	11	2	227	6	10	1	1.8	.959	OF-123
1980		88	.213	.333	216	46	9	5	3	1.4	29	20	19	46	4	24	1	161	9	3	7	2.0	.983	OF-56, 1B-11
1981	2 teams		HOU N (7G – .167)		SF N (37G – .307)																			
"	total	44	.290	.510	145	42	12	4	4	2.8	21	29	12	25	5	6	1	152	5	1	5	3.6	.994	1B-30, OF-7
1982	SF N	80	.259	.421	278	72	16	1	9	3.2	32	49	19	65	18	2	1	137	2	9	0	1.9	.939	OF-74, 1B-1
1983		139	.279	.461	516	144	17	7	21	4.1	74	87	35	116	26	4	2	253	17	7	2	2.0	.975	OF-136
1984		136	.302	.484	514	155	27	2	21	4.1	76	86	47	123	17	4	0	247	14	8	4	2.0	.970	OF-131
1985		133	.241	.393	507	122	20	6	17	3.4	49	107	21	107	11	7	1	203	10	5	0	1.6	.977	OF-126
1986		89	.279	.381	341	95	11	3	6	1.8	48	42	20	62	16	4	2	158	4	5	1	1.9	.970	OF-87
1987		131	.280	.467	503	141	29	4	19	3.8	70	63	21	68	16	11	6	193	7	7	2	1.6	.966	OF-127

Year	Team	Games	BA	SA	AB	H	2B	3B	HR	HR%	R	RBI	BB	SO	SB	Pinch Hit AB	Pinch Hit H	PO	A	E	DP	TC/G	FA	G by Pos

Jeffrey Leonard *continued*

Year	Team	Games	BA	SA	AB	H	2B	3B	HR	HR%	R	RBI	BB	SO	SB	PH AB	PH H	PO	A	E	DP	TC/G	FA	G by Pos
1988	2 teams	SF	N	(44G –	.256)		MIL	A	(94G –	.235)														
"	total	138	.242	.352	534	129	27	1	10	1.9	57	64	25	92	17	3	0	265	4	4	1	2.0	.985	OF-134, DH-2
1989	SEA A	150	.254	.420	566	144	20	1	24	4.2	69	93	38	125	6	2	0	54	2	1	0	0.4	.982	DH-123, OF-26
13 yrs.		1281	.268	.416	4567	1222	203	37	134	2.9	575	648	305	903	159	82	21	2073	81	60	24	1.7	.973	OF-1045, DH-125, 1B-42

LEAGUE CHAMPIONSHIP SERIES

Year	Team	Games	BA	SA	AB	H	2B	3B	HR	HR%	R	RBI	BB	SO	SB	PH AB	PH H	PO	A	E	DP	TC/G	FA	G by Pos
1980	HOU N	3	.000	.000	3	0	0	0	0	0.0	0	0	0	2	0	2	0	2	1	0	1	1.0	1.000	OF-1
1987	SF N	7	.417	.917	24	10	0	0	4	16.7	5	5	3	4	0	0	0	14	1	0	0	2.1	1.000	OF-7
2 yrs.		10	.370	.815	27	10	0	0	4	14.8	5	5	3	6	0	2	0	16	2	0	1	1.8	1.000	OF-8

Joe Leonard

LEONARD, JOSEPH HOWARD
B. Nov. 15, 1894, West Chicago, Ill. D. May 1, 1920, Washington, D. C.   BL TR 5'7½" 156 lbs.

Year	Team	Games	BA	SA	AB	H	2B	3B	HR	HR%	R	RBI	BB	SO	SB	PH AB	PH H	PO	A	E	DP	TC/G	FA	G by Pos
1914	PIT N	53	.198	.246	126	25	2	2	0	0.0	17	4	12	21	4	7	0	29	52	8	2	1.7	.910	3B-38, SS-1
1916	2 teams	CLE	A	(3G –	.000)		WAS	A	(42G –	.274)														
"	total	45	.271	.312	170	46	7	0	0	0.0	21	14	22	24	4	1	0	54	66	6	6	2.8	.952	3B-42, 2B-1
1917	WAS A	99	.192	.259	297	57	6	7	0	0.0	30	23	45	40	6	9	3	252	134	16	32	4.1	.960	3B-67, 1B-20, OF-1, SS-1
1919		71	.258	.359	198	51	8	3	2	1.0	26	20	20	28	3	6	1	112	99	8	14	3.1	.963	2B-28, 3B-25, 1B-4, OF-1
1920		1			0	0	0	0	0	–	0		0			0	0	0	0	0	0	0.0	–	
5 yrs.		269	.226	.293	791	179	23	12	2	0.3	94	61	99	113	17	23	4	447	351	38	54	3.1	.955	3B-172, 2B-29, 1B-24, OF-2, SS-2

John Leovich

LEOVICH, JOHN JOSEPH
B. May 5, 1918, Portland, Ore.   BR TR 6'½" 200 lbs.

Year	Team	Games	BA	SA	AB	H	2B	3B	HR	HR%	R	RBI	BB	SO	SB	PH AB	PH H	PO	A	E	DP	TC/G	FA	G by Pos
1941	PHI A	1	.500	1.000	2	1	1	0	0	0.0	0	0	0	0	0	0	0	0	0	0	0	0.0	–	C-1

Ted Lepcio

LEPCIO, THADDEUS STANLEY
B. July 28, 1930, Utica, N. Y.   BR TR 5'10" 177 lbs.

Year	Team	Games	BA	SA	AB	H	2B	3B	HR	HR%	R	RBI	BB	SO	SB	PH AB	PH H	PO	A	E	DP	TC/G	FA	G by Pos
1952	BOS A	84	.263	.394	274	72	17	2	5	1.8	34	26	24	41	3	0	0	164	212	14	46	4.6	.964	2B-57, 3B-25, SS-1
1953		66	.236	.360	161	38	4	2	4	2.5	17	11	17	24	0	4	1	96	155	6	37	3.9	.977	2B-34, SS-20, 3B-11
1954		116	.256	.384	398	102	19	4	8	2.0	42	45	42	62	3	2	0	276	297	21	64	5.1	.965	2B-80, 3B-24, SS-14
1955		51	.231	.433	134	31	9	0	6	4.5	19	15	13	36	1	4	0	48	84	8	6	2.7	.943	3B-45
1956		83	.261	.454	284	74	10	0	15	5.3	34	51	30	77	1	9	3	170	206	13	51	4.7	.967	2B-57, 3B-22
1957		79	.241	.418	232	56	10	2	9	3.9	24	37	29	61	0	10	2	136	194	8	58	4.3	.976	2B-68
1958		50	.199	.353	136	27	3	0	6	4.4	10	14	12	47	0	10	3	93	99	4	27	3.9	.980	2B-40
1959	2 teams	BOS	A	(3G –	.333)		DET	A	(76G –	.279)														
"	total	79	.280	.417	218	61	9	0	7	3.2	26	25	17	51	2	16	5	96	144	11	30	3.2	.956	SS-35, 2B-25, 3B-11
1960	PHI N	69	.227	.319	141	32	7	0	2	1.4	16	8	17	41	0	9	1	50	74	9	6	1.9	.932	3B-50, SS-14, 2B-5
1961	2 teams	CHI	A	(5G –	.000)		MIN	A	(47G –	.170)														
"	total	52	.167	.395	114	19	3	1	7	6.1	11	19	9	31	1	1	0	53	77	7	20	2.6	.949	3B-36, 2B-22, SS-6
10 yrs.		729	.245	.398	2092	512	91	11	69	3.3	233	251	210	471	11	69	15	1182	1542	101	345	3.9	.964	2B-388, 3B-224, SS-90

Pete LePine

LePINE, LOUIS JOSEPH
B. Sept. 5, 1876, Montreal, Que., Canada D. Dec. 3, 1949, Woonsocket, R. I.   BL TL

Year	Team	Games	BA	SA	AB	H	2B	3B	HR	HR%	R	RBI	BB	SO	SB	PH AB	PH H	PO	A	E	DP	TC/G	FA	G by Pos
1902	DET A	30	.208	.313	96	20	3	2	1	1.0	8	19	8		1	2	0	77	9	3	6	3.0	.966	OF-19, 1B-8

Don Leppert

LEPPERT, DON EUGENE (Tiger)
B. Nov. 20, 1930, Memphis, Tenn.   BL TR 5'8" 175 lbs.

Year	Team	Games	BA	SA	AB	H	2B	3B	HR	HR%	R	RBI	BB	SO	SB	PH AB	PH H	PO	A	E	DP	TC/G	FA	G by Pos
1955	BAL A	40	.114	.143	70	8	0	1	0	0.0	6	2	9	10	1	2	0	52	37	6	11	2.4	.937	2B-35

Don Leppert

LEPPERT, DONALD GEORGE
B. Oct. 19, 1931, Indianapolis, Ind.   BL TR 6'2" 220 lbs.

Year	Team	Games	BA	SA	AB	H	2B	3B	HR	HR%	R	RBI	BB	SO	SB	PH AB	PH H	PO	A	E	DP	TC/G	FA	G by Pos
1961	PIT N	22	.267	.483	60	16	2	1	3	5.0	6	5	1	11	0	2	0	80	11	3	1	4.3	.968	C-21
1962		45	.266	.388	139	37	6	1	3	2.2	14	18	12	21	0	1	0	243	23	3	2	6.0	.989	C-44
1963	WAS A	73	.237	.374	211	50	11	0	6	2.8	20	24	20	29	0	14	6	281	20	5	4	4.2	.984	C-60
1964		50	.156	.254	122	19	3	0	3	2.5	6	12	11	32	0	7	1	191	14	2	2	4.1	.990	C-43
4 yrs.		190	.229	.363	532	122	22	2	15	2.8	46	59	44	93	0	24	7	795	68	13	9	4.6	.985	C-168

Dutch Lerchen

LERCHEN, BERTRAM ROE
Father of George Lerchen.
B. Apr. 4, 1889, Detroit, Mich. D. Jan. 7, 1962, Detroit, Mich.   BR TR 5'8" 160 lbs.

Year	Team	Games	BA	SA	AB	H	2B	3B	HR	HR%	R	RBI	BB	SO	SB	PH AB	PH H	PO	A	E	DP	TC/G	FA	G by Pos
1910	BOS A	6	.000	.000	15	0	0	0	0	0.0	1	0	1			0	0	9	4	1	1	2.3	.929	SS-6

George Lerchen

LERCHEN, GEORGE EDWARD
Son of Dutch Lerchen.
B. Dec. 1, 1922, Detroit, Mich.   BB TR 5'11" 175 lbs.
BL 1953

Year	Team	Games	BA	SA	AB	H	2B	3B	HR	HR%	R	RBI	BB	SO	SB	PH AB	PH H	PO	A	E	DP	TC/G	FA	G by Pos
1952	DET A	14	.156	.281	32	5	1	0	1	3.1	1	3	7	10	1	7	2	15	0	0	0	1.1	1.000	OF-7
1953	CIN N	22	.294	.353	17	5	1	0	0	0.0	2	2	5	6	0	17	6	1	0	0	0	0.0	1.000	OF-1
2 yrs.		36	.204	.306	49	10	2	0	1	2.0	3	5	12	16	1	24	8	16	0	0	0	0.4	1.000	OF-8

Walt Lerian

LERIAN, WALTER IRVIN (Peck)
B. Feb. 10, 1903, Baltimore, Md. D. Oct. 22, 1929, Baltimore, Md.   BR TR 6' 190 lbs.

Year	Team	Games	BA	SA	AB	H	2B	3B	HR	HR%	R	RBI	BB	SO	SB	PH AB	PH H	PO	A	E	DP	TC/G	FA	G by Pos
1928	PHI N	96	.272	.381	239	65	16	2	2	0.8	28	25	41	29	1	17	4	239	61	7	12	3.2	.977	C-74
1929		105	.223	.363	273	61	13	2	7	2.6	28	25	53	37	0	2	0	271	69	5	13	3.3	.986	C-103
2 yrs.		201	.246	.371	512	126	29	4	9	1.8	56	50	94	66	1	19	4	510	130	12	25	3.2	.982	C-177

Roy Leslie

LESLIE, ROY REID
B. Aug. 23, 1894, Bailey, Tex. D. Apr. 9, 1972, Sherman, Tex.   BR TR 6'1" 175 lbs.

Year	Team	Games	BA	SA	AB	H	2B	3B	HR	HR%	R	RBI	BB	SO	SB	PH AB	PH H	PO	A	E	DP	TC/G	FA	G by Pos
1917	CHI N	7	.211	.211	19	4	0	0	0	0.0	1	1	1	5	1	1	0	59	3	2	3	9.1	.969	1B-6
1919	STL N	12	.208	.250	24	5	1	0	0	0.0	2	4	4	3	0	1	0	62	4	3	5	5.8	.957	1B-9

Year	Team		Games	BA	SA	AB	H	2B	3B	HR	HR%	R	RBI	BB	SO	SB	Pinch Hit AB	H	PO	A	E	DP	TC/G	FA	G by Pos

Carlos Lezcano

LEZCANO, CARLOS MANUEL
Born Carlos Manuel Lezcano y Rubio.
B. Sept. 30, 1955, Arecibo, Puerto Rico
BR TR 6'2" 185 lbs.

Year	Team		Games	BA	SA	AB	H	2B	3B	HR	HR%	R	RBI	BB	SO	SB	PH AB	PH H	PO	A	E	DP	TC/G	FA	G by Pos
1980	CHI	N	42	.205	.375	88	18	4	1	3	3.4	15	12	11	29	1	2	0	70	3	4	0	1.8	.948	OF-39
1981			7	.071	.071	14	1	0	0	0	0.0	1	2	0	4	0	2	0	7	0	0	0	1.0	1.000	OF-5
2 yrs.			49	.186	.333	102	19	4	1	3	2.9	16	14	11	33	1	4	0	77	3	4	0	1.7	.952	OF-44

Sixto Lezcano

LEZCANO, SIXTO JOAQUIN
Born Sixto Joaquin Lezcano y Curras.
B. Nov. 28, 1953, Arecibo, Puerto Rico
BR TR 5'10" 165 lbs.

Year	Team		Games	BA	SA	AB	H	2B	3B	HR	HR%	R	RBI	BB	SO	SB	PH AB	PH H	PO	A	E	DP	TC/G	FA	G by Pos
1974	MIL	A	15	.241	.389	54	13	2	0	2	3.7	5	9	4	9	1	4	0	32	3	1	1	2.4	.972	OF-15
1975			134	.247	.382	429	106	19	3	11	2.6	55	43	46	93	5	4	0	240	10	6	1	1.9	.977	OF-129, DH-2
1976			145	.285	.382	513	146	19	5	7	1.4	53	56	51	112	14	0	0	345	10	10	3	2.5	.973	OF-142, DH-3
1977			109	.273	.503	400	109	21	4	21	5.3	50	49	52	78	6	0	0	238	11	3	2	2.3	.988	OF-108
1978			132	.292	.459	442	129	21	4	15	3.4	62	61	64	83	3	2	1	262	18	6	5	2.2	.979	OF-127, DH-3
1979			138	.321	.573	473	152	29	3	28	5.9	84	101	77	74	4	1	0	281	10	4	2	2.1	.986	OF-135, DH-1
1980			112	.229	.421	411	94	19	3	18	4.4	51	55	39	75	1	0	0	228	8	4	2	2.1	.983	OF-108, DH-4
1981	STL	N	72	.266	.393	214	57	8	2	5	2.3	26	28	40	40	0	4	1	103	5	3	1	1.5	.973	OF-65
1982	SD	N	138	.289	.472	470	136	26	6	16	3.4	73	84	78	69	2	2	0	275	16	3	8	2.1	.990	OF-134
1983	2 teams		SD	N (97G – .233)						PHI	N (18G – .282)														
"	total		115	.239	.351	356	85	12	2	8	2.2	49	56	52	75	1	14	5	176	9	7	1	1.7	.964	OF-106
1984	PHI	N	109	.277	.480	256	71	6	2	14	5.5	36	40	38	43	0	27	6	151	3	3	0	1.4	.981	OF-87
1985	PIT	N	72	.207	.302	116	24	2	0	3	2.6	16	9	35	17	0	27	6	57	2	2	0	0.8	.967	OF-40
12 yrs.			1291	.271	.440	4134	1122	184	34	148	3.6	560	591	576	768	37	81	19	2388	105	52	28	2.0	.980	OF-1196, DH-13

LEAGUE CHAMPIONSHIP SERIES

Year	Team		Games	BA	SA	AB	H	2B	3B	HR	HR%	R	RBI	BB	SO	SB	PH AB	PH H	PO	A	E	DP	TC/G	FA	G by Pos
1983	PHI	N	4	.308	.538	13	4	0	0	1	7.7	2	2	1	1	0	1	0	5	1	1	0	1.8	.857	OF-4

WORLD SERIES

Year	Team		Games	BA	SA	AB	H	2B	3B	HR	HR%	R	RBI	BB	SO	SB	PH AB	PH H	PO	A	E	DP	TC/G	FA	G by Pos
1983	PHI	N	4	.125	.125	8	1	0	0	0	0.0	0	0	0	2	0	1	0	2	0	0	0	0.5	1.000	OF-3

Steve Libby

LIBBY, STEPHEN AUGUSTUS
B. Dec. 8, 1853, Scarborough, Me. Deceased.
6'1½" 168 lbs.

Year	Team		Games	BA	SA	AB	H	2B	3B	HR	HR%	R	RBI	BB	SO	SB	PH AB	PH H	PO	A	E	DP	TC/G	FA	G by Pos
1879	BUF	N	1	.000	.000	2	0	0	0	0	0.0	0	0	0	1	0	0	0	8	0	0	0	8.0	1.000	1B-1

Al Libke

LIBKE, ALBERT WALTER (Big Al)
B. Sept. 12, 1918, Tacoma, Wash.
BL TR 6'4" 215 lbs.

Year	Team		Games	BA	SA	AB	H	2B	3B	HR	HR%	R	RBI	BB	SO	SB	PH AB	PH H	PO	A	E	DP	TC/G	FA	G by Pos
1945	CIN	N	130	.283	.383	449	127	23	5	4	0.9	41	53	34	62	6	15	3	236	15	9	7	2.0	.965	OF-108, P-4, 1B-2
1946			124	.253	.343	431	109	22	1	5	1.2	32	42	43	50	0	8	2	191	14	6	4	1.7	.972	OF-115, P-1
2 yrs.			254	.268	.364	880	236	45	6	9	1.0	73	95	77	112	6	23	5	427	29	15	11	1.9	.968	OF-223, P-5, 1B-2

Francisco Libran

LIBRAN, FRANCISCO
Born Francisco Libran y Rosas.
B. May 6, 1948, Mayaguez, Puerto Rico
BR TR 6' 168 lbs.

Year	Team		Games	BA	SA	AB	H	2B	3B	HR	HR%	R	RBI	BB	SO	SB	PH AB	PH H	PO	A	E	DP	TC/G	FA	G by Pos
1969	SD	N	10	.100	.200	10	1	1	0	0	0.0	1	1	1	2	0	0	0	4	10	0	1	1.4	1.000	SS-9

John Lickert

LICKERT, JOHN WILBUR
B. Apr. 4, 1960, Pittsburgh, Pa.
BR TR 5'11" 175 lbs.

Year	Team		Games	BA	SA	AB	H	2B	3B	HR	HR%	R	RBI	BB	SO	SB	PH AB	PH H	PO	A	E	DP	TC/G	FA	G by Pos
1981	BOS	A	1	–	–	0	0	0	0	0	–	0	0	0	0	0	0	0	1	0	0	0	1.0	1.000	C-1

Fred Liese

LIESE, FREDERICK RICHARD
B. Oct. 7, 1885, Wis. D. June 30, 1967, Los Angeles, Calif.
TL

Year	Team		Games	BA	SA	AB	H	2B	3B	HR	HR%	R	RBI	BB	SO	SB	PH AB	PH H	PO	A	E	DP	TC/G	FA	G by Pos
1910	BOS	N	5	.000	.000	4	0	0	0	0	0.0	0	0	1	2	0	4	0	0	0	0	0	0.0	–	

Bill Lillard

LILLARD, WILLIAM BEVERLY
Brother of Gene Lillard.
B. Jan. 10, 1918, Goleta, Calif.
BR TR 5'10" 170 lbs.

Year	Team		Games	BA	SA	AB	H	2B	3B	HR	HR%	R	RBI	BB	SO	SB	PH AB	PH H	PO	A	E	DP	TC/G	FA	G by Pos
1939	PHI	A	7	.316	.368	19	6	1	0	0	0.0	4	3	1	1	0	0	0	12	25	1	3	5.4	.974	SS-7
1940			73	.238	.311	206	49	8	2	1	0.5	26	21	28	28	0	1	0	113	157	23	28	4.0	.922	SS-69, 2B-1
2 yrs.			80	.244	.316	225	55	9	2	1	0.4	30	22	31	29	0	1	0	125	182	24	31	4.1	.927	SS-76, 2B-1

Gene Lillard

LILLARD, ROBERT EUGENE
Brother of Bill Lillard.
B. Nov. 12, 1913, Santa Barbara, Calif.
BR TR 5'10½" 178 lbs.

Year	Team		Games	BA	SA	AB	H	2B	3B	HR	HR%	R	RBI	BB	SO	SB	PH AB	PH H	PO	A	E	DP	TC/G	FA	G by Pos
1936	CHI	N	19	.206	.235	34	7	1	0	0	0.0	6	2	3	8	0	10	3	11	13	2	2	1.4	.923	SS-4, 3B-3
1939			23	.100	.100	10	1	0	0	0	0.0	3	0	6	3	0	0	0	2	11	0	0	0.6	1.000	P-20
1940	STL	N	2	–	–	0	0	0	0	0	–	0	0	0	0	0	0	0	0	1	0	0	0.5	1.000	P-2
3 yrs.			44	.182	.205	44	8	1	0	0	0.0	9	2	9	11	0	10	3	13	25	2	2	0.9	.950	P-22, SS-4, 3B-3

Jim Lillie

LILLIE, JAMES J. (Grasshopper)
B. 1862, New Haven, Conn. D. Nov. 9, 1890, Kansas City, Mo.

Year	Team		Games	BA	SA	AB	H	2B	3B	HR	HR%	R	RBI	BB	SO	SB	PH AB	PH H	PO	A	E	DP	TC/G	FA	G by Pos
1883	BUF	N	50	.234	.313	201	47	7	3	1	0.5	25		1	31		0	0	84	13	22	3	2.4	.815	OF-47, P-3, C-2, SS-1, 3B-1, 2B-1
1884			114	.223	.289	471	105	12	5	3	0.6	68		5	71		0	0	190	46	40	7	2.4	.855	OF-114, P-2
1885			112	.249	.307	430	107	13	3	2	0.5	49	30	6	39		0	0	196	31	35	5	2.3	.866	OF-112, SS-3, 1B-1
1886	KC	N	114	.175	.197	416	73	9	0	0	0.0	37	22	11	80		0	0	199	32	30	3	2.3	.885	OF-114, P-1
4 yrs.			390	.219	.272	1518	332	41	11	6	0.4	179	52	23	221		0	0	669	122	127	18	2.4	.862	OF-387, P-6, SS-4, C-2, 3B-1, 2B-1, 1B-1

Bob Lillis

LILLIS, ROBERT PERRY (Flea)
B. June 2, 1930, Altadena, Calif.
Manager 1982-85.
BR TR 5'11" 160 lbs.

Year	Team		Games	BA	SA	AB	H	2B	3B	HR	HR%	R	RBI	BB	SO	SB	Pinch Hit AB	Pinch Hit H	PO	A	E	DP	TC/G	FA	G by Pos

Bob Lillis *continued*

Year	Team		Games	BA	SA	AB	H	2B	3B	HR	HR%	R	RBI	BB	SO	SB	AB	H	PO	A	E	DP	TC/G	FA	G by Pos
1958	LA	N	20	.391	.507	69	27	3	1	1	1.4	10	5	4	2	1	1	1	29	52	3	10	4.2	.964	SS-19
1959			30	.229	.271	48	11	2	0	0	0.0	7	2	3	4	0	1	1	27	52	7	10	2.9	.919	SS-20
1960			48	.267	.333	60	16	4	0	0	0.0	6	6	2	6	2	3	0	40	52	1	11	1.9	.989	SS-23, 3B-14, 2B-1
1961	2 teams		LA	N	(19G –	.111)			STL	N	(86G –	.217)													
"	total		105	.213	.230	239	51	4	0	0	0.0	24	22	8	14	3	3	0	123	201	19	33	3.3	.945	SS-57, 2B-25, 3B-12
1962	HOU	N	129	.249	.300	457	114	12	4	1	0.2	38	30	28	23	7	1	1	223	378	15	72	4.8	.976	SS-99, 2B-33, 3B-9
1963			147	.198	.237	469	93	13	1	1	0.2	31	19	15	35	3	3	0	249	375	26	59	4.4	.960	SS-124, 2B-19, 3B-6
1964			109	.268	.313	332	89	11	2	0	0.0	31	17	11	10	4	13	3	169	236	10	40	3.8	.976	2B-52, SS-43, 3B-12
1965			124	.221	.255	408	90	12	1	0	0.0	34	20	20	10	2	5	3	206	304	16	52	4.2	.970	SS-104, 3B-9, 2B-6
1966			68	.232	.268	164	38	6	0	0	0.0	14	11	7	4	1	8	1	99	109	10	24	3.2	.954	2B-35, SS-18, 3B-6
1967			37	.244	.256	82	20	1	0	0	0.0	3	5	1	8	0	9	1	27	66	7	9	2.7	.930	SS-23, 2B-3, 3B-2
10 yrs.			817	.236	.277	2328	549	68	9	3	0.1	198	137	99	116	23	47	11	1192	1825	114	320	3.8	.964	SS-530, 2B-174, 3B-70

Lou Limmer

LIMMER, LOUIS
B. Mar. 10, 1925, New York, N.Y.
BL TL 6'2" 190 lbs.

Year	Team		Games	BA	SA	AB	H	2B	3B	HR	HR%	R	RBI	BB	SO	SB	AB	H	PO	A	E	DP	TC/G	FA	G by Pos
1951	PHI	A	94	.159	.280	214	34	9	1	5	2.3	25	30	28	40	1	31	5	450	40	6	54	5.3	.988	1B-58
1954			115	.231	.415	316	73	10	3	14	4.4	41	32	35	37	2	30	8	597	56	8	63	5.7	.988	1B-79
2 yrs.			209	.202	.360	530	107	19	4	19	3.6	66	62	63	77	3	61	13	1047	96	14	117	5.5	.988	1B-137

Rufino Linares

LINARES, RUFINO
Born Rufino de la Cruz y Linares.
B. Feb. 28, 1951, Ingerio Quiqueya, Dominican Republic
BR TR 6' 170 lbs.

Year	Team		Games	BA	SA	AB	H	2B	3B	HR	HR%	R	RBI	BB	SO	SB	AB	H	PO	A	E	DP	TC/G	FA	G by Pos
1981	ATL	N	78	.265	.375	253	67	9	2	5	2.0	27	25	9	28	8	24	5	124	6	5	1	1.7	.963	OF-60
1982			77	.298	.377	191	57	7	1	2	1.0	28	17	7	29	5	31	8	92	4	0	1	1.2	1.000	OF-53
1984			34	.207	.310	58	12	3	0	1	1.7	4	10	6	12	0	20	5	21	2	1	0	0.7	.958	OF-13
1985	CAL	A	18	.256	.512	43	11	2	0	3	7.0	7	11	2	5	2	5	1	1	0	0	0	0.1	1.000	DH-14, OF-2
4 yrs.			207	.270	.380	545	147	21	3	11	2.0	66	63	24	74	15	80	19	238	12	6	2	1.2	.977	OF-128, DH-14

Carl Lind

LIND, HENRY CARL
B. Sept. 19, 1903, New Orleans, La.   D. Aug. 2, 1946, New York, N.Y.
BR TR 6' 160 lbs.

Year	Team		Games	BA	SA	AB	H	2B	3B	HR	HR%	R	RBI	BB	SO	SB	AB	H	PO	A	E	DP	TC/G	FA	G by Pos
1927	CLE	A	12	.135	.135	37	5	0	0	0	0.0	2	1	5	7	1	0	0	21	41	2	6	5.3	.969	2B-11, SS-1
1928			154	.294	.375	650	191	42	4	1	0.2	102	54	36	48	8	0	0	390	505	37	116	6.1	.960	2B-154
1929			66	.241	.286	224	54	8	1	0	0.0	19	13	13	17	0	1	0	190	211	18	60	6.3	.957	2B-64, 3B-1
1930			24	.246	.290	69	17	3	0	0	0.0	8	6	3	7	0	1	0	48	77	8	19	5.5	.940	SS-22, 2B-1
4 yrs.			256	.272	.340	980	267	53	5	1	0.1	131	74	57	79	9	2	0	649	834	65	201	6.0	.958	2B-230, SS-23, 3B-1

Jack Lind

LIND, JACKSON HUGH
B. June 8, 1946, Denver, Colo.
BB TR 6' 170 lbs.

Year	Team		Games	BA	SA	AB	H	2B	3B	HR	HR%	R	RBI	BB	SO	SB	AB	H	PO	A	E	DP	TC/G	FA	G by Pos
1974	MIL	A	9	.235	.353	17	4	2	0	0	0.0	4	1	3	2	0	0	0	15	16	1	3	3.6	.969	SS-5, 2B-4
1975			17	.050	.050	20	1	0	0	0	0.0	1	0	2	12	1	0	0	19	27	3	3	2.9	.939	SS-9, 3B-6, 1B-1
2 yrs.			26	.135	.189	37	5	2	0	0	0.0	5	1	5	14	1	0	0	34	43	4	6	3.1	.951	SS-14, 3B-6, 2B-4, 1B-1

Jose Lind

LIND, JOSE
Born Jose Lind y Salgado.
B. May 1, 1964, Toabaja, Puerto Rico
BR TR 5'11" 155 lbs.

Year	Team		Games	BA	SA	AB	H	2B	3B	HR	HR%	R	RBI	BB	SO	SB	AB	H	PO	A	E	DP	TC/G	FA	G by Pos
1987	PIT	N	35	.322	.434	143	46	8	4	0	0.0	21	11	8	12	2	0	0	53	139	1	12	5.5	.995	2B-35
1988			154	.262	.324	611	160	24	4	2	0.3	82	49	42	75	15	4	2	333	473	11	73	5.3	.987	2B-153
1989			153	.232	.289	578	134	21	3	2	0.3	52	48	39	64	15	5	2	309	438	18	81	5.0	.976	2B-151
3 yrs.			342	.255	.321	1332	340	53	11	4	0.3	155	108	89	151	32	9	4	695	1050	30	166	5.2	.983	2B-339

Em Lindbeck

LINDBECK, EMERIT DESMOND
B. Aug. 27, 1935, Kewanee, Ill.
BL TR 6' 185 lbs.

Year	Team		Games	BA	SA	AB	H	2B	3B	HR	HR%	R	RBI	BB	SO	SB	AB	H	PO	A	E	DP	TC/G	FA	G by Pos
1960	DET	A	2	.000	.000	1	0	0	0	0	0.0	0	0	1	0	0	1	0	0	0	0	0	0.0	—	

Johnny Lindell

LINDELL, JOHN HARLAN
B. Aug. 30, 1916, Greeley, Colo.   D. Aug. 27, 1985, Newport Beach, Calif.
BR TR 6'4½" 217 lbs.

Year	Team		Games	BA	SA	AB	H	2B	3B	HR	HR%	R	RBI	BB	SO	SB	AB	H	PO	A	E	DP	TC/G	FA	G by Pos
1941	NY	A	1	.000	.000	1	0	0	0	0	0.0	0	0	0	0	0	0	0	0	0	0	0	0.0	—	
1942			27	.250	.292	24	6	1	0	0	0.0	1	4	0	5	0	5	2	5	7	1	2	0.5	.923	P-23
1943			122	.245	.365	441	108	17	12	4	0.9	53	51	51	55	2	1	0	269	11	10	1	2.4	.966	OF-122
1944			149	.300	.500	594	178	33	16	18	3.0	91	103	44	56	5	0	0	468	9	7	3	3.2	.986	OF-149
1945			41	.283	.377	159	45	6	3	1	0.6	26	20	17	10	2	0	0	108	2	2	0	2.7	.982	OF-41
1946			102	.259	.410	332	86	10	5	10	3.0	41	40	32	47	4	14	3	275	12	6	18	2.9	.980	OF-74, 1B-14
1947			127	.275	.412	476	131	18	7	11	2.3	66	67	32	70	1	7	3	308	6	7	1	2.5	.978	OF-118
1948			88	.317	.511	309	98	17	2	13	4.2	58	55	35	50	0	7	0	165	7	1	1	2.0	.994	OF-79
1949			78	.242	.374	211	51	10	0	6	2.8	33	27	35	27	3	13	2	114	4	2	1	1.5	.983	OF-65
1950	2 teams		NY	A	(7G –	.190)			STL	N	(36G –	.186)													
"	total		43	.187	.366	134	25	6	2	5	3.7	18	18	19	26	0	4	0	67	1	2	1	1.6	.971	OF-39
1953	2 teams		PIT	N	(58G –	.286)			PHI	N	(11G –	.389)													
"	total		69	.303	.495	109	33	7	1	4	3.7	14	17	22	17	0	26	8	22	45	4	2	1.0	.944	P-32, OF-2, 1B-2
1954	PHI	N	7	.200	.200	5	1	0	0	0	0.0	2	0	2	3	0	5	1	0	0	0	0	0.0		
12 yrs.			854	.273	.429	2795	762	124	48	72	2.6	401	404	289	366	17	83	19	1801	104	42	30	2.3	.978	OF-689, P-55, 1B-16

WORLD SERIES

Year	Team		Games	BA	SA	AB	H	2B	3B	HR	HR%	R	RBI	BB	SO	SB	AB	H	PO	A	E	DP	TC/G	FA	G by Pos
1943	NY	A	4	.111	.111	9	1	0	0	0	0.0	1	0	1	0	0	0	0	8	0	0	0	2.0	1.000	OF-4
1947			6	.500	.778	18	9	3	1	0	0.0	3	7	5	2	0	0	0	11	0	0	0	1.8	1.000	OF-6
1949			2	.143	.143	7	1	0	0	0	0.0	0	0	0	2	0	0	0	2	1	1	0	2.0	.750	OF-2
3 yrs.			12	.324	.471	34	11	3	1	0	0.0	4	7	6	4	0	0	0	21	1	1	0	1.9	.957	OF-12

Jim Lindeman

LINDEMAN, JAMES WILLIAM
B. Jan. 10, 1962, Evanston, Ill.
BR TR 6'1" 200 lbs.

Year	Team		Games	BA	SA	AB	H	2B	3B	HR	HR%	R	RBI	BB	SO	SB	AB	H	PO	A	E	DP	TC/G	FA	G by Pos
1986	STL	N	19	.255	.327	55	14	1	0	1	1.8	7	6	2	10	1	2	1	118	10	1	8	6.8	.992	1B-17, OF-1, 3B-1

Year	Team		Games	BA	SA	AB	H	2B	3B	HR	HR%	R	RBI	BB	SO	SB	Pinch Hit AB	Pinch Hit H	PO	A	E	DP	TC/G	FA	G by Pos

Jim Lindeman *continued*

Year	Team		Games	BA	SA	AB	H	2B	3B	HR	HR%	R	RBI	BB	SO	SB	AB	H	PO	A	E	DP	TC/G	FA	G by Pos
1987			75	.208	.386	207	43	13	0	8	3.9	20	28	11	56	3	13	2	196	14	3	13	2.8	.986	OF-49, 1B-20
1988			17	.209	.372	43	9	1	0	2	4.7	3	7	2	9	0	4	2	36	2	1	2	2.3	.974	OF-12, 1B-3
1989			73	.111	.133	45	5	1	0	0	0.0	8	2	3	18	0	26	1	93	6	1	7	1.4	.990	1B-42, OF-5
4 yrs.			184	.203	.343	350	71	16	0	11	3.1	38	43	18	93	4	45	7	443	32	6	30	2.6	.988	1B-82, OF-67, 3B-1

LEAGUE CHAMPIONSHIP SERIES

| 1987 | STL | N | 5 | .308 | .538 | 13 | 4 | 0 | 0 | 1 | 7.7 | 1 | 3 | 0 | 3 | 0 | 1 | 0 | 33 | 2 | 0 | 3 | 7.0 | 1.000 | 1B-5 |

WORLD SERIES

| 1987 | STL | N | 6 | .333 | .400 | 15 | 5 | 1 | 0 | 0 | 0.0 | 3 | 2 | 0 | 3 | 0 | 1 | 0 | 28 | 2 | 3 | 2 | 5.5 | .909 | 1B-6, OF-1 |

Bob Lindemann

LINDEMANN, JOHN FREDERICK MANN
B. June 5, 1881, Philadelphia, Pa. D. Dec. 19, 1951, Williamsport, Pa.   BB TR 6' 175 lbs.

| 1901 | PHI | A | 3 | .111 | .111 | 9 | 1 | 0 | 0 | 0 | 0.0 | 0 | 0 | 0 | | 0 | 0 | 0 | 2 | 1 | 2 | 0 | 1.7 | .600 | OF-3 |

Walt Linden

LINDEN, WALTER CHARLES
B. Mar. 27, 1924, Chicago, Ill.   BR TR 6'1" 190 lbs.

| 1950 | BOS | N | 3 | .400 | .600 | 5 | 2 | 1 | 0 | 0 | 0.0 | 0 | 1 | 0 | 0 | 0 | 0 | 0 | 5 | 0 | 0 | 0 | 1.7 | 1.000 | C-3 |

Bill Lindsay

LINDSAY, WILLIAM GIBBONS
B. Feb. 24, 1881, Madison, N. C. D. July 14, 1963, Greensboro, N. C.   BL TR 5'10½" 165 lbs.

| 1911 | CLE | A | 19 | .242 | .273 | 66 | 16 | 0 | 0 | 0 | 0.0 | 6 | 5 | 1 | | 2 | 1 | 1 | 14 | 41 | 7 | 1 | 3.3 | .887 | 3B-15, 2B-1 |

Pinky Lindsay

LINDSAY, CHRISTIAN HALLER (Chris Crab)
B. July 24, 1878, Baker's Yard, Pa. D. Jan. 25, 1941, Cleveland, Ohio   BR TR 6' 190 lbs.

1905	DET	A	88	.267	.316	329	88	14	1	0	0.0	38	31	18		10	0	0	761	57	18	40	9.5	.978	1B-88
1906			141	.224	.265	499	112	16	2	0	0.0	59	33	45		18	2	0	1162	104	36	59	9.2	.972	1B-122, 2B-17, 3B-1
2 yrs.			229	.242	.285	828	200	30	3	0	0.0	97	64	63		28	2	0	1923	161	54	99	9.3	.975	1B-210, 2B-17, 3B-1

Bill Lindsey

LINDSEY, WILLIAM DONALD
B. Apr. 12, 1960, Staten Island, N. Y.   BR TR 6'3" 195 lbs.

| 1987 | CHI | A | 9 | .188 | .188 | 16 | 3 | 0 | 0 | 0 | 0.0 | 2 | 1 | 0 | 3 | 0 | 0 | 0 | 28 | 4 | 0 | 1 | 3.6 | 1.000 | C-9 |

Charlie Lindstrom

LINDSTROM, CHARLES WILLIAM
Son of Freddie Lindstrom.
B. Sept. 7, 1936, Chicago, Ill.   BR TR 5'11" 175 lbs.

| 1958 | CHI | A | 1 | 1.000 | 3.000 | 1 | 1 | 0 | 1 | 0 | 0.0 | 1 | 1 | 1 | 0 | 0 | 0 | 0 | 2 | 0 | 0 | 0 | 2.0 | 1.000 | C-1 |

Freddie Lindstrom

LINDSTROM, FREDERICK CHARLES (Lindy)
Father of Charlie Lindstrom.
B. Nov. 21, 1905, Chicago, Ill. D. Oct. 4, 1981, Chicago, Ill.   BR TR 5'11" 170 lbs.
Hall of Fame 1976.

1924	NY	N	52	.253	.316	79	20	3	1	0	0.0	19	4	6	10	3	6	2	34	53	6	7	1.8	.935	2B-23, 3B-11
1925			104	.287	.430	356	102	15	12	4	1.1	43	33	22	20	5	2	1	127	154	14	10	2.8	.953	3B-96, SS-1, 2B-1
1926			140	.302	.420	543	164	19	9	9	1.7	90	76	39	21	11	1	1	152	251	16	23	3.0	.962	3B-138, OF-1
1927			138	.306	.436	562	172	36	8	7	1.2	107	58	40	40	10	1	1	182	181	12	12	2.7	.968	3B-87, OF-51
1928			153	.358	.511	646	**231**	39	9	14	2.2	99	107	25	21	15	0	0	145	340	21	34	3.3	.958	3B-153
1929			130	.319	.464	549	175	23	6	15	2.7	99	91	30	28	10	2	0	134	258	14	24	3.1	.966	3B-128
1930			148	.379	.575	609	231	39	7	22	3.6	127	106	48	33	15	0	0	132	291	21	24	3.0	.953	3B-148
1931			78	.300	.429	303	91	12	6	5	1.7	38	36	26	12	5	1	0	158	8	7	3	2.2	.960	OF-73, 2B-4
1932			144	.271	.407	595	161	26	5	15	2.5	83	92	27	28	6	0	0	326	33	10	3	2.6	.973	OF-128, 1B-15
1933	PIT	N	138	.310	.448	538	167	39	10	5	0.9	70	55	33	22	1	8	3	388	7	5	2	2.9	.988	OF-130
1934			97	.290	.405	383	111	24	4	4	1.0	59	49	23	21	1	4	1	181	8	2	1	2.0	.990	OF-92
1935	CHI	N	90	.275	.389	342	94	22	4	3	0.9	49	62	10	13	1	6	1	167	40	7	7	2.4	.967	OF-50, 3B-33
1936	BKN	N	26	.264	.302	106	28	4	0	0	0.0	12	10	5	7	1	0	0	51	6	1	0	2.2	.982	OF-26
13 yrs.			1438	.311	.449	5611	1747	301	81	103	1.8	895	779	334	276	84	31	9	2177	1628	136	150	2.7	.965	3B-809, OF-551, 2B-28, SS-1

WORLD SERIES

1924	NY	N	7	.333	.400	30	10	2	0	0	0.0	0	4	3	6	0	0	0	7	18	0	0	3.6	1.000	3B-7
1935	CHI	N	4	.200	.267	15	3	1	0	0	0.0	1	0	1	1	0	0	0	1	0	1	0	0.5	.500	OF-4, 3B-1
2 yrs.			11	.289	.356	45	13	3	0	0	0.0	1	4	4	7	0	0	0	8	18	1	0	2.5	.963	3B-8, OF-4

Carl Linhart

LINHART, CARL JAMES
B. Dec. 14, 1929, Zborov, Czechoslovakia   BL TR 5'11" 184 lbs.

| 1952 | DET | A | 3 | .000 | .000 | 2 | 0 | 0 | 0 | 0 | 0.0 | 0 | 0 | 0 | 0 | 0 | 2 | 0 | 0 | 0 | 0 | 0 | 0.0 | — | |

Bob Linton

LINTON, CLAUD CLARENCE
B. Apr. 18, 1903, Emerson, Ark. D. Apr. 3, 1980, Destin, Fla.   BL TR 6' 185 lbs.

| 1929 | PIT | N | 17 | .111 | .111 | 18 | 2 | 0 | 0 | 0 | 0.0 | 0 | 1 | 0 | 1 | 0 | 8 | 1 | 6 | 3 | 0 | 0 | 0.5 | 1.000 | C-8 |

Larry Lintz

LINTZ, LARRY
B. Oct. 10, 1949, Martinez, Calif.   BR TR 5'10" 150 lbs.

1973	MON	N	52	.250	.259	116	29	1	0	0	0.0	20	3	17	18	12	1	0	63	114	9	19	3.6	.952	2B-34, SS-15
1974			113	.238	.276	319	76	10	1	0	0.0	60	20	44	50	50	0	0	169	252	18	48	3.9	.959	2B-67, SS-31, 3B-1
1975 2 teams		MON N (46G – .197) STL N (27G – .278)																							
" total			73	.207	.213	150	31	1	0	0	0.0	24	4	26	20	21	0	0	101	132	9	21	3.3	.963	2B-45, SS-8
1976	OAK	A	68	.000	.000	1	0	0	0	0	0.0	21	0	2	0	31	0	0	2	2	0	0	0.1	1.000	DH-19, 2B-5, OF-3
1977			41	.133	.167	30	4	1	0	0	0.0	11	0	8	13	13	0	0	29	37	1	9	1.6	.985	2B-28, DH-5, SS-2, 3B-1

Year	Team	Games	BA	SA	AB	H	2B	3B	HR	HR%	R	RBI	BB	SO	SB	Pinch Hit AB	H	PO	A	E	DP	TC/G	FA	G by Pos

Larry Lintz *continued*

Year	Team	Games	BA	SA	AB	H	2B	3B	HR	HR%	R	RBI	BB	SO	SB	AB	H	PO	A	E	DP	TC/G	FA	G by Pos
1978	CLE A	3	–	–	0	0	0	0	0	–	1	0	0	0	1	0	0	0	0	0	0	0.0	–	DH-1
6 yrs.		350	.227	.252	616	140	13	1	0	0.0	137	27	97	101	128	2	1	364	537	37	97	2.7	.961	2B-179, SS-56, DH-25, OF-3, 3B-2

Phil Linz

LINZ, PHILIP FRANCIS (Supersub)
B. June 4, 1939, Baltimore, Md.
BR TR 6'1" 180 lbs.

Year	Team	Games	BA	SA	AB	H	2B	3B	HR	HR%	R	RBI	BB	SO	SB	AB	H	PO	A	E	DP	TC/G	FA	G by Pos
1962	NY A	71	.287	.372	129	37	8	0	1	0.8	28	14	6	17	6	16	7	53	59	9	10	1.7	.926	SS-21, 3B-8, 2B-5, OF-2
1963		72	.269	.349	186	50	9	0	2	1.1	22	12	15	18	1	15	2	69	103	4	17	2.4	.977	SS-22, 3B-13, OF-12, 2B-6
1964		112	.250	.364	368	92	21	3	5	1.4	63	25	43	61	3	9	0	126	282	20	43	3.8	.953	SS-55, 3B-41, 2B-5, OF-3
1965		99	.207	.277	285	59	12	1	2	0.7	37	16	30	33	2	8	1	144	221	17	30	3.9	.955	SS-71, OF-4, 3B-4, 2B-1
1966	PHI N	40	.200	.243	70	14	3	0	0	0.0	4	6	2	14	0	15	0	18	29	2	4	1.2	.959	3B-14, SS-6, 2B-3
1967	2 teams	PHI N	(23G – .222)		NY N	(24G – .207)																		
"	total	47	.211	.303	76	16	4	0	1	1.3	12	6	6	11	0	15	2	40	39	3	8	1.7	.963	SS-15, 2B-11, 3B-2, OF-1
1968	NY N	78	.209	.236	258	54	7	0	0	0.0	19	17	10	41	1	9	1	136	162	10	36	3.9	.968	2B-71
7 yrs.		519	.235	.311	1372	322	64	4	11	0.8	185	96	112	195	13	87	13	586	895	65	148	3.0	.958	SS-190, 2B-102, 3B-82, OF-22

WORLD SERIES

Year	Team	Games	BA	SA	AB	H	2B	3B	HR	HR%	R	RBI	BB	SO	SB	AB	H	PO	A	E	DP	TC/G	FA	G by Pos
1963	NY A	3	.333	.333	3	1	0	0	0	0.0	0	0	0	1	0	3	1	0	0	0	0	0.0	–	
1964		7	.226	.452	31	7	1	0	2	6.5	5	2	2	5	0	0	0	7	21	2	5	4.3	.933	SS-7
2 yrs.		10	.235	.441	34	8	1	0	2	5.9	5	2	2	6	0	3	1	7	21	2	5	3.0	.933	SS-7

Johnny Lipon

LIPON, JOHN JOSEPH (Skids)
B. Nov. 10, 1922, Martin's Ferry, Ohio
Manager 1971.
BR TR 6' 175 lbs.

Year	Team	Games	BA	SA	AB	H	2B	3B	HR	HR%	R	RBI	BB	SO	SB	AB	H	PO	A	E	DP	TC/G	FA	G by Pos
1942	DET A	34	.191	.206	131	25	2	0	0	0.0	5	9	7	7	1	0	0	85	103	11	24	5.9	.945	SS-34
1946		14	.300	.300	20	6	0	0	0	0.0	4	1	5	3	0	1	0	14	15	2	5	2.2	.935	SS-8, 3B-1
1948		121	.290	.397	458	133	18	8	5	1.1	65	52	68	22	4	1	0	212	347	17	63	4.8	.970	SS-117, 3B-1, 2B-1
1949		127	.251	.330	439	110	14	6	3	0.7	57	59	75	24	2	5	0	240	364	22	92	4.9	.965	SS-120
1950		147	.293	.368	601	176	27	6	2	0.3	104	63	81	26	9	0	0	273	483	33	126	5.4	.958	SS-147
1951		129	.265	.300	487	129	15	1	0	0.0	56	38	49	27	7	2	0	244	364	33	80	5.0	.949	SS-125
1952	2 teams	DET A	(39G – .221)		BOS A	(79G – .205)																		
"	total	118	.211	.259	370	78	12	3	0	0.0	42	30	48	26	4	1	0	202	330	11	67	4.6	.980	SS-108, 3B-7
1953	2 teams	BOS A	(60G – .214)		STL A	(7G – .222)																		
"	total	67	.214	.260	154	33	7	0	0	0.0	18	14	14	17	1	2	0	89	154	12	26	3.8	.953	SS-58, 3B-6, 2B-1
1954	CIN N		.000	.000	1	0	0	0	0	0.0	0	0	0	0	0	1	0	0	0	0	0	0.0	–	
9 yrs.		758	.259	.324	2661	690	95	24	10	0.4	351	266	347	152	28	13	0	1359	2160	141	483	4.8	.961	SS-717, 3B-15, 2B-2

Nig Lipscomb

LIPSCOMB, GERARD
B. Feb. 24, 1911, Rutherfordton, N. C. D. Feb. 27, 1978, Huntersville, N. C.
BR TR 6' 175 lbs.

Year	Team	Games	BA	SA	AB	H	2B	3B	HR	HR%	R	RBI	BB	SO	SB	AB	H	PO	A	E	DP	TC/G	FA	G by Pos
1937	STL A	36	.323	.438	96	31	9	1	0	0.0	11	8	11	10	0	4	1	73	82	6	28	4.5	.963	2B-27, P-3, 3B-1

Bob Lipski

LIPSKI, ROBERT PETER
B. July 7, 1938, Scranton, Pa.
BL TR 6'1" 180 lbs.

Year	Team	Games	BA	SA	AB	H	2B	3B	HR	HR%	R	RBI	BB	SO	SB	AB	H	PO	A	E	DP	TC/G	FA	G by Pos
1963	CLE A	2	.000	.000	1	0	0	0	0	0.0	0	0	0	1	0	0	0	3	0	0	0	1.5	1.000	C-2

Nelson Liriano

LIRIANO, NELSON ARTURO
Born Nelson Arturo Liriano y Bonilla.
B. June 3, 1964, Santo Domingo, Dominican Republic
BB TR 5'10" 165 lbs.

Year	Team	Games	BA	SA	AB	H	2B	3B	HR	HR%	R	RBI	BB	SO	SB	AB	H	PO	A	E	DP	TC/G	FA	G by Pos
1987	TOR A	37	.241	.342	158	38	6	2	2	1.3	29	10	16	22	13	1	1	83	107	1	28	5.2	.995	2B-37
1988		99	.264	.333	276	73	6	2	3	1.1	36	23	11	40	12	16	4	121	177	12	48	3.1	.961	2B-80, DH-11, 3B-1
1989		132	.263	.376	418	110	26	3	5	1.2	51	53	43	51	16	7	4	267	330	12	76	4.6	.980	2B-122, DH-5
3 yrs.		268	.259	.356	852	221	38	7	10	1.2	116	86	70	113	41	24	9	471	614	25	152	4.1	.977	2B-239, DH-16, 3B-1

LEAGUE CHAMPIONSHIP SERIES

Year	Team	Games	BA	SA	AB	H	2B	3B	HR	HR%	R	RBI	BB	SO	SB	AB	H	PO	A	E	DP	TC/G	FA	G by Pos
1989	TOR A	3	.429	.429	7	3	0	0	0	0.0	1	1	2	0	3	0	0	4	3	1	1	2.7	.875	2B-3

Joe Lis

LIS, JOSEPH ANTHONY
B. Aug. 15, 1946, Somerville, N. J.
BR TR 6' 195 lbs.

Year	Team	Games	BA	SA	AB	H	2B	3B	HR	HR%	R	RBI	BB	SO	SB	AB	H	PO	A	E	DP	TC/G	FA	G by Pos
1970	PHI N	13	.189	.324	37	7	2	0	1	2.7	1	4	5	11	0	4	0	18	0	1	0	1.5	.947	OF-9
1971		59	.211	.407	123	26	6	0	6	4.9	16	16	16	43	0	22	3	42	2	1	0	0.8	.978	OF-35
1972		62	.243	.414	140	34	6	0	6	4.3	13	18	30	34	0	19	4	242	16	2	19	4.2	.992	1B-30, OF-14
1973	MIN A	103	.245	.403	253	62	11	1	9	3.6	37	25	28	66	0	4	1	626	48	9	59	6.6	.987	1B-96, DH-1
1974	2 teams	MIN A	(24G – .195)		CLE A	(57G – .202)																		
"	total	81	.200	.340	150	30	3	0	6	4.0	20	19	19	42	1	15	4	297	27	4	24	4.0	.988	1B-49, DH-9, 3B-9, OF-1
1975	CLE A	9	.308	.923	13	4	2	0	2	15.4	4	8	3	3	0	0	0	39	2	0	2	4.6	1.000	1B-8, DH-1
1976		20	.314	.451	51	16	1	0	2	3.9	4	7	8	8	0	3	0	107	8	0	10	5.8	1.000	1B-17, DH-1
1977	SEA A	9	.231	.231	13	3	0	0	0	0.0	1	1	1	2	0	1	1	24	1	0	3	2.8	1.000	1B-4, C-1
8 yrs.		356	.233	.399	780	182	31	1	32	4.1	96	92	110	209	1	69	13	1395	104	17	117	4.3	.989	1B-204, OF-59, DH-12, 3B-9, C-1

Rick Lisi

LISI, RICARDO PATRICK EMILO
B. Mar. 17, 1956, Halifax, Nova Scotia, Canada
BR TR 6' 175 lbs.

Year	Team	Games	BA	SA	AB	H	2B	3B	HR	HR%	R	RBI	BB	SO	SB	AB	H	PO	A	E	DP	TC/G	FA	G by Pos
1981	TEX A	9	.313	.313	16	5	0	0	0	0.0	6	1	4	0	0	2	0	9	0	0	0	1.0	1.000	OF-8

Pete Lister

LISTER, MORRIS ELMER
B. July 21, 1881, Savanna, Ill. D. Mar. 27, 1947, St. Petersburg, Fla.
BR TR

Year	Team	Games	BA	SA	AB	H	2B	3B	HR	HR%	R	RBI	BB	SO	SB	AB	H	PO	A	E	DP	TC/G	FA	G by Pos
1907	CLE A	22	.277	.308	65	18	2	0	0	0.0	5	4	3		2	0	0	219	10	6	12	10.7	.974	1B-22

Bryan Little

LITTLE, RICHARD BRYAN
B. Oct. 8, 1959, Houston, Tex.
BB TR 5'11" 155 lbs.

Year	Team		Games	BA	SA	AB	H	2B	3B	HR	HR%	R	RBI	BB	SO	SB	Pinch Hit AB	Pinch Hit H	PO	A	E	DP	TC/G	FA	G by Pos

Bryan Little *continued*

1982	MON	N	29	.214	.214	42	9	0	0	0	0.0	6	3	4	6	2	2	0	21	32	1	2	1.9	.981	2B-16, SS-10
1983			106	.260	.329	350	91	15	3	1	0.3	48	34	50	22	4	4	1	181	248	9	44	4.1	.979	SS-66, 2B-51
1984			85	.244	.293	266	65	11	1	0	0.0	31	9	34	19	2	7	3	137	199	6	44	4.0	.982	2B-77, SS-2
1985	CHI	A	73	.250	.340	188	47	9	1	2	1.1	35	27	26	21	0	3	0	101	165	5	33	3.7	.982	2B-68, 3B-2, SS-1
1986	2 teams		CHI A (20G – .171)			NY A (14G – .195)																			
"	total		34	.184	.211	76	14	2	0	0	0.0	6	2	6	11	0	3	0	69	69	2	15	4.1	.986	2B-26, SS-7, 3B-1
	5 yrs.		327	.245	.306	922	226	37	5	3	0.3	126	77	120	79	8	19	4	509	713	23	138	3.8	.982	2B-238, SS-86, 3B-3

Harry Little

LITTLE, HARRY A.
B. St. Louis, Mo.   TR

| 1877 | 2 teams | | STL N (3G – .167) | | | LOU N (1G – .000) | | | | | | | | | | | | | | | | | | | |
| " | total | | 4 | .133 | .133 | 15 | 2 | 0 | 0 | 0 | 0.0 | 2 | 0 | 2 | 7 | | 0 | 0 | 7 | 5 | 1 | 0 | 3.3 | .923 | OF-3, 2B-1 |

Jack Little

LITTLE, WILLIAM ARTHUR
B. Mar. 12, 1891, Mart, Tex.   D. July 27, 1961, Dallas, Tex.   BR TR 5'11" 175 lbs.

| 1912 | NY | A | 3 | .250 | .250 | 12 | 3 | 0 | 0 | 0 | 0.0 | 0 | 1 | 0 | 2 | 0 | 0 | 0 | 6 | 1 | 0 | 0 | 2.3 | 1.000 | OF-3 |

Scott Little

LITTLE, DENNIS SCOTT
B. Jan. 19, 1963, East St. Louis, Ill.   BR TR 6' 198 lbs.

| 1989 | PIT | N | 3 | .250 | .250 | 4 | 1 | 0 | 0 | 0 | 0.0 | 0 | 0 | 0 | 1 | 0 | 2 | 0 | 1 | 1 | 0 | 1 | 0.7 | 1.000 | OF-1 |

Dennis Littlejohn

LITTLEJOHN, DENNIS GERALD
B. Oct. 4, 1954, Santa Monica, Calif.   BR TR 6'2" 200 lbs.

1978	SF	N	2	–	–	0	0	0	0	0	–	0	0	0	0	0	0	0	0	0	0	0	0.0	–	C-2
1979			63	.197	.254	193	38	6	1	0	0.5	15	13	21	46	0	0	0	366	43	6	7	6.6	.986	C-63
1980			13	.241	.276	29	7	1	0	0	0.0	2	2	7	7	0	3	0	51	8	1	1	4.6	.983	C-10
	3 yrs.		78	.203	.257	222	45	7	1	1	0.5	17	15	28	53	0	3	0	417	51	7	8	6.1	.985	C-75

Larry Littleton

LITTLETON, LARRY MARVIN
B. Apr. 3, 1954, Charlotte, N. C.   BR TR 6'1" 185 lbs.

| 1981 | CLE | A | 26 | .000 | .000 | 23 | 0 | 0 | 0 | 0 | 0.0 | 2 | 1 | 3 | 6 | 0 | 4 | 0 | 11 | 0 | 0 | 0 | 0.4 | 1.000 | OF-24 |

Greg Litton

LITTON, JON GREGORY
B. July 13, 1964, New Orleans, La.   BR TR 6' 175 lbs.

| 1989 | SF | N | 71 | .252 | .413 | 143 | 36 | 5 | 3 | 4 | 2.8 | 12 | 17 | 7 | 29 | 0 | 27 | 9 | 44 | 66 | 3 | 5 | 1.6 | .973 | 3B-34, 2B-15, SS-9, OF-6, C-2 |

LEAGUE CHAMPIONSHIP SERIES

| 1989 | SF | N | 1 | 1.000 | 1.000 | 1 | 1 | 0 | 0 | 0 | 0.0 | 0 | 0 | 0 | 0 | 0 | 1 | 1 | 0 | 0 | 0 | 0 | 0.0 | – | |

WORLD SERIES

| 1989 | SF | N | 2 | .500 | 1.167 | 6 | 3 | 1 | 0 | 1 | 16.7 | 0 | 3 | 0 | 0 | 0 | 1 | 1 | 2 | 3 | 0 | 0 | 2.5 | 1.000 | 2B-2, 3B-1 |

Jack Littrell

LITTRELL, JACK NAPIER
B. Jan. 22, 1929, Louisville, Ky.   BR TR 6' 179 lbs.

1952	PHI	A	4	.000	.000	2	0	0	0	0	0.0	0	0	1	2	0	1	0	0	2	0	1	0.5	1.000	SS-2, 3B-1
1954			9	.300	.467	30	9	2	0	1	3.3	7	3	6	3	1	0	0	19	22	1	8	4.7	.976	SS-9
1955	KC	A	37	.200	.229	70	14	0	1	0	0.0	7	1	4	12	0	6	0	55	51	6	12	3.0	.946	SS-22, 1B-6, 2B-4
1957	CHI	N	61	.190	.261	153	29	4	2	1	0.7	8	13	9	43	0	2	1	84	131	12	23	3.7	.947	SS-47, 2B-6, 3B-5
	4 yrs.		111	.204	.275	255	52	6	3	2	0.8	22	17	20	60	1	9	1	158	206	19	44	3.5	.950	SS-80, 2B-10, 3B-6, 1B-6

Danny Litwhiler

LITWHILER, DANIEL WEBSTER
B. Aug. 31, 1916, Ringtown, Pa.   BR TR 5'10½" 198 lbs.

1940	PHI	N	36	.345	.493	142	49	2	2	5	3.5	19	17	3	13	1	2	0	68	4	1	1	2.0	.986	OF-36
1941			151	.305	.466	590	180	29	6	18	3.1	72	66	39	43	1	1	0	393	12	15	3	2.8	.964	OF-150
1942			151	.271	.389	591	160	25	9	9	1.5	59	56	27	42	2	0	0	308	9	0	0	2.1	1.000	OF-151
1943	2 teams		PHI N (36G – .259)			STL N (80G – .279)																			
"	total		116	.272	.428	397	108	20	3	12	3.0	63	48	30	45	2	8	0	225	12	1	2	2.1	.996	OF-104
1944	STL	N	140	.264	.427	492	130	25	5	15	3.0	53	82	37	56	2	3	1	294	6	8	1	2.2	.974	OF-136
1946	2 teams		STL N (6G – .000)			BOS N (79G – .291)																			
"	total		85	.286	.444	252	72	12	2	8	3.2	29	38	20	24	1	17	5	128	7	2	0	1.6	.985	OF-65, 3B-2
1947	BOS	N	91	.261	.394	226	59	6	2	7	3.1	38	31	25	43	1	23	4	119	2	3	0	1.4	.976	OF-66
1948	2 teams		BOS N (13G – .273)			CIN N (106G – .275)																			
"	total		119	.275	.456	371	102	21	2	14	3.8	51	50	52	43	1	15	5	200	38	3	4	2.0	.988	OF-91, 3B-15
1949	CIN	N	102	.291	.473	292	85	18	1	11	3.8	35	48	44	42	0	14	3	147	12	3	2	1.6	.981	OF-82, 3B-3
1950			54	.259	.455	112	29	4	0	6	5.4	15	12	20	21	0	9	4	46	0	2	0	0.9	.958	OF-29
1951			12	.276	.517	29	8	1	0	2	6.9	3	3	2	5	0	4	2	14	0	1	0	1.3	.933	OF-7
	11 yrs.		1057	.281	.438	3494	982	162	32	107	3.1	428	451	299	377	11	106	24	1942	99	39	13	2.0	.981	OF-917, 3B-20

WORLD SERIES

1943	STL	N	5	.267	.333	15	4	1	0	0	0.0	0	2	2	4	0	1	0	11	0	0	0	2.2	1.000	OF-4
1944			5	.200	.400	20	4	1	0	1	5.0	2	1	2	7	0	0	1	5	0	0	0	1.0	1.000	OF-5
	2 yrs.		10	.229	.371	35	8	2	0	1	2.9	2	3	4	11	0	1	1	16	0	0	0	1.6	1.000	OF-9

Mickey Livingston

LIVINGSTON, THOMPSON ORVILLE
B. Nov. 15, 1914, Newberry, S. C.   D. Apr. 3, 1983, Newberry, S. C.   BR TR 6'1½" 185 lbs.

1938	WAS	A	2	.750	1.250	4	3	0	0	0	0.0	2	0	0	0	0	0	0	2	0	1	0	1.5	.667	C-2
1941	PHI	N	95	.203	.242	207	42	6	1	0	0.0	16	18	20	38	2	18	4	263	34	8	5	3.2	.974	C-71, 1B-1
1942			89	.205	.264	239	49	6	1	2	0.8	20	22	25	20	0	6	2	334	37	5	13	4.2	.987	C-78, 1B-6

Year	Team	Games	BA	SA	AB	H	2B	3B	HR	HR%	R	RBI	BB	SO	SB	Pinch Hit AB	Pinch Hit H	PO	A	E	DP	TC/G	FA	G by Pos

Mickey Livingston *continued*

Year	Team	Games	BA	SA	AB	H	2B	3B	HR	HR%	R	RBI	BB	SO	SB	AB	H	PO	A	E	DP	TC/G	FA	G by Pos
1943	2 teams	PHI N (84G – .249)			CHI N (36G – .261)																			
"	total	120	.253	.362	376	95	14	3	7	1.9	36	34	31	26	2	2	0	422	66	4	11	4.1	.992	C-115, 1B-6
1945	CHI N	71	.254	.317	224	57	4	2	2	0.9	19	23	19	6	2	2	0	264	27	3	2	4.1	.990	C-68, 1B-1
1946		66	.256	.369	176	45	14	0	2	1.1	14	20	20	19	0	8	1	239	25	5	3	4.1	.981	C-56
1947	2 teams	CHI N (19G – .212)			NY N (5G – .167)																			
"	total	24	.205	.256	39	8	0	0	0	0.0	2	3	2	7	0	14	5	30	2	1	0	1.4	.970	C-9
1948	NY N	45	.212	.333	99	21	4	1	2	2.0	9	12	21	11	1	3	1	135	10	3	2	3.3	.980	C-42
1949	2 teams	NY N (19G – .298)			BOS N (28G – .234)																			
"	total	47	.264	.413	121	32	4	1	4	3.3	12	18	5	13	0	6	0	136	14	3	0	3.3	.980	C-41
1951	BKN N	2	.400	.400	5	2	0	0	0	0.0	0	2	1	0	0	0	0	3	2	0	1	2.5	1.000	C-2
10 yrs.		561	.238	.326	1490	354	56	9	19	1.3	128	153	144	141	7	59	13	1828	217	33	37	3.7	.984	C-484, 1B-14
WORLD SERIES																								
1945	CHI N	6	.364	.500	22	8	3	0	0	0.0	3	4	1	1	0	0	0	22	4	0	0	4.3	1.000	C-6

Paddy Livingston

LIVINGSTON, PATRICK JOSEPH
B. Jan. 14, 1880, Cleveland, Ohio   D. Sept. 19, 1977, Cleveland, Ohio
BR TR 5'8" 197 lbs.

Year	Team	Games	BA	SA	AB	H	2B	3B	HR	HR%	R	RBI	BB	SO	SB	AB	H	PO	A	E	DP	TC/G	FA	G by Pos
1901	CLE A	1	.000	.000	2	0	0	0	0	0.0	0	0	0		0	0	0	1	0	0		1.0	1.000	C-1
1906	CIN N	50	.158	.223	139	22	1	4	0	0.0	8	8	12		0	3	0	202	62	11	5	5.5	.960	C-47
1909	PHI A	64	.234	.314	175	41	6	4	0	0.0	15	15	15		4	0	0	306	106	13	6	6.6	.969	C-64
1910		37	.208	.292	120	25	4	3	0	0.0	11	9	6		2	0	0	205	68	9	5	7.6	.968	C-37
1911		27	.239	.296	71	17	4	0	0	0.0	9	8	7		1	1	0	133	36	4	1	6.4	.977	C-26
1912	CLE A	19	.234	.319	47	11	2	1	0	0.0	5	3	1		0	6	0	63	18	2	0	4.4	.976	C-13
1917	STL N	7	.200	.200	20	4	0	0	0	0.0	0	2	0		1	2	1	0	26	6	0	4.6	1.000	C-6
7 yrs.		205	.209	.280	574	120	17	12	0	0.0	48	45	41		1	9	11	0	935	297	39	17	6.2	.969	C-194

Abel Lizotte

LIZOTTE, ABEL
B. Apr. 13, 1870, Lewiston, Me.   D. Dec. 4, 1926, Wilkes-Barre, Pa.

Year	Team	Games	BA	SA	AB	H	2B	3B	HR	HR%	R	RBI	BB	SO	SB	AB	H	PO	A	E	DP	TC/G	FA	G by Pos
1896	PIT N	7	.103	.103	29	3	0	0	0	0.0	3	3	2	2	1	0	0	53	6	3	3	8.9	.952	1B-7

Winston Llenas

LLENAS, WINSTON ENRIQUILLO (Chilote)
Born Winston Enriquillo Llenas y Davilla.
B. Sept. 23, 1943, Santiago, Dominican Republic
BR TR 5'10" 165 lbs.

Year	Team	Games	BA	SA	AB	H	2B	3B	HR	HR%	R	RBI	BB	SO	SB	AB	H	PO	A	E	DP	TC/G	FA	G by Pos
1968	CAL A	16	.128	.154	39	5	1	0	0	0.0	5	1	2	5	0	7	0	9	15	6	0	1.9	.800	3B-9
1969		34	.170	.213	47	8	2	0	0	0.0	4	0	2	10	0	26	7	2	11	1	1	0.4	.929	3B-9
1972		44	.266	.313	64	17	3	0	0	0.0	3	7	3	8	0	28	7	7	16	2	2	0.6	.920	3B-10, OF-2, 2B-2
1973		78	.269	.300	130	35	1	0	1	0.8	16	25	10	16	0	56	16	42	37	1	3	1.0	.988	2B-20, 3B-11, OF-4
1974		72	.261	.348	138	36	6	0	2	1.4	16	17	11	19	0	33	7	48	11	0	2	0.8	1.000	OF-32, 2B-15, DH-10, 3B-2
1975		56	.186	.221	113	21	4	0	0	0.0	6	11	10	11	0	24	7	76	36	0	16	2.0	1.000	2B-12, OF-10, DH-6, 1B-6, 3B-3
6 yrs.		300	.230	.279	531	122	17	0	3	0.6	50	61	38	69	0	174	44	184	126	10	24	1.1	.969	2B-49, OF-48, 3B-44, DH-16, 1B-6

Mike Loan

LOAN, WILLIAM JOSEPH
B. Sept. 27, 1894, Philadelphia, Pa.   D. Nov. 21, 1966, Springfield, Pa.
BR TR 5'11" 185 lbs.

Year	Team	Games	BA	SA	AB	H	2B	3B	HR	HR%	R	RBI	BB	SO	SB	AB	H	PO	A	E	DP	TC/G	FA	G by Pos
1912	PHI N	1	.500	.500	2	1	0	0	0	0.0	1	0	0	0	0	0	0	1	0	0	0	1.0	1.000	C-1

Bobby Loane

LOANE, ROBERT KENNETH
B. Aug. 6, 1914, Berkeley, Calif.
BR TR 6' 190 lbs.

Year	Team	Games	BA	SA	AB	H	2B	3B	HR	HR%	R	RBI	BB	SO	SB	AB	H	PO	A	E	DP	TC/G	FA	G by Pos
1939	WAS A	3	.000	.000	9	0	0	0	0	0.0	2	1	4	4	0	0	0	8	2	1	1	3.7	.909	OF-3
1940	BOS N	13	.227	.364	22	5	3	0	0	0.0	4	1	2	5	2	1	1	19	2	0	1	1.6	1.000	OF-10
2 yrs.		16	.161	.258	31	5	3	0	0	0.0	6	2	6	9	2	1	1	27	4	1	2	2.0	.969	OF-13

Frank Lobert

LOBERT, FRANK JOHN
Brother of Hans Lobert.
B. Nov. 26, 1883, Williamsport, Pa.   D. May 29, 1932, Pittsburgh, Pa.
BR TR 6' 180 lbs.

Year	Team	Games	BA	SA	AB	H	2B	3B	HR	HR%	R	RBI	BB	SO	SB	AB	H	PO	A	E	DP	TC/G	FA	G by Pos
1914	BAL F	11	.200	.267	30	6	0	1	0	0.0	3	2	0		0	1	0	17	5	3	1	2.3	.880	3B-7, 2B-1

Hans Lobert

LOBERT, JOHN BERNARD (Honus)
Brother of Frank Lobert.
B. Oct. 18, 1881, Wilmington, Del.   D. Sept. 14, 1968, Philadelphia, Pa.
Manager 1938, 1942.
BR TR 5'9" 170 lbs.

Year	Team	Games	BA	SA	AB	H	2B	3B	HR	HR%	R	RBI	BB	SO	SB	AB	H	PO	A	E	DP	TC/G	FA	G by Pos
1903	PIT N	5	.077	.154	13	1	1	0	0		1	0	1		1	0	0	6	8	3	1	3.4	.824	3B-3, SS-1, 2B-1
1905	CHI N	14	.196	.239	46	9	2	0	0	0.0	7	1	3		4	0	0	20	25	4	2	3.5	.918	3B-13, OF-1
1906	CIN N	79	.310	.366	268	83	5	5	0	0.0	39	19	19		20	4	1	118	178	20	8	4.0	.937	3B-35, SS-31, 2B-10, OF-1
1907		148	.246	.313	537	132	9	12	1	0.2	61	41	37		30	1	0	311	392	46	53	5.1	.939	SS-142, 3B-5
1908		155	.293	.407	570	167	17	18	4	0.7	71	63	46		47	0	0	222	270	42	16	3.4	.921	3B-99, SS-35, OF-21
1909		122	.212	.294	425	90	13	5	4	0.9	50	52	48		30	0	0	182	204	33	16	3.4	.921	3B-122
1910		93	.309	.395	314	97	6	6	3	1.0	43	40	30	9	41	0	0	123	164	21	11	3.3	.932	3B-90
1911	PHI N	147	.285	.405	541	154	20	9	9	1.7	94	72	66	31	40	0	0	202	213	20	13	3.0	.954	3B-147
1912		65	.327	.436	257	84	12	5	2	0.8	37	33	19	13	13	1	0	80	86	4	3	2.6	.976	3B-65
1913		150	.300	.424	573	172	28	11	7	1.2	98	55	42	34	41	1	0	184	228	11	13	2.8	.974	3B-145, SS-3, 2B-1
1914		135	.275	.349	505	139	24	5	1	0.2	83	52	49	32	31	0	0	194	178	22	10	2.9	.944	3B-133, SS-2
1915	NY N	106	.251	.319	386	97	18	4	0	0.0	46	38	25	24	14	3	1	109	192	16	9	3.0	.950	3B-106
1916		48	.224	.316	76	17	3	2	0	0.0	6	11	5	8	2	24	6	14	35	2	2	1.1	.961	3B-20
1917		50	.192	.269	52	10	1	0	1	1.9	4	5	5	5	2	24	3	10	19	3	2	0.6	.906	3B-21
14 yrs.		1317	.274	.366	4563	1252	159	82	32	0.7	640	482	395	156	316	58	11	1775	2192	247	159	3.2	.941	3B-1003, SS-214, OF-23, 2B-12

Year	Team		Games	BA	SA	AB	H	2B	3B	HR	HR%	R	RBI	BB	SO	SB	Pinch Hit AB	Pinch Hit H	PO	A	E	DP	TC/G	FA	G by Pos

Harry Lochhead

LOCHHEAD, ROBERT HENRY
B. Mar. 29, 1876, Stockton, Calif. D. Aug. 22, 1909, Stockton, Calif. TR

1899	CLE	N	148	.238	.261	541	129	7	1	1	0.2	52	43	21		23	0	0	320	493	81	54	6.0	.909	SS-146, 2B-1, P-1
1901	2 teams			DET A (1G – .500)		PHI A (9G – .088)																			
"	total		10	.132	.132	38	5	0	0	0	0.0	5	2	3		0	0	0	12	22	10	1	4.4	.773	SS-10
2 yrs.			158	.231	.252	579	134	7	1	1	0.2	57	45	24		23	0	0	332	515	91	55	5.9	.903	SS-156, 2B-1, P-1

Don Lock

LOCK, DON WILSON
B. July 27, 1936, Wichita, Kans. BR TR 6'2" 195 lbs.

1962	WAS	A	71	.253	.458	225	57	6	2	12	5.3	30	37	30	63	4	3	1	144	2	4	0	2.1	.973	OF-67
1963			149	.252	.446	531	134	20	1	27	5.1	71	82	70	151	7	5	2	377	14	8	6	2.7	.980	OF-146
1964			152	.248	.461	512	127	17	4	28	5.5	73	80	79	137	4	6	1	354	19	5	3	2.5	.987	OF-149
1965			143	.215	.371	418	90	15	1	16	3.8	52	39	57	115	1	8	3	278	6	9	3	2.0	.969	OF-136
1966			138	.233	.396	386	90	13	1	16	4.1	52	48	57	126	2	13	5	295	8	7	1	2.2	.977	OF-129
1967	PHI	N	112	.252	.435	313	79	13	1	14	4.5	46	51	43	98	9	25	2	172	8	5	2	1.7	.973	OF-97
1968			99	.210	.351	248	52	7	2	8	3.2	27	34	26	64	3	25	3	145	2	7	1	1.6	.955	OF-78
1969	2 teams			PHI N (4G – .000)		BOS A (53G – .224)																			
"	total		57	.210	.274	62	13	1	0	1	1.6	8	2	11	22	0	22	0	34	2	0	0	0.6	1.000	OF-29, 1B-4
8 yrs.			921	.238	.417	2695	642	92	12	122	4.5	359	373	373	776	30	107	19	1799	61	45	16	2.1	.976	OF-831, 1B-4

Marshall Locke

LOCKE, MARSHALL
B. Indianapolis, Ind. Deceased.

| 1884 | IND | AA | 7 | .241 | .310 | 29 | 7 | 0 | 1 | 0 | 0.0 | 5 | | 0 | | | 0 | 0 | 7 | 1 | 2 | 0 | 1.4 | .800 | OF-7 |

Gene Locklear

LOCKLEAR, GENE
B. July 19, 1949, Lumberton, N. C. BL TR 5'10" 165 lbs.

1973	2 teams			CIN N (29G – .192)		SD N (67G – .240)																			
"	total		96	.233	.328	180	42	6	1	3	1.7	26	25	23	27	9	44	9	81	2	4	0	0.9	.954	OF-42
1974	SD	N	39	.270	.405	74	20	3	2	1	1.4	7	3	4	12	0	25	7	22	1	0	0	0.6	1.000	OF-12
1975			100	.321	.439	237	76	11	1	5	2.1	31	27	22	26	4	48	14	92	4	3	1	1.0	.970	OF-51
1976	2 teams			SD N (43G – .224)		NY A (13G – .219)																			
"	total		56	.222	.263	99	22	4	0	0	0.0	11	9	6	22	0	33	9	24	0	1	0	0.4	.960	OF-14, DH-6
1977	NY	A	1	.600	.600	5	3	0	0	0	0.0	1	2	0	0	0	0	0	2	0	1	0	3.0	.667	OF-1
5 yrs.			292	.274	.373	595	163	24	4	9	1.5	76	66	55	87	13	150	39	221	7	9	1	0.8	.962	OF-120, DH-6

Stu Locklin

LOCKLIN, STUART CARLTON
B. July 22, 1928, Appleton, Wis. BL TL 6'1½" 190 lbs.

1955	CLE	A	16	.167	.222	18	3	1	0	0	0.0	4	0	3	4	1	6	1	3	0	0	0	0.2	1.000	OF-7
1956			9	.167	.167	6	1	0	0	0	0.0	0	0	0	1	0	4	0	1	0	0	0	0.1	1.000	OF-1
2 yrs.			25	.167	.208	24	4	1	0	0	0.0	4	0	3	5	1	10	1	4	0	0	0	0.2	1.000	OF-8

Whitey Lockman

LOCKMAN, CARROLL WALTER
B. July 25, 1926, Lowell, N. C.
Manager 1972-74. BL TR 6'1" 175 lbs.

1945	NY	N	32	.341	.481	129	44	9	0	3	2.3	16	18	13	10	1	0	0	72	1	3	1	2.4	.961	OF-32
1947			2	.500	.500	2	1	0	0	0	0.0	0	0	1	0	0	2	1	0	0	0	0	0.0	–	
1948			146	.286	.454	584	167	24	10	18	3.1	117	59	68	63	8	1	0	388	6	5	0	2.7	.987	OF-144
1949			151	.301	.429	617	186	32	7	11	1.8	97	65	62	31	12	0	0	353	10	10	1	2.5	.973	OF-151
1950			129	.295	.490	532	157	28	5	6	1.1	72	52	42	29	1	1	0	305	11	7	3	2.5	.978	OF-128
1951			153	.282	.407	614	173	27	7	12	2.0	85	73	50	32	4	0	0	1120	92	17	115	8.0	.986	1B-119, OF-34
1952			154	.290	.396	606	176	17	4	13	2.1	99	58	67	52	2	0	0	1435	111	13	155	10.1	.992	1B-154
1953			150	.295	.389	607	179	22	4	9	1.5	85	61	52	36	3	3	1	1106	102	13	96	8.1	.989	1B-120, OF-30
1954			148	.251	.375	570	143	17	3	16	2.8	73	60	59	31	2	1	0	1265	88	18	122	9.3	.987	1B-145, OF-2
1955			147	.273	.384	576	157	19	0	15	2.6	76	49	39	34	3	2	0	780	38	6	62	5.6	.993	OF-81, 1B-68
1956	2 teams			NY N (48G – .272)		STL N (70G – .249)																			
"	total		118	.260	.304	362	94	7	3	1	0.3	27	20	34	25	2	17	4	234	7	11	3	2.1	.956	OF-96, 1B-9
1957	NY	N	133	.248	.331	456	113	9	4	7	1.5	51	30	39	19	5	8	0	1022	72	14	94	8.3	.987	1B-102, OF-27
1958	SF	N	92	.238	.328	122	29	1	3	2	1.6	15	7	13	8	1	45	11	100	21	2	10	1.3	.984	OF-25, 2B-15, 1B-7
1959	2 teams			BAL A (38G – .217)		CIN N (52G – .262)																			
"	total		90	.242	.307	153	37	6	2	0	0.0	17	9	12	10	0	33	4	227	33	5	30	2.9	.981	1B-42, 2B-11, OF-2, 3B-1
1960	CIN	N	21	.200	.500	10	2	0	0	1	10.0	6	1	2	3	0	8	1	10	0	0	2	0.5	1.000	1B-5
15 yrs.			1666	.279	.391	5940	1658	222	49	114	1.9	836	563	552	383	43	121	22	8417	592	124	694	5.5	.986	1B-771, OF-752, 2B-26, 3B-1

WORLD SERIES

1951	NY	N	6	.240	.440	25	6	1	0	1	4.0	1	4	1	2	0	0	0	48	5	2	4	9.2	.964	1B-6
1954			4	.111	.111	18	2	0	0	0	0.0	2	0	1	2	0	0	0	40	0	0	2	10.0	1.000	1B-4
2 yrs.			10	.186	.302	43	8	2	0	1	2.3	3	4	2	4	0	0	0	88	5	2	6	9.5	.979	1B-10

Skip Lockwood

LOCKWOOD, CLAUDE EDWARD
B. Aug. 17, 1946, Roslindale, Mass. BR TR 6'1" 175 lbs.

1965	KC	A	42	.121	.121	33	4	0	0	0	0.0	7	11	0	25	3	9	4	0	1	0.3	1.000	3B-7
1969	SEA	A	6	.000	.000	7	0	0	0	0	0.0	0	0	0	2	0	2	5	0	1	1.2	1.000	P-6
1970	MIL	A	27	.226	.302	53	12	1	0	1	1.9	2	2	1	11	0	14	18	1	1	1.2	.970	P-27
1971			36	.081	.145	62	5	1	0	1	1.6	2	4	5	20	0	9	18	0	2	0.8	1.000	P-33
1972			31	.132	.132	53	7	0	0	0	0.0	3	0	3	12	0	10	13	1	1	0.8	.958	P-29
1973			37	–	–	0	0	0	0	0	–	0	0	0	0	0	11	23	2	1	1.0	.944	P-37
1974	CAL	A	37	–	–	0	0	0	0	0	–	0	0	0	0	0	3	11	0	1	0.4	1.000	P-37
1975	NY	N	24	.167	.167	6	1	0	0	0	0.0	1	1	0	1	0	1	3	1	0	0.2	.800	P-24
1976			56	.333	.389	18	6	1	0	0	0.0	2	3	2	6	0	2	11	2	1	0.3	.867	P-56
1977			63	.200	.200	15	3	0	0	0	0.0	1	1	0	4	0	1	6	1	0	0.1	.875	P-63
1978			57	.182	.545	11	2	1	0	1	9.1	2	1	0	5	0	4	5	1	0	0.2	.900	P-57
1979			28	.000	.000	2	0	0	0	0	0.0	0	0	0	1	0	3	1	1	0	0.2	.800	P-27

Year	Team	Games	BA	SA	AB	H	2B	3B	HR	HR%	R	RBI	BB	SO	SB	Pinch Hit AB	H	PO	A	E	DP	TC/G	FA	G by Pos

Skip Lockwood *continued*

Year	Team	Games	BA	SA	AB	H	2B	3B	HR	HR%	R	RBI	BB	SO	SB	PH AB	PH H	PO	A	E	DP	TC/G	FA	G by Pos
1980	BOS A	24	–	–	0	0	0	0	0	–	0	0	0	0	0	0	0	3	3	0	0	0.3	1.000	P-24
13 yrs.		468	.154	.204	260	40	4	0	3	1.2	15	11	18	66	0	25	3	70	123	10	11	0.4	.951	P-420, 3B-7

Dario Lodigiani

LODIGIANI, DARIO ANTONIO (Lodi)
B. July 16, 1916, San Francisco, Calif. BR TR 5'8" 150 lbs.

Year	Team	Games	BA	SA	AB	H	2B	3B	HR	HR%	R	RBI	BB	SO	SB	PH AB	PH H	PO	A	E	DP	TC/G	FA	G by Pos
1938	PHI A	93	.280	.388	325	91	15	1	6	1.8	36	44	34	25	3	0	0	210	259	25	48	5.3	.949	2B-80, 3B-13
1939		121	.260	.382	393	102	22	4	6	1.5	46	44	42	18	2	4	1	159	263	27	24	3.7	.940	3B-89, 2B-28
1940		1	.000	.000	1	0	0	0	0	0.0	0	0	0	0	0	1	0	0	0	0	0	0.0	–	
1941	CHI A	87	.239	.348	322	77	19	2	4	1.2	39	40	31	19	0	0	0	120	187	12	22	3.7	.962	3B-86
1942		59	.280	.321	168	47	7	0	0	0.0	9	15	18	10	5	1	0	55	118	9	9	3.1	.951	3B-43, 2B-7
1946		44	.245	.297	155	38	8	0	0	0.0	12	13	16	14	4	0	0	41	88	9	4	3.1	.935	3B-44
6 yrs.		405	.260	.358	1364	355	71	7	16	1.2	142	156	141	86	12	10	2	585	915	82	107	3.9	.948	3B-275, 2B-115

George Loepp

LOEPP, GEORGE HERBERT
B. Sept. 11, 1901, Detroit, Mich. D. Sept. 4, 1967, Los Angeles, Calif. BR TR 5'11" 170 lbs.

Year	Team	Games	BA	SA	AB	H	2B	3B	HR	HR%	R	RBI	BB	SO	SB	PH AB	PH H	PO	A	E	DP	TC/G	FA	G by Pos
1928	BOS A	15	.176	.275	51	9	3	1	0	0.0	6	3	5	12	0	1	0	35	2	2	1	2.6	.949	OF-14
1930	WAS A	50	.276	.343	134	37	7	1	0	0.0	23	14	20	9	0	1	0	89	3	4	0	1.9	.958	OF-48
2 yrs.		65	.249	.324	185	46	10	2	0	0.0	29	17	25	21	0	2	0	124	5	6	1	2.1	.956	OF-62

Dick Loftus

LOFTUS, RICHARD JOSEPH
B. Mar. 7, 1901, Concord, Mass. D. Jan. 21, 1972, Concord, Mass. BL TR 6' 155 lbs.

Year	Team	Games	BA	SA	AB	H	2B	3B	HR	HR%	R	RBI	BB	SO	SB	PH AB	PH H	PO	A	E	DP	TC/G	FA	G by Pos
1924	BKN N	46	.272	.346	81	22	6	0	0	0.0	18	8	7	2	1	7	3	51	1	0	1	1.1	1.000	OF-29, 1B-1
1925		51	.237	.282	131	31	6	0	0	0.0	16	13	5	5	2	10	1	82	4	2	1	1.7	.977	OF-38
2 yrs.		97	.250	.307	212	53	12	0	0	0.0	34	21	12	7	3	17	4	133	5	2	2	1.4	.986	OF-67, 1B-1

Tom Loftus

LOFTUS, THOMAS JOSEPH
B. Nov. 15, 1856, St. Louis, Mo. D. Apr. 16, 1910, Dubuque, Iowa BR 168 lbs.
Manager 1884, 1888-91, 1900-03.

Year	Team	Games	BA	SA	AB	H	2B	3B	HR	HR%	R	RBI	BB	SO	SB	PH AB	PH H	PO	A	E	DP	TC/G	FA	G by Pos
1877	STL N	3	.182	.182	11	2	0	0	0	0.0	2		0	1		0	0	4	3	2	0	3.0	.778	OF-3
1883	STL AA	6	.182	.182	22	4	0	0	0	0.0	1		2			0	0	15	0	2	0	2.8	.882	OF-6
2 yrs.		9	.182	.182	33	6	0	0	0	0.0	3		2	1		0	0	19	3	4	0	2.9	.846	OF-9

Johnny Logan

LOGAN, JOHN (Yatcha)
B. Mar. 23, 1927, Endicott, N.Y. BR TR 5'11" 175 lbs.

Year	Team	Games	BA	SA	AB	H	2B	3B	HR	HR%	R	RBI	BB	SO	SB	PH AB	PH H	PO	A	E	DP	TC/G	FA	G by Pos
1951	BOS N	62	.219	.272	169	37	7	1	0	0.0	14	16	18	13	0	3	0	98	155	11	31	4.3	.958	SS-58
1952		117	.283	.368	456	129	21	3	4	0.9	56	42	31	33	1	0	0	247	385	18	81	5.6	.972	SS-117
1953	MIL N	150	.273	.398	611	167	27	8	11	1.8	100	73	41	33	2	0	0	295	481	20	104	5.3	.975	SS-150
1954		154	.275	.373	560	154	17	7	8	1.4	66	66	51	51	2	0	0	324	489	26	104	5.4	.969	SS-154
1955		154	.297	.442	595	177	37	5	13	2.2	95	83	58	58	3	0	0	268	511	30	100	5.3	.963	SS-154
1956		148	.281	.431	545	153	27	5	15	2.8	69	46	46	49	3	0	0	266	467	24	94	5.1	.968	SS-148
1957		129	.273	.401	494	135	19	7	10	2.0	59	49	31	49	5	1	1	263	440	29	94	5.7	.960	SS-129
1958		145	.226	.326	530	120	20	0	11	2.1	54	53	40	57	1	1	1	273	481	32	99	5.4	.959	SS-144
1959		138	.291	.411	470	137	17	0	13	2.8	59	50	57	45	1	0	0	260	431	18	78	5.1	.975	SS-138
1960		136	.245	.334	482	118	14	4	7	1.5	52	42	43	40	1	0	0	235	417	30	77	5.0	.956	SS-136
1961	2 teams	MIL N (18G – .105)			PIT N (27G – .231)																			
"	total	45	.197	.268	71	14	5	0	0	0.0	5	6	5	11	0	30	8	12	29	1	6	0.9	.976	SS-8, 3B-7
1962	PIT N	44	.300	.375	80	24	3	0	1	1.3	7	12	7	6	0	23	3	13	35	1	5	1.1	.980	3B-19
1963		81	.232	.254	181	42	2	1	0	0.0	15	9	23	27	0	30	7	77	126	17	29	2.7	.923	SS-44, 3B-4
13 yrs.		1503	.268	.378	5244	1407	216	41	93	1.8	651	547	451	472	19	88	20	2631	4447	257	902	4.9	.965	SS-1380, 3B-30

WORLD SERIES

Year	Team	Games	BA	SA	AB	H	2B	3B	HR	HR%	R	RBI	BB	SO	SB	PH AB	PH H	PO	A	E	DP	TC/G	FA	G by Pos
1957	MIL N	7	.185	.333	27	5	1	0	1	3.7	5	2	3	6	0	0	0	13	25	0	6	5.4	1.000	SS-7
1958		7	.120	.200	25	3	2	0	0	0.0	3	2	2	4	0	0	0	10	24	2	2	5.1	.944	SS-7
2 yrs.		14	.154	.269	52	8	3	0	1	1.9	8	4	5	10	0	0	0	23	49	2	8	5.3	.973	SS-14

Pete Lohman

LOHMAN, GEORGE F.
B. Oct. 21, 1864, Lake Elmo, Minn. D. Nov. 21, 1928, Los Angeles, Calif.

Year	Team	Games	BA	SA	AB	H	2B	3B	HR	HR%	R	RBI	BB	SO	SB	PH AB	PH H	PO	A	E	DP	TC/G	FA	G by Pos
1891	WAS AA	32	.193	.303	109	21	4	1	1	0.9	18	11	16	17	1	0	0	125	35	18	4	5.6	.899	C-21, OF-8, 3B-4, SS-1, 2B-1

Howard Lohr

LOHR, HOWARD SYLVESTER
B. June 3, 1892, Philadelphia, Pa. D. June 9, 1977, Philadelphia, Pa. BR TR 6' 165 lbs.

Year	Team	Games	BA	SA	AB	H	2B	3B	HR	HR%	R	RBI	BB	SO	SB	PH AB	PH H	PO	A	E	DP	TC/G	FA	G by Pos
1914	CIN N	18	.213	.277	47	10	1	1	0	0.0	6	7	0	8	2	1	0	24	1	2	1	1.5	.926	OF-17
1916	CLE A	3	.143	.143	7	1	0	0	0	0.0	0	1	0	1	1	0	0	3	0	0	0	1.0	1.000	OF-3
2 yrs.		21	.204	.259	54	11	1	1	0	0.0	6	8	0	9	3	1	0	27	1	2	1	1.4	.933	OF-20

Lucky Lohrke

LOHRKE, JACK WAYNE
B. Feb. 25, 1924, Los Angeles, Calif. BR TR 6' 180 lbs.

Year	Team	Games	BA	SA	AB	H	2B	3B	HR	HR%	R	RBI	BB	SO	SB	PH AB	PH H	PO	A	E	DP	TC/G	FA	G by Pos
1947	NY N	112	.240	.401	329	79	12	4	11	3.3	44	35	46	29	3	1	0	118	187	20	20	2.9	.938	3B-111
1948		97	.250	.364	280	70	15	1	5	1.8	35	31	30	30	3	9	0	125	170	22	21	3.3	.931	3B-50, 2B-36
1949		55	.267	.456	180	48	11	4	5	2.8	32	22	16	12	3	3	1	86	143	9	13	4.3	.962	2B-23, 3B-19, SS-15
1950		30	.186	.186	43	8	0	0	0	0.0	4	4	4	8	0	13	2	10	18	1	3	1.0	.966	3B-16, 2B-1
1951		23	.200	.275	40	8	0	0	1	2.5	3	2	10	2	0	5	0	11	23	2	2	1.6	.944	3B-17, SS-1
1952	PHI N	25	.207	.207	29	6	0	0	0	0.0	4	1	4	3	0	12	4	7	15	1	3	0.9	.957	SS-5, 3B-3, 2B-1
1953		12	.154	.154	13	2	0	0	0	0.0	3	1	1	2	0	5	2	2	8	2	1	1.0	.833	SS-2, 2B-2, 3B-1
7 yrs.		354	.242	.375	914	221	38	9	22	2.4	125	96	111	86	9	48	9	359	564	57	63	2.8	.942	3B-217, 2B-63, SS-23

WORLD SERIES

Year	Team	Games	BA	SA	AB	H	2B	3B	HR	HR%	R	RBI	BB	SO	SB	PH AB	PH H	PO	A	E	DP	TC/G	FA	G by Pos
1951	NY N	2	.000	.000	2	0	0	0	0	0.0	0	0	0	1	0	2	0	0	0	0	0	0.0	–	

Year	Team	Games	BA	SA	AB	H	2B	3B	HR	HR%	R	RBI	BB	SO	SB	Pinch Hit AB	Pinch Hit H	PO	A	E	DP	TC/G	FA	G by Pos

Al Lois

LOIS, ALBERTO
Born Alberto Louis y Pie.
B. May 6, 1956, Hato Mayor, Dominican Republic
BR TR 5'9" 175 lbs.

Year	Team	Games	BA	SA	AB	H	2B	3B	HR	HR%	R	RBI	BB	SO	SB	PH AB	PH H	PO	A	E	DP	TC/G	FA	G by Pos
1978	PIT	N	3	.250	.750	4	1	0	1	0	0.0	0	0	0	0	1	0	0	0	4	0	0	0	1.3	1.000	OF-2
1979		11	–	–	0	0	0	0	0	–	6	0	0	0	1	0	0	0	0	0	0	0.0	–	OF-2
2 yrs.		14	.250	.750	4	1	0	1	0	0.0	6	0	0	1	1	0	0	4	0	0	0	0.3	1.000	OF-2

Ron Lolich

LOLICH, RONALD JOHN
B. Sept. 19, 1946, Portland, Ore.
BR TR 6'1" 185 lbs.

Year	Team	Games	BA	SA	AB	H	2B	3B	HR	HR%	R	RBI	BB	SO	SB	PH AB	PH H	PO	A	E	DP	TC/G	FA	G by Pos
1971	CHI	A	2	.125	.250	8	1	1	0	0	0.0	0	0	0	2	0	0	0	1	0	0	0	0.5	1.000	OF-2
1972	CLE	A	24	.188	.275	80	15	1	0	2	2.5	4	8	4	20	0	3	0	39	1	0	0	1.7	1.000	OF-22
1973		61	.229	.321	140	32	7	0	2	1.4	16	15	7	27	0	19	4	38	2	4	0	0.7	.909	OF-32, DH-12
3 yrs.		87	.211	.303	228	48	9	0	4	1.8	20	23	11	49	0	22	4	78	3	4	0	1.0	.953	OF-56, DH-12

Sherm Lollar

LOLLAR, JOHN SHERMAN
B. Aug. 23, 1924, Durham, Ark. D. Sept. 24, 1977, Springfield, Mo.
BR TR 6'1" 185 lbs.

Year	Team	Games	BA	SA	AB	H	2B	3B	HR	HR%	R	RBI	BB	SO	SB	PH AB	PH H	PO	A	E	DP	TC/G	FA	G by Pos
1946	CLE	A	28	.242	.387	62	15	6	0	1	1.6	7	9	5	4	0	4	1	89	9	1	1	3.5	.990	C-24
1947	NY	A	11	.219	.375	32	7	1	0	1	3.1	4	6	1	5	0	2	0	44	3	0	0	4.3	1.000	C-9
1948		22	.211	.211	38	8	0	0	0	0.0	0	4	1	6	0	12	4	36	4	1	1	1.9	.976	C-10
1949	STL	A	109	.261	.384	284	74	9	1	8	2.8	28	49	32	22	0	15	2	279	39	4	3	3.0	.988	C-93
1950		126	.280	.449	396	111	22	3	13	3.3	55	65	64	25	2	13	4	367	48	8	9	3.4	.981	C-109
1951	CHI	A	98	.252	.397	310	78	21	0	8	2.6	44	44	43	26	1	10	2	361	48	2	8	4.2	.995	C-85, 3B-1
1952		132	.240	.384	375	90	15	0	13	3.5	35	50	54	34	1	11	2	590	53	7	4	4.9	.989	C-120
1953		113	.287	.416	334	96	19	0	8	2.4	46	54	47	29	1	5	1	473	51	3	2	4.7	.994	C-107, 1B-1
1954		107	.244	.351	316	77	13	0	7	2.2	31	34	37	28	0	15	3	395	38	3	8	4.1	.993	C-93
1955		138	.261	.408	426	111	13	1	16	3.8	61	67	68	34	2	4	1	664	62	4	12	5.3	.995	C-136
1956		136	.293	.438	450	132	28	2	11	2.4	55	75	53	34	2	5	2	679	40	5	6	5.3	.993	C-132
1957		101	.256	.393	351	90	11	2	11	3.1	33	70	35	24	2	9	3	454	45	1	5	5.0	.998	C-96
1958		127	.273	.454	421	115	16	0	20	4.8	53	84	57	37	2	13	5	597	63	9	8	5.3	.987	C-116
1959		140	.265	.451	505	134	22	3	22	4.4	63	84	55	49	4	5	3	800	68	6	33	6.2	.993	C-122, 1B-24
1960		129	.252	.356	421	106	23	0	7	1.7	43	46	42	39	2	7	2	555	54	3	12	4.7	.995	C-123
1961		116	.282	.380	337	95	10	1	7	2.1	38	41	37	22	0	10	4	464	48	1	6	4.4	.998	C-107
1962		84	.268	.350	220	59	12	0	2	0.9	17	26	32	23	1	19	2	298	23	3	0	3.9	.991	C-66
1963		35	.233	.288	73	17	4	0	0	0.0	4	6	8	7	0	11	2	98	9	2	2	3.1	.982	C-23, 1B-2
18 yrs.		1752	.264	.402	5351	1415	244	14	155	2.9	623	808	671	453	20	170	43	7243	705	63	120	4.6	.992	C-1571, 1B-27, 3B-1

WORLD SERIES

Year	Team	Games	BA	SA	AB	H	2B	3B	HR	HR%	R	RBI	BB	SO	SB	PH AB	PH H	PO	A	E	DP	TC/G	FA	G by Pos
1947	NY	A	2	.750	1.250	4	3	2	0	0	0.0	3	1	0	0	0	0	0	2	1	0	0	1.5	1.000	C-2
1959	CHI	A	6	.227	.364	22	5	0	0	1	4.5	3	5	1	3	0	0	0	28	5	0	0	5.5	1.000	C-6
2 yrs.		8	.308	.500	26	8	2	0	1	3.8	6	6	1	3	0	0	0	30	6	0	0	4.5	1.000	C-8

Doug Loman

LOMAN, DOUGLAS EDWARD
B. May 9, 1958, Bakersfield, Calif.
BL TL 5'11½" 185 lbs.

Year	Team	Games	BA	SA	AB	H	2B	3B	HR	HR%	R	RBI	BB	SO	SB	PH AB	PH H	PO	A	E	DP	TC/G	FA	G by Pos
1984	MIL	A	23	.276	.408	76	21	4	0	2	2.6	13	12	15	7	0	0	0	54	4	2	0	2.6	.967	OF-23
1985		24	.212	.318	66	14	3	2	0	0.0	10	7	1	12	0	7	2	41	4	0	2	1.9	1.000	OF-20
2 yrs.		47	.246	.366	142	35	7	2	2	1.4	23	19	16	19	0	7	2	95	8	2	2	2.2	.981	OF-43

Ernie Lombardi

LOMBARDI, ERNESTO NATALI (Schnozz, Bocci)
B. Apr. 6, 1908, Oakland, Calif. D. Sept. 26, 1977, Santa Cruz, Calif.
Hall of Fame 1986.
BR TR 6'3" 230 lbs.

Year	Team	Games	BA	SA	AB	H	2B	3B	HR	HR%	R	RBI	BB	SO	SB	PH AB	PH H	PO	A	E	DP	TC/G	FA	G by Pos
1931	BKN	N	73	.297	.412	182	54	7	1	4	2.2	20	23	12	12	1	21	7	218	23	4	5	3.4	.984	C-50
1932	CIN	N	118	.303	.479	413	125	22	9	11	2.7	43	68	41	19	0	7	2	288	76	14	6	3.2	.963	C-108
1933		107	.283	.383	350	99	21	1	4	1.1	30	47	16	17	2	10	2	223	52	8	3	2.6	.972	C-95
1934		132	.305	.434	417	127	19	4	9	2.2	42	62	16	22	0	19	4	383	61	5	8	3.4	.989	C-111
1935		120	.343	.539	332	114	23	3	12	3.6	36	64	16	6	0	36	8	298	49	6	4	2.9	.983	C-82
1936		121	.333	.496	387	129	23	2	12	3.1	42	68	19	16	1	15	3	330	54	15	10	3.3	.962	C-105
1937		120	.334	.473	368	123	22	1	9	2.4	41	59	14	17	1	28	5	333	58	11	3	3.4	.973	C-90
1938		129	**.342**	.524	489	167	30	1	19	3.9	60	95	40	14	0	6	3	512	73	9	8	4.6	.985	C-123
1939		130	.287	.487	450	129	26	2	20	4.4	43	85	35	19	0	8	1	536	63	10	7	4.7	.984	C-120
1940		109	.319	.489	376	120	22	0	14	3.7	50	74	31	14	0	7	2	397	46	5	5	4.1	.989	C-101
1941		117	.264	.374	398	105	12	1	10	2.5	33	60	36	14	0	1	0	496	70	10	9	4.9	.983	C-116
1942	BOS	N	105	**.330**	.482	309	102	14	0	11	3.6	32	46	37	12	1	16	2	251	41	6	3	2.8	.980	C-85
1943	NY	N	104	.305	.431	295	90	7	0	10	3.4	19	51	16	11	0	28	7	296	36	10	8	3.3	.971	C-73
1944		117	.255	.370	373	95	13	0	10	2.7	37	58	33	25	0	14	3	350	47	13	11	3.5	.968	C-100
1945		115	.307	.481	368	113	7	1	19	5.2	19	70	43	11	0	18	4	425	49	8	8	4.2	.983	C-96
1946		88	.290	.466	238	69	4	1	12	5.0	19	39	18	24	0	24	6	272	36	7	7	3.6	.978	C-63
1947		48	.282	.436	110	31	5	0	4	3.6	8	21	7	9	0	23	7	86	11	2	2	2.1	.980	C-24
17 yrs.		1853	.306	.460	5855	1792	277	27	190	3.2	601	990	430	262	8	281	66	5694	845	143	107	3.6	.979	C-1542

WORLD SERIES

Year	Team	Games	BA	SA	AB	H	2B	3B	HR	HR%	R	RBI	BB	SO	SB	PH AB	PH H	PO	A	E	DP	TC/G	FA	G by Pos
1939	CIN	N	4	.214	.214	14	3	0	0	0	0.0	0	2	1	0	0	0	0	22	1	1	0	6.0	.958	C-4
1940		2	.333	.667	3	1	1	0	0	0.0	0	0	0	1	0	0	0	4	0	0	0	2.0	1.000	C-1
2 yrs.		6	.235	.294	17	4	1	0	0	0.0	0	2	1	1	0	0	0	26	1	1	0	4.7	.964	C-5

Phil Lombardi

LOMBARDI, PHILLIP ARDEN
B. Feb. 20, 1963, Abilene, Tex.
BR TR 6'2" 200 lbs.

Year	Team	Games	BA	SA	AB	H	2B	3B	HR	HR%	R	RBI	BB	SO	SB	PH AB	PH H	PO	A	E	DP	TC/G	FA	G by Pos
1986	NY	A	20	.278	.528	36	10	3	0	2	5.6	6	6	4	7	0	9	3	22	3	3	0	1.4	.893	OF-8, C-3
1987		5	.125	.125	8	1	0	0	0	0.0	0	0	0	2	0	5	0	7	1	0	0	1.6	1.000	C-3
1989	NY	N	18	.229	.313	48	11	1	0	1	2.1	4	3	5	8	0	3	0	93	5	2	1	5.6	.980	C-16, 1B-1
3 yrs.		43	.239	.380	92	22	4	0	3	3.3	10	9	9	17	0	17	3	122	9	5	1	3.2	.963	C-22, OF-8, 1B-1

Year	Team		Games	BA	SA	AB	H	2B	3B	HR	HR%	R	RBI	BB	SO	SB	Pinch Hit AB	H	PO	A	E	DP	TC/G	FA	G by Pos

Steve Lombardozzi

LOMBARDOZZI, STEPHEN PAUL (Lombo)
B. Apr. 26, 1960, Malden, Mass. BR TR 6' 175 lbs.

Year	Team	Games	BA	SA	AB	H	2B	3B	HR	HR%	R	RBI	BB	SO	SB	PH AB	PH H	PO	A	E	DP	TC/G	FA	G by Pos
1985	MIN A	28	.370	.481	54	20	4	1	0	0.0	10	6	6	6	3	1	0	31	80	2	16	4.0	.982	2B-26
1986		156	.227	.347	453	103	20	5	8	1.8	53	33	52	76	3	0	0	289	407	6	102	4.5	.991	2B-155
1987		136	.238	.352	432	103	19	3	8	1.9	51	38	33	66	5	0	0	245	356	14	77	4.5	.977	2B-133
1988		103	.209	.307	287	60	15	2	3	1.0	34	27	35	48	2	1	1	152	237	5	54	3.8	.987	2B-90, SS-12, 3B-5
1989	HOU N	21	.216	.432	37	8	3	1	1	2.7	5	3	4	9	0	2	0	20	28	4	5	2.5	.923	2B-18, 3B-1
5 yrs.		444	.233	.348	1263	294	61	12	20	1.6	153	107	130	205	13	4	1	737	1108	31	254	4.2	.983	2B-422, SS-12, 3B-6

LEAGUE CHAMPIONSHIP SERIES

Year	Team	Games	BA	SA	AB	H	2B	3B	HR	HR%	R	RBI	BB	SO	SB	PH AB	PH H	PO	A	E	DP	TC/G	FA	G by Pos
1987	MIN A	5	.267	.267	15	4	0	0	0	0.0	2	1	2	2	0	0	0	8	9	1	3	3.6	.944	2B-5

WORLD SERIES

Year	Team	Games	BA	SA	AB	H	2B	3B	HR	HR%	R	RBI	BB	SO	SB	PH AB	PH H	PO	A	E	DP	TC/G	FA	G by Pos
1987	MIN A	6	.412	.647	17	7	1	0	1	5.9	3	4	2	2	0	0	0	9	24	0	3	5.5	1.000	2B-6

Walt Lonergan

LONERGAN, WALTER E.
B. Sept. 22, 1885, Boston, Mass. D. Jan. 23, 1958, Lexington, Mass. BR TR 5'7" 156 lbs.

Year	Team	Games	BA	SA	AB	H	2B	3B	HR	HR%	R	RBI	BB	SO	SB	PH AB	PH H	PO	A	E	DP	TC/G	FA	G by Pos
1911	BOS A	10	.269	.269	26	7	0	0	0	0.0	2	1	1		1	0	0	19	17	3	2	3.9	.923	2B-7, SS-1, 3B-1

Dale Long

LONG, RICHARD DALE
B. Feb. 6, 1926, Springfield, Mo. BL TL 6'4" 205 lbs.

Year	Team	Games	BA	SA	AB	H	2B	3B	HR	HR%	R	RBI	BB	SO	SB	PH AB	PH H	PO	A	E	DP	TC/G	FA	G by Pos
1951	2 teams	PIT N (10G – .167)			STL A	(34G – .238)																		
"	total	44	.231	.368	117	27	5	1	3	2.6	12	12	10	25	0	13	1	235	19	3	23	5.8	.988	1B-29, OF-1
1955	PIT N	131	.291	.513	419	122	19	13	16	3.8	59	79	48	72	0	13	4	968	97	13	114	8.2	.988	1B-119
1956		148	.263	.485	547	136	20	7	27	5.2	64	91	54	85	1	12	2	1201	99	24	92	8.9	.982	1B-138
1957	2 teams	PIT N (7G – .182)			CHI N	(123G – .305)																		
"	total	130	.298	.496	419	125	20	0	21	5.0	55	67	56	73	1	18	6	962	77	5	87	8.0	.995	1B-111
1958	CHI N	142	.271	.467	480	130	26	4	20	4.2	68	75	66	64	2	5	2	1173	85	10	130	8.9	.992	1B-137, C-2
1959		110	.236	.432	296	70	10	3	14	4.7	34	37	31	53	0	27	6	731	49	12	63	7.2	.985	1B-85
1960	2 teams	SF N (37G – .167)			NY A	(26G – .366)																		
"	total	63	.253	.495	95	24	1	0	6	6.3	10	16	12	13	0	39	11	73	6	0	5	1.3	1.000	1B-21
1961	WAS A	123	.249	.459	377	94	20	4	17	4.5	52	49	39	41	0	24	3	827	62	15	87	7.3	.983	1B-95
1962	2 teams	WAS A (67G – .241)			NY A	(41G – .298)																		
"	total	108	.260	.386	285	74	12	0	8	2.8	29	41	36	31	6	28	3	468	35	2	68	4.7	.996	1B-82
1963	NY A	14	.200	.200	15	3	0	0	0	0.0	1	0	1	3	0	11	2	11	0	1	1	0.9	.917	1B-2
10 yrs.		1013	.267	.464	3020	805	135	33	132	4.4	384	467	353	460	10	190	40	6649	529	85	670	7.2	.988	1B-819, C-2, OF-1

WORLD SERIES

Year	Team	Games	BA	SA	AB	H	2B	3B	HR	HR%	R	RBI	BB	SO	SB	PH AB	PH H	PO	A	E	DP	TC/G	FA	G by Pos
1960	NY A	3	.333	.333	3	1	0	0	0	0.0	0	0	0	0	0	3	1	0	0	0	0	–		
1962		2	.200	.200	5	1	0	0	0	0.0	0	1	0	1	0	0	0	9	3	0	1	6.0	1.000	1B-2
2 yrs.		5	.250	.250	8	2	0	0	0	0.0	0	1	0	1	0	3	1	9	3	0	1	2.4	1.000	1B-2

Dan Long

LONG, DANIEL W.
B. Aug. 27, 1867, Boston, Mass. D. Apr. 30, 1929, Sausalito, Calif.

Year	Team	Games	BA	SA	AB	H	2B	3B	HR	HR%	R	RBI	BB	SO	SB	PH AB	PH H	PO	A	E	DP	TC/G	FA	G by Pos
1888	LOU AA	1	.000	.000	2	0	0	0	0	0.0	0	0	1		0	0	0	0	0	0	0	0.0	–	OF-1
1890	BAL AA	21	.156	.156	77	12	0	0	0	0.0	19		14		16	0	0	26	5	2	0	1.6	.939	OF-21
2 yrs.		22	.152	.152	79	12	0	0	0	0.0	19		15		16	0	0	26	5	2	0	1.5	.939	OF-22

Herman Long

LONG, HERMAN C. (Germany)
B. Apr. 13, 1866, Chicago, Ill. D. Sept. 17, 1909, Denver, Colo. BL TR 5'8½" 160 lbs.

Year	Team	Games	BA	SA	AB	H	2B	3B	HR	HR%	R	RBI	BB	SO	SB	PH AB	PH H	PO	A	E	DP	TC/G	FA	G by Pos
1889	KC AA	136	.279	.371	574	160	32	6	3	0.5	137	60	64	63	89	0	0	355	506	122	59	7.2	.876	SS-128, 2B-8, OF-1
1890	BOS N	101	.251	.355	431	108	15	3	8	1.9	95	52	40	34	49	0	0	230	352	66	40	6.4	.898	SS-101
1891		139	.282	.404	577	163	21	11	9	1.6	129	74	80	51	60	0	0	345	441	85	60	6.3	.902	SS-139
1892		151	.280	.378	646	181	33	6	6	0.9	115	77	44	36	57	0	0	313	502	102	60	6.1	.889	SS-141, OF-12, 3B-1
1893		128	.288	.382	552	159	22	6	6	1.1	149	58	73	32	38	0	0	282	487	100	68	6.8	.885	SS-123, 2B-5
1894		104	.324	.505	475	154	28	11	12	2.5	137	79	35	17	24	0	0	239	365	78	53	6.6	.886	SS-98, OF-5, 2B-3
1895		124	.316	.447	535	169	23	10	9	1.7	109	75	31	12	35	0	0	289	412	84	49	6.3	.893	SS-122, 2B-2
1896		120	.343	.463	501	172	26	8	6	1.2	108	100	26	16	36	0	0	311	415	83	52	6.7	.897	SS-120
1897		107	.322	.444	450	145	32	7	3	0.7	89	69	23		22	0	0	274	353	66	40	6.5	.905	SS-107, OF-1
1898		144	.265	.365	589	156	21	10	6	1.0	99	99	39		20	0	0	333	479	67	65	6.1	.924	SS-142, 2B-2
1899		145	.265	.375	578	153	30	8	6	1.0	91	100	45		20	0	0	371	437	60	69	6.0	.931	SS-143, 1B-2
1900		125	.261	.391	486	127	19	4	12	2.5	80	66	44		26	0	0	257	454	48	34	6.1	.937	SS-125
1901		138	.228	.295	518	118	14	6	3	0.6	55	68	25		20	0	0	304	468	44	55	5.9	.946	SS-138
1902		118	.228	.268	429	98	11	0	2	0.5	39	44	31		24	0	0	320	395	44	52	6.4	.942	SS-105, 2B-13
1903	2 teams	NY A (22G – .188)			DET A	(69G – .222)																		
"	total	91	.213	.260	319	68	15	0	0	0.0	27	31	12		14	1	1	213	258	46	24	5.7	.911	SS-60, 2B-31
1904	PHI N	1	.250	.250	4	1	0	0	0	0.0	0	0	0		0	0	0	4	0	1	0	9.0	.889	2B-1
16 yrs.		1872	.278	.383	7664	2132	342	96	91	1.2	1459	1052	612	261	534	1	1	4440	6328	96	785	5.0	.991	SS-1792, 2B-65, OF-19, 1B-2, 3B-1

Jeoff Long

LONG, JEOFFREY KEITH
B. Oct. 9, 1941, Covington, Ky. BR TR 6'1" 200 lbs.

Year	Team	Games	BA	SA	AB	H	2B	3B	HR	HR%	R	RBI	BB	SO	SB	PH AB	PH H	PO	A	E	DP	TC/G	FA	G by Pos
1963	STL N	5	.200	.200	5	1	0	0	0	0.0	0	0	0	1	0	5	1	0	0	0	0	0.0	–	
1964	2 teams	STL N (28G – .233)			CHI A	(23G – .143)																		
"	total	51	.192	.244	78	15	1	0	1	1.3	5	9	10	33	0	28	4	69	4	3	7	1.5	.961	OF-9, 1B-8
2 yrs.		56	.193	.241	83	16	1	0	1	1.2	5	9	10	34	0	33	5	69	4	3	7	1.4	.961	OF-9, 1B-8

Jim Long

LONG, JAMES ALBERT
B. June 29, 1898, Fort Dodge, Iowa D. Sept. 14, 1970, Fort Dodge, Iowa BR TR 5'11" 160 lbs.

Year	Team	Games	BA	SA	AB	H	2B	3B	HR	HR%	R	RBI	BB	SO	SB	PH AB	PH H	PO	A	E	DP	TC/G	FA	G by Pos
1922	CHI A	3	.000	.000	3	0	0	0	0	0.0	0	0	1	0	0	1	0	1	0	0	0	0.3	1.000	C-2

Jim Long

LONG, JAMES M.
B. Nov. 15, 1862, Louisville, Ky. D. Dec. 12, 1932, Louisville, Ky.

Year	Team		Games	BA	SA	AB	H	2B	3B	HR	HR%	R	RBI	BB	SO	SB	Pinch Hit AB	Pinch Hit H	PO	A	E	DP	TC/G	FA	G by Pos

Jim Long *continued*

Year	Team		Games	BA	SA	AB	H	2B	3B	HR	HR%	R	RBI	BB	SO	SB	PH AB	PH H	PO	A	E	DP	TC/G	FA	G by Pos
1891	LOU	AA	6	.240	.240	25	6	0	0	0	0.0	5	4	3	6	1	0	0	10	2	2	1	2.3	.857	OF-6
1893	BAL	N	55	.212	.283	226	48	8	1	2	0.9	31	25	16	27	23	0	0	109	8	14	1	2.4	.893	OF-55
2 yrs.			61	.215	.279	251	54	8	1	2	0.8	36	29	19	33	24	0	0	119	10	16	2	2.4	.890	OF-61

Red Long

LONG, NELSON — BR TR 6'1" 190 lbs.
B. Sept. 28, 1876, Burlington, Ont., Canada   D. Aug. 11, 1929, Hamilton, Ont., Canada

Year	Team		Games	BA	SA	AB	H	2B	3B	HR	HR%	R	RBI	BB	SO	SB	PH AB	PH H	PO	A	E	DP	TC/G	FA	G by Pos
1902	BOS	N	3	.273	.273	11	3	0	0	0	0.0	1	0	0		0	0	0	8	6	0	0	4.7	1.000	SS-2, P-1

Tommy Long

LONG, THOMAS AUGUSTUS — BR TR 5'10½" 165 lbs.
B. June 1, 1890, Mitchum, Ala.   D. June 15, 1972, Mobile, Ala.

Year	Team		Games	BA	SA	AB	H	2B	3B	HR	HR%	R	RBI	BB	SO	SB	PH AB	PH H	PO	A	E	DP	TC/G	FA	G by Pos
1911	WAS	A	14	.229	.292	48	11	3	0	0	0.0	1	5	1		4	1	0	13	1	2	0	1.1	.875	OF-13
1912			1	.000	.000	1	0	0	0	0	0.0	0	0	0		0	1	0	0	0	0	0	0.0	–	
1915	STL	N	140	.294	.446	507	149	21	25	2	0.4	61	61	31	50	19	4	2	236	18	20	1	2.0	.927	OF-140
1916			119	.293	.377	403	118	11	10	1	0.2	37	33	10	43	21	12	2	143	13	9	2	1.4	.945	OF-106
1917			144	.232	.325	530	123	12	14	3	0.6	49	41	37	44	21	7	1	173	9	16	2	1.4	.919	OF-137
5 yrs.			418	.269	.379	1489	401	47	49	6	0.4	148	140	79	137	65	25	5	565	41	47	5	1.6	.928	OF-396

Joe Lonnett

LONNETT, JOSEPH PAUL — BR TR 5'10" 180 lbs.
B. Feb. 7, 1927, Beaver Falls, Pa.

Year	Team		Games	BA	SA	AB	H	2B	3B	HR	HR%	R	RBI	BB	SO	SB	PH AB	PH H	PO	A	E	DP	TC/G	FA	G by Pos
1956	PHI	N	16	.182	.182	22	4	1	0	0	0.0	2	2	2	7	0	8	1	24	2	0	1	1.6	1.000	C-7
1957			67	.169	.294	160	27	5	0	5	3.1	12	15	22	39	0	2	0	305	16	1	3	4.8	.997	C-65
1958			17	.140	.180	50	7	2	0	0	0.0	2	2	2	11	0	2	0	78	7	1	3	5.1	.988	C-15
1959			43	.172	.215	93	16	1	0	1	1.1	8	10	14	17	0	0	0	171	4	3	0	4.1	.983	C-43
4 yrs.			143	.166	.246	325	54	8	0	6	1.8	22	27	40	74	0	12	1	578	29	5	7	4.3	.992	C-130

Bruce Look

LOOK, BRUCE MICHAEL — BL TR 5'11" 183 lbs.
Brother of Dean Look.
B. June 9, 1943, Lansing, Mich.

Year	Team		Games	BA	SA	AB	H	2B	3B	HR	HR%	R	RBI	BB	SO	SB	PH AB	PH H	PO	A	E	DP	TC/G	FA	G by Pos
1968	MIN	A	59	.246	.280	118	29	4	0	0	0.0	7	9	20	24	0	16	3	202	20	1	5	3.8	.996	C-41

Dean Look

LOOK, DEAN ZACHARY — BR TR 5'11" 185 lbs.
Brother of Bruce Look.
B. July 23, 1937, Lansing, Mich.

Year	Team		Games	BA	SA	AB	H	2B	3B	HR	HR%	R	RBI	BB	SO	SB	PH AB	PH H	PO	A	E	DP	TC/G	FA	G by Pos
1961	CHI	A	3	.000	.000	6	0	0	0	0	0.0	0	0	0	2	0	0	0	1	0	0	0	0.3	1.000	OF-1

Stan Lopata

LOPATA, STANLEY EDWARD — BR TR 6'2" 210 lbs.
B. Sept. 12, 1925, Delray, Mich.

Year	Team		Games	BA	SA	AB	H	2B	3B	HR	HR%	R	RBI	BB	SO	SB	PH AB	PH H	PO	A	E	DP	TC/G	FA	G by Pos
1948	PHI	N	6	.133	.200	15	2	1	0	0	0.0	2	2	0	4	0	2	0	17	1	0	1	3.0	1.000	C-4
1949			83	.271	.425	240	65	9	2	8	3.3	31	27	21	44	1	19	4	236	19	7	2	3.2	.973	C-58
1950			58	.209	.279	129	27	2	2	1	0.8	10	11	22	25	1	5	1	176	13	5	3	3.3	.974	C-51
1951			3	.000	.000	5	0	0	0	0	0.0	0	0	0	2	0	2	0	6	0	0	0	2.0	1.000	C-1
1952			57	.274	.402	179	49	9	1	4	2.2	25	27	36	33	1	3	0	274	21	4	6	5.2	.987	C-55
1953			81	.239	.419	234	56	12	3	8	3.4	34	31	28	39	3	1	0	344	27	5	2	4.6	.987	C-80
1954			86	.290	.544	259	75	14	5	14	5.4	42	42	33	37	1	8	3	336	27	4	1	4.3	.989	C-75, 1B-1
1955			99	.271	.538	303	82	9	3	22	7.3	49	58	58	62	4	8	2	480	50	3	16	5.4	.984	C-66, 1B-24
1956			146	.267	.535	535	143	33	7	32	6.0	96	95	75	93	5	5	2	873	40	16	41	6.4	.983	C-102, 1B-39
1957			116	.237	.433	388	92	18	2	18	4.6	50	67	56	81	2	7	2	634	36	8	9	5.8	.988	C-108
1958	MIL	N	86	.248	.388	258	64	9	0	9	3.5	36	33	60	63	0	6	2	418	28	6	6	5.3	.987	C-80
1959			25	.104	.104	48	5	0	0	0	0.0	0	4	3	13	0	11	2	49	0	0	1	2.0	1.000	C-11, 1B-2
1960			7	.125	.125	8	1	0	0	0	0.0	0	0	1	3	0	3	1	17	0	1	0	2.6	.944	C-4
13 yrs.			853	.254	.452	2601	661	116	25	116	4.5	375	397	393	497	18	80	19	3860	262	59	88	4.9	.986	C-695, 1B-66

WORLD SERIES

Year	Team		Games	BA	SA	AB	H	2B	3B	HR	HR%	R	RBI	BB	SO	SB	PH AB	PH H	PO	A	E	DP	TC/G	FA	G by Pos
1950	PHI	N	2	.000	.000	1	0	0	0	0	0.0	0	0	0	0	0	1	0	1	0	0	0	0.5	1.000	C-1

Davey Lopes

LOPES, DAVID EARL — BR TR 5'9" 170 lbs.
B. May 3, 1945, East Providence, R. I.

Year	Team		Games	BA	SA	AB	H	2B	3B	HR	HR%	R	RBI	BB	SO	SB	PH AB	PH H	PO	A	E	DP	TC/G	FA	G by Pos
1972	LA	N	11	.214	.310	42	9	4	0	0	0.0	6	1	7	6	4	0	0	27	27	2	5	5.1	.964	2B-11
1973			142	.275	.351	535	147	13	5	6	1.1	77	37	62	77	36	1	0	323	380	11	90	5.0	.985	2B-135, OF-5, SS-2, 3B-1
1974			145	.266	.383	530	141	26	3	10	1.9	95	35	66	71	59	0	0	309	360	24	71	4.8	.965	2B-143
1975			155	.262	.359	618	162	24	6	8	1.3	108	41	91	93	77	0	0	360	386	16	60	4.9	.979	2B-137, OF-24, SS-14
1976			117	.241	.342	427	103	17	4	4	0.9	72	20	56	49	63	0	0	254	268	19	56	4.6	.965	2B-100, OF-19
1977			134	.283	.406	502	142	19	5	11	2.2	85	53	73	47	47	1	1	287	380	14	74	5.1	.979	2B-130
1978			151	.278	.421	587	163	25	4	17	2.9	93	58	71	70	45	1	1	340	424	20	88	5.2	.974	2B-147, OF-2
1979			153	.265	.464	582	154	20	6	28	4.8	109	73	97	88	44	1	0	341	384	14	82	4.8	.981	2B-152
1980			141	.251	.344	553	139	15	3	10	1.8	79	49	58	71	23	0	0	304	416	15	85	5.2	.980	2B-140
1981			58	.206	.285	214	44	2	0	5	2.3	35	17	22	35	20	3	0	129	161	2	30	5.0	.993	2B-55
1982	OAK	A	128	.242	.371	450	109	19	3	11	2.4	58	42	40	51	28	0	3	295	338	15	82	5.1	.977	2B-123, DH-12, OF-7, 3B-5
1983			147	.277	.423	494	137	19	3	17	3.4	64	67	51	61	22	10	3	267	287	9	83	3.8	.984	2B-125, OF-6
1984	2 teams	OAK A (72G – .257)			CHI N (16G – .235)																				
"	total		88	.255	.421	247	63	12	1	9	3.6	37	36	37	41	15	7	2	105	49	6	10	1.8	.963	OF-51, 2B-19, DH-9, 3B-5
1985	CHI	N	99	.284	.444	275	78	11	0	11	4.0	52	44	46	37	47	22	4	115	6	1	1	1.2	.992	OF-79, 3B-4, 2B-1
1986	2 teams	CHI N (59G – .299)			HOU N (37G – .235)																				
"	total		96	.275	.420	255	70	10	3	7	2.7	49	35	43	25	25	19	4	96	65	8	5	1.8	.953	OF-41, 3B-37
1987	HOU	N	47	.233	.349	43	10	2	0	1	2.3	4	6	13	8	2	28	7	6	0	1	0	0.1	.857	OF-5
16 yrs.			1812	.263	.388	6354	1671	232	50	155	2.4	1023	614	833	852	557	93	22	3558	3931	177	822	4.2	.977	2B-1418, OF-239, 3B-52, DH-21, SS-16

DIVISIONAL PLAYOFF SERIES

Year	Team		Games	BA	SA	AB	H	2B	3B	HR	HR%	R	RBI	BB	SO	SB	PH AB	PH H	PO	A	E	DP	TC/G	FA	G by Pos
1981	LA	N	5	.200	.250	20	4	1	0	0	0.0	0	3	1	0	3	7	1	0	0	0	0	0.0	–	2B-5

Year	Team		Games	BA	SA	AB	H	2B	3B	HR	HR%	R	RBI	BB	SO	SB	Pinch Hit AB	H	PO	A	E	DP	TC/G	FA	G by Pos

Davey Lopes *continued*

LEAGUE CHAMPIONSHIP SERIES

Year	Team		Games	BA	SA	AB	H	2B	3B	HR	HR%	R	RBI	BB	SO	SB	Pinch Hit AB	H	PO	A	E	DP	TC/G	FA	G by Pos
1974	LA	N	4	.267	.400	15	4	0	1	0	0.0	4	3	5	0	3	0	0	9	18	1	4	7.0	.964	2B-4
1977			4	.235	.235	17	4	0	0	0	0.0	2	3	2	0	0	0	0	9	10	1	1	5.0	.950	2B-4
1978			4	.389	.889	18	7	1	1	2	11.1	3	5	0	1	1	0	0	10	10	2	3	5.5	.909	2B-4
1981			5	.278	.278	18	5	0	0	0	0.0	0	0	1	3	5	0	0	0	0	0	0	0.0	—	2B-5
1984	CHI	N	2	.000	.000	1	0	0	0	0	0.0	0	0	0	0	0	0	1	0	0	0	0	0.0	—	OF-1
1986	HOU	N	3	.000	.000	2	0	0	0	0	0.0	1	0	1	0	0	0	2	0	0	0	0	0.0	—	
6 yrs.			22	.282	.437	71	20	1	2	2	2.8	10	11	9	5	9	3	0	28	38	4	8	3.2	.943	2B-17, OF-1

WORLD SERIES

Year	Team		Games	BA	SA	AB	H	2B	3B	HR	HR%	R	RBI	BB	SO	SB	Pinch Hit AB	H	PO	A	E	DP	TC/G	FA	G by Pos
1974	LA	N	5	.111	.111	18	2	0	0	0	0.0	2	0	3	4	2	0	0	19	9	0	3	5.6	1.000	2B-5
1977			6	.167	.375	24	4	0	1	1	4.2	3	2	4	3	2	0	0	12	22	0	2	5.7	1.000	2B-6
1978			6	.308	.654	26	8	0	0	3	11.5	7	7	2	1	0	0	0	10	19	1	4	5.0	.967	2B-6
1981			6	.227	.273	22	5	1	0	0	0.0	6	2	4	3	4	0	0	26	14	6	5	7.7	.870	2B-6
4 yrs.			23	.211	.378	90	19	1	1	4	4.4	18	11	13	11	10 3rd	0	0	67	64	7	14	6.0	.949	2B-23

Al Lopez

LOPEZ, ALFONSO RAYMOND
B. Aug. 20, 1908, Tampa, Fla.
Manager 1951-65, 1968-69.
Hall of Fame 1977.

BR TR 5'11" 165 lbs.

Year	Team		Games	BA	SA	AB	H	2B	3B	HR	HR%	R	RBI	BB	SO	SB	Pinch Hit AB	H	PO	A	E	DP	TC/G	FA	G by Pos
1928	BKN	N	3	.000	.000	12	0	0	0	0	0.0	0	0	0	0	0	0	0	9	0	0	0	3.0	1.000	C-3
1930			128	.309	.418	421	130	20	4	6	1.4	60	57	33	35	3	1	1	465	66	9	9	4.2	.983	C-126
1931			111	.269	.328	360	97	13	4	0	0.0	38	40	28	33	1	5	1	390	69	11	6	4.2	.977	C-105
1932			126	.275	.356	404	111	18	6	1	0.2	44	43	34	35	3	1	0	456	82	13	10	4.4	.976	C-125
1933			126	.301	.376	372	112	11	4	3	0.8	39	41	21	39	10	1	1	452	88	5	15	4.3	.991	C-124, 2B-1
1934			140	.273	.383	439	120	23	2	7	1.6	58	54	49	44	2	1	0	548	68	11	6	4.5	.982	C-137, 3B-2, 2B-2
1935			128	.251	.327	379	95	14	4	3	0.8	50	39	35	36	2	1	0	472	65	11	8	4.3	.980	C-126
1936	BOS	N	128	.242	.345	426	103	12	4	8	1.9	46	50	41	41	1	1	0	448	107	14	9	4.4	.975	C-127, 1B-1
1937			105	.204	.269	334	68	11	1	3	0.9	31	38	35	57	3	1	1	342	83	7	5	4.1	.984	C-102
1938			71	.267	.314	236	63	6	1	1	0.4	19	14	11	24	5	0	0	240	42	3	4	4.0	.989	C-71
1939			131	.252	.369	412	104	22	1	8	1.9	32	49	40	45	1	0	0	424	72	7	11	3.8	.986	C-129
1940	2 teams					BOS	N	(36G —	.294)		PIT	N	(59G —	.259)										
"	total		95	.273	.355	293	80	9	3	3	1.0	35	41	19	21	6	0	0	343	62	4	11	4.3	.990	C-95
1941	PIT	N	114	.265	.347	317	84	9	1	5	1.6	33	43	31	23	0	0	0	345	54	8	5	3.6	.980	C-114
1942			103	.256	.308	289	74	8	2	1	0.3	17	26	34	17	0	2	2	327	53	2	14	3.7	.995	C-99
1943			118	.263	.317	372	98	9	4	1	0.3	40	39	49	25	2	1	0	378	67	5	9	3.8	.989	C-116, 3B-1
1944			115	.230	.281	331	76	12	1	1	0.3	27	34	34	24	4	0	0	372	52	7	6	3.7	.984	C-115
1945			91	.218	.251	243	53	8	0	1	0.4	22	18	35	12	1	0	0	326	38	3	7	4.0	.992	C-91
1946			56	.307	.340	150	46	2	0	1	0.7	13	12	23	14	1	0	0	173	30	4	4	3.7	.985	C-56
1947	CLE	A	61	.262	.270	126	33	1	0	0	0.0	9	14	9	13	1	4	0	144	28	0	1	2.8	1.000	C-57
19 yrs.			1950	.261	.337	5916	1547	206	42	52	0.9	613	652	561	538	46	19	6	6654	1126	123	140	4.1	.984	C-1918, 3B-3, 2B-3, 1B-1

Art Lopez

LOPEZ, ARTURO
Born Arturo Lopez y Rodriguez.
B. June 8, 1937, Mayaguez, Puerto Rico

BL TL 5'9" 170 lbs.

Year	Team		Games	BA	SA	AB	H	2B	3B	HR	HR%	R	RBI	BB	SO	SB	Pinch Hit AB	H	PO	A	E	DP	TC/G	FA	G by Pos
1965	NY	A	38	.143	.143	49	7	0	0	0	0.0	5	0	1	6	0	13	1	23	0	1	0	0.6	.958	OF-16

Carlos Lopez

LOPEZ, CARLOS ANTONIO
Born Carlos Antonio Lopez y Morales.
B. Sept. 27, 1950, Mazatlan, Mexico

BR TR 6' 190 lbs.

Year	Team		Games	BA	SA	AB	H	2B	3B	HR	HR%	R	RBI	BB	SO	SB	Pinch Hit AB	H	PO	A	E	DP	TC/G	FA	G by Pos
1976	CAL	A	9	.000	.000	10	0	0	0	0	0.0	1	0	2	3	2	0	0	4	0	0	0	0.4	1.000	OF-4, DH-1
1977	SEA	A	99	.283	.431	297	84	18	1	8	2.7	39	34	14	61	16	5	1	160	11	5	3	1.8	.972	OF-90, DH-2
1978	BAL	A	129	.238	.332	193	46	6	0	4	2.1	21	20	9	34	5	14	1	151	7	2	2	1.2	.988	OF-114, DH-1
3 yrs.			237	.260	.384	500	130	24	1	12	2.4	61	54	25	98	23	19	2	315	18	7	5	1.4	.979	OF-208, DH-4

Hector Lopez

LOPEZ, HECTOR HEADLEY
Born Hector Headley Lopez y Swainson.
B. July 9, 1929, Colon, Panama

BR TR 5'11" 182 lbs.

Year	Team		Games	BA	SA	AB	H	2B	3B	HR	HR%	R	RBI	BB	SO	SB	Pinch Hit AB	H	PO	A	E	DP	TC/G	FA	G by Pos
1955	KC	A	128	.290	.422	483	140	15	2	15	3.1	50	68	33	58	1	1	0	197	331	29	58	4.4	.948	3B-93, 2B-36
1956			151	.273	.428	561	153	27	3	18	3.2	91	69	63	73	4	5	2	218	282	30	32	3.5	.943	3B-121, OF-20, 2B-8, SS-4
1957			121	.294	.448	391	115	19	4	11	2.8	51	35	41	66	1	8	3	125	229	23	21	3.1	.939	3B-111, 2B-4, OF-3
1958			151	.261	.415	564	147	28	4	17	3.0	84	73	49	61	2	4	1	309	377	21	86	4.7	.970	2B-96, 3B-55, OF-1, SS-1
1959	2 teams		148	KC	A	(36G —	.281)		NY	A	(112G —	.283)												
"	total		148	.283	.471	541	153	26	5	22	4.1	82	93	36	77	4	5	0	209	219	31	31	3.1	.932	3B-76, OF-35, 2B-33
1960	NY	A	131	.284	.414	408	116	14	6	9	2.2	66	42	46	64	1	26	2	204	9	7	2	1.7	.968	OF-106, 2B-5, 3B-1
1961			93	.222	.305	243	54	7	2	3	1.2	27	22	24	38	1	16	4	123	7	3	0	1.4	.977	OF-72
1962			106	.275	.391	335	92	19	1	6	1.8	45	48	33	53	0	24	5	177	5	3	0	1.7	.984	OF-84, 3B-1, 2B-1
1963			130	.249	.395	433	108	13	4	14	3.2	54	52	35	71	1	9	2	188	11	9	2	1.6	.957	OF-124, 2B-1
1964			127	.260	.418	285	74	9	3	10	3.5	34	34	24	54	1	22	7	131	4	4	1	1.1	.971	OF-103, 3B-1
1965			111	.261	.392	283	74	12	2	7	2.5	25	39	26	61	0	28	5	100	3	7	1	1.0	.936	OF-75, 1B-2
1966			54	.214	.368	117	25	4	1	4	3.4	14	16	8	20	0	20	7	43	1	2	1	0.9	.936	OF-29
12 yrs.			1451	.269	.415	4644	1251	193	37	136	2.9	623	591	418	696	16	168	38	2024	1478	170	234	2.5	.954	OF-652, 3B-459, 2B-184, SS-5, 1B-2

WORLD SERIES

Year	Team		Games	BA	SA	AB	H	2B	3B	HR	HR%	R	RBI	BB	SO	SB	Pinch Hit AB	H	PO	A	E	DP	TC/G	FA	G by Pos
1960	NY	A	3	.429	.429	7	3	0	0	0	0.0	0	0	0	0	0	2	2	0	1	0	0	0.3	1.000	OF-1
1961			4	.333	.889	9	3	0	1	1	11.1	3	7	2	3	0	0	0	8	0	0	0	2.0	1.000	OF-3
1962			2	.000	.000	2	0	0	0	0	0.0	0	0	0	2	0	0	0	0	0	0	0	0.0	—	OF-3
1963			3	.250	.500	8	2	0	1	0	0.0	1	0	0	1	0	0	0	3	0	0	0	0.7	1.000	OF-2

Year Team	Games	BA	SA	AB	H	2B	3B	HR	HR%	R	RBI	BB	SO	SB	Pinch Hit AB	H	PO	A	E	DP	TC/G	FA	G by Pos

Hector Lopez *continued*

Year Team	Games	BA	SA	AB	H	2B	3B	HR	HR%	R	RBI	BB	SO	SB	AB	H	PO	A	E	DP	TC/G	FA	G by Pos
1964	3	.000	.000	2	0	0	0	0	0.0	0	0	0	2	0	2	0	0	0	0	0	0.0	–	OF-1
5 yrs.	15	.286	.536	28	8	2	1	1	3.6	4	7	2	6	0	7	2	10	1	0	0	0.7	1.000	OF-7
																	6th						

Bris Lord

LORD, BRISCOE ROBOTHAM (The Human Eyeball)
B. Sept. 21, 1883, Upland, Pa. D. Nov. 13, 1964, Annapolis, Md.

BR TR 5'9" 185 lbs.

Year Team	Games	BA	SA	AB	H	2B	3B	HR	HR%	R	RBI	BB	SO	SB	AB	H	PO	A	E	DP	TC/G	FA	G by Pos
1905 PHI A	66	.239	.298	238	57	14	0	0	0.0	41	13	14		3	5	1	94	9	4	3	1.6	.963	OF-60, 3B-1
1906	118	.233	.302	434	101	13	7	1	0.2	50	44	27		12	2	1	212	13	14	4	2.0	.941	OF-115
1907	57	.182	.218	170	31	3	0	1	0.6	12	11	14		2	4	1	91	6	5	0	1.8	.951	OF-53, P-1
1909 CLE A	69	.269	.333	249	67	7	3	1	0.4	26	25	8		10	2	0	110	13	1	4	1.8	.992	OF-69
1910 2 teams		CLE A	(56G – .219)		PHI A	(72G – .278)																	
" total	128	.254	.376	489	124	21	18	1	0.2	76	37	35		10	2	1	219	20	7	6	1.9	.972	OF-126
1911 PHI A	134	.310	.429	574	178	37	11	3	0.5	92	55	35		15	2	1	271	17	11	5	2.2	.963	OF-132
1912	96	.238	.317	378	90	12	9	0	0.0	63	25	34		15	0	0	148	15	10	5	1.8	.942	OF-96
1913 BOS N	73	.251	.387	235	59	12	1	6	2.6	22	26	8	22	7	11	1	81	4	8	2	1.3	.914	OF-62
8 yrs.	741	.256	.348	2767	707	119	49	13	0.5	382	236	175	22	74	28	6	1226	97	60	27	1.9	.957	OF-713, 3B-1, P-1

WORLD SERIES

Year Team	Games	BA	SA	AB	H	2B	3B	HR	HR%	R	RBI	BB	SO	SB	AB	H	PO	A	E	DP	TC/G	FA	G by Pos
1905 PHI A	5	.100	.100	20	2	0	0	0	0.0	0	2	1	5	0	0	0	11	1	0	0	2.4	1.000	OF-5
1910	5	.182	.273	22	4	2	0	0	0.0	3	1	1	3	0	0	0	8	0	0	0	1.6	1.000	OF-5
1911	6	.185	.259	27	5	2	0	0	0.0	2	1	0	5	0	0	0	14	1	0	0	2.5	1.000	OF-6
3 yrs.	16	.159	.217	69	11	4	0	0	0.0	5	4	1	13	0	0	0	33	2	0	0	2.2	1.000	OF-16

Carlton Lord

LORD, WILLIAM CARLTON
B. Jan. 7, 1900, Philadelphia, Pa. D. Aug. 15, 1947, Chester, Pa.

BR TR 5'11" 170 lbs.

Year Team	Games	BA	SA	AB	H	2B	3B	HR	HR%	R	RBI	BB	SO	SB	AB	H	PO	A	E	DP	TC/G	FA	G by Pos
1923 PHI N	17	.234	.277	47	11	2	0	0	0.0	3	2	2	3	0	3	1	12	23	7	1	2.5	.833	3B-14

Harry Lord

LORD, HARRY DONALD
B. Mar. 8, 1882, Porter, Me. D. Aug. 9, 1948, Westbrook, Me.
Manager 1915.

BL TR 5'10½" 165 lbs.

Year Team	Games	BA	SA	AB	H	2B	3B	HR	HR%	R	RBI	BB	SO	SB	AB	H	PO	A	E	DP	TC/G	FA	G by Pos
1907 BOS A	10	.158	.184	38	6	1	0	0	0.0	4	3	1		1	0	0	12	22	3	0	3.7	.919	3B-10
1908	145	.260	.319	558	145	15	6	2	0.4	61	37	22		23	1	0	181	271	47	13	3.4	.906	3B-143
1909	136	.311	.360	534	166	12	7	0	0.0	85	31	20		36	1	0	180	268	34	10	3.5	.929	3B-134
1910 2 teams		BOS A	(77G – .250)		CHI A	(44G – .297)																	
" total	121	.267	.333	453	121	11	8	1	0.2	51	42	28		34	3	1	136	219	27	15	3.2	.929	3B-114, SS-1
1911 CHI A	141	.321	.433	561	180	18	18	3	0.5	103	61	32		43	2	0	175	226	25	21	3.0	.941	3B-138
1912	151	.267	.368	570	152	19	12	5	0.9	81	54	52		28	0	0	188	177	38	14	2.7	.906	3B-106, OF-45
1913	150	.263	.346	547	144	18	12	1	0.2	62	42	45	39	24	0	0	142	221	30	13	2.6	.924	3B-150
1914	21	.188	.275	69	13	1	1	1	1.4	8	3	5	3	2	0	0	10	32	3	0	2.1	.933	3B-19, OF-1
1915 BUF F	97	.270	.345	359	97	12	6	1	0.3	50	21	21		15	3	1	86	158	14	13	2.7	.946	3B-92, OF-1
9 yrs.	972	.278	.356	3689	1024	107	70	14	0.4	505	294	226	42	206	10	2	1110	1594	221	99	3.0	.924	3B-906, OF-47, SS-1

Scott Loucks

LOUCKS, SCOTT GREGORY
B. Nov. 11, 1956, Anchorage, Alaska

BR TR 6' 178 lbs.

Year Team	Games	BA	SA	AB	H	2B	3B	HR	HR%	R	RBI	BB	SO	SB	AB	H	PO	A	E	DP	TC/G	FA	G by Pos
1980 HOU N	8	.333	.333	3	1	0	0	0	0.0	4	0	0	2	1	1	0	1	0	0	0	0.1	1.000	OF-4
1981	10	.571	.571	7	4	0	0	0	0.0	2	0	1	3	1	0	0	5	0	0	0	0.5	1.000	OF-5
1982	44	.224	.265	49	11	2	0	0	0.0	6	3	3	17	4	5	0	41	3	1	1	1.0	.978	OF-37
1983	7	.214	.214	14	3	0	0	0	0.0	2	0	1	4	2	1	0	12	0	0	0	1.9	1.000	OF-6
1985 PIT N	4	.286	.571	7	2	2	0	0	0.0	1	1	2	2	0	1	1	2	0	0	0	0.5	1.000	OF-4
5 yrs.	73	.263	.313	80	21	4	0	0	0.0	15	4	7	28	7	8	1	61	3	1	1	0.9	.985	OF-56

Baldy Louden

LOUDEN, WILLIAM P.
B. Aug. 27, 1885, Piedmont, W. Va. D. Dec. 8, 1935, Piedmont, W. Va.

BR TR 5'11" 175 lbs.

Year Team	Games	BA	SA	AB	H	2B	3B	HR	HR%	R	RBI	BB	SO	SB	AB	H	PO	A	E	DP	TC/G	FA	G by Pos
1907 NY A	5	.111	.111	9	1	0	0	0	0.0	4	0	2		1	0	0	4	8	4	0	3.2	.750	3B-3
1912 DET A	121	.241	.298	403	97	12	4	1	0.2	57	36	58		28	2	1	242	370	39	25	5.4	.940	2B-86, 3B-26, SS-5
1913	72	.241	.314	191	46	4	5	0	0.0	28	23	24	22	6	2	0	76	146	17	11	3.3	.929	2B-32, 3B-26, SS-6, OF-5
1914 BUF F	126	.313	.399	431	135	11	4	6	1.4	73	63	52		35	10	4	299	285	43	34	5.0	.931	SS-115
1915	141	.281	.367	469	132	18	5	4	0.9	67	48	64		30	2	0	283	391	27	51	5.0	.961	2B-88, SS-27, 3B-19
1916 CIN N	134	.219	.280	439	96	16	4	1	0.2	38	32	54	54	12	5	0	279	417	25	51	5.4	.965	2B-108, SS-23
6 yrs.	599	.261	.334	1942	507	61	22	12	0.6	267	202	254	76	112	21	5	1183	1617	155	172	4.9	.948	2B-314, SS-176, 3B-74, OF-5

Charlie Loudenslager

LOUDENSLAGER, CHARLES EDWARD
B. May 21, 1881, Baltimore, Md. D. Oct. 31, 1933, Baltimore, Md.

TR 5'9" 186 lbs.

Year Team	Games	BA	SA	AB	H	2B	3B	HR	HR%	R	RBI	BB	SO	SB	AB	H	PO	A	E	DP	TC/G	FA	G by Pos
1904 BKN N	1	.000	.000	2	0	0	0	0	0.0	0	0	0		0	0	0	1	0	0	0	1.0	1.000	2B-1

Bill Loughlin

LOUGHLIN, WILLIAM H.
B. Baltimore, Md. Deceased.

Year Team	Games	BA	SA	AB	H	2B	3B	HR	HR%	R	RBI	BB	SO	SB	AB	H	PO	A	E	DP	TC/G	FA	G by Pos
1883 BAL AA	1	.400	.400	5	2	0	0	0	0.0	0				0	0	0	0	0	0	0	0.0	–	OF-1

Loughran

LOUGHRAN,
B. New York, N. Y. Deceased.

Year Team	Games	BA	SA	AB	H	2B	3B	HR	HR%	R	RBI	BB	SO	SB	AB	H	PO	A	E	DP	TC/G	FA	G by Pos
1884 NY N	9	.103	.207	29	3	1	1	0	0.0	4		7	11		0	0	46	8	10	1	7.1	.844	C-9, OF-1

Tom Lovelace

LOVELACE, THOMAS RIVERS
B. Oct. 19, 1897, Wolfe City, Tex. D. July 12, 1979, Dallas, Tex.

BR TR 5'11" 170 lbs.

Year Team	Games	BA	SA	AB	H	2B	3B	HR	HR%	R	RBI	BB	SO	SB	AB	H	PO	A	E	DP	TC/G	FA	G by Pos
1922 PIT N	1	.000	.000	1	0	0	0	0	0.0	0	0	0	0	0	1	0	0	0	0	0	0.0	–	

Mem Lovett

LOVETT, MERRITT MARWOOD
B. June 15, 1912, Chicago, Ill.

BR TR 5'9½" 165 lbs.

Mem Lovett *continued*

Year Team	Games	BA	SA	AB	H	2B	3B	HR	HR%	R	RBI	BB	SO	SB	Pinch Hit AB	Pinch Hit H	PO	A	E	DP	TC/G	FA	G by Pos
1933 CHI A	1	.000	.000	1	0	0	0	0	0.0	0	0	0	0	0	1	0	0	0	0	0	0.0	—	

Jay Loviglio

LOVIGLIO, JOHN PAUL
B. May 30, 1956, Freeport, N. Y. — BR TR 5'9" 160 lbs.

Year Team	Games	BA	SA	AB	H	2B	3B	HR	HR%	R	RBI	BB	SO	SB	Pinch Hit AB	Pinch Hit H	PO	A	E	DP	TC/G	FA	G by Pos
1980 PHI N	16	.000	.000	5	0	0	0	0	0.0	7	0	1	0	1	0	0	3	2	0	0	0.3	1.000	2B-1
1981 CHI A	14	.267	.267	15	4	0	0	0	0.0	5	2	1	1	2	0	0	9	10	3	2	1.6	.864	3B-4, 2B-3, DH-2
1982	15	.194	.194	31	6	0	0	0	0.0	5	2	1	4	2	0	0	24	30	2	5	3.7	.964	2B-13, DH-2
1983 CHI N	1	.000	.000	1	0	0	0	0	0.0	0	0	0	1	0	1	0	0	0	0	0	0.0		
4 yrs.	46	.192	.192	52	10	0	0	0	0.0	17	4	3	6	5	1	0	36	42	5	7	1.8	.940	2B-17, DH-4, 3B-4

Joe Lovitto

LOVITTO, JOSEPH JR.
B. Jan. 6, 1951, San Pedro, Calif. — BB TR 6' 185 lbs.

Year Team	Games	BA	SA	AB	H	2B	3B	HR	HR%	R	RBI	BB	SO	SB	Pinch Hit AB	Pinch Hit H	PO	A	E	DP	TC/G	FA	G by Pos
1972 TEX A	117	.224	.267	330	74	9	1	1	0.3	23	19	37	54	13	7	1	233	7	6	2	2.1	.976	OF-103
1973	26	.136	.159	44	6	1	0	0	0.0	3	0	5	7	1	0	0	26	21	5	3	2.0	.904	3B-20, OF-3
1974	113	.223	.297	283	63	9	3	2	0.7	27	26	25	36	6	1	0	224	7	6	4	2.1	.975	OF-107, 1B-5
1975	50	.208	.264	106	22	3	0	1	0.9	17	8	13	16	2	7	1	71	3	1	1	1.5	.987	OF-38, DH-2, 1B-1, C-1
4 yrs.	306	.216	.271	763	165	22	4	4	0.5	70	53	80	113	22	15	2	554	38	18	10	2.0	.970	OF-251, 3B-20, 1B-6, DH-2, C-1

Torey Lovullo

LOVULLO, SALVATORE ANTHONY
B. July 25, 1965, Santa Monica, Calif. — BB TR 6' 185 lbs.

Year Team	Games	BA	SA	AB	H	2B	3B	HR	HR%	R	RBI	BB	SO	SB	Pinch Hit AB	Pinch Hit H	PO	A	E	DP	TC/G	FA	G by Pos
1988 DET A	12	.381	.667	21	8	1	1	1	4.8	2	2	1	2	0	0	0	12	19	0	2	2.6	1.000	2B-9, 3B-3
1989	29	.115	.172	87	10	2	0	1	1.1	8	4	14	20	0	4	0	134	24	1	15	5.5	.994	1B-18, 3B-11
2 yrs.	41	.167	.269	108	18	3	1	2	1.9	10	6	15	22	0	4	0	146	43	1	17	4.6	.995	1B-18, 3B-14, 2B-9

Fletcher Low

LOW, FLETCHER
B. Apr. 7, 1893, Essex, Mass. D. June 6, 1973, Hanover, N. H. — BR TR 5'10½" 175 lbs.

Year Team	Games	BA	SA	AB	H	2B	3B	HR	HR%	R	RBI	BB	SO	SB	Pinch Hit AB	Pinch Hit H	PO	A	E	DP	TC/G	FA	G by Pos
1915 BOS N	1	.250	.750	4	1	0	1	0	0.0	1	1	0	0	0	0	0	2	1	0	0	3.0	1.000	3B-1

Bobby Lowe

LOWE, ROBERT LINCOLN (Link)
B. July 10, 1868, Pittsburg, Pa. D. Dec. 8, 1951, Detroit, Mich. — BR TR 5'10" 150 lbs.
Manager 1904.

Year Team	Games	BA	SA	AB	H	2B	3B	HR	HR%	R	RBI	BB	SO	SB	Pinch Hit AB	Pinch Hit H	PO	A	E	DP	TC/G	FA	G by Pos
1890 BOS N	52	.280	.391	207	58	13	2	2	1.0	35	21	26	32	15	0	0	103	82	11	2	3.8	.944	SS-24, OF-15, 3B-12
1891	125	.260	.354	497	129	19	5	6	1.2	92	74	53	54	43	1	0	214	70	24	5	2.5	.922	OF-107, 2B-17, SS-2, 3B-1, P-1
1892	124	.242	.324	475	115	16	7	3	0.6	79	57	37	46	36	0	0	264	119	37	18	3.4	.912	OF-90, 3B-14, SS-13, 2B-10
1893	126	.298	.428	526	157	19	5	13	2.5	130	89	55	29	22	0	0	320	425	52	59	6.3	.935	2B-121, SS-5
1894	133	.346	.520	613	212	34	11	17	2.8	158	115	50	25	23	0	0	348	408	59	63	6.1	.928	2B-130, SS-2, 3B-1
1895	99	.296	.410	412	122	12	7	7	1.7	101	62	40	16	24	0	0	265	336	29	50	6.4	.954	2B-99
1896	73	.321	.403	305	98	11	4	2	0.7	59	48	20	11	15	0	0	193	280	17	31	6.7	.965	2B-73
1897	123	.309	.419	499	154	24	8	5	1.0	87	106	32		16	0	0	270	404	34	33	5.8	.952	2B-123
1898	147	.272	.338	559	152	11	7	4	0.7	65	94	26		12	0	0	405	467	38	64	6.2	.958	2B-145, SS-2
1899	152	.272	.335	559	152	5	9	4	0.7	81	88	35		17	0	0	366	473	40	66	5.8	.954	2B-148, SS-4
1900	127	.278	.342	474	132	11	5	3	0.6	65	71	26		15	0	0	323	335	34	38	5.4	.951	2B-127
1901	129	.255	.299	491	125	11	1	3	0.6	47	47	17		22	0	0	201	244	38	21	3.7	.921	3B-111, 2B-18
1902 CHI N	121	.246	.286	472	116	13	3	0	0.0	41	31	11		16	0	0	329	410	33	59	6.4	.957	2B-117, 3B-2
1903	32	.267	.371	105	28	5	3	0	0.0	14	15	4		5	1	1	91	80	11	13	5.7	.940	2B-22, 1B-6, 3B-1
1904 2 teams	PIT N (1G – .000)			DET A (140G – .208)																			
" total	141	.207	.258	507	105	14	6	0	0.0	47	40	17		15	1	0	328	402	27	44	5.4	.964	2B-140
1905 DET A	60	.193	.254	181	35	7	2	0	0.0	17	9	13		3	2	0	93	54	4	1	2.5	.974	OF-25, 3B-22, 2B-6, SS-4, 1B-1
1906	41	.207	.248	145	30	3	0	1	0.7	11	12	4		3	0	0	99	136	16	3	6.1	.936	SS-19, 2B-17, 3B-5
1907	17	.243	.297	37	9	2	0	0	0.0	2	5	4		0	2	0	7	17	3	0	1.6	.889	3B-10, OF-4, SS-2
18 yrs.	1822	.273	.359	7064	1929	230	85	70	1.0	1131	984	473	213	302	9	1	4219	4742	507	570	5.2	.946	2B-1313, OF-241, 3B-179, SS-77, 1B-7, P-1

Dickie Lowe

LOWE, RICHARD ALVERN
B. Jan. 28, 1854, Evansville, Wis. D. June 28, 1922, Jansesville, Wis.

Year Team	Games	BA	SA	AB	H	2B	3B	HR	HR%	R	RBI	BB	SO	SB	Pinch Hit AB	Pinch Hit H	PO	A	E	DP	TC/G	FA	G by Pos
1884 DET N	1	.333	.333	3	1	0	0	0	0.0	0		0	1		0	0	0	1	7	0	8.0	.125	C-1

John Lowenstein

LOWENSTEIN, JOHN LEE
B. Jan. 27, 1947, Wolf Point, Mont. — BL TR 6' 175 lbs.

Year Team	Games	BA	SA	AB	H	2B	3B	HR	HR%	R	RBI	BB	SO	SB	Pinch Hit AB	Pinch Hit H	PO	A	E	DP	TC/G	FA	G by Pos
1970 CLE A	17	.256	.442	43	11	3	1	1	2.3	5	6	1	9	1	3	0	15	37	2	6	3.2	.963	2B-10, OF-2, 3B-2, SS-1
1971	58	.186	.307	140	26	5	0	4	2.9	15	9	16	28	1	9	2	103	66	4	18	3.0	.977	2B-29, OF-18, SS-3
1972	68	.212	.397	151	32	8	1	6	4.0	16	21	20	43	2	11	3	82	7	0	3	1.3	1.000	OF-58, 1B-2
1973	98	.292	.410	305	89	16	1	6	2.0	42	40	23	41	5	20	7	124	85	7	22	2.2	.968	OF-51, DH-25, 2B-25, 3B-8, 1B-1
1974	140	.242	.325	508	123	14	2	8	1.6	65	48	53	85	36	2	1	314	84	6	11	2.9	.985	OF-100, 3B-28, 1B-12, 2B-4
1975	91	.242	.404	265	64	5	1	12	4.5	37	33	28	28	15	14	4	61	16	2	1	0.9	.975	OF-36, DH-31, 3B-8, 2B-2
1976	93	.205	.284	229	47	8	2	2	0.9	33	14	25	35	11	16	2	178	10	7	9	2.1	.964	OF-61, DH-11, 1B-1
1977	81	.242	.376	149	36	6	1	4	2.7	24	12	21	29	4	25	4	63	1	0	0	0.8	1.000	OF-39, DH-19, 1B-1
1978 TEX A	77	.222	.386	176	39	8	3	5	2.8	28	21	28	37	16	22	6	34	42	6	2	1.1	.927	3B-25, DH-21, OF-16
1979 BAL A	97	.254	.482	197	50	8	2	11	5.6	33	34	30	37	16	23	5	124	7	1	3	1.4	.992	OF-72, DH-3, 3B-1, 1B-1
1980	104	.311	.413	196	61	8	0	4	2.0	38	27	32	29	7	12	5	128	3	1	0	1.3	.992	OF-91, DH-3
1981	83	.249	.381	189	47	7	0	6	3.2	19	20	22	32	7	10	3	100	3	1	0	1.1	.990	OF-73, DH-4
1982	122	.320	.602	322	103	15	2	24	7.5	69	66	54	59	7	17	5	202	2	0	0	1.7	1.000	OF-111
1983	122	.281	.481	310	87	13	2	15	4.8	52	60	49	55	3	16	4	155	8	3	1	1.4	.982	OF-107, DH-1, 2B-1
1984	105	.237	.374	270	64	13	0	8	3.0	34	28	33	54	6	26	6	113	5	3	2	1.2	.975	OF-67, DH-22, 1B-2

Year	Team	Games	BA	SA	AB	H	2B	3B	HR	HR%	R	RBI	BB	SO	SB	Pinch Hit AB	Pinch Hit H	PO	A	E	DP	TC/G	FA	G by Pos

John Lowenstein *continued*

Year	Team	Games	BA	SA	AB	H	2B	3B	HR	HR%	R	RBI	BB	SO	SB	PH AB	PH H	PO	A	E	DP	TC/G	FA	G by Pos
1985		12	.077	.077	26	2	0	0	0	0.0	0	2	2	3	0	3	0	7	0	0	0	0.6	1.000	DH-6, OF-4
16 yrs.		1368	.253	.403	3476	881	137	18	116	3.3	510	441	446	596	128	229	55	1803	376	43	78	1.6	.981	OF-906, DH-146, 3B-72, 2B-71, 1B-28, SS-4

LEAGUE CHAMPIONSHIP SERIES

Year	Team	Games	BA	SA	AB	H	2B	3B	HR	HR%	R	RBI	BB	SO	SB	PH AB	PH H	PO	A	E	DP	TC/G	FA	G by Pos
1979	BAL A	4	.167	.667	6	1	0	0	1	16.7	2	3	2	2	0	2	1	6	0	0	0	1.5	1.000	OF-3
1983		2	.167	.333	6	1	1	0	0	0.0	0	2	1	2	0	0	0	4	0	0	0	2.0	1.000	OF-2, DH-1
2 yrs.		6	.167	.500	12	2	1	0	1	8.3	2	5	3	4	0	2	1	10	0	0	0	1.7	1.000	OF-5, DH-1

WORLD SERIES

Year	Team	Games	BA	SA	AB	H	2B	3B	HR	HR%	R	RBI	BB	SO	SB	PH AB	PH H	PO	A	E	DP	TC/G	FA	G by Pos
1979	BAL A	6	.231	.308	13	3	0	0	0	0.0	2	3	1	3	0	3	2	6	0	1	0	1.2	.857	OF-3
1983		4	.385	.692	13	5	1	0	1	7.7	2	1	0	3	0	0	0	4	0	1	0	1.3	.800	OF-4
2 yrs.		10	.308	.500	26	8	2	0	1	3.8	4	4	1	6	0	3	2	10	0	2	0	1.2	.833	OF-7

Peanuts Lowrey

LOWREY, HARRY LEE
B. Aug. 27, 1918, Culver City, Calif. D. July 2, 1986, Inglewood, Calif.

BR TR 5'8½" 170 lbs.

Year	Team	Games	BA	SA	AB	H	2B	3B	HR	HR%	R	RBI	BB	SO	SB	PH AB	PH H	PO	A	E	DP	TC/G	FA	G by Pos
1942	CHI N	27	.190	.241	58	11	0	0	0		1.7	4	4	4	4	0	3	0	43	2	1	1	1.7	.978	OF-19
1943		130	.292	.400	480	140	25	12	1	0.2	59	63	35	24	13	4	1	341	62	10	11	3.2	.976	OF-113, SS-16, 2B-3
1945		143	.283	.392	523	148	22	7	7	1.3	72	89	48	27	11	5	1	281	19	5	1	2.9	.984	OF-138, SS-2
1946		144	.257	.343	540	139	24	5	4	0.7	75	54	56	22	10	0	0	330	49	12	5	2.7	.969	OF-126, 3B-20
1947		115	.281	.375	448	126	17	5	5	1.1	56	37	38	26	2	1	0	138	200	17	21	3.1	.952	3B-91, OF-25, 2B-6
1948		129	.294	.349	435	128	12	3	2	0.5	47	54	34	31	2	13	3	238	29	5	4	2.1	.982	OF-103, 3B-9, 2B-2, SS-1
1949	2 teams		CHI N	(38G – .270)					CIN N	(89G – .275)														
"	total	127	.274	.362	420	115	21	2	4	1.0	66	35	46	19	4	16	6	259	9	4	2	2.1	.985	OF-109, 3B-1
1950	2 teams		CIN N	(91G – .227)					STL N	(17G – .268)														
"	total	108	.234	.297	320	75	14	0	2	0.6	44	15	42	8	0	14	2	184	36	4	8	2.1	.982	OF-76, 2B-7, 3B-5
1951	STL N	114	.303	.422	370	112	19	5	5	1.4	52	40	35	12	0	19	5	230	25	9	5	2.3	.966	OF-85, 3B-11, 2B-3
1952		132	.286	.353	374	107	18	2	1	0.3	48	48	34	13	3	27	13	176	20	7	2	1.5	.966	OF-106, 3B-6
1953		104	.269	.423	182	49	9	2	5	2.7	26	27	15	21	1	59	22	64	20	3	6	0.8	.966	OF-38, 2B-10, 3B-1
1954		74	.115	.197	61	7	1	2	0	0.0	9	9	9	9	0	53	7	5	0	0	0	0.1	1.000	OF-12
1955	PHI N	54	.189	.226	106	20	4	0	0	0.0	9	8	7	10	2	16	2	44	6	1	2	0.9	.980	OF-28, 2B-2, 1B-1
13 yrs.		1401	.273	.362	4317	1177	186	45	37	0.9	564	479	403	226	48	230	62	2333	477	78	68	2.1	.973	OF-978, 3B-144, 2B-33, SS-19, 1B-1

WORLD SERIES

Year	Team	Games	BA	SA	AB	H	2B	3B	HR	HR%	R	RBI	BB	SO	SB	PH AB	PH H	PO	A	E	DP	TC/G	FA	G by Pos
1945	CHI N	7	.310	.345	29	9	1	0	0	0.0	4	0	1	2	1	0	0	21	1	0	0	3.1	1.000	OF-7

Dwight Lowry

LOWRY, DWIGHT
Born Dwight Lowery.
B. Oct. 23, 1957, Lumberton, N. C.

BL TR 6'3" 210 lbs.

Year	Team	Games	BA	SA	AB	H	2B	3B	HR	HR%	R	RBI	BB	SO	SB	PH AB	PH H	PO	A	E	DP	TC/G	FA	G by Pos
1984	DET A	32	.244	.422	45	11	2	0	2	4.4	8	7	3	11	0	4	1	87	8	0	2	3.0	1.000	C-31
1986		56	.307	.393	150	46	4	0	3	2.0	21	18	17	19	0	0	0	250	17	2	2	4.8	.993	C-55, OF-1, 1B-1
1987		13	.200	.280	25	5	2	0	0	0.0	0	1	0	6	0	1	0	40	2	0	0	3.2	1.000	C-12, 1B-1
1988	MIN A	7	.000	.000	7	0	0	0	0	0.0	0	0	0	2	0	2	0	12	1	0	0	1.9	1.000	C-5
4 yrs.		108	.273	.374	227	62	8	0	5	2.2	29	26	20	38	0	7	1	389	28	2	4	3.9	.995	C-103, 1B-2, OF-1

Willie Lozado

LOZADO, WILLIAM
B. May 12, 1959, New York, N. Y.

BR TR 6'1" 170 lbs.

Year	Team	Games	BA	SA	AB	H	2B	3B	HR	HR%	R	RBI	BB	SO	SB	PH AB	PH H	PO	A	E	DP	TC/G	FA	G by Pos
1984	MIL A	43	.271	.411	107	29	8	1	1	0.9	15	20	12	23	0	2	0	26	61	7	7	2.2	.926	3B-36, SS-6, DH-1, 2B-1

Steve Lubratich

LUBRATICH, STEVEN GEORGE
B. May 1, 1955, Oakland, Calif.

BR TR 6' 170 lbs.

Year	Team	Games	BA	SA	AB	H	2B	3B	HR	HR%	R	RBI	BB	SO	SB	PH AB	PH H	PO	A	E	DP	TC/G	FA	G by Pos
1981	CAL A	7	.143	.190	21	3	1	0	0	0.0	2	1	0	2	1	0	0	2	17	0	2	2.7	1.000	3B-6
1983		57	.218	.276	156	34	9	0	0	0.0	12	7	4	17	0	0	0	91	149	7	34	4.3	.972	SS-23, 3B-22, 2B-14
2 yrs.		64	.209	.266	177	37	10	0	0	0.0	14	8	4	19	1	0	0	93	166	7	36	4.2	.974	3B-28, SS-23, 2B-14

Hugh Luby

LUBY, HUGH MAX (Hal)
B. June 13, 1913, Blackfoot, Ida. D. May 4, 1986, Eugene, Ore.

BR TR 5'10" 185 lbs.

Year	Team	Games	BA	SA	AB	H	2B	3B	HR	HR%	R	RBI	BB	SO	SB	PH AB	PH H	PO	A	E	DP	TC/G	FA	G by Pos
1936	PHI A	9	.184	.211	38	7	1	0	0	0.0	3	3	0	7	0	0	0	16	28	6	3	5.6	.880	2B-9
1944	NY N	111	.254	.316	323	82	10	2	2	0.6	30	35	52	15	2	2	0	179	244	19	35	4.0	.957	3B-65, 2B-45, 1B-1
2 yrs.		120	.247	.305	361	89	11	2	2	0.6	33	38	52	22	2	2	0	195	272	25	38	4.1	.949	3B-65, 2B-54, 1B-1

Pat Luby

LUBY, JOHN PERKINS
B. 1868, Charleston, S. C. D. Apr. 24, 1899, Charleston, S. C.

TR 6' 185 lbs.

Year	Team	Games	BA	SA	AB	H	2B	3B	HR	HR%	R	RBI	BB	SO	SB	PH AB	PH H	PO	A	E	DP	TC/G	FA	G by Pos
1890	CHI N	36	.267	.440	116	31	5	3	3	2.6	27	17	9	6	3	0	0	31	44	3	0	2.2	.962	P-34, 1B-2
1891		32	.245	.408	98	24	2	4	2	2.0	19	24	8	16	3	0	0	14	42	3	2	1.8	.949	P-30, OF-2, 1B-1
1892		45	.190	.270	163	31	3	2	2	1.2	14	20	12	27	3	0	0	28	62	9	3	2.2	.909	P-31, OF-16
1895	LOU N	19	.283	.396	53	15	2	2	0	0.0	6	9	8	3	2	0	0	54	25	5	5	4.4	.940	P-11, 1B-5, OF-2
4 yrs.		132	.235	.363	430	101	12	11	7	1.6	66	70	37	52	11	0	0	127	173	20	10	2.4	.938	P-106, OF-20, 1B-8

Johnny Lucadello

LUCADELLO, JOHN
B. Feb. 22, 1919, Thurber, Tex.

BB TR 5'11" 160 lbs.

Year	Team	Games	BA	SA	AB	H	2B	3B	HR	HR%	R	RBI	BB	SO	SB	PH AB	PH H	PO	A	E	DP	TC/G	FA	G by Pos
1938	STL A	7	.150	.200	20	3	1	0	0	0.0	1	0	0	0	0	1	0	5	5	1	0	1.6	.909	3B-6
1939		9	.233	.300	30	7	2	0	0	0.0	4	4	2	4	0	2	1	16	15	3	3	3.8	.912	2B-7
1940		17	.317	.508	63	20	4	2	2	3.2	15	10	6	4	1	1	0	37	53	3	14	5.5	.968	2B-16
1941		107	.279	.382	351	98	22	4	2	0.6	58	31	48	23	5	22	2	195	209	22	40	4.0	.948	2B-70, SS-12, 3B-6, OF-1
1946		87	.248	.305	210	52	7	1	0	0.5	21	15	36	20	0	25	7	84	102	7	14	2.2	.964	2B-37, 2B-19
1947	NY A	12	.083	.083	12	1	0	0	0	0.0	1	0	1	5	0	7	1	3	0	0	0	0.3	1.000	2B-5
6 yrs.		239	.264	.359	686	181	36	7	5	0.7	95	60	93	56	6	58	11	340	384	36	71	3.2	.953	2B-117, 3B-49, SS-12, OF-1

Year Team	Games	BA	SA	AB	H	2B	3B	HR	HR%	R	RBI	BB	SO	SB	Pinch Hit AB	Pinch Hit H	PO	A	E	DP	TC/G	FA	G by Pos

Fritz Lucas

LUCAS, FREDERICK WARRINGTON
B. Jan. 19, 1903, Vineland, N. J.   D. Mar. 11, 1987, Cambridge, Md.
BR TR 5'10"   165 lbs.

Year Team	Games	BA	SA	AB	H	2B	3B	HR	HR%	R	RBI	BB	SO	SB	PH AB	PH H	PO	A	E	DP	TC/G	FA	G by Pos
1935 PHI N	20	.265	.265	34	9	0	0	0	0.0	1	2	3	6	0	8	1	17	0	1	0	0.9	.944	OF-10

Johnny Lucas

LUCAS, JOHN CHARLES (Buster)
B. Feb. 10, 1903, Glen Carbon, Ill.   D. Oct. 31, 1970, Maryville, Ill.
BR TL 5'10"   186 lbs.

Year Team	Games	BA	SA	AB	H	2B	3B	HR	HR%	R	RBI	BB	SO	SB	PH AB	PH H	PO	A	E	DP	TC/G	FA	G by Pos
1931 BOS A	3	.000	.000	2	0	0	0	0	0.0	0	0	0	1	0	0	0	0	0	0	0	0.0	–	OF-2
1932	1	.000	.000	1	0	0	0	0	0.0	0	0	0	0	0	1	0	0	0	0	0	0.0	–	
2 yrs.	4	.000	.000	3	0	0	0	0	0.0	0	0	0	1	0	1	0	0	0	0	0	0.0	–	OF-2

Red Lucas

LUCAS, CHARLES FREDERICK (The Nashville Narcissus)
B. Apr. 28, 1902, Columbia, Tenn.   D. July 9, 1986, Nashville, Tenn.
BL TR 5'9½"   170 lbs.

Year Team	Games	BA	SA	AB	H	2B	3B	HR	HR%	R	RBI	BB	SO	SB	PH AB	PH H	PO	A	E	DP	TC/G	FA	G by Pos
1923 NY N	3	.000	.000	2	0	0	0	0	0.0	0	0	0	1	0	0	0	1	3	0	0	1.3	1.000	P-3
1924 BOS N	33	.333	.364	33	11	1	0	0	0.0	5	5	1	4	0	3	0	5	23	0	1	0.8	1.000	P-27, 3B-2
1925	6	.150	.150	20	3	0	0	0	0.0	1	2	2	4	0	0	0	9	21	1	3	5.2	.968	2B-6
1926 CIN N	66	.303	.461	76	23	4	4	0	0.0	15	14	10	13	0	21	5	6	36	0	1	0.6	1.000	P-39, 2B-1
1927	80	.313	.373	150	47	5	2	0	0.0	14	28	12	10	0	27	6	14	63	4	4	1.0	.951	P-37, 2B-5, SS-3, OF-1
1928	39	.315	.370	73	23	2	1	0	0.0	8	7	4	6	0	12	4	8	37	0	3	1.2	1.000	P-27
1929	76	.293	.336	140	41	6	0	0	0.0	15	13	13	15	1	42	13	12	63	4	3	1.0	.949	P-32
1930	80	.336	.442	113	38	4	1	2	1.8	18	19	17	4	0	39	14	8	30	0	0	0.5	1.000	P-33
1931	97	.281	.307	153	43	4	0	0	0.0	15	17	12	9	0	60	15	8	54	1	3	0.6	.984	P-29
1932	76	.287	.387	150	43	11	2	0	0.0	13	19	10	9	0	42	10	17	55	2	4	1.0	.973	P-31
1933	75	.287	.377	122	35	6	1	1	0.8	14	15	12	6	0	41	13	3	52	0	5	0.7	1.000	P-29
1934 PIT N	68	.219	.286	105	23	5	1	0	0.0	11	8	6	16	1	34	8	7	24	2	2	0.5	.939	P-29
1935	47	.318	.409	66	21	6	0	0	0.0	6	10	7	11	0	22	8	7	23	1	1	0.7	.968	P-20
1936	69	.241	.296	108	26	4	1	0	0.0	11	14	8	17	0	40	9	8	33	1	4	0.6	.976	P-27
1937	59	.268	.305	82	22	3	0	0	0.0	8	17	7	6	0	37	9	9	19	0	1	0.5	1.000	P-20
1938	33	.109	.109	46	5	0	0	0	0.0	1	2	3	2	0	17	0	3	14	0	1	0.5	1.000	P-13
16 yrs.	907	.281	.347	1439	404	61	13	3	0.2	155	190	124	133	2	437 **6th**	114 **6th**	125	550	16	36	0.8	.977	P-396, 2B-12, SS-3, 3B-2, OF-1

Frank Luce

LUCE, FRANK EDWARD
B. Dec. 6, 1896, Spencer, Ohio   D. Feb. 3, 1942, Milwaukee, Wis.
BL TR 5'11"   180 lbs.

Year Team	Games	BA	SA	AB	H	2B	3B	HR	HR%	R	RBI	BB	SO	SB	PH AB	PH H	PO	A	E	DP	TC/G	FA	G by Pos
1923 PIT N	9	.500	.500	12	6	0	0	0	0.0	2	3	2	2	2	3	0	4	0	0	0	0.4	1.000	OF-5

Fred Luderus

LUDERUS, FREDERICK WILLIAM
B. Sept. 12, 1885, Milwaukee, Wis.   D. Jan. 4, 1961, Milwaukee, Wis.
BL TR 5'11½"   185 lbs.

Year Team	Games	BA	SA	AB	H	2B	3B	HR	HR%	R	RBI	BB	SO	SB	PH AB	PH H	PO	A	E	DP	TC/G	FA	G by Pos
1909 CHI N	11	.297	.459	37	11	1	1	1	2.7	8	9	3		0	0	0	110	4	6	4	10.9	.950	1B-11
1910 2 teams	45					CHI N (24G – .204)			PHI N (21G – .294)														
" total	45	.254	.352	122	31	6	3	0	0.0	15	17	13	8	2	8	2	335	19	7	22	8.0	.981	1B-36
1911 PHI N	146	.301	.472	551	166	24	11	16	2.9	69	99	40	76	6	0	0	1373	77	22	85	10.1	.985	1B-146
1912	148	.257	.381	572	147	31	5	10	1.7	77	69	44	65	8	2	0	1421	104	15	77	10.4	.990	1B-146
1913	155	.262	.432	588	154	32	7	18	3.1	67	86	34	51	5	0	0	1533	92	26	76	10.7	.984	1B-155
1914	121	.248	.388	443	110	16	5	12	2.7	55	55	33	31	2	0	0	1102	76	30	49	10.0	.975	1B-121
1915	141	.315	.457	499	157	36	7	7	1.4	55	62	42	36	9	0	0	1409	99	11	76	10.8	.993	1B-141
1916	146	.281	.374	508	143	26	3	5	1.0	52	53	41	32	8	0	0	1499	71	28	83	10.9	.982	1B-146
1917	154	.261	.351	522	136	24	4	5	1.0	57	72	65	35	5	0	0	1597	91	16	91	11.1	.991	1B-154
1918	125	.288	.378	468	135	23	2	5	1.1	54	67	42	33	4	0	0	1307	98	17	74	11.4	.988	1B-125
1919	138	.293	.405	509	149	30	6	5	1.0	60	54	54	48	6	0	0	1385	108	22	82	11.0	.985	1B-138
1920	16	.156	.219	32	5	2	0	0	0.0	1	4	3	6	0	9	2	55	4	1	6	3.8	.983	1B-7
12 yrs.	1346	.277	.403	4851	1344	251	54	84	1.7	570	647	414	421	55	19	4	13126	843	201	725	10.5	.986	1B-1326

WORLD SERIES

Year Team	Games	BA	SA	AB	H	2B	3B	HR	HR%	R	RBI	BB	SO	SB	PH AB	PH H	PO	A	E	DP	TC/G	FA	G by Pos
1915 PHI N	5	.438	.750	16	7	1	0	1	6.3	1	6	1	4	0	0	0	40	4	1	2	9.0	.978	1B-5

Bill Ludwig

LUDWIG, WILLIAM LAWRENCE
B. May 27, 1882, Louisville, Ky.   D. Sept. 5, 1947, Louisville, Ky.
BR TR

Year Team	Games	BA	SA	AB	H	2B	3B	HR	HR%	R	RBI	BB	SO	SB	PH AB	PH H	PO	A	E	DP	TC/G	FA	G by Pos
1908 STL N	66	.182	.214	187	34	2	2	0	0.0	15	8	16		3	4	0	227	87	16	2	5.0	.952	C-62

Roy Luebbe

LUEBBE, ROY JOHN
B. Sept. 17, 1900, Parkersburg, Iowa   D. Aug. 21, 1985, Papillon, Neb.
BB TR 6'   175 lbs.

Year Team	Games	BA	SA	AB	H	2B	3B	HR	HR%	R	RBI	BB	SO	SB	PH AB	PH H	PO	A	E	DP	TC/G	FA	G by Pos
1925 NY A	8	.000	.000	15	0	0	0	0	0.0	1	3	2	6	0	0	0	26	4	0	0	3.8	1.000	C-8

Henry Luff

LUFF, HENRY T.
B. Sept. 14, 1856, Philadelphia, Pa.   D. Oct. 11, 1916, Philadelphia, Pa.
5'11"   175 lbs.

Year Team	Games	BA	SA	AB	H	2B	3B	HR	HR%	R	RBI	BB	SO	SB	PH AB	PH H	PO	A	E	DP	TC/G	FA	G by Pos
1882 2 teams	31					DET N (3G – .273)			CIN AA (28G – .233)														
" total	31	.237	.298	131	31	4	2	0	0.0	17		2			0	0	273	15	29	15	10.2	.909	1B-27, 2B-3, OF-2
1883 LOU AA	6	.174	.174	23	4	0	0	0	0.0	1		0			0	0	36	1	7	1	7.3	.841	1B-4, OF-2
1884 2 teams	31					PHI U (26G – .270)			KC U (5G – .053)														
" total	31	.238	.300	130	31	4	2	0	0.0	9		5			0	0	95	26	40	4	5.2	.752	OF-16, 3B-9, 1B-6, 2B-3
3 yrs.	68	.232	.289	284	66	8	4	0	0.0	27	1	7			0	0	404	42	76	20	7.7	.854	1B-37, OF-20, 3B-9, 2B-6

Eddie Lukon

LUKON, EDWARD PAUL (Mongoose)
B. Aug. 5, 1920, Burgettstown, Pa.
BL TL 5'10"   168 lbs.

Year Team	Games	BA	SA	AB	H	2B	3B	HR	HR%	R	RBI	BB	SO	SB	PH AB	PH H	PO	A	E	DP	TC/G	FA	G by Pos
1941 CIN N	23	.267	.302	86	23	3	0	0	0.0	6	3	6	6	1	0	0	47	2	1	1	2.2	.980	OF-22
1945	2	.125	.125	8	1	0	0	0	0.0	0	1	0	1	0	0	0	6	0	0	0	3.0	1.000	OF-2
1946	102	.250	.442	312	78	8	8	12	3.8	31	34	26	29	3	18	2	190	5	3	1	1.9	.985	OF-83
1947	86	.205	.410	200	41	6	1	11	5.5	26	33	28	36	0	28	6	103	4	0	2	1.2	1.000	OF-55
4 yrs.	213	.236	.408	606	143	17	9	23	3.8	64	70	60	72	4	46	8	346	11	4	4	1.7	.989	OF-162

Year	Team		Games	BA	SA	AB	H	2B	3B	HR	HR%	R	RBI	BB	SO	SB	Pinch Hit AB	Pinch Hit H	PO	A	E	DP	TC/G	FA	G by Pos

Mike Lum

LUM, MICHAEL KEN-WAI
B. Oct. 27, 1945, Honolulu, Hawaii — BL TL 6' 180 lbs.

Year	Team		Games	BA	SA	AB	H	2B	3B	HR	HR%	R	RBI	BB	SO	SB	PH AB	PH H	PO	A	E	DP	TC/G	FA	G by Pos
1967	ATL	N	9	.231	.231	26	6	0	0	0	0.0	1	0	1	4	0	3	1	16	1	1	0	2.0	.944	OF-6
1968			122	.224	.319	232	52	7	3	3	1.3	22	21	14	35	3	27	8	115	7	3	0	1.0	.976	OF-95
1969			121	.268	.333	168	45	8	0	1	0.6	20	22	16	18	0	31	9	119	2	1	1	1.0	.992	OF-89
1970			123	.254	.399	291	74	17	2	7	2.4	25	28	17	43	3	28	9	168	3	2	0	1.4	.988	OF-98
1971			145	.269	.390	454	122	14	1	13	2.9	56	55	47	43	0	14	2	287	11	3	2	2.1	.990	OF-125, 1B-1
1972			123	.228	.350	369	84	14	2	9	2.4	40	38	50	52	1	15	6	247	6	6	1	2.1	.977	OF-109, 1B-2
1973			138	.294	.462	513	151	26	6	16	3.1	74	82	41	89	2	9	0	833	45	9	64	6.4	.990	1B-84, OF-64
1974			106	.233	.366	361	84	11	2	11	3.0	50	50	45	49	0	10	1	554	26	4	44	5.5	.993	1B-60, OF-50
1975			124	.228	.327	364	83	8	2	8	2.2	32	36	39	38	2	26	4	657	34	5	41	5.6	.993	1B-60, OF-38
1976	CIN	N	84	.228	.346	136	31	5	1	3	2.2	15	20	22	24	0	39	10	48	0	0	0	0.6	1.000	OF-38
1977			81	.160	.288	125	20	1	0	5	4.0	14	16	9	33	2	47	5	83	2	1	4	1.1	.988	OF-24, 1B-8
1978			86	.267	.452	146	39	7	1	6	4.1	15	23	22	18	0	36	11	100	8	2	2	1.3	.982	OF-43, 1B-7
1979	ATL	N	111	.249	.359	217	54	6	0	6	2.8	27	27	18	34	0	52	17	420	30	1	36	4.1	.998	1B-51, OF-3
1980			93	.205	.241	83	17	3	0	0	0.0	7	5	18	19	0	50	12	58	4	0	1	0.7	1.000	OF-19, 1B-10
1981	2 teams		ATL N (10G – .091)				CHI N (41G – .241)																		
"	total		51	.217	.319	69	15	1	0	2	2.9	6	7	7	7	0	31	8	16	0	1	0	0.3	.941	OF-15, 1B-1
	15 yrs.		1517	.247	.370	3554	877	128	20	90	2.5	404	431	366	506	13	418	103	3721	179	39	196	2.6	.990	OF-816, 1B-284
																	8th	10th							

LEAGUE CHAMPIONSHIP SERIES

Year	Team		Games	BA	SA	AB	H	2B	3B	HR	HR%	R	RBI	BB	SO	SB	PH AB	PH H	PO	A	E	DP	TC/G	FA	G by Pos
1969	ATL	N	2	1.000	1.500	2	2	1	0	0	0.0	0	0	0	0	0	1	1	0	0	0	0	0.0	–	OF-1
1976	CIN	N	1	.000	.000	1	0	0	0	0	0.0	0	0	0	0	0	1	0	0	0	0	0	0.0	–	
	2 yrs.		3	.667	1.000	3	2	1	0	0	0.0	0	0	0	0	0	2	1	0	0	0	0	0.0	–	OF-1

Harry Lumley

LUMLEY, HARRY G
B. Sept. 29, 1880, Forest City, Pa. D. May 22, 1938, Binghamton, N. Y. — BL TR 5'10" 183 lbs.
Manager 1909.

Year	Team		Games	BA	SA	AB	H	2B	3B	HR	HR%	R	RBI	BB	SO	SB	PH AB	PH H	PO	A	E	DP	TC/G	FA	G by Pos
1904	BKN	N	150	.279	.428	577	161	23	18	9	1.6	79	78	41		30	0	0	228	26	12	8	1.8	.955	OF-150
1905			130	.293	.412	505	148	19	10	7	1.4	50	47	36		22	1	1	177	21	19	4	1.7	.912	OF-129
1906			133	.324	.477	484	157	23	12	9	1.9	72	61	48		35	2	0	231	13	13	5	1.9	.949	OF-131
1907			127	.267	.425	454	121	23	11	9	2.0	47	66	31		18	9	1	171	15	8	7	1.5	.959	OF-118
1908			127	.216	.327	440	95	13	12	4	0.9	36	39	29		4	11	2	157	13	8	6	1.4	.955	OF-116
1909			55	.250	.331	172	43	8	3	0	0.0	13	14	16		1	3	1	83	9	5	1	1.8	.948	OF-52
1910			8	.143	.143	21	3	0	0	0	0.0	3	0	3	6	0	2	0	5	0	1	0	0.8	.833	OF-4
	7 yrs.		730	.274	.408	2653	728	109	66	38	1.4	300	305	204	6	110	28	5	1052	97	66	31	1.7	.946	OF-700

Jerry Lumpe

LUMPE, JERRY DEAN
B. June 2, 1933, Lincoln, Mo. — BL TR 6'2" 185 lbs.

Year	Team		Games	BA	SA	AB	H	2B	3B	HR	HR%	R	RBI	BB	SO	SB	PH AB	PH H	PO	A	E	DP	TC/G	FA	G by Pos
1956	NY	A	20	.258	.306	62	16	3	0	0	0.0	12	4	5	11	1	4	0	33	56	8	15	4.9	.918	SS-17, 3B-1
1957			40	.340	.437	103	35	6	2	0	0.0	15	11	9	13	2	7	2	22	57	4	8	2.1	.952	3B-30, SS-6
1958			81	.254	.362	232	59	8	4	3	1.3	34	32	23	21	1	16	4	63	135	11	15	2.6	.947	3B-65, SS-6
1959	2 teams		NY A (18G – .222)				KC A (108G – .243)																		
"	total		126	.241	.308	448	108	11	5	3	0.7	49	30	47	39	2	4	1	231	343	13	86	4.7	.978	2B-62, SS-60, 3B-16
1960	KC	A	146	.272	.357	574	156	19	3	8	1.4	69	53	48	49	1	5	0	383	408	16	112	5.5	.980	2B-134, SS-15
1961			148	.293	.392	569	167	29	9	3	0.5	81	54	48	39	1	1	0	403	426	18	105	5.7	.979	2B-147
1962			156	.301	.432	641	193	34	10	10	1.6	89	83	44	38	0	1	1	344	435	11	97	5.1	.986	2B-156, SS-2
1963			157	.271	.363	595	161	26	7	5	0.8	75	59	58	44	3	2	0	341	452	10	92	5.1	.988	2B-155
1964	DET	A	158	.256	.338	624	160	21	6	6	1.0	75	46	50	61	2	0	0	339	394	13	95	4.7	.983	2B-158
1965			145	.257	.323	502	129	15	3	4	0.8	72	39	56	34	7	10	1	281	308	9	69	4.1	.985	2B-139
1966			113	.231	.291	385	89	14	3	1	0.3	30	26	24	44	0	20	2	202	223	4	51	3.8	.991	2B-95
1967			81	.232	.322	177	41	4	0	4	2.3	19	17	16	18	0	29	3	73	93	7	12	2.1	.960	2B-54, 3B-6
	12 yrs.		1371	.268	.356	4912	1314	190	52	47	1.0	620	454	428	411	20	99	14	2715	3330	124	757	4.5	.980	2B-1100, 3B-118, SS-105

WORLD SERIES

Year	Team		Games	BA	SA	AB	H	2B	3B	HR	HR%	R	RBI	BB	SO	SB	PH AB	PH H	PO	A	E	DP	TC/G	FA	G by Pos
1957	NY	A	6	.286	.286	14	4	0	0	0	0.0	0	2	1	1	0	3	2	3	6	0	0	1.5	1.000	3B-3
1958			6	.167	.167	12	2	0	0	0	0.0	0	0	1	2	0	3	0	2	4	0	0	1.0	1.000	3B-3, SS-2
	2 yrs.		12	.231	.231	26	6	0	0	0	0.0	0	2	2	3	0	6	2	5	10	0	0	1.3	1.000	3B-6, SS-2

Don Lund

LUND, DONALD ANDREW
B. May 18, 1923, Detroit, Mich. — BR TR 6' 200 lbs.

Year	Team		Games	BA	SA	AB	H	2B	3B	HR	HR%	R	RBI	BB	SO	SB	PH AB	PH H	PO	A	E	DP	TC/G	FA	G by Pos
1945	BKN	N	4	.000	.000	3	0	0	0	0	0.0	0	0	1	1	0	3	0	0	0	0	0	0.0	–	
1947			11	.300	.700	20	6	2	0	2	10.0	5	5	3	7	0	5	2	11	0	0	0	1.0	1.000	OF-5
1948	2 teams		BKN N (27G – .188)				STL A (63G – .248)																		
"	total		90	.230	.365	230	53	11	4	4	1.7	30	30	15	33	1	16	0	113	5	1	0	1.3	.992	OF-70
1949	DET	A	2	.000	.000	2	0	0	0	0	0.0	0	0	0	1	0	2	0	0	0	0	0	0.0	–	
1952			8	.304	.304	23	7	0	0	0	0.0	1	1	3	3	0	1	0	10	1	0	0	1.4	1.000	OF-7
1953			131	.257	.390	421	108	21	4	9	2.1	51	47	39	65	1	3	2	275	12	6	0	2.2	.980	OF-123
1954			35	.130	.167	54	7	2	0	0	0.0	4	3	4	3	1	9	1	32	1	1	0	1.0	.971	OF-31
	7 yrs.		281	.240	.369	753	181	36	8	15	2.0	91	86	65	113	5	44	5	441	19	8	0	1.7	.983	OF-236

Gordon Lund

LUND, GORDON THOMAS
B. Feb. 23, 1941, Iron Mountain, Mich. — BR TR 5'11" 170 lbs.

Year	Team		Games	BA	SA	AB	H	2B	3B	HR	HR%	R	RBI	BB	SO	SB	PH AB	PH H	PO	A	E	DP	TC/G	FA	G by Pos
1967	CLE	A	3	.250	.375	8	2	1	0	0	0.0	1	0	0	2	0	1	0	1	3	2	2	2.0	.667	SS-2
1969	SEA	A	20	.263	.263	38	10	0	0	0	0.0	4	1	5	7	1	0	0	15	38	5	7	2.9	.914	SS-17, 3B-1, 2B-1
	2 yrs.		23	.261	.283	46	12	1	0	0	0.0	5	1	5	9	1	1	0	16	41	7	9	2.8	.891	SS-19, 3B-1, 2B-1

Tom Lundstedt

LUNDSTEDT, THOMAS ROBERT
B. Apr. 10, 1949, Davenport, Iowa — BR TR 6'4" 195 lbs.

Year	Team		Games	BA	SA	AB	H	2B	3B	HR	HR%	R	RBI	BB	SO	SB	PH AB	PH H	PO	A	E	DP	TC/G	FA	G by Pos
1973	CHI	N	4	.000	.000	5	0	0	0	0	0.0	0	0	1	1	0	0	0	10	1	0	0	2.8	1.000	C-4
1974			22	.094	.094	32	3	0	0	0	0.0	1	0	5	7	0	0	0	70	4	1	0	3.4	.987	C-22

Year	Team	Games	BA	SA	AB	H	2B	3B	HR	HR%	R	RBI	BB	SO	SB	Pinch Hit AB	Pinch Hit H	PO	A	E	DP	TC/G	FA	G by Pos

Tom Lundstedt *continued*

Year	Team	Games	BA	SA	AB	H	2B	3B	HR	HR%	R	RBI	BB	SO	SB	PH AB	PH H	PO	A	E	DP	TC/G	FA	G by Pos
1975	MIN A	18	.107	.107	28	3	0	0	0	0.0	2	1	4	5	0	3	1	46	3	0	2	2.7	1.000	C-14, DH-2
3 yrs.		44	.092	.092	65	6	0	0	0	0.0	3	1	9	13	0	3	1	126	8	1	2	3.1	.993	C-40, DH-2

Harry Lunte

LUNTE, HARRY AUGUST
B. Sept. 15, 1892, St. Louis, Mo.   D. July 27, 1965, St. Louis, Mo.

BR TR 5'11½" 165 lbs.

Year	Team	Games	BA	SA	AB	H	2B	3B	HR	HR%	R	RBI	BB	SO	SB	PH AB	PH H	PO	A	E	DP	TC/G	FA	G by Pos
1919	CLE A	26	.195	.221	77	15	2	0	0	0.0	2	2	1	7	0	2	0	37	64	7	5	4.2	.935	SS-24
1920		28	.197	.197	71	14	0	0	0	0.0	6	7	5	6	0	0	0	31	66	2	7	3.5	.980	SS-21, 2B-3
2 yrs.		54	.196	.209	148	29	2	0	0	0.0	8	9	6	13	0	2	0	68	130	9	12	3.8	.957	SS-45, 2B-3

WORLD SERIES

Year	Team	Games	BA	SA	AB	H	2B	3B	HR	HR%	R	RBI	BB	SO	SB	PH AB	PH H	PO	A	E	DP	TC/G	FA	G by Pos
1920	CLE A	1	–	–	0	0	0	0	0	–	0	0	0	0	0	0	0	0	0	0	0	0.0	–	SS-1

Tony Lupien

LUPIEN, ULYSSES JOHN
B. Apr. 23, 1917, Chelmsford, Mass.

BL TL 5'10½" 185 lbs.

Year	Team	Games	BA	SA	AB	H	2B	3B	HR	HR%	R	RBI	BB	SO	SB	PH AB	PH H	PO	A	E	DP	TC/G	FA	G by Pos
1940	BOS A	10	.474	.842	19	9	3	2	0	0.0	5	4	1	1	0	2	1	37	2	0	4	3.9	1.000	1B-8
1942		128	.281	.384	463	130	25	7	3	0.6	63	70	50	20	10	6	0	1091	68	9	99	9.1	.992	1B-121
1943		154	.255	.339	608	155	21	9	4	0.7	65	47	54	23	16	1	0	1487	118	12	149	10.5	.993	1B-153
1944	PHI N	153	.283	.377	597	169	23	9	5	0.8	82	52	56	29	18	1	1	1453	103	13	114	10.3	.992	1B-151
1945		15	.315	.333	54	17	1	0	0	0.0	1	3	6	0	2	0	0	129	16	0	11	9.7	1.000	1B-15
1948	CHI A	154	.246	.316	617	152	19	3	6	1.0	69	54	74	38	11	0	0	1436	92	11	155	10.0	.993	1B-154
6 yrs.		614	.268	.355	2358	632	92	30	18	0.8	285	230	241	111	57	10	2	5633	399	45	532	9.9	.993	1B-602

Al Luplow

LUPLOW, ALVIN DAVID
B. Mar. 13, 1939, Saginaw, Mich.

BL TR 5'10" 175 lbs.

Year	Team	Games	BA	SA	AB	H	2B	3B	HR	HR%	R	RBI	BB	SO	SB	PH AB	PH H	PO	A	E	DP	TC/G	FA	G by Pos
1961	CLE A	5	.056	.056	18	1	0	0	0	0.0	2	6	0	0	0	0	0	9	2	0	1	2.2	1.000	OF-5
1962		97	.277	.475	318	88	15	3	14	4.4	54	45	36	44	1	13	4	162	4	7	0	1.8	.960	OF-86
1963		100	.234	.339	295	69	6	2	7	2.4	34	27	33	62	4	18	1	157	7	1	1	1.7	.994	OF-85
1964		19	.111	.111	18	2	0	0	0	0.0	1	1	1	8	0	15	1	5	0	0	0	0.3	1.000	OF-5
1965		53	.133	.244	45	6	2	0	1	2.2	3	4	3	14	0	44	6	3	0	0	0	0.1	1.000	OF-6
1966	NY N	111	.251	.347	334	84	9	1	7	2.1	31	31	38	46	2	19	5	147	4	2	1	1.4	.987	OF-101
1967	2 teams	NY N	(41G – .205)		PIT N	(55G – .184)																		
"	total	96	.195	.260	215	42	2	0	4	1.9	24	17	14	33	1	41	7	100	5	4	1	1.1	.963	OF-58
7 yrs.		481	.235	.352	1243	292	34	6	33	2.7	147	125	127	213	8	150	24	583	22	14	4	1.3	.977	OF-346

Scott Lusader

LUSADER, SCOTT EDWARD
B. Sept. 30, 1964, Chicago, Ill.

BL TL 5'10" 165 lbs.

Year	Team	Games	BA	SA	AB	H	2B	3B	HR	HR%	R	RBI	BB	SO	SB	PH AB	PH H	PO	A	E	DP	TC/G	FA	G by Pos
1987	DET A	23	.319	.489	47	15	3	1	1	2.1	8	8	5	7	1	0	0	29	0	1	0	1.3	.967	OF-22, DH-1
1988		16	.063	.250	16	1	0	0	1	6.3	3	3	1	4	0	5	0	7	0	0	0	0.4	1.000	DH-6, OF-4
1989		40	.252	.320	103	26	4	0	1	1.0	15	9	9	21	3	8	1	56	0	4	0	1.5	.933	OF-33, DH-1
3 yrs.		79	.253	.361	166	42	7	1	3	1.8	26	19	15	32	4	13	1	92	0	5	0	1.2	.948	OF-59, DH-8

Billy Lush

LUSH, WILLIAM LUCAS
Brother of Ernie Lush.
B. Nov. 10, 1873, Bridgeport, Conn.   D. Aug. 28, 1951, Hawthorne, N. Y.

BB TR 5'8" 165 lbs.

Year	Team	Games	BA	SA	AB	H	2B	3B	HR	HR%	R	RBI	BB	SO	SB	PH AB	PH H	PO	A	E	DP	TC/G	FA	G by Pos
1895	WAS N	5	.333	.333	18	6	0	0	0	0.0	2	2	2	1	0	0	0	9	0	4	0	2.6	.692	OF-5
1896		97	.247	.369	352	87	9	11	4	1.1	74	45	66	49	28	3	1	145	23	23	4	2.0	.880	OF-91, 2B-3
1897		3	.000	.000	12	0	0	0	0	0.0	1	0	2		0	0	0	5	1	0	0	2.0	1.000	OF-3
1901	BOS N	7	.185	.296	27	5	1	1	0	0.0	2	3	3		0	0	0	22	2	1	1	3.6	.960	OF-7
1902		120	.223	.262	413	92	8	1	2	0.5	68	19	76		30	3	1	251	26	14	5	2.4	.952	OF-116, 3B-1
1903	DET A	119	.274	.390	423	116	18	14	1	0.2	71	33	70		14	1	0	257	43	15	6	2.6	.952	OF-101, 3B-12, SS-3, 2B-3
1904	CLE A	138	.258	.325	477	123	13	8	1	0.2	76	50	72		12	0	0	269	11	12	4	2.1	.959	OF-138
7 yrs.		489	.249	.332	1722	429	49	35	8	0.5	294	152	291	50	84	7	2	958	106	69	20	2.3	.939	OF-461, 3B-13, 2B-6, SS-3

Ernie Lush

LUSH, ERNEST BENJAMIN
Brother of Billy Lush.
B. Oct. 31, 1884, Bridgeport, Conn.   D. Feb. 26, 1937, Detroit, Mich.

BR TL

Year	Team	Games	BA	SA	AB	H	2B	3B	HR	HR%	R	RBI	BB	SO	SB	PH AB	PH H	PO	A	E	DP	TC/G	FA	G by Pos
1910	STL N	1	.000	.000	4	0	0	0	0	0.0	0	0	1	1	0	0	0	1	0	0	0	1.0	1.000	OF-1

Johnny Lush

LUSH, JOHN CHARLES
B. Oct. 8, 1885, Williamsport, Pa.   D. Nov. 18, 1946, Beverly Hills, Calif.

BL TL 5'9½" 165 lbs.

Year	Team	Games	BA	SA	AB	H	2B	3B	HR	HR%	R	RBI	BB	SO	SB	PH AB	PH H	PO	A	E	DP	TC/G	FA	G by Pos
1904	PHI N	106	.276	.369	369	102	22	3	2	0.5	39	42	27		12	4	1	583	44	35	28	6.2	.947	1B-62, OF-33, P-7
1905		6	.313	.313	16	5	0	0	0	0.0	3	1	1		0	1	1	6	6	4	0	2.7	.750	OF-3, P-2
1906		76	.264	.307	212	56	7	1	0	0.0	28	15	14		6	14	1	75	95	13	3	2.4	.929	P-37, OF-22, 1B-2
1907	2 teams	PHI N	(17G – .200)		STL N	(27G – .280)																		
"	total	44	.254	.344	122	31	3	4	0	0.0	11	10	6		5	13	2	19	54	7	4	1.8	.913	P-28, OF-11
1908	STL N	45	.169	.191	89	15	2	0	0	0.0	7	2	7		1	6	1	15	73	7	0	2.1	.926	P-38
1909		45	.239	.293	92	22	5	0	0	0.0	11	14	6		2	7	0	9	64	4	0	1.7	.948	P-34, OF-3
1910		47	.226	.301	93	21	1	3	0	0.0	9	10	8	11	2	10	4	8	56	5	2	1.5	.928	P-36
7 yrs.		369	.254	.322	993	252	40	11	2	0.2	107	94	69	11	28	55	10	715	392	75	37	3.2	.937	P-182, OF-72, 1B-64

Charlie Luskey

LUSKEY, CHARLES MELTON
B. Apr. 6, 1876, Washington, D. C.   D. Dec. 20, 1962, Bethesda, Md.

BR TR 5'7" 165 lbs.

Year	Team	Games	BA	SA	AB	H	2B	3B	HR	HR%	R	RBI	BB	SO	SB	PH AB	PH H	PO	A	E	DP	TC/G	FA	G by Pos
1901	WAS A	11	.195	.317	41	8	3	1	0	0.0	8	3	2		0	0	0	25	1	7	0	3.0	.788	OF-8, C-3

Luke Lutenberg

LUTENBERG, CHARLES WILLIAM
B. Oct. 4, 1864, Quincy, Ill.   D. Dec. 24, 1938, Quincy, Ill.

BR TR 6'2" 225 lbs.

Year	Team	Games	BA	SA	AB	H	2B	3B	HR	HR%	R	RBI	BB	SO	SB	PH AB	PH H	PO	A	E	DP	TC/G	FA	G by Pos
1894	LOU N	69	.192	.264	250	48	10	4	0	0.0	42	23	23	21	4	0	0	597	43	15	55	9.5	.977	1B-67, 2B-2

Year	Team	Games	BA	SA	AB	H	2B	3B	HR	HR%	R	RBI	BB	SO	SB	PH AB	PH H	PO	A	E	DP	TC/G	FA	G by Pos

Lyle Luttrell

LUTTRELL, LYLE KENNETH
B. Feb. 22, 1930, Bloomington, Ill. D. July 11, 1984, Chattanooga, Tenn.
BR TR 6' 180 lbs.

Year	Team	Games	BA	SA	AB	H	2B	3B	HR	HR%	R	RBI	BB	SO	SB	PH AB	PH H	PO	A	E	DP	TC/G	FA	G by Pos
1956	WAS A	38	.189	.328	122	23	5	3	2	1.6	17	9	8	19	5	1	0	69	100	11	19	4.7	.939	SS-37
1957		19	.200	.289	45	9	4	0	0	0.0	4	5	3	8	0	2	0	23	28	4	5	2.9	.927	SS-17
2 yrs.		57	.192	.317	167	32	9	3	2	1.2	21	14	11	27	5	3	0	92	128	15	24	4.1	.936	SS-54

Joe Lutz

LUTZ, ROLLIN JOSEPH
B. Feb. 18, 1925, Keokuk, Iowa
BL TL 6' 195 lbs.

Year	Team	Games	BA	SA	AB	H	2B	3B	HR	HR%	R	RBI	BB	SO	SB	PH AB	PH H	PO	A	E	DP	TC/G	FA	G by Pos
1951	STL A	14	.167	.222	36	6	0	1	0	0.0	7	2	6	9	0	3	1	76	4	0	9	5.7	1.000	1B-11

Red Lutz

LUTZ, LOUIS WILLIAM
B. Dec. 17, 1898, Cincinnati, Ohio D. Feb. 22, 1984, Cincinnati, Ohio
BR TR 5'10" 170 lbs.

Year	Team	Games	BA	SA	AB	H	2B	3B	HR	HR%	R	RBI	BB	SO	SB	PH AB	PH H	PO	A	E	DP	TC/G	FA	G by Pos
1922	CIN N	1	1.000	2.000	1	1	1	0	0	0.0	0	0	0	0	0	0	0	0	0	0	0	0.0	—	C-1

Rube Lutzke

LUTZKE, WALTER JOHN
B. Nov. 17, 1897, Milwaukee, Wis. D. Mar. 6, 1938, Granville, Wis.
BR TR 5'11" 175 lbs.

Year	Team	Games	BA	SA	AB	H	2B	3B	HR	HR%	R	RBI	BB	SO	SB	PH AB	PH H	PO	A	E	DP	TC/G	FA	G by Pos
1923	CLE A	143	.256	.337	511	131	20	6	3	0.6	71	65	59	57	10	0	0	186	358	35	23	4.0	.940	3B-143
1924		106	.243	.314	341	83	18	3	0	0.0	37	42	38	46	4	0	0	161	241	22	26	4.0	.948	3B-103, 2B-3
1925		81	.218	.269	238	52	9	0	1	0.4	31	16	26	29	2	2	1	83	156	14	14	3.1	.945	3B-69, 2B-10
1926		142	.261	.345	475	124	28	6	0	0.0	42	59	34	35	6	0	0	160	302	19	27	3.4	.960	3B-142
1927		100	.251	.309	311	78	12	3	0	0.0	35	41	22	29	2	2	0	120	199	21	24	3.4	.938	3B-98
5 yrs.		572	.249	.321	1876	468	87	18	4	0.2	216	223	179	196	24	4	1	710	1256	111	114	3.6	.947	3B-555, 2B-13

Greg Luzinski

LUZINSKI, GREGORY MICHAEL (The Bull)
B. Nov. 22, 1950, Chicago, Ill.
BR TR 6'1" 220 lbs.

Year	Team	Games	BA	SA	AB	H	2B	3B	HR	HR%	R	RBI	BB	SO	SB	PH AB	PH H	PO	A	E	DP	TC/G	FA	G by Pos
1970	PHI N	8	.167	.167	12	2	0	0	0	0.0	0	0	3	5	0	5	1	20	3	0	1	2.9	1.000	1B-3
1971		28	.300	.470	100	30	8	0	3	3.0	13	15	12	32	2	1	0	247	34	1	16	10.1	.996	1B-28
1972		150	.281	.453	563	158	33	5	18	3.2	66	68	42	114	0	4	1	257	9	12	2	1.9	.957	OF-145, 1B-2
1973		161	.285	.484	610	174	26	4	29	4.8	76	97	51	135	3	4	2	262	7	2	1	1.7	.993	OF-159
1974		85	.272	.394	302	82	14	1	7	2.3	29	48	29	76	3	4	0	146	10	3	0	1.9	.981	OF-82
1975		161	.300	.540	596	179	35	3	34	5.7	85	**120**	89	151	3	2	0	248	10	9	0	1.7	.966	OF-159
1976		149	.304	.478	533	162	28	1	21	3.9	74	95	50	107	1	5	0	204	8	8	0	1.5	.964	OF-144
1977		149	.309	.594	554	171	35	3	39	7.0	99	130	80	**140**	3	1	0	205	11	8	2	1.5	.964	OF-148
1978		155	.265	.526	540	143	32	2	35	6.5	85	101	100	135	8	1	0	232	7	4	2	1.6	.984	OF-154
1979		137	.252	.427	452	114	23	1	18	4.0	47	81	56	103	3	9	1	156	3	9	1	1.2	.946	OF-125
1980		106	.228	.440	368	84	19	1	19	5.2	44	56	60	100	3	1	0	137	2	1	0	1.3	.993	OF-105
1981	CHI A	104	.265	.476	378	100	15	1	21	5.6	55	62	58	80	0	0	0	0	0	0	0	0.0	—	DH-103
1982		159	.292	.451	583	170	37	1	18	3.1	87	102	89	120	1	2	0	0	0	0	0	0.0	—	DH-156
1983		144	.255	.502	502	128	26	1	32	6.4	73	95	70	117	2	2	0	6	1	0	1	0.0	1.000	DH-139, 1B-2
1984		125	.238	.364	412	98	13	0	13	3.2	47	58	56	80	5	11	3	0	0	0	0	0.0	—	DH-114
15 yrs.		1821	.276	.478	6505	1795	344	24	307	4.7	880	1128	845	1495	37	51	9	2120	105	57	26	1.3	.975	OF-1221, DH-512, 1B-35

LEAGUE CHAMPIONSHIP SERIES

Year	Team	Games	BA	SA	AB	H	2B	3B	HR	HR%	R	RBI	BB	SO	SB	PH AB	PH H	PO	A	E	DP	TC/G	FA	G by Pos
1976	PHI N	3	.273	.727	11	3	2	0	1	9.1	2	3	1	4	0	0	0	6	0	0	0	2.0	1.000	OF-3
1977		4	.286	.571	14	4	1	0	1	7.1	2	2	3	3	1	0	0	4	1	0	0	1.3	1.000	OF-4
1978		4	.375	.875	16	6	0	1	2	12.5	3	3	1	2	0	0	0	5	0	0	0	1.3	1.000	OF-4
1980		5	.294	.588	17	5	2	0	1	5.9	3	4	0	6	0	1	1	5	0	1	0	1.2	.833	OF-4
1983	CHI A	4	.133	.200	15	2	1	0	0	0.0	0	0	1	5	0	0	0	0	0	0	0	0.0	—	DH-4
5 yrs.		20	.274	.589	73	20	6	1	5	6.8	10	12	6	20	1	1	1	20	1	1	0	1.1	.955	OF-15, DH-4

WORLD SERIES

Year	Team	Games	BA	SA	AB	H	2B	3B	HR	HR%	R	RBI	BB	SO	SB	PH AB	PH H	PO	A	E	DP	TC/G	FA	G by Pos
1980	PHI N	3	.000	.000	9	0	0	0	0	0.0	0	0	0	5	0	0	0	1	0	0	0	0.3	1.000	DH-2, OF-1

Dummy Lynch

LYNCH, MATTHEW DANIEL
B. Feb. 7, 1927, Dallas, Tex. D. June 30, 1978, Plano, Tex.
BR TR 5'11" 174 lbs.

Year	Team	Games	BA	SA	AB	H	2B	3B	HR	HR%	R	RBI	BB	SO	SB	PH AB	PH H	PO	A	E	DP	TC/G	FA	G by Pos
1948	CHI N	7	.286	.714	7	2	0	0	1	14.3	3	1	1	1	0	4	1	0	2	0	0	0.3	1.000	2B-1

Henry Lynch

LYNCH, HENRY W.
B. Apr. 8, 1866, Worcester, Mass. D. Nov. 23, 1925, Worcester, Mass.
5'7" 143 lbs.

Year	Team	Games	BA	SA	AB	H	2B	3B	HR	HR%	R	RBI	BB	SO	SB	PH AB	PH H	PO	A	E	DP	TC/G	FA	G by Pos
1893	CHI N	4	.214	.357	14	3	2	0	0	0.0	0	2	1		0	0	0	5	0	1	0	1.5	.833	OF-4

Jerry Lynch

LYNCH, GERALD THOMAS
B. July 17, 1930, Bay City, Mich.
BL TR 6'1" 185 lbs.

Year	Team	Games	BA	SA	AB	H	2B	3B	HR	HR%	R	RBI	BB	SO	SB	PH AB	PH H	PO	A	E	DP	TC/G	FA	G by Pos
1954	PIT N	98	.239	.373	284	68	14	8	8	2.8	27	36	20	43	2	15	2	127	10	5	2	1.4	.965	OF-83
1955		88	.284	.443	282	80	18	6	5	1.8	43	28	22	33	2	18	4	112	13	6	3	1.5	.954	OF-71, C-2
1956		19	.158	.263	19	3	0	1	0	0.0	0	1	0	4	0	16	3	3	0	0	0	0.2	1.000	OF-1
1957	CIN N	67	.258	.403	124	32	4	1	4	3.2	11	13	6	18	0	42	6	40	0	0	0	0.6	1.000	OF-24, C-2
1958		122	.312	.498	420	131	20	5	16	3.8	58	68	18	54	1	25	9	154	5	5	2	1.3	.970	OF-101
1959		117	.269	.462	379	102	16	3	17	4.5	49	58	29	50	2	19	7	180	5	4	3	1.6	.979	OF-98
1960		102	.289	.478	159	46	8	2	6	3.8	23	27	16	25	0	66	19	41	1	4	1	0.5	.913	OF-32
1961		96	.315	.624	181	57	13	2	13	7.2	33	50	27	25	2	47	19	53	2	3	0	0.6	.948	OF-44
1962		114	.281	.486	288	81	15	4	12	4.2	41	57	24	38	3	38	9	89	7	3	1	0.9	.970	OF-73
1963	2 teams	CIN N (22G – .250)			PIT N (88G – .266)																			
"	total	110	.264	.454	269	71	9	3	12	4.5	31	45	23	33	1	37	12	75	2	3	0	0.7	.963	OF-71
1964	PIT N	114	.273	.495	297	81	14	2	16	5.4	35	66	26	57	1	34	7	59	0	1	0	0.5	.983	OF-78
1965		73	.281	.413	121	34	1	0	5	4.1	7	16	8	26	0	41	7	27	1	3	0	0.4	.903	OF-26
1966		64	.214	.286	56	12	1	0	1	1.8	5	6	4	10	0	49	10	5	0	0	0	0.1	1.000	OF-4
13 yrs.		1184	.277	.463	2879	798	123	34	115	4.0	364	470	224	416	12	447 / 4th	116 / 5th	965	46	37	12	0.9	.965	OF-706, C-4

WORLD SERIES

Year	Team	Games	BA	SA	AB	H	2B	3B	HR	HR%	R	RBI	BB	SO	SB	PH AB	PH H	PO	A	E	DP	TC/G	FA	G by Pos
1961	CIN N	4	.000	.000	3	0	0	0	0	0.0	0	0	1	1	0	3	0	0	0	0	0	0.0	—	

Year Team	Games	BA	SA	AB	H	2B	3B	HR	HR%	R	RBI	BB	SO	SB	Pinch Hit AB	H	PO	A	E	DP	TC/G	FA	G by Pos

Mike Lynch

LYNCH, MICHAEL JOSEPH
B. Sept. 10, 1875, St. Paul, Minn. D. Apr. 1, 1947, Jennings Lodge, Ore. TR 6'2" 170 lbs.

| 1902 CHI N | 7 | .143 | .143 | 28 | 4 | 0 | 0 | 0 | 0.0 | 4 | 0 | 2 | | 0 | 0 | 0 | 12 | 1 | 1 | 0 | 2.0 | .929 | OF-7 |

Tom Lynch

LYNCH, THOMAS JAMES
B. Apr. 3, 1860, Bennington, Vt. D. Mar. 28, 1955, Cohoes, N. Y. BL TR 5'10½" 170 lbs.

1884 2 teams		WIL	U	(16G – .276)			PHI	N	(13G – .313)														
" total	29	.292	.415	106	31	7	3	0	0.0	13		9	5		0	0	101	29	17	3	5.1	.884	OF-15, C-15, 1B-1
1885 PHI N	13	.189	.245	53	10	3	0	0	0.0	7		10	3		0	0	26	5	6	1	2.8	.838	OF-13
2 yrs.	42	.258	.358	159	41	10	3	0	0.0	20		19	8		0	0	127	34	23	4	4.4	.875	OF-28, C-15, 1B-1

Walt Lynch

LYNCH, WALTER EDWARD
B. Apr. 15, 1897, Buffalo, N. Y. D. Dec. 21, 1976, Daytona Beach, Fla. BR TR 6' 176 lbs.

| 1922 BOS A | 3 | .500 | .500 | 2 | 1 | 0 | 0 | 0 | 0.0 | 1 | 0 | 0 | 0 | 0 | 0 | 0 | 1 | 1 | 0 | 0 | 0.7 | 1.000 | C-3 |

Byrd Lynn

LYNN, BYRD
B. Mar. 13, 1889, Unionville, Ill. D. Feb. 5, 1940, Napa, Calif. BR TR 5'11" 165 lbs.

1916 CHI A	31	.225	.250	40	9	1	0	0	0.0	4	3	4	7	2	15	3	56	24	4	0	2.7	.952	C-13
1917	35	.222	.250	72	16	2	0	0	0.0	7	5	7	11	1	6	1	104	13	5	4	3.5	.959	C-29
1918	5	.250	.250	8	2	0	0	0	0.0	0	0	2	1	0	1	1	6	3	0	0	1.8	1.000	C-4
1919	29	.227	.288	66	15	4	0	0	0.0	4	4	4	9	0	1	1	87	20	2	5	3.8	.982	C-28
1920	16	.320	.480	25	8	2	1	0	0.0	0	3	1	3	0	2	2	27	5	0	0	2.0	1.000	C-14
5 yrs.	116	.237	.289	211	50	9	1	0	0.0	15	15	18	31	3	25	8	280	65	11	9	3.1	.969	C-88

WORLD SERIES

1917 CHI A	1	.000	.000	1	0	0	0	0	0.0	0	0	0	1	0	1	0	0	0	0	0	0.0	–	
1919	1	.000	.000	1	0	0	0	0	0.0	0	0	0	0	0	0	0	1	0	0	0	1.0	1.000	C-1
2 yrs.	2	.000	.000	2	0	0	0	0	0.0	0	0	0	1	0	1	0	1	0	0	0	0.5	1.000	C-1

Fred Lynn

LYNN, FREDRIC MICHAEL
B. Feb. 3, 1952, Chicago, Ill. BL TL 6'1" 185 lbs.

1974 BOS A	15	.419	.698	43	18	2	2	2	4.7	5	10	6	6	0	2	0	18	2	0	0	1.3	1.000	OF-15, DH-1
1975	145	.331	.566	528	175	47	7	21	4.0	103	105	62	90	10	2	1	404	11	7	1	2.9	.983	OF-144
1976	132	.314	.467	507	159	32	8	10	2.0	76	65	48	67	14	1	0	367	13	6	4	2.9	.984	OF-128, DH-5
1977	129	.260	.447	497	129	29	5	18	3.6	81	76	51	63	2	3	0	333	7	2	1	2.7	.994	OF-125, DH-1
1978	150	.298	.492	541	161	33	3	22	4.1	75	82	75	50	3	0	0	408	11	7	2	2.8	.984	OF-149
1979	147	.333	.637	531	177	42	1	39	7.3	116	122	82	79	2	4	1	381	10	5	4	2.7	.987	OF-143, DH-1
1980	110	.301	.480	415	125	32	3	12	2.9	67	61	58	39	12	0	0	302	11	2	4	2.9	.994	OF-110
1981 CAL A	76	.219	.316	256	56	8	1	5	2.0	28	31	38	42	1	9	1	176	4	4	1	2.4	.978	OF-69
1982	138	.299	.517	472	141	38	1	21	4.4	89	86	58	72	7	10	5	317	6	3	3	2.4	.991	OF-133
1983	117	.272	.483	437	119	20	3	22	5.0	56	74	55	83	2	3	0	274	8	2	4	2.4	.993	OF-113, DH-2
1984	142	.271	.474	517	140	28	4	23	4.4	84	79	77	98	2	5	2	321	12	6	5	2.4	.982	OF-140
1985 BAL A	124	.263	.449	448	118	12	1	23	5.1	59	68	53	100	7	1	0	314	6	2	1	2.6	.994	OF-123
1986	112	.287	.499	397	114	13	1	23	5.8	67	67	53	59	2	7	3	244	2	4	1	2.2	.984	OF-107, DH-1
1987	111	.253	.487	396	100	24	1	23	5.8	49	60	39	72	3	4	1	229	2	2	1	2.1	.991	OF-101, DH-8
1988 2 teams		BAL	A	(87G – .252)			DET	A	(27G – .222)														
" total	114	.246	.478	391	96	14	1	25	6.4	46	56	33	82	2	7	2	257	3	2	0	2.3	.992	OF-105, DH-5
1989 DET A	117	.241	.371	353	85	11	1	11	3.1	44	46	47	71	1	17	3	119	5	1	0	1.1	.992	OF-68, DH-46
16 yrs.	1879	.284	.488	6729	1913	385	42	300	4.5	1045	1088	835	1073	70	75	19	4464	113	55	33	2.5	.988	OF-1773, DH-70

LEAGUE CHAMPIONSHIP SERIES

1975 BOS A	3	.364	.455	11	4	1	0	0	0.0	1	3	0	0	0	0	0	12	1	1	1	4.7	.929	OF-3
1982 CAL A	5	.611	.889	18	11	2	0	1	5.6	4	5	2	3	0	0	0	0	0	1	0	0.2	–	OF-5
2 yrs.	8	.517	.724	29	15	3	0	1	3.4	5	8	2	3	0	0	0	12	1	2	1	1.9	.867	OF-8

WORLD SERIES

| 1975 BOS A | 7 | .280 | .440 | 25 | 7 | 0 | 1 | 1 | 4.0 | 3 | 5 | 3 | 5 | 0 | 0 | 0 | 23 | 1 | 0 | 0 | 3.4 | 1.000 | OF-7 |

Jerry Lynn

LYNN, JEROME EDWARD
B. Apr. 14, 1916, Scranton, Pa. D. Sept. 25, 1972, Scranton, Pa. BR TR 5'10" 164 lbs.

| 1937 WAS A | 1 | .667 | 1.000 | 3 | 2 | 1 | 0 | 0 | 0.0 | 0 | 0 | 0 | 0 | 0 | 0 | 0 | 4 | 3 | 0 | 2 | 7.0 | 1.000 | 2B-1 |

Russ Lyon

LYON, RUSSELL MAYO
B. June 26, 1913, Ball Ground, Ga. BR TR 6'1" 230 lbs.

| 1944 CLE A | 7 | .182 | .182 | 11 | 2 | 0 | 0 | 0 | 0.0 | 1 | 0 | 1 | 1 | 0 | 4 | 0 | 7 | 3 | 1 | 0 | 1.6 | .909 | C-3 |

Barry Lyons

LYONS, BARRY STEPHEN
B. June 3, 1960, Biloxi, Miss. BR TR 6'1" 205 lbs.

1986 NY N	6	.000	.000	9	0	0	0	0	0.0	1	2	1	2	0	2	0	16	0	1	0	2.8	.941	C-3
1987	53	.254	.392	130	33	4	1	4	3.1	15	24	8	24	0	4	1	223	17	4	0	4.6	.984	C-49
1988	50	.231	.330	91	21	7	1	0	0.0	5	11	3	12	0	18	3	130	9	3	0	2.8	.979	C-32, 1B-1
1989	79	.247	.340	235	58	13	0	3	1.3	15	27	11	28	0	8	2	463	29	10	4	6.4	.980	C-76
4 yrs.	188	.241	.346	465	112	24	2	7	1.5	36	64	23	66	0	32	6	832	55	18	4	4.8	.980	C-160, 1B-1

Bill Lyons

LYONS, WILLIAM ALLEN
B. Apr. 26, 1958, Alton, Ill. BR TR 6'1" 175 lbs.

1983 STL N	42	.167	.217	60	10	1	1	0	0.0	3	3	1	11	3	11	1	30	44	1	7	1.8	.987	2B-23, 3B-8, SS-2
1984	46	.219	.260	73	16	3	0	0	0.0	13	3	9	13	3	8	1	58	74	1	21	2.9	.992	2B-25, SS-11, 3B-3
2 yrs.	88	.195	.241	133	26	4	1	0	0.0	16	6	10	24	6	19	2	88	118	2	28	2.4	.990	2B-48, SS-13, 3B-11

Denny Lyons

LYONS, DENNIS PATRICK ALOYSIUS
B. Mar. 12, 1866, Cincinnati, Ohio D. Jan. 3, 1929, West Covington, Ky. BR TR 5'10" 185 lbs.

Year	Team	Games	BA	SA	AB	H	2B	3B	HR	HR%	R	RBI	BB	SO	SB	Pinch Hit AB	Pinch Hit H	PO	A	E	DP	TC/G	FA	G by Pos

Denny Lyons *continued*

Year	Team	Games	BA	SA	AB	H	2B	3B	HR	HR%	R	RBI	BB	SO	SB	PH AB	PH H	PO	A	E	DP	TC/G	FA	G by Pos
1885	PRO N	4	.125	.188	16	2	1	0	0	0.0	3	1	0	3		0	0	6	8	3	0	4.3	.824	3B-4
1886	PHI AA	32	.211	.252	123	26	3	1	0	0.0	22		8			0	0	35	53	21	1	3.4	.807	3B-32
1887		137	.367	.523	570	209	43	14	6	1.1	128		47		73	0	0	255	215	73	29	4.0	.866	3B-137
1888		111	.296	.406	456	135	22	5	6	1.3	93	83	41		39	0	0	159	193	49	11	3.6	.878	3B-111
1889		131	.329	.469	510	168	36	4	9	1.8	135	82	79	44	10	0	0	209	291	81	29	4.4	.861	3B-130, 1B-1
1890		88	.354	**.531**	339	120	29	5	7	2.1	79		57		21	0	0	147	203	35	14	4.4	.909	3B-88
1891	STL AA	120	.315	.455	451	142	24	3	11	2.4	124	84	88	58	9	0	0	151	246	59	16	3.8	.871	3B-120
1892	NY N	108	.257	.396	389	100	16	7	8	2.1	71	51	59	36	11	0	0	152	206	53	13	3.8	.871	3B-108
1893	PIT N	131	.306	.429	490	150	19	16	3	0.6	103	105	97	29	19	0	0	214	303	46	23	4.3	.918	3B-131
1894		71	.323	.457	254	82	14	4	4	1.6	51	50	42	12	14	0	0	119	155	31	11	4.3	.898	3B-71
1895	STL N	33	.295	.388	129	38	6	0	2	1.6	24	25	14	5	3	0	0	61	49	13	2	3.7	.894	3B-33
1896	PIT N	118	.307	.420	436	134	25	6	4	0.9	77	71	67	25	13	2	0	165	201	44	15	3.5	.893	3B-116
1897		37	.206	.359	131	27	6	4	2	1.5	22	17	22		5	0	0	345	19	4	14	9.9	.989	1B-35, 3B-2
13 yrs.		1121	.310	.443	4294	1333	244	69	62	1.4	932	569	621	212	217	2	0	2018	2142	512	178	4.2	.890	3B-1083, 1B-36

Ed Lyons

LYONS, EDWARD HOYTE (Mouse)
B. May 12, 1923, Winston-Salem, N. C.
BR TR 5'9" 165 lbs.

Year	Team	Games	BA	SA	AB	H	2B	3B	HR	HR%	R	RBI	BB	SO	SB	PH AB	PH H	PO	A	E	DP	TC/G	FA	G by Pos
1947	WAS A	7	.154	.154	26	4	0	0	0	0.0	2	0	2	2	0	0	0	19	28	0	7	6.7	1.000	2B-7

Harry Lyons

LYONS, HARRY P.
B. Mar. 25, 1866, Chester, Pa. D. June 30, 1912, Mauricetown, N. J.
BR TR 5'10½" 157 lbs.

Year	Team	Games	BA	SA	AB	H	2B	3B	HR	HR%	R	RBI	BB	SO	SB	PH AB	PH H	PO	A	E	DP	TC/G	FA	G by Pos
1887	2 teams	PHI N (1G – .000)			STL AA (2G – .125)																			
"	total	3	.083	.083	12	1	0	0	0	0.0	2		1		2	0	0	4	5	1	1	3.3	.900	OF-2, 2B-1
1888	STL AA	123	.194	.259	499	97	10	5	4	0.8	66	63	20		36	0	0	237	35	36	4	2.5	.883	OF-122, 3B-2, SS-1, 2B-1
1889	NY N	5	.100	.200	20	2	0	1	0	0.0	1	2	2	0	0	0	0	5	0	0	0	1.0	1.000	OF-5
1890	ROC AA	133	.260	.332	584	152	11	11	3	0.5	83		27		47	0	0	265	30	27	4	2.4	.916	OF-132, 3B-2, C-1, P-1
1892	NY N	96	.238	.260	411	98	5	2	0	0.0	67	53	33	29	25	0	0	186	16	20	1	2.3	.910	OF-96
1893		47	.273	.321	187	51	5	2	0	0.0	27	21	14	6	10	0	0	113	9	11	3	2.8	.917	OF-47
6 yrs.		407	.234	.289	1713	401	31	21	7	0.4	246	139	97	35	120	0	0	810	95	95	13	2.5	.905	OF-404, 3B-4, 2B-2, SS-1, C-1, P-1

Pat Lyons

LYONS, PATRICK JERRY
B. 1860, Canada D. Jan. 20, 1914, Springfield, Ohio
TR

Year	Team	Games	BA	SA	AB	H	2B	3B	HR	HR%	R	RBI	BB	SO	SB	PH AB	PH H	PO	A	E	DP	TC/G	FA	G by Pos
1890	CLE N	11	.053	.079	38	2	1	0	0	0.0	2	1	4	4	0	0	0	24	28	10	2	5.6	.839	2B-11

Steve Lyons

LYONS, STEPHEN JOHN (Psycho)
B. June 3, 1960, Tacoma, Wash.
BL TR 6'3" 190 lbs.

Year	Team	Games	BA	SA	AB	H	2B	3B	HR	HR%	R	RBI	BB	SO	SB	PH AB	PH H	PO	A	E	DP	TC/G	FA	G by Pos
1985	BOS A	133	.264	.358	371	98	14	3	5	1.3	52	30	32	64	12	13	2	253	6	7	0	2.0	.974	OF-114, DH-5, SS-1, 3B-1
1986	2 teams	BOS A (59G – .250)			CHI A (42G – .203)																			
"	total	101	.227	.300	247	56	9	1	1	0.4	30	20	19	47	4	7	1	175	11	4	1	1.9	.979	OF-90, 3B-3, DH-1, 1B-1
1987	CHI A	76	.280	.363	193	54	11	1	1	0.5	26	19	12	37	3	4	0	69	101	4	12	2.3	.977	3B-51, OF-15, 2B-1
1988		146	.269	.373	472	127	28	3	5	1.1	59	45	32	59	1	3	1	128	243	29	38	2.7	.928	3B-128, OF-14, 2B-4, C-2, 1B-1
1989		140	.264	.339	443	117	21	3	2	0.5	51	50	35	68	9	14	5	414	245	15	73	4.8	.978	2B-70, 1B-40, 3B-28, OF-20, SS-3, DH-1, C-1
5 yrs.		596	.262	.349	1726	452	83	13	14	0.8	218	164	130	275	29	41	9	1039	606	59	124	2.9	.965	OF-253, 3B-211, 2B-75, 1B-42, DH-7, SS-4, C-3

Ted Lyons

LYONS, THEODORE AMAR
B. Dec. 28, 1900, Lake Charles, La.
D. July 25, 1986, Sulphur, La.
Manager 1946-48.
Hall of Fame 1955.
BB TR 5'11" 200 lbs.
BR 1925-27

Year	Team	Games	BA	SA	AB	H	2B	3B	HR	HR%	R	RBI	BB	SO	SB	PH AB	PH H	PO	A	E	DP	TC/G	FA	G by Pos
1923	CHI A	9	.200	.200	5	1	0	0	0	0.0	0	1	1	3	0	0	0	3	7	0	1	1.1	1.000	P-9
1924		41	.221	.247	77	17	0	1	0	0.0	10	6	5	13	0	0	0	3	45	5	2	1.3	.906	P-41
1925		43	.186	.216	97	18	3	0	0	0.0	6	7	3	13	0	0	0	8	80	4	3	2.1	.957	P-43
1926		41	.212	.240	104	22	1	1	0	0.0	7	3	1	10	0	1	0	16	91	5	3	2.7	.955	P-39
1927		41	.255	.373	110	28	6	2	1	0.9	16	9	6	17	0	0	0	13	79	2	3	2.3	.979	P-39
1928		49	.253	.275	91	23	2	0	0	0.0	10	8	1	9	0	0	0	20	60	7	6	1.8	.920	P-39
1929		40	.220	.264	91	20	4	0	0	0.0	7	11	9	13	0	0	0	21	66	5	4	2.3	.946	P-37, OF-1
1930		57	.311	.434	122	38	6	3	1	0.8	20	15	2	18	0	9	3	14	77	6	5	1.7	.938	P-42
1931		42	.152	.152	33	5	0	0	0	0.0	0	3	2	1	0	2	0	4	18	1	3	0.5	.957	P-22
1932		49	.260	.356	73	19	2	1	1	1.4	11	10	4	10	0	1	0	11	42	2	1	1.1	.964	P-33
1933		51	.286	.363	91	26	2	1	1	1.1	11	11	4	6	0	7	1	10	49	1	3	1.2	.983	P-36
1934		50	.206	.278	97	20	4	0	1	1.0	9	16	3	19	0	17	3	12	50	4	4	1.3	.939	P-30
1935		29	.220	.268	82	18	4	0	0	0.0	5	4	3	4	0	6	1	9	31	0	2	1.4	1.000	P-23
1936		26	.157	.157	70	11	0	0	0	0.0	2	5	5	12	0	0	0	12	38	0	2	1.9	1.000	P-26
1937		23	.211	.211	57	12	0	0	0	0.0	6	3	7	9	0	0	0	6	33	0	3	1.7	1.000	P-22
1938		24	.194	.222	72	14	2	0	0	0.0	9	4	2	7	0	0	0	9	46	1	1	2.3	.982	P-23
1939		21	.295	.344	61	18	3	0	0	0.0	5	8	5	7	0	0	0	9	22	3	3	1.6	.912	P-21
1940		22	.240	.293	75	18	4	0	0	0.0	4	7	2	7	0	0	0	12	24	3	1	1.8	.923	P-22
1941		22	.270	.297	74	20	2	0	0	0.0	8	6	3	6	0	0	0	17	36	1	3	2.5	.981	P-22
1942		20	.239	.299	67	16	4	0	0	0.0	10	10	3	7	0	0	0	8	41	1	4	2.5	.980	P-20
1946		5	.000	.000	14	0	0	0	0	0.0	0	0	1	3	0	0	0	2	10	0	0	2.4	1.000	P-5
21 yrs.		705	.233	.285	1563	364	49	9	5	0.3	162	149	73	201	0	44	9	219	945	51	57	1.7	.958	P-594, OF-1

Terry Lyons

LYONS, TERENCE HILBERT
B. Dec. 14, 1908, New Holland, Ohio D. Sept. 9, 1959, Dayton, Ohio
BR TR 6'½" 165 lbs.

Year	Team	Games	BA	SA	AB	H	2B	3B	HR	HR%	R	RBI	BB	SO	SB	PH AB	PH H	PO	A	E	DP	TC/G	FA	G by Pos
1929	PHI N	1	–	–	0	0	0	0	0	–	0	0	0	0	0	0	0	0	0	0	0	0.0	–	1B-1

Year	Team	Games	BA	SA	AB	H	2B	3B	HR	HR%	R	RBI	BB	SO	SB	Pinch Hit AB	H	PO	A	E	DP	TC/G	FA	G by Pos

Pop Lyttle

LYTLE, EDWARD BENSON (Dad)
B. Mar. 10, 1862, Racine, Wis. D. Dec. 21, 1950, Long Beach, Calif.

BR TR 5'11" 160 lbs.

Year	Team	Games	BA	SA	AB	H	2B	3B	HR	HR%	R	RBI	BB	SO	SB	AB	H	PO	A	E	DP	TC/G	FA	G by Pos
1890	2 teams				CHI N (1G – .000)				PIT N (15G – .145)															
"	total	16	.136	.153	59	8	1	0	0	0.0	3	0	8	10	0	0	0	28	22	10	0	3.8	.833	OF-8, 2B-8

Jim Lyttle

LYTTLE, JAMES LAWRENCE
B. May 20, 1946, Hamilton, Ohio

BL TR 6' 180 lbs.

Year	Team	Games	BA	SA	AB	H	2B	3B	HR	HR%	R	RBI	BB	SO	SB	AB	H	PO	A	E	DP	TC/G	FA	G by Pos
1969	NY A	28	.181	.229	83	15	4	0	0	0.0	7	4	4	19	1	1	0	55	3	1	1	2.1	.983	OF-28
1970		87	.310	.452	126	39	7	1	3	2.4	20	14	10	26	3	7	3	84	2	1	0	1.0	.989	OF-70
1971		49	.198	.291	86	17	5	0	1	1.2	7	7	8	18	0	15	1	47	1	0	0	1.0	1.000	OF-29
1972	CHI A	44	.232	.341	82	19	5	2	0	0.0	8	5	1	28	0	21	6	32	1	0	1	0.8	1.000	OF-21
1973	MON N	49	.259	.422	116	30	5	1	4	3.4	12	19	9	14	0	11	2	73	3	2	1	1.6	.974	OF-36
1974		25	.333	.333	9	3	0	0	0	0.0	1	2	1	3	0	6	1	6	1	0	0	0.3	1.000	OF-18
1975		44	.273	.345	55	15	4	0	0	0.0	7	6	13	6	0	19	4	17	1	0	0	0.4	1.000	OF-16
1976	2 teams				MON N (42G – .271)				LA N (23G – .221)															
"	total	65	.248	.327	153	38	7	1	1	0.7	9	13	15	25	0	20	5	87	8	1	4	1.5	.990	OF-47
8 yrs.		391	.248	.352	710	176	37	5	9	1.3	71	70	61	139	4	100	23	401	20	5	7	1.1	.988	OF-265

Harvey MacDonald

MacDONALD, HARVEY FORSYTH
B. May 18, 1898, New York, N. Y. D. Oct. 4, 1965, Manoa, Pa.

BL TL 5'11" 170 lbs.

Year	Team	Games	BA	SA	AB	H	2B	3B	HR	HR%	R	RBI	BB	SO	SB	AB	H	PO	A	E	DP	TC/G	FA	G by Pos
1928	PHI N	13	.250	.250	16	4	0	0	0	0.0	0	2	2	3	0	9	4	3	0	0	0	0.2	1.000	OF-2

Macey

MACEY,
B. Columbus, Ohio Deceased.

Year	Team	Games	BA	SA	AB	H	2B	3B	HR	HR%	R	RBI	BB	SO	SB	AB	H	PO	A	E	DP	TC/G	FA	G by Pos
1890	PHI AA	1	.000	.000	1	0	0	0	0	0.0	0		0		0	0	0	1	0	0	0	1.0	1.000	C-1

Mike Macfarlane

MACFARLANE, MICHAEL ANDREW (Mac)
B. Apr. 12, 1964, Stockton, Calif.

BR TR 6'1" 200 lbs.

Year	Team	Games	BA	SA	AB	H	2B	3B	HR	HR%	R	RBI	BB	SO	SB	AB	H	PO	A	E	DP	TC/G	FA	G by Pos
1987	KC A	8	.211	.263	19	4	1	0	0	0.0	0	3	2	2	0	0	0	29	2	0	0	3.9	1.000	C-8
1988		70	.265	.393	211	56	15	0	4	1.9	25	26	21	37	0	4	0	309	18	2	3	4.7	.994	C-68
1989		69	.223	.299	157	35	6	0	2	1.3	13	19	7	27	0	12	2	249	17	1	4	3.9	.996	C-59, DH-4
3 yrs.		147	.245	.349	387	95	22	0	6	1.6	38	48	30	66	0	16	2	587	37	3	7	4.3	.995	C-135, DH-4

Ed MacGamwell

MacGAMWELL, EDWARD M.
B. Jan. 10, 1879, Buffalo, N. Y. D. May 26, 1924, Albany, N. Y.

BL TL

Year	Team	Games	BA	SA	AB	H	2B	3B	HR	HR%	R	RBI	BB	SO	SB	AB	H	PO	A	E	DP	TC/G	FA	G by Pos
1905	BKN N	4	.250	.250	16	4	0	0	0	0.0	1		0		0	0	0	37	2	2	0	10.3	.951	1B-4

Ken Macha

MACHA, KENNETH EDWARD
Brother of Mike Macha.
B. Sept. 29, 1950, Monroeville, Pa.

BR TR 6'2" 215 lbs.

Year	Team	Games	BA	SA	AB	H	2B	3B	HR	HR%	R	RBI	BB	SO	SB	AB	H	PO	A	E	DP	TC/G	FA	G by Pos
1974	PIT N	5	.600	.800	5	3	1	0	0	0.0	1	1	0	0	0	5	3	1	0	0	0	0.2	1.000	C-1
1977		35	.274	.316	95	26	4	0	0	0.0	2	11	6	17	1	6	0	72	25	1	5	2.8	.990	3B-17, 1B-11, OF-4
1978		29	.212	.269	52	11	1	1	0	0.0	5	5	12	10	2	7	1	11	21	1	3	1.1	.970	3B-21
1979	MON N	25	.278	.417	36	10	3	1	0	0.0	8	4	2	9	0	7	1	22	18	0	2	1.6	1.000	3B-13, OF-2, 1B-2, C-1
1980		49	.290	.383	107	31	5	1	1	0.9	10	8	11	17	0	11	2	31	43	6	5	1.6	.925	3B-33, 1B-2, OF-1, C-1
1981	TOR A	37	.200	.224	85	17	2	0	0	0.0	4	6	8	15	1	1	0	99	36	5	17	3.8	.964	3B-19, 1B-16, DH-2, C-1
6 yrs.		180	.258	.324	380	98	16	3	1	0.3	30	35	39	68	4	37	7	236	143	13	32	2.2	.967	3B-103, 1B-31, OF-7, C-4, DH-2

Mike Macha

MACHA, MICHAEL WILLIAM
Brother of Ken Macha.
B. Feb. 17, 1954, Victoria, Tex.

BR TR 5'11" 180 lbs.

Year	Team	Games	BA	SA	AB	H	2B	3B	HR	HR%	R	RBI	BB	SO	SB	AB	H	PO	A	E	DP	TC/G	FA	G by Pos
1979	ATL N	6	.154	.154	13	2	0	0	0	0.0	1	5	0	2	0	2	0	2	8	3	0	2.2	.769	3B-3
1980	TOR A	5	.000	.000	8	0	0	0	0	0.0	0	0	0	1	0	2	0	2	5	2	1	1.8	.778	3B-2, C-1
2 yrs.		11	.095	.095	21	2	0	0	0	0.0	1	5	0	3	0	4	0	4	13	5	1	2.0	.773	3B-5, C-1

Dave Machemer

MACHEMER, DAVID RITCHIE
B. May 24, 1951, St. Joseph, Mich.

BR TR 5'11½" 180 lbs.

Year	Team	Games	BA	SA	AB	H	2B	3B	HR	HR%	R	RBI	BB	SO	SB	AB	H	PO	A	E	DP	TC/G	FA	G by Pos
1978	CAL A	10	.273	.455	22	6	1	0	1	4.5	6	2	3	1	0	0	0	6	12	2	0	2.0	.900	2B-5, 3B-3, SS-1
1979	DET A	19	.192	.231	26	5	1	0	0	0.0	8	2	2	2	0	0	0	18	20	1	6	2.1	.974	2B-11, DH-1, OF-1
2 yrs.		29	.229	.333	48	11	2	0	1	2.1	14	4	5	3	0	0	0	24	32	3	6	2.0	.949	2B-16, 3B-3, DH-1, OF-1, SS-1

Connie Mack

MACK, CORNELIUS ALEXANDER (The Tall Tactician)
Born Cornelius Alexander McGilicuddy. Father of Earle Mack.
B. Dec. 22, 1862, E. Brookfield, Mass. D. Feb. 8, 1956, Germantown, Pa.
Manager 1894-96, 1901-50.
Hall of Fame 1937.

BR TR 6'1" 170 lbs.

Year	Team	Games	BA	SA	AB	H	2B	3B	HR	HR%	R	RBI	BB	SO	SB	AB	H	PO	A	E	DP	TC/G	FA	G by Pos
1886	WAS N	10	.361	.472	36	13	2	1	0	0.0	4	5	0	2			0	0	88	22	5	2	11.5	.957	C-10
1887		82	.201	.226	314	63	6	1	0	0.0	35	20	8	17	26	0	0	403	127	55	16	7.1	.906	C-76, OF-5, 2B-2
1888		85	.187	.273	300	56	5	6	3	1.0	49	29	17	18	31	0	0	384	155	48	8	6.9	.918	C-79, OF-4, SS-1, 1B-1
1889		98	.293	.339	386	113	16	1	0	0.0	51	42	15	12	26	0	0	432	100	57	22	6.0	.903	C-45, OF-34, 1B-22
1890	BUF P	123	.266	.344	503	134	15	12	0	0.0	95	53	47	13	16	0	0	500	147	50	14	5.7	.928	C-112, OF-9, 1B-5
1891	PIT N	75	.214	.250	280	60	10	0	0	0.0	43	29	19	11	4	0	0	385	79	35	1	6.7	.930	C-72, 1B-3
1892		97	.243	.301	346	84	9	4	1	0.3	39	31	21	22	11	0	1	415	143	29	11	6.1	.951	C-92, OF-3, 1B-1
1893		37	.286	.323	133	38	3	1	0	0.0	22	15	10	9	4	0	0	128	47	11	5	5.0	.941	C-37
1894		69	.250	.303	228	57	7	1	1	0.4	32	21	20	14	8	0	0	274	67	19	6	5.2	.947	C-69
1895		14	.306	.347	49	15	2	0	0	0.0	12	4	7	1	1	0	0	48	10	2	6	4.3	.967	C-12, 1B-1
1896		33	.217	.267	120	26	4	1	0	0.0	9	16	5		1	0	0	261	19	7	14	8.7	.976	1B-28, C-5
11 yrs.		723	.245	.300	2695	659	79	28	5	0.2	391	265	169	127	127	2	1	3318	916	318	101	6.3	.930	C-609, 1B-61, OF-55, 2B-2, SS-1

Year	Team	Games	BA	SA	AB	H	2B	3B	HR	HR%	R	RBI	BB	SO	SB	Pinch Hit AB	H	PO	A	E	DP	TC/G	FA	G by Pos

Denny Mack

MACK, DENNIS JOSEPH
Born Dennis Joseph McGee.
B. 1851, Easton, Pa. D. Apr. 10, 1888, Wilkes-Barre, Pa.
Manager 1882.

BR TR 5'7" 164 lbs.

Year	Team	Games	BA	SA	AB	H	2B	3B	HR	HR%	R	RBI	BB	SO	SB	PH AB	PH H	PO	A	E	DP	TC/G	FA	G by Pos
1876	STL	N	48	.217	.261	180	39	5	0	1	0.6	32	-	7	11	5			0	0	59	124	26	8	4.4	.876	SS-41, 2B-5, OF-2
1880	BUF	N	17	.203	.203	59	12	0	0	0	0.0	5	3		5	7			0	0	19	46	4	3	4.1	.942	SS-16, 2B-1
1882	LOU	AA	72	.182	.201	264	48	3	1	0	0.0	41		16				0	0	108	220	49	20	5.2	.870	SS-49, 2B-24, OF-5
1883	PIT	AA	60	.196	.246	224	44	5	3	0	0.0	26		13				0	0	256	123	34	18	6.9	.918	SS-38, 1B-25, 2B-1
4 yrs.		197	.197	.230	727	143	13	4	1	0.1	104	10	45	12			0	0	442	513	113	49	5.4	.894	SS-144, 2B-31, 1B-25, OF-7

Earle Mack

MACK, EARLE THADDEUS
Born Earle Thaddeus McGillicuddy. Son of Connie Mack.
B. Feb. 1, 1890, Spencer, Mass. D. Feb. 4, 1967, Upper Darby, Pa.
Manager 1937, 1939.

BL TR 5'8" 140 lbs.

Year	Team	Games	BA	SA	AB	H	2B	3B	HR	HR%	R	RBI	BB	SO	SB	PH AB	PH H	PO	A	E	DP	TC/G	FA	G by Pos
1910	PHI	A	1	.500	1.000	4	2	0	1	0	0.0	0	0	0	0	0	0	0	3	2	0	0	5.0	1.000	C-1
1911		2	.000	.000	4	0	0	0	0	0.0	0	0	0	0	0	0	0	0	0	0	0	0.0	—	3B-2
1914		2	.000	.000	8	0	0	0	0	0.0	0	1	0	0	1	0	0	19	1	0	0	10.0	1.000	1B-2
3 yrs.		5	.125	.250	16	2	0	1	0	0.0	0	1	0	0	1	0	0	22	3	0	0	5.0	1.000	3B-2, 1B-2, C-1

Joe Mack

MACK, JOSEPH JOHN
Born Joseph John Maciarz.
B. Jan. 4, 1912, Chicago, Ill.

BB TL 5'11½" 185 lbs.

Year	Team	Games	BA	SA	AB	H	2B	3B	HR	HR%	R	RBI	BB	SO	SB	PH AB	PH H	PO	A	E	DP	TC/G	FA	G by Pos
1945	BOS	N	66	.231	.323	260	60	13	1	3	1.2	30	44	34	39	1	1	0	635	48	6	48	10.4	.991	1B-65

Ray Mack

MACK, RAYMOND JAMES
Born Raymond James Mlckovsky.
B. Aug. 31, 1916, Cleveland, Ohio D. May 7, 1969, Bucyrus, Ohio

BR TR 6' 200 lbs.

Year	Team	Games	BA	SA	AB	H	2B	3B	HR	HR%	R	RBI	BB	SO	SB	PH AB	PH H	PO	A	E	DP	TC/G	FA	G by Pos
1938	CLE	A	2	.333	.667	6	2	0	0	0	0.0	2	2	0	1	0			8	6	0	0	7.0	1.000	2B-2
1939		36	.152	.232	112	17	4	1	1	0.9	12	6	12	19	0	2	0	80	87	4	25	4.8	.977	2B-34, 3B-1
1940		146	.283	.409	530	150	21	5	12	2.3	60	69	51	77	4	0	0	323	417	27	109	5.3	.965	2B-146
1941		145	.228	.341	501	114	22	4	9	1.8	54	44	54	69	8	0	0	363	386	23	109	5.3	.970	2B-145
1942		143	.225	.291	481	108	14	6	2	0.4	43	45	41	51	9	0	0	340	434	25	105	5.6	.969	2B-143
1943		153	.220	.312	545	120	25	2	7	1.3	56	62	47	61	8	0	0	381	444	28	123	5.6	.967	2B-153
1944		83	.232	.306	284	66	15	3	0	0.0	24	29	28	45	4	0	0	226	243	24	73	5.9	.951	2B-83
1946		61	.205	.281	171	35	6	3	1	0.6	13	9	23	27	2	0	0	118	142	8	37	4.4	.970	2B-61
1947	2 teams	NY A (1G – .000)	CHI N (21G – .218)																					
"	total	22	.218	.372	78	17	6	0	2	2.6	9	12	5	15	0	0	0	58	78	5	15	6.4	.965	2B-21
9 yrs.		791	.232	.329	2708	629	113	24	34	1.3	273	278	261	365	35	2	0	1897	2237	144	596	5.4	.966	2B-788, 3B-1

Reddy Mack

MACK, JOSEPH
Born Joseph McNamara.
B. May 2, 1866, Ireland D. Dec. 30, 1916, Newport, Ky.

Year	Team	Games	BA	SA	AB	H	2B	3B	HR	HR%	R	RBI	BB	SO	SB	PH AB	PH H	PO	A	E	DP	TC/G	FA	G by Pos
1885	LOU	AA	11	.244	.268	41	10	1	0	0	0.0	7		2			0	0	33	36	9	9	7.1	.885	2B-11
1886		137	.244	.344	483	118	23	11	1	0.2	82		68			0	0	350	446	88	60	6.5	.900	2B-137
1887		128	.308	.395	478	147	23	8	1	0.2	117		83		22	0	0	366	395	73	48	6.5	.912	2B-128
1888		112	.217	.289	446	97	13	5	3	0.7	77	34	52		18	0	0	307	344	67	35	6.4	.907	2B-112
1889	BAL	AA	136	.241	.320	519	125	24	7	1	0.2	84	87	60	69	23	0	0	372	358	83	70	6.0	.898	2B-135, OF-1
1890		26	.284	.421	95	27	3	5	0	0.0	14		10		7	0	0	62	76	10	7	5.7	.932	2B-26
6 yrs.		550	.254	.340	2062	524	87	36	6	0.3	381	121	275	69	70	0	0	1490	1655	330	229	6.3	.905	2B-549, OF-1

Shane Mack

MACK, SHANE LEE
B. Dec. 7, 1963, Los Angeles, Calif.

BR TR 6' 185 lbs.

Year	Team	Games	BA	SA	AB	H	2B	3B	HR	HR%	R	RBI	BB	SO	SB	PH AB	PH H	PO	A	E	DP	TC/G	FA	G by Pos
1987	SD	N	105	.239	.361	238	57	11	3	4	1.7	28	25	18	47	4	20	3	159	1	3	0	1.6	.982	OF-91
1988		56	.244	.269	119	29	3	0	0	0.0	13	12	14	21	5	0	0	110	4	2	1	2.1	.983	OF-55
2 yrs.		161	.241	.331	357	86	14	3	4	1.1	41	37	32	68	9	20	3	269	5	5	1	1.7	.982	OF-146

Pete Mackanin

MACKANIN, PETER, JR.
B. Aug. 1, 1951, Chicago, Ill.

BR TR 6'2" 190 lbs.

Year	Team	Games	BA	SA	AB	H	2B	3B	HR	HR%	R	RBI	BB	SO	SB	PH AB	PH H	PO	A	E	DP	TC/G	FA	G by Pos
1973	TEX	A	44	.100	.122	90	9	2	0	0	0.0	3	2	4	26	0	2	0	39	88	7	15	3.0	.948	SS-33, 3B-10
1974		2	.167	.500	6	1	0	1	0	0.0	0	0	0	2	0	1	0	3	8	0	3	5.5	1.000	SS-2
1975	MON	N	130	.225	.375	448	101	19	6	12	2.7	59	44	31	99	11	4	0	300	411	26	100	5.7	.965	2B-127, SS-1, 3B-1
1976		114	.224	.337	380	85	15	2	8	2.1	36	33	15	66	6	4	1	203	307	19	64	4.6	.964	2B-100, 3B-8, SS-3, OF-1
1977		55	.224	.329	85	19	2	2	1	1.2	9	6	4	17	3	29	7	34	44	4	11	1.5	.951	2B-9, SS-8, 3B-5, OF-4
1978	PHI	N	5	.250	.250	8	2	0	0	0	0.0	0	0	1	0	4	4	1	6	2	0	0	1.6	1.000	3B-1, 1B-1
1979		13	.111	.444	9	1	0	0	1	11.1	2	2	1	2	0	6	0	9	0	0	0	0.8	1.000	SS-2, 3B-2, 2B-2
1980	MIN	A	108	.266	.361	319	85	18	0	4	1.3	31	35	14	34	6	15	5	168	285	18	75	4.4	.962	2B-71, SS-30, DH-5, 1B-4, 3B-3
1981		77	.231	.324	225	52	7	1	4	1.8	21	18	7	40	1	2	0	171	149	12	40	4.3	.964	2B-31, SS-28, 1B-10, DH-6, 3B-4
9 yrs.		548	.226	.339	1570	355	63	12	30	1.9	161	141	76	290	27	74	16	925	1303	86	308	4.2	.963	2B-340, SS-107, 3B-34, 1B-15, DH-11, OF-5

Eric MacKenzie

MacKENZIE, ERIC HUGH
B. Aug. 29, 1932, Glendon, Alta., Canada

BL TR 6' 185 lbs.

Year	Team	Games	BA	SA	AB	H	2B	3B	HR	HR%	R	RBI	BB	SO	SB	PH AB	PH H	PO	A	E	DP	TC/G	FA	G by Pos
1955	KC	A	1	.000	.000	1	0	0	0	0	0.0	0	0	0	0	0	0	0	0	0	0	0	0.0	—	C-1

Gordon MacKenzie

MacKENZIE, HENRY GORDON
B. July 9, 1937, St. Petersburg, Fla.

BR TR 5'11" 175 lbs.

Year	Team	Games	BA	SA	AB	H	2B	3B	HR	HR%	R	RBI	BB	SO	SB	PH AB	PH H	PO	A	E	DP	TC/G	FA	G by Pos
1961	KC	A	11	.125	.125	24	3	0	0	0	0.0	1	1	1	6	0	6	1	22	3	0	2	2.3	1.000	C-7

Year	Team		Games	BA	SA	AB	H	2B	3B	HR	HR%	R	RBI	BB	SO	SB	Pinch Hit AB	H	PO	A	E	DP	TC/G	FA	G by Pos

Felix Mackiewicz

MACKIEWICZ, FELIX THADDEUS
B. Nov. 20, 1917, Chicago, Ill.　　　　　BR TR 6'2" 195 lbs.

Year	Team		Games	BA	SA	AB	H	2B	3B	HR	HR%	R	RBI	BB	SO	SB	PH AB	PH H	PO	A	E	DP	TC/G	FA	G by Pos
1941	PHI	A	5	.286	.429	14	4	0	1	0	0.0	3	0	1	0	0	1	0	5	0	0	0	1.0	1.000	OF-3
1942			6	.214	.357	14	3	2	0	0	0.0	3	2	0	4	0	3	1	6	1	0	0	1.2	1.000	OF-3
1943			9	.063	.063	16	1	0	0	0	0.0	1	0	2	8	0	3	0	9	0	0	0	1.0	1.000	OF-3
1945	CLE	A	120	.273	.368	359	98	14	7	2	0.6	42	37	44	41	5	7	0	288	11	4	4	2.5	.987	OF-112
1946			78	.260	.349	258	67	15	4	0	0.0	35	16	16	32	5	5	1	172	2	3	1	2.3	.983	OF-72
1947	2 teams		CLE A (2G – .000)			WAS A (3G – .167)																			
"	total		5	.091	.182	11	1	0	0	0	0.0	1	0	0	3	0	0	0	8	0	0	0	1.6	1.000	OF-5
6 yrs.			223	.259	.351	672	174	32	12	2	0.3	85	55	63	88	10	19	2	488	14	7	5	2.3	.986	OF-198

Steve Macko

MACKO, STEVEN JOSEPH
B. Sept. 6, 1954, Burlington, Iowa　D. Nov. 15, 1981, Arlington, Tex.　　BL TR 5'10" 160 lbs.

Year	Team		Games	BA	SA	AB	H	2B	3B	HR	HR%	R	RBI	BB	SO	SB	PH AB	PH H	PO	A	E	DP	TC/G	FA	G by Pos
1979	CHI	N	19	.225	.250	40	9	1	0	0	0.0	2	3	4	8	0	5	0	21	33	0	4	2.8	1.000	2B-10, 3B-4
1980			6	.300	.400	20	6	2	0	0	0.0	2	2	0	3	0	0	0	11	14	0	4	4.2	1.000	SS-3, 3B-2, 2B-1
2 yrs.			25	.250	.300	60	15	3	0	0	0.0	4	5	4	11	0	5	0	32	47	0	8	3.2	1.000	2B-11, 3B-6, SS-3

Max Macon

MACON, MAX CULLEN
B. Oct. 14, 1915, Pensacola, Fla.　D. Aug. 5, 1989, Jupiter, Fla.　　BL TL 6'3" 175 lbs.

Year	Team		Games	BA	SA	AB	H	2B	3B	HR	HR%	R	RBI	BB	SO	SB	PH AB	PH H	PO	A	E	DP	TC/G	FA	G by Pos
1938	STL	N	46	.306	.306	36	11	0	0	0	0.0	5	3	2	4	0	2	0	3	32	2	2	0.8	.946	P-38, OF-1
1940	BKN	N	2	1.000	1.000	1	1	0	0	0	0.0	0	0	0	0	0	0	0	0	0	0	0	0.0	–	P-2
1942			26	.279	.372	43	12	2	1	0	0.0	4	1	2	4	1	11	5	9	15	1	0	1.0	.960	P-14
1943			45	.164	.164	55	9	0	0	0	0.0	7	6	0	1	1	13	1	14	19	1	4	0.8	.971	P-25, 1B-3
1944	BOS	N	106	.273	.355	366	100	15	3	3	0.8	38	36	12	23	7	10	2	671	51	17	62	7.0	.977	1B-72, OF-22, P-1
1947			1	.000	.000	1	0	0	0	0	0.0	0	0	0	0	0	0	0	0	1	0	0	1.0	1.000	P-1
6 yrs.			226	.265	.333	502	133	17	4	3	0.6	54	46	16	32	9	36	8	697	118	21	68	3.7	.975	P-81, 1B-75, OF-23

Waddy MacPhee

MacPHEE, WALTER SCOTT
B. Dec. 23, 1899, Brooklyn, N. Y.　D. Jan. 20, 1980, Charlotte, N. C.　　BR TR 5'8" 140 lbs.

Year	Team		Games	BA	SA	AB	H	2B	3B	HR	HR%	R	RBI	BB	SO	SB	PH AB	PH H	PO	A	E	DP	TC/G	FA	G by Pos
1922	NY	N	2	.286	.571	7	2	0	1	0	0.0	2	0	1	0	0	0	0	3	5	1	0	4.5	.889	3B-2

Jimmy Macullar

MACULLAR, JAMES F. (Little Mac)
B. Jan. 16, 1855, Boston, Mass.　D. Apr. 8, 1924, Baltimore, Md.
Manager 1879.　　BR TL

Year	Team		Games	BA	SA	AB	H	2B	3B	HR	HR%	R	RBI	BB	SO	SB	PH AB	PH H	PO	A	E	DP	TC/G	FA	G by Pos
1879	SYR	N	64	.211	.248	246	52	9	0	0	0.0	24	13	3	27		0	0	139	120	42	9	4.7	.860	SS-37, OF-26, 2B-4, 3B-1
1882	CIN	AA	79	.234	.294	299	70	6	6	0	0.0	44		14			0	0	141	13	13	2	2.1	.922	OF-79
1883			14	.167	.208	48	8	2	0	0	0.0	4		4			0	0	17	2	4	0	1.6	.826	OF-14, SS-1
1884	BAL	AA	107	.204	.316	358	73	16	6	4	1.1	73	35				0	0	119	317	67	23	4.7	.867	SS-107
1885			100	.191	.278	320	61	7	6	3	0.9	52	49				0	0	178	311	68	28	5.6	.878	SS-98, OF-2
1886			85	.205	.239	268	55	7	1	0	0.0	49	49				0	0	120	213	58	19	4.6	.852	SS-82, OF-2, 2B-1, P-1
6 yrs.			449	.207	.276	1539	319	47	19	7	0.5	246	13	154	27		0	0	714	976	252	81	4.3	.870	SS-325, OF-123, 2B-5, 3B-1, P-1

Frank Madden

MADDEN, FRANCIS A. (Red)
B. Oct. 17, 1892, Pittsburgh, Pa.　D. Apr. 30, 1952, Pittsburgh, Pa.

Year	Team		Games	BA	SA	AB	H	2B	3B	HR	HR%	R	RBI	BB	SO	SB	PH AB	PH H	PO	A	E	DP	TC/G	FA	G by Pos
1914	PIT	F	2	.500	.500	2	1	0	0	0	0.0	0	1	0		0	0	1	0	0	0	0	0.0	–	C-1

Bunny Madden

MADDEN, THOMAS JOSEPH
B. July 31, 1883, Philadelphia, Pa.　D. July 26, 1930, Philadelphia, Pa.　　BL TL 5'11" 160 lbs.

Year	Team		Games	BA	SA	AB	H	2B	3B	HR	HR%	R	RBI	BB	SO	SB	PH AB	PH H	PO	A	E	DP	TC/G	FA	G by Pos
1906	BOS	N	4	.267	.267	15	4	0	0	0	0.0	1	0	1		0	0	0	3	0	0	0	1.0	1.000	OF-4
1910	NY	A	1	.000	.000	1	0	0	0	0	0.0	0	0	0	1	0	1	0	0	1	0	0	1.0	1.000	
2 yrs.			5	.250	.250	16	4	0	0	0	0.0	1	0	1	1	0	1	0	3	1	0	0	0.8	1.000	OF-4

Gene Madden

MADDEN, EUGENE
B. June 5, 1890, Elm Grove, W. Va.　D. Apr. 6, 1949, Utica, N. Y.　　BL TR 5'10" 155 lbs.

Year	Team		Games	BA	SA	AB	H	2B	3B	HR	HR%	R	RBI	BB	SO	SB	PH AB	PH H	PO	A	E	DP	TC/G	FA	G by Pos
1916	PIT	N	1	.000	.000	1	0	0	0	0	0.0	0	0	0	0	0	1	0	0	0	0	0	0.0	–	

Tom Madden

MADDEN, THOMAS FRANCIS
B. Sept. 14, 1882, Boston, Mass.　D. Jan. 20, 1954, Cambridge, Mass.　　BR TR 5'10" 190 lbs.

Year	Team		Games	BA	SA	AB	H	2B	3B	HR	HR%	R	RBI	BB	SO	SB	PH AB	PH H	PO	A	E	DP	TC/G	FA	G by Pos
1909	BOS	A	10	.235	.235	17	4	0	0	0	0.0	0	1	0		0	3	1	27	5	2	0	3.4	.941	C-7
1910			14	.371	.457	35	13	3	0	0	0.0	4	4	3		0	2	1	50	11	4	0	4.6	.938	C-12
1911	2 teams		BOS A (4G – .200)			PHI N (28G – .276)																			
"	total		32	.264	.297	91	24	1	1	0	0.0	6	6	2	13	0	1	1	130	36	12	3	5.6	.933	C-26
3 yrs.			56	.287	.329	143	41	4	1	0	0.0	10	11	5	13	0	6	3	207	52	18	3	4.9	.935	C-45

Clarence Maddern

MADDERN, CLARENCE JAMES
B. Sept. 26, 1921, Bisbee, Ariz.　D. Aug. 9, 1986, Tucson, Ariz.　　BR TR 6'1" 185 lbs.

Year	Team		Games	BA	SA	AB	H	2B	3B	HR	HR%	R	RBI	BB	SO	SB	PH AB	PH H	PO	A	E	DP	TC/G	FA	G by Pos
1946	CHI	N	3	.000	.000	3	0	0	0	0	0.0	0	0	0	0	0	1	0	4	0	0	0	1.3	1.000	OF-2
1948			80	.252	.374	214	54	12	1	4	1.9	16	27	10	25	0	23	5	98	6	2	0	1.3	.981	OF-55
1949			10	.333	.667	9	3	0	1	1	11.1	1	2	0	0	0	7	1	2	1	0	0	0.3	1.000	1B-1
1951	CLE	A	11	.167	.167	12	2	0	0	0	0.0	0	0	1	0	0	9	1	2	0	1	0	0.3	.667	OF-1
4 yrs.			104	.248	.370	238	59	12	1	5	2.1	17	29	12	26	0	40	7	106	7	3	0	1.1	.974	OF-58, 1B-1

Elliott Maddox

MADDOX, ELLIOTT
B. Dec. 21, 1947, East Orange, N. J.　　BR TR 5'11" 180 lbs.

Year	Team		Games	BA	SA	AB	H	2B	3B	HR	HR%	R	RBI	BB	SO	SB	PH AB	PH H	PO	A	E	DP	TC/G	FA	G by Pos
1970	DET	A	109	.248	.364	258	64	13	4	3	1.2	30	24	30	42	2	20	2	104	100	14	10	2.0	.936	3B-40, OF-37, SS-19, 2B-1
1971	WAS	A	128	.217	.275	258	56	8	2	1	0.4	38	18	51	42	10	19	7	201	21	3	4	1.8	.987	OF-103, 3B-12
1972	TEX	A	98	.252	.289	294	74	7	2	0	0.0	40	10	49	53	20	1	0	199	7	2	4	2.1	.990	OF-94
1973			100	.238	.262	172	41	1	0	1	0.6	24	17	29	28	5	3	0	148	14	3	2	1.7	.982	OF-89, 3B-7, DH-1
1974	NY	A	137	.303	.386	466	141	26	2	3	0.6	75	45	69	48	6	3	2	336	19	5	4	2.6	.986	OF-135, 2B-2, 3B-1
1975			55	.307	.394	218	67	10	3	1	0.5	36	23	21	24	9	0	0	158	5	0	3	3.0	1.000	OF-55, 2B-1

Year	Team		Games	BA	SA	AB	H	2B	3B	HR	HR%	R	RBI	BB	SO	SB	Pinch Hit AB	Pinch Hit H	PO	A	E	DP	TC/G	FA	G by Pos

Elliott Maddox *continued*

Year	Team		Games	BA	SA	AB	H	2B	3B	HR	HR%	R	RBI	BB	SO	SB	AB	H	PO	A	E	DP	TC/G	FA	G by Pos
1976			18	.217	.261	46	10	2	0	0	0.0	4	3	4	3	0	2	1	21	2	0	1	1.3	1.000	OF-13, DH-2
1977	BAL	A	49	.262	.383	107	28	7	0	2	1.9	14	9	13	9	2	2	0	99	0	1	0	2.0	.990	OF-45, 3B-1
1978	NY	N	119	.257	.329	389	100	18	2	2	0.5	43	39	71	38	2	7	0	196	80	9	8	2.4	.968	OF-79, 3B-43, 1B-1
1979			86	.268	.339	224	60	13	0	1	0.4	21	12	20	27	3	21	8	131	22	3	1	1.8	.981	OF-65, 3B-11
1980			130	.246	.319	411	101	16	1	4	1.0	35	34	52	44	1	11	2	111	211	14	19	2.6	.958	3B-115, OF-4, 1B-2
11 yrs.			1029	.261	.334	2843	742	121	16	18	0.6	360	234	409	358	60	89	22	1704	481	54	56	2.2	.976	OF-719, 3B-230, SS-19, 2B-4, DH-3, 1B-3

LEAGUE CHAMPIONSHIP SERIES

Year	Team		Games	BA	SA	AB	H	2B	3B	HR	HR%	R	RBI	BB	SO	SB	AB	H	PO	A	E	DP	TC/G	FA	G by Pos
1976	NY	A	3	.222	.333	9	2	1	0	0	0.0	0	1	0	1	0	0	0	9	0	0	0	3.0	1.000	OF-3

WORLD SERIES

Year	Team		Games	BA	SA	AB	H	2B	3B	HR	HR%	R	RBI	BB	SO	SB	AB	H	PO	A	E	DP	TC/G	FA	G by Pos
1976	NY	A	2	.200	.600	5	1	0	1	0	0.0	0	0	1	2	0	0	0	0	0	0	0	0.0	—	DH-1, OF-1

Garry Maddox

MADDOX, GARRY LEE
B. Sept. 1, 1949, Cincinnati, Ohio

BR TR 6'3" 175 lbs.

Year	Team		Games	BA	SA	AB	H	2B	3B	HR	HR%	R	RBI	BB	SO	SB	AB	H	PO	A	E	DP	TC/G	FA	G by Pos
1972	SF	N	125	.266	.432	458	122	26	7	12	2.6	62	58	14	97	13	2	0	279	7	6	3	2.3	.979	OF-121
1973			144	.319	.460	587	187	30	10	11	1.9	81	76	24	73	24	2	1	370	4	12	0	2.7	.969	OF-140
1974			135	.284	.398	538	153	31	3	8	1.5	74	50	29	64	21	6	2	345	3	5	0	2.6	.986	OF-131
1975	2 teams			SF	N	(17G – .135)			PHI	N	(99G – .291)														
"	total		116	.272	.406	426	116	26	4	5	1.2	54	50	42	57	25	5	0	325	13	5	4	3.0	.985	OF-110
1976	PHI	N	146	.330	.456	531	175	37	6	6	1.1	75	68	42	59	29	2	0	441	10	5	0	3.1	.989	OF-144
1977			139	.292	.448	571	167	27	10	14	2.5	85	74	24	58	22	2	0	383	7	9	2	2.9	.977	OF-138
1978			155	.288	.410	598	172	34	3	11	1.8	62	68	39	89	33	1	0	444	7	8	1	3.0	.983	OF-154
1979			148	.281	.425	548	154	28	6	13	2.4	70	61	17	71	26	6	1	433	13	2	2	3.0	.996	OF-140
1980			143	.259	.386	549	142	31	3	11	2.0	59	73	18	52	25	1	0	405	7	10	0	3.0	.976	OF-143
1981			94	.263	.337	323	85	7	1	5	1.5	37	40	17	42	9	1	0	251	8	6	4	2.8	.977	OF-94
1982			119	.284	.417	412	117	27	2	8	1.9	39	61	12	32	7	9	2	253	8	2	1	2.2	.992	OF-111
1983			97	.275	.367	324	89	14	2	4	1.2	27	32	17	31	7	11	3	216	1	5	0	2.3	.977	OF-95
1984			77	.282	.390	241	68	11	0	5	2.1	29	19	13	29	3	14	0	160	3	0	1	2.1	1.000	OF-69
1985			105	.239	.339	218	52	8	1	4	1.8	22	23	13	26	4	25	4	143	3	3	0	1.4	.980	OF-94
1986			6	.429	.429	7	3	0	0	0	0.0	1	1	2	1	0	3	1	1	0	0	0	0.2	1.000	OF-5
15 yrs.			1749	.285	.413	6331	1802	337	62	117	1.8	777	754	323	781	248	90	14	4449	94	78	21	2.6	.983	OF-1687

DIVISIONAL PLAYOFF SERIES

Year	Team		Games	BA	SA	AB	H	2B	3B	HR	HR%	R	RBI	BB	SO	SB	AB	H	PO	A	E	DP	TC/G	FA	G by Pos
1981	PHI	N	2	.333	.667	3	1	1	0	0	0.0	0	0	0	0	0	0	0	0	0	0	0	0.0	—	OF-2

LEAGUE CHAMPIONSHIP SERIES

Year	Team		Games	BA	SA	AB	H	2B	3B	HR	HR%	R	RBI	BB	SO	SB	AB	H	PO	A	E	DP	TC/G	FA	G by Pos
1976	PHI	N	3	.231	.308	13	3	1	0	0	0.0	2	1	1	0	0	0	0	9	0	0	0	3.0	1.000	OF-3
1977			4	.429	.429	7	3	0	0	0	0.0	1	2	0	1	0	0	0	6	0	0	0	1.5	1.000	OF-4
1978			4	.263	.263	19	5	0	0	0	0.0	1	2	0	3	0	0	0	16	0	1	0	4.3	.941	OF-4
1980			5	.300	.400	20	6	2	0	0	0.0	2	3	2	2	2	0	0	23	0	0	0	4.6	1.000	OF-5
1983			3	.273	.364	11	3	1	0	0	0.0	0	1	0	1	0	0	0	8	0	1	0	3.0	.889	OF-3
5 yrs.			19	.286	.343	70	20	4	0	0	0.0	6	9	3	7	2	0	0	62	0	2	0	3.4	.969	OF-17

WORLD SERIES

Year	Team		Games	BA	SA	AB	H	2B	3B	HR	HR%	R	RBI	BB	SO	SB	AB	H	PO	A	E	DP	TC/G	FA	G by Pos
1980	PHI	N	6	.227	.318	22	5	2	0	0	0.0	1	1	1	3	0	0	0	11	1	0	1	2.0	1.000	OF-6
1983			4	.250	.583	12	3	1	0	1	8.3	1	1	0	2	0	1	0	7	0	0	0	1.8	1.000	OF-4
2 yrs.			10	.235	.412	34	8	3	0	1	2.9	2	2	1	5	0	1	0	18	1	0	1	1.9	1.000	OF-9

Jerry Maddox

MADDOX, JERRY GLENN
B. July 28, 1953, Whittier, Calif.

BR TR 6'2" 200 lbs.

Year	Team		Games	BA	SA	AB	H	2B	3B	HR	HR%	R	RBI	BB	SO	SB	AB	H	PO	A	E	DP	TC/G	FA	G by Pos
1978	ATL	N	7	.214	.214	14	3	0	0	0	0.0	1	1	2	0	2	1	3	7	1	0	1.6	.909	3B-5	

Art Madison

MADISON, ARTHUR M.
B. Jan. 14, 1872, Clarksburg, Mass. D. Jan. 27, 1933, North Adams, Mass.

BR TR 5'9" 165 lbs.

Year	Team		Games	BA	SA	AB	H	2B	3B	HR	HR%	R	RBI	BB	SO	SB	AB	H	PO	A	E	DP	TC/G	FA	G by Pos
1895	PHI	N	11	.353	.441	34	12	3	0	0	0.0	6	8	1		4	0	0	17	23	6	2	4.2	.870	SS-6, 2B-3, 3B-2
1899	PIT	N	42	.271	.356	118	32	2	4	0	0.0	20	19	11		1	6	3	72	87	12	10	4.1	.930	2B-19, SS-15, 3B-2
2 yrs.			53	.289	.375	152	44	5	4	0	0.0	26	27	12		5	6	3	89	110	18	12	4.1	.917	2B-22, SS-21, 3B-4

Scotti Madison

MADISON, CHARLES SCOTT
B. Sept. 12, 1959, Pensacola, Fla.

BB TR 5'11" 185 lbs.

Year	Team		Games	BA	SA	AB	H	2B	3B	HR	HR%	R	RBI	BB	SO	SB	AB	H	PO	A	E	DP	TC/G	FA	G by Pos
1985	DET	A	6	.000	.000	11	0	0	0	0	0.0	1	2	0	2	0	2	0	1	0	0	0	0.2	1.000	DH-3, C-1
1986			2	.000	.000	7	0	0	0	0	0.0	0	1	0	3	0	0	0	1	1	1	1	1.5	.667	DH-1, 3B-1
1987	KC	A	7	.267	.467	15	4	3	0	0	0.0	4	0	1	5	0	1	0	28	3	3	4	4.9	.912	1B-4, C-3
1988			16	.171	.229	35	6	2	0	0	0.0	4	2	4	5	1	6	0	23	1	0	0	1.5	1.000	C-4, OF-3, 1B-2
1989	CIN	N	40	.173	.276	98	17	7	0	1	1.0	13	7	8	9	0	16	1	19	44	0	3	1.6	1.000	3B-26
5 yrs.			71	.163	.253	166	27	12	0	1	0.6	21	11	15	22	1	25	1	72	49	4	8	1.8	.968	3B-27, C-8, 1B-6, DH-4, OF-3

Ed Madjeski

MADJESKI, EDWARD WILLIAM
Born Edward William Majewski.
B. July 24, 1909, Far Rockaway, N. Y.

BR TR 5'11" 178 lbs.

Year	Team		Games	BA	SA	AB	H	2B	3B	HR	HR%	R	RBI	BB	SO	SB	AB	H	PO	A	E	DP	TC/G	FA	G by Pos
1932	PHI	A	17	.229	.229	35	8	0	0	0	0.0	4	3	3	6	0	8	2	30	7	0	3	2.2	1.000	C-8
1933			51	.282	.310	142	40	4	0	0	0.0	17	17	4	21	0	12	4	122	14	6	3	2.8	.958	C-41
1934	2 teams			PHI	A	(8G – .375)			CHI	A	(85G – .221)														
"	total		93	.225	.343	289	65	15	2	5	1.7	37	34	14	32	2	11	3	348	49	12	11	4.4	.971	C-80
1937	NY	N	5	.200	.200	15	3	0	0	0	0.0	0	2	0	2	0	0	0	8	2	0	1	2.0	1.000	C-5
4 yrs.			166	.241	.320	481	116	19	2	5	1.0	58	56	21	61	2	31	9	508	72	18	18	3.6	.970	C-134

Bill Madlock

MADLOCK, WILLIAM, JR. (Mad Dog)
B. Jan. 2, 1951, Memphis, Tenn.

BR TR 5'11" 185 lbs.

Year	Team		Games	BA	SA	AB	H	2B	3B	HR	HR%	R	RBI	BB	SO	SB	AB	H	PO	A	E	DP	TC/G	FA	G by Pos
1973	TEX	A	21	.351	.532	77	27	5	3	1	1.3	16	5	7	9	3	0	0	13	32	4	2	2.3	.918	3B-21

Year	Team		Games	BA	SA	AB	H	2B	3B	HR	HR%	R	RBI	BB	SO	SB	Pinch Hit AB	Pinch Hit H	PO	A	E	DP	TC/G	FA	G by Pos

Bill Madlock *continued*

Year	Team		Games	BA	SA	AB	H	2B	3B	HR	HR%	R	RBI	BB	SO	SB	PH AB	PH H	PO	A	E	DP	TC/G	FA	G by Pos
1974	CHI	N	128	.313	.442	453	142	21	5	9	2.0	65	54	42	39	11	8	4	84	229	18	14	2.6	.946	3B-121
1975			130	**.354**	.479	514	182	29	7	7	1.4	77	64	42	34	9	0	0	79	250	20	14	2.7	.943	3B-128
1976			142	**.339**	.500	514	174	36	1	15	2.9	68	84	56	27	15	5	1	107	234	14	21	2.5	.961	3B-136
1977	SF	N	140	.302	.426	533	161	28	1	12	2.3	70	46	43	33	13	8	1	101	234	18	18	2.5	.949	3B-126, 2B-6
1978			122	.309	.481	447	138	26	3	15	3.4	76	44	48	39	16	8	1	234	300	14	49	4.5	.974	2B-114, 1B-3
1979	2 teams			SF N	(69G – .261)		PIT N	(85G – .328)																		
"	total		154	.298	.438	560	167	26	5	14	2.5	85	85	52	41	32	5	2	147	151	7	36	2.0	.977	3B-85, 2B-63, 1B-5
1980	PIT	N	137	.277	.399	494	137	22	4	10	2.0	62	53	45	33	16	3	1	159	217	17	25	2.9	.957	3B-127, 1B-12
1981			82	**.341**	.495	279	95	23	1	6	2.2	35	45	34	17	18	4	0	50	147	9	17	2.5	.956	3B-78
1982			154	.319	.488	568	181	33	3	19	3.3	92	95	48	39	18	7	2	114	267	18	25	2.6	.955	3B-146, 1B-3
1983			130	**.323**	.444	473	153	21	0	12	2.5	68	68	49	24	3	4	1	59	193	11	20	2.0	.958	3B-126
1984			103	.253	.323	403	102	16	0	4	1.0	38	44	26	29	3	3	0	76	176	15	17	2.6	.944	3B-98, 1B-1
1985	2 teams			PIT N	(110G – .251)		LA N	(34G – .360)																		
"	total		144	.275	.402	513	141	27	1	12	2.3	69	56	49	30	10	5	4	133	189	14	13	2.3	.958	3B-130, 1B-12
1986	LA	N	111	.280	.404	379	106	17	0	10	2.6	38	60	30	43	3	9	1	79	171	26	8	2.5	.906	3B-101, 1B-2
1987	2 teams			LA N	(21G – .180)		DET A	(87G – .279)																		
"	total		108	.264	.442	387	102	18	0	17	4.4	61	57	34	50	4	6	0	8	23	3	2	0.3	.912	DH-64, 1B-3, 3B-17
	15 yrs.		1806	.305	.442	6594	2008	348	34	163	2.5	920	860	605	510	174	75	18	1443	2813	208	281	2.5	.953	3B-1440, 2B-183, DH-64, 1B-61

LEAGUE CHAMPIONSHIP SERIES

Year	Team		Games	BA	SA	AB	H	2B	3B	HR	HR%	R	RBI	BB	SO	SB	PH AB	PH H	PO	A	E	DP	TC/G	FA	G by Pos
1979	PIT	N	3	.250	.500	12	3	0	0	1	8.3	1	2	2	0	2	0	0	1	7	0	1	2.7	1.000	3B-3
1985	LA	N	6	.333	.750	24	8	1	0	3	12.5	5	7	0	2	1	0	0	6	9	0	0	2.5	1.000	3B-6
1987	DET	A	1	.000	.000	5	0	0	0	0	0.0	0	0	0	3	0	0	0	0	0	0	0	0.0	–	DH-1
	3 yrs.		10	.268	.585	41	11	1	0	4	9.8	6	9	2	5	3	0	0	7	16	0	1	2.3	1.000	3B-9, DH-1

WORLD SERIES

Year	Team		Games	BA	SA	AB	H	2B	3B	HR	HR%	R	RBI	BB	SO	SB	PH AB	PH H	PO	A	E	DP	TC/G	FA	G by Pos
1979	PIT	N	9	.375	.417	24	9	1	0	0	0.0	2	3	5	1	0	0	0	3	10	1	4	1.6	.929	3B-7

Sal Madrid

MADRID, SALVADOR
B. June 9, 1920, El Paso, Tex.   D. Feb. 24, 1977, Fort Wayne, Ind.

BR TR 5'9"   165 lbs.

Year	Team		Games	BA	SA	AB	H	2B	3B	HR	HR%	R	RBI	BB	SO	SB	PH AB	PH H	PO	A	E	DP	TC/G	FA	G by Pos
1947	CHI	N	8	.125	.167	24	3	1	0	0	0.0	0	1	1	6	0	0	0	16	27	2	5	5.6	.956	SS-8

Dave Magadan

MAGADAN, DAVID JOSEPH
B. Sept. 30, 1962, Tampa, Fla.

BL TR 6'3"   190 lbs.

Year	Team		Games	BA	SA	AB	H	2B	3B	HR	HR%	R	RBI	BB	SO	SB	PH AB	PH H	PO	A	E	DP	TC/G	FA	G by Pos
1986	NY	N	10	.444	.444	18	8	0	0	0	0.0	3	3	3	1	0	1	1	48	5	0	5	5.3	1.000	1B-9
1987			85	.318	.443	192	61	13	1	3	1.6	21	24	22	22	0	30	6	88	92	4	9	2.2	.978	3B-50, 1B-13
1988			112	.277	.334	314	87	15	0	1	0.3	39	35	60	39	0	12	1	459	99	10	42	5.1	.982	1B-71, 3B-48
1989			127	.286	.393	374	107	22	3	4	1.1	47	41	49	37	1	23	5	587	89	7	54	5.4	.990	1B-87, 3B-28
	4 yrs.		334	.293	.384	898	263	50	4	8	0.9	110	103	134	99	1	66	13	1182	285	21	110	4.5	.986	1B-180, 3B-126

LEAGUE CHAMPIONSHIP SERIES

Year	Team		Games	BA	SA	AB	H	2B	3B	HR	HR%	R	RBI	BB	SO	SB	PH AB	PH H	PO	A	E	DP	TC/G	FA	G by Pos
1988	NY	N	3	.000	.000	3	0	0	0	0	0.0	0	0	0	2	0	3	0	0	0	0	0	0.0	–	

Lee Magee

MAGEE, LEO CHRISTOPHER
Born Leopold Christopher Hoernschemeyer.
B. June 4, 1889, Cincinnati, Ohio   D. Mar. 14, 1966, Columbus, Ohio
Manager 1915.

BB TR 5'11"   165 lbs.

Year	Team		Games	BA	SA	AB	H	2B	3B	HR	HR%	R	RBI	BB	SO	SB	PH AB	PH H	PO	A	E	DP	TC/G	FA	G by Pos
1911	STL	N	26	.261	.304	69	18	1	1	0	0.0	9	8	8	8	4	2	0	45	44	5	6	3.6	.947	2B-18, SS-3
1912			128	.290	.354	458	133	13	8	0	0.0	60	40	39	29	16	8	3	299	101	20	17	3.3	.952	OF-85, 2B-23, 1B-6, SS-1
1913			136	.265	.327	529	140	13	7	2	0.4	53	31	34	30	23	0	0	374	86	9	17	3.4	.981	OF-107, 2B-21, 1B-6, SS-2
1914			162	.284	.353	529	150	23	4	2	0.4	59	40	42	24	36	0	0	626	51	8	25	4.2	.988	OF-102, 1B-40, 2B-6
1915	BKN	F	121	.323	.436	452	146	19	10	4	0.9	87	49	22		34	4	0	290	322	41	47	5.4	.937	2B-115, 1B-2
1916	NY	A	131	.257	.325	510	131	18	4	0	0.0	57	45	50	31	29	1	0	305	26	8	3	2.6	.976	OF-128, 2B-2
1917	2 teams			NY A	(51G – .220)		STL A	(36G – .170)																		
"	total		87	.200	.225	285	57	5	1	0	0.0	28	12	19	24	6	3	1	164	80	8	9	2.9	.968	OF-51, 3B-20, 2B-6, 1B-5
1918	CIN	N	119	.290	.394	459	133	22	13	0	0.0	62	28	28	19	19	1	0	281	364	29	74	5.7	.957	2B-114, 3B-3
1919	2 teams			BKN N	(45G – .238)		CHI N	(79G – .292)																		
"	total		124	.270	.346	448	121	19	6	1	0.2	52	24	23	24	19	7	2	213	226	27	15	3.8	.942	OF-44, 2B-43, 3B-19, SS-13
	9 yrs.		1034	.275	.349	3739	1029	133	54	12	0.3	467	277	265	189	186	26	6	2597	1300	155	213	3.9	.962	OF-517, 2B-348, 1B-59, 3B-42, SS-19

Sherry Magee

MAGEE, SHERWOOD ROBERT
B. Aug. 6, 1884, Clarendon, Pa.   D. Mar. 13, 1929, Philadelphia, Pa.

BR TR 5'11"   179 lbs.

Year	Team		Games	BA	SA	AB	H	2B	3B	HR	HR%	R	RBI	BB	SO	SB	PH AB	PH H	PO	A	E	DP	TC/G	FA	G by Pos
1904	PHI	N	95	.277	.409	364	101	15	12	3	0.8	51	57	14		11	0	0	156	19	15	3	2.0	.921	OF-94, 1B-1
1905			155	.299	.420	603	180	24	17	5	0.8	100	98	44		48	0	0	341	19	14	6	2.4	.963	OF-155
1906			154	.282	.407	563	159	36	8	6	1.1	77	67	52		55	0	0	316	18	6	2	2.2	.982	OF-154
1907			140	.328	.455	503	165	28	12	4	0.8	75	**85**	53		46	1	0	297	13	7	7	2.3	.978	OF-139
1908			143	.283	.417	508	144	30	16	2	0.4	79	57	49		40	0	0	279	15	9	5	2.1	.970	OF-142
1909			143	.270	.398	522	141	33	14	2	0.4	60	66	43		38	0	0	283	11	9	0	2.1	.970	OF-143
1910			154	**.331**	**.507**	519	172	39	17	6	1.2	**110**	**123**	94	36	49	0	0	285	9	8	2	2.0	.974	OF-154
1911			121	.288	.483	445	128	32	5	15	3.4	79	94	49	33	22	1	0	248	14	5	3	2.2	.981	OF-120
1912			132	.306	.438	464	142	25	9	6	1.3	79	72	55	54	30	5	2	312	8	12	4	2.5	.964	OF-124, 1B-6
1913			138	.306	.479	470	144	36	6	11	2.3	92	70	38	36	23	12	3	257	8	9	4	2.0	.967	OF-123, 1B-4
1914			146	.314	**.509**	544	**171**	39	11	15	2.8	96	103	55	42	25	2	2	549	187	37	20	5.3	.952	OF-67, SS-39, 1B-32, 2B-8
1915	BOS	N	156	.280	.392	571	160	34	12	2	0.4	72	87	54	39	15	0	0	524	26	7	11	3.6	.987	OF-134, 1B-22
1916			120	.241	.327	419	101	17	5	2	0.7	44	54	44	52	10	1	0	231	9	5	0	2.0	.980	OF-120, 1B-2, SS-1
1917	2 teams			BOS N	(72G – .256)		CIN N	(45G – .321)																		
"	total		117	.279	.371	383	107	16	4	1	0.3	41	52	29	30	11	5	1	253	17	9	7	2.4	.968	OF-106, 1B-4
1918	CIN	N	115	.298	.415	400	119	15	13	2	0.5	46	**76**	37	18	14	5	0	692	56	15	41	6.6	.980	1B-66, OF-38, 2B-6

Sherry Magee *continued*

Year Team	Games	BA	SA	AB	H	2B	3B	HR	HR%	R	RBI	BB	SO	SB	PH AB	PH H	PO	A	E	DP	TC/G	FA	G by Pos
1919	56	.215	.264	163	35	6	1	0	0.0	11	21	26	19	4	6	2	102	4	1	1	1.9	.991	OF-47, 3B-1, 2B-1
16 yrs.	2085	.291	.427	7441	2169	425	166	83	1.1	1112	1182	736	359	441	39	11	5125	433	168	116	2.7	.971	OF-1860, 1B-137, SS-40, 2B-15, 3B-1

WORLD SERIES

Year Team	Games	BA	SA	AB	H	2B	3B	HR	HR%	R	RBI	BB	SO	SB	PH AB	PH H	PO	A	E	DP	TC/G	FA	G by Pos
1919 CIN N	2	.500	.500	2	1	0	0	0	0.0	0	0	0	0	0	2	1	0	0	0	0	0.0	—	

Harl Maggert

MAGGERT, HARL VESTIN
Father of Harl Maggert.
B. Feb. 13, 1883, Cromwell, Ind. D. Jan. 7, 1963, Fresno, Calif.
BL TR 5'8" 155 lbs.

Year Team	Games	BA	SA	AB	H	2B	3B	HR	HR%	R	RBI	BB	SO	SB	PH AB	PH H	PO	A	E	DP	TC/G	FA	G by Pos
1907 PIT N	3	.000	.000	6	0	0	0	0	0.0	1	0	2		1	1	0	6	0	0	0	2.0	1.000	OF-2
1912 PHI A	72	.256	.351	242	62	8	6	1	0.4	39	13	36		10	11	3	103	5	7	0	1.6	.939	OF-61
2 yrs.	75	.250	.343	248	62	8	6	1	0.4	40	13	38		11	12	3	109	5	7	0	1.6	.942	OF-63

Harl Maggert

MAGGERT, HARL WARREN
Son of Harl Maggert.
B. May 14, 1914, Los Angeles, Calif. D. July 10, 1986, Citrus Heights, Calif.
BR TR 6' 190 lbs.

Year Team	Games	BA	SA	AB	H	2B	3B	HR	HR%	R	RBI	BB	SO	SB	PH AB	PH H	PO	A	E	DP	TC/G	FA	G by Pos
1938 BOS N	66	.281	.416	89	25	3	0	3	3.4	12	19	10	20	0	43	10	24	13	2	1	0.6	.949	OF-10, 3B-8

John Magner

MAGNER, WILLIAM JOHN
B. 1855

Year Team	Games	BA	SA	AB	H	2B	3B	HR	HR%	R	RBI	BB	SO	SB	PH AB	PH H	PO	A	E	DP	TC/G	FA	G by Pos
1879 CIN N	1	.000	.000	4	0	0	0	0	0.0	0	1	0	1		0	0	1	0	1	0	2.0	.500	OF-1

Stubby Magner

MAGNER, EDMUND BURKE
B. Feb. 20, 1888, Kalamazoo, Mich. D. Sept. 6, 1956, Chillicothe, Ohio
BR TR 5'3" 135 lbs.

Year Team	Games	BA	SA	AB	H	2B	3B	HR	HR%	R	RBI	BB	SO	SB	PH AB	PH H	PO	A	E	DP	TC/G	FA	G by Pos
1911 NY A	13	.212	.212	33	7	0	0	0	0.0	3	4	4		1	0	0	15	32	2	3	3.8	.959	SS-6, 2B-5

George Magoon

MAGOON, GEORGE HENRY (Topsy, maggie)
B. Mar. 27, 1875, St. Albans, Me. D. Dec. 6, 1943, Rochester, N. H.
BR TR 5'10" 165 lbs.

Year Team	Games	BA	SA	AB	H	2B	3B	HR	HR%	R	RBI	BB	SO	SB	PH AB	PH H	PO	A	E	DP	TC/G	FA	G by Pos
1898 BKN N	93	.224	.254	343	77	7	0	1	0.3	35	39	30		7	0	0	199	357	45	38	6.5	.925	SS-93
1899 2 teams BAL N (62G – .256) CHI N (59G – .228)																							
" total	121	.242	.295	396	96	13	4	0	0.0	50	52	50		12	0	0	281	431	71	53	6.5	.909	SS-121
1901 CIN N	127	.252	.324	460	116	16	7	1	0.2	47	53	52		15	0	0	284	382	57	42	5.7	.921	SS-112, 2B-15
1902	45	.272	.352	162	44	9	2	0	0.0	29	23	13		7	1	0	92	152	20	19	5.9	.924	2B-41, SS-3
1903 2 teams CIN N (42G – .216) CHI A (94G – .228)																							
" total	136	.224	.273	473	106	17	3	0	0.0	38	34	49		6	1	0	287	366	40	37	5.1	.942	2B-126, 3B-9
5 yrs.	522	.239	.294	1834	439	62	16	2	0.1	199	201	194		47	2	0	1143	1688	233	189	5.9	.924	SS-329, 2B-182, 3B-9

Tom Magrann

MAGRANN, THOMAS JOSEPH
B. Dec. 9, 1963, Hollywood, Fla.
BR TR 6'3" 177 lbs.

Year Team	Games	BA	SA	AB	H	2B	3B	HR	HR%	R	RBI	BB	SO	SB	PH AB	PH H	PO	A	E	DP	TC/G	FA	G by Pos
1989 CLE A	9	.000	.000	10	0	0	0	0	0.0	0	0	0	4	0	0	0	30	2	0	0	3.6	1.000	C-9

Freddie Maguire

MAGUIRE, FREDERICK EDWARD
B. May 10, 1899, Roxbury, Mass. D. Nov. 3, 1961, Boston, Mass.
BR TR 5'11" 155 lbs.

Year Team	Games	BA	SA	AB	H	2B	3B	HR	HR%	R	RBI	BB	SO	SB	PH AB	PH H	PO	A	E	DP	TC/G	FA	G by Pos
1922 NY N	5	.333	.333	12	4	0	0	0	0.0	4	1	0	1	3	1	0	4	13	1	1	3.6	.944	2B-3
1923	41	.200	.233	30	6	1	0	0	0.0	11	2	2	4	1	1	0	21	31	7	7	1.4	.881	2B-16, 3B-1
1928 CHI N	140	.279	.350	574	160	24	7	1	0.2	67	41	25	38	6	2	1	410	524	23	126	6.8	.976	2B-138
1929 BOS N	138	.252	.337	496	125	26	8	0	0.0	54	41	19	40	8	0	0	387	476	28	104	6.5	.969	2B-138, SS-1
1930	146	.267	.328	516	138	21	5	0	0.0	54	52	20	22	4	0	0	372	478	21	94	6.0	.976	2B-146
1931	148	.228	.272	492	112	18	2	0	0.0	36	26	16	26	1	0	0	335	438	23	94	5.4	.971	2B-148
6 yrs.	618	.257	.322	2120	545	90	22	1	0.0	226	163	82	131	23	4	1	1529	1960	103	426	5.8	.971	2B-589, SS-1, 3B-1

WORLD SERIES

Year Team	Games	BA	SA	AB	H	2B	3B	HR	HR%	R	RBI	BB	SO	SB	PH AB	PH H	PO	A	E	DP	TC/G	FA	G by Pos
1923 NY N	2	—	—	0	0	0	0	0	—	1	0	0	0	0	0	0	0	0	0	0	0.0	—	

Jack Maguire

MAGUIRE, JACK
B. Feb. 5, 1925, St. Louis, Mo.
BR TR 5'11" 165 lbs.

Year Team	Games	BA	SA	AB	H	2B	3B	HR	HR%	R	RBI	BB	SO	SB	PH AB	PH H	PO	A	E	DP	TC/G	FA	G by Pos
1950 NY N	29	.175	.225	40	7	2	0	0	0.0	3	3	3	13	0	16	3	31	5	0	2	1.2	1.000	OF-9, 1B-2
1951 3 teams NY N (16G – .400) PIT N (8G – .000) STL A (41G – .244)																							
" total	65	.257	.342	152	39	3	2	2	1.3	22	18	15	23	1	13	2	85	18	4	1	1.6	.963	OF-34, 3B-6, 2B-3
2 yrs.	94	.240	.318	192	46	5	2	2	1.0	25	21	18	36	1	29	5	116	23	4	3	1.5	.972	OF-43, 3B-6, 2B-3, 1B-2

Jim Mahady

MAHADY, JAMES BERNARD
B. Apr. 22, 1901, Cortland, N. Y. D. Aug. 9, 1936, Cortland, N. Y.
BR TR 5'11" 170 lbs.

Year Team	Games	BA	SA	AB	H	2B	3B	HR	HR%	R	RBI	BB	SO	SB	PH AB	PH H	PO	A	E	DP	TC/G	FA	G by Pos
1921 NY N	1	—	—	0	0	0	0	0	—	0	0	0	0	0	0	0	0	1	0	0	1.0	1.000	2B-1

Art Mahan

MAHAN, ARTHUR LEO
B. June 8, 1913, Somerville, Mass.
BL TL 5'11" 178 lbs.

Year Team	Games	BA	SA	AB	H	2B	3B	HR	HR%	R	RBI	BB	SO	SB	PH AB	PH H	PO	A	E	DP	TC/G	FA	G by Pos
1940 PHI N	146	.244	.318	544	133	24	5	2	0.4	55	39	40	37	4	0	0	1380	102	12	120	10.2	.992	1B-145, P-1

Frank Mahar

MAHAR, FRANK EDWARD
B. Dec. 4, 1878, Natick, Mass. D. Dec. 5, 1961, Somerville, Mass.
TR 5'10½"

Year Team	Games	BA	SA	AB	H	2B	3B	HR	HR%	R	RBI	BB	SO	SB	PH AB	PH H	PO	A	E	DP	TC/G	FA	G by Pos
1902 PHI N	1	.000	.000	1	0	0	0	0	0.0	0	0	0		0	0	0	0	0	0	0	0.0	—	—

Billy Maharg

MAHARG, WILLIAM JOSEPH
Born William Joseph Graham.
B. Mar. 19, 1881, Philadelphia, Pa. D. Nov. 20, 1953, Philadelphia, Pa.
BR TR 5'4½"

Year Team	Games	BA	SA	AB	H	2B	3B	HR	HR%	R	RBI	BB	SO	SB	PH AB	PH H	PO	A	E	DP	TC/G	FA	G by Pos
1912 DET A	1	.000	.000	1	0	0	0	0	0.0	0	0	0		0	0	0	2	0	0	0	2.0	1.000	3B-1

Year	Team	Games	BA	SA	AB	H	2B	3B	HR	HR%	R	RBI	BB	SO	SB	Pinch Hit AB	H	PO	A	E	DP	TC/G	FA	G by Pos

Billy Maharg *continued*

Year	Team	Games	BA	SA	AB	H	2B	3B	HR	HR%	R	RBI	BB	SO	SB	AB	H	PO	A	E	DP	TC/G	FA	G by Pos
1916	PHI N	1	.000	.000	1	0	0	0	0	0.0	0	0	0	0	0	0	0	0	0	0	0	0.0	–	OF-1
2 yrs.		2	.000	.000	2	0	0	0	0	0.0	0	0	0	0	0	0	0	0	2	0	0	1.0	1.000	OF-1, 3B-1

Tom Maher
MAHER, THOMAS FRANCIS
B. Philadelphia, Pa.

Year	Team	Games	BA	SA	AB	H	2B	3B	HR	HR%	R	RBI	BB	SO	SB	AB	H	PO	A	E	DP	TC/G	FA	G by Pos
1902	PHI N	1	–	–	0	0	0	0	0	–	0	0	0	0	0	0	0	0	0	0	0.0	–	

Greg Mahlberg
MAHLBERG, GREGORY JOHN
B. Aug. 8, 1952, Milwaukee, Wis.   BR TR 5'10" 180 lbs.

Year	Team	Games	BA	SA	AB	H	2B	3B	HR	HR%	R	RBI	BB	SO	SB	AB	H	PO	A	E	DP	TC/G	FA	G by Pos
1978	TEX A	1	.000	.000	1	0	0	0	0	0.0	0	0	0	0	0	0	0	2	0	0	0	2.0	1.000	C-1
1979		7	.118	.294	17	2	0	0	1	5.9	2	1	2	4	0	0	0	22	1	0	0	3.3	1.000	C-7
2 yrs.		8	.111	.278	18	2	0	0	1	5.6	2	1	2	4	0	0	0	24	1	0	0	3.1	1.000	C-8

Dan Mahoney
MAHONEY, DANIEL J.
B. Mar. 20, 1864, Springfield, Mass. D. Feb. 1, 1904, Springfield, Mass.   BR TR 5'9½" 165 lbs.

Year	Team	Games	BA	SA	AB	H	2B	3B	HR	HR%	R	RBI	BB	SO	SB	AB	H	PO	A	E	DP	TC/G	FA	G by Pos
1892	CIN N	5	.190	.286	21	4	0	1	0	0.0	1	1	0		0			23	10	2	0	7.0	.943	C-5
1895	WAS N	6	.167	.167	12	2	0	0	0	0.0	2	1	0	0	0	3	1	14	1	1	1	2.7	.938	C-2, 1B-1
2 yrs.		11	.182	.242	33	6	0	1	0	0.0	3	2	1		4	3	1	37	11	3	1	4.6	.941	C-7, 1B-1

Danny Mahoney
MAHONEY, DANIEL JOSEPH
B. Sept. 6, 1888, Haverhill, Mass. D. Sept. 28, 1960, Utica, N. Y.   BR TR 5'6½" 145 lbs.

Year	Team	Games	BA	SA	AB	H	2B	3B	HR	HR%	R	RBI	BB	SO	SB	AB	H	PO	A	E	DP	TC/G	FA	G by Pos
1911	CIN N	1	–	–	0	0	0	0	0	–	0	0	0	0	0	0	0	0	0	0	0	0.0	–	

Jim Mahoney
MAHONEY, JAMES THOMAS (Moe)
B. May 26, 1934, Englewood, N. J.   BR TR 6' 175 lbs.

Year	Team	Games	BA	SA	AB	H	2B	3B	HR	HR%	R	RBI	BB	SO	SB	AB	H	PO	A	E	DP	TC/G	FA	G by Pos
1959	BOS A	31	.130	.261	23	3	0	0	1	4.3	10	4	3	7	0	0	0	24	39	4	5	2.2	.940	SS-30
1961	WAS A	43	.241	.259	108	26	0	1	0	0.0	10	6	5	23	1	1	0	59	97	5	26	3.7	.969	SS-31, 2B-2
1962	CLE A	41	.243	.419	74	18	4	0	3	4.1	12	5	3	14	0	1	0	44	70	3	14	2.9	.974	SS-23, 2B-8, 3B-1
1965	HOU N	5	.200	.200	5	1	0	0	0	0.0	0	0	0	3	0	0	0	5	2	0	3	1.4	1.000	SS-5
4 yrs.		120	.229	.314	210	48	4	1	4	1.9	32	15	11	47	1	2	0	132	208	12	48	2.9	.966	SS-89, 2B-10, 3B-1

Mike Mahoney
MAHONEY, GEORGE W.
B. Dec. 5, 1873, Boston, Mass. D. Jan. 3, 1940, Boston, Mass.   6'4" 220 lbs.

Year	Team	Games	BA	SA	AB	H	2B	3B	HR	HR%	R	RBI	BB	SO	SB	AB	H	PO	A	E	DP	TC/G	FA	G by Pos
1897	BOS N	2	.500	.500	2	1	0	0	0	0.0	1	1	0		0	0	0	1	0	1	0	1.0	1.000	C-1, P-1
1898	STL N	2	.000	.000	7	0	0	0	0	0.0	0	0	0		0	0	0	22	1	2	1	12.5	.920	1B-2
2 yrs.		4	.111	.111	9	1	0	0	0	0.0	1	1	0		0	0	0	23	1	2	1	6.8	.926	1B-2, C-1, P-1

Bob Maier
MAIER, ROBERT PHILLIP
B. Sept. 5, 1915, Dunellen, N. J.   BR TR 5'8" 180 lbs.

Year	Team	Games	BA	SA	AB	H	2B	3B	HR	HR%	R	RBI	BB	SO	SB	AB	H	PO	A	E	DP	TC/G	FA	G by Pos
1945	DET A	132	.263	.350	486	128	25	7	1	0.2	58	34	37	32	7	2	1	144	226	25	19	3.0	.937	3B-124, OF-5

WORLD SERIES

Year	Team	Games	BA	SA	AB	H	2B	3B	HR	HR%	R	RBI	BB	SO	SB	AB	H	PO	A	E	DP	TC/G	FA	G by Pos
1945	DET A	1	1.000	1.000	1	1	0	0	0	0.0	0	0	0	0	0	1	1	0	0	0	0	0.0	–	

Emil Mailho
MAILHO, EMIL PIERRE (Lefty)
B. Dec. 16, 1909, Berkeley, Calif.   BL TL 5'10" 165 lbs.

Year	Team	Games	BA	SA	AB	H	2B	3B	HR	HR%	R	RBI	BB	SO	SB	AB	H	PO	A	E	DP	TC/G	FA	G by Pos
1936	PHI A	21	.056	.056	18	1	0	0	0	0.0	5	0	5	3	0	16	1	2	0	0	0	0.1	1.000	OF-1

Charlie Maisel
MAISEL, CHARLES LOUIS
B. Apr. 21, 1894, Cantonsville, Md. D. Aug. 25, 1953, Baltimore, Md.   BR TR 6'1"

Year	Team	Games	BA	SA	AB	H	2B	3B	HR	HR%	R	RBI	BB	SO	SB	AB	H	PO	A	E	DP	TC/G	FA	G by Pos
1915	BAL F	1	.000	.000	4	0	0	0	0	0.0	0	0	0	0	0	0	0	6	2	0	0	8.0	1.000	C-1

Fritz Maisel
MAISEL, FREDERICK CHARLES (Flash)
Brother of George Maisel.
B. Dec. 23, 1889, Catonsville, Md. D. Apr. 22, 1967, Baltimore, Md.   BR TR 5'7½" 170 lbs.

Year	Team	Games	BA	SA	AB	H	2B	3B	HR	HR%	R	RBI	BB	SO	SB	AB	H	PO	A	E	DP	TC/G	FA	G by Pos
1913	NY A	51	.257	.310	187	48	4	3	0	0.0	33	12	34	20	25	0	0	70	83	8	3	3.2	.950	3B-51
1914		149	.239	.325	548	131	23	9	2	0.4	78	47	76	69	74	0	0	206	245	35	17	3.3	.928	3B-148
1915		135	.281	.357	530	149	16	6	4	0.8	77	46	48	35	51	1	1	184	223	26	20	3.2	.940	3B-134
1916		53	.228	.259	158	36	5	0	0	0.0	18	7	20	18	4	6	1	71	32	4	4	2.0	.963	OF-26, 3B-11, 2B-4
1917		113	.198	.228	404	80	4	4	0	0.0	46	20	36	18	29	5	2	231	295	19	37	4.8	.965	2B-100, 3B-7
1918	STL A	90	.232	.261	284	66	4	2	0	0.0	43	16	46	17	11	5	0	108	154	14	10	3.1	.949	3B-79, OF-1
6 yrs.		591	.242	.299	2111	510	56	24	6	0.3	295	148	260	177	194	17	4	870	1032	106	91	3.4	.947	3B-430, 2B-104, OF-27

George Maisel
MAISEL, GEORGE JOHN
Brother of Fritz Maisel.
B. Mar. 12, 1892, Catonsville, Md. D. Nov. 20, 1968, Baltimore, Md.   BR TR 5'10½" 180 lbs.

Year	Team	Games	BA	SA	AB	H	2B	3B	HR	HR%	R	RBI	BB	SO	SB	AB	H	PO	A	E	DP	TC/G	FA	G by Pos
1913	STL A	11	.167	.278	18	3	2	0	0	0.0	2	1	1	7	0	5	1	5	0	1	0	0.5	.833	OF-5
1916	DET A	7	.000	.000	5	0	0	0	0	0.0	2	0	0	2	0	0	0	1	0	1	1	1.0	.857	3B-3
1921	CHI N	111	.310	.338	393	122	7	2	0	0.0	54	43	11	13	17	1	1	259	12	6	2	2.5	.978	OF-108
1922		38	.190	.226	84	16	1	1	0	0.0	9	6	8	2	1	5	1	50	2	0	0	1.4	1.000	OF-38
4 yrs.		167	.282	.314	500	141	10	3	0	0.0	67	50	20	24	18	11	3	315	19	8	3	2.0	.977	OF-151, 3B-3

Hank Majeski
MAJESKI, HENRY (Heeney)
B. Dec. 13, 1916, Staten Island, N. Y.   BR TR 5'9" 174 lbs.

Year	Team	Games	BA	SA	AB	H	2B	3B	HR	HR%	R	RBI	BB	SO	SB	AB	H	PO	A	E	DP	TC/G	FA	G by Pos
1939	BOS N	106	.272	.379	367	100	16	1	7	1.9	35	54	18	30	2	7	2	111	196	18	19	3.1	.945	3B-99
1940		3	.000	.000	3	0	0	0	0	0.0	0	0	0	0	0	3	0	0	0	0	0	0.0	–	
1941		19	.145	.236	55	8	5	0	0	0.0	5	3	1	13	0	8	1	15	26	4	2	2.4	.911	3B-11

Year	Team		Games	BA	SA	AB	H	2B	3B	HR	HR%	R	RBI	BB	SO	SB	Pinch Hit AB	Pinch Hit H	PO	A	E	DP	TC/G	FA	G by Pos

Hank Majeski *continued*

Year	Team		Games	BA	SA	AB	H	2B	3B	HR	HR%	R	RBI	BB	SO	SB	AB	H	PO	A	E	DP	TC/G	FA	G by Pos
1946	2 teams	NY A (8G – .083)			PHI A (78G – .250)																				
"	total		86	.243	.333	276	67	14	4	1	0.4	26	25	26	16	3	11	0	79	161	9	22	2.9	.964	3B-74
1947	PHI	A	141	.280	.405	479	134	26	5	8	1.7	54	72	53	31	1	2	0	170	283	5	32	3.2	.989	3B-134, SS-4, 2B-1
1948			148	.310	.454	590	183	41	4	12	2.0	88	120	48	43	2	0	0	176	292	12	23	3.2	.975	3B-142, SS-8
1949			114	.277	.417	448	124	26	5	9	2.0	62	67	29	23	0	1	0	117	219	15	37	3.1	.957	3B-113
1950	CHI	A	122	.309	.406	414	128	18	2	6	1.4	47	46	42	34	1	9	1	115	246	11	31	3.0	.970	3B-112
1951	2 teams	CHI A (12G – .257)			PHI A (89G – .285)																				
"	total		101	.282	.411	358	101	23	4	5	1.4	45	48	36	24	1	5	2	86	232	9	19	3.2	.972	3B-97
1952	2 teams	PHI A (34G – .256)			CLE A (36G – .296)																				
"	total		70	.269	.351	171	46	4	2	2	1.2	21	29	26	17	0	23	6	48	105	5	16	2.3	.968	3B-45, 2B-3
1953	CLE	A	50	.300	.440	50	15	1	0	2	4.0	6	12	3	8	0	31	11	9	11	0	2	0.4	1.000	2B-10, 3B-7, OF-1
1954			57	.281	.388	121	34	4	0	3	2.5	10	17	7	14	0	26	8	67	64	3	11	2.4	.978	2B-25, 3B-10
1955	2 teams	CLE A (36G – .188)			BAL A (16G – .171)																				
"	total		52	.180	.281	89	16	3	0	2	2.2	5	8	10	7	0	23	1	22	29	0	4	1.0	1.000	3B-17, 2B-9
13 yrs.			1069	.279	.398	3421	956	181	27	57	1.7	404	501	299	260	10	149	32	1015	1864	91	218	2.8	.969	3B-861, 2B-48, SS-12, OF-1

WORLD SERIES

Year	Team		Games	BA	SA	AB	H	2B	3B	HR	HR%	R	RBI	BB	SO	SB	AB	H	PO	A	E	DP	TC/G	FA	G by Pos
1954	CLE	A	4	.167	.667	6	1	0	0	1	16.7	1	3	0	1	0	2	1	2	1	0	0	0.8	1.000	3B-1

Charlie Malay

MALAY, CHARLES FRANCIS
Father of Joe Malay.
B. June 13, 1879, Brooklyn, N. Y.   D. Sept. 18, 1949, Brooklyn, N. Y.

BB TR 5'11½" 175 lbs.

Year	Team		Games	BA	SA	AB	H	2B	3B	HR	HR%	R	RBI	BB	SO	SB	AB	H	PO	A	E	DP	TC/G	FA	G by Pos
1905	BKN	N	102	.252	.292	349	88	7	2	1	0.3	33	31	22		13	1	0	188	220	32	17	4.3	.927	2B-75, OF-25, SS-1

Joe Malay

MALAY, JOSEPH CHARLES
Son of Charlie Malay.
B. Oct. 25, 1905, Brooklyn, N. Y.   D. Mar. 19, 1989, Bridgeport, Conn.

BL TL 6'   175 lbs.

Year	Team		Games	BA	SA	AB	H	2B	3B	HR	HR%	R	RBI	BB	SO	SB	AB	H	PO	A	E	DP	TC/G	FA	G by Pos
1933	NY	N	8	.125	.125	24	3	0	0	0	0.0	0	2	0	0	0	0	0	56	7	0	2	7.9	1.000	1B-8
1935			1	1.000	1.000	1	1	0	0	0	0.0	0	0	0	0	0	1	1	0	0	0	0	0.0	–	
2 yrs.			9	.160	.160	25	4	0	0	0	0.0	0	2	0	0	0	1	1	56	7	0	2	7.0	1.000	1B-8

Candy Maldonado

MALDONADO, CANDIDO
Born Candido Maldonado y Guadarrama.
B. Sept. 5, 1960, Humacao, Puerto Rico

BR TR 6'   185 lbs.

Year	Team		Games	BA	SA	AB	H	2B	3B	HR	HR%	R	RBI	BB	SO	SB	AB	H	PO	A	E	DP	TC/G	FA	G by Pos
1981	LA	N	11	.083	.083	12	1	0	0	0	0.0	0	0	0	5	0	4	0	8	0	0	0	0.7	1.000	OF-9
1982			6	.000	.000	4	0	0	0	0	0.0	0	0	1	2	0	2	0	5	0	0	0	0.8	1.000	OF-3
1983			42	.194	.290	62	12	1	1	1	1.6	5	6	5	14	0	9	2	26	0	0	0	0.6	1.000	OF-33
1984			116	.268	.382	254	68	14	1	5	2.0	25	28	19	29	0	31	9	124	5	8	0	1.2	.942	OF-102, 3B-4
1985			121	.225	.338	213	48	7	1	5	2.3	20	19	19	40	1	31	7	121	6	2	0	1.1	.984	OF-113
1986	SF	N	133	.252	.477	405	102	31	3	18	4.4	49	85	20	77	4	40	17	161	11	3	0	1.3	.983	OF-101, 3B-1
1987			118	.292	.509	442	129	28	4	20	4.5	69	85	34	78	8	4	1	176	7	5	0	1.6	.973	OF-116
1988			142	.255	.377	499	127	23	1	12	2.4	53	68	37	89	6	5	0	251	5	10	1	1.9	.962	OF-139
1989			129	.217	.362	345	75	23	0	9	2.6	39	41	37	69	4	30	7	181	6	5	1	1.5	.974	OF-116
9 yrs.			818	.251	.411	2236	562	127	10	70	3.1	260	332	172	403	23	156	43	1053	40	33	2	1.4	.971	OF-732, 3B-5

LEAGUE CHAMPIONSHIP SERIES

Year	Team		Games	BA	SA	AB	H	2B	3B	HR	HR%	R	RBI	BB	SO	SB	AB	H	PO	A	E	DP	TC/G	FA	G by Pos
1983	LA	N	2	.000	.000	2	0	0	0	0	0.0	0	0	0	0	0	2	0	0	0	0	0	0.0	–	
1985			4	.143	.143	7	1	0	0	0	0.0	0	1	0	3	0	1	0	4	0	1	0	1.3	.800	OF-3
1987	SF	N	5	.211	.263	19	4	1	0	0	0.0	2	2	0	3	0	0	0	7	0	0	0	1.4	1.000	OF-5
1989			3	.000	.000	3	0	0	0	0	0.0	0	1	1	2	0	0	0	2	0	0	0	0.7	1.000	OF-3
4 yrs.			14	.161	.194	31	5	1	0	0	0.0	3	4	2	7	0	4	0	13	0	1	0	1.0	.929	OF-11

WORLD SERIES

Year	Team		Games	BA	SA	AB	H	2B	3B	HR	HR%	R	RBI	BB	SO	SB	AB	H	PO	A	E	DP	TC/G	FA	G by Pos
1989	SF	N	4	.091	.273	11	1	0	1	0	0.0	1	0	0	4	0	1	1	5	0	0	0	1.3	1.000	OF-3

Jim Maler

MALER, JAMES MICHAEL
B. Aug. 16, 1958, New York, N. Y.

BR TR 6'4" 230 lbs.

Year	Team		Games	BA	SA	AB	H	2B	3B	HR	HR%	R	RBI	BB	SO	SB	AB	H	PO	A	E	DP	TC/G	FA	G by Pos
1981	SEA	A	12	.348	.391	23	8	1	0	0	0.0	1	2	2	1	1	7	3	36	2	0	5	3.2	1.000	1B-5, DH-2
1982			64	.226	.344	221	50	8	3	4	1.8	18	26	12	35	0	5	1	529	41	5	45	9.0	.991	1B-57, DH-5
1983			26	.182	.242	66	12	1	0	1	1.5	5	3	5	11	0	4	1	152	9	0	8	6.2	1.000	1B-19, DH-5
3 yrs.			102	.226	.326	310	70	10	3	5	1.6	24	31	19	47	1	16	5	717	52	5	58	7.6	.994	1B-81, DH-12

Tony Malinosky

MALINOSKY, ANTHONY FRANCIS
B. Oct. 5, 1909, Collinsville, Ill.

BR TR 5'10½" 165 lbs.

Year	Team		Games	BA	SA	AB	H	2B	3B	HR	HR%	R	RBI	BB	SO	SB	AB	H	PO	A	E	DP	TC/G	FA	G by Pos
1937	BKN	N	35	.228	.253	79	18	2	0	0	0.0	7	3	9	11	0	0	0	15	28	9	2	1.5	.827	3B-13, SS-11

Bobby Malkmus

MALKMUS, ROBERT EDWARD
B. July 4, 1931, Newark, N. J.

BR TR 5'9" 175 lbs.

Year	Team		Games	BA	SA	AB	H	2B	3B	HR	HR%	R	RBI	BB	SO	SB	AB	H	PO	A	E	DP	TC/G	FA	G by Pos
1957	MIL	N	13	.091	.182	22	2	0	1	0	0.0	6	0	3	3	0	3	0	16	19	1	4	2.8	.972	2B-7
1958	WAS	A	41	.186	.243	70	13	2	1	0	0.0	5	3	4	15	0	11	4	55	54	4	14	2.8	.965	2B-26, 3B-2, SS-1
1959			6	–	–	0	0	0	0	0	–	0	0	0	0	0	0	0	0	0	0	0	0.0	–	
1960	PHI	N	79	.211	.278	133	28	4	1	1	0.8	16	12	11	28	2	6	0	68	101	2	20	2.2	.988	2B-58, SS-34, 3B-25
1961			121	.231	.327	342	79	8	2	7	2.0	39	31	20	43	1	6	0	210	299	12	67	4.3	.977	SS-1
1962			8	.200	.400	5	1	1	0	0	0.0	3	0	0	1	0	3	0	1	4	0	1	0.6	1.000	
6 yrs.			268	.215	.301	572	123	15	5	8	1.4	69	46	38	90	3	28	4	350	477	19	106	3.2	.978	2B-114, SS-65, 3B-39

Jerry Mallett

MALLETT, GERALD GORDON
B. Sept. 18, 1935, Bonne Terre, Mo.

BR TR 6'5" 208 lbs.

Year	Team		Games	BA	SA	AB	H	2B	3B	HR	HR%	R	RBI	BB	SO	SB	AB	H	PO	A	E	DP	TC/G	FA	G by Pos
1959	BOS	A	4	.267	.267	15	4	0	0	0	0.0	1	1	1	3	0	0	0	14	2	0	2	4.0	1.000	OF-4

Year	Team		Games	BA	SA	AB	H	2B	3B	HR	HR%	R	RBI	BB	SO	SB	Pinch Hit AB	Pinch Hit H	PO	A	E	DP	TC/G	FA	G by Pos

Les Mallon
MALLON, LESLIE CLYDE
B. Nov. 21, 1905, Sweetwater, Tex.
BR TR 5'8" 160 lbs.

1931	PHI	N	122	.309	.379	375	116	19	2	1	0.3	41	45	29	40	0	9	2	270	308	28	62	5.0	.954	2B-97, 1B-5, SS-3, 3B-3
1932			103	.259	.349	347	90	16	0	5	1.4	44	31	28	28	1	9	3	202	233	22	42	4.4	.952	2B-88, 3B-5
1934	BOS	N	42	.295	.343	166	49	6	1	0	0.0	23	18	15	12	0	0	0	92	145	8	17	5.8	.967	2B-42
1935			116	.274	.357	412	113	24	2	2	0.5	48	25	28	37	3	5	3	201	281	18	34	4.3	.964	2B-73, 3B-36, OF-1
4 yrs.			383	.283	.359	1300	368	65	5	8	0.6	156	119	100	117	4	23	8	765	967	76	155	4.7	.958	2B-300, 3B-44, 1B-5, SS-3, OF-1

Ben Mallonee
MALLONEE, HOWARD BENNETT (Lefty)
B. Mar. 31, 1894, Baltimore, Md. D. Feb. 19, 1978, Baltimore, Md.
BL TL 5'6" 150 lbs.

| 1921 | PHI | A | 6 | .250 | .292 | 24 | 6 | 1 | 0 | 0 | 0.0 | 2 | 0 | 1 | 1 | 1 | 0 | 0 | 15 | 1 | 0 | 0 | 2.7 | 1.000 | OF-6 |

Jule Mallonee
MALLONEE, JULIUS NORRIS
B. Apr. 4, 1900, Charlotte, N. C. D. Dec. 26, 1934, Charlotte, N. C.
BL TR 6'2" 180 lbs.

| 1925 | CHI | A | 2 | .000 | .000 | 3 | 0 | 0 | 0 | 0 | 0.0 | 1 | 0 | 1 | 0 | 0 | 1 | 0 | 1 | 0 | 0 | 0 | 0.5 | 1.000 | OF-1 |

Jim Mallory
MALLORY, JAMES BAUGH (Sunny Jim)
B. Sept. 1, 1918, Lawrenceville, Va.
BR TR 6'1" 170 lbs.

1940	WAS	A	4	.167	.167	12	2	0	0	0	0.0	2	0	1	1	0	0	0	10	0	0	0	2.5	1.000	OF-3
1945	2 teams		STL N (13G – .233)			NY N (37G – .298)																			
"	total		50	.277	.299	137	38	3	0	0	0.0	13	14	6	9	1	11	3	67	3	3	1	1.5	.959	OF-32
2 yrs.			54	.268	.289	149	40	3	0	0	0.0	15	14	7	10	1	11	3	77	3	3	1	1.5	.964	OF-35

Sheldon Mallory
MALLORY, SHELDON
B. July 16, 1953, Argo, Ill.
BL TL 6'2" 175 lbs.

| 1977 | OAK | A | 64 | .214 | .262 | 126 | 27 | 4 | 1 | 0 | 0.0 | 19 | 5 | 11 | 18 | 12 | 6 | 2 | 96 | 3 | 3 | 0 | 1.6 | .971 | OF-45, DH-7, 1B-4 |

Harry Malmberg
MALMBERG, HARRY WILLIAM (Swede)
B. July 31, 1926, Fairfield, Ala. D. Oct. 29, 1976, San Francisco, Calif.
BR TR 6'1" 170 lbs.

| 1955 | DET | A | 67 | .216 | .260 | 208 | 45 | 5 | 2 | 0 | 0.0 | 25 | 19 | 29 | 19 | 0 | 0 | 0 | 155 | 181 | 5 | 42 | 5.1 | .985 | 2B-65 |

Eddie Malone
MALONE, EDWARD RUSSELL
B. June 16, 1920, Chicago, Ill.
BR TR 5'10" 175 lbs.

1949	CHI	A	55	.271	.353	170	46	7	2	1	0.6	17	16	29	19	2	3	1	186	22	2	2	3.8	.990	C-51
1950			31	.225	.254	71	16	2	0	0	0.0	2	10	10	8	0	10	2	79	10	0	3	2.9	1.000	C-21
2 yrs.			86	.257	.324	241	62	9	2	1	0.4	19	26	39	27	2	13	3	265	32	2	5	3.5	.993	C-72

Fergy Malone
MALONE, FERGUSON G.
B. 1842, Ireland D. Jan. 1, 1905, Seattle, Wash.
Manager 1873-74, 1884.
BR TL 5'8" 156 lbs.

1876	PHI	N	22	.229	.250	96	22	2	0	0	0.0	14	6	0	1			0	0	82	32	32	0	6.6	.781	C-20, OF-3, SS-1
1884	PHI	U	1	.250	.250	4	1	0	0	0	0.0	0	0	0	0			0	0	9	0	2	0	11.0	.818	C-1
2 yrs.			23	.230	.250	100	23	2	0	0	0.0	14	6	0	1			0	0	91	32	34	0	6.8	.783	C-21, OF-3, SS-1

Lew Malone
MALONE, LEWIS ALOYSIUS
Played as Lew Ryan in 1915.
B. Mar. 13, 1897, Baltimore, Md. D. Feb. 17, 1972, Brooklyn, N. Y.
BR TR 5'11" 175 lbs.

1915	PHI	A	76	.204	.279	201	41	4	4	1	0.5	17	17	21	40	1	7	3	133	126	28	10	3.8	.902	2B-43, 3B-12, OF-4, SS-2
1916			5	.000	.000	4	0	0	0	0	0.0	0	0	1	2	0	3	0	1	0	0	0	0.2	1.000	SS-1
1917	BKN	N	1			0	0	0	0	0	–	1	0	0	0	0	1	0	0	0	0	0	0.0		
1919			51	.204	.284	162	33	7	3	0	0.0	9	11	6	18	1	0	0	62	82	11	5	3.0	.929	3B-47, SS-2, 2B-2
4 yrs.			133	.202	.278	367	74	11	7	1	0.3	28	28	28	60	3	16	3	196	208	39	15	3.3	.912	3B-59, 2B-45, SS-5, OF-4

Billy Maloney
MALONEY, WILLIAM ALPHONSE
B. June 5, 1878, Lewiston, Me. D. Sept. 2, 1960, Breckenridge, Tex.
BL TR 5'10" 177 lbs.

1901	MIL	A	86	.293	.331	290	85	3	4	0	0.0	42	22	7			11	5	302	111	23	6	5.1	.947	C-72, OF-8
1902	2 teams		STL A (30G – .205)			CIN N (27G – .247)																			
"	total		57	.224	.274	201				1	0.5	21	18	8			8		103	19	13	3	2.4	.904	OF-41, C-14
1905	CHI	N	145	.260	.351	558	145	17	14	2	0.4	78	56	43			59	0	0	251	18	13	4	1.9	.954	OF-145
1906	BKN	N	151	.221	.272	566	125	15	7	0	0.0	71	32	49			38	0	0	355	19	13	6	2.6	.966	OF-151
1907			144	.229	.283	502	115	7	10	0	0.0	51	32	31			25	0	0	336	18	12	5	2.5	.967	OF-144
1908			113	.195	.273	359	70	5	7	3	0.0	31	17	24			14	6	1	255	19	14	4	2.5	.951	OF-103, C-4
6 yrs.			696	.236	.299	2476	585	54	42	6	0.2	294	177	162			155	14	3	1602	204	88	28	2.7	.954	OF-592, C-90

John Maloney
MALONEY, JOHN
D. July 21, 1890

1876	NY	N	2	.286	.571	7	2	0	1	0	0.0	2		0	1			0	0	4	0	1	0	2.5	.800	OF-2
1877	HAR	N	1	.250	.250	4	1	0	0	0	0.0	0		0	0			0	0	1	0	3	0	4.0	.250	OF-1
2 yrs.			3	.273	.455	11	3	0	1	0	0.0	2		0	1			0	0	5	0	4	0	3.0	.556	OF-3

Pat Maloney
MALONEY, PATRICK WILLIAM
B. Jan. 19, 1888, Grosvenordale, Conn. D. June 27, 1979, Pawtucket, R. I.
BR TR 6' 150 lbs.

| 1912 | NY | A | 22 | .215 | .228 | 79 | 17 | 1 | 0 | 0 | 0.0 | 9 | 4 | 6 | | | 3 | 0 | 0 | 61 | 2 | 5 | 0 | 3.1 | .926 | OF-20 |

Frank Malzone
MALZONE, FRANK JAMES
B. Feb. 28, 1930, Bronx, N. Y.
BR TR 5'10" 180 lbs.

1955	BOS	A	6	.350	.400	20	7	1	0	0	0.0	2	1	1	3	0	1	0	2	15	0	1	2.8	1.000	3B-4
1956			27	.165	.272	103	17	3	1	2	1.9	15	11	9	8	1	1	0	24	57	6	4	3.2	.931	3B-26
1957			153	.292	.427	634	185	31	5	15	2.4	82	103	31	41	2	0	0	151	370	25	31	3.6	.954	3B-153

Year	Team	Games	BA	SA	AB	H	2B	3B	HR	HR%	R	RBI	BB	SO	SB	Pinch Hit AB	H	PO	A	E	DP	TC/G	FA	G by Pos

Frank Malzone *continued*

Year	Team	Games	BA	SA	AB	H	2B	3B	HR	HR%	R	RBI	BB	SO	SB	AB	H	PO	A	E	DP	TC/G	FA	G by Pos
1958		155	.295	.421	**627**	185	30	2	15	2.4	76	87	33	53	1	0	0	139	378	27	36	3.5	.950	3B-155
1959		154	.280	.437	604	169	34	2	19	3.1	90	92	42	58	6	0	0	134	357	24	40	3.3	.953	3B-154
1960		152	.271	.398	595	161	30	2	14	2.4	60	79	36	42	2	1	0	159	318	26	36	3.3	.948	3B-151
1961		151	.266	.386	590	157	21	4	14	2.4	74	87	44	49	1	2	0	136	304	23	45	3.1	.950	3B-149
1962		156	.283	.426	619	175	20	3	21	3.4	74	95	35	43	0	0	0	154	313	16	32	3.1	.967	3B-156
1963		151	.291	.419	580	169	25	2	15	2.6	66	71	31	45	0	3	0	151	283	16	18	3.0	.964	3B-148
1964		148	.264	.372	537	142	19	0	13	2.4	62	56	37	43	0	5	1	141	259	17	24	2.8	.959	3B-143
1965		106	.239	.319	364	87	20	0	3	0.8	40	34	28	38	1	16	3	79	170	8	19	2.4	.969	3B-96
1966	CAL A	82	.206	.277	155	32	5	0	2	1.3	6	12	10	11	0	43	10	38	60	8	3	1.3	.925	3B-35
12 yrs.		1441	.274	.399	5428	1486	239	21	133	2.5	647	728	337	434	14	71	14	1308	2884	196	289	3.0	.955	3B-1370

Frank Mancuso

MANCUSO, FRANK OCTAVIUS   BR TR 6'   195 lbs.
Brother of Gus Mancuso.
B. May 23, 1918, Houston, Tex.

Year	Team	Games	BA	SA	AB	H	2B	3B	HR	HR%	R	RBI	BB	SO	SB	AB	H	PO	A	E	DP	TC/G	FA	G by Pos
1944	STL A	88	.205	.262	244	50	11	0	1	0.4	19	24	20	32	1	1	0	311	35	17	9	4.1	.953	C-87
1945		119	.268	.329	365	98	13	3	1	0.3	39	38	46	44	0	3	0	467	55	6	10	4.4	.989	C-115
1946		87	.240	.328	262	63	8	3	3	1.1	22	23	30	31	1	1	0	298	31	9	3	3.9	.973	C-85
1947	WAS A	43	.229	.282	131	30	5	1	0	0.0	5	13	5	11	0	7	2	144	15	7	1	3.9	.958	C-35
4 yrs.		337	.241	.306	1002	241	37	7	5	0.5	85	98	101	118	2	12	2	1220	136	39	23	4.1	.972	C-322

WORLD SERIES

Year	Team	Games	BA	SA	AB	H	2B	3B	HR	HR%	R	RBI	BB	SO	SB	AB	H	PO	A	E	DP	TC/G	FA	G by Pos
1944	STL A	2	.667	.667	3	2	0	0	0	0.0	0	1	0	0	0	1	1	3	0	0	0	1.5	1.000	C-1

Gus Mancuso

MANCUSO, AUGUST RODNEY (Blackie)   BR TR 5'10"   185 lbs.
Brother of Frank Mancuso.
B. Dec. 5, 1905, Galveston, Tex.   D. Oct. 26, 1984, Houston, Tex.

Year	Team	Games	BA	SA	AB	H	2B	3B	HR	HR%	R	RBI	BB	SO	SB	AB	H	PO	A	E	DP	TC/G	FA	G by Pos
1928	STL N	11	.184	.237	38	7	0	1	0	0.0	2	3	0	5	0	0	0	54	7	1	0	5.6	.984	C-11
1930		76	.366	.551	227	83	17	2	7	3.1	39	59	18	16	1	12	3	277	33	10	2	4.2	.969	C-61
1931		67	.262	.374	187	49	16	1	1	0.5	13	23	18	13	2	10	1	239	40	8	6	4.3	.972	C-56
1932		103	.284	.413	310	88	23	1	5	1.6	25	43	30	15	0	19	6	454	53	12	7	5.0	.977	C-82
1933	NY N	144	.264	.345	481	127	17	2	6	1.2	39	56	48	21	0	2	1	580	83	19	15	4.7	.972	C-142
1934		122	.245	.337	383	94	14	0	7	1.8	32	46	27	19	0	0	0	448	67	12	7	4.3	.977	C-122
1935		128	.298	.380	447	133	18	2	5	1.1	33	56	30	16	1	2	0	484	71	16	4	4.5	.972	C-126
1936		139	.301	.405	519	156	21	3	9	1.7	55	63	39	28	0	1	0	524	104	15	15	4.6	.977	C-138
1937		86	.279	.387	287	80	17	1	4	1.4	30	39	17	20	1	5	0	410	69	9	4	5.7	.982	C-81
1938		52	.348	.437	158	55	8	0	2	1.3	19	15	17	13	0	3	2	184	24	5	5	4.1	.977	C-44
1939	CHI N	80	.231	.295	251	58	10	0	2	0.8	17	17	24	19	0	3	0	333	36	7	6	4.7	.981	C-76
1940	BKN N	60	.229	.285	144	33	8	0	1	0.7	16	16	13	7	0	4	1	193	26	4	6	3.7	.982	C-56
1941	STL N	106	.229	.293	328	75	13	1	2	0.6	25	37	37	19	0	1	0	482	58	6	6	5.2	.989	C-105
1942	2 teams		STL	N	(5G – .077)						NY	N	(39G – .193)											
"	total	44	.180	.205	122	22	1	0	0	0.0	4	9	14	7	1	3	0	151	21	4	2	4.0	.977	C-41
1943	NY N	94	.198	.242	252	50	5	0	2	0.8	11	20	28	16	0	15	3	336	40	10	1	4.1	.974	C-77
1944		78	.251	.297	195	49	4	1	1	0.5	15	25	30	20	0	4	2	249	37	7	4	3.8	.976	C-72
1945	PHI N	70	.199	.227	176	35	5	0	0	0.0	11	16	28	10	2	0	0	215	34	3	4	3.6	.988	C-70
17 yrs.		1460	.265	.351	4505	1194	197	16	53	1.2	386	543	418	264	8	89	19	5613	803	148	94	4.5	.977	C-1360

WORLD SERIES

Year	Team	Games	BA	SA	AB	H	2B	3B	HR	HR%	R	RBI	BB	SO	SB	AB	H	PO	A	E	DP	TC/G	FA	G by Pos
1930	STL N	2	.286	.286	7	2	0	0	0	0.0	1	0	1	2	0	0	0	12	1	0	0	6.5	1.000	C-2
1931		2	.000	.000	1	0	0	0	0	0.0	0	0	0	0	0	1	0	2	0	0	0	1.0	1.000	C-1
1933	NY N	5	.118	.176	17	2	1	0	0	0.0	2	3	0	1	0	0	0	31	4	0	2	7.0	1.000	C-5
1936		6	.263	.368	19	5	2	0	0	0.0	3	1	3	0	0	0	0	40	5	0	2	7.5	1.000	C-6
1937		3	.000	.000	8	0	0	0	0	0.0	0	0	1	1	0	0	0	8	1	0	0	3.0	1.000	C-2
5 yrs.		18	.173	.231	52	9	3	0	0	0.0	6	4	7	6	0	1	0	93	11	0	4	5.8	1.000	C-16

Carl Manda

MANDA, CARL ALAN   BR TR 5'10"   170 lbs.
B. Nov. 16, 1888, Little River, Kans.   D. Mar. 9, 1983, Artesia, N. M.

Year	Team	Games	BA	SA	AB	H	2B	3B	HR	HR%	R	RBI	BB	SO	SB	AB	H	PO	A	E	DP	TC/G	FA	G by Pos
1914	CHI A	9	.267	.267	15	4	0	0	0	0.0	2	1	3	3	1	0	0	10	23	1	1	3.8	.971	2B-7

Jim Mangan

MANGAN, JAMES DANIEL   BR TR 5'10"   190 lbs.
B. Sept. 24, 1929, San Francisco, Calif.

Year	Team	Games	BA	SA	AB	H	2B	3B	HR	HR%	R	RBI	BB	SO	SB	AB	H	PO	A	E	DP	TC/G	FA	G by Pos
1952	PIT N	11	.154	.154	13	2	0	0	0	0.0	1	2	1	3	0	7	0	3	2	1	0	0.5	.833	C-4
1954		14	.192	.192	26	5	0	0	0	0.0	2	2	4	9	0	7	1	24	3	0	1	1.9	1.000	C-7
1956	NY N	20	.100	.100	20	2	0	0	0	0.0	2	1	4	6	0	3	1	34	1	0	1	1.8	1.000	C-15
3 yrs.		45	.153	.153	59	9	0	0	0	0.0	5	5	9	18	0	17	2	61	6	1	2	1.5	.985	C-26

Angel Mangual

MANGUAL, ANGEL LUIS   BR TR 5'10"   178 lbs.
Born Angel Luis Mangual y Guilbe.   Brother of Pepe Mangual.
B. Mar. 19, 1947, Juana Diaz, Puerto Rico

Year	Team	Games	BA	SA	AB	H	2B	3B	HR	HR%	R	RBI	BB	SO	SB	AB	H	PO	A	E	DP	TC/G	FA	G by Pos
1969	PIT N	6	.250	.500	4	1	1	0	0	0.0	1	0	0	0	0	3	1	0	0	1	0	0.2	—	OF-3
1971	OAK A	94	.286	.362	287	82	8	1	4	1.4	32	30	17	27	1	14	2	163	3	2	1	1.8	.988	OF-81
1972		91	.246	.364	272	67	13	2	5	1.8	19	32	14	48	0	16	6	166	4	5	2	1.9	.971	OF-74
1973		74	.224	.302	192	43	4	1	3	1.6	20	13	9	34	0	13	0	88	2	5	0	1.3	.947	OF-50, 1B-2, 2B-1
1974		115	.233	.367	365	85	14	4	9	2.5	37	43	17	59	3	11	3	142	1	6	0	1.3	.961	OF-74, DH-37, 3B-1
1975		62	.220	.275	109	24	3	0	1	0.9	13	6	3	18	0	17	4	44	1	1	0	0.7	.978	OF-39, DH-15
1976		8	.167	.250	12	2	1	0	0	0.0	0	1	0	1	0	1	0	4	1	0	0	0.6	1.000	OF-7
7 yrs.		450	.245	.346	1241	304	44	8	22	1.8	122	125	59	187	5	75	16	607	16	20	4	1.4	.969	OF-328, DH-52, 1B-2, 3B-1, 2B-1

LEAGUE CHAMPIONSHIP SERIES

Year	Team	Games	BA	SA	AB	H	2B	3B	HR	HR%	R	RBI	BB	SO	SB	AB	H	PO	A	E	DP	TC/G	FA	G by Pos
1971	OAK A	3	.167	.417	12	2	1	0	1	0.0	1	2	0	1	0	0	0	6	0	0	0	2.0	1.000	OF-3
1972		3	.000	.000	3	0	0	0	0	0.0	0	0	0	2	0	2	0	0	0	0	0	0.0	—	OF-3
1973		3	.111	.111	9	1	0	0	0	0.0	0	0	0	1	0	0	0	2	0	0	0	0.7	1.000	OF-3

Year	Team	Games	BA	SA	AB	H	2B	3B	HR	HR%	R	RBI	BB	SO	SB	Pinch Hit AB	Pinch Hit H	PO	A	E	DP	TC/G	FA	G by Pos

Angel Mangual *continued*

Year	Team	Games	BA	SA	AB	H	2B	3B	HR	HR%	R	RBI	BB	SO	SB	PH AB	PH H	PO	A	E	DP	TC/G	FA	G by Pos
1974		1	.250	.250	4	1	0	0	0	0.0	0	0	0	0	0	0	0	0	0	0	0	0.0	–	DH-1
4 yrs.		10	.143	.250	28	4	1	1	0	0.0	2	2	0	5	0	4	0	8	0	0	0	0.8	1.000	OF-6, DH-1
WORLD SERIES																								
1972	OAK A	4	.300	.300	10	3	0	0	0	0.0	1	1	0	0	0	2	1	6	0	1	0	1.8	.857	OF-2
1973		5	.000	.000	6	0	0	0	0	0.0	0	0	0	3	0	5	0	1	0	0	0	0.2	1.000	OF-1
1974		1	.000	.000	1	0	0	0	0	0.0	0	0	0	1	0	1	0	0	0	0	0	0.0	–	
3 yrs.		10	.176	.176	17	3	0	0	0	0.0	1	1	0	4	0	8	1	7	0	1	0	0.8	.875	OF-3

(3rd)

Pepe Mangual

MANGUAL, JOSE MANUEL
Also known as Jose Manuel Mangual y Guilbe. Brother of Angel Mangual.
B. May 23, 1952, Ponce, Puerto Rico

BR TR 5'10" 157 lbs.

Year	Team	Games	BA	SA	AB	H	2B	3B	HR	HR%	R	RBI	BB	SO	SB	PH AB	PH H	PO	A	E	DP	TC/G	FA	G by Pos
1972	MON N	8	.273	.273	11	3	0	0	0	0.0	2	0	1	5	0	1	0	2	0	0	0	0.3	1.000	OF-3
1973		33	.177	.387	62	11	2	1	3	4.8	9	7	6	18	2	7	1	28	0	1	0	0.9	.966	OF-22
1974		23	.311	.361	61	19	3	0	0	0.0	10	4	5	15	5	2	1	22	0	0	0	1.0	1.000	OF-22
1975		140	.245	.337	514	126	16	2	9	1.8	84	45	74	115	33	6	3	308	8	9	2	2.3	.972	OF-138
1976	2 teams	MON N (66G – .260)		NY N (41G – .186)																				
"	total	107	.237	.338	317	75	14	3	4	1.3	49	25	60	81	24	4	0	210	5	6	2	2.1	.973	OF-100
1977	NY N	8	.143	.143	7	1	0	0	0	0.0	1	2	1	4	0	0	0	5	0	1	0	0.8	.833	OF-4
6 yrs.		319	.242	.340	972	235	35	6	16	1.6	155	83	147	238	64	20	4	575	13	17	4	1.9	.972	OF-289

George Mangus

MANGUS, GEORGE GRAHAM
B. May 22, 1890, Red Creek, N. Y. D. Aug. 10, 1933, Rutland, Mass.

BL TR 5'11½" 165 lbs.

Year	Team	Games	BA	SA	AB	H	2B	3B	HR	HR%	R	RBI	BB	SO	SB	PH AB	PH H	PO	A	E	DP	TC/G	FA	G by Pos
1912	PHI N	10	.200	.320	25	5	3	0	0	0.0	2	3	1	6	0	4	0	9	0	3	0	1.2	.750	OF-5

Clyde Manion

MANION, CLYDE JENNINGS (Pete)
B. Oct. 30, 1896, Jefferson City, Mo. D. Sept. 4, 1967, Detroit, Mich.

BR TR 5'11" 175 lbs.

Year	Team	Games	BA	SA	AB	H	2B	3B	HR	HR%	R	RBI	BB	SO	SB	PH AB	PH H	PO	A	E	DP	TC/G	FA	G by Pos
1920	DET A	32	.275	.350	80	22	4	1	0	0.0	4	8	4	7	0	2	1	83	27	7	3	3.7	.940	C-30
1921		12	.111	.111	18	2	0	0	0	0.0	2	2	2	2	0	6	1	5	3	0	0	0.7	1.000	C-4
1922		42	.275	.362	69	19	4	1	0	0.0	9	12	4	6	0	13	4	61	8	5	0	1.8	.932	C-21, 1B-1
1923		23	.136	.136	22	3	0	0	0	0.0	0	2	2	2	0	17	2	5	1	1	0	0.3	.857	C-3, 1B-1
1924		14	.231	.231	13	3	0	0	0	0.0	1	2	1	1	0	9	3	4	0	1	0	0.4	.800	C-3, 1B-1
1926		75	.199	.222	176	35	4	0	0	0.0	15	14	24	16	1	1	0	227	48	8	2	3.8	.972	C-74
1927		1	–	–	0	0	0	0	0	–	0	0	1	0	0	1	0	0	0	0	0	0.0	–	
1928	STL A	76	.226	.280	243	55	5	1	0	0.0	25	31	15	18	3	5	2	302	49	7	10	4.7	.980	C-71
1929		35	.243	.261	111	27	2	0	0	0.0	16	11	15	3	1	1	0	141	22	4	2	4.8	.976	C-34
1930		57	.216	.243	148	32	1	0	1	0.7	12	11	24	17	0	1	0	214	44	4	4	4.6	.985	C-56
1932	CIN N	49	.207	.237	135	28	4	0	0	0.0	7	12	14	16	0	1	0	137	23	5	3	3.4	.970	C-47
1933		36	.167	.179	84	14	1	0	0	0.0	3	3	8	7	0	2	0	84	19	2	2	2.9	.981	C-34
1934		25	.185	.185	54	10	0	0	0	0.0	4	4	4	7	0	1	0	57	13	0	2	2.8	1.000	C-24
13 yrs.		477	.217	.252	1153	250	25	3	3	0.3	96	112	118	102	5	60	13	1320	257	44	28	3.4	.973	C-401, 1B-3

Phil Mankowski

MANKOWSKI, PHILLIP ANTHONY
B. Jan. 9, 1953, Buffalo, N. Y.

BL TR 6' 180 lbs.

Year	Team	Games	BA	SA	AB	H	2B	3B	HR	HR%	R	RBI	BB	SO	SB	PH AB	PH H	PO	A	E	DP	TC/G	FA	G by Pos
1976	DET A	24	.271	.353	85	23	2	1	1	1.2	9	4	4	8	0	1	0	20	47	2	8	2.9	.971	3B-23
1977		94	.276	.353	286	79	7	3	3	1.0	21	27	16	41	1	10	3	73	196	10	15	3.0	.964	3B-85, 2B-1
1978		88	.275	.365	222	61	8	0	4	1.8	28	20	22	28	2	9	2	42	129	5	17	2.0	.972	3B-80, DH-1
1979		42	.222	.263	99	22	4	0	0	0.0	11	8	10	16	0	9	1	22	56	3	6	1.9	.963	3B-36, DH-1
1980	NY N	8	.167	.250	12	2	1	0	0	0.0	1	1	2	4	0	4	0	0	4	3	0	0.9	.571	3B-3
1982		13	.229	.257	35	8	1	0	0	0.0	2	4	1	6	0	0	0	2	20	1	2	1.8	.957	3B-13
6 yrs.		269	.264	.338	739	195	23	4	8	1.1	72	64	55	103	3	33	6	159	452	24	48	2.4	.962	3B-240, DH-2, 2B-1

Charlie Manlove

MANLOVE, CHARLES HENRY (Chick)
B. Oct. 8, 1862, Philadelphia, Pa. D. Feb. 12, 1952, Altoona, Pa.

BR TR 5'9" 165 lbs.

Year	Team	Games	BA	SA	AB	H	2B	3B	HR	HR%	R	RBI	BB	SO	SB	PH AB	PH H	PO	A	E	DP	TC/G	FA	G by Pos
1884	2 teams	ALT U (2G – .429)		NY N (3G – .000)																				
"	total	5	.176	.176	17	3	0	0	0	0.0	1		0	4		0	0	17	5	4	2	5.2	.846	C-4, OF-2

Ben Mann

MANN, BEN GARTH (Red)
B. Nov. 16, 1915, Brandon, Tex.

BR TR 6' 155 lbs.

Year	Team	Games	BA	SA	AB	H	2B	3B	HR	HR%	R	RBI	BB	SO	SB	PH AB	PH H	PO	A	E	DP	TC/G	FA	G by Pos
1944	CHI N	1	–	–	0	0	0	0	0	–	0	1	0	0	0	0	0	0	0	0	0	0.0	–	

Fred Mann

MANN, FRED J.
B. Apr. 1, 1858, Sutton, Vt. D. Apr. 16, 1916, Springfield, Mass.

BL 5'10½" 178 lbs.

Year	Team	Games	BA	SA	AB	H	2B	3B	HR	HR%	R	RBI	BB	SO	SB	PH AB	PH H	PO	A	E	DP	TC/G	FA	G by Pos
1882	2 teams	WOR N (19G – .234)		PHI AA (29G – .231)																				
"	total	48	.232	.333	198	46	12	4	0	0.0	25		6	15		0	0	67	68	40	5	3.6	.771	3B-47, 1B-1
1883	COL AA	96	.249	.368	394	98	18	13	1	0.3	61		18			0	0	217	29	38	5	3.0	.866	OF-82, 1B-9, 3B-6, SS-1
1884		99	.276	.464	366	101	12	18	7	1.9	70		25			0	0	126	18	23	3	1.7	.862	OF-97, 2B-2
1885	PIT AA	99	.253	.327	391	99	17	6	0	0.0	60		31			0	0	159	13	18	2	1.9	.905	OF-97, 3B-3
1886		116	.250	.364	440	110	16	14	2	0.5	85		45			0	0	203	13	30	2	2.1	.878	OF-116
1887	2 teams	CLE AA (64G – .309)		PHI AA (55G – .275)																				
"	total	119	.293	.418	488	143	29	13	2	0.4	87		38		41	0	0	215	18	27	6	2.2	.896	OF-119
6 yrs.		577	.262	.383	2277	597	104	68	12	0.5	388		163	15	41	0	0	987	159	176	23	2.3	.867	OF-511, 3B-56, 1B-10, 2B-2, SS-1

Johnny Mann

MANN, JOHN LEO
B. Feb. 4, 1898, Fontanet, Ind. D. Mar. 31, 1977, Terre Haute, Ind.

BR TR 5'11" 160 lbs.

Year	Team	Games	BA	SA	AB	H	2B	3B	HR	HR%	R	RBI	BB	SO	SB	PH AB	PH H	PO	A	E	DP	TC/G	FA	G by Pos
1928	CHI A	6	.333	.333	6	2	0	0	0	0.0	1	0	1	0	0	1	0	2	0	0	0	0.5	1.000	3B-2

Year	Team		Games	BA	SA	AB	H	2B	3B	HR	HR%	R	RBI	BB	SO	SB	Pinch Hit AB	Pinch Hit H	PO	A	E	DP	TC/G	FA	G by Pos

Kelly Mann

MANN, KELLY JOHN
B. Aug. 17, 1967, Santa Monica, Calif.   BR TR 6'3" 215 lbs.

Year	Team		Games	BA	SA	AB	H	2B	3B	HR	HR%	R	RBI	BB	SO	SB	PH AB	PH H	PO	A	E	DP	TC/G	FA	G by Pos
1989	ATL	N	7	.208	.292	24	5	2	0	0	0.0	1	1	0	6	0	0	0	48	5	0	0	7.6	1.000	C-7

Les Mann

MANN, LESLIE
B. Nov. 18, 1893, Lincoln, Neb.   D. Jan. 14, 1962, Pasadena, Calif.   BR TR 5'9" 172 lbs.

Year	Team		Games	BA	SA	AB	H	2B	3B	HR	HR%	R	RBI	BB	SO	SB	PH AB	PH H	PO	A	E	DP	TC/G	FA	G by Pos
1913	BOS	N	120	.253	.369	407	103	24	7	3	0.7	54	51	18	73	7	0	0	250	14	11	2	2.3	.960	OF-120
1914			126	.247	.375	389	96	16	11	4	1.0	44	40	24	50	9	3	0	273	24	15	8	2.5	.952	OF-123
1915	CHI	F	135	.306	.438	470	144	12	19	4	0.9	74	58	36		18	4	2	269	17	9	3	2.2	.969	OF-130, SS-1
1916	CHI	N	127	.272	.361	415	113	13	9	2	0.5	46	29	19	31	11	9	1	200	9	6	1	1.7	.972	OF-115
1917			117	.273	.367	444	121	19	10	1	0.2	63	44	27	46	14	1	0	203	20	11	2	2.0	.953	OF-116
1918			129	.288	.384	489	141	27	7	2	0.4	69	55	38	45	21	0	0	229	15	10	3	2.0	.961	OF-129
1919	2 teams		CHI	N (80G – .227)		BOS	N	(40G – .283)																	
"	total		120	.245	.358	444	109	14	12	4	0.9	46	42	20	43	19	1	0	237	19	10	3	2.2	.962	OF-118
1920	BOS	N	110	.276	.351	424	117	7	8	3	0.7	48	32	38	42	7	3	0	228	13	5	1	2.2	.980	OF-110
1921	STL	N	97	.328	.512	256	84	12	7	7	2.7	57	30	23	28	5	5	1	174	11	6	2	2.0	.969	OF-79
1922			84	.347	.497	147	51	14	1	2	1.4	42	20	16	12	0	2	0	87	3	2	1	1.1	.978	OF-57
1923	2 teams		STL	N (38G – .371)		CIN	N	(8G – .000)																	
"	total		46	.367	.633	90	33	5	2	5	5.6	21	11	9	5	0	1	0	44	3	1	0	1.0	.979	OF-26
1924	BOS	N	32	.275	.402	102	28	7	4	0	0.0	13	10	8	10	1	3	1	59	4	0	0	2.0	1.000	OF-28
1925			60	.342	.478	184	63	11	4	2	1.1	27	20	5	11	6	2	1	116	7	1	1	2.1	.992	OF-57
1926			50	.302	.419	129	39	8	2	1	0.8	23	20	9	9	5	3	0	79	5	3	0	1.7	.966	OF-46
1927	2 teams		BOS	N (29G – .258)		NY	N	(29G – .328)																	
"	total		58	.293	.421	133	39	7	2	2	1.5	21	16	16	10	4	5	1	65	6	2	1	1.3	.973	OF-46
1928	NY	N	82	.264	.342	193	51	14	7	2	1.0	29	25	18	9	2	1	0	97	3	5	1	1.3	.952	OF-68
16 yrs.			1493	.282	.398	4716	1332	203	106	44	0.9	677	503	324	424	129	43	7	2610	173	97	29	1.9	.966	OF-1368, SS-1

WORLD SERIES

Year	Team		Games	BA	SA	AB	H	2B	3B	HR	HR%	R	RBI	BB	SO	SB	PH AB	PH H	PO	A	E	DP	TC/G	FA	G by Pos
1914	BOS	N	3	.286	.286	7	2	0	0	0	0.0	1	1	0	1	0	1	0	1	0	0	0	0.3	1.000	OF-2
1918	CHI	N	6	.227	.318	22	5	2	0	0	0.0	0	2	0	0	0	0	0	7	0	0	0	1.2	1.000	OF-6
2 yrs.			9	.241	.310	29	7	2	0	0	0.0	1	3	0	1	0	1	0	8	0	0	0	0.9	1.000	OF-8

Jack Manning

MANNING, JOHN E.
B. Dec. 20, 1853, Braintree, Mass.   D. Aug. 15, 1929, Boston, Mass.   BR TR 5'8½" 158 lbs.

Year	Team		Games	BA	SA	AB	H	2B	3B	HR	HR%	R	RBI	BB	SO	SB	PH AB	PH H	PO	A	E	DP	TC/G	FA	G by Pos
1876	BOS	N	70	.264	.330	288	76	13	2	0	0.7	52	25	7	5		0	0	85	37	26	3	2.1	.824	OF-56, P-34, SS-1, 2B-1
1877	CIN	N	57	.317	.437	252	80	16	7	0	0.0	47	36	5	6		0	0	233	84	51	8	6.5	.861	SS-26, 1B-17, OF-12, P-10, 2B-2
1878	BOS	N	60	.254	.302	248	63	10	1	0	0.0	41	23	10	16		0	0	61	12	23	1	1.6	.760	OF-59, P-3
1880	CIN	N	48	.216	.311	190	41	6	3	2	1.1	20	17	7	15		0	0	64	12	20	1	2.0	.792	OF-47, 1B-1
1881	BUF	N	1	.000	.000	1	0	0	0	0	0.0	0	0	0	0		0	0	0	1	0	0	1.0	1.000	OF-1
1883	PHI	N	98	.267	.364	420	112	31	5	0	0.0	60		20	37		0	0	155	37	33	5	2.3	.853	OF-98
1884			104	.271	.394	424	115	29	4	5	1.2	71		40	67		0	0	140	26	30	7	1.9	.847	OF-104
1885			107	.256	.348	445	114	24	4	3	0.7	61		37	27		0	0	134	21	18	3	1.6	.896	OF-107
1886	BAL	AA	137	.223	.286	556	124	18	7	1	0.2	78		50			0	0	165	16	23	3	1.5	.887	OF-137
9 yrs.			682	.257	.345	2824	725	147	31	13	0.5	430	101	176	173		0	0	1037	246	224	31	2.2	.851	OF-621, P-47, SS-27, 1B-18, 2B-3

Jimmy Manning

MANNING, JAMES H.
B. Jan. 31, 1862, Fall River, Mass.   D. Oct. 22, 1929, Edinburg, Tex.   TR 157 lbs.
Manager 1901.

Year	Team		Games	BA	SA	AB	H	2B	3B	HR	HR%	R	RBI	BB	SO	SB	PH AB	PH H	PO	A	E	DP	TC/G	FA	G by Pos
1884	BOS	N	89	.241	.316	345	83	8	6	2	0.6	52		19	47		0	0	139	61	29	7	2.6	.873	OF-73, SS-9, 2B-9, 3B-3
1885	2 teams		BOS	N (84G – .206)		DET	N	(20G – .269)																	
"	total		104	.219	.320	384	84	12	9	3	0.8	49	36	23	46		0	0	184	75	40	10	2.9	.866	OF-83, SS-21
1886	DET	N	26	.186	.268	97	18	2	3	0	0.0	14	7	6	10		0	0	32	5	2	1	1.5	.949	OF-26, SS-1
1887			13	.192	.212	52	10	1	0	0	0.0	5	3	5	4	3	0	0	16	7	8	0	2.4	.742	OF-10, SS-3
1889	KC	AA	132	.204	.281	506	103	16	7	3	0.6	68	68	54	61	58	0	0	238	206	44	25	3.7	.910	OF-69, 2B-63, SS-1, 3B-1
5 yrs.			364	.215	.297	1384	298	39	25	8	0.6	188	114	107	168	61	0	0	609	354	123	43	3.0	.887	OF-261, 2B-72, SS-35, 3B-4

Rick Manning

MANNING, RICHARD EUGENE
B. Sept. 2, 1954, Niagara Falls, N.Y.   BL TR 6'1" 180 lbs.

Year	Team		Games	BA	SA	AB	H	2B	3B	HR	HR%	R	RBI	BB	SO	SB	PH AB	PH H	PO	A	E	DP	TC/G	FA	G by Pos
1975	CLE	A	120	.285	.358	480	137	16	5	3	0.6	69	35	44	62	19	1	0	331	12	9	2	2.9	.974	OF-118, DH-1
1976			138	.292	.393	552	161	24	7	6	1.1	73	43	41	75	16	2	1	359	8	5	1	2.7	.987	OF-136
1977			68	.226	.337	252	57	7	3	5	2.0	33	18	21	35	9	0	0	191	2	2	0	2.9	.990	OF-68
1978			148	.263	.342	566	149	27	3	3	0.5	65	50	38	62	14	2	1	377	7	2	1	2.6	.995	OF-144
1979			144	.259	.304	560	145	12	2	3	0.5	67	51	55	48	30	3	1	417	9	6	2	3.0	.986	OF-141, DH-1
1980			140	.234	.306	471	110	17	4	3	0.6	55	52	63	66	12	0	0	379	7	4	1	2.8	.990	OF-139
1981			103	.244	.336	360	88	15	3	4	1.1	47	33	40	57	25	0	0	305	6	4	3	3.1	.987	OF-103
1982			152	.270	.352	562	152	18	2	8	1.4	71	44	54	60	12	0	0	387	10	9	1	2.7	.978	OF-152
1983	2 teams		CLE	A (50G – .278)		MIL	A	(108G – .229)																	
"	total		158	.246	.346	569	140	20	4	4	0.7	60	43	38	62	18	0	0	471	2	5	0	3.0	.990	OF-158
1984	MIL	A	119	.249	.370	341	85	10	5	7	2.1	53	31	34	32	5	11	3	231	2	3	2	2.0	.987	OF-114, DH-1
1985			79	.218	.296	216	47	9	1	2	0.9	19	18	14	19	1	9	0	160	2	4	0	2.1	.976	OF-74, DH-2
1986			89	.254	.434	205	52	7	3	8	3.9	31	27	17	20	5	2	0	155	3	2	0	1.8	.988	OF-83, DH-2
1987			97	.228	.307	114	26	7	1	0	0.0	21	13	12	18	4	16	6	68	1	3	0	0.7	.958	OF-78, DH-2
13 yrs.			1555	.257	.341	5248	1349	189	43	56	1.1	664	458	471	616	168	51	13	3831	71	58	13	2.5	.985	OF-1508, DH-12

Tim Manning

MANNING, TIMOTHY EDWARD
B. Dec. 3, 1853, Henley-On-Thames, England   D. June 11, 1934, Oak Park, Ill.   BR TR 5'10" 170 lbs.

Year	Team		Games	BA	SA	AB	H	2B	3B	HR	HR%	R	RBI	BB	SO	SB	PH AB	PH H	PO	A	E	DP	TC/G	FA	G by Pos
1882	PRO	N	21	.105	.105	76	8	0	0	0	0.0	7		5	13		0	0	32	42	20	3	4.5	.787	SS-17, C-4
1883	BAL	AA	35	.215	.256	121	26	5	0	0	0.0	23		14			0	0	105	106	20	8	6.6	.913	2B-35
1884			91	.205	.293	341	70	14	5	2	0.6	49		26			0	0	228	277	52	28	6.1	.907	2B-91

Year	Team	Games	BA	SA	AB	H	2B	3B	HR	HR%	R	RBI	BB	SO	SB	Pinch Hit AB	Pinch Hit H	PO	A	E	DP	TC/G	FA	G by Pos

Tim Manning *continued*

Year	Team	Games	BA	SA	AB	H	2B	3B	HR	HR%	R	RBI	BB	SO	SB	PH AB	PH H	PO	A	E	DP	TC/G	FA	G by Pos
1885	2 teams				BAL AA (43G – .204)				PRO N (10G – .057)															
"	total	53	.177	.234	192	34	9	1	0	0.0	20		11	11		0	0	139	159	29	21	6.2	.911	2B-41, SS-10, 3B-3
	4 yrs.	200	.189	.252	730	138	28	6	2	0.3	99		56	24		0	0	504	584	121	60	6.0	.900	2B-167, SS-27, C-4, 3B-3

Don Manno

MANNO, DONALD D.
B. May 15, 1915, Williamsport, Pa.

BR TR 6'1" 190 lbs.

Year	Team	Games	BA	SA	AB	H	2B	3B	HR	HR%	R	RBI	BB	SO	SB	PH AB	PH H	PO	A	E	DP	TC/G	FA	G by Pos
1940	BOS N	3	.286	.714	7	2	0	0	1	14.3	1	4	0	2	0	1	0	5	0	0	0	1.7	1.000	OF-2
1941		22	.167	.200	30	5	1	0	0	0.0	2	4	3	7	0	13	2	13	0	0	0	0.6	1.000	OF-5, 3B-3, 1B-1
	2 yrs.	25	.189	.297	37	7	1	0	1	2.7	3	8	3	9	0	14	2	18	0	0	0	0.7	1.000	OF-7, 3B-3, 1B-1

Fred Manrique

MANRIQUE, FRED ELOY
Born Fred Eloy Manrique y Reyes.
B. May 11, 1961, Edo Bolivar, Venezuela

BR TR 6'1" 175 lbs.

Year	Team	Games	BA	SA	AB	H	2B	3B	HR	HR%	R	RBI	BB	SO	SB	PH AB	PH H	PO	A	E	DP	TC/G	FA	G by Pos
1981	TOR A	14	.143	.143	28	4	0	0	0	0.0	1	1	0	12	0	2	1	10	27	3	7	2.9	.925	SS-11, 3B-2, DH-1
1984		10	.333	.333	9	3	0	0	0	0.0	1	1	0	1	0	1	0	5	10	1	3	1.6	.938	2B-9, DH-1
1985	MON N	9	.308	.769	13	4	1	1	1	7.7	5	1	1	3	0	4	2	5	10	0	1	1.7	1.000	SS-2, 2B-2, 3B-1
1986	STL N	13	.176	.353	17	3	0	0	1	5.9	2	1	1	1	1	7	1	3	0	0	0	0.3	1.000	3B-4, 2B-1
1987	CHI A	115	.258	.362	298	77	13	3	4	1.3	30	29	19	69	5	5	0	176	286	7	64	4.1	.985	2B-92, SS-23
1988		140	.235	.342	345	81	10	6	5	1.4	43	37	21	54	6	5	1	241	343	13	83	4.3	.978	2B-129, SS-12
1989	2 teams				CHI A (65G – .299)				TEX A (54G – .288)															
"	total	119	.294	.397	378	111	25	1	4	1.1	46	52	17	63	4	8	3	177	250	21	61	3.8	.953	2B-74, SS-39, 3B-7, DH-1
	7 yrs.	420	.260	.367	1088	283	49	11	15	1.4	127	122	59	203	16	28	8	615	929	45	219	3.8	.972	2B-307, SS-87, 3B-14, DH-3

John Mansell

MANSELL, JOHN
Brother of Tom Mansell. Brother of Mike Mansell.
B. 1861, Auburn, N. Y. D. Feb. 20, 1925, Willard, N. Y.

BL

Year	Team	Games	BA	SA	AB	H	2B	3B	HR	HR%	R	RBI	BB	SO	SB	PH AB	PH H	PO	A	E	DP	TC/G	FA	G by Pos
1882	PHI AA	31	.238	.278	126	30	3	1	0	0.0	17		4			0	0	49	4	14	0	2.2	.791	OF-31

Mike Mansell

MANSELL, MICHAEL R.
Brother of John Mansell. Brother of Tom Mansell.
B. Jan. 15, 1858, Auburn, N. Y. D. Dec. 4, 1902, Auburn, N. Y.

BL

Year	Team	Games	BA	SA	AB	H	2B	3B	HR	HR%	R	RBI	BB	SO	SB	PH AB	PH H	PO	A	E	DP	TC/G	FA	G by Pos
1879	SYR N	67	.215	.260	242	52	4	2	1	0.4	24	13	5	45		0	0	204	11	29	2	3.6	.881	OF-67
1880	CIN N	53	.193	.278	187	36	6	2	2	1.1	22	12	4	37		0	0	147	13	25	5	3.5	.865	OF-53
1882	PIT AA	79	.277	.438	347	96	18	16	2	0.6	59		7			0	0	159	16	36	1	2.7	.829	OF-79
1883		96	.257	.371	412	106	12	13	3	0.7	90		25			0	0	186	11	26	1	2.3	.883	OF-96
1884	3 teams				PIT AA (27G – .140)				PHI AA (20G – .200)				RIC AA (29G – .301)											
"	total	76	.219	.304	283	62	3	9	1	0.4	42		20			0	0	92	10	29	2	1.7	.779	OF-76, 1B-1
	5 yrs.	371	.239	.344	1471	352	43	42	9	0.6	237	25	61	82		0	0	788	61	145	11	2.7	.854	OF-371, 1B-1

Tom Mansell

MANSELL, THOMAS E.
Brother of Mike Mansell. Brother of John Mansell.
B. Jan. 1, 1855, Auburn, N. Y. D. Oct. 6, 1934, Auburn, N. Y.

BL TL 5'8" 160 lbs.

Year	Team	Games	BA	SA	AB	H	2B	3B	HR	HR%	R	RBI	BB	SO	SB	PH AB	PH H	PO	A	E	DP	TC/G	FA	G by Pos
1879	2 teams				TRO N (40G – .243)				SYR N (1G – .250)															
"	total	41	.243	.276	181	44	6	0	0	0.0	29	11	3	9		0	0	65	3	23	1	2.2	.747	OF-41
1883	2 teams				DET N (34G – .221)				STL AA (28G – .402)															
"	total	62	.305	.370	243	74	12	2	0	0.0	45		15	13		0	0	68	13	25	1	1.7	.764	OF-62, P-1
1884	2 teams				CIN AA (65G – .248)				COL AA (23G – .195)															
"	total	88	.236	.303	343	81	5	9	0	0.0	58		21			0	0	99	6	37	0	1.6	.739	OF-87, 3B-1
	3 yrs.	191	.259	.318	767	199	23	11	0	0.0	132	11	39	22		0	0	232	22	85	2	1.8	.749	OF-190, 3B-1, P-1

Felix Mantilla

MANTILLA, FELIX
Born Felix Mantilla y Lamela.
B. July 29, 1934, Isabela, Puerto Rico

BR TR 6' 160 lbs.

Year	Team	Games	BA	SA	AB	H	2B	3B	HR	HR%	R	RBI	BB	SO	SB	PH AB	PH H	PO	A	E	DP	TC/G	FA	G by Pos
1956	MIL N	35	.283	.340	53	15	1	1	0	0.0	9	3	1	8	0	5	2	21	45	1	8	1.9	.985	SS-15, 3B-3
1957		71	.236	.363	182	43	9	1	4	2.2	28	21	14	34	2	7	0	87	136	12	28	3.3	.948	SS-35, 2B-13, 3B-7, OF-1
1958		85	.221	.345	226	50	5	1	7	3.1	37	19	20	20	2	7	1	122	61	4	15	2.2	.979	OF-43, 2B-21, SS-5, 3B-2
1959		103	.215	.271	251	54	5	0	3	1.2	26	19	16	31	6	4	0	136	211	17	40	3.5	.953	2B-60, SS-23, 3B-9, OF-7
1960		63	.257	.365	148	38	7	0	3	2.0	21	11	7	16	3	7	2	80	85	9	15	2.8	.948	2B-26, SS-25, OF-8
1961		45	.215	.280	93	20	3	0	1	1.1	13	5	10	16	1	5	0	47	48	3	7	2.2	.969	SS-19, OF-10, 2B-10, 3B-6
1962	NY N	141	.275	.399	466	128	17	4	11	2.4	54	59	37	51	3	17	3	139	251	20	36	2.9	.951	3B-95, SS-25, 2B-14
1963	BOS A	66	.315	.461	178	56	8	0	6	3.4	27	15	20	14	2	16	2	83	74	4	19	2.4	.975	SS-27, OF-11, 2B-5
1964		133	.289	.553	425	123	20	1	30	7.1	69	64	41	46	0	25	6	173	146	5	29	2.4	.985	OF-48, 3B-45, 2B-3, SS-6
1965		150	.275	.416	534	147	17	2	18	3.4	60	92	79	84	7	1	1	296	288	16	64	4.0	.973	2B-123, OF-27, 1B-2
1966	HOU N	77	.219	.371	151	33	5	0	6	4.0	16	22	11	32	1	38	10	124	46	4	11	2.3	.977	3B-14, 1B-8, 2B-9, OF-1
	11 yrs.	969	.261	.403	2707	707	97	10	89	3.3	360	330	256	352	27	132	27	1308	1391	95	272	2.9	.966	2B-326, SS-180, OF-156, 3B-143, 1B-16

WORLD SERIES

Year	Team	Games	BA	SA	AB	H	2B	3B	HR	HR%	R	RBI	BB	SO	SB	PH AB	PH H	PO	A	E	DP	TC/G	FA	G by Pos
1957	MIL N	4	.000	.000	10	0	0	0	0	0.0	1		1	0	0	0	0	6	8	0	1	3.5	1.000	2B-3
1958		4	–	–	0	0	0	0	0	–	1		0	0	0	0	0	0	0	0	0	0.0		2B-3
	2 yrs.	8	.000	.000	10	0	0	0	0	0.0	2		1	0	0	0	0	6	8	0	1	1.8	1.000	2B-3

Mickey Mantle

MANTLE, MICKEY CHARLES (The Commerce Comet)
B. Oct. 20, 1931, Spavinaw, Okla.
Hall of Fame 1974.

BB TR 5'11½" 195 lbs.

Year	Team	Games	BA	SA	AB	H	2B	3B	HR	HR%	R	RBI	BB	SO	SB	PH AB	PH H	PO	A	E	DP	TC/G	FA	G by Pos
1951	NY A	96	.267	.443	341	91	11	5	13	3.8	61	65	43	74	8	8	1	135	4	6	1	1.5	.959	OF-86
1952		142	.311	.530	549	171	37	7	23	4.2	94	87	75	111	4	1	0	348	16	14	5	2.7	.963	OF-141, 3B-1
1953		127	.295	.497	461	136	24	3	21	4.6	105	92	79	90	8	1	0	322	10	6	2	2.7	.982	OF-121, SS-1
1954		146	.300	.525	543	163	17	12	27	5.0	129	102	102	107	5	1	0	334	25	9	6	2.5	.976	OF-144, SS-4, 2B-1
1955		147	.306	.611	517	158	25	11	37	7.2	121	99	113	97	8	3	1	376	11	2	2	2.6	.995	OF-145, SS-2

Year	Team	Games	BA	SA	AB	H	2B	3B	HR	HR%	R	RBI	BB	SO	SB	Pinch Hit AB	Pinch Hit H	PO	A	E	DP	TC/G	FA	G by Pos

Mickey Mantle *continued*

Year	Team	Games	BA	SA	AB	H	2B	3B	HR	HR%	R	RBI	BB	SO	SB	PH AB	PH H	PO	A	E	DP	TC/G	FA	G by Pos
1956		150	.353	.705	533	188	22	5	52	9.8	132	130	112	99	10	4	1	370	10	4	3	2.6	.990	OF-144
1957		144	.365	.665	474	173	28	6	34	7.2	121	94	146	75	16	4	1	324	6	7	1	2.3	.979	OF-139
1958		150	.304	.592	519	158	21	1	42	8.1	127	97	129	120	18	0	0	331	5	8	2	2.3	.977	OF-150
1959		144	.285	.514	541	154	23	4	31	5.7	104	75	94	126	21	0	0	366	7	2	3	2.6	.995	OF-143
1960		153	.275	.558	527	145	17	6	40	7.6	119	94	111	125	14	2	0	326	9	3	1	2.2	.991	OF-150
1961		153	.317	.687	514	163	16	6	54	10.5	132	128	126	112	12	2	0	351	6	6	0	2.4	.983	OF-117
1962		123	.321	.605	377	121	15	1	30	8.0	96	89	122	78	9	6	1	214	4	5	1	1.8	.978	OF-123
1963		65	.314	.622	172	54	8	0	15	8.7	40	35	40	32	2	10	3	99	2	1	0	1.6	.990	OF-52
1964		143	.303	.591	465	141	25	2	35	7.5	92	111	99	102	6	11	2	217	3	5	1	1.6	.978	OF-132
1965		122	.255	.452	361	92	12	1	19	5.3	44	46	73	76	4	14	0	165	3	6	0	1.4	.966	OF-108
1966		108	.288	.538	333	96	12	1	23	6.9	40	56	57	76	1	11	1	172	2	0	0	1.6	1.000	OF-97
1967		144	.245	.434	440	108	17	0	22	5.0	63	55	107	113	1	12	5	1089	91	8	82	8.3	.993	1B-131
1968		144	.237	.398	435	103	14	1	18	4.1	57	54	106	97	6	9	4	1195	76	15	91	8.9	.988	1B-131
18 yrs.		2401	.298	.557	8102	2415	344	72	536	6.6	1677	1509	1734	1710	153	106	25	6734	290	107	201	3.0	.985	OF-2019, 1B-262, SS-7, 3B-1, 2B-1
										8th	6th			5th	8th									

WORLD SERIES

Year	Team	Games	BA	SA	AB	H	2B	3B	HR	HR%	R	RBI	BB	SO	SB	PH AB	PH H	PO	A	E	DP	TC/G	FA	G by Pos
1951	NY A	2	.200	.200	5	1	0	0	0	0.0	1	0	2	1	0	0	0	4	0	0	0	2.0	1.000	OF-2
1952		7	.345	.655	29	10	1	1	2	6.9	5	3	3	4	0	0	0	16	0	0	0	2.3	1.000	OF-7
1953		6	.208	.458	24	5	0	0	2	8.3	3	7	3	8	0	0	0	14	0	0	0	2.3	1.000	OF-6
1955		3	.200	.500	10	2	0	0	1	10.0	1	1	0	2	0	1	0	4	0	0	0	1.3	1.000	OF-2
1956		7	.250	.667	24	6	1	0	3	12.5	6	4	6	5	1	0	0	18	1	0	0	2.7	1.000	OF-7
1957		6	.263	.421	19	5	0	1	1	5.3	3	2	3	1	0	0	0	8	0	1	0	1.5	.889	OF-5
1958		7	.250	.583	24	6	0	1	2	8.3	4	3	7	4	0	0	0	16	0	0	0	2.3	1.000	OF-7
1960		7	.400	.800	25	10	1	0	3	12.0	8	11	8	9	0	0	0	15	0	0	0	2.1	1.000	OF-7
1961		2	.167	.167	6	1	0	0	0	0.0	0	0	0	2	0	0	0	2	0	0	0	1.0	1.000	OF-2
1962		7	.120	.160	25	3	1	0	0	0.0	2	0	4	5	2	0	0	11	0	0	0	1.6	1.000	OF-7
1963		4	.133	.333	15	2	0	0	1	6.7	1	1	1	5	0	0	0	6	0	0	0	1.5	1.000	OF-4
1964		7	.333	.792	24	8	2	0	3	12.5	8	8	6	8	0	0	0	13	0	2	0	2.1	.867	OF-7
12 yrs.		65	.257	.535	230	59	6	2	18	7.8	42	40	43	54	3	1	0	127	1	3	0	2.0	.977	OF-63
			2nd			2nd		2nd			1st	8th	1st	1st										

Chuck Manuel

MANUEL, CHARLES FUQUA
B. Jan. 4, 1944, North Fork, W. Va.

BL TR 6'4" 195 lbs.

Year	Team	Games	BA	SA	AB	H	2B	3B	HR	HR%	R	RBI	BB	SO	SB	PH AB	PH H	PO	A	E	DP	TC/G	FA	G by Pos
1969	MIN A	83	.207	.280	164	34	6	2	2	1.2	14	24	28	33	1	37	3	57	2	2	0	0.7	.967	OF-46
1970		59	.188	.234	64	12	0	1	1	1.6	4	7	6	17	0	43	9	7	0	0	0	0.1	1.000	OF-11
1971		18	.125	.188	16	2	1	0	0	0.0	1	1	1	8	0	16	2	0	0	0	0	0.0	–	OF-1
1972		63	.205	.270	122	25	5	0	1	0.8	6	8	4	16	0	33	7	39	4	1	0	0.7	.977	OF-28
1974	LA N	4	.333	.333	3	1	0	0	0	0.0	0	1	1	0	0	3	1	0	0	0	0	0.0	–	
1975		15	.133	.133	15	2	0	0	0	0.0	0	2	0	3	0	15	2	0	0	0	0	0.0	–	
6 yrs.		242	.198	.260	384	76	12	3	4	1.0	25	43	40	77	1	147	24	103	6	3	0	0.5	.973	OF-86

LEAGUE CHAMPIONSHIP SERIES

Year	Team	Games	BA	SA	AB	H	2B	3B	HR	HR%	R	RBI	BB	SO	SB	PH AB	PH H	PO	A	E	DP	TC/G	FA	G by Pos
1969	MIN A	1	–	–	0	0	0	0	0	–	0	0	1	0	0	0	0	0	0	0	0	0.0	–	
1970		1	.000	.000	1	0	0	0	0	0.0	0	0	0	1	0	1	0	0	0	0	0	0.0	–	
2 yrs.		2	.000	.000	1	0	0	0	0	0.0	0	0	1	1	0	1	0	0	0	0	0	0.0	–	

Jerry Manuel

MANUEL, JERRY
B. Dec. 23, 1953, Hahira, Ga.

BB TR 6' 158 lbs.

Year	Team	Games	BA	SA	AB	H	2B	3B	HR	HR%	R	RBI	BB	SO	SB	PH AB	PH H	PO	A	E	DP	TC/G	FA	G by Pos
1975	DET A	6	.056	.056	18	1	0	0	0	0.0	0	0	0	4	0	0	0	11	23	2	4	6.0	.944	2B-6
1976		54	.140	.163	43	6	1	0	0	0.0	4	2	3	9	1	0	0	40	64	8	8	2.1	.929	2B-47, SS-4, DH-1
1980	MON N	7	.000	.000	6	0	0	0	0	0.0	0	0	0	2	0	0	0	5	11	1	0	2.4	.941	SS-7
1981		27	.200	.455	55	11	5	0	3	5.5	10	10	6	11	0	0	0	37	41	1	10	2.9	.987	2B-23, SS-2
1982	SD N	2	.200	.600	5	1	0	1	0	0.0	0	1	1	0	0	0	0	1	1	0	1	1.0	1.000	SS-1, 3B-1, 2B-1
5 yrs.		96	.150	.283	127	19	6	1	3	2.4	14	13	10	26	1	0	0	94	140	12	23	2.6	.951	2B-77, SS-14, DH-1, 3B-1

DIVISIONAL PLAYOFF SERIES

Year	Team	Games	BA	SA	AB	H	2B	3B	HR	HR%	R	RBI	BB	SO	SB	PH AB	PH H	PO	A	E	DP	TC/G	FA	G by Pos
1981	MON N	5	.071	.071	14	1	0	0	0	0.0	0	0	2	5	0	0	0	0	0	3	0	0.6	–	2B-5

LEAGUE CHAMPIONSHIP SERIES

Year	Team	Games	BA	SA	AB	H	2B	3B	HR	HR%	R	RBI	BB	SO	SB	PH AB	PH H	PO	A	E	DP	TC/G	FA	G by Pos
1981	MON N	1	–	–	0	0	0	0	0	–	0	0	0	0	0	0	0	0	0	0	0	0.0	–	

Frank Manush

MANUSH, FRANK BENJAMIN
Brother of Heinie Manush.
B. Sept. 18, 1883, Tuscumbia, Ala.   D. Jan. 5, 1965, Laguna Beach, Calif.

BR TR 5'10½" 175 lbs.

Year	Team	Games	BA	SA	AB	H	2B	3B	HR	HR%	R	RBI	BB	SO	SB	PH AB	PH H	PO	A	E	DP	TC/G	FA	G by Pos
1908	PHI A	23	.156	.208	77	12	2	1	0	0.0	6	0	2			2	1	0	28	29	6	3	2.7	.905	3B-20, 2B-2

Heinie Manush

MANUSH, HENRY EMMETT
Brother of Frank Manush.
B. July 20, 1901, Tuscumbia, Ala.   D. May 12, 1971, Sarasota, Fla.
Hall of Fame 1964.

BL TL 6'1" 200 lbs.

Year	Team	Games	BA	SA	AB	H	2B	3B	HR	HR%	R	RBI	BB	SO	SB	PH AB	PH H	PO	A	E	DP	TC/G	FA	G by Pos
1923	DET A	109	.334	.471	308	103	20	5	4	1.3	59	54	20	21	3	27	6	158	6	8	0	1.6	.953	OF-79
1924		120	.289	.448	422	122	24	8	9	2.1	83	68	27	30	14	11	1	225	4	5	1	2.0	.979	OF-106, 1B-1
1925		99	.303	.430	277	84	14	3	5	1.8	46	47	24	21	8	22	6	153	7	3	0	1.6	.982	OF-73
1926		136	.378	.564	498	188	35	8	14	2.8	95	86	31	28	11	14	5	283	7	10	3	2.2	.967	OF-120
1927		152	.298	.442	593	177	31	18	6	1.0	102	80	47	29	12	1	1	361	9	11	3	2.5	.971	OF-150
1928	STL A	154	.378	.575	638	241	47	20	13	2.0	104	108	39	14	17	0	0	355	6	3	2	2.4	.992	OF-154
1929		142	.355	.500	574	204	45	10	6	1.0	85	81	43	24	9	1	0	293	11	4	3	2.2	.987	OF-141
1930	2 teams		STL A (49G – .328)		WAS A (88G – .362)																			
"	total	137	.350	.531	554	194	49	12	9	1.6	100	94	31	24	7	3	0	255	10	3	0	2.0	.989	OF-134
1931	WAS A	146	.307	.438	616	189	41	11	6	1.0	110	70	36	27	3	3	0	245	5	6	1	1.8	.977	OF-143
1932		149	.342	.520	625	214	41	14	14	2.2	121	116	36	29	7	3	1	318	6	4	3	2.2	.988	OF-146
1933		153	.336	.459	658	221	32	17	5	0.8	115	95	36	18	6	3	0	325	10	6	1	2.2	.982	OF-150

Year	Team		Games	BA	SA	AB	H	2B	3B	HR	HR%	R	RBI	BB	SO	SB	Pinch Hit AB	Pinch Hit H	PO	A	E	DP	TC/G	FA	G by Pos

Heinie Manush *continued*

Year	Team		Games	BA	SA	AB	H	2B	3B	HR	HR%	R	RBI	BB	SO	SB	PH AB	PH H	PO	A	E	DP	TC/G	FA	G by Pos
1934			137	.349	.523	556	194	42	11	11	2.0	88	89	36	23	7	7	1	293	5	6	2	2.2	.980	OF-131
1935			119	.273	.390	479	131	26	9	4	0.8	68	56	35	17	2	7	1	251	8	4	5	2.2	.985	OF-111
1936	BOS	A	82	.291	.371	313	91	15	5	0	0.0	43	45	17	11	1	9	4	110	3	4	1	1.4	.966	OF-72
1937	BKN	N	132	.333	.442	466	155	25	7	4	0.9	57	73	40	24	6	9	3	187	7	6	1	1.5	.970	OF-123
1938	2 teams		BKN	N	(17G – .235)		PIT	N	(15G – .308)																
"	total		32	.250	.375	64	16	4	2	0	0.0	11	10	7	4	1	18	5	29	1	0	0	0.9	1.000	OF-12
1939	PIT	N	10	.000	.000	12	0	0	0	0	0.0	0	1	1	1	0	8	0	1	0	0	0	0.1	1.000	OF-1
17 yrs.			2009	.330	.479	7653	2524	491	160	110	1.4	1287	1173	506	345	114	146	36	3842	105	83	26	2.0	.979	OF-1846, 1B-1

WORLD SERIES

Year	Team		Games	BA	SA	AB	H	2B	3B	HR	HR%	R	RBI	BB	SO	SB	PH AB	PH H	PO	A	E	DP	TC/G	FA	G by Pos
1933	WAS	A	5	.111	.111	18	2	0	0	0	0.0	2	0	2	1	0	0	0	10	0	0	0	2.0	1.000	OF-5

Kirt Manwaring

MANWARING, KIRT DEAN
B. July 15, 1965, Elmira, N. Y.

BR TR 6'1" 195 lbs.

Year	Team		Games	BA	SA	AB	H	2B	3B	HR	HR%	R	RBI	BB	SO	SB	PH AB	PH H	PO	A	E	DP	TC/G	FA	G by Pos
1987	SF	N	6	.143	.143	7	1	0	0	0	0.0	0	0	1	0	0	0	0	9	1	1	0	1.8	.909	C-6
1988			40	.250	.336	116	29	7	0	1	0.9	12	15	2	21	0	0	0	162	24	4	2	4.8	.979	C-40
1989			85	.210	.250	200	42	4	2	0	0.0	14	18	11	28	2	9	2	289	32	6	3	3.8	.982	C-81
3 yrs.			131	.223	.279	323	72	11	2	1	0.3	26	33	13	50	2	9	2	460	57	11	5	4.0	.979	C-127

LEAGUE CHAMPIONSHIP SERIES

Year	Team		Games	BA	SA	AB	H	2B	3B	HR	HR%	R	RBI	BB	SO	SB	PH AB	PH H	PO	A	E	DP	TC/G	FA	G by Pos
1989	SF	N	3	.000	.000	2	0	0	0	0	0.0	0	0	0	0	0	1	0	5	0	0	0	1.7	1.000	C-3

WORLD SERIES

Year	Team		Games	BA	SA	AB	H	2B	3B	HR	HR%	R	RBI	BB	SO	SB	PH AB	PH H	PO	A	E	DP	TC/G	FA	G by Pos
1989	SF	N	1	1.000	2.000	1	1	1	0	0	0.0	1	0	0	0	0	0	0	0	0	0	0	0.0	–	C-1

Cliff Mapes

MAPES, CLIFFORD FRANKLIN (Tiger)
B. Mar. 13, 1922, Sutherland, Neb.

BL TR 6'3" 205 lbs.

Year	Team		Games	BA	SA	AB	H	2B	3B	HR	HR%	R	RBI	BB	SO	SB	PH AB	PH H	PO	A	E	DP	TC/G	FA	G by Pos
1948	NY	A	53	.250	.432	88	22	11	1	1	1.1	19	12	6	13	1	26	4	42	4	2	1	0.9	.958	OF-21
1949			111	.247	.378	304	75	13	3	7	2.3	56	38	58	50	6	4	0	228	14	6	4	2.2	.976	OF-108
1950			108	.247	.421	356	88	14	6	12	3.4	60	61	47	61	1	6	2	183	8	10	4	1.9	.950	OF-102
1951	2 teams		NY	A	(45G – .216)		STL	A	(56G – .274)																
"	total		101	.262	.433	252	66	10	2	9	3.6	38	38	30	47	0	13	5	136	4	2	1	1.4	.986	OF-87
1952	DET	A	86	.197	.373	193	38	7	0	9	4.7	26	23	27	42	0	23	6	86	3	3	1	1.1	.967	OF-62
5 yrs.			459	.242	.406	1193	289	55	13	38	3.2	199	172	168	213	8	72	17	675	33	23	11	1.6	.969	OF-380

WORLD SERIES

Year	Team		Games	BA	SA	AB	H	2B	3B	HR	HR%	R	RBI	BB	SO	SB	PH AB	PH H	PO	A	E	DP	TC/G	FA	G by Pos
1949	NY	A	4	.100	.200	10	1	1	0	0	0.0	3	2	2	4	0	0	0	8	0	1	0	2.3	.889	OF-4
1950			1	.000	.000	4	0	0	0	0	0.0	0	0	0	1	0	0	0	3	0	0	0	3.0	1.000	OF-1
2 yrs.			5	.071	.143	14	1	1	0	0	0.0	3	2	2	5	0	0	0	11	0	1	0	2.4	.917	OF-5

Howard Maple

MAPLE, HOWARD ALBERT
B. July 20, 1903, Adrian, Mo. D. Nov. 9, 1970, Portland, Ore.

BL TR 5'7" 175 lbs.

Year	Team		Games	BA	SA	AB	H	2B	3B	HR	HR%	R	RBI	BB	SO	SB	PH AB	PH H	PO	A	E	DP	TC/G	FA	G by Pos
1932	WAS	A	44	.244	.293	41	10	0	1	0	0.0	6	7	7	7	0	2	0	34	5	0	2	0.9	1.000	C-41

George Mappes

MAPPES, GEORGE RICHARD (Dick)
B. Dec. 25, 1865, St. Louis, Mo. D. Feb. 20, 1934, St. Louis, Mo.

Year	Team		Games	BA	SA	AB	H	2B	3B	HR	HR%	R	RBI	BB	SO	SB	PH AB	PH H	PO	A	E	DP	TC/G	FA	G by Pos
1885	BAL	AA	6	.211	.316	19	4	0	1	0	0.0	2		1		0	0	0	16	12	4	1	5.3	.875	2B-6
1886	STL	N	6	.143	.143	14	2	0	0	0	0.0	1	0	1	5	0	0	0	18	5	4	0	4.5	.852	C-3, 3B-2, 2B-1
2 yrs.			12	.182	.242	33	6	0	1	0	0.0	3	0	2	5	0	0	0	34	17	8	1	4.9	.864	2B-7, C-3, 3B-2

Rabbit Maranville

MARANVILLE, WALTER JAMES VINCENT
B. Nov. 11, 1891, Springfield, Mass. D. Jan. 5, 1954, New York, N. Y.
Manager 1925.
Hall of Fame 1954.

BR TR 5'5" 155 lbs.

Year	Team		Games	BA	SA	AB	H	2B	3B	HR	HR%	R	RBI	BB	SO	SB	PH AB	PH H	PO	A	E	DP	TC/G	FA	G by Pos
1912	BOS	N	26	.209	.233	86	18	2	0	0	0.0	8	8	9	14	1	0	0	46	97	11	11	5.9	.929	SS-26
1913			143	.247	.308	571	141	13	8	2	0.4	68	48	68	62	25	0	0	317	475	43	49	5.8	.949	SS-143
1914			156	.246	.326	586	144	23	6	4	0.7	74	78	45	56	28	0	0	407	574	65	92	6.7	.938	SS-156
1915			149	.244	.324	509	124	23	6	2	0.4	51	43	45	65	18	0	0	391	486	55	63	6.3	.941	SS-149
1916			155	.235	.325	604	142	16	13	4	0.7	79	38	50	69	32	0	0	386	515	50	79	6.1	.947	SS-155
1917			142	.260	.357	561	146	19	13	3	0.5	69	43	40	47	27	0	0	341	474	46	67	6.1	.947	SS-142
1918			11	.316	.368	38	12	0	1	0	0.0	3	3	4	0	1	0	0	34	34	5	2	6.6	.932	SS-11
1919			131	.267	.377	480	128	18	10	5	1.0	44	43	36	23	12	0	0	361	488	53	74	6.9	.941	SS-131
1920			134	.266	.371	493	131	19	15	1	0.2	48	43	28	24	14	1	0	354	462	45	62	6.4	.948	SS-133
1921	PIT	N	153	.294	.379	612	180	25	12	1	0.2	90	70	47	38	25	0	0	325	529	34	72	5.8	.962	SS-153
1922			155	.295	.378	672	198	26	15	0	0.0	115	63	61	43	24	0	0	419	512	36	93	6.3	.963	SS-138, 2B-18
1923			141	.277	.346	581	161	19	9	1	0.2	78	41	42	34	14	0	0	332	505	30	94	6.1	.965	SS-141
1924			152	.266	.399	594	158	33	20	2	0.3	62	71	35	53	18	0	0	365	568	26	109	6.3	.973	2B-152
1925	CHI	N	75	.233	.293	266	62	10	3	0	0.0	37	23	29	20	6	1	0	162	261	20	51	5.9	.955	SS-74
1926	BKN	N	78	.235	.312	234	55	8	5	0	0.0	32	24	26	24	7	0	0	161	246	19	30	5.5	.955	SS-60, 2B-18
1927	STL	N	9	.241	.276	29	7	1	0	0	0.0	0	0	2	2	0	0	0	17	34	2	6	5.9	.962	SS-9
1928			112	.240	.342	366	88	14	10	1	0.3	40	34	36	27	3	0	0	237	364	19	58	5.5	.969	SS-112, 2B-2
1929	BOS	N	146	.284	.366	560	159	26	10	0	0.0	87	55	47	33	13	0	0	324	537	35	104	6.1	.961	SS-146, 2B-1
1930			142	.281	.367	558	157	26	8	2	0.4	85	43	48	23	9	0	0	349	450	29	98	5.8	.965	SS-138, 3B-4
1931			145	.260	.317	562	146	22	5	0	0.0	69	33	56	34	9	1	0	289	453	41	98	5.4	.948	SS-137, 2B-11
1932			149	.235	.284	571	134	20	4	0	0.0	67	37	46	28	4	0	0	402	473	22	91	6.0	.975	2B-149
1933			143	.218	.266	478	104	15	4	0	0.0	46	38	36	34	2	1	1	362	384	22	82	5.4	.971	2B-142
1935			23	.149	.179	67	10	2	0	0	0.0	3	5	3	3	0	3	0	32	46	3	10	3.5	.963	2B-20
23 yrs.			2670	.258	.340	10078	2605	380	177	28	0.3	1255	884	839	756	291	7	1	6413	8967	711	1495	6.0	.956	SS-2154, 2B-513, 3B-4

WORLD SERIES

Year	Team		Games	BA	SA	AB	H	2B	3B	HR	HR%	R	RBI	BB	SO	SB	PH AB	PH H	PO	A	E	DP	TC/G	FA	G by Pos
1914	BOS	N	4	.308	.308	13	4	0	0	0	0.0	1	3	1	1	2	0	0	7	13	1	2	5.3	.952	SS-4

Year	Team	Games	BA	SA	AB	H	2B	3B	HR	HR%	R	RBI	BB	SO	SB	Pinch Hit AB	H	PO	A	E	DP	TC/G	FA	G by Pos

Rabbit Maranville *continued*

Year	Team	Games	BA	SA	AB	H	2B	3B	HR	HR%	R	RBI	BB	SO	SB	AB	H	PO	A	E	DP	TC/G	FA	G by Pos
1928	STL N	4	.308	.385	13	4	1	0	0	0.0	2	0	1	1	1	0	0	11	3	1	2	3.8	.933	SS-4
2 yrs.		8	.308	.346	26	8	1	0	0	0.0	3	3	2	2	3	0	0	18	16	2	4	4.5	.944	SS-8

Johnny Marcum

MARCUM, JOHN ALFRED (Footsie) BL TR 5'11" 197 lbs.
B. Sept. 9, 1909, Campbellsburg, Ky.   D. Sept. 10, 1984, Louisville, Ky.

Year	Team	Games	BA	SA	AB	H	2B	3B	HR	HR%	R	RBI	BB	SO	SB	AB	H	PO	A	E	DP	TC/G	FA	G by Pos
1933	PHI A	5	.167	.167	12	2	0	0	0	0.0	2	0	2	1	0	0	0	5	6	0	0	2.2	1.000	P-5
1934		58	.268	.330	112	30	4	0	1	0.9	13	13	3	5	0	20	3	14	42	3	2	1.0	.949	P-37
1935		64	.311	.395	119	37	2	1	2	1.7	13	17	9	5	0	23	7	11	32	5	1	0.8	.896	P-39
1936	BOS A	48	.205	.307	88	18	3	0	2	2.3	6	7	3	5	0	18	0	7	31	2	3	0.8	.950	P-31
1937		51	.267	.360	86	23	8	0	0	0.0	12	13	7	4	0	13	2	13	38	1	1	1.0	.981	P-37
1938		19	.135	.135	37	5	0	0	0	0.0	3	3	6	9	0	3	0	3	15	0	0	0.9	1.000	P-15
1939	2 teams	STL A	(16G –	.455)		CHI A	(38G –	.281)																
"	total	54	.329	.342	79	26	1	0	0	0.0	10	17	6	3	0	22	5	8	17	1	2	0.5	.962	P-31
7 yrs.		299	.265	.330	533	141	18	1	5	0.9	56	70	36	32	0	99	17	61	181	12	9	0.8	.953	P-195

Marty Marion

MARION, MARTIN WHITFORD (Slats, The Octopus) BR TR 6'2" 170 lbs.
Brother of Red Marion.
B. Dec. 1, 1917, Richburg, S. C.
Manager 1951-56.

Year	Team	Games	BA	SA	AB	H	2B	3B	HR	HR%	R	RBI	BB	SO	SB	AB	H	PO	A	E	DP	TC/G	FA	G by Pos
1940	STL N	125	.278	.345	435	121	18	1	3	0.7	44	46	21	34	9	0	0	245	366	33	76	5.2	.949	SS-125
1941		155	.252	.320	547	138	23	3	3	0.5	50	58	42	48	8	0	0	299	489	38	85	5.3	.954	SS-155
1942		147	.276	.375	485	134	38	5	0	0.0	66	54	48	50	8	0	0	296	448	31	87	5.3	.960	SS-147
1943		129	.280	.337	418	117	15	3	1	0.2	38	52	32	37	1	1	0	232	424	20	93	5.2	.970	SS-128
1944		144	.267	.362	506	135	26	4	6	1.2	50	63	43	50	1	0	0	268	461	21	90	5.2	.972	SS-144
1945		123	.277	.370	430	119	27	5	1	0.2	63	59	39	39	2	0	0	237	372	21	70	5.1	.967	SS-122
1946		146	.233	.325	498	116	29	4	3	0.6	51	46	59	53	1	1	0	290	480	21	105	5.4	.973	SS-145
1947		149	.272	.352	540	147	19	6	4	0.7	57	74	49	58	3	0	0	329	452	15	104	5.3	.981	SS-149
1948		144	.252	.333	567	143	26	4	4	0.7	70	43	37	54	1	2	0	263	445	19	80	5.0	.974	SS-142
1949		134	.272	.369	515	140	31	2	5	1.0	61	70	37	42	0	0	0	242	441	17	74	5.2	.976	SS-134
1950		106	.247	.317	372	92	10	2	4	1.1	36	40	44	55	1	5	1	180	313	11	73	4.8	.978	SS-101
1952	STL A	67	.247	.339	186	46	11	0	2	1.1	16	19	19	17	0	4	2	105	138	5	41	3.7	.980	SS-63
1953		3	.000	.000	7	0	0	0	0	0.0	0	0	0	0	0	1	0	1	0	0	0	0.3	1.000	3B-2
13 yrs.		1572	.263	.345	5506	1448	272	37	36	0.7	602	624	470	537	35	14	3	2987	4829	252	978	5.1	.969	SS-1555, 3B-2

WORLD SERIES

Year	Team	Games	BA	SA	AB	H	2B	3B	HR	HR%	R	RBI	BB	SO	SB	AB	H	PO	A	E	DP	TC/G	FA	G by Pos
1942	STL N	5	.111	.222	18	2	0	1	0	0.0	2	3	1	2	0	0	0	13	16	0	3	5.8	1.000	SS-5
1943		5	.357	.714	14	5	2	0	1	7.1	2	2	3	1	0	0	0	8	14	1	4	4.6	.957	SS-5
1944		6	.227	.364	22	5	3	0	0	0.0	1	2	2	3	0	0	0	7	22	0	2	4.8	1.000	SS-6
1946		7	.250	.333	24	6	2	0	0	0.0	4	4	1	1	0	0	0	12	22	2	3	5.1	.944	SS-7
4 yrs.		23	.231	.385	78	18	7	1	1	1.3	5	11	7	7	0	0	0	40	74	3	12	5.1	.974	SS-23
							9th																	

Red Marion

MARION, JOHN WYETH BR TR 6'2" 175 lbs.
Brother of Marty Marion.
B. Mar. 14, 1914, Richburg, S. C.   D. Mar. 13, 1975, San Jose, Calif.

Year	Team	Games	BA	SA	AB	H	2B	3B	HR	HR%	R	RBI	BB	SO	SB	AB	H	PO	A	E	DP	TC/G	FA	G by Pos
1935	WAS A	4	.182	.545	11	2	1	0	1	9.1	1	1	0	2	0	0	0	4	1	1	0	1.5	.833	OF-3
1943		14	.176	.176	17	3	0	0	0	0.0	2	1	3	1	0	9	1	7	0	0	0	0.5	1.000	OF-4
2 yrs.		18	.179	.321	28	5	1	0	1	3.6	3	2	3	3	0	9	1	11	1	1	0	0.7	.923	OF-7

Roger Maris

MARIS, ROGER EUGENE BL TR 6' 197 lbs.
Born Roger Eugene Maras.
B. Sept. 10, 1934, Hibbing, Minn.   D. Dec. 14, 1985, Houston, Tex.

Year	Team	Games	BA	SA	AB	H	2B	3B	HR	HR%	R	RBI	BB	SO	SB	AB	H	PO	A	E	DP	TC/G	FA	G by Pos
1957	CLE A	116	.235	.405	358	84	9	5	14	3.9	61	51	60	79	8	5	2	266	10	7	2	2.4	.975	OF-112
1958	2 teams	150	CLE A	(51G –	.225)		KC A	(99G –	.247)															
"	total	150	.240	.431	583	140	19	4	28	4.8	87	80	45	85	4	6	0	303	15	9	4	2.2	.972	OF-146
1959	KC A	122	.273	.464	433	118	21	7	16	3.7	69	72	58	53	2	5	2	231	7	6	4	2.0	.975	OF-117
1960	NY A	136	.283	.581	499	141	18	7	39	7.8	98	112	70	65	2	4	1	263	6	4	1	2.0	.985	OF-131
1961		161	.269	.620	590	159	16	4	61	10.3	132	142	94	67	0	1	0	266	9	9	1	1.8	.968	OF-160
1962		157	.256	.485	590	151	34	1	33	5.6	92	100	87	78	1	3	0	316	4	3	0	2.1	.991	OF-154
1963		90	.269	.542	312	84	14	1	23	7.4	53	53	35	40	1	5	2	162	6	2	1	1.9	.988	OF-86
1964		141	.281	.464	513	144	12	2	26	5.1	86	71	62	78	3	6	1	250	6	1	0	1.8	.996	OF-137
1965		46	.239	.439	155	37	7	0	8	5.2	22	27	29	29	0	1	0	66	1	2	0	1.5	.971	OF-43
1966		119	.233	.382	348	81	9	2	13	3.7	37	43	36	60	0	20	6	133	3	1	0	1.2	.993	OF-95
1967	STL N	125	.261	.405	410	107	18	7	9	2.2	64	55	52	61	0	19	2	224	5	2	1	1.8	.991	OF-118
1968		100	.255	.374	310	79	18	2	5	1.6	25	45	24	38	0	21	6	169	4	3	1	1.8	.983	OF-84
12 yrs.		1463	.260	.476	5101	1325	195	42	275	5.4	826	851	652	733	21	99	23	2649	76	49	15	1.9	.982	OF-1383

WORLD SERIES

Year	Team	Games	BA	SA	AB	H	2B	3B	HR	HR%	R	RBI	BB	SO	SB	AB	H	PO	A	E	DP	TC/G	FA	G by Pos
1960	NY A	7	.267	.500	30	8	1	0	2	6.7	6	2	2	4	0	0	0	11	0	1	0	1.7	.917	OF-7
1961		5	.105	.316	19	2	1	0	1	5.3	4	2	4	6	0	0	0	11	1	0	0	2.4	1.000	OF-5
1962		7	.174	.348	23	4	1	0	1	4.3	4	5	5	2	0	0	0	11	1	0	0	1.7	1.000	OF-7
1963		2	.000	.000	5	0	0	0	0	0.0	0	0	0	1	0	0	0	3	0	0	0	1.5	1.000	OF-2
1964		7	.200	.300	30	6	0	0	1	3.3	4	1	1	4	0	0	0	19	0	0	0	2.7	1.000	OF-7
1967	STL N	7	.385	.538	26	10	1	0	1	3.8	3	7	3	1	0	0	0	15	0	1	0	2.3	.938	OF-7
1968		6	.158	.211	19	3	1	0	0	0.0	5	3	3	3	0	1	0	8	0	0	0	1.3	1.000	OF-5
7 yrs.		41	.217	.368	152	33	4	0	6	3.9	26	18	18	21	0	1	0	78	2	2	0	2.0	.976	OF-40
			10th		10th								6th											

Gene Markland

MARKLAND, CLENETH EUGENE (Mousey) BR TR 5'10" 160 lbs.
B. Dec. 26, 1919, Detroit, Mich.

Year	Team	Games	BA	SA	AB	H	2B	3B	HR	HR%	R	RBI	BB	SO	SB	AB	H	PO	A	E	DP	TC/G	FA	G by Pos
1950	PHI A	5	.125	.125	8	1	0	0	0	0.0	2	0	3	0	0	0	0	12	9	0	1	4.2	1.000	2B-5

Year Team	Games	BA	SA	AB	H	2B	3B	HR	HR%	R	RBI	BB	SO	SB	Pinch Hit AB	Pinch Hit H	PO	A	E	DP	TC/G	FA	G by Pos

Hal Marnie

MARNIE, HARRY SYLVESTER
B. July 6, 1918, Philadelphia, Pa. — BR TR 6'1" 178 lbs.

Year Team	Games	BA	SA	AB	H	2B	3B	HR	HR%	R	RBI	BB	SO	SB	PH AB	PH H	PO	A	E	DP	TC/G	FA	G by Pos
1940 PHI N	11	.176	.176	34	6	0	0	0	0.0	4	4	4	2	0	0	0	19	42	1	8	5.6	.984	2B-11
1941	61	.241	.297	158	38	3	3	0	0.0	12	11	13	25	0	2	0	129	108	3	24	3.9	.988	2B-39, SS-16, 3B-3
1942	24	.167	.167	30	5	0	0	0	0.0	3	0	1	1	1	2	0	30	32	4	9	2.8	.939	2B-11, SS-7, 3B-1
3 yrs.	96	.221	.261	222	49	3	3	0	0.0	19	15	18	28	1	4	0	178	182	8	41	3.8	.978	2B-61, SS-23, 3B-4

Fred Marolewski

MAROLEWSKI, FRED DANIEL (Fritz)
B. Oct. 6, 1928, Chicago, Ill. — BR TR 6'2½" 205 lbs.

Year Team	Games	BA	SA	AB	H	2B	3B	HR	HR%	R	RBI	BB	SO	SB	PH AB	PH H	PO	A	E	DP	TC/G	FA	G by Pos
1953 STL N	1	–	–	0	0	0	0	0	–	0	0	0	0	0	0	0	0	0	0	0	0.0	–	1B-1

Ollie Marquardt

MARQUARDT, ALBERT LUDWIG
B. Sept. 22, 1902, Toledo, Ohio   D. Feb. 7, 1968, Port Clinton, Ohio — BR TR 5'9" 156 lbs.

Year Team	Games	BA	SA	AB	H	2B	3B	HR	HR%	R	RBI	BB	SO	SB	PH AB	PH H	PO	A	E	DP	TC/G	FA	G by Pos
1931 BOS A	17	.179	.205	39	7	1	0	0	0.0	4	2	3	4	0	1	0	20	33	3	4	3.3	.946	2B-13

Gonzalo Marquez

MARQUEZ, GONZALO ENRIQUE
Born Gonzalo Enrique Marquez y Mora.
B. Mar. 31, 1946, Carupano, Venezuela   D. Dec. 20, 1984, Valencia, Venezuela — BL TL 5'11" 180 lbs.

Year Team	Games	BA	SA	AB	H	2B	3B	HR	HR%	R	RBI	BB	SO	SB	PH AB	PH H	PO	A	E	DP	TC/G	FA	G by Pos
1972 OAK A	23	.381	.381	21	8	0	0	0	0.0	2	4	3	4	1	16	7	12	1	1	1	0.6	.929	1B-2
1973 2 teams	OAK A (23G – .240)			CHI N (19G – .224)																			
" total	42	.229	.301	83	19	3	0	1	1.2	6	6	3	8	0	20	5	156	15	1	14	4.1	.994	1B-19, 2B-2
1974 CHI N	11	.000	.000	11	0	0	0	0	0.0	1	0	1	2	0	10	0	2	0	0	0	0.2	1.000	1B-1
3 yrs.	76	.235	.287	115	27	3	0	1	0.9	9	10	7	14	1	46	12	170	16	2	15	2.5	.989	1B-22, 2B-2

LEAGUE CHAMPIONSHIP SERIES

Year Team	Games	BA	SA	AB	H	2B	3B	HR	HR%	R	RBI	BB	SO	SB	PH AB	PH H	PO	A	E	DP	TC/G	FA	G by Pos
1972 OAK A	3	.667	.667	3	2	0	0	0	0.0	1	1	0	0	0	3	2	0	0	0	0	0.0	–	

WORLD SERIES

Year Team	Games	BA	SA	AB	H	2B	3B	HR	HR%	R	RBI	BB	SO	SB	PH AB	PH H	PO	A	E	DP	TC/G	FA	G by Pos
1972 OAK A	5	.600	.600	5	3	0	0	0	0.0	0	1	0	0	0	5	3	0	0	0	0	0.0	–	

1st

Luis Marquez

MARQUEZ, LUIS ANGEL (Canena)
Born Luis Angel Marquez y Sanchez.
B. Oct. 28, 1925, Aguadilla, Puerto Rico   D. Mar. 1, 1988, Aguadilla, Puerto Rico — BR TR 5'10½" 174 lbs.

Year Team	Games	BA	SA	AB	H	2B	3B	HR	HR%	R	RBI	BB	SO	SB	PH AB	PH H	PO	A	E	DP	TC/G	FA	G by Pos
1951 BOS N	68	.197	.254	122	24	5	1	0	0.0	19	11	10	20	4	9	2	100	2	0	0	1.5	1.000	OF-43
1954 2 teams	CHI N (17G – .083)			PIT N (14G – .111)																			
" total	31	.095	.095	21	2	0	0	0	0.0	5	0	6	4	3	5	1	20	0	0	0	0.6	1.000	OF-18
2 yrs.	99	.182	.231	143	26	5	1	0	0.0	24	11	16	24	7	14	3	120	2	0	0	1.2	1.000	OF-61

Bob Marquis

MARQUIS, ROBERT RUDOLPH
B. Dec. 23, 1924, Oklahoma City, Okla. — BL TL 6'1" 170 lbs.

Year Team	Games	BA	SA	AB	H	2B	3B	HR	HR%	R	RBI	BB	SO	SB	PH AB	PH H	PO	A	E	DP	TC/G	FA	G by Pos
1953 CIN N	40	.273	.477	44	12	1	1	2	4.5	9	3	4	11	0	26	5	19	0	2	0	0.5	.905	OF-10

Roger Marquis

MARQUIS, ROGER JULIAN (Noonie)
B. Apr. 5, 1937, Holyoke, Mass. — BL TL 6' 190 lbs.

Year Team	Games	BA	SA	AB	H	2B	3B	HR	HR%	R	RBI	BB	SO	SB	PH AB	PH H	PO	A	E	DP	TC/G	FA	G by Pos
1955 BAL A	1	.000	.000	1	0	0	0	0	0.0	0	0	0	0	0	0	0	0	0	0	0	0.0	–	OF-1

Lefty Marr

MARR, CHARLES W.
B. Sept. 19, 1862, Cincinnati, Ohio   D. Jan. 11, 1912, New Britain, Conn. — BL TL

Year Team	Games	BA	SA	AB	H	2B	3B	HR	HR%	R	RBI	BB	SO	SB	PH AB	PH H	PO	A	E	DP	TC/G	FA	G by Pos
1886 CIN AA	8	.276	.379	29	8	1	1	0	0.0	2					0	0	15	1	7	0	2.9	.696	OF-8
1889 COL AA	139	.306	.414	546	167	26	15	1	0.2	110	75	87	32	29	0	0	254	253	90	22	4.3	.849	3B-66, OF-47, SS-26, 1B-1, C-1
1890 CIN N	130	.300	.389	527	158	17	12	2	0.4	91	73	46	29	44	0	0	140	144	39	8	2.5	.879	OF-64, 3B-63, SS-3
1891 2 teams	CIN N (72G – .259)			CIN AA (14G – .193)																			
" total	86	.248	.318	343	85	10	7	0	0.0	41	36	32	19	18	0	0	98	7	18	2	1.4	.854	OF-86
4 yrs.	363	.289	.381	1445	418	54	35	3	0.2	244	184	166	80	91	0	0	507	405	154	32	2.9	.856	OF-205, 3B-129, SS-29, 1B-1, C-1

Bill Marriott

MARRIOTT, WILLIAM EARL
B. Apr. 18, 1893, Pratt, Kans.   D. Aug. 11, 1969, Berkeley, Calif. — BL TR 6' 170 lbs.

Year Team	Games	BA	SA	AB	H	2B	3B	HR	HR%	R	RBI	BB	SO	SB	PH AB	PH H	PO	A	E	DP	TC/G	FA	G by Pos
1917 CHI N	2	.000	.000	6	0	0	0	0	0.0	0	0	0	1	0	2	0	2	0	1	0	1.5	.667	OF-1
1920	14	.279	.465	43	12	4	2	0	0.0	7	5	6	5	1	0	0	26	40	8	2	5.3	.892	2B-14
1921	30	.316	.395	38	12	1	1	0	0.0	3	7	4	1	0	20	4	11	13	5	2	1.0	.828	2B-6, OF-1, SS-1, 3B-1
1925 BOS N	103	.268	.305	370	99	9	1	1	0.3	37	40	28	26	3	8	1	100	187	22	13	3.0	.929	3B-89, OF-1
1926 BKN N	109	.267	.378	360	96	13	9	3	0.8	39	42	17	20	12	4	0	80	173	20	6	2.5	.927	3B-104
1927	6	.111	.333	9	1	0	1	0	0.0	0	1	2	2	0	4	0	3	5	1	0	1.5	.889	3B-2
6 yrs.	264	.266	.347	826	220	27	14	4	0.5	86	95	57	55	16	38	5	222	418	57	23	2.6	.918	3B-196, 2B-20, OF-3, SS-1

Armando Marsans

MARSANS, ARMANDO
B. Oct. 3, 1887, Matanzas, Cuba   D. Sept. 3, 1960, Havana, Cuba — BR TR 5'10" 157 lbs.

Year Team	Games	BA	SA	AB	H	2B	3B	HR	HR%	R	RBI	BB	SO	SB	PH AB	PH H	PO	A	E	DP	TC/G	FA	G by Pos
1911 CIN N	58	.261	.304	138	36	2	2	0	0.0	17	11	15	11	11	19	3	64	2	3	0	1.2	.957	OF-34, 3B-1, 1B-1
1912	110	.317	.404	416	132	19	7	1	0.2	59	38	20	17	35	2	2	265	12	8	2	2.6	.972	OF-98, 1B-6
1913	118	.297	.340	435	129	7	6	0	0.0	49	38	17	25	37	1	0	402	26	15	21	3.8	.966	OF-94, 1B-22, 3B-2, SS-1
1914 2 teams	CIN N (36G – .298)			STL F (9G – .350)																			
" total	45	.311	.354	164	51	3	2	0	0.0	21	24	17	6	17	0	0	98	28	12	9	3.1	.913	OF-36, 2B-7, SS-2
1915 STL F	36	.177	.202	124	22	3	0	0	0.0	16	6	14		5	1	0	71	8	3	3	2.3	.975	OF-35
1916 STL A	151	.254	.286	528	134	12	1	1	0.2	51	60	57	41	46	1	1	351	25	9	7	2.5	.977	OF-150
1917 2 teams	STL A (75G – .230)			NY A (25G – .227)																			
" total	100	.229	.275	345	79	16	0	0	0.0	41	35	28	9	17	1	1	232	24	9	3	2.7	.966	OF-92, 3B-5, 2B-1
1918 NY A	37	.236	.293	123	29	5	1	0	0.0	13	9	5	3	3	1	0	64	2	4	0	1.9	.943	OF-36
8 yrs.	655	.269	.318	2273	612	67	19	2	0.1	267	221	173	112	171	26	7	1547	127	62	45	2.7	.964	OF-575, 1B-29, 3B-8, 2B-8, SS-3

Year	Team		Games	BA	SA	AB	H	2B	3B	HR	HR%	R	RBI	BB	SO	SB	Pinch Hit AB	Pinch Hit H	PO	A	E	DP	TC/G	FA	G by Pos

Freddie Marsh

MARSH, FRED FRANCIS
B. Jan. 5, 1924, Valley Falls, Kans.
BR TR 5'10" 180 lbs.

Year	Team		Games	BA	SA	AB	H	2B	3B	HR	HR%	R	RBI	BB	SO	SB	PH AB	PH H	PO	A	E	DP	TC/G	FA	G by Pos
1949	CLE	A	1	–	–	0	0	0	0	0	–	0	0	0	0	0	0	0	0	0	0	0	0.0	–	
1951	STL	A	130	.243	.335	445	108	21	4	4	0.9	44	43	36	56	4	10	2	141	231	29	33	3.1	.928	3B-117, SS-3, 2B-2
1952	3 teams	STL A (11G – .217)				WAS A (9G – .042)				STL A (76G – .286)															
"	total		96	.258	.321	271	70	9	1	2	0.7	29	28	28	37	3	3	2	114	183	19	45	3.3	.940	SS-60, 3B-21, 2B-14, OF-2
1953	CHI	A	67	.200	.274	95	19	1	0	2	2.1	22	2	13	26	0	11	2	61	71	6	12	2.1	.957	3B-32, SS-17, 1B-5, 2B-2
1954			62	.306	.398	98	30	5	2	0	0.0	21	4	9	16	4	2	0	41	86	4	8	2.1	.969	3B-36, SS-3, 1B-2, OF-1
1955	BAL	A	89	.218	.267	303	66	7	1	2	0.7	30	19	35	33	1	1	0	216	193	14	55	4.8	.967	2B-76, 3B-18, SS-16
1956			20	.125	.125	24	3	0	0	0	0.0	2	0	4	3	1	0	0	17	18	3	5	1.9	.921	SS-8, 3B-8, 2B-5
7 yrs.			465	.239	.311	1236	296	43	8	10	0.8	148	96	125	171	13	27	6	590	782	75	158	3.1	.948	3B-232, SS-107, 2B-99, 1B-7, OF-3

Bill Marshall

MARSHALL, WILLIAM HENRY
B. Feb. 14, 1911, Dorchester, Mass. D. May 5, 1977, Sacramento, Calif.
BR TR 5'8½" 156 lbs.

Year	Team		Games	BA	SA	AB	H	2B	3B	HR	HR%	R	RBI	BB	SO	SB	PH AB	PH H	PO	A	E	DP	TC/G	FA	G by Pos
1931	BOS	A	1	–	–	0	0	0	0	0	–	1	0	0	0	0	0	0	0	0	0	0	0.0	–	
1934	CIN	N	6	.125	.125	8	1	0	0	0	0.0	0	0	0	2	0	3	1	2	5	1	0	1.3	.875	2B-2
2 yrs.			7	.125	.125	8	1	0	0	0	0.0	1	0	0	2	0	3	1	2	5	1	0	1.1	.875	2B-2

Charlie Marshall

MARSHALL, CHARLES ANTHONY
Born Charles Anthony Marcziewicz.
B. Aug. 28, 1919, Wilmington, Del.
BR TR 5'10½" 178 lbs.

Year	Team		Games	BA	SA	AB	H	2B	3B	HR	HR%	R	RBI	BB	SO	SB	PH AB	PH H	PO	A	E	DP	TC/G	FA	G by Pos
1941	STL	N	1	–	–	0	0	0	0	0	–	0	0	0	0	0	0	0	1	0	0	0	1.0	1.000	C-1

Dave Marshall

MARSHALL, DAVID LEWIS
B. Jan. 14, 1943, Artesia, Calif.
BL TR 6'1" 182 lbs.

Year	Team		Games	BA	SA	AB	H	2B	3B	HR	HR%	R	RBI	BB	SO	SB	PH AB	PH H	PO	A	E	DP	TC/G	FA	G by Pos
1967	SF	N	1	–	–	0	0	0	0	0	–	0	0	0	0	0	0	0	0	0	0	0	0.0	–	
1968			76	.264	.322	174	46	5	1	1	0.6	17	16	20	37	2	23	7	58	3	5	3	0.9	.924	OF-50
1969			110	.232	.288	267	62	7	1	2	0.7	32	33	40	68	1	20	4	106	3	5	0	1.0	.956	OF-87
1970	NY	N	92	.243	.402	189	46	10	1	6	3.2	21	29	17	43	4	44	11	71	2	2	0	0.8	.973	OF-43
1971			100	.238	.332	214	51	9	1	3	1.4	28	21	26	54	1	36	8	92	2	1	0	1.0	.989	OF-64
1972			72	.250	.359	156	39	5	0	4	2.6	21	11	22	28	5	29	3	70	0	2	0	1.0	.972	OF-42
1973	SD	N	39	.286	.388	49	14	5	0	0	0.0	4	4	8	9	0	24	5	14	0	0	0	0.4	1.000	OF-8
7 yrs.			490	.246	.338	1049	258	41	4	16	1.5	123	114	133	239	13	176	38	411	10	15	3	0.9	.966	OF-294

Doc Marshall

MARSHALL, EDWARD HERBERT
B. June 4, 1906, New Albany, Miss.
BR TR 5'11" 150 lbs.

Year	Team		Games	BA	SA	AB	H	2B	3B	HR	HR%	R	RBI	BB	SO	SB	PH AB	PH H	PO	A	E	DP	TC/G	FA	G by Pos
1929	NY	N	5	.400	.533	15	6	2	0	0	0.0	6	2	1	1	0	0	0	7	11	0	0	3.6	1.000	2B-5
1930			78	.309	.359	223	69	5	3	0	0.0	33	21	13	9	0	5	3	109	179	13	29	3.9	.957	SS-45, 2B-17, 3B-5
1931			68	.201	.253	194	39	6	2	0	0.0	15	10	8	8	1	3	1	124	160	14	31	4.4	.953	2B-47, SS-11, 3B-3
1932			68	.248	.292	226	56	8	1	0	0.0	18	28	6	11	1	0	0	119	199	27	37	5.1	.922	SS-63
4 yrs.			219	.258	.309	658	170	21	6	0	0.0	72	61	28	28	2	8	4	359	549	54	97	4.4	.944	SS-119, 2B-69, 3B-8

Doc Marshall

MARSHALL, WILLIAM RIDDLE
B. Sept. 22, 1875, Butler, Pa. D. Dec. 11, 1959, Clinton, Ill.
BR TR 6' 185 lbs.

Year	Team		Games	BA	SA	AB	H	2B	3B	HR	HR%	R	RBI	BB	SO	SB	PH AB	PH H	PO	A	E	DP	TC/G	FA	G by Pos
1904	3 teams	PHI N (8G – .100)				NY N (11G – .353)				BOS N (13G – .209)															
"	total		32	.213	.250	80	17	1	1	0	0.0	7	5	3		2	7	0	82	42	8	4	4.1	.939	C-20, OF-3, 2B-1
1906	2 teams	NY N (38G – .167)				STL N (39G – .276)																			
"	total		77	.227	.284	225	51	7	3	0	0.0	14	17	13		8	9	1	270	73	10	5	4.6	.972	C-51, OF-16, 1B-2
1907	STL	N	84	.201	.269	268	54	8	2	2	0.7	19	18	12		2	1	0	374	142	26	9	6.5	.952	C-83
1908	2 teams	STL N (6G – .071)				CHI N (12G – .300)																			
"	total		18	.206	.265	34	7	0	1	0	0.0	4	4	0		0	2	1	48	10	1	2	3.3	.983	C-10, OF-3
1909	BKN	N	50	.201	.262	149	30	7	1	0	0.0	7	10	6		3	1	0	110	61	9	2	3.6	.950	C-49, OF-1
5 yrs.			261	.210	.270	756	159	23	8	2	0.3	51	54	34		15	20	2	884	328	54	22	4.9	.957	C-213, OF-23, 1B-2, 2B-1

Jim Marshall

MARSHALL, RUFUS JAMES
B. May 25, 1931, Danville, Ill.
Manager 1974-76, 1979.
BL TL 6'1" 190 lbs.

Year	Team		Games	BA	SA	AB	H	2B	3B	HR	HR%	R	RBI	BB	SO	SB	PH AB	PH H	PO	A	E	DP	TC/G	FA	G by Pos
1958	2 teams	BAL A (85G – .215)				CHI N (26G – .272)																			
"	total		111	.232	.386	272	63	6	3	10	3.7	29	30	30	43	4	36	6	504	27	1	48	4.8	.998	1B-67, OF-19
1959	CHI	N	108	.252	.405	294	74	10	1	11	3.7	39	40	33	39	0	33	8	565	52	2	52	5.7	.997	1B-72, OF-6
1960	SF	N	75	.237	.339	118	28	2	2	2	1.7	19	13	17	24	0	38	8	177	9	6	13	2.6	.969	1B-28, OF-6
1961			44	.222	.306	36	8	0	0	1	2.8	5	7	3	8	0	32	7	9	1	0	1	0.2	1.000	1B-4, OF-2
1962	2 teams	NY N (17G – .344)				PIT N (55G – .220)																			
"	total		72	.250	.424	132	33	6	1	5	3.8	19	16	18	25	1	32	6	229	20	0	27	3.5	1.000	1B-31, OF-1
5 yrs.			410	.242	.388	852	206	24	7	29	3.4	111	106	101	139	5	171	35	1484	109	9	141	3.9	.994	1B-202, OF-36

Joe Marshall

MARSHALL, JOSEPH HANLEY (Home Run Joe)
B. Feb. 19, 1876, Audubon, Minn. D. Sept. 11, 1931, Santa Monica, Calif.
BR TR

Year	Team		Games	BA	SA	AB	H	2B	3B	HR	HR%	R	RBI	BB	SO	SB	PH AB	PH H	PO	A	E	DP	TC/G	FA	G by Pos
1903	PIT	N	10	.261	.478	23	6	1	2	0	0.0	2	2	0		0	3	0	8	8	1	1	1.7	.941	OF-3, SS-3, 2B-1
1906	STL	N	33	.158	.211	95	15	1	2	0	0.0	2	7	6		0	5	1	54	9	6	3	2.1	.913	OF-23, 1B-4, SS-3, 2B-1
2 yrs.			43	.178	.263	118	21	2	4	0	0.0	4	9	6		0	8	1	62	17	7	4	2.0	.919	OF-26, 1B-4, SS-3, 2B-1

Keith Marshall

MARSHALL, KEITH ALAN
B. July 2, 1951, San Francisco, Calif.
BR TR 6'2" 175 lbs.

Year	Team		Games	BA	SA	AB	H	2B	3B	HR	HR%	R	RBI	BB	SO	SB	PH AB	PH H	PO	A	E	DP	TC/G	FA	G by Pos
1973	KC	A	8	.222	.333	9	2	1	0	0	0.0	3	1	0	4	0	0	0	6	0	0	0	0.8	1.000	OF-8

Max Marshall

MARSHALL, MILO MAX
B. Sept. 18, 1913, Shenandoah, Iowa
BL TR 6'1" 180 lbs.

Year	Team		Games	BA	SA	AB	H	2B	3B	HR	HR%	R	RBI	BB	SO	SB	PH AB	PH H	PO	A	E	DP	TC/G	FA	G by Pos
1942	CIN	N	131	.255	.349	530	135	17	6	7	1.3	49	43	34	38	4	1	0	245	3	6	2	1.9	.976	OF-129
1943			132	.236	.313	508	120	11	8	4	0.8	55	39	34	52	8	3	1	240	12	5	4	1.9	.981	OF-129

Year	Team	Games	BA	SA	AB	H	2B	3B	HR	HR%	R	RBI	BB	SO	SB	Pinch Hit AB	Pinch Hit H	PO	A	E	DP	TC/G	FA	G by Pos

Max Marshall *continued*

Year	Team	Games	BA	SA	AB	H	2B	3B	HR	HR%	R	RBI	BB	SO	SB	PH AB	PH H	PO	A	E	DP	TC/G	FA	G by Pos
1944		66	.245	.371	229	56	13	2	4	1.7	36	23	21	10	3	7	1	131	6	5	3	2.2	.965	OF-59
3 yrs.		329	.245	.339	1267	311	41	16	15	1.2	140	105	89	100	15	11	2	616	21	16	9	2.0	.975	OF-317

Mike Marshall

MARSHALL, MICHAEL ALLEN (Bigfoot)
B. Jan. 12, 1960, Libertyville, Ill.
BR TR 6'5" 215 lbs.

Year	Team	Games	BA	SA	AB	H	2B	3B	HR	HR%	R	RBI	BB	SO	SB	PH AB	PH H	PO	A	E	DP	TC/G	FA	G by Pos
1981	LA N	14	.200	.320	25	5	3	0	0	0.0	2	1	1	4	0	7	3	14	2	0	2	1.1	1.000	3B-3, 1B-3, OF-2
1982		49	.242	.432	95	23	3	0	5	5.3	10	9	13	23	2	20	3	122	5	2	6	2.6	.984	OF-19, 1B-13
1983		140	.284	.434	465	132	17	1	17	3.7	47	65	43	127	7	6	1	395	21	6	16	3.0	.986	OF-109, 1B-33
1984		134	.257	.438	495	127	27	0	21	4.2	69	65	40	93	4	7	2	331	17	5	12	2.6	.986	OF-118, 1B-15
1985		135	.293	.515	518	152	27	2	28	5.4	72	95	37	137	3	3	0	265	12	4	9	2.1	.986	OF-125, 1B-7
1986		103	.233	.439	330	77	11	0	19	5.8	47	53	27	90	4	1	0	149	8	6	1	1.6	.963	OF-97
1987		104	.294	.460	402	118	19	0	16	4.0	45	72	18	79	0	2	1	147	4	2	0	1.5	.987	OF-102
1988		144	.277	.445	542	150	27	2	20	3.7	63	82	24	93	4	0	0	605	49	7	31	4.6	.989	OF-143
1989		105	.260	.408	377	98	21	1	11	2.9	41	42	33	78	2	5	2	179	2	4	0	1.8	.978	OF-102
9 yrs.		928	.271	.449	3249	882	155	6	137	4.2	396	484	236	724	26	55	12	2207	120	36	77	2.5	.985	OF-817, 1B-71, 3B-3

DIVISIONAL PLAYOFF SERIES

Year	Team	Games	BA	SA	AB	H	2B	3B	HR	HR%	R	RBI	BB	SO	SB	PH AB	PH H	PO	A	E	DP	TC/G	FA	G by Pos
1981	LA N	1	.000	.000	1	0	0	0	0	0.0	0	0	0	1	0	1	0	0	0	0	0	0.0	—	

LEAGUE CHAMPIONSHIP SERIES

Year	Team	Games	BA	SA	AB	H	2B	3B	HR	HR%	R	RBI	BB	SO	SB	PH AB	PH H	PO	A	E	DP	TC/G	FA	G by Pos
1983	LA N	4	.133	.400	15	2	1	0	1	6.7	1	2	1	6	0	0	0	18	2	0	0	5.0	1.000	1B-3, OF-2
1985		6	.217	.435	23	5	2	0	1	4.3	1	3	1	3	0	0	0	8	0	0	0	1.3	1.000	OF-6
1988		7	.233	.333	30	7	1	0	0	0.0	3	5	2	9	0	0	0	14	0	0	0	2.0	1.000	OF-7
3 yrs.		17	.206	.382	68	14	4	0	2	2.9	5	10	4	18	0	0	0	40	2	0	0	2.5	1.000	OF-15, 1B-3

WORLD SERIES

Year	Team	Games	BA	SA	AB	H	2B	3B	HR	HR%	R	RBI	BB	SO	SB	PH AB	PH H	PO	A	E	DP	TC/G	FA	G by Pos
1988	LA N	5	.231	.615	13	3	0	1	1	7.7	2	3	0	5	0	0	0	6	0	0	0	1.2	1.000	OF-5

Willard Marshall

MARSHALL, WILLARD WARREN
B. Feb. 8, 1921, Richmond, Va.
BL TR 6'1" 205 lbs.

Year	Team	Games	BA	SA	AB	H	2B	3B	HR	HR%	R	RBI	BB	SO	SB	PH AB	PH H	PO	A	E	DP	TC/G	FA	G by Pos
1942	NY N	116	.257	.372	401	103	9	2	11	2.7	41	59	26	20	1	8	2	222	13	6	4	2.1	.975	OF-107
1946		131	.282	.406	510	144	18	3	13	2.5	63	48	33	29	3	7	2	253	14	6	2	2.1	.978	OF-125
1947		155	.291	.528	587	171	19	6	36	6.1	102	107	67	30	3	0	0	334	19	10	6	2.3	.972	OF-155
1948		143	.272	.419	537	146	21	8	14	2.6	72	86	64	34	2	0	0	266	16	5	2	2.0	.983	OF-142
1949		141	.307	.429	499	153	19	3	12	2.4	81	70	78	20	4	3	1	292	13	8	3	2.2	.974	OF-138
1950	BOS N	105	.235	.332	298	70	10	2	5	1.7	38	40	36	5	1	20	4	150	11	7	2	1.6	.958	OF-85
1951		136	.281	.433	469	132	24	7	11	2.3	65	62	48	18	0	7	1	220	11	0	3	1.7	1.000	OF-127
1952	2 teams	BOS N	(21G – .227)		CIN N	(107G – .267)																		
"	total	128	.261	.393	463	121	27	2	10	2.2	57	57	41	25	0	9	0	215	16	5	5	1.8	.979	OF-121
1953	CIN N	122	.266	.482	357	95	14	6	17	4.8	51	62	41	28	0	33	4	187	11	1	1	1.6	.995	OF-95
1954	CHI A	47	.254	.324	71	18	2	0	1	1.4	7	7	11	9	0	19	4	23	1	1	0	0.5	.960	OF-29
1955		22	.171	.171	41	7	0	0	0	0.0	6	6	13	1	0	7	0	22	0	1	0	1.0	.957	OF-12
11 yrs.		1246	.274	.423	4233	1160	163	39	130	3.1	583	604	458	219	14	113	18	2184	125	50	28	1.9	.979	OF-1136

Marty Martel

MARTEL, LEON ALPHONSE (Doc)
B. Jan. 29, 1883, Weymouth, Mass. D. Oct. 11, 1947, Washington, D. C.
BR TR 6' 185 lbs.

Year	Team	Games	BA	SA	AB	H	2B	3B	HR	HR%	R	RBI	BB	SO	SB	PH AB	PH H	PO	A	E	DP	TC/G	FA	G by Pos
1909	PHI N	24	.268	.390	41	11	3	1	0	0.0	1		7	4		10	3	56	19	2	1	3.2	.974	C-12
1910	BOS N	10	.129	.129	31	4	0	0	0	0.0	0	1	2	3	0	1	0	92	5	2	5	9.9	.980	1B-10
2 yrs.		34	.208	.278	72	15	3	1	0	0.0	1	8	6	3	0	11	3	148	24	4	6	5.2	.977	C-12, 1B-10

Babe Martin

MARTIN, BORIS MICHAEL
Born Boris Michael Martinovich.
B. Mar. 28, 1920, Seattle, Wash.
BR TR 5'11½" 194 lbs.

Year	Team	Games	BA	SA	AB	H	2B	3B	HR	HR%	R	RBI	BB	SO	SB	PH AB	PH H	PO	A	E	DP	TC/G	FA	G by Pos
1944	STL A	2	.750	1.000	4	3	0	0	0	0.0	0	0	0	0	0	1	1	1	0	0	0	0.5	1.000	OF-1
1945		54	.200	.281	185	37	5	2	2	1.1	13	16	11	24	0	1	1	152	11	3	3	3.1	.982	OF-48, 1B-6
1946		3	.222	.222	9	2	0	0	0	0.0	0	1	1	2	0	1	1	18	0	0	0	6.0	1.000	C-2
1948	BOS A	4	.500	.500	4	2	0	0	0	0.0	0	0	0	1	0	1	1	0	0	0	0	0.0	—	C-1
1949		2	.000	.000	2	0	0	0	0	0.0	0	0	0	0	0	1	0	0	0	0	0	0.0	—	C-1
1953	STL A	4	.000	.000	2	0	0	0	0	0.0	0	0	1	0	0	2	0	0	0	0	0	0.0	—	C-1
6 yrs.		69	.214	.291	206	44	6	2	2	1.0	13	18	13	27	0	9	4	171	11	3	3	2.7	.984	OF-49, 1B-6, C-5

Bill Martin

MARTIN, WILLIAM LLOYD
B. Feb. 13, 1894, Washington, D. C. D. Sept. 14, 1949, Arlington, Va.
BR TR 5'8½" 170 lbs.

Year	Team	Games	BA	SA	AB	H	2B	3B	HR	HR%	R	RBI	BB	SO	SB	PH AB	PH H	PO	A	E	DP	TC/G	FA	G by Pos
1914	BOS N	1	.000	.000	3	0	0	0	0	0.0	0	0	0	0	0	0	0	0	1	1	0	2.0	.500	SS-1

Billy Martin

MARTIN, ALFRED MANUEL (The Kid)
Born Alfred Manuel Pesano.
B. May 16, 1928, Berkeley, Calif. D. Dec. 25, 1989, Johnson City, N. Y.
Manager 1969, 1971-83, 1985, 1988.
BR TR 5'11½" 165 lbs.

Year	Team	Games	BA	SA	AB	H	2B	3B	HR	HR%	R	RBI	BB	SO	SB	PH AB	PH H	PO	A	E	DP	TC/G	FA	G by Pos
1950	NY A	34	.250	.361	36	9	1	0	1	2.8	10	8	3	3	0	10	2	24	16	1	5	1.2	.976	2B-22, 3B-1
1951		51	.259	.345	58	15	1	2	0	0.0	10	2	4	9	0	10	0	45	62	4	17	2.2	.964	2B-23, SS-6, 3B-2, OF-1
1952		109	.267	.344	363	97	13	3	3	0.8	32	33	22	31	3	1	0	244	323	9	92	5.3	.984	2B-107
1953		149	.257	.395	587	151	24	6	15	2.6	72	75	43	56	6	1	0	389	409	14	126	5.4	.983	2B-146, SS-18
1955		20	.300	.371	70	21	2	0	1	1.4	8	9	7	9	1	0	0	46	50	3	20	5.0	.970	2B-17, SS-3
1956		121	.264	.397	458	121	24	5	9	2.0	76	49	30	56	7	1	0	253	288	15	87	4.6	.973	2B-105, 3B-16
1957	2 teams	NY A	(43G – .241)		KC A	(73G – .257)																		
"	total	116	.251	.383	410	103	14	5	10	2.4	45	39	15	34	9	5	0	220	232	13	53	4.0	.972	2B-78, 3B-33, SS-2
1958	DET A	131	.255	.339	498	127	19	4	7	1.4	56	42	16	62	5	2	0	206	288	20	63	3.9	.961	SS-88, 3B-41
1959	CLE A	73	.260	.401	242	63	7	0	9	3.7	37	24	7	18	0	1	0	150	153	2	37	4.2	.993	2B-67, 3B-4
1960	CIN N	103	.246	.334	317	78	17	1	3	0.9	34	16	27	34	0	4	0	228	207	11	52	4.3	.975	2B-97

Year	Team		Games	BA	SA	AB	H	2B	3B	HR	HR%	R	RBI	BB	SO	SB	Pinch Hit AB	Pinch Hit H	PO	A	E	DP	TC/G	FA	G by Pos

Billy Martin *continued*

Year	Team		Games	BA	SA	AB	H	2B	3B	HR	HR%	R	RBI	BB	SO	SB	AB	H	PO	A	E	DP	TC/G	FA	G by Pos
1961	2 teams	MIL N (6G – .000)				MIN A (108G – .246)																				
"	total		114	.242	.355	380	92	15	5	6	1.6	45	36	13	43	3	9	1	217	224	17	61	4.0	.963	2B-105, SS-1
	11 yrs.		1021	.257	.369	3419	877	137	28	64	1.9	425	333	187	355	34	44	3	2022	2252	109	613	4.3	.975	2B-767, SS-118, 3B-97, OF-1

WORLD SERIES

Year	Team		Games	BA	SA	AB	H	2B	3B	HR	HR%	R	RBI	BB	SO	SB	AB	H	PO	A	E	DP	TC/G	FA	G by Pos
1951	NY	A	1	–	–	0	0	0	0	0	–	1	0	0	0	0	0	0	0	0	0	0	0.0	–	
1952			7	.217	.348	23	5	0	0	1	4.3	2	4	2	2	0	0	0	16	16	1	5	4.7	.970	2B-7
1953			6	.500	.958	24	12	1	2	2	8.3	5	8	1	2	1	0	0	13	15	0	3	4.7	1.000	2B-6
1955			7	.320	.440	25	8	1	1	0	0.0	2	4	1	5	0	0	0	17	20	0	7	5.3	1.000	2B-7
1956			7	.296	.519	27	8	0	0	2	7.4	5	3	1	6	0	0	0	12	18	0	4	4.3	1.000	2B-7, 3B-2
	5 yrs.		28	.333	.566	99	33	2	3	5	5.1	15	19	5	15	1	0	0	58	69	1	19	4.6	.992	2B-27, 3B-2
									4th																	

Frank Martin

MARTIN, FRANK
B. 1877, Chicago, Ill. Deceased.

Year	Team		Games	BA	SA	AB	H	2B	3B	HR	HR%	R	RBI	BB	SO	SB	AB	H	PO	A	E	DP	TC/G	FA	G by Pos
1897	LOU	N	2	.250	.250	8	2	0	0	0	0.0	1	0	0		0	0	0	4	9	3	0	8.0	.813	2B-2
1898	CHI	N	1	.000	.000	4	0	0	0	0	0.0	0	0	0		0	0	0	5	2	0	0	7.0	1.000	2B-1
1899	NY	N	17	.259	.296	54	14	2	0	0	0.0	5	1	2		0	0	0	24	37	13	5	4.4	.824	3B-17
	3 yrs.		20	.242	.273	66	16	2	0	0	0.0	6	1	2		0	0	0	33	48	16	5	4.9	.835	3B-17, 2B-3

Gene Martin

MARTIN, THOMAS EUGENE
B. Jan. 12, 1947, Americus, Ga.   BL TR 6'½" 190 lbs.

Year	Team		Games	BA	SA	AB	H	2B	3B	HR	HR%	R	RBI	BB	SO	SB	AB	H	PO	A	E	DP	TC/G	FA	G by Pos
1968	WAS	A	9	.364	.727	11	4	1	0	1	9.1	1	1	0	1	0	7	3	0	0	0	0	0.0	–	OF-2

Hersh Martin

MARTIN, HERSHEL RAY
B. Sept. 19, 1909, Birmingham, Ala.   D. Nov. 17, 1980, Cuba, Mo.   BB TR 6'2" 190 lbs.

Year	Team		Games	BA	SA	AB	H	2B	3B	HR	HR%	R	RBI	BB	SO	SB	AB	H	PO	A	E	DP	TC/G	FA	G by Pos
1937	PHI	N	141	.283	.409	579	164	35	7	8	1.4	102	49	69	66	11	2	0	353	9	8	1	2.6	.978	OF-139
1938			120	.298	.421	466	139	36	6	3	0.6	58	39	34	48	8	4	3	298	7	11	2	2.6	.965	OF-116
1939			111	.282	.387	393	111	28	5	1	0.3	59	22	42	27	4	14	3	276	5	7	1	2.6	.979	OF-95
1940			33	.253	.349	83	21	6	1	0	0.0	10	5	9	9	1	10	4	42	4	1	0	1.4	.979	OF-23
1944	NY	A	85	.302	.445	328	99	12	4	9	2.7	49	47	34	26	5	5	1	177	8	7	4	2.3	.964	OF-80
1945			117	.267	.392	408	109	18	6	7	1.7	53	53	65	31	4	14	5	233	8	4	1	2.1	.984	OF-102
	6 yrs.		607	.285	.408	2257	643	135	29	28	1.2	331	215	253	207	33	49	16	1379	41	38	9	2.4	.974	OF-555

J. C. Martin

MARTIN, JOSEPH CLIFTON
B. Dec. 13, 1936, Axton, Va.   BL TR 6'2" 188 lbs.

Year	Team		Games	BA	SA	AB	H	2B	3B	HR	HR%	R	RBI	BB	SO	SB	AB	H	PO	A	E	DP	TC/G	FA	G by Pos
1959	CHI	A	3	.250	.250	4	1	0	0	0	0.0	0	1	0	1	0	0	0	0	0	0	0	1.0	.667	3B-2
1960			4	.100	.150	20	2	1	0	0	0.0	0	2	0	6	0	0	0	8	8	0	0	4.0	1.000	3B-5, 1B-1
1961			110	.230	.336	274	63	8	3	5	1.8	26	32	21	31	1	11	2	353	118	10	38	4.4	.979	1B-60, 3B-36
1962			18	.077	.077	26	2	0	0	0	0.0	0	2	0	3	0	11	0	19	2	0	0	1.2	1.000	C-6, 3B-1, 1B-1
1963			105	.205	.313	259	53	11	1	5	1.9	25	28	26	35	0	12	3	476	49	9	9	5.1	.983	C-98, 1B-3, 3B-1
1964			122	.197	.279	294	58	10	4	4	1.4	23	22	16	30	0	6	0	530	43	8	6	4.8	.986	C-120
1965			119	.261	.339	230	60	12	0	2	0.9	21	21	24	29	2	15	3	385	43	7	7	3.7	.984	C-112, 1B-4, 3B-2
1966			67	.255	.363	157	40	5	3	2	1.3	13	20	14	24	0	4	1	243	23	5	3	4.0	.982	C-63
1967			101	.234	.337	252	59	12	1	4	1.6	22	22	30	41	4	6	1	479	39	7	3	5.2	.987	C-96, 1B-1
1968	NY	N	78	.225	.316	244	55	9	2	3	1.2	20	31	21	31	0	8	1	458	31	6	11	6.3	.987	C-53, 1B-14
1969			66	.209	.316	177	37	5	1	4	2.3	12	21	12	32	1	18	0	279	9	1	2	4.5	.997	C-48, 1B-2
1970	CHI	N	40	.156	.208	77	12	1	0	1	1.3	11	4	20	1	0	3	0	164	16	5	2	4.6	.973	C-36, 1B-3
1971			47	.264	.352	125	33	5	0	2	1.6	13	17	12	16	1	5	0	218	21	1	2	5.1	.996	C-43, OF-1
1972			25	.240	.300	50	12	3	0	0	0.0	3	7	5	9	1	9	2	60	4	2	1	2.6	.970	C-17
	14 yrs.		905	.222	.315	2189	487	82	12	32	1.5	189	230	201	299	9	109	16	3672	408	62	84	4.6	.985	C-692, 1B-89, 3B-47, OF-1

LEAGUE CHAMPIONSHIP SERIES

Year	Team		Games	BA	SA	AB	H	2B	3B	HR	HR%	R	RBI	BB	SO	SB	AB	H	PO	A	E	DP	TC/G	FA	G by Pos
1969	NY	N	2	.500	.500	2	1	0	0	0	0.0	0	2	0	0	0	2	1	0	0	0	0	0.0	–	

WORLD SERIES

Year	Team		Games	BA	SA	AB	H	2B	3B	HR	HR%	R	RBI	BB	SO	SB	AB	H	PO	A	E	DP	TC/G	FA	G by Pos
1969	NY	N	1	–	–	0	0	0	0	0	–	0	0	0	0	0	0	0	0	0	0	0	0.0	–	

Jack Martin

MARTIN, JOHN CHRISTOPHER
B. Apr. 19, 1887, Plainfield, N. J.   D. July 4, 1980, Bronx, N. Y.   BR TR 5'9" 159 lbs.

Year	Team		Games	BA	SA	AB	H	2B	3B	HR	HR%	R	RBI	BB	SO	SB	AB	H	PO	A	E	DP	TC/G	FA	G by Pos
1912	NY	A	69	.225	.260	231	52	6	1	0	0.0	30	17	37		14	0	0	127	217	39	18	5.6	.898	SS-64, 3B-4, 2B-1
1914	2 teams	BOS N (33G – .212)				PHI N (83G – .253)																				
"	total		116	.244	.279	377	92	7	3	0	0.0	36	26	33	36	6	3	0	217	294	38	29	4.7	.931	SS-83, 3B-27, 2B-1, 1B-1
	2 yrs.		185	.237	.271	608	144	13	4	0	0.0	66	43	70	36	20	3	0	344	511	77	47	5.0	.917	SS-147, 3B-31, 2B-2, 1B-1

Jerry Martin

MARTIN, JERRY LINDSEY
Son of Barney Martin.
B. May 11, 1949, Columbia, S. C.   BR TR 6'1" 195 lbs.

Year	Team		Games	BA	SA	AB	H	2B	3B	HR	HR%	R	RBI	BB	SO	SB	AB	H	PO	A	E	DP	TC/G	FA	G by Pos
1974	PHI	N	13	.214	.286	14	3	1	0	0	0.0	2	1	1	5	0	4	1	5	0	0	0	0.4	1.000	OF-11
1975			57	.212	.345	113	24	7	1	2	1.8	15	11	11	16	2	9	1	90	3	2	1	1.7	.979	OF-49
1976			130	.248	.355	121	30	7	0	2	1.7	30	15	7	28	3	22	6	85	0	2	0	0.7	.977	OF-110, 1B-1
1977			116	.260	.447	215	56	16	3	6	2.8	34	28	18	42	6	18	5	117	4	2	1	1.1	.984	OF-106, 1B-1
1978			128	.271	.451	266	72	13	4	9	3.4	40	36	28	65	9	24	5	148	8	2	1	1.2	.987	OF-112
1979	CHI	N	150	.272	.453	534	145	34	3	19	3.6	74	73	38	85	22	2	2	297	11	6	4	2.1	.981	OF-144
1980			141	.227	.419	494	112	22	2	23	4.7	57	73	38	107	8	11	2	262	8	6	0	2.0	.978	OF-129
1981	SF	N	72	.241	.336	241	58	5	3	4	1.7	23	25	21	52	6	7	0	138	4	1	1	2.0	.993	OF-64
1982	KC	A	147	.266	.399	519	138	22	1	15	2.9	52	65	38	138	1	7	1	333	4	5	1	2.3	.980	OF-142, DH-3
1983			13	.318	.500	44	14	2	0	2	4.5	4	13	1	7	1	0	0	22	0	1	0	1.8	.957	OF-13
1984	NY	N	51	.154	.264	91	14	1	0	3	3.3	6	5	6	29	0	24	3	56	1	0	5	1.2	1.000	OF-30, 1B-3
	11 yrs.		1018	.251	.409	2652	666	130	17	85	3.2	337	345	207	574	38	134	26	1553	45	29	17	1.6	.982	OF-910, 1B-5, DH-3

Year	Team	Games	BA	SA	AB	H	2B	3B	HR	HR%	R	RBI	BB	SO	SB	Pinch Hit AB	H	PO	A	E	DP	TC/G	FA	G by Pos

Jerry Martin *continued*
LEAGUE CHAMPIONSHIP SERIES

Year	Team	Games	BA	SA	AB	H	2B	3B	HR	HR%	R	RBI	BB	SO	SB	AB	H	PO	A	E	DP	TC/G	FA	G by Pos
1976	PHI N	1	.000	.000	1	0	0	0	0	0.0	1	0	0	0	0	0	0	1	0	0	0	1.0	1.000	OF-1
1977		3	.000	.000	4	0	0	0	0	0.0	0	0	0	2	0	1	0	1	0	0	0	0.3	1.000	OF-1
1978		4	.222	.667	9	2	1	0	1	11.1	1	2	1	3	0	2	1	7	0	0	0	1.8	1.000	OF-3
3 yrs.		8	.143	.429	14	2	1	0	1	7.1	2	2	1	5	0	3	1	9	0	0	0	1.1	1.000	OF-5

Joe Martin
MARTIN, JOSEPH SAMUEL (Silent Joe)
B. Jan. 1, 1876, Hollidaysburg, Pa. D. May 25, 1964, Altoona, Pa.
BL TR 5'9½" 155 lbs.

Year	Team	Games	BA	SA	AB	H	2B	3B	HR	HR%	R	RBI	BB	SO	SB	AB	H	PO	A	E	DP	TC/G	FA	G by Pos
1903 **2 teams**					WAS A (35G – .227)				STL A	(44G – .214)														
" total		79	.219	.315	292	64	10	9	0	0.0	29	14	11		2	1	1	119	82	21	9	2.8	.905	OF-45, 2B-21, 3B-14

Joe Martin
MARTIN, WILLIAM JOSEPH (Smokey Joe)
B. Aug. 28, 1911, Seymour, Mo. D. Sept. 28, 1960, Buffalo, N. Y.
BR TR 5'11½" 181 lbs.

Year	Team	Games	BA	SA	AB	H	2B	3B	HR	HR%	R	RBI	BB	SO	SB	AB	H	PO	A	E	DP	TC/G	FA	G by Pos
1936	NY N	7	.267	.333	15	4	1	0	0	0.0	0	2	0	4	0	0	0	5	8	0	1	1.9	1.000	3B-7
1938	CHI A	1	–	–	0	0	0	0	0	–	0	0	0	0	0	0	0	0	0	0	0	0.0	–	
2 yrs.		8	.267	.333	15	4	1	0	0	0.0	0	2	0	4	0	0	0	5	8	0	1	1.6	1.000	3B-7

Mike Martin
MARTIN, JOSEPH MICHAEL
B. Dec. 3, 1958, Portland, Ore.
BL TR 6'2" 193 lbs.

Year	Team	Games	BA	SA	AB	H	2B	3B	HR	HR%	R	RBI	BB	SO	SB	AB	H	PO	A	E	DP	TC/G	FA	G by Pos
1986	CHI N	8	.077	.154	13	1	1	0	0	0.0	1	0	2	4	0	1	0	18	5	0	0	2.9	1.000	C-8

Pepper Martin
MARTIN, JOHN LEONARD ROOSEVELT (The Wild Hoss Of The Osage)
B. Feb. 29, 1904, Temple, Okla. D. Mar. 5, 1965, McAlester, Okla.
BR TR 5'8" 170 lbs.

Year	Team	Games	BA	SA	AB	H	2B	3B	HR	HR%	R	RBI	BB	SO	SB	AB	H	PO	A	E	DP	TC/G	FA	G by Pos
1928	STL N	39	.308	.308	13	4	0	0	0	0.0	11	0	1	2	2	12	3	2	0	0	0	0.1	1.000	OF-4
1930		6	.000	.000	1	0	0	0	0	0.0	5	0	0	0	0	1	0	0	0	0	0	0.0	–	
1931		123	.300	.467	413	124	33	8	7	1.7	68	75	30	40	16	7	4	282	10	10	2	2.5	.967	OF-110
1932		85	.238	.372	323	77	19	6	4	1.2	47	34	30	31	9	0	0	169	28	5	4	2.4	.975	OF-69, 3B-15
1933		145	.316	.456	599	189	36	12	8	1.3	**122**	57	67	46	**26**	0	0	139	273	25	14	3.0	.943	3B-145
1934		110	.289	.425	454	131	25	11	5	1.1	76	49	32	41	23	1	0	85	196	19	7	2.7	.937	3B-107, P-1
1935		135	.299	.447	539	161	41	6	9	1.7	121	54	33	58	20	5	0	145	171	32	17	2.6	.908	3B-114, OF-16
1936		143	.309	.469	572	177	36	11	11	1.9	121	76	58	66	23	1	0	239	25	13	6	1.9	.953	OF-127, 3B-15, P-1
1937		98	.304	.475	339	103	27	8	5	1.5	60	38	33	50	9	9	2	210	20	7	5	2.4	.970	OF-82, 3B-5
1938		91	.294	.398	269	79	18	2	2	0.7	34	38	18	34	4	23	5	139	4	2	1	1.6	.986	OF-62, 3B-1
1939		88	.306	.448	281	86	17	7	3	1.1	48	37	30	35	6	10	0	128	34	7	2	1.9	.959	OF-51, 3B-22
1940		86	.316	.456	228	72	15	4	3	1.3	28	39	22	24	6	17	4	106	13	3	0	1.4	.975	OF-63, 3B-2
1944		40	.279	.395	86	24	4	0	2	2.3	15	4	15	11	2	5	1	48	1	1	0	1.3	.980	OF-29
13 yrs.		1189	.298	.443	4117	1227	270	75	59	1.4	756	501	369	438	146	91	19	1692	775	124	58	2.2	.952	OF-613, 3B-429, P-2

WORLD SERIES

Year	Team	Games	BA	SA	AB	H	2B	3B	HR	HR%	R	RBI	BB	SO	SB	AB	H	PO	A	E	DP	TC/G	FA	G by Pos
1928	STL N	1	–	–	0	0	0	0	0	–	1	0	0	0	0	0	0	0	0	0	0	0.0	–	
1931		7	.500	.792	24	12	4	0	1	4.2	5	5	2	3	5	0	0	10	0	0	0	1.4	1.000	OF-7
1934		7	.355	.516	31	11	3	1	0	0.0	8	3	3	3	2	0	0	6	9	4	0	2.7	.789	3B-7
3 yrs.		15	.418	.636	55	23	7	1	1	1.8	14	8	5	6	7	0	0	16	9	4	0	1.9	.862	OF-7, 3B-7
			1st	7th			9th								9th									

Stu Martin
MARTIN, STUART McGUIRE
B. Nov. 17, 1913, Rich Square, N. C.
BL TR 6' 155 lbs.

Year	Team	Games	BA	SA	AB	H	2B	3B	HR	HR%	R	RBI	BB	SO	SB	AB	H	PO	A	E	DP	TC/G	FA	G by Pos
1936	STL N	92	.298	.440	332	99	21	4	6	1.8	63	41	29	27	17	4	0	173	250	22	52	4.8	.951	2B-83, SS-3
1937		90	.260	.309	223	58	6	1	1	0.4	34	17	32	18	3	28	6	168	138	14	30	3.6	.956	2B-48, 1B-9, SS-1
1938		114	.278	.357	417	116	26	2	1	0.2	54	27	30	28	4	15	3	225	301	18	59	4.8	.967	2B-99
1939		120	.268	.384	425	114	26	7	3	0.7	60	30	33	40	4	11	0	249	305	13	62	4.7	.977	2B-107, 1B-1
1940		112	.238	.336	369	88	12	6	4	1.1	45	32	33	33	5	9	1	99	160	7	14	2.4	.974	3B-73, 2B-33
1941	PIT N	88	.305	.378	233	71	13	2	0	0.0	37	19	10	17	2	28	6	134	157	9	26	3.4	.970	2B-53, 3B-2, 1B-1
1942		42	.225	.317	120	27	4	2	1	0.8	16	12	8	10	1	10	0	69	70	3	14	3.4	.979	2B-30, SS-1, 1B-1
1943	CHI N	64	.220	.254	118	26	4	0	0	0.0	13	5	15	10	1	25	5	64	69	2	11	2.1	.985	2B-22, 3B-8, 1B-2
8 yrs.		722	.268	.361	2237	599	112	24	16	0.7	322	183	190	185	36	130	21	1181	1450	88	268	3.8	.968	2B-475, 3B-83, 1B-14, SS-5

Buck Martinez
MARTINEZ, JOHN ALBERT
B. Nov. 7, 1948, Redding, Calif.
BR TR 5'10" 190 lbs.

Year	Team	Games	BA	SA	AB	H	2B	3B	HR	HR%	R	RBI	BB	SO	SB	AB	H	PO	A	E	DP	TC/G	FA	G by Pos
1969	KC A	72	.229	.327	205	47	6	1	4	2.0	14	23	8	25	0	18	4	292	26	9	8	4.5	.972	C-55, OF-1
1970		6	.111	.111	9	1	0	0	0	0.0	1	0	2	1	0	1	0	20	3	1	0	4.0	.958	C-5
1971		22	.152	.196	46	7	2	0	0	0.0	3	1	5	9	0	1	0	84	6	3	0	4.2	.968	C-21
1973		14	.250	.375	32	8	1	0	1	3.1	2	4	4	5	0	0	0	52	4	2	1	4.1	.966	C-14
1974		43	.215	.290	107	23	3	1	1	0.9	10	8	14	19	0	4	2	151	16	4	1	4.0	.977	C-38
1975		80	.226	.323	226	51	9	2	3	1.3	15	23	21	28	1	1	0	361	39	8	4	5.1	.980	C-79
1976		95	.228	.356	267	61	13	2	5	1.9	24	34	16	45	0	4	1	420	40	4	4	4.9	.991	C-94
1977		29	.225	.313	80	18	4	0	1	1.3	9	9	3	12	0	2	0	133	8	1	0	4.9	.993	C-29
1978	MIL A	89	.219	.277	256	56	10	1	1	0.4	26	20	14	42	1	0	0	327	32	8	7	4.1	.978	C-89
1979		69	.270	.372	196	53	8	0	4	2.0	17	26	8	25	0	0	0	198	39	8	2	3.6	.967	C-68, P-1
1980		76	.224	.306	219	49	9	0	3	1.4	16	17	12	33	1	0	0	293	33	5	0	4.4	.985	C-76
1981	TOR A	45	.227	.398	128	29	8	1	4	3.1	13	21	11	16	1	0	0	192	22	2	3	4.8	.991	C-45
1982		96	.242	.423	260	63	17	0	10	3.8	26	37	24	34	1	10	4	382	35	5	8	4.4	.988	C-93
1983		88	.253	.452	221	56	14	0	10	4.5	27	33	29	39	0	12	4	331	25	4	3	4.1	.989	C-85
1984		102	.220	.349	232	51	13	1	5	2.2	24	37	29	49	0	18	0	360	34	2	5	3.9	.995	C-98, DH-1
1985		42	.162	.313	99	16	1	0	4	4.0	11	14	10	12	0	1	0	155	16	2	5	4.1	.988	C-42
1986		81	.181	.269	160	29	8	0	2	1.3	13	12	20	25	0	17	4	289	19	2	6	3.8	.994	C-78, DH-1
17 yrs.		1049	.225	.343	2743	618	128	10	58	2.1	245	321	230	419	5	92	21	4040	397	70	57	4.3	.984	C-1009, DH-2, OF-1, P-1

LEAGUE CHAMPIONSHIP SERIES

Year	Team	Games	BA	SA	AB	H	2B	3B	HR	HR%	R	RBI	BB	SO	SB	AB	H	PO	A	E	DP	TC/G	FA	G by Pos
1976	KC A	5	.333	.333	15	5	0	0	0	0.0	0	4	0	3	0	0	0	15	4	0	1	3.8	1.000	C-5

Year	Team		Games	BA	SA	AB	H	2B	3B	HR	HR%	R	RBI	BB	SO	SB	Pinch Hit AB	Pinch Hit H	PO	A	E	DP	TC/G	FA	G by Pos

Carlos Martinez

MARTINEZ, CARLOS ALBERTO
Born Carlos Alberto Escobar y Martinez.
B. Aug. 11, 1964, LaGuaira, Venezuela

BR TR 6'5" 175 lbs.

Year	Team		Games	BA	SA	AB	H	2B	3B	HR	HR%	R	RBI	BB	SO	SB	PH AB	PH H	PO	A	E	DP	TC/G	FA	G by Pos
1988	CHI	A	17	.164	.182	55	9	1	0	0	0.0	5	0	0	12	1	0	0	7	33	4	1	2.6	.909	3B-15
1989			109	.300	.406	350	105	22	0	5	1.4	44	32	21	57	4	5	2	283	134	20	25	4.0	.954	3B-68, 1B-34, OF-10, DH-1
2 yrs.			126	.281	.375	405	114	23	0	5	1.2	49	32	21	69	5	5	2	290	167	24	26	3.8	.950	3B-83, 1B-34, OF-10, DH-1

Carmelo Martinez

MARTINEZ, CARMELO
Born Carmelo Martinez y Salgado.
B. July 28, 1960, Dorado, Puerto Rico

BR TR 6'2" 185 lbs.

Year	Team		Games	BA	SA	AB	H	2B	3B	HR	HR%	R	RBI	BB	SO	SB	PH AB	PH H	PO	A	E	DP	TC/G	FA	G by Pos
1983	CHI	N	29	.258	.494	89	23	3	0	6	6.7	8	16	4	19	0	4	1	233	17	2	18	8.7	.992	1B-26, OF-1, 3B-1
1984	SD	N	149	.250	.395	488	122	28	2	13	2.7	64	66	68	82	1	4	0	317	15	8	4	2.3	.976	OF-142, 1B-2
1985			150	.253	.434	514	130	28	1	21	4.1	64	72	87	82	0	0	0	302	14	7	5	2.2	.978	OF-150, 1B-3
1986			113	.238	.389	244	58	10	0	9	3.7	28	25	35	46	1	36	8	142	14	2	4	1.4	.987	OF-60, 1B-26, 3B-1
1987			139	.273	.430	447	122	21	2	15	3.4	59	70	70	82	5	7	1	591	42	9	41	4.6	.986	OF-78, 1B-65
1988			121	.236	.416	365	86	12	0	18	4.9	48	65	35	57	1	28	8	430	32	4	31	3.9	.991	OF-64, 1B-41
1989			111	.221	.348	267	59	12	2	6	2.2	23	39	32	54	0	32	7	225	18	2	11	2.2	.992	OF-65, 1B-32
7 yrs.			812	.249	.411	2414	600	114	7	88	3.6	294	353	331	422	8	111	25	2240	152	34	114	3.0	.986	OF-560, 1B-195, 3B-2
LEAGUE CHAMPIONSHIP SERIES																									
1984	SD	N	5	.176	.176	17	3	0	0	0	0.0	1	0	2	4	0	0	0	6	0	0	0	1.2	1.000	OF-5
WORLD SERIES																									
1984	SD	N	5	.176	.176	17	3	0	0	0	0.0	0	0	0	9	0	0	0	7	0	1	0	1.6	.875	OF-5

Dave Martinez

MARTINEZ, DAVID
B. Sept. 26, 1964, New York, N. Y.

BL TL 5'10" 150 lbs.

Year	Team		Games	BA	SA	AB	H	2B	3B	HR	HR%	R	RBI	BB	SO	SB	PH AB	PH H	PO	A	E	DP	TC/G	FA	G by Pos
1986	CHI	N	53	.139	.194	108	15	1	1	1	0.9	13	7	6	22	4	5	1	77	2	1	1	1.5	.988	OF-46
1987			142	.292	.418	459	134	18	8	8	1.7	70	36	57	96	16	11	3	283	10	6	1	2.1	.980	OF-139
1988	2 teams		CHI N (75G – .254)			MON N (63G – .257)																			
"	total		138	.255	.351	447	114	13	6	6	1.3	51	46	38	94	23	11	4	281	4	6	1	2.1	.979	OF-132
1989	MON	N	126	.274	.382	361	99	16	7	3	0.8	41	27	27	57	23	11	1	199	7	7	1	1.7	.967	OF-118
4 yrs.			459	.263	.369	1375	362	48	22	18	1.3	175	116	128	269	66	38	8	840	23	20	4	1.9	.977	OF-435

Edgar Martinez

MARTINEZ, EDGAR
B. Jan. 2, 1963, New York, N. Y.

BR TR 6' 175 lbs.

Year	Team		Games	BA	SA	AB	H	2B	3B	HR	HR%	R	RBI	BB	SO	SB	PH AB	PH H	PO	A	E	DP	TC/G	FA	G by Pos
1987	SEA	A	13	.372	.581	43	16	5	2	0	0.0	6	5	2	5	0	1	0	13	19	0	1	2.5	1.000	3B-12, DH-1
1988			14	.281	.406	32	9	4	0	0	0.0	0	5	4	7	0	1	1	5	8	1	1	1.0	.929	3B-13
1989			65	.240	.304	171	41	5	0	2	1.2	20	20	17	26	2	8	1	40	72	6	9	1.8	.949	3B-61
3 yrs.			92	.268	.366	246	66	14	2	2	0.8	26	30	23	38	2	10	2	58	99	7	11	1.8	.957	3B-86, DH-1

Hector Martinez

MARTINEZ, RODOLFO HECTOR
B. May 11, 1939, Las Villas, Cuba

BR TR 5'10" 160 lbs.

Year	Team		Games	BA	SA	AB	H	2B	3B	HR	HR%	R	RBI	BB	SO	SB	PH AB	PH H	PO	A	E	DP	TC/G	FA	G by Pos
1962	KC	A	1	.000	.000	1	0	0	0	0	0.0	0	0	0	1	0	1	0	0	0	0	0	0.0	–	
1963			6	.286	.500	14	4	0	0	1	7.1	2	3	1	3	0	3	0	7	0	0	0	1.2	1.000	OF-3
2 yrs.			7	.267	.467	15	4	0	0	1	6.7	2	3	1	4	0	4	0	7	0	0	0	1.0	1.000	OF-3

Jose Martinez

MARTINEZ, JOSE
Born Jose Martinez y Azcuiz.
B. July 26, 1942, Cardenas, Cuba

BR TR 6' 178 lbs.

Year	Team		Games	BA	SA	AB	H	2B	3B	HR	HR%	R	RBI	BB	SO	SB	PH AB	PH H	PO	A	E	DP	TC/G	FA	G by Pos
1969	PIT	N	77	.268	.321	168	45	6	0	1	0.6	20	16	9	32	1	6	2	86	132	6	31	2.9	.973	2B-42, SS-20, 3B-5, OF-2
1970			19	.050	.050	20	1	0	0	0	0.0	1	0	1	5	0	3	0	12	17	3	4	1.7	.906	3B-7, 2B-4, SS-1
2 yrs.			96	.245	.293	188	46	6	0	1	0.5	21	16	10	37	1	9	2	98	149	9	35	2.7	.965	2B-46, SS-21, 3B-12, OF-2

Marty Martinez

MARTINEZ, ORLANDO
Born Orlando Martinez y Oliva.
B. Aug. 23, 1941, Havana, Cuba
Manager 1986.

BB TR 6' 170 lbs.
BR 1962

Year	Team		Games	BA	SA	AB	H	2B	3B	HR	HR%	R	RBI	BB	SO	SB	PH AB	PH H	PO	A	E	DP	TC/G	FA	G by Pos
1962	MIN	A	37	.167	.278	18	3	0	1	0	0.0	13	3	3	4	0	0	0	6	18	2	2	0.7	.923	SS-11, 3B-1
1967	ATL	N	44	.288	.342	73	21	2	1	0	0.0	14	5	11	11	0	0	0	45	73	9	16	2.9	.929	SS-25, 2B-9, C-3, 3B-2, 1B-1
1968			113	.230	.261	356	82	5	3	0	0.0	34	12	29	28	6	1	0	169	264	18	44	4.0	.960	SS-54, 3B-37, 2B-16, C-14
1969	HOU	N	78	.308	.374	198	61	5	4	0	0.0	14	15	10	21	0	18	4	77	66	11	8	2.9	.929	OF-21, SS-17, 3B-15, C-7, 2B-1, P-1
1970			75	.220	.240	150	33	3	0	0	0.0	12	12	9	22	0	38	9	57	78	2	10	1.8	.985	SS-29, 3B-10, C-6, 2B-4
1971			32	.258	.339	62	16	3	1	0	0.0	4	4	3	6	1	13	4	29	37	1	7	2.1	.985	2B-9, SS-7, 1B-4, 3B-3
1972	3 teams		STL N (9G – .429)			TEX A (26G – .146)			OAK A (22G – .125)																
"	total		57	.159	.193	88	14	1	1	0	0.0	6	6	5	15	0	19	4	44	56	7	11	1.9	.935	2B-20, SS-14, 3B-6
7 yrs.			436	.243	.287	945	230	19	11	0	0.0	97	57	70	107	7	89	21	427	592	50	98	2.5	.953	SS-157, 3B-74, 2B-59, C-30, OF-21, 1B-5, P-1

Teddy Martinez

MARTINEZ, TEODORO NOEL
Born Teodoro Noel Martinez y Encarnacion.
B. Dec. 10, 1947, Bahrahona, Dominican Republic

BR TR 6' 165 lbs.

Year	Team		Games	BA	SA	AB	H	2B	3B	HR	HR%	R	RBI	BB	SO	SB	PH AB	PH H	PO	A	E	DP	TC/G	FA	G by Pos
1970	NY	N	4	.063	.063	16	1	0	0	0	0.0	0	0	0	3	0	0	0	9	11	0	4	5.0	1.000	2B-4, SS-1
1971			38	.288	.384	125	36	5	2	1	0.8	16	10	4	22	6	1	0	45	80	3	17	3.4	.977	SS-23, 2B-13, 3B-3, OF-1
1972			103	.224	.279	330	74	5	5	1	0.3	22	19	12	49	7	4	0	175	194	5	30	3.6	.987	2B-47, SS-42, OF-15, 3B-2
1973			92	.255	.308	263	67	11	0	1	0.4	34	14	13	38	3	1	0	119	139	12	15	2.9	.956	SS-44, OF-21, 3B-14, 2B-5
1974			116	.219	.323	334	73	15	7	2	0.6	32	43	14	40	3	8	1	164	257	20	38	3.8	.955	SS-75, 3B-12, 2B-11, OF-10

Year	Team	Games	BA	SA	AB	H	2B	3B	HR	HR%	R	RBI	BB	SO	SB	Pinch Hit AB	Pinch Hit H	PO	A	E	DP	TC/G	FA	G by Pos

Teddy Martinez *continued*

Year	Team	Games	BA	SA	AB	H	2B	3B	HR	HR%	R	RBI	BB	SO	SB	PH AB	PH H	PO	A	E	DP	TC/G	FA	G by Pos
1975	2 teams	STL N (16G – .190)		OAK A (86G – .172)																				
"	total	102	.176	.194	108	19	2	0	0	0.0	8	5	2	11	1	11	1	12	4	1	0	0.2	.941	SS-46, 2B-33, 3B-15, OF-7
1977	LA N	67	.299	.380	137	41	6	1	1	0.7	21	10	2	20	3	4	0	80	96	3	29	2.7	.983	2B-27, SS-13, 3B-12
1978		54	.255	.327	55	14	1	0	1	1.8	13	5	4	14	3	4	0	39	51	5	7	1.8	.947	SS-17, 3B-16, 2B-10
1979		81	.268	.330	112	30	5	1	0	0.0	19	2	4	16	3	4	0	45	69	5	7	1.5	.958	3B-23, SS-21, 2B-18
9 yrs.		657	.240	.309	1480	355	50	16	7	0.5	165	108	55	213	29	37	2	688	901	54	147	2.5	.967	SS-282, 2B-168, 3B-97, OF-54

LEAGUE CHAMPIONSHIP SERIES

| 1975 | OAK A | 3 | – | – | 0 | 0 | 0 | 0 | 0 | – | 0 | 0 | 0 | 0 | 0 | 0 | 0 | 1 | 1 | 0 | 0 | 0.7 | 1.000 | 2B-3 |

WORLD SERIES

| 1973 | NY N | 2 | – | – | 0 | 0 | 0 | 0 | 0 | – | 0 | 0 | 0 | 0 | 0 | 0 | 0 | 0 | 0 | 0 | 0 | 0.0 | – | |

Tony Martinez

MARTINEZ, GABRIEL ANTONIO
Born Gabriel Antonio Martinez y Diaz.
B. Mar. 18, 1941, Perico, Cuba

BR TR 5'10" 165 lbs.

Year	Team	Games	BA	SA	AB	H	2B	3B	HR	HR%	R	RBI	BB	SO	SB	PH AB	PH H	PO	A	E	DP	TC/G	FA	G by Pos
1963	CLE A	43	.156	.184	141	22	4	0	0	0.0	10	8	5	18	1	0	0	59	90	6	17	3.6	.961	SS-41
1964		9	.214	.286	14	3	1	0	0	0.0	1	2	0	2	0	1	0	11	11	0	6	2.4	1.000	2B-4, SS-1
1965		4	.000	.000	3	0	0	0	0	0.0	0	0	0	0	0	3	0	0	0	0	0	0.0	–	
1966		17	.294	.294	17	5	0	0	0	0.0	2	0	1	6	1	6	3	10	8	1	1	1.1	.947	SS-5, 2B-4
4 yrs.		73	.171	.200	175	30	5	0	0	0.0	13	10	6	26	2	10	3	80	109	7	24	2.7	.964	SS-47, 2B-8

Joe Marty

MARTY, JOSEPH ANTON
B. Sept. 1, 1913, Sacramento, Calif.   D. Oct. 4, 1984, Sacramento, Calif.

BR TR 6' 182 lbs.

Year	Team	Games	BA	SA	AB	H	2B	3B	HR	HR%	R	RBI	BB	SO	SB	PH AB	PH H	PO	A	E	DP	TC/G	FA	G by Pos
1937	CHI N	88	.290	.414	290	84	17	2	5	1.7	41	44	28	30	3	3	2	196	4	5	0	2.3	.976	OF-84
1938		76	.243	.391	235	57	8	3	7	3.0	32	35	18	26	0	7	0	143	6	2	1	2.0	.987	OF-68
1939	2 teams	CHI N (23G – .132)		PHI N (91G – .254)																				
"	total	114	.229	.384	375	86	13	6	11	2.9	38	54	28	40	3	12	3	200	13	7	3	1.9	.968	OF-100, P-1
1940	PHI N	123	.270	.437	455	123	21	8	13	2.9	52	50	17	50	2	4	1	296	7	8	0	2.5	.974	OF-118
1941		137	.268	.371	477	128	19	3	8	1.7	60	39	51	41	6	5	0	286	7	11	0	2.2	.964	OF-132
5 yrs.		538	.261	.400	1832	478	78	22	44	2.4	223	222	142	187	14	31	6	1121	37	33	4	2.2	.972	OF-502, P-1

WORLD SERIES

| 1938 | CHI N | 3 | .500 | .833 | 12 | 6 | 1 | 0 | 1 | 8.3 | 1 | 5 | 0 | 2 | 0 | 0 | 0 | 7 | 0 | 0 | 0 | 2.3 | 1.000 | OF-3 |

Bob Martyn

MARTYN, ROBERT GORDON
B. Aug. 15, 1930, Weiser, Ida.

BL TR 6' 176 lbs.

Year	Team	Games	BA	SA	AB	H	2B	3B	HR	HR%	R	RBI	BB	SO	SB	PH AB	PH H	PO	A	E	DP	TC/G	FA	G by Pos
1957	KC A	58	.267	.366	131	35	2	4	1	0.8	10	12	11	20	1	8	0	77	3	2	0	1.4	.976	OF-49
1958		95	.261	.394	226	59	10	7	2	0.9	25	23	26	36	1	28	7	112	4	4	2	1.3	.967	OF-63
1959		1	.000	.000	1	0	0	0	0	0.0	0	0	0	0	0	1	0	0	0	0	0	0.0	–	
3 yrs.		154	.263	.383	358	94	12	11	3	0.8	35	35	37	56	2	37	7	189	7	6	2	1.3	.970	OF-112

Gary Martz

MARTZ, GARY ARTHUR
B. Jan. 10, 1951, Spokane, Wash.

BR TR 6'4" 210 lbs.

Year	Team	Games	BA	SA	AB	H	2B	3B	HR	HR%	R	RBI	BB	SO	SB	PH AB	PH H	PO	A	E	DP	TC/G	FA	G by Pos
1975	KC A	1	.000	.000	1	0	0	0	0	0.0	0	0	0	0	0	1	0	1	0	0	0	1.0	1.000	OF-1

John Marzano

MARZANO, JOHN ROBERT
B. Feb. 14, 1963, Philadelphia, Pa.

BR TR 5'11" 185 lbs.

Year	Team	Games	BA	SA	AB	H	2B	3B	HR	HR%	R	RBI	BB	SO	SB	PH AB	PH H	PO	A	E	DP	TC/G	FA	G by Pos
1987	BOS A	52	.244	.399	168	41	11	0	5	3.0	20	24	7	41	0	1	0	337	24	5	7	7.0	.986	C-52
1988		10	.138	.172	29	4	1	0	0	0.0	3	1	1	3	0	0	0	77	4	0	0	8.1	1.000	C-10
1989		7	.444	.778	18	8	3	0	1	5.6	5	3	0	2	0	1	1	29	4	0	0	4.7	1.000	C-7
3 yrs.		69	.247	.400	215	53	15	0	6	2.8	28	28	8	46	0	2	1	443	32	5	7	7.0	.990	C-69

Clyde Mashore

MASHORE, CLYDE WAYNE
B. May 29, 1945, Concord, Calif.

BR TR 6' 182 lbs.

Year	Team	Games	BA	SA	AB	H	2B	3B	HR	HR%	R	RBI	BB	SO	SB	PH AB	PH H	PO	A	E	DP	TC/G	FA	G by Pos
1969	CIN N	2	.000	.000	1	0	0	0	0	0.0	1	0	0	0	0	1	0	0	0	0	0	0.0	–	
1970	MON N	13	.160	.280	25	4	0	0	1	4.0	2	3	4	11	0	4	0	12	0	0	0	0.9	1.000	OF-10
1971		66	.193	.263	114	22	5	0	1	0.9	20	7	10	22	1	12	1	60	0	2	0	0.9	.968	OF-47, 3B-1
1972		93	.227	.330	176	40	7	1	3	1.7	23	23	14	41	6	19	3	80	3	1	0	0.9	.988	OF-74
1973		67	.204	.320	103	21	3	0	3	2.9	12	14	15	28	4	15	3	65	4	3	0	1.1	.958	OF-44, 2B-1
5 yrs.		241	.208	.305	419	87	15	1	8	1.9	58	47	43	102	11	51	8	217	7	6	0	1.0	.974	OF-175, 3B-1, 2B-1

Phil Masi

MASI, PHILIP SAMUEL
B. Jan. 6, 1917, Chicago, Ill.

BR TR 5'10" 177 lbs.

Year	Team	Games	BA	SA	AB	H	2B	3B	HR	HR%	R	RBI	BB	SO	SB	PH AB	PH H	PO	A	E	DP	TC/G	FA	G by Pos
1939	BOS N	46	.254	.377	114	29	7	2	1	0.9	14	14	9	15	0	3	0	104	15	5	0	2.7	.960	C-42
1940		63	.196	.261	138	27	4	1	1	0.7	11	14	14	9	3	3	0	137	32	6	2	2.8	.966	C-52
1941		87	.222	.339	180	40	8	2	3	1.7	17	18	16	13	4	3	1	194	31	5	3	2.6	.978	C-83
1942		57	.218	.276	87	19	3	1	0	0.0	14	9	12	4	2	1	0	82	21	4	1	1.9	.963	C-39, OF-4
1943		80	.273	.345	238	65	9	1	2	0.8	27	28	27	20	7	1	1	192	40	2	1	2.9	.991	C-73
1944		89	.275	.402	251	69	13	5	3	1.2	33	23	31	20	4	8	1	298	46	7	12	3.9	.980	C-63, 1B-12, 3B-2
1945		111	.272	.418	371	101	25	4	7	1.9	55	46	42	32	9	9	1	390	54	10	8	4.1	.978	C-95, 1B-7
1946		133	.267	.358	397	106	17	5	3	0.8	52	62	55	41	5	5	2	470	56	10	5	4.0	.981	C-124
1947		126	.304	.443	411	125	22	4	9	2.2	54	50	47	27	7	3	1	411	58	8	5	3.8	.989	C-123
1948		113	.253	.343	376	95	19	2	5	1.3	43	44	35	26	2	1	0	458	39	6	5	4.5	.988	C-109
1949	2 teams	BOS N (37G – .210)		PIT N (48G – .274)																				
"	total	85	.246	.313	240	59	14	1	2	0.8	29	19	31	26	1	3	0	308	37	2	11	4.1	.994	C-81, 1B-2
1950	CHI A	122	.279	.390	377	105	17	2	7	1.9	38	55	49	36	2	9	1	440	52	2	9	4.0	.996	C-114
1951		84	.271	.391	225	61	11	2	4	1.8	24	28	27	21	1	3	0	299	24	7	3	3.9	.979	C-78
1952		30	.254	.302	63	16	1	1	0	0.0	9	7	10	10	1	3	1	101	7	5	2	3.8	.956	C-25
14 yrs.		1226	.264	.370	3468	917	164	31	47	1.4	420	417	410	311	45	61	12	3884	512	76	67	3.6	.983	C-1101, 1B-21, OF-4, 3B-2

Year	Team		Games	BA	SA	AB	H	2B	3B	HR	HR%	R	RBI	BB	SO	SB	Pinch Hit AB	H	PO	A	E	DP	TC/G	FA	G by Pos

Phil Masi *continued*

WORLD SERIES

| 1948 | BOS | N | 5 | .125 | .250 | 8 | 1 | 1 | 0 | 0 | 0.0 | 1 | 1 | 0 | 0 | 0 | 1 | 1 | 10 | 1 | 0 | 0 | 2.2 | 1.000 | C-5 |

Harry Maskrey

MASKREY, HARRY H.
Brother of Leech Maskrey.
B. Dec. 21, 1861, Mercer, Pa.   D. Aug. 17, 1930, Mercer, Pa.

| 1882 | LOU | AA | 1 | .000 | .000 | 4 | 0 | 0 | 0 | 0 | 0.0 | 0 | | 0 | | | 0 | 0 | 0 | 0 | 1 | 0 | 1.0 | — | OF-1 |

Leech Maskrey

MASKREY, SAMUEL LEECH   BR TR 5'8"   150 lbs.
Brother of Harry Maskrey.
B. Feb. 11, 1854, Mercer, Pa.   D. Apr. 1, 1922, Mercer, Pa.
Manager 1882-83.

1882	LOU	AA	76	.226	.288	288	65	14	2	0	0.0	30		9			0	0	137	13	18	1	2.2	.893	OF-76, 2B-1
1883			96	.202	.291	361	73	13	8	1	0.3	50		10			0	0	193	19	20	1	2.4	.914	OF-96, SS-1
1884			105	.250	.301	412	103	13	4	0	0.0	48		17			0	0	141	20	19	2	1.7	.894	OF-103, 3B-3, SS-1
1885			109	.229	.307	423	97	8	11	1	0.2	54		19			0	0	169	12	21	2	1.9	.896	OF-108, 3B-3
1886	2 teams			LOU	AA (5G – .158)			CIN	AA	(27G –	.194)														
"	total		32	.188	.239	117	22	4	1	0	0.0	8		6			0	0	54	9	8	1	2.2	.887	OF-31, 3B-2
5 yrs.			418	.225	.294	1601	360	52	26	2	0.1	190		61			0	0	694	73	86	7	2.0	.899	OF-414, 3B-8, SS-2, 2B-1

Charlie Mason

MASON, CHARLES E.   TR
B. June 25, 1853, New Orleans, La.   D. Oct. 21, 1936, Philadelphia, Pa.
Manager 1882, 1884-85, 1887.

| 1883 | PHI | AA | 1 | .500 | .500 | 2 | 1 | 0 | 0 | 0 | 0.0 | 0 | | 0 | | | 0 | 0 | 0 | 0 | 0 | 0 | 0.0 | — | OF-1 |

Don Mason

MASON, DONALD STETSON   BL TR 5'11"   160 lbs.
B. Dec. 20, 1944, Boston, Mass.

1966	SF	N	42	.120	.240	25	3	0	0	1	4.0	8	1	0	2	0	13	1	10	9	2	1	0.5	.905	2B-9
1967			4	.000	.000	3	0	0	0	0	0.0	0	0	0	0	0	0	0	0	3	0	0	0.8	1.000	2B-2
1968			10	.158	.158	19	3	0	0	0	0.0	3	1	1	4	1	0	0	9	9	0	1.8	1.000	2B-5, SS-4, 3B-2
1969			104	.228	.260	250	57	4	2	0	0.0	43	13	36	29	1	18	5	135	179	20	37	3.2	.940	2B-51, 3B-21, SS-7
1970			46	.139	.139	36	5	0	0	0	0.0	4	1	5	7	0	20	1	11	8	1	1	0.4	.950	2B-14
1971	SD	N	113	.212	.270	344	73	12	1	2	0.6	43	11	27	35	6	17	6	189	233	16	47	3.9	.963	2B-90, 3B-3
1972			9	.182	.182	11	2	0	0	0	0.0	1	0	1	1	0	2	0	3	6	4	0	1.4	.692	2B-3
1973			8	.000	.000	8	0	0	0	0	0.0	0	0	0	2	0	6	0	1	2	1	1	0.5	.750	2B-1
8 yrs.			336	.205	.250	696	143	16	3	3	0.4	102	27	70	80	8	78	14	358	449	44	87	2.5	.948	2B-175, 3B-26, SS-11

Jim Mason

MASON, JAMES PERCY   BL TR 6'2"   185 lbs.
B. Aug. 14, 1950, Mobile, Ala.

1971	WAS	A	3	.333	.333	9	3	0	0	0	0.0	0	0	1	3	0	0	0	8	13	1	1	7.3	.955	SS-3
1972	TEX	A	46	.197	.218	147	29	3	0	0	0.0	10	10	9	39	0	3	0	58	106	10	14	3.8	.943	SS-32, 3B-10
1973			92	.206	.290	238	49	7	2	3	1.3	23	19	23	48	0	1	0	143	230	20	51	4.3	.949	SS-74, 2B-19, 3B-1
1974	NY	A	152	.250	.352	440	110	18	6	5	1.1	41	37	35	87	1	0	0	241	430	25	87	4.6	.964	SS-152
1975			94	.152	.211	223	34	3	2	2	0.9	17	16	22	49	0	1	0	134	209	16	45	3.8	.955	SS-93, 2B-1
1976			93	.180	.235	217	39	7	1	1	0.5	17	14	9	37	0	0	0	128	245	13	47	4.2	.966	SS-93
1977	2 teams			TOR	A (22G – .165)			TEX	A	(36G –	.218)														
"	total		58	.187	.254	134	25	6	0	1	0.7	19	9	13	20	1	1	0	75	108	6	20	3.3	.968	SS-54, DH-3, 3B-1
1978	TEX	A	55	.190	.229	105	20	4	0	0	0.0	10	3	5	17	0	2	0	47	92	10	14	2.7	.933	SS-42, 3B-11, DH-1, 2B-1
1979	MON	N	40	.183	.282	71	13	5	1	0	0.0	3	6	7	16	0	4	0	35	62	3	10	2.5	.970	SS-33, 3B-6
9 yrs.			633	.203	.275	1584	322	53	12	12	0.8	140	114	124	316	2	11	0	869	1495	104	289	3.9	.958	SS-576, 3B-29, 2B-21, DH-4

LEAGUE CHAMPIONSHIP SERIES

| 1976 | NY | A | 2 | — | — | 0 | 0 | 0 | 0 | 0 | 0.0 | 0 | 0 | 0 | 0 | 0 | 0 | 0 | 1 | 2 | 0 | 0 | 1.5 | 1.000 | SS-2 |

WORLD SERIES

| 1976 | NY | A | 3 | 1.000 | 4.000 | 1 | 1 | 0 | 0 | 1 | 0.0 | 1 | 1 | 0 | 0 | 0 | 0 | 0 | 1 | 2 | 0 | 0 | 1.0 | 1.000 | SS-3 |

Gordon Massa

MASSA, GORDON RICHARD (Moose, Duke)   BL TR 6'3"   210 lbs.
B. Sept. 2, 1935, Cincinnati, Ohio

1957	CHI	N	6	.467	.533	15	7	1	0	0	0.0	2	3	4	3	0	0	0	21	0	0	0	3.5	1.000	C-6
1958			2	.000	.000	2	0	0	0	0	0.0	0	0	0	2	0	2	0	0	0	0	0	0.0	—	
2 yrs.			8	.412	.471	17	7	1	0	0	0.0	2	3	4	5	0	2	0	21	0	0	0	2.6	1.000	C-6

Bill Massey

MASSEY, WILLIAM HENRY (Big Bill)   BR   5'11"   168 lbs.
B. Jan., 1871, Philadelphia, Pa.   D. Oct. 9, 1940, Manila, Philippines

| 1894 | CIN | N | 13 | .283 | .340 | 53 | 15 | 3 | 0 | 0 | 0.0 | 7 | 5 | 3 | 2 | 0 | 0 | 0 | 123 | 11 | 6 | 17 | 10.8 | .957 | 1B-10, 2B-2, 3B-1 |

Mike Massey

MASSEY, WILLIAM HERBERT   BB TR 6'   195 lbs.
B. Sept. 28, 1893, Galveston, Tex.   D. Oct. 17, 1971, Shreveport, La.

| 1917 | BOS | N | 31 | .198 | .198 | 91 | 18 | 0 | 0 | 0 | 0.0 | 12 | 2 | 15 | 15 | 2 | 0 | 0 | 40 | 68 | 12 | 10 | 3.9 | .900 | 2B-25 |

Roy Massey

MASSEY, ROY HARDEE (Red)   BB TR 5'11"   170 lbs.
B. Oct. 9, 1890, Sevierville, Tenn.   D. June 23, 1954, Atlanta, Ga.

| 1918 | BOS | N | 66 | .291 | .340 | 203 | 59 | 6 | 2 | 0 | 0.0 | 20 | 18 | 23 | 20 | 1 | 12 | 0 | 107 | 6 | 6 | 3 | 1.8 | .950 | OF-45, 1B-4, SS-1, 3B-1 |

Vic Mata

MATA, VICTOR JOSE   BR TR 6'1"   165 lbs.
Born Victor Jose Mata y Abreu.
B. June 17, 1961, Santiago, Dominican Republic

Year	Team	Games	BA	SA	AB	H	2B	3B	HR	HR%	R	RBI	BB	SO	SB	Pinch Hit AB	Pinch Hit H	PO	A	E	DP	TC/G	FA	G by Pos

Vic Mata *continued*

Year	Team		Games	BA	SA	AB	H	2B	3B	HR	HR%	R	RBI	BB	SO	SB	AB	H	PO	A	E	DP	TC/G	FA	G by Pos
1984	NY	A	30	.329	.443	70	23	5	0	1	1.4	8	6	0	12	1	4	2	49	0	3	0	1.7	.942	OF-28
1985			6	.143	.143	7	1	0	0	0	0.0	1	0	0	0	0	2	0	1	0	0	0	0.2	1.000	OF-3
2 yrs.			36	.312	.416	77	24	5	0	1	1.3	9	6	0	12	1	6	2	50	0	3	0	1.5	.943	OF-31

Tom Matchick   MATCHICK, JOHN THOMAS
B. Sept. 7, 1943, Hazelton, Pa.   BL TR 6'1" 173 lbs.

Year	Team		Games	BA	SA	AB	H	2B	3B	HR	HR%	R	RBI	BB	SO	SB	AB	H	PO	A	E	DP	TC/G	FA	G by Pos
1967	DET	A	8	.167	.167	6	1	0	0	0	0.0	1	0	0	2	0	5	0	1	0	0	0	0.1	1.000	SS-1
1968			80	.203	.286	227	46	6	2	3	1.3	18	14	10	46	0	13	5	106	154	10	31	3.4	.963	SS-59, 2B-13, 1B-6
1969			94	.242	.292	298	72	11	2	0	0.0	25	32	15	51	3	16	8	121	176	8	36	3.2	.974	2B-47, 3B-27, SS-6, 1B-2
1970	2 teams		KC A (55G – .196)			BOS A (10G – .071)																			
"	total		65	.186	.227	172	32	3	2	0	0.0	13	11	7	25	0	12	0	87	155	3	39	3.8	.988	SS-44, 2B-11, 3B-3
1971	MIL	A	42	.219	.254	114	25	1	0	1	0.9	6	7	7	23	3	0	0	31	62	2	6	2.3	.979	3B-41, 2B-1
1972	BAL	A	3	.222	.222	9	2	0	0	0	0.0	0	0	0	1	0	0	0	2	4	1	0	2.3	.857	3B-3
6 yrs.			292	.215	.270	826	178	21	6	4	0.5	63	64	39	148	6	46	13	348	551	24	112	3.2	.974	SS-110, 3B-74, 2B-72, 1B-8

WORLD SERIES

Year	Team		Games	BA	SA	AB	H	2B	3B	HR	HR%	R	RBI	BB	SO	SB	AB	H	PO	A	E	DP	TC/G	FA	G by Pos
1968	DET	A	3	.000	.000	3	0	0	0	0	0.0	0	0	0	1	0	3	0	0	0	0	0	0.0	–	

Joe Mathes   MATHES, JOSEPH JOHN
B. July 28, 1891, Milwaukee, Wis. D. Dec. 21, 1978, St. Louis, Mo.   BB TR 6'½" 180 lbs.

Year	Team		Games	BA	SA	AB	H	2B	3B	HR	HR%	R	RBI	BB	SO	SB	AB	H	PO	A	E	DP	TC/G	FA	G by Pos
1912	PHI	A	4	.143	.143	14	2	0	0	0	0.0	0	0	0	0	0	0	0	1	7	1	0	2.3	.889	3B-4
1914	STL	F	26	.294	.329	85	25	3	0	0	0.0	10	6	9		1	1	1	48	57	7	5	4.3	.938	2B-23
1916	BOS	N	2	–	–	0	0	0	0	0	–	0	0	0	0	0	0	0	0	0	2	0	1.0	–	2B-2
3 yrs.			32	.273	.303	99	27	3	0	0	0.0	10	6	9	0	1	1	1	49	64	10	5	3.8	.919	2B-25, 3B-4

Bobby Mathews   MATHEWS, ROBERT T.
B. Nov. 21, 1851, Baltimore, Md. D. Apr. 17, 1898, Baltimore, Md.   BR TR 5'5½" 140 lbs.

Year	Team		Games	BA	SA	AB	H	2B	3B	HR	HR%	R	RBI	BB	SO	SB	AB	H	PO	A	E	DP	TC/G	FA	G by Pos
1876	NY	N	56	.183	.211	218	40	4	1	0	0.0	19	9	3	2		0	0	41	78	28	0	2.6	.810	P-56, OF-1
1877	CIN	N	15	.169	.169	59	10	0	0	0	0.0	5	0	1	2		0	0	8	19	7	0	2.3	.794	P-15, OF-1, SS-1
1879	PRO	N	43	.202	.231	173	35	2	0	1	0.6	25	10	7	12		0	0	24	46	13	1	1.9	.843	P-27, OF-21, 3B-5
1881	2 teams		PRO N (16G – .193)			BOS N (19G – .169)																			
"	total		35	.180	.203	128	23	0	0	0	0.0	8	8	5	11		0	0	30	21	11	2	1.8	.823	OF-23, P-19
1882	BOS	N	45	.225	.260	169	38	6	0	0	0.0	17	13	8	18		0	0	11	34	12	1	1.3	.789	P-34, OF-13, SS-1
1883	PHI	AA	45	.186	.198	167	31	2	0	0	0.0	15	4			0	0	0	15	68	12	2	2.1	.874	P-44, OF-3
1884			49	.185	.223	184	34	5	1	0	0.0	26	7			0	0	0	8	78	25	1	2.3	.775	P-49, OF-1
1885			48	.168	.184	179	30	3	0	0	0.0	22	10			0	0	0	8	67	10	1	1.8	.882	P-48, OF-1
1886			24	.239	.273	88	21	3	0	0	0.0	16	3			0	0	0	5	46	9	3	2.5	.850	P-24, OF-1
1887			7	.200	.200	25	5	0	0	0	0.0	5	4		0	0	0	0	2	14	2	1	2.6	.889	P-7
10 yrs.			367	.192	.217	1390	267	28	2	1	0.1	158	40	52	45	0	0	0	152	471	129	12	2.0	.828	P-323, OF-65, 3B-5, SS-2

Eddie Mathews   MATHEWS, EDWIN LEE
B. Oct. 13, 1931, Texarkana, Tex.
Manager 1972-74.
Hall of Fame 1978.   BL TR 6'1" 190 lbs.

Year	Team		Games	BA	SA	AB	H	2B	3B	HR	HR%	R	RBI	BB	SO	SB	AB	H	PO	A	E	DP	TC/G	FA	G by Pos
1952	BOS	N	145	.242	.447	528	128	23	5	25	4.7	80	58	59	115	6	2	0	160	259	19	21	3.0	.957	3B-142
1953	MIL	N	154	.302	.627	579	175	31	8	47	8.1	110	135	99	83	1	0	0	154	311	30	33	3.2	.939	3B-157
1954			138	.290	.603	476	138	21	4	40	8.4	96	103	113	61	10	2	0	133	254	15	28	2.9	.963	3B-127, OF-10
1955			141	.289	.601	499	144	23	5	41	8.2	108	101	109	98	3	2	1	140	280	21	23	3.1	.952	3B-137
1956			151	.272	.518	552	150	21	2	37	6.7	103	95	91	86	6	2	0	133	287	25	22	2.9	.944	3B-150
1957			148	.292	.540	572	167	28	9	32	5.6	109	94	90	79	3	0	0	131	299	16	27	3.0	.964	3B-147
1958			149	.251	.458	546	137	18	1	31	5.7	97	77	85	85	5	0	0	116	351	22	24	3.3	.955	3B-149
1959			148	.306	.593	594	182	16	8	46	7.7	118	114	80	71	2	0	0	144	305	18	21	3.2	.961	3B-148
1960			153	.277	.551	548	152	19	7	39	7.1	108	124	111	113	7	0	0	141	280	22	23	2.9	.950	3B-153
1961			152	.306	.535	572	175	23	6	32	5.6	103	91	93	95	12	1	0	168	281	18	30	3.1	.961	3B-151
1962			152	.265	.496	536	142	25	6	29	5.4	106	90	101	90	4	3	0	208	285	16	29	3.3	.969	3B-140, 1B-7
1963			158	.263	.453	547	144	27	4	23	4.2	82	84	124	119	3	1	0	176	277	19	23	3.0	.960	3B-121, OF-42
1964			141	.233	.412	502	117	19	1	23	4.6	83	74	85	100	2	6	1	184	252	17	23	3.2	.962	3B-128, 1B-7
1965			156	.251	.469	546	137	23	0	32	5.9	77	95	73	110	1	8	1	113	301	19	19	2.8	.956	3B-153
1966	ATL	N	134	.250	.420	452	113	21	4	16	3.5	72	53	63	82	1	12	4	114	237	20	31	2.8	.946	3B-127
1967	2 teams		HOU N (101G – .238)			DET A (36G – .231)																			
"	total		137	.236	.392	436	103	16	2	16	3.7	53	57	63	88	2	15	2	714	113	15	62	6.1	.982	1B-92, 3B-45
1968	DET	A	31	.212	.385	52	11	0	0	3	5.8	4	8	5	12	0	16	3	37	14	1	5	1.7	.981	3B-6, 1B-6
17 yrs.			2388	.271	.509	8537	2315	354	72	512	6.0	1509	1453	1444	1487	68	70	12	2966	4386	313	444	3.2	.959	3B-2181, 1B-112, OF-52

WORLD SERIES

Year	Team		Games	BA	SA	AB	H	2B	3B	HR	HR%	R	RBI	BB	SO	SB	AB	H	PO	A	E	DP	TC/G	FA	G by Pos
1957	MIL	N	7	.227	.500	22	5	3	0	1	4.5	4	4	8	5	0	0	0	9	19	1	1	4.1	.966	3B-7
1958			7	.160	.240	25	4	2	0	0	0.0	3	3	6	11	1	0	0	5	13	1	0	2.7	.947	3B-7
1968	DET	A	2	.333	.333	3	1	0	0	0	0.0	0	0	1	1	0	0	0	0	1	1	0	1.0	.500	3B-1
3 yrs.			16	.200	.360	50	10	5	0	1	2.0	7	7	15	17	1	0	0	14	33	3	1	3.1	.940	3B-15

Nelson Mathews   MATHEWS, NELSON ELMER
B. July 21, 1941, Columbia, Ill.   BR TR 6'4" 195 lbs.

Year	Team		Games	BA	SA	AB	H	2B	3B	HR	HR%	R	RBI	BB	SO	SB	AB	H	PO	A	E	DP	TC/G	FA	G by Pos
1960	CHI	N	3	.250	.250	8	2	0	0	0	0.0	1	0	0	2	0	1	0	5	0	0	0	1.7	1.000	OF-2
1961			3	.111	.111	9	1	0	0	0	0.0	0	0	0	2	0	1	0	5	0	0	0	1.7	1.000	OF-2
1962			15	.306	.469	49	15	2	0	2	4.1	5	13	5	4	3	1	0	25	0	1	0	1.7	.962	OF-14
1963			61	.155	.277	155	24	3	2	4	2.6	12	10	16	49	3	8	0	91	1	2	1	1.5	.979	OF-46
1964	KC	A	157	.239	.377	573	137	27	5	14	2.4	58	60	43	143	2	1	0	384	5	13	2	2.6	.968	OF-154
1965			67	.212	.359	184	39	7	7	2	1.1	17	15	24	49	0	10	2	103	1	2	0	1.6	.981	OF-57
6 yrs.			306	.223	.359	978	218	39	14	22	2.2	93	98	88	248	8	22	2	613	7	18	3	2.1	.972	OF-275

Jimmy Mathison   MATHISON, JAMES I.
B. Nov., 1878, Baltimore, Md. D. July 4, 1911, Baltimore, Md.   TR

Year	Team		Games	BA	SA	AB	H	2B	3B	HR	HR%	R	RBI	BB	SO	SB	Pinch Hit AB	Pinch Hit H	PO	A	E	DP	TC/G	FA	G by Pos

Jimmy Mathison *continued*

Year	Team		Games	BA	SA	AB	H	2B	3B	HR	HR%	R	RBI	BB	SO	SB	AB	H	PO	A	E	DP	TC/G	FA	G by Pos
1902	BAL	A	29	.264	.308	91	24	2	1	0	0.0	12	7	9		2	0	0	43	53	12	4	3.7	.889	3B-28, SS-1

John Matias

MATIAS, JOHN ROY
B. Aug. 15, 1944, Honolulu, Hawaii — BL TL 5'11" 170 lbs.

| 1970 | CHI | A | 58 | .188 | .256 | 117 | 22 | 2 | 0 | 2 | 1.7 | 7 | 6 | 3 | 22 | 1 | 27 | 5 | 132 | 12 | 3 | 14 | 2.5 | .980 | OF-22, 1B-18 |

Bob Matthews

MATTHEWS, ROBERT
B. Camden, N. J. Deceased.

| 1891 | PHI | AA | 1 | .333 | .333 | 3 | 1 | 0 | 0 | 0 | 0.0 | 1 | 0 | 0 | 1 | 0 | 0 | 0 | 0 | 0 | 0 | 0 | 0.0 | — | OF-1 |

Gary Matthews

MATTHEWS, GARY NATHANIEL (Sarge)
B. July 5, 1950, San Fernando, Calif. — BR TR 6'2" 185 lbs.

1972	SF	N	20	.290	.532	62	18	1	1	4	6.5	11	14	7	13	0	1	0	34	0	1	0	1.8	.971	OF-19
1973			148	.300	.444	540	162	22	10	12	2.2	74	58	58	83	17	1	1	277	11	5	0	2.0	.983	OF-145
1974			154	.287	.442	561	161	27	6	16	2.9	87	82	70	69	11	4	0	281	9	9	2	1.9	.970	OF-151
1975			116	.280	.431	425	119	23	3	12	2.8	67	58	65	53	13	3	1	225	11	8	2	2.1	.967	OF-113
1976			156	.279	.443	587	164	28	4	20	3.4	79	84	75	94	12	1	0	265	8	7	0	1.8	.975	OF-156
1977	ATL	N	148	.283	.438	555	157	25	5	17	3.1	89	64	67	90	22	2	1	262	11	10	1	1.9	.965	OF-145
1978			129	.285	.462	474	135	20	5	18	3.8	75	62	61	92	8	3	0	238	10	8	0	2.0	.969	OF-127
1979			156	.304	.502	631	192	34	5	27	4.3	97	90	60	75	18	0	0	292	12	8	4	2.0	.974	OF-156
1980			155	.278	.419	571	159	17	3	19	3.3	79	75	42	93	11	8	2	258	8	11	3	1.8	.960	OF-143
1981	PHI		101	.301	.451	359	108	21	3	9	2.5	62	67	59	42	15	2	0	170	11	7	1	1.9	.963	OF-100
1982			162	.281	.427	616	173	31	1	19	3.1	89	83	66	87	21	1	0	268	14	10	2	1.8	.966	OF-162
1983			132	.258	.374	446	115	18	2	10	2.2	66	50	69	81	13	9	2	174	11	5	2	1.4	.974	OF-122
1984	CHI	N	147	.291	.428	491	143	21	2	14	2.9	101	82	103	97	17	3	0	224	7	11	0	1.6	.955	OF-145
1985			97	.235	.406	298	70	12	0	13	4.4	45	40	59	64	2	11	2	119	7	3	2	1.3	.977	OF-85
1986			123	.259	.478	370	96	16	1	21	5.7	49	46	60	59	3	16	0	137	5	9	1	1.2	.940	OF-105
1987	2 teams			CHI	N	(44G – .262)				SEA	A	(45G – .235)													
"	total		89	.242	.323	161	39	4	0	3	1.9	13	23	19	33	0	49	11	2	0	0	0	0.0	1.000	DH-45, OF-2
	16 yrs.		2033	.281	.439	7147	2011	319	51	234	3.3	1083	978	940	1125	183	114	20	3226	135	112	17	1.7	.968	OF-1876, DH-45

DIVISIONAL PLAYOFF SERIES

| 1981 | PHI | N | 5 | .400 | .650 | 20 | 8 | 0 | 1 | 1 | 5.0 | 3 | 1 | 0 | 2 | 0 | 0 | 0 | 0 | 0 | 0 | 0 | 0.0 | — | OF-5 |

LEAGUE CHAMPIONSHIP SERIES

1983	PHI	N	4	.429	1.071	14	6	0	0	3	21.4	4	8	2	1	1	0	0	6	0	0	0	1.5	1.000	OF-4
1984	CHI	N	5	.200	.600	15	3	0	0	2	13.3	4	5	6	4	1	0	0	10	0	0	0	2.0	1.000	OF-5
	2 yrs.		9	.310	.828	29	9	0	0	5	17.2	8	13	8	5	2	0	0	16	0	0	0	1.8	1.000	OF-9

WORLD SERIES

| 1983 | PHI | N | 5 | .250 | .438 | 16 | 4 | 0 | 0 | 1 | 6.3 | 1 | 1 | 2 | 2 | 0 | 0 | 0 | 15 | 0 | 0 | 0 | 3.0 | 1.000 | OF-5 |

Wid Matthews

MATTHEWS, WID CURRY
B. Oct. 20, 1896, Raleigh, Ill. D. Oct. 5, 1965, Hollywood, Calif. — BL TL 5'8½" 155 lbs.

1923	PHI	A	129	.274	.328	485	133	11	6	1	0.2	52	25	50	27	16	1	0	316	3	18	0	2.6	.947	OF-127
1924	WAS	A	53	.302	.408	169	51	10	4	0	0.0	25	13	11	4	3	6	4	121	7	2	2	2.5	.985	OF-44
1925			10	.444	.444	9	4	0	0	0	0.0	2	1	0	1	0	7	3	1	0	0	0	0.1	1.000	OF-1
	3 yrs.		192	.284	.350	663	188	21	10	1	0.2	79	39	61	32	19	14	7	438	10	20	2	2.4	.957	OF-172

Steve Matthias

MATTHIAS, DALE WESLEY
B. May 15, 1923, Catasauqua, Pa. D. Feb. 20, 1984, Blairsville, Ga. — BR TR 5'11½" 145 lbs.

1884	CHI	U	37	.275	.338	142	39	7	1	0	0.0	24		5		0	0	0	33	101	25	5	4.3	.843	SS-36, OF-2
1943	PHI	N	12	.000	.000	2	0	0	0	0	0.0	0	0	0	1	0	0	0	1	4	0	1	0.4	1.000	P-11
1944			17	.333	.333	3	1	0	0	0	0.0	0	0	0	0	0	0	0	3	5	1	0	0.5	.889	P-17
	3 yrs.		66	.272	.333	147	40	7	1	0	0.0	24		5	1	0	0	0	37	110	26	6	2.6	.850	SS-36, P-28, OF-2

Bobby Mattick

MATTICK, ROBERT JAMES
Son of Wally Mattick.
B. Dec. 5, 1915, Sioux City, Iowa
Manager 1980-81. — BR TR 5'11" 178 lbs.

1938	CHI	N	1	1.000	1.000	1	1	0	0	0	0.0	0	1	0	0	0	0	0	0	0	0	0	0.0	—	SS-1
1939			51	.287	.365	178	51	12	1	0	0.0	16	23	6	19	1	1	0	102	179	22	28	5.9	.927	SS-48
1940			128	.218	.252	441	96	15	1	0	0.0	30	33	19	33	5	1	0	233	431	38	76	5.5	.946	SS-126, 3B-1
1941	CIN	N	20	.183	.233	60	11	3	0	0	0.0	8	7	8	7	1	2	0	28	42	1	6	3.6	.986	SS-12, 3B-5, 2B-1
1942			6	.200	.300	10	2	1	0	0	0.0	0	0	0	1	0	0	0	7	6	0	1	2.2	1.000	SS-3
	5 yrs.		206	.233	.281	690	161	31	1	0	0.0	54	64	33	60	7	4	0	370	658	61	111	5.3	.944	SS-190, 3B-6, 2B-1

Wally Mattick

MATTICK, WALTER JOSEPH (Chick)
Father of Bobby Mattick.
B. Mar. 12, 1887, St. Louis, Mo. D. Nov. 5, 1968, Los Altos, Calif. — BR TR 5'10" 180 lbs.

1912	CHI	A	88	.260	.358	285	74	7	9	1	0.4	45	35	27		15	8	3	154	8	3	1	1.9	.982	OF-78
1913			68	.188	.237	207	39	8	1	0	0.0	15	11	18	16	3	3	1	116	14	3	2	2.0	.977	OF-63
1918	STL	N	8	.143	.143	14	2	0	0	0	0.0	0	1	2	3	0	5	1	5	1	0	0	0.8	1.000	OF-3
	3 yrs.		164	.227	.302	506	115	15	10	1	0.2	60	47	47	19	18	16	5	275	23	6	3	1.9	.980	OF-144

Mike Mattimore

MATTIMORE, MICHAEL JOSEPH
B. 1859, Renovo, Pa. D. Apr. 28, 1931, Butte, Mont. — BL TL 5'8½" 160 lbs.

| 1887 | NY | N | 8 | .250 | .281 | 32 | 8 | 1 | 0 | 0 | 0.0 | 5 | 4 | 0 | 6 | 11 | 0 | 0 | 8 | 5 | 1 | 0 | 1.8 | .929 | P-7, OF-2 |
| 1888 | PHI | AA | 41 | .268 | .380 | 142 | 38 | 6 | 5 | 0 | 0.0 | 22 | 12 | 12 | | 16 | 0 | 0 | 32 | 71 | 10 | 6 | 2.8 | .912 | P-26, OF-16 |

Year	Team		Games	BA	SA	AB	H	2B	3B	HR	HR%	R	RBI	BB	SO	SB	Pinch Hit AB	Pinch Hit H	PO	A	E	DP	TC/G	FA	G by Pos

Mike Mattimore *continued*

Year	Team		Games	BA	SA	AB	H	2B	3B	HR	HR%	R	RBI	BB	SO	SB	PH AB	PH H	PO	A	E	DP	TC/G	FA	G by Pos
1889	2 teams	PHI AA (23G – .233)																							KC AA (19G – .160)
"	total		42	.196	.270	148	29	2	3	1	0.7	16	13	12	23	6	0	0	98	12	15	2	3.0	.880	OF-31, 1B-7, P-6
1890	BKN	AA	33	.132	.155	129	17	1	1	0	0.0	14		16		11	0	0	20	38	12	0	2.1	.829	P-19, OF-14
4 yrs.			124	.204	.273	451	92	10	9	1	0.2	57	29	40	29	34	0	0	158	126	38	8	2.6	.882	OF-63, P-58, 1B-7

Don Mattingly

MATTINGLY, DONALD ARTHUR
B. Apr. 20, 1961, Evansville, Ind.
BL TL 6'   185 lbs.

Year	Team	Games	BA	SA	AB	H	2B	3B	HR	HR%	R	RBI	BB	SO	SB	PH AB	PH H	PO	A	E	DP	TC/G	FA	G by Pos
1982	NY A	7	.167	.167	12	2	0	0	0	0.0	0	1	0	1	0	1	0	15	1	0	0	2.3	1.000	OF-6, 1B-1
1983		91	.283	.409	279	79	15	4	4	1.4	34	32	21	31	0	8	1	350	15	3	31	4.0	.992	OF-48, 1B-42, 2B-1
1984		153	**.343**	.537	603	**207**	44	2	23	3.8	91	110	41	33	1	3	1	1143	126	6	136	8.3	.995	1B-133, OF-19
1985		159	.324	.567	652	211	48	3	35	5.4	107	**145**	56	41	2	0	0	1318	87	7	154	8.9	.995	1B-159
1986		162	.352	**.573**	677	**238**	53	2	31	4.6	117	113	53	35	0	0	0	1378	111	7	134	9.2	.995	1B-160, 3B-3, DH-1
1987		141	.327	.559	569	186	38	2	30	5.3	93	115	51	38	1	1	0	1239	91	5	122	9.5	.996	1B-140, DH-1
1988		144	.311	.462	599	186	37	0	18	3.0	94	88	41	29	1	1	0	1250	99	9	131	9.4	.993	1B-143, DH-1, OF-1
1989		158	.303	.477	631	191	37	2	23	3.6	79	113	51	30	3	0	0	1276	87	7	143	8.7	.995	1B-145, DH-17, OF-1
8 yrs.		1015	.323	.521	4022	1300	272	15	164	4.1	615	717	314	238	8	14	2	7969	617	44	851	8.5	.995	1B-923, OF-75, DH-20, 3B-3, 2B-1

Ralph Mattis

MATTIS, RALPH L. (Matty)
B. Aug. 24, 1890, Roxborough, Pa.   D. Sept. 13, 1960, Williamsport, Pa.
BR TR 5'11"   172 lbs.

Year	Team	Games	BA	SA	AB	H	2B	3B	HR	HR%	R	RBI	BB	SO	SB	PH AB	PH H	PO	A	E	DP	TC/G	FA	G by Pos
1914	PIT F	36	.247	.318	85	21	4	1	0	0.0	14	8	9		2	11	3	39	6	3	1	1.3	.938	OF-24

Cloy Mattox

MATTOX, CLOY MITCHELL (Monk)
Brother of Jim Mattox.
B. Nov. 24, 1902, Leesville, Va.   D. Aug. 31, 1985, Danville, Va.
BL TL 5'8"   168 lbs.

Year	Team	Games	BA	SA	AB	H	2B	3B	HR	HR%	R	RBI	BB	SO	SB	PH AB	PH H	PO	A	E	DP	TC/G	FA	G by Pos
1929	PHI A	3	.167	.167	6	1	0	0	0	0.0	0	0	1	1	0	0	0	5	2	1	0	2.7	.875	C-3

Jim Mattox

MATTOX, JAMES POWELL
Brother of Cloy Mattox.
B. Dec. 17, 1896, Leesville, Va.   D. Oct. 12, 1973, Myrtle Beach, S. C.
BL TR 5'9½"   168 lbs.

Year	Team	Games	BA	SA	AB	H	2B	3B	HR	HR%	R	RBI	BB	SO	SB	PH AB	PH H	PO	A	E	DP	TC/G	FA	G by Pos
1922	PIT N	29	.294	.353	51	15	1	1	0	0.0	11	3	3	3	0	4	3	52	11	1	2	2.2	.984	C-21
1923		22	.188	.281	32	6	1	1	0	0.0	4	1	0	5	0	14	2	16	8	1	0	1.1	.960	C-8
2 yrs.		51	.253	.325	83	21	2	2	0	0.0	15	4	1	8	0	18	5	68	19	2	2	1.7	.978	C-29

Len Matuszek

MATUSZEK, LEONARD JAMES
B. Sept. 27, 1954, Toledo, Ohio
BL TR 6'2"   190 lbs.

Year	Team		Games	BA	SA	AB	H	2B	3B	HR	HR%	R	RBI	BB	SO	SB	PH AB	PH H	PO	A	E	DP	TC/G	FA	G by Pos
1981	PHI N		13	.273	.364	11	3	1	0	0	0.0	3	1	3	0	9	3	5	4	0	1	0.7	1.000	3B-1, 1B-1
1982			25	.077	.103	39	3	1	0	0	0.0	1	3	1	10	0	17	1	12	8	3	1	0.9	.870	3B-8, 1B-3
1983			28	.275	.525	80	22	6	1	4	5.0	12	16	1	14	0	6	1	144	9	0	8	5.5	1.000	1B-21
1984			101	.248	.458	262	65	17	1	12	4.6	40	43	39	54	4	24	10	644	55	8	40	7.0	.989	1B-81, OF-1
1985	2 teams	TOR A (62G – .212)																							LA N (43G – .222)
"	total		105	.215	.350	214	46	8	3	5	2.3	33	28	19	38	2	29	4	66	4	0	3	0.7	1.000	DH-54, OF-17, 1B-15, 3B-1
1986	LA	N	91	.261	.432	199	52	7	0	9	4.5	26	28	21	47	2	25	4	235	22	5	18	2.9	.981	OF-37, 1B-31
1987			16	.067	.067	15	1	0	0	0	0.0	0	0	1	4	0	13	0	4	1	0	0	0.3	1.000	1B-3
7 yrs.			379	.234	.405	820	192	40	5	30	3.7	113	119	88	168	8	123	23	1110	103	16	71	3.2	.987	1B-155, OF-55, DH-54, 3B-10

LEAGUE CHAMPIONSHIP SERIES

Year	Team	Games	BA	SA	AB	H	2B	3B	HR	HR%	R	RBI	BB	SO	SB	PH AB	PH H	PO	A	E	DP	TC/G	FA	G by Pos
1985	LA N	3	1.000	1.000	1	1	0	0	0	0.0	1	0	0	0	1	1	1	0	0	0	0	0.0	–	OF-1, 1B-1

Gene Mauch

MAUCH, GENE WILLIAM (Skip)
B. Nov. 18, 1925, Salina, Kans.
Manager 1960-82, 1985-87.
BR TR 5'10"   165 lbs.

Year	Team		Games	BA	SA	AB	H	2B	3B	HR	HR%	R	RBI	BB	SO	SB	PH AB	PH H	PO	A	E	DP	TC/G	FA	G by Pos
1944	BKN	N	5	.133	.200	15	2	1	0	0	0.0	2	2	2	3	0	0	0	7	9	0	3	3.2	1.000	SS-5
1947	PIT	N	16	.300	.300	30	9	0	0	0	0.0	8	1	7	6	0	0	0	18	20	3	1	2.6	.927	2B-6, SS-4
1948	2 teams	BKN N (12G – .154)																							CHI N (53G – .203)
"	total		65	.199	.265	151	30	3	2	1	0.7	19	7	27	14	1	1	0	90	105	12	26	3.2	.942	2B-33, SS-20
1949	CHI	N	72	.247	.333	150	37	6	2	1	0.7	15	7	21	15	3	13	4	98	125	9	27	3.2	.961	2B-25, SS-19, 3B-7
1950	BOS	N	48	.231	.298	121	28	5	0	1	0.8	17	15	14	9	1	3	2	83	85	7	18	3.6	.960	2B-28, 3B-7, SS-5
1951			19	.100	.100	20	2	0	0	0	0.0	5	1	7	4	0	2	0	16	16	1	2	1.7	.970	SS-10, 3B-3, 2B-2
1952	STL	N	7	.000	.000	3	0	0	0	0	0.0	0	0	1	2	0	1	0	1	0	1	0	0.3	.500	SS-2
1956	BOS	A	7	.320	.320	25	8	0	0	0	0.0	4	3	3	3	0	0	0	12	17	2	4	4.4	.935	2B-6
1957			65	.270	.369	222	60	10	3	2	0.9	23	28	22	26	1	7	3	127	153	11	41	4.5	.962	2B-58
9 yrs.			304	.239	.312	737	176	25	7	5	0.7	93	62	104	82	6	38	9	452	530	46	122	3.4	.955	2B-158, SS-65, 3B-17

Al Maul

MAUL, ALBERT JOSEPH (Smiling Al)
B. Oct. 9, 1865, Philadelphia, Pa.   D. May 3, 1958, Philadelphia, Pa.
BR TR 6'   175 lbs.

Year	Team		Games	BA	SA	AB	H	2B	3B	HR	HR%	R	RBI	BB	SO	SB	PH AB	PH H	PO	A	E	DP	TC/G	FA	G by Pos
1884	PHI	U	1	.000	.000	4	0	0	0	0	0.0	0		0			0	0	1	0	0	0	1.0	1.000	P-1
1887	PHI	N	16	.304	.464	56	17	2	2	1	1.8	15	4	15	10	5	0	0	30	10	5	2	2.8	.889	OF-8, P-7, 1B-2
1888	PIT	N	74	.208	.274	259	54	9	4	0	0.0	21	31	21	45	9	0	0	450	20	16	22	6.6	.967	1B-38, OF-34, P-3
1889			68	.276	.393	257	71	6	6	4	1.6	37	44	29	41	18	0	0	125	32	10	5	2.5	.940	OF-64, P-15, SS-1
1890	PIT	P	45	.259	.321	162	42	6	2	0	0.0	31	21	22	12	5	0	0	51	84	16	5	3.4	.894	P-30, OF-15, SS-1
1891	PIT	N	47	.188	.255	149	28	2	4	0	0.0	15	14	20	28	4	0	0	61	13	9	3	1.8	.892	OF-40, P-8
1893	WAS	N	44	.254	.373	134	34	8	4	0	0.0	10	12	33	14	1	2	0	28	70	12	1	2.5	.891	P-37, OF-7
1894			41	.242	.363	124	30	3	3	2	1.6	23	20	14	11	1	2	0	30	51	9	1	2.2	.900	P-28, OF-12
1895			22	.250	.375	72	18	5	2	0	0.0	9	16	6	7	0	2	1	18	32	4	3	2.5	.926	P-16, OF-4
1896			8	.286	.393	28	8	1	1	0	0.0	6	6	5		3	0	0	2	10	1	1	1.6	.923	P-8
1897	2 teams	WAS N (1G – .000)																							BAL N (2G – .333)
"	total		3	.250	.250	4	1	0	0	0	0.0	0		0			0	0	0	2	0	0	0.7	1.000	P-3
1898	BAL	N	29	.204	.280	93	19	3	2	0	0.0	21	10	16		1	0	0	9	38	2	0	1.7	.959	P-28, OF-1
1899	BKN	N	4	.273	.273	11	3	0	0	0	0.0	2	0	1			0	0	0	9	1	0	2.5	.900	P-4

Year	Team		Games	BA	SA	AB	H	2B	3B	HR	HR%	R	RBI	BB	SO	SB	Pinch Hit AB	Pinch Hit H	PO	A	E	DP	TC/G	FA	G by Pos

Al Maul *continued*

Year	Team		Games	BA	SA	AB	H	2B	3B	HR	HR%	R	RBI	BB	SO	SB	PH AB	PH H	PO	A	E	DP	TC/G	FA	G by Pos
1900	PHI	N	5	.200	.200	15	3	0	0	0	0.0	2	1	2		0	0	0	0	11	1	0	2.4	.917	P-5
1901	NY	N	3	.375	.375	8	3	0	0	0	0.0	1	1	0		0	0	0	1	7	0	0	2.7	1.000	P-3
15 yrs.			410	.241	.332	1376	331	45	30	7	0.5	193	179	182	170	44	6	1	805	390	86	43	3.1	.933	P-187, OF-185, 1B-40, SS-1

Mark Mauldin

MAULDIN, MARSHALL REESE   BR TR 5'11" 170 lbs.
B. Nov. 5, 1914, Atlanta, Ga.

Year	Team		Games	BA	SA	AB	H	2B	3B	HR	HR%	R	RBI	BB	SO	SB	PH AB	PH H	PO	A	E	DP	TC/G	FA	G by Pos
1934	CHI	A	10	.263	.395	38	10	2	0	1	2.6	3	3	0	3	0	0	0	12	17	3	3	3.2	.906	3B-10

Carmen Mauro

MAURO, CARMEN LOUIS   BL TR 6' 167 lbs.
B. Nov. 10, 1926, St. Paul, Minn.

Year	Team		Games	BA	SA	AB	H	2B	3B	HR	HR%	R	RBI	BB	SO	SB	PH AB	PH H	PO	A	E	DP	TC/G	FA	G by Pos
1948	CHI	N	3	.200	.800	5	1	0	0	1	20.0	2	1	2	0	0	0	0	7	0	0	0	2.3	1.000	OF-2
1950			62	.227	.297	185	42	4	3	1	0.5	19	10	13	31	3	9	1	86	2	5	0	1.5	.946	OF-49
1951			13	.172	.207	29	5	1	0	0	0.0	3	3	2	6	0	6	1	17	1	2	0	1.5	.900	OF-6
1953	3 teams	BKN	N (8G – .000)			WAS	A (17G – .174)			PHI	A (64G – .267)														
"	total		89	.244	.315	197	48	4	5	0	0.0	16	19	20	28	3	31	8	130	6	4	0	1.6	.971	OF-56, 3B-1
4 yrs.			167	.231	.305	416	96	9	8	2	0.5	40	33	37	65	6	46	10	240	9	11	0	1.6	.958	OF-113, 3B-1

Bob Mavis

MAVIS, ROBERT HENRY   BL TR 5'7" 160 lbs.
B. Apr. 8, 1918, Milwaukee, Wis.

Year	Team		Games	BA	SA	AB	H	2B	3B	HR	HR%	R	RBI	BB	SO	SB	PH AB	PH H	PO	A	E	DP	TC/G	FA	G by Pos
1949	DET	A	1	–	–	0	0	0	0	0	–	0	0	0	0	0	0	0	0	0	0	0	0.0	–	

Dal Maxvill

MAXVILL, CHARLES DALLAN   BR TR 5'11" 157 lbs.
B. Feb. 18, 1939, Granite City, Ill.

Year	Team		Games	BA	SA	AB	H	2B	3B	HR	HR%	R	RBI	BB	SO	SB	PH AB	PH H	PO	A	E	DP	TC/G	FA	G by Pos
1962	STL	N	79	.222	.265	189	42	3	1	1	0.5	20	18	17	39	1	3	0	111	169	11	41	3.7	.962	SS-76, 3B-1
1963			53	.235	.275	51	12	2	0	0	0.0	12	3	6	11	0	3	0	25	40	2	10	1.3	.970	SS-24, 2B-9, 3B-3
1964			37	.231	.231	26	6	0	0	0	0.0	4	4	0	7	1	1	0	27	19	1	5	1.3	.979	2B-15, SS-13, OF-1, 3B-1
1965			68	.135	.202	89	12	2	2	0	0.0	10	10	7	15	0	2	0	74	86	2	23	2.4	.988	2B-49, SS-12
1966			134	.244	.294	394	96	14	3	0	0.0	25	24	37	61	3	2	0	223	434	22	91	5.1	.968	SS-128, 2B-5, OF-1
1967			152	.227	.279	476	108	14	4	1	0.2	37	41	48	66	1	0	0	241	486	19	78	4.9	.975	SS-148, 2B-7
1968			151	.253	.298	459	116	8	5	1	0.2	51	24	52	71	0	0	0	232	458	22	81	4.7	.969	SS-151
1969			132	.175	.228	372	65	10	2	2	0.5	27	32	44	52	1	0	0	216	408	20	78	4.9	.969	SS-131
1970			152	.201	.223	399	80	5	2	0	0.0	35	28	51	56	0	0	0	260	485	13	91	5.0	.983	SS-136, 2B-22
1971			142	.225	.258	356	80	10	1	0	0.0	31	24	43	45	1	1	0	188	413	13	71	4.3	.979	SS-140
1972	2 teams	STL	N (105G – .221)			OAK	A (27G – .250)																		
"	total		132	.224	.263	312	70	7	1	1	0.3	24	24	32	58	0	1	0	173	274	10	60	3.5	.978	SS-99, 2B-35
1973	2 teams	OAK	A (29G – .211)			PIT	N (74G – .189)																		
"	total		103	.191	.233	236	45	4	3	0	0.0	19	18	23	43	0	2	0	119	257	12	51	3.8	.969	SS-92, 2B-11, 3B-1
1974	2 teams	PIT	N (8G – .182)			OAK	A (60G – .192)																		
"	total		68	.189	.189	74	14	0	0	0	0.0	6	2	10	14	0	0	0	14	24	2	9	0.6	.950	SS-37, 2B-30, 3B-1
1975	OAK	A	20	.200	.200	10	2	0	0	0	0.0	1	0	0	0	0	0	0	10	13	1	1	1.2	.958	SS-20, 2B-2
14 yrs.			1423	.217	.259	3443	748	79	24	6	0.2	302	252	370	538	7	15	0	1913	3566	150	690	4.0	.973	SS-1207, 2B-185, 3B-7, OF-2

LEAGUE CHAMPIONSHIP SERIES

Year	Team		Games	BA	SA	AB	H	2B	3B	HR	HR%	R	RBI	BB	SO	SB	PH AB	PH H	PO	A	E	DP	TC/G	FA	G by Pos
1972	OAK	A	5	.125	.125	8	1	0	0	0	0.0	0	0	1	2	0	0	0	0	1	0	0	0.2	1.000	SS-4, 2B-1
1974			1	.000	.000	1	0	0	0	0	0.0	0	0	0	1	0	0	0	2	1	0	1	3.0	1.000	2B-1
2 yrs.			6	.111	.111	9	1	0	0	0	0.0	0	0	1	3	0	0	0	2	2	0	1	0.7	1.000	SS-4, 2B-2

WORLD SERIES

Year	Team		Games	BA	SA	AB	H	2B	3B	HR	HR%	R	RBI	BB	SO	SB	PH AB	PH H	PO	A	E	DP	TC/G	FA	G by Pos
1964	STL	N	7	.200	.250	20	4	1	0	0	0.0	0	1	1	4	0	0	0	13	15	0	5	4.0	1.000	2B-7
1967			7	.158	.263	19	3	0	1	0	0.0	1	1	4	1	0	0	0	13	17	0	3	4.3	1.000	SS-7
1968			7	.000	.000	22	0	0	0	0	0.0	1	0	3	5	0	0	0	15	14	0	6	4.1	1.000	SS-7
1974	OAK	A	2	–	–	0	0	0	0	0	–	0	0	0	0	0	0	0	0	0	0	0	0.0	–	2B-2
4 yrs.			23	.115	.164	61	7	1	1	0	0.0	2	2	8	10	0	0	0	41	46	0	14	3.8	1.000	SS-14, 2B-9

Charlie Maxwell

MAXWELL, CHARLES RICHARD (Smokey)   BL TL 5'11" 185 lbs.
B. Apr. 8, 1927, Lawton, Mich.

Year	Team		Games	BA	SA	AB	H	2B	3B	HR	HR%	R	RBI	BB	SO	SB	PH AB	PH H	PO	A	E	DP	TC/G	FA	G by Pos
1950	BOS	A	3	.000	.000	8	0	0	0	0	0.0	1	0	1	3	0	1	0	6	0	0	0	2.0	1.000	OF-2
1951			49	.188	.313	80	15	1	0	3	3.8	8	12	9	18	0	31	7	25	0	2	0	0.6	.926	OF-13
1952			8	.067	.133	15	1	1	0	0	0.0	0	3	11	0	3	0	30	5	1	1	4.5	.972	OF-3, 1B-3
1954			74	.250	.308	104	26	4	1	0	0.0	9	5	12	21	3	45	12	25	1	0	0	0.4	1.000	OF-27
1955	2 teams	BAL	A (4G – .000)			DET	A (55G – .266)																		
"	total		59	.257	.522	113	29	7	1	7	6.2	19	18	8	21	0	30	7	76	5	3	0	1.4	.964	OF-26, 1B-2
1956	DET	A	141	.326	.534	500	163	14	3	28	5.6	96	87	79	74	1	7	4	281	12	4	1	2.1	.987	OF-136
1957			138	.276	.482	492	136	23	3	24	4.9	75	82	76	84	3	3	3	317	6	1	1	2.3	.997	OF-137
1958			131	.272	.426	397	108	14	4	13	3.3	56	65	64	54	6	8	1	290	8	4	9	2.3	.987	OF-114, 1B-14
1959			145	.251	.461	518	130	12	2	31	6.0	81	95	81	91	0	8	3	285	6	4	1	2.0	.986	OF-136
1960			134	.237	.440	482	114	16	5	24	5.0	70	81	58	75	1	14	1	254	5	1	1	1.9	.996	OF-120
1961			79	.229	.405	131	30	4	1	5	3.8	11	11	20	24	1	45	12	53	2	2	0	0.7	.965	OF-25
1962	2 teams	DET	A (30G – .194)			CHI	A (69G – .296)																		
"	total		99	.271	.440	273	74	10	0	10	3.7	35	52	42	42	0	20	3	176	6	3	7	1.9	.984	OF-71, 1B-7
1963	CHI	A	71	.231	.362	130	30	4	1	3	2.3	17	17	31	27	0	21	3	136	7	0	15	2.0	1.000	OF-24, 1B-17
1964			2	.000	.000	2	0	0	0	0	0.0	0	0	0	0	0	0	0	0	0	0	0	0.0	–	
14 yrs.			1133	.264	.451	3245	856	110	26	148	4.6	478	532	484	545	18	238	56	1954	63	25	35	1.8	.988	OF-834, 1B-43

Carlos May

MAY, CARLOS   BL TR 5'11" 200 lbs.
Brother of Lee May.
B. May 17, 1948, Birmingham, Ala.

Year	Team		Games	BA	SA	AB	H	2B	3B	HR	HR%	R	RBI	BB	SO	SB	PH AB	PH H	PO	A	E	DP	TC/G	FA	G by Pos
1968	CHI	A	17	.179	.194	67	12	1	0	0	0.0	4	1	3	15	0	0	0	24	0	1	0	1.5	.960	OF-17
1969			100	.281	.488	367	103	18	2	18	4.9	62	62	58	66	1	2	1	154	10	3	0	1.7	.982	OF-100
1970			150	.285	.414	555	158	28	4	12	2.2	83	68	79	96	12	2	0	276	23	4	8	2.0	.987	OF-141, 1B-7

Year	Team	Games	BA	SA	AB	H	2B	3B	HR	HR%	R	RBI	BB	SO	SB	Pinch Hit AB	H	PO	A	E	DP	TC/G	FA	G by Pos

Carlos May *continued*

Year	Team	Games	BA	SA	AB	H	2B	3B	HR	HR%	R	RBI	BB	SO	SB	PH AB	PH H	PO	A	E	DP	TC/G	FA	G by Pos
1971		141	.294	.406	500	147	21	7	7	1.4	64	70	62	61	16	5	2	1206	72	19	90	9.2	.985	1B-130, OF-9
1972		148	.308	.438	523	161	26	3	12	2.3	83	68	79	70	23	0	0	247	15	5	2	1.8	.981	OF-145, 1B-5
1973		149	.268	.412	553	148	20	0	20	3.6	62	96	53	73	8	2	0	129	8	1	0	0.9	.993	DH-75, OF-70, 1B-2
1974		149	.249	.334	551	137	19	2	8	1.5	66	58	46	76	8	10	0	245	11	3	1	1.7	.988	OF-129, DH-13
1975		128	.271	.374	454	123	19	2	8	1.8	55	53	67	46	12	1	0	580	52	8	55	5.0	.988	1B-63, OF-46, DH-19
1976 2 teams	CHI A (20G – .175)			NY A (87G – .278)																				
" total		107	.259	.333	351	91	13	2	3	0.9	45	43	43	37	5	15	5	41	0	1	0	0.4	.976	DH-81, OF-16, 1B-1
1977 2 teams	NY A (65G – .227)			CAL A (11G – .333)																				
" total		76	.236	.312	199	47	7	1	2	1.0	21	17	22	25	0	14	6	18	2	0	1	0.3	1.000	DH-54, OF-4, 1B-3
10 yrs.		1165	.274	.392	4120	1127	172	23	90	2.2	545	536	512	565	85	51	14	2920	193	45	157	2.7	.986	OF-677, DH-242, 1B-211

LEAGUE CHAMPIONSHIP SERIES

| 1976 | NY A | 3 | .200 | .300 | 10 | 2 | 1 | 0 | 0 | 0.0 | 1 | 0 | 1 | 4 | 0 | 1 | 0 | 0 | 0 | 0 | 0 | 0.0 | – | DH-3 |

WORLD SERIES

| 1976 | NY A | 4 | .000 | .000 | 9 | 0 | 0 | 0 | 0 | 0.0 | 0 | 0 | 0 | 1 | 0 | 2 | 0 | 0 | 0 | 0 | 0 | 0.0 | – | DH-4 |

Dave May

MAY, DAVID LaFRANCE
B. Dec. 23, 1943, New Castle, Del.

BL TR 5'10½" 186 lbs.

Year	Team	Games	BA	SA	AB	H	2B	3B	HR	HR%	R	RBI	BB	SO	SB	PH AB	PH H	PO	A	E	DP	TC/G	FA	G by Pos
1967	BAL A	36	.235	.306	85	20	1	0	1	1.2	12	7	6	13	0	15	3	30	1	0	0	0.9	.969	OF-19
1968		84	.191	.270	152	29	6	3	0	0.0	15	7	19	27	3	26	3	62	1	1	0	0.8	.984	OF-61
1969		78	.242	.367	120	29	6	0	3	2.5	8	10	9	23	2	32	8	43	4	3	0	0.6	.940	OF-40
1970 2 teams	BAL A (25G – .194)			MIL A (101G – .240)																				
" total		126	.236	.332	373	88	8	2	8	2.1	42	37	48	60	8	15	1	260	6	3	0	2.1	.989	OF-108
1971	MIL A	144	.277	.425	501	139	20	3	16	3.2	74	65	50	59	15	3	0	342	10	9	3	2.5	.985	OF-142
1972		143	.238	.340	500	119	20	2	9	1.8	49	45	47	56	11	7	3	376	9	6	3	2.7	.985	OF-138
1973		156	.303	.473	624	189	23	4	25	4.0	96	93	44	78	6	3	3	401	9	9	3	2.7	.979	OF-152, DH-2
1974		135	.226	.325	477	108	15	1	10	2.1	56	42	28	73	4	8	1	249	10	3	2	1.9	.989	OF-121, DH-8
1975	ATL N	82	.276	.493	203	56	8	0	12	5.9	28	40	25	27	1	26	7	103	3	4	2	1.3	.964	OF-53
1976		105	.215	.308	214	46	5	3	3	1.4	27	23	26	31	5	44	8	98	5	3	1	1.0	.972	OF-60
1977	TEX A	120	.241	.350	340	82	14	1	7	2.1	46	42	32	43	1	11	2	181	8	6	2	1.6	.969	OF-111, DH-5
1978 2 teams	MIL A (39G – .195)			PIT N (5G – .000)																				
" total		44	.185	.309	81	15	4	0	2	2.5	9	11	10	11	1	18	4	32	2	2	1	0.8	.944	OF-16, DH-8
12 yrs.		1253	.251	.375	3670	920	130	20	96	2.6	462	422	344	501	60	208	43	2177	68	50	17	1.8	.978	OF-1021, DH-23

LEAGUE CHAMPIONSHIP SERIES

| 1969 | BAL A | 1 | .000 | .000 | 1 | 0 | 0 | 0 | 0 | 0.0 | 0 | 0 | 0 | 0 | 0 | 1 | 0 | 0 | 0 | 0 | 0 | 0.0 | – | |

WORLD SERIES

| 1969 | BAL A | 2 | .000 | .000 | 1 | 0 | 0 | 0 | 0 | 0.0 | 0 | 0 | 1 | 1 | 0 | 1 | 0 | 0 | 0 | 0 | 0 | 0.0 | – | |

Jerry May

MAY, JERRY LEE
B. Dec. 14, 1943, Staunton, Va.

BR TR 6'2" 190 lbs.

Year	Team	Games	BA	SA	AB	H	2B	3B	HR	HR%	R	RBI	BB	SO	SB	PH AB	PH H	PO	A	E	DP	TC/G	FA	G by Pos
1964	PIT N	11	.258	.258	31	8	0	0	0	0.0	1	3	3	9	0	0	0	80	5	1	0	7.8	.988	C-11
1965		4	.500	.500	2	1	0	0	0	0.0	0	1	0	0	0	0	0	2	0	0	0	0.5	1.000	C-4
1966		42	.250	.385	52	13	4	0	1	1.9	6	2	2	15	0	4	0	114	12	2	3	3.0	.984	C-41
1967		110	.271	.351	325	88	13	2	3	0.9	23	22	36	55	0	1	0	550	52	4	9	5.5	.993	C-110
1968		137	.219	.272	416	91	15	2	1	0.2	26	33	41	80	0	1	0	752	70	10	10	6.1	.988	C-135
1969		62	.232	.384	190	44	8	0	7	3.7	21	23	9	53	1	11	2	325	22	2	3	5.6	.994	C-52
1970		51	.209	.288	139	29	4	2	1	0.7	13	16	21	25	0	4	2	280	32	2	6	6.2	.994	C-45
1971	KC A	71	.252	.344	218	55	13	2	1	0.5	16	24	27	37	0	2	0	314	38	1	6	5.0	.997	C-71
1972		53	.190	.276	116	22	5	1	1	0.9	10	4	14	13	0	11	1	175	13	4	1	3.6	.979	C-41
1973 2 teams	KC A (11G – .133)			NY N (4G – .250)																				
" total		15	.158	.237	38	6	1	1	0	0.0	4	2	4	6	0	0	0	57	4	3	2	4.3	.953	C-15
10 yrs.		556	.234	.318	1527	357	63	10	15	1.0	120	130	157	293	1	34	5	2649	248	29	36	5.3	.990	C-525

Lee May

MAY, LEE ANDREW
Brother of Carlos May.
B. Mar. 23, 1943, Birmingham, Ala.

BR TR 6'3" 195 lbs.

Year	Team	Games	BA	SA	AB	H	2B	3B	HR	HR%	R	RBI	BB	SO	SB	PH AB	PH H	PO	A	E	DP	TC/G	FA	G by Pos
1965	CIN N	5	.000	.000	4	0	0	0	0	0.0	1	0	0	1	0	4	0	0	0	0	0	0.0	–	
1966		25	.333	.507	75	25	5	1	2	2.7	14	10	0	14	0	9	1	132	9	4	15	5.8	.972	1B-16
1967		127	.265	.422	438	116	29	2	12	2.7	54	57	19	80	4	8	0	703	46	6	50	5.9	.992	1B-81, OF-48
1968		146	.290	.469	559	162	32	4	22	3.9	78	80	34	100	4	3	1	1094	73	9	86	8.0	.996	1B-122, OF-33
1969		158	.278	.529	607	169	32	3	38	6.3	85	110	45	142	5	1	0	1395	102	11	128	9.5	.993	1B-156, OF-7
1970		153	.253	.484	605	153	34	2	34	5.6	78	94	38	125	1	0	0	1362	109	10	143	9.7	.993	1B-153
1971		147	.278	.532	553	154	17	3	39	7.1	85	98	42	113	3	4	1	1261	78	8	118	9.2	.994	1B-143
1972	HOU N	148	.284	.490	592	168	31	2	29	4.9	87	98	52	**145**	3	2	1	1318	76	6	133	9.5	.996	1B-146
1973		148	.270	.479	545	147	24	3	28	5.1	65	105	34	122	1	4	0	1220	78	9	112	8.8	.993	1B-144
1974		152	.268	.444	556	149	26	0	24	4.3	59	85	17	97	1	8	1	1253	88	8	116	8.9	.994	1B-145
1975	BAL A	146	.262	.424	580	152	28	2	20	3.4	67	99	36	91	1	1	0	1312	106	10	138	9.8	.993	1B-144, DH-2
1976		148	.258	.447	530	137	17	4	25	4.7	61	**109**	41	104	4	4	1	722	62	3	61	5.3	.996	1B-94, DH-52
1977		150	.253	.426	585	148	16	2	27	4.6	75	99	38	119	2	2	0	907	56	5	101	6.5	.995	1B-110, DH-39
1978		148	.246	.414	556	137	16	1	25	4.5	56	80	31	110	5	6	1	34	2	1	3	0.3	.973	DH-140, 1B-4
1979		124	.254	.412	456	116	15	0	19	4.2	59	69	28	100	3	7	3	21	0	2	0	0.2	.913	DH-117, 1B-2
1980		78	.243	.401	222	54	10	2	7	3.2	20	31	15	53	2	27	11	57	3	0	4	0.8	1.000	DH-58, 1B-7
1981	KC A	26	.291	.345	55	16	3	0	0	0.0	3	8	3	14	0	13	4	63	2	0	7	2.5	1.000	1B-8, DH-4
1982		42	.308	.505	91	28	5	2	3	3.3	12	12	14	18	0	9	1	175	10	2	18	4.5	.989	1B-32, DH-2
18 yrs.		2071	.267	.459	7609	2031	340	31	354	4.7	959	1244	487	1570	39	112	27	13029	900	90	1236	6.8	.994	1B-1507, DH-414, OF-88
														10th										

DIVISIONAL PLAYOFF SERIES

| 1981 | KC A | 1 | – | – | 0 | 0 | 0 | 0 | 0 | – | 0 | 0 | 0 | 0 | 0 | 0 | 0 | 0 | 0 | 0 | 0 | 0.0 | – | 1B-1 |

LEAGUE CHAMPIONSHIP SERIES

| 1970 | CIN N | 3 | .167 | .250 | 12 | 2 | 1 | 0 | 0 | 0.0 | 0 | 2 | 0 | 2 | 0 | 0 | 0 | 31 | 1 | 0 | 1 | 10.7 | 1.000 | 1B-3 |

Year	Team	Games	BA	SA	AB	H	2B	3B	HR	HR%	R	RBI	BB	SO	SB	Pinch Hit AB	Pinch Hit H	PO	A	E	DP	TC/G	FA	G by Pos

Lee May continued

Year	Team		Games	BA	SA	AB	H	2B	3B	HR	HR%	R	RBI	BB	SO	SB	AB	H	PO	A	E	DP	TC/G	FA	G by Pos
1979	BAL	A	2	.143	.143	7	1	0	0	0	0.0	0	1	1	3	0	0	0	0	0	0	0	0.0	–	DH-2
	2 yrs.		5	.158	.211	19	3	1	0	0	0.0	1	3	1	5	0	0	0	31	1	0	1	6.4	1.000	1B-3, DH-2

WORLD SERIES

1970	CIN	N	5	.389	.833	18	7	2	0	2	11.1	6	8	2	2	0	0	0	48	3	0	3	10.2	1.000	1B-5
1979	BAL	A	2	.000	.000	1	0	0	0	0	0.0	0	0	1	1	0	1	0	0	0	0	0	0.0	–	
	2 yrs.		7	.368	.789	19	7	2	0	2	10.5	6	8	3	3	0	1	0	48	3	0	3	7.3	1.000	1B-5

Milt May

MAY, MILTON SCOTT
Son of Pinky May.
B. Aug. 1, 1950, Gary, Ind.

BL TR 6' 190 lbs.

Year	Team		Games	BA	SA	AB	H	2B	3B	HR	HR%	R	RBI	BB	SO	SB	AB	H	PO	A	E	DP	TC/G	FA	G by Pos
1970	PIT	N	5	.500	.750	4	2	1	0	0	0.0	1	2	0	0	0	4	2	0	0	0	0	0.0	–	C-31
1971			49	.278	.429	126	35	1	0	6	4.8	15	25	9	16	0	17	3	168	12	0	3	3.7	1.000	C-31
1972			57	.281	.353	139	39	10	0	0	0.0	12	14	10	13	0	18	4	179	21	3	2	3.6	.985	C-33
1973			101	.269	.378	283	76	8	1	7	2.5	29	31	34	26	0	18	2	402	36	12	4	4.5	.973	C-79
1974	HOU	N	127	.289	.402	405	117	17	4	7	1.7	47	54	39	33	0	9	2	525	63	4	10	4.7	.993	C-116
1975			111	.241	.316	386	93	15	1	4	1.0	29	52	26	41	1	8	3	568	70	9	8	5.8	.986	C-102
1976	DET	A	6	.280	.320	25	7	1	0	0	0.0	2	1	0	1	0	0	0	33	5	0	0	6.3	1.000	C-6
1977			115	.249	.378	397	99	9	3	12	3.0	32	46	26	31	0	5	2	551	78	9	12	5.5	.986	C-111
1978			105	.250	.361	352	88	9	0	10	2.8	24	37	27	26	0	12	1	406	58	10	5	4.5	.979	C-94
1979	2 teams		DET A (6G – .273)			CHI A (65G – .252)																			
"	total		71	.254	.423	213	54	15	0	7	3.3	24	31	15	28	0	2	0	296	28	6	1	4.6	.982	C-70
1980	SF	N	111	.260	.366	358	93	16	2	6	1.7	27	50	25	40	0	15	6	500	59	8	12	5.1	.986	C-103
1981			97	.310	.383	316	98	17	0	2	0.6	20	33	34	29	1	9	5	468	48	6	4	5.4	.989	C-93
1982			114	.263	.380	395	104	19	0	9	2.3	29	39	28	38	0	13	6	552	61	8	5	5.4	.987	C-110
1983	2 teams		SF N (66G – .247)			PIT N (7G – .250)																			
"	total		73	.247	.369	198	49	6	0	8	4.0	18	20	22	24	2	13	3	308	35	6	5	4.8	.983	C-60
1984	PIT	N	50	.177	.240	96	17	2	0	1	1.0	4	8	10	15	0	18	3	135	15	1	2	3.0	.993	C-26
	15 yrs.		1192	.263	.371	3693	971	147	11	77	2.1	313	443	305	361	4	161	42	5091	589	82	73	4.8	.986	C-1034

LEAGUE CHAMPIONSHIP SERIES

1971	PIT	N	1	.000	.000	1	0	0	0	0	0.0	0	0	0	1	0	1	0	0	0	0	0	0.0	–	C-1
1972			1	.500	.500	2	1	0	0	0	0.0	0	1	0	0	0	0	0	8	1	0	1	9.0	1.000	C-1
	2 yrs.		2	.333	.333	3	1	0	0	0	0.0	0	1	0	1	0	1	0	8	1	0	1	4.5	1.000	C-1

WORLD SERIES

| 1971 | PIT | N | 2 | .500 | .500 | 2 | 1 | 0 | 0 | 0 | 0.0 | 0 | 1 | 0 | 0 | 0 | 2 | 1 | 0 | 0 | 0 | 0 | 0.0 | – | |

Pinky May

MAY, MERRILL GLEND
Father of Milt May.
B. Jan. 18, 1911, Laconia, Ind.

BR TR 5'11½" 165 lbs.

Year	Team		Games	BA	SA	AB	H	2B	3B	HR	HR%	R	RBI	BB	SO	SB	AB	H	PO	A	E	DP	TC/G	FA	G by Pos
1939	PHI	N	135	.287	.371	464	133	27	3	2	0.4	49	62	41	20	4	3	1	153	263	19	28	3.2	.956	3B-132
1940			136	.293	.355	501	147	24	2	1	0.2	59	48	58	33	2	0	0	140	303	22	13	3.4	.953	3B-135, SS-1
1941			142	.267	.318	490	131	17	4	0	0.0	46	39	55	30	2	2	1	194	324	15	31	3.8	.972	3B-140
1942			115	.238	.281	345	82	15	0	0	0.0	25	18	51	17	3	7	0	109	227	13	23	3.0	.963	3B-107
1943			137	.282	.345	415	117	19	2	1	0.2	31	48	56	21	2	5	3	142	280	16	20	3.2	.963	3B-132
	5 yrs.		665	.275	.337	2215	610	102	11	4	0.2	210	215	261	121	13	17	5	738	1397	85	115	3.3	.962	3B-646, SS-1

John Mayberry

MAYBERRY, JOHN CLAIBORN
B. Feb. 18, 1949, Detroit, Mich.

BL TL 6'3" 215 lbs.

Year	Team		Games	BA	SA	AB	H	2B	3B	HR	HR%	R	RBI	BB	SO	SB	AB	H	PO	A	E	DP	TC/G	FA	G by Pos
1968	HOU	N	4	.000	.000	9	0	0	0	0	0.0	0	0	0	2	0	2	0	25	0	0	1	6.3	1.000	1B-2
1969			5	.000	.000	4	0	0	0	0	0.0	0	0	1	1	0	3	0	0	0	0	0	0.0	–	
1970			50	.216	.365	148	32	3	2	5	3.4	23	14	21	33	1	6	1	371	35	2	29	8.2	.995	1B-45
1971			46	.182	.350	137	25	0	1	7	5.1	16	14	13	32	0	10	1	317	15	1	20	7.2	.997	1B-37
1972	KC	A	149	.298	.507	503	150	24	3	25	5.0	65	100	78	74	0	4	2	1338	82	7	141	9.5	.995	1B-146
1973			152	.278	.478	510	142	20	2	26	5.1	87	100	122	79	3	4	2	1457	81	9	156	10.2	.994	1B-149, DH-1
1974			126	.234	.424	427	100	13	1	22	5.2	63	69	77	72	4	7	2	963	61	10	101	8.2	.990	1B-106, DH-16
1975			156	.291	.547	554	161	38	1	34	6.1	95	106	119	73	5	1	0	1199	100	16	105	8.4	.988	1B-131, DH-27
1976			161	.232	.342	594	138	22	2	13	2.2	76	95	82	73	3	1	0	1484	105	7	132	9.9	.995	1B-160, DH-9
1977			153	.230	.401	543	125	22	1	23	4.2	73	82	83	86	1	2	1	1296	81	7	118	9.0	.995	1B-145, DH-8
1978	TOR	A	152	.250	.416	515	129	15	2	22	4.3	51	70	60	57	1	10	2	1143	52	8	120	7.9	.993	1B-139, DH-7
1979			137	.274	.461	464	127	22	1	21	4.5	61	74	69	60	1	6	2	1192	74	6	129	9.3	.995	1B-135
1980			149	.248	.473	501	124	19	2	30	6.0	62	82	77	80	2	5	1	1243	79	8	138	8.9	.994	1B-136, DH-8
1981			94	.248	.452	290	72	6	1	17	5.9	34	43	44	45	1	7	2	647	36	5	65	7.3	.993	1B-80, DH-10
1982	2 teams		TOR A (17G – .273)			NY A (69G – .209)																			
"	total		86	.218	.367	248	54	7	0	10	4.0	27	30	35	43	0	6	1	494	26	2	52	6.1	.996	1B-67, DH-17
	15 yrs.		1620	.253	.439	5447	1379	211	19	255	4.7	733	879	881	810	20	73	20	13169	827	88	1307	8.7	.994	1B-1478, DH-103

LEAGUE CHAMPIONSHIP SERIES

1976	KC	A	5	.222	.389	18	4	0	0	1	5.6	4	3	1	0	0	0	0	48	1	0	4	9.8	1.000	1B-5
1977			4	.167	.500	12	2	1	0	1	8.3	1	3	1	2	0	0	0	29	1	2	0	8.0	.938	1B-4
	2 yrs.		9	.200	.433	30	6	1	0	2	6.7	5	6	2	2	0	0	0	77	2	2	4	9.0	.975	1B-9

Lee Maye

MAYE, ARTHUR LEE
B. Dec. 11, 1934, Tuscaloosa, Ala.

BL TR 6'2" 190 lbs.

Year	Team		Games	BA	SA	AB	H	2B	3B	HR	HR%	R	RBI	BB	SO	SB	AB	H	PO	A	E	DP	TC/G	FA	G by Pos
1959	MIL	N	51	.300	.436	140	42	5	1	4	2.9	17	16	7	26	2	7	4	80	3	2	1	1.7	.976	OF-44
1960			41	.301	.373	83	25	6	0	0	0.0	14	2	7	21	5	17	2	29	1	1	0	0.8	.968	OF-19
1961			110	.271	.440	373	101	11	5	14	3.8	68	41	36	50	10	17	5	169	6	5	0	1.6	.972	OF-96
1962			99	.244	.358	349	85	10	0	10	2.9	40	41	25	58	9	8	1	209	2	5	1	2.2	.977	OF-94
1963			124	.271	.428	442	120	21	7	11	2.5	67	34	36	52	14	18	3	231	4	4	1	1.9	.983	OF-111
1964			153	.304	.447	588	179	44	5	10	1.7	96	74	34	54	5	13	2	268	9	11	1	1.9	.962	OF-135, 3B-5

Year	Team	Games	BA	SA	AB	H	2B	3B	HR	HR%	R	RBI	BB	SO	SB	Pinch Hit AB	Pinch Hit H	PO	A	E	DP	TC/G	FA	G by Pos

Lee Maye *continued*

Year	Team	Games	BA	SA	AB	H	2B	3B	HR	HR%	R	RBI	BB	SO	SB	PH AB	PH H	PO	A	E	DP	TC/G	FA	G by Pos
1965	2 teams	MIL N (15G – .302)			HOU N	(108G – .251)																		
"	total	123	.256	.359	468	120	19	7	5	1.1	46	43	22	43	1	8	1	200	8	10	1	1.8	.954	OF-116
1966	HOU N	115	.288	.419	358	103	12	4	9	2.5	38	36	20	26	4	20	4	145	4	8	0	1.4	.949	OF-97
1967	CLE A	115	.259	.444	297	77	20	4	9	3.0	43	27	26	47	3	42	10	102	2	2	0	0.9	.981	OF-77, 2B-1
1968		109	.281	.378	299	84	13	2	4	1.3	20	26	15	24	0	30	9	123	4	3	0	1.2	.977	OF-80, 1B-1
1969	2 teams	CLE A (43G – .250)			WAS A	(71G – .290)																		
"	total	114	.277	.422	346	96	14	3	10	2.9	50	41	28	40	2	24	4	155	2	7	1	1.4	.957	OF-93, 3B-1
1970	2 teams	WAS A (96G – .263)			CHI A	(6G – .167)																		
"	total	102	.261	.395	261	68	12	1	7	2.7	28	31	21	33	4	39	7	75	5	0	1	0.8	1.000	OF-68, 3B-1
1971	CHI A	32	.205	.318	44	9	2	0	1	2.3	6	7	5	7	0	17	5	11	1	0	0	0.4	1.000	OF-10
13 yrs.		1288	.274	.410	4048	1109	190	39	94	2.3	533	419	282	481	59	260	57	1797	51	58	7	1.5	.970	OF-1040, 3B-7, 2B-1, 1B-1

Ed Mayer

MAYER, EDWARD H   B. Aug. 16, 1866, Marshall, Ill.   D. May 18, 1913, Chicago, Ill.   5'8½"   155 lbs.

Year	Team	Games	BA	SA	AB	H	2B	3B	HR	HR%	R	RBI	BB	SO	SB	PH AB	PH H	PO	A	E	DP	TC/G	FA	G by Pos
1890	PHI N	117	.242	.320	484	117	25	5	1	0.2	49	70	22	36	20	0	0	173	224	55	22	3.9	.878	3B-117
1891		68	.187	.224	268	50	2	4	0	0.0	24	31	14	29	7	0	0	100	105	29	4	3.4	.876	3B-31, OF-29, SS-7, 2B-1
2 yrs.		185	.222	.286	752	167	27	9	1	0.1	73	101	36	65	27	0	0	273	329	84	26	3.7	.878	3B-148, OF-29, SS-7, 2B-1

Sam Mayer

MAYER, SAMUEL FRANKEL   Born Samuel Frankel Erskine.   Brother of Erskine Mayer.   BR TL 5'10"   164 lbs.
B. Feb. 28, 1893, Atlanta, Ga.   D. July 1, 1962, Atlanta, Ga.

Year	Team	Games	BA	SA	AB	H	2B	3B	HR	HR%	R	RBI	BB	SO	SB	PH AB	PH H	PO	A	E	DP	TC/G	FA	G by Pos
1915	WAS A	11	.241	.345	29	7	0	0	1	3.4	5	4	4	2	1	0	0	14	1	0	1	1.4	1.000	OF-9, 1B-1, P-1

Wally Mayer

MAYER, WALTER A.   B. July 8, 1890, Cincinnati, Ohio   D. Nov. 18, 1951, Minneapolis, Minn.   BR TR 5'11"   168 lbs.

Year	Team	Games	BA	SA	AB	H	2B	3B	HR	HR%	R	RBI	BB	SO	SB	PH AB	PH H	PO	A	E	DP	TC/G	FA	G by Pos
1911	CHI A	1	.000	.000	3	0	0	0	0	0.0	0	0	2		0	0	0	7	2	1	0	10.0	.900	C-1
1912		7	.000	.000	9	0	0	0	0	0.0	1	0	1		0	0	0	13	1	0	0	2.0	1.000	C-6
1914		39	.165	.224	85	14	3	1	0	0.0	7	5	14	23	1	5	0	138	47	7	3	4.9	.964	C-33, 3B-1
1915		22	.222	.315	54	12	3	1	0	0.0	5	8	5	8	0	2	0	89	15	1	0	4.8	.990	C-20
1917	BOS A	4	.167	.167	12	2	0	0	0	0.0	2	0	5		0	0	0	19	8	1	1	7.0	.964	C-4
1918		26	.224	.306	49	11	4	0	0	0.0	7	5	7	7	0	3	0	63	18	3	0	3.2	.964	C-23
1919	STL A	30	.226	.323	62	14	4	1	0	0.0	2	5	8	11	0	5	1	84	33	5	1	4.1	.959	C-25
7 yrs.		129	.193	.266	274	53	14	4	0	0.0	22	20	42	51	1	16	1	413	124	18	5	4.3	.968	C-112, 3B-1

Paddy Mayes

MAYES, ADAIR BUSHYHEAD   B. Mar. 17, 1885, Locust Grove, Okla.   D. May 28, 1962, Fayetteville, Ark.   BL TR 5'11"   160 lbs.

Year	Team	Games	BA	SA	AB	H	2B	3B	HR	HR%	R	RBI	BB	SO	SB	PH AB	PH H	PO	A	E	DP	TC/G	FA	G by Pos
1911	PHI N	5	.000	.000	5	0	0	0	0	0.0	1	0	1	2	0	1	0	2	0	0	0	0.4	1.000	OF-2

Buster Maynard

MAYNARD, JAMES WALTER   B. Mar. 25, 1913, Henderson, N. C.   D. Sept. 7, 1977, Durham, N. C.   BR TR 5'11"   170 lbs.

Year	Team	Games	BA	SA	AB	H	2B	3B	HR	HR%	R	RBI	BB	SO	SB	PH AB	PH H	PO	A	E	DP	TC/G	FA	G by Pos
1940	NY N	7	.276	.586	29	8	2	2	1	3.4	6	2	2	6	0	0	0	13	0	1	0	2.0	.929	OF-7
1942		89	.247	.342	190	47	4	1	4	2.1	17	32	19	19	3	15	3	116	28	5	5	1.7	.966	OF-58, 3B-10, 2B-1
1943		121	.206	.305	393	81	8	2	9	2.3	43	32	24	27	3	19	1	177	57	7	2	2.0	.971	OF-74, 3B-22
1946		7	.000	.000	4	0	0	0	0	0.0	2	0	1	1	0	1	0	3	0	1	0	0.6	.750	OF-3
4 yrs.		224	.221	.328	616	136	14	5	14	2.3	68	66	46	53	6	35	4	309	85	14	7	1.8	.966	OF-142, 3B-32, 2B-1

Chick Maynard

MAYNARD, LEROY EVANS   B. Nov. 2, 1896, Turner Falls, Mass.   D. Jan. 31, 1957, Bangor, Me.   BL TR 5'9"   150 lbs.

Year	Team	Games	BA	SA	AB	H	2B	3B	HR	HR%	R	RBI	BB	SO	SB	PH AB	PH H	PO	A	E	DP	TC/G	FA	G by Pos
1922	BOS A	12	.125	.125	24	3	0	0	0	0.0	1	0	3	2	0	0	0	13	21	5	1	3.3	.872	SS-12

Eddie Mayo

MAYO, EDWARD JOSEPH   Born Edward Joseph Mayoski.   BL TR 5'11"   178 lbs.
B. Apr. 15, 1910, Holyoke, Mass.

Year	Team	Games	BA	SA	AB	H	2B	3B	HR	HR%	R	RBI	BB	SO	SB	PH AB	PH H	PO	A	E	DP	TC/G	FA	G by Pos
1936	NY N	46	.199	.262	141	28	4	1	1	0.7	11	8	11	12	0	3	1	32	69	2	8	2.2	.981	3B-40
1937	BOS N	65	.227	.291	172	39	6	1	1	0.6	19	18	15	20	1	14	4	57	73	6	2	2.1	.956	3B-50
1938		8	.214	.429	14	3	0	0	1	7.1	2	4	1	0	0	0	0	6	10	1	3	2.1	.941	3B-6, SS-2
1943	PHI A	128	.219	.244	471	103	10	1	0	0.0	49	28	34	32	2	5	0	176	223	10	18	3.2	.976	3B-123
1944	DET A	154	.249	.313	607	151	18	3	5	0.8	76	63	57	23	9	0	0	401	498	21	125	6.0	.977	2B-143, SS-11
1945		134	.285	.405	501	143	24	3	10	2.0	71	54	48	29	7	9	4	326	393	15	91	5.5	.980	2B-124
1946		51	.252	.317	202	51	9	2	0	0.0	21	22	14	12	6	2	0	96	128	8	28	4.5	.965	2B-49
1947		142	.279	.379	535	149	28	4	6	1.1	66	48	48	28	3	1	1	326	365	12	80	5.0	.983	2B-142
1948		106	.249	.324	370	92	20	1	2	0.5	35	42	30	19	1	10	2	211	242	11	49	4.4	.976	2B-86, 3B-10
9 yrs.		834	.252	.328	3013	759	119	16	26	0.9	350	287	258	175	29	44	12	1631	1998	86	404	4.5	.977	2B-544, 3B-229, SS-13
WORLD SERIES																								
1936	NY N	1	.000	.000	1	0	0	0	0	0.0	0	0	0	0	0	0	0	0	0	0	0	0.0	–	3B-1
1945	DET A	7	.250	.286	28	7	1	0	0	0.0	4	2	2	2	0	0	0	18	13	1	4	4.6	.969	2B-7
2 yrs.		8	.241	.276	29	7	1	0	0	0.0	4	2	2	2	0	0	0	18	13	1	4	4.0	.969	2B-7, 3B-1

Jackie Mayo

MAYO, JOHN LEWIS   B. July 26, 1925, Litchfield, Ill.   BL TR 6'1"   190 lbs.

Year	Team	Games	BA	SA	AB	H	2B	3B	HR	HR%	R	RBI	BB	SO	SB	PH AB	PH H	PO	A	E	DP	TC/G	FA	G by Pos
1948	PHI N	12	.229	.343	35	8	2	1	0	0.0	7	3	7	7	1	1	0	27	1	0	0	2.3	1.000	OF-11
1949		45	.128	.128	39	5	0	0	0	0.0	3	2	4	9	0	15	0	23	1	3	0	0.6	.889	OF-25
1950		18	.222	.306	36	8	3	0	0	0.0	1	3	2	5	0	3	0	23	0	1	0	1.3	.958	OF-15
1951		9	.143	.143	7	1	0	0	0	0.0	1	0	0	0	0	4	0	5	0	0	0	0.4	1.000	OF-5
1952		50	.244	.311	119	29	5	0	1	0.8	13	4	12	17	1	15	0	108	10	0	4	2.4	1.000	OF-27, 1B-6
1953		5	.000	.000	4	0	0	0	0	0.0	0	0	0	1	0	4	0	0	0	0	0	0.0	–	OF-1
6 yrs.		139	.213	.275	240	51	10	1	1	0.4	25	12	25	35	2	42	1	185	12	4	4	1.4	.980	OF-84, 1B-6
WORLD SERIES																								
1950	PHI N	3	–	–	0	0	0	0	0	–	0	0	1	0	0	0	0	1	0	0	0	0.3	1.000	OF-1

Year	Team		Games	BA	SA	AB	H	2B	3B	HR	HR%	R	RBI	BB	SO	SB	Pinch Hit AB	H	PO	A	E	DP	TC/G	FA	G by Pos

Jim McAnany *continued*

WORLD SERIES

Year	Team		Games	BA	SA	AB	H	2B	3B	HR	HR%	R	RBI	BB	SO	SB	AB	H	PO	A	E	DP	TC/G	FA	G by Pos
1959	CHI	A	3	.000	.000	5	0	0	0	0	0.0	0	0	1	0	0	0	0	5	0	0	0	1.7	1.000	OF-3

Ike McAuley

McAULEY, JAMES EARL
B. Aug. 19, 1891, Wichita, Kans. D. Apr. 6, 1928, Des Moines, Iowa
BR TR 5'9½'' 150 lbs.

Year	Team		Games	BA	SA	AB	H	2B	3B	HR	HR%	R	RBI	BB	SO	SB	AB	H	PO	A	E	DP	TC/G	FA	G by Pos
1914	PIT	N	15	.125	.125	24	3	0	0	0	0.0	3	0	0	8	0	0	1	9	19	4	4	2.1	.875	SS-5, 3B-3, 2B-2
1915			5	.133	.200	15	2	1	0	0	0.0	0	0	0	6	0	2	0	3	8	1	1	2.4	.917	SS-5
1916			4	.250	.250	8	2	0	0	0	0.0	1	1	0	1	0	0	0	8	7	1	2	4.0	.938	SS-4
1917	STL	N	3	.286	.286	7	2	0	0	0	0.0	0	1	0	1	0	0	0	2	3	1	0	2.0	.833	SS-3
1925	CHI	N	37	.280	.368	125	35	7	2	0	0.0	10	11	11	12	1	0	0	94	93	10	21	5.3	.949	SS-37
5 yrs.			64	.246	.313	179	44	8	2	0	0.0	14	13	11	28	1	3	0	116	130	17	28	4.1	.935	SS-54, 3B-3, 2B-2

Dick McAuliffe

McAULIFFE, RICHARD JOHN
B. Nov. 29, 1939, Hartford, Conn.
BL TR 5'11'' 176 lbs.

Year	Team		Games	BA	SA	AB	H	2B	3B	HR	HR%	R	RBI	BB	SO	SB	AB	H	PO	A	E	DP	TC/G	FA	G by Pos
1960	DET	A	8	.259	.333	27	7	0	1	0	0.0	2	1	2	6	0	0	0	12	26	5	7	5.4	.884	SS-7
1961			80	.256	.389	285	73	12	4	6	2.1	36	33	24	39	2	7	3	92	154	19	32	3.3	.928	SS-55, 3B-22
1962			139	.263	.403	471	124	20	5	12	2.5	50	63	64	76	4	6	1	260	257	30	45	3.9	.945	2B-70, 3B-49, SS-16
1963			150	.262	.384	568	149	18	6	13	2.3	77	61	64	75	11	2	1	256	388	24	76	4.5	.964	SS-133, 2B-15
1964			162	.241	.427	557	134	18	7	24	4.3	85	66	77	96	8	2	1	262	467	32	84	4.7	.958	SS-160
1965			113	.260	.433	404	105	13	6	15	3.7	61	54	49	62	6	2	0	190	286	22	58	4.4	.956	SS-112
1966			124	.274	.509	430	118	16	8	23	5.3	83	56	66	80	5	8	3	174	321	19	52	4.1	.963	SS-105, 3B-15
1967			153	.239	.411	557	133	16	7	22	3.9	92	65	105	118	6	0	0	300	374	28	82	4.6	.960	2B-145, SS-43
1968			151	.249	.411	570	142	24	10	16	2.8	95	56	82	99	8	3	2	292	352	9	80	4.3	.986	2B-148, SS-5
1969			74	.262	.458	271	71	10	5	11	4.1	49	33	47	41	2	2	1	167	196	9	40	5.0	.976	2B-72
1970			146	.234	.345	530	124	21	1	12	2.3	73	50	101	62	5	8	0	299	391	21	83	4.9	.970	2B-127, SS-15, 3B-12
1971			128	.208	.379	477	99	16	6	18	3.8	67	57	53	67	4	4	2	326	310	8	87	5.0	.988	2B-123, SS-7
1972			122	.240	.353	408	98	16	3	8	2.0	47	30	59	59	0	8	0	267	251	13	63	4.4	.976	2B-116, SS-3, 3B-1
1973			106	.274	.437	343	94	18	1	12	3.5	39	47	49	52	0	6	2	217	266	7	63	4.6	.986	2B-102, SS-2, DH-1
1974	BOS	A	100	.210	.320	272	57	13	1	5	1.8	32	24	39	40	2	9	1	151	178	11	38	3.4	.968	2B-53, 3B-40, DH-3, SS-3
1975			7	.133	.133	15	2	0	0	0	0.0	0	1	1	2	0	0	0	2	8	3	1	1.9	.769	3B-7
16 yrs.			1763	.247	.403	6185	1530	231	71	197	3.2	888	697	882	974	63	67	16	3267	4225	260	891	4.4	.966	2B-971, SS-666, 3B-146, DH-4

LEAGUE CHAMPIONSHIP SERIES

| 1972 | DET | A | 5 | .200 | .350 | 20 | 4 | 0 | 0 | 1 | 5.0 | 3 | 1 | 1 | 4 | 0 | 0 | 0 | 2 | 3 | 1 | 1 | 1.2 | .833 | SS-4, 2B-1 |

WORLD SERIES

| 1968 | DET | A | 7 | .222 | .333 | 27 | 6 | 0 | 0 | 1 | 3.7 | 5 | 3 | 4 | 6 | 0 | 0 | 0 | 11 | 16 | 0 | 2 | 3.9 | 1.000 | 2B-7 |

Gene McAuliffe

McAULIFFE, EUGENE LEO
B. Feb. 28, 1872, Randolph, Mass. D. Apr. 29, 1953, Randolph, Mass.
BR TR 6'1'' 180 lbs.

| 1904 | BOS | N | 1 | .500 | .500 | 2 | 1 | 0 | 0 | 0 | 0.0 | 0 | 0 | 0 | 0 | 0 | 0 | 0 | 1 | 1 | 1 | 0 | 3.0 | .667 | C-1 |

George McAvoy

McAVOY, GEORGE H.
B. Unknown.

| 1914 | PHI | N | 1 | .000 | .000 | 1 | 0 | 0 | 0 | 0 | 0.0 | 0 | 0 | 0 | 0 | 0 | 1 | 0 | 0 | 0 | 0 | 0 | 0.0 | — | |

Wickey McAvoy

McAVOY, JAMES EUGENE
B. Oct. 20, 1894, Rochester, N. Y. D. July 5, 1973, Rochester, N. Y.
BR TR 5'11'' 172 lbs.

1913	PHI	A	4	.111	.111	9	1	0	0	0	0.0	0	0	0	4	0	0	0	14	7	0	0	5.3	1.000	C-4
1914			8	.125	.250	16	2	0	1	0	0.0	1	0	0	4	0	0	0	25	8	1	0	4.3	.971	C-8
1915			68	.190	.250	184	35	7	2	0	0.0	12	6	11	32	0	4	0	235	130	25	8	5.7	.936	C-64
1917			10	.250	.417	24	6	1	0	1	4.2	1	4	0	3	0	2	0	27	15	2	0	4.4	.955	C-8
1918			83	.244	.284	271	66	5	3	0	0.0	14	32	13	23	5	6	1	242	123	15	15	4.6	.961	C-74, OF-1, 1B-1, P-1
1919			62	.141	.194	170	24	5	2	0	0.0	10	11	14	21	1	4	0	182	73	7	6	4.2	.973	C-57
6 yrs.			235	.199	.254	674	134	18	8	1	0.1	38	53	38	87	6	16	1	725	356	50	30	4.8	.956	C-215, OF-1, 1B-1, P-1

Algie McBride

McBRIDE, ALGERNON GRIGGS
B. May 23, 1869, Washington, D. C. D. Jan. 10, 1956, Georgetown, Ohio
BL TL 5'9'' 152 lbs.

1896	CHI	N	9	.241	.448	29	7	1	1	1	3.4	2	7	7		3	0	0	21	1	2	0	2.7	.917	OF-9
1898	CIN	N	120	.302	.393	486	147	14	12	2	0.4	94	43	51		16	0	0	288	18	13	3	2.7	.959	OF-120
1899			64	.347	.446	251	87	12	5	1	0.4	57	23	30		5	0	0	124	8	7	2	2.2	.950	OF-64
1900			112	.275	.374	436	120	15	8	4	0.9	57	59	25		12	3	0	163	10	16	5	1.7	.915	OF-109
1901	2 teams		CIN	N	(30G – .236)		NY	N	(68G – .280)																
"	total		98	.266	.344	387	103	18	0	4	1.0	46	47	19		3	5	2	143	9	7	3	1.6	.956	OF-93
5 yrs.			403	.292	.385	1589	464	60	26	12	0.8	256	179	132	3	36	8	2	739	46	45	13	2.1	.946	OF-395

Bake McBride

McBRIDE, ARNOLD RAY
B. Feb. 3, 1949, Fulton, Mo.
BL TR 6'2'' 190 lbs.

1973	STL	N	40	.302	.349	63	19	3	0	0	0.0	8	5	4	10	0	17	6	39	1	1	0	1.0	.976	OF-17
1974			150	.309	.394	559	173	19	5	6	1.1	81	56	43	57	30	7	3	395	9	4	1	2.7	.990	OF-144
1975			116	.300	.404	413	124	10	9	5	1.2	70	36	34	52	26	11	3	289	4	3	1	2.6	.990	OF-107
1976			72	.335	.445	272	91	13	4	3	1.1	40	24	18	28	10	7	2	201	5	4	0	2.9	.981	OF-66
1977	2 teams		STL	N	(43G – .262)		PHI	N	(85G – .339)																
"	total		128	.316	.520	402	127	25	6	15	3.7	76	61	32	44	36	21	5	54	4	0	1	0.5	1.000	OF-106
1978	PHI	N	122	.269	.392	472	127	20	4	10	2.1	68	49	28	68	28	6	1	234	8	1	3	2.0	.996	OF-119
1979			151	.280	.411	582	163	16	12	12	2.1	82	60	41	77	25	9	3	341	12	4	3	2.4	.989	OF-147
1980			137	.309	.453	554	171	33	10	9	1.6	68	87	26	58	13	3	2	282	6	3	1	2.1	.990	OF-133
1981			58	.271	.385	221	60	17	1	2	0.9	26	21	11	25	5	9	1	76	2	1	1	1.4	.987	OF-56
1982	CLE	A	27	.365	.471	85	31	3	0	0	0.0	8	13	2	12	2	5	2	37	0	0	0	1.4	1.000	OF-22

Year	Team		Games	BA	SA	AB	H	2B	3B	HR	HR%	R	RBI	BB	SO	SB	Pinch Hit AB	H	PO	A	E	DP	TC/G	FA	G by Pos

Bake McBride *continued*

| 1983 | | | 70 | .291 | .348 | 230 | 67 | 8 | 1 | 1 | 0.4 | 21 | 18 | 9 | 26 | 8 | 10 | 2 | 81 | 4 | 2 | 1 | 1.2 | .977 | OF-46, DH-15 |
| 11 yrs. | | | 1071 | .299 | .420 | 3853 | 1153 | 167 | 55 | 63 | 1.6 | 548 | 430 | 248 | 457 | 183 | 105 | 32 | 2029 | 55 | 23 | 12 | 2.0 | .989 | OF-963, DH-15 |

DIVISIONAL PLAYOFF SERIES

| 1981 | PHI | N | 4 | .200 | .267 | 15 | 3 | 1 | 0 | 0 | 0.0 | 1 | 0 | 0 | 5 | 0 | 0 | 0 | 0 | 0 | 0 | 0 | 0.0 | — | OF-4 |

LEAGUE CHAMPIONSHIP SERIES

1977	PHI	N	4	.222	.389	18	4	0	0	1	5.6	2	2	0	2	0	0	0	6	2	0	1	2.0	1.000	OF-4
1978			3	.222	.556	9	2	0	0	1	11.1	2	1	0	2	0	1	1	1	0	0	0	0.3	1.000	OF-2
1980			5	.238	.238	21	5	0	0	0	0.0	0	0	1	5	2	0	0	11	3	1	2	3.0	.933	OF-5
3 yrs.			12	.229	.354	48	11	0	0	2	4.2	4	3	1	9	2	1	1	18	5	1	3	2.0	.958	OF-11

WORLD SERIES

| 1980 | PHI | N | 6 | .304 | .478 | 23 | 7 | 1 | 0 | 1 | 4.3 | 3 | 5 | 2 | 1 | 0 | 0 | 0 | 13 | 1 | 0 | 0 | 2.3 | 1.000 | OF-6 |

George McBride

McBRIDE, GEORGE FLORIAN
B. Nov. 20, 1880, Milwaukee, Wis. D. July 2, 1973, Milwaukee, Wis.
Manager 1921.

BR TR 5'11" 170 lbs.

1901	MIL	A	3	.167	.167	12	2	0	0	0	0.0	0	0	1		0	0	0	5	7	0	2	4.0	1.000	SS-3
1905	2 teams			PIT	N	(27G – .218)		STL	N	(81G – .217)															
"	total		108	.217	.258	368	80	5	2	0	0.5	31	41	20		12	0	0	176	321	36	35	4.9	.932	SS-88, 3B-17, 1B-1
1906	STL	N	90	.169	.208	313	53	8	2	0	0.0	24	13	17		5	0	0	194	310	30	33	5.9	.944	SS-90
1908	WAS	A	155	.232	.274	518	120	10	6	0	0.0	47	34	41		12	0	0	372	568	52	58	6.4	.948	SS-155
1909			155	.234	.266	504	118	16	0	0	0.0	38	34	36		17	0	0	341	499	58	56	5.8	.935	SS-155
1910			154	.230	.288	514	118	19	4	1	0.2	54	55	61		11	0	0	370	518	58	57	6.1	.939	SS-154
1911			154	.235	.269	557	131	11	4	0	0.0	58	59	52		15	0	0	353	546	56	60	6.2	.941	SS-154
1912			152	.226	.284	521	118	13	7	1	0.2	56	52	38		17	0	0	349	498	53	55	5.9	.941	SS-152
1913			150	.214	.285	499	107	18	7	1	0.2	52	52	43	46	12	0	0	316	490	34	62	5.6	.960	SS-150
1914			156	.203	.243	503	102	12	4	0	0.0	49	24	43	70	12	0	0	367	460	36	72	5.5	.958	SS-156
1915			146	.204	.252	476	97	8	6	1	0.2	54	30	29	60	10	0	0	326	422	25	47	5.3	.968	SS-146
1916			139	.227	.283	466	106	15	4	1	0.2	36	36	23	58	8	0	0	282	438	32	64	5.4	.957	SS-139
1917			50	.191	.213	141	27	3	0	0	0.0	6	9	10	17	1	1	0	78	122	11	15	4.2	.948	SS-41, 3B-6, 2B-2
1918			18	.132	.132	53	7	0	0	0	0.0	2	1	0	11	1	1	0	29	45	1	4	4.2	.987	SS-14, 2B-2
1919			15	.200	.275	40	8	1	1	0	0.0	3	4	3	6	0	0	0	29	40	5	2	4.9	.932	SS-15
1920			13	.220	.244	41	9	1	0	0	0.0	6	3	2	3	0	0	0	24	32	2	3	4.5	.966	SS-13
16 yrs.			1658	.218	.264	5526	1203	140	47	7	0.1	516	447	419	271	133	4	0	3611	5316	489	614	5.7	.948	SS-1625, 3B-23, 2B-4, 1B-1

John McBride

McBRIDE, JOHN F.
Deceased.

| 1890 | PHI | AA | 1 | .000 | .000 | 2 | 0 | 0 | 0 | 0 | 0.0 | | 0 | | 0 | 0 | 0 | 1 | 1 | 0 | 0 | 2.0 | 1.000 | OF-1 |

Tom McBride

McBRIDE, THOMAS RAYMOND
B. Nov. 2, 1914, Bonham, Tex.

BR TR 6'½" 188 lbs.

1943	BOS	A	26	.240	.292	96	23	3	1	0	0.0	11	7	7	3	2	2	0	60	2	1	1	2.4	.984	OF-24
1944			71	.245	.306	216	53	7	3	0	0.0	29	24	8	13	4	7	3	159	10	2	7	2.4	.988	OF-57, 1B-5
1945			100	.305	.387	344	105	11	7	1	0.3	38	47	26	17	2	9	2	281	18	3	15	3.0	.990	OF-81, 1B-11
1946			61	.301	.359	153	46	5	2	0	0.0	21	19	9	6	0	17	5	61	1	0	0	1.0	1.000	OF-43
1947	2 teams			BOS	A	(2G – .200)		WAS	A	(56G – .271)															
"	total		58	.269	.316	171	46	4	2	0	0.0	19	15	15	9	3	8	2	105	3	3	0	1.9	.973	OF-52, 3B-1
1948	WAS	A	92	.257	.325	206	53	9	1	1	0.5	22	29	28	15	2	33	5	108	7	2	3	1.3	.983	OF-55
6 yrs.			408	.275	.340	1186	326	39	16	2	0.2	140	141	93	63	13	76	17	774	41	11	26	2.0	.987	OF-312, 1B-16, 3B-1

WORLD SERIES

| 1946 | BOS | A | 5 | .167 | .167 | 12 | 2 | 0 | 0 | 0 | 0.0 | 0 | 1 | 0 | 1 | 0 | 3 | 0 | 4 | 0 | 1 | 0 | 1.0 | .800 | OF-2 |

Bill McCabe

McCABE, WILLIAM FRANCIS
B. Oct. 28, 1892, Chicago, Ill. D. Sept. 2, 1966, Chicago, Ill.

BB TR 5'9½" 180 lbs.

1918	CHI	N	29	.178	.222	45	8	0	1	0	0.0	9	4	5	4	7	2	6	1	23	42	4	1	2.4	.942	2B-13, OF-4
1919			33	.155	.214	84	13	3	1	0	0.0	8	5	9	15	3	3	0	43	10	4	3	1.7	.930	OF-19, SS-4, 3B-1
1920	2 teams			CHI	N	(3G – .500)		BKN	N	(41G – .147)															
"	total		44	.157	.157	70	11	0	0	0	0.0	11	3	2	6	1	1	0	0	0	0	0	0.0	—	SS-13, OF-6, 2B-4, 3B-3
3 yrs.			106	.161	.196	199	32	3	2	0	0.0	28	13	15	28	6	13	2	66	52	8	4	1.2	.937	OF-29, SS-17, 2B-17, 3B-4

WORLD SERIES

1918	CHI	N	3	.000	.000	1	0	0	0	0	0.0	1	0	0	0	1	0	0	0	0	0	0	0.0	—	
1920	BKN	N	1		—	0	0	0	0	0	0.0	0	0	0	0	0	1	0	0	0	0	0	0.0	—	
2 yrs.			4	.000	.000	1	0	0	0	0	0.0	1	0	0	0	1	1	0	0	0	0	0	0.0	—	

Joe McCabe

McCABE, JOSEPH ROBERT
B. Aug. 27, 1938, Indianapolis, Ind.

BR TR 6' 190 lbs.

1964	MIN	A	14	.158	.158	19	3	0	0	0	0.0	1	2	0	8	0	1	0	34	2	0	1	2.6	1.000	C-12
1965	WAS	A	14	.185	.296	27	5	0	0	1	3.7	1	5	4	13	1	4	2	30	5	1	0	2.6	.972	C-11
2 yrs.			28	.174	.239	46	8	0	0	1	2.2	2	7	4	21	1	5	2	64	7	1	1	2.6	.986	C-23

Swat McCabe

McCABE, JAMES ARTHUR
B. Nov. 20, 1881, Towanda, Pa. D. Dec. 9, 1944, Bristol, Conn.

BL TR 5'10"

1909	CIN	N	3	.545	.636	11	6	1	0	0	0.0	2	0	1		0	0	0	5	0	3	0	2.7	.625	OF-3
1910			13	.257	.286	35	9	1	0	0	0.0	3	5	1	2	0	4	1	14	2	0	1	1.2	1.000	OF-9
2 yrs.			16	.326	.370	46	15	2	0	0	0.0	5	5	1	2	1	4	1	19	2	3	1	1.5	.875	OF-12

Harry McCaffrey

McCAFFREY, HARRY CHARLES
B. Nov. 25, 1858, St. Louis, Mo. D. Apr. 19, 1928, St. Louis, Mo.

BR TR 5'10½" 185 lbs.

Year	Team		Games	BA	SA	AB	H	2B	3B	HR	HR%	R	RBI	BB	SO	SB	Pinch Hit AB	Pinch Hit H	PO	A	E	DP	TC/G	FA	G by Pos

Harry McCaffrey *continued*

Year	Team		Games	BA	SA	AB	H	2B	3B	HR	HR%	R	RBI	BB	SO	SB	AB	H	PO	A	E	DP	TC/G	FA	G by Pos
1882	2 teams	STL AA (38G – .275)								LOU AA (1G – .250)																
"	total		39	.274	.401	157	43	8	6	0	0.0	24		3			0	0	74	50	17	5	3.6	.879	OF-23, 2B-9, 3B-7, 1B-1
1883	STL	AA	5	.056	.056	18	1	0	0	0	0.0	0		1			0	0	6	3	1	2	2.0	.900	OF-5
1885	CIN	AA	1	.000	.000	5	0	0	0	0	0.0	0		0			0	0	0	0	1	0	1.0	–	P-1
3 yrs.			45	.244	.356	180	44	8	6	0	0.0	24		4			0	0	80	53	19	7	3.4	.875	OF-28, 2B-9, 3B-7, 1B-1, P-1

Sparrow McCaffrey

McCAFFREY, CHARLES P.
B. Philadelphia, Pa. D. Apr. 29, 1894, Philadelphia, Pa.

Year	Team		Games	BA	SA	AB	H	2B	3B	HR	HR%	R	RBI	BB	SO	SB	AB	H	PO	A	E	DP	TC/G	FA	G by Pos
1889	COL	AA	2	1.000	1.000	1	1	0	0	0	0.0	1		0	1	0	0	0	0	0	0	0	0.0	–	C-2

Brian McCall

McCALL, BRIAN ALLEN (Bam)
B. June 25, 1943, Kentfield, Calif.   BL TL 5'10" 170 lbs.

Year	Team		Games	BA	SA	AB	H	2B	3B	HR	HR%	R	RBI	BB	SO	SB	AB	H	PO	A	E	DP	TC/G	FA	G by Pos
1962	CHI	A	4	.375	1.125	8	3	0	0	2	25.0	2	3	0	3	0	3	1	4	0	0	0	1.0	1.000	OF-1
1963			3	.000	.000	7	0	0	0	0	0.0	1	0	1	2	0	0	0	3	0	0	0	1.0	1.000	OF-2
2 yrs.			7	.200	.600	15	3	0	0	2	13.3	3	3	1	4	0	3	1	7	0	0	0	1.0	1.000	OF-3

Scott McCandless

McCANDLESS, SCOTT COOK (Cook)
B. May 5, 1891, Pittsburgh, Pa. D. Aug. 17, 1961, Pittsburgh, Pa.   BL TR 6' 170 lbs.

Year	Team		Games	BA	SA	AB	H	2B	3B	HR	HR%	R	RBI	BB	SO	SB	AB	H	PO	A	E	DP	TC/G	FA	G by Pos
1914	BAL	F	11	.258	.323	31	8	0	0	0	0.0	5	1	3		0	2	0	10	1	0	0	1.0	1.000	OF-8
1915			117	.214	.300	406	87	6	7	5	1.2	47	34	41		9	9	1	209	16	13	8	2.0	.945	OF-105
2 yrs.			128	.217	.302	437	95	6	8	5	1.1	52	35	44		9	11	1	219	17	13	8	1.9	.948	OF-113

Emmett McCann

McCANN, ROBERT EMMETT
B. Mar. 4, 1902, Philadelphia, Pa. D. Apr. 15, 1937, Philadelphia, Pa.   BR TR 6' 175 lbs.

Year	Team		Games	BA	SA	AB	H	2B	3B	HR	HR%	R	RBI	BB	SO	SB	AB	H	PO	A	E	DP	TC/G	FA	G by Pos
1920	PHI	A	13	.265	.353	34	9	1	1	0	0.0	4	3	3	1	0	1	0	20	29	5	3	4.2	.907	SS-11
1921			52	.223	.255	157	35	5	0	0	0.0	15	15	4	6	2	6	1	64	119	11	13	3.7	.943	SS-32, 3B-9, 2B-2, 1B-1, C-1
1926	BOS	A	6	.000	.000	3	0	0	0	0	0.0	0	0	1	1	0	1	0	2	0	0	0	0.3	1.000	SS-1, 3B-1
3 yrs.			71	.227	.268	194	44	6	1	0	0.0	19	18	8	8	2	8	1	86	148	16	16	3.5	.936	SS-44, 3B-10, 2B-2, 1B-1, C-1

Roger McCardell

McCARDELL, ROGER MORTON
B. Aug. 29, 1932, Gorsuch Mills, Md.   BR TR 6' 200 lbs.

Year	Team		Games	BA	SA	AB	H	2B	3B	HR	HR%	R	RBI	BB	SO	SB	AB	H	PO	A	E	DP	TC/G	FA	G by Pos
1959	SF	N	4	.000	.000	4	0	0	0	0	0.0	0	0	0	0	0	1	0	9	0	0	0	1.5	1.000	C-3

Bill McCarren

McCARREN, WILLIAM JOSEPH
B. Nov. 4, 1895, Fortenia, Pa. D. Sept. 11, 1983, Denver, Colo.   BR TR 5'11½" 170 lbs.

Year	Team		Games	BA	SA	AB	H	2B	3B	HR	HR%	R	RBI	BB	SO	SB	AB	H	PO	A	E	DP	TC/G	FA	G by Pos
1923	BKN	N	69	.245	.343	216	53	10	1	3	1.4	28	27	22	39	1	1	0	72	106	14	11	2.8	.927	3B-66, OF-1

Alex McCarthy

McCARTHY, ALEXANDER GEORGE
B. May 12, 1888, Chicago, Ill. D. Mar. 12, 1978, Salisbury, Md.   BR TR 5'9" 150 lbs.

Year	Team		Games	BA	SA	AB	H	2B	3B	HR	HR%	R	RBI	BB	SO	SB	AB	H	PO	A	E	DP	TC/G	FA	G by Pos
1910	PIT	N	3	.083	.250	12	1	0	1	0	0.0	1	0	0	2	0	0	0	4	10	2	2	5.3	.875	SS-3
1911			50	.240	.327	150	36	5	1	2	1.3	18	31	14	24	4	2	0	94	127	5	20	4.5	.978	SS-33, 2B-11, OF-1, 3B-1
1912			111	.277	.334	401	111	12	4	1	0.2	53	41	30	36	8	2	0	242	325	22	53	5.3	.963	2B-105, 3B-4
1913			31	.203	.270	74	15	5	0	0	0.0	7	10	7	7	1	1	0	33	55	5	4	3.0	.946	SS-12, 3B-12, 2B-6
1914			57	.150	.179	173	26	0	1	1	0.6	14	14	6	17	2	1	0	63	136	11	10	3.7	.948	3B-36, 2B-10, SS-6
1915	2 teams	PIT N (21G – .204)									CHI N (23G – .264)															
"	total		44	.240	.306	121	29	3	1	1	0.8	7	9	10	17	3	2	1	83	109	5	17	4.5	.975	2B-21, 3B-16, SS-6, 1B-1
1916	2 teams	CHI N (37G – .243)									PIT N (50G – .199)															
"	total		87	.217	.261	253	55	5	3	0	0.0	21	9	26	17	4	2	0	156	212	21	27	4.5	.946	SS-42, 2B-41, 3B-5
1917	PIT	N	49	.219	.245	151	33	4	0	0	0.0	15	8	11	13	1	0	0	85	115	6	18	4.2	.971	SS-26, 2B-13, SS-9
8 yrs.			432	.229	.282	1335	306	34	11	5	0.4	136	122	104	133	23	10	1	760	1089	77	151	4.5	.960	2B-207, SS-111, 3B-100, OF-1, 1B-1

Bill McCarthy

McCARTHY, WILLIAM JOHN
B. Boston, Mass. D. Feb. 4, 1928, Washington, D. C.   TR

Year	Team		Games	BA	SA	AB	H	2B	3B	HR	HR%	R	RBI	BB	SO	SB	AB	H	PO	A	E	DP	TC/G	FA	G by Pos
1905	BOS	N	1	.000	.000	3	0	0	0	0	0.0	0	0	0		0	0	0	5	1	3	0	9.0	.667	C-1
1907	CIN	N	3	.125	.125	8	1	0	0	0	0.0	1	0	0		0	0	0	6	4	0	0	3.3	1.000	C-3
2 yrs.			4	.091	.091	11	1	0	0	0	0.0	1	0	0		0	0	0	11	5	3	0	4.8	.842	C-4

Jack McCarthy

McCARTHY, JOHN ARTHUR
B. Mar. 26, 1869, Gilbertville, Mass. D. Sept. 11, 1931, Chicago, Ill.   BL TL 5'9" 155 lbs.

Year	Team		Games	BA	SA	AB	H	2B	3B	HR	HR%	R	RBI	BB	SO	SB	AB	H	PO	A	E	DP	TC/G	FA	G by Pos
1893	CIN	N	49	.282	.354	195	55	8	3	0	0.0	28	22	22	7	6	0	0	111	9	13	1	2.7	.902	OF-47, 1B-2
1894			40	.269	.335	167	45	9	1	0	0.0	29	21	17	6	3	0	0	193	19	13	12	5.6	.942	OF-25, 1B-15
1898	PIT	N	137	.289	.380	537	155	13	12	4	0.7	75	78	34		7	0	0	296	19	22	4	2.5	.935	OF-137
1899			138	.305	.421	560	171	22	17	3	0.5	108	67	39		28	0	0	281	18	12	5	2.2	.961	OF-138
1900	CHI	N	124	.294	.354	503	148	16	7	0	0.0	68	48	24		22	1	0	233	20	15	4	2.2	.944	OF-123
1901	CLE	A	86	.321	.402	343	110	14	7	0	0.0	60	32	30		9	0	0	157	9	9	5	2.0	.949	OF-86
1902			95	.284	.398	359	102	31	5	0	0.0	45	41	24		12	0	0	178	6	11	0	2.1	.944	OF-95
1903	2 teams	CLE A (108G – .265)									CHI N (24G – .277)															
"	total		132	.267	.347	516	138	25	8	0	0.0	58	57	23		23	0	0	211	13	9	6	1.8	.961	OF-132
1904	CHI	N	115	.264	.306	432	114	14	2	0	0.0	36	51	23		14	0	0	213	8	9	7	2.0	.961	OF-115
1905			59	.276	.335	170	47	4	3	0	0.0	16	14	10		8	15	6	107	12	4	9	2.1	.967	OF-37, 1B-6
1906	BKN	N	91	.304	.351	322	98	13	0	0	0.0	23	35	20		9	5	1	158	13	14	1	2.0	.924	OF-86
1907			25	.220	.242	91	20	2	0	0	0.0	8	8	2		1	0	0	38	0	0	0	1.5	1.000	OF-25
12 yrs.			1091	.287	.364	4195	1203	171	66	7	0.2	550	474	268	13	145	21	7	2176	146	131	47	2.2	.947	OF-1046, 1B-23

Jerry McCarthy

McCARTHY, JEROME FRANCIS
B. May 23, 1923, Brooklyn, N. Y. D. Oct. 3, 1965, Oceanside, N. Y.   BL TL 6'1" 205 lbs.

Year	Team		Games	BA	SA	AB	H	2B	3B	HR	HR%	R	RBI	BB	SO	SB	Pinch Hit AB	Pinch Hit H	PO	A	E	DP	TC/G	FA	G by Pos

Jerry McCarthy *continued*

Year	Team		Games	BA	SA	AB	H	2B	3B	HR	HR%	R	RBI	BB	SO	SB	Pinch Hit AB	Pinch Hit H	PO	A	E	DP	TC/G	FA	G by Pos
1948	STL	A	2	.333	.333	3	1	0	0	0	0.0	0	0	0	0	0	1	0	3	0	2	0	2.5	.600	1B-2

Joe McCarthy

McCARTHY, JOSEPH N.
B. Dec. 25, 1881, Syracuse, N. Y. D. Jan. 12, 1937, Syracuse, N. Y.

BR TR

Year	Team		Games	BA	SA	AB	H	2B	3B	HR	HR%	R	RBI	BB	SO	SB	Pinch Hit AB	Pinch Hit H	PO	A	E	DP	TC/G	FA	G by Pos
1905	NY	A	1	.000	.000	2	0	0	0	0	0.0	0	0	0	0	0	0	0	2	1	0	0	3.0	1.000	C-1
1906	STL	N	15	.243	.297	37	9	2	0	0	0.0	3	2	2			0	0	0	47	14	1	2	4.1	.984	C-15
2 yrs.			16	.231	.282	39	9	2	0	0	0.0	3	2	2			0	0	0	49	15	1	2	4.1	.985	C-16

Johnny McCarthy

McCARTHY, JOHN JOSEPH
B. Jan. 7, 1910, Chicago, Ill. D. Sept. 13, 1973, Mundelein, Ill.

BL TL 6'1½" 185 lbs.

Year	Team		Games	BA	SA	AB	H	2B	3B	HR	HR%	R	RBI	BB	SO	SB	Pinch Hit AB	Pinch Hit H	PO	A	E	DP	TC/G	FA	G by Pos
1934	BKN	N	17	.179	.308	39	7	1	0	1	2.6	7	5	2	9	0	3	0	89	9	4	13	6.0	.961	1B-13
1935			22	.250	.313	48	12	1	0	0	0.0	9	4	2	9	0	3	0	110	0	2	11	5.1	.982	1B-19
1936	NY	N	4	.438	.625	16	7	0	0	1	6.3	1	2	0	1	1	0	0	45	6	1	5	13.0	.981	1B-4
1937			114	.279	.410	420	117	19	3	10	2.4	53	65	24	37	1	4	0	1123	82	16	89	10.7	.987	1B-110
1938			134	.272	.368	470	128	13	4	8	1.7	55	59	39	28	3	8	3	1315	77	10	111	10.5	.993	1B-125
1939			50	.263	.400	80	21	6	1	1	1.3	12	11	3	8	0	33	8	114	4	0	13	2.4	1.000	1B-12, OF-4, P-1
1940			51	.239	.299	67	16	4	0	0	0.0	6	5	2	8	0	43	11	57	5	0	6	1.2	1.000	1B-6
1941			14	.325	.400	40	13	3	0	0	0.0	1	12	3	0	0	5	2	68	7	1	4	5.4	.987	1B-8, OF-1
1943	BOS	N	78	.304	.438	313	95	24	6	2	0.6	32	33	10	19	1	0	0	839	53	4	51	11.5	.996	1B-78
1946			2	.143	.143	7	1	0	0	0	0.0	0	1	2	0	0	0	0	18	0	1	0	9.0	1.000	1B-2
1948	NY	N	56	.263	.404	57	15	0	1	2	3.5	6	12	3	2	0	45	13	27	1	1	2	0.5	.966	1B-6
11 yrs.			542	.277	.392	1557	432	72	16	25	1.6	182	209	90	114	7	144	37	3805	244	39	305	7.5	.990	1B-383, OF-5, P-1

WORLD SERIES

Year	Team		Games	BA	SA	AB	H	2B	3B	HR	HR%	R	RBI	BB	SO	SB	Pinch Hit AB	Pinch Hit H	PO	A	E	DP	TC/G	FA	G by Pos
1937	NY	N	5	.211	.263	19	4	1	0	0	0.0	1	1	1	2	0	0	0	38	1	2	4	8.2	.951	1B-5

Tommy McCarthy

McCARTHY, THOMAS FRANCIS MICHAEL
B. July 24, 1863, Boston, Mass. D. Aug. 5, 1922, Boston, Mass.
Manager 1890.
Hall of Fame 1946.

BR TR 5'7" 170 lbs.

Year	Team		Games	BA	SA	AB	H	2B	3B	HR	HR%	R	RBI	BB	SO	SB	Pinch Hit AB	Pinch Hit H	PO	A	E	DP	TC/G	FA	G by Pos
1884	BOS	U	53	.215	.249	209	45	3	2	0	0.0	37		6			0	0	45	30	18	2	1.8	.806	OF-48, P-7
1885	BOS	N	40	.182	.196	148	27	2	0	0	0.0	16	11	5	25		0	0	69	8	12	0	2.2	.865	OF-40
1886	PHI	N	8	.185	.333	27	5	2	1	0	0.0	6	3	2	3		0	0	8	1	2	0	1.4	.818	OF-8, P-1
1887			18	.186	.243	70	13	4	0	0	0.0	7	6	2	5	15	0	0	40	11	7	1	3.8	.750	OF-8, 2B-5, SS-3, 3B-2
1888	STL	AA	131	.274	.331	511	140	20	3	1	0.2	107	68	38		93	0	0	243	44	21	12	2.4	.932	OF-131, P-2
1889			140	.291	.364	604	176	24	7	2	0.3	136	63	46	26	57	0	0	230	39	33	11	2.2	.891	OF-140, 2B-2, P-1
1890			133	.350	.467	548	192	28	9	6	1.1	137		66		83	0	0	205	95	43	11	2.6	.875	OF-102, 3B-32, 2B-1
1891			136	.310	.415	578	179	21	8	8	1.4	127	95	50	19	37	0	0	228	93	48	14	2.7	.870	OF-113, 2B-14, SS-12, 3B-3, P-1
1892	BOS	N	152	.242	.310	603	146	19	5	4	0.7	119	63	93	29	53	0	0	219	29	34	4	1.8	.883	OF-152
1893			116	.346	.465	462	160	28	6	5	1.1	107	111	64	10	46	0	0	228	49	32	9	2.7	.896	OF-108, 2B-7, SS-3
1894			127	.349	.490	539	188	21	8	13	2.4	118	126	59	17	43	0	0	291	33	34	10	2.8	.905	OF-127, SS-2, 2B-1, P-1
1895			117	.290	.341	452	131	13	2	2	0.4	90	73	72	12	18	0	0	212	35	33	3	2.4	.882	OF-109, 2B-9
1896	BKN	N	104	.249	.316	377	94	8	4	3	0.8	62	47	34	17	22	0	0	175	20	17	6	2.0	.920	OF-103
13 yrs.			1275	.292	.377	5128	1496	193	55	44	0.9	1069	666	537	163	467	0	0	2193	487	343	83	2.4	.887	OF-1189, 2B-39, 3B-37, SS-20, P-13

Lew McCarty

McCARTY, GEORGE LEWIS
B. Nov. 17, 1888, Milton, Pa. D. June 9, 1930, Reading, Pa.

BR TR 5'11½" 192 lbs.

Year	Team		Games	BA	SA	AB	H	2B	3B	HR	HR%	R	RBI	BB	SO	SB	Pinch Hit AB	Pinch Hit H	PO	A	E	DP	TC/G	FA	G by Pos
1913	BKN	N	9	.231	.231	26	6	0	0	0	0.0	1	2	2	2	0	0	0	37	10	0	1	5.2	1.000	C-9
1914			90	.254	.327	284	72	14	2	1	0.4	20	30	14	22	1	6	2	398	117	16	9	5.9	.970	C-84
1915			84	.239	.301	276	66	9	4	0	0.0	19	19	7	23	3	1	1	310	101	13	5	5.0	.969	C-84
1916	2 teams		80	BKN N (55G – .313)		NY N (25G – .397)																				
"	total		80	.339	.427	218	74	9	5	0	0.0	23	22	21	25	4	10	4	357	68	6	13	5.4	.986	C-51, 1B-17
1917	NY	N	56	.247	.327	162	40	3	2	2	1.2	15	19	14	6	1	2	1	235	43	6	0	5.1	.979	C-54
1918			86	.268	.319	257	69	7	3	0	0.0	16	24	17	13	3	7	2	288	67	9	3	4.2	.975	C-75
1919			85	.281	.371	210	59	5	4	2	1.0	17	21	18	15	2	24	7	203	56	8	1	3.1	.970	C-59
1920	2 teams		41	NY N (36G – .132)		STL N (5G – .286)																				
"	total		41	.156	.156	45	7	0	0	0	0.0	2	0	9	2	2	29	5	21	10	0	1	0.8	1.000	C-8
1921	STL	N	1	.000	.000	1	0	0	0	0	0.0	0	0	0	1	0	1	0	0	0	0	0	0.0	—	C-1
9 yrs.			532	.266	.335	1479	393	47	20	5	0.3	113	137	102	109	20	82	22	1849	472	58	33	4.5	.976	C-424, 1B-17

WORLD SERIES

Year	Team		Games	BA	SA	AB	H	2B	3B	HR	HR%	R	RBI	BB	SO	SB	Pinch Hit AB	Pinch Hit H	PO	A	E	DP	TC/G	FA	G by Pos
1917	NY	N	3	.400	.800	5	2	0	1	0	0.0	1	1	0	0	0	1	0	7	1	1	0	3.0	.889	C-2

Tim McCarver

McCARVER, JAMES TIMOTHY
B. Oct. 16, 1941, Memphis, Tenn.

BL TR 6' 183 lbs.

Year	Team		Games	BA	SA	AB	H	2B	3B	HR	HR%	R	RBI	BB	SO	SB	Pinch Hit AB	Pinch Hit H	PO	A	E	DP	TC/G	FA	G by Pos
1959	STL	N	8	.167	.208	24	4	1	0	0	0.0	3	2	2	1	0	1	0	32	2	1	0	4.4	.971	C-6
1960			10	.200	.200	10	2	0	0	0	0.0	3	0	1	2	0	4	1	9	0	0	0	0.9	1.000	C-5
1961			22	.239	.343	67	16	2	1	1	1.5	5	6	0	5	0	2	2	86	9	3	0	4.5	.969	C-20
1963			127	.289	.383	405	117	12	7	4	1.0	39	51	27	43	5	5	1	722	55	5	7	6.2	.994	C-126
1964			143	.288	.400	465	134	19	3	9	1.9	53	52	40	44	2	7	1	762	43	11	9	5.7	.987	C-137
1965			113	.276	.408	409	113	17	2	11	2.7	48	48	31	26	5	5	1	687	43	4	4	6.5	.995	C-111
1966			150	.274	.424	543	149	19	13	12	2.2	50	68	36	38	9	5	1	841	62	7	7	6.1	.992	C-148
1967			138	.295	.452	471	139	26	3	14	3.0	68	69	54	32	8	11	4	819	67	7	10	6.4	.992	C-130
1968			128	.253	.350	434	110	15	6	5	1.2	35	48	26	31	4	19	4	708	54	11	6	6.0	.986	C-109
1969			138	.260	.365	515	134	27	3	7	1.4	46	51	49	26	4	1	0	925	66	14	10	7.3	.986	C-136
1970	PHI	N	44	.287	.439	164	47	11	4	2	2.4	16	14	14	10	2	0	0	314	18	3	2	7.6	.991	C-44
1971			134	.278	.392	474	132	20	5	8	1.7	51	46	43	26	5	14	3	673	51	11	8	5.5	.985	C-125

Year	Team		Games	BA	SA	AB	H	2B	3B	HR	HR%	R	RBI	BB	SO	SB	Pinch Hit AB	H	PO	A	E	DP	TC/G	FA	G by Pos

Tim McCarver *continued*

1972	2 teams	PHI N (45G – .237)				MON	N	(77G – .251)																		
"	total		122	.246	.338	391	96	13	1	7	1.8	33	34	36	29	5	18	2	561	47	8	3	5.0	.987	C-85, OF-14, 3B-6
1973	STL	N	130	.266	.366	331	88	16	4	3	0.9	30	49	38	31	2	39	8	608	34	9	48	5.0	.986	1B-77, C-11
1974	2 teams	STL N (74G – .217)				BOS	A	(11G – .250)																		
"	total		85	.224	.246	134	30	1	1	0	0.0	16	12	26	7	1	43	7	163	16	4	1	2.2	.978	C-29, 1B-6, DH-2
1975	2 teams	BOS A (12G – .381)				PHI	N	(47G – .254)																		
"	total		59	.288	.400	80	23	4	1	1	1.3	7	10	15	10	0	39	10	83	9	2	2	1.6	.979	C-17, 1B-2
1976	PHI	N	90	.277	.432	155	43	11	2	3	1.9	26	29	35	14	2	42	9	265	9	0	1	3.0	1.000	C-41, 1B-2
1977			93	.320	.527	169	54	13	2	6	3.6	28	30	28	11	3	36	9	238	14	3	5	2.7	.988	C-42, 1B-3
1978			90	.247	.342	146	36	9	1	1	0.7	18	14	28	24	2	41	8	215	14	2	5	2.6	.991	C-34, 1B-11
1979			79	.241	.314	137	33	5	1	1	0.7	13	12	19	12	0	39	10	174	12	2	0	2.4	.989	C-31, OF-1
1980			6	.200	.400	5	1	0	0	0	0.0	2	2	1	0	0	2	0	8	0	0	0	1.3	1.000	1B-2
21 yrs.			1909	.271	.388	5529	1501	242	57	97	1.8	590	645	548	422	61	373	82	8893	625	103	128	5.0	.989	C-1387, 1B-103, OF-15, 3B-6, DH-2

LEAGUE CHAMPIONSHIP SERIES

1976	PHI	N	2	.000	.000	4	0	0	0	0	0.0	0	0	0	1	0	1	0	6	0	0	0	3.0	1.000	C-1
1977			3	.167	.167	6	1	0	0	0	0.0	1	0	1	3	0	1	0	7	0	0	0	2.3	1.000	C-2
1978			2	.000	.000	4	0	0	0	0	0.0	2	1	2	0	0	1	0	8	0	0	0	4.0	1.000	C-1
3 yrs.			7	.071	.071	14	1	0	0	0	0.0	3	1	3	4	0	3	0	21	0	0	0	3.0	1.000	C-4

WORLD SERIES

1964	STL	N	7	.478	.739	23	11	1	1	1	4.3	4	5	5	1	1	0	0	57	1	0	0	8.3	1.000	C-7
1967			7	.125	.167	24	3	1	0	0	0.0	3	2	2	2	0	0	0	55	4	0	1	8.4	1.000	C-7
1968			7	.333	.593	27	9	0	2	1	3.7	3	4	3	2	0	0	0	61	1	0	0	8.9	1.000	C-7
3 yrs.			21	.311	.500	74	23	2	3	2	2.7	10	11	10	5	1	0	0	173	6	0	1	8.5	1.000	C-21
											4th														

Al McCauley

McCAULEY, ALLEN A.
B. Mar. 4, 1863, Indianapolis, Ind. D. Aug. 24, 1917, Indianapolis, Ind.

BL TL 6' 180 lbs.

1884	IND	AA	17	.189	.226	53	10	0	1	0	0.0	7		12			0	0	40	23	4	4	3.9	.940	P-10, 1B-5, OF-3
1890	PHI	N	112	.244	.344	418	102	25	7	1	0.2	63	42	57	38	8	0	0	1053	26	30	68	9.9	.973	1B-112
1891	WAS	AA	59	.282	.398	206	58	5	8	1	0.5	36	31	30	13	9	0	0	541	22	18	27	9.8	.969	1B-59
3 yrs.			188	.251	.352	677	170	30	16	2	0.3	106	73	99	51	17	0	0	1634	71	52	99	9.3	.970	1B-176, P-10, OF-3

Bill McCauley

McCAULEY, WILLIAM H.
B. Dec. 20, 1869, Washington, D. C. D. Jan. 27, 1926, Washington, D. C.

| 1895 | WAS | N | 1 | .000 | .000 | 2 | 0 | 0 | 0 | 0 | 0.0 | 0 | 0 | 0 | 0 | 0 | 0 | 0 | 1 | 4 | 2 | 0 | 7.0 | .714 | SS-1 |

Jim McCauley

McCAULEY, JAMES A.
B. Mar. 24, 1863, Stanley, N. Y. D. Sept. 14, 1930, Canandaigua, N. Y.

BL TR 6' 180 lbs.

1884	STL	AA	1	.000	.000	2	0	0	0	0	0.0	0		0			0	0	7	2	2	0	11.0	.818	C-1
1885	2 teams	BUF N (24G – .179)				CHI	N	(3G – .167)																		
"	total		27	.178	.222	90	16	2	1	0	0.0	5	7	13	15		0	0	104	39	11	1	5.7	.929	C-23, OF-6
1886	BKN	AA	11	.233	.267	30	7	1	0	0	0.0	5		11			0	0	61	16	14	2	8.3	.846	C-11
3 yrs.			39	.189	.230	122	23	3	1	0	0.0	10	7	24	15		0	0	172	57	27	3	6.6	.895	C-35, OF-6

Pat McCauley

McCAULEY, PATRICK M.
B. June 10, 1870, Ware, Mass. D. Jan. 23, 1917, Newark, N. J.

TR

1893	STL	N	5	.063	.063	16	1	0	0	0	0.0	0	1	0		0	0	0	15	6	5	1	5.2	.808	C-5
1896	WAS	N	26	.250	.357	84	21	3	0	2	2.4	14	11	7	8	3	1	0	73	27	9	2	4.2	.917	C-24, OF-1
1903	NY	A	6	.053	.053	19	1	0	0	0	0.0	0	0	0	0	0	0	0	20	3	2	0	4.2	.920	C-6
3 yrs.			37	.193	.269	119	23	3	0	2	1.7	14	12	7	9	3	1	0	108	36	16	3	4.3	.900	C-35, OF-1

Harry McChesney

McCHESNEY, HARRY VINCENT (Pud)
B. June 1, 1880, Pittsburgh, Pa. D. Aug. 11, 1960, Pittsburgh, Pa.

BR TR 5'9" 165 lbs.

| 1904 | CHI | N | 22 | .261 | .375 | 88 | 23 | 6 | 2 | 0 | 0.0 | 9 | 11 | 4 | | 2 | 0 | 0 | 27 | 2 | 1 | 1 | 1.4 | .967 | OF-22 |

Pete McClanahan

McCLANAHAN, ROBERT HUGH
B. Oct. 24, 1906, Cold Springs, Tex. D. Oct. 28, 1987, Mont Belvieu, Tex.

BR TR 5'9" 170 lbs.

| 1931 | PIT | N | 7 | .500 | .500 | 4 | 2 | 0 | 0 | 0 | 0.0 | 2 | 0 | 2 | 0 | 0 | 4 | 2 | 0 | 0 | 0 | 0 | 0.0 | – | |

Bill McClellan

McCLELLAN, WILLIAM HENRY
B. Mar. 22, 1856, Chicago, Ill. D. July 2, 1929, Chicago, Ill.

BL TL 156 lbs.

1878	CHI	N	48	.224	.263	205	46	6	1	0	0.0	26	29	2	13		0	0	89	159	40	15	6.0	.861	2B-42, SS-5, OF-1
1881	PRO	N	68	.166	.185	259	43	3	1	0	0.0	30	16	15	21		0	0	82	153	39	18	4.0	.858	SS-50, OF-17, 2B-1
1883	PHI	N	80	.230	.328	326	75	21	4	1	0.3	42		19	18		0	0	157	256	75	25	6.1	.846	SS-78, OF-2, 3B-1
1884			111	.258	.316	450	116	13	2	3	0.7	71		28	43		0	0	165	313	84	22	5.1	.851	SS-111, OF-1
1885	BKN	AA	112	.267	.345	464	124	22	7	0	0.0	85		28			0	0	237	261	67	29	5.0	.881	3B-57, 2B-55
1886			141	.255	.346	595	152	33	9	1	0.2	131		56			0	0	423	435	88	64	6.7	.907	2B-141
1887			136	.263	.334	548	144	24	6	1	0.2	109		80		70	0	0	366	397	105	52	6.4	.879	2B-136
1888	2 teams	BKN AA (74G – .205)				CLE	AA	(22G – .222)																		
"	total		96	.209	.246	350	73	7	3	0	0.0	39	26	46		19	0	0	202	175	44	26	4.4	.895	2B-61, OF-33, SS-2
8 yrs.			792	.242	.308	3197	773	129	33	6	0.2	533	71	274	95	89	0	0	1721	2149	542	251	5.6	.877	2B-436, SS-246, 3B-58, OF-54

Harvey McClellan

McCLELLAN, HARVEY McDOWELL (Little Mac)
B. Dec. 22, 1894, Cynthiana, Ky. D. Nov. 6, 1925, Cynthiana, Ky.

BR TR 5'9½" 143 lbs.

1919	CHI	A	7	.333	.333	12	4	0	0	0	0.0	2	1	1	1	0	2	0	6	7	1	1	2.0	.929	3B-3, SS-2
1920			10	.333	.500	18	6	1	1	0	0.0	4	5	4	1	2	2	0	7	6	1	0	1.4	.929	SS-4, 3B-2
1921			63	.179	.224	196	35	4	1	1	0.5	20	14	14	18	2	3	0	112	141	8	23	4.1	.969	2B-20, OF-15, SS-15, 3B-5
1922			91	.226	.322	301	68	17	3	2	0.7	28	28	16	32	3	5	4	94	180	12	17	3.1	.958	3B-71, SS-8, 2B-2, OF-1

Year	Team	Games	BA	SA	AB	H	2B	3B	HR	HR%	R	RBI	BB	SO	SB	Pinch Hit AB	Pinch Hit H	PO	A	E	DP	TC/G	FA	G by Pos

Harvey McClellan *continued*

Year	Team	Games	BA	SA	AB	H	2B	3B	HR	HR%	R	RBI	BB	SO	SB	AB	H	PO	A	E	DP	TC/G	FA	G by Pos
1923		141	.235	.304	550	129	29	3	1	0.2	67	41	27	44	14	1	1	222	399	27	65	4.6	.958	SS-138, 2B-2
1924		32	.176	.212	85	15	3	0	0	0.0	9	9	6	7	2	1	0	36	87	7	7	4.1	.946	SS-21, 2B-7, OF-1, 3B-1
6 yrs.		344	.221	.292	1162	257	54	8	4	0.3	130	98	68	103	23	13	5	477	820	56	113	3.9	.959	SS-188, 3B-82, 2B-31, OF-17

Lloyd McClendon

McCLENDON, LLOYD GLENN
B. Jan. 11, 1959, Gary, Ind.   BR TR 5'10"   190 lbs.

Year	Team	Games	BA	SA	AB	H	2B	3B	HR	HR%	R	RBI	BB	SO	SB	AB	H	PO	A	E	DP	TC/G	FA	G by Pos
1987	CIN N	45	.208	.361	72	15	5	0	2	2.8	8	13	4	15	1	24	6	80	5	2	3	1.9	.977	C-12, 1B-5, OF-1, 3B-1
1988		72	.219	.314	137	30	4	0	3	2.2	9	14	15	22	4	24	6	197	13	4	11	3.0	.981	C-23, OF-17, 1B-12, 3B-2
1989	CHI N	92	.286	.479	259	74	12	1	12	4.6	47	40	37	31	6	16	5	310	18	6	21	3.6	.982	OF-45, 1B-28, 3B-6, C-5
3 yrs.		209	.254	.412	468	119	21	1	17	3.6	64	67	56	68	11	64	17	587	36	12	35	3.0	.981	OF-63, 1B-45, C-40, 3B-9

LEAGUE CHAMPIONSHIP SERIES

Year	Team	Games	BA	SA	AB	H	2B	3B	HR	HR%	R	RBI	BB	SO	SB	AB	H	PO	A	E	DP	TC/G	FA	G by Pos
1989	CHI N	3	.667	.667	3	2	0	0	0	0.0	0	0	1	0	0	2	1	3	0	0	0	1.0	1.000	C-2, OF-1

Jeff McCleskey

McCLESKEY, JEFFERSON LAMAR
B. Nov. 6, 1891, Americus, Ga.   D. May 11, 1971, Americus, Ga.   BL TR 5'11"   160 lbs.

Year	Team	Games	BA	SA	AB	H	2B	3B	HR	HR%	R	RBI	BB	SO	SB	AB	H	PO	A	E	DP	TC/G	FA	G by Pos
1913	BOS N	2	.000	.000	3	0	0	0	0	0.0	0	0	1	0	0	0	0	2	1	1	0	2.0	.750	3B-2

Bill McCloskey

McCLOSKEY, WILLIAM GEORGE
B. May, 1854, Philadelphia, Pa.   Deceased.   5'8"   155 lbs.

Year	Team	Games	BA	SA	AB	H	2B	3B	HR	HR%	R	RBI	BB	SO	SB	AB	H	PO	A	E	DP	TC/G	FA	G by Pos
1884	WIL U	9	.100	.100	30	3	0	0	0	0.0	0		0			0	0	38	7	13	1	6.4	.776	OF-5, C-5

Hal McClure

McCLURE, HAROLD MURRAY (Mac)
B. Aug. 8, 1859, Lewisburg, Pa.   D. June 5, 1919, Wilkes-Barre, Pa.   BR TR 6'   165 lbs.

Year	Team	Games	BA	SA	AB	H	2B	3B	HR	HR%	R	RBI	BB	SO	SB	AB	H	PO	A	E	DP	TC/G	FA	G by Pos
1882	BOS N	2	.333	.333	6	2	0	0	0	0.0	1	0	1	0	1	0	0	3	0	1	0	2.0	.750	OF-2

Larry McClure

McCLURE, LAWRENCE LEDWITH
B. Oct. 3, 1885, Wayne, W. Va.   D. Aug. 31, 1949, Huntington, W. Va.   BR TR 5'6½"   130 lbs.

Year	Team	Games	BA	SA	AB	H	2B	3B	HR	HR%	R	RBI	BB	SO	SB	AB	H	PO	A	E	DP	TC/G	FA	G by Pos
1910	NY A	1	.000	.000	1	0	0	0	0	0.0	0	0	0	0	0	0	0	0	0	0	0	0.0	—	OF-1

Amby McConnell

McCONNELL, AMBROSE MOSES
B. Apr. 29, 1883, North Powell, Vt.   D. May 20, 1942, Utica, N. Y.   BL TR 5'7"   150 lbs.

Year	Team	Games	BA	SA	AB	H	2B	3B	HR	HR%	R	RBI	BB	SO	SB	AB	H	PO	A	E	DP	TC/G	FA	G by Pos
1908	BOS A	140	.279	.335	502	140	10	6	2	0.4	77	34	38		31	10	5	238	355	41	33	4.5	.935	2B-126, SS-3
1909		121	.238	.289	453	108	7	8	0	0.0	59	36	34		26	0	0	251	389	31	43	5.5	.954	2B-121
1910	2 teams		BOS A	(12G – .167)					CHI A	(32G – .277)														
"	total	44	.252	.303	155	39	2	3	0	0.0	19	6	12		8	0	0	78	108	9	10	4.4	.954	2B-42
1911	CHI A	104	.280	.341	396	111	11	5	1	0.3	45	34	23		7	1	0	189	280	13	31	4.6	.973	2B-103
4 yrs.		409	.264	.319	1506	398	30	22	3	0.2	200	119	107		72	13	5	756	1132	94	117	4.8	.953	2B-392, SS-3

George McConnell

McCONNELL, GEORGE NEELY
B. Sept. 16, 1877, Shelbyville, Tenn.   D. May 10, 1964, Chattanooga, Tenn.   BR TR 6'3"   190 lbs.

Year	Team	Games	BA	SA	AB	H	2B	3B	HR	HR%	R	RBI	BB	SO	SB	AB	H	PO	A	E	DP	TC/G	FA	G by Pos
1909	NY A	13	.209	.256	43	9	0	1	0	0.0	4	5	1		1	0	0	124	14	5	7	11.0	.965	1B-11, P-2
1912		42	.297	.385	91	27	4	2	0	0.0	11	8	4		0	17	6	24	75	8	3	2.5	.925	P-23, 1B-2
1913		39	.179	.209	67	12	2	0	0	0.0	4	2	0	11	0	3	0	11	74	3	2	2.3	.966	P-35, 1B-1
1914	CHI N	1	.000	.000	2	0	0	0	0	0.0	0	0	1		0	0	0	0	3	0	0	3.0	1.000	P-1
1915	CHI F	53	.248	.352	125	31	6	2	1	0.8	14	18	6		2	8	2	8	105	3	4	2.2	.974	P-44
1916	CHI N	48	.158	.158	57	9	0	0	0	0.0	2	0	2	4	2	0	0	9	50	3	3	1.3	.952	P-28
6 yrs.		196	.229	.294	385	88	12	5	1	0.3	35	33	7	16	3	28	8	176	321	22	19	2.6	.958	P-133, 1B-14

Sammy McConnell

McCONNELL, SAMUEL FAULKNER
B. June 8, 1895, Philadelphia, Pa.   D. June 27, 1981, Phoenixville, Pa.   BL TR 5'6½"   150 lbs.

Year	Team	Games	BA	SA	AB	H	2B	3B	HR	HR%	R	RBI	BB	SO	SB	AB	H	PO	A	E	DP	TC/G	FA	G by Pos
1915	PHI A	6	.182	.273	11	2	1	0	0	0.0	1	0	1	3	0	0	0	6	10	3	0	3.2	.842	3B-5

Don McCormack

McCORMACK, DONALD ROSS
B. Sept. 18, 1955, Omak, Wash.   BR TR 6'3"   205 lbs.

Year	Team	Games	BA	SA	AB	H	2B	3B	HR	HR%	R	RBI	BB	SO	SB	AB	H	PO	A	E	DP	TC/G	FA	G by Pos
1980	PHI N	2	1.000	1.000	1	1	0	0	0	0.0	0	0	0	0	0	0	0	6	0	0	0	3.0	1.000	C-2
1981		3	.250	.250	4	1	0	0	0	0.0	0	0	0	1	0	0	0	4	2	0	0	2.0	1.000	C-3
2 yrs.		5	.400	.400	5	2	0	0	0	0.0	0	0	0	1	0	0	0	10	2	0	0	2.4	1.000	C-5

Barry McCormick

McCORMICK, WILLIAM J.
B. Dec. 25, 1874, Maysville, Ky.   D. Jan. 28, 1956, Cincinnati, Ohio   TR 5'9"

Year	Team	Games	BA	SA	AB	H	2B	3B	HR	HR%	R	RBI	BB	SO	SB	AB	H	PO	A	E	DP	TC/G	FA	G by Pos
1895	LOU N	3	.250	.417	12	3	0	1	0	0.0	2	0	0		0	0	0	4	7	1	1	4.0	.917	SS-2, 2B-1
1896	CHI N	45	.220	.268	168	37	3	1	1	0.6	22	23	14	30	9	0	0	51	98	31	12	4.0	.828	3B-35, SS-6, 2B-3, OF-1
1897		101	.267	.348	419	112	8	10	2	0.5	87	55	33		0	0	0	171	269	59	26	4.9	.882	3B-56, SS-46, 2B-1
1898		137	.247	.321	530	131	15	9	2	0.4	76	78	47		15	0	0	155	326	63	31	4.0	.884	3B-136, SS-1, 2B-1
1899		102	.258	.324	376	97	15	2	2	0.5	48	52	25		14	0	0	205	351	37	49	5.8	.938	2B-99, SS-3
1900		110	.219	.303	379	83	13	5	3	0.8	35	48	38		8	0	0	198	378	64	34	5.8	.900	SS-84, 3B-21, 2B-5
1901		115	.234	.304	427	100	15	6	1	0.2	45	32	31		12	0	0	206	411	60	47	5.9	.911	SS-112, 3B-3
1902	STL A	139	.246	.308	504	124	14	4	3	0.6	55	51	37		10	0	0	159	298	45	28	3.6	.910	3B-132, SS-7, OF-1
1903	2 teams		STL A	(61G – .217)					WAS A	(63G – .215)														
"	total	124	.216	.282	426	92	16	3	2	0.5	27	40	28		8	0	0	217	347	25	49	4.8	.958	3B-91, 1B-28, SS-4
1904	WAS A	113	.218	.250	404	88	11	1	0	0.0	36	39	27		9	0	0	204	355	37	39	5.3	.938	2B-113
10 yrs.		989	.238	.304	3645	867	110	42	16	0.4	433	418	280	30	130	0	0	1570	2840	422	310	4.9	.913	3B-411, 2B-314, SS-265, OF-2

Frank McCormick

McCORMICK, FRANK ANDREW (Buck)
B. June 9, 1911, New York, N. Y.   D. Nov. 21, 1982, Manhasset, N. Y.   BR TR 6'4"   205 lbs.

Year	Team	Games	BA	SA	AB	H	2B	3B	HR	HR%	R	RBI	BB	SO	SB	AB	H	PO	A	E	DP	TC/G	FA	G by Pos
1934	CIN N	12	.313	.563	16	5	2	1	0	0.0	1	5	0	1	0	10	4	16	0	1	1	1.4	.941	1B-2

Year	Team		Games	BA	SA	AB	H	2B	3B	HR	HR%	R	RBI	BB	SO	SB	Pinch Hit AB	Pinch Hit H	PO	A	E	DP	TC/G	FA	G by Pos

Frank McCormick *continued*

Year	Team		Games	BA	SA	AB	H	2B	3B	HR	HR%	R	RBI	BB	SO	SB	AB	H	PO	A	E	DP	TC/G	FA	G by Pos
1937			24	.325	.386	83	27	5	0	0	0.0	5	9	2	4	1	0	0	199	18	1	20	9.1	.995	1B-20, 2B-4, OF-1
1938			151	.327	.425	640	209	40	4	5	0.8	89	106	18	17	1	0	0	1441	95	7	127	10.2	.995	1B-151
1939			156	.332	.495	630	209	41	4	18	2.9	99	128	40	16	1	0	0	1518	100	7	153	10.4	.995	1B-156
1940			155	.309	.482	618	191	44	3	19	3.1	93	127	52	26	2	0	0	1587	98	8	146	10.9	.995	1B-155
1941			154	.269	.421	603	162	31	5	17	2.8	77	97	40	13	2	0	0	1464	92	8	130	10.2	.995	1B-154
1942			145	.277	.388	564	156	24	0	13	2.3	58	89	45	18	1	1	0	1403	101	10	132	10.4	.993	1B-144
1943			126	.303	.413	472	143	28	0	8	1.7	56	59	29	15	2	6	0	1156	85	6	116	9.9	.995	1B-120
1944			153	.305	.482	581	177	37	3	20	3.4	85	102	57	17	7	0	0	1508	135	13	130	10.8	.992	1B-153
1945			152	.276	.384	580	160	33	0	10	1.7	68	81	56	22	6	1	0	1469	118	9	104	10.5	.994	1B-151
1946	PHI	N	135	.284	.397	504	143	20	2	11	2.2	46	66	36	21	2	1	0	1185	98	1	92	9.5	.999	1B-134
1947	2 teams		PHI N (15G – .225)			BOS N (81G – .354)																			
"	total		96	.333	.464	252	84	20	2	3	1.2	31	51	14	10	2	36	13	514	30	3	40	5.7	.995	1B-60
1948	BOS	N	75	.250	.389	180	45	9	2	4	2.2	14	34	10	9	0	22	4	343	33	5	30	5.1	.987	1B-50
13 yrs.			1534	.299	.434	5723	1711	334	26	128	2.2	722	954	399	189	27	77	21	13803	1003	79	1221	9.7	.995	1B-1450, 2B-4, OF-1

WORLD SERIES

Year	Team		Games	BA	SA	AB	H	2B	3B	HR	HR%	R	RBI	BB	SO	SB	AB	H	PO	A	E	DP	TC/G	FA	G by Pos
1939	CIN	N	4	.400	.467	15	6	1	0	0	0.0	1	1	0	1	0	0	0	32	2	0	1	8.5	1.000	1B-4
1940			7	.214	.250	28	6	1	0	0	0.0	2	0	1	1	0	0	0	59	4	2	7	9.3	.969	1B-7
1948	BOS	N	3	.200	.200	5	1	0	0	0	0.0	0	0	0	2	0	2	0	5	1	0	1	2.0	1.000	1B-1
3 yrs.			14	.271	.313	48	13	2	0	0	0.0	3	1	1	4	0	2	0	96	7	2	9	7.5	.981	1B-12

Jerry McCormick

McCORMICK, JOHN
B. Philadelphia, Pa.   D. Sept. 19, 1905, Philadelphia, Pa.

Year	Team		Games	BA	SA	AB	H	2B	3B	HR	HR%	R	RBI	BB	SO	SB	AB	H	PO	A	E	DP	TC/G	FA	G by Pos
1883	BAL	AA	93	.262	.334	389	102	16	6	0	0.0	40		2			0	0	138	196	84	10	4.5	.799	3B-93
1884	2 teams		PHI U (67G – .285)			WAS U (42G – .217)																			
"	total		109	.261	.323	452	118	20	4	0	0.0	64		5			0	0	161	208	82	18	4.1	.818	3B-92, SS-7, OF-5, 2B-5, P-1
2 yrs.			202	.262	.328	841	220	36	10	0	0.0	104		7			0	0	299	404	166	28	4.3	.809	3B-185, SS-7, OF-5, 2B-5, P-1

Jim McCormick

McCORMICK, JAMES
B. 1856, Glasgow, Scotland   D. Mar. 10, 1918, Paterson, N. J.
Manager 1879-82.

BR TR 5'10½" 215 lbs.

Year	Team		Games	BA	SA	AB	H	2B	3B	HR	HR%	R	RBI	BB	SO	SB	AB	H	PO	A	E	DP	TC/G	FA	G by Pos
1878	IND	N	15	.143	.161	56	8	0	0	0	0.0	5	0	0	2		0	0	9	33	3	3	3.0	.933	P-14, OF-3
1879	CLE	N	75	.220	.270	282	62	10	2	0	0.0	35	20	1	9		0	0	97	120	15	4	3.1	.935	P-62, OF-13, 1B-4
1880			78	.246	.284	289	71	11	0	0	0.0	34	26	5	5		0	0	38	135	26	4	2.6	.869	P-74, OF-5
1881			70	.256	.311	309	79	9	4	0	0.0	45	26	5	16		0	0	55	92	18	4	2.4	.891	P-59, OF-10, 3B-1, 2B-1
1882			70	.218	.290	262	57	7	3	2	0.8	35	15	2	22		0	0	45	100	15	1	2.3	.906	P-68, OF-4
1883			43	.236	.274	157	37	2	2	0	0.0	21		2	14		0	0	28	101	17	4	3.4	.884	P-85, OF-1
1884	2 teams		CLE N (49G – .263)			CIN U (27G – .245)																			
"	total		76	.257	.317	300	77	8	5	0	0.0	27	23	1	11		0	0	54	119	9	6	2.4	.951	P-66, OF-11
1885	2 teams		PRO N (4G – .214)			CHI N (25G – .223)																			
"	total		29	.222	.308	117	26	2	4	0	0.0	15	16	2	18		0	0	23	75	5	3	3.6	.951	P-28, OF-1
1886	CHI	N	42	.236	.345	174	41	9	2	2	1.1	17	21	2	30		0	0	22	75	6	3	2.5	.942	P-42, OF-4
1887	PIT	N	36	.243	.294	136	33	7	0	0	0.0	12	18	2	0	9	0	0	13	88	8	1	3.0	.927	P-36
10 yrs.			534	.236	.294	2082	491	66	22	4	0.2	246	165	22	127	9	0	0	384	938	122	33	2.7	.916	P-534, OF-52, 1B-4, 3B-1, 2B-1

Jim McCormick

McCORMICK, JAMES AMBROSE
B. Nov. 2, 1868, Spencer, Mass.   D. Feb. 1, 1948, Saco, Me.

BR TR 6'1" 160 lbs.

Year	Team		Games	BA	SA	AB	H	2B	3B	HR	HR%	R	RBI	BB	SO	SB	AB	H	PO	A	E	DP	TC/G	FA	G by Pos
1892	STL	N	3	.000	.000	11	0	0	0	0	0.0	0	0	1	5	0	0	0	4	8	0	0	4.0	1.000	2B-2, 3B-1

Mike McCormick

McCORMICK, MICHAEL J.
B. 1883, Jersey City, N. J.   D. Nov. 18, 1953, Jersey City, N. J.

BR TR 5'9"

Year	Team		Games	BA	SA	AB	H	2B	3B	HR	HR%	R	RBI	BB	SO	SB	AB	H	PO	A	E	DP	TC/G	FA	G by Pos
1904	BKN	N	105	.184	.222	347	64	5	4	0	0.0	28	27	43		22	0	0	139	190	31	21	3.4	.914	3B-104, 2B-1

Mike McCormick

McCORMICK, MYRON WINTHROP
B. May 6, 1917, Angel's Camp, Calif.   D. Apr. 14, 1976, Ventura, Calif.

BR TR 6' 195 lbs.

Year	Team		Games	BA	SA	AB	H	2B	3B	HR	HR%	R	RBI	BB	SO	SB	AB	H	PO	A	E	DP	TC/G	FA	G by Pos
1940	CIN	N	110	.300	.355	417	125	20	0	1	0.2	48	30	13	36	8	2	0	266	9	4	2	2.5	.986	OF-107
1941			110	.287	.382	369	106	17	3	4	1.1	52	31	30	24	4	4	0	240	9	6	2	2.3	.976	OF-101
1942			40	.237	.319	135	32	2	3	1	0.7	18	11	13	7	0	1	0	93	2	1	1	2.4	.990	OF-38
1943			4	.133	.133	15	2	0	0	0	0.0	0	0	2	0	0	1	0	10	0	1	0	2.8	.909	OF-4
1946	2 teams		CIN N (23G – .216)			BOS N (59G – .262)																			
"	total		82	.248	.311	238	59	8	2	1	0.4	33	21	19	12	0	10	2	165	2	3	0	2.1	.982	OF-69
1947	BOS	N	92	.285	.412	284	81	13	7	3	1.1	42	36	20	21	1	12	4	155	4	3	0	1.8	.981	OF-79
1948			115	.303	.417	343	104	22	7	1	0.3	45	39	32	34	1	14	6	187	7	5	3	1.7	.975	OF-100
1949	BKN	N	55	.209	.302	139	29	5	1	2	1.4	17	14	14	12	1	6	2	75	3	0	0	1.4	1.000	OF-49
1950	2 teams		NY N (4G – .000)			CHI A (55G – .232)																			
"	total		59	.225	.296	142	32	4	3	0	0.0	16	10	16	8	0	11	1	105	4	2	0	1.9	.982	OF-44
1951	WAS	A	81	.288	.362	243	70	9	3	1	0.4	31	23	29	20	1	15	7	134	7	5	0	1.8	.966	OF-62
10 yrs.			748	.275	.361	2325	640	100	29	14	0.6	302	215	188	174	16	75	22	1430	47	30	10	2.0	.980	OF-653

WORLD SERIES

Year	Team		Games	BA	SA	AB	H	2B	3B	HR	HR%	R	RBI	BB	SO	SB	AB	H	PO	A	E	DP	TC/G	FA	G by Pos
1940	CIN	N	7	.310	.414	29	9	3	0	0	0.0	1	2	1	6	0	0	0	24	1	1	0	3.7	.962	OF-7
1948	BOS	N	6	.261	.261	23	6	0	0	0	0.0	1	2	0	4	0	0	0	17	0	0	0	2.8	1.000	OF-6
1949	BKN	N	1	–	–	0	0	0	0	0	–	0	0	0	0	0	0	0	1	0	0	0	1.0	1.000	OF-1
3 yrs.			14	.288	.346	52	15	3	0	0	0.0	2	4	1	10	0	0	0	42	1	1	0	3.1	.977	OF-14

Moose McCormick

McCORMICK, HARRY ELWOOD
B. Feb. 28, 1881, Philadelphia, Pa.   D. July 9, 1962, Lewisburg, Pa.

BL TL 5'11" 180 lbs.

Year	Team	Games	BA	SA	AB	H	2B	3B	HR	HR%	R	RBI	BB	SO	SB	Pinch Hit AB	Pinch Hit H	PO	A	E	DP	TC/G	FA	G by Pos

Moose McCormick *continued*

Year	Team		Games	BA	SA	AB	H	2B	3B	HR	HR%	R	RBI	BB	SO	SB	PH AB	PH H	PO	A	E	DP	TC/G	FA	G by Pos
1904	2 teams	NY N (59G – .266)				PIT N (66G – .290)																			
"	total		125	.279	.392	441	123	19	11	3	0.7	53	49	26		19	4	2	182	10	15	2	1.7	.928	OF-121
1908	2 teams	PHI N (11G – .091)				NY N (73G – .302)																			
"	total		84	.285	.365	274	78	16	3	0	0.0	31	34	6		6	10	3	108	3	11	2	1.5	.910	OF-70
1909	NY	N	110	.291	.402	413	120	21	8	3	0.7	68	27	49		4	10	2	144	13	13	6	1.5	.924	OF-109
1912			42	.333	.487	39	13	4	1	0	0.0	4	8	6	9	1	30	11	3	0	1	0	0.1	.750	OF-6, 1B-1
1913			57	.275	.375	80	22	2	3	0	0.0	9	15	5	13	1	39	10	19	1	2	1	0.4	.909	OF-15
5 yrs.			418	.285	.391	1247	356	62	26	6	0.5	165	133	92	22	30	93	28	456	27	42	11	1.3	.920	OF-321, 1B-1

WORLD SERIES

Year	Team		Games	BA	SA	AB	H	2B	3B	HR	HR%	R	RBI	BB	SO	SB	PH AB	PH H	PO	A	E	DP	TC/G	FA	G by Pos
1912	NY	N	5	.250	.250	4	1	0	0	0	0.0	0	0	0	0	0	4	1	0	0	0	0	0.0		–
1913			2	.500	.500	2	1	0	0	0	0.0	1	0	0	0	0	2	1	0	0	0	0	0.0		–
2 yrs.			7	.333	.333	6	2	0	0	0	0.0	1	1	0	0	0	6	2	0	0	0	0	0.0		–

Barney McCosky

McCOSKY, WILLIAM BARNEY
B. Apr. 11, 1918, Coal Run, Pa.
BL TR 6'1" 184 lbs.

Year	Team		Games	BA	SA	AB	H	2B	3B	HR	HR%	R	RBI	BB	SO	SB	PH AB	PH H	PO	A	E	DP	TC/G	FA	G by Pos
1939	DET	A	147	.311	.430	611	190	33	14	4	0.7	120	58	70	45	20	2	1	428	7	6	2	3.0	.986	OF-145
1940			143	.340	.491	589	200	39	19	4	0.7	123	57	67	41	13	2	1	349	7	6	2	2.5	.983	OF-141
1941			127	.324	.425	494	160	25	8	3	0.6	80	55	61	33	8	4	4	328	6	5	2	2.7	.985	OF-122
1942			154	.293	.412	600	176	28	11	7	1.2	75	50	68	37	11	0	0	351	7	7	2	2.4	.981	OF-154
1946	2 teams	DET A (25G – .198)				PHI A (92G – .354)																			
"	total		117	.318	.409	399	127	22	7	2	0.5	44	45	60	22	2	5	1	263	3	6	0	2.3	.978	OF-109
1947	PHI	A	137	.328	.399	546	179	22	7	1	0.2	77	52	57	29	1	1	0	346	8	6	2	2.6	.983	OF-136
1948			135	.326	.386	515	168	21	5	0	0.0	95	46	68	22	1	1	1	277	9	3	1	2.1	.990	OF-134
1950			66	.240	.307	179	43	10	1	0	0.0	19	11	22	12	0	23	5	73	1	1	1	1.1	.987	OF-42
1951	3 teams	PHI A (12G – .296)				CIN N (25G – .320)				CLE A (31G – .213)															
"	total		68	.268	.377	138	37	7	1	2	1.4	14	14	15	11	1	32	7	58	0	0	0	0.9	1.000	OF-34
1952	CLE	A	54	.213	.325	80	17	4	1	1	1.3	14	6	8	5	1	30	9	17	0	1	0	0.3	.944	OF-19
1953			22	.190	.333	21	4	3	0	0	0.0	3	3	1	4	0	21	4	0	0	0	0	0.0		OF-19
11 yrs.			1170	.312	.414	4172	1301	214	71	24	0.6	664	397	497	261	58	121	33	2490	48	41	12	2.2	.984	OF-1036

WORLD SERIES

Year	Team		Games	BA	SA	AB	H	2B	3B	HR	HR%	R	RBI	BB	SO	SB	PH AB	PH H	PO	A	E	DP	TC/G	FA	G by Pos
1940	DET	A	7	.304	.348	23	7	1	0	0	0.0	5	1	7	0	0	0	0	19	0	0	0	2.7	1.000	OF-7

Willie McCovey

McCOVEY, WILLIE LEE (Stretch)
B. Jan. 10, 1938, Mobile, Ala.
Hall of Fame 1986.
BL TL 6'4" 198 lbs.

Year	Team		Games	BA	SA	AB	H	2B	3B	HR	HR%	R	RBI	BB	SO	SB	PH AB	PH H	PO	A	E	DP	TC/G	FA	G by Pos
1959	SF	N	52	.354	.656	192	68	9	5	13	6.8	32	38	22	35	2	2	2	424	29	5	29	8.8	.989	1B-51
1960			101	.238	.469	260	62	15	3	13	5.0	37	51	45	53	1	32	7	557	39	9	42	6.0	.985	1B-71
1961			106	.271	.491	328	89	12	3	18	5.5	59	50	37	60	1	21	4	669	55	11	55	6.9	.985	1B-84
1962			91	.293	.590	229	67	6	1	20	8.7	41	54	29	35	3	17	4	186	9	3	13	2.2	.985	OF-57, 1B-17
1963			152	.280	.566	564	158	19	5	44	7.8	103	102	50	119	1	5	0	363	21	15	5	2.6	.962	OF-135, 1B-23
1964			130	.220	.412	364	80	14	1	18	4.9	55	54	61	73	2	23	4	273	19	14	20	2.4	.954	OF-83, 1B-26
1965			160	.276	.539	540	149	17	4	39	7.2	93	92	88	118	0	6	1	1310	87	13	93	8.8	.991	1B-156
1966			150	.295	.586	502	148	26	6	36	7.2	85	96	76	100	2	7	2	1287	81	22	91	9.3	.984	1B-145
1967			135	.276	.535	456	126	17	4	31	6.8	73	91	71	110	3	9	2	1221	81	15	102	9.8	.985	1B-127
1968			148	.293	.545	523	153	16	4	36	6.9	81	105	72	71	4	2	1	1305	103	21	91	9.7	.985	1B-146
1969			149	.320	.656	491	157	26	2	45	9.2	101	126	121	66	0	1	0	1392	79	12	116	10.0	.992	1B-148
1970			152	.289	.612	495	143	39	2	39	7.9	98	126	137	75	0	5	2	1217	134	15	117	9.0	.989	1B-146
1971			105	.277	.480	329	91	13	0	18	5.5	45	70	64	57	0	8	3	828	63	15	80	8.6	.983	1B-95
1972			81	.213	.403	263	56	8	0	14	5.3	30	35	38	45	0	7	2	617	32	9	52	8.1	.986	1B-74
1973			130	.266	.546	383	102	14	3	29	7.6	52	75	105	78	1	9	1	930	76	12	89	7.8	.988	1B-117
1974	SD	N	128	.253	.506	344	87	19	1	22	6.4	53	63	96	76	1	18	7	815	47	11	59	6.8	.987	1B-104
1975			122	.252	.460	413	104	17	0	23	5.6	43	68	57	80	1	4	2	979	73	15	94	8.7	.986	1B-115
1976	2 teams	SD N (71G – .203)				OAK A (11G – .208)																			
"	total		82	.204	.336	226	46	9	0	7	3.1	20	36	24	43	0	21	6	420	44	4	39	5.7	.991	1B-51, DH-9
1977	SF	N	141	.280	.500	478	134	21	0	28	5.9	54	86	67	106	3	4	0	1072	60	13	93	8.1	.989	1B-136
1978			108	.228	.396	351	80	19	2	12	3.4	32	64	36	57	1	9	2	721	44	10	49	7.2	.987	1B-97
1979			117	.249	.402	353	88	9	0	15	4.2	34	57	36	70	0	28	11	740	48	10	60	6.8	.987	1B-89
1980			48	.204	.301	113	23	8	0	1	0.9	8	16	13	23	0	17	2	241	12	2	18	5.3	.992	1B-27
22 yrs.			2588	.270	.515	8197	2211	353	46	521	6.4	1229	1555	1345	1550	26	254	66	17567	1236	256	1407	7.4	.987	1B-2045, OF-275, DH-9
										10th	10th														

LEAGUE CHAMPIONSHIP SERIES

Year	Team		Games	BA	SA	AB	H	2B	3B	HR	HR%	R	RBI	BB	SO	SB	PH AB	PH H	PO	A	E	DP	TC/G	FA	G by Pos
1971	SF	N	4	.429	.857	14	6	0	0	2	14.3	2	6	4	2	0	0	0	34	3	1	0	9.5	.974	1B-4

WORLD SERIES

Year	Team		Games	BA	SA	AB	H	2B	3B	HR	HR%	R	RBI	BB	SO	SB	PH AB	PH H	PO	A	E	DP	TC/G	FA	G by Pos
1962	SF	N	4	.200	.533	15	3	0	1	1	6.7	2	1	1	3	0	0	0	23	4	2	2	7.3	.931	OF-2, 1B-2

Art McCoy

McCOY, ARTHUR GRAY
B. 1865, Danville, Pa. D. Mar. 22, 1904, Danville, Pa.
168 lbs.

Year	Team		Games	BA	SA	AB	H	2B	3B	HR	HR%	R	RBI	BB	SO	SB	PH AB	PH H	PO	A	E	DP	TC/G	FA	G by Pos
1889	WAS	N	2	.000	.000	6	0	0	0	0	0.0	2	1	0		0	0	0	6	2	1	0	4.5	.889	2B-2

Benny McCoy

McCOY, BENJAMIN JENISON
B. Nov. 9, 1915, Jenison, Mich.
BL TR 5'9" 170 lbs.

Year	Team		Games	BA	SA	AB	H	2B	3B	HR	HR%	R	RBI	BB	SO	SB	PH AB	PH H	PO	A	E	DP	TC/G	FA	G by Pos
1938	DET	A	7	.200	.267	15	3	1	0	0	0.0	2	0	1	2	0	0	0	10	16	3	4	4.1	.897	2B-6, 3B-1
1939			55	.302	.448	192	58	13	6	1	0.5	38	33	29	26	3	5	0	108	150	11	25	4.9	.959	2B-34, SS-16
1940	PHI	A	134	.257	.373	490	126	26	4	7	1.4	56	62	65	44	2	4	2	262	393	35	82	5.1	.949	2B-130, 3B-1
1941			141	.271	.368	517	140	12	7	8	1.5	86	61	95	50	3	5	0	285	423	27	87	5.2	.963	2B-135
4 yrs.			337	.269	.381	1214	327	52	18	16	1.3	182	156	190	122	8	14	2	665	982	76	198	5.1	.956	2B-305, SS-16, 3B-2

Tom McCraw

McCRAW, TOMMY LEE
B. Nov. 21, 1940, Malvern, Ark.
BL TL 6' 183 lbs.

Year	Team	Games	BA	SA	AB	H	2B	3B	HR	HR%	R	RBI	BB	SO	SB	Pinch Hit AB	Pinch Hit H	PO	A	E	DP	TC/G	FA	G by Pos

Tom McCraw *continued*

Year	Team	Games	BA	SA	AB	H	2B	3B	HR	HR%	R	RBI	BB	SO	SB	AB	H	PO	A	E	DP	TC/G	FA	G by Pos
1963	CHI A	102	.254	.379	280	71	11	3	6	2.1	38	33	21	46	15	3	1	673	47	5	65	7.1	.993	1B-97
1964		125	.261	.367	368	96	11	5	6	1.6	47	36	32	65	15	20	2	637	41	7	57	5.5	.990	1B-84, OF-36
1965		133	.238	.344	273	65	12	1	5	1.8	38	21	25	48	12	22	7	336	24	4	18	2.7	.989	1B-72, OF-64
1966		151	.229	.329	389	89	16	4	5	1.3	49	48	29	40	20	7	1	893	68	9	56	6.4	.991	1B-121, OF-41
1967		125	.236	.362	453	107	18	3	11	2.4	55	45	33	55	24	2	0	1177	110	11	92	10.4	.992	1B-123, OF-6
1968		136	.235	.375	477	112	16	12	9	1.9	51	44	36	58	20	3	0	1285	93	20	103	10.3	.986	1B-135
1969		93	.258	.350	240	62	12	2	2	0.8	21	25	21	24	1	17	4	302	15	3	21	3.4	.991	1B-44, OF-41
1970		129	.220	.319	332	73	11	2	6	1.8	39	31	21	50	12	32	8	427	35	9	34	3.7	.981	1B-59, OF-49
1971	WAS A	122	.213	.382	207	44	6	4	7	3.4	33	25	19	38	3	40	9	134	2	5	3	1.2	.965	OF-60, 1B-30
1972	CLE A	129	.258	.371	391	101	13	5	7	1.8	43	33	41	47	12	12	2	504	28	3	29	4.1	.994	1B-84, OF-38
1973	CAL A	99	.265	.326	264	70	7	0	3	1.1	25	24	30	42	3	23	5	268	25	1	28	3.0	.997	OF-34, 1B-25, DH-8
1974	2 teams		CAL A	(56G –	.286)		CLE	A	(45G –	.304)														
"	total	101	.294	.442	231	68	16	0	6	2.6	38	34	17	24	2	23	6	448	38	3	39	4.8	.994	1B-67, OF-13, DH-2
1975	CLE A	23	.275	.451	51	14	1	1	2	3.9	7	5	7	7	4	4	2	112	6	1	9	5.2	.992	1B-16, OF-3
13 yrs.		1468	.246	.362	3956	972	150	42	75	1.9	484	404	332	544	143	208	47	7196	532	81	554	5.3	.990	1B-911, OF-431, DH-10

Frank McCrea

McCREA, FRANCIS WILLIAM
B. Sept. 6, 1896, Jersey City, N. J.   D. Feb. 25, 1981, Dover, N. J.
BR TR 5'9" 155 lbs.

Year	Team	Games	BA	SA	AB	H	2B	3B	HR	HR%	R	RBI	BB	SO	SB	AB	H	PO	A	E	DP	TC/G	FA	G by Pos
1925	CLE A	1	.200	.200	5	1	0	0	0	0.0	1	0	0	0	0	0	0	4	0	0	0	4.0	1.000	C-1

Walt McCreedie

McCREEDIE, WALTER HENRY
B. Nov. 29, 1876, Manchester, Iowa   D. July 29, 1934, Portland, Ore.
BL TR 6'2" 195 lbs.

Year	Team	Games	BA	SA	AB	H	2B	3B	HR	HR%	R	RBI	BB	SO	SB	AB	H	PO	A	E	DP	TC/G	FA	G by Pos
1903	BKN N	56	.324	.347	213	69	5	0	0	0.0	40	20	24		10	0	0	68	6	6	3	1.4	.925	OF-56

Tom McCreery

McCREERY, THOMAS LIVINGSTON
B. Oct. 19, 1874, Beaver, Pa.   D. July 3, 1941, Beaver, Pa.
BB TR 5'11" 180 lbs.

Year	Team	Games	BA	SA	AB	H	2B	3B	HR	HR%	R	RBI	BB	SO	SB	AB	H	PO	A	E	DP	TC/G	FA	G by Pos
1895	LOU N	31	.324	.370	108	35	3	1	0	0.0	18	10	8	15	3	0	0	31	23	10	4	2.1	.844	OF-18, P-8, SS-4, 3B-1, 1B-1
1896		115	.351	.546	441	155	23	21	7	1.6	87	65	42	58	26	2	1	180	22	18	5	1.9	.918	OF-111, 2B-1, P-1
1897	2 teams		LOU	N	(89G –	.284)	NY	N	(49G –	.299)														
"	total	138	.289	.386	515	149	13	11	5	1.0	91	68	60		28	2	1	186	32	33	4	1.8	.869	OF-134, 2B-3
1898	2 teams		NY	N	(35G –	.198)	PIT	N	(53G –	.311)														
"	total	88	.267	.389	311	83	9	10	3	1.0	48	37	45		6	2	1	144	10	17	1	1.9	.901	OF-86
1899	PIT N	118	.323	.422	455	147	21	9	2	0.4	76	64	47		11	5	2	234	55	34	5	2.7	.895	OF-97, SS-9, 2B-7
1900		43	.220	.318	132	29	4	3	1	0.8	20	13	16		2	5	0	62	10	9	2	1.9	.889	OF-35, P-1
1901	BKN N	91	.290	.433	335	97	11	14	3	0.9	47	53	32		13	3	1	217	15	14	6	2.7	.943	OF-82, 1B-4, SS-2
1902		112	.244	.309	430	105	8	4	4	0.9	49	57	29		16	0	0	1036	60	23	54	10.0	.979	1B-108, OF-4
1903	2 teams		BKN	N	(40G –	.262)	BOS	N	(23G –	.217)														
"	total	63	.246	.317	224	55	7	3	1	0.4	28	20	29		11	2	1	106	6	13	3	2.0	.896	OF-61
9 yrs.		799	.290	.401	2951	855	99	76	26	0.9	464	387	308	73	116	21	7	2196	233	171	84	3.3	.934	OF-628, 1B-113, SS-15, 2B-11, P-10, 3B-1

Frank McCue

McCUE, FRANK ALOYSIUS
B. Oct. 4, 1898, Chicago, Ill.   D. July 5, 1953, Evergreen Park, Ill.
BB TR 5'9" 150 lbs.

Year	Team	Games	BA	SA	AB	H	2B	3B	HR	HR%	R	RBI	BB	SO	SB	AB	H	PO	A	E	DP	TC/G	FA	G by Pos
1922	PHI A	2	.000	.000	5	0	0	0	0	0.0	0	0	0	0	0	0	0	0	0	0	0	0.0	–	3B-2

Clyde McCullough

McCULLOUGH, CLYDE EDWARD
B. Mar. 4, 1917, Nashville, Tenn.   D. Sept. 18, 1982, San Francisco, Calif.
BR TR 5'11½" 180 lbs.

Year	Team	Games	BA	SA	AB	H	2B	3B	HR	HR%	R	RBI	BB	SO	SB	AB	H	PO	A	E	DP	TC/G	FA	G by Pos
1940	CHI N	9	.154	.192	26	4	1	0	0	0.0	4	1	5	5	0	2	0	44	4	0	1	5.3	1.000	C-7
1941		125	.227	.323	418	95	9	2	9	2.2	41	53	34	67	5	5	1	481	64	10	6	4.4	.982	C-119
1942		109	.282	.398	337	95	22	1	5	1.5	39	31	25	47	7	4	0	386	61	9	10	4.2	.980	C-97
1943		87	.237	.293	266	63	5	2	2	0.8	20	23	24	33	6	4	0	271	25	7	2	3.5	.977	C-81
1946		95	.287	.417	307	88	18	5	4	1.3	38	34	22	39	2	5	0	390	40	4	4	4.6	.991	C-89
1947		86	.252	.376	234	59	12	4	3	1.3	25	30	20	20	1	17	3	280	35	5	3	3.7	.984	C-64
1948		69	.209	.273	172	36	4	2	1	0.6	10	7	15	25	0	15	2	225	25	7	5	3.7	.973	C-51
1949	PIT N	91	.237	.349	241	57	9	3	4	1.7	30	21	24	30	1	1	0	363	39	6	8	4.5	.985	C-90
1950		103	.254	.405	279	71	16	4	6	2.2	28	34	31	35	3	2	0	362	45	6	10	4.0	.985	C-100
1951		92	.297	.440	259	77	9	2	8	3.1	26	39	27	31	2	7	4	364	52	5	10	4.6	.988	C-86
1952		66	.233	.291	172	40	1	0	1	0.6	15	10	18	10	1	0	0	227	38	5	4	4.1	.981	C-61, 1B-1
1953	CHI N	77	.258	.367	229	59	3	2	6	2.6	21	23	15	23	0	4	1	273	31	4	7	4.0	.987	C-26, 3B-3
1954		31	.259	.457	81	21	7	0	3	3.7	9	17	5	5	0	2	0	105	7	2	1	3.7	.982	C-37
1955		44	.198	.198	81	16	0	0	0	0.0	7	10	8	15	0	7	1	160	12	0	0	3.9	1.000	C-7
1956		14	.211	.263	19	4	1	0	0	0.0	0	1	0	4	0	7	1	24	3	0	0	1.9	1.000	C-7
15 yrs.		1098	.252	.358	3121	785	121	28	52	1.7	308	339	265	398	27	90	18	3955	481	72	67	4.1	.984	C-988, 3B-3, 1B-1

WORLD SERIES

Year	Team	Games	BA	SA	AB	H	2B	3B	HR	HR%	R	RBI	BB	SO	SB	AB	H	PO	A	E	DP	TC/G	FA	G by Pos
1945	CHI N	1	.000	.000	1	0	0	0	0	0.0	0	0	0	0	0	1	0	0	0	0	0	0.0	–	

Harry McCurdy

McCURDY, HARRY HENRY
B. Sept. 15, 1899, Stevens Point, Wis.   D. July 21, 1972, Houston, Tex.
BL TR 5'11" 187 lbs.

Year	Team	Games	BA	SA	AB	H	2B	3B	HR	HR%	R	RBI	BB	SO	SB	AB	H	PO	A	E	DP	TC/G	FA	G by Pos
1922	STL N	13	.296	.519	27	8	2	2	0	0.0	3	5	1	1	0	3	0	24	5	1	2	2.3	.967	C-9, 1B-2
1923		67	.265	.346	185	49	11	2	0	0.0	17	15	11	11	3	9	0	157	30	6	4	2.9	.969	C-58
1926	CHI A	44	.326	.488	86	28	7	2	1	1.2	16	11	6	10	0	11	2	84	13	3	3	2.3	.970	C-25, 1B-8
1927		86	.286	.393	262	75	19	3	1	0.4	34	27	32	24	6	3	0	261	55	9	8	3.8	.972	C-82
1928		49	.262	.417	103	27	10	2	2	1.9	12	13	8	15	0	14	3	95	11	4	2	2.2	.964	C-34
1930	PHI N	80	.331	.419	148	49	6	2	1	0.7	23	25	15	12	0	32	8	97	16	4	1	1.5	.966	C-41
1931		66	.287	.367	150	43	9	0	1	0.7	21	25	23	16	2	17	7	157	27	6	1	2.9	.968	C-45
1932		62	.235	.316	136	32	6	1	1	0.7	13	14	17	13	0	15	2	132	14	4	3	2.5	.974	C-42
1933		73	.278	.407	54	15	1	0	2	3.7	9	12	16	6	0	52	15	0	0	0	0	–		C-2

Year	Team	Games	BA	SA	AB	H	2B	3B	HR	HR%	R	RBI	BB	SO	SB	Pinch Hit AB	Pinch Hit H	PO	A	E	DP	TC/G	FA	G by Pos

Harry McCurdy *continued*

Year	Team	Games	BA	SA	AB	H	2B	3B	HR	HR%	R	RBI	BB	SO	SB	AB	H	PO	A	E	DP	TC/G	FA	G by Pos
1934	CIN N	3	.000	.000	6	0	0	0	0	0.0	0	1	0	0	0	2	0	11	2	0	2	4.3	1.000	1B-3
10 yrs.		543	.282	.387	1157	326	71	12	9	0.8	148	148	129	108	12	158	37	1018	176	37	26	2.3	.970	C-338, 1B-13

Mickey McDermott

McDERMOTT, MAURICE JOSEPH
B. Aug. 29, 1928, Poughkeepsie, N. Y. BL TL 6'2" 170 lbs.

Year	Team	Games	BA	SA	AB	H	2B	3B	HR	HR%	R	RBI	BB	SO	SB	AB	H	PO	A	E	DP	TC/G	FA	G by Pos
1948	BOS A	7	.375	.500	8	3	1	0	0	0.0	2	0	0	0	0	0	0	1	8	0	0	1.3	1.000	P-7
1949		13	.212	.303	33	7	3	0	0	0.0	3	6	3	6	0	0	0	2	14	1	0	1.3	.941	P-12
1950		39	.364	.477	44	16	5	0	0	0.0	11	12	9	3	0	0	0	5	25	2	1	0.8	.938	P-38
1951		43	.273	.364	66	18	1	1	1	1.5	8	6	3	14	0	3	0	4	34	2	5	0.9	.950	P-34
1952		36	.226	.323	62	14	1	1	1	1.6	10	7	4	11	0	1	0	10	24	2	1	1.0	.944	P-30
1953		45	.301	.419	93	28	8	0	1	1.1	9	13	2	13	0	12	1	5	40	2	3	1.0	.957	P-32
1954	WAS A	54	.200	.232	95	19	3	0	0	0.0	7	4	7	12	0	19	3	3	39	2	2	0.8	.955	P-30
1955		70	.263	.337	95	25	4	0	1	1.1	10	10	6	16	1	38	9	3	30	2	1	0.5	.943	P-31
1956	NY A	46	.212	.269	52	11	0	0	1	1.9	4	4	8	13	0	19	4	2	13	0	2	0.3	1.000	P-23
1957	KC A	58	.245	.510	49	12	1	0	4	8.2	6	7	9	16	0	24	5	12	17	2	0	0.5	.935	P-29, 1B-2
1958	DET A	4	.333	.333	3	1	0	0	0	0.0	0	1	0	2	0	2	1	0	0	0	0	0.0	—	P-2
1961	2 teams	STL N	(22G – .071)		KC A	(7G – .200)																		P-23
"	total	29	.105	.211	19	2	2	0	0	0.0	1	4	1	6	0	9	2	2	3	1	0	0.2	.833	P-23
12 yrs.		444	.252	.349	619	156	29	2	9	1.5	71	74	52	112	1	127	25	49	247	16	15	0.7	.949	P-291, 1B-2

WORLD SERIES

Year	Team	Games	BA	SA	AB	H	2B	3B	HR	HR%	R	RBI	BB	SO	SB	AB	H	PO	A	E	DP	TC/G	FA	G by Pos
1956	NY A	1	1.000	1.000	1	1	0	0	0	0.0	0	0	0	0	0	0	0	0	0	0	0	0.0	—	P-1

Red McDermott

McDERMOTT, FRANK A.
B. Nov. 12, 1889, Philadelphia, Pa. D. Sept. 11, 1964, Philadelphia, Pa. BR TR 5'6" 150 lbs.

Year	Team	Games	BA	SA	AB	H	2B	3B	HR	HR%	R	RBI	BB	SO	SB	AB	H	PO	A	E	DP	TC/G	FA	G by Pos
1912	DET A	5	.267	.333	15	4	1	0	0	0.0	2	0	0		1	0	0	7	1	0	0	1.6	1.000	OF-5

Terry McDermott

McDERMOTT, TERRENCE MICHAEL
B. Mar. 20, 1951, Rockville Center, N. Y. BR TR 6'3" 205 lbs.

Year	Team	Games	BA	SA	AB	H	2B	3B	HR	HR%	R	RBI	BB	SO	SB	AB	H	PO	A	E	DP	TC/G	FA	G by Pos
1972	LA N	9	.130	.130	23	3	0	0	0	0.0	2	0	2	8	0	3	1	46	2	0	4	5.3	1.000	1B-7

Tom McDermott

McDERMOTT, THOMAS NATHANIEL
B. Mar. 15, 1856, Zanesville, Ohio D. Nov. 23, 1922, Mansfield, Ohio

Year	Team	Games	BA	SA	AB	H	2B	3B	HR	HR%	R	RBI	BB	SO	SB	AB	H	PO	A	E	DP	TC/G	FA	G by Pos
1885	BAL AA	1	—	—	0	0	0	0	0	—	0		0		0	0	0	0	0	0	0	0.0	—	2B-1

Dave McDonald

McDONALD, DAVID BRUCE
B. May 20, 1943, New Albany, Ind. BL TR 6'3" 215 lbs.

Year	Team	Games	BA	SA	AB	H	2B	3B	HR	HR%	R	RBI	BB	SO	SB	AB	H	PO	A	E	DP	TC/G	FA	G by Pos
1969	NY A	9	.217	.261	23	5	1	0	0	0.0	0	2	2	5	0	3	0	45	3	2	2	5.6	.960	1B-7
1971	MON N	24	.103	.231	39	4	2	0	1	2.6	3	4	4	19	0	17	1	53	4	1	9	2.4	.983	1B-8, OF-1
2 yrs.		33	.145	.242	62	9	3	0	1	1.6	3	6	6	19	0	20	1	98	7	3	11	3.3	.972	1B-15, OF-1

Ed McDonald

McDONALD, EDWARD C.
B. Oct. 28, 1886, Albany, N. Y. D. Mar. 11, 1946, Albany, N. Y. BR TR 6' 180 lbs.

Year	Team	Games	BA	SA	AB	H	2B	3B	HR	HR%	R	RBI	BB	SO	SB	AB	H	PO	A	E	DP	TC/G	FA	G by Pos
1911	BOS N	54	.206	.297	175	36	7	3	1	0.6	28	21	40	39	11	0	0	65	86	7	10	2.9	.956	3B-53, SS-1
1912		121	.259	.349	459	119	23	6	2	0.4	70	34	70	91	22	3	1	147	216	23	18	3.2	.940	3B-118
1913	CHI N	1	—	—	0	0	0	0	0	—	0	0	0	0	0	0	0	0	0	0	0	0.0	—	
3 yrs.		176	.244	.334	634	155	30	9	3	0.5	98	55	110	130	33	3	1	212	302	30	28	3.1	.945	3B-171, SS-1

Jim McDonald

McDONALD, JAMES
B. Philadelphia, Pa. Deceased. BR TR 6' 180 lbs.

Year	Team	Games	BA	SA	AB	H	2B	3B	HR	HR%	R	RBI	BB	SO	SB	AB	H	PO	A	E	DP	TC/G	FA	G by Pos
1902	NY N	2	.333	.333	9	3	0	0	0	0.0	0	1	0		0	0	0	2	0	0	0	1.0	1.000	OF-2

Jim McDonald

McDONALD, JAMES A.
B. Aug. 6, 1860, San Francisco, Calif. D. Sept. 14, 1914, San Francisco, Calif.

Year	Team	Games	BA	SA	AB	H	2B	3B	HR	HR%	R	RBI	BB	SO	SB	AB	H	PO	A	E	DP	TC/G	FA	G by Pos
1884	2 teams	PIT AA	(38G – .159)		WAS U	(2G – .167)																		3B-22, OF-16, 2B-1, C-1
"	total	40	.159	.179	151	24	3	0	0	0.0	11		2		0	0	0	50	42	24	2	2.9	.793	
1885	BUF N	5	.000	.000	14	0	0	0	0	0.0	0		0	4	0	0	0	6	12	2	1	4.0	.900	SS-4, OF-1
2 yrs.		45	.145	.164	165	24	3	0	0	0.0	11	0	2	4	0	0	0	56	54	26	3	3.0	.809	3B-22, OF-17, SS-4, 2B-1, C-1

Joe McDonald

McDONALD, MALCOLM JOSEPH (Tex)
B. Apr. 9, 1888, Galveston, Tex. D. May 30, 1963, Baytown, Tex. BR TR 5'11" 175 lbs.

Year	Team	Games	BA	SA	AB	H	2B	3B	HR	HR%	R	RBI	BB	SO	SB	AB	H	PO	A	E	DP	TC/G	FA	G by Pos
1910	STL A	10	.156	.156	32	5	0	0	0	0.0	4	1	1		0	0	0	10	13	5	2	2.8	.821	3B-10

Tex McDonald

McDONALD, CHARLES C.
Born Charles C. Crabtree.
B. Jan. 31, 1891, Farmersville, Tex. D. Mar. 31, 1943, Houston, Tex. BL TR 5'10" 160 lbs.

Year	Team	Games	BA	SA	AB	H	2B	3B	HR	HR%	R	RBI	BB	SO	SB	AB	H	PO	A	E	DP	TC/G	FA	G by Pos
1912	CIN N	61	.257	.357	140	36	3	4	1	0.7	16	15	13	24	5	15	5	84	89	16	7	3.1	.915	SS-42
1913	2 teams	CIN N	(11G – .300)		BOS N	(62G – .359)																		
"	total	73	.355	.432	155	55	4	4	0	0.0	25	20	15	18	4	26	9	39	76	16	9	1.8	.878	3B-31, 2B-6, OF-1, SS-1
1914	2 teams	PIT F	(67G – .318)		BUF F	(69G – .296)																		
"	total	136	.307	.461	473	145	29	13	6	1.3	59	61	33		20	8	1	201	126	22	15	2.6	.937	OF-90, 2B-37, SS-5
1915	BUF F	87	.271	.426	251	68	9	6	6	2.4	31	39	27		5	20	7	93	4	8	1	1.2	.924	OF-65
4 yrs.		357	.298	.434	1019	304	45	27	13	1.3	131	135	88	42	34	69	22	417	295	62	32	2.2	.920	OF-156, SS-48, 2B-43, 3B-31

Jim McDonnell

McDONNELL, JAMES WILLIAM (Mack)
B. Aug. 15, 1922, Gagetown, Mich. BL TR 5'11" 165 lbs.

Year	Team	Games	BA	SA	AB	H	2B	3B	HR	HR%	R	RBI	BB	SO	SB	AB	H	PO	A	E	DP	TC/G	FA	G by Pos
1943	CLE A	2	.000	.000	1	0	0	0	0	0.0	1	0	2	1	0	0	0	1	0	0	0	0.5	1.000	C-1

Year	Team	Games	BA	SA	AB	H	2B	3B	HR	HR%	R	RBI	BB	SO	SB	Pinch Hit AB	H	PO	A	E	DP	TC/G	FA	G by Pos

Jim McDonnell *continued*

1944		20	.233	.233	43	10	0	0	0	0.0	5	4	4	3	0	7	0	40	5	5	1	2.5	.900	C-13
1945		28	.196	.235	51	10	2	0	0	0.0	3	8	2	4	0	5	0	85	12	2	4	3.5	.980	C-23
3 yrs.		50	.211	.232	95	20	2	0	0	0.0	9	12	8	8	0	12	0	126	17	7	5	3.0	.953	C-37

Ed McDonough

McDONOUGH, EDWARD SEBASTIAN
B. Sept. 11, 1886, Elgin, Ill. D. Sept. 2, 1926, Elgin, Ill.

BR TR 6' 160 lbs.

1909	PHI N	1	.000	.000	1	0	0	0	0	0.0	0	0	0	0	0	1	0	1	1	0	0	2.0	1.000	C-1
1910		5	.111	.111	9	1	0	0	0	0.0	1	0	0	1	0	1	0	11	1	0	0	2.4	1.000	C-4
2 yrs.		6	.100	.100	10	1	0	0	0	0.0	1	0	0	1	0	1	0	12	2	0	0	2.3	1.000	C-5

Gil McDougald

McDOUGALD, GILBERT JAMES
B. May 19, 1928, San Francisco, Calif.

BR TR 6' 175 lbs.

1951	NY A	131	.306	.488	402	123	23	4	14	3.5	72	63	56	54	14	4	0	174	249	14	46	3.3	.968	3B-82, 2B-55
1952		152	.263	.369	555	146	16	5	11	2.0	65	78	57	73	6	1	0	233	372	18	69	4.1	.971	3B-117, 2B-38
1953		141	.285	.416	541	154	27	7	10	1.8	82	83	60	65	3	1	0	170	332	23	45	3.7	.956	3B-136, 2B-26
1954		126	.259	.416	394	102	22	2	12	3.0	66	48	62	64	3	4	0	240	286	8	88	4.2	.985	2B-92, 3B-35
1955		141	.285	.407	533	152	10	8	13	2.4	79	53	65	77	6	0	0	367	382	13	123	5.4	.983	2B-126, 3B-17
1956		120	.311	.443	438	136	13	3	13	3.0	79	56	68	59	3	2	0	239	363	17	109	5.2	.973	SS-92, 2B-31, 3B-5
1957		141	.289	.442	539	156	25	9	13	2.4	87	62	59	71	2	1	0	313	451	17	123	5.5	.978	SS-121, 2B-21, 3B-7
1958		138	.250	.376	503	126	19	1	14	2.8	69	65	59	75	6	6	1	299	357	16	111	4.9	.976	2B-115, SS-19
1959		127	.251	.353	434	109	16	8	4	0.9	44	34	35	40	0	2	0	190	345	10	70	4.3	.982	2B-53, SS-52, 3B-25
1960		119	.258	.401	337	87	16	4	8	2.4	54	34	38	45	2	20	9	127	236	13	31	3.2	.965	3B-84, 2B-42
10 yrs.		1336	.276	.410	4676	1291	187	51	112	2.4	697	576	559	623	45	41	10	2352	3373	149	815	4.4	.975	2B-599, 3B-508, SS-284

WORLD SERIES

1951	NY A	6	.261	.435	23	6	1	0	1	4.3	2	7	2	7	0	0	0	10	14	1	4	4.2	.960	3B-5, 2B-4
1952		7	.200	.320	25	5	0	0	1	4.0	5	3	5	2	1	0	0	4	15	4	2	3.3	.826	3B-7
1953		6	.167	.500	24	4	0	1	2	8.3	2	4	1	3	0	0	0	5	14	0	0	3.2	1.000	3B-6
1955		7	.259	.370	27	7	0	0	1	3.7	2	1	2	6	0	0	0	6	13	1	1	2.9	.950	3B-7
1956		7	.143	.143	21	3	0	0	0	0.0	0	1	3	6	0	0	0	16	16	0	4	4.6	1.000	SS-7
1957		7	.250	.250	24	6	0	0	0	0.0	3	2	3	3	1	0	0	13	24	1	5	5.4	.974	SS-7
1958		7	.321	.607	28	9	2	0	2	7.1	5	4	2	4	0	0	0	18	23	0	3	5.9	1.000	2B-7
1960		6	.278	.333	18	5	1	0	0	0.0	4	2	2	0	0	0	0	5	7	1	0	2.2	.923	3B-6
8 yrs.		53	.237	.379	190	45	4	1	7	3.7	23	24	20	29	2	0	0	77	126	8	19	4.0	.962	3B-31, SS-14, 2B-11
		4th			5th	7th			10th		8th	8th	9th	5th										

Oddibe McDowell

McDOWELL, ODDIBE, JR.
B. Aug. 25, 1962, Hollywood, Fla.

BL TL 5'9" 165 lbs.

1985	TEX A	111	.239	.431	406	97	14	5	18	4.4	63	42	36	85	25	8	2	282	9	2	2	2.6	.993	OF-103, DH-4
1986		154	.266	.427	572	152	24	7	18	3.1	105	49	65	112	33	8	2	325	13	3	3	2.2	.991	OF-148, DH-1
1987		128	.241	.428	407	98	26	4	14	3.4	65	52	51	99	24	11	1	263	5	3	1	2.1	.989	OF-125
1988		120	.247	.355	437	108	19	5	6	1.4	55	37	41	89	33	9	2	267	2	2	1	2.3	.989	OF-113, DH-3
1989	2 teams				CLE A (69G – .222)				ATL N	(76G – .304)														
"	total	145	.266	.391	519	138	23	6	10	1.9	89	46	52	73	27	9	3	303	7	5	1	2.2	.984	OF-132, DH-2
5 yrs.		658	.253	.406	2341	593	106	27	66	2.8	377	226	245	458	142	45	10	1440	36	16	8	2.3	.989	OF-621, DH-10

Pryor McElveen

McELVEEN, PRYOR MYNATT (Humpy)
B. Nov. 5, 1883, Atlanta, Ga. D. Oct. 27, 1951, Pleasant Hill, Tenn.

BR TR 5'10" 168 lbs.

1909	BKN N	81	.198	.271	258	51	8	1	3	1.2	22	25	14		6	13	4	147	107	14	11	3.3	.948	3B-37, OF-13, SS-10, 2B-5, 1B-5
1910		74	.225	.305	213	48	8	3	1	0.5	19	26	22	47	6	9	3	89	105	12	14	2.8	.942	3B-54, SS-6, 2B-3, C-1
1911		16	.194	.194	31	6	0	0	0	0.0	1	5	0	3	0	10	3	16	10	2	4	1.8	.929	2B-5, SS-1
3 yrs.		171	.209	.281	502	105	16	4	4	0.8	42	56	36	50	12	32	10	252	222	28	29	2.9	.944	3B-91, SS-17, OF-13, 2B-13, 1B-5, C-1

Lee McElwee

McELWEE, LELAND STANFORD (Mac)
B. May 23, 1894, La Mesa, Calif. D. Feb. 8, 1957, Union, Me.

BR TR 5'10½" 160 lbs.

| 1916 | PHI A | 54 | .265 | .284 | 155 | 41 | 3 | 0 | 0 | 0.0 | 9 | 10 | 8 | 17 | 0 | 9 | 1 | 57 | 68 | 14 | 7 | 2.6 | .899 | 3B-30, OF-9, 2B-2, SS-1, 1B-1 |

Frank McElyea

McELYEA, FRANK
B. Aug. 4, 1918, Carmi, Ill.

BR TR 6'6" 221 lbs.

| 1942 | BOS N | 7 | .000 | .000 | 4 | 0 | 0 | 0 | 0 | 0.0 | 2 | 0 | 0 | 0 | 0 | 1 | 0 | 2 | 0 | 0 | 0 | 0.3 | 1.000 | OF-1 |

Guy McFadden

McFADDEN, GUY G.
B. 1873, Topeka, Kans.

| 1895 | STL N | 4 | .214 | .214 | 14 | 3 | 0 | 0 | 0 | 0.0 | 1 | 2 | 0 | 2 | 0 | 0 | 0 | 30 | 0 | 1 | 3 | 7.8 | .968 | 1B-4 |

Leon McFadden

McFADDEN, LEON
B. Apr. 26, 1944, Little Rock, Ark.

BR TR 6'2" 195 lbs.

1968	HOU N	16	.277	.298	47	13	1	0	0	0.0	2	1	6	10	1	1	1	16	44	2	3	3.9	.968	SS-16
1969		44	.176	.203	74	13	2	0	0	0.0	3	3	4	9	1	11	1	25	17	2	0	1.0	.955	OF-17, SS-8
1970		2	–	–	0	0	0	0	0	–	0	0	0	0	0	0	0	0	0	0	0	0.0	–	
3 yrs.		62	.215	.240	121	26	3	0	0	0.0	5	4	10	19	2	12	2	41	61	4	3	1.7	.962	SS-24, OF-17

Alex McFarlan

McFARLAN, ALEXANDER SHEPERD
Brother of Dan McFarlan.
B. Oct. 11, 1869, St. Louis, Mo. D. Mar. 2, 1939, Pewee Valley, Ky.

| 1892 | LOU N | 14 | .167 | .167 | 42 | 7 | 0 | 0 | 0 | 0.0 | 2 | 1 | 8 | 11 | 1 | 0 | 0 | 21 | 6 | 7 | 1 | 2.4 | .794 | OF-12, 2B-2 |

Year	Team		Games	BA	SA	AB	H	2B	3B	HR	HR%	R	RBI	BB	SO	SB	PH AB	PH H	PO	A	E	DP	TC/G	FA	G by Pos

Chris McFarland

McFARLAND, CHRISTOPHER
B. Aug. 17, 1861, Fall River, Mass. D. May 24, 1918, New Bedford, Mass. 5'9" 170 lbs.

Year	Team		Games	BA	SA	AB	H	2B	3B	HR	HR%	R	RBI	BB	SO	SB	PH AB	PH H	PO	A	E	DP	TC/G	FA	G by Pos
1884	BAL	U	3	.214	.286	14	3	1	0	0	0.0	2		0			0	0	4	0	3	0	2.3	.571	OF-3, P-1

Ed McFarland

McFARLAND, EDWARD WILLIAM
B. Aug. 3, 1874, Cleveland, Ohio D. Nov. 28, 1959, Cleveland, Ohio BR TR 5'10" 180 lbs.

Year	Team		Games	BA	SA	AB	H	2B	3B	HR	HR%	R	RBI	BB	SO	SB	PH AB	PH H	PO	A	E	DP	TC/G	FA	G by Pos
1893	CLE	N	8	.409	.591	22	9	2	1	0	0.0	5	6	1		0	0	0	4	4	1	0	1.1	.889	OF-5, 3B-2, C-1
1896	STL	N	83	.241	.345	290	70	13	4	3	1.0	48	36	15	17	7	1	0	276	117	16	6	4.9	.961	C-80, OF-2
1897	2 teams		STL N (31G – .327)		PHI N (38G – .223)																				
"	total		69	.270	.388	237	64	8	7	2	0.8	32	33	22			4	2	228	77	18	4	4.7	.944	C-60, OF-3, 1B-3, 2B-1
1898	PHI	N	121	.282	.375	429	121	21	5	3	0.7	65	71	44		4	0	0	420	136	23	7	4.8	.960	C-121
1899			96	.333	.472	324	108	22	10	1	0.3	59	57	36		9	2	0	305	125	14	14	4.6	.968	C-94
1900			94	.305	.392	344	105	14	8	0	0.0	50	38	29		9	1	0	280	137	16	9	4.6	.963	C-93, 3B-1
1901			74	.285	.356	295	84	14	2	1	0.3	33	32	18		11	0	0	316	102	13	2	5.8	.970	C-74
1902	CHI	A	73	.230	.295	244	56	9	2	1	0.4	29	25	19		8	2	0	291	71	12	7	5.1	.968	C-69, 1B-1
1903			61	.209	.279	201	42	7	2	1	0.5	15	19	14		3	4	1	244	65	10	7	5.2	.969	C-56, 1B-1
1904			50	.275	.381	160	44	11	3	0	0.0	22	20	17		2	1	1	195	39	6	2	4.8	.975	C-49
1905			80	.280	.364	250	70	13	4	0	0.0	24	31	23		5	9	4	343	88	12	8	5.5	.973	C-70
1906			7	.136	.182	22	3	1	0	0	0.0	0	3	3		0	3	1	32	4	1	0	5.3	.973	C-3
1907			52	.283	.362	138	39	9	1	0	0.0	11	8	12		3	7	2	192	47	7	4	4.7	.972	C-43
1908	BOS	A	19	.208	.292	48	10	2	1	0	0.0	5	4	1		0	6	2	63	24	2	3	4.7	.978	C-13
14 yrs.			887	.275	.369	3004	825	146	50	12	0.4	398	383	254	19	65	38	11	3189	1036	151	73	4.9	.965	C-826, OF-10, 1B-5, 3B-3, 2B-1

WORLD SERIES

Year	Team		Games	BA	SA	AB	H	2B	3B	HR	HR%	R	RBI	BB	SO	SB	PH AB	PH H	PO	A	E	DP	TC/G	FA	G by Pos
1906	CHI	A	1	.000	.000	1	0	0	0	0	0.0	0	0	0	0	0	1	0	0	0	0	0	0.0	—	

Herm McFarland

McFARLAND, HERMAS WALTER
B. Mar. 11, 1870, Des Moines, Iowa D. Sept. 21, 1935, Richmond, Va. BL TR 5'6" 150 lbs.

Year	Team		Games	BA	SA	AB	H	2B	3B	HR	HR%	R	RBI	BB	SO	SB	PH AB	PH H	PO	A	E	DP	TC/G	FA	G by Pos
1896	LOU	N	30	.191	.273	110	21	4	1	1	0.9	11	12	9	14	4	1	0	54	6	15	3	2.5	.800	OF-28, C-1
1898	CIN	N	19	.281	.391	64	18	1	3	0	0.0	10	11	7		3	1	0	29	1	1	0	1.6	.968	OF-17
1901	CHI	A	132	.275	.383	473	130	21	9	4	0.8	83	59	75		33	0	0	283	14	17	3	2.4	.946	OF-132
1902	2 teams		CHI A (9G – .172)		BAL A (61G – .322)																				
"	total		70	.306	.454	271	83	19	6	3	1.1	59	40	38		11	2	0	165	12	6	1	2.6	.967	OF-68
1903	NY	A	103	.243	.378	362	88	16	9	5	1.4	41	45	46		13	0	0	207	9	14	2	2.2	.939	OF-103
5 yrs.			354	.266	.388	1280	340	61	28	13	1.0	204	167	175	14	64	4	0	738	42	53	9	2.4	.936	OF-348, C-1

Howie McFarland

McFARLAND, HOWARD ALEXANDER
B. Mar. 7, 1911, El Reno, Okla. BR TR 6' 175 lbs.

Year	Team		Games	BA	SA	AB	H	2B	3B	HR	HR%	R	RBI	BB	SO	SB	PH AB	PH H	PO	A	E	DP	TC/G	FA	G by Pos
1945	WAS	A	6	.091	.091	11	1	0	0	0	0.0	0	2	0	3	0	3	0	2	1	0	0	0.5	1.000	OF-3

Orlando McFarlane

McFARLANE, ORLANDO DeJESUS
Born Orlando DeJesus McFarlane y Quesada.
B. June 28, 1938, Oriente, Cuba BR TR 6' 180 lbs.

Year	Team		Games	BA	SA	AB	H	2B	3B	HR	HR%	R	RBI	BB	SO	SB	PH AB	PH H	PO	A	E	DP	TC/G	FA	G by Pos
1962	PIT	N	8	.087	.087	23	2	0	0	0	0.0	0	1	0	4	0	0	0	44	5	0	1	6.1	1.000	C-8
1964			37	.244	.308	78	19	5	0	0	0.0	5	1	4	27	0	3	1	106	12	2	2	3.2	.983	C-35, OF-1
1966	DET	A	49	.254	.413	138	35	7	0	5	3.6	16	13	9	46	0	15	2	205	21	2	2	4.7	.991	C-33
1967	CAL	A	12	.227	.227	22	5	0	0	0	0.0	0	3	1	7	0	5	1	28	1	2	0	2.6	.935	C-6
1968			18	.290	.290	31	9	0	0	0	0.0	1	2	5	9	0	10	3	36	6	1	1	2.4	.977	C-9
5 yrs.			124	.240	.332	292	70	12	0	5	1.7	22	20	20	93	0	33	7	419	45	7	6	3.8	.985	C-91, OF-1

Patsy McGaffigan

McGAFFIGAN, MARK ANDREW
B. Sept. 12, 1888, Carlyle, Ill. D. Dec. 22, 1940, Carlyle, Ill. BR TR 5'8" 140 lbs.

Year	Team		Games	BA	SA	AB	H	2B	3B	HR	HR%	R	RBI	BB	SO	SB	PH AB	PH H	PO	A	E	DP	TC/G	FA	G by Pos
1917	PHI	N	19	.167	.183	60	10	1	0	0	0.0	5	6	0	7	1	0	0	32	49	7	5	4.6	.920	SS-17, OF-1
1918			54	.203	.255	192	39	3	2	1	0.5	17	8	16	23	4	0	0	100	158	14	19	5.0	.949	2B-53, SS-1
2 yrs.			73	.194	.238	252	49	4	2	1	0.4	22	14	16	30	4	0	0	132	207	21	24	4.9	.942	2B-53, SS-18, OF-1

Ed McGah

McGAH, EDWARD JOSEPH
B. Sept. 30, 1921, Oakland, Calif. BR TR 6' 183 lbs.

Year	Team		Games	BA	SA	AB	H	2B	3B	HR	HR%	R	RBI	BB	SO	SB	PH AB	PH H	PO	A	E	DP	TC/G	FA	G by Pos
1946	BOS	A	15	.216	.297	37	8	1	1	0	0.0	2	1	7	7	0	1	0	47	5	1	0	3.5	.981	C-14
1947			9	.000	.000	14	0	0	0	0	0.0	1	2	3	0	0	1	0	24	3	1	1	3.1	.964	C-7
2 yrs.			24	.157	.216	51	8	1	1	0	0.0	3	3	10	7	0	2	0	71	8	2	1	3.4	.975	C-21

Dan McGann

McGANN, DENNIS LAWRENCE (Cap)
B. July 15, 1871, Shelbyville, Ky. D. Dec. 13, 1910, Louisville, Ky. BB TR 6' 190 lbs.

Year	Team		Games	BA	SA	AB	H	2B	3B	HR	HR%	R	RBI	BB	SO	SB	PH AB	PH H	PO	A	E	DP	TC/G	FA	G by Pos
1895	LOU	N	20	.288	.411	73	21	5	2	0	0.0	9	9	8	6	6	1	0	35	39	12	1	4.3	.860	SS-8, 3B-6, OF-5
1896	BOS	N	43	.322	.474	171	55	6	7	2	1.2	25	30	12	10	2	0	0	88	111	21	10	5.1	.905	2B-43
1898	BAL	N	145	.301	.393	535	161	18	8	5	0.9	99	106	53		33	0	0	1416	68	26	78	10.4	.983	1B-145
1899	2 teams		BKN N (63G – .243)		WAS N (76G – .343)																				
"	total		139	.300	.431	494	148	20	12	4	0.8	114	90	35		27	2	0	1312	67	17	86	10.0	.988	1B-137
1900	STL	N	121	.297	.387	444	132	10	9	4	0.9	79	58	32		26	0	0	1215	59	13	41	10.6	.990	1B-121, 2B-1
1901			103	.289	.411	426	123	14	10	6	1.4	73	56	16		17	0	0	1030	50	18	64	10.7	.984	1B-103
1902	2 teams		BAL A (68G – .316)		NY N (61G – .300)																				
"	total		129	.308	.403	477	147	15	15	0	0.0	67	63	31		29	0	0	1292	80	22	90	10.8	.984	1B-129
1903	NY	N	129	.270	.357	482	130	21	6	3	0.6	75	50	32		36	0	0	1188	64	15	58	9.8	.988	1B-129
1904			141	.286	.387	517	148	22	6	6	1.2	81	71	36		42	0	0	1481	94	15	62	11.3	.991	1B-141
1905			136	.299	.434	491	147	23	14	5	1.0	88	75	55		22	0	0	1350	86	13	59	10.7	.991	1B-136
1906			134	.237	.304	451	107	14	8	0	0.0	62	37	60		30	0	0	1391	83	8	61	11.1	.995	1B-133
1907			81	.298	.363	262	78	9	1	2	0.8	29	36	29		9	0	0	781	55	5	36	10.4	.994	1B-81
1908	BOS	N	135	.240	.291	475	114	8	5	2	0.4	52	55	38		9	5	1	1247	117	18	66	10.2	.987	1B-121, 2B-9
13 yrs.			1456	.285	.383	5298	1511	185	103	42	0.8	853	736	437	16	288	9	1	13826	973	203	712	10.3	.986	1B-1376, 2B-53, SS-8, 3B-6, OF-5

Year	Team	Games	BA	SA	AB	H	2B	3B	HR	HR%	R	RBI	BB	SO	SB	Pinch Hit AB	H	PO	A	E	DP	TC/G	FA	G by Pos

Dan McGann *continued*

WORLD SERIES

| 1905 | NY | N | 5 | .235 | .353 | 17 | 4 | 2 | 0 | 0 | 0.0 | 1 | 4 | 2 | 7 | 0 | 0 | 0 | 55 | 2 | 1 | 2 | 11.6 | .983 | 1B-5 |

Chippy McGarr

McGARR, JAMES B.
B. May 10, 1863, Worcester, Mass.   D. June 6, 1904, Worcester, Mass.   BR TR

1884	CHI	U	19	.157	.186	70	11	3	0	0	0.0	10				0	0	0	35	25	8	2	3.6	.882	2B-13, OF-6
1886	PHI	AA	71	.266	.345	267	71	9	3	2	0.7	41		9			0	0	109	231	60	25	5.6	.850	SS-71
1887			137	.295	.366	536	158	23	6	1	0.2	93		23		84	0	0	198	402	86	42	5.0	.875	SS-137
1888	STL	AA	34	.235	.242	132	31	1	0	0	0.0	17	13	6		25	0	0	70	102	22	11	5.7	.887	2B-33, SS-1
1889	2 teams		KC	AA	(25G – .287)		BAL	AA	(3G – .143)																
"	total		28	.278	.304	115	32	3	0	0	0.0	23	16	7	12	12	0	0	51	47	20	12	4.2	.831	3B-11, OF-6, SS-6, 2B-5
1890	BOS	N	121	.236	.296	487	115	12	7	1	0.2	68	51	34	38	39	0	0	160	243	30	15	3.6	.931	3B-115, SS-5, OF-1
1893	CLE	N	63	.309	.357	249	77	12	0	0	0.0	38	28	20	15	24	0	0	93	147	31	7	4.3	.886	3B-63
1894			128	.275	.356	523	144	24	6	2	0.4	94	74	28	29	31	0	0	170	242	45	17	3.6	.902	3B-128
1895			112	.265	.322	419	111	14	2	2	0.5	85	59	34	33	19	0	0	123	228	29	20	3.4	.924	3B-113, C-1
1896			113	.268	.327	455	122	16	4	1	0.2	68	53	22	30	16	0	0	137	222	52	14	3.7	.873	3B-108, 2B-4
	10 yrs.		826	.268	.329	3253	872	116	28	9	0.3	537	294	183	157	250	0	0	1146	1889	383	165	4.1	.888	3B-538, SS-220, 2B-55, OF-13, C-1

Jim McGarr

McGARR, JAMES VINCENT (Reds)
B. Nov. 9, 1888, Philadelphia, Pa.   D. July 21, 1981, Miami, Fla.   BR TR 5'9½" 170 lbs.

| 1912 | DET | A | 1 | .000 | .000 | 4 | 0 | 0 | 0 | 0 | 0.0 | 0 | 0 | 0 | 0 | 0 | 0 | 0 | 1 | 3 | 1 | 0 | 5.0 | .800 | 2B-1 |

Dan McGarvey

McGARVEY, DANIEL FRANCIS
B. Dec. 2, 1887, Philadelphia, Pa.   D. Mar. 7, 1947, Philadelphia, Pa.

| 1912 | DET | A | 1 | .000 | .000 | 3 | 0 | 0 | 0 | 0 | 0.0 | 0 | 0 | 1 | | | 0 | 0 | 1 | 1 | 1 | 0 | 3.0 | .667 | OF-1 |

Jack McGeachy

McGEACHY, JOHN CHARLES
B. May 13, 1864, Clinton, Mass.   D. Apr. 5, 1930, Cambridge, Mass.   BR TR 5'8" 165 lbs.

1886	2 teams		DET	N	(6G – .333)		STL	N	(59G – .204)																
"	total		65	.217	.320	253	55	12	4	2	0.8	34	28	1	40		0	0	102	28	22	5	2.3	.855	OF-61, 3B-2, 2B-2
1887	IND	N	99	.269	.333	405	109	17	3	1	0.2	49	56	5	16	27	0	0	231	25	33	3	2.9	.886	OF-98, SS-1, P-1
1888			118	.219	.261	452	99	15	2	0	0.0	45	30	5	21	49	0	0	194	28	16	5	2.0	.933	OF-117, SS-1, P-1
1889			131	.267	.342	532	142	31	1	2	0.4	83	63	9	39	37	0	0	189	36	20	8	1.9	.918	OF-131, P-3
1890	BKN	P	104	.244	.323	443	108	24	4	1	0.2	84	65	19	12	21	0	0	206	16	23	1	2.4	.906	OF-104
1891	2 teams		PHI	AA	(50G – .229)		BOS	AA	(41G – .253)																
"	total		91	.240	.301	379	91	6	4	3	0.8	50	34	18	20	20	0	0	139	14	14	0	1.8	.916	OF-91
	6 yrs.		608	.245	.314	2464	604	106	18	9	0.4	345	276	57	148	154	0	0	1061	147	128	22	2.2	.904	OF-602, P-5, 3B-3, 2B-2, SS-1

Mike McGeary

McGEARY, MICHAEL HENRY
B. 1851, Philadelphia, Pa.   Deceased.
Manager 1875, 1880-81.   BR TR 5'7" 138 lbs.

1876	STL	N	61	.261	.272	276	72	3	0	0	0.0	48	30	2	1		0	0	146	185	44	17	6.1	.883	2B-56, C-5, OF-1, 3B-1
1877			57	.252	.279	258	65	3	2	0	0.0	35	20	2	6		0	0	164	181	42	12	6.8	.891	2B-39, 3B-19
1879	PRO	N	85	.275	.305	374	103	7	2	0	0.0	62	35	5	13		0	0	238	290	67	25	7.0	.887	2B-73, 3B-12
1880	2 teams		PRO	N	(18G – .136)		CLE	N	(31G – .252)																
"	total		49	.212	.235	170	36	2	1	0	0.0	19	4	4	9		0	0	57	95	22	6	3.6	.874	3B-46, OF-2, 2B-2, SS-1
1881	CLE	N	11	.220	.220	41	9	0	0	0	0.0	1	5	0	6		0	0	8	13	8	1	2.6	.724	3B-11
1882	DET	N	34	.143	.188	133	19	4	1	0	0.0	14	2	2	20		0	0	64	120	16	5	5.9	.920	SS-33, 2B-1
	6 yrs.		297	.243	.268	1252	304	19	6	0	0.0	179	96	15	55		0	0	677	884	199	66	5.9	.887	2B-173, 3B-89, SS-34, C-5, OF-3

Dan McGee

McGEE, DANIEL ALOYSIUS
B. Sept. 29, 1913, New York, N. Y.   BR TR 5'8½" 152 lbs.

| 1934 | BOS | N | 7 | .136 | .136 | 22 | 3 | 0 | 0 | 0 | 0.0 | 2 | 1 | 3 | 6 | 0 | 0 | 0 | 14 | 25 | 2 | 3 | 5.9 | .951 | SS-7 |

Tubby McGee

McGEE, FRANCIS D.
B. Apr. 28, 1899, Columbus, Ohio   D. Jan. 30, 1934, Columbus, Ohio   BR TR 5'11½" 175 lbs.

| 1925 | WAS | A | 2 | .000 | .000 | 3 | 0 | 0 | 0 | 0 | 0.0 | 0 | 0 | 0 | 1 | 0 | 0 | 0 | 11 | 1 | 0 | 1 | 6.0 | 1.000 | 1B-2 |

Willie McGee

McGEE, WILLIE DEAN
B. Nov. 2, 1958, San Francisco, Calif.   BB TR 6'1" 176 lbs.

1982	STL	N	123	.296	.391	422	125	12	8	4	0.9	43	56	12	58	24	15	6	245	3	11	0	2.1	.958	OF-117
1983			147	.286	.374	601	172	22	8	5	0.8	75	75	26	98	39	3	2	385	7	5	1	2.7	.987	OF-145
1984			145	.291	.394	571	166	19	11	6	1.1	82	50	29	80	43	5	0	374	10	6	4	2.7	.985	OF-141
1985			152	**.353**	.503	612	**216**	26	**18**	10	1.6	114	82	34	86	56	4	2	382	11	9	2	2.6	.978	OF-149
1986			124	.256	.370	497	127	22	7	7	1.4	65	48	37	82	19	2	0	325	9	3	0	2.7	.991	OF-121
1987			153	.285	.434	620	177	37	11	11	1.8	76	105	24	90	16	2	1	354	10	7	1	2.4	.981	OF-152, SS-1
1988			137	.292	.372	562	164	24	6	3	0.5	73	50	32	84	41	2	1	348	9	9	0	2.1	.976	OF-47
1989			58	.236	.352	199	47	10	2	3	1.5	23	17	10	34	8	10	2	118	2	3	0	2.1	.976	OF-135
	8 yrs.		1039	.292	.405	4084	1194	172	71	49	1.2	551	483	204	612	246	43	14	2531	61	53	8	2.5	.980	OF-1007, SS-1

LEAGUE CHAMPIONSHIP SERIES

1982	STL	N	3	.308	.846	13	4	0	2	1	7.7	4	5	0	5	0	0	0	0	0	1	0	0.3	—	OF-3
1985			6	.269	.308	26	7	1	0	0	0.0	6	3	3	6	2	0	0	17	0	0	0	2.8	1.000	OF-6
1987			7	.308	.423	26	8	1	1	0	0.0	2	2	0	5	0	0	0	16	0	1	0	2.3	1.000	OF-7
	3 yrs.		16	.292	.462	65	19	2	3	1	1.5	12	10	3	16	2	0	0	33	0	1	0	2.1	.971	OF-16

WORLD SERIES

| 1982 | STL | N | 6 | .240 | .480 | 25 | 6 | 0 | 0 | 2 | 8.0 | 6 | 5 | 1 | 3 | 2 | 0 | 0 | 24 | 0 | 0 | 0 | 4.0 | 1.000 | OF-6 |

Year Team	Games	BA	SA	AB	H	2B	3B	HR	HR%	R	RBI	BB	SO	SB	PH AB	PH H	PO	A	E	DP	TC/G	FA	G by Pos

Willie McGee continued

Year Team	Games	BA	SA	AB	H	2B	3B	HR	HR%	R	RBI	BB	SO	SB	PH AB	PH H	PO	A	E	DP	TC/G	FA	G by Pos
1985	7	.259	.444	27	7	2	0	1	3.7	2	2	1	3	1	0	0	15	0	0	0	2.1	1.000	OF-7
1987	7	.370	.444	27	10	2	0	0	0.0	2	4	0	9	0	0	0	21	1	1	0	3.3	.957	OF-7
3 yrs.	20	.291	.456	79	23	4	0	3	3.8	10	11	2	15	3	0	0	60	1	1	0	3.1	.984	OF-20

Dan McGeehan

McGEEHAN, DANIEL DeSALES
Brother of Connie McGeehan.
B. June 7, 1885, Jeddo, Pa. D. July 12, 1955, Hazleton, Pa.   BR TR 5'6" 135 lbs.

Year Team	Games	BA	SA	AB	H	2B	3B	HR	HR%	R	RBI	BB	SO	SB	PH AB	PH H	PO	A	E	DP	TC/G	FA	G by Pos
1911 STL N	3	.222	.222	9	2	0	0	0	0.0	0	1	0	1	0	0	0	4	5	2	0	3.7	.818	2B-3

Bill McGhee

McGHEE, WILLIAM MAC (Fibber)
B. Sept. 5, 1908, Shawmut, Ala.   BL TL 5'10½" 185 lbs.

Year Team	Games	BA	SA	AB	H	2B	3B	HR	HR%	R	RBI	BB	SO	SB	PH AB	PH H	PO	A	E	DP	TC/G	FA	G by Pos
1944 PHI A	77	.289	.341	287	83	12	1	0	0.3	27	19	21	20	2	2	0	701	46	8	51	9.8	.989	1B-75
1945	93	.252	.284	250	63	6	1	0	0.0	24	19	24	16	3	31	9	143	9	1	7	1.6	.993	OF-48, 1B-8
2 yrs.	170	.272	.315	537	146	18	1	1	0.2	51	38	45	36	5	33	9	844	55	9	58	5.3	.990	1B-83, OF-48

Ed McGhee

McGHEE, WARREN EDWARD
B. Sept. 29, 1924, Perry, Ark. D. Feb. 13, 1986, Memphis, Tenn.   BR TR 5'11" 170 lbs.

Year Team	Games	BA	SA	AB	H	2B	3B	HR	HR%	R	RBI	BB	SO	SB	PH AB	PH H	PO	A	E	DP	TC/G	FA	G by Pos
1950 CHI A	3	.167	.500	6	1	0	1	0	0.0	0	0	0	1	0	0	0	1	0	0	0	0.3	1.000	OF-1
1953 PHI A	104	.263	.324	358	94	11	4	1	0.3	36	29	32	43	4	7	2	319	4	6	0	3.2	.982	OF-99
1954 2 teams	PHI A (21G – .208)			CHI A (42G – .227)																			
" total	63	.219	.289	128	28	3	0	2	1.6	17	14	16	16	5	11	1	93	4	4	1	1.6	.960	OF-47
1955 CHI A	26	.077	.077	13	1	0	0	0	0.0	6	0	6	1	2	2	1	12	0	1	0	0.5	.923	OF-17
4 yrs.	196	.246	.311	505	124	14	5	3	0.6	59	43	54	61	11	21	4	425	8	11	1	2.3	.975	OF-164

Bill McGilvray

McGILVRAY, WILLIAM ALEXANDER (Big Bill)
B. Apr. 29, 1883, Portland, Ore. D. May 23, 1952, Denver, Colo.   BL TL 6' 160 lbs.

Year Team	Games	BA	SA	AB	H	2B	3B	HR	HR%	R	RBI	BB	SO	SB	PH AB	PH H	PO	A	E	DP	TC/G	FA	G by Pos
1908 CIN N	2	.000	.000	2	0	0	0	0	0.0	0	0	0	2	0	0	0	0	0	0	0	0.0	–	

Tim McGinley

McGINLEY, TIMOTHY S.
B. Philadelphia, Pa. D. Nov. 2, 1899, Oakland, Calif.   5'9½" 155 lbs.

Year Team	Games	BA	SA	AB	H	2B	3B	HR	HR%	R	RBI	BB	SO	SB	PH AB	PH H	PO	A	E	DP	TC/G	FA	G by Pos
1876 BOS N	9	.150	.150	40	6	0	0	0	0.0	5	2	0	1		0	0	26	3	16	1	5.0	.644	OF-6, C-3

Frank McGinn

McGINN, FRANK J.
B. Cincinnati, Ohio D. Nov. 19, 1897, Cincinnati, Ohio

Year Team	Games	BA	SA	AB	H	2B	3B	HR	HR%	R	RBI	BB	SO	SB	PH AB	PH H	PO	A	E	DP	TC/G	FA	G by Pos
1890 PIT N	1	.000	.000	4	0	0	0	0	0.0	0	0	0	2	0	0	0	1	0	0	0	1.0	1.000	OF-1

John McGlone

McGLONE, JOHN T.
B. 1864, Brooklyn, N. Y. D. Nov. 24, 1927, Brooklyn, N. Y.

Year Team	Games	BA	SA	AB	H	2B	3B	HR	HR%	R	RBI	BB	SO	SB	PH AB	PH H	PO	A	E	DP	TC/G	FA	G by Pos
1886 WAS N	4	.067	.067	15	1	0	0	0	0.0	2	1	0	3		0	0	7	4	2	0	3.3	.846	3B-4
1887 CLE AA	21	.253	.304	79	20	1	0	0	0.0	14		7		15	0	0	42	40	14	3	4.6	.854	3B-21
1888	55	.182	.232	203	37	1	3	1	0.5	22	22	16		26	0	0	81	95	45	5	4.0	.796	3B-48, OF-7
3 yrs.	80	.195	.242	297	58	3	4	1	0.3	38	23	23	3	41	0	0	130	139	61	8	4.1	.815	3B-73, OF-7

Art McGovern

McGOVERN, ARTHUR JOHN
B. Feb. 27, 1882, St. John, N. B., Canada D. Nov. 14, 1915, Thornton, R. I.   BR TR 160 lbs.

Year Team	Games	BA	SA	AB	H	2B	3B	HR	HR%	R	RBI	BB	SO	SB	PH AB	PH H	PO	A	E	DP	TC/G	FA	G by Pos
1905 BOS A	15	.114	.136	44	5	1	0	0	0.0	1	1	4		0	0	0	67	11	4	1	5.5	.951	C-15

Frank McGowan

McGOWAN, FRANK BERNARD (Beauty)
B. Nov. 8, 1901, Branford, Conn. D. May 6, 1982, Hamden, Conn.   BL TR 5'11" 190 lbs.

Year Team	Games	BA	SA	AB	H	2B	3B	HR	HR%	R	RBI	BB	SO	SB	PH AB	PH H	PO	A	E	DP	TC/G	FA	G by Pos
1922 PHI A	99	.230	.307	300	69	10	5	1	0.3	36	20	40	46	6	12	4	210	13	8	2	2.3	.965	OF-82
1923	95	.254	.303	287	73	9	1	1	0.3	41	19	36	25	4	7	0	154	12	5	1	1.8	.971	OF-79
1928 STL A	47	.363	.524	168	61	13	4	2	1.2	35	18	16	15	2	0	0	99	3	4	1	2.3	.962	OF-47
1929	125	.254	.354	441	112	26	6	2	0.5	62	51	61	34	5	7	0	257	16	7	5	2.2	.975	OF-117
1937 BOS N	9	.083	.083	12	1	0	0	0	0.0	0	0	1	2		6	0	2	0	0	0	0.2	1.000	OF-2
5 yrs.	375	.262	.351	1208	316	58	16	6	0.5	174	108	154	122	17	32	4	722	44	24	9	2.1	.970	OF-327

John McGraw

McGRAW, JOHN JOSEPH (Little Napoleon)
B. Apr. 7, 1873, Truxton, N. Y. D. Feb. 25, 1934, New Rochelle, N. Y.
Manager 1899, 1901-32.
Hall of Fame 1937.   BL TR 5'7" 155 lbs.

Year Team	Games	BA	SA	AB	H	2B	3B	HR	HR%	R	RBI	BB	SO	SB	PH AB	PH H	PO	A	E	DP	TC/G	FA	G by Pos
1891 BAL AA	33	.270	.383	115	31	3	5	0	0.0	17	14	12	17	4	0	0	47	52	21	7	3.6	.825	SS-21, OF-9, 2B-3
1892 BAL N	79	.269	.339	286	77	13	2	1	0.3	41	26	32	21	15	0	0	165	144	28	16	4.3	.917	OF-34, 2B-34, SS-8, 3B-3
1893	127	.321	.413	480	154	9	10	5	1.0	123	64	101	11	38	0	0	234	350	68	40	5.1	.896	SS-117, OF-11
1894	124	.340	.436	512	174	18	14	1	0.2	156	92	91	12	78	0	0	143	265	48	17	3.7	.895	3B-118, 2B-6
1895	96	.369	.448	388	143	13	6	2	0.5	110	48	60	9	61	0	0	100	239	47	19	4.0	.878	3B-95, 2B-1
1896	23	.325	.403	77	25	2	2	0	0.0	20	14	11	4	13	3	0	32	38	12	4	3.6	.854	3B-18, 1B-1
1897	106	.325	.379	391	127	15	3	0	0.0	90	48	99		44	1	0	112	182	38	16	3.1	.886	3B-105
1898	143	.342	.396	515	176	8	10	0	0.0	143	53	112		43	1	0	148	271	47	16	3.3	.899	3B-137, OF-3
1899	117	.391	.446	399	156	13	3	1	0.3	140	33	124		73	0	0	142	270	24	14	3.7	.945	3B-117
1900 STL N	99	.344	.416	334	115	10	4	2	0.6	84	33	85		29	0	0	106	213	32	7	3.5	.909	3B-99
1901 BAL A	73	.349	.487	232	81	14	9	0	0.0	71	28	61		24	3	0	80	107	23	5	2.9	.890	3B-69
1902 2 teams	BAL A (20G – .286)			NY N (35G – .224)																			
" total	55	.247	.306	170	42	3	2	1	0.6	27	8	43		12	2	0	85	140	22	18	4.5	.911	SS-34, 3B-19
1903 NY N	12	.273	.273	11	3	0	0	0	0.0	2	1	1		1	6	2	2	1	1	0	0.3	.750	OF-2, 2B-2, SS-1, 3B-1
1904	5	.333	.333	12	4	0	0	0	0.0	0	0	3		1	0	0	12	17	2	3	6.2	.935	SS-2, 2B-2
1905	3	–	–	0	0	0	0	0	0.0	0	0	0		1	0	0	0	0	0	0	0.0	–	OF-1
1906	4	.000	.000	2	0	0	0	0	0.0	0	0	0		2	0	0	0	0	0	0	0.0	–	3B-1
16 yrs.	1099	.333	.410	3924	1308	121	70	13	0.3	1024	462	836	74	436	19	2	1408	2289	413	182	3.7	.900	3B-782, SS-183, OF-60, 2B-48, 1B-1

Year	Team		Games	BA	SA	AB	H	2B	3B	HR	HR%	R	RBI	BB	SO	SB	Pinch Hit AB	Pinch Hit H	PO	A	E	DP	TC/G	FA	G by Pos

Fred McGriff

McGRIFF, FREDERICK STANLEY
B. Oct. 31, 1963, Tampa, Fla.   BL TL 6'3"   200 lbs.

Year	Team		Games	BA	SA	AB	H	2B	3B	HR	HR%	R	RBI	BB	SO	SB	PH AB	PH H	PO	A	E	DP	TC/G	FA	G by Pos
1986	TOR	A	3	.200	.200	5	1	0	0	0	0.0	1	0	0	2	0	0	0	3	0	0	0	1.0	1.000	DH-2, 1B-1
1987			107	.247	.505	295	73	16	0	20	6.8	58	43	60	104	3	14	1	108	7	2	5	1.1	.983	DH-90, 1B-14
1988			154	.282	.552	536	151	35	4	34	6.3	100	82	79	149	6	5	2	1344	93	5	143	9.4	.997	1B-153
1989			161	.269	.525	551	148	27	3	36	6.5	98	92	119	132	7	1	0	1460	115	17	148	9.9	.989	1B-159, DH-2
4 yrs.			425	.269	.530	1387	373	78	7	90	6.5	257	217	258	387	16	20	3	2915	215	24	296	7.4	.992	1B-327, DH-94

LEAGUE CHAMPIONSHIP SERIES

| 1989 | TOR | A | 5 | .143 | .143 | 21 | 3 | 0 | 0 | 0 | 0.0 | 1 | 3 | 0 | 4 | 0 | 0 | 0 | 35 | 2 | 1 | 3 | 7.6 | .974 | 1B-5 |

Terry McGriff

McGRIFF, TERENCE ROY
B. Sept. 23, 1963, Fort Pierce, Fla.   BR TR 6'2"   190 lbs.

Year	Team		Games	BA	SA	AB	H	2B	3B	HR	HR%	R	RBI	BB	SO	SB	PH AB	PH H	PO	A	E	DP	TC/G	FA	G by Pos
1987	CIN	N	34	.225	.326	89	20	3	0	2	2.2	6	11	8	17	0	0	0	160	14	3	1	5.2	.983	C-33
1988			35	.198	.260	96	19	3	0	1	1.0	9	4	12	31	1	1	0	177	14	2	1	5.5	.990	C-32
1989			6	.273	.273	11	3	0	0	0	0.0	1	2	2	3	0	0	0	23	3	2	0	4.7	.929	C-6
3 yrs.			75	.214	.291	196	42	6	0	3	1.5	16	17	22	51	1	1	0	360	31	7	2	5.3	.982	C-71

Mark McGrillis

McGRILLIS, MARK A.
B. Oct. 22, 1872, Philadelphia, Pa.   D. May 16, 1935, Philadelphia, Pa.

Year	Team		Games	BA	SA	AB	H	2B	3B	HR	HR%	R	RBI	BB	SO	SB	PH AB	PH H	PO	A	E	DP	TC/G	FA	G by Pos
1892	STL	N	1	.000	.000	3	0	0	0	0	0.0	0	0	0	1	0	0	0	0	2	0	0	2.0	1.000	3B-1

Joe McGuckin

McGUCKIN, JOSEPH W.
B. 1862, Paterson, N. J.   D. Dec. 31, 1903, Yonkers, N. Y.

Year	Team		Games	BA	SA	AB	H	2B	3B	HR	HR%	R	RBI	BB	SO	SB	PH AB	PH H	PO	A	E	DP	TC/G	FA	G by Pos
1890	BAL	AA	11	.108	.108	37	4	0	0	0	0.0	2		6		3	0	0	21	4	1	1	2.4	.962	OF-11

John McGuinness

McGUINNESS, JOHN JAMES
B. 1857, Ireland   D. Dec. 19, 1916, Binghamton, N. Y.

Year	Team		Games	BA	SA	AB	H	2B	3B	HR	HR%	R	RBI	BB	SO	SB	PH AB	PH H	PO	A	E	DP	TC/G	FA	G by Pos
1876	NY	N	1	.000	.000	4	0	0	0	0	0.0	0	0	0	0		0	0	1	1	4	0	6.0	.333	2B-1, C-1
1879	SYR	N	12	.294	.353	51	15	1	1	0	0.0	7	4	0	6		0	0	113	3	9	8	10.4	.928	1B-12
1884	PHI	U	53	.236	.282	220	52	8	1	0	0.0	25		5			0	0	569	25	28	22	11.7	.955	1B-48, 2B-5, SS-1
3 yrs.			66	.244	.291	275	67	9	2	0	0.0	32	4	5	6		0	0	683	29	41	30	11.4	.946	1B-60, 2B-6, SS-1, C-1

Bill McGuire

McGUIRE, WILLIAM PATRICK (Moose)
B. Feb. 14, 1964, Omaha, Neb.   BR TR 6'3"   205 lbs.

Year	Team		Games	BA	SA	AB	H	2B	3B	HR	HR%	R	RBI	BB	SO	SB	PH AB	PH H	PO	A	E	DP	TC/G	FA	G by Pos
1988	SEA	A	9	.188	.188	16	3	0	0	0	0.0	1	2	3	2	0	0	0	29	3	0	0	3.6	1.000	C-9
1989			14	.179	.286	28	5	0	0	1	3.6	2	4	2	6	0	0	0	62	6	0	0	4.9	1.000	C-14
2 yrs.			23	.182	.250	44	8	0	0	1	2.3	3	6	5	8	0	0	0	91	9	0	0	4.3	1.000	C-23

Deacon McGuire

McGUIRE, JAMES THOMAS
B. Nov. 18, 1863, Youngstown, Ohio   D. Oct. 31, 1936, Albion, Mich.   BR TL 6'1"   185 lbs.
Manager 1898, 1907-11.

Year	Team		Games	BA	SA	AB	H	2B	3B	HR	HR%	R	RBI	BB	SO	SB	PH AB	PH H	PO	A	E	DP	TC/G	FA	G by Pos
1884	TOL	AA	45	.185	.252	151	28	7	0	1	0.7	12		5			0	0	231	61	32	1	7.2	.901	C-41, OF-4, SS-3
1885	DET	N	34	.190	.256	121	23	4	2	0	0.0	11	9	5	23		0	0	252	52	26	2	9.7	.921	C-31, OF-3
1886	PHI	N	50	.198	.287	167	33	7	1	2	1.2	25	18	19	25		0	0	299	51	41	3	7.8	.895	C-49, OF-1
1887			41	.307	.467	150	46	6	6	2	1.3	22	23	11	8	3	0	0	214	52	35	6	7.3	.884	C-41
1888	3 teams		41	PHI N (12G – .333)		DET N (3G – .000)				CLE AA (26G – .255)															
"	total		41	.259	.373	158	41	5	5	1	0.6	22	24	11	13	2	0	0	223	47	38	4	7.5	.877	C-30, 1B-6, OF-3, 3B-2
1890	ROC	AA	87	.299	.408	331	99	16	4	4	1.2	46		21		8	0	0	543	103	35	15	7.8	.949	C-71, 1B-15, OF-3, P-1
1891	WAS	AA	114	.303	.426	413	125	22	10	3	0.7	55	66	43	34	10	0	0	463	140	65	9	5.9	.903	C-98, OF-18, 3B-3, 1B-1
1892	WAS	N	97	.232	.340	315	73	14	4	4	1.3	44	43	61	48	7	0	0	453	101	33	10	6.1	.944	C-89, OF-1
1893			63	.262	.359	237	62	14	3	1	0.4	29	26	26	12	3	0	0	287	56	34	14	6.0	.910	C-50, 1B-12
1894			104	.306	.419	425	130	18	6	6	1.4	67	78	33	19	11	0	0	288	114	36	8	4.2	.918	C-104
1895			132	.336	.478	533	179	30	8	10	1.9	89	97	40	18	16	0	0	408	181	41	11	4.8	.935	C-132, SS-1
1896			108	.321	.416	389	125	25	3	2	0.5	60	70	30	14	12	0	0	351	88	30	14	4.3	.936	C-98, 1B-1
1897			93	.343	.474	327	112	17	7	4	1.2	51	53	21		9	11	3	355	88	22	8	5.2	.953	C-73, 1B-6
1898			131	.268	.323	489	131	18	3	1	0.2	59	57	24		10	3	2	707	120	29	37	6.5	.966	C-93, 1B-37
1899	2 teams		105	WAS N (59G – .271)		BKN N (46G – .318)																			
"	total		105	.292	.371	356	104	15	5	1	0.3	47	35	28		7	2	0	334	129	14	5	4.5	.971	C-102, 1B-1
1900	BKN	N	71	.286	.365	241	69	15	2	0	0.0	20	34	19		2	1	0	218	77	15	7	4.4	.952	C-69
1901			85	.296	.375	301	89	16	4	0	0.0	28	40	18		4	1	0	439	94	21	6	6.5	.962	C-81, 1B-3
1902	DET	A	73	.227	.323	229	52	14	1	2	0.9	27	23	24		0	2	0	210	65	14	6	4.0	.952	C-70
1903			72	.250	.306	248	62	12	1	0	0.0	15	21	19		3	2	0	331	73	18	9	5.9	.957	C-69, 1B-1
1904	NY	A	101	.208	.258	322	67	12	2	0	0.0	17	20	27		2	2	2	536	120	20	11	6.7	.970	C-97, 1B-1
1905			72	.219	.268	228	50	7	2	0	0.0	9	33	18		3	1	1	366	69	11	4	6.2	.975	C-71
1906			51	.299	.333	144	43	5	0	0	0.0	11	14	12		3	1	0	226	38	10	2	5.4	.964	C-49, 1B-1
1907	2 teams		7	NY A (1G – .000)		BOS A (6G – .750)																			
"	total		7	.600	1.200	5	3	0	0	1	20.0	1	1	0		0	4	3	3	1	0	0	0.6	1.000	C-1
1908	2 teams		2	BOS A (1G – .000)		CLE A (1G – .250)																			
"	total		2	.200	.400	5	1	0	0	0	0.0	0	2	0		0	0	0	10	0	0	0	5.0	1.000	1B-1
1910	CLE	A	1	.333	.333	3	1	0	0	0	0.0	0	0	0		0	1	0	2	1	0	0	3.0	1.000	C-1
1912	DET	A	1	.500	.500	2	1	0	0	0	0.0	1	0	0		0	0	0	2	3	2	0	7.0	.714	C-1
26 yrs.			1781	.278	.372	6290	1749	300	79	45	0.7	770	787	515	214	115	41	14	7751	1924	622	192	5.8	.940	C-1611, 1B-94, OF-33, 3B-5, SS-4, P-1

Jim McGuire

McGUIRE, JAMES A.
B. Feb. 4, 1875, Dunkirk, N. Y.   D. Jan. 26, 1917, Buffalo, N. Y.   TR

Year	Team		Games	BA	SA	AB	H	2B	3B	HR	HR%	R	RBI	BB	SO	SB	PH AB	PH H	PO	A	E	DP	TC/G	FA	G by Pos
1901	CLE	A	18	.232	.261	69	16	2	0	0	0.0	4	3	0		0	0	0	40	54	9	10	5.7	.913	SS-18

Mickey McGuire

McGUIRE, MICKEY C.
B. Jan. 18, 1941, Dayton, Ohio   BR TR 5'10"   170 lbs.

Year	Team		Games	BA	SA	AB	H	2B	3B	HR	HR%	R	RBI	BB	SO	SB	PH AB	PH H	PO	A	E	DP	TC/G	FA	G by Pos
1962	BAL	A	6	.000	.000	4	0	0	0	0	0.0	0	0	0	0	0	1	0	2	2	0	0	0.7	1.000	SS-5

Year	Team		Games	BA	SA	AB	H	2B	3B	HR	HR%	R	RBI	BB	SO	SB	Pinch Hit AB	Pinch Hit H	PO	A	E	DP	TC/G	FA	G by Pos

Mickey McGuire *continued*

Year	Team		Games	BA	SA	AB	H	2B	3B	HR	HR%	R	RBI	BB	SO	SB	PH AB	PH H	PO	A	E	DP	TC/G	FA	G by Pos
1967			10	.235	.235	17	4	0	0	0	0.0	2	2	0	2	0	6	1	3	3	0	0	0.6	1.000	2B-4
2 yrs.			16	.190	.190	21	4	0	0	0	0.0	2	2	0	2	0	7	1	5	5	0	0	0.6	1.000	SS-5, 2B-4

Bill McGunnigle

McGUNNIGLE, WILLIAM HENRY (Gunner)
B. Jan. 1, 1855, Boston, Mass.   D. Mar. 9, 1899, Brockton, Mass.
Manager 1880, 1888-91, 1896.

BR TR 5'9"   155 lbs.

Year	Team		Games	BA	SA	AB	H	2B	3B	HR	HR%	R	RBI	BB	SO	SB	PH AB	PH H	PO	A	E	DP	TC/G	FA	G by Pos
1879	BUF	N	47	.175	.187	171	30	5	1	0	0.0	22	5	5	24		0	0	64	35	9	2	2.3	.917	OF-34, P-14
1880	2 teams		BUF N	(7G – .182)		WOR N	(1G – .000)																		
"	total		8	.154	.154	26	4	0	0	0	0.0	0	1	0	6		0	0	6	4	2	0	1.5	.833	P-5, OF-4
1882	CLE	N	1	.200	.200	5	1	0	0	0	0.0	2	0	0	1		0	0	0	0	0	0	0.0	—	OF-1
3 yrs.			56	.173	.183	202	35	0	1	0	0.0	24	6	5	31		0	0	70	39	11	2	2.1	.908	OF-39, P-19

Mark McGwire

McGWIRE, MARK DAVID
B. Oct. 1, 1963, Pomona, Calif.

BR TR 6'5"   215 lbs.

Year	Team		Games	BA	SA	AB	H	2B	3B	HR	HR%	R	RBI	BB	SO	SB	PH AB	PH H	PO	A	E	DP	TC/G	FA	G by Pos
1986	OAK	A	18	.189	.377	53	10	1	0	3	5.7	10	9	4	18	0	3	1	10	20	6	1	2.0	.833	3B-16
1987			151	.289	.618	557	161	28	4	49	8.8	97	118	71	131	1	2	1	1176	101	13	91	8.5	.990	1B-145, 3B-8, OF-3
1988			155	.260	.478	550	143	22	1	32	5.8	87	99	76	117	0	4	2	1228	88	9	118	8.5	.993	1B-154, OF-1
1989			143	.231	.467	490	113	17	0	33	6.7	74	95	83	94	1	1	0	1170	114	6	122	9.0	.995	1B-141, DH-2
4 yrs.			467	.259	.519	1650	427	68	5	117	7.1	268	321	234	360	2	10	4	3584	323	34	332	8.4	.991	1B-440, 3B-24, OF-4, DH-2

LEAGUE CHAMPIONSHIP SERIES

Year	Team		Games	BA	SA	AB	H	2B	3B	HR	HR%	R	RBI	BB	SO	SB	PH AB	PH H	PO	A	E	DP	TC/G	FA	G by Pos
1988	OAK	A	4	.333	.533	15	5	0	0	1	6.7	4	3	1	5	0	0	0	24	2	0	4	6.5	1.000	1B-4
1989			5	.389	.611	18	7	1	0	1	5.6	3	3	1	4	0	0	0	46	1	1	4	9.6	.979	1B-5
2 yrs.			9	.364	.576	33	12	1	0	2	6.1	7	6	2	9	0	0	0	70	3	1	8	8.2	.986	1B-9

WORLD SERIES

Year	Team		Games	BA	SA	AB	H	2B	3B	HR	HR%	R	RBI	BB	SO	SB	PH AB	PH H	PO	A	E	DP	TC/G	FA	G by Pos
1988	OAK	A	5	.059	.235	17	1	0	0	1	5.9	1	1	3	4	0	0	0	40	3	0	2	8.6	1.000	1B-5
1989			4	.294	.353	17	5	1	0	0	0.0	0	1	1	3	0	0	0	28	2	0	1	7.5	1.000	1B-4
2 yrs.			9	.176	.294	34	6	1	0	1	2.9	1	2	4	7	0	0	0	68	5	0	3	8.1	1.000	1B-9

Bob McHale

McHALE, ROBERT EMMET
B. Feb. 7, 1870, Sacramento, Calif.   D. June 9, 1952, Sacramento, Calif.

Year	Team		Games	BA	SA	AB	H	2B	3B	HR	HR%	R	RBI	BB	SO	SB	PH AB	PH H	PO	A	E	DP	TC/G	FA	G by Pos
1898	WAS	N	11	.182	.242	33	6	2	0	0	0.0	5	7	1		1	1	0	19	2	3	2	2.2	.875	OF-9, SS-1, 1B-1

Jim McHale

McHALE, JAMES BERNARD
B. Dec. 17, 1875, Miners Mills, Pa.   D. June 17, 1959, Los Angeles, Calif.

BR TR 5'11"   165 lbs.

Year	Team		Games	BA	SA	AB	H	2B	3B	HR	HR%	R	RBI	BB	SO	SB	PH AB	PH H	PO	A	E	DP	TC/G	FA	G by Pos
1908	BOS	A	21	.224	.313	67	15	2	2	0	0.0	9	7	4		4	0	0	30	2	1	0	1.6	.970	OF-19

John McHale

McHALE, JOHN JOSEPH
B. Sept. 21, 1921, Detroit, Mich.

BL TR 6'   200 lbs.

Year	Team		Games	BA	SA	AB	H	2B	3B	HR	HR%	R	RBI	BB	SO	SB	PH AB	PH H	PO	A	E	DP	TC/G	FA	G by Pos
1943	DET	A	4	.000	.000	3	0	0	0	0	0.0	1	1	0	3	0	3	0	0	0	0	0	0.0	—	
1944			1	.000	.000	1	0	0	0	0	0.0	0	0	0	1	0	1	0	0	0	0	0	0.0	—	
1945			19	.143	.143	14	2	0	0	0	0.0	1	4	0	4	0	14	2	5	1	0	0	0.3	1.000	1B-3
1947			39	.211	.316	95	20	1	0	3	3.2	10	11	7	24	1	15	4	195	12	1	12	5.3	.995	1B-25
1948			1	.000	.000	1	0	0	0	0	0.0	0	0	0	0	0	1	0	0	0	0	0	0.0	—	
5 yrs.			64	.193	.281	114	22	1	0	3	2.6	10	12	9	29	1	34	7	200	13	1	12	3.3	.995	1B-28

WORLD SERIES

Year	Team		Games	BA	SA	AB	H	2B	3B	HR	HR%	R	RBI	BB	SO	SB	PH AB	PH H	PO	A	E	DP	TC/G	FA	G by Pos
1945	DET	A	3	.000	.000	3	0	0	0	0	0.0	0	0	0	1	0	3	0	0	0	0	0	0.0	—	

Austin McHenry

McHENRY, AUSTIN BUSH (Mac)
B. Sept. 22, 1895, Wrightsville, Ohio   D. Nov. 27, 1922, Jefferson, Ohio

BR TR 6'   175 lbs.

Year	Team		Games	BA	SA	AB	H	2B	3B	HR	HR%	R	RBI	BB	SO	SB	PH AB	PH H	PO	A	E	DP	TC/G	FA	G by Pos
1918	STL	N	80	.261	.360	272	71	12	6	1	0.4	32	29	21	24	8	0	0	145	14	8	3	2.1	.952	OF-80
1919			110	.286	.404	371	106	19	11	1	0.3	41	47	19	57	7	4	0	183	20	3	3	1.9	.985	OF-103
1920			137	.282	.423	504	142	19	11	10	2.0	66	65	25	73	8	3	1	297	21	16	1	2.4	.952	OF-133
1921			152	.350	.531	574	201	37	8	17	3.0	92	102	38	48	10	0	0	371	13	14	3	2.6	.965	OF-152
1922			64	.303	.466	238	72	18	3	5	2.1	31	43	14	27	2	2	1	132	13	10	3	2.4	.935	OF-61
5 yrs.			543	.302	.448	1959	592	105	39	34	1.7	262	286	117	229	35	9	2	1128	81	51	13	2.3	.960	OF-529

Vance McHenry

McHENRY, VANCE LOREN
B. July 10, 1956, Chico, Calif.

BR TR 5'9"   165 lbs.

Year	Team		Games	BA	SA	AB	H	2B	3B	HR	HR%	R	RBI	BB	SO	SB	PH AB	PH H	PO	A	E	DP	TC/G	FA	G by Pos
1981	SEA	A	15	.222	.222	18	4	0	0	0	0.0	3	2	1	1	0	2	1	7	18	3	6	1.9	.893	SS-13, DH-1
1982			3	.000	.000	1	0	0	0	0	0.0	0	0	0	0	0	1	0	1	0	1	0	0.7	.500	DH-1, SS-1
2 yrs.			18	.211	.211	19	4	0	0	0	0.0	3	2	1	1	0	3	1	8	18	4	6	1.7	.867	SS-14, DH-2

Irish McIlveen

McILVEEN, HENRY COOKE
B. July 27, 1880, Belfast, Ireland   D. Oct. 18, 1960, Lorain, Ohio

BL TL 5'11½"   180 lbs.

Year	Team		Games	BA	SA	AB	H	2B	3B	HR	HR%	R	RBI	BB	SO	SB	PH AB	PH H	PO	A	E	DP	TC/G	FA	G by Pos
1906	PIT	N	5	.400	.400	5	2	0	0	0	0.0	1					1	0	2	0	0	0	0.6	1.000	P-2
1908	NY	A	44	.213	.266	169	36	3	3	0	0.0	17	8	14		6	2	0	70	4	4	0	1.8	.949	OF-44
1909			4	.000	.000	3	0	0	0	0	0.0	0				1	3	0	0	0	0	0	0.0	—	
3 yrs.			53	.215	.266	177	38	3	3	0	0.0	18	8	15		6	5	1	71	6	4	0	1.5	.951	OF-44, P-2

Stuffy McInnis

McINNIS, JOHN PHALEN
B. Sept. 19, 1890, Gloucester, Mass.   D. Feb. 16, 1960, Ipswich, Mass.
Manager 1927.

BR TR 5'9½"   162 lbs.

Year	Team		Games	BA	SA	AB	H	2B	3B	HR	HR%	R	RBI	BB	SO	SB	PH AB	PH H	PO	A	E	DP	TC/G	FA	G by Pos
1909	PHI	A	19	.239	.304	46	11	0	0	1	2.2	4	4	2		0	5	2	34	44	10	5	4.6	.886	SS-14
1910			38	.301	.438	73	22	2	4	0	0.0	10	12	7		3	10	3	33	39	5	3	2.0	.935	SS-17, 2B-5, 3B-4, OF-1
1911			126	.321	.425	468	150	20	10	3	0.6	76	77	25		23	4	1	1105	101	35	58	9.8	.972	1B-97, SS-24
1912			153	.327	.433	568	186	25	13	3	0.5	83	101	49		27	0	0	1533	100	27	88	10.8	.984	1B-153
1913			148	.326	.418	543	177	30	4	4	0.7	79	90	45	31	16	0	0	1504	80	12	85	10.8	.992	1B-148
1914			149	.314	.368	576	181	12	8	1	0.2	74	95	19	27	25	0	0	1423	85	7	89	10.2	.995	1B-149

Year	Team	Games	BA	SA	AB	H	2B	3B	HR	HR%	R	RBI	BB	SO	SB	Pinch Hit AB	Pinch Hit H	PO	A	E	DP	TC/G	FA	G by Pos

Stuffy McInnis *continued*

Year	Team	Games	BA	SA	AB	H	2B	3B	HR	HR%	R	RBI	BB	SO	SB	AB	H	PO	A	E	DP	TC/G	FA	G by Pos
1915		119	.314	.362	456	143	14	4	0	0.0	44	49	14	17	8	0	0	1123	83	13	63	10.2	.989	1B-119
1916		140	.295	.361	512	151	25	3	1	0.2	42	60	25	19	7	0	0	1404	96	12	87	10.8	.992	1B-140
1917		150	.303	.351	567	172	19	4	0	0.0	50	44	33	19	18	0	0	1658	95	12	81	11.8	.993	1B-150
1918	BOS A	117	.272	.322	423	115	11	5	0	0.0	40	56	19	10	10	0	0	1100	113	10	53	10.5	.992	1B-94, 3B-23
1919		120	.305	.361	440	134	12	5	1	0.2	32	58	23	11	8	2	1	1236	82	7	84	11.0	.995	1B-118
1920		148	.297	.356	559	166	21	3	2	0.4	50	71	18	19	6	0	0	1586	91	7	101	11.4	.996	1B-148
1921		152	.307	.394	584	179	31	10	0	0.0	72	74	21	9	2	0	0	1549	102	1	109	10.9	.999	1B-152
1922	CLE A	142	.305	.389	537	164	28	7	1	0.2	58	78	15	5	1	1	0	1376	73	5	96	10.2	.997	1B-140, C-1
1923	BOS N	154	.315	.392	607	191	23	9	2	0.3	70	95	26	12	7	0	0	1500	89	14	136	10.4	.991	1B-154
1924		146	.291	.360	581	169	23	7	1	0.2	57	59	15	6	9	0	0	1435	95	10	129	10.5	.994	1B-146
1925	PIT N	59	.368	.484	155	57	10	4	0	0.0	19	24	17	1	1	13	4	377	24	3	40	6.8	.993	1B-46
1926		47	.299	.362	127	38	6	1	0	0.0	12	13	7	3	1	7	2	300	17	4	32	6.8	.988	1B-40
1927	PHI N	1	–	–	0	0	0	0	0	–	0	0	0	0	0	0	0	1	0	0	0	1.0	1.000	1B-1
19 yrs.		2128	.308	.381	7822	2406	312	101	20	0.3	872	1060	380	189	172	42	13	20277	1409	194	1339	10.3	.991	1B-1995, SS-55, 3B-27, 2B-5, OF-1, C-1

WORLD SERIES

Year	Team	Games	BA	SA	AB	H	2B	3B	HR	HR%	R	RBI	BB	SO	SB	AB	H	PO	A	E	DP	TC/G	FA	G by Pos
1911	PHI A	1	–	–	0	0	0	0	0	–	0	0	0	0	0	0	0	1	0	0	0	1.0	1.000	1B-1
1913		5	.118	.176	17	2	1	0	0	0.0	1	2	0	1	0	0	0	45	0	0	4	9.0	1.000	1B-5
1914		4	.143	.214	14	2	1	0	0	0.0	2	0	3	3	0	0	0	50	2	1	4	13.3	.981	1B-4
1918	BOS A	6	.250	.250	20	5	0	0	0	0.0	2	1	1	1	0	0	0	71	2	0	3	12.2	1.000	1B-6
1925	PIT N	4	.286	.286	14	4	0	0	0	0.0	0	1	0	2	0	1	0	30	3	0	0	8.3	1.000	1B-3
5 yrs.		20	.200	.231	65	13	2	0	0	0.0	5	4	4	8	0	1	0	197	7	1	11	10.3	.995	1B-19

Matty McIntyre

McINTYRE, MATTHEW W.
B. June 12, 1880, Stonington, Conn. D. Apr. 2, 1920, Detroit, Mich.

BL TL 5'11" 175 lbs.

Year	Team	Games	BA	SA	AB	H	2B	3B	HR	HR%	R	RBI	BB	SO	SB	AB	H	PO	A	E	DP	TC/G	FA	G by Pos
1901	PHI A	82	.276	.341	308	85	12	4	0	0.0	38	46	30		11	0	0	155	8	14	0	2.2	.921	OF-82
1904	DET A	152	.253	.317	578	146	11	10	2	0.3	74	46	44		11	0	0	334	16	15	4	2.4	.959	OF-152
1905		131	.263	.325	495	130	21	5	0	0.0	59	30	48		9	0	0	286	18	10	6	2.4	.968	OF-131
1906		133	.260	.343	493	128	19	11	0	0.0	63	39	56		29	0	0	254	25	5	8	2.1	.982	OF-133
1907		20	.284	.321	81	23	1	1	0	0.0	6	9	7		6	0	0	43	3	0	1	2.3	1.000	OF-20
1908		151	.295	.383	569	168	24	13	0	0.0	105	28	83		20	0	0	329	17	8	4	2.3	.977	OF-151
1909		125	.244	.326	476	116	18	9	1	0.2	65	34	54		13	2	0	217	14	6	1	1.9	.975	OF-122
1910		83	.236	.318	305	72	15	5	0	0.0	40	25	39		6	1	0	147	12	9	2	2.0	.946	OF-77
1911	CHI A	146	.323	.401	569	184	19	11	1	0.2	102	52	64		17	0	0	235	18	14	5	1.8	.948	OF-146
1912		45	.167	.167	84	14	0	0	0	0.0	10	10	14		3	0	0	37	2	0	0	0.9	1.000	OF-45
10 yrs.		1068	.269	.343	3958	1066	140	69	4	0.1	562	319	439		120	8	0	2037	133	81	31	2.1	.964	OF-1059

WORLD SERIES

Year	Team	Games	BA	SA	AB	H	2B	3B	HR	HR%	R	RBI	BB	SO	SB	AB	H	PO	A	E	DP	TC/G	FA	G by Pos
1908	DET A	5	.222	.278	18	4	1	0	0	0.0	2	0	3	2	1	0	0	10	0	1	0	2.2	.909	OF-5
1909		4	.000	.000	3	0	0	0	0	0.0	0	0	0	1	0	3	0	0	0	0	0	0.0	–	OF-1
2 yrs.		9	.190	.238	21	4	1	0	0	0.0	2	0	3	3	1	3	0	10	0	1	0	1.2	.909	OF-6

Otto McIvor

McIVOR, EDWARD OTTO
B. July 26, 1884, Greenville, Tex. D. May 4, 1954, Dallas, Tex.

BB TL 5'11½" 175 lbs.

Year	Team	Games	BA	SA	AB	H	2B	3B	HR	HR%	R	RBI	BB	SO	SB	AB	H	PO	A	E	DP	TC/G	FA	G by Pos
1911	STL N	30	.226	.339	62	14	2	1	1	1.6	11	9	9	14	0	7	0	24	1	2	0	0.9	.926	OF-17

Dave McKay

McKAY, DAVID LAWRENCE
B. Mar. 14, 1950, Vancouver, B.c., Canada

BB TR 6'1" 195 lbs.

Year	Team	Games	BA	SA	AB	H	2B	3B	HR	HR%	R	RBI	BB	SO	SB	AB	H	PO	A	E	DP	TC/G	FA	G by Pos
1975	MIN A	33	.256	.352	125	32	4	1	2	1.6	8	16	6	14	1	0	0	38	70	9	12	3.5	.923	3B-33
1976		45	.203	.217	138	28	2	0	0	0.0	8	8	9	27	1	3	1	27	77	10	13	2.5	.912	3B-41, SS-2, DH-1
1977	TOR A	95	.197	.266	274	54	4	3	3	1.1	18	22	7	51	2	0	0	141	205	14	36	3.8	.961	2B-40, 3B-32, SS-20, DH-2
1978		145	.238	.351	504	120	20	8	7	1.4	59	45	20	91	4	0	0	310	414	12	96	5.1	.984	2B-140, SS-3, 3B-2, DH-1
1979		47	.218	.276	156	34	9	0	0	0.0	19	12	7	19	1	0	0	119	150	7	37	5.9	.975	2B-46, 3B-2
1980	OAK A	123	.244	.315	295	72	16	1	1	0.3	29	29	10	57	1	1	1	155	242	10	33	3.3	.975	2B-62, 3B-54, SS-10
1981		79	.263	.375	224	59	11	1	4	1.8	25	21	16	43	4	3	0	118	172	13	26	3.8	.957	3B-43, 2B-38, SS-7
1982		78	.198	.283	212	42	4	1	4	1.9	25	17	11	35	6	2	0	120	153	11	24	3.6	.961	2B-59, 3B-16, SS-3
8 yrs.		645	.229	.313	1928	441	70	15	21	1.1	191	170	86	337	20	9	2	1028	1483	86	277	4.0	.967	2B-385, 3B-223, SS-45, DH-4

DIVISIONAL PLAYOFF SERIES

Year	Team	Games	BA	SA	AB	H	2B	3B	HR	HR%	R	RBI	BB	SO	SB	AB	H	PO	A	E	DP	TC/G	FA	G by Pos
1981	OAK A	3	.273	.545	11	3	0	0	1	9.1	1	1	1	1	0	0	0	0	0	1	0	0.3	–	2B-3

LEAGUE CHAMPIONSHIP SERIES

Year	Team	Games	BA	SA	AB	H	2B	3B	HR	HR%	R	RBI	BB	SO	SB	AB	H	PO	A	E	DP	TC/G	FA	G by Pos
1981	OAK A	3	.273	.273	11	3	0	0	0	0.0	0	1	0	2	0	0	0	0	0	1	0	0.3	–	2B-3

Ed McKean

McKEAN, EDWIN JOHN (Mack)
B. June 6, 1864, Grafton, Ohio D. Aug. 16, 1919, Cleveland, Ohio

BR TR 5'9" 160 lbs.

Year	Team	Games	BA	SA	AB	H	2B	3B	HR	HR%	R	RBI	BB	SO	SB	AB	H	PO	A	E	DP	TC/G	FA	G by Pos
1887	CLE AA	132	.286	.375	539	154	16	13	2	0.4	97		60		76	0	0	220	369	105	34	5.3	.849	SS-123, 2B-8, OF-4
1888		131	.299	.425	548	164	21	15	6	1.1	94	68	28		52	0	0	226	271	56	19	4.2	.899	SS-78, OF-48, 2B-9, 3B-1
1889	CLE N	123	.318	.418	500	159	22	8	4	0.8	88	75	42	25	35	0	0	209	401	62	42	5.5	.908	SS-122, 2B-1
1890		136	.296	.417	530	157	15	14	7	1.3	95	61	87	25	23	0	0	268	439	75	47	5.8	.904	SS-134, 2B-3
1891		141	.282	.373	603	170	13	12	6	1.0	115	69	64	19	14	0	0	248	463	91	42	5.7	.887	SS-141
1892		129	.262	.326	531	139	14	10	0	0.0	76	93	49	28	19	0	0	207	369	92	29	5.2	.862	SS-129
1893		125	.310	.473	545	169	29	24	4	0.7	103	133	50	14	16	0	0	247	431	74	55	6.0	.902	SS-125
1894		130	.357	.509	554	198	30	15	8	1.4	116	128	49	12	33	0	0	269	411	71	43	5.8	.905	SS-130
1895		131	.342	.501	565	193	32	17	8	1.4	131	119	45	25	12	0	0	246	424	67	42	5.6	.909	SS-131
1896		133	.338	.468	571	193	29	12	7	1.2	100	112	45	9	13	0	0	214	400	57	57	5.0	.915	SS-133
1897		125	.273	.379	523	143	21	14	2	0.4	83	78	40		15	0	0	226	385	53	36	5.3	.920	SS-125
1898		151	.285	.371	604	172	23	1	9	1.5	89	94	56	11	0	0	0	304	425	53	47	5.2	.932	SS-151
1899	STL N	67	.260	.339	277	72	7	3	3	1.1	40	40	20		4	0	0	254	156	34	25	6.6	.923	SS-42, 1B-15, 2B-10
13 yrs.		1654	.302	.416	6890	2083	272	158	66	1.0	1227	1070	635	157	323	0	0	3138	4944	890	518	5.4	.901	SS-1564, OF-52, 2B-31, 1B-15, 3B-1

Year	Team	Games	BA	SA	AB	H	2B	3B	HR	HR%	R	RBI	BB	SO	SB	Pinch Hit AB	Pinch Hit H	PO	A	E	DP	TC/G	FA	G by Pos

Bill McKechnie

McKECHNIE, WILLIAM BOYD (Deacon)
B. Aug. 7, 1886, Wilkinsburg, Pa.   D. Oct. 29, 1965, Bradenton, Fla.
Manager 1915, 1922-26, 1928-46.
Hall of Fame 1962.

BB TR 5'10"   160 lbs.

Year	Team	Games	BA	SA	AB	H	2B	3B	HR	HR%	R	RBI	BB	SO	SB	PH AB	PH H	PO	A	E	DP	TC/G	FA	G by Pos
1907	PIT N	3	.125	.125	8	1	0	0	0	0.0	0	0	0		0	0	0	1	4	0	0	1.7	1.000	3B-2, 2B-1
1910		71	.217	.241	212	46	1	2	0	0.0	23	12	11	23	4	8	2	146	166	12	20	4.6	.963	2B-36, SS-14, 3B-8, 1B-4
1911		104	.227	.315	321	73	8	7	2	0.6	40	37	28	18	9	5	2	598	109	21	49	7.0	.971	1B-57, 2B-17, SS-12, 3B-6
1912		24	.247	.274	73	18	0	1	0	0.0	8	2	1	2	1	0	0	23	42	3	4	2.8	.956	3B-15, SS-4, 2B-3, 1B-2
1913	2 teams	BOS N	(1G – .000)		NY A	(44G – .134)																		
"	total	45	.129	.129	116	15	0	0	0	0.0	8	8	8	18	2	4	0	77	94	12	13	4.1	.934	2B-27, SS-7, 3B-2, OF-1
1914	IND F	149	.304	.377	570	173	24	6	2	0.4	107	38	53		47	0	0	195	327	34	28	3.7	.939	3B-149
1915	NWK F	127	.251	.328	451	113	22	5	1	0.2	49	43	41		28	8	3	184	226	19	17	3.4	.956	3B-117, OF-1
1916	2 teams	NY N	(71G – .246)		CIN N	(37G – .277)																		
"	total	108	.256	.292	390	100	12	1	0	0.0	26	27	10	32	11	2	0	108	193	17	14	2.9	.947	3B-106
1917	CIN N	48	.254	.291	134	34	3	1	0	0.0	11	15	7	7	5	4	1	76	94	15	15	3.9	.919	2B-26, SS-13, 3B-4
1918	PIT N	126	.255	.340	435	111	13	9	2	0.5	34	43	24	22	12	0	0	162	261	15	26	3.5	.966	3B-126
1920		40	.218	.278	133	29	3	1	1	0.8	13	13	4	7	3	0	0	56	84	8	11	3.7	.946	3B-20, SS-10, 2B-6, 1B-1
11 yrs.		845	.251	.313	2843	713	86	33	8	0.3	319	240	188	128	127	35	8	1626	1600	156	197	4.0	.954	3B-555, 2B-116, 1B-64, SS-60, OF-2

Frank McKee

McKEE, FRANK
B. Philadelphia, Pa.   Deceased.

Year	Team	Games	BA	SA	AB	H	2B	3B	HR	HR%	R	RBI	BB	SO	SB	PH AB	PH H	PO	A	E	DP	TC/G	FA	G by Pos
1884	WAS U	4	.176	.176	17	3	0	0	0	0.0	2	0	1	0	0	0	0	1	1	4	0	1.5	.333	OF-3, 3B-2, C-1

Red McKee

McKEE, RAYMOND ELLIS
B. July 20, 1890, Shawnee, Ohio   D. Aug. 5, 1972, Saginaw, Mich.

BL TR 5'11"   180 lbs.

Year	Team	Games	BA	SA	AB	H	2B	3B	HR	HR%	R	RBI	BB	SO	SB	PH AB	PH H	PO	A	E	DP	TC/G	FA	G by Pos
1913	DET A	67	.283	.358	187	53	3	4	1	0.5	18	20	21	21	7	6	0	237	84	17	5	5.0	.950	C-61
1914		32	.188	.234	64	12	1	1	0	0.0	7	8	14	16	1	5	1	87	20	4	2	3.5	.964	C-27
1915		55	.274	.349	106	29	5	0	1	0.9	10	17	13	16	1	15	2	116	30	7	4	2.8	.954	C-35
1916		32	.211	.276	76	16	1	2	0	0.0	3	4	6	11	0	6	2	76	31	5	3	3.5	.955	C-26
4 yrs.		186	.254	.323	433	110	10	7	2	0.5	38	49	54	64	9	32	5	516	165	33	14	3.8	.954	C-149

Jim McKeever

McKEEVER, JAMES
B. Apr. 19, 1861, Newfoundland, Canada   D. Aug. 19, 1897, Boston, Mass.

Year	Team	Games	BA	SA	AB	H	2B	3B	HR	HR%	R	RBI	BB	SO	SB	PH AB	PH H	PO	A	E	DP	TC/G	FA	G by Pos
1884	BOS U	16	.136	.136	66	9	0	0	0	0.0	13		0			0	0	96	12	16	1	7.8	.871	C-12, OF-4

Russ McKelvey

McKELVEY, RUSSELL ERRETT
B. Sept. 8, 1856, Meadville, Pa.   D. Oct. 19, 1915, Omaha, Neb.

BR TR

Year	Team	Games	BA	SA	AB	H	2B	3B	HR	HR%	R	RBI	BB	SO	SB	PH AB	PH H	PO	A	E	DP	TC/G	FA	G by Pos
1878	IND N	63	.225	.289	253	57	4	3	2	0.8	33	36	5	38		0	0	121	27	28	2	2.8	.841	OF-62, P-4
1882	PIT AA	1	.000	.000	4	0	0	0	0	0.0	0	0	0	0		0	0	0	0	0	0	0.0	–	OF-1
2 yrs.		64	.222	.284	257	57	4	3	2	0.8	33	36	5	38		0	0	121	27	28	2	2.8	.841	OF-63, P-4

Ed McKenna

McKENNA, EDWARD J.
B. St. Louis, Mo.   Deceased.

Year	Team	Games	BA	SA	AB	H	2B	3B	HR	HR%	R	RBI	BB	SO	SB	PH AB	PH H	PO	A	E	DP	TC/G	FA	G by Pos
1877	STL N	1	.200	.200	5	1	0	0	0	0.0	0		0	1		0	0	1	0	0	0	1.0	1.000	OF-1
1884	WAS U	32	.188	.197	117	22	1	0	0	0.0	19		4			0	0	124	46	35	5	6.4	.829	C-23, OF-10, 3B-7
2 yrs.		33	.189	.197	122	23	1	0	0	0.0	19		4	1		0	0	125	46	35	5	6.2	.830	C-23, OF-11, 3B-7

Dave McKeough

McKEOUGH, DAVID J.
B. Dec. 1, 1863, Utica, N.Y.   D. July 11, 1901, Utica, N.Y.

5'7"   158 lbs.

Year	Team	Games	BA	SA	AB	H	2B	3B	HR	HR%	R	RBI	BB	SO	SB	PH AB	PH H	PO	A	E	DP	TC/G	FA	G by Pos
1890	ROC AA	62	.225	.248	218	49	5	0	0	0.0	38		29		14	0	0	205	124	31	8	5.8	.914	C-47, SS-13, 2B-2, 3B-1
1891	PHI AA	15	.259	.315	54	14	1	1	0	0.0	4	3	8	6	0	0	0	55	17	13	5	5.7	.847	C-14, SS-1
2 yrs.		77	.232	.261	272	63	6	1	0	0.0	42	3	37	6	14	0	0	260	141	44	13	5.8	.901	C-61, SS-14, 2B-2, 3B-1

Bob McKinney

McKINNEY, ROBERT FRANCIS
B. Oct. 4, 1875, McSherrystown, Pa.   D. Aug. 19, 1946, Chicago, Ill.

BR TR 5'7"   165 lbs.

Year	Team	Games	BA	SA	AB	H	2B	3B	HR	HR%	R	RBI	BB	SO	SB	PH AB	PH H	PO	A	E	DP	TC/G	FA	G by Pos
1901	PHI A	2	.000	.000	2	0	0	0	0	0.0	0	0	0			0	0	0	0	1	0	0.5	–	3B-1, 2B-1

Rich McKinney

McKINNEY, CHARLES RICHARD
B. Nov. 22, 1946, Piqua, Ohio

BR TR 5'11"   185 lbs.

Year	Team	Games	BA	SA	AB	H	2B	3B	HR	HR%	R	RBI	BB	SO	SB	PH AB	PH H	PO	A	E	DP	TC/G	FA	G by Pos
1970	CHI A	43	.168	.311	119	20	4	0	4	3.4	12	17	11	25	3	6	1	34	81	6	9	2.8	.950	3B-23, SS-11
1971		114	.271	.377	369	100	11	2	8	2.2	35	46	35	37	0	19	11	195	171	11	34	3.3	.971	2B-67, OF-25, 3B-5
1972	NY A	37	.215	.256	121	26	2	0	1	0.8	10	7	7	13	0	4	0	17	71	8	5	2.6	.917	3B-33
1973	OAK A	48	.246	.338	65	16	3	0	1	1.5	9	7	7	4	0	19	2	13	19	2	4	0.7	.941	3B-17, 2B-7, DH-6, OF-3
1974		5	.143	.143	7	1	0	0	0	0.0	0	0	0	0	0	0	0	1	0	0	0	0.2	1.000	2B-3
1975		8	.143	.143	7	1	0	0	0	0.0	0	2	1	2	0	4	0	1	0	0	0	0.1	1.000	DH-2, 1B-1
1977		86	.177	.303	198	35	6	0	6	3.0	13	21	16	43	1	31	6	213	27	9	22	2.9	.964	1B-32, DH-18, 3B-7, OF-5, 2B-3
7 yrs.		341	.225	.328	886	199	28	2	20	2.3	79	100	77	124	4	88	20	474	369	36	74	2.6	.959	3B-85, 2B-80, OF-33, 1B-33, DH-26, SS-11

Alex McKinnon

McKINNON, ALEXANDER J.
B. Aug. 14, 1856, Boston, Mass.   D. July 24, 1887, Charlestown, Mass.
Manager 1885.

BR 5'11½"

Year	Team	Games	BA	SA	AB	H	2B	3B	HR	HR%	R	RBI	BB	SO	SB	PH AB	PH H	PO	A	E	DP	TC/G	FA	G by Pos
1884	NY N	116	.272	.394	470	128	21	12	4	0.9	66		8	62		0	0	1097	31	53	57	10.2	.955	1B-116
1885	STL N	100	.294	.382	411	121	21	6	0	0.2	42	44	8	31		0	0	1102	26	25	50	11.5	.978	1B-100
1886		122	.301	.428	491	148	24	7	8	1.6	75	72	21	23		0	0	1175	35	47	61	10.3	.963	1B-119, OF-3
1887	PIT N	48	.340	.475	200	68	16	4	1	0.5	26	30	8	9	6	0	0	483	25	12	27	10.8	.977	1B-48
4 yrs.		386	.296	.412	1572	465	82	29	14	0.9	209	146	45	125	6	0	0	3857	117	137	195	10.7	.967	1B-383, OF-3

Year	Team		Games	BA	SA	AB	H	2B	3B	HR	HR%	R	RBI	BB	SO	SB	Pinch Hit AB	H	PO	A	E	DP	TC/G	FA	G by Pos

Jeff McKnight

McKNIGHT, JEFFERSON ALAN
Son of Jim McKnight.
B. Feb. 18, 1963, Conway, Ark.   BB TR 6' 170 lbs.

| 1989 | NY | N | 6 | .250 | .250 | 12 | 3 | 0 | 0 | 0 | 0.0 | 2 | 0 | 2 | 1 | 0 | 3 | 1 | 4 | 5 | 1 | 1 | 1.7 | .900 | 2B-4, SS-1, 3B-1, 1B-1 |

Jim McKnight

McKNIGHT, JAMES ARTHUR
Father of Jeff McKnight.
B. July 1, 1936, Bee Branch, Ark.   BR TR 6'1" 185 lbs.

1960	CHI	N	3	.333	.333	6	2	0	0	0	0.0	0	1	0	1	0	1	0	0	2	1	1	1.0	.667	OF-1, 2B-1
1962			60	.224	.247	85	19	0	1	0	0.0	6	5	2	13	0	49	11	17	20	2	5	0.7	.949	3B-9, OF-5, 2B-2
2 yrs.			63	.231	.253	91	21	0	1	0	0.0	6	6	2	14	0	50	11	17	22	3	6	0.7	.929	3B-9, OF-6, 2B-3

Ed McLane

McLANE, EDWARD CAMERON
B. Aug. 20, 1881, Weston, Mass.   Deceased.   5'10" 179 lbs.

| 1907 | BKN | N | 1 | .000 | .000 | 2 | 0 | 0 | 0 | 0 | 0.0 | 0 | 0 | 0 | | 0 | 0 | 0 | 1 | 0 | 2 | 0 | 3.0 | .333 | OF-1 |

Art McLarney

McLARNEY, ARTHUR JAMES
B. Dec. 20, 1908, Fort Worden, Wash.   D. Dec. 20, 1984, Seattle, Wash.   BB TR 6' 168 lbs.

| 1932 | NY | N | 9 | .130 | .174 | 23 | 3 | 1 | 0 | 0 | 0.0 | 2 | 3 | 1 | 3 | 0 | 0 | 0 | 13 | 17 | 0 | 3 | 3.3 | 1.000 | SS-9 |

Polly McLarry

McLARRY, HOWARD ZELL
B. Mar. 25, 1891, Leonard, Tex.   D. Nov. 4, 1971, Bonham, Tex.   BL TR 6' 185 lbs.

1912	CHI	A	2	.000	.000	2	0	0	0	0	0.0	0	0	0	2	0	2	0	0	0	0	0	0.0	–	
1915	CHI	N	68	.197	.244	127	25	3	0	1	0.8	16	12	14	20	2	21	2	208	55	8	8	4.0	.970	1B-25, 2B-20
2 yrs.			70	.194	.240	129	25	3	0	1	0.8	16	12	14	20	2	23	2	208	55	8	8	3.9	.970	1B-25, 2B-20

Barney McLaughlin

McLAUGHLIN, BERNARD
Brother of Frank McLaughlin.
B. 1857, Ireland   D. Feb. 13, 1921, Lowell, Mass.   BR TR 5'8" 163 lbs.

1884	KC	U	42	.228	.309	162	37	7	3	0	0.0	15		9			0	0	58	49	24	8	3.1	.817	OF-24, 2B-12, P-7, SS-2
1887	PHI	N	50	.220	.302	205	45	8	3	1	0.5	26	26	11	27	2	0	0	106	156	36	15	6.0	.879	2B-50
1890	SYR	AA	86	.264	.313	329	87	8	1	2	0.6	43		47		13	0	0	120	258	41	22	4.9	.902	SS-86
3 yrs.			178	.243	.309	696	169	23	7	3	0.4	84	26	67	27	15	0	0	284	463	101	45	4.8	.881	SS-88, 2B-62, OF-24, P-7

Frank McLaughlin

McLAUGHLIN, FRANCIS EDWARD
Brother of Barney McLaughlin.
B. June 19, 1856, Lowell, Mass.   D. Apr. 5, 1917, Lowell, Mass.   BR TR 5'9" 160 lbs.

1882	WOR	N	15	.218	.345	55	12	0	2	1	1.8	7	4	0	11		0	0	17	40	20	2	5.1	.740	SS-14, OF-1
1883	PIT	AA	29	.219	.263	114	25	2	0	1	0.9	15		6			0	0	24	85	25	4	4.6	.813	SS-25, OF-4, 2B-2, P-2
1884	3 teams			CIN U (16G – .239)		CHI U (15G – .239)			KC U (32G – .228)																
"	total		63	.233	.358	257	60	19	2	3	1.2	38		12			0	0	114	133	62	15	4.9	.799	2B-24, SS-22, OF-11, 3B-9, P-2
3 yrs.			107	.228	.331	426	97	21	4	5	1.2	60	4	18	11		0	0	155	258	107	21	4.9	.794	SS-61, 2B-26, OF-16, 3B-9, P-4

Jim McLaughlin

McLAUGHLIN, JAMES C.
B. 1860, Cleveland, Ohio   D. Nov. 16, 1895, Cleveland, Ohio   TL

| 1884 | 2 teams | | | WAS U (10G – .189) | | BAL AA (5G – .227) | | | | | | | | | | | | | | | | | | |
| " | total | | 15 | .203 | .305 | 59 | 12 | 6 | 4 | 0 | 0.0 | 6 | | 0 | | | 0 | 0 | 15 | 28 | 18 | 0 | 4.1 | .705 | SS-9, OF-3, P-3, 3B-1 |

Jim McLaughlin

McLAUGHLIN, JAMES ROBERT
B. Jan. 3, 1902, St. Louis, Mo.   D. Dec. 18, 1968, Mount Vernon, Ill.   BR TR 5'10½" 170 lbs.

| 1932 | STL | A | 1 | .000 | .000 | 1 | 0 | 0 | 0 | 0 | 0.0 | 0 | 1 | 0 | 0 | 0 | 0 | 0 | 0 | 0 | 0 | 0 | 0.0 | – | 3B-1 |

Kid McLaughlin

McLAUGHLIN, JAMES ANSON (Sunshine)
B. Apr. 12, 1888, Randolph, N. Y.   D. Nov. 13, 1934, Allegany, N. Y.   BL TR 5'8½" 158 lbs.

| 1914 | CIN | N | 3 | .000 | .000 | 2 | 0 | 0 | 0 | 0 | 0.0 | 0 | 0 | 0 | 1 | 0 | 1 | 0 | 1 | 0 | 0 | 0 | 0.3 | 1.000 | OF-2 |

Tom McLaughlin

McLAUGHLIN, THOMAS
B. Mar. 28, 1860, Louisville, Ky.   D. July 21, 1921, Louisville, Ky.   TR

1883	LOU	AA	42	.192	.226	146	28	1	2	0	0.0	16		5			0	0	105	72	27	8	4.9	.868	SS-19, OF-17, 1B-5, 3B-2, 2B-2
1884			98	.200	.272	335	67	11	5	1	0.3	41		22			0	0	126	346	57	36	5.4	.892	SS-93, 3B-4, 2B-2
1885			112	.212	.302	411	87	13	9	2	0.5	49		15			0	0	351	330	88	50	6.9	.886	2B-93, SS-19
1886	NY	AA	74	.136	.156	250	34	3	1	0	0.0	27		26			0	0	126	233	43	17	5.4	.893	SS-63, 2B-10, OF-1
1891	WAS	AA	14	.268	.317	41	11	0	1	0	0.0	9	3	7	6	3	0	0	25	36	9	6	5.0	.871	SS-14
5 yrs.			340	.192	.254	1183	227	28	18	3	0.3	142	3	75	6	3	0	0	733	1017	224	117	5.8	.887	SS-208, 2B-107, OF-18, 3B-6, 1B-5

Ralph McLaurin

McLAURIN, RALPH EDGAR
B. May 23, 1885, Kissimmee, Fla.   D. Feb. 11, 1943, McColl, S. C.

| 1908 | STL | N | 8 | .227 | .227 | 22 | 5 | 0 | 0 | 0 | 0.0 | 2 | 0 | 0 | | 0 | 2 | 0 | 14 | 0 | 2 | 0 | 2.0 | .875 | OF-6 |

Larry McLean

McLEAN, JOHN BANNERMAN
B. July 18, 1881, Cambridge, Mass.   D. Mar. 24, 1921, Boston, Mass.   BR TR 6'5" 228 lbs.

1901	BOS	A	9	.211	.263	19	4	1	0	0	0.0	4	2	0		1	4	2	38	2	0	2	4.4	1.000	1B-5
1903	CHI	N	1	.000	.000	4	0	0	0	0	0.0	0	1	0		0	0	0	7	1	1	0	9.0	.889	C-1
1904	STL	N	27	.167	.214	84	14	2	1	0	0.0	5	4	4		1	2	0	126	20	7	1	5.7	.954	C-24
1906	CIN	N	12	.200	.257	35	7	2	0	0	0.0	3	2	4		0	0	0	49	13	3	0	5.4	.954	C-12
1907			113	.289	.361	374	108	9	9	0	0.0	35	54	13		4	11	2	476	113	15	22	5.3	.975	C-89, 1B-13

Year	Team		Games	BA	SA	AB	H	2B	3B	HR	HR%	R	RBI	BB	SO	SB	Pinch Hit AB	H	PO	A	E	DP	TC/G	FA	G by Pos

Larry McLean *continued*

Year	Team		Games	BA	SA	AB	H	2B	3B	HR	HR%	R	RBI	BB	SO	SB	AB	H	PO	A	E	DP	TC/G	FA	G by Pos
1908			99	.217	.282	309	67	9	4	1	0.3	24	28	15		2	10	2	445	87	22	11	5.6	.960	C-69, 1B-19
1909			95	.256	.324	324	83	12	2	2	0.6	26	36	21		1	0	0	379	119	11	16	5.4	.978	C-95
1910			127	.298	.378	423	126	14	7	2	0.5	27	71	26	23	4	9	2	485	158	11	18	5.1	.983	C-119
1911			107	.287	.320	328	94	7	2	0	0.0	24	34	20	18	1	8	0	414	138	18	16	5.3	.968	C-98
1912			102	.243	.303	333	81	15	1	1	0.3	17	27	18	15	1	4	2	425	124	15	16	5.5	.973	C-98
1913	2 teams	STL N (48G – .270)				NY	N	(30G – .320)																	
"	total		78	.286	.344	227	65	13	0	0	0.0	10	21	10	13	1	8	2	155	64	4	8	2.9	.982	C-70
1914	NY N		79	.260	.299	154	40	6	0	0	0.0	8	14	4	9	4	4	0	211	42	7	8	3.3	.973	C-74
1915			13	.152	.152	33	5	0	0	0	0.0	0	4	0	1	0	1	0	47	18	1	0	5.1	.985	C-12
13 yrs.			862	.262	.323	2647	694	90	26	6	0.2	183	298	136	79	20	61	12	3257	899	115	118	5.0	.973	C-761, 1B-37

WORLD SERIES

| 1913 | NY N | | 5 | .500 | .500 | 12 | 6 | 0 | 0 | 0 | 0.0 | 0 | 2 | 0 | 0 | 0 | '1 | 0 | 12 | 4 | 0 | 0 | 3.2 | 1.000 | C-4 |

Mark McLemore

McLEMORE, MARK TREMELL
B. Oct. 4, 1964, San Diego, Calif.

BB TR 5'11" 175 lbs.

Year	Team		Games	BA	SA	AB	H	2B	3B	HR	HR%	R	RBI	BB	SO	SB	AB	H	PO	A	E	DP	TC/G	FA	G by Pos
1986	CAL A		5	.000	.000	4	0	0	0	0	0.0	1	0	0	0	0	0	0	3	10	0	1	2.6	1.000	2B-2
1987			138	.236	.300	433	102	13	3	3	0.7	61	41	48	72	25	1	0	293	363	17	98	4.9	.975	2B-132, SS-6, DH-3
1988			77	.240	.330	233	56	11	2	2	0.9	38	16	25	28	13	9	3	108	178	6	53	3.8	.979	2B-63, 3B-5, DH-1
1989			32	.243	.291	103	25	3	1	0	0.0	12	14	7	19	6	1	0	55	88	5	24	4.6	.966	2B-27, DH-1
4 yrs.			252	.237	.307	773	183	27	6	5	0.6	111	71	81	121	44	11	3	459	639	28	176	4.5	.975	2B-224, SS-6, DH-5, 3B-5

Jim McLeod

McLEOD, SOULE JAMES
B. Sept. 12, 1908, Jones, La. D. Aug. 3, 1981, Little Rock, Ark.

BR TR 6' 187 lbs.

Year	Team		Games	BA	SA	AB	H	2B	3B	HR	HR%	R	RBI	BB	SO	SB	AB	H	PO	A	E	DP	TC/G	FA	G by Pos
1930	WAS A		18	.265	.294	34	9	1	0	0	0.0	3	1	1	5	1	0	0	10	19	2	1	1.7	.935	3B-10, SS-7
1932			7	—	—	0	0	0	0	0	—	1	0	1	0	0	0	0	0	1	0	0	0.1	1.000	SS-1
1933	PHI N		67	.194	.228	232	45	6	1	0	0.0	20	15	12	25	1	0	0	60	120	17	8	2.9	.914	3B-67, SS-1
3 yrs.			92	.203	.237	266	54	7	1	0	0.0	24	16	14	30	2	0	0	70	140	19	9	2.5	.917	3B-77, SS-9

Ralph McLeod

McLEOD, RALPH ALTON
B. Oct. 19, 1916, West Quincy, Mass.

BL TL 6' 170 lbs.

Year	Team		Games	BA	SA	AB	H	2B	3B	HR	HR%	R	RBI	BB	SO	SB	AB	H	PO	A	E	DP	TC/G	FA	G by Pos
1938	BOS N		6	.286	.429	7	2	1	0	0	0.0	1	0	2	0	0	5	2	1	0	0	0	0.2	1.000	OF-1

Jack McMahon

McMAHON, JOHN HENRY
B. Oct. 15, 1869, Waterbury, Conn. D. Dec. 30, 1894, Bridgeport, Conn.

BR TL 5'10" 165 lbs.

Year	Team		Games	BA	SA	AB	H	2B	3B	HR	HR%	R	RBI	BB	SO	SB	AB	H	PO	A	E	DP	TC/G	FA	G by Pos
1892	NY N		40	.224	.374	147	33	5	7	1	0.7	21	24	10	9	3	0	0	331	16	11	14	9.0	.969	1B-36, C-5
1893			11	.333	.467	30	10	2	1	0	0.0	5	4	2	0	0	0	0	33	8	5	0	4.2	.891	C-11
2 yrs.			51	.243	.390	177	43	7	8	1	0.6	26	28	12	9	3	0	0	364	24	16	14	7.9	.960	1B-36, C-16

Frank McManus

McMANUS, FRANCIS E.
B. Sept. 21, 1875, Lawrence, Mass. D. Sept. 1, 1923, Syracuse, N. Y.

TR 5'10"

Year	Team		Games	BA	SA	AB	H	2B	3B	HR	HR%	R	RBI	BB	SO	SB	AB	H	PO	A	E	DP	TC/G	FA	G by Pos
1899	WAS N		7	.381	.429	21	8	1	0	0	0.0	3	2	2			3	0	15	12	2	1	4.1	.931	C-7
1903	BKN N		2	.000	.000	7	0	0	0	0	0.0	0	0	0			0	0	9	4	1	0	7.0	.929	C-2
1904	2 teams	DET A (1G – .000)				NY	A	(4G – .000)																	
"	total		5	.000	.000	7	0	0	0	0	0.0	0	0	0			0	0	9	0	1	0	2.0	.900	C-5
3 yrs.			14	.229	.257	35	8	1	0	0	0.0	3	2	2			3	0	33	16	4	1	3.8	.925	C-14

Jim McManus

McMANUS, JAMES MICHAEL
B. July 20, 1936, Brookline, Mass.

BL TL 6'4" 215 lbs.

Year	Team		Games	BA	SA	AB	H	2B	3B	HR	HR%	R	RBI	BB	SO	SB	AB	H	PO	A	E	DP	TC/G	FA	G by Pos
1960	KC A		5	.308	.538	13	4	0	0	1	7.7	3	2	1	2	0	2	0	29	1	0	1	6.0	1.000	1B-3

Marty McManus

McMANUS, MARTIN JOSEPH
B. Mar. 14, 1900, Chicago, Ill. D. Feb. 18, 1966, St. Louis, Mo.
Manager 1932-33.

BR TR 5'10½" 160 lbs.

Year	Team		Games	BA	SA	AB	H	2B	3B	HR	HR%	R	RBI	BB	SO	SB	AB	H	PO	A	E	DP	TC/G	FA	G by Pos
1920	STL A		1	.333	1.000	3	1	0	1	0	0.0	0	0	0	0	0	0	0	0	2	1	0	3.0	.667	3B-1
1921			121	.260	.367	412	107	19	8	3	0.7	49	64	27	30	5	0	0	290	312	32	54	5.2	.950	2B-96, 3B-13, 1B-10, SS-2
1922			154	.312	.459	606	189	34	11	11	1.8	88	109	38	41	9	0	0	404	468	33	103	5.9	.964	2B-153, 1B-1
1923			154	.309	.481	582	180	35	10	15	2.6	86	94	49	50	14	1	0	555	385	32	102	6.3	.967	2B-133, 1B-20
1924			123	.333	.441	442	147	23	5	5	1.1	71	80	54	40	13	4	1	324	365	20	67	5.8	.972	2B-118
1925			154	.288	.457	587	169	44	8	13	2.2	108	90	73	69	5	0	0	430	479	31	93	6.1	.967	2B-154, OF-1
1926			149	.284	.424	549	156	30	10	9	1.6	102	68	55	62	5	0	0	332	399	27	68	5.1	.964	3B-84, 2B-61, 1B-4
1927	DET A		108	.268	.431	369	99	19	7	9	2.4	60	69	34	38	8	9	4	245	263	17	54	4.9	.968	SS-39, 2B-35, 3B-22, 1B-6
1928			139	.288	.430	500	144	37	5	8	1.6	78	73	51	32	11	4	1	490	213	19	45	5.2	.974	3B-92, 1B-45, SS-1
1929			154	.280	.451	599	168	32	8	18	3.0	99	90	60	52	17	0	0	219	308	15	31	3.5	.972	3B-150, SS-9
1930			132	.320	.475	484	155	40	4	9	1.9	74	89	59	28	23	0	0	156	249	14	26	3.2	.967	3B-130, SS-3, 1B-1
1931	2 teams	DET A (107G – .271)				BOS	A	(17G – .290)																	
"	total		124	.274	.366	424	116	21	3	4	0.9	47	62	57	23	8	5	0	162	303	21	37	3.9	.957	3B-90, 2B-28, 1B-1
1932	BOS A		93	.235	.374	302	71	19	4	5	1.7	39	24	36	30	1	15	1	151	228	18	28	4.3	.955	2B-49, 3B-30, SS-2, 1B-1
1933			106	.284	.413	366	104	30	4	3	0.8	51	36	49	21	3	3	1	143	207	14	20	3.4	.962	3B-76, 2B-26, 1B-4
1934	BOS N		119	.276	.372	435	120	18	0	6	1.8	56	47	32	42	5	8	2	188	326	22	45	4.5	.959	2B-73, 3B-37
15 yrs.			1831	.289	.430	6660	1926	401	88	120	1.8	1008	996	674	558	127	49	10	4089	4507	316	773	4.9	.965	2B-926, 3B-725, 1B-93, SS-56, OF-1

Jimmy McMath

McMATH, JIMMY LEE
B. Aug. 10, 1949, Tuscaloosa, Ala.

BL TL 6'1½" 195 lbs.

Year	Team		Games	BA	SA	AB	H	2B	3B	HR	HR%	R	RBI	BB	SO	SB	AB	H	PO	A	E	DP	TC/G	FA	G by Pos
1968	CHI N		6	.143	.143	14	2	0	0	0	0.0	2	0	0	6	0	3	0	6	0	0	0	1.0	1.000	OF-3

George McMillan

McMILLAN, GEORGE A. (Reddy)
B. Evansville, Ind. Deceased.

5'8" 175 lbs.

Year	Team		Games	BA	SA	AB	H	2B	3B	HR	HR%	R	RBI	BB	SO	SB	AB	H	PO	A	E	DP	TC/G	FA	G by Pos
1890	NY N		10	.143	.143	35	5	0	0	0	0.0	4	1	7	4	1	0	0	11	1	3	0	1.5	.800	OF-10

Year	Team		Games	BA	SA	AB	H	2B	3B	HR	HR%	R	RBI	BB	SO	SB	Pinch Hit AB	Pinch Hit H	PO	A	E	DP	TC/G	FA	G by Pos

Norm McMillan

McMILLAN, NORMAN ALEXIS (Bub)
B. Oct. 5, 1895, Latta, S. C. D. Sept. 28, 1969, Marion, S. C.
BR TR 6' 175 lbs.

Year	Team		Games	BA	SA	AB	H	2B	3B	HR	HR%	R	RBI	BB	SO	SB	AB	H	PO	A	E	DP	TC/G	FA	G by Pos
1922	NY	A	33	.256	.321	78	20	1	2	0	0.0	7	11	6	10	4	1	0	37	1	3	0	1.2	.927	OF-23, 3B-5
1923	BOS	A	131	.253	.327	459	116	24	5	0	0.0	37	42	28	44	13	2	0	261	327	35	48	4.8	.944	3B-67, 2B-35, SS-28
1924	STL	A	76	.279	.358	201	56	12	2	0	0.0	25	27	12	17	6	8	4	132	122	11	19	3.5	.958	2B-37, 3B-17, SS-6, 1B-2
1928	CHI	N	49	.220	.293	123	27	2	2	1	0.8	11	12	13	19	0	9	1	44	84	5	10	2.7	.962	2B-19, 3B-18
1929			124	.271	.392	495	134	35	5	5	1.0	77	55	36	43	13	3	2	131	226	21	21	3.0	.944	3B-120
5 yrs.			413	.260	.352	1356	353	74	16	6	0.4	157	147	95	133	36	23	7	605	760	75	101	3.5	.948	SS-227, 2B-91, SS-34, OF-23, 1B-2

WORLD SERIES

Year	Team		Games	BA	SA	AB	H	2B	3B	HR	HR%	R	RBI	BB	SO	SB	AB	H	PO	A	E	DP	TC/G	FA	G by Pos
1922	NY	A	1	.000	.000	2	0	0	0	0	0.0	0	0	0	0	0	1	0	1	0	0	0	1.0	1.000	OF-1
1929	CHI	N	5	.100	.100	20	2	0	0	0	0.0	0	0	2	6	1	0	0	6	9	0	0	3.0	1.000	3B-5
2 yrs.			6	.091	.091	22	2	0	0	0	0.0	0	0	2	6	1	1	0	7	9	0	0	2.7	1.000	3B-5, OF-1

Roy McMillan

McMILLAN, ROY DAVID
B. July 17, 1930, Bonham, Tex.
Manager 1972, 1975.
BR TR 5'11" 170 lbs.

Year	Team		Games	BA	SA	AB	H	2B	3B	HR	HR%	R	RBI	BB	SO	SB	AB	H	PO	A	E	DP	TC/G	FA	G by Pos
1951	CIN	N	85	.211	.246	199	42	4	0	1	0.5	21	8	17	26	0	8	3	92	160	9	28	3.1	.966	SS-54, 3B-12, 2B-1
1952			154	.244	.350	540	132	32	2	7	1.3	60	57	45	81	4	0	0	297	495	24	101	5.3	.972	SS-154
1953			155	.233	.302	557	130	15	4	5	0.9	51	43	43	52	2	0	0	288	519	23	114	5.4	.972	SS-155
1954			154	.250	.313	588	147	21	4	2	0.3	86	42	47	54	4	0	0	290	495	34	129	5.4	.959	SS-154
1955			151	.268	.328	470	126	21	2	1	0.2	50	37	66	33	4	0	0	319	511	21	105	5.7	.975	SS-150
1956			150	.263	.344	479	126	16	7	3	0.6	51	62	76	54	4	0	0	253	418	16	86	4.5	.977	SS-151
1957			151	.272	.357	448	122	25	5	1	0.2	50	55	66	44	4	0	0	278	394	14	81	4.7	.980	SS-145
1958			145	.229	.298	393	90	18	3	1	0.3	48	25	47	33	5	0	0	163	205	10	50	4.8	.974	SS-73
1959			79	.264	.447	246	65	14	2	9	3.7	38	24	27	27	0	0	0	174	329	19	70	4.2	.964	SS-116, 2B-10
1960			124	.236	.351	399	94	12	2	10	2.5	42	42	35	40	2	0	0	257	496	19	110	5.0	.975	SS-154
1961	MIL	N	154	.220	.293	505	111	16	0	7	1.4	42	48	61	86	2	0	0	243	424	19	85	5.0	.972	SS-135
1962			137	.246	.350	468	115	13	0	12	2.6	66	41	60	53	2	2	1	143	283	9	60	4.4	.979	SS-94
1963			100	.250	.325	320	80	10	1	4	1.3	35	29	17	25	1	4	2							
1964	2 teams		MIL	N	(8G – .308)		NY	N	(113G – .211)															
"	total		121	.214	.253	392	84	8	2	1	0.3	31	27	14	18	4	4	0	224	360	15	66	5.0	.975	SS-119
1965	NY	N	157	.242	.292	528	128	19	2	1	0.2	44	42	24	60	1	4	0	248	477	27	80	4.8	.964	SS-153
1966			76	.214	.277	220	47	9	1	1	0.5	24	12	20	25	1	5	2	112	203	8	35	4.3	.975	SS-71
16 yrs.			2093	.243	.321	6752	1639	253	35	68	1.0	739	594	665	711	41	25	8	3722	6233	292	1311	4.9	.972	SS-2028, 3B-12, 2B-11

Tommy McMillan

McMILLAN, THOMAS ERWIN
B. Sept. 13, 1951, Richmond, Va.
BR TR 5'9" 165 lbs.

Year	Team		Games	BA	SA	AB	H	2B	3B	HR	HR%	R	RBI	BB	SO	SB	AB	H	PO	A	E	DP	TC/G	FA	G by Pos
1977	SEA	A	2	.000	.000	5	0	0	0	0	0.0	0	0	0	0	0	0	0	2	3	0	1	2.5	1.000	SS-2

Tommy McMillan

McMILLAN, THOMAS LAW (Rebel)
B. Apr. 18, 1888, Pittston, Pa. D. July 15, 1966, Orlando, Fla.
BR TR 5'5" 130 lbs.

Year	Team		Games	BA	SA	AB	H	2B	3B	HR	HR%	R	RBI	BB	SO	SB	AB	H	PO	A	E	DP	TC/G	FA	G by Pos
1908	BKN	N	43	.238	.259	147	35	3	0	0	0.0	9	3	9		5	0	0	82	86	22	10	4.4	.884	SS-29, OF-14
1909			108	.212	.257	373	79	15	1	0	0.0	18	24	20		11	1	0	197	314	48	33	5.2	.914	SS-105, 2B-2, 3B-1
1910	2 teams		BKN	N	(23G – .176)		CIN	N	(82G – .185)															
"	total		105	.183	.205	322	59	1	3	0	0.0	22	15	37	33	11	0	0	210	336	47	39	5.6	.921	SS-105
1912	NY	A	41	.228	.242	149	34	2	0	0	0.0	24	12	15		18	0	0	74	109	10	12	4.7	.948	SS-41
4 yrs.			297	.209	.238	991	207	21	4	0	0.0	73	54	81	33	45	1	0	563	845	127	94	5.2	.917	SS-280, OF-14, 2B-2, 3B-1

Hugh McMullen

McMULLEN, HUGH RAPHAEL
B. Dec. 16, 1901, La Cygne, Kans.
D. May 23, 1986, Whittier, Calif.
BR TR 6'1" 180 lbs.
BB 1928-29

Year	Team		Games	BA	SA	AB	H	2B	3B	HR	HR%	R	RBI	BB	SO	SB	AB	H	PO	A	E	DP	TC/G	FA	G by Pos
1925	NY	N	5	.133	.200	15	2	1	0	0	0.0	1	0	1	3	0	0	0	12	0	0	0	2.4	1.000	C-5
1926			57	.187	.209	91	17	2	0	0	0.0	5	6	2	18	1	1	0	107	22	8	3	2.4	.942	C-56
1928	WAS	A	1	.000	.000	1	0	0	0	0	0.0	0	0	0	1	0	1	0	0	0	0	0	0.0	–	
1929	CIN	N	1	.000	.000	1	0	0	0	0	0.0	0	0	0	0	0	0	0	2	0	0	0	2.0	1.000	C-1
4 yrs.			64	.176	.204	108	19	3	0	0	0.0	6	6	3	22	1	2	0	121	22	8	3	2.4	.947	C-62

Ken McMullen

McMULLEN, KENNETH LEE
B. June 1, 1942, Oxnard, Calif.
BR TR 6'3" 190 lbs.

Year	Team		Games	BA	SA	AB	H	2B	3B	HR	HR%	R	RBI	BB	SO	SB	AB	H	PO	A	E	DP	TC/G	FA	G by Pos
1962	LA	N	6	.273	.273	11	3	0	0	0	0.0	0	0	0	3	0	4	1	1	0	0	0	0.2	1.000	OF-2
1963			79	.236	.339	233	55	9	0	5	2.1	16	28	20	46	1	8	1	48	134	13	8	2.5	.933	3B-71, OF-1, 2B-1
1964			24	.209	.254	67	14	0	0	1	1.5	3	2	3	7	0	6	0	106	9	3	7	4.9	.975	1B-13, 3B-4, OF-3
1965	WAS	A	150	.263	.414	555	146	18	6	18	3.2	75	54	47	90	2	5	0	169	300	22	29	3.3	.955	3B-142, OF-8, 1B-1
1966			147	.233	.399	524	122	19	4	13	2.5	48	54	44	89	3	2	1	190	284	21	33	3.4	.958	3B-141, 1B-8, OF-1
1967			146	.245	.377	563	138	22	2	16	2.8	73	67	46	84	5	0	0	153	348	18	38	3.6	.965	3B-145
1968			151	.248	.382	557	138	11	2	20	3.6	66	62	63	66	1	0	0	194	302	19	26	3.4	.963	3B-145, SS-11
1969			158	.272	.425	562	153	25	2	19	3.4	83	87	70	103	4	5	1	185	347	13	35	3.4	.976	3B-158
1970	2 teams		WAS	A	(15G – .203)		CAL	A	(124G – .232)															
"	total		139	.229	.351	481	110	11	3	14	2.9	55	64	64	91	1	3	1	154	306	19	39	3.4	.960	3B-137
1971	CAL	A	160	.250	.395	593	148	19	2	21	3.5	63	68	53	74	1	1	0	137	344	17	27	3.1	.966	3B-158
1972			137	.269	.369	472	127	18	1	9	1.9	36	34	48	59	2	0	0	89	267	11	26	2.7	.970	3B-137
1973	LA	N	42	.247	.482	85	21	5	0	5	5.9	6	18	6	13	0	35	9	5	54	5	1	1.5	.922	3B-24
1974			44	.250	.417	60	15	1	0	3	5.0	5	12	2	12	0	35	9	10	14	0	1	0.5	1.000	3B-7, 2B-3
1975			39	.239	.435	46	11	1	1	2	4.3	4	14	7	12	0	25	6	26	12	0	1	1.0	1.000	3B-11, 1B-3
1976	OAK	A	98	.220	.355	186	41	6	2	5	2.7	20	23	22	33	1	31	9	222	39	2	20	2.7	.992	3B-35, 1B-26, DH-23, OF-5, 2B-1
1977	MIL	A	63	.228	.404	136	31	7	1	5	3.7	15	19	15	33	1	24	5	80	15	2	10	1.5	.979	DH-29, 1B-11, 3B-7
16 yrs.			1583	.248	.383	5131	1273	172	26	156	3.0	568	606	510	815	20	176	41	1769	2775	165	302	3.0	.965	3B-1318, 1B-62, DH-52, OF-20, SS-11, 2B-5

LEAGUE CHAMPIONSHIP SERIES

Year	Team		Games	BA	SA	AB	H	2B	3B	HR	HR%	R	RBI	BB	SO	SB	AB	H	PO	A	E	DP	TC/G	FA	G by Pos
1974	LA	N	1	.000	.000	1	0	0	0	0	0.0	0	0	0	1	0	1	0	0	0	0	0	0.0	–	

Year	Team	Games	BA	SA	AB	H	2B	3B	HR	HR%	R	RBI	BB	SO	SB	Pinch Hit AB	Pinch Hit H	PO	A	E	DP	TC/G	FA	G by Pos

Fred McMullin

McMULLIN, FREDERICK WILLIAM
B. Oct. 13, 1891, Scammon, Kans. D. Nov. 21, 1952, Los Angeles, Calif.
BR TR 5'11" 170 lbs.

Year	Team	Games	BA	SA	AB	H	2B	3B	HR	HR%	R	RBI	BB	SO	SB	PH AB	PH H	PO	A	E	DP	TC/G	FA	G by Pos
1914	DET A	1	.000	.000	1	0	0	0	0	0.0	0	0	0	1	0	0	0	1	1	1	0	3.0	.667	SS-1
1916	CHI A	68	.257	.273	187	48	3	0	0	0.0	8	10	19	30	9	2	1	78	116	10	11	3.0	.951	3B-63, SS-2, 2B-1
1917		59	.237	.258	194	46	2	1	0	0.0	35	12	27	17	9	5	1	63	92	15	4	2.9	.912	3B-52, SS-2
1918		70	.277	.319	235	65	7	0	1	0.4	32	16	25	26	7	0	0	74	151	14	9	3.4	.941	3B-69, 2B-1
1919		60	.294	.388	170	50	8	4	0	0.0	31	19	11	18	4	8	4	54	96	11	11	2.7	.932	3B-46, 2B-5
1920		46	.197	.268	127	25	1	4	0	0.0	14	13	9	13	1	11	1	31	56	3	5	2.0	.967	3B-29, 2B-3, SS-1
6 yrs.		304	.256	.302	914	234	21	9	1	0.1	120	70	91	105	30	26	7	301	512	54	40	2.9	.938	3B-259, 2B-10, SS-6

WORLD SERIES

1917	CHI A	6	.125	.167	24	3	1	0	0	0.0	1	2	1	6	0	0	0	2	14	0	2	2.7	1.000	3B-6
1919		2	.500	.500	2	1	0	0	0	0.0	0	0	0	0	0	2	1	0	0	0	0	0.0	—	
2 yrs.		8	.154	.192	26	4	1	0	0	0.0	1	2	1	6	0	2	1	2	14	0	2	2.0	1.000	3B-6

Carl McNabb

McNABB, CARL MAC (Skinny)
B. Jan. 25, 1917, Stevenson, Ala.
BR TR 5'9" 155 lbs.

Year	Team	Games	BA	SA	AB	H	2B	3B	HR	HR%	R	RBI	BB	SO	SB	PH AB	PH H	PO	A	E	DP	TC/G	FA	G by Pos
1945	DET A	1	.000	.000	1	0	0	0	0	0.0	0	0	0	1	0	1	0	0	0	0	0	0.0	—	

Eric McNair

McNAIR, DONALD ERIC (Boob)
B. Apr. 12, 1909, Meridian, Miss. D. Mar. 11, 1949, Meridian, Miss.
BR TR 5'8" 160 lbs.

Year	Team	Games	BA	SA	AB	H	2B	3B	HR	HR%	R	RBI	BB	SO	SB	PH AB	PH H	PO	A	E	DP	TC/G	FA	G by Pos
1929	PHI A	4	.500	.625	8	4	1	0	0	0.0	2	3	0	1	0	0	0	6	5	0	0	2.8	1.000	SS-4
1930		78	.266	.333	237	63	12	2	0	0.0	27	34	9	19	5	7	1	100	110	17	13	2.9	.925	SS-31, 3B-29, 2B-5, OF-1
1931		79	.271	.368	280	76	10	1	5	1.8	41	33	11	19	1	3	1	97	155	19	36	3.4	.930	3B-47, 2B-16, SS-13
1932		135	.285	.478	554	158	47	3	18	3.2	87	95	28	29	8	2	0	242	391	31	89	4.9	.953	SS-133
1933		89	.261	.403	310	81	15	4	7	2.3	57	48	15	32	2	16	5	169	216	17	39	4.5	.958	SS-46, 2B-28
1934		151	.280	.412	599	168	20	4	17	2.8	80	82	35	42	7	0	0	305	489	41	109	5.5	.951	SS-151
1935		137	.270	.342	526	142	22	2	4	0.8	55	57	35	33	3	3	0	270	364	28	80	4.8	.958	SS-121, 3B-11, 1B-2
1936	BOS A	128	.285	.391	494	141	36	2	4	0.8	68	74	27	34	3	3	0	272	346	23	67	5.0	.964	SS-84, 2B-35, 3B-11
1937		126	.292	.453	455	133	29	4	12	2.6	60	76	30	33	10	9	2	256	344	27	72	5.0	.957	2B-106, SS-9, 3B-4, 1B-1
1938		46	.156	.188	96	15	1	1	0	0.0	9	7	3	6	0	14	2	43	69	10	15	2.7	.918	SS-15, 2B-14, 3B-3
1939	CHI A	129	.324	.426	479	155	18	5	7	1.5	62	82	38	41	17	1	0	151	299	25	43	3.7	.947	3B-89, 2B-19, SS-9
1940		66	.227	.371	251	57	13	1	7	2.8	26	31	12	26	1	0	0	130	171	17	27	4.8	.947	2B-65, 3B-1
1941	DET A	23	.186	.203	59	11	1	0	0	0.0	5	3	4	4	1	8	1	14	24	2	1	1.7	.950	3B-11, SS-3
1942 2 teams	DET A (26G – .162)				PHI A	(34G – .243)																		
" total		60	.211	.251	171	36	4	0	1	0.6	13	8	14	10	1	8	1	77	101	15	16	3.2	.922	SS-50, 2B-1
14 yrs.		1251	.274	.392	4519	1240	229	29	82	1.8	592	633	261	328	59	72	15	2132	3084	272	607	4.4	.950	SS-669, 2B-289, 3B-220, 1B-3, OF-1

WORLD SERIES

1930	PHI A	1	.000	.000	1	0	0	0	0	0.0	0	0	0	1	0	1	0	0	0	0	0	0.0	—	
1931		2	.000	.000	2	0	0	0	0	0.0	0	0	1	0	0	1	0	1	1	0	0	1.0	1.000	2B-1
2 yrs.		3	.000	.000	3	0	0	0	0	0.0	1	0	1	0	0	2	0	1	1	0	0	0.7	1.000	2B-1

Mike McNally

McNALLY, MICHAEL JOSEPH
B. Sept. 9, 1892, Minooka, Pa. D. May 29, 1965, Bethlehem, Pa.
BR TR 5'11" 150 lbs.

Year	Team	Games	BA	SA	AB	H	2B	3B	HR	HR%	R	RBI	BB	SO	SB	PH AB	PH H	PO	A	E	DP	TC/G	FA	G by Pos
1915	BOS A	23	.151	.189	53	8	0	1	0	0.0	7	0	3	7	0	0	0	20	28	5	4	2.3	.906	3B-18, 2B-5
1916		87	.170	.170	135	23	0	0	0	0.0	28	9	10	19	9	2	0	63	112	11	10	2.1	.941	2B-35, 3B-14, SS-7, OF-1
1917		42	.300	.320	50	15	1	0	0	0.0	9	2	6	3	3	1	1	21	48	3	3	1.7	.958	3B-14, SS-9, 2B-6
1919		33	.262	.357	42	11	4	0	0	0.0	10	6	1	2	4	1	0	21	42	3	3	2.0	.955	SS-11, 3B-11, 2B-3
1920		93	.256	.279	312	80	5	1	0	0.0	42	23	31	24	13	1	1	230	246	32	40	5.5	.937	2B-76, SS-8, 1B-6
1921	NY A	71	.260	.312	215	56	4	2	1	0.5	36	24	14	15	5	1	0	80	169	9	12	3.6	.965	3B-48, 2B-16
1922		52	.252	.294	143	36	2	2	0	0.0	20	18	16	14	2	0	0	61	96	4	7	3.1	.975	3B-32, 2B-9, SS-4, 1B-1
1923		30	.211	.211	38	8	0	0	0	0.0	5	1	3	4	2	3	0	10	27	2	1	1.3	.949	SS-13, 3B-7, 2B-5
1924		49	.246	.246	69	17	0	0	0	0.0	11	2	7	5	1	2	1	48	62	2	7	2.3	.982	2B-25, 3B-13, SS-6
1925	WAS A	12	.143	.143	21	3	0	0	0	0.0	2	2	1	0	0	1	0	11	10	2	1	1.9	.913	3B-7, SS-2, 2B-1
10 yrs.		492	.238	.267	1078	257	16	6	1	0.1	169	85	92	97	39	11	3	565	840	73	91	3.0	.951	2B-181, 3B-164, SS-60, 1B-7, OF-1

WORLD SERIES

1916	BOS A	1	—	—	0	0	0	0	0	—	1	0	0	0	0	0	0	0	0	0	0	0.0	—	
1921	NY A	7	.200	.250	20	4	1	0	0	0.0	3	1	1	3	2	0	0	5	10	3	2	2.6	.833	3B-7
1922		1	—	—	0	0	0	0	0	0.0	0	0	0	0	0	0	0	1	1	0	0	2.0	1.000	2B-1
3 yrs.		9	.200	.250	20	4	1	0	0	0.0	4	1	1	3	2	0	0	6	11	3	2	2.2	.850	3B-7, 2B-1

Bob McNamara

McNAMARA, ROBERT MAXEY
B. Sept. 19, 1916, Denver, Colo.
BR TR 5'10" 170 lbs.

Year	Team	Games	BA	SA	AB	H	2B	3B	HR	HR%	R	RBI	BB	SO	SB	PH AB	PH H	PO	A	E	DP	TC/G	FA	G by Pos
1939	PHI A	9	.222	.333	9	2	1	0	0	0.0	0	3	1	1	0	0	0	5	5	0	0	1.1	1.000	3B-5, SS-2, 2B-1, 1B-1

Dinny McNamara

McNAMARA, JOHN RAYMOND
B. Sept. 16, 1905, Lexington, Mass. D. Dec. 20, 1963, Arlington, Mass.
BL TR 5'9" 165 lbs.

Year	Team	Games	BA	SA	AB	H	2B	3B	HR	HR%	R	RBI	BB	SO	SB	PH AB	PH H	PO	A	E	DP	TC/G	FA	G by Pos
1927	BOS N	11	.000	.000	9	0	0	0	0	0.0	3	0	0	3	0	0	0	10	0	0	0	0.9	1.000	OF-3
1928		9	.250	.250	4	1	0	0	0	0.0	2	0	0	1	0	1	0	7	0	0	0	0.8	1.000	OF-3
2 yrs.		20	.077	.077	13	1	0	0	0	0.0	5	0	0	4	0	1	0	17	0	0	0	0.9	1.000	OF-6

George McNamara

McNAMARA, GEORGE FRANCIS
B. Jan. 11, 1903, Chicago, Ill.
BL TR 6' 175 lbs.

Year	Team	Games	BA	SA	AB	H	2B	3B	HR	HR%	R	RBI	BB	SO	SB	PH AB	PH H	PO	A	E	DP	TC/G	FA	G by Pos
1922	WAS A	3	.273	.273	11	3	0	0	0	0.0	3	1	1	1	2	0	0	3	0	0	0	1.0	1.000	OF-3

Tom McNamara

McNAMARA, THOMAS HENRY
B. Nov. 5, 1895, Roxbury, Mass. D. May 5, 1974, Danvers, Mass.
BR TR 6'2" 200 lbs.

Year	Team	Games	BA	SA	AB	H	2B	3B	HR	HR%	R	RBI	BB	SO	SB	PH AB	PH H	PO	A	E	DP	TC/G	FA	G by Pos
1922	PIT N	1	.000	.000	1	0	0	0	0	0.0	0	0	0	0	0	1	0	0	0	0	0	0.0	—	

Year	Team	Games	BA	SA	AB	H	2B	3B	HR	HR%	R	RBI	BB	SO	SB	Pinch Hit AB	H	PO	A	E	DP	TC/G	FA	G by Pos

Rusty McNealy

McNEALY, ROBERT LEE
B. Aug. 12, 1958, Sacramento, Calif.
BL TL 5'8" 160 lbs.

Year	Team	Games	BA	SA	AB	H	2B	3B	HR	HR%	R	RBI	BB	SO	SB	AB	H	PO	A	E	DP	TC/G	FA	G by Pos
1983	OAK A	15	.000	.000	4	0	0	0	0	0.0	5	0	0	0	0	0	0	6	0	0	0	0.4	1.000	DH-7, OF-5

Earl McNeely

McNEELY, GEORGE EARL
B. May 12, 1898, Sacramento, Calif.   D. July 16, 1971, Sacramento, Calif.
BR TR 5'9" 155 lbs.

Year	Team	Games	BA	SA	AB	H	2B	3B	HR	HR%	R	RBI	BB	SO	SB	AB	H	PO	A	E	DP	TC/G	FA	G by Pos
1924	WAS A	43	.330	.425	179	59	5	6	0	0.0	31	15	5	21	3	1	0	105	3	3	1	2.6	.973	OF-42
1925		122	.286	.356	385	110	14	2	3	0.8	76	37	48	54	14	1	0	262	13	7	3	2.3	.975	OF-112, 1B-1
1926		124	.303	.403	442	134	20	12	0	0.0	84	48	44	28	18	2	0	274	9	9	3	2.4	.969	OF-120
1927		73	.276	.373	185	51	10	4	0	0.0	40	16	11	13	11	11	2	118	5	4	1	1.7	.969	OF-47, 1B-4
1928	STL A	127	.236	.319	496	117	27	7	0	0.0	66	44	37	39	8	7	2	229	19	4	2	2.0	.984	OF-120
1929		69	.243	.300	230	56	8	1	1	0.4	27	18	7	13	2	6	0	96	4	2	0	1.5	.980	OF-62
1930		76	.272	.362	235	64	19	1	0	0.0	33	20	22	14	8	3	1	302	18	8	30	4.3	.976	OF-38, 1B-27
1931		49	.225	.265	102	23	4	0	0	0.0	12	15	9	5	4	4	0	59	3	2	1	1.3	.969	OF-36
8 yrs.		683	.272	.354	2254	614	107	33	4	0.2	369	213	183	187	68	35	5	1445	74	39	41	2.3	.975	OF-577, 1B-32

WORLD SERIES

Year	Team	Games	BA	SA	AB	H	2B	3B	HR	HR%	R	RBI	BB	SO	SB	AB	H	PO	A	E	DP	TC/G	FA	G by Pos
1924	WAS A	7	.222	.333	27	6	3	0	0	0.0	4	1	4	4	1	0	0	8	0	1	0	1.3	.889	OF-6
1925		4	—	—	0	0	0	0	0	—	2	0	0	0	1	0	0	3	0	0	0	0.8	1.000	OF-2
2 yrs.		11	.222	.333	27	6	3	0	0	0.0	6	1	4	4	2	0	0	11	0	1	0	1.1	.917	OF-8

Norm McNeil

McNEIL, NORMAN FRANCIS
B. Oct. 22, 1892, Chicago, Ill.   D. Apr. 11, 1942, Buffalo, N. Y.
BR TR 5'11" 180 lbs.

Year	Team	Games	BA	SA	AB	H	2B	3B	HR	HR%	R	RBI	BB	SO	SB	AB	H	PO	A	E	DP	TC/G	FA	G by Pos
1919	BOS A	5	.333	.333	9	3	0	0	0	0.0	1	0	1	0	0	0	0	8	1	2	0	2.2	.818	C-5

Jerry McNertney

McNERTNEY, GERALD EDWARD
B. Aug. 7, 1936, Boone, Iowa
BR TR 6' 180 lbs.

Year	Team	Games	BA	SA	AB	H	2B	3B	HR	HR%	R	RBI	BB	SO	SB	AB	H	PO	A	E	DP	TC/G	FA	G by Pos
1964	CHI A	73	.215	.290	186	40	5	0	3	1.6	16	23	19	24	0	6	1	360	30	5	5	5.4	.987	C-69
1966		44	.220	.220	59	13	0	0	0	0.0	3	1	7	6	1	5	0	112	14	4	0	3.0	.969	C-37
1967		56	.228	.350	123	28	6	0	3	2.4	8	13	6	14	0	1	1	229	41	1	4	4.8	.996	C-52
1968		74	.219	.308	169	37	4	1	3	1.8	18	18	18	29	1	11	3	301	39	5	9	4.7	.986	C-64, 1B-1
1969	SEA A	128	.241	.349	410	99	18	1	8	2.0	39	55	29	63	1	7	3	697	67	9	13	6.0	.988	C-122
1970	MIL A	111	.243	.348	296	72	11	1	6	2.0	27	22	22	33	1	18	4	461	53	8	6	4.7	.985	C-94, 1B-13
1971	STL N	56	.289	.445	128	37	4	2	4	3.1	15	22	12	14	0	16	5	192	7	3	1	3.6	.985	C-36
1972		39	.208	.313	48	10	3	1	0	0.0	3	9	6	16	0	28	4	50	4	1	0	1.4	.982	C-10
1973	PIT N	9	.250	.250	4	1	0	0	0	0.0	0	0	0	0	0	0	0	11	0	0	0	1.2	1.000	C-9
9 yrs.		590	.237	.338	1423	337	51	6	27	1.9	129	163	119	199	3	92	20	2413	255	36	38	4.6	.987	C-493, 1B-14

Bill McNulty

McNULTY, WILLIAM FRANCIS
B. Aug. 29, 1946, Sacramento, Calif.
BR TR 6'4" 205 lbs.

Year	Team	Games	BA	SA	AB	H	2B	3B	HR	HR%	R	RBI	BB	SO	SB	AB	H	PO	A	E	DP	TC/G	FA	G by Pos
1969	OAK A	5	.000	.000	17	0	0	0	0	0.0	0	0	0	10	0	0	0	9	2	0	0	2.2	1.000	OF-5
1972		4	.100	.100	10	1	0	0	0	0.0	0	0	2	1	0	1	0	2	2	1	0	1.3	.800	3B-3
2 yrs.		9	.037	.037	27	1	0	0	0	0.0	0	0	2	11	0	1	0	11	4	1	0	1.8	.938	OF-5, 3B-3

Pat McNulty

McNULTY, PATRICK HOWARD
B. Feb. 27, 1899, Cleveland, Ohio   D. May 4, 1963, Hollywood, Calif.
BL TR 5'11" 160 lbs.

Year	Team	Games	BA	SA	AB	H	2B	3B	HR	HR%	R	RBI	BB	SO	SB	AB	H	PO	A	E	DP	TC/G	FA	G by Pos
1922	CLE A	22	.271	.339	59	16	2	1	0	0.0	10	5	9	5	4	0	0	43	0	2	0	2.0	.956	OF-22
1924		101	.268	.347	291	78	13	5	0	0.0	46	26	33	22	10	15	3	137	9	6	2	1.5	.961	OF-75
1925		118	.314	.421	373	117	18	2	6	1.6	70	43	47	23	7	5	3	206	16	8	2	1.9	.965	OF-111
1926		48	.250	.321	56	14	2	1	0	0.0	3	6	5	9	0	31	7	8	2	1	0	0.2	.909	OF-9
1927		19	.317	.341	41	13	1	0	0	0.0	3	4	4	3	1	5	2	28	1	3	1	1.7	.906	OF-12
5 yrs.		308	.290	.378	820	238	36	9	6	0.7	132	84	98	62	22	56	15	422	28	20	5	1.5	.957	OF-229

Bid McPhee

McPHEE, JOHN ALEXANDER
B. Nov. 1, 1859, Massena, N. Y.   D. Jan. 3, 1943, San Diego, Calif.
Manager 1901-02.
BR TR 5'8" 152 lbs.

Year	Team	Games	BA	SA	AB	H	2B	3B	HR	HR%	R	RBI	BB	SO	SB	AB	H	PO	A	E	DP	TC/G	FA	G by Pos
1882	CIN AA	78	.228	.309	311	71	8	7	1	0.3	43		11			0	0	274	207	42	36	6.7	.920	2B-78
1883		96	.245	.343	367	90	10	10	2	0.5	61		18			0	0	314	277	46	48	6.6	.928	2B-96
1884		112	.278	.360	450	125	8	7	5	1.1	107		27			0	0	415	365	64	74	7.5	.924	2B-112
1885		110	.265	.311	431	114	12	4	0	0.0	78		19			0	0	339	354	47	57	6.7	.936	2B-110
1886		140	.266	.388	560	149	23	12	7	1.3	139		59			0	0	529	464	65	90	7.6	.939	2B-140
1887		129	.289	.407	540	156	20	19	2	0.4	137		55		95	0	0	442	434	72	76	7.3	.924	2B-129
1888		111	.240	.336	458	110	12	10	4	0.9	88	51	43		54	0	0	369	365	47	65	7.0	.940	2B-109, OF-1, 3B-1
1889		135	.269	.368	543	146	25	7	5	0.9	109	57	60	29	63	0	0	430	450	52	85	6.9	.944	2B-135, 3B-1
1890	CIN N	132	.256	.386	528	135	16	22	3	0.6	125	39	82	26	55	0	0	404	431	51	62	6.7	.942	2B-132
1891		138	.256	.345	562	144	14	16	6	1.1	107	38	74	35	33	0	0	389	492	42	72	6.7	.954	2B-138
1892		144	.274	.370	573	157	19	12	4	0.7	111	60	84	48	44	0	0	451	471	51	86	6.8	.948	2B-144
1893		127	.281	.379	491	138	17	11	3	0.6	101	68	94	20	25	0	0	396	455	41	101	7.0	.954	2B-126
1894		128	.320	.432	481	154	21	9	5	1.0	113	88	90	23	33	0	0	389	446	49	72	6.9	.945	2B-126
1895		115	.299	.417	432	129	24	12	1	0.2	107	75	73	30	30	0	0	355	366	34	57	6.6	.955	2B-115
1896		117	.305	.386	433	132	18	7	1	0.2	81	87	51	18	48	0	0	297	357	15	56	5.7	.978	2B-117
1897		81	.301	.408	282	85	13	7	1	0.4	45	39	35		9	0	0	209	267	17	34	6.1	.966	2B-81
1898		133	.249	.346	486	121	26	9	1	0.2	72	60	66		21	0	0	302	396	34	74	5.5	.954	2B-130, OF-3
1899		111	.279	.370	373	104	17	7	1	0.3	60	65	40		18	5	3	245	312	26	41	5.3	.955	2B-106
18 yrs.		2137	.272	.373	8301	2260	303	188	52	0.6	1684	727	981	229	528	5	3	6549	6909	795	1186	6.7	.944	2B-2125, OF-4, 3B-2

Marty McQuaid

McQUAID, MORTIMER MARTIN
B. June 28, 1861, Chicago, Ill.   D. Mar. 5, 1928, Chicago, Ill.

Year	Team	Games	BA	SA	AB	H	2B	3B	HR	HR%	R	RBI	BB	SO	SB	AB	H	PO	A	E	DP	TC/G	FA	G by Pos
1891	STL AA	4	.364	.545	11	4	2	0	0	0.0	1	1	0	1	0	0	0	6	6	0	1	3.0	1.000	2B-3, OF-1
1898	WAS N	1	.000	.000	4	0	0	0	0	0.0	0	0	1		0	0	0	1	0	2	0	3.0	.333	OF-1
2 yrs.		5	.267	.400	15	4	2	0	0	0.0	1	1	1	1	0	0	0	7	6	2	1	3.0	.867	2B-3, OF-2

Year	Team		Games	BA	SA	AB	H	2B	3B	HR	HR%	R	RBI	BB	SO	SB	Pinch Hit AB	Pinch Hit H	PO	A	E	DP	TC/G	FA	G by Pos

Jerry McQuaig

McQUAIG, GERALD JOSEPH
B. Jan. 31, 1912, Douglas, Ga.

BR TR 5'11" 183 lbs.

Year	Team		Games	BA	SA	AB	H	2B	3B	HR	HR%	R	RBI	BB	SO	SB	AB	H	PO	A	E	DP	TC/G	FA	G by Pos
1934	PHI	A	7	.063	.063	16	1	0	0	0	0.0	2	1	2	4	0	0	0	8	0	1	0	1.3	.889	OF-6

Mox McQuery

McQUERY, WILLIAM THOMAS
B. June 28, 1861, Garrard County, Ky.   D. June 12, 1900, Covington, Ky.

6'4"

Year	Team		Games	BA	SA	AB	H	2B	3B	HR	HR%	R	RBI	BB	SO	SB	AB	H	PO	A	E	DP	TC/G	FA	G by Pos
1884	CIN	U	35	.280	.364	132	37	5	0	2	1.5	31		8			0	0	340	8	8	9	10.2	.978	1B-35
1885	DET	N	70	.273	.388	278	76	15	4	3	1.1	34	30	8	29		0	0	714	29	18	33	10.9	.976	1B-69, OF-1
1886	KC	N	122	.247	.352	449	111	27	4	4	0.9	62	38	36	44		0	0	1295	50	43	61	11.4	.969	1B-122
1890	SYR	AA	122	.308	.384	461	142	17	6	2	0.4	64	53			26	0	0	1146	45	34	63	10.0	.972	1B-122
1891	WAS	AA	68	.241	.330	261	63	9	4	2	0.8	40	37	18	19	3	0	0	701	30	17	39	11.0	.977	1B-68
5 yrs.			417	.271	.365	1581	429	73	18	13	0.8	231	105	123	92	29	0	0	4196	162	120	205	10.7	.973	1B-416, OF-1

Glenn McQuillen

McQUILLEN, GLENN RICHARD (Red)
B. Apr. 19, 1915, Strasburg, Va.

BR TR 6' 198 lbs.

Year	Team		Games	BA	SA	AB	H	2B	3B	HR	HR%	R	RBI	BB	SO	SB	AB	H	PO	A	E	DP	TC/G	FA	G by Pos
1938	STL	A	43	.284	.319	116	33	4	0	0	0.0	14	13	4	12	0	12	3	66	0	2	0	1.6	.971	OF-30
1941			7	.333	.524	21	7	2	1	0	0.0	4	3	1	2	0	1	0	14	0	1	0	2.1	.933	OF-6
1942			100	.283	.425	339	96	15	12	3	0.9	40	47	10	17	1	23	4	156	2	5	0	1.6	.969	OF-77
1946			59	.241	.313	166	40	3	3	1	0.6	24	12	19	18	0	9	1	77	8	2	0	1.5	.977	OF-48
1947			1	.000	.000	1	0	0	0	0	0.0	0	0	0	0	0	1	0	0	0	0	0	0.0		
5 yrs.			210	.274	.379	643	176	24	16	4	0.6	82	75	34	49	1	46	8	313	10	10	0	1.6	.970	OF-161

George McQuinn

McQUINN, GEORGE HARTLEY
B. May 29, 1910, Arlington, Va.   D. June 8, 1989, Gardenville, Md.

BL TL 5'11" 165 lbs.

Year	Team		Games	BA	SA	AB	H	2B	3B	HR	HR%	R	RBI	BB	SO	SB	AB	H	PO	A	E	DP	TC/G	FA	G by Pos
1936	CIN	N	38	.201	.284	134	27	3	4	0	0.0	5	13	10	22	0	0	0	336	27	3	30	9.6	.992	1B-38
1938	STL	A	148	.324	.477	602	195	42	7	12	2.0	100	82	58	49	4	0	0	1207	90	10	134	8.8	.992	1B-148
1939			154	.316	.515	617	195	37	13	20	3.2	101	94	65	42	6	0	0	1377	110	11	122	9.8	.993	1B-154
1940			151	.279	.460	594	166	39	10	16	2.7	78	84	57	58	3	1	0	1436	124	13	157	10.4	.992	1B-150
1941			130	.297	.479	495	147	28	4	18	3.6	93	80	74	30	5	4	0	1138	109	6	109	9.6	.995	1B-125
1942			145	.262	.403	554	145	32	5	12	2.2	86	78	60	77	1	1	0	1384	105	13	116	10.4	.991	1B-144
1943			125	.243	.374	449	109	19	2	12	2.7	53	74	56	65	4	3	0	1072	86	9	88	9.3	.992	1B-122
1944			146	.250	.376	516	129	26	3	11	2.1	83	72	85	74	4	0	0	1332	72	9	116	9.7	.994	1B-146
1945			139	.277	.398	483	134	31	3	7	1.4	69	61	65	51	1	4	0	1143	105	11	87	9.1	.991	1B-136
1946	PHI	A	136	.225	.316	484	109	23	6	3	0.6	47	35	64	62	1	2	1	1098	99	15	107	8.9	.988	1B-134
1947	NY	A	144	.304	.437	517	157	24	4	13	2.5	84	80	78	66	0	2	1	1198	93	8	120	9.0	.994	1B-142
1948			94	.248	.421	302	75	11	4	11	3.6	33	41	40	38	0	7	1	693	48	5	79	7.9	.993	1B-90
12 yrs.			1550	.276	.424	5747	1588	315	64	135	2.3	832	794	712	634	32	24	7	13414	1074	113	1265	9.4	.992	1B-1529

WORLD SERIES

Year	Team		Games	BA	SA	AB	H	2B	3B	HR	HR%	R	RBI	BB	SO	SB	AB	H	PO	A	E	DP	TC/G	FA	G by Pos
1944	STL	A	6	.438	.750	16	7	2	0	1	6.3	2	5	7	2	0	0	0	50	2	0	3	8.7	1.000	1B-6
1947	NY	A	7	.130	.130	23	3	0	0	0	0.0	3	1	5	8	0	0	0	48	4	1	3	7.6	.981	1B-7
2 yrs.			13	.256	.385	39	10	2	0	1	2.6	5	6	12	10	0	0	0	98	6	1	6	8.1	.990	1B-13

Hal McRae

McRAE, HAROLD ABRAHAM
B. July 10, 1945, Avon Park, Fla.

BR TR 5'11" 180 lbs.

Year	Team		Games	BA	SA	AB	H	2B	3B	HR	HR%	R	RBI	BB	SO	SB	AB	H	PO	A	E	DP	TC/G	FA	G by Pos
1968	CIN	N	17	.196	.216	51	10	1	0	0	0.0	1	2	4	14	1	0	0	33	30	5	8	4.0	.926	2B-16
1970			70	.248	.442	165	41	6	1	8	4.8	18	23	15	23	0	19	5	53	7	1	1	0.9	.984	OF-46, 3B-6, 2B-1
1971			99	.264	.427	337	89	24	2	9	2.7	39	34	11	35	3	13	2	167	6	6	1	1.8	.966	OF-91
1972			61	.278	.474	97	27	4	0	5	5.2	9	26	2	14	0	40	10	16	14	6	1	0.6	.833	OF-12, 3B-11
1973	KC	A	106	.234	.385	338	79	18	3	9	2.7	36	50	34	38	2	10	2	101	6	5	2	1.1	.955	OF-64, DH-37, 3B-2
1974			148	.310	.475	539	167	36	4	15	2.8	71	88	54	68	11	0	0	132	3	7	2	1.0	.951	OF-90, OF-56, 3B-1
1975			126	.306	.442	480	147	38	6	5	1.0	58	71	47	47	11	0	0	207	7	3	2	1.7	.986	OF-114, DH-12, 3B-1
1976			149	.332	.461	527	175	34	5	8	1.5	75	73	64	43	22	3	1	63	2	2	0	0.4	.970	DH-117, OF-31
1977			162	.298	.515	641	191	54	11	21	3.3	104	92	59	43	18	1	1	81	8	4	1	0.6	.957	DH-116, OF-46
1978			156	.273	.429	623	170	39	5	16	2.6	90	72	51	62	17	0	0	3	1	0	0	0.0	1.000	DH-153, OF-3
1979			101	.288	.466	393	113	32	4	10	2.5	55	74	38	46	5	2	1	0	0	0	0	0.0	—	DH-100
1980			124	.297	.483	489	145	39	5	14	2.9	73	83	29	56	10	4	2	10	0	0	0	0.1	1.000	DH-110, OF-9
1981			101	.272	.396	389	106	23	2	7	1.8	38	36	34	33	3	0	0	10	0	1	0	0.1	.909	DH-97, OF-4
1982			159	.308	.542	613	189	46	7	27	4.4	91	133	55	61	4	0	0	1	0	0	0	0.0	.500	DH-158, OF-1
1983			157	.311	.462	589	183	41	6	12	2.0	84	82	50	68	2	1	0	0	0	0	0	0.0	—	DH-156
1984			106	.303	.397	317	96	13	4	3	0.9	30	42	34	47	0	20	4	0	0	0	0	0.0	—	DH-94
1985			112	.259	.450	320	83	19	4	14	4.4	41	70	44	45	0	24	4	0	0	0	0	0.0	—	DH-106
1986			112	.252	.378	278	70	14	0	7	2.5	22	37	18	39	0	47	15	0	0	0	0	0.0	—	DH-75
1987			18	.313	.500	32	10	3	0	1	3.1	5	9	5	1	0	11	4	0	0	0	0	0.0	—	DH-7
19 yrs.			2084	.290	.454	7218	2091	484	66	191	2.6	940	1097	648	779	109	198	51	884	84	41	18	0.5	.959	DH-1428, OF-477, 3B-21, 2B-17

DIVISIONAL PLAYOFF SERIES

Year	Team		Games	BA	SA	AB	H	2B	3B	HR	HR%	R	RBI	BB	SO	SB	AB	H	PO	A	E	DP	TC/G	FA	G by Pos
1981	KC	A	3	.091	.182	11	1	1	0	0	0.0	0	0	1	1	0	0	0	0	0	0	0	0.0	—	DH-3

LEAGUE CHAMPIONSHIP SERIES

Year	Team		Games	BA	SA	AB	H	2B	3B	HR	HR%	R	RBI	BB	SO	SB	AB	H	PO	A	E	DP	TC/G	FA	G by Pos
1970	CIN	N	2	.000	.000	4	0	0	0	0	0.0	0	0	0	1	0	0	0	2	0	0	0	1.0	1.000	OF-1
1972			1	—	—	0	0	0	0	0	—	0	0	0	0	0	1	0	0	0	0	0	0.0	—	
1976	KC	A	5	.118	.294	17	2	1	0	1	5.9	2	1	1	4	0	0	0	5	1	0	0	1.2	1.000	DH-3, OF-2
1977			5	.444	.778	18	8	3	0	1	5.6	6	2	3	1	0	0	0	2	1	0	0	0.6	1.000	DH-3, OF-2
1978			4	.214	.214	14	3	0	0	0	0.0	0	2	2	2	0	0	0	0	0	0	0	0.0	—	DH-4
1980			3	.200	.200	10	2	0	0	0	0.0	1	3	0	0	0	0	0	0	0	0	0	0.0	—	DH-3
1984			2	1.000	1.500	2	2	1	0	0	0.0	0	1	0	0	0	0	0	0	0	0	0	0.0	—	
1985			6	.261	.348	23	6	2	0	0	0.0	1	3	1	6	0	0	0	0	0	0	0	0.0	—	DH-6
8 yrs.			28	.261	.398	88	23	7	1	1	1.1	9	9	8	17	0	1	3	2	9	2	0	0	0.4	1.000	DH-19, OF-5

WORLD SERIES

Year	Team		Games	BA	SA	AB	H	2B	3B	HR	HR%	R	RBI	BB	SO	SB	AB	H	PO	A	E	DP	TC/G	FA	G by Pos
1970	CIN	N	3	.455	.636	11	5	2	0	0	0.0	1	3	0	1	0	0	0	2	1	0	0	1.0	1.000	OF-3
1972			5	.444	.556	9	4	1	0	0	0.0	2	1	0	2	0	2	0	4	0	0	0	0.8	1.000	OF-2

Year	Team	Games	BA	SA	AB	H	2B	3B	HR	HR%	R	RBI	BB	SO	SB	Pinch Hit AB	H	PO	A	E	DP	TC/G	FA	G by Pos

Hal McRae *continued*

1980	KC A	6	.375	.500	24	9	3	0	0	0.0	3	1	2	2	0	0	0	0	0	0	0	0.0	–	DH-6
1985		3	.000	.000	1	0	0	0	0	0.0	0	0	1	0	0	1	0	0	0	0	0	0.0	–	
4 yrs.		17	.400	.533	45	18	6	0	0	0.0	5	6	3	4	0	3	2	6	1	0	0	0.4	1.000	DH-6, OF-5

McRemer

McREMER, Deceased.

1884	WAS U	1	.000	.000	3	0	0	0	0	0.0	0		0			0	0	2	0	0	0	2.0	1.000	OF-1

Kevin McReynolds

McREYNOLDS, WALTER KEVIN (Big Mac)
B. Oct. 16, 1959, Little Rock, Ark.　　　　　　　　　　　BR TR 6'1"　205 lbs.

1983	SD N	39	.221	.343	140	31	3	1	4	2.9	15	14	12	29	2	2	1	87	4	1	1	2.4	.989	OF-38
1984		147	.278	.465	525	146	26	6	20	3.8	68	75	34	69	3	5	1	422	10	4	1	3.0	.991	OF-143
1985		152	.234	.371	564	132	24	4	15	2.7	61	75	43	81	4	2	0	430	12	3	3	2.9	.993	OF-150
1986		158	.288	.504	560	161	31	6	26	4.6	89	96	66	83	8	4	1	332	9	8	4	2.2	.977	OF-150
1987	NY N	151	.276	.495	590	163	32	5	29	4.9	86	95	39	70	14	3	2	286	8	4	0	2.0	.987	OF-150
1988		147	.288	.496	552	159	30	2	27	4.9	82	99	38	56	21	3	1	252	18	4	5	1.9	.985	OF-147
1989		148	.272	.450	545	148	25	3	22	4.0	74	85	46	74	15	3	1	307	10	10	3	2.2	.969	OF-145
7 yrs.		942	.270	.459	3476	940	171	27	143	4.1	475	539	278	462	67	22	7	2116	71	34	17	2.4	.985	OF-927

LEAGUE CHAMPIONSHIP SERIES

1984	SD N	4	.300	.600	10	3	0	0	1	10.0	2	4	3	1	0	0	0	10	0	0	0	2.5	1.000	OF-4
1988	NY N	7	.250	.536	28	7	2	0	2	7.1	4	4	3	5	2	0	0	19	0	0	0	2.7	1.000	OF-7
2 yrs.		11	.263	.553	38	10	2	0	3	7.9	6	8	6	6	2	0	0	29	0	0	0	2.6	1.000	OF-11

Pete McShannic

McSHANNIC, PETER ROBERT
B. Mar. 20, 1864, Pittsburgh, Pa.　D. Nov. 30, 1946, Toledo, Ohio　　　BB TR 5'7"　190 lbs.

1888	PIT N	26	.194	.204	98	19	1	0	0	0.0	5		5	1	9	0	0	39	49	9	1	3.7	.907	3B-26

Trick McSorley

McSORLEY, JOHN BERNARD
B. Dec. 16, 1858, St. Louis, Mo.　D. Feb. 9, 1936, St. Louis, Mo.　　　TR 5'4"　142 lbs.

1884	TOL AA	21	.250	.265	68	17	1	0	0	0.0	12		3			0	0	154	10	7	13	8.1	.959	1B-16, OF-5, 3B-1, P-1
1885	STL N	2	.500	.667	6	3	1	0	0	0.0	2	1	2		1	0	0	1	1	3	0	2.5	.400	3B-2
1886	STL AA	5	.150	.300	20	3	3	0	0	0.0	1		0			0	0	4	9	4	0	3.4	.765	SS-5
3 yrs.		28	.245	.298	94	23	5	0	0	0.0	15	1	5		1	0	0	159	20	14	13	6.9	.927	1B-16, OF-5, SS-5, 3B-3, P-1

Paul McSweeney

McSWEENEY, PAUL A.
B. Apr. 3, 1867, St. Louis, Mo.　D. Aug. 12, 1951, St. Louis, Mo.

1891	STL AA	3	.250	.333	12	3	1	0	0	0.0	2	2	0		1	0	0	7	6	8	0	7.0	.619	2B-3, 3B-1

Jim McTamany

McTAMANY, JAMES EDWARD
B. July 1, 1863, Philadelphia, Pa.　D. Apr. 16, 1916, Lenni, Pa.　　　BR TR 5'8"　190 lbs.

1885	BKN AA	35	.275	.382	131	36	7	2	1	0.8	21		9			0	0	43	0	5	0	1.4	.896	OF-35
1886		111	.254	.371	418	106	23	10	2	0.5	86		54			0	0	215	27	29	5	2.4	.893	OF-111
1887		134	.258	.344	520	134	22	10	1	0.2	123		76	66		0	0	281	32	28	8	2.5	.918	OF-134
1888	KC AA	130	.246	.331	516	127	12	10	1	0.2	94	41	67	55		0	0	245	27	26	5	2.3	.913	OF-130
1889	COL AA	139	.276	.365	529	146	21	7	4	0.8	113	52	116	66	40	0	0	247	28	30	8	2.2	.902	OF-139
1890		125	.258	.352	466	120	27	7	1	0.2	**140**		**112**		43	0	0	232	17	16	8	2.1	.940	OF-125
1891	2 teams		COL AA (81G – .250)			PHI AA (58G – .225)																			
"	total	139	.239	.364	522	125	23	12	6	1.1	116	56	101	92	33	0	0	279	20	27	5	2.3	.917	OF-139
7 yrs.		813	.256	.355	3102	794	135	58	19	0.6	693	149	535	158	237	0	0	1542	151	161	39	2.3	.913	OF-813

Cal McVey

McVEY, CALVIN ALEXANDER
B. Aug. 30, 1850, Montrose, Iowa　D. Aug. 20, 1926, San Francisco, Calif.
Manager 1873, 1878-79.　　　BR TR 5'9"　170 lbs.

1876	CHI N	63	.347	.406	308	107	15	0	1	0.3	62	53	2	4		0	0	511	24	27	21	8.9	.952	1B-55, P-11, C-6, OF-1, 3B-1
1877		60	.368	.455	266	98	9	7	0	0.0	58	36	8	11		0	0	179	75	42	4	4.9	.858	C-40, 3B-17, P-17, 2B-1, 1B-1
1878	CIN N	61	.306	.395	271	83	10	4	2	0.7	43	28	5	10		0	0	83	107	42	6	3.8	.819	3B-61, C-3
1879		81	.297	.381	354	105	18	6	0	0.0	64	55	8	13		0	0	752	8	44	33	9.9	.945	1B-72, OF-7, P-3, 3B-1, C-1
4 yrs.		265	.328	.407	1199	393	52	17	3	0.3	227	172	23	38		0	0	1525	214	155	64	7.1	.918	1B-128, 3B-80, C-50, P-31, OF-8, 2B-1

George McVey

McVEY, GEORGE W.
B. 1864, Port Jervis, N. Y.　D. May 3, 1896, Quincy, Ill.　　　6'1"　185 lbs.

1885	BKN AA	6	.143	.143	21	3	0	0	0	0.0	2		2			0	0	45	4	3	3	8.7	.942	1B-3, C-3

Bill McWilliams

McWILLIAMS, WILLIAM HENRY
B. Nov. 28, 1910, Dubuque, Iowa　　　BR TR 6'1"　180 lbs.

1931	BOS A	2	.000	.000	2	0	0	0	0	0.0	0	0	0	1	0	2	0	0	0	0	0	0.0	–	

Bobby Meacham

MEACHAM, ROBERT ANDREW
B. Aug. 25, 1960, Los Angeles, Calif.　　　BB TR 6'1"　180 lbs.

1983	NY A	22	.235	.275	51	12	0	0	0	0.0	5	4	4	10	8	0	0	16	64	6	9	3.9	.930	SS-18, 3B-4
1984		99	.253	.328	360	91	13	4	2	0.6	62	25	32	70	9	0	0	140	272	19	52	4.4	.956	SS-96, 2B-2
1985		156	.218	.266	481	105	16	2	1	0.2	70	47	54	102	25	0	0	236	390	24	103	4.2	.963	SS-155
1986		56	.224	.280	161	36	7	1	0	0.0	19	10	17	39	3	0	0	70	149	12	31	4.1	.948	SS-56

Year	Team	Games	BA	SA	AB	H	2B	3B	HR	HR%	R	RBI	BB	SO	SB	Pinch Hit AB	Pinch Hit H	PO	A	E	DP	TC/G	FA	G by Pos

Bobby Meacham *continued*

Year	Team	Games	BA	SA	AB	H	2B	3B	HR	HR%	R	RBI	BB	SO	SB	AB	H	PO	A	E	DP	TC/G	FA	G by Pos
1987		77	.271	.409	203	55	11	1	5	2.5	28	21	19	33	6	1	1	110	184	10	36	3.9	.967	SS-56, 2B-25
1988		47	.217	.296	115	25	9	0	0	0.0	18	7	14	22	7	1	0	56	85	7	19	3.1	.953	SS-24, 2B-21, 3B-5
6 yrs.		457	.236	.308	1371	324	58	8	8	0.6	202	114	140	276	58	2	1	628	1144	78	250	4.0	.958	SS-405, 2B-48, 3B-9

Charlie Mead

MEAD, CHARLES RICHARD
B. Apr. 9, 1921, Vermilion, Alta., Canada — BL TR 6'1" 185 lbs.

Year	Team	Games	BA	SA	AB	H	2B	3B	HR	HR%	R	RBI	BB	SO	SB	AB	H	PO	A	E	DP	TC/G	FA	G by Pos
1943	NY N	37	.274	.349	146	40	6	1	1	0.7	9	13	10	15	3	0	0	77	3	2	3	2.2	.976	OF-37
1944		39	.179	.231	78	14	1	0	1	1.3	5	8	5	7	0	14	2	47	4	1	2	1.3	.981	OF-23
1945		11	.270	.378	37	10	1	0	1	2.7	4	6	5	2	0	0	0	22	3	1	1	2.4	.962	OF-11
3 yrs.		87	.245	.318	261	64	8	1	3	1.1	18	27	20	24	3	14	2	146	10	4	6	1.8	.975	OF-71

Louie Meadows

MEADOWS, MICHAEL RAY
B. Apr. 29, 1961, Maysville, N. C. — BL TL 5'11" 190 lbs.

Year	Team	Games	BA	SA	AB	H	2B	3B	HR	HR%	R	RBI	BB	SO	SB	AB	H	PO	A	E	DP	TC/G	FA	G by Pos
1986	HOU N	6	.333	.333	6	2	0	0	0	0.0	1	0	0	0	1	6	2	0	0	0	0	0.0	–	OF-1
1988		35	.190	.381	42	8	0	1	2	4.8	5	3	6	8	4	18	3	18	1	0	0	0.5	1.000	OF-10
1989		31	.176	.353	51	9	0	0	3	5.9	5	10	1	14	1	20	2	13	0	0	0	0.4	1.000	OF-14, 1B-1
3 yrs.		72	.192	.364	99	19	0	1	5	5.1	11	13	7	22	6	44	7	31	1	0	0	0.4	1.000	OF-25, 1B-1

Pat Meaney

MEANEY, PATRICK J.
B. 1892, Philadelphia, Pa. D. Oct. 20, 1922, Philadelphia, Pa. — TR

Year	Team	Games	BA	SA	AB	H	2B	3B	HR	HR%	R	RBI	BB	SO	SB	AB	H	PO	A	E	DP	TC/G	FA	G by Pos
1912	DET A	1	.000	.000	2	0	0	0	0	0.0	0	0	1		0	0	0	3	2	1		6.0	.833	SS-1

Charlie Meara

MEARA, CHARLES EDWARD (Goggy)
B. Apr. 13, 1891, New York, N. Y. D. Feb. 8, 1962, Bronx, N. Y. — BL TR 5'10" 160 lbs.

Year	Team	Games	BA	SA	AB	H	2B	3B	HR	HR%	R	RBI	BB	SO	SB	AB	H	PO	A	E	DP	TC/G	FA	G by Pos
1914	NY A	4	.286	.286	7	2	0	0	0	0.0	2	1	2	2	0	0	0	4	0	0	0	1.0	1.000	OF-3

Ray Medeiros

MEDEIROS, RAY ANTONE (Pep)
B. May 9, 1926, Oakland, Calif. — BR TR 5'10" 163 lbs.

Year	Team	Games	BA	SA	AB	H	2B	3B	HR	HR%	R	RBI	BB	SO	SB	AB	H	PO	A	E	DP	TC/G	FA	G by Pos
1945	CIN N	1	–	–	0	0	0	0	0		0	0	0	0	0	0	0	0	0	0	0	0.0	–	

Luis Medina

MEDINA, LUIS MAIN
B. Mar. 26, 1963, Santa Monica, Calif. — BR TL 6'4" 200 lbs.

Year	Team	Games	BA	SA	AB	H	2B	3B	HR	HR%	R	RBI	BB	SO	SB	AB	H	PO	A	E	DP	TC/G	FA	G by Pos
1988	CLE A	16	.255	.608	51	13	0	0	6	11.8	10	8	2	18	0	1	0	137	9	0	14	9.1	1.000	1B-16
1989		30	.205	.361	83	17	1	0	4	4.8	8	8	6	35	0	3	2	4	0	2	0	0.2	.667	DH-25, OF-3, 1B-1
2 yrs.		46	.224	.455	134	30	1	0	10	7.5	18	16	8	53	0	4	2	141	9	2	14	3.3	.987	DH-25, 1B-17, OF-3

Joe Medwick

MEDWICK, JOSEPH MICHAEL (Ducky, Muscles)
B. Nov. 24, 1911, Carteret, N. J. D. Mar. 21, 1975, St. Petersburg, Fla. — BR TR 5'10" 187 lbs.
Hall of Fame 1968.

Year	Team	Games	BA	SA	AB	H	2B	3B	HR	HR%	R	RBI	BB	SO	SB	AB	H	PO	A	E	DP	TC/G	FA	G by Pos
1932	STL N	26	.349	.538	106	37	12	1	2	1.9	13	12	2	10	3	0	0	63	2	2	1	2.6	.970	OF-26
1933		148	.306	.497	595	182	40	10	18	3.0	92	98	26	56	5	1	0	318	17	7	2	2.3	.980	OF-147
1934		149	.319	.529	620	198	40	18	18	2.9	110	106	21	83	3	0	0	322	10	14	1	2.3	.960	OF-149
1935		154	.353	.576	634	224	46	13	23	3.6	132	126	30	59	4	0	0	352	8	13	0	2.4	.965	OF-154
1936		155	.351	.577	636	223	64	13	18	2.8	115	138	34	33	3	0	0	367	16	6	4	2.5	.985	OF-155
1937		156	**.374**	**.641**	**633**	**237**	56	10	**31**	4.9	**111**	**154**	41	50	4	0	0	329	9	4	1	2.2	.988	OF-156
1938		146	.322	.536	590	190	47	8	21	3.6	100	122	42	41	0	2	0	330	12	9	6	2.4	.974	OF-144
1939		150	.332	.507	606	201	48	8	14	2.3	98	117	45	44	6	1	0	313	10	8	1	2.2	.976	OF-149
1940	2 teams	STL N	(37G – .304)		BKN N	(106G – .300)																		
"	total	143	.301	.482	581	175	30	10	17	2.9	83	86	32	36	2	3	0	321	8	6	0	2.3	.982	OF-140
1941	BKN N	133	.318	.517	538	171	33	10	18	3.3	100	88	38	35	2	2	1	270	11	5	2	2.2	.983	OF-131
1942		142	.300	.403	553	166	37	4	4	0.7	69	96	32	25	2	2	0	287	5	3	1	2.1	.990	OF-140
1943	2 teams	BKN N	(48G – .272)		NY N	(78G – .281)																		
"	total	126	.278	.380	497	138	30	3	5	1.0	54	70	19	22	1	6	2	221	12	7	3	1.9	.971	OF-117, 1B-3
1944	NY N	128	.337	.441	490	165	24	3	7	1.4	64	85	38	24	2	6	1	290	8	2	2	2.3	.993	OF-122
1945	2 teams	NY N	(26G – .304)		BOS N	(66G – .284)																		
"	total	92	.290	.374	310	90	17	0	3	1.0	31	37	14	14	5	17	3	248	11	1	8	2.8	.996	OF-61, 1B-15
1946	BKN N	41	.312	.442	77	24	4	0	2	2.6	7	18	6	5	0	18	4	38	0	2	2	1.0	.950	OF-18, 1B-1
1947	STL N	75	.307	.467	150	46	12	0	4	2.7	19	28	16	12	0	31	7	56	3	0	2	0.8	1.000	OF-43
1948		20	.211	.211	19	4	0	0	0	0.0	0	2	1	2	0	18	4	0	0	0	0	0.0	–	OF-1
17 yrs.		1984	.324	.505	7635	2471	540	113	205	2.7	1198	1383	437	551	42	107	22	4125	142	89	36	2.2	.980	OF-1853, 1B-19

WORLD SERIES

Year	Team	Games	BA	SA	AB	H	2B	3B	HR	HR%	R	RBI	BB	SO	SB	AB	H	PO	A	E	DP	TC/G	FA	G by Pos
1934	STL N	7	.379	.552	29	11	0	1	1	3.4	4	5	1	7	0	0	0	9	0	0	0	1.3	1.000	OF-7
1941	BKN N	5	.235	.294	17	4	1	0	0	0.0	1	0	1	2	0	0	0	8	0	0	0	1.6	1.000	OF-5
2 yrs.		12	.326	.457	46	15	1	1	1	2.2	5	5	2	9	0	0	0	17	0	0	0	1.4	1.000	OF-12

Tommy Mee

MEE, THOMAS WILLIAM (Judge)
B. Mar. 18, 1890, Chicago, Ill. D. May 16, 1981, Chicago, Ill. — BR TR 5'8" 165 lbs.

Year	Team	Games	BA	SA	AB	H	2B	3B	HR	HR%	R	RBI	BB	SO	SB	AB	H	PO	A	E	DP	TC/G	FA	G by Pos
1910	STL A	8	.158	.263	19	3	2	0	0	0.0	1	1	0		0	0	0	8	18	5	0	3.9	.839	SS-6, 3B-1, 2B-1

Dad Meek

MEEK, FRANK J.
B. St. Louis, Mo. D. Dec. 26, 1922, St. Louis, Mo.

Year	Team	Games	BA	SA	AB	H	2B	3B	HR	HR%	R	RBI	BB	SO	SB	AB	H	PO	A	E	DP	TC/G	FA	G by Pos
1889	STL AA	2	.500	.500	2	1	0	0	0	0.0	2		1		0	0	0	0	2	1	0	1.5	.667	C-2
1890		4	.313	.313	16	5	0	0	0	0.0	3		1	0	0	0	0	33	9	4	0	11.5	.913	C-4
2 yrs.		6	.333	.333	18	6	0	0	0	0.0	5		2	0	0	0	0	33	11	5	0	8.2	.898	C-6

Sammy Meeks

MEEKS, SAMUEL MACK
B. Apr. 23, 1923, Anderson, S. C. — BR TR 5'9" 160 lbs.

Year	Team	Games	BA	SA	AB	H	2B	3B	HR	HR%	R	RBI	BB	SO	SB	AB	H	PO	A	E	DP	TC/G	FA	G by Pos
1948	WAS A	24	.121	.152	33	4	1	0	0	0.0	4	2	1	12	0	9	0	13	18	2	6	1.4	.939	SS-10, 2B-1
1949	CIN N	16	.306	.528	36	11	2	0	2	5.6	10	6	2	6	1	3	1	24	33	0	12	3.6	1.000	2B-8, SS-3

Year	Team		Games	BA	SA	AB	H	2B	3B	HR	HR%	R	RBI	BB	SO	SB	Pinch Hit AB	Pinch Hit H	PO	A	E	DP	TC/G	FA	G by Pos

Sammy Meeks *continued*

Year	Team		Games	BA	SA	AB	H	2B	3B	HR	HR%	R	RBI	BB	SO	SB	AB	H	PO	A	E	DP	TC/G	FA	G by Pos
1950			39	.284	.368	95	27	5	0	1	1.1	7	8	6	14	1	7	3	35	68	5	13	2.8	.954	SS-29, 3B-2
1951			23	.229	.229	35	8	0	0	0	0.0	4	2	0	4	1	18	3	9	4	1	2	0.6	.929	3B-4, SS-1
4 yrs.			102	.251	.337	199	50	8	0	3	1.5	25	18	9	36	3	37	7	81	123	8	33	2.1	.962	SS-43, 2B-9, 3B-6

Dave Meier

MEIER, DAVID KEITH
B. Aug. 8, 1959, Helena, Mont.

BR TR 6' 195 lbs.

Year	Team		Games	BA	SA	AB	H	2B	3B	HR	HR%	R	RBI	BB	SO	SB	AB	H	PO	A	E	DP	TC/G	FA	G by Pos
1984	MIN	A	59	.238	.306	147	35	8	1	0	0.0	18	13	6	9	0	9	1	87	2	2	0	1.5	.978	OF-50, DH-4, 3B-1
1985			71	.260	.346	104	27	6	0	1	1.0	15	8	18	12	0	11	0	77	1	1	1	1.1	.987	OF-63, DH-3
1987	TEX	A	13	.286	.333	21	6	1	0	0	0.0	4	0	0	4	0	3	1	11	0	1	0	0.9	.917	OF-8
1988	CHI	N	2	.400	.400	5	2	0	0	0	0.0	0	1	0	1	0	1	0	1	0	0	0	0.5	1.000	3B-1
4 yrs.			145	.253	.325	277	70	15	1	1	0.4	37	22	24	26	0	24	2	176	3	4	1	1.3	.978	OF-121, DH-7, 3B-2

Dutch Meier

MEIER, ARTHUR ERNST
B. Mar. 30, 1879, St. Louis, Mo. D. Mar. 23, 1948, Chicago, Ill.

BR TR 5'10" 175 lbs.

Year	Team		Games	BA	SA	AB	H	2B	3B	HR	HR%	R	RBI	BB	SO	SB	AB	H	PO	A	E	DP	TC/G	FA	G by Pos
1906	PIT	N	82	.256	.326	273	70	11	4	0	0.0	32	16	13		4	13	2	115	43	11	6	2.1	.935	OF-52, SS-17

Walt Meinert

MEINERT, WALTER HENRY
B. Dec. 11, 1890, New York, N.Y. D. Nov. 9, 1958, Decatur, Ill.

BL TL 5'7½" 150 lbs.

Year	Team		Games	BA	SA	AB	H	2B	3B	HR	HR%	R	RBI	BB	SO	SB	AB	H	PO	A	E	DP	TC/G	FA	G by Pos
1913	STL	A	4	.375	.375	8	3	0	0	0	0.0	1	0	1	3	1	1	1	3	0	0	0	0.8	1.000	OF-2

Bob Meinke

MEINKE, ROBERT BERNARD
Son of Frank Meinke.
B. June 25, 1887, Chicago, Ill. D. Dec. 29, 1952, Chicago, Ill.

BR TR 5'10" 135 lbs.

Year	Team		Games	BA	SA	AB	H	2B	3B	HR	HR%	R	RBI	BB	SO	SB	AB	H	PO	A	E	DP	TC/G	FA	G by Pos
1910	CIN	N	2	.000	.000	1	0	0	0	0	0.0	0	0	1	0	0	0	0	3	4	0	0	3.5	1.000	SS-2

Frank Meinke

MEINKE, FRANK LOUIS
Father of Bob Meinke.
B. Oct. 18, 1863, Chicago, Ill. D. Nov. 8, 1931, Chicago, Ill.

5'10½" 172 lbs.

Year	Team		Games	BA	SA	AB	H	2B	3B	HR	HR%	R	RBI	BB	SO	SB	AB	H	PO	A	E	DP	TC/G	FA	G by Pos
1884	DET	N	92	.164	.273	341	56	5	7	6	1.8	28		6	89		0	0	80	214	44	20	3.7	.870	SS-51, P-35, OF-4, 3B-3, 2B-3
1885			1	.000	.000	3	0	0	0	0	0.0	0	0	0	1		0	0	1	2	0	0	3.0	1.000	OF-1, P-1
2 yrs.			93	.163	.270	344	56	5	7	6	1.7	28	0	6	90		0	0	81	216	44	20	3.7	.871	SS-51, P-36, OF-5, 3B-3, 2B-3

George Meister

MEISTER, GEORGE B.
B. June 5, 1864, Germany D. Aug. 24, 1908, Glenwood, Pa.

Year	Team		Games	BA	SA	AB	H	2B	3B	HR	HR%	R	RBI	BB	SO	SB	AB	H	PO	A	E	DP	TC/G	FA	G by Pos
1884	TOL	AA	34	.193	.244	119	23	6	0	0	0.0	9		3			0	0	27	40	15	3	2.4	.817	3B-34

John Meister

MEISTER, JOHN F.
B. May 10, 1863, Altoona, Pa. D. Jan. 28, 1923, Philadelphia, Pa.

Year	Team		Games	BA	SA	AB	H	2B	3B	HR	HR%	R	RBI	BB	SO	SB	AB	H	PO	A	E	DP	TC/G	FA	G by Pos
1886	NY	AA	45	.237	.339	186	44	7	3	2	1.1	35		4			0	0	130	121	26	18	6.2	.906	2B-45
1887			39	.222	.304	158	35	6	2	1	0.6	24		16		9	0	0	68	43	13	9	3.2	.895	OF-22, 2B-14, 3B-3, SS-1
2 yrs.			84	.230	.323	344	79	13	5	3	0.9	59		20		9	0	0	198	164	39	27	4.8	.903	2B-59, OF-22, 3B-3, SS-1

Karl Meister

MEISTER, KARL DANIEL (Dutch)
B. May 15, 1891, Marietta, Ohio D. Aug. 15, 1967, Marietta, Ohio

BR TR 6' 178 lbs.

Year	Team		Games	BA	SA	AB	H	2B	3B	HR	HR%	R	RBI	BB	SO	SB	AB	H	PO	A	E	DP	TC/G	FA	G by Pos
1913	CIN	N	4	.286	.429	7	2	1	0	0	0.0	1	2	0	4	0	0	0	2	0	1	0	0.8	.667	OF-4

Moxie Meixell

MEIXELL, MERTON MERRILL
B. Oct. 18, 1887, Lake Crystal, Minn. D. Aug. 17, 1982, Los Angeles, Calif.

BL TL 5'10" 168 lbs.

Year	Team		Games	BA	SA	AB	H	2B	3B	HR	HR%	R	RBI	BB	SO	SB	AB	H	PO	A	E	DP	TC/G	FA	G by Pos
1912	CLE	A	2	.500	.500	2	1	0	0	0	0.0	0	0	0		0	2	1	0	0	0	0	0.0	—	

Roman Mejias

MEJIAS, ROMAN
Born Roman Mejias y Gomez.
B. Aug. 9, 1930, Abreus, Cuba

BR TR 6' 175 lbs.

Year	Team		Games	BA	SA	AB	H	2B	3B	HR	HR%	R	RBI	BB	SO	SB	AB	H	PO	A	E	DP	TC/G	FA	G by Pos
1955	PIT	N	71	.216	.329	167	36	8	1	3	1.8	14	21	9	13	1	20	4	67	8	6	2	1.1	.926	OF-43
1957			58	.275	.423	142	39	7	4	2	1.4	12	15	6	13	2	17	3	60	6	0	0	1.1	1.000	OF-42
1958			76	.268	.408	157	42	3	2	5	3.2	17	19	2	27	0	21	5	104	3	3	0	1.4	.973	OF-57
1959			96	.236	.341	276	65	6	1	7	2.5	28	28	21	48	1	4	1	155	8	5	2	1.8	.970	OF-85
1960			3	.000	.000	0	0	0	0	0	0.0	1	0	1	0	0	1	0	0	0	0	0	0.0	—	
1961			4	.000	.000	1	0	0	0	0	0.0	0	1	0	1	0	1	0	1	0	0	0	0.3	1.000	OF-2
1962	HOU	N	146	.286	.445	566	162	12	3	24	4.2	82	76	30	83	12	5	0	217	10	13	2	1.6	.946	OF-142
1963	BOS	A	111	.227	.370	357	81	18	0	11	3.1	43	39	14	36	4	24	4	177	6	5	1	1.7	.973	OF-86
1964			62	.238	.347	101	24	3	1	2	2.0	14	4	7	16	0	16	4	49	2	2	0	0.9	.962	OF-37
9 yrs.			627	.254	.391	1768	449	57	12	54	3.1	212	202	89	238	20	109	21	830	43	34	7	1.4	.963	OF-494

Sam Mejias

MEJIAS, SAMUEL ELIAS
B. May 9, 1952, Santiago, Dominican Republic

BR TR 6' 170 lbs.

Year	Team		Games	BA	SA	AB	H	2B	3B	HR	HR%	R	RBI	BB	SO	SB	AB	H	PO	A	E	DP	TC/G	FA	G by Pos
1976	STL	N	18	.143	.190	21	3	1	0	0	0.0	1	1	2	2	1	2	1	0	19	1	0	0	1.1	1.000	OF-17
1977	MON	N	74	.228	.376	101	23	4	1	3	3.0	14	8	2	17	1	20	4	55	2	2	1	0.8	.966	OF-56
1978			67	.232	.250	56	13	1	0	0	0.0	9	6	2	5	0	10	3	35	2	2	0	0.6	.949	OF-52, P-1
1979	2 teams		CHI N (31G – .182)				CHI N (7G – .500)																			
"	total		38	.231	.231	13	3	0	0	0	0.0	5	0	2	5	0	7	1	8	0	1	0	0.2	.889	OF-28
1980	CIN	N	71	.278	.370	108	30	5	1	1	0.9	16	10	6	13	4	7	2	89	4	1	1	1.3	.989	OF-67
1981			66	.286	.327	49	14	2	0	0	0.0	6	7	2	9	1	8	1	34	1	1	0	0.5	.972	OF-58
6 yrs.			334	.247	.330	348	86	13	2	4	1.1	51	31	16	51	7	53	12	240	10	7	2	0.8	.973	OF-278, P-1

Year	Team		Games	BA	SA	AB	H	2B	3B	HR	HR%	R	RBI	BB	SO	SB	Pinch Hit AB	Pinch Hit H	PO	A	E	DP	TC/G	FA	G by Pos

Dutch Mele

MELE, ALBERT ERNEST
B. Jan. 11, 1915, New York, N. Y. D. Feb. 12, 1975, Hollywood, Calif.
BL TL 6'½" 195 lbs.

| 1937 | CIN | N | 6 | .143 | .214 | 14 | 2 | 1 | 0 | 0 | 0.0 | 1 | 1 | 1 | 1 | 0 | 1 | 0 | 1 | 0 | 0 | 0 | 0.2 | 1.000 | OF-5 |

Sam Mele

MELE, SABATH ANTHONY
B. Jan. 21, 1923, Astoria, N. Y.
Manager 1961-67.
BR TR 6'1" 183 lbs.

1947	BOS	A	123	.302	.448	453	137	14	8	12	2.6	71	73	37	35	0	6	3	238	10	2	1	2.0	.992	OF-115, 1B-1
1948			66	.233	.344	180	42	12	1	2	1.1	25	25	13	21	1	9	1	99	2	3	0	1.6	.971	OF-55
1949	2 teams	BOS A (18G – .196)				WAS A (78G – .242)																			
"	total		96	.235	.326	310	73	13	3	3	1.0	22	32	24	48	4	15	2	207	13	6	12	2.4	.973	OF-74, 1B-11
1950	WAS	A	126	.274	.432	435	119	21	6	12	2.8	57	86	51	40	2	10	4	341	26	4	13	2.9	.989	OF-99, 1B-16
1951			143	.274	.391	558	153	36	7	5	0.9	58	94	32	31	2	6	1	385	15	2	12	2.8	.995	OF-124, 1B-15
1952	2 teams	WAS A (9G – .429)				CHI A (123G – .248)																			
"	total		132	.259	.421	451	117	21	2	16	3.5	48	69	49	42	1	12	2	178	8	1	1	1.4	.995	OF-119, 1B-3
1953	CHI	A	140	.274	.437	481	132	26	8	12	2.5	64	82	58	47	3	6	3	217	14	1	1	1.7	.996	OF-138, 1B-2
1954	2 teams	BAL A (72G – .239)				BOS A (42G – .318)																			
"	total		114	.268	.431	362	97	15	4	12	3.3	39	55	30	38	1	19	7	285	14	6	19	2.7	.980	OF-75, 1B-22
1955	2 teams	BOS A (14G – .129)				CIN N (35G – .210)																			
"	total		49	.183	.280	93	17	3	0	2	2.2	5	8	5	20	1	25	1	38	3	1	0	0.9	.976	OF-20, 1B-1
1956	CLE	A	57	.254	.421	114	29	7	0	4	3.5	17	20	12	20	0	28	8	88	7	1	5	1.7	.990	OF-20, 1B-8
10 yrs.			1046	.267	.408	3437	916	168	39	80	2.3	406	544	311	342	15	136	32	2076	112	27	64	2.1	.988	OF-839, 1B-79

Francisco Melendez

MELENDEZ, FRANCISCO JAVIER
Born Francisco Javier Melendez y Villegas.
B. Jan. 25, 1964, Rio Piedras, Puerto Rico
BL TL 6' 170 lbs.

1984	PHI	N	21	.130	.130	23	3	0	0	0	0.0	0	2	1	5	0	13	1	37	4	0	1	2.0	1.000	1B-10
1986			9	.250	.250	8	2	0	0	0	0.0	0	0	0	2	0	7	1	1	0	0	0	0.1	1.000	1B-2
1987	SF	N	12	.313	.500	16	5	0	0	1	6.3	2	1	0	3	0	10	1	19	0	0	0	1.6	1.000	1B-5
1988			23	.192	.192	26	5	0	0	0	0.0	1	3	3	2	0	16	4	27	0	0	2	1.2	1.000	1B-6, OF-1
1989	BAL	A	9	.273	.273	11	3	0	0	0	0.0	1	3	1	2	0	4	1	25	2	0	4	3.0	1.000	1B-5
5 yrs.			74	.214	.250	84	18	0	0	1	1.2	4	9	5	14	0	50	8	109	6	0	7	1.6	1.000	1B-28, OF-1

Luis Melendez

MELENDEZ, LUIS ANTONIO
Born Luis Antonio Melendez y Santana.
B. Aug. 11, 1949, Aibonito, Puerto Rico
BR TR 6' 165 lbs.

1970	STL	N	21	.300	.314	70	21	1	0	0	0.0	11	8	2	12	3	3	0	31	2	0	0	1.6	1.000	OF-18
1971			88	.225	.254	173	39	3	1	0	0.0	25	11	24	29	2	22	4	90	3	4	0	1.1	.959	OF-66
1972			118	.238	.334	332	79	11	3	5	1.5	32	28	25	34	5	21	2	206	5	9	0	1.9	.959	OF-105
1973			121	.267	.343	341	91	18	1	2	0.6	35	35	27	50	2	21	8	196	8	2	4	1.7	.990	OF-95
1974			83	.218	.298	124	27	4	3	0	0.0	15	8	11	9	2	31	4	84	1	2	0	1.0	.977	OF-46, SS-1
1975			110	.265	.347	291	77	8	5	2	0.7	33	27	16	25	3	35	8	169	3	3	1	1.6	.983	OF-89
1976	2 teams	STL N (20G – .125)				SD N (72G – .244)																			
"	total		92	.224	.259	143	32	5	0	0	0.0	15	5	3	15	1	25	4	99	0	1	0	1.1	.990	OF-68
1977	SD	N	8	.000	.000	3	0	0	0	0	0.0	1	0	1	1	0	3	0	1	0	0	0	0.1	1.000	OF-2
8 yrs.			641	.248	.318	1477	366	50	13	9	0.6	167	122	109	175	18	161	30	876	22	21	5	1.4	.977	OF-489, SS-1

Oscar Melillo

MELILLO, OSCAR DONALD (Ski, Spinach)
B. Aug. 4, 1899, Chicago, Ill. D. Nov. 14, 1963, Chicago, Ill.
BR TR 5'8" 150 lbs.

1926	STL	A	99	.255	.335	385	98	18	5	1	0.3	54	30	32	31	6	0	0	238	324	22	71	5.9	.962	2B-88, 3B-11
1927			107	.225	.287	356	80	18	2	0	0.0	45	26	25	28	3	5	1	229	293	36	72	5.2	.935	2B-101
1928			51	.189	.205	132	25	2	0	0	0.0	9	9	9	11	2	2	0	79	104	6	15	3.7	.968	2B-28, 3B-19
1929			141	.296	.401	494	146	17	10	5	1.0	57	67	29	30	11	0	0	342	519	24	98	6.3	.973	2B-141
1930			149	.256	.369	574	147	30	10	5	0.9	62	59	23	44	15	1	0	384	572	21	107	6.6	.979	2B-148
1931			151	.306	.407	617	189	34	11	2	0.3	89	75	37	29	7	0	0	428	543	32	118	6.6	.968	2B-151
1932			154	.242	.324	612	148	19	11	3	0.5	71	66	36	42	6	1	0	393	526	18	110	6.1	.981	2B-153
1933			132	.292	.381	496	145	23	6	3	0.6	50	79	29	18	12	0	0	362	451	7	110	6.2	.991	2B-130
1934			144	.241	.297	552	133	19	3	2	0.4	54	55	28	27	4	3	0	412	462	17	110	6.2	.981	2B-141
1935	2 teams	STL A (19G – .206)				BOS A (106G – .261)																			
"	total		125	.253	.303	462	117	16	2	1	0.2	53	44	46	26	3	1	0	324	432	21	94	6.2	.973	2B-123
1936	BOS	A	98	.226	.287	327	74	12	4	0	0.0	39	32	28	16	0	4	2	239	242	10	59	5.0	.980	2B-93
1937			26	.250	.286	56	14	2	0	0	0.0	8	6	5	4	0	2	1	33	35	4	8	2.8	.944	2B-19, SS-2, 3B-2
12 yrs.			1377	.260	.340	5063	1316	210	64	22	0.4	591	548	327	306	69	19	4	3463	4503	218	972	5.9	.973	2B-1316, 3B-32, SS-2

Joe Mellana

MELLANA, JOSEPH PETER
B. Mar. 11, 1905, Oakland, Calif. D. Nov. 1, 1969, Larkspur, Calif.
BR TR 5'10" 180 lbs.

| 1927 | PHI | A | 4 | .286 | .286 | 7 | 2 | 0 | 0 | 0 | 0.0 | 1 | 2 | 0 | 1 | 0 | 0 | 0 | 0 | 8 | 1 | 1 | 2.3 | .889 | 3B-2 |

Bill Mellor

MELLOR, WILLIAM HARPIN
B. June 6, 1874, Camden, N. J. D. Nov. 5, 1940, Bridgeton, R. I.
BR TR 6' 190 lbs.

| 1902 | BAL | A | 10 | .361 | .444 | 36 | 13 | 3 | 0 | 0 | 0.0 | 4 | 5 | 3 | | 1 | 0 | 0 | 87 | 2 | 2 | 1 | 9.1 | .978 | 1B-10 |

Paul Meloan

MELOAN, PAUL B. (Molly)
B. Aug. 23, 1888, Paynesville, Mo. D. Feb. 11, 1950, Taft, Calif.
BL TR 5'10½" 175 lbs.

1910	CHI	A	65	.243	.324	222	54	6	6	0	0.0	23	23	17		4	0	0	76	16	5	1	1.5	.948	OF-65
1911	2 teams	CHI A (1G – .333)				STL A (64G – .262)																			
"	total		65	.263	.378	209	55	11	2	3	1.4	30	15	15		7	9	0	69	6	9	1	1.3	.893	OF-55
2 yrs.			130	.253	.350	431	109	17	8	3	0.7	53	38	32		11	9	0	145	22	14	2	1.4	.923	OF-120

Bill Melton

MELTON, WILLIAM EDWIN
B. July 7, 1945, Gulfport, Miss.
BR TR 6'2" 200 lbs.

| 1968 | CHI | A | 34 | .266 | .394 | 109 | 29 | 8 | 0 | 2 | 1.8 | 5 | 16 | 10 | 32 | 1 | 1 | 0 | 17 | 75 | 3 | 5 | 2.8 | .968 | 3B-33 |

Year	Team		Games	BA	SA	AB	H	2B	3B	HR	HR%	R	RBI	BB	SO	SB	Pinch Hit AB	H	PO	A	E	DP	TC/G	FA	G by Pos

Bill Melton *continued*

Year	Team		Games	BA	SA	AB	H	2B	3B	HR	HR%	R	RBI	BB	SO	SB	AB	H	PO	A	E	DP	TC/G	FA	G by Pos
1969			157	.255	.433	556	142	26	2	23	4.1	67	87	56	106	1	4	1	125	325	22	36	3.0	.953	3B-148, OF-11
1970			141	.263	.488	514	135	15	1	33	6.4	74	96	56	107	2	0	0	158	187	18	22	2.6	.950	OF-71, 3B-70
1971			150	.269	.492	543	146	18	2	33	6.1	72	86	61	87	3	0	0	116	371	16	26	3.4	.968	3B-148
1972			57	.245	.370	208	51	5	0	7	3.4	22	30	23	31	1	1	0	47	125	12	12	3.2	.935	3B-56
1973			152	.277	.439	560	155	29	1	20	3.6	83	87	75	66	4	0	0	115	347	23	31	3.2	.953	3B-151, DH-1
1974			136	.242	.404	495	120	17	0	21	4.2	63	63	59	60	3	1	0	100	272	24	29	2.9	.939	3B-123, DH-11
1975			149	.240	.359	512	123	16	0	15	2.9	62	70	78	106	5	0	0	131	313	26	23	3.2	.945	3B-138, DH-11
1976	CAL	A	118	.208	.328	341	71	17	3	6	1.8	31	42	44	53	2	26	7	227	36	3	22	2.3	.989	DH-51, 1B-30, 3B-21
1977	CLE	A	50	.241	.323	133	32	11	0	0	0.0	17	14	17	21	1	10	3	142	28	2	11	3.4	.988	1B-15, DH-14, 3B-13
10 yrs.			1144	.253	.419	3971	1004	162	9	160	4.0	496	591	479	669	23	43	11	1178	2079	149	217	3.0	.956	3B-901, DH-88, OF-82, 1B-45

Dave Melton

MELTON, DAVID OLIN
B. Oct. 3, 1928, Pampa, Tex.

BR TR 6' 185 lbs.

Year	Team		Games	BA	SA	AB	H	2B	3B	HR	HR%	R	RBI	BB	SO	SB	AB	H	PO	A	E	DP	TC/G	FA	G by Pos
1956	KC	A	3	.333	.333	3	1	0	0	0	0.0	0	0	0	0	0	0	0	3	0	0	0	1.0	1.000	OF-3
1958			9	.000	.000	6	0	0	0	0	0.0	0	0	0	5	0	6	0	2	0	0	0	0.2	1.000	OF-2
2 yrs.			12	.111	.111	9	1	0	0	0	0.0	0	0	0	5	0	6	0	5	0	0	0	0.4	1.000	OF-5

Bob Melvin

MELVIN, ROBERT PAUL
B. Oct. 28, 1961, Palo Alto, Calif.

BR TR 6'4" 205 lbs.

Year	Team		Games	BA	SA	AB	H	2B	3B	HR	HR%	R	RBI	BB	SO	SB	AB	H	PO	A	E	DP	TC/G	FA	G by Pos
1985	DET	A	41	.220	.293	82	18	4	1	0	0.0	10	4	3	21	0	0	0	175	13	2	1	4.6	.989	C-41
1986	SF	N	89	.224	.347	268	60	14	2	5	1.9	24	25	15	69	3	6	1	443	60	6	7	5.7	.988	C-84, 3B-1
1987			84	.199	.366	246	49	8	0	11	4.5	31	31	17	44	0	8	1	414	44	1	8	5.5	.998	C-78, 1B-1
1988			92	.234	.377	273	64	13	1	8	2.9	23	27	13	46	1	4	1	406	31	7	4	4.8	.984	C-89, 1B-1
1989	BAL	A	85	.241	.295	278	67	10	1	1	0.4	22	32	15	53	0	5	0	303	20	3	1	3.8	.991	C-75, DH-9
5 yrs.			391	.225	.342	1147	258	49	5	25	2.2	110	119	63	233	4	23	3	1741	168	19	21	4.9	.990	C-367, DH-9, 1B-2, 3B-1

LEAGUE CHAMPIONSHIP SERIES

Year	Team		Games	BA	SA	AB	H	2B	3B	HR	HR%	R	RBI	BB	SO	SB	AB	H	PO	A	E	DP	TC/G	FA	G by Pos
1987	SF	N	3	.429	.429	7	3	0	0	0	0.0	0	0	1	1	0	1	0	14	1	0	0	5.0	1.000	C-2

Mario Mendoza

MENDOZA, MARIO
Born Mario Mendoza y Aizpuru.
B. Dec. 26, 1950, Chihuahua, Mexico.

BR TR 5'11" 170 lbs.

Year	Team		Games	BA	SA	AB	H	2B	3B	HR	HR%	R	RBI	BB	SO	SB	AB	H	PO	A	E	DP	TC/G	FA	G by Pos
1974	PIT	N	91	.221	.252	163	36	1	2	0	0.0	10	15	8	35	1	1	0	77	187	10	21	3.0	.964	SS-87
1975			56	.180	.200	50	9	1	0	0	0.0	8	2	3	17	0	0	0	29	70	5	10	1.9	.952	SS-53, 3B-1
1976			50	.185	.239	92	17	5	0	0	0.0	6	12	4	15	0	1	0	42	105	5	19	3.0	.967	SS-45, 3B-2, 2B-1
1977			70	.198	.235	81	16	3	0	0	0.0	5	4	3	10	0	4	2	41	87	10	13	2.0	.928	SS-45, 3B-19, P-1
1978			57	.218	.291	55	12	1	0	1	1.8	5	3	2	9	3	2	1	28	61	5	4	1.6	.947	2B-21, 3B-18, SS-14
1979	SEA	A	148	.198	.249	373	74	10	3	1	0.3	26	29	9	62	3	0	0	177	422	20	91	4.2	.968	SS-148
1980			114	.245	.310	277	68	6	3	2	0.7	27	14	16	42	3	0	0	149	290	19	68	4.0	.959	SS-114
1981	TEX	A	88	.231	.266	229	53	6	1	0	0.0	18	22	7	25	2	0	0	114	270	12	47	4.5	.970	SS-88
1982			12	.118	.118	17	2	0	0	0	0.0	1	0	0	4	0	0	0	14	16	4	6	2.8	.882	SS-12
9 yrs.			686	.215	.262	1337	287	33	9	4	0.3	106	101	52	219	12	8	3	671	1508	90	279	3.3	.960	SS-606, 3B-40, 2B-22, P-1

LEAGUE CHAMPIONSHIP SERIES

Year	Team		Games	BA	SA	AB	H	2B	3B	HR	HR%	R	RBI	BB	SO	SB	AB	H	PO	A	E	DP	TC/G	FA	G by Pos
1974	PIT	N	3	.200	.200	5	1	0	0	0	0.0	0	1	1	0	0	0	0	4	7	0	0	3.7	1.000	SS-3

Mike Mendoza

MENDOZA, MICHAEL JOSEPH
B. Nov. 26, 1955, Inglewood, Calif.

BR TR 6'5" 215 lbs.

Year	Team		Games	BA	SA	AB	H	2B	3B	HR	HR%	R	RBI	BB	SO	SB	AB	H	PO	A	E	DP	TC/G	FA	G by Pos
1979	HOU	N	2	-	-	0	0	0	0	0	0.0	0	0	0	0	0	0	0	0	0	0	0	0.0	-	P-1

Minnie Mendoza

MENDOZA, CRISTOBAL RIGABERTO
Born Cristobal Rigoberto Mendoza y Carreras.
B. Nov. 16, 1933, Ceiba Del Agua, Cuba.

BR TR 6' 180 lbs.

Year	Team		Games	BA	SA	AB	H	2B	3B	HR	HR%	R	RBI	BB	SO	SB	AB	H	PO	A	E	DP	TC/G	FA	G by Pos
1970	MIN	A	16	.188	.188	16	3	0	0	0	0.0	2	2	0	1	0	9	2	8	5	0	0	0.8	1.000	3B-5, 2B-4

Jock Menefee

MENEFEE, JOHN
B. Jan. 15, 1868, West Virginia D. Mar. 11, 1953, Belle Vernon, Pa.

BR TR 6'

Year	Team		Games	BA	SA	AB	H	2B	3B	HR	HR%	R	RBI	BB	SO	SB	AB	H	PO	A	E	DP	TC/G	FA	G by Pos
1892	PIT	N	2	.000	.000	3	0	0	0	0	0.0	0	0	0	0	0	0	0	1	2	0	0	1.5	1.000	OF-1, P-1
1893	LOU	N	22	.274	.329	73	20	2	1	0	0.0	10	12	13	5	2	0	0	19	38	5	2	2.8	.919	P-15, OF-7
1894	2 teams		42				LOU N (29G – .165)				PIT N (13G – .255)															
"	total		42	.198	.246	126	25	2	2	0	0.0	13	11	11	10	4	0	0	30	79	8	0	2.8	.932	P-41, 2B-1
1895	PIT	N	2	-	-	0	0	0	0	0	-	0	0	0	0	0	0	0	1	1	0	0	1.5	.667	P-2
1898	NY	N	1	.000	.000	5	0	0	0	0	0.0	0	0	0	0	0	0	0	0	3	1	0	4.0	.750	P-1
1900	CHI	N	17	.109	.109	46	5	0	0	0	0.0	5	4	2		0	1	0	3	21	3	1	1.6	.889	P-16
1901			48	.257	.329	152	39	5	3	0	0.0	19	13	8		4	1	0	67	48	12	2	2.6	.906	OF-24, P-21, 1B-2, 2B-1
1902			65	.231	.259	216	50	4	1	0	0.0	24	15	15		4	0	0	230	57	13	7	4.6	.957	OF-23, P-22, 1B-18, 3B-2, 2B-1
1903			22	.203	.250	64	13	3	0	0	0.0	3	2	3		0	0	0	31	56	8	0	4.3	.916	P-20, 1B-2
9 yrs.			221	.222	.266	685	152	16	7	0	0.0	74	57	52	15	14	2	0	382	305	51	12	3.3	.931	P-139, OF-55, 1B-22, 2B-3, 3B-2

Denis Menke

MENKE, DENIS JOHN
B. July 21, 1940, Algona, Iowa.

BR TR 6' 185 lbs.

Year	Team		Games	BA	SA	AB	H	2B	3B	HR	HR%	R	RBI	BB	SO	SB	AB	H	PO	A	E	DP	TC/G	FA	G by Pos
1962	MIL	N	50	.192	.267	146	28	3	1	2	1.4	12	16	16	38	0	2	0	87	109	8	23	4.1	.961	2B-20, 3B-15, SS-9, 1B-2, OF-1
1963			146	.234	.344	518	121	16	4	11	2.1	58	50	37	106	6	2	0	234	398	24	67	4.5	.963	SS-82, 3B-51, 2B-22, OF-1, 1B-1
1964			151	.283	.479	505	143	29	5	20	4.0	79	65	68	77	4	2	1	283	455	27	84	5.1	.965	SS-141, 2B-15, 3B-6
1965			71	.243	.392	181	44	13	1	4	2.2	16	18	18	28	1	12	2	110	146	9	27	3.7	.966	SS-54, 1B-8, 3B-4
1966	ATL	N	138	.251	.412	454	114	20	4	15	3.3	55	60	71	87	0	3	1	228	341	24	56	4.3	.960	SS-106, 3B-39, 1B-7

Year	Team		Games	BA	SA	AB	H	2B	3B	HR	HR%	R	RBI	BB	SO	SB	Pinch Hit AB	Pinch Hit H	PO	A	E	DP	TC/G	FA	G by Pos

Denis Menke *continued*

Year	Team		Games	BA	SA	AB	H	2B	3B	HR	HR%	R	RBI	BB	SO	SB	PH AB	PH H	PO	A	E	DP	TC/G	FA	G by Pos
1967			129	.227	.325	418	95	14	3	7	1.7	37	39	65	62	5	0	0	183	350	19	65	4.3	.966	SS-124, 3B-3
1968	HOU	N	150	.249	.347	542	135	23	6	6	1.1	56	56	64	81	5	1	0	346	384	15	71	5.0	.980	2B-119, SS-35, 1B-5, 3B-4
1969			154	.269	.387	553	149	25	5	10	1.8	72	90	87	87	2	0	0	257	414	27	75	4.5	.961	SS-131, 2B-23, 1B-9, 3B-1
1970			154	.304	.441	562	171	26	6	13	2.3	82	92	82	80	6	1	0	262	460	30	81	4.9	.960	SS-133, 2B-21, 3B-5, 1B-5, OF-3
1971			146	.246	.320	475	117	26	3	1	0.2	57	43	59	68	4	9	1	892	151	10	88	7.2	.991	1B-101, 3B-32, SS-17, 2B-5
1972	CIN	N	140	.233	.345	447	104	19	2	9	2.0	41	50	58	76	0	3	1	125	260	16	25	2.9	.960	3B-130, 1B-11
1973			139	.191	.270	241	46	10	0	3	1.2	38	26	69	53	1	8	1	80	197	9	20	2.1	.969	3B-123, SS-7, 2B-5, 1B-1
1974	HOU	N	30	.103	.138	29	3	1	0	0	0.0	2	1	4	10	0	8	2	21	23	0	5	1.5	1.000	1B-12, 3B-7, 2B-3, SS-2
13 yrs.			1598	.250	.370	5071	1270	225	40	101	2.0	605	606	698	853	34	51	9	3108	3688	218	687	4.4	.969	SS-841, 3B-420, 2B-233, 1B-162, OF-5

LEAGUE CHAMPIONSHIP SERIES

Year	Team		Games	BA	SA	AB	H	2B	3B	HR	HR%	R	RBI	BB	SO	SB	PH AB	PH H	PO	A	E	DP	TC/G	FA	G by Pos
1972	CIN	N	5	.250	.313	16	4	1	0	0	0.0	1	0	4	3	0	0	0	3	11	0	0	2.8	1.000	3B-5
1973			3	.222	.556	9	2	0	0	1	11.1	1	1	1	2	0	1	0	0	4	0	0	1.3	1.000	3B-2, SS-1
2 yrs.			8	.240	.400	25	6	1	0	1	4.0	2	1	5	5	0	1	0	3	15	0	0	2.3	1.000	3B-7, SS-1

WORLD SERIES

Year	Team		Games	BA	SA	AB	H	2B	3B	HR	HR%	R	RBI	BB	SO	SB	PH AB	PH H	PO	A	E	DP	TC/G	FA	G by Pos
1972	CIN	N	7	.083	.208	24	2	0	0	1	4.2	1	2	2	6	0	0	0	6	23	0	0	4.1	1.000	3B-7

Mike Menosky

MENOSKY, MICHAEL WILLIAM (Leaping Mike)
B. Oct. 16, 1894, Glen Campbell, Pa.   D. Apr. 11, 1983, Detroit, Mich.   BL TR 5'10" 163 lbs.

Year	Team		Games	BA	SA	AB	H	2B	3B	HR	HR%	R	RBI	BB	SO	SB	PH AB	PH H	PO	A	E	DP	TC/G	FA	G by Pos
1914	PIT	F	68	.264	.350	140	37	4	1	2	1.4	26	9	16		5	17	6	60	5	4	0	1.0	.942	OF-41
1915			17	.095	.095	21	2	0	0	0	0.0	3	1	2		2	5	0	11	0	1	0	0.7	.917	OF-9
1916	WAS	A	10	.162	.243	37	6	1	1	0	0.0	5	3	1	10	1	1	0	17	3	1	2	2.1	.952	OF-9
1917			114	.258	.366	322	83	12	10	1	0.3	46	34	45	55	22	13	4	208	15	4	3	2.0	.982	OF-94
1919			116	.287	.401	342	98	15	3	6	1.8	62	39	44	46	13	7	3	222	7	5	1	2.0	.979	OF-103
1920	BOS	A	141	.297	.393	532	158	24	9	3	0.6	80	64	65	52	23	0	0	281	17	12	2	2.2	.961	OF-141
1921			133	.300	.377	477	143	18	5	3	0.6	77	43	60	45	12	0	0	278	12	9	3	2.2	.970	OF-133
1922			126	.283	.369	406	115	16	5	3	0.7	61	32	40	33	9	21	7	240	14	6	3	2.1	.977	OF-103
1923			84	.229	.314	188	43	8	4	0	0.0	22	25	22	19	3	23	6	103	12	10	1	1.5	.920	OF-49
9 yrs.			809	.278	.370	2465	685	98	38	18	0.7	382	250	295	260	90	87	26	1420	85	52	15	1.9	.967	OF-682

Ed Mensor

MENSOR, EDWARD (The Midget)
B. Nov. 7, 1886, Woodville, Ontario, Canada   D. Apr. 20, 1970, Salem, Ore.   BB TR 5'6" 145 lbs.

Year	Team		Games	BA	SA	AB	H	2B	3B	HR	HR%	R	RBI	BB	SO	SB	PH AB	PH H	PO	A	E	DP	TC/G	FA	G by Pos
1912	PIT	N	39	.263	.333	99	26	3	2	0	0.0	19	1	23	12	10	5	1	60	3	3	0	1.7	.955	OF-32
1913			44	.179	.196	56	10	1	0	0	0.0	9	1	8	13	2	15	4	31	4	1	1	0.8	.972	OF-18, SS-1, 2B-1
1914			44	.202	.281	89	18	2	1	1	1.1	15	6	22	13	2	6	0	61	2	2	0	1.5	.969	OF-25
3 yrs.			127	.221	.283	244	54	6	3	1	0.4	43	8	53	38	14	26	5	152	9	6	1	1.3	.964	OF-75, SS-1, 2B-1

Ted Menze

MENZE, THEODORE CHARLES
B. Nov. 4, 1897, St. Louis, Mo.   D. Dec. 23, 1969, St. Louis, Mo.   BR TR 5'9" 172 lbs.

Year	Team		Games	BA	SA	AB	H	2B	3B	HR	HR%	R	RBI	BB	SO	SB	PH AB	PH H	PO	A	E	DP	TC/G	FA	G by Pos
1918	STL	N	1	.000	.000	3	0	0	0	0	0.0	0	0	0	2	0	0	0	1	0	0	0	1.0	1.000	OF-1

Rudi Meoli

MEOLI, RUDOLPH BARTHOLOMEW
B. May 1, 1951, Troy, N. Y.   BL TR 5'9" 165 lbs.

Year	Team		Games	BA	SA	AB	H	2B	3B	HR	HR%	R	RBI	BB	SO	SB	PH AB	PH H	PO	A	E	DP	TC/G	FA	G by Pos
1971	CAL	A	7	.000	.000	3	0	0	0	0	0.0	0	0	0	1	0	3	0	0	0	0	0	0.0	—	
1973			120	.223	.289	305	68	12	1	2	0.7	36	23	31	38	2	1	1	142	284	30	57	3.8	.934	SS-95, 3B-13, 2B-8
1974			36	.244	.267	90	22	2	0	0	0.0	9	3	8	10	2	5	0	15	67	5	6	2.4	.943	3B-20, SS-8, 2B-1, 1B-1
1975			70	.214	.246	126	27	2	1	0	0.0	12	6	15	20	3	8	1	39	97	10	13	2.1	.932	SS-28, 3B-15, 2B-11, DH-3
1978	CHI	N	47	.103	.172	29	3	0	1	0	0.0	10	2	6	4	1	19	2	6	14	1	0	0.4	.952	2B-6, 3B-5
1979	PHI	N	30	.178	.260	73	13	4	1	0	0.0	2	6	9	15	2	2	0	37	75	2	12	3.8	.982	SS-16, 2B-15, 3B-1
6 yrs.			310	.212	.267	626	133	20	4	2	0.3	69	40	69	88	10	38	4	239	537	48	88	2.7	.942	SS-147, 3B-54, 2B-41, DH-3, 1B-1

Orlando Mercado

MERCADO, ORLANDO
Born Orlando Mercado y Rodriguez.
B. Nov. 7, 1961, Arecibo, Puerto Rico   BR TR 6' 180 lbs.

Year	Team		Games	BA	SA	AB	H	2B	3B	HR	HR%	R	RBI	BB	SO	SB	PH AB	PH H	PO	A	E	DP	TC/G	FA	G by Pos
1982	SEA	A	9	.118	.294	17	2	0	0	1	5.9	1	6	0	5	0	0	0	31	1	0	0	3.6	1.000	C-8, DH-1
1983			66	.197	.298	178	35	11	2	1	0.6	10	16	14	27	2	2	0	342	27	2	2	5.6	.995	C-65
1984			30	.218	.282	78	17	3	1	0	0.0	5	5	4	12	1	3	1	118	10	1	0	4.3	.992	C-29
1986	TEX	A	46	.235	.294	102	24	1	1	1	1.0	7	7	6	13	0	1	0	240	25	1	5	5.8	.996	C-45
1987	2 teams		DET A (10G - .136)			LA	N	(7G -	.600)																
"	total		17	.222	.259	27	6	1	0	0	0.0	3	2	3	1	0	0	0	53	8	1	1	3.6	.984	C-17
1988	OAK	A	16	.125	.250	24	3	0	0	1	4.2	3	1	3	8	0	0	0	45	2	2	0	3.1	.959	C-16
1989	MIN	A	19	.105	.105	38	4	0	0	0	0.0	1	1	4	4	1	0	0	73	9	0	2	4.3	1.000	C-19
7 yrs.			203	.196	.274	464	91	16	4	4	0.9	30	38	34	70	4	6	1	902	82	7	10	4.9	.993	C-199, DH-1

John Mercer

MERCER, JOHN LOCKE
B. June 22, 1892, Taylortown, La.   D. Dec. 22, 1982, Shreveport, La.   BL TL 5'10½" 155 lbs.

Year	Team		Games	BA	SA	AB	H	2B	3B	HR	HR%	R	RBI	BB	SO	SB	PH AB	PH H	PO	A	E	DP	TC/G	FA	G by Pos
1912	STL	N	1	.000	.000	1	0	0	0	0	0.0	0	0	0	0	0	0	0	1	0	1	0	2.0	.500	1B-1

Win Mercer

MERCER, GEORGE BARCLAY
B. June 20, 1874, Chester, W. Va.   D. Jan. 12, 1903, San Francisco, Calif.   BR TR 5'7" 140 lbs.

Year	Team		Games	BA	SA	AB	H	2B	3B	HR	HR%	R	RBI	BB	SO	SB	PH AB	PH H	PO	A	E	DP	TC/G	FA	G by Pos
1894	WAS	N	52	.284	.377	162	46	5	2	2	1.2	27	29	9	20	9	0	0	20	69	6	1	1.8	.937	P-49, OF-4
1895			63	.255	.327	196	50	9	1	1	0.5	26	26	12	32	7	5	2	44	76	25	3	2.3	.828	P-43, SS-7, OF-5, 3B-3, 2B-1
1896			49	.244	.282	156	38	1	1	1	0.6	23	14	9	18	9	2	1	37	89	21	3	3.0	.857	P-46, OF-1
1897			48	.319	.407	135	43	2	5	0	0.0	22	19	6	7	2	0	0	0	0	0	0	0.0	—	P-45
1898			80	.321	.398	249	80	3	5	2	0.8	38	25	18		14	2	1	91	116	29	8	3.0	.877	P-33, SS-23, OF-19, 3B-5, 2B-1
1899			108	.299	.360	375	112	6	7	1	0.3	73	35	32		16	6	3	109	156	40	8	2.8	.869	3B-62, P-23, OF-16, SS-1, 1B-1

Year	Team	Games	BA	SA	AB	H	2B	3B	HR	HR%	R	RBI	BB	SO	SB	Pinch Hit AB	Pinch Hit H	PO	A	E	DP	TC/G	FA	G by Pos

Win Mercer *continued*

Year	Team	Games	BA	SA	AB	H	2B	3B	HR	HR%	R	RBI	BB	SO	SB	AB	H	PO	A	E	DP	TC/G	FA	G by Pos
1900	NY N	75	.294	.310	248	73	4	0	0	0.0	31	27	26		15	1	0	75	149	32	11	3.4	.875	P-32, 3B-19, OF-14, SS-7, 2B-3
1901	WAS A	51	.300	.379	140	42	7	2	0	0.0	26	16	23		10	4	0	92	57	15	10	3.2	.909	P-24, OF-16, 1B-7, SS-1, 3B-1
1902	DET A	35	.180	.200	100	18	2	0	0	0.0	8	6	6		1	0	0	13	103	8	2	3.5	.935	P-35
9 yrs.		561	.285	.345	1761	502	39	23	7	0.4	274	197	141	70	88	22	4	481	815	176	46	2.6	.880	P-330, 3B-90, OF-75, SS-39, 1B-8, 2B-5

Andy Merchant

MERCHANT, JAMES ANDERSON
B. Aug. 30, 1950, Mobile, Ala.
BL TR 5'11" 185 lbs.

Year	Team	Games	BA	SA	AB	H	2B	3B	HR	HR%	R	RBI	BB	SO	SB	AB	H	PO	A	E	DP	TC/G	FA	G by Pos
1975	BOS A	1	.500	.500	4	2	0	0	0	0.0	1	0	1	0	0	0	0	2	1	0	0	3.0	1.000	C-1
1976		2	.000	.000	2	0	0	0	0	0.0	0	0	0	2	0	2	0	1	0	0	0	0.5	1.000	C-1
2 yrs.		3	.333	.333	6	2	0	0	0	0.0	1	0	1	2	0	2	0	3	1	0	0	1.3	1.000	C-2

Art Merewether

MEREWETHER, ARTHUR FRANCIS (Merry)
B. July 1, 1902, East Providence, R. I.
BR TR 5'9½" 155 lbs.

Year	Team	Games	BA	SA	AB	H	2B	3B	HR	HR%	R	RBI	BB	SO	SB	AB	H	PO	A	E	DP	TC/G	FA	G by Pos
1922	PIT N	1	.000	.000	1	0	0	0	0	0.0	0	0	0	0	0	1	0	0	0	0	0	0.0	—	

Fred Merkle

MERKLE, FREDERICK CHARLES
B. Dec. 20, 1888, Watertown, Wis. D. Mar. 2, 1956, Daytona Beach, Fla.
BR TR 6'1" 190 lbs.

Year	Team	Games	BA	SA	AB	H	2B	3B	HR	HR%	R	RBI	BB	SO	SB	AB	H	PO	A	E	DP	TC/G	FA	G by Pos
1907	NY N	15	.255	.277	47	12	1	0	0	0.0	0	5	1		0	0	0	122	7	7	4	9.1	.949	1B-15
1908		38	.268	.439	41	11	2	1	1	2.4	6	7	4		0	16	6	65	3	0	3	1.8	1.000	1B-11, OF-5, 3B-1, 2B-1
1909		78	.191	.237	236	45	9	1	0	0.0	15	20	16		7	8	3	622	30	16	29	8.6	.976	1B-69, 2B-1
1910		144	.292	.441	506	148	35	14	4	0.8	75	70	44	59	23	0	0	1390	84	29	87	10.4	.981	1B-144
1911		149	.283	.438	541	153	24	12	12	2.2	80	84	43	60	49	0	0	1375	117	22	73	10.2	.985	1B-148
1912		129	.309	.449	479	148	22	6	11	2.3	82	84	42	70	37	0	0	1229	72	27	77	10.3	.980	1B-129
1913		153	.261	.373	563	147	30	12	3	0.5	78	69	41	60	35	0	0	1463	76	22	86	10.2	.986	1B-153
1914		146	.258	.375	512	132	25	7	7	1.4	71	63	52	80	23	0	0	1463	88	16	80	10.7	.990	1B-146
1915		140	.299	.384	505	151	25	3	4	0.8	52	62	36	39	20	1	0	1191	58	15	63	9.0	.988	1B-111, OF-29
1916	2 teams		NY N	(112G – .237)		BKN N	(23G – .232)																		
"	total	135	.236	.336	470	111	20	3	7	1.5	51	46	40	50	19	5	2	1192	59	21	61	9.4	.983	1B-127, OF-4
1917	2 teams		BKN N	(2G – .125)		CHI N	(146G – .266)																		
"	total	148	.264	.368	557	147	31	9	3	0.5	66	57	42	61	13	1	0	1453	69	26	86	10.5	.983	1B-142, OF-6
1918	CHI N	129	.297	.388	482	143	25	5	3	0.6	55	65	35	36	21	0	0	1388	82	15	69	11.5	.990	1B-129
1919		133	.267	.349	498	133	20	6	3	0.6	52	62	33	35	20	0	0	1494	56	23	66	11.8	.985	1B-132
1920		92	.285	.397	330	94	20	4	3	0.9	33	38	24	32	3	6	0	906	54	15	52	10.6	.985	1B-85, OF-1
1925	NY A	7	.385	.462	13	5	1	0	0	0.0	4	1	1	1	0	2	1	28	1	0	3	4.1	1.000	1B-5
1926		1	.000	.000	2	0	0	0	0	0.0	0	0	0	0	0	0	0	6	0	0	0	6.0	1.000	1B-1
16 yrs.		1637	.273	.384	5782	1580	290	83	61	1.1	720	733	454	583	271	39	8	15387	856	254	839	10.1	.985	1B-1547, OF-45, 2B-2, 3B-1

WORLD SERIES

Year	Team	Games	BA	SA	AB	H	2B	3B	HR	HR%	R	RBI	BB	SO	SB	AB	H	PO	A	E	DP	TC/G	FA	G by Pos
1911	NY N	6	.150	.200	20	3	1	0	0	0.0	1	1	2	6	0	0	0	62	4	2	0	11.3	.971	1B-6
1912		8	.273	.394	33	9	2	1	0	0.0	5	3	0	7	1	0	0	83	1	3	2	10.9	.966	1B-8
1913		4	.231	.462	13	3	0	0	1	7.7	3	3	1	2	0	0	0	38	1	2	0	10.3	.951	1B-4
1916	BKN N	3	.250	.250	4	1	0	0	0	0.0	0	0	2	0	0	1	0	9	1	1	0	3.7	.909	1B-1
1918	CHI N	6	.278	.278	18	5	0	0	0	0.0	1	1	4	3	0	0	0	52	9	0	6	10.2	1.000	1B-6
5 yrs.		27	.239	.330	88	21	3	1	1	1.1	10	8	9	18	1	1	0	244	16	8	8	9.9	.970	1B-25

Ed Merrill

MERRILL, EDWARD MASON
B. 1860, Chicago, Ill. D. Aug. 18, 1924, Chicago, Ill.
5'11" 176 lbs.

Year	Team	Games	BA	SA	AB	H	2B	3B	HR	HR%	R	RBI	BB	SO	SB	AB	H	PO	A	E	DP	TC/G	FA	G by Pos
1882	WOR N	2	.125	.125	8	1	0	0	0	0.0	0	4	0	1		0	0	1	4	2	0	3.5	.714	3B-2
1884	IND AA	55	.179	.204	196	35	3	1	0	0.0	14	6				0	0	144	162	34	15	6.2	.900	2B-55
2 yrs.		57	.176	.201	204	36	3	1	0	0.0	14	6	1	1		0	0	145	166	36	15	6.1	.896	2B-55, 3B-2

Lloyd Merriman

MERRIMAN, LLOYD ARCHER (Citation)
B. Aug. 2, 1924, Clovis, Calif.
BL TL 6' 190 lbs.

Year	Team	Games	BA	SA	AB	H	2B	3B	HR	HR%	R	RBI	BB	SO	SB	AB	H	PO	A	E	DP	TC/G	FA	G by Pos
1949	CIN N	103	.230	.348	287	66	12	5	4	1.4	35	26	21	36	2	11	1	214	7	7	1	2.2	.969	OF-86
1950		92	.258	.349	298	77	15	3	2	0.7	44	31	30	23	6	4	1	181	4	2	1	2.0	.989	OF-84
1951		114	.242	.359	359	87	23	5	5	1.4	34	36	31	34	8	14	4	309	5	1	2	2.8	.997	OF-102
1954		73	.268	.357	112	30	8	1	0	0.0	12	16	23	10	3	38	11	51	0	1	0	0.7	.981	OF-25
1955	2 teams		CHI A	(1G – .000)		CHI N	(72G – .214)																		
"	total	73	.212	.288	146	31	6	1	1	0.7	15	8	21	21	1	20	4	82	2	2	2	1.2	.977	OF-49
5 yrs.		455	.242	.345	1202	291	64	12	12	1.0	140	117	126	124	20	87	21	837	18	13	6	1.9	.985	OF-346

Bill Merritt

MERRITT, WILLIAM HENRY
B. July 30, 1870, Lowell, Mass. D. Nov. 17, 1937, Lowell, Mass.
BR TR 5'7" 160 lbs.

Year	Team	Games	BA	SA	AB	H	2B	3B	HR	HR%	R	RBI	BB	SO	SB	AB	H	PO	A	E	DP	TC/G	FA	G by Pos
1891	CHI N	11	.214	.238	42	9	1	0	0	0.0	4	4	2	2	0	0	0	41	11	3	2	5.0	.945	C-11, 1B-1
1892	LOU N	46	.196	.262	168	33	4	2	1	0.6	22	13	11	15	3	0	0	175	58	15	6	5.4	.940	C-46
1893	BOS N	39	.348	.496	141	49	6	3	2	1.4	30	26	13	13	3	0	0	130	25	9	6	4.2	.945	C-37, OF-2
1894	3 teams		BOS N	(10G – .231)		PIT N	(36G – .275)		CIN N	(29G – .327)															
"	total	75	.294	.375	248	73	8	3	2	0.8	38	45	32	10	6	4	0	202	78	17	8	4.0	.943	C-60, 1B-5, OF-4, 3B-3
1895	2 teams		CIN N	(22G – .177)		PIT N	(67G – .285)																		
"	total	89	.258	.286	318	82	7	1	0	0.0	41	39	24	21	4	1	0	342	79	27	12	5.0	.940	C-83, 1B-2, 2B-1
1896	PIT N	77	.291	.344	282	82	8	2	1	0.4	26	42	18	10	3	3	1	286	95	25	8	5.3	.938	C-62, 3B-5, 2B-3, 1B-3, SS-2
1897		62	.263	.316	209	55	6	1	1	0.5	21	26	9		2	2	0	270	47	15	10	5.4	.955	C-53, 1B-7
1899	BOS N	1	.000	.000	2	0	0	0	0	0.0	0	0	0	0		0	0	4	2	1	0	4.0	1.000	C-1
8 yrs.		400	.272	.334	1410	383	40	12	8	0.6	182	195	109	71	21	10	1	1448	395	111	52	4.9	.943	C-353, 1B-18, 3B-8, OF-6, 2B-4, SS-2

Year	Team		Games	BA	SA	AB	H	2B	3B	HR	HR%	R	RBI	BB	SO	SB	Pinch Hit AB	H	PO	A	E	DP	TC/G	FA	G by Pos

George Merritt

MERRITT, GEORGE WASHINGTON
B. Apr. 14, 1880, Paterson, N. J. D. Feb. 21, 1938, Memphis, Tenn. TR 6' 160 lbs.

1901	PIT	N	4	.273	.455	11	3	0	1	0	0.0	2		0		0		1	0	1	5	0	0	1.5	1.000	P-3
1902			2	.333	.444	9	3	0	0	0	0.0	2	2	0		0		0	0	4	1	0	0	2.5	1.000	OF-2
1903			9	.148	.222	27	4	0	1	0	0.0	4	3	2		1		0	0	9	0	1	0	1.1	.900	OF-7, P-1
3 yrs.			15	.213	.319	47	10	1	2	0	0.0	8	5	2		1		1	0	14	6	1	0	1.4	.952	OF-9, P-4

Herm Merritt

MERRITT, HERMAN G.
B. Nov. 12, 1900, Independence, Kans. D. May 26, 1957, Kansas City, Mo. BR TR

| 1921 | DET | A | 20 | .370 | .478 | 46 | 17 | 1 | 2 | 0 | 0.0 | 3 | 6 | 1 | 5 | 1 | | 1 | 0 | 25 | 20 | 6 | 0 | 2.6 | .882 | SS-17 |

Howard Merritt

MERRITT, JOHN HOWARD (Lefty)
B. Oct. 6, 1894, Tupelo, Miss. D. Nov. 3, 1955, Tupelo, Miss. BR TL 5'11" 170 lbs.

| 1913 | NY | N | 1 | – | – | 0 | 0 | 0 | 0 | 0 | – | 0 | 0 | 0 | 0 | 0 | | 0 | 0 | 0 | 0 | 0 | 0 | 0.0 | – | OF-1 |

Jack Merson

MERSON, JOHN WARREN
B. Jan. 17, 1922, Elk Ridge, Md. BR TR 5'11" 175 lbs.

1951	PIT	N	13	.360	.540	50	18	2	2	1	2.0	6	14	1	7	0		0	0	30	46	1	7	5.9	.987	2B-13
1952			111	.246	.344	398	98	20	2	5	1.3	41	38	22	38	1		3	0	220	266	12	62	4.5	.976	2B-81, 3B-27
1953	BOS	A	1	.000	.000	4	0	0	0	0	0.0	0	0	0	0	0		0	0	3	4	1	0	8.0	.875	2B-1
3 yrs.			125	.257	.363	452	116	22	4	6	1.3	47	52	23	45	1		3	0	253	316	14	69	4.7	.976	2B-95, 3B-27

Sam Mertes

MERTES, SAMUEL BLAIR (Sandow)
B. Aug. 6, 1872, San Francisco, Calif. D. Mar. 11, 1945, San Francisco, Calif. BR TR 5'10" 185 lbs.

1896	PHI	N	37	.238	.322	143	34	4	4		0	20	14	8		10		1	0	86	5	9	1	2.7	.910	OF-35, SS-1, 2B-1
1898	CHI	N	83	.297	.383	269	80	4	8	1	0.4	45	47	34		27		5	0	128	53	27	16	2.5	.870	OF-60, SS-14, 2B-4, 1B-2
1899			117	.298	.467	426	127	13	16	9	2.1	83	81	33		45		5	1	223	27	21	9	2.3	.923	OF-108, 1B-3, SS-1
1900			127	.295	.407	481	142	25	4	7	1.5	72	60	42		38		0	0	532	49	28	24	4.8	.954	OF-88, 1B-33, SS-7
1901	CHI	A	137	.277	.396	545	151	16	17	5	0.9	94	98	52		46		0	0	357	396	47	54	5.8	.941	2B-132, OF-5
1902			129	.282	.362	497	140	23	7	1	0.2	60	79	37		46		0	0	263	45	23	9	2.6	.931	OF-120, SS-5, C-2, 3B-1, 2B-1, 1B-1, P-1
1903	NY	N	138	.280	.437	517	145	32	14	7	1.4	100	104	61		45		0	0	274	25	9	5	2.2	.971	OF-137, 1B-1, C-1
1904			148	.276	.393	532	147	28	11	4	0.8	83	78	54		47		0	0	248	19	12	1	1.9	.957	OF-147, SS-1
1905			150	.279	.417	551	154	27	17	5	0.9	81	108	56		52		0	0	230	10	10	3	1.7	.960	OF-150
1906	2 teams		124	NY N (71G – .237)		STL N	(53G – .246)																			
"	total		124	.241	.329	444	107	16	10	1	0.2	57	52	45		31		0	0	196	14	14	0	1.8	.938	OF-124
10 yrs.			1190	.279	.398	4405	1227	188	108	40	0.9	695	721	422	10	396		11	0	2537	643	200	120	2.8	.941	OF-974, 2B-138, 1B-40, SS-29, C-3, 3B-1, P-1

WORLD SERIES

| 1905 | NY | N | 5 | .176 | .235 | 17 | 3 | 1 | 0 | 0 | 0.0 | 2 | 3 | 1 | | 0 | | 0 | 0 | 3 | 1 | 0 | 0 | 0.8 | 1.000 | OF-5 |

Lennie Merullo

MERULLO, LEONARD RICHARD
B. May 5, 1917, Boston, Mass. BR TR 5'11½" 166 lbs.

1941	CHI	N	7	.353	.412	17	6	1	0	0	0.0	3	1	2	0	1		0	0	12	18	1	5	4.4	.968	SS-7
1942			143	.256	.324	515	132	23	3	2	0.4	53	37	35	45	14		0	0	299	438	42	80	5.4	.946	SS-143
1943			129	.254	.313	453	115	18	3	1	0.2	37	25	26	42	7		0	0	222	396	39	68	5.1	.941	SS-125, 3B-2, 2B-1
1944			66	.212	.280	193	41	8	1	1	0.5	20	16	16	8	6		1	0	116	167	19	26	4.6	.937	SS-56, 1B-1
1945			121	.239	.299	394	94	18	0	2	0.5	40	37	31	30	7		0	0	209	336	30	49	4.8	.948	SS-118
1946			65	.151	.214	126	19	8	0	0	0.0	14	7	11	13	2		1	0	78	131	12	23	3.4	.946	SS-44
1947			108	.241	.290	373	90	16	1	0	0.0	24	29	15	26	4		0	0	219	322	29	77	5.3	.949	SS-108
7 yrs.			639	.240	.301	2071	497	92	8	6	0.3	191	152	136	174	38		7	1	1155	1808	172	328	4.9	.945	SS-601, 3B-2, 2B-1, 1B-1

WORLD SERIES

| 1945 | CHI | N | 3 | .000 | .000 | 2 | 0 | 0 | 0 | 0 | 0.0 | 0 | 0 | 0 | 1 | 0 | | 0 | 0 | 4 | 2 | 0 | 0 | 2.0 | 1.000 | SS-3 |

Matt Merullo

MERULLO, MATTHEW BATES
B. Aug. 4, 1965, Winchester, Mass. BL TR 6'2" 200 lbs.

| 1989 | CHI | A | 31 | .222 | .272 | 81 | 18 | 1 | 0 | 1 | 1.2 | 5 | 8 | 6 | 14 | 0 | | 7 | 3 | 100 | 10 | 3 | 0 | 3.6 | .973 | C-27, DH-1 |

Steve Mesner

MESNER, STEPHEN MATHIAS
B. Jan. 13, 1918, Los Angeles, Calif. D. Apr. 6, 1981, San Diego, Calif. BR TR 5'9" 178 lbs.

1938	CHI	N	2	.250	.250	4	1	0	0	0	0.0	2	0	1	1	0		1	0	0	2	1	0	1.5	.667	SS-1
1939			17	.279	.372	43	12	4	0	0	0.0	7	6	3	4	0		3	0	16	43	4	8	3.7	.937	SS-12, 3B-1, 2B-1
1941	STL	N	24	.145	.159	69	10	1	0	0	0.0	8	10	5	6	0		1	0	23	45	3	8	3.0	.958	3B-22
1943	CIN	N	137	.272	.327	504	137	26	1	0	0.0	53	52	26	20	6		7	4	132	274	24	29	3.1	.944	3B-130
1944			121	.242	.309	414	100	17	4	1	0.2	31	47	34	20	1		1	0	120	246	19	21	3.2	.951	3B-120
1945			150	.254	.298	540	137	19	1	1	0.2	52	52	52	18	4		0	0	173	329	15	36	3.4	.971	3B-148, 2B-3
6 yrs.			451	.252	.306	1574	397	67	6	2	0.1	153	167	121	69	11		13	4	464	939	66	102	3.3	.955	3B-421, SS-13, 2B-4

Bobby Messenger

MESSENGER, CHARLES WALTER
B. Mar. 19, 1884, Bangor, Me. D. July 10, 1951, Bath, Me. BB TR 5'10½" 165 lbs.

1909	CHI	A	31	.170	.196	112	19	1	1	0	0.0	18	0	13		7		0	0	34	4	2	1	1.3	.950	OF-31
1910			9	.231	.308	26	6	0	1	0	0.0	7	4	3		1		0	0	9	2	2	0	1.4	.846	OF-9
1911			13	.118	.235	17	2	0	1	0	0.0	4	0	3		0	9	2	0	7	0	1	0	0.6	.875	OF-4
1914	STL	A	1	.000	.000	2	0	0	0	0	0.0	0	0	0		0		0	0	0	0	0	0	0.0	–	OF-1
4 yrs.			54	.172	.217	157	27	1	3	0	0.0	29	4	20		10		2	0	50	6	5	1	1.1	.918	OF-45

Tom Messitt

MESSITT, THOMAS JOHN
B. July 27, 1874, Frankfort, Pa. D. Sept. 22, 1934, Chicago, Ill. 5'9" 177 lbs.

| 1899 | LOU | N | 3 | .091 | .091 | 11 | 1 | 0 | 0 | 0 | 0.0 | 0 | 0 | 0 | | 0 | | 0 | 0 | 5 | 7 | 0 | 0 | 4.0 | 1.000 | C-3 |

Year	Team	Games	BA	SA	AB	H	2B	3B	HR	HR%	R	RBI	BB	SO	SB	Pinch Hit AB	H	PO	A	E	DP	TC/G	FA	G by Pos

Scat Metha

METHA, FRANK JOSEPH
B. Dec. 13, 1913, Los Angeles, Calif.   D. Mar. 2, 1975, Fountain Valley, Calif.
BR TR 5'11" 165 lbs.

Year	Team	Games	BA	SA	AB	H	2B	3B	HR	HR%	R	RBI	BB	SO	SB	AB	H	PO	A	E	DP	TC/G	FA	G by Pos
1940	DET A	26	.243	.297	37	9	0	1	0	0.0	6	3	2	8	0	2	0	10	27	2	3	1.5	.949	2B-10, 3B-6

Bud Metheny

METHENY, ARTHUR BEAUREGARD
B. June 1, 1915, St. Louis, Mo.
BL TL 5'11" 190 lbs.

Year	Team	Games	BA	SA	AB	H	2B	3B	HR	HR%	R	RBI	BB	SO	SB	AB	H	PO	A	E	DP	TC/G	FA	G by Pos
1943	NY A	103	.261	.397	360	94	18	2	9	2.5	51	36	39	34	2	10	1	156	1	6	0	1.6	.963	OF-91
1944		137	.239	.355	518	124	16	1	14	2.7	72	67	56	57	5	4	0	232	8	11	2	1.8	.956	OF-132
1945		133	.248	.338	509	126	18	2	8	1.6	64	53	54	31	5	4	0	227	12	4	2	1.8	.984	OF-128
1946		3	.000	.000	3	0	0	0	0	0.0	0	0	0	0	0	3	0	0	0	0	0	0.0	–	
4 yrs.		376	.247	.359	1390	344	52	5	31	2.2	187	156	149	122	12	21	1	615	21	21	4	1.7	.968	OF-351

WORLD SERIES

Year	Team	Games	BA	SA	AB	H	2B	3B	HR	HR%	R	RBI	BB	SO	SB	AB	H	PO	A	E	DP	TC/G	FA	G by Pos
1943	NY A	2	.125	.125	8	1	0	0	0	0.0	0	0	0	0	0	2	0	3	0	0	0	1.5	1.000	OF-2

Catfish Metkovich

METKOVICH, GEORGE MICHAEL
B. Oct. 8, 1921, Angel's Camp, Calif.
BL TL 6'1" 185 lbs.

Year	Team	Games	BA	SA	AB	H	2B	3B	HR	HR%	R	RBI	BB	SO	SB	AB	H	PO	A	E	DP	TC/G	FA	G by Pos
1943	BOS A	78	.246	.361	321	79	14	4	5	1.6	34	27	19	38	1	0	0	206	9	9	5	2.9	.960	OF-76, 1B-2
1944		134	.277	.406	549	152	28	8	9	1.6	94	59	31	57	13	2	1	711	41	16	40	5.7	.978	OF-82, 1B-50
1945		138	.260	.347	539	140	26	3	5	0.9	65	62	51	70	19	3	0	1022	78	16	96	8.1	.986	1B-97, OF-42
1946		86	.246	.356	281	69	15	2	4	1.4	42	25	36	39	8	3	0	125	3	7	0	1.6	.948	OF-81
1947	CLE A	126	.254	.362	473	120	22	7	5	1.1	68	40	32	51	5	6	2	350	3	4	2	2.8	.989	OF-119, 1B-1
1949	CHI A	93	.237	.331	338	80	9	4	5	1.5	50	40	41	24	5	5	1	212	1	7	0	2.4	.968	OF-87
1951	PIT N	120	.293	.378	423	124	21	3	3	0.7	51	40	28	23	3	13	6	477	31	4	32	4.3	.992	1B-37, OF-69
1952		125	.271	.391	373	101	18	3	7	1.9	41	41	32	29	1	20	4	602	34	7	59	5.1	.989	1B-72, OF-33
1953	2 teams	PIT N (26G – .146)			CHI N (61G – .234)																			
"	total	87	.212	.333	165	35	9	1	3	1.8	24	19	22	13	2	33	8	158	3	2	4	1.9	.988	OF-42, 1B-12
1954	MIL N	68	.276	.358	123	34	5	1	1	0.8	7	15	15	15	0	31	9	160	17	0	15	2.6	1.000	1B-18, OF-13
10 yrs.		1055	.261	.367	3585	934	167	36	47	1.3	476	373	307	359	61	116	31	4023	220	73	253	4.1	.983	OF-644, 1B-289

WORLD SERIES

Year	Team	Games	BA	SA	AB	H	2B	3B	HR	HR%	R	RBI	BB	SO	SB	AB	H	PO	A	E	DP	TC/G	FA	G by Pos
1946	BOS A	2	.500	1.000	2	1	0	0	0	0.0	1	0	0	0	0	2	1	0	0	0	0	0.0	–	

Charlie Metro

METRO, CHARLES
Born Charles Moreskonich.
B. Apr. 28, 1919, Nanty-Glo, Pa.
Manager 1962, 1970.
BR TR 5'11½" 178 lbs.

Year	Team	Games	BA	SA	AB	H	2B	3B	HR	HR%	R	RBI	BB	SO	SB	AB	H	PO	A	E	DP	TC/G	FA	G by Pos
1943	DET A	44	.200	.200	40	8	0	0	0	0.0	12	2	3	6	1	2	0	28	0	1	0	0.7	.966	OF-14
1944	2 teams	DET A (38G – .192)			PHI A (24G – .100)																			
"	total	62	.161	.178	118	19	0	1	0	0.0	12	6	10	16	1	8	2	64	11	1	3	1.2	.987	OF-31, 3B-5, 2B-2
1945	PHI A	65	.210	.315	200	42	10	1	3	1.5	18	15	23	33	1	9	3	100	5	3	0	1.7	.972	OF-57
3 yrs.		171	.193	.257	358	69	10	2	3	0.8	42	23	36	55	3	19	5	192	16	5	3	1.2	.977	OF-102, 3B-5, 2B-2

Lenny Metz

METZ, LEONARD RAYMOND
B. July 6, 1899, Louisville, Colo.   D. Feb. 24, 1953, Denver, Colo.
BR TR 5'10½" 170 lbs.

Year	Team	Games	BA	SA	AB	H	2B	3B	HR	HR%	R	RBI	BB	SO	SB	AB	H	PO	A	E	DP	TC/G	FA	G by Pos
1923	PHI N	12	.216	.216	37	8	0	0	0	0.0	4	3	4	0	0	0	0	28	32	2	7	5.2	.968	SS-6, 2B-6
1924		7	.286	.286	7	2	0	0	0	0.0	1	1	0	0	0	0	0	3	8	1	1	1.9	.846	SS-6
1925		11	.000	.000	14	0	0	0	0	0.0	1	0	0	0	0	0	0	9	16	1	0	2.4	.962	SS-9, 2B-2
3 yrs.		30	.172	.172	58	10	0	0	0	0.0	6	4	5	5	0	0	0	40	56	5	8	3.4	.950	SS-21, 2B-8

Roger Metzger

METZGER, ROGER HENRY
B. Oct. 10, 1947, Fredericksburg, Tex.
BB TR 6' 165 lbs.

Year	Team	Games	BA	SA	AB	H	2B	3B	HR	HR%	R	RBI	BB	SO	SB	AB	H	PO	A	E	DP	TC/G	FA	G by Pos
1970	CHI N	1	.000	.000	2	0	0	0	0	0.0	0	0	0	0	0	0	0	1	4	1	1	6.0	.833	SS-1
1971	HOU N	150	.235	.299	562	132	14	11	0	0.0	64	26	44	50	15	1	1	275	459	17	91	5.0	.977	SS-148
1972		153	.222	.259	641	142	12	3	2	0.3	84	38	60	71	23	0	0	238	504	22	101	5.0	.971	SS-153
1973		154	.250	.322	580	145	11	14	1	0.2	67	35	39	70	10	1	0	231	429	17	83	4.4	.982	SS-149
1974		143	.253	.320	572	145	18	10	0	0.0	66	30	37	73	9	0	0	238	451	17	85	4.9	.976	SS-143
1975		127	.227	.296	450	102	7	9	2	0.4	54	26	41	39	4	2	1	186	441	15	83	5.1	.977	SS-126
1976		152	.210	.270	481	101	13	8	0	0.0	37	29	52	63	1	0	0	258	468	10	93	4.8	.986	SS-150, 2B-1
1977		97	.186	.264	269	50	9	6	0	0.0	24	16	32	24	2	1	0	130	260	11	45	4.1	.973	SS-96, 2B-1
1978	2 teams	HOU N (45G – .220)			SF N (75G – .260)																			
"	total	120	.246	.285	358	88	10	2	0	0.0	28	23	24	26	8	4	1	171	289	14	51	4.0	.970	SS-116, 2B-1
1979	SF N	94	.251	.340	259	65	7	8	0	0.0	24	31	23	31	11	6	1	122	237	15	38	4.0	.960	SS-78, 2B-10, 3B-1
1980		28	.074	.074	27	2	0	0	0	0.0	5	0	3	2	0	8	1	14	19	1	4	1.2	.971	SS-13, 2B-1
11 yrs.		1219	.231	.293	4201	972	101	71	5	0.1	453	254	355	449	83	23	5	1864	3561	135	675	4.6	.976	SS-1173, 2B-15, 3B-1

Bill Metzig

METZIG, WILLIAM ANDREW
B. Dec. 4, 1918, Fort Dodge, Iowa
BR TR 6'1" 180 lbs.

Year	Team	Games	BA	SA	AB	H	2B	3B	HR	HR%	R	RBI	BB	SO	SB	AB	H	PO	A	E	DP	TC/G	FA	G by Pos
1944	CHI A	5	.125	.125	16	2	0	0	0	0.0	1	1	1	4	0	0	0	13	15	0	2	5.6	1.000	2B-5

Alex Metzler

METZLER, ALEXANDER
B. Jan. 4, 1903, Fresno, Calif.   D. Nov. 30, 1973, Fresno, Calif.
BL TR 5'9" 167 lbs.

Year	Team	Games	BA	SA	AB	H	2B	3B	HR	HR%	R	RBI	BB	SO	SB	AB	H	PO	A	E	DP	TC/G	FA	G by Pos
1925	CHI N	9	.184	.237	38	7	2	0	0	0.0	2	2	3	7	1	0	0	24	3	0	0	3.0	1.000	OF-9
1926	PHI A	20	.239	.284	67	16	3	0	0	0.0	8	12	7	5	1	3	1	34	3	0	1	1.9	1.000	OF-17
1927	CHI A	134	.319	.429	543	173	29	11	3	0.6	87	61	61	39	15	0	0	397	16	15	6	3.2	.965	OF-134
1928		139	.304	.422	464	141	18	14	3	0.6	71	55	77	30	16	6	2	288	11	10	3	2.2	.968	OF-134
1929		146	.275	.371	568	156	23	13	2	0.4	80	49	80	45	11	4	3	316	16	14	3	2.4	.960	OF-141
1930	2 teams	CHI A (56G – .177)			STL A (56G – .258)																			
"	total	112	.236	.302	288	68	10	3	1	0.3	42	28	32	18	5	24	4	144	3	7	0	1.4	.955	OF-83
6 yrs.		560	.285	.384	1968	561	85	41	9	0.5	290	207	260	144	48	37	7	1203	52	46	13	2.3	.965	OF-518

Year	Team	Games	BA	SA	AB	H	2B	3B	HR	HR%	R	RBI	BB	SO	SB	Pinch Hit AB	Pinch Hit H	PO	A	E	DP	TC/G	FA	G by Pos

Hensley Meulens

MEULENS, HENSLEY FILEMON ACASIO (Bam-Bam)
B. June 23, 1967, Curacao, Netherlands, Ant.
BR TR 6'4" 200 lbs.

Year	Team	Games	BA	SA	AB	H	2B	3B	HR	HR%	R	RBI	BB	SO	SB	PH AB	PH H	PO	A	E	DP	TC/G	FA	G by Pos
1989	NY A	8	.179	.179	28	5	0	0	0	0.0	2	1	2	8	0	0	0	5	23	4	1	4.0	.875	3B-8

Bob Meusel

MEUSEL, ROBERT WILLIAM (Long Bob)
Brother of Irish Meusel.
B. July 19, 1896, San Jose, Calif. D. Nov. 28, 1977, Downey, Calif.
BR TR 6'3" 190 lbs.

Year	Team	Games	BA	SA	AB	H	2B	3B	HR	HR%	R	RBI	BB	SO	SB	PH AB	PH H	PO	A	E	DP	TC/G	FA	G by Pos
1920	NY A	119	.328	.517	460	151	40	7	11	2.4	75	83	20	72	4	8	5	162	85	20	17	2.2	.925	OF-64, 3B-45, 1B-2
1921		149	.318	.559	598	190	40	16	24	4.0	104	135	34	88	17	2	2	253	28	20	8	2.0	.934	OF-147
1922		121	.319	.522	473	151	26	11	16	3.4	61	84	40	58	13	0	0	202	24	12	0	2.0	.950	OF-121
1923		132	.313	.478	460	144	29	10	9	2.0	59	91	31	52	13	9	4	206	17	11	2	1.8	.953	OF-121
1924		143	.325	.494	579	188	40	11	12	2.1	93	120	32	43	26	0	0	252	17	14	4	2.0	.951	OF-143, 3B-2
1925		156	.290	.542	624	181	34	12	33	5.3	101	138	54	55	10	0	0	271	55	6	8	2.1	.982	OF-131, 3B-27
1926		108	.315	.470	413	130	22	3	12	2.9	73	81	37	32	16	1	0	211	4	9	1	2.1	.960	OF-107
1927		135	.337	.510	516	174	47	9	8	1.6	75	103	45	58	24	3	1	249	15	14	1	2.1	.950	OF-131
1928		131	.297	.467	518	154	45	5	11	2.1	77	113	39	56	6	0	0	259	16	7	6	2.2	.975	OF-131
1929		100	.261	.391	391	102	15	3	10	2.6	46	57	17	42	2	3	0	206	9	7	2	2.2	.968	OF-96
1930	CIN N	113	.289	.460	443	128	30	8	10	2.3	62	62	26	63	9	1	0	223	8	9	3	2.1	.963	OF-112
11 yrs.		1407	.309	.497	5475	1693	368	95	156	2.8	826	1067	375	619	140	27	12	2494	278	129	52	2.1	.956	OF-1304, 3B-74, 1B-2

WORLD SERIES

Year	Team	Games	BA	SA	AB	H	2B	3B	HR	HR%	R	RBI	BB	SO	SB	PH AB	PH H	PO	A	E	DP	TC/G	FA	G by Pos
1921	NY A	8	.200	.267	30	6	2	0	0	0.0	3	3	2	5	1	0	0	10	2	0	0	1.5	1.000	OF-8
1922		5	.300	.350	20	6	1	0	0	0.0	2	2	1	3	1	0	0	7	1	0	0	1.6	1.000	OF-5
1923		6	.269	.462	26	7	1	2	0	0.0	1	8	0	3	0	0	0	14	0	0	0	2.3	1.000	OF-6
1926		7	.238	.381	21	5	1	0	0	0.0	3	0	6	1	0	0	0	13	0	1	0	2.0	.929	OF-7
1927		4	.118	.118	17	2	0	0	0	0.0	1	1	1	7	1	0	0	8	0	1	0	2.3	.889	OF-4
1928		4	.200	.467	15	3	1	0	1	6.7	5	3	2	5	2	0	0	4	0	0	0	1.0	1.000	OF-4
6 yrs.		34	.225	.341	129	29	6	3	1	0.8	15	17	12	24	5	0	0	56	3	2	0	1.8	.967	OF-34
						4th						8th												

Irish Meusel

MEUSEL, EMIL FREDERICK
Brother of Bob Meusel.
B. June 9, 1893, Oakland, Calif. D. Mar. 1, 1963, Long Beach, Calif.
BR TR 5'11½" 178 lbs.

Year	Team	Games	BA	SA	AB	H	2B	3B	HR	HR%	R	RBI	BB	SO	SB	PH AB	PH H	PO	A	E	DP	TC/G	FA	G by Pos
1914	WAS A	1	.000	.000	2	0	0	0	0	0.0	0	0	0	0	0	0	0	1	0	0	0	1.0	1.000	OF-1
1918	PHI N	124	.279	.383	473	132	25	6	4	0.8	48	62	30	21	18	0	0	303	25	12	4	2.7	.965	OF-120, 2B-4
1919		135	.305	.411	521	159	26	7	5	1.0	65	59	15	13	24	5	1	256	14	9	4	2.1	.968	OF-128
1920		138	.309	.473	518	160	27	8	14	2.7	75	69	32	27	17	7	1	283	17	21	8	2.3	.935	OF-129, 1B-3
1921	2 teams		PHI	N (89G – .353)		NY	N	(62G – .329)																
"	total	151	.343	.515	586	201	33	13	14	2.4	96	87	33	29	13	0	0	161	20	13	4	1.3	.933	OF-147
1922	NY N	154	.331	.509	617	204	28	17	16	2.6	100	132	35	33	12	0	0	279	15	6	1	1.9	.980	OF-154
1923		146	.297	.477	595	177	22	14	19	3.2	102	125	38	16	8	1	0	268	10	15	2	2.0	.949	OF-145
1924		139	.310	.423	549	170	26	9	6	1.1	75	102	33	18	11	1	1	287	4	10	0	2.2	.967	OF-138
1925		135	.328	.548	516	169	35	8	21	4.1	82	111	26	19	5	8	2	244	16	11	2	2.0	.959	OF-126
1926		129	.292	.432	449	131	25	10	6	1.3	51	65	16	18	5	15	2	197	10	9	1	1.7	.958	OF-112
1927	BKN N	42	.243	.351	74	18	3	1	1	1.4	7	7	11	5	0	23	6	28	2	0	1	0.7	1.000	OF-17
11 yrs.		1294	.310	.464	4900	1521	250	93	106	2.2	701	819	269	199	113	60	13	2307	133	106	27	2.0	.958	OF-1217, 2B-4, 1B-3

WORLD SERIES

Year	Team	Games	BA	SA	AB	H	2B	3B	HR	HR%	R	RBI	BB	SO	SB	PH AB	PH H	PO	A	E	DP	TC/G	FA	G by Pos
1921	NY N	8	.345	.586	29	10	1	1	1	3.4	4	7	2	3	1	0	0	8	2	0	0	1.3	1.000	OF-8
1922		5	.250	.400	20	5	0	0	1	5.0	3	7	0	1	0	0	0	3	0	0	0	0.6	1.000	OF-5
1923		6	.280	.520	25	7	1	1	1	4.0	3	2	0	2	0	0	0	13	0	0	0	2.2	1.000	OF-6
1924		4	.154	.154	13	2	0	0	0	0.0	0	1	2	0	0	1	0	5	0	1	0	1.5	.833	OF-4
4 yrs.		23	.276	.460	87	24	3	2	3	3.4	10	17	4	6	1	1	0	29	2	1	0	1.4	.969	OF-23

Benny Meyer

MEYER, BERNHARD (Earache)
B. Jan. 1, 1888, Hematite, Mo. D. Feb. 6, 1974, Festus, Mo.
BR TR 5'9" 170 lbs.

Year	Team	Games	BA	SA	AB	H	2B	3B	HR	HR%	R	RBI	BB	SO	SB	PH AB	PH H	PO	A	E	DP	TC/G	FA	G by Pos
1913	BKN N	38	.195	.253	87	17	1	1	1	1.1	12	10	10	14	8	2	0	47	3	6	0	1.4	.943	OF-27, C-1
1914	BAL F	143	.304	.410	500	152	18	10	5	1.0	76	40	71		23	5	1	179	22	18	6	1.5	.918	OF-132, SS-4
1915	2 teams		BAL	F (35G – .242)		BUF	F	(93G – .231)																
"	total	128	.234	.289	453	106	10	6	1	0.2	57	34	77		15	7	2	187	10	12	1	1.6	.943	OF-122
1925	PHI N	1	1.000	2.000	1	1	1	0	0	0.0	1	0	0	0	0	0	0	0	0	0	0	0.0	–	2B-1
4 yrs.		310	.265	.346	1041	276	29	17	7	0.7	146	84	158	14	46	14	3	413	35	33	7	1.6	.931	OF-281, SS-4, 2B-1, C-1

Billy Meyer

MEYER, WILLIAM ADAM
B. Jan. 14, 1892, Knoxville, Tenn. D. Mar. 31, 1957, Knoxville, Tenn.
Manager 1948-52.
BR TR 5'9½" 170 lbs.

Year	Team	Games	BA	SA	AB	H	2B	3B	HR	HR%	R	RBI	BB	SO	SB	PH AB	PH H	PO	A	E	DP	TC/G	FA	G by Pos
1913	CHI A	1	1.000	1.000	1	1	0	0	0	0.0	0	0	0	0	0	0	0	5	1	1	0	7.0	.857	C-1
1916	PHI A	50	.232	.297	138	32	2	2	1	0.7	6	12	8	11	3	2	0	217	79	12	5	6.2	.961	C-48
1917		62	.235	.278	162	38	5	1	0	0.0	9	9	7	14	0	7	0	235	66	12	2	5.0	.962	C-55
3 yrs.		113	.236	.289	301	71	7	3	1	0.3	15	21	15	25	3	9	0	457	146	25	7	5.6	.960	C-104

Dan Meyer

MEYER, DANIEL THOMAS
B. Aug. 3, 1952, Hamilton, Ohio.
BL TR 5'11" 180 lbs.

Year	Team	Games	BA	SA	AB	H	2B	3B	HR	HR%	R	RBI	BB	SO	SB	PH AB	PH H	PO	A	E	DP	TC/G	FA	G by Pos
1974	DET A	13	.200	.440	50	10	1	1	3	6.0	5	7	1	1	1	1	0	29	0	1	0	2.3	.967	OF-12
1975		122	.236	.336	470	111	17	3	8	1.7	56	47	26	25	8	2	1	571	41	12	39	5.1	.981	OF-74, 1B-46
1976		105	.252	.327	294	74	8	4	2	0.7	37	16	17	22	10	36	8	244	14	2	16	2.5	.992	OF-47, 1B-19
1977	SEA A	159	.273	.442	582	159	24	4	22	3.8	75	90	43	51	11	2	0	1407	109	12	134	9.6	.992	1B-159
1978		123	.227	.327	444	101	18	4	8	1.8	38	56	24	39	7	1	0	1107	79	13	119	9.7	.989	1B-121, OF-2, DH-1
1979		144	.278	.459	525	146	21	7	20	3.8	72	74	29	35	11	7	2	198	205	22	27	3.0	.948	3B-101, OF-31, 1B-15
1980		146	.275	.407	531	146	25	6	11	2.1	56	71	31	42	8	17	3	219	22	10	7	1.7	.960	OF-123, DH-7, 3B-5, 1B-4
1981		83	.262	.345	252	66	10	1	3	1.2	26	22	10	16	4	19	3	79	88	7	15	2.1	.960	3B-49, OF-14, DH-3, 1B-3
1982	OAK A	120	.240	.363	383	92	17	3	8	2.1	28	59	19	33	1	29	4	387	32	5	38	3.5	.988	1B-58, DH-38, OF-11
1983		69	.189	.260	169	32	9	0	1	0.6	15	13	19	11	0	7	1	305	16	4	28	4.7	.988	1B-41, DH-12, OF-11, 3B-1
1984		20	.318	.545	22	7	3	1	0	0.0	1	4	0	2	0	17	4	15	2	1	1	0.9	.944	1B-3, DH-2

Year	Team		Games	BA	SA	AB	H	2B	3B	HR	HR%	R	RBI	BB	SO	SB	Pinch Hit AB	Pinch Hit H	PO	A	E	DP	TC/G	FA	G by Pos

Dan Meyer *continued*

| 1985 | | | 14 | .000 | .000 | 12 | 0 | 0 | 0 | 0 | 0.0 | 2 | 0 | 1 | 0 | 0 | 12 | 0 | 1 | 0 | 0 | 0 | 0.1 | 1.000 | DH-1, OF-1, 3B-1 |
| 12 yrs. | | | 1118 | .253 | .379 | 3734 | 944 | 153 | 31 | 86 | 2.3 | 411 | 459 | 220 | 277 | 61 | 150 | 26 | 4562 | 608 | 89 | 424 | 4.7 | .983 | 1B-469, OF-326, 3B-157, DH-64 |

Dutch Meyer

MEYER, LAMBERT DALTON BR TR 5'10½" 181 lbs.
B. Oct. 6, 1915, Waco, Tex.

1937	CHI	N	1	–	–	0	0	0	0	0	0.0	0	0	0	0	0	0	0	0	0	0	0	0.0	–	
1940	DET	A	23	.259	.310	58	15	3	0	0	0.0	12	6	4	10	2	3	0	28	44	3	6	3.3	.960	2B-21
1941			46	.190	.281	153	29	9	1	1	0.7	12	14	8	13	1	6	2	107	101	6	19	4.7	.972	2B-40
1942			14	.327	.500	52	17	3	0	2	3.8	5	9	4	4	0	0	0	31	56	1	14	6.3	.989	2B-14
1945	CLE	A	130	.292	.418	524	153	29	8	7	1.3	71	48	40	32	2	0	0	317	313	14	66	5.0	.978	2B-130
1946			72	.232	.285	207	48	5	3	0	0.0	13	16	26	16	0	7	1	110	150	6	26	3.7	.977	2B-64
6 yrs.			286	.264	.367	994	262	49	12	10	1.0	113	93	82	75	5	16	3	593	664	30	131	4.5	.977	2B-269

George Meyer

MEYER, GEORGE FRANCIS BR TR 5'9" 160 lbs.
B. Aug. 3, 1909, Chicago, Ill.

| 1938 | CHI | A | 24 | .296 | .370 | 81 | 24 | 2 | 2 | 0 | 0.0 | 10 | 9 | 11 | 17 | 3 | 0 | 0 | 61 | 86 | 5 | 12 | 6.3 | .967 | 2B-24 |

Joey Meyer

MEYER, TANNER JOE BR TR 6'3" 260 lbs.
B. May 10, 1962, Honolulu, Hawaii

1988	MIL	A	103	.263	.419	327	86	18	0	11	3.4	22	45	23	88	0	4	1	190	18	3	19	2.0	.986	DH-66, 1B-33
1989			53	.224	.408	147	33	6	0	7	4.8	13	29	12	36	1	6	1	100	7	2	14	2.1	.982	DH-31, 1B-18
2 yrs.			156	.251	.416	474	119	24	0	18	3.8	35	74	35	124	1	10	2	290	25	5	33	2.1	.984	DH-97, 1B-51

Leo Meyer

MEYER, LEO TR

| 1909 | BKN | N | 7 | .130 | .130 | 23 | 3 | 0 | 0 | 0 | 0.0 | 1 | 0 | 2 | | 0 | 0 | 0 | 22 | 23 | 6 | 2 | 7.3 | .882 | SS-7 |

Scott Meyer

MEYER, SCOTT WILLIAM BR TR 6'1" 195 lbs.
B. Aug. 19, 1957, Evergreen Park, Ill.

| 1978 | OAK | A | 8 | .111 | .222 | 9 | 1 | 1 | 0 | 0 | 0.0 | 1 | 0 | 1 | 4 | 0 | 0 | 0 | 11 | 0 | 0 | 0 | 1.4 | 1.000 | C-7, DH-1 |

Levi Meyerle

MEYERLE, LEVI SAMUEL (Long Levi) BR TR 6'1" 177 lbs.
B. July, 1845, Philadelphia, Pa. D. Nov. 4, 1921, Philadelphia, Pa.

1876	PHI	N	55	.340	.449	256	87	12	8	0	0.0	46	34	3	2		0	0	98	110	52	5	4.7	.800	3B-49, OF-3, 2B-3, P-2
1877	CIN	N	27	.327	.430	107	35	7	2	0	0.0	11	15	0	4		0	0	55	86	24	5	6.1	.855	SS-18, 2B-12, OF-1
1884	PHI	U	3	.091	.182	11	1	1	0	0	0.0	0		0			0	0	15	0	4	1	6.3	.789	1B-2, OF-1
3 yrs.			85	.329	.436	374	123	20	10	0	0.0	57	49	3	6		0	0	168	196	80	11	5.2	.820	3B-49, SS-18, 2B-15, OF-5, 1B-2, P-2

Chief Meyers

MEYERS, JOHN TORTES BR TR 5'11" 194 lbs.
B. July 29, 1880, Riverside, Calif. D. July 25, 1971, San Bernardino, Calif.

1909	NY	N	90	.277	.382	220	61	10	5	1	0.5	15	30	22		3	24	8	376	71	17	4	5.2	.963	C-64
1910			127	.285	.342	365	104	18	0	1	0.3	25	62	40	18	5	9	1	638	154	25	16	6.4	.969	C-117
1911			133	.332	.432	391	130	18	9	1	0.3	48	61	25	33	7	4	1	729	108	18	11	6.4	.979	C-128
1912			126	.358	.477	371	133	16	5	6	1.6	60	54	47	20	8	7	1	576	111	19	10	5.6	.973	C-122
1913			120	.312	.410	378	118	18	5	3	0.8	37	47	37	21	7	2	1	579	143	25	12	6.2	.967	C-116
1914			134	.286	.354	381	109	13	5	1	0.3	33	55	34	25	4	7	3	487	150	20	16	4.9	.970	C-126
1915			110	.232	.311	289	67	10	5	1	0.3	24	26	26	18	4	11	1	464	90	8	15	5.1	.986	C-110
1916	BKN	N	80	.247	.314	239	59	10	3	0	0.0	21	21	26	15	2	5	0	389	95	8	9	6.2	.984	C-74
1917	2 teams		BKN	N	(47G – .212)		BOS	N	(25G – .250)																
"	total		72	.225	.300	200	45	7	4	0	0.0	13	7	17	11	4	4	0	299	74	6	6	5.3	.984	C-68
9 yrs.			992	.291	.378	2834	826	120	41	14	0.5	276	363	274	162	44	68	16	4537	996	146	99	5.7	.974	C-925

WORLD SERIES

1911	NY	N	6	.300	.400	20	6	2	0	0	0.0	2	2	0	3	0	0	0	37	12	0	1	8.2	1.000	C-6
1912			8	.357	.429	28	10	0	1	0	0.0	2	3	2	3	1	0	0	42	4	1	0	5.9	.979	C-8
1913			1	.000	.000	4	0	0	0	0	0.0	0	0	0	0	0	0	0	4	2	0	0	6.0	1.000	C-1
1916	BKN	N	3	.200	.400	10	2	0	1	0	0.0	0	1	1	0	0	0	0	21	8	0	0	9.7	1.000	C-3
4 yrs.			18	.290	.387	62	18	2	2	0	0.0	4	6	3	6	1	0	0	104	26	1	1	7.3	.992	C-18

Henry Meyers

MEYERS, HENRY L.
B. 1860, Philadelphia, Pa. D. June 28, 1898, Harrisburg, Pa.

| 1890 | PHI | AA | 5 | .158 | .158 | 19 | 3 | 0 | 0 | 0 | 0.0 | 2 | | 1 | | 2 | 0 | 0 | 6 | 7 | 6 | 0 | 3.8 | .684 | 3B-5 |

Lew Meyers

MEYERS, LEWIS HENRY BR TR 5'11" 165 lbs.
B. Dec. 9, 1859, Cincinnati, Ohio D. Nov. 30, 1920, Cincinnati, Ohio

| 1884 | CIN | U | 2 | .000 | .000 | 3 | 0 | 0 | 0 | 0 | 0.0 | 1 | | 1 | | | 0 | 0 | 1 | 1 | 1 | 0 | 1.5 | .667 | C-2, OF-1 |

Bob Micelotta

MICELOTTA, ROBERT PETER (Mickey) BR TR 5'11" 185 lbs.
B. Oct. 20, 1928, Corona, N. Y.

1954	PHI	N	13	.000	.000	3	0	0	0	0	0.0	2	0	1	1	0	2	0	0	1	1	0	0.1	1.000	SS-1
1955			4	.000	.000	4	0	0	0	0	0.0	0	0	0	1	0	2	0	2	2	0	1	1.0	1.000	SS-2
2 yrs.			17	.000	.000	7	0	0	0	0	0.0	2	0	1	2	0	4	0	2	3	1	1	0.3	1.000	SS-3

Gene Michael

MICHAEL, EUGENE RICHARD (Stick) BB TR 6'2" 183 lbs.
B. June 2, 1938, Kent, Ohio
Manager 1981-82, 1986-87.

| 1966 | PIT | N | 30 | .152 | .273 | 33 | 5 | 2 | 1 | 0 | 0.0 | 9 | 2 | 0 | 7 | 0 | 10 | 3 | 10 | 20 | 3 | 7 | 1.1 | .909 | SS-8, 2B-2, 3B-1 |
| 1967 | LA | N | 98 | .202 | .224 | 223 | 45 | 3 | 1 | 0 | 0.0 | 20 | 7 | 11 | 30 | 1 | 2 | 0 | 117 | 204 | 17 | 30 | 3.4 | .950 | SS-83 |

Year	Team		Games	BA	SA	AB	H	2B	3B	HR	HR%	R	RBI	BB	SO	SB	Pinch Hit AB	H	PO	A	E	DP	TC/G	FA	G by Pos

Gene Michael *continued*

Year	Team		Games	BA	SA	AB	H	2B	3B	HR	HR%	R	RBI	BB	SO	SB	PH AB	PH H	PO	A	E	DP	TC/G	FA	G by Pos
1968	NY	A	61	.198	.250	116	23	3	0	1	0.9	8	8	2	23	3	0	0	68	103	11	15	3.0	.940	SS-43, P-1
1969			119	.272	.364	412	112	24	4	2	0.5	41	31	43	56	7	1	0	205	365	19	64	4.9	.968	SS-118
1970			134	.214	.255	435	93	10	1	2	0.5	42	38	50	93	3	6	4	259	390	28	79	5.1	.959	SS-123, 3B-4, 2B-3
1971			139	.224	.276	456	102	15	0	3	0.7	36	35	48	64	3	6	2	243	474	20	88	5.3	.973	SS-136
1972			126	.233	.279	391	91	7	4	1	0.3	29	32	32	45	4	5	2	218	437	21	89	5.4	.969	SS-121
1973			129	.225	.278	418	94	11	1	3	0.7	30	47	26	51	1	0	0	208	433	23	84	5.1	.965	SS-129
1974			81	.260	.311	177	46	9	0	0	0.0	19	13	14	24	0	1	1	122	170	9	40	3.7	.970	2B-45, SS-39, 3B-2
1975	DET	A	56	.214	.290	145	31	2	0	3	2.1	15	13	8	28	0	1	1	63	125	10	28	3.5	.949	SS-44, 2B-7, 3B-4
10 yrs.			973	.229	.284	2806	642	86	12	15	0.5	249	226	234	421	22	32	13	1513	2721	161	524	4.5	.963	SS-844, 2B-57, 3B-11, P-1

Cass Michaels

MICHAELS, CASIMIR EUGENE
Born Casimir Eugene Kwietniewski.
B. Mar. 4, 1926, Detroit, Mich.   D. Nov. 12, 1982, Grosse Pointe, Mich.

BR TR 5'11" 175 lbs.

Year	Team		Games	BA	SA	AB	H	2B	3B	HR	HR%	R	RBI	BB	SO	SB	PH AB	PH H	PO	A	E	DP	TC/G	FA	G by Pos
1943	CHI	A	2	.000	.000	7	0	0	0	0	0.0	0	0	0	0	0	0	0	1	1	0	0	1.0	1.000	3B-2
1944			27	.176	.265	68	12	4	1	0	0.0	4	5	2	5	0	1	0	37	71	8	12	4.3	.931	SS-21, 3B-3
1945			129	.245	.299	445	109	8	5	2	0.4	47	54	37	28	8	2	0	260	428	47	74	5.7	.936	SS-126, 2B-1
1946			91	.258	.296	291	75	8	0	1	0.3	37	22	29	36	9	3	0	213	235	22	62	5.2	.953	2B-66, 3B-13, SS-6
1947			110	.273	.363	355	97	15	4	3	0.8	31	34	39	28	10	3	0	210	267	15	61	4.5	.970	2B-60, 3B-44, SS-2
1948			145	.248	.329	484	120	12	6	5	1.0	47	56	69	42	8	4	2	313	456	28	115	5.5	.965	SS-85, 2B-55, OF-1
1949			154	.308	.421	561	173	27	9	6	1.1	73	83	101	50	5	0	0	392	484	22	135	5.8	.976	2B-154
1950	2 teams			CHI A	(36G – .312)		WAS A	(106G – .250)																		
"	total		142	.266	.365	526	140	14	7	8	1.5	69	66	68	47	2	3	2	399	401	23	127	5.8	.972	2B-139
1951	WAS	A	138	.258	.340	485	125	20	4	4	0.8	59	45	61	41	1	7	2	258	391	24	86	4.9	.964	2B-128
1952	3 teams			WAS A	(22G – .233)		STL A	(55G – .265)		PHI A	(55G – .250)														
"	total		132	.252	.356	452	114	10	1	5	1.1	53	50	53	42	4	6	2	258	308	17	62	4.4	.971	2B-85, 3B-42
1953	PHI	A	117	.251	.363	411	103	10	0	12	2.9	53	42	51	56	7	6	2	304	302	19	81	5.3	.970	2B-110
1954	CHI	A	101	.262	.397	282	74	13	2	7	2.5	35	44	56	31	10	7	0	96	182	12	10	2.9	.959	3B-91, 2B-2
12 yrs.			1288	.262	.353	4367	1142	147	46	53	1.2	508	501	566	406	64	42	10	2741	3526	237	825	5.0	.964	2B-800, SS-240, 3B-195, OF-1

Ralph Michaels

MICHAELS, RALPH JOSEPH
B. May 3, 1902, Etna, Pa.

BR TR 5'10½" 178 lbs.

Year	Team		Games	BA	SA	AB	H	2B	3B	HR	HR%	R	RBI	BB	SO	SB	PH AB	PH H	PO	A	E	DP	TC/G	FA	G by Pos
1924	CHI	N	8	.364	.364	11	4	0	0	0	0.0	0	2	0	1	0	3	1	6	7	1	1	1.8	.929	SS-4
1925			22	.280	.300	50	14	1	0	0	0.0	10	6	6	9	1	3	0	26	26	1	4	2.4	.981	3B-15, SS-1, 2B-1, 1B-1
1926			2	–	–	0	0	0	0	0	–	1	0	0	0	0	0	0	0	0	0	0	0.0	–	
3 yrs.			32	.295	.311	61	18	1	0	0	0.0	11	8	6	10	1	6	1	32	33	2	5	2.1	.970	3B-15, SS-5, 2B-1, 1B-1

Ed Mickelson

MICKELSON, EDWARD ALLEN
B. Sept. 9, 1926, Ottawa, Ill.

BR TR 6'3" 205 lbs.

Year	Team		Games	BA	SA	AB	H	2B	3B	HR	HR%	R	RBI	BB	SO	SB	PH AB	PH H	PO	A	E	DP	TC/G	FA	G by Pos
1950	STL	N	5	.100	.100	10	1	0	0	0	0.0	1	0	2	3	0	1	0	36	4	0	1	8.0	1.000	1B-4
1953	STL	A	7	.133	.200	15	2	0	0	0	0.0	0	2	2	6	0	3	0	20	2	0	2	3.1	1.000	1B-3
1957	CHI	N	6	.000	.000	12	0	0	0	0	0.0	0	1	0	4	0	4	0	21	3	0	3	4.0	1.000	1B-3
3 yrs.			18	.081	.108	37	3	1	0	0	0.0	2	3	4	13	0	8	0	77	9	0	6	4.8	1.000	1B-9

Ezra Midkiff

MIDKIFF, EZRA MILLINGTON (Salt Rock)
B. Nov. 13, 1882, Salt Rock, W. Va.   D. Mar. 20, 1957, Huntington, W. Va.

BL TR 5'10" 180 lbs.

Year	Team		Games	BA	SA	AB	H	2B	3B	HR	HR%	R	RBI	BB	SO	SB	PH AB	PH H	PO	A	E	DP	TC/G	FA	G by Pos
1909	CIN	N	1	.000	.000	2	0	0	0	0	0.0	0	0	0		0	0	0	0	0	1	0	1.0	–	3B-1
1912	NY	A	21	.244	.256	86	21	0	0	0	0.0	9	9	7	4	0	0	0	21	52	8	1	3.9	.901	3B-21
1913			83	.197	.236	284	56	9	1	0	0.0	22	14	12	33	9	1	0	113	193	13	12	3.8	.959	3B-76, SS-4, 2B-2
3 yrs.			105	.207	.239	372	77	10	1	0	0.0	31	23	19	33	13	1	0	134	245	22	13	3.8	.945	3B-98, SS-4, 2B-2

Ed Mierkowicz

MIERKOWICZ, EDWARD FRANK (Butch)
B. Mar. 6, 1924, Wyandotte, Mich.

BR TR 6'4" 205 lbs.

Year	Team		Games	BA	SA	AB	H	2B	3B	HR	HR%	R	RBI	BB	SO	SB	PH AB	PH H	PO	A	E	DP	TC/G	FA	G by Pos
1945	DET	A	10	.133	.267	15	2	2	0	0	0.0	2	1	1	3	0	3	1	8	0	0	0	0.8	1.000	OF-6
1947			21	.190	.286	42	8	1	0	1	2.4	6	1	1	12	1	9	1	18	0	1	0	0.9	.947	OF-10
1948			3	.200	.200	5	1	0	0	0	0.0	0	0	2	2	0	2	0	4	0	0	0	1.3	1.000	OF-1
1950	STL	N	1	.000	.000	1	0	0	0	0	0.0	0	0	0	1	0	1	0	0	0	0	0	0.0	–	
4 yrs.			35	.175	.270	63	11	3	0	1	1.6	6	4	4	18	1	15	2	30	0	1	0	0.9	.968	OF-17

WORLD SERIES

Year	Team		Games	BA	SA	AB	H	2B	3B	HR	HR%	R	RBI	BB	SO	SB	PH AB	PH H	PO	A	E	DP	TC/G	FA	G by Pos
1945	DET	A	1	–	–	0	0	0	0	0	0.0	0	0	0	0	0	0	0	0	0	0	0	0.0	–	OF-1

Larry Miggins

MIGGINS, LAWRENCE EDWARD (Irish)
B. Aug. 20, 1925, Bronx, N. Y.

BR TR 6'4" 198 lbs.

Year	Team		Games	BA	SA	AB	H	2B	3B	HR	HR%	R	RBI	BB	SO	SB	PH AB	PH H	PO	A	E	DP	TC/G	FA	G by Pos
1948	STL	N	1	.000	.000	1	0	0	0	0	0.0	1	0	0	0	0	0	0	0	0	0	0	0.0	–	
1952			42	.229	.365	96	22	5	1	2	2.1	7	10	3	19	0	16	4	30	0	1	0	0.7	.968	OF-25, 1B-1
2 yrs.			43	.227	.361	97	22	5	1	2	2.1	8	10	3	19	0	17	4	30	0	1	0	0.7	.968	OF-25, 1B-1

John Mihalic

MIHALIC, JOHN MICHAEL
B. Nov. 13, 1911, Cleveland, Ohio   D. Apr. 24, 1987, Ft. Ogelthorpe, Ga.

BR TR 5'11" 172 lbs.

Year	Team		Games	BA	SA	AB	H	2B	3B	HR	HR%	R	RBI	BB	SO	SB	PH AB	PH H	PO	A	E	DP	TC/G	FA	G by Pos
1935	WAS	A	6	.227	.364	22	5	3	0	0	0.0	4	0	2	3	1	0	0	11	17	1	5	4.8	.966	SS-6
1936			25	.239	.284	88	21	2	1	0	0.0	15	8	14	14	2	0	0	59	79	4	23	5.7	.972	2B-25
1937			38	.252	.336	107	27	5	2	0	0.0	13	8	17	9	2	5	0	75	90	3	25	4.4	.982	2B-28, SS-3
3 yrs.			69	.244	.318	217	53	10	3	0	0.0	32	22	33	26	5	5	0	145	186	8	53	4.9	.976	2B-53, SS-9

Eddie Miksis

MIKSIS, EDWARD THOMAS
B. Sept. 11, 1926, Burlington, N. J.

BR TR 6'½" 185 lbs.

Year	Team	Games	BA	SA	AB	H	2B	3B	HR	HR%	R	RBI	BB	SO	SB	Pinch Hit AB	H	PO	A	E	DP	TC/G	FA	G by Pos

Eddie Miksis *continued*

Year	Team	Games	BA	SA	AB	H	2B	3B	HR	HR%	R	RBI	BB	SO	SB	AB	H	PO	A	E	DP	TC/G	FA	G by Pos
1944	BKN N	26	.220	.242	91	20	2	0	0	0.0	12	11	6	11	4	1	0	41	44	8	13	3.6	.914	3B-15, SS-10
1946		23	.146	.146	48	7	0	0	0	0.0	3	5	3	3	0	3	0	13	20	1	0	1.5	.971	3B-13, 2B-1
1947		45	.267	.419	86	23	1	0	4	4.7	18	10	9	8	0	12	1	54	29	1	4	1.9	.988	2B-11, OF-11, 3B-5, SS-2
1948		86	.213	.281	221	47	7	1	2	0.9	28	16	19	27	5	3	1	125	148	9	20	3.3	.968	2B-54, 3B-22, SS-5
1949		50	.221	.292	113	25	5	0	1	0.9	17	6	7	8	3	8	0	33	66	2	4	2.0	.980	3B-29, SS-4, 2B-3, 1B-1
1950		51	.250	.382	76	19	2	1	2	2.6	13	10	5	10	3	4	1	57	55	6	10	2.3	.949	SS-15, 2B-15, 3B-7
1951	2 teams		BKN N	(19G – .200)		CHI N		(102G – .266)																
"	total	121	.265	.339	431	114	14	3	4	0.9	54	35	34	38	11	5	1	282	321	19	73	5.1	.969	2B-103, 3B-6
1952	CHI N	93	.232	.305	383	89	20	1	2	0.5	44	19	20	32	4	1	0	207	254	18	43	5.2	.962	2B-54, SS-40
1953		142	.251	.343	577	145	17	6	8	1.4	61	39	33	59	13	0	0	315	406	35	96	5.3	.954	2B-92, SS-53
1954		38	.202	.293	99	20	3	0	2	2.0	9	3	3	9	1	10	0	64	63	5	16	3.5	.962	2B-21, 3B-2, OF-1
1955		131	.235	.328	481	113	14	2	9	1.9	52	41	32	55	3	2	0	290	52	6	6	2.7	.983	OF-111, 3B-18
1956		114	.239	.360	356	85	10	3	9	2.5	54	27	32	40	4	13	6	144	151	7	14	2.6	.977	3B-48, OF-33, 2B-19, SS-2
1957	2 teams		STL N	(49G – .211)		BAL A		(1G – .000)																
"	total	50	.205	.282	39	8	0	1			1	2.6	3	2	7	7	0	15	3	13	0	0	0	0.3	1.000	OF-31
1958	2 teams		BAL A	(3G – .000)		CIN N		(69G – .140)																
"	total	72	.135	.135	52	7	0	0	0	0.0	15	4	5	6	1	5	0	41	32	4	2	1.1	.948	OF-32, 3B-14, 2B-7, SS-6, 1B-1
14 yrs.		1042	.236	.322	3053	722	95	17	44	1.4	383	228	215	313	52	82	13	1679	1641	121	301	3.3	.965	2B-382, OF-219, 3B-179, SS-137, 1B-2

WORLD SERIES

Year	Team	Games	BA	SA	AB	H	2B	3B	HR	HR%	R	RBI	BB	SO	SB	AB	H	PO	A	E	DP	TC/G	FA	G by Pos
1947	BKN N	5	.250	.250	4	1	0	0	0	0.0	1	0	0	1	0	3	0	3	1	1	2	1.0	.800	OF-2, 2B-1
1949		3	.286	.429	7	2	1	0	0	0.0	0	0	0	1	0	1	1	3	3	1	0	2.3	.857	3B-2
2 yrs.		8	.273	.364	11	3	1	0	0	0.0	1	0	0	2	0	4	1	6	4	2	2	1.5	.833	OF-2, 3B-2, 2B-1

Clyde Milan

MILAN, JESSE CLYDE (Deerfoot)
Brother of Horace Milan.
B. Mar. 25, 1887, Linden, Tenn. D. Mar. 3, 1953, Orlando, Fla.
Manager 1922.

BL TR 5'9" 168 lbs.

Year	Team	Games	BA	SA	AB	H	2B	3B	HR	HR%	R	RBI	BB	SO	SB	AB	H	PO	A	E	DP	TC/G	FA	G by Pos
1907	WAS A	48	.279	.328	183	51	5	2	0	0.0	22	9	8		8	1	0	80	12	7	1	2.1	.929	OF-47
1908		130	.239	.315	485	116	10	12	1	0.2	55	32	38		29	8	1	265	18	12	6	2.3	.959	OF-122
1909		130	.200	.258	400	80	12	4	1	0.3	36	15	31		10	9	3	222	19	7	3	1.9	.972	OF-120
1910		142	.279	.333	531	148	17	6	0	0.0	89	16	71		44	0	0	267	30	17	10	2.2	.946	OF-142
1911		154	.315	.394	616	194	24	8	3	0.5	109	35	74		58	0	0	347	33	17	2	2.6	.957	OF-154
1912		154	.306	.379	601	184	19	11	1	0.2	105	79	63		88	0	0	326	31	25	6	2.5	.935	OF-154
1913		154	.301	.378	579	174	18	9	3	0.5	92	54	58	25	75	0	0	296	20	23	7	2.2	.932	OF-154
1914		115	.295	.396	437	129	19	11	1	0.2	63	39	32	26	38	2	0	230	10	13	0	2.2	.949	OF-113
1915		153	.288	.346	573	165	13	7	2	0.3	83	66	53	32	40	1	0	352	13	21	3	2.5	.946	OF-149
1916		150	.273	.313	565	154	14	3	1	0.2	58	45	56	31	34	0	0	372	27	16	8	2.8	.961	OF-150
1917		155	.294	.333	579	170	15	4	0	0.0	60	48	58	26	20	2	0	339	18	14	3	2.4	.962	OF-153
1918		128	.290	.346	503	146	18	5	0	0.0	56	56	36	14	26	4	1	299	17	9	3	2.5	.972	OF-124
1919		88	.287	.361	321	92	12	6	0	0.0	43	37	40	16	11	2	1	195	9	10	2	2.4	.953	OF-86
1920		126	.322	.403	506	163	22	5	3	0.6	70	41	28	12	10	3	0	291	15	9	1	2.5	.971	OF-123
1921		112	.288	.397	406	117	19	11	1	0.2	55	40	37	13	12	4	0	196	19	16	2	2.1	.931	OF-98
1922		42	.230	.297	74	17	5	0	0	0.0	8	5	2	2	0	29	4	18	3	0	1	0.5	1.000	OF-11
16 yrs.		1981	.285	.353	7359	2100	242	104	17	0.2	1004	617	685	197	495	74	14	4095	294	216	58	2.3	.953	OF-1901

Horace Milan

MILAN, HORACE ROBERT
Brother of Clyde Milan.
B. Apr. 7, 1894, Linden, Tenn. D. June 29, 1955, Texarkana, Ark.

BR TR 5'9" 175 lbs.

Year	Team	Games	BA	SA	AB	H	2B	3B	HR	HR%	R	RBI	BB	SO	SB	AB	H	PO	A	E	DP	TC/G	FA	G by Pos
1915	WAS A	11	.407	.519	27	11	1	1	0	0.0	6	7	8	7	2	0	0	10	0	0	0	0.9	1.000	OF-10
1917		31	.288	.356	73	21	3	1	0	0.0	8	9	4	9	4	8	2	41	0	3	0	1.4	.932	OF-23
2 yrs.		42	.320	.400	100	32	4	2	0	0.0	14	16	12	16	6	8	2	51	0	3	0	1.3	.944	OF-33

Larry Milbourne

MILBOURNE, LAWRENCE WILLIAM
B. Feb. 14, 1951, Port Norris, N. J.

BB TR 6' 161 lbs.

Year	Team	Games	BA	SA	AB	H	2B	3B	HR	HR%	R	RBI	BB	SO	SB	AB	H	PO	A	E	DP	TC/G	FA	G by Pos
1974	HOU N	112	.279	.309	136	38	2	1	0	0.0	31	9	10	14	6	1	0	102	148	7	24	2.3	.973	2B-87, SS-8, OF-4
1975		73	.212	.265	151	32	1	2	1	0.7	17	9	6	14	1	4	1	95	136	10	35	3.3	.959	2B-43, SS-22
1976		59	.248	.276	145	36	4	0	0	0.0	22	7	14	10	6	18	3	67	100	6	19	2.9	.965	2B-32
1977	SEA A	86	.219	.285	242	53	10	0	2	0.8	24	21	6	20	3	9	1	120	209	11	46	4.0	.968	2B-41, SS-40, DH-1, 3B-1
1978		93	.226	.295	234	53	6	2	2	0.9	31	20	9	6	5	3	2	92	169	9	27	2.9	.967	3B-32, SS-23, 2B-15, DH-10
1979		123	.278	.354	356	99	13	4	2	0.6	40	26	19	20	5	30	12	144	265	12	57	3.4	.971	SS-65, 2B-49, 3B-11
1980		106	.264	.333	258	68	6	6	0	0.0	31	26	19	13	7	19	3	103	195	8	50	2.9	.974	2B-38, SS-34, DH-8, 3B-6
1981	NY A	61	.313	.399	163	51	7	2	1	0.6	24	12	9	14	1	2	2	74	121	8	26	3.3	.961	SS-39, 2B-14, DH-3, 3B-3
1982	3 teams		NY A	(14G – .148)		MIN A		(29G – .235)		CLE A		(82G – .275)											
"	total	125	.257	.327	416	107	13	5	2	0.5	40	26	20	32	3	8	1	210	297	18	59	4.2	.966	2B-92, SS-30, 3B-12, DH-1
1983	2 teams		PHI N	(41G – .242)		NY A		(31G – .200)																
"	total	72	.221	.265	136	30	4	1	0	0.0	8	6	9	17	3	9	1	86	105	4	17	2.7	.979	2B-46, SS-14, 3B-7
1984	SEA A	79	.265	.313	211	56	5	1	1	0.5	22	22	12	16	0	23	8	53	86	12	14	1.9	.921	3B-40, 2B-14, DH-6, SS-5
11 yrs.		989	.254	.317	2448	623	71	24	11	0.4	290	184	133	176	41	127	34	1146	1831	105	374	3.1	.966	2B-471, SS-280, 3B-112, DH-29, OF-4

DIVISIONAL PLAYOFF SERIES

Year	Team	Games	BA	SA	AB	H	2B	3B	HR	HR%	R	RBI	BB	SO	SB	AB	H	PO	A	E	DP	TC/G	FA	G by Pos
1981	NY A	5	.316	.368	19	6	1	0	0	0.0	4	0	0	1	0	0	0	0	0	0	0	0.0	–	SS-5

LEAGUE CHAMPIONSHIP SERIES

Year	Team	Games	BA	SA	AB	H	2B	3B	HR	HR%	R	RBI	BB	SO	SB	AB	H	PO	A	E	DP	TC/G	FA	G by Pos
1981	NY A	3	.462	.462	13	6	0	0	0	0.0	4	1	0	0	0	0	0	0	0	0	0	0.0	–	SS-3

WORLD SERIES

Year	Team	Games	BA	SA	AB	H	2B	3B	HR	HR%	R	RBI	BB	SO	SB	AB	H	PO	A	E	DP	TC/G	FA	G by Pos
1981	NY A	6	.250	.350	20	5	2	0	0	0.0	2	3	4	0	0	0	0	5	16	2	1	3.8	.913	SS-6

Year	Team	Games	BA	SA	AB	H	2B	3B	HR	HR%	R	RBI	BB	SO	SB	Pinch Hit AB	Pinch Hit H	PO	A	E	DP	TC/G	FA	G by Pos

Dee Miles

MILES, WILSON DANIEL
B. Feb. 15, 1909, Kellerman, Ala.   D. Nov. 2, 1976, Birmingham, Ala.
BL TR 6' 175 lbs.

Year	Team	Games	BA	SA	AB	H	2B	3B	HR	HR%	R	RBI	BB	SO	SB	PH AB	PH H	PO	A	E	DP	TC/G	FA	G by Pos
1935	WAS A	60	.264	.306	216	57	5	2	0	0.0	28	29	7	13	6	13	4	92	5	3	1	1.7	.970	OF-45
1936		25	.237	.322	59	14	1	2	0	0.0	8	7	1	5	0	14	1	22	1	1	0	1.0	.958	OF-10
1939	PHI A	106	.300	.400	320	96	17	6	1	0.3	49	37	15	17	3	29	7	146	4	5	1	1.5	.968	OF-77
1940		88	.301	.403	236	71	9	4	1	0.4	26	23	8	18	1	33	8	117	3	7	0	1.4	.945	OF-50
1941		80	.312	.365	170	53	7	1	0	0.0	14	15	4	8	0	45	15	79	2	0	1	1.0	1.000	OF-35
1942		99	.272	.335	346	94	12	5	0	0.0	41	22	12	10	5	10	3	177	6	3	0	1.9	.984	OF-81
1943	BOS A	45	.215	.264	121	26	2	2	0	0.0	9	10	3	3	0	21	5	58	3	2	1	1.4	.968	OF-25
7 yrs.		503	.280	.353	1468	411	53	24	2	0.1	175	143	50	74	15	165	43	691	24	21	4	1.5	.971	OF-323

Don Miles

MILES, DONALD RAY
B. Mar. 13, 1936, Indianapolis, Ind.
BL TL 6'1" 210 lbs.

Year	Team	Games	BA	SA	AB	H	2B	3B	HR	HR%	R	RBI	BB	SO	SB	PH AB	PH H	PO	A	E	DP	TC/G	FA	G by Pos
1958	LA N	8	.182	.182	22	4	0	0	0	0.0	2	0	0	6	0	3	0	16	0	0	0	2.0	1.000	OF-5

Mike Miley

MILEY, MICHAEL WILFRED
B. Mar. 30, 1953, Yazoo City, Miss.   D. Jan. 6, 1977, Baton Rouge, La.
BB TR 6'1" 185 lbs.

Year	Team	Games	BA	SA	AB	H	2B	3B	HR	HR%	R	RBI	BB	SO	SB	PH AB	PH H	PO	A	E	DP	TC/G	FA	G by Pos
1975	CAL A	70	.174	.259	224	39	3	2	4	1.8	17	26	16	54	0	0	0	107	186	19	53	4.5	.939	SS-70
1976		14	.184	.237	38	7	2	0	0	0.0	4	4	4	8	1	0	0	22	30	1	9	3.8	.981	SS-14
2 yrs.		84	.176	.256	262	46	5	2	4	1.5	21	30	20	62	1	0	0	129	216	20	62	4.3	.945	SS-84

Felix Millan

MILLAN, FELIX BERNARDO
Born Felix Bernardo Millan y Martinez.
B. Aug. 21, 1943, Yabucoa, Puerto Rico
BR TR 5'11" 172 lbs.

Year	Team	Games	BA	SA	AB	H	2B	3B	HR	HR%	R	RBI	BB	SO	SB	PH AB	PH H	PO	A	E	DP	TC/G	FA	G by Pos
1966	ATL N	37	.275	.341	91	25	6	0	0	0.0	20	5	2	3	3	0	0	57	56	3	13	3.1	.974	2B-25, SS-1, 3B-1
1967		41	.235	.346	136	32	3	3	2	1.5	13	6	4	10	0	0	0	84	125	6	24	5.2	.972	2B-41
1968		149	.289	.340	570	165	22	2	1	0.2	49	33	22	26	6	0	0	330	438	16	91	5.3	.980	2B-145
1969		162	.267	.345	652	174	23	5	6	0.9	98	57	34	35	14	0	0	373	444	17	72	5.1	.980	2B-162
1970		142	.310	.380	590	183	25	5	2	0.3	100	37	35	23	16	0	0	337	359	15	83	5.0	.979	2B-142
1971		143	.289	.362	577	167	20	8	2	0.3	65	45	37	22	11	1	1	373	437	15	120	5.8	.982	2B-141
1972		125	.257	.313	498	128	19	3	1	0.2	46	38	23	28	6	5	1	273	339	8	67	5.0	.987	2B-120
1973	NY N	153	.290	.353	638	185	23	4	3	0.5	82	37	35	22	2	0	0	410	411	9	99	5.4	.989	2B-153
1974		136	.268	.311	518	139	15	2	1	0.2	50	33	31	14	5	1	1	374	315	15	81	5.2	.979	2B-134
1975		162	.283	.348	676	191	37	2	1	0.1	81	56	36	28	1	0	0	379	420	23	95	5.1	.972	2B-162
1976		139	.282	.343	531	150	25	2	1	0.2	55	35	41	19	2	4	1	311	315	15	68	4.6	.977	2B-136
1977		91	.248	.315	314	78	11	2	2	0.6	40	21	18	9	1	0	0	197	188	9	43	4.3	.977	2B-89
12 yrs.		1480	.279	.343	5791	1617	229	38	22	0.4	699	403	318	242	67	14	4	3498	3847	151	856	5.1	.980	2B-1450, SS-1, 3B-1

LEAGUE CHAMPIONSHIP SERIES

Year	Team	Games	BA	SA	AB	H	2B	3B	HR	HR%	R	RBI	BB	SO	SB	PH AB	PH H	PO	A	E	DP	TC/G	FA	G by Pos
1969	ATL N	3	.333	.417	12	4	1	0	0	0.0	2	0	3	0	0	0	0	3	9	1	1	4.3	.923	2B-3
1973	NY N	5	.316	.316	19	6	0	0	0	0.0	5	2	3	1	0	0	0	9	11	0	2	4.0	1.000	2B-5
2 yrs.		8	.323	.355	31	10	1	0	0	0.0	7	2	6	1	0	0	0	12	20	1	3	4.1	.970	2B-8

WORLD SERIES

Year	Team	Games	BA	SA	AB	H	2B	3B	HR	HR%	R	RBI	BB	SO	SB	PH AB	PH H	PO	A	E	DP	TC/G	FA	G by Pos
1973	NY N	7	.188	.281	32	6	1	0	0	0.0	1	1	1	1	0	0	0	16	13	3	3	4.6	.906	2B-7

Frank Millard

MILLARD, FRANK E.
B. July 4, 1865, E. St. Louis, Ill.   D. July 4, 1892, Galveston, Tex.

Year	Team	Games	BA	SA	AB	H	2B	3B	HR	HR%	R	RBI	BB	SO	SB	PH AB	PH H	PO	A	E	DP	TC/G	FA	G by Pos
1890	STL AA	1	.000	.000	1	0	0	0	0	0.0	1		0			0	0	1	4	3	0	8.0	.625	2B-1

Bill Miller

MILLER, WILLIAM A.
B. Cleveland, Ohio   Deceased.
6'5"

Year	Team	Games	BA	SA	AB	H	2B	3B	HR	HR%	R	RBI	BB	SO	SB	PH AB	PH H	PO	A	E	DP	TC/G	FA	G by Pos
1902	PIT N	1	.200	.200	5	1	0	0	0	0.0	0	2	0		0	0	0	0	0	0	0	0.0	—	OF-1

Bing Miller

MILLER, EDMUND JOHN
Brother of Ralph Miller.
B. Aug. 30, 1894, Vinton, Iowa   D. May 7, 1966, Philadelphia, Pa.
BR TR 6' 185 lbs.

Year	Team	Games	BA	SA	AB	H	2B	3B	HR	HR%	R	RBI	BB	SO	SB	PH AB	PH H	PO	A	E	DP	TC/G	FA	G by Pos
1921	WAS A	114	.288	.457	420	121	28	8	9	2.1	57	71	25	50	3	5	2	247	13	15	4	2.4	.945	OF-109
1922	PHI A	143	.336	.553	535	180	29	12	21	3.9	90	90	24	42	10	4	1	314	19	8	3	2.4	.977	OF-139
1923		123	.299	.450	458	137	25	4	12	2.6	68	64	27	34	9	3	0	262	10	6	0	2.3	.978	OF-119
1924		113	.342	.462	398	136	22	4	6	1.5	62	62	12	24	11	9	3	238	18	7	11	2.3	.973	OF-94, 1B-7
1925		124	.319	.485	474	151	29	10	10	2.1	78	81	19	14	11	3	0	245	13	7	7	2.1	.974	OF-115, 1B-12
1926	2 teams	PHI A	(38G – .291)		STL A	(94G – .331)																		
"	total	132	.322	.462	463	149	33	7	6	1.3	73	63	33	18	11	2	1	273	13	15	3	2.3	.950	OF-128, 1B-1
1927	STL A	144	.325	.449	492	160	32	7	5	1.0	83	75	30	26	9	16	6	309	9	10	3	2.3	.970	OF-126
1928	PHI A	139	.329	.471	510	168	34	7	8	1.6	76	85	27	24	10	5	0	298	8	10	2	2.3	.968	OF-133
1929		147	.335	.493	556	186	32	16	8	1.4	84	93	40	25	1	0	0	311	10	10	3	2.3	.970	OF-145
1930		154	.303	.438	585	177	38	7	9	1.5	89	100	47	22	13	0	0	309	10	8	3	2.1	.976	OF-154
1931		137	.281	.425	534	150	43	5	8	1.5	76	77	36	16	5	0	0	305	7	4	1	2.3	.987	OF-137
1932		95	.295	.449	305	90	17	3	8	2.6	40	58	20	11	7	8	2	180	3	4	0	2.0	.979	OF-84
1933		67	.275	.400	120	33	7	1	2	1.7	22	17	12	7	1	30	7	62	2	1	2	1.0	.985	OF-30, 1B-6
1934		81	.243	.339	177	43	10	2	1	0.6	22	22	16	14	1	33	10	72	2	0	1	0.9	1.000	OF-46
1935	BOS A	78	.304	.442	138	42	8	1	3	2.2	18	26	10	8	0	43	13	48	2	0	1	0.7	1.000	OF-29
1936		30	.298	.447	47	14	2	1	1	2.1	9	6	5	5	0	13	1	14	0	0	0	0.5	1.000	OF-13
16 yrs.		1821	.312	.462	6212	1937	389	95	117	1.9	947	990	383	340	128	175	46	3487	140	107	45	2.1	.971	OF-1601, 1B-26

WORLD SERIES

Year	Team	Games	BA	SA	AB	H	2B	3B	HR	HR%	R	RBI	BB	SO	SB	PH AB	PH H	PO	A	E	DP	TC/G	FA	G by Pos
1929	PHI A	5	.368	.421	19	7	1	0	0	0.0	1	4	0	2	0	0	0	13	0	1	0	2.8	.929	OF-5
1930		6	.143	.238	21	3	2	0	0	0.0	0	1	0	4	0	0	0	12	0	0	0	2.0	1.000	OF-6
1931		7	.269	.308	26	7	1	0	0	0.0	3	1	0	4	0	0	0	12	0	0	0	1.7	1.000	OF-7
3 yrs.		18	.258	.318	66	17	4	0	0	0.0	4	8	0	10	0	0	0	37	0	1	0	2.1	.974	OF-18

Year	Team		Games	BA	SA	AB	H	2B	3B	HR	HR%	R	RBI	BB	SO	SB	Pinch Hit AB	H	PO	A	E	DP	TC/G	FA	G by Pos

Bruce Miller

MILLER, CHARLES BRUCE
B. Mar. 4, 1947, Ft. Wayne, Ind.
BR TR 6'1" 185 lbs.

Year	Team		Games	BA	SA	AB	H	2B	3B	HR	HR%	R	RBI	BB	SO	SB	AB	H	PO	A	E	DP	TC/G	FA	G by Pos
1973	SF	N	12	.143	.143	21	3	0	0	0	0.0	1	2	2	3	0	4	0	7	14	2	0	1.9	.913	3B-4, 2B-3, SS-1
1974			73	.278	.323	198	55	7	1	0	0.0	19	16	11	15	1	10	3	55	161	12	11	3.1	.947	3B-41, SS-13, 2B-9
1975			99	.239	.288	309	74	6	3	1	0.3	22	31	15	26	0	12	1	114	186	15	31	3.2	.952	3B-68, 2B-21, SS-6
1976			12	.160	.200	25	4	1	0	0	0.0	1	2	2	5	0	2	0	9	16	2	3	2.3	.926	2B-8, 3B-2
4 yrs.			196	.246	.291	553	136	14	4	1	0.2	43	51	30	49	1	28	4	185	377	31	45	3.0	.948	3B-115, 2B-41, SS-20

Charlie Miller

MILLER, CHARLES ELMER
B. Jan. 4, 1892, Warrensburg, Mo. D. Apr. 23, 1972, Warrensburg, Mo.
TR

Year	Team		Games	BA	SA	AB	H	2B	3B	HR	HR%	R	RBI	BB	SO	SB	AB	H	PO	A	E	DP	TC/G	FA	G by Pos
1912	STL	A	1	.000	.000	2	0	0	0	0	0.0	0	0	0	0	0			0	2	0	0	2.0	1.000	SS-1

Charlie Miller

MILLER, CHARLES HESS
B. Dec. 30, 1877, Conestoga Center, Pa. D. Jan. 13, 1951, Millersville, Pa.
BR TR 6' 190 lbs.

Year	Team		Games	BA	SA	AB	H	2B	3B	HR	HR%	R	RBI	BB	SO	SB	AB	H	PO	A	E	DP	TC/G	FA	G by Pos
1915	BAL	F	1	.000	.000	1	0	0	0	0	0.0	0	0	0	0	0	1	0	0	0	0	0	0.0	—	

Charlie Miller

MILLER, CHARLES MARION
B. Sept. 18, 1889, Woodville, Ohio D. June 16, 1961, Houston, Tex.
BL TL 5'8½" 155 lbs.

Year	Team		Games	BA	SA	AB	H	2B	3B	HR	HR%	R	RBI	BB	SO	SB	AB	H	PO	A	E	DP	TC/G	FA	G by Pos
1913	STL	N	4	.167	.167	12	2	0	0	0	0.0	0	1	0	2	0	1	0	4	0	0	0	1.0	1.000	OF-3
1914			36	.194	.222	36	7	1	0	0	0.0	4	2	3	9	2	11	2	11	1	0	0	0.3	1.000	OF-19
2 yrs.			40	.188	.208	48	9	1	0	0	0.0	4	3	3	11	2	12	2	15	1	0	0	0.4	1.000	OF-22

Dakin Miller

MILLER, DAKIN EVANS
B. Sept. 2, 1877, Malvern, Iowa D. Apr. 20, 1950, Stockton, Calif.
BL TR 5'10" 175 lbs.

Year	Team		Games	BA	SA	AB	H	2B	3B	HR	HR%	R	RBI	BB	SO	SB	AB	H	PO	A	E	DP	TC/G	FA	G by Pos
1902	CHI	N	51	.246	.278	187	46	4	1	0	0.0	17	13	7		10	0	0	97	9	5	0	2.2	.955	OF-51

Darrell Miller

MILLER, DARRELL KEITH
B. Feb. 26, 1958, Washington, D. C.
BR TR 6'2" 200 lbs.

Year	Team		Games	BA	SA	AB	H	2B	3B	HR	HR%	R	RBI	BB	SO	SB	AB	H	PO	A	E	DP	TC/G	FA	G by Pos
1984	CAL	A	17	.171	.171	41	7	0	0	0	0.0	5	1	4	9	0	1	0	92	7	1	12	5.9	.990	1B-16, OF-1
1985			51	.375	.583	48	18	2	1	2	4.2	8	7	1	10	0	6	3	39	3	2	0	0.9	.955	OF-45, DH-4, 3B-1, C-1
1986			33	.228	.298	57	13	2	1	0	0.0	6	4	4	8	0	5	2	30	3	0	0	1.0	1.000	OF-23, C-10, DH-2
1987			53	.241	.398	108	26	5	0	4	3.7	14	16	9	13	1	9	4	131	15	2	1	2.8	.986	C-33, OF-18, 3B-1
1988			70	.221	.307	140	31	4	1	2	1.4	21	7	9	29	2	9	2	229	18	4	1	3.6	.984	C-53, OF-8, DH-1
5 yrs.			224	.241	.350	394	95	13	3	8	2.0	54	35	27	69	3	30	11	521	46	9	14	2.6	.984	C-97, OF-95, 1B-16, DH-7, 3B-2

Doc Miller

MILLER, ROY OSCAR
B. 1883, Chatham, Ont., Canada D. July 31, 1938, Jersey City, N. J.
BL TL 5'10½" 170 lbs.

Year	Team		Games	BA	SA	AB	H	2B	3B	HR	HR%	R	RBI	BB	SO	SB	AB	H	PO	A	E	DP	TC/G	FA	G by Pos
1910	2 teams				CHI N (1G – .000)			BOS N (130G – .286)																	
"	total		131	.286	.377	483	138	27	4	3	0.6	48	55	33	52	17	1	0	203	9	11	3	1.7	.951	OF-130
1911	BOS	N	146	.333	.442	577	192	36	3	7	1.2	69	91	43	43	32	0	0	243	26	11	4	1.9	.961	OF-146
1912	2 teams				BOS N (51G – .234)			PHI N (67G – .288)																	
"	total		118	.259	.360	378	98	20	6	2	0.5	50	45	23	30	9	28	7	140	21	6	5	1.4	.964	OF-90
1913	PHI	N	69	.345	.414	87	30	6	0	0	0.0	9	11	6	6	2	56	20	8	0	2	0	0.1	.800	OF-12
1914	CIN	N	47	.255	.313	192	49	7	2	0	0.0	8	33	16	18	4	35	12	79	2	2	1	1.8	.976	OF-47
5 yrs.			511	.295	.390	1717	507	96	15	12	0.7	184	235	121	149	64	120	39	673	58	32	13	1.5	.958	OF-425

Doggie Miller

MILLER, GEORGE FREDERICK (Foghorn, Calliope)
B. Aug. 15, 1864, Brooklyn, N. Y. D. Apr. 6, 1909, Brooklyn, N. Y.
BR TR 5'6"

Year	Team		Games	BA	SA	AB	H	2B	3B	HR	HR%	R	RBI	BB	SO	SB	AB	H	PO	A	E	DP	TC/G	FA	G by Pos
1884	PIT	AA	89	.225	.265	347	78	10	2	0	0.0	46		13			0	0	252	62	49	4	4.1	.865	OF-49, C-36, 3B-3, 2B-1
1885			42	.163	.193	166	27	3	1	0	0.0	19		4			0	0	185	60	33	4	6.6	.881	C-33, OF-6, SS-2, 3B-2
1886			83	.252	.325	317	80	15	1	2	0.6	70		43			0	0	286	63	34	1	4.6	.911	C-61, OF-23, 2B-1
1887	PIT	N	87	.243	.325	342	83	17	4	1	0.3	58	34	35	13	33	0	0	294	61	31	2	4.4	.920	C-73, OF-14, 3B-1
1888			103	.277	.344	404	112	17	5	0	0.0	50	36	18	16	27	0	0	331	92	44	8	4.5	.906	C-68, OF-32, 3B-4
1889			104	.268	.384	422	113	25	3	6	1.4	77	56	31	11	16	0	0	357	101	53	9	4.9	.896	C-76, OF-27, 3B-3
1890			138	.273	.350	549	150	24	3	4	0.7	85	66	68	11	32	0	0	236	285	82	21	4.4	.864	3B-88, OF-25, SS-13, C-10, 2B-6
1891			135	.285	.363	548	156	19	3	4	0.7	80	57	59	26	35	0	0	339	238	80	13	4.9	.878	C-41, SS-37, 3B-34, OF-24, 1B-1
1892			149	.254	.326	623	158	15	12	2	0.3	103	59	69	14	28	0	0	413	145	44	22	4.0	.927	OF-76, C-63, SS-19, 3B-2
1893			41	.182	.234	154	28	6	1	0	0.0	23	17	17	8	3	1	0	141	45	17	3	5.0	.916	C-40
1894	STL	N	127	.339	.453	481	163	9	11	8	1.7	93	86	58	9	17	2	0	361	191	60	17	4.8	.902	3B-52, C-41, 2B-18, 1B-12, OF-4, SS-1
1895			121	.292	.369	490	143	19	4	5	1.0	81	74	25	12	18	0	0	276	145	55	16	3.9	.884	3B-46, C-46, OF-21, SS-9, 1B-6
1896	LOU	N	98	.275	.361	324	89	17	4	1	0.3	54	33	27	9	16	9	6	202	130	31	14	3.7	.915	C-48, 2B-25, OF-8, 3B-8, 1B-3, SS-2
13 yrs.			1317	.267	.345	5167	1380	192	57	33	0.6	839	518	467	129	225	12	6	3673	1618	613	134	4.5	.896	C-636, OF-309, 3B-243, SS-83, 2B-51, 1B-22

Dots Miller

MILLER, JOHN BARNEY
B. Sept. 9, 1886, Kearny, N. J. D. Sept. 5, 1923, Saranac Lake, N. Y.
BR TR 5'11½" 170 lbs.

Year	Team		Games	BA	SA	AB	H	2B	3B	HR	HR%	R	RBI	BB	SO	SB	AB	H	PO	A	E	DP	TC/G	FA	G by Pos
1909	PIT	N	151	.279	.396	560	156	31	13	3	0.5	71	87	39		14	1	0	260	426	34	50	4.8	.953	2B-150
1910			120	.227	.309	444	101	13	10	1	0.2	45	48	33	41	11	1	0	266	321	33	45	5.2	.947	2B-117, SS-2
1911			137	.268	.377	470	126	17	8	6	1.3	82	78	51	48	17	5	1	273	357	38	65	4.9	.943	2B-129
1912			148	.275	.397	567	156	33	12	4	0.7	74	87	37	45	18	1	0	1385	85	23	93	10.1	.985	1B-147
1913			154	.272	.419	580	158	24	20	7	1.2	75	90	37	52	20	0	0	1406	82	25	68	9.8	.983	1B-150, SS-3
1914	STL	N	155	.290	.393	573	166	27	10	4	0.7	67	88	34	52	16	0	0	1176	247	30	67	9.4	.979	1B-98, SS-53, 2B-5
1915			150	.264	.342	553	146	17	10	4	0.7	73	72	43	49	27	0	0	1142	215	20	83	9.2	.985	1B-83, 2B-55, 3B-9, SS-3
1916			143	.238	.315	505	120	22	7	1	0.2	47	46	40	49	18	0	0	1056	200	19	84	8.9	.985	1B-93, 2B-38, SS-21, 3B-1
1917			148	.248	.320	544	135	15	9	2	0.4	61	45	33	52	14	0	0	755	362	28	100	7.7	.976	2B-92, 1B-46, SS-11
1919			101	.231	.292	346	80	10	4	1	0.3	38	24	13	23	6	1	0	756	127	22	47	9.0	.976	1B-68, 2B-28

Dots Miller *continued*

Year	Team		Games	BA	SA	AB	H	2B	3B	HR	HR%	R	RBI	BB	SO	SB	Pinch Hit AB	Pinch Hit H	PO	A	E	DP	TC/G	FA	G by Pos
1920	PHI	N	98	.254	.309	343	87	12	2	1	0.3	41	27	16	17	13	2	0	254	234	27	48	5.3	.948	2B-59, 3B-17, SS-12, 1B-9, OF-1
1921			84	.297	.350	320	95	11	3	0	0.0	37	23	15	27	3	1	0	441	113	19	36	6.8	.967	3B-41, 1B-38, 2B-6
12 yrs.			1589	.263	.357	5805	1526	232	108	32	0.6	711	715	391	454	177	16	3	9170	2769	318	786	7.7	.974	1B-732, 2B-679, SS-105, 3B-68, OF-1

WORLD SERIES

Year	Team		Games	BA	SA	AB	H	2B	3B	HR	HR%	R	RBI	BB	SO	SB	Pinch Hit AB	Pinch Hit H	PO	A	E	DP	TC/G	FA	G by Pos
1909	PIT	N	7	.250	.286	28	7	1	0	0	0.0	2	4	2	4	3	0	0	17	13	3	1	4.7	.909	2B-7

Dusty Miller   MILLER, CHARLES BRADLEY
B. Sept. 10, 1868, Oil City, Pa.   D. Sept. 3, 1945, Memphis, Tenn.   BL TR 5'11½" 170 lbs.

Year	Team		Games	BA	SA	AB	H	2B	3B	HR	HR%	R	RBI	BB	SO	SB	Pinch Hit AB	Pinch Hit H	PO	A	E	DP	TC/G	FA	G by Pos
1889	BAL	AA	11	.150	.225	40	6	1	1	0	0.0	4	6	2	11	3	0	0	11	21	16	0	4.4	.667	SS-8, OF-3
1890	STL	AA	26	.219	.365	96	21	5	3	1	1.0	17		8		4	0	0	35	16	7	3	2.2	.879	OF-24, SS-3
1895	CIN	N	132	.335	.507	529	177	31	18	8	1.5	103	112	33	34	43	0	0	243	25	18	8	2.2	.937	OF-132
1896			125	.321	.468	504	162	38	12	4	0.8	91	93	33	30	76	0	0	199	21	24	7	2.0	.902	OF-125
1897			119	.316	.409	440	139	27	1	4	0.9	83	70	48		29	0	0	203	18	17	2	2.0	.929	OF-119
1898			152	.299	.396	586	175	24	12	3	0.5	99	90	38		32	0	0	292	23	24	4	2.2	.929	OF-152
1899	2 teams					CIN N (80G – .251)			STL N (10G – .205)																
"	total		90	.246	.309	362	89	13	5	0	0.0	47	40	12		19	0	0	168	19	16	5	2.3	.921	OF-90
7 yrs.			655	.301	.419	2557	769	139	52	20	0.8	444	411	174	75	206	0	0	1151	143	122	29	2.2	.914	OF-645, SS-11

Ed Miller   MILLER, EDWIN J.
B. Nov. 24, 1888, Annville, Pa.   D. Apr. 17, 1980, Lebanon, Pa.   BR TR 6' 180 lbs.

Year	Team		Games	BA	SA	AB	H	2B	3B	HR	HR%	R	RBI	BB	SO	SB	Pinch Hit AB	Pinch Hit H	PO	A	E	DP	TC/G	FA	G by Pos
1912	STL	A	13	.196	.217	46	9	1	0	0	0.0	4	5	2		1	0	0	90	11	8	3	8.4	.927	1B-8, SS-5
1914			34	.138	.172	58	8	0	1	0	0.0	8	4	4	13	1	1	0	60	14	6	4	2.4	.927	1B-8, OF-5, 2B-5, 3B-2
1918	CLE	A	32	.229	.333	96	22	4	3	0	0.0	9	3	12	10	2	2	0	236	20	6	16	8.2	.977	1B-22, OF-4
3 yrs.			79	.195	.260	200	39	5	4	0	0.0	21	12	18	23	4	10	0	386	45	20	23	5.7	.956	1B-38, OF-9, SS-5, 2B-5, 3B-2

Ed Miller   MILLER, L. EDWARD
B. Tecumseh, Mich.   Deceased.

Year	Team		Games	BA	SA	AB	H	2B	3B	HR	HR%	R	RBI	BB	SO	SB	Pinch Hit AB	Pinch Hit H	PO	A	E	DP	TC/G	FA	G by Pos
1884	TOL	AA	8	.250	.250	24	6	0	0	0	0.0		2	1		0	0	0	5	3	5	0	1.6	.615	OF-8

Eddie Miller   MILLER, EDWARD LEE
B. June 29, 1957, San Pablo, Calif.   BB TR 5'9" 175 lbs.

Year	Team		Games	BA	SA	AB	H	2B	3B	HR	HR%	R	RBI	BB	SO	SB	Pinch Hit AB	Pinch Hit H	PO	A	E	DP	TC/G	FA	G by Pos
1977	TEX	A	17	.333	.333	6	2	0	0	0	0.0	9	1	1	3	1	3	0	4	0	0	0	0.2	1.000	DH-3, OF-2
1978	ATL	N	6	.143	.190	21	3	1	0	0	0.0	5	2	2	4	3	0	0	7	0	0	0	1.2	1.000	OF-5
1979			27	.310	.319	113	35	1	0	0	0.0	12	5	5	24	15	0	0	79	1	1	0	3.0	.988	OF-27
1980			11	.158	.158	19	3	0	0	0	0.0	3	0	0	5	1	0	0	6	0	0	0	0.5	1.000	OF-9
1981			50	.231	.269	134	31	3	1	0	0.0	29	7	7	29	28	6	2	65	2	1	0	1.4	.985	OF-36
1982	DET	A	14	.040	.040	25	1	0	0	0	0.0	3	0	4	4	0	1	0	13	1	0	0	1.0	1.000	OF-8, DH-1
1984	SD	N	13	.286	.643	14	4	0	1	1	7.1	2	2	4	4	1	0		5	2	0	0	0.5	1.000	OF-8
7 yrs.			138	.238	.274	332	79	5	2	1	0.3	63	17	19	71	49	9	2	179	6	2	0	1.4	.989	OF-95, DH-4

Eddie Miller   MILLER, EDWARD ROBERT (Eppie)
B. Nov. 26, 1916, Pittsburgh, Pa.   BR TR 5'9" 180 lbs.

Year	Team		Games	BA	SA	AB	H	2B	3B	HR	HR%	R	RBI	BB	SO	SB	Pinch Hit AB	Pinch Hit H	PO	A	E	DP	TC/G	FA	G by Pos
1936	CIN	N	5	.100	.100	10	1	0	0	0	0.0	1	1	0	0	0	0	0	5	10	1	1	3.2	.938	SS-4, 2B-1
1937			36	.150	.233	60	9	3	1	0	0.0	3	5	3	8	0	2	0	46	69	9	16	3.4	.927	SS-30, 3B-4
1939	BOS	N	77	.267	.361	296	79	12	2	4	1.4	32	31	16	21	4	0	0	183	275	14	76	6.1	.970	SS-77
1940			151	.276	.418	569	157	33	3	14	2.5	78	79	41	43	8	0	0	405	487	28	122	6.1	.966	SS-151
1941			154	.239	.326	585	140	27	3	6	1.0	54	68	35	72	8	0	0	336	485	29	112	5.5	.966	SS-154
1942			144	.243	.337	534	130	28	6	6	1.1	47	47	22	42	11	0	0	285	450	13	78	5.2	.983	SS-144
1943	CIN	N	154	.224	.293	576	129	26	4	2	0.3	49	71	33	43	8	0	0	335	543	19	123	5.8	.979	SS-154
1944			155	.209	.289	536	112	21	5	4	0.7	48	55	41	41	9	0	0	357	546	17	100	6.0	.981	SS-155
1945			115	.238	.404	421	100	27	5	13	3.1	46	49	18	38	4	0	0	245	382	16	61	5.6	.975	SS-115
1946			91	.194	.288	299	58	10	6	2	0.6	30	36	25	34	5	0	0	184	297	15	79	5.5	.970	SS-88
1947			151	.268	.457	545	146	**38**	4	19	3.5	69	87	49	40	5	0	0	295	445	21	88	5.0	.972	SS-151
1948	PHI	N	130	.246	.382	468	115	20	1	14	3.0	45	61	19	40	1	7	0	229	341	20	63	4.5	.966	SS-122
1949			85	.207	.320	266	55	10	1	6	2.3	21	29	29	21	1	3	1	240	189	6	54	5.1	.986	2B-82, SS-1
1950	STL	N	64	.227	.326	172	39	8	0	3	1.7	17	22	19	21	0	11	1	75	176	5	31	4.0	.980	SS-51, 2B-1
14 yrs.			1512	.238	.352	5337	1270	263	28	97	1.8	539	640	351	465	64	26	3	3220	4693	223	1004	5.4	.973	SS-1397, 2B-84, 3B-4

Elmer Miller   MILLER, ELMER
B. July 28, 1890, Sandusky, Ohio   D. Nov. 28, 1944, Beloit, Wis.   BR TR 6' 175 lbs.

Year	Team		Games	BA	SA	AB	H	2B	3B	HR	HR%	R	RBI	BB	SO	SB	Pinch Hit AB	Pinch Hit H	PO	A	E	DP	TC/G	FA	G by Pos
1912	STL	N	12	.189	.216	37	7	1	0	0	0.0	5	3	4	9	1	0	0	24	1	0	0	2.1	1.000	OF-11
1915	NY	A	26	.145	.157	83	12	1	0	0	0.0	4	3	4	14	0	1	0	41	1	2	0	1.7	.955	OF-26
1916			43	.224	.289	152	34	3	2	1	0.7	12	18	11	18	8	0	0	84	9	3	5	2.2	.969	OF-42
1917			114	.251	.319	379	95	11	3	3	0.8	43	35	40	44	11	1	0	204	13	9	5	2.0	.961	OF-112
1918			67	.243	.322	202	49	9	2	1	0.5	18	22	19	17	2	4	0	149	13	9	0	2.6	.947	OF-62
1921			56	.298	.450	242	72	9	8	4	1.7	41	36	19	16	2	0	0	134	10	8	2	2.7	.947	OF-56
1922	2 teams					NY A (51G – .267)			BOS A (44G – .190)																
"	total		95	.232	.357	319	74	7	2	7	2.2	47	34	16	22	5	9	1	186	10	6	2	2.1	.970	OF-83
7 yrs.			413	.243	.335	1414	343	43	20	16	1.1	170	151	113	140	29	15	1	822	60	37	12	2.2	.960	OF-392

WORLD SERIES

Year	Team		Games	BA	SA	AB	H	2B	3B	HR	HR%	R	RBI	BB	SO	SB	Pinch Hit AB	Pinch Hit H	PO	A	E	DP	TC/G	FA	G by Pos
1921	NY	A	8	.161	.194	31	5	1	0	0	0.0	3	2	2	5	0	0	0	10	1	0	0	1.4	1.000	OF-8

Elmer Miller   MILLER, ELMER JOSEPH
B. Apr. 17, 1904, Detroit, Mich.   D. Jan. 8, 1987, Corona, Calif.   BL TL 5'11" 189 lbs.

Year	Team		Games	BA	SA	AB	H	2B	3B	HR	HR%	R	RBI	BB	SO	SB	Pinch Hit AB	Pinch Hit H	PO	A	E	DP	TC/G	FA	G by Pos
1929	PHI	N	31	.237	.342	38	9	1	0	1	2.6	3	4	1	5	0	17	2	11	5	1	0	0.5	.941	P-8, OF-4

Year Team	Games	BA	SA	AB	H	2B	3B	HR	HR%	R	RBI	BB	SO	SB	Pinch Hit AB	Pinch Hit H	PO	A	E	DP	TC/G	FA	G by Pos

George Miller
MILLER, GEORGE C.
B. Feb. 19, 1853, Newport, Ky.   D. July 24, 1929, Norwood, Ohio
BR TR 5'5"   160 lbs.

Year Team	Games	BA	SA	AB	H	2B	3B	HR	HR%	R	RBI	BB	SO	SB	PH AB	PH H	PO	A	E	DP	TC/G	FA	G by Pos
1877 CIN N	11	.162	.189	37	6	1	0	0	0.0	4	3	5	2		0	0	56	11	6	0	6.6	.918	C-11
1884 CIN AA	6	.250	.400	20	5	1	1	0	0.0	6		1			0	0	30	9	1	1	6.7	.975	C-6
2 yrs.	17	.193	.263	57	11	2	1	0	0.0	10	3	6	2		0	0	86	20	7	1	6.6	.938	C-17

Hack Miller
MILLER, JAMES ELDRIDGE
B. Feb. 13, 1913, Celeste, Tex.   D. Nov. 21, 1966, Dallas, Tex.
BR TR 5'11½"   215 lbs.

Year Team	Games	BA	SA	AB	H	2B	3B	HR	HR%	R	RBI	BB	SO	SB	PH AB	PH H	PO	A	E	DP	TC/G	FA	G by Pos
1944 DET A	5	.200	.800	5	1	0	0	1	20.0	0	3	1	1	0	0	0	7	1	0	0	1.6	1.000	C-5
1945	2	.750	.750	4	3	0	0	0	0.0	0	1	0	0	0	0	0	4	1	0	0	2.5	1.000	C-2
2 yrs.	7	.444	.778	9	4	0	0	1	11.1	0	4	1	1	0	0	0	11	2	0	0	1.9	1.000	C-7

Hack Miller
MILLER, LAWRENCE H.
B. Jan. 1, 1894, New York, N. Y.   D. Sept. 17, 1971, Oakland, Calif.
BR TR 5'9"   195 lbs.

Year Team	Games	BA	SA	AB	H	2B	3B	HR	HR%	R	RBI	BB	SO	SB	PH AB	PH H	PO	A	E	DP	TC/G	FA	G by Pos
1916 BKN N	3	.333	1.000	3	1	0	1	0	0.0	0	1	1	1		0	0	1	0	0	0	0.3	1.000	OF-3
1918 BOS A	12	.276	.345	29	8	2	0	0	0.0	2	4	0	4		0	0	10	0	0	0	0.8	1.000	OF-10
1922 CHI N	122	.352	.511	466	164	28	5	12	2.6	61	78	26	39	3	6	2	219	15	10	3	2.0	.959	OF-116
1923	135	.301	.482	485	146	24	2	20	4.1	74	88	27	39	6	4	4	256	17	6	4	2.1	.978	OF-129
1924	53	.336	.504	131	44	8	1	4	3.1	17	25	8	11	1	20	7	54	1	3	0	1.1	.948	OF-32
1925	24	.279	.430	86	24	3	2	2	2.3	10	9	2	9	0	3	2	35	1	5	0	1.7	.878	OF-21
6 yrs.	349	.323	.490	1200	387	65	11	38	3.2	164	205	64	103	10	35	15	575	34	24	7	1.8	.962	OF-311

WORLD SERIES

Year Team	Games	BA	SA	AB	H	2B	3B	HR	HR%	R	RBI	BB	SO	SB	PH AB	PH H	PO	A	E	DP	TC/G	FA	G by Pos
1918 BOS A	1	.000	.000	1	0	0	0	0	0.0	0	0	0	0	0	1	0	0	0	0	0	0.0	—	

Hughie Miller
MILLER, HUGH STANLEY (Cotton)
B. Dec. 28, 1887, St. Louis, Mo.   D. Dec. 24, 1945, Jefferson Barracks, Mo.
BR TR 6'1½"   175 lbs.

Year Team	Games	BA	SA	AB	H	2B	3B	HR	HR%	R	RBI	BB	SO	SB	PH AB	PH H	PO	A	E	DP	TC/G	FA	G by Pos
1911 PHI N	1	—	—	0	0	0	0	0	—	0	0	0	0		0	0	0	0	0	0	0.0	—	
1914 STL F	132	.222	.284	490	109	20	5	0	0.0	51	46	27		4	2	1	1256	65	14	48	10.1	.990	1B-130
1915	7	.500	.667	6	3	1	0	0	0.0	0	3	0			1	1	13	0	0	0	1.9	1.000	1B-6
3 yrs.	140	.226	.288	496	112	21	5	0	0.0	51	49	27		4	3	1	1269	65	14	48	9.6	.990	1B-136

Jake Miller
MILLER, JACOB GEORGE
Born Jacob George Munzing.
B. Dec. 1, 1895, Baltimore, Md.   D. Aug. 24, 1974, Towson, Md.
BR TR 5'10"   170 lbs.

Year Team	Games	BA	SA	AB	H	2B	3B	HR	HR%	R	RBI	BB	SO	SB	PH AB	PH H	PO	A	E	DP	TC/G	FA	G by Pos
1922 PIT N	3	.091	.091	11	1	0	0	0	0.0	0	2	0	1	0	0	0	8	0	1	0	3.0	.889	OF-3

Jim Miller
MILLER, JAMES McCURDY (Rabbit)
B. Oct. 2, 1880, Pittsburgh, Pa.   D. Feb. 7, 1937, Pittsburgh, Pa.
BR TR 5'8"   165 lbs.

Year Team	Games	BA	SA	AB	H	2B	3B	HR	HR%	R	RBI	BB	SO	SB	PH AB	PH H	PO	A	E	DP	TC/G	FA	G by Pos
1901 NY N	18	.138	.138	58	8	0	0	0	0.0	3	3	6		1	0	0	26	47	5	6	4.3	.936	2B-18

Joe Miller
MILLER, JOSEPH A.
B. Feb. 17, 1861, Baltimore, Md.   D. Apr. 23, 1928, Wheeling, W. Va.
5'9½"   165 lbs.

Year Team	Games	BA	SA	AB	H	2B	3B	HR	HR%	R	RBI	BB	SO	SB	PH AB	PH H	PO	A	E	DP	TC/G	FA	G by Pos
1884 TOL AA	105	.239	.312	423	101	12	8	1	0.2	46		26			0	0	125	320	70	26	4.9	.864	SS-105
1885 LOU AA	98	.183	.239	339	62	9	5	0	0.0	44		28			0	0	123	329	68	26	5.3	.869	SS-79, 3B-11, 2B-8
2 yrs.	203	.214	.280	762	163	21	13	1	0.1	90		54			0	0	248	649	138	52	5.1	.867	SS-184, 3B-11, 2B-8

John Miller
MILLER, JOHN ALLEN
B. Mar. 14, 1944, Alhambra, Calif.
BR TR 5'11"   195 lbs.

Year Team	Games	BA	SA	AB	H	2B	3B	HR	HR%	R	RBI	BB	SO	SB	PH AB	PH H	PO	A	E	DP	TC/G	FA	G by Pos
1966 NY A	6	.087	.217	23	2	0	0	1	4.3	1	2	0	9	0	0	0	20	0	0	1	3.3	1.000	OF-3, 1B-3
1969 LA N	26	.211	.316	38	8	1	0	1	2.6	3	1	2	9	0	15	3	30	4	0	2	1.3	1.000	OF-6, 1B-8, 3B-2, 2B-1
2 yrs.	32	.164	.279	61	10	1	0	2	3.3	4	3	2	18	0	15	3	50	4	0	3	1.7	1.000	OF-9, 1B-8, 3B-2, 2B-1

Keith Miller
MILLER, KEITH ALAN
B. June 12, 1963, Midland, Mich.
BR TR 5'11"   175 lbs.

Year Team	Games	BA	SA	AB	H	2B	3B	HR	HR%	R	RBI	BB	SO	SB	PH AB	PH H	PO	A	E	DP	TC/G	FA	G by Pos
1987 NY N	25	.373	.490	51	19	2	2	0	0.0	14	1	2	6	8	0	0	21	38	2	6	2.4	.967	2B-16
1988	40	.214	.300	70	15	1	1	1	1.4	9	5	6	10	0	9	2	34	24	5	3	1.6	.921	2B-16, SS-8, 3B-6, OF-1
1989	57	.231	.301	143	33	7	0	1	0.7	15	7	5	27	6	7	2	90	52	5	8	2.6	.966	2B-23, OF-14, SS-8, 3B-2
3 yrs.	122	.254	.337	264	67	10	3	2	0.8	38	13	13	43	14	16	4	145	114	12	17	2.2	.956	2B-55, SS-16, OF-15, 3B-8

Keith Miller
MILLER, NEAL KEITH
B. Mar. 7, 1963, Dallas, Tex.
BB TR 5'11"   175 lbs.

Year Team	Games	BA	SA	AB	H	2B	3B	HR	HR%	R	RBI	BB	SO	SB	PH AB	PH H	PO	A	E	DP	TC/G	FA	G by Pos
1988 PHI N	47	.167	.229	48	8	3	0	0	0.0	4	6	5	13	0	37	6	3	2	1	1	0.1	.833	OF-4, 3B-3, SS-1
1989	8	.300	.400	10	3	1	0	0	0.0	0	0	0	3	0	6	1	2	0	0	0	0.3	1.000	OF-2
2 yrs.	55	.190	.259	58	11	4	0	0	0.0	4	6	5	16	0	43	7	5	2	1	1	0.1	.875	OF-6, 3B-3, SS-1

Kohly Miller
MILLER, FRANK A.
B. Philadelphia, Pa.   Deceased.

Year Team	Games	BA	SA	AB	H	2B	3B	HR	HR%	R	RBI	BB	SO	SB	PH AB	PH H	PO	A	E	DP	TC/G	FA	G by Pos
1892 2 teams	WAS N (1G – .000)			STL N (1G – .000)																			
" total	2	.000	.000	7	0	0	0	0	0.0	0	0	0	0	0	0	0	1	2	4	0	3.5	.429	SS-1, 3B-1
1897 PHI N	3	.182	.182	11	2	0	0	0	0.0	2	1	2	0	0	0	0	8	4	2	1	4.7	.857	2B-3
2 yrs.	5	.111	.111	18	2	0	0	0	0.0	2	1	2	0	0	0	0	9	6	6	1	4.2	.714	2B-3, SS-1, 3B-1

Lemmie Miller
MILLER, LEMMIE EARL
B. June 2, 1960, Dallas, Tex.
BR TR 6'1"   190 lbs.

Year Team	Games	BA	SA	AB	H	2B	3B	HR	HR%	R	RBI	BB	SO	SB	PH AB	PH H	PO	A	E	DP	TC/G	FA	G by Pos
1984 LA N	8	.167	.167	12	2	0	0	0	0.0	1	0	1	2	0	5	1	3	0	0	0	0.4	1.000	OF-5

Norm Miller
MILLER, NORMAN CALVIN
B. Feb. 5, 1946, Los Angeles, Calif.
BL TR 5'10"   185 lbs.

Year Team	Games	BA	SA	AB	H	2B	3B	HR	HR%	R	RBI	BB	SO	SB	PH AB	PH H	PO	A	E	DP	TC/G	FA	G by Pos
1965 HOU N	11	.200	.333	15	3	0	1	0	0.0	2	1	1	7	0	7	1	2	0	0	0	0.2	1.000	OF-2

Year	Team	Games	BA	SA	AB	H	2B	3B	HR	HR%	R	RBI	BB	SO	SB	Pinch Hit AB	Pinch Hit H	PO	A	E	DP	TC/G	FA	G by Pos

Norm Miller *continued*

Year	Team	Games	BA	SA	AB	H	2B	3B	HR	HR%	R	RBI	BB	SO	SB	AB	H	PO	A	E	DP	TC/G	FA	G by Pos
1966		11	.147	.235	34	5	0	0	1	2.9	1	3	2	8	0	2	0	15	4	1	2	1.8	.950	OF-8, 3B-2
1967		64	.205	.300	190	39	9	3	1	0.5	15	14	19	42	2	13	2	84	3	3	1	1.4	.967	OF-53
1968		79	.237	.393	257	61	18	2	6	2.3	35	28	22	48	6	6	2	131	1	4	1	1.7	.971	OF-74
1969		119	.264	.364	409	108	21	4	4	1.0	58	50	47	77	4	2	0	172	7	3	3	1.5	.984	OF-114
1970		90	.239	.332	226	54	9	0	4	1.8	29	29	41	33	3	19	5	103	6	6	1	1.3	.948	OF-72, C-1
1971		45	.257	.405	74	19	5	0	2	2.7	5	10	5	13	0	28	9	23	0	0	0	0.5	1.000	OF-20, C-1
1972		67	.243	.393	107	26	4	0	4	3.7	18	13	13	23	1	31	10	35	1	0	1	0.5	1.000	OF-29
1973	2 teams	HOU	N	(3G – .000)		ATL	N	(9G – .375)																
"	total	12	.273	.636	11	3	1	0	1	9.1	2	6	3	5	0	8	1	2	0	1	0	0.3	.667	OF-2
1974	ATL N	42	.171	.268	41	7	1	0	1	2.4	1	5	7	9	0	31	6	3	1	0	0	0.1	1.000	OF-4
10 yrs.		540	.238	.356	1364	325	68	10	24	1.8	166	159	160	265	16	147	36	570	23	18	9	1.1	.971	OF-378, 3B-2, C-2

Otto Miller

MILLER, LOWELL OTTO (Moonie)
B. June 1, 1889, Minden, Neb.   D. Mar. 29, 1962, Brooklyn, N. Y.   BR TR 6'   196 lbs.

Year	Team	Games	BA	SA	AB	H	2B	3B	HR	HR%	R	RBI	BB	SO	SB	AB	H	PO	A	E	DP	TC/G	FA	G by Pos
1910	BKN N	31	.167	.212	66	11	3	0	0	0.0	5	2	2	19	1	3	0	116	37	2	2	5.0	.987	C-28
1911		25	.210	.306	62	13	2	2	0	0.0	7	8	0	4	2	2	0	61	28	7	0	3.8	.927	C-22
1912		98	.278	.351	316	88	18	1	1	0.3	35	31	18	50	11	2	2	455	141	15	11	6.2	.975	C-94
1913		104	.272	.350	320	87	11	7	0	0.0	26	26	10	31	7	0	0	460	148	18	14	6.0	.971	C-103, 1B-1
1914		54	.231	.278	169	39	6	1	0	0.0	17	9	7	20	0	3	1	236	66	11	5	5.8	.965	C-50
1915		84	.224	.287	254	57	4	6	0	0.0	20	25	6	28	3	1	0	363	91	9	8	5.5	.981	C-84
1916		73	.255	.329	216	55	9	2	1	0.5	16	17	7	29	6	4	2	311	85	13	6	5.6	.968	C-69
1917		92	.230	.288	274	63	5	4	1	0.4	19	17	14	29	5	0	0	412	95	11	8	5.6	.979	C-91
1918		75	.193	.228	228	44	6	1	0	0.0	8	8	9	20	1	11	1	289	78	10	7	5.0	.973	C-62, 1B-1
1919		51	.226	.256	164	37	5	0	0	0.0	18	5	7	14	2	0	0	223	58	10	5	5.7	.966	C-51
1920		90	.289	.332	301	87	9	2	0	0.0	16	33	9	18	0	1	0	418	65	7	8	5.4	.986	C-89
1921		91	.234	.315	286	67	8	6	1	0.3	22	27	9	26	2	0	0	338	107	13	10	5.0	.972	C-91
1922		59	.261	.350	180	47	11	1	1	0.6	20	23	6	13	0	2	1	216	56	9	3	4.8	.968	C-57
13 yrs.		927	.245	.308	2836	695	97	33	5	0.2	229	231	104	301	40	29	7	3898	1055	135	87	5.5	.973	C-891, 1B-2

WORLD SERIES

Year	Team	Games	BA	SA	AB	H	2B	3B	HR	HR%	R	RBI	BB	SO	SB	AB	H	PO	A	E	DP	TC/G	FA	G by Pos
1916	BKN N	2	.125	.125	8	1	0	0	0	0.0	0	0	0	1	0	0	0	8	3	0	1	5.5	1.000	C-2
1920		6	.143	.143	14	2	0	0	0	0.0	0	0	1	2	0	0	0	17	6	0	0	3.8	1.000	C-6
2 yrs.		8	.136	.136	22	3	0	0	0	0.0	0	0	1	3	0	0	0	25	9	0	1	4.3	1.000	C-8

Otto Miller

MILLER, OTIS LOUIS
B. Feb. 2, 1901, Belleville, Ill.   D. July 26, 1959, Belleville, Ill.   BR TR 5'10½" 168 lbs.

Year	Team	Games	BA	SA	AB	H	2B	3B	HR	HR%	R	RBI	BB	SO	SB	AB	H	PO	A	E	DP	TC/G	FA	G by Pos
1927	STL A	51	.224	.289	76	17	5	0	0	0.0	8	8	8	8	0	5	0	29	54	6	9	1.7	.933	SS-35, 3B-11
1930	BOS A	112	.286	.373	370	106	22	5	0	0.0	49	40	26	21	2	13	5	97	201	17	20	2.8	.946	3B-83, 2B-15
1931		107	.272	.308	389	106	12	1	0	0.0	38	43	15	20	1	10	1	135	230	16	27	3.6	.958	3B-75, 2B-25
1932		2	.000	.000	2	0	0	0	0	0.0	0	0	0	0	0	2	0	0	0	0	0	0.0	–	
4 yrs.		272	.274	.335	837	229	39	6	0	0.0	95	91	49	46	3	30	6	261	485	39	56	2.9	.950	3B-169, 2B-40, SS-35

Ralph Miller

MILLER, RALPH JOSEPH
B. Feb. 29, 1896, Fort Wayne, Ind.   D. Mar. 18, 1939, Fort Wayne, Ind.   BR TR 6'   190 lbs.

Year	Team	Games	BA	SA	AB	H	2B	3B	HR	HR%	R	RBI	BB	SO	SB	AB	H	PO	A	E	DP	TC/G	FA	G by Pos
1920	PHI N	97	.219	.266	338	74	14	1	0	0.0	28	28	11	32	3	0	0	105	183	18	16	3.2	.941	3B-91, 1B-3, SS-2, OF-1
1921		57	.304	.397	204	62	10	0	3	1.5	19	26	6	10	3	2	1	107	164	30	24	5.3	.900	SS-46, 3B-10
1924	WAS A	9	.133	.133	15	2	0	0	0	0.0	1	0	1	1	0	6	0	5	11	1	1	1.9	.941	2B-3
3 yrs.		163	.248	.311	557	138	24	1	3	0.5	48	54	18	43	6	8	1	217	358	49	41	3.8	.921	3B-101, SS-48, 2B-3, 1B-3, OF-1

WORLD SERIES

Year	Team	Games	BA	SA	AB	H	2B	3B	HR	HR%	R	RBI	BB	SO	SB	AB	H	PO	A	E	DP	TC/G	FA	G by Pos
1924	WAS A	4	.182	.182	11	2	0	0	0	0.0	0	2	1	0	0	0	0	6	4	2	0	3.0	.833	3B-4

Ray Miller

MILLER, RAYMOND PETER
B. Feb. 12, 1888, Pittsburgh, Pa.   D. Apr. 7, 1927, Pittsburgh, Pa.   BL TL 5'10" 168 lbs.

Year	Team	Games	BA	SA	AB	H	2B	3B	HR	HR%	R	RBI	BB	SO	SB	AB	H	PO	A	E	DP	TC/G	FA	G by Pos
1917	2 teams	CLE	A	(19G – .190)		PIT	N	(6G – .148)																
"	total	25	.167	.208	48	8	2	0	0	0.0	2	2	10	6	0	12	2	94	9	0	5	4.1	1.000	1B-10

Rick Miller

MILLER, RICHARD ALAN
B. Apr. 19, 1948, Grand Rapids, Mich.   BL TL 6'   175 lbs.

Year	Team	Games	BA	SA	AB	H	2B	3B	HR	HR%	R	RBI	BB	SO	SB	AB	H	PO	A	E	DP	TC/G	FA	G by Pos
1971	BOS A	15	.333	.576	33	11	5	0	1	3.0	9	7	8	8	0	0	0	30	1	1	0	2.1	.969	OF-14
1972		89	.214	.367	98	21	4	1	3	3.1	13	15	11	27	0	7	0	80	7	3	0	1.0	.967	OF-75
1973		143	.261	.372	441	115	17	7	6	1.4	65	43	51	59	12	3	1	301	4	7	1	2.2	.978	OF-137
1974		114	.261	.350	280	73	8	1	5	1.8	41	22	37	47	13	1	0	253	7	3	3	2.3	.989	OF-105
1975		77	.194	.231	108	21	2	1	0	0.0	21	15	21	20	3	9	1	101	2	1	1	1.4	.991	OF-65
1976		105	.283	.361	269	76	15	3	0	0.0	40	27	34	47	11	17	5	220	4	2	1	2.2	.991	OF-82, DH-4
1977		86	.254	.333	189	48	9	3	0	0.0	34	24	22	30	11	6	2	118	5	1	3	1.4	.992	OF-79, DH-1
1978	CAL A	132	.263	.339	475	125	25	4	1	0.2	66	37	54	70	3	5	1	353	9	4	5	2.8	.989	OF-129
1979		120	.293	.365	427	125	15	5	2	0.5	60	28	50	69	5	1	0	349	3	4	1	3.0	.989	OF-117, DH-2
1980		129	.274	.337	412	113	14	5	2	0.5	52	38	48	71	7	10	4	299	11	5	3	2.4	.984	OF-118
1981	BOS A	97	.291	.377	316	92	17	2	2	0.6	38	33	28	36	3	3	1	219	5	3	0	2.3	.987	OF-95
1982		135	.254	.325	409	104	13	2	4	1.0	50	38	40	41	5	8	2	277	6	5	2	2.1	.983	OF-127
1983		104	.286	.363	262	75	10	2	2	0.8	41	21	28	30	3	35	16	151	5	1	2	1.5	.994	OF-66, DH-2, 1B-2
1984		95	.260	.317	123	32	5	1	0	0.0	17	12	17	22	1	53	14	80	5	1	0	0.9	.988	OF-31, 1B-8
1985		41	.333	.378	45	15	2	0	0	0.0	5	9	5	6	1	31	7	9	0	0	0	0.2	1.000	OF-8, DH-4
15 yrs.		1482	.269	.350	3887	1046	161	35	28	0.7	552	369	454	583	78	189	54	2840	74	42	23	2.0	.986	OF-1248, DH-13, 1B-10

LEAGUE CHAMPIONSHIP SERIES

Year	Team	Games	BA	SA	AB	H	2B	3B	HR	HR%	R	RBI	BB	SO	SB	AB	H	PO	A	E	DP	TC/G	FA	G by Pos
1979	CAL A	4	.250	.250	16	4	0	0	0	0.0	2	0	0	1	0	0	0	14	2	0	2	4.0	1.000	OF-4

WORLD SERIES

Year	Team	Games	BA	SA	AB	H	2B	3B	HR	HR%	R	RBI	BB	SO	SB	AB	H	PO	A	E	DP	TC/G	FA	G by Pos
1975	BOS A	3	.000	.000	2	0	0	0	0	0.0	0	0	0	0	0	0	0	1	0	0	0	0.3	1.000	OF-2

Year	Team		Games	BA	SA	AB	H	2B	3B	HR	HR%	R	RBI	BB	SO	SB	Pinch Hit AB	H	PO	A	E	DP	TC/G	FA	G by Pos

Fred Mitchell *continued*

Year	Team		Games	BA	SA	AB	H	2B	3B	HR	HR%	R	RBI	BB	SO	SB	AB	H	PO	A	E	DP	TC/G	FA	G by Pos
1902	2 teams	BOS A (1G – .000)				PHI A (20G – .188)																			
"	total		21	.184	.245	49	9	1	1	0	0.0	7	3	1		1	1	0	6	45	4	4	2.6	.927	P-19, OF-1
1903	PHI N		29	.200	.242	95	19	4	0	0	0.0	11	10	0		0	1	1	10	50	10	3	2.4	.857	P-28
1904	2 teams	PHI N (25G – .207)				BKN N (8G – .292)																			
"	total		33	.226	.302	106	24	4	2	0	0.0	12	9	6		1	0	0	85	83	11	5	5.4	.939	P-21, 1B-9, 3B-2, OF-1
1905	BKN N		27	.190	.190	79	15	0	0	0	0.0	4	8	4		0	2	1	71	44	13	2	4.7	.898	P-12, 1B-7, 3B-4, OF-1, SS-1
1910	NY A		68	.230	.286	196	45	7	2	0	0.0	16	18	9		6	6	2	262	69	11	2	5.0	.968	C-68
1913	BOS N		4	.333	.333	3	1	0	0	0	0.0	0	0	0	2	0	3	1	0	0	0	0	0.0	–	
7 yrs.			202	.210	.262	572	120	16	7	0	0.0	55	52	22	2	8	13	5	436	325	55	18	4.0	.933	P-97, C-68, 1B-16, 3B-6, OF-3, SS-2, 2B-2

Johnny Mitchell

MITCHELL, JOHN FRANKLIN
B. Aug. 9, 1894, Detroit, Mich. D. Nov. 4, 1965, Birmingham, Mich.

BB TR 5'8'' 155 lbs.

Year	Team		Games	BA	SA	AB	H	2B	3B	HR	HR%	R	RBI	BB	SO	SB	AB	H	PO	A	E	DP	TC/G	FA	G by Pos
1921	NY A		13	.262	.286	42	11	1	0	0	0.0	4	2	4	1	1	0	0	13	26	6	1	3.5	.867	SS-7, 2B-5
1922	2 teams	NY A (4G – .000)				BOS A (59G – .251)																			
"	total		63	.246	.290	207	51	4	1	1	0.5	21	8	16	18	1	1	0	98	185	11	31	4.7	.963	SS-62
1923	BOS A		92	.225	.291	347	78	15	4	0	0.0	40	19	34	18	7	0	0	194	271	18	40	5.3	.963	SS-87, 2B-5
1924	BKN N		64	.263	.317	243	64	10	3	1	0.4	42	16	37	22	3	0	0	131	216	18	30	5.7	.951	SS-64
1925			97	.250	.292	336	84	8	0	0	0.0	45	18	28	19	2	1	0	184	266	25	49	4.9	.947	SS-90
5 yrs.			329	.245	.296	1175	288	38	8	2	0.2	152	63	119	81	14	2	0	620	964	78	151	5.1	.953	SS-310, 2B-10

Kevin Mitchell

MITCHELL, KEVIN DARNELL (Mitch, World)
B. Jan. 13, 1962, San Diego, Calif.

BR TR 5'10'' 185 lbs.

Year	Team		Games	BA	SA	AB	H	2B	3B	HR	HR%	R	RBI	BB	SO	SB	AB	H	PO	A	E	DP	TC/G	FA	G by Pos
1984	NY N		7	.214	.214	14	3	0	0	0	0.0	0	1	0	3	0	4	1	1	4	1	2	0.9	.833	3B-5
1986			108	.277	.466	328	91	22	2	12	3.7	51	43	33	61	3	20	3	158	69	10	10	2.2	.958	OF-68, SS-24, 3B-7, 1B-2
1987	2 teams	SD N (62G – .245)				SF N (69G – .306)																			
"	total		131	.280	.474	464	130	20	2	22	4.7	68	70	48	88	9	9	2	76	240	15	19	2.5	.955	3B-119, OF-6, SS-1
1988	SF N		148	.251	.442	505	127	25	7	19	3.8	60	80	48	85	5	10	2	118	205	22	18	2.3	.936	3B-102, OF-40
1989			154	.291	.635	543	158	34	6	47	8.7	100	125	87	115	3	3	1	305	10	7	0	2.1	.978	OF-147, 3B-2
5 yrs.			548	.275	.509	1854	509	101	17	100	5.4	279	319	216	352	20	46	9	658	528	55	49	2.3	.956	OF-261, 3B-235, SS-25, 1B-2

LEAGUE CHAMPIONSHIP SERIES

Year	Team		Games	BA	SA	AB	H	2B	3B	HR	HR%	R	RBI	BB	SO	SB	AB	H	PO	A	E	DP	TC/G	FA	G by Pos
1986	NY N		2	.250	.250	8	2	0	0	0	0.0	1	0	0	1	0	0	0	3	0	0	0	1.5	1.000	OF-2
1987	SF N		7	.267	.400	30	8	1	0	1	3.3	2	2	0	3	1	0	0	4	10	1	1	2.1	.933	3B-7
1989			5	.353	.706	17	6	0	0	2	11.8	5	7	3	3	0	0	0	15	1	1	1	3.4	.941	OF-5
3 yrs.			14	.291	.473	55	16	1	0	3	5.5	8	9	3	7	1	0	0	22	11	2	2	2.5	.943	OF-7, 3B-7

WORLD SERIES

Year	Team		Games	BA	SA	AB	H	2B	3B	HR	HR%	R	RBI	BB	SO	SB	AB	H	PO	A	E	DP	TC/G	FA	G by Pos
1986	NY N		5	.250	.250	8	2	0	0	0	0.0	1	0	0	3	0	2	0	10	0	1	0	2.8	.909	OF-4
1989	SF N		4	.294	.471	17	5	0	0	1	5.9	2	2	0	3	0	0	0	10	2	1	0	1.4	.923	OF-6, DH-1
2 yrs.			9	.280	.400	25	7	0	0	1	4.0	3	2	0	6	0	2	1	10	2	2	0	1.4	.923	

Mike Mitchell

MITCHELL, MICHAEL FRANCIS
B. Dec. 12, 1879, Springfield, Ohio D. July 16, 1961, Phoenix, Ariz.

BR TR 6'1'' 185 lbs.

Year	Team		Games	BA	SA	AB	H	2B	3B	HR	HR%	R	RBI	BB	SO	SB	AB	H	PO	A	E	DP	TC/G	FA	G by Pos
1907	CIN N		148	.292	.382	558	163	17	12	3	0.5	64	47	37			18	0	0	280	39	14	10	2.3	.958	OF-146, 1B-2
1908			119	.222	.281	406	90	9	6	1	0.2	41	37	46			18	0	0	201	16	9	2	1.9	.960	OF-118, 1B-1
1909			145	.310	.430	523	162	17	17	4	0.8	83	86	57			37	0	0	262	20	11	3	2.0	.962	OF-144, 1B-1
1910			156	.286	.401	583	167	16	18	5	0.9	79	88	59		56	35	0	0	314	22	13	9	2.2	.963	OF-149, 1B-7
1911			142	.291	.427	529	154	22	22	2	0.4	74	84	44	34	35	2	0	280	23	9	8	2.2	.971	OF-140
1912			157	.283	.377	552	156	14	13	4	0.7	60	78	41	43	23	2	1	251	18	15	8	1.8	.947	OF-144
1913	2 teams	CHI N (81G – .259)				PIT N (54G – .271)																			
"	total		135	.264	.369	477	126	19	8	5	1.0	62	51	46	48	23	0	0	326	23	21	0	2.7	.943	OF-135
1914	2 teams	PIT N (76G – .234)				WAS A (55G – .285)																			
"	total		131	.255	.343	466	119	16	8	3	0.6	51	43	38	35	14	2	0	273	22	8	6	2.3	.974	OF-129
8 yrs.			1133	.278	.380	4094	1137	130	104	27	0.7	514	514	368	216	202	6	1	2187	183	100	46	2.2	.960	OF-1105, 1B-11

Ralph Mitterling

MITTERLING, RALPH (Sarge)
B. Apr. 19, 1890, Freeburg, Pa. D. Jan. 22, 1956, Pittsburgh, Pa.

BR TR 5'10'' 165 lbs.

Year	Team		Games	BA	SA	AB	H	2B	3B	HR	HR%	R	RBI	BB	SO	SB	AB	H	PO	A	E	DP	TC/G	FA	G by Pos
1916	PHI A		13	.154	.154	39	6	0	0	0	0.0	1	2	3	6	0	1	0	16	1	1	1	1.4	.944	OF-12

George Mitterwald

MITTERWALD, GEORGE EUGENE
B. June 7, 1945, Berkeley, Calif.

BR TR 6'2'' 195 lbs.

Year	Team		Games	BA	SA	AB	H	2B	3B	HR	HR%	R	RBI	BB	SO	SB	AB	H	PO	A	E	DP	TC/G	FA	G by Pos
1966	MIN A		3	.200	.200	5	1	0	0	0	0.0	0	0	0	0	0	0	0	13	0	0	0	4.3	1.000	C-3
1968			11	.206	.235	34	7	1	0	0	0.0	1	1	3	8	0	1	0	69	4	3	0	6.9	.961	C-10
1969			69	.257	.380	187	48	8	0	5	2.7	18	13	17	47	0	6	1	340	33	5	6	5.5	.987	C-63, OF-1
1970			117	.222	.388	369	82	12	2	15	4.1	36	46	34	84	3	1	0	740	62	3	8	6.9	.996	C-117
1971			125	.250	.389	388	97	13	1	13	3.4	38	44	39	104	3	7	2	656	53	10	7	5.8	.986	C-120
1972			64	.184	.239	163	30	4	1	1	0.6	12	8	9	37	0	4	1	272	33	5	4	4.8	.984	C-61
1973			125	.259	.405	432	112	15	0	16	3.7	50	64	39	111	3	3	0	676	59	6	6	5.9	.992	C-122, DH-3
1974	CHI N		78	.251	.381	215	54	7	0	7	3.3	17	28	18	42	1	11	3	335	40	10	4	4.9	.974	C-68
1975			84	.220	.345	200	44	4	3	5	2.5	19	26	19	46	0	15	3	315	38	8	10	4.3	.978	C-59, 1B-10
1976			101	.215	.287	303	65	5	1	7	1.7	19	28	16	63	1	16	1	512	50	6	13	5.6	.986	C-64, 1B-25
1977			110	.238	.378	349	83	22	0	9	2.6	40	43	28	69	3	2	0	623	78	6	13	6.4	.989	C-109, 1B-1
11 yrs.			887	.236	.362	2645	623	93	7	76	2.9	251	301	222	607	14	66	11	4551	450	66	71	5.7	.987	C-796, 1B-36, DH-3, OF-1

LEAGUE CHAMPIONSHIP SERIES

Year	Team		Games	BA	SA	AB	H	2B	3B	HR	HR%	R	RBI	BB	SO	SB	AB	H	PO	A	E	DP	TC/G	FA	G by Pos
1969	MIN A		2	.143	.143	7	1	0	0	0	0.0	0	0	1	3	0	0	0	10	4	0	0	7.0	1.000	C-2
1970			3	.500	.625	8	4	1	0	0	0.0	2	2	0	2	0	0	0	16	1	0	2	5.7	1.000	C-2
2 yrs.			5	.333	.400	15	5	1	0	0	0.0	2	2	1	5	0	0	0	26	5	0	2	6.2	1.000	C-4

Year	Team	Games	BA	SA	AB	H	2B	3B	HR	HR%	R	RBI	BB	SO	SB	Pinch Hit AB	Pinch Hit H	PO	A	E	DP	TC/G	FA	G by Pos

Johnny Mize

MIZE, JOHN ROBERT (The Big Cat)
B. Jan. 7, 1913, Demorest, Ga.
Hall of Fame 1981.

BL TR 6'2" 215 lbs.

Year	Team	Games	BA	SA	AB	H	2B	3B	HR	HR%	R	RBI	BB	SO	SB	PH AB	PH H	PO	A	E	DP	TC/G	FA	G by Pos
1936	STL N	126	.329	.577	414	136	30	8	19	4.6	76	93	50	32	1	15	7	909	67	6	63	7.8	.994	1B-97, OF-8
1937		145	.364	.595	560	204	40	7	25	4.5	103	113	56	57	2	1	0	1308	67	17	104	9.6	.988	1B-144
1938		149	.337	.614	531	179	34	16	27	5.1	85	102	74	47	0	7	1	1297	93	15	117	9.4	.989	1B-140
1939		153	.349	.626	564	197	44	14	28	5.0	104	108	92	49	0	1	0	1348	90	19	123	9.5	.987	1B-152
1940		155	.314	.636	579	182	31	13	43	7.4	111	137	82	49	7	2	1	1376	80	14	105	9.5	.990	1B-153
1941		126	.317	.535	473	150	39	8	16	3.4	67	100	70	45	4	4	1	1157	82	8	104	9.9	.994	1B-122
1942	NY N	142	.305	.521	541	165	25	7	26	4.8	97	110	60	39	3	3	0	1393	74	8	98	10.4	.995	1B-138
1946		101	.337	.576	377	127	18	3	22	5.8	70	70	62	26	3	0	0	928	83	11	80	10.1	.989	1B-101
1947		154	.302	.614	586	177	26	2	51	8.7	137	138	74	42	2	0	0	1380	117	6	120	9.8	.996	1B-154
1948		152	.289	.564	560	162	26	4	40	7.1	110	125	94	37	4	0	0	1359	111	13	114	9.8	.991	1B-152
1949	2 teams	NY N (106G – .263)			NY A (13G – .261)																			
"	total	119	.263	.440	411	108	16	0	19	4.6	63	64	54	21	1	8	2	906	65	6	77	8.2	.994	1B-107
1950	NY A	90	.277	.595	274	76	12	0	25	9.1	43	72	29	24	0	16	3	490	31	2	73	5.8	.996	1B-72
1951		113	.259	.398	332	86	14	1	10	3.0	37	49	36	24	1	21	9	632	44	4	86	6.0	.994	1B-93
1952		78	.263	.416	137	36	9	0	4	2.9	9	29	11	15	0	48	10	218	18	3	32	3.1	.987	1B-27
1953		81	.250	.394	104	26	3	0	4	3.8	6	27	12	17	0	61	19	113	7	0	19	1.5	1.000	1B-15
15 yrs.		1884	.312	.562 8th	6443	2011	367	83	359	5.6	1118	1337	856	524	28	187	53	14814	1029	132	1315	8.5	.992	1B-1667, OF-8

WORLD SERIES

Year	Team	Games	BA	SA	AB	H	2B	3B	HR	HR%	R	RBI	BB	SO	SB	PH AB	PH H	PO	A	E	DP	TC/G	FA	G by Pos
1949	NY A	2	1.000	1.000	2	2	0	0	0	0.0	0	2	0	0	0	2	2	0	0	0	0	0.0	–	
1950		4	.133	.133	15	2	0	0	0	0.0	0	0	0	1	0	0	0	27	3	0	2	7.5	1.000	1B-4
1951		4	.286	.429	7	2	1	0	0	0.0	2	1	2	0	0	2	0	12	0	0	4	3.0	1.000	1B-2
1952		5	.400	1.067	15	6	1	0	3	20.0	3	6	3	1	0	0	0	25	3	0	4	5.6	1.000	1B-4
1953		3	.000	.000	3	0	0	0	0	0.0	0	0	0	1	0	3	0	0	0	0	0	0.0		
5 yrs.		18	.286	.548	42	12	2	0	3	7.1	5	9	5	3	0	8 3rd	3 1st	64	6	0	10	3.9	1.000	1B-10

John Mizerock

MIZEROCK, JOHN JOSEPH
B. Dec. 8, 1960, Punxsutawney, Pa.

BL TR 6' 180 lbs.

Year	Team	Games	BA	SA	AB	H	2B	3B	HR	HR%	R	RBI	BB	SO	SB	PH AB	PH H	PO	A	E	DP	TC/G	FA	G by Pos
1983	HOU N	33	.153	.259	85	13	4	1	1	1.2	8	10	12	15	0	0	0	154	24	6	5	5.6	.967	C-33
1985		15	.237	.342	38	9	4	0	0	0.0	6	6	2	8	0	0	0	77	8	3	1	5.9	.966	C-15
1986		44	.185	.259	81	15	1	1	1	1.2	9	6	24	16	0	3	0	221	12	3	0	5.4	.987	C-42
1989	ATL N	11	.222	.222	27	6	0	0	0	0.0	1	2	0	3	0	0	0	48	4	0	0	4.7	1.000	C-11
4 yrs.		103	.186	.268	231	43	9	2	2	0.9	24	24	38	42	0	3	0	500	48	12	6	5.4	.979	C-101

Bill Mizeur

MIZEUR, WILLIAM FRANCIS (Bad Bill)
B. June 22, 1897, Nokomis, Ill. D. Aug. 27, 1976, Decatur, Ill.

BL TR 6' 180 lbs.

Year	Team	Games	BA	SA	AB	H	2B	3B	HR	HR%	R	RBI	BB	SO	SB	PH AB	PH H	PO	A	E	DP	TC/G	FA	G by Pos
1923	STL A	1	.000	.000	1	0	0	0	0	0.0	0	0	0	0	0	1	0	0	0	0	0	0.0	–	
1924		1	.000	.000	1	0	0	0	0	0.0	0	0	0	0	0	1	0	0	0	0	0	0.0	–	
2 yrs.		2	.000	.000	2	0	0	0	0	0.0	0	0	0	0	0	2	0	0	0	0	0	0.0		

Dave Moates

MOATES, DAVID ALLEN
B. Jan. 30, 1948, Great Lakes, Ill.

BL TL 5'9" 163 lbs.

Year	Team	Games	BA	SA	AB	H	2B	3B	HR	HR%	R	RBI	BB	SO	SB	PH AB	PH H	PO	A	E	DP	TC/G	FA	G by Pos
1974	TEX A	1	–	–	0	0	0	0	0	–	0	0	0	0	0	0	0	0	0	0	0	0.0	–	
1975		54	.274	.377	175	48	9	0	3	1.7	21	14	13	15	9	0	0	114	6	2	1	2.3	.984	OF-51, DH-1
1976		85	.241	.307	137	33	7	1	0	0.0	21	13	11	18	6	7	3	106	4	1	2	1.3	.991	OF-66, DH-7
3 yrs.		140	.260	.346	312	81	16	1	3	1.0	42	27	24	33	15	7	3	220	10	3	3	1.7	.987	OF-117, DH-8

Danny Moeller

MOELLER, DANIEL EDWARD
B. Mar. 23, 1885, DeWitt, Iowa D. Apr. 14, 1951, Florence, Ala.

BB TR 5'11" 165 lbs.

Year	Team	Games	BA	SA	AB	H	2B	3B	HR	HR%	R	RBI	BB	SO	SB	PH AB	PH H	PO	A	E	DP	TC/G	FA	G by Pos
1907	PIT N	11	.286	.357	42	12	1	1	0	0.0	4	3	4		2	0	0	11	1	3	1	1.4	.800	OF-11
1908		36	.193	.239	109	21	3	1	0	0.0	14	9	9		4	7	0	38	0	2	0	1.1	.950	OF-27
1912	WAS A	132	.276	.399	519	143	26	10	6	1.2	90	46	52		30	0	0	227	25	15	5	2.0	.944	OF-132
1913		153	.236	.321	589	139	15	10	5	0.8	88	42	72	103	62	0	0	249	27	22	4	1.9	.926	OF-153
1914		151	.250	.324	571	143	19	10	1	0.2	83	45	71	89	26	1	0	208	19	17	4	1.6	.930	OF-150
1915		118	.226	.311	438	99	11	10	2	0.5	65	23	59	63	32	1	0	167	13	9	6	1.6	.952	OF-116
1916	2 teams	WAS A (78G – .246)			CLE A (25G – .067)																			
"	total	103	.226	.274	270	61	8	1	1	0.4	35	24	35	41	15	21	4	105	13	4	4	1.2	.967	OF-73, 2B-1
7 yrs.		704	.243	.328	2538	618	83	43	15	0.6	379	192	302	296	171	30	4	1005	98	72	24	1.7	.939	OF-662, 2B-1

Joe Moffett

MOFFETT, JOSEPH W.
Brother of Sam Moffett.
B. June, 1859, Wheeling, W. Va. Deceased.

6'

Year	Team	Games	BA	SA	AB	H	2B	3B	HR	HR%	R	RBI	BB	SO	SB	PH AB	PH H	PO	A	E	DP	TC/G	FA	G by Pos
1884	TOL AA	56	.201	.255	204	41	5	3	0	0.0	17		2			0	0	421	42	33	23	8.9	.933	1B-38, 3B-12, OF-3, 2B-3

Sam Moffett

MOFFETT, SAMUEL R.
Brother of Joe Moffett.
B. Mar. 14, 1857, Wheeling, W. Va. D. May 5, 1907, Butte, Mont.

TR

Year	Team	Games	BA	SA	AB	H	2B	3B	HR	HR%	R	RBI	BB	SO	SB	PH AB	PH H	PO	A	E	DP	TC/G	FA	G by Pos
1884	CLE N	67	.184	.246	256	47	12	2	0	0.0	26	14	8	56		0	0	102	68	23	4	2.9	.881	OF-42, P-24, 1B-2, 3B-1, 2B-1
1887	IND N	11	.122	.146	41	5	1	0	0	0.0	6	1	1	6		0	0	8	7	3	0	1.6	.833	P-6, OF-5
1888		10	.114	.114	35	4	0	0	0	0.0	6		5	4		0	0	4	5	3	1	1.2	.750	P-7, OF-3
3 yrs.		88	.169	.220	332	56	13	2	0	0.0	38	15	14	66		2	0	114	80	29	5	2.5	.870	OF-50, P-37, 1B-2, 3B-1, 2B-1

John Mohardt

MOHARDT, JOHN HENRY
B. Jan. 21, 1898, Pittsburgh, Pa. D. Nov. 24, 1961, La Jolla, Calif.

BR TR 5'10" 165 lbs.

Year	Team	Games	BA	SA	AB	H	2B	3B	HR	HR%	R	RBI	BB	SO	SB	PH AB	PH H	PO	A	E	DP	TC/G	FA	G by Pos
1922	DET A	5	1.000	1.000	1	1	0	0	0	0.0	2	0	1	0	0	0	0	1	0	0	0	0.2	1.000	OF-3

Year Team	Games	BA	SA	AB	H	2B	3B	HR	HR%	R	RBI	BB	SO	SB	Pinch Hit AB	Pinch Hit H	PO	A	E	DP	TC/G	FA	G by Pos

Kid Mohler

MOHLER, ERNEST FOLLETTE
B. Dec. 13, 1874, Oneida, Ill. D. Nov. 4, 1961, San Francisco, Calif.
BL TL 5'4½" 145 lbs.

Year Team	Games	BA	SA	AB	H	2B	3B	HR	HR%	R	RBI	BB	SO	SB	PH AB	PH H	PO	A	E	DP	TC/G	FA	G by Pos
1894 WAS N	3	.111	.111	9	1	0	0	0	0.0	0	0	2	4	0	0	0	10	10	1	1	7.0	.952	2B-3

Johnny Mokan

MOKAN, JOHN LEO
B. Sept. 23, 1895, Buffalo, N. Y. D. Feb. 10, 1985, Buffalo, N. Y.
BR TR 5'7" 165 lbs.

Year Team	Games	BA	SA	AB	H	2B	3B	HR	HR%	R	RBI	BB	SO	SB	PH AB	PH H	PO	A	E	DP	TC/G	FA	G by Pos
1921 PIT N	19	.269	.404	52	14	3	2	0	0.0	7	9	5	3	0	3	0	35	0	2	0	1.9	.946	OF-13
1922 2 teams		PIT N (31G – .258)		PHI N (47G – .252)																			
" total	78	.254	.350	240	61	10	2	3	1.3	29	35	25	28	1	14	3	90	9	11	3	1.4	.900	OF-54, 3B-2
1923 PHI N	113	.313	.460	400	125	23	3	10	2.5	76	48	53	31	6	6	1	237	19	8	0	2.3	.970	OF-105, 3B-1
1924	96	.260	.363	366	95	15	1	7	1.9	50	44	30	27	7	2	1	195	9	3	1	2.2	.986	OF-94
1925	75	.330	.488	209	69	11	2	6	2.9	30	42	27	9	3	6	1	120	1	2	0	1.6	.984	OF-68
1926	127	.303	.414	456	138	23	5	6	1.3	68	62	41	31	4	2	1	221	16	8	4	1.9	.967	OF-123
1927	74	.286	.366	213	61	13	2	0	0.0	22	33	25	21	5	9	2	97	5	4	0	1.4	.962	OF-63
7 yrs.	582	.291	.409	1936	563	98	17	32	1.7	282	273	206	150	26	42	9	995	59	38	8	1.9	.965	OF-520, 3B-3

Fenton Mole

MOLE, FENTON LeROY (Muscles)
B. June 14, 1925, San Leandro, Calif.
BL TL 6'1½" 200 lbs.

Year Team	Games	BA	SA	AB	H	2B	3B	HR	HR%	R	RBI	BB	SO	SB	PH AB	PH H	PO	A	E	DP	TC/G	FA	G by Pos
1949 NY A	10	.185	.333	27	5	2	1	0	0.0	3	5	0	3	0	2	1	59	6	0	12	6.5	1.000	1B-8

Bob Molinaro

MOLINARO, ROBERT JOSEPH (Molly)
B. May 21, 1950, Newark, N. J.
BL TR 6' 180 lbs.

Year Team	Games	BA	SA	AB	H	2B	3B	HR	HR%	R	RBI	BB	SO	SB	PH AB	PH H	PO	A	E	DP	TC/G	FA	G by Pos
1975 DET A	6	.263	.368	19	5	0	1	0	0.0	2	1	1	0	0	0	0	8	1	0	0	1.5	1.000	OF-6
1977 2 teams		DET A (4G – .250)		CHI A (1G – .500)																			
" total	5	.333	.500	6	2	0	0	0	0.0	0	0	0	3	1	4	1	1	0	0	0	0.2	1.000	OF-1
1978 CHI A	105	.262	.378	286	75	5	5	6	2.1	39	27	19	12	22	12	4	88	2	0	0	0.9	1.000	OF-62, DH-32
1979 BAL A	8	.000	.000	6	0	0	0	0	0.0	0	0	1	3	1	1	0	7	0	0	0	0.9	1.000	OF-5
1980 CHI A	119	.291	.404	344	100	16	4	5	1.5	48	36	26	29	18	21	7	85	3	4	0	0.8	.957	OF-49, DH-47
1981	47	.262	.405	42	11	1	1	1	2.4	7	9	8	1	1	**35**	9	3	0	0	0	0.1	1.000	DH-4, OF-2
1982 2 teams		CHI N (65G – .197)		PHI N (19G – .286)																			
" total	84	.213	.263	80	17	1	0	1	1.3	6	14	9	6	2	**67**	14	2	0	0	0	0.0	1.000	OF-4
1983 2 teams		PHI N (19G – .111)		DET A (8G – .000)																			
" total	27	.100	.300	20	2	1	0	1	5.0	4	3	1	3	1	20	2	0	0	0	0	0.0	–	DH-1
8 yrs.	401	.264	.375	803	212	25	11	14	1.7	106	90	65	57	46	160	37	194	6	4	0	0.5	.980	OF-129, DH-84

Paul Molitor

MOLITOR, PAUL LEO
B. Aug. 22, 1956, St. Paul, Minn.
BR TR 6' 185 lbs.

Year Team	Games	BA	SA	AB	H	2B	3B	HR	HR%	R	RBI	BB	SO	SB	PH AB	PH H	PO	A	E	DP	TC/G	FA	G by Pos
1978 MIL A	125	.273	.372	521	142	26	4	6	1.2	73	45	19	54	30	3	0	253	401	22	74	5.4	.967	2B-91, SS-31, DH-2, 3B-1
1979	140	.322	.469	584	188	27	16	9	1.5	88	62	48	48	33	2	0	309	440	16	84	5.5	.979	2B-122, SS-10, DH-8
1980	111	.304	.438	450	137	29	2	9	2.0	81	37	48	48	34	2	1	260	336	20	90	5.5	.968	2B-91, SS-12, DH-7, 3B-1
1981	64	.267	.335	251	67	11	0	2	0.8	45	19	25	29	10	1	0	119	4	3	1	2.0	.976	OF-46, DH-16
1982	160	.302	.450	666	201	26	8	19	2.9	136	71	69	93	41	0	0	134	350	32	48	3.2	.938	3B-150, DH-6, SS-4
1983	152	.270	.410	608	164	28	6	15	2.5	95	47	59	74	41	2	0	105	343	16	37	3.1	.966	3B-146, DH-2
1984	13	.217	.239	46	10	1	0	0	0.0	3	6	2	8	1	2	0	7	21	2	3	2.3	.933	3B-7, DH-4
1985	140	.297	.408	576	171	28	3	10	1.7	93	48	54	80	21	1	0	126	263	19	30	2.9	.953	3B-135, DH-4
1986	105	.281	.426	437	123	24	6	9	2.1	62	55	40	81	20	0	0	86	171	15	25	2.6	.945	3B-91, DH-10, OF-4
1987	118	.353	.566	465	164	**41**	5	16	3.4	114	75	69	67	45	1	0	60	113	5	24	1.5	.972	DH-58, 3B-41, 2B-19
1988	154	.312	.452	609	190	34	6	13	2.1	115	60	71	54	41	0	0	87	188	17	15	1.9	.942	3B-105, DH-49, 2B-1
1989	155	.315	.439	615	194	35	4	11	1.8	84	56	64	67	27	0	0	106	287	18	27	2.7	.956	3B-112, DH-28, 2B-16
12 yrs.	1437	.300	.435	5828	1751	310	60	119	2.0	989	581	568	703	344	14	1	1652	2917	185	458	3.3	.961	3B-789, 2B-340, DH-194, SS-57, OF-50

DIVISIONAL PLAYOFF SERIES

Year Team	Games	BA	SA	AB	H	2B	3B	HR	HR%	R	RBI	BB	SO	SB	PH AB	PH H	PO	A	E	DP	TC/G	FA	G by Pos
1981 MIL A	5	.250	.400	20	5	0	1	1	5.0	2	1	2	5	0	0	0	0	0	0	0	0.0	–	OF-5

LEAGUE CHAMPIONSHIP SERIES

Year Team	Games	BA	SA	AB	H	2B	3B	HR	HR%	R	RBI	BB	SO	SB	PH AB	PH H	PO	A	E	DP	TC/G	FA	G by Pos
1982 MIL A	5	.316	.684	19	6	1	0	2	10.5	4	5	2	3	1	0	0	0	2	0	0	0.4	1.000	3B-5

WORLD SERIES

Year Team	Games	BA	SA	AB	H	2B	3B	HR	HR%	R	RBI	BB	SO	SB	PH AB	PH H	PO	A	E	DP	TC/G	FA	G by Pos
1982 MIL A	7	.355	.355	31	11	0	0	0	0.0	5	2	2	4	1	0	0	4	9	0	1	1.9	1.000	3B-7

Fred Mollenkamp

MOLLENKAMP, FREDERICK HENRY
B. Mar. 15, 1890, Cincinnati, Ohio D. Nov. 1, 1948, Cincinnati, Ohio

Year Team	Games	BA	SA	AB	H	2B	3B	HR	HR%	R	RBI	BB	SO	SB	PH AB	PH H	PO	A	E	DP	TC/G	FA	G by Pos
1914 PHI N	3	.125	.125	8	1	0	0	0	0.0	0	0	2	0	0	1	0	23	0	0	2	9.3	1.000	1B-3

Fritz Mollwitz

MOLLWITZ, FREDERICK AUGUST (Zip)
B. June 16, 1890, Koburg, Germany D. Oct. 3, 1967, Bradenton, Fla.
BR TR 6'2" 170 lbs.

Year Team	Games	BA	SA	AB	H	2B	3B	HR	HR%	R	RBI	BB	SO	SB	PH AB	PH H	PO	A	E	DP	TC/G	FA	G by Pos
1913 CHI N	2	.429	.429	7	3	0	0	0	0.0	1	0	0	0	0	0	0	19	0	0	0	9.5	1.000	1B-2
1914 2 teams		CHI N (13G – .150)		CIN N (32G – .162)																			
" total	45	.160	.176	131	21	2	0	0	0.0	12	6	3	12	3	6	0	339	21	4	19	8.1	.989	1B-36, OF-1
1915 CIN N	153	.259	.316	525	136	21	3	1	0.2	36	51	15	49	19	0	0	1545	79	7	107	10.7	.996	1B-153
1916 2 teams		CIN N (65G – .224)		CHI N (33G – .268)																			
" total	98	.236	.291	254	60	4	0	0	0.0	13	27	12	18	10	20	5	606	30	14	35	6.6	.978	1B-73, OF-6
1917 PIT N	36	.257	.300	140	36	4	1	0	0.0	15	12	8	8	2	0	0	341	17	2	16	10.0	.994	1B-36, 2B-1
1918	119	.269	.322	432	116	12	7	0	0.0	43	45	23	24	23	0	0	1252	73	13	67	11.2	.990	1B-119
1919 2 teams		PIT N (56G – .173)		STL N (25G – .229)																			
" total	81	.191	.243	251	48	5	4	0	0.0	18	17	22	21	11	2	1	778	34	6	41	10.1	.994	1B-77, OF-2
7 yrs.	534	.241	.294	1740	420	50	19	1	0.1	138	158	83	132	70	28	6	4880	254	45	285	9.7	.991	1B-496, OF-9, 2B-1

Blas Monaco

MONACO, BLAS
B. Nov. 16, 1915, San Antonio, Tex.
BB TR 5'11" 170 lbs.

Year Team	Games	BA	SA	AB	H	2B	3B	HR	HR%	R	RBI	BB	SO	SB	PH AB	PH H	PO	A	E	DP	TC/G	FA	G by Pos
1937 CLE A	5	.286	.571	7	2	0	1	0	0.0	0	2	0	2	0	2	1	4	5	0	0	1.8	1.000	2B-3

Year	Team	Games	BA	SA	AB	H	2B	3B	HR	HR%	R	RBI	BB	SO	SB	Pinch Hit AB	Pinch Hit H	PO	A	E	DP	TC/G	FA	G by Pos

Blas Monaco *continued*

Year	Team	Games	BA	SA	AB	H	2B	3B	HR	HR%	R	RBI	BB	SO	SB	AB	H	PO	A	E	DP	TC/G	FA	G by Pos
1946		12	.000	.000	6	0	0	0	0	0.0	2	0	1	1	0	6	0	0	0	0	0	0.0	–	
2 yrs.		17	.154	.308	13	2	0	1	0	0.0	2	2	1	3	0	8	1	4	5	0	0	0.5	1.000	2B-3

Freddie Moncewicz

MONCEWICZ, FREDERICK ALFRED
B. Sept. 1, 1903, Brockton, Mass. D. Apr. 23, 1969, Brockton, Mass.   BR TR 5'8½" 175 lbs.

Year	Team	Games	BA	SA	AB	H	2B	3B	HR	HR%	R	RBI	BB	SO	SB	AB	H	PO	A	E	DP	TC/G	FA	G by Pos
1928	BOS A	3	.000	.000	1	0	0	0	0	0.0	0	0	0	1	0	0	0	1	1	0	0	0.7	1.000	SS-2

Al Monchak

MONCHAK, ALEX
B. Mar. 5, 1917, Bayonne, N. J.   BR TR 6' 180 lbs.

Year	Team	Games	BA	SA	AB	H	2B	3B	HR	HR%	R	RBI	BB	SO	SB	AB	H	PO	A	E	DP	TC/G	FA	G by Pos
1940	PHI N	19	.143	.143	14	2	0	0	0	0.0	1	0	0	6	1	1	0	5	5	2	1	0.6	.833	SS-9, 2B-1

Rick Monday

MONDAY, ROBERT JAMES
B. Nov. 20, 1945, Batesville, Ark.   BL TL 6'3" 195 lbs.

Year	Team	Games	BA	SA	AB	H	2B	3B	HR	HR%	R	RBI	BB	SO	SB	AB	H	PO	A	E	DP	TC/G	FA	G by Pos
1966	KC A	17	.098	.171	41	4	1	1	0	0.0	4	2	6	16	1	1	0	26	1	1	0	1.6	.964	OF-15
1967		124	.251	.419	406	102	14	6	14	3.4	52	58	42	107	3	13	2	260	14	8	6	2.3	.972	OF-113
1968	OAK A	148	.274	.402	482	132	24	7	8	1.7	56	49	72	143	14	6	2	299	11	7	3	2.1	.978	OF-144
1969		122	.271	.424	399	108	17	4	12	3.0	57	54	72	100	12	5	1	262	3	10	4	2.3	.964	OF-119
1970		112	.290	.457	376	109	19	7	10	2.7	63	37	58	99	17	1	0	257	3	5	2	2.4	.981	OF-109
1971		116	.245	.439	355	87	9	3	18	5.1	53	56	49	93	6	7	2	238	6	4	1	2.1	.984	OF-111
1972	CHI N	138	.249	.399	434	108	22	5	11	2.5	68	42	78	102	12	3	0	268	6	1	2	2.0	.996	OF-134
1973		149	.267	.469	554	148	24	5	26	4.7	93	56	92	124	5	3	1	317	9	9	2	2.2	.973	OF-148
1974		142	.294	.467	538	158	19	7	20	3.7	84	58	70	94	7	4	0	302	10	5	5	2.2	.984	OF-139
1975		136	.267	.446	491	131	29	4	17	3.5	89	60	83	95	8	4	1	315	6	9	0	2.4	.973	OF-131
1976		137	.272	.507	534	145	20	5	32	6.0	107	77	60	125	5	4	1	587	26	5	17	4.5	.992	OF-103, 1B-32
1977	LA N	118	.230	.383	392	90	13	1	15	3.8	47	48	60	109	1	6	0	221	5	2	0	1.9	.991	OF-115, 1B-3
1978		119	.254	.468	342	87	14	1	19	5.6	54	57	49	100	2	16	2	217	3	1	1	1.9	.995	OF-103, 1B-1
1979		12	.303	.303	33	10	0	0	0	0.0	2	2	5	6	0	1	1	27	0	1	0	2.3	.964	OF-10
1980		96	.268	.469	194	52	7	1	10	5.2	25	25	28	49	2	36	8	92	1	3	0	1.0	.969	OF-50
1981		66	.315	.608	130	41	1	2	11	8.5	24	25	24	42	1	23	8	50	1	2	0	0.8	.962	OF-41
1982		104	.257	.481	210	54	6	4	11	5.2	37	42	39	51	2	35	4	86	7	4	2	0.9	.959	OF-57, 1B-4
1983		99	.247	.399	178	44	7	1	6	3.4	21	20	29	42	0	42	8	80	2	3	1	0.9	.965	OF-44, 1B-4
1984		31	.191	.298	47	9	2	0	1	2.1	4	7	8	16	0	17	3	74	4	1	3	2.5	.987	1B-10, OF-2
19 yrs.		1986	.264	.443	6136	1619	248	64	241	3.9	950	775	924	1513	98	227	44	3978	118	81	45	2.1	.981	OF-1688, 1B-54

DIVISIONAL PLAYOFF SERIES

Year	Team	Games	BA	SA	AB	H	2B	3B	HR	HR%	R	RBI	BB	SO	SB	AB	H	PO	A	E	DP	TC/G	FA	G by Pos
1981	LA N	5	.214	.214	14	3	0	0	0	0.0	1	1	2	4	0	0	0	0	0	0	0	0.0	–	OF-5

LEAGUE CHAMPIONSHIP SERIES

Year	Team	Games	BA	SA	AB	H	2B	3B	HR	HR%	R	RBI	BB	SO	SB	AB	H	PO	A	E	DP	TC/G	FA	G by Pos
1971	OAK A	1	.000	.000	3	0	0	0	0	0.0	0	0	1	0	0	0	0	4	0	0	0	4.0	1.000	OF-1
1977	LA N	3	.286	.429	7	2	1	0	0	0.0	1	0	2	1	0	1	0	6	0	0	0	2.0	1.000	OF-3
1978		3	.200	.400	10	2	0	1	0	0.0	2	0	1	5	0	1	0	6	0	0	0	2.0	1.000	OF-3
1981		3	.333	.667	9	3	0	0	1	11.1	2	1	0	4	0	1	0	0	0	0	0	0.0	–	OF-2
1983		1	–	–	0	0	0	0	0	–	0	0	0	0	0	0	0	0	0	0	0	0.0	–	
5 yrs.		11	.241	.448	29	7	1	1	1	3.4	5	1	4	12	0	3	0	16	0	0	0	1.5	1.000	OF-9

WORLD SERIES

Year	Team	Games	BA	SA	AB	H	2B	3B	HR	HR%	R	RBI	BB	SO	SB	AB	H	PO	A	E	DP	TC/G	FA	G by Pos
1977	LA N	4	.167	.167	12	2	0	0	0	0.0	0	0	0	3	0	0	0	5	0	0	0	1.3	1.000	OF-4
1978		5	.154	.231	13	2	1	0	0	0.0	2	0	4	3	0	0	0	5	0	0	0	1.0	1.000	OF-4, DH-1
1981		5	.231	.308	13	3	1	0	0	0.0	1	0	3	6	0	1	0	9	0	0	0	1.8	1.000	OF-4
3 yrs.		14	.184	.237	38	7	2	0	0	0.0	3	0	7	12	0	1	0	19	0	0	0	1.4	1.000	OF-12, DH-1

Don Money

MONEY, DONALD WAYNE (Brooks)
B. June 7, 1947, Washington, D. C.   BR TR 6'1" 170 lbs.

Year	Team	Games	BA	SA	AB	H	2B	3B	HR	HR%	R	RBI	BB	SO	SB	AB	H	PO	A	E	DP	TC/G	FA	G by Pos
1968	PHI N	4	.231	.385	13	3	2	0	0	0.0	1	2	2	4	0	0	0	6	8	0	3	3.5	1.000	SS-4
1969		127	.229	.327	450	103	22	2	6	1.3	41	42	43	83	1	1	0	212	443	21	82	5.3	.969	SS-126
1970		120	.295	.463	447	132	25	4	14	3.1	66	66	43	68	4	0	0	133	236	15	28	3.2	.961	SS-119, SS-2
1971		121	.223	.358	439	98	22	8	7	1.6	40	38	31	80	4	5	0	167	197	11	21	3.1	.971	3B-68, OF-40, 2B-20
1972		152	.222	.343	536	119	16	2	15	2.8	54	52	41	92	5	1	0	140	316	10	31	3.1	.979	3B-151, SS-2
1973	MIL A	145	.284	.401	556	158	28	2	11	2.0	75	61	53	53	22	2	0	146	276	13	41	3.0	.970	3B-124, SS-21
1974		159	.283	.415	629	178	32	3	15	2.4	85	65	62	80	19	0	0	131	336	5	42	3.0	.989	3B-157, DH-1, 2B-1
1975		109	.277	.432	405	112	16	1	15	3.7	58	43	31	51	7	5	1	109	194	15	24	2.9	.953	3B-99, SS-7
1976		117	.267	.408	439	117	18	4	12	2.7	51	62	47	50	6	8	1	96	202	13	21	2.7	.958	3B-103, DH-10, SS-1
1977		152	.279	.470	570	159	28	3	25	4.4	86	83	57	70	8	2	2	306	390	16	83	4.7	.978	2B-116, OF-23, 3B-15, DH-7
1978		137	.293	.440	518	152	30	2	14	2.7	88	54	48	70	3	5	2	705	216	9	88	6.8	.990	1B-61, 2B-36, 3B-25, DH-15, SS-2
1979		92	.237	.351	350	83	20	1	6	1.7	52	38	40	47	1	3	1	240	117	2	33	3.9	.994	DH-33, 3B-26, 1B-19, 2B-16
1980		86	.256	.498	289	74	17	1	17	5.9	39	46	40	36	0	5	2	176	129	12	35	3.7	.962	3B-55, DH-14, 1B-14, 2B-2
1981		60	.216	.286	185	40	7	0	2	1.1	17	14	19	27	0	3	1	33	100	3	9	2.3	.978	3B-56, DH-2, 1B-1
1982		96	.284	.531	275	78	14	3	16	5.8	40	55	32	38	0	21	2	72	49	4	11	1.3	.968	DH-66, 3B-16, 1B-11, 2B-1
1983		43	.149	.219	114	17	5	0	1	0.9	5	8	11	17	0	12	1	25	33	1	2	1.4	.983	DH-28, 3B-11, 1B-2
16 yrs.		1720	.261	.406	6215	1623	302	36	176	2.8	798	729	600	866	80	73	14	2697	3242	150	554	3.5	.975	3B-1025, 2B-192, DH-176, SS-165, 1B-108, OF-63

DIVISIONAL PLAYOFF SERIES

Year	Team	Games	BA	SA	AB	H	2B	3B	HR	HR%	R	RBI	BB	SO	SB	AB	H	PO	A	E	DP	TC/G	FA	G by Pos
1981	MIL A	2	.000	.000	3	0	0	0	0	0.0	0	0	0	0	0	2	0	0	0	0	0	0.0	–	DH-1, 2B-1

LEAGUE CHAMPIONSHIP SERIES

Year	Team	Games	BA	SA	AB	H	2B	3B	HR	HR%	R	RBI	BB	SO	SB	AB	H	PO	A	E	DP	TC/G	FA	G by Pos
1982	MIL A	4	.182	.182	11	2	0	0	0	0.0	2	1	3	1	0	0	0	0	0	0	0	0.0	–	DH-4

WORLD SERIES

Year	Team	Games	BA	SA	AB	H	2B	3B	HR	HR%	R	RBI	BB	SO	SB	AB	H	PO	A	E	DP	TC/G	FA	G by Pos
1982	MIL A	5	.231	.308	13	3	1	0	0	0.0	4	1	2	3	0	1	0	0	0	0	0	0.0	–	DH-4

Year	Team		Games	BA	SA	AB	H	2B	3B	HR	HR%	R	RBI	BB	SO	SB	Pinch Hit AB	Pinch Hit H	PO	A	E	DP	TC/G	FA	G by Pos

Charlie Moore *continued*

Year	Team		Games	BA	SA	AB	H	2B	3B	HR	HR%	R	RBI	BB	SO	SB	AB	H	PO	A	E	DP	TC/G	FA	G by Pos
1986			80	.260	.374	235	61	12	3	3	1.3	24	39	21	38	5	2	1	429	45	4	7	6.0	.992	C-72, OF-4, DH-2, 2B-1
1987	TOR	A	51	.215	.355	107	23	10	1	1	0.9	15	7	13	12	0	3	2	237	11	5	0	5.0	.980	C-44, OF-5
15 yrs.			1334	.261	.355	4033	1052	187	43	36	0.9	456	408	346	470	51	91	32	4481	471	101	54	3.8	.980	C-894, OF-396, DH-18, 2B-4, 3B-1

DIVISIONAL PLAYOFF SERIES

| 1981 | MIL | A | 4 | .222 | .222 | 9 | 2 | 0 | 0 | 0 | 0.0 | 0 | 1 | 1 | 2 | 0 | 0 | 0 | 0 | 0 | 0 | 0 | 0.0 | – | DH-2, OF-2 |

LEAGUE CHAMPIONSHIP SERIES

| 1982 | MIL | A | 5 | .462 | .462 | 13 | 6 | 0 | 0 | 0 | 0.0 | 3 | 0 | 1 | 0 | 0 | 0 | 0 | 0 | 0 | 0 | 0 | 0.0 | – | OF-5 |

WORLD SERIES

| 1982 | MIL | A | 7 | .346 | .462 | 26 | 9 | 3 | 0 | 0 | 0.0 | 3 | 2 | 1 | 0 | 0 | 0 | 0 | 13 | 0 | 0 | 0 | 1.9 | 1.000 | OF-7 |

Dee Moore

MOORE, D C
B. Apr. 6, 1914, Hedley, Tex.   BR TR 6' 200 lbs.

Year	Team		Games	BA	SA	AB	H	2B	3B	HR	HR%	R	RBI	BB	SO	SB	AB	H	PO	A	E	DP	TC/G	FA	G by Pos
1936	CIN	N	6	.400	.800	10	4	2	1	0	0.0	4	1	0	3	0	4	1	5	3	1	0	1.5	.889	P-2, C-1
1937			7	.077	.077	13	1	0	0	0	0.0	2	0	1	2	0	1	0	23	4	2	1	4.1	.931	C-6
1943	2 teams						BKN N (37G – .253)				PHI N (37G – .239)														
"	total		74	.245	.307	192	47	7	1	1	0.5	21	20	26	16	1	13	1	156	41	8	7	2.8	.961	C-36, 3B-14, OF-6, 1B-1
1946	PHI	N	11	.077	.077	13	1	0	0	0	0.0	2	1	7	3	0	2	0	24	2	1	3	2.5	.963	C-6, 1B-2
4 yrs.			98	.232	.303	228	53	9	2	1	0.4	29	22	34	24	1	20	2	208	50	12	11	2.8	.956	C-49, 3B-14, OF-6, 1B-3, P-2

Eddie Moore

MOORE, GRAHAM EDWARD
B. Jan. 18, 1899, Barlow, Ky.   D. Feb. 10, 1976, Ft. Myers, Fla.   BR TR 5'7" 165 lbs.

Year	Team		Games	BA	SA	AB	H	2B	3B	HR	HR%	R	RBI	BB	SO	SB	AB	H	PO	A	E	DP	TC/G	FA	G by Pos
1923	PIT	N	6	.269	.308	26	7	1	0	0	0.0	6	1	2	3	1	0	0	12	12	2	2	4.3	.923	SS-6
1924			72	.359	.464	209	75	8	4	2	1.0	47	13	27	12	6	8	4	93	34	1	2	1.8	.992	OF-35, 3B-14, 2B-4
1925			142	.298	.413	547	163	29	8	6	1.1	106	77	73	26	19	2	2	340	407	39	82	5.5	.950	2B-122, OF-15, 3B-3
1926	2 teams						PIT N (43G – .227)				BOS N (54G – .266)														
"	total		97	.250	.304	316	79	11	3	0	0.0	36	34	28	18	9	9	3	170	245	25	49	4.5	.943	2B-62, SS-15, 3B-10
1927	BOS	N	112	.302	.363	411	124	14	4	1	0.2	53	32	39	17	5	6	3	200	223	16	36	3.9	.964	3B-52, 2B-39, OF-16, SS-1
1928			68	.237	.307	215	51	9	0	2	0.9	27	18	19	12	7	5	0	131	8	6	3	2.1	.959	OF-54, 2B-1
1929	BKN	N	111	.296	.371	402	119	18	6	1	0.2	48	48	44	16	3	1	1	205	348	28	52	5.2	.952	2B-74, SS-36, OF-2, 3B-1
1930			76	.281	.372	196	55	13	1	1	0.5	24	20	21	7	1	9	5	117	115	10	23	3.2	.959	2B-23, SS-17, 3B-1
1932	NY	N	37	.264	.333	87	23	3	0	1	1.1	9	6	9	5	1	4	0	52	81	9	13	3.8	.937	SS-21, 3B-6, 2B-5
1934	CLE	A	27	.154	.185	65	10	2	0	0	0.0	4	8	10	4	0	3	0	56	47	7	11	4.1	.936	2B-18, 3B-3, SS-2
10 yrs.			748	.285	.366	2474	706	108	26	13	0.5	360	257	272	121	52	47	18	1376	1520	143	273	4.1	.953	2B-348, OF-145, SS-98, 3B-90

WORLD SERIES

| 1925 | PIT | N | 7 | .231 | .385 | 26 | 6 | 1 | 0 | 1 | 3.8 | 7 | 2 | 5 | 2 | 0 | 0 | 0 | 16 | 13 | 1 | 2 | 4.3 | .967 | 2B-7 |

Ferdie Moore

MOORE, FERDINAND DePAGE
B. Feb. 21, 1896, Camden, N. J.   D. May 6, 1947, Atlantic City, N. J.

| 1914 | PHI | A | 2 | .500 | .500 | 4 | 2 | 0 | 0 | 0 | 0.0 | 1 | 1 | 0 | 2 | 0 | 0 | 0 | 17 | 0 | 2 | 0 | 9.5 | .895 | 1B-2 |

Gary Moore

MOORE, GARY DOUGLAS
B. Feb. 24, 1945, Tulsa, Okla.   BR TL 5'10" 175 lbs.

| 1970 | LA | N | 7 | .188 | .438 | 16 | 3 | 0 | 2 | 0 | 0.0 | 2 | 0 | 0 | 1 | 1 | 2 | 1 | 9 | 0 | 0 | 0 | 1.3 | 1.000 | OF-5, 1B-1 |

Gene Moore

MOORE, EUGENE, JR. (Rowdy)
Son of Gene Moore.
B. Aug. 26, 1909, Lancaster, Tex.   D. Mar. 12, 1978, Jackson, Miss.   BL TL 5'11" 175 lbs.

Year	Team		Games	BA	SA	AB	H	2B	3B	HR	HR%	R	RBI	BB	SO	SB	AB	H	PO	A	E	DP	TC/G	FA	G by Pos
1931	CIN	N	4	.143	.214	14	2	1	0	0	0.0	2	1	0	0	0	1	0	8	0	0	0	2.0	1.000	OF-3
1933	STL	N	11	.395	.579	38	15	3	2	0	0.0	6	8	4	10	1	1	0	29	0	1	0	2.7	.967	OF-10
1934			9	.278	.333	18	5	1	0	0	0.0	2	1	2	2	0	6	2	12	0	1	0	1.4	.923	OF-3
1935			3	.000	.000	3	0	0	0	0	0.0	0	0	0	3	0	0	0	0	0	0	0	0.0	–	
1936	BOS	N	151	.290	.449	637	185	38	12	13	2.0	91	67	40	80	6	0	0	314	32	8	0	2.3	.977	OF-151
1937			148	.283	.456	561	159	29	10	16	2.9	88	70	61	73	11	0	0	340	21	8	1	2.5	.978	OF-148
1938			54	.272	.400	180	49	8	3	3	1.7	27	19	16	20	1	5	1	97	4	2	0	1.9	.981	OF-47
1939	BKN	N	107	.225	.337	306	69	13	6	3	1.0	45	39	40	50	4	18	3	141	8	6	3	1.4	.961	OF-86, 1B-1
1940	2 teams						BKN N (10G – .269)				BOS N (103G – .292)														
"	total		113	.290	.401	389	113	26	1	5	1.3	49	41	26	35	2	11	0	206	11	3	1	1.9	.986	OF-100
1941	BOS	N	129	.272	.393	397	108	17	8	5	1.3	42	43	45	37	5	16	3	229	13	8	2	1.9	.968	OF-110
1942	WAS	A	1	.000	.000	2	0	0	0	0	0.0	0	0	0	1	0	0	0	0	0	0	0	0.0	–	OF-1
1943			92	.268	.370	254	68	14	3	2	0.8	41	39	19	29	0	30	12	125	5	2	0	1.4	.985	OF-57, 1B-1
1944	STL	A	110	.238	.349	390	93	13	6	6	1.5	56	58	24	37	0	11	5	210	5	8	3	2.0	.964	OF-98, 1B-1
1945			110	.260	.359	354	92	16	2	5	1.4	48	50	40	26	1	10	0	184	10	6	0	1.8	.970	OF-100
14 yrs.			1042	.270	.400	3543	958	179	53	58	1.6	497	436	317	401	31	112	27	1895	109	53	12	2.0	.974	OF-914, 1B-3

WORLD SERIES

| 1944 | STL | A | 6 | .182 | .182 | 22 | 4 | 0 | 0 | 0 | 0.0 | 4 | 0 | 3 | 6 | 0 | 0 | 0 | 8 | 0 | 0 | 0 | 1.3 | 1.000 | OF-6 |

Henry Moore

MOORE, HENRY S.
Deceased.

| 1884 | WAS | U | 111 | .336 | .414 | 461 | 155 | 23 | 5 | 1 | 0.2 | 77 | | 19 | | | 0 | 0 | 141 | 24 | 45 | 6 | 1.9 | .786 | OF-105, SS-8 |

Jackie Moore

MOORE, JACKIE SPENCER
B. Feb. 19, 1939, Jay, Fla.
Manager 1984-86.   BR TR 6' 180 lbs.

| 1965 | DET | A | 21 | .094 | .094 | 53 | 5 | 0 | 0 | 0 | 0.0 | 2 | 2 | 6 | 12 | 0 | 1 | 0 | 128 | 6 | 2 | 1 | 6.5 | .985 | C-20 |

Year	Team	Games	BA	SA	AB	H	2B	3B	HR	HR%	R	RBI	BB	SO	SB	Pinch Hit AB	H	PO	A	E	DP	TC/G	FA	G by Pos

Jerry Moore

MOORE, JEREMIAH S.
B. Detroit, Mich.   D. Sept. 26, 1908, Wayne, Mich.   BL

1884	2 teams	ALT U (20G – .313)			CLE N	(9G – .200)																		
"	total	29	.282	.355	110	31	3	1	1	0.9	11	10	0	5		0	0	118	27	29	0	6.0	.833	C-21, OF-9
1885	DET N	6	.174	.217	23	4	1	0	0	0.0	2	0	1	3		0	0	24	12	9	0	7.5	.800	C-6
2 yrs.		35	.263	.331	133	35	4	1	1	0.8	13	10	1	8		0	0	142	39	38	0	6.3	.826	C-27, OF-9

Jimmy Moore

MOORE, JAMES WILLIAM
B. Apr. 24, 1903, Paris, Tenn.   D. Mar. 7, 1986, Memphis, Tenn.   BR TR 6'1½" 187 lbs.

1930	2 teams	CHI A (16G – .205)			PHI A	(15G – .380)																		
"	total	31	.303	.427	89	27	5	1	2	2.2	14	14	8	7	1	9	4	38	3	3	2	1.4	.932	OF-22
1931	PHI A	49	.224	.315	143	32	5	1	2	1.4	18	21	11	13	0	11	0	70	3	2	2	1.5	.973	OF-36
2 yrs.		80	.254	.358	232	59	10	2	4	1.7	32	35	19	20	1	20	4	108	6	5	4	1.5	.958	OF-58

WORLD SERIES

1930	PHI A	3	.333	.333	3	1	0	0	0	0.0	0	0	1	1	0	1	1	0	0	0	0	0.0	–	OF-1
1931		2	.333	.333	3	1	0	0	0	0.0	0	0	0	1	0	1	0	1	0	0	0	0.5	1.000	OF-1
2 yrs.		5	.333	.333	6	2	0	0	0	0.0	0	0	1	2	0	-2	1	1	0	0	0	0.2	1.000	OF-2

Joe Moore

MOORE, JOSEPH GREGG (Jo-Jo, The Gause Ghost)
B. Dec. 25, 1908, Gause, Tex.   BL TR 5'11" 155 lbs.

1930	NY N	3	.200	.200	5	1	0	0	0	0.0	1	0	1	1	0	2	1	2	0	0	0	0.7	1.000	OF-1
1931		4	.250	.375	8	2	1	0	0	0.0	0	3	0	1	1	3	0	2	0	0	0	0.5	1.000	OF-1
1932		86	.305	.374	361	110	15	2	2	0.6	53	27	20	18	4	0	0	160	6	3	10	2.0	.982	OF-86
1933		132	.292	.342	524	153	16	5	0	0.0	56	42	21	27	4	0	0	266	19	10	6	2.2	.966	OF-132
1934		139	.331	.486	580	192	37	4	15	2.6	106	61	31	23	5	8	1	242	8	12	1	1.9	.954	OF-131
1935		155	.295	.429	681	201	28	9	15	2.2	108	71	53	24	5	0	0	342	11	10	2	2.3	.972	OF-155
1936		152	.316	.421	649	205	29	9	7	1.1	110	63	37	27	2	3	0	291	25	6	3	2.1	.981	OF-149
1937		142	.310	.440	580	180	37	10	6	1.0	89	57	46	37	7	2	0	226	12	6	0	1.7	.975	OF-140
1938		125	.302	.437	506	153	23	6	11	2.2	76	56	22	27	2	10	1	214	8	5	1	1.8	.978	OF-114
1939		138	.269	.370	562	151	23	2	10	1.8	80	47	45	17	5	2	1	260	13	4	2	2.0	.986	OF-136
1940		138	.276	.385	543	150	33	4	6	1.1	83	46	43	30	7	3	0	259	9	5	1	2.0	.982	OF-133
1941		121	.273	.369	428	117	16	2	7	1.6	47	40	30	15	4	3	1	237	5	7	0	2.1	.972	OF-116
12 yrs.		1335	.298	.408	5427	1615	258	53	79	1.5	809	513	348	247	46	36	5	2501	116	68	26	2.0	.975	OF-1294

WORLD SERIES

1933	NY N	5	.227	.273	22	5	1	0	0	0.0	1	1	1	3	0	0	0	13	1	0	1	2.8	1.000	OF-5
1936		6	.214	.393	28	6	2	0	1	3.6	4	1	1	4	0	0	0	9	0	0	0	1.5	1.000	OF-6
1937		5	.391	.435	23	9	1	0	0	0.0	1	1	0	1	0	0	0	13	0	0	0	2.6	1.000	OF-5
3 yrs.		16	.274	.370	73	20	4	0	1	1.4	6	3	2	8	0	0	0	35	1	0	1	2.3	1.000	OF-16

Johnny Moore

MOORE, JOHN FRANCIS
B. Mar. 23, 1902, Waterville, Conn.   BL TR 5'10½" 175 lbs.

1928	CHI N	4	.000	.000	4	0	0	0	0	0.0	0	0	0	0	0	4	0	0	0	0	0	0.0	–	
1929		37	.286	.397	63	18	1	0	2	3.2	13	8	4	6	0	15	5	32	1	1	0	0.9	.971	OF-15
1931		39	.240	.346	104	25	3	1	2	1.9	19	16	7	5	1	15	3	51	3	2	0	1.4	.964	OF-22
1932		119	.305	.470	443	135	24	5	13	2.9	59	64	22	38	4	10	4	272	12	5	2	2.4	.983	OF-109
1933	CIN N	135	.263	.325	514	135	19	5	1	0.2	60	44	29	16	4	3	1	329	12	9	4	2.6	.974	OF-132
1934	2 teams	CIN N (16G – .190)			PHI N	(116G – .343)																		
"	total	132	.330	.494	500	165	35	7	11	2.2	73	98	43	20	7	6	1	267	18	5	2	2.2	.983	OF-125
1935	PHI N	153	.323	.483	600	194	33	3	19	3.2	84	93	45	50	4	3	0	233	18	7	6	1.7	.973	OF-150
1936		124	.328	.494	472	155	24	3	16	3.4	85	68	26	22	1	10	4	214	5	12	1	1.9	.948	OF-112
1937		96	.319	.472	307	98	16	2	9	2.9	46	59	18	18	2	20	7	124	9	8	1	1.5	.943	OF-72
1945	CHI N	7	.167	.167	6	1	0	0	0	0.0	0	0	2	1	0	6	1	0	0	0	0	0.0	–	
10 yrs.		846	.307	.449	3013	926	155	26	73	2.4	439	452	195	176	23	92	26	1522	78	49	16	1.9	.970	OF-737

WORLD SERIES

| 1932 | CHI N | 2 | .000 | .000 | 7 | 0 | 0 | 0 | 0 | 0.0 | 1 | 0 | 2 | 1 | 0 | 0 | 0 | 4 | 0 | 0 | 0 | 2.0 | 1.000 | OF-2 |

Junior Moore

MOORE, ALVIN EARL
B. Jan. 25, 1953, Waskom, Tex.   BR TR 5'11" 195 lbs.

1976	ATL N	20	.269	.308	26	7	1	0	0	0.0	1	2	4	4	0	12	4	7	10	1	1	0.9	.944	3B-6, OF-1, 2B-1
1977		112	.260	.343	361	94	9	3	5	1.4	41	34	33	29	4	10	3	86	189	17	10	2.6	.942	3B-104, 2B-1
1978	CHI A	24	.292	.323	65	19	0	1	0	0.0	8	4	6	7	1	5	2	12	9	2	2	1.0	.913	DH-12, 3B-6, OF-5
1979		88	.264	.328	201	53	6	2	1	0.5	24	23	12	20	0	25	6	83	5	3	0	1.0	.967	OF-61, DH-10, 2B-2
1980		45	.256	.331	121	31	4	1	1	0.8	9	10	7	11	0	4	2	30	65	7	6	2.3	.931	3B-34, OF-3, DH-2, 1B-1
5 yrs.		289	.264	.335	774	204	20	7	7	0.9	83	73	62	71	5	56	17	218	278	30	19	1.8	.943	3B-150, OF-70, DH-24, 2B-4, 1B-1

Kelvin Moore

MOORE, KELVIN ORLANDO
B. Sept. 26, 1957, LeRoy, Ala.   BR TL 6'1" 195 lbs.

1981	OAK A	14	.255	.362	47	12	1	0	2	2.1	5	3	5	15	1	1	0	99	7	0	9	7.6	1.000	1B-13
1982		21	.224	.358	67	15	1	0	2	3.0	6	6	3	23	0	1	0	123	9	4	9	6.5	.971	1B-20
1983		41	.210	.363	124	26	4	0	5	4.0	12	16	10	39	2	0	0	293	16	2	38	7.6	.994	1B-40
3 yrs.		76	.223	.361	238	53	5	2	8	3.4	23	25	18	77	3	2	0	515	32	6	56	7.3	.989	1B-73

DIVISIONAL PLAYOFF SERIES

| 1981 | OAK A | 2 | .000 | .000 | 8 | 0 | 0 | 0 | 0 | 0.0 | 0 | 0 | 0 | 2 | 0 | 0 | 0 | 0 | 0 | 0 | 0 | 0.0 | – | 1B-2 |

LEAGUE CHAMPIONSHIP SERIES

| 1981 | OAK A | 3 | .222 | .222 | 9 | 2 | 0 | 0 | 0 | 0.0 | 0 | 0 | 0 | 1 | 0 | 0 | 0 | 0 | 0 | 0 | 0 | 0.0 | – | 1B-3 |

Randy Moore

MOORE, RANDOLPH EDWARD
B. June 21, 1905, Naples, Tex.   BL TR 6' 185 lbs.

Year	Team		Games	BA	SA	AB	H	2B	3B	HR	HR%	R	RBI	BB	SO	SB	Pinch Hit AB	Pinch Hit H	PO	A	E	DP	TC/G	FA	G by Pos

Randy Moore *continued*

Year	Team		Games	BA	SA	AB	H	2B	3B	HR	HR%	R	RBI	BB	SO	SB	AB	H	PO	A	E	DP	TC/G	FA	G by Pos
1927	CHI	A	6	.000	.000	15	0	0	0	0	0.0	0	0	0	2	0	2	0	8	1	0	0	1.5	1.000	OF-4
1928			24	.213	.311	61	13	4	1	0	0.0	6	5	3	5	0	6	2	34	1	2	0	1.5	.946	OF-16
1930	BOS	N	83	.288	.366	191	55	9	0	2	1.0	24	34	10	13	3	30	6	79	27	6	3	1.3	.946	OF-34, 3B-13
1931			83	.260	.359	192	50	8	1	3	1.6	19	34	13	3	1	32	6	71	39	6	3	1.4	.948	OF-29, 3B-22, 2B-1
1932			107	.293	.390	351	103	21	2	3	0.9	41	43	15	11	1	14	4	258	67	5	34	3.1	.985	OF-41, 3B-31, 1B-22, C-1
1933			135	.302	.425	497	150	23	7	8	1.6	64	70	40	16	3	6	1	355	12	7	5	2.8	.981	OF-122, 1B-10
1934			123	.284	.393	422	120	21	2	7	1.7	55	64	40	16	2	13	5	496	23	12	24	4.3	.977	OF-72, 1B-37
1935			125	.275	.373	407	112	20	4	4	1.0	42	42	26	16	1	23	5	370	20	13	14	3.2	.968	OF-78, 1B-21
1936	BKN	N	42	.239	.273	88	21	3	0	0	0.0	4	14	8	1	0	18	7	27	0	1	0	0.7	.964	OF-21
1937	2 teams		BKN N	(13G –	.136)			STL N	(8G –	.000)																
"	total		21	.103	.138	29	3	1	0	0	0.0	3	2	3	2	0	9	0	27	5	4	0	1.7	.889	C-10, OF-1
10 yrs.			749	.278	.378	2253	627	110	17	27	1.2	258	308	158	85	11	153	36	1725	195	56	83	2.6	.972	OF-418, 1B-90, 3B-66, C-11, 2B-1

Scrappy Moore

MOORE, WILLIAM ALLEN
B. Dec. 16, 1892, St. Louis, Mo.   D. Oct. 13, 1964, Little Rock, Ark.   BR TR 5'8" 153 lbs.

Year	Team		Games	BA	SA	AB	H	2B	3B	HR	HR%	R	RBI	BB	SO	SB	AB	H	PO	A	E	DP	TC/G	FA	G by Pos
1917	STL	A	4	.125	.125	8	1	0	0	0	0.0	1	0	1	0	0	2	1	2	4	2	2	2.0	.750	3B-2

Terry Moore

MOORE, TERRY BLUFORD
B. May 27, 1912, Vernon, Ala.
Manager 1954.   BR TR 5'11" 195 lbs.

Year	Team		Games	BA	SA	AB	H	2B	3B	HR	HR%	R	RBI	BB	SO	SB	AB	H	PO	A	E	DP	TC/G	FA	G by Pos
1935	STL	N	119	.287	.414	456	131	34	3	6	1.3	63	53	15	40	13	0	0	354	11	6	3	3.1	.984	OF-117
1936			143	.264	.369	590	156	39	4	5	0.8	85	47	37	52	9	7	2	418	14	10	7	3.1	.977	OF-133
1937			115	.267	.349	461	123	17	3	5	1.1	76	43	32	41	13	8	1	307	9	4	2	2.8	.988	OF-106
1938			94	.272	.397	312	85	21	3	4	1.3	49	21	46	19	9	9	1	228	21	6	2	2.7	.977	OF-75, 3B-6
1939			130	.295	.487	417	123	25	2	17	4.1	65	77	43	38	6	7	2	291	17	2	1	2.4	.994	OF-121, P-1
1940			136	.304	.475	537	163	33	4	17	3.2	92	64	42	44	18	3	0	383	11	5	4	2.9	.987	OF-133
1941			122	.294	.400	493	145	26	4	6	1.2	86	68	52	31	3	1	0	293	14	5	3	2.6	.984	OF-121
1942			130	.288	.391	489	141	26	3	6	1.2	80	49	56	26	10	4	2	271	9	5	0	2.2	.982	OF-126, 3B-1
1946			91	.263	.353	278	73	14	1	3	1.1	32	28	18	26	0	25	6	158	5	3	0	1.8	.982	OF-66
1947			127	.283	.370	460	130	17	1	7	1.5	61	45	38	39	1	6	1	292	6	5	2	2.4	.983	OF-120
1948			91	.232	.343	207	48	11	0	4	1.9	30	18	27	12	0	17	4	131	2	1	0	1.5	.993	OF-71
11 yrs.			1298	.280	.399	4700	1318	263	28	80	1.7	719	513	406	368	82	87	19	3126	119	52	24	2.5	.984	OF-1189, 3B-7, P-1

WORLD SERIES

Year	Team		Games	BA	SA	AB	H	2B	3B	HR	HR%	R	RBI	BB	SO	SB	AB	H	PO	A	E	DP	TC/G	FA	G by Pos
1942	STL	N	5	.294	.353	17	5	1	0	0	0.0	2	2	2	3	0	0	0	15	0	0	0	3.0	1.000	OF-5
1946			7	.148	.148	27	4	0	0	0	0.0	1	2	2	6	0	0	0	17	1	0	0	2.6	1.000	OF-7
2 yrs.			12	.205	.227	44	9	1	0	0	0.0	3	4	4	9	0	0	0	32	1	0	0	2.8	1.000	OF-12

Andres Mora

MORA, ANDRES IBARA
Born Andres Mora y Ibara.
B. May 25, 1955, Rio Bravo, Mexico   BR TR 6' 180 lbs.

Year	Team		Games	BA	SA	AB	H	2B	3B	HR	HR%	R	RBI	BB	SO	SB	AB	H	PO	A	E	DP	TC/G	FA	G by Pos
1976	BAL	A	73	.218	.350	220	48	11	0	6	2.7	18	25	13	49	1	10	4	55	3	3	0	0.8	.951	DH-34, OF-31
1977			77	.245	.464	233	57	8	2	13	5.6	32	44	5	53	0	16	5	66	2	0	0	0.9	1.000	OF-57, DH-5, 3B-1
1978			76	.214	.354	229	49	8	0	8	3.5	21	14	13	47	0	13	0	129	4	3	0	1.8	.978	OF-69, DH-1
1980	CLE	A	9	.111	.111	18	2	0	0	0	0.0	0	0	0	0	0	6	1	6	0	0	0	0.7	1.000	OF-3
4 yrs.			235	.223	.383	700	156	27	2	27	3.9	71	83	31	149	1	45	12	256	9	6	0	1.2	.978	OF-160, DH-40, 3B-1

Jerry Morales

MORALES, JULIO RUBEN
Born Julio Ruben Morales y Torres.
B. Feb. 18, 1949, Yabucoa, Puerto Rico   BR TR 5'10" 155 lbs.

Year	Team		Games	BA	SA	AB	H	2B	3B	HR	HR%	R	RBI	BB	SO	SB	AB	H	PO	A	E	DP	TC/G	FA	G by Pos
1969	SD	N	19	.195	.317	41	8	2	0	1	2.4	5	6	5	7	0	2	0	27	2	0	1	1.5	1.000	OF-19
1970			28	.155	.241	58	9	0	1	1	1.7	6	4	3	11	0	2	0	25	0	2	0	1.0	.926	OF-26
1971			12	.118	.118	17	2	0	0	0	0.0	0	1	2	2	1	2	0	8	0	0	0	0.7	1.000	OF-7
1972			115	.239	.357	347	83	15	7	4	1.2	38	18	35	54	4	19	3	214	8	4	2	2.0	.982	OF-96, 3B-4
1973			122	.281	.420	388	109	23	2	9	2.3	47	34	27	55	6	22	9	214	5	2	1	1.8	.991	OF-100
1974	CHI	N	151	.273	.423	534	146	21	7	15	2.8	70	82	46	63	4	8	2	266	5	7	2	1.8	.975	OF-143
1975			153	.270	.369	578	156	21	4	12	2.1	62	91	50	65	3	2	2	273	11	6	1	1.9	.979	OF-151
1976			140	.274	.395	537	147	17	0	16	3.0	66	67	41	49	5	5	1	273	12	5	6	2.1	.983	OF-136
1977			136	.290	.447	490	142	34	5	11	2.2	56	69	43	75	0	11	3	247	8	4	3	1.9	.985	OF-128
1978	STL	N	130	.239	.341	457	109	19	8	4	0.9	44	46	33	44	4	8	1	254	5	6	0	2.0	.977	OF-126
1979	DET	A	129	.211	.364	440	93	23	1	14	3.2	50	56	30	56	10	7	0	206	6	3	2	1.7	.986	OF-119, DH-7
1980	NY	N	94	.254	.347	193	49	7	1	3	1.6	19	30	13	31	2	30	7	107	3	3	1	1.2	.973	OF-63
1981	CHI	N	84	.286	.339	245	70	6	2	1	0.4	27	25	22	29	1	12	3	142	2	1	1	1.7	.986	OF-72
1982			65	.284	.440	116	33	2	2	4	3.4	14	30	9	7	1	30	10	72	5	0	1	1.2	1.000	OF-41
1983			63	.195	.299	87	17	9	0	0	0.0	11	11	7	19	0	41	8	29	1	0	0	0.5	1.000	OF-29
15 yrs.			1441	.259	.382	4528	1173	199	36	95	2.1	516	570	366	567	37	199	49	2357	73	44	21	1.7	.982	OF-1256, DH-7, 3B-4

Jose Morales

MORALES, JOSE MANUEL
B. Dec. 30, 1944, Frederiksted, Virgin Islands   BR TR 5'11" 187 lbs.

Year	Team		Games	BA	SA	AB	H	2B	3B	HR	HR%	R	RBI	BB	SO	SB	AB	H	PO	A	E	DP	TC/G	FA	G by Pos
1973	2 teams		OAK A	(6G –	.286)			MON N	(5G –	.400)																
"	total		11	.316	.368	19	6	1	0	0	0.0	0	1	1	5	0	7	3	0	0	0	0	0.0	–	DH-3
1974	MON	N	25	.269	.538	26	7	4	0	1	3.8	3	5	1	7	0	22	5	3	1	1	0	0.2	.800	C-2
1975			93	.301	.387	163	49	6	1	2	1.2	18	24	14	21	0	51	15	234	28	4	19	2.9	.985	1B-27, OF-6, C-5
1976			104	.316	.462	158	50	11	0	4	2.5	12	37	3	20	0	78	25¹	137	21	3	9	1.5	.981	1B-21, C-12
1977			65	.203	.324	74	15	4	1	1	1.4	9	9	5	12	0	52	10	52	3	0	4	0.8	1.000	1B-8, C-8
1978	MIN	A	101	.314	.401	242	76	13	1	2	0.8	22	38	20	35	0	46	14	1	0	0	0	0.0	1.000	DH-77, OF-1, 1B-1, C-1
1979			92	.267	.335	191	51	5	1	2	1.0	21	27	14	27	0	42	9	2	0	0	0	0.0	1.000	DH-77, 1B-1
1980			97	.303	.490	241	73	17	2	8	3.3	36	36	22	19	0	36	13	19	0	0	2	0.2	1.000	DH-86, 1B-2, C-2
1981	BAL	A	38	.244	.349	86	21	3	0	2	2.3	6	14	3	13	0	19	5	13	0	0	1	0.3	1.000	DH-22, 1B-3

Year	Team		Games	BA	SA	AB	H	2B	3B	HR	HR%	R	RBI	BB	SO	SB	Pinch Hit AB	Pinch Hit H	PO	A	E	DP	TC/G	FA	G by Pos

Jose Morales *continued*

1982	2 teams	BAL A (3G – .000)				LA	N	(35G – .300)																		
"	total		38	.273	.394	33	9	1	0	1	3.0	1	8	4	10	0	33	9	0	0	0	0	0.0	–	
1983	LA	N	47	.283	.509	53	15	3	0	3	5.7	4	8	1	11	0	40	12	37	2	2	2	0.9	.951	1B-4
1984			22	.158	.158	19	3	0	0	0	0.0	0	0	1	2	0	19	3	0	0	0	0	0.0	–	
12 yrs.			733	.287	.408	1305	375	68	6	26	2.0	126	207	89	182	0	445 5th	123 4th	498	57	10	37	0.8	.982	DH-265, 1B-67, C-30, OF-7

LEAGUE CHAMPIONSHIP SERIES

| 1983 | LA | N | 2 | .000 | .000 | 2 | 0 | 0 | 0 | 0 | 0.0 | 0 | 0 | 0 | 1 | 0 | 2 | 0 | 0 | 0 | 0 | 0 | 0.0 | – | |

Rich Morales

MORALES, RICHARD ANGELO
B. Sept. 20, 1943, San Francisco, Calif.　　　　　BR TR 5'11" 170 lbs.

1967	CHI	A	8	.000	.000	10	0	0	0	0	0.0	0	0	0	2	0	0	0	6	11	1	1	2.3	.944	SS-7
1968			10	.172	.172	29	5	0	0	0	0.0	2	0	2	5	0	0	0	17	26	1	5	4.4	.977	SS-7, 2B-5
1969			55	.215	.231	121	26	0	1	0	0.0	12	6	7	18	1	3	1	77	118	4	22	3.6	.980	2B-38, SS-13, 3B-1
1970			62	.161	.205	112	18	2	0	1	0.9	6	2	9	16	1	9	1	49	91	7	14	2.4	.952	SS-24, 3B-20, 2B-12
1971			84	.243	.319	185	45	8	0	2	1.1	19	14	22	26	2	12	3	75	159	9	18	2.9	.963	SS-57, 3B-18, 2B-3, OF-1
1972			110	.206	.258	287	59	7	1	2	0.7	24	20	19	49	2	5	1	133	248	11	38	3.6	.972	SS-86, 2B-16, 3B-14
1973	2 teams	CHI A (7G – .000)				SD	N	(90G – .164)																		
"	total		97	.161	.194	248	40	6	1	0	0.0	10	17	28	37	0	2	0	194	268	5	49	4.8	.989	2B-81, SS-10, 3B-5
1974	SD	N	54	.197	.295	61	12	3	0	1	1.6	8	5	8	6	1	2	1	54	61	6	11	2.2	.950	SS-29, 2B-18, 3B-6, 1B-1
8 yrs.			480	.195	.242	1053	205	26	3	6	0.6	81	64	95	159	7	33	7	605	982	44	158	3.4	.973	SS-233, 2B-173, 3B-64, OF-1, 1B-1

Al Moran

MORAN, RICHARD ALAN
B. Dec. 5, 1938, Detroit, Mich.　　　　　BR TR 6'1½" 190 lbs.

1963	NY	N	119	.193	.230	331	64	5	2	1	0.3	26	23	36	60	3	1	0	190	332	27	57	4.6	.951	SS-116, 3B-1
1964			16	.227	.227	22	5	0	0	0	0.0	2	4	2	2	0	0	0	15	31	2	5	3.0	.958	SS-15, 3B-1
2 yrs.			135	.195	.229	353	69	5	2	1	0.3	28	27	38	62	3	1	0	205	363	29	62	4.4	.951	SS-131, 3B-2

Bill Moran

MORAN, WILLIAM L.
B. Oct. 10, 1869, Joliet, Ill. D. Apr. 8, 1916, Joliet, Ill.　　　　　175 lbs.

1892	STL	N	24	.136	.148	81	11	1	0	0	0.0	2	5	2	12	0	0	0	91	23	14	0	5.3	.891	C-22
1895	CHI	N	15	.164	.291	55	9	2	1	1	1.8	8	9	3	2	2	0	0	49	18	14	0	5.4	.827	C-15
2 yrs.			39	.147	.206	136	20	3	1	1	0.7	10	14	5	14	2	0	0	140	41	28	0	5.4	.866	C-37

Billy Moran

MORAN, WILLIAM NELSON
B. Nov. 27, 1933, Montgomery, Ala.　　　　　BR TR 5'11" 185 lbs.

1958	CLE	A	115	.226	.280	257	58	11	0	1	0.4	26	18	13	23	3	4	0	174	210	15	56	3.5	.962	2B-74, SS-38
1959			11	.294	.294	17	5	0	0	0	0.0	1	2	0	1	0	0	0	13	9	1	2	2.1	.957	2B-6, SS-5
1961	LA	A	54	.260	.347	173	45	7	1	2	1.2	17	22	17	16	0	0	0	109	120	9	31	4.4	.962	2B-51, SS-2
1962			160	.282	.407	659	186	25	3	17	2.6	90	74	39	80	5	0	0	422	477	13	103	5.7	.986	2B-160
1963			153	.275	.375	597	164	29	5	7	1.2	67	65	31	57	1	2	1	352	455	22	98	5.4	.973	2B-151
1964	2 teams	LA A (50G – .268)				CLE	A	(69G – .205)																		
"	total		119	.241	.301	349	84	16	1	1	0.3	40	21	31	36	1	12	2	105	177	14	13	2.5	.953	3B-89, 2B-18, 1B-2, SS-1
1965	CLE	A	22	.125	.125	24	3	0	0	0	0.0	1	0	2	5	0	13	2	6	11	0	2	0.8	1.000	2B-7, SS-1
7 yrs.			634	.263	.355	2076	545	88	10	28	1.3	242	202	133	218	10	31	5	1181	1459	74	305	4.3	.973	2B-467, 3B-89, SS-47, 1B-2

Charley Moran

MORAN, CHARLES BARTHELL (Uncle Charlie)
B. Feb. 22, 1878, Nashville, Tenn. D. June 14, 1949, Horse Cave, Ky.　　　　　BR TR 5'8" 180 lbs.

1903	STL	N	4	.429	.429	14	6	0	0	0	0.0	2	1	0			1	0	2	4	0	0	1.5	1.000	P-3, SS-1
1908			21	.175	.254	63	11	1	2	0	0.0	2	2	0			5	2	58	26	9	1	4.4	.903	C-16
2 yrs.			25	.221	.286	77	17	1	2	0	0.0	4	3	0		1	5	2	60	30	9	1	4.0	.909	C-16, P-3, SS-1

Charlie Moran

MORAN, CHARLES VINCENT
B. Mar. 26, 1879, Washington, D. C. D. Apr. 11, 1934, Washington, D. C.　　　　　TR

1903	WAS	A	98	.225	.298	373	84	14	5	1	0.3	41	24	33		8	0	0	220	310	32	39	5.7	.943	SS-96, 2B-2
1904	2 teams	WAS A (62G – .222)				STL	A	(82G – .173)																		
"	total		144	.196	.225	515	101	13	1	0	0.0	42	21	48		9	0	0	185	343	41	19	4.0	.928	3B-82, SS-61, OF-1
1905	STL	A	28	.195	.207	82	16	1	0	0	0.0	6	5	10		3	2	1	43	52	9	7	3.7	.913	2B-21, 3B-7
3 yrs.			270	.207	.252	970	201	28	6	1	0.1	89	50	91		20	2	1	448	705	82	65	4.6	.934	SS-157, 3B-89, 2B-23, OF-1

Herbie Moran

MORAN, JOHN HERBERT
B. Feb. 16, 1884, Costello, Pa. D. Sept. 21, 1954, Clarkson, N. Y.　　　　　BL TR 5'5" 150 lbs.

1908	2 teams	PHI A (19G – .153)				BOS	N	(8G – .276)																		
"	total		27	.193	.193	88	17	0	0	0	0.0	7	6	8			2	0	58	3	2	3	2.3	.968	OF-27
1909	BOS	N	8	.226	.258	31	7	1	0	0	0.0	8	0	5			0	0	14	1	0	0	1.9	1.000	OF-8
1910			20	.119	.119	67	8	0	0	0	0.0	11	3	13	14		6	0	39	7	2	3	2.4	.958	OF-20
1912	BKN	N	130	.276	.356	508	140	18	10	1	0.2	77	40	69	38	28	0	0	273	24	12	5	2.4	.961	OF-129
1913			132	.266	.315	515	137	15	5	0	0.0	71	26	45	29	21	0	0	231	15	13	7	2.0	.950	OF-129
1914	2 teams	CIN N (107G – .235)				BOS	N	(41G – .266)																		
"	total		148	.244	.295	549	134	13	6	1	0.2	67	39	58	40	30	0	0	177	11	10	4	1.3	.949	OF-148
1915	BOS	N	130	.200	.255	419	84	13	5	0	0.0	59	21	66	41	16	6	1	168	17	7	3	1.5	.964	OF-123
7 yrs.			595	.242	.296	2177	527	60	26	2	0.1	300	135	264	162	103	9	1	960	78	46	25	1.8	.958	OF-584

WORLD SERIES

| 1914 | BOS | N | 3 | .077 | .154 | 13 | 1 | 1 | 0 | 0 | 0.0 | 2 | 0 | 1 | 1 | 1 | 0 | 0 | 2 | 0 | 1 | 0 | 1.0 | .667 | OF-3 |

Pat Moran

MORAN, PATRICK JOSEPH
B. Feb. 7, 1876, Fitchburg, Mass. D. Mar. 7, 1924, Orlando, Fla.
Manager 1915-23.　　　　　BR TR 5'10" 180 lbs.

Year	Team		Games	BA	SA	AB	H	2B	3B	HR	HR%	R	RBI	BB	SO	SB	Pinch Hit AB	H	PO	A	E	DP	TC/G	FA	G by Pos

Pat Moran *continued*

Year	Team		Games	BA	SA	AB	H	2B	3B	HR	HR%	R	RBI	BB	SO	SB	AB	H	PO	A	E	DP	TC/G	FA	G by Pos
1901	BOS	N	53	.211	.283	180	38	5	1	2	1.1	12	18	3		3	0	0	299	37	14	8	6.6	.960	C-28, 1B-13, 3B-4, OF-3, SS-3, 2B-1
1902			80	.239	.311	251	60	5	5	1	0.4	22	24	17		6	6	1	339	95	8	5	5.5	.982	C-71, 1B-3, OF-1
1903			109	.262	.406	389	102	25	5	7	**1.8**	40	54	29		8	1	0	408	214	24	17	5.9	.963	C-107, 1B-1
1904			113	.226	.299	398	90	11	3	4	1.0	26	34	18		10	2	0	391	200	37	16	5.6	.941	C-72, 3B-39, 1B-2
1905			85	.240	.341	267	64	11	5	2	0.7	22	22	8		3	7	0	389	113	7	5	6.0	.986	C-78
1906	CHI	N	70	.252	.319	226	57	13	1	0	0.0	22	35	7		6	9	0	335	78	9	6	6.0	.979	C-61
1907			65	.227	.278	198	45	5	1	1	0.5	8	19	10		5	6	2	258	72	9	9	5.2	.973	C-59
1908			50	.260	.307	150	39	5	1	0	0.0	12	12	13		6	4	0	242	56	10	5	6.2	.968	C-45
1909			77	.220	.285	246	54	11	1	1	0.4	18	23	16		2	2	1	181	97	8	3	3.7	.972	C-74
1910	PHI	N	68	.236	.281	199	47	7	1	0	0.0	13	11	17	16	6	11	1	278	83	4	5	5.4	.989	C-56
1911			34	.184	.214	103	19	3	0	0	0.0	2	8	3	13	0	1	0	148	41	3	4	5.6	.984	C-32
1912			13	.115	.154	26	3	1	0	0	0.0	1	1	1	7	0	4	1	35	7	2	1	3.4	.955	C-13
1913			1	.000	.000	1	0	0	0	0	0.0	0	0	0	0	0	1	0	0	0	0	0	0.0	–	
1914			1	–	–	0	0	0	0	0	–	0	0	0	0	0	0	0	0	0	0	0	0.0	–	C-1
14 yrs.			819	.235	.312	2634	618	102	24	18	0.7	198	262	142	36	55	54	6	3303	1093	135	84	5.5	.970	C-697, 3B-43, 1B-19, OF-4, SS-3, 2B-1

WORLD SERIES

Year	Team		Games	BA	SA	AB	H	2B	3B	HR	HR%	R	RBI	BB	SO	SB	AB	H	PO	A	E	DP	TC/G	FA	G by Pos
1906	CHI	N	2	.000	.000	2	0	0	0	0	0.0	0	0	0	0	0	2	0	0	0	0	0	0.0	–	
1907			1	–	–	0	0	0	0	0	0.0	0	0	0	0	0	0	0	0	0	0	0	0.0	–	
2 yrs.			3	.000	.000	2	0	0	0	0	0.0	0	0	0	0	0	2	0	0	0	0	0	0.0	–	

Roy Moran

MORAN, ROY ELLIS (Deedle)
B. Sept. 17, 1884, Vincennes, Ind.   D. July 18, 1966, Atlanta, Ga.   BR TR 5'8"   155 lbs.

Year	Team		Games	BA	SA	AB	H	2B	3B	HR	HR%	R	RBI	BB	SO	SB	AB	H	PO	A	E	DP	TC/G	FA	G by Pos
1912	WAS	A	5	.154	.154	13	2	0	0	0	0.0	0	8	3	0	0	7	1	1	0	1.8	.889	OF-5

Ray Morehart

MOREHART, RAYMOND ANDERSON
B. Dec. 2, 1899, Abner, Tex.   D. Jan. 13, 1989, Dallas, Tex.   BL TR 5'9"   157 lbs.

Year	Team		Games	BA	SA	AB	H	2B	3B	HR	HR%	R	RBI	BB	SO	SB	AB	H	PO	A	E	DP	TC/G	FA	G by Pos
1924	CHI	A	31	.200	.280	100	20	4	2	0	0.0	10	8	17	7	3	2	0	39	70	16	12	4.0	.872	SS-27, 2B-2
1926			73	.318	.401	192	61	10	3	0	0.0	27	21	11	15	3	17	6	71	136	11	13	3.0	.950	2B-48
1927	NY	A	73	.256	.328	195	50	7	2	1	0.5	45	20	29	18	4	14	2	101	175	16	27	4.0	.945	2B-53
3 yrs.			177	.269	.347	487	131	21	7	1	0.2	82	49	57	40	10	33	8	211	381	43	52	3.6	.932	2B-103, SS-27

Dan Morejon

MOREJON, DANIEL
Born Daniel Morejon y Torres.
B. July 21, 1930, Havana, Cuba   BR TR 6'1"   175 lbs.

Year	Team		Games	BA	SA	AB	H	2B	3B	HR	HR%	R	RBI	BB	SO	SB	AB	H	PO	A	E	DP	TC/G	FA	G by Pos
1958	CIN	N	12	.192	.192	26	5	0	0	0	0.0	4	1	9	2	1	1	0	14	0	0	0	1.2	1.000	OF-11

Keith Moreland

MORELAND, BOBBY KEITH
B. May 2, 1954, Dallas, Tex.   BR TR 6'   190 lbs.

Year	Team		Games	BA	SA	AB	H	2B	3B	HR	HR%	R	RBI	BB	SO	SB	AB	H	PO	A	E	DP	TC/G	FA	G by Pos
1978	PHI	N	1	.000	.000	2	0	0	0	0	0.0	0	0	0	0	0	0	0	4	0	0	0	4.0	1.000	C-1
1979			14	.375	.521	48	18	3	2	0	0.0	3	8	3	5	0	1	0	71	3	0	1	5.3	1.000	C-13
1980			62	.314	.440	159	50	8	0	4	2.5	13	29	8	14	3	17	7	188	24	8	7	3.5	.964	C-39, 3B-4, OF-2
1981			61	.255	.383	196	50	4	0	6	3.1	16	37	15	13	1	5	1	267	31	9	4	5.0	.971	C-50, 3B-7, OF-2, 1B-2
1982	CHI	N	138	.261	.399	476	124	17	2	15	3.2	50	68	46	71	1	6	1	384	38	8	2	3.1	.981	OF-86, C-44, 3B-2
1983			154	.302	.460	533	161	30	3	16	3.0	76	70	68	73	0	2	0	244	7	6	1	1.7	.977	OF-151, C-3
1984			140	.279	.422	495	138	17	3	16	3.2	59	80	34	71	1	15	2	393	30	10	19	3.1	.977	OF-103, 1B-29, 3B-8, C-3
1985			161	.307	.440	587	180	30	3	14	2.4	74	106	68	58	12	2	1	313	29	13	7	2.2	.963	OF-148, 1B-12, 3B-11, C-2
1986			156	.271	.384	586	159	30	0	12	2.0	72	79	53	48	3	4	1	340	58	9	16	2.6	.978	OF-121, 3B-24, C-13, 1B-12
1987			153	.266	.465	563	150	29	1	27	4.8	63	88	39	66	3	1	0	99	300	28	27	2.8	.934	3B-150, 1B-1
1988	SD	N	143	.256	.331	511	131	23	0	5	1.0	40	64	40	51	2	3	1	747	58	7	55	5.7	.991	1B-73, OF-64, 3B-2
1989	2 teams		DET A	(90G – .299)		BAL A	(33G – .215)																		
"	total		123	.278	.367	425	118	20	0	6	1.4	45	45	31	45	3	17	4	243	32	4	23	2.3	.986	DH-80, 1B-31, 3B-12, C-1
12 yrs.			1306	.279	.411	4581	1279	214	14	121	2.6	511	674	405	515	28	73	18	3293	610	102	162	3.1	.975	OF-677, 3B-220, C-169, 1B-160, DH-80

DIVISIONAL PLAYOFF SERIES

Year	Team		Games	BA	SA	AB	H	2B	3B	HR	HR%	R	RBI	BB	SO	SB	AB	H	PO	A	E	DP	TC/G	FA	G by Pos
1981	PHI	N	4	.462	.692	13	6	0	0	1	7.7	2	3	1	1	0	0	0	0	0	1	0	0.3	–	C-4

LEAGUE CHAMPIONSHIP SERIES

Year	Team		Games	BA	SA	AB	H	2B	3B	HR	HR%	R	RBI	BB	SO	SB	AB	H	PO	A	E	DP	TC/G	FA	G by Pos
1980	PHI	N	2	.000	.000	1	0	0	0	0	0.0	0	1	0	0	0	0	0	0	0	0	0	0.0	–	C-1
1984	CHI	N	5	.333	.444	18	6	2	0	0	0.0	3	2	1	1	0	0	0	9	0	0	0	1.8	1.000	OF-5
2 yrs.			7	.316	.421	19	6	2	0	0	0.0	3	3	1	1	0	1	0	9	0	0	0	1.3	1.000	OF-5, C-1

WORLD SERIES

Year	Team		Games	BA	SA	AB	H	2B	3B	HR	HR%	R	RBI	BB	SO	SB	AB	H	PO	A	E	DP	TC/G	FA	G by Pos
1980	PHI	N	3	.333	.333	12	4	0	0	0	0.0	1	1	0	1	0	0	0	0	0	0	0	0.0	–	DH-3

Harry Morelock

MORELOCK, A. HARRY
B. Philadelphia, Pa.   Deceased.

Year	Team		Games	BA	SA	AB	H	2B	3B	HR	HR%	R	RBI	BB	SO	SB	AB	H	PO	A	E	DP	TC/G	FA	G by Pos
1891	PHI	N	4	.071	.071	14	1	0	0	0	0.0	1	0	3	3	0	0	0	5	9	3	0	4.3	.824	SS-4
1892			1	.000	.000	3	0	0	0	0	0.0	0	0	1	0	0	0	0	2	1	2	0	5.0	.600	3B-1
2 yrs.			5	.059	.059	17	1	0	0	0	0.0	1	0	4	3	0	0	0	7	10	5	0	4.4	.773	SS-4, 3B-1

Jose Moreno

MORENO, JOSE de los SANTOS
Born Jose de los Santos Mauricio y Moreno.
B. Nov. 1, 1957, Santo Domingo, Dominican Republic   BB TR 6'   175 lbs.

Year	Team		Games	BA	SA	AB	H	2B	3B	HR	HR%	R	RBI	BB	SO	SB	AB	H	PO	A	E	DP	TC/G	FA	G by Pos
1980	NY	N	37	.196	.413	46	9	2	2	2	4.3	6	9	3	12	1	26	4	11	11	3	3	0.7	.880	3B-4, 2B-4
1981	SD	N	34	.229	.271	48	11	2	0	0	0.0	5	6	1	8	4	23	6	15	2	0	1	0.5	1.000	OF-9, 2B-1

Year Team	Games	BA	SA	AB	H	2B	3B	HR	HR%	R	RBI	BB	SO	SB	Pinch Hit AB	H	PO	A	E	DP	TC/G	FA	G by Pos

Jose Moreno *continued*

Year Team	Games	BA	SA	AB	H	2B	3B	HR	HR%	R	RBI	BB	SO	SB	AB	H	PO	A	E	DP	TC/G	FA	G by Pos
1982 CAL A	11	.000	.000	3	0	0	0	0	0.0	3	0	2	0	0	0	0	2	2	0	0	0.4	1.000	2B-2, DH-1
3 yrs.	82	.206	.330	97	20	4	1	2	2.1	14	15	6	20	5	49	10	28	15	3	4	0.6	.935	OF-9, 2B-7, 3B-4, DH-1

Omar Moreno

MORENO, OMAR RENAN
Born Omar Renan Moreno y Quintero.
B. Oct. 24, 1952, Puerto Armuelles, Panama

BL TL 6'2" 180 lbs.

Year Team	Games	BA	SA	AB	H	2B	3B	HR	HR%	R	RBI	BB	SO	SB	AB	H	PO	A	E	DP	TC/G	FA	G by Pos
1975 PIT N	6	.167	.167	6	1	0	0	0	0.0	0	0	1	1	1	2	0	0	0	1	0	0.2	—	OF-1
1976	48	.270	.369	122	33	4	1	2	1.6	24	12	16	24	15	4	2	93	3	4	1	2.1	.960	OF-42
1977	150	.240	.358	492	118	19	9	7	1.4	69	34	38	102	53	6	0	366	10	9	4	2.6	.977	OF-147
1978	155	.235	.303	515	121	15	7	2	0.4	95	33	81	104	71	4	1	409	9	7	2	2.7	.984	OF-152
1979	162	.282	.381	695	196	21	12	8	1.2	110	69	51	104	77	0	0	490	11	13	3	3.2	.975	OF-162
1980	162	.249	.325	676	168	20	13	2	0.3	87	36	57	101	96	0	0	479	15	5	2	3.1	.990	OF-162
1981	103	.276	.362	434	120	18	8	1	0.2	62	35	26	76	39	0	0	302	6	1	1	3.0	.997	OF-103
1982	158	.245	.315	645	158	18	9	3	0.5	82	44	44	121	60	1	0	396	10	7	3	2.6	.983	OF-157
1983 2 teams		HOU N	(97G – .242)		NY A	(48G – .250)																	
" total	145	.244	.330	557	136	21	12	1	0.2	65	42	30	103	37	0	0	371	9	7	4	2.7	.982	OF-145
1984 NY A	117	.259	.361	355	92	12	6	4	1.1	37	38	18	48	20	0	0	262	9	4	2	2.4	.985	OF-108, DH-1
1985 2 teams		NY A	(34G – .197)		KC A	(24G – .243)																	
" total	58	.221	.382	136	30	5	4	3	2.2	21	16	4	24	1	12	0	86	3	0	1	1.5	1.000	OF-47, DH-1
1986 ATL N	118	.234	.351	359	84	18	6	4	1.1	46	27	21	77	17	25	7	151	8	5	3	1.4	.970	OF-97
12 yrs.	1382	.252	.343	4992	1257	171	87	37	0.7	699	386	387	885	487	54	10	3405	93	63	26	2.6	.982	OF-1323, DH-2

LEAGUE CHAMPIONSHIP SERIES

Year Team	Games	BA	SA	AB	H	2B	3B	HR	HR%	R	RBI	BB	SO	SB	AB	H	PO	A	E	DP	TC/G	FA	G by Pos
1979 PIT N	3	.250	.417	12	3	0	1	0	0.0	0	3	0	2	1	0	0	7	0	0	0	2.3	1.000	OF-3

WORLD SERIES

Year Team	Games	BA	SA	AB	H	2B	3B	HR	HR%	R	RBI	BB	SO	SB	AB	H	PO	A	E	DP	TC/G	FA	G by Pos
1979 PIT N	7	.333	.394	33	11	2	0	0	0.0	4	3	1	7	0	0	0	20	1	0	0	3.0	1.000	OF-7

Bill Morgan

MORGAN, HENRY WILLIAM
B. Brooklyn, N. Y. Deceased.

Year Team	Games	BA	SA	AB	H	2B	3B	HR	HR%	R	RBI	BB	SO	SB	AB	H	PO	A	E	DP	TC/G	FA	G by Pos
1878 MIL N	14	.196	.196	56	11	0	0	0	0.0	2	5	3	9		0	0	14	9	7	0	2.1	.767	OF-13, 3B-3, 2B-1
1882 PIT AA	17	.258	.318	66	17	2	1	0	0.0	10		4			0	0	38	7	15	1	3.5	.750	OF-11, C-7
1884 2 teams		BAL U	(2G – .222)		RIC AA	(11G – .167)																	
" total	13	.178	.222	45	8	0	1	0	0.0	3		3			0	0	36	18	13	1	5.2	.806	P-5, C-4, OF-3, 2B-2
3 yrs.	44	.216	.251	167	36	2	2	0	0.0	15	5	10	9		0	0	88	34	35	2	3.6	.777	OF-27, C-11, P-5, 3B-3, 2B-3

Bill Morgan

MORGAN, WILLIAM

Year Team	Games	BA	SA	AB	H	2B	3B	HR	HR%	R	RBI	BB	SO	SB	AB	H	PO	A	E	DP	TC/G	FA	G by Pos
1883 PIT AA	32	.158	.193	114	18	1	1	0	0.0	12		7		0	0	0	59	72	25	4	4.9	.840	SS-21, OF-6, C-5, 2B-2
1884 WAS AA	45	.173	.191	162	28	1	1	0	0.0	8		8		0	0	0	117	27	26	2	3.8	.847	OF-31, 2B-14, SS-2
2 yrs.	77	.167	.192	276	46	3	2	0	0.0	20		15		0	0	0	176	99	51	6	4.2	.844	OF-37, SS-23, 2B-16, C-5

Bobby Morgan

MORGAN, ROBERT MORRIS
B. June 29, 1926, Oklahoma City, Okla.

BR TR 5'9" 175 lbs.

Year Team	Games	BA	SA	AB	H	2B	3B	HR	HR%	R	RBI	BB	SO	SB	AB	H	PO	A	E	DP	TC/G	FA	G by Pos
1950 BKN N	67	.226	.412	199	45	10	3	7	3.5	38	21	32	43	0	5	1	43	145	8	20	2.9	.959	3B-52, SS-10
1952	67	.236	.387	191	45	8	0	7	3.7	36	16	46	35	2	2	0	61	115	7	11	2.7	.962	3B-60, 2B-5, SS-4
1953	69	.260	.418	196	51	6	2	7	3.6	35	33	33	47	2	9	0	71	105	10	19	2.7	.946	3B-36, SS-21
1954 PHI N	135	.262	.418	455	119	25	2	14	3.1	58	50	70	68	3	0	0	251	381	30	73	4.9	.955	SS-129, 3B-8, 2B-5
1955	136	.232	.344	483	112	20	2	10	2.1	61	49	73	72	6	6	2	291	332	18	70	4.7	.972	2B-88, SS-41, 3B-6, 1B-1
1956 2 teams		PHI N	(8G – .200)		STL N	(61G – .195)																	
" total	69	.196	.312	138	27	7	0	3	2.2	15	21	21	28	0	29	5	56	74	9	8	2.0	.935	3B-16, 2B-16, SS-6
1957 2 teams		PHI N	(2G – .000)		CHI N	(125G – .207)																	
" total	127	.207	.299	425	88	20	2	5	1.2	43	27	52	87	5	0	0	236	361	15	59	4.8	.975	2B-118, 3B-12
1958 CHI N	1	.000	.000	1	0	0	0	0	0.0	0	0	0	1	0	1	0	0	0	0	0	0.0	—	
8 yrs.	671	.233	.366	2088	487	96	11	53	2.5	286	217	327	381	18	52	8	1009	1513	97	260	3.9	.963	2B-232, SS-211, 3B-190, 1B-1

WORLD SERIES

Year Team	Games	BA	SA	AB	H	2B	3B	HR	HR%	R	RBI	BB	SO	SB	AB	H	PO	A	E	DP	TC/G	FA	G by Pos
1952 BKN N	2	.000	.000	1	0	0	0	0	0.0	0	0	0	0	0	1	0	0	1	0	0	0.5	1.000	3B-2
1953	1	.000	.000	1	0	0	0	0	0.0	0	0	0	0	0	0	0	0	0	0	0	0.0	—	
2 yrs.	3	.000	.000	2	0	0	0	0	0.0	0	0	0	0	0	2	0	0	1	0	0	0.3	1.000	3B-2

Chet Morgan

MORGAN, CHESTER COLLINS (Chick)
B. June 6, 1910, Cleveland, Miss.

BL TR 5'9" 160 lbs.

Year Team	Games	BA	SA	AB	H	2B	3B	HR	HR%	R	RBI	BB	SO	SB	AB	H	PO	A	E	DP	TC/G	FA	G by Pos
1935 DET A	14	.174	.217	23	4	1	0	0	0.0	2	1	5	0	0	9	1	10	0	1	0	0.8	.909	OF-4
1938	74	.284	.310	306	87	6	1	0	0.0	50	27	20	12	5	0	0	192	6	4	2	2.7	.980	OF-74
2 yrs.	88	.277	.304	329	91	7	1	0	0.0	52	28	25	12	5	9	1	202	6	5	2	2.4	.977	OF-78

Ed Morgan

MORGAN, EDWARD CARRE
B. May 22, 1904, Cairo, Ill. D. Apr. 9, 1980, New Orleans, La.

BR TR 6'½" 180 lbs.

Year Team	Games	BA	SA	AB	H	2B	3B	HR	HR%	R	RBI	BB	SO	SB	AB	H	PO	A	E	DP	TC/G	FA	G by Pos
1928 CLE A	76	.313	.494	265	83	24	6	4	1.5	42	54	21	17	5	1	1	387	69	18	41	6.2	.962	1B-36, OF-21, 3B-14
1929	93	.318	.469	318	101	19	10	3	0.9	60	37	37	23	4	12	4	100	8	11	1	1.3	.908	OF-81
1930	150	.349	.601	584	204	47	11	26	4.5	122	136	62	66	8	2	0	1298	80	18	116	9.3	.987	1B-150, OF-19
1931	131	.351	.511	462	162	33	4	11	2.4	87	86	83	46	4	10	2	1117	80	20	102	9.3	.984	1B-117, 3B-3
1932	144	.293	.402	532	156	32	7	4	0.8	96	68	94	44	7	1	0	1430	74	23	100	10.6	.985	1B-142
1933	39	.264	.364	121	32	3	3	1	0.8	10	13	7	9	1	7	2	302	21	1	14	8.3	.997	1B-32, OF-1
1934 BOS A	138	.267	.352	528	141	28	4	3	0.6	95	79	81	46	7	1	0	1283	56	16	111	9.8	.988	1B-137
7 yrs.	771	.313	.467	2810	879	186	45	52	1.9	512	473	385	251	36	34	9	5917	388	107	485	8.3	.983	1B-614, OF-122, 3B-17

Eddie Morgan

MORGAN, EDWIN WILLIS (Pepper)
B. Nov. 19, 1914, Brady Lake, Ohio D. June 27, 1982, Lakewood, Ohio

BL TL 5'10" 160 lbs.

Year	Team		Games	BA	SA	AB	H	2B	3B	HR	HR%	R	RBI	BB	SO	SB	Pinch Hit AB	H	PO	A	E	DP	TC/G	FA	G by Pos

Eddie Morgan *continued*

Year	Team		Games	BA	SA	AB	H	2B	3B	HR	HR%	R	RBI	BB	SO	SB	AB	H	PO	A	E	DP	TC/G	FA	G by Pos
1936	STL	N	8	.278	.444	18	5	0	0	1	5.6	4	3	2	4	0	3	2	8	0	1	0	1.1	.889	OF-4
1937	BKN	N	31	.188	.250	48	9	3	0	0	0.0	4	5	9	7	0	8	1	68	2	3	4	2.4	.959	OF-7, 1B-7
2 yrs.			39	.212	.303	66	14	3	0	1	1.5	8	8	11	11	0	11	3	76	2	4	4	2.1	.951	OF-11, 1B-7

Joe Morgan

MORGAN, JOE LEONARD
B. Sept. 19, 1943, Bonham, Tex.

BL TR 5'7" 150 lbs.

Year	Team		Games	BA	SA	AB	H	2B	3B	HR	HR%	R	RBI	BB	SO	SB	AB	H	PO	A	E	DP	TC/G	FA	G by Pos
1963	HOU	N	8	.240	.320	25	6	0	1	0	0.0	5	3	5	5	1	1	0	15	15	3	2	4.1	.909	2B-7
1964			10	.189	.189	37	7	0	0	0	0.0	4	0	6	7	0	0	0	31	25	3	4	5.9	.949	2B-10
1965			157	.271	.418	601	163	22	12	14	2.3	100	40	97	77	20	0	0	348	492	27	82	5.5	.969	2B-157
1966			122	.285	.391	425	121	14	8	5	1.2	60	42	89	43	11	4	1	256	316	21	61	4.9	.965	2B-117
1967			133	.275	.411	494	136	27	11	6	1.2	73	42	81	51	29	3	0	299	344	14	67	4.9	.979	2B-130, OF-1
1968			10	.250	.350	20	5	0	1	0	0.0	6	0	7	4	3	3	0	10	6	2	2	1.8	.889	2B-5, OF-1
1969			147	.236	.372	535	126	18	5	15	2.8	94	43	110	74	49	2	1	315	328	18	79	4.5	.973	2B-132, OF-14
1970			144	.268	.396	548	147	28	9	8	1.5	102	52	102	55	42	2	1	349	430	17	98	5.5	.979	2B-142
1971			160	.256	.407	583	149	27	11	13	2.2	87	56	88	52	40	4	1	336	482	12	93	5.2	.986	2B-157
1972	CIN	N	149	.292	.435	552	161	23	4	16	2.9	122	73	115	44	58	1	1	370	436	8	92	5.5	.990	2B-149
1973			157	.290	.493	576	167	35	2	26	4.5	116	82	111	61	67	3	3	417	440	9	106	5.5	.990	2B-154
1974			149	.293	.494	512	150	31	3	22	4.3	107	67	120	69	58	6	2	344	385	13	92	5.0	.982	2B-142
1975			146	.327	.508	498	163	27	6	17	3.4	107	94	132	52	67	4	1	356	425	11	96	5.4	.986	2B-142
1976			141	.320	.576	472	151	30	5	27	5.7	113	111	114	41	60	6	0	342	335	13	85	4.9	.981	2B-133
1977			153	.288	.478	521	150	21	6	22	4.2	113	78	117	58	49	2	0	351	359	5	100	4.7	.993	2B-151
1978			132	.236	.385	441	104	27	0	13	2.9	68	75	79	40	19	9	2	252	290	11	49	4.2	.980	2B-124
1979			127	.250	.376	436	109	26	1	9	2.1	70	32	93	45	28	3	0	259	329	12	74	4.7	.980	2B-121
1980	HOU	N	141	.243	.373	461	112	17	5	11	2.4	66	49	93	47	24	21	4	244	348	7	68	4.2	.988	2B-130
1981	SF		90	.240	.377	308	74	16	1	8	2.6	47	31	66	37	14	3	1	177	258	6	61	4.9	.991	2B-87
1982			134	.289	.438	463	134	19	4	14	3.0	68	61	85	60	24	12	4	255	366	8	69	4.7	.987	2B-120, 3B-3
1983	PHI	N	123	.230	.403	404	93	20	1	16	4.0	72	59	89	54	18	10	3	231	331	17	63	4.7	.971	2B-117
1984	OAK	A	116	.244	.351	365	89	21	0	6	1.6	50	43	66	39	8	12	2	201	229	10	62	3.8	.977	2B-100
22 yrs.			2649	.271	.427	9277	2517	449	96	268	2.9	1650	1133	1865 **3rd**	1015 **7th**	689	111	27	5758	6969	245	1505	4.9	.981	2B-2527, OF-16, 3B-3

LEAGUE CHAMPIONSHIP SERIES

Year	Team		Games	BA	SA	AB	H	2B	3B	HR	HR%	R	RBI	BB	SO	SB	AB	H	PO	A	E	DP	TC/G	FA	G by Pos
1972	CIN	N	5	.263	.579	19	5	0	0	2	10.5	5	3	1	2	1	0	0	11	18	0	3	5.8	1.000	2B-5
1973			5	.100	.150	20	2	1	0	0	0.0	1	1	2	2	0	0	0	12	27	0	3	7.8	1.000	2B-5
1975			3	.273	.545	11	3	0	0	0	0.0	2	1	3	2	4	0	0	2	9	0	1	3.7	1.000	2B-3
1976			3	.000	.000	7	0	0	0	0	0.0	2	0	6	1	1	0	0	9	5	0	2	4.7	1.000	2B-3
1979			3	.000	.000	11	0	0	0	0	0.0	0	0	3	1	1	0	0	12	11	0	2	7.7	1.000	2B-3
1980	HOU	N	4	.154	.385	13	2	1	1	0	0.0	1	0	6	1	0	0	0	9	8	0	3	4.3	1.000	2B-4
1983	PHI	N	4	.067	.067	15	1	0	0	0	0.0	1	0	2	1	0	0	0	8	7	0	0	3.8	1.000	2B-4
7 yrs.			27	.135	.271	96	13	5	1	2	2.1	12	5	23	10	8	0	0	63	85	0	14	5.5	1.000	2B-27

WORLD SERIES

Year	Team		Games	BA	SA	AB	H	2B	3B	HR	HR%	R	RBI	BB	SO	SB	AB	H	PO	A	E	DP	TC/G	FA	G by Pos
1972	CIN	N	7	.125	.208	24	3	0	0	0	0.0	4	1	6	3	2	0	0	18	18	1	3	5.3	.973	2B-7
1975			7	.259	.296	27	7	1	0	0	0.0	4	3	5	1	2	0	0	17	28	0	4	6.4	1.000	2B-7
1976			4	.333	.733	15	5	1	1	1	6.7	3	2	2	2	0	0	0	13	10	2	3	6.3	.920	2B-4
1983	PHI	N	5	.263	.684	19	5	0	1	2	10.5	3	2	2	3	1	0	0	8	10	0	3	3.6	1.000	2B-5
4 yrs.			23	.235	.435	85	20	4	2	3	3.5	14	8	15 **9th**	9	7	0	0	56	66	3	13	5.4	.976	2B-23

Joe Morgan

MORGAN, JOSEPH MICHAEL
B. Nov. 19, 1930, Walpole, Mass.
Manager 1988-89.

BL TR 5'10" 170 lbs.

Year	Team		Games	BA	SA	AB	H	2B	3B	HR	HR%	R	RBI	BB	SO	SB	AB	H	PO	A	E	DP	TC/G	FA	G by Pos
1959	2 teams	MIL N (13G – .217)																							KC A (20G – .190)
"	total		33	.205	.273	44	9	1	1	0	0.0	4	4	5	11	0	22	5	10	14	2	1	0.8	.923	2B-7, 3B-2
1960	2 teams	PHI N (26G – .133)																							CLE A (22G – .298)
"	total		48	.192	.300	130	25	4	2	2	1.5	11	6	12	15	0	10	1	35	64	6	4	2.2	.943	3B-36, OF-2
1961	CLE	A	4	.200	.200	10	2	0	0	0	0.0	0	0	1	3	0	2	0	6	0	0	0	1.5	1.000	OF-2
1964	STL	N	3	.000	.000	3	0	0	0	0	0.0	0	0	0	2	0	3	0	0	0	0	0	–		
4 yrs.			88	.193	.283	187	36	5	3	2	1.1	15	10	18	31	0	37	6	51	78	8	5	1.6	.942	3B-38, 2B-7, OF-4

Ray Morgan

MORGAN, RAYMOND CARYLL
B. June 14, 1889, Baltimore, Md. D. Feb. 15, 1940, Baltimore, Md.

BR TR 5'8½" 155 lbs.

Year	Team		Games	BA	SA	AB	H	2B	3B	HR	HR%	R	RBI	BB	SO	SB	AB	H	PO	A	E	DP	TC/G	FA	G by Pos
1911	WAS	A	25	.213	.236	89	19	2	0	0	0.0	11	5	4		2	0	0	29	43	8	1	3.2	.900	3B-25
1912			80	.238	.337	273	65	10	7	1	0.4	40	30	29		11	0	0	157	181	23	23	4.5	.936	2B-75, SS-4, 3B-1
1913			137	.272	.345	481	131	19	8	0	0.0	58	57	68	63	19	0	0	261	372	33	61	4.9	.950	2B-133, SS-4
1914			147	.257	.340	491	126	22	8	1	0.2	50	49	62	34	24	0	0	290	379	37	58	4.8	.948	2B-146
1915			62	.233	.301	193	45	5	4	0	0.0	21	21	30	15	6	1	0	105	179	13	24	4.8	.956	2B-57, SS-2, 3B-2
1916			99	.267	.340	315	84	12	4	1	0.3	41	29	59	29	14	3	0	184	246	22	37	4.6	.951	2B-82, SS-9, 1B-3, 3B-1
1917			101	.266	.308	338	90	9	1	1	0.3	32	33	40	29	7	2	0	210	249	20	45	4.7	.958	2B-95, 3B-3
1918			88	.233	.277	300	70	11	1	0	0.0	25	30	28	14	4	1	1	175	251	18	30	5.0	.959	2B-80, OF-2
8 yrs.			739	.254	.322	2480	630	90	33	4	0.2	278	254	320	184	87	11	1	1411	1900	174	279	4.7	.950	2B-668, 3B-32, SS-19, 1B-3, OF-2

Red Morgan

MORGAN, JAMES EDWARD
B. Oct. 6, 1883, Neola, Iowa   Deceased.

TR

Year	Team		Games	BA	SA	AB	H	2B	3B	HR	HR%	R	RBI	BB	SO	SB	AB	H	PO	A	E	DP	TC/G	FA	G by Pos
1906	BOS	A	88	.215	.264	307	66	6	3	1	0.3	20	21	16		7	0	0	126	139	41	8	3.5	.866	3B-88

Vern Morgan

MORGAN, VERNON THOMAS
B. Aug. 8, 1928, Emporia, Va. D. Nov. 8, 1975, Minneapolis, Minn.

BL TR 6'1" 190 lbs.

Year	Team		Games	BA	SA	AB	H	2B	3B	HR	HR%	R	RBI	BB	SO	SB	AB	H	PO	A	E	DP	TC/G	FA	G by Pos
1954	CHI	N	24	.234	.266	64	15	2	0	0	0.0	3	2	1	10	0	7	1	8	26	4	1	1.6	.895	3B-15

Year	Team		Games	BA	SA	AB	H	2B	3B	HR	HR%	R	RBI	BB	SO	SB	Pinch Hit AB	Pinch Hit H	PO	A	E	DP	TC/G	FA	G by Pos

Vern Morgan *continued*

| 1955 | | | 7 | .143 | .143 | 7 | 1 | 0 | 0 | 0 | 0.0 | 1 | 1 | 3 | 4 | 0 | 3 | 0 | 2 | 2 | 2 | 0 | 0.9 | .667 | 3B-2 |
| 2 yrs. | | | 31 | .225 | .254 | 71 | 16 | 2 | 0 | 0 | 0.0 | 4 | 3 | 4 | 14 | 0 | 10 | 1 | 10 | 28 | 6 | 1 | 1.4 | .864 | 3B-17 |

Moe Morhardt

MORHARDT, MEREDITH GOODWIN
B. Jan. 16, 1937, Manchester, Conn.
BL TL 6'1" 185 lbs.

1961	CHI	N	7	.278	.278	18	5	0	0	0	0.0	3	1	3	5	0	0	0	72	3	3	9	11.1	.962	1B-7
1962			18	.125	.125	16	2	0	0	0	0.0	2	2	2	8	0	16	2	0	0	0	0		—	
2 yrs.			25	.206	.206	34	7	0	0	0	0.0	5	3	5	13	0	16	2	72	3	3	9	3.1	.962	1B-7

Gene Moriarity

MORIARITY, EUGENE JOHN
B. Holyoke, Mass. Deceased.
BL TL 5'8" 190 lbs.

1884	2 teams		BOS	N	(4G – .063)		IND	AA	(10G – .216)																
"	total		14	.170	.245	53	9	0	2	0	0.0	5		0	8		0	0	16	7	6	0	2.1	.793	OF-11, P-2, 3B-1
1885	DET	N	11	.026	.051	39	1	0	0	0	0.0	1	0	0	10		0	0	23	12	9	0	4.0	.795	OF-6, 3B-4, SS-1, P-1
1892	STL	N	47	.175	.260	177	31	4	1	3	1.7	20	19	4	37	7	0	0	96	9	23	0	2.7	.820	OF-47
3 yrs.			72	.152	.227	269	41	5	3	3	1.1	26	19	4	55	7	0	0	135	28	38	0	2.8	.811	OF-64, 3B-5, P-3, SS-1

Bill Moriarty

MORIARTY, WILLIAM JOSEPH
Brother of George Moriarty.
B. 1883, Chicago, Ill. D. Dec. 25, 1916, Elgin, Ill.
BR TR 6'2" 180 lbs.

| 1909 | CIN | N | 6 | .200 | .250 | 20 | 4 | 1 | 0 | 0 | 0.0 | 1 | 1 | 0 | | 2 | 0 | 0 | 18 | 16 | 2 | 2 | 6.0 | .944 | SS-6 |

Ed Moriarty

MORIARTY, EDWARD JEROME
B. Oct. 12, 1912, Holyoke, Mass.
BR TR 5'10½" 180 lbs.

1935	BOS	N	8	.324	.529	34	11	2	1	1	2.9	4	1	0	6	0	0	0	11	25	3	0	4.9	.923	2B-8
1936			6	.167	.167	6	1	0	0	0	0.0	0	0	0	1	0	6	1	0	0	0	0	0.0	—	
2 yrs.			14	.300	.475	40	12	2	1	1	2.5	4	1	0	7	0	6	1	11	25	3	0	2.8	.923	2B-8

George Moriarty

MORIARTY, GEORGE JOSEPH
Brother of Bill Moriarty.
B. July 7, 1884, Chicago, Ill. D. Apr. 8, 1964, Miami, Fla.
Manager 1927-28.
BR TR 6' 185 lbs.

1903	CHI	N	1	.000	.000	5	0	0	0	0	0.0	1	0	0			0	0	3	1	0	0	4.0	1.000	3B-1
1904			4	.000	.000	13	0	0	0	0	0.0	0	0	1			0	0	8	3	3	0	3.5	.786	OF-2, 3B-2
1906	NY	A	65	.234	.340	197	46	7	7	0	0.0	22	23	17		8	4	1	129	84	17	5	3.5	.926	3B-39, OF-15, 1B-5, 2B-1
1907			126	.277	.336	437	121	16	5	0	0.0	51	43	25		28	1	0	372	186	43	20	4.8	.928	3B-91, 1B-22, OF-9, 2B-8, SS-1
1908			101	.236	.276	348	82	12	1	0	0.0	25	27	11		22	8	2	609	117	24	30	7.4	.968	1B-52, 3B-28, OF-10, 2B-4
1909	DET	A	133	.273	.338	473	129	20	4	1	0.2	43	39	24		34	3	1	400	265	27	23	5.2	.961	3B-106, 1B-24
1910			136	.251	.324	490	123	24	3	2	0.4	53	60	33		33	1	0	165	302	37	17	3.7	.927	3B-134
1911			130	.243	.308	478	116	20	4	1	0.2	51	60	27		28	0	0	162	274	33	11	3.6	.930	3B-129, 1B-1
1912			105	.248	.315	375	93	23	1	0	0.0	38	54	26		27	1	1	842	97	19	25	9.1	.980	1B-71, 3B-33
1913			102	.239	.265	347	83	5	2	0	0.0	29	30	24	25	33	0	0	136	183	21	9	3.3	.938	3B-93, OF-7
1914			130	.254	.323	465	118	19	5	1	0.2	56	40	39	27	34	0	0	151	313	20	16	3.7	.959	3B-126, 1B-3
1915			31	.211	.237	38	8	1	0	0	0.0	2	5	5	7	1	10	2	11	14	3	1	0.9	.893	3B-12, OF-1, 2B-1, 1B-1
1916	CHI	A	7	.200	.200	5	1	0	0	0	0.0	1	0	2	0	0	3	1	2	0	0	0	0.6	1.000	3B-1, 1B-1
13 yrs.			1071	.251	.312	3671	920	147	32	5	0.1	372	376	234	59	248	31	8	2990	1841	247	157	4.7	.951	3B-795, 1B-180, OF-44, 2B-14, SS-1

WORLD SERIES

| 1909 | DET | A | 7 | .273 | .318 | 22 | 6 | 1 | 0 | 0 | 0.0 | 4 | 1 | 3 | 1 | 0 | 0 | 0 | 7 | 14 | 0 | 2 | 3.0 | 1.000 | 3B-7 |

Bill Morley

MORLEY, WILLIAM M.
Born William Morley Jennings.
B. Jan. 23, 1890, Holland, Mich. D. May 14, 1985, Lubbock, Tex.
BR TR 5'11" 170 lbs.

| 1913 | WAS | A | 2 | .000 | .000 | 3 | 0 | 0 | 0 | 0 | 0.0 | 0 | 0 | 0 | 0 | 0 | 0 | 0 | 0 | 0 | 0 | 0 | 0.0 | — | 2B-1 |

Russ Morman

MORMAN, RUSSELL LEE
B. Apr. 28, 1962, Independence, Mo.
BR TR 6'4" 215 lbs.

1986	CHI	A	49	.252	.358	159	40	5	0	4	2.5	18	17	16	36	1	1	0	342	26	4	31	7.6	.989	1B-47
1988			40	.240	.267	75	18	2	0	0	0.0	8	3	3	17	0	5	2	114	5	2	8	3.0	.983	1B-22, OF-10, DH-3
1989			37	.224	.259	58	13	2	0	0	0.0	5	8	6	16	1	2	2	157	13	2	21	4.6	.988	1B-35, DH-1
3 yrs.			126	.243	.315	292	71	9	0	4	1.4	31	28	25	69	2	8	4	613	44	8	60	5.3	.988	1B-104, OF-10, DH-4

Jeff Moronko

MORONKO, JEFFREY ROBERT
B. Aug. 17, 1959, Houston, Tex.
BR TR 6'2" 190 lbs.

1984	CLE	A	7	.158	.211	19	3	1	0	0	0.0	1	3	3	5	0	1	0	10	7	2	2	2.7	.895	3B-6, DH-1
1987	NY	A	7	.091	.091	11	1	0	0	0	0.0	0	0	0	2	0	0	0	1	9	0	1	1.4	1.000	3B-3, OF-2, SS-2
2 yrs.			14	.133	.167	30	4	1	0	0	0.0	1	3	3	7	0	1	0	11	16	2	3	2.1	.931	3B-9, OF-2, SS-2, DH-1

John Morrill

MORRILL, JOHN FRANCIS (Honest John)
B. Feb. 19, 1855, Boston, Mass. D. Apr. 2, 1932, Boston, Mass.
Manager 1882-89.
BR TR 5'10½" 155 lbs.

1876	BOS	N	66	.263	.295	278	73	5	2	0	0.0	38	26	3	5		0	0	238	160	78	21	7.2	.836	2B-37, C-23, OF-5, 1B-3
1877			61	.302	.331	242	73	5	1	0	0.0	47	28	6	15		0	0	223	61	38	14	5.3	.882	3B-30, 1B-18, OF-11, 2B-3
1878			60	.240	.270	233	56	5	1	0	0.0	26	23	5	16		0	0	608	30	36	36	11.1	.955	1B-59, OF-1, 3B-1
1879			84	.282	.362	348	98	18	5	0	0.0	56	49	14	32		0	0	383	112	34	25	6.3	.936	1B-51, 3B-33
1880			86	.237	.348	342	81	16	8	2	0.6	51	44	11	37		0	0	479	98	38	30	7.2	.938	1B-46, 3B-40, P-3
1881			81	.289	.379	311	90	19	3	1	0.3	47	39	12	30		0	0	764	61	26	33	10.5	.969	1B-74, 2B-4, P-3, 3B-2
1882			83	.289	.424	349	101	19	11	2	0.6	73	54	18	29		0	0	752	34	34	23	9.9	.959	1B-76, SS-3, 2B-2, OF-1, 3B-1, P-2

Year	Team		Games	BA	SA	AB	H	2B	3B	HR	HR%	R	RBI	BB	SO	SB	Pinch Hit AB	Pinch Hit H	PO	A	E	DP	TC/G	FA	G by Pos

John Morrill *continued*

Year	Team		Games	BA	SA	AB	H	2B	3B	HR	HR%	R	RBI	BB	SO	SB	AB	H	PO	A	E	DP	TC/G	FA	G by Pos
1883			97	.319	.525	404	129	33	16	6	1.5	83	68	15	68		0	0	819	44	31	34	9.2	.965	1B-81, OF-7, 3B-6, SS-2, 2B-2, P-2
1884			111	.260	.356	438	114	19	7	3	0.7	80		30	87		0	0	1006	86	41	37	10.2	.964	1B-91, 2B-17, P-7, 3B-2, OF-1
1885			111	.226	.343	394	89	20	7	4	1.0	74	44	64	78		0	0	1010	87	41	61	10.3	.964	1B-92, 2B-17, 3B-2
1886			117	.247	.381	430	106	25	6	7	1.6	86	69	56	81		0	0	535	245	61	44	7.2	.927	SS-55, 1B-42, 2B-20, P-1
1887			127	.280	.438	504	141	32	6	12	2.4	79	81	37	**86**	19	0	0	1231	50	21	76	10.3	.984	1B-127
1888			135	.198	.288	486	96	18	7	4	0.8	60	39	55	68	21	0	0	1401	79	33	67	11.2	.978	1B-133, 2B-2
1889	WAS	N	44	.185	.260	146	27	5	0	2	1.4	20	16	30	23	12	0	0	373	23	13	16	9.3	.968	1B-40, 3B-3, 2B-1, P-1
1890	BOS	P	2	.143	.143	7	1	0	0	0	0.0	1	2	2	1	0	0	0	16	2	1	0	9.5	.947	SS-1, 1B-1
15 yrs.			1265	.260	.367	4912	1275	239	80	43	0.9	821	582	358	656	52	0	0	9838	1167	520	517	9.1	.955	1B-916, 3B-138, 2B-105, SS-61, OF-26, C-23, P-18

Doyt Morris

MORRIS, DOYT THEODORE
B. July 15, 1916, Stanley, N. C. D. July 4, 1984, Gastonia, N. C.

BR TR 6'4"   195 lbs.

Year	Team		Games	BA	SA	AB	H	2B	3B	HR	HR%	R	RBI	BB	SO	SB	AB	H	PO	A	E	DP	TC/G	FA	G by Pos
1937	PHI	A	6	.154	.154	13	2	0	0	0	0.0	0	0	0	3	0	3	1	7	0	0	0	1.2	1.000	OF-3

Hal Morris

MORRIS, WILLIAM HAROLD
B. Apr. 9, 1965, Fort Rucker, Ala.

BL TL 6'3"   200 lbs.

Year	Team		Games	BA	SA	AB	H	2B	3B	HR	HR%	R	RBI	BB	SO	SB	AB	H	PO	A	E	DP	TC/G	FA	G by Pos
1988	NY	A	15	.100	.100	20	2	0	0	0	0.0	0	0	0	9	0	10	2	7	0	0	0	0.5	1.000	OF-4, DH-1
1989			15	.278	.278	18	5	0	0	0	0.0	2	4	1	4	0	9	1	12	0	0	2	0.8	1.000	OF-5, 1B-2, DH-1
2 yrs.			30	.184	.184	38	7	0	0	0	0.0	3	4	1	13	0	19	3	19	0	0	2	0.6	1.000	OF-9, DH-2, 1B-2

John Morris

MORRIS, JOHN DANIEL
B. Feb. 23, 1961, Freeport, N. Y.

BL TL 6'1"   185 lbs.

Year	Team		Games	BA	SA	AB	H	2B	3B	HR	HR%	R	RBI	BB	SO	SB	AB	H	PO	A	E	DP	TC/G	FA	G by Pos
1986	STL	N	39	.240	.290	100	24	0	1	1	1.0	8	14	7	15	6	11	3	68	0	1	0	1.8	.986	OF-31
1987			101	.261	.408	157	41	6	4	3	1.9	22	23	11	22	5	30	10	86	0	1	0	0.9	.989	OF-74
1988			20	.289	.395	38	11	2	1	0	0.0	3	3	1	7	0	6	2	12	0	2	0	0.7	.857	OF-16
1989			96	.239	.342	117	28	4	1	2	1.7	8	14	4	22	1	41	9	45	0	0	0	0.5	1.000	OF-51
4 yrs.			256	.252	.359	412	104	12	7	6	1.5	41	54	23	66	12	88	24	211	0	4	0	0.8	.981	OF-172

LEAGUE CHAMPIONSHIP SERIES

Year	Team		Games	BA	SA	AB	H	2B	3B	HR	HR%	R	RBI	BB	SO	SB	AB	H	PO	A	E	DP	TC/G	FA	G by Pos
1987	STL	N	2	.000	.000	3	0	0	0	0	0.0	0	0	0	0	0	0	0	1	0	0	0	0.5	1.000	OF-2

WORLD SERIES

Year	Team		Games	BA	SA	AB	H	2B	3B	HR	HR%	R	RBI	BB	SO	SB	AB	H	PO	A	E	DP	TC/G	FA	G by Pos
1987	STL	N	1	.000	.000	2	0	0	0	0	0.0	0	0	0	0	0	0	0	2	0	0	0	2.0	1.000	OF-1

P. Morris

MORRIS, P.
B. Rockford, Ill. Deceased.

Year	Team		Games	BA	SA	AB	H	2B	3B	HR	HR%	R	RBI	BB	SO	SB	AB	H	PO	A	E	DP	TC/G	FA	G by Pos
1884	WAS	U	1	.000	.000	3	0	0	0	0	0.0	0		0		0	0	0	0	3	1	0	4.0	.750	SS-1

Walter Morris

MORRIS, JOHN WALTER
B. Jan. 31, 1880, Rockwall, Tex. D. Aug. 2, 1961, Dallas, Tex.

BR TR 5'11"

Year	Team		Games	BA	SA	AB	H	2B	3B	HR	HR%	R	RBI	BB	SO	SB	AB	H	PO	A	E	DP	TC/G	FA	G by Pos
1908	STL	N	23	.178	.219	73	13	1	1	0	0.0	1	2	0		1	1	0	47	75	8	8	5.7	.938	SS-23

William Morris

Playing record listed under John Fluhrer

Jim Morrison

MORRISON, JAMES FORREST
B. Sept. 23, 1952, Pensacola, Fla.

BR TR 5'11"   175 lbs.

Year	Team		Games	BA	SA	AB	H	2B	3B	HR	HR%	R	RBI	BB	SO	SB	AB	H	PO	A	E	DP	TC/G	FA	G by Pos
1977	PHI	N	5	.429	.429	7	3	0	0	0	0.0	3	1	1	1	0	0	0	0	7	1	0	1.6	.875	3B-5
1978			53	.157	.269	108	17	1	1	3	2.8	12	10	10	21	1	12	0	88	97	6	22	3.6	.969	2B-31, 3B-3, OF-1
1979	CHI	A	67	.275	.508	240	66	14	0	14	5.8	38	35	15	48	11	4	0	121	185	9	38	4.7	.971	2B-48, 3B-29
1980			162	.283	.424	604	171	40	0	15	2.5	66	57	36	74	9	0	0	422	482	29	117	5.8	.969	2B-161, DH-1, SS-1
1981			90	.234	.372	290	68	8	1	10	3.4	27	34	10	29	3	2	0	64	200	12	15	3.1	.957	3B-87, DH-1, 2B-1
1982	2 teams					CHI A (51G – .223)				PIT N (44G – .279)															
"	total		95	.242	.448	252	61	11	4	11	4.4	27	34	18	29	2	16	0	36	130	12	12	1.9	.933	3B-76, OF-2, DH-1, SS-1, 2B-1
1983	PIT	N	66	.304	.487	158	48	7	2	6	3.8	16	25	9	25	2	15	4	55	99	7	21	2.4	.957	2B-28, 3B-25, SS-7
1984			100	.286	.454	304	87	14	2	11	3.6	38	45	20	52	0	13	1	86	166	10	21	2.6	.962	3B-61, 2B-26, SS-2, 1B-1
1985			92	.254	.348	244	62	11	0	4	1.6	17	22	8	44	3	19	4	73	121	5	14	2.2	.975	3B-59, 2B-15, OF-1
1986			154	.274	.482	537	147	35	4	23	4.3	58	88	47	88	9	4	1	92	258	20	12	2.4	.946	3B-151, SS-1, 2B-1
1987	2 teams					PIT N (96G – .264)				DET A (34G – .205)															
"	total		130	.249	.391	465	116	23	2	13	2.8	56	65	29	83	10	11	2	73	202	7	24	2.2	.975	3B-98, SS-20, 2B-12, DH-8, OF-3, 1B-1
1988	2 teams					DET A (24G – .216)				ATL N (51G – .152)															
"	total		75	.181	.259	166	30	7	0	2	1.2	13	19	10	27	0	31	6	57	30	0	3	1.2	.956	3B-24, DH-14, OF-6, 1B-4, P-3, SS-1
12 yrs.			1089	.260	.419	3375	876	171	16	112	3.3	371	435	213	521	50	127	21	1167	1977	122	299	3.0	.963	3B-618, 2B-324, SS-33, DH-25, OF-13, 1B-6, P-3

LEAGUE CHAMPIONSHIP SERIES

Year	Team		Games	BA	SA	AB	H	2B	3B	HR	HR%	R	RBI	BB	SO	SB	AB	H	PO	A	E	DP	TC/G	FA	G by Pos
1978	PHI	N	1	.000	.000	1	0	0	0	0	0.0	0	0	0	1	0	1	0	0	0	0	0	0.0	—	DH-1
1987	DET	A	2	.400	.400	5	2	0	0	0	0.0	1	0	0	1	0	0	0	1	2	0	0	1.5	1.000	DH-1, 3B-1
2 yrs.			3	.333	.333	6	2	0	0	0	0.0	1	0	0	2	0	1	0	1	2	0	0	1.0	1.000	DH-1, 3B-1

Jon Morrison

MORRISON, JONATHAN W.
B. 1859, Port Huron, Mich. Deceased.

Year	Team		Games	BA	SA	AB	H	2B	3B	HR	HR%	R	RBI	BB	SO	SB	AB	H	PO	A	E	DP	TC/G	FA	G by Pos
1884	IND	AA	44	.264	.401	182	48	6	8	1	0.5	26		7			0	0	78	9	24	4	2.5	.784	OF-44
1887	NY	AA	9	.118	.118	34	4	0	0	0	0.0	7		6			0	0	12	0	8	0	2.2	.600	OF-9
2 yrs.			53	.241	.356	216	52	6	8	1	0.5	33		13			0	0	90	9	32	4	2.5	.756	OF-53

Year	Team		Games	BA	SA	AB	H	2B	3B	HR	HR%	R	RBI	BB	SO	SB	Pinch Hit AB	Pinch Hit H	PO	A	E	DP	TC/G	FA	G by Pos

Tom Morrison

MORRISON, THOMAS J.
B. 1875, St. Louis, Mo.   5'3"   145 lbs.

Year	Team		Games	BA	SA	AB	H	2B	3B	HR	HR%	R	RBI	BB	SO	SB	PH AB	PH H	PO	A	E	DP	TC/G	FA	G by Pos
1895	LOU	N	6	.273	.455	22	6	0	2	0	0.0	3	4	1	1	0	0	0	7	9	2	1	3.0	.889	SS-3, 3B-3
1896			8	.148	.185	27	4	1	0	0	0.0	3	0	4	4	0	0	0	7	16	3	1	3.3	.885	3B-5, OF-2, SS-1
2 yrs.			14	.204	.306	49	10	1	2	0	0.0	6	4	5	5	0	0	0	14	25	5	2	3.1	.886	3B-8, SS-4, OF-2

Jack Morrissey

MORRISSEY, JOHN ALBERT (King)
B. May 2, 1876, Lansing, Mich.   D. Oct. 30, 1936, Lansing, Mich.   BB TR 5'10"   160 lbs.

Year	Team		Games	BA	SA	AB	H	2B	3B	HR	HR%	R	RBI	BB	SO	SB	PH AB	PH H	PO	A	E	DP	TC/G	FA	G by Pos
1902	CIN	N	12	.282	.359	39	11	1	0	0	0.0	5	3	4		0	0	0	24	26	3	3	4.4	.943	2B-11, OF-1
1903			29	.247	.258	89	22	1	0	0	0.0	14	9	14		3	2	0	48	38	16	7	3.5	.843	2B-17, OF-8, SS-2
2 yrs.			41	.258	.289	128	33	2	1	0	0.0	19	12	18		3	2	0	72	64	19	10	3.8	.877	2B-28, OF-9, SS-2

Jo-Jo Morrissey

MORRISSEY, JOSEPH ANSELM
B. Jan. 16, 1904, Warren, R.I.   D. May 2, 1950, Worcester, Mass.   BR TR 6'1½"   178 lbs.

Year	Team		Games	BA	SA	AB	H	2B	3B	HR	HR%	R	RBI	BB	SO	SB	PH AB	PH H	PO	A	E	DP	TC/G	FA	G by Pos
1932	CIN	N	89	.242	.286	269	65	10	1	0	0.0	15	13	14	15	2	1	0	144	240	8	38	4.4	.980	SS-45, 2B-42, 3B-12, OF-1
1933			148	.230	.268	534	123	20	0	0	0.0	43	26	20	22	5	1	1	300	461	40	76	5.4	.950	2B-88, SS-63, 3B-15
1936	CHI	A	17	.184	.211	38	7	1	0	0	0.0	3	6	2	3	0	4	2	17	22	3	2	2.5	.929	3B-9, SS-4, 2B-1
3 yrs.			254	.232	.271	841	195	31	1	0	0.0	61	45	36	40	7	6	3	461	723	51	116	4.9	.959	2B-131, SS-112, 3B-36, OF-1

John Morrissey

MORRISSEY, JOHN J.
Brother of Tom Morrissey.
B. 1856, Janesville, Wis.   D. Apr. 29, 1884, Janesville, Wis.

Year	Team		Games	BA	SA	AB	H	2B	3B	HR	HR%	R	RBI	BB	SO	SB	PH AB	PH H	PO	A	E	DP	TC/G	FA	G by Pos
1881	BUF	N	12	.213	.255	47	10	2	0	0	0.0	3		3	3	0	0	0	10	22	5	0	3.1	.865	3B-12
1882	DET	N	2	.286	.286	7	2	0	0	0	0.0	1	0	0	2	0	0	0	4	1	2	0	3.5	.714	3B-2
2 yrs.			14	.222	.259	54	12	2	0	0	0.0	4	3	3	5	0	0	0	14	23	7	0	3.1	.841	3B-14

Tom Morrissey

MORRISSEY, THOMAS J.
Brother of John Morrissey.
B. 1861, Janesville, Wis.   D. Sept. 23, 1941, Janesville, Wis.

Year	Team		Games	BA	SA	AB	H	2B	3B	HR	HR%	R	RBI	BB	SO	SB	PH AB	PH H	PO	A	E	DP	TC/G	FA	G by Pos
1884	MIL	U	12	.170	.213	47	8	2	0	0	0.0	3		0			0	0	7	15	9	1	2.6	.710	3B-12

Bud Morse

MORSE, NEWELL OBEDIAH
B. Sept. 4, 1904, Berkeley, Calif.   D. Apr. 6, 1987, Sparks, Nev.   BR TR 5'8"   160 lbs.

Year	Team		Games	BA	SA	AB	H	2B	3B	HR	HR%	R	RBI	BB	SO	SB	PH AB	PH H	PO	A	E	DP	TC/G	FA	G by Pos
1929	PHI	A	8	.074	.074	27	2	0	0	0	0.0	1	0	0	2	0	0	0	17	22	1	3	5.0	.975	2B-8

Hap Morse

MORSE, PETER RAYMOND
B. Dec. 6, 1886, St. Paul, Minn.   D. June 19, 1974, St. Paul, Minn.   BR TR 5'8"   160 lbs.

Year	Team		Games	BA	SA	AB	H	2B	3B	HR	HR%	R	RBI	BB	SO	SB	PH AB	PH H	PO	A	E	DP	TC/G	FA	G by Pos
1911	STL	N	4	.000	.000	8	0	0	0	0	0.0	0	0	1	2	0	1	0	6	5	3	0	3.5	.786	SS-2, OF-1

Bubba Morton

MORTON, WYCLIFFE NATHANIEL
B. Dec. 13, 1931, Washington, D.C.   BR TR 5'10"   175 lbs.

Year	Team		Games	BA	SA	AB	H	2B	3B	HR	HR%	R	RBI	BB	SO	SB	PH AB	PH H	PO	A	E	DP	TC/G	FA	G by Pos
1961	DET	A	77	.287	.407	108	31	5	1	2	1.9	26	19	9	25	3	37	11	39	1	2	1	0.5	.952	OF-30
1962			90	.262	.385	195	51	6	3	4	2.1	30	17	32	32	1	21	5	124	4	1	1	1.4	.992	OF-62, 1B-3
1963	2 teams		21	.154	.154	DET A (6G – .091)		MIL N (15G – .179)																	OF-12
"	total		21	.154	.154	39	6	0	0	0	0.0	3	6	4	4	0	10	1	21	0	1	0	1.0	.955	OF-12
1966	CAL	A	15	.220	.240	50	11	1	0	0	0.0	4	2	2	6	1	0	0	25	1	0	0	1.7	1.000	OF-14
1967			80	.313	.388	201	63	9	3	0	0.0	23	32	22	29	2	25	8	83	1	0	0	1.1	1.000	OF-61
1968			81	.270	.325	163	44	6	0	1	0.6	13	18	14	18	2	33	10	64	1	1	1	0.8	.985	OF-50, 3B-1
1969			87	.244	.436	172	42	10	1	7	4.1	18	32	28	29	0	34	10	72	5	0	1	0.9	1.000	OF-49, 1B-1
7 yrs.			451	.267	.370	928	248	37	8	14	1.5	117	128	111	143	7	160	45	428	13	5	4	1.0	.989	OF-278, 1B-4, 3B-1

Charlie Morton

MORTON, CHARLES HAZEN
B. Oct. 12, 1854, Kingsville, Ohio   D. Dec. 9, 1921, Massillon, Ohio   TR
Manager 1884-85, 1890.

Year	Team		Games	BA	SA	AB	H	2B	3B	HR	HR%	R	RBI	BB	SO	SB	PH AB	PH H	PO	A	E	DP	TC/G	FA	G by Pos
1882	2 teams					PIT AA (25G – .282)		STL AA (9G – .063)																	
"	total		34	.230	.289	135	31	0	4	0	0.0	14		7		0	0		42	25	18	1	2.5	.788	OF-28, 2B-7, 3B-3, SS-1
1884	TOL	AA	32	.162	.252	111	18	6	2	0	0.0	11		7		0	0		33	26	8	1	2.1	.881	3B-16, OF-15, P-3, 2B-1
1885	DET	N	22	.177	.241	79	14	1	2	0	0.0	9	3	5	10	0	0		23	57	22	4	4.6	.784	3B-18, SS-4
3 yrs.			88	.194	.265	325	63	7	8	0	0.0	34	3	19	10	0	0		98	108	48	6	2.9	.811	OF-43, 3B-37, 2B-8, SS-5, P-3

Guy Morton

MORTON, GUY, JR. (Moose)
Son of Guy Morton.
B. Nov. 4, 1930, Tuscaloosa, Ala.   BR TR 6'2"   200 lbs.

Year	Team		Games	BA	SA	AB	H	2B	3B	HR	HR%	R	RBI	BB	SO	SB	PH AB	PH H	PO	A	E	DP	TC/G	FA	G by Pos
1954	BOS	A	1	.000	.000	1	0	0	0	0	0.0	0	1	0	1	0	1	0	0	0	0	0	0.0	–	

Walt Moryn

MORYN, WALTER JOSEPH (Moose)
B. Apr. 12, 1926, St. Paul, Minn.   BL TR 6'2"   205 lbs.

Year	Team		Games	BA	SA	AB	H	2B	3B	HR	HR%	R	RBI	BB	SO	SB	PH AB	PH H	PO	A	E	DP	TC/G	FA	G by Pos
1954	BKN	N	48	.275	.429	91	25	4	2	2	2.2	16	14	7	11	0	23	5	34	3	5	1	0.9	.881	OF-21
1955			11	.263	.474	19	5	1	0	1	5.3	3	3	5	4	0	4	0	5	0	1	0	0.5	.833	OF-7
1956	CHI	N	147	.285	.478	529	151	27	3	23	4.3	69	67	50	67	4	6	0	268	18	5	2	2.0	.983	OF-141
1957			149	.289	.447	568	164	33	3	19	3.3	76	88	50	90	0	4	1	276	13	12	3	2.0	.960	OF-147
1958			143	.264	.494	512	135	26	7	26	5.1	77	77	62	83	1	6	4	265	4	6	1	1.9	.978	OF-141
1959			117	.234	.386	381	89	14	1	14	3.7	41	48	44	66	0	13	5	175	9	2	1	1.6	.989	OF-104
1960	2 teams					CHI N (38G – .294)		STL N (75G – .245)																	OF-92
"	total		113	.262	.434	309	81	8	3	13	4.2	36	46	30	57	2	22	3	152	6	3	1	1.4	.981	OF-92
1961	2 teams					STL N (17G – .125)		PIT N (40G – .200)																	OF-18
"	total		57	.175	.299	97	17	3	0	3	3.1	6	11	3	15	0	36	6	25	2	2	1	0.5	.931	OF-18
8 yrs.			785	.266	.446	2506	667	116	16	101	4.0	324	354	251	393	7	114	24	1200	55	36	10	1.6	.972	OF-671

Year	Team	Games	BA	SA	AB	H	2B	3B	HR	HR%	R	RBI	BB	SO	SB	Pinch Hit AB	Pinch Hit H	PO	A	E	DP	TC/G	FA	G by Pos

Ross Moschitto
MOSCHITTO, ROSAIRE ALLEN
B. Feb. 15, 1945, Fresno, Calif.
BR TR 6'2" 175 lbs.

Year	Team	Games	BA	SA	AB	H	2B	3B	HR	HR%	R	RBI	BB	SO	SB	PH AB	PH H	PO	A	E	DP	TC/G	FA	G by Pos
1965	NY A	96	.185	.296	27	5	0	0	1	3.7	12	3	0	12	0	1	0	48	0	3	0	0.5	.941	OF-89
1967		14	.111	.111	9	1	0	0	0	0.0	1	0	1	2	0	6	0	2	1	0	0	0.2	1.000	OF-8
2 yrs.		110	.167	.250	36	6	0	0	1	2.8	13	3	1	14	0	7	0	50	1	3	0	0.5	.944	OF-97

Lloyd Moseby
MOSEBY, LLOYD ANTHONY
B. Nov. 5, 1959, Portland, Ark.
BL TR 6'3" 200 lbs.

Year	Team	Games	BA	SA	AB	H	2B	3B	HR	HR%	R	RBI	BB	SO	SB	PH AB	PH H	PO	A	E	DP	TC/G	FA	G by Pos
1980	TOR A	114	.229	.365	389	89	24	1	9	2.3	44	46	25	85	4	2	0	208	12	4	1	2.0	.982	OF-104, DH-6
1981		100	.233	.357	378	88	16	2	9	2.4	36	43	24	86	11	2	0	259	4	3	0	2.7	.989	OF-100
1982		147	.236	.370	487	115	20	9	9	1.8	51	52	33	106	11	7	3	361	4	3	0	2.5	.992	OF-145
1983		151	.315	.499	539	170	31	7	18	3.3	104	81	51	85	27	9	4	399	10	7	1	2.8	.983	OF-147
1984		158	.280	.470	592	166	28	15	18	3.0	97	92	78	122	39	3	1	473	8	5	2	3.1	.990	OF-156
1985		152	.259	.426	584	151	30	7	18	3.1	92	71	76	91	37	1	0	394	7	8	1	2.7	.980	OF-152
1986		152	.253	.418	589	149	24	5	21	3.6	89	86	64	122	32	4	0	371	6	6	1	2.5	.984	OF-147, DH-3
1987		155	.282	.473	592	167	27	4	26	4.4	106	96	70	124	39	0	0	294	7	6	1	2.0	.980	OF-153, DH-2
1988		128	.239	.369	472	113	17	7	10	2.1	77	42	70	93	31	3	0	304	2	5	1	2.4	.984	OF-125, DH-1
1989		135	.221	.349	502	111	25	3	11	2.2	72	43	56	101	24	4	1	288	3	4	1	2.2	.986	OF-120, DH-14
10 yrs.		1392	.257	.415	5124	1319	242	60	149	2.9	768	652	547	1015	255	35	9	3351	63	51	9	2.5	.985	OF-1349, DH-26

LEAGUE CHAMPIONSHIP SERIES

Year	Team	Games	BA	SA	AB	H	2B	3B	HR	HR%	R	RBI	BB	SO	SB	PH AB	PH H	PO	A	E	DP	TC/G	FA	G by Pos
1985	TOR A	7	.226	.258	31	7	1	0	0	0.0	5	4	2	3	1	0	0	10	0	0	0	1.4	1.000	OF-7
1989		5	.313	.500	16	5	0	1	1	6.3	4	2	5	2	1	0	0	15	0	0	0	3.0	1.000	OF-5
2 yrs.		12	.255	.340	47	12	1	1	1	2.1	9	6	7	5	2	0	0	25	0	0	0	2.1	1.000	OF-12

Arnie Moser
MOSER, ARNOLD ROBERT
B. Aug. 9, 1915, Houston, Tex.
BR TR 5'11" 165 lbs.

Year	Team	Games	BA	SA	AB	H	2B	3B	HR	HR%	R	RBI	BB	SO	SB	PH AB	PH H	PO	A	E	DP	TC/G	FA	G by Pos
1937	CIN N	5	.000	.000	5	0	0	0	0	0.0	0	0	0	2	0	5	0	0	0	0	0	0.0	—	

Gerry Moses
MOSES, GERALD BRAHEEN
B. Aug. 9, 1946, Yazoo City, Miss.
BR TR 6'3" 210 lbs.

Year	Team	Games	BA	SA	AB	H	2B	3B	HR	HR%	R	RBI	BB	SO	SB	PH AB	PH H	PO	A	E	DP	TC/G	FA	G by Pos
1965	BOS A	4	.250	1.000	4	1	0	0	1	25.0	1	1	0	4	0	4	1	0	0	0	0	0.0	—	
1968		6	.333	.667	18	6	0	0	2	11.1	2	4	1	4	0	0	0	26	0	1	0	4.5	.963	C-6
1969		53	.304	.474	135	41	9	1	4	3.0	13	17	5	23	0	17	2	191	11	4	1	3.9	.981	C-36
1970		92	.263	.384	315	83	18	1	6	1.9	26	35	21	45	1	5	2	578	45	9	3	6.8	.990	C-88, OF-1
1971	CAL A	69	.227	.359	181	41	8	2	4	2.2	12	15	10	34	0	8	0	299	38	8	3	5.0	.977	C-63, OF-1
1972	CLE A	52	.220	.326	141	31	3	0	4	2.8	9	14	11	29	0	10	2	220	17	5	8	4.7	.979	C-39, 1B-3
1973	NY A	21	.254	.288	59	15	2	0	0	0.0	5	3	2	6	0	3	1	93	9	0	0	4.9	1.000	C-17, DH-1
1974	DET A	74	.237	.359	198	47	6	3	4	2.0	19	14	11	38	0	1	0	377	26	6	6	5.5	.985	C-74
1975	2 teams		CHI A (2G — .500)		SD N (13G — .158)																			
"	total	15	.190	.381	21	4	2	1	0	0.0	2	1	2	3	0	6	1	18	1	2	0	1.4	.905	C-5, DH-1, 1B-1
9 yrs.		386	.251	.381	1072	269	48	8	25	2.3	89	109	63	184	1	54	9	1802	147	32	21	5.1	.984	C-328, 1B-4, DH-2, OF-2

John Moses
MOSES, JOHN WILLIAM
B. Aug. 9, 1957, Los Angeles, Calif.
BB TL 5'10" 165 lbs.

Year	Team	Games	BA	SA	AB	H	2B	3B	HR	HR%	R	RBI	BB	SO	SB	PH AB	PH H	PO	A	E	DP	TC/G	FA	G by Pos
1982	SEA A	22	.318	.545	44	14	5	1	1	2.3	7	3	4	5	5	2	1	16	2	1	0	0.9	.947	OF-19
1983		93	.208	.254	130	27	4	1	0	0.0	19	6	12	20	11	4	1	87	8	2	1	1.0	.979	OF-71, DH-10
1984		19	.343	.429	35	12	1	1	0	0.0	3	2	2	5	1	0	0	26	1	0	0	1.4	1.000	OF-19, DH-1
1985		33	.194	.194	62	12	0	0	0	0.0	4	3	2	8	5	0	0	35	1	0	0	1.1	1.000	OF-29
1986		103	.256	.333	399	102	16	3	3	0.8	56	34	34	65	25	2	0	249	11	5	4	2.6	.981	OF-93, 1B-7, DH-4
1987		116	.246	.331	390	96	16	4	3	0.8	58	38	29	49	23	3	1	271	7	4	3	2.4	.986	OF-100, 1B-16, DH-5
1988	MIN A	105	.316	.422	206	65	10	3	2	1.0	33	12	15	21	11	21	6	123	1	0	0	1.2	1.000	OF-82, DH-7
1989		129	.281	.368	242	68	12	3	1	0.4	33	31	19	23	14	30	8	168	3	2	0	1.3	.988	OF-108, DH-3, 1B-2, P-1
8 yrs.		620	.263	.346	1508	396	64	16	10	0.7	213	129	117	196	95	62	17	975	34	14	8	1.7	.986	OF-521, DH-25, 1B-25, P-1

Wally Moses
MOSES, WALLACE
B. Oct. 8, 1910, Uvalda, Ga.
BL TL 5'10" 160 lbs.

Year	Team	Games	BA	SA	AB	H	2B	3B	HR	HR%	R	RBI	BB	SO	SB	PH AB	PH H	PO	A	E	DP	TC/G	FA	G by Pos
1935	PHI A	85	.325	.446	345	112	21	3	5	1.4	60	35	25	18	3	6	4	157	7	10	1	2.0	.943	OF-80
1936		146	.345	.479	585	202	35	11	7	1.2	96	66	62	32	12	2	0	396	11	11	3	2.9	.974	OF-144
1937		154	.320	.550	649	208	48	13	25	3.9	113	86	54	38	9	0	0	323	16	15	4	2.3	.958	OF-154
1938		142	.307	.424	589	181	29	8	8	1.4	86	49	58	31	15	3	1	304	11	11	3	2.3	.966	OF-139
1939		115	.307	.423	437	134	28	7	3	0.7	68	33	44	23	7	11	2	209	10	8	2	2.0	.965	OF-103
1940		142	.309	.469	537	166	41	9	9	1.7	91	50	75	44	6	6	1	295	10	8	1	2.2	.974	OF-133
1941		116	.301	.418	438	132	31	4	4	0.9	78	35	62	27	3	6	1	263	12	7	5	2.4	.975	OF-109
1942	CHI A	146	.270	.369	577	156	28	4	7	1.2	73	49	74	27	16	1	0	323	14	7	3	2.4	.980	OF-145
1943		150	.245	.337	599	147	22	12	3	0.5	82	48	55	47	56	2	0	370	12	8	2	2.6	.979	OF-148
1944		136	.280	.379	535	150	26	4	3	0.6	82	34	52	22	21	1	0	267	7	7	2	2.1	.975	OF-134
1945		140	.295	.420	569	168	35	15	2	0.4	79	50	69	33	11	1	0	329	12	8	1	2.5	.977	OF-139
1946	2 teams	CHI A (56G — .274)		BOS A (48G — .206)																				
"	total	104	.239	.373	343	82	20	4	4	1.7	43	33	31	35	4	24	4	89	2	0	0	0.9	1.000	OF-80
1947	BOS A	90	.275	.384	255	70	18	2	2	0.8	32	27	27	16	3	29	5	109	2	3	0	1.3	.974	OF-58
1948		78	.259	.365	189	49	12	1	2	1.1	26	29	21	19	5	27	6	101	2	1	1	1.3	.981	OF-45
1949	PHI A	110	.276	.367	308	85	19	3	1	0.3	49	25	51	19	1	17	5	169	7	3	3	1.6	.983	OF-92
1950		88	.264	.385	265	70	16	5	2	0.8	47	21	40	17	0	21	4	147	7	2	2	1.8	.987	OF-62
1951		70	.191	.235	136	26	6	0	0	0.0	17	9	21	9	2	34	4	62	1	1	0	0.9	.984	OF-27
17 yrs.		2012	.291	.416	7356	2138	435	110	89	1.2	1124	679	821	457	174	193	37	3913	144	111	34	2.1	.973	OF-1792

WORLD SERIES

Year	Team	Games	BA	SA	AB	H	2B	3B	HR	HR%	R	RBI	BB	SO	SB	PH AB	PH H	PO	A	E	DP	TC/G	FA	G by Pos
1946	BOS A	4	.417	.417	12	5	0	0	0	0.0	1	0	1	2	0	0	0	5	0	0	0	1.3	1.000	OF-4

Doc Moskiman
MOSKIMAN, WILLIAM BANKHEAD
B. Dec. 20, 1879, Oakland, Calif. D. Jan. 11, 1953, San Leandro, Calif.
BR TR 6' 170 lbs.

Year	Team	Games	BA	SA	AB	H	2B	3B	HR	HR%	R	RBI	BB	SO	SB	PH AB	PH H	PO	A	E	DP	TC/G	FA	G by Pos
1910	BOS A	5	.111	.111	9	1	0	0	0	0.0	1	1	2		0	0	0	20	1	0	1	4.2	1.000	1B-2, OF-1

Year	Team		Games	BA	SA	AB	H	2B	3B	HR	HR%	R	RBI	BB	SO	SB	Pinch Hit AB	Pinch Hit H	PO	A	E	DP	TC/G	FA	G by Pos

Jim Mosolf

MOSOLF, JAMES FREDERICK
B. Aug. 21, 1905, Puyallup, Wash.   D. Dec. 28, 1979, Dallas, Ore.
BL TR 5'10" 186 lbs.

Year	Team		Games	BA	SA	AB	H	2B	3B	HR	HR%	R	RBI	BB	SO	SB	PH AB	PH H	PO	A	E	DP	TC/G	FA	G by Pos
1929	PIT	N	8	.462	.692	13	6	1	1	0	0.0	3	2	1	1	0	4	2	7	0	0	0	0.9	1.000	OF-3
1930			40	.333	.412	51	17	2	1	0	0.0	16	9	8	7	0	22	8	12	1	4	0	0.4	.765	OF-12, P-1
1931			39	.250	.341	44	11	1	0	1	2.3	7	8	8	5	0	30	6	5	0	0	0	0.1	1.000	OF-4
1933	CHI	N	31	.268	.390	82	22	5	1	1	1.2	13	9	5	8	0	8	3	51	2	2	0	1.8	.964	OF-22
4 yrs.			118	.295	.405	190	56	9	3	2	1.1	39	28	22	21	0	64	19	75	3	6	0	0.7	.929	OF-41, P-1

Charlie Moss

MOSS, CHARLES CROSBY
B. Mar. 20, 1911, Meridian, Miss.
BR TR 5'10" 160 lbs.

Year	Team		Games	BA	SA	AB	H	2B	3B	HR	HR%	R	RBI	BB	SO	SB	PH AB	PH H	PO	A	E	DP	TC/G	FA	G by Pos
1934	PHI	A	10	.200	.200	10	2	0	0	0	0.0	3	1	0	0	0	4	1	3	1	0	0	0.4	1.000	C-6
1935			4	.333	.333	3	1	0	0	0	0.0	1	1	1	0	0	2	1	0	0	0	0	0.0	—	C-1
1936			33	.250	.318	44	11	1	1	0	0.0	2	10	6	5	1	14	2	35	4	3	0	1.3	.929	C-19
3 yrs.			47	.246	.298	57	14	1	1	0	0.0	6	12	7	5	1	20	4	38	5	3	0	1.0	.935	C-26

Howie Moss

MOSS, HOWARD GLENN
B. Oct. 17, 1919, Gastonia, N. C.   D. May 7, 1989, Baltimore, Md.
BR TR 5'11½" 185 lbs.

Year	Team		Games	BA	SA	AB	H	2B	3B	HR	HR%	R	RBI	BB	SO	SB	PH AB	PH H	PO	A	E	DP	TC/G	FA	G by Pos
1942	NY	N	7	.000	.000	14	0	0	0	0	0.0	0	0	0	4	0	4	0	7	0	0	0	1.0	1.000	OF-3
1946	2 teams		CIN	N	(7G – .192)		CLE	A	(8G – .063)																
"	total		15	.121	.121	58	7	0	0	0	0.0	3	1	3	13	0	1	0	23	19	5	0	3.1	.894	3B-8, OF-6
2 yrs.			22	.097	.097	72	7	0	0	0	0.0	3	1	3	17	0	5	0	30	19	5	0	2.5	.907	OF-9, 3B-8

Les Moss

MOSS, JOHN LESTER
B. May 14, 1925, Tulsa, Okla.
Manager 1968, 1979.
BR TR 5'11" 205 lbs.

Year	Team		Games	BA	SA	AB	H	2B	3B	HR	HR%	R	RBI	BB	SO	SB	PH AB	PH H	PO	A	E	DP	TC/G	FA	G by Pos
1946	STL	A	12	.371	.457	35	13	3	0	0	0.0	4	5	3	5	1	0	0	55	5	2	1	5.2	.968	C-12
1947			96	.157	.255	274	43	5	2	6	2.2	17	27	35	48	0	1	0	362	43	7	6	4.3	.983	C-96
1948			107	.257	.424	335	86	12	1	14	4.2	35	46	39	50	0	5	0	357	52	5	8	3.9	.988	C-103
1949			97	.291	.439	278	81	11	0	10	3.6	28	39	49	32	0	12	2	283	41	10	9	3.4	.970	C-83
1950			84	.266	.401	222	59	6	0	8	3.6	24	34	26	32	0	19	5	204	20	10	4	2.8	.957	C-60
1951	2 teams		STL	A	(16G – .170)		BOS	A	(71G – .198)																
"	total		87	.193	.273	249	48	8	0	4	1.6	23	23	31	42	1	6	0	335	36	7	5	4.3	.981	C-81
1952	STL	A	52	.246	.347	118	29	3	0	3	2.5	11	12	15	13	0	13	4	118	17	6	3	2.7	.957	C-39
1953			78	.276	.368	239	66	14	1	2	0.8	21	28	18	31	0	6	0	296	21	7	4	4.2	.978	C-71
1954	BAL	A	50	.246	.270	126	31	3	0	0	0.0	7	5	14	16	0	12	2	159	16	5	4	3.6	.972	C-38
1955	2 teams		BAL	A	(29G – .339)		CHI	A	(32G – .254)																
"	total		61	.296	.426	115	34	3	0	4	3.5	10	13	13	14	0	12	2	156	10	1	5	2.7	.994	C-48
1956	CHI	A	56	.244	.512	127	31	4	0	10	7.9	20	22	18	15	0	8	1	149	10	1	1	2.9	.994	C-49
1957			42	.270	.348	115	31	3	0	2	1.7	10	12	20	18	0	4	0	138	8	3	2	3.5	.980	C-39
1958			2	.000	.000	1	0	0	0	0	0.0	0	0	1	0	0	1	0	0	0	0	0	0.0	—	
13 yrs.			824	.247	.369	2234	552	75	4	63	2.8	210	276	282	316	2	99	18	2612	279	64	52	3.6	.978	C-719

Johnny Mostil

MOSTIL, JOHN ANTHONY
B. June 1, 1896, Chicago, Ill.   D. Dec. 10, 1970, Midlothian, Ill.
BR TR 5'8½" 168 lbs.

Year	Team		Games	BA	SA	AB	H	2B	3B	HR	HR%	R	RBI	BB	SO	SB	PH AB	PH H	PO	A	E	DP	TC/G	FA	G by Pos
1918	CHI	A	10	.273	.455	33	9	2	2	0	0.0	4	4	1	6	1	0	0	15	21	3	4	3.9	.923	2B-9
1921			100	.301	.436	326	98	21	7	3	0.9	43	42	28	35	10	5	2	215	14	13	1	2.4	.946	OF-91, 2B-1
1922			132	.303	.472	458	139	28	14	7	1.5	74	70	38	39	14	9	4	333	9	12	2	2.7	.966	OF-132
1923			153	.291	.430	546	159	37	15	3	0.5	91	64	62	51	41	4	0	434	34	15	7	3.2	.969	OF-143, 3B-6, SS-1
1924			118	.325	.439	385	125	22	5	4	1.0	75	49	45	41	7	14	5	281	13	8	2	2.6	.974	OF-102
1925			153	.299	.421	605	181	36	16	2	0.3	135	50	90	52	43	0	0	446	11	7	5	3.0	.985	OF-153
1926			148	.328	.467	600	197	41	15	4	0.7	120	42	79	55	35	0	0	440	15	15	4	3.2	.968	OF-147
1927			13	.125	.125	16	2	0	0	0	0.0	3	1	0	1	1	1	0	5	1	1	0	0.5	.857	OF-6
1928			133	.270	.340	503	136	19	8	0	0.0	69	51	66	54	23	2	0	394	18	10	3	3.2	.976	OF-131
1929			12	.229	.314	35	8	3	0	0	0.0	4	3	6	2	1	1	1	25	1	1	1	2.3	.963	OF-11
10 yrs.			972	.301	.427	3507	1054	209	82	23	0.7	618	376	415	336	176	35	11	2588	137	85	29	2.9	.970	OF-916, 2B-10, 3B-6, SS-1

Manny Mota

MOTA, MANUEL RAFAEL
Born Manuel Rafael Mota y Geronimo.
B. Feb. 18, 1938, Santo Domingo, Dominican Republic
BR TR 5'10" 160 lbs.

Year	Team		Games	BA	SA	AB	H	2B	3B	HR	HR%	R	RBI	BB	SO	SB	PH AB	PH H	PO	A	E	DP	TC/G	FA	G by Pos
1962	SF	N	47	.176	.189	74	13	1	0	0	0.0	9	9	7	8	3	15	1	38	18	2	2	1.2	.966	OF-27, 3B-7, 2B-3
1963	PIT	N	59	.270	.333	126	34	2	3	0	0.0	20	7	7	18	0	22	6	40	1	2	0	0.7	.953	OF-37, 2B-1
1964			115	.277	.384	271	75	8	3	5	1.8	43	32	10	31	4	21	5	122	5	5	1	1.1	.962	OF-93, 2B-1, C-1
1965			121	.279	.384	294	82	7	6	4	1.4	47	29	22	32	2	32	11	127	5	2	1	1.1	.985	OF-95
1966			116	.332	.472	322	107	16	7	5	1.6	54	46	25	28	7	26	10	152	4	1	0	1.4	.994	OF-96, 3B-4
1967			120	.321	.441	349	112	14	8	4	1.1	53	56	14	46	3	30	5	156	14	2	3	1.4	.988	OF-99, 3B-2
1968			111	.281	.332	331	93	10	2	1	0.3	35	33	20	19	4	21	5	150	8	3	2	1.5	.981	OF-92, 3B-1, 2B-1
1969	2 teams		MON	N	(31G – .315)		LA	N	(85G – .323)																
"	total		116	.321	.389	383	123	7	5	3	0.8	41	30	32	36	6	16	2	157	8	3	2	1.5	.954	OF-102
1970	LA	N	124	.305	.384	417	127	12	6	3	0.7	63	37	47	37	11	16	6	172	9	5	3	1.5	.973	OF-111, 3B-1
1971			91	.312	.398	269	84	13	5	0	0.0	24	34	20	20	4	15	5	108	3	4	1	1.3	.965	OF-80
1972			118	.323	.434	371	120	16	5	5	1.3	57	48	27	15	4	25	10	141	3	1	1	1.2	.993	OF-99
1973			89	.314	.365	293	92	11	2	0	0.0	33	23	25	12	1	14	5	96	4	0	0	1.1	1.000	OF-74
1974			66	.281	.316	57	16	2	0	0	0.0	5	16	5	4	0	53	15	1	0	0	0	0.0	1.000	OF-3
1975			52	.265	.286	49	13	1	0	0	0.0	3	10	5	1	0	40	10	9	0	0	0	0.2	1.000	OF-5
1976			50	.288	.346	52	15	3	0	0	0.0	1	13	7	5	0	40	12	11	1	0	0	0.2	1.000	OF-6
1977			49	.395	.500	38	15	1	0	1	2.6	5	4	10	0	1	36	14	1	0	0	0	0.0	1.000	OF-1
1978			37	.303	.333	33	10	1	0	0	0.0	1	3	3	3	0	33	10	0	0	0	0	0.0	—	
1979			47	.357	.357	42	15	0	0	0	0.0	1	3	4	3	0	42	15	0	0	0	0	0.0	—	OF-1
1980			7	.429	.429	7	3	0	0	0	0.0	0	2	0	0	0	7	3	0	0	0	0	0.0	—	
1982			1	.000	.000	1	0	0	0	0	0.0	0	0	0	0	0	1	0	0	0	0	0	0.0	—	
20 yrs.			1536	.304	.389	3779	1149	125	52	31	0.8	496	438	289	320	50	505	150	1481	83	35	16	1.0	.978	OF-1021, 3B-15, 2B-6, C-1
																	3rd	**1st**							

Year	Team		Games	BA	SA	AB	H	2B	3B	HR	HR%	R	RBI	BB	SO	SB	Pinch Hit AB	Pinch Hit H	PO	A	E	DP	TC/G	FA	G by Pos

Manny Mota *continued*

LEAGUE CHAMPIONSHIP SERIES

1974	LA	N	3	.333	.333	3	1	0	0	0	0.0	0	1	0	0	0	3	1	1	0	0	0	0.3	1.000	OF-1
1977			1	1.000	2.000	1	1	1	0	0	0.0	1	0	0	0	0	1	1	0	0	0	0	0.0		
1978			2	1.000	2.000	1	1	1	0	0	0.0	0	0	0	0	0	1	1	0	0	0	0	0.0		OF-1
3 yrs.			6	.600	1.000	5	3	2	0	0	0.0	1	1	0	0	0	5	3	1	0	0	0	0.2	1.000	OF-1

WORLD SERIES

1977	LA	N	3	.000	.000	3	0	0	0	0	0.0	0	0	0	1	0	3	0	0	0	0	0	0.0	—	
1978			1	—	—	0	0	0	0	0	—	0	0	1	0	0	0	0	0	0	0	0	0.0		
2 yrs.			4	.000	.000	3	0	0	0	0	0.0	0	0	1	1	0	3	0	0	0	0	0	0.0		

Darryl Motley

MOTLEY, DARRYL DeWAYNE
B. Jan. 21, 1960, Muskogee, Okla.

BR TR 5'9" 196 lbs.

1981	KC	A	42	.232	.312	125	29	4	0	2	1.6	15	8	7	15	1	3	0	88	3	3	1	2.2	.968	OF-39
1983			19	.235	.441	68	16	1	2	3	4.4	9	11	2	8	2	1	1	42	2	1	0	2.4	.978	OF-18, DH-1
1984			146	.284	.439	522	148	24	6	15	2.9	64	70	28	73	10	9	1	301	7	5	2	2.1	.984	OF-138
1985			123	.222	.413	383	85	20	1	17	4.4	45	49	18	57	6	9	2	198	4	7	1	1.7	.967	OF-114, DH-7
1986	2 teams	KC	A (72G – .203)		ATL	N	(5G – .200)																			
"	total		77	.203	.348	227	46	10	1	7	3.1	23	20	12	32	0	12	4	97	2	2	1	1.3	.980	OF-69, DH-2
1987	ATL	N	6	.000	.000	8	0	0	0	0	0.0	0	1	0	1	0	4	0	2	0	0	0	0.3	1.000	OF-2
6 yrs.			413	.243	.401	1333	324	59	10	44	3.3	156	159	67	186	19	38	8	728	18	18	5	1.8	.976	OF-380, DH-10

LEAGUE CHAMPIONSHIP SERIES

1984	KC	A	3	.167	.167	12	2	0	0	0	0.0	0	1	1	3	0	0	0	11	0	0	0	3.7	1.000	OF-3
1985			2	.333	.333	3	1	0	0	0	0.0	0	1	1	2	0	0	0	4	0	0	0	2.0	1.000	OF-2
2 yrs.			5	.200	.200	15	3	0	0	0	0.0	0	2	2	5	0	0	0	15	0	0	0	3.0	1.000	OF-5

WORLD SERIES

| 1985 | KC | A | 5 | .364 | .636 | 11 | 4 | 0 | 0 | 1 | 9.1 | 1 | 3 | 0 | 1 | 0 | 0 | 0 | 4 | 0 | 0 | 0 | 0.8 | 1.000 | OF-4 |

Bitsy Mott

MOTT, ELISHA MATTHEW
B. June 12, 1918, Arcadia, Fla.

BR TR 5'8" 155 lbs.

| 1945 | PHI | N | 90 | .221 | .249 | 289 | 64 | 8 | 0 | 0 | 0.0 | 21 | 22 | 27 | 25 | 2 | 0 | 0 | 184 | 257 | 27 | 53 | 5.2 | .942 | SS-63, 2B-27, 3B-7 |

Curt Motton

MOTTON, CURTELL HOWARD
B. Sept. 24, 1940, Darnell, La.

BR TR 5'8" 164 lbs.

1967	BAL	A	27	.200	.323	65	13	2	0	2	3.1	5	9	5	14	0	11	1	36	0	1	0	1.4	.973	OF-18
1968			83	.198	.341	217	43	7	0	8	3.7	27	25	31	43	1	27	5	91	2	1	0	1.1	.989	OF-54
1969			56	.303	.573	89	27	6	0	6	6.7	15	21	13	10	3	25	8	26	0	0	0	0.5	1.000	OF-20
1970			52	.226	.393	84	19	3	1	3	3.6	16	19	18	20	1	26	4	32	1	0	0	0.6	1.000	OF-20
1971			38	.189	.434	53	10	1	0	4	7.5	13	8	10	12	0	15	3	20	1	0	0	0.6	1.000	OF-16
1972	2 teams	MIL	A (6G – .167)		CAL	A	(42G – .154)																			
"	total		48	.156	.244	45	7	1	0	1	2.2	7	3	6	14	0	18	1	15	0	0	0	0.3	1.000	OF-12
1973	BAL	A	5	.333	.833	6	2	0	0	1	16.7	2	4	1	1	0	2	0	0	0	0	0	0.0	—	DH-1, OF-1
1974			7	.000	.000	8	0	0	0	0	0.0	0	0	2	2	0	3	0	4	0	0	0	0.6	1.000	OF-2, DH-1
8 yrs.			316	.213	.384	567	121	20	1	25	4.4	85	89	86	116	5	127	22	224	4	2	0	0.7	.991	OF-143, DH-2

LEAGUE CHAMPIONSHIP SERIES

1969	BAL	A	2	.500	.500	2	1	0	0	0	0.0	0	1	0	0	0	2	1	0	0	0	0	0.0	—	
1971			1	1.000	2.000	1	1	1	0	0	0.0	0	0	0	1	0	1	1	0	0	0	0	0.0	—	
1974			1	.000	.000	1	0	0	0	0	0.0	0	1	0	1	0	1	0	0	0	0	0	0.0	—	
3 yrs.			4	.500	.750	4	2	1	0	0	0.0	0	2	0	2	0	4	2	0	0	0	0	0.0	—	

WORLD SERIES

| 1969 | BAL | A | 1 | .000 | .000 | 1 | 0 | 0 | 0 | 0 | 0.0 | 0 | 0 | 0 | 0 | 0 | 1 | 0 | 0 | 0 | 0 | 0 | 0.0 | — | |

Frank Motz

MOTZ, FRANK H.
B. Oct. 1, 1868, Freeburg, Pa. D. Mar. 18, 1944, Akron, Ohio

6' 160 lbs.

1890	PHI	N	1	.000	.000	2	0	0	0	0	0.0	1	3	1	1	0	0	0	8	1	0	2	9.0	1.000	1B-1
1893	CIN	N	43	.256	.353	156	40	7	1	2	1.3	16	25	19	10	3	0	0	426	38	9	27	11.0	.981	1B-43
1894			18	.203	.261	69	14	4	0	0	0.0	8	12	9	1	2	0	0	186	18	1	10	11.4	.995	1B-18
3 yrs.			62	.238	.322	227	54	11	1	2	0.9	25	40	29	12	6	0	0	620	57	10	39	11.1	.985	1B-62

Ollie Moulton

MOULTON, ALBERT THEODORE
B. Jan. 16, 1886, Medway, Mass. D. July 10, 1968, Peabody, Mass.

BR TR 5'6" 155 lbs.

| 1911 | STL | A | 4 | .067 | .067 | 15 | 1 | 0 | 0 | 0 | 0.0 | 4 | 1 | 4 | | 0 | 0 | 0 | 2 | 13 | 1 | 0 | 4.0 | .938 | 2B-4 |

Frank Mountain

MOUNTAIN, FRANK HENRY
B. May 17, 1860, Ft. Edward, N. Y. D. Nov. 19, 1939, Schenectady, N. Y.

BR TR 5'11" 185 lbs.

1880	TRO	N	2	.222	.222	9	2	0	0	0	0.0	1		0		0	0	0	0	4	0	0	2.0	1.000	P-2
1881	DET	N	7	.160	.280	25	4	1	0	0	0.0	4		2	8	0	0	0	6	6	1	0	1.9	.923	P-7
1882	3 teams	WOR	N (5G – .063)		PHI	AA	(9G – .333)			WOR	N	(20G – .271)														
"	total		34	.262	.385	122	32	5	2	2	1.6	14	6	5	23	0	0	0	31	54	10	3	2.8	.895	P-26, OF-7, 1B-2, SS-1
1883	COL	AA	70	.217	.337	276	60	14	5	3	1.1	36		9		0	0	0	55	106	26	3	2.7	.861	P-59, OF-12
1884			58	.238	.357	210	50	7	3	4	1.9	26		9		0	0	0	30	90	10	0	2.2	.923	P-42, OF-17
1885	PIT	AA	5	.100	.100	20	2	0	1	0	0.0	1		1		0	0	0	1	10	2	0	2.6	.846	P-5
1886			18	.145	.200	55	8	1	1	0	0.0	6		13		0	0	0	160	9	9	6	9.9	.949	1B-16, P-2
7 yrs.			194	.220	.333	717	158	28	13	9	1.3	84	10	39	35	0	0	0	283	279	58	12	3.2	.906	P-143, OF-36, 1B-18, SS-1

Ray Mowe

MOWE, RAYMOND BENJAMIN
B. July 12, 1889, Rochester, Ind. D. Aug. 14, 1968, Sarasota, Fla.

BL TR 5'7½" 160 lbs.

| 1913 | BKN | N | 5 | .111 | .111 | 9 | 1 | 0 | 0 | 0 | 0.0 | 0 | 0 | 0 | 1 | 0 | 1 | 0 | 7 | 9 | 1 | 1 | 3.4 | .941 | SS-2 |

Year	Team		Games	BA	SA	AB	H	2B	3B	HR	HR%	R	RBI	BB	SO	SB	Pinch Hit AB	Pinch Hit H	PO	A	E	DP	TC/G	FA	G by Pos

Mike Mowrey

MOWREY, HARRY HARLAN
B. Apr. 20, 1884, Brown's Mill, Pa. D. Mar. 20, 1947, Chambersburg, Pa.
BR TR 5'10" 180 lbs.

Year	Team		Games	BA	SA	AB	H	2B	3B	HR	HR%	R	RBI	BB	SO	SB	PH AB	PH H	PO	A	E	DP	TC/G	FA	G by Pos
1905	CIN	N	7	.267	.300	30	8	1	0	0	0.0	4	6	1		0	0	0	6	16	7	1	4.1	.759	3B-7
1906			21	.321	.377	53	17	3	0	0	0.0	3	6	5		2	4	1	21	37	4	1	3.0	.935	3B-15, SS-1, 2B-1
1907			138	.252	.321	448	113	16	6	1	0.2	43	44	35		10	0	0	178	245	35	14	3.3	.924	3B-127, SS-11
1908			77	.220	.269	227	50	9	1	0	0.0	17	23	12		5	12	2	64	117	15	6	2.5	.923	3B-56, OF-3, SS-3
1909	2 teams			CIN	N (38G – .191)		STL	N	(12G – .241)																
"	total		50	.201	.243	144	29	6	0	0	0.0	13	9	24		3	6	1	66	99	15	11	3.6	.917	3B-24, SS-13, 2B-7
1910	STL	N	143	.282	.368	489	138	24	6	2	0.4	69	70	67	38	21	0	0	171	301	37	30	3.6	.927	3B-141
1911			137	.268	.359	471	126	29	7	0	0.0	59	61	59	46	15	1	0	175	267	26	19	3.4	.944	3B-134, SS-1
1912			114	.255	.341	408	104	13	8	2	0.5	59	50	46	29	19	4	1	131	220	26	22	3.3	.931	3B-108
1913			131	.258	.316	449	116	18	4	0	0.0	61	33	53	40	21	0	0	143	284	21	23	3.4	.953	3B-130
1914	PIT	N	79	.254	.324	284	72	7	5	1	0.4	24	25	22	20	8	0	0	83	156	10	8	3.2	.960	3B-78
1915	PIT	F	151	.280	.359	521	146	26	6	1	0.2	56	49	66		40	0	0	174	268	19	15	3.1	.959	3B-151
1916	BKN	N	144	.244	.313	495	121	22	6	0	0.0	57	60	50	60	16	0	0	154	291	16	17	3.2	.965	3B-144
1917			83	.214	.284	271	58	9	5	0	0.0	20	25	29	25	7	1	0	77	170	12	14	3.1	.954	3B-80, 2B-2
13 yrs.			1275	.256	.329	4290	1098	183	54	7	0.2	485	461	469	258	167	28	5	1443	2471	243	181	3.3	.942	3B-1195, SS-29, 2B-10, OF-3

WORLD SERIES

Year	Team		Games	BA	SA	AB	H	2B	3B	HR	HR%	R	RBI	BB	SO	SB	PH AB	PH H	PO	A	E	DP	TC/G	FA	G by Pos
1916	BKN	N	5	.176	.176	17	3	0	0	0	0.0	2	1	3	2	0	0	0	8	15	2	1	5.0	.920	3B-5

Joe Mowry

MOWRY, JOSEPH ALOYSIUS
B. Apr. 6, 1908, St. Louis, Mo.
BB TR 6' 198 lbs.

Year	Team		Games	BA	SA	AB	H	2B	3B	HR	HR%	R	RBI	BB	SO	SB	PH AB	PH H	PO	A	E	DP	TC/G	FA	G by Pos
1933	BOS	N	86	.221	.293	249	55	8	5	0	0.0	25	20	15	22	1	20	7	155	2	1	0	1.8	.994	OF-64
1934			25	.215	.291	79	17	3	0	1	1.3	9	4	3	13	0	3	0	45	5	1	2	2.0	.980	OF-20, 2B-1
1935			81	.265	.360	136	36	8	1	1	0.7	17	13	11	13	0	30	10	62	3	2	0	0.8	.970	OF-45
3 yrs.			192	.233	.313	464	108	19	6	2	0.4	51	37	29	48	1	53	17	262	10	4	2	1.4	.986	OF-129, 2B-1

Mike Moynahan

MOYNAHAN, MICHAEL
B. 1856, Chicago, Ill. D. Apr. 9, 1899, Chicago, Ill.
BL TR

Year	Team		Games	BA	SA	AB	H	2B	3B	HR	HR%	R	RBI	BB	SO	SB	PH AB	PH H	PO	A	E	DP	TC/G	FA	G by Pos
1880	BUF	N	27	.330	.400	100	33	5	1	0	0.0	12	14	6	9		0	0	30	70	16	7	4.3	.862	SS-27
1881	2 teams			CLE	N (33G – .230)		DET	N	(1G – .250)																
"	total		34	.230	.281	139	32	5	1	0	0.0	13	8	3	15		0	0	68	6	11	2	2.5	.871	OF-32, 3B-2
1883	PHI	AA	95	.308	.410	400	123	18	10	1	0.3	90		30			0	0	105	268	75	14	4.7	.833	SS-95
1884	2 teams			PHI	AA (1G – .000)		CLE	N	(12G – .289)																
"	total		13	.265	.347	49	13	2	1	0	0.0	9	6	7	11		0	0	16	27	11	1	4.2	.796	2B-6, OF-4, SS-3
4 yrs.			169	.292	.378	688	201	30	13	1	0.1	124	28	46	35		0	0	219	371	113	24	4.2	.839	SS-125, OF-36, 2B-6, 3B-2

Bill Mueller

MUELLER, WILLIAM LAWRENCE (Hawk)
B. Nov. 9, 1920, Bay City, Mich.
BR TR 6'1½" 180 lbs.

Year	Team		Games	BA	SA	AB	H	2B	3B	HR	HR%	R	RBI	BB	SO	SB	PH AB	PH H	PO	A	E	DP	TC/G	FA	G by Pos
1942	CHI	A	26	.165	.176	85	14	1	0	0	0.0	5	5	12	9	2	1	0	81	7	2	1	3.5	.978	OF-26
1945			13	.000	.000	9	0	0	0	0	0.0	3	0	2	1	1	1	0	7	0	2	0	0.7	.778	OF-7
2 yrs.			39	.149	.160	94	14	1	0	0	0.0	8	5	14	10	3	2	0	88	7	4	1	2.5	.960	OF-33

Don Mueller

MUELLER, DONALD FREDERICK (Mandrake the Magician)
Son of Walter Mueller.
B. Apr. 14, 1927, St. Louis, Mo.
BL TR 6' 185 lbs.

Year	Team		Games	BA	SA	AB	H	2B	3B	HR	HR%	R	RBI	BB	SO	SB	PH AB	PH H	PO	A	E	DP	TC/G	FA	G by Pos
1948	NY	N	36	.358	.469	81	29	4	1	1	1.2	12	9	0	3	0	14	6	33	3	1	0	1.0	.973	OF-22
1949			51	.232	.304	56	13	4	0	0	0.0	5	1	5	6	0	42	7	8	0	0	0	0.2	1.000	OF-6
1950			132	.291	.383	525	153	15	6	7	1.3	60	84	10	26	1	6	2	205	7	3	2	1.6	.986	OF-125
1951			122	.277	.431	469	130	10	7	16	3.4	58	69	19	13	1	7	1	233	5	4	1	2.0	.983	OF-115
1952			126	.281	.421	456	128	14	7	12	2.6	61	49	34	24	2	4	0	221	8	3	4	1.8	.987	OF-120
1953			131	.333	.404	480	160	12	2	6	1.3	56	60	19	13	2	8	4	203	7	6	0	1.6	.972	OF-122
1954			153	.342	.444	619	212	35	8	4	0.6	90	71	22	17	2	1	1	263	14	6	5	1.8	.979	OF-153
1955			147	.306	.393	605	185	21	4	8	1.3	67	83	19	12	1	1	1	239	5	6	1	1.7	.976	OF-146
1956			138	.269	.333	453	122	12	1	5	1.1	38	41	15	7	0	21	6	180	4	2	1	1.3	.989	OF-117
1957			135	.258	.318	450	116	7	1	6	1.3	45	37	13	16	2	23	6	174	13	2	4	1.4	.989	OF-115
1958	CHI	A	70	.253	.283	166	42	5	0	0	0.0	7	16	11	9	0	26	9	57	3	2	1	0.9	.968	OF-43
1959			4	.500	.500	4	2	0	0	0	0.0	0	0	0	0	0	4	2	0	0	0	0	0.0	—	
12 yrs.			1245	.296	.390	4364	1292	139	37	65	1.5	499	520	167	146	11	157	44	1816	69	35	20	1.5	.982	OF-1084

WORLD SERIES

Year	Team		Games	BA	SA	AB	H	2B	3B	HR	HR%	R	RBI	BB	SO	SB	PH AB	PH H	PO	A	E	DP	TC/G	FA	G by Pos
1954	NY	N	4	.389	.389	18	7	0	0	0	0.0	4	1	0	1	0	0	0	3	0	2	0	1.3	.600	OF-4

Emmett Mueller

MUELLER, EMMETT JEROME (Heinie)
B. July 20, 1912, St. Louis, Mo. D. Oct. 3, 1986, Orlando, Fla.
BB TR 5'6" 167 lbs.

Year	Team		Games	BA	SA	AB	H	2B	3B	HR	HR%	R	RBI	BB	SO	SB	PH AB	PH H	PO	A	E	DP	TC/G	FA	G by Pos
1938	PHI	N	136	.250	.322	444	111	12	4	4	0.9	53	34	64	43	2	7	1	249	306	23	48	4.3	.960	2B-111, 3B-21
1939			115	.279	.437	341	95	19	4	9	2.6	46	43	33	34	4	26	8	163	166	11	38	3.0	.968	2B-51, OF-17, SS-1
1940			97	.247	.346	263	65	13	2	3	1.1	24	28	37	23	2	18	4	146	96	5	13	2.5	.980	2B-34, OF-31, 3B-13, 1B-2
1941			93	.227	.296	233	53	11	1	1	0.4	21	22	22	24	2	24	2	114	107	6	21	2.4	.974	2B-29, OF-21, 3B-19
4 yrs.			441	.253	.353	1281	324	55	11	17	1.3	144	127	156	124	10	75	15	672	675	45	120	3.2	.968	2B-225, 3B-70, OF-69, 1B-2, SS-1

Heinie Mueller

MUELLER, CLARENCE FRANCIS
Brother of Walter Mueller.
B. Sept. 16, 1899, Creve Coeur, Mo. D. Jan. 23, 1975, Desoto, Mo.
BL TL 5'8" 158 lbs.

Year	Team		Games	BA	SA	AB	H	2B	3B	HR	HR%	R	RBI	BB	SO	SB	PH AB	PH H	PO	A	E	DP	TC/G	FA	G by Pos
1920	STL	N	4	.318	.364	22	7	1	0	0	0.0	0	1	2	4	1	0	0	12	0	0	0	3.0	1.000	OF-4
1921			55	.352	.494	176	62	10	6	1	0.6	25	34	11	22	2	1	0	117	5	3	1	2.3	.976	OF-54
1922			61	.270	.396	159	43	7	2	3	1.9	20	26	14	18	2	17	5	83	6	5	2	1.5	.947	OF-44
1923			78	.343	.528	265	91	16	9	5	1.9	39	41	18	16	4	4	3	197	9	8	3	2.7	.963	OF-74
1924			92	.264	.365	296	78	12	6	2	0.7	39	37	19	16	8	10	1	335	15	9	17	3.9	.975	OF-53, 1B-27
1925			78	.313	.424	243	76	16	4	1	0.4	33	26	17	11	0	5	2	165	6	8	3	2.3	.955	OF-72

Year	Team	Games	BA	SA	AB	H	2B	3B	HR	HR%	R	RBI	BB	SO	SB	Pinch Hit AB	Pinch Hit H	PO	A	E	DP	TC/G	FA	G by Pos

Heinie Mueller *continued*

Year	Team		Games	BA	SA	AB	H	2B	3B	HR	HR%	R	RBI	BB	SO	SB	AB	H	PO	A	E	DP	TC/G	FA	G by Pos
1926	2 teams	STL N (52G – .267)				NY	N (85G – .249)																		
"	total		137	.256	.353	496	127	13	7	7	1.4	72	57	32	23	15	3	2	300	20	17	5	2.5	.950	OF-133
1927	NY N	84	.289	.379	190	55	6	1	3	1.6	33	19	25	12	2	18	3	117	2	6	3	1.5	.952	OF-56, 1B-1
1928	BOS N	42	.225	.258	151	34	3	1	0	0.0	25	19	17	9	1	1	1	127	6	2	1	3.2	.985	OF-41
1929		46	.204	.247	93	19	2	1	0	0.0	10	11	12	12	2	16	4	45	1	0	0	1.0	1.000	OF-24
1935	STL A	16	.185	.222	27	5	1	0	0	0.0	0	1	1	4	0	11	3	19	3	2	3	1.5	.917	1B-3, OF-2
11 yrs.		693	.282	.389	2118	597	87	37	22	1.0	296	272	168	147	37	86	24	1517	73	60	38	2.4	.964	OF-557, 1B-31

Ray Mueller

MUELLER, RAY COLEMAN (Iron Man)
B. Mar. 8, 1912, Pittsburg, Kans.   BR TR 5'9" 175 lbs.

Year	Team	Games	BA	SA	AB	H	2B	3B	HR	HR%	R	RBI	BB	SO	SB	AB	H	PO	A	E	DP	TC/G	FA	G by Pos
1935	BOS N	42	.227	.371	97	22	5	0	3	3.1	10	11	3	11	0	2	0	64	27	2	6	2.2	.978	C-40
1936		24	.197	.254	71	14	4	0	0	0.0	5	5	5	17	0	1	0	66	7	1	2	3.1	.986	C-23
1937		64	.251	.353	187	47	9	2	2	1.1	21	26	18	36	1	6	0	169	44	1	6	3.3	.995	C-57
1938		83	.237	.354	274	65	8	6	4	1.5	23	35	16	28	3	8	2	239	47	2	4	3.5	.993	C-75
1939	PIT N	86	.233	.322	180	42	8	1	2	1.1	14	18	14	22	0	3	1	203	32	7	5	2.8	.971	C-81
1940		4	.333	.333	3	1	0	0	0	0.0	1	1	2	0	0	0	0	7	2	0	0	2.3	1.000	C-4
1943	CIN N	141	.260	.379	427	111	19	4	8	1.9	50	52	56	42	1	1	0	579	100	8	17	4.9	.988	C-140
1944		155	.286	.398	555	159	24	4	10	1.8	54	73	53	47	4	0	0	471	65	9	5	3.6	.983	C-155
1946		111	.254	.386	378	96	18	4	8	2.1	35	42	27	37	0	14	0	405	65	3	12	4.3	.994	C-100
1947		71	.250	.401	192	48	11	0	6	3.1	17	33	16	25	1	12	5	221	28	4	2	3.6	.984	C-55
1948		14	.206	.235	34	7	1	0	0	0.0	2	2	4	3	0	4	1	51	5	1	0	4.1	.982	C-10
1949	2 teams	CIN N (32G – .274)				NY	N (56G – .224)																		
"	total	88	.243	.344	276	67	6	2	6	2.2	24	36	18	27	2	1	0	307	36	4	3	3.9	.988	C-87
1950	2 teams	NY N (4G – .091)				PIT	N (67G – .269)																		
"	total	71	.257	.413	167	43	8	0	6	3.6	17	24	11	16	2	4	1	228	30	1	3	3.6	.996	C-67
1951	BOS N	28	.157	.229	70	11	2	0	1	1.4	8	9	7	11	0	4	1	85	15	0	3	3.6	1.000	C-23
14 yrs.		982	.252	.368	2911	733	123	23	56	1.9	281	373	250	322	14	60	11	3095	503	43	68	3.7	.988	C-917

Walter Mueller

MUELLER, WALTER JOHN
Father of Don Mueller. Brother of Heinie Mueller.
B. Dec. 6, 1894, Central, Mo. D. Aug. 16, 1971, St. Louis, Mo.   BR TR 5'8" 160 lbs.

Year	Team	Games	BA	SA	AB	H	2B	3B	HR	HR%	R	RBI	BB	SO	SB	AB	H	PO	A	E	DP	TC/G	FA	G by Pos
1922	PIT N	32	.270	.377	122	33	5	1	2	1.6	21	18	5	7	1	0	0	74	8	2	1	2.6	.976	OF-31
1923		40	.306	.414	111	34	4	4	0	0.0	11	20	4	6	2	14	6	62	2	4	0	1.7	.941	OF-26
1924		30	.260	.320	50	13	1	1	0	0.0	6	8	4	4	1	14	2	20	4	0	0	0.8	1.000	OF-15
1926		19	.242	.274	62	15	0	1	0	0.0	8	3	0	2	0	4	0	29	2	1	0	1.7	.969	OF-15
4 yrs.		121	.275	.362	345	95	10	7	2	0.6	46	49	13	19	4	32	8	185	16	7	1	1.7	.966	OF-87

Mike Muldoon

MULDOON, MICHAEL D.
B. 1860, Hartford, Conn. Deceased.   5'8" 165 lbs.

Year	Team	Games	BA	SA	AB	H	2B	3B	HR	HR%	R	RBI	BB	SO	SB	AB	H	PO	A	E	DP	TC/G	FA	G by Pos
1882	CLE N	84	.246	.378	341	84	17	5	6	1.8	50	45	10	28		0	0	132	137	37	12	3.6	.879	3B-61, OF-23
1883		98	.228	.302	378	86	23	3	0	0.0	54		10	39		0	0	123	170	62	9	3.6	.825	3B-98, OF-2
1884		110	.239	.320	422	101	16	6	2	0.5	46	38	18	67		0	0	130	207	67	16	3.7	.834	3B-109, OF-1, 2B-1
1885	BAL AA	102	.251	.344	410	103	20	6	2	0.5	47		20			0	0	106	184	44	17	3.3	.868	3B-101, 2B-1
1886		101	.199	.276	381	76	13	8	0	0.0	57		34			0	0	177	270	58	22	5.0	.885	2B-57, 3B-44
5 yrs.		495	.233	.323	1932	450	88	28	10	0.5	254	83	92	134		0	0	668	968	268	76	3.8	.859	3B-413, 2B-59, OF-26

Tony Mullane

MULLANE, ANTHONY JOHN (Count, The Apollo of the Box)
B. Jan. 30, 1859, Cork, Ireland
D. Apr. 25, 1944, Chicago, Ill.   BB TB 5'10½" 165 lbs.
BL 1882

Year	Team	Games	BA	SA	AB	H	2B	3B	HR	HR%	R	RBI	BB	SO	SB	AB	H	PO	A	E	DP	TC/G	FA	G by Pos
1881	DET N	5	.263	.263	19	5	0	0	0	0.0	0	1	0			0	0	8	7	2	0	3.4	.882	P-5
1882	LOU AA	77	.257	.307	303	78	13	1	0	0.0	46		13			0	0	187	191	24	10	5.2	.940	P-55, 1B-13, OF-12, 2B-2
1883	STL AA	83	.225	.300	307	69	11	6	0	0.0	38		13			0	0	66	108	27	6	2.4	.866	P-53, OF-30, 2B-3, 1B-2
1884	TOL AA	95	.276	.372	352	97	19	3	3	0.9	49		33			0	0	139	161	41	10	3.6	.880	P-68, OF-18, 1B-7, 3B-6, SS-1, 2B-1
1886	CIN AA	91	.225	.293	324	73	12	5	0	0.0	59		25			0	0	114	117	27	10	2.8	.895	P-63, OF-27, 1B-4, 3B-2, SS-1, 2B-1
1887		56	.221	.327	199	44	6	3	3	1.5	35		16		20	0	0	40	73	7	6	2.1	.942	P-48, OF-9
1888		51	.251	.337	175	44	4	4	1	0.6	27	16	8		12	0	0	62	85	14	2	3.2	.913	P-44, 1B-4, OF-3, 2B-2
1889		63	.296	.418	196	58	16	4	0	0.0	53	29	27	21	24	0	0	78	80	22	10	2.9	.878	P-33, 3B-18, OF-12, 1B-4
1890	CIN N	81	.276	.364	286	79	9	8	0	0.0	41	34	39	30	19	0	0	114	116	37	7	3.3	.861	OF-28, P-25, 3B-21, SS-10, 1B-1
1891		64	.148	.172	209	31	1	2	0	0.0	16		19	33	4	0	0	33	100	9	3	2.2	.937	P-51, OF-12, 3B-3
1892		39	.169	.212	118	20	3	1	0	0.0	14	9	9	8	4	0	0	38	87	9	6	3.4	.933	P-37, 1B-2
1893	2 teams	CIN N (16G – .288)				BAL	N (38G – .228)																		
"	total	54	.247	.289	166	41	2	1	1	0.6	26	20	10	17	6	0	0	27	90	8	3	2.3	.936	P-49, OF-2, 3B-1, 1B-1
1894	2 teams	BAL N (21G – .396)				CLE	N (4G – .077)																		
"	total	25	.333	.379	66	22	3	0	0	0.0	8	9	3		3	0	0	10	31	4	2	1.8	.911	P-25
13 yrs.		784	.243	.316	2720	661	99	38	8	0.3	407	128	221	114	92	1	0	916	1246	231	75	3.1	.903	P-556, OF-153, 3B-51, 1B-38, SS-12, 2B-9

Greg Mulleavy

MULLEAVY, GREGORY THOMAS (Moe)
B. Sept. 25, 1905, Detroit, Mich. D. Feb. 1, 1980, Arcadia, Calif.   BR TR 5'9" 167 lbs.

Year	Team	Games	BA	SA	AB	H	2B	3B	HR	HR%	R	RBI	BB	SO	SB	AB	H	PO	A	E	DP	TC/G	FA	G by Pos
1930	CHI A	77	.263	.346	289	76	14	5	0	0.0	27	28	20	23	5	4	1	137	219	32	41	5.0	.918	SS-73
1932		1	.000	.000	3	0	0	0	0	0.0	0	0	0	0	0	0	0	2	2	0	1	4.0	1.000	2B-1
1933	BOS A	1	–		0	0	0	0	0	–	1	0	0	0	0	0	0	0	0	0	0	0.0	–	
3 yrs.		79	.260	.342	292	76	14	5	0	0.0	28	28	20	23	5	4	1	139	221	32	42	5.0	.918	SS-73, 2B-1

Billy Mullen

MULLEN, WILLIAM JOHN
B. Jan. 23, 1896, St. Louis, Mo. D. May 4, 1971, St. Louis, Mo.   BR TR 5'8" 160 lbs.

Year	Team	Games	BA	SA	AB	H	2B	3B	HR	HR%	R	RBI	BB	SO	SB	AB	H	PO	A	E	DP	TC/G	FA	G by Pos
1920	STL A	1	.000	.000	1	0	0	0	0	0.0	0	0	0	0	0	0	0	0	0	0	0	0.0	–	
1921		4	.000	.000	4	0	0	0	0	0.0	0	0	2	1	0	2	0	2	2	0	0	1.0	1.000	3B-2
1923	BKN N	4	.273	.273	11	3	0	0	0	0.0	1	0	0	0	0	0	0	1	6	1	0	2.0	.875	3B-4

Billy Mullen *continued*

Year	Team	Games	BA	SA	AB	H	2B	3B	HR	HR%	R	RBI	BB	SO	SB	PH AB	PH H	PO	A	E	DP	TC/G	FA	G by Pos
1926	DET A	11	.077	.077	13	1	0	0	0	0.0	2	0	5		1	2	0	6	8	2	0	1.5	.875	3B-9
1928	STL A	15	.389	.444	18	7	1	0	0	0.0	2	2	3	4	0	8	3	4	9	2	1	1.0	.867	3B-6
5 yrs.		35	.234	.255	47	11	1	0	0	0.0	5	2	10	6	1	13	3	13	25	5	1	1.2	.884	3B-21

Charlie Mullen

MULLEN, CHARLES GEORGE
B. Mar. 15, 1889, Seattle, Wash.   D. June 6, 1963, Seattle, Wash.
BR TR 5'10½" 155 lbs.

Year	Team	Games	BA	SA	AB	H	2B	3B	HR	HR%	R	RBI	BB	SO	SB	PH AB	PH H	PO	A	E	DP	TC/G	FA	G by Pos
1910	CHI A	41	.195	.228	123	24	2	1	0	0.0	15	13	4		4	1	1	365	23	7	21	9.6	.982	1B-37, OF-2
1911		20	.203	.271	59	12	2	1	0	0.0	7	5	5		1	0	0	176	12	6	2	9.7	.969	1B-20
1914	NY A	93	.260	.285	323	84	8	0	0	0.0	33	44	33	55	11	0	0	898	62	6	54	10.4	.994	1B-93
1915		40	.267	.278	90	24	1	0	0	0.0	11	7	10	12	5	10	3	201	15	4	0	5.5	.982	1B-27
1916		59	.267	.342	146	39	9	1	0	0.0	11	18	9	13	7	14	5	191	46	6	7	4.1	.975	2B-20, 1B-17, OF-6
5 yrs.		253	.247	.285	741	183	22	3	0	0.0	77	87	61	80	28	25	9	1831	158	29	84	8.0	.986	1B-194, 2B-20, OF-8

John Mullen

MULLEN, JOHN
B. Philadelphia, Pa.   Deceased.
BL TL

Year	Team	Games	BA	SA	AB	H	2B	3B	HR	HR%	R	RBI	BB	SO	SB	PH AB	PH H	PO	A	E	DP	TC/G	FA	G by Pos
1876	PHI N	1	.000	.000	3	0	0	0	0	0.0	0	0	0		0	0	0	3	2	2	0	7.0	.714	C-1

Moon Mullen

MULLEN, FORD PARKER
B. Feb. 9, 1917, Olympia, Wash.
BL TR 5'9" 165 lbs.

Year	Team	Games	BA	SA	AB	H	2B	3B	HR	HR%	R	RBI	BB	SO	SB	PH AB	PH H	PO	A	E	DP	TC/G	FA	G by Pos
1944	PHI N	118	.267	.304	464	124	9	4	0	0.0	51	31	28	32	4	3	0	295	323	25	53	5.4	.961	2B-114, 3B-1, C-1

Freddie Muller

MULLER, FREDERICK WILLIAM
B. Dec. 21, 1907, Newark, Calif.   D. Oct. 20, 1976, Davis, Calif.
BR TR 5'10" 170 lbs.

Year	Team	Games	BA	SA	AB	H	2B	3B	HR	HR%	R	RBI	BB	SO	SB	PH AB	PH H	PO	A	E	DP	TC/G	FA	G by Pos
1933	BOS A	15	.188	.250	48	9	1	1	0	0.0	6	3	5	5	1	1	0	24	36	5	6	4.3	.923	2B-14
1934		2	.000	.000	1	0	0	0	0	0.0	1	0	1	0	0	0	0	3	1	1	0	2.5	.800	3B-1, 2B-1
2 yrs.		17	.184	.245	49	9	1	1	0	0.0	7	3	6	5	1	1	0	27	37	6	6	4.1	.914	2B-15, 3B-1

Mulligan

MULLIGAN,
B. Philadelphia, Pa.   Deceased.

Year	Team	Games	BA	SA	AB	H	2B	3B	HR	HR%	R	RBI	BB	SO	SB	PH AB	PH H	PO	A	E	DP	TC/G	FA	G by Pos
1884	WAS U	1	.250	.250	4	1	0	0	0	0.0	2		0		0	0	0	4	3	0	0	7.0	1.000	3B-1

Eddie Mulligan

MULLIGAN, EDWARD JOSEPH
B. Aug. 27, 1894, St. Louis, Mo.   D. Mar. 15, 1982, San Rafael, Calif.
BR TR 5'9" 152 lbs.

Year	Team	Games	BA	SA	AB	H	2B	3B	HR	HR%	R	RBI	BB	SO	SB	PH AB	PH H	PO	A	E	DP	TC/G	FA	G by Pos
1915	CHI N	11	.364	.409	22	8	1	0	0	0.0	5		5	1	2	0	0	23	26	5	9	4.9	.907	SS-10, 3B-1
1916		58	.153	.212	189	29	3	4	0	0.0	13	9	8	30	1	0	0	116	200	40	27	6.1	.888	SS-58
1921	CHI A	152	.251	.330	609	153	21	12	1	0.2	82	45	32	53	13	0	0	162	308	22	28	3.2	.955	3B-152, SS-1
1922		103	.234	.315	372	87	14	8	0	0.0	39	31	22	32	7	10	2	104	216	13	17	3.2	.961	3B-86, SS-7
1928	PIT N	27	.233	.279	43	10	2	0	0	0.0	4	1	3	4	0	9	5	18	18	2	7	1.4	.947	3B-6, 2B-4
5 yrs.		351	.232	.307	1235	287	41	24	1	0.1	143	88	70	120	23	19	7	423	768	82	88	3.6	.936	3B-245, SS-76, 2B-4

George Mullin

MULLIN, GEORGE JOSEPH (Wabash George)
B. July 4, 1880, Toledo, Ohio   D. Jan. 7, 1944, Wabash, Ind.
BR TR 5'11" 188 lbs.

Year	Team	Games	BA	SA	AB	H	2B	3B	HR	HR%	R	RBI	BB	SO	SB	PH AB	PH H	PO	A	E	DP	TC/G	FA	G by Pos
1902	DET A	40	.325	.408	120	39	4	3	0	0.0	20	11	8		1	2	0	30	79	9	3	3.0	.924	P-35, OF-4
1903		46	.278	.389	126	35	9	1	1	0.8	11	12	2		1	4	1	38	108	10	1	3.4	.936	P-41, OF-1
1904		53	.298	.397	151	45	11	2	0	0.0	14	8	10		1	6	2	28	163	13	5	3.8	.936	P-45, OF-2
1905		47	.259	.289	135	35	4	0	0	0.0	15	12	12		1	2	0	20	134	6	7	3.4	.963	P-44
1906		50	.225	.324	142	32	6	4	0	0.0	13	6	4		2	8	3	21	113	6	2	2.8	.957	P-40
1907		70	.217	.287	157	34	5	3	0	0.0	16	13	12		2	20	5	15	133	6	1	2.2	.961	P-46
1908		55	.256	.328	125	32	2	1	1	0.8	13	8	7		2	14	3	21	102	5	2	2.3	.961	P-39
1909		53	.214	.270	126	27	7	0	0	0.0	13	17	13		2	10	1	12	99	3	2	2.2	.974	P-40, OF-2
1910		50	.256	.357	129	33	6	2	1	0.8	15	11	8		1	9	0	22	97	8	1	2.5	.937	P-38, OF-2
1911		40	.286	.398	98	28	7	2	0	0.0	13	12	5		1	8	2	9	55	4	2	1.7	.941	P-30
1912		38	.278	.356	90	25	5	1	0	0.0	13	12	17		0	8	1	8	70	6	1	2.2	.929	P-30
1913	2 teams	DET A (12G – .350)		WAS A (12G – .190)																				
"	total	24	.268	.268	41	11	0	0	0	0.0	5	1	6		1	3	1	2	41	2	1	1.9	.956	P-19
1914	IND F	43	.312	.455	77	24	5	3	0	0.0	11	21	11		0	6	1	9	45	5	1	1.4	.915	P-36
1915	NWK F	6	.100	.100	10	1	0	0	0	0.0	0	0	2		0	1	0	1	5	0	0	1.0	1.000	P-5
14 yrs.		615	.263	.345	1527	401	71	23	3	0.2	163	137	122	6	18	101	20	236	1244	83	30	2.5	.947	P-488, OF-11

WORLD SERIES

Year	Team	Games	BA	SA	AB	H	2B	3B	HR	HR%	R	RBI	BB	SO	SB	PH AB	PH H	PO	A	E	DP	TC/G	FA	G by Pos
1907	DET A	2	.000	.000	6	0	0	0	0	0.0	0	0	0	1	0	0	0	1	4	0	0	2.5	1.000	P-2
1908		1	.333	.333	3	1	0	0	0	0.0	1	1	0		0	0	0	1	2	0	0	2.0	1.000	P-1
1909		6	.188	.250	16	3	1	0	0	0.0	1	1	3		0	0	0		12	0	0	2.0	1.000	P-4
3 yrs.		9	.160	.200	25	4	1	0	0	0.0	2	2	4		0	2	0	1	18	0	0	2.1	1.000	P-7

Henry Mullin

MULLIN, HENRY
B. Boston, Mass.   Deceased.
BR

Year	Team	Games	BA	SA	AB	H	2B	3B	HR	HR%	R	RBI	BB	SO	SB	PH AB	PH H	PO	A	E	DP	TC/G	FA	G by Pos
1884	2 teams	WAS AA (34G – .142)		BOS U (2G – .000)																				
"	total	36	.133	.172	128	17	3	1	0	0.0	14		8		0	0	0	52	10	8	1	1.9	.886	OF-36, 3B-1

Jim Mullin

MULLIN, JAMES HENRY
B. Oct. 16, 1883, New York, N.Y.   D. Jan. 24, 1925, Philadelphia, Pa.
BR TR 5'10" 173 lbs.

Year	Team	Games	BA	SA	AB	H	2B	3B	HR	HR%	R	RBI	BB	SO	SB	PH AB	PH H	PO	A	E	DP	TC/G	FA	G by Pos
1904	2 teams	PHI A (41G – .218)		WAS A (27G – .186)																				
"	total	68	.203	.250	212	43	3	2	1	0.5	19	13	9		7	6	0	304	114	11	17	6.3	.974	2B-32, 1B-26, SS-2, OF-1
1905	WAS A	50	.190	.307	163	31	7	6	0	0.0	18	13	5		5	4	0	129	101	16	8	4.9	.935	2B-39, 1B-7
2 yrs.		118	.197	.275	375	74	10	8	1	0.3	37	26	14		12	10	0	433	215	27	25	5.7	.960	2B-71, 1B-33, SS-2, OF-1

Pat Mullin

MULLIN, PATRICK JOSEPH
B. Nov. 1, 1917, Trotter, Pa.
BL TR 6'2" 190 lbs.

Year	Team	Games	BA	SA	AB	H	2B	3B	HR	HR%	R	RBI	BB	SO	SB	PH AB	PH H	PO	A	E	DP	TC/G	FA	G by Pos
1940	DET A	4	.000	.000	4	0	0	0	0	0.0	0	0	0	0	0	0	0	3	0	0	0	0.0	–	OF-1

Year	Team	Games	BA	SA	AB	H	2B	3B	HR	HR%	R	RBI	BB	SO	SB	Pinch Hit AB	Pinch Hit H	PO	A	E	DP	TC/G	FA	G by Pos

Pat Mullin *continued*

Year	Team	Games	BA	SA	AB	H	2B	3B	HR	HR%	R	RBI	BB	SO	SB	AB	H	PO	A	E	DP	TC/G	FA	G by Pos
1941		54	.345	.509	220	76	11	5	5	2.3	42	23	18	18	5	2	0	117	2	7	0	2.3	.944	OF-51
1946		93	.246	.355	276	68	13	4	3	1.1	34	35	25	36	3	14	1	121	8	7	1	1.5	.949	OF-75
1947		116	.256	.470	398	102	28	6	15	3.8	62	62	63	66	3	9	3	229	10	3	2	2.1	.988	OF-106
1948		138	.288	.504	496	143	16	11	23	4.6	91	80	77	57	1	4	0	274	7	8	0	2.1	.972	OF-131
1949		104	.268	.448	310	83	8	6	12	3.9	55	59	42	29	1	26	6	169	4	2	0	1.7	.989	OF-79
1950		69	.218	.380	142	31	5	0	6	4.2	16	23	20	23	1	33	6	62	4	0	1	1.0	1.000	OF-32
1951		110	.281	.481	295	83	11	6	12	4.1	41	51	40	38	2	30	5	151	4	10	1	1.5	.939	OF-83
1952		97	.251	.424	255	64	13	5	7	2.7	29	35	31	30	1	30	6	131	6	3	2	1.4	.979	OF-65
1953		79	.268	.402	97	26	1	0	4	4.1	11	17	14	15	0	57	13	16	1	1	0	0.2	.944	OF-14
10 yrs.		864	.271	.453	2493	676	106	43	87	3.5	381	385	330	312	20	208	40	1270	46	41	7	1.6	.970	OF-637

Rance Mulliniks

MULLINIKS, STEVEN RANCE
B. Jan. 15, 1956, Tulare, Calif.

BL TR 5'11" 162 lbs.

Year	Team	Games	BA	SA	AB	H	2B	3B	HR	HR%	R	RBI	BB	SO	SB	AB	H	PO	A	E	DP	TC/G	FA	G by Pos
1977	CAL A	78	.269	.365	271	73	13	2	1	1.1	36	21	23	36	1	1	0	112	229	13	37	4.5	.963	SS-77
1978		50	.185	.252	119	22	3	1	1	0.8	6	6	8	23	2	1	0	68	93	8	22	3.4	.953	SS-47, DH-2
1979		22	.147	.191	68	10	3	0	1	1.5	7	8	4	14	0	0	0	46	43	4	13	4.2	.957	SS-22
1980	KC A	36	.259	.315	54	14	3	0	0	0.0	8	6	7	10	0	0	0	30	53	1	9	2.3	.988	SS-18, 2B-14
1981		24	.227	.295	44	10	3	0	0	0.0	6	5	2	7	0	0	0	25	39	5	9	2.9	.928	2B-10, SS-7, 3B-5
1982	TOR A	112	.244	.363	311	76	25	0	4	1.3	32	35	37	49	3	22	3	69	154	14	16	2.1	.941	3B-102, SS-15
1983		129	.275	.467	364	100	34	3	10	2.7	54	49	57	43	0	23	10	77	185	7	19	2.1	.974	3B-116, SS-15, 2B-2
1984		125	.324	.440	343	111	21	5	3	0.9	41	42	33	44	2	18	6	67	152	8	10	1.8	.965	3B-119
1985		129	.295	.454	366	108	26	1	10	2.7	55	56	55	54	1	19	9	75	162	7	16	1.9	.971	3B-110, DH-5, 2B-1
1986		117	.259	.417	348	90	22	0	11	3.2	50	45	43	60	1	16	2	60	176	6	13	1.9	.975	3B-110, DH-5, 2B-1
1987		124	.310	.500	332	103	28	1	11	3.3	37	44	34	55	1	24	8	29	137	13	14	1.4	.927	3B-96, DH-22, SS-1
1988		119	.300	.475	337	101	21	1	12	3.6	49	48	56	57	1	17	6	3	5	0	0	0.1	1.000	DH-108, 3B-7
1989		103	.238	.326	273	65	11	2	3	1.1	25	29	34	40	0	18	3	15	50	1	9	0.6	.985	DH-73, 3B-29
13 yrs.		1168	.273	.412	3230	883	210	16	69	2.1	406	394	393	492	13	159	47	676	1478	87	187	1.9	.961	3B-703, DH-210, SS-206, 2B-28

LEAGUE CHAMPIONSHIP SERIES

Year	Team	Games	BA	SA	AB	H	2B	3B	HR	HR%	R	RBI	BB	SO	SB	AB	H	PO	A	E	DP	TC/G	FA	G by Pos
1985	TOR A	5	.364	.727	11	4	1	0	1	9.1	1	3	2	2	0	2	1	1	4	0	0	1.0	1.000	3B-5
1989		1	.000	.000	1	0	0	0	0	0.0	0	0	0	1	0	1	0	0	0	0	0	0.0	—	
2 yrs.		6	.333	.667	12	4	1	0	1	8.3	1	3	2	3	0	3	1	1	4	0	0	0.8	1.000	3B-5

Fran Mullins

MULLINS, FRANCIS JOSEPH
B. May 14, 1957, Oakland, Calif.

BR TR 6' 180 lbs.

Year	Team	Games	BA	SA	AB	H	2B	3B	HR	HR%	R	RBI	BB	SO	SB	AB	H	PO	A	E	DP	TC/G	FA	G by Pos
1980	CHI A	21	.194	.258	62	12	4	0	0	0.0	9	8	3	9	0	0	0	15	36	1	7	2.5	.981	3B-21
1984	SF N	57	.218	.345	110	24	8	0	2	1.8	8	9	9	29	3	3	2	39	101	5	14	2.5	.966	SS-28, 3B-28, 2B-4
1986	CLE A	28	.175	.275	40	7	4	0	0	0.0	3	1	8	10	0	3	1	23	46	4	6	2.6	.945	2B-13, SS-11, DH-1, 1B-1
3 yrs.		106	.203	.307	212	43	16	0	2	0.9	20	18	20	48	3	6	3	77	183	10	27	2.5	.963	3B-49, SS-39, 2B-17, DH-1, 1B-1

Joe Mulvey

MULVEY, JOSEPH H.
B. Oct. 27, 1858, Providence, R. I.   D. Aug. 21, 1928, Philadelphia, Pa.

BR TR 5'11½" 178 lbs.

Year	Team	Games	BA	SA	AB	H	2B	3B	HR	HR%	R	RBI	BB	SO	SB	AB	H	PO	A	E	DP	TC/G	FA	G by Pos
1883	2 teams		PRO N	(4G – .125)		PHI N	(3G – .500)																	
"	total	7	.286	.357	28	8	1	1	0	0.0	3		0	2		0	0	10	11	8	1	4.1	.724	SS-4, 3B-3
1884	PHI N	100	.229	.282	401	92	11	2	2	0.5	47		4	49		0	0	151	216	73	20	4.4	.834	3B-100
1885		107	.269	.393	443	119	25	6	6	1.4	74		3	18		0	0	144	201	62	12	3.8	.848	3B-107
1886		107	.267	.365	430	115	16	10	2	0.5	71	53	15	31		0	0	99	191	40	2	3.1	.879	3B-107, OF-1
1887		111	.287	.369	474	136	21	6	2	0.4	93	78	21	14	43	0	0	123	197	50	18	3.3	.865	3B-111
1888		100	.216	.261	398	86	12	3	0	0.0	37	39	9	33	18	0	0	87	174	32	9	2.9	.891	3B-100
1889		129	.289	.393	544	157	21	9	6	1.1	77	77	23	25	23	0	0	165	284	54	20	3.9	.893	3B-129
1890	PHI P	120	.287	.430	519	149	26	15	6	1.2	96	87	27	36	20	0	0	144	227	62	15	3.6	.857	3B-113
1891	PHI AA	113	.254	.364	453	115	9	13	5	1.1	62	66	17	32	11	0	0	172	241	49	18	4.1	.894	3B-113
1892	PHI N	25	.143	.173	98	14	1	1	0	0.0	9	4	6	7	4	0	0	40	58	13	5	4.4	.883	3B-25
1893	WAS N	55	.235	.310	226	53	9	4	0	0.0	21	19	7	8	2	0	0	76	140	31	10	4.5	.874	3B-55
1895	BKN N	13	.306	.429	49	15	4	1	0	0.0	8	8	2			0	0	25	30	5	1	4.6	.917	3B-13
12 yrs.		987	.261	.355	4063	1059	157	70	29	0.7	598	431	134	257	120	0	0	1236	1970	479	131	3.7	.870	3B-983, SS-4, OF-1

Jerry Mumphrey

MUMPHREY, JERRY WAYNE
B. Sept. 9, 1952, Tyler, Tex.

BB TR 6'2" 185 lbs.

Year	Team	Games	BA	SA	AB	H	2B	3B	HR	HR%	R	RBI	BB	SO	SB	AB	H	PO	A	E	DP	TC/G	FA	G by Pos
1974	STL N	5	.000	.000	2	0	0	0	0	0.0	2	0	0	0	0	0	0	0	0	0	0	0.0	—	OF-1
1975		11	.375	.500	16	6	2	0	0	0.0	2	1	4	3	0	4	2	9	0	0	0	0.8	1.000	OF-3
1976		112	.258	.331	384	99	15	5	1	0.3	51	26	37	53	22	10	3	261	6	2	1	2.4	.993	OF-94
1977		145	.287	.387	463	133	20	10	2	0.4	73	38	47	70	22	16	5	291	8	9	1	2.1	.971	OF-133
1978		125	.262	.335	367	96	13	4	2	0.5	41	37	30	40	14	16	5	178	10	1	1	1.5	.984	OF-116
1979		124	.295	.369	339	100	10	3	3	0.9	53	32	26	39	8	16	5	180	3	3	0	1.5	.984	OF-114
1980	SD N	160	.298	.372	564	168	24	3	4	0.7	61	59	49	90	52	6	1	398	10	11	1	2.6	.974	OF-153
1981	NY A	80	.307	.429	319	98	11	5	6	1.9	44	32	24	27	14	0	0	219	5	8	0	2.9	.966	OF-79
1982		123	.300	.449	477	143	24	10	9	1.9	76	68	50	66	11	0	0	336	5	5	2	2.8	.986	OF-123
1983	2 teams	NY A	(83G – .262)		HOU N	(44G – .336)																		
"	total	127	.288	.427	410	118	21	6	8	2.0	58	53	50	56	7	2	0	330	8	5	1	2.7	.985	OF-126
1984	HOU N	151	.290	.391	524	152	20	3	9	1.7	66	83	56	79	15	13	5	317	5	4	2	2.2	.988	OF-137
1985		130	.277	.396	444	123	25	2	8	1.8	52	61	37	57	6	10	4	248	6	8	1	2.0	.969	OF-126
1986	CHI N	111	.304	.401	309	94	11	2	5	1.6	37	32	26	45	2	29	10	161	3	5	1	1.5	.982	OF-92
1987		118	.333	.534	309	103	19	2	13	4.2	41	44	35	47	1	35	12	124	5	1	0	1.1	.992	OF-85
1988		63	.136	.167	66	9	2	0	0	0.0	3	9	7	16	0	50	5	5	0	0	0	0.1	1.000	OF-4
15 yrs.		1585	.289	.396	4993	1442	217	55	70	1.4	660	575	478	688	174	207	55	3057	74	60	13	2.0	.981	OF-1386

DIVISIONAL PLAYOFF SERIES

Year	Team	Games	BA	SA	AB	H	2B	3B	HR	HR%	R	RBI	BB	SO	SB	AB	H	PO	A	E	DP	TC/G	FA	G by Pos
1981	NY A	5	.095	.095	21	2	0	0	0	0.0	2	0	0	1	0	0	0	0	0	0	0	0.0	—	OF-5

Year	Team	Games	BA	SA	AB	H	2B	3B	HR	HR%	R	RBI	BB	SO	SB	Pinch Hit AB	Pinch Hit H	PO	A	E	DP	TC/G	FA	G by Pos

Jerry Mumphrey *continued*

LEAGUE CHAMPIONSHIP SERIES

| 1981 | NY | A | 3 | .500 | .583 | 12 | 6 | 1 | 0 | 0 | 0.0 | 2 | 0 | 3 | 2 | 0 | 0 | 0 | 0 | 0 | 0 | 0 | 0.0 | – | OF-3 |

WORLD SERIES

| 1981 | NY | A | 5 | .200 | .200 | 15 | 3 | 0 | 0 | 0 | 0.0 | 2 | 0 | 3 | 2 | 1 | 0 | 0 | 6 | 0 | 0 | 0 | 1.2 | 1.000 | OF-5 |

John Munce

MUNCE, JOHN LEWIS   6'
B. Nov. 18, 1857, Philadelphia, Pa.   D. Mar. 15, 1917, Philadelphia, Pa.

| 1884 | WIL | U | 7 | .190 | .190 | 21 | 4 | 0 | 0 | 0 | 0.0 | 1 | | 1 | | | 0 | 0 | 4 | 2 | 3 | 0 | 1.3 | .667 | OF-7 |

Jake Munch

MUNCH, JACOB FERDINAND   BL TL 6'2½" 170 lbs.
B. Nov. 16, 1890, Morton, Pa.   D. June 8, 1966, Lansdowne, Pa.

| 1918 | PHI | A | 22 | .267 | .333 | 30 | 8 | 0 | 1 | 0 | 0.0 | 3 | 0 | 0 | 5 | 0 | 17 | 4 | 19 | 1 | 2 | 1 | 1.0 | .909 | OF-2, 1B-2 |

George Mundinger

MUNDINGER, GEORGE (Mundy)   BR TR 6'2" 200 lbs.
B. Nov. 20, 1854, New Orleans, La.   D. Oct. 12, 1910, Covington, Ky.

| 1884 | IND | AA | 3 | .250 | .250 | 8 | 2 | 0 | 0 | 0 | 0.0 | | | | | | 0 | 0 | 4 | 2 | 2 | 0 | 2.7 | .750 | C-3 |

Bill Mundy

MUNDY, WILLIAM EDWARD   BL TL 5'10" 154 lbs.
B. June 28, 1889, Salineville, Ohio   D. Sept. 23, 1958, Kalamazoo, Mich.

| 1913 | BOS | A | 15 | .255 | .255 | 47 | 12 | 0 | 0 | 0 | 0.0 | 4 | 4 | 4 | 12 | 0 | 0 | 0 | 134 | 4 | 7 | 4 | 9.7 | .952 | 1B-14 |

Joe Munson

MUNSON, JOSEPH MARTIN NAPOLEON   BL TR 5'9" 184 lbs.
Born Joseph Martin Napoleon Carlson.
B. Nov. 6, 1899, Renovo, Pa.

1925	CHI	N	9	.371	.514	35	13	3	1	0	0.0	5	3	3	1	1	0	0	17	1	0	1	2.0	1.000	OF-9
1926			33	.257	.406	101	26	2	2	3	3.0	17	15	8	4	0	4	1	51	2	6	1	1.8	.898	OF-28
2 yrs.			42	.287	.434	136	39	5	3	3	2.2	22	18	11	5	1	4	1	68	3	6	2	1.8	.922	OF-37

Red Munson

MUNSON, CLARENCE HANFORD   TR
B. July 31, 1883, Cincinnati, Ohio   D. Feb. 19, 1957, Mishawaka, Ind.

| 1905 | PHI | N | 9 | .115 | .154 | 26 | 3 | 1 | 0 | 0 | 0.0 | 1 | 2 | 0 | | 0 | 1 | 0 | 32 | 10 | 7 | 0 | 5.4 | .857 | C-8 |

Thurman Munson

MUNSON, THURMAN LEE   BR TR 5'11" 190 lbs.
B. June 7, 1947, Akron, Ohio   D. Aug. 2, 1979, Canton, Ohio

1969	NY	A	26	.256	.349	86	22	1	2	1	1.2	9	9	10	10	0	1	0	119	18	2	0	5.3	.986	C-25
1970			132	.302	.415	453	137	25	4	6	1.3	59	53	57	56	5	9	3	631	80	8	11	5.4	.989	C-125
1971			125	.251	.368	451	113	15	4	10	2.2	71	42	52	65	6	10	3	547	67	1	4	4.9	.998	C-117, OF-1
1972			140	.280	.364	511	143	16	3	7	1.4	54	46	47	58	6	8	2	575	71	15	11	4.7	.977	C-132
1973			147	.301	.487	519	156	29	4	20	3.9	80	74	48	64	4	2	0	673	80	12	11	5.2	.984	C-142
1974			144	.261	.381	517	135	19	2	13	2.5	64	60	44	66	2	2	0	743	75	22	10	5.8	.974	C-137, DH-4
1975			157	.318	.429	597	190	24	3	12	2.0	83	102	45	52	3	1	0	725	95	23	15	5.4	.973	C-130, DH-22, OF-2, 1B-2, 3B-1
1976			152	.302	.432	616	186	27	1	17	2.8	79	105	29	38	14	4	3	546	78	14	8	4.2	.978	C-121, DH-21, OF-11
1977			149	.308	.462	595	183	28	5	18	3.0	85	100	39	55	5	2	0	657	73	12	4	5.0	.984	C-136, DH-10
1978			154	.297	.373	617	183	27	1	6	1.0	73	71	35	70	2	1	1	698	61	11	4	5.0	.986	C-125, DH-14, OF-13
1979			97	.288	.374	382	110	18	3	3	0.8	42	39	32	37	1	1	0	428	44	10	7	5.0	.979	C-88, DH-5, 1B-3
11 yrs.			1423	.292	.410	5344	1558	229	32	113	2.1	696	701	438	571	48	41	12	6342	742	130	85	5.1	.982	C-1278, DH-76, OF-27, 1B-5, 3B-1

LEAGUE CHAMPIONSHIP SERIES

1976	NY	A	5	.435	.522	23	10	2	0	0	0.0	3	3	0	1	0	0	0	18	6	2	0	5.2	.923	C-5
1977			5	.286	.476	21	6	1	0	1	4.8	3	5	0	2	0	0	0	24	4	0	0	5.6	1.000	C-5
1978			4	.278	.500	18	5	1	0	1	5.6	2	2	0	0	0	0	0	22	4	0	0	6.5	1.000	C-4
3 yrs.			14	.339	.500	62	21	4	0	2	3.2	8	10	0	3	0	0	0	64	14	2	0	5.7	.975	C-14

WORLD SERIES

1976	NY	A	4	.529	.529	17	9	0	0	0	0.0	2	2	0	1	0	0	0	21	7	0	0	7.0	1.000	C-4
1977			6	.320	.520	25	8	2	0	1	4.0	4	3	2	8	0	0	0	40	5	0	0	7.5	1.000	C-6
1978			6	.320	.440	25	8	3	0	0	0.0	5	7	3	7	1	0	0	33	5	0	1	6.3	1.000	C-6
3 yrs.			16	.373	.493	67	25	5	0	1	1.5	11	12	5	16	1	0	0	94	17	0	1	6.9	1.000	C-16
				3rd																					

John Munyan

MUNYAN, JOHN B.
B. Nov. 14, 1860, Chester, Pa.   D. Feb. 18, 1945, Endicott, N. Y.

1887	CLE	AA	16	.241	.293	58	14	1	0	0	0.0	9		3		4	0	0	30	12	11	2	3.3	.792	OF-12, C-3, 3B-2
1890	2 teams		COL AA (2G – .143)		STL AA (96G – .266)																				
"	total		98	.264	.381	349	92	15	4	4	1.1	62		32		11	0	0	477	136	45	10	6.7	.932	C-83, OF-9, 2B-5, 3B-3, SS-1
1891	STL	AA	62	.231	.286	182	42	4	3	0	0.0	44	20	43	39	13	0	0	207	55	25	4	4.6	.913	C-45, OF-12, SS-5, 3B-3
3 yrs.			176	.251	.343	589	148	20	11	4	0.7	115	20	78	39	28	0	0	714	203	81	16	5.7	.919	C-131, OF-33, 3B-8, SS-6, 2B-5

Bobby Murcer

MURCER, BOBBY RAY   BL TR 5'11" 160 lbs.
B. May 20, 1946, Oklahoma City, Okla.

1965	NY	A	11	.243	.378	37	9	0	1	2	2.7	2	4	5	12	0	0	0	28	41	5	14	6.7	.932	SS-11
1966			21	.174	.217	69	12	1	1	0	0.0	3	5	4	5	2	1	0	31	50	6	4	4.1	.931	SS-18
1969			152	.259	.454	564	146	24	4	26	4.6	82	82	50	103	7	5	0	235	81	22	11	2.2	.935	OF-118, 3B-31
1970			159	.251	.420	581	146	23	3	23	4.0	95	78	87	100	15	2	1	375	15	3	3	2.5	.992	OF-155
1971			146	.331	.543	529	175	25	6	25	4.7	94	94	91	60	14	4	1	317	10	5	1	2.3	.985	OF-143
1972			153	.292	.537	585	171	30	7	33	5.6	102	96	63	67	11	3	2	382	11	3	1	2.6	.992	OF-151

Year	Team		Games	BA	SA	AB	H	2B	3B	HR	HR%	R	RBI	BB	SO	SB	Pinch Hit AB	Pinch Hit H	PO	A	E	DP	TC/G	FA	G by Pos

Bobby Murcer *continued*

Year	Team		Games	BA	SA	AB	H	2B	3B	HR	HR%	R	RBI	BB	SO	SB	AB	H	PO	A	E	DP	TC/G	FA	G by Pos
1973			160	.304	.464	616	187	29	2	22	3.6	83	95	50	67	6	0	0	380	14	6	2	2.5	.985	OF-160
1974			156	.274	.378	606	166	25	4	10	1.7	69	88	57	59	14	1	0	297	21	7	2	2.1	.978	OF-156
1975	SF	N	147	.298	.432	526	157	29	4	11	2.1	80	91	91	45	9	3	2	201	10	4	3	1.5	.981	OF-144
1976			147	.259	.433	533	138	20	2	23	4.3	73	90	84	78	12	2	0	282	11	12	2	2.1	.961	OF-146
1977	CHI	N	154	.265	.455	554	147	18	3	27	4.9	90	89	80	77	16	5	2	238	11	5	5	1.6	.980	OF-150, SS-1, 2B-1
1978			146	.281	.403	499	140	22	6	9	1.8	66	64	80	57	14	10	4	225	8	5	0	1.6	.979	OF-138
1979	2 teams				CHI	N	(58G – .258)			NY	A	(74G – .273)													
"	total		132	.267	.405	454	121	16	1	15	3.3	64	55	61	52	3	5	1	279	8	3	0	2.2	.990	OF-124
1980	NY	A	100	.269	.438	297	80	9	1	13	4.4	41	57	34	28	2	22	7	82	2	4	0	0.9	.955	OF-59, DH-33
1981			50	.265	.470	117	31	6	0	6	5.1	14	24	12	15	0	22	6	0	0	0	0	0.0	–	DH-33
1982			65	.227	.418	141	32	6	0	7	5.0	12	30	12	15	2	30	6	0	0	0	0	0.0	–	DH-47
1983			9	.182	.409	22	4	2	0	1	4.5	2	1	1	1	0	4	0	0	0	0	0	0.0	–	DH-5
17 yrs.			1908	.277	.445	6730	1862	285	45	252	3.7	972	1043	862	841	127	119	32	3352	293	90	48	2.0	.976	OF-1644, DH-118, 3B-31, SS-30, 2B-1

DIVISIONAL PLAYOFF SERIES

Year	Team		Games	BA	SA	AB	H	2B	3B	HR	HR%	R	RBI	BB	SO	SB	AB	H	PO	A	E	DP	TC/G	FA	G by Pos
1981	NY	A	2	.000	.000	1	0	0	0	0	0.0	0	0	1	0	0	1	0	0	0	0	0	0.0	–	

LEAGUE CHAMPIONSHIP SERIES

Year	Team		Games	BA	SA	AB	H	2B	3B	HR	HR%	R	RBI	BB	SO	SB	AB	H	PO	A	E	DP	TC/G	FA	G by Pos
1980	NY	A	1	.000	.000	4	0	0	0	0	0.0	0	0	0	2	0	0	0	0	0	0	0	0.0	–	DH-1
1981			1	.333	.333	3	1	0	0	0	0.0	0	0	1	1	0	0	0	0	0	0	0	0.0	–	DH-1
2 yrs.			2	.143	.143	7	1	0	0	0	0.0	0	0	1	3	0	0	0	0	0	0	0	0.0	–	DH-2

WORLD SERIES

Year	Team		Games	BA	SA	AB	H	2B	3B	HR	HR%	R	RBI	BB	SO	SB	AB	H	PO	A	E	DP	TC/G	FA	G by Pos
1981	NY	A	4	.000	.000	3	0	0	0	0	0.0	0	0	0	1	0	3	0	0	0	0	0	0.0	–	

Simmy Murch

MURCH, SIMEON AUGUSTUS
B. Nov. 21, 1880, Castine, Me.   D. June 6, 1939, Exeter, N. H.

BR TR 6'4" 220 lbs.

Year	Team		Games	BA	SA	AB	H	2B	3B	HR	HR%	R	RBI	BB	SO	SB	AB	H	PO	A	E	DP	TC/G	FA	G by Pos
1904	STL	N	13	.137	.157	51	7	1	0	0	0.0	3	1	1		0	0	0	13	27	2	2	3.2	.952	3B-6, 2B-6, SS-1
1905			3	.111	.111	9	1	0	0	0	0.0			1		0	1	0	6	1	2	0	3.0	.778	2B-2, SS-1
1908	BKN	N	6	.182	.273	11	2	1	0	0	0.0	1	0	1		0	4	0	27	0	1	1	4.7	.964	1B-2
3 yrs.			22	.141	.169	71	10	2	0	0	0.0	4	1	2		0	5	0	46	28	5	3	3.6	.937	2B-8, 3B-6, SS-2, 1B-2

Wilbur Murdoch

MURDOCH, WILBUR EDWIN
B. Mar. 14, 1875, Avon, N. Y.   D. Oct. 29, 1941, Los Angeles, Calif.

Year	Team		Games	BA	SA	AB	H	2B	3B	HR	HR%	R	RBI	BB	SO	SB	AB	H	PO	A	E	DP	TC/G	FA	G by Pos
1908	STL	N	27	.258	.306	62	16	3	0	0	0.0	5	5	3		4	9	2	21	0	2	0	0.9	.913	OF-16

Tim Murnane

MURNANE, TIMOTHY HAYES
B. June 4, 1852, Naugatuck, Conn.   D. Feb. 7, 1917, Boston, Mass.
Manager 1884.

BL TR 5'9½" 172 lbs.

Year	Team		Games	BA	SA	AB	H	2B	3B	HR	HR%	R	RBI	BB	SO	SB	AB	H	PO	A	E	DP	TC/G	FA	G by Pos
1876	BOS	N	69	.282	.334	308	87	4	3	2	0.6	60	34	8	12		0	0	697	9	56	30	11.0	.927	1B-65, OF-3, 2B-1
1877			35	.279	.364	140	39	7	1	1	0.7	23	15	6	7		0	0	78	9	13	3	2.9	.870	OF-30, 1B-5
1878	PRO	N	49	.239	.282	188	45	6	1	0	0.0	35	14	8	12		0	0	545	22	38	25	12.3	.937	1B-48, OF-1
1884	BOS	U	76	.235	.264	311	73	5	2	0	0.0	55		22			0	0	603	10	35	8	8.5	.946	1B-63, OF-16
4 yrs.			229	.258	.305	947	244	22	7	3	0.3	173	63	44	31		0	0	1923	50	142	66	9.2	.933	1B-181, OF-50, 2B-1

Billy Murphy

MURPHY, WILLIAM EUGENE
B. May 7, 1944, Pineville, La.

BR TR 6'1" 191 lbs.

Year	Team		Games	BA	SA	AB	H	2B	3B	HR	HR%	R	RBI	BB	SO	SB	AB	H	PO	A	E	DP	TC/G	FA	G by Pos
1966	NY	N	84	.230	.341	135	31	4	1	3	2.2	15	13	7	34	1	25	5	57	6	3	1	0.8	.955	OF-57

Buzz Murphy

MURPHY, ROBERT R.
B. Apr. 26, 1895, Denver, Colo.   D. May 11, 1938, Denver, Colo.

BL TL 5'8½" 155 lbs.

Year	Team		Games	BA	SA	AB	H	2B	3B	HR	HR%	R	RBI	BB	SO	SB	AB	H	PO	A	E	DP	TC/G	FA	G by Pos
1918	BOS	N	9	.375	.719	32	12	2	3	1	3.1	6	9	3	5	0	0	0	13	0	0	0	1.4	1.000	OF-9
1919	WAS	A	79	.262	.321	252	66	7	4	0	0.0	19	28	19	32	5	6	1	177	8	8	2	2.4	.959	OF-73
2 yrs.			88	.275	.366	284	78	9	7	1	0.4	25	37	22	37	5	6	1	190	8	8	2	2.3	.961	OF-82

Clarence Murphy

MURPHY, CLARENCE
Deceased.

Year	Team		Games	BA	SA	AB	H	2B	3B	HR	HR%	R	RBI	BB	SO	SB	AB	H	PO	A	E	DP	TC/G	FA	G by Pos
1886	LOU	AA	1	.000	.000	3	0	0	0	0	0.0			0		0	0	0	2	0	0	0	2.0	1.000	OF-1

Connie Murphy

MURPHY, CORNELIUS DAVID
B. Nov. 1, 1870, Northfield, Mass.   D. Dec. 14, 1945, New Bedford, Mass.

BL TR 5'8" 155 lbs.

Year	Team		Games	BA	SA	AB	H	2B	3B	HR	HR%	R	RBI	BB	SO	SB	AB	H	PO	A	E	DP	TC/G	FA	G by Pos
1893	CIN	N	6	.176	.235	17	3	1	0	0	0.0	3	2	1	2	0	2	0	10	1	1	0	2.0	.917	C-4
1894			1	.000	.000	4	0	0	0	0	0.0			1	1	0	0	0	0	1	1	0	2.0	.500	C-1
2 yrs.			7	.143	.190	21	3	1	0	0	0.0	3	2	2	3	0	2	0	10	2	2	0	2.0	.857	C-5

Dale Murphy

MURPHY, DALE BRYAN
B. Mar. 12, 1956, Portland, Ore.

BR TR 6'4" 210 lbs.

Year	Team		Games	BA	SA	AB	H	2B	3B	HR	HR%	R	RBI	BB	SO	SB	AB	H	PO	A	E	DP	TC/G	FA	G by Pos
1976	ATL	N	19	.262	.354	65	17	6	0	0	0.0	3	9	7	9	0	0	0	100	13	3	0	6.1	.974	C-19
1977			18	.316	.526	76	24	8	1	2	2.6	5	14	0	8	0	0	0	114	11	6	2	7.3	.954	C-18
1978			151	.226	.394	530	120	14	3	23	4.3	66	79	42	145	11	7	3	1220	105	23	84	8.9	.983	1B-129, C-21
1979			104	.276	.469	384	106	7	2	21	5.5	53	57	38	67	6	2	0	812	57	20	63	8.5	.978	1B-76, C-27
1980			156	.281	.510	569	160	27	2	33	5.8	98	89	59	133	9	1	0	384	15	6	4	2.6	.985	OF-154, 1B-1
1981			104	.247	.390	369	91	12	1	13	3.5	43	50	44	72	14	2	0	264	11	5	5	2.7	.982	OF-103, 1B-3
1982			162	.281	.507	598	168	23	2	36	6.0	113	109	93	134	23	1	1	407	6	9	2	2.6	.979	OF-162
1983			162	.302	.540	589	178	24	4	36	6.1	131	121	90	110	30	2	0	373	10	6	0	2.4	.985	OF-160
1984			162	.290	.547	607	176	32	8	36	5.9	94	100	79	134	19	2	0	369	10	5	1	2.4	.987	OF-160
1985			162	.300	.539	616	185	32	2	37	6.0	118	111	90	141	10	0	0	334	8	7	4	2.2	.980	OF-161
1986			160	.265	.477	614	163	29	7	29	4.7	89	83	75	141	7	1	1	303	6	6	1	2.0	.981	OF-159
1987			159	.295	.580	566	167	27	1	44	7.8	115	105	115	136	16	0	0	325	14	8	1	2.2	.977	OF-159
1988			156	.226	.421	592	134	35	4	24	4.1	77	77	74	125	3	1	0	340	15	3	4	2.3	.992	OF-156

Year	Team	Games	BA	SA	AB	H	2B	3B	HR	HR%	R	RBI	BB	SO	SB	Pinch Hit AB	Pinch Hit H	PO	A	E	DP	TC/G	FA	G by Pos

Dale Murphy *continued*

Year	Team	Games	BA	SA	AB	H	2B	3B	HR	HR%	R	RBI	BB	SO	SB	PH AB	PH H	PO	A	E	DP	TC/G	FA	G by Pos
1989		154	.228	.361	574	131	16	0	20	3.5	60	84	65	142	3	2	0	331	5	5	0	2.2	.985	OF-151
14 yrs.		1829	.270	.481	6749	1820	292	37	354	5.2	1065	1088	871	1497	151	21	5	5676	286	112	171	3.3	.982	OF-1525, 1B-209, C-85

LEAGUE CHAMPIONSHIP SERIES

Year	Team		Games	BA	SA	AB	H	2B	3B	HR	HR%	R	RBI	BB	SO	SB	PH AB	PH H	PO	A	E	DP	TC/G	FA	G by Pos
1982	ATL	N	3	.273	.273	11	3	0	0	0	0.0	1	0	0	2	1	0	0	0	0	0	0	0.0	–	OF-3

Danny Murphy

MURPHY, DANIEL FRANCIS
B. Aug. 11, 1876, Philadelphia, Pa. D. Nov. 22, 1955, Jersey City, N. J.
BR TR 5'9" 175 lbs.

Year	Team		Games	BA	SA	AB	H	2B	3B	HR	HR%	R	RBI	BB	SO	SB	PH AB	PH H	PO	A	E	DP	TC/G	FA	G by Pos
1900	NY	N	22	.270	.284	74	20	1	0	0	0.0	12	6	8		4	0	0	46	49	12	9	4.9	.888	2B-22
1901			28	.186	.216	102	19	3	0	0	0.0	12	6	4		1	0	0	44	73	20	3	4.9	.854	2B-28
1902	PHI	A	76	.313	.416	291	91	11	8	1	0.3	48	48	13		12	0	0	167	197	14	22	5.0	.963	2B-76
1903			133	.273	.382	513	140	31	11	1	0.2	65	60	13		17	0	0	241	349	32	34	4.7	.949	2B-133
1904			150	.287	.440	557	160	30	17	7	1.3	78	77	22		22	0	0	280	455	46	35	5.2	.941	2B-150
1905			150	.278	.390	533	148	34	4	6	1.1	71	71	42		23	0	0	287	387	31	29	4.7	.956	2B-150
1906			119	.301	.404	448	135	28	6	2	0.4	48	60	21		17	0	0	239	308	26	38	4.8	.955	2B-119
1907			124	.271	.345	469	127	23	3	2	0.4	51	57	30		11	1	0	271	386	24	28	5.5	.965	2B-122
1908			142	.265	.364	525	139	28	6	4	0.8	51	66	32		16	0	0	308	173	18	18	3.5	.964	OF-84, 2B-56, 1B-2
1909			149	.281	.412	541	152	28	14	5	0.9	61	69	35		19	0	0	191	17	5	5	1.4	.977	OF-149
1910			151	.300	.436	560	168	28	18	4	0.7	70	64	31		18	0	0	209	15	6	5	1.5	.974	OF-151
1911			141	.329	.461	508	167	27	11	6	1.2	104	66	50		22	1	0	164	46	8	8	1.5	.963	OF-136, 2B-4
1912			36	.323	.446	130	42	6	2	2	1.5	27	20	16		8	0	0	39	2	5	2	1.3	.891	OF-36
1913			40	.322	.441	59	19	5	1	0	0.0	3	6	4	8	0	31	8	5	0	0	1	0.1	1.000	OF-9
1914	BKN	F	52	.304	.435	161	49	9	0	4	2.5	16	32	17		4	6	0	65	8	1	2	1.4	.986	OF-46
1915			5	.167	.167	6	1	0	0	0	0.0	0	0	0		0	3	1	0	1	0	0	0.2	1.000	OF-1, 2B-1
16 yrs.			1518	.288	.402	5477	1577	292	101	44	0.8	711	708	338	8	194	42	9	2556	2466	248	239	3.5	.953	2B-861, OF-612, 1B-2

WORLD SERIES

Year	Team		Games	BA	SA	AB	H	2B	3B	HR	HR%	R	RBI	BB	SO	SB	PH AB	PH H	PO	A	E	DP	TC/G	FA	G by Pos
1905	PHI	A	5	.188	.250	16	3	1	0	0	0.0	0	0	0	2	0	0	0	4	10	4	0	3.6	.778	2B-5
1910			5	.350	.650	20	7	3	0	1	5.0	6	8	1	0	1	0	0	6	2	0	2	1.6	1.000	OF-5
1911			6	.304	.435	23	7	3	0	0	0.0	4	2	0	3	0	0	0	8	0	1	0	1.5	.889	OF-6
3 yrs.			16	.288	.458	59	17	7	0	1	1.7	10	10	1	5	1	0	0	18	12	5	2	2.2	.857	OF-11, 2B-5
							9th																		

Danny Murphy

MURPHY, DANIEL FRANCIS
B. Aug. 23, 1942, Beverly, Mass.
BL TR 5'11" 185 lbs.

Year	Team		Games	BA	SA	AB	H	2B	3B	HR	HR%	R	RBI	BB	SO	SB	PH AB	PH H	PO	A	E	DP	TC/G	FA	G by Pos
1960	CHI	N	31	.120	.187	75	9	2	0	1	1.3	7	6	4	13	0	7	0	40	1	1	1	1.4	.976	OF-21
1961			4	.385	.846	13	5	0	0	2	15.4	3	3	1	5	0	0	0	5	1	0	0	1.5	1.000	OF-4
1962			14	.200	.343	35	7	3	1	0	0.0	5	3	2	9	0	6	0	5	0	0	0	0.4	1.000	OF-9
1969	CHI	A	17	.000	.000	1	0	0	0	0	0.0	0	0	2	0	0	0	0	0	4	0	0	0.2	1.000	P-17
1970			51	.333	.833	6	2	0	0	1	16.7	3	1	2	2	0	0	0	4	10	1	1	0.3	.933	P-51
5 yrs.			117	.177	.323	130	23	5	1	4	3.1	18	13	11	29	0	13	0	54	16	2	2	0.6	.972	P-68, OF-34

Danny Murphy

MURPHY, DANIEL JOSEPH (Handsome Dan)
B. Sept. 10, 1864, Brooklyn, N. Y. D. Dec. 14, 1915, Brooklyn, N. Y.

Year	Team		Games	BA	SA	AB	H	2B	3B	HR	HR%	R	RBI	BB	SO	SB	PH AB	PH H	PO	A	E	DP	TC/G	FA	G by Pos
1892	NY	N	8	.115	.115	26	3	0	0	0	0.0	2	0	5	4	0	0	0	39	6	5	1	6.3	.900	C-8

Dave Murphy

MURPHY, DAVID FRANCIS (Dirty Dave)
B. May 4, 1876, Adams, Mass. D. Apr. 8, 1940, Adams, Mass.
TR

Year	Team		Games	BA	SA	AB	H	2B	3B	HR	HR%	R	RBI	BB	SO	SB	PH AB	PH H	PO	A	E	DP	TC/G	FA	G by Pos
1905	BOS	N	3	.182	.182	11	2	0	0	0	0.0	0	1	0		0	0	0	2	5	2	0	3.0	.778	SS-2, 3B-1

Dick Murphy

MURPHY, RICHARD LEE
B. Oct. 25, 1931, Cincinnati, Ohio
BL TL 5'11" 170 lbs.

Year	Team		Games	BA	SA	AB	H	2B	3B	HR	HR%	R	RBI	BB	SO	SB	PH AB	PH H	PO	A	E	DP	TC/G	FA	G by Pos
1954	CIN	N	6	.000	.000	1	0	0	0	0	0.0	1	0	0	1	0	1	0	0	0	0	0	0.0	–	

Dummy Murphy

MURPHY, HERBERT COURTLAND
B. Dec. 18, 1886, Olney, Ill. D. Aug. 10, 1962, Tallahassee, Fla.
BR TR 5'10" 165 lbs.

Year	Team		Games	BA	SA	AB	H	2B	3B	HR	HR%	R	RBI	BB	SO	SB	PH AB	PH H	PO	A	E	DP	TC/G	FA	G by Pos
1914	PHI	N	9	.154	.192	26	4	1	0	0	0.0	1	3	0	4	0	0	0	23	28	8	2	6.6	.864	SS-9

Dwayne Murphy

MURPHY, DWAYNE KEITH
B. Mar. 18, 1955, Merced, Calif.
BL TR 6'1" 180 lbs.

Year	Team		Games	BA	SA	AB	H	2B	3B	HR	HR%	R	RBI	BB	SO	SB	PH AB	PH H	PO	A	E	DP	TC/G	FA	G by Pos
1978	OAK	A	60	.192	.231	52	10	2	0	0	0.0	15	5	7	14	6	4	1	49	1	0	1	0.8	1.000	OF-45, DH-5
1979			121	.255	.387	388	99	10	4	11	2.8	57	40	84	80	15	2	1	322	10	4	0	2.8	.988	OF-118
1980			159	.274	.380	573	157	18	2	13	2.3	86	68	102	96	26	0	0	507	13	5	0	3.3	.990	OF-158
1981			107	.251	.408	390	98	10	3	15	3.8	58	60	73	91	10	0	0	326	6	5	0	3.1	.985	OF-106, DH-1
1982			151	.238	.418	543	129	15	1	27	5.0	84	94	93	122	26	3	0	452	18	8	3	3.2	.983	OF-147, DH-1, SS-1
1983			130	.227	.380	471	107	17	2	17	3.6	55	75	62	105	7	1	0	365	7	8	0	2.9	.979	OF-124, DH-7
1984			153	.256	.472	559	143	18	2	33	5.9	93	88	74	111	4	0	0	474	14	6	2	3.2	.988	OF-153
1985			152	.233	.400	523	122	21	3	20	3.8	77	59	84	123	4	0	0	432	6	5	1	2.9	.989	OF-150
1986			98	.252	.386	329	83	11	3	9	2.7	50	39	56	80	3	2	2	276	6	2	3	2.9	.993	OF-97, DH-1
1987			82	.233	.374	219	51	7	0	8	3.7	39	35	58	61	4	5	0	187	2	3	0	2.3	.984	OF-79, 2B-1, 1B-1
1988	DET	A	49	.250	.368	144	36	5	0	4	2.8	14	19	24	26	1	4	1	122	1	0	0	2.5	1.000	OF-43, DH-3
1989	PHI	N	98	.218	.423	156	34	5	0	9	5.8	20	27	29	44	0	43	9	69	1	1	1	0.7	.986	OF-52
12 yrs.			1360	.246	.402	4347	1069	139	20	166	3.8	648	609	746	953	100	64	14	3581	85	47	11	2.7	.987	OF-1272, DH-18, SS-1, 2B-1, 1B-1

DIVISIONAL PLAYOFF SERIES

Year	Team		Games	BA	SA	AB	H	2B	3B	HR	HR%	R	RBI	BB	SO	SB	PH AB	PH H	PO	A	E	DP	TC/G	FA	G by Pos
1981	OAK	A	3	.545	.909	11	6	1	0	1	9.1	4	2	1	1	0	0	0	0	0	0	0	0.0	–	OF-3

LEAGUE CHAMPIONSHIP SERIES

Year	Team		Games	BA	SA	AB	H	2B	3B	HR	HR%	R	RBI	BB	SO	SB	PH AB	PH H	PO	A	E	DP	TC/G	FA	G by Pos
1981	OAK	A	3	.250	.375	8	2	1	0	0	0.0	1	1	2	3	0	0	0	0	0	0	0	0.0	–	OF-3

Year	Team		Games	BA	SA	AB	H	2B	3B	HR	HR%	R	RBI	BB	SO	SB	Pinch Hit AB	H	PO	A	E	DP	TC/G	FA	G by Pos

Ed Murphy
MURPHY, EDWARD JOSEPH
B. Aug. 23, 1918, Joliet, Ill.
BR TR 5'11" 190 lbs.

| 1942 | PHI | N | 13 | .250 | .321 | 28 | 7 | 2 | 0 | 0 | 0.0 | 2 | 4 | 2 | 4 | 0 | 5 | 1 | 69 | 3 | 0 | 7 | 5.5 | 1.000 | 1B-8 |

Eddie Murphy
MURPHY, JOHN EDWARD (Honest Eddie)
B. Oct. 2, 1891, Hancock, N. Y.   D. Feb. 21, 1969, Dunmore, Pa.
BL TR 5'9" 155 lbs.

1912	PHI	A	33	.317	.359	142	45	4	1	0	0.0	24	6	11		7	0	0	48	6	3	1	1.7	.947	OF-33
1913			136	.295	.356	508	150	14	7	1	0.2	105	30	70	44	21	1	0	166	14	11	2	1.4	.942	OF-135
1914			148	.272	.340	573	156	12	9	3	0.5	101	43	87	46	36	0	0	194	15	13	4	1.5	.941	OF-148
1915	2 teams																								
	PHI	A	(68G – .231)		CHI	A	(70G – .315)																		
"	total		138	.274	.334	533	146	14	9	0	0.0	88	43	68	27	33	4	0	177	30	16	0	1.6	.928	OF-128, 3B-6
1916	CHI	A	51	.210	.276	105	22	5	1	0	0.0	14	4	9	5	3	20	4	28	2	1	0	0.6	.968	OF-24, 3B-1
1917			53	.314	.392	51	16	2	1	0	0.0	9	16	5	1	4	32	12	2	0	0	0	1.000	OF-9
1918			91	.297	.350	286	85	9	3	0	0.0	36	23	22	18	6	18	4	124	18	7	2	1.6	.953	OF-63, 2B-8
1919			30	.486	.600	35	17	4	0	0	0.0	8	5	7	0	0	21	8	10	1	1	0	0.4	.917	OF-6
1920			58	.339	.373	118	40	2	1	0	0.0	22	19	12	4	1	33	13	27	13	5	2	0.8	.889	OF-19, 3B-3
1921			6	.200	.200	5	1	0	0	0	0.0	0	0	0	0	0	5	1	0	0	0	0	0.3	1.000	OF-3
1926	PIT	N	16	.118	.118	17	2	0	0	0	0.0	3	6	3	0	0	11	1	5	0	0	0	1.2	.939	OF-3
	11 yrs.		760	.287	.346	2373	680	66	32	4	0.2	411	195	294	145	111	145	43	781	99	57	11	1.2	.939	OF-568, 3B-10, 2B-8

WORLD SERIES

1913	PHI	A	5	.227	.227	22	5	0	0	0	0.0	2	2	0		0	0	0	15	0	0	0	3.0	1.000	OF-5
1914			4	.188	.313	16	3	2	0	0	0.0	2	2	2	2	0	0	0	4	0	0	0	1.0	1.000	OF-4
1919	CHI	A	3	.000	.000	2	0	0	0	0	0.0	0	0	0	1	0	2	0	0	0	0	0	0.0	–	OF-9
	3 yrs.		12	.200	.250	40	8	2	0	0	0.0	4	4	3		0	2	0	19	0	0	0	1.6	1.000	OF-9

Frank Murphy
MURPHY, FRANK MORTON
B. 1880, Hackensack, N. J.   D. Nov. 2, 1912, New York, N. Y.

1901	2 teams																								
	BOS	N	(45G – .261)		NY	N	(12G – .125)																		
"	total		57	.232	.295	224	52	5	3	1	0.4	17	20	7		7	0	0	114	11	8	1	2.3	.940	OF-57

Howard Murphy
MURPHY, HOWARD
B. Jan. 1, 1882, Birmingham, Ala.   D. Oct. 5, 1926, Fort Worth, Tex.
BL TR 5'8½" 150 lbs.

| 1909 | STL | N | 25 | .200 | .200 | 60 | 12 | 0 | 0 | 0 | 0.0 | 3 | 3 | 4 | | 1 | 5 | 1 | 35 | 2 | 3 | 0 | 1.6 | .925 | OF-19 |

Jerry Murphy
MURPHY, JEREMIAH FRANCIS
B. 1871, Pawtucket, R. I.   D. June 1, 1914, Baker, Ore.

| 1903 | DET | A | 5 | .182 | .227 | 22 | 4 | 1 | 0 | 0 | 0.0 | 1 | 1 | 0 | 0 | 0 | 0 | 0 | 7 | 16 | 4 | 1 | 5.4 | .852 | SS-5 |

John Murphy
MURPHY, JOHN PATRICK
B. 1879, New Haven, Conn.   Deceased.

| 1902 | STL | N | 1 | .667 | 1.000 | 3 | 2 | 1 | 0 | 0 | 0.0 | 1 | 1 | 1 | | 0 | 0 | 0 | 2 | 0 | 0 | 0 | 2.0 | 1.000 | 3B-1 |

Larry Murphy
MURPHY, LAWRENCE PATRICK
Deceased.
BL

| 1891 | WAS | AA | 101 | .265 | .325 | 400 | 106 | 15 | 3 | 1 | 0.3 | 73 | 35 | 63 | 27 | 29 | 0 | 0 | 164 | 10 | 25 | 3 | 2.0 | .874 | OF-101 |

Leo Murphy
MURPHY, LEO JOSEPH (Red)
B. Jan. 7, 1889, Terre Haute, Ind.   D. Aug. 12, 1960, Racine, Wis.
BR TR 6'1" 179 lbs.

| 1915 | PIT | N | 34 | .098 | .098 | 41 | 4 | 0 | 0 | 0 | 0.0 | 4 | 4 | 4 | 12 | 0 | 9 | 1 | 29 | 12 | 3 | 2 | 1.3 | .932 | C-34 |

Mike Murphy
MURPHY, MICHAEL JEROME
B. Aug. 19, 1888, Forestville, Pa.   D. Oct. 26, 1952, Johnson City, N. Y.
BR TR 5'9" 170 lbs.

1912	STL	N	1	.000	.000	1	0	0	0	0	0.0	0	1	0	0	0	0	0	0	0	0	0	0.0	–	C-1
1916	PHI	A	14	.111	.111	27	3	0	0	0	0.0	0	1	1	3	0	2	0	29	9	1	0	2.8	.974	C-12
	2 yrs.		15	.107	.107	28	3	0	0	0	0.0	0	2	1	3	0	2	0	29	9	1	0	2.6	.974	C-13

Morg Murphy
MURPHY, MORGAN EDWARD
B. Feb. 12, 1867, E. Providence, R. I.   D. Oct. 3, 1938, Providence, R. I.
BR TR 5'8" 160 lbs.

1890	BOS	P	68	.228	.309	246	56	10	2	2	0.8	38	32	24	31	16	0	0	257	62	34	8	5.2	.904	C-67, SS-2, OF-1, 3B-1
1891	BOS	AA	106	.216	.294	402	87	11	4	4	1.0	60	54	36	58	17	0	0	533	118	31	8	6.4	.955	C-104, OF-4
1892	CIN	N	74	.197	.274	234	46	8	2	2	0.9	29	24	25	57	4	0	0	315	67	18	6	5.4	.955	C-74
1893			57	.235	.285	200	47	5	1	0	0.0	25	19	14	35	1	0	0	169	47	15	6	4.1	.935	C-56, 1B-1
1894			75	.275	.322	255	70	9	0	1	0.4	42	37	26	34	6	0	0	196	76	30	5	4.0	.901	C-74, SS-1, 3B-1
1895			25	.268	.293	82	22	2	0	0	0.0	15	16	11	8	6	0	0	70	18	9	1	3.9	.907	C-25
1896	STL	N	49	.257	.309	175	45	5	2	0	0.0	12	11	8	14	1	1	0	178	48	18	5	5.0	.926	C-48
1897			62	.169	.179	207	35	2	0	0	0.0	13	12	6		1	0	0	191	66	11	6	4.3	.959	C-53, 1B-8
1898	2 teams																								
	PIT	N	(5G – .125)		PHI	N	(25G – .198)																		
"	total		30	.186	.216	102	19	3	0	0	0.0	6	13	7		0	0	0	91	38	5	3	4.5	.963	C-30
1900	PHI	N	11	.278	.333	36	10	0	1	0	0.0	2	3	0		0	0	0	33	15	1	1	4.5	.980	C-11
1901	PHI	A	9	.214	.250	28	6	1	0	0	0.0	5	6	5		1	0	0	39	7	5	1	5.7	.902	C-8, 1B-1
	11 yrs.		566	.225	.281	1967	443	56	12	10	0.5	247	227	157	237	53	1	0	2072	562	177	50	5.0	.937	C-550, 1B-10, OF-5, SS-3, 3B-2

Pat Murphy
MURPHY, PATRICK J.
B. Jan. 2, 1857, Auburn, Mass.   D. May 16, 1927, Worcester, Mass.
5'10" 160 lbs.

1887	NY	N	17	.214	.250	56	12	2	0	0	0.0	4	4	2		4	1	0	79	26	19	3	7.3	.847	C-17
1888			28	.170	.179	106	18	1	0	0	0.0	11	4	6	11	3	0	0	186	56	23	3	9.5	.913	C-28
1889			9	.357	.571	28	10	1	1	1	3.6	5	4	2		0	0	0	26	8	5	0	4.3	.872	C-9

Year	Team		Games	BA	SA	AB	H	2B	3B	HR	HR%	R	RBI	BB	SO	SB	Pinch Hit AB	Pinch Hit H	PO	A	E	DP	TC/G	FA	G by Pos

Pat Murphy *continued*

Year	Team		Games	BA	SA	AB	H	2B	3B	HR	HR%	R	RBI	BB	SO	SB	AB	H	PO	A	E	DP	TC/G	FA	G by Pos
1890			32	.235	.294	119	28	5	1	0	0.0	14	9	14	13	3	0	0	157	33	22	2	6.6	.896	C-29, OF-3, SS-1
4 yrs.			86	.220	.272	309	68	9	2	1	0.3	34	21	24	28	7	0	0	448	123	69	8	7.4	.892	C-83, OF-3, SS-1

Tony Murphy

MURPHY, FRANK J.
B. Brooklyn, N. Y. Deceased.

| 1884 | NY | AA | 1 | .333 | .333 | 3 | 1 | 0 | 0 | 0 | 0.0 | 1 | | 0 | | | 0 | 0 | 3 | 0 | 0 | 0 | 3.0 | 1.000 | C-1 |

Willie Murphy

MURPHY, WILLIAM N. (Gentle Willie)   5'11"   198 lbs.
B. 1865, Boston, Mass. Deceased.

| 1884 | 3 teams | | CLE N | (42G – .226) | | WAS AA | (5G – .476) | | | BOS U | (1G – .000) | | | | | | | | | | | | | | |
| " | total | | 48 | .250 | .313 | 192 | 48 | 3 | 3 | 1 | 0.5 | 21 | 9 | 3 | 23 | | 0 | 0 | 70 | 14 | 33 | 0 | 2.4 | .718 | OF-47, 3B-1, C-1 |

Yale Murphy

MURPHY, WILLIAM HENRY (Tot Midget)   BL TR 5'3"   125 lbs.
B. Nov. 11, 1869, Southville, Mass. D. Feb. 14, 1906, Southville, Mass.

1894	NY	N	74	.271	.307	280	76	6	2	0	0.0	64	28	51	23	28	0	0	150	157	35	15	4.6	.898	SS-49, OF-20, 3B-3, 2B-1, 1B-1
1895			51	.201	.255	184	37	6	2	0	0.0	35	16	27	13	7	0	0	82	39	18	4	2.7	.871	OF-33, SS-8, 3B-8, 2B-1
1897			5	.000	.000	8	0	0	0	0	0.0	1	1	2		0	0	0	3	3	1	0	1.4	.857	SS-3, 2B-2
3 yrs.			130	.239	.282	472	113	12	4	0	0.0	100	45	80	36	35	0	0	235	199	54	19	3.8	.889	SS-60, OF-53, 3B-11, 2B-4, 1B-1

Bill Murray

MURRAY, WILLIAM ALLENWOOD (Dasher)   BB TR 5'11"   165 lbs.
B. Sept. 6, 1893, Vinalhaven, Me. D. Sept. 14, 1943, Boston, Mass.

| 1917 | WAS | A | 8 | .143 | .238 | 21 | 3 | 0 | 1 | 0 | 0.0 | 2 | 4 | 2 | 2 | 1 | 0 | 0 | 11 | 14 | 3 | 2 | 3.5 | .893 | 2B-6, SS-1 |

Bobby Murray

MURRAY, ROBERT HAYES   BL TR 5'7"   155 lbs.
B. July 4, 1898, St. Albans, Vt. D. Jan. 4, 1979, Nashua, N. H.

| 1923 | WAS | A | 10 | .179 | .205 | 39 | 7 | 1 | 0 | 0 | 0.0 | 2 | 1 | 2 | 4 | 1 | 0 | 0 | 11 | 26 | 0 | 0 | 3.7 | 1.000 | 3B-10 |

Ed Murray

MURRAY, EDWARD FRANCIS   BR TR 5'6"   145 lbs.
B. May 8, 1895, Mystic, Conn. D. Nov. 8, 1970, Cheyenne, Wyo.

| 1917 | STL | A | 1 | .000 | .000 | 1 | 0 | 0 | 0 | 0 | 0.0 | 0 | 0 | 0 | 1 | 0 | 0 | 0 | 0 | 0 | 0 | 0 | 0.0 | – | SS-1 |

Eddie Murray

MURRAY, EDDIE CLARENCE   BB TR 6'2"   190 lbs.
Brother of Rich Murray.
B. Feb. 24, 1956, Los Angeles, Calif.

1977	BAL	A	160	.283	.470	611	173	29	2	27	4.4	81	88	48	104	0	4	0	375	17	3	34	2.5	.992	DH-111, 1B-42, OF-3
1978			161	.285	.480	610	174	32	3	27	4.4	85	95	70	97	6	0	0	1507	112	6	144	10.1	.996	1B-157, 3B-3, DH-1
1979			159	.295	.475	606	179	30	2	25	4.1	90	99	72	78	10	0	0	1456	107	10	135	9.9	.994	1B-157, DH-2
1980			158	.300	.519	621	186	36	2	32	5.2	100	116	54	71	7	3	1	1369	77	9	158	9.2	.994	1B-154, DH-1
1981			99	.294	.534	378	111	21	2	22	5.8	57	78	40	43	2	0	0	899	91	1	98	10.0	.999	1B-99
1982			151	.316	.549	550	174	30	1	32	5.8	87	110	70	82	7	0	0	1269	97	4	106	9.1	.997	1B-149, DH-2
1983			156	.306	.538	582	178	30	3	33	5.7	115	111	86	90	5	2	0	1393	114	10	136	9.7	.993	1B-153, DH-2
1984			162	.306	.509	588	180	26	3	29	4.9	97	110	107	87	10	0	0	1538	143	13	152	10.5	.992	1B-159, DH-3
1985			156	.297	.523	583	173	37	1	31	5.3	111	124	84	68	5	0	0	1338	152	19	154	9.7	.987	1B-154, DH-2
1986			137	.305	.463	495	151	25	1	17	3.4	61	84	78	49	3	2	0	1045	88	13	100	8.4	.989	1B-119, DH-16
1987			160	.277	.477	618	171	28	3	30	4.9	89	91	73	80	1	0	0	1371	145	10	146	9.5	.993	1B-156, DH-4
1988			161	.284	.474	603	171	27	2	28	4.6	75	84	75	78	5	0	0	867	106	11	101	6.1	.989	1B-103, DH-58
1989	LA	N	160	.247	.401	594	147	29	1	20	3.4	66	88	87	85	7	1	1	1316	137	6	122	9.1	.996	1B-159, 3B-2
13 yrs.			1980	.291	.492	7439	2168	380	26	353	4.7	1114	1278	944	1012	68	12	2	15743	1386	115	1586	8.7	.993	1B-1761, DH-202, 3B-5, OF-3

LEAGUE CHAMPIONSHIP SERIES

1979	BAL	A	4	.417	.667	12	5	0	0	1	8.3	3	5	5	2	0	0	0	44	3	2	4	12.3	.959	1B-4
1983			4	.267	.467	15	4	0	0	1	6.7	5	3	3	3	1	0	0	36	2	1	2	9.8	.974	1B-4
2 yrs.			8	.333	.556	27	9	0	0	2	7.4	8	8	8	5	1	0	0	80	5	3	6	11.0	.966	1B-8

WORLD SERIES

1979	BAL	A	7	.154	.308	26	4	1	0	1	3.8	3	2	4	4	1	0	0	60	7	0	5	9.6	1.000	1B-7
1983			5	.250	.550	20	5	0	0	2	10.0	2	3	1	4	0	0	0	46	1	1	5	9.6	.979	1B-5
2 yrs.			12	.196	.413	46	9	1	0	3	6.5	5	5	5	8	1	0	0	106	8	1	10	9.6	.991	1B-12

Jim Murray

MURRAY, JAMES OSCAR   BR TL 5'10"   180 lbs.
B. Jan. 16, 1878, Galveston, Tex. D. Apr. 25, 1945, Galveston, Tex.

1902	CHI	N	12	.170	.170	47	8	0	0	0	0.0	3	1	2		0	0	0	17	1	0	0	1.5	1.000	OF-12
1911	STL	A	31	.186	.324	102	19	5	0	3	2.9	8	11	5		0	6	1	39	4	3	1	1.5	.935	OF-25
1914	BOS	N	39	.232	.304	112	26	4	2	0	0.0	10	12	6	24	2	6	2	31	1	2	0	0.9	.941	OF-32
3 yrs.			82	.203	.287	261	53	9	2	3	1.1	21	24	13	24	2	12	3	87	6	5	1	1.2	.949	OF-69

Larry Murray

MURRAY, LARRY   BB TR 5'11"   179 lbs.
B. Mar. 1, 1953, Chicago, Ill.

1974	NY	A	6	.000	.000	1	0	0	0	0	0.0	1	0	0	0	0	0	0	0	0	0	0	0.0	–	OF-3
1975			6	.000	.000	1	0	0	0	0	0.0	1	0	0	0	0	0	0	1	0	0	0	0.2	1.000	OF-4
1976			8	.100	.100	10	1	0	0	0	0.0	2	2	1	2	2	0	0	9	1	0	0	1.3	1.000	OF-7
1977	OAK	A	90	.179	.253	162	29	5	2	1	0.6	19	9	17	36	12	3	1	114	3	1	3	1.3	.992	OF-78, DH-3, SS-1
1978			11	.083	.083	12	1	0	0	0	0.0	1	0	3	2	0	2	0	6	0	0	0	0.5	1.000	OF-6
1979			105	.186	.279	226	42	11	2	2	0.9	25	20	28	34	6	1	0	174	8	7	2	1.8	.963	OF-90, 2B-3
6 yrs.			226	.177	.257	412	73	16	4	3	0.7	49	31	49	74	20	6	1	304	12	8	5	1.4	.975	OF-188, DH-3, 2B-3, SS-1

Year	Team	Games	BA	SA	AB	H	2B	3B	HR	HR%	R	RBI	BB	SO	SB	Pinch Hit AB	H	PO	A	E	DP	TC/G	FA	G by Pos

Miah Murray

MURRAY, JEREMIAH J.
B. Jan. 1, 1865, Boston, Mass.   D. Jan. 11, 1922, Boston, Mass.
BR TR 5'11½" 170 lbs.

Year	Team	Games	BA	SA	AB	H	2B	3B	HR	HR%	R	RBI	BB	SO	SB	AB	H	PO	A	E	DP	TC/G	FA	G by Pos
1884	PRO N	8	.185	.185	27	5	0	0	0	0.0	1		1	8		0	0	44	4	11	0	7.4	.814	C-7, OF-1, 1B-1
1885	LOU AA	12	.186	.186	43	8	0	0	0	0.0	4	2				0	0	72	19	14	1	8.8	.867	C-12, 1B-2
1888	WAS N	12	.095	.119	42	4	1	0	0	0.0	1	3	1	7		0	0	58	14	8	3	6.7	.900	C-10, 1B-2
1891	WAS AA	2	.000	.000	8	0	0	0	0	0.0	0		0	1		0	0	22	2	0	0	12.0	1.000	C-2
4 yrs.		34	.142	.150	120	17	1	0	0	0.0	6	3	4	16	0	0	0	196	39	33	4	7.9	.877	C-31, 1B-5, OF-1

Ray Murray

MURRAY, RAYMOND LEE (Deacon)
B. Oct. 12, 1917, Spring Hope, N. C.
BR TR 6'3" 204 lbs.

Year	Team	Games	BA	SA	AB	H	2B	3B	HR	HR%	R	RBI	BB	SO	SB	AB	H	PO	A	E	DP	TC/G	FA	G by Pos
1948	CLE A	4	.000	.000	4	0	0	0	0	0.0	0	0	0	3	0	4	0	0	0	0	0	0.0	—	
1950		55	.273	.381	139	38	8	2	1	0.7	16	13	12	13	1	8	2	156	15	5	2	3.2	.972	C-45
1951	2 teams	CLE A (1G – 1.000)			PHI A (40G – .213)																			
"	total	41	.220	.268	123	27	6	0	0	0.0	10	14	14	8	0	1	0	111	25	2	5	3.4	.986	C-40
1952	PHI A	44	.206	.265	136	28	5	0	1	0.7	14	10	9	13	0	2	1	175	35	1	3	4.8	.995	C-42
1953		84	.284	.425	268	76	14	3	6	2.2	25	41	18	25	0	6	2	330	45	4	8	4.5	.989	C-78
1954	BAL A	22	.246	.344	61	15	4	1	0	0.0	4	2	2	5	0	0	0	83	9	1	3	4.2	.989	C-21
6 yrs.		250	.252	.352	731	184	37	6	8	1.1	69	80	55	67	1	21	5	855	129	13	21	4.0	.987	C-226

Red Murray

MURRAY, JOHN JOSEPH
B. Mar. 4, 1884, Arnot, Pa.   D. Dec. 4, 1958, Sayre, Pa.
BR TR 5'10½" 190 lbs.

Year	Team	Games	BA	SA	AB	H	2B	3B	HR	HR%	R	RBI	BB	SO	SB	AB	H	PO	A	E	DP	TC/G	FA	G by Pos
1906	STL N	46	.257	.438	144	37	9	7	1	0.7	18	16	9		5	5	0	73	17	5	2	2.1	.947	OF-34, C-7
1907		132	.262	.367	485	127	10	10	7	1.4	46	46	24		23	1	1	232	25	18	4	2.1	.935	OF-131
1908		154	.282	.400	593	167	19	15	7	1.2	64	62	37		48	0	0	274	22	28	4	2.1	.914	OF-154
1909	NY N	149	.263	.368	570	150	15	12	7	1.2	74	91	44		48	0	0	222	30	14	1	1.8	.947	OF-148
1910		149	.277	.376	553	153	27	8	4	0.7	78	87	52	51	57	1	1	246	26	15	3	1.9	.948	OF-148
1911		140	.291	.426	488	142	27	15	3	0.6	70	78	43	37	48	6	1	196	12	10	1	1.6	.954	OF-131
1912		143	.277	.413	549	152	26	20	3	0.5	83	92	27	45	38	0	0	255	20	9	7	2.0	.968	OF-143
1913		147	.267	.331	520	139	21	3	2	0.4	70	59	34	28	35	0	0	279	24	11	3	2.1	.965	OF-147
1914		86	.223	.309	139	31	6	3	0	0.0	19	23	9	7	11	26	4	56	2	0	0	0.7	1.000	OF-49
1915	2 teams	NY N (45G – .220)			CHI N (51G – .299)																			
"	total	96	.262	.343	271	71	7	3	3	1.1	32	22	15	23	8	17	8	148	12	6	2	1.7	.964	OF-73, 2B-1
1917	NY N	22	.045	.091	22	1	1	0	0	0.0	1	3	4	3	0	8	0	13	0	0	0	0.6	1.000	OF-11, C-1
11 yrs.		1264	.270	.379	4334	1170	168	96	37	0.9	555	579	298	194	321	64	15	1994	190	116	27	1.8	.950	OF-1169, C-8, 2B-1

WORLD SERIES

Year	Team	Games	BA	SA	AB	H	2B	3B	HR	HR%	R	RBI	BB	SO	SB	AB	H	PO	A	E	DP	TC/G	FA	G by Pos
1911	NY N	6	.000	.000	21	0	0	0	0	0.0	0	0	2	5	0	0	0	4	1	3	0	1.3	.625	OF-6
1912		8	.323	.516	31	10	4	1	0	0.0	5	5	2	2	0	0	0	23	1	0	0	3.0	1.000	OF-8
1913		5	.250	.250	16	4	0	0	0	0.0	2	1	2	2	2	0	0	9	0	0	0	1.8	1.000	OF-5
3 yrs.		19	.206	.294	68	14	4	1	0	0.0	7	6	6	9	2	0	0	36	2	3	0	2.2	.927	OF-19

Rich Murray

MURRAY, RICHARD DALE
Brother of Eddie Murray.
B. July 6, 1957, Los Angeles, Calif.
BR TR 6'4" 195 lbs.

Year	Team	Games	BA	SA	AB	H	2B	3B	HR	HR%	R	RBI	BB	SO	SB	AB	H	PO	A	E	DP	TC/G	FA	G by Pos
1980	SF N	53	.216	.340	194	42	8	2	4	2.1	19	24	11	48	2	0	0	508	35	7	32	10.4	.987	1B-53
1983		4	.200	.200	10	2	0	0	0	0.0	0	1	0	3	0	1	0	20	1	0	1	5.3	1.000	1B-3
2 yrs.		57	.216	.333	204	44	8	2	4	2.0	19	25	11	51	2	1	0	528	36	7	33	10.0	.988	1B-56

Tom Murray

MURRAY, THOMAS W.
B. 1866, Savannah, Ga.   Deceased.

Year	Team	Games	BA	SA	AB	H	2B	3B	HR	HR%	R	RBI	BB	SO	SB	AB	H	PO	A	E	DP	TC/G	FA	G by Pos
1894	PHI N	1	.000	.000	2	0	0	0	0	0.0	0	0	0	2	0	0	0	4	1	1	0	6.0	.833	SS-1

Tony Murray

MURRAY, ANTHONY JOSEPH
B. Apr. 30, 1904, Chicago, Ill.   D. Mar. 19, 1974, Chicago, Ill.
BR TR 5'10½" 154 lbs.

Year	Team	Games	BA	SA	AB	H	2B	3B	HR	HR%	R	RBI	BB	SO	SB	AB	H	PO	A	E	DP	TC/G	FA	G by Pos
1923	CHI N	2	.250	.250	4	1	0	0	0	0.0	0	0	0	0	0	0	0	2	0	0	0	1.0	1.000	OF-2

Ivan Murrell

MURRELL, IVAN AUGUSTUS
Born Ivan Augustus Murrell y Peters.
B. Apr. 24, 1945, Almirante, Panama
BR TR 6'2" 195 lbs.

Year	Team	Games	BA	SA	AB	H	2B	3B	HR	HR%	R	RBI	BB	SO	SB	AB	H	PO	A	E	DP	TC/G	FA	G by Pos
1963	HOU N	2	.200	.200	5	1	0	0	0	0.0	1	0	0	2	0	0	0	3	0	0	0	1.5	1.000	OF-2
1964		10	.143	.214	14	2	1	0	0	0.0	1	1	0	6	0	3	0	2	0	0	0	0.2	1.000	OF-5
1967		10	.310	.310	29	9	0	0	0	0.0	2	1	1	9	1	4	0	11	0	2	0	1.3	.846	OF-6
1968		32	.102	.153	59	6	1	1	0	0.0	3	3	1	17	0	12	2	24	3	2	2	0.9	.931	OF-15
1969	SD N	111	.255	.381	247	63	10	6	3	1.2	19	25	11	65	3	36	5	152	4	6	3	1.5	.963	OF-72, 1B-2
1970		125	.245	.392	347	85	9	3	12	3.5	43	35	17	93	9	24	4	184	8	6	3	1.6	.970	OF-101, 1B-1
1971		103	.235	.365	255	60	6	3	7	2.7	23	24	7	60	5	33	3	133	2	3	0	1.3	.978	OF-72
1972		5	.143	.143	7	1	0	0	0	0.0	0	1	0	3	0	3	0	2	0	0	0	0.4	1.000	OF-1
1973		93	.229	.429	210	48	13	1	9	4.3	23	21	2	52	2	35	2	249	16	5	14	2.9	.981	OF-32, 1B-24
1974	ATL N	73	.248	.316	133	33	1	1	2	1.5	11	12	5	35	0	30	5	161	9	1	11	2.3	.994	OF-32, 1B-13
10 yrs.		564	.236	.366	1306	308	41	15	33	2.5	126	123	44	342	20	180	21	921	42	25	33	1.8	.975	OF-343, 1B-40

Danny Murtaugh

MURTAUGH, DANIEL EDWARD
B. Oct. 8, 1917, Chester, Pa.   D. Dec. 2, 1976, Chester, Pa.
Manager 1957-64, 1967, 1970-71, 1973-76.
BR TR 5'9" 165 lbs.

Year	Team	Games	BA	SA	AB	H	2B	3B	HR	HR%	R	RBI	BB	SO	SB	AB	H	PO	A	E	DP	TC/G	FA	G by Pos
1941	PHI N	85	.219	.248	347	76	8	1	0	0.0	34	11	26	31	18	0	0	234	247	11	49	5.8	.978	2B-85, SS-1
1942		144	.241	.289	506	122	16	4	0	0.0	48	27	49	39	13	2	0	302	377	43	61	5.0	.941	SS-60, 3B-53, 2B-32
1943		113	.273	.335	451	123	17	4	1	0.2	65	35	57	23	4	0	0	321	345	18	76	6.1	.974	2B-113
1946		6	.211	.421	19	4	1	0	1	5.3	1	3	2	2	0	0	0	13	10	1	0	4.0	.958	2B-6
1947	BOS N	3	.125	.125	8	1	0	0	0	0.0	0	0	0	1	0	0	0	7	6	0	1	4.3	1.000	2B-2
1948	PIT N	146	.290	.356	514	149	21	5	1	0.2	56	71	60	40	10	0	0	375	412	17	95	5.5	.979	2B-146
1949		75	.203	.275	236	48	7	2	2	0.8	16	24	29	17	2	1	1	202	182	10	58	5.3	.975	2B-74
1950		118	.294	.392	367	108	20	5	2	0.5	34	37	47	42	2	9	4	273	292	14	84	4.9	.976	2B-108

Year	Team	Games	BA	SA	AB	H	2B	3B	HR	HR%	R	RBI	BB	SO	SB	Pinch Hit AB	Pinch Hit H	PO	A	E	DP	TC/G	FA	G by Pos

Danny Murtaugh *continued*

| 1951 | | 77 | .199 | .265 | 151 | 30 | 7 | 0 | 1 | 0.7 | 9 | 11 | 16 | 19 | 0 | 13 | 3 | 110 | 117 | 8 | 35 | 3.1 | .966 | 2B-65, 3B-3 |
| 9 yrs. | | 767 | .254 | .317 | 2599 | 661 | 97 | 21 | 8 | 0.3 | 263 | 219 | 287 | 215 | 49 | 25 | 8 | 1837 | 1988 | 122 | 459 | 5.1 | .969 | 2B-631, SS-61, 3B-56 |

Tony Muser

MUSER, ANTHONY JOSEPH   BL TL 6'2" 180 lbs.
B. Aug. 1, 1947, Van Nuys, Calif.

1969	BOS A	2	.111	.111	9	1	0	0	0	0.0	0	1	1	1	0	0	0	17	3	0	3	10.0	1.000	1B-2
1971	CHI A	11	.313	.438	16	5	0	1	0	0.0	2	0	1	1	0	7	2	23	3	1	1	2.5	.963	1B-4
1972		44	.279	.426	61	17	2	2	1	1.6	6	9	2	6	1	12	4	135	7	2	12	3.3	.986	1B-29, OF-1
1973		109	.285	.388	309	88	14	3	4	1.3	38	30	33	36	8	9	4	681	38	6	70	6.7	.992	1B-89, OF-2
1974		103	.291	.340	206	60	5	1	1	0.5	16	18	6	22	1	13	3	419	13	1	46	4.2	.998	1B-80, DH-13
1975	2 teams		CHI A	(43G – .243)		BAL A	(80G – .317)																	
"	total	123	.275	.306	193	53	6	0	0	0.0	22	17	15	17	2	18	6	476	37	3	58	4.2	.994	1B-103
1976	BAL A	136	.227	.264	326	74	7	1	1	0.3	25	30	21	34	1	16	4	693	63	7	65	5.6	.991	1B-109, OF-12, DH-10
1977		120	.229	.280	118	27	6	0	0	0.0	14	7	13	16	1	31	6	232	20	3	36	2.1	.988	1B-77, OF-11, DH-1
1978	MIL A	15	.133	.233	30	4	1	1	0	0.0	0	5	3	5	0	3	0	79	5	1	4	5.7	.988	1B-12
9 yrs.		663	.259	.323	1268	329	41	9	7	0.6	123	117	95	138	14	109	29	2755	189	24	295	4.5	.992	1B-505, OF-26, DH-24

Stan Musial

MUSIAL, STANLEY FRANK (Stan the Man)   BL TL 6' 175 lbs.
B. Nov. 21, 1920, Donora, Pa.
Hall of Fame 1969.

1941	STL N	12	.426	.574	47	20	4	0	1	2.1	8	7	2	1	1	1	0	20	1	0	0	1.8	1.000	OF-11
1942		140	.315	.490	467	147	32	10	10	2.1	87	72	62	25	6	2	0	296	6	5	0	2.2	.984	OF-135
1943		157	**.357**	**.562**	617	**220**	48	**20**	13	2.1	108	81	72	18	9	2	1	376	15	7	4	2.5	.982	OF-155
1944		146	.347	**.549**	568	**197**	51	14	12	2.1	112	94	90	28	7	0	0	353	16	5	2	2.6	.987	OF-146
1946		156	**.365**	~	**.587**	624	228	50	20	16	2.6	**124**	103	73	31	7	0	0	1166	69	15	119	8.0	.988	1B-114, OF-42
1947		149	.312	.504	587	183	30	13	19	3.2	113	95	80	24	4	0	0	1360	77	8	138	9.7	.994	1B-149
1948		155	**.376**	**.702**	611	**230**	46	18	39	6.4	135	131	79	34	7	0	0	354	11	7	3	2.4	.981	OF-155, 1B-2
1949		157	.338	.624	612	**207**	41	13	36	5.9	128	123	107	38	3	0	0	337	11	3	5	2.2	.991	OF-156, 1B-1
1950		146	.346	.596	555	192	41	7	28	5.0	105	109	87	36	5	1	0	760	39	8	67	5.5	.990	OF-77, 1B-69
1951		152	.355	.614	578	205	30	**12**	32	5.5	**124**	108	98	40	4	1	1	816	45	10	64	5.7	.989	OF-91, 1B-60
1952		154	**.336**	.538	578	**194**	42	6	21	3.6	105	91	96	29	7	0	0	502	18	5	15	3.4	.990	OF-135, 1B-25, P-1
1953		157	.337	.609	593	200	**53**	9	30	5.1	127	113	**105**	32	3	0	0	294	9	5	1	2.0	.984	OF-157
1954		153	.330	.607	591	195	**41**	9	35	5.9	120	126	103	39	1	0	0	307	15	5	8	2.1	.985	OF-152, 1B-10
1955		154	.319	.566	562	179	30	5	33	5.9	97	108	80	39	5	0	0	1000	94	9	93	7.2	.992	1B-110, OF-51
1956		156	.310	.522	594	184	33	6	27	4.5	87	**109**	75	39	2	0	0	954	95	8	96	6.8	.992	1B-103, OF-53
1957		134	**.351**	.612	502	176	38	3	29	5.8	82	102	66	34	1	4	2	1167	99	10	131	9.5	.994	1B-130
1958		135	.337	.528	472	159	35	2	17	3.6	64	62	72	26	0	12	5	1019	100	13	127	8.4	.989	1B-124
1959		115	.255	.428	341	87	13	2	14	4.1	37	44	60	25	0	22	5	624	63	7	72	6.0	.990	1B-90, OF-3
1960		116	.275	.486	331	91	17	1	17	5.1	49	63	41	34	1	28	4	300	19	3	16	2.8	.991	OF-59, 1B-29
1961		123	.288	.489	372	107	22	4	15	4.0	46	70	52	35	0	19	5	149	9	1	0	1.3	.994	OF-103
1962		135	.330	.508	433	143	18	1	19	4.4	57	82	64	46	3	13	8	164	6	4	1	1.3	.977	OF-119
1963		124	.255	.404	337	86	10	2	12	3.6	34	58	35	43	2	21	4	121	1	4	0	1.0	.968	OF-96
22 yrs.		3026	.331	.559	10972	3630	725	177	475	4.3	1949	1951	1599	696	78	126	35	12439	818	142	962	4.4	.989	OF-1896, 1B-1016, P-1
			5th		9th	5th	4th	3rd			6th	5th	9th											

WORLD SERIES

1942	STL N	5	.222	.278	18	4	1	0	0	0.0	2	2	4	0	0	0	0	13	0	0	0	2.6	1.000	OF-5
1943		5	.278	.278	18	5	0	0	0	0.0	2	0	2	2	0	0	0	7	2	0	0	1.8	1.000	OF-5
1944		6	.304	.522	23	7	2	0	1	4.3	2	2	2	0	0	0	0	11	0	1	0	2.0	.917	OF-6
1946		7	.222	.444	27	6	4	1	0	0.0	3	4	4	2	1	0	0	60	2	0	6	8.9	1.000	1B-7
4 yrs.		23	.256	.395	86	22	7	1	1	1.2	9	8	12	4	1	0	0	91	4	1	6	4.2	.990	OF-16, 1B-7
							9th																	

Danny Musser

MUSSER, WILLIAM DANIEL   BL TR 5'9½" 160 lbs.
B. Sept. 5, 1905, Zion, Pa.

| 1932 | WAS A | 1 | .500 | .500 | 2 | 1 | 0 | 0 | 0 | 0.0 | 0 | 0 | 0 | 0 | 0 | 0 | 0 | 0 | 0 | 0 | 0 | 0.0 | – | 3B-1 |

George Myatt

MYATT, GEORGE EDWARD (Mercury, Stud, Foghorn)   BL TR 5'11" 167 lbs.
B. June 14, 1914, Denver, Colo.
Manager 1968-69.

1938	NY N	43	.306	.382	170	52	1	3	3	1.8	27	10	14	13	10	0	0	77	128	17	24	5.2	.923	SS-24, 3B-19
1939		22	.189	.226	53	10	2	0	0	0.0	7	3	6	6	2	5	0	10	29	4	3	2.0	.907	3B-14
1943	WAS A	42	.245	.302	53	13	3	0	0	0.0	11	3	13	7	3	12	1	27	35	5	4	1.6	.925	2B-11, SS-2, 3B-2
1944		140	.284	.342	538	153	19	6	0	0.0	86	40	54	44	26	0	0	384	339	41	90	5.5	.946	2B-121, SS-15, OF-3
1945		133	.296	.365	490	145	17	7	1	0.2	81	39	63	43	30	1	0	293	255	18	50	4.3	.968	2B-94, OF-32, 3B-6, SS-1
1946		15	.235	.265	34	8	1	0	0	0.0	7	4	2	3	1	4	1	10	12	2	1	1.6	.917	3B-7, 2B-2
1947		12	.000	.000	7	0	0	0	0	0.0	1	0	4	4	0	6	0	0	1	0	0	0.1	1.000	2B-1
7 yrs.		407	.283	.346	1345	381	44	14	4	0.3	220	99	156	120	72	28	2	801	799	87	172	4.1	.948	2B-229, 3B-48, SS-42, OF-35

Glenn Myatt

MYATT, GLENN CALVIN   BL TR 5'11" 165 lbs.
B. July 9, 1897, Argenta, Ark.   D. Aug. 9, 1969, Houston, Tex.

1920	PHI A	70	.250	.321	196	49	8	3	0	0.0	14	18	12	22	1	8	1	83	22	10	3	1.6	.913	OF-37, C-21
1921		44	.203	.232	69	14	2	0	0	0.0	6	5	6	7	1	7	1	59	18	5	2	1.9	.939	C-27
1923	CLE A	92	.286	.414	220	63	7	6	3	1.4	36	40	16	18	0	18	6	188	37	16	3	2.6	.934	C-69
1924		105	.342	.518	342	117	22	7	8	2.3	55	73	33	12	6	9	2	248	63	7	7	3.0	.978	C-95
1925		106	.271	.455	358	97	15	9	11	3.1	51	54	29	24	2	5	1	273	53	9	2	3.2	.973	C-98, OF-1
1926		56	.248	.325	117	29	5	2	0	0.0	14	13	13	13	1	18	3	94	18	0	0	2.0	1.000	C-35
1927		55	.245	.372	94	23	6	0	2	2.1	15	8	12	7	1	25	5	67	20	2	4	1.7	.978	C-26
1928		58	.288	.400	125	36	7	2	1	0.8	9	15	13	13	0	26	8	72	15	3	2	1.6	.967	C-30
1929		59	.233	.302	129	30	4	1	1	0.8	14	17	7	5	0	14	1	99	24	3	3	2.1	.976	C-41

Year	Team	Games	BA	SA	AB	H	2B	3B	HR	HR%	R	RBI	BB	SO	SB	Pinch Hit AB	Pinch Hit H	PO	A	E	DP	TC/G	FA	G by Pos

Glenn Myatt *continued*

Year	Team	Games	BA	SA	AB	H	2B	3B	HR	HR%	R	RBI	BB	SO	SB	AB	H	PO	A	E	DP	TC/G	FA	G by Pos
1930		86	.294	.419	265	78	23	2	2	0.8	30	37	18	17	2	13	3	214	43	6	8	3.1	.977	C-71
1931		65	.246	.354	195	48	14	2	1	0.5	21	29	21	13	2	9	3	176	34	2	2	3.3	.991	C-58
1932		82	.246	.397	252	62	12	1	8	3.2	45	46	28	21	2	16	3	211	32	3	3	3.0	.988	C-65
1933		40	.234	.286	77	18	4	0	0	0.0	10	7	15	8	0	12	3	65	17	3	2	2.1	.965	C-27
1934		36	.318	.393	107	34	6	1	0	0.0	18	12	13	5	1	0	0	132	14	3	3	4.1	.980	C-34
1935	2 teams	CLE A			(10G – .083)			NY N	(13G – .222)																
"	total	23	.130	.241	54	7	1	1	1	1.9	3	8	4	6	0	9	1	48	4	0	0	2.3	1.000	C-14
1936	DET A	27	.218	.231	78	17	1	0	0	0.0	5	5	9	4	0	1	1	79	12	0	1	3.4	1.000	C-27
16 yrs.		1004	.270	.391	2678	722	137	37	38	1.4	346	387	249	195	18	190	42	2108	426	72	45	2.6	.972	C-738, OF-38

Buddy Myer

MYER, CHARLES SOLOMON
B. Mar. 16, 1904, Ellisville, Miss. D. Oct. 31, 1974, Baton Rouge, La.

BL TR 5'10½" 163 lbs.

Year	Team	Games	BA	SA	AB	H	2B	3B	HR	HR%	R	RBI	BB	SO	SB	AB	H	PO	A	E	DP	TC/G	FA	G by Pos
1925	WAS A	4	.250	.250	8	2	0	0	0	0.0	1	0	1	0	0			1	3	0	0	1.0	1.000	SS-4
1926		132	.304	.380	434	132	18	6	1	0.2	66	62	45	19	10	3	2	226	304	42	47	4.3	.927	SS-117, 3B-8
1927	2 teams	WAS A			(15G – .216)			BOS A	(133G – .288)																
"	total	148	.281	.379	520	146	23	11	2	0.4	66	54	56	18	12	8	1	305	384	44	78	5.0	.940	SS-116, 3B-14, OF-10, 2B-1
1928	BOS A	147	.313	.390	536	168	26	6	1	0.2	78	44	53	28	**30**	1	1	137	306	14	35	3.1	.969	3B-144
1929	WAS A	141	.300	.403	563	169	29	10	3	0.5	80	82	63	33	18	1	1	274	363	32	64	4.7	.952	2B-88, 3B-53
1930		138	.303	.377	541	164	18	8	2	0.4	97	61	58	31	14	0	0	330	405	27	89	5.5	.965	2B-134, OF-2
1931		139	.293	.406	591	173	33	11	4	0.7	114	56	58	42	11	0	0	333	398	12	87	5.3	.984	2B-137
1932		143	.279	.426	577	161	38	16	5	0.9	120	52	69	33	12	3	1	352	426	20	97	5.6	.975	2B-139
1933		131	.302	.436	530	160	29	15	4	0.8	95	61	60	29	6	1	0	356	417	17	92	6.0	.978	2B-129
1934		139	.305	.435	524	160	33	8	3	0.6	103	57	102	32	6	4	1	367	420	20	101	5.8	.975	2B-135
1935		151	**.349**	.468	616	215	36	11	5	0.8	115	100	96	40	7	0	0	460	473	20	138	6.3	.979	2B-151
1936		51	.269	.327	156	42	5	2	0	0.0	31	15	42	11	7	7	1	120	143	4	31	5.2	.985	2B-43
1937		125	.293	.384	430	126	16	10	1	0.2	54	65	78	41	2	5	1	308	338	23	90	5.4	.966	2B-119, OF-1
1938		127	.336	.465	437	147	22	8	6	1.4	79	71	93	32	9	5	1	308	355	12	91	5.3	.982	2B-121
1939		83	.302	.376	258	78	10	3	1	0.4	33	32	40	18	4	17	3	175	188	12	48	4.5	.968	2B-65
1940		71	.290	.395	210	61	14	4	0	0.0	28	29	34	10	6	14	1	119	176	10	34	4.3	.967	2B-54
1941		53	.252	.299	107	27	3	1	0	0.0	14	9	18	10	2	25	6	53	54	2	12	2.1	.982	2B-24
17 yrs.		1923	.303	.406	7038	2131	353	130	38	0.5	1174	850	965	428	156	94	20	4224	5153	311	1134	5.0	.968	2B-1340, SS-237, 3B-219, OF-13

WORLD SERIES

Year	Team	Games	BA	SA	AB	H	2B	3B	HR	HR%	R	RBI	BB	SO	SB	AB	H	PO	A	E	DP	TC/G	FA	G by Pos
1925	WAS A	3	.250	.250	8	2	0	0	0	0.0	0	1	0	2	0	0	0	1	1	0	0	0.7	1.000	3B-3
1933		5	.300	.350	20	6	1	0	0	0.0	2	2	3	3	0	0	0	15	12	3	3	6.0	.900	2B-5
2 yrs.		8	.286	.321	28	8	1	0	0	0.0	2	2	3	5	0	0	0	16	13	3	3	4.0	.906	2B-5, 3B-3

Al Myers

MYERS, JAMES ALBERT (Cod)
B. Oct. 22, 1863, Danville, Ill. D. Dec. 24, 1927, Marshall, Ill.

BR TR 5'8½" 165 lbs.

Year	Team	Games	BA	SA	AB	H	2B	3B	HR	HR%	R	RBI	BB	SO	SB	AB	H	PO	A	E	DP	TC/G	FA	G by Pos
1884	MIL U	12	.326	.457	46	15	6	0	0	0.0	6		0			0	0	26	30	10	1	5.5	.848	2B-12
1885	PHI N	93	.204	.261	357	73	13	2	1	0.3	25		11	41		0	0	201	287	64	31	5.9	.884	2B-93
1886	KC N	118	.277	.387	473	131	22	9	4	0.8	69	51	22	42		0	0	298	384	65	50	6.3	.913	2B-118
1887	WAS N	105	.232	.301	362	84	9	5	2	0.6	45	36	40	26	18	0	0	244	341	77	29	6.3	.884	2B-78, SS-27
1888		132	.207	.271	502	104	12	7	2	0.4	46	46	37	46	20	0	0	271	399	60	37	5.5	.918	2B-132
1889	2 teams	WAS N			(46G – .261)			PHI N	(75G – .269)																
"	total	121	.266	.310	481	128	17	2	0	0.0	76	48	58	16	18	0	0	339	409	96	59	7.0	.886	2B-121
1890	PHI N	117	.277	.378	487	135	29	7	2	0.4	95	81	57	46	44	0	0	347	352	38	62	6.3	.948	2B-117
1891		135	.230	.302	514	118	27	2	2	0.4	67	69	69	46	8	0	0	354	438	53	67	6.3	.937	2B-135
8 yrs.		833	.245	.320	3222	788	135	34	13	0.4	429	331	294	263	108	0	0	2080	2640	463	336	6.2	.911	2B-806, SS-27

Bert Myers

MYERS, JAMES ALBERT
B. Apr. 8, 1874, Frederick, Md. D. Oct. 12, 1915, Washington, D. C.

BR TR 5'10"

Year	Team	Games	BA	SA	AB	H	2B	3B	HR	HR%	R	RBI	BB	SO	SB	AB	H	PO	A	E	DP	TC/G	FA	G by Pos
1896	STL N	122	.256	.317	454	116	12	8	0	0.0	47	37	40	32	8	0	0	165	243	62	16	3.9	.868	3B-121, SS-1
1898	WAS N	31	.264	.345	110	29	1	4	0	0.0	14	13	13		2	0	0	35	61	19	6	3.7	.835	3B-31
1900	PHI N	7	.179	.214	28	5	1	0	0	0.0	5	2	3		1	0	0	6	24	3	3	4.7	.909	3B-7
3 yrs.		160	.253	.318	592	150	14	12	0	0.0	66	52	56	32	11	0	0	206	328	84	25	3.9	.864	3B-159, SS-1

Billy Myers

MYERS, WILLIAM HARRISON
Brother of Lynn Myers.
B. Aug. 14, 1910, Enola, Pa.

BR TR 5'8" 168 lbs.

Year	Team	Games	BA	SA	AB	H	2B	3B	HR	HR%	R	RBI	BB	SO	SB	AB	H	PO	A	E	DP	TC/G	FA	G by Pos
1935	CIN N	117	.267	.380	445	119	15	10	5	1.1	60	36	29	81	10	0	0	230	335	37	77	5.1	.939	SS-112
1936		98	.269	.390	323	87	9	6	6	1.9	45	27	28	56	6	0	0	225	304	35	73	5.8	.938	SS-98
1937		124	.251	.370	335	84	13	3	7	2.1	35	43	44	57	0	0	0	198	368	30	68	4.8	.950	SS-121, 2B-6
1938		134	.253	.403	442	112	18	6	12	2.7	57	47	41	80	2	0	0	283	411	47	75	5.5	.937	SS-123, 2B-11
1939		151	.281	.393	509	143	18	6	9	1.8	79	56	71	90	4	0	0	309	512	42	110	5.7	.951	SS-151
1940		90	.202	.319	282	57	14	2	5	1.8	33	30	30	56	0	0	0	155	269	17	62	4.9	.961	SS-88
1941	CHI N	24	.222	.286	63	14	1	0	1	1.6	10	4	7	25	1	0	0	37	66	6	13	4.5	.945	SS-19, 2B-1
7 yrs.		738	.257	.377	2399	616	88	33	45	1.9	319	243	250	445	23	0	0	1437	2265	214	478	5.3	.945	SS-712, 2B-18

WORLD SERIES

Year	Team	Games	BA	SA	AB	H	2B	3B	HR	HR%	R	RBI	BB	SO	SB	AB	H	PO	A	E	DP	TC/G	FA	G by Pos
1939	CIN N	4	.333	.500	12	4	0	1	0	0.0	2	0	2	2	0	0	0	10	9	2	1	5.3	.905	SS-4
1940		7	.130	.130	23	3	0	0	0	0.0	0	2	2	5	0	0	0	14	18	2	5	4.9	.941	SS-7
2 yrs.		11	.200	.257	35	7	0	1	0	0.0	2	2	4	8	0	0	0	24	27	4	6	5.0	.927	SS-11

George Myers

MYERS, GEORGE D.
B. Nov. 13, 1860, Buffalo, N. Y. D. Dec. 14, 1926, Buffalo, N. Y.

BR TR

Year	Team	Games	BA	SA	AB	H	2B	3B	HR	HR%	R	RBI	BB	SO	SB	AB	H	PO	A	E	DP	TC/G	FA	G by Pos
1884	BUF N	78	.182	.240	325	59	9	2	2	0.6	34		13	33		0	0	320	61	78	5	5.9	.830	C-49, OF-34
1885		89	.206	.329	326	67	7	2	2	0.6	40	19	23	40		0	0	341	96	53	4	5.5	.892	C-69, OF-23
1886	STL N	79	.190	.234	295	56	7	3	0	0.0	26	27	18	42		0	0	378	82	38	8	6.3	.924	C-72, OF-6, 3B-1
1887	IND N	69	.217	.272	235	51	8	1	1	0.4	25	20	22	7	26	0	0	236	63	19	13	4.6	.940	C-50, OF-15, 1B-6, 3B-1
1888		66	.238	.298	248	59	9	0	2	0.8	36	16	16	14	28	0	0	235	85	32	6	5.3	.909	C-47, 3B-14, OF-10, 1B-1

Year	Team		Games	BA	SA	AB	H	2B	3B	HR	HR%	R	RBI	BB	SO	SB	Pinch Hit AB	Pinch Hit H	PO	A	E	DP	TC/G	FA	G by Pos

George Myers *continued*

Year	Team		Games	BA	SA	AB	H	2B	3B	HR	HR%	R	RBI	BB	SO	SB	PH AB	PH H	PO	A	E	DP	TC/G	FA	G by Pos
1889			43	.195	.215	149	29	3	0	0	0.0	22	12	17	13	12	0	0	106	37	18	1	3.7	.888	OF-23, C-18, 1B-1
6 yrs.			424	.203	.250	1578	321	43	8	5	0.3	183	94	109	149	66	0	0	1616	424	238	37	5.4	.896	C-305, OF-111, 3B-16, 1B-8

Greg Myers

MYERS, GREGORY RICHARD
B. Apr. 14, 1966, Riverside, Calif. BL TR 6'1" 200 lbs.

Year	Team		Games	BA	SA	AB	H	2B	3B	HR	HR%	R	RBI	BB	SO	SB	PH AB	PH H	PO	A	E	DP	TC/G	FA	G by Pos
1987	TOR	A	7	.111	.111	9	1	0	0	0	0.0	1	0	0	3	0	0	0	24	1	0	0	3.6	1.000	C-7
1989			17	.114	.159	44	5	2	0	0	0.0	0	1	2	9	0	1	0	46	6	0	1	3.1	1.000	C-11, DH-6
2 yrs.			24	.113	.151	53	6	2	0	0	0.0	1	1	2	12	0	1	0	70	7	0	1	3.2	1.000	C-18, DH-6

Hap Myers

MYERS, RALPH EDWARD
B. Apr. 8, 1888, San Francisco, Calif. D. June 30, 1967, San Francisco, Calif. BR TR 6'3" 175 lbs.

Year	Team		Games	BA	SA	AB	H	2B	3B	HR	HR%	R	RBI	BB	SO	SB	PH AB	PH H	PO	A	E	DP	TC/G	FA	G by Pos
1910	BOS	A	3	.333	.333	6	2	0	0	0	0.0	0	0	0		0	1	0	1	1	0	0	0.7	1.000	OF-2
1911	2 teams		STL	A	(11G – .297)		BOS	A	(13G – .368)																
"	total		24	.333	.373	75	25	3	0	0	0.0	7	1	5		4	0	0	223	9	9	10	10.0	.963	1B-23
1913	BOS	N	140	.273	.326	524	143	20	1	2	0.4	74	50	38	48	57	5	3	1344	85	19	57	10.3	.987	1B-135
1914	BKN	F	92	.220	.295	305	67	10	5	1	0.3	61	29	44	43	0	0	0	784	44	9	47	9.1	.989	1B-88
1915			118	.287	.328	341	98	9	1	1	0.3	61	36	32		28	7	1	961	56	10	52	8.7	.990	1B-107
5 yrs.			377	.268	.322	1251	335	42	7	4	0.3	203	116	119	48	132	13	4	3313	195	47	166	9.4	.987	1B-353, OF-2

Henry Myers

MYERS, HENRY C.
B. May, 1858, Philadelphia, Pa. D. Apr. 18, 1895, Philadelphia, Pa. BR TR 5'9" 159 lbs.
Manager 1882.

Year	Team		Games	BA	SA	AB	H	2B	3B	HR	HR%	R	RBI	BB	SO	SB	PH AB	PH H	PO	A	E	DP	TC/G	FA	G by Pos
1881	PRO	N	1	.000	.000	4	0	0	0	0	0.0	0	0	0		2	0	0	1	2	0	0	3.0	1.000	SS-1
1882	BAL	AA	69	.180	.190	294	53	3	0	0	0.0	43		12		0	0	0	66	264	70	15	5.8	.825	SS-68, P-6
1884	WIL	U	6	.125	.125	24	3	0	0	0	0.0	3		0		0	0	0	12	21	3	3	6.0	.917	SS-5, 2B-1
3 yrs.			76	.174	.183	322	56	3	0	0	0.0	46		12	2	0	0	0	79	287	73	18	5.8	.834	SS-74, P-6, 2B-1

Hy Myers

MYERS, HENRY HARRISON
B. Apr. 27, 1889, East Liverpool, Ohio D. May 1, 1965, Minerva, Ohio BR TR 5'9½" 175 lbs.

Year	Team		Games	BA	SA	AB	H	2B	3B	HR	HR%	R	RBI	BB	SO	SB	PH AB	PH H	PO	A	E	DP	TC/G	FA	G by Pos
1909	BKN	N	6	.227	.273	22	5	1	0	0	0.0	1	6	2		1	0	0	9	0	0	0	1.5	1.000	OF-6
1911			13	.163	.186	43	7	1	0	0	0.0	2	0	2	3	1	0	0	22	2	3	0	2.1	.889	OF-13
1914			70	.286	.379	227	65	3	9	0	0.0	35	17	7	24	2	5	2	102	4	4	0	1.6	.964	OF-60
1915			153	.248	.316	605	150	21	7	2	0.3	69	46	17	51	19	0	0	352	13	14	5	2.5	.964	OF-153
1916			113	.262	.381	412	108	12	14	3	0.7	54	36	21	35	17	6	1	242	11	8	5	2.3	.969	OF-106
1917			120	.268	.348	471	126	15	10	1	0.2	37	41	18	25	5	3	0	410	102	19	15	4.4	.964	OF-66, 1B-22, 2B-19, 3B-15
1918			107	.256	.346	407	104	9	8	4	1.0	36	40	20	26	17	0	0	294	17	8	7	3.0	.975	OF-107
1919			133	.307	**.436**	512	157	23	**14**	5	1.0	62	**73**	23	34	13	0	0	358	13	8	5	2.8	.979	OF-131
1920			154	.304	.462	582	177	36	**22**	4	0.7	83	80	35	54	9	0	0	388	19	9	5	2.7	.978	OF-152, 3B-2
1921			144	.288	.350	549	158	14	4	4	0.7	51	68	22	51	8	0	0	318	78	14	16	2.8	.966	OF-124, 2B-21, 3B-1
1922			153	.317	.408	618	196	20	9	6	1.0	82	89	13	26	9	0	0	399	21	12	2	2.8	.972	OF-153, 2B-1
1923	STL	N	96	.300	.385	330	99	18	2	2	0.6	29	48	12	19	5	6	1	239	15	6	0	2.7	.977	OF-87
1924			43	.210	.290	124	26	5	1	1	0.8	12	15	3	10	1	5	0	61	25	6	1	2.1	.935	OF-22, 3B-12, 2B-3
1925	3 teams		STL	N	(1G – .000)		CIN	N	(3G – .167)		STL	N	(1G – 1.000)											
"	total		5	.250	.375	8	2	1	0	0	0.0	2	0	0		2	1	5	0	0	0	1.0	1.000	OF-3
14 yrs.			1310	.281	.378	4910	1380	179	100	32	0.7	555	559	195	358	107	27	5	3199	330	111	61	2.8	.970	OF-1183, 2B-44, 3B-30, 1B-22

WORLD SERIES

Year	Team		Games	BA	SA	AB	H	2B	3B	HR	HR%	R	RBI	BB	SO	SB	PH AB	PH H	PO	A	E	DP	TC/G	FA	G by Pos
1916	BKN	N	5	.182	.318	22	4	0	0	1	4.5	2	3	0	3	0	0	0	9	1	0	1	2.0	1.000	OF-5
1920			7	.231	.231	26	6	0	0	0	0.0	0	1	0	1	0	0	0	15	1	0	1	2.3	1.000	OF-7
2 yrs.			12	.208	.271	48	10	0	0	1	2.1	2	4	0	4	0	0	0	24	2	0	2	2.2	1.000	OF-12

Lynn Myers

MYERS, LYNNWOOD LINCOLN
Brother of Billy Myers.
B. Feb. 23, 1914, Enola, Pa. BR TR 5'6½" 145 lbs.

Year	Team		Games	BA	SA	AB	H	2B	3B	HR	HR%	R	RBI	BB	SO	SB	PH AB	PH H	PO	A	E	DP	TC/G	FA	G by Pos
1938	STL	N	70	.242	.317	227	55	10	2	1	0.4	18	19	9	25	9	0	0	110	195	18	36	4.6	.944	SS-69
1939			74	.239	.308	117	28	6	1	0	0.0	24	10	12	23	1	5	3	65	94	17	25	2.4	.903	SS-36, 2B-13, 3B-5
2 yrs.			144	.241	.314	344	83	16	3	1	0.3	42	29	21	48	10	5	3	175	289	35	61	3.5	.930	SS-105, 2B-13, 3B-5

Richie Myers

MYERS, RICHARD
B. Apr. 7, 1930, Sacramento, Calif. BR TR 5'6" 150 lbs.

Year	Team		Games	BA	SA	AB	H	2B	3B	HR	HR%	R	RBI	BB	SO	SB	PH AB	PH H	PO	A	E	DP	TC/G	FA	G by Pos
1956	CHI	N	4	.000	.000	1	0	0	0	0	0.0	1	0	0		0	1	0	0	0	0	0	0.0	–	

Bill Nagel

NAGEL, WILLIAM TAYLOR
B. Aug. 19, 1915, Memphis, Tenn. D. Oct. 8, 1981, Freehold, N. J. BR TR 6'1" 190 lbs.

Year	Team		Games	BA	SA	AB	H	2B	3B	HR	HR%	R	RBI	BB	SO	SB	PH AB	PH H	PO	A	E	DP	TC/G	FA	G by Pos
1939	PHI	A	105	.252	.437	341	86	19	4	12	3.5	39	39	25	86	2	4	0	134	218	21	32	3.6	.944	2B-56, 3B-43, P-1
1941	PHI	N	17	.143	.196	56	8	1	1	0	0.0	2	6	3	14	0	2	0	29	38	4	7	4.2	.944	2B-12, OF-2, 3B-1
1945	CHI	A	67	.209	.323	220	46	10	3	3	1.4	21	27	15	41	3	9	0	503	35	9	42	8.2	.984	1B-57, 3B-1
3 yrs.			189	.227	.374	617	140	30	8	15	2.4	62	72	43	141	5	15	0	666	291	34	81	5.2	.966	2B-68, 1B-57, 3B-45, OF-2, P-1

Lou Nagelsen

NAGELSEN, LOUIS MARCELLUS
Born Louis Marcellus Nageleisen.
B. June 29, 1887, Piqua, Ohio D. Oct. 22, 1965, Fort Wayne, Ind. BR TR 6'2" 180 lbs.

Year	Team		Games	BA	SA	AB	H	2B	3B	HR	HR%	R	RBI	BB	SO	SB	PH AB	PH H	PO	A	E	DP	TC/G	FA	G by Pos
1912	CLE	A	2	.000	.000	3	0	0	0	0	0.0	0	0	0		0	0	0	2	0	0	0	1.0	1.000	C-2

Russ Nagelson

NAGELSON, RUSSELL CHARLES (Rusty)
B. Sept. 19, 1944, Cincinnati, Ohio BL TR 6' 205 lbs.

Year	Team	Games	BA	SA	AB	H	2B	3B	HR	HR%	R	RBI	BB	SO	SB	Pinch Hit AB	Pinch Hit H	PO	A	E	DP	TC/G	FA	G by Pos

Russ Nagelson *continued*

Year	Team	Games	BA	SA	AB	H	2B	3B	HR	HR%	R	RBI	BB	SO	SB	PH AB	PH H	PO	A	E	DP	TC/G	FA	G by Pos
1968	CLE A	5	.333	.333	3	1	0	0	0	0.0	0	0	2	2	0	3	1	0	0	0	0	0.0	–	OF-3, 1B-1
1969		12	.353	.353	17	6	0	0	0	0.0	1	0	3	3	0	7	1	11	1	0	1	1.0	1.000	OF-3, 1B-1
1970	2 teams	CLE A (17G – .125)						DET A (28G – .188)																
"	total	45	.161	.232	56	9	1	0	1	1.8	8	4	8	15	0	31	6	13	0	0	0	0.3	1.000	OF-8, 1B-1
3 yrs.		62	.211	.263	76	16	1	0	1	1.3	9	4	13	20	0	41	8	24	1	0	1	0.4	1.000	OF-11, 1B-2

Tom Nagle

NAGLE, THOMAS EDWARD
B. Oct. 30, 1865, Milwaukee, Wis. D. Mar. 9, 1946, Milwaukee, Wis. BR TR 5'10" 150 lbs.

Year	Team	Games	BA	SA	AB	H	2B	3B	HR	HR%	R	RBI	BB	SO	SB	PH AB	PH H	PO	A	E	DP	TC/G	FA	G by Pos
1890	CHI N	38	.271	.340	144	39	5	1	1	0.7	21	11	7	24	4	0	0	167	25	13	0	5.4	.937	C-33, OF-6
1891		8	.120	.120	25	3	0	0	0	0.0	3	1	1	3	0	0	0	25	4	3	1	4.0	.906	C-7, OF-1
2 yrs.		46	.249	.308	169	42	5	1	1	0.6	24	12	8	27	4	0	0	192	29	16	1	5.2	.932	C-40, OF-7

Bill Nahorodny

NAHORODNY, WILLIAM GERARD
B. Aug. 31, 1953, Hamtramck, Mich. BR TR 6'2" 200 lbs.

Year	Team	Games	BA	SA	AB	H	2B	3B	HR	HR%	R	RBI	BB	SO	SB	PH AB	PH H	PO	A	E	DP	TC/G	FA	G by Pos
1976	PHI N	3	.200	.400	5	1	1	0	0	0.0	0	0	0	2	0	2	0	7	0	0	0	2.3	1.000	C-2
1977	CHI A	7	.261	.435	23	6	1	0	1	4.3	3	4	2	3	0	0	0	29	6	0	2	5.0	1.000	C-7
1978		107	.236	.349	347	82	11	2	8	2.3	29	35	23	52	1	1	0	509	55	11	6	5.4	.981	C-104, 1B-4, DH-1
1979		65	.257	.413	179	46	10	0	6	3.4	20	29	18	23	0	11	6	223	25	7	3	3.9	.973	C-60, DH-3
1980	ATL N	59	.242	.414	157	38	12	0	5	3.2	14	18	8	21	0	6	1	178	24	2	2	3.5	.990	C-54, 1B-1
1981		14	.231	.308	13	3	1	0	0	0.0	0	2	1	3	0	9	3	7	0	0	0	0.5	1.000	C-3, 1B-1
1982	CLE A	39	.223	.426	94	21	5	1	4	4.3	6	18	7	2	0	7	2	111	11	0	0	3.1	1.000	C-35
1983	DET A	2	.000	.000	1	0	0	0	0	0.0	0	0	1	0	0	1	0	0	0	0	0	0.0	–	
1984	SEA A	12	.240	.360	25	6	0	1	1	4.0	2	3	1	7	0	1	0	41	2	1	2	3.7	.977	C-10, 1B-1
9 yrs.		308	.241	.385	844	203	41	3	25	3.0	74	109	56	118	1	38	12	1105	123	21	17	4.1	.983	C-275, 1B-7, DH-4

Frank Naleway

NALEWAY, FRANK (Chick)
B. July 5, 1902, Chicago, Ill. D. Jan. 28, 1949, Chicago, Ill. BR TR 5'9½" 165 lbs.

Year	Team	Games	BA	SA	AB	H	2B	3B	HR	HR%	R	RBI	BB	SO	SB	PH AB	PH H	PO	A	E	DP	TC/G	FA	G by Pos
1924	CHI A	1	.000	.000	2	0	0	0	0	0.0	0	0	1	0	0	0	0	1	2	1	0	4.0	.750	SS-1

Doc Nance

NANCE, WILLIAM G. (Kid)
Born William G. Cooper.
B. Aug. 2, 1876, Fort Worth, Tex. D. May 28, 1958, Fort Worth, Tex. BR TR

Year	Team	Games	BA	SA	AB	H	2B	3B	HR	HR%	R	RBI	BB	SO	SB	PH AB	PH H	PO	A	E	DP	TC/G	FA	G by Pos
1897	LOU N	35	.242	.408	120	29	5	3	3	2.5	25	17	20		3	0	0	60	8	1	4	2.0	.986	OF-35
1898		22	.316	.421	76	24	5	0	1	1.3	13	16	12		2	0	0	28	7	2	2	1.7	.946	OF-22
1901	DET A	132	.280	.373	461	129	24	5	3	0.7	72	66	51		9	0	0	240	20	19	6	2.1	.932	OF-132
1904	STL A	1	.333	.333	3	1	0	0	0	0.0	0	0	0		0	0	0	0	0	0	0	–		OF-1
4 yrs.		190	.277	.385	660	183	34	8	7	1.1	110	99	83		14	0	0	328	35	22	12	2.0	.943	OF-190

Al Naples

NAPLES, ALOYSIUS FRANCIS
B. Aug. 29, 1927, St. George, N. Y. BR TR 5'9" 168 lbs.

Year	Team	Games	BA	SA	AB	H	2B	3B	HR	HR%	R	RBI	BB	SO	SB	PH AB	PH H	PO	A	E	DP	TC/G	FA	G by Pos
1949	STL A	2	.143	.286	7	1	1	0	0	0.0	0	0	0	1	0	0	0	1	6	1	0	4.0	.875	SS-2

Danny Napoleon

NAPOLEON, DANIEL
B. Jan. 11, 1942, Claysburg, Pa. BR TR 5'11" 190 lbs.

Year	Team	Games	BA	SA	AB	H	2B	3B	HR	HR%	R	RBI	BB	SO	SB	PH AB	PH H	PO	A	E	DP	TC/G	FA	G by Pos
1965	NY N	68	.144	.175	97	14	1	1	0	0.0	5	7	8	23	0	45	9	33	1	2	0	0.5	.944	OF-15, 3B-7
1966		12	.212	.273	33	7	2	0	0	0.0	2	0	1	10	0	1	0	12	1	1	0	1.2	.929	OF-10
2 yrs.		80	.162	.200	130	21	3	1	0	0.0	7	7	9	33	0	46	9	45	2	3	0	0.6	.940	OF-25, 3B-7

Hal Naragon

NARAGON, HAROLD RICHARD
B. Oct. 1, 1928, Zanesville, Ohio BL TR 6' 160 lbs.

Year	Team	Games	BA	SA	AB	H	2B	3B	HR	HR%	R	RBI	BB	SO	SB	PH AB	PH H	PO	A	E	DP	TC/G	FA	G by Pos
1951	CLE A	3	.250	.250	8	2	0	0	0	0.0	0	0	1	1	0	1	1	12	1	1	1	4.7	.929	C-2
1954		46	.238	.297	101	24	2	2	0	0.0	10	12	9	12	0	1	0	132	14	0	1	3.2	1.000	C-45
1955		57	.323	.449	127	41	9	2	1	0.8	12	14	15	8	0	13	3	199	15	2	3	3.8	.991	C-52
1956		53	.287	.402	122	35	3	1	3	2.5	11	18	13	9	0	14	5	162	7	2	0	3.2	.988	C-48
1957		57	.256	.281	121	31	1	1	0	0.0	12	8	12	9	0	24	4	179	14	2	2	3.4	.990	C-39
1958		9	.333	.556	9	3	0	1	0	0.0	2	0	0	0	0	9	3	0	0	0	0	0.0	–	
1959	2 teams	CLE A (14G – .278)						WAS A (71G – .241)																
"	total	85	.247	.303	231	57	7	3	0	0.0	18	16	11	11	0	24	3	313	16	2	1	3.9	.994	C-64
1960	WAS A	33	.207	.228	92	19	2	0	0	0.0	7	5	8	4	0	4	0	119	14	3	1	4.1	.978	C-29
1961	MIN A	57	.302	.374	139	42	2	1	2	1.4	10	11	4	8	0	20	3	168	12	1	4	3.2	.994	C-36
1962		24	.229	.257	35	8	1	0	0	0.0	1	3	3	1	0	15	1	41	0	0	1	1.7	1.000	C-9
10 yrs.		424	.266	.334	985	262	27	11	6	0.6	83	87	76	62	1	125	23	1325	93	13	14	3.4	.991	C-324

WORLD SERIES

Year	Team	Games	BA	SA	AB	H	2B	3B	HR	HR%	R	RBI	BB	SO	SB	PH AB	PH H	PO	A	E	DP	TC/G	FA	G by Pos
1954	CLE A	1	–	–	0	0	0	0	0	–	0	0	1	0	0	0	0	0	0	0	0	1.0	1.000	C-1

Bill Narleski

NARLESKI, WILLIAM EDWARD (Cap)
Father of Ray Narleski.
B. June 9, 1899, Perth Amboy, N. J. D. July 22, 1964, Laurel Springs, N. J. BR TR 5'9" 160 lbs.

Year	Team	Games	BA	SA	AB	H	2B	3B	HR	HR%	R	RBI	BB	SO	SB	PH AB	PH H	PO	A	E	DP	TC/G	FA	G by Pos
1929	BOS A	96	.277	.346	260	72	16	1	0	0.0	31	25	21	22	4	3	1	146	200	15	41	3.8	.958	SS-51, 2B-28, 3B-10
1930		39	.235	.327	98	23	9	0	0	0.0	11	7	7	5	0	0	0	50	52	6	10	2.8	.944	SS-19, 3B-14, 2B-5
2 yrs.		135	.265	.341	358	95	25	1	0	0.0	42	32	28	27	4	3	1	196	252	21	51	3.5	.955	SS-70, 2B-33, 3B-24

Jerry Narron

NARRON, JERRY AUSTIN
B. Jan. 15, 1956, Goldsboro, N. C. BL TR 6'3" 205 lbs.

Year	Team	Games	BA	SA	AB	H	2B	3B	HR	HR%	R	RBI	BB	SO	SB	PH AB	PH H	PO	A	E	DP	TC/G	FA	G by Pos
1979	NY A	61	.171	.309	123	21	3	0	4	3.3	17	18	9	26	0	4	0	167	15	5	2	3.1	.973	C-56, DH-1
1980	SEA A	48	.196	.336	107	21	3	0	4	3.7	7	18	13	18	0	4	1	115	11	1	0	2.6	.992	C-39, DH-1
1981		76	.222	.291	203	45	5	0	3	1.5	13	17	16	35	0	15	3	248	11	1	3	3.4	.996	C-65
1983	CAL A	10	.136	.273	22	3	0	0	1	4.5	1	4	1	3	0	6	0	14	3	2	0	1.9	.895	C-6, DH-1
1984		69	.247	.340	150	37	5	0	3	2.0	9	17	8	12	0	29	7	184	12	1	6	2.9	.995	C-46, 1B-7

Year	Team		Games	BA	SA	AB	H	2B	3B	HR	HR%	R	RBI	BB	SO	SB	Pinch Hit AB	H	PO	A	E	DP	TC/G	FA	G by Pos

Jerry Narron *continued*

Year	Team		Games	BA	SA	AB	H	2B	3B	HR	HR%	R	RBI	BB	SO	SB	AB	H	PO	A	E	DP	TC/G	FA	G by Pos
1985			67	.220	.364	132	29	4	0	5	3.8	12	14	11	17	0	22	5	146	14	0	4	2.4	1.000	C-45, DH-7, 1B-1
1986			57	.221	.305	95	21	3	1	1	1.1	5	8	9	14	0	11	2	155	14	2	3	3.0	.988	C-51, DH-2
1987	SEA	A	4	.000	.000	8	0	0	0	0	0.0	0	0	0	2	0	1	0	9	0	0	0	2.3	1.000	C-3
8 yrs.			392	.211	.318	840	177	23	2	21	2.5	64	96	67	127	0	102	20	1038	80	12	18	2.9	.989	C-311, DH-12, 1B-8

LEAGUE CHAMPIONSHIP SERIES

| 1986 | CAL | A | 4 | .500 | .500 | 2 | 1 | 0 | 0 | 0 | 0.0 | 1 | 0 | 1 | 1 | 0 | 1 | 0 | 0 | 0 | 0 | 0 | 0.0 | — | C-3 |

Sam Narron

NARRON, SAMUEL
B. Aug. 25, 1913, Middlesex, N. C.   BR TR 5'10" 180 lbs.

1935	STL	N	4	.429	.429	7	3	0	0	0	0.0	0	0	0	0	0	3	2	5	0	0	0	1.3	1.000	C-1
1942			10	.400	.400	10	4	0	0	0	0.0	0	1	0	2	0	8	3	2	0	0	0	0.2	1.000	C-2
1943			10	.091	.091	11	1	0	0	0	0.0	0	0	1	2	0	7	1	8	1	0	0	0.9	1.000	C-3
3 yrs.			24	.286	.286	28	8	0	0	0	0.0	0	1	1	4	0	18	6	15	1	0	0	0.7	1.000	C-6

WORLD SERIES

| 1943 | STL | N | 1 | .000 | .000 | 1 | 0 | 0 | 0 | 0 | 0.0 | 0 | 0 | 0 | 0 | 0 | 0 | 1 | 0 | 0 | 0 | 0 | 0.0 | — | |

Billy Nash

NASH, WILLIAM MITCHELL
B. June 24, 1865, Richmond, Va.   D. Nov. 15, 1929, East Orange, N. J.   BR TR 5'8½" 167 lbs.
Manager 1896.

1884	RIC	AA	45	.199	.361	166	33	8	8	1	0.6	31		12			0	0	77	87	34	8	4.4	.828	3B-45
1885	BOS	N	26	.255	.298	94	24	4	0	0	0.0	9	11	2	9		0	0	34	43	12	6	3.4	.865	3B-19, 2B-8
1886			109	.281	.353	417	117	11	8	1	0.2	61	45	24	28		0	0	160	217	61	14	4.0	.861	3B-90, SS-17
1887			121	.295	.440	475	140	24	12	7	1.5	100	94	60	30	43	0	0	220	243	60	19	4.3	.885	3B-117, OF-5
1888			135	.283	.397	526	149	18	15	4	0.8	71	75	50	46	20	0	0	229	358	58	31	4.8	.910	3B-105, 2B-31
1889			128	.274	.343	481	132	20	2	3	0.6	84	76	79	44	26	0	0	205	274	50	25	4.1	.905	3B-128, P-1
1890	BOS	P	129	.266	.379	488	130	28	6	5	1.0	103	90	88	43	26	0	0	198	307	78	37	4.5	.866	3B-129, P-1
1891	BOS	N	140	.276	.382	537	148	24	9	5	0.9	92	95	74	50	28	0	0	213	264	53	20	3.8	.900	3B-140
1892			135	.260	.350	526	137	25	5	4	0.8	94	95	59	41	31	0	0	197	351	62	23	4.5	.898	3B-135, OF-1
1893			128	.291	.433	485	141	27	6	10	2.1	115	123	85	29	30	0	0	189	300	41	23	4.1	.923	3B-128
1894			132	.289	.404	512	148	23	6	8	1.6	132	87	91	23	20	0	0	204	267	34	24	3.8	.933	3B-132
1895			132	.289	.417	508	147	23	6	10	2.0	97	108	74	19	18	0	0	193	246	59	26	3.8	.882	3B-132
1896	PHI	N	65	.247	.335	227	56	9	1	3	1.3	29	30	34	21	3	0	0	87	148	23	12	4.0	.911	3B-65
1897			104	.258	.329	337	87	20	2	0	0.0	45	39	60		4	1	1	172	206	38	17	4.0	.909	3B-79, SS-19, 2B-4
1898			20	.243	.300	70	17	2	1	0	0.0	9	9	11			0	0	35	33	3	6	3.6	.958	3B-20
15 yrs.			1549	.275	.381	5849	1606	266	87	61	1.0	1072	977	803	383	249	1	1	2413	3344	666	291	4.1	.896	3B-1464, 2B-43, SS-36, OF-6, P-2

Cotton Nash

NASH, CHARLES FRANCIS
B. July 24, 1942, Jersey City, N. J.   BR TR 6'6" 220 lbs.

1967	CHI	A	3	.000	.000	3	0	0	0	0	0.0	1		1			0	0	10	0	2	3	4.0	.833	1B-3
1969	MIN	A	6	.222	.222	9	2	0	0	0	0.0	0	0	1	2	0	0	0	29	5	0	0	5.7	1.000	1B-6, OF-1
1970			4	.250	.250	4	1	0	0	0	0.0	1	2	1	1	0	2	0	11	0	0	2	2.8	1.000	1B-2
3 yrs.			13	.188	.188	16	3	0	0	0	0.0	2	2	3	3	0	2	0	50	5	2	5	4.4	.965	1B-11, OF-1

Ken Nash

NASH, KENNETH LELAND
Played as J. A. Costello in 1912. Also known as Kenneth Leland Costello.   BB TR 5'8" 140 lbs.
B. July 14, 1888, South Weymouth, Mass.   D. Feb. 16, 1977, Epsom, N. H.

1912	CLE	A	11	.174	.174	23	4	0	0	0	0.0	2	0		3		0	3	6	13	4	1	2.1	.826	SS-8
1914	STL	N	24	.275	.373	51	14	3	1	0	0.0	4	6	6	10	0	5	1	15	25	8	2	2.0	.833	3B-10, 2B-6, SS-3
2 yrs.			35	.243	.311	74	18	3	1	0	0.0	6	6	9	10	0	8	1	21	38	12	3	2.0	.831	SS-11, 3B-10, 2B-6

Pete Naton

NATON, PETER ALPHONSUS
B. Sept. 9, 1931, Flushing, N. Y.   BR TR 6'1" 200 lbs.

| 1953 | PIT | N | 6 | .167 | .167 | 12 | 2 | 0 | 0 | 0 | 0.0 | 2 | 1 | 2 | 1 | 0 | 1 | 0 | 13 | 0 | 0 | 0 | 2.2 | 1.000 | C-4 |

Sandy Nava

NAVA, VINCENT P.
Born Irwin Sandy.   5'6" 155 lbs.
B. Apr. 12, 1850, San Francisco, Calif.   D. June 15, 1906, Baltimore, Md.

1882	PRO	N	28	.206	.227	97	20	2	0	0	0.0	15		1	13		0	0	112	31	22	6	5.9	.867	C-27, OF-1
1883			29	.240	.320	100	24	4	2	0	0.0	18		3	17		0	0	100	41	32	4	6.0	.815	C-27, OF-2
1884			34	.095	.095	116	11	0	0	0	0.0	10		11	35		0	0	183	54	31	3	7.9	.884	C-27, SS-6, 2B-1
1885	BAL	AA	8	.185	.222	27	5	1	0	0	0.0	2		1			0	0	26	7	7	0	5.0	.825	C-8
1886			2	.200	.200	5	1	0	0	0	0.0	0					0	0	5	2	2	0	4.5	.778	SS-1, C-1
5 yrs.			101	.177	.209	345	61	7	2	0	0.0	45		16	65		0	0	426	135	94	13	6.5	.856	C-90, SS-7, OF-3, 2B-1

Earl Naylor

NAYLOR, EARL EUGENE
B. May 19, 1919, Kansas City, Mo.   BR TR 6' 190 lbs.

1942	PHI	N	76	.196	.232	168	33	4	1	0	0.0	9	14	11	18	1	17	5	68	11	1	0	1.1	.988	OF-34, P-20, 1B-1
1943			33	.175	.267	120	21	2	0	3	2.5	12	14	12	16	1	0	0	101	6	4	2	3.4	.964	OF-33
1946	BKN	N	3	.000	.000	2	0	0	0	0	0.0	1	0	0	1	0	2	0	0	0	0	0	0.0	—	
3 yrs.			112	.186	.245	290	54	6	1	3	1.0	22	28	23	35	2	19	5	169	17	5	2	1.7	.974	OF-67, P-20, 1B-1

Jack Neagle

NEAGLE, JOHN HENRY
B. Jan. 2, 1858, Syracuse, N. Y.   D. Sept. 20, 1904, Syracuse, N. Y.   BR TR 5'6" 155 lbs.

1879	CIN	N	3	.167	.167	12	2	0	0	0	0.0	0		0			0	0	1	2	2	0	1.7	.600	OF-2, P-2
1883	3 teams			PHI N (18G – .164)		BAL AA (9G – .286)					PIT AA (27G – .188)														
"	total		54	.196	.230	209	41	1	0	0	0.0	23		8	9		0	0	45	40	19	0	1.9	.817	OF-32, P-30

Year	Team	Games	BA	SA	AB	H	2B	3B	HR	HR%	R	RBI	BB	SO	SB	Pinch Hit AB	Pinch Hit H	PO	A	E	DP	TC/G	FA	G by Pos

Jack Neagle *continued*

Year	Team	Games	BA	SA	AB	H	2B	3B	HR	HR%	R	RBI	BB	SO	SB	PH AB	PH H	PO	A	E	DP	TC/G	FA	G by Pos
1884	PIT AA	43	.149	.189	148	22	6	0	0	0.0	13		6			0	0	25	57	29	1	2.6	.739	P-38, OF-6
3 yrs.		100	.176	.211	369	65	11	1	0	0.0	37	2	14	9		0	0	71	99	50	1	2.2	.773	P-70, OF-40

Charlie Neal

NEAL, CHARLES LENARD
B. Jan. 30, 1931, Longview, Tex.
BR TR 5'10'' 165 lbs.

Year	Team	Games	BA	SA	AB	H	2B	3B	HR	HR%	R	RBI	BB	SO	SB	PH AB	PH H	PO	A	E	DP	TC/G	FA	G by Pos
1956	BKN N	62	.287	.382	136	39	5	1	2	1.5	14	14	14	19	2	8	3	70	104	5	24	2.9	.972	2B-51, SS-1
1957		128	.270	.411	448	121	13	7	12	2.7	62	62	53	83	11	1	1	182	340	27	66	4.3	.951	SS-100, 3B-23, 2B-3
1958	LA N	140	.254	.438	473	120	9	6	22	4.7	87	65	61	91	7	2	1	344	361	19	123	5.2	.974	2B-132, 3B-9
1959		151	.287	.464	616	177	30	11	19	3.1	103	83	43	86	17	0	0	386	415	9	110	5.4	.989	2B-151, SS-1
1960		139	.256	.363	477	122	23	2	8	1.7	60	40	48	75	5	2	0	251	296	13	79	4.0	.977	2B-136, SS-3
1961		108	.235	.346	341	80	6	1	10	2.9	40	48	30	49	3	4	1	211	246	11	63	4.3	.976	2B-104
1962	NY N	136	.260	.388	508	132	14	9	11	2.2	59	58	56	90	2	0	0	256	389	28	85	4.9	.958	2B-85, SS-39, 3B-12
1963	2 teams		NY N	(72G – .225)		CIN N	(34G – .156)																	
"	total	106	.211	.287	317	67	13	1	3	0.9	28	21	32	64	1	15	3	98	167	12	17	2.6	.957	3B-85, SS-9, 2B-1
8 yrs.		970	.259	.394	3316	858	113	38	87	2.6	461	391	337	557	48	32	9	1798	2318	124	567	4.4	.971	2B-663, SS-153, 3B-129

WORLD SERIES

Year	Team	Games	BA	SA	AB	H	2B	3B	HR	HR%	R	RBI	BB	SO	SB	PH AB	PH H	PO	A	E	DP	TC/G	FA	G by Pos
1956	BKN N	1	.000	.000	4	0	0	0	0	0.0	0	0	0	1	0	0	0	2	2	1	1	5.0	.800	2B-1
1959	LA N	6	.370	.667	27	10	2	0	2	7.4	4	6	0	1	0	0	0	18	19	1	7	6.3	.974	2B-6
2 yrs.		7	.323	.581	31	10	2	0	2	6.5	4	6	0	1	0	0	0	20	21	2	8	6.1	.953	2B-7

Offa Neal

NEAL, THEOPHILUS FOUNTAIN
B. June 5, 1876, Logan, Ill. D. Apr. 12, 1950, Mt. Vernon, Ill.
BL TR 6' 185 lbs.

Year	Team	Games	BA	SA	AB	H	2B	3B	HR	HR%	R	RBI	BB	SO	SB	PH AB	PH H	PO	A	E	DP	TC/G	FA	G by Pos
1905	NY N	4	.000	.000	13	0	0	0	0	0.0	0	0	0		0	0	0	5	4	0	2	2.3	1.000	3B-3, 2B-1

Greasy Neale

NEALE, ALFRED EARLE
B. Nov. 5, 1891, Parkersburg, W. Va. D. Nov. 2, 1973, Lake Worth, Fla.
BL TR 6' 170 lbs.

Year	Team	Games	BA	SA	AB	H	2B	3B	HR	HR%	R	RBI	BB	SO	SB	PH AB	PH H	PO	A	E	DP	TC/G	FA	G by Pos
1916	CIN N	138	.262	.306	530	139	13	5	0	0.0	53	20	19	79	17	3	0	307	20	9	6	2.4	.973	OF-133
1917		121	.294	.400	385	113	14	9	3	0.8	40	33	24	36	25	2	0	216	13	5	1	1.9	.979	OF-119
1918		107	.270	.367	371	100	11	11	0	0.3	59	32	24	38	23	4	0	249	11	5	2	2.5	.981	OF-102
1919		139	.242	.316	500	121	10	12	1	0.2	57	54	47	51	28	1	0	285	16	13	4	2.3	.959	OF-138
1920		150	.255	.317	530	135	10	7	3	0.6	55	46	45	48	29	0	0	347	19	5	7	2.5	.987	OF-150
1921	2 teams		PHI N	(22G – .211)		CIN N	(63G – .241)																	
"	total	85	.235	.305	298	70	11	5	0	0.0	46	13	36	25	12	3	0	144	7	8	2	1.9	.950	OF-82
1922	CIN N	25	.233	.326	43	10	2	1	0	0.0	11	2	6	3	5	3	1	18	1	3	0	0.9	.864	OF-10
1924		3	.000	.000	4	0	0	0	0	0.0	0	0	0	0	0	0	0	3	0	0	0	1.0	1.000	OF-2
8 yrs.		768	.259	.332	2661	688	71	50	8	0.3	321	200	201	281	139	16	1	1569	87	48	22	2.2	.972	OF-736

WORLD SERIES

Year	Team	Games	BA	SA	AB	H	2B	3B	HR	HR%	R	RBI	BB	SO	SB	PH AB	PH H	PO	A	E	DP	TC/G	FA	G by Pos
1919	CIN N	8	.357	.464	28	10	1	0	0	0.0	3	4	2	5	1	0	0	20	0	1	0	2.6	.952	OF-8

Jim Nealon

NEALON, JAMES JOSEPH
B. Dec. 15, 1884, Sacramento, Calif. D. Apr. 2, 1910, San Francisco, Calif.
6'1½''

Year	Team	Games	BA	SA	AB	H	2B	3B	HR	HR%	R	RBI	BB	SO	SB	PH AB	PH H	PO	A	E	DP	TC/G	FA	G by Pos
1906	PIT N	154	.255	.353	556	142	21	12	3	0.5	82	83	53		15	0	0	1592	102	23	90	11.1	.987	1B-154
1907		105	.257	.325	381	98	10	8	0	0.0	29	47	23		11	1	0	998	68	24	35	10.4	.978	1B-104
2 yrs.		259	.256	.342	937	240	31	20	3	0.3	111	130	76		26	1	0	2590	170	47	125	10.8	.983	1B-258

Tom Needham

NEEDHAM, THOMAS J. (Deerfoot)
B. Apr. 7, 1879, Ireland D. Dec. 13, 1926, Steubenville, Ohio
BR TR 5'10'' 180 lbs.

Year	Team	Games	BA	SA	AB	H	2B	3B	HR	HR%	R	RBI	BB	SO	SB	PH AB	PH H	PO	A	E	DP	TC/G	FA	G by Pos
1904	BOS N	84	.260	.372	269	70	12	3	4	1.5	18	19	11		3	6	0	326	140	27	8	5.9	.945	C-77, OF-1
1905		83	.218	.269	271	59	6	1	2	0.7	21	17	24		3	1	0	311	135	24	7	5.7	.949	C-77, OF-3, 1B-2
1906		83	.189	.242	285	54	8	2	1	0.4	11	12	13		3	2	0	342	131	20	11	5.9	.959	C-76, 2B-5, 1B-2, OF-1, 3B-1
1907		86	.196	.246	260	51	6	2	1	0.4	19	19	18		4	5	0	288	101	13	9	4.7	.968	C-78, 1B-1
1908	NY N	54	.209	.242	91	19	3	0	0	0.0	8	11	12		0	5	0	168	30	5	2	3.8	.975	C-47
1909	CHI N	13	.143	.143	28	4	0	0	0	0.0	3	0	0		0	6	2	43	5	1	0	3.8	.980	C-7
1910		31	.184	.250	76	14	3	1	0	0.0	9	10	10	10	1	3	0	133	31	3	6	5.4	.982	C-27, 1B-1
1911		27	.194	.226	62	12	2	0	0	0.0	4	5	9	14	2	3	0	94	32	2	2	4.7	.984	C-23
1912		33	.178	.233	90	16	5	0	0	0.0	12	10	7	13	3	1	0	116	39	1	3	4.7	.994	C-32
1913		20	.238	.381	42	10	4	1	0	0.0	5	11	4	8	0	4	0	53	24	3	4	4.0	.963	C-14, 1B-1
1914		9	.118	.176	17	2	1	0	0	0.0	3	3	1	4	1	2	0	22	11	2	0	3.9	.943	C-7
11 yrs.		523	.209	.272	1491	311	50	10	8	0.5	113	117	109	49	20	38	2	1896	679	101	46	5.1	.962	C-465, 1B-7, OF-5, 2B-5, 3B-1

WORLD SERIES

Year	Team	Games	BA	SA	AB	H	2B	3B	HR	HR%	R	RBI	BB	SO	SB	PH AB	PH H	PO	A	E	DP	TC/G	FA	G by Pos
1910	CHI N	1	.000	.000	1	0	0	0	0	0.0	0	0	0	0	0	1	0	0	0	0	0	0.0	–	

Cal Neeman

NEEMAN, CALVIN AMANDUS
B. Feb. 18, 1929, Valmeyer, Ill.
BR TR 6'1'' 192 lbs.

Year	Team	Games	BA	SA	AB	H	2B	3B	HR	HR%	R	RBI	BB	SO	SB	PH AB	PH H	PO	A	E	DP	TC/G	FA	G by Pos
1957	CHI N	122	.258	.376	415	107	17	1	10	2.4	37	39	22	87	0	4	0	703	56	8	13	6.3	.990	C-118
1958		76	.259	.473	201	52	7	0	12	6.0	30	29	21	41	0	6	0	340	25	3	6	4.8	.992	C-71
1959		44	.162	.267	105	17	2	0	3	2.9	7	9	11	23	0	5	0	158	9	1	1	3.8	.994	C-38
1960	2 teams		CHI N	(9G – .154)		PHI N	(59G – .181)																	
"	total	68	.179	.312	173	31	7	2	4	2.3	13	13	16	47	1	4	0	286	35	6	3	4.8	.982	C-61
1961	PHI N	19	.226	.258	31	7	1	0	0	0.0	0	2	4	8	1	0	0	63	5	1	0	3.6	.986	C-19
1962	PIT N	24	.180	.300	50	9	1	1	2	2.0	5	5	3	10	0	0	0	103	12	2	1	5.0	.983	C-24
1963	2 teams		CLE A	(9G – .000)		WAS A	(14G – .056)																	
"	total	23	.037	.037	27	1	0	0	0	0.0	1	0	2	5	0	2	0	61	5	1	4	2.9	.985	C-21
7 yrs.		376	.224	.356	1002	224	35	4	30	3.0	93	97	79	221	1	23	0	1714	150	22	28	5.0	.988	C-352

Doug Neff

NEFF, DOUGLAS WILLIAMS
B. Oct. 8, 1891, Harrisonburg, Va. D. May 23, 1932, Cape Charles, Va.
BR TR 5'9'' 141 lbs.

Year	Team		Games	BA	SA	AB	H	2B	3B	HR	HR%	R	RBI	BB	SO	SB	Pinch Hit AB	H	PO	A	E	DP	TC/G	FA	G by Pos

Doug Neff *continued*

1914	WAS	A	3	.000	.000	2	0	0	0	0	0.0	0	0	0	0	0	0	0	3	5	1	0	3.0	.889	SS-3
1915			30	.167	.183	60	10	1	0	0	0.0	1	4	4	6	1	0	0	23	41	13	4	2.6	.831	3B-12, 2B-10, SS-7
2 yrs.			33	.161	.177	62	10	1	0	0	0.0	1	4	4	6	1	0	0	26	46	14	4	2.6	.837	3B-12, SS-10, 2B-10

Bob Neighbors

NEIGHBORS, ROBERT OTIS
B. Nov. 9, 1917, Talahina, Okla. D. Aug. 8, 1952, North Korea
BR TR 5'11" 165 lbs.

| 1939 | STL | A | 7 | .182 | .455 | 11 | 2 | 0 | 0 | 1 | 9.1 | 3 | 1 | 0 | 1 | 0 | 0 | 0 | 5 | 6 | 1 | 1 | 1.7 | .917 | SS-5 |

Cy Neighbors

NEIGHBORS, FLEMON CECIL
B. Sept. 23, 1880, Fayetteville, Mo. D. May 20, 1964, Tacoma, Wash.
BR

| 1908 | PIT | N | 1 | – | – | 0 | 0 | 0 | 0 | 0 | – | 0 | 0 | 0 | 0 | 0 | 0 | 0 | 0 | 0 | 0 | 0 | 0.0 | – | OF-1 |

Tommy Neill

NEILL, THOMAS WHITE
B. Nov. 7, 1919, Hartselle, Ala.
BL TR 6'2" 200 lbs.

1946	BOS	N	13	.267	.311	45	12	2	0	0	0.0	8	7	2	1	0	0	0	19	1	0	0	1.5	1.000	OF-13
1947			7	.200	.400	10	2	0	1	0	0.0	1	0	1	2	0	4	2	2	0	0	0	0.3	1.000	OF-7
2 yrs.			20	.255	.327	55	14	2	1	0	0.0	9	7	3	3	0	4	2	21	1	0	0	1.1	1.000	OF-20

Bernie Neis

NEIS, BERNARD EDMUND
B. Sept. 26, 1895, Bloomington, Ill.
D. Nov. 29, 1972, Inverness, Fla.
BB TR 5'7" 160 lbs.
BR 1920-21,1926

1920	BKN	N	95	.253	.337	249	63	11	2	2	0.8	38	22	26	35	9	4	0	145	11	7	4	1.7	.957	OF-83
1921			102	.257	.365	230	59	5	4	4	1.7	34	34	25	41	9	16	6	126	14	8	1	1.5	.946	OF-77, 2B-1
1922			61	.229	.357	70	16	4	1	1	1.4	15	9	13	8	3	9	1	32	3	4	0	0.6	.897	OF-27
1923			126	.274	.364	445	122	17	4	5	1.1	78	37	36	38	8	8	1	268	20	18	3	2.4	.941	OF-111
1924			80	.303	.427	211	64	8	3	4	1.9	43	26	27	17	4	11	2	114	5	8	1	1.6	.937	OF-62
1925	BOS	N	106	.285	.394	355	101	20	2	5	1.4	47	45	38	19	8	14	6	282	8	9	1	2.8	.970	OF-87
1926			30	.215	.312	93	20	5	2	0	0.0	16	8	10	8	4	2	0	60	2	5	1	2.2	.925	OF-23
1927	2 teams		CLE A	(32G – .302)		CHI A	(45G – .289)																		
"	total		77	.297	.448	172	51	14	0	4	2.3	26	29	28	18	1	20	5	119	7	5	1	1.7	.962	OF-50
8 yrs.			677	.272	.379	1825	496	84	18	25	1.4	297	210	201	186	46	84	21	1146	70	64	12	1.9	.950	OF-520, 2B-1

WORLD SERIES

| 1920 | BKN | N | 4 | .000 | .000 | 5 | 0 | 0 | 0 | 0 | 0.0 | 0 | 0 | 1 | 0 | 0 | 1 | 0 | 3 | 0 | 0 | 0 | 0.8 | 1.000 | OF-2 |

Ernie Neitzke

NEITZKE, ERNEST FREDERICK
B. Nov. 13, 1894, Toledo, Ohio D. Apr. 27, 1977, Sylvania, Ohio
BR TR 5'10" 180 lbs.

| 1921 | BOS | A | 11 | .240 | .240 | 25 | 6 | 0 | 0 | 0 | 0.0 | 3 | 1 | 4 | 1 | 0 | 0 | 0 | 13 | 4 | 2 | 0 | 1.7 | .895 | OF-8, P-2 |

Bob Nelson

NELSON, ROBERT SIDNEY (Tex, Babe)
B. Aug. 7, 1936, Dallas, Tex.
BL TL 6'3" 205 lbs.

1955	BAL	A	25	.194	.194	31	6	0	0	0	0.0	4	1	7	13	0	16	3	15	3	3	3	0.8	.857	OF-6, 1B-2
1956			39	.206	.235	68	14	2	0	0	0.0	5	5	7	22	0	15	4	28	3	2	0	0.8	.939	OF-24
1957			15	.217	.391	23	5	0	2	0	0.0	2	5	1	5	0	6	3	6	0	0	0	0.4	1.000	OF-8
3 yrs.			79	.205	.254	122	25	2	2	0	0.0	11	11	15	40	0	37	10	49	6	5	3	0.8	.917	OF-38, 1B-2

Candy Nelson

NELSON, JOHN W.
B. Mar. 12, 1854, Portland, Me. D. Sept. 4, 1910, Brooklyn, N. Y.
BL TR 5'6" 145 lbs.

1878	IND	N	19	.131	.143	84	11	1	0	0	0.0	12	5	5	11		0	0	19	50	13	1	4.3	.841	SS-19
1879	TRO	N	28	.264	.349	106	28	7	1	0	0.0	17	10	8	4		0	0	42	90	25	8	5.6	.841	SS-24, OF-4
1881	WOR	N	24	.282	.320	103	29	1	0	1	1.0	13	15	5	6		0	0	20	94	13	6	5.3	.898	SS-24
1883	NY	AA	97	.305	.379	417	127	19	6	0	0.0	75		31			0	0	98	232	47	18	3.9	.875	SS-97
1884			111	.255	.310	432	110	15	3	1	0.2	114		74			0	0	120	292	56	16	4.2	.880	SS-110, 2B-1
1885			107	.255	.310	420	107	12	4	1	0.2	98		61			0	0	153	370	63	33	5.5	.892	SS-107, 3B-1
1886			109	.225	.252	413	93	7	2	0	0.0	89		64			0	0	159	219	60	19	4.0	.863	SS-73, OF-36
1887	2 teams		NY	AA	(68G – .245)		NY	N	(1G – .000)																
"	total		69	.243	.270	259	63	5	1	0	0.0	61		48	1	29	0	0	121	111	27	18	3.8	.896	OF-37, SS-32, 3B-1, 2B-1
1890	BKN	AA	60	.251	.283	223	56	3	2	0	0.0	44		35		12	0	0	67	198	40	20	5.1	.869	SS-57, OF-4
9 yrs.			624	.254	.302	2457	624	70	19	3	0.1	523	30	331	22	41	0	0	799	1656	344	139	4.5	.877	SS-543, OF-81, 3B-2, 2B-2

Dave Nelson

NELSON, DAVID EARL
B. June 20, 1944, Fort Sill, Okla.
BR TR 5'10" 160 lbs.

1968	CLE	A	88	.233	.307	189	44	4	5	0	0.0	26	19	17	35	23	2	0	124	127	4	27	2.9	.984	2B-59, SS-14
1969			52	.203	.203	123	25	0	0	0	0.0	11	6	9	26	4	5	0	79	94	6	28	3.4	.966	2B-33, OF-2
1970	WAS	A	47	.159	.168	107	17	1	0	0	0.0	5	4	7	24	2	11	2	64	79	2	19	3.1	.986	2B-33
1971			85	.280	.377	329	92	11	3	5	1.5	47	33	23	29	17	3	0	63	150	14	15	2.7	.938	3B-84, 2B-1
1972	TEX	A	145	.226	.283	499	113	16	3	2	0.4	68	28	67	81	51	6	0	131	222	22	25	2.6	.941	3B-119, OF-15
1973			142	.286	.378	576	165	24	4	7	1.2	71	48	34	78	43	2	2	327	364	11	98	4.9	.984	2B-140
1974			121	.236	.287	474	112	13	1	3	0.6	71	42	34	72	25	0	0	295	337	20	74	5.4	.969	2B-120, DH-1
1975			28	.213	.300	80	17	1	0	2	2.5	9	10	8	10	6	2	1	56	60	5	16	4.3	.959	2B-23, DH-1
1976	KC	A	78	.235	.307	153	36	4	2	1	0.7	24	17	14	26	15	16	0	79	90	4	17	2.2	.977	2B-46, DH-22, 1B-3
1977			27	.188	.292	48	9	3	1	0	0.0	8	4	7	11	1	5	2	11	14	2	3	1.0	.926	2B-11, DH-7
10 yrs.			813	.244	.312	2578	630	77	19	20	0.8	340	211	220	392	187	52	7	1229	1537	90	322	3.5	.968	2B-466, 3B-203, DH-31, OF-17, SS-14, 1B-3

LEAGUE CHAMPIONSHIP SERIES

| 1976 | KC | A | 2 | .000 | .000 | 2 | 0 | 0 | 0 | 0 | 0.0 | 0 | 0 | 0 | 0 | 1 | 0 | 2 | 0 | 0 | 0 | 0 | 0.0 | – | |

Jamie Nelson

NELSON, JAMES VICTOR
B. Sept. 5, 1959, Clinton, Okla.
BR TR 5'11" 180 lbs.

Year	Team	Games	BA	SA	AB	H	2B	3B	HR	HR%	R	RBI	BB	SO	SB	Pinch Hit AB	Pinch Hit H	PO	A	E	DP	TC/G	FA	G by Pos

Jamie Nelson *continued*
| 1983 | SEA A | 40 | .219 | .281 | 96 | 21 | 3 | 0 | 1 | 1.0 | 9 | 5 | 13 | 12 | 4 | 1 | 0 | 202 | 16 | 5 | 2 | 5.6 | .978 | C-39 |

Lynn Nelson
NELSON, LYNN BERNARD (Line Drive)
B. Feb. 24, 1905, Sheldon, N. D. D. Feb. 15, 1955, Kansas City, Mo.
BL TR 5'10½" 170 lbs.

1930	CHI N	37	.222	.389	18	4	1	1	0	0.0	0	2	0	1	0	0	0	6	22	1	1	0.8	.966	P-37
1933		29	.238	.381	21	5	1	1	0	0.0	5	1	3	0	0	0	0	1	20	0	1	0.7	1.000	P-24
1934		2	–	–	0	0	0	0	0	–	0	0	0	0	0	0	0	0	0	0	0	0	–	P-2
1937	PHI A	74	.354	.549	113	40	6	2	4	3.5	18	29	6	13	1	38	9	19	15	0	0	0.5	1.000	P-30, OF-6
1938		67	.277	.277	112	31	0	0	0	0.0	12	15	7	12	0	32	6	4	36	2	0	0.6	.952	P-32
1939		40	.188	.213	80	15	2	0	0	0.0	3	5	2	13	0	5	1	11	27	2	6	1.0	.950	P-35
1940	DET A	19	.348	.478	23	8	0	0	1	4.3	4	3	0	6	0	14	5	0	3	0	0	0.2	1.000	P-6
7 yrs.		268	.281	.371	367	103	10	4	5	1.4	42	55	16	48	1	89	21	41	123	5	8	0.6	.970	P-166, OF-6

Ray Nelson
NELSON, RAYMOND (Kell)
Born Raymond Nelson Kellogg.
B. Aug. 4, 1875, Holyoke, Mass. D. Jan. 8, 1961, Mount Vernon, N. Y.
BR TR 5'9" 150 lbs.

| 1901 | NY N | 39 | .200 | .215 | 130 | 26 | 2 | 0 | 0 | 0.0 | 12 | 7 | 10 | | 3 | 0 | 0 | 44 | 125 | 22 | 10 | 4.9 | .885 | 2B-39 |

Ricky Nelson
NELSON, RICKY LEE
B. May 8, 1959, Eloy, Ariz.
BL TR 6' 200 lbs.

1983	SEA A	98	.254	.371	291	74	13	3	5	1.7	32	36	17	50	7	12	5	122	10	4	1	1.4	.971	OF-91, DH-1
1984		9	.200	.400	15	3	0	0	1	6.7	2	2	2	4	0	5	1	2	0	0	0	0.2	1.000	DH-3, OF-2
1985		6	.000	.000	2	0	0	0	0	0.0	2	0	0	1	0	1	0	1	0	0	0	0.2	1.000	OF-3
1986		10	.167	.167	12	2	0	0	0	0.0	2	1	0	4	1	4	1	2	0	1	0	0.3	.667	DH-4, OF-1
4 yrs.		123	.247	.363	320	79	13	3	6	1.9	38	39	19	59	8	22	7	127	10	5	1	1.2	.965	OF-97, DH-8

Rob Nelson
NELSON, ROBERT AUGUSTUS
B. May 17, 1964, Pasadena, Calif.
BL TL 6'4" 215 lbs.

1986	OAK A	5	.222	.333	9	2	1	0	0	0.0	1	0	1	4	0	2	1	3	1	1	1	1.0	.800	1B-2, DH-1
1987	2 teams		OAK A (7G – .167)		SD N (10G – .091)																			
"	total	17	.143	.171	35	5	1	0	0	0.0	1	1	1	20	0	7	1	63	11	2	7	4.5	.974	1B-9
1988	SD N	7	.190	.333	21	4	0	0	1	4.8	4	3	2	9	0	2	0	48	5	1	5	7.7	.981	1B-5
1989		42	.195	.329	82	16	0	1	3	3.7	6	7	20	29	1	11	1	201	23	2	17	5.4	.991	1B-31
4 yrs.		71	.184	.293	147	27	2	1	4	2.7	12	11	24	62	1	22	3	315	40	6	30	5.1	.983	1B-47, DH-1

Rocky Nelson
NELSON, GLENN RICHARD
B. Nov. 18, 1924, Portsmouth, Ohio
BL TL 5'10½" 175 lbs.

1949	STL N	82	.221	.336	244	54	8	4	4	1.6	28	32	11	12	1	8	2	564	24	0	48	7.2	1.000	1B-70
1950		76	.247	.336	235	58	10	4	4	1.7	26	26	9		1	4	1	596	51	5	66	8.6	.992	1B-70
1951	3 teams		STL N (9G – .222)		PIT N (71G – .267)		CHI A (6G – .000)																	
"	total	86	.257	.344	218	56	4	1	1	0.5	32	15	12	7	0	31	6	326	26	3	37	4.1	.992	1B-36, OF-13
1952	BKN N	37	.256	.282	39	10	1	0	0	0.0	6	3	7	4	0	27	7	16	0	0	2	0.4	1.000	1B-5
1954	CLE A	4	.000	.000	4	0	0	0	0	0.0	0	1	0	0	0	3	0	6	0	0	1	1.5	1.000	1B-2
1956	2 teams		BKN N (31G – .208)		STL N (38G – .232)																			
"	total	69	.217	.401	152	33	7	0	7	4.6	13	23	10	16	0	26	3	254	27	2	26	4.1	.993	1B-39, OF-8
1959	PIT N	98	.291	.457	175	51	11	0	6	3.4	31	32	23	19	0	33	13	339	18	3	45	3.7	.992	1B-56, OF-2
1960		93	.300	.470	200	60	11	1	7	3.5	34	35	24	15	1	18	4	463	37	2	48	5.4	.996	1B-73
1961		75	.197	.370	127	25	5	1	5	3.9	15	13	17	11	0	37	5	231	15	1	26	3.3	.996	1B-35
9 yrs.		620	.249	.379	1394	347	61	14	31	2.2	186	173	130	94	6	187	41	2795	198	16	299	4.9	.995	1B-386, OF-23

WORLD SERIES
1952	BKN N	4	.000	.000	3	0	0	0	0	0.0	0	0	1	2	0	3	0	0	0	0	0	0.0	–	
1960	PIT N	4	.333	.667	9	3	0	0	1	11.1	2	2	1	1	0	1	0	13	3	0	0	4.0	1.000	1B-3
2 yrs.		8	.250	.500	12	3	0	0	1	8.3	2	2	2	3	0	4	0	13	3	0	0	2.0	1.000	1B-3

Tom Nelson
NELSON, TOM COUSINEAU
B. May 1, 1917, Chicago, Ill. D. Sept. 24, 1973, San Diego, Calif.
BR TR 6' 180 lbs.

| 1945 | BOS N | 40 | .165 | .182 | 121 | 20 | 2 | 0 | 0 | 0.0 | 6 | 6 | 4 | 13 | 1 | 8 | 1 | 39 | 64 | 11 | 9 | 2.9 | .904 | 3B-20, 2B-12 |

Dick Nen
NEN, RICHARD LeROY
B. Sept. 24, 1939, South Gate, Calif.
BL TL 6'2" 200 lbs.

1963	LA N	7	.125	.500	8	1	0	0	1	12.5	1	3	3	3	0	4	0	22	0	0	0	3.1	1.000	1B-5
1965	WAS A	69	.260	.370	246	64	7	1	6	2.4	18	31	19	47	1	5	1	519	61	4	48	8.5	.993	1B-65
1966		94	.213	.323	235	50	8	0	6	2.6	20	30	28	46	0	20	3	566	38	6	44	6.5	.990	1B-76
1967		110	.218	.332	238	52	7	1	6	2.5	21	29	21	39	0	40	6	516	42	3	49	5.1	.995	1B-65, OF-1
1968	CHI A	81	.181	.277	94	17	1	1	2	2.1	8	16	6	17	0	28	4	219	11	3	12	2.9	.987	1B-52
1970	WAS A	6	.200	.200	5	1	0	0	0	0.0	0	0	0	0	0	5	1	4	0	0	0	0.8	1.000	1B-1
6 yrs.		367	.224	.335	826	185	23	3	21	2.5	70	107	77	152	1	102	15	1846	153	16	153	5.5	.992	1B-264, OF-1

Jack Ness
NESS, JOHN CHARLES
B. Nov. 11, 1885, Chicago, Ill. D. Dec. 3, 1957, DeLand, Fla.
BR TR 6'2" 165 lbs.

1911	DET A	12	.154	.154	39	6	0	0	0	0.0	6	2	2		0	0	0	119	9	3	4	10.9	.977	1B-12
1916	CHI A	75	.267	.345	258	69	7	5	1	0.4	32	34	9	32	4	6	3	655	31	15	45	9.3	.979	1B-69
2 yrs.		87	.253	.320	297	75	7	5	1	0.3	38	36	11	32	4	6	3	774	40	18	49	9.6	.978	1B-81

Graig Nettles
NETTLES, GRAIG
Brother of Jim Nettles.
B. Aug. 20, 1944, San Diego, Calif.
BL TR 6' 180 lbs.

| 1967 | MIN A | 3 | .333 | .667 | 3 | 1 | 1 | 0 | 0 | 0.0 | 0 | 0 | 0 | 0 | 0 | 1 | 0 | 0 | 0 | 0 | 0 | 0.0 | – | |
| 1968 | | 22 | .224 | .474 | 76 | 17 | 2 | 1 | 5 | 6.6 | 13 | 8 | 7 | 20 | 0 | 0 | 0 | 50 | 9 | 2 | 2 | 2.8 | .967 | OF-16, 3B-5, 1B-3 |

Year	Team		Games	BA	SA	AB	H	2B	3B	HR	HR%	R	RBI	BB	SO	SB	Pinch Hit AB	Pinch Hit H	PO	A	E	DP	TC/G	FA	G by Pos

Graig Nettles *continued*

Year	Team		Games	BA	SA	AB	H	2B	3B	HR	HR%	R	RBI	BB	SO	SB	PH AB	PH H	PO	A	E	DP	TC/G	FA	G by Pos
1969			96	.222	.373	225	50	9	2	7	3.1	27	26	32	47	1	28	4	88	44	2	3	1.4	.985	OF-54, 3B-21
1970	CLE	A	157	.235	.404	549	129	13	1	26	4.7	81	62	81	77	3	5	1	135	358	17	40	3.2	.967	3B-154, OF-3
1971			158	.261	.435	598	156	18	1	28	4.7	78	86	82	56	7	0	0	159	412	16	54	3.7	.973	3B-158
1972			150	.253	.395	557	141	28	0	17	3.1	65	70	57	50	2	0	0	114	358	21	27	3.3	.957	3B-150
1973	NY	A	160	.234	.386	552	129	18	0	22	4.0	65	81	78	76	0	1	0	117	410	26	39	3.5	.953	3B-157, DH-2
1974			155	.246	.403	566	139	21	1	22	3.9	74	75	59	75	1	1	0	147	377	21	29	3.5	.961	3B-154, SS-1
1975			157	.267	.430	581	155	24	4	21	3.6	71	91	51	88	1	0	0	135	379	19	31	3.4	.964	3B-157
1976			158	.254	.475	583	148	29	2	32	5.5	88	93	62	94	11	1	0	137	384	19	30	3.4	.965	3B-158, SS-1
1977			158	.255	.496	589	150	23	4	37	6.3	99	107	68	79	2	0	0	132	321	12	31	2.9	.974	3B-156, SS-1
1978			159	.276	.460	587	162	23	2	27	4.6	81	93	59	69	1	0	0	110	326	11	30	2.8	.975	3B-159, SS-2
1979			145	.253	.401	521	132	15	1	20	3.8	71	73	59	53	1	2	0	110	339	16	30	3.2	.966	3B-144
1980			89	.244	.435	324	79	14	0	16	4.9	52	45	42	42	0	3	1	59	182	10	18	2.8	.960	3B-88, SS-1
1981			103	.244	.398	349	85	7	1	15	4.3	46	46	47	49	0	3	1	63	214	8	14	2.8	.972	3B-97, DH-4
1982			122	.232	.402	405	94	11	2	18	4.4	47	55	51	49	1	10	1	73	255	23	23	2.9	.934	3B-113, DH-3
1983			129	.266	.446	462	123	17	3	20	4.3	56	75	51	65	0	6	3	78	273	16	18	2.8	.956	3B-126, DH-1
1984	SD	N	124	.228	.413	395	90	11	1	20	5.1	56	65	58	55	0	13	3	93	201	20	14	2.5	.936	3B-119
1985			137	.261	.420	440	115	23	1	15	3.4	66	61	72	59	0	9	2	122	229	15	16	2.7	.959	3B-130
1986			126	.218	.379	354	77	9	0	16	4.5	36	55	41	62	0	19	5	83	174	16	14	2.2	.941	3B-114
1987	ATL	N	112	.209	.350	177	37	8	1	5	2.8	16	33	22	25	1	72	13	61	56	3	13	1.1	.975	3B-40, 1B-6
1988	MON	N	80	.172	.247	93	16	4	0	1	1.1	5	14	9	19	0	54	13	32	14	1	4	0.6	.902	3B-12, 1B-5
22 yrs.			2700	.248	.421	8986	2225	328	28	390	4.3	1193	1314	1088	1209	32	230	48	2098	5315	298	480	2.9	.961	3B-2412, OF-73, 1B-14, DH-11, SS-5

DIVISIONAL PLAYOFF SERIES

Year	Team		Games	BA	SA	AB	H	2B	3B	HR	HR%	R	RBI	BB	SO	SB	PH AB	PH H	PO	A	E	DP	TC/G	FA	G by Pos
1981	NY	A	5	.059	.059	17	1	0	0	0	0.0	1	1	3	1	0	0	0	0	0	0	0	0.0	–	3B-5

LEAGUE CHAMPIONSHIP SERIES

Year	Team		Games	BA	SA	AB	H	2B	3B	HR	HR%	R	RBI	BB	SO	SB	PH AB	PH H	PO	A	E	DP	TC/G	FA	G by Pos
1969	MIN	A	1	1.000	1.000	1	1	0	0	0	0.0	0	0	0	0	0	1	1	0	0	0	0	0.0	–	
1976	NY	A	5	.235	.647	17	4	1	0	2	11.8	2	4	3	3	0	0	0	5	14	0	0	3.8	1.000	3B-5
1977			5	.150	.150	20	3	0	0	0	0.0	1	1	0	3	0	0	0	2	12	0	2	2.8	1.000	3B-5
1978			4	.333	.667	15	5	0	1	1	6.7	3	2	0	1	0	0	0	6	7	0	2	3.3	1.000	3B-4
1980			2	.167	.667	6	1	0	0	1	16.7	1	1	0	1	0	1	0	2	0	0	0	1.0	1.000	3B-2
1981			3	.500	.917	12	6	2	0	1	8.3	2	9	1	0	0	0	0	0	1	0	0	0.3	1.000	3B-3
1984	SD	N	4	.143	.143	14	2	0	0	0	0.0	1	2	1	1	0	0	0	5	7	0	0	3.0	1.000	3B-4
7 yrs.			24	.259	.494	85	22	3	1	5	5.9	10	19	5	9	0	2	1	18	42	1	4	2.5	.984	3B-23

WORLD SERIES

Year	Team		Games	BA	SA	AB	H	2B	3B	HR	HR%	R	RBI	BB	SO	SB	PH AB	PH H	PO	A	E	DP	TC/G	FA	G by Pos
1976	NY	A	4	.250	.250	12	3	0	0	0	0.0	0	2	3	1	0	0	0	8	8	0	2	4.0	1.000	3B-4
1977			6	.190	.238	21	4	1	0	0	0.0	1	2	2	3	0	0	0	2	20	1	0	3.8	.957	3B-6
1978			6	.160	.160	25	4	0	0	0	0.0	2	1	0	6	0	0	0	8	18	0	4	4.3	1.000	3B-6
1981			3	.400	.500	10	4	1	0	0	0.0	1	0	1	1	0	0	0	3	10	1	0	4.7	.929	3B-3
1984	SD	N	5	.250	.250	12	3	0	0	0	0.0	2	2	5	0	0	0	0	7	12	0	1	3.8	1.000	3B-5
5 yrs.			24	.225	.250	80	18	2	0	0	0.0	6	7	11	11	0	0	0	28	68	2	7	4.1	.980	3B-24

Jim Nettles

NETTLES, JAMES WILLIAM
Brother of Graig Nettles.
B. Mar. 2, 1947, San Diego, Calif.

BL TL 6'   186 lbs.

Year	Team		Games	BA	SA	AB	H	2B	3B	HR	HR%	R	RBI	BB	SO	SB	PH AB	PH H	PO	A	E	DP	TC/G	FA	G by Pos
1970	MIN	A	13	.250	.250	20	5	0	0	0	0.0	3	0	1	5	0	1	0	8	0	0	0	0.6	1.000	OF-11
1971			70	.250	.399	168	42	5	1	6	3.6	17	24	19	24	3	8	2	139	3	2	1	2.1	.986	OF-62
1972			102	.204	.294	235	48	5	2	4	1.7	28	15	32	52	4	20	7	157	5	3	1	1.6	.982	OF-78, 1B-1
1974	DET	A	43	.227	.404	141	32	5	1	6	4.3	20	17	15	26	1	1	1	80	1	0	0	1.9	1.000	OF-41
1979	KC	A	11	.087	.087	23	2	0	0	0	0.0	0	1	3	2	0	2	0	21	0	0	0	1.9	1.000	OF-8, 1B-1
1981	OAK	A	1	–	–	0	0	0	0	0	–	0	0	0	0	0	0	0	0	0	0	0	0.0	–	OF-1
6 yrs.			240	.220	.341	587	129	15	4	16	2.7	68	57	70	109	10	32	10	405	9	5	2	1.7	.988	OF-201, 1B-2

Morris Nettles

NETTLES, MORRIS, JR.
B. Jan. 26, 1952, Los Angeles, Calif.

BL TL 6'1"   170 lbs.

Year	Team		Games	BA	SA	AB	H	2B	3B	HR	HR%	R	RBI	BB	SO	SB	PH AB	PH H	PO	A	E	DP	TC/G	FA	G by Pos
1974	CAL	A	56	.274	.297	175	48	4	0	0	0.0	27	8	17	38	20	2	1	99	0	1	0	1.8	.990	OF-54
1975			112	.231	.269	294	68	11	0	0	0.0	50	23	26	57	22	6	2	186	4	5	0	1.7	.974	OF-90, DH-9
2 yrs.			168	.247	.279	469	116	15	0	0	0.0	77	31	43	95	42	8	3	285	4	6	0	1.8	.980	OF-144, DH-9

Milo Netzel

NETZEL, MILES A.
B. May 12, 1886, Eldred, Pa.   D. Mar. 18, 1938, Oxnard, Calif.

TL

Year	Team		Games	BA	SA	AB	H	2B	3B	HR	HR%	R	RBI	BB	SO	SB	PH AB	PH H	PO	A	E	DP	TC/G	FA	G by Pos
1909	CLE	A	10	.189	.216	37	7	1	0	0	0.0	2	3	3		1	1	1	5	9	4	1	1.8	.778	3B-6, OF-2

Otto Neu

NEU, OTTO ADAM (Ott)
B. Sept. 24, 1894, Springfield, Ohio   D. Sept. 19, 1932, Kenton, Ohio

BR TR 5'11"   170 lbs.

Year	Team		Games	BA	SA	AB	H	2B	3B	HR	HR%	R	RBI	BB	SO	SB	PH AB	PH H	PO	A	E	DP	TC/G	FA	G by Pos
1917	STL	A	1	–	–	0	0	0	0	0	–	0	0	0	0	0	0	0	0	0	0	0	0.0	–	SS-1

Johnny Neun

NEUN, JOHN HENRY
B. Oct. 28, 1900, Baltimore, Md.
Manager 1946-48.

BB TL 5'10½"   175 lbs.

BR 1928

Year	Team		Games	BA	SA	AB	H	2B	3B	HR	HR%	R	RBI	BB	SO	SB	PH AB	PH H	PO	A	E	DP	TC/G	FA	G by Pos
1925	DET	A	60	.267	.387	75	20	3	3	0	0.0	15	4	9	12	2	33	8	99	4	1	5	1.7	.990	1B-13
1926			97	.298	.388	242	72	14	4	0	0.0	47	15	27	26	4	42	12	433	22	3	34	4.7	.993	1B-49
1927			79	.324	.407	204	66	9	4	0	0.0	38	27	35	13	22	17	6	548	30	12	45	7.5	.980	1B-53
1928			36	.213	.259	108	23	3	1	0	0.0	15	5	7	10	2	11	3	180	16	5	16	5.6	.975	1B-25
1930	BOS	N	81	.325	.429	212	69	12	2	2	0.9	39	23	21	18	9	23	8	431	31	4	46	5.8	.991	1B-55
1931			79	.221	.288	104	23	1	3	0	0.0	17	11	11	14	2	34	4	159	9	1	15	2.1	.994	1B-36
6 yrs.			432	.289	.376	945	273	42	17	2	0.2	171	85	110	93	41	160	41	1850	112	26	161	4.6	.987	1B-231

Don Newcombe

NEWCOMBE, DONALD (Newk)
B. June 14, 1926, Madison, N.J.

BL TR 6'4"   220 lbs.

Year	Team		Games	BA	SA	AB	H	2B	3B	HR	HR%	R	RBI	BB	SO	SB	Pinch Hit AB	Pinch Hit H	PO	A	E	DP	TC/G	FA	G by Pos

Don Newcombe *continued*

Year	Team		Games	BA	SA	AB	H	2B	3B	HR	HR%	R	RBI	BB	SO	SB	PH AB	PH H	PO	A	E	DP	TC/G	FA	G by Pos
1949	BKN	N	39	.229	.271	96	22	4	0	0	0.0	8	10	5	16	0	1	0	17	40	0	2	1.5	1.000	P-38
1950			40	.247	.330	97	24	3	1	1	1.0	8	8	10	19	0	0	0	19	43	2	3	1.6	.969	P-40
1951			40	.223	.272	103	23	3	1	0	0.0	11	8	8	9	0	0	0	24	45	3	3	1.8	.958	P-40
1954			31	.319	.340	47	15	1	0	0	0.0	6	4	4	6	0	1	0	11	16	2	2	0.9	.931	P-29
1955			57	.359	.632	117	42	9	1	7	6.0	18	23	6	18	1	21	8	15	24	4	5	0.8	.907	P-34
1956			52	.234	.342	111	26	6	0	2	1.8	13	16	12	18	1	12	0	25	39	1	5	1.3	.985	P-38
1957			34	.230	.297	74	17	2	0	1	1.4	8	7	11	11	0	3	0	13	41	2	1	1.6	.964	P-28
1958	2 teams		50	LA N (11G – .417)		CIN N (39G – .350)																			
"	total		50	.361	.417	72	26	1	0	1	1.4	11	9	10	12	0	16	6	11	19	0	2	0.6	1.000	P-31
1959	CIN	N	61	.305	.410	105	32	2	0	3	2.9	10	21	17	23	0	21	5	14	31	1	4	0.8	.978	P-30
1960	2 teams		48	CIN N (24G – .139)		CLE A (24G – .300)																			
"	total		48	.196	.232	56	11	2	0	0	0.0	1	2	4	15	0	12	1	10	15	3	0	0.6	.893	P-36
10 yrs.			452	.271	.367	878	238	33	3	15	1.7	94	108	87	147	2	87	20	159	313	18	27	1.1	.963	P-344

WORLD SERIES

Year	Team		Games	BA	SA	AB	H	2B	3B	HR	HR%	R	RBI	BB	SO	SB	PH AB	PH H	PO	A	E	DP	TC/G	FA	G by Pos
1949	BKN	N	2	.000	.000	4	0	0	0	0	0.0	0	0	0	3	0	0	0	1	1	0	0	1.0	1.000	P-2
1955			1	.000	.000	3	0	0	0	0	0.0	0	0	0	0	0	0	0	0	1	0	0	1.0	1.000	P-1
1956			2	.000	.000	1	0	0	0	0	0.0	0	0	0	0	0	0	0	0	2	0	0	1.0	1.000	P-2
3 yrs.			5	.000	.000	8	0	0	0	0	0.0	0	0	0	3	0	0	0	1	4	0	0	1.0	1.000	P-5

John Newell

NEWELL, JOHN A.
B. Jan. 14, 1868, Wilmington, Del.   D. Jan. 28, 1919, Wilmington, Del.   BR TL

Year	Team		Games	BA	SA	AB	H	2B	3B	HR	HR%	R	RBI	BB	SO	SB	PH AB	PH H	PO	A	E	DP	TC/G	FA	G by Pos
1891	PIT	N	5	.111	.111	18	2	0	0	0	0.0	1	0	2	0	0	0	0	1	10	2	0	2.6	.846	3B-5

T. E. Newell

NEWELL, T. E.
B. St. Louis, Mo.   Deceased.

Year	Team		Games	BA	SA	AB	H	2B	3B	HR	HR%	R	RBI	BB	SO	SB	PH AB	PH H	PO	A	E	DP	TC/G	FA	G by Pos
1877	STL	N	1	.000	.000	3	0	0	0	0	0.0	0	0	0	0	0	0	0	2	3	1	0	6.0	.833	SS-1

Al Newman

NEWMAN, ALBERT DWAYNE
B. June 30, 1960, Kansas City, Mo.   BB TR 5'9"   175 lbs.

Year	Team		Games	BA	SA	AB	H	2B	3B	HR	HR%	R	RBI	BB	SO	SB	PH AB	PH H	PO	A	E	DP	TC/G	FA	G by Pos
1985	MON	N	25	.172	.207	29	5	1	0	0	0.0	7	1	3	4	2	2	0	19	36	0	7	2.2	1.000	2B-15, SS-2
1986			95	.200	.232	185	37	3	0	1	0.5	23	8	21	20	11	14	2	98	161	11	35	2.8	.959	2B-59, SS-22
1987	MIN	A	110	.221	.303	307	68	15	5	0	0.0	44	29	34	27	15	6	0	120	225	5	44	3.2	.986	SS-55, 2B-47, 3B-12, DH-5, OF-2
1988			105	.223	.250	260	58	7	0	0	0.0	35	19	29	34	12	3	0	97	155	6	33	2.5	.977	3B-60, SS-28, 2B-23
1989			141	.253	.303	446	113	18	2	0	0.0	62	38	59	46	25	9	2	191	282	16	58	3.5	.967	2B-84, 3B-37, SS-31, OF-4, DH-2
5 yrs.			476	.229	.279	1227	281	44	7	1	0.1	171	95	146	131	65	34	4	525	859	38	177	3.0	.973	2B-228, SS-138, 3B-109, DH-7, OF-6

LEAGUE CHAMPIONSHIP SERIES

Year	Team		Games	BA	SA	AB	H	2B	3B	HR	HR%	R	RBI	BB	SO	SB	PH AB	PH H	PO	A	E	DP	TC/G	FA	G by Pos
1987	MIN	A	1	.000	.000	2	0	0	0	0	0.0	0	0	0	0	0	0	0	1	0	0	0	1.0	1.000	2B-1

WORLD SERIES

Year	Team		Games	BA	SA	AB	H	2B	3B	HR	HR%	R	RBI	BB	SO	SB	PH AB	PH H	PO	A	E	DP	TC/G	FA	G by Pos
1987	MIN	A	4	.200	.200	5	1	0	0	0	0.0	0	0	1	1	0	1	0	1	2	0	0	0.8	1.000	2B-3

Charlie Newman

NEWMAN, CHARLES
B. Nov. 5, 1868, Juda, Wis.   D. Nov. 23, 1947, San Diego, Calif.   BR TR 5'11"   160 lbs.

Year	Team		Games	BA	SA	AB	H	2B	3B	HR	HR%	R	RBI	BB	SO	SB	PH AB	PH H	PO	A	E	DP	TC/G	FA	G by Pos
1892	2 teams		19	NY N (3G – .333)		CHI N (16G – .164)																			
"	total		19	.192	.192	73	14	0	0	0	0.0	5	3	3	6	5	0	0	20	2	2	1	1.3	.917	OF-19

Jeff Newman

NEWMAN, JEFFREY LYNN
B. Sept. 11, 1948, Ft. Worth, Tex.
Manager 1986.   BR TR 6'2"   215 lbs.

Year	Team		Games	BA	SA	AB	H	2B	3B	HR	HR%	R	RBI	BB	SO	SB	PH AB	PH H	PO	A	E	DP	TC/G	FA	G by Pos
1976	OAK	A	43	.195	.247	77	15	4	0	0	0.0	5	4	4	12	0	5	1	140	18	3	1	3.7	.981	C-43
1977			94	.222	.352	162	36	9	0	4	2.5	17	15	4	24	2	1	0	251	36	9	5	3.1	.970	C-94, P-1
1978			105	.239	.373	268	64	7	1	9	3.4	25	32	18	40	0	24	6	399	41	12	20	4.3	.973	C-61, 1B-36, DH-2
1979			143	.231	.399	516	119	17	2	22	4.3	53	71	27	88	2	9	2	730	95	18	38	5.9	.979	C-81, 1B-46, DH-7, 3B-7
1980			127	.233	.384	438	102	19	1	15	3.4	37	56	25	81	3	12	5	675	54	15	28	5.9	.980	1B-60, C-55, DH-9, 3B-2, 2B-1
1981			68	.231	.329	216	50	12	0	3	1.4	17	15	9	28	0	5	0	367	28	2	14	5.8	.995	C-37, 1B-30
1982			72	.199	.315	251	50	11	0	6	2.4	19	30	14	49	0	1	1	347	28	5	6	5.3	.987	C-67, 1B-3, DH-1, 3B-1
1983	BOS	A	59	.189	.288	132	25	4	0	3	2.3	11	7	10	31	0	4	1	171	19	2	3	3.3	.990	C-51, DH-6
1984			24	.222	.302	63	14	2	0	1	1.6	5	3	5	16	0	0	0	118	8	1	0	5.3	.992	C-24
9 yrs.			735	.224	.357	2123	475	85	4	63	3.0	189	233	116	369	7	56	15	3198	327	67	115	4.9	.981	C-513, 1B-175, DH-25, 3B-10, 2B-1, P-1

DIVISIONAL PLAYOFF SERIES

Year	Team		Games	BA	SA	AB	H	2B	3B	HR	HR%	R	RBI	BB	SO	SB	PH AB	PH H	PO	A	E	DP	TC/G	FA	G by Pos
1981	OAK	A	1	.000	.000	3	0	0	0	0	0.0	0	0	0	1	0	0	0	0	0	0	0	–		C-1

LEAGUE CHAMPIONSHIP SERIES

Year	Team		Games	BA	SA	AB	H	2B	3B	HR	HR%	R	RBI	BB	SO	SB	PH AB	PH H	PO	A	E	DP	TC/G	FA	G by Pos
1981	OAK	A	2	.000	.000	5	0	0	0	0	0.0	0	0	0	2	0	0	0	0	0	0	0	0.0		C-2

Pat Newnam

NEWNAM, PATRICK HENRY
B. Dec. 10, 1880, Hempstead, Tex.   D. June 20, 1938, San Antonio, Tex.   BR TR 6'   180 lbs.

Year	Team		Games	BA	SA	AB	H	2B	3B	HR	HR%	R	RBI	BB	SO	SB	PH AB	PH H	PO	A	E	DP	TC/G	FA	G by Pos
1910	STL	A	103	.216	.281	384	83	3	8	2	0.5	45	26	29		16	0	0	1041	56	32	53	11.0	.972	1B-103
1911			20	.194	.258	62	12	4	0	0	0.0	11	5	12		4	0	0	200	14	3	11	10.9	.986	1B-20
2 yrs.			123	.213	.278	446	95	7	8	2	0.4	56	31	41		20	0	0	1241	70	35	64	10.9	.974	1B-123

Skeeter Newsome

NEWSOME, LAMAR ASHBY
B. Oct. 18, 1910, Phenix City, Ala.   BR TR 5'9"   155 lbs.

Year	Team		Games	BA	SA	AB	H	2B	3B	HR	HR%	R	RBI	BB	SO	SB	PH AB	PH H	PO	A	E	DP	TC/G	FA	G by Pos
1935	PHI	A	59	.207	.290	145	30	7	1	1	0.7	18	10	5	9	2	7	0	79	110	9	25	3.4	.955	SS-24, 2B-13, 3B-4, OF-1
1936			127	.225	.265	471	106	15	2	0	0.0	41	46	25	27	13	2	0	274	418	31	87	5.7	.957	SS-123, 2B-2, OF-1, 3B-1

Year	Team		Games	BA	SA	AB	H	2B	3B	HR	HR%	R	RBI	BB	SO	SB	Pinch Hit AB	Pinch Hit H	PO	A	E	DP	TC/G	FA	G by Pos

Skeeter Newsome *continued*

Year	Team		Games	BA	SA	AB	H	2B	3B	HR	HR%	R	RBI	BB	SO	SB	AB	H	PO	A	E	DP	TC/G	FA	G by Pos
1937			122	.253	.315	438	111	22	1	1	0.2	53	30	37	22	11	0	0	256	408	32	76	5.7	.954	SS-122
1938			17	.271	.354	48	13	4	0	0	0.0	7	7	1	4	1	0	0	24	43	2	7	4.1	.971	SS-15
1939			99	.222	.266	248	55	9	1	0	0.0	22	17	19	12	5	1	0	178	221	21	44	4.2	.950	SS-93, 2B-2
1941	BOS	A	93	.225	.278	227	51	6	0	2	0.9	28	17	22	11	10	0	0	141	204	13	36	3.8	.964	SS-69, 2B-23
1942			29	.274	.337	95	26	6	0	0	0.0	7	9	9	5	2	0	0	56	67	7	13	4.5	.946	3B-12, 2B-10, SS-7
1943			114	.265	.327	449	119	21	2	1	0.2	48	22	21	21	5	0	0	245	346	21	71	5.4	.966	SS-98, 3B-15
1944			136	.242	.309	472	114	26	3	0	0.0	41	41	33	21	4	0	0	270	447	30	87	5.5	.960	SS-126, 2B-8, 3B-1
1945			125	.290	.370	438	127	30	1	1	0.2	45	48	20	15	6	1	0	276	376	22	78	5.4	.967	2B-82, SS-33, 3B-11
1946	PHI	N	112	.232	.277	375	87	10	2	1	0.3	35	23	30	23	4	3	0	181	321	24	53	4.7	.954	SS-107, 2B-3, 3B-2
1947			95	.229	.287	310	71	8	2	2	0.6	36	22	24	24	4	1	1	136	252	12	60	4.2	.970	SS-85, 2B-6, 3B-1
12 yrs.			1128	.245	.304	3716	910	164	15	9	0.2	381	292	246	194	67	15	1	2116	3213	224	637	4.9	.960	SS-902, 2B-149, 3B-47, OF-2

Gus Niarhos

NIARHOS, CONSTANTINE GREGORY
B. Dec. 6, 1920, Birmingham, Ala.

BR TR 6' 160 lbs.

Year	Team		Games	BA	SA	AB	H	2B	3B	HR	HR%	R	RBI	BB	SO	SB	AB	H	PO	A	E	DP	TC/G	FA	G by Pos
1946	NY	A	37	.225	.300	40	9	1	1	0	0.0	11	2	11	2	1	2	0	76	10	1	1	2.4	.989	C-29
1948			83	.268	.338	228	61	12	2	0	0.0	41	19	52	15	1	0	0	376	33	4	7	5.0	.990	C-82
1949			32	.279	.372	43	12	2	1	0	0.0	7	6	13	8	0	2	1	84	7	0	2	2.8	1.000	C-30
1950 2 teams		NY A (1G – .000)				CHI A (41G – .324)																			
" total			42	.324	.362	105	34	4	0	0	0.0	17	16	14	6	0	2	0	167	14	4	2	4.4	.978	C-36
1951	CHI	A	66	.256	.310	168	43	6	0	1	0.6	27	10	47	9	4	4	2	240	31	4	5	4.2	.985	C-59
1952	BOS	A	29	.103	.103	58	6	0	0	0	0.0	4	4	12	9	0	3	0	107	12	1	2	4.1	.992	C-25
1953			16	.200	.286	35	7	1	1	0	0.0	6	2	4	0	0	0	0	61	5	1	2	4.2	.985	C-16
1954	PHI	N	3	.200	.200	5	1	0	0	0	0.0	0	0	0	1	0	0	0	9	1	0	0	3.3	1.000	C-3
1955			7	.111	.111	9	1	0	0	0	0.0	1	0	0	2	0	0	0	13	2	0	0	2.1	1.000	C-7
9 yrs.			315	.252	.308	691	174	26	5	1	0.1	114	59	153	56	6	13	3	1133	115	15	21	4.0	.988	C-287

WORLD SERIES

| 1949 | NY | A | 1 | – | – | 0 | 0 | 0 | 0 | 0 | – | 0 | 0 | 0 | 0 | 0 | 0 | 0 | 0 | 0 | 0 | 0 | 0.0 | – | C-1 |

Sam Nichol

NICHOL, SAMUEL ANDERSON
B. Apr. 20, 1869, Ireland D. Apr. 19, 1937, Steubenville, Ohio

BR TR 5'10" 178 lbs.

Year	Team		Games	BA	SA	AB	H	2B	3B	HR	HR%	R	RBI	BB	SO	SB	AB	H	PO	A	E	DP	TC/G	FA	G by Pos
1888	PIT	N	8	.045	.045	22	1	0	0	0	0.0	3		2	2	0	0	0	19	1	1	0	2.6	.952	OF-8
1890	COL	AA	14	.161	.161	56	9	0	0	0	0.0	7		2		3	0	0	23	5	3	2	2.2	.903	OF-14
2 yrs.			22	.128	.128	78	10	0	0	0	0.0	10		4	2	3	0	0	42	6	4	2	2.4	.923	OF-22

Don Nicholas

NICHOLAS, DONALD LEIGH
B. Oct. 30, 1930, Phoenix, Ariz.

BL TR 5'7" 150 lbs.

Year	Team		Games	BA	SA	AB	H	2B	3B	HR	HR%	R	RBI	BB	SO	SB	AB	H	PO	A	E	DP	TC/G	FA	G by Pos
1952	CHI	A	3	.000	.000	2	0	0	0	0	0.0	0	0	0	0	0	2	0	0	0	0	0	0.0	–	OF-3
1954			7	–		0	0	0	0	0	–	3	0	1	0	0	0	0	0	0	0	0	0.0	–	OF-7
2 yrs.			10	.000	.000	2	0	0	0	0	0.0	3	0	1	0	0	2	0	0	0	0	0	0.0	–	OF-10

Simon Nicholls

NICHOLLS, SIMON BURDETTE
B. July 18, 1882, Germantown, Md. D. Mar. 12, 1911, Baltimore, Md.

BL TR

Year	Team		Games	BA	SA	AB	H	2B	3B	HR	HR%	R	RBI	BB	SO	SB	AB	H	PO	A	E	DP	TC/G	FA	G by Pos
1903	DET	A	2	.375	.375	8	3	0	0	0	0.0	0	0	0		0	0	0	3	3	4	0	5.0	.600	SS-2
1906	PHI	A	12	.182	.205	44	8	1	0	0	0.0	1	1	3		0	0	0	22	33	2	4	4.8	.965	SS-12
1907			126	.302	.337	460	139	12	2	0	0.0	75	23	24		13	2	0	227	337	48	17	4.9	.922	SS-82, 2B-28, 3B-13
1908			150	.216	.280	550	119	17	3	4	0.7	58	31	35		14	0	0	280	434	63	33	5.2	.919	SS-120, 2B-23, 3B-7
1909			21	.211	.268	71	15	2	1	0	0.0	10	3	3		0	1	0	39	49	9	5	4.6	.907	SS-14, 3B-5, 1B-1
1910	CLE	A	3	–	–	0	0	0	0	0	–	0	0	0		0	0	0	0	0	1	0	0.3	–	SS-3
6 yrs.			314	.251	.300	1133	284	32	6	4	0.4	144	58	65		27	3	0	571	856	127	59	4.9	.918	SS-233, 2B-51, 3B-25, 1B-1

Al Nichols

NICHOLS, ALFRED H.
B. Brooklyn, N. Y. Deceased.

5'11" 180 lbs.

Year	Team		Games	BA	SA	AB	H	2B	3B	HR	HR%	R	RBI	BB	SO	SB	AB	H	PO	A	E	DP	TC/G	FA	G by Pos
1876	NY	N	57	.179	.198	212	38	4	0	0	0.0	20	9	2	3		0	0	123	135	73	1	5.8	.779	3B-57
1877	LOU	N	6	.211	.316	19	4	0	1	0	0.0	1	0	0	2		0	0	12	22	5	2	6.5	.872	2B-3, SS-1, 3B-1, 1B-1
2 yrs.			63	.182	.208	231	42	4	1	0	0.0	21	9	2	5		0	0	135	157	78	3	5.9	.789	3B-58, 2B-3, SS-1, 1B-1

Art Nichols

NICHOLS, ARTHUR FRANCIS
Born Arthur Francis Meikle.
B. July 14, 1871, Manchester, N. H. D. Aug. 9, 1945, Willimantic, Conn.

BR TR 5'10" 175 lbs.

Year	Team		Games	BA	SA	AB	H	2B	3B	HR	HR%	R	RBI	BB	SO	SB	AB	H	PO	A	E	DP	TC/G	FA	G by Pos
1898	CHI	N	14	.286	.310	42	12	1	0	0	0.0	7	6	4		6	0	0	47	13	2	1	4.4	.968	C-14
1899			17	.255	.362	47	12	2	0	1	2.1	5	11	0		3	2	0	44	10	4	3	3.4	.931	C-15
1900			8	.200	.200	25	5	0	0	0	0.0	1	0	3		1	1	0	21	9	2	0	4.0	.938	C-7
1901	STL	N	93	.244	.308	308	75	11	3	1	0.3	50	33	10		14	6	1	256	60	13	9	3.5	.960	C-47, OF-40
1902			73	.267	.327	251	67	12	0	1	0.4	36	31	21		18	2	0	615	33	13	28	9.1	.980	1B-56, C-11, OF-4
1903			36	.192	.208	120	23	2	0	0	0.0	13	9	12		9	1	0	294	9	10	12	8.7	.968	1B-25, OF-7, C-2
6 yrs.			241	.245	.299	793	194	28	3	3	0.4	112	90	50		51	12	1	1277	134	44	53	6.0	.970	C-96, 1B-81, OF-51

Carl Nichols

NICHOLS, CARL EDWARD
B. Oct. 14, 1962, Los Angeles, Calif.

BR TR 6' 184 lbs.

Year	Team		Games	BA	SA	AB	H	2B	3B	HR	HR%	R	RBI	BB	SO	SB	AB	H	PO	A	E	DP	TC/G	FA	G by Pos
1986	BAL	A	5	.000	.000	5	0	0	0	0	0.0	1	4	0	0	0	0	0	11	0	0	0	2.2	1.000	C-5
1987			13	.381	.429	21	8	1	0	0	0.0	4	3	1	4	0	0	0	39	3	0	1	3.2	1.000	C-13
1988			18	.191	.213	47	9	1	0	0	0.0	2	1	3	10	0	1	0	71	13	1	2	4.7	.988	C-13, OF-3
1989	HOU	N	8	.077	.077	13	1	0	0	0	0.0	0	2	0	3	0	4	0	16	1	0	0	2.1	1.000	C-6
4 yrs.			44	.209	.233	86	18	2	0	0	0.0	6	6	5	21	0	5	0	137	17	1	3	3.5	.994	C-37, OF-3

Kid Nichols

NICHOLS, CHARLES AUGUSTUS (Nick)
B. Sept. 14, 1869, Madison, Wis. D. Apr. 11, 1953, Kansas City, Mo.
Manager 1904-05.
Hall of Fame 1949.

BB TR 5'10½" 175 lbs.

Year	Team		Games	BA	SA	AB	H	2B	3B	HR	HR%	R	RBI	BB	SO	SB	Pinch Hit AB	Pinch Hit H	PO	A	E	DP	TC/G	FA	G by Pos

Kid Nichols *continued*

Year	Team		Games	BA	SA	AB	H	2B	3B	HR	HR%	R	RBI	BB	SO	SB	AB	H	PO	A	E	DP	TC/G	FA	G by Pos
1890	BOS	N	49	.247	.287	174	43	5	1	0	0.0	18	23	11	36	2	0	0	15	85	14	1	2.3	.877	P-48, OF-2
1891			52	.197	.230	183	36	6	0	0	0.0	21	27	12	31	1	0	0	30	100	7	5	2.6	.949	P-52
1892			57	.198	.279	197	39	6	2	2	1.0	21	21	16	51	3	0	0	36	88	5	4	2.3	.961	P-53, OF-5
1893			53	.220	.294	177	39	3	2	2	1.1	25	26	15	22	4	0	0	22	81	7	5	2.1	.936	P-52, OF-1
1894			51	.294	.382	170	50	11	2	0	0.0	39	34	16	24	1	0	0	35	67	7	3	2.1	.936	P-50, OF-1
1895			49	.236	.280	157	37	3	2	0	0.0	23	18	14	28	0	0	0	29	73	4	2	2.2	.962	P-48, OF-1
1896			51	.190	.272	147	28	3	3	1	0.7	27	24	12	18	2	0	0	23	92	1	3	2.3	.991	P-49, OF-2
1897			46	.265	.361	147	39	5	0	3	2.0	20	28	7		4	0	0	29	62	3	1	2.0	.968	P-46
1898			51	.241	.335	158	38	3	3	2	1.3	26	23	4		0	0	0	28	78	5	1	2.2	.955	P-50, 1B-1
1899			42	.191	.235	136	26	3	0	1	0.7	13	12	6		1	0	0	25	71	5	5	2.4	.950	P-42
1900			29	.200	.233	90	18	0	0	1	1.1	14	7	7		1	0	0	19	48	1	1	2.3	.985	P-29
1901			55	.282	.491	163	46	8	7	4	2.5	16	28	8		0	4	2	73	72	10	4	2.8	.935	P-38, OF-7, 1B-5
1904	STL	N	36	.156	.202	109	17	1	2	0	0.0	7	5	7		0	0	0	13	84	5	1	2.8	.951	P-36
1905	2 teams	STL	N (8G – .227)			PHI	N	(17G – .189)																	
"	total		25	.200	.213	75	15	1	0	0	0.0	3	2	2		0	0	0	5	32	5	1	1.7	.881	P-24, OF-1
1906	PHI	N	4	.000	.000	3	0	0	0	0	0.0	0	0	0		0	0	0	0	1	0	0	0.3	1.000	P-4
	15 yrs.		650	.226	.300	2086	471	58	24	16	0.8	273	278	137	210	19	4	2	382	1034	79	37	2.3	.947	P-621, OF-20, 1B-6

Reid Nichols

NICHOLS, THOMAS REID
B. Aug. 5, 1958, Ocala, Fla.   BR TR 5'11" 165 lbs.

Year	Team		Games	BA	SA	AB	H	2B	3B	HR	HR%	R	RBI	BB	SO	SB	AB	H	PO	A	E	DP	TC/G	FA	G by Pos
1980	BOS	A	12	.222	.278	36	8	1	0	0	0.0	5	3	3	8	0	0	0	24	1	1	0	2.2	.962	OF-9, DH-1
1981			39	.188	.229	48	9	0	1	0	0.0	13	3	2	6	0	1	0	35	4	0	1	1.0	1.000	OF-27, DH-7, 3B-1
1982			92	.302	.461	245	74	16	1	7	2.9	35	33	14	28	5	6	0	169	9	2	4	2.0	.989	OF-82, DH-4
1983			100	.285	.438	274	78	22	1	6	2.2	35	22	26	36	7	19	6	168	5	1	1	1.7	.994	OF-72, DH-18, SS-1
1984			73	.226	.306	124	28	5	1	1	0.8	14	14	12	18	2	20	5	79	3	1	0	1.1	.988	OF-48, DH-1
1985	2 teams	BOS	A (21G – .188)			CHI	A	(51G – .297)																	
"	total		72	.273	.380	150	41	8	1	2	1.3	23	18	17	17	6	17	5	85	2	1	1	1.2	.989	OF-58, DH-5, 2B-3
1986	CHI	A	74	.228	.301	136	31	4	0	2	1.5	9	18	11	23	5	16	6	90	4	1	0	1.3	.989	OF-53, DH-3, 2B-2
1987	MON	N	77	.265	.429	147	39	4	2	4	2.7	22	20	14	13	2	16	3	98	5	2	0	1.4	.981	OF-59, 3B-3
	8 yrs.		539	.266	.391	1160	308	63	8	22	1.9	156	131	99	149	27	95	25	748	33	9	7	1.5	.989	OF-408, DH-39, 2B-5, 3B-4, SS-1

Roy Nichols

NICHOLS, ROY
B. Mar. 3, 1921, Little Rock, Ark.   BR TR 5'11" 155 lbs.

Year	Team		Games	BA	SA	AB	H	2B	3B	HR	HR%	R	RBI	BB	SO	SB	AB	H	PO	A	E	DP	TC/G	FA	G by Pos
1944	NY	N	11	.222	.333	9	2	1	0	0	0.0	3	0	2	2	0	1	0	3	4	0	0	0.6	1.000	3B-1, 2B-1

Tricky Nichols

NICHOLS, FREDERICK C.
B. July 26, 1850, Bridgeport, Conn.   D. Aug. 22, 1897, Bridgeport Conn.,   BR TR 5'7½" 150 lbs.

Year	Team		Games	BA	SA	AB	H	2B	3B	HR	HR%	R	RBI	BB	SO	SB	AB	H	PO	A	E	DP	TC/G	FA	G by Pos
1876	BOS	N	1	.000	.000	4	0	0	0	0	0.0	0	0	0		0	0	0	0	2	0	1	2.0	1.000	P-1
1877	STL	N	51	.167	.210	186	31	4	2	0	0.0	22	9	3	15	0	0	0	32	62	8	1	2.0	.922	P-42, OF-16
1878	PRO	N	11	.184	.224	49	9	2	0	0	0.0	2	2	2	10	0	0	0	6	27	1	2	3.1	.971	P-11
1880	WOR	N	2	.000	.000	7	0	0	0	0	0.0	0	0	0		0	0	0	0	3	3	0	3.0	.500	P-2
1882	BAL	AA	26	.158	.168	95	15	1	0	0	0.0	4		7		0	0	0	26	36	13	0	2.9	.827	P-16, OF-14
	5 yrs.		91	.161	.194	341	55	7	2	0	0.0	28	11	12	25	0	0	0	64	130	25	3	2.4	.886	P-72, OF-30

Bill Nicholson

NICHOLSON, WILLIAM BECK (Swish)
B. Dec. 11, 1914, Chestertown, Md.   BL TR 6' 205 lbs.

Year	Team		Games	BA	SA	AB	H	2B	3B	HR	HR%	R	RBI	BB	SO	SB	AB	H	PO	A	E	DP	TC/G	FA	G by Pos
1936	PHI	A	11	.000	.000	12	0	0	0	0	0.0	2	0	0	5	0	10	0	1	0	0	0	0.1	1.000	OF-1
1939	CHI	N	58	.295	.464	220	65	12	5	5	2.3	37	38	20	29	0	0	0	123	5	6	0	2.3	.955	OF-58
1940			135	.297	.534	491	146	27	7	25	5.1	78	98	50	67	2	9	2	235	10	13	2	1.9	.950	OF-123
1941			147	.254	.453	532	135	26	1	26	4.9	74	98	82	91	1	4	0	293	10	9	2	2.1	.971	OF-143
1942			152	.294	.476	588	173	22	11	21	3.6	83	78	76	80	8	1	0	327	18	5	2	2.3	.986	OF-151
1943			154	.309	.531	608	188	30	9	29	4.8	95	128	71	78	4	0	0	340	16	8	2	2.4	.978	OF-154
1944			156	.287	.545	582	167	35	8	33	5.7	116	122	93	71	3	0	0	305	18	7	4	2.1	.979	OF-156
1945			151	.243	.377	559	136	28	4	13	2.3	82	88	92	73	4	0	0	300	12	3	4	2.1	.990	OF-151
1946			105	.220	.358	296	65	13	2	8	2.7	36	41	44	44	1	18	6	179	4	5	1	1.8	.973	OF-80
1947			148	.244	.466	487	119	28	1	26	5.3	69	75	87	83	1	7	0	281	7	3	1	2.0	.990	OF-140
1948			143	.261	.445	494	129	24	5	19	3.8	68	67	81	60	2	4	3	244	7	5	1	1.8	.980	OF-136
1949	PHI	N	98	.234	.391	299	70	8	3	11	3.7	42	40	45	53	1	7	0	185	10	1	1	2.0	.995	OF-91
1950			41	.224	.448	58	13	2	1	3	5.2	3	10	8	16	0	24	5	20	0	1	0	0.5	.952	OF-15
1951			85	.241	.459	170	41	9	2	8	4.7	23	30	25	24	0	36	11	75	1	1	0	0.9	.987	OF-41
1952			55	.273	.511	88	24	3	0	6	6.8	17	19	14	26	0	31	8	33	0	0	0	0.6	1.000	OF-19
1953			38	.210	.419	62	13	5	1	2	3.2	12	16	12	20	0	23	2	13	0	0	0	0.3	1.000	OF-12
	16 yrs.		1677	.268	.465	5546	1484	272	60	235	4.2	837	948	800	820	27	174	37	2954	118	67	20	1.9	.979	OF-1471

WORLD SERIES

Year	Team		Games	BA	SA	AB	H	2B	3B	HR	HR%	R	RBI	BB	SO	SB	AB	H	PO	A	E	DP	TC/G	FA	G by Pos
1945	CHI	N	7	.214	.321	28	6	1	1	0	0.0	1	8	2	5	0	0	0	9	0	1	0	1.4	.900	OF-7

Dave Nicholson

NICHOLSON, DAVID LAWRENCE
B. Aug. 29, 1939, St. Louis, Mo.   BR TR 6'2" 215 lbs.

Year	Team		Games	BA	SA	AB	H	2B	3B	HR	HR%	R	RBI	BB	SO	SB	AB	H	PO	A	E	DP	TC/G	FA	G by Pos
1960	BAL	A	54	.186	.345	113	21	1	1	5	4.4	17	11	20	55	0	9	0	51	3	1	1	1.0	.982	OF-44
1962			97	.173	.364	173	30	4	1	9	5.2	25	15	27	76	3	4	0	111	4	2	0	1.2	.983	OF-80
1963	CHI	A	126	.229	.419	449	103	11	4	22	4.9	53	70	63	175	2	1	0	213	10	7	1	1.8	.970	OF-123
1964			97	.204	.364	294	60	6	1	13	4.4	40	39	52	126	0	7	1	136	4	4	0	1.5	.972	OF-92
1965			54	.153	.271	85	13	2	1	2	2.4	11	12	9	40	0	12	0	30	0	0	0	0.6	1.000	OF-36
1966	HOU	N	100	.246	.411	280	69	8	4	10	3.6	36	31	46	92	0	16	2	139	11	5	0	1.6	.968	OF-90
1967	ATL	N	10	.200	.200	25	5	0	0	0	0.0	2	1	2	9	0	3	0	10	1	0	0	1.1	1.000	OF-7
	7 yrs.		538	.212	.381	1419	301	32	12	61	4.3	184	179	219	573	6	52	4	690	33	19	2	1.4	.974	OF-472

Fred Nicholson

NICHOLSON, FRED
B. Sept. 1, 1894, Honey Grove, Tex.   D. Jan. 23, 1972, Kilgore, Tex.   BR TR 5'10½" 173 lbs.

Year	Team		Games	BA	SA	AB	H	2B	3B	HR	HR%	R	RBI	BB	SO	SB	Pinch Hit AB	Pinch Hit H	PO	A	E	DP	TC/G	FA	G by Pos

Fred Nicholson *continued*

Year	Team		Games	BA	SA	AB	H	2B	3B	HR	HR%	R	RBI	BB	SO	SB	PH AB	PH H	PO	A	E	DP	TC/G	FA	G by Pos
1917	DET	A	13	.286	.357	14	4	1	0	0	0.0	4	1	1	2	0	4	1	3	0	0	0	0.2	1.000	OF-3
1919	PIT	N	30	.273	.409	66	18	2	2	1	1.5	8	6	6	11	2	11	2	43	3	2	2	1.6	.958	OF-17, 1B-1
1920			99	.360	.530	247	89	16	7	4	1.6	33	30	18	31	9	38	12	125	9	6	2	1.6	.957	OF-58
1921	BOS	N	83	.327	.490	245	80	11	7	5	2.0	36	41	17	29	5	15	3	138	11	6	4	1.9	.961	OF-59, 1B-4, 2B-2
1922			78	.252	.342	222	56	4	5	2	0.9	31	29	23	24	5	12	3	125	5	12	0	1.8	.915	OF-63
5 yrs.			303	.311	.452	794	247	34	21	12	1.5	112	107	65	97	21	80	21	434	28	26	8	1.6	.947	OF-200, 1B-5, 2B-2

Ovid Nicholson

NICHOLSON, OVID EDWARD
B. Dec. 30, 1888, Salem, Ind. D. Mar. 24, 1968, Salem, Ind.

BL TR 5'9½" 155 lbs.

Year	Team		Games	BA	SA	AB	H	2B	3B	HR	HR%	R	RBI	BB	SO	SB	PH AB	PH H	PO	A	E	DP	TC/G	FA	G by Pos
1912	PIT	N	6	.455	.455	11	5	0	0	0	0.0	2	3	1	2	0	0	0	8	0	0	0	1.3	1.000	OF-4

Parson Nicholson

NICHOLSON, THOMAS C. (Beacon)
B. Apr. 14, 1863, Blaine, Ohio D. Feb. 28, 1917, Bellaire, Ohio

6'6" 190 lbs.

Year	Team		Games	BA	SA	AB	H	2B	3B	HR	HR%	R	RBI	BB	SO	SB	PH AB	PH H	PO	A	E	DP	TC/G	FA	G by Pos
1888	DET	N	24	.259	.388	85	22	2	3	1	1.2	11	9	2	7	6	0	0	44	71	8	5	5.1	.935	2B-24
1890	TOL	AA	134	.268	.363	523	140	16	11	4	0.8	78		42		46	0	0	294	385	52	45	5.5	.929	2B-134, C-1
1895	WAS	N	10	.184	.289	38	7	2	1	0	0.0	7	5	7	4	6	0	0	17	34	13	4	6.4	.797	SS-10
3 yrs.			168	.262	.362	646	169	20	15	5	0.8	96	14	51	11	58	0	0	355	490	73	54	5.5	.920	2B-158, SS-10, C-1

George Nicol

NICOL, GEORGE EDWARD
B. Oct. 17, 1870, Barry, Ill. D. Aug. 10, 1924, Milwaukee, Wis.

TL 5'7" 155 lbs.

Year	Team		Games	BA	SA	AB	H	2B	3B	HR	HR%	R	RBI	BB	SO	SB	PH AB	PH H	PO	A	E	DP	TC/G	FA	G by Pos
1890	STL	AA	3	.286	.429	7	2	1	0	0	0.0	4		4		0	0	0	2	0	0	0	0.7	1.000	P-3
1891	CHI	N	3	.333	.667	6	2	0	1	0	0.0	0	3	0	1	0	0	0	0	0	3	0	1.0	–	P-3
1894	2 teams		PIT	N	(8G –	.450)		LOU	N	(27G –	.352)															
"	total		35	.367	.484	128	47	7	4	0	0.0	20	22	2	4	4	0	0	32	9	10	1	1.5	.804	OF-26, P-9
3 yrs.			41	.362	.489	141	51	8	5	0	0.0	24	25	6	5	4	0	0	34	9	13	1	1.4	.768	OF-26, P-15

Hugh Nicol

NICOL, HUGH N.
B. Jan. 1, 1858, Campsie, Scotland D. June 27, 1921, Lafayette, Ind.
Manager 1897.

BR TR 5'4" 145 lbs.

Year	Team		Games	BA	SA	AB	H	2B	3B	HR	HR%	R	RBI	BB	SO	SB	PH AB	PH H	PO	A	E	DP	TC/G	FA	G by Pos
1881	CHI	N	26	.204	.222	108	22	2	0	0	0.0	13	7	4	12		0	0	45	12	5	1	2.4	.919	OF-26, SS-1
1882			47	.199	.274	186	37	9	1	1	0.5	19	16	7	29		0	0	62	35	15	2	2.4	.866	OF-47, SS-8
1883	STL	AA	94	.288	.340	368	106	13	3	0	0.0	73		18			0	0	162	63	27	7	2.7	.893	OF-84, 2B-11
1884			110	.260	.314	442	115	14	5	0	0.0	79		22			0	0	205	123	45	15	3.4	.879	OF-87, 2B-23, SS-1, 3B-1
1885			112	.207	.238	425	88	11	1	0	0.0	59		34			0	0	214	35	31	2	2.5	.889	OF-111, 3B-1
1886			67	.206	.253	253	52	6	3	0	0.0	44		26			0	0	103	40	19	2	2.4	.883	OF-57, SS-8, 2B-4
1887	CIN	AA	125	.215	.267	475	102	18	2	1	0.2	122		86		138	0	0	194	20	19	1	1.9	.918	OF-125
1888			135	.239	.270	548	131	10	2	1	0.2	112	35	67		103	0	0	217	43	12	9	2.0	.956	OF-125, 2B-12, SS-1
1889			122	.255	.316	474	121	7	8	2	0.4	82	58	54	35	80	0	0	193	39	19	7	2.1	.924	OF-115, 2B-7, 3B-3
1890	CIN	N	50	.210	.258	186	39	1	4	0	0.0	28	19	19	12	24	0	0	66	15	13	3	1.9	.862	OF-46, SS-3, 2B-1
10 yrs.			888	.235	.282	3465	813	91	29	5	0.1	631	135	337	88	345	0	0	1461	425	205	49	2.4	.902	OF-823, 2B-58, SS-22, 3B-5

Steve Nicosia

NICOSIA, STEVEN RICHARD
B. Aug. 6, 1955, Paterson, N. J.

BR TR 5'10" 185 lbs.

Year	Team		Games	BA	SA	AB	H	2B	3B	HR	HR%	R	RBI	BB	SO	SB	PH AB	PH H	PO	A	E	DP	TC/G	FA	G by Pos
1978	PIT	N	3	.000	.000	5	0	0	0	0	0.0	0	0	1	0	0	1	0	8	1	0	0	3.0	1.000	C-1
1979			70	.288	.435	191	55	16	0	4	2.1	22	13	23	17	0	6	0	320	25	3	4	5.0	.991	C-65
1980			60	.216	.278	176	38	8	0	1	0.6	16	22	19	16	0	2	0	284	25	5	4	5.2	.984	C-58
1981			54	.231	.337	169	39	10	1	2	1.2	21	18	13	10	3	2	0	257	23	5	2	5.3	.982	C-52
1982			39	.280	.340	100	28	3	0	1	1.0	6	7	11	13	0	2	1	183	22	2	1	5.3	.990	C-35, OF-3
1983	2 teams		PIT	N	(21G –	.130)		SF	N	(15G –	.333)															
"	total		36	.215	.278	79	17	2	0	1	1.3	8	7	4	9	0	9	3	131	9	2	0	3.9	.986	C-24
1984	SF	N	48	.303	.462	132	40	11	2	2	1.5	9	19	8	14	1	10	4	190	11	3	1	4.3	.985	C-41
1985	2 teams		MON	N	(42G –	.169)		TOR	A	(6G –	.267)															
"	total		48	.186	.209	86	16	2	0	0	0.0	4	2	7	11	1	18	2	109	7	1	2	2.4	.991	C-29, 1B-2
8 yrs.			358	.248	.345	938	233	52	3	11	1.2	86	88	86	90	5	50	10	1482	123	21	14	4.5	.987	C-305, OF-3, 1B-2

WORLD SERIES

Year	Team		Games	BA	SA	AB	H	2B	3B	HR	HR%	R	RBI	BB	SO	SB	PH AB	PH H	PO	A	E	DP	TC/G	FA	G by Pos
1979	PIT	N	4	.063	.063	16	1	0	0	0	0.0	1	0	0	2	0	0	0	23	2	0	0	6.3	1.000	C-4

Charlie Niebergall

NIEBERGALL, CHARLES ARTHUR (Nig)
B. May 23, 1899, New York, N. Y. D. Aug. 29, 1982, Holiday, Fla.

BR TR 5'10" 160 lbs.

Year	Team		Games	BA	SA	AB	H	2B	3B	HR	HR%	R	RBI	BB	SO	SB	PH AB	PH H	PO	A	E	DP	TC/G	FA	G by Pos
1921	STL	N	5	.167	.167	6	1	0	0	0	0.0	1	0	0	0	0	2	1	2	1	0	0	0.6	1.000	C-3
1923			9	.107	.143	28	3	1	0	0	0.0	2	1	2	2	0	1	0	28	5	0	0	3.7	1.000	C-7
1924			40	.293	.397	58	17	6	0	0	0.0	6	7	3	9	0	6	2	57	20	4	1	2.0	.951	C-34
3 yrs.			54	.228	.304	92	21	7	0	0	0.0	9	8	5	11	0	9	3	87	26	4	1	2.2	.966	C-44

Al Niehaus

NIEHAUS, ALBERT BERNARD
B. June 1, 1899, Cincinnati, Ohio D. Oct. 14, 1931, Cincinnati, Ohio

BR TR 5'11" 175 lbs.

Year	Team		Games	BA	SA	AB	H	2B	3B	HR	HR%	R	RBI	BB	SO	SB	PH AB	PH H	PO	A	E	DP	TC/G	FA	G by Pos
1925	2 teams		PIT	N	(17G –	.219)		CIN	N	(51G –	.299)															
"	total		68	.275	.379	211	58	10	2	0	0.0	23	21	14	15	1	8	3	544	33	11	50	8.6	.981	1B-60

Bert Niehoff

NIEHOFF, JOHN ALBERT
B. May 13, 1884, Louisville, Colo. D. Dec. 8, 1974, Inglewood, Calif.

BR TR 5'10½" 170 lbs.

Year	Team		Games	BA	SA	AB	H	2B	3B	HR	HR%	R	RBI	BB	SO	SB	PH AB	PH H	PO	A	E	DP	TC/G	FA	G by Pos
1913	CIN	N	2	.000	.000	8	0	0	0	0	0.0	0	0	0	0	0	0	0	9	2	1	0	6.0	.917	3B-2
1914			142	.242	.337	484	117	16	9	4	0.8	46	49	38	77	20	5	2	157	281	35	15	3.3	.926	3B-134, 2B-3
1915	PHI	N	148	.238	.308	529	126	27	2	2	0.4	61	49	30	63	21	0	2	307	411	41	55	5.1	.946	2B-148
1916			146	.243	.356	548	133	42	4	4	0.7	65	61	37	57	20	0	0	287	441	50	65	5.3	.936	2B-146, 3B-1
1917			114	.255	.341	361	92	17	4	2	0.6	30	42	23	29	8	7	0	219	345	31	42	5.2	.948	2B-96, 1B-7, 3B-6

Year	Team	Games	BA	SA	AB	H	2B	3B	HR	HR%	R	RBI	BB	SO	SB	Pinch Hit AB	Pinch Hit H	PO	A	E	DP	TC/G	FA	G by Pos

Bert Niehoff *continued*

Year	Team	Games	BA	SA	AB	H	2B	3B	HR	HR%	R	RBI	BB	SO	SB	PH AB	PH H	PO	A	E	DP	TC/G	FA	G by Pos
1918 2 teams	STL N (22G – .179)				NY N (7G – .261)																			
" total		29	.196	.215	107	21	2	0	0	0.0	8	6	3	14	2	0	0	68	78	7	13	5.3	.954	2B-29
6 yrs.		581	.240	.327	2037	489	104	19	12	0.6	210	207	131	242	71	12	2	1040	1565	165	190	4.8	.940	2B-422, 3B-143, 1B-7

WORLD SERIES

Year	Team	Games	BA	SA	AB	H	2B	3B	HR	HR%	R	RBI	BB	SO	SB	PH AB	PH H	PO	A	E	DP	TC/G	FA	G by Pos
1915 PHI N		5	.063	.063	16	1	0	0	0	0.0	1	0	1	5	0	0	0	10	10	0	0	4.0	1.000	2B-5

Milt Nielsen

NIELSEN, MILTON ROBERT
B. Feb. 8, 1925, Tyler, Minn. BL TL 5'11" 190 lbs.

Year	Team	Games	BA	SA	AB	H	2B	3B	HR	HR%	R	RBI	BB	SO	SB	PH AB	PH H	PO	A	E	DP	TC/G	FA	G by Pos
1949 CLE A		3	.111	.111	9	1	0	0	0	0.0	1	0	2	4	0	0	0	6	0	0	0	2.0	1.000	OF-3
1951		16	.000	.000	6	0	0	0	0	0.0	1	0	1	1	0	6	0	0	0	0	0	0.0	–	
2 yrs.		19	.067	.067	15	1	0	0	0	0.0	2	0	3	5	0	6	0	6	0	0	0	0.3	1.000	OF-3

Bob Nieman

NIEMAN, ROBERT CHARLES
B. Jan. 26, 1927, Cincinnati, Ohio D. Mar. 10, 1985, Corona, Calif. BR TR 5'11" 195 lbs.

Year	Team	Games	BA	SA	AB	H	2B	3B	HR	HR%	R	RBI	BB	SO	SB	PH AB	PH H	PO	A	E	DP	TC/G	FA	G by Pos
1951 STL A		12	.372	.628	43	16	3	1	2	4.7	6	8	3	5	0	1	1	24	1	1	0	2.2	.962	OF-11
1952		131	.289	.456	478	138	22	2	18	3.8	66	74	46	73	0	9	1	230	10	6	5	1.9	.976	OF-125
1953 DET A		142	.281	.453	508	143	32	5	15	3.0	72	69	57	57	0	7	1	271	10	6	1	2.0	.979	OF-135
1954		91	.263	.422	251	66	14	1	8	3.2	24	35	22	32	0	26	8	119	2	2	0	1.4	.984	OF-62
1955 CHI A		99	.283	.460	272	77	11	2	11	4.0	36	53	36	37	1	24	7	118	4	3	2	1.3	.976	OF-78
1956 2 teams	CHI A (14G – .300)				BAL A (114G – .322)																			
" total		128	.320	.495	428	137	21	6	14	3.3	63	68	90	63	1	1	1	267	4	5	1	2.2	.982	OF-124
1957 BAL A		129	.276	.449	445	123	17	6	13	2.9	61	70	63	86	4	9	0	237	6	5	0	1.9	.980	OF-120
1958		105	.325	.522	366	119	20	2	16	4.4	56	60	44	57	2	6	1	145	3	6	0	1.5	.961	OF-100
1959		118	.292	.528	360	105	18	2	21	5.8	49	60	42	55	1	17	4	171	6	5	0	1.5	.973	OF-97
1960 STL N		81	.287	.473	188	54	13	5	4	2.1	19	31	24	31	0	26	4	63	0	4	0	0.8	.940	OF-55
1961 2 teams	STL N (6G – .471)				CLE A (39G – .354)																			
" total		45	.378	.537	82	31	7	0	2	2.4	2	12	7	6	1	27	9	25	1	1	0	0.6	.963	OF-16
1962 2 teams	CLE A (2G – .000)				SF N (30G – .300)																			
" total		32	.290	.452	31	9	2	0	1	3.2	1	4	1	10	0	30	8	2	0	0	0	0.1	1.000	OF-3
12 yrs.		1113	.295	.474	3452	1018	180	32	125	3.6	455	544	435	512	10	183	45	1672	47	44	9	1.6	.975	OF-926

WORLD SERIES

Year	Team	Games	BA	SA	AB	H	2B	3B	HR	HR%	R	RBI	BB	SO	SB	PH AB	PH H	PO	A	E	DP	TC/G	FA	G by Pos
1962 SF N		1	–	–	0	0	0	0	0	0.0	0	0	1	0	0	0	0	0	0	0	0	0.0	–	

Butch Nieman

NIEMAN, ELMER LeROY
B. Feb. 8, 1918, Herkimer, Kans. BL TL 6'2" 195 lbs.

Year	Team	Games	BA	SA	AB	H	2B	3B	HR	HR%	R	RBI	BB	SO	SB	PH AB	PH H	PO	A	E	DP	TC/G	FA	G by Pos
1943 BOS N		101	.251	.406	335	84	15	8	7	2.1	39	46	39	39	4	2	0	195	12	8	1	2.1	.963	OF-93
1944		134	.265	.427	468	124	16	6	16	3.4	65	65	47	47	5	9	2	261	13	7	2	2.1	.975	OF-126
1945		97	.247	.478	247	61	15	0	14	5.7	43	56	43	33	11	36	11	132	4	10	1	1.5	.932	OF-57
3 yrs.		332	.256	.432	1050	269	46	14	37	3.5	147	167	129	119	20	47	13	588	29	25	4	1.9	.961	OF-276

Al Niemiec

NIEMIEC, ALFRED JOSEPH
B. May 18, 1911, Meriden, Conn. BR TR 5'11" 158 lbs.

Year	Team	Games	BA	SA	AB	H	2B	3B	HR	HR%	R	RBI	BB	SO	SB	PH AB	PH H	PO	A	E	DP	TC/G	FA	G by Pos
1934 BOS A		9	.219	.219	32	7	0	0	0	0.0	2	3	3	4	0	0	0	25	33	0	8	6.4	1.000	2B-9
1936 PHI A		69	.197	.246	203	40	3	2	1	0.5	22	20	26	16	2	10	1	150	196	11	35	5.2	.969	2B-52, SS-5
2 yrs.		78	.200	.243	235	47	3	2	1	0.4	24	23	29	20	2	10	1	175	229	11	43	5.3	.973	2B-61, SS-5

Tom Nieto

NIETO, THOMAS ANDREW
B. Oct. 27, 1960, Downey, Calif. BR TR 6'1" 205 lbs.

Year	Team	Games	BA	SA	AB	H	2B	3B	HR	HR%	R	RBI	BB	SO	SB	PH AB	PH H	PO	A	E	DP	TC/G	FA	G by Pos
1984 STL N		33	.279	.430	86	24	4	0	3	3.5	7	12	5	18	0	2	0	135	18	1	0	4.7	.994	C-32
1985		95	.225	.281	253	57	10	2	0	0.0	15	34	26	37	0	1	0	384	28	4	3	4.4	.990	C-95
1986 MON N		30	.200	.323	65	13	3	1	1	1.5	5	7	6	21	0	1	1	123	11	3	1	4.6	.978	C-30
1987 MIN A		41	.200	.314	105	21	7	1	1	1.0	7	12	8	24	0	1	1	210	17	1	5	5.6	.996	C-40, DH-1
1988		24	.067	.067	60	4	0	0	0	0.0	1	0	1	17	0	0	0	108	6	1	1	4.8	.991	C-24
1989 PHI N		11	.150	.150	20	3	0	0	0	0.0	1	0	6	7	0	0	0	63	2	0	0	5.9	1.000	C-11
6 yrs.		234	.207	.287	589	122	24	4	5	0.8	36	65	52	124	0	5	2	1023	82	10	10	4.8	.991	C-232, DH-1

LEAGUE CHAMPIONSHIP SERIES

Year	Team	Games	BA	SA	AB	H	2B	3B	HR	HR%	R	RBI	BB	SO	SB	PH AB	PH H	PO	A	E	DP	TC/G	FA	G by Pos
1985 STL N		1	.000	.000	3	0	0	0	0	0.0	1	0	1	2	0	0	0	0	0	0	0	0.0	–	C-1

WORLD SERIES

Year	Team	Games	BA	SA	AB	H	2B	3B	HR	HR%	R	RBI	BB	SO	SB	PH AB	PH H	PO	A	E	DP	TC/G	FA	G by Pos
1985 STL N		2	.000	.000	5	0	0	0	0	0.0	0	1	1	2	0	0	0	23	1	0	0	12.0	1.000	C-2

Tom Niland

NILAND, THOMAS JAMES (Honest Tom)
B. Apr. 14, 1870, Brookfield, Mass. D. Apr. 30, 1950, Lynn, Mass. BR TR 5'11" 160 lbs.

Year	Team	Games	BA	SA	AB	H	2B	3B	HR	HR%	R	RBI	BB	SO	SB	PH AB	PH H	PO	A	E	DP	TC/G	FA	G by Pos
1896 STL N		18	.176	.206	68	12	0	0	0	0.0	3	3	5	4	0	0	0	23	16	7	1	2.6	.848	OF-13, SS-5

Billy Niles

NILES, WILLIAM E.
B. Jan., 1874, Vt. D. July 3, 1936, Springfield, Ohio 160 lbs.

Year	Team	Games	BA	SA	AB	H	2B	3B	HR	HR%	R	RBI	BB	SO	SB	PH AB	PH H	PO	A	E	DP	TC/G	FA	G by Pos
1895 PIT N		11	.216	.216	37	8	0	0	0	0.0	2	0	5	2	2	0	0	23	20	4	1	4.3	.915	3B-10, 2B-1

Harry Niles

NILES, HERBERT CLYDE
B. Sept. 10, 1880, Buchanan, Mich. D. Apr. 18, 1953, Sturgis, Mich. BR TR 5'8" 175 lbs.

Year	Team	Games	BA	SA	AB	H	2B	3B	HR	HR%	R	RBI	BB	SO	SB	PH AB	PH H	PO	A	E	DP	TC/G	FA	G by Pos
1906 STL A		142	.229	.281	541	124	14	4	2	0.4	71	31	46		30	0	0	189	88	15	8	2.1	.949	OF-108, 3B-34
1907		120	.289	.339	492	142	9	5	2	0.4	65	35	28		19	3	2	282	352	34	41	5.6	.949	2B-116, OF-1
1908 2 teams	NY A (96G – .249)				BOS A (17G – .273)																			
" total		113	.251	.355	394	99	14	6	5	1.3	47	27	31		21	5	0	195	249	30	17	4.2	.937	2B-93, OF-7, SS-2
1909 BOS A		145	.245	.291	546	134	12	5	1	0.2	64	38	39		27	1	1	240	87	28	9	2.4	.921	OF-117, 3B-13, SS-9, 2B-5

Year	Team	Games	BA	SA	AB	H	2B	3B	HR	HR%	R	RBI	BB	SO	SB	Pinch Hit AB	Pinch Hit H	PO	A	E	DP	TC/G	FA	G by Pos

Harry Niles *continued*

Year	Team	Games	BA	SA	AB	H	2B	3B	HR	HR%	R	RBI	BB	SO	SB	PH AB	PH H	PO	A	E	DP	TC/G	FA	G by Pos
1910	2 teams	BOS A (18G – .211)			CLE A (70G – .213)																			
"	total	88	.212	.290	297	63	9	4	2	0.7	31	21	19		10	8	2	109	38	10	5	1.8	.936	OF-71, SS-7, 3B-5
	5 yrs.	608	.248	.310	2270	562	58	24	12	0.5	278	152	163		107	17	5	1015	814	117	80	3.2	.940	OF-304, 2B-214, 3B-52, SS-18

Rabbit Nill

NILL, GEORGE CHARLES
B. July 14, 1881, Fort Wayne, Ind. D. May 24, 1962, Fort Wayne, Ind.

BR TR 5'7" 160 lbs.

Year	Team	Games	BA	SA	AB	H	2B	3B	HR	HR%	R	RBI	BB	SO	SB	PH AB	PH H	PO	A	E	DP	TC/G	FA	G by Pos
1904	WAS A	15	.167	.208	48	8	0	1	0	0.0	4	3	5		0	0	0	29	36	9	3	4.9	.878	2B-15
1905		103	.182	.251	319	58	7	3	3	0.9	46	31	33		12	10	3	146	200	29	15	3.6	.923	3B-54, 2B-33, SS-6
1906		89	.235	.273	315	74	8	2	0	0.0	37	15	47		16	2	0	148	211	36	21	4.4	.909	SS-31, 2B-25, OF-15, 3B-15
1907	2 teams	WAS A (66G – .219)			CLE A (12G – .279)																			
"	total	78	.229	.283	258	59	8	3	0	0.0	26	27	18		8	8	2	127	134	16	10	3.6	.942	2B-32, OF-25, 3B-10, SS-2
1908	CLE A	10	.217	.217	23	5	0	0	0	0.0	3	1	0		0	1	0	13	25	6	2	4.4	.864	SS-6, OF-2, 2B-1
	5 yrs.	295	.212	.264	963	204	23	9	3	0.3	116	77	103		36	21	5	463	606	96	51	3.9	.918	2B-106, 3B-79, SS-45, OF-42

Al Nixon

NIXON, ALBERT RICHARD
B. Apr. 11, 1886, Atlantic City, N. J. D. Nov. 9, 1960, Opelousas, La.

BR TL 5'7½" 164 lbs.

Year	Team	Games	BA	SA	AB	H	2B	3B	HR	HR%	R	RBI	BB	SO	SB	PH AB	PH H	PO	A	E	DP	TC/G	FA	G by Pos
1915	BKN N	14	.231	.269	26	6	1	0	0	0.0	3	2	2		1	0	0	11	1	0	1	0.9	1.000	OF-14
1916		1	1.000	1.000	2	2	0	0	0	0.0	0	0	0		0	0	0	0	0	0	0	0.0	–	OF-1
1918		6	.455	.455	11	5	0	0	0	0.0	1	0	0		0	1	1	6	0	0	0	1.0	1.000	OF-4
1921	BOS N	55	.239	.348	138	33	6	3	1	0.7	25	9	7	11	3	6	1	92	4	2	1	1.8	.980	OF-45
1922		86	.264	.352	318	84	14	4	2	0.6	35	22	9	19	6	6	2	189	6	5	0	2.3	.975	OF-79
1923		88	.274	.336	321	88	12	4	0	0.0	53	19	24	14	2	1	0	214	14	3	4	2.6	.987	OF-80
1926	PHI N	93	.293	.402	311	91	18	2	4	1.3	38	41	13	20	5	3	0	206	7	3	3	2.3	.977	OF-88
1927		54	.312	.357	154	48	7	0	0	0.0	18	18	5	5	1	5	1	121	3	4	0	2.4	.969	OF-44
1928		25	.234	.266	64	15	2	0	0	0.0	7	7	6	4	1	3	0	40	1	0	0	1.6	1.000	OF-20
	9 yrs.	422	.277	.356	1345	372	60	13	7	0.5	180	118	66	77	19	27	7	879	36	19	9	2.2	.980	OF-375

Donell Nixon

NIXON, ROBERT DONELL
Brother of Otis Nixon.
B. Dec. 31, 1961, Evergreen, N. C.

BR TR 6'1" 185 lbs.

Year	Team	Games	BA	SA	AB	H	2B	3B	HR	HR%	R	RBI	BB	SO	SB	PH AB	PH H	PO	A	E	DP	TC/G	FA	G by Pos
1987	SEA A	46	.250	.348	132	33	4	0	3	2.3	17	12	13	28	21	0	0	76	1	0	0	1.7	1.000	OF-32, DH-6
1988	SF N	59	.346	.385	78	27	3	0	0	0.0	15	6	10	12	11	5	1	59	0	1	0	1.0	.983	OF-46
1989		95	.265	.295	166	44	2	0	1	0.6	23	15	11	30	10	25	5	87	0	3	0	0.9	.967	OF-64
	3 yrs.	200	.277	.332	376	104	9	0	4	1.1	55	33	34	70	42	30	6	222	1	4	0	1.1	.982	OF-142, DH-6

LEAGUE CHAMPIONSHIP SERIES

Year	Team	Games	BA	SA	AB	H	2B	3B	HR	HR%	R	RBI	BB	SO	SB	PH AB	PH H	PO	A	E	DP	TC/G	FA	G by Pos
1989	SF N	3	.000	.000	3	0	0	0	0	0.0	0	0	0	1	1	0	0	2	0	1	0	1.0	.667	OF-2

WORLD SERIES

Year	Team	Games	BA	SA	AB	H	2B	3B	HR	HR%	R	RBI	BB	SO	SB	PH AB	PH H	PO	A	E	DP	TC/G	FA	G by Pos
1989	SF N	2	.200	.200	5	1	0	0	0	0.0	1	0	1	1	0	1	0	2	0	0	0	1.0	1.000	OF-2

Otis Nixon

NIXON, OTIS JUNIOR
Brother of Donell Nixon.
B. Jan. 9, 1959, Evergreen, N. C.

BB TR 6'2" 175 lbs.

Year	Team	Games	BA	SA	AB	H	2B	3B	HR	HR%	R	RBI	BB	SO	SB	PH AB	PH H	PO	A	E	DP	TC/G	FA	G by Pos
1983	NY A	13	.143	.143	14	2	0	0	0	0.0	2	0	1	5	2	0	0	14	1	1	0	1.2	.938	OF-9
1984	CLE A	49	.154	.154	91	14	0	0	0	0.0	16	1	8	11	12	0	0	81	3	0	0	1.7	1.000	OF-46
1985		104	.235	.315	162	38	4	0	3	1.9	34	9	8	27	20	2	0	129	5	4	1	1.3	.971	OF-80, DH-11
1986		105	.263	.326	95	25	4	1	0	0.0	33	8	13	12	23	3	1	90	3	3	0	0.9	.969	OF-95, DH-5
1987		19	.059	.059	17	1	0	0	0	0.0	2	1	3	4	2	0	0	21	0	0	0	1.1	1.000	OF-17
1988	MON N	90	.244	.288	271	66	8	2	0	0.0	47	15	28	42	46	11	6	176	2	1	1	2.0	.994	OF-82
1989		126	.217	.260	258	56	7	2	0	0.0	41	21	33	36	37	21	2	160	2	2	0	1.3	.988	OF-98
	7 yrs.	506	.222	.269	908	202	23	5	3	0.3	175	55	94	137	142	37	9	671	16	11	2	1.4	.984	OF-427, DH-16

Russ Nixon

NIXON, RUSSELL EUGENE
B. Feb. 19, 1935, Cleves, Ohio
Manager 1982-83, 1988-89.

BL TR 6'1" 195 lbs.

Year	Team	Games	BA	SA	AB	H	2B	3B	HR	HR%	R	RBI	BB	SO	SB	PH AB	PH H	PO	A	E	DP	TC/G	FA	G by Pos
1957	CLE A	62	.281	.362	185	52	7	1	2	1.1	15	18	12	12	0	8	1	268	31	5	5	4.9	.984	C-57
1958		113	.301	.439	376	113	17	4	9	2.4	42	46	13	38	0	18	4	499	31	5	4	4.7	.991	C-101
1959		82	.240	.314	258	62	10	3	1	0.4	23	29	15	28	0	9	2	374	31	6	8	5.0	.985	C-74
1960	2 teams	CLE A (25G – .244)			BOS A (80G – .298)																			
"	total	105	.285	.415	354	101	22	3	6	1.7	30	39	19	29	0	11	2	488	34	6	5	5.0	.989	C-99
1961	BOS A	87	.289	.368	242	70	12	2	1	0.4	24	19	13	19	0	18	8	330	24	9	2	4.2	.975	C-66
1962		65	.278	.371	151	42	7	2	1	0.7	11	19	8	14	0	28	10	201	7	0	1	3.2	1.000	C-38
1963		98	.268	.390	287	77	18	1	5	1.7	27	30	22	32	0	25	6	483	22	4	1	5.2	.992	C-76
1964		81	.233	.294	163	38	7	0	1	0.6	10	20	14	29	0	34	9	273	11	3	3	3.5	.990	C-45
1965		59	.270	.321	137	37	5	1	0	0.0	11	11	6	23	0	24	7	200	10	4	0	3.6	.981	C-38
1966	MIN A	51	.260	.302	96	25	2	1	0	0.0	5	7	7	13	0	22	5	137	5	2	0	2.8	.986	C-32
1967		74	.235	.300	170	40	6	1	1	0.6	16	22	18	29	0	19	4	308	26	2	1	4.5	.994	C-69
1968	BOS A	29	.153	.176	85	13	2	0	0	0.0	1	6	7	13	0	2	1	147	6	1	1	5.3	.994	C-27
	12 yrs.	906	.268	.361	2504	670	115	19	27	1.1	215	266	154	279	0	218	59	3708	238	47	31	4.4	.988	C-722

Ray Noble

NOBLE, RAFAEL MIGUEL (Ray)
Born Rafael Miguel Noble y Magee.
B. Mar. 15, 1919, Central Hatillo, Cuba

BR TR 5'11" 210 lbs.

Year	Team	Games	BA	SA	AB	H	2B	3B	HR	HR%	R	RBI	BB	SO	SB	PH AB	PH H	PO	A	E	DP	TC/G	FA	G by Pos
1951	NY N	55	.234	.383	141	33	6	0	5	3.5	16	26	6	26	0	18	3	144	8	4	3	2.8	.974	C-41
1952		6	.000	.000	5	0	0	0	0	0.0	0	0	0	1	0	1	0	4	1	0	0	0.8	1.000	C-5
1953		46	.206	.351	97	20	0	1	4	4.1	15	14	19	14	1	4	0	152	13	3	0	3.7	.982	C-41
	3 yrs.	107	.218	.362	243	53	6	1	9	3.7	31	40	25	41	1	23	3	300	22	7	3	3.1	.979	C-87

Year	Team		Games	BA	SA	AB	H	2B	3B	HR	HR%	R	RBI	BB	SO	SB	Pinch Hit AB	Pinch Hit H	PO	A	E	DP	TC/G	FA	G by Pos

Ray Noble *continued*

WORLD SERIES

| 1951 | NY | N | 2 | .000 | .000 | 2 | 0 | 0 | 0 | 0 | 0.0 | 0 | 0 | 0 | 1 | 0 | 2 | 0 | 0 | 1 | 0 | 0 | 0.5 | 1.000 | C-2 |

Junior Noboa

NOBOA, MILCIADES ARTURO
Born Milciades Arturo Noboa y Diaz.
B. Nov. 10, 1964, Azua, Dominican Republic

BR TR 5'10" 155 lbs.

1984	CLE	A	23	.364	.364	11	4	0	0	0	0.0	2	1	0	1	0	0	0	7	13	0	4	0.9	1.000	2B-19, DH-1
1987			39	.225	.275	80	18	2	1	0	0.0	7	7	3	6	1	2	0	28	66	3	8	2.5	.969	2B-21, SS-8, 3B-5
1988	CAL	A	21	.063	.063	16	1	0	0	0	0.0	4	0	0	1	0	0	0	8	24	1	7	1.6	.970	2B-9, SS-3, 3B-2
1989	MON	N	21	.227	.227	44	10	0	0	0	0.0	3	1	1	3	0	5	3	17	45	0	7	3.0	1.000	2B-13, SS-4, 3B-1
4 yrs.			104	.219	.245	151	33	2	1	0	0.0	17	8	4	12	2	7	3	60	148	4	26	2.0	.981	2B-62, SS-15, 3B-8, DH-1

Paul Noce

NOCE, PAUL DAVID
B. Dec. 16, 1959, San Francisco, Calif.

BR TR 5'10" 175 lbs.

| 1987 | CHI | N | 70 | .228 | .350 | 180 | 41 | 9 | 2 | 3 | 1.7 | 17 | 14 | 6 | 49 | 5 | 2 | 0 | 117 | 157 | 5 | 39 | 4.0 | .982 | 2B-36, SS-35, 3B-2 |

George Noftsker

NOFTSKER, GEORGE WASHINGTON
B. Aug. 24, 1859, Shippensburg, Pa. D. May 8, 1931, Shippensburg, Pa.

BR TR 5'8" 135 lbs.

| 1884 | ALT | U | 7 | .040 | .040 | 25 | 1 | 0 | 0 | 0 | 0.0 | 0 | | 0 | | | 0 | 0 | 21 | 9 | 5 | 1 | 5.0 | .857 | OF-5, C-3 |

Matt Nokes

NOKES, MATTHEW DODGE
B. Oct. 31, 1963, San Diego, Calif.

BL TR 6'1" 180 lbs.

1985	SF	N	19	.208	.358	53	11	2	0	2	3.8	3	5	1	5	0	5	0	84	2	2	0	4.6	.977	C-14
1986	DET	A	7	.333	.500	24	8	1	0	1	4.2	2	2	1	1	0	0	0	43	2	0	2	6.4	1.000	C-7
1987			135	.289	.536	461	133	14	2	32	6.9	69	87	35	70	2	19	4	600	32	5	2	4.7	.992	C-109, OF-3, 3B-2
1988			122	.251	.424	382	96	18	0	16	4.2	53	53	34	58	0	16	3	574	45	7	8	5.1	.989	C-110, DH-4
1989			87	.250	.388	268	67	10	0	9	3.4	15	39	17	37	1	11	1	235	26	6	3	3.1	.978	C-51, DH-33
5 yrs.			370	.265	.458	1188	315	45	2	60	5.1	142	186	88	175	3	51	8	1536	107	20	15	4.5	.988	C-291, DH-37, OF-3, 3B-2

LEAGUE CHAMPIONSHIP SERIES

| 1987 | DET | A | 5 | .143 | .357 | 14 | 2 | 0 | 0 | 1 | 7.1 | 2 | 2 | 1 | 4 | 0 | 2 | 0 | 11 | 2 | 0 | 0 | 2.6 | 1.000 | C-3, DH-2 |

Joe Nolan

NOLAN, JOSEPH WILLIAM JR.
B. May 12, 1951, St. Louis, Mo.

BL TR 5'11" 175 lbs.

1972	NY	N	4	.000	.000	10	0	0	0	0	0.0	0	0	1	0	0	1	0	12	3	1	0	4.0	.938	C-3
1975	ATL	N	4	.250	.250	4	1	0	0	0	0.0	0	0	1	0	0	3	0	2	0	0	0	0.5	1.000	C-1
1977			62	.280	.427	82	23	3	0	3	3.7	13	9	13	12	1	39	14	80	7	0	2	1.4	1.000	C-19
1978			95	.230	.347	213	49	7	3	4	1.9	22	22	34	28	1	34	6	295	24	7	3	3.4	.979	C-61
1979			89	.248	.365	230	57	9	3	4	1.7	28	21	27	28	1	14	1	328	27	6	2	4.1	.983	C-74
1980	2 teams		ATL N (17G – .273)			CIN N (53G – .312)																			
"	total		70	.307	.403	176	54	8	0	3	1.7	16	26	15	15	0	15	3	271	26	5	7	4.3	.983	C-57
1981	CIN	N	81	.309	.407	236	73	18	1	1	0.4	25	26	24	19	1	9	3	393	18	2	2	5.1	.995	C-81
1982	BAL	A	77	.233	.356	219	51	7	1	6	2.7	24	35	16	35	1	12	2	292	22	7	2	4.2	.978	C-72
1983			73	.277	.429	184	51	11	1	5	2.7	25	24	16	31	0	12	2	223	16	5	2	3.3	.980	C-65
1984			35	.290	.387	62	18	1	1	1	1.6	2	9	12	10	0	15	4	22	3	1	0	0.7	.962	DH-11, C-6
1985			31	.132	.184	38	5	2	0	0	0.0	1	6	5	5	0	22	2	22	2	0	0	0.8	1.000	C-5, DH-4
11 yrs.			621	.263	.378	1454	382	66	10	27	1.9	156	178	164	183	7	176	37	1940	148	34	20	3.4	.984	C-444, DH-15

LEAGUE CHAMPIONSHIP SERIES

| 1983 | BAL | A | 1 | – | – | 0 | 0 | 0 | 0 | 0 | – | 0 | 1 | 0 | 0 | 0 | 0 | 0 | 0 | 0 | 0 | 0 | 0.0 | – | |

WORLD SERIES

| 1983 | BAL | A | 2 | .000 | .000 | 2 | 0 | 0 | 0 | 0 | 0.0 | 0 | 1 | 0 | 1 | 0 | 0 | 0 | 3 | 0 | 0 | 0 | 1.5 | 1.000 | C-2 |

The Only Nolan

NOLAN, EDWARD SYLVESTER
B. Nov. 7, 1857, Paterson, N. J. D. May 18, 1913, Paterson, N. J.

BL TR 5'8" 171 lbs.

1878	IND	N	38	.243	.296	152	37	8	0	0	0.0	11	16	2	10		0	0	19	80	11	5	2.9	.900	P-38, OF-1
1881	CLE	N	41	.244	.286	168	41	5	1	0	0.0	12	18	4	13		0	0	32	37	9	2	1.9	.885	P-22, OF-14, 3B-6
1883	PIT	AA	7	.308	.346	26	8	1	0	0	0.0	4		1			0	0	2	11	5	0	2.6	.722	P-7, OF-1
1884	WIL	U	9	.273	.394	33	9	2	1	0	0.0	5		2			0	0	5	11	1	0	1.9	.941	P-5, OF-4
1885	PHI	N	7	.077	.115	26	2	1	0	0	0.0	1		3	8		0	0	1	11	3	0	2.1	.800	P-7, OF-1
5 yrs.			102	.240	.291	405	97	17	2	0	0.0	33	34	12	31		0	0	59	150	29	7	2.3	.878	P-79, OF-21, 3B-6

Red Nonnenkamp

NONNENKAMP, LEO WILLIAM
B. July 7, 1911, St. Louis, Mo.

BL TL 5'11" 165 lbs.

1933	PIT	N	1	.000	.000	1	0	0	0	0	0.0	0	0	0	1	0	1	0	0	0	0	0	0.0	–	
1938	BOS	A	87	.283	.317	180	51	4	1	0	0.0	37	18	21	13	6	34	10	101	5	3	2	1.3	.972	OF-39, 1B-5
1939			58	.240	.293	75	18	2	1	0	0.0	12	5	12	6	0	34	9	25	0	1	0	0.4	.962	OF-15
1940			9	.000	.000	7	0	0	0	0	0.0	0	1	1	4	0	7	0	0	0	0	0	0.0	–	
4 yrs.			155	.262	.300	263	69	6	2	0	0.0	49	24	34	24	6	76	19	126	5	4	2	0.9	.970	OF-54, 1B-5

Pete Noonan

NOONAN, PETER JOHN
B. Nov. 24, 1881, W. Stockbridge, Mass. D. Feb. 11, 1965, Great Barrington, Mass.

BR TR 6' 180 lbs.

1904	PHI	A	39	.202	.298	114	23	3	1	2	1.8	13	13	1		1	6	1	205	27	5	6	6.1	.979	C-22, 1B-10
1906	2 teams		CHI N (5G – .333)			STL N (44G – .168)																			
"	total		49	.172	.250	128	22	1	3	1	0.8	8	9	11		1	8	1	271	48	14	6	6.8	.958	C-23, 1B-17
1907	STL	N	74	.225	.292	236	53	7	3	1	0.4	19	16	9		3	5	1	369	98	24	12	6.6	.951	C-70
3 yrs.			162	.205	.282	478	98	11	7	4	0.8	40	38	21		5	19	4	845	173	43	24	6.5	.959	C-115, 1B-27

Tim Nordbrook

NORDBROOK, TIMOTHY CHARLES
B. July 7, 1949, Baltimore, Md.

BR TR 6'1" 180 lbs.

Year	Team	Games	BA	SA	AB	H	2B	3B	HR	HR%	R	RBI	BB	SO	SB	Pinch Hit AB	Pinch Hit H	PO	A	E	DP	TC/G	FA	G by Pos

Tim Nordbrook *continued*

Year	Team	Games	BA	SA	AB	H	2B	3B	HR	HR%	R	RBI	BB	SO	SB	PH AB	PH H	PO	A	E	DP	TC/G	FA	G by Pos
1974	BAL A	6	.267	.267	15	4	0	0	0	0.0	4	1	2	2	1	0	0	6	17	0	5	3.8	1.000	SS-5, 2B-1
1975		40	.118	.147	34	4	1	0	0	0.0	6	0	7	7	0	0	0	19	51	2	7	1.8	.972	SS-37, 2B-3
1976	2 teams		BAL A (27G – .227)		CAL A (5G – .000)																			
"	total	32	.167	.167	30	5	0	0	0	0.0	5	0	4	8	1	0	0	23	33	1	6	1.8	.982	SS-16, 2B-15, DH-1
1977	2 teams		CHI A (15G – .000)		TOR A (24G – .175)																			
"	total	39	.193	.217	83	16	0	1	0	0.0	11	2	11	15	2	12	3	52	74	7	13	3.4	.947	SS-35, DH-2, 3B-1
1978	2 teams		TOR A (7G – .000)		MIL A (2G – .000)																			
"	total	9	.000	.000	5	0	0	0	0	0.0	1	0	1	1	0	0	0	2	14	1	0	1.9	.941	SS-9
1979	MIL A	2	.500	.500	2	1	0	0	0	0.0	0	0	0	0	0	0	0	1	0	0	0	0.5	1.000	SS-2
6 yrs.		128	.178	.195	169	30	1	1	0	0.0	27	3	25	33	4	12	3	103	189	11	31	2.4	.964	SS-104, 2B-19, DH-3, 3B-1

Wayne Nordhagen

NORDHAGEN, WAYNE OREN
B. July 4, 1948, Thief River Falls, Minn. BR TR 6'2" 205 lbs.

Year	Team	Games	BA	SA	AB	H	2B	3B	HR	HR%	R	RBI	BB	SO	SB	PH AB	PH H	PO	A	E	DP	TC/G	FA	G by Pos
1976	CHI A	22	.189	.226	53	10	2	0	0	0.0	6	5	4	12	0	2	0	35	3	1	0	1.8	.974	OF-10, DH-6, C-5
1977		52	.315	.516	124	39	7	3	4	3.2	16	22	2	12	1	7	2	52	1	5	2	1.1	.914	OF-46, C-3, DH-2
1978		68	.301	.451	206	62	16	0	5	2.4	28	35	5	18	0	15	6	87	12	6	2	1.5	.943	OF-36, DH-16, C-12
1979		78	.280	.466	193	54	15	0	7	3.6	20	25	13	22	0	21	7	28	4	3	0	0.4	.914	DH-47, OF-12, C-5, P-2
1980		123	.277	.458	415	115	22	4	15	3.6	45	59	10	45	0	21	5	120	6	4	1	1.1	.969	OF-74, DH-32
1981		65	.308	.442	208	64	8	1	6	2.9	19	33	10	25	0	7	1	85	4	5	1	1.4	.947	OF-60
1982	2 teams		TOR A (72G – .270)		PIT N (1G – .500)																			
"	total	73	.275	.323	189	52	6	0	1	0.5	12	22	10	23	0	26	11	17	1	0	1	0.2	1.000	DH-60, 1B-10, OF-1
1983	CHI N	21	.143	.257	35	5	1	0	1	2.9	1	4	0	5	0	15	2	7	0	0	0	0.3	1.000	OF-7
8 yrs.		502	.282	.429	1423	401	77	8	39	2.7	147	205	54	162	1	114	34	431	31	24	7	1.0	.951	OF-246, DH-163, C-25, 1B-10, P-2

Lou Nordyke

NORDYKE, LOUIS ELLIS
B. Aug. 7, 1876, Brighton, Iowa D. Sept. 27, 1945, Los Angeles, Calif. BR TR 6' 185 lbs.

Year	Team	Games	BA	SA	AB	H	2B	3B	HR	HR%	R	RBI	BB	SO	SB	PH AB	PH H	PO	A	E	DP	TC/G	FA	G by Pos
1906	STL A	25	.245	.264	53	13	1	0	0	0.0	4	7	10		3	12	3	125	4	8	12	5.5	.942	1B-12

Irv Noren

NOREN, IRVING ARNOLD
B. Nov. 29, 1924, Jamestown, N. Y. BL TL 6' 190 lbs.

Year	Team	Games	BA	SA	AB	H	2B	3B	HR	HR%	R	RBI	BB	SO	SB	PH AB	PH H	PO	A	E	DP	TC/G	FA	G by Pos
1950	WAS A	138	.295	.459	542	160	27	10	14	2.6	80	98	67	77	5	0	0	500	34	13	21	4.0	.976	OF-121, 1B-17
1951		129	.279	.411	509	142	33	5	8	1.6	82	86	51	35	10	3	0	420	15	10	1	3.4	.978	OF-126
1952	2 teams		WAS A (12G – .245)		NY A (93G – .235)																			
"	total	105	.237	.352	321	76	16	3	5	1.6	40	23	32	37	5	18	3	44	2	0	0	0.4	1.000	OF-72, 1B-19
1953	NY A	109	.267	.388	345	92	12	6	6	1.7	55	46	42	39	3	15	3	208	11	2	1	2.0	.991	OF-96
1954		125	.319	.481	426	136	21	6	12	2.8	70	66	43	38	4	12	3	243	10	5	2	2.1	.981	OF-116, 1B-1
1955		132	.253	.375	371	94	19	1	8	2.2	49	59	43	33	5	11	1	238	9	5	0	1.9	.980	OF-126
1956		29	.216	.243	37	8	1	0	0	0.0	4	6	12	7	0	13	4	10	2	1	0	0.4	.923	OF-10, 1B-1
1957	2 teams		KC A (81G – .213)		STL N (17G – .367)																			
"	total	98	.237	.358	190	45	12	1	3	1.6	11	26	15	25	0	54	14	204	13	2	24	2.2	.991	1B-25, OF-14
1958	STL N	117	.264	.393	178	47	9	1	4	2.2	24	22	13	21	0	43	8	75	1	2	0	0.7	.974	OF-77
1959	2 teams		STL N (8G – .125)		CHI N (65G – .321)																			
"	total	73	.311	.451	164	51	7	2	4	2.4	27	19	13	26	2	29	12	85	0	0	2	1.2	1.000	OF-42, 1B-2
1960	2 teams		CHI N (12G – .091)		LA N (26G – .200)																			
"	total	38	.167	.250	36	6	0	0	1	2.8	1	2	4	12	0	32	5	6	0	1	1	0.2	.857	OF-1, 1B-1
11 yrs.		1093	.275	.410	3119	857	157	35	65	2.1	443	453	335	350	34	230	52	2033	101	41	52	2.0	.981	OF-801, 1B-66

WORLD SERIES

Year	Team	Games	BA	SA	AB	H	2B	3B	HR	HR%	R	RBI	BB	SO	SB	PH AB	PH H	PO	A	E	DP	TC/G	FA	G by Pos
1952	NY A	4	.300	.300	10	3	0	0	0	0.0	0	1	1	3	0	1	1	2	0	0	0	0.5	1.000	OF-3
1953		2	.000	.000	1	0	0	0	0	0.0	0	0	1	0	0	1	0	0	0	0	0	0.0	–	
1955		5	.063	.063	16	1	0	0	0	0.0	0	1	1	1	0	0	0	13	0	0	0	2.6	1.000	OF-5
3 yrs.		11	.148	.148	27	4	0	0	0	0.0	0	2	3	4	0	2	1	15	0	0	0	1.4	1.000	OF-8

Bill Norman

NORMAN, HENRY WILLIS PATRICK
B. July 16, 1910, St. Louis, Mo. D. Apr. 21, 1962, Milwaukee, Wis. BR TR 6'2" 190 lbs.
Manager 1958-59.

Year	Team	Games	BA	SA	AB	H	2B	3B	HR	HR%	R	RBI	BB	SO	SB	PH AB	PH H	PO	A	E	DP	TC/G	FA	G by Pos
1931	CHI A	24	.182	.218	55	10	2	0	0	0.0	7	6	4	10	0	4	0	41	1	3	0	1.9	.933	OF-17
1932		13	.229	.333	48	11	3	1	0	0.0	6	2	2	3	0	0	0	20	2	2	0	1.8	.917	OF-13
2 yrs.		37	.204	.272	103	21	5	1	0	0.0	13	8	6	13	0	4	0	61	3	5	0	1.9	.928	OF-30

Dan Norman

NORMAN, DANIEL EDMUND
B. Jan. 11, 1955, Los Angeles, Calif. BR TR 6'2" 195 lbs.

Year	Team	Games	BA	SA	AB	H	2B	3B	HR	HR%	R	RBI	BB	SO	SB	PH AB	PH H	PO	A	E	DP	TC/G	FA	G by Pos
1977	NY N	7	.250	.313	16	4	1	0	0	0.0	2	0	4	2	0	1	0	8	0	0	0	1.1	1.000	OF-6
1978		19	.266	.484	64	17	0	1	4	6.3	7	10	2	14	1	1	0	33	1	0	0	1.8	1.000	OF-18
1979		44	.245	.373	110	27	3	1	3	2.7	9	11	10	26	2	13	3	54	4	2	0	1.4	.967	OF-33
1980		69	.185	.283	92	17	1	1	2	2.2	5	9	6	14	5	47	9	19	1	0	0	0.3	1.000	OF-19
1982	MON N	53	.212	.348	66	14	3	0	2	3.0	6	7	7	20	0	21	3	30	1	1	0	0.6	.969	OF-31
5 yrs.		192	.227	.362	348	79	8	3	11	3.2	29	37	29	76	8	83	14	144	7	3	0	0.8	.981	OF-107

Nelson Norman

NORMAN, NELSON AUGUSTO (Gus)
B. May 23, 1958, San Pedro de Macoris, Dominican Republic BR TR 6'2" 160 lbs.

Year	Team	Games	BA	SA	AB	H	2B	3B	HR	HR%	R	RBI	BB	SO	SB	PH AB	PH H	PO	A	E	DP	TC/G	FA	G by Pos
1978	TEX A	23	.265	.324	34	9	2	0	0	0.0	1	1	0	5	0	0	0	16	50	1	2	2.9	.985	SS-18, 3B-6
1979		147	.222	.265	343	76	9	3	0	0.0	36	21	19	41	4	1	0	177	302	24	64	3.4	.952	SS-142, 2B-1
1980		17	.219	.219	32	7	0	0	0	0.0	4	1	1	1	0	0	0	21	45	4	12	4.1	.943	SS-17
1981		7	.231	.308	13	3	1	0	0	0.0	1	2	1	2	0	0	0	5	21	1	5	3.9	.963	SS-5
1982	PIT N	3	.000	.000	3	0	0	0	0	0.0	0	0	0	0	0	0	0	1	2	0	0	1.0	1.000	2B-2, SS-1
1987	MON N	1	.000	.000	4	0	0	0	0	0.0	0	0	0	1	0	0	0	1	1	1	0	3.0	.667	SS-1
6 yrs.		198	.221	.263	429	95	12	3	0	0.0	42	25	21	50	4	1	0	221	421	31	83	3.4	.954	SS-184, 3B-6, 2B-3

Jim Norris

NORRIS, JAMES FRANCIS
B. Dec. 20, 1948, Brooklyn, N. Y. BL TL 5'10" 175 lbs.

Year Team	Games	BA	SA	AB	H	2B	3B	HR	HR%	R	RBI	BB	SO	SB	Pinch Hit AB	H	PO	A	E	DP	TC/G	FA	G by Pos

Jim Norris *continued*

Year Team	Games	BA	SA	AB	H	2B	3B	HR	HR%	R	RBI	BB	SO	SB	AB	H	PO	A	E	DP	TC/G	FA	G by Pos
1977 CLE A	133	.270	.364	440	119	23	6	2	0.5	59	37	64	57	26	10	5	326	9	6	2	2.6	.982	OF-124, 1B-3
1978	113	.283	.378	315	89	14	5	2	0.6	41	27	42	20	12	20	5	196	8	2	6	1.8	.990	OF-78, DH-15, 1B-6
1979	124	.246	.348	353	87	15	6	3	0.8	50	30	44	35	15	18	4	214	2	4	0	1.8	.982	OF-93, DH-13
1980 TEX A	119	.247	.276	174	43	5	0	0	0.0	23	16	23	16	6	31	9	96	4	0	1	0.8	1.000	OF-82, 1B-10, DH-1
4 yrs.	489	.264	.351	1282	338	57	17	7	0.5	173	110	173	128	59	79	23	832	23	12	9	1.8	.986	OF-377, DH-29, 1B-19

Leo Norris

NORRIS, LEO JOHN
B. May 17, 1908, Bay St. Louis, Miss. D. Feb. 13, 1987, Zachary, La.

BR TR 5'11" 165 lbs.

Year Team	Games	BA	SA	AB	H	2B	3B	HR	HR%	R	RBI	BB	SO	SB	AB	H	PO	A	E	DP	TC/G	FA	G by Pos
1936 PHI N	154	.265	.382	581	154	27	4	11	1.9	64	76	39	79	4	0	0	414	475	53	98	6.1	.944	SS-121, 2B-38
1937	116	.257	.407	381	98	24	3	9	2.4	45	36	21	53	3	5	0	212	264	22	43	4.3	.956	2B-74, 3B-24, SS-20
2 yrs.	270	.262	.392	962	252	51	7	20	2.1	109	112	60	132	7	5	0	626	739	75	141	5.3	.948	SS-141, 2B-112, 3B-24

Billy North

NORTH, WILLIAM ALEX
B. May 15, 1948, Seattle, Wash.

BB TR 5'11" 185 lbs.

Year Team	Games	BA	SA	AB	H	2B	3B	HR	HR%	R	RBI	BB	SO	SB	AB	H	PO	A	E	DP	TC/G	FA	G by Pos
1971 CHI N	8	.375	.375	16	6	0	0	0	0.0	3	0	4	6	1	0	0	4	0	0	0	0.5	1.000	OF-6
1972	66	.181	.244	127	23	2	3	0	0.0	22	4	13	33	6	13	3	61	3	3	1	1.0	.955	OF-48
1973 OAK A	146	.285	.348	554	158	10	5	5	0.9	98	34	78	89	53	2	0	429	14	9	5	3.1	.980	OF-138, DH-6
1974	149	.260	.337	543	141	20	5	4	0.7	79	33	69	86	54	1	1	437	9	4	2	3.0	.991	OF-138, DH-8
1975	140	.273	.330	524	143	17	5	1	0.2	74	43	81	80	30	1	1	420	10	11	1	3.2	.975	OF-138, DH-1
1976	154	.276	.337	590	163	20	5	2	0.3	91	31	73	95	75	1	0	397	8	9	1	2.7	.978	OF-144, DH-8
1977	56	.261	.326	184	48	3	3	1	0.5	32	9	32	25	17	4	0	112	1	2	0	2.1	.983	OF-52, DH-1
1978 2 teams			OAK A (24G – .212)				LA N (110G – .234)																
" total	134	.230	.270	356	82	14	0	0	0.0	59	15	74	61	30	9	4	263	3	6	1	2.0	.978	OF-120
1979 SF N	142	.259	.341	460	119	15	4	5	1.1	87	30	96	84	58	11	1	300	8	4	2	2.2	.987	OF-130
1980	128	.251	.292	415	104	12	1	0	0.2	73	19	81	78	45	19	5	313	6	6	1	2.5	.982	OF-115
1981	46	.221	.298	131	29	7	0	1	0.8	22	12	26	28	26	7	1	84	1	3	1	1.9	.966	OF-37
11 yrs.	1169	.261	.323	3900	1016	120	31	20	0.5	640	230	627	665	395	68	16	2820	63	57	15	2.5	.981	OF-1066, DH-24

LEAGUE CHAMPIONSHIP SERIES

Year Team	Games	BA	SA	AB	H	2B	3B	HR	HR%	R	RBI	BB	SO	SB	AB	H	PO	A	E	DP	TC/G	FA	G by Pos
1974 OAK A	4	.063	.125	16	1	1	0	0	0.0	3	0	2	1	0	0	0	14	0	0	0	3.5	1.000	OF-4
1975	3	.000	.000	10	0	0	0	0	0.0	0	1	2	0	0	0	0	6	1	1	0	2.7	.875	OF-3
1978 LA N	4	.000	.000	8	0	0	0	0	0.0	0	0	0	1	0	0	0	9	0	0	0	2.3	1.000	OF-4
3 yrs.	11	.029	.059	34	1	1	0	0	0.0	3	1	4	2	1	0	0	29	1	1	0	2.8	.968	OF-11

WORLD SERIES

Year Team	Games	BA	SA	AB	H	2B	3B	HR	HR%	R	RBI	BB	SO	SB	AB	H	PO	A	E	DP	TC/G	FA	G by Pos
1974 OAK A	5	.059	.059	17	1	0	0	0	0.0	3	0	2	5	1	0	0	17	0	1	0	3.6	.944	OF-5
1978 LA N	4	.125	.250	8	1	1	0	0	0.0	2	2	1	0	1	1	1	0	0	0	0	—		OF
2 yrs.	9	.080	.120	25	2	1	0	0	0.0	5	2	3	5	2	1	1	17	0	1	0	2.0	.944	OF-5

Hub Northen

NORTHEN, HUBBARD ELWIN
B. Aug. 16, 1885, Atlanta, Tex. D. Oct. 1, 1947, Shreveport, La.

BL TL 5'8" 175 lbs.

Year Team	Games	BA	SA	AB	H	2B	3B	HR	HR%	R	RBI	BB	SO	SB	AB	H	PO	A	E	DP	TC/G	FA	G by Pos
1910 STL A	26	.198	.208	96	19	1	0	0	0.0	6	16	5		2	0	0	48	2	4	0	2.1	.926	OF-26
1911 2 teams	20	CIN N (1G – .000)		BKN N (19G – .316)																			
" total	20	.316	.395	76	24	2	2	0	0.0	16	1	14	9	4	0	0	46	5	5	0	2.8	.911	OF-19
1912 BKN N	118	.282	.388	412	116	26	6	2	0.5	54	46	41	46	8	15	4	178	11	10	3	1.7	.950	OF-102
3 yrs.	164	.272	.360	584	159	29	8	2	0.3	76	63	60	55	14	15	4	272	18	19	3	1.9	.939	OF-147

Ron Northey

NORTHEY, RONALD JAMES (The Round Man)
Father of Scott Northey.
B. Apr. 26, 1920, Mahanoy City, Pa. D. Apr. 16, 1971, Pittsburgh, Pa.

BL TR 5'10" 195 lbs.

Year Team	Games	BA	SA	AB	H	2B	3B	HR	HR%	R	RBI	BB	SO	SB	AB	H	PO	A	E	DP	TC/G	FA	G by Pos
1942 PHI N	127	.251	.331	402	101	13	2	5	1.2	31	31	28	33	2	17	4	206	12	11	2	1.8	.952	OF-109
1943	147	.278	.430	586	163	31	5	16	2.7	72	68	51	52	2	2	0	292	19	7	6	2.2	.978	OF-145
1944	152	.288	.496	570	164	35	9	22	3.9	72	104	67	51	1	1	0	286	24	6	7	2.1	.981	OF-151
1946	128	.249	.441	438	109	24	6	16	3.7	55	62	39	59	1	14	5	194	7	6	3	1.6	.971	OF-111
1947 2 teams		PHI N (13G – .255)		STL N (110G – .293)																			
" total	123	.288	.492	358	103	22	3	15	4.2	59	66	54	32	1	13	3	143	16	8	2	1.4	.952	OF-107, 3B-2
1948 STL N	96	.321	.528	246	79	10	1	13	5.3	40	64	38	25	0	25	11	85	2	1	0	0.9	.989	OF-67
1949	90	.260	.423	265	69	18	2	7	2.6	28	50	31	15	0	12	0	93	4	2	2	1.1	.980	OF-73
1950 2 teams		CIN N (27G – .260)		CHI N (53G – .281)																			
" total	80	.272	.487	191	52	14	0	9	4.7	22	29	25	15	0	27	5	59	3	2	1	0.8	.969	OF-51
1952 CHI N	1	.000	.000	1	0	0	0	0	0.0	0	0	0	0	0	1	0	0	0	0	0	0.0	—	
1955 CHI A	14	.357	.714	14	5	2	0	1	7.1	1	4	3	3	0	10	4	1	0	0	0	0.1	1.000	OF-2
1956	53	.354	.583	48	17	2	0	3	6.3	4	23	8	1	0	39	15	4	1	0	0	0.1	1.000	OF-4
1957 2 teams		CHI A (40G – .185)		PHI N (33G – .269)																			
" total	73	.226	.302	53	12	1	0	1	1.9	4	12	17	11	0	53	12	0	0	0	0	0.0	—	
12 yrs.	1084	.276	.450	3172	874	172	28	108	3.4	385	513	361	297	7	214	59	1363	88	43	24	1.4	.971	OF-820, 3B-2

Scott Northey

NORTHEY, SCOTT RICHARD
Son of Ron Northey.
B. Oct. 15, 1946, Philadelphia, Pa.

BR TR 6' 175 lbs.

Year Team	Games	BA	SA	AB	H	2B	3B	HR	HR%	R	RBI	BB	SO	SB	AB	H	PO	A	E	DP	TC/G	FA	G by Pos
1969 KC A	20	.262	.410	61	16	2	1	2	1.6	11	7	7	19	6	0	0	35	1	1	0	1.9	.973	OF-18

Jim Northrup

NORTHRUP, JAMES THOMAS
B. Nov. 24, 1939, Breckenridge, Mich.

BL TR 6'3" 190 lbs.

Year Team	Games	BA	SA	AB	H	2B	3B	HR	HR%	R	RBI	BB	SO	SB	AB	H	PO	A	E	DP	TC/G	FA	G by Pos
1964 DET A	5	.083	.167	12	1	1	0	0	0.0	0	1	0	3	1	3	0	4	0	0	0	0.8	1.000	OF-2
1965	80	.205	.315	219	45	12	3	2	0.9	20	16	12	50	1	24	3	82	0	2	0	1.1	.976	OF-54
1966	123	.265	.465	419	111	24	6	16	3.8	53	58	33	52	4	10	4	241	8	5	1	2.1	.980	OF-113
1967	144	.271	.392	495	134	18	6	10	2.0	63	61	43	83	7	5	1	271	3	8	1	2.0	.972	OF-143
1968	154	.264	.447	580	153	29	7	21	3.6	76	90	50	87	4	4	0	321	7	7	1	2.2	.979	OF-151
1969	148	.295	.508	543	160	31	5	25	4.6	79	66	52	83	4	5	0	323	8	5	2	2.3	.985	OF-143
1970	139	.262	.458	504	132	21	3	24	4.8	71	80	58	68	3	3	1	284	4	2	1	2.1	.993	OF-136
1971	136	.270	.442	459	124	27	4	16	3.5	72	71	60	43	7	14	5	441	20	9	23	3.5	.981	OF-108, 1B-32

Year	Team	Games	BA	SA	AB	H	2B	3B	HR	HR%	R	RBI	BB	SO	SB	Pinch Hit AB	H	PO	A	E	DP	TC/G	FA	G by Pos

Jim Northrup *continued*

Year	Team	Games	BA	SA	AB	H	2B	3B	HR	HR%	R	RBI	BB	SO	SB	AB	H	PO	A	E	DP	TC/G	FA	G by Pos
1972		134	.261	.362	426	111	15	2	8	1.9	40	42	38	47	4	14	2	224	9	5	2	1.8	.979	OF-127, 1B-2
1973		119	.307	.465	404	124	14	7	12	3.0	55	44	38	41	4	8	2	207	6	4	2	1.8	.982	OF-116
1974 3 teams	DET A (97G – .237)			MON N	(21G – .241)				BAL A	(8G – .571)														
" total		126	.243	.373	437	106	13	1	14	3.2	46	53	43	56	0	10	2	226	6	6	0	1.9	.975	OF-116
1975 BAL	A	84	.273	.418	194	53	13	0	5	2.6	27	29	22	22	0	22	8	91	2	2	0	1.1	.979	OF-58, DH-3
12 yrs.		1392	.267	.429	4692	1254	218	42	153	3.3	603	610	449	635	39	122	28	2715	73	55	33	2.0	.981	OF-1267, 1B-34, DH-3

LEAGUE CHAMPIONSHIP SERIES

Year	Team	Games	BA	SA	AB	H	2B	3B	HR	HR%	R	RBI	BB	SO	SB	AB	H	PO	A	E	DP	TC/G	FA	G by Pos
1972 DET	A	5	.357	.357	14	5	0	0	0	0.0	0	1	2	3	0	0	0	12	0	0	0	2.4	1.000	OF-5

WORLD SERIES

Year	Team	Games	BA	SA	AB	H	2B	3B	HR	HR%	R	RBI	BB	SO	SB	AB	H	PO	A	E	DP	TC/G	FA	G by Pos
1968 DET	A	7	.250	.536	28	7	0	1	2	7.1	4	8	1	5	0	0	0	22	0	2	0	3.4	.917	OF-7

Willie Norwood

NORWOOD, WILLIE
B. Nov. 7, 1950, Green County, Ala.   BR TR 6' 185 lbs.

Year	Team	Games	BA	SA	AB	H	2B	3B	HR	HR%	R	RBI	BB	SO	SB	AB	H	PO	A	E	DP	TC/G	FA	G by Pos
1977 MIN	A	39	.229	.373	83	19	3	0	3	3.6	15	9	6	17	6	7	1	59	0	3	0	1.6	.952	OF-28, DH-5
1978		125	.255	.376	428	109	23	3	8	1.9	56	46	28	64	25	8	2	227	7	14	1	2.0	.944	OF-115, DH-12
1979		96	.248	.385	270	67	13	3	6	2.2	32	30	20	51	9	14	5	147	4	4	0	1.6	.974	OF-71, DH-14
1980		34	.164	.233	73	12	2	0	1	1.4	6	8	3	13	1	7	2	42	0	0	0	1.2	1.000	OF-17, DH-9
4 yrs.		294	.242	.367	854	207	40	6	18	2.1	109	93	57	145	41	36	10	475	11	21	1	1.7	.959	OF-231, DH-40

Joe Nossek

NOSSEK, JOSEPH RUDOLPH
B. Nov. 8, 1940, Cleveland, Ohio   BR TR 6' 178 lbs.

Year	Team	Games	BA	SA	AB	H	2B	3B	HR	HR%	R	RBI	BB	SO	SB	AB	H	PO	A	E	DP	TC/G	FA	G by Pos
1964 MIN	A	7	.000	.000	1	0	0	0	0	0.0	0	0	0	1	0	1	0	0	0	0	0	0.0	–	OF-2
1965		87	.218	.306	170	37	9	0	2	1.2	19	16	7	22	2	28	7	72	26	4	1	1.2	.961	OF-48, 3B-9
1966 2 teams	MIN	A (4G – .000)		KC	A	(87G – .261)																		
" total		91	.261	.343	230	60	10	3	1	0.4	13	27	8	21	4	17	8	161	8	3	1	1.9	.983	OF-80, 3B-1
1967 KC	A	87	.205	.253	166	34	6	1	0	0.0	12	10	4	26	2	28	1	105	2	2	0	1.3	.982	OF-63
1969 2 teams	OAK	A (13G – .000)		STL	N	(9G – .200)																		
" total		22	.091	.091	11	1	0	0	0	0.0	2	0	0	3	0	4	1	9	0	0	0	0.4	1.000	OF-13
1970 STL	N	1	.000	.000	1	0	0	0	0	0.0	0	0	0	0	0	1	0	0	0	0	0	0.0	–	
6 yrs.		295	.228	.301	579	132	25	4	3	0.5	47	53	19	72	8	79	17	347	36	9	2	1.3	.977	OF-206, 3B-10

WORLD SERIES

Year	Team	Games	BA	SA	AB	H	2B	3B	HR	HR%	R	RBI	BB	SO	SB	AB	H	PO	A	E	DP	TC/G	FA	G by Pos
1965 MIN	A	6	.200	.200	20	4	0	0	0	0.0	0	0	0	1	0	1	1	13	0	0	0	2.2	1.000	OF-5

Lou Novikoff

NOVIKOFF, LOUIS ALEXANDER (The Mad Russian)
B. Oct. 12, 1915, Glendale, Ariz.   D. Sept. 30, 1970, South Gate, Calif.   BR TR 5'10" 185 lbs.

Year	Team	Games	BA	SA	AB	H	2B	3B	HR	HR%	R	RBI	BB	SO	SB	AB	H	PO	A	E	DP	TC/G	FA	G by Pos
1941 CHI	N	62	.241	.355	203	49	8	0	5	2.5	22	24	11	15	0	8	3	92	3	0	0	1.5	1.000	OF-54
1942		128	.300	.416	483	145	25	5	7	1.4	48	64	24	28	3	8	2	232	11	9	2	2.0	.964	OF-120
1943		78	.279	.335	233	65	7	3	0	0.0	22	28	18	15	0	15	6	96	2	2	1	1.3	.980	OF-61
1944		71	.281	.403	139	39	4	2	3	2.2	15	19	10	11	1	39	12	39	1	1	0	0.6	.976	OF-29
1946 PHI	N	17	.304	.348	23	7	1	0	0	0.0	0	3	1	2	0	14	6	9	0	0	0	0.5	1.000	OF-3
5 yrs.		356	.282	.384	1081	305	45	10	15	1.4	107	138	64	71	4	84	29	468	17	12	3	1.4	.976	OF-267

Rube Novotney

NOVOTNEY, RALPH JOSEPH
B. Aug. 5, 1924, Streator, Ill.   BR TR 6' 187 lbs.

Year	Team	Games	BA	SA	AB	H	2B	3B	HR	HR%	R	RBI	BB	SO	SB	AB	H	PO	A	E	DP	TC/G	FA	G by Pos
1949 CHI	N	22	.269	.328	67	18	2	1	0	0.0	4	6	3	11	0	2	1	82	9	4	3	4.3	.958	C-20

Les Nunamaker

NUNAMAKER, LESLIE GRANT
B. Jan. 25, 1889, Malcolm, Neb.   D. Nov. 14, 1938, Hastings, Neb.   BR TR 6'2" 190 lbs.

Year	Team	Games	BA	SA	AB	H	2B	3B	HR	HR%	R	RBI	BB	SO	SB	AB	H	PO	A	E	DP	TC/G	FA	G by Pos
1911 BOS	A	62	.257	.311	183	47	4	3	0	0.0	18	19	12		1	3	0	309	79	11	8	6.4	.972	C-59
1912		35	.252	.340	103	26	5	2	0	0.0	15	6	6		2	0	0	166	33	6	3	5.9	.971	C-35
1913		29	.215	.354	65	14	5	2	0	0.0	9	9	8	8	2	1	0	147	23	4	1	6.0	.977	C-27
1914 2 teams	BOS	A (4G – .200)		NY	A	(87G – .265)																		
" total		91	.263	.347	262	69	10	3	2	0.8	19	29	23	34	11	10	3	329	131	15	13	5.2	.968	C-72, 1B-6
1915 NY	A	87	.225	.273	249	56	6	3	0	0.0	24	17	23	24	3	6	2	350	100	16	9	5.4	.966	C-77, 1B-2
1916		91	.296	.404	260	77	14	7	0	0.0	25	28	34	21	4	11	6	353	102	8	13	5.1	.983	C-79
1917		104	.261	.303	310	81	9	2	0	0.0	22	33	21	25	5	13	7	372	113	12	12	4.8	.976	C-91
1918 STL	A	85	.259	.307	274	71	9	2	0	0.0	22	22	28	16	6	3	3	322	108	12	10	5.2	.973	C-81, OF-1, 1B-1
1919 CLE	A	26	.250	.304	56	14	1	1	0	0.0	6	7	2	6	0	10	3	39	12	4	0	2.1	.927	C-16
1920		34	.333	.500	54	18	3	3	0	0.0	10	14	4	5	1	10	1	69	13	4	1	2.5	.953	C-17, 1B-6
1921		46	.359	.443	131	47	7	2	0	0.0	16	24	11	8	1	0	0	166	31	6	3	4.4	.970	C-46
1922		25	.302	.349	43	13	2	0	0	0.0	8	7	4	3	0	11	3	38	5	3	0	1.8	.935	C-15
12 yrs.		715	.268	.339	1990	533	75	30	2	0.1	194	215	176	150	36	78	28	2660	750	101	73	4.9	.971	C-615, 1B-15, OF-1

WORLD SERIES

Year	Team	Games	BA	SA	AB	H	2B	3B	HR	HR%	R	RBI	BB	SO	SB	AB	H	PO	A	E	DP	TC/G	FA	G by Pos
1920 CLE	A	2	.500	.500	2	1	0	0	0	0.0	0	0	0	0	0	2	1	0	0	0	0	0.0	–	C-1

Emory Nusz

NUSZ, EMORY MOBERLY
B. Apr. 2, 1866, Frederick, Md.   D. Aug. 3, 1898, Point of Rocks, Md.

Year	Team	Games	BA	SA	AB	H	2B	3B	HR	HR%	R	RBI	BB	SO	SB	AB	H	PO	A	E	DP	TC/G	FA	G by Pos
1884 WAS	U	1	.000	.000	4	0	0	0	0	0.0	1		0			0	0	2	0	2	0	4.0	.500	OF-1

Dizzy Nutter

NUTTER, EVERETT CLARENCE
B. Aug. 27, 1893, Roseville, Ohio   D. July 25, 1958, Battle Creek, Mich.   BL TR 5'9" 160 lbs.

Year	Team	Games	BA	SA	AB	H	2B	3B	HR	HR%	R	RBI	BB	SO	SB	AB	H	PO	A	E	DP	TC/G	FA	G by Pos
1919 BOS	N	18	.212	.212	52	11	0	0	0	0.0	4	3	4	5	1	5	0	29	3	0	1	1.8	1.000	OF-12

Charlie Nyce

NYCE, CHARLES REIFF
Born Charles Reiff Nice
B. July 1, 1870, Philadelphia, Pa.   D. May 9, 1908, Philadelphia, Pa.   5'8" 160 lbs.

Year	Team	Games	BA	SA	AB	H	2B	3B	HR	HR%	R	RBI	BB	SO	SB	AB	H	PO	A	E	DP	TC/G	FA	G by Pos
1895 BOS	N	9	.229	.543	35	8	5	0	1	2.9	7	9	4	2	0	0	0	18	30	6	4	6.0	.889	SS-9

Year	Team		Games	BA	SA	AB	H	2B	3B	HR	HR%	R	RBI	BB	SO	SB	Pinch Hit AB	H	PO	A	E	DP	TC/G	FA	G by Pos

Chris Nyman

NYMAN, CHRISTOPHER CURTIS
Brother of Nyls Nyman.
B. June 6, 1955, Pomona, Calif.

BR TR 6'4" 200 lbs.

Year	Team		Games	BA	SA	AB	H	2B	3B	HR	HR%	R	RBI	BB	SO	SB	PH AB	PH H	PO	A	E	DP	TC/G	FA	G by Pos
1982	CHI	A	28	.246	.262	65	16	1	0	0	0.0	6	2	3	9	3	5	0	161	12	1	16	6.2	.994	1B-24, OF-2
1983			21	.286	.500	28	8	0	0	2	7.1	12	4	4	7	2	0	0	87	5	0	8	4.4	1.000	DH-10, 1B-10
2 yrs.			49	.258	.333	93	24	1	0	2	2.2	18	6	7	16	5	5	0	248	17	1	24	5.4	.996	1B-34, DH-10, OF-2

Nyls Nyman

NYMAN, NYLS WALLACE REX
Brother of Chris Nyman.
B. Mar. 7, 1954, Detroit, Mich.

BL TR 6' 170 lbs.

Year	Team		Games	BA	SA	AB	H	2B	3B	HR	HR%	R	RBI	BB	SO	SB	PH AB	PH H	PO	A	E	DP	TC/G	FA	G by Pos
1974	CHI	A	5	.643	.929	14	9	1	0	0	0.0	5	4	0	1	1	1	1	6	1	0	1	1.4	1.000	OF-3
1975			106	.226	.281	327	74	6	3	2	0.6	36	28	11	34	10	3	1	177	6	8	0	1.8	.958	OF-94, DH-4
1976			8	.133	.200	15	2	1	0	0	0.0	2	1	0	3	1	0	0	13	0	0	0	1.6	1.000	OF-7
1977			1	.000	.000	0	0	0	0	0	0.0	0	0	0	0	0	0	0	0	0	0	0	0.0	—	
4 yrs.			120	.238	.303	357	85	9	4	2	0.6	43	33	11	38	12	4	2	196	7	8	1	1.8	.962	OF-104, DH-4

Rebel Oakes

OAKES, ENNIS TELFAIR
B. Dec. 17, 1886, Homer, La. D. Feb. 29, 1948, Rocky Springs, La.
Manager 1914-15.

BL TR 5'8" 170 lbs.

Year	Team		Games	BA	SA	AB	H	2B	3B	HR	HR%	R	RBI	BB	SO	SB	PH AB	PH H	PO	A	E	DP	TC/G	FA	G by Pos
1909	CIN	N	120	.270	.340	415	112	10	5	3	0.7	55	31	40		23	7	2	218	15	5	3	2.0	.979	OF-113
1910	STL	N	131	.252	.308	468	118	14	6	0	0.0	50	43	38	38	18	3	1	266	12	18	3	2.3	.939	OF-127
1911			154	.263	.319	551	145	13	6	2	0.4	69	59	41	35	25	2	1	364	26	16	8	2.6	.961	OF-151
1912			136	.281	.358	495	139	19	5	3	0.6	57	58	31	24	26	1	1	324	15	19	5	2.6	.947	OF-136
1913			146	.291	.335	537	156	14	5	0	0.0	59	49	43	32	22	2	1	321	16	11	2	2.4	.968	OF-144
1914	PIT	F	145	.312	.415	571	178	18	10	7	1.2	82	75	35		28	0	0	313	23	14	2	2.4	.960	OF-145
1915			153	.278	.336	580	161	24	5	0	0.0	55	82	37		21	0	0	348	12	10	2	2.4	.973	OF-153
7 yrs.			985	.279	.346	3617	1009	112	42	15	0.4	427	397	265	129	163	15	6	2154	119	93	25	2.4	.961	OF-969

Prince Oana

OANA, HENRY KAUHANE
B. Jan. 22, 1908, Waipahu, Hawaii D. June 19, 1976, Austin, Tex.

BR TR 6'2" 193 lbs.

Year	Team		Games	BA	SA	AB	H	2B	3B	HR	HR%	R	RBI	BB	SO	SB	PH AB	PH H	PO	A	E	DP	TC/G	FA	G by Pos
1934	PHI	N	6	.238	.286	21	5	0	0	0	0.0	3	3	0		0	1	0	14	0	0	0	2.3	1.000	OF-4
1943	DET	A	20	.385	.654	26	10	2	1	1	3.8	5	7	1	2	0	9	3	0	6	2	2	0.4	.750	P-10
1945			4	.200	.200	5	1	0	0	0	0.0	0	0	0	1	0	0	0	0	1	0	0	0.3	1.000	P-3
3 yrs.			30	.308	.462	52	16	3	1	1	1.9	8	10	1	3	0	12	4	14	7	2	2	0.8	.913	P-13, OF-4

Johnny Oates

OATES, JOHNNY LANE
B. Jan. 21, 1946, Sylva, N. C.

BL TR 5'11" 188 lbs.

Year	Team		Games	BA	SA	AB	H	2B	3B	HR	HR%	R	RBI	BB	SO	SB	PH AB	PH H	PO	A	E	DP	TC/G	FA	G by Pos
1970	BAL	A	5	.278	.389	18	5	0	1	0	0.0	2	2	2	0	0	1	1	30	1	2	1	6.6	.939	C-4
1972			85	.261	.364	253	66	12	1	4	1.6	20	21	28	31	5	10	1	391	31	2	4	5.0	.995	C-82
1973	ATL	N	93	.248	.304	322	80	6	0	4	1.2	27	27	22	31	1	6	2	409	57	9	6	5.1	.981	C-86
1974			100	.223	.268	291	65	10	0	1	0.3	22	21	23	24	2	15	4	434	55	4	4	4.9	.992	C-91
1975 2 teams	ATL	N (8G – .222)			PHI N (90G – .286)																				
" total			98	.282	.345	287	81	15	0	1	0.3	28	25	34	33	1	13	2	450	45	5	10	5.1	.990	C-88
1976	PHI	N	37	.253	.273	99	25	2	0	0	0.0	10	8	8	12	0	8	2	155	15	1	1	4.6	.994	C-33
1977	LA	N	60	.269	.353	156	42	4	0	3	1.9	18	11	11	11	1	6	0	258	37	4	3	5.0	.987	C-56
1978			40	.307	.320	75	23	1	0	0	0.0	5	6	3	4	1	14	3	77	10	4	1	2.3	.956	C-24
1979			26	.130	.174	46	6	2	0	0	0.0	1	0	1	6	1	6	1	64	13	2	2	3.0	.975	C-20
1980	NY	A	39	.188	.281	64	12	3	0	1	1.6	6	3	2	3	1	1	0	99	10	1	1	2.8	.991	C-39
1981			10	.192	.231	26	5	1	0	0	0.0	4	0	2	0	0	0	0	49	3	2	0	5.4	.963	C-10
11 yrs.			593	.250	.313	1637	410	56	2	14	0.9	146	126	141	149	11	79	16	2416	277	36	33	4.6	.987	C-533

LEAGUE CHAMPIONSHIP SERIES

Year	Team		Games	BA	SA	AB	H	2B	3B	HR	HR%	R	RBI	BB	SO	SB	PH AB	PH H	PO	A	E	DP	TC/G	FA	G by Pos
1976	PHI	N	1	.000	.000	1	0	0	0	0	0.0	0	0	0	0	0	0	0	1	0	0	0	1.0	1.000	C-1

WORLD SERIES

Year	Team		Games	BA	SA	AB	H	2B	3B	HR	HR%	R	RBI	BB	SO	SB	PH AB	PH H	PO	A	E	DP	TC/G	FA	G by Pos
1977	LA	N	1	.000	.000	1	0	0	0	0	0.0	0	0	0	1	0	1	0	1	0	0	0	1.0	1.000	C-1
1978			1	1.000	1.000	1	1	0	0	0	0.0	0	0	0	0	0	0	0	3	1	0	0	4.0	1.000	C-1
2 yrs.			2	.500	.500	2	1	0	0	0	0.0	0	0	0	1	0	1	0	4	1	0	0	2.5	1.000	C-2

Henry Oberbeck

OBERBECK, HENRY A.
B. May 17, 1858, St. Louis, Mo. D. Aug. 26, 1921, St. Louis, Mo.

Year	Team		Games	BA	SA	AB	H	2B	3B	HR	HR%	R	RBI	BB	SO	SB	PH AB	PH H	PO	A	E	DP	TC/G	FA	G by Pos
1883 2 teams	PIT	AA (2G – .222)			STL	AA (4G – .000)																			
" total			6	.087	.130	23	2	1	0	0	0.0	1		0			0	0	28	2	1	3	5.2	.968	OF-4, 1B-2
1884 2 teams	BAL	U (33G – .184)			KC	U (27G – .189)																			
" total			60	.186	.219	215	40	7	0	0	0.0	26		10			0	0	107	59	26	3	3.2	.865	OF-35, 3B-23, P-8, 1B-3
2 yrs.			66	.176	.210	238	42	8	0	0	0.0	27		10			0	0	135	61	27	6	3.4	.879	OF-39, 3B-23, P-8, 1B-5

Ken Oberkfell

OBERKFELL, KENNETH RAY (Obie)
B. May 4, 1956, Highland, Ill.

BL TR 6' 175 lbs.

Year	Team		Games	BA	SA	AB	H	2B	3B	HR	HR%	R	RBI	BB	SO	SB	PH AB	PH H	PO	A	E	DP	TC/G	FA	G by Pos
1977	STL	N	9	.111	.111	9	1	0	0	0	0.0	0	1	0	3	0	3	0	3	4	0	1	0.8	1.000	2B-6
1978			24	.120	.140	50	6	1	0	0	0.0	7	0	3	1	0	3	0	30	48	1	8	3.3	.987	2B-17, 3B-4
1979			135	.301	.388	369	111	19	5	1	0.3	53	35	57	35	4	13	3	223	343	9	67	4.3	.984	2B-117, 3B-17, SS-2
1980			116	.303	.417	422	128	27	6	3	0.7	58	46	51	23	4	1	0	227	340	7	64	4.9	.988	2B-101, 3B-16
1981			102	.293	.372	376	110	12	6	2	0.5	43	45	37	28	13	1	0	77	247	15	23	3.3	.956	3B-102, SS-1
1982			137	.289	.370	470	136	22	5	2	0.4	55	34	40	31	11	3	1	80	305	11	23	2.9	.972	3B-135, 2B-1
1983			151	.293	.385	488	143	26	5	3	0.6	62	38	61	27	12	8	3	132	303	18	44	3.0	.960	3B-127, 2B-32, SS-1
1984 2 teams	STL	N (50G – .309)			ATL	N (50G – .233)																			
" total			100	.269	.349	324	87	19	2	1	0.3	38	21	31	27	2	6	1	64	173	8	15	2.5	.967	3B-91, 2B-6, SS-1
1985	ATL	N	134	.272	.359	412	112	19	4	3	0.7	30	35	51	38	1	10	2	88	257	12	26	2.7	.966	3B-117, 2B-16
1986			151	.270	.360	503	136	24	3	5	1.0	62	48	83	40	7	4	1	116	335	11	39	3.1	.976	3B-130, 2B-41
1987			135	.280	.362	508	142	29	2	3	0.6	59	48	48	29	3	5	0	89	265	7	23	2.7	.981	3B-126, 2B-11

Year	Team		Games	BA	SA	AB	H	2B	3B	HR	HR%	R	RBI	BB	SO	SB	Pinch Hit AB	H	PO	A	E	DP	TC/G	FA	G by Pos

Ken Oberkfell *continued*

Year	Team		Games	BA	SA	AB	H	2B	3B	HR	HR%	R	RBI	BB	SO	SB	AB	H	PO	A	E	DP	TC/G	FA	G by Pos
1988	**2 teams**		ATL N (120G – .277)			PIT N (20G – .222)																			
"	total		140	.271	.353	476	129	22	4	3	0.6	49	42	37	34	4	15	2	107	237	15	24	2.6	.958	3B-115, 2B-12, SS-3, 1B-1
1989	**2 teams**		PIT N (14G – .125)			SF N (83G – .319)																			
"	total		97	.269	.359	156	42	6	1	2	1.3	19	17	10	10	0	50	**18**	131	47	4	11	1.9	.978	3B-38, 1B-16, 2B-10
	13 yrs.		1431	.281	.368	4563	1283	226	43	28	0.6	535	410	509	326	61	122	31	1367	2904	118	368	3.1	.973	3B-1018, 2B-370, 1B-17, SS-8

LEAGUE CHAMPIONSHIP SERIES

Year	Team		Games	BA	SA	AB	H	2B	3B	HR	HR%	R	RBI	BB	SO	SB	AB	H	PO	A	E	DP	TC/G	FA	G by Pos
1982	STL	N	3	.200	.200	15	3	0	0	0	0.0	1	2	0	0	0	0	0	0	0	1	0	0.3	–	3B-3
1989	SF	N	3	.000	.000	4	0	0	0	0	0.0	0	0	0	0	0	3	0	0	1	0	0	0.3	1.000	3B-1
	2 yrs.		6	.158	.158	19	3	0	0	0	0.0	1	2	0	0	0	3	0	0	1	1	0	0.3	.500	3B-4

WORLD SERIES

Year	Team		Games	BA	SA	AB	H	2B	3B	HR	HR%	R	RBI	BB	SO	SB	AB	H	PO	A	E	DP	TC/G	FA	G by Pos
1982	STL	N	7	.292	.333	24	7	1	0	0	0.0	4	1	2	1	2	0	0	3	21	1	2	3.6	.960	3B-7
1989	SF	N	4	.333	.333	6	2	0	0	0	0.0	1	0	3	0	0	1	1	0	5	1	1	1.5	.833	3B-4
	2 yrs.		11	.300	.333	30	9	1	0	0	0.0	5	1	5	1	2	1	1	3	26	2	3	2.8	.935	3B-11

Mike O'Berry

O'BERRY, PRESTON MICHAEL
B. Apr. 20, 1954, Birmingham, Ala.
BR TR 6'2" 190 lbs.

Year	Team		Games	BA	SA	AB	H	2B	3B	HR	HR%	R	RBI	BB	SO	SB	AB	H	PO	A	E	DP	TC/G	FA	G by Pos
1979	BOS	A	43	.169	.237	59	10	1	0	1	1.7	8	4	5	16	0	0	0	103	7	5	1	2.7	.957	C-43
1980	CHI	N	19	.208	.229	48	10	1	0	0	0.0	7	5	5	13	0	0	0	94	16	2	2	5.9	.982	C-19
1981	CIN	N	55	.180	.252	111	20	3	1	1	0.9	6	5	14	19	0	0	0	208	22	4	2	4.3	.983	C-55
1982			21	.222	.267	45	10	2	0	0	0.0	10	3	10	13	0	0	0	84	12	1	2	4.6	.990	C-21
1983	CAL	A	26	.167	.233	60	10	1	0	1	1.7	7	5	3	11	0	0	1	77	8	0	0	3.3	1.000	C-26
1984	NY	N	13	.250	.313	32	8	2	0	0	0.0	3	5	2	2	0	1	0	53	5	0	1	4.5	1.000	C-12, 3B-1
1985	MON	N	20	.190	.190	21	4	0	0	0	0.0	2	0	4	3	1	0	0	53	6	0	2	3.0	1.000	C-20
	7 yrs.		197	.191	.247	376	72	10	1	3	0.8	38	27	43	77	1	2	0	672	76	12	10	3.9	.984	C-196, 3B-1

Jim O'Bradovich

O'BRADOVICH, JAMES THOMAS
B. Sept. 13, 1949, Ft. Campbell, Ky.
BL TL 6'2" 200 lbs.

Year	Team		Games	BA	SA	AB	H	2B	3B	HR	HR%	R	RBI	BB	SO	SB	AB	H	PO	A	E	DP	TC/G	FA	G by Pos
1978	HOU	N	10	.176	.294	17	3	0	1	0	0.0	3	2	1	3	0	6	0	28	1	0	0	2.9	1.000	1B-3

Billy O'Brien

O'BRIEN, WILLIAM SMITH
B. Mar. 14, 1860, Albany, N. Y. D. May 26, 1911, Kansas City, Mo.
BR 6' 185 lbs.

Year	Team		Games	BA	SA	AB	H	2B	3B	HR	HR%	R	RBI	BB	SO	SB	AB	H	PO	A	E	DP	TC/G	FA	G by Pos
1884	**2 teams**		STP U (8G – .233)			KC U (4G – .235)																			
"	total		12	.234	.298	47	11	3	0	0	0.0	3		0			0	0	25	28	11	1	5.3	.828	3B-11, P-2, 1B-1
1887	WAS	N	113	.278	.492	453	126	16	12	**19**	4.2	71	73	21	17	11	0	0	1175	39	34	53	11.0	.973	1B-104, OF-4, 3B-4, 2B-2
1888			133	.225	.313	528	119	15	2	9	1.7	42	66	9	70	10	0	0	1273	39	33	55	10.1	.973	1B-132, 3B-1
1889			2	.000	.000	8	0	0	0	0	0.0	1	0	1	1	0	0	0	19	0	0	0	9.5	1.000	1B-2
1890	BKN	AA	96	.278	.415	388	108	25	8	4	1.0	47		28		5	0	0	1015	35	29	66	11.2	.973	1B-96
	5 yrs.		356	.256	.395	1424	364	59	22	32	2.2	164	139	59	88	26	0	0	3507	141	107	175	10.5	.972	1B-335, 3B-16, OF-4, 2B-2, P-2

Charlie O'Brien

O'BRIEN, CHARLES HUGH
B. May 1, 1960, Tulsa, Okla.
BR TR 6'2" 195 lbs.

Year	Team		Games	BA	SA	AB	H	2B	3B	HR	HR%	R	RBI	BB	SO	SB	AB	H	PO	A	E	DP	TC/G	FA	G by Pos
1985	OAK	A	16	.273	.364	11	3	1	0	0	0.0	3	1	3	3	0	0	0	23	0	1	0	1.5	.958	C-16
1987	MIL	A	10	.200	.343	35	7	3	1	0	0.0	2	0	4	4	0	0	0	78	11	0	0	8.9	1.000	C-10
1988			40	.220	.322	118	26	6	0	2	1.7	12	9	5	16	0	0	0	210	20	2	4	5.8	.991	C-40
1989			62	.234	.383	188	44	10	0	6	3.2	22	35	21	11	0	0	0	314	36	5	5	5.7	.986	C-62
	4 yrs.		128	.227	.358	352	80	20	1	8	2.3	39	45	33	34	0	0	0	625	67	8	9	5.5	.989	C-128

Darby O'Brien

O'BRIEN, WILLIAM D.
B. Sept. 1, 1863, Peoria, Ill. D. June 15, 1893, Peoria, Ill.
BR TR 6'1" 186 lbs.

Year	Team		Games	BA	SA	AB	H	2B	3B	HR	HR%	R	RBI	BB	SO	SB	AB	H	PO	A	E	DP	TC/G	FA	G by Pos
1887	NY	AA	127	.301	.437	522	157	30	13	5	1.0	97	40		49	0	0	0	312	28	31	9	2.9	.916	OF-121, 1B-10, SS-2, 3B-1, P-1
1888	BKN	AA	136	.280	.365	532	149	27	6	2	0.4	105	65	30		55	0	0	231	15	18	1	1.9	.932	OF-136
1889			136	.300	.418	567	170	31	11	5	0.9	146	80	61	76	91	0	0	255	14	28	5	2.2	.906	OF-136
1890	BKN	N	85	.314	.446	350	110	28	6	2	0.6	78	63	32	43	38	0	0	176	14	8	2	2.3	.960	OF-85
1891			103	.253	.367	395	100	18	6	5	1.3	79	57	39	53	31	0	0	203	11	11	1	2.2	.951	OF-103
1892			122	.243	.298	490	119	14	5	1	0.2	72	56	29	52	57	0	0	222	16	11	3	2.0	.956	OF-122
	6 yrs.		709	.282	.387	2856	805	147	47	20	0.7	577	321	231	224	321	0	0	1399	98	107	21	2.3	.933	OF-703, 1B-10, SS-2, 3B-1, P-1

Eddie O'Brien

O'BRIEN, EDWARD JOSEPH
Brother of Johnny O'Brien.
B. Dec. 11, 1930, South Amboy, N. J.
BR TR 5'9" 165 lbs.

Year	Team		Games	BA	SA	AB	H	2B	3B	HR	HR%	R	RBI	BB	SO	SB	AB	H	PO	A	E	DP	TC/G	FA	G by Pos
1953	PIT	N	89	.238	.280	261	62	5	3	0	0.0	21	14	17	30	6	4	0	122	207	23	39	4.0	.935	SS-81
1955			75	.233	.254	236	55	3	1	0	0.0	26	8	18	13	4	3	1	144	19	4	1	2.2	.976	OF-56, 3B-7, SS-4
1956			63	.264	.302	53	14	2	0	0	0.0	17	3	2	2	1	1	0	38	54	2	14	1.5	.979	SS-23, OF-6, 3B-4, 2B-2, P-1
1957			3	.000	.000	4	0	0	0	0	0.0	0	0	0	0	0	0	0	0	2	0	1	0.7	1.000	P-3
1958			1	–	–	0	0	0	0	0	–	0	0	0	0	0	0	0	0	0	0	0	0.0	–	P-1
	5 yrs.		231	.236	.269	554	131	10	4	0	0.0	64	25	37	45	11	8	1	304	282	29	55	2.7	.953	SS-108, OF-62, 3B-11, P-5, 2B-2

George O'Brien

O'BRIEN, GEORGE JOSEPH
B. Nov. 4, 1889, Cleveland, Ohio D. Mar. 24, 1966, Columbus, Ohio
BR TR 6' 185 lbs.

Year	Team		Games	BA	SA	AB	H	2B	3B	HR	HR%	R	RBI	BB	SO	SB	AB	H	PO	A	E	DP	TC/G	FA	G by Pos
1915	STL	A	3	.222	.222	9	2	0	0	0	0.0	1	0	1	2	0	0	0	11	3	1	0	5.0	.933	C-3

Jack O'Brien

O'BRIEN, JOHN JOSEPH
B. Feb. 5, 1873, Watervliet, N. Y. D. June 10, 1933, Watervliet, N. Y.
BL TR 6'1" 165 lbs.

Year	Team		Games	BA	SA	AB	H	2B	3B	HR	HR%	R	RBI	BB	SO	SB	Pinch Hit AB	H	PO	A	E	DP	TC/G	FA	G by Pos

Jack O'Brien *continued*

1899	WAS	N	127	.282	.365	468	132	11	5	6	1.3	68	51	31		17	1	0	271	31	29	6	2.6	.912	OF-121, 3B-4
1901	2 teams		WAS	A	(11G – .178)		CLE	A	(92G – .283)																
"	total		103	.271	.329	420	114	14	5	0	0.0	59	44	25		15	0	0	177	11	12	4	1.9	.940	OF-103, 3B-1
1903	BOS	A	96	.210	.302	338	71	14	4	3	0.9	44	38	21		10	9	2	142	31	13	5	1.9	.930	OF-71, 3B-11, 2B-4, SS-1
3 yrs.			326	.259	.335	1226	317	39	14	9	0.7	171	133	77		42	10	2	590	73	54	15	2.2	.925	OF-295, 3B-16, 2B-4, SS-1

WORLD SERIES

| 1903 | BOS | A | 2 | .000 | .000 | 2 | 0 | 0 | 0 | 0 | 0.0 | 0 | 0 | 0 | | 1 | 0 | 2 | 0 | 0 | 0 | 0 | 0.0 | – | |

Jack O'Brien

O'BRIEN, JOHN K
Born John K Byrne.
B. June 12, 1860, Philadelphia, Pa. D. Nov. 2, 1910, Philadelphia, Pa.

BR TR 5'10" 186 lbs.

1882	PHI	AA	62	.303	.419	241	73	13	3	3	1.2	44		13			0	0	234	81	28	1	5.5	.918	C-45, OF-18, 3B-1, 1B-1
1883			94	.290	.377	390	113	14	10	0	0.0	74		25			0	0	372	89	76	8	5.7	.858	C-58, OF-25, 3B-19, SS-1
1884			36	.283	.362	138	39	6	1	1	0.7	25		9			0	0	195	45	19	8	7.2	.927	C-30, OF-5, 1B-1
1885			62	.267	.342	225	60	9	1	2	0.9	35		20			0	0	276	95	38	10	6.6	.907	C-43, SS-9, 1B-7, OF-3, 3B-2
1886			105	.253	.345	423	107	25	7	0	0.0	65		38			0	0	426	170	70	26	6.3	.895	C-36, 3B-27, 1B-24, SS-10, 2B-7, OF-3
1887	BKN	AA	30	.228	.301	123	28	4	1	1	0.8	18		6		8	0	0	98	42	27	4	5.6	.838	C-25, OF-4, 2B-1
1888	BAL	AA	57	.224	.332	196	44	11	5	0	0.0	25	18	17		14	0	0	286	43	26	9	6.2	.927	C-37, OF-13, 1B-7
1890	PHI	AA	109	.261	.409	433	113	24	14	4	0.9	80		52		31	0	0	1021	54	27	63	10.1	.975	1B-109, OF-1, C-1
8 yrs.			555	.266	.369	2169	577	106	42	11	0.5	366	18	180		53	0	0	2908	619	311	129	6.9	.919	C-275, 1B-149, OF-72, 3B-49, SS-20, 2B-8

Jerry O'Brien

O'BRIEN, JEREMIAH
B. Feb. 2, 1864, New York D. July 5, 1911, Binghampton, Pa.

| 1887 | WAS | N | 1 | .000 | .000 | 4 | 0 | 0 | 0 | 0 | 0.0 | 0 | | 0 | | 2 | 0 | 0 | 0 | 5 | 2 | 0 | 7.0 | .714 | 2B-1 |

John O'Brien

O'BRIEN, JOHN E.
B. Oct. 22, 1851, Columbus, Ohio D. Dec. 31, 1914, Fall River, Mass.

TR 5'11½" 187 lbs.

| 1884 | BAL | U | 18 | .247 | .286 | 77 | 19 | 1 | 0 | 0 | 0.0 | 7 | | 2 | | 0 | 0 | 0 | 29 | 3 | 5 | 2 | 2.1 | .865 | OF-18 |

John O'Brien

O'BRIEN, JOHN J. (Chewing Gum)
B. July 14, 1870, St. John, N. B., Canada D. May 13, 1913, Lewiston, Me.

BL TR 175 lbs.

1891	BKN	N	43	.246	.293	167	41	4	2	0	0.0	22	26	12	17	4	0	0	85	102	32	13	5.1	.854	2B-43
1893	CHI	N	4	.357	.500	14	5	0	1	0	0.0	3	1	2	2	1	0	0	10	8	2	1	5.0	.900	2B-4
1895	LOU	N	128	.256	.295	539	138	10	4	1	0.2	82	50	45	20	15	0	0	339	397	47	58	6.1	.940	2B-125, 1B-3
1896	2 teams		LOU	N	(49G – .339)		WAS	N	(73G – .267)																
"	total		122	.296	.386	456	135	12	6	6	1.3	62	57	40	19	8	0	0	291	375	44	52	5.8	.938	2B-122
1897	WAS	N	86	.244	.322	320	78	12	2	3	0.9	37	45	19		6	0	0	223	260	30	43	6.0	.942	2B-86
1899	2 teams		BAL	N	(39G – .193)		PIT	N	(79G – .226)																
"	total		118	.215	.263	414	89	6	4	2	0.5	40	50	36		12	0	0	309	375	34	53	6.1	.953	2B-118
6 yrs.			501	.254	.316	1910	486	47	17	12	0.6	246	229	154	58	45	0	0	1257	1517	189	220	5.9	.936	2B-498, 1B-3

Johnny O'Brien

O'BRIEN, JOHN THOMAS
Brother of Eddie O'Brien.
B. Dec. 11, 1930, South Amboy, N. J.

BR TR 5'9" 170 lbs.

1953	PIT	N	89	.247	.330	279	69	13	2	2	0.7	28	22	21	36	1	5	0	172	210	7	48	4.4	.982	2B-77, SS-1
1955			84	.299	.378	278	83	15	2	1	0.4	22	25	20	19	1	5	0	185	220	13	53	5.0	.969	2B-78
1956			73	.173	.183	104	18	1	0	0	0.0	13	3	5	7	0	8	1	67	99	9	17	2.4	.949	2B-53, P-8, SS-1
1957			34	.314	.429	35	11	2	1	0	0.0	7	1	1	4	0	3	1	14	16	4	2	1.0	.882	P-16, SS-8, 2B-2
1958	2 teams		PIT	N	(3G – .000)		STL	N	(12G – .000)																
"	total		15	.000	.000	3	0	0	0	0	0.0	0	4	0	1	0	0	0	3	1	0	0	0.3	1.000	SS-5, 2B-1, P-1
1959	MIL	N	44	.198	.259	116	23	4	0	1	0.9	16	8	11	15	0	0	0	70	83	2	24	3.5	.987	2B-37
6 yrs.			339	.250	.320	815	204	35	5	4	0.5	90	59	59	82	2	23	2	511	629	35	144	3.5	.970	2B-248, P-25, SS-15

Mickey O'Brien

O'BRIEN, FRANK ALOYSIUS
B. Sept. 13, 1894, San Francisco, Calif. D. Nov. 4, 1971, Monterey Park, Calif.

BR TR 5'8" 160 lbs.

| 1923 | PHI | N | 15 | .333 | .429 | 21 | 7 | 2 | 0 | 0 | 0.0 | 3 | 0 | 2 | 1 | 0 | 6 | 2 | 13 | 7 | 2 | 0 | 1.5 | .909 | C-9 |

Pete O'Brien

O'BRIEN, PETER J.
B. June 17, 1877, Binghampton, N. Y. D. Jan. 31, 1917, Jersey City, N. J.

BL TR 5'7" 170 lbs.

1901	CIN	N	16	.204	.278	54	11	1	0	1	1.9	1	3	2		0	1	0	35	37	9	6	5.1	.889	2B-15
1906	STL	A	151	.233	.277	524	122	9	4	2	0.4	44	57	42		25	0	0	297	338	42	32	4.5	.938	2B-120, 3B-20, SS-11
1907	2 teams		CLE	A	(43G – .228)		WAS	A	(39G – .187)																
"	total		82	.208	.258	279	58	3	0	0	0.0	15	18	19		5	4	1	102	199	30	13	4.0	.909	3B-40, SS-22, 2B-18
3 yrs.			249	.223	.271	857	191	18	7	3	0.4	60	78	63		30	5	1	434	574	81	51	4.4	.926	2B-153, 3B-60, SS-33

Pete O'Brien

O'BRIEN, PETER JAMES
B. June 16, 1867, Chicago, Ill. D. June 30, 1937, York, Ill.

BR TR 5'9½" 165 lbs.

| 1890 | CHI | N | 27 | .283 | .434 | 106 | 30 | 7 | 0 | 3 | 2.8 | 15 | 16 | 5 | 10 | 4 | 0 | 0 | 65 | 80 | 11 | 11 | 5.8 | .929 | 2B-27 |

Pete O'Brien

O'BRIEN, PETER MICHAEL
B. Feb. 9, 1958, Santa Monica, Calif.

BL TL 6' 180 lbs.

1982	TEX	A	20	.239	.507	67	16	4	1	4	6.0	13	13	6	8	1	0	0	39	3	0	5	2.1	1.000	OF-11, DH-4, 1B-3
1983			154	.237	.347	524	124	24	5	8	1.5	53	53	58	62	5	6	2	1191	121	11	105	8.6	.992	1B-133, OF-27, DH-1
1984			142	.287	.448	520	149	26	2	18	3.5	57	80	53	50	3	2	1	1271	105	11	103	9.8	.992	1B-141, OF-1
1985			159	.267	.452	573	153	34	3	22	3.8	69	92	69	53	5	3	0	1457	98	8	125	9.8	.995	1B-159
1986			156	.290	.468	551	160	23	3	23	4.2	86	90	87	66	4	3	1	1224	115	11	123	8.7	.992	1B-155
1987			159	.286	.457	569	163	26	1	23	4.0	84	88	59	61	0	3	0	1233	146	11	118	8.7	.992	1B-158, OF-2

Year	Team		Games	BA	SA	AB	H	2B	3B	HR	HR%	R	RBI	BB	SO	SB	Pinch Hit AB	Pinch Hit H	PO	A	E	DP	TC/G	FA	G by Pos

Pete O'Brien *continued*

Year	Team		Games	BA	SA	AB	H	2B	3B	HR	HR%	R	RBI	BB	SO	SB	PH AB	PH H	PO	A	E	DP	TC/G	FA	G by Pos
1988			156	.272	.408	547	149	24	1	16	2.9	57	71	72	73	1	5	1	1346	140	8	124	9.6	.995	1B-155, DH-1
1989	CLE	A	155	.260	.372	554	144	24	1	12	2.2	75	55	83	48	3	4	0	1359	114	9	111	9.6	.994	1B-154, DH-1
8 yrs.			1101	.271	.424	3905	1058	185	17	126	3.2	494	542	487	421	22	26	5	9120	842	69	814	9.1	.993	1B-1058, OF-41, DH-7

Ray O'Brien

O'BRIEN, RAYMOND JOSEPH   BL TL 5'9" 175 lbs.
B. Oct. 31, 1892, St. Louis, Mo. D. Mar. 31, 1942, St. Louis, Mo.

Year	Team		Games	BA	SA	AB	H	2B	3B	HR	HR%	R	RBI	BB	SO	SB	PH AB	PH H	PO	A	E	DP	TC/G	FA	G by Pos
1916	PIT	N	16	.211	.333	57	12	3	2	0	0.0	5	3	1	14	0	1	0	16	3	3	1	1.4	.864	OF-14

Syd O'Brien

O'BRIEN, SYDNEY LLOYD   BR TR 6'1" 185 lbs.
B. Dec. 18, 1944, Compton, Calif.

Year	Team		Games	BA	SA	AB	H	2B	3B	HR	HR%	R	RBI	BB	SO	SB	PH AB	PH H	PO	A	E	DP	TC/G	FA	G by Pos
1969	BOS	A	100	.243	.422	263	64	10	5	9	3.4	47	29	15	37	2	18	5	65	143	15	30	2.2	.933	3B-53, SS-15, 2B-12
1970	CHI	A	121	.247	.340	441	109	13	2	8	1.8	48	44	22	62	3	8	2	158	271	25	50	3.8	.945	3B-68, 2B-43, SS-5
1971	CAL	A	90	.199	.299	251	50	8	1	5	2.0	25	21	15	33	0	20	6	115	173	11	38	3.3	.963	SS-52, 2B-7, 3B-6, OF-1, 1B-1
1972	2 teams			CAL	A	(36G – .179)				MIL	A	(31G – .207)													
"	total		67	.196	.299	97	19	4	0	2	2.1	15	6	8	23	0	22	4	21	48	8	8	1.1	.896	3B-17, 2B-10, SS-4, 1B-1
4 yrs.			378	.230	.347	1052	242	35	8	24	2.3	135	100	60	155	5	68	17	359	635	59	126	2.8	.944	3B-144, SS-76, 2B-72, 1B-2, OF-1

Tom O'Brien

O'BRIEN, THOMAS EDWARD
B. Feb. 20, 1873, Verona, Pa. D. July 25, 1959, Boston, Mass.

Year	Team		Games	BA	SA	AB	H	2B	3B	HR	HR%	R	RBI	BB	SO	SB	PH AB	PH H	PO	A	E	DP	TC/G	FA	G by Pos
1897	BAL	N	50	.252	.293	147	37	6	0	0	0.0	25	32	20		7	2	1	243	15	9	9	5.3	.966	1B-25, OF-24
1898	2 teams			BAL	N	(18G – .217)				PIT	N	(107G – .259)													
"	total		125	.254	.315	473	120	10	8	1	0.2	62	59	35		13	2	0	398	66	40	23	4.0	.921	OF-85, 1B-21, 3B-8, 2B-7, SS-4
1899	NY	N	150	.297	.400	573	170	21	10	6	1.0	100	77	44		23	0	0	269	66	30	12	2.4	.918	OF-127, 3B-21, SS-2, 2B-1, 1B-1
1900	PIT	N	102	.290	.404	376	109	22	6	3	0.8	60	61	21		12	5	1	726	36	33	39	7.8	.958	1B-65, OF-25, 2B-4, SS-2
4 yrs.			427	.278	.365	1569	436	59	24	10	0.6	247	229	120		55	9	2	1636	183	112	83	4.5	.942	OF-261, 1B-112, 3B-29, 2B-12, SS-8

Tom O'Brien

O'BRIEN, THOMAS H.   BR TR
B. June 22, 1860, Salem, Mass. D. Apr. 21, 1921, Worcester, Mass.

Year	Team		Games	BA	SA	AB	H	2B	3B	HR	HR%	R	RBI	BB	SO	SB	PH AB	PH H	PO	A	E	DP	TC/G	FA	G by Pos
1882	WOR	N	22	.202	.236	89	18	1	1	0	0.0	9	7	1	10		0	0	47	9	17	2	3.3	.767	OF-20, 2B-2, 3B-1
1883	BAL	AA	33	.268	.370	138	37	6	4	0	0.0	16		5			0	0	83	93	36	8	6.4	.830	2B-29, OF-4
1884	BOS	U	103	.263	.394	449	118	31	8	4	0.9	80		12			0	0	290	267	91	23	6.3	.860	2B-99, OF-3, 1B-2, C-1
1885	BAL	AA	8	.212	.303	33	7	3	0	0	0.0	4		2			0	0	41	13	4	1	7.3	.931	1B-6, 2B-2
1887	NY	AA	31	.194	.248	129	25	3	2	0	0.0	13		2		10	0	0	203	10	11	10	7.2	.951	1B-20, OF-8, 3B-2, 2B-2, P-1
1890	ROC	AA	73	.190	.249	273	52	6	5	0	0.0	36		30		6	0	0	689	41	28	43	10.4	.963	1B-68, 2B-8
6 yrs.			270	.231	.323	1111	257	50	20	4	0.4	158	7	52	10	16	0	0	1353	433	187	87	7.3	.905	2B-142, 1B-96, OF-35, 3B-3, C-1, P-1

Tommy O'Brien

O'BRIEN, THOMAS EDWARD (Obie)   BR TR 5'11" 195 lbs.
B. Dec. 19, 1918, Anniston, Ala. D. Nov. 5, 1978, Anniston, Ala.

Year	Team		Games	BA	SA	AB	H	2B	3B	HR	HR%	R	RBI	BB	SO	SB	PH AB	PH H	PO	A	E	DP	TC/G	FA	G by Pos
1943	PIT	N	89	.310	.448	232	72	12	7	2	0.9	35	26	15	24	0	27	7	87	23	6	0	1.3	.948	OF-48, 3B-9
1944			85	.250	.372	156	39	6	2	3	1.9	27	20	21	33	5	33	5	50	6	2	1	0.7	.966	OF-48
1945			58	.335	.435	161	54	6	5	0	0.0	23	18	9	13	0	12	3	72	2	3	0	1.2	.961	OF-45
1949	BOS	A	49	.224	.336	125	28	5	0	3	2.4	24	10	21	12	1	12	1	58	2	1	0	1.2	.984	OF-32
1950	2 teams			BOS	A	(9G – .129)				WAS	A	(3G – .111)													
"	total		12	.125	.150	40	5	1	0	0	0.0	1	4	4	5	0	0	0	21	2	0	0	1.9	1.000	OF-12
5 yrs.			293	.277	.392	714	198	30	14	8	1.1	110	78	70	66	2	84	16	288	35	12	1	1.1	.964	OF-185, 3B-9

Whitey Ock

OCK, HAROLD DAVID   BR TR 5'11" 180 lbs.
B. Mar. 17, 1912, Brooklyn, N. Y. D. Mar. 18, 1975, Mount Kisco, N. Y.

Year	Team		Games	BA	SA	AB	H	2B	3B	HR	HR%	R	RBI	BB	SO	SB	PH AB	PH H	PO	A	E	DP	TC/G	FA	G by Pos
1935	BKN	N	1	.000	.000	3	0	0	0	0	0.0	0	0	1	2	0	0	0	3	0	0	0	3.0	1.000	C-1

Danny O'Connell

O'CONNELL, DANIEL FRANCIS   BR TR 5'11" 168 lbs.
B. Jan. 21, 1927, Paterson, N. J. D. Oct. 2, 1969, Clifton, N. J.

Year	Team		Games	BA	SA	AB	H	2B	3B	HR	HR%	R	RBI	BB	SO	SB	PH AB	PH H	PO	A	E	DP	TC/G	FA	G by Pos
1950	PIT	N	79	.292	.425	315	92	16	1	8	2.5	39	32	24	33	7	2	0	162	267	11	49	5.6	.975	SS-65, 3B-12
1953			149	.294	.401	588	173	26	8	7	1.2	88	55	57	42	3	0	0	226	370	23	43	4.2	.963	3B-104, 2B-47
1954	MIL	N	146	.279	.357	541	151	28	4	2	0.4	61	37	38	46	2	4	3	351	386	12	97	5.1	.984	2B-103, 3B-35, 1B-8, SS-1
1955			124	.225	.316	453	102	15	4	6	1.3	47	40	28	43	2	6	1	317	362	14	78	5.6	.980	2B-114, 3B-7, SS-1
1956			139	.239	.321	498	119	17	9	2	0.4	71	42	76	42	1	0	0	299	384	11	99	5.0	.984	2B-138, 3B-4, SS-1
1957	2 teams			MIL	N	(48G – .235)				NY	N	(95G – .266)													
"	total		143	.256	.364	547	140	27	4	8	1.5	86	36	52	50	9	1	0	317	408	16	99	5.2	.978	2B-116, 3B-30
1958	SF	N	107	.232	.314	306	71	12	2	3	1.0	44	23	51	35	2	0	0	222	278	7	70	4.7	.986	2B-104, 3B-3
1959			34	.190	.241	58	11	3	0	0	0.0	6	0	5	15	0	0	0	31	45	4	4	2.4	.950	3B-26, 2B-8
1961	WAS	A	138	.260	.331	493	128	30	1	1	0.2	61	37	77	62	15	5	4	219	343	23	66	4.2	.961	3B-73, 2B-61
1962			84	.263	.335	236	62	7	2	2	0.8	24	18	23	28	5	20	8	70	141	10	21	2.6	.955	3B-41, 2B-22
10 yrs.			1143	.260	.351	4035	1049	181	35	39	1.0	527	320	431	396	48	39	16	2214	2984	131	626	4.7	.975	2B-713, 3B-335, SS-68, 1B-8

Jimmy O'Connell

O'CONNELL, JAMES JOSEPH   BL TR 5'10½" 175 lbs.
B. Feb. 11, 1901, Sacramento, Calif. D. Nov. 11, 1976, Bakersfield, Calif.

Year	Team		Games	BA	SA	AB	H	2B	3B	HR	HR%	R	RBI	BB	SO	SB	PH AB	PH H	PO	A	E	DP	TC/G	FA	G by Pos
1923	NY	N	87	.250	.373	252	63	9	2	6	2.4	42	39	34	32	7	10	0	213	3	4	7	2.5	.982	OF-64, 1B-8
1924			52	.317	.452	104	33	4	2	2	1.9	24	18	11	16	2	15	4	41	6	3	0	1.0	.940	OF-29, 2B-1
2 yrs.			139	.270	.396	356	96	13	4	8	2.2	66	57	45	48	9	25	4	254	9	7	7	1.9	.974	OF-93, 1B-8, 2B-1

WORLD SERIES

Year	Team		Games	BA	SA	AB	H	2B	3B	HR	HR%	R	RBI	BB	SO	SB	PH AB	PH H	PO	A	E	DP	TC/G	FA	G by Pos
1923	NY	N	2	.000	.000	1	0	0	0	0	0.0	0	0	0	1	0	1	0	0	0	0	0	0.0	–	

Year	Team		Games	BA	SA	AB	H	2B	3B	HR	HR%	R	RBI	BB	SO	SB	Pinch Hit AB	Pinch Hit H	PO	A	E	DP	TC/G	FA	G by Pos

John O'Connell

O'CONNELL, JOHN CHARLES
B. June 13, 1904, Pittsburgh, Pa. — BR TR 6' 170 lbs.

Year	Team		Games	BA	SA	AB	H	2B	3B	HR	HR%	R	RBI	BB	SO	SB	PH AB	PH H	PO	A	E	DP	TC/G	FA	G by Pos
1928	PIT	N	1	.000	.000	1	0	0	0	0	0.0	0	0	0	0	0	0	0	1	2	0	0	3.0	1.000	C-1
1929			2	.143	.286	7	1	1	0	0	0.0	1	0	1	1	0	0	0	7	0	0	0	3.5	1.000	C-2
2 yrs.			3	.125	.250	8	1	1	0	0	0.0	1	0	1	1	0	0	0	8	2	0	0	3.3	1.000	C-3

John O'Connell

O'CONNELL, JOHN JOSEPH (Jack)
B. May 16, 1872, Lawrence, Mass. D. May 14, 1908, Derry, N. H.

Year	Team		Games	BA	SA	AB	H	2B	3B	HR	HR%	R	RBI	BB	SO	SB	PH AB	PH H	PO	A	E	DP	TC/G	FA	G by Pos
1891	BAL	AA	8	.172	.207	29	5	1	0	0	0.0	2	7	3	6	2	0	0	13	15	5	1	4.1	.848	SS-3, 2B-3, OF-2
1902	DET	A	8	.182	.182	22	4	0	0	0	0.0	1	0	3	0	0	0	0	37	20	3	3	7.5	.950	2B-6, 1B-2
2 yrs.			16	.176	.196	51	9	1	0	0	0.0	3	7	6	6	2	0	0	50	35	8	4	5.8	.914	2B-9, SS-3, OF-2, 1B-2

Pat O'Connell

O'CONNELL, PATRICK H.
B. June 10, 1861, Bangor, Me. D. Jan. 24, 1943, Lewiston, Me. — BL TR 5'10" 175 lbs.

Year	Team		Games	BA	SA	AB	H	2B	3B	HR	HR%	R	RBI	BB	SO	SB	PH AB	PH H	PO	A	E	DP	TC/G	FA	G by Pos
1886	BAL	AA	42	.181	.223	166	30	3	2	0	0.0	20		11		0			65	4	17	0	2.0	.802	OF-41, 1B-1, P-1
1890	BKN	AA	11	.225	.325	40	9	2	1	0	0.0	7	0	7	0	3	0	0	22	23	8	3	4.8	.849	3B-10, 1B-1
2 yrs.			53	.189	.243	206	39	5	3	0	0.0	27	0	18	0	3	0	0	87	27	25	3	2.6	.820	OF-41, 3B-10, 1B-2, P-1

Bucky O'Connor

O'CONNOR, JOHN CHARLES (Okie)
B. Dec. 1, 1891, Cahersiveen, Ireland D. May 30, 1982, Bonner Springs, Kans. — BR TR 5'9"

Year	Team		Games	BA	SA	AB	H	2B	3B	HR	HR%	R	RBI	BB	SO	SB	PH AB	PH H	PO	A	E	DP	TC/G	FA	G by Pos
1916	CHI	N	1	–	–	0	0	0	0	0	–	0	0	0	0	0	0	0	0	0	0	0	0.0	–	C-1

Dan O'Connor

O'CONNOR, DANIEL CORNELIUS
B. Aug., 1868, Guelph, Ont., Canada D. Mar. 3, 1942, Guelph, Ont., Canada — BL TR 6'2" 185 lbs.

Year	Team		Games	BA	SA	AB	H	2B	3B	HR	HR%	R	RBI	BB	SO	SB	PH AB	PH H	PO	A	E	DP	TC/G	FA	G by Pos
1890	LOU	AA	6	.462	.577	26	12	1	0	0	0.0	3		1		5	0	0	58	0	0	3	9.7	1.000	1B-6

Jack O'Connor

O'CONNOR, JOHN JOSEPH (Peach Pie)
B. June 2, 1869, St. Louis, Mo. D. Nov. 14, 1937, St. Louis, Mo. — BR TR 5'10" 170 lbs.
Manager 1910.

Year	Team		Games	BA	SA	AB	H	2B	3B	HR	HR%	R	RBI	BB	SO	SB	PH AB	PH H	PO	A	E	DP	TC/G	FA	G by Pos
1887	CIN	AA	12	.100	.100	40	4	0	0	0	0.0	4		2		3	0	0	29	15	7	1	4.3	.863	OF-7, C-5
1888			36	.204	.263	137	28	3	1	1	0.7	14	17	6		12	0	0	68	17	20	0	2.9	.810	OF-34, C-2
1889	COL	AA	107	.269	.377	398	107	17	7	4	1.0	69	60	33	37	26	0	0	492	135	35	11	6.2	.947	C-84, OF-19, 2B-4, 1B-3
1890			121	.324	.411	457	148	14	10	2	0.4	89		38		29	0	0	572	164	35	20	6.4	.954	C-106, OF-9, SS-8, 2B-2, 3B-1
1891			56	.266	.345	229	61	12	3	0	0.0	28	37	11	14	10	0	0	135	37	11	5	3.3	.940	OF-40, C-21
1892	CLE	N	140	.248	.309	572	142	22	5	1	0.2	71	58	25	48	17	1	0	310	61	19	8	2.8	.951	OF-106, C-34
1893			96	.286	.375	384	110	23	1	3	0.8	72	75	29	12	29	0	0	252	70	19	2	3.6	.944	C-56, OF-44
1894			86	.315	.445	330	104	23	7	2	0.6	67	51	15	7	15	1	0	304	46	21	8	4.3	.943	C-45, OF-33, 1B-7
1895			89	.291	.391	340	99	14	10	0	0.0	51	58	30	22	11	0	0	522	66	16	24	6.8	.974	C-47, 1B-41, 3B-1
1896			68	.297	.359	256	76	11	1	1	0.4	41	43	15	12	15	3	2	242	40	7	13	4.3	.976	C-37, 1B-17, OF-12
1897			103	.290	.378	397	115	21	4	2	0.5	49	69	26		20	4	3	477	23	16	10	5.0	.969	OF-52, 1B-36, C-13
1898			131	.249	.308	478	119	17	4	1	0.2	50	56	26		8	1	0	761	92	20	36	6.7	.977	1B-69, C-48, OF-15
1899	STL	N	84	.253	.311	289	73	5	6	0	0.0	33	43	15		7	2	0	427	76	18	20	6.2	.965	C-57, 1B-26
1900	2 teams			STL	N (10G – .219)			PIT		N	(43G – .238)														
"	total		53	.235	.268	179	42	4	1	0	0.0	19	25	5		5	5	1	161	56	11	5	4.3	.952	C-50, 1B-2
1901	PIT	N	61	.193	.257	202	39	7	3	0	0.0	16	22	10		2	2	0	256	59	7	5	5.3	.978	C-59
1902			49	.294	.341	170	50	1	2	1	0.6	13	28	3		2	1	0	243	50	6	5	6.1	.980	C-42, 1B-6, OF-1
1903	NY	A	64	.203	.231	212	43	4	1	0	0.0	13	12	8		4	0	0	287	56	4	6	5.4	.988	C-63, 1B-1
1904	STL	A	14	.213	.234	47	10	1	0	0	0.0	4	2	2		0	0	0	55	11	4	0	5.0	.943	C-14
1906			58	.190	.190	174	33	0	0	0	0.0	8	11	2		4	4	0	248	64	3	2	5.4	.990	C-54
1907			25	.157	.180	89	14	2	0	0	0.0	2	4	0		0	4	1	87	29	1	4	4.7	.991	C-25
1910			1	–	–	0	0	0	0	0	–	0	0	0		0	0	0	1	0	0	0	1.0	1.000	C-1
21 yrs.			1454	.263	.335	5380	1417	201	66	18	0.3	713	671	301	152	219	19	5	5929	1167	280	185	5.1	.962	C-863, OF-372, 1B-208, SS-8, 2B-6, 3B-2

Paddy O'Connor

O'CONNOR, PATRICK FRANCIS
B. Aug. 4, 1879, County Kerry, Ireland D. Aug. 17, 1950, Springfield, Mass. — BR TR 5'8" 168 lbs.

Year	Team		Games	BA	SA	AB	H	2B	3B	HR	HR%	R	RBI	BB	SO	SB	PH AB	PH H	PO	A	E	DP	TC/G	FA	G by Pos
1908	PIT	N	12	.188	.188	16	3	0	0	0	0.0	1	2	0		0	7	2	6	2	1	0	0.8	.889	C-4
1909			9	.313	.375	16	5	1	0	0	0.0	1	3	0		0	5	0	7	2	3	1	1.3	.750	C-3, 3B-1
1910			6	.250	.250	4	1	0	0	0	0.0	0	0	0		0	4	1	1	0	0	0	0.2	1.000	C-1
1914	STL	N	10	.000	.000	9	0	0	0	0	0.0	0	0	2	2	0	2	0	9	3	0	0	1.2	1.000	C-7
1915	PIT	F	70	.228	.283	219	50	10	1	0	0.0	15	16	14		4	4	1	275	112	5	4	5.6	.987	C-66
1918	NY	A	1	.333	.333	3	1	0	0	0	0.0	0	0	0	1	0	0	0	2	1	0	0	3.0	1.000	C-1
6 yrs.			108	.225	.273	267	60	11	1	0	0.0	17	21	17	4	4	22	4	300	120	9	5	4.0	.979	C-82, 3B-1

WORLD SERIES

Year	Team		Games	BA	SA	AB	H	2B	3B	HR	HR%	R	RBI	BB	SO	SB	PH AB	PH H	PO	A	E	DP	TC/G	FA	G by Pos
1909	PIT	N	1	.000	.000	1	0	0	0	0	0.0	0	0	0	1	0	1	0	0	0	0	0	0.0	–	

Hank O'Day

O'DAY, HENRY FRANCIS (Peep)
B. July 8, 1862, Chicago, Ill. D. July 2, 1935, Chicago, Ill. — TR
Manager 1912, 1914.

Year	Team		Games	BA	SA	AB	H	2B	3B	HR	HR%	R	RBI	BB	SO	SB	PH AB	PH H	PO	A	E	DP	TC/G	FA	G by Pos
1884	TOL	AA	64	.211	.256	242	51	4	1	0	0.0	23		10		0	0	0	61	95	20	5	2.8	.886	P-39, OF-24, 3B-3, 1B-3
1885	PIT	AA	13	.245	.327	49	12	2	1	0	0.0	7		1		0	0	0	8	19	4	2	2.4	.871	P-12, OF-3
1886	WAS	N	6	.053	.053	19	1	0	0	0	0.0	0		0		0	0	0	4	14	2	1	3.3	.900	P-6
1887			36	.198	.224	116	23	3	0	0	0.0	10	7	7	15	1	0	0	15	59	6	4	2.2	.925	P-30, SS-6, OF-2
1888			47	.139	.151	166	23	2	0	0	0.0	6	8	4	41	3	0	0	19	67	8	1	2.0	.915	P-46, SS-2
1889	2 teams			WAS	N (13G – .182)			NY		N	(10G – .097)														
"	total		23	.147	.160	75	11	1	0	0	0.0	6	7	7	17	1	0	0	12	34	3	1	2.1	.939	P-23
1890	NY	P	43	.227	.273	150	34	2	1	1	0.7	24	23	10	27	1	0	0	11	71	7	0	2.1	.921	P-43
7 yrs.			232	.190	.224	817	155	19	3	1	0.1	76	43	39	109	7	0	0	130	359	50	14	2.3	.907	P-199, OF-29, SS-8, 3B-3, 1B-3

Year	Team		Games	BA	SA	AB	H	2B	3B	HR	HR%	R	RBI	BB	SO	SB	Pinch Hit AB	H	PO	A	E	DP	TC/G	FA	G by Pos

Ken O'Dea

O'DEA, JAMES KENNETH   BL TR 6'   180 lbs.
B. Mar. 16, 1913, Lima, N. Y.   D. Dec. 17, 1985, Lima, N. Y.

Year	Team		Games	BA	SA	AB	H	2B	3B	HR	HR%	R	RBI	BB	SO	SB	PH AB	H	PO	A	E	DP	TC/G	FA	G by Pos
1935	CHI	N	76	.257	.431	202	52	13	2	6	3.0	30	38	26	18	0	9	1	213	27	9	3	3.3	.964	C-63
1936			80	.307	.423	189	58	10	3	2	1.1	36	38	38	18	0	22	7	211	27	5	1	3.0	.979	C-55
1937			83	.301	.434	219	66	7	5	4	1.8	31	32	24	26	1	13	3	234	29	4	4	3.2	.985	C-64
1938			86	.263	.356	247	65	12	1	3	1.2	22	33	12	18	1	13	2	294	32	10	3	3.9	.970	C-71
1939	NY	N	52	.175	.278	97	17	1	0	3	3.1	7	11	10	16	0	26	3	78	11	5	1	1.8	.947	C-30
1940			48	.240	.302	96	23	4	1	0	0.0	9	12	16	15	0	14	2	89	29	1	1	2.5	.992	C-31
1941			59	.213	.393	89	19	5	1	3	3.4	13	17	8	20	0	42	9	62	9	0	0	1.2	1.000	C-14
1942	STL	N	58	.234	.359	192	45	7	1	5	2.6	22	32	17	23	0	9	1	247	37	6	6	5.0	.979	C-49
1943			71	.281	.399	203	57	11	2	3	1.5	15	25	19	25	0	14	4	237	32	3	6	3.8	.989	C-56
1944			85	.249	.374	265	66	11	2	6	2.3	35	37	37	29	1	14	4	326	34	2	4	4.3	.994	C-69
1945			100	.254	.365	307	78	18	2	4	1.3	36	43	50	31	0	8	0	321	50	2	14	3.7	.995	C-91
1946	2 teams	STL	N (22G – .123)			BOS	N (12G – .219)																		
"	total		34	.157	.213	89	14	2	0	1	1.1	6	5	16	12	0	0	0	138	19	1	1	4.6	.994	C-34
12 yrs.			832	.255	.374	2195	560	101	20	40	1.8	262	323	273	251	3	184	36	2450	336	48	44	3.4	.983	C-627

WORLD SERIES

Year	Team		Games	BA	SA	AB	H	2B	3B	HR	HR%	R	RBI	BB	SO	SB	PH AB	H	PO	A	E	DP	TC/G	FA	G by Pos
1935	CHI	N	1	1.000	1.000	1	1	0	0	0	0.0	0	1	0	0	0	1	1	0	0	0	0	0.0	—	
1938			3	.200	.800	5	1	0	0	1	20.0	1	2	1	0	0	2	0	5	0	0	0	1.7	1.000	C-1
1942	STL	N	1	1.000	1.000	1	1	0	0	0	0.0	0	0	0	0	0	1	1	0	0	0	0	0.0	—	
1943			2	.667	.667	3	2	0	0	0	0.0	0	0	0	0	0	1	0	2	0	0	0	1.0	1.000	C-1
1944			3	.333	.333	3	1	0	0	0	0.0	0	2	0	0	0	3	1	0	0	0	0	0.0	—	
5 yrs.			10	.462	.692	13	6	0	0	1	7.7	1	6	1	0	0	8	3	7	0	0	0	0.7	1.000	C-2
																	3rd	1st							

Paul O'Dea

O'DEA, PAUL (Lefty)   BL TL 6'   200 lbs.
B. July 3, 1920, Cleveland, Ohio   D. Dec. 11, 1978, Cleveland, Ohio

Year	Team		Games	BA	SA	AB	H	2B	3B	HR	HR%	R	RBI	BB	SO	SB	PH AB	H	PO	A	E	DP	TC/G	FA	G by Pos
1944	CLE	A	76	.318	.370	173	55	9	0	0	0.0	25	13	23	21	2	25	5	93	3	5	3	1.3	.950	OF-41, 1B-3, P-3
1945			87	.235	.276	221	52	2	2	1	0.5	21	21	20	26	3	30	7	118	5	1	2	1.4	.992	OF-53, P-1
2 yrs.			163	.272	.317	394	107	11	2	1	0.3	46	34	43	47	5	55	12	211	8	6	5	1.4	.973	OF-94, P-4, 1B-3

Heinie Odom

ODOM, HERMAN BOYD   BB TR 6'   170 lbs.
B. Oct. 13, 1900, Rusk, Tex.   D. Aug. 31, 1970, Rusk, Tex.

Year	Team		Games	BA	SA	AB	H	2B	3B	HR	HR%	R	RBI	BB	SO	SB	PH AB	H	PO	A	E	DP	TC/G	FA	G by Pos
1925	NY	A	1	1.000	1.000	1	1	0	0	0	0.0	0	0	0	0	0	0	0	0	1	0	0	1.0	1.000	3B-1

O'Donnell

O'DONNELL,
B. Littlestown, Pa.   Deceased.

Year	Team		Games	BA	SA	AB	H	2B	3B	HR	HR%	R	RBI	BB	SO	SB	PH AB	H	PO	A	E	DP	TC/G	FA	G by Pos
1884	PHI	U	1	.250	.250	4	1	0	0	0	0.0	0		0			0	0	2	4	5	0	11.0	.545	C-1

Harry O'Donnell

O'DONNELL, HARRY HERMAN   BR TR 5'10"   180 lbs.
B. Apr. 2, 1894, Philadelphia, Pa.   D. Jan. 31, 1958, Philadelphia, Pa.

Year	Team		Games	BA	SA	AB	H	2B	3B	HR	HR%	R	RBI	BB	SO	SB	PH AB	H	PO	A	E	DP	TC/G	FA	G by Pos
1927	PHI	N	16	.063	.063	16	1	0	0	0	0.0	1	2	2	2	0	0	0	16	3	0	1	1.2	1.000	C-12

Lefty O'Doul

O'DOUL, FRANCIS JOSEPH   BL TL 6'   180 lbs.
B. Mar. 4, 1897, San Francisco, Calif.   D. Dec. 7, 1969, San Francisco, Calif.

Year	Team		Games	BA	SA	AB	H	2B	3B	HR	HR%	R	RBI	BB	SO	SB	PH AB	H	PO	A	E	DP	TC/G	FA	G by Pos
1919	NY	A	19	.250	.250	16	4	0	0	0	0.0	0	2	1	2	0	14	4	1	1	0	0	0.1	1.000	P-3, OF-1
1920			13	.167	.250	12	2	1	0	0	0.0	2	1	1	1	0	9	1	0	0	0	0	0.0	—	P-2, OF-1
1922			8	.333	.444	9	3	1	0	0	0.0	0	4	0	2	0	2	1	1	4	0	1	0.6	1.000	P-6
1923	BOS	A	36	.143	.143	35	5	0	0	0	0.0	2	4	2	3	0	12	2	2	21	1	0	0.7	.958	P-23
1928	NY	N	114	.319	.463	354	113	19	4	8	2.3	67	46	30	8	9	8	4	149	4	6	0	1.4	.962	OF-94
1929	PHI	N	154	**.398**	.622	638	**254**	35	6	32	5.0	152	122	76	19	2	0	0	320	14	10	5	2.2	.971	OF-154
1930			140	.383	.604	528	202	37	7	22	4.2	122	97	63	21	3	8	3	262	3	13	1	2.0	.953	OF-131
1931	BKN	N	134	.336	.482	512	172	32	11	7	1.4	85	75	48	16	5	2	2	285	4	14	0	2.3	.954	OF-132
1932			148	**.368**	.555	595	219	32	8	21	3.5	120	90	50	20	11	0	0	317	4	7	0	2.2	.979	OF-148
1933	2 teams	BKN	N (43G – .252)			NY	N (78G – .306)																		
"	total		121	.284	.438	388	110	14	2	14	3.6	45	56	44	23	3	14	5	197	5	8	0	1.7	.962	OF-104
1934	NY	N	83	.316	.525	177	56	4	3	9	5.1	27	46	18	7	2	37	10	60	1	2	0	0.8	.968	OF-38
11 yrs.			970	.349	.532	3264	1140	175	41	113	3.5	624	542	333	122	36	106	32	1594	61	61	4	1.8	.964	OF-803, P-34

WORLD SERIES

Year	Team		Games	BA	SA	AB	H	2B	3B	HR	HR%	R	RBI	BB	SO	SB	PH AB	H	PO	A	E	DP	TC/G	FA	G by Pos
1933	NY	N	1	1.000	1.000	1	1	0	0	0	0.0	1	2	0	0	0	1	1	0	0	0	0	0.0	—	

Fred Odwell

ODWELL, FREDERICK WILLIAM (Fritz)   BL TR 5'9½"   160 lbs.
B. Sept. 25, 1872, Downsville, N. Y.   D. Aug. 19, 1948, Downsville, N. Y.

Year	Team		Games	BA	SA	AB	H	2B	3B	HR	HR%	R	RBI	BB	SO	SB	PH AB	H	PO	A	E	DP	TC/G	FA	G by Pos
1904	CIN	N	129	.284	.380	468	133	22	10	1	0.2	75	58	26		30	2	1	285	18	14	6	2.5	.956	OF-126, 2B-1
1905			130	.241	.359	468	113	10	9	9	1.9	79	65	26		21	4	3	216	18	8	5	1.9	.967	OF-126
1906			58	.223	.287	202	45	5	4	0	0.0	20	21	15		11	1	0	94	10	4	0	1.9	.963	OF-57
1907			94	.270	.339	274	74	5	7	0	0.0	24	24	22		10	5	0	187	9	6	2	2.1	.970	OF-84, 2B-1
4 yrs.			411	.258	.352	1412	365	42	30	10	0.7	198	168	89		72	12	4	782	55	32	13	2.1	.963	OF-393, 2B-2

Chuck Oertel

OERTEL, CHARLES FRANK (Ducky, Snuffy)   BL TR 5'8"   165 lbs.
B. Mar. 12, 1931, Coffeyville, Kans.

Year	Team		Games	BA	SA	AB	H	2B	3B	HR	HR%	R	RBI	BB	SO	SB	PH AB	H	PO	A	E	DP	TC/G	FA	G by Pos
1958	BAL	A	14	.167	.417	12	2	0	0	1	8.3	4	1	1	1	0	8	0	1	0	0	0	0.1	1.000	OF-2

Ron Oester

OESTER, RONALD JOHN   BB TR 6'2"   185 lbs.
B. May 5, 1956, Cincinnati, Ohio

Year	Team		Games	BA	SA	AB	H	2B	3B	HR	HR%	R	RBI	BB	SO	SB	PH AB	H	PO	A	E	DP	TC/G	FA	G by Pos
1978	CIN	N	6	.375	.375	8	3	0	0	0	0.0	1	1	0	2	0	0	0	3	9	0	2	2.0	1.000	SS-6
1979			6	.000	.000	3	0	0	0	0	0.0	0	0	1	1	0	1	0	1	2	0	0	0.5	1.000	SS-2
1980			100	.277	.363	303	84	16	2	2	0.7	40	20	26	44	6	10	3	161	224	10	46	4.0	.975	2B-79, SS-17, 3B-3
1981			105	.271	.398	354	96	16	7	5	1.4	45	42	42	49	2	0	0	213	341	11	64	5.4	.981	2B-103, SS-9
1982			151	.260	.359	549	143	19	4	9	1.6	63	47	35	82	5	6	1	304	403	22	87	4.8	.970	2B-118, SS-29, 3B-13

Year	Team	Games	BA	SA	AB	H	2B	3B	HR	HR%	R	RBI	BB	SO	SB	Pinch Hit AB	Pinch Hit H	PO	A	E	DP	TC/G	FA	G by Pos

Ron Oester *continued*

Year	Team	Games	BA	SA	AB	H	2B	3B	HR	HR%	R	RBI	BB	SO	SB	PH AB	PH H	PO	A	E	DP	TC/G	FA	G by Pos
1983		157	.264	.384	549	145	23	5	11	2.0	63	58	49	106	2	5	2	315	413	17	80	4.7	.977	2B-154
1984		150	.242	.316	553	134	26	3	3	0.5	54	38	41	97	7	6	2	357	388	15	75	5.1	.980	2B-147, SS-1
1985		152	.295	.361	526	155	26	3	1	0.2	59	34	51	65	5	2	0	366	457	9	100	5.5	.989	2B-149
1986		153	.258	.356	523	135	23	2	8	1.5	52	44	52	84	9	4	0	367	475	19	100	5.6	.978	2B-151
1987		69	.253	.367	237	60	9	6	2	0.8	28	23	22	51	2	0	0	183	186	10	37	5.5	.974	2B-69
1988		54	.280	.327	150	42	7	0	0	0.0	20	10	9	24	0	3	1	110	113	1	26	4.1	.996	2B-49, SS-5
1989		109	.246	.305	305	75	15	0	1	0.3	23	14	32	47	1	8	3	215	249	7	44	4.3	.985	2B-102, SS-2
12 yrs.		1212	.264	.355	4060	1072	180	32	42	1.0	448	331	359	652	39	45	12	2595	3260	121	661	4.9	.980	2B-1121, SS-71, 3B-16

Bob O'Farrell

O'FARRELL, ROBERT ARTHUR
B. Oct. 19, 1896, Waukegan, Ill.   D. Feb. 20, 1988, Waukegan, Ill.
Manager 1927, 1934.

BR TR 5'9½" 180 lbs.

Year	Team	Games	BA	SA	AB	H	2B	3B	HR	HR%	R	RBI	BB	SO	SB	PH AB	PH H	PO	A	E	DP	TC/G	FA	G by Pos
1915	CHI N	2	.333	.333	3	1	0	0	0	0.0	0	0	0	0	0	0	0	1	1	1	0	1.5	.667	C-2
1916		1	–	–	0	0	0	0	0	–	0	0	0	0	0	0	0	0	0	0	0	0.0	–	C-1
1917		3	.375	.625	8	3	2	0	0	0.0	1	1	1	0	0	1	0	9	1	0	1	3.3	1.000	C-3
1918		52	.283	.425	113	32	7	3	1	0.9	9	14	10	15	0	7	2	115	36	4	3	3.0	.974	C-45
1919		49	.216	.280	125	27	4	2	0	0.0	11	9	7	10	2	9	1	119	48	6	5	3.5	.965	C-38
1920		94	.248	.352	270	67	11	4	3	1.1	29	19	34	23	1	8	1	317	100	19	6	4.6	.956	C-86
1921		96	.250	.396	260	65	12	7	4	1.5	32	32	18	14	2	6	1	269	87	12	8	3.8	.967	C-90
1922		128	.324	.441	392	127	18	8	4	1.0	68	60	79	34	5	2	1	446	143	14	22	4.7	.977	C-125
1923		131	.319	.471	452	144	25	4	12	2.7	73	84	67	38	10	6	3	418	118	13	11	4.2	.976	C-124
1924		71	.240	.344	183	44	6	2	3	1.6	25	18	30	13	2	10	3	204	40	4	5	3.5	.984	C-57
1925 2 teams	CHI					N (17G – .182)				STL		N	(94G – .278)											
" total		111	.271	.354	339	92	13	3	7	2.1	39	35	48	31	0	14	4	330	67	10	5	3.7	.975	C-95
1926	STL N	147	.293	.433	492	144	30	9	7	1.4	63	68	61	44	1	1	1	466	117	10	12	4.0	.983	C-146
1927		61	.264	.331	178	47	10	1	0	0.0	19	18	23	22	3	6	2	141	45	4	5	3.1	.979	C-53
1928 2 teams	STL					N (16G – .212)				NY		N	(75G – .195)											
" total		91	.200	.270	185	37	7	0	2	1.1	29	24	47	25	4	9	1	199	31	3	2	2.6	.987	C-77
1929	NY N	91	.306	.435	248	76	14	3	4	1.6	35	42	28	30	3	4	2	254	22	6	2	3.1	.979	C-84
1930		94	.301	.446	249	75	16	4	4	1.6	37	54	31	21	1	23	6	259	34	8	0	3.2	.973	C-69
1931		85	.224	.322	174	39	8	3	1	0.6	11	19	21	23	0	5	0	223	27	5	1	3.0	.980	C-80
1932		50	.239	.284	67	16	0	0	0	0.0	7	8	11	10	0	5	1	85	9	3	2	1.9	.969	C-41
1933	STL N	55	.239	.325	163	39	4	2	2	1.2	16	20	15	25	0	4	1	211	19	7	1	4.3	.970	C-50
1934 2 teams	CIN					N (44G – .224)				CHI		N	(22G – .224)											
" total		66	.237	.342	190	45	11	3	1	0.5	13	14	14	30	0	2	0	217	35	1	4	3.8	.996	C-64
1935	STL N	14	.000	.000	10	0	0	0	0	0.0	0	0	2	0	0	4	0	12	0	0	0	0.9	1.000	C-8
21 yrs.		1492	.273	.388	4101	1120	201	58	51	1.2	517	549	547	408	35	125	29	4295	980	130	95	3.6	.976	C-1338

WORLD SERIES

Year	Team	Games	BA	SA	AB	H	2B	3B	HR	HR%	R	RBI	BB	SO	SB	PH AB	PH H	PO	A	E	DP	TC/G	FA	G by Pos
1918	CHI N	3	.000	.000	3	0	0	0	0	0.0	0	0	0	0	0	3	0	0	0	0	0	0.0	–	C-1
1926	STL N	7	.304	.348	23	7	1	0	0	0.0	2	2	2	2	0	0	0	35	8	0	1	6.1	1.000	C-7
2 yrs.		10	.269	.308	26	7	1	0	0	0.0	2	2	2	2	0	3	0	35	8	0	1	4.3	1.000	C-8

Rowland Office

OFFICE, ROWLAND JOHNIE
B. Oct. 25, 1952, Sacramento, Calif.

BL TL 6' 170 lbs.

Year	Team	Games	BA	SA	AB	H	2B	3B	HR	HR%	R	RBI	BB	SO	SB	PH AB	PH H	PO	A	E	DP	TC/G	FA	G by Pos
1972	ATL N	2	.400	.400	5	2	0	0	0	0.0	1	0	1	0	0	0	0	3	0	0	0	1.5	1.000	OF-1
1974		131	.246	.355	248	61	16	1	3	1.2	20	31	16	30	5	11	4	171	0	1	0	1.3	.994	OF-119
1975		126	.290	.361	355	103	14	1	3	0.8	30	30	23	41	2	20	7	229	6	8	0	1.9	.967	OF-107
1976		99	.281	.368	359	101	17	1	4	1.1	51	34	37	49	2	5	2	204	3	3	2	2.1	.986	OF-92
1977		124	.241	.311	428	103	13	1	5	1.2	42	39	23	58	2	20	5	250	8	3	3	2.1	.989	OF-104, 1B-1
1978		146	.250	.354	404	101	13	1	9	2.2	40	40	22	52	8	18	3	291	4	3	2	2.0	.990	OF-136
1979		124	.249	.336	277	69	14	2	2	0.7	35	37	27	33	5	21	5	164	4	2	0	1.4	.988	OF-97
1980	MON N	116	.267	.401	292	78	13	4	6	2.1	36	30	36	39	3	17	6	150	2	1	0	1.3	.987	OF-97
1981		26	.175	.175	40	7	0	0	0	0.0	4	0	4	6	0	13	1	15	0	1	0	0.6	.938	OF-15
1982		3	.333	.667	3	1	1	0	0	0.0	0	0	0	1	0	2	0	2	0	0	0	0.7	1.000	OF-1
1983	NY A	2	.000	.000	2	0	0	0	0	0.0	0	1	0	0	0	2	0	0	0	0	0	1.0	1.000	OF-2
11 yrs.		899	.259	.350	2413	626	101	11	32	1.3	259	242	189	311	27	129	35	1481	27	23	8	1.7	.985	OF-771, 1B-1

Jim Oglesby

OGLESBY, JAMES DORN
B. Aug. 10, 1905, Schofield, Mo.   D. Sept. 1, 1955, Tulsa, Okla.

BL TL 6' 190 lbs.

Year	Team	Games	BA	SA	AB	H	2B	3B	HR	HR%	R	RBI	BB	SO	SB	PH AB	PH H	PO	A	E	DP	TC/G	FA	G by Pos
1936	PHI A	3	.182	.182	11	2	0	0	0	0.0	0	2	2	0	0	0	0	23	2	0	2	8.3	1.000	1B-3

Ben Oglivie

OGLIVIE, BENJAMIN AMBROSIO
B. Feb. 11, 1949, Colon, Panama

BL TL 6'2" 160 lbs.

Year	Team	Games	BA	SA	AB	H	2B	3B	HR	HR%	R	RBI	BB	SO	SB	PH AB	PH H	PO	A	E	DP	TC/G	FA	G by Pos
1971	BOS A	14	.263	.342	38	10	3	0	0	0.0	2	4	0	5	0	5	0	22	1	1	1	1.7	.958	OF-11
1972		94	.241	.391	253	61	10	2	8	3.2	27	30	18	61	1	24	9	98	5	2	2	1.1	.981	OF-65
1973		58	.218	.333	147	32	9	1	2	1.4	16	9	9	32	1	10	2	56	2	1	0	1.0	.983	OF-32, DH-13
1974	DET A	92	.270	.385	252	68	11	3	4	1.6	28	29	34	38	12	19	5	162	11	5	13	1.9	.972	OF-63, 1B-10, DH-4
1975		100	.286	.416	332	95	14	1	9	2.7	45	36	16	62	11	3	0	232	8	5	5	2.5	.980	OF-86, 1B-5, DH-2
1976		115	.285	.492	305	87	12	3	15	4.9	36	47	11	44	9	38	9	234	8	3	13	2.1	.988	OF-64, 1B-9, DH-1
1977		132	.262	.464	450	118	24	2	21	4.7	63	61	40	80	1	12	4	236	10	6	3	1.9	.976	OF-118, DH-2
1978	MIL A	128	.303	.497	469	142	29	4	18	3.8	71	72	52	69	11	6	1	275	8	6	4	2.3	.979	OF-89, DH-27, 1B-11
1979		139	.282	.501	514	145	30	4	29	5.6	88	81	48	56	12	6	3	320	10	5	3	2.4	.985	OF-120, DH-13, 1B-9
1980		156	.304	.563	592	180	26	2	41	6.9	94	118	54	71	11	0	0	384	18	9	3	2.6	.978	OF-152, DH-4
1981		107	.243	.395	400	97	15	2	14	3.5	53	72	37	49	2	1	1	211	3	4	1	2.0	.982	OF-101, DH-6
1982		159	.244	.453	602	147	22	1	34	5.6	92	102	70	81	3	1	1	359	15	7	3	2.4	.982	OF-159
1983		125	.280	.436	411	115	19	3	13	3.2	49	66	60	64	4	10	3	259	8	4	1	2.2	.985	OF-113, DH-8
1984		131	.262	.384	461	121	16	2	12	2.6	49	60	44	56	0	10	3	256	6	8	4	2.1	.970	OF-125, DH-1
1985		101	.290	.440	341	99	17	2	10	2.9	40	61	37	51	0	9	1	190	4	5	2	2.0	.975	OF-91, DH-4
1986		103	.283	.390	346	98	20	1	5	1.4	31	53	30	33	1	8	1	105	4	1	1	1.1	.991	OF-50, DH-42
16 yrs.		1754	.273	.450	5913	1615	277	33	235	4.0	784	901	560	852	87	162	42	3399	121	74	54	2.0	.979	OF-1439, DH-127, 1B-44

Year	Team	Games	BA	SA	AB	H	2B	3B	HR	HR%	R	RBI	BB	SO	SB	Pinch Hit AB	Pinch Hit H	PO	A	E	DP	TC/G	FA	G by Pos

Ben Oglivie *continued*

DIVISIONAL PLAYOFF SERIES

| 1981 | MIL A | 5 | .167 | .222 | 18 | 3 | 1 | 0 | 0 | 0.0 | 0 | 1 | 0 | 7 | 0 | 0 | 0 | 0 | 0 | 0 | 0 | 0.0 | – | OF-5 |

LEAGUE CHAMPIONSHIP SERIES

| 1982 | MIL A | 4 | .133 | .333 | 15 | 2 | 0 | 0 | 1 | 6.7 | 1 | 1 | 0 | 3 | 0 | 0 | 0 | 0 | 0 | 2 | 0 | 0.5 | – | OF-4 |

WORLD SERIES

| 1982 | MIL A | 7 | .222 | .407 | 27 | 6 | 0 | 1 | 1 | 3.7 | 4 | 1 | 2 | 4 | 0 | 0 | 0 | 13 | 0 | 1 | 0 | 2.0 | .929 | OF-7 |

Brusie Ogrodowski

OGRODOWSKI, AMBROSE FRANCIS   BR TR 5'11" 175 lbs.
B. Feb. 17, 1912, Hoytville, Pa.   D. Mar. 5, 1956, San Francisco, Calif.

1936	STL N	94	.228	.312	237	54	15	1	1	0.4	28	20	10	20	1	0	9	1	314	32	4	6	3.7	.989	C-85
1937		90	.233	.323	279	65	10	3	3	1.1	37	31	11	17	2	3	2		387	50	7	2	4.9	.984	C-87
2 yrs.		184	.231	.318	516	119	25	4	4	0.8	65	51	21	37	2	12	3		701	82	11	8	4.3	.986	C-172

Hal O'Hagen

O'HAGEN, HARRY P.   6' 173 lbs.
B. Sept. 30, 1873, Washington, D. C.   D. Jan. 14, 1913, Newark, N. J.

1892	WAS N	1	.250	.250	4	1	0	0	0	0.0	1	0	0	2	0	0	0	3	3	0	1	6.0	1.000	C-1
1902 3 teams	CHI N (31G – .194)				NY N (26G – .143)					CLE A (3G – .385)														1B-52, OF-8
" total	60	.185	.249	205	38	5	4	0	0.0	17	19	13		13	0	0	533	38	12	30	9.7	.979	1B-52, OF-8
2 yrs.		61	.187	.249	209	39	5	4	0	0.0	18	19	13	2	13	0	0	536	41	12	31	9.7	.980	1B-52, OF-8, C-1

Bill O'Hara

O'HARA, WILLIAM ALEXANDER   BL TR 5'10"
B. Aug. 14, 1883, Toronto, Ont., Canada   D. June 15, 1931, Jersey City, N. J.

1909	NY N	115	.236	.286	360	85	9	3	1	0.3	48	30	41		31	0	0	202	19	5	4	2.0	.978	OF-115
1910	STL N	9	.150	.150	20	3	0	0	0	0.0	1	2	1	3	0	0	0	14	1	0	0	1.7	1.000	OF-4, 1B-1, P-1
2 yrs.		124	.232	.279	380	88	9	3	1	0.3	49	32	42	3	31	0	0	216	20	5	4	1.9	.979	OF-119, 1B-1, P-1

Kid O'Hara

O'HARA, JAMES FRANCIS   BB TR 5'7½" 152 lbs.
B. Dec. 19, 1875, Wilkes-Barre, Pa.   D. Dec. 1, 1954, Canton, Ohio

| 1904 | BOS N | 8 | .207 | .207 | 29 | 6 | 0 | 0 | 0 | 0.0 | 3 | 0 | 4 | | 1 | 0 | 0 | 10 | 2 | 1 | 0 | 1.6 | .923 | OF-8 |

Tom O'Hara

O'HARA, THOMAS F
B. July 13, 1885, Waverly, N. Y.   D. June 8, 1954, Denver, Colo.

1906	STL N	14	.302	.321	53	16	1	0	0	0.0	8	0	3		3	0	0	24	0	3	0	1.9	.889	OF-14
1907		48	.237	.260	173	41	2	1	0	0.0	11	5	12		1	1	0	78	5	5	2	1.8	.943	OF-47
2 yrs.		62	.252	.274	226	57	3	1	0	0.0	19	5	15		4	1	0	102	5	8	2	1.9	.930	OF-61

Len Okrie

OKRIE, LEONARD JOSEPH   BR TR 6' 185 lbs.
Son of Frank Okrie.
B. July 16, 1923, Detroit, Mich.

1948	WAS A	19	.238	.286	42	10	0	1	0	0.0	1	1	1	7	0	2	0	43	10	1	1	2.8	.981	C-17
1950		17	.222	.222	27	6	0	0	0	0.0	1	2	6	7	0	0	0	34	6	0	3	2.4	1.000	C-17
1951		5	.125	.250	8	1	1	0	0	0.0	1	0	2	1	0	0	0	13	4	3	0	4.0	.850	C-5
1952	BOS A	1	.000	.000	1	0	0	0	0	0.0	0	0	0	1	0	0	0	1	0	0	0	1.0	1.000	C-1
4 yrs.		42	.218	.256	78	17	1	1	0	0.0	3	3	9	16	0	2	0	91	20	4	4	2.7	.965	C-40

Dave Oldfield

OLDFIELD, DAVID   BB TL 5'7" 175 lbs.
B. Dec. 18, 1864, Philadelphia, Pa.   D. Aug. 28, 1939, Philadelphia, Pa.

1883	BAL AA	1	.000	.000	4	0	0	0	0	0.0	0		0			0	0	6	0	3	0	9.0	.667	C-1
1885	BKN AA	10	.320	.360	25	8	1	0	0	0.0	2		3			0	0	47	10	9	0	6.6	.864	C-9, OF-2
1886 2 teams	BKN AA (14G – .236)				WAS N (21G – .141)																			C-25, OF-10, SS-1
" total	35	.183	.206	126	23	3	0	0	0.0	9	2	7	15		0	0	141	37	28	1	5.9	.864	C-25, OF-10, SS-1
3 yrs.		46	.200	.226	155	31	4	0	0	0.0	11	2	10	15		0	0	194	47	40	1	6.1	.858	C-35, OF-12, SS-1

John Oldham

OLDHAM, JOHN HARDIN   BR TL 6'3" 198 lbs.
B. Nov. 6, 1932, Salinas, Calif.

| 1956 | CIN N | 1 | – | – | 0 | 0 | 0 | 0 | 0 | – | 0 | 0 | 0 | 0 | 0 | 0 | 0 | 0 | 0 | 0 | 0 | 0.0 | – | |

Bob Oldis

OLDIS, ROBERT CARL   BR TR 6'1" 185 lbs.
B. Jan. 5, 1928, Preston, Iowa

1953	WAS A	7	.250	.250	16	4	0	0	0	0.0	1	3	1	2	0	0	0	23	3	0	1	3.7	1.000	C-7
1954		11	.333	.375	24	8	1	0	0	0.0	1	1	1	3	0	1	0	30	2	2	0	3.1	.941	C-8, 3B-2
1955		6	.000	.000	6	0	0	0	0	0.0	1	0	1	0	0	0	0	12	1	0	0	2.2	1.000	C-6
1960	PIT N	22	.200	.250	20	4	1	0	0	0.0	1	1	1	2	0	4	0	42	2	0	0	2.0	1.000	C-22
1961		4	.000	.000	5	0	0	0	0	0.0	0	0	0	0	0	0	0	11	3	0	3	3.5	1.000	C-4
1962	PHI N	38	.263	.313	80	21	1	0	1	1.3	9	10	13	10	0	7	2	134	14	2	4	3.9	.987	C-30
1963		47	.224	.259	85	19	2	0	0	0.0	8	8	3	5	0	11	3	170	15	4	4	4.0	.979	C-43
7 yrs.		135	.237	.275	236	56	6	0	1	0.4	20	22	20	22	0	19	5	422	40	8	12	3.5	.983	C-120, 3B-2

WORLD SERIES

| 1960 | PIT N | 2 | – | – | 0 | 0 | 0 | 0 | 0 | – | 0 | 0 | 0 | 0 | 0 | 0 | 0 | 0 | 0 | 0 | 0 | 0.0 | – | C-2 |

Rube Oldring

OLDRING, REUBEN HENRY   BR TR 5'10" 186 lbs.
B. May 30, 1884, New York, N. Y.   D. Sept. 9, 1961, Bridgeton, N. J.

1905	NY A	8	.300	.467	30	9	1	0	1	3.3	2	6	2			2		24	24	2	4	6.3	.960	SS-8
1906	PHI A	59	.241	.310	174	42	10	1	0	0.0	15	19	2		7	2	0	65	90	17	5	2.9	.901	3B-49, SS-3, 2B-2, 1B-1
1907		117	.286	.395	441	126	27	9	1	0.2	48	40	7		29	0	0	180	10	5	0	1.7	.974	OF-117
1908		116	.221	.270	434	96	14	2	1	0.2	39	39	18		13	0	0	246	9	16	3	2.3	.941	OF-116
1909		90	.230	.328	326	75	13	8	1	0.3	39	28	20		17	0	0	175	7	8	1	2.1	.958	OF-89, 1B-1

Year	Team	Games	BA	SA	AB	H	2B	3B	HR	HR%	R	RBI	BB	SO	SB	Pinch Hit AB	Pinch Hit H	PO	A	E	DP	TC/G	FA	G by Pos

Rube Oldring *continued*

Year	Team	Games	BA	SA	AB	H	2B	3B	HR	HR%	R	RBI	BB	SO	SB	PH AB	PH H	PO	A	E	DP	TC/G	FA	G by Pos
1910		134	.308	.430	546	168	27	14	4	0.7	79	57	23		17	0	0	249	14	6	6	2.0	.978	OF-134
1911		121	.297	.394	495	147	11	14	3	0.6	84	59	21		21	1	0	225	13	5	2	2.0	.979	OF-119
1912		98	.301	.370	395	119	14	5	1	0.3	61	24	10		17	1	0	214	8	6	1	2.3	.974	OF-97
1913		136	.283	.394	538	152	27	9	5	0.9	101	71	34	37	40	0	0	248	20	9	3	2.0	.968	OF-136, SS-5
1914		119	.277	.371	466	129	21	7	3	0.6	68	49	18	35	14	2	0	215	7	8	5	1.9	.965	OF-117
1915		107	.248	.363	408	101	23	3	6	1.5	49	42	22	21	11	3	2	224	23	9	6	2.4	.965	OF-96, 3B-8
1916 **2 teams**	PHI A (40G – .247)				NY A (43G – .234)																			
" total		83	.240	.322	304	73	16	3	1	0.3	27	26	21	22	7	0	0	130	7	11	5	1.8	.926	OF-83
1918 PHI	A	49	.233	.263	133	31	2	1	0	0.0	5	11	8	10	0	15	4	39	9	3	3	1.0	.941	OF-30, 3B-2, 2B-2
13 yrs.		1237	.270	.364	4690	1268	205	77	27	0.6	616	471	206	125	197	24	6	2234	241	105	44	2.1	.959	OF-1134, 3B-59, SS-16, 2B-4, 1B-2

WORLD SERIES

Year	Team	Games	BA	SA	AB	H	2B	3B	HR	HR%	R	RBI	BB	SO	SB	PH AB	PH H	PO	A	E	DP	TC/G	FA	G by Pos
1911 PHI	A	6	.200	.400	25	5	2	0	1	4.0	2	3	0	6	0	0	0	8	0	1	0	1.5	.889	OF-6
1913		5	.273	.364	22	6	0	1	0	0.0	5	0	1	1	0	0	0	10	0	0	0	2.0	1.000	OF-5
1914		4	.067	.067	15	1	0	0	0	0.0	0	0	0	5	0	0	0	6	0	0	0	1.5	1.000	OF-4
3 yrs.		15	.194	.306	62	12	2	1	1	1.6	7	3	0	12	1	0	0	24	0	1	0	1.7	.960	OF-15

Charley O'Leary

O'LEARY, CHARLES TIMOTHY
B. Oct. 15, 1882, Chicago, Ill. D. Jan. 6, 1941, Chicago, Ill.　　　　BR TR 5'7" 165 lbs.

Year	Team	Games	BA	SA	AB	H	2B	3B	HR	HR%	R	RBI	BB	SO	SB	PH AB	PH H	PO	A	E	DP	TC/G	FA	G by Pos
1904 DET	A	135	.213	.254	456	97	10	3	1	0.2	39	16	21		9	0	0	308	439	54	48	5.9	.933	SS-135
1905		148	.213	.248	512	109	13	1	1	0.2	47	33	29		13	0	0	358	411	55	40	5.6	.933	SS-148
1906		128	.219	.271	443	97	13	2	2	0.5	34	34	17		8	1	1	326	398	58	37	6.1	.926	SS-127
1907		139	.241	.286	465	112	19	1	0	0.0	61	34	32		11	1	0	353	448	44	35	6.1	.948	SS-138
1908		65	.251	.322	211	53	9	3	0	0.0	21	17	9		4	0	0	131	179	27	15	5.2	.920	SS-64, 2B-1
1909		76	.203	.241	261	53	10	0	0	0.0	29	13	6		9	0	0	104	162	18	8	3.7	.937	3B-54, 2B-15, SS-4, OF-2
1910		65	.242	.284	211	51	7	1	0	0.0	23	9	9		7	2	0	121	167	16	15	4.7	.947	2B-38, SS-16, 3B-6
1911		74	.266	.313	256	68	8	2	0	0.0	29	25	21		10	0	0	178	212	14	22	5.5	.965	2B-67, 3B-6
1912		3	.200	.200	10	2	0	0	0	0.0	1	1	0		0	0	0	5	11	0	1	5.3	1.000	2B-3
1913 STL	N	120	.218	.280	404	88	15	5	0	0.0	32	31	20	34	3	1	0	218	338	28	33	4.9	.952	SS-102, 2B-15
1934 STL	A	1	1.000	1.000	1	1	0	0	0	0.0	1	0	0	0	0	1	1	0	0	0	0	0.0		
11 yrs.		954	.226	.273	3230	731	104	18	4	0.1	317	213	164	34	74	6	2	2102	2765	314	253	5.4	.939	SS-734, 2B-139, 3B-66, OF-2

WORLD SERIES

Year	Team	Games	BA	SA	AB	H	2B	3B	HR	HR%	R	RBI	BB	SO	SB	PH AB	PH H	PO	A	E	DP	TC/G	FA	G by Pos
1907 DET	A	5	.059	.059	17	1	0	0	0	0.0	0	0	0	3	0	0	0	9	18	2	0	5.8	.931	SS-5
1908		5	.158	.158	19	3	0	0	0	0.0	0	0	0	3	0	0	0	7	12	1	3	4.0	.950	SS-5
1909		1	.000	.000	3	0	0	0	0	0.0	0	0	0	0	0	0	0	1	1	0	0	2.0	1.000	3B-1
3 yrs.		11	.103	.103	39	4	0	0	0	0.0	2	0	1	6	0	0	0	17	31	3	3	4.6	.941	SS-10, 3B-1

Dan O'Leary

O'LEARY, DANIEL (Hustling Dan)
B. Oct. 22, 1856, Detroit, Mich. D. June 24, 1922, Chicago, Ill.　　BL
Manager 1884.

Year	Team	Games	BA	SA	AB	H	2B	3B	HR	HR%	R	RBI	BB	SO	SB	PH AB	PH H	PO	A	E	DP	TC/G	FA	G by Pos
1879 PRO	N	2	.429	.429	7	3	0	0	0	0.0	0	2	0		0	0	0	0	0	0	0	0.0	–	OF-2
1880 BOS	N	3	.250	.417	12	3	2	0	0	0.0	1	1	0	3	0	0	0	1	0	0	0	0.3	1.000	OF-3
1881 DET	N	2	.000	.000	8	0	0	0	0	0.0	0	0	0	2	0	0	0	5	0	2	0	3.5	.714	OF-2
1882 WOR	U	6	.182	.227	22	4	1	0	0	0.0	2	2	5	5	0	0	0	8	0	2	0	1.7	.800	OF-6
1884 CIN	U	32	.258	.311	132	34	0	2	1	0.8	14		5		0	0	0	48	8	9	0	2.0	.862	OF-32
5 yrs.		45	.243	.298	181	44	3	2	1	0.6	18	5	10	10	0	0	0	62	8	13	0	1.8	.843	OF-45

John Olerud

OLERUD, JOHN GARRETT
B. Aug. 5, 1968, Bellevue, Wash.　　　　BL TL 6'5" 205 lbs.

Year	Team	Games	BA	SA	AB	H	2B	3B	HR	HR%	R	RBI	BB	SO	SB	PH AB	PH H	PO	A	E	DP	TC/G	FA	G by Pos
1989 TOR	A	6	.375	.375	8	3	0	0	0	0.0	2	0	0	1	0	1	0	19	2	0	0	3.5	1.000	1B-5, DH-1

Frank Olin

OLIN, FRANKLIN WALTER
B. Jan. 9, 1860, Woodford, Vt. D. May 20, 1951, St. Louis, Mo.　　　　BL

Year	Team	Games	BA	SA	AB	H	2B	3B	HR	HR%	R	RBI	BB	SO	SB	PH AB	PH H	PO	A	E	DP	TC/G	FA	G by Pos
1884 **3 teams**	WAS AA (21G – .386)				WAS U (1G – .000)				TOL AA (26G – .256)															
" total		48	.312	.376	173	54	4	2	1	0.6	28		13			0	0	67	33	24	3	2.6	.806	OF-38, 2B-12
1885 DET	N	1	.500	.500	4	2	0	0	0	0.0	1	0	0	0		0	0	2	2	2	0	6.0	.667	3B-1
2 yrs.		49	.316	.379	177	56	4	2	1	0.6	29	0	13	0		0	0	69	35	26	3	2.7	.800	OF-38, 2B-12, 3B-1

Tony Oliva

OLIVA, PEDRO
Born Pedro Oliva y Lopez.
B. July 20, 1940, Pinar del Rio, Cuba　　　　BL TR 6'1" 175 lbs.

Year	Team	Games	BA	SA	AB	H	2B	3B	HR	HR%	R	RBI	BB	SO	SB	PH AB	PH H	PO	A	E	DP	TC/G	FA	G by Pos
1962 MIN	A	9	.444	.556	9	4	1	0	0	0.0	3	3	3	2	0	5	2	3	0	0	0	0.3	1.000	OF-2
1963		7	.429	.429	7	3	0	0	0	0.0	0	1	0	2	0	7	3	0	0	0	0	0.0	–	
1964		161	.323	.557	672	217	43	9	32	4.8	109	94	34	68	12	2	1	313	5	6	0	2.0	.981	OF-159
1965		149	.321	.491	576	185	40	5	16	2.8	107	98	55	64	19	1	0	284	10	11	3	2.0	.964	OF-147
1966		159	.307	.502	622	191	32	7	25	4.0	99	87	42	72	13	1	1	335	9	10	3	2.2	.972	OF-159
1967		146	.289	.463	557	161	34	6	17	3.1	76	83	44	61	11	1	1	286	8	4	2	2.0	.987	OF-146
1968		128	.289	.477	470	136	24	5	18	3.8	54	68	45	61	10	2	0	227	7	4	1	1.9	.983	OF-126
1969		153	.309	.496	637	197	39	4	24	3.8	97	101	45	66	10	1	1	311	14	6	3	2.2	.982	OF-152
1970		157	.325	.514	628	204	36	7	23	3.7	96	107	38	67	5	1	1	351	12	12	4	2.4	.968	OF-157
1971		126	.337	.546	487	164	30	3	22	4.5	73	81	25	44	4	5	0	216	6	7	3	1.8	.969	OF-121
1972		10	.321	.357	28	9	1	0	0	0.0	1	1	2	5	0	1	0	6	0	1	0	0.7	.857	OF-9
1973		146	.291	.410	571	166	20	0	16	2.8	63	92	45	44	2	4	2	0	0	0	0	0.0	–	DH-142
1974		127	.285	.414	459	131	16	2	13	2.8	43	57	27	31	0	13	1	0	0	0	0	0.0	–	DH-112
1975		131	.270	.378	455	123	10	0	13	2.9	46	58	41	45	0	10	5	0	0	0	0	0.0	–	DH-120
1976		67	.211	.260	123	26	3	0	1	0.8	3	16	2	13	0	32	7	0	0	0	0	0.0	–	DH-32
15 yrs.		1676	.304	.476	6301	1917	329	48	220	3.5	870	947	448	645	86	86	30	2332	71	61	19	1.5	.975	OF-1178, DH-406

LEAGUE CHAMPIONSHIP SERIES

Year	Team	Games	BA	SA	AB	H	2B	3B	HR	HR%	R	RBI	BB	SO	SB	PH AB	PH H	PO	A	E	DP	TC/G	FA	G by Pos
1969 MIN	A	3	.385	.769	13	5	2	0	1	7.7	3	2	1	3	1	0	0	6	1	2	0	3.0	.778	OF-3

Tony Oliva *continued*

Year Team	Games	BA	SA	AB	H	2B	3B	HR	HR%	R	RBI	BB	SO	SB	PH AB	PH H	PO	A	E	DP	TC/G	FA	G by Pos
1970	3	.500	.917	12	6	2	0	1	8.3	2	1	0	1	0	0	0	10	2	0	1	4.0	1.000	OF-3
2 yrs.	6	.440	.840	25	11	4	0	2	8.0	5	3	1	4	1	0	0	16	3	2	1	3.5	.905	OF-6

WORLD SERIES

Year Team	Games	BA	SA	AB	H	2B	3B	HR	HR%	R	RBI	BB	SO	SB	PH AB	PH H	PO	A	E	DP	TC/G	FA	G by Pos
1965 MIN A	7	.192	.346	26	5	1	0	1	3.8	2	2	1	6	0	0	0	20	0	1	0	3.0	.952	OF-7

Ed Olivares — OLIVARES, EDWARD
Born Edward Olivares y Balzac.
B. Nov. 5, 1938, Mayaguez, Puerto Rico

BR TR 5'11" 180 lbs.

Year Team	Games	BA	SA	AB	H	2B	3B	HR	HR%	R	RBI	BB	SO	SB	PH AB	PH H	PO	A	E	DP	TC/G	FA	G by Pos
1960 STL N	3	.000	.000	5	0	0	0	0	0.0	0	0	0	3	0	2	0	0	1	1	0	0.7	.500	2B-1
1961	21	.167	.167	30	5	0	0	0	0.0	2	1	0	4	1	11	1	8	0	0	0	0.4	1.000	OF-10
2 yrs.	24	.143	.143	35	5	0	0	0	0.0	2	1	0	7	1	13	1	8	1	1	0	0.4	.900	OF-10, 2B-1

Al Oliver — OLIVER, ALBERT (Scoop)
B. Oct. 14, 1946, Portsmouth, Ohio

BL TL 6' 195 lbs.

Year Team	Games	BA	SA	AB	H	2B	3B	HR	HR%	R	RBI	BB	SO	SB	PH AB	PH H	PO	A	E	DP	TC/G	FA	G by Pos
1968 PIT N	4	.125	.125	8	1	0	0	0	0.0	0	1	0	0	0	3	0	3	0	0	0	0.8	1.000	OF-1
1969	129	.285	.445	463	132	19	2	17	3.7	55	70	21	38	8	7	0	911	50	9	87	7.5	.991	1B-106, OF-21
1970	151	.270	.414	551	149	33	5	12	2.2	63	83	35	35	1	4	2	718	52	9	69	5.2	.988	OF-80, 1B-77
1971	143	.282	.446	529	149	31	7	14	2.6	69	64	27	72	4	6	0	497	15	6	18	3.6	.988	OF-116, 1B-25
1972	140	.312	.437	565	176	27	4	12	2.1	88	89	34	44	2	1	0	353	4	5	4	2.6	.986	OF-138, 1B-3
1973	158	.292	.463	654	191	38	7	20	3.1	90	99	22	52	6	2	0	692	36	13	42	4.7	.982	OF-109, 1B-50
1974	147	.321	.475	617	198	38	12	11	1.8	96	85	33	58	10	2	1	702	26	7	29	5.0	.990	OF-98, 1B-49
1975	155	.280	.454	628	176	39	8	18	2.9	90	84	25	73	4	1	0	409	6	5	6	2.7	.988	OF-153, 1B-4
1976	121	.323	.476	443	143	22	5	12	2.7	62	61	26	29	6	11	3	327	4	5	5	2.8	.985	OF-106, 1B-3
1977	154	.308	.481	568	175	29	6	19	3.3	75	82	40	38	13	6	3	305	6	6	1	2.1	.981	OF-148
1978 TEX A	133	.324	.490	525	170	35	5	14	2.7	65	89	31	41	8	0	0	219	8	3	1	1.7	.987	OF-107, DH-26
1979	136	.323	.470	492	159	28	4	12	2.4	69	76	34	34	4	13	5	260	9	7	2	2.0	.975	OF-119, DH-10
1980	163	.319	.480	656	209	43	3	19	2.9	96	117	39	47	5	2	1	315	9	9	2	2.0	.973	OF-157, DH-4, 1B-1
1981	102	.309	.411	421	130	29	1	4	1.0	53	55	24	28	3	1	1	2	0	0	0		1.000	DH-101, 1B-1
1982 MON N	160	**.331**	.514	617	**204**	**43**	2	22	3.6	90	**109**	61	59	5	1	1	1286	92	19	96	8.7	.986	1B-159
1983	157	.300	.410	614	184	**38**	3	8	1.3	70	84	44	44	1	4	2	1207	118	13	93	8.5	.990	1B-153, OF-1
1984 2 teams	SF N (91G – .298)			PHI N (28G – .312)																			
" total	119	.301	.370	432	130	26	2	0	0.0	36	48	27	36	3	16	4	818	61	13	58	7.5	.985	1B-101, OF-5
1985 2 teams	LA N (35G – .253)			TOR A (61G – .251)																			
" total	96	.252	.357	266	67	11	1	5	1.9	21	31	12	24	1	28	6	13	2	2	0	0.2	.882	DH-59, OF-17, 1B-1
18 yrs.	2368	.303	.451	9049	2743	529	77	219	2.4	1189	1326	535	756	84	108	29	9037	498	131	513	4.1	.986	OF-1376, 1B-733, DH-200

LEAGUE CHAMPIONSHIP SERIES

Year Team	Games	BA	SA	AB	H	2B	3B	HR	HR%	R	RBI	BB	SO	SB	PH AB	PH H	PO	A	E	DP	TC/G	FA	G by Pos
1970 PIT N	2	.250	.250	8	2	0	0	0	0.0	0	1	1	0	0	0	0	22	1	0	1	11.5	1.000	1B-2
1971	4	.250	.500	12	3	0	0	1	8.3	2	5	1	3	0	0	0	5	0	0	0	1.3	1.000	OF-4
1972	5	.250	.600	20	5	2	1	1	5.0	3	3	0	4	0	0	0	17	1	0	0	3.6	1.000	OF-5
1974	4	.143	.143	14	2	0	0	0	0.0	1	1	2	2	0	0	0	9	0	0	0	2.3	1.000	OF-4
1975	3	.182	.455	11	2	0	0	1	9.1	1	2	2	0	0	0	0	5	0	0	0	1.7	1.000	OF-3
1985 TOR A	4	.375	.500	8	3	1	0	0	0.0	0	3	0	0	0	2	1	0	0	0	0	0.0	–	DH-3
6 yrs.	22	.233	.425	73	17	3	1	3	4.1	7	15	6	9	0	2	1	58	2	0	1	2.7	1.000	OF-16, DH-3, 1B-2

WORLD SERIES

Year Team	Games	BA	SA	AB	H	2B	3B	HR	HR%	R	RBI	BB	SO	SB	PH AB	PH H	PO	A	E	DP	TC/G	FA	G by Pos
1971 PIT N	5	.211	.316	19	4	0	0			1	2	2	5	0	1	0	11	0	1	0	2.4	.917	OF-4

Bob Oliver — OLIVER, ROBERT LEE
B. Feb. 8, 1943, Shreveport, La.

BR TR 6'3" 205 lbs.

Year Team	Games	BA	SA	AB	H	2B	3B	HR	HR%	R	RBI	BB	SO	SB	PH AB	PH H	PO	A	E	DP	TC/G	FA	G by Pos
1965 PIT N	3	.000	.000	2	0	0	0	0	0.0	0	0	1	0	0	0	0	3	0	0	0	1.0	1.000	OF-3
1969 KC A	118	.254	.393	394	100	8	4	13	3.3	43	43	21	74	5	7	2	276	25	8	10	2.6	.974	OF-98, 1B-12, 3B-8
1970	160	.260	.451	612	159	24	6	27	4.4	83	99	42	126	3	2	0	1077	145	14	111	7.7	.989	1B-115, 3B-46
1971	128	.244	.351	373	91	12	2	8	2.1	35	52	14	88	0	22	5	566	37	9	52	4.8	.985	1B-68, OF-48, 3B-2
1972 2 teams	CAL A (134G – .269)			KC A (16G – .270)																			
" total	150	.269	.430	572	154	22	5	20	3.5	54	76	29	109	5	1	0	1136	55	10	93	8.0	.992	1B-127, OF-24
1973 CAL A	151	.265	.412	544	144	24	1	18	3.3	51	89	33	100	1	12	2	396	121	11	26	3.5	.979	3B-49, OF-47, 1B-32, DH-12
1974 2 teams	CAL A (110G – .248)			BAL A (9G – .150)																			
" total	119	.243	.340	379	92	11	1	8	2.1	23	59	16	56	3	24	4	438	90	14	47	4.6	.974	1B-61, 3B-46, OF-4, DH-2
1975 NY A	18	.132	.158	38	5	1	0	0	0.0	3	1	1	9	0	6	1	39	4	0	9	2.4	1.000	1B-8, DH-3, 3B-1
8 yrs.	847	.256	.400	2914	745	102	19	94	3.2	293	419	156	562	17	74	14	3931	477	66	348	5.3	.985	1B-423, OF-224, 3B-152, DH-17

Dave Oliver — OLIVER, DAVID JACOB
B. Apr. 7, 1951, Stockton, Calif.

BL TR 5'11" 175 lbs.

Year Team	Games	BA	SA	AB	H	2B	3B	HR	HR%	R	RBI	BB	SO	SB	PH AB	PH H	PO	A	E	DP	TC/G	FA	G by Pos
1977 CLE A	7	.318	.409	22	7	0	1	0	0.0	2	3	4	0	0	1	0	20	17	2	7	5.6	.949	2B-7

Gene Oliver — OLIVER, EUGENE GEORGE
B. Mar. 22, 1935, Moline, Ill.

BR TR 6'2" 225 lbs.

Year Team	Games	BA	SA	AB	H	2B	3B	HR	HR%	R	RBI	BB	SO	SB	PH AB	PH H	PO	A	E	DP	TC/G	FA	G by Pos
1959 STL N	68	.244	.401	172	42	9	0	6	3.5	14	28	7	41	3	18	4	125	5	4	1	2.0	.970	OF-42, C-9, 1B-5
1961	22	.269	.538	52	14	2	0	4	7.7	7	8	6	10	0	5	1	77	6	1	4	3.8	.988	C-15, OF-1
1962	122	.258	.441	345	89	19	1	14	4.1	42	45	50	59	5	19	6	514	47	5	9	4.6	.991	C-98, OF-8, 1B-3
1963 2 teams	STL N (39G – .225)			MIL N (95G – .250)																			
" total	134	.244	.422	398	97	16	2	17	4.3	44	65	40	78	4	16	2	668	33	13	40	5.3	.982	1B-55, C-37, OF-35
1964 MIL N	93	.276	.477	279	77	15	1	13	4.7	45	49	17	41	3	23	3	625	35	12	50	7.2	.982	1B-76, C-1
1965	122	.270	.482	392	106	20	0	21	5.4	56	58	36	61	3	12	3	750	71	17	37	6.9	.980	C-64, 1B-52, OF-1
1966 ATL N	76	.194	.377	191	37	9	1	8	4.2	19	28	16	43	2	24	5	308	26	3	6	4.4	.991	C-48, 1B-5, OF-2
1967 2 teams	ATL N (17G – .196)			PHI N (85G – .224)																			
" total	102	.220	.373	314	69	18	0	10	3.2	37	40	35	64	2	11	0	515	41	9	8	5.5	.984	C-93, 1B-2

Year	Team		Games	BA	SA	AB	H	2B	3B	HR	HR%	R	RBI	BB	SO	SB	Pinch Hit AB	Pinch Hit H	PO	A	E	DP	TC/G	FA	G by Pos

Gene Oliver *continued*

1968	2 teams	BOS A (16G – .143)								CHI N (8G – .364)															
"	total		24	.196	.196	46	9	0	0	0	0.0	3	2	7	14	0	10	3	83	4	1	0	3.7	.989	C-11, OF-2, 1B-2
1969	CHI	N	23	.222	.333	27	6	3	0	0	0.0	0	0	1	9	0	14	4	28	2	0	1	1.3	1.000	C-6
10 yrs.			786	.246	.427	2216	546	111	5	93	4.2	268	320	215	420	24	152	31	3693	270	65	156	5.1	.984	C-382, 1B-200, OF-91

Joe Oliver

OLIVER, JOSEPH MELTON
B. July 24, 1965, Memphis, Tenn.

BR TR 6'3" 215 lbs.

| 1989 | CIN | N | 49 | .272 | .384 | 151 | 41 | 8 | 0 | 3 | 2.0 | 13 | 23 | 6 | 28 | 0 | 7 | 2 | 260 | 21 | 4 | 1 | 5.8 | .986 | C-47 |

Nate Oliver

OLIVER, NATHANIEL (Pee Wee)
B. Dec. 13, 1940, St. Petersburg, Fla.

BR TR 5'10" 160 lbs.

1963	LA	N	65	.239	.307	163	39	4	3	1	0.6	23	9	13	25	3	6	0	111	114	9	26	3.6	.962	2B-57, SS-2
1964			99	.243	.271	321	78	9	4	0	0.0	28	21	31	57	7	1	0	194	247	15	44	4.6	.967	2B-98, SS-1
1965			8	1.000	1.000	1	1	0	0	0	0.0	3	0	0	0	1	0	0	2	1	0	0	0.4	1.000	2B-2
1966			80	.193	.210	119	23	2	0	0	0.0	17	3	13	17	3	3	1	99	114	6	29	2.7	.973	2B-68, SS-2, 3B-1
1967			77	.237	.280	232	55	6	2	0	0.0	18	7	13	50	3	12	3	125	157	12	35	3.8	.959	2B-39, SS-32, OF-1
1968	SF	N	36	.178	.205	73	13	2	0	0	0.0	3	1	1	13	0	4	0	25	58	10	11	2.6	.892	2B-14, SS-13, 3B-1
1969	2 teams	NY A (1G – .000)								CHI N (44G – .159)															
"	total		45	.156	.289	45	7	3	0	1	2.2	15	4	1	10	0	4	0	22	31	0	9	1.2	1.000	2B-13
7 yrs.			410	.226	.268	954	216	24	5	2	0.2	107	45	72	172	17	29	4	578	722	52	147	3.3	.962	2B-291, SS-50, 3B-2, OF-1

WORLD SERIES

| 1966 | LA | N | 1 | – | – | 0 | 0 | 0 | 0 | 0 | – | 0 | 0 | 0 | 0 | 0 | 0 | 0 | 0 | 0 | 0 | 0 | 0.0 | – | |

Tom Oliver

OLIVER, THOMAS NOBLE (Rebel)
B. Jan. 15, 1903, Montgomery, Ala. D. Feb. 26, 1988, Montgomery, Ala.

BR TR 6' 168 lbs.

1930	BOS	A	154	.293	.351	646	189	34	2	0	0.0	86	46	42	25	6	0	0	477	9	9	3	3.2	.982	OF-154
1931			148	.276	.353	586	162	35	5	0	0.0	52	70	25	17	4	0	0	433	15	3	4	3.0	.993	OF-148
1932			122	.264	.327	455	120	23	3	0	0.0	39	37	25	12	1	5	1	328	12	6	4	2.8	.983	OF-116
1933			90	.258	.303	244	63	9	1	0	0.0	25	23	13	7	1	2	1	187	9	3	3	2.2	.985	OF-86
4 yrs.			514	.277	.340	1931	534	101	11	0	0.0	202	176	105	61	12	7	2	1425	45	21	14	2.9	.986	OF-504

Luis Olmo

OLMO, LUIS FRANCISCO RODRIGUEZ (Jibaro)
Born Luis Francisco Rodriguez y Olmo.
B. Aug. 11, 1919, Arecibo, Puerto Rico

BR TR 5'11½" 185 lbs.

1943	BKN	N	57	.303	.412	238	72	6	4	4	1.7	39	37	8	20	3	0	0	128	6	6	0	2.5	.957	OF-57
1944			136	.258	.367	520	134	20	5	9	1.7	65	85	17	37	10	6	3	316	138	27	18	3.5	.944	OF-64, 2B-42, 3B-31
1945			141	.313	.462	556	174	27	13	10	1.8	62	110	36	33	15	3	0	253	43	19	7	2.2	.940	OF-106, 3B-31, 2B-1
1949			38	.305	.390	105	32	4	1	1	1.0	15	14	5	11	2	4	2	54	3	3	0	1.6	.950	OF-34
1950	BOS	N	69	.227	.383	154	35	7	1	5	3.2	23	22	18	23	3	12	0	74	2	2	0	1.1	.974	OF-55, 3B-1
1951			21	.196	.250	56	11	1	1	0	0.0	4	4	4	4	0	3	0	23	2	0	0	1.2	1.000	OF-16
6 yrs.			462	.281	.405	1629	458	65	25	29	1.8	208	272	88	128	33	28	5	848	194	57	25	2.4	.948	OF-332, 3B-63, 2B-43

WORLD SERIES

| 1949 | BKN | N | 4 | .273 | .545 | 11 | 3 | 0 | 0 | 1 | 9.1 | 2 | 2 | 0 | 2 | 0 | 0 | 0 | 6 | 1 | 0 | 0 | 1.8 | 1.000 | OF-4 |

Barney Olsen

OLSEN, BERNARD CHARLES
B. Sept. 11, 1919, Everett, Mass. D. Mar. 30, 1977, Everett, Mass.

BR TR 5'11" 179 lbs.

| 1941 | CHI | N | 24 | .288 | .438 | 73 | 21 | 6 | 1 | 1 | 1.4 | 13 | 4 | 4 | 11 | 0 | 1 | 0 | 51 | 3 | 3 | 1 | 2.4 | .947 | OF-23 |

Greg Olson

OLSON, GREGORY WILLIAM
B. Sept. 6, 1960, Marshall, Minn.

BR TR 6' 200 lbs.

| 1989 | MIN | A | 3 | .500 | .500 | 2 | 1 | 0 | 0 | 0 | 0.0 | 0 | 0 | 0 | 0 | 0 | 0 | 0 | 4 | 0 | 0 | 0 | 1.3 | 1.000 | C-3 |

Ivy Olson

OLSON, IVAN MASSIE
B. Oct. 14, 1885, Kansas City, Mo. D. Sept. 1, 1965, Inglewood, Calif.

BR TR 5'10½" 175 lbs.

1911	CLE	A	140	.261	.332	545	142	20	8	1	0.2	89	50	34		20	0	0	293	430	73	51	5.7	.908	SS-139, 3B-1
1912			123	.253	.285	467	118	13	1	0	0.0	68	33	21		16	8	1	230	318	44	18	4.8	.926	SS-56, 3B-35, 2B-21, OF-3
1913			104	.249	.300	370	92	13	3	0	0.0	47	32	22	28	7	7	2	308	158	21	25	4.7	.957	3B-73, 1B-22, 2B-1
1914			89	.242	.284	310	75	6	2	1	0.3	22	20	13	24	15	6	0	197	197	17	20	4.6	.959	SS-31, 2B-23, 3B-19, OF-6, 1B-3
1915	2 teams	CIN N (63G – .232)								BKN N (18G – .077)															
"	total		81	.215	.279	233	50	5	5	0	0.0	20	17	13	13	10	8	0	186	181	22	22	4.8	.943	2B-47, 3B-16, SS-7, 1B-7, OF-1
1916	BKN	N	108	.254	.322	351	89	13	4	1	0.3	29	38	21	27	14	1	0	243	307	48	28	5.5	.920	SS-105, 2B-3, 1B-1
1917			139	.269	.328	580	156	18	5	2	0.3	64	38	14	34	6	0	0	287	438	51	53	5.6	.934	SS-133, 3B-6
1918			126	.239	.292	506	121	16	4	0	0.2	63	17	27	18	21	0	0	265	388	58	42	5.6	.918	SS-126
1919			140	.278	.337	590	164	14	9	1	0.2	73	38	30	12	26	0	0	349	445	44	57	6.0	.947	SS-140
1920			143	.254	.314	637	162	13	11	1	0.2	71	46	20	19	4	0	0	326	482	54	68	6.0	.937	SS-125, 2B-21
1921			151	.267	.345	652	174	22	10	3	0.5	88	35	28	26	4	0	0	379	530	56	83	6.4	.942	SS-133, 2B-20
1922			136	.272	.347	551	150	26	6	1	0.2	63	47	25	10	8	0	0	332	432	33	82	5.9	.959	2B-85, SS-51
1923			82	.260	.315	292	76	11	1	1	0.3	33	35	14	10	5	2	2	168	245	12	36	5.2	.972	2B-72, 3B-3, SS-2, 1B-1
1924			10	.222	.259	27	6	1	0	0	0.0	0	0	3		3	1	0	16	17	2	6	3.5	.943	SS-8, 2B-2
14 yrs.			1572	.258	.318	6111	1575	191	69	13	0.2	730	446	285	222	156	33	5	3579	4568	535	591	5.5	.938	SS-1054, 2B-295, 3B-153, 1B-34, OF-10

WORLD SERIES

1916	BKN	N	5	.250	.375	16	4	0	1	0	0.0	1	2	2	2	0	0	0	9	12	4	0	5.0	.840	SS-5
1920			7	.320	.360	25	8	1	0	0	0.0	2	0	3	1	0	0	0	12	20	0	3	4.6	1.000	SS-7
2 yrs.			12	.293	.366	41	12	1	1	0	0.0	3	2	5	3	0	0	0	21	32	4	3	4.8	.930	SS-12

Year	Team	Games	BA	SA	AB	H	2B	3B	HR	HR%	R	RBI	BB	SO	SB	Pinch Hit AB	Pinch Hit H	PO	A	E	DP	TC/G	FA	G by Pos

Karl Olson

OLSON, KARL ARTHUR (Ole)
B. July 6, 1930, Ross, Calif.　　　　BR TR 6'3" 205 lbs.

Year	Team	Games	BA	SA	AB	H	2B	3B	HR	HR%	R	RBI	BB	SO	SB	AB	H	PO	A	E	DP	TC/G	FA	G by Pos
1951	BOS A	5	.100	.100	10	1	0	0	0	0.0	0	0	0	3	0	0	0	8	0	0	0	1.6	1.000	OF-5
1953		25	.123	.211	57	7	2	0	1	1.8	5	6	1	9	0	1	0	31	1	1	0	1.3	.970	OF-24
1954		101	.260	.344	227	59	12	2	1	0.4	25	20	12	23	2	21	3	122	10	6	1	1.4	.957	OF-78
1955		26	.250	.354	48	12	1	2	0	0.0	7	1	1	10	0	3	2	27	1	0	0	1.1	1.000	OF-21
1956	WAS A	106	.246	.329	313	77	10	2	4	1.3	34	22	28	41	1	10	2	192	4	2	0	1.9	.990	OF-101
1957	2 teams		WAS	A (8G – .167)		DET	A	(8G – .143)																
"	total	16	.154	.154	26	4	0	0	0	0.0	3	1	1	8	0	5	0	16	0	0	0	1.0	1.000	OF-11
6 yrs.		279	.235	.316	681	160	25	6	6	0.9	74	50	43	94	3	40	7	396	16	9	1	1.5	.979	OF-240

Marv Olson

OLSON, MARVIN CLEMENT (Sparky)
B. May 28, 1907, Gayville, S. D.　　　　BR TR 5'7" 160 lbs.

Year	Team	Games	BA	SA	AB	H	2B	3B	HR	HR%	R	RBI	BB	SO	SB	AB	H	PO	A	E	DP	TC/G	FA	G by Pos
1931	BOS A	15	.189	.208	53	10	1	0	0	0.0	8	5	9	3	0	0	0	49	55	4	9	7.2	.963	2B-15
1932		115	.248	.313	403	100	14	6	0	0.0	58	25	61	26	1	7	2	266	327	28	68	5.4	.955	2B-106, 3B-1
1933		3	.000	.000	1	0	0	0	0	0.0	1	0	0	1	0	0	0	0	0	0	0	0.0	–	2B-1
3 yrs.		133	.241	.300	457	110	15	6	0	0.0	67	30	70	30	1	7	2	315	382	32	77	5.5	.956	2B-122, 3B-1

Tom O'Malley

O'MALLEY, THOMAS PATRICK
B. Dec. 25, 1960, Orange, N. J.　　　　BL TR 6' 170 lbs.

Year	Team	Games	BA	SA	AB	H	2B	3B	HR	HR%	R	RBI	BB	SO	SB	AB	H	PO	A	E	DP	TC/G	FA	G by Pos
1982	SF N	92	.275	.364	291	80	12	4	2	0.7	26	27	33	39	0	9	3	60	161	8	10	2.5	.965	3B-83, SS-1, 2B-1
1983		135	.259	.339	410	106	16	1	5	1.2	40	45	52	47	2	17	5	70	213	18	12	2.2	.940	3B-117
1984	2 teams		SF	N (13G – .120)		CHI	A	(12G – .125)																
"	total	25	.122	.122	41	5	0	0	0	0.0	2	3	2	7	0	13	2	7	9	0	1	0.6	1.000	3B-13
1985	BAL A	8	.071	.286	14	1	0	0	1	7.1	2	2	0	5	0	5	0	2	3	1	0	0.8	.833	3B-3
1986		56	.254	.320	181	46	9	0	1	0.6	19	18	17	21	0	4	0	37	98	9	8	2.6	.938	3B-55
1987	TEX A	45	.274	.368	117	32	8	0	1	0.9	10	12	15	9	0	8	2	21	56	3	3	1.8	.963	3B-40, 2B-1
1988	MON N	14	.259	.259	27	7	0	0	0	0.0	3	2	3	4	0	5	1	4	15	2	0	1.5	.905	3B-7
1989	NY N	9	.545	.727	11	6	2	0	0	0.0	2	8	0	2	0	7	4	2	1	0	0	0.3	1.000	3B-3
8 yrs.		384	.259	.339	1092	283	47	5	10	0.9	103	117	122	131	2	68	17	203	556	41	34	2.1	.949	3B-321, 2B-2, SS-1

Ollie O'Mara

O'MARA, OLIVER EDWARD
B. Mar. 8, 1891, St. Louis, Mo.　D. Oct. 24, 1989, Reno, Nev.　　　　BR TR 5'9" 155 lbs.

Year	Team	Games	BA	SA	AB	H	2B	3B	HR	HR%	R	RBI	BB	SO	SB	AB	H	PO	A	E	DP	TC/G	FA	G by Pos
1912	DET A	1	.000	.000	4	0	0	0	0	0.0	0	0	0	0	0	0	0	2	4	1	0	7.0	.857	SS-1
1914	BKN N	67	.263	.332	247	65	10	2	1	0.4	41	7	16	26	14	0	0	110	183	26	17	4.8	.918	SS-63
1915		149	.244	.300	577	141	26	3	0	0.0	77	31	51	40	11	0	0	319	431	78	44	5.6	.906	SS-149
1916		72	.202	.249	193	39	5	2	0	0.0	18	15	12	20	10	11	1	117	148	30	13	4.1	.898	SS-51
1918		121	.213	.242	450	96	8	1	1	0.2	29	24	7	18	11	0	0	126	262	20	15	3.4	.951	3B-121
1919		2	.000	.000	7	0	0	0	0	0.0	1	0	0	0	0	0	0	4	3	1	0	4.0	.875	3B-2
6 yrs.		412	.231	.279	1478	341	49	8	2	0.1	166	77	86	104	46	11	1	678	1031	156	89	4.5	.916	SS-264, 3B-123

WORLD SERIES

Year	Team	Games	BA	SA	AB	H	2B	3B	HR	HR%	R	RBI	BB	SO	SB	AB	H	PO	A	E	DP	TC/G	FA	G by Pos
1916	BKN N	1	.000	.000	1	0	0	0	0	0.0	0	0	0	1	0	1	0	0	0	0	0	0.0	–	

Tom O'Meara

O'MEARA, THOMAS EDWARD
B. Dec. 12, 1872, Chicago, Ill.　D. Feb. 16, 1902, Ft. Wayne, Ind.

Year	Team	Games	BA	SA	AB	H	2B	3B	HR	HR%	R	RBI	BB	SO	SB	AB	H	PO	A	E	DP	TC/G	FA	G by Pos
1895	CLE N	1	.000	.000	1	0	0	0	0	0.0	1	0	1	0	0	0	0	0	1	1	0	2.0	.500	C-1
1896		12	.152	.152	33	5	0	0	0	0.0	5	0	5	7	0	2	0	29	6	3	0	3.2	.921	C-9, 1B-1
2 yrs.		13	.147	.147	34	5	0	0	0	0.0	6	0	6	7	0	2	0	29	7	4	0	3.1	.900	C-10, 1B-1

John O'Neil

O'NEIL, JOHN FRANCIS
B. Apr. 19, 1920, Shelbiana, Ky.　　　　BR TR 5'9" 155 lbs.

Year	Team	Games	BA	SA	AB	H	2B	3B	HR	HR%	R	RBI	BB	SO	SB	AB	H	PO	A	E	DP	TC/G	FA	G by Pos
1946	PHI N	46	.266	.298	94	25	3	0	0	0.0	12	9	5	12	0	3	0	51	75	8	15	2.9	.940	SS-32

Mickey O'Neil

O'NEIL, GEORGE MICHAEL
B. Apr. 12, 1900, St. Louis, Mo.　D. Apr. 8, 1964, St. Louis, Mo.　　　　BR TR 5'10" 185 lbs.

Year	Team	Games	BA	SA	AB	H	2B	3B	HR	HR%	R	RBI	BB	SO	SB	AB	H	PO	A	E	DP	TC/G	FA	G by Pos
1919	BOS N	11	.214	.214	28	6	0	0	0	0.0	3	1	1	7	0	0	0	33	19	1	3	4.8	.981	C-11
1920		112	.283	.326	304	86	5	4	0	0.0	19	28	21	20	4	7	3	304	153	18	10	4.2	.962	C-105, 2B-1
1921		98	.249	.332	277	69	9	4	2	0.7	26	29	23	21	2	3	0	276	117	13	8	4.1	.968	C-95
1922		83	.223	.259	251	56	5	2	0	0.0	18	26	14	11	1	3	0	239	70	7	3	3.8	.978	C-79
1923		96	.212	.261	306	65	7	4	0	0.0	29	20	17	14	3	1	0	298	104	11	5	4.3	.973	C-95
1924		106	.246	.262	362	89	4	1	0	0.0	32	22	14	27	4	0	0	362	108	7	8	4.5	.985	C-106
1925		70	.257	.356	222	57	6	5	2	0.9	29	30	21	16	1	1	0	208	31	7	3	3.5	.972	C-69
1926	BKN N	75	.209	.264	201	42	5	3	0	0.0	19	20	23	8	3	1	0	247	53	11	5	4.1	.965	C-74
1927	2 teams		WAS	A (5G – .000)		NY	N	(16G – .132)																
"	total	21	.114	.114	44	5	0	0	0	0.0	2	3	5	3	0	1	0	53	15	2	2	3.3	.971	C-20
9 yrs.		672	.238	.288	1995	475	41	23	4	0.2	177	179	139	127	18	17	3	2020	670	77	47	4.1	.972	C-654, 2B-1

Bill O'Neill

O'NEILL, WILLIAM JOHN
B. Jan. 22, 1880, St. John, N. B., Canada　D. July 27, 1920, St. John, N. B., Canada　　　　BB TR 5'11" 175 lbs.

Year	Team	Games	BA	SA	AB	H	2B	3B	HR	HR%	R	RBI	BB	SO	SB	AB	H	PO	A	E	DP	TC/G	FA	G by Pos
1904	2 teams		BOS	A (17G – .196)		WAS	A	(95G – .244)																
"	total	112	.238	.276	416	99	11	4	1	0.2	40	21	24		22	6	2	160	25	26	1	1.9	.877	OF-102, 2B-3, SS-2
1906	CHI A	94	.248	.276	330	82	4	1	1	0.3	37	21	22		19	1	0	118	12	7	1	1.5	.949	OF-93
2 yrs.		206	.243	.276	746	181	15	2	2	0.3	77	42	46		41	7	2	278	37	33	2	1.7	.905	OF-195, 2B-3, SS-2

WORLD SERIES

Year	Team	Games	BA	SA	AB	H	2B	3B	HR	HR%	R	RBI	BB	SO	SB	AB	H	PO	A	E	DP	TC/G	FA	G by Pos
1906	CHI A	1	.000	.000	1	0	0	0	0	0.0	0	0	1	0	0	0	0	1	0	0	0	1.0	1.000	OF-1

Dennie O'Neill

O'NEILL, DENNIS
B. Nov. 22, 1866, Holyoke, Mass.　D. Nov. 15, 1912, Rushville, Ind.　　　　TL 6'2½" 200 lbs.

Year	Team	Games	BA	SA	AB	H	2B	3B	HR	HR%	R	RBI	BB	SO	SB	AB	H	PO	A	E	DP	TC/G	FA	G by Pos
1893	STL N	7	.120	.120	25	3	0	0	0	0.0	3	2	4	0	3	0	0	68	0	1	3	9.9	.986	1B-7

Year	Team		Games	BA	SA	AB	H	2B	3B	HR	HR%	R	RBI	BB	SO	SB	Pinch Hit AB	H	PO	A	E	DP	TC/G	FA	G by Pos

Fred O'Neill

O'NEILL, FREDERICK JAMES
B. 1865, London, Ont., Canada D. Mar. 7, 1892, London, Ont., Canada   5'7" 142 lbs.

Year	Team		Games	BA	SA	AB	H	2B	3B	HR	HR%	R	RBI	BB	SO	SB	AB	H	PO	A	E	DP	TC/G	FA	G by Pos
1887	NY	AA	6	.308	.423	26	8	1	1	0	0.0	4		1		3	0	0	3	1	1	0	0.8	.800	OF-6

Harry O'Neill

O'NEILL, HARRY MINK
B. May 8, 1917, Philadelphia, Pa. D. Mar. 6, 1945, Iwo Jima, Marianas Is.   BR TR 6'3" 205 lbs.

Year	Team		Games	BA	SA	AB	H	2B	3B	HR	HR%	R	RBI	BB	SO	SB	AB	H	PO	A	E	DP	TC/G	FA	G by Pos
1939	PHI	A	1	–	–	0	0	0	0	0	–	0	0	0	0	0	0	0	0	0	0	0	0.0	–	C-1

Jack O'Neill

O'NEILL, JOHN JOSEPH
Brother of Jim O'Neill. Brother of Steve O'Neill.
Brother of Mike O'Neill.
B. Jan. 10, 1873, Galway, Ireland D. June 29, 1935, Scranton, Pa.   BR TR 5'10" 165 lbs.

Year	Team		Games	BA	SA	AB	H	2B	3B	HR	HR%	R	RBI	BB	SO	SB	AB	H	PO	A	E	DP	TC/G	FA	G by Pos
1902	STL	N	63	.141	.156	192	27	1	1	0	0.0	13	12	13		2	4	0	246	79	9	5	5.3	.973	C-59
1903			75	.236	.280	246	58	9	1	0	0.0	23	27	13		11	1	0	348	135	14	8	6.6	.972	C-74
1904	CHI	N	51	.214	.262	168	36	5	0	1	0.6	8	19	6		1	2	0	256	62	6	5	6.4	.981	C-49
1905			53	.198	.244	172	34	4	2	0	0.0	16	12	8		6	3	0	276	63	9	8	6.6	.974	C-50
1906	BOS	N	61	.180	.222	167	30	5	1	0	0.0	14	4	12		0	7	2	279	75	11	7	6.0	.970	C-48, 1B-2, OF-1
5 yrs.			303	.196	.235	945	185	24	5	1	0.1	74	74	52		20	17	2	1405	414	49	33	6.2	.974	C-280, 1B-2, OF-1

Jim O'Neill

O'NEILL, JAMES LEO
Brother of Steve O'Neill. Brother of Mike O'Neill.
Brother of Jack O'Neill.
B. Feb. 23, 1893, Minooka, Pa. D. Sept. 5, 1976, Chambersburg, Pa.   BR TR 5'10½" 165 lbs.

Year	Team		Games	BA	SA	AB	H	2B	3B	HR	HR%	R	RBI	BB	SO	SB	AB	H	PO	A	E	DP	TC/G	FA	G by Pos
1920	WAS	A	86	.289	.405	294	85	17	7	1	0.3	27	40	13	30	7	2	0	135	256	23	23	4.8	.944	SS-80, 2B-2
1923			23	.273	.303	33	9	1	0	0	0.0	6	3	1	3	0	2	0	19	26	3	5	2.1	.938	2B-8, 3B-6, OF-1
2 yrs.			109	.287	.394	327	94	18	7	1	0.3	33	43	14	33	7	4	0	154	282	26	28	4.2	.944	SS-80, 2B-10, 3B-6, OF-1

John O'Neill

O'NEILL, JOHN J
B. New York, N. Y.   TR

Year	Team		Games	BA	SA	AB	H	2B	3B	HR	HR%	R	RBI	BB	SO	SB	AB	H	PO	A	E	DP	TC/G	FA	G by Pos
1899	NY	N	2	.000	.000	7	0	0	0	0	0.0	0	0	0		0	0	0	9	4	1	1	7.0	.929	C-2
1902			2	.000	.000	8	0	0	0	0	0.0	0	0	0		0	0	0	10	4	1	0	7.5	.933	C-2
2 yrs.			4	.000	.000	15	0	0	0	0	0.0	0	0	0		0	0	0	19	8	2	1	7.3	.931	C-4

Mike O'Neill

O'NEILL, MICHAEL JOYCE
Played as Mike Joyce in 1901. Brother of Jim O'Neill.
Brother of Jack O'Neill. Brother of Steve O'Neill.
B. Sept. 7, 1877, Galway, Ireland D. Aug. 12, 1959, Scranton, Pa.   BR TR 5'11" 185 lbs.

Year	Team		Games	BA	SA	AB	H	2B	3B	HR	HR%	R	RBI	BB	SO	SB	AB	H	PO	A	E	DP	TC/G	FA	G by Pos
1901	STL	N	6	.400	.400	15	6	0	0	0	0.0	3	2	3		0	1	1	1	6	1	0	1.3	.875	P-5
1902			51	.319	.444	135	43	5	3	2	1.5	21	15	2		0	12	1	24	73	8	0	2.1	.924	P-36, OF-3
1903			41	.227	.282	110	25	2	2	0	0.0	12	6	8		3	7	3	28	41	6	3	1.8	.920	P-19, OF-13
1904			30	.231	.352	91	21	7	2	0	0.0	9	16	5		0	2	1	16	69	8	3	3.1	.914	P-25, OF-3
1907	CIN	N	9	.069	.207	29	2	0	2	0	0.0	5	2	2		1	0	0	18	1	3	0	2.4	.864	OF-9
5 yrs.			137	.255	.355	380	97	14	9	2	0.5	50	41	20		4	22	6	87	190	26	6	2.2	.914	P-85, OF-28

Paul O'Neill

O'NEILL, PAUL ANDREW
B. Feb. 25, 1963, Columbus, Ohio   BL TL 6'4" 200 lbs.

Year	Team		Games	BA	SA	AB	H	2B	3B	HR	HR%	R	RBI	BB	SO	SB	AB	H	PO	A	E	DP	TC/G	FA	G by Pos
1985	CIN	N	5	.333	.417	12	4	1	0	0	0.0	1	1	0	2	0	3	1	3	1	0	0	0.8	1.000	OF-2
1986			3	.000	.000	2	0	0	0	0	0.0	0	0	1	1	0	2	0	0	0	0	0	0.0	–	
1987			84	.256	.488	160	41	14	1	7	4.4	24	28	18	29	2	37	11	90	2	4	2	1.1	.958	OF-42, 1B-2, P-1
1988			145	.252	.414	485	122	25	3	16	3.3	58	73	38	65	8	11	0	410	13	6	14	3.0	.986	OF-139
1989			117	.276	.446	428	118	24	2	15	3.5	49	74	46	64	20	3	3	223	7	4	1	2.0	.983	OF-115
5 yrs.			354	.262	.437	1087	285	64	6	38	3.5	132	176	103	161	30	56	15	726	23	14	17	2.2	.982	OF-298, 1B-2, P-1

Peaches O'Neill

O'NEILL, PHILIP BERNARD
B. Aug. 30, 1879, Anderson, Ind. D. Aug. 2, 1955, Anderson, Ind.   BR TR 5'11" 165 lbs.

Year	Team		Games	BA	SA	AB	H	2B	3B	HR	HR%	R	RBI	BB	SO	SB	AB	H	PO	A	E	DP	TC/G	FA	G by Pos
1904	CIN	N	8	.267	.267	15	4	0	0	0	0.0	0	1	1		0	2	0	7	2	1	0	1.3	.900	C-5, 1B-1

Steve O'Neill

O'NEILL, STEPHEN FRANCIS
Brother of Jim O'Neill. Brother of Jack O'Neill.
Brother of Mike O'Neill.
B. July 6, 1891, Minooka, Pa. D. Jan. 26, 1962, Cleveland, Ohio   BR TR 5'10" 165 lbs.
Manager 1935-37, 1943-48, 1950-54.

Year	Team		Games	BA	SA	AB	H	2B	3B	HR	HR%	R	RBI	BB	SO	SB	AB	H	PO	A	E	DP	TC/G	FA	G by Pos
1911	CLE	A	9	.148	.185	27	4	1	0	0	0.0	1	4			2	0	0	55	17	1	1	8.1	.986	C-9
1912			68	.228	.247	215	49	4	0	0	0.0	17	14	12		2	1	0	316	108	17	9	6.5	.961	C-67
1913			78	.295	.376	234	69	13	3	0	0.0	19	29	10	24	1	4	1	353	119	13	9	6.2	.973	C-78
1914			86	.253	.312	269	68	12	2	0	0.0	28	20	15	35	1	4	1	394	134	24	23	6.4	.957	C-81, 1B-1
1915			121	.236	.298	386	91	14	2	2	0.5	32	34	26	41	2	6	1	556	175	24	17	6.2	.968	C-115
1916			130	.235	.296	378	89	23	0	0	0.0	30	29	24	33	2	2	1	540	154	21	36	5.5	.971	C-128
1917			129	.184	.222	370	68	10	2	0	0.0	21	29	41	55	2	2	1	446	145	12	19	4.7	.980	C-127
1918			114	.242	.312	359	87	8	7	1	0.3	34	35	48	22	5	1	0	409	154	10	10	5.0	.983	C-113
1919			125	.289	.427	398	115	35	7	2	0.5	46	47	48	21	4	2	0	472	125	14	13	4.9	.977	C-123
1920			149	.321	.440	489	157	39	5	3	0.6	63	55	69	39	3	1	0	576	128	17	1	4.8	.976	C-148
1921			106	.322	.403	335	108	22	1	0	0.0	39	50	57	22	0	1	0	393	92	9	8	4.7	.982	C-105
1922			133	.311	.416	392	122	27	4	2	0.5	33	65	73	25	2	2	0	450	116	15	9	4.4	.974	C-130
1923			113	.248	.285	330	82	12	0	0	0.0	31	50	64	34	2	0	0	354	68	14	3	3.9	.968	C-111
1924	BOS	A	106	.238	.293	307	73	15	1	0	0.0	29	38	63	23	0	14	2	342	75	13	2	4.1	.970	C-92
1925	NY	A	35	.286	.374	91	26	5	0	1	1.1	7	13	10	3	0	3	0	113	27	8	8	4.2	.946	C-31
1927	STL	A	74	.230	.283	191	44	7	0	1	0.5	14	22	20	6	0	13	5	180	57	4	8	3.3	.983	C-60

Year	Team		Games	BA	SA	AB	H	2B	3B	HR	HR%	R	RBI	BB	SO	SB	Pinch Hit AB	H	PO	A	E	DP	TC/G	FA	G by Pos

Steve O'Neill *continued*

Year	Team		Games	BA	SA	AB	H	2B	3B	HR	HR%	R	RBI	BB	SO	SB	AB	H	PO	A	E	DP	TC/G	FA	G by Pos
1928			10	.292	.333	24	7	1	0	0	0.0	4	6	8	0	0	0	0	19	4	1	0	2.4	.958	C-10
17 yrs.			1586	.263	.337	4795	1259	248	34	13	0.3	448	537	592	383	30	54	10	5968	1698	217	176	5.0	.972	C-1528, 1B-1

WORLD SERIES

| 1920 | CLE | A | 7 | .333 | .476 | 21 | 7 | 3 | 0 | 0 | 0.0 | 1 | 2 | 4 | 3 | 0 | 0 | 0 | 23 | 6 | 1 | 2 | 4.3 | .967 | C-7 |

Tip O'Neill

O'NEILL, JAMES EDWARD
B. May 25, 1858, Woodstock, Ont., Canada D. Dec. 31, 1915, Montreal Que., Canada
BR TR 6'1½" 167 lbs.

1883	NY	N	23	.197	.237	76	15	3	0	0	0.0	8		3	15		0	0	17	24	5	0	2.0	.891	P-19, OF-7
1884	STL	AA	78	.276	.424	297	82	13	11	3	1.0	49		12			0	0	75	37	22	1	1.7	.836	OF-64, P-17, 1B-1
1885			52	.350	.466	206	72	7	4	3	1.5	44		13			0	0	83	6	12	1	1.9	.881	OF-52
1886			138	.328	.440	579	190	28	14	3	0.5	106		47			0	0	279	14	23	4	2.3	.927	OF-138
1887			124	**.435**	**.691**	517	**225**	**52**	**19**	**14**	2.7	**167**		50		30	0	0	247	8	30	2	2.3	.895	OF-124
1888			130	**.335**	.446	529	**177**	24	10	5	0.9	96	98	44		26	0	0	231	8	16	1	2.0	.937	OF-130
1889			134	.335	.478	534	179	33	8	9	1.7	123	110	72	37	28	0	0	264	12	19	3	2.2	.936	OF-134
1890	CHI	P	137	.302	.407	577	174	20	16	3	0.5	112	75	65	36	29	0	0	231	8	19	1	1.9	.926	OF-137
1891	STL	AA	129	.321	.447	521	167	28	4	10	1.9	112	95	62	33	25	0	0	197	5	14	0	1.7	.935	OF-129
1892	CIN	N	109	.251	.327	419	105	14	6	2	0.5	63	52	53	25	14	0	0	188	13	17	3	2.0	.922	OF-109
10 yrs.			1054	.326	.458	4255	1386	222	92	52	1.2	880	430	421	146	152	0	0	1812	135	177	16	2.0	.917	OF-1024, P-36, 1B-1

Curly Onis

ONIS, MANUEL DOMINGUEZ (Ralph)
B. Oct. 24, 1908, Tampa, Fla.
BR TR 5'9" 180 lbs.

| 1935 | BKN | N | 1 | 1.000 | 1.000 | 1 | 1 | 0 | 0 | 0 | 0.0 | 0 | 0 | 0 | 0 | 0 | 0 | 0 | 1 | 0 | 1 | 0 | 2.0 | .500 | C-1 |

Eddie Onslow

ONSLOW, EDWARD JOSEPH
Brother of Jack Onslow.
B. Feb. 17, 1893, Meadville, Pa. D. May 8, 1981, Dennison, Ohio
BL TL 6' 170 lbs.

1912	DET	A	35	.227	.289	128	29	1	2	1	0.8	11	13	3		3	0	0	408	15	12	19	12.4	.972	1B-35
1913			17	.255	.273	55	14	1	0	0	0.0	7	8	5	9	1	0	0	191	7	2	9	11.8	.990	1B-17
1918	CLE	A	2	.167	.167	6	1	0	0	0	0.0	0	0	0	1	0	0	0	0	0	1	0	0.5	—	OF-1
1927	WAS	A	9	.222	.278	18	4	1	0	0	0.0	1	1	1	0	0	3	0	29	2	0	3	3.4	1.000	1B-5
4 yrs.			63	.232	.280	207	48	3	2	1	0.5	19	22	9	10	4	4	0	628	24	15	31	10.6	.978	1B-57, OF-1

Jack Onslow

ONSLOW, JOHN JAMES
Brother of Eddie Onslow.
B. Oct. 13, 1888, Scottdale, Pa. D. Dec. 22, 1960, Concord, Mass.
Manager 1949-50.
BR TR 5'11" 180 lbs.

1912	DET	A	31	.159	.174	69	11	1	0	0	0.0	7	4	10		1	0	0	109	38	8	4	5.0	.948	C-31
1917	NY	N	9	.250	.375	8	2	1	0	0	0.0	1	0	0		0	0	0	11	2	1	0	1.6	.929	C-9
2 yrs.			40	.169	.195	77	13	2	0	0	0.0	8	4	10		1	0	0	120	40	9	4	4.2	.947	C-40

Steve Ontiveros

ONTIVEROS, STEVEN ROBERT
B. Oct. 26, 1951, Bakersfield, Calif.
BB TR 6' 185 lbs.

1973	SF	N	24	.242	.333	33	8	0	0	1	3.0	3	5	4	7	0	17	5	36	6	0	2	1.8	1.000	1B-5, OF-1
1974			120	.265	.350	343	91	15	1	4	1.2	45	33	57	41	0	23	4	225	158	19	30	3.4	.953	3B-75, 1B-19, OF-2
1975			108	.289	.366	325	94	16	0	3	0.9	31	31	55	44	2	11	2	80	189	21	15	2.7	.928	3B-89, OF-8, 1B-4
1976			59	.176	.216	74	13	3	0	0	0.0	8	5	6	11	0	44	8	18	8	2	2	0.5	.929	OF-7, 3B-7, 1B-4
1977	CHI	N	156	.299	.423	546	163	32	3	10	1.8	54	68	81	69	3	3	1	100	324	20	24	2.8	.955	3B-155
1978			82	.243	.333	276	67	14	4	1	0.4	34	22	34	33	0	4	2	64	194	9	16	3.3	.966	3B-77, 1B-1
1979			152	.285	.370	519	148	28	2	4	0.8	58	57	58	68	0	9	3	105	269	23	28	2.6	.942	3B-142, 1B-1
1980			31	.208	.286	77	16	3	0	1	1.3	7	3	14	17	0	6	0	13	39	4	1	1.8	.929	3B-24
8 yrs.			732	.274	.366	2193	600	111	10	24	1.1	230	224	309	290	5	117	25	641	1187	98	118	2.6	.949	3B-569, 1B-34, OF-18

Jose Oquendo

OQUENDO, JOSE MANUEL
Born Jose Manuel Oquendo y Contreras.
B. July 4, 1963, Rio Peidras, Puerto Rico
BB TR 5'10" 160 lbs.
BR 1984

1983	NY	N	120	.213	.244	328	70	7	0	1	0.3	29	17	19	60	8	1	0	182	326	21	65	4.4	.960	SS-116
1984			81	.222	.249	189	42	5	0	0	0.0	23	10	15	26	10	3	2	95	152	7	33	3.1	.972	SS-67
1986	STL	N	76	.297	.341	138	41	4	1	0	0.0	20	13	15	20	2	27	6	52	94	8	23	2.0	.948	SS-29, 2B-21, OF-1, 3B-1
1987			116	.286	.335	248	71	9	0	1	0.4	43	24	54	29	4	26	10	149	133	4	31	2.5	.986	OF-46, 2B-32, SS-23, 3B-8, 1B-3, P-1
1988			148	.277	.350	451	125	10	1	7	1.6	36	46	52	40	4	10	2	268	315	11	61	4.0	.981	2B-69, 3B-47, SS-17, 1B-16, OF-15, C-1, P-1
1989			163	.291	.372	556	162	28	7	1	0.2	59	48	79	59	3	1	1	356	523	6	108	5.4	.993	2B-156, SS-7, 1B-1
6 yrs.			704	.268	.326	1910	511	63	9	10	0.5	210	158	234	234	31	68	21	1102	1543	57	321	3.8	.979	2B-278, SS-259, OF-62, 3B-56, 1B-20, P-2, C-1

LEAGUE CHAMPIONSHIP SERIES

| 1987 | STL | N | 5 | .167 | .417 | 12 | 2 | 0 | 0 | 1 | 8.3 | 3 | 4 | 3 | 4 | 0 | 0 | 0 | 7 | 0 | 0 | 0 | 1.4 | 1.000 | OF-5, 3B-1 |

WORLD SERIES

| 1987 | STL | N | 7 | .250 | .250 | 24 | 6 | 0 | 0 | 0 | 0.0 | 2 | 2 | 1 | 4 | 0 | 0 | 0 | 8 | 10 | 0 | 0 | 2.6 | 1.000 | 3B-4, OF-3 |

Ernie Oravetz

ORAVETZ, ERNEST EUGENE
B. Jan. 24, 1932, Johnstown, Pa.
BB TL 5'4" 145 lbs.

1955	WAS	A	100	.270	.297	263	71	5	1	0	0.0	24	25	26	19	1	35	6	117	1	4	0	1.2	.967	OF-57
1956			88	.248	.299	137	34	3	2	0	0.0	20	11	27	20	1	**49**	11	51	2	3	0	0.6	.946	OF-31
2 yrs.			188	.263	.298	400	105	8	3	0	0.0	44	36	53	39	2	84	17	168	3	7	0	0.9	.961	OF-88

Tony Ordenana

ORDENANA, ANTONIO
Born Antonio Ordenana y Rodriguez.
B. Oct. 30, 1918, Guanabacoa, Cuba D. Sept. 29, 1988, Miami, Fla.
BR TR 5'9" 158 lbs.

Year	Team		Games	BA	SA	AB	H	2B	3B	HR	HR%	R	RBI	BB	SO	SB	Pinch Hit AB	Pinch Hit H	PO	A	E	DP	TC/G	FA	G by Pos

Tony Ordenana *continued*

Year	Team		Games	BA	SA	AB	H	2B	3B	HR	HR%	R	RBI	BB	SO	SB	AB	H	PO	A	E	DP	TC/G	FA	G by Pos
1943	PIT	N	1	.500	.500	4	2	0	0	0	0.0	0	3	0	0	0	0	0	2	5	0	1	7.0	1.000	SS-1

Joe Orengo

ORENGO, JOSEPH CHARLES
B. Nov. 29, 1914, San Francisco, Calif. D. July 24, 1988, San Francisco, Calif.
BR TR 6' 185 lbs.

Year	Team		Games	BA	SA	AB	H	2B	3B	HR	HR%	R	RBI	BB	SO	SB	AB	H	PO	A	E	DP	TC/G	FA	G by Pos
1939	STL	N	7	.000	.000	3	0	0	0	0	0.0	0	0	0	0	0	0	0	3	3	3	0	1.3	.667	SS-7
1940			129	.287	.412	415	119	23	4	7	1.7	58	56	65	90	9	0	0	281	318	29	65	4.9	.954	2B-77, 3B-34, SS-19
1941	NY	N	77	.214	.321	252	54	11	2	4	1.6	23	25	28	49	1	3	1	117	189	10	22	4.1	.968	3B-59, SS-9, 2B-6
1943	2 teams		NY	N (83G – .218)			BKN	N	(7G – .200)																	
"	total		90	.217	.331	281	61	10	2	6	2.1	29	30	40	48	1	2	2	734	70	6	49	9.0	.993	1B-82, 3B-6
1944	DET	A	46	.201	.266	154	31	10	0	0	0.0	14	10	20	29	1	1	0	124	124	20	24	5.8	.925	SS-29, 3B-11, 1B-5, 2B-2
1945	CHI	A	17	.067	.067	15	1	0	0	0	0.0	5	1	3	2	0	5	0	5	7	1	0	0.8	.923	3B-7, 2B-1
6 yrs.			366	.238	.346	1120	266	54	8	17	1.5	129	122	156	219	12	11	3	1264	711	69	160	5.6	.966	3B-117, 1B-87, 2B-86, SS-64

George Orme

ORME, GEORGE WILLIAM
B. Sept. 16, 1891, Lebanon, Ind. D. Mar. 16, 1962, Indianapolis, Ind.
BR TR 5'10" 160 lbs.

Year	Team		Games	BA	SA	AB	H	2B	3B	HR	HR%	R	RBI	BB	SO	SB	AB	H	PO	A	E	DP	TC/G	FA	G by Pos
1920	BOS	A	4	.333	.333	6	2	0	0	0	0.0	4	1	3	0	0	0	0	8	0	0	0	2.0	1.000	OF-3

Jess Orndorff

ORNDORFF, JESSE WALWORTH THAYER
B. Jan. 15, 1881, Chicago, Ill. D. Sept. 28, 1960, Cardiff-By-The-Sea, Calif.
BB TR 6' 168 lbs.

Year	Team		Games	BA	SA	AB	H	2B	3B	HR	HR%	R	RBI	BB	SO	SB	AB	H	PO	A	E	DP	TC/G	FA	G by Pos
1907	BOS	N	5	.118	.118	17	2	0	0	0	0.0	0		0	0	0	0	0	11	7	2	0	4.0	.900	C-5

Charlie O'Rourke

O'ROURKE, JAMES PATRICK
B. June 22, 1937, Walla Walla, Wash.
BR TR 6'2" 195 lbs.

Year	Team		Games	BA	SA	AB	H	2B	3B	HR	HR%	R	RBI	BB	SO	SB	AB	H	PO	A	E	DP	TC/G	FA	G by Pos
1959	STL	N	2	.000	.000	2	0	0	0	0	0.0	0	0	0	0	0	2	0	0	0	0	0	0.0	—	

Frank O'Rourke

O'ROURKE, JAMES FRANCIS (Blackie)
B. Nov. 28, 1894, Hamilton, Ont., Canada D. May 14, 1986, Chatham, N. J.
BR TR 5'10½" 165 lbs.

Year	Team		Games	BA	SA	AB	H	2B	3B	HR	HR%	R	RBI	BB	SO	SB	AB	H	PO	A	E	DP	TC/G	FA	G by Pos
1912	BOS	N	61	.122	.148	196	24	3	1	0	0.0	11	16	11	50	1	0	0	92	167	24	16	4.6	.915	SS-59
1917	BKN	N	64	.237	.283	198	47	7	1	0	0.0	18	15	14	25	11	4	0	72	134	10	6	3.4	.954	3B-58
1918			4	.167	.167	12	2	0	0	0	0.0	0	2	1	3	0	1	1	3	11	2	1	4.0	.875	2B-2, OF-1
1920	WAS	A	14	.296	.315	54	16	1	0	0	0.0	8	5	2	5	2	0	0	38	47	4	12	6.4	.955	SS-13, 3B-1
1921			123	.234	.329	444	104	17	8	3	0.7	51	54	26	56	6	0	0	272	378	55	52	5.7	.922	SS-122
1922	BOS	A	67	.264	.370	216	57	14	3	1	0.5	28	17	20	28	6	0	0	98	170	24	18	4.4	.918	SS-48, 3B-19
1924	DET	A	47	.276	.359	181	50	11	2	0	0.0	28	19	12	19	7	0	0	127	165	11	28	6.4	.964	2B-40, SS-7
1925			124	.293	.436	482	141	40	7	5	1.0	88	57	32	37	5	0	0	316	391	22	67	5.9	.970	2B-118, 3B-6
1926			111	.242	.300	363	88	16	1	1	0.3	43	41	35	33	8	0	0	191	264	24	43	4.3	.950	3B-58, 2B-41, SS-10
1927	STL	A	140	.268	.331	538	144	25	3	1	0.2	85	39	64	43	19	2	0	246	299	23	47	4.1	.960	3B-120, 2B-16, 1B-3
1928			99	.263	.348	391	103	24	3	1	0.3	54	62	21	19	10	3	0	150	162	15	13	3.3	.954	3B-96, SS-2
1929			154	.251	.332	585	147	23	9	2	0.3	81	62	41	28	14	0	0	184	255	25	32	3.0	.946	3B-151, 2B-3, SS-2
1930			115	.268	.333	400	107	15	4	1	0.3	52	41	35	30	11	4	1	167	235	19	30	3.7	.955	3B-84, SS-23, 1B-3
1931			8	.222	.222	9	2	0	0	0	0.0	0	0	0	1	1	3	1	15	3	0	0	2.3	1.000	SS-2, 1B-1
14 yrs.			1131	.254	.333	4069	1032	196	42	15	0.4	547	430	314	377	101	20	2	1971	2681	258	365	4.3	.947	3B-593, SS-288, 2B-220, 1B-7, OF-1

Jim O'Rourke

O'ROURKE, JAMES HENRY (Orator Jim)
Brother of John O'Rourke.
B. Sept. 1, 1850, Bridgeport, Conn. D. Jan. 8, 1919, Bridgeport, Conn.
Manager 1881-84, 1893.
Hall of Fame 1945.
BR TR 5'8" 185 lbs.

Year	Team		Games	BA	SA	AB	H	2B	3B	HR	HR%	R	RBI	BB	SO	SB	AB	H	PO	A	E	DP	TC/G	FA	G by Pos
1876	BOS	N	70	.327	.420	312	102	17	3	2	0.6	61	43	15	17		0	0	170	7	28	1	2.9	.863	OF-68, 1B-2, C-1
1877			61	.362	.445	265	96	14	4	0	0.0	68	23	20	9		0	0	118	9	23	2	2.5	.847	OF-60, 1B-1
1878			60	.278	.412	255	71	17	7	1	0.4	44	29	5	21		0	0	124	17	22	5	2.7	.865	OF-57, 1B-2, C-2
1879	PRO	N	81	.348	.459	362	126	19	9	1	0.3	69	46	13	10		0	0	302	29	34	6	4.5	.907	OF-56, 1B-20, C-5, 3B-3
1880	BOS	N	86	.275	.441	363	100	20	11	6	1.7	71	45	21	16		0	0	268	96	43	18	4.7	.894	OF-37, 1B-19, SS-17, 3B-10, C-9
1881	BUF	N	83	.302	.402	348	105	21	7	0	0.0	71	30	27	18		0	0	148	97	47	8	3.5	.839	3B-56, OF-18, C-8, SS-3, 1B-1
1882			84	.281	.370	370	104	15	6	2	0.5	62		13	13		0	0	149	17	26	3	2.3	.865	OF-81, SS-2, C-2, 3B-1
1883			94	.328	.438	436	143	29	8	1	0.2	102		15	13		0	0	226	61	39	2	3.5	.880	OF-61, C-33, 3B-8, SS-3, P-2
1884			108	.347	.480	467	162	33	7	5	1.1	119		35	17		0	0	350	23	30	12	3.7	.926	OF-86, 1B-18, C-10, P-4, 3B-1
1885	NY	N	112	.300	.442	477	143	21	16	5	1.0	119		40	21		0	0	182	13	15	0	1.9	.929	OF-112, C-8
1886			105	.309	.402	440	136	26	6	1	0.2	106	34	39	21		0	0	369	96	28	5	4.7	.943	OF-63, C-47, 1B-2
1887			103	.285	.411	397	113	15	13	3	0.8	73	50	36	11	46	0	0	248	127	48	7	4.1	.887	C-40, 3B-38, OF-28, 2B-2
1888			107	.274	.372	409	112	16	4	4	1.0	50	50	24	30	25	0	0	251	40	14	4	2.9	.954	OF-87, C-15, 1B-4, 3B-2
1889			128	.321	.438	502	161	36	7	3	0.6	89	81	40	34	33	0	0	166	20	22	2	1.6	.894	OF-128, C-1
1890	NY	P	111	.360	.515	478	172	37	5	9	1.9	112	115	33	20	23	0	0	175	25	15	3	1.9	.930	OF-111
1891	NY	N	136	.295	.398	555	164	28	7	5	0.9	92	95	26	29	19	0	0	244	44	26	3	2.3	.917	OF-126, C-14
1892			115	.304	.388	448	136	28	5	0	0.0	62	56	30	30	16	0	0	168	17	17	2	1.8	.916	OF-111, C-4, 1B-1
1893	WAS	N	129	.287	.362	547	157	22	5	3	0.5	75	95	49	26	15	0	0	487	52	27	19	4.4	.952	OF-87, 1B-33, C-9
1904	NY	N	1	.250	.250	4	1	0	0	0	0.0	1	0	0	1	0	0	0	5	0	0	0	5.0	.800	C-1
19 yrs.			1774	.310	.422	7435	2304	414	132	51	0.7	1446	830	481	348	177	0	0	4149	790	505	102	3.1	.907	OF-1377, C-209, 3B-119, 1B-103, SS-25, P-6, 2B-2

Joe O'Rourke

O'ROURKE, JOSEPH LEO, JR.
Son of Patsy O'Rourke.
B. Oct. 28, 1904, Philadelphia, Pa.
BL TR 5'7" 145 lbs.

Year	Team		Games	BA	SA	AB	H	2B	3B	HR	HR%	R	RBI	BB	SO	SB	AB	H	PO	A	E	DP	TC/G	FA	G by Pos
1929	PHI	N	3	.000	.000	3	0	0	0	0	0.0	0	0	0	1	0	3	0	0	0	0	0	0.0	—	

Year	Team		Games	BA	SA	AB	H	2B	3B	HR	HR%	R	RBI	BB	SO	SB	Pinch Hit AB	H	PO	A	E	DP	TC/G	FA	G by Pos

John O'Rourke

O'ROURKE, JOHN
Brother of Jim O'Rourke.
B. Aug. 23, 1849, Bridgeport, Conn. D. June 23, 1911, Boston, Mass.
BL TL 6' 190 lbs.

1879	BOS	N	72	.341	.521	317	108	17	11	6	1.9	69	62	8	32		0	0	147	10	21	2	2.5	.882	OF-71
1880			81	.275	.425	313	86	22	8	3	1.0	30	36	18	32		0	0	156	19	26	0	2.5	.871	OF-81
1883	NY	AA	77	.270	.381	315	85	19	5	2	0.6	49		21			0	0	104	12	21	2	1.8	.847	OF-76, 1B-1
3 yrs.			230	.295	.442	945	279	58	24	11	1.2	148	98	47	64		0	0	407	41	68	4	2.2	.868	OF-228, 1B-1

Patsy O'Rourke

O'ROURKE, JOSEPH LEO, SR.
Father of Joe O'Rourke.
B. Apr. 13, 1881, Philadelphia, Pa. D. Apr. 18, 1956, Philadelphia, Pa.
BR TR 5'7" 160 lbs.

| 1908 | STL | N | 53 | .195 | .244 | 164 | 32 | 4 | 2 | 0 | 0.0 | 8 | 16 | 14 | | | 2 | 0 | 80 | 171 | 41 | 10 | 5.5 | .860 | SS-53 |

Queenie O'Rourke

O'ROURKE, JAMES STEPHEN
Son of Jim O'Rourke.
B. Dec. 26, 1883, Bridgeport, Conn. D. Dec. 22, 1955, Sparrows Point, Md.
BR TR 5'7" 150 lbs.

| 1908 | NY | A | 34 | .231 | .241 | 108 | 25 | 1 | 0 | 0 | 0.0 | 5 | 3 | 4 | | | 4 | 2 | 0 | 43 | 44 | 6 | 4 | 2.7 | .935 | OF-14, SS-11, 2B-4, 3B-3 |

Tim O'Rourke

O'ROURKE, TIMOTHY PATRICK (Voiceless Tim)
B. May 18, 1864, Chicago, Ill. D. Apr. 20, 1938, Seattle, Wash.
BL TR 5'10" 170 lbs.

1890	SYR	AA	87	.283	.367	332	94	13	6	1	0.3	48		36		22	0	0	117	168	44	9	3.8	.866	3B-87
1891	COL	AA	34	.279	.331	136	38	1	3	0	0.0	22	12	15	7	9	0	0	48	76	17	7	4.1	.879	3B-34
1892	BAL	N	63	.310	.377	239	74	8	4	0	0.0	40	35	24	19	12	0	0	105	181	45	17	5.3	.864	SS-58, OF-4, 3B-1
1893	2 teams	BAL N (31G – .363)		LOU N (92G – .281)																					
"	total		123	.304	.349	487	148	12	5	0	0.0	102	72	89	19	27	0	0	203	202	55	28	3.7	.880	SS-61, OF-51, 3B-11
1894	3 teams	LOU N (55G – .277)		STL N (18G – .282)		WAS N (7G – .200)																			
"	total		80	.272	.332	316	86	9	5	0	0.0	60	39	33	13	11	0	0	369	94	36	39	6.2	.928	1B-30, 3B-21, OF-18, SS-6, 2B-5
5 yrs.			387	.291	.352	1510	440	43	23	1	0.1	272	158	197	58	81	0	0	842	721	197	100	4.5	.888	3B-154, SS-125, OF-73, 1B-30, 2B-5

Tom O'Rourke

O'ROURKE, THOMAS JOSEPH
B. 1863, New York, N. Y. D. July 19, 1929, New York, N. Y.
TR 5'9" 158 lbs.

1887	BOS	N	22	.154	.192	78	12	3	0	0	0.0	12	10	7	6	4	0	0	81	29	32	3	6.5	.775	C-21, OF-1, 3B-1
1888			20	.176	.176	74	13	0	0	0	0.0	3	4	1	9	2	0	0	89	37	17	1	7.2	.881	C-20, OF-1
1890	2 teams	NY N (2G – .000)		SYR AA (41G – .216)																					
"	total		43	.206	.256	160	33	8	0	0	0.0	17		13		2	0	0	213	54	27	6	6.8	.908	C-42, 1B-1
3 yrs.			85	.186	.221	312	58	11	0	0	0.0	32	14	21	15	8	0	0	383	120	76	10	6.8	.869	C-83, OF-2, 3B-1, 1B-1

Bill Orr

ORR, WILLIAM JOHN
B. Apr. 22, 1891, San Francisco, Calif. D. Mar. 10, 1967, Santarium, Calif.
BR TR 5'11" 168 lbs.

1913	PHI	A	27	.194	.239	67	13	1	1	0	0.0	6	7	4	10	1	1	0	57	41	6	3	3.9	.942	SS-16, 1B-3, 3B-2, 2B-2
1914			10	.167	.292	24	4	1	1	0	0.0	3	1	2	5	1	3	1	4	13	5	0	2.2	.773	SS-6, 3B-1
2 yrs.			37	.187	.253	91	17	2	2	0	0.0	9	8	6	15	2	4	1	61	54	11	3	3.4	.913	SS-22, 3B-3, 1B-3, 2B-2

Dave Orr

ORR, DAVID L.
B. Sept. 29, 1859, New York, N. Y. D. June 3, 1915, Brooklyn, N. Y.
Manager 1887.
BL TR 5'11" 250 lbs.

1883	2 teams	NY AA (13G – .320)		NY N (1G – .000)																					
"	total		14	.302	.604	53	16	4	3	2	3.8	6		0	1		0	0	148	1	9	4	11.3	.943	1B-13, OF-1
1884	NY	AA	110	.354	.539	458	162	32	13	9	2.0	82		5			0	0	1163	24	49	30	11.2	.960	1B-110, OF-3
1885			107	.342	.543	444	152	29	21	6	1.4	76		8			0	0	1089	20	39	48	10.7	.966	1B-107, P-3
1886			136	.338	.527	571	193	25	31	7	1.2	93		17			0	0	1445	34	28	62	11.1	.981	1B-136
1887			84	.368	.516	345	127	25	10	2	0.6	63		22		17	0	0	810	28	28	41	10.3	.968	1B-81, OF-3
1888	BKN	AA	99	.305	.388	394	120	20	5	1	0.3	57	59	7		11	0	0	976	44	22	41	10.5	.979	1B-99
1889	COL	AA	134	.327	.446	560	183	31	12	4	0.7	70	87	9	38	12	0	0	1291	61	23	64	10.3	.983	1B-134
1890	BKN	P	107	.373	.537	464	173	32	13	6	1.3	89	124	30	11	10	0	0	1009	42	30	67	10.1	.972	1B-107
8 yrs.			791	.342	.502	3289	1126	198	108	37	1.1	536	270	98	50	50	0	0	7931	254	228	357	10.6	.973	1B-787, OF-7, P-3

Ernie Orsatti

ORSATTI, ERNEST RALPH
B. Sept. 8, 1902, Los Angeles, Calif. D. Sept. 4, 1968, Canoga Park, Calif.
BL TL 5'7½" 154 lbs.

1927	STL	N	27	.315	.457	92	29	7	3	0	0.0	15	12	11	12	2	1	0	56	3	5	2	2.4	.922	OF-26
1928			27	.304	.522	69	21	6	0	3	4.3	10	15	10	11	0	3	0	70	3	1	2	2.7	.986	OF-17, 1B-5
1929			113	.332	.460	346	115	21	7	3	0.9	64	39	33	43	7	17	6	259	14	6	9	2.5	.978	OF-77, 1B-10
1930			48	.321	.466	131	42	8	4	1	0.8	24	15	12	18	1	12	3	210	19	3	19	4.8	.987	1B-22, OF-11
1931			78	.291	.468	158	46	16	6	0	0.0	27	19	14	16	1	15	2	94	1	2	0	1.2	.979	OF-45, 1B-1
1932			101	.336	.456	375	126	27	6	2	0.5	44	44	18	29	5	3	2	207	3	6	1	2.1	.972	OF-96, 1B-1
1933			120	.298	.374	436	130	21	6	0	0.0	55	38	33	33	14	9	3	299	5	5	3	2.6	.984	OF-101, 1B-3
1934			105	.300	.365	337	101	14	4	0	0.0	39	31	27	31	6	10	2	207	5	3	0	2.0	.986	OF-90
1935			90	.240	.321	221	53	9	3	1	0.5	28	24	18	26	5	23	5	115	3	3	2	1.3	.975	OF-60
9 yrs.			709	.306	.416	2165	663	129	39	10	0.5	306	237	176	218	46	93	23	1517	56	34	38	2.3	.979	OF-523, 1B-42
WORLD SERIES																									
1928	STL	N	4	.286	.429	7	2	1	0	0	0.0	1	0	1	3	0	2	0	4	0	0	0	1.0	1.000	OF-1
1930			1	.000	.000	1	0	0	0	0	0.0	0	0	0	0	0	1	0	0	0	0	0	0.0	–	
1931			1	.000	.000	3	0	0	0	0	0.0	0	0	0	3	0	0	0	1	0	0	0	1.0	1.000	OF-1
1934			7	.318	.409	22	7	0	1	0	0.0	3	1	3	1	0	1	0	16	1	2	0	2.7	.895	OF-6
4 yrs.			13	.273	.364	33	9	1	1	0	0.0	4	2	4	7	0	4	0	21	1	2	0	1.8	.917	OF-8

John Orsino

ORSINO, JOHN JOSEPH (Horse)
B. Apr. 22, 1938, Teaneck, N. J.
BR TR 6'3" 215 lbs.

| 1961 | SF | N | 25 | .277 | .506 | 83 | 23 | 3 | 2 | 4 | 4.8 | 5 | 12 | 3 | 13 | 0 | 3 | 2 | 130 | 9 | 6 | 4 | 5.8 | .959 | C-25 |

Year	Team	Games	BA	SA	AB	H	2B	3B	HR	HR%	R	RBI	BB	SO	SB	Pinch Hit AB	Pinch Hit H	PO	A	E	DP	TC/G	FA	G by Pos

John Orsino *continued*

Year	Team	Games	BA	SA	AB	H	2B	3B	HR	HR%	R	RBI	BB	SO	SB	AB	H	PO	A	E	DP	TC/G	FA	G by Pos
1962		18	.271	.313	48	13	2	0	0	0.0	4	4	5	11	0	3	1	72	6	3	1	4.5	.963	C-16
1963	BAL A	116	.272	.475	379	103	18	1	19	5.0	53	56	38	53	2	5	2	656	38	7	10	6.0	.990	C-109, 1B-3
1964		81	.222	.359	248	55	10	0	8	3.2	21	23	23	55	0	12	3	426	32	10	7	5.8	.976	C-66, 1B-5
1965		77	.233	.409	232	54	10	2	9	3.9	30	28	23	51	1	14	4	372	26	6	4	5.2	.985	C-62, 1B-5
1966	WAS A	14	.174	.217	23	4	1	0	0	0.0	1	0	0	7	1	7	1	28	2	0	3	2.1	1.000	1B-5, C-2
1967		1	.000	.000	0	0	0	0	0	0.0	0	0	0	1	0	1	0	0	0	0	0	0.0	—	—
7 yrs.		332	.249	.420	1014	252	44	5	40	3.9	114	123	92	191	3	45	13	1684	113	32	29	5.5	.983	C-280, 1B-18

WORLD SERIES
| 1962 | SF N | 1 | .000 | .000 | 1 | 0 | 0 | 0 | 0 | 0.0 | 0 | 0 | 0 | 0 | 0 | 0 | 0 | 0 | 0 | 0 | 0 | 0.0 | — | C-1 |

Joe Orsulak

ORSULAK, JOSEPH MICHAEL
B. May 31, 1962, Glen Ridge, N. J.

BL TL 6'1" 185 lbs.

Year	Team	Games	BA	SA	AB	H	2B	3B	HR	HR%	R	RBI	BB	SO	SB	AB	H	PO	A	E	DP	TC/G	FA	G by Pos
1983	PIT N	7	.182	.182	11	2	0	0	0	0.0	0	0	0	2	0	3	0	2	2	0	0	0.6	1.000	OF-4
1984		32	.254	.328	67	17	1	2	0	0.0	12	3	1	7	3	6	1	41	1	0	0	1.3	1.000	OF-25
1985		121	.300	.365	397	119	14	6	0	0.0	54	21	26	27	24	8	4	229	10	6	1	2.0	.976	OF-115
1986		138	.249	.342	401	100	19	6	2	0.5	60	19	28	38	24	22	4	193	11	4	2	1.5	.981	OF-120
1988	BAL A	125	.288	.422	379	109	21	3	8	2.1	48	27	23	30	9	17	4	228	6	5	2	1.9	.979	OF-117
1989		123	.285	.421	390	111	22	5	7	1.8	59	55	41	35	5	15	6	250	10	4	2	2.1	.985	OF-109, DH-5
6 yrs.		546	.278	.383	1645	458	77	22	17	1.0	233	126	119	139	65	71	19	943	40	19	7	1.8	.981	OF-490, DH-5

Jorge Orta

ORTA, JORGE
Born Jorge Orta y Nunez.
B. Nov. 26, 1950, Mazatlan, Mexico

BL TR 5'10" 170 lbs.

Year	Team	Games	BA	SA	AB	H	2B	3B	HR	HR%	R	RBI	BB	SO	SB	AB	H	PO	A	E	DP	TC/G	FA	G by Pos
1972	CHI A	51	.202	.315	124	25	3	1	3	2.4	20	11	6	37	3	11	1	50	85	8	23	2.8	.944	SS-18, 2B-14, 3B-9
1973		128	.266	.376	425	113	9	10	6	1.4	46	40	37	87	8	5	2	255	301	18	75	4.5	.969	2B-122, SS-1
1974		139	.316	.440	525	166	31	2	10	1.9	73	67	40	88	9	7	1	297	313	18	93	4.5	.971	2B-123, DH-10, SS-3
1975		140	.304	.450	542	165	26	10	11	2.0	64	83	48	67	16	3	2	354	354	16	95	5.2	.978	2B-135, DH-2
1976		158	.274	.410	636	174	29	8	14	2.2	74	72	38	77	24	3	0	187	111	15	10	2.0	.952	OF-77, 3B-49, DH-31
1977		144	.282	.417	564	159	27	8	11	2.0	71	84	46	49	4	7	1	287	335	19	64	4.5	.970	2B-139
1978		117	.274	.421	420	115	19	2	13	3.1	45	53	42	39	1	3	1	275	290	9	62	4.9	.984	2B-114, DH-2
1979		113	.262	.437	325	85	18	3	11	3.4	49	46	44	33	1	22	4	57	75	3	17	1.2	.978	DH-62, 2B-41
1980	CLE A	129	.291	.403	481	140	18	3	10	2.1	78	64	71	44	6	2	0	269	10	5	1	2.2	.982	2B-120, DH-7
1981		86	.272	.376	338	92	14	3	5	1.5	50	34	21	43	4	5	2	150	11	1	2	1.8	.994	OF-86
1982	LA N	86	.217	.313	115	25	5	0	2	1.7	13	8	12	13	0	60	9	35	1	2	1	0.4	.947	OF-17
1983	TOR A	103	.237	.408	245	58	6	3	10	4.1	30	38	19	29	1	26	5	16	1	0	1	0.2	1.000	DH-69, OF-17
1984	KC A	122	.298	.457	403	120	23	7	9	2.2	50	50	28	39	0	13	4	48	0	1	0	0.4	.980	DH-83, OF-26, 2B-1
1985		110	.267	.383	300	80	21	1	4	1.3	32	45	22	28	2	29	8	0	0	0	0	0.0	—	DH-85
1986		106	.277	.411	336	93	14	2	9	2.7	35	46	23	34	0	21	6	0	0	0	0	0.0	—	DH-87
1987		21	.180	.380	50	9	4	0	2	4.0	3	4	3	8	0	9	2	0	0	0	0	0.0	—	DH-12
16 yrs.		1755	.278	.412	5829	1619	267	63	130	2.2	733	745	500	715	79	226	48	2280	1887	115	444	2.4	.973	2B-689, DH-450, OF-343, 3B-58, SS-22

LEAGUE CHAMPIONSHIP SERIES
Year	Team	Games	BA	SA	AB	H	2B	3B	HR	HR%	R	RBI	BB	SO	SB	AB	H	PO	A	E	DP	TC/G	FA	G by Pos
1984	KC A	3	.100	.300	10	1	0	1	0	0.0	1	0	0	2	0	0	0	0	0	0	0	0.0	—	DH-3
1985		2	.000	.000	5	0	0	0	0	0.0	0	1	0	1	0	1	0	0	0	0	0	0.0	—	DH-1
2 yrs.		5	.067	.200	15	1	0	1	0	0.0	1	1	0	3	0	1	0	0	0	0	0	0.0	—	DH-4

WORLD SERIES
| 1985 | KC A | 3 | .333 | .333 | 3 | 1 | 0 | 0 | 0 | 0.0 | 0 | 0 | 0 | 0 | 0 | 3 | 1 | 0 | 0 | 0 | 0 | 0.0 | — | |

Frank Ortenzio

ORTENZIO, FRANK JOSEPH JR.
B. Feb. 24, 1951, Fresno, Calif.

BR TR 6'2" 215 lbs.

Year	Team	Games	BA	SA	AB	H	2B	3B	HR	HR%	R	RBI	BB	SO	SB	AB	H	PO	A	E	DP	TC/G	FA	G by Pos
1973	KC A	9	.280	.480	25	7	2	0	1	4.0	1	6	2	6	0	1	0	51	6	1	4	6.4	.983	1B-7, DH-1

Al Orth

ORTH, ALBERT LEWIS (The Curveless Wonder)
B. Sept. 5, 1872, Tipton, Ind.   D. Oct. 8, 1948, Lynchburg, Va.

BL TR 6' 200 lbs.

Year	Team	Games	BA	SA	AB	H	2B	3B	HR	HR%	R	RBI	BB	SO	SB	AB	H	PO	A	E	DP	TC/G	FA	G by Pos
1895	PHI N	11	.356	.511	45	16	4	0	1	2.2	8	13	1	6	0	0	0	2	14	3	0	1.7	.842	P-11
1896		25	.256	.402	82	21	3	3	1	1.2	12	13	3	11	2	0	0	10	54	7	2	2.8	.901	P-25
1897		53	.329	.447	152	50	7	4	1	0.7	26	17	3		5	11	1	20	70	7	1	1.8	.928	P-36, OF-6
1898		39	.293	.431	123	36	4	1	1	0.8	17	14	3		1	6	2	9	63	3	1	1.9	.960	P-32, OF-1
1899		22	.210	.339	62	13	3	1	1	1.6	5	5	1		2	0	0	5	19	6	0	1.4	.800	P-21, OF-1
1900		39	.310	.380	129	40	4	1	0	0.8	6	21	2		2	3	0	23	68	5	3	2.5	.948	P-33, OF-3
1901		41	.281	.352	128	36	6	0	1	0.8	14	15	3		3	2	1	25	83	6	2	2.8	.947	P-35, OF-4
1902	WAS A	56	.217	.291	175	38	3	2	2	1.1	20	10	9		2	1	1	46	97	12	3	2.8	.923	P-38, OF-13, SS-1, 1B-1
1903		55	.302	.444	162	49	9	7	0	0.0	19	11	4		3	6	0	55	98	15	3	3.1	.911	P-36, SS-7, OF-4, 1B-2
1904	2 teams	WAS A (31G – .216)		NY A (26G – .297)																				
"	total	57	.247	.295	166	41	4	2	0	0.0	13	18	1		4	4	1	53	74	10	1	2.4	.927	P-30, OF-20
1905	NY A	54	.183	.244	131	24	3	1	1	0.8	13	8	4		2	11	2	31	98	10	1	2.6	.928	P-40, OF-1, 1B-1
1906		47	.274	.341	135	37	2	2	1	0.7	12	17	4		1	0	0	13	103	8	1	2.6	.935	P-45, OF-1
1907		44	.324	.410	105	34	6	0	1	1.0	11	13	4		1	5	0	9	95	9	1	2.6	.920	P-36, OF-1
1908		38	.290	.362	69	20	1	2	0	0.0	4	4	2		0	13	4	6	42	1	2	1.3	.980	P-21
1909		22	.265	.324	34	9	1	0	0	0.0	3	5	5		1	13	5	10	16	0	0	1.2	1.000	2B-6, P-1
15 yrs.		603	.273	.366	1698	464	61	30	12	0.7	183	184	51	17	30	78	17	317	994	102	21	2.3	.928	P-440, OF-55, SS-8, 2B-6, 1B-4

Jose Ortiz

ORTIZ, JOSE LUIS
Born Jose Luis Ortiz y Irizarry.
B. June 25, 1947, Ponce, Puerto Rico

BR TR 5'9½" 155 lbs.

Year	Team	Games	BA	SA	AB	H	2B	3B	HR	HR%	R	RBI	BB	SO	SB	AB	H	PO	A	E	DP	TC/G	FA	G by Pos
1969	CHI A	16	.273	.364	11	3	1	0	0	0.0	0	2	1	0	0	1	0	4	1	0	0	0.3	1.000	OF-8
1970		15	.333	.375	24	8	1	0	0	0.0	4	1	2	2	1	1	0	10	3	0	0	0.9	1.000	OF-8

Year	Team	Games	BA	SA	AB	H	2B	3B	HR	HR%	R	RBI	BB	SO	SB	Pinch Hit AB	Pinch Hit H	PO	A	E	DP	TC/G	FA	G by Pos

Jose Ortiz *continued*

Year	Team	Games	BA	SA	AB	H	2B	3B	HR	HR%	R	RBI	BB	SO	SB	PH AB	PH H	PO	A	E	DP	TC/G	FA	G by Pos
1971	CHI N	36	.295	.398	88	26	7	1	0	0.0	10	3	4	10	2	1	0	53	1	0	1	1.5	1.000	OF-20
3 yrs.		67	.301	.390	123	37	9	1	0	0.0	14	6	7	12	3	3	0	67	5	0	1	1.1	1.000	OF-36

Junior Ortiz

ORTIZ, ADALBERTO
Born Adalberto Ortiz y Colon.
B. Oct. 24, 1959, Humacao, Puerto Rico

BR TR 5'11" 174 lbs.

Year	Team	Games	BA	SA	AB	H	2B	3B	HR	HR%	R	RBI	BB	SO	SB	PH AB	PH H	PO	A	E	DP	TC/G	FA	G by Pos
1982	PIT N	7	.200	.267	15	3	1	0	0	0.0	1	0	1	3	0	0	0	27	3	0	0	4.3	1.000	C-7
1983 2 teams	PIT N (5G - .125)				NY N (68G - .254)																			
" total		73	.249	.275	193	48	5	0	0	0.0	11	12	4	34	1	5	2	293	31	11	2	4.6	.967	C-71
1984	NY N	40	.198	.231	91	18	3	0	0	0.0	6	11	5	15	1	10	1	136	13	3	3	3.8	.980	C-32
1985	PIT N	23	.292	.361	72	21	2	0	1	1.4	4	5	3	17	1	1	0	115	14	2	3	5.7	.985	C-23
1986		49	.336	.391	110	37	6	0	0	0.0	11	14	9	13	0	11	3	165	13	3	2	3.7	.983	C-36
1987		75	.271	.339	192	52	8	1	1	0.5	16	22	15	23	0	8	2	313	39	9	2	4.8	.975	C-72
1988		49	.280	.381	118	33	6	0	2	1.7	8	18	9	9	1	12	3	152	23	3	2	3.6	.983	C-40
1989		91	.217	.265	230	50	6	1	1	0.4	16	22	20	20	2	13	1	334	32	2	2	4.0	.995	C-84
8 yrs.		407	.257	.311	1021	262	37	2	5	0.5	73	104	66	134	6	60	12	1535	168	33	16	4.3	.981	C-365

Roberto Ortiz

ORTIZ, ROBERTO GONZALO
Born Roberto Gonzalo Ortiz y Nunez. Brother of Baby Ortiz.
B. June 30, 1915, Camaguey, Cuba D. Sept. 15, 1971, Miami, Fla.

BR TR 6'4" 200 lbs.

Year	Team	Games	BA	SA	AB	H	2B	3B	HR	HR%	R	RBI	BB	SO	SB	PH AB	PH H	PO	A	E	DP	TC/G	FA	G by Pos
1941	WAS A	22	.329	.430	79	26	1	2	1	1.3	10	17	3	10	0	1	0	34	3	6	0	2.0	.860	OF-21
1942		20	.167	.405	42	7	1	3	1	2.4	4	4	5	11	0	7	0	15	1	1	0	0.9	.941	OF-9
1943		1	.250	.250	4	1	0	0	0	0.0	0	0	0	0	0	0	0	3	0	0	0	3.0	1.000	OF-1
1944		85	.253	.361	316	80	11	4	5	1.6	36	35	19	47	4	5	1	165	2	9	1	2.1	.949	OF-80
1949		40	.279	.326	129	36	3	0	1	0.8	12	11	9	12	0	8	4	48	5	3	1	1.4	.946	OF-32
1950 2 teams	WAS A (39G - .227)				PHI A (6G - .071)																			
" total		45	.202	.247	89	18	2	1	0	0.0	5	11	7	15	0	21	2	29	2	0	0	0.7	1.000	OF-22
6 yrs.		213	.255	.349	659	168	18	10	8	1.2	67	78	43	95	4	42	7	294	13	19	2	1.5	.942	OF-165

John Orton

ORTON, JOHN ANDREW
B. Dec. 8, 1965, Santa Cruz, Calif.

BR TR 6'1" 195 lbs.

Year	Team	Games	BA	SA	AB	H	2B	3B	HR	HR%	R	RBI	BB	SO	SB	PH AB	PH H	PO	A	E	DP	TC/G	FA	G by Pos
1989	CAL A	16	.179	.205	39	7	1	0	0	0.0	4	4	2	17	0	0	0	76	7	1	3	5.3	.988	C-16

Ossie Orwoll

ORWOLL, OSWALD CHRISTIAN
B. Nov. 17, 1900, Portland, Ore. D. May 8, 1967, Decorah, Iowa

BL TL 6' 174 lbs.

Year	Team	Games	BA	SA	AB	H	2B	3B	HR	HR%	R	RBI	BB	SO	SB	PH AB	PH H	PO	A	E	DP	TC/G	FA	G by Pos
1928	PHI A	64	.306	.406	170	52	13	2	0	0.0	28	22	16	24	3	1	1	328	41	7	32	5.9	.981	1B-34, P-27
1929		30	.255	.333	51	13	2	1	0	0.0	6	6	2	11	0	8	2	18	6	0	1	0.8	1.000	P-12, OF-9
2 yrs.		94	.294	.389	221	65	15	3	0	0.0	34	28	18	35	3	9	3	346	47	7	33	4.3	.983	P-39, 1B-34, OF-9

Fred Osborn

OSBORN, WILFRED PEARL
B. Nov. 28, 1883, Nevada, Ohio D. Sept. 2, 1954, Upper Sandusky, Ohio

BL TR 5'9" 178 lbs.

Year	Team	Games	BA	SA	AB	H	2B	3B	HR	HR%	R	RBI	BB	SO	SB	PH AB	PH H	PO	A	E	DP	TC/G	FA	G by Pos
1907	PHI N	56	.276	.325	163	45	2	3	0	0.0	22	9	3			4	19	7	68	2	0	1	1.3	1.000	OF-36, 1B-1
1908		152	.267	.355	555	148	19	12	2	0.4	62	44	30			16	0	0	359	14	12	3	2.5	.969	OF-152
1909		58	.185	.217	189	35	4	1	0	0.0	14	19	12			6	6	1	126	14	3	3	2.5	.979	OF-54
3 yrs.		266	.251	.321	907	228	25	16	2	0.2	98	72	45			26	25	8	553	30	15	7	2.2	.975	OF-242, 1B-1

Bobo Osborne

OSBORNE, LAWRENCE SIDNEY
Son of Tiny Osborne.
B. Oct. 12, 1935, Chattahoochee, Ga.

BL TR 6'1" 205 lbs.

Year	Team	Games	BA	SA	AB	H	2B	3B	HR	HR%	R	RBI	BB	SO	SB	PH AB	PH H	PO	A	E	DP	TC/G	FA	G by Pos
1957	DET A	11	.148	.185	27	4	1	0	0	0.0	4	3	3	7	0	2	0	28	1	0	1	2.6	1.000	OF-5, 1B-4
1958		2	.000	.000	2	0	0	0	0	0.0	0	0	0	0	0	2	0	0	0	0	0	0.0		
1959		86	.191	.278	209	40	7	1	3	1.4	27	21	16	41	1	23	0	378	27	8	36	4.8	.981	1B-56, OF-1
1961		71	.215	.355	93	20	7	0	2	2.2	8	13	20	15	1	41	10	60	15	1	6	1.1	.987	1B-11, 3B-8
1962		64	.230	.243	74	17	1	0	0	0.0	12	7	16	25	0	29	6	22	21	5	0	0.8	.896	3B-13, 1B-7, C-1
1963	WAS A	125	.212	.358	358	76	14	1	12	3.4	42	44	49	83	0	22	5	719	81	13	69	6.5	.984	1B-81, 3B-16
6 yrs.		359	.206	.317	763	157	30	2	17	2.2	93	86	104	171	2	119	21	1207	145	27	112	3.8	.980	1B-159, 3B-37, OF-6, C-1

Fred Osborne

OSBORNE, FREDERICK W.
B. May, 1865, Canada Deceased.

TL

Year	Team	Games	BA	SA	AB	H	2B	3B	HR	HR%	R	RBI	BB	SO	SB	PH AB	PH H	PO	A	E	DP	TC/G	FA	G by Pos
1890	PIT N	41	.238	.339	168	40	8	3	1	0.6	24	14	6	18	0	0	0	67	19	18	0	2.5	.827	OF-35, P-8

Harry Ostdiek

OSTDIEK, HENRY GIRARD
B. Apr. 12, 1881, Ottumwa, Iowa D. May 6, 1956, Minneapolis, Minn.

BR TR 5'11" 185 lbs.

Year	Team	Games	BA	SA	AB	H	2B	3B	HR	HR%	R	RBI	BB	SO	SB	PH AB	PH H	PO	A	E	DP	TC/G	FA	G by Pos
1904	CLE A	7	.167	.278	18	3	0	1	0	0.0	1	3	3			1	0	0	29	6	2	1	5.3	.946	C-7
1908	BOS A	1	.000	.000	3	0	0	0	0	0.0	0	0	0			0	0	0	7	1	1	0	9.0	.889	C-1
2 yrs.		8	.143	.238	21	3	0	1	0	0.0	1	3	3			1	0	0	36	7	3	1	5.8	.935	C-8

Champ Osteen

OSTEEN, JAMES CHAMPLIN
B. Feb. 24, 1877, Hendersonville, N. C. D. Dec. 14, 1962, Greenville, S. C.

BL TR 5'8" 150 lbs.

Year	Team	Games	BA	SA	AB	H	2B	3B	HR	HR%	R	RBI	BB	SO	SB	PH AB	PH H	PO	A	E	DP	TC/G	FA	G by Pos
1903	WAS A	10	.200	.300	40	8	0	2	0	0.0	4	4	2			0	0	0	28	32	4	4	6.4	.938	SS-10
1904	NY A	28	.196	.336	107	21	4	4	2	1.9	15	9	1			0	0	0	66	56	8	3	4.6	.938	3B-17, SS-8, 1B-4
1908	STL N	29	.196	.232	112	22	4	0	0	0.0	2	11	0			0	0	0	44	63	14	6	4.2	.884	SS-17, 3B-12
1909		16	.200	.222	45	9	1	0	0	0.0	6	7	7			1	0	0	17	41	8	1	4.1	.879	SS-16
4 yrs.		83	.197	.276	304	60	6	6	2	0.7	27	31	10			1	0	0	155	192	34	14	4.6	.911	SS-51, 3B-29, 1B-4

Red Ostergard

OSTERGARD, ROY LUND
B. May 16, 1896, Denmark, Wis. D. Jan. 13, 1977, Hemet, Calif.

BR TR 5'10½" 175 lbs.

Year	Team	Games	BA	SA	AB	H	2B	3B	HR	HR%	R	RBI	BB	SO	SB	PH AB	PH H	PO	A	E	DP	TC/G	FA	G by Pos
1921	CHI A	12	.364	.364	11	4	0	0	0	0.0	2	0	2	0	2	0	11	4	0	0	0	0	0.0	–	

Year	Team	Games	BA	SA	AB	H	2B	3B	HR	HR%	R	RBI	BB	SO	SB	Pinch Hit AB	Pinch Hit H	PO	A	E	DP	TC/G	FA	G by Pos

Charlie Osterhout

OSTERHOUT, CHARLES H. (Ostey)
B. 1856, Syracuse, N. Y.   D. May 21, 1933, Syracuse, N. Y.
TR

| 1879 | SYR | N | 2 | .000 | .000 | 8 | 0 | 0 | 0 | 0 | 0.0 | 0 | 0 | 0 | 0 | 0 | 0 | 0 | 6 | 2 | 1 | 0 | 4.5 | .889 | OF-1, C-1 |

Brian Ostrosser

OSTROSSER, BRIAN LEONARD
B. June 17, 1949, Hamilton, Ont., Canada
BL TR 6'   175 lbs.

| 1973 | NY | N | 4 | .000 | .000 | 5 | 0 | 0 | 0 | 0 | 0.0 | 0 | 0 | 0 | 2 | 0 | 0 | 0 | 1 | 4 | 0 | 0 | 1.3 | 1.000 | SS-4 |

John Ostrowski

OSTROWSKI, JOHN THADDEUS
B. Oct. 17, 1917, Chicago, Ill.
BR TR 5'10½" 170 lbs.

1943	CHI	N	10	.207	.276	29	6	0	1	0	0.0	2	3	3	8	0	0	0	11	5	2	1	1.8	.889	OF-5, 3B-4
1944			8	.154	.231	13	2	1	0	0	0.0	2	2	1	4	0	5	2	1	0	1	0	0.3	.500	OF-2
1945			7	.300	.500	10	3	2	0	0	0.0	4	1	0	4	0	2	0	1	2	1	0	0.6	.750	3B-4
1946			64	.213	.319	160	34	4	2	3	1.9	20	12	20	31	1	10	0	35	82	8	5	2.0	.936	3B-50, 2B-1
1948	BOS	A	1	.000	.000	1	0	0	0	0	0.0	0	0	0	1	0	1	0	0	0	0	0	0.0	—	
1949	CHI	A	49	.266	.468	158	42	9	4	5	3.2	19	31	15	41	4	0	0	85	12	6	0	2.1	.942	OF-41, 3B-8
1950	2 teams			CHI	A	(21G – .222)		WAS	A	(55G – .227)															
"	total		76	.226	.360	186	42	3	2	6	3.2	25	25	28	40	2	16	0	132	4	6	1	1.9	.958	OF-60
7 yrs.			215	.232	.373	557	129	19	9	14	2.5	72	74	67	125	7	40	3	265	105	24	7	1.8	.939	OF-108, 3B-66, 2B-1

Reggie Otero

OTERO, REGINO JOSE
Born Regino Jose Otero y Gomez.
B. Sept. 7, 1915, Havana, Cuba   D. Oct. 21, 1988, Hialeah, Fla.
BL TR 5'11" 160 lbs.

| 1945 | CHI | N | 14 | .391 | .391 | 23 | 9 | 0 | 0 | 0 | 0.0 | 1 | 5 | 2 | 0 | 0 | 6 | 0 | 54 | 4 | 2 | 4 | 4.3 | .967 | 1B-8 |

Amos Otis

OTIS, AMOS JOSEPH
B. Apr. 26, 1947, Mobile, Ala.
BR TR 5'11½" 165 lbs.

1967	NY	N	19	.220	.254	59	13	2	0	0	0.0	6	1	5	13	0	0	0	23	2	0	1	1.3	1.000	OF-16, 3B-1
1969			48	.151	.204	93	14	3	1	0	0.0	6	4	6	27	1	10	1	49	6	1	0	1.2	.982	OF-35, 3B-3
1970	KC	A	159	.284	.424	620	176	36	9	11	1.8	91	58	68	67	33	1	1	388	15	4	6	2.6	.990	OF-159
1971			147	.301	.443	555	167	26	4	15	2.7	80	79	40	74	52	4	0	404	10	4	4	2.8	.990	OF-144
1972			143	.293	.413	540	158	28	2	11	2.0	75	54	50	59	28	5	1	351	6	3	3	2.5	.992	OF-137
1973			148	.300	.484	583	175	21	4	26	4.5	89	93	63	47	13	0	0	330	10	5	4	2.3	.986	OF-135, DH-14
1974			146	.284	.438	552	157	31	9	12	2.2	87	73	58	67	18	3	1	425	8	6	3	3.0	.986	OF-143, DH-2
1975			132	.247	.385	470	116	26	6	9	1.9	87	46	66	48	39	4	0	310	9	4	3	2.4	.988	OF-130
1976			153	.279	.444	592	165	40	2	18	3.0	93	86	55	100	26	0	0	373	5	3	1	2.5	.992	OF-152
1977			142	.251	.433	478	120	20	8	17	3.6	85	78	71	88	23	3	1	326	10	3	0	2.4	.991	OF-140
1978			141	.298	.525	486	145	30	7	22	4.5	74	96	66	54	32	3	0	382	9	2	1	2.8	.995	OF-136, DH-1
1979			151	.295	.444	577	170	28	2	18	3.1	100	90	68	92	30	1	1	385	11	3	5	2.6	.992	OF-146, DH-4
1980			107	.251	.383	394	99	16	3	10	2.5	56	53	39	70	16	2	1	310	6	4	1	3.0	.988	OF-105
1981			99	.269	.417	372	100	22	3	9	2.4	49	57	31	59	16	2	1	294	6	2	1	3.1	.993	OF-97, DH-1
1982			125	.286	.421	475	136	25	3	11	2.3	73	88	37	65	9	1	0	308	5	1	1	2.5	.997	OF-125
1983			96	.261	.357	356	93	16	3	4	1.1	35	41	27	63	5	2	1	233	6	1	1	2.5	.996	OF-96, DH-1
1984	PIT	N	40	.165	.206	97	16	4	0	0	0.0	6	10	7	15	0	7	2	49	5	2	0	1.4	.964	OF-32
17 yrs.			1996	.277	.425	7299	2020	374	66	193	2.6	1092	1007	757	1008	341	48	11	4940	129	48	35	2.6	.991	OF-1928, DH-23, 3B-4

DIVISIONAL PLAYOFF SERIES

| 1981 | KC | A | 3 | .000 | .000 | 12 | 0 | 0 | 0 | 0 | 0.0 | 0 | 1 | 0 | 4 | 0 | 0 | 0 | 0 | 0 | 0 | 0 | 0.0 | — | OF-3 |

LEAGUE CHAMPIONSHIP SERIES

1976	KC	A	1	.000	.000	1	0	0	0	0	0.0	0	0	0	0	0	0	0	0	0	0	0	0.0	—	OF-1
1977			5	.125	.188	16	2	1	0	0	0.0	1	2	2	3	2	1	1	11	1	0	0	2.4	1.000	OF-5
1978			4	.429	.571	14	6	2	0	0	0.0	2	1	3	5	4	0	0	8	0	1	0	2.3	.889	OF-4
1980			3	.333	.417	12	4	1	0	0	0.0	2	0	0	3	2	0	0	11	0	0	0	3.7	1.000	OF-3
4 yrs.			13	.279	.372	43	12	4	0	0	0.0	5	3	5	11	8	1	1	30	1	1	0	2.5	.969	OF-13

WORLD SERIES

| 1980 | KC | A | 6 | .478 | .957 | 23 | 11 | 2 | 0 | 3 | 13.0 | 4 | 7 | 3 | 3 | 0 | 0 | 0 | 21 | 0 | 0 | 0 | 3.5 | 1.000 | OF-6 |

Bill Otis

OTIS, PAUL FRANKLIN
B. Dec. 24, 1889, Scituate, Mass.
BL TR 5'10½" 150 lbs.

| 1912 | NY | A | 4 | .050 | .050 | 20 | 1 | 0 | 0 | 0 | 0.0 | 1 | 2 | 3 | | | 0 | 0 | 10 | 1 | 1 | 0 | 3.0 | .917 | OF-4 |

Billy Ott

OTT, WILLIAM JOSEPH
B. Nov. 23, 1940, New York, N. Y.
BB TR 6'1" 180 lbs.

1962	CHI	N	12	.143	.250	28	4	0	0	1	3.6	3	2	2	10	0	5	1	9	1	0	0	0.8	1.000	OF-7
1964			20	.179	.256	39	7	3	0	0	0.0	4	1	3	10	0	10	2	12	0	0	0	0.6	1.000	OF-10
2 yrs.			32	.164	.254	67	11	3	0	1	1.5	7	3	5	20	0	15	3	21	1	0	0	0.7	1.000	OF-17

Ed Ott

OTT, NATHAN EDWARD
B. July 11, 1951, Muncy, Pa.
BL TR 5'10" 190 lbs.

1974	PIT	N	7	.000	.000	5	0	0	0	0	0.0	1	0	0	1	0	5	0	1	0	0	0	0.1	1.000	OF-2
1975			5	.200	.200	5	1	0	0	0	0.0	0	0	0	0	0	3	0	2	0	0	0	0.4	1.000	C-2
1976			27	.308	.359	39	12	2	0	0	0.0	2	5	3	5	0	17	6	20	6	0	1	1.0	1.000	C-8
1977			104	.264	.395	311	82	14	3	7	2.3	40	38	32	41	7	18	3	455	49	9	6	4.9	.982	C-90
1978			112	.269	.409	379	102	18	4	9	2.4	49	48	27	56	4	15	5	547	43	16	7	5.4	.974	C-97, OF-4
1979			117	.273	.385	403	110	20	2	7	1.7	49	51	26	62	0	3	1	612	53	4	6	5.7	.994	C-116
1980			120	.260	.357	392	102	14	0	8	2.0	35	41	33	47	1	7	1	571	73	11	5	5.5	.983	C-117, OF-3
1981	CAL	A	75	.217	.279	258	56	8	1	2	0.8	20	22	17	42	2	5	0	287	36	7	1	4.4	.979	C-72
8 yrs.			567	.259	.368	1792	465	76	10	33	1.8	196	195	138	254	14	73	16	2495	260	47	26	4.9	.983	C-502, OF-9

LEAGUE CHAMPIONSHIP SERIES

| 1979 | PIT | N | 3 | .231 | .231 | 13 | 3 | 0 | 0 | 0 | 0.0 | 0 | 0 | 0 | 2 | 0 | 0 | 0 | 25 | 3 | 0 | 0 | 9.3 | 1.000 | C-3 |

Year	Team		Games	BA	SA	AB	H	2B	3B	HR	HR%	R	RBI	BB	SO	SB	Pinch Hit AB	H	PO	A	E	DP	TC/G	FA	G by Pos

Ed Ott *continued*

WORLD SERIES

Year	Team		Games	BA	SA	AB	H	2B	3B	HR	HR%	R	RBI	BB	SO	SB	PH AB	H	PO	A	E	DP	TC/G	FA	G by Pos
1979	PIT	N	3	.333	.417	12	4	1	0	0	0.0	2	3	0	2	0	0	0	20	0	0	1	6.7	1.000	C-3

Mel Ott

OTT, MELVIN THOMAS (Master Melvin)
B. Mar. 2, 1909, Gretna, La.   D. Nov. 21, 1958, New Orleans, La.
Manager 1942-48.
Hall of Fame 1951.

BL TR 5'9"   170 lbs.

Year	Team		Games	BA	SA	AB	H	2B	3B	HR	HR%	R	RBI	BB	SO	SB	PH AB	H	PO	A	E	DP	TC/G	FA	G by Pos
1926	NY	N	35	.383	.417	60	23	0	0	0	0.0	7	4	1	9	1	24	9	18	3	2	0	0.7	.913	OF-10
1927			82	.282	.380	163	46	7	3	1	0.6	23	19	13	9	2	46	11	52	2	1	1	0.7	.982	OF-32
1928			124	.322	.524	435	140	26	4	18	4.1	69	77	52	36	3	3	0	228	29	8	8	2.1	.970	OF-115, 2B-5, 3B-1
1929			150	.328	.635	545	179	37	2	42	7.7	138	152	113	38	6	0	0	339	27	11	12	2.5	.971	OF-149, 2B-1
1930			148	.349	.578	521	182	34	5	25	4.8	122	119	103	35	9	1	0	320	23	11	6	2.4	.969	OF-146
1931			138	.292	.545	497	145	23	8	29	5.8	104	115	80	44	10	1	1	332	20	7	4	2.6	.981	OF-137
1932			154	.318	.601	566	180	30	8	38	6.7	119	123	100	39	6	0	0	347	11	6	5	2.4	.984	OF-154
1933			152	.283	.467	580	164	36	1	23	4.0	98	103	75	48	1	0	0	283	12	5	3	2.0	.983	OF-152
1934			153	.326	.591	582	190	29	10	35	6.0	119	135	85	43	0	0	0	286	12	8	1	2.0	.974	OF-153
1935			152	.322	.555	593	191	33	6	31	5.2	113	114	82	58	7	0	0	304	42	6	10	2.3	.983	OF-137, 3B-15
1936			150	.328	.588	534	175	28	6	33	6.2	120	135	111	41	6	1	1	250	20	4	3	1.8	.985	OF-148
1937			151	.294	.523	545	160	28	2	31	5.7	99	95	102	69	7	1	0	198	126	10	6	2.2	.970	OF-91, 3B-60
1938			154	.311	.583	527	164	23	6	36	6.8	116	116	118	47	2	1	0	163	241	15	14	2.7	.964	3B-113, OF-37
1939			125	.308	.581	396	122	23	2	27	6.8	85	80	100	50	2	9	2	190	45	11	6	2.0	.955	OF-96, 3B-20
1940			151	.289	.457	536	155	27	3	19	3.5	89	79	100	50	6	0	0	240	92	12	10	2.3	.965	OF-111, 3B-42
1941			148	.286	.495	525	150	29	0	27	5.1	89	90	100	68	5	2	0	256	19	9	3	1.9	.968	OF-145
1942			152	.295	.497	549	162	21	0	30	5.5	118	93	109	61	6	0	0	269	15	3	3	1.9	.990	OF-152
1943			125	.234	.418	380	89	12	2	18	4.7	65	47	95	48	7	6	1	219	12	6	1	1.9	.975	OF-111, 3B-1
1944			120	.288	.544	399	115	16	4	26	6.5	91	82	90	47	2	10	2	200	19	7	0	1.9	.969	OF-103, 3B-4
1945			135	.308	.499	451	139	23	0	21	4.7	73	79	71	41	1	15	4	217	11	4	1	1.7	.983	OF-118
1946			31	.074	.132	68	5	1	0	1	1.5	2	4	8	15	0	13	1	23	2	0	1	0.8	1.000	OF-16
1947			4	.000	.000	4	0	0	0	0	0.0	0	0	0	0	0	4	0	0	0	0	0	–		
22 yrs.			2734	.304	.533	9456	2876	488	72	511	5.4	1859	1861	1708	896	89	137	32	4734	783	146	98	2.1	.974	OF-2313, 3B-256, 2B-6
												9th	8th	6th											

WORLD SERIES

Year	Team		Games	BA	SA	AB	H	2B	3B	HR	HR%	R	RBI	BB	SO	SB	PH AB	H	PO	A	E	DP	TC/G	FA	G by Pos
1933	NY	N	5	.389	.722	18	7	0	0	2	11.1	3	4	4	4	0	0	0	10	0	0	0	2.0	1.000	OF-5
1936			6	.304	.522	23	7	2	0	1	4.3	4	3	3	1	0	0	0	12	0	1	0	2.2	.923	OF-6
1937			5	.200	.350	20	4	0	0	1	5.0	1	3	1	4	0	0	0	5	9	1	1	3.0	.933	3B-5
3 yrs.			16	.295	.525	61	18	2	0	4	6.6	8	10	8	9	0	0	0	27	9	2	1	2.4	.947	OF-11, 3B-5

Joe Otten

OTTEN, JOSEPH G.
B. Murphysboro, Ill.   Deceased.

TR

Year	Team		Games	BA	SA	AB	H	2B	3B	HR	HR%	R	RBI	BB	SO	SB	PH AB	H	PO	A	E	DP	TC/G	FA	G by Pos
1895	STL	N	26	.241	.241	87	21	0	0	0	0.0	8	8	5	8	2	0	0	75	15	6	3	3.7	.938	C-24, OF-2

Billy Otterson

OTTERSON, WILLIAM JOHN
B. May 4, 1862, Pittsburgh, Pa.   D. Sept. 21, 1940, Pittsburgh, Pa.

BR TR 5'7"   135 lbs.

Year	Team		Games	BA	SA	AB	H	2B	3B	HR	HR%	R	RBI	BB	SO	SB	PH AB	H	PO	A	E	DP	TC/G	FA	G by Pos
1887	BKN	AA	30	.200	.320	100	20	4	1	2	2.0	16		8		8	0	0	41	93	22	11	5.2	.859	SS-30

Phil Ouellette

OUELLETTE, PHILIP ROLAND
B. Nov. 10, 1961, Salem, Ore.

BB TR 6'   190 lbs.

Year	Team		Games	BA	SA	AB	H	2B	3B	HR	HR%	R	RBI	BB	SO	SB	PH AB	H	PO	A	E	DP	TC/G	FA	G by Pos
1986	SF	N	10	.174	.174	23	4	0	0	0	0.0	1	0	3	3	0	3	0	42	3	0	0	4.5	1.000	C-9

Johnny Oulliber

OULLIBER, JOHN ANDREW
B. Feb. 24, 1911, New Orleans, La.   D. Dec. 26, 1980, New Orleans, La.

BR TR 5'11"   165 lbs.

Year	Team		Games	BA	SA	AB	H	2B	3B	HR	HR%	R	RBI	BB	SO	SB	PH AB	H	PO	A	E	DP	TC/G	FA	G by Pos
1933	CLE	A	22	.267	.280	75	20	1	0	0	0.0	9	3	4	5	0	4	0	25	0	0	0	1.1	1.000	OF-18

Chink Outen

OUTEN, WILLIAM AUSTIN
B. June 17, 1905, Mt. Holly, N. C.   D. Sept. 11, 1961, Durham, N. C.

BL TR 6'   200 lbs.

Year	Team		Games	BA	SA	AB	H	2B	3B	HR	HR%	R	RBI	BB	SO	SB	PH AB	H	PO	A	E	DP	TC/G	FA	G by Pos
1933	BKN	N	93	.248	.392	153	38	10	0	4	2.6	20	17	20	15	1	31	1	98	11	2	1	1.2	.982	C-56

Jimmy Outlaw

OUTLAW, JAMES PAULUS
B. Jan. 20, 1913, Orme, Tenn.

BR TR 5'8"   165 lbs.

Year	Team		Games	BA	SA	AB	H	2B	3B	HR	HR%	R	RBI	BB	SO	SB	PH AB	H	PO	A	E	DP	TC/G	FA	G by Pos
1937	CIN	N	49	.273	.352	165	45	7	3	0	0.0	18	11	3	31	2	4	0	41	87	12	4	2.9	.914	3B-41
1938			4	–		0	0	0	0	0	–	0	1	0	0	0	0	0	0	0	0	0	0.0		
1939	BOS	N	65	.263	.278	133	35	2	0	0	0.0	15	5	10	14	1	16	4	83	1	3	0	1.3	.966	OF-39, 3B-2
1943	DET	A	20	.269	.328	67	18	1	0	1	1.5	8	6	8	4	0	4	1	32	2	0	0	1.7	1.000	OF-16
1944			139	.273	.350	535	146	20	6	3	0.6	69	57	41	40	7	3	0	254	14	10	2	2.0	.964	OF-137
1945			132	.271	.330	446	121	16	5	0	0.0	56	34	45	33	6	7	0	210	55	11	11	2.1	.960	OF-105, 3B-21
1946			92	.261	.341	299	78	14	2	2	0.7	36	31	29	24	5	5	1	101	64	7	4	1.9	.959	OF-43, 3B-38
1947			70	.228	.299	127	29	7	1	0	0.0	20	15	21	14	3	3	0	69	7	2	0	1.1	.974	OF-37, 3B-9
1948			74	.283	.343	198	56	12	0	0	0.0	33	25	31	15	0	11	4	58	88	11	8	2.1	.930	3B-47, OF-13
1949			5	.250	.250	4	1	0	0	0	0.0	1	0	0	1	0	4	1	0	0	0	0	0.0		
10 yrs.			650	.268	.334	1974	529	79	17	6	0.3	257	184	188	176	24	57	11	848	318	56	29	1.9	.954	OF-390, 3B-158

WORLD SERIES

Year	Team		Games	BA	SA	AB	H	2B	3B	HR	HR%	R	RBI	BB	SO	SB	PH AB	H	PO	A	E	DP	TC/G	FA	G by Pos
1945	DET	A	7	.179	.179	28	5	0	0	0	0.0	1	3	2	1	1	0	0	5	15	0	0	2.9	1.000	3B-7

Dave Owen

OWEN, DAVID
Brother of Spike Owen.
B. Apr. 25, 1958, Cleburne, Tex.

BB TR 6'1"   175 lbs.

Year	Team		Games	BA	SA	AB	H	2B	3B	HR	HR%	R	RBI	BB	SO	SB	PH AB	H	PO	A	E	DP	TC/G	FA	G by Pos
1983	CHI	N	16	.091	.182	22	2	0	1	0	0.0	1	2	2	7	1	0	0	10	29	0	5	2.4	1.000	SS-14, 3B-3

Year	Team	Games	BA	SA	AB	H	2B	3B	HR	HR%	R	RBI	BB	SO	SB	Pinch Hit AB	Pinch Hit H	PO	A	E	DP	TC/G	FA	G by Pos

Dave Owen *continued*

Year	Team	Games	BA	SA	AB	H	2B	3B	HR	HR%	R	RBI	BB	SO	SB	AB	H	PO	A	E	DP	TC/G	FA	G by Pos
1984		47	.194	.290	93	18	2	2	1	1.1	8	10	8	15	1	3	2	40	91	7	19	2.9	.949	SS-35, 3B-6, 2B-4
1985		22	.368	.368	19	7	0	0	0	0.0	6	4	1	5	1	3	0	6	14	2	2	1.0	.909	SS-7, 3B-7, 2B-4
1988	KC A	7	.000	.000	5	0	0	0	0	0.0	0	0	0	3	0	0	0	7	9	1	6	2.4	.941	SS-7
4 yrs.		92	.194	.273	139	27	2	3	1	0.7	15	16	11	30	3	6	2	63	143	10	32	2.3	.954	SS-63, 3B-16, 2B-8

Larry Owen

OWEN, LAWRENCE THOMAS
B. May 31, 1955, Cleveland, Ohio

BR TR 5'11" 185 lbs.

Year	Team	Games	BA	SA	AB	H	2B	3B	HR	HR%	R	RBI	BB	SO	SB	AB	H	PO	A	E	DP	TC/G	FA	G by Pos
1981	ATL N	13	.000	.000	16	0	0	0	0	0.0	0	0	1	4	0	4	0	23	4	1	2	2.2	.964	C-10
1982		2	.333	.667	3	1	1	0	0	0.0	1	0	0	1	0	0	0	2	1	0	0	1.5	1.000	C-2
1983		17	.118	.118	17	2	0	0	0	0.0	0	1	0	2	0	1	0	30	2	1	1	1.9	.970	C-16
1985		26	.239	.366	71	17	3	0	2	2.8	7	12	8	17	0	2	0	129	11	5	1	5.6	.966	C-25
1987	KC A	76	.189	.317	164	31	6	0	5	3.0	17	14	16	51	0	0	0	370	38	7	4	5.5	.983	C-76
1988		37	.210	.259	81	17	1	0	1	1.2	5	3	9	23	0	0	0	168	13	2	1	4.9	.989	C-37
6 yrs.		171	.193	.293	352	68	11	0	8	2.3	30	30	34	98	0	7	0	722	69	16	9	4.7	.980	C-166

Marv Owen

OWEN, MARVIN JAMES
B. Mar. 22, 1906, Agnew, Calif.

BR TR 6'1" 175 lbs.

Year	Team	Games	BA	SA	AB	H	2B	3B	HR	HR%	R	RBI	BB	SO	SB	AB	H	PO	A	E	DP	TC/G	FA	G by Pos
1931	DET A	105	.223	.308	377	84	11	6	3	0.8	35	39	29	38	2	3	1	308	220	24	46	5.3	.957	SS-37, 3B-37, 1B-27, 2B-4
1933		138	.262	.349	550	144	24	9	2	0.4	77	65	44	56	2	1	0	143	226	22	19	2.8	.944	3B-136
1934		154	.317	.451	565	179	34	9	8	1.4	79	96	59	37	3	0	0	202	253	21	33	3.1	.956	3B-154
1935		134	.263	.346	483	127	24	5	2	0.4	52	71	43	37	1	2	1	148	215	16	19	2.8	.958	3B-131
1936		154	.295	.389	583	172	20	4	9	1.5	72	105	53	41	9	0	0	202	281	24	29	3.3	.953	3B-153, 1B-2
1937		107	.288	.376	396	114	22	5	1	0.3	48	45	41	24	3	1	0	108	219	10	17	3.1	.970	3B-106
1938	CHI A	141	.281	.373	577	162	23	6	6	1.0	84	55	45	31	6	1	0	136	305	24	29	3.3	.948	3B-140
1939		58	.237	.284	194	46	9	0	0	0.0	22	15	16	15	4	2	0	63	99	8	11	2.9	.953	3B-55
1940	BOS A	20	.211	.211	57	12	0	0	0	0.0	4	6	8	4	0	3	0	62	24	2	12	4.4	.977	3B-9, 1B-8
9 yrs.		1011	.275	.367	3782	1040	167	44	31	0.8	473	497	338	283	30	13	2	1372	1842	151	215	3.3	.955	3B-921, SS-37, 1B-37, 2B-4

WORLD SERIES

Year	Team	Games	BA	SA	AB	H	2B	3B	HR	HR%	R	RBI	BB	SO	SB	AB	H	PO	A	E	DP	TC/G	FA	G by Pos
1934	DET A	7	.069	.069	29	2	0	0	0	0.0	0	1	0	5	1	0	0	9	9	2	1	2.9	.900	3B-7
1935		6	.050	.050	20	1	0	0	0	0.0	2	1	2	3	0	0	0	46	5	1	4	8.7	.981	1B-4, 3B-2
2 yrs.		13	.061	.061	49	3	0	0	0	0.0	2	2	2	8	1	0	0	55	14	3	5	5.5	.958	3B-9, 1B-4

Mickey Owen

OWEN, ARNOLD MALCOLM
B. Apr. 4, 1916, Nixa, Mo.

BR TR 5'10" 190 lbs.

Year	Team	Games	BA	SA	AB	H	2B	3B	HR	HR%	R	RBI	BB	SO	SB	AB	H	PO	A	E	DP	TC/G	FA	G by Pos
1937	STL N	80	.231	.265	234	54	4	2	0	0.0	17	20	15	13	1	2	0	287	49	9	6	4.3	.974	C-78
1938		122	.267	.370	397	106	25	2	4	1.0	45	36	32	14	2	5	1	463	67	11	8	4.4	.980	C-116
1939		131	.259	.349	344	89	18	2	3	0.9	32	35	43	28	6	5	0	452	52	9	7	3.9	.982	C-126
1940		117	.264	.329	307	81	16	2	0	0.0	27	27	34	13	4	4	2	378	56	9	8	3.8	.980	C-113
1941	BKN N	128	.231	.288	386	89	15	2	1	0.3	32	44	34	14	1	0	0	530	64	3	7	4.7	.995	C-128
1942		133	.259	.311	421	109	16	3	0	0.0	53	44	44	17	10	0	0	595	66	9	12	5.0	.987	C-133
1943		106	.260	.301	365	95	11	2	0	0.0	31	54	25	15	4	5	1	421	57	7	11	4.6	.986	C-100, 3B-3, SS-1
1944		130	.273	.336	461	126	20	3	1	0.2	43	42	36	17	4	4	1	507	57	12	8	4.4	.979	C-125, 2B-1
1945		24	.286	.393	84	24	9	0	0	0.0	5	11	10	2	0	0	0	92	13	4	2	4.5	.963	C-24
1949	CHI N	62	.273	.379	198	54	9	3	2	1.0	15	18	12	13	1	3	1	219	35	8	5	4.2	.969	C-59
1950		86	.243	.309	259	63	11	0	2	0.8	22	21	13	16	2	1	0	318	39	8	8	4.2	.978	C-86
1951		58	.184	.232	125	23	6	0	0	0.0	10	15	19	13	1	1	0	188	28	7	6	3.8	.969	C-57
1954	BOS A	32	.235	.324	68	16	3	0	1	1.5	6	11	9	6	0	1	1	85	8	1	4	2.9	.989	C-30
13 yrs.		1209	.255	.322	3649	929	163	21	14	0.4	338	378	326	181	36	31	7	4535	591	97	92	4.3	.981	C-1175, 3B-3, SS-1, 2B-1

WORLD SERIES

Year	Team	Games	BA	SA	AB	H	2B	3B	HR	HR%	R	RBI	BB	SO	SB	AB	H	PO	A	E	DP	TC/G	FA	G by Pos
1941	BKN N	5	.167	.333	12	2	0	1	0	0.0	1	2	3	0	0	0	0	20	4	1	1	5.0	.960	C-5

Spike Owen

OWEN, SPIKE DEE
Brother of Dave Owen.
B. Apr. 19, 1961, Cleburne, Tex.

BB TR 5'9" 160 lbs.

Year	Team	Games	BA	SA	AB	H	2B	3B	HR	HR%	R	RBI	BB	SO	SB	AB	H	PO	A	E	DP	TC/G	FA	G by Pos
1983	SEA A	80	.196	.271	306	60	11	3	2	0.7	36	21	24	44	10	1	0	122	233	11	45	4.6	.970	SS-80
1984		152	.245	.326	530	130	18	8	3	0.6	67	43	46	63	16	1	1	245	463	17	86	4.8	.977	SS-151
1985		118	.259	.372	352	91	10	6	6	1.7	41	37	34	27	11	0	0	196	361	14	76	4.8	.975	SS-117
1986	2 teams	SEA A (112G – .246)						BOS A (42G – .183)																
"	total	154	.231	.309	528	122	24	7	1	0.2	67	45	51	51	4	1	0	221	393	22	101	4.1	.965	SS-154
1987	BOS A	132	.259	.343	437	113	17	7	2	0.5	50	48	53	43	11	1	1	176	336	13	69	4.0	.975	SS-130
1988		89	.249	.300	257	64	14	1	1	0.4	19	18	40	18	0	6	1	102	192	10	34	3.4	.967	SS-76, DH-7
1989	MON N	142	.233	.332	437	102	17	4	6	1.4	52	41	76	44	3	1	0	232	388	13	65	4.5	.979	SS-142
7 yrs.		867	.240	.330	2847	682	111	36	25	0.9	353	253	311	299	55	10	2	1294	2366	100	476	4.3	.973	SS-850, DH-7

LEAGUE CHAMPIONSHIP SERIES

Year	Team	Games	BA	SA	AB	H	2B	3B	HR	HR%	R	RBI	BB	SO	SB	AB	H	PO	A	E	DP	TC/G	FA	G by Pos
1986	BOS A	7	.429	.524	21	9	0	1	0	0.0	5	3	2	1	0	0	0	12	21	5	2	5.4	.868	SS-7
1988		1	—	—	0	0	0	0	0	—	0	0	1	0	0	0	0	0	0	0	0	0.0	—	
2 yrs.		8	.429	.524	21	9	0	1	0	0.0	5	3	3	1	0	0	0	12	21	5	2	4.8	.868	SS-7

WORLD SERIES

Year	Team	Games	BA	SA	AB	H	2B	3B	HR	HR%	R	RBI	BB	SO	SB	AB	H	PO	A	E	DP	TC/G	FA	G by Pos
1986	BOS A	7	.300	.300	20	6	0	0	0	0.0	2	2	5	6	0	0	0	10	13	0	3	3.3	1.000	SS-7

Frank Owens

OWENS, FRANK WALTER
B. Jan. 26, 1886, Toronto, Ont., Canada   D. July 2, 1958, Minneapolis, Minn.

BR TR 6' 170 lbs.

Year	Team	Games	BA	SA	AB	H	2B	3B	HR	HR%	R	RBI	BB	SO	SB	AB	H	PO	A	E	DP	TC/G	FA	G by Pos
1905	BOS A	1	.000	.000	2	0	0	0	0	0.0	0	0	0		0	0	0	2	0	0	0	3.0	1.000	C-1
1909	CHI A	64	.201	.236	174	35	4	1	0	0.0	12	17	8		3	6	1	266	62	14	2	5.3	.959	C-57
1914	BKN F	58	.277	.380	184	51	7	3	2	1.1	15	20	9		2	0	0	228	67	10	10	5.3	.967	C-58
1915	BAL F	99	.251	.362	334	84	14	7	3	0.9	32	28	17		4	0	0	462	146	15	19	6.3	.976	C-99
4 yrs.		222	.245	.334	694	170	25	11	5	0.7	59	65	34		9	6	1	958	276	39	31	5.7	.969	C-215

Year Team	Games	BA	SA	AB	H	2B	3B	HR	HR%	R	RBI	BB	SO	SB	Pinch Hit AB	Pinch Hit H	PO	A	E	DP	TC/G	FA	G by Pos

Jack Owens

OWENS, FURMAN LEE   BR TR 6'1" 186 lbs.
B. May 6, 1908, Converse, S. C.   D. Nov. 14, 1958, Greenville, S. C.

Year Team	Games	BA	SA	AB	H	2B	3B	HR	HR%	R	RBI	BB	SO	SB	PH AB	PH H	PO	A	E	DP	TC/G	FA	G by Pos
1935 PHI A	2	.250	.250	8	2	0	0	0	0.0	0	1	0	1	0	0	0	8	1	1	0	5.0	.900	C-2

Red Owens

OWENS, THOMAS LLEWELLYN   BR TR
B. Nov. 1, 1874, Pottsville, Pa.   D. Aug. 20, 1952, Harrisburg, Pa.

Year Team	Games	BA	SA	AB	H	2B	3B	HR	HR%	R	RBI	BB	SO	SB	PH AB	PH H	PO	A	E	DP	TC/G	FA	G by Pos
1899 PHI N	8	.048	.048	21	1	0	0	0	0.0	0	1	2		0	0	0	13	19	3	2	4.4	.914	2B-8
1905 BKN N	43	.214	.292	168	36	6	2	1	0.6	14	20	6		1	0	0	102	132	18	19	5.9	.929	2B-43
2 yrs.	51	.196	.265	189	37	6	2	1	0.5	14	21	8		1	0	0	115	151	21	21	5.6	.927	2B-51

Henry Oxley

OXLEY, HENRY HAVELOCK
B. Jan. 4, 1858, Covehead, P. E. I., Canada   D. Oct. 12, 1945, Somerville, Mass.

Year Team	Games	BA	SA	AB	H	2B	3B	HR	HR%	R	RBI	BB	SO	SB	PH AB	PH H	PO	A	E	DP	TC/G	FA	G by Pos
1884 2 teams		NY	N (3G – .000)		NY	AA (1G – .000)																	
" total	4	.000	.000	7	0	0	0	0	0.0	0		1	2		0	0	11	6	2	0	4.8	.895	C-3

Andy Oyler

OYLER, ANDREW PAUL (Pepper)   BR -TR 5'6½" 138 lbs.
B. May 5, 1880, Newville, Pa.   D. Oct. 24, 1970, Cumberland County, Pa.

Year Team	Games	BA	SA	AB	H	2B	3B	HR	HR%	R	RBI	BB	SO	SB	PH AB	PH H	PO	A	E	DP	TC/G	FA	G by Pos
1902 BAL A	27	.221	.273	77	17	1	0	1	1.3	9	6	8		3	2	0	34	30	4	2	2.5	.941	3B-20, OF-3, SS-2, 2B-1

Ray Oyler

OYLER, RAYMOND FRANCIS   BR TR 5'11" 165 lbs.
B. Aug. 4, 1938, Indianapolis, Ind.   D. Jan. 26, 1981, Redmond, Wash.

Year Team	Games	BA	SA	AB	H	2B	3B	HR	HR%	R	RBI	BB	SO	SB	PH AB	PH H	PO	A	E	DP	TC/G	FA	G by Pos
1965 DET A	82	.186	.294	194	36	6	0	5	2.6	22	13	21	61	1	11	3	92	166	11	18	3.3	.959	SS-57, 2B-11, 3B-1, 1B-1
1966	71	.171	.252	210	36	8	3	1	0.5	16	9	23	62	0	1	0	107	194	11	42	4.4	.965	SS-69
1967	148	.207	.264	367	76	14	2	1	0.3	33	29	37	91	0	0	0	185	374	21	61	3.9	.964	SS-146
1968	111	.135	.186	215	29	6	1	1	0.5	13	12	20	59	0	0	0	139	207	8	31	3.2	.977	SS-111
1969 SEA A	106	.165	.267	255	42	5	0	7	2.7	24	22	31	80	1	0	0	143	266	15	47	4.0	.965	SS-106
1970 CAL A	24	.083	.083	24	2	0	0	0	0.0	2	1	3	6	0	7	0	7	12	0	1	0.8	1.000	SS-13, 3B-2
6 yrs.	542	.175	.251	1265	221	39	6	15	1.2	110	86	135	359	2	19	3	673	1219	66	200	3.6	.966	SS-502, 2B-11, 3B-3, 1B-1

WORLD SERIES

Year Team	Games	BA	SA	AB	H	2B	3B	HR	HR%	R	RBI	BB	SO	SB	PH AB	PH H	PO	A	E	DP	TC/G	FA	G by Pos
1968 DET A	4	–	–	0	0	0	0	0	–	0	0	0	0	0	0	0	2	0	0	0	0.5	1.000	SS-4

Ed Pabst

PABST, EDWARD D. A.   5'11" 170 lbs.
B. 1868, St. Louis, Mo.   D. June 19, 1940, St. Louis, Mo.

Year Team	Games	BA	SA	AB	H	2B	3B	HR	HR%	R	RBI	BB	SO	SB	PH AB	PH H	PO	A	E	DP	TC/G	FA	G by Pos
1890 2 teams		PHI	AA (8G – .400)		STL	AA (4G – .143)																	
" total	12	.308	.410	39	12	2	1	0	0.0	8		5		3	0	0	29	6	1	0	3.0	.972	OF-12

Jim Paciorek

PACIOREK, JAMES JOSEPH   BR TR 6'3" 205 lbs.
Brother of John Paciorek. Brother of Tom Paciorek.
B. June 7, 1960, Detroit, Mich.

Year Team	Games	BA	SA	AB	H	2B	3B	HR	HR%	R	RBI	BB	SO	SB	PH AB	PH H	PO	A	E	DP	TC/G	FA	G by Pos
1987 MIL A	48	.228	.337	101	23	5	2	2.0		16	10	12	20	1	8	3	113	22	8	12	3.0	.944	1B-21, 3B-15, OF-5

John Paciorek

PACIOREK, JOHN FRANCIS   BR TR 6'2" 200 lbs.
Brother of Tom Paciorek. Brother of Jim Paciorek.
B. Feb. 11, 1945, Detroit, Mich.

Year Team	Games	BA	SA	AB	H	2B	3B	HR	HR%	R	RBI	BB	SO	SB	PH AB	PH H	PO	A	E	DP	TC/G	FA	G by Pos
1963 HOU N	1	1.000	1.000	3	3	0	0	0	0.0	4	3	2	0	0	0	0	2	0	0	0	2.0	1.000	OF-1

Tom Paciorek

PACIOREK, THOMAS MARIAN   BR TR 6'4" 215 lbs.
Brother of John Paciorek. Brother of Jim Paciorek.
B. Nov. 2, 1946, Detroit, Mich.

Year Team	Games	BA	SA	AB	H	2B	3B	HR	HR%	R	RBI	BB	SO	SB	PH AB	PH H	PO	A	E	DP	TC/G	FA	G by Pos
1970 LA N	8	.222	.333	9	2	1	0	0	0.0	2	0	0	3	0	5	1	1	0	0	0	0.1	1.000	OF-3
1971	2	.500	.500	2	1	0	0	0	0.0	0	1	0	0	0	2	1	1	0	0	0	0.5	1.000	OF-1
1972	11	.255	.404	47	12	4	0	1	2.1	4	6	1	7	1	0	0	53	5	1	4	5.4	.983	OF-6, 1B-6
1973	96	.262	.379	195	51	8	0	5	2.6	26	18	11	35	3	17	4	117	3	2	3	1.3	.984	OF-77, 1B-4
1974	85	.240	.371	175	42	8	6	1	0.6	23	24	10	32	1	18	6	85	1	5	1	1.1	.945	OF-77, 1B-1
1975	62	.193	.269	145	28	8	0	1	0.7	14	5	11	29	4	10	2	69	0	2	0	1.1	.972	OF-54
1976 ATL N	111	.290	.383	324	94	10	4	4	1.2	39	36	19	57	2	20	8	216	10	3	8	2.1	.987	OF-84, 1B-12, 3B-1
1977	72	.239	.348	155	37	8	0	3	1.9	20	15	6	46	1	32	6	248	16	5	20	3.7	.981	1B-32, OF-9, 3B-1
1978 2 teams		ATL	N (5G – .333)		SEA	A (70G – .299)																	
" total	75	.300	.446	260	78	20	3	4	1.5	34	30	15	40	2	7	2	136	5	2	2	1.9	.986	OF-54, DH-12, 1B-5
1979 SEA A	103	.287	.445	310	89	23	4	6	1.9	38	42	28	62	6	17	4	237	12	1	12	2.4	.996	OF-75, 1B-15
1980	126	.273	.431	418	114	19	1	15	3.6	44	59	17	67	3	14	2	360	22	5	25	3.1	.987	OF-60, 1B-36, DH-23
1981	104	.326	.509	405	132	28	2	14	3.5	50	66	35	65	13	1	1	253	10	7	1	2.6	.974	OF-103
1982 CHI A	104	.312	.490	382	119	27	4	11	2.9	49	55	24	53	3	0	0	835	66	6	85	8.7	.993	1B-102, OF-6
1983	115	.307	.462	420	129	32	3	9	2.1	65	63	25	58	6	9	3	629	38	1	42	5.8	.999	1B-67, OF-55, DH-2
1984	115	.256	.358	363	93	21	2	4	1.1	35	29	25	69	6	18	7	596	25	6	50	5.6	.990	1B-67, OF-41
1985 2 teams		CHI	A (46G – .246)		NY	N (46G – .284)																	
" total	92	.265	.307	238	63	5	1	1	0.4	28	20	14	36	3	27	5	152	9	1	6	1.8	.994	OF-52, 1B-14, DH-12
1986 TEX A	88	.286	.376	213	61	7	0	4	1.9	17	22	3	41	1	15	5	178	45	4	16	2.6	.982	OF-25, 1B-23, 3B-21, DH-9, 1B-1
1987	27	.283	.483	60	17	3	0	3	5.0	6	12	1	19	0	4	1	82	7	1	9	3.3	.989	OF-12, 1B-12, DH-3
18 yrs.	1392	.282	.415	4121	1162	232	30	86	2.1	494	503	245	704	55	219	58	4248	274	52	284	3.3	.989	OF-794, 1B-396, DH-61, 3B-23, SS-1

LEAGUE CHAMPIONSHIP SERIES

Year Team	Games	BA	SA	AB	H	2B	3B	HR	HR%	R	RBI	BB	SO	SB	PH AB	PH H	PO	A	E	DP	TC/G	FA	G by Pos
1974 LA N	1	1.000	1.000	1	1	0	0	0	0.0	0	0	0	0	0	1	1	0	0	0	0	0.0	–	OF-1
1983 CHI A	4	.250	.250	16	4	0	0	0	0.0	1	1	1	2	0	0	0	30	2	0	2	8.0	1.000	1B-3, OF-2
2 yrs.	5	.294	.294	17	5	0	0	0	0.0	1	1	1	2	0	1	1	30	2	0	2	6.4	1.000	OF-3, 1B-3

WORLD SERIES

Year Team	Games	BA	SA	AB	H	2B	3B	HR	HR%	R	RBI	BB	SO	SB	PH AB	PH H	PO	A	E	DP	TC/G	FA	G by Pos
1974 LA N	3	.500	1.000	2	1	1	0	0	0.0	1	0	0	0	0	2	1	0	0	0	0	0.0	–	

Year	Team	Games	BA	SA	AB	H	2B	3B	HR	HR%	R	RBI	BB	SO	SB	Pinch Hit AB	Pinch Hit H	PO	A	E	DP	TC/G	FA	G by Pos

Frankie Pack

PACK, FRANK
B. Apr. 10, 1928, Morristown, Tenn.   BL TR 6'   190 lbs.

Year	Team	Games	BA	SA	AB	H	2B	3B	HR	HR%	R	RBI	BB	SO	SB	PH AB	PH H	PO	A	E	DP	TC/G	FA	G by Pos
1949	STL A	1	.000	.000	1	0	0	0	0	0.0	0	0	0	1	0	1	0	0	0	0	0	0.0	–	

Dick Padden

PADDEN, RICHARD JOSEPH (Brains)
B. Sept. 17, 1870, Martin's Ferry, Ohio   D. Oct. 31, 1922, Martin's Ferry, Ohio   BR TR 5'10½" 165 lbs.

Year	Team	Games	BA	SA	AB	H	2B	3B	HR	HR%	R	RBI	BB	SO	SB	PH AB	PH H	PO	A	E	DP	TC/G	FA	G by Pos
1896	PIT N	61	.242	.361	219	53	4	8	2	0.9	33	24	14		8	0	0	176	149	24	14	5.7	.931	2B-61
1897		134	.282	.364	517	146	16	10	2	0.4	84	58	38		18	0	0	369	402	48	36	6.1	.941	2B-134
1898		128	.257	.311	463	119	7	6	2	0.4	61	43	35		11	0	0	301	407	40	46	5.8	.947	2B-128
1899	WAS N	134	.277	.366	451	125	20	7	2	0.4	66	61	24		27	1	1	341	405	64	45	6.0	.921	SS-85, 2B-48
1901	STL N	123	.256	.332	488	125	17	7	2	0.4	71	62	31		26	0	0	301	360	40	49	5.7	.943	2B-115, SS-8
1902	STL A	117	.264	.349	413	109	26	3	1	0.2	54	40	30		11	0	0	288	363	22	64	5.8	.967	2B-117
1903		29	.202	.234	94	19	3	0	0	0.0	7	6	9		5	0	0	57	93	7	17	5.4	.955	2B-29
1904		132	.238	.298	453	108	19	4	0	0.0	42	36	40		23	0	0	288	373	28	31	5.2	.959	2B-132
1905		16	.172	.224	58	10	1	1	0	0.0	5	4	3		3	0	0	32	44	4	2	5.0	.950	2B-16
9 yrs.		874	.258	.333	3156	814	113	46	11	0.3	423	334	224		132	1	1	2153	2596	277	304	5.8	.945	2B-780, SS-93

Tom Padden

PADDEN, THOMAS FRANCIS
B. Oct. 6, 1908, Manchester, N. H.   D. June 11, 1973, Manchester, N. H.   BR TR 5'11½" 170 lbs.

Year	Team	Games	BA	SA	AB	H	2B	3B	HR	HR%	R	RBI	BB	SO	SB	PH AB	PH H	PO	A	E	DP	TC/G	FA	G by Pos
1932	PIT N	47	.263	.331	118	31	6	1	0	0.0	13	10	9	7	0	3	1	111	19	2	1	2.8	.985	C-43
1933		30	.211	.233	90	19	2	0	0	0.0	8	6	2	6	0	3	0	100	22	2	1	4.1	.984	C-27
1934		82	.321	.388	237	76	12	2	0	0.0	27	22	30	23	3	4	1	297	20	7	3	4.0	.978	C-76
1935		97	.272	.318	302	82	9	1	1	0.3	35	30	48	26	1	3	1	425	64	17	2	5.2	.966	C-94
1936		88	.249	.306	281	70	9	2	1	0.4	22	31	22	41	0	1	0	342	62	10	6	4.7	.976	C-87
1937		35	.286	.306	98	28	2	0	0	0.0	14	8	13	11	1	1	0	143	28	3	4	5.0	.983	C-34
1943	2 teams	PHI N	(17G – .293)		WAS A	(3G – .000)																		
"	total	20	.273	.273	44	12	0	0	0	0.0	6	1	3	1	0	2	0	64	7	0	2	3.6	1.000	C-18
7 yrs.		399	.272	.321	1170	318	40	6	2	0.2	122	110	127	121	5	17	3	1482	222	41	19	4.4	.977	C-379

Del Paddock

PADDOCK, DELMAR HAROLD
B. June 8, 1887, Volga, S. D.   D. Feb. 6, 1952, Remer, Minn.   BL TR 5'9"   165 lbs.

Year	Team	Games	BA	SA	AB	H	2B	3B	HR	HR%	R	RBI	BB	SO	SB	PH AB	PH H	PO	A	E	DP	TC/G	FA	G by Pos
1912	2 teams	CHI A	(1G – .000)		NY A	(45G – .288)																		
"	total	46	.287	.376	157	45	5	3	1	0.6	26	14	23		9	2	0	55	73	16	4	3.1	.889	3B-41, 2B-2, OF-1

Don Padgett

PADGETT, DON WILSON (Red)
B. Dec. 5, 1911, Caroleen, N. C.   D. Dec. 9, 1980, High Point, N. C.   BL TR 6'   190 lbs.

Year	Team	Games	BA	SA	AB	H	2B	3B	HR	HR%	R	RBI	BB	SO	SB	PH AB	PH H	PO	A	E	DP	TC/G	FA	G by Pos
1937	STL N	123	.314	.457	446	140	22	6	10	2.2	62	74	30	43	4	13	4	225	9	11	5	2.0	.955	OF-109
1938		110	.271	.425	388	105	26	5	8	2.1	59	65	18	28	0	18	6	295	27	9	15	3.0	.973	OF-71, 1B-16, C-6
1939		92	.399	.554	233	93	15	3	5	2.1	38	53	18	11	1	21	4	276	18	7	6	3.3	.977	C-61, 1B-6
1940		93	.242	.388	240	58	15	1	6	2.5	24	41	26	16	1	16	3	244	34	11	5	3.1	.962	C-72, 1B-2
1941		107	.247	.349	324	80	18	0	5	1.5	39	44	21	16	0	22	3	189	7	9	1	1.9	.956	OF-62, C-18, 1B-2
1946	2 teams	BKN N	(19G – .167)		BOS N	(44G – .255)																		
"	total	63	.234	.336	128	30	4	0	3	2.3	8	30	9	11	0	27	4	89	15	5	2	1.7	.954	C-36
1947	PHI N	75	.316	.380	158	50	8	1	0	0.0	14	24	16	5	0	31	8	111	16	5	1	1.8	.962	C-39
1948		36	.230	.270	74	17	3	0	0	0.0	3	7	3	2	0	13	2	64	2	3	0	1.9	.957	C-19
8 yrs.		699	.288	.415	1991	573	111	16	37	1.9	247	338	141	130	6	161	34	1493	128	60	35	2.4	.964	C-251, OF-242, 1B-26

Ernie Padgett

PADGETT, ERNEST KITCHEN (Red)
B. Mar. 1, 1899, Philadelphia, Pa.   D. Apr. 15, 1957, East Orange, N. J.   BR TR 5'8"   155 lbs.

Year	Team	Games	BA	SA	AB	H	2B	3B	HR	HR%	R	RBI	BB	SO	SB	PH AB	PH H	PO	A	E	DP	TC/G	FA	G by Pos
1923	BOS N	4	.182	.182	11	2	0	0	0	0.0	2		0	1	0	1	0	14	12	1	4	6.8	.963	SS-2, 2B-1
1924		138	.255	.347	502	128	25	9	1	0.2	42	46	37	56	4	0	0	155	288	17	35	3.3	.963	3B-113, 2B-29
1925		86	.305	.395	256	78	9	7	0	0.0	31	29	14	14	3	15	4	127	160	13	30	3.5	.957	2B-47, SS-18, 3B-7
1926	CLE A	36	.210	.242	62	13	0	1	0	0.0	7	6	3	1	0	3	0	13	46	4	4	1.8	.937	3B-29, SS-2
1927		7	.286	.286	7	2	0	0	0	0.0	1	0	0	2	1	3	1	3	2	0	0	0.7	1.000	2B-4
5 yrs.		271	.266	.351	838	223	34	17	1	0.1	84	81	61	75	8	22	5	312	508	35	73	3.2	.959	3B-149, 2B-81, SS-22

Dennis Paepke

PAEPKE, DENNIS RAY
B. Apr. 17, 1945, Long Beach, Calif.   BR TR 6'   202 lbs.

Year	Team	Games	BA	SA	AB	H	2B	3B	HR	HR%	R	RBI	BB	SO	SB	PH AB	PH H	PO	A	E	DP	TC/G	FA	G by Pos
1969	KC A	12	.111	.148	27	3	1	0	0	0.0	2	3	0	4	0			56	2	0	0	4.8	1.000	C-8
1971		60	.204	.283	152	31	6	0	2	1.3	11	14	8	29	0	16	3	160	15	3	1	3.0	.983	C-32, OF-17
1972		2	.000	.000	6	0	0	0	0	0.0	0	0	1	1	0	0	0	14	2	3	0	9.5	.842	C-2
1974		6	.167	.167	12	2	0	0	0	0.0	0	1	0	2	0	1	0	10	2	0	1	2.0	1.000	C-4, OF-1
4 yrs.		80	.183	.249	197	36	7	0	2	1.0	13	14	12	36	0	21	3	240	21	6	2	3.3	.978	C-46, OF-18

Andy Pafko

PAFKO, ANDREW (Pruschka, Handy Andy)
B. Feb. 25, 1921, Boyceville, Wis.   BR TR 6'   190 lbs.

Year	Team	Games	BA	SA	AB	H	2B	3B	HR	HR%	R	RBI	BB	SO	SB	PH AB	PH H	PO	A	E	DP	TC/G	FA	G by Pos
1943	CHI N	13	.379	.431	58	22	3	0	0	0.0	7	10	2	5	1	0	0	25	0	0	0	1.9	1.000	OF-13
1944		128	.269	.406	469	126	16	2	6	1.3	47	62	28	23	2	5	1	333	24	6	4	2.8	.983	OF-123
1945		144	.298	.455	534	159	24	12	12	2.2	64	110	45	36	5	4	1	371	11	2	0	2.7	.995	OF-140
1946		65	.282	.380	234	66	6	4	3	1.3	18	39	27	15	4	1	0	165	13	4	4	2.8	.978	OF-64
1947		129	.302	.454	513	155	25	7	13	2.5	68	66	31	39	4	2	0	327	9	5	3	2.6	.985	OF-127
1948		142	.312	.516	548	171	30	2	26	4.7	82	101	50	50	3	1	0	125	314	29	29	3.3	.938	3B-139
1949		144	.281	.449	519	146	29	2	18	3.5	79	69	63	33	4	1	1	257	109	13	12	2.6	.966	OF-98, 3B-49
1950		146	.304	.591	514	156	24	8	36	7.0	95	92	69	32	4	2	0	342	12	8	1	2.5	.978	OF-144
1951	2 teams	CHI N	(49G – .264)		BKN N	(84G – .249)																		
"	total	133	.255	.501	455	116	16	3	30	6.6	68	93	52	37	2	6	0	263	14	2	3	2.1	.993	OF-126
1952	BKN N	150	.287	.439	551	158	17	5	19	3.4	76	85	64	48	4	4	1	244	37	6	5	1.9	.979	OF-139, 3B-13
1953	MIL N	140	.297	.455	516	153	23	4	17	3.3	70	72	37	33	2	1	0	241	5	6	1	1.8	.976	OF-139
1954		138	.286	.427	510	146	22	4	14	2.7	61	69	61	36	1	0	0	245	9	8	3	1.9	.969	OF-138
1955		86	.266	.377	252	67	3	5	5	2.0	29	34	7	23	1	22	3	105	27	3	1	1.6	.978	OF-58, 3B-12
1956		45	.258	.376	93	24	5	0	2	2.2	15	9	10	13	1	12	3	43	1	1	1	1.0	.978	OF-37
1957		83	.277	.423	220	61	6	3	8	3.6	31	27	10	22	1	22	5	108	1	1	2	1.3	.982	OF-69

Year	Team		Games	BA	SA	AB	H	2B	3B	HR	HR%	R	RBI	BB	SO	SB	Pinch Hit AB	Pinch Hit H	PO	A	E	DP	TC/G	FA	G by Pos

Andy Pafko *continued*

Year	Team		Games	BA	SA	AB	H	2B	3B	HR	HR%	R	RBI	BB	SO	SB	AB	H	PO	A	E	DP	TC/G	FA	G by Pos
1958			95	.238	.348	164	39	7	1	3	1.8	17	23	15	17	0	13	3	107	2	0	0	1.1	1.000	OF-93
1959			71	.218	.324	142	31	8	2	1	0.7	17	15	14	15	0	13	2	87	1	2	0	1.3	.978	OF-64
17 yrs.			1852	.285	.449	6292	1796	264	62	213	3.4	844	976	561	477	38	110	20	3388	590	97	67	2.2	.976	OF-1572, 3B-213

WORLD SERIES

Year	Team		Games	BA	SA	AB	H	2B	3B	HR	HR%	R	RBI	BB	SO	SB	AB	H	PO	A	E	DP	TC/G	FA	G by Pos
1945	CHI	N	7	.214	.357	28	6	2	1	0	0.0	5	2	2	5	0	0	0	24	2	1	0	3.9	.963	OF-7
1952	BKN	N	7	.190	.190	21	4	0	0	0	0.0	0	2	0	4	0	2	0	12	1	0	0	1.9	1.000	OF-5
1957	MIL	N	6	.214	.214	14	3	0	0	0	0.0	1	0	0	1	0	1	0	9	0	0	0	1.5	1.000	OF-5
1958			4	.333	.444	9	3	1	0	0	0.0	0	1	0	0	0	0	0	8	0	0	0	2.0	1.000	OF-4
4 yrs.			24	.222	.292	72	16	3	1	0	0.0	6	5	2	10	0	3	0	53	3	1	0	2.4	.982	OF-21

Jose Pagan

PAGAN, JOSE ANTONIO
Born Jose Antonio Pagan y Rodriguez.
B. May 5, 1935, Barceloneta, Puerto Rico

BR TR 5'9" 160 lbs.

Year	Team		Games	BA	SA	AB	H	2B	3B	HR	HR%	R	RBI	BB	SO	SB	AB	H	PO	A	E	DP	TC/G	FA	G by Pos
1959	SF	N	31	.174	.196	46	8	1	0	0	0.0	7	1	2	8	1	4	0	17	26	4	3	1.5	.915	3B-18, SS-5, 2B-3
1960			18	.286	.408	49	14	2	2	0	0.0	8	2	1	6	2	6	0	16	17	3	2	2.0	.917	SS-11, 3B-1
1961			134	.253	.332	434	110	15	2	5	1.2	38	46	31	45	8	1	1	230	334	21	55	4.4	.964	SS-132, OF-4
1962			164	.259	.359	580	150	25	6	7	1.2	73	57	47	77	13	0	0	286	461	21	84	4.7	.973	SS-164
1963			148	.234	.300	483	113	12	1	6	1.2	46	39	26	67	10	4	1	262	375	20	69	4.4	.970	SS-143, OF-1, 2B-1
1964			134	.223	.264	367	82	10	1	1	0.3	33	28	35	66	5	0	0	210	303	22	52	4.0	.959	SS-132, OF-8
1965	2 teams		SF N (26G – .205)			PIT N (42G – .237)																			
"	total		68	.215	.256	121	26	5	0	0	0.0	16	6	9	16	1	10	2	47	97	12	12	2.3	.923	SS-33, 3B-15
1966	PIT	N	109	.264	.370	368	97	15	6	4	1.1	44	54	13	38	0	10	2	86	219	18	26	3.0	.944	3B-83, SS-18, OF-3, 2B-3
1967			81	.289	.351	211	61	6	2	1	0.5	17	19	10	28	1	13	4	73	109	7	14	2.3	.963	3B-25, OF-23, SS-16, 2B-2, C-1
1968			80	.221	.350	163	36	7	1	4	2.5	24	21	11	32	2	22	5	40	65	7	7	1.4	.938	3B-30, OF-19, SS-8, 2B-2, 1B-1
1969			108	.285	.453	274	78	11	4	9	3.3	29	42	17	46	1	42	19	56	78	5	7	1.3	.964	3B-44, OF-23, 2B-1
1970			95	.265	.426	230	61	14	1	7	3.0	21	29	20	24	1	35	9	46	91	6	14	1.5	.958	3B-53, OF-4, 2B-1, 1B-1
1971			57	.241	.342	158	38	1	0	5	3.2	16	15	16	25	0	12	2	53	62	2	9	2.1	.983	3B-41, OF-3, 1B-2
1972			53	.252	.394	127	32	9	0	3	2.4	11	8	5	17	0	22	6	27	37	7	3	1.3	.901	3B-32, OF-2
1973	PHI	N	46	.205	.269	78	16	5	0	0	0.0	4	5	1	15	0	29	6	21	18	1	2	0.9	.975	3B-16, 1B-5, OF-2, 2B-1
15 yrs.			1326	.250	.344	3689	922	138	26	52	1.4	387	372	244	510	46	207	56	1470	2292	156	359	3.0	.960	SS-662, 3B-358, OF-92, 2B-14, 1B-9, C-1

LEAGUE CHAMPIONSHIP SERIES

Year	Team		Games	BA	SA	AB	H	2B	3B	HR	HR%	R	RBI	BB	SO	SB	AB	H	PO	A	E	DP	TC/G	FA	G by Pos
1970	PIT	N	1	.333	.333	3	1	0	0	0	0.0	0	1	0	1	0	0	0	0	4	0	0	4.0	1.000	3B-1
1971			1	.000	.000	1	0	0	0	0	0.0	0	0	0	0	0	0	0	1	2	0	0	3.0	1.000	3B-1
2 yrs.			2	.250	.250	4	1	0	0	0	0.0	0	1	0	1	0	0	0	1	6	0	0	3.5	1.000	3B-2

WORLD SERIES

Year	Team		Games	BA	SA	AB	H	2B	3B	HR	HR%	R	RBI	BB	SO	SB	AB	H	PO	A	E	DP	TC/G	FA	G by Pos
1962	SF	N	7	.368	.526	19	7	0	0	1	5.3	2	2	0	1	0	0	0	8	14	1	2	3.3	.957	SS-7
1971	PIT	N	4	.267	.400	15	4	2	0	0	0.0	0	2	0	1	0	0	0	2	8	0	1	2.5	1.000	3B-4
2 yrs.			11	.324	.471	34	11	2	0	1	2.9	2	4	0	2	0	0	0	10	22	1	3	3.0	.970	SS-7, 3B-4

Mike Page

PAGE, MICHAEL RANDY
B. July 12, 1940, Woodruff, S. C.

BL TR 6'2½" 210 lbs.

Year	Team		Games	BA	SA	AB	H	2B	3B	HR	HR%	R	RBI	BB	SO	SB	AB	H	PO	A	E	DP	TC/G	FA	G by Pos
1968	ATL	N	20	.179	.179	28	5	0	0	0	0.0	1	1	1	9	0	13	1	5	0	0	0	0.3	1.000	OF-6

Mitchell Page

PAGE, MITCHELL OTIS
B. Oct. 15, 1951, Los Angeles, Calif.

BL TR 6'2" 205 lbs.

Year	Team		Games	BA	SA	AB	H	2B	3B	HR	HR%	R	RBI	BB	SO	SB	AB	H	PO	A	E	DP	TC/G	FA	G by Pos
1977	OAK	A	145	.307	.521	501	154	28	8	21	4.2	85	75	78	95	42	6	2	279	11	14	0	2.1	.954	OF-133, DH-8
1978			147	.285	.459	516	147	25	7	17	3.3	62	70	53	95	23	1	0	211	4	6	0	1.5	.973	OF-114, DH-33
1979			133	.247	.335	478	118	11	2	9	1.9	51	42	52	93	17	1	0	6	0	0	0	0.0	1.000	DH-126, OF-4
1980			110	.244	.443	348	85	10	4	17	4.9	58	51	35	87	14	19	2	0	0	0	0	0.0	–	DH-101
1981			34	.141	.283	92	13	1	0	4	4.3	9	13	7	29	2	4	1	0	0	0	0	0.0	–	DH-29
1982			31	.256	.474	78	20	5	0	4	5.1	14	7	7	24	3	3	0	0	0	0	0	0.0	–	DH-24
1983			57	.241	.278	79	19	3	0	0	0.0	16	1	10	22	3	12	3	12	0	0	0	0.2	1.000	DH-34, OF-10
1984	PIT	N	16	.333	.417	12	4	1	0	0	0.0	2	0	3	4	0	12	4	0	0	0	0	0.0	–	DH-5, OF-1
8 yrs.			673	.266	.429	2104	560	84	21	72	3.4	297	259	245	449	104	58	12	508	15	20	0	0.8	.963	DH-355, OF-261

Karl Pagel

PAGEL, KARL DOUGLAS
B. Mar. 29, 1955, Madison, Wis.

BL TL 6'2" 188 lbs.

Year	Team		Games	BA	SA	AB	H	2B	3B	HR	HR%	R	RBI	BB	SO	SB	AB	H	PO	A	E	DP	TC/G	FA	G by Pos
1978	CHI	N	2	.000	.000	2	0	0	0	0	0.0	0	0	0	2	0	2	0	0	0	0	0	0.0	–	
1979			1	.000	.000	1	0	0	0	0	0.0	0	0	0	1	0	1	0	0	0	0	0	0.0	–	
1981	CLE	A	14	.267	.733	15	4	0	2	1	6.7	3	4	4	1	0	5	1	28	6	0	5	2.4	1.000	1B-6, DH-1
1982			23	.167	.167	18	3	0	0	0	0.0	3	2	7	11	0	8	2	30	2	1	2	1.4	.970	1B-10, DH-1
1983			8	.300	.300	20	6	0	0	0	0.0	1	1	0	5	0	3	1	0	0	1	0	0.1	–	DH-5, OF-1
5 yrs.			48	.232	.357	56	13	0	2	1	1.8	7	7	11	20	0	19	4	58	8	2	7	1.4	.971	1B-16, DH-7, OF-1

Jim Pagliaroni

PAGLIARONI, JAMES VINCENT (Pag)
B. Dec. 8, 1937, Dearborn, Mich.

BR TR 6'4" 210 lbs.

Year	Team		Games	BA	SA	AB	H	2B	3B	HR	HR%	R	RBI	BB	SO	SB	AB	H	PO	A	E	DP	TC/G	FA	G by Pos
1955	BOS	A	1	–	–	0	0	0	0	0		0	0	0	0	0	0	0	0	0	0	0	0.0	–	C-1
1960			28	.306	.548	62	19	5	2	2	3.2	7	9	13	11	0	7	1	91	5	1	0	3.5	.990	C-18
1961			120	.242	.415	376	91	17	0	16	4.3	50	58	55	74	1	14	3	586	39	10	5	5.3	.984	C-108
1962			90	.258	.438	260	67	14	0	11	4.2	39	37	36	55	2	13	2	411	33	6	4	5.0	.987	C-73
1963	PIT	N	92	.230	.381	252	58	5	0	11	4.4	27	26	36	57	0	9	3	435	56	6	4	5.4	.988	C-85
1964			97	.295	.454	302	89	12	3	10	3.3	33	36	41	56	1	1	0	584	42	5	5	6.5	.992	C-96
1965			134	.268	.432	403	108	15	0	17	4.2	42	65	41	84	0	4	1	669	42	4	14	5.3	.994	C-131
1966			123	.235	.377	374	88	20	0	11	2.9	37	49	50	71	0	7	1	613	37	2	6	5.3	.997	C-118
1967			44	.200	.230	100	20	1	1	0	0.0	4	9	16	26	0	7	0	172	13	3	6	4.3	.984	C-38
1968	OAK	A	66	.246	.357	199	49	4	0	6	3.0	19	20	24	42	0	3	1	375	16	1	3	5.9	.997	C-63

Year Team	Games	BA	SA	AB	H	2B	3B	HR	HR%	R	RBI	BB	SO	SB	Pinch Hit AB	Pinch Hit H	PO	A	E	DP	TC/G	FA	G by Pos

Jim Pagliaroni *continued*

Year Team	Games	BA	SA	AB	H	2B	3B	HR	HR%	R	RBI	BB	SO	SB	AB	H	PO	A	E	DP	TC/G	FA	G by Pos
1969 2 teams		OAK A (14G – .148)				SEA A		(40G – .264)															
" total	54	.241	.423	137	33	5	1	6	4.4	11	16	18	18	0	16	6	216	19	3	3	4.4	.987	C-36, 1B-2, OF-1
11 yrs.	849	.252	.407	2465	622	98	7	90	3.7	269	326	330	494	4	81	18	4152	302	41	50	5.3	.991	C-767, 1B-2, OF-1

Mike Pagliarulo

PAGLIARULO, MICHAEL TIMOTHY (Pags)
B. Mar. 15, 1960, Medford, Mass.
BL TR 6'2" 195 lbs.

Year Team	Games	BA	SA	AB	H	2B	3B	HR	HR%	R	RBI	BB	SO	SB	AB	H	PO	A	E	DP	TC/G	FA	G by Pos
1984 NY A	67	.239	.448	201	48	15	3	7	3.5	24	34	15	46	0	0	0	44	106	7	16	2.3	.955	3B-67
1985	138	.239	.442	380	91	16	2	19	5.0	55	62	45	86	0	19	6	67	187	13	15	1.9	.951	3B-134
1986	149	.238	.464	504	120	24	3	28	5.6	71	71	54	120	4	9	1	104	283	19	25	2.7	.953	3B-143, SS-2
1987	150	.234	.479	522	122	26	3	32	6.1	76	87	53	111	1	8	0	97	297	17	35	2.7	.959	3B-147, 1B-1
1988	125	.216	.367	444	96	20	1	15	3.4	46	67	37	104	1	9	0	82	232	19	16	2.7	.943	3B-124
1989 2 teams		NY A (74G – .197)			SD N	(50G – .196)																	
" total	124	.197	.299	371	73	17	0	7	1.9	31	30	37	82	3	10	1	44	205	17	9	2.1	.936	3B-118, DH-1
6 yrs.	753	.227	.419	2422	550	118	12	108	4.5	303	351	241	549	9	55	8	438	1310	92	116	2.4	.950	3B-733, SS-2, DH-1, 1B-1

Tom Pagnozzi

PAGNOZZI, THOMAS ALAN
B. July 30, 1962, Tucson, Ariz.
BR TR 6' 190 lbs.

Year Team	Games	BA	SA	AB	H	2B	3B	HR	HR%	R	RBI	BB	SO	SB	AB	H	PO	A	E	DP	TC/G	FA	G by Pos
1987 STL N	27	.188	.333	48	9	1	0	2	4.2	8	9	4	13	1	7	1	61	5	0	2	2.4	1.000	C-25, 1B-1
1988	81	.282	.328	195	55	9	0	0	0.0	17	15	11	32	0	26	4	340	30	4	11	4.6	.989	1B-28, C-28, 3B-5
1989	52	.150	.175	80	12	2	0	0	0.0	3	3	6	19	0	15	2	100	9	2	1	2.1	.982	C-38, 1B-2, 3B-1
3 yrs.	160	.235	.291	323	76	12	0	2	0.6	28	27	21	64	1	48	8	501	44	6	14	3.4	.989	C-91, 1B-31, 3B-6

LEAGUE CHAMPIONSHIP SERIES

Year Team	Games	BA	SA	AB	H	2B	3B	HR	HR%	R	RBI	BB	SO	SB	AB	H	PO	A	E	DP	TC/G	FA	G by Pos
1987 STL N	1	.000	.000	1	0	0	0	0	0.0	0	0	0	0	0	1	0	0	0	0	0	0.0	–	

WORLD SERIES

Year Team	Games	BA	SA	AB	H	2B	3B	HR	HR%	R	RBI	BB	SO	SB	AB	H	PO	A	E	DP	TC/G	FA	G by Pos
1987 STL N	2	.250	.250	4	1	0	0	0	0.0	0	0	0	0	0	1	0	0	0	0	0	0.0	–	DH-1

Rey Palacios

PALACIOS, ROBERT REY
B. Nov. 8, 1962, Brooklyn, N. Y.
BR TR 5'10" 190 lbs.

Year Team	Games	BA	SA	AB	H	2B	3B	HR	HR%	R	RBI	BB	SO	SB	AB	H	PO	A	E	DP	TC/G	FA	G by Pos
1988 KC A	5	.091	.091	11	1	0	0	0	0.0	2	0	0	4	0	1	0	17	1	0	0	3.6	1.000	C-3, 3B-1
1989	55	.170	.277	47	8	2	0	1	2.1	12	8	2	14	0	1	0	96	15	2	8	2.1	.982	3B-21, 1B-18, C-13, DH-2, OF-1
2 yrs.	60	.155	.241	58	9	2	0	1	1.7	14	8	2	18	0	2	0	113	16	2	8	2.2	.985	3B-22, 1B-18, C-16, DH-2, OF-1

Rafael Palmeiro

PALMEIRO, RAFAEL
Born Rafael Palmeiro y Corrales.
B. Sept. 24, 1964, Havana, Cuba
BL TL 6' 180 lbs.

Year Team	Games	BA	SA	AB	H	2B	3B	HR	HR%	R	RBI	BB	SO	SB	AB	H	PO	A	E	DP	TC/G	FA	G by Pos
1986 CHI N	22	.247	.425	73	18	4	0	3	4.1	9	12	4	6	1	2	0	34	2	1	1	1.8	.900	OF-20
1987	84	.276	.543	221	61	15	1	14	6.3	32	30	20	26	2	27	5	176	9	1	16	2.2	.995	OF-45, 1B-18
1988	152	.307	.436	580	178	41	5	8	1.4	75	53	38	34	12	5	0	322	11	5	2	2.2	.985	OF-152
1989 TEX A	156	.275	.374	559	154	23	4	8	1.4	76	64	63	48	4	3	1	1167	119	12	106	8.3	.991	1B-147, DH-6
4 yrs.	414	.287	.428	1433	411	83	10	33	2.3	192	159	125	114	19	37	6	1699	141	22	125	4.5	.988	OF-217, 1B-165, DH-6

Dean Palmer

PALMER, DEAN WILLIAM
B. Dec. 27, 1968, Tallahassee, Fla.
BR TR 6'1" 175 lbs.

Year Team	Games	BA	SA	AB	H	2B	3B	HR	HR%	R	RBI	BB	SO	SB	AB	H	PO	A	E	DP	TC/G	FA	G by Pos
1989 TEX A	16	.105	.211	19	2	2	0	0	0.0	0	1	0	12	0	6	0	3	4	2	0	0.6	.778	DH-6, 3B-6, OF-1, SS-1

Eddie Palmer

PALMER, EDWIN HENRY (Baldy)
B. June 1, 1893, Petty, Tex. D. Jan. 9, 1983, Marlow, Okla.
BR TR 5'9½" 175 lbs.

Year Team	Games	BA	SA	AB	H	2B	3B	HR	HR%	R	RBI	BB	SO	SB	AB	H	PO	A	E	DP	TC/G	FA	G by Pos
1917 PHI A	16	.212	.231	52	11	1	0	0	0.0	7	5	7	7	1	2	0	16	32	6	1	3.4	.889	3B-13, SS-1

Joe Palmisano

PALMISANO, JOSEPH
B. Nov. 19, 1902, West Point, Ga. D. Nov. 5, 1971, Albuquerque, N. M.
BR TR 5'8" 160 lbs.

Year Team	Games	BA	SA	AB	H	2B	3B	HR	HR%	R	RBI	BB	SO	SB	AB	H	PO	A	E	DP	TC/G	FA	G by Pos
1931 PHI A	19	.227	.273	44	10	2	0	0	0.0	5	4	6	3	0	2	0	45	4	2	2	2.7	.961	C-16, 2B-1

Stan Palys

PALYS, STANLEY FRANCIS
B. May 1, 1930, Blakely, Pa.
BR TR 6'2" 190 lbs.

Year Team	Games	BA	SA	AB	H	2B	3B	HR	HR%	R	RBI	BB	SO	SB	AB	H	PO	A	E	DP	TC/G	FA	G by Pos
1953 PHI N	2	.000	.000	2	0	0	0	0	0.0	0	0	1	0	0	1	0	0	0	0	0	0.0	–	OF-1
1954	2	.250	.250	4	1	0	0	0	0.0	0	0	1	1	0	1	0	2	0	0	0	1.0	1.000	OF-1
1955 2 teams		PHI N (15G – .288)			CIN N	(79G – .230)																	
" total	94	.241	.391	274	66	17	0	8	2.9	37	38	18	40	1	22	4	146	4	1	0	1.6	.993	OF-70, 1B-1
1956 CIN N	40	.226	.340	53	12	0	0	2	3.8	5	5	6	13	0	24	6	13	0	1	0	0.4	.929	OF-10
4 yrs.	138	.237	.378	333	79	17	0	10	3.0	42	43	26	54	2	47	10	161	4	2	0	1.2	.988	OF-82, 1B-1

Jim Pankovits

PANKOVITS, JAMES FRANKLIN
B. Aug. 6, 1955, Pennington Gap, Va.
BR TR 5'10" 170 lbs.

Year Team	Games	BA	SA	AB	H	2B	3B	HR	HR%	R	RBI	BB	SO	SB	AB	H	PO	A	E	DP	TC/G	FA	G by Pos
1984 HOU N	53	.284	.407	81	23	7	0	1	1.2	6	14	2	20	2	40	9	22	22	3	7	0.9	.936	2B-15, SS-4, OF-3
1985	75	.244	.331	172	42	3	0	4	2.3	24	14	17	29	1	23	5	81	38	2	8	1.6	.983	OF-33, 2B-21, SS-1, 3B-1
1986	70	.283	.381	113	32	6	1	1	0.9	12	7	11	25	1	38	11	42	58	4	10	1.5	.962	2B-26, OF-5, C-1
1987	50	.230	.311	61	14	2	0	1	1.6	7	8	6	13	2	32	7	19	15	0	3	0.7	1.000	2B-9, OF-6, 3B-4
1988	68	.221	.329	140	31	7	1	2	1.4	13	12	8	28	2	27	2	48	80	11	20	2.0	.921	2B-31, 3B-11, 1B-2
5 yrs.	316	.250	.349	567	142	25	2	9	1.6	62	55	44	115	8	160	34	212	213	20	48	1.4	.955	2B-102, OF-47, 3B-16, SS-5, 1B-2, C-1

LEAGUE CHAMPIONSHIP SERIES

Year Team	Games	BA	SA	AB	H	2B	3B	HR	HR%	R	RBI	BB	SO	SB	AB	H	PO	A	E	DP	TC/G	FA	G by Pos
1986 HOU N	2	.000	.000	2	0	0	0	0	0.0	0	0	0	1	0	2	0	0	0	0	0	0.0	–	

Ken Pape

PAPE, KENNETH WAYNE
B. Oct. 1, 1951, San Antonio, Tex.
BR TR 5'11" 195 lbs.

Year	Team	Games	BA	SA	AB	H	2B	3B	HR	HR%	R	RBI	BB	SO	SB	Pinch Hit AB	Pinch Hit H	PO	A	E	DP	TC/G	FA	G by Pos

Ken Pape *continued*

Year	Team	Games	BA	SA	AB	H	2B	3B	HR	HR%	R	RBI	BB	SO	SB	AB	H	PO	A	E	DP	TC/G	FA	G by Pos
1976	TEX A	21	.217	.391	23	5	1	0	1	4.3	7	4	3	2	0	1	0	9	23	2	4	1.6	.941	SS-6, 3B-4, DH-3, 2B-1

Stan Papi

PAPI, STANLEY GERARD
B. Feb. 4, 1951, Fresno, Calif.

BR TR 6' 170 lbs.

Year	Team	Games	BA	SA	AB	H	2B	3B	HR	HR%	R	RBI	BB	SO	SB	AB	H	PO	A	E	DP	TC/G	FA	G by Pos
1974	STL N	8	.250	.250	4	1	0	0	0	0.0	0	0	0	0	0	1	0	6	3	0	3	1.1	1.000	SS-7, 2B-1
1977	MON N	13	.233	.326	43	10	2	1	0	0.0	5	4	1	9	1	0	0	10	15	2	0	2.1	.926	3B-10, SS-2, 2B-1
1978		67	.230	.303	152	35	11	0	0	0.0	15	11	10	28	0	24	3	56	88	6	13	2.2	.960	SS-22, 3B-15, 2B-5
1979	BOS A	50	.188	.282	117	22	8	0	1	0.9	9	6	5	20	0	3	0	61	118	3	24	3.6	.984	2B-26, SS-21, DH-1
1980	2 teams	BOS	A (1G – .000)		DET	A	(46G – .237)																	
"	total	47	.237	.412	114	27	3	4	3	2.6	12	12	5	24	0	4	1	68	80	5	19	3.3	.967	2B-31, 3B-12, SS-5, 1B-1
1981	DET A	40	.204	.344	93	19	2	1	3	3.2	8	12	3	18	1	4	1	16	51	4	3	1.8	.944	3B-32, DH-3, OF-1, 2B-1, 1B-1
6 yrs.		225	.218	.331	523	114	26	6	7	1.3	49	51	24	99	1	36	5	217	355	20	62	2.6	.966	3B-69, 2B-65, SS-57, DH-4, 1B-2, OF-1

Al Pardo

PARDO, ALBERTO JUDAS
B. Sept. 8, 1962, Oviedo, Spain

BB TR 6'2" 187 lbs.

Year	Team	Games	BA	SA	AB	H	2B	3B	HR	HR%	R	RBI	BB	SO	SB	AB	H	PO	A	E	DP	TC/G	FA	G by Pos
1985	BAL A	34	.133	.147	75	10	1	0	0	0.0	3	3	15	0	0	7	0	131	7	3	0	4.1	.979	C-29
1986		16	.137	.216	51	7	1	0	1	2.0	3	3	0	14	0	1	0	70	5	1	1	4.8	.987	C-14, DH-1
1988	PHI N	2	.000	.000	2	0	0	0	0	0.0	0	0	0	2	0	0	0	2	0	0	0	1.0	1.000	C-2
1989		1	.000	.000	1	0	0	0	0	0.0	0	0	0	0	0	0	0	3	0	0	0	3.0	1.000	C-1
4 yrs.		53	.132	.171	129	17	2	0	1	0.8	6	4	3	31	0	8	0	206	12	4	1	4.2	.982	C-46, DH-1

Johnny Paredes

PAREDES, JHONNY ALFONSO
Born Jhonny Alfonso Paredes y Isambert.
B. Sept. 2, 1962, Maracaibo, Venezuela

BR TR 5'11" 165 lbs.

Year	Team	Games	BA	SA	AB	H	2B	3B	HR	HR%	R	RBI	BB	SO	SB	AB	H	PO	A	E	DP	TC/G	FA	G by Pos
1988	MON N	35	.187	.242	91	17	2	0	1	1.1	6	10	9	17	5	2	0	46	77	3	18	3.6	.976	2B-28, OF-1

Freddy Parent

PARENT, FREDERICK ALFRED
B. Nov. 25, 1875, Biddeford, Me.   D. Nov. 2, 1972, Sanford, Me.

BR TR 5'7" 154 lbs.

Year	Team	Games	BA	SA	AB	H	2B	3B	HR	HR%	R	RBI	BB	SO	SB	AB	H	PO	A	E	DP	TC/G	FA	G by Pos
1899	STL N	2	.125	.125	8	1	0	0	0	0.0	0	1	0			0	0	3	5	1	1	4.5	.889	2B-2
1901	BOS A	138	.306	.408	517	158	23	9	4	0.8	87	59	41			16	0	260	446	63	52	5.6	.918	SS-138
1902		138	.275	.374	567	156	31	8	3	0.5	91	62	24			16	0	287	496	58	60	6.1	.931	SS-138
1903		139	.304	.441	560	170	31	17	4	0.7	83	80	13			24	0	296	456	57	36	5.8	.930	SS-139
1904		155	.291	.389	591	172	22	9	6	1.0	85	77	28			20	0	327	493	63	44	5.7	.929	SS-155
1905		153	.234	.277	602	141	16	5	0	0.0	55	33	47			25	0	294	461	66	48	5.4	.920	SS-153
1906		149	.235	.297	600	141	14	10	1	0.2	67	49	31			16	0	320	480	59	49	5.8	.931	SS-143, 2B-6
1907		119	.276	.355	409	113	19	5	1	0.2	51	26	22			12	12	2	195	191	25	20	3.6	.939	OF-47, SS-43, 3B-7, 2B-5
1908	CHI A	119	.207	.251	391	81	7	5	0	0.0	28	35	50			9	0	212	442	49	33	5.9	.930	SS-118
1909		136	.261	.303	472	123	10	5	0	0.0	61	30	46			32	0	255	363	41	34	4.8	.938	SS-98, OF-37, 2B-1
1910		81	.178	.221	258	46	6	1	1	0.4	23	16	29			14	0	119	55	7	5	2.2	.961	OF-62, 2B-11, SS-4, 3B-1
1911		3	.444	.556	9	4	1	0	0	0.0	2	3	2			0	0	5	10	0	0	5.0	1.000	2B-3
12 yrs.		1327	.262	.340	4984	1306	180	74	20	0.4	633	471	333			184	12	2	2573	3898	489	382	5.2	.930	SS-1129, OF-146, 2B-28, 3B-8

WORLD SERIES

Year	Team	Games	BA	SA	AB	H	2B	3B	HR	HR%	R	RBI	BB	SO	SB	AB	H	PO	A	E	DP	TC/G	FA	G by Pos
1903	BOS A	8	.281	.469	32	9	0	3	0	0.0	8	3	1	1	0	0	0	18	30	2	2	6.3	.960	SS-8

4th

Mark Parent

PARENT, MARK ALAN
B. Sept. 16, 1961, Ashland, Ore.

BR TR 6'5" 215 lbs.

Year	Team	Games	BA	SA	AB	H	2B	3B	HR	HR%	R	RBI	BB	SO	SB	AB	H	PO	A	E	DP	TC/G	FA	G by Pos
1986	SD N	8	.143	.143	14	2	0	0	0	0.0	1	3	0	4	0	1	0	16	0	2	0	2.3	.889	C-3
1987		12	.080	.080	25	2	0	0	0	0.0	0	2	0	9	0	2	0	36	3	0	0	3.3	1.000	C-10
1988		41	.195	.373	118	23	3	0	6	5.1	9	15	6	23	0	3	1	203	15	3	3	5.4	.986	C-36
1989		52	.191	.369	141	27	4	0	7	5.0	12	21	8	34	1	9	2	246	17	0	2	5.1	1.000	C-41, 1B-1
4 yrs.		113	.181	.336	298	54	7	0	13	4.4	22	38	15	69	1	18	3	501	35	5	5	4.8	.991	C-90, 1B-1

Kelly Paris

PARIS, KELLY JAY
B. Oct. 17, 1957, Encino, Calif.

BB TR 6' 175 lbs.

Year	Team	Games	BA	SA	AB	H	2B	3B	HR	HR%	R	RBI	BB	SO	SB	AB	H	PO	A	E	DP	TC/G	FA	G by Pos
1982	STL N	12	.103	.103	29	3	0	0	0	0.0	1	0	7	0	0	3	1	9	25	4	4	3.2	.895	3B-5, SS-4
1983	CIN N	56	.250	.300	120	30	6	0	0	0.0	13	7	15	22	8	11	1	60	62	6	7	2.3	.953	3B-16, 2B-10, SS-7, 1B-3
1985	BAL A	4	.000	.000	8	0	0	0	0	0.0	0	0	0	1	0	1	0	3	3	1	0	1.8	.857	DH-2, 2B-2
1986		5	.200	.200	10	2	0	0	0	0.0	0	1	0	3	0	1	0	0	6	1	1	1.4	.857	3B-3, DH-2
1988	CHI A	14	.250	.455	44	11	0	0	3	6.8	6	6	0	6	0	2	0	60	12	1	9	5.2	.986	1B-9, 3B-4
5 yrs.		91	.218	.289	211	46	6	0	3	1.4	20	14	15	39	8	18	2	132	108	13	21	2.8	.949	3B-28, 2B-12, 1B-12, SS-11, DH-4

Tony Parisse

PARISSE, LOUIS PETER
B. June 25, 1911, Philadelphia, Pa.   D. June 2, 1956, Philadelphia, Pa.

BR TR 5'10" 165 lbs.

Year	Team	Games	BA	SA	AB	H	2B	3B	HR	HR%	R	RBI	BB	SO	SB	AB	H	PO	A	E	DP	TC/G	FA	G by Pos
1943	PHI A	6	.176	.176	17	3	0	0	0	0.0	0	1	2	2	0	1	0	16	1	0	0	3.8	1.000	C-5
1944		4	.000	.000	4	0	0	0	0	0.0	0	0	0	1	0	2	0	1	0	1	0	0.5	.500	C-2
2 yrs.		10	.143	.143	21	3	0	0	0	0.0	0	1	2	3	0	3	0	17	1	1	0	2.5	.960	C-7

Ace Parker

PARKER, CLARENCE McKAY
B. May 17, 1912, Portsmouth, Va.

BR TR 6' 180 lbs.

Year	Team	Games	BA	SA	AB	H	2B	3B	HR	HR%	R	RBI	BB	SO	SB	AB	H	PO	A	E	DP	TC/G	FA	G by Pos
1937	PHI A	38	.117	.202	94	11	0	1	2	2.1	8	13	4	17	0	3	2	54	60	10	12	3.3	.919	SS-19, 2B-9, OF-5
1938		56	.230	.274	113	26	5	0	0	0.0	12	12	10	16	1	4	1	54	75	5	10	2.4	.963	SS-26, 3B-9, 2B-9
2 yrs.		94	.179	.242	207	37	5	1	2	1.0	20	25	14	33	1	7	3	108	135	15	22	2.7	.942	SS-45, 2B-18, 3B-9, OF-5

Year	Team		Games	BA	SA	AB	H	2B	3B	HR	HR%	R	RBI	BB	SO	SB	Pinch Hit AB	Pinch Hit H	PO	A	E	DP	TC/G	FA	G by Pos

Billy Parker

PARKER, WILLIAM DAVID
B. Jan. 14, 1947, Hayneville, Ala.
BR TR 5'8" 168 lbs.

Year	Team		Games	BA	SA	AB	H	2B	3B	HR	HR%	R	RBI	BB	SO	SB	PH AB	PH H	PO	A	E	DP	TC/G	FA	G by Pos
1971	CAL	A	20	.229	.300	70	16	0	1	1	1.4	4	6	2	20	1	0	0	39	52	4	13	4.8	.958	2B-20
1972			36	.213	.313	80	17	2	0	2	2.5	11	8	9	17	0	1	0	29	43	2	8	2.1	.973	3B-21, 2B-9, OF-5, SS-1
1973			38	.225	.265	102	23	2	1	0	0.0	14	7	8	23	0	1	0	82	61	6	15	3.9	.960	2B-32, SS-3
3 yrs.			94	.222	.290	252	56	4	2	3	1.2	29	21	19	60	1	2	0	150	156	12	36	3.4	.962	2B-61, 3B-21, OF-5, SS-4

Dave Parker

PARKER, DAVID GENE (The Cobra)
B. June 9, 1951, Calhoun, Miss.
BL TR 6'5" 230 lbs.

Year	Team		Games	BA	SA	AB	H	2B	3B	HR	HR%	R	RBI	BB	SO	SB	PH AB	PH H	PO	A	E	DP	TC/G	FA	G by Pos
1973	PIT	N	54	.288	.453	139	40	9	1	4	2.9	17	14	2	27	1	15	4	77	3	3	1	1.5	.964	OF-39
1974			73	.282	.409	220	62	10	3	4	1.8	27	29	10	53	3	21	4	154	8	4	10	2.3	.976	OF-49, 1B-6
1975			148	.308	.541	558	172	35	10	25	4.5	75	101	38	89	8	7	4	311	7	9	2	2.2	.972	OF-141
1976			138	.313	.475	537	168	28	10	13	2.4	82	90	30	80	19	4	2	294	12	14	0	2.3	.956	OF-134
1977			159	.338	.531	637	215	44	8	21	3.3	107	88	58	107	17	0	0	389	26	15	0	2.7	.965	OF-158, 2B-1
1978			148	.334	.585	581	194	32	12	30	5.2	102	117	57	92	20	0	0	302	12	13	3	2.2	.960	OF-147
1979			158	.310	.526	622	193	45	7	25	4.0	109	94	67	101	20	0	0	341	15	15	1	2.3	.960	OF-158
1980			139	.295	.458	518	153	31	1	17	3.3	71	79	25	69	10	7	2	235	14	9	0	1.9	.965	OF-130
1981			67	.258	.454	240	62	14	3	9	3.8	29	48	9	25	6	6	3	110	1	7	0	1.8	.941	OF-60
1982			73	.270	.447	244	66	19	3	6	2.5	41	29	22	45	7	7	2	108	2	5	1	1.6	.957	OF-63
1983			144	.279	.411	552	154	29	4	12	2.2	68	69	28	89	12	2	0	282	3	8	2	2.0	.973	OF-142
1984	CIN	N	156	.285	.410	607	173	28	0	16	2.6	73	94	41	89	11	6	0	296	6	8	1	2.0	.974	OF-151
1985			160	.312	.551	635	198	42	4	34	5.4	88	125	52	80	5	2	1	329	12	10	1	2.2	.972	OF-159
1986			162	.273	.477	637	174	31	3	31	4.9	89	116	56	126	1	3	1	278	9	9	2	1.8	.970	OF-159
1987			153	.253	.433	589	149	28	0	26	4.4	77	97	44	104	7	3	0	354	17	11	10	2.5	.971	OF-142, 1B-9
1988	OAK	A	101	.257	.406	377	97	18	1	12	3.2	43	55	32	70	0	9	4	63	5	3	0	0.7	.958	DH-61, OF-34, 1B-1
1989			144	.264	.432	553	146	27	0	22	4.0	56	97	38	91	0	7	0	2	0	0	0	0.0	1.000	DH-140, OF-1
17 yrs.			2177	.293	.479	8246	2416	470	70	307	3.7	1154	1342	609	1337	147	99	27	3925	152	143	34	1.9	.966	OF-1867, DH-201, 1B-16, 2B-1

LEAGUE CHAMPIONSHIP SERIES

Year	Team		Games	BA	SA	AB	H	2B	3B	HR	HR%	R	RBI	BB	SO	SB	PH AB	PH H	PO	A	E	DP	TC/G	FA	G by Pos
1974	PIT	N	3	.125	.125	8	1	0	0	0	0.0	0	0	0	1	0	1	0	4	1	0	0	1.7	1.000	OF-2
1975			3	.000	.000	10	0	0	0	0	0.0	2	0	1	3	0	0	0	13	1	0	1	4.7	1.000	OF-3
1979			3	.333	.333	12	4	0	0	0	0.0	2	2	3	3	1	0	0	9	0	0	0	3.0	1.000	OF-3
1988	OAK	A	3	.250	.333	12	3	1	0	0	0.0	1	0	0	4	0	0	0	1	0	1	0	0.7	.500	DH-2, OF-1
1989			4	.188	.563	16	3	0	0	2	12.5	2	3	0	0	0	0	0	0	0	0	0	0.0	—	DH-4
5 yrs.			16	.190	.310	58	11	1	0	2	3.4	7	5	3	11	1	1	0	27	2	1	1	1.9	.967	OF-9, DH-6

WORLD SERIES

Year	Team		Games	BA	SA	AB	H	2B	3B	HR	HR%	R	RBI	BB	SO	SB	PH AB	PH H	PO	A	E	DP	TC/G	FA	G by Pos
1979	PIT	N	7	.345	.448	29	10	3	0	0	0.0	2	4	2	7	0	0	0	13	1	1	1	2.1	.933	OF-7
1988	OAK	A	4	.200	.200	15	3	0	0	0	0.0	0	0	2	4	0	0	0	4	0	0	0	1.0	1.000	DH-2, OF-2
1989			3	.222	.667	9	2	1	0	1	11.1	2	2	0	2	0	1	0	0	0	0	0	0.0	—	DH-2
3 yrs.			14	.283	.415	53	15	4	0	1	1.9	4	6	4	13	0	1	0	17	1	1	1	1.4	.947	OF-9, DH-4

Dixie Parker

PARKER, DOUGLAS WOOLLEY
B. Apr. 24, 1895, Forest Home, Ala.   D. May 15, 1972, Tuscaloosa, Ala.
BL TR 5'11" 160 lbs.

Year	Team		Games	BA	SA	AB	H	2B	3B	HR	HR%	R	RBI	BB	SO	SB	PH AB	PH H	PO	A	E	DP	TC/G	FA	G by Pos
1923	PHI	N	4	.200	.200	5	1	0	0	0	0.0	0	0	1	0	1	0	1	8	1	0	1	0	0.5	.500	C-2

Pat Parker

PARKER, CLARENCE PERKINS
B. May 22, 1893, Somerville, Mass.   D. Mar. 21, 1967, Claremont, N. H.
BR TR 5'7" 160 lbs.

Year	Team		Games	BA	SA	AB	H	2B	3B	HR	HR%	R	RBI	BB	SO	SB	PH AB	PH H	PO	A	E	DP	TC/G	FA	G by Pos
1915	STL	A	3	.167	.167	6	1	0	0	0	0.0	0	1	0	3	0	1	0	3	0	0	0	1.0	1.000	OF-2

Salty Parker

PARKER, FRANCIS JAMES
B. July 8, 1913, East St. Louis, Ill.
Manager 1967, 1972.
BR TR 6' 173 lbs.

Year	Team		Games	BA	SA	AB	H	2B	3B	HR	HR%	R	RBI	BB	SO	SB	PH AB	PH H	PO	A	E	DP	TC/G	FA	G by Pos
1936	DET	A	11	.280	.360	25	7	2	0	0	0.0	6	4	2	3	0	0	0	30	21	3	6	4.9	.944	SS-7, 1B-2

Wes Parker

PARKER, MAURICE WESLEY
B. Nov. 13, 1939, Evanston, Ill.
BB TL 6'1" 180 lbs.

Year	Team		Games	BA	SA	AB	H	2B	3B	HR	HR%	R	RBI	BB	SO	SB	PH AB	PH H	PO	A	E	DP	TC/G	FA	G by Pos
1964	LA	N	124	.257	.341	214	55	7	1	3	1.4	29	10	14	45	5	30	6	326	26	6	18	2.9	.983	OF-69, 1B-31
1965			154	.238	.352	542	129	24	7	8	1.5	80	51	75	95	13	1	1	1434	95	5	112	10.0	.997	1B-154, OF-1
1966			156	.253	.385	475	120	17	5	12	2.5	67	51	69	83	7	1	1	1149	70	9	74	7.9	.993	1B-140, OF-14
1967			139	.247	.346	413	102	16	5	5	1.2	56	31	65	83	10	13	5	949	70	5	72	7.4	.995	1B-112, OF-18
1968			135	.239	.314	468	112	22	2	3	0.6	42	27	49	87	4	6	0	980	70	2	74	7.8	.998	1B-114, OF-28
1969			132	.278	.427	471	131	23	4	13	2.8	76	68	56	46	4	5	3	1190	79	6	87	9.7	.995	1B-128, OF-2
1970			161	.319	.458	614	196	47	4	10	1.6	84	111	79	70	8	1	1	1498	125	7	116	10.1	.996	1B-161
1971			157	.274	.356	533	146	24	1	6	1.1	69	62	63	63	6	1	1	1240	98	5	114	8.6	.996	1B-148, OF-18
1972			130	.279	.354	427	119	14	3	4	0.9	45	59	62	43	3	8	2	1085	68	4	91	8.9	.997	1B-120, OF-5
9 yrs.			1288	.267	.375	4157	1110	194	32	64	1.5	548	470	532	615	60	71	19	9851	701	49	758	8.2	.995	1B-1108, OF-155

WORLD SERIES

Year	Team		Games	BA	SA	AB	H	2B	3B	HR	HR%	R	RBI	BB	SO	SB	PH AB	PH H	PO	A	E	DP	TC/G	FA	G by Pos
1965	LA	N	7	.304	.522	23	7	0	1	1	4.3	3	2	3	2	2	0	0	55	4	0	6	8.4	1.000	1B-7
1966			4	.231	.385	13	3	0	0	0	0.0	0	0	1	3	0	0	0	31	2	0	4	8.3	1.000	1B-4
2 yrs.			11	.278	.472	36	10	0	1	1	2.8	3	2	4	5	2	0	0	86	6	0	10	8.4	1.000	1B-11

Frank Parkinson

PARKINSON, FRANK JOSEPH
B. Mar. 23, 1895, Dickson City, Pa.   D. July 4, 1960, Trenton, N. J.
BR TR 5'11" 175 lbs.

Year	Team		Games	BA	SA	AB	H	2B	3B	HR	HR%	R	RBI	BB	SO	SB	PH AB	PH H	PO	A	E	DP	TC/G	FA	G by Pos
1921	PHI	N	108	.253	.353	391	99	20	2	5	1.3	36	32	13	81	3	1	0	234	405	47	55	6.4	.931	SS-105, 3B-1
1922			141	.275	.413	545	150	18	6	15	2.8	86	70	55	93	3	2	0	323	562	34	78	6.5	.963	2B-139
1923			67	.242	.338	219	53	12	0	3	1.4	21	28	13	31	0	5	1	118	175	18	36	4.6	.942	2B-37, SS-15, 3B-11
1924			62	.212	.276	156	33	7	0	1	0.6	14	19	14	28	3	5	1	63	127	7	23	3.2	.964	3B-28, SS-21, 2B-10
4 yrs.			378	.256	.366	1311	335	57	8	24	1.8	157	149	95	233	9	13	2	738	1269	106	192	5.6	.950	2B-186, SS-141, 3B-40

Art Parks

PARKS, ARTIE WILLIAM
B. Nov. 1, 1911, Paris, Ark.
BL TR 5'9" 170 lbs.

Year	Team		Games	BA	SA	AB	H	2B	3B	HR	HR%	R	RBI	BB	SO	SB	AB	H	PO	A	E	DP	TC/G	FA	G by Pos
1937	BKN	N	7	.313	.438	16	5	2	0	0	0.0	2	0	2	2	0	3	0	4	1	0	1	0.7	1.000	OF-4
1939			71	.272	.356	239	65	13	2	1	0.4	27	19	28	14	2	4	2	125	2	3	0	1.8	.977	OF-65
2 yrs.			78	.275	.361	255	70	15	2	1	0.4	29	19	30	16	2	7	2	129	3	3	1	1.7	.978	OF-69

Bill Parks

PARKS, WILLIAM ROBERT
B. June 4, 1849, Easton, Pa. D. Oct. 10, 1911, Easton, Pa.
Manager 1875.
BR TR 5'8" 150 lbs.

Year	Team		Games	BA	SA	AB	H	2B	3B	HR	HR%	R	RBI	BB	SO	SB	AB	H	PO	A	E	DP	TC/G	FA	G by Pos
1876	BOS	N	1	.000	.000	4	0	0	0	0	0.0	0	0	0	0		0	0	3	0	1	0	4.0	.750	OF-1

Sam Parrilla

PARRILLA, SAMUEL
B. June 12, 1943, Santurce, Puerto Rico
BR TR 5'11" 185 lbs.

Year	Team		Games	BA	SA	AB	H	2B	3B	HR	HR%	R	RBI	BB	SO	SB	AB	H	PO	A	E	DP	TC/G	FA	G by Pos
1970	PHI	N	11	.125	.188	16	2	1	0	0	0.0	0	0	1	4	0	7	1	5	0	0	0	0.5	1.000	OF-3

Lance Parrish

PARRISH, LANCE MICHAEL
B. June 15, 1956, Clairton, Pa.
BR TR 6'3" 210 lbs.

Year	Team		Games	BA	SA	AB	H	2B	3B	HR	HR%	R	RBI	BB	SO	SB	AB	H	PO	A	E	DP	TC/G	FA	G by Pos
1977	DET	A	12	.196	.435	46	9	2	0	3	6.5	10	7	5	12	0	0	0	76	6	0	0	6.8	1.000	C-12
1978			85	.219	.424	288	63	11	3	14	4.9	37	41	11	71	0	6	1	353	39	5	5	4.7	.987	C-79
1979			143	.276	.456	493	136	26	3	19	3.9	65	65	49	105	6	3	1	707	79	9	10	5.6	.989	C-142
1980			144	.286	.499	553	158	34	6	24	4.3	79	82	31	109	6	4	1	607	67	7	15	4.7	.990	C-121, DH-16, OF-5, 1B-5
1981			96	.244	.394	348	85	18	2	10	2.9	39	46	34	52	2	0	0	407	40	3	6	4.7	.993	C-90, DH-5
1982			133	.284	.529	486	138	19	2	32	6.6	75	87	40	99	3	2	1	627	76	8	8	5.3	.989	C-132, OF-1
1983			155	.269	.483	605	163	42	3	27	4.5	80	114	44	106	1	2	0	695	73	4	8	5.0	.995	C-131, DH-27
1984			147	.237	.443	578	137	16	2	33	5.7	75	98	41	120	2	3	1	720	67	7	11	5.4	.991	C-127, DH-22
1985			140	.273	.479	549	150	27	1	28	5.1	64	98	41	90	2	5	1	695	53	5	9	5.4	.993	C-120, DH-22
1986			91	.257	.483	327	84	6	1	22	6.7	53	62	38	83	0	4	0	483	48	6	5	5.9	.989	C-85, DH-6
1987	PHI	N	130	.245	.399	466	114	21	0	17	3.6	42	67	47	104	0	4	0	724	66	9	1	6.1	.989	C-127
1988			123	.215	.370	424	91	17	2	15	3.5	44	60	47	93	0	3	2	640	73	9	12	5.9	.988	C-117, 1B-1
1989	CAL	A	124	.238	.388	433	103	12	1	17	3.9	48	50	42	104	1	2	0	638	63	5	7	5.7	.993	C-122, DH-2
13 yrs.			1523	.256	.450	5596	1431	251	26	261	4.7	711	877	470	1148	23	34	8	7372	750	77	97	5.4	.991	C-1405, DH-100, OF-6, 1B-6

LEAGUE CHAMPIONSHIP SERIES

Year	Team		Games	BA	SA	AB	H	2B	3B	HR	HR%	R	RBI	BB	SO	SB	AB	H	PO	A	E	DP	TC/G	FA	G by Pos
1984	DET	A	3	.250	.583	12	3	1	0	1	8.3	1	3	0	3	0	0	0	21	2	0	0	7.7	1.000	C-3

WORLD SERIES

Year	Team		Games	BA	SA	AB	H	2B	3B	HR	HR%	R	RBI	BB	SO	SB	AB	H	PO	A	E	DP	TC/G	FA	G by Pos
1984	DET	A	5	.278	.500	18	5	1	0	1	5.6	3	2	3	2	1	0	0	30	3	1	1	6.8	.971	C-5

Larry Parrish

PARRISH, LARRY ALTON
B. Nov. 10, 1953, Winter Haven, Fla.
BR TR 6'3" 190 lbs.

Year	Team		Games	BA	SA	AB	H	2B	3B	HR	HR%	R	RBI	BB	SO	SB	AB	H	PO	A	E	DP	TC/G	FA	G by Pos
1974	MON	N	25	.203	.275	69	14	5	0	0	0.0	9	4	6	19	0	1	0	20	51	1	3	2.9	.986	3B-24
1975			145	.274	.410	532	146	32	5	10	1.9	50	65	28	74	4	5	1	105	291	35	33	3.0	.919	3B-143, SS-1, 2B-1
1976			154	.232	.363	543	126	28	5	11	2.0	65	61	41	91	2	1	0	122	310	25	35	3.0	.945	3B-153
1977			123	.246	.386	402	99	19	2	11	2.7	50	46	37	71	2	14	4	81	225	21	11	2.7	.936	3B-115
1978			144	.277	.454	520	144	39	4	15	2.9	68	70	32	103	2	5	3	122	288	23	20	3.0	.947	3B-139
1979			153	.307	.551	544	167	39	2	30	5.5	83	82	41	101	5	0	0	119	290	23	25	2.8	.931	3B-153
1980			126	.254	.427	452	115	27	3	15	3.3	55	72	36	80	2	1	0	106	231	18	15	2.9	.949	3B-124
1981			97	.244	.384	349	85	19	3	8	2.3	41	44	28	73	0	1	0	91	141	16	7	2.6	.935	3B-95
1982	TEX	A	128	.264	.414	440	116	15	0	17	3.9	59	62	30	84	5	5	2	190	12	8	4	1.6	.962	OF-124, 3B-3, DH-2
1983			145	.272	.474	555	151	26	4	26	4.7	76	88	46	91	0	0	0	215	11	9	1	1.6	.962	OF-132, DH-13
1984			156	.285	.465	613	175	42	1	22	3.6	73	101	42	116	2	1	0	155	35	4	6	1.2	.979	OF-81, DH-63, 3B-12
1985			94	.249	.434	346	86	11	1	17	4.9	44	51	33	77	0	1	0	111	7	1	0	1.3	.992	OF-69, DH-22, 3B-2
1986			129	.276	.509	464	128	22	1	28	6.0	67	94	52	114	3	2	0	23	34	4	2	0.5	.935	DH-99, 3B-30
1987			152	.268	.483	557	149	22	1	32	5.7	79	100	49	154	3	5	1	19	26	4	6	0.3	.918	DH-122, 3B-28, OF-1
1988	2 teams					TEX A (68G – .190)							BOS A (52G – .259)												
"	total		120	.217	.360	406	88	14	1	14	3.4	32	52	28	111	0	5	2	7	0	0	0	0.1	1.000	DH-81, 1B-36
15 yrs.			1891	.263	.439	6792	1789	360	33	256	3.8	851	992	529	1359	30	47	13	1486	1953	192	168	1.9	.947	3B-1021, OF-407, DH-402, 1B-36, SS-1, 2B-1

DIVISIONAL PLAYOFF SERIES

Year	Team		Games	BA	SA	AB	H	2B	3B	HR	HR%	R	RBI	BB	SO	SB	AB	H	PO	A	E	DP	TC/G	FA	G by Pos
1981	MON	N	5	.150	.200	20	3	1	0	0	0.0	3	1	1	3	0	0	0	0	0	0	0	0.0	–	3B-5

LEAGUE CHAMPIONSHIP SERIES

Year	Team		Games	BA	SA	AB	H	2B	3B	HR	HR%	R	RBI	BB	SO	SB	AB	H	PO	A	E	DP	TC/G	FA	G by Pos
1981	MON	N	5	.263	.368	19	5	2	0	0	0.0	2	2	1	1	0	0	0	0	0	1	0	0.2	–	3B-5
1988	BOS	A	4	.000	.000	6	0	0	0	0	0.0	0	0	0	2	0	3	0	7	0	0	0	1.8	1.000	1B-2, DH-1
2 yrs.			9	.200	.280	25	5	2	0	0	0.0	2	2	1	3	0	3	0	7	0	1	0	0.9	.875	3B-5, 1B-2, DH-1

Jiggs Parrott

PARROTT, WALTER EDWARD
Brother of Tom Parrott.
B. July 14, 1871, Portland, Ore. D. Apr. 16, 1898, Phoenix, Ariz.
5'11" 160 lbs.

Year	Team		Games	BA	SA	AB	H	2B	3B	HR	HR%	R	RBI	BB	SO	SB	AB	H	PO	A	E	DP	TC/G	FA	G by Pos
1892	CHI	N	78	.201	.273	333	67	8	5	2	0.6	38	22	8	30	7	0	0	115	164	34	7	4.0	.891	3B-78
1893			110	.244	.312	455	111	10	9	1	0.2	54	65	13	25	25	0	0	163	274	45	23	4.4	.907	3B-99, 2B-7, OF-4
1894			127	.261	.344	532	139	17	9	3	0.6	83	64	16	35	30	0	0	287	380	49	56	5.6	.932	2B-123, 3B-1
1895			3	.250	.250	4	1	0	0	0	0.0	0	0	0	0	0	0	0	2	1	0	0	1.0	1.000	OF-1, SS-1, 1B-1
4 yrs.			318	.240	.315	1324	318	35	23	6	0.5	175	151	37	90	62	0	0	567	819	128	86	4.8	.915	3B-178, 2B-130, OF-5, SS-1, 1B-1

Tom Parrott

PARROTT, THOMAS WILLIAM (Tacky Tom)
Brother of Jiggs Parrott.
B. Apr. 10, 1868, Portland, Ore. D. Jan. 1, 1932, Dundee, Ore.
BR TR 5'10½" 170 lbs.

Year	Team	Games	BA	SA	AB	H	2B	3B	HR	HR%	R	RBI	BB	SO	SB	Pinch Hit AB	Pinch Hit H	PO	A	E	DP	TC/G	FA	G by Pos

Tom Parrott *continued*

Year	Team	Games	BA	SA	AB	H	2B	3B	HR	HR%	R	RBI	BB	SO	SB	AB	H	PO	A	E	DP	TC/G	FA	G by Pos
1893	2 teams	CHI N (7G – .259)		CIN N (24G – .191)																				
"	total	31	.211	.284	95	20	2	1	1	1.1	9	12	2	11	0	1	0	20	47	6	1	2.4	.918	P-26, 3B-2, OF-1, 2B-1
1894	CIN N	68	.323	.480	229	74	12	6	4	1.7	51	40	17	10	4	3	2	143	87	22	10	3.7	.913	P-41, OF-13, 1B-12, SS-1, 3B-1, 2B-1
1895		64	.343	.522	201	69	13	7	3	1.5	35	41	11	8	10	0	0	151	70	13	12	3.7	.944	P-41, 1B-14, OF-9
1896	STL N	118	.291	.414	474	138	13	12	7	1.5	62	70	11	24	12	0	0	334	27	18	7	3.2	.953	OF-108, P-7, 1B-6
4 yrs.		281	.301	.438	999	301	40	26	15	1.5	157	163	41	53	26	4	2	648	231	59	30	3.3	.937	OF-131, P-115, 1B-32, 3B-3, 2B-2, SS-1

Casey Parsons

PARSONS, CASEY ROBERT
B. Apr. 14, 1954, Wenatchee, Wash.
BL TR 6'1" 180 lbs.

Year	Team	Games	BA	SA	AB	H	2B	3B	HR	HR%	R	RBI	BB	SO	SB	AB	H	PO	A	E	DP	TC/G	FA	G by Pos
1981	SEA A	36	.227	.409	22	5	1	0	1	4.5	6	5	1	4	0	8	1	22	2	0	1	0.7	1.000	OF-24, 1B-1
1983	CHI A	8	.200	.200	5	1	0	0	0	0.0	1	0	2	1	0	4	0	3	0	0	0	0.4	1.000	OF-3, DH-2
1984		1	.000	.000	1	0	0	0	0	0.0	0	0	0	1	0	1	0	0	0	0	0	0.0	–	
1987	CLE A	18	.160	.280	25	4	0	0	1	4.0	2	5	0	5	0	14	4	4	0	0	0	0.2	1.000	DH-5, OF-2, 1B-1
4 yrs.		63	.189	.321	53	10	1	0	2	3.8	9	10	3	11	0	27	5	29	2	0	1	0.5	1.000	OF-29, DH-7, 1B-2

Dixie Parsons

PARSONS, EDWARD DIXON
B. May 12, 1916, Talladega, Ala.
BR TR 6'2" 180 lbs.

Year	Team	Games	BA	SA	AB	H	2B	3B	HR	HR%	R	RBI	BB	SO	SB	AB	H	PO	A	E	DP	TC/G	FA	G by Pos
1939	DET A	5	.000	.000	1	0	0	0	0	0.0	0	1	1	0	1	0	1	0	2	0	0	0	0.4	1.000	C-4
1942		63	.197	.250	188	37	4	0	2	1.1	8	11	13	22	1	1	0	274	44	6	6	5.1	.981	C-62
1943		40	.142	.170	106	15	3	0	0	0.0	2	4	6	16	0	0	0	167	31	5	2	5.1	.975	C-40
3 yrs.		108	.176	.220	295	52	7	0	2	0.7	10	15	20	39	1	2	0	443	75	11	8	4.9	.979	C-106

John Parsons

PARSONS, JOHN S.
B. Napoleon, Ohio Deceased.

Year	Team	Games	BA	SA	AB	H	2B	3B	HR	HR%	R	RBI	BB	SO	SB	AB	H	PO	A	E	DP	TC/G	FA	G by Pos
1884	CIN AA	1	.000	.000	3	0	0	0	0		0		0			0	0	1	0	0	0	1.0	1.000	OF-1

Roy Partee

PARTEE, ROY ROBERT
B. Sept. 7, 1917, Los Angeles, Calif.
BR TR 5'10" 180 lbs.

Year	Team	Games	BA	SA	AB	H	2B	3B	HR	HR%	R	RBI	BB	SO	SB	AB	H	PO	A	E	DP	TC/G	FA	G by Pos
1943	BOS A	96	.281	.341	299	84	14	2	0	0.0	30	31	39	33	0	5	2	349	57	7	11	4.3	.983	C-91
1944		89	.243	.307	280	68	12	4	2	0.7	18	41	37	29	0	5	1	326	40	4	5	4.2	.989	C-85
1946		40	.315	.396	111	35	5	2	0	0.0	13	9	13	14	0	1	1	139	12	4	1	3.9	.974	C-38
1947		60	.231	.243	169	39	2	0	0	0.0	14	16	18	23	0	6	0	207	26	6	4	4.0	.975	C-54
1948	STL A	82	.203	.247	231	47	8	1	0	0.0	14	17	25	21	2	6	0	297	22	6	7	4.0	.982	C-76
5 yrs.		367	.250	.303	1090	273	41	5	2	0.2	89	114	132	120	2	23	4	1318	157	27	28	4.1	.982	C-344

WORLD SERIES

Year	Team	Games	BA	SA	AB	H	2B	3B	HR	HR%	R	RBI	BB	SO	SB	AB	H	PO	A	E	DP	TC/G	FA	G by Pos
1946	BOS A	5	.100	.100	10	1	0	0	0	0.0	1	1	1	1	0	1	0	14	1	0	1	3.0	1.000	C-5

Steve Partenheimer

PARTENHEIMER, HAROLD PHILIP
Father of Stan Partenheimer.
B. Aug. 30, 1891, Greenfield, Mass. D. June 16, 1971, Mansfield, Ohio
BR TR 5'8½" 145 lbs.

Year	Team	Games	BA	SA	AB	H	2B	3B	HR	HR%	R	RBI	BB	SO	SB	AB	H	PO	A	E	DP	TC/G	FA	G by Pos
1913	DET A	1	.000	.000	2	0	0	0	0	0.0	0	0	0	0	0	0	0	0	3	1	0	4.0	.750	3B-1

Jay Partridge

PARTRIDGE, JAMES BUGG
B. Nov. 15, 1902, Mountville, Ga. D. Jan. 14, 1974, Nashville, Tenn.
BL TR 5'11" 160 lbs.

Year	Team	Games	BA	SA	AB	H	2B	3B	HR	HR%	R	RBI	BB	SO	SB	AB	H	PO	A	E	DP	TC/G	FA	G by Pos
1927	BKN N	146	.260	.348	572	149	17	6	7	1.2	72	40	20	36	9	6	1	330	454	52	63	5.7	.938	2B-140
1928		37	.247	.274	73	18	0	1	0	0.0	18	12	13	6	2	11	4	40	44	9	7	2.5	.903	2B-18, 3B-2
2 yrs.		183	.259	.340	645	167	17	7	7	1.1	90	52	33	42	11	17	5	370	498	61	70	5.1	.934	2B-158, 3B-2

Ben Paschal

PASCHAL, BENJAMIN EDWIN
B. Oct. 13, 1895, Enterprise, Ala. D. Nov. 10, 1974, Charlotte, N. C.
BR TR 5'11" 185 lbs.

Year	Team	Games	BA	SA	AB	H	2B	3B	HR	HR%	R	RBI	BB	SO	SB	AB	H	PO	A	E	DP	TC/G	FA	G by Pos
1915	CLE A	9	.111	.111	9	1	0	0	0	0.0	0	0	0	3	0	9	1	0	0	0	0	0.0		
1920	BOS A	9	.357	.357	28	10	0	0	0	0.0	5	5	5	2	1	2	1	10	1	0	0	1.2	1.000	OF-7
1924	NY A	4	.250	.333	12	3	1	0	0	0.0	2	3	1	0	0	1	0	4	1	0	1	1.3	1.000	OF-4
1925		89	.360	.611	247	89	16	5	12	4.9	49	56	22	29	14	21	5	117	6	6	0	1.4	.953	OF-66
1926		96	.287	.438	258	74	12	3	7	2.7	46	33	26	35	7	18	6	134	10	10	0	1.6	.935	OF-74
1927		50	.317	.549	82	26	9	2	2	2.4	16	16	4	10	0	22	5	39	1	1	0	0.8	.976	OF-27
1928		65	.316	.456	79	25	6	1	1	1.3	12	15	8	11	1	35	8	26	1	0	0	0.4	1.000	OF-25
1929		42	.208	.333	72	15	3	0	2	2.8	13	11	6	3	1	20	3	37	2	2	0	1.0	.951	OF-20
8 yrs.		364	.309	.488	787	243	47	11	24	3.0	143	139	72	93	24	128	29	367	22	19	1	1.1	.953	OF-223

WORLD SERIES

Year	Team	Games	BA	SA	AB	H	2B	3B	HR	HR%	R	RBI	BB	SO	SB	AB	H	PO	A	E	DP	TC/G	FA	G by Pos
1926	NY A	5	.250	.250	4	1	0	0	0	0.0	0	1	1	1	0	4	1	0	0	0	0	0.0	–	
1928		3	.200	.200	10	2	0	0	0	0.0	1	1	1	0	0	1	1	8	0	0	0	2.7	1.000	OF-3
2 yrs.		8	.214	.214	14	3	0	0	0	0.0	1	2	2	1	0	5	2	8	0	0	0	1.0	1.000	OF-3

Johnny Pasek

PASEK, JOHN PAUL
B. June 25, 1905, Niagara Falls, N. Y. D. Mar. 13, 1976, Niagara Falls, N. Y.
BR TR 5'10" 175 lbs.

Year	Team	Games	BA	SA	AB	H	2B	3B	HR	HR%	R	RBI	BB	SO	SB	AB	H	PO	A	E	DP	TC/G	FA	G by Pos
1933	DET A	28	.246	.311	61	15	4	0	0	0.0	6	4	7	7	2	0	0	75	13	1	3	3.2	.989	C-28
1934	CHI A	4	.333	.333	9	3	0	0	0	0.0	1	0	1	1	0	0	0	12	1	0	0	3.3	1.000	C-4
2 yrs.		32	.257	.314	70	18	4	0	0	0.0	7	4	8	8	2	0	0	87	14	1	3	3.2	.990	C-32

Dode Paskert

PASKERT, GEORGE HENRY
B. Aug. 28, 1881, Cleveland, Ohio D. Feb. 12, 1959, Cleveland, Ohio
BR TR 5'11" 165 lbs.

Year	Team	Games	BA	SA	AB	H	2B	3B	HR	HR%	R	RBI	BB	SO	SB	AB	H	PO	A	E	DP	TC/G	FA	G by Pos
1907	CIN N	16	.280	.420	50	14	4	4	1	2.0	10	8	2		2	0	0	33	3	1	0	2.3	.973	OF-16
1908		118	.243	.306	395	96	14	4	1	0.3	40	36	27		25	3	1	251	15	13	3	2.4	.953	OF-116
1909		104	.252	.298	322	81	7	4	0	0.0	49	33	34		23	16	3	207	12	6	9	2.2	.973	OF-82, 1B-6
1910		144	.300	.374	506	152	21	5	2	0.4	63	46	70	60	51	2	0	367	25	19	4	2.9	.954	OF-139, 1B-2
1911	PHI N	153	.273	.345	560	153	18	5	4	0.7	96	47	70	70	28	0	0	361	20	8	6	2.5	.979	OF-153

Year	Team		Games	BA	SA	AB	H	2B	3B	HR	HR%	R	RBI	BB	SO	SB	Pinch Hit AB	Pinch Hit H	PO	A	E	DP	TC/G	FA	G by Pos

Dode Paskert *continued*

Year	Team		Games	BA	SA	AB	H	2B	3B	HR	HR%	R	RBI	BB	SO	SB	PH AB	PH H	PO	A	E	DP	TC/G	FA	G by Pos
1912			145	.315	.413	540	170	37	5	2	0.4	102	43	91	67	36	0	0	342	25	13	4	2.6	.966	OF-141, 2B-2, 3B-1
1913			124	.262	.374	454	119	21	9	4	0.9	83	29	65	69	12	4	0	330	19	10	8	2.9	.972	OF-120
1914			132	.264	.366	451	119	25	6	3	0.7	59	44	56	68	23	3	0	309	26	18	5	2.7	.949	OF-128, SS-4
1915			109	.244	.348	328	80	17	4	3	0.9	51	39	35	38	9	10	3	231	14	7	3	2.3	.972	OF-104, 1B-5
1916			149	.279	.402	555	155	30	7	8	1.4	82	46	54	76	22	2	1	334	16	6	4	2.4	.983	OF-146, SS-1
1917			141	.251	.363	546	137	27	11	4	0.7	78	43	62	63	19	1	1	286	19	5	4	2.2	.984	OF-138
1918	CHI	N	127	.286	.371	461	132	24	3	3	0.7	69	59	53	49	20	0	0	289	26	9	3	2.6	.972	OF-121, 3B-6
1919			87	.196	.281	270	53	11	3	2	0.7	21	29	28	33	7	8	1	146	12	5	1	1.9	.969	OF-80
1920			139	.279	.396	487	136	22	10	5	1.0	57	71	64	58	16	1	0	306	23	15	3	2.5	.956	OF-137
1921	CIN	N	27	.174	.207	92	16	1	1	0	0.0	8	4	4	8	0	1	0	60	2	1	2	2.3	.984	OF-24
15 yrs.			1715	.268	.361	6017	1613	279	77	42	0.7	868	577	715	659	293	51	10	3852	257	136	59	2.5	.968	OF-1645, 1B-13, 3B-7, SS-5, 2B-2

WORLD SERIES

Year	Team		Games	BA	SA	AB	H	2B	3B	HR	HR%	R	RBI	BB	SO	SB	PH AB	PH H	PO	A	E	DP	TC/G	FA	G by Pos
1915	PHI	N	5	.158	.158	19	3	0	0	0	0.0	2	0	1	2	0	0	0	17	0	0	0	3.4	1.000	OF-5
1918	CHI	N	6	.190	.238	21	4	1	0	0	0.0	0	2	2	2	0	0	0	17	0	0	0	2.8	1.000	OF-6
2 yrs.			11	.175	.200	40	7	1	0	0	0.0	2	2	3	4	0	0	0	34	0	0	0	3.1	1.000	OF-11

Kevin Pasley

PASLEY, KEVIN PATRICK
B. July 22, 1953, Brooklyn, N. Y.   BR TR 6'   185 lbs.

Year	Team		Games	BA	SA	AB	H	2B	3B	HR	HR%	R	RBI	BB	SO	SB	PH AB	PH H	PO	A	E	DP	TC/G	FA	G by Pos
1974	LA	N	1	–	–	0	0	0	0	0		0	0	0	0	0	0	0	1	0	0	0	1.0	1.000	C-1
1976			23	.231	.269	52	12	2	0	0	0.0	4	2	3	7	0	0	0	86	15	3	0	4.5	.971	C-23
1977	2 teams		LA N (2G – .333)			SEA A (4G – .385)																			
"	total		6	.375	.375	16	6	0	0	0	0.0	1	2	1	2	0	0	0	24	1	0	0	4.2	1.000	C-6
1978	SEA	A	25	.241	.389	54	13	5	0	1	1.9	3	5	2	4	0	0	0	85	4	0	0	3.6	1.000	C-25
4 yrs.			55	.254	.336	122	31	7	0	1	0.8	8	9	6	13	0	0	0	196	20	3	0	4.0	.986	C-55

Dan Pasqua

PASQUA, DANIEL ANTHONY
B. Oct. 17, 1961, Yonkers, N. Y.   BL TL 6' ·   205 lbs.

Year	Team		Games	BA	SA	AB	H	2B	3B	HR	HR%	R	RBI	BB	SO	SB	PH AB	PH H	PO	A	E	DP	TC/G	FA	G by Pos
1985	NY	A	60	.209	.426	148	31	3	1	9	6.1	17	25	16	38	0	15	2	72	2	0	0	1.2	1.000	OF-37, DH-14
1986			102	.293	.525	280	82	17	0	16	5.7	44	45	47	78	2	22	7	172	4	2	6	1.7	.989	OF-81, 1B-5, DH-3
1987			113	.233	.421	318	74	7	1	17	5.3	42	42	40	99	0	22	3	214	10	2	2	2.0	.991	OF-74, DH-20, 1B-12
1988	CHI	A	129	.227	.417	422	96	16	2	20	4.7	48	50	46	100	1	15	1	316	14	2	13	2.6	.994	OF-119, DH-2
1989			73	.248	.427	246	61	9	1	11	4.5	26	47	25	58	1	3	2	149	3	1	2	2.1	.993	OF-66, DH-5
5 yrs.			477	.243	.442	1414	344	52	5	73	5.2	177	209	174	373	4	77	15	923	33	7	23	2.0	.993	OF-377, DH-44, 1B-17

Mike Pasquariello

PASQUARIELLO, MICHAEL JOHN (Toney)
B. Nov. 7, 1898, Philadelphia, Pa.   D. Apr. 5, 1965, Bridgeport, Conn.   BR TR 5'11"   167 lbs.

Year	Team		Games	BA	SA	AB	H	2B	3B	HR	HR%	R	RBI	BB	SO	SB	PH AB	PH H	PO	A	E	DP	TC/G	FA	G by Pos
1919	2 teams		PHI N (1G – 1.000)			STL N (1G – .000)																			
"	total		2	.500	.500	2	1	0	0	0	0.0	1	0	0	1	0	1	0	0	0	0	0	0.0	–	1B-1

Cliff Pastornicky

PASTORNICKY, CLIFFORD SCOT
B. Nov. 18, 1958, Seattle, Wash.   BR TR 6'   180 lbs.

Year	Team		Games	BA	SA	AB	H	2B	3B	HR	HR%	R	RBI	BB	SO	SB	PH AB	PH H	PO	A	E	DP	TC/G	FA	G by Pos
1983	KC	A	10	.125	.313	32	4	0	0	2	6.3	4	5	0	3	0	0	0	5	21	2	0	2.8	.929	3B-10

Bob Pate

PATE, ROBERT WAYNE
B. Dec. 3, 1953, Los Angeles, Calif.   BR TR 6'3½"   200 lbs.

Year	Team		Games	BA	SA	AB	H	2B	3B	HR	HR%	R	RBI	BB	SO	SB	PH AB	PH H	PO	A	E	DP	TC/G	FA	G by Pos
1980	MON	N	23	.256	.308	39	10	2	0	0	0.0	3	5	3	6	0	5	1	18	0	0	0	0.8	1.000	OF-18
1981			8	.333	.333	6	2	0	0	0	0.0	0	0	1	0	0	2	0	3	0	0	0	0.4	1.000	OF-5
2 yrs.			31	.267	.311	45	12	2	0	0	0.0	3	5	4	6	0	7	1	21	0	0	0	0.7	1.000	OF-23

Freddie Patek

PATEK, FREDERICK JOSEPH (The Flea, Moochie)
B. Oct. 9, 1944, Sequin, Tex.   BR TR 5'5"   148 lbs.

Year	Team		Games	BA	SA	AB	H	2B	3B	HR	HR%	R	RBI	BB	SO	SB	PH AB	PH H	PO	A	E	DP	TC/G	FA	G by Pos
1968	PIT	N	61	.255	.322	208	53	4	2	2	1.0	31	18	12	37	18	1	0	90	166	6	23	4.3	.977	SS-52, OF-5, 3B-1
1969			147	.239	.296	460	110	9	1	5	1.1	48	32	53	86	15	0	0	227	399	30	81	4.5	.954	SS-146
1970			84	.245	.342	237	58	10	5	1	0.4	42	19	29	46	8	11	3	122	212	10	42	4.1	.971	SS-65
1971	KC	A	147	.267	.371	591	158	21	11	6	1.0	86	36	44	80	49	1	0	301	459	25	107	5.3	.968	SS-147
1972			136	.212	.276	518	110	25	4	0	0.0	59	32	47	64	33	0	0	230	510	22	113	5.6	.971	SS-136
1973			135	.234	.321	501	117	19	5	5	1.0	82	45	54	63	36	0	0	242	503	26	115	5.7	.966	SS-135
1974			149	.225	.298	537	121	18	6	3	0.6	72	38	77	69	33	0	0	250	493	25	108	5.2	.967	SS-149
1975			136	.228	.308	483	110	14	5	5	1.0	58	45	42	65	32	1	0	231	405	27	78	4.9	.959	SS-136, DH-1
1976			144	.241	.306	432	104	19	3	1	0.2	58	43	50	63	51	0	0	233	426	26	87	4.8	.962	SS-143, DH-1
1977			154	.262	.368	497	130	26	6	5	1.0	72	60	41	84	53	0	0	252	413	29	70	4.5	.958	SS-154
1978			138	.248	.318	440	109	23	1	2	0.5	54	46	42	56	38	1	1	240	350	32	84	4.5	.949	SS-137
1979			106	.252	.317	306	77	17	0	1	0.3	30	37	16	42	11	0	0	153	249	19	54	4.0	.955	SS-104
1980	CAL	A	86	.264	.392	273	72	10	5	5	1.8	41	34	15	26	7	4	0	129	199	16	42	4.0	.953	SS-81
1981			27	.234	.298	47	11	1	1	0	0.0	3	5	1	6	1	1	1	27	42	2	8	2.6	.972	2B-16, 3B-7, SS-3
14 yrs.			1650	.242	.324	5530	1340	216	55	41	0.7	736	490	523	787	385	20	5	2727	4826	295	1012	4.8	.962	SS-1588, 2B-16, 3B-8, OF-5, DH-2

LEAGUE CHAMPIONSHIP SERIES

Year	Team		Games	BA	SA	AB	H	2B	3B	HR	HR%	R	RBI	BB	SO	SB	PH AB	PH H	PO	A	E	DP	TC/G	FA	G by Pos
1970	PIT	N	1	.000	.000	3	0	0	0	0	0.0	0	0	1	2	0	0	0	1	2	0	0	3.0	1.000	SS-1
1976	KC	A	5	.389	.500	18	7	2	0	0	0.0	2	4	0	1	0	0	0	13	18	0	3	6.2	1.000	SS-5
1977			5	.389	.667	18	7	3	1	0	0.0	4	5	1	2	0	0	0	8	18	1	0	5.4	.963	SS-5
1978			4	.077	.308	13	1	0	0	1	7.7	2	2	1	4	0	0	0	9	8	2	2	4.8	.895	SS-4
4 yrs.			15	.288	.481	52	15	5	1	1	1.9	8	11	3	9	0	0	0	31	46	3	5	5.3	.963	SS-15

Bob Patrick

PATRICK, ROBERT LEE
B. Oct. 27, 1917, Fort Smith, Ark.   BR TR 6'2"   190 lbs.

Year	Team		Games	BA	SA	AB	H	2B	3B	HR	HR%	R	RBI	BB	SO	SB	PH AB	PH H	PO	A	E	DP	TC/G	FA	G by Pos
1941	DET	A	5	.286	.286	7	2	0	0	0	0.0	2	0	0	1	0	2	1	3	0	1	0	0.8	.750	OF-3

Year	Team		Games	BA	SA	AB	H	2B	3B	HR	HR%	R	RBI	BB	SO	SB	Pinch Hit AB	Pinch Hit H	PO	A	E	DP	TC/G	FA	G by Pos

Bob Patrick *continued*

Year	Team		Games	BA	SA	AB	H	2B	3B	HR	HR%	R	RBI	BB	SO	SB	AB	H	PO	A	E	DP	TC/G	FA	G by Pos
1942			4	.250	.750	8	2	1	0	1	12.5	1	3	1	0	0	1	0	5	0	0	0	1.3	1.000	OF-3
2 yrs.			9	.267	.533	15	4	1	0	1	6.7	3	3	1	1	0	3	1	8	0	1	0	1.0	.889	OF-6

Harry Pattee   **PATTEE, HARRY ERNEST**   BL TR 5'8"   149 lbs.
B. Jan. 17, 1882, Charlestown, Mass.   D. July 17, 1971, Lynchburg, Va.

| 1908 | BKN | N | 80 | .216 | .250 | 264 | 57 | 5 | 2 | 0 | 0.0 | 19 | 9 | 25 | | 24 | 6 | 1 | 158 | 246 | 15 | 15 | 5.2 | .964 | 2B-74 |

Claire Patterson   **PATTERSON, LORENZO CLAIRE**   BL TR 6'   180 lbs.
B. Oct. 5, 1887, Arkansas City, Kans.   D. Mar. 28, 1913, Mojave, Calif.

| 1909 | CIN | N | 4 | .125 | .125 | 8 | 1 | 0 | 0 | 0 | 0.0 | 0 | 1 | 0 | | 0 | 2 | 0 | 4 | 0 | 0 | 0 | 1.0 | 1.000 | OF-2 |

Ham Patterson   **PATTERSON, HAMILTON**   BR TR 6'2"   185 lbs.
Brother of Pat Patterson.
B. Oct. 13, 1877, Belleville, Ill.   D. Nov. 25, 1945, E. St. Louis, Ill.

| 1909 | 2 teams | | | STL A (17G – .204) | | CHI A | (1G – .000) | | | | | | | | | | | | | | | | | | |
| " | total | | 18 | .192 | .212 | 52 | 10 | 1 | 0 | 0 | 0.0 | 4 | 5 | 1 | | 1 | 5 | 0 | 76 | 4 | 0 | 2 | 4.4 | 1.000 | 1B-7, OF-6 |

Hank Patterson   **PATTERSON, HENRY JOSEPH**   BR TR 5'11½"   170 lbs.
B. July 17, 1907, San Francisco, Calif.   D. Sept. 30, 1970, Panorama City, Calif.

| 1932 | BOS | A | 1 | .000 | .000 | 1 | 0 | 0 | 0 | 0 | 0.0 | 0 | 0 | 0 | 0 | 0 | 0 | 0 | 0 | 0 | 0 | 0 | 0.0 | – | C-1 |

Mike Patterson   **PATTERSON, MICHAEL LEE**   BL TR 5'10"   170 lbs.
B. Jan. 26, 1958, Santa Monica, Calif.

1981	2 teams			OAK A (12G – .348)		NY A	(4G – .222)																		
"	total		16	.313	.531	32	10	1	3	0	0.0	6	1	2	5	0	5	2	13	0	0	0	0.8	1.000	OF-9, DH-2
1982	NY	A	11	.188	.438	16	3	1	0	1	6.3	3	1	2	6	1	0	0	5	0	0	0	0.5	1.000	OF-9, DH-3
2 yrs.			27	.271	.500	48	13	2	3	1	2.1	9	2	4	11	1	5	2	18	0	0	0	0.7	1.000	OF-18, DH-3

Pat Patterson   **PATTERSON, WILLIAM JENNINGS BRYAN**   BR TR 6'   175 lbs.
Brother of Ham Patterson.
B. Jan. 29, 1901, Belleville, Ill.   D. Oct. 1, 1977, St. Louis, Mo.

| 1921 | NY | N | 23 | .400 | .486 | 35 | 14 | 0 | 0 | 1 | 2.9 | 5 | 5 | 2 | 5 | 0 | 2 | 0 | 11 | 29 | 2 | 0 | 1.8 | .952 | 3B-14, SS-7 |

George Pattison   **PATTISON, GEORGE**
Deceased.

| 1884 | PHI | U | 2 | .143 | .143 | 7 | 1 | 0 | 0 | 0 | 0.0 | 0 | | 0 | | | 0 | 0 | 1 | 1 | 2 | 0 | 2.0 | .500 | OF-2 |

Bill Patton   **PATTON, GEORGE WILLIAM**   BR TR 6'2"   180 lbs.
B. Oct. 7, 1912, Cornwall, Pa.   D. Mar. 15, 1986, Philadelphia, Pa.

| 1935 | PHI | A | 9 | .300 | .400 | 10 | 3 | 1 | 0 | 0 | 0.0 | 1 | 2 | 2 | 3 | 0 | 4 | 1 | 4 | 3 | 0 | 1 | 0.8 | 1.000 | C-3 |

Gene Patton   **PATTON, GENE TUNNEY**   BL TR 5'10"   165 lbs.
B. July 8, 1926, Coatesville, Pa.

| 1944 | BOS | N | 1 | – | – | 0 | 0 | 0 | 0 | 0 | 0.0 | 0 | 0 | 0 | 0 | 0 | 0 | 0 | 0 | 0 | 0 | 0 | 0.0 | – | |

Tom Patton   **PATTON, THOMAS ALLEN**   BR TR 5'9½"   185 lbs.
B. Sept. 5, 1935, Honey Brook, Pa.

| 1957 | BAL | A | 1 | .000 | .000 | 2 | 0 | 0 | 0 | 0 | 0.0 | 0 | 0 | 0 | 2 | 0 | 0 | 0 | 4 | 2 | 0 | 1 | 6.0 | 1.000 | C-1 |

Lou Paul   **PAUL, LOUIS**   BR TR
B. Unknown.   Deceased.

| 1876 | PHI | N | 3 | .167 | .250 | 12 | 2 | 1 | 0 | 0 | 0.0 | 2 | 0 | 0 | | 0 | 0 | 0 | 5 | 4 | 5 | 0 | 4.7 | .643 | C-3 |

Carlos Paula   **PAULA, CARLOS**   BR TR 6'3"   195 lbs.
Born Carlos Paula y Conill.
B. Nov. 28, 1927, Havana, Cuba   D. Apr. 25, 1983, Miami, Fla.

1954	WAS	A	9	.167	.208	24	4	1	0	0	0.0	2	2	2	4	0	0	0	14	1	0	0	1.7	1.000	OF-6
1955			115	.299	.447	351	105	20	7	6	1.7	34	45	17	43	2	28	8	154	5	10	3	1.5	.941	OF-85
1956			33	.183	.341	82	15	2	1	3	3.7	8	13	8	15	0	11	3	37	0	1	0	1.2	.974	OF-20
3 yrs.			157	.271	.416	457	124	23	8	9	2.0	44	60	27	62	2	42	11	205	6	11	3	1.4	.950	OF-111

Gene Paulette   **PAULETTE, EUGENE EDWARD**   BR TR 6'   150 lbs.
B. May 26, 1891, Centralia, Ill.   D. Feb. 8, 1966, Little Rock, Ark.

1911	NY	N	10	.167	.167	12	2	0	0	0	0.0	1		1		0	0	0	29	1	2	0	3.2	.938	1B-7, SS-1, 3B-1
1916	STL	A	5	.500	.500	4	2	0	0	0	0.0	1	0	1	1	0	4	2	0	0	0	0	0.0	–	
1917	2 teams			STL A (12G – .182)		STL N	(95G – .265)																		
"	total		107	.260	.359	354	92	21	7	0	0.0	35	34	19	19	9	6	1	1186	55	12	85	11.7	.990	1B-98, 2B-3, 3B-1
1918	STL	N	125	.273	.319	461	126	15	3	0	0.0	33	52	27	16	11	3	0	1171	129	26	77	10.6	.980	1B-97, SS-12, 2B-7, OF-6, 3B-2, P-1
1919	2 teams			STL N (43G – .215)		PHI N	(67G – .259)																		
"	total		110	.243	.302	387	94	14	3	1	0.3	31	42	28	16	14	3	0	554	209	20	54	7.1	.974	2B-53, 1B-16, OF-10, SS-3
1920	PHI	N	143	.288	.343	562	162	16	6	1	0.2	59	36	33	16	9	2	1	1432	103	18	95	10.9	.988	1B-139, SS-2
6 yrs.			500	.269	.330	1780	478	66	19	2	0.1	160	165	108	69	43	18	4	4372	497	78	311	9.9	.984	1B-377, 2B-63, SS-18, OF-16, 3B-4, P-1

Si Pauxtis   **PAUXTIS, SIMON FRANCIS**   BR TR 6'   175 lbs.
B. July 20, 1885, Pittston, Pa.   D. Mar. 13, 1961, Philadelphia, Pa.

Year	Team	Games	BA	SA	AB	H	2B	3B	HR	HR%	R	RBI	BB	SO	SB	Pinch Hit AB	Pinch Hit H	PO	A	E	DP	TC/G	FA	G by Pos

Si Pauxtis *continued*

| 1909 | CIN N | 4 | .125 | .125 | 8 | 1 | 0 | 0 | 0 | 0.0 | 2 | 0 | 0 | | 0 | 0 | 0 | 11 | 1 | 0 | 0 | 3.0 | 1.000 | C-4 |

Don Pavletich

PAVLETICH, DONALD STEPHEN BR TR 5'11" 190 lbs.
B. July 13, 1938, Milwaukee, Wis.

1957	CIN N	1	.000	.000	1	0	0	0	0	0.0	0	0	0	0	0	1	0	0	0	0	0	0.0	–	
1959		1	–	–	0	0	0	0	0	–	1	0	0	0	0	0	0	0	0	0	0	0.0	–	
1962		34	.222	.317	63	14	3	0	1	1.6	7	7	8	18	0	11	3	167	11	0	12	5.2	1.000	1B-25, C-2
1963		71	.208	.350	183	38	11	0	5	2.7	18	18	17	12	0	16	0	409	20	3	21	6.1	.993	1B-57, C-13
1964		34	.242	.451	91	22	4	0	5	5.5	12	11	10	17	0	7	1	168	8	3	2	5.3	.983	C-27, 1B-1
1965		68	.319	.513	191	61	11	1	8	4.2	25	32	23	27	1	11	4	391	18	6	14	6.1	.986	C-54, 1B-9
1966		83	.294	.519	235	69	13	2	12	5.1	29	38	18	37	1	23	6	379	32	9	10	5.1	.979	C-55, 1B-10
1967		74	.238	.403	231	55	14	3	6	2.6	25	34	21	38	2	8	1	414	34	7	8	6.1	.985	C-66, 1B-6, 3B-1
1968		46	.286	.398	98	28	3	1	2	2.0	11	11	8	23	0	20	4	185	13	0	14	4.3	1.000	1B-22, C-5
1969	CHI A	78	.245	.404	188	46	12	0	6	3.2	26	33	28	45	0	19	4	285	27	7	16	4.1	.978	C-51, 1B-13
1970	BOS A	32	.138	.185	65	9	1	1	0	0.0	4	6	10	15	1	7	1	123	12	0	11	4.2	1.000	1B-16, C-10
1971		14	.259	.407	27	7	1	0	1	3.7	5	3	5	5	0	5	1	35	1	1	1	2.6	.973	C-8
12 yrs.		536	.254	.420	1373	349	73	8	46	3.4	163	193	148	237	5	128	25	2556	177	36	109	5.2	.987	C-291, 1B-159, 3B-1

Ted Pawelek

PAWELEK, THEODORE JOHN (Porky) BL TR 5'10½" 202 lbs.
B. Aug. 15, 1919, Chicago Heights, Ill. D. Feb. 12, 1964, Chicago Heights, Ill.

| 1946 | CHI N | 4 | .250 | .500 | 4 | 1 | 1 | 0 | 0 | 0.0 | 0 | 0 | 0 | 0 | 0 | 3 | 1 | 0 | 0 | 0 | 0 | 0.0 | – | C-1 |

Stan Pawloski

PAWLOSKI, STANLEY WALTER BR TR 6'1" 175 lbs.
B. Sept. 6, 1931, Wanamie, Pa.

| 1955 | CLE A | 2 | .125 | .125 | 8 | 1 | 0 | 0 | 0 | 0.0 | 0 | 0 | 0 | 2 | 0 | 0 | 0 | 3 | 8 | 0 | 0 | 5.5 | 1.000 | 2B-2 |

Fred Payne

PAYNE, FREDERICK THOMAS BR TR 5'10" 162 lbs.
B. Sept. 2, 1880, Camden, N. Y. D. Jan. 16, 1954, Camden, N. Y.

1906	DET A	72	.270	.338	222	60	5	5	0	0.0	23	20	13		4	7	3	213	54	9	6	3.8	.967	C-47, OF-17
1907		53	.166	.201	169	28	2	2	0	0.0	17	14	7		4	1	0	213	56	5	5	5.2	.982	C-46, OF-5
1908		20	.067	.067	45	3	0	0	0	0.0	3	2	3		1	2	0	54	10	3	1	3.4	.955	C-16, OF-2
1909	CHI A	32	.244	.268	82	20	2	0	0	0.0	8	12	5		0	2	1	111	38	2	5	4.7	.987	C-27, OF-3
1910		91	.218	.268	257	56	5	4	0	0.0	17	19	11		6	9	2	410	106	14	11	5.8	.974	C-78, OF-2
1911		66	.203	.256	133	27	2	1	1	0.8	14	19	8		6	9	3	213	48	10	10	4.1	.963	C-56
6 yrs.		334	.214	.261	908	194	16	12	1	0.1	82	86	47		21	30	9	1214	312	43	38	4.7	.973	C-270, OF-29

WORLD SERIES

| 1907 | DET A | 2 | .250 | .250 | 4 | 1 | 0 | 0 | 0 | 0.0 | 0 | 1 | 0 | | 0 | 0 | 0 | 5 | 1 | 1 | 0 | 3.5 | .857 | C-1 |

George Paynter

PAYNTER, GEORGE WASHINGTON BR TR 5'9" 125 lbs.
Born George Washington Paner.
B. July 6, 1871, Cincinnati, Ohio D. Oct. 1, 1950, Cincinnati, Ohio

| 1894 | STL N | 1 | .000 | .000 | 4 | 0 | 0 | 0 | 0 | 0.0 | 1 | 0 | 1 | | 0 | 1 | 0 | 1 | 2 | 0 | 0 | 3.0 | 1.000 | OF-1 |

Johnny Peacock

PEACOCK, JOHN GASTON BL TR 5'11" 165 lbs.
B. Jan. 10, 1910, Fremont, N. C. D. Oct. 17, 1981, Wilson, N. C.

1937	BOS A	9	.313	.438	32	10	2	0	0	0.0	3	6	1	0	0	0	0	42	8	1	1	5.7	.980	C-9
1938		72	.303	.364	195	59	7	1	1	0.5	29	39	17	4	4	15	4	187	12	4	4	2.8	.980	C-57, OF-1, 1B-1
1939		92	.277	.347	274	76	11	4	0	0.0	33	36	29	11	1	10	3	314	33	10	6	3.9	.972	C-84
1940		63	.282	.328	131	37	4	1	0	0.0	20	13	23	10	1	12	3	159	13	1	0	2.7	.994	C-48
1941		79	.284	.368	261	74	20	1	0	0.0	28	27	21	3	2	9	3	298	33	4	7	4.2	.988	C-70
1942		88	.266	.311	286	76	7	3	0	0.0	17	25	21	11	1	8	1	280	44	4	8	3.7	.988	C-82
1943		48	.202	.246	114	23	3	1	0	0.0	7	7	10	9	1	14	2	121	18	4	2	3.0	.972	C-32
1944	2 teams		BOS A	(4G – .000)	PHI N	(83G – .225)																		
"	total	87	.222	.280	257	57	9	3	0	0.0	21	21	31	5	1	12	4	275	41	3	4	3.7	.991	C-75, 2B-1
1945	2 teams		PHI N	(33G – .203)	BKN N	(48G – .255)																		
"	total	81	.234	.304	184	43	11	1	0	0.0	17	20	30	10	3	19	4	197	20	6	9	2.8	.973	C-61
9 yrs.		619	.262	.325	1734	455	74	16	1	0.1	175	194	183	63	14	99	24	1873	222	37	41	3.4	.983	C-518, OF-1, 2B-1, 1B-1

Elias Peak

PEAK, ELIAS
B. May 23, 1859, Philadelphia, Pa. D. Dec. 17, 1916, Philadelphia, Pa.

| 1884 | 2 teams | | BOS U | (1G – .667) | PHI U | (54G – .195) | | | | | | | | | | | | | | | | | | |
| " | total | 55 | .202 | .266 | 218 | 44 | 6 | 4 | 0 | 0.0 | 37 | | 8 | | | 0 | 0 | 154 | 141 | 70 | 14 | 6.6 | .808 | 2B-47, OF-6, SS-2 |

Dickey Pearce

PEARCE, RICHARD J. BR TR 5'3½" 161 lbs.
B. Feb. 29, 1836, Brooklyn, N. Y. D. Oct. 12, 1908, Onset, Mass.
Manager 1872, 1875.

1876	STL N	25	.206	.216	102	21	1	0	0	0.0	12	10	3	5		0	0	27	88	14	6	5.2	.891	SS-23, OF-1, 2B-1
1877		8	.172	.172	29	5	0	0	0	0.0	1	4	1	4		0	0	7	31	2	3	5.0	.950	SS-8
2 yrs.		33	.198	.206	131	26	1	0	0	0.0	13	14	4	9		0	0	34	119	16	9	5.1	.905	SS-31, OF-1, 2B-1

Ducky Pearce

PEARCE, WILLIAM C. BR TR 6'1" 185 lbs.
B. Mar. 17, 1885, Corning, Ohio D. May 22, 1933, Brownstown, Ind.

1908	CIN N	2	.000	.000	2	0	0	0	0	0.0	0	0	0		0	0	0	5	3	0	0	4.0	1.000	C-2
1909		2	.000	.000	2	0	0	0	0	0.0	0	0	0		0	0	0	3	0	0	0	1.5	1.000	C-2
2 yrs.		4	.000	.000	4	0	0	0	0	0.0	0	0	0		0	0	0	8	3	0	0	2.8	1.000	C-4

Harry Pearce

PEARCE, HARRY JAMES BR TR 5'9" 158 lbs.
B. July 12, 1889, Philadelphia, Pa. D. Jan. 8, 1942, Philadelphia, Pa.

Year	Team		Games	BA	SA	AB	H	2B	3B	HR	HR%	R	RBI	BB	SO	SB	Pinch Hit AB	H	PO	A	E	DP	TC/G	FA	G by Pos

Harry Pearce *continued*

Year	Team		Games	BA	SA	AB	H	2B	3B	HR	HR%	R	RBI	BB	SO	SB	AB	H	PO	A	E	DP	TC/G	FA	G by Pos
1917	PHI	N	7	.250	.438	16	4	3	0	0	0.0	2	2	0	4	0	0	0	7	22	1	1	4.3	.967	SS-4
1918			60	.244	.287	164	40	3	2	0	0.0	16	18	9	31	5	2	0	100	157	17	18	4.6	.938	2B-46, SS-2, 3B-1, 1B-1
1919			68	.180	.217	244	44	3	3	0	0.0	24	9	8	27	6	0	0	130	202	17	30	5.1	.951	2B-43, SS-23, 3B-2
3 yrs.			135	.208	.252	424	88	9	5	0	0.0	42	29	17	62	11	2	0	237	381	35	49	4.8	.946	2B-89, SS-29, 3B-3, 1B-1

Albie Pearson

PEARSON, ALBERT GREGORY
B. Sept. 12, 1934, Alhambra, Calif.   BL TL 5'5"   140 lbs.

Year	Team		Games	BA	SA	AB	H	2B	3B	HR	HR%	R	RBI	BB	SO	SB	AB	H	PO	A	E	DP	TC/G	FA	G by Pos
1958	WAS	A	146	.275	.358	530	146	25	5	3	0.6	63	33	64	31	7	4	2	338	6	7	1	2.4	.980	OF-141
1959	2 teams				WAS A (25G – .188)			BAL A (80G – .232)																	
"	total		105	.216	.257	218	47	5	2	0	0.0	31	8	27	8	5	29	6	112	2	2	0	1.1	.983	OF-71
1960	BAL	A	48	.244	.305	82	20	2	0	1	1.2	17	6	17	3	4	13	4	38	1	1	0	0.8	.975	OF-32
1961	LA	A	144	.288	.400	427	123	21	3	7	1.6	92	41	96	40	11	23	9	233	7	11	2	1.7	.956	OF-113
1962			160	.261	.352	614	160	29	6	5	0.8	115	42	95	36	15	0	0	366	8	4	0	2.4	.989	OF-160
1963			154	.304	.398	578	176	26	5	6	1.0	92	47	92	37	17	4	0	340	10	6	5	2.3	.983	OF-148
1964			107	.223	.272	265	59	5	1	2	0.8	34	16	35	22	6	31	7	132	1	3	1	1.3	.978	OF-66
1965	CAL	A	122	.278	.369	360	100	17	2	4	1.1	41	21	51	17	12	27	6	166	5	2	1	1.4	.988	OF-101
1966			2	.000	.000	3	0	0	0	0	0.0	0	0	0	1	0	2	0	0	0	0	0	0.0	–	OF-1
9 yrs.			988	.270	.355	3077	831	130	24	28	0.9	485	214	477	195	77	133	34	1725	40	36	10	1.8	.980	OF-833

Charlie Pechous

PECHOUS, CHARLES EDWARD
B. Oct. 5, 1896, Chicago, Ill.   D. Sept. 13, 1980, Kenosha, Wis.   BR TR 6'   170 lbs.

Year	Team		Games	BA	SA	AB	H	2B	3B	HR	HR%	R	RBI	BB	SO	SB	AB	H	PO	A	E	DP	TC/G	FA	G by Pos
1915	CHI	F	18	.176	.235	51	9	3	0	0	0.0	4	4	4		1	0	0	13	32	3	2	2.7	.938	3B-18
1916	CHI	N	22	.145	.188	69	10	1	1	0	0.0	5	4	3	21	1	0	0	22	56	5	2	3.8	.940	3B-22
1917			13	.244	.244	41	10	0	0	0	0.0	2	1	2	9	1	0	0	19	23	4	2	3.5	.913	3B-7, SS-5
3 yrs.			53	.180	.217	161	29	4	1	0	0.0	11	9	9	30	3	0	0	54	111	12	4	3.3	.932	3B-47, SS-5

Hal Peck

PECK, HAROLD ARTHUR
B. Apr. 20, 1917, Big Bend, Wis.   BL TL 5'11"   175 lbs.

Year	Team		Games	BA	SA	AB	H	2B	3B	HR	HR%	R	RBI	BB	SO	SB	AB	H	PO	A	E	DP	TC/G	FA	G by Pos
1943	BKN	N	1	.000	.000	1	0	0	0	0	0.0	0	0	0	0	0	1	0	0	0	0	0	0.0		
1944	PHI	A	2	.250	.250	8	2	0	0	0	0.0	0	1	0	2	0	0	0	3	0	0	0	1.5	1.000	OF-2
1945			112	.276	.399	449	124	22	9	5	1.1	51	39	37	28	5	2	0	190	9	12	3	1.9	.943	OF-110
1946			48	.247	.367	150	37	8	2	2	1.3	14	11	16	14	1	12	3	47	4	1	1	1.1	.981	OF-35
1947	CLE	A	114	.293	.411	392	115	18	2	8	2.0	58	44	27	31	3	11	4	166	5	3	3	1.5	.983	OF-97
1948			45	.286	.333	63	18	3	0	0	0.0	12	8	4	8	1	30	8	13	0	0	0	0.3	1.000	OF-9
1949			33	.310	.345	29	9	1	0	0	0.0	1	9	3	3	0	28	8	1	0	0	0	0.0	1.000	OF-2
7 yrs.			355	.279	.392	1092	305	52	13	15	1.4	136	112	87	86	10	84	23	420	18	16	7	1.3	.965	OF-255

WORLD SERIES

Year	Team		Games	BA	SA	AB	H	2B	3B	HR	HR%	R	RBI	BB	SO	SB	AB	H	PO	A	E	DP	TC/G	FA	G by Pos
1948	CLE	A	1	–	–	0	0	0	0	0	0.0	0	0	0	0	0	0	0	0	0	0	0	0.0	–	OF-1

Roger Peckinpaugh

PECKINPAUGH, ROGER THORPE
B. Feb. 5, 1891, Wooster, Ohio   D. Nov. 17, 1977, Cleveland, Ohio
Manager 1914, 1928-33, 1941.   BR TR 5'10½" 165 lbs.

Year	Team		Games	BA	SA	AB	H	2B	3B	HR	HR%	R	RBI	BB	SO	SB	AB	H	PO	A	E	DP	TC/G	FA	G by Pos
1910	CLE	A	15	.200	.200	45	9	0	0	0	0.0	1	6	1		3	0	0	20	38	6	3	4.3	.906	SS-14
1912			69	.212	.250	236	50	4	1	1	0.4	18	22	16		11	2	0	127	188	26	16	4.9	.924	SS-67
1913	2 teams				CLE A (1G – .000)			NY A (95G – .268)																	
"	total		96	.268	.347	340	91	10	7	1	0.3	36	32	24	47	19	1	0	184	303	36	30	5.4	.931	SS-94
1914	NY	A	157	.223	.284	570	127	14	6	3	0.5	55	51	51	73	38	0	0	356	500	39	45	5.7	.956	SS-157
1915			142	.220	.307	540	119	18	7	5	0.9	67	44	49	72	19	0	0	291	468	47	60	5.7	.942	SS-142
1916			146	.255	.346	552	141	22	8	4	0.7	65	58	62	50	18	0	0	285	468	43	50	5.5	.946	SS-146
1917			148	.260	.330	543	141	24	7	0	0.0	63	41	64	46	17	0	0	292	467	54	84	5.5	.934	SS-148
1918			122	.231	.278	446	103	15	3	0	0.0	59	43	43	41	12	0	0	260	439	28	75	6.0	.961	SS-122
1919			122	.305	.404	453	138	20	2	7	1.5	89	33	59	37	10	1	0	271	434	43	57	6.1	.943	SS-121
1920			139	.270	.386	534	144	26	6	8	1.5	109	54	72	47	8	0	0	263	441	28	56	5.3	.962	SS-137
1921			149	.288	.397	577	166	25	7	8	1.4	128	71	84	44	2	0	0	318	443	42	75	5.4	.948	SS-149
1922	WAS	A	147	.254	.308	520	132	14	4	2	0.4	62	48	55	36	11	0	0	265	524	41	93	5.6	.951	SS-147
1923			154	.264	.320	568	150	18	4	2	0.4	73	62	64	30	10	0	0	311	510	45	105	5.6	.948	SS-154
1924			155	.272	.340	523	142	20	5	2	0.4	72	73	72	45	11	0	0	278	487	29	81	5.1	.963	SS-155
1925			126	.294	.379	422	124	16	4	4	0.9	67	64	49	23	13	0	0	219	346	28	71	4.7	.953	SS-124, 1B-1
1926			57	.238	.299	147	35	4	1	1	0.7	19	14	28	12	3	9	2	89	109	9	21	3.6	.957	SS-46, 1B-1
1927	CHI	A	68	.295	.350	217	64	6	3	0	0.0	23	23	21	6	2	7	2	101	170	10	30	4.1	.964	SS-60
17 yrs.			2012	.259	.335	7233	1876	256	75	48	0.7	1006	739	814	609	207	22	4	3930	6335	554	952	5.4	.949	SS-1983, 1B-2

WORLD SERIES

Year	Team		Games	BA	SA	AB	H	2B	3B	HR	HR%	R	RBI	BB	SO	SB	AB	H	PO	A	E	DP	TC/G	FA	G by Pos
1921	NY	A	8	.179	.214	28	5	1	0	0	0.0	2	0	4	3	0	0	0	18	28	1	4	5.9	.979	SS-8
1924	WAS	A	4	.417	.583	12	5	2	0	0	0.0	1	2	1	0	1	0	0	7	14	0	3	5.3	1.000	SS-4
1925			7	.250	.417	24	6	1	0	1	4.2	1	2	1	2	1	0	0	10	22	8	3	5.7	.800	SS-7
3 yrs.			19	.250	.359	64	16	4	0	1	1.6	4	4	6	5	2	0	0	35	64	9	10	5.7	.917	SS-19

Bill Pecota

PECOTA, WILLIAM JOSEPH
B. Feb. 16, 1960, Redwood City, Calif.   BR TR 6'2"   195 lbs.

Year	Team		Games	BA	SA	AB	H	2B	3B	HR	HR%	R	RBI	BB	SO	SB	AB	H	PO	A	E	DP	TC/G	FA	G by Pos
1986	KC	A	12	.207	.276	29	6	2	0	0	0.0	3	2	3	3	0	0	0	7	31	1	1	3.3	.974	3B-12, SS-2
1987			66	.276	.378	156	43	5	1	3	1.9	22	14	15	25	5	7	0	67	135	6	28	3.2	.971	SS-36, 3B-17, 2B-15
1988			90	.208	.275	178	37	3	3	1	0.6	25	15	18	34	7	1	1	98	145	6	25	2.8	.976	SS-41, 3B-21, 1B-11, OF-9, DH-4, 2B-3, C-1
1989			65	.205	.410	83	17	4	2	3	3.6	21	5	7	9	5	0	0	50	79	2	14	2.0	.985	SS-29, OF-15, 2B-12, 3B-7, 1B-4, DH-1
4 yrs.			233	.231	.336	446	103	14	6	7	1.6	71	36	43	71	17	8	1	222	390	15	68	2.7	.976	SS-108, 3B-57, 2B-30, OF-24, 1B-15, DH-5, C-1

Les Peden

PEDEN, LESLIE EARL
B. Sept. 17, 1923, Azle, Tex.   BR TR 6'1½" 212 lbs.

Year	Team	Games	BA	SA	AB	H	2B	3B	HR	HR%	R	RBI	BB	SO	SB	Pinch Hit AB	Pinch Hit H	PO	A	E	DP	TC/G	FA	G by Pos

Les Peden *continued*

1953	WAS A	9	.250	.393	28	7	1	0	1	3.6	4	1	4	3	0	1	1	26	5	0	1	3.4	1.000	C-8

Stu Pederson

PEDERSON, STUART RUSSELL
B. Jan. 28, 1960, Palo Alto, Calif.

BL TL 6' 190 lbs.

1985	LA N	8	.000	.000	4	0	0	0	0	0.0	1	1	0	2	0	3	0	2	0	0	0	0.3	1.000	OF-5

Al Pedrique

PEDRIQUE, ALFREDO JOSE
Born Alfredo Jose Pedrique y Garcia.
B. Aug. 11, 1960, Aragua, Venezuela

BR TR 6' 155 lbs.

1987	2 teams	NY	N (5G – .000)	PIT	N (88G – .301)																			
"	total	93	.294	.353	252	74	10	1	1	0.4	24	27	19	29	5	7	0	118	196	11	43	3.5	.966	SS-80, 3B-3, 2B-3
1988	PIT N	50	.180	.219	128	23	5	0	0	0.0	7	4	8	17	0	1	0	65	124	5	23	3.9	.974	SS-46, 3B-5
1989	DET A	31	.203	.246	69	14	3	0	0	0.0	1	5	2	15	0	1	0	35	62	3	14	3.2	.970	SS-12, 3B-12, 2B-8
3 yrs.		174	.247	.298	449	111	18	1	1	0.2	32	36	29	61	5	10	0	218	382	19	80	3.6	.969	SS-138, 3B-20, 2B-11

Chick Pedroes

PEDROES, CHARLES P.
B. Oct. 27, 1869, Chicago, Ill.   D. Aug. 6, 1927, Chicago, Ill.

1902	CHI N	2	.000	.000	6	0	0	0	0	0.0	0	0	0	0	0	0	0	2	0	0	0	1.0	1.000	OF-2

Homer Peel

PEEL, HOMER HEFNER
B. Oct. 10, 1902, Fort Sullivan, Tex.

BR TR 5'9½" 170 lbs.

1927	STL N	2	.000	.000	2	0	0	0	0	0.0	0	1	0	1	0	0	0	0	0	0	0	0.0	–	OF-1
1929	PHI N	53	.269	.359	156	42	12	1	0	0.0	16	19	12	7	1	13	1	100	5	3	2	2.0	.972	OF-39, 1B-1
1930	STL N	26	.164	.192	73	12	2	0	0	0.0	9	10	3	4	0	4	1	30	0	1	0	1.2	.968	OF-21
1933	NY N	84	.257	.297	148	38	1	1	1	0.7	16	12	14	10	0	35	9	49	1	2	0	0.6	.962	OF-45
1934		21	.195	.268	41	8	0	1	1	2.4	7	3	1	2	0	10	2	13	0	1	0	0.7	.929	OF-10
5 yrs.		186	.238	.298	420	100	15	2	2	0.5	48	44	30	24	1	63	13	192	6	7	2	1.1	.966	OF-116, 1B-1

WORLD SERIES

1933	NY N	2	.500	.500	2	1	0	0	0	0.0	0	0	0	0	0	1	1	0	0	0	0	0.0	–	OF-1

Jack Peerson

PEERSON, JACK CHILES
B. Aug. 28, 1910, Brunswick, Ga.   D. Oct. 23, 1966, Fort Walton Beach, Fla.

BR TR 5'11" 175 lbs.

1935	PHI A	10	.316	.368	19	6	1	0	0	0.0	3	1	1	1	0	4	1	7	13	1	0	2.1	.952	SS-4
1936		8	.324	.412	34	11	1	1	0	0.0	7	5	0	3	0	0	0	19	33	3	5	6.9	.945	SS-7, 2B-1
2 yrs.		18	.321	.396	53	17	2	1	0	0.0	10	6	1	4	0	4	1	26	46	4	5	4.2	.947	SS-11, 2B-1

Charlie Peete

PEETE, CHARLES (Mule)
B. Feb. 22, 1929, Franklin, Va.   D. Nov. 27, 1956, Caracas, Venezuela

BL TR 5'9½" 190 lbs.

1956	STL N	23	.192	.308	52	10	2	2	0	0.0	3	6	6	10	0	4	1	37	3	0	1	1.7	1.000	OF-21

Heinie Peitz

PEITZ, HENRY CLEMENT
Brother of Joe Peitz.
B. Nov. 28, 1870, St. Louis, Mo.   D. Oct. 23, 1943, Cincinnati, Ohio

BR TR 5'11" 165 lbs.

1892	STL N	1	.000	.000	3	0	0	0	0	0.0	0	0	0	0	0	0	0	3	0	0	0	3.0	1.000	C-1
1893		96	.254	.345	362	92	12	9	1	0.3	53	45	54	20	12	0	0	388	116	33	16	5.6	.939	C-74, SS-11, OF-10, 1B-5
1894		99	.263	.399	338	89	19	9	3	0.9	52	49	43	21	14	0	0	320	136	33	18	4.9	.933	3B-47, C-39, 1B-14, P-1
1895	CIN N	90	.284	.416	334	95	14	12	2	0.6	44	65	29	20	9	0	0	348	93	32	17	5.3	.932	C-71, 1B-11, 3B-10
1896		68	.299	.431	211	63	12	5	2	0.9	33	34	30	15	7	1	0	201	42	8	6	3.7	.968	C-67
1897		77	.293	.398	266	78	11	7	1	0.4	35	44	18		3	4	0	261	72	7	8	4.4	.979	C-71, P-2
1898		105	.273	.358	330	90	15	5	1	0.3	49	43	35		9	3	1	323	90	24	12	4.2	.945	C-101
1899		93	.272	.341	290	79	13	2	1	0.3	45	43	45		11	2	0	331	91	10	12	4.6	.977	C-91, P-1
1900		91	.255	.330	294	75	14	1	2	0.7	34	34	20		5	4	0	373	127	9	14	5.7	.962	C-80, 1B-8
1901		82	.305	.401	269	82	13	5	1	0.4	24	34	23		3	6	2	321	127	9	14	5.6	.980	C-49, 2B-21, 3B-6, 1B-2
1902		112	.315	.406	387	122	22	5	1	0.3	54	60	24		7	5	1	376	209	33	40	5.5	.947	2B-48, C-47, 3B-6, 1B-6
1903		105	.260	.318	358	93	15	3	0	0.0	45	42	37		7	2	1	496	129	18	17	6.1	.972	C-78, 1B-11, 3B-9, 2B-4
1904		84	.243	.316	272	66	13	1	0	0.4	28	30	14		1	2	1	425	100	9	17	6.4	.983	C-64, 1B-18, 3B-1
1905	PIT N	88	.223	.259	278	62	10	0	0	0.0	18	27	24		2	2	0	338	105	16	14	5.2	.965	C-87, 2B-1
1906		40	.240	.304	125	30	5	1	0	0.0	13	20	13		1	2	0	186	45	5	2	5.9	.979	C-38
1913	STL N	3	.250	.750	4	1	0	1	0	0.0	1	0	0		0	0	0	3	2	3	0	2.7	.625	C-2, OF-1
16 yrs.		1234	.271	.361	4121	1117	191	66	16	0.4	532	560	409	76	91	33	6	4693	1484	260	207	5.2	.960	C-960, 3B-79, 1B-75, 2B-74, OF-11, SS-11, P-4

Joe Peitz

PEITZ, JOSEPH
Brother of Heinie Peitz.
B. Nov. 8, 1869, St. Louis, Mo.   D. Dec. 4, 1919, St. Louis, Mo.

1894	STL N	7	.423	.731	26	11	2	3	0	0.0	10	3	6	1	2	0	0	17	1	4	1	3.1	.818	OF-7

Eddie Pellagrini

PELLAGRINI, EDWARD CHARLES
B. Mar. 13, 1918, Boston, Mass.

BR TR 5'9" 160 lbs.

1946	BOS A	22	.211	.366	71	15	3	1	2	2.8	7	4	3	18	1	0	0	29	40	10	8	3.6	.873	3B-14, SS-9
1947		74	.203	.299	231	47	8	1	4	1.7	29	19	23	35	2	3	0	73	142	14	17	3.1	.939	3B-42, SS-26
1948	STL A	105	.238	.307	290	69	8	3	2	0.7	31	27	34	40	1	2	1	194	292	18	85	4.8	.964	SS-98
1949		79	.238	.306	235	56	8	1	2	0.9	26	15	14	24	2	1	0	164	227	16	52	5.2	.961	SS-76
1951	PHI N	86	.234	.381	197	46	4	5	5	2.5	31	30	23	25	5	12	2	104	132	5	23	2.8	.979	2B-53, SS-8, 3B-6
1952	CIN N	46	.170	.220	100	17	2	1	1	1.0	15	3	8	18	1	6	1	119	67	2	20	4.1	.989	2B-22, 1B-8, SS-1, 3B-1
1953	PIT N	78	.253	.362	174	44	3	2	4	2.3	16	19	14	20	1	32	8	76	98	6	13	2.3	.967	2B-31, 3B-12, SS-3

Year	Team		Games	BA	SA	AB	H	2B	3B	HR	HR%	R	RBI	BB	SO	SB	Pinch Hit AB	H	PO	A	E	DP	TC/G	FA	G by Pos

Eddie Pellagrini *continued*

1954			73	.216	.264	125	27	6	0	0	0.0	12	16	9	21	0	34	7	42	60	2	10	1.4	.981	3B-31, 2B-7, SS-1
8 yrs.			563	.226	.316	1423	321	42	13	20	1.4	167	133	128	201	13	90	19	801	1058	73	228	3.4	.962	SS-222, 2B-113, 3B-106, 1B-8

Bill Pelouze

PELOUZE, WILLIAM NELSON
B. Sept. 12, 1865, Washington, D. C.   D. June 20, 1943, Lake Geneva, Wis.

BR TR 5'8"   170 lbs.

1886	STL	N	1	.000	.000	3	0	0	0	0	0.0	0	0	0	2		0	0	4	0	0	0	4.0	1.000	OF-1

John Peltz

PELTZ, JOHN
B. Apr. 23, 1861, New Orleans, La.   D. Feb. 27, 1906, New Orleans, La.

BR TR

1884	IND	AA	106	.219	.361	393	86	13	17	3	0.8	40		7			0	0	155	16	38	1	2.0	.818	OF-106
1888	BAL	AA	1	.250	.250	4	1	0	0	0	0.0		0		1		0	0	1	0	1	0	2.0	.500	OF-1
1890	3 teams		BKN	AA (98G – .227)		SYR	AA (5G – .176)			TOL	AA (20G – .247)														
"	total		123	.228	.297	474	108	12	9	1	0.2	65		38		17	0	0	239	23	29	8	2.4	.900	OF-123
3 yrs.			230	.224	.326	871	195	25	26	4	0.5	106		45		18	0	0	395	39	68	9	2.2	.865	OF-230

Brock Pemberton

PEMBERTON, BROCK
B. Nov. 5, 1953, Tulsa, Okla.

BB TL 6'3"   190 lbs.

1974	NY	N	11	.182	.182	22	4	0	0	0	0.0	0	1	0	3	0	7	3	31	4	0	4	3.2	1.000	1B-4
1975			2	.000	.000	2	0	0	0	0	0.0	0	0	0	1	0	2	0	0	0	0	0	0.0	–	1B-4
2 yrs.			13	.167	.167	24	4	0	0	0	0.0	0	1	0	4	0	9	3	31	4	0	4	2.7	1.000	1B-4

Bert Pena

PENA, ADELBERTO
Born Adelberto Pena y Rivera.
B. July 11, 1959, Santurce, Puerto Rico

BR TR 5'11"   165 lbs.

1981	HOU	N	4	.500	.500	2	1	0	0	0	0.0	0	0	0	2	0	1	1	1	1	0	1	0.5	1.000	SS-3
1983			4	.125	.125	8	1	0	0	0	0.0	0	0	2	2	0	0	0	1	7	0	2	2.0	1.000	SS-4
1984			24	.205	.308	39	8	1	0	1	2.6	3	4	3	8	0	2	0	26	39	3	5	2.8	.956	SS-21
1985			20	.276	.345	29	8	2	0	0	0.0	3	7	4	6	0	3	2	9	15	1	2	1.3	.960	3B-7, SS-6, 2B-2
1986			15	.207	.241	29	6	1	0	0	0.0	3	2	5	5	1	1	0	20	24	4	2	3.2	.917	SS-10, 3B-2, 2B-1
1987			21	.152	.152	46	7	0	0	0	0.0	5	2	7	7	0	1	0	19	35	1	3	2.6	.982	SS-19, 3B-1
6 yrs.			88	.203	.248	153	31	4	0	1	0.7	18	10	13	28	1	9	3	76	121	9	15	2.3	.956	SS-63, 3B-10, 2B-3

Roberto Pena

PENA, ROBERTO CESAR
Born Roberto Cesar Zapata y Pena.
B. Apr. 17, 1937, Santo Domingo, Dominican Republic
D. July 23, 1982, Santiago, Dominican Republic

BR TR 5'8"   170 lbs.

1965	CHI	N	51	.218	.294	170	37	5	1	2	1.2	17	12	16	19	1	1	0	74	151	17	29	4.7	.930	SS-50
1966			6	.176	.294	17	3	2	0	0	0.0	0	1	0	4	0	2	0	10	12	1	2	3.8	.957	SS-5
1968	PHI	N	138	.260	.300	500	130	13	2	1	0.2	56	38	34	63	3	1	1	230	434	32	93	5.0	.954	SS-133
1969	SD	N	139	.250	.322	472	118	16	3	4	0.8	44	30	21	63	0	18	5	289	285	13	54	4.2	.978	SS-65, 2B-33, 3B-27, 1B-12
1970	2 teams		OAK	A (19G – .259)					MIL	A (121G – .238)															
"	total		140	.241	.306	474	114	20	1	3	0.6	40	45	28	49	4	11	2	222	339	14	68	4.1	.976	SS-111, 1B-7, 3B-5
1971	MIL	A	113	.237	.325	274	65	9	3	3	1.1	17	28	15	37	2	29	5	290	112	4	38	3.6	.990	1B-50, 3B-37, SS-23, 2B-1
6 yrs.			587	.245	.310	1907	467	65	10	13	0.7	174	154	114	235	10	62	13	1115	1333	81	284	4.3	.968	SS-387, 3B-69, 1B-69, 2B-49

Tony Pena

PENA, ANTONIO FRANCESCO
Born Antonio Francesco Pena y Padilla.   Brother of Ramon Pena.
B. June 4, 1957, Monte Cristi, Dominican Republic

BR TR 6'   175 lbs.

1980	PIT	N	8	.429	.571	21	9	1	1	0	0.0	1	1	0	4	0	2	1	38	2	2	0	5.3	.952	C-6
1981			66	.300	.381	210	63	9	1	2	1.0	16	17	8	23	1	2	1	286	41	5	10	5.0	.985	C-64
1982			138	.296	.435	497	147	28	4	11	2.2	53	63	17	57	2	0	0	763	89	16	6	6.3	.982	C-137
1983			151	.301	.435	542	163	22	3	15	2.8	51	70	31	73	6	2	1	976	90	9	9	7.1	.992	C-149
1984			147	.286	.425	546	156	27	2	15	2.7	77	78	36	79	12	1	1	895	95	9	15	6.8	.991	C-146
1985			147	.249	.361	546	136	27	2	10	1.8	53	59	29	67	12	0	0	925	102	12	9	7.1	.988	C-146, 1B-1
1986			144	.288	.406	510	147	26	2	10	2.0	56	52	53	69	9	7	1	824	99	18	13	6.5	.981	C-139, 1B-4
1987	STL	N	116	.214	.307	384	82	13	4	5	1.3	40	44	36	54	6	4	1	624	51	8	8	5.9	.988	C-112, 1B-4, OF-2
1988			149	.263	.372	505	133	23	1	10	2.0	55	51	33	60	6	8	1	796	72	6	9	5.9	.993	C-142, 1B-3
1989			141	.259	.337	424	110	17	2	4	0.9	36	37	35	33	5	7	1	675	70	2	13	5.3	.997	C-134, OF-1
10 yrs.			1207	.274	.389	4185	1146	193	22	82	2.0	438	472	278	519	59	33	8	6802	711	87	92	6.3	.989	C-1175, 1B-12, OF-3

LEAGUE CHAMPIONSHIP SERIES

1987	STL	N	7	.381	.476	21	8	0	1	0	0.0	5	0	3	4	1	0	0	55	5	0	0	8.6	1.000	C-7

WORLD SERIES

1987	STL	N	7	.409	.455	22	9	1	0	0	0.0	2	4	3	2	1	0	0	32	1	1	0	4.9	.971	C-6, DH-1

Elmer Pence

PENCE, ELMER CLAIR
B. Aug. 17, 1900, Valley Springs, Calif.   D. Sept. 17, 1968, San Francisco, Calif.

BR TR 6'   185 lbs.

1922	CHI	A	1	–	–	0	0	0	0	0	–	0	0	0	0	0	0	0	0	0	0	0	1.0	1.000	OF-1

Jim Pendleton

PENDLETON, JAMES EDWARD
B. Jan. 7, 1924, St. Charles, Mo.

BR TR 6'   185 lbs.

1953	MIL	N	120	.299	.462	251	75	12	4	7	2.8	48	27	7	36	6	5	0	152	35	6	4	1.6	.969	OF-105, SS-7
1954			71	.220	.266	173	38	3	1	1	0.6	20	16	4	21	2	16	3	90	5	5	0	1.4	.950	OF-50
1955			8	.000	.000	10	0	0	0	0	0.0	0	0	0	5	0	6	0	6	0	0	0	0.8	1.000	SS-3, 3B-2, 2B-1, 1B-1
1956			14	.000	.000	11	0	0	0	0	0.0	0	0	1	3	0	9	0	3	3	0	0	0.4	1.000	OF-9, 3B-2, SS-1
1957	PIT	N	46	.305	.356	59	18	1	1	0	0.0	9	9	9	14	1	24	6	12	3	2	0	0.4	.882	OF-9, 3B-2, SS-1
1958			3	.333	.333	3	1	0	0	0	0.0	0	0	0	0	0	3	1	0	0	0	0	0.0	–	
1959	CIN	N	65	.257	.354	113	29	6	3	3	2.7	13	9	8	18	1	19	6	45	31	3	4	1.2	.962	OF-24, 3B-16, SS-3

Year	Team		Games	BA	SA	AB	H	2B	3B	HR	HR%	R	RBI	BB	SO	SB	Pinch Hit AB	Pinch Hit H	PO	A	E	DP	TC/G	FA	G by Pos

Jim Pendleton *continued*

Year	Team		Games	BA	SA	AB	H	2B	3B	HR	HR%	R	RBI	BB	SO	SB	AB	H	PO	A	E	DP	TC/G	FA	G by Pos
1962	HOU	N	117	.246	.371	321	79	12	2	8	2.5	30	36	14	57	0	23	7	181	5	7	5	1.6	.964	OF-90, 1B-8, 3B-3, SS-2
8 yrs.			444	.255	.365	941	240	30	8	19	2.0	120	97	43	151	11	104	23	489	82	23	10	1.3	.961	OF-279, 3B-24, SS-17, 1B-9, 2B-1

Terry Pendleton

PENDLETON, TERRY LEE
B. July 16, 1960, Los Angeles, Calif.

BB TR 5'9" 180 lbs.

Year	Team		Games	BA	SA	AB	H	2B	3B	HR	HR%	R	RBI	BB	SO	SB	AB	H	PO	A	E	DP	TC/G	FA	G by Pos
1984	STL	N	67	.324	.420	262	85	16	3	1	0.4	37	33	16	32	20	1	0	59	155	13	10	3.4	.943	3B-66
1985			149	.240	.306	559	134	16	3	5	0.9	56	69	37	75	17	2	1	129	361	18	26	3.4	.965	3B-149
1986			159	.239	.306	578	138	26	5	1	0.2	56	59	34	59	24	3	0	133	371	20	36	3.3	.962	3B-156, OF-1
1987			159	.286	.412	583	167	29	4	12	2.1	82	96	70	74	19	1	1	117	369	26	27	3.2	.949	3B-158
1988			110	.253	.361	391	99	20	2	6	1.5	44	53	21	51	3	11	4	75	239	12	13	3.0	.963	3B-101
1989			162	.264	.390	613	162	28	5	13	2.1	83	74	44	81	9	3	0	113	392	15	25	3.2	.971	3B-161
6 yrs.			806	.263	.361	2986	785	135	22	38	1.3	358	384	222	372	92	21	6	626	1887	104	137	3.2	.960	3B-791, OF-1

LEAGUE CHAMPIONSHIP SERIES

Year	Team		Games	BA	SA	AB	H	2B	3B	HR	HR%	R	RBI	BB	SO	SB	AB	H	PO	A	E	DP	TC/G	FA	G by Pos
1985	STL	N	6	.208	.250	24	5	1	0	0	0.0	2	4	1	2	0	0	0	6	18	1	2	4.2	.960	3B-6
1987			6	.211	.316	19	4	0	1	0	0.0	3	1	0	6	0	0	0	3	11	0	1	2.3	1.000	3B-6
2 yrs.			12	.209	.279	43	9	1	1	0	0.0	5	5	1	8	0	0	0	9	29	1	3	3.3	.974	3B-12

WORLD SERIES

Year	Team		Games	BA	SA	AB	H	2B	3B	HR	HR%	R	RBI	BB	SO	SB	AB	H	PO	A	E	DP	TC/G	FA	G by Pos
1985	STL	N	7	.261	.391	23	6	1	1	0	0.0	3	3	3	2	0	0	0	6	14	1	0	3.0	.952	3B-7
1987			3	.429	.429	7	3	0	0	0	0.0	2	1	1	1	2	0	0	0	0	0	0	0.0	–	DH-2
2 yrs.			10	.300	.400	30	9	1	1	0	0.0	5	4	4	3	2	0	0	6	14	1	3	2.1	.952	3B-7, DH-2

Jimmy Peoples

PEOPLES, JAMES ELSWORTH
B. Oct. 8, 1863, Big Beaver, Mich.   D. Aug. 29, 1920, Detroit, Mich.

TR 5'8" 200 lbs.

Year	Team		Games	BA	SA	AB	H	2B	3B	HR	HR%	R	RBI	BB	SO	SB	AB	H	PO	A	E	DP	TC/G	FA	G by Pos
1884	CIN	AA	69	.169	.199	267	45	2	3	0	0.0	28			6		0	0	142	168	46	21	5.2	.871	SS-47, C-14, OF-10, 3B-1, 1B-1
1885 2 teams	CIN	AA (7G – .182)				BKN		AA	(41G – .199)																
" total			48	.197	.249	173	34	4	1	1	0.6	22			6		0	0	200	78	32	7	6.5	.897	C-42, OF-2, SS-2, P-2, 3B-1, 1B-1
1886	BKN	AA	93	.218	.282	340	74	7	3	3	0.9	43		20			0	0	419	190	87	14	7.5	.875	C-76, SS-14, OF-8, 3B-1
1887			73	.254	.332	268	68	14	2	1	0.4	36		16		22	0	0	265	122	66	5	6.2	.854	C-57, OF-8, SS-4, 1B-4, 2B-1
1888			32	.194	.301	103	20	3	3	0	0.0	15	17	8		10	0	0	181	56	29	7	8.3	.891	C-25, SS-5, OF-2
1889	COL	AA	29	.230	.360	100	23	6	2	1	1.0	13	16	6	8	3	0	0	120	37	16	1	6.0	.908	C-22, OF-5, 2B-2, SS-1
6 yrs.			344	.211	.278	1251	264	38	14	6	0.5	157	33	62	33	35	0	0	1327	651	276	55	6.6	.878	C-236, SS-73, OF-35, 1B-6, 3B-3, 2B-3, P-2

Joe Pepitone

PEPITONE, JOSEPH ANTHONY (Pepi)
B. Oct. 9, 1940, Brooklyn, N. Y.

BL TL 6'2" 185 lbs.

Year	Team		Games	BA	SA	AB	H	2B	3B	HR	HR%	R	RBI	BB	SO	SB	AB	H	PO	A	E	DP	TC/G	FA	G by Pos
1962	NY	A	63	.239	.442	138	33	3	2	7	5.1	14	17	3	21	1	19	5	126	11	2	9	2.2	.986	OF-32, 1B-16
1963			157	.271	.448	580	157	16	3	27	4.7	79	89	23	63	3	9	1	1166	104	8	111	8.1	.994	1B-143, OF-16
1964			160	.251	.418	613	154	12	3	28	4.6	71	100	24	63	2	3	1	1346	121	18	128	9.3	.988	1B-155, OF-30
1965			143	.247	.394	531	131	18	3	18	3.4	51	62	43	59	4	2	0	1081	75	4	104	8.1	.997	1B-115, OF-41
1966			152	.255	.463	585	149	21	4	31	5.3	85	83	29	58	4	1	0	1126	97	9	94	8.1	.993	1B-119, OF-55
1967			133	.251	.377	501	126	18	3	13	2.6	45	64	34	62	1	4	1	321	13	8	6	2.6	.977	OF-123, 1B-6
1968			108	.245	.403	380	93	9	3	15	3.9	41	56	37	45	8	4	1	318	8	4	11	3.1	.988	OF-92, 1B-12
1969			135	.242	.442	513	124	19	3	27	5.3	49	70	30	42	8	4	2	1254	74	7	118	9.9	.995	1B-132
1970 2 teams	HOU	N (75G – .251)				CHI		N	(56G – .268)																
" total			131	.258	.482	492	127	18	7	26	5.3	82	79	33	43	5	2	0	576	33	4	45	4.7	.993	OF-84, 1B-63
1971	CHI	N	115	.307	.482	427	131	19	4	16	3.7	50	61	24	41	1	2	1	904	64	10	75	8.5	.990	1B-95, OF-23
1972			66	.262	.397	214	56	5	0	8	3.7	23	21	13	22	1	5	1	552	31	2	51	8.9	.997	1B-66
1973 2 teams	CHI	N (31G – .268)				ATL		N	(3G – .364)																
" total			34	.276	.374	123	34	3	0	3	2.4	16	19	9	7	3	3	1	266	19	5	33	8.5	.983	1B-31
12 yrs.			1397	.258	.432	5097	1315	158	35	219	4.3	606	721	302	526	41	58	13	9036	650	81	785	7.0	.992	1B-953, OF-496

WORLD SERIES

Year	Team		Games	BA	SA	AB	H	2B	3B	HR	HR%	R	RBI	BB	SO	SB	AB	H	PO	A	E	DP	TC/G	FA	G by Pos
1963	NY	A	4	.154	.154	13	2	0	0	0	0.0	0	0	1	3	0	0	0	37	6	1	8	11.0	.977	1B-4
1964			7	.154	.308	26	4	1	0	1	3.8	1	5	2	3	0	0	0	64	5	0	6	9.9	1.000	1B-7
2 yrs.			11	.154	.256	39	6	1	0	1	2.6	1	5	3	6	0	0	0	101	11	1	14	10.3	.991	1B-11

Henry Peploski

PEPLOSKI, HENRY STEPHEN (Pep)
Brother of Pepper Peploski.
B. Sept. 15, 1905, Garlin, Poland   D. Jan. 28, 1982, Dover, N. J.

BL TR 5'9" 155 lbs.

Year	Team		Games	BA	SA	AB	H	2B	3B	HR	HR%	R	RBI	BB	SO	SB	AB	H	PO	A	E	DP	TC/G	FA	G by Pos
1929	BOS	N	6	.200	.200	10	2	0	0	0	0.0	1	1	1	3	0	4	1	2	3	0	2	0.8	1.000	3B-2

Pepper Peploski

PEPLOSKI, JOSEPH ALOYSIUS
Brother of Henry Peploski.
B. Sept. 12, 1891, Brooklyn, N. Y.

BR TR 5'8" 155 lbs.

Year	Team		Games	BA	SA	AB	H	2B	3B	HR	HR%	R	RBI	BB	SO	SB	AB	H	PO	A	E	DP	TC/G	FA	G by Pos
1913	DET	A	2	.500	.500	4	2	0	0	0	0.0	1	0	0	0	0	0	0	1	0	1	0	0.5	1.000	3B-2

Don Pepper

PEPPER, DONALD HOYTE
B. Oct. 8, 1943, Saratoga Springs, N. Y.

BL TL 6'4½" 215 lbs.

Year	Team		Games	BA	SA	AB	H	2B	3B	HR	HR%	R	RBI	BB	SO	SB	AB	H	PO	A	E	DP	TC/G	FA	G by Pos
1966	DET	A	4	.000	.000	3	0	0	0	0	0.0	0	0	1	0	0	1	0	2	0	0	0	0.5	1.000	1B-1

Ray Pepper

PEPPER, RAYMOND WATSON
B. Aug. 5, 1905, Decatur, Ala.

BR TR 6'2" 195 lbs.

Year	Team		Games	BA	SA	AB	H	2B	3B	HR	HR%	R	RBI	BB	SO	SB	AB	H	PO	A	E	DP	TC/G	FA	G by Pos
1932	STL	N	21	.246	.316	57	14	2	1	0	0.0	5	7	5	13	1	4	0	33	1	1	0	1.7	.971	OF-17
1933			3	.222	.556	9	2	0	1	1	11.1	2	2	0	1	0	1	0	3	0	0	0	1.0	1.000	OF-2
1934	STL	A	148	.298	.399	564	168	24	6	7	1.2	71	101	29	67	1	12	2	299	15	12	4	2.2	.963	OF-136
1935			92	.253	.379	261	66	15	3	4	1.5	20	37	20	32	0	34	7	103	5	2	1	1.2	.982	OF-57

Year	Team		Games	BA	SA	AB	H	2B	3B	HR	HR%	R	RBI	BB	SO	SB	Pinch Hit AB	Pinch Hit H	PO	A	E	DP	TC/G	FA	G by Pos

Ray Pepper *continued*

Year	Team		Games	BA	SA	AB	H	2B	3B	HR	HR%	R	RBI	BB	SO	SB	AB	H	PO	A	E	DP	TC/G	FA	G by Pos
1936			75	.282	.371	124	35	5	0	2	1.6	13	23	5	23	0	54	18	31	1	2	0	0.5	.941	OF-18
5 yrs.			339	.281	.387	1015	285	46	10	14	1.4	109	170	59	136	2	105	27	469	22	17	5	1.5	.967	OF-230

Jack Perconte

PERCONTE, JOHN PATRICK
B. Aug. 31, 1954, Joliet, Ill.

BL TR 5'10" 160 lbs.

Year	Team		Games	BA	SA	AB	H	2B	3B	HR	HR%	R	RBI	BB	SO	SB	AB	H	PO	A	E	DP	TC/G	FA	G by Pos
1980	LA	N	14	.235	.235	17	4	0	0	0	0.0	2	2	2	1	3	3	0	13	18	0	3	2.2	1.000	2B-9
1981			8	.222	.444	9	2	0	1	0	0.0	2	1	2	2	1	5	2	4	13	0	3	2.1	1.000	2B-2
1982	CLE	A	93	.237	.292	219	52	4	4	0	0.0	27	15	22	25	9	7	1	131	199	8	23	3.6	.976	2B-82, DH-2
1983			14	.269	.308	26	7	1	0	0	0.0	1	0	5	2	3	2	1	20	37	3	12	4.3	.950	2B-13
1984	SEA	A	155	.294	.346	612	180	24	4	0	0.0	93	31	57	47	29	4	1	303	438	14	90	4.9	.981	2B-150
1985			125	.264	.340	485	128	17	7	2	0.4	60	23	50	36	31	2	1	244	381	9	91	5.1	.986	2B-125
1986	CHI	A	24	.219	.233	73	16	1	0	0	0.0	6	4	11	10	2	0	0	46	54	1	12	4.2	.990	2B-24
7 yrs.			433	.270	.329	1441	389	47	16	2	0.1	191	76	149	123	78	23	6	761	1140	35	234	4.5	.982	2B-405, DH-2

Marty Perez

PEREZ, MARTIN ROMAN
B. Feb. 28, 1947, Visalia, Calif.

BR TR 5'11" 160 lbs.

Year	Team		Games	BA	SA	AB	H	2B	3B	HR	HR%	R	RBI	BB	SO	SB	AB	H	PO	A	E	DP	TC/G	FA	G by Pos
1969	CAL	A	13	.231	.231	13	3	0	0	0	0.0	3	0	2	1	0	0	0	12	19	0	6	2.4	1.000	SS-7, 3B-2, 2B-2
1970			3	.000	.000	3	0	0	0	0	0.0	0	1	0	0	0	0	0	3	2	1	1	2.0	.833	SS-2
1971	ATL	N	130	.227	.307	410	93	15	3	4	1.0	28	32	25	44	1	2	0	195	382	28	91	4.7	.954	SS-126, 2B-1
1972			141	.228	.265	479	109	13	1	1	0.2	33	28	30	55	0	1	0	220	378	27	73	4.4	.957	SS-141
1973			141	.250	.347	501	125	15	5	8	1.6	66	57	49	66	2	5	2	215	416	25	78	4.7	.962	SS-139
1974			127	.260	.340	447	116	20	5	2	0.4	51	34	35	51	2	8	1	236	333	10	69	4.6	.983	2B-102, SS-14, 3B-6
1975			120	.275	.328	461	127	14	2	2	0.4	50	34	37	44	2	0	0	262	349	10	75	5.2	.984	2B-116, SS-7
1976 2 teams	ATL	N	(31G – .250)		SF	N	(93G – .259)																		
" total			124	.257	.322	428	110	17	1	3	0.7	49	32	38	37	3	5	1	256	357	14	71	5.1	.978	2B-107, SS-22, 3B-2
1977 2 teams	NY	A	(1G – .500)		OAK	A	(115G – .231)																		
" total			116	.233	.313	377	88	14	5	2	0.5	32	23	29	66	1	3	1	207	318	16	54	4.7	.970	2B-105, 3B-13, SS-4
1978	OAK	A	16	.000	.000	12	0	0	0	0	0.0	0	0	0	5	0	0	0	4	12	1	1	1.1	.941	3B-11, SS-3, 2B-1
10 yrs.			931	.246	.316	3131	771	108	22	22	0.7	313	241	245	369	11	24	5	1610	2566	132	519	4.6	.969	SS-465, 2B-434, 3B-34

Tony Perez

PEREZ, ATANASIO
Born Atanasio Perez y Rigal.
B. May 14, 1942, Camaguey, Cuba

BR TR 6'2" 175 lbs.

Year	Team		Games	BA	SA	AB	H	2B	3B	HR	HR%	R	RBI	BB	SO	SB	AB	H	PO	A	E	DP	TC/G	FA	G by Pos
1964	CIN	N	12	.080	.120	25	2	1	0	0	0.0	1	1	3	9	0	6	0	51	0	1	2	4.3	.981	1B-6
1965			104	.260	.466	281	73	14	4	12	4.3	40	47	21	67	0	25	6	525	40	6	55	5.5	.989	1B-93
1966			99	.265	.381	257	68	10	4	4	1.6	25	39	14	44	1	28	5	530	23	6	46	5.6	.989	1B-75
1967			156	.290	.490	600	174	28	7	26	4.3	78	102	33	102	0	0	0	249	234	13	26	3.2	.974	3B-139, 1B-18, 2B-1
1968			160	.282	.430	625	176	25	7	18	2.9	93	92	51	92	3	0	0	151	343	25	33	3.2	.952	3B-160
1969			160	.294	.526	629	185	31	2	37	5.9	103	122	63	131	4	0	0	136	342	32	35	3.2	.937	3B-160
1970			158	.317	.589	587	186	28	6	40	6.8	107	129	83	134	8	1	0	167	292	35	38	3.1	.929	3B-153, 1B-8
1971			158	.269	.438	609	164	22	3	25	4.1	72	91	51	120	4	1	0	281	308	20	42	3.9	.967	3B-148, 1B-44
1972			136	.283	.497	515	146	33	7	21	4.1	64	90	55	121	4	2	0	1207	68	9	111	9.4	.993	1B-136
1973			151	.314	.527	564	177	33	3	27	4.8	73	101	74	117	3	1	0	1318	85	13	131	9.4	.991	1B-151
1974			158	.265	.460	596	158	28	2	28	4.7	81	101	61	112	1	1	0	1292	75	6	111	8.7	.996	1B-157
1975			137	.282	.466	511	144	28	3	20	3.9	74	109	54	101	1	4	0	1192	72	9	113	9.3	.993	1B-132
1976			139	.260	.452	527	137	32	6	19	3.6	77	91	50	88	10	8	3	1158	73	5	110	8.9	.996	1B-136
1977	MON	N	154	.283	.463	559	158	32	6	19	3.4	71	91	63	111	4	6	1	1312	110	11	88	9.3	.992	1B-148
1978			148	.290	.449	544	158	38	3	14	2.6	63	78	38	104	2	3	1	1181	82	11	116	8.6	.991	1B-145
1979			132	.270	.425	489	132	29	4	13	2.7	58	73	38	82	2	3	1	1114	65	11	81	9.0	.991	1B-129
1980	BOS	A	151	.275	.467	585	161	31	3	25	4.3	73	105	41	93	1	1	0	1301	87	10	150	9.3	.993	1B-137, DH-13
1981			84	.252	.395	306	77	11	3	9	2.9	35	39	27	66	0	5	2	519	37	4	63	6.7	.993	1B-56, DH-23
1982			69	.260	.444	196	51	14	2	6	3.1	18	31	19	48	0	21	5	5	1	1	0	0.1	.857	DH-46, 1B-2
1983	PHI	N	91	.241	.372	253	61	11	2	6	2.4	18	43	28	57	1	19	4	514	40	1	36	6.1	.998	1B-69
1984	CIN	N	71	.241	.343	137	33	6	1	2	1.5	9	15	11	21	0	38	11	186	12	2	17	2.8	.990	1B-31
1985			72	.328	.470	183	60	8	0	6	3.3	25	33	22	22	0	20	4	340	22	2	34	5.1	.995	1B-50
1986			77	.255	.355	200	51	12	1	2	1.0	14	29	25	25	0	22	5	398	29	7	46	5.6	.984	1B-55
23 yrs.			2777	.279	.463	9778	2732	505	79	379	3.9	1272	1652	925	1867 4th	49	214	47	15127	2440	240	1484	6.4	.987	1B-1778, 3B-760, DH-82, 2B-1

LEAGUE CHAMPIONSHIP SERIES

Year	Team		Games	BA	SA	AB	H	2B	3B	HR	HR%	R	RBI	BB	SO	SB	AB	H	PO	A	E	DP	TC/G	FA	G by Pos
1970	CIN	N	3	.333	.750	12	4	2	0	1	8.3	1	2	1	1	0	0	0	1	0	0	0	0.3	1.000	3B-3, 1B-1
1972			5	.200	.250	20	4	1	0	0	0.0	0	2	0	7	0	0	0	45	3	0	2	9.6	1.000	1B-5
1973			5	.091	.227	22	2	0	0	1	4.5	1	2	0	4	0	0	0	47	4	0	3	10.2	1.000	1B-5
1975			3	.417	.667	12	5	0	0	1	8.3	3	4	1	2	0	0	0	27	5	0	1	10.7	1.000	1B-3
1976			3	.200	.200	10	2	0	0	0	0.0	1	3	1	2	0	0	0	27	2	1	2	10.0	.967	1B-3
1983	PHI	N	1	1.000	1.000	1	1	0	0	0	0.0	0	0	0	0	0	1	1	0	0	0	0	0.0	—	
6 yrs.			20	.234	.390	77	18	3	0	3	3.9	6	13	3	16	0	1	1	147	14	1	9	8.1	.994	1B-17, 3B-3

WORLD SERIES

Year	Team		Games	BA	SA	AB	H	2B	3B	HR	HR%	R	RBI	BB	SO	SB	AB	H	PO	A	E	DP	TC/G	FA	G by Pos
1970	CIN	N	5	.056	.056	18	1	0	0	0	0.0	2	0	3	4	0	0	0	3	13	1	0	3.4	.941	3B-5
1972			7	.435	.522	23	10	2	0	0	0.0	3	2	4	4	0	0	0	73	3	1	3	11.0	.987	1B-7
1975			7	.179	.500	28	5	0	0	3	10.7	4	7	3	9	1	0	0	66	5	1	5	10.3	.986	1B-7
1976			4	.313	.375	16	5	1	0	0	0.0	1	2	1	2	0	0	0	32	4	0	2	9.0	1.000	1B-4
1983	PHI	N	4	.200	.200	10	2	0	0	0	0.0	0	0	0	2	0	2	1	13	1	0	1	3.5	1.000	1B-2
5 yrs.			27	.242	.368	95	23	3	0	3	3.2	10	11	11	21	1	2	1	187	26	3	14	8.0	.986	1B-20, 3B-5

Tony Perezchica

PEREZCHICA, ANTONIO LLAMAS
B. Apr. 20, 1966, Mexicali, Mexico

BR TR 5'11" 165 lbs.

Year	Team		Games	BA	SA	AB	H	2B	3B	HR	HR%	R	RBI	BB	SO	SB	AB	H	PO	A	E	DP	TC/G	FA	G by Pos
1988	SF	N	7	.125	.125	8	1	0	0	0	0.0	1	1	2	1	0	0	0	5	5	0	0	1.4	1.000	2B-6

Broderick Perkins

PERKINS, BRODERICK PHILLIP
B. Nov. 23, 1954, Pittsburg, Calif.

BL TL 5'10" 180 lbs.

Year	Team		Games	BA	SA	AB	H	2B	3B	HR	HR%	R	RBI	BB	SO	SB	Pinch Hit AB	Pinch Hit H	PO	A	E	DP	TC/G	FA	G by Pos

Broderick Perkins *continued*

Year	Team		Games	BA	SA	AB	H	2B	3B	HR	HR%	R	RBI	BB	SO	SB	AB	H	PO	A	E	DP	TC/G	FA	G by Pos
1978	SD	N	62	.240	.341	217	52	14	1	2	0.9	14	33	5	29	4	5	0	538	41	4	56	9.4	.993	1B-59
1979			57	.264	.264	87	23	0	0	0	0.0	8	8	8	12	0	26	4	155	10	3	16	2.9	.982	1B-28
1980			43	.370	.520	100	37	9	0	2	2.0	18	14	11	10	2	12	4	159	9	3	14	4.0	.982	1B-20, OF-10
1981			92	.280	.398	254	71	18	3	2	0.8	27	40	14	16	0	14	4	602	38	3	56	7.0	.995	1B-80, OF-3
1982			125	.271	.340	347	94	10	4	2	0.6	32	34	26	20	2	29	11	831	64	6	61	7.2	.993	1B-98, OF-11
1983	CLE	A	79	.272	.326	184	50	10	0	0	0.0	23	24	9	19	1	28	5	148	6	2	12	2.0	.987	1B-19, OF-17, DH-16
1984			58	.197	.212	66	13	1	0	0	0.0	5	4	7	10	0	41	6	8	0	0	2	0.1	1.000	DH-10, 1B-2
7 yrs.			516	.271	.352	1255	340	62	8	8	0.6	127	157	80	116	9	155	34	2441	168	21	217	5.1	.992	1B-306, OF-41, DH-26

Cy Perkins

PERKINS, RALPH FOSTER
B. Feb. 27, 1896, Gloucester, Mass. D. Oct. 2, 1963, Philadelphia, Pa.   BR TR 5'10½" 158 lbs.

Year	Team		Games	BA	SA	AB	H	2B	3B	HR	HR%	R	RBI	BB	SO	SB	AB	H	PO	A	E	DP	TC/G	FA	G by Pos
1915	PHI	A	7	.200	.250	20	4	1	0	0	0.0	2	0	3	3	0	1	0	38	8	4	0	7.1	.920	C-6
1917			6	.167	.167	18	3	0	0	0	0.0	1	2	2	1	0	0	0	31	14	1	1	7.7	.978	C-6
1918			68	.188	.229	218	41	4	1	1	0.5	9	14	8	15	1	7	1	201	103	3	11	4.5	.990	C-60
1919			101	.252	.357	305	77	12	7	2	0.7	22	29	27	22	2	6	1	357	153	16	16	5.2	.970	C-87, SS-8
1920			148	.260	.363	493	128	24	6	5	1.0	40	52	28	35	5	1	0	528	182	15	16	4.9	.979	C-146, 2B-1
1921			141	.288	.428	538	155	31	4	12	2.2	58	73	32	32	5	0	0	540	137	20	16	4.9	.971	C-141
1922			148	.267	.366	505	135	20	6	6	1.2	58	69	40	30	1	7	1	432	130	9	10	3.9	.984	C-141
1923			143	.270	.370	500	135	34	5	2	0.4	53	65	65	30	1	4	1	475	102	17	12	4.2	.971	C-137
1924			128	.242	.311	392	95	19	4	0	0.0	31	32	31	20	3	0	0	415	102	9	9	4.1	.983	C-128
1925			65	.307	.400	140	43	10	0	1	0.7	21	18	26	6	0	4	1	213	36	5	3	3.9	.980	C-58, 3B-1
1926			63	.291	.331	148	43	6	0	0	0.0	14	19	18	7	0	7	4	205	38	4	5	3.9	.984	C-55
1927			59	.255	.358	137	35	7	2	1	0.7	11	15	12	8	0	2	0	162	29	4	2	3.3	.979	C-54, 1B-1
1928			19	.172	.172	29	5	0	0	0	0.0	1	1	1	1	0	0	0	47	7	1	0	2.9	.982	C-19
1929			38	.211	.263	76	16	4	0	0	0.0	4	9	5	4	0	0	0	85	15	1	1	2.7	.990	C-38
1930			20	.158	.211	38	6	2	0	0	0.0	1	4	2	3	0	0	0	52	3	2	1	2.9	.965	C-19, 1B-1
1931	NY	A	16	.255	.277	47	12	1	0	0	0.0	3	7	1	4	0	0	0	51	7	0	0	3.6	1.000	C-16
1934	DET	A	1	.000	.000	1	0	0	0	0	0.0	0	0	0	0	0	1	0	0	0	0	0	0.0	—	
17 yrs.			1171	.259	.352	3605	933	175	35	30	0.8	329	409	301	221	18	40	9	3832	1066	111	103	4.3	.978	C-1111, SS-8, 1B-2, 3B-1, 2B-1

Sam Perlozzo

PERLOZZO, SAMUEL BENEDICT
B. Mar. 4, 1951, Cumberland, Md.   BR TR 5'9" 170 lbs.

Year	Team		Games	BA	SA	AB	H	2B	3B	HR	HR%	R	RBI	BB	SO	SB	AB	H	PO	A	E	DP	TC/G	FA	G by Pos
1977	MIN	A	10	.292	.458	24	7	0	2	0	0.0	6	0	2	3	0	2	0	12	17	0	2	2.9	1.000	2B-10, 3B-1
1979	SD	N	2	.000	.000	2	0	0	0	0	0.0	0	0	1	0	0	0	0	1	0	1	0	1.0	.500	2B-2
2 yrs.			12	.269	.423	26	7	0	2	0	0.0	6	0	3	3	0	2	0	13	17	1	2	2.6	.968	2B-12, 3B-1

Jack Perrin

PERRIN, JOHN STEPHENSON
B. Feb. 4, 1898, Escanaba, Mich. D. June 24, 1969, Detroit, Mich.   BL TR 5'9" 160 lbs.

Year	Team		Games	BA	SA	AB	H	2B	3B	HR	HR%	R	RBI	BB	SO	SB	AB	H	PO	A	E	DP	TC/G	FA	G by Pos
1921	BOS	A	4	.231	.231	13	3	0	0	0	0.0	3	1	0	3	0	0	0	1	0	0	0	0.3	1.000	OF-4

Nig Perrine

PERRINE, JOHN GROVER
B. Jan. 14, 1885, Clinton, Wis. D. Aug. 13, 1948, Kansas City, Mo.   BR TR 5'9" 160 lbs.

Year	Team		Games	BA	SA	AB	H	2B	3B	HR	HR%	R	RBI	BB	SO	SB	AB	H	PO	A	E	DP	TC/G	FA	G by Pos
1907	WAS	A	44	.171	.212	146	25	4	1	0	0.0	13	15	13		10	0	0	90	117	14	13	5.0	.937	2B-24, SS-18, 3B-2

George Perring

PERRING, GEORGE WILSON
B. Aug. 13, 1884, Sharon, Wis. D. Aug. 20, 1960, Beloit, Wis.   BR TR 6' 190 lbs.

Year	Team		Games	BA	SA	AB	H	2B	3B	HR	HR%	R	RBI	BB	SO	SB	AB	H	PO	A	E	DP	TC/G	FA	G by Pos
1908	CLE	A	89	.216	.274	310	67	8	5	0	0.0	23	19	16		0	0	133	236	29	16	4.5	.927	SS-48, 3B-41
1909			88	.223	.322	283	63	10	9	0	0.0	26	20	19		6	0	105	188	22	11	3.6	.930	3B-66, SS-11, 2B-8
1910			39	.221	.320	122	27	6	3	0	0.0	14	8	3		3	2	87	69	9	7	4.2	.945	3B-33, 1B-4
1914	KC	F	144	.278	.387	496	138	28	10	2	0.4	68	69	59		7	6	486	242	28	46	5.3	.963	3B-101, 1B-41, SS-1, P-1
1915			153	.259	.358	553	143	23	7	6	1.1	67	67	55		10	0	454	334	24	38	5.3	.970	3B-102, 2B-31, 1B-31, SS-1
5 yrs.			513	.248	.343	1764	438	75	34	8	0.5	198	183	152		26	8	1265	1069	112	118	4.8	.954	3B-343, 1B-76, SS-61, 2B-39, P-1

Bob Perry

PERRY, MELVIN GRAY
B. Sept. 14, 1934, New Bern, N. C.   BR TR 6'2" 180 lbs.

Year	Team		Games	BA	SA	AB	H	2B	3B	HR	HR%	R	RBI	BB	SO	SB	AB	H	PO	A	E	DP	TC/G	FA	G by Pos
1963	LA	A	61	.253	.361	166	42	9	0	3	1.8	16	14	9	31	1	4	2	86	1	5	0	1.5	.946	OF-55
1964			70	.276	.362	221	61	8	1	3	1.4	19	16	14	52	1	7	0	115	2	3	0	1.7	.975	OF-62
2 yrs.			131	.266	.362	387	103	17	1	6	1.6	35	30	23	83	2	11	2	201	3	8	0	1.6	.962	OF-117

Boyd Perry

PERRY, BOYD GLENN
B. Mar. 21, 1914, Snow Camp, N. C.   BR TR 5'10" 158 lbs.

Year	Team		Games	BA	SA	AB	H	2B	3B	HR	HR%	R	RBI	BB	SO	SB	AB	H	PO	A	E	DP	TC/G	FA	G by Pos
1941	DET	A	36	.181	.241	83	15	5	0	0	0.0	9	11	10	9	1	0	0	46	62	4	12	3.1	.964	SS-25, 2B-11

Clay Perry

PERRY, CLAYTON SHIELDS
B. Dec. 18, 1881, Rice Lake, Wis. D. Jan. 16, 1954, Rice Lake, Wis.   BR TR 5'10½" 175 lbs.

Year	Team		Games	BA	SA	AB	H	2B	3B	HR	HR%	R	RBI	BB	SO	SB	AB	H	PO	A	E	DP	TC/G	FA	G by Pos
1908	DET	A	5	.182	.182	11	2	0	0	0	0.0	0	0		0	0	0	0	4	7	1	1	2.4	.917	3B-5

Gerald Perry

PERRY, GERALD JUNE
B. Oct. 30, 1960, Savannah, Ga.   BL TR 5'11" 172 lbs.

Year	Team		Games	BA	SA	AB	H	2B	3B	HR	HR%	R	RBI	BB	SO	SB	AB	H	PO	A	E	DP	TC/G	FA	G by Pos
1983	ATL	N	27	.359	.487	39	14	2	0	1	2.6	5	6	5	4	0	16	7	55	0	1	5	2.1	.982	1B-7, OF-1
1984			122	.265	.372	347	92	12	2	7	2.0	52	47	61	38	15	16	8	550	28	12	41	4.8	.980	1B-64, OF-53
1985			110	.214	.273	238	51	5	0	3	1.3	22	13	23	28	9	44	6	541	37	9	48	5.3	.985	1B-55, OF-1
1986			29	.271	.386	70	19	2	0	2	2.9	6	11	8	4	0	11	3	24	1	2	2	0.9	.926	OF-21, 1B-1
1987			142	.270	.411	533	144	35	2	12	2.3	77	74	48	63	42	5	1	1297	72	14	118	9.7	.990	1B-136, OF-7
1988			141	.300	.400	547	164	29	1	8	1.5	61	74	36	49	29	0	0	1282	106	17	102	10.0	.988	1B-141

Year	Team	Games	BA	SA	AB	H	2B	3B	HR	HR%	R	RBI	BB	SO	SB	PH AB	PH H	PO	A	E	DP	TC/G	FA	G by Pos

Gerald Perry *continued*

Year	Team	Games	BA	SA	AB	H	2B	3B	HR	HR%	R	RBI	BB	SO	SB	PH AB	PH H	PO	A	E	DP	TC/G	FA	G by Pos
1989		72	.252	.338	266	67	11	0	4	1.5	24	21	32	28	10	0	0	618	51	9	49	9.4	.987	1B-72
7 yrs.		643	.270	.376	2040	551	96	5	37	1.8	247	246	213	214	105	92	25	4367	295	64	365	7.3	.986	1B-476, OF-83

Hank Perry

PERRY, WILLIAM HENRY (Socks)
B. July 28, 1886, Howell, Mich. D. July 18, 1956, Pontiac, Mich.
BL TR 5'11" 190 lbs.

Year	Team	Games	BA	SA	AB	H	2B	3B	HR	HR%	R	RBI	BB	SO	SB	PH AB	PH H	PO	A	E	DP	TC/G	FA	G by Pos
1912	DET A	13	.167	.194	36	6	1	0	0	0.0	3	0	3	0	0	6	3	20	2	0	0	1.7	1.000	OF-7

Johnny Pesky

PESKY, JOHN MICHAEL
Born John Michael Paveskovich.
B. Sept. 27, 1919, Portland, Ore.
Manager 1963-64, 1980.
BL TR 5'9" 168 lbs.

Year	Team	Games	BA	SA	AB	H	2B	3B	HR	HR%	R	RBI	BB	SO	SB	PH AB	PH H	PO	A	E	DP	TC/G	FA	G by Pos
1942	BOS A	147	.331	.416	620	205	29	9	2	0.3	105	51	42	36	12	0	0	320	465	37	94	5.6	.955	SS-147
1946		153	.335	.427	621	208	43	4	2	0.3	115	55	65	29	9	0	0	296	479	25	96	5.2	.969	SS-153
1947		155	.324	.392	638	207	27	8	0	0.0	106	39	72	22	12	0	0	276	429	17	97	4.7	.976	SS-133, 3B-22
1948		143	.281	.365	565	159	26	6	3	0.5	124	55	99	32	3	2	1	121	303	22	35	3.1	.951	3B-141
1949		148	.306	.384	604	185	27	7	2	0.3	111	69	100	19	8	0	0	184	333	16	48	3.6	.970	3B-148
1950		127	.312	.388	490	153	22	6	1	0.2	112	49	104	31	2	2	0	183	289	13	36	3.8	.973	3B-116, SS-8
1951		131	.313	.398	480	150	20	6	3	0.6	93	41	84	15	2	9	3	223	370	26	79	4.7	.958	SS-106, 3B-11, 2B-5
1952	2 teams				BOS A (25G – .149)				DET A (69G – .254)																
"	total	94	.225	.262	244	55	6		0	0.4	36	11	57	16	1	14	1	126	172	15	38	3.3	.952	SS-43, 3B-22, 2B-22
1953	DET A	103	.292	.390	308	90	22	1	2	0.6	43	24	27	10	3	30	12	166	183	3	49	3.4	.991	2B-73
1954	2 teams				DET A (20G – .176)				WAS A (49G – .253)																
"	total	69	.246	.320	175	43	4	1		0.6	22	10	13	8	1	29	4	92	91	4	22	2.7	.979	2B-37, SS-1
10 yrs.		1270	.307	.386	4745	1455	226	50	17	0.4	867	404	663	218	53	86	21	1987	3114	178	594	4.2	.966	SS-591, 3B-460, 2B-137

WORLD SERIES

Year	Team	Games	BA	SA	AB	H	2B	3B	HR	HR%	R	RBI	BB	SO	SB	PH AB	PH H	PO	A	E	DP	TC/G	FA	G by Pos
1946	BOS A	7	.233	.233	30	7	0	0	0	0.0	2	0	1	3	1	0	0	13	16	4	5	4.7	.879	SS-7

Bill Peterman

PETERMAN, WILLIAM DAVID
B. Apr. 20, 1921, Philadelphia, Pa.
BR TR 6'2" 185 lbs.

Year	Team	Games	BA	SA	AB	H	2B	3B	HR	HR%	R	RBI	BB	SO	SB	PH AB	PH H	PO	A	E	DP	TC/G	FA	G by Pos
1942	PHI N	1	1.000	1.000	1	1	0	0	0	0.0	0	0	0	0	0	0	0	0	0	0	0	0.0	–	C-1

Gary Peters

PETERS, GARY CHARLES
B. Apr. 21, 1937, Grove City, Pa.
BL TL 6'2" 200 lbs.

Year	Team	Games	BA	SA	AB	H	2B	3B	HR	HR%	R	RBI	BB	SO	SB	PH AB	PH H	PO	A	E	DP	TC/G	FA	G by Pos
1959	CHI A	2	–	–	0	0	0	0	0	–	0	0	0	0	0	0	0	0	0	0	0	0.0	–	P-2
1960		2	–	–	0	0	0	0	0	–	0	0	0	0	0	0	0	0	0	0	0	0.0	–	P-2
1961		3	.333	.333	3	1	0	0	0	0.0	1	0	0	1	0	0	0	3	6	0	1	3.0	1.000	P-3
1962		5	–	–	0	0	0	0	0	–	0	0	0	0	0	0	0	0	2	0	0	0.4	1.000	P-5
1963		50	.259	.444	81	21	4	1	3	3.7	12	12	3	19	0	1	0	17	30	2	4	1.0	.959	P-41
1964		54	.208	.367	120	25	7	0	4	3.3	9	19	2	29	0	15	4	16	41	3	4	1.1	.950	P-37
1965		42	.181	.236	72	13	1	0	1	1.4	2	6	2	15	0	7	3	12	32	1	0	1.1	.978	P-33
1966		38	.235	.358	81	19	3	2	1	1.2	12	9	0	19	0	5	1	7	41	1	4	1.3	.980	P-38
1967		48	.212	.313	99	21	0	2	2	2.0	10	13	2	23	0	6	1	15	50	2	5	1.4	.970	P-38
1968		46	.208	.361	72	15	1	2	2	2.8	10	8	6	13	0	14	2	12	21	0	3	0.7	1.000	P-31
1969		37	.169	.310	71	12	4	0	2	2.8	9	4	2	15	0	0	0	6	25	1	1	0.9	.969	P-36
1970	BOS A	37	.244	.341	82	20	3	1	1	1.2	12	11	2	8	0	0	0	7	27	3	1	1.0	.919	P-34
1971		53	.271	.406	96	26	4	0	3	3.1	7	19	3	20	0	18	5	13	27	2	2	0.8	.952	P-34
1972		33	.200	.267	30	6	2	0	0	0.0	2	1	1	0	0	0	0	3	10	0	0	0.4	1.000	P-33
14 yrs.		450	.222	.348	807	179	31	7	19	2.4	86	102	29	172	0	66	16	111	312	15	27	1.0	.966	P-359

John Peters

PETERS, JOHN WILLIAM (Shotgun, Big Pete)
B. July 14, 1893, Kansas City, Kans. D. Feb. 21, 1932, Kansas City, Mo.
BR TR 6' 192 lbs.

Year	Team	Games	BA	SA	AB	H	2B	3B	HR	HR%	R	RBI	BB	SO	SB	PH AB	PH H	PO	A	E	DP	TC/G	FA	G by Pos
1915	DET A	1	.000	.000	3	0	0	0	0	0.0	0	0	0	0	0	0	0	6	3	0	0	9.0	1.000	C-1
1918	CLE A	1	.000	.000	0	0	0	0	0	–	0	0	1	0	0	0	0	3	1	4	0	8.0	.500	C-1
1921	PHI N	55	.290	.374	155	45	4	0	3	1.9	7	23	6	13	1	10	5	116	24	10	0	2.7	.933	C-44
1922		55	.245	.406	143	35	9	1	4	2.8	15	24	9	18	0	15	3	118	24	7	3	2.7	.953	C-39
4 yrs.		112	.265	.384	302	80	13	1	7	2.3	22	47	16	33	1	25	8	243	52	21	3	2.8	.934	C-85

Johnny Peters

PETERS, JOHN PAUL
B. Apr. 8, 1850, Louisiana, Mo. D. Jan. 4, 1924, St. Louis, Mo.
BR TR 180 lbs.

Year	Team	Games	BA	SA	AB	H	2B	3B	HR	HR%	R	RBI	BB	SO	SB	PH AB	PH H	PO	A	E	DP	TC/G	FA	G by Pos
1876	CHI N	66	.351	.418	316	111	14	2	1	0.3	70	47	3	2		0	0	95	193	21	16	4.7	.932	SS-66, P-1
1877		60	.317	.377	265	84	10	3	0	0.0	45	41	7	7		0	0	124	215	45	23	6.4	.883	SS-60
1878	MIL N	55	.309	.341	246	76	6	1	0	0.0	33	22	5	8		0	0	130	205	53	18	7.1	.863	2B-34, SS-22
1879	CHI N	83	.245	.298	379	93	13	2	1	0.3	45	31	1	19		0	0	94	271	71	14	5.3	.837	SS-83
1880	PRO N	86	.228	.242	359	82	5	0	0	0.0	30	24	5	15		0	0	111	268	42	26	4.9	.900	SS-86
1881	BUF N	54	.214	.258	229	49	4	1	0	0.0	21	25	3	12		0	0	105	185	47	17	6.2	.861	SS-53, OF-1
1882	PIT AA	78	.288	.324	333	96	10	1	0	0.0		46		4		0	0	92	282	51	21	5.4	.880	SS-77, 2B-1
1883		8	.107	.107	28	3	0	0	0	0.0	3		0			0	0	9	27	8	3	5.5	.818	SS-8
1884		1	.000	.000	4	0	0	0	0	0.0	0		0			0	0	1	1	1	0	3.0	.667	SS-1
9 yrs.		491	.275	.318	2159	594	66	10	2	0.1	293	190	22	63		0	0	761	1647	339	138	5.6	.877	SS-456, 2B-35, OF-1, P-1

Ricky Peters

PETERS, RICHARD DEVIN
B. Nov. 21, 1955, Lynwood, Calif.
BB TR 5'9" 170 lbs.

Year	Team	Games	BA	SA	AB	H	2B	3B	HR	HR%	R	RBI	BB	SO	SB	PH AB	PH H	PO	A	E	DP	TC/G	FA	G by Pos
1979	DET A	12	.263	.263	19	5	0	0	0	0.0	3	2	5	3	0	1	0	4	0	2	0	0.5	.667	DH-3, 3B-3, 2B-2, OF-1
1980		133	.291	.373	477	139	19	7	2	0.4	79	42	54	48	13	13	3	296	1	7	1	2.3	.977	OF-109, DH-11
1981		63	.256	.319	207	53	7	3	0	0.0	26	15	29	28	1	5	1	103	3	1	0	1.7	.991	OF-38, DH-19
1983	OAK A	55	.287	.326	178	51	7	0	0	0.0	20	20	12	21	4	2	1	141	3	2	1	2.7	.986	OF-47, DH-8
1986		44	.184	.211	38	7	0	0	0	0.0	7	1	7	7	2	9	3	29	1	0	1	0.7	1.000	OF-27, DH-4, 2B-1
5 yrs.		307	.277	.343	919	255	34	10	2	0.2	135	80	107	107	20	30	8	573	8	12	4	1.9	.980	OF-222, DH-45, 3B-3, 2B-3

Year	Team		Games	BA	SA	AB	H	2B	3B	HR	HR%	R	RBI	BB	SO	SB	Pinch Hit AB	Pinch Hit H	PO	A	E	DP	TC/G	FA	G by Pos

Rusty Peters

PETERS, RUSSELL DIXON
B. Dec. 14, 1914, Roanoke, Va.
BR TR 5'11" 170 lbs.

Year	Team		Games	BA	SA	AB	H	2B	3B	HR	HR%	R	RBI	BB	SO	SB	AB	H	PO	A	E	DP	TC/G	FA	G by Pos
1936	PHI	A	45	.218	.353	119	26	3	2	3	2.5	12	16	4	28	1	7	0	51	82	14	15	3.3	.905	SS-25, 3B-10, OF-2, 2B-1
1937			116	.260	.372	339	88	17	6	3	0.9	39	43	41	59	4	6	3	191	266	29	39	4.2	.940	2B-70, 3B-31, SS-13
1938			2	.000	.000	7	0	0	0	0	0.0	0	0	0	1	0	0	0	3	2	2	0	3.5	.714	SS-2
1940	CLE	A	30	.239	.338	71	17	3	2	0	0.0	5	7	4	14	1	9	3	32	44	8	8	2.8	.905	2B-9, SS-6, 3B-6, 1B-1
1941			29	.206	.238	63	13	2	0	0	0.0	6	2	7	10	0	1	0	26	45	10	9	2.8	.877	SS-11, 3B-9, 2B-3
1942			34	.224	.345	58	13	5	1	0	0.0	6	2	2	14	0	5	1	21	46	4	8	2.1	.944	SS-24, 3B-1, 2B-1
1943			79	.219	.279	215	47	6	2	1	0.5	22	19	18	29	1	11	2	66	98	11	17	2.2	.937	3B-46, SS-14, 2B-6, OF-2
1944			88	.223	.301	282	63	13	3	1	0.4	23	24	15	35	2	5	1	180	209	9	52	4.5	.977	2B-63, SS-13, 3B-8
1946			9	.286	.286	21	6	0	0	0	0.0	0	1	1	1	0	0	0	11	13	0	3	2.7	1.000	SS-7
1947	STL	A	39	.340	.426	47	16	4	0	0	0.0	10	2	6	8	0	11	6	34	31	3	9	1.7	.956	2B-13, SS-2
10 yrs.			471	.236	.326	1222	289	53	16	8	0.7	123	117	98	199	9	57	17	615	836	90	160	3.3	.942	2B-166, SS-117, 3B-111, OF-4, 1B-1

Bob Peterson

PETERSON, EVESHAM N. J.
B. July 16, 1884, Philadelphia, Pa.   D. Nov. 27, 1962, Evesham Township, N. J.
BR TR 6'1" 160 lbs.

Year	Team		Games	BA	SA	AB	H	2B	3B	HR	HR%	R	RBI	BB	SO	SB	AB	H	PO	A	E	DP	TC/G	FA	G by Pos
1906	BOS	A	39	.203	.254	118	24	1	1	1	0.8	10	9	11			1	2	0	136	52	21	2	5.4	.900	C-30, 2B-3, 1B-2, OF-1
1907			4	.077	.077	13	1	0	0	0	0.0	1	0	0			0	0	0	18	5	0	0	5.8	1.000	C-4
2 yrs.			43	.191	.237	131	25	1	1	1	0.8	11	9	11			1	2	0	154	57	21	2	5.4	.909	C-34, 2B-3, 1B-2, OF-1

Buddy Peterson

PETERSON, CARL FRANCIS
B. Apr. 23, 1925, Portland, Ore.
BR TR 5'9½" 170 lbs.

Year	Team		Games	BA	SA	AB	H	2B	3B	HR	HR%	R	RBI	BB	SO	SB	AB	H	PO	A	E	DP	TC/G	FA	G by Pos
1955	CHI	A	6	.286	.333	21	6	1	0	0	0.0	3	2	3	2	0	1	1	10	15	1	4	4.3	.962	SS-6
1957	BAL	A	7	.176	.294	17	3	2	0	0	0.0	1	0	2	2	0	1	0	12	14	1	3	3.9	.963	SS-7
2 yrs.			13	.237	.316	38	9	3	0	0	0.0	8	2	5	4	0	2	1	22	29	2	7	4.1	.962	SS-13

Cap Peterson

PETERSON, CHARLES ANDREW
B. Aug. 15, 1942, Tacoma, Wash.   D. May 16, 1980, Tacoma, Wash.
BR TR 6'2" 195 lbs.

Year	Team		Games	BA	SA	AB	H	2B	3B	HR	HR%	R	RBI	BB	SO	SB	AB	H	PO	A	E	DP	TC/G	FA	G by Pos
1962	SF	N	4	.167	.167	6	1	0	0	0	0.0	1	0	1	4	0	3	0	1	2	0	1	0.8	1.000	SS-2
1963			22	.259	.352	54	14	2	0	1	1.9	7	2	2	13	0	8	1	16	24	5	0	2.0	.889	2B-8, 3B-5, OF-3, SS-1
1964			66	.203	.284	74	15	1	1	1	1.4	8	8	3	20	0	55	12	11	1	0	0	0.2	1.000	OF-10, 1B-2, 3B-1, 2B-1
1965			63	.248	.400	105	26	7	0	3	2.9	14	15	10	16	0	38	5	22	1	0	0	0.4	1.000	OF-27
1966			89	.237	.311	190	45	6	1	2	1.1	13	19	11	32	2	37	5	73	4	1	3	0.9	.987	OF-51, 1B-2
1967	WAS	A	122	.240	.351	405	97	17	2	8	2.0	35	46	32	61	0	21	3	190	5	6	1	1.6	.970	OF-101
1968			94	.204	.288	226	46	8	1	3	1.3	20	18	18	31	2	39	11	82	2	0	0	0.9	1.000	OF-52
1969	CLE	A	76	.227	.282	110	25	3	0	1	0.9	8	14	24	18	0	39	9	40	2	1	1	0.6	.977	OF-30, 3B-4
8 yrs.			536	.230	.325	1170	269	44	5	19	1.6	106	122	101	195	4	240	46	435	41	13	6	0.9	.973	OF-274, 3B-10, 2B-9, 1B-4, SS-3

Hardy Peterson

PETERSON, HARDING WILLIAM
B. Oct. 17, 1929, Perth Amboy, N. J.
BR TR 6' 205 lbs.

Year	Team		Games	BA	SA	AB	H	2B	3B	HR	HR%	R	RBI	BB	SO	SB	AB	H	PO	A	E	DP	TC/G	FA	G by Pos
1955	PIT	N	32	.247	.358	81	20	6	0	1	1.2	7	10	7	7	0	2	0	117	21	5	4	4.5	.965	C-31
1957			30	.301	.438	73	22	2	1	2	2.7	10	11	9	10	0	0	0	116	14	2	3	4.4	.985	C-30
1958			2	.333	.333	6	2	0	0	0	0.0	0	0	1	0	0	0	0	7	1	0	0	4.0	1.000	C-2
1959			2	.000	.000	1	0	0	0	0	0.0	0	0	0	0	0	0	0	4	0	0	0	2.0	1.000	C-2
4 yrs.			66	.273	.391	161	44	8	1	3	1.9	17	21	17	17	0	2	0	244	36	7	7	4.3	.976	C-65

Ted Petoskey

PETOSKEY, FREDERICK LEE
B. Jan. 5, 1911, St. Charles, Mich.
BR TR 5'11½" 183 lbs.

Year	Team		Games	BA	SA	AB	H	2B	3B	HR	HR%	R	RBI	BB	SO	SB	AB	H	PO	A	E	DP	TC/G	FA	G by Pos
1934	CIN	N	6	.000	.000	7	0	0	0	0	0.0	0	1	0	5	0	4	0	6	1	0	1	1.2	1.000	OF-2
1935			4	.400	.400	5	2	0	0	0	0.0	0	0	0	1	1	1	1	1	0	0	0	0.3	1.000	OF-2
2 yrs.			10	.167	.167	12	2	0	0	0	0.0	0	1	0	6	1	5	1	7	1	0	1	0.8	1.000	OF-4

Geno Petralli

PETRALLI, EUGENE JAMES
B. Sept. 25, 1959, Sacramento, Calif.
BB TR 6'2" 185 lbs.

Year	Team		Games	BA	SA	AB	H	2B	3B	HR	HR%	R	RBI	BB	SO	SB	AB	H	PO	A	E	DP	TC/G	FA	G by Pos
1982	TOR	A	16	.364	.409	44	16	2	0	0	0.0	3	1	4	6	0	3	1	51	4	1	0	3.5	.982	C-12, 3B-3
1983			6	.000	.000	4	0	0	0	0	0.0	0	0	1	1	1	1	0	7	0	0	0	1.2	1.000	C-5, DH-1
1984			3	.000	.000	3	0	0	0	0	0.0	0	0	0	2	0	1	0	1	1	0	0	0.7	1.000	DH-1, C-1
1985	TEX	A	42	.270	.290	100	27	2	0	0	0.0	7	11	8	12	1	3	0	179	16	2	6	4.7	.990	C-41
1986			69	.255	.409	137	35	9	3	2	1.5	17	18	5	14	3	22	4	163	14	4	2	2.6	.978	C-41, 3B-15, DH-2, 2B-2
1987			101	.302	.480	202	61	11	2	7	3.5	28	31	27	29	0	26	5	370	34	5	4	4.0	.988	C-63, 3B-1, 1B-5, 2B-4, OF-3, DH-2
1988			129	.282	.393	351	99	14	2	7	2.0	35	36	41	52	0	23	6	421	54	10	8	3.8	.979	C-85, DH-23, 3B-9, 2B-2, 1B-2
1989			70	.304	.408	184	56	7	0	4	2.2	18	23	17	24	0	15	4	258	15	3	3	3.9	.989	C-49, DH-16
8 yrs.			436	.287	.403	1025	294	45	7	20	2.0	108	120	103	138	5	95	20	1450	138	25	23	3.7	.985	C-297, DH-45, 3B-44, 2B-8, 1B-7, OF-3

Rico Petrocelli

PETROCELLI, AMERICO PETER
B. June 27, 1943, Brooklyn, N. Y.
BR TR 6' 175 lbs.

Year	Team		Games	BA	SA	AB	H	2B	3B	HR	HR%	R	RBI	BB	SO	SB	AB	H	PO	A	E	DP	TC/G	FA	G by Pos
1963	BOS	A	1	.250	.500	4	1	1	0	0	0.0	0	1	0	1	0	0	0	3	2	1	0	6.0	.833	SS-1
1965			103	.232	.412	323	75	15	2	13	4.0	38	33	36	71	0	8	0	151	278	19	45	4.3	.958	SS-93
1966			139	.238	.383	522	124	20	1	18	3.4	58	59	41	99	1	6	0	211	390	28	72	4.5	.955	SS-127, 3B-5
1967			142	.259	.420	491	127	24	2	17	3.5	53	66	49	93	2	1	0	223	432	19	73	4.7	.972	SS-141
1968			123	.234	.374	406	95	17	2	12	3.0	41	46	31	73	0	4	1	178	361	12	68	4.5	.978	SS-117, 1B-1
1969			154	.297	.589	535	159	32	2	40	7.5	92	97	98	68	3	0	0	269	469	15	103	4.9	.980	SS-153, 3B-1
1970			157	.261	.473	583	152	31	3	29	5.0	82	103	67	82	1	1	0	276	430	21	80	4.6	.971	SS-141, 3B-18
1971			158	.251	.461	553	139	24	4	28	5.1	82	89	91	108	2	2	1	118	334	11	37	2.9	.976	3B-156
1972			147	.240	.363	521	125	15	2	15	2.9	62	75	78	91	0	1	1	146	278	13	38	3.0	.970	3B-146
1973			100	.244	.396	356	87	13	1	13	3.7	44	45	47	64	0	1	0	73	224	6	22	3.0	.980	3B-99
1974			129	.267	.421	454	121	23	1	15	3.3	53	76	48	74	1	5	1	83	219	12	23	2.4	.962	3B-116, DH-9

Year	Team		Games	BA	SA	AB	H	2B	3B	HR	HR%	R	RBI	BB	SO	SB	Pinch Hit AB	Pinch Hit H	PO	A	E	DP	TC/G	FA	G by Pos

Rico Petrocelli *continued*

Year	Team		Games	BA	SA	AB	H	2B	3B	HR	HR%	R	RBI	BB	SO	SB	AB	H	PO	A	E	DP	TC/G	FA	G by Pos
1975			115	.239	.333	402	96	15	1	7	1.7	31	59	41	66	0	1	0	85	229	13	13	2.8	.960	3B-113, DH-1
1976			85	.213	.288	240	51	7	1	3	1.3	17	24	34	36	0	2	0	70	134	6	15	2.5	.971	3B-73, 2B-5, DH-4, SS-1, 1B-1
13 yrs.			1553	.251	.420	5390	1352	237	22	210	3.9	653	773	661	926	10	32	4	1886	3780	176	589	3.8	.970	SS-774, 3B-727, DH-14, 2B-5, 1B-2

LEAGUE CHAMPIONSHIP SERIES

| 1975 | BOS | A | 3 | .167 | .417 | 12 | 2 | 0 | 0 | 1 | 8.3 | 1 | 2 | 0 | 3 | 0 | 0 | 0 | 4 | 3 | 0 | 1 | 2.3 | 1.000 | 3B-3 |

WORLD SERIES

1967	BOS	A	7	.200	.550	20	4	1	0	2	10.0	3	3.	3	8	0	0	0	11	21	2	1	4.9	.941	SS-7
1975			7	.308	.346	26	8	1	0	0	0.0	3	4	3	6	0	0	0	7	15	0	1	3.1	1.000	3B-7
2 yrs.			14	.261	.435	46	12	2	0	2	4.3	6	7	6	14	0	0	0	18	36	2	2	4.0	.964	SS-7, 3B-7

Pat Pettee

PETTEE, PATRICK E.
B. Jan. 10, 1863, Natick, Mass.   D. Oct. 9, 1934, Natick, Mass.

BR TR 5'10''   170 lbs.

| 1891 | LOU | AA | 2 | .000 | .000 | 5 | 0 | 0 | 0 | 0 | 0.0 | 1 | 0 | 3 | 1 | 1 | 0 | 0 | 3 | 6 | 2 | 1 | 5.5 | .818 | 2B-2 |

Ned Pettigrew

PETTIGREW, JIM NED
B. Aug. 25, 1881, Honey Grove, Tex.   D. Aug. 20, 1952, Duncan, Okla.

BR TR 5'11''   175 lbs.

| 1914 | BUF | F | 2 | .000 | .000 | 2 | 0 | 0 | 0 | 0 | 0.0 | 0 | 0 | 0 | 0 | 0 | 2 | 0 | 0 | 0 | 0 | 0 | 0.0 | — | |

Joe Pettini

PETTINI, JOSEPH PAUL
B. Jan. 26, 1955, Wheeling, W. Va.

BR TR 5'9''   165 lbs.

1980	SF	N	63	.232	.274	190	44	3	1	1	0.5	19	9	17	33	5	2	1	66	147	8	24	3.5	.964	SS-42, 3B-18, 2B-8
1981			35	.069	.103	29	2	1	0	0	0.0	3	2	4	5	1	1	0	13	37	6	4	1.6	.893	SS-12, 2B-12, 3B-9
1982			29	.205	.231	39	8	1	0	0	0.0	5	2	3	4	0	2	0	24	33	4	5	2.1	.934	SS-26, 3B-1
1983			61	.186	.209	86	16	0	1	0	0.0	11	7	9	11	4	3	0	44	82	6	16	2.2	.955	SS-26, 2B-14, 3B-12
4 yrs.			188	.203	.238	344	70	5	2	1	0.3	38	20	33	53	10	8	1	147	299	24	49	2.5	.949	SS-106, 3B-40, 2B-34

Gary Pettis

PETTIS, GARY GEORGE
B. Apr. 3, 1958, Oakland, Calif.

BB TR 6'1''   165 lbs.

1982	CAL	A	10	.200	.800	5	1	0	0	1	20.0	5	1	0	2	0	0	0	5	1	0	0	0.6	1.000	OF-8
1983			22	.294	.494	85	25	2	3	3	3.5	19	6	7	15	8	0	0	49	5	1	2	2.5	.982	OF-21
1984			140	.227	.300	397	90	11	6	2	0.5	63	29	60	115	48	2	0	337	11	6	4	2.5	.983	OF-134
1985			125	.257	.323	443	114	10	8	1	0.2	67	32	62	125	56	0	0	368	13	4	5	3.1	.990	OF-122
1986			154	.258	.343	539	139	23	4	5	0.9	93	58	69	132	50	0	0	462	9	7	3	3.1	.985	OF-153, DH-1
1987			133	.208	.259	394	82	13	2	1	0.3	49	17	52	124	24	0	0	344	2	7	2	2.7	.980	OF-131
1988	DET	A	129	.210	.277	458	96	14	4	3	0.7	65	36	47	85	44	2	0	361	5	5	0	2.9	.987	OF-126, DH-2
1989			119	.257	.309	444	114	8	6	1	0.2	77	18	84	106	43	0	0	325	1	4	0	2.8	.988	OF-119
8 yrs.			832	.239	.311	2765	661	81	33	17	0.6	438	197	381	704	273	5	0	2251	47	34	16	2.8	.985	OF-814, DH-3

LEAGUE CHAMPIONSHIP SERIES

| 1986 | CAL | A | 7 | .346 | .500 | 26 | 9 | 1 | 0 | 1 | 3.8 | 4 | 4 | 3 | 5 | 0 | 0 | 0 | 24 | 0 | 1 | 0 | 3.6 | .960 | OF-7 |

Bob Pettit

PETTIT, ROBERT HENRY
B. July 19, 1861, Williamstown, Mass.   D. Nov. 1, 1910, Derby, Conn.

BL TR 5'9''   160 lbs.

1887	CHI	N	32	.261	.370	138	36	3	3	2	1.4	29	12	8	15	16	0	0	35	8	6	0	1.5	.878	OF-32, C-1, P-1
1888			43	.254	.379	169	43	1	4	4	2.4	23	23	7	9	7	0	0	46	8	4	3	1.3	.931	OF-43
1891	MIL	AA	21	.175	.263	80	14	4	0	1	1.3	10	5	7	7	2	0	0	22	35	6	1	3.0	.905	2B-9, OF-7, 3B-6
3 yrs.			96	.240	.351	387	93	8	7	7	1.8	62	40	22	31	25	0	0	103	51	16	4	1.8	.906	OF-82, 2B-9, 3B-6, C-1, P-1

Marty Pevey

PEVEY, MARTY ASHLEY
B. Dec. 25, 1962, Savannah, Ga.

BL TR 6'1''   185 lbs.

| 1989 | MON | N | 13 | .220 | .293 | 41 | 9 | 1 | 1 | 0 | 0.0 | 2 | 3 | 0 | 8 | 0 | 2 | 0 | 58 | 7 | 1 | 0 | 5.1 | .985 | C-11, OF-1 |

Larry Pezold

PEZOLD, LORENZ JOHANNES
B. June 22, 1893, New Orleans, La.   D. Oct. 22, 1957, Baton Rouge, La.

BR TR 5'9½''   175 lbs.

| 1914 | CLE | A | 23 | .225 | .254 | 71 | 16 | 0 | 1 | 0 | 0.0 | 4 | 5 | 9 | 6 | 3 | 2 | 0 | 21 | 41 | 13 | 2 | 3.3 | .827 | 3B-20, OF-1 |

Big Jeff Pfeffer

PFEFFER, FRANCIS XAVIER
Brother of Jeff Pfeffer.
B. Mar. 31, 1882, Champaign, Ill.   D. Dec. 19, 1954, Kankakee, Ill.

BR TR 6'   185 lbs.

1905	CHI	N	15	.200	.275	40	8	3	0	0	0.0	4	3	0		2	0	0	4	24	0	0	1.9	1.000	P-15
1906	BOS	N	60	.196	.272	158	31	3	3	1	0.6	10	11	5		2	8	0	32	93	5	1	2.2	.962	P-35, OF-14
1907			21	.250	.300	60	15	3	0	0	0.0	1	6	2		2	0	0	4	38	2	0	2.1	.955	P-19
1908			4	.000	.000	2	0	0	0	0	0.0	0	0	0		0	0	0	0	1	0	0	0.3	1.000	P-4
1910	CHI	N	14	.176	.353	17	3	1	1	0	0.0	1	2	1	1	0	0	0	1	10	0	0	0.8	1.000	P-13, OF-1
1911	BOS	N	33	.196	.304	46	9	2	0	1	2.2	4	6	5	7	0	3	0	10	25	0	1	1.1	1.000	P-26, OF-3, 1B-1
6 yrs.			147	.204	.285	323	66	12	4	2	0.6	20	28	13	8	4	13	0	51	191	7	1	1.7	.972	P-112, OF-18, 1B-1

Fred Pfeffer

PFEFFER, NATHANIEL FREDERICK (Dandelion, Fritz)
B. Mar. 17, 1860, Louisville, Ky.   D. Apr. 10, 1932, Chicago, Ill.
Manager 1892.

BR TR 5'10½''   184 lbs.

1882	TRO	N	85	.218	.273	330	72	7	4	1	0.3	26	31	1	24		0	0	169	282	76	35	6.2	.856	SS-83, 2B-2
1883	CHI	N	96	.235	.340	371	87	22	7	1	0.3	41		8	50		0	0	281	328	86	56	7.2	.876	2B-79, SS-18, 3B-1, 1B-1
1884			112	.289	.514	467	135	10	10	25	5.4	105		25	47		0	0	395	422	88	85	8.1	.903	2B-112, P-1
1885			112	.241	.330	469	113	12	6	6	1.3	90	71	26	47		0	0	328	397	86	66	7.2	.894	2B-109, P-5, OF-1
1886			118	.264	.378	474	125	17	8	7	1.5	88	95	36	46		0	0	344	340	73	66	6.4	.904	2B-118, 1B-1
1887			123	.278	.447	479	133	21	6	16	3.3	95	89	34	20	57	0	0	394	402	72	68	7.1	.917	2B-123, OF-2

Year	Team		Games	BA	SA	AB	H	2B	3B	HR	HR%	R	RBI	BB	SO	SB	Pinch Hit AB	Pinch Hit H	PO	A	E	DP	TC/G	FA	G by Pos

Fred Pfeffer *continued*

Year	Team		Games	BA	SA	AB	H	2B	3B	HR	HR%	R	RBI	BB	SO	SB	AB	H	PO	A	E	DP	TC/G	FA	G by Pos
1888			135	.250	.377	517	129	22	10	8	1.5	90	57	32	38	64	0	0	421	457	65	78	7.0	.931	2B-135
1889			134	.228	.322	531	121	15	7	7	1.3	85	77	53	51	45	0	0	452	483	56	69	7.4	.943	2B-134
1890	CHI	P	124	.257	.361	499	128	21	8	5	1.0	86	80	44	23	27	0	0	441	387	76	73	7.3	.916	2B-124
1891	CHI	N	137	.247	.349	498	123	12	9	7	1.4	93	77	79	60	40	0	0	429	474	77	78	7.2	.921	2B-137
1892	LOU	N	124	.257	.338	470	121	14	9	2	0.4	78	76	67	36	27	0	0	401	384	58	75	6.8	.931	2B-116, 1B-10, OF-1, P-1
1893			125	.254	.376	508	129	29	12	3	0.6	85	75	51	18	32	0	0	355	398	49	74	6.4	.939	2B-125
1894			104	.308	.443	409	126	12	14	5	1.2	68	59	30	14	31	0	0	282	340	48	67	6.4	.928	2B-90, SS-15, P-1
1895			11	.289	.311	45	13	1	0	0	0.0	8	5	5	3	2	0	0	53	22	12	6	7.9	.862	SS-5, 2B-3, 1B-3
1896	2 teams			NY	N (4G – .143)		CHI	N	(94G –	.244)															
"	total		98	.241	.337	374	90	16	7	2	0.5	46	56	24	21	22	0	0	236	317	36	43	6.0	.939	2B-98
1897	CHI	N	32	.228	.246	114	26	0	1	0	0.0	10	11	12		5	0	0	73	93	22	12	5.9	.883	2B-32
16 yrs.			1670	.255	.370	6555	1671	231	118	95	1.4	1094	859	527	498	352	0	0	5054	5526	980	951	6.9	.915	2B-1537, SS-121, 1B-15, P-8, OF-4, 3B-1

Monte Pfeffer

PFEFFER, MONTE
Born Monte Pfeiffer.
B. Oct. 8, 1891, New York, N. Y.   D. Sept. 27, 1941, New York, N. Y.

BR TR 5'4½" 147 lbs.

Year	Team		Games	BA	SA	AB	H	2B	3B	HR	HR%	R	RBI	BB	SO	SB	AB	H	PO	A	E	DP	TC/G	FA	G by Pos
1913	PHI	A	1	.000	.000	3	0	0	0	0	0.0	0	0	0	1	0	1	0	0	4	1	0	5.0	.800	SS-1

Bobby Pfeil

PFEIL, ROBERT RAYMOND
B. Nov. 13, 1943, Passaic, N. J.

BR TR 6'1" 180 lbs.

Year	Team		Games	BA	SA	AB	H	2B	3B	HR	HR%	R	RBI	BB	SO	SB	AB	H	PO	A	E	DP	TC/G	FA	G by Pos
1969	NY	N	62	.232	.275	211	49	0	0	0	0.0	20	10	7	27	0	9	5	53	105	4	12	2.6	.975	3B-49, 2B-11, OF-2
1971	PHI	N	44	.271	.400	70	19	3	0	2	2.9	5	9	6	9	1	17	3	15	27	1	7	1.0	.977	3B-15, C-4, OF-3, SS-1, 2B-1, 1B-1
2 yrs.			106	.242	.306	281	68	12	0	2	0.7	25	19	13	36	1	26	8	68	132	5	19	1.9	.976	3B-64, 2B-12, OF-5, C-4, SS-1, 1B-1

George Pfister

PFISTER, GEORGE EDWARD
B. Sept. 4, 1918, Bound Brook, N. J.

BR TR 6' 200 lbs.

Year	Team		Games	BA	SA	AB	H	2B	3B	HR	HR%	R	RBI	BB	SO	SB	AB	H	PO	A	E	DP	TC/G	FA	G by Pos
1941	BKN	N	1	.000	.000	2	0	0	0	0	0.0	0	0	0	0	0	0	0	3	2	0	1	5.0	1.000	C-1

Monte Pfyl

PFYL, MEINHARD CHARLES
B. May 11, 1884, St. Louis, Mo.   D. Oct. 18, 1945, San Francisco, Calif.

BL TL 6'3" 190 lbs.

Year	Team		Games	BA	SA	AB	H	2B	3B	HR	HR%	R	RBI	BB	SO	SB	AB	H	PO	A	E	DP	TC/G	FA	G by Pos
1907	NY	N	1	–	–	0	0	0	0	0	–	0	0	0		0	0	0	0	0	0	0	0.0	–	1B-1

Art Phelan

PHELAN, ARTHUR THOMAS (Dugan)
B. Aug. 14, 1887, Niantic, Ill.   D. Dec. 27, 1964, Fort Worth, Tex.

BR TR 5'8" 160 lbs.

Year	Team		Games	BA	SA	AB	H	2B	3B	HR	HR%	R	RBI	BB	SO	SB	AB	H	PO	A	E	DP	TC/G	FA	G by Pos
1910	CIN	N	23	.214	.214	42	9	0	0	0	0.0	7	4	7	6	5	2	0	19	20	0	1	1.7	1.000	3B-8, 2B-5, OF-3, SS-1
1912			130	.243	.330	461	112	9	11	3	0.7	56	54	46	37	25	0	0	155	255	33	18	3.4	.926	3B-127, 2B-3
1913	CHI	N	90	.251	.363	259	65	11	6	2	0.8	41	35	29	25	8	7	3	102	148	19	12	3.0	.929	2B-46, 3B-38, SS-1
1914			25	.283	.370	46	13	2	1	0	0.0	5	3	4	3	0	13	6	12	21	3	1	1.4	.917	3B-7, 2B-3, SS-2
1915			133	.219	.306	448	98	16	7	3	0.7	41	35	55	42	12	0	0	197	267	28	19	3.7	.943	3B-110, 2B-24
5 yrs.			401	.236	.326	1256	297	38	25	8	0.6	150	131	141	113	50	22	9	485	711	83	51	3.2	.935	3B-290, 2B-81, SS-4, OF-3

Dan Phelan

PHELAN, DANIEL T.
B. July, 1865, Thomaston, Conn.   D. Dec. 7, 1945, West Haven, Conn.

Year	Team		Games	BA	SA	AB	H	2B	3B	HR	HR%	R	RBI	BB	SO	SB	AB	H	PO	A	E	DP	TC/G	FA	G by Pos
1890	LOU	AA	8	.250	.344	32	8	1	1	0	0.0	4		0		1	0	0	76	3	2	0	10.1	.975	1B-8

Dick Phelan

PHELAN, JAMES DICKSON
B. Dec. 10, 1854, Towanda, Pa.   D. Feb. 13, 1931, San Antonio, Tex.

Year	Team		Games	BA	SA	AB	H	2B	3B	HR	HR%	R	RBI	BB	SO	SB	AB	H	PO	A	E	DP	TC/G	FA	G by Pos
1884	BAL	U	101	.246	.316	402	99	13	3	3	0.7	63		12		0	0	0	277	256	80	34	6.1	.869	2B-100, 3B-5, OF-1
1885	2 teams		6				BUF	N	(4G – .125)			STL	N	(2G –	.250)										
"	total		6	.150	.350	20	3	1	0	1	5.0	3	4	0	5	0	0	0	8	15	5	2	4.7	.821	2B-4, 3B-2
2 yrs.			107	.242	.318	422	102	14	3	4	0.9	66	4	12	5	0	0	0	285	271	85	36	6.0	.867	2B-104, 3B-7, OF-1

Babe Phelps

PHELPS, ERNEST GORDON (Blimp)
B. Apr. 19, 1908, Odenton, Md.

BL TR 6'2" 225 lbs.

Year	Team		Games	BA	SA	AB	H	2B	3B	HR	HR%	R	RBI	BB	SO	SB	AB	H	PO	A	E	DP	TC/G	FA	G by Pos
1931	WAS	A	3	.333	.333	3	1	0	0	0	0.0	0	0	0	0	0	3	1	0	0	0	0	0.0	–	
1933	CHI	N	3	.286	.286	7	2	0	0	0	0.0	0	2	0	1	0	1	0	6	2	0	1	2.7	1.000	C-2
1934			44	.286	.500	70	20	5	2	2	2.9	7	12	1	8	0	26	9	44	7	1	0	1.2	.981	C-18
1935	BKN	N	47	.364	.579	121	44	7	2	5	4.1	17	22	9	10	0	12	6	118	16	4	4	3.0	.971	C-34
1936			115	.367	.498	319	117	23	2	5	1.6	36	57	27	18	1	15	5	337	49	9	6	3.4	.977	C-98, OF-1
1937			121	.313	.469	409	128	37	3	7	1.7	42	58	25	28	2	8	1	465	76	16	10	4.6	.971	C-111
1938			66	.308	.457	208	64	12	2	5	2.4	33	46	23	15	2	9	1	218	25	5	5	3.8	.980	C-55
1939			98	.285	.418	323	92	21	2	6	1.9	33	42	24	24	0	6	1	361	40	8	6	4.2	.980	C-92
1940			118	.295	.492	370	109	24	5	13	3.5	47	61	30	27	2	16	2	436	35	11	4	4.1	.977	C-99, 1B-1
1941			16	.233	.533	30	7	3	0	2	6.7	3	4	1	2	0	5	1	33	1	1	0	2.2	.971	C-11
1942	PIT	N	95	.284	.440	257	73	11	1	9	3.5	21	41	20	21	2	22	7	244	40	12	5	3.1	.959	C-72
11 yrs.			726	.310	.472	2117	657	143	19	54	2.6	239	345	160	154	9	123	34	2262	291	69	41	3.6	.974	C-592, OF-1, 1B-1

Ed Phelps

PHELPS, EDWARD JAYKILL
B. Mar. 3, 1879, Albany, N. Y.   D. Jan. 31, 1942, East Greenbush, N. Y.

BR TR 5'11" 185 lbs.

Year	Team		Games	BA	SA	AB	H	2B	3B	HR	HR%	R	RBI	BB	SO	SB	AB	H	PO	A	E	DP	TC/G	FA	G by Pos
1902	PIT	N	18	.213	.230	61	13	1	0	0	0.0	5	6	4		2	0	0	89	11	3	3	5.7	.971	C-13, 1B-5
1903			81	.282	.352	273	77	7	3	2	0.7	32	31	17		2	1	0	345	83	8	7	5.4	.982	C-76, 1B-3
1904			94	.242	.278	302	73	5	3	0	0.0	29	28	15		2	1	0	372	97	17	8	5.2	.965	C-91, 1B-1
1905	CIN	N	44	.231	.301	156	36	5	3	0	0.0	18	18	12		4	0	0	189	55	13	6	5.8	.949	C-44
1906	2 teams			CIN	N (12G – .275)		PIT	N	(43G –	.237)															
"	total		55	.247	.323	158	39	3	1	1	0.6	12	17	12		3	2	0	231	45	7	4	5.1	.975	C-52
1907	PIT	N	43	.212	.221	113	24	1	0	0	0.0	11	12	9		1	6	0	156	39	4	3	4.6	.980	C-35, 1B-1
1908			34	.234	.328	64	15	2	1	0	0.0	3	11	2		0	12	7	69	15	2	0	2.5	.977	C-20

Year	Team		Games	BA	SA	AB	H	2B	3B	HR	HR%	R	RBI	BB	SO	SB	Pinch Hit AB	H	PO	A	E	DP	TC/G	FA	G by Pos

Ed Phelps *continued*

Year	Team		Games	BA	SA	AB	H	2B	3B	HR	HR%	R	RBI	BB	SO	SB	Pinch Hit AB	H	PO	A	E	DP	TC/G	FA	G by Pos
1909	STL	N	100	.248	.297	306	76	13	1	0	0.0	43	22	39		7	19	3	330	87	20	11	4.4	.954	C-82
1910			93	.263	.293	270	71	4	2	0	0.0	25	37	36	29	9	13	3	320	84	10	10	4.5	.976	C-80
1912	BKN	N	52	.288	.378	111	32	4	3	0	0.0	8	23	16	15	1	20	4	130	35	4	4	3.3	.976	C-32
1913			15	.222	.222	18	4	0	0	0	0.0	0	0	1	2	0	10	1	6	1	1	0	0.5	.875	C-4
11 yrs.			629	.251	.302	1832	460	45	20	3	0.2	186	205	163	46	31	84	19	2237	552	89	55	4.6	.969	C-529, 1B-10

WORLD SERIES

Year	Team		Games	BA	SA	AB	H	2B	3B	HR	HR%	R	RBI	BB	SO	SB	Pinch Hit AB	H	PO	A	E	DP	TC/G	FA	G by Pos
1903	PIT	N	8	.231	.308	26	6	2	0	0	0.0	1	2	1	6	0	1	0	36	4	2	0	5.3	.952	C-7

Ken Phelps

PHELPS, KENNETH ALLEN
B. Aug. 6, 1954, Seattle, Wash.

BL TL 6'1" 209 lbs.

Year	Team		Games	BA	SA	AB	H	2B	3B	HR	HR%	R	RBI	BB	SO	SB	Pinch Hit AB	H	PO	A	E	DP	TC/G	FA	G by Pos
1980	KC	A	3	.000	.000	4	0	0	0	0	0.0	0	0	0	2	0	1	0	14	0	0	2	4.7	1.000	1B-2
1981			21	.136	.227	22	3	0	1	0	0.0	1	1	1	13	0	15	1	4	1	0	0	0.2	1.000	DH-4, 1B-2
1982	MON	N	10	.250	.250	8	2	0	0	0	0.0	0	0	0	3	0	8	2	0	0	0	0	0.0	—	—
1983	SEA	A	50	.236	.449	127	30	4	1	7	5.5	10	16	13	25	0	11	3	164	16	0	11	3.6	1.000	1B-22, DH-19
1984			101	.241	.521	290	70	9	0	24	8.3	52	51	61	73	3	15	2	72	4	1	7	0.8	.987	DH-84, 1B-9
1985			61	.207	.466	116	24	3	0	9	7.8	18	24	24	33	2	25	5	31	2	0	5	0.5	1.000	DH-25, 1B-8
1986			125	.247	.526	344	85	16	4	24	7.0	69	64	88	96	2	16	3	487	34	9	58	4.2	.983	1B-55, DH-52
1987			120	.259	.548	332	86	13	1	27	8.1	68	68	80	75	1	12	2	8	0	0	0	0.1	1.000	DH-114, 1B-1
1988	2 teams			SEA	A (72G – .284)			NY	A	(45G – .224)															
"	total		117	.263	.549	297	78	13	0	24	8.1	54	54	70	61	1	17	2	18	2	1	2	0.2	.952	DH-92, 1B-4
1989	2 teams			NY	A (86G – .249)			OAK	A	(11G – .111)															
"	total		97	.242	.371	194	47	4	0	7	3.6	26	29	31	47	0	**38**	**11**	56	2	1	5	0.6	.983	DH-56, 1B-9
10 yrs.			705	.245	.500	1734	425	62	7	122	7.0	298	307	368	428	9	158	32	854	61	12	90	1.3	.987	DH-446, 1B-112

LEAGUE CHAMPIONSHIP SERIES

Year	Team		Games	BA	SA	AB	H	2B	3B	HR	HR%	R	RBI	BB	SO	SB	Pinch Hit AB	H	PO	A	E	DP	TC/G	FA	G by Pos
1989	OAK	A	1	1.000	2.000	1	1	1	0	0	0.0	0	0	0	0	0	1	1	0	0	0	0	0.0	—	—

WORLD SERIES

Year	Team		Games	BA	SA	AB	H	2B	3B	HR	HR%	R	RBI	BB	SO	SB	Pinch Hit AB	H	PO	A	E	DP	TC/G	FA	G by Pos
1989	OAK	A	1	.000	.000	1	0	0	0	0	0.0	0	0	0	0	0	1	0	0	0	0	0	0.0	—	—

Neal Phelps

PHELPS, CORNELIUS CARMAN
B. Nov. 19, 1840, New York, N. Y. D. Feb. 12, 1885, New York, N. Y.

Year	Team		Games	BA	SA	AB	H	2B	3B	HR	HR%	R	RBI	BB	SO	SB	Pinch Hit AB	H	PO	A	E	DP	TC/G	FA	G by Pos
1876	2 teams			NY	N (1G – .000)			PHI	N	(1G – .000)															
"	total		2	.000	.000	7	0	0	0	0	0.0	0	0	0	1		0	0	5	1	4		5.0	.600	OF-1, C-1

Dave Philley

PHILLEY, DAVID EARL
B. May 16, 1920, Paris, Tex.

BB TR 6' 188 lbs.

Year	Team		Games	BA	SA	AB	H	2B	3B	HR	HR%	R	RBI	BB	SO	SB	Pinch Hit AB	H	PO	A	E	DP	TC/G	FA	G by Pos
1941	CHI	A	7	.222	.333	9	2	1	0	0	0.0	4	0	3	3	0	4	0	0	0	0	0	0.0	—	OF-2
1946			17	.353	.471	68	24	2	3	0	0.0	10	17	4	4	5	0	0	55	3	1	0	3.5	.983	OF-17
1947			143	.258	.354	551	142	25	11	2	0.4	55	45	35	39	21	6	2	356	15	5	3	2.6	.987	OF-133, 3B-4
1948			137	.287	.387	488	140	28	3	5	1.0	51	42	50	33	8	8	1	381	22	9	6	3.0	.978	OF-128
1949			146	.286	.346	598	171	20	8	0	0.0	84	44	54	51	13	1	0	282	16	7	3	2.1	.977	OF-145
1950			156	.242	.360	619	150	21	5	14	2.3	69	80	52	57	6	1	0	367	19	8	8	2.5	.980	OF-154
1951	2 teams			CHI	A (7G – .240)			PHI	A	(125G – .263)															
"	total		132	.262	.373	493	129	20	7	7	1.4	71	61	65	41	10	5	1	314	15	8	4	2.6	.976	OF-126
1952	PHI	A	151	.263	.355	586	154	25	4	7	1.2	80	71	59	35	11	0	0	445	16	4	3	3.1	.991	OF-149, 3B-2
1953			157	.303	.424	620	188	30	9	9	1.5	80	59	51	35	13	1	0	296	18	6	0	2.0	.981	OF-157, 3B-1
1954	CLE	A	133	.226	.347	452	102	13	3	12	2.7	48	60	57	51	1	1	0	237	6	4	0	1.9	.984	OF-129
1955	2 teams			CLE	A (43G – .298)			BAL	A	(83G – .299)															
"	total		126	.299	.422	415	124	17	5	8	1.9	65	50	46	48	1	10	4	198	7	6	4	1.7	.972	OF-116, 3B-2
1956	2 teams			BAL	A (32G – .205)			CHI	A	(86G – .265)															
"	total		118	.247	.351	396	98	18	4	5	1.3	57	64	48	40	4	12	0	407	25	12	34	3.8	.973	OF-61, 1B-51, 3B-5
1957	2 teams			CHI	A (22G – .324)			DET	A	(65G – .283)															
"	total		87	.295	.377	244	72	12	1	2	0.8	24	25	11	26	4	29	12	273	25	3	21	3.5	.990	OF-29, 1B-29, 3B-1
1958	PHI	N	91	.309	.444	207	64	11	4	3	1.4	30	31	15	20	1	44	**18**	183	12	1	12	2.2	.995	OF-24, 1B-18
1959			99	.291	.461	254	74	18	2	7	2.8	32	37	18	27	1	38	15	238	15	4	18	2.6	.984	OF-34, 1B-24
1960	3 teams			PHI	N (14G – .333)			SF	N	(39G – .164)			BAL	A (14G – .265)										
"	total		67	.218	.327	110	24	4	1	2	1.8	13	16	13	21	1	48	11	32	0	1	1	0.5	.970	OF-21, 3B-4, 1B-2
1961	BAL	A	99	.250	.361	144	36	9	2	1	0.7	13	23	10	20	2	**72**	**24**	24	0	0	0	0.2	1.000	OF-25, 1B-1
1962	BOS	A	38	.143	.190	42	6	2	0	0	0.0	3	4	5	3	0	37	6	6	0	0	0	0.2	1.000	OF-4
18 yrs.			1904	.270	.377	6296	1700	276	72	84	1.3	789	729	596	551	102	311	93	4094	214	79	117	2.3	.982	OF-1454, 1B-125, 3B-19

WORLD SERIES

Year	Team		Games	BA	SA	AB	H	2B	3B	HR	HR%	R	RBI	BB	SO	SB	Pinch Hit AB	H	PO	A	E	DP	TC/G	FA	G by Pos
1954	CLE	A	4	.125	.125	8	1	0	0	0	0.0	0	0	1	3	0	2	0	1	0	0	0	0.3	1.000	OF-2

Adolfo Phillips

PHILLIPS, ADOLFO EMILIO
Born Adolfo Emilio Phillips y Lopez.
B. Dec. 16, 1941, Bethania, Panama

BR TR 6'1" 175 lbs.

Year	Team		Games	BA	SA	AB	H	2B	3B	HR	HR%	R	RBI	BB	SO	SB	Pinch Hit AB	H	PO	A	E	DP	TC/G	FA	G by Pos
1964	PHI	N	13	.231	.231	13	3	0	0	0	0.0	4	0	3	3	0	6	2	5	0	0	0	0.5	1.000	OF-4
1965			41	.230	.379	87	20	4	0	3	3.4	14	5	5	34	3	6	1	46	0	0	0	1.1	1.000	OF-32
1966	2 teams			PHI	N (2G – .000)			CHI	N	(116G – .262)															
"	total		118	.260	.449	419	109	29	1	16	3.8	69	36	43	135	32	4	1	260	14	6	2	2.4	.979	OF-112
1967	CHI	N	144	.268	.458	448	120	20	7	17	3.8	66	70	80	93	24	2	0	340	13	7	0	2.5	.981	OF-141
1968			143	.241	.399	439	106	20	5	13	3.0	49	33	47	90	9	2	0	311	11	7	3	2.3	.979	OF-141
1969	2 teams			CHI	N (28G – .224)			MON	N	(58G – .216)															
"	total		86	.218	.335	248	54	7	5	4	1.6	30	8	35	77	7	4	0	142	3	4	0	1.7	.973	OF-78
1970	MON	N	92	.238	.379	214	51	6	3	6	2.8	36	21	36	51	7	18	3	130	1	2	0	1.4	.985	OF-75
1972	CLE	A	12	.000	.000	7	0	0	0	0	0.0	2	0	2	2	0	3	0	6	0	0	0	0.6	1.000	OF-10
8 yrs.			649	.247	.410	1875	463	86	21	59	3.1	270	173	251	485	82	45	7	1241	43	26	5	2.0	.980	OF-593

Bill Phillips

PHILLIPS, WILLIAM B.
B. 1857, St. John, N. B., Canada D. Oct. 7, 1900, Chicago, Ill.

BR TR 202 lbs.

Year	Team		Games	BA	SA	AB	H	2B	3B	HR	HR%	R	RBI	BB	SO	SB	Pinch Hit AB	H	PO	A	E	DP	TC/G	FA	G by Pos

Bill Phillips *continued*

Year	Team		Games	BA	SA	AB	H	2B	3B	HR	HR%	R	RBI	BB	SO	SB	AB	H	PO	A	E	DP	TC/G	FA	G by Pos
1879	CLE	N	81	.271	.334	365	99	15	4	0	0.0	58	29	2	20		0	0	775	32	54	25	10.6	.937	1B-75, C-11, OF-2
1880			85	.254	.365	334	85	14	10	1	0.3	41	36	6	29		0	0	842	25	33	37	10.6	.963	1B-85
1881			85	.272	.387	357	97	18	10	1	0.3	51	44	5	19		0	0	806	24	29	51	10.1	.966	1B-85
1882			78	.260	.388	335	87	17	7	4	1.2	40	47	7	18		0	0	830	25	25	55	11.3	.972	1B-78, C-1
1883			97	.246	.380	382	94	29	8	2	0.5	42		8	49		0	0	953	22	33	53	10.4	.967	1B-97
1884			111	.276	.401	464	128	25	12	3	0.6	58	46	18	80		0	0	1107	30	48	59	10.7	.959	1B-111
1885	BKN	AA	99	.302	.422	391	118	16	11	3	0.8	65		27			0	0	1109	24	32	40	11.8	.973	1B-99
1886			141	.274	.369	585	160	26	15	0	0.0	68		33			0	0	1395	33	32	65	10.4	.978	1B-141
1887			132	.266	.383	533	142	34	11	2	0.4	82		45		16	0	0	1299	46	24	62	10.4	.982	1B-132
1888	KC	AA	129	.236	.320	509	120	20	10	1	0.2	57	56	27		10	0	0	1476	55	32	66	12.1	.980	1B-129
10 yrs.			1038	.266	.374	4255	1130	214	98	17	0.4	562	258	178	215	26	0	0	10592	316	342	513	10.8	.970	1B-1032, C-12, OF-2

Bubba Phillips

PHILLIPS, JOHN MELVIN
B. Feb. 24, 1930, West Point, Miss.

BR TR 5'9" 180 lbs.

Year	Team		Games	BA	SA	AB	H	2B	3B	HR	HR%	R	RBI	BB	SO	SB	AB	H	PO	A	E	DP	TC/G	FA	G by Pos
1955	DET	A	95	.234	.304	184	43	4	0	3	1.6	18	23	14	20	2	17	1	131	11	3	1	1.5	.979	OF-65, 3B-4
1956	CHI	A	67	.273	.394	99	27	6	0	2	2.0	16	11	6	12	1	13	4	61	4	0	2	1.0	1.000	OF-35, 3B-2
1957			121	.270	.372	393	106	13	3	7	1.8	38	42	28	32	5	3	0	147	230	14	17	3.2	.964	3B-97, OF-20
1958			84	.273	.369	260	71	10	0	5	1.9	26	30	15	14	3	4	0	122	87	8	13	2.6	.963	3B-47, OF-37
1959			117	.264	.380	379	100	27	1	5	1.3	43	40	27	28	1	1	0	127	202	15	13	2.9	.956	3B-100, OF-23
1960	CLE	A	113	.207	.299	304	63	14	1	4	1.3	34	33	14	37		5	0	109	135	13	18	2.3	.949	3B-85, OF-25, SS-1
1961			143	.264	.408	546	144	23	1	18	3.3	64	72	29	61	1	0	0	188	246	19	23	3.2	.958	3B-143
1962			148	.258	.358	562	145	26	0	10	1.8	53	54	20	55	4	1	0	183	243	11	16	3.0	.975	3B-145, OF-3, 2B-1
1963	DET	A	128	.246	.310	464	114	11	2	5	1.1	42	45	19	42	6	6	2	125	226	15	26	2.9	.959	3B-117, OF-5
1964			46	.253	.368	87	22	1	0	3	3.4	14	6	10	13	1	17	4	18	40	1	5	1.3	.983	3B-22, OF-1
10 yrs.			1062	.255	.358	3278	835	135	8	62	1.9	348	356	182	314	25	67	11	1211	1424	99	134	2.6	.964	3B-762, OF-214, SS-1, 2B-1

WORLD SERIES

Year	Team		Games	BA	SA	AB	H	2B	3B	HR	HR%	R	RBI	BB	SO	SB	AB	H	PO	A	E	DP	TC/G	FA	G by Pos
1959	CHI	A	3	.300	.400	10	3	1	0	0	0.0	0	0	0	0	0	0	0	6	3	0	0	3.0	1.000	3B-3, OF-1

Damon Phillips

PHILLIPS, DAMON ROSWELL (Dee)
B. June 8, 1919, Corsicanna, Tex.

BR TR 6' 176 lbs.

Year	Team		Games	BA	SA	AB	H	2B	3B	HR	HR%	R	RBI	BB	SO	SB	AB	H	PO	A	E	DP	TC/G	FA	G by Pos
1942	CIN	N	28	.202	.226	84	17	2	0	0	0.0	4	6	7	5	0	1	0	49	84	5	17	4.9	.964	SS-27
1944	BOS	N	140	.258	.329	489	126	30	1	1	0.2	35	53	28	34	1	0	0	206	336	33	55	4.1	.943	3B-90, SS-60
1946			2	.500	.500	2	1	0	0	0	0.0	0	0	0	0	0	2	1	0	0	0	0	0.0		
3 yrs.			170	.250	.315	575	144	32	1	1	0.2	39	59	35	39	1	3	1	255	420	38	72	4.2	.947	3B-90, SS-87

Dick Phillips

PHILLIPS, RICHARD EUGENE
B. Nov. 24, 1931, Racine, Wis.

BL TR 6' 180 lbs.

Year	Team		Games	BA	SA	AB	H	2B	3B	HR	HR%	R	RBI	BB	SO	SB	AB	H	PO	A	E	DP	TC/G	FA	G by Pos
1962	SF	N	5	.000	.000	3	0	0	0	0	0.0	1	1	1	1		3	0	1	0	0	0	0.2	1.000	1B-1
1963	WAS	A	124	.237	.355	321	76	8	0	10	3.1	33	32	29	35	1	39	8	657	64	4	73	5.8	.994	1B-68, 2B-5, 3B-4
1964			109	.231	.291	234	54	6	1	2	0.9	17	23	27	22	1	39	5	475	43	3	50	4.8	.994	1B-61, 3B-4
1966			25	.162	.162	37	6	0	0	0	0.0	3	4	2	5	0	18	2	46	2	0	2	1.9	1.000	1B-5
4 yrs.			263	.229	.316	595	136	14	1	12	2.0	54	60	59	63	2	99	15	1179	109	7	125	4.9	.995	1B-135, 3B-8, 2B-5

Ed Phillips

PHILLIPS, HOWARD EDWARD
B. July 8, 1931, St. Louis, Mo.

BB TR 6'1" 180 lbs.

Year	Team		Games	BA	SA	AB	H	2B	3B	HR	HR%	R	RBI	BB	SO	SB	AB	H	PO	A	E	DP	TC/G	FA	G by Pos
1953	STL	N	9	—	—	0	0	0	0	0	—	4	0	0	0	0	0	0	0	0	0	0	0.0	—	

Eddie Phillips

PHILLIPS, EDWARD DAVID
B. Feb. 17, 1901, Worcester, Mass. D. Jan. 26, 1968, Buffalo, N. Y.

BR TR 6' 178 lbs.

Year	Team		Games	BA	SA	AB	H	2B	3B	HR	HR%	R	RBI	BB	SO	SB	AB	H	PO	A	E	DP	TC/G	FA	G by Pos
1924	BOS	N	3	.000	.000	3	0	0	0	0	0.0	0	0	0	2	0	2	0	0	1	0	0	0.3	1.000	C-1
1929	DET	A	68	.235	.330	221	52	13	1	2	0.9	24	21	20	16	0	4	1	255	34	10	4	4.4	.967	C-63
1931	PIT	N	106	.232	.360	353	82	18	3	7	2.0	30	44	41	49	1	1	0	293	49	5	12	3.3	.986	C-103
1932	NY	A	9	.290	.516	31	9	1	0	2	6.5	4	4	2	3	1	0	0	46	6	0	0	5.8	1.000	C-9
1934	WAS	A	56	.195	.278	169	33	6	1	2	1.2	6	16	26	24	1	3	0	162	21	3	4	3.3	.984	C-53
1935	CLE	A	70	.273	.368	220	60	16	1	1	0.5	18	41	15	21	0	1	0	233	18	5	3	3.7	.980	C-69
6 yrs.			312	.237	.345	997	236	54	6	14	1.4	82	126	104	115	3	11	1	989	129	23	23	3.7	.980	C-298

Jack Phillips

PHILLIPS, JACK DORN (Stretch)
B. Sept. 6, 1921, Clarence, N. Y.

BR TR 6'4" 193 lbs.

Year	Team		Games	BA	SA	AB	H	2B	3B	HR	HR%	R	RBI	BB	SO	SB	AB	H	PO	A	E	DP	TC/G	FA	G by Pos
1947	NY	A	16	.278	.417	36	10	1	1	1	2.8	5	5	3	5	0	4	0	71	1	1	8	4.6	.986	1B-10
1948			1	.000	.000	2	0	0	0	0	0.0	0	0	0	1	0	0	0	8	0	1	0	9.0	.889	1B-1
1949	2 teams	NY A (45G – .308)				PIT N (18G – .232)																			
"	total		63	.279	.374	147	41	7	2	1	0.7	22	13	16	14	2	7	2	380	22	6	42	6.5	.985	1B-54, 3B-1
1950	PIT	N	69	.293	.457	208	61	7	6	5	2.4	25	34	20	17	1	11	3	455	47	9	47	7.4	.982	1B-54, 3B-3, P-1
1951			70	.237	.321	156	37	7	3	0	0.0	12	12	15	17	1	12	2	324	28	4	38	5.1	.989	1B-53, 3B-4
1952			1	.000	.000	1	0	0	0	0	0.0	0	0	0	0	0	0	0	2	0	0	1	2.0	1.000	1B-1
1955	DET	A	55	.316	.444	117	37	8	2	1	0.9	15	20	10	12	0	17	8	239	15	2	16	4.7	.992	1B-35, 3B-3
1956			67	.295	.384	224	66	13	2	1	0.4	31	20	21	19	1	9	3	425	32	10	49	7.0	.979	1B-56, OF-1, 2B-1
1957			1	.000	.000	1	0	0	0	0	0.0	0	0	0	0	0	1	0	0	0	0	0	0.0	—	
9 yrs.			343	.283	.396	892	252	42	16	9	1.0	111	101	85	86	5	61	18	1904	145	33	201	6.1	.984	1B-264, 3B-11, OF-1, 2B-1, P-1

WORLD SERIES

Year	Team		Games	BA	SA	AB	H	2B	3B	HR	HR%	R	RBI	BB	SO	SB	AB	H	PO	A	E	DP	TC/G	FA	G by Pos
1947	NY	A	2	.000	.000	2	0	0	0	0	0.0	0	0	0	0	0	1	0	4	0	0	1	2.0	1.000	1B-1

John Phillips

PHILLIPS, JOHN STEPHEN
B. May 24, 1919, St. Louis, Mo. D. June 16, 1958, St. Louis, Mo.

BR TR 6'1" 185 lbs.

Year	Team		Games	BA	SA	AB	H	2B	3B	HR	HR%	R	RBI	BB	SO	SB	AB	H	PO	A	E	DP	TC/G	FA	G by Pos
1945	NY	N	2	.500	.500	2	1	0	0	0	0.0	1	0	0	0	0	0	0	1	0	0	0	0.5	1.000	P-1

Year	Team	Games	BA	SA	AB	H	2B	3B	HR	HR%	R	RBI	BB	SO	SB	Pinch Hit AB	Pinch Hit H	PO	A	E	DP	TC/G	FA	G by Pos

Marr Phillips

PHILLIPS, MARR B.
B. June 16, 1857, Pittsburgh, Pa.   D. Apr. 1, 1928, Pittsburgh, Pa.

Year	Team	Games	BA	SA	AB	H	2B	3B	HR	HR%	R	RBI	BB	SO	SB	PH AB	PH H	PO	A	E	DP	TC/G	FA	G by Pos
1884	IND AA	97	.269	.351	413	111	18	8	0	0.0	41		5			0	0	108	335	71	16	5.3	.862	SS-97
1885	2 teams	DET N (33G – .209)		PIT AA (4G – .267)																				
"	total	37	.214	.247	154	33	5	0	0	0.0	14	17	2	13		0	0	37	132	23	8	5.2	.880	SS-37
1890	ROC AA	64	.206	.237	257	53	8	0	0	0.0	18		16		10	0	0	101	222	29	24	5.5	.918	SS-64
	3 yrs.	198	.239	.296	824	197	31	8	0	0.0	73	17	23	13	10	0	0	246	689	123	48	5.3	.884	SS-198

Mike Phillips

PHILLIPS, MICHAEL DWAINE
B. Aug. 19, 1950, Beaumont, Tex.

BL TR 6'   170 lbs.

Year	Team	Games	BA	SA	AB	H	2B	3B	HR	HR%	R	RBI	BB	SO	SB	PH AB	PH H	PO	A	E	DP	TC/G	FA	G by Pos
1973	SF N	63	.240	.375	104	25	3	4	1	1.0	18	9	6	17	0	5	1	42	69	6	9	1.9	.949	3B-28, SS-20, 2B-7
1974		100	.219	.269	283	62	6	1	2	0.7	19	20	14	37	4	13	2	125	195	19	33	3.4	.944	3B-34, 2B-30, SS-23
1975	2 teams	SF N (10G – .194)		NY N (116G – .256)																				
"	total	126	.251	.316	414	104	10	7	1	0.2	34	29	31	51	4	3	0	203	364	32	56	4.8	.947	SS-115, 2B-7, 3B-6
1976	NY N	87	.256	.363	262	67	4	6	4	1.5	30	29	25	29	2	13	3	115	191	11	26	3.6	.965	SS-53, 2B-19, 3B-10
1977	2 teams	NY N (38G – .209)		STL N (48G – .241)																				
"	total	86	.225	.306	173	39	5	3	1	0.6	22	12	20	36	1	24	0	90	126	7	31	2.6	.969	2B-35, SS-29, 3B-14
1978	STL N	76	.268	.348	164	44	8	1	1	0.6	14	28	13	25	0	19	1	107	135	7	31	3.3	.972	2B-55, SS-10, 3B-1
1979		44	.227	.309	97	22	3	1	1	1.0	10	6	10	9	0	1	0	54	107	4	16	3.8	.976	SS-25, 2B-16, 3B-1
1980		63	.234	.273	128	30	5	0	0	0.0	13	7	9	17	0	9	2	63	130	9	27	3.2	.955	SS-37, 2B-9, 3B-8
1981	2 teams	SD N (14G – .207)		MON N (34G – .218)																				
"	total	48	.214	.262	84	18	2	1	0	0.0	6	4	5	18	1	5	1	23	24	1	7	1.0	.979	SS-27, 2B-15
1982	MON N	14	.125	.125	8	1	0	0	0	0.0	0	0	1	3	0	1	0	8	10	0	1	1.3	1.000	2B-10, SS-2
1983		5	.000	.000	2	0	0	0	0	0.0	0	0	0	0	0	0	0	0	0	1	0	0.2	–	SS-3, 3B-2
	11 yrs.	712	.240	.314	1719	412	46	24	11	0.6	166	145	133	242	12	93	10	830	1351	97	237	3.2	.957	SS-344, 2B-203, 3B-104

DIVISIONAL PLAYOFF SERIES

Year	Team	Games	BA	SA	AB	H	2B	3B	HR	HR%	R	RBI	BB	SO	SB	PH AB	PH H	PO	A	E	DP	TC/G	FA	G by Pos
1981	MON N	1	.000	.000	1	0	0	0	0	0.0	0	0	0	0	0	0	0	0	0	0	0	0.0	–	2B-1

Tony Phillips

PHILLIPS, KEITH ANTHONY
B. Apr. 25, 1959, Atlanta, Ga.

BB TR 5'9"   155 lbs.

Year	Team	Games	BA	SA	AB	H	2B	3B	HR	HR%	R	RBI	BB	SO	SB	PH AB	PH H	PO	A	E	DP	TC/G	FA	G by Pos
1982	OAK A	40	.210	.284	81	17	2	2	0	0.0	11	8	12	26	2	0	0	46	95	7	17	3.7	.953	SS-39
1983		148	.248	.320	412	102	12	3	4	1.0	54	35	48	70	16	1	1	218	383	30	85	4.3	.952	SS-101, 2B-63, 3B-4, DH-1
1984		154	.266	.359	451	120	24	3	4	0.9	62	37	42	86	10	2	0	255	391	28	90	4.4	.958	SS-91, 2B-90, OF-1
1985		42	.280	.453	161	45	12	2	4	2.5	23	17	13	34	3	1	0	54	103	3	13	3.8	.981	3B-31, 2B-24
1986		118	.256	.345	441	113	14	5	5	1.1	76	52	76	82	15	0	0	191	326	13	43	4.5	.975	2B-88, 3B-30, OF-4, DH-2, SS-1
1987		111	.240	.372	379	91	20	0	10	2.6	48	46	57	76	7	6	1	179	299	14	47	4.4	.972	2B-87, 3B-11, SS-9, OF-2
1988		79	.203	.307	212	43	8	4	2	0.9	32	17	36	50	0	5	1	84	80	10	18	2.2	.943	3B-32, OF-31, 2B-27, SS-10, 1B-3
1989		143	.262	.348	451	118	15	6	4	0.9	48	47	58	66	3	10	3	184	321	15	54	3.6	.971	2B-84, 3B-49, SS-17, OF-16, 1B-1
	8 yrs.	835	.251	.350	2588	649	107	25	33	1.3	354	259	342	490	56	25	6	1211	1998	120	367	4.0	.964	2B-463, SS-268, 3B-157, OF-54, 1B-4, DH-3

LEAGUE CHAMPIONSHIP SERIES

Year	Team	Games	BA	SA	AB	H	2B	3B	HR	HR%	R	RBI	BB	SO	SB	PH AB	PH H	PO	A	E	DP	TC/G	FA	G by Pos
1988	OAK A	2	.286	.429	7	2	1	0	0	0.0	0	0	1	3	0	0	0	10	0	0	1	5.0	1.000	OF-2, 2B-1
1989		5	.167	.222	18	3	1	0	0	0.0	1	1	2	4	2	0	0	4	14	0	2	3.6	1.000	3B-3, 2B-3
	2 yrs.	7	.200	.280	25	5	2	0	0	0.0	1	1	3	7	2	0	0	14	14	0	3	4.0	1.000	2B-4, 3B-3, OF-2

WORLD SERIES

Year	Team	Games	BA	SA	AB	H	2B	3B	HR	HR%	R	RBI	BB	SO	SB	PH AB	PH H	PO	A	E	DP	TC/G	FA	G by Pos
1988	OAK A	2	.250	.250	4	1	0	0	0	0.0	1	0	1	0	0	0	0	3	5	0	1	4.0	1.000	OF-1, 2B-1
1989		4	.235	.471	17	4	1	0	1	5.9	2	3	0	3	0	0	0	8	15	0	1	5.8	1.000	2B-4, 3B-2, OF-1
	2 yrs.	6	.238	.429	21	5	1	0	1	4.8	3	3	1	5	0	0	0	11	20	0	2	5.2	1.000	2B-5, OF-2, 3B-2

Rob Picciolo

PICCIOLO, ROBERT MICHAEL
B. Feb. 4, 1953, Santa Monica, Calif.

BR TR 6'2"   185 lbs.

Year	Team	Games	BA	SA	AB	H	2B	3B	HR	HR%	R	RBI	BB	SO	SB	PH AB	PH H	PO	A	E	DP	TC/G	FA	G by Pos
1977	OAK A	148	.200	.258	419	84	12	3	2	0.5	35	22	9	55	1	0	0	213	381	21	70	4.2	.966	SS-148
1978		78	.226	.301	93	21	1	0	2	2.2	16	7	2	13	1	0	0	74	90	7	19	2.2	.959	SS-41, 2B-19, 3B-13
1979		115	.253	.328	348	88	16	2	2	0.6	37	27	3	45	2	1	1	203	288	17	55	4.4	.967	SS-105, 2B-6, 3B-4, OF-1
1980		95	.240	.343	271	65	9	2	5	1.8	32	18	2	63	1	1	0	164	208	6	39	4.0	.984	SS-49, 2B-47, OF-1
1981		82	.268	.397	179	48	5	3	4	2.2	23	13	5	22	0	0	0	99	157	5	30	3.2	.981	SS-82
1982	2 teams	OAK A (18G – .224)		MIL A (22G – .286)																				
"	total	40	.243	.271	70	17	2	0	0	0.0	10	4	2	14	1	5	2	47	72	3	11	3.1	.975	SS-24, 2B-11, DH-1
1983	MIL A	14	.222	.333	27	6	3	0	0	0.0	2	1	0	4	0	2	0	27	20	1	7	3.4	.979	SS-7, 3B-2, 2B-2, DH-1, 1B-1
1984	CAL A	87	.202	.277	119	24	6	1	0	0.0	18	9	0	21	0	1	0	69	135	6	22	2.4	.971	3B-19, 2B-17, 1B-13, DH-10, SS-9, OF-2
1985	OAK A	71	.275	.324	102	28	2	0	1	1.0	19	8	2	17	3	9	3	56	66	5	12	1.8	.961	3B-19, 2B-17, 1B-13, DH-12, SS-9, OF-2
	9 yrs.	730	.234	.312	1628	381	56	10	17	1.0	192	109	25	254	9	20	6	952	1417	71	268	3.3	.971	SS-531, 2B-111, 3B-51, 1B-14, DH-12, OF-5

DIVISIONAL PLAYOFF SERIES

Year	Team	Games	BA	SA	AB	H	2B	3B	HR	HR%	R	RBI	BB	SO	SB	PH AB	PH H	PO	A	E	DP	TC/G	FA	G by Pos
1981	OAK A	1	.333	.333	3	1	0	0	0	0.0	0	0	0	0	0	0	0	0	0	0	0	0.0	–	SS-1

LEAGUE CHAMPIONSHIP SERIES

Year	Team	Games	BA	SA	AB	H	2B	3B	HR	HR%	R	RBI	BB	SO	SB	PH AB	PH H	PO	A	E	DP	TC/G	FA	G by Pos
1981	OAK A	2	.200	.200	5	1	0	0	0	0.0	0	1	0	2	0	0	0	0	1	0	0	0.5	–	SS-2

Nick Picciuto

PICCIUTO, NICHOLAS THOMAS
B. Aug. 27, 1921, Newark, N. J.

BR TR 5'8½"   165 lbs.

Year	Team	Games	BA	SA	AB	H	2B	3B	HR	HR%	R	RBI	BB	SO	SB	PH AB	PH H	PO	A	E	DP	TC/G	FA	G by Pos
1945	PHI N	36	.135	.202	89	12	6	0	0	0.0	7	6	6	17	0	2	0	32	38	10	2	2.2	.875	3B-30, 2B-4

Val Picinich

PICINICH, VALENTINE JOHN
B. Sept. 8, 1896, New York, N. Y.   D. Dec. 5, 1942, Nobleboro, Me.

BR TR 5'9"   165 lbs.

Year	Team	Games	BA	SA	AB	H	2B	3B	HR	HR%	R	RBI	BB	SO	SB	PH AB	PH H	PO	A	E	DP	TC/G	FA	G by Pos
1916	PHI A	40	.195	.237	118	23	3	1	0	0.0	8	5	6	33	1	3	2	179	52	8	6	6.0	.967	C-37
1917		2	.333	.333	6	2	0	0	0	0.0	0	0	1	2	0	1	0	10	1	3	0	7.0	.786	C-2

Year	Team	Games	BA	SA	AB	H	2B	3B	HR	HR%	R	RBI	BB	SO	SB	Pinch Hit AB	Pinch Hit H	PO	A	E	DP	TC/G	FA	G by Pos

Val Picinich *continued*

Year	Team	Games	BA	SA	AB	H	2B	3B	HR	HR%	R	RBI	BB	SO	SB	AB	H	PO	A	E	DP	TC/G	FA	G by Pos
1918	WAS A	47	.230	.297	148	34	3	2	1	0.7	13	12	9	25	0	1	0	216	48	11	5	5.9	.960	C-46
1919		80	.274	.401	212	58	12	3	3	1.4	18	22	17	43	6	11	2	303	92	9	5	5.1	.978	C-69
1920		48	.203	.346	133	27	6	2	3	2.3	14	14	9	33	0	2	0	185	41	5	6	4.8	.978	C-45
1921		45	.277	.340	141	39	9	0	0	0.0	10	12	16	21	0	0	0	197	29	8	1	5.2	.966	C-45
1922		76	.229	.305	210	48	12	2	0	0.0	16	19	23	33	1	0	0	273	55	8	4	4.4	.976	C-76
1923	BOS A	87	.276	.384	268	74	21	1	2	0.7	33	31	46	32	3	6	0	247	89	15	7	4.0	.957	C-81
1924		68	.266	.354	158	42	5	3	1	0.6	24	24	28	19	5	16	3	155	36	10	2	3.0	.950	C-51
1925		90	.255	.351	251	64	21	0	1	0.4	31	25	33	21	2	11	3	242	54	10	6	3.4	.967	C-74, 1B-2
1926	CIN N	89	.263	.363	240	63	16	1	2	0.8	33	31	29	22	4	2	2	240	52	10	6	3.4	.967	C-86
1927		65	.254	.335	173	44	8	3	0	0.0	16	12	24	15	3	4	0	218	31	5	8	3.9	.980	C-61
1928		96	.302	.420	324	98	15	1	7	2.2	29	35	20	25	1	2	0	279	65	6	6	3.6	.983	C-93
1929	BKN N	93	.260	.407	273	71	16	6	4	1.5	28	31	34	24	3	6	1	311	62	8	8	4.1	.979	C-85
1930		35	.217	.283	46	10	3	0	0	0.0	4	3	5	6	1	1	0	43	8	3	0	1.5	.944	C-22
1931		24	.267	.422	45	12	4	0	1	2.2	5	4	4	9	1	5	2	55	4	2	1	2.5	.967	C-24
1932		41	.257	.386	70	18	6	0	1	1.4	8	11	4	8	0	16	3	59	6	1	1	1.6	.985	C-24
1933	2 teams	BKN	N	(6G – .167)				PIT	N	(16G – .250)														
"	total	22	.241	.379	58	14	5	0	1	1.7	7	7	5	11	0	0	0	54	8	2	0	2.9	.969	C-22
18 yrs.		1048	.258	.361	2874	741	165	25	27	0.9	297	298	313	382	31	86	18	3266	733	124	70	3.9	.970	C-943, 1B-2

Charlie Pick

PICK, CHARLES THOMAS
B. Apr. 10, 1888, Brookneal, Va. D. June 26, 1954, Lynchburg, Va. BL TR 5'10" 160 lbs.

Year	Team	Games	BA	SA	AB	H	2B	3B	HR	HR%	R	RBI	BB	SO	SB	AB	H	PO	A	E	DP	TC/G	FA	G by Pos
1914	WAS A	10	.391	.391	23	9	0	0	0	0.0	0	1	4	4	1	0	0	8	2	0	0	1.2	.833	OF-7
1915		3	.000	.000	2	0	0	0	0	0.0	0	0	0	0	0	2	0	0	0	0	0	0.0	–	
1916	PHI A	121	.241	.281	398	96	10	3	0	0.0	29	20	40	24	25	5	1	156	232	44	25	3.6	.898	3B-108, OF-8
1918	CHI N	29	.326	.393	89	29	4	1	0	0.0	13	12	14	4	7	0	0	45	77	7	6	4.4	.946	2B-20, 3B-8
1919	2 teams	CHI	N	(75G – .242)				BOS	N	(34G – .254)														
"	total	109	.245	.313	383	94	9	7	1	0.3	39	25	21	17	21	3	1	209	324	33	42	5.2	.942	2B-92, 3B-8, OF-3, 1B-2
1920	BOS N	95	.274	.363	383	105	16	6	2	0.5	34	28	23	11	10	1	1	219	333	28	45	6.1	.952	2B-94
6 yrs.		367	.261	.325	1278	333	39	17	3	0.2	115	86	102	60	64	13	4	637	968	114	118	4.7	.934	2B-206, 3B-124, OF-18, 1B-2

WORLD SERIES

Year	Team	Games	BA	SA	AB	H	2B	3B	HR	HR%	R	RBI	BB	SO	SB	AB	H	PO	A	E	DP	TC/G	FA	G by Pos
1918	CHI N	6	.389	.444	18	7	1	0	0	0.0	2	0	1	1	0	0	0	12	11	0	3	3.8	1.000	2B-6

Eddie Pick

PICK, EDGAR EVERETT
B. May 7, 1899, Attleboro, Mass. D. May 13, 1967, Santa Monica, Calif. BB TR 6' 185 lbs.

Year	Team	Games	BA	SA	AB	H	2B	3B	HR	HR%	R	RBI	BB	SO	SB	AB	H	PO	A	E	DP	TC/G	FA	G by Pos
1923	CIN N	9	.375	.375	8	3	0	0	0	0.0	2	2	3	3	0	2	0	2	0	0	0	0.2	1.000	OF-4
1924		3	.000	.000	2	0	0	0	0	0.0	0	0	0	1	0	1	0	1	0	0	0	0.3	1.000	OF-1
1927	CHI N	54	.171	.254	181	31	5	2	2	1.1	23	15	20	26	0	0	0	61	73	13	9	2.7	.912	3B-49, OF-1, 2B-1
3 yrs.		66	.178	.257	191	34	5	2	2	1.0	25	17	23	30	0	3	0	64	73	13	9	2.3	.913	3B-49, OF-6, 2B-1

Ollie Pickering

PICKERING, OLIVER DANIEL (Pick, Von Der Ahe)
B. Apr. 9, 1870, Olney, Ill. D. Jan. 20, 1952, Vincennes, Ind. BL TR 5'11" 170 lbs.

Year	Team	Games	BA	SA	AB	H	2B	3B	HR	HR%	R	RBI	BB	SO	SB	AB	H	PO	A	E	DP	TC/G	FA	G by Pos
1896	LOU N	45	.303	.406	165	50	6	4	1	0.6	28	22	12	11	13	0	0	97	12	12	4	2.7	.901	OF-45
1897	2 teams	LOU	N	(63G – .252)				CLE	N	(46G – .352)														
"	total	109	.294	.350	428	126	10	4	2	0.5	67	43	36		38	1	0	244	20	16	3	2.6	.943	OF-108, 2B-1
1901	CLE A	137	.309	.377	547	169	25	6	0	0.0	102	40	58		36	0	0	315	22	18	9	2.6	.949	OF-137
1902		69	.256	.317	293	75	5	4	3	1.0	46	26	19		22	2	2	155	5	4	2	2.4	.976	OF-64, 1B-2
1903	PHI A	137	.281	.346	512	144	18	6	1	0.2	93	36	53		40	2	0	272	17	9	5	2.2	.970	OF-135
1904		124	.226	.262	455	103	10	3	0	0.0	56	30	45		17	2	0	217	13	15	2	2.0	.939	OF-121
1907	STL A	151	.276	.337	576	159	15	10	0	0.0	63	60	35		15	1	0	210	14	12	5	1.6	.949	OF-151
1908	WAS A	113	.225	.282	373	84	7	4	2	0.5	45	30	28		13	14	3	135	6	9	1	1.3	.940	OF-98
8 yrs.		885	.272	.332	3349	910	96	39	9	0.3	500	287	286	11	194	22	5	1645	109	95	31	2.1	.949	OF-859, 1B-2, 2B-1

Urbane Pickering

PICKERING, URBANE HENRY (Dick)
B. June 3, 1899, Hoxie, Kans. D. May 13, 1970, Modesto, Calif. BR TR 5'10" 180 lbs.

Year	Team	Games	BA	SA	AB	H	2B	3B	HR	HR%	R	RBI	BB	SO	SB	AB	H	PO	A	E	DP	TC/G	FA	G by Pos
1931	BOS A	103	.252	.393	341	86	13	4	9	2.6	48	52	33	53	3	12	3	129	189	16	12	3.2	.952	3B-74, 2B-16
1932		132	.260	.357	457	119	28	5	2	0.4	47	40	39	71	3	5	2	111	222	22	22	2.7	.938	3B-126, C-1
2 yrs.		235	.257	.372	798	205	41	9	11	1.4	95	92	72	124	6	17	5	240	411	38	34	2.9	.945	3B-200, 2B-16, C-1

Dave Pickett

PICKETT, DAVID T.
B. May 26, 1874, Brookline, Mass. D. Apr. 22, 1950, Easton, Mass. 5'7½" 170 lbs.

Year	Team	Games	BA	SA	AB	H	2B	3B	HR	HR%	R	RBI	BB	SO	SB	AB	H	PO	A	E	DP	TC/G	FA	G by Pos
1898	BOS N	14	.279	.302	43	12	1	0	0	0.0	3	3	6		2	0	0	20	1	1	0	1.6	.955	OF-14

John Pickett

PICKETT, JOHN THOMAS
B. Feb. 20, 1866, Chicago, Ill. D. July 4, 1922, Chicago, Ill. BR TR

Year	Team	Games	BA	SA	AB	H	2B	3B	HR	HR%	R	RBI	BB	SO	SB	AB	H	PO	A	E	DP	TC/G	FA	G by Pos
1889	KC AA	53	.224	.259	201	45	7	0	0	0.0	20	12	11	21	7	0	0	77	44	23	4	2.7	.840	OF-28, 3B-14, 2B-11
1890	PHI P	100	.280	.371	407	114	7	9	4	1.0	82	64	40	17	12	0	0	236	284	62	46	5.8	.893	2B-100
1892	BAL N	36	.213	.291	141	30	2	3	1	0.7	13	12	7	10	2	0	0	86	109	18	9	5.9	.915	2B-36
3 yrs.		189	.252	.326	749	189	16	12	5	0.7	115	88	58	48	21	0	0	399	437	103	59	5.0	.890	2B-147, OF-28, 3B-14

Ty Pickup

PICKUP, CLARENCE WILLIAM
B. Oct. 29, 1897, Philadelphia, Pa. D. Aug. 2, 1974, Philadelphia, Pa. BR TR 6' 180 lbs.

Year	Team	Games	BA	SA	AB	H	2B	3B	HR	HR%	R	RBI	BB	SO	SB	AB	H	PO	A	E	DP	TC/G	FA	G by Pos
1918	PHI N	1	1.000	1.000	1	1	0	0	0	0.0	0	0	0	0	0	0	0	0	0	0	0	1.0	1.000	OF-1

Gracie Pierce

PIERCE, GRAYSON S.
B. New York, N. Y. D. Aug. 29, 1894, New York, N. Y. BL TR 5'11" 176 lbs.

Year	Team	Games	BA	SA	AB	H	2B	3B	HR	HR%	R	RBI	BB	SO	SB	AB	H	PO	A	E	DP	TC/G	FA	G by Pos
1882	2 teams	LOU	AA	(9G – .303)				BAL	AA	(41G – .199)														
"	total	50	.217	.245	184	40	3	1	0	0.0	11		4		0	0	0	154	127	65	21	6.9	.812	2B-47, OF-3, SS-1

Year	Team		Games	BA	SA	AB	H	2B	3B	HR	HR%	R	RBI	BB	SO	SB	Pinch Hit AB	H	PO	A	E	DP	TC/G	FA	G by Pos

Gracie Pierce *continued*

Year	Team		Games	BA	SA	AB	H	2B	3B	HR	HR%	R	RBI	BB	SO	SB	AB	H	PO	A	E	DP	TC/G	FA	G by Pos
1883	2 teams	COL AA (11G – .171)				NY	N	(18G – .081)																	
"	total		29	.117	.136	103	12	0	1	0	0.0	8		1	9		0	0	67	13	17	4	3.3	.825	OF-23, 2B-7
1884	NY	AA	5	.250	.300	20	5	1	0	0	0.0	2		0			0	0	10	2	7	0	3.8	.632	OF-3, 2B-3
3 yrs.			84	.186	.212	307	57	4	2	0	0.0	21		5	9		0	0	231	142	89	25	5.5	.807	2B-57, OF-29, SS-1

Jack Pierce

PIERCE, LAVERN JACK
B. June 2, 1948, Laurel, Miss.

BL TR 6' 210 lbs.

Year	Team		Games	BA	SA	AB	H	2B	3B	HR	HR%	R	RBI	BB	SO	SB	AB	H	PO	A	E	DP	TC/G	FA	G by Pos
1973	ATL	N	11	.050	.050	20	1	0	0	0	0.0	0	1	8		0	5		42	4	0	1	4.2	1.000	1B-6
1974			6	.111	.111	9	1	0	0	0	0.0	1	0	1	0	0	3	1	21	2	1	1	4.0	.958	1B-2
1975	DET	A	53	.235	.424	170	40	6	1	8	4.7	19	22	20	40	0	4	0	407	26	13	38	8.4	.971	1B-49
3 yrs.			70	.211	.372	199	42	6	1	8	4.0	20	22	22	48	0	12	1	470	32	14	40	7.4	.973	1B-57

Maury Pierce

PIERCE, MAURICE
B. Baltimore, Md. Deceased.

Year	Team		Games	BA	SA	AB	H	2B	3B	HR	HR%	R	RBI	BB	SO	SB	AB	H	PO	A	E	DP	TC/G	FA	G by Pos
1884	WAS	U	2	.143	.143	7	1	0	0	0	0.0	0		0			0	0	5	2	2	0	4.5	.778	3B-2

Andy Piercy

PIERCY, ANDREW J.
B. Aug., 1856, San Jose, Calif. D. Dec. 27, 1932, San Jose, Calif.

TR

Year	Team		Games	BA	SA	AB	H	2B	3B	HR	HR%	R	RBI	BB	SO	SB	AB	H	PO	A	E	DP	TC/G	FA	G by Pos
1881	CHI	N	2	.250	.250	8	2	0	0	0	0.0	1	0	0	1		0	0	6	3	3	0	6.0	.750	3B-1, 2B-1

Dick Pierre

PIERRE, RICHARD J.
B. Grand Haven, Mich. Deceased.

Year	Team		Games	BA	SA	AB	H	2B	3B	HR	HR%	R	RBI	BB	SO	SB	AB	H	PO	A	E	DP	TC/G	FA	G by Pos
1883	PHI	N	5	.158	.158	19	3	0	0	0	0.0	1		0	2		0	0	6	9	11	1	5.2	.577	SS-5

Jimmy Piersall

PIERSALL, JAMES ANTHONY
B. Nov. 14, 1929, Waterbury, Conn.

BR TR 6' 175 lbs.

Year	Team		Games	BA	SA	AB	H	2B	3B	HR	HR%	R	RBI	BB	SO	SB	AB	H	PO	A	E	DP	TC/G	FA	G by Pos
1950	BOS	A	6	.286	.286	7	2	0	0	0	0.0	4	0	4	0	0	1	1	9	0	0	0	1.5	1.000	OF-2
1952			56	.267	.335	161	43	8	0	1	0.6	28	16	28	26	3	0	0	79	79	10	13	3.0	.940	SS-30, OF-22, 3B-1
1953			151	.272	.354	585	159	21	9	3	0.5	76	52	41	52	11	0	0	352	15	5	7	2.5	.987	OF-151
1954			133	.285	.395	474	135	24	2	8	1.7	77	38	36	42	5	6	0	249	10	4	2	2.0	.985	OF-126
1955			149	.283	.427	515	146	25	5	13	2.5	68	62	67	52	6	2	1	425	7	3	2	2.9	.993	OF-147
1956			155	.293	.449	601	176	**40**	6	14	2.3	91	87	58	48	7	0	0	455	10	4	1	3.0	.991	OF-155
1957			151	.261	.415	609	159	27	5	19	3.1	103	63	62	54	14	0	0	397	12	4	0	2.7	.990	OF-151
1958			130	.237	.350	417	99	13	5	8	1.9	55	48	42	43	12	5	1	314	8	5	2	2.5	.985	OF-125
1959	CLE	A	100	.246	.338	317	78	13	2	4	1.3	42	30	24	31	6	6	1	216	4	4	2	2.2	.982	OF-91, 3B-1
1960			138	.282	.434	486	137	12	4	18	3.7	70	66	24	38	18	7	1	355	5	3	0	2.6	.992	OF-134
1961			121	.322	.442	484	156	26	7	6	1.2	81	40	43	46	8	1	1	328	9	3	3	2.8	.991	OF-120
1962	WAS	A	135	.244	.329	471	115	20	4	4	0.8	38	31	39	53	12	5	1	308	5	1	0	2.3	.997	OF-132
1963	3 teams	WAS A (29G – .245)				NY	N	(40G – .194)		LA	A	(20G – .308)													
"	total		89	.233	.285	270	63	6	1	2	0.7	26	19	21	30	5	7	2	158	3	0	0	1.8	1.000	OF-77
1964	LA	A	87	.314	.380	255	80	11	0	2	0.8	28	13	16	32	5	13	2	115	2	0	2	1.3	1.000	OF-72
1965	CAL	A	53	.268	.402	112	30	5	2	2	1.8	10	12	5	15	2	14	3	62	0	1	0	1.2	.984	OF-41
1966			75	.211	.252	123	26	0	0	0	0.0	14	14	13	19	1	15	4	69	3	2	0	1.0	.973	OF-63
1967			5	.000	.000	3	0	0	0	0	0.0	0	0	0	2	0	3	0	1	0	0	0	0.2	1.000	OF-1
17 yrs.			1734	.272	.386	5890	1604	256	52	104	1.8	811	591	523	583	115	85	18	3892	172	49	34	2.4	.988	OF-1610, SS-30, 3B-2

Dave Pierson

PIERSON, DAVID P.
Brother of Dick Pierson.
B. Aug. 20, 1855, Wilkes-Barre, Pa. D. Nov. 11, 1922, Trenton, N. J.

BR TR 5'7" 142 lbs.

Year	Team		Games	BA	SA	AB	H	2B	3B	HR	HR%	R	RBI	BB	SO	SB	AB	H	PO	A	E	DP	TC/G	FA	G by Pos
1876	CIN	N	57	.236	.262	233	55	4	1	0	0.0	33	13	1	9		0	0	159	58	59	6	4.8	.786	C-31, OF-30, SS-1, 3B-1, 2B-1, P-1

Dick Pierson

PIERSON, EDMUND DANA
Brother of Dave Pierson.
B. Oct. 24, 1857, Wilkes - Barre, Pa. D. July 20, 1922, Newark, N. J.

TR

Year	Team		Games	BA	SA	AB	H	2B	3B	HR	HR%	R	RBI	BB	SO	SB	AB	H	PO	A	E	DP	TC/G	FA	G by Pos
1885	NY	AA	3	.111	.111	9	1	0	0	0	0.0	1		2			0	0	9	6	7	1	7.3	.682	2B-3

Tony Piet

PIET, ANTHONY FRANCIS
Born Anthony Francis Pietruszka.
B. Dec. 7, 1906, Berwick, Pa. D. Dec. 1, 1981, Hinsdale, Ill.

BR TR 6' 175 lbs.

Year	Team		Games	BA	SA	AB	H	2B	3B	HR	HR%	R	RBI	BB	SO	SB	AB	H	PO	A	E	DP	TC/G	FA	G by Pos
1931	PIT	N	44	.299	.419	167	50	12	4	0	0.0	22	24	13	24	10	0	0	103	134	3	17	5.5	.988	2B-44, SS-1
1932			154	.282	.390	574	162	25	8	7	1.2	66	85	46	56	19	0	0	378	454	26	80	5.6	.970	2B-154
1933			107	.323	.417	362	117	21	5	1	0.3	45	42	19	28	12	9	2	241	305	26	61	5.3	.955	2B-97
1934	CIN	N	106	.259	.337	421	109	20	5	1	0.2	58	38	23	44	6	4	2	171	245	25	34	4.2	.943	3B-51, 2B-49
1935	2 teams	CIN N (6G – .200)				CHI	A	(77G – .298)																	
"	total		83	.296	.421	297	88	18	5	3	1.0	49	29	33	27	2	1	0	151	245	12	33	4.9	.971	2B-59, 3B-17, OF-1
1936	CHI	A	109	.273	.386	352	96	15	2	7	2.0	69	42	66	48	15	7	1	167	317	18	49	4.6	.964	2B-68, 3B-32
1937			100	.235	.322	332	78	15	1	4	1.2	34	38	32	36	14	1	1	119	207	16	24	3.4	.953	3B-86, 2B-13
1938	DET	A	41	.213	.288	80	17	6	0	0	0.0	9	14	15	11	2	12	5	45	45	3	5	1.5	.919	3B-18, 2B-1
8 yrs.			744	.277	.378	2585	717	132	30	23	0.9	352	312	247	274	80	39	11	1342	1952	131	301	4.6	.962	2B-485, 3B-204, OF-1, SS-1

Sandy Piez

PIEZ, CHARLES WILLIAM
B. Oct. 13, 1892, New York, N. Y. D. Dec. 29, 1930, Atlantic City, N. J.

BR TR 5'10" 170 lbs.

Year	Team		Games	BA	SA	AB	H	2B	3B	HR	HR%	R	RBI	BB	SO	SB	AB	H	PO	A	E	DP	TC/G	FA	G by Pos
1914	NY	N	35	.375	.625	8	3	0	1	0	0.0	9	3	0	1	4	0	0	8	0	0	0	0.2	1.000	OF-4

Joe Pignatano

PIGNATANO, JOSEPH BENJAMIN
B. Aug. 4, 1929, Brooklyn, N. Y.

BR TR 5'10" 180 lbs.

Year	Team		Games	BA	SA	AB	H	2B	3B	HR	HR%	R	RBI	BB	SO	SB	AB	H	PO	A	E	DP	TC/G	FA	G by Pos
1957	BKN	N	8	.214	.286	14	3	1	0	0	0.0	1	0	5	0	0	0	0	36	1	0	0	4.6	1.000	C-6

Year	Team		Games	BA	SA	AB	H	2B	3B	HR	HR%	R	RBI	BB	SO	SB	Pinch Hit AB	Pinch Hit H	PO	A	E	DP	TC/G	FA	G by Pos

Joe Pignatano *continued*

1958	LA	N	63	.218	.437	142	31	4	0	9	6.3	18	17	16	26	4	3	0	286	18	0	3	4.8	1.000	C-57
1959			52	.237	.302	139	33	4	1	1	0.7	17	11	21	15	1	0	0	322	17	1	8	6.5	.997	C-49
1960			58	.233	.344	90	21	4	0	2	2.2	11	9	15	17	1	5	3	231	21	4	2	4.4	.984	C-40
1961	KC	A	92	.243	.358	243	59	10	3	4	1.6	31	22	36	42	2	7	1	380	35	9	7	4.6	.979	C-83, 3B-2
1962	2 teams		SF	N	(7G – .200)		NY	N	(27G – .232)																
"	total		34	.230	.262	61	14	2	0	0	0.0	4	2	6	11	0	5	0	107	13	1	2	3.6	.992	C-32
6 yrs.			307	.234	.351	689	161	25	4	16	2.3	81	62	94	116	8	20	4	1362	105	15	22	4.8	.990	C-267, 3B-2

WORLD SERIES

| 1959 | LA | N | 1 | – | – | 0 | 0 | 0 | 0 | 0 | – | 0 | 0 | 0 | 0 | 0 | 0 | 0 | 1 | 0 | 0 | 0 | 1.0 | 1.000 | C-1 |

Jay Pike

PIKE, JACOB EMANUEL
Brother of Lip Pike.
B. Brooklyn, N. Y.   Deceased.

| 1877 | HAR | N | 1 | .250 | .250 | 4 | 1 | 0 | 0 | 0 | 0.0 | 0 | 0 | 0 | 0 | 0 | 0 | 0 | 0 | 0 | 1 | 0 | 1.0 | – | OF-1 |

Jess Pike

PIKE, JESS WILLARD
B. July 31, 1915, Dustin, Okla.   D. Mar. 28, 1984, San Diego, Calif.

BL TL 6'3"   175 lbs.

| 1946 | NY | N | 16 | .171 | .317 | 41 | 7 | 1 | 1 | 1 | 2.4 | 4 | 6 | 6 | 9 | 0 | 4 | 0 | 13 | 0 | 1 | 0 | 0.9 | .929 | OF-10 |

Lip Pike

PIKE, LIPMAN EMANUEL (The Iron Batter)
Brother of Jay Pike.
B. May 25, 1845, New York, N. Y.   D. Oct. 10, 1893, Brooklyn, N. Y.
Manager 1871, 1874, 1877.

BL TL 5'8"   158 lbs.

1876	STL	N	63	.323	.472	282	91	19	10	1	0.4	55	50	8	9		0	0	90	16	13	7	1.9	.891	OF-62, 2B-2
1877	CIN	N	58	.298	.420	262	78	12	4	4	1.5	45	23	9	7		0	0	144	75	51	7	4.7	.811	OF-38, 2B-22, SS-2
1878	2 teams		CIN	N	(31G – .324)		PRO	N	(5G – .227)																
"	total		36	.311	.365	167	52	5	2	0	0.0	32	15	5	10		0	0	51	17	16	1	2.3	.810	OF-31, 2B-5
1881	WOR	N	5	.111	.111	18	2	0	0	0	0.0	1	0	4	3		0	0	10	1	6	1	3.4	.647	OF-5
1887	NY	AA	1	.000	.000	4	0	0	0	0	0.0	0	0	0		0	0	0	2	0	0	0	2.0	1.000	OF-1
5 yrs.			163	.304	.417	733	223	36	16	5	0.7	133	88	26	29	0	0	0	297	109	86	16	3.0	.825	OF-137, 2B-29, SS-2

Al Pilarcik

PILARCIK, ALFRED JAMES
B. July 3, 1930, Whiting, Ind.

BL TL 5'10"   180 lbs.

1956	KC	A	69	.251	.351	239	60	10	1	4	1.7	28	22	30	32	9	4	1	154	9	4	1	2.4	.976	OF-67
1957	BAL	A	142	.278	.398	407	113	16	3	9	2.2	52	49	53	28	14	15	3	234	15	1	2	1.8	.996	OF-126
1958			141	.243	.306	379	92	21	0	1	0.3	40	24	42	37	7	24	7	213	5	3	0	1.6	.986	OF-118
1959			130	.282	.366	273	77	12	1	3	1.1	37	16	30	25	9	21	7	133	3	3	1	1.1	.978	OF-106
1960			104	.247	.345	194	48	5	1	4	2.1	30	17	15	16	0	23	6	75	4	0	0	0.8	1.000	OF-75
1961	2 teams		KC	A	(35G – .200)		CHI	A	(47G – .177)																
"	total		82	.189	.246	122	23	1	1	1	0.8	18	15	15	12	2	28	6	63	4	2	0	0.8	.971	OF-38
6 yrs.			668	.256	.346	1614	413	66	7	22	1.4	205	143	185	150	41	115	30	872	40	13	5	1.4	.986	OF-530

Andy Pilney

PILNEY, ANTONE JAMES
B. Jan. 19, 1913, Frontenac, Kans.

BR TR 5'11"   174 lbs.

| 1936 | BOS | N | 3 | .000 | .000 | 2 | 0 | 0 | 0 | 0 | 0.0 | 0 | 0 | 0 | 1 | 0 | 2 | 0 | 0 | 0 | 0 | 0 | 0.0 | – | |

George Pinckney

PINCKNEY, GEORGE BURTON
B. Jan. 11, 1862, Orange Prairie, Ill.   D. Nov. 10, 1926, Peoria, Ill.

BR TR 5'7"   160 lbs.

1884	CLE	N	36	.313	.375	144	45	9	0	0	0.0	18	16	10	7		0	0	73	110	32	11	6.0	.851	2B-25, SS-11
1885	BKN	AA	110	.277	.336	447	124	16	5	0	0.0	77		27			0	0	207	267	56	20	4.8	.894	2B-57, 3B-51, SS-3
1886			141	.261	.322	597	156	22	7	0	0.0	119		70			0	0	184	234	69	17	3.5	.858	3B-141, P-1
1887			138	.267	.348	580	155	26	6	3	0.5	133		61		59	0	0	197	294	60	26	4.0	.891	3B-136, SS-2
1888			143	.271	.351	575	156	18	8	4	0.7	134	52	66		51	0	0	189	234	48	14	3.3	.898	3B-143
1889			138	.246	.339	545	134	25	7	4	0.7	103	82	59	43	47	0	0	183	278	53	19	3.7	.897	3B-138
1890	BKN	N	126	.309	.431	485	150	20	9	7	1.4	115	83	80	19	47	0	0	179	222	29	15	3.4	.933	3B-126
1891			135	.273	.347	501	137	19	6	2	0.4	80	71	66	32	44	0	0	152	276	46	10	3.5	.903	3B-130, SS-5
1892	STL	N	78	.172	.197	290	50	3	2	0	0.0	31	25	36	26	4	0	0	84	161	31	12	3.5	.888	3B-78
1893	LOU	N	118	.235	.296	446	105	12	6	1	0.2	64	62	50	8	12	0	0	126	279	34	26	3.8	.923	3B-118
10 yrs.			1163	.263	.338	4610	1212	170	56	21	0.5	874	391	525	135	264	0	0	1574	2355	458	170	3.8	.896	3B-1061, 2B-82, SS-21, P-1

Babe Pinelli

PINELLI, RALPH ARTHUR
Born Rinaldo Angelo Paolinelli.
B. Oct. 18, 1895, San Francisco, Calif.   D. Oct. 22, 1984, Daly City, Calif.

BR TR 5'9"   165 lbs.

1918	CHI	A	24	.231	.308	78	18	1	1	1	1.3	7	7	7	8	3	0	0	28	33	11	4	3.0	.847	3B-24
1920	DET	A	102	.229	.282	284	65	9	3	0	0.0	33	21	25	16	6	4	0	144	226	23	20	3.9	.941	3B-74, SS-18, 2B-1
1922	CIN	N	156	.305	.371	547	167	19	7	1	0.2	77	72	48	37	17	0	0	204	350	32	16	3.8	.945	3B-156
1923			117	.277	.333	423	117	14	5	0	0.0	44	51	27	29	10	0	0	131	250	25	17	3.5	.938	3B-116
1924			144	.306	.365	510	156	16	7	0	0.0	61	70	32	22	23	1	1	182	318	23	21	3.5	.956	3B-143
1925			130	.283	.386	492	139	33	6	2	0.4	68	49	22	28	8	6	2	151	321	30	36	3.9	.940	3B-109, SS-17
1926			71	.222	.295	207	46	7	4	0	0.0	26	24	15	5	2	3	1	58	150	12	9	3.1	.945	3B-40, SS-27, 2B-3
1927			30	.197	.263	76	15	2	0	1	1.3	11	4	6	7	2	0	0	33	54	2	5	3.0	.978	3B-15, SS-9, 2B-5
8 yrs.			774	.276	.346	2617	723	101	33	5	0.2	327	298	182	162	71	14	4	931	1702	158	131	3.6	.943	3B-677, SS-71, 2B-9

Lou Piniella

PINIELLA, LOUIS VICTOR (Sweet Lou)
B. Aug. 28, 1943, Tampa, Fla.
Manager 1986-88.

BR TR 6'   182 lbs.

1964	BAL	A	4	.000	.000	1	0	0	0	0	0.0	0	0	0	0	0	1	0	0	0	0	0	0.0	–	
1968	CLE	A	6	.000	.000	5	0	0	0	0	0.0	1	1	0	0	0	2	0	1	0	0	0	0.2	1.000	OF-2
1969	KC	A	135	.282	.416	493	139	21	6	11	2.2	43	68	33	56	2	9	3	278	13	7	1	2.2	.977	OF-129

Lou Piniella *continued*

Year	Team	Games	BA	SA	AB	H	2B	3B	HR	HR%	R	RBI	BB	SO	SB	Pinch Hit AB	H	PO	A	E	DP	TC/G	FA	G by Pos
1970		144	.301	.424	542	163	24	5	11	2.0	54	88	35	42	3	4	1	250	6	4	2	1.8	.985	OF-139, 1B-1
1971		126	.279	.368	448	125	21	5	3	0.7	43	51	21	43	5	13	3	201	6	3	2	1.7	.986	OF-115
1972		151	.312	.441	574	179	33	4	11	1.9	65	72	34	59	7	1	0	275	8	7	2	1.9	.976	OF-150
1973		144	.250	.361	513	128	28	1	9	1.8	53	69	30	65	5	7	1	196	9	3	3	1.4	.986	OF-128, DH-9
1974	NY A	140	.305	.407	518	158	26	0	9	1.7	71	70	32	58	1	2	1	270	16	3	0	2.1	.990	OF-130, DH-6, 1B-1
1975		74	.196	.226	199	39	4	1	0	0.0	7	22	16	22	0	19	4	65	5	1	0	1.0	.986	OF-46, DH-12
1976		100	.281	.394	327	92	16	6	3	0.9	36	38	18	34	0	14	4	106	4	2	0	1.1	.982	OF-49, DH-38
1977		103	.330	.510	339	112	19	3	12	3.5	47	45	20	31	2	11	2	86	3	2	1	0.9	.978	OF-51, DH-43, 1B-1
1978		130	.314	.445	472	148	34	5	6	1.3	67	69	34	36	3	9	4	213	4	7	0	1.7	.969	OF-103, DH-23
1979		130	.297	.425	461	137	22	2	11	2.4	49	69	17	31	3	12	6	204	13	4	1	1.7	.982	OF-112, DH-16
1980		116	.287	.361	321	92	18	0	2	0.6	39	27	29	20	0	24	4	157	8	5	1	1.5	.971	OF-104, DH-7
1981		60	.277	.428	159	44	9	0	5	3.1	16	18	13	9	0	9	1	69	2	1	1	1.2	.986	OF-36, DH-19
1982		102	.307	.448	261	80	17	1	6	2.3	33	37	18	18	0	25	9	68	2	0	1	0.7	1.000	DH-55, OF-40
1983		53	.291	.405	148	43	9	1	2	1.4	19	16	11	12	1	10	3	67	4	3	2	1.4	.959	OF-43, DH-1
1984		29	.302	.407	86	26	4	1	1	1.2	8	6	7	5	0	3	0	40	3	0	0	1.5	1.000	OF-24, DH-2
18 yrs.		1747	.291	.409	5867	1705	305	41	102	1.7	651	766	368	541	32	175	46	2546	106	52*	17	1.5	.981	OF-1401, DH-231, 1B-3

DIVISIONAL PLAYOFF SERIES

Year	Team	Games	BA	SA	AB	H	2B	3B	HR	HR%	R	RBI	BB	SO	SB	Pinch Hit AB	H	PO	A	E	DP	TC/G	FA	G by Pos
1981	NY A	4	.200	.600	10	2	1	0	1	10.0	1	3	0	0	0	2	1	0	0	0	0	0.0	–	DH-4

LEAGUE CHAMPIONSHIP SERIES

Year	Team	Games	BA	SA	AB	H	2B	3B	HR	HR%	R	RBI	BB	SO	SB	Pinch Hit AB	H	PO	A	E	DP	TC/G	FA	G by Pos
1976	NY A	4	.273	.364	11	3	1	0	0	0.0	1	0	0	0	0	1	0	0	0	0	0		–	DH-3
1977		5	.333	.476	21	7	3	0	0	0.0	0	2	0	1	0	0	0	9	1	0	0	2.0	1.000	OF-4, DH-1
1978		4	.235	.235	17	4	0	0	0	0.0	2	0	0	3	0	0	0	13	0	0	0	3.3	1.000	OF-4
1980		2	.200	.800	5	1	0	0	1	20.0	1	1	2	1	0	0	0	5	0	0	0	2.5	1.000	OF-2
1981		3	.600	1.200	5	3	0	0	1	20.0	2	3	0	0	0	2	2	0	0	0	0		–	DH-2, OF-1
5 yrs.		18	.305	.475	59	18	4	0	2	3.4	7	6	2	6	0	3	2	27	1	0	0	1.6	1.000	OF-11, DH-6

WORLD SERIES

Year	Team	Games	BA	SA	AB	H	2B	3B	HR	HR%	R	RBI	BB	SO	SB	Pinch Hit AB	H	PO	A	E	DP	TC/G	FA	G by Pos
1976	NY A	4	.333	.444	9	3	1	0	0	0.0	1	2	0	0	0	2	0	1	0	0	0	0.3	1.000	DH-3, OF-2
1977		6	.273	.273	22	6	0	0	0	0.0	1	3	0	3	0	0	0	16	1	1	0	3.0	.944	OF-6
1978		6	.280	.280	25	7	0	0	0	0.0	3	4	0	1	0	0	0	14	0	0	1	2.5	1.000	OF-6
1981		6	.438	.500	16	7	1	0	0	0.0	2	1	0	0	1	0	0	7	0	0	0	1.2	1.000	OF-3
4 yrs.		22	.319	.347	72	23	2	0	0	0.0	7	10	0	4	2	2	0	38	2	1	1	1.9	.976	OF-17, DH-3

Vada Pinson

PINSON, VADA EDWARD
B. Aug. 11, 1936, Memphis, Tenn.   BL TL 5'11" 170 lbs.

Year	Team	Games	BA	SA	AB	H	2B	3B	HR	HR%	R	RBI	BB	SO	SB	Pinch Hit AB	H	PO	A	E	DP	TC/G	FA	G by Pos
1958	CIN N	27	.271	.375	96	26	7	0	1	1.0	20	8	11	18	2	0	0	50	4	0	1	2.0	1.000	OF-27
1959		154	.316	.509	648	205	47	9	20	3.1	131	84	55	98	21	0	0	423	11	7	4	2.9	.984	OF-154
1960		154	.287	.472	652	187	37	12	20	3.1	107	61	47	96	32	0	0	401	11	8	1	2.7	.981	OF-154
1961		154	.343	.504	607	208	34	8	16	2.6	101	87	39	63	23	1	1	391	19	10	4	2.7	.976	OF-153
1962		155	.292	.477	619	181	31	7	23	3.7	107	100	45	68	26	3	1	344	13	4	1	2.3	.989	OF-152
1963		162	.313	.514	652	204	37	14	22	3.4	96	106	36	80	27	0	0	357	9	8	0	2.3	.979	OF-162
1964		156	.266	.448	625	166	23	11	23	3.7	99	84	42	99	8	1	0	299	14	9	1	2.1	.972	OF-156
1965		159	.305	.484	669	204	34	10	22	3.3	97	94	43	81	21	0	0	354	9	3	1	2.3	.992	OF-159
1966		156	.288	.442	618	178	35	6	16	2.6	70	76	33	83	18	3	2	344	9	13	1	2.3	.964	OF-154
1967		158	.288	.454	650	187	28	13	18	2.8	90	66	26	86	26	2	0	341	4	5	1	2.2	.986	OF-157
1968		130	.271	.383	499	135	29	6	5	1.0	60	48	32	59	17	10	2	258	7	6	0	2.1	.978	OF-123
1969	STL N	132	.255	.384	495	126	22	6	10	2.0	58	70	35	63	4	8	1	218	6	1	2	1.7	.996	OF-124
1970	CLE A	148	.286	.481	574	164	28	6	24	4.2	74	82	28	69	7	8	1	284	9	5	5	2.0	.983	OF-141, 1B-7
1971		146	.263	.376	566	149	23	4	11	1.9	60	35	21	58	25	7	2	315	11	7	4	2.3	.979	OF-141, 1B-3
1972	CAL A	136	.275	.376	484	133	24	2	7	1.4	56	49	30	54	17	7	1	207	11	2	3	1.6	.991	OF-134, 1B-1
1973		124	.260	.367	466	121	14	6	8	1.7	56	57	20	55	5	4	1	210	11	8	2	1.8	.965	OF-110
1974	KC A	115	.276	.374	406	112	18	2	6	1.5	46	41	21	45	21	9	3	198	9	4	2	1.8	.981	OF-110, DH-2, 1B-1
1975		103	.223	.335	319	71	14	5	4	1.3	38	22	10	21	5	17	2	151	6	1	0	1.5	.994	OF-82, DH-5, 1B-4
18 yrs.		2469	.286	.442	9645	2757	485	127	256	2.7	1366	1170	574	1196	305	80	17	5145	173	101	33	2.2	.981	OF-2403, 1B-16, DH-7

WORLD SERIES

Year	Team	Games	BA	SA	AB	H	2B	3B	HR	HR%	R	RBI	BB	SO	SB	Pinch Hit AB	H	PO	A	E	DP	TC/G	FA	G by Pos
1961	CIN N	5	.091	.136	22	2	1	0	0	0.0	0	0	0	1	0	0	0	18	1	1	0	4.0	.950	OF-5

Wally Pipp

PIPP, WALTER CLEMENT
B. Feb. 17, 1893, Chicago, Ill.   D. Jan. 11, 1965, Grand Rapids, Mich.   BL TL 6'1" 180 lbs.

Year	Team	Games	BA	SA	AB	H	2B	3B	HR	HR%	R	RBI	BB	SO	SB	Pinch Hit AB	H	PO	A	E	DP	TC/G	FA	G by Pos
1913	DET A	12	.161	.355	31	5	0	3	0	0.0	3	5	2	6	0	2	0	80	4	2	6	7.2	.977	1B-10
1915	NY A	136	.246	.367	479	118	20	13	4	0.8	59	60	66	81	18	2	2	1396	85	12	85	11.0	.992	1B-134
1916		151	.262	.417	545	143	20	14	12	2.2	70	93	54	82	16	1	1	1513	99	13	89	10.8	.992	1B-148
1917		155	.244	.380	587	143	29	12	9	1.5	82	70	60	66	11	0	0	1609	109	17	97	11.2	.990	1B-155
1918		91	.304	.415	349	106	15	9	2	0.6	48	44	22	34	11	0	0	918	61	12	75	10.9	.988	1B-91
1919		138	.275	.398	523	144	23	10	7	1.3	74	50	39	42	9	0	0	1488	94	15	77	11.6	.991	1B-138
1920		153	.280	.430	610	171	30	14	11	1.8	109	76	48	54	4	0	0	1649	100	15	101	11.5	.991	1B-153
1921		153	.296	.427	588	174	35	9	8	1.4	96	97	45	28	17	0	0	1624	89	16	116	11.3	.991	1B-153
1922		152	.329	.466	577	190	32	10	9	1.6	96	90	56	32	7	0	0	1667	88	13	106	11.6	.993	1B-152
1923		144	.304	.397	569	173	19	8	6	1.1	79	108	36	21	6	0	0	1461	81	12	97	10.8	.992	1B-144
1924		153	.295	.457	589	174	30	19	9	1.5	88	113	51	36	12	0	0	1447	106	9	106	10.2	.994	1B-153
1925		62	.230	.348	178	41	6	3	3	1.7	19	24	13	12	3	9	0	399	38	4	40	7.1	.991	1B-47
1926	CIN N	155	.291	.413	574	167	22	15	6	1.0	72	99	49	26	8	0	0	1710	92	15	140	11.7	.992	1B-155
1927		122	.260	.343	443	115	19	6	2	0.5	49	41	32	11	2	7	3	1145	66	5	86	10.0	.996	1B-114
1928		95	.283	.368	272	77	11	3	2	0.7	30	26	23	13	1	20	6	673	40	8	69	7.6	.989	1B-72
15 yrs.		1872	.281	.408	6914	1941	311	148	90	1.3	974	996	596	551	125	41	12	18779	1152	168	1290	10.7	.992	1B-1819

WORLD SERIES

Year	Team	Games	BA	SA	AB	H	2B	3B	HR	HR%	R	RBI	BB	SO	SB	Pinch Hit AB	H	PO	A	E	DP	TC/G	FA	G by Pos
1921	NY A	8	.154	.192	26	4	1	0	0	0.0	1	2	2	3	1	0	0	91	1	0	5	11.5	1.000	1B-8
1922		5	.286	.333	21	6	1	0	0	0.0	0	3	0	2	1	0	0	51	4	0	7	11.0	1.000	1B-5

Year	Team		Games	BA	SA	AB	H	2B	3B	HR	HR%	R	RBI	BB	SO	SB	Pinch Hit AB	H	PO	A	E	DP	TC/G	FA	G by Pos

Wally Pipp *continued*

Year	Team		Games	BA	SA	AB	H	2B	3B	HR	HR%	R	RBI	BB	SO	SB	AB	H	PO	A	E	DP	TC/G	FA	G by Pos
1923			6	.250	.250	20	5	0	0	0	0.0	2	2	4	1	0	0	0	63	3	0	6	11.0	1.000	1B-6
3 yrs.			19	.224	.254	67	15	2	0	0	0.0	3	7	6	6	2	0	0	205	8	0	18	11.2	1.000	1B-19

Jim Pisoni

PISONI, JAMES PETE
B. Aug. 14, 1929, St. Louis, Mo.
BR TR 5'10" 169 lbs.

Year	Team		Games	BA	SA	AB	H	2B	3B	HR	HR%	R	RBI	BB	SO	SB	AB	H	PO	A	E	DP	TC/G	FA	G by Pos
1953	STL	A	3	.083	.333	12	1	0	0	1	8.3	1	1	0	5	0	0	0	7	0	0	0	2.3	1.000	OF-3
1956	KC	A	10	.267	.467	30	8	0	0	2	6.7	4	5	2	8	0	1	0	24	4	1	1	2.9	.966	OF-9
1957			44	.237	.392	97	23	2	2	3	3.1	14	12	10	17	0	0	0	88	3	1	1	2.1	.989	OF-44
1959	2 teams		MIL N (9G – .167)			NY	A	(17G – .176)																	
"	total		26	.171	.244	41	7	1	1	0	0.0	6	1	3	15	0	1	0	32	1	1	0	1.3	.971	OF-24
1960	NY	A	20	.111	.111	9	1	0	0	0	0.0	1	1	1	2	0	0	0	15	0	1	0	0.8	.938	OF-18
5 yrs.			103	.212	.354	189	40	3	3	6	3.2	26	20	16	47	0	2	0	166	8	4	2	1.7	.978	OF-98

Alex Pitko

PITKO, ALEXANDER (Spunk)
B. Nov. 22, 1914, Burlington, N. J.
BR TR 5'10" 180 lbs.

Year	Team		Games	BA	SA	AB	H	2B	3B	HR	HR%	R	RBI	BB	SO	SB	AB	H	PO	A	E	DP	TC/G	FA	G by Pos
1938	PHI	N	7	.316	.368	19	6	1	0	0	0.0	2	2	3	3	1	0	0	8	0	1	0	1.3	.889	OF-7
1939	WAS	A	4	.125	.125	8	1	0	0	0	0.0	0	1	1	3	0	0	0	3	0	0	0	0.8	1.000	OF-3
2 yrs.			11	.259	.296	27	7	1	0	0	0.0	2	3	4	6	1	0	0	11	0	1	0	1.1	.917	OF-10

Jake Pitler

PITLER, JACOB ALBERT
B. Apr. 22, 1894, New York, N. Y.   D. Feb. 3, 1968, Binghamton, N. Y.
BR TR 5'8" 150 lbs.

Year	Team		Games	BA	SA	AB	H	2B	3B	HR	HR%	R	RBI	BB	SO	SB	AB	H	PO	A	E	DP	TC/G	FA	G by Pos
1917	PIT	N	109	.233	.280	382	89	8	5	0	0.0	39	23	30	24	6	0	0	286	277	20	46	5.3	.966	2B-106, OF-3
1918			2	.000	.000	1	0	0	0	0	0.0	1	0	1	0	2	0	0	2	2	2	0	3.0	.667	2B-1
2 yrs.			111	.232	.279	383	89	8	5	0	0.0	40	23	31	24	8	0	0	288	279	22	46	5.3	.963	2B-107, OF-3

Chris Pittaro

PITTARO, CHRISTOPHER FRANCIS
B. Sept. 16, 1961, Trenton, N. J.
BB TR 5'11" 170 lbs.

Year	Team		Games	BA	SA	AB	H	2B	3B	HR	HR%	R	RBI	BB	SO	SB	AB	H	PO	A	E	DP	TC/G	FA	G by Pos
1985	DET	A	27	.242	.323	62	15	3	1	0	0.0	10	7	5	13	1	0	0	15	36	6	5	2.1	.895	3B-22, 2B-4, DH-1
1986	MIN	A	11	.095	.095	21	2	0	0	0	0.0	0	8	1	0	0	0	0	15	19	1	8	3.2	.971	2B-8, SS-4
1987			14	.333	.333	12	4	0	0	0	0.0	6	0	1	0	1	0	0	10	6	0	3	1.1	1.000	2B-8
3 yrs.			52	.221	.274	95	21	3	1	0	0.0	16	7	6	21	2	1	0	40	61	7	16	2.1	.935	3B-22, 2B-20, SS-4, DH-1

Pinky Pittenger

PITTENGER, CLARKE ALONZO
B. Feb. 24, 1899, Hudson, Mich.   D. Nov. 4, 1977, Ft. Lauderdale, Fla.
BR TR 5'10" 160 lbs.

Year	Team		Games	BA	SA	AB	H	2B	3B	HR	HR%	R	RBI	BB	SO	SB	AB	H	PO	A	E	DP	TC/G	FA	G by Pos
1921	BOS	A	40	.198	.209	91	18	1	0	0	0.0	6	5	4	13	3	6	1	66	13	1	1	2.0	.988	OF-27, 3B-3, SS-2, 2B-1
1922			66	.258	.274	186	48	3	0	0	0.0	16	7	9	10	2	1	0	88	148	21	19	3.9	.915	3B-31, SS-29
1923			60	.215	.243	177	38	5	0	0	0.0	15	15	5	10	3	2	0	97	112	8	13	3.6	.963	2B-42, SS-10, 3B-3
1925	CHI	N	59	.312	.376	173	54	7	2	0	0.0	21	15	12	7	5	6	1	71	127	11	13	3.5	.947	SS-24, 3B-24
1927	CIN	N	31	.274	.369	84	23	5	0	1	1.2	17	10	2	5	4	0	0	55	83	8	19	4.7	.945	2B-20, SS-9, 3B-2
1928			40	.237	.289	38	9	0	1	0	0.0	12	4	0	1	2	3	0	15	33	4	7	1.3	.923	SS-12, 3B-4, 2B-4
1929			77	.295	.348	210	62	11	0	0	0.0	31	27	5	4	8	0	0	117	179	14	40	4.0	.955	SS-50, 3B-8, 2B-4
7 yrs.			373	.263	.306	959	252	32	3	1	0.1	118	83	37	50	27	18	2	509	695	68	112	3.4	.947	SS-136, 3B-75, 2B-71, OF-27

Joe Pittman

PITTMAN, JOSEPH WAYNE
B. Jan. 1, 1954, Houston, Tex.
BR TR 6'1" 180 lbs.

Year	Team		Games	BA	SA	AB	H	2B	3B	HR	HR%	R	RBI	BB	SO	SB	AB	H	PO	A	E	DP	TC/G	FA	G by Pos
1981	HOU	N	52	.281	.341	135	38	4	2	0	0.0	11	7	11	16	4	16	4	59	92	3	14	3.0	.981	2B-35, 3B-4
1982	2 teams		HOU N (15G – .200)			SD	N	(55G – .254)																	
"	total		70	.250	.273	128	32	3	0	0	0.0	16	7	9	15	8	15	2	52	97	6	18	2.2	.961	2B-30, SS-13, 3B-3, OF-1
1984	SF	N	17	.227	.227	22	5	0	0	0	0.0	2	2	0	6	1	3	0	5	13	1	1	1.1	.947	SS-6, 2B-5, 3B-2
3 yrs.			139	.263	.302	285	75	7	2	0	0.0	29	16	20	37	13	34	6	116	202	10	33	2.4	.970	2B-70, SS-19, 3B-9, OF-1

DIVISIONAL PLAYOFF SERIES

Year	Team		Games	BA	SA	AB	H	2B	3B	HR	HR%	R	RBI	BB	SO	SB	AB	H	PO	A	E	DP	TC/G	FA	G by Pos
1981	HOU	N	2	.000	.000	2	0	0	0	0	0.0	0	0	0	2	0	0	0	0	0	0	0		—	

Gaylen Pitts

PITTS, GAYLEN RICHARD
B. June 6, 1946, Wichita, Kans.
BR TR 6'1" 175 lbs.

Year	Team		Games	BA	SA	AB	H	2B	3B	HR	HR%	R	RBI	BB	SO	SB	AB	H	PO	A	E	DP	TC/G	FA	G by Pos
1974	OAK	A	18	.244	.317	41	10	3	0	0	0.0	4	3	5	4	0	1	1	22	28	4	3	3.0	.926	3B-11, 2B-6, 1B-1
1975			10	.333	.667	3	1	1	0	0	0.0	1	1	0	0	0	0	0	4	6	1	1	1.1	.909	3B-6, SS-2, 2B-1
2 yrs.			28	.250	.341	44	11	4	0	0	0.0	5	4	5	4	0	1	1	26	34	5	4	2.3	.923	3B-17, 2B-7, SS-2, 1B-1

Herman Pitz

PITZ, HERMAN
B. July 18, 1865, Brooklyn, N. Y.   D. Sept. 3, 1924, Far Rockaway, N. Y.
5'6" 140 lbs.

Year	Team		Games	BA	SA	AB	H	2B	3B	HR	HR%	R	RBI	BB	SO	SB	AB	H	PO	A	E	DP	TC/G	FA	G by Pos
1890	2 teams		BKN AA (61G – .138)			SYR	AA	(29G – .221)																	
"	total		90	.165	.165	284	47	0	0	0	0.0	43		58		39	0	0	268	134	55	8	5.1	.880	C-61, 3B-16, OF-10, SS-1

Don Plarski

PLARSKI, DONALD JOSEPH
B. Nov. 9, 1929, Chicago, Ill.   D. Dec. 29, 1981, St. Louis, Mo.
BR TR 5'6" 160 lbs.

Year	Team		Games	BA	SA	AB	H	2B	3B	HR	HR%	R	RBI	BB	SO	SB	AB	H	PO	A	E	DP	TC/G	FA	G by Pos
1955	KC	A	8	.091	.091	11	1	0	0	0	0.0	0	0	2	1	1	0	0	7	0	0	0	0.9	1.000	OF-6

Elmo Plaskett

PLASKETT, ELMO ALEXANDER
B. June 27, 1938, Frederiksted, Virgin Islands
BR TR 5'10" 195 lbs.

Year	Team		Games	BA	SA	AB	H	2B	3B	HR	HR%	R	RBI	BB	SO	SB	AB	H	PO	A	E	DP	TC/G	FA	G by Pos
1962	PIT	N	7	.286	.500	14	4	0	0	1	7.1	2	3	1	3	0	4	0	13	1	0	0	2.0	1.000	C-4
1963			10	.143	.143	21	3	0	0	0	0.0	1	2	0	5	0	5	1	18	2	0	0	2.0	1.000	C-5, 3B-1
2 yrs.			17	.200	.286	35	7	0	0	1	2.9	3	5	1	8	0	9	1	31	3	0	0	2.0	1.000	C-9, 3B-1

Whitey Platt

PLATT, MIZELL GEORGE
B. Aug. 21, 1920, West Palm Beach, Fla.   D. July 27, 1970, West Palm Beach, Fla.
BR TR 6'1½" 190 lbs.

Year	Team		Games	BA	SA	AB	H	2B	3B	HR	HR%	R	RBI	BB	SO	SB	AB	H	PO	A	E	DP	TC/G	FA	G by Pos
1942	CHI	N	4	.063	.063	16	1	0	0	0	0.0	1	2	0	3	0	0	0	7	1	0	0	2.0	1.000	OF-4

Year Team	Games	BA	SA	AB	H	2B	3B	HR	HR%	R	RBI	BB	SO	SB	Pinch Hit AB	Pinch Hit H	PO	A	E	DP	TC/G	FA	G by Pos

Whitey Platt *continued*

Year Team	Games	BA	SA	AB	H	2B	3B	HR	HR%	R	RBI	BB	SO	SB	AB	H	PO	A	E	DP	TC/G	FA	G by Pos
1943	20	.171	.244	41	7	3	0	0	0.0	2	2	1	7	0	4	1	20	0	1	0	1.1	.952	OF-14
1946 CHI A	84	.251	.360	247	62	8	5	3	1.2	28	32	17	34	1	24	6	130	4	4	1	1.6	.971	OF-61
1948 STL A	123	.271	.410	454	123	22	10	7	1.5	57	82	39	51	1	8	2	230	5	13	2	2.0	.948	OF-114
1949	102	.258	.344	244	63	8	2	3	1.2	29	29	24	27	0	34	7	156	5	3	1	1.6	.982	OF-59, 1B-2
5 yrs.	333	.255	.369	1002	256	41	17	13	1.3	117	147	81	122	2	70	16	543	15	21	4	1.7	.964	OF-252, 1B-2

Al Platte

PLATTE, ALFRED FREDERICK JOSEPH
B. Apr. 13, 1890, Grand Rapids, Mich.   D. Aug. 29, 1976, Grand Rapids, Mich.   BL TL 5'7"   160 lbs.

Year Team	Games	BA	SA	AB	H	2B	3B	HR	HR%	R	RBI	BB	SO	SB	AB	H	PO	A	E	DP	TC/G	FA	G by Pos
1913 DET A	7	.111	.167	18	2	1	0	0	0.0	1	0	1	1	0	2	0	8	0	2	0	1.4	.800	OF-5

Rance Pless

PLESS, RANCE
B. Dec. 6, 1925, Greeneville, Tenn.   BR TR 6'   195 lbs.

Year Team	Games	BA	SA	AB	H	2B	3B	HR	HR%	R	RBI	BB	SO	SB	AB	H	PO	A	E	DP	TC/G	FA	G by Pos
1956 KC A	48	.271	.329	85	23	3	1	0	0.0	4	9	10	13	0	26	7	142	20	0	20	3.4	1.000	1B-15, 3B-5

Herb Plews

PLEWS, HERBERT EUGENE
B. June 14, 1928, Helena, Mont.   BL TR 5'11"   160 lbs.

Year Team	Games	BA	SA	AB	H	2B	3B	HR	HR%	R	RBI	BB	SO	SB	AB	H	PO	A	E	DP	TC/G	FA	G by Pos
1956 WAS A	91	.270	.375	256	69	10	7	1	0.4	24	25	26	40	1	24	4	140	175	18	39	3.7	.946	2B-66, SS-5, 3B-2
1957	104	.271	.362	329	89	19	4	1	0.3	51	26	28	39	0	25	5	203	188	11	43	3.9	.973	2B-79, 3B-11, SS-4
1958	111	.258	.337	380	98	12	6	2	0.5	46	29	17	45	2	22	4	156	208	16	45	3.4	.958	2B-64, 3B-36
1959 2 teams	WAS A (27G – .225)			BOS A (13G – .083)																			
" total	40	.192	.212	52	10	1	0	0	0.0	4	2	3	9	0	32	7	21	18	2	3	3.3	.951	2B-8
4 yrs.	346	.262	.348	1017	266	42	17	4	0.4	125	82	74	133	3	103	20	520	589	47	130	3.3	.959	2B-217, 3B-49, SS-9

Walter Plock

PLOCK, WALTER S.
B. July 2, 1869, Philadelphia, Pa.   D. Apr. 28, 1900, Richmond, Va.   6'3"

Year Team	Games	BA	SA	AB	H	2B	3B	HR	HR%	R	RBI	BB	SO	SB	AB	H	PO	A	E	DP	TC/G	FA	G by Pos
1891 PHI N	2	.400	.400	5	2	0	0	0	0.0	2	0	0	1	0	0	0	0	0	1	0	0.5	–	OF-2

Bill Plummer

PLUMMER, WILLIAM FRANCIS
B. Mar. 21, 1947, Oakland, Calif.   BR TR 6'1"   190 lbs.

Year Team	Games	BA	SA	AB	H	2B	3B	HR	HR%	R	RBI	BB	SO	SB	AB	H	PO	A	E	DP	TC/G	FA	G by Pos
1968 CHI N	2	.000	.000	2	0	0	0	0	0.0	0	0	0	1	0	2	0	2	0	0	0	1.0	1.000	C-1
1970 CIN N	4	.125	.125	8	1	0	0	0	0.0	0	0	0	2	0	0	0	6	0	1	0	1.8	.857	C-4
1971	10	.000	.000	19	0	0	0	0	0.0	0	0	0	4	0	3	0	8	6	0	0	1.4	1.000	C-4, 3B-2
1972	38	.186	.284	102	19	4	0	2	2.0	8	9	4	20	0	0	0	156	9	1	3	4.4	.994	C-35, 3B-1, 1B-1
1973	50	.151	.227	119	18	3	0	2	1.7	8	11	18	26	1	2	0	172	10	2	3	3.7	.989	C-42, 3B-5
1974	50	.225	.333	120	27	7	0	2	1.7	7	10	6	21	1	1	0	208	14	6	1	4.6	.974	C-49, 3B-1
1975	65	.182	.245	159	29	9	0	1	0.6	17	19	24	28	1	4	1	186	14	2	5	3.1	.990	C-63
1976	56	.248	.379	153	38	6	1	4	2.6	16	19	14	36	0	3	2	235	21	6	1	4.7	.977	C-54
1977	51	.137	.205	117	16	5	0	1	0.9	10	7	17	34	1	2	0	194	15	3	3	4.2	.986	C-40
1978 SEA A	41	.215	.333	93	20	5	0	2	2.2	6	7	12	19	0	1	0	127	9	3	1	3.4	.978	C-40
10 yrs.	367	.188	.279	892	168	37	1	14	1.6	72	82	95	191	4	17	3	1294	98	24	17	3.9	.983	C-342, 3B-9, 1B-1

Biff Pocoroba

POCOROBA, BIFF BENEDICT
B. July 25, 1953, Burbank, Calif.   BB TR 5'10"   175 lbs.

Year Team	Games	BA	SA	AB	H	2B	3B	HR	HR%	R	RBI	BB	SO	SB	AB	H	PO	A	E	DP	TC/G	FA	G by Pos
1975 ATL N	67	.255	.319	188	48	7	1	1	0.5	15	22	20	11	0	8	3	237	25	8	2	4.0	.970	C-62
1976	54	.241	.282	174	42	7	0	0	0.0	16	14	19	12	1	2	0	273	39	7	5	5.9	.978	C-54
1977	113	.290	.445	321	93	24	1	8	2.5	46	44	57	27	3	20	3	542	78	7	8	5.5	.989	C-100
1978	92	.242	.332	289	70	8	0	6	2.1	21	34	29	14	0	13	2	454	43	5	1	5.5	.990	C-79
1979	28	.316	.421	38	12	4	0	0	0.0	6	4	7	0	1	16	6	39	3	3	0	1.6	.933	C-7
1980	70	.265	.386	83	22	4	0	2	2.4	7	7	11	11	1	53	15	56	1	4	0	0.9	.934	C-10
1981	57	.180	.213	122	22	4	0	0	0.0	4	8	12	15	0	26	4	43	34	3	6	1.4	.963	3B-21, C-9
1982	56	.275	.383	120	33	7	0	2	1.7	5	22	13	12	0	17	4	144	16	2	2	2.9	.988	C-36, 3B-2
1983	55	.267	.367	120	32	6	0	2	1.7	11	16	12	7	0	20	1	166	12	3	1	3.3	.983	C-34
1984	4	.000	.000	2	0	0	0	0	0.0	1	0	2	0	0	0	0	0	0	0	0	0.0	–	
10 yrs.	596	.257	.351	1457	374	71	2	21	1.4	132	172	182	109	6	177	38	1954	251	42	25	3.8	.981	C-391, 3B-23

LEAGUE CHAMPIONSHIP SERIES

Year Team	Games	BA	SA	AB	H	2B	3B	HR	HR%	R	RBI	BB	SO	SB	AB	H	PO	A	E	DP	TC/G	FA	G by Pos
1982 ATL N	1	.000	.000	1	0	0	0	0	0.0	0	0	0	0	0	1	0	0	0	0	0	0.0	–	

Mike Poepping

POEPPING, MICHAEL HAROLD
B. Aug. 7, 1950, Little Falls, Minn.   BR TR 6'6"   230 lbs.

Year Team	Games	BA	SA	AB	H	2B	3B	HR	HR%	R	RBI	BB	SO	SB	AB	H	PO	A	E	DP	TC/G	FA	G by Pos
1975 MIN A	14	.135	.162	37	5	1	0	0	0.0	1	5	0	7	0	1	0	18	1	1	0	1.4	.950	OF-13

Jimmy Pofahl

POFAHL, JAMES WILLARD
B. June 18, 1917, Faribault, Minn.   D. Sept. 14, 1984, Owatonna, Minn.   BR TR 5'11"   185 lbs.

Year Team	Games	BA	SA	AB	H	2B	3B	HR	HR%	R	RBI	BB	SO	SB	AB	H	PO	A	E	DP	TC/G	FA	G by Pos
1940 WAS A	119	.234	.330	406	95	23	5	2	0.5	34	36	37	55	2	2	0	200	317	25	73	4.6	.954	SS-112, 2B-4
1941	22	.187	.280	75	14	3	2	0	0.0	9	6	10	11	1	1	0	30	55	6	8	4.1	.934	SS-21
1942	84	.208	.247	283	59	7	2	0	0.0	22	28	29	30	4	6	2	166	204	18	45	4.6	.954	SS-49, 2B-15, 3B-14
3 yrs.	225	.220	.295	764	168	33	9	2	0.3	65	70	76	96	7	8	2	396	576	49	126	4.5	.952	SS-182, 2B-19, 3B-14

John Poff

POFF, JOHN WILLIAM
B. Oct. 23, 1952, Chillicothe, Ohio   BL TL 6'2"   190 lbs.

Year Team	Games	BA	SA	AB	H	2B	3B	HR	HR%	R	RBI	BB	SO	SB	AB	H	PO	A	E	DP	TC/G	FA	G by Pos
1979 PHI N	12	.105	.158	19	2	1	0	0	0.0	2	1	1	6	0	6	0	8	0	1	0	0.8	.889	OF-4, 1B-1
1980 MIL A	19	.250	.368	68	17	1	2	1	1.5	7	7	3	7	0	2	1	38	0	1	0	2.1	.974	DH-7, OF-7, 1B-3
2 yrs.	31	.218	.322	87	19	2	2	1	1.1	9	8	4	11	0	8	1	46	0	2	0	1.5	.958	OF-11, DH-7, 1B-4

Aaron Pointer

POINTER, AARON ELTON (Hawk)
B. Apr. 19, 1942, Little Rock, Ark.   BR TR 6'2"   185 lbs.

Year Team	Games	BA	SA	AB	H	2B	3B	HR	HR%	R	RBI	BB	SO	SB	AB	H	PO	A	E	DP	TC/G	FA	G by Pos
1963 HOU N	2	.200	.200	5	1	0	0	0	0.0	0	0	0	1	0	0	0	1	0	0	0	0.5	1.000	OF-1
1966	11	.346	.500	26	9	1	0	1	3.8	5	5	5	6	1	1	0	13	3	0	1	1.5	1.000	OF-11

Year	Team		Games	BA	SA	AB	H	2B	3B	HR	HR%	R	RBI	BB	SO	SB	Pinch Hit AB	Pinch Hit H	PO	A	E	DP	TC/G	FA	G by Pos

Aaron Pointer *continued*

Year	Team		Games	BA	SA	AB	H	2B	3B	HR	HR%	R	RBI	BB	SO	SB	AB	H	PO	A	E	DP	TC/G	FA	G by Pos
1967			27	.157	.257	70	11	4	0	1	1.4	6	10	13	26	1	3	0	37	2	2	0	1.5	.951	OF-22
3 yrs.			40	.208	.317	101	21	5	0	2	2.0	11	15	18	33	2	4	0	51	5	2	1	1.5	.966	OF-34

Hugh Poland

POLAND, HUGH REID
B. Jan. 19, 1913, Tompkinsville, Ky.   D. Mar. 30, 1984, Guthrie, Ky.
BL TR 5'11½" 185 lbs.

Year	Team		Games	BA	SA	AB	H	2B	3B	HR	HR%	R	RBI	BB	SO	SB	AB	H	PO	A	E	DP	TC/G	FA	G by Pos
1943	2 teams		NY N (4G – .083)			BOS N (44G – .191)																			
"	total		48	.183	.242	153	28	7	1	0	0.0	5	15	5	11	0	5	1	143	11	5	3	3.3	.969	C-42
1944	BOS	N	8	.130	.174	23	3	1	0	0	0.0	1	2	0	1	0	2	0	31	0	2	0	4.1	.939	C-6
1946			4	.167	.333	6	1	1	0	0	0.0	0	0	0	0	0	2	1	6	0	0	0	1.5	1.000	C-2
1947	2 teams		PHI N (4G – .000)			CIN N (16G – .333)																			
"	total		20	.231	.269	26	6	1	0	0	0.0	1	2	1	4	0	14	4	11	2	2	0	0.8	.867	C-5
1948	CIN	N	3	.333	.333	3	1	0	0	0	0.0	0	0	0	0	0	3	1	0	0	0	0	0.0	–	
5 yrs.			83	.185	.242	211	39	10	1	0	0.0	7	19	6	16	0	26	7	191	13	9	3	2.6	.958	C-55

Mark Polhemus

POLHEMUS, MARK S. (Humpty Dumpty)
B. Oct. 4, 1862, Brooklyn, N. Y.   D. Nov. 12, 1923, Lynn, Mass.
5'6½" 185 lbs.

Year	Team		Games	BA	SA	AB	H	2B	3B	HR	HR%	R	RBI	BB	SO	SB	AB	H	PO	A	E	DP	TC/G	FA	G by Pos
1887	IND	N	20	.240	.253	75	18	1	0	0	0.0	6	8	2	9	4	0	0	21	8	10	0	2.0	.744	OF-20

Gus Polidor

POLIDOR, GUSTAVO ADOLFO
Born Gustavo Adolfo Polidor y Gonzalez.
B. Oct. 26, 1961, Caracas, Venezuela
BR TR 6' 170 lbs.

Year	Team		Games	BA	SA	AB	H	2B	3B	HR	HR%	R	RBI	BB	SO	SB	AB	H	PO	A	E	DP	TC/G	FA	G by Pos
1985	CAL	A	2	1.000	1.000	1	1	0	0	0	0.0	1	0	0	0	0	0	0	0	2	0	0	1.0	1.000	OF-1, SS-1
1986			6	.263	.316	19	5	1	0	0	0.0	1	1	1	0	0	0	0	10	13	0	2	3.8	1.000	2B-4, SS-1, 3B-1
1987			63	.263	.328	137	36	3	0	2	1.5	12	15	2	15	0	3	1	46	92	2	14	2.2	.986	SS-46, 3B-11, 2B-3
1988			54	.148	.185	81	12	3	0	0	0.0	4	4	3	11	0	8	2	31	54	1	9	1.6	.988	SS-25, 3B-22, 2B-3
1989	MIL	A	79	.194	.234	175	34	7	0	0	0.0	15	14	6	18	3	3	0	78	123	12	20	2.7	.944	3B-30, 2B-29, SS-21, DH-2
5 yrs.			204	.213	.262	413	88	14	0	2	0.5	33	34	12	44	3	14	3	165	284	15	45	2.3	.968	SS-94, 3B-64, 2B-39, DH-2, OF-1

Nick Polly

POLLY, NICHOLAS
Born Nicholas Polachanin.
B. Apr. 18, 1917, Chicago, Ill.
BR TR 5'11" 190 lbs.

Year	Team		Games	BA	SA	AB	H	2B	3B	HR	HR%	R	RBI	BB	SO	SB	AB	H	PO	A	E	DP	TC/G	FA	G by Pos
1937	BKN	N	10	.222	.222	18	4	0	0	0	0.0	2	2	0	1	0	3	1	4	13	3	0	2.0	.850	3B-7
1945	BOS	A	4	.143	.143	7	1	0	0	0	0.0	0	1	0	1	0	2	0	1	2	0	0	0.8	1.000	3B-2
2 yrs.			14	.200	.200	25	5	0	0	0	0.0	2	3	0	2	0	5	1	5	15	3	0	1.6	.870	3B-9

Luis Polonia

POLONIA, LUIS ANDREW
Born Luis Andrew Polonia y Almonte.
B. Dec. 10, 1964, Santiago, Dominican Republic
BB TL 5'8" 155 lbs.

Year	Team		Games	BA	SA	AB	H	2B	3B	HR	HR%	R	RBI	BB	SO	SB	AB	H	PO	A	E	DP	TC/G	FA	G by Pos
1987	OAK	A	125	.287	.398	435	125	16	10	4	0.9	78	49	32	64	29	8	3	235	2	5	1	1.9	.979	OF-104, DH-18
1988			84	.292	.378	288	84	11	4	2	0.7	51	27	21	40	24	9	2	155	3	2	1	1.9	.988	OF-76, DH-2
1989	2 teams		OAK A (59G – .286)			NY A (66G – .313)																			
"	total		125	.300	.388	433	130	17	6	3	0.7	70	46	25	44	22	14	6	231	9	4	2	2.0	.984	OF-108, DH-9
3 yrs.			334	.293	.389	1156	339	44	20	9	0.8	199	122	78	148	75	31	11	621	14	11	4	1.9	.983	OF-288, DH-29

LEAGUE CHAMPIONSHIP SERIES

Year	Team		Games	BA	SA	AB	H	2B	3B	HR	HR%	R	RBI	BB	SO	SB	AB	H	PO	A	E	DP	TC/G	FA	G by Pos
1988	OAK	A	3	.400	.400	5	2	0	0	0	0.0	0	0	1	0	0	0	0	2	0	0	0	0.7	1.000	OF-1

WORLD SERIES

Year	Team		Games	BA	SA	AB	H	2B	3B	HR	HR%	R	RBI	BB	SO	SB	AB	H	PO	A	E	DP	TC/G	FA	G by Pos
1988	OAK	A	3	.111	.111	9	1	0	0	0	0.0	1	0	0	2	0	2	0	2	0	0	0	0.7	1.000	OF-2

Carlos Ponce

PONCE, CARLOS ANTONIO
Born Carlos Antonio Ponce y Diaz.
B. Feb. 7, 1959, Rio Piedras, Puerto Rico
BR TR 5'10" 170 lbs.

Year	Team		Games	BA	SA	AB	H	2B	3B	HR	HR%	R	RBI	BB	SO	SB	AB	H	PO	A	E	DP	TC/G	FA	G by Pos
1985	MIL	A	21	.161	.242	62	10	2	0	1	1.6	4	5	1	9	0	3	0	67	3	0	7	3.3	1.000	1B-15, OF-6, DH-3

Ralph Pond

POND, RALPH BENJAMIN
B. May 4, 1888, Eau Claire, Wis.   D. Sept. 8, 1947, Cleveland, Ohio

Year	Team		Games	BA	SA	AB	H	2B	3B	HR	HR%	R	RBI	BB	SO	SB	AB	H	PO	A	E	DP	TC/G	FA	G by Pos
1910	BOS	A	1	.250	.250	4	1	0	0	0	0.0	0	0	0		1	0	0	0	0	1	0	1.0	–	OF-1

Harlin Pool

POOL, HARLON WELTY (Samson)
B. Mar. 12, 1908, Lakeport, Calif.   D. Feb. 15, 1963, Rodeo, Calif.
BL TR 5'10" 195 lbs.

Year	Team		Games	BA	SA	AB	H	2B	3B	HR	HR%	R	RBI	BB	SO	SB	AB	H	PO	A	E	DP	TC/G	FA	G by Pos
1934	CIN	N	99	.327	.433	358	117	22	5	2	0.6	38	50	17	18	3	6	3	196	8	10	1	2.2	.953	OF-94
1935			28	.176	.324	68	12	6	2	0	0.0	8	11	2	2	0	9	1	24	1	1	0	0.9	.962	OF-18
2 yrs.			127	.303	.415	426	129	28	7	2	0.5	46	61	19	20	3	15	4	220	9	11	1	1.9	.954	OF-112

Jim Poole

POOLE, JAMES ROBERT (Easy)
B. May 12, 1895, Taylorsville, N. C.   D. Jan. 2, 1975, Hickory, N. C.
BL TR 6' 175 lbs.

Year	Team		Games	BA	SA	AB	H	2B	3B	HR	HR%	R	RBI	BB	SO	SB	AB	H	PO	A	E	DP	TC/G	FA	G by Pos
1925	PHI	A	133	.298	.423	480	143	29	8	5	1.0	65	67	27	37	5	6	2	1166	65	23	102	9.4	.982	1B-123
1926			112	.294	.452	361	106	23	5	8	2.2	49	63	23	25	4	9	2	888	55	8	71	8.5	.992	1B-101, OF-1
1927			38	.222	.242	99	22	2	0	0	0.0	4	10	9	6	0	8	0	264	17	2	14	7.4	.993	1B-31
3 yrs.			283	.288	.415	940	271	54	13	13	1.4	118	140	59	68	9	23	4	2318	137	33	187	8.8	.987	1B-255, OF-1

Ray Poole

POOLE, RAYMOND HERMAN
B. Jan. 16, 1920, Salisbury, N. C.
BL TR 6' 180 lbs.

Year	Team		Games	BA	SA	AB	H	2B	3B	HR	HR%	R	RBI	BB	SO	SB	AB	H	PO	A	E	DP	TC/G	FA	G by Pos
1941	PHI	A	2	.000	.000	2	0	0	0	0	0.0	0	0	0	1	0	2	0	0	0	0	0	0.0	–	
1947			13	.231	.231	13	3	0	0	0	0.0	1	1	1	4	0	13	3	0	0	0	0	0.0	–	
2 yrs.			15	.200	.200	15	3	0	0	0	0.0	1	1	1	5	0	15	3	0	0	0	0	0.0	–	

Year	Team	Games	BA	SA	AB	H	2B	3B	HR	HR%	R	RBI	BB	SO	SB	Pinch Hit AB	H	PO	A	E	DP	TC/G	FA	G by Pos

Tom Poorman

POORMAN, THOMAS IVERSON
B. Oct. 14, 1857, Lock Haven, Pa.   D. Feb. 18, 1905, Lock Haven, Pa.

BL TR 5'10½" 170 lbs.

Year	Team	Games	BA	SA	AB	H	2B	3B	HR	HR%	R	RBI	BB	SO	SB	AB	H	PO	A	E	DP	TC/G	FA	G by Pos
1880	2 teams	BUF N (19G – .157)			CHI N (7G – .200)																			
"	total	26	.168	.232	95	16	2	2	0	0.0	8	1	0	15		0	0	19	25	9	0	2.0	.830	OF-17, P-13
1884	TOL AA	94	.233	.291	382	89	8	7	0	0.0	56			10		0	0	130	31	30	5	2.0	.843	OF-93, P-1
1885	BOS N	56	.238	.326	227	54	5	3	3	1.3	44	25	7	32		0	0	82	9	14	1	1.9	.867	OF-56
1886		96	.261	.361	371	97	16	6	3	0.8	72	41	19	52		0	0	145	21	18	6	1.9	.902	OF-96
1887	PHI AA	135	.265	.381	585	155	18	19	4	0.7	140		35		88	0	0	237	18	25	6	2.1	.911	OF-135, 2B-2, P-1
1888		97	.227	.316	383	87	16	6	2	0.5	76	44	31	46		0	0	115	8	14	1	1.4	.898	OF-97
6 yrs.		504	.244	.335	2043	498	65	43	12	0.6	396	111	102	99	134	0	0	728	112	110	19	1.9	.884	OF-494, P-15, 2B-2

Dave Pope

POPE, DAVID
B. June 17, 1925, Talladega, Ala.

BL TR 5'10½" 170 lbs.

Year	Team	Games	BA	SA	AB	H	2B	3B	HR	HR%	R	RBI	BB	SO	SB	AB	H	PO	A	E	DP	TC/G	FA	G by Pos
1952	CLE A	12	.294	.471	34	10	1	1	1	2.9	9	4	1	7	0	3	0	13	0	0	0	1.1	1.000	OF-10
1954		60	.294	.451	102	30	2	1	4	3.9	21	13	10	22	2	19	5	45	1	0	0	0.8	1.000	OF-29
1955	2 teams	CLE A (35G – .298)			BAL A (86G – .248)																			
"	total	121	.264	.393	326	86	13	4	7	2.1	38	52	28	65	5	31	12	214	3	3	1	1.8	.986	OF-104
1956	2 teams	BAL A (12G – .158)			CLE A (25G – .243)																			
"	total	37	.225	.281	89	20	3	1	0	0.0	7	4	1	19	0	13	2	37	1	0	0	1.0	1.000	OF-22
4 yrs.		230	.265	.390	551	146	19	7	12	2.2	75	73	40	113	7	66	19	309	5	3	1	1.4	.991	OF-165

WORLD SERIES

Year	Team	Games	BA	SA	AB	H	2B	3B	HR	HR%	R	RBI	BB	SO	SB	AB	H	PO	A	E	DP	TC/G	FA	G by Pos
1954	CLE A	3	.000	.000	3	0	0	0	0	0.0	0	0	1	1	0	3	0	0	0	0	0	0.0	–	OF-2

Paul Popovich

POPOVICH, PAUL EDWARD
B. Aug. 18, 1940, Flemington, W. Va.

BB TR 6' 175 lbs.
BB 1968

Year	Team	Games	BA	SA	AB	H	2B	3B	HR	HR%	R	RBI	BB	SO	SB	AB	H	PO	A	E	DP	TC/G	FA	G by Pos
1964	CHI N	1	1.000	1.000	1	1	0	0	0	0.0	0	0	0	0	0	1	1	0	0	0	0	0.0	–	2B-2
1966		2	.000	.000	6	0	0	0	0	0.0	0	0	0	2	0	0	0	5	3	1	1	4.5	.889	2B-2
1967		49	.214	.239	159	34	4	0	0	0.0	18	2	9	12	0	5	0	66	116	5	23	3.8	.973	SS-31, 2B-17, 3B-2
1968	LA N	134	.232	.270	418	97	8	1	2	0.5	35	25	29	37	1	4	0	232	349	11	68	4.4	.981	2B-89, SS-45, 3B-7
1969	2 teams	LA N (28G – .200)			CHI N (60G – .312)																			
"	total	88	.284	.328	204	58	6	0	1	0.5	31	18	19	18	0	25	8	93	136	6	30	2.7	.974	2B-48, SS-10, 3B-6, OF-1
1970	CHI N	78	.253	.355	186	47	5	1	4	2.2	22	20	18	18	0	26	2	75	97	4	26	2.3	.977	2B-22, SS-17, 3B-16
1971		89	.217	.310	226	49	7	1	4	1.8	24	28	14	17	0	30	2	78	146	4	27	2.6	.981	2B-40, SS-16, SS-1
1972		58	.194	.271	129	25	3	2	1	0.8	8	11	12	8	0	12	2	77	127	4	30	3.6	.981	2B-36, SS-8, 3B-1
1973		99	.236	.300	280	66	6	3	2	0.7	24	24	18	27	3	9	1	179	262	8	58	4.5	.982	2B-84, SS-9, 3B-1
1974	PIT N	59	.217	.265	83	18	2	1	0	0.0	9	5	5	10	0	38	9	24	38	2	9	1.1	.969	2B-12, SS-10
1975		25	.200	.225	40	8	1	0	0	0.0	5	1	3	2	0	15	3	17	21	1	3	1.6	.974	SS-8, 2B-8
11 yrs.		682	.233	.292	1732	403	42	9	14	0.8	176	134	127	151	4	165	28	846	1295	46	275	3.2	.979	2B-358, SS-139, 3B-49, OF-1

LEAGUE CHAMPIONSHIP SERIES

Year	Team	Games	BA	SA	AB	H	2B	3B	HR	HR%	R	RBI	BB	SO	SB	AB	H	PO	A	E	DP	TC/G	FA	G by Pos
1974	PIT N	3	.600	.600	5	3	0	0	0	0.0	0	0	1	0	0	3	3	2	0	0	0	0.7	1.000	SS-3

Tom Poquette

POQUETTE, THOMAS ARTHUR
B. Oct. 30, 1951, Eau Claire, Wis.

BL TR 5'10" 175 lbs.

Year	Team	Games	BA	SA	AB	H	2B	3B	HR	HR%	R	RBI	BB	SO	SB	AB	H	PO	A	E	DP	TC/G	FA	G by Pos
1973	KC A	21	.214	.250	28	6	1	0	0	0.0	4	3	1	4	1	0	0	19	1	3	0	1.1	.870	OF-20
1976		104	.302	.430	344	104	18	10	2	0.6	43	34	29	31	6	7	1	188	1	4	0	1.9	.979	OF-98, DH-2
1977		106	.292	.412	342	100	23	6	2	0.6	43	33	19	21	1	12	1	177	4	0	1	1.7	1.000	OF-96
1978		80	.216	.338	204	44	9	2	4	2.0	16	30	14	9	2	21	6	144	5	7	0	2.0	.955	OF-63, DH-1
1979	2 teams	KC A (21G – .192)			BOS A (63G – .331)																			
"	total	84	.311	.394	180	56	9	0	1	0.6	2	1.1	15	26	9	11	2	28	4	80	3	4	2	1.0	.954	OF-53, DH-4
1981	2 teams	BOS A (3G – .000)			TEX A (30G – .156)																			
"	total	33	.152	.167	66	10	1	0	0	0.0	2	7	5	1	0	12	3	26	0	1	0	0.8	.963	OF-20
1982	KC A	24	.145	.161	62	9	1	0	0	0.0	4	3	4	5	1	3	0	44	1	2	0	2.0	.957	OF-23
7 yrs.		452	.268	.373	1226	329	62	18	10	0.8	127	136	81	82	13	83	15	678	15	21	3	1.6	.971	OF-373, DH-7

LEAGUE CHAMPIONSHIP SERIES

Year	Team	Games	BA	SA	AB	H	2B	3B	HR	HR%	R	RBI	BB	SO	SB	AB	H	PO	A	E	DP	TC/G	FA	G by Pos
1976	KC A	5	.188	.313	16	3	2	0	0	0.0	1	4	2	3	0	0	0	13	0	0	0	2.6	1.000	OF-5
1977		2	.167	.167	6	1	0	0	0	0.0	0	0	0	0	0	1	0	3	0	0	0	1.5	1.000	OF-2
1978		1	.000	.000	1	0	0	0	0	0.0	0	0	0	0	0	0	0	0	0	0	0	0.0	–	OF-7
3 yrs.		8	.174	.261	23	4	2	0	0	0.0	1	4	2	3	0	1	0	16	0	0	0	2.0	1.000	OF-7

Bob Porter

PORTER, ROBERT LEE, JR.
B. July 22, 1959, Yuma, Ariz.

BL TL 5'10" 180 lbs.

Year	Team	Games	BA	SA	AB	H	2B	3B	HR	HR%	R	RBI	BB	SO	SB	AB	H	PO	A	E	DP	TC/G	FA	G by Pos
1981	ATL N	17	.286	.357	14	4	1	0	0	0.0	2	4	2	1	0	14	4	0	0	0	0	0.0	–	OF-4, 1B-1
1982		24	.111	.111	27	3	0	0	0	0.0	1	0	1	9	0	16	3	7	0	0	1	0.3	1.000	OF-4, 1B-1
2 yrs.		41	.171	.195	41	7	1	0	0	0.0	3	4	3	10	0	30	5	7	0	0	1	0.2	1.000	OF-4, 1B-1

Dan Porter

PORTER, DANIEL EDWARD
B. Oct. 17, 1931, Decatur, Ill.

BL TL 6' 164 lbs.

Year	Team	Games	BA	SA	AB	H	2B	3B	HR	HR%	R	RBI	BB	SO	SB	AB	H	PO	A	E	DP	TC/G	FA	G by Pos
1951	WAS A	13	.211	.211	19	4	0	0	0	0.0	2	0	2	4	0	9	2	4	0	0	0	0.3	1.000	OF-3

Darrell Porter

PORTER, DARRELL RAY
B. Jan. 17, 1952, Joplin, Mo.

BL TR 6' 193 lbs.

Year	Team	Games	BA	SA	AB	H	2B	3B	HR	HR%	R	RBI	BB	SO	SB	AB	H	PO	A	E	DP	TC/G	FA	G by Pos
1971	MIL A	22	.214	.329	70	15	2	0	2	2.9	4	9	9	20	2	1	0	108	18	3	2	5.9	.977	C-22
1972		18	.125	.196	56	7	1	0	1	1.8	2	2	5	21	0	0	0	113	8	3	3	6.9	.976	C-18
1973		117	.254	.457	350	89	19	2	16	4.6	50	67	57	85	5	9	4	372	47	10	9	3.7	.977	C-90, DH-19
1974		131	.241	.377	432	104	15	4	12	2.8	59	56	50	88	8	5	1	484	60	12	8	4.2	.978	C-117, DH-9
1975		130	.232	.418	409	95	12	5	18	4.4	66	60	89	77	2	2	0	532	82	13	10	4.8	.979	C-124, DH-2
1976		119	.208	.288	389	81	14	1	5	1.3	43	32	51	61	2	7	1	491	52	14	7	4.7	.975	C-111, DH-2
1977	KC A	130	.275	.452	425	117	21	3	16	3.8	61	60	53	70	1	5	2	663	61	13	4	5.7	.982	C-125, DH-1
1978		150	.265	.444	520	138	27	6	18	3.5	77	78	75	75	0	5	2	608	62	8	10	4.5	.988	C-145, DH-4
1979		157	.291	.484	533	155	23	10	20	3.8	101	112	121	65	3	0	0	628	68	13	15	4.5	.982	C-141, DH-15

Year	Team		Games	BA	SA	AB	H	2B	3B	HR	HR%	R	RBI	BB	SO	SB	Pinch Hit AB	Pinch Hit H	PO	A	E	DP	TC/G	FA	G by Pos

Darrell Porter *continued*

Year	Team	Lg	Games	BA	SA	AB	H	2B	3B	HR	HR%	R	RBI	BB	SO	SB	PH AB	PH H	PO	A	E	DP	TC/G	FA	G by Pos
1980			118	.249	.342	418	104	14	2	7	1.7	51	51	69	50	1	4	0	322	37	8	6	3.1	.978	C-81, DH-34
1981	STL	N	61	.224	.408	174	39	10	2	6	3.4	22	31	39	32	1	6	0	206	31	5	2	4.0	.979	C-52
1982			120	.231	.402	373	86	18	5	12	3.2	46	48	66	66	1	8	1	469	64	9	8	4.5	.983	C-111
1983			145	.262	.431	443	116	24	3	15	3.4	57	66	68	94	1	19	6	578	70	7	8	4.5	.989	C-133
1984			127	.232	.363	422	98	16	3	11	2.6	56	68	60	79	5	11	2	620	58	11	6	5.4	.984	C-122
1985			84	.221	.413	240	53	12	2	10	4.2	30	36	41	48	6	6	2	386	26	4	4	5.0	.990	C-82
1986	TEX	A	68	.265	.535	155	41	6	0	12	7.7	21	29	22	51	1	18	5	165	9	1	2	2.6	.994	C-25, DH-19
1987			85	.238	.423	130	31	3	0	7	5.4	19	21	30	43	0	36	7	21	2	0	2	0.3	1.000	DH-35, C-7, 1B-5
17 yrs.			1782	.247	.409	5539	1369	237	48	188	3.4	765	826	905	1025	39	142	33	6766	755	134	106	4.3	.982	C-1506, DH-140, 1B-5

LEAGUE CHAMPIONSHIP SERIES

Year	Team	Lg	Games	BA	SA	AB	H	2B	3B	HR	HR%	R	RBI	BB	SO	SB	PH AB	PH H	PO	A	E	DP	TC/G	FA	G by Pos
1977	KC	A	5	.333	.333	15	5	0	0	0	0.0	3	0	3	0	0	0	0	18	0	0	0	3.6	1.000	C-5
1978			4	.357	.429	14	5	1	0	0	0.0	1	3	2	0	0	0	0	21	1	0	1	5.5	1.000	C-4
1980			3	.100	.100	10	1	0	0	0	0.0	2	0	1	0	0	0	0	17	1	0	0	6.0	1.000	C-3
1982	STL	N	3	.556	.889	9	5	3	0	0	0.0	3	1	5	2	0	0	0	0	0	0	0	0.0	—	C-3
1985			5	.267	.333	15	4	1	0	0	0.0	1	0	5	4	0	0	0	25	2	1	1	5.6	.964	C-5
5 yrs.			20	.317	.397	63	20	5	0	0	0.0	10	4	16	6	0	0	0	81	4	1	2	4.3	.988	C-20

WORLD SERIES

Year	Team	Lg	Games	BA	SA	AB	H	2B	3B	HR	HR%	R	RBI	BB	SO	SB	PH AB	PH H	PO	A	E	DP	TC/G	FA	G by Pos
1980	KC	A	5	.143	.143	14	2	0	0	0	0.0	1	0	3	4	0	0	0	13	2	0	0	3.0	1.000	C-4
1982	STL	N	7	.286	.464	28	8	2	0	1	3.6	1	5	1	4	0	0	0	33	2	0	1	5.0	1.000	C-7
1985			5	.133	.133	15	2	0	0	0	0.0	0	0	2	5	0	0	0	36	4	1	1	8.0	1.000	C-5
3 yrs.			17	.211	.298	57	12	2	0	1	1.8	2	5	6	13	0	1	0	82	8	1	2	5.3	1.000	C-16

Dick Porter

PORTER, RICHARD TWILLEY (Twitchy)
B. Dec. 30, 1901, Princess Anne, Md. D. Sept. 24, 1974, Philadelphia, Pa.

BL TR 5'10" 170 lbs.

Year	Team	Lg	Games	BA	SA	AB	H	2B	3B	HR	HR%	R	RBI	BB	SO	SB	PH AB	PH H	PO	A	E	DP	TC/G	FA	G by Pos
1929	CLE	A	71	.328	.479	192	63	16	5	1	0.5	26	24	17	14	3	20	9	95	63	8	8	2.3	.952	OF-30, 2B-22
1930			119	.350	.498	480	168	43	8	4	0.8	100	57	55	31	3	1	1	189	12	8	4	1.8	.962	OF-118
1931			114	.312	.391	414	129	24	3	1	0.2	82	38	56	36	6	4	1	187	12	6	0	1.8	.971	OF-109, 2B-1
1932			146	.308	.420	621	191	42	8	4	0.6	106	62	64	43	2	1	0	269	2	5	0	1.9	.982	OF-145
1933			132	.267	.329	499	133	19	6	0	0.0	73	41	51	42	4	6	2	236	9	1	3	1.9	.996	OF-124
1934	2 teams			CLE A	(13G – .227)			BOS A	(80G – .302)																	
"	total		93	.291	.395	309	90	15	7	1	0.3	40	62	25	20	5	16	2	123	1	7	1	1.4	.947	OF-85
6 yrs.			675	.308	.414	2515	774	159	37	11	0.4	427	284	268	186	23	48	15	1099	99	35	16	1.8	.972	OF-611, 2B-23

Irv Porter

PORTER, IRVING MARBLE
B. May 17, 1888, Lynn, Mass. D. Feb. 20, 1971, Lynn, Mass.

BB TR 5'9" 155 lbs.

Year	Team	Lg	Games	BA	SA	AB	H	2B	3B	HR	HR%	R	RBI	BB	SO	SB	PH AB	PH H	PO	A	E	DP	TC/G	FA	G by Pos
1914	CHI	A	1	.250	.250	4	1	0	0	0	0.0	1	0	0	0	0	0	0	1	0	0	0	1.0	1.000	OF-1

J. W. Porter

PORTER, J. W. (Jay)
B. Jan. 17, 1933, Shawnee, Okla.

BR TR 6'2" 180 lbs.

Year	Team	Lg	Games	BA	SA	AB	H	2B	3B	HR	HR%	R	RBI	BB	SO	SB	PH AB	PH H	PO	A	E	DP	TC/G	FA	G by Pos
1952	STL	A	33	.250	.308	104	26	4	1	0	0.0	12	7	10	10	4	1	0	74	4	3	0	2.5	.963	OF-29, 3B-2
1955	DET	A	24	.236	.273	55	13	2	0	0	0.0	6	3	8	15	0	8	2	72	2	0	5	3.1	1.000	1B-6, OF-4, C-4
1956			14	.095	.095	21	2	0	0	0	0.0	0	3	0	8	0	10	0	9	0	1	1	0.7	.900	OF-2, C-2
1957			58	.250	.350	140	35	8	0	2	1.4	14	18	14	20	0	17	4	118	11	6	5	2.3	.956	OF-27, C-12, 1B-3
1958	CLE	A	40	.200	.353	85	17	1	0	4	4.7	13	19	9	23	0	17	3	108	10	0	1	3.0	1.000	C-20, 1B-4, 3B-1
1959	2 teams			WAS A	(37G – .226)			STL N	(23G – .212)																	
"	total		60	.223	.317	139	31	7	0	2	1.4	13	12	12	20	0	6	2	198	25	1	4	3.7	.996	C-53, 1B-3
6 yrs.			229	.228	.316	544	124	22	1	8	1.5	58	62	53	96	4	59	11	579	52	11	16	2.8	.983	C-91, OF-62, 1B-16, 3B-3

Matt Porter

PORTER, MATTHEW S.
B. 1859, N. Y.

Year	Team	Lg	Games	BA	SA	AB	H	2B	3B	HR	HR%	R	RBI	BB	SO	SB	PH AB	PH H	PO	A	E	DP	TC/G	FA	G by Pos
1884	KC	U	3	.083	.167	12	1	1	0	0	0.0	1		0	0		0	0	4	3	2	1	3.0	.778	OF-3

Leo Posada

POSADA, LEOPOLDO JESUS (Popy)
Born Leopoldo Jesus Posada y Hernandez.
B. Apr. 15, 1936, Havana, Cuba

BR TR 5'11" 175 lbs.

Year	Team	Lg	Games	BA	SA	AB	H	2B	3B	HR	HR%	R	RBI	BB	SO	SB	PH AB	PH H	PO	A	E	DP	TC/G	FA	G by Pos
1960	KC	A	10	.361	.556	36	13	0	2	1	2.8	8	2	3	7	1	1	0	11	1	0	0	1.2	1.000	OF-9
1961			116	.253	.366	344	87	10	4	7	2.0	37	53	36	84	0	12	5	205	8	6	0	1.9	.973	OF-102
1962			29	.196	.261	46	9	1	1	0	0.0	6	3	7	14	0	16	3	15	1	0	1	0.6	1.000	OF-11
3 yrs.			155	.256	.371	426	109	11	7	8	1.9	51	58	46	105	1	29	8	231	10	6	1	1.6	.976	OF-122

Lew Post

POST, LEWIS G.
B. Apr. 12, 1875, Hastings, Mich. D. Aug. 21, 1944, Chicago, Ill.

Year	Team	Lg	Games	BA	SA	AB	H	2B	3B	HR	HR%	R	RBI	BB	SO	SB	PH AB	PH H	PO	A	E	DP	TC/G	FA	G by Pos
1902	DET	A	3	.083	.083	12	1	0	0	0	0.0	2	2	0		0	0	0	4	0	1	0	1.7	.800	OF-3

Sam Post

POST, SAMUEL GILBERT
B. Nov. 17, 1896, Richmond, Va. D. Mar. 31, 1971, Portsmouth, Va.

BL TL 6'1½" 170 lbs.

Year	Team	Lg	Games	BA	SA	AB	H	2B	3B	HR	HR%	R	RBI	BB	SO	SB	PH AB	PH H	PO	A	E	DP	TC/G	FA	G by Pos
1922	BKN	N	9	.280	.280	25	7	0	0	0	0.0	3	4	4	4	1	1	1	54	1	1	1	6.2	.982	1B-8

Wally Post

POST, WALTER CHARLES
B. July 9, 1929, St. Wendelin, Ohio D. Jan. 6, 1982, St. Henry, Ohio

BR TR 6'1" 190 lbs.

Year	Team	Lg	Games	BA	SA	AB	H	2B	3B	HR	HR%	R	RBI	BB	SO	SB	PH AB	PH H	PO	A	E	DP	TC/G	FA	G by Pos
1949	CIN	N	6	.250	.250	8	2	0	0	0	0.0	1	1	0	3	0	1	0	3	0	1	0	0.7	.750	OF-3
1951			15	.220	.366	41	9	3	0	1	2.4	6	7	3	4	0	2	1	25	1	1	0	1.8	.963	OF-9
1952			19	.155	.276	58	9	1	0	2	3.4	5	7	4	20	0	3	0	38	1	0	0	2.1	1.000	OF-16
1953			11	.242	.364	33	8	1	0	1	3.0	3	4	4	4	1	0	0	22	2	1	0	2.3	.960	OF-11
1954			130	.255	.435	451	115	21	3	18	4.0	46	83	26	70	2	13	3	231	13	11	2	2.0	.957	OF-116
1955			154	.309	.574	601	186	33	3	40	6.7	116	109	60	102	7	0	0	298	13	7	2	2.1	.978	OF-154
1956			143	.249	.506	539	134	25	3	36	6.7	94	83	37	124	0	6	0	292	16	10	1	2.2	.969	OF-136
1957			134	.244	.437	467	114	26	2	20	4.3	68	74	33	84	2	10	2	252	12	4	4	2.0	.985	OF-124
1958	PHI	N	110	.282	.449	379	107	21	3	12	3.2	51	62	32	74	0	20	5	185	12	10	1	1.9	.952	OF-91

Year	Team	Games	BA	SA	AB	H	2B	3B	HR	HR%	R	RBI	BB	SO	SB	Pinch Hit AB	Pinch Hit H	PO	A	E	DP	TC/G	FA	G by Pos

Wally Post *continued*

Year	Team	Games	BA	SA	AB	H	2B	3B	HR	HR%	R	RBI	BB	SO	SB	PH AB	PH H	PO	A	E	DP	TC/G	FA	G by Pos
1959		132	.254	.457	468	119	17	6	22	4.7	62	94	36	**101**	0	12	3	226	12	2	3	1.8	.992	OF-120
1960	2 teams		PHI N	(34G – .286)		CIN N	(77G – .281)																	
"	total	111	.282	.520	333	94	20	1	19	5.7	47	50	37	75	0	24	2	168	9	2	0	1.6	.989	OF-89
1961	CIN N	99	.294	.585	282	83	16	3	20	7.1	44	57	22	61	0	25	7	133	7	6	3	1.5	.959	OF-81
1962		109	.263	.498	285	75	10	3	17	6.0	43	62	32	67	1	27	9	110	5	8	0	1.1	.935	OF-90
1963	2 teams		CIN N	(5G – .000)		MIN A	(21G – .191)																	
"	total	26	.167	.315	54	9	0	1	2	3.7	7	6	2	18	0	12	0	17	0	0	0	0.7	1.000	OF-13
1964	CLE A	5	.000	.000	8	0	0	0	0	0.0	1	0	3	4	0	3	0	2	0	1	0	0.6	.667	OF-2
15 yrs.		1204	.266	.485	4007	1064	194	28	210	5.2	594	699	331	813	19	159	34	2002	103	64	15	1.8	.970	OF-1055

WORLD SERIES

Year	Team	Games	BA	SA	AB	H	2B	3B	HR	HR%	R	RBI	BB	SO	SB	PH AB	PH H	PO	A	E	DP	TC/G	FA	G by Pos
1961	CIN N	5	.333	.556	18	6	1	0	1	5.6	3	2	0	1	0	0	0	8	0	0	0	1.6	1.000	OF-5

Mike Potter

POTTER, MICHAEL GARY
B. May 16, 1951, Montebello, Calif.

BR TR 6'1" 190 lbs.

Year	Team	Games	BA	SA	AB	H	2B	3B	HR	HR%	R	RBI	BB	SO	SB	PH AB	PH H	PO	A	E	DP	TC/G	FA	G by Pos
1976	STL N	9	.000	.000	16	0	0	0	0	0.0	0	6	0	5	0	5	0	9	0	0	0	1.0	1.000	OF-4
1977		5	.000	.000	7	0	0	0	0	0.0	0	0	1	2	0	5	0	0	0	0	0	0.0	–	OF-1
2 yrs.		14	.000	.000	23	0	0	0	0	0.0	0	0	1	8	0	10	0	9	0	0	0	0.6	1.000	OF-5

Dan Potts

POTTS, DANIEL
B. Kent, Ohio   Deceased.

Year	Team	Games	BA	SA	AB	H	2B	3B	HR	HR%	R	RBI	BB	SO	SB	PH AB	PH H	PO	A	E	DP	TC/G	FA	G by Pos
1892	WAS N	1	.250	.250	4	1	0	0	0	0.0	0	0	0	1	0	0	0	4	3	0	0	7.0	1.000	C-1

John Potts

POTTS, JOHN FREDERICK (Fred)
B. Feb. 6, 1887, Tipp City, Ohio   D. Sept. 5, 1962, Cleveland, Ohio

BL TR 5'7" 165 lbs.

Year	Team	Games	BA	SA	AB	H	2B	3B	HR	HR%	R	RBI	BB	SO	SB	PH AB	PH H	PO	A	E	DP	TC/G	FA	G by Pos
1914	KC F	41	.265	.333	102	27	4	0	1	1.0	14	9	25		7	8	1	40	2	3	2	1.1	.933	OF-31

Ken Poulsen

POULSEN, KEN STERLING
B. Aug. 4, 1947, Van Nuys, Calif.

BL TR 6'1" 190 lbs.

Year	Team	Games	BA	SA	AB	H	2B	3B	HR	HR%	R	RBI	BB	SO	SB	PH AB	PH H	PO	A	E	DP	TC/G	FA	G by Pos
1967	BOS A	5	.200	.400	5	1	1	0	0	0.0	0	0	0	2	0	2	0	0	2	1	0	0.6	.667	3B-2, SS-1

Abner Powell

POWELL, CHARLES ABNER
B. Dec. 15, 1860, Shenandoah, Pa.   D. Aug. 7, 1953, New Orleans, La.

BR TR 5'7" 160 lbs.

Year	Team	Games	BA	SA	AB	H	2B	3B	HR	HR%	R	RBI	BB	SO	SB	PH AB	PH H	PO	A	E	DP	TC/G	FA	G by Pos
1884	WAS U	48	.283	.387	191	54	10	5	0	0.0	36		3			0	0	55	46	18	0	2.5	.849	OF-30, P-18, 3B-2, SS-1, 2B-1
1886	2 teams		BAL AA	(11G – .179)		CIN AA	(19G – .230)																	
"	total	30	.212	.274	113	24	3	2	0	0.0	17		5			0	0	30	48	17	4	3.2	.821	OF-17, P-11, SS-6
2 yrs.		78	.257	.345	304	78	13	7	0	0.0	53		8			0	0	85	94	35	4	2.7	.836	OF-47, P-29, SS-7, 3B-2, 2B-1

Alonzo Powell

POWELL, ALONZO SIDNEY
B. Dec. 12, 1964, San Francisco, Calif.

BR TR 6'2" 190 lbs.

Year	Team	Games	BA	SA	AB	H	2B	3B	HR	HR%	R	RBI	BB	SO	SB	PH AB	PH H	PO	A	E	DP	TC/G	FA	G by Pos
1987	MON N	14	.195	.268	41	8	3	0	0	0.0	3	4	5	17	0	4	0	13	0	0	0	0.9	1.000	OF-11

Bob Powell

POWELL, ROBERT LEROY
B. Oct. 17, 1933, Flint, Mich.

BR TR 6'1" 190 lbs.

Year	Team	Games	BA	SA	AB	H	2B	3B	HR	HR%	R	RBI	BB	SO	SB	PH AB	PH H	PO	A	E	DP	TC/G	FA	G by Pos
1955	CHI A	1	–	–	0	0	0	0	0	–	0	0	0	0	0	0	0	0	0	0	0	0.0	–	
1957		1	–	–	0	0	0	0	0	–	1	0	0	0	0	0	0	0	0	0	0	0.0	–	
2 yrs.		2	–	–	0	0	0	0	0	–	1	0	0	0	0	0	0	0	0	0	0	0.0	–	

Boog Powell

POWELL, JOHN WESLEY
B. Aug. 17, 1941, Lakeland, Fla.

BL TR 6'4½" 230 lbs.

Year	Team	Games	BA	SA	AB	H	2B	3B	HR	HR%	R	RBI	BB	SO	SB	PH AB	PH H	PO	A	E	DP	TC/G	FA	G by Pos
1961	BAL A	4	.077	.077	13	1	0	0	0	0.0	0	1	0	2	0	1	0	3	0	0	0	0.8	1.000	OF-3
1962		124	.243	.398	400	97	13	2	15	3.8	44	53	38	79	1	10	2	194	6	6	0	1.6	.970	OF-112, 1B-1
1963		140	.265	.470	491	130	22	2	25	5.1	67	82	49	87	1	3	1	316	18	9	11	2.5	.974	OF-121, 1B-23
1964		134	.290	**.606**	424	123	17	0	39	9.2	74	99	76	91	0	12	2	223	19	5	6	1.8	.980	OF-124, 1B-5
1965		144	.248	.407	472	117	20	2	17	3.6	54	72	71	93	1	8	1	658	53	5	50	5.0	.993	1B-78, OF-71
1966		140	.287	.532	491	141	18	0	34	6.9	78	109	67	125	0	4	2	1094	68	13	96	8.4	.989	1B-136
1967		125	.234	.366	415	97	14	1	13	3.1	53	55	55	94	1	13	4	903	64	14	82	7.8	.986	1B-114
1968		154	.249	.411	550	137	21	1	22	4.0	60	85	73	97	7	4	1	1293	79	14	102	9.0	.990	1B-149
1969		152	.304	.559	533	162	25	0	37	6.9	83	121	72	76	1	7	1	1192	84	7	105	8.4	.995	1B-144
1970		154	.297	.549	526	156	28	0	35	6.7	82	114	104	80	1	8	2	1209	89	10	107	8.5	.992	1B-145
1971		128	.256	.459	418	107	19	0	22	5.3	59	92	82	64	1	4	1	1031	67	5	97	8.6	.995	1B-124
1972		140	.252	.434	465	117	20	1	21	4.5	53	81	65	92	4	7	1	1116	70	15	111	8.6	.988	1B-133
1973		114	.265	.395	370	98	13	1	11	3.0	52	54	85	64	0	6	3	988	77	12	95	9.4	.989	1B-111
1974		110	.265	.413	344	91	13	1	12	3.5	37	45	52	58	0	8	1	866	61	4	102	8.5	.996	1B-102, DH-1
1975	CLE A	134	.297	.524	435	129	18	0	27	6.2	64	86	59	72	1	11	4	997	69	3	92	8.0	.997	1B-121, DH-5
1976		95	.215	.338	293	63	9	0	9	3.1	29	33	41	43	1	10	3	698	61	10	76	8.1	.987	1B-89
1977	LA N	50	.244	.244	41	10	0	0	0	0.0	0	5	12	9	0	36	8	15	0	1	1	0.3	.938	1B-4
17 yrs.		2042	.266	.462	6681	1776	270	11	339	5.1	889	1187	1001	1226	20	152	37	12796	880	133	1133	6.8	.990	1B-1479, OF-431, DH-6

LEAGUE CHAMPIONSHIP SERIES

Year	Team	Games	BA	SA	AB	H	2B	3B	HR	HR%	R	RBI	BB	SO	SB	PH AB	PH H	PO	A	E	DP	TC/G	FA	G by Pos
1969	BAL A	3	.385	.615	13	5	0	0	1	7.7	2	2	2	0	0	0	0	34	0	0	2	11.3	1.000	1B-3
1970		3	.429	.786	14	6	2	0	1	7.1	2	6	0	3	0	0	0	24	1	0	3	8.3	1.000	1B-3
1971		3	.300	.900	10	3	0	0	2	20.0	4	3	3	3	0	0	0	28	2	0	3	10.0	1.000	1B-3
1973		1	.000	.000	4	0	0	0	0	0.0	0	1	0	0	0	0	0	7	0	0	0	7.0	1.000	1B-1
1974		2	.125	.125	8	1	0	0	0	0.0	1	1	0	1	0	0	0	22	1	0	1	11.5	1.000	1B-2
5 yrs.		12	.306	.592	49	15	2	0	4	8.2	9	11	5	7	0	0	0	115	4	0	9	9.9	1.000	1B-12

WORLD SERIES

Year	Team	Games	BA	SA	AB	H	2B	3B	HR	HR%	R	RBI	BB	SO	SB	PH AB	PH H	PO	A	E	DP	TC/G	FA	G by Pos
1966	BAL A	4	.357	.429	14	5	1	0	0	0.0	1	1	0	1	0	0	0	27	1	0	3	7.0	1.000	1B-4

Year	Team	Games	BA	SA	AB	H	2B	3B	HR	HR%	R	RBI	BB	SO	SB	Pinch Hit AB	H	PO	A	E	DP	TC/G	FA	G by Pos

Boog Powell *continued*

Year	Team	Games	BA	SA	AB	H	2B	3B	HR	HR%	R	RBI	BB	SO	SB	AB	H	PO	A	E	DP	TC/G	FA	G by Pos
1969		5	.263	.263	19	5	0	0	0	0.0	0	0	1	4	0	0	0	46	2	1	3	9.8	.980	1B-5
1970		5	.294	.706	17	5	1	0	2	11.8	6	5	5	2	0	0	0	38	2	0	3	8.0	1.000	1B-5
1971		7	.111	.111	27	3	0	0	0	0.0	1	1	1	3	0	0	0	52	4	1	1	8.1	.982	1B-7
4 yrs.		21	.234	.338	77	18	2	0	2	2.6	8	7	7	10	0	0	0	163	9	2	10	8.3	.989	1B-21

Hosken Powell

POWELL, HOSKEN
B. May 14, 1955, Selma, Ala.

BL TL 6'1" 175 lbs.

Year	Team	Games	BA	SA	AB	H	2B	3B	HR	HR%	R	RBI	BB	SO	SB	AB	H	PO	A	E	DP	TC/G	FA	G by Pos
1978	MIN A	121	.247	.333	381	94	20	2	3	0.8	55	31	45	31	11	7	2	219	9	4	2	1.9	.983	OF-117
1979		104	.293	.379	338	99	17	3	2	0.6	49	36	33	25	5	15	2	165	6	4	3	1.7	.977	OF-93, DH-5
1980		137	.262	.355	485	127	17	5	6	1.2	58	35	32	46	14	14	2	265	11	9	1	2.1	.968	OF-129
1981		80	.239	.326	264	63	11	3	2	0.8	30	25	17	31	7	11	3	122	6	4	1	1.7	.970	OF-64, DH-8
1982	TOR A	112	.275	.389	265	73	13	4	3	1.1	43	26	12	23	4	30	10	111	2	3	0	1.0	.974	OF-75, DH-19
1983		40	.169	.205	83	14	0	0	1	1.2	6	7	5	8	2	12	2	52	1	1	1	1.4	.981	OF-33, DH-1, 1B-1
6 yrs.		594	.259	.349	1816	470	78	17	17	0.9	241	160	144	164	43	89	21	934	35	25	8	1.7	.975	OF-511, DH-33, 1B-1

Jake Powell

POWELL, ALVIN JACOB
B. July 15, 1908, Silver Spring, Md. D. Nov. 4, 1948, Washington, D. C.

BR TR 5'11½" 180 lbs.

Year	Team	Games	BA	SA	AB	H	2B	3B	HR	HR%	R	RBI	BB	SO	SB	AB	H	PO	A	E	DP	TC/G	FA	G by Pos
1930	WAS A	3	.000	.000	4	0	0	0	0	0.0	1	0	0	1	0	1	0	3	0	0	0	1.0	1.000	OF-2
1934		9	.286	.343	35	10	2	0	0	0.0	6	1	4	2	1	0	0	18	3	1	0	2.4	.955	OF-9
1935		139	.312	.428	551	172	26	10	6	1.1	88	98	37	37	15	2	0	361	12	9	4	2.7	.976	OF-136, 2B-2
1936	2 teams		WAS A (53G – .290)		NY A	(87G – .306)																		
"	total	140	.299	.418	538	161	24	8	8	1.5	102	78	52	51	26	4	3	127	2	6	1	1.0	.956	OF-137
1937	NY A	97	.263	.364	365	96	23	3	3	0.8	54	45	25	36	7	3	0	201	5	4	2	2.2	.981	OF-94
1938		45	.256	.378	164	42	12	1	2	1.2	27	20	15	20	3	1	0	86	1	2	0	2.0	.978	OF-43
1939		31	.244	.349	86	21	4	1	1	1.2	12	9	3	8	1	2	0	56	1	1	0	1.9	.983	OF-23
1940		12	.185	.185	27	5	0	0	0	0.0	3	2	1	4	0	2	0	15	1	0	0	1.3	1.000	OF-7
1943	WAS A	37	.265	.371	132	35	10	2	0	0.0	14	20	5	13	3	3	1	83	4	2	0	2.4	.978	OF-33
1944		96	.240	.278	367	88	9	1	1	0.3	29	37	16	26	7	5	0	196	5	4	3	2.1	.980	OF-90, 3B-1
1945	2 teams		WAS A (31G – .194)		PHI N	(48G – .231)																		
"	total	79	.218	.255	271	59	7	0	1	0.4	17	17	16	21	2	4	1	123	6	4	3	1.7	.970	OF-71
11 yrs.		688	.271	.363	2540	689	116	26	22	0.9	353	327	174	219	65	29	6	1269	40	33	10	2.0	.975	OF-645, 2B-2, 3B-1

WORLD SERIES

Year	Team	Games	BA	SA	AB	H	2B	3B	HR	HR%	R	RBI	BB	SO	SB	AB	H	PO	A	E	DP	TC/G	FA	G by Pos
1936	NY A	6	.455	.636	22	10	1	0	1	4.5	8	5	4	4	1	0	0	12	0	0	0	2.0	1.000	OF-6
1937		1	.000	.000	1	0	0	0	0	0.0	0	0	0	1	0	1	0	0	0	0	0	0.0	—	
1938		1			0	0	0	0	0	—	0	0	0	0	0	0	0	0	0	0	0	0.0	—	OF-1
3 yrs.		8	.435	.609	23	10	1	0	1	4.3	8	5	4	5	1	1	0	12	0	0	0	1.5	1.000	OF-7

Jim Powell

POWELL, JAMES E.
B. Aug., 1859, Richmond, Va. Deceased.

5'10" 170 lbs.

Year	Team	Games	BA	SA	AB	H	2B	3B	HR	HR%	R	RBI	BB	SO	SB	AB	H	PO	A	E	DP	TC/G	FA	G by Pos
1884	RIC AA	41	.245	.351	151	37	8	4	0	0.0	23		7			0	0	380	18	24	15	10.3	.943	1B-41

Martin Powell

POWELL, MARTIN J.
B. Mar. 25, 1856, Fitchburg, Mass. D. Feb. 5, 1888, Fitchburg, Mass.

BL TL 6'4½"

Year	Team	Games	BA	SA	AB	H	2B	3B	HR	HR%	R	RBI	BB	SO	SB	AB	H	PO	A	E	DP	TC/G	FA	G by Pos
1881	DET N	55	.338	.429	219	74	9	4	1	0.5	47	38	15	9		0	0	513	17	31	47	10.2	.945	1B-55, C-1
1882		80	.240	.287	338	81	13	0	1	0.3	44	29	19	27		0	0	680	14	44	27	9.2	.940	1B-80
1883		101	.273	.344	421	115	17	5	1	0.2	76		28	23		0	0	995	32	54	62	10.7	.950	1B-101
1884	CIN U	43	.319	.378	185	59	4	2	1	0.5	46		13			0	0	463	11	30	19	11.7	.940	1B-43
1885	PHI AA	19	.160	.240	75	12	0	3	0	0.0	5		1			0	0	178	3	5	6	9.8	.973	1B-19
5 yrs.		298	.275	.342	1238	341	43	14	4	0.3	218	67	76	59		0	0	2829	77	164	161	10.3	.947	1B-298, C-1

Paul Ray Powell

POWELL, PAUL RAY
B. Mar. 19, 1948, San Angelo, Tex.

BR TR 5'11" 185 lbs.

Year	Team	Games	BA	SA	AB	H	2B	3B	HR	HR%	R	RBI	BB	SO	SB	AB	H	PO	A	E	DP	TC/G	FA	G by Pos
1971	MIN A	20	.161	.258	31	5	0	0	1	3.2	7	2	3	12	0	2	0	24	0	0	0	1.2	1.000	OF-15
1973	LA N	2	.000	.000	1	0	0	0	0	0.0	0	0	0	1	0	1	0	0	0	0	0	0.0	—	OF-1
1975		8	.200	.300	10	2	1	0	0	0.0	2	0	1	2	0	0	0	18	3	1	1	2.8	.955	C-7, OF-1
3 yrs.		30	.167	.262	42	7	1	0	1	2.4	9	2	4	15	0	3	0	42	3	1	1	1.5	.978	OF-17, C-7

Ray Powell

POWELL, RAYMOND RAETH (Rabbit)
B. Nov. 20, 1888, Siloam Springs, Ark. D. Oct. 16, 1962, Chillicothe, Mo.

BL TR 5'9" 160 lbs.

Year	Team	Games	BA	SA	AB	H	2B	3B	HR	HR%	R	RBI	BB	SO	SB	AB	H	PO	A	E	DP	TC/G	FA	G by Pos
1913	DET A	2	—	—	0	0	0	0	0	—	0	0	0	0	0	0	0	0	0	0	0	0.0	—	OF-1
1917	BOS N	88	.272	.356	357	97	10	4	4	1.1	42	30	24	54	12	0	0	231	14	6	2	2.9	.976	OF-88
1918		53	.213	.303	188	40	7	5	0	0.0	31	20	29	30	2	0	0	121	8	7	2	2.6	.949	OF-53
1919		123	.236	.326	470	111	12	12	2	0.4	51	33	41	79	16	1	0	213	21	12	7	2.0	.951	OF-122
1920		147	.225	.314	609	137	12	12	6	1.0	69	29	44	82	10	0	0	370	25	18	5	2.8	.956	OF-147
1921		149	.306	.462	624	191	25	18	12	1.9	114	74	58	85	6	0	0	377	21	19	3	2.8	.954	OF-149
1922		142	.296	.409	550	163	22	11	6	1.1	82	37	59	66	3	5	0	377	18	8	2	2.8	.980	OF-136
1923		97	.302	.420	338	102	20	4	4	1.2	57	38	45	36	1	8	3	214	8	14	0	2.4	.941	OF-84
1924		74	.261	.335	188	49	9	1	1	0.5	21	15	21	28	1	23	6	117	9	7	3	1.8	.947	OF-46
9 yrs.		875	.268	.375	3324	890	117	67	35	1.1	467	276	321	461	51	37	9	2020	124	91	24	2.6	.959	OF-826

Tom Power

POWER, THOMAS E.
B. San Francisco, Calif. D. Feb. 25, 1898, San Francisco, Calif.

5'11" 164 lbs.

Year	Team	Games	BA	SA	AB	H	2B	3B	HR	HR%	R	RBI	BB	SO	SB	AB	H	PO	A	E	DP	TC/G	FA	G by Pos
1890	BAL AA	38	.208	.248	125	26	3	1	0	0.0	11		13		6	0	0	289	39	20	12	9.2	.943	1B-26, 2B-12

Vic Power

POWER, VICTOR
Born Victor Pellot y Power.
B. Nov. 1, 1931, Arecibo, Puerto Rico

BR TR 6' 186 lbs.

Year	Team	Games	BA	SA	AB	H	2B	3B	HR	HR%	R	RBI	BB	SO	SB	AB	H	PO	A	E	DP	TC/G	FA	G by Pos
1954	PHI A	127	.255	.366	462	118	17	5	8	1.7	36	38	19	19	2	7	3	406	26	6	20	3.4	.986	OF-101, 1B-21, SS-1, 3B-1
1955	KC A	147	.319	.505	596	190	34	10	19	3.2	91	76	35	27	0	3	1	1281	130	10	140	9.7	.993	1B-144
1956		127	.309	.447	530	164	21	5	14	2.6	77	63	24	16	2	4	2	807	200	12	113	8.0	.988	1B-76, 2B-47, OF-7

Year	Team		Games	BA	SA	AB	H	2B	3B	HR	HR%	R	RBI	BB	SO	SB	Pinch Hit AB	Pinch Hit H	PO	A	E	DP	TC/G	FA	G by Pos

Vic Power *continued*

Year	Team		Games	BA	SA	AB	H	2B	3B	HR	HR%	R	RBI	BB	SO	SB	PH AB	PH H	PO	A	E	DP	TC/G	FA	G by Pos
1957			129	.259	.385	467	121	15	1	14	3.0	48	42	19	21	3	10	2	992	106	3	95	8.5	.997	1B-113, OF-6, 2B-4
1958 2 teams	KC	A (52G – .302)		CLE	A	(93G – .317)																			
" total			145	.312	.490	590	184	37	10	16	2.7	98	80	20	14	3	3	0	806	220	12	122	7.2	.988	1B-91, 3B-42, 2B-28, SS-2, OF-1
1959	CLE	A	147	.289	.412	595	172	31	6	10	1.7	102	60	40	22	9	0	0	1094	174	10	105	8.7	.992	1B-121, 2B-21, 3B-7
1960			147	.288	.395	580	167	26	3	10	1.7	69	84	24	20	9	0	0	1184	151	5	146	9.1	.996	1B-147, SS-5, 3B-4
1961			147	.268	.369	563	151	34	4	5	0.9	64	63	38	16	4	0	0	1174	164	10	108	9.2	.993	1B-141, 2B-7
1962	MIN	A	144	.290	.481	611	177	28	2	16	2.6	80	63	22	35	7	3	2	1195	134	10	133	9.3	.993	1B-142, 2B-2
1963			138	.270	.384	541	146	28	2	10	1.8	65	52	22	24	3	7	2	947	129	12	95	7.9	.989	1B-124, 2B-18, 3B-5
1964 3 teams	MIN	A (19G – .222)		LA	A	(68G – .249)			PHI	N	(18G – .208)														
" total			105	.239	.306	314	75	12	0	3	1.0	24	17	11	20	1	14	2	517	104	5	43	6.0	.992	1B-77, 3B-28, 2B-6
1965	CAL	A	124	.259	.320	197	51	7	1	1	0.5	11	20	5	13	2	15	2	430	54	2	38	3.9	.996	1B-107, 2B-6, 3B-2
12 yrs.			1627	.284	.411	6046	1716	290	49	126	2.1	765	658	279	247	45	66	16	10833	1592	97	1158	7.7	.992	1B-1304, 2B-139, OF-115, 3B-89, SS-8

Johnny Powers

POWERS, JOHN CALVIN
B. July 8, 1929, Birmingham, Ala.

BL TR 6'1" 185 lbs.

Year	Team		Games	BA	SA	AB	H	2B	3B	HR	HR%	R	RBI	BB	SO	SB	PH AB	PH H	PO	A	E	DP	TC/G	FA	G by Pos
1955	PIT	N	2	.250	.250	4	1	0	0	0	0.0	0	0	0	0	0			4	0	0	0	2.0	1.000	OF-2
1956			11	.048	.048	21	1	0	0	0	0.0	0	0	1	4	0	6	0	9	0	0	0	0.8	1.000	OF-5
1957			20	.286	.543	35	10	3	0	2	5.7	7	8	5	9	0	9	3	14	1	0	0	0.8	1.000	OF-8, 2B-1
1958			57	.183	.268	82	15	1	0	2	2.4	6	2	8	19	0	38	8	27	1	0	0	0.5	1.000	OF-14
1959	CIN	N	43	.256	.488	43	11	2	1	2	4.7	8	4	3	13	0	36	8	4	0	0	0	0.1	1.000	OF-5
1960 2 teams	BAL	A (10G – .111)		CLE	A	(8G – .167)																			
" total			18	.133	.233	30	4	1	0	0	0.0	5	0	5	3	0	9	0	13	0	1	0	0.8	.929	OF-9
6 yrs.			151	.195	.330	215	42	7	2	6	2.8	26	14	22	48	0	98	19	71	2	1	0	0.5	.986	OF-43, 2B-1

Les Powers

POWERS, LESLIE EDWIN
B. Nov. 5, 1909, Ballard, Wash.   D. Nov. 13, 1978, Santa Monica, Calif.

BL TL 6' 175 lbs.

Year	Team		Games	BA	SA	AB	H	2B	3B	HR	HR%	R	RBI	BB	SO	SB	PH AB	PH H	PO	A	E	DP	TC/G	FA	G by Pos
1938	NY	N	3	.000	.000	3	0	0	0	0	0.0	0	0	0	0	0	0	0	0	0	0	0	0.0	–	
1939	PHI	N	19	.346	.404	52	18	1	1	0	0.0	7	2	4	6	0	4	1	112	4	2	10	6.2	.983	1B-13
2 yrs.			22	.327	.382	55	18	1	1	0	0.0	7	2	4	7	0	7	1	112	4	2	10	5.4	.983	1B-13

Mike Powers

POWERS, ELLIS FOREE
B. Mar. 2, 1906, Crestwood, Ky.   D. Dec. 2, 1983, Louisville, Ky.

BL TL 6'1" 185 lbs.

Year	Team		Games	BA	SA	AB	H	2B	3B	HR	HR%	R	RBI	BB	SO	SB	PH AB	PH H	PO	A	E	DP	TC/G	FA	G by Pos
1932	CLE	A	14	.182	.303	33	6	4	0	0	0.0	4	5	2	2	0	5	0	11	0	1	0	0.9	.917	OF-8
1933			24	.277	.362	47	13	2	1	0	0.0	6	2	6	6	2	11	3	20	0	1	0	0.9	.952	OF-11
2 yrs.			38	.238	.338	80	19	6	1	0	0.0	10	7	8	8	2	16	3	31	0	2	0	0.9	.939	OF-19

Mike Powers

POWERS, MICHAEL RILEY
B. Sept. 22, 1870, Pittsfield, Mass.   D. Apr. 26, 1909, Philadelphia, Pa.

BR TR

Year	Team		Games	BA	SA	AB	H	2B	3B	HR	HR%	R	RBI	BB	SO	SB	PH AB	PH H	PO	A	E	DP	TC/G	FA	G by Pos
1898	LOU	N	34	.273	.404	99	27	4	3	1	1.0	13	19	5		1	5	0	112	21	4	3	4.0	.971	C-22, 1B-6, OF-1
1899 2 teams	LOU	N (49G – .207)		WAS	N	(14G – .263)																			
" total			63	.217	.285	207	45	10	2	0	0.0	18	25	7		1	5	0	208	41	16	6	4.2	.940	C-50, 1B-8
1901	PHI	A	116	.251	.341	431	108	26	5	1	0.2	53	47	18		10	2	1	430	137	29	7	5.1	.951	C-111, 1B-3
1902			71	.264	.325	246	65	7	1	2	0.8	35	39	14		3	1	0	250	112	18	6	5.4	.953	C-68, 1B-3
1903			75	.227	.279	247	56	11	1	0	0.0	19	23	5		1	2	0	398	88	9	6	6.6	.982	C-66, 1B-7
1904			57	.190	.207	184	35	3	0	0	0.0	11	11	6		3	0	0	339	52	14	6	7.1	.965	C-56, OF-1
1905 3 teams	PHI	A (19G – .131)		NY	A	(11G – .182)			PHI	A	(21G – .183)														
" total			51	.162	.169	154	25	1	0	0	0.0	11	12	4		4	0	0	290	54	14	6	7.0	.961	C-44, 1B-7
1906	PHI	A	58	.157	.162	185	29	1	0	0	0.0	5	7	1		2	0	0	299	79	10	2	6.7	.974	C-57, 1B-1
1907			59	.182	.201	159	29	3	0	0	0.0	9	9	7		1	0	0	313	80	7	8	6.8	.983	C-59
1908			62	.180	.227	172	31	6	1	0	0.0	8	7	5		1	0	0	309	76	13	3	6.4	.967	C-60, 1B-2
1909			1	.250	.250	4	1	0	0	0	0.0	1	0	0		0	0	0	9	1	0	0	10.0	1.000	C-1
11 yrs.			647	.216	.269	2088	451	72	13	4	0.2	183	199	72		27	15	1	2957	741	134	53	5.9	.965	C-594, 1B-37, OF-2

WORLD SERIES

Year	Team		Games	BA	SA	AB	H	2B	3B	HR	HR%	R	RBI	BB	SO	SB	PH AB	PH H	PO	A	E	DP	TC/G	FA	G by Pos
1905	PHI	A	3	.143	.286	7	1	0	0	0	0.0	0	0	0	0	0	0	0	13	4	0	1	5.7	1.000	C-3

Phil Powers

POWERS, PHILLIP B. (Grandmother)
B. July 26, 1854, New York, N. Y.   D. Dec. 22, 1914, New York, N. Y.

BR TR 5'7" 166 lbs.

Year	Team		Games	BA	SA	AB	H	2B	3B	HR	HR%	R	RBI	BB	SO	SB	PH AB	PH H	PO	A	E	DP	TC/G	FA	G by Pos
1878	CHI	N	8	.161	.258	31	5	1	1	0	0.0	2	2	1	5		0	0	47	19	5		8.9	.930	C-8
1880	BOS	N	37	.143	.183	126	18	5	0	0	0.0	11	10	5	15		0	0	152	59	37	6	6.7	.851	C-37, OF-2
1881	CLE	N	5	.067	.067	15	1	0	0	0	0.0	1	0	1	2		0	0	17	5	1	1	4.6	.957	C-4, 3B-1
1882	CIN	AA	16	.217	.267	60	13	1	1	0	0.0	4		3			0	0	89	13	7	3	6.8	.936	C-10, 1B-5, OF-1
1883			30	.246	.325	114	28	1	4	0	0.0	16		3			0	0	74	20	12	0	3.5	.887	C-17, OF-13
1884			34	.138	.146	130	18	1	0	0	0.0	10		5			0	0	160	56	26	5	7.1	.893	C-31, OF-2, 1B-2
1885 2 teams	CIN	AA (15G – .267)		BAL	AA	(9G – .118)																			
" total			24	.213	.245	94	20	3	0	0	0.0	12		1			0	0	101	30	25	1	6.5	.840	C-23, OF-1
7 yrs.			154	.181	.223	570	103	12	6	0	0.0	56	12	19	22		0	0	640	202	113	16	6.2	.882	C-130, OF-19, 1B-7, 3B-1

Carl Powis

POWIS, CARL EDGAR (Jug)
B. Jan. 11, 1928, Philadelphia, Pa.

BR TR 6' 185 lbs.

Year	Team		Games	BA	SA	AB	H	2B	3B	HR	HR%	R	RBI	BB	SO	SB	PH AB	PH H	PO	A	E	DP	TC/G	FA	G by Pos
1957	BAL	A	15	.195	.317	41	8	3	1	0	0.0	4	2	7	9	2	2	0	19	1	2	0	1.5	.909	OF-13

Johnny Pramesa

PRAMESA, JOHN STEVEN
B. Aug. 28, 1925, Barton, Ohio

BR TR 6'2" 210 lbs.

Year	Team		Games	BA	SA	AB	H	2B	3B	HR	HR%	R	RBI	BB	SO	SB	PH AB	PH H	PO	A	E	DP	TC/G	FA	G by Pos
1949	CIN	N	17	.240	.400	25	6	1	0	1	4.0	2	2	3	5	0	4	1	27	1	1	0	1.7	.966	C-13
1950			74	.307	.425	228	70	10	1	5	2.2	14	30	19	15	0	1	0	328	37	7	2	5.0	.981	C-73
1951			72	.229	.348	227	52	5	2	6	2.6	12	22	5	17	0	9	2	241	27	9	4	3.8	.968	C-63
1952	CHI	N	22	.283	.370	46	13	1	0	1	2.2	1	5	4	4	0	19	5	62	6	3	3	3.2	.958	C-17
4 yrs.			185	.268	.386	526	141	17	3	13	2.5	29	59	31	41	0	19	5	658	71	20	9	4.0	.973	C-166

Year	Team	Games	BA	SA	AB	H	2B	3B	HR	HR%	R	RBI	BB	SO	SB	Pinch Hit AB	Pinch Hit H	PO	A	E	DP	TC/G	FA	G by Pos

Del Pratt

PRATT, DERRILL BURNHAM
B. Jan. 10, 1888, Walhalla, S. C.   D. Sept. 30, 1977, Texas City, Tex.
BR TR 5'11" 175 lbs.

Year	Team	Games	BA	SA	AB	H	2B	3B	HR	HR%	R	RBI	BB	SO	SB	AB	H	PO	A	E	DP	TC/G	FA	G by Pos
1912	STL A	151	.302	.426	570	172	26	15	5	0.9	76	69	36		24	0	0	339	407	51	61	5.3	.936	2B-121, SS-21, OF-8, 3B-1
1913		155	.296	.402	592	175	31	13	2	0.3	60	87	40	57	37	0	0	440	431	42	60	5.9	.954	2B-146, 1B-9
1914		158	.283	.411	584	165	34	13	5	0.9	85	65	50	45	37	0	0	372	425	46	48	5.3	.945	2B-152, OF-5, SS-1
1915		159	.291	.394	602	175	31	11	3	0.5	61	78	26	43	32	0	0	417	441	31	82	5.6	.965	2B-158
1916		158	.267	.391	596	159	35	12	5	0.8	64	103	54	56	26	0	0	438	491	33	74	6.1	.966	2B-158
1917		123	.247	.338	450	111	22	8	1	0.2	40	53	33	36	18	0	0	346	355	29	64	5.9	.960	2B-119, 1B-4
1918	NY A	126	.275	.356	477	131	19	7	2	0.4	65	55	35	26	12	0	0	340	386	23	82	5.9	.969	2B-126
1919		140	.292	.393	527	154	27	7	4	0.8	69	56	36	24	22	0	0	315	491	26	64	5.9	.969	2B-140
1920		154	.314	.427	574	180	37	8	4	0.7	84	97	50	24	12	0	0	354	515	26	77	5.8	.971	2B-154
1921	BOS A	135	.324	.461	521	169	36	10	5	1.0	80	100	44	10	8	1	0	283	408	28	90	5.3	.961	2B-134
1922		154	.301	.427	607	183	44	7	6	1.0	73	86	53	20	7	0	0	362	484	30	80	5.7	.966	2B-154
1923	DET A	101	.310	.391	297	92	18	3	0	0.0	43	40	25	9	5	8	4	281	179	18	32	4.7	.962	2B-60, 1B-17, 3B-12
1924		121	.303	.399	429	130	32	3	1	0.2	56	77	31	10	6	1	0	621	225	23	73	7.2	.974	2B-63, 1B-51, 3B-4
13 yrs.		1835	.292	.403	6826	1996	392	117	43	0.6	856	966	513	360	246	10	4	4908	5238	406	887	5.8	.962	2B-1685, 1B-81, SS-22, 3B-17, OF-13

Frank Pratt

PRATT, FRANCIS BRUCE (Truckhorse)
B. Aug. 24, 1897, Blocton, Ala.   D. Mar. 8, 1974, Centreville, Ala.
BL TR 5'9½" 155 lbs.

Year	Team	Games	BA	SA	AB	H	2B	3B	HR	HR%	R	RBI	BB	SO	SB	AB	H	PO	A	E	DP	TC/G	FA	G by Pos
1921	CHI A	1	.000	.000	1	0	0	0	0	0.0	0	0	0	0	0	1	0	0	0	0	0	0.0	—	

Larry Pratt

PRATT, LESTER JOHN
B. Oct. 8, 1886, Gibson City, Ill.   D. Jan. 8, 1969, Peoria, Ill.
BR TR 6' 183 lbs.

Year	Team	Games	BA	SA	AB	H	2B	3B	HR	HR%	R	RBI	BB	SO	SB	AB	H	PO	A	E	DP	TC/G	FA	G by Pos
1914	BOS A	5	.000	.000	4	0	0	0	0	0.0	0	0	0	4	0	0	0	7	5	1	0	2.6	.923	C-5
1915	2 teams	BKN F (20G – .184)			NWK F (5G – .500)																			
"	total	25	.208	.321	53	11	3	0	1	1.9	7	2	5		4	4	0	59	22	4	0	3.4	.953	C-20
2 yrs.		30	.193	.298	57	11	3	0	1	1.8	7	2	5	4	4	4	0	66	27	5	0	3.3	.949	C-25

Mel Preibisch

PREIBISCH, MELVIN ALOYSIUS (Primo)
B. Nov. 23, 1914, Sealy, Tex.   D. Apr. 12, 1980, Sealy, Tex.
BR TR 5'11" 185 lbs.

Year	Team	Games	BA	SA	AB	H	2B	3B	HR	HR%	R	RBI	BB	SO	SB	AB	H	PO	A	E	DP	TC/G	FA	G by Pos
1940	BOS N	11	.225	.275	40	9	2	0	0	0.0	3	5	2	4	0	0	0	29	1	0	0	2.7	1.000	OF-11
1941		5	.000	.000	4	0	0	0	0	0.0	0	0	1	2	0	2	0	1	0	0	0	0.2	1.000	OF-2
2 yrs.		16	.205	.250	44	9	2	0	0	0.0	3	5	3	6	0	2	0	30	1	0	0	1.9	1.000	OF-13

Bobby Prescott

PRESCOTT, GEORGE BERTRAND
B. Mar. 27, 1931, Colon, Panama
BR TR 5'11" 180 lbs.

Year	Team	Games	BA	SA	AB	H	2B	3B	HR	HR%	R	RBI	BB	SO	SB	AB	H	PO	A	E	DP	TC/G	FA	G by Pos
1961	KC A	10	.083	.083	12	1	0	0	0	0.0	0	0	2	5	0	7	1	0	0	0	0	0.0	—	OF-2

Jim Presley

PRESLEY, JAMES ARTHUR
B. Oct. 23, 1961, Pensacola, Fla.
BR TR 6'1" 176 lbs.

Year	Team	Games	BA	SA	AB	H	2B	3B	HR	HR%	R	RBI	BB	SO	SB	AB	H	PO	A	E	DP	TC/G	FA	G by Pos
1984	SEA A	70	.227	.402	251	57	12	1	10	4.0	27	36	6	63	1	1	0	48	113	7	12	2.4	.958	3B-69, DH-1
1985		155	.275	.484	570	157	33	1	28	4.9	71	84	44	100	2	1	0	82	335	17	24	2.8	.961	3B-154
1986		155	.265	.463	616	163	33	4	27	4.4	83	107	32	172	0	0	0	110	308	15	31	2.8	.965	3B-155
1987		152	.247	.433	575	142	23	6	24	4.2	78	88	38	157	2	1	1	113	315	21	29	3.0	.953	3B-148, SS-4, DH-1
1988		150	.230	.355	544	125	26	0	14	2.6	50	62	36	114	3	0	0	112	234	22	25	2.5	.940	3B-146, DH-4
1989		117	.236	.385	390	92	20	1	12	3.1	42	41	21	107	0	6	1	222	169	18	29	3.5	.956	3B-90, 1B-30, DH-1
6 yrs.		799	.250	.426	2946	736	147	13	115	3.9	351	418	177	713	8	9	2	687	1474	100	150	2.8	.956	3B-762, 1B-30, DH-7, SS-4

Walt Preston

PRESTON, WALTER B.
B. 1870, Richmond, Va.   Deceased.
BL TR 6' 175 lbs.

Year	Team	Games	BA	SA	AB	H	2B	3B	HR	HR%	R	RBI	BB	SO	SB	AB	H	PO	A	E	DP	TC/G	FA	G by Pos
1895	LOU N	50	.279	.365	197	55	6	4	1	0.5	42	24	17	17	11	0	0	71	54	33	5	3.2	.791	OF-26, 3B-25

Jackie Price

PRICE, JOHN THOMAS REID
B. Nov. 13, 1912, Winborn, Miss.   D. Oct. 2, 1967, San Francisco, Calif.
BL TR 5'10½" 150 lbs.

Year	Team	Games	BA	SA	AB	H	2B	3B	HR	HR%	R	RBI	BB	SO	SB	AB	H	PO	A	E	DP	TC/G	FA	G by Pos
1946	CLE A	7	.231	.231	13	3	0	0	0	0.0	1	0	0	0	0	2	1	7	11	1	1	2.7	.947	SS-4

Jim Price

PRICE, JIMMIE WILLIAM
B. Oct. 13, 1941, Harrisburg, Pa.
BR TR 6' 192 lbs.

Year	Team	Games	BA	SA	AB	H	2B	3B	HR	HR%	R	RBI	BB	SO	SB	AB	H	PO	A	E	DP	TC/G	FA	G by Pos
1967	DET A	44	.261	.304	92	24	4	0	0	0.0	9	8	4	10	0	20	5	139	8	4	1	3.4	.974	C-24
1968		64	.174	.273	132	23	4	0	3	2.3	12	13	13	14	0	22	5	223	14	1	1	3.7	.996	C-42
1969		72	.234	.417	192	45	8	0	9	4.7	21	28	18	20	0	21	2	337	18	4	1	5.0	.989	C-51
1970		52	.182	.326	132	24	2	0	5	3.8	12	15	21	23	0	12	1	266	8	6	2	5.4	.979	C-38
1971		29	.241	.333	54	13	2	0	1	1.9	4	7	6	3	0	2	0	99	7	2	2	3.7	.981	C-25
5 yrs.		261	.214	.341	602	129	22	0	18	3.0	58	71	62	70	0	77	13	1064	55	17	10	4.4	.985	C-180

WORLD SERIES

| 1968 | DET A | 2 | .000 | .000 | 2 | 0 | 0 | 0 | 0 | 0.0 | 0 | 0 | 0 | 1 | 0 | 2 | 0 | 0 | 0 | 0 | 0 | 0.0 | — | |

Joe Price

PRICE, JOSEPH PRESTON (Lumber)
B. Apr. 10, 1897, Milligan College, Tenn.   D. Jan. 15, 1961, Washington, D. C.
BR TR 6'1½" 187 lbs.

Year	Team	Games	BA	SA	AB	H	2B	3B	HR	HR%	R	RBI	BB	SO	SB	AB	H	PO	A	E	DP	TC/G	FA	G by Pos
1928	NY N	1	.000	.000	1	0	0	0	0	0.0	0	0	0	0	0	0	0	0	0	0	0	0.0	—	OF-1

Bob Prichard

PRICHARD, ROBERT ALEXANDER
B. Oct. 21, 1917, Paris, Tex.
BL TL 6'1" 195 lbs.

Year	Team	Games	BA	SA	AB	H	2B	3B	HR	HR%	R	RBI	BB	SO	SB	AB	H	PO	A	E	DP	TC/G	FA	G by Pos
1939	WAS A	26	.235	.294	85	20	5	0	0	0.0	8	8	19	16	0	0	0	251	13	2	30	10.2	.992	1B-26

Gerry Priddy

PRIDDY, GERALD EDWARD
B. Nov. 9, 1919, Los Angeles, Calif.   D. Mar. 3, 1980, North Hollywood, Calif.
BR TR 5'11½" 180 lbs.

Year	Team	Games	BA	SA	AB	H	2B	3B	HR	HR%	R	RBI	BB	SO	SB	AB	H	PO	A	E	DP	TC/G	FA	G by Pos
1941	NY A	56	.213	.270	174	37	7	0	1	0.6	18	26	18	16	4	2	1	167	119	8	46	5.3	.973	2B-31, 3B-14, 1B-10

Year	Team	Games	BA	SA	AB	H	2B	3B	HR	HR%	R	RBI	BB	SO	SB	Pinch Hit AB	Pinch Hit H	PO	A	E	DP	TC/G	FA	G by Pos

Gerry Priddy *continued*

Year	Team	Games	BA	SA	AB	H	2B	3B	HR	HR%	R	RBI	BB	SO	SB	PH AB	PH H	PO	A	E	DP	TC/G	FA	G by Pos
1942		59	.280	.381	189	53	9	2	2	1.1	23	28	31	27	0	3	1	146	114	9	26	4.6	.967	3B-35, 1B-11, 2B-8, SS-3
1943	WAS A	149	.271	.359	560	152	31	3	4	0.7	68	62	67	76	5	0	0	398	451	27	111	5.9	.969	2B-134, SS-15, 3B-1
1946		138	.254	.364	511	130	22	8	6	1.2	54	58	57	73	9	0	0	378	428	32	105	6.1	.962	2B-138
1947		147	.214	.283	505	108	20	3	3	0.6	42	49	62	79	7	1	0	382	405	16	89	5.5	.980	2B-146
1948	STL A	151	.296	.443	560	166	40	9	8	1.4	96	79	86	71	6	3	0	407	471	29	132	6.0	.968	2B-146
1949		145	.290	.414	544	158	26	4	11	2.0	83	63	80	81	5	0	0	407	415	27	96	5.9	.968	2B-145
1950	DET A	157	.277	.401	618	171	26	6	13	2.1	104	75	95	95	2	0	0	440	542	19	150	6.4	.981	2B-154, SS-1
1951		154	.260	.360	584	152	22	6	8	1.4	73	57	69	73	4	0	0	438	464	18	118	6.0	.980	2B-75
1952		75	.283	.430	279	79	23	3	4	1.4	37	20	42	29	1	0	0	211	209	14	48	5.8	.968	2B-45, 1B-11, 3B-2
1953		65	.235	.301	196	46	6	2	1	0.5	14	24	17	19	1	9	2	203	118	5	35	5.0	.985	
11 yrs.		1296	.265	.373	4720	1252	232	46	61	1.3	612	541	624	639	44	18	4	3577	3736	204	956	5.8	.973	2B-1179, 3B-52, 1B-32, SS-19

WORLD SERIES

Year	Team	Games	BA	SA	AB	H	2B	3B	HR	HR%	R	RBI	BB	SO	SB	PH AB	PH H	PO	A	E	DP	TC/G	FA	G by Pos
1942	NY A	3	.100	.200	10	1	1	0	0	0.0	0	1	1	0	0	0	0	22	4	1	1	9.0	.963	1B-3, 3B-1

Johnnie Priest

PRIEST, JOHN GOODING B. June 23, 1886, St. Joseph, Mo. D. Nov. 4, 1979, Washington, D. C. BR TR 5'11" 170 lbs.

Year	Team	Games	BA	SA	AB	H	2B	3B	HR	HR%	R	RBI	BB	SO	SB	PH AB	PH H	PO	A	E	DP	TC/G	FA	G by Pos
1911	NY A	7	.143	.143	21	3	0	0	0	0.0	2	2	2		3	0	0	8	10	3	0	3.0	.857	2B-5, 3B-2
1912		2	.500	.500	2	1	0	0	0	0.0	1	1	0		0	2	1	0	0	0	0	0.0		
2 yrs.		9	.174	.174	23	4	0	0	0	0.0	3	3	2		3	2	1	8	10	3	0	2.3	.857	2B-5, 3B-2

Tom Prince

PRINCE, THOMAS ALBERT B. Aug. 13, 1964, Kankakee, Ill. BR TR 5'11" 185 lbs.

Year	Team	Games	BA	SA	AB	H	2B	3B	HR	HR%	R	RBI	BB	SO	SB	PH AB	PH H	PO	A	E	DP	TC/G	FA	G by Pos
1987	PIT N	4	.222	.667	9	2	1	0	1	11.1	1	2	0	2	0	0	0	14	3	0	0	4.3	1.000	C-4
1988		29	.176	.203	74	13	2	0	0	0.0	3	6	4	15	0	2	0	108	8	2	1	4.1	.983	C-28
1989		21	.135	.212	52	7	4	0	0	0.0	1	5	6	12	1	0	0	85	11	4	1	4.8	.960	C-21
3 yrs.		54	.163	.237	135	22	7	0	1	0.7	5	13	10	29	1	2	0	207	22	6	2	4.4	.974	C-53

Walter Prince

PRINCE, WALTER FARR B. May 9, 1861, Amherst, N. H. D. Mar. 2, 1938, Bristol, N. H. BL TR 5'9" 150 lbs.

Year	Team	Games	BA	SA	AB	H	2B	3B	HR	HR%	R	RBI	BB	SO	SB	PH AB	PH H	PO	A	E	DP	TC/G	FA	G by Pos
1883	LOU AA	4	.182	.182	11	2	0	0	0	0.0	1		0			0	0	14	2	6	0	5.5	.727	OF-2, 1B-2, SS-1
1884 3 teams	DET N (7G – .143)							WAS AA (43G – .217)			WAS U (1G – .250)													
" total		51	.209	.246	191	40	3	2	0	0.0	22		16	4		0	0	417	4	33	19	8.9	.927	1B-44, OF-7
2 yrs.		55	.208	.243	202	42	3	2	0	0.0	23		16	4		0	0	431	6	39	19	8.7	.918	1B-46, OF-9, SS-1

Buddy Pritchard

PRITCHARD, HAROLD WILLIAM B. Jan. 25, 1936, South Gate, Calif. BR TR 6'1" 195 lbs.

Year	Team	Games	BA	SA	AB	H	2B	3B	HR	HR%	R	RBI	BB	SO	SB	PH AB	PH H	PO	A	E	DP	TC/G	FA	G by Pos
1957	PIT N	23	.091	.091	11	1	0	0	0	0.0	4	0	5	0	0	11	8	1	3	0.9	.950	SS-10, 2B-3

George Proeser

PROESER, GEORGE (White Wings) B. May 30, 1864, Cincinnati, Ohio D. Oct. 14, 1941, New Burlington, Ohio BL TL 5'10" 190 lbs.

Year	Team	Games	BA	SA	AB	H	2B	3B	HR	HR%	R	RBI	BB	SO	SB	PH AB	PH H	PO	A	E	DP	TC/G	FA	G by Pos
1888	CLE AA	7	.304	.391	23	7	0	0	0	0.0	5	1	1					0	11	0		1.9	.846	P-7
1890	SYR AA	13	.245	.358	53	13	1	1	1	1.9	11		10			1	0	16	1	2	0	1.5	.895	OF-13
2 yrs.		20	.263	.368	76	20	3	1	1	1.3	16	1	11			1	0	16	12	4	0	1.6	.875	OF-13, P-7

Jake Propst

PROPST, WILLIAM JACOB B. Mar. 10, 1895, Kennedy, Ala. D. Feb. 24, 1967, Columbus, Miss. BL TR 5'10" 165 lbs.

Year	Team	Games	BA	SA	AB	H	2B	3B	HR	HR%	R	RBI	BB	SO	SB	PH AB	PH H	PO	A	E	DP	TC/G	FA	G by Pos
1923	WAS A	1	.000	.000	1	0	0	0	0	0.0	0	0	0	0	0	1	0	0	0	0	0	0.0	–	

Doc Prothro

PROTHRO, JAMES THOMPSON B. July 16, 1893, Memphis, Tenn. D. Oct. 14, 1971, Memphis, Tenn. Manager 1939-41. BR TR 5'10½" 170 lbs.

Year	Team	Games	BA	SA	AB	H	2B	3B	HR	HR%	R	RBI	BB	SO	SB	PH AB	PH H	PO	A	E	DP	TC/G	FA	G by Pos
1920	WAS A	6	.385	.385	13	5	0	0	0	0.0	2	2	0	4	0	2	1	4	5	0	4	1.5	1.000	SS-2, 3B-2
1923		6	.250	.500	8	2	0	1	0	0.0	2	3	1	3	0	0	0	5	11	0	0	2.7	1.000	3B-6
1924		46	.333	.465	159	53	11	5	0	0.0	17	24	15	11	4	0	0	40	68	10	6	2.6	.915	3B-45
1925	BOS A	119	.313	.383	415	130	23	3	0	0.0	44	51	52	21	9	7	0	122	216	20	17	3.0	.944	3B-108, SS-3
1926	CIN N	3	.200	.600	5	1	0	1	0	0.0	1	1	1	1	0	1	0	0	2	0	0	0.7	1.000	3B-2
5 yrs.		180	.318	.408	600	191	34	10	0	0.0	66	81	69	40	13	10	1	171	302	30	27	2.8	.940	3B-163, SS-5

Gibby Pruess

PRUESS, EARL HENRY B. Apr. 2, 1895, Chicago, Ill. D. Aug. 28, 1979, Branson, Mo. BR TR 5'10½" 170 lbs.

Year	Team	Games	BA	SA	AB	H	2B	3B	HR	HR%	R	RBI	BB	SO	SB	PH AB	PH H	PO	A	E	DP	TC/G	FA	G by Pos
1920	STL A	1	–	–	0	0	0	0	0	–	1	0	1	0	0	1	0	2	0	0	0	2.0	1.000	OF-1

Jim Pruett

PRUETT, JAMES CALVIN B. Dec. 16, 1917, Nashville, Tenn. BR TR 5'10" 178 lbs.

Year	Team	Games	BA	SA	AB	H	2B	3B	HR	HR%	R	RBI	BB	SO	SB	PH AB	PH H	PO	A	E	DP	TC/G	FA	G by Pos
1944	PHI A	3	.250	.250	4	1	0	0	0	0.0	1	0	1	0	0	1	0	7	1	0	1	2.7	1.000	C-2
1945		6	.222	.222	9	2	0	0	0	0.0	1	0	1	2	0	2	0	12	1	0	0	2.2	1.000	C-4
2 yrs.		9	.231	.231	13	3	0	0	0	0.0	2	0	2	2	0	3	0	19	2	0	1	2.3	1.000	C-6

Ron Pruitt

PRUITT, RONALD RALPH (Do-It) B. Oct. 21, 1951, Flint, Mich. BR TR 6' 185 lbs.

Year	Team	Games	BA	SA	AB	H	2B	3B	HR	HR%	R	RBI	BB	SO	SB	PH AB	PH H	PO	A	E	DP	TC/G	FA	G by Pos
1975	TEX A	14	.176	.176	17	3	0	0	0	0.0	1	3	0	0	0	21	5	0	0	1.9	1.000	C-13, OF-1
1976	CLE A	47	.267	.302	86	23	1	1	0	0.0	7	5	16	8	2	7	3	73	16	1	2	1.9	.989	OF-26, 3B-6, C-6, DH-4, 1B-1
1977		78	.288	.379	219	63	10	2	2	0.9	29	32	28	22	2	8	1	113	6	3	0	1.6	.975	OF-69, DH-4, C-4, 3B-1
1978		71	.235	.374	187	44	6	1	6	3.2	17	17	16	20	3	10	3	199	15	4	4	3.1	.982	C-48, OF-16, DH-5, 3B-2
1979		64	.283	.361	166	47	9	0	2	1.2	23	21	19	21	2	18	6	66	5	2	1	1.1	.973	OF-29, DH-14, C-11, 3B-3

Year	Team		Games	BA	SA	AB	H	2B	3B	HR	HR%	R	RBI	BB	SO	SB	Pinch Hit AB	Pinch Hit H	PO	A	E	DP	TC/G	FA	G by Pos

Ron Pruitt *continued*

Year	Team		Games	BA	SA	AB	H	2B	3B	HR	HR%	R	RBI	BB	SO	SB	PH AB	PH H	PO	A	E	DP	TC/G	FA	G by Pos
1980	2 teams	CLE A (23G – .306)				CHI A (33G – .300)																			
"	total		56	.302	.387	106	32	3	0	2	1.9	9	15	12	13	0	20	5	34	2	1	1	0.7	.973	OF-17, DH-9, 3B-5, C-5, 1B-1
1981	CLE	A	5	.000	.000	9	0	0	0	0	0.0	0	0	1	2	0	2	0	3	0	0	0	0.6	1.000	OF-3, DH-1, C-1
1982	SF	N	5	.500	.750	4	2	1	0	0	0.0	1	2	1	1	0	2	1	5	0	0	0	1.0	1.000	OF-1, C-1
1983			1	.000	.000	1	0	0	0	0	0.0	0	0	0	0	0	1	0	0	0	0	0	0.0		
9 yrs.			341	.269	.360	795	214	28	4	12	1.5	88	92	94	90	8	68	19	514	49	11	8	1.7	.981	OF-162, C-89, DH-37, 3B-17, 1B-2

Greg Pryor

PRYOR, GREGORY RUSSELL
B. Oct. 2, 1949, Marietta, Ohio

BR TR 6' 180 lbs.

Year	Team		Games	BA	SA	AB	H	2B	3B	HR	HR%	R	RBI	BB	SO	SB	PH AB	PH H	PO	A	E	DP	TC/G	FA	G by Pos
1976	TEX	A	5	.375	.375	8	3	0	0	0	0.0	1	1	0	1	0	0	0	4	8	0	1	2.4	1.000	2B-3, SS-1, 1B-1
1978	CHI	A	82	.261	.338	222	58	11	0	2	0.9	27	15	11	18	3	0	0	100	202	11	31	3.8	.965	2B-35, SS-28, 3B-20
1979			143	.275	.355	476	131	23	3	3	0.6	60	34	35	41	3	1	0	218	447	26	69	4.8	.962	SS-119, 2B-25, 3B-22
1980			122	.240	.325	338	81	18	4	1	0.3	32	29	12	35	2	5	1	130	344	15	55	4.0	.967	SS-76, 3B-41, 2B-5, DH-1
1981			47	.224	.237	76	17	1	0	0	0.0	4	6	6	8	0	1	0	27	65	6	8	2.1	.939	3B-27, SS-13, 2B-5
1982	KC	A	73	.270	.388	152	41	10	1	2	1.3	23	12	10	20	2	3	0	78	112	5	18	2.7	.974	3B-40, 2B-15, 1B-14, SS-7
1983			68	.217	.278	115	25	4	0	1	0.9	9	14	7	8	0	1	0	38	100	5	10	2.1	.965	3B-60, 1B-6, 2B-3
1984			123	.263	.356	270	71	11	1	4	1.5	32	25	12	28	0	3	1	87	190	8	27	2.3	.972	3B-105, 2B-22, SS-2, DH-1, 1B-1
1985			63	.219	.272	114	25	3	0	1	0.9	8	8	8	12	1	6	0	47	87	5	16	2.2	.964	3B-26, 2B-20, SS-13, DH-1, 1B-1
1986			63	.170	.205	112	19	4	0	0	0.0	7	7	3	14	1	4	0	30	88	6	15	2.0	.952	3B-35, SS-17, 2B-12, 1B-1
10 yrs.			789	.250	.327	1883	471	85	9	14	0.7	204	146	104	185	11	24	3	759	1643	88	250	3.2	.965	3B-377, SS-276, 2B-145, 1B-23, DH-3

LEAGUE CHAMPIONSHIP SERIES

| 1984 | KC | A | 1 | – | – | 0 | 0 | 0 | 0 | 0 | – | 0 | 0 | 0 | 0 | 0 | 0 | 0 | 1 | 0 | 0 | 0 | 1.0 | 1.000 | 3B-1 |

WORLD SERIES

| 1985 | KC | A | 1 | – | – | 0 | 0 | 0 | 0 | 0 | – | 0 | 0 | 0 | 0 | 0 | 0 | 0 | 0 | 1 | 0 | 0 | 1.0 | 1.000 | 3B-1 |

George Puccinelli

PUCCINELLI, GEORGE LAWRENCE (Count)
B. June 22, 1907, San Francisco, Calif. D. Apr. 16, 1956, San Francisco, Calif.

BR TR 6½" 190 lbs.

Year	Team		Games	BA	SA	AB	H	2B	3B	HR	HR%	R	RBI	BB	SO	SB	PH AB	PH H	PO	A	E	DP	TC/G	FA	G by Pos
1930	STL	N	11	.563	1.188	16	9	1	0	3	18.8	5	8	0	1	0	8	4	2	0	0	0	0.2	1.000	OF-3
1932			31	.278	.435	108	30	8	0	3	2.8	17	11	12	13	1	1	0	59	6	4	1	2.2	.942	OF-30
1934	STL	A	10	.231	.500	26	6	1	0	2	7.7	4	5	1	8	0	4	0	15	1	1	0	1.7	.941	OF-6
1936	PHI	A	135	.278	.429	457	127	30	3	11	2.4	83	78	65	70	2	17	3	245	11	14	1	2.0	.948	OF-117
4 yrs.			187	.283	.453	607	172	40	3	19	3.1	109	102	78	92	3	30	7	321	18	19	2	1.9	.947	OF-156

WORLD SERIES

| 1930 | STL | N | 1 | .000 | .000 | 1 | 0 | 0 | 0 | 0 | 0.0 | 0 | 0 | 0 | 0 | 0 | 1 | 0 | 0 | 0 | 0 | 0 | 0.0 | – | |

Kirby Puckett

PUCKETT, KIRBY
B. Mar. 14, 1961, Chicago, Ill.

BR TR 5'8" 178 lbs.

Year	Team		Games	BA	SA	AB	H	2B	3B	HR	HR%	R	RBI	BB	SO	SB	PH AB	PH H	PO	A	E	DP	TC/G	FA	G by Pos
1984	MIN	A	128	.296	.336	557	165	12	5	0	0.0	63	31	16	69	14	0	0	438	16	3	4	3.6	.993	OF-128
1985			161	.288	.385	691	199	29	13	4	0.6	80	74	41	87	21	1	0	465	19	8	5	3.1	.984	OF-161
1986			161	.328	.537	680	223	37	6	31	4.6	119	96	34	99	20	4	1	429	8	6	3	2.8	.986	OF-160
1987			157	.332	.534	624	207	32	5	28	4.5	96	99	32	91	12	2	0	341	8	5	2	2.3	.986	OF-147, DH-8
1988			158	.356	.545	657	234	42	5	24	3.7	109	121	23	83	6	1	0	450	12	3	4	2.9	.994	OF-158
1989			159	.339	.465	635	215	45	4	9	1.4	75	85	41	59	11	2	1	438	13	4	3	2.9	.991	OF-157, DH-2
6 yrs.			924	.323	.469	3844	1243	197	38	96	2.5	542	506	187	488	84	10	2	2561	76	29	21	2.9	.989	OF-911, DH-10

LEAGUE CHAMPIONSHIP SERIES

| 1987 | MIN | A | 5 | .208 | .375 | 24 | 5 | 1 | 0 | 1 | 4.2 | 3 | 3 | 0 | 5 | 1 | 0 | 0 | 7 | 0 | 0 | 0 | 1.4 | 1.000 | OF-5 |

WORLD SERIES

| 1987 | MIN | A | 7 | .357 | .464 | 28 | 10 | 1 | 1 | 0 | 0.0 | 5 | 3 | 2 | 1 | 1 | 0 | 0 | 15 | 1 | 1 | 0 | 2.4 | .941 | OF-7 |

John Puhl

PUHL, JOHN
B. 1875, Bayonne, N. J. D. Aug. 24, 1900, Bayonne, N. J.

Year	Team		Games	BA	SA	AB	H	2B	3B	HR	HR%	R	RBI	BB	SO	SB	PH AB	PH H	PO	A	E	DP	TC/G	FA	G by Pos
1898	NY	N	2	.222	.222	9	2	0	0	0	0.0	1	0	1		0	0	0	1	5	3	1	4.5	.667	3B-2
1899			1	.000	.000	2	0	0	0	0	0.0	0	0	0		0	0	0	0	2	1	0	3.0	.667	3B-1
2 yrs.			3	.182	.182	11	2	0	0	0	0.0	1	0	1		0	0	0	1	7	4	1	4.0	.667	3B-3

Terry Puhl

PUHL, TERRY STEPHEN
B. July 8, 1956, Melville, Sask., Canada

BL TR 6'2" 195 lbs.

Year	Team		Games	BA	SA	AB	H	2B	3B	HR	HR%	R	RBI	BB	SO	SB	PH AB	PH H	PO	A	E	DP	TC/G	FA	G by Pos
1977	HOU	N	60	.301	.402	229	69	13	5	0	0.0	40	10	30	31	10	0	0	119	3	1	0	2.1	.992	OF-59
1978			149	.289	.368	585	169	25	6	3	0.5	87	35	48	46	32	1	1	386	6	3	2	2.7	.992	OF-148
1979			157	.287	.377	600	172	22	4	8	1.3	87	49	58	46	30	5	1	352	7	0	4	2.3	1.000	OF-152
1980			141	.282	.419	535	151	24	5	13	2.4	75	55	60	52	27	6	0	311	14	3	3	2.3	.991	OF-135
1981			96	.251	.354	350	88	19	4	3	0.9	43	28	31	49	22	8	1	185	5	0	1	2.0	1.000	OF-88
1982			145	.262	.379	507	133	17	9	8	1.6	64	50	51	49	17	7	3	257	4	3	3	1.8	.989	OF-138
1983			137	.292	.428	465	136	25	7	8	1.7	66	44	36	48	24	15	4	220	4	2	1	1.6	.991	OF-124
1984			132	.301	.434	449	135	19	7	9	2.0	66	55	59	45	13	5	2	213	6	3	4	1.7	.986	OF-126
1985			57	.284	.418	194	55	14	3	2	1.0	34	23	18	23	6	3	1	92	3	0	1	1.7	1.000	OF-53
1986			81	.244	.355	172	42	10	4	3	1.7	17	14	15	24	3	28	8	65	0	0	0	0.8	1.000	OF-47
1987			90	.230	.320	122	28	5	0	2	1.6	9	15	11	16	1	52	15	48	0	1	0	0.5	.980	OF-40
1988			113	.303	.389	234	71	7	2	3	1.3	42	19	35	30	22	36	11	116	2	2	0	1.1	.983	OF-78
1989			121	.271	.364	354	96	25	4	0	0.0	41	27	45	39	9	15	4	212	3	0	1	1.8	1.000	OF-103, 1B-3
13 yrs.			1479	.280	.389	4796	1345	225	56	62	1.3	671	424	497	498	216	181	51	2576	57	18	19	1.8	.993	OF-1291, 1B-3

DIVISIONAL PLAYOFF SERIES

| 1981 | HOU | N | 5 | .190 | .238 | 21 | 4 | 1 | 0 | 0 | 0.0 | 2 | 0 | 0 | 1 | 0 | 0 | 0 | 0 | 0 | 0 | 0 | 0.0 | – | OF-5 |

Year	Team		Games	BA	SA	AB	H	2B	3B	HR	HR%	R	RBI	BB	SO	SB	Pinch Hit AB	H	PO	A	E	DP	TC/G	FA	G by Pos

Terry Puhl *continued*

LEAGUE CHAMPIONSHIP SERIES

1980	HOU	N	5	.526	.632	19	10	2	0	0	0.0	4	3	3	2	2	1	0	13	0	0	0	2.6	1.000	OF-4
1986			3	.667	.667	3	2	0	0	0	0.0	0	0	0	0	1	3	2	0	0	0	0			OF-4
2 yrs.			8	.545	.636	22	12	2	0	0	0.0	4	3	3	2	3	4	2	13	0	0	0	1.6	1.000	OF-4

Rich Puig

PUIG, RICHARD GERALD
B. Mar. 16, 1953, Tampa, Fla.

BL TR 5'10" 165 lbs.

| 1974 | NY | N | 4 | .000 | .000 | 10 | 0 | 0 | 0 | 0 | 0.0 | 0 | 0 | 1 | 2 | 0 | 0 | 0 | 7 | 6 | 1 | 2 | 3.5 | .929 | 2B-3, 3B-1 |

Luis Pujols

PUJOLS, LUIS BIENVENIDO
Born Luis Bienvenido Pujols y Toribio.
B. Nov. 18, 1955, Santiago, Dominican Republic

BR TR 6'2" 175 lbs.

1977	HOU	N	6	.067	.067	15	1	0	0	0	0.0	0	0	0	0	0	0	0	18	4	0	0	3.7	1.000	C-6
1978			56	.131	.216	153	20	8	1	1	0.7	11	11	12	45	0	0	0	272	33	6	2	5.6	.981	C-55, 1B-1
1979			26	.227	.280	75	17	2	1	0	0.0	7	8	2	14	0	0	0	136	6	1	0	5.5	.993	C-26
1980			78	.199	.235	221	44	6	1	0	0.0	15	20	13	29	0	7	0	349	35	4	5	5.0	.990	C-75, 3B-1
1981			40	.239	.308	117	28	3	1	1	0.9	5	14	10	17	1	3	1	192	14	1	1	5.2	.995	C-39
1982			65	.199	.324	176	35	6	2	4	2.3	8	15	10	40	0	1	0	295	39	3	3	5.2	.991	C-64
1983			40	.195	.218	87	17	2	0	0	0.0	4	12	5	14	0	0	0	180	20	6	0	5.2	.971	C-39
1984	KC	A	4	.200	.200	5	1	0	0	0	0.0	0	1	0	0	0	1	0	9	0	0	0	2.3	1.000	C-4
1985	TEX	A	1	1.000	1.000	1	1	0	0	0	0.0	0	0	0	0	0	0	0	1	0	0	0	1.0	1.000	C-1
9 yrs.			316	.193	.260	850	164	27	6	6	0.7	50	81	52	164	1	12	1	1452	151	21	11	5.1	.987	C-309, 3B-1, 1B-1

DIVISIONAL PLAYOFF SERIES

| 1981 | HOU | N | 2 | .000 | .000 | 6 | 0 | 0 | 0 | 0 | 0.0 | 0 | 0 | 0 | 0 | 0 | 0 | 0 | 0 | 0 | 0 | 0 | 0.0 | — | C-2 |

LEAGUE CHAMPIONSHIP SERIES

| 1980 | HOU | N | 4 | .100 | .300 | 10 | 1 | 0 | 1 | 0 | 0.0 | 1 | 0 | 3 | 0 | 0 | 0 | 0 | 21 | 2 | 0 | 0 | 5.8 | 1.000 | C-4 |

Blondie Purcell

PURCELL, WILLIAM ALOYSIUS
B. Mar. 16, 1854, Paterson, N. J. D. Feb. 20, 1912, Trenton N. J.,
Manager 1883.

BR TR 5'9½" 159 lbs.

1879	2 teams		SYR	N (63G – .260)		CIN	N (12G – .220)																		
"	total		75	.254	.291	327	83	6	3	0	0.0	42	29	3	16		0	0	98	41	33	0	2.3	.808	OF-57, P-24, C-1
1880	CIN	N	77	.292	.378	325	95	13	6	1	0.3	48	24	5	13		0	0	88	54	25	1	2.2	.850	OF-55, P-25, SS-1
1881	2 teams		CLE	N (20G – .175)		BUF	N (30G – .292)																		
"	total		50	.244	.321	193	47	9	3	0	0.0	18	21	14	16		0	0	74	24	29	0	2.5	.772	OF-45, P-6
1882	BUF	N	84	.276	.371	380	105	18	6	2	0.5	79		14	27		0	0	144	21	35	0	2.4	.825	OF-82, P-6
1883	PHI	N	97	.268	.346	425	114	20	5	1	0.2	70		13	26		0	0	130	146	66	9	3.5	.807	3B-46, OF-44, P-11
1884			103	.252	.318	428	108	11	7	1	0.2	67		29	30		0	0	182	12	28	1	2.2	.874	OF-103, P-1
1885	2 teams		PHI	AA (66G – .296)		BOS	N (21G – .218)																		
"	total		87	.279	.350	391	109	16	6	0	0.0	80	3	19	15		0	0	97	16	19	1	1.5	.856	OF-87, P-1
1886	BAL	AA	26	.224	.247	85	19	0	1	0	0.0	17		17			0	0	35	4	6	0	1.7	.867	OF-26, SS-1, P-1
1887			140	.250	.344	567	142	25	8	4	0.7	101		46		88	0	0	203	18	18	5	1.7	.925	OF-140, P-1
1888	2 teams		BAL	AA (101G – .236)		PHI	AA (18G – .167)																		
"	total		119	.227	.286	472	107	12	5	2	0.4	63	45	32		26	0	0	172	14	20	4	1.7	.903	OF-117, SS-2, 3B-1, 1B-1
1889	PHI	AA	129	.316	.381	507	160	19	7	0	0.0	72	85	50	27	22	0	0	172	15	20	3	1.6	.903	OF-129
1890			110	.276	.363	463	128	28	3	2	0.4	110		43		48	0	0	170	17	10	3	1.8	.949	OF-110
12 yrs.			1097	.267	.340	4563	1217	177	60	13	0.3	767	207	285	170	184	0	0	1565	382	309	27	2.1	.863	OF-995, P-79, 3B-47, SS-4, 1B-1, C-1

Pid Purdy

PURDY, EVERETT VIRGIL
B. June 15, 1904, Beatrice, Neb. D. Jan. 16, 1951, Beatrice, Neb.

BL TR 5'6" 150 lbs.

1926	CHI	A	11	.182	.303	33	6	2	1	0	0.0	5	6	2		0	2	0	17	1	0	0	1.6	1.000	OF-9
1927	CIN	N	18	.355	.565	62	22	2	4	1	1.6	15	12	4	3	0	2	1	35	0	2	0	2.1	.946	OF-16
1928			70	.309	.368	223	69	11	1	0	0.0	32	25	23	13	1	8	6	137	3	5	1	2.1	.966	OF-61
1929			82	.271	.381	181	49	7	5	1	0.6	22	16	19	8	2	33	8	84	3	2	0	1.1	.978	OF-42
4 yrs.			181	.293	.393	499	146	22	11	2	0.4	74	59	48	25	3	45	15	273	7	9	1	1.6	.969	OF-128

Jesse Purnell

PURNELL, JESSE RHOADES (Scrappy)
B. May 11, 1881, Glenside, Pa. D. July 4, 1966, Philadelphia, Pa.

BL TR 5'5½" 140 lbs.

| 1904 | PHI | N | 7 | .105 | .105 | 19 | 2 | 0 | 0 | 0 | 0.0 | 2 | 1 | 4 | | 1 | 0 | 0 | 7 | 12 | 3 | 0 | 3.1 | .864 | 3B-7 |

Billy Purtell

PURTELL, WILLIAM PATRICK
B. Jan. 6, 1886, Columbus, Ohio D. Mar. 17, 1962, Bradenton, Fla.

BR TR 5'9" 170 lbs.

1908	CHI	A	26	.130	.159	69	9	2	0	0	0.0	3	2	2		2	1	0	18	60	5	5	3.2	.940	3B-25
1909			103	.258	.299	361	93	9	3	0	0.0	34	40	19		14	0	0	162	248	24	24	4.2	.945	3B-71, 2B-32
1910	2 teams		CHI	A (102G – .234)		BOS	A (49G – .208)																		
"	total		151	.226	.267	536	121	6	5	2	0.4	36	51	39		7	0	0	166	341	52	20	3.7	.907	3B-143, SS-8
1911	BOS	A	27	.280	.415	82	23	5	3	0	0.0	5	7	1		1	5	1	29	35	10	1	2.7	.865	3B-16, SS-3, 2B-3, OF-1
1914	DET	A	26	.171	.224	76	13	4	0	0	0.0	4	3	2	7	0	1	0	21	36	4	2	2.3	.934	3B-16, SS-1, 2B-1
5 yrs.			333	.230	.278	1124	259	26	11	2	0.2	82	104	63	7	24	14	2	396	720	95	52	3.6	.922	3B-271, 2B-36, SS-12, OF-1

Ed Putman

PUTMAN, EDDY WILLIAM
B. Sept. 25, 1953, Los Angeles, Calif.

BR TR 6'1" 190 lbs.

1976	CHI	N	5	.429	.429	7	3	0	0	0	0.0	0	0	0	2	0	2	1	16	0	0	0	3.2	1.000	C-3, 1B-1
1978			17	.200	.200	25	5	0	0	0	0.0	2	3	4	6	0	5	2	15	13	2	1	1.8	.933	3B-8, 1B-3, C-2
1979	DET	A	21	.231	.462	39	9	3	0	2	5.1	4	4	4	12	0	3	0	75	7	1	5	4.0	.988	C-16, 1B-5
3 yrs.			43	.239	.366	71	17	3	0	2	2.8	6	7	8	18	0	10	3	106	20	3	6	3.0	.977	C-21, 1B-9, 3B-8

Year Team	Games	BA	SA	AB	H	2B	3B	HR	HR%	R	RBI	BB	SO	SB	Pinch Hit AB	Pinch Hit H	PO	A	E	DP	TC/G	FA	G by Pos

Pat Putnam

PUTNAM, PATRICK EDWARD
B. Dec. 3, 1953, Bethel, Vt.   BL TR 6' 205 lbs.

Year Team	Games	BA	SA	AB	H	2B	3B	HR	HR%	R	RBI	BB	SO	SB	PH AB	PH H	PO	A	E	DP	TC/G	FA	G by Pos
1977 TEX A	11	.308	.462	26	8	4	0	0	0.0	3	3	1	4	0	2	1	35	1	0	3	3.3	1.000	1B-7, DH-3
1978	20	.152	.239	46	7	1	0	1	2.2	4	2	2	5	0	5	1	15	1	0	1	0.8	1.000	DH-12, 1B-4
1979	139	.277	.458	426	118	19	2	18	4.2	57	64	23	50	1	21	8	832	62	5	65	6.5	.994	1B-96, DH-32
1980	147	.263	.407	410	108	16	2	13	3.2	42	55	36	49	0	18	8	979	80	9	107	7.3	.992	1B-137, DH-1, 3B-1
1981	95	.266	.418	297	79	17	2	8	2.7	33	35	17	38	4	2	0	771	64	7	65	8.9	.992	1B-94, OF-3
1982	43	.230	.344	122	28	8	0	2	1.6	14	9	10	18	0	6	1	287	24	3	26	7.3	.990	1B-39, OF-1, 3B-1
1983 SEA A	144	.269	.448	469	126	23	2	19	4.1	58	67	39	57	2	12	4	1067	85	7	105	8.0	.994	1B-125, DH-11
1984 2 teams	SEA A (64G – .200)		MIN A (14G – .079)																				
" total	78	.176	.244	193	34	7	0	2	1.0	12	20	16	39	3	25	4	46	6	1	7	0.7	.981	DH-14, OF-13, 1B-6
8 yrs.	677	.255	.406	1989	508	95	8	63	3.2	223	255	144	260	10	91	27	4032	323	32	379	6.5	.993	1B-508, DH-73, OF-17, 3B-2

Jim Pyburn

PYBURN, JAMES EDWARD
B. Nov. 1, 1932, Fairfield, Ala.   BR TR 6' 190 lbs.

Year Team	Games	BA	SA	AB	H	2B	3B	HR	HR%	R	RBI	BB	SO	SB	PH AB	PH H	PO	A	E	DP	TC/G	FA	G by Pos
1955 BAL A	39	.204	.265	98	20	2	2	0	0.0	5	7	8	24	1	6	1	27	36	0	1	1.6	1.000	3B-33, OF-1
1956	84	.173	.269	156	27	3	3	2	1.3	23	11	17	26	4	7	2	114	5	3	3	1.5	.975	OF-77
1957	35	.225	.300	40	9	0	0	1	2.5	8	2	9	6	1	5	1	41	3	0	0	1.3	1.000	OF-28, C-1
3 yrs.	158	.190	.272	294	56	5	5	3	1.0	36	20	34	56	6	18	4	182	44	3	4	1.4	.987	OF-106, 3B-33, C-1

Frankie Pytlak

PYTLAK, FRANK ANTHONY
B. July 30, 1908, Buffalo, N.Y.   D. May 8, 1977, Buffalo, N.Y.   BR TR 5'7½" 160 lbs.

Year Team	Games	BA	SA	AB	H	2B	3B	HR	HR%	R	RBI	BB	SO	SB	PH AB	PH H	PO	A	E	DP	TC/G	FA	G by Pos
1932 CLE A	12	.241	.345	29	7	1	1	0	0.0	5	4	3	2	1	0	0	40	7	0	0	3.9	1.000	C-12
1933	80	.310	.423	248	77	10	6	2	0.8	36	33	17	10	3	6	3	246	57	0	11	3.8	1.000	C-69
1934	91	.260	.329	289	75	12	4	0	0.0	46	35	36	11	11	3	1	325	38	4	4	4.0	.989	C-88
1935	55	.295	.369	149	44	6	1	1	0.7	14	12	11	4	3	7	3	166	20	3	2	3.4	.984	C-48
1936	75	.321	.424	224	72	15	4	0	0.0	35	31	24	11	5	15	3	224	35	1	6	3.5	.996	C-58
1937	125	.315	.390	397	125	15	6	1	0.3	60	44	52	15	16	9	4	559	80	9	13	5.2	.986	C-115
1938	113	.308	.393	364	112	14	7	1	0.3	46	43	36	15	9	15	2	475	56	7	11	4.8	.987	C-99
1939	63	.268	.333	183	49	2	5	0	0.0	20	14	20	5	4	5	3	227	24	0	5	4.0	1.000	C-51
1940	62	.141	.168	149	21	2	1	0	0.0	16	16	17	5	0	3	1	235	30	1	5	4.3	.996	C-58, OF-1
1941 BOS A	106	.271	.363	336	91	23	1	2	0.6	36	39	28	19	5	11	4	416	41	4	7	4.3	.991	C-91
1945	9	.118	.118	17	2	0	0	0	0.0	1	0	3	0	0	2	0	17	6	0	0	2.6	1.000	C-6
1946	4	.143	.143	14	2	0	0	0	0.0	0	1	0	0	0	0	0	28	1	0	0	7.3	1.000	C-4
12 yrs.	795	.282	.363	2399	677	100	36	7	0.3	316	272	247	97	56	76	24	2958	395	29	64	4.3	.991	C-699, OF-1

Tim Pyznarski

PYZNARSKI, TIMOTHY MATTHEW
B. Feb. 4, 1960, Chicago, Ill.   BR TR 6'2" 195 lbs.

Year Team	Games	BA	SA	AB	H	2B	3B	HR	HR%	R	RBI	BB	SO	SB	PH AB	PH H	PO	A	E	DP	TC/G	FA	G by Pos
1986 SD N	15	.238	.262	42	10	1	0	0	0.0	3	0	4	11	2	1	0	118	8	3	11	8.6	.977	1B-13

Jimmy Qualls

QUALLS, JAMES ROBERT
B. Oct. 9, 1946, Exeter, Calif.   BB TR 5'10" 158 lbs.

Year Team	Games	BA	SA	AB	H	2B	3B	HR	HR%	R	RBI	BB	SO	SB	PH AB	PH H	PO	A	E	DP	TC/G	FA	G by Pos
1969 CHI N	43	.250	.342	120	30	5	3	0	0.0	12	9	2	14	2	4	2	62	5	0	2	1.6	1.000	OF-35, 2B-4
1970 MON N	9	.111	.111	9	1	0	0	0	0.0	1	1	0	0	0	5	1	2	2	0	0	0.4	1.000	OF-2, 2B-2
1972 CHI A	11	.000	.000	10	0	0	0	0	0.0	0	0	0	2	0	7	0	3	0	0	0	0.3	1.000	OF-1
3 yrs.	63	.223	.302	139	31	5	3	0	0.0	13	10	2	16	2	16	3	67	7	0	2	1.2	1.000	OF-38, 2B-6

Billy Queen

QUEEN, WILLIAM EDDLEMAN (Doc)
B. Nov. 28, 1928, Gastonia, N.C.   BR TR 6'1" 185 lbs.

Year Team	Games	BA	SA	AB	H	2B	3B	HR	HR%	R	RBI	BB	SO	SB	PH AB	PH H	PO	A	E	DP	TC/G	FA	G by Pos
1954 MIL N	3	.000	.000	2	0	0	0	0	0.0	0	0	0	2	0	2	0	1	0	0	0	0.3	1.000	OF-1

Mel Queen

QUEEN, MELVIN DOUGLAS
Son of Mel Queen.
B. Mar. 26, 1942, Johnson City, N.Y.   BL TR 6'1" 189 lbs.

Year Team	Games	BA	SA	AB	H	2B	3B	HR	HR%	R	RBI	BB	SO	SB	PH AB	PH H	PO	A	E	DP	TC/G	FA	G by Pos
1964 CIN N	48	.200	.284	95	19	2	0	2	2.1	7	12	4	19	0	26	5	42	0	1	0	0.9	.977	OF-20
1965	5	.000	.000	3	0	0	0	0	0.0	0	0	0	1	0	3	0	1	0	0	0	0.2	1.000	OF-1
1966	56	.127	.145	55	7	1	0	0	0.0	4	5	10	17	3	17	3	35	2	0	0	0.7	1.000	OF-32, P-7
1967	49	.210	.259	81	17	4	0	0	0.0	6	5	4	10	2	13	1	15	17	2	2	0.7	.941	P-31
1968	10	.125	.125	8	1	0	0	0	0.0	2	0	1	3	0	3	0	0	4	0	0	0.4	1.000	P-5
1969	2	.167	.167	6	1	0	0	0	0.0	0	0	1	2	0	0	0	0	1	0	0	0.5	1.000	P-2
1970 CAL A	37	.250	.250	16	4	0	0	0	0.0	1	1	0	4	0	3	1	1	5	0	0	0.2	1.000	P-34
1971	45	.000	.000	8	0	0	0	0	0.0	0	1	1	0	0	2	0	1	8	1	0	0.2	.900	P-44
1972	17	.000	.000	2	0	0	0	0	0.0	0	1	0	1	0	0	0	0	0	0	0	0.3	1.000	P-17
9 yrs.	269	.179	.226	274	49	7	0	2	0.7	20	25	21	50	2	68	12	96	41	4	2	0.5	.972	P-140, OF-53

George Quellich

QUELLICH, GEORGE WILLIAM
B. Feb. 10, 1903, Johnsville, Calif.   D. Aug. 31, 1958, Johnsville, Calif.   BR TR 6'1" 180 lbs.

Year Team	Games	BA	SA	AB	H	2B	3B	HR	HR%	R	RBI	BB	SO	SB	PH AB	PH H	PO	A	E	DP	TC/G	FA	G by Pos
1931 DET A	13	.222	.370	54	12	5	0	1	1.9	6	11	3	4	1	0	0	27	2	0	0	2.2	1.000	OF-13

Joe Quest

QUEST, JOSEPH L.
B. Nov., 1851, New Castle, Pa.   Deceased.   BR TR 5'6" 150 lbs.

Year Team	Games	BA	SA	AB	H	2B	3B	HR	HR%	R	RBI	BB	SO	SB	PH AB	PH H	PO	A	E	DP	TC/G	FA	G by Pos
1878 IND N	62	.205	.230	278	57	3	0	0	0.0	45	13	12	24		0	0	228	196	60	27	7.8	.876	2B-62
1879 CHI N	83	.207	.260	334	69	16	1	0	0.0	38	22	9	33		0	0	263	331	48	30	7.7	.925	2B-83
1880	82	.237	.283	300	71	12	1	0	0.0	37	27	8	16		0	0	226	278	60	26	6.9	.894	2B-80, SS-2, 3B-1
1881	78	.246	.276	293	72	6	0	1	0.3	35	26	2	29		0	0	242	252	37	28	6.8	.930	2B-77, SS-1
1882	42	.201	.258	159	32	9	0	0	0.0	24	16	2	16		0	0	113	128	35	18	6.6	.873	2B-41, SS-1
1883 2 teams	DET N (37G – .234)		STL AA (19G – .256)																				
" total	56	.242	.321	215	52	11	3	0	0.0	34		11	18		0	0	162	161	38	29	6.4	.895	2B-56

Year	Team		Games	BA	SA	AB	H	2B	3B	HR	HR%	R	RBI	BB	SO	SB	Pinch Hit AB	H	PO	A	E	DP	TC/G	FA	G by Pos

Joe Quest *continued*

Year	Team		Games	BA	SA	AB	H	2B	3B	HR	HR%	R	RBI	BB	SO	SB	AB	H	PO	A	E	DP	TC/G	FA	G by Pos
1884	2 teams	STL AA (81G – .206)				PIT AA (12G – .209)																			
"	total		93	.207	.269	353	73	12	5	0	0.0	48		19			0	0	261	286	64	45	6.6	.895	2B-87, SS-5, OF-1
1885	DET	N	55	.195	.255	200	39	8	2	0	0.0	24	21	14	25		0	0	117	169	37	13	5.9	.885	2B-39, SS-15, OF-1
1886	PHI	AA	42	.207	.247	150	31	4	1	0	0.0	14		20			0	0	63	146	39	16	5.9	.843	SS-41, 2B-2
9 yrs.			593	.217	.267	2282	496	77	17	1	0.0	299	124	103	161		0	0	1675	1947	418	232	6.8	.897	2B-527, SS-65, OF-2, 3B-1

Hal Quick

QUICK, JAMES HAROLD (Blondie)
B. Oct. 4, 1917, Rome, Ga.   D. Mar. 9, 1974, Swansea, Ill.   BR TR 5'10"   165 lbs.

Year	Team		Games	BA	SA	AB	H	2B	3B	HR	HR%	R	RBI	BB	SO	SB	AB	H	PO	A	E	DP	TC/G	FA	G by Pos
1939	WAS	A	12	.244	.268	41	10	1	0	0	0.0	3	1	1	1	1	0	0	18	33	4	6	4.6	.927	SS-10

Frank Quilici

QUILICI, FRANCIS RALPH (Guido)
B. May 11, 1939, Chicago, Ill.   BR TR 6'1"   170 lbs.
Manager 1972-75.

Year	Team		Games	BA	SA	AB	H	2B	3B	HR	HR%	R	RBI	BB	SO	SB	AB	H	PO	A	E	DP	TC/G	FA	G by Pos
1965	MIN	A	56	.208	.255	149	31	5	1	0	0.0	16	7	15	33	1	2	0	96	120	2	34	3.9	.991	2B-52, SS-4
1967			23	.105	.158	19	2	1	0	0	0.0	2	0	3	4	0	2	0	10	13	1	4	1.0	.958	2B-13, 3B-8, SS-1
1968			97	.245	.341	229	56	11	4	1	0.4	22	22	21	45	0	6	1	130	176	5	34	3.2	.984	2B-48, 3B-40, SS-6, 1B-1
1969			118	.174	.250	144	25	3	1	2	1.4	19	12	12	22	2	7	2	99	139	6	17	2.1	.975	3B-84, 2B-36, SS-1
1970			111	.227	.291	141	32	3	0	2	1.4	19	12	15	16	0	3	1	114	133	6	26	2.3	.976	2B-73, 3B-27, SS-1
5 yrs.			405	.214	.287	682	146	23	6	5	0.7	78	53	66	120	3	20	4	449	581	20	115	2.6	.981	2B-222, 3B-159, SS-13, 1B-1

LEAGUE CHAMPIONSHIP SERIES

Year	Team		Games	BA	SA	AB	H	2B	3B	HR	HR%	R	RBI	BB	SO	SB	AB	H	PO	A	E	DP	TC/G	FA	G by Pos
1970	MIN	A	3	.000	.000	2	0	0	0	0	0.0	0	0	1	0	0	1	0	1	1	0	1	0.7	1.000	2B-2

WORLD SERIES

Year	Team		Games	BA	SA	AB	H	2B	3B	HR	HR%	R	RBI	BB	SO	SB	AB	H	PO	A	E	DP	TC/G	FA	G by Pos
1965	MIN	A	7	.200	.300	20	4	2	0	0	0.0	2	1	4	3	0	0	0	14	19	2	0	5.0	.943	2B-7

Lee Quillen

QUILLEN, LEON ABNER
B. May 5, 1882, North Branch, Minn.   D. Mar. 14, 1965, White Bear Lake, Minn.   BR TR 5'10"   165 lbs.

Year	Team		Games	BA	SA	AB	H	2B	3B	HR	HR%	R	RBI	BB	SO	SB	AB	H	PO	A	E	DP	TC/G	FA	G by Pos
1906	CHI	A	4	.333	.333	9	3	0	0	0	0.0	1	0			1	1	0	4	5	6	1	3.8	.600	SS-3
1907			49	.192	.225	151	29	5	0	0	0.0	17	14	10		8	0	0	45	103	22	4	3.5	.871	3B-48
2 yrs.			53	.200	.231	160	32	5	0	0	0.0	18	14	10		9	1	0	49	108	28	5	3.5	.849	3B-48, SS-3

Finners Quinlan

QUINLAN, THOMAS FINNERS
B. Oct. 21, 1887, Scranton, Pa.   D. Feb. 17, 1966, Scranton, Pa.   BL TL 5'8"   154 lbs.

Year	Team		Games	BA	SA	AB	H	2B	3B	HR	HR%	R	RBI	BB	SO	SB	AB	H	PO	A	E	DP	TC/G	FA	G by Pos
1913	STL	N	13	.160	.160	50	8	0	0	0	0.0	1	1	1	9	0	1	0	23	3	3	2	2.2	.897	OF-12
1915	CHI	A	42	.193	.219	114	22	3	0	0	0.0	11	7	4	11	3	4	0	43	5	0	2	1.1	1.000	OF-32
2 yrs.			55	.183	.201	164	30	3	0	0	0.0	12	8	5	20	3	5	0	66	8	3	4	1.4	.961	OF-44

Frank Quinlan

QUINLAN, FRANCIS PATRICK
B. Mar. 9, 1869, Marlboro, Mass.   D. May 4, 1904, Brockton, Mass.

Year	Team		Games	BA	SA	AB	H	2B	3B	HR	HR%	R	RBI	BB	SO	SB	AB	H	PO	A	E	DP	TC/G	FA	G by Pos
1891	BOS	AA	2	.000	.000	5	0	0	0	0	0.0	0	0	0	2	0	0	0	5	1	0	0	3.0	1.000	OF-1, C-1

Frank Quinn

QUINN, FRANK J.
B. 1876, Grand Rapids, Mich.   D. Feb. 17, 1920, Camden, Ind.   5'8"

Year	Team		Games	BA	SA	AB	H	2B	3B	HR	HR%	R	RBI	BB	SO	SB	AB	H	PO	A	E	DP	TC/G	FA	G by Pos
1899	CHI	N	12	.176	.235	34	6	0	1	0	0.0	6		6		1	1	0	10	1	1	0	1.0	.917	OF-10, 2B-1

Joe Quinn

QUINN, JOSEPH C.
B. 1851, Chicago, Ill.   D. Jan. 2, 1909, Chicago, Ill.   5'8½"   148 lbs.

Year	Team		Games	BA	SA	AB	H	2B	3B	HR	HR%	R	RBI	BB	SO	SB	AB	H	PO	A	E	DP	TC/G	FA	G by Pos
1877	CHI	N	4	.071	.071	14	1	0	0	0	0.0	1	0	1	0		0	0	7	1	4	0	3.0	.667	OF-4

Joe Quinn

QUINN, JOSEPH J. (Uncle Joe, Ol' Reliable)
B. Dec. 25, 1864, Sydney, Australia   D. Nov. 12, 1940, St. Louis, Mo.   BR TR 5'7"   158 lbs.
Manager 1895, 1899.

Year	Team		Games	BA	SA	AB	H	2B	3B	HR	HR%	R	RBI	BB	SO	SB	AB	H	PO	A	E	DP	TC/G	FA	G by Pos
1884	STL	U	103	.270	.324	429	116	21	1	0	0.0	74		9			0	0	1039	36	64	55	11.1	.944	1B-100, OF-3, SS-1
1885	STL	N	97	.213	.248	343	73	8	2	0	0.0	27	15	9	38		0	0	229	76	35	4	3.5	.897	OF-57, 3B-31, 1B-11
1886			75	.232	.306	271	63	11	3	1	0.4	33	21	8	31		0	0	199	55	34	13	3.8	.882	OF-48, 2B-15, 1B-7, 3B-4, SS-2
1888	BOS	N	38	.301	.468	156	47	8	3	4	2.6	19	29	2	5	12	0	0	97	115	20	11	6.1	.914	2B-38
1889			112	.261	.327	444	116	13	5	2	0.5	57	69	25	21	24	0	0	174	314	59	36	4.9	.892	SS-63, 2B-47, 3B-2
1890	BOS	P	130	.301	.411	509	153	19	8	7	1.4	87	82	44	24	29	0	0	431	395	51	70	6.7	.942	2B-130
1891	BOS	N	124	.240	.313	508	122	8	10	3	0.6	70	63	28	28	24	0	0	275	364	42	44	5.5	.938	2B-124
1892			143	.218	.254	532	116	14	1	1	0.2	63	59	35	40	17	0	0	356	426	40	75	5.7	.951	2B-143
1893	STL	N	135	.230	.285	547	126	18	6	0	0.0	71	33	7	24	0	0	354	366	44	63	5.7	.942	2B-135
1894			106	.286	.365	405	116	18	4	4	1.0	59	61	24	8	25	0	0	341	339	34	74	6.7	.952	2B-106
1895			134	.311	.390	543	169	19	9	2	0.4	84	74	36	6	22	0	0	359	390	43	63	5.9	.946	2B-134
1896	2 teams	STL N (48G – .209)				BAL N (24G – .329)																			
"	total		72	.245	.297	273	67	7	4	1	0.4	41	22	15	6	14	2	0	123	206	16	10	4.8	.954	2B-56, OF-8, 3B-5, SS-1
1897	BAL	N	75	.260	.337	285	74	11	4	1	0.4	33	45	13		12	2	0	142	176	16	22	4.5	.952	3B-37, SS-21, 2B-11, OF-6, 1B-2
1898	2 teams	BAL N (12G – .250)				STL N (103G – .251)																			
"	total		115	.251	.302	407	102	11	5	0	0.0	40	41	25		13	1	0	235	356	35	31	5.4	.944	2B-63, SS-41, 3B-8, OF-2
1899	CLE	N	147	.286	.345	615	176	24	6	0	0.0	73	72	21		22	0	0	350	440	31	61	5.6	.962	2B-147
1900	2 teams	STL N (22G – .263)				CIN N (74G – .274)																			
"	total		96	.272	.312	346	94	7	2	1	0.3	30	36	26		11	1	1	198	215	24	28	4.6	.945	2B-88, SS-6, 3B-1
1901	WAS	A	66	.252	.342	266	67	11	2	3	1.1	30	33	11	7		0	0	158	177	16	17	5.3	.954	2B-66
17 yrs.			1768	.261	.328	6879	1797	228	70	30	0.4	891	796	364	214	256	6	1	5060	4446	604	677	5.7	.940	2B-1303, SS-135, OF-124, 1B-120, 3B-88

John Quinn

QUINN, JOHN EDWARD (Pit)
B. Sept. 12, 1885, Framingham, Mass.   D. Apr. 9, 1956, Marlboro, Mass.   BR TR 5'11"   150 lbs.

Year	Team		Games	BA	SA	AB	H	2B	3B	HR	HR%	R	RBI	BB	SO	SB	Pinch Hit AB	Pinch Hit H	PO	A	E	DP	TC/G	FA	G by Pos

John Quinn *continued*

Year	Team		Games	BA	SA	AB	H	2B	3B	HR	HR%	R	RBI	BB	SO	SB	AB	H	PO	A	E	DP	TC/G	FA	G by Pos
1911	PHI	N	1	.000	.000	2	0	0	0	0	0.0	0	0	0	0	0	0	0	3	1	0	0	4.0	1.000	C-1

Paddy Quinn
QUINN, PATRICK
B. Boston, Mass. D. Mar., 1893

Year	Team		Games	BA	SA	AB	H	2B	3B	HR	HR%	R	RBI	BB	SO	SB	AB	H	PO	A	E	DP	TC/G	FA	G by Pos
1881	2 teams		BOS N (1G – .000)				WOR N (2G – .143)																			
"	total		3	.091	.091	11	1	0	0	0	0.0	0	1	1	2		0	0	15	1	2	0	6.0	.889	C-2, 1B-1

Tom Quinn
QUINN, THOMAS OSCAR
B. Apr. 25, 1864, Annapolis, Md. D. July 24, 1932, Pittsburgh, Pa. BR TR 5'8" 180 lbs.

Year	Team		Games	BA	SA	AB	H	2B	3B	HR	HR%	R	RBI	BB	SO	SB	AB	H	PO	A	E	DP	TC/G	FA	G by Pos
1886	PIT	AA	3	.000	.000	11	0	0	0	0	0.0	0		0			0	0	10	3	1	0	4.7	.929	C-3
1889	BAL	AA	55	.175	.211	194	34	2	1	1	0.5	18	15	19	22	6	0	0	290	81	30	10	7.3	.925	C-55
1890	PIT	P	55	.213	.275	207	44	4	3	1	0.5	23	15	17	8	1	0	0	203	58	33	3	5.3	.888	C-55
3 yrs.			113	.189	.238	412	78	6	4	2	0.5	42	30	36	30	7	0	0	503	142	64	13	6.3	.910	C-113

Luis Quinones
QUINONES, LUIS RAUL
Born Luis Raul Quinones y Torruellas.
B. Apr. 28, 1962, Ponce, Puerto Rico BB TR 5'11" 165 lbs.

Year	Team		Games	BA	SA	AB	H	2B	3B	HR	HR%	R	RBI	BB	SO	SB	AB	H	PO	A	E	DP	TC/G	FA	G by Pos
1983	OAK	A	19	.190	.286	42	8	2	1	0	0.0	5	4	1	4	1	1	1	22	24	1	7	2.5	.979	2B-6, DH-4, OF-4, 3B-4, SS-3
1986	SF	N	71	.179	.245	106	19	1	3	0	0.0	13	11	3	17	3	7	0	28	66	8	10	1.4	.922	SS-33, 3B-31, 2B-8
1987	CHI	N	49	.218	.277	101	22	6	0	0	0.0	12	8	10	16	0	23	4	35	58	3	10	2.0	.969	SS-28, 2B-4, 3B-1
1988	CIN	N	23	.231	.346	52	12	3	0	1	1.9	4	11	2	11	1	6	1	15	37	2	5	2.3	.963	SS-10, 3B-4, 2B-4
1989			97	.244	.412	340	83	13	4	12	3.5	43	34	25	46	2	5	1	112	213	10	25	3.5	.970	2B-53, 3B-50, SS-5
5 yrs.			259	.225	.349	641	144	25	8	13	2.0	77	68	41	94	7	42	7	212	398	24	57	2.4	.962	3B-90, SS-79, 2B-75, DH-4, OF-4

Rey Quinones
QUINONES, REY FRANCISCO
Born Rey Francisco Quinones y Santiago.
B. Nov. 11, 1963, Rio Piedras, Puerto Rico BR TR 5'11" 160 lbs.

Year	Team		Games	BA	SA	AB	H	2B	3B	HR	HR%	R	RBI	BB	SO	SB	AB	H	PO	A	E	DP	TC/G	FA	G by Pos
1986	2 teams		BOS A (62G – .237)				SEA A (36G – .189)																			
"	total		98	.218	.295	312	68	16	1	2	0.6	32	22	24	57	4	0	0	143	247	24	54	4.2	.942	SS-98
1987	SEA	A	135	.276	.397	478	132	18	2	12	2.5	55	56	26	71	1	0	0	204	384	25	76	4.5	.959	SS-135
1988			140	.248	.393	499	124	30	3	12	2.4	63	52	23	71	0	2	0	202	396	23	103	4.4	.963	SS-135, DH-4
1989	2 teams		SEA A (7G – .105)				PIT N (71G – .209)																			
"	total		78	.201	.283	244	49	11	0	3	1.2	23	29	16	41	0	2	0	99	193	22	27	4.0	.930	SS-76
4 yrs.			451	.243	.357	1533	373	75	6	29	1.9	173	159	89	240	5	4	0	648	1220	94	260	4.4	.952	SS-444, DH-4

Carlos Quintana
QUINTANA, CARLOS NARCIS
Born Carlos Narcis Quintana y Hernandez.
B. Aug. 26, 1965, Estado, Mirana, Venezuela BR TR 6' 175 lbs.

Year	Team		Games	BA	SA	AB	H	2B	3B	HR	HR%	R	RBI	BB	SO	SB	AB	H	PO	A	E	DP	TC/G	FA	G by Pos
1988	BOS	A	5	.333	.333	6	2	0	0	0	0.0	1	2	3	3	0	0	0	4	0	0	0	0.8	1.000	OF-3, DH-1
1989			34	.208	.273	77	16	5	0	0	0.0	6	6	7	12	0	7	2	31	0	2	0	1.0	.939	OF-21, DH-7, 1B-1
2 yrs.			39	.217	.277	83	18	5	0	0	0.0	7	8	9	15	0	7	2	35	0	2	0	0.9	.946	OF-24, DH-8, 1B-1

Marshall Quinton
QUINTON, MARSHALL J.
B. Philadelphia, Pa. Deceased. 5'11" 190 lbs.

Year	Team		Games	BA	SA	AB	H	2B	3B	HR	HR%	R	RBI	BB	SO	SB	AB	H	PO	A	E	DP	TC/G	FA	G by Pos
1884	RIC	AA	26	.234	.287	94	22	5	0	0	0.0	12		0			0	0	64	26	12	3	3.9	.882	C-14, OF-10, SS-2
1885	PHI	AA	7	.207	.241	29	6	1	0	0	0.0	6		1			0	0	40	13	8	0	8.7	.869	C-7
2 yrs.			33	.228	.276	123	28	6	0	0	0.0	18		1			0	0	104	39	20	3	4.9	.877	C-21, OF-10, SS-2

Jamie Quirk
QUIRK, JAMES PATRICK
B. Oct. 22, 1954, Whittier, Calif. BL TR 6'4" 190 lbs.

Year	Team		Games	BA	SA	AB	H	2B	3B	HR	HR%	R	RBI	BB	SO	SB	AB	H	PO	A	E	DP	TC/G	FA	G by Pos
1975	KC	A	14	.256	.333	39	10	0	0	1	2.6	2	5	2	7	0	1	1	19	3	2	0	1.7	.917	OF-10, 3B-2, DH-1
1976			64	.246	.325	114	28	6	0	1	0.9	11	15	2	22	0	32	7	9	14	2	2	0.4	.920	DH-19, SS-12, 3B-11, 1B-2
1977	MIL	A	93	.217	.330	221	48	14	1	3	1.4	16	13	8	47	0	29	5	19	4	2	2	0.3	.920	DH-53, OF-10, 3B-8
1978	KC	A	17	.207	.276	29	6	2	0	0	0.0	3	2	5	4	0	4	2	11	16	2	1	1.7	.931	3B-10, SS-2, DH-1
1979			51	.304	.443	79	24	6	1	1	1.3	8	11	5	13	0	30	8	16	9	1	0	0.5	.962	DH-9, C-9, SS-5, 3B-3
1980			62	.276	.399	163	45	9	0	5	3.1	13	21	7	24	3	12	1	72	66	8	3	2.4	.945	3B-28, C-15, 1B-1
1981			46	.250	.320	100	25	7	0	0	0.0	8	10	6	17	0	18	4	63	23	4	2	2.0	.956	C-22, 3B-8, DH-1, 2B-1
1982			36	.231	.308	78	18	3	0	1	1.3	8	5	3	15	0	7	1	110	12	0	1	3.4	1.000	C-29, 1B-6, OF-1, 3B-1
1983	STL	N	48	.209	.326	86	18	2	1	2	2.3	3	11	3	27	0	17	1	68	13	6	1	1.8	.931	C-22, 3B-7, SS-1
1984	2 teams		CHI A (3G – .000)				CLE A (1G – 1.000)																			
"	total		4	.333	1.333	3	1	0	0	1	33.3	1	2	1	0	0	2	0	1	0	0	0	0.3	1.000	3B-1, C-1
1985	KC	A	19	.281	.368	57	16	3	1	0	0.0	3	2	9	4	0	4	0	66	8	1	1	3.9	.987	C-17, 1B-1
1986			80	.215	.370	219	47	10	0	8	3.7	24	26	17	41	0	20	4	303	64	4	13	4.6	.989	C-41, SS-24, 1B-6, OF-1
1987			109	.236	.345	296	70	17	0	5	1.7	24	33	28	56	1	5	2	532	40	8	3	5.3	.986	C-108, SS-1
1988			84	.240	.408	196	47	7	1	8	4.1	22	25	28	41	1	7	0	412	34	8	5	5.4	.982	C-79, 3B-1, 1B-1
1989	3 teams		NY A (13G – .083)				OAK A (9G – .200)					BAL A (25G – .216)													
"	total		47	.176	.235	85	15	2	0	1	1.2	6	10	12	20	0	11	1	129	15	1	3	3.1	.993	C-32, 3B-3, DH-1, OF-1, SS-1, 1B-1
15 yrs.			774	.237	.353	1765	418	84	5	37	2.1	152	193	131	345	5	199	37	1830	321	49	37	2.8	.978	C-375, DH-85, 3B-83, SS-46, OF-23, 1B-18, 2B-1

LEAGUE CHAMPIONSHIP SERIES

Year	Team		Games	BA	SA	AB	H	2B	3B	HR	HR%	R	RBI	BB	SO	SB	AB	H	PO	A	E	DP	TC/G	FA	G by Pos
1976	KC	A	4	.143	.429	7	1	0	1	0	0.0	0	1	0	2	0	1	0	0	0	0	0	0.0	–	DH-2
1985			1	.000	.000	1	0	0	0	0	0.0	0	0	0	0	0	1	0	0	0	0	0	0.0	–	
2 yrs.			5	.125	.375	8	1	0	1	0	0.0	0	1	0	2	0	2	0	0	0	0	0	0.0	–	DH-2

Johnny Rabb
RABB, JOHN ANDREW
B. June 23, 1960, Los Angeles, Calif. BR TR 6'1" 179 lbs.

Year	Team		Games	BA	SA	AB	H	2B	3B	HR	HR%	R	RBI	BB	SO	SB	AB	H	PO	A	E	DP	TC/G	FA	G by Pos
1982	SF	N	2	.500	1.500	2	1	0	1	0	0.0	0	0	0	1	0	1	0	1	0	0	0	0.5	1.000	OF-1

Year	Team		Games	BA	SA	AB	H	2B	3B	HR	HR%	R	RBI	BB	SO	SB	Pinch Hit AB	Pinch Hit H	PO	A	E	DP	TC/G	FA	G by Pos

Johnny Rabb *continued*

Year	Team		Games	BA	SA	AB	H	2B	3B	HR	HR%	R	RBI	BB	SO	SB	PH AB	PH H	PO	A	E	DP	TC/G	FA	G by Pos
1983			40	.231	.346	104	24	9	0	1	1.0	10	14	9	17	1	6	2	176	13	5	2	4.9	.974	C-31, OF-2
1984			54	.195	.317	82	16	1	0	3	3.7	10	9	10	33	1	28	2	107	7	3	3	2.2	.974	1B-13, OF-8, C-6
1985	ATL	N	3	.000	.000	2	0	0	0	0	0.0	0	0	0	1	0	2	0	0	0	0	0	0.0	—	OF-1
1988	SEA	A	9	.357	.500	14	5	2	0	0	0.0	2	4	0	1	0	3	0	5	0	0	0	0.6	1.000	DH-5, OF-2, 1B-1
5 yrs.			108	.225	.353	204	46	12	1	4	2.0	22	27	19	53	2	40	4	289	20	8	5	2.9	.975	C-37, OF-14, 1B-14, DH-5

Joe Rabbitt

RABBITT, JOSEPH PATRICK
B. Jan. 15, 1900, Frontenac, Kans. D. Dec. 5, 1969, Norwalk, Conn. BL TR 5'10" 165 lbs.

Year	Team		Games	BA	SA	AB	H	2B	3B	HR	HR%	R	RBI	BB	SO	SB	PH AB	PH H	PO	A	E	DP	TC/G	FA	G by Pos
1922	CLE	A	2	.333	.333	3	1	0	0	0	0.0	1	0	0	1	0	0	0	1	0	0	0	0.5	1.000	OF-1

Marv Rackley

RACKLEY, MARVIN EUGENE
B. July 25, 1921, Seneca, S. C. BL TL 5'10" 170 lbs.

Year	Team		Games	BA	SA	AB	H	2B	3B	HR	HR%	R	RBI	BB	SO	SB	PH AB	PH H	PO	A	E	DP	TC/G	FA	G by Pos
1947	BKN	N	18	.222	.222	9	2	0	0	0	0.0	2	1	0	5	1	7	0	0	0	0.4	1.000	OF-2
1948			88	.327	.409	281	92	13	5	0	0.0	55	15	19	25	8	11	3	143	7	8	1	1.8	.949	OF-74
1949	3 teams					BKN N	(9G – .444)			PIT N	(11G – .314)			BKN N	(54G – .291)										
"	total		74	.303	.368	185	56	7	1	1	0.5	30	17	16	11	2	17	6	24	0	0	0	0.3	1.000	OF-55
1950	CIN	N	5	.500	.500	2	1	0	0	0	0.0	0	0	0	0	2	1	0	0	0	0.0	—	
4 yrs.			185	.317	.390	477	151	20	6	1	0.2	87	35	36	36	10	35	11	174	7	8	1	1.0	.958	OF-131

WORLD SERIES

Year	Team		Games	BA	SA	AB	H	2B	3B	HR	HR%	R	RBI	BB	SO	SB	PH AB	PH H	PO	A	E	DP	TC/G	FA	G by Pos
1949	BKN	N	2	.000	.000	5	0	0	0	0	0.0	0	0	0	2	0	0	2	0	0	0	1.0	1.000	OF-2

Old Hoss Radbourn

RADBOURN, CHARLES GARDNER
Brother of George Radbourn.
B. Dec. 11, 1854, Rochester, N. Y. D. Feb. 5, 1897, Bloomington, Ill.
Hall of Fame 1939. BB TR 5'9" 168 lbs.

Year	Team		Games	BA	SA	AB	H	2B	3B	HR	HR%	R	RBI	BB	SO	SB	PH AB	PH H	PO	A	E	DP	TC/G	FA	G by Pos
1880	BUF	N	6	.143	.143	21	3	0	0	0	0.0	1	1	0	1		0	0	15	16	3	2	5.7	.912	OF-3, 2B-3
1881	PRO	N	72	.219	.252	270	59	9	0	0	0.0	27	28	10	15		0	0	57	121	30	8	2.9	.856	P-41, OF-25, SS-13
1882			83	.239	.282	326	78	11	0	1	0.3	30		12	22		0	0	71	105	16	5	2.3	.917	P-55, OF-31, SS-1
1883			89	.283	.352	381	108	11	3	3	0.8	59		14	16		0	0	74	142	22	8	2.7	.908	P-76, OF-20, 1B-2
1884			87	.230	.263	361	83	7	1	1	0.3	48		26	42		0	0	69	131	25	4	2.6	.889	P-75, OF-7, 1B-5, SS-2, 2B-1
1885	BOS	N	66	.233	.285	249	58	9	2	0	0.0	34	22	36	27		0	0	40	122	22	9	2.8	.880	P-49, OF-16, 2B-2
1886			66	.237	.289	253	60	5	1	2	0.8	30	22	17	36		0	0	39	107	12	8	2.4	.924	P-58
1887			51	.229	.280	175	40	2	2	1	0.6	25	24	18	21	6	0	0	15	69	16	3	2.0	.840	P-50, OF-2
1888			24	.215	.228	79	17	1	0	0	0.0	6	6	3	14	4	0	0	14	37	6	1	2.4	.895	P-24
1889			35	.189	.221	122	23	1	0	1	0.8	14	14	9	19	3	0	0	19	58	2	6	2.3	.975	P-33, OF-2, 3B-1
1890	BOS	P	45	.253	.292	154	39	6	0	0	0.0	20	16	9	20	7	0	0	16	99	8	4	2.7	.935	P-41, OF-4, 1B-1
1891	CIN	N	29	.177	.240	96	17	2	2	0	0.0	11	10	4	11	1	0	0	9	40	7	1	1.9	.875	P-26, OF-2, 3B-1
12 yrs.			653	.235	.281	2487	585	64	11	9	0.4	308	142	158	244	21	0	0	438	1047	169	59	2.5	.898	P-528, OF-112, SS-16, 1B-8, 2B-6, 3B-2

Rip Radcliff

RADCLIFF, RAYMOND ALLEN
B. Jan. 19, 1906, Kiowa, Okla. D. May 23, 1962, Enid, Okla. BL TL 5'10" 170 lbs.

Year	Team		Games	BA	SA	AB	H	2B	3B	HR	HR%	R	RBI	BB	SO	SB	PH AB	PH H	PO	A	E	DP	TC/G	FA	G by Pos
1934	CHI	A	14	.268	.339	56	15	2	1	0	0.0	7	5	0	2	1	0	0	35	0	2	0	2.6	.946	OF-14
1935			146	.286	.404	623	178	28	8	10	1.6	95	68	53	21	4	2	0	231	8	8	1	1.7	.968	OF-142
1936			138	.335	.447	618	207	31	7	8	1.3	120	82	44	12	6	6	3	213	6	15	2	1.7	.936	OF-132
1937			144	.325	.445	584	190	38	10	4	0.7	105	79	53	25	6	6	0	273	9	10	5	2.0	.966	OF-139
1938			129	.330	.429	503	166	23	6	5	1.0	64	81	36	17	5	7	2	466	15	10	25	3.8	.980	OF-99, 1B-23
1939			113	.264	.353	397	105	25	2	2	0.5	49	53	26	21	6	13	1	300	12	6	11	2.8	.981	OF-78, 1B-20
1940	STL	A	150	.342	.466	584	200	33	9	7	1.2	83	81	47	20	6	5	1	307	10	9	4	2.2	.972	OF-139, 1B-4
1941	2 teams			STL A	(19G – .282)			DET A	(96G – .317)																	
"	total		115	.311	.411	450	140	16	7	5	1.1	59	53	29	14	5	8	0	205	7	5	3	1.9	.977	OF-101, 1B-3
1942	DET	A	62	.250	.306	144	36	5	0	1	0.7	13	20	9	6	0	29	3	83	6	1	1	1.5	.989	OF-24, 1B-4
1943			70	.261	.296	115	30	4	0	0	0.0	3	10	13	3	1	44	11	39	3	0	1	0.6	1.000	OF-19, 1B-1
10 yrs.			1081	.311	.417	4074	1267	205	50	42	1.0	598	532	310	141	40	119	24	2152	76	66	53	2.1	.971	OF-887, 1B-55

Dave Rader

RADER, DAVID MARTIN
B. Dec. 26, 1948, Claremore, Okla. BL TR 5'11" 165 lbs.

Year	Team		Games	BA	SA	AB	H	2B	3B	HR	HR%	R	RBI	BB	SO	SB	PH AB	PH H	PO	A	E	DP	TC/G	FA	G by Pos
1971	SF	N	3	.000	.000	4	0	0	0	0	0.0	0	0	0	0	0	3	0	1	0	0	0	0.3	1.000	C-1
1972			133	.259	.333	459	119	14	1	6	1.3	44	41	29	31	1	9	2	661	45	11	7	5.4	.985	C-127
1973			148	.229	.338	462	106	15	4	9	1.9	59	41	63	22	0	4	3	701	48	7	5	5.1	.991	C-148
1974			113	.291	.362	323	94	16	2	1	0.3	26	26	31	21	1	13	4	461	38	8	4	4.5	.984	C-109
1975			98	.291	.394	292	85	15	0	5	1.7	39	31	32	30	1	1	1	457	37	8	7	5.1	.984	C-94
1976			88	.263	.333	255	67	15	0	1	0.4	25	22	27	21	2	12	2	349	32	6	4	4.4	.984	C-81
1977	STL	N	66	.263	.368	114	30	7	1	1	0.9	15	16	9	10	3	28	9	147	13	4	2	2.5	.976	C-38
1978	CHI	N	116	.203	.295	305	62	13	3	3	1.0	29	36	34	26	1	13	4	412	51	11	7	4.1	.977	C-114
1979	PHI	N	31	.204	.315	54	11	1	1	1	1.9	6	6	7	0	1	1	62	6	1	4	2.4	.932	C-25
1980	BOS	A	50	.328	.474	137	45	11	0	3	2.2	14	17	14	12	1	9	2	140	15	3	4	3.2	.981	C-34, DH-9
10 yrs.			846	.257	.349	2405	619	107	12	30	1.2	254	235	245	180	10	105	28	3391	285	63	41	4.4	.983	C-771, DH-9

Don Rader

RADER, DONALD RUSSELL
B. Sept. 5, 1893, Wolcott, Ind. D. June 26, 1983, Walla Walla, Wash. BL TR 5'10" 164 lbs.

Year	Team		Games	BA	SA	AB	H	2B	3B	HR	HR%	R	RBI	BB	SO	SB	PH AB	PH H	PO	A	E	DP	TC/G	FA	G by Pos
1913	CHI	A	2	.333	.667	3	1	1	0	0	0.0	1	0	0	0	0	2	0	1	0	1.5	.667	OF-1, 3B-1
1921	PHI	N	9	.281	.344	32	9	2	0	0	0.0	4	3	3	5	0	0	0	15	22	3	3	4.1	1.000	SS-9
2 yrs.			11	.286	.371	35	10	3	0	0	0.0	5	3	3	5	0	0	0	17	22	3	3.6	.975	SS-9, OF-1, 3B-1

Doug Rader

RADER, DOUGLAS LEE (Rojo, The Red Rooster)
B. July 30, 1944, Chicago, Ill.
Manager 1983-86, 1989. BR TR 6'2" 208 lbs.

Year	Team		Games	BA	SA	AB	H	2B	3B	HR	HR%	R	RBI	BB	SO	SB	PH AB	PH H	PO	A	E	DP	TC/G	FA	G by Pos
1967	HOU	N	47	.333	.481	162	54	10	4	2	1.2	24	26	7	31	0	6	1	270	33	8	27	6.6	.974	1B-36, 3B-7

Doug Rader *continued*

Year	Team		Games	BA	SA	AB	H	2B	3B	HR	HR%	R	RBI	BB	SO	SB	Pinch Hit AB	Pinch Hit H	PO	A	E	DP	TC/G	FA	G by Pos
1968			98	.267	.393	333	89	16	4	6	1.8	42	43	31	51	2	7	3	130	171	22	18	3.3	.932	3B-86, 1B-5
1969			155	.246	.359	569	140	25	3	11	1.9	62	83	62	103	1	0	0	140	307	26	36	3.1	.945	3B-154, 1B-4
1970			156	.252	.436	576	145	25	3	25	4.3	90	87	57	102	3	1	0	149	357	18	39	3.4	.966	3B-154, 1B-1
1971			135	.244	.378	484	118	21	4	12	2.5	51	56	40	112	5	1	0	93	275	21	28	2.9	.946	3B-135
1972			152	.237	.425	553	131	24	7	22	4.0	70	90	57	120	5	0	0	119	340	20	31	3.2	.958	3B-152
1973			154	.254	.409	574	146	26	0	21	3.7	79	89	46	97	4	2	0	134	296	25	24	3.0	.945	3B-152
1974			152	.257	.415	533	137	27	3	17	3.2	61	78	60	131	7	0	0	128	347	17	28	3.2	.965	3B-152
1975			129	.223	.364	448	100	23	2	12	2.7	41	48	42	101	5	4	2	114	259	11	25	3.0	.971	3B-124, SS-2
1976	SD	N	139	.257	.378	471	121	22	4	9	1.9	45	55	55	102	3	2	0	109	318	20	22	3.2	.955	3B-137
1977	2 teams				SD	N	(52G – .271)			TOR	A	(96G – .240)													
"	total		148	.251	.437	483	121	26	5	18	3.7	66	67	71	105	2	11	1	140	210	13	12	2.5	.964	3B-96, DH-34, 1B-7, OF-1
11 yrs.			1465	.251	.403	5186	1302	245	39	155	3.0	631	722	528	1055	37	34	7	1526	2913	201	290	3.2	.957	3B-1349, 1B-53, DH-34, SS-2, OF-1

Paul Radford

RADFORD, PAUL REVERE
B. Oct. 14, 1861, Roxbury, Mass.   D. Feb. 21, 1945, Boston, Mass.

BR TR 5'6"   148 lbs.

Year	Team		Games	BA	SA	AB	H	2B	3B	HR	HR%	R	RBI	BB	SO	SB	Pinch Hit AB	Pinch Hit H	PO	A	E	DP	TC/G	FA	G by Pos
1883	BOS	N	72	.205	.252	258	53	6	3	0	0.0	46	14	9	26		0	0	86	16	20	2	1.7	.836	OF-72
1884	PRO	N	97	.197	.248	355	70	11	2	1	0.3	56		25	43		0	0	146	29	24	4	2.1	.879	OF-96, P-2
1885			105	.243	.302	371	90	12	5	0	0.0	55	32	33	43		0	0	156	73	40	7	2.6	.851	OF-88, SS-16, P-3, 2B-1
1886	KC	N	122	.229	.284	493	113	17	5	0	0.0	78	20	58	48		0	0	179	136	46	13	3.0	.873	OF-92, SS-30, 2B-1
1887	NY	AA	128	.265	.342	486	129	15	5	4	0.8	127	106		73		0	0	226	294	89	36	4.8	.854	SS-76, OF-37, 2B-18, P-2
1888	BKN	AA	90	.218	.286	308	67	9	3	2	0.6	48	29	35		33	0	0	186	28	12	3	2.5	.947	OF-88, 2B-2
1889	CLE	N	136	.238	.308	487	116	21	5	1	0.2	94	46	91	37	30	0	0	205	24	14	6	1.8	.942	OF-136, 3B-1
1890	CLE	P	122	.292	.408	466	136	24	12	2	0.4	98	62	82	28	25	0	0	228	176	42	19	3.7	.906	OF-80, SS-36, 3B-7, 2B-4, P-1
1891	BOS	AA	133	.259	.305	456	118	11	5	0	0.0	102	65	96	36	55	0	0	239	455	71	52	5.8	.907	SS-131, OF-4, P-1
1892	WAS	N	137	.255	.314	510	130	19	4	1	0.2	93	37	86	47	35	0	0	186	198	66	22	3.3	.853	SS-70, 2B-36, OF-20, 2B-2
1893			124	.228	.293	464	106	18	3	2	0.4	87	34	105	42	32	0	0	198	33	25	4	2.1	.902	OF-123, 2B-1, P-1
1894			95	.240	.311	325	78	13	5	0	0.0	61	49	65	23	24	0	0	219	247	73	23	5.7	.865	SS-47, 2B-25, OF-24
12 yrs.			1361	.242	.308	4979	1206	176	57	13	0.3	945	388	791	373	307	0	0	2254	1709	522	191	3.3	.884	OF-902, SS-356, 3B-62, 2B-54, P-10

Jack Radtke

RADTKE, JACK WILLIAM
B. Apr. 14, 1913, Denver, Colo.

BB TR 5'8"   155 lbs.

Year	Team		Games	BA	SA	AB	H	2B	3B	HR	HR%	R	RBI	BB	SO	SB	Pinch Hit AB	Pinch Hit H	PO	A	E	DP	TC/G	FA	G by Pos
1936	BKN	N	33	.097	.097	31	3	0	0	0	0.0	8	2	4	9	3	1	0	18	28	4	3	1.5	.920	2B-14, 3B-5, SS-4

Jack Rafter

RAFTER, JOHN CORNELIUS
B. Feb. 20, 1875, Troy, N. Y.   D. Jan. 5, 1943, Troy, N. Y.

BR TR 5'8"   165 lbs.

Year	Team		Games	BA	SA	AB	H	2B	3B	HR	HR%	R	RBI	BB	SO	SB	Pinch Hit AB	Pinch Hit H	PO	A	E	DP	TC/G	FA	G by Pos
1904	PIT	N	1	.000	.000	3	0	0	0	0	0.0	0	0	0		0	0	0	3	1	0	0	4.0	1.000	C-1

Tom Raftery

RAFTERY, THOMAS FRANCIS
B. Oct. 5, 1881, Boston, Mass.   D. Dec. 31, 1954, Boston, Mass.

BR TR 5'10½" 175 lbs.

Year	Team		Games	BA	SA	AB	H	2B	3B	HR	HR%	R	RBI	BB	SO	SB	Pinch Hit AB	Pinch Hit H	PO	A	E	DP	TC/G	FA	G by Pos
1909	CLE	A	8	.219	.344	32	7	2	1	0	0.0	6	0	4		1	0	0	12	0	0	0	1.5	1.000	OF-8

Tom Ragland

RAGLAND, THOMAS
B. June 16, 1946, Talladega, Ala.

BR TR 5'10"   155 lbs.

Year	Team		Games	BA	SA	AB	H	2B	3B	HR	HR%	R	RBI	BB	SO	SB	Pinch Hit AB	Pinch Hit H	PO	A	E	DP	TC/G	FA	G by Pos
1971	WAS	A	10	.174	.174	23	4	0	0	0	0.0	0	0	0	5	0	0	0	18	15	0	3	3.3	1.000	2B-10
1972	TEX	A	25	.172	.207	58	10	2	0	0	0.0	3	2	5	11	0	4	0	30	34	1	6	2.6	.985	2B-13, 3B-5, SS-3
1973	CLE	A	67	.257	.306	183	47	7	1	0	0.0	16	12	8	31	2	2	0	136	166	5	43	4.6	.984	2B-65, SS-2
3 yrs.			102	.231	.273	264	61	9	1	0	0.0	20	14	13	47	2	6	0	184	215	6	52	4.0	.985	2B-88, SS-5, 3B-5

Larry Raines

RAINES, LAWRENCE GLENN HOPE
B. Mar. 9, 1930, St. Albans, W. Va.   D. Jan. 28, 1978, Lansing, Mich.

BR TR 5'10"   165 lbs.

Year	Team		Games	BA	SA	AB	H	2B	3B	HR	HR%	R	RBI	BB	SO	SB	Pinch Hit AB	Pinch Hit H	PO	A	E	DP	TC/G	FA	G by Pos
1957	CLE	A	96	.262	.344	244	64	14	0	2	0.8	39	16	19	40	5	21	5	84	109	13	15	2.1	.937	3B-27, SS-25, 2B-10, OF-8
1958			7	.000	.000	9	0	0	0	0	0.0	0	0	0	5	0	2	0	6	8	1	4	2.1	.933	2B-2
2 yrs.			103	.253	.332	253	64	14	0	2	0.8	39	16	19	45	5	23	5	90	117	14	19	2.1	.937	3B-27, SS-25, 2B-12, OF-8

Tim Raines

RAINES, TIMOTHY (Rock)
B. Sept. 16, 1959, Sanford, Fla.

BB TR 5'8"   160 lbs.

Year	Team		Games	BA	SA	AB	H	2B	3B	HR	HR%	R	RBI	BB	SO	SB	Pinch Hit AB	Pinch Hit H	PO	A	E	DP	TC/G	FA	G by Pos
1979	MON	N	6	–	–	0	0	0	0	0		3	0	0	0	2	0	0	0	0	0	0	0.0	–	
1980			15	.050	.050	20	1	0	0	0	0.0	5	0	6	3	5	0	0	15	16	0	2	2.1	1.000	2B-7, OF-1
1981			88	.304	.438	313	95	13	7	5	1.6	61	37	45	31	71	0	0	162	8	4	0	2.0	.977	OF-81, 2B-1
1982			156	.277	.369	647	179	32	8	4	0.6	90	43	75	83	78	0	0	293	126	8	12	2.7	.981	OF-120, 2B-36
1983			156	.298	.429	615	183	32	8	11	1.8	133	71	97	70	90	1	1	314	23	4	3	2.2	.988	OF-154, 2B-7
1984			160	.309	.437	622	192	38	9	8	1.3	106	60	87	69	75	0	0	420	8	6	1	2.7	.986	OF-160, 2B-2
1985			150	.320	.475	575	184	30	13	11	1.9	115	41	81	60	70	7	0	284	8	2	4	2.0	.993	OF-145
1986			151	.334	.476	580	194	35	10	9	1.6	91	62	78	60	70	4	1	270	13	6	1	1.9	.979	OF-147
1987			139	.330	.526	530	175	34	8	18	3.4	123	68	90	52	50	0	0	297	9	4	1	2.2	.987	OF-139
1988			109	.270	.431	429	116	19	7	12	2.8	66	48	53	44	33	1	0	235	5	3	1	2.2	.988	OF-108
1989			145	.286	.418	517	148	29	6	9	1.7	76	60	93	48	41	4	3	253	7	1	0	1.8	.996	OF-139
11 yrs.			1275	.303	.442	4848	1467	262	76	87	1.8	869	490	705	520	585	17	5	2543	223	38	25	2.2	.986	OF-1194, 2B-53

LEAGUE CHAMPIONSHIP SERIES

Year	Team		Games	BA	SA	AB	H	2B	3B	HR	HR%	R	RBI	BB	SO	SB	Pinch Hit AB	Pinch Hit H	PO	A	E	DP	TC/G	FA	G by Pos
1981	MON	N	5	.238	.333	21	5	0	0	0	0.0	1	1	0	3	0	0	0	0	0	0	0	0.0	–	OF-5

John Rainey

RAINEY, JOHN PAUL
B. July 26, 1864, Birmingham, Mich.   D. Nov. 11, 1912, Detroit, Mich.

BL TR 6'1½"   164 lbs.

Year	Team		Games	BA	SA	AB	H	2B	3B	HR	HR%	R	RBI	BB	SO	SB	Pinch Hit AB	Pinch Hit H	PO	A	E	DP	TC/G	FA	G by Pos
1887	NY	N	17	.293	.345	58	17	3	0	0	0.0	6	12	5	6	0	0	0	19	26	10	3	3.2	.818	3B-17
1890	BUF	P	42	.235	.295	166	39	5	1	1	0.6	29	20	24	15	12	0	0	72	42	17	8	3.1	.870	OF-28, SS-7, 3B-6, 2B-2
2 yrs.			59	.250	.308	224	56	8	1	1	0.4	35	32	29	21	12	0	0	91	68	27	11	3.2	.855	OF-28, 3B-23, SS-7, 2B-2

Year	Team		Games	BA	SA	AB	H	2B	3B	HR	HR%	R	RBI	BB	SO	SB	Pinch Hit AB	H	PO	A	E	DP	TC/G	FA	G by Pos

Gary Rajsich

RAJSICH, GARY LOUIS
Brother of Dave Rajsich.
B. Oct. 28, 1954, Youngstown, Ohio

BL TL 6'2" 190 lbs.

Year	Team		Games	BA	SA	AB	H	2B	3B	HR	HR%	R	RBI	BB	SO	SB	AB	H	PO	A	E	DP	TC/G	FA	G by Pos
1982	NY	N	80	.259	.383	162	42	8	3	2	1.2	17	12	17	40	1	35	2	70	1	0	1	0.9	1.000	OF-35, 1B-2
1983			11	.333	.500	36	12	3	0	1	2.8	5	3	3	1	0	1	0	94	6	0	9	9.1	1.000	OF-10
1984	STL	N	7	.143	.143	7	1	0	0	0	0.0	1	2	2	1	0	4	1	13	0	0	1	1.9	1.000	1B-3
1985	SF	N	51	.165	.231	91	15	6	0	0	0.0	5	10	17	22	0	23	1	185	11	2	17	3.9	.990	1B-23
4 yrs.			149	.236	.345	296	70	17	3	3	1.0	28	27	39	64	1	63	4	362	18	2	29	2.6	.995	OF-45, 1B-28

Doc Ralston

RALSTON, SAMUEL BERYL
B. Aug. 3, 1885, Pierpont, Ohio   D. Aug. 29, 1950, Lancaster, Pa.

BR TR 6' 185 lbs.

Year	Team		Games	BA	SA	AB	H	2B	3B	HR	HR%	R	RBI	BB	SO	SB	AB	H	PO	A	E	DP	TC/G	FA	G by Pos
1910	WAS	A	22	.205	.219	73	15	1	0	0	0.0	4	3	3		2	0	0	38	3	1	1	1.9	.976	OF-22

Bob Ramazzotti

RAMAZZOTTI, ROBERT LOUIS
B. Jan. 16, 1917, Elanora, Pa.

BR TR 5'8½" 175 lbs.

Year	Team		Games	BA	SA	AB	H	2B	3B	HR	HR%	R	RBI	BB	SO	SB	AB	H	PO	A	E	DP	TC/G	FA	G by Pos
1946	BKN	N	62	.208	.242	120	25	4	0	0	0.0	10	7	9	13	0	15	1	52	64	4	9	1.9	.967	3B-30, 2B-16
1948			4	.000	.000	3	0	0	0	0	0.0	0	0	0	1	0	2	0	2	1	0	0	0.8	1.000	3B-2, 2B-1
1949	2 teams			BKN	N (5G – .154)					CHI	N (65G – .179)														
"	total		70	.177	.217	203	36	3	1	1	0.5	15	9	5	36	9	11	2	61	130	7	20	2.8	.965	3B-39, SS-12, 2B-4
1950	CHI	N	61	.262	.345	145	38	3	3	1	0.7	19	6	4	16	3	6	2	73	92	9	19	2.9	.948	2B-31, 3B-10, SS-3
1951			73	.247	.323	158	39	5	2	1	0.6	13	15	10	23	4	9	2	83	152	11	35	3.4	.955	SS-51, 2B-6, 3B-1
1952			50	.284	.361	183	52	5	3	1	0.5	26	12	14	14	3	0	0	90	143	5	28	4.8	.979	2B-50
1953			26	.154	.205	39	6	2	0	0	0.0	3	4	3	4	0	3	0	28	23	5	6	2.2	.911	2B-18
7 yrs.			346	.230	.291	851	196	22	9	4	0.5	86	53	45	107	15	46	7	389	605	41	117	3.0	.960	2B-126, 3B-82, SS-66

Mario Ramirez

RAMIREZ, MARIO
Born Mario Ramirez y Torres.
B. Sept. 12, 1957, Yauco, Puerto Rico

BR TR 5'9" 155 lbs.

Year	Team		Games	BA	SA	AB	H	2B	3B	HR	HR%	R	RBI	BB	SO	SB	AB	H	PO	A	E	DP	TC/G	FA	G by Pos
1980	NY	N	18	.208	.208	24	5	0	0	0	0.0	2	0	1	7	0	0	0	13	21	0	6	1.9	1.000	SS-7, 2B-4, 3B-3
1981	SD	N	13	.077	.077	13	1	0	0	0	0.0	1	1	2	5	0	3	1	5	11	0	1	1.2	1.000	SS-2, 2B-2
1982			13	.174	.217	23	4	1	0	0	0.0	1	2	4	4	0	5	1	10	21	1	3	2.5	.969	SS-8, 3B-1, 2B-1
1983			55	.196	.308	107	21	6	3	0	0.0	11	12	20	23	0	15	0	50	86	2	14	2.5	.986	SS-38, 3B-1
1984			48	.119	.237	59	7	1	0	2	3.4	12	9	13	14	0	3	0	34	45	3	12	1.7	.963	SS-33, 3B-6, 2B-2
1985			37	.283	.383	60	17	0	0	2	3.3	6	5	3	11	0	5	3	25	38	5	9	1.8	.926	SS-27, 2B-7
6 yrs.			184	.192	.283	286	55	8	3	4	1.4	33	28	41	64	0	31	5	137	222	11	45	2.0	.970	SS-115, 2B-14, 3B-13

LEAGUE CHAMPIONSHIP SERIES

Year	Team		Games	BA	SA	AB	H	2B	3B	HR	HR%	R	RBI	BB	SO	SB	AB	H	PO	A	E	DP	TC/G	FA	G by Pos
1984	SD	N	2	.000	.000	2	0	0	0	0	0.0	0	0	0		0	2	0	0	0	0	0	0.0	–	

Milt Ramirez

RAMIREZ, MILTON
Born Milton Ramirez y Barboza.
B. Apr. 2, 1950, Mayaguez, Puerto Rico

BR TR 5'9" 150 lbs.

Year	Team		Games	BA	SA	AB	H	2B	3B	HR	HR%	R	RBI	BB	SO	SB	AB	H	PO	A	E	DP	TC/G	FA	G by Pos
1970	STL	N	62	.190	.241	79	15	2	1	0	0.0	8	3	8	9	1	0	0	63	92	14	25	2.7	.917	SS-59, 3B-1
1971			4	.273	.273	11	3	0	0	0	0.0	2	0	2	0	0	0	0	11	7	1	1	4.8	.947	SS-4
1979	OAK	A	28	.161	.210	62	10	1	1	0	0.0	4	3	3	8	0	0	0	25	43	5	5	2.6	.932	3B-12, 2B-11, SS-8
3 yrs.			94	.184	.230	152	28	3	2	0	0.0	14	6	13	18	1	0	0	99	142	20	31	2.8	.923	SS-71, 3B-13, 2B-11

Orlando Ramirez

RAMIREZ, ORLANDO
Born Orlando Ramirez y Leal.
B. Dec. 18, 1951, Cartagena, Colombia

BR TR 5'10" 175 lbs.

Year	Team		Games	BA	SA	AB	H	2B	3B	HR	HR%	R	RBI	BB	SO	SB	AB	H	PO	A	E	DP	TC/G	FA	G by Pos
1974	CAL	A	31	.163	.163	86	14	0	0	0	0.0	4	7	6	23	2	0	0	41	90	6	20	4.4	.956	SS-31
1975			44	.240	.300	100	24	4	1	0	0.0	10	4	11	22	9	1	0	62	90	16	27	3.8	.905	SS-40
1976			30	.200	.214	70	14	1	0	0	0.0	3	5	6	11	3	0	0	30	82	4	11	3.9	.966	SS-30
1977			25	.077	.077	13	1	0	0	0	0.0	6	0	1	3	1	0	0	6	17	1	2	1.0	.958	2B-5, SS-3, DH-1
1979			13	.000	.000	12	0	0	0	0	0.0	1	0	0	6	1	0	0	7	20	5	3	2.5	.844	SS-10, DH-1
5 yrs.			143	.189	.214	281	53	5	1	0	0.0	24	16	24	65	16	1	0	146	299	32	63	3.3	.933	SS-114, 2B-5, DH-2

Rafael Ramirez

RAMIREZ, RAFAEL EMILIO (Raffy)
Born Rafael Emilio Ramirez y Peguero.
B. Feb. 18, 1958, San Pedro de Macoris, Dominican Republic

BR TR 6' 170 lbs.

Year	Team		Games	BA	SA	AB	H	2B	3B	HR	HR%	R	RBI	BB	SO	SB	AB	H	PO	A	E	DP	TC/G	FA	G by Pos
1980	ATL	N	50	.267	.352	165	44	6	1	2	1.2	17	11	2	33	2	0	0	63	140	11	25	4.3	.949	SS-46
1981			95	.218	.303	307	67	16	2	2	0.7	30	20	24	47	7	0	0	181	306	30	55	5.4	.942	SS-95
1982			157	.278	.379	609	169	24	4	10	1.6	74	52	36	49	27	0	0	300	528	38	130	5.5	.956	SS-157
1983			152	.297	.368	622	185	13	5	7	1.1	82	58	36	48	16	1	0	232	490	39	116	5.0	.949	SS-152
1984			145	.266	.327	591	157	22	4	2	0.3	51	48	26	70	14	0	0	251	443	30	94	5.0	.959	SS-145
1985			138	.248	.333	568	141	25	4	5	0.9	54	58	20	63	2	3	2	214	451	32	115	5.1	.954	SS-133
1986			134	.240	.335	496	119	21	1	8	1.6	57	33	21	60	19	5	1	156	371	29	68	4.1	.948	SS-86, 3B-57, OF-3
1987			56	.263	.346	179	47	12	0	1	0.6	22	21	8	16	6	8	2	66	110	10	33	3.3	.946	SS-38, 3B-12
1988	HOU	N	155	.276	.378	566	156	30	5	6	1.1	51	59	18	61	3	4	3	232	408	23	68	4.3	.965	SS-154
1989			151	.246	.324	537	132	20	2	6	1.1	46	54	29	64	3	5	1	189	326	30	60	3.6	.945	SS-149
10 yrs.			1233	.262	.347	4640	1217	189	28	49	1.1	484	414	220	511	99	26	9	1884	3573	272	764	4.6	.953	SS-1155, 3B-69, OF-3

LEAGUE CHAMPIONSHIP SERIES

Year	Team		Games	BA	SA	AB	H	2B	3B	HR	HR%	R	RBI	BB	SO	SB	AB	H	PO	A	E	DP	TC/G	FA	G by Pos
1982	ATL	N	3	.182	.182	11	2	0	0	0	0.0	1	1	0	1	1	0	0	0	1	0	1	0.3	–	SS-3

Bobby Ramos

RAMOS, ROBERTO
B. Nov. 5, 1955, Calabazar de Sagua, Cuba

BR TR 5'11" 190 lbs.

Year	Team		Games	BA	SA	AB	H	2B	3B	HR	HR%	R	RBI	BB	SO	SB	AB	H	PO	A	E	DP	TC/G	FA	G by Pos
1978	MON	N	2	.000	.000	4	0	0	0	0	0.0	0	0	0	1	0	0	0	3	0	0	0	2.0	1.000	C-1
1980			13	.156	.219	32	5	2	0	0	0.0	5	2	5	5	0	1	1	47	7	2	0	4.3	.964	C-12
1981			26	.195	.293	41	8	1	0	1	2.4	4	3	3	5	0	3	2	70	5	2	2	3.0	.974	C-23
1982	NY	A	4	.091	.364	11	1	0	0	1	9.1	1	2	0	3	0	0	0	21	1	0	0	5.5	1.000	C-4
1983	MON	N	27	.230	.311	61	14	3	1	0	0.0	2	5	8	11	0	0	0	111	14	2	0	4.7	.984	C-25

Year Team	Games	BA	SA	AB	H	2B	3B	HR	HR%	R	RBI	BB	SO	SB	Pinch Hit AB	H	PO	A	E	DP	TC/G	FA	G by Pos

Bobby Ramos *continued*

Year Team	Games	BA	SA	AB	H	2B	3B	HR	HR%	R	RBI	BB	SO	SB	AB	H	PO	A	E	DP	TC/G	FA	G by Pos
1984	31	.193	.277	83	16	1	0	2	2.4	8	5	6	13	0	0	0	138	22	3	1	5.3	.982	C-31
6 yrs.	103	.190	.280	232	44	7	1	4	1.7	20	17	22	38	0	5	3	390	50	9	3	4.4	.980	C-96

Chucho Ramos

RAMOS, JESUS MANUEL
Born Jesus Manuel Ramos y Garcia.
B. Apr. 12, 1918, Maturin, Venezuela

BR TL 5'10½" 167 lbs.

Year Team	Games	BA	SA	AB	H	2B	3B	HR	HR%	R	RBI	BB	SO	SB	AB	H	PO	A	E	DP	TC/G	FA	G by Pos
1944 CIN N	4	.500	.600	10	5	1	0	0	0.0	1	0	0	0	0	0	0	5	0	0	0	1.3	1.000	OF-3

Domingo Ramos

RAMOS, DOMINGO ANTONIO
Born Domingo Antonio Ramos y DeRamos.
B. Mar. 29, 1958, Santiago, Dominican Republic

BR TR 5'10" 154 lbs.

Year Team	Games	BA	SA	AB	H	2B	3B	HR	HR%	R	RBI	BB	SO	SB	AB	H	PO	A	E	DP	TC/G	FA	G by Pos
1978 NY A	1	–	–	0	0	0	0	0	–	0	0	0	0	0	0	0	0	0	0	0	0.0	–	SS-1
1980 TOR A	5	.125	.125	16	2	0	0	0	0.0	0	0	2	5	0	0	0	5	10	0	3	3.0	1.000	SS-2, 2B-2, DH-1
1982 SEA A	8	.154	.231	26	4	2	0	0	0.0	3	1	3	2	0	0	0	9	14	2	0	3.1	.920	SS-8
1983	53	.283	.362	127	36	4	0	2	1.6	14	10	7	12	3	9	1	51	109	8	22	3.2	.952	SS-28, 3B-8, 2B-8, DH-2
1984	59	.185	.210	81	15	2	0	0	0.0	6	2	5	12	2	2	0	51	49	5	10	1.8	.952	3B-38, SS-13, 1B-5, 2B-3
1985	75	.196	.250	168	33	6	0	1	0.6	19	23	17	23	0	2	0	87	119	10	26	2.9	.954	SS-36, 2B-20, 1B-14, 3B-7
1986	49	.182	.202	99	18	2	0	0	0.0	8	5	8	13	0	1	0	55	93	6	16	3.1	.961	SS-21, 2B-16, 3B-8, DH-2
1987	42	.311	.427	103	32	6	0	2	1.9	9	11	3	12	0	1	0	47	88	5	19	3.3	.964	SS-25, 3B-7, 2B-6
1988 2 teams	CLE A	(22G –	.261)	CAL A	(10G –	.133)																	
" total	32	.230	.246	61	14	1	0	0	0.0	10	5	3	7	0	4	1	37	43	1	8	2.5	.988	2B-11, 3B-10, 1B-5, SS-4, OF-1
1989 CHI N	85	.263	.335	179	47	6	2	1	0.6	18	19	17	23	1	14	6	49	142	11	20	2.4	.946	SS-42, 3B-30
10 yrs.	409	.234	.293	860	201	29	2	6	0.7	87	68	65	109	6	32	8	391	667	48	124	2.7	.957	SS-180, 3B-108, 2B-66, 1B-24, DH-5, OF-1

LEAGUE CHAMPIONSHIP SERIES

Year Team	Games	BA	SA	AB	H	2B	3B	HR	HR%	R	RBI	BB	SO	SB	AB	H	PO	A	E	DP	TC/G	FA	G by Pos
1989 CHI N	1	.000	.000	1	0	0	0	0	0.0	0	0	0	0	0	1	0	0	0	0	0	0.0	–	–

Bill Ramsey

RAMSEY, WILLIAM THRACE (Square Jaw)
B. Feb. 20, 1921, Osceola, Ark.

BR TR 6'1" 190 lbs.

Year Team	Games	BA	SA	AB	H	2B	3B	HR	HR%	R	RBI	BB	SO	SB	AB	H	PO	A	E	DP	TC/G	FA	G by Pos
1945 BOS N	78	.292	.372	137	40	8	0	1	0.7	16	12	4	22	1	29	5	78	1	3	0	1.1	.963	OF-43

Mike Ramsey

RAMSEY, MICHAEL JAMES
B. July 8, 1960, Thomson, Ga.

BB TL 6' 170 lbs.

Year Team	Games	BA	SA	AB	H	2B	3B	HR	HR%	R	RBI	BB	SO	SB	AB	H	PO	A	E	DP	TC/G	FA	G by Pos
1987 LA N	48	.232	.296	125	29	4	2	0	0.0	18	12	10	32	2	0	0	70	1	2	0	1.5	.973	OF-43

Mike Ramsey

RAMSEY, MICHAEL JEFFREY
B. May 29, 1954, Roanoke, Va.

BB TR 6'1" 170 lbs.

Year Team	Games	BA	SA	AB	H	2B	3B	HR	HR%	R	RBI	BB	SO	SB	AB	H	PO	A	E	DP	TC/G	FA	G by Pos
1978 STL N	12	.200	.200	5	1	0	0	0	0.0	4	0	1	0	0	1	0	4	6	1	3	0.9	.909	SS-4
1980	59	.262	.341	126	33	8	1	0	0.0	11	8	3	17	0	18	6	62	94	9	19	2.8	.945	2B-24, SS-20, 3B-8
1981	47	.258	.282	124	32	3	0	0	0.0	19	9	8	16	4	7	1	56	126	6	21	4.0	.968	SS-35, 3B-5, OF-1, 2B-1
1982	112	.230	.289	256	59	8	2	1	0.4	18	21	22	34	6	16	4	135	219	10	42	3.3	.973	2B-43, 3B-28, SS-22, OF-2
1983	97	.263	.337	175	46	4	3	1	0.6	25	16	12	23	4	6	1	94	149	8	34	2.6	.968	2B-66, SS-20, 3B-8, OF-1
1984 2 teams	STL N	(21G –	.067)	MON N	(37G –	.214)																	
" total	58	.188	.212	85	16	2	0	0	0.0	3	3	1	16	0	2	0	44	79	3	19	2.2	.976	SS-33, 2B-19, 3B-1
1985 LA N	9	.133	.200	15	2	1	0	0	0.0	1	0	2	4	0	5	1	5	11	2	1	2.0	.889	SS-4, 2B-2
7 yrs.	394	.240	.296	786	189	26	6	2	0.3	81	57	48	111	14	55	13	400	684	39	139	2.9	.965	2B-155, SS-138, 3B-50, OF-4

WORLD SERIES

Year Team	Games	BA	SA	AB	H	2B	3B	HR	HR%	R	RBI	BB	SO	SB	AB	H	PO	A	E	DP	TC/G	FA	G by Pos
1982 STL N	3	.000	.000	1	0	0	0	0	0.0	1	0	0	1	0	0	0	0	0	0	0	0.0	–	3B-2

Dick Rand

RAND, RICHARD HILTON
B. Mar. 7, 1931, South Gate, Calif.

BR TR 6'2" 185 lbs.

Year Team	Games	BA	SA	AB	H	2B	3B	HR	HR%	R	RBI	BB	SO	SB	AB	H	PO	A	E	DP	TC/G	FA	G by Pos
1953 STL N	9	.290	.323	31	9	1	0	0	0.0	1	2	6	0	0	0	0	56	7	1	0	7.1	.984	C-9
1955	3	.300	.600	10	3	0	0	1	10.0	1	3	1	1	0	0	0	9	1	0	0	3.3	1.000	C-3
1957 PIT N	60	.219	.286	105	23	2	1	1	1.0	7	9	11	24	0	3	1	172	11	5	5	3.1	.973	C-57
3 yrs.	72	.240	.315	146	35	3	1	2	1.4	11	13	14	31	0	3	1	237	19	6	5	3.6	.977	C-69

Bob Randall

RANDALL, ROBERT LEE
B. June 6, 1949, Norton, Kans.

BR TR 6'2" 175 lbs.

Year Team	Games	BA	SA	AB	H	2B	3B	HR	HR%	R	RBI	BB	SO	SB	AB	H	PO	A	E	DP	TC/G	FA	G by Pos
1976 MIN A	153	.267	.328	475	127	18	4	1	0.2	55	34	28	38	3	0	0	327	423	24	124	5.1	.969	2B-153
1977	103	.239	.294	306	73	13	2	0	0.0	36	22	15	25	1	5	1	222	297	8	74	5.1	.985	2B-101, DH-4, 3B-1, 1B-1
1978	119	.270	.321	330	89	11	3	0	0.0	36	21	24	22	5	11	2	231	345	10	81	4.9	.983	2B-116, 3B-2, DH-1
1979	80	.246	.281	199	49	7	0	0	0.0	25	14	15	17	2	13	2	130	169	5	48	3.8	.984	2B-71, 3B-7, OF-1, SS-1
1980	5	.200	.267	15	3	1	0	0	0.0	2	0	1	0	0	1	0	1	10	1	1	2.4	.917	3B-4, 2B-1
5 yrs.	460	.257	.311	1325	341	50	9	1	0.1	154	91	83	102	11	30	5	911	1244	48	328	4.8	.978	2B-442, 3B-14, DH-5, OF-1, SS-1, 1B-1

Jim Randall

RANDALL, JAMES ODELL
B. Aug. 19, 1960, Mobile, Ala.

BB TR 5'11" 195 lbs.

Year Team	Games	BA	SA	AB	H	2B	3B	HR	HR%	R	RBI	BB	SO	SB	AB	H	PO	A	E	DP	TC/G	FA	G by Pos
1988 CHI A	4	.000	.000	12	0	0	0	0	0.0	1	1	2	3	0	0	0	15	2	0	2	4.3	1.000	1B-2, DH-1, OF-1

Newt Randall

RANDALL, NEWTON J.
B. Feb. 3, 1880, New Lowell, Ont., Canada   D. May 3, 1955, Duluth, Minn.

BR TR 5'10"

Year Team	Games	BA	SA	AB	H	2B	3B	HR	HR%	R	RBI	BB	SO	SB	AB	H	PO	A	E	DP	TC/G	FA	G by Pos
1907 2 teams	CHI N	(22G –	.205)	BOS N	(75G –	.213)																	
" total	97	.211	.271	336	71	10	5	0	0.0	22	19	27		6	3	0	150	12	15	2	1.8	.915	OF-94

Year	Team		Games	BA	SA	AB	H	2B	3B	HR	HR%	R	RBI	BB	SO	SB	Pinch Hit AB	Pinch Hit H	PO	A	E	DP	TC/G	FA	G by Pos

Lenny Randle

RANDLE, LEONARD SHENOFF
B. Feb. 12, 1949, Long Beach, Calif.   BR TR 5'10" 169 lbs.

Year	Team		Games	BA	SA	AB	H	2B	3B	HR	HR%	R	RBI	BB	SO	SB	PH AB	PH H	PO	A	E	DP	TC/G	FA	G by Pos
1971	WAS	A	75	.219	.298	215	47	11	0	2	0.9	27	13	24	56	1	6	0	178	178	12	50	4.9	.967	2B-66
1972	TEX	A	74	.193	.269	249	48	13	0	2	0.8	23	21	13	51	4	4	0	161	177	20	39	4.8	.944	2B-65, SS-4, OF-2
1973			10	.207	.414	29	6	1	1	1	3.4	3	1	0	2	0	0	0	19	9	2	3	3.0	.933	2B-5, OF-2
1974			151	.302	.356	520	157	17	4	1	0.2	65	49	29	43	26	2	2	218	285	23	53	3.5	.956	3B-89, 2B-40, OF-21, DH-2, SS-1
1975			156	.276	.359	601	166	24	7	4	0.7	85	57	57	80	16	4	1	376	270	16	68	4.2	.976	2B-79, OF-66, 3B-17, DH-3, SS-1, C-1
1976			142	.224	.273	539	121	11	6	1	0.2	53	51	46	63	30	2	0	354	324	20	63	4.9	.971	2B-113, OF-30, 3B-2, DH-1
1977	NY	N	136	.304	.404	513	156	22	7	5	1.0	78	27	65	70	33	5	0	152	261	15	33	3.1	.965	3B-110, 2B-20, OF-6, SS-1
1978			132	.233	.320	437	102	16	8	2	0.5	53	35	64	57	14	15	5	111	215	11	21	2.6	.967	3B-124, 2B-5
1979	NY	A	20	.179	.179	39	7	0	0	0	0.0	2	3	3	2	0	5	1	19	2	0	0	1.1	1.000	OF-11, DH-2
1980	CHI	N	130	.276	.370	489	135	19	6	5	1.0	67	39	50	55	19	8	4	119	273	25	12	3.2	.940	3B-111, 2B-17, OF-6
1981	SEA	A	82	.231	.315	273	63	9	1	4	1.5	22	25	17	22	11	5	0	89	178	5	23	3.3	.982	3B-59, 2B-21, OF-5, SS-3
1982			30	.174	.217	46	8	2	0	0	0.0	10	1	4	4	2	1	1	10	27	3	3	1.3	.925	DH-13, 3B-9, 2B-6
12 yrs.			1138	.257	.335	3950	1016	145	40	27	0.7	488	322	372	505	156	57	14	1806	2199	152	368	3.7	.963	3B-521, 2B-437, OF-149, DH-21, SS-10, C-1

Willie Randolph

RANDOLPH, WILLIE LARRY
B. July 6, 1954, Holly Hill, S. C.   BR TR 5'11" 165 lbs.

Year	Team		Games	BA	SA	AB	H	2B	3B	HR	HR%	R	RBI	BB	SO	SB	PH AB	PH H	PO	A	E	DP	TC/G	FA	G by Pos
1975	PIT	N	30	.164	.180	61	10	1	0	0	0.0	9	3	7	6	1	8	2	34	45	6	8	2.8	.929	2B-14, 3B-1
1976	NY	A	125	.267	.328	430	115	15	4	1	0.2	59	40	58	39	37	1	0	307	415	19	87	5.9	.974	2B-124
1977			147	.274	.387	551	151	28	11	4	0.7	91	40	64	53	13	0	0	350	454	16	108	5.6	.980	2B-147
1978			134	.279	.357	499	139	18	6	3	0.6	87	42	82	51	36	0	0	296	400	16	80	5.3	.978	2B-134
1979			153	.270	.368	574	155	15	13	5	0.9	98	61	95	39	33	0	0	355	478	13	128	5.5	.985	2B-153
1980			138	.294	.407	513	151	23	7	7	1.4	99	46	119	45	30	0	0	361	401	19	97	5.7	.976	2B-138
1981			93	.232	.305	357	83	14	3	2	0.6	59	24	57	24	14	0	0	205	268	11	74	5.2	.977	2B-93
1982			144	.280	.349	553	155	21	4	3	0.5	85	36	75	35	16	0	0	352	380	14	100	5.2	.981	2B-142, DH-1
1983			104	.279	.348	420	117	21	1	2	0.5	73	38	53	32	12	0	0	265	298	12	77	5.5	.979	2B-104
1984			142	.287	.348	564	162	24	2	2	0.4	86	31	86	42	10	0	0	334	419	13	112	5.4	.983	2B-142
1985			143	.276	.356	497	137	21	2	5	1.0	75	40	85	39	16	0	0	303	425	11	104	5.2	.985	2B-143
1986			141	.276	.346	492	136	15	2	5	1.0	76	50	94	49	15	2	1	313	381	20	94	5.1	.972	2B-139, DH-1
1987			120	.305	.414	449	137	24	2	7	1.6	96	67	82	25	11	0	0	286	338	12	89	5.3	.981	2B-119, DH-1
1988			110	.230	.300	404	93	20	1	2	0.5	43	34	55	39	8	0	0	254	339	7	83	5.5	.988	2B-110
1989	LA	N	145	.282	.326	549	155	18	0	2	0.4	62	36	71	51	7	3	0	260	412	9	85	4.7	.987	2B-140
15 yrs.			1869	.274	.353	6913	1896	278	58	50	0.7	1098	588	1083	569	259	14	3	4275	5453	198	1326	5.3	.980	2B-1842, DH-3, 3B-1

DIVISIONAL PLAYOFF SERIES

Year	Team		Games	BA	SA	AB	H	2B	3B	HR	HR%	R	RBI	BB	SO	SB	PH AB	PH H	PO	A	E	DP	TC/G	FA	G by Pos
1981	NY	N	5	.200	.200	20	4	0	0	0	0.0	0	1	1	1	0	0	0	0	0	0	0	0.0	—	2B-5

LEAGUE CHAMPIONSHIP SERIES

Year	Team		Games	BA	SA	AB	H	2B	3B	HR	HR%	R	RBI	BB	SO	SB	PH AB	PH H	PO	A	E	DP	TC/G	FA	G by Pos
1975	PIT	N	2	.000	.000	2	0	0	0	0	0.0	1	0	0	1	0	0	0	0	1	0	0	0.5	1.000	2B-1
1976	NY	A	5	.118	.118	17	2	0	0	0	0.0	0	1	3	1	1	0	0	8	14	0	2	4.4	1.000	2B-5
1977			5	.278	.333	18	5	1	0	0	0.0	0	2	1	0	0	0	0	13	9	0	2	4.4	1.000	2B-5
1980			3	.385	.538	13	5	2	0	0	0.0	0	1	1	3	0	0	0	2	9	0	2	3.7	1.000	2B-3
1981			3	.333	.583	12	4	0	0	1	8.3	2	2	0	1	0	0	0	0	0	0	0	0.0	—	2B-3
5 yrs.			18	.258	.355	62	16	3	0	1	1.6	7	6	5	6	1	0	0	23	33	0	6	3.1	1.000	2B-17

WORLD SERIES

Year	Team		Games	BA	SA	AB	H	2B	3B	HR	HR%	R	RBI	BB	SO	SB	PH AB	PH H	PO	A	E	DP	TC/G	FA	G by Pos
1976	NY	A	4	.071	.071	14	1	0	0	0	0.0	1	0	1	3	0	0	0	13	8	0	5	5.3	1.000	2B-4
1977			6	.160	.360	25	4	2	0	1	4.0	5	1	2	2	0	0	0	13	14	0	1	4.5	1.000	2B-6
1981			6	.222	.722	18	4	1	1	2	11.1	5	3	9	0	1	0	0	13	11	0	2	4.0	1.000	2B-6
3 yrs.			16	.158	.404	57	9	3	1	3	5.3	11	4	12	5	1	0	0	39	33	0	8	4.5	1.000	2B-16

Merritt Ranew

RANEW, MERRITT THOMAS
B. May 10, 1938, Albany, Ga.   BL TR 5'11" 170 lbs.

Year	Team		Games	BA	SA	AB	H	2B	3B	HR	HR%	R	RBI	BB	SO	SB	PH AB	PH H	PO	A	E	DP	TC/G	FA	G by Pos
1962	HOU	N	71	.234	.390	218	51	6	8	4	1.8	26	24	14	43	2	15	1	357	35	8	1	5.6	.980	C-58
1963	CHI	N	78	.338	.461	154	52	8	1	3	1.9	18	15	9	32	1	41	17	213	19	3	14	3.0	.987	C-37, 1B-7
1964	2 teams		CHI N (16G – .091)			MIL N (9G – .118)																			
"	total		25	.100	.100	50	5	0	0	0	0.0	1	1	2	1	0	11	0	53	10	0	0	2.5	1.000	C-12
1965	CAL	A	41	.209	.286	91	19	4	0	1	1.1	12	10	7	22	0	17	2	78	7	1	1	2.1	.988	C-24
1969	SEA	A	54	.247	.272	81	20	2	0	0	0.0	11	4	10	14	0	31	6	62	4	2	2	1.3	.971	C-13, OF-3, 3B-1
5 yrs.			269	.247	.352	594	147	20	9	8	1.3	68	54	42	120	3	115	28	763	75	14	18	3.2	.984	C-144, 1B-7, OF-3, 3B-1

Jeff Ransom

RANSOM, JEFFREY DEAN
B. Nov. 11, 1960, Fresno, Calif.   BB TR 5'11" 185 lbs.

Year	Team		Games	BA	SA	AB	H	2B	3B	HR	HR%	R	RBI	BB	SO	SB	PH AB	PH H	PO	A	E	DP	TC/G	FA	G by Pos
1981	SF	N	5	.267	.333	15	4	1	0	0	0.0	2	1	1	1	0	0	0	28	5	0	0	6.6	1.000	C-5
1982			15	.159	.159	44	7	0	0	0	0.0	5	3	6	7	0	1	0	71	8	1	1	5.3	.988	C-14
1983			6	.200	.350	20	4	0	0	1	5.0	3	3	4	7	0	0	0	32	3	2	0	6.2	.946	C-6
3 yrs.			26	.190	.241	79	15	1	0	1	1.3	10	7	11	15	0	1	0	131	16	3	1	5.8	.980	C-25

Earl Rapp

RAPP, EARL WELLINGTON
B. May 20, 1921, Corunna, Mich.   BL TR 6'2" 185 lbs.

Year	Team		Games	BA	SA	AB	H	2B	3B	HR	HR%	R	RBI	BB	SO	SB	PH AB	PH H	PO	A	E	DP	TC/G	FA	G by Pos
1949	2 teams		DET A (1G – .000)			CHI A (19G – .259)																			
"	total		20	.259	.315	54	14	1	1	0	0.0	3	11	6	6	1	5	1	36	2	1	0	2.0	.974	OF-13
1951	2 teams		NY N (13G – .091)			STL A (26G – .327)																			
"	total		39	.303	.459	109	33	5	3	2	1.8	14	15	13	14	1	12	1	45	2	1	0	1.2	.979	OF-25
1952	2 teams		STL A (30G – .143)			WAS A (46G – .284)																			
"	total		76	.224	.310	116	26	10	0	0	0.0	10	13	6	21	0	54	10	23	0	1	0	0.3	.958	OF-17
3 yrs.			135	.262	.369	279	73	16	4	2	0.7	27	39	25	41	2	71	12	104	4	3	0	0.8	.973	OF-55

Goldie Rapp

RAPP, JOSEPH ALOYSIUS
B. Feb. 6, 1892, Cincinnati, Ohio   D. July 1, 1966, La Mesa, Calif.   BB TR 5'10" 165 lbs.

Year	Team		Games	BA	SA	AB	H	2B	3B	HR	HR%	R	RBI	BB	SO	SB	Pinch Hit AB	Pinch Hit H	PO	A	E	DP	TC/G	FA	G by Pos

Goldie Rapp *continued*

1921	2 teams	NY N (58G – .215)				PHI N (52G – .277)																			
"	total		110	.248	.308	383	95	16	2	1	0.3	49	25	29	21	9	1	0	117	226	20	19	3.3	.945	3B-106, 2B-1
1922	PHI	N	119	.253	.317	502	127	26	3	0	0.0	58	38	32	29	6	0	0	123	254	22	20	3.4	.945	3B-117, SS-2
1923			47	.263	.307	179	47	5	0	1	0.6	27	10	14	14	1	2	1	58	84	8	9	3.2	.947	3B-45
3 yrs.			276	.253	.312	1064	269	47	5	2	0.2	134	73	75	64	16	3	1	298	564	50	48	3.3	.945	3B-268, SS-2, 2B-1

Bill Rariden

RARIDEN, WILLIAM ANGEL (Bedford Bill)
B. Feb. 4, 1888, Bedford, Ind. D. Aug. 28, 1942, Bedford, Ind.   BR TR 5'10" 168 lbs.

1909	BOS	N	13	.143	.167	42	6	1	0	0	0.0	1	1	4		1	0	0	47	15	6	2	5.2	.912	C-13
1910			49	.226	.299	137	31	5	1	0	0.0	15	14	12	22	1	0	0	177	75	10	6	5.3	.962	C-49
1911			70	.228	.264	246	56	9	1	0	0.7	22	21	21	18	3	1	0	293	120	22	12	6.2	.949	C-65, 3B-3, 2B-1
1912			79	.223	.255	247	55	3	1	1	0.4	27	14	18	35	3	6	2	297	103	15	6	5.3	.964	C-73
1913			95	.236	.325	246	58	9	2	3	1.2	31	30	30	21	5	5	1	377	111	12	6	5.3	.976	C-87
1914	IND	F	131	.235	.298	396	93	15	5	0	0.0	44	47	61		12	1	0	714	215	18	14	7.2	.981	C-130
1915	NWK	F	142	.270	.369	444	120	30	7	0	0.0	49	40	60		8	0	0	709	238	21	18	6.8	.978	C-142
1916	NY	N	120	.222	.274	351	78	9	3	1	0.3	23	29	55	32	4	1	1	576	144	21	10	6.2	.972	C-119
1917			104	.271	.316	266	72	10	1	0	0.0	20	25	42	17	3	0	0	354	74	13	7	4.2	.971	C-100
1918			69	.224	.262	183	41	5	1	0	0.0	15	17	15	15	1	4	0	195	45	4	3	3.5	.984	C-63
1919	CIN	N	75	.216	.284	218	47	6	3	1	0.5	16	24	17	19	4	4	2	283	67	6	5	4.7	.983	C-70
1920			39	.248	.277	101	25	3	0	0	0.0	9	10	5	9	2	2	0	107	34	4	3	3.7	.972	C-37
12 yrs.			986	.237	.298	2877	682	105	24	7	0.2	272	272	340	179	47	24	6	4129	1241	152	92	5.6	.972	C-948, 3B-3, 2B-1

WORLD SERIES

1917	NY	N	5	.385	.385	13	5	0	0	0	0.0	2	2	2	1	0	0	0	25	10	0	1	7.0	1.000	C-5
1919	CIN	N	5	.211	.211	19	4	0	0	0	0.0	0	2	0	0	1	0	0	25	3	1	0	5.8	.966	C-5
2 yrs.			10	.281	.281	32	9	0	0	0	0.0	2	4	2	1	1	0	0	50	13	1	1	6.4	.984	C-10

Morrie Rath

RATH, MORRIS CHARLES
B. Dec. 25, 1886, Mobeetie, Tex. D. Nov. 18, 1945, Upper Darby, Pa.   BL TR 5'8½" 160 lbs.

1909	PHI	A	7	.269	.308	26	7	1	0	0	0.0	4	3	2		1	0	0	20	18	7	2	6.4	.844	SS-4, 3B-2
1910	2 teams	PHI A (18G – .154)				CLE A (24G – .194)																			
"	total		42	.183	.215	93	17	3	0	0	0.0	8	1	15		2	3	0	36	60	5	5	2.4	.950	3B-33, 2B-3, SS-1
1912	CHI	A	157	.272	.301	591	161	10	2	1	0.2	104	19	95		30	0	0	353	463	31	46	5.4	.963	2B-157
1913			90	.200	.207	295	59	2	0	0	0.0	37	12	46	22	22	2	1	159	251	16	32	4.7	.962	2B-86
1919	CIN	N	138	.264	.298	537	142	13	1	1	0.2	77	29	64	24	17	0	0	345	452	21	59	5.9	.974	2B-138
1920			129	.267	.308	506	135	7	4	2	0.4	61	28	36	24	10	1	0	312	400	17	60	5.7	.977	2B-126, OF-1, 3B-1
6 yrs.			563	.254	.285	2048	521	36	7	4	0.2	291	92	258	70	82	6	1	1225	1644	97	204	5.3	.967	2B-510, 3B-36, SS-5, OF-1

WORLD SERIES

| 1919 | CIN | N | 8 | .226 | .258 | 31 | 7 | 1 | 0 | 0 | 0.0 | 5 | 2 | 4 | 1 | 2 | 0 | 0 | 22 | 17 | 2 | 3 | 5.1 | .951 | 2B-8 |

Gene Ratliff

RATLIFF, KELLY EUGENE
B. Sept. 28, 1945, Macon, Ga.   BR TR 6'5" 185 lbs.

| 1965 | HOU | N | 4 | .000 | .000 | 4 | 0 | 0 | 0 | 0 | 0.0 | 0 | 0 | 0 | 4 | 0 | 0 | 0 | 0 | 0 | 0 | 0 | 0.0 | – | |

Paul Ratliff

RATLIFF, PAUL HAWTHORNE
B. Jan. 23, 1944, San Diego, Calif.   BL TR 6'2" 190 lbs.

1963	MIN	A	10	.190	.381	21	4	1	0	1	4.8	2	3	2	7	0	4	2	37	4	1	1	4.2	.976	C-7
1970			69	.268	.443	149	40	7	2	5	3.4	19	22	15	51	0	22	4	183	11	4	4	2.9	.980	C-53
1971	2 teams	MIN A (21G – .159)				MIL A (23G – .171)																			
"	total		44	.165	.365	85	14	2	0	5	5.9	6	13	9	38	0	16	1	126	9	2	1	3.1	.985	C-28
1972	MIL	A	22	.071	.143	42	3	0	0	1	2.4	1	4	2	23	0	10	0	38	5	0	0	2.0	1.000	C-13
4 yrs.			145	.205	.374	297	61	10	2	12	4.0	28	42	28	119	0	52	7	384	29	7	6	2.9	.983	C-101

LEAGUE CHAMPIONSHIP SERIES

| 1970 | MIN | A | 1 | .250 | .250 | 4 | 1 | 0 | 0 | 0 | 0.0 | 0 | 0 | 0 | 1 | 0 | 0 | 0 | 7 | 0 | 1 | 0 | 8.0 | .875 | C-1 |

Tommy Raub

RAUB, THOMAS JEFFERSON
B. Dec. 1, 1870, Raubsville, Pa. D. Feb. 16, 1949, Phillipsburg, N. J.   BR TR 5'10" 155 lbs.

1903	CHI	N	36	.226	.310	84	19	3	2	0	0.0	6	7	5		3	8	3	90	20	15	3	3.5	.880	C-12, 1B-6, OF-5, 3B-4
1906	STL	N	24	.282	.410	78	22	2	4	0	0.0	9	2	4		2	0	0	81	30	5	1	4.8	.957	C-22
2 yrs.			60	.253	.358	162	41	5	6	0	0.0	15	9	9		5	8	3	171	50	20	4	4.0	.917	C-34, 1B-6, OF-5, 3B-4

Bob Raudman

RAUDMAN, ROBERT JOYCE (Shorty)
B. Mar. 14, 1942, Erie, Pa.   BL TL 5'9½" 185 lbs.

1966	CHI	N	8	.241	.310	29	7	2	0	0	0.0	1	2	1	4	0	0	0	8	2	1	0	1.4	.909	OF-8
1967			8	.154	.154	26	4	0	0	0	0.0	1	1	1	4	0	0	0	13	1	2	1	2.0	.875	OF-8
2 yrs.			16	.200	.236	55	11	2	0	0	0.0	1	3	2	8	0	0	0	21	3	3	1	1.7	.889	OF-16

Johnny Rawlings

RAWLINGS, JOHN WILLIAM
B. Aug. 17, 1892, Bloomfield, Iowa D. Oct. 16, 1972, Inglewood, Calif.   BR TR 5'8" 158 lbs.

1914	2 teams	CIN N (33G – .217)				KC F (61G – .212)																			
"	total		94	.213	.229	253	54	4	0	0	0.0	28	23	28	8	7	1	0	138	264	30	27	4.6	.931	SS-66, 3B-10, 2B-7
1915	KC	F	120	.216	.263	399	86	9	2	2	0.5	40	24	27		17	0	0	209	366	46	36	5.2	.926	SS-120
1917	BOS	N	122	.256	.318	371	95	9	4	2	0.5	37	31	38	32	12	5	1	207	347	15	46	4.7	.974	2B-96, SS-17, OF-1, 3B-1
1918			111	.207	.239	410	85	7	3	0	0.0	32	21	30	31	10	1	0	208	309	19	34	4.8	.965	SS-71, 2B-20, OF-18
1919			77	.255	.309	275	70	8	2	1	0.4	30	16	16	20	11	3	0	127	185	12	22	4.2	.963	2B-58, OF-12, SS-5
1920	2 teams	BOS N (5G – .000)				PHI N (98G – .234)																			
"	total		103	.233	.315	387	90	19	2	3	0.8	39	32	22	26	9	2	0	222	322	17	53	5.4	.970	2B-98

Year	Team	Games	BA	SA	AB	H	2B	3B	HR	HR%	R	RBI	BB	SO	SB	Pinch Hit AB	Pinch Hit H	PO	A	E	DP	TC/G	FA	G by Pos

Johnny Rawlings *continued*

Year	Team	Games	BA	SA	AB	H	2B	3B	HR	HR%	R	RBI	BB	SO	SB	AB	H	PO	A	E	DP	TC/G	FA	G by Pos
1921	2 teams		PHI	N (60G – .291)		NY	N (86G – .267)																		
"	total	146	.278	.339	561	156	22	3	2	0.4	60	46	26	31	8	0	0	158	242	17	37	2.9	.959	2B-146, SS-1
1922	NY	N	88	.282	.386	308	87	13	8	1	0.3	46	30	23	15	7	5	1	169	253	7	45	4.9	.984	2B-77, 3B-5
1923	PIT	N	119	.284	.347	461	131	18	4	1	0.2	53	45	25	29	9	0	0	294	388	30	68	6.0	.958	2B-119
1924		3	.333	.333	3	1	0	0	0	0.0	0	2	0	0	0	3	1	0	0	0	0	0.0	–	
1925		36	.282	.400	110	31	7	0	2	1.8	17	13	8	8	0	3	0	60	91	3	12	4.3	.981	2B-29
1926		61	.232	.265	181	42	6	0	0	0.0	27	20	14	10	3	2	1	126	164	9	25	4.9	.970	2B-59
	12 yrs.	1080	.250	.309	3719	928	122	28	14	0.4	409	303	257	210	92	31	5	1918	2931	205	405	4.7	.959	2B-709, SS-280, OF-31, 3B-16

WORLD SERIES

Year	Team	Games	BA	SA	AB	H	2B	3B	HR	HR%	R	RBI	BB	SO	SB	AB	H	PO	A	E	DP	TC/G	FA	G by Pos
1921	NY	N	8	.333	.433	30	10	3	0	0	0.0	2	4	0	3	0	0	0	20	27	0	5	5.9	1.000	2B-8

Irv Ray — RAY, IRVING BURTON (Stubby)
B. Jan. 22, 1864, Harrington, Me. D. Feb. 21, 1948, Harrington, Me. TL 5'6"

Year	Team	Games	BA	SA	AB	H	2B	3B	HR	HR%	R	RBI	BB	SO	SB	AB	H	PO	A	E	DP	TC/G	FA	G by Pos
1888	BOS	N	50	.248	.316	206	51	2	3	2	1.0	26	26	6	11	7	0	0	61	133	30	6	4.5	.866	SS-48, 2B-3
1889	2 teams		BOS	N (9G – .303)		BAL	AA (26G – .340)																		
"	total	35	.331	.381	139	46	5	1	0	0.0	28	19	11	6	13	0	0	45	72	28	10	4.1	.807	SS-25, OF-6, 3B-4
1890	BAL	AA	38	.360	.453	139	50	6	2	1	0.7	28		15		11	0	0	40	104	17	7	4.2	.894	SS-38
1891		103	.278	.342	418	116	17	5	0	0.0	72	58	54	18	28	0	0	168	114	42	10	3.1	.870	OF-64, SS-40
	4 yrs.	226	.292	.359	902	263	30	11	3	0.3	154	103	86	35	59	0	0	314	423	117	33	3.8	.863	SS-151, OF-70, 3B-4, 2B-3

Johnny Ray — RAY, JOHNNY CORNELIUS
B. Mar. 1, 1957, Chouteau, Okla. BB TR 5'11" 170 lbs.

Year	Team	Games	BA	SA	AB	H	2B	3B	HR	HR%	R	RBI	BB	SO	SB	AB	H	PO	A	E	DP	TC/G	FA	G by Pos
1981	PIT	N	31	.245	.353	102	25	11	0	0	0.0	6	9	0	2	1	0	0	52	96	2	22	4.8	.987	2B-31
1982		162	.281	.382	647	182	30	7	7	1.1	79	63	36	34	16	0	0	381	512	21	89	5.6	.977	2B-162
1983		151	.283	.399	576	163	**38**	5	9	0.9	68	53	35	26	18	5	1	320	452	13	102	5.2	.983	2B-151, 3B-1
1984		155	.312	.434	555	173	**38**	6	6	1.1	75	67	37	31	11	9	3	331	400	12	90	4.8	.984	2B-149
1985		154	.274	.375	594	163	33	3	7	1.2	67	70	46	24	13	4	1	305	423	18	89	4.8	.976	2B-151
1986		155	.301	.394	579	174	33	0	7	1.2	67	78	58	47	6	8	2	280	479	5	89	4.9	.993	2B-151
1987	2 teams		PIT	N (123G – .273)		CAL	A (30G – .346)																		
"	total	153	.289	.374	599	173	30	3	5	0.8	64	69	44	46	4	6	1	300	448	14	103	5.0	.982	2B-148, DH-1
1988	CAL	A	153	.306	.429	602	184	42	7	6	1.0	75	83	36	38	4	4	2	269	328	20	64	4.0	.984	2B-104, OF-40, DH-6
1989		134	.289	.358	530	153	16	3	5	0.9	52	62	36	30	6	4	2	279	403	11	98	5.2	.984	2B-130
	9 yrs.	1248	.291	.392	4784	1390	271	36	48	1.0	557	551	334	285	78	42	13	2517	3541	116	746	4.9	.981	2B-1177, OF-40, DH-7, 3B-1

Larry Ray — RAY, LARRY DALE
B. Mar. 11, 1958, Madison, Ind. BL TR 6'1" 195 lbs.

Year	Team	Games	BA	SA	AB	H	2B	3B	HR	HR%	R	RBI	BB	SO	SB	AB	H	PO	A	E	DP	TC/G	FA	G by Pos
1982	HOU	N	5	.167	.167	6	1	0	0	0	0.0	0	1	0	4	0	4	1	1	0	0	0	0.2	1.000	OF-1

Floyd Rayford — RAYFORD, FLOYD KINNARD
B. July 27, 1957, Memphis, Tenn. BR TR 5'10" 190 lbs.

Year	Team	Games	BA	SA	AB	H	2B	3B	HR	HR%	R	RBI	BB	SO	SB	AB	H	PO	A	E	DP	TC/G	FA	G by Pos
1980	BAL	A	8	.222	.222	18	4	0	0	0	0.0	1	1	0	5	0	2	1	3	11	2	0	2.0	.875	3B-4, DH-1, 2B-1
1982		34	.132	.302	53	7	0	0	3	5.7	7	5	6	14	0	1	1	11	43	6	2	1.8	.900	3B-27, DH-2, C-2
1983	STL	N	56	.212	.337	104	22	4	0	3	2.9	5	14	10	27	1	26	5	13	40	7	3	1.1	.883	3B-33
1984	BAL	A	86	.256	.360	250	64	14	0	4	1.6	24	27	12	51	0	4	1	310	67	6	5	4.5	.984	C-66, 3B-22, 1B-1
1985		105	.306	.521	359	110	21	1	18	5.0	55	48	10	69	3	9	2	176	152	7	13	3.2	.979	3B-78, C-29, DH-1
1986		81	.176	.310	210	37	4	0	8	3.8	15	19	15	50	0	3	0	72	117	16	15	2.5	.922	3B-72, C-10, DH-1
1987		20	.220	.340	50	11	0	0	2	4.0	5	3	2	9	0	2	1	94	10	3	4	5.4	.972	C-17, DH-1, 3B-1
	7 yrs.	390	.244	.397	1044	255	43	1	38	3.6	112	117	55	225	4	47	11	679	440	47	42	3.0	.960	3B-237, C-124, DH-6, 2B-1, 1B-1

Fred Raymer — RAYMER, FREDERICK CHARLES
B. Nov. 12, 1875, Leavenworth, Kans. D. June 11, 1957, Los Angeles, Calif. BR TR 5'11" 185 lbs.

Year	Team	Games	BA	SA	AB	H	2B	3B	HR	HR%	R	RBI	BB	SO	SB	AB	H	PO	A	E	DP	TC/G	FA	G by Pos
1901	CHI	N	120	.233	.272	463	108	14	2	0	0.0	41	43	11		18	1	0	186	235	42	15	3.9	.909	3B-82, SS-29, 1B-5, 2B-3
1904	BOS	N	114	.210	.260	419	88	12	3	1	0.2	28	27	13		17	0	0	272	351	27	38	5.7	.958	2B-114
1905		137	.211	.247	498	105	14	2	0	0.0	26	31	8		15	1	0	270	381	34	33	5.0	.950	2B-134, OF-1, 1B-1
	3 yrs.	371	.218	.259	1380	301	40	7	1	0.1	95	101	32		50	2	1	728	967	103	86	4.8	.943	2B-251, 3B-82, SS-29, 1B-6, OF-1

Harry Raymond — RAYMOND, HARRY H.
Also known as Harry H. Truman.
B. Feb. 20, 1862, Utica, N. Y. D. Mar. 21, 1925, San Diego, Calif. 5'9" 179 lbs.

Year	Team	Games	BA	SA	AB	H	2B	3B	HR	HR%	R	RBI	BB	SO	SB	AB	H	PO	A	E	DP	TC/G	FA	G by Pos
1888	LOU	AA	32	.211	.228	123	26	2	0	0	0.0	8	13	1		7	0	0	59	55	15	1	4.0	.884	3B-31, OF-1
1889		130	.239	.297	515	123	12	9	0	0.0	58	47	19	45	19	0	0	207	261	60	23	4.1	.886	3B-129, OF-1, P-1
1890		123	.259	.299	521	135	7	4	2	0.4	91		22		18	0	0	195	267	62	22	4.3	.882	3B-119, SS-4
1891		14	.203	.237	59	12	0	0	0	0.0	4	2	5	6	3	0	0	37	51	10	9	7.0	.898	SS-14
1892	2 teams		PIT	N (12G – .082)		WAS	N (4G – .067)																		
"	total	16	.078	.109	64	5	0	0	0	0.0	6	2	7	10	2	0	0	18	39	11	1	4.3	.838	3B-16
	5 yrs.	315	.235	.279	1282	301	23	14	2	0.2	167	64	54	61	49	0	0	516	673	158	56	4.3	.883	3B-295, SS-18, OF-2, P-1

Lou Raymond — RAYMOND, LOUIS ANTHONY
Born Louis Anthony Raymondjack.
B. Dec. 11, 1894, Buffalo, N. Y. D. May 2, 1979, Rochester, N. Y. BR TR 5'10½" 187 lbs.

Year	Team	Games	BA	SA	AB	H	2B	3B	HR	HR%	R	RBI	BB	SO	SB	AB	H	PO	A	E	DP	TC/G	FA	G by Pos
1919	PHI	N	1	.500	.500	2	1	0	0	0	0.0	0	0	0	0	0	0	0	0	0	0	0	0.0	–	2B-1

Randy Ready — READY, RANDY MAX
B. Jan. 8, 1960, San Mateo, Calif. BR TR 5'11" 175 lbs.

Year	Team	Games	BA	SA	AB	H	2B	3B	HR	HR%	R	RBI	BB	SO	SB	AB	H	PO	A	E	DP	TC/G	FA	G by Pos
1983	MIL	A	12	.405	.676	37	15	3	2	1	2.7	8	6	6	3	1	0	0	5	8	0	1	1.1	1.000	DH-6, 3B-4
1984		37	.187	.325	123	23	6	1	3	2.4	13	13	14	18	1	0	0	29	76	6	4	3.0	.946	3B-36

Year	Team		Games	BA	SA	AB	H	2B	3B	HR	HR%	R	RBI	BB	SO	SB	Pinch Hit AB	Pinch Hit H	PO	A	E	DP	TC/G	FA	G by Pos

Randy Ready *continued*

1985			48	.265	.387	181	48	9	5	1	0.6	29	21	14	23	0	2	0	93	14	1	1	2.3	.991	OF-37, 3B-7, 2B-3, DH-2
1986	2 teams	MIL A (23G – .190)				SD	N	(1G – .000)																	
"	total		24	.183	.268	82	15	4	0	1	1.2	8	4	9	10	2	2	0	35	23	4	4	2.6	.935	OF-11, 2B-7, 3B-4, DH-1
1987	SD	N	124	.309	.520	350	108	26	6	12	3.4	69	54	67	44	7	25	6	124	220	15	35	2.9	.958	3B-52, 2B-51, OF-16
1988			114	.266	.390	331	88	16	2	7	2.1	43	39	39	38	6	24	5	112	153	11	22	2.4	.960	3B-57, 2B-26, OF-16
1989	2 teams	SD N (28G – .254)				PHI	N	(72G – .267)																	
"	total		100	.264	.425	254	67	13	2	8	3.1	37	26	42	37	4	28	6	80	72	9	13	1.6	.944	OF-37, 3B-32, 2B-9
7 yrs.			459	.268	.424	1358	364	77	18	33	2.4	207	163	191	173	19	83	17	478	566	46	80	2.4	.958	3B-192, OF-117, 2B-96, DH-9

Leroy Reams

REAMS, LEROY
B. Aug. 11, 1943, Pine Bluff, Ark.

BL TR 6'2" 175 lbs.

| 1969 | PHI | N | 1 | .000 | .000 | 1 | 0 | 0 | 0 | 0 | 0.0 | 0 | 0 | 0 | 1 | 0 | 1 | 0 | 0 | 0 | 0 | 0 | 0.0 | – | |

Phil Reardon

REARDON, PHILIP MICHAEL
B. Oct. 3, 1883, Brooklyn, N. Y.   D. Sept. 28, 1920, Brooklyn, N. Y.

BR TR

| 1906 | BKN | N | 5 | .071 | .071 | 14 | 1 | 0 | 0 | 0 | 0.0 | 0 | | 0 | | 0 | 1 | 0 | 10 | 1 | 1 | 1 | 2.4 | .917 | OF-4 |

Art Rebel

REBEL, ARTHUR ANTHONY
B. Mar. 4, 1915, Cincinnati, Ohio

BL TL 5'8" 180 lbs.

1938	PHI	N	7	.222	.222	9	2	0	0	0	0.0	2	1	1	1	0	4	0	3	0	0	0	0.4	1.000	OF-3
1945	STL	N	26	.347	.403	72	25	4	0	0	0.0	12	5	6	4	1	8	1	37	4	1	0	1.6	.976	OF-18
2 yrs.			33	.333	.383	81	27	4	0	0	0.0	14	6	7	5	1	12	1	40	4	1	0	1.4	.978	OF-21

John Reccius

RECCIUS, JOHN
Brother of Phil Reccius.
B. June 7, 1862, Louisville, Ky.   D. Sept. 1, 1930, Louisville, Ky.

5'6½"

1882	LOU	AA	74	.237	.316	266	63	12	3	1	0.4	46		23		0	0		91	40	23	3	2.1	.851	OF-65, P-13
1883			18	.143	.175	63	9	2	0	0	0.0	10		7		0	0		35	3	7	1	2.5	.844	OF-18, P-1
2 yrs.			92	.219	.289	329	72	14	3	1	0.3	56		30		0	0		126	43	30	4	2.2	.849	OF-83, P-14

Phil Reccius

RECCIUS, PHILIP
Brother of John Reccius.
B. June 7, 1862, Louisville, Ky.   D. Feb. 15, 1903, Louisville, Ky.

5'9" 163 lbs.

1882	LOU	AA	4	.133	.133	15	2	0	0	0	0.0	0		0		0	0		6	1	2	0	2.3	.778	OF-4
1883			1	.333	.667	3	1	1	0	0	0.0	1		0		0	0		1	0	0	0	1.0	1.000	OF-1
1884			73	.240	.323	263	63	9	2	3	1.1	23		5		0	0		56	147	31	7	3.2	.868	3B-51, P-18, SS-10
1885			102	.241	.318	402	97	8	10	1	0.2	57		13		0	0		107	193	59	18	3.5	.836	3B-97, P-7
1886			13	.308	.538	13	4	1	0	0	0.0	4		3		0	0		6	2	1	0	1.8	.889	OF-5, P-1
1887	2 teams	LOU AA (11G – .243)				CLE	AA	(62G – .205)																	
"	total		73	.211	.263	266	56	8	3	0	0.0	32		32		12	0		109	144	34	18	3.9	.882	3B-62, OF-10, SS-1, P-1
1888	LOU	AA	2	.222	.333	9	2	1	0	0	0.0	1		0	4	0	0		0	3	1	0	2.0	.750	3B-2
1890	ROC	AA	1	.000	.000	4	0	0	0	0	0.0	0		0		0	0		0	0	0	0	0.0	–	OF-1
8 yrs.			261	.231	.305	975	225	28	16	4	0.4	117	4	54		12	0		285	490	128	43	3.5	.858	3B-212, P-27, OF-21, SS-11

Johnny Reder

REDER, JOHN ANTHONY
B. Sept. 24, 1909, Lublin, Poland

BR TR 6' 184 lbs.

| 1932 | BOS | A | 17 | .135 | .162 | 37 | 5 | 1 | 0 | 0 | 0.0 | 4 | 3 | 6 | 6 | 0 | 4 | 0 | 89 | 8 | 2 | 11 | 5.8 | .980 | 1B-10, 3B-1 |

Buck Redfern

REDFERN, GEORGE HOWARD
B. Apr. 7, 1902, Asheville, N. C.   D. Sept. 8, 1964, Asheville, N. C.

BR TR 5'11" 165 lbs.

1928	CHI	A	86	.234	.280	261	61	6	3	0	0.0	22	35	12	19	8	1	0	167	223	24	39	4.8	.942	2B-45, SS-33, 3B-1
1929			21	.136	.136	44	6	0	0	0	0.0	0	3	3	3	1	1	0	23	22	2	2	2.2	.957	2B-11, 3B-5, SS-4
2 yrs.			107	.220	.259	305	67	6	3	0	0.0	22	38	15	22	9	2	0	190	245	26	41	4.3	.944	2B-56, SS-37, 3B-6

Joe Redfield

REDFIELD, JOSEPH RANDALL
B. Jan. 14, 1961, Doylestown, Pa.

BR TR 6'2" 190 lbs.

| 1988 | CAL | A | 1 | .000 | .000 | 2 | 0 | 0 | 0 | 0 | 0.0 | 0 | 0 | 0 | 0 | 0 | 0 | 0 | 1 | 0 | 0 | 1 | 1.0 | 1.000 | 3B-1 |

Glenn Redmon

REDMON, GLENN VINCENT
B. Jan. 11, 1948, Detroit, Mich.

BR TR 5'11" 180 lbs.

| 1974 | SF | N | 7 | .235 | .412 | 17 | 4 | 3 | 0 | 0 | 0.0 | 0 | 4 | 1 | 3 | 0 | 2 | 0 | 12 | 9 | 1 | 2 | 3.1 | .955 | 2B-4 |

Billy Redmond

REDMOND, WILLIAM T.
B. Brooklyn, N. Y.   Deceased.

BL TL

1877	CIN	N	3	.250	.333	12	3	1	0	0	0.0	1	3	1	1		0	0	6	14	4	0	8.0	.833	SS-3
1878	MIL	N	48	.230	.273	187	43	8	0	0	0.0	16	21	8	13		0	0	45	106	41	5	4.0	.786	SS-39, OF-7, 3B-3, C-1
2 yrs.			51	.231	.276	199	46	9	0	0	0.0	17	24	9	14		0	0	51	120	45	5	4.2	.792	SS-42, OF-7, 3B-3, C-1

Harry Redmond

REDMOND, HARRY JOHN
B. Sept. 13, 1887, Cleveland, Ohio   D. July 10, 1960, Cleveland, Ohio

TR

| 1909 | BKN | N | 6 | .000 | .000 | 19 | 0 | 0 | 0 | 0 | 0.0 | 3 | | 0 | | | 0 | 1 | 0 | 12 | 21 | 4 | 2 | 6.2 | .892 | 2B-5 |

Jack Redmond

REDMOND, JOHN McKITTRICK, JR. (Red)
B. Sept. 3, 1910, Florence, Ariz.   D. July 27, 1968, Garland, Tex.

BL TR 5'11" 185 lbs.

| 1935 | WAS | A | 22 | .176 | .294 | 34 | 6 | 1 | 0 | 1 | 2.9 | 8 | 7 | 3 | 1 | 0 | 8 | 1 | 39 | 5 | 1 | 3 | 2.0 | .978 | C-15 |

Year	Team	Games	BA	SA	AB	H	2B	3B	HR	HR%	R	RBI	BB	SO	SB	Pinch Hit AB	Pinch Hit H	PO	A	E	DP	TC/G	FA	G by Pos

Wayne Redmond

REDMOND, HOWARD WAYNE
B. Nov. 25, 1945, Athens, Ala.
BR TR 5'10" 165 lbs.

Year	Team		Games	BA	SA	AB	H	2B	3B	HR	HR%	R	RBI	BB	SO	SB	AB	H	PO	A	E	DP	TC/G	FA	G by Pos
1965	DET	A	4	.000	.000	4	0	0	0	0	0.0	1	0	1	2	0	0	0	3	0	0	0	0.8	1.000	OF-2
1969			5	.000	.000	3	0	0	0	0	0.0	0	0	0	1	0	3	0	0	0	0	0	–	–	
2 yrs.			9	.000	.000	7	0	0	0	0	0.0	1	0	1	3	0	3	0	3	0	0	0	0.3	1.000	OF-2

Gary Redus

REDUS, GARY EUGENE
B. Nov. 1, 1956, Tanner, Ala.
BR TR 6'1" 180 lbs.

Year	Team		Games	BA	SA	AB	H	2B	3B	HR	HR%	R	RBI	BB	SO	SB	AB	H	PO	A	E	DP	TC/G	FA	G by Pos
1982	CIN	N	20	.217	.337	83	18	3	2	1	1.2	12	7	5	21	11	0	0	29	3	1	0	1.7	.970	OF-20
1983			125	.247	.444	453	112	20	9	17	3.8	90	51	71	111	39	4	2	235	11	7	0	2.0	.972	OF-120
1984			123	.254	.376	394	100	21	3	7	1.8	69	22	52	71	48	10	3	200	6	7	3	1.7	.967	OF-114
1985			101	.252	.415	246	62	14	4	6	2.4	51	28	44	52	48	17	6	140	3	2	0	1.4	.986	OF-85
1986	PHI	N	90	.247	.432	340	84	22	4	11	3.2	62	33	47	78	25	2	0	185	8	4	2	2.2	.980	OF-89
1987	CHI	A	130	.236	.392	475	112	26	6	12	2.5	78	48	69	90	52	0	0	262	13	6	4	2.2	.979	OF-123, DH-4
1988	2 teams		CHI A (77G – .263)			PIT N (30G – .197)																			
"	total		107	.249	.381	333	83	12	4	8	2.4	54	38	48	71	31	16	4	182	9	4	1	1.8	.979	OF-87, DH-2
1989	PIT	N	98	.283	.462	279	79	18	7	6	2.2	42	33	40	51	25	12	3	583	55	9	43	6.6	.986	1B-72, OF-16
8 yrs.			794	.250	.410	2603	650	136	39	68	2.6	458	260	376	545	279	61	18	1816	108	40	53	2.5	.980	OF-654, 1B-72, DH-6

Bob Reece

REECE, ROBERT SCOTT
B. Jan. 5, 1951, Sacramento, Calif.
BR TR 6'1" 190 lbs.

Year	Team		Games	BA	SA	AB	H	2B	3B	HR	HR%	R	RBI	BB	SO	SB	AB	H	PO	A	E	DP	TC/G	FA	G by Pos
1978	MON	N	9	.182	.273	11	2	1	0	0	0.0	2	3	0	4	0	0	0	16	2	1	1	2.1	.947	C-9

Bill Reed

REED, WILLIAM JOSEPH
B. Nov. 12, 1922, Shawano, Wis.
BL TR 5'10½" 175 lbs.

Year	Team		Games	BA	SA	AB	H	2B	3B	HR	HR%	R	RBI	BB	SO	SB	AB	H	PO	A	E	DP	TC/G	FA	G by Pos
1952	BOS	N	15	.250	.250	52	13	0	0	0	0.0	4	0	5	0	1	0	0	22	32	4	6	3.9	.931	2B-14

Jack Reed

REED, JOHN BURWELL
B. Feb. 2, 1933, Silver City, Miss.
BR TR 6' 185 lbs.

Year	Team		Games	BA	SA	AB	H	2B	3B	HR	HR%	R	RBI	BB	SO	SB	AB	H	PO	A	E	DP	TC/G	FA	G by Pos
1961	NY	A	28	.154	.154	13	2	0	0	0	0.0	4	1	1	0	0	1	0	14	0	1	0	0.5	.933	OF-27
1962			88	.302	.465	43	13	2	1	1	2.3	17	4	4	7	2	2	0	48	0	3	0	0.6	.941	OF-75
1963			106	.205	.274	73	15	3	1	0	0.0	18	1	9	14	5	6	0	73	2	0	0	0.7	1.000	OF-89
3 yrs.			222	.233	.326	129	30	5	2	1	0.8	39	6	14	22	7	8	0	135	2	4	0	0.6	.972	OF-191

WORLD SERIES

Year	Team		Games	BA	SA	AB	H	2B	3B	HR	HR%	R	RBI	BB	SO	SB	AB	H	PO	A	E	DP	TC/G	FA	G by Pos
1961	NY	A	3	–	–	0	0	0	0	0	–	0	0	0	0	0	0	0	0	0	0	0	0.0	–	OF-3

Jeff Reed

REED, JEFFREY SCOTT
B. Nov. 12, 1962, Joliet, Ill.
BL TR 6'2" 190 lbs.

Year	Team		Games	BA	SA	AB	H	2B	3B	HR	HR%	R	RBI	BB	SO	SB	AB	H	PO	A	E	DP	TC/G	FA	G by Pos
1984	MIN	A	18	.143	.286	21	3	0	0	1	4.8	2	6	1	2	0	0	0	41	2	1	1	2.4	.977	C-18
1985			7	.200	.200	10	2	0	0	0	0.0	2	0	0	3	0	1	0	9	3	0	0	1.7	1.000	C-7
1986			68	.236	.321	165	39	6	1	2	1.2	13	9	16	19	1	7	3	332	19	2	5	5.2	.994	C-64
1987	MON	N	75	.213	.280	207	44	11	0	1	0.5	15	21	12	20	1	5	1	357	36	12	6	5.4	.970	C-74
1988	2 teams		MON N (43G – .220)			CIN N (49G – .232)																			
"	total		92	.226	.287	265	60	9	2	1	0.4	20	16	28	41	0	6	1	468	38	3	3	5.5	.994	C-88
1989	CIN	N	102	.223	.293	287	64	11	0	3	1.0	16	23	34	46	0	5	0	504	50	7	2	5.5	.988	C-99
6 yrs.			362	.222	.292	955	212	40	3	7	0.7	69	70	92	135	2	24	5	1711	148	25	17	5.2	.987	C-350

Jody Reed

REED, JODY ERIC
B. July 26, 1962, Tampa, Fla.
BR TR 5'9" 170 lbs.

Year	Team		Games	BA	SA	AB	H	2B	3B	HR	HR%	R	RBI	BB	SO	SB	AB	H	PO	A	E	DP	TC/G	FA	G by Pos
1987	BOS	A	9	.300	.400	30	9	1	1	0	0.0	4	8	4	0	1	0	0	11	26	0	9	4.1	1.000	SS-6, 2B-2, 3B-1
1988			109	.293	.376	338	99	23	1	1	0.3	60	28	45	21	1	0	0	147	282	11	57	4.0	.975	SS-94, 2B-11, 3B-4
1989			146	.288	.393	524	151	42	2	3	0.6	76	40	73	44	4	3	1	255	423	19	88	4.8	.973	SS-77, 2B-70, 3B-4, DH-1, OF-1
3 yrs.			264	.290	.387	892	259	66	4	4	0.4	140	76	122	65	6	3	1	413	731	30	154	4.4	.974	SS-177, 2B-83, 3B-9, DH-1, OF-1

LEAGUE CHAMPIONSHIP SERIES

Year	Team		Games	BA	SA	AB	H	2B	3B	HR	HR%	R	RBI	BB	SO	SB	AB	H	PO	A	E	DP	TC/G	FA	G by Pos
1988	BOS	A	4	.273	.364	11	3	1	0	0	0.0	0	0	2	1	0	0	0	3	10	0	2	3.3	1.000	SS-4

Milt Reed

REED, MILTON D.
B. July 4, 1890, Atlanta, Ga. D. July 27, 1938, Atlanta, Ga.
BL TR 5'9½" 150 lbs.

Year	Team		Games	BA	SA	AB	H	2B	3B	HR	HR%	R	RBI	BB	SO	SB	AB	H	PO	A	E	DP	TC/G	FA	G by Pos
1911	STL	N	1	.000	.000	1	0	0	0	0	0.0	0	0	0	0	0	0	0	0	0	0	0	0.0	–	
1913	PHI	N	13	.250	.292	24	6	1	0	0	0.0	4	0	1	5	1	1	1	7	14	3	0	1.8	.875	SS-9, 2B-3
1914			44	.206	.243	107	22	2	1	0	0.0	10	2	10	13	4	6	2	41	54	11	4	2.4	.896	SS-22, 2B-11, 3B-1
1915	BKN	F	10	.290	.387	31	9	1	1	0	0.0	2	8	2	0	2	0	0	18	20	6	2	4.4	.864	SS-10
4 yrs.			68	.227	.276	163	37	4	2	0	0.0	16	10	13	18	7	8	3	66	88	20	6	2.6	.885	SS-41, 2B-14, 3B-1

Ted Reed

REED, RALPH EDWIN
B. Oct. 18, 1890, Beaver, Pa. D. Feb. 16, 1959, Beaver, Pa.
BR TR 5'11" 190 lbs.

Year	Team		Games	BA	SA	AB	H	2B	3B	HR	HR%	R	RBI	BB	SO	SB	AB	H	PO	A	E	DP	TC/G	FA	G by Pos
1915	NWK	F	20	.260	.325	77	20	1	2	0	0.0	5	4	2		1	0	0	36	33	11	4	4.0	.863	3B-20

Icicle Reeder

REEDER, EDWARD JAMES
B. May, 1859, Cincinnati, Ohio Deceased.
BR

Year	Team		Games	BA	SA	AB	H	2B	3B	HR	HR%	R	RBI	BB	SO	SB	AB	H	PO	A	E	DP	TC/G	FA	G by Pos
1884	2 teams		CIN AA (3G – .143)			WAS U (3G – .167)																			
"	total		6	.154	.154	26	4	0	0	0	0.0	0		0			0	0	5	0	2	0	1.2	.714	OF-6

Nick Reeder

REEDER, NICHOLAS (Old Emergency No. 2)
Born Nicholas Herchenroeder.
B. Mar. 22, 1867, Louisville, Ky. D. Sept. 26, 1894, Louisville, Ky.
BR TR 5'9" 189 lbs.

Year	Team		Games	BA	SA	AB	H	2B	3B	HR	HR%	R	RBI	BB	SO	SB	AB	H	PO	A	E	DP	TC/G	FA	G by Pos
1891	LOU	AA	1	.000	.000	2	0	0	0	0	0.0	0	0	0	1	0	0	0	0	1	0	0	1.0	1.000	3B-1

Year	Team	Games	BA	SA	AB	H	2B	3B	HR	HR%	R	RBI	BB	SO	SB	Pinch Hit AB	Pinch Hit H	PO	A	E	DP	TC/G	FA	G by Pos

Andy Reese

REESE, ANDREW JACKSON
B. Feb. 7, 1904, Tupelo, Miss.　D. Jan. 10, 1966, Tupelo, Miss.

BR TR 5'11" 180 lbs.

Year	Team	Games	BA	SA	AB	H	2B	3B	HR	HR%	R	RBI	BB	SO	SB	PH AB	PH H	PO	A	E	DP	TC/G	FA	G by Pos
1927	NY N	97	.265	.349	355	94	14	2	4	1.1	43	21	13	52	5	12	2	92	128	18	15	2.5	.924	3B-64, OF-16, 1B-1
1928		109	.308	.416	406	125	18	4	6	1.5	61	44	13	24	7	4	0	232	136	16	21	3.5	.958	OF-64, 2B-26, SS-6, 3B-6, 1B-6
1929		58	.263	.344	209	55	11	3	0	0.0	36	21	15	19	8	2	0	117	168	11	24	5.1	.963	2B-44, OF-8, 3B-4
1930		67	.273	.390	172	47	4	2	4	2.3	26	25	10	12	1	17	3	70	13	5	1	1.3	.943	OF-32, 3B-10
4 yrs.		331	.281	.378	1142	321	47	11	14	1.2	166	111	51	107	21	35	5	511	445	50	61	3.0	.950	OF-120, 3B-84, 2B-70, 1B-7, SS-6

Jimmy Reese

REESE, JAMES HARRISON
Born James Harrison Solomon.
B. Oct. 1, 1905, Los Angeles, Calif.

BL TR 5'11½" 165 lbs.

Year	Team	Games	BA	SA	AB	H	2B	3B	HR	HR%	R	RBI	BB	SO	SB	PH AB	PH H	PO	A	E	DP	TC/G	FA	G by Pos
1930	NY A	77	.346	.489	188	65	14	2	3	1.6	44	18	11	8	1	20	10	93	105	5	26	2.6	.975	2B-48, 3B-5
1931		65	.241	.335	245	59	10	2	3	1.2	41	26	17	10	2	3	1	173	168	10	44	5.4	.972	2B-61
1932	STL N	90	.265	.333	309	82	15	0	2	0.6	38	26	20	19	4	10	4	209	220	9	48	4.9	.979	2B-77
3 yrs.		232	.278	.373	742	206	39	4	8	1.1	123	70	48	37	7	33	15	475	493	24	118	4.3	.976	2B-186, 3B-5

Pee Wee Reese

REESE, HAROLD HENRY (The Little Colonel)
B. July 23, 1918, Ekron, Ky.
Hall of Fame 1984.

BR TR 5'10" 160 lbs.

Year	Team	Games	BA	SA	AB	H	2B	3B	HR	HR%	R	RBI	BB	SO	SB	PH AB	PH H	PO	A	E	DP	TC/G	FA	G by Pos
1940	BKN N	84	.272	.372	312	85	8	4	5	1.6	58	28	45	42	15	0	0	190	238	18	41	5.3	.960	SS-83
1941		152	.229	.294	595	136	23	5	2	0.3	76	46	68	56	10	1	0	346	473	47	76	5.7	.946	SS-151
1942		151	.255	.332	564	144	24	5	3	0.5	87	53	82	55	15	0	0	337	482	35	99	5.7	.959	SS-151
1946		152	.284	.378	542	154	16	10	5	0.9	79	60	87	71	10	0	0	285	463	26	104	5.1	.966	SS-152
1947		142	.284	.426	476	135	24	4	12	2.5	81	73	104	67	7	0	0	266	441	25	99	5.2	.966	SS-142
1948		151	.274	.390	566	155	31	4	9	1.6	96	75	79	63	25	2	0	335	453	31	93	5.4	.962	SS-149
1949		155	.279	.410	617	172	27	3	16	2.6	132	73	116	59	26	0	0	316	454	18	93	5.1	.977	SS-155
1950		141	.260	.380	531	138	21	5	11	2.1	97	52	91	62	17	0	0	291	414	26	95	5.2	.964	SS-134, 3B-7
1951		154	.286	.393	616	176	20	8	10	1.6	94	84	81	57	20	0	0	292	422	35	106	4.9	.953	SS-154
1952		149	.272	.365	559	152	18	8	6	1.1	94	58	86	59	30	4	1	282	376	21	89	4.6	.969	SS-145
1953		140	.271	.420	524	142	25	7	13	2.5	108	61	82	61	22	3	0	265	380	23	83	4.8	.966	SS-135
1954		141	.309	.455	554	171	35	8	10	1.8	98	69	90	62	8	1	1	270	426	25	74	5.1	.965	SS-140
1955		145	.282	.403	553	156	29	4	10	1.8	99	61	78	60	8	3	0	239	404	23	86	4.6	.965	SS-142
1956		147	.257	.344	572	147	19	2	9	1.6	85	46	56	69	13	1	0	269	388	25	80	4.6	.963	SS-136, 3B-12
1957		103	.224	.248	330	74	3	1	1	0.3	33	29	39	32	5	4	1	97	228	19	21	3.3	.945	3B-75, SS-23
1958	LA N	59	.224	.381	147	33	7	2	4	2.7	21	17	26	15	1	15	1	44	89	10	16	2.4	.930	SS-22, 3B-21
16 yrs.		2166	.269	.377	8058	2170	330	80	126	1.6	1338	885	1210	890	232	34	4	4124	6131	407	1255	4.9	.962	SS-2014, 3B-115

WORLD SERIES

Year	Team	Games	BA	SA	AB	H	2B	3B	HR	HR%	R	RBI	BB	SO	SB	PH AB	PH H	PO	A	E	DP	TC/G	FA	G by Pos
1941	BKN N	5	.200	.200	20	4	0	0	0	0.0	1	2	0	0	0	0	0	13	14	3	4	6.0	.900	SS-5
1947		7	.304	.348	23	7	1	0	0	0.0	5	4	6	3	3	0	0	8	15	1	5	3.4	.958	SS-7
1949		5	.316	.526	19	6	1	0	1	5.3	2	2	1	0	1	0	0	5	9	1	0	3.0	.933	SS-5
1952		7	.345	.448	29	10	0	0	1	3.4	4	4	2	2	1	0	0	15	18	2	3	5.0	.943	SS-7
1953		6	.208	.292	24	5	0	1	0	0.0	4	1	0	4	1	0	0	7	14	0	0	3.5	1.000	SS-6
1955		7	.296	.333	27	8	1	0	0	0.0	5	2	3	5	0	0	0	15	23	1	7	5.6	.974	SS-7
1956		7	.222	.296	27	6	0	1	0	0.0	3	2	2	6	0	0	0	14	21	1	7	5.1	.972	SS-7
7 yrs.		44	.272	.349	169	46	3	2	2	1.2	24	17	14	25	6	0	0	77	114	9	26	4.5	.955	SS-44
	9th				9th	5th									5									

Rich Reese

REESE, RICHARD BENJAMIN
B. Sept. 29, 1941, Leipsic, Ohio

BL TL 6'3" 185 lbs.

Year	Team	Games	BA	SA	AB	H	2B	3B	HR	HR%	R	RBI	BB	SO	SB	PH AB	PH H	PO	A	E	DP	TC/G	FA	G by Pos
1964	MIN A	10	.000	.000	7	0	0	0	0	0.0	0	1	0	7	0	3	0	0	0	0.3	1.000	1B-1
1965		14	.286	.429	7	2	1	0	0	0.0	0	0	2	2	0	4	1	14	1	0	1	1.1	1.000	1B-6, OF-1
1966		3	.000	.000	2	0	0	0	0	0.0	0	0	1	2	0	2	0	0	0	0	0	0.0	—	
1967		95	.248	.416	101	25	5	0	4	4.0	13	20	8	17	0	41	13	107	4	1	5	1.2	.991	1B-36, OF-10
1968		126	.259	.352	332	86	15	2	4	1.2	40	28	18	36	3	30	6	642	38	6	36	5.4	.991	1B-87, OF-15
1969		132	.322	.513	419	135	24	4	16	3.8	52	69	23	57	1	17	4	929	57	7	97	7.5	.993	1B-117, OF-5
1970		153	.261	.371	501	131	15	5	10	2.0	63	56	48	70	5	12	4	1118	82	10	94	7.9	.992	1B-146
1971		120	.219	.353	329	72	8	3	10	3.0	40	39	20	35	7	20	6	679	44	4	71	6.1	.994	1B-95, OF-9
1972		132	.218	.330	197	43	3	2	5	2.5	23	26	25	27	0	26	7	419	30	7	55	3.5	.985	1B-98, OF-13
1973	2 teams		DET A	(59G – .137)		MIN A	(22G – .174)																	
"	total	81	.144	.248	125	18	2	1	3	2.4	17	7	13	23	0	15	3	198	13	1	15	2.6	.995	1B-54, OF-21
10 yrs.		866	.253	.384	2020	512	73	17	52	2.6	248	245	158	270	16	174	44	4109	269	36	373	5.1	.992	1B-640, OF-74

LEAGUE CHAMPIONSHIP SERIES

Year	Team	Games	BA	SA	AB	H	2B	3B	HR	HR%	R	RBI	BB	SO	SB	PH AB	PH H	PO	A	E	DP	TC/G	FA	G by Pos
1969	MIN A	3	.167	.167	12	2	0	0	0	0.0	0	2	1	1	0	0	0	26	5	0	3	10.3	1.000	1B-3
1970		2	.143	.143	7	1	0	0	0	0.0	0	0	1	1	0	0	0	16	2	0	3	9.0	1.000	1B-2
2 yrs.		5	.158	.158	19	3	0	0	0	0.0	0	2	2	2	0	0	0	42	7	0	6	9.8	1.000	1B-5

Bobby Reeves

REEVES, ROBERT EDWIN (Gunner)
B. June 24, 1904, Hill City, Tenn.

BR TR 5'11" 170 lbs.

Year	Team	Games	BA	SA	AB	H	2B	3B	HR	HR%	R	RBI	BB	SO	SB	PH AB	PH H	PO	A	E	DP	TC/G	FA	G by Pos
1926	WAS A	20	.224	.265	49	11	0	1	0	0.0	4	7	6	9	1	1	0	23	29	3	4	2.8	.945	3B-16, SS-1, 2B-1
1927		112	.255	.318	380	97	11	5	1	0.3	37	39	21	53	3	0	0	207	315	46	37	5.1	.919	SS-96, 3B-12, 2B-2
1928		102	.303	.419	353	107	16	8	3	0.8	44	42	24	47	4	2	1	231	265	45	40	5.3	.917	SS-66, 2B-22, 3B-8, OF-1
1929	BOS A	140	.248	.311	460	114	19	2	2	0.4	66	28	60	57	7	1	0	152	242	38	27	3.1	.912	3B-132, 2B-2, 1B-1
1930		92	.217	.294	272	59	7	4	2	0.7	41	18	50	36	6	4	1	123	183	27	32	3.6	.919	3B-62, SS-15, 2B-11
1931		36	.167	.238	84	14	2	2	0	0.0	11	1	14	16	0	2	0	64	64	12	11	3.9	.914	2B-29, P-1
6 yrs.		502	.252	.329	1598	402	55	22	8	0.5	203	135	175	218	21	10	2	800	1098	171	151	4.1	.917	3B-230, SS-178, 2B-67, OF-1, 1B-1, P-1

Rudy Regalado

REGALADO, RUDOLPH VALENTINO
B. May 21, 1930, Los Angeles, Calif.

BR TR 6'1" 185 lbs.

Year	Team	Games	BA	SA	AB	H	2B	3B	HR	HR%	R	RBI	BB	SO	SB	PH AB	PH H	PO	A	E	DP	TC/G	FA	G by Pos
1954	CLE A	65	.250	.311	180	45	5	0	2	1.1	21	24	19	16	0	8	1	62	86	5	7	2.4	.967	3B-50, 2B-2

Year	Team	Games	BA	SA	AB	H	2B	3B	HR	HR%	R	RBI	BB	SO	SB	Pinch Hit AB	Pinch Hit H	PO	A	E	DP	TC/G	FA	G by Pos

Rudy Regalado *continued*

Year	Team	Games	BA	SA	AB	H	2B	3B	HR	HR%	R	RBI	BB	SO	SB	AB	H	PO	A	E	DP	TC/G	FA	G by Pos
1955		10	.269	.346	26	7	2	0	0	0.0	2	5	2	4	0	1	0	8	15	1	2	2.4	.958	3B-8, 2B-1
1956		16	.234	.255	47	11	1	0	0	0.0	4	2	4	1	0	1	0	10	10	5	3	1.6	.800	3B-14, 1B-1
3 yrs.		91	.249	.304	253	63	8	0	2	0.8	27	31	25	21	0	10	1	80	111	11	12	2.2	.946	3B-72, 2B-3, 1B-1

WORLD SERIES

| 1954 | CLE A | 4 | .333 | .333 | 3 | 1 | 0 | 0 | 0 | 0.0 | 0 | 1 | 0 | 0 | 0 | 2 | 1 | 0 | 0 | 0 | 0 | 0.0 | — | 3B-1 |

Bill Regan

REGAN, WILLIAM WRIGHT
B. Jan. 23, 1899, Pittsburgh, Pa. D. June 11, 1968, Pittsburgh, Pa.   BR TR 5'10" 155 lbs.

1926	BOS A	108	.263	.360	403	106	21	3	4	1.0	40	34	23	37	6	2	0	264	392	24	66	6.3	.965	2B-106
1927		129	.274	.408	468	128	37	10	2	0.4	43	66	26	51	10	7	1	283	397	28	76	5.5	.960	2B-121
1928		138	.264	.387	511	135	30	6	7	1.4	53	75	21	40	9	0	0	294	467	29	87	5.7	.963	2B-137, OF-1
1929		104	.288	.407	371	107	27	7	1	0.3	38	54	22	38	7	2	1	203	296	21	68	5.0	.960	2B-91, 3B-10, 1B-1
1930		134	.266	.393	507	135	35	10	3	0.6	54	53	25	60	4	5	2	309	440	29	92	5.8	.963	2B-127, 3B-2
1931	PIT N	28	.202	.308	104	21	8	0	1	1.0	8	10	5	19	2	0	0	63	90	9	14	5.8	.944	2B-28
6 yrs.		641	.267	.387	2364	632	158	36	18	0.8	236	292	122	245	38	16	4	1416	2082	140	403	5.7	.962	2B-610, 3B-12, OF-1, 1B-1

Joe Regan

REGAN, JOSEPH CHARLES
B. July 12, 1872, Seymour, Conn. D. Nov. 18, 1948, Hartford, Conn.   BR TR 6'1"

| 1898 | NY N | 2 | .200 | .200 | 5 | 1 | 0 | 0 | 0 | 0.0 | 1 | 2 | 0 | | 0 | 0 | 0 | 1 | 0 | 0 | 0 | 0.5 | 1.000 | OF-2 |

Tony Rego

REGO, ANTONE (Mighty Midget)
Born Antone DoRego.
B. Oct. 31, 1897, Wailuku, Hawaii   D. Jan. 6, 1978, Tulsa, Okla.   BR TR 5'4" 140 lbs.

1924	STL A	23	.224	.241	58	13	1	0	0	0.0	5	5	1	3	0	1	1	57	12	2	2	3.1	.972	C-22
1925		20	.406	.531	32	13	2	1	0	0.0	5	3	3	2	0	1	0	35	12	1	1	2.4	.979	C-19
2 yrs.		43	.289	.344	90	26	3	1	0	0.0	10	8	4	5	0	2	1	92	24	3	3	2.8	.975	C-41

Wally Rehg

REHG, WALTER PHILLIP
B. Aug. 31, 1888, Summerfield, Ill. D. Apr. 5, 1946, Burbank, Calif.   BR TR 5'8" 160 lbs.

1912	PIT N	8	.000	.000	9	0	0	0	0	0.0	0	0	0		0	0	0	2	0	0	0	0.3	1.000	OF-2
1913	BOS A	30	.277	.347	101	28	3	2	0	0.0	14	9	2	7	4	2	1	30	3	2	0	1.2	.943	OF-27
1914		84	.219	.272	151	33	4	2	0	0.0	14	11	18	11	5	36	10	45	4	1	3	0.6	.980	OF-42
1915		5	.200	.200	5	1	0	0	0	0.0	2	0	1	0	0	0	0	1	0	0	0	0.2	1.000	OF-1
1917	BOS N	86	.270	.349	341	92	12	6	1	0.3	48	31	24	32	13	0	0	122	9	6	2	1.6	.956	OF-86
1918		40	.241	.316	133	32	5	1	1	0.8	6	12	5	14	3	2	0	75	6	1	1	2.1	.988	OF-38
1919	CIN N	5	.167	.167	12	2	0	0	0	0.0	1	3	1	0	0	0	0	5	2	1	0	1.6	.875	OF-5
7 yrs.		258	.250	.319	752	188	24	11	2	0.3	86	66	52	66	26	47	12	280	24	11	6	1.2	.965	OF-201

Frank Reiber

REIBER, FRANK BERNARD (Tubby)
B. Sept. 19, 1909, Huntington, W. Va.   BR TR 5'8½" 169 lbs.

1933	DET A	13	.278	.556	18	5	0	1	1	5.6	3	3	2	3	0	6	1	13	0	1	0	1.1	.929	C-6
1934		3	.000	.000	1	0	0	0	0	0.0	0	0	2	0	0	0	0	0	0	0	0	0.0	—	
1935		8	.273	.273	11	3	0	0	0	0.0	3	1	3	3	0	2	0	10	0	0	1	1.3	1.000	C-5
1936		20	.273	.364	55	15	2	0	1	1.8	7	5	5	7	0	2	0	47	7	1	0	2.8	.982	C-17, OF-1
4 yrs.		44	.271	.388	85	23	2	1	2	2.4	13	9	12	13	0	11	1	70	7	2	1	1.8	.975	C-28, OF-1

Herm Reich

REICH, HERMAN CHARLES
B. Nov. 23, 1917, Bell, Calif.   BR TL 6'2" 200 lbs.

| 1949 | 3 teams | WAS A (2G – .000) | | | | | CLE A (1G – .500) | | | | CHI N (108G – .280) | | | | | | | | | | | | | |
| " | total | 111 | .279 | .359 | 390 | 109 | 18 | 2 | 3 | 0.8 | 43 | 34 | 14 | 33 | 4 | 10 | 1 | 786 | 87 | 10 | 58 | 8.0 | .989 | 1B-85, OF-17 |

Rick Reichardt

REICHARDT, FREDERIC CARL
B. Mar. 16, 1943, Madison, Wis.   BR TR 6'3" 210 lbs.

1964	LA A	11	.162	.162	37	6	0	0	0	0.0	0	0	1	12	1	0	0	26	0	0	0	2.4	1.000	OF-11
1965	CAL A	20	.267	.360	75	20	4	0	1	1.3	8	6	5	12	4	0	0	38	1	1	1	2.0	.975	OF-20
1966		89	.288	.480	319	92	5	4	16	5.0	48	44	27	61	8	2	1	153	8	4	1	1.9	.976	OF-87
1967		146	.265	.404	498	132	14	2	17	3.4	56	69	35	90	5	9	2	254	10	7	4	1.9	.974	OF-138
1968		151	.255	.421	534	136	20	4	21	3.9	62	73	42	118	4	1	0	267	9	3	2	1.8	.989	OF-148
1969		137	.254	.371	493	125	11	4	13	2.6	60	68	43	100	3	0	0	270	16	5	5	2.1	.983	OF-136, 1B-3
1970	2 teams	CAL A (9G – .167)					WAS A (107G – .253)																	
"	total	116	.251	.473	283	71	14	2	15	5.3	43	47	26	69	2	41	8	135	0	2	0	1.2	.985	OF-80, 3B-1
1971	CHI A	138	.278	.429	496	138	14	2	19	3.8	53	62	37	90	5	7	2	333	7	5	2	2.5	.986	OF-128, 1B-9
1972		101	.251	.409	291	73	14	4	8	2.7	31	43	28	63	2	10	1	157	2	3	1	1.6	.981	OF-90
1973	2 teams	CHI A (46G – .275)					KC A (41G – .220)																	
"	total	87	.250	.382	280	70	13	3	6	2.1	30	33	19	57	2	9	3	68	2	0	1	0.8	1.000	OF-44, DH-37
1974	KC A	1	1.000	1.000	1	1	0	0	0	0.0	0	0	0	0	0	1	1	0	0	0	0	0.0	—	
11 yrs.		997	.261	.414	3307	864	109	24	116	3.5	391	445	263	672	40	84	19	1701	55	30	17	1.8	.983	OF-882, DH-37, 1B-12, 3B-1

Dick Reichle

REICHLE, RICHARD WENDELL
B. Nov. 23, 1896, Lincoln, Ill. D. June 13, 1967, St. Louis, Mo.   BL TR 6' 185 lbs.

1922	BOS A	6	.250	.292	24	6	1	0	0	0.0	3	0	0	0	0	0	0	15	0	0	0	2.5	1.000	OF-6
1923		122	.258	.330	361	93	17	3	1	0.3	40	39	22	34	3	19	5	190	10	5	2	1.7	.976	OF-93
2 yrs.		128	.257	.327	385	99	18	3	1	0.3	43	39	22	36	3	19	5	205	10	5	2	1.7	.977	OF-99

Billy Reid

REID, WILLIAM ALEXANDER
B. May 17, 1857, London, Ont., Canada   D. June 26, 1940, London, Ont., Canada   BR TR 6' 170 lbs.

| 1883 | BAL AA | 24 | .278 | .309 | 97 | 27 | 3 | 0 | 0 | 0.0 | 14 | | 4 | | | 0 | 0 | 61 | 65 | 24 | 7 | 6.3 | .840 | 2B-23, SS-1 |

Year	Team		Games	BA	SA	AB	H	2B	3B	HR	HR%	R	RBI	BB	SO	SB	Pinch Hit AB	Pinch Hit H	PO	A	E	DP	TC/G	FA	G by Pos

Billy Reid *continued*

Year	Team		Games	BA	SA	AB	H	2B	3B	HR	HR%	R	RBI	BB	SO	SB	AB	H	PO	A	E	DP	TC/G	FA	G by Pos
1884	PIT	AA	19	.243	.271	70	17	2	0	0	0.0	11		4			0	0	24	2	11	0	1.9	.703	OF-17, 3B-1, 2B-1, 1B-1
2 yrs.			43	.263	.293	167	44	5	0	0	0.0	25		8			0	0	85	67	35	7	4.3	.813	2B-24, OF-17, SS-1, 3B-1, 1B-1

Jessie Reid

REID, JESSIE THOMAS
B. June 1, 1962, Honolulu, Hawaii   BL TL 6'1" 200 lbs.

1987	SF	N	6	.125	.500	8	1	0	0	1	12.5	1	1	1	5	0	5	0	3	0	0	0	0.5	1.000	OF-3
1988			2	.000	.000	2	0	0	0	0	0.0	0	0	0	1	0	2	0	0	0	0	0	0.0	—	
2 yrs.			8	.100	.400	10	1	0	0	1	10.0	1	1	1	6	0	7	0	3	0	0	0	0.4	1.000	OF-3

Scott Reid

REID, SCOTT DONALD
B. Jan. 7, 1947, Chicago, Ill.   BL TR 6'1" 195 lbs.

1969	PHI	N	13	.211	.211	19	4	0	0	0	0.0	5	0	7	5	0	5	1	7	0	0	0	0.5	1.000	OF-5
1970			25	.122	.143	49	6	1	0	0	0.0	5	1	11	22	0	4	0	28	6	0	1	1.4	1.000	OF-18
2 yrs.			38	.147	.162	68	10	1	0	0	0.0	10	1	18	27	0	9	1	35	6	0	1	1.1	1.000	OF-23

Charlie Reilley

REILLEY, CHARLES E.
B. 1856, Hartford, Conn. D. 1888   BR TR 5'8" 160 lbs.

1879	TRO	N	62	.229	.258	236	54	5	1	0	0.0	17	19	1	20		0	0	354	51	53	6	7.4	.884	C-49, 1B-11, OF-2
1880	CIN	N	30	.204	.214	103	21	1	0	0	0.0	8	9	0	5		0	0	68	16	14	0	3.3	.857	OF-16, C-13, 3B-4
1881	2 teams		DET N (19G – .171)						WOR N (2G – .375)																
"	total		21	.192	.218	78	15	2	0	0	0.0	10	4	0	11		0	0	65	29	19	2	5.4	.832	C-12, OF-4, SS-3, 3B-3, 1B-1
1882	PRO	N	3	.182	.182	11	2	0	0	0	0.0	0		1	2		0	0	14	1	6	0	7.0	.714	C-3
4 yrs.			116	.215	.238	428	92	8	1	0	0.0	35	32	2	38		0	0	501	97	92	8	5.9	.867	C-77, OF-22, 1B-12, 3B-7, SS-3

Duke Reilley

REILLEY, ALEXANDER ALOYSIUS (Midget)
B. Aug. 25, 1884, Chicago, Ill. D. Mar. 4, 1968, Indianapolis, Ind.   BB TR 5'4½" 148 lbs.

| 1909 | CLE | A | 20 | .210 | .210 | 62 | 13 | 0 | 0 | 0 | 0.0 | 10 | 0 | 4 | | 5 | 0 | 0 | 46 | 1 | 1 | 1 | 2.4 | .979 | OF-18 |

Arch Reilly

REILLY, ARCHER EDWIN
B. Aug. 17, 1891, Alton, Ill. D. Nov. 29, 1963, Columbus, Ohio   BR TR 5'10" 163 lbs.

| 1917 | PIT | N | 1 | — | — | 0 | 0 | 0 | 0 | 0 | — | 0 | 0 | 0 | 0 | 0 | 0 | 0 | 1 | 0 | 0 | 0 | 1.0 | 1.000 | 3B-1 |

Barney Reilly

REILLY, BERNARD EUGENE
B. Feb. 7, 1884, Brockton, Mass. D. Nov. 15, 1934, St. Joseph, Mo.   BR TR 6' 175 lbs.

| 1909 | CHI | A | 12 | .200 | .200 | 25 | 5 | 0 | 0 | 0 | 0.0 | 3 | 3 | 3 | | 2 | 0 | 0 | 18 | 33 | 2 | 0 | 4.4 | .962 | 2B-11, OF-1 |

Charlie Reilly

REILLY, CHARLES THOMAS (Princeton Charlie)
B. June 24, 1855, Princeton, N. J. D. Dec. 16, 1937, Los Angeles, Calif.   BB TR 5'11" 190 lbs.

1889	COL	AA	6	.478	.913	23	11	1	0	3	13.0	5	6	2	2	9	0	0	7	17	2	0	4.3	.923	3B-6
1890			137	.266	.343	530	141	23	3	4	0.8	75		35		43	0	0	206	354	67	26	4.6	.893	3B-136, 2B-1
1891	PIT	N	114	.219	.284	415	91	8	5	3	0.7	43	44	29	58	20	0	0	156	261	67	10	4.2	.862	3B-99, SS-11, OF-4
1892	PHI	N	91	.196	.245	331	65	7	3	1	0.3	42	24	18	43	13	2	1	136	178	31	13	3.8	.910	3B-70, OF-15, 2B-4
1893			104	.245	.346	416	102	16	7	4	1.0	64	56	33	36	13	0	0	164	235	47	21	4.3	.895	3B-104
1894			39	.296	.333	135	40	1	2	0	0.0	21	19	16	10	9	0	0	53	71	16	4	3.6	.886	3B-28, OF-5, 2B-4, SS-1, 1B-1
1895			49	.268	.313	179	48	6	1	0	0.0	28	25	13	12	7	0	0	82	133	23	15	4.9	.903	SS-34, 3B-11, 2B-3, OF-1
1897	WAS	N	101	.276	.362	351	97	18	3	2	0.6	64	60	34		18	0	0	149	224	39	17	4.1	.905	3B-101
8 yrs.			641	.250	.325	2380	595	80	24	17	0.7	342	234	180	161	132	2	1	953	1473	292	106	4.2	.893	3B-555, SS-46, OF-25, 2B-12, 1B-1

Hal Reilly

REILLY, HAROLD J.
B. Unknown.

| 1919 | CHI | N | 1 | .000 | .000 | 3 | 0 | 0 | 0 | 0 | 0.0 | 0 | 0 | 0 | 1 | 0 | 0 | 0 | 0 | 0 | 0 | 0 | 0.0 | — | OF-1 |

Joe Reilly

REILLY, JOSEPH J.
B. New York, N. Y. Deceased.   5'10" 140 lbs.

1884	BOS	U	3	.000	.000	11	0	0	0	0	0.0		1				0	0	3	0	1	0	1.3	.750	OF-2, 3B-1
1885	NY	AA	10	.175	.250	40	7	3	0	0	0.0	6		2			0	0	33	29	11	3	7.3	.849	2B-8, 3B-2
2 yrs.			13	.137	.196	51	7	3	0	0	0.0	7		3			0	0	36	29	12	3	5.9	.844	2B-8, 3B-3, OF-2

Josh Reilly

REILLY, CHARLES
B. 1868, San Francisco, Calif. D. June 13, 1938, San Francisco, Calif.

| 1896 | CHI | N | 9 | .214 | .238 | 42 | 9 | 1 | 0 | 0 | 0.0 | 6 | 2 | 1 | 1 | 2 | 0 | 0 | 21 | 32 | 11 | 1 | 7.1 | .828 | 2B-8, SS-1 |

Long John Reilly

REILLY, JOHN GOOD
B. Oct. 5, 1858, Cincinnati, Ohio D. May 31, 1937, Cincinnati, Ohio   BR TR 6'3" 178 lbs.

1880	CIN	N	73	.206	.265	272	56	8	4	0	0.0	21	16	3	36		0	0	616	13	36	36	9.1	.946	1B-72, OF-3
1883	CIN	AA	98	.311	.485	437	136	21	14	9	2.1	103		9			0	0	960	19	40	50	10.4	.961	1B-98, OF-1
1884			105	.339	.551	448	152	24	19	11	2.5	114		5			0	0	979	26	30	60	9.9	.962	1B-103, OF-3, SS-1
1885			111	.297	.411	482	143	18	11	5	1.0	92		11			0	0	1042	22	42	59	10.0	.962	1B-107, OF-7
1886			115	.265	.370	441	117	12	11	4	0.9	92		31			0	0	1126	38	42	80	10.5	.965	1B-110, OF-6
1887			134	.309	.477	551	170	35	14	10	1.8	106		22		50	0	0	1291	34	26	84	10.1	.981	1B-127, OF-9
1888			127	.321	.501	527	169	28	14	13	2.5	112	103	17		82	0	0	1275	45	31	73	10.0	.977	1B-117, OF-10
1889			111	.260	.412	427	111	24	13	5	1.2	84	66	34	37	43	0	0	1145	30	19	76	10.8	.984	1B-109, OF-2
1890	CIN	N	133	.300	.472	553	166	25	26	6	1.1	114	86	16	41	29	0	0	1393	38	33	77	11.0	.977	1B-132, OF-1

Year Team	Games	BA	SA	AB	H	2B	3B	HR	HR%	R	RBI	BB	SO	SB	Pinch Hit AB	Pinch Hit H	PO	A	E	DP	TC/G	FA	G by Pos

Long John Reilly *continued*

Year Team	Games	BA	SA	AB	H	2B	3B	HR	HR%	R	RBI	BB	SO	SB	AB	H	PO	A	E	DP	TC/G	FA	G by Pos
1891	135	.242	.348	546	132	20	13	4	0.7	60	64	9	42	22	0	0	1161	34	27	61	9.1	.978	1B-100, OF-36
10 yrs.	1142	.289	.437	4684	1352	215	139	67	1.4	898	335	157	156	226	0	0	10988	299	326	656	10.2	.972	1B-1075, OF-78, SS-1

Tom Reilly

REILLY, THOMAS HENRY
B. Aug. 3, 1884, St. Louis, Mo.   D. Oct. 18, 1918, New Orleans, La.

BR TR 5'10"

Year Team	Games	BA	SA	AB	H	2B	3B	HR	HR%	R	RBI	BB	SO	SB	AB	H	PO	A	E	DP	TC/G	FA	G by Pos
1908 STL N	29	.173	.222	81	14	1	0	1	1.2	5	3	2		4	0	0	34	69	16	10	4.1	.866	SS-29
1909	5	.286	.571	7	2	0	1	0	0.0	0	2	0	0	0	0	0	2	7	0	0	1.8	1.000	SS-5
1914 CLE A	1	.000	.000	1	0	0	0	0	0.0	0	0	0	0	0	1	0	0	0	0	0	0.0	–	
3 yrs.	35	.180	.247	89	16	1	1	1	1.1	5	5	2	0	4	1	0	36	76	16	10	3.7	.875	SS-34

Kevin Reimer

REIMER, KEVIN MICHAEL
B. June 28, 1964, Macon, Ga.

BL TR 6'2"   215 lbs.

Year Team	Games	BA	SA	AB	H	2B	3B	HR	HR%	R	RBI	BB	SO	SB	AB	H	PO	A	E	DP	TC/G	FA	G by Pos
1988 TEX A	12	.120	.240	25	3	0	0	1	4.0	2	2	0	6	0	5	0	0	0	0	0	0.0	–	DH-7, OF-1
1989	3	.000	.000	5	0	0	0	0	0.0	0	0	0	1	0	2	0	0	0	0	0	0.0	–	DH-1
2 yrs.	15	.100	.200	30	3	0	0	1	3.3	2	2	0	7	0	7	0	0	0	0	0	0.0	–	DH-8, OF-1

Mike Reinbach

REINBACH, MICHAEL WAYNE
B. Aug. 6, 1949, San Diego, Calif.

BL TR 6'2"   195 lbs.

Year Team	Games	BA	SA	AB	H	2B	3B	HR	HR%	R	RBI	BB	SO	SB	AB	H	PO	A	E	DP	TC/G	FA	G by Pos
1974 BAL A	12	.250	.300	20	5	1	0	0	0.0	2	2	5	0	7	1	3	0	0	0	0	0.3	1.000	DH-3, OF-3

Wally Reinecker

REINECKER, WALTER JOSEPH
Born Walter Joseph Smith.
B. Apr. 21, 1890, Pittsburgh, Pa.   D. Apr. 18, 1957, Pittsburgh, Pa.

BR TR 5'6"   150 lbs.

Year Team	Games	BA	SA	AB	H	2B	3B	HR	HR%	R	RBI	BB	SO	SB	AB	H	PO	A	E	DP	TC/G	FA	G by Pos
1915 BAL F	3	.125	.125	8	1	0	0	0	0.0	0		0	0	0	0	0	3	1	3	0	2.3	.571	3B-3

Art Reinholz

REINHOLZ, ARTHUR AUGUST
B. Jan. 27, 1903, Detroit, Mich.   D. Dec. 29, 1980, New Port Richey, Fla.

BR TR 5'10½" 175 lbs.

Year Team	Games	BA	SA	AB	H	2B	3B	HR	HR%	R	RBI	BB	SO	SB	AB	H	PO	A	E	DP	TC/G	FA	G by Pos
1928 CLE A	2	.333	.333	3	1	0	0	0	0.0	0	0	0	0	0	0	0	1	4	1	0	3.0	.833	3B-2

Charlie Reipschlager

REIPSCHLAGER, CHARLES W.
Deceased.

BR TR 5'6½" 160 lbs.

Year Team	Games	BA	SA	AB	H	2B	3B	HR	HR%	R	RBI	BB	SO	SB	AB	H	PO	A	E	DP	TC/G	FA	G by Pos
1883 NY AA	37	.186	.241	145	27	4	2	0	0.0	8		4			0	0	212	46	17	1	7.4	.938	C-29, OF-8
1884	59	.240	.313	233	56	13	2	0	0.0	21		1			0	0	378	111	42	4	9.0	.921	C-51, OF-8
1885	72	.243	.291	268	65	11	1	0	0.0	29		9			0	0	277	135	57	8	6.5	.878	C-59, OF-6, 3B-6, SS-1, 2B-1
1886	65	.211	.280	232	49	4	6	0	0.0	21		9			0	0	280	107	52	5	6.8	.882	C-57, OF-9
1887 CLE AA	63	.212	.273	231	49	8	3	0	0.0	20		11	7		0	0	314	106	45	13	7.4	.903	C-48, 1B-16
5 yrs.	296	.222	.283	1109	246	40	14	0	0.0	99		34	7		0	0	1461	505	213	31	7.4	.902	C-244, OF-31, 1B-16, 3B-6, SS-1, 2B-1

Bobby Reis

REIS, ROBERT JOSEPH THOMAS
B. Jan. 2, 1909, Woodside, N. Y.   D. May 1, 1973, St. Paul, Minn.

BR TR 6'1"   175 lbs.

Year Team	Games	BA	SA	AB	H	2B	3B	HR	HR%	R	RBI	BB	SO	SB	AB	H	PO	A	E	DP	TC/G	FA	G by Pos
1931 BKN N	6	.294	.294	17	5	0	0	0	0.0	3	2	2	0	0	0	0	7	7	1	0	2.5	.933	3B-6
1932	1	.250	.250	4	1	0	0	0	0.0	0	0	0	1	0	0	0	0	1	1	0	2.0	.500	3B-1
1935	52	.247	.329	85	21	3	2	0	0.0	10	4	6	13	2	9	3	42	28	2	6	1.4	.972	OF-21, P-14, 2B-4, 3B-1, 1B-1
1936 BOS N	37	.217	.250	60	13	2	0	0	0.0	3	5	3	6	0	0	0	14	47	0	2	1.6	1.000	OF-18, 1B-4, P-4
1937	45	.244	.302	86	21	5	0	0	0.0	10	6	13	12	2	13	4	74	2	1	1	1.7	.987	P-16, OF-10, SS-3, 2B-1, C-1
1938	34	.184	.184	49	9	0	0	0	0.0	6	4	1	3	1	2	0	17	17	1	0	1.0	.971	P-18, OF-2
6 yrs.	175	.233	.279	301	70	10	2	0	0.0	32	21	25	35	5	24	7	154	102	6	9	1.5	.977	P-69, OF-51, 3B-8, 2B-5, 1B-5, SS-3, C-1

Pete Reiser

REISER, HAROLD PATRICK (Pistol Pete)
B. Mar. 17, 1919, St. Louis, Mo.
D. Oct. 25, 1981, Palm Springs, Calif.

BL TR 5'11"   185 lbs.
BB 1948-51

Year Team	Games	BA	SA	AB	H	2B	3B	HR	HR%	R	RBI	BB	SO	SB	AB	H	PO	A	E	DP	TC/G	FA	G by Pos
1940 BKN N	58	.293	.418	225	66	11	4	3	1.3	34	20	15	33	2	6	0	72	70	7	8	2.6	.953	3B-30, OF-17, SS-5
1941	137	.343	.558	536	184	39	17	14	2.6	117	76	46	71	4	1	0	356	14	7	0	2.8	.981	OF-133
1942	125	.310	.463	480	149	33	5	10	2.1	89	64	48	45	20	0	0	277	9	9	2	2.4	.975	OF-125
1946	122	.277	.428	423	117	21	5	11	2.6	75	73	55	58	34	10	3	221	50	7	4	2.3	.975	OF-97, 3B-15
1947	110	.309	.418	388	120	23	2	5	1.3	68	46	68	41	14	2	0	240	3	3	0	2.2	.988	OF-108
1948	64	.236	.354	127	30	8	2	1	0.8	17	19	29	21	4	21	10	56	8	2	1	1.0	.970	OF-30, 3B-4
1949 BOS N	84	.271	.443	221	60	8	3	8	3.6	32	40	33	42	3	10	4	142	10	4	4	1.9	.974	OF-63, 3B-4
1950	53	.205	.269	78	16	2	0	1	1.3	12	10	18	22	1	24	3	46	0	1	0	0.9	.979	OF-27, 3B-5
1951 PIT N	74	.271	.421	140	38	9	3	2	1.4	22	13	27	20	4	33	11	56	8	0	0	0.9	1.000	OF-10
1952 CLE A	34	.136	.364	44	6	1	0	3	6.8	7	7	4	16	1	15	1	20	0	0	0	0.6	1.000	OF-10
10 yrs.	861	.295	.450	2662	786	155	41	58	2.2	473	368	343	369	87	122	32	1486	172	42	20	2.0	.975	OF-634, 3B-59, SS-5

WORLD SERIES

Year Team	Games	BA	SA	AB	H	2B	3B	HR	HR%	R	RBI	BB	SO	SB	AB	H	PO	A	E	DP	TC/G	FA	G by Pos
1941 BKN N	5	.200	.500	20	4	1	1	1	5.0	1	3	1	6	0	0	0	14	1	0	0	3.0	1.000	OF-5
1947	5	.250	.250	8	2	0	0	0	0.0	1	0	3	1	0	2	1	7	1	1	0	1.6	.875	OF-3
2 yrs.	10	.214	.429	28	6	1	1	1	3.6	2	3	4	7	0	2	1	21	2	1	0	2.3	.957	OF-8

Charlie Reising

REISING, CHARLES (Pop)
B. Aug. 28, 1861, Indiana   D. July 26, 1915, Louisville, Ky.

Year Team	Games	BA	SA	AB	H	2B	3B	HR	HR%	R	RBI	BB	SO	SB	AB	H	PO	A	E	DP	TC/G	FA	G by Pos
1884 IND AA	2	.000	.000	8	0	0	0	0	0.0	0		0			0	0	2	0	3	0	2.5	.400	OF-2

Al Reiss

REISS, ALBERT ALLEN
B. Jan. 8, 1909, Elizabeth, N. J.   D. May 13, 1989, Red Bank, N. J.

BB TR 5'10½" 165 lbs.

Year Team	Games	BA	SA	AB	H	2B	3B	HR	HR%	R	RBI	BB	SO	SB	AB	H	PO	A	E	DP	TC/G	FA	G by Pos
1932 PHI A	9	.200	.200	5	1	0	0	0	0.0	0	1	1	1	0	2	0	2	3	0	0	0.6	1.000	SS-6

Year	Team		Games	BA	SA	AB	H	2B	3B	HR	HR%	R	RBI	BB	SO	SB	Pinch Hit AB	H	PO	A	E	DP	TC/G	FA	G by Pos

Heinie Reitz

REITZ, HENRY P.
B. June 29, 1867, Chicago, Ill. D. Nov. 10, 1914, San Francisco, Calif.
BL TR 5'7½" 160 lbs.

Year	Team		Games	BA	SA	AB	H	2B	3B	HR	HR%	R	RBI	BB	SO	SB	AB	H	PO	A	E	DP	TC/G	FA	G by Pos
1893	BAL	N	130	.286	.380	490	140	17	13	1	0.2	90	76	65	32	24	0	0	315	421	48	62	6.0	.939	2B-130
1894			108	.303	.504	446	135	22	31	2	0.4	86	105	42	24	18	0	0	278	373	25	53	6.3	.963	2B-97, 3B-12
1895			71	.294	.396	245	72	15	5	0	0.0	45	29	18	11	15	3	0	138	162	21	26	4.5	.935	2B-48, 3B-18, SS-1
1896			120	.287	.371	464	133	15	6	4	0.9	76	106	49	32	28	0	0	259	342	31	54	5.3	.951	2B-118, SS-3
1897			128	.289	.358	477	138	15	6	2	0.4	76	84	50		23	0	0	280	449	29	62	5.9	.962	2B-128
1898	WAS	N	132	.303	.364	489	148	20	2	2	0.4	62	47	32		11	0	0	323	401	31	56	5.7	.959	2B-132
1899	PIT	N	34	.262	.323	130	34	4	2	0	0.0	11	15	10		3	0	0	86	110	5	8	5.9	.975	2B-34
7 yrs.			723	.292	.391	2741	800	108	65	11	0.4	446	462	266	99	122	3	0	1679	2258	190	321	5.7	.954	2B-687, 3B-30, SS-4

Ken Reitz

REITZ, KENNETH JOHN
B. June 24, 1951, San Francisco, Calif.
BR TR 6' 180 lbs.

Year	Team		Games	BA	SA	AB	H	2B	3B	HR	HR%	R	RBI	BB	SO	SB	AB	H	PO	A	E	DP	TC/G	FA	G by Pos
1972	STL	N	21	.359	.410	78	28	4	0	0	0.0	5	10	2	4	0	1	0	17	26	2	3	2.1	.956	3B-20
1973			147	.235	.333	426	100	20	2	6	1.4	40	42	9	25	0	12	2	88	213	8	20	2.1	.974	3B-135, SS-1
1974			154	.271	.363	579	157	28	2	7	1.2	48	54	23	63	0	3	1	131	281	12	29	2.8	.972	3B-151, SS-2
1975			161	.269	.340	592	159	25	1	5	0.8	43	63	22	54	1	1	0	124	279	23	21	2.6	.946	3B-160
1976	SF	N	155	.267	.333	577	154	21	1	5	0.9	40	66	24	48	5	0	0	141	304	19	33	3.0	.959	3B-155, SS-1
1977	STL	N	157	.261	.412	587	153	36	1	17	2.9	58	79	19	74	2	0	0	121	320	9	35	2.9	.980	3B-157
1978			150	.246	.357	540	133	26	2	10	1.9	41	75	23	61	1	4	4	111	314	12	18	2.9	.973	3B-150
1979			159	.268	.382	605	162	41	2	8	1.3	42	73	25	85	1	2	0	124	290	12	26	2.7	.972	3B-158
1980			151	.270	.379	523	141	33	0	8	1.5	39	58	22	44	0	1	0	86	293	8	25	2.6	.979	3B-150
1981	CHI	N	82	.215	.281	260	56	9	1	2	0.8	10	28	15	56	0	1	0	57	157	5	11	2.7	.977	3B-81
1982	PIT	N	7	.000	.000	10	0	0	0	0	0.0	0	0	0	4	0	3	0	6	0	0	0	0.9	1.000	3B-4
11 yrs.			1344	.260	.359	4777	1243	243	12	68	1.4	366	548	184	518	10	28	7	1000	2483	110	221	2.7	.969	3B-1321, SS-4

Butch Rementer

REMENTER, WILLIS J.
B. Mar. 14, 1878, Philadelphia, Pa. D. Sept. 23, 1922, Philadelphia, Pa.
TR

Year	Team		Games	BA	SA	AB	H	2B	3B	HR	HR%	R	RBI	BB	SO	SB	AB	H	PO	A	E	DP	TC/G	FA	G by Pos
1904	PHI	N	1	.000	.000	2	0	0	0	0	0.0	0	0	0		0	0	0	3	0	0	0	3.0	1.000	C-1

Jack Remsen

REMSEN, JOHN J.
B. Apr., 1851, Brooklyn, N. Y. Deceased.
BR TR 5'11" 170 lbs.

Year	Team		Games	BA	SA	AB	H	2B	3B	HR	HR%	R	RBI	BB	SO	SB	AB	H	PO	A	E	DP	TC/G	FA	G by Pos
1876	HAR	N	69	.275	.352	324	89	12	5	1	0.3	62	30	1	15		0	0	177	12	24	5	3.1	.887	OF-69
1877	STL	N	33	.260	.350	123	32	3	4	0	0.0	14	13	4	3		0	0	73	4	8	0	2.6	.906	OF-33
1878	CHI	N	56	.232	.304	224	52	11	1	1	0.4	32	19	17	33		0	0	103	14	7	5	2.2	.944	OF-56
1879			42	.217	.270	152	33	4	2	0	0.0	14	8	2	23		0	0	187	9	23	3	5.2	.899	OF-31, 1B-11
1881	CLE	N	48	.174	.233	172	30	4	1	0	0.0	14	13	9	31		0	0	117	7	18	1	3.0	.873	OF-48
1884	2 teams		PHI	N	(12G –	.209)		BKN	AA	(81G –	.223)														
"	total		93	.221	.305	344	76	4	3	3	0.9	54		29	9		0	0	169	10	16	2	2.1	.918	OF-93
6 yrs.			341	.233	.307	1339	312	42	21	5	0.4	190	83	62	114		0	0	826	56	95	16	2.9	.903	OF-330, 1B-11

Jerry Remy

REMY, GERALD PETER
B. Nov. 8, 1952, Fall River, Mass.
BL TR 5'9" 165 lbs.

Year	Team		Games	BA	SA	AB	H	2B	3B	HR	HR%	R	RBI	BB	SO	SB	AB	H	PO	A	E	DP	TC/G	FA	G by Pos
1975	CAL	A	147	.258	.311	569	147	17	5	1	0.2	82	46	45	55	34	0	0	336	427	14	111	5.3	.982	2B-147
1976			143	.263	.303	502	132	14	3	0	0.0	64	28	38	43	35	1	1	279	406	16	77	4.9	.977	2B-133, DH-5
1977	BOS	A	154	.252	.341	575	145	19	10	4	0.7	74	44	59	59	41	0	0	307	420	19	90	4.8	.975	2B-152, 3B-1
1978			148	.278	.350	583	162	24	6	2	0.3	87	44	40	55	30	0	0	328	446	13	114	5.3	.983	2B-140, DH-4, SS-1
1979			80	.297	.346	306	91	11	2	0	0.0	49	29	26	25	14	1	0	147	205	11	43	4.5	.970	2B-76
1980			63	.313	.361	230	72	7	2	0	0.0	24	9	10	14	14	4	1	109	189	7	30	4.8	.977	2B-60, OF-1
1981			88	.307	.338	358	110	9	1	0	0.0	55	31	36	30	9	1	0	162	272	7	58	5.0	.984	2B-87
1982			155	.280	.324	636	178	22	3	0	0.0	89	47	55	77	16	1	0	290	432	13	104	4.7	.982	2B-154
1983			146	.275	.319	592	163	16	5	0	0.0	73	43	40	35	11	2	0	295	376	7	104	4.6	.990	2B-144
1984			30	.250	.279	104	26	1	1	0	0.0	8	8	7	11	4	5	0	40	70	3	13	3.8	.973	2B-24
10 yrs.			1154	.275	.328	4455	1226	140	38	7	0.2	605	329	356	404	208	16	2	2293	3243	110	744	4.9	.981	2B-1117, DH-9, OF-1, SS-1, 3B-1

Rick Renick

RENICK, WARREN RICHARD
B. Mar. 16, 1944, London, Ohio
BR TR 6' 188 lbs.

Year	Team		Games	BA	SA	AB	H	2B	3B	HR	HR%	R	RBI	BB	SO	SB	AB	H	PO	A	E	DP	TC/G	FA	G by Pos
1968	MIN	A	42	.216	.402	97	21	5	2	3	3.1	16	13	9	42	0	1	0	50	91	8	13	3.5	.946	SS-40
1969			71	.245	.374	139	34	3	0	5	3.6	21	17	12	32	0	25	8	34	59	10	7	1.5	.903	3B-30, OF-10, SS-6
1970			81	.229	.391	179	41	8	0	7	3.9	20	25	22	29	0	26	7	52	54	2	5	1.3	.981	3B-30, OF-25, SS-1
1971			27	.222	.333	45	10	2	0	1	2.2	4	8	5	14	0	13	1	11	8	2	0	0.8	.905	OF-7, 3B-7
1972			55	.172	.323	93	16	2	0	4	4.3	10	8	15	25	0	24	2	39	10	1	9	0.9	.980	OF-21, 1B-6, 3B-4, SS-1
5 yrs.			276	.221	.373	553	122	20	2	20	3.6	71	71	63	142	0	89	18	186	222	23	34	1.6	.947	3B-71, OF-63, SS-48, 1B-6

LEAGUE CHAMPIONSHIP SERIES

Year	Team		Games	BA	SA	AB	H	2B	3B	HR	HR%	R	RBI	BB	SO	SB	AB	H	PO	A	E	DP	TC/G	FA	G by Pos
1969	MIN	A	1	.000	.000	1	0	0	0	0	0.0	0	0	0	0	0	1	0	0	0	0	0	0.0	—	
1970			2	.200	.200	5	1	0	0	0	0.0	0	0	0	1	0	1	0	1	3	0	0	2.0	1.000	3B-1
2 yrs.			3	.167	.167	6	1	0	0	0	0.0	0	0	0	1	0	2	0	1	3	0	0	1.3	1.000	3B-1

Bill Renna

RENNA, WILLIAM BENEDITTO (Big Bill)
B. Oct. 14, 1924, Hanford, Calif.
BR TR 6'3" 218 lbs.

Year	Team		Games	BA	SA	AB	H	2B	3B	HR	HR%	R	RBI	BB	SO	SB	AB	H	PO	A	E	DP	TC/G	FA	G by Pos
1953	NY	A	61	.314	.463	121	38	6	3	2	1.7	19	13	13	31	0	17	5	57	0	1	0	1.0	.983	OF-40
1954	PHI	A	123	.232	.379	422	98	15	4	13	3.1	52	53	41	60	1	9	3	226	13	7	5	2.0	.972	OF-115
1955	KC	A	100	.213	.349	249	53	7	3	7	2.8	33	28	31	42	0	23	4	118	5	1	2	1.2	.992	OF-79
1956			33	.271	.458	48	13	3	0	2	4.2	12	5	3	10	0	9	2	18	1	1	0	0.6	.950	OF-25
1958	BOS	A	39	.268	.571	56	15	5	4	4	7.1	5	18	6	14	0	25	7	17	0	0	0	0.4	1.000	OF-11
1959			14	.091	.091	22	2	0	0	0	0.0	2	2	5	9	0	8	1	5	0	0	0	0.4	1.000	OF-7
6 yrs.			370	.239	.391	918	219	36	10	28	3.1	123	119	99	166	2	91	22	441	19	10	7	1.3	.979	OF-277

Tony Rensa

RENSA, GEORGE ANTHONY (Pug)
B. Sept. 29, 1901, Parsons, Pa. D. Jan. 4, 1987, Wilkes-Barre, Pa.
BR TR 5'10" 180 lbs.

Year	Team	Games	BA	SA	AB	H	2B	3B	HR	HR%	R	RBI	BB	SO	SB	Pinch Hit AB	Pinch Hit H	PO	A	E	DP	TC/G	FA	G by Pos

Tony Rensa *continued*

Year	Team	Games	BA	SA	AB	H	2B	3B	HR	HR%	R	RBI	BB	SO	SB	AB	H	PO	A	E	DP	TC/G	FA	G by Pos
1930	2 teams	DET A (20G – .270)			PHI N (54G – .285)																			
"	total	74	.282	.431	209	59	13	3	4	1.9	37	34	16	25	1	6	1	177	27	13	6	2.9	.940	C-67
1931	PHI N	19	.103	.138	29	3	1	0	0	0.0	2	2	6	2	0	2	0	35	11	2	2	2.5	.958	C-17
1933	NY A	8	.310	.448	29	9	2	1	0	0.0	4	3	1	3	0	0	0	39	4	1	1	5.5	.977	C-8
1937	CHI A	26	.298	.421	57	17	5	1	0	0.0	10	5	8	6	3	2	1	70	9	2	3	3.1	.975	C-23
1938		59	.248	.333	165	41	5	0	3	1.8	15	19	25	16	1	2	0	185	36	4	4	3.8	.982	C-57
1939		14	.200	.200	25	5	0	0	0	0.0	3	2	1	2	0	1	1	29	6	1	0	2.6	.972	C-13
6 yrs.		200	.261	.372	514	134	26	5	7	1.4	71	65	57	54	5	13	3	535	93	23	16	3.3	.965	C-185

Rich Renteria

RENTERIA, RICHARD AVINA   BR TR 5'9"   172 lbs.
B. Dec. 25, 1961, Harbor City, Calif.

Year	Team	Games	BA	SA	AB	H	2B	3B	HR	HR%	R	RBI	BB	SO	SB	AB	H	PO	A	E	DP	TC/G	FA	G by Pos
1986	PIT N	10	.250	.333	12	3	1	0	0	0.0	2	1	0	4	0	9	1	1	2	2	0	0.5	.600	3B-1
1987	SEA A	12	.100	.200	10	1	1	0	0	0.0	2	1	1	2	1	3	0	3	4	1	1	0.7	.875	DH-4, 2B-4, SS-1
1988		31	.205	.307	88	18	9	0	0	0.0	6	6	2	8	1	7	1	33	44	3	10	2.6	.963	SS-11, 3B-5, 2B-4
3 yrs.		53	.200	.300	110	22	11	0	0	0.0	10	7	3	14	2	19	3	37	50	6	11	1.8	.935	SS-12, 2B-8, 3B-6, DH-4

Bob Repass

REPASS, ROBERT WILLIS   BR TR 6'1"   185 lbs.
B. Nov. 6, 1917, West Pittston, Pa.

Year	Team	Games	BA	SA	AB	H	2B	3B	HR	HR%	R	RBI	BB	SO	SB	AB	H	PO	A	E	DP	TC/G	FA	G by Pos
1939	STL N	3	.333	.500	6	2	1	0	0	0.0	0	1	0	2	0	1	1	1	5	0	1	2.0	1.000	2B-2
1942	WAS A	81	.239	.313	259	62	11	1	2	0.8	30	23	33	30	6	6	1	142	178	12	21	4.1	.964	2B-33, 3B-29, SS-11
2 yrs.		84	.242	.317	265	64	12	1	2	0.8	30	24	33	32	6	7	2	143	183	12	22	4.0	.964	2B-35, 3B-29, SS-11

Roger Repoz

REPOZ, ROGER ALLEN   BL TL 6'3"   190 lbs.
B. Aug. 3, 1940, Bellingham, Wash.

Year	Team	Games	BA	SA	AB	H	2B	3B	HR	HR%	R	RBI	BB	SO	SB	AB	H	PO	A	E	DP	TC/G	FA	G by Pos
1964	NY A	11	.000	.000	1	0	0	0	0	0.0	0	1	0	1	0	1	0	1	0	0	0	0.1	1.000	OF-9
1965		79	.220	.454	218	48	7	4	12	5.5	34	28	25	57	1	11	0	133	1	1	0	1.7	.993	OF-69
1966	2 teams	NY A (37G – .349)			KC A (101G – .216)																			
"	total	138	.232	.384	362	84	14	4	11	3.0	44	43	48	88	3	16	2	466	22	5	27	3.6	.990	OF-82, 1B-45
1967	2 teams	KC A (40G – .241)			CAL A (74G – .250)																			
"	total	114	.247	.399	263	65	15	2	7	2.7	34	28	31	57	6	23	4	167	6	5	0	1.6	.972	OF-94
1968	CAL A	133	.240	.371	375	90	8	1	13	3.5	30	54	38	83	8	25	6	226	4	3	1	1.8	.987	OF-114
1969		103	.164	.288	219	36	1	1	8	3.7	25	19	32	52	1	24	2	296	2	2	26	3.1	.994	OF-48, 1B-31
1970		137	.238	.442	407	97	17	6	18	4.4	50	47	45	90	4	20	3	330	9	2	11	2.5	.994	OF-110, 1B-18
1971		113	.199	.374	297	59	11	1	13	4.4	39	42	60	69	3	8	1	227	9	0	5	2.1	1.000	OF-97, 1B-13
1972		3	.333	.333	3	1	0	0	0	0.0	0	0	0	2	0	3	1	0	0	0	0	0.0	–	
9 yrs.		831	.224	.390	2145	480	73	19	82	3.8	257	261	280	499	26	131	19	1846	73	18	70	2.3	.991	OF-623, 1B-107

Rip Repulski

REPULSKI, ELDON JOHN   BR TR 6'   195 lbs.
B. Oct. 4, 1927, Sauk Rapids, Minn.

Year	Team	Games	BA	SA	AB	H	2B	3B	HR	HR%	R	RBI	BB	SO	SB	AB	H	PO	A	E	DP	TC/G	FA	G by Pos
1953	STL N	153	.275	.413	567	156	25	4	15	2.6	75	66	33	71	3	0	0	361	7	5	1	2.4	.987	OF-153
1954		152	.283	.454	619	175	39	5	19	3.1	99	79	43	75	8	0	0	302	4	8	0	2.1	.975	OF-152
1955		147	.270	.467	512	138	28	2	23	4.5	64	73	49	66	5	10	3	260	5	7	1	1.9	.974	OF-141
1956		112	.277	.428	376	104	18	3	11	2.9	44	55	24	46	2	17	7	187	3	5	0	1.7	.974	OF-100
1957	PHI N	134	.260	.436	516	134	23	4	20	3.9	65	68	19	74	7	3	0	264	6	9	2	2.1	.968	OF-130
1958		85	.244	.479	238	58	9	4	13	5.5	33	40	15	47	0	30	8	90	3	5	0	1.2	.949	OF-56
1959	LA N	53	.255	.362	94	24	4	0	2	2.1	11	14	13	23	0	25	6	30	0	0	0	0.6	1.000	OF-31
1960	2 teams	LA N (4G – .200)			BOS A (73G – .243)																			
"	total	77	.241	.362	141	34	4	1	3	2.1	14	20	10	39	0	39	4	57	0	0	0	0.7	1.000	OF-35
1961	BOS A	15	.280	.320	25	7	1	0	0	0.0	1	1	1	5	0	10	3	4	0	0	0	0.3	1.000	OF-4
9 yrs.		928	.269	.436	3088	830	153	23	106	3.4	407	416	207	433	25	134	38	1555	28	39	4	1.7	.976	OF-802

WORLD SERIES

Year	Team	Games	BA	SA	AB	H	2B	3B	HR	HR%	R	RBI	BB	SO	SB	AB	H	PO	A	E	DP	TC/G	FA	G by Pos
1959	LA N	1	–	–	0	0	0	0	0	–	0	0	1	0	0	0	0	0	0	0	0	0.0	–	OF-1

Dino Restelli

RESTELLI, DINO PAUL (Dingo)   BR TR 6'1½"   191 lbs.
B. Sept. 23, 1924, St. Louis, Mo.

Year	Team	Games	BA	SA	AB	H	2B	3B	HR	HR%	R	RBI	BB	SO	SB	AB	H	PO	A	E	DP	TC/G	FA	G by Pos
1949	PIT N	72	.250	.453	232	58	11	0	12	5.2	41	40	35	26	3	8	2	169	5	7	2	2.5	.961	OF-61, 1B-1
1951		21	.184	.289	38	7	1	0	1	2.6	1	3	2	4	0	8	1	22	1	2	1	1.2	.920	OF-11
2 yrs.		93	.241	.430	270	65	12	0	13	4.8	42	43	37	30	3	16	3	191	6	9	3	2.2	.956	OF-72, 1B-1

Merv Rettenmund

RETTENMUND, MERVIN WELDON   BR TR 5'10"   190 lbs.
B. June 6, 1943, Flint, Mich.

Year	Team	Games	BA	SA	AB	H	2B	3B	HR	HR%	R	RBI	BB	SO	SB	AB	H	PO	A	E	DP	TC/G	FA	G by Pos
1968	BAL A	31	.297	.469	64	19	5	0	2	3.1	10	7	18	20	1	6	3	29	1	0	0	1.0	1.000	OF-23
1969		95	.247	.395	190	47	10	3	4	2.1	29	25	28	28	6	17	2	107	3	1	0	1.2	.991	OF-78
1970		106	.322	.544	338	109	17	2	18	5.3	60	58	38	59	13	17	5	201	6	5	1	2.0	.976	OF-93
1971		141	.318	.448	491	156	23	4	11	2.2	81	75	87	60	15	3	0	292	7	7	4	2.2	.977	OF-134
1972		102	.233	.339	301	70	10	2	6	2.0	40	21	41	37	6	10	3	174	6	2	1	1.8	.989	OF-98
1973		95	.262	.411	321	84	17	2	9	2.8	59	44	57	38	11	11	5	196	4	3	1	2.1	.985	OF-90
1974	CIN N	80	.216	.332	208	45	6	0	6	2.9	30	28	37	39	5	14	3	103	3	0	0	1.3	1.000	OF-69
1975		93	.239	.314	188	45	6	1	2	1.1	24	19	35	22	5	30	6	99	2	1	1	1.1	1.000	OF-61, 3B-1
1976	SD N	86	.229	.321	140	32	7	0	2	1.4	16	11	29	23	4	40	12	79	6	2	1	1.0	.977	OF-43
1977		107	.286	.444	126	36	6	1	4	3.2	23	17	33	28	1	**67**	**21**	30	0	0	0	0.3	1.000	OF-27, 3B-1
1978	CAL A	50	.269	.361	108	29	5	1	1	0.9	16	14	30	13	0	15	2	30	0	1	0	0.6	.968	OF-22, DH-18
1979		35	.263	.329	76	20	1	1	2	1.3	7	10	11	14	1	10	4	6	0	0	0	0.2	1.000	DH-11, OF-9
1980		2	.250	.250	4	1	0	0	0	0.0	0	0	1	1	0	1	0	0	0	0	0	0.0	–	DH-1
13 yrs.		1023	.271	.406	2555	693	114	16	66	2.6	393	329	445	382	68	241	66	1346	38	21	10	1.4	.985	OF-747, DH-36, 3B-2

LEAGUE CHAMPIONSHIP SERIES

Year	Team	Games	BA	SA	AB	H	2B	3B	HR	HR%	R	RBI	BB	SO	SB	AB	H	PO	A	E	DP	TC/G	FA	G by Pos
1969	BAL A	1	–	–	0	0	0	0	0	–	1	1	0	1	0	0	0	0	0	0	0	0.0	–	
1970			.333	.333	3	1	0	0	0	0.0	1	1	2	1	1	0	0	3	1	0	0	4.0	1.000	OF-1
1971		3	.250	.375	8	2	1	0	0	0.0	1	0	0	3	0	0	0	7	0	0	0	2.3	1.000	OF-3
1973		3	.091	.091	11	1	0	0	0	0.0	1	0	3	2	0	0	0	3	0	0	0	1.0	1.000	OF-3

Year	Team	Games	BA	SA	AB	H	2B	3B	HR	HR%	R	RBI	BB	SO	SB	Pinch Hit AB	Pinch Hit H	PO	A	E	DP	TC/G	FA	G by Pos

Merv Rettenmund *continued*

Year	Team	Games	BA	SA	AB	H	2B	3B	HR	HR%	R	RBI	BB	SO	SB	AB	H	PO	A	E	DP	TC/G	FA	G by Pos
1975	CIN N	2	.000	.000	1	0	0	0	0	0.0	0	0	1	0	0	1	0	0	0	0	0	0.0	–	
1979	CAL A	2	.000	.000	2	0	0	0	0	0.0	0	0	2	1	0	0	0	0	0	0	0	0.0	–	DH-2
6 yrs.		12	.160	.200	25	4	1	0	0	0.0	2	2	8	7	1	1	0	13	1	0	0	1.2	1.000	OF-7, DH-2

WORLD SERIES

Year	Team	Games	BA	SA	AB	H	2B	3B	HR	HR%	R	RBI	BB	SO	SB	AB	H	PO	A	E	DP	TC/G	FA	G by Pos
1969	BAL A	1	–	–	0	0	0	0	0	–	0	0	0	0	0	0	0	0	0	0	0	0.0		
1970		2	.400	1.000	5	2	0	0	1	20.0	2	2	1	0	0	1	0	3	0	0	0	1.5	1.000	OF-1
1971		7	.185	.296	27	5	0	0	1	3.7	3	4	0	4	0	1	0	17	0	0	0	2.4	1.000	OF-6
1975	CIN N	3	.000	.000	3	0	0	0	0	0.0	0	0	0	1	0	3	0	0	0	0	0	0.0		
4 yrs.		13	.200	.371	35	7	0	0	2	5.7	5	6	1	5	0	5	0	20	0	0	0	1.5	1.000	OF-7

Ken Retzer

RETZER, KENNETH LEO
B. Apr. 30, 1934, Wood River, Ill.

BL TR 6' 185 lbs.

Year	Team	Games	BA	SA	AB	H	2B	3B	HR	HR%	R	RBI	BB	SO	SB	AB	H	PO	A	E	DP	TC/G	FA	G by Pos
1961	WAS A	16	.340	.472	53	18	4	0	1	1.9	7	3	4	5	1	0	0	71	8	1	2	5.0	.988	C-16
1962		109	.285	.400	340	97	11	2	8	2.4	36	39	26	21	2	11	2	488	44	8	5	5.0	.985	C-99
1963		95	.242	.336	265	64	10	0	5	1.9	21	31	17	20	2	15	2	320	35	7	5	3.8	.981	C-81
1964		17	.094	.094	32	3	0	0	0	0.0	1	1	5	4	0	4	2	56	10	2	1	4.0	.971	C-13
4 yrs.		237	.264	.367	690	182	25	2	14	2.0	65	72	52	50	5	30	6	935	97	18	13	4.4	.983	C-209

Dave Revering

REVERING, DAVID ALLEN
B. Feb. 12, 1953, Roseville, Calif.

BL TR 6'4" 210 lbs.

Year	Team	Games	BA	SA	AB	H	2B	3B	HR	HR%	R	RBI	BB	SO	SB	AB	H	PO	A	E	DP	TC/G	FA	G by Pos
1978	OAK A	152	.271	.415	521	141	21	3	16	3.1	49	46	26	55	0	12	3	1013	110	13	98	7.5	.989	1B-138, DH-3
1979		125	.288	.483	472	136	25	5	19	4.0	63	65	34	65	1	3	2	828	80	13	77	7.4	.986	1B-104, DH-18
1980		106	.290	.492	376	109	21	5	15	4.0	48	62	32	37	1	11	4	724	67	9	56	7.5	.989	1B-95, DH-5
1981	2 teams				OAK A	(31G – .230)			NY A	(45G – .235)														
"	total	76	.233	.335	206	48	3	2	4	1.9	20	17	22	22	0	11	1	188	13	1	12	2.7	.995	1B-73, DH-2
1982	3 teams				NY A	(14G – .150)			TOR A	(55G – .215)		SEA A	(29G – .207)											
"	total	98	.202	.346	257	52	11	1	8	3.1	25	32	34	51	0	20	2	351	15	3	33	3.8	.992	DH-50, 1B-44
5 yrs.		557	.265	.430	1832	486	83	16	62	3.4	205	234	148	240	2	57	12	3104	285	39	276	6.2	.989	1B-454, DH-78

DIVISIONAL PLAYOFF SERIES

Year	Team	Games	BA	SA	AB	H	2B	3B	HR	HR%	R	RBI	BB	SO	SB	AB	H	PO	A	E	DP	TC/G	FA	G by Pos
1981	NY A	2	–	–	0	0	0	0	0	–	0	0	0	0	0	0	0	0	0	0	0	0.0	–	1B-2

LEAGUE CHAMPIONSHIP SERIES

Year	Team	Games	BA	SA	AB	H	2B	3B	HR	HR%	R	RBI	BB	SO	SB	AB	H	PO	A	E	DP	TC/G	FA	G by Pos
1981	NY A	2	.500	.500	2	1	0	0	0	0.0	0	0	0	0	0	0	0	0	0	0	0	0.0	–	1B-2

Gilberto Reyes

REYES, GILBERTO ROLANDO
Born Gilberto Rolando Reyes y Polanco.
B. Dec. 10, 1963, Santo Domingo, Dominican Republic

BR TR 6'3" 195 lbs.

Year	Team	Games	BA	SA	AB	H	2B	3B	HR	HR%	R	RBI	BB	SO	SB	AB	H	PO	A	E	DP	TC/G	FA	G by Pos
1983	LA N	19	.161	.226	31	5	2	0	0	0.0	0	0	0	5	0	0	0	59	9	4	2	3.8	.944	C-19
1984		4	.000	.000	5	0	0	0	0	0.0	0	0	0	3	0	2	0	5	0	0	0	1.3	1.000	C-2
1985		6	.000	.000	1	0	0	0	0	0.0	0	1	1	1	0	1	0	6	4	0	0	1.7	1.000	C-6
1987		1	–	–	0	0	0	0	0	0.0	0	0	0	0	0	0	0	2	0	0	0	2.0	1.000	C-1
1988		5	.111	.111	9	1	0	0	0	0.0	1	0	0	3	0	0	0	16	0	0	1	3.2	1.000	C-5
1989	MON N	4	.200	.200	5	1	0	0	0	0.0	0	0	0	1	0	1	0	10	1	0	0	2.8	1.000	C-4
6 yrs.		39	.137	.176	51	7	2	0	0	0.0	2	1	1	13	0	4	0	98	14	4	3	3.0	.966	C-37

Nap Reyes

REYES, NAPOLEON AGUILERA
Born Napoleon Reyes y Aguilera.
B. Nov. 24, 1919, Santiago, Cuba

BR TR 6' 195 lbs.

Year	Team	Games	BA	SA	AB	H	2B	3B	HR	HR%	R	RBI	BB	SO	SB	AB	H	PO	A	E	DP	TC/G	FA	G by Pos
1943	NY N	40	.256	.320	125	32	4	2	0	0.0	13	13	4	12	2	1	0	340	9	2	25	8.8	.994	1B-38, 3B-1
1944		116	.289	.422	374	108	16	5	8	2.1	38	53	15	24	2	11	4	585	120	12	49	6.2	.983	1B-63, 3B-37, OF-3
1945		122	.288	.376	431	124	15	4	5	1.2	39	44	25	26	1	3	0	170	233	14	13	3.4	.966	3B-115, 1B-5
1950		1	.000	.000	1	0	0	0	0	0.0	0	0	0	0	0	0	0	2	0	1	0	3.0	.667	1B-1
4 yrs.		279	.284	.387	931	264	35	11	13	1.4	90	110	44	62	5	15	4	1097	362	29	87	5.3	.981	3B-153, 1B-107, OF-3

Bill Reynolds

REYNOLDS, WILLIAM DEE
B. Aug. 14, 1884, Eastland, Tex. D. June 5, 1924, Carnegie, Okla.

BR TR 6' 185 lbs.

Year	Team	Games	BA	SA	AB	H	2B	3B	HR	HR%	R	RBI	BB	SO	SB	AB	H	PO	A	E	DP	TC/G	FA	G by Pos
1913	NY A	5	.000	.000	5	0	0	0	0	0.0	0	0	0	1	0	0	0	10	1	1	0	2.4	.917	C-5
1914		4	.400	.400	5	2	0	0	0	0.0	0	0	0	3	0	3	1	4	1	0	0	1.3	1.000	C-1
2 yrs.		9	.200	.200	10	2	0	0	0	0.0	0	0	0	4	0	3	1	14	2	1	0	1.9	.941	C-6

Carl Reynolds

REYNOLDS, CARL NETTLES
B. Feb. 1, 1903, LaRue, Tex. D. May 29, 1978, Houston, Tex.

BR TR 6' 194 lbs.

Year	Team	Games	BA	SA	AB	H	2B	3B	HR	HR%	R	RBI	BB	SO	SB	AB	H	PO	A	E	DP	TC/G	FA	G by Pos
1927	CHI A	14	.214	.357	42	9	3	0	1	2.4	7	5	7	7	1	1	0	37	1	0	0	2.7	1.000	OF-13
1928		84	.323	.491	291	94	21	11	2	0.7	51	36	17	13	15	10	6	135	6	3	2	1.7	.979	OF-74
1929		131	.317	.474	517	164	24	12	11	2.1	81	67	20	37	19	0	6	268	13	15	5	2.3	.949	OF-131
1930		138	.359	.584	563	202	25	18	22	3.9	103	100	20	39	16	5	0	336	11	9	1	2.6	.975	OF-132
1931		118	.290	.442	462	134	24	14	6	1.3	71	77	24	26	17	9	3	233	10	13	3	2.2	.949	OF-109
1932	WAS A	102	.305	.475	406	124	28	7	9	2.2	53	63	14	19	8	3	0	229	3	4	0	2.3	.983	OF-95
1933	STL A	135	.286	.451	475	136	26	14	8	1.7	81	71	50	25	5	13	3	269	8	10	3	2.1	.965	OF-124
1934	BOS A	113	.303	.438	413	125	26	9	4	1.0	61	86	27	28	5	14	3	244	6	6	3	2.3	.977	OF-100
1935		78	.270	.430	244	66	13	4	6	2.5	33	35	24	20	4	11	2	146	7	4	0	2.0	.975	OF-64
1936	WAS A	89	.276	.392	293	81	18	2	4	1.4	41	41	21	22	8	15	3	142	8	5	0	1.7	.968	OF-72
1937	CHI N	7	.273	.364	11	3	1	0	0	0.0	1	2	2	2	0	4	1	4	0	1	0	0.7	.800	OF-2
1938		125	.302	.416	497	150	28	10	3	0.6	59	67	22	32	9	0	0	328	10	6	4	2.8	.983	OF-125
1939		88	.246	.367	281	69	10	6	4	1.4	33	44	16	38	5	14	3	168	5	5	1	2.0	.972	OF-72
13 yrs.		1222	.302	.458	4495	1357	247	107	80	1.8	672	695	262	308	112	100	25	2539	88	81	22	2.2	.970	OF-1113

WORLD SERIES

Year	Team	Games	BA	SA	AB	H	2B	3B	HR	HR%	R	RBI	BB	SO	SB	AB	H	PO	A	E	DP	TC/G	FA	G by Pos
1938	CHI N	4	.000	.000	12	0	0	0	0	0.0	0	0	1	3	0	1	0	7	0	0	0	1.8	1.000	OF-3

Year	Team		Games	BA	SA	AB	H	2B	3B	HR	HR%	R	RBI	BB	SO	SB	Pinch Hit AB	Pinch Hit H	PO	A	E	DP	TC/G	FA	G by Pos

Charlie Reynolds

REYNOLDS, CHARLES LAWRENCE
B. May 1, 1865, Williamsburgh, Ind.   D. July 3, 1944, Denver, Colo.

5'9"   175 lbs.

Year	Team		Games	BA	SA	AB	H	2B	3B	HR	HR%	R	RBI	BB	SO	SB	AB	H	PO	A	E	DP	TC/G	FA	G by Pos
1889	2 teams	KC AA (1G – .250)				BKN AA (12G – .214)																			
"	total		13	.217	.283	46	10	1	1	0	0.0	6	4	1	7	2	0	0	49	18	8	0	5.8	.893	C-13

Craig Reynolds

REYNOLDS, GORDON CRAIG
B. Dec. 27, 1952, Houston, Tex.

BL TR 6'1"   175 lbs.

Year	Team		Games	BA	SA	AB	H	2B	3B	HR	HR%	R	RBI	BB	SO	SB	AB	H	PO	A	E	DP	TC/G	FA	G by Pos
1975	PIT	N	31	.224	.263	76	17	3	0	0	0.0	8	4	3	5	0	1	1	43	82	4	12	4.2	.969	SS-30
1976			7	.250	1.000	4	1	0	0	1	25.0	1	1	0	0	0	0	0	2	6	1	1	1.3	.889	SS-4, 2B-1
1977	SEA	A	135	.248	.319	420	104	12	3	4	1.0	41	28	15	23	6	2	1	197	397	28	86	4.6	.955	SS-134
1978			148	.292	.374	548	160	16	7	5	0.9	57	44	36	41	9	1	0	243	461	29	102	5.0	.960	SS-146
1979	HOU	N	146	.265	.333	555	147	20	9	0	0.0	63	39	21	49	12	5	1	208	428	23	88	4.5	.965	SS-143
1980			137	.226	.304	381	86	9	6	3	0.8	34	28	20	39	2	2	0	162	362	17	59	3.9	.969	SS-135
1981			87	.260	.402	323	84	10	12	4	1.2	43	31	12	31	3	2	1	139	261	11	36	4.7	.973	SS-85
1982			54	.254	.347	118	30	2	1	1	0.8	16	7	11	9	3	5	0	45	98	6	15	2.8	.960	SS-35, 3B-7
1983			65	.214	.276	98	21	3	0	1	1.0	10	6	6	10	0	12	2	37	57	3	15	1.5	.969	2B-26, 3B-15, SS-8, OF-1
1984			146	.260	.364	527	137	15	11	6	1.1	61	60	22	53	7	4	2	212	473	25	91	4.9	.965	SS-143, 3B-1
1985			107	.272	.393	379	103	18	8	4	1.1	43	32	12	30	4	10	3	159	319	11	65	4.6	.978	SS-102, 2B-1
1986			114	.249	.348	313	78	7	3	6	1.9	32	41	12	31	3	22	9	124	209	7	38	3.0	.979	SS-98, 1B-5, 3B-4, OF-2, P-1
1987			135	.254	.348	374	95	17	3	4	1.1	35	28	30	44	5	12	3	160	292	14	43	3.5	.970	SS-129, 3B-2
1988			78	.255	.317	161	41	7	0	1	0.6	20	14	8	23	3	22	4	88	81	9	20	2.3	.949	SS-22, 3B-19, 2B-11, 1B-10
1989			101	.201	.254	189	38	4	0	2	1.1	16	14	19	18	1	37	5	86	136	8	24	2.3	.965	2B-29, SS-26, 3B-10, 1B-5, OF-1, P-1
15 yrs.			1491	.256	.345	4466	1142	143	65	42	0.9	480	377	227	406	58	137	32	1905	3662	196	695	3.9	.966	SS-1240, 2B-68, 3B-58, 1B-20, OF-4, P-2

DIVISIONAL PLAYOFF SERIES

Year	Team		Games	BA	SA	AB	H	2B	3B	HR	HR%	R	RBI	BB	SO	SB	AB	H	PO	A	E	DP	TC/G	FA	G by Pos
1981	HOU	N	2	.333	.333	3	1	0	0	0	0.0	1	0	0	1	0	1	1	0	0	0	0	0.0	–	SS-1

LEAGUE CHAMPIONSHIP SERIES

Year	Team		Games	BA	SA	AB	H	2B	3B	HR	HR%	R	RBI	BB	SO	SB	AB	H	PO	A	E	DP	TC/G	FA	G by Pos
1975	PIT	N	2	.000	.000	1	0	0	0	0	0.0	0	0	0	0	0	0	0	0	0	1	0	0.5	–	SS-1
1980	HOU	N	4	.154	.231	13	2	1	0	0	0.0	2	0	3	0	0	0	0	8	12	1	1	5.3	.952	SS-4
1986			4	.333	.333	12	4	0	0	0	0.0	1	0	1	3	0	1	0	7	8	2	0	4.3	.882	SS-4
3 yrs.			10	.231	.269	26	6	1	0	0	0.0	3	0	4	4	0	1	0	15	20	4	1	3.9	.897	SS-9

Danny Reynolds

REYNOLDS, DANIEL VANCE (Squirrel)
B. Nov. 27, 1919, Stony Point, N. C.

BR TR 5'11"   158 lbs.

Year	Team		Games	BA	SA	AB	H	2B	3B	HR	HR%	R	RBI	BB	SO	SB	AB	H	PO	A	E	DP	TC/G	FA	G by Pos
1945	CHI	A	29	.167	.222	72	12	2	1	0	0.0	6	4	3	8	1	4	0	39	62	4	13	3.6	.962	SS-14, 2B-11

Don Reynolds

REYNOLDS, DONALD EDWARD
Brother of Harold Reynolds.
B. Apr. 16, 1953, Arkadelphia, Ark.

BR TR 5'8"   178 lbs.

Year	Team		Games	BA	SA	AB	H	2B	3B	HR	HR%	R	RBI	BB	SO	SB	AB	H	PO	A	E	DP	TC/G	FA	G by Pos
1978	SD	N	57	.253	.276	87	22	2	0	0	0.0	8	10	15	14	1	30	7	22	2	2	0	0.5	.923	OF-25
1979			30	.222	.333	45	10	1	2	0	0.0	6	6	7	6	0	12	0	17	2	1	1	0.7	.950	OF-14
2 yrs.			87	.242	.295	132	32	3	2	0	0.0	14	16	22	20	1	42	7	39	4	3	1	0.5	.935	OF-39

Harold Reynolds

REYNOLDS, HAROLD CRAIG
Brother of Don Reynolds.
B. Nov. 26, 1960, Eugene, Ore.

BB TR 5'11"   165 lbs.

Year	Team		Games	BA	SA	AB	H	2B	3B	HR	HR%	R	RBI	BB	SO	SB	AB	H	PO	A	E	DP	TC/G	FA	G by Pos
1983	SEA	A	20	.203	.305	59	12	4	1	0	0.0	8	2	9	2	0	0	0	30	48	2	14	4.0	.975	2B-18
1984			10	.300	.300	10	3	0	0	0	0.0	3	0	0	1	1	1	0	8	12	0	3	2.0	1.000	2B-6
1985			66	.144	.192	104	15	3	1	0	0.0	15	6	17	14	3	2	0	69	123	8	22	3.0	.960	2B-61
1986			126	.222	.290	445	99	19	4	1	0.2	46	24	29	42	30	0	0	278	415	16	111	5.6	.977	2B-126
1987			160	.275	.370	530	146	31	8	1	0.2	73	35	39	34	**60**	0	0	347	507	20	111	5.5	.977	2B-160
1988			158	.283	.383	598	169	26	11	4	0.7	61	41	51	51	35	0	0	303	471	18	111	5.0	.977	2B-158
1989			153	.300	.369	613	184	24	9	0	0.0	87	43	55	45	25	2	0	311	506	17	109	5.5	.980	2B-151, DH-1
7 yrs.			693	.266	.348	2359	628	107	34	6	0.3	293	150	193	196	154	4	0	1346	2082	81	481	5.1	.977	2B-680, DH-1

R. J. Reynolds

REYNOLDS, ROBERT JAMES
B. Apr. 19, 1959, Sacramento, Calif.

BB TR 6'   180 lbs.

Year	Team		Games	BA	SA	AB	H	2B	3B	HR	HR%	R	RBI	BB	SO	SB	AB	H	PO	A	E	DP	TC/G	FA	G by Pos
1983	LA	N	24	.236	.345	55	13	0	0	2	3.6	5	11	3	11	5	7	2	25	2	2	1	1.2	.931	OF-18
1984			73	.258	.350	240	62	12	2	2	0.8	23	24	14	38	7	13	5	104	4	3	1	1.5	.973	OF-63
1985	2 teams	LA N (73G – .266)	104	.282	.395	337	95	15	7	3	0.9	44	42	22	49	18	19	3	159	6	6	0	1.6	.965	OF-85
"	total	PIT N (31G – .308)																							
1986	PIT	N	118	.269	.420	402	108	30	6	9	2.2	63	48	40	78	16	11	2	190	2	9	0	1.7	.955	OF-112
1987			117	.260	.400	335	87	24	1	7	2.1	47	51	34	80	14	23	6	134	7	1	2	1.2	.993	OF-99
1988			130	.248	.359	323	80	14	2	6	1.9	35	51	20	62	15	42	9	142	7	4	2	1.2	.974	OF-95
1989			125	.270	.375	363	98	16	2	6	1.7	45	48	34	66	22	31	9	200	6	2	3	1.7	.990	OF-98
7 yrs.			691	.264	.385	2055	543	111	16	35	1.7	262	275	167	384	97	146	36	954	34	27	9	1.5	.973	OF-570

Ronn Reynolds

REYNOLDS, RONN DWAYNE
B. Sept. 28, 1958, Wichita, Kans.

BR TR 6'   200 lbs.

Year	Team		Games	BA	SA	AB	H	2B	3B	HR	HR%	R	RBI	BB	SO	SB	AB	H	PO	A	E	DP	TC/G	FA	G by Pos
1982	NY	N	2	.000	.000	4	0	0	0	0	0.0	0	0	1	1	0	0	0	3	0	0	0	1.5	1.000	C-2
1983			24	.197	.212	66	13	1	0	0	0.0	4	2	8	12	0	0	0	99	14	7	2	5.0	.942	C-24
1985			28	.209	.256	43	9	2	0	0	0.0	4	1	0	18	0	2	0	86	9	1	2	3.4	.990	C-25
1986	PHI	N	43	.214	.317	126	27	4	0	3	2.4	8	10	5	30	0	1	1	198	16	2	3	5.0	.991	C-42
1987	HOU	N	38	.167	.235	102	17	4	0	1	1.0	5	7	3	29	0	0	0	216	16	6	1	6.3	.975	C-38
5 yrs.			135	.194	.261	341	66	11	0	4	1.2	21	20	17	90	0	3	1	602	55	16	8	5.0	.976	C-131

Tommie Reynolds

REYNOLDS, THOMAS D.
B. Aug. 15, 1941, Arizona, La.

BR TR 6'2"   190 lbs.
BB 1967

Year	Team		Games	BA	SA	AB	H	2B	3B	HR	HR%	R	RBI	BB	SO	SB	Pinch Hit AB	H	PO	A	E	DP	TC/G	FA	G by Pos

Tommie Reynolds *continued*

1963	KC	A	8	.053	.105	19	1	1	0	0	0.0	1	0	1	7	0	3	0	8	0	2	0	1.3	.800	OF-5
1964			31	.202	.277	94	19	1	0	2	2.1	11	9	10	22	0	5	2	39	5	3	0	1.5	.936	OF-25, 3B-3
1965			90	.237	.311	270	64	11	3	1	0.4	34	22	36	41	9	7	1	154	8	3	2	1.8	.982	OF-83, 3B-1
1967	NY	N	101	.206	.257	136	28	1	0	2	1.5	16	9	11	26	1	22	5	69	6	2	1	0.8	.974	OF-72, 3B-5, C-1
1969	OAK	A	107	.257	.308	315	81	10	0	2	0.6	51	20	34	29	1	20	6	184	5	4	2	1.8	.979	OF-89
1970	CAL	A	59	.250	.317	120	30	3	1	1	0.8	11	6	6	10	1	24	4	63	1	2	0	1.1	.970	OF-32, 3B-1
1971			45	.186	.291	86	16	3	0	2	2.3	4	8	9	6	0	21	4	44	3	1	1	1.1	.979	OF-26, 3B-1
1972	MIL	A	72	.200	.300	130	26	5	1	2	1.5	13	13	10	25	0	32	7	77	2	3	0	1.1	.963	OF-41, 3B-1, 1B-1
8 yrs.			513	.226	.296	1170	265	35	5	12	1.0	141	87	117	166	12	134	29	638	30	20	6	1.3	.971	OF-373, 3B-12, 1B-1, C-1

Bobby Rhawn

RHAWN, ROBERT JOHN (Rocky)
B. Feb. 13, 1919, Catawissa, Pa.   D. June 9, 1984, Danville, Pa.
BR TR 5'8"   180 lbs.

1947	NY	N	13	.311	.444	45	14	3	0	1	2.2	7	3	8	1	0	0	0	19	37	4	6	4.6	.933	2B-8, 3B-5
1948			36	.273	.432	44	12	2	1	2	2.3	11	8	8	6	3	4	2	17	28	5	4	1.4	.900	SS-14, 3B-7
1949	3 teams		NY N (14G – .172)			PIT N (3G – .143)						CHI A (24G – .205)													
"	total		41	.193	.248	109	21	4	1	0	0.0	20	7	19	10	1	3	1	52	82	7	12	3.4	.950	3B-21, 2B-8, SS-3
3 yrs.			90	.237	.333	198	47	9	2	2	1.0	38	18	35	17	4	7	3	88	147	16	22	2.8	.936	3B-33, SS-17, 2B-16

Cy Rheam

RHEAM, KENNETH JOHNSTON
B. Sept. 28, 1893, Pittsburgh, Pa.   D. Oct. 23, 1947, Pittsburgh, Pa.
BR TR 6'   175 lbs.

1914	PIT	F	73	.210	.262	214	45	5	3	0	0.0	15	20	9		6	5	1	431	55	16	16	6.9	.968	1B-43, 3B-13, 2B-11, OF-1
1915			34	.174	.217	69	12	0	0	1	1.4	10	5	1		4	4	1	51	2	2	0	1.6	.964	OF-22, 1B-1
2 yrs.			107	.201	.251	283	57	5	3	1	0.4	25	25	10		10	9	2	482	57	18	16	5.2	.968	1B-44, OF-23, 3B-13, 2B-11

Billy Rhiel

RHIEL, WILLIAM JOSEPH
B. Aug. 16, 1900, Youngstown, Ohio   D. Aug. 16, 1946, Youngstown, Ohio
BR TR 5'11"   175 lbs.

1929	BKN	N	76	.278	.420	205	57	9	4	4	2.0	27	25	19	25	0	14	2	105	159	7	18	3.6	.974	2B-47, 3B-7, SS-2
1930	BOS	N	20	.170	.255	47	8	4	0	0	0.0	3	4	2	5	0	3	0	8	13	1	2	1.1	.955	3B-13, 2B-2
1932	DET	A	84	.280	.392	250	70	13	3	3	1.2	30	38	17	23	2	27	13	150	65	5	21	2.6	.977	3B-36, 1B-12, OF-8, 2B-1
1933			19	.176	.294	17	3	0	1	0	0.0	1	1	5	4	0	13	3	4	0	0	0	0.2	1.000	OF-1
4 yrs.			199	.266	.387	519	138	26	8	7	1.3	61	68	43	57	2	57	18	267	237	13	41	2.6	.975	3B-56, 2B-50, 1B-12, OF-9, SS-2

Dusty Rhodes

RHODES, JAMES LAMAR
B. May 13, 1927, Mathews, Ala.
BL TR 6'   178 lbs.

1952	NY	N	67	.250	.477	176	44	8	1	10	5.7	34	36	23	33	1	9	1	97	3	9	0	1.6	.917	OF-56
1953			76	.233	.479	163	38	7	0	11	6.7	18	30	10	28	0	29	5	76	6	3	4	1.1	.965	OF-47
1954			82	.341	.695	164	56	7	3	15	9.1	31	50	18	25	1	45	15	62	1	1	0	0.8	.984	OF-37
1955			94	.305	.449	187	57	5	2	6	3.2	22	32	27	26	1	44	11	68	2	1	0	0.8	.986	OF-45
1956			111	.217	.381	244	53	10	3	8	3.3	20	33	30	41	0	39	7	85	6	4	1	0.9	.958	OF-68
1957			92	.205	.305	190	39	5	1	4	2.1	20	19	18	34	0	46	7	63	0	0	0	0.7	1.000	OF-44
1959	SF		54	.188	.229	48	9	2	0	0	0.0	1	7	5	9	0	48	9	0	0	0	0	0.0	–	
7 yrs.			576	.253	.445	1172	296	44	10	54	4.6	146	207	131	196	3	260	55	451	18	18	5	0.8	.963	OF-297

WORLD SERIES

| 1954 | NY | N | 3 | .667 | 1.667 | 6 | 4 | 0 | 0 | 2 | 33.3 | 2 | 7 | 1 | 2 | 0 | 3 | 3 | 4 | 0 | 0 | 0 | 1.3 | 1.000 | OF-2 |

1st

Kevin Rhomberg

RHOMBERG, KEVIN JAY
B. Nov. 22, 1955, Dubuque, Iowa
BR TR 6'   175 lbs.

1982	CLE	A	16	.333	.500	18	6	0	0	1	5.6	3	1	2	4	0	2	0	9	2	1	1	0.8	.917	OF-7, DH-4, 3B-1
1983			12	.476	.476	21	10	0	0	0	0.0	2	2	2	4	1	1	0	10	0	0	0	0.8	1.000	OF-9, DH-1
1984			13	.250	.250	8	2	0	0	0	0.0	0	0	0	3	0	3	0	7	1	0	0	0.6	1.000	OF-7, DH-1, 2B-1, 1B-1
3 yrs.			41	.383	.447	47	18	0	0	1	2.1	5	3	4	11	1	6	0	26	3	1	1	0.7	.967	OF-23, DH-6, 3B-1, 2B-1, 1B-1

Hal Rhyne

RHYNE, HAROLD J.
B. Mar. 30, 1899, Paso Robles, Calif.   D. Jan. 7, 1971, Orangevale, Calif.
BR TR 5'8½"   163 lbs.

1926	PIT	N	109	.251	.322	366	92	14	3	2	0.5	46	39	35	21	1	0	0	271	346	26	80	5.9	.960	2B-66, SS-44, 3B-1
1927			62	.274	.304	168	46	5	0	0	0.0	21	17	14	9	0	1	0	118	122	11	22	4.0	.956	2B-45, 3B-10, SS-7
1929	BOS	A	120	.251	.350	346	87	24	5	0	0.0	41	38	25	14	4	1	0	220	298	36	71	4.6	.935	SS-114, OF-1, 3B-1
1930			107	.203	.264	296	60	8	5	0	0.0	34	23	25	19	1	0	0	188	284	28	63	4.7	.944	SS-107
1931			147	.273	.343	565	154	34	3	0	0.0	75	51	57	41	3	0	0	295	502	31	74	5.6	.963	SS-147
1932			71	.227	.333	207	47	12	5	0	0.0	26	14	23	14	3	10	3	99	168	10	31	3.9	.964	SS-55, 3B-4, 2B-1
1933	CHI	A	39	.265	.301	83	22	1	1	0	0.0	9	10	5	9	1	6	1	48	72	7	13	3.3	.945	2B-19, 3B-13, SS-2
7 yrs.			655	.250	.323	2031	508	98	22	2	0.1	252	192	184	127	13	18	4	1239	1792	149	354	4.9	.953	SS-476, 2B-131, 3B-29, OF-1

WORLD SERIES

| 1927 | PIT | N | 1 | .000 | .000 | 4 | 0 | 0 | 0 | 0 | 0.0 | 0 | 0 | 0 | 0 | 0 | 0 | 0 | 0 | 6 | 0 | 0 | 6.0 | 1.000 | 2B-1 |

Bob Rice

RICE, ROBERT TURNBULL
B. May 28, 1899, Philadelphia, Pa.   D. Feb. 20, 1986, Elizabethtown, Pa.
BR TR 5'10"   170 lbs.

| 1926 | PHI | N | 19 | .148 | .185 | 54 | 8 | 0 | 1 | 0 | 0.0 | 3 | 10 | 3 | 10 | 0 | 0 | 0 | 17 | 33 | 6 | 8 | 2.9 | .893 | 3B-15, SS-2, 2B-2 |

Del Rice

RICE, DELBERT W.
B. Oct. 27, 1922, Portsmouth, Ohio   D. Jan. 26, 1983, Buena Park, Calif.
Manager 1972.
BR TR 6'2"   190 lbs.

| 1945 | STL | N | 83 | .261 | .364 | 253 | 66 | 17 | 3 | 1 | 0.4 | 27 | 28 | 16 | 33 | 0 | 6 | 0 | 284 | 39 | 2 | 6 | 3.9 | .994 | C-77 |
| 1946 | | | 55 | .273 | .367 | 139 | 38 | 8 | 1 | 1 | 0.7 | 10 | 12 | 8 | 16 | 0 | 2 | 0 | 196 | 12 | 5 | 0 | 3.9 | .977 | C-53 |

Year	Team	Games	BA	SA	AB	H	2B	3B	HR	HR%	R	RBI	BB	SO	SB	Pinch Hit AB	Pinch Hit H	PO	A	E	DP	TC/G	FA	G by Pos

Del Rice *continued*

Year	Team	Games	BA	SA	AB	H	2B	3B	HR	HR%	R	RBI	BB	SO	SB	AB	H	PO	A	E	DP	TC/G	FA	G by Pos
1947		97	.218	.406	261	57	7	3	12	4.6	28	44	36	40	1	3	0	380	33	8	7	4.3	.981	C-94
1948		100	.197	.279	290	57	10	1	4	1.4	24	34	37	46	1	0	0	447	46	2	5	5.0	.996	C-99
1949		92	.236	.342	284	67	16	1	4	1.4	25	29	30	40	0	0	0	355	29	3	4	4.2	.992	C-92
1950		130	.244	.372	414	101	20	3	9	2.2	39	54	43	65	0	0	0	572	63	10	12	5.0	.984	C-130
1951		122	.251	.364	374	94	13	1	9	2.4	34	47	34	26	0	3	0	447	66	8	12	4.3	.985	C-120
1952		147	.259	.388	495	128	27	2	11	2.2	43	65	33	38	0	1	0	677	81	6	8	5.2	.992	C-147
1953		135	.236	.337	419	99	22	1	6	1.4	32	37	48	49	0	0	0	627	60	8	6	5.1	.988	C-135
1954		56	.252	.374	147	37	10	1	2	1.4	13	16	16	21	0	4	2	248	20	4	2	4.9	.985	C-52
1955	2 teams	STL N	(20G –	.203)		MIL	N	(27G –	.197)															
"	total	47	.200	.308	130	26	3	1	3	2.3	11	14	13	18	0	7	0	164	18	5	3	4.0	.973	C-40
1956	MIL N	71	.213	.319	188	40	9	1	3	1.6	15	17	18	34	0	5	1	271	21	5	2	4.2	.983	C-65
1957		54	.229	.438	144	33	1	1	9	6.3	15	20	17	37	0	6	1	235	14	2	3	4.6	.992	C-48
1958		43	.223	.306	121	27	7	0	1	0.8	10	9	8	30	0	6	2	174	13	1	1	4.4	.995	C-38
1959		13	.207	.207	29	6	0	0	0	0.0	3	1	2	3	0	4	1	42	1	2	1	3.5	.956	C-9
1960	3 teams	CHI N	(18G –	.231)		STL	N	(1G –	.000)		BAL	A	(1G –	.000)										
"	total	20	.218	.273	55	12	3	0	0	0.0	2	4	3	7	0	0	0	90	7	3	0	5.0	.970	C-20
1961	LA A	44	.241	.434	83	20	4	0	4	4.8	11	11	20	19	0	15	4	144	14	1	0	3.6	.994	C-30
	17 yrs.	1309	.237	.356	3826	908	177	20	79	2.1	342	441	382	522	2	62	12	5353	537	75	72	4.6	.987	C-1249

WORLD SERIES

Year	Team	Games	BA	SA	AB	H	2B	3B	HR	HR%	R	RBI	BB	SO	SB	AB	H	PO	A	E	DP	TC/G	FA	G by Pos
1946	STL N	3	.500	.667	6	3	1	0	0	0.0	2	2	2	0	0	0	0	9	1	0	0	3.3	1.000	C-3
1957	MIL N	2	.167	.167	6	1	0	0	0	0.0	0	0	1	2	0	0	0	15	2	0	2	8.5	1.000	C-2
	2 yrs.	5	.333	.417	12	4	1	0	0	0.0	2	2	3	2	0	0	0	24	3	0	2	5.4	1.000	C-5

Hal Rice

RICE, HAROLD HOUSTEN (Hoot)
B. Feb. 11, 1924, Morganette, W. Va.

BL TR 6'1" 195 lbs.

Year	Team	Games	BA	SA	AB	H	2B	3B	HR	HR%	R	RBI	BB	SO	SB	AB	H	PO	A	E	DP	TC/G	FA	G by Pos
1948	STL N	8	.323	.484	31	10	1	2	0	0.0	3	3	2	4	0	0	0	16	0	0	0	2.0	1.000	OF-8
1949		40	.196	.348	46	9	2	1	1	2.2	3	9	3	7	0	27	6	8	1	0	0	0.2	1.000	OF-10
1950		44	.211	.297	128	27	3	1	2	1.6	12	11	10	10	0	6	1	67	3	2	0	1.6	.972	OF-37
1951		69	.254	.364	236	60	12	1	4	1.7	20	38	24	22	1	5	1	116	6	6	0	1.9	.953	OF-63
1952		98	.288	.441	295	85	14	5	7	2.4	37	45	16	26	1	19	3	132	5	4	0	1.4	.972	OF-81
1953	2 teams	STL N	(8G –	.250)		PIT	N	(78G –	.311)															
"	total	86	.310	.412	294	91	16	1	4	1.4	39	42	17	25	0	17	3	167	14	5	2	2.2	.973	OF-70
1954	2 teams	PIT N	(28G –	.173)		CHI	N	(51G –	.153)															
"	total	79	.163	.222	153	25	4	1	1	0.7	15	14	22	39	0	29	2	79	5	3	2	1.1	.966	OF-48
	7 yrs.	424	.260	.372	1183	307	52	12	19	1.6	129	162	94	133	1	103	16	585	34	20	4	1.5	.969	OF-317

Harry Rice

RICE, HARRY FRANCIS
B. Nov. 22, 1901, Ware Station, Ill. D. Jan. 1, 1971, Portland, Ore.

BL TR 5'9" 185 lbs.

Year	Team	Games	BA	SA	AB	H	2B	3B	HR	HR%	R	RBI	BB	SO	SB	AB	H	PO	A	E	DP	TC/G	FA	G by Pos
1923	STL A	4	.000	.000	3	0	0	0	0	0.0	0	0	0	0	0	3	0	0	0	0	0	—		—
1924		43	.283	.359	92	26	7	0	0	0.0	19	15	7	5	1	22	7	26	38	7	6	1.7	.901	3B-15, 2B-4, OF-2, SS-2, 1B-2
1925		103	.359	.568	354	127	25	8	11	3.1	87	47	54	15	8	14	6	207	18	7	4	2.3	.970	OF-85, 3B-3, 1B-1, 2B-1, C-1
1926		148	.313	.441	578	181	27	10	9	1.6	86	59	63	40	10	4	2	322	49	16	7	2.6	.959	OF-133, 3B-7, 2B-4, SS-2
1927		137	.287	.412	520	149	26	9	7	1.3	90	68	50	21	6	0	0	281	36	23	9	2.5	.932	OF-130, 3B-2
1928	DET A	131	.302	.425	510	154	21	12	6	1.2	87	81	44	27	20	2	0	347	10	14	0	2.8	.962	OF-129, 3B-2
1929		130	.304	.425	536	163	33	7	6	1.1	97	69	61	23	6	1	0	347	20	15	6	2.9	.961	OF-127, 3B-3
1930	2 teams	DET A	(37G –	.305)		NY	A	(100G –	.298)															
"	total	137	.300	.426	474	142	23	5	9	1.9	78	98	50	29	3	8	1	326	12	13	5	2.4	.963	OF-122, 1B-6, 3B-1
1931	WAS A	47	.265	.370	162	43	5	6	0	0.0	32	15	12	10	2	5	3	89	3	3	0	2.0	.968	OF-42
1933	CIN N	143	.261	.322	510	133	19	6	0	0.0	44	54	35	24	4	1	0	315	14	3	3	2.3	.991	OF-141, 3B-1
	10 yrs.	1023	.299	.421	3739	1118	186	63	48	1.3	620	506	376	194	60	60	19	2260	200	101	40	2.5	.961	OF-911, 3B-37, 1B-11, 2B-9, SS-4, C-1

Jim Rice

RICE, JAMES EDWARD
B. Mar. 8, 1953, Anderson, S. C.

BR TR 6'2" 200 lbs.

Year	Team	Games	BA	SA	AB	H	2B	3B	HR	HR%	R	RBI	BB	SO	SB	AB	H	PO	A	E	DP	TC/G	FA	G by Pos
1974	BOS A	24	.269	.373	67	18	2	1	1	1.5	6	13	4	12	0	6	0	4	0	1	0	0.2	.800	DH-16, OF-3
1975		144	.309	.491	564	174	29	4	22	3.9	92	102	36	122	10	0	0	162	6	0	0	1.2	1.000	OF-90, DH-54
1976		153	.282	.482	581	164	25	8	25	4.3	75	85	28	123	8	3	1	199	8	7	0	1.4	.967	OF-98, DH-54
1977		160	.320	**.593**	644	206	29	15	39	6.1	104	114	53	120	5	0	0	83	4	4	1	0.6	.956	OF-114, DH-44
1978		163	.315	**.600**	677	213	25	15	46	6.8	121	139	58	126	7	0	0	245	13	3	1	1.6	.989	OF-114, DH-49
1979		158	.325	.596	619	201	39	6	39	6.3	117	130	57	97	9	1	0	241	8	4	1	1.6	.984	OF-125, DH-33
1980		124	.294	.504	504	148	22	6	24	4.8	81	86	30	87	8	0	0	233	10	3	2	2.0	.988	OF-109, DH-15
1981		108	.284	.441	451	128	18	1	17	3.8	51	62	34	76	2	0	0	237	9	3	0	2.3	.988	OF-108
1982		145	.309	.494	573	177	24	5	24	4.2	86	97	55	98	0	0	0	273	10	9	3	2.0	.969	OF-145
1983		155	.305	.550	626	191	34	1	**39**	6.2	90	**126**	52	102	0	0	0	339	21	6	5	2.4	.984	OF-151, DH-4
1984		159	.280	.467	657	184	25	7	28	4.3	98	122	44	102	4	0	0	336	12	4	3	2.2	.989	OF-157, DH-2
1985		140	.291	.487	546	159	20	3	27	4.9	85	103	51	75	2	2	0	236	8	9	1	1.8	.964	OF-130, DH-7
1986		157	.324	.490	618	200	39	2	20	3.2	98	110	62	78	0	0	0	330	16	8	0	2.3	.977	OF-156, DH-1
1987		108	.277	.408	404	112	14	0	13	3.2	66	62	45	77	1	2	1	155	12	4	2	1.6	.977	OF-94, DH-12
1988		135	.264	.406	485	128	18	3	15	3.1	57	72	48	89	1	5	2	30	0	1	0	0.2	.968	DH-112, OF-19
1989		56	.234	.344	209	49	10	2	3	1.4	22	28	13	39	1	3	1	0	0	0	0	0.0	—	DH-55
	16 yrs.	2089	.298	.502	8225	2452	373	79	382	4.6	1249	1451	670	1423	58	22	5	3103	137	66	19	1.6	.980	OF-1543, DH-530

LEAGUE CHAMPIONSHIP SERIES

Year	Team	Games	BA	SA	AB	H	2B	3B	HR	HR%	R	RBI	BB	SO	SB	AB	H	PO	A	E	DP	TC/G	FA	G by Pos
1986	BOS A	7	.161	.387	31	5	1	0	2	6.5	8	6	1	6	0	0	0	13	1	0	0	2.0	1.000	OF-7
1988		4	.154	.154	13	2	0	0	0	0.0	0	1	2	4	0	0	0	0	0	0	0	0.0	—	DH-4
	2 yrs.	11	.159	.318	44	7	1	0	2	4.5	8	7	3	12	0	0	0	13	1	0	0	1.3	1.000	OF-7, DH-4

WORLD SERIES

Year	Team	Games	BA	SA	AB	H	2B	3B	HR	HR%	R	RBI	BB	SO	SB	AB	H	PO	A	E	DP	TC/G	FA	G by Pos
1986	BOS A	7	.333	.444	27	9	1	0	0	0.0	6	0	6	9	0	0	0	16	2	0	1	2.6	1.000	OF-7

Year	Team	Games	BA	SA	AB	H	2B	3B	HR	HR%	R	RBI	BB	SO	SB	Pinch Hit AB	Pinch Hit H	PO	A	E	DP	TC/G	FA	G by Pos

Len Rice

RICE, LEONARD OLIVER
B. Sept. 2, 1918, Lead, S. D.   BR TR 6'   180 lbs.

Year	Team	Games	BA	SA	AB	H	2B	3B	HR	HR%	R	RBI	BB	SO	SB	PH AB	PH H	PO	A	E	DP	TC/G	FA	G by Pos
1944	CIN N	10	.000	.000	4	0	0	0	0	0.0	1	0	0	0	0	1	0	4	0	0	0	0.4	1.000	C-5
1945	CHI N	32	.232	.263	99	23	3	0	0	0.0	10	7	5	8	2	2	0	115	8	3	1	3.9	.976	C-29
2 yrs.		42	.223	.252	103	23	3	0	0	0.0	11	7	5	8	2	3	0	119	8	3	1	3.1	.977	C-34

Sam Rice

RICE, EDGAR CHARLES
B. Feb. 20, 1890, Morocco, Ind.   D. Oct. 13, 1974, Rossmor, Md.
Hall of Fame 1963.   BL TR 5'9"   150 lbs.

Year	Team	Games	BA	SA	AB	H	2B	3B	HR	HR%	R	RBI	BB	SO	SB	PH AB	PH H	PO	A	E	DP	TC/G	FA	G by Pos
1915	WAS A	4	.375	.375	8	3	0	0	0	0.0	1	0	0	1	0	0	0	1	7	1	1	2.3	.889	P-4
1916		58	.299	.386	197	59	8	3	1	0.5	26	17	15	13	4	6	2	83	11	4	1	1.7	.959	OF-46, P-5
1917		155	.302	.369	586	177	25	7	0	0.0	77	69	50	41	35	0	0	265	26	12	5	2.0	.960	OF-155
1918		7	.348	.391	23	8	1	0	0	0.0	3	2	2	0	1	1	0	11	4	0	1	2.1	1.000	OF-6
1919		141	.321	.411	557	179	23	9	3	0.5	80	71	42	26	26	0	0	285	18	12	3	2.2	.962	OF-141
1920		153	.338	.428	624	211	29	9	3	0.5	83	80	39	23	63	0	0	454	24	20	5	3.3	.960	OF-153
1921		143	.330	.467	561	185	39	13	4	0.7	83	79	38	10	25	1	0	380	18	15	3	2.9	.964	OF-141
1922		154	.295	.423	633	187	37	13	6	0.9	91	69	48	13	20	0	0	385	23	21	3	2.8	.951	OF-154
1923		148	.316	.450	595	188	35	18	3	0.5	117	75	57	12	20	1	0	307	21	10	8	2.3	.970	OF-147
1924		154	.334	.441	646	216	38	14	1	0.2	106	76	46	24	24	0	0	331	18	12	4	2.3	.967	OF-154
1925		152	.350	.442	649	227	31	13	1	0.2	111	87	37	10	26	0	0	339	20	12	7	2.4	.968	OF-152
1926		152	.337	.445	641	216	32	14	3	0.5	98	76	42	20	25	0	0	342	25	15	5	2.5	.961	OF-152
1927		142	.297	.408	603	179	33	14	2	0.3	98	65	36	11	19	3	0	258	12	7	2	2.0	.975	OF-139
1928		148	.328	.438	616	202	32	15	2	0.3	95	55	49	15	16	0	0	240	11	7	5	1.7	.973	OF-147
1929		150	.323	.424	616	199	39	10	1	0.2	119	62	55	9	16	2	0	272	20	9	5	2.0	.970	OF-147
1930		147	.349	.457	593	207	35	13	1	0.2	121	73	55	14	13	0	0	297	13	12	4	2.2	.963	OF-145
1931		120	.310	.400	413	128	21	8	0	0.0	81	42	35	11	6	7	1	221	7	7	2	2.0	.970	OF-105
1932		106	.323	.438	288	93	16	7	1	0.3	58	34	32	6	7	33	5	132	7	4	2	1.3	.972	OF-69
1933		73	.294	.447	85	25	4	3	1	1.2	19	12	5	3	7	28	7	41	4	0	2	0.6	1.000	OF-39
1934	CLE A	97	.293	.364	335	98	19	1	1	0.3	48	33	28	9	5	23	5	129	2	5	0	1.4	.963	OF-78
20 yrs.		2404	.322	.427	9269	2987	497	184	34	0.4	1515	1078	709	275	351	105	20	4773	291	185	68	2.2	.965	OF-2270, P-9

WORLD SERIES

Year	Team	Games	BA	SA	AB	H	2B	3B	HR	HR%	R	RBI	BB	SO	SB	PH AB	PH H	PO	A	E	DP	TC/G	FA	G by Pos
1924	WAS A	7	.207	.207	29	6	0	0	0	0.0	2	1	3	2	0	0	0	13	4	1	1	2.6	.944	OF-7
1925		7	.364	.364	33	12	0	0	0	0.0	5	3	0	1	0	0	0	17	0	0	0	2.4	1.000	OF-7
1933		1	1.000	1.000	1	1	0	0	0	0.0	0	0	0	0	0	1	1	0	0	0	0	0.0	—	
3 yrs.		15	.302	.302	63	19	0	0	0	0.0	7	4	3	3	2	1	1	30	4	1	1	2.3	.971	OF-14

Lee Richard

RICHARD, LEE EDWARD (Bee Bee)
B. Sept. 18, 1948, Lafayette, La.   BR TR 5'11"   165 lbs.

Year	Team	Games	BA	SA	AB	H	2B	3B	HR	HR%	R	RBI	BB	SO	SB	PH AB	PH H	PO	A	E	DP	TC/G	FA	G by Pos
1971	CHI A	87	.231	.304	260	60	7	3	2	0.8	38	17	20	46	8	6	0	107	213	27	31	4.0	.922	SS-68, OF-16
1972		11	.241	.241	29	7	0	0	0	0.0	5	1	0	7	1	1	1	8	2	0	1	0.9	1.000	OF-6, SS-1
1974		32	.164	.179	67	11	1	0	0	0.0	5	1	5	8	0	0	0	14	40	5	11	1.8	.915	3B-12, SS-6, DH-5, 2B-3, OF-1
1975		43	.200	.244	45	9	0	0	0	0.0	11	5	4	7	2	0	0	20	33	3	3	1.3	.946	3B-12, SS-9, DH-5, 2B-5
1976	STL N	66	.176	.264	91	16	4	2	0	0.0	12	5	4	9	1	3	0	71	71	7	18	2.3	.953	2B-26, SS-12, 3B-1
5 yrs.		239	.209	.270	492	103	12	6	2	0.4	71	29	33	77	12	10	1	220	359	42	64	2.6	.932	SS-96, 2B-34, 3B-25, OF-23, DH-10

Fred Richards

RICHARDS, FRED CHARLES (Fuzzy)
B. Nov. 3, 1927, Warren, Ohio   BL TL 6'1½"   185 lbs.

Year	Team	Games	BA	SA	AB	H	2B	3B	HR	HR%	R	RBI	BB	SO	SB	PH AB	PH H	PO	A	E	DP	TC/G	FA	G by Pos
1951	CHI N	10	.296	.370	27	8	2	0	0	0.0	4	4	2	3	0	1	0	62	8	0	3	7.0	1.000	1B-9

Gene Richards

RICHARDS, EUGENE
B. Sept. 29, 1953, Monticello, S. C.   BL TL 6'   175 lbs.

Year	Team	Games	BA	SA	AB	H	2B	3B	HR	HR%	R	RBI	BB	SO	SB	PH AB	PH H	PO	A	E	DP	TC/G	FA	G by Pos
1977	SD N	146	.290	.390	525	152	16	11	5	1.0	79	32	60	80	56	14	4	416	35	13	23	3.2	.972	OF-109, 1B-32
1978		154	.308	.420	555	171	26	12	4	0.7	90	45	64	80	37	9	1	421	20	17	23	3.0	.963	OF-124, 1B-26
1979		150	.279	.365	545	152	17	9	4	0.7	77	41	47	62	24	20	3	320	7	9	2	2.2	.973	OF-132
1980		158	.301	.385	642	193	26	8	4	0.6	91	41	61	73	61	2	1	307	21	7	4	2.1	.979	OF-156
1981		104	.288	.407	393	113	14	12	3	0.8	47	42	53	44	20	2	1	178	14	5	1	1.9	.975	OF-102
1982		132	.286	.359	521	149	13	8	3	0.6	63	28	36	52	30	3	0	423	20	11	18	3.4	.976	OF-103, 1B-25
1983		95	.275	.386	233	64	11	3	3	1.3	37	22	17	17	14	36	6	96	2	2	0	1.1	.980	OF-54
1984	SF N.	87	.252	.281	135	34	4	0	0	0.0	18	4	18	28	5	48	10	46	1	3	0	0.6	.940	OF-26
8 yrs.		1026	.290	.383	3549	1028	127	63	26	0.7	502	255	356	436	247	134	26	2207	120	67	71	2.3	.972	OF-806, 1B-83

Paul Richards

RICHARDS, PAUL RAPIER
B. Nov. 21, 1908, Waxahachie, Tex.   D. May 4, 1986, Waxahachie, Tex.
Manager 1951-61, 1976.   BR TR 6'1½"   180 lbs.

Year	Team	Games	BA	SA	AB	H	2B	3B	HR	HR%	R	RBI	BB	SO	SB	PH AB	PH H	PO	A	E	DP	TC/G	FA	G by Pos
1932	BKN N	3	.000	.000	8	0	0	0	0	0.0	0	0	0	2	0	0	0	21	3	0	0	8.0	1.000	C-3
1933	NY N	51	.195	.230	87	17	3	0	0	0.0	4	10	3	12	0	14	2	74	17	1	2	1.8	.989	C-36
1934		42	.160	.173	75	12	1	0	0	0.0	10	3	13	8	0	3	2	86	15	0	3	2.4	1.000	C-37
1935	2 teams		NY N	(7G – .250)				PHI A	(85G – .245)																
"	total	92	.245	.337	261	64	10	1	4	1.5	31	29	26	13	0	6	2	300	42	8	5	3.8	.977	C-83
1943	DET A	100	.220	.297	313	69	7	1	5	1.6	32	33	38	35	1	0	0	537	86	9	12	6.3	.986	C-100
1944		95	.237	.310	300	71	13	0	3	1.0	24	37	35	30	8	3	0	413	60	10	13	5.1	.979	C-90
1945		83	.256	.355	234	60	12	1	3	1.3	26	32	19	31	4	0	0	361	44	2	7	4.9	.995	C-83
1946		57	.201	.266	139	28	5	2	0	0.0	13	11	23	18	2	3	2	311	35	1	6	6.1	.997	C-54
8 yrs.		523	.227	.301	1417	321	51	5	15	1.1	140	155	157	149	15	29	8	2103	302	31	48	4.7	.987	C-486

WORLD SERIES

Year	Team	Games	BA	SA	AB	H	2B	3B	HR	HR%	R	RBI	BB	SO	SB	PH AB	PH H	PO	A	E	DP	TC/G	FA	G by Pos
1945	DET A	7	.211	.316	19	4	2	0	0	0.0	0	6	4	3	0	0	0	46	5	1	1	7.4	.981	C-7

Bill Richardson

RICHARDSON, WILLIAM HEZEKIAH
B. Sept. 24, 1878, Salem, Ind.   D. Nov. 6, 1949, Sullivan, Ind.

Year	Team	Games	BA	SA	AB	H	2B	3B	HR	HR%	R	RBI	BB	SO	SB	Pinch Hit AB	Pinch Hit H	PO	A	E	DP	TC/G	FA	G by Pos

Bill Richardson *continued*

Year	Team	Games	BA	SA	AB	H	2B	3B	HR	HR%	R	RBI	BB	SO	SB	Pinch Hit AB	Pinch Hit H	PO	A	E	DP	TC/G	FA	G by Pos
1901	STL N	15	.212	.365	52	11	2	0	2	3.8	7	7	6		1	0	0	154	5	3	7	10.8	.981	1B-15

Bobby Richardson

RICHARDSON, ROBERT CLINTON
B. Aug. 19, 1935, Sumter, S. C.
BR TR 5'9" 170 lbs.

Year	Team	Games	BA	SA	AB	H	2B	3B	HR	HR%	R	RBI	BB	SO	SB	Pinch Hit AB	Pinch Hit H	PO	A	E	DP	TC/G	FA	G by Pos
1955	NY A	11	.154	.154	26	4	0	0	0	0.0	2	3	2	0	1	0	0	14	9	3	2	2.4	.885	2B-6, SS-4
1956		5	.143	.143	7	1	0	0	0	0.0	1	0	0	1	0	0	0	15	4	0	2	3.8	1.000	2B-5
1957		97	.256	.298	305	78	11	4	0	0.0	36	19	9	26	1	1	0	206	223	9	60	4.5	.979	2B-93
1958		73	.247	.302	182	45	6	2	0	0.0	18	14	8	5	1	0	0	115	141	8	38	3.6	.970	2B-51, 3B-13, SS-2
1959		134	.301	.377	469	141	18	6	2	0.4	53	33	26	20	5	0	0	269	336	22	94	4.7	.965	2B-109, SS-14, 3B-12
1960		150	.252	.298	460	116	12	3	1	0.2	45	26	35	19	6	1	0	318	350	18	103	4.6	.974	2B-141, 3B-11
1961		162	.261	.316	662	173	17	5	3	0.5	80	49	30	23	9	1	0	413	376	18	136	5.0	.978	2B-161
1962		161	.302	.406	692	**209**	38	5	8	1.2	99	59	37	24	11	0	0	378	452	15	116	5.2	.982	2B-161
1963		151	.265	.330	**630**	167	20	6	3	0.5	72	48	25	22	15	1	0	335	424	12	105	5.1	.984	2B-150
1964		159	.267	.333	**679**	181	25	4	4	0.6	90	50	28	36	11	2	1	402	413	15	109	5.2	.982	2B-157, SS-1
1965		160	.247	.322	664	164	28	2	6	0.9	76	47	37	39	7	3	0	372	403	15	121	4.9	.981	2B-158
1966		149	.251	.330	610	153	21	3	7	1.1	71	42	25	28	6	2	0	322	410	15	91	5.0	.980	2B-147, 3B-2
12 yrs.		1412	.266	.335	5386	1432	196	37	34	0.6	643	390	262	243	73	11	1	3159	3541	150	977	4.9	.978	2B-1339, 3B-38, SS-21

WORLD SERIES

Year	Team	Games	BA	SA	AB	H	2B	3B	HR	HR%	R	RBI	BB	SO	SB	Pinch Hit AB	Pinch Hit H	PO	A	E	DP	TC/G	FA	G by Pos
1957	NY A	2	–	–	0	0	0	0	0	–	0	0	0	0	0	0	0	0	0	0	0	0.0	–	2B-1
1958		4	.000	.000	5	0	0	0	0	0.0	0	0	0	0	0	0	0	0	1	0	0	0.3	1.000	3B-4
1960		7	.367	.667	30	11	2	2	1	3.3	8	12	1	1	0	0	0	21	28	2	7	7.3	.961	2B-7
1961		5	.391	.435	23	9	1	0	0	0.0	2	0	0	1	0	0	0	10	16	0	1	5.2	1.000	2B-5
1962		7	.148	.148	27	4	0	0	0	0.0	3	0	3	1	0	0	0	19	19	1	4	5.6	.974	2B-7
1963		4	.214	.286	14	3	1	0	0	0.0	0	0	1	3	0	0	0	7	14	0	5	5.3	1.000	2B-7
1964		7	.406	.469	32	13	2	0	0	0.0	3	3	0	2	1	0	0	19	19	2	5	5.7	.950	2B-7
7 yrs.		36	.305	.405	131	40	6	2	1	0.8	16	15	5	7	2	0	0	76	97	5	22	4.9	.972	2B-31, 3B-4

Danny Richardson

RICHARDSON, DANIEL
B. Jan. 25, 1863, Elmira, N. Y.   D. Sept. 12, 1926, New York, N. Y.
Manager 1892.
BR TR 5'8" 165 lbs.

Year	Team	Games	BA	SA	AB	H	2B	3B	HR	HR%	R	RBI	BB	SO	SB	Pinch Hit AB	Pinch Hit H	PO	A	E	DP	TC/G	FA	G by Pos
1884	NY N	74	.253	.300	277	70	8	1	1	0.4	36		16	17		0	0	110	54	24	9	2.5	.872	OF-55, SS-19
1885		49	.263	.338	198	52	9	3	0	0.0	26		10	14		0	0	52	58	5	1	2.3	.957	OF-22, 3B-21, P-9
1886		68	.232	.291	237	55	9	1	1	0.4	43	27	17	21		0	0	103	26	6	3	2.0	.956	OF-64, P-5, SS-1, 3B-1, 2B-1
1887		122	.278	.384	450	125	19	10	3	0.7	79	62	36	25	41	0	0	273	413	59	47	6.1	.921	2B-108, 3B-14, P-1
1888		135	.226	.323	561	127	16	7	8	1.4	82	61	15	35	35	0	0	321	423	46	43	5.9	.942	2B-135
1889		125	.280	.398	497	139	22	8	7	1.4	88	100	46	37	32	0	0	332	416	53	60	6.4	.934	2B-125
1890	NY P	123	.256	.335	528	135	12	9	4	0.8	102	80	37	19	37	0	0	301	430	72	54	6.5	.910	SS-68, 2B-56
1891	NY N	123	.269	.353	516	139	18	5	5	1.0	85	51	33	27	28	0	0	358	461	46	64	7.0	.947	2B-114, SS-9
1892	WAS N	142	.240	.294	551	132	13	4	3	0.5	48	58	25	45	25	0	0	389	541	60	69	7.0	.939	SS-93, 2B-49, 3B-1
1893	BKN N	54	.223	.272	206	46	6	2	0	0.0	36	27	13	18	7	0	0	130	129	14	21	5.1	.949	2B-46, 3B-5, SS-3
1894	LOU N	116	.253	.309	430	109	17	2	1	0.2	51	40	35	31	8	0	0	267	388	57	64	6.1	.920	SS-107, 2B-10
11 yrs.		1131	.254	.333	4451	1129	149	52	33	0.7	676	506	283	289	213	0	0	2636	3339	442	435	5.7	.931	2B-644, SS-300, OF-141, 3B-42, P-15

Ezra Richardson

RICHARDSON, ARTHUR L.
B. 1862, Hamilton, Ontario, Canada   Deceased,

Year	Team	Games	BA	SA	AB	H	2B	3B	HR	HR%	R	RBI	BB	SO	SB	Pinch Hit AB	Pinch Hit H	PO	A	E	DP	TC/G	FA	G by Pos
1884	CHI U	1	.000	.000	4	0	0	0	0	0.0	0		0			0	0	1	1	1	0	3.0	.667	2B-1

Hardy Richardson

RICHARDSON, ABRAM HARDING (Old True Blue)
B. Apr. 21, 1855, Clarksboro, N. J.   D. Jan. 14, 1931, Utica, N. Y.
BR TR 5'9½" 170 lbs.

Year	Team	Games	BA	SA	AB	H	2B	3B	HR	HR%	R	RBI	BB	SO	SB	Pinch Hit AB	Pinch Hit H	PO	A	E	DP	TC/G	FA	G by Pos
1879	BUF N	79	.283	.396	336	95	18	10	0	0.0	54	37	16	30		0	0	94	153	44	13	3.7	.849	3B-78, C-1
1880		83	.259	.359	343	89	18	8	0	0.0	48	17	14	37		0	0	123	163	52	6	4.1	.846	3B-81, C-5
1881		83	.291	.413	344	100	18	9	2	0.6	62	53	12	27		0	0	195	62	24	6	3.4	.915	OF-79, 2B-5, SS-1, 3B-1
1882		83	.271	.390	354	96	20	8	2	0.6	61		11	33		0	0	289	280	63	28	7.4	.898	2B-83
1883		92	.311	.439	399	124	34	7	1	0.3	73		22	20		0	0	289	344	68	33	7.6	.903	2B-92
1884		102	.301	.444	439	132	27	9	6	1.4	85		22	41		0	0	275	258	57	21	5.8	.903	2B-71, OF-24, 3B-5, 1B-3
1885		96	.319	.458	426	136	19	11	6	1.4	90	44	20	22		0	0	284	179	49	19	5.3	.904	2B-50, OF-48, SS-1, P-1
1886	DET N	125	.351	.504	**538**	**189**	27	11	**11**	2.0	125	61	46	27		0	0	242	153	32	17	3.4	.925	OF-80, 2B-42, P-4, SS-3, 3B-2
1887		120	.328	.501	543	178	25	18	11	2.0	131	94	31	40	29	0	0	328	223	37	28	4.9	.938	2B-64, OF-59
1888		58	.289	.444	266	77	18	1	7	2.6	60	32	17	23	13	0	0	173	185	29	21	6.7	.925	2B-58
1889	BOS N	132	.304	.438	536	163	33	9	7	1.3	122	79	48	44	47	0	0	320	316	51	45	5.2	.926	2B-86, OF-46
1890	BOS P	130	.326	.483	555	181	26	14	11	2.0	126	**143**	52	46	42	0	0	260	37	13	8	2.4	.958	OF-124, SS-6, 1B-1
1891	BOS AA	74	.255	.392	278	71	9	4	7	2.5	45	51	40	26	16	0	0	141	36	10	5	2.5	.947	OF-60, 3B-9, SS-4, 1B-3
1892	2 teams	WAS N (10G – .108)				NY N (64G – .214)																			
"	total	74	.200	.295	285	57	11	5	2	0.7	38	34	26	29	16	0	0	237	140	25	16	5.4	.938	2B-34, OF-24, 1B-9, SS-6, 3B-2
14 yrs.		1331	.299	.436	5642	1688	303	124	73	1.3	1120	645	377	445	163	0	0	3236	2529	554	266	4.7	.912	2B-585, OF-544, 3B-178, SS-21, 1B-16, C-6, P-5

Jeff Richardson

RICHARDSON, JEFFREY SCOTT
B. Aug. 26, 1965, Grand Island, Neb.
BR TR 6'2"

Year	Team	Games	BA	SA	AB	H	2B	3B	HR	HR%	R	RBI	BB	SO	SB	Pinch Hit AB	Pinch Hit H	PO	A	E	DP	TC/G	FA	G by Pos
1989	CIN N	53	.168	.248	125	21	4	0	2	1.6	10	11	10	23	1	5	2	50	81	4	16	2.5	.970	SS-39, 3B-8

Ken Richardson

RICHARDSON, KENNETH FRANKLIN
B. May 2, 1915, Orleans, Ind.   D. Dec. 7, 1987, Woodland Hills, Calif.
BR TR 5'10½" 187 lbs.

Year	Team	Games	BA	SA	AB	H	2B	3B	HR	HR%	R	RBI	BB	SO	SB	Pinch Hit AB	Pinch Hit H	PO	A	E	DP	TC/G	FA	G by Pos
1942	PHI A	6	.067	.067	15	1	0	0	0	0.0	1	0	2	0	0	1	0	18	2	1	1	3.5	.952	OF-3, 3B-1, 1B-1

Year	Team	Games	BA	SA	AB	H	2B	3B	HR	HR%	R	RBI	BB	SO	SB	Pinch Hit AB	H	PO	A	E	DP	TC/G	FA	G by Pos

Ken Richardson *continued*

Year	Team	Games	BA	SA	AB	H	2B	3B	HR	HR%	R	RBI	BB	SO	SB	AB	H	PO	A	E	DP	TC/G	FA	G by Pos
1946	PHI N	6	.150	.200	20	3	1	0	0	0.0	1	2	0	2	0	0	0	16	15	2	0	5.5	.939	2B-6
2 yrs.		12	.114	.143	35	4	1	0	0	0.0	2	2	2	2	0	1	0	34	17	3	1	4.5	.944	2B-6, OF-3, 3B-1, 1B-1

Nolen Richardson

RICHARDSON, CLIFFORD NOLEN
B. Jan. 18, 1903, Chattanooga, Tenn.   D. Sept. 25, 1951, Athens, Ga.   BR TR 6'1½" 170 lbs.

Year	Team	Games	BA	SA	AB	H	2B	3B	HR	HR%	R	RBI	BB	SO	SB	AB	H	PO	A	E	DP	TC/G	FA	G by Pos
1929	DET A	13	.190	.190	21	4	0	0	0	0.0	2	2	2	1	0	0	0	15	11	5	2	2.4	.839	SS-13
1931		38	.270	.358	148	40	9	2	0	0.0	13	16	6	3	2	0	0	31	75	6	2	2.9	.946	3B-38
1932		69	.219	.277	155	34	5	2	0	0.0	13	12	9	13	5	0	0	56	102	3	9	2.3	.981	3B-65, SS-4
1935	NY A	12	.217	.283	46	10	1	1	0	0.0	3	5	3	1	0	0	0	23	24	4	4	4.3	.922	SS-12
1938	CIN N	35	.290	.330	100	29	4	0	0	0.0	8	10	3	4	0	0	0	56	87	5	13	4.2	.966	SS-35
1939		1	.000	.000	3	0	0	0	0	0.0	0	0	0	0	0	0	0	4	3	0	1	7.0	1.000	SS-1
6 yrs.		168	.247	.309	473	117	19	5	0	0.0	39	45	23	22	8	0	0	185	302	23	31	3.0	.955	3B-103, SS-65

Tom Richardson

RICHARDSON, THOMAS MITCHELL
B. Aug. 7, 1883, Louisville, Ill.   D. Nov. 15, 1939, Onawa, Iowa   BR TR 6' 190 lbs.

Year	Team	Games	BA	SA	AB	H	2B	3B	HR	HR%	R	RBI	BB	SO	SB	AB	H	PO	A	E	DP	TC/G	FA	G by Pos
1917	STL A	1	.000	.000	1	0	0	0	0	0.0	0	0	0	1	0	0	0	0	0	0	0	0.0	—	

Mike Richardt

RICHARDT, MICHAEL ANTHONY
B. May 24, 1958, North Hollywood, Calif.   BR TR 6' 170 lbs.

Year	Team	Games	BA	SA	AB	H	2B	3B	HR	HR%	R	RBI	BB	SO	SB	AB	H	PO	A	E	DP	TC/G	FA	G by Pos
1980	TEX A	22	.225	.254	71	16	2	0	0	0.0	2	8	3	7	0	0	0	32	55	2	11	4.0	.978	2B-20, DH-1
1982		119	.241	.289	402	97	10	0	3	0.7	34	43	23	42	9	1	0	253	279	6	68	4.5	.989	2B-98, DH-15, OF-6
1983		22	.157	.241	83	13	2	1	1	1.2	9	7	2	11	2	2	0	56	61	1	16	5.4	.992	2B-20
1984	2 teams	TEX A (7G – .111)			HOU N	(16G –	.267)																	
"	total	23	.208	.250	24	5	0	0	0	0.0	1	2	1	2	0	17	4	5	6	0	4	0.5	1.000	2B-4
4 yrs.		186	.226	.276	580	131	15	1	4	0.7	46	60	27	62	11	20	4	346	401	9	99	4.1	.988	2B-142, DH-16, OF-6

Lance Richbourg

RICHBOURG, LANCE CLAYTON
B. Dec. 18, 1897, DeFuniak Springs, Fla.   D. Sept. 10, 1975, Crestview, Fla.   BL TR 5'10½" 160 lbs.

Year	Team	Games	BA	SA	AB	H	2B	3B	HR	HR%	R	RBI	BB	SO	SB	AB	H	PO	A	E	DP	TC/G	FA	G by Pos
1921	PHI N	10	.200	.400	5	1	1	0	0	0.0	2	0	0	3	1	1	2	3	4	0	0	0.7	1.000	2B-4
1924	WAS A	15	.281	.406	32	9	2	1	0	0.0	3	1	2	6	0	6	4	11	2	0	1	0.9	1.000	OF-7
1927	BOS N	115	.309	.389	450	139	12	9	2	0.4	57	34	22	30	24	4	1	233	10	12	0	2.2	.953	OF-110
1928		148	.337	.428	612	206	26	12	2	0.3	105	52	62	39	11	0	0	367	8	11	1	2.6	.972	OF-148
1929		139	.305	.411	557	170	24	13	3	0.5	76	56	42	26	7	3	0	323	14	10	2	2.5	.971	OF-134
1930		130	.304	.395	529	161	23	8	3	0.6	81	54	19	31	13	2	1	294	9	9	4	2.4	.971	OF-128
1931		97	.287	.388	286	82	11	6	2	0.7	39	19	19	14	9	22	5	154	3	3	2	1.6	.981	OF-71
1932	CHI N	44	.257	.318	148	38	2	2	1	0.7	22	21	8	4	0	10	3	70	2	1	1	1.7	.986	OF-33
8 yrs.		698	.308	.400	2619	806	101	51	13	0.5	378	247	174	153	65	49	14	1455	52	46	11	2.2	.970	OF-631, 2B-4

Rob Richie

RICHIE, ROBERT EUGENE
B. Sept. 5, 1965, Reno, Nev.   BL TR 6'2" 190 lbs.

Year	Team	Games	BA	SA	AB	H	2B	3B	HR	HR%	R	RBI	BB	SO	SB	AB	H	PO	A	E	DP	TC/G	FA	G by Pos
1989	DET A	19	.265	.490	49	13	4	2	1	2.0	6	10	5	10	0	4	0	21	1	2	0	1.3	.917	OF-13, DH-4

Don Richmond

RICHMOND, DONALD LESTER
B. Oct. 27, 1919, Gillett, Pa.   D. May 24, 1981, Elmira, N. Y.   BL TR 6'1" 175 lbs.

Year	Team	Games	BA	SA	AB	H	2B	3B	HR	HR%	R	RBI	BB	SO	SB	AB	H	PO	A	E	DP	TC/G	FA	G by Pos
1941	PHI A	9	.200	.286	35	7	1	1	0	0.0	3	5	0	5	0	0	0	6	16	1	3	2.6	.957	3B-9
1946		16	.290	.387	62	18	3	0	1	1.6	3	9	0	10	1	0	0	19	28	3	1	3.1	.940	3B-16
1947		19	.190	.333	21	4	1	1	0	0.0	2	4	3	3	0	11	2	1	3	2	0	0.3	.667	3B-4, 2B-1
1951	STL N	12	.088	.206	34	3	1	0	1	2.9	3	4	3	3	0	0	0	14	28	0	3	3.5	1.000	3B-11
4 yrs.		56	.211	.316	152	32	6	2	2	1.3	11	22	6	17	1	11	2	40	75	6	7	2.2	.950	3B-40, 2B-1

John Richmond

RICHMOND, JOHN H.
B. 1854, Pennsylvania   Deceased.   TR

Year	Team	Games	BA	SA	AB	H	2B	3B	HR	HR%	R	RBI	BB	SO	SB	AB	H	PO	A	E	DP	TC/G	FA	G by Pos
1879	SYR N	62	.213	.287	254	54	8	4	1	0.4	31	23	4	24		0	0	132	75	30	5	3.8	.873	OF-35, SS-28, C-2
1880	BOS N	32	.248	.287	129	32	3	1	0	0.0	12	9	2	18		0	0	31	73	19	14	3.8	.846	SS-31, OF-1
1881		27	.276	.367	98	27	2	2	1	1.0	13	12	6	7		0	0	62	10	5	1	2.9	.935	OF-25, SS-2
1882	2 teams	CLE N	(41G – .171)		PHI AA	(18G –	.185)																	
"	total	59	.176	.254	205	36	8	4	0	0.0	20	11	22	27		0	0	94	16	11	0	2.1	.909	OF-59
1883	COL AA	92	.283	.343	385	109	7	8	0	0.0	63		25			0	0	122	306	60	19	5.3	.877	SS-91, OF-2
1884		105	.251	.342	398	100	13	7	3	0.8	57		35			0	0	96	306	62	26	4.4	.866	SS-105
1885	PIT AA	34	.206	.252	131	27	2	2	0	0.0	14		8			0	0	27	66	17	6	3.2	.845	SS-23, OF-11
7 yrs.		411	.241	.312	1600	385	43	28	5	0.3	210	55	102	76		0	0	564	852	204	71	3.9	.874	SS-280, OF-133, C-2

Lee Richmond

RICHMOND, J. LEE
B. May 5, 1857, Sheffield, Ohio   D. Oct. 1, 1929, Toledo, Ohio   TL 5'10" 142 lbs.

Year	Team	Games	BA	SA	AB	H	2B	3B	HR	HR%	R	RBI	BB	SO	SB	AB	H	PO	A	E	DP	TC/G	FA	G by Pos
1879	BOS N	1	.333	.333	6	2	0	0	1	0	0	1	0	0		0	0	0	2	0	0	2.0	1.000	P-1
1880	WOR N	77	.227	.278	309	70	8	4	0	0.0	44	34	9	32		0	0	17	99	26	1	1.8	.817	P-74, OF-20
1881		61	.250	.278	252	63	5	1	0	0.0	31	28	10	10		0	0	26	101	13	4	2.3	.907	P-53, OF-11
1882	PRO N	55	.281	.421	228	64	8	9	2	0.9	50	28	9	11		0	0	23	101	19	2	2.6	.867	P-48, OF-11
1883	PRO N	49	.284	.402	194	55	8	6	1	0.5	41		15	19		0	0	49	22	22	0	1.9	.763	OF-41, P-12
1886	CIN AA	8	.276	.276	29	8	0	0	0	0.0	3		3			0	0	6	4	6	0	1.8	.571	OF-7, P-3
6 yrs.		251	.257	.334	1018	262	29	20	3	0.3	169	91	46	73		0	0	121	327	86	7	2.1	.839	P-191, OF-90

Al Richter

RICHTER, ALLEN GORDON
B. Feb. 7, 1927, Norfolk, Va.   BR TR 6' 175 lbs.

Year	Team	Games	BA	SA	AB	H	2B	3B	HR	HR%	R	RBI	BB	SO	SB	AB	H	PO	A	E	DP	TC/G	FA	G by Pos
1951	BOS A	5	.091	.091	11	1	0	0	0	0.0	1	0	3	0	0	2	0	8	10	0	5	3.6	1.000	SS-3
1953		1	–	–	0	0	0	0	0	–	0	0	0	0	0	0	0	1	1	0	1	2.0	1.000	SS-1
2 yrs.		6	.091	.091	11	1	0	0	0	0.0	1	0	3	0	0	2	0	9	11	0	6	3.3	1.000	SS-4

John Richter

RICHTER, JOHN M.
B. Feb. 8, 1873, Louisville, Ky.   D. Oct. 4, 1927, Louisville, Ky.

Year	Team		Games	BA	SA	AB	H	2B	3B	HR	HR%	R	RBI	BB	SO	SB	Pinch Hit AB	H	PO	A	E	DP	TC/G	FA	G by Pos

John Richter *continued*

| 1898 | LOU | N | 3 | .154 | .154 | 13 | 2 | 0 | 0 | 0 | 0.0 | 1 | 0 | 0 | | 0 | | 0 | 0 | 5 | 8 | 1 | 1 | 4.7 | .929 | 3B-3 |

Joe Rickert

RICKERT, JOSEPH FRANCIS (Diamond Joe)
B. Dec. 12, 1876, London, Ohio D. Oct. 15, 1943, Springfield, Ohio

BR TR 5'10½" 165 lbs.

1898	PIT	N	2	.167	.167	6	1	0	0	0	0.0	0		0			0	0	10	0	0	0	5.0	1.000	OF-2
1901	BOS	N	13	.167	.250	60	10	1	2	0	0.0	6	1	3		1	0	0	35	2	1	1	2.9	.974	OF-13
2 yrs.			15	.167	.242	66	11	1	2	0	0.0	6	1	3		1	0	0	45	2	1	1	3.2	.979	OF-15

Marv Rickert

RICKERT, MARVIN AUGUST (Twitch)
B. Jan. 8, 1921, Long Branch, Wash. D. June 3, 1978, Oakville, Wash.

BL TR 6'2" 195 lbs.

1942	CHI	N	8	.269	.269	26	7	0	0	0	0.0	5	1	1	5	0	1	0	18	0	0	0	2.4	1.000	OF-6
1946			111	.263	.378	392	103	18	3	7	1.8	44	47	28	54	3	6	0	200	5	6	1	1.9	.972	OF-104
1947			71	.146	.190	137	20	0	0	2	1.5	7	15	15	17	0	27	6	123	8	1	8	1.9	.992	OF-30, 1B-7
1948	2 teams			CIN N	(8G – .167)				BOS	N	(3G – .231)														
"	total		11	.211	.316	19	4	0	1	0	0.0	1	0	2	0	0	6	1	20	0	0	0	1.8	1.000	OF-3
1949	BOS	N	100	.292	.444	277	81	18	3	6	2.2	44	49	23	38	1	12	3	223	14	6	8	2.4	.975	OF-75, 1B-12
1950	2 teams			PIT N	(17G – .150)				CHI	A	(84G – .237)														
"	total		101	.232	.315	298	69	9	2	4	1.3	38	31	21	46	0	20	1	154	3	5	1	1.6	.969	OF-81, 1B-1
6 yrs.			402	.247	.352	1149	284	45	9	19	1.7	139	145	88	161	4	72	11	738	31	18	18	2.0	.977	OF-299, 1B-20

WORLD SERIES

| 1948 | BOS | N | 5 | .211 | .368 | 19 | 4 | 0 | 0 | 1 | 5.3 | 2 | 2 | 0 | 4 | 0 | 0 | 0 | 20 | 0 | 0 | 0 | 4.0 | 1.000 | OF-5 |

Dave Ricketts

RICKETTS, DAVID WILLIAM
Brother of Dick Ricketts.
B. July 12, 1935, Pottstown, Pa.

BB TR 6' 190 lbs.

1963	STL	N	3	.250	.250	8	2	0	0	0	0.0	0	0	0	2	0	0	0	14	0	0	0	4.7	1.000	C-3
1965			11	.241	.241	29	7	0	0	0	0.0	1	0	1	3	0	1	0	41	2	1	0	4.0	.977	C-11
1967			52	.273	.384	99	27	8	0	1	1.0	11	14	4	7	0	32	7	111	10	0	0	2.3	1.000	C-21
1968			20	.136	.136	22	3	0	0	0	0.0	1	1	0	3	0	19	2	5	0	0	0	0.3	1.000	C-1
1969			30	.273	.295	44	12	1	0	0	0.0	2	5	4	5	0	18	5	57	1	1	0	2.0	.983	C-8
1970	PIT	N	14	.182	.182	11	2	0	0	0	0.0	0	0	1	3	0	7	1	8	2	1	0	0.8	.909	C-7
6 yrs.			130	.249	.305	213	53	9	0	1	0.5	15	20	10	23	0	77	15	236	15	3	0	2.0	.988	C-51

WORLD SERIES

1967	STL	N	3	.000	.000	3	0	0	0	0	0.0	0	0	0	0	0	3	0	0	0	0	0	0.0	–	
1968			1	1.000	1.000	1	1	0	0	0	0.0	0	0	0	0	0	1	1	0	0	0	0	0.0	–	
2 yrs.			4	.250	.250	4	1	0	0	0	0.0	0	0	0	0	0	4	1	0	0	0	0	0.0	–	

Branch Rickey

RICKEY, WESLEY BRANCH (The Mahatma)
B. Dec. 20, 1881, Stockdale, Ohio D. Dec. 9, 1965, Columbia, Mo.
Manager 1913-15, 1919-25.
Hall of Fame 1967.

BL TR 5'9" 175 lbs.

1905	STL	A	1	.000	.000	3	0	0	0	0	0.0	0	0	0		0	0	0	2	1	0	0	3.0	1.000	C-1
1906			64	.284	.393	201	57	7	3	3	1.5	22	24	16		4	7	2	234	58	14	2	4.8	.954	C-54, OF-1
1907	NY	A	52	.182	.241	137	25	2	3	0	0.0	16	15	11		4	12	1	159	16	17	5	3.7	.911	OF-22, C-11, 1B-9
1914	STL	A	2	.000	.000	2	0	0	0	0	0.0	0	0	0	1	0	2	0	0	0	0	0	0.0	–	
4 yrs.			119	.239	.327	343	82	9	6	3	0.9	38	39	27	1	8	21	3	395	75	31	7	4.2	.938	C-66, OF-23, 1B-9

Chris Rickley

RICKLEY, CHRISTIAN
B. Oct. 7, 1859, Philadelphia, Pa. D. Oct. 25, 1911, Philadelphia, Pa.

5'8" 160 lbs.

| 1884 | PHI | U | 6 | .200 | .280 | 25 | 5 | 2 | 0 | 0 | 0.0 | 5 | | 0 | | 0 | 0 | 0 | 7 | 21 | 9 | 2 | 6.2 | .757 | SS-6 |

John Ricks

RICKS, JOHN
Deceased.

1891	STL	AA	5	.167	.167	18	3	0	0	0	0.0	3		0	2	0	0	0	11	6	4	0	4.2	.810	3B-5
1894	STL	N	1	.000	.000	1	0	0	0	0	0.0	0		0	0	0	0	0	1	0	3	0	4.0	.250	3B-1
2 yrs.			6	.158	.158	19	3	0	0	0	0.0	3		0	2	0	0	0	12	6	7	0	4.2	.720	3B-6

Art Rico

RICO, ARTHUR RAYMOND
B. July 23, 1896, Roxbury, Mass. D. Jan. 3, 1919, Boston, Mass.

BR TR 5'9½" 185 lbs.

1916	BOS	N	4	.000	.000	4	0	0	0	0	0.0	0		0	0	0	0	0	5	1	0	0	1.5	1.000	C-4
1917			13	.286	.357	14	4	1	0	0	0.0	1	2	0	2	0	0	0	15	4	1	1	1.5	.950	C-11, OF-2
2 yrs.			17	.222	.278	18	4	1	0	0	0.0	1	2	0	2	0	0	0	20	5	1	1	1.5	.962	C-15, OF-2

Fred Rico

RICO, ALFREDO CRUZ
B. July 4, 1944, Jerome, Ariz.

BR TR 5'10" 180 lbs.

| 1969 | KC | A | 12 | .231 | .308 | 26 | 6 | 2 | 0 | 0 | 0.0 | 2 | 2 | 9 | 10 | 0 | 1 | 0 | 27 | 4 | 0 | 0 | 2.6 | 1.000 | OF-9, 3B-1 |

Harry Riconda

RICONDA, HENRY PAUL
B. Mar. 17, 1897, New York, N. Y. D. Nov. 15, 1958, Mahopac, N. Y.

BR TR 5'10" 175 lbs.

1923	PHI	A	55	.263	.371	175	46	11	4	0	0.0	23	12	12	18	4	4	0	46	118	16	9	3.3	.911	3B-47, SS-2
1924			83	.253	.342	281	71	16	3	1	0.4	34	21	27	43	3	4	0	97	148	19	14	3.2	.928	3B-73, SS-2, C-1
1926	BOS	N	4	.167	.167	12	2	0	0	0	0.0	1	0	2	2	0	0	0	6	3	2	0	2.8	.818	3B-4
1928	BKN	N	92	.224	.338	281	63	15	4	3	1.1	22	35	20	28	6	1	0	181	222	20	25	4.6	.953	3B-53, SS-21, SS-16
1929	PIT	N	8	.467	.600	15	7	2	0	0	0.0	3	2	0	3	1	3	1	12	9	4	3	3.1	.840	SS-4
1930	CIN	N	1	.000	.000	1	0	0	0	0	0.0	0	0	0	0	0	0	0	0	0	0	0	0.0	–	
6 yrs.			243	.247	.349	765	189	44	11	4	0.5	83	70	61	91	13	13	1	342	500	61	51	3.7	.932	3B-145, 2B-53, SS-24, C-1

Year	Team	Games	BA	SA	AB	H	2B	3B	HR	HR%	R	RBI	BB	SO	SB	Pinch Hit AB	Pinch Hit H	PO	A	E	DP	TC/G	FA	G by Pos

John Riddle

RIDDLE, JOHN H.
B. Feb., 1864, Philadelphia, Pa.   Deceased.
BR TR

Year	Team	Games	BA	SA	AB	H	2B	3B	HR	HR%	R	RBI	BB	SO	SB	PH AB	PH H	PO	A	E	DP	TC/G	FA	G by Pos
1889	WAS N	11	.216	.297	37	8	3	0	0	0.0	3	3	2	8	0	0	0	40	15	11	1	6.0	.833	C-9, OF-2
1890	PHI AA	27	.082	.106	85	7	0	1	0	0.0	7	17	4	0	0	0	0	76	25	15	2	4.3	.871	C-13, OF-12, 2B-2, 3B-1
2 yrs.		38	.123	.164	122	15	3	1	0	0.0	10	3	19	8	4	0	0	116	40	26	3	4.8	.857	C-22, OF-14, 2B-2, 3B-1

Johnny Riddle

RIDDLE, JOHN LUDY (Mutt)
Brother of Elmer Riddle.
B. Oct. 3, 1905, Clinton, S. C.
BR TR 5'11" 190 lbs.

Year	Team	Games	BA	SA	AB	H	2B	3B	HR	HR%	R	RBI	BB	SO	SB	PH AB	PH H	PO	A	E	DP	TC/G	FA	G by Pos
1930	CHI A	25	.241	.328	58	14	3	1	0	0.0	7	4	3	6	0	0	0	48	13	0	3	2.4	1.000	C-25
1937 2 teams	WAS A (8G – .269)				BOS N	(2G – .000)																		
" total		10	.241	.241	29	7	0	0	0	0.0	2	3	1	2	0	0	0	32	8	1	1	4.1	.976	C-10
1938	BOS N	19	.281	.298	57	16	1	0	0	0.0	6	2	4	2	0	0	0	63	15	4	4	4.3	.951	C-19
1941	CIN N	10	.300	.300	10	3	0	0	0	0.0	2	0	0	1	0	0	0	18	1	0	1	1.9	1.000	C-10
1944		1	–	–	0	0	0	0	0	–	0	0	0	0	0	0	0	0	0	0	0	0.0	–	C-1
1945		23	.178	.178	45	8	0	0	0	0.0	0	2	4	6	0	1	0	51	11	0	3	2.7	1.000	C-23
1948	PIT N	10	.200	.200	15	3	0	0	0	0.0	1	0	1	2	0	0	0	18	3	0	1	2.1	1.000	C-10
7 yrs.		98	.238	.266	214	51	4	1	0	0.0	18	11	13	19	0	1	0	230	51	5	12	2.9	.983	C-98

Hank Riebe

RIEBE, HARVEY DONALD
B. Oct. 10, 1921, Cleveland, Ohio
BR TR 5'9½" 175 lbs.

Year	Team	Games	BA	SA	AB	H	2B	3B	HR	HR%	R	RBI	BB	SO	SB	PH AB	PH H	PO	A	E	DP	TC/G	FA	G by Pos
1942	DET A	11	.314	.371	35	11	2	0	0	0.0	1	2	0	6	0	0	0	42	5	0	1	4.3	1.000	C-11
1947		8	.000	.000	7	0	0	0	0	0.0	0	2	0	2	0	5	0	2	0	0	0	0.3	1.000	C-3
1948		25	.194	.194	62	12	0	0	0	0.0	0	5	3	5	0	1	0	90	6	0	1	3.8	1.000	C-24
1949		17	.182	.242	33	6	2	0	0	0.0	1	2	0	5	1	6	1	21	3	1	1	1.5	.960	C-11
4 yrs.		61	.212	.241	137	29	4	0	0	0.0	2	11	3	18	1	12	1	155	14	1	3	2.8	.994	C-49

Joe Riggert

RIGGERT, JOSEPH ALOYSIUS
B. Dec. 11, 1886, Janesville, Wis.   D. Dec. 10, 1973, Kansas City, Mo.
BR TR 5'9½" 170 lbs.

Year	Team	Games	BA	SA	AB	H	2B	3B	HR	HR%	R	RBI	BB	SO	SB	PH AB	PH H	PO	A	E	DP	TC/G	FA	G by Pos
1911	BOS A	50	.212	.336	146	31	4	4	2	1.4	19	13	12		5	8	3	63	2	5	1	1.4	.929	OF-38
1914 2 teams	BKN N (27G – .193)				STL N	(34G – .213)																		
" total		61	.203	.331	172	35	6	5	2	1.2	15	14	9	34	6	8	1	78	6	3	1	1.4	.966	OF-50
1919	BOS N	63	.283	.408	240	68	8	5	4	1.7	34	17	25	30	9	0	0	165	6	9	2	2.9	.950	OF-61
3 yrs.		174	.240	.366	558	134	18	14	8	1.4	68	44	46	64	20	16	3	306	14	17	4	1.9	.950	OF-149

Lew Riggs

RIGGS, LEWIS SIDNEY
B. Apr. 22, 1910, Mebane, N. C.   D. Aug. 12, 1975, Durham, N. C.
BL TR 6' 175 lbs.

Year	Team	Games	BA	SA	AB	H	2B	3B	HR	HR%	R	RBI	BB	SO	SB	PH AB	PH H	PO	A	E	DP	TC/G	FA	G by Pos
1934	STL N	2	.000	.000	1	0	0	0	0	0.0	0	0	0	1	0	1	0	0	0	0	0	0.0	–	3B-135
1935	CIN N	142	.278	.385	532	148	26	8	5	0.9	73	46	43	32	8	2	0	132	269	31	21	3.0	.928	3B-135
1936		141	.257	.372	538	138	20	12	6	1.1	69	57	38	33	5	1	1	122	267	13	19	2.9	.968	3B-140
1937		122	.242	.359	384	93	17	5	6	1.6	43	45	24	17	4	17	4	112	226	21	16	2.9	.942	3B-100, 2B-4, SS-1
1938		142	.252	.352	531	134	21	13	2	0.4	53	55	40	28	3	2	0	146	280	24	18	3.2	.947	3B-142
1939		22	.158	.184	38	6	1	0	0	0.0	5	1	5	4	1	6	1	6	16	1	1	1.0	.957	3B-11
1940		41	.292	.458	72	21	7	1	1	1.4	8	9	2	4	0	27	8	10	23	2	2	0.9	.943	3B-11
1941	BKN N	77	.305	.487	197	60	13	4	5	2.5	27	36	16	12	1	29	10	55	78	10	6	1.9	.930	3B-43, 2B-1, 1B-1
1942		70	.278	.356	180	50	5	0	3	1.7	20	22	13	9	0	21	8	37	65	6	7	1.5	.944	3B-46, 1B-1
1946		1	.000	.000	4	0	0	0	0	0.0	0	0	0	0	0	0	0	2	2	0	0	4.0	1.000	3B-1
10 yrs.		760	.262	.375	2477	650	110	43	28	1.1	298	271	181	140	22	106	32	622	1226	108	90	2.6	.945	3B-629, 2B-5, 1B-2, SS-1

WORLD SERIES

Year	Team	Games	BA	SA	AB	H	2B	3B	HR	HR%	R	RBI	BB	SO	SB	PH AB	PH H	PO	A	E	DP	TC/G	FA	G by Pos
1940	CIN N	3	.000	.000	3	0	0	0	0	0.0	1	0	0	3	0	3	0	0	0	0	0	0.0	–	
1941	BKN N	3	.250	.250	8	2	0	0	0	0.0	0	1	1	0	0	1	1	1	5	0	1	2.0	1.000	3B-2
2 yrs.		6	.182	.182	11	2	0	0	0	0.0	1	1	1	3	0	4	1	1	5	0	1	1.0	1.000	3B-2

Bill Rigney

RIGNEY, WILLIAM JOSEPH (Specs, The Cricket)
B. Jan. 29, 1918, Alameda, Calif.
Manager 1956-72, 1976.
BR TR 6'1" 178 lbs.

Year	Team	Games	BA	SA	AB	H	2B	3B	HR	HR%	R	RBI	BB	SO	SB	PH AB	PH H	PO	A	E	DP	TC/G	FA	G by Pos
1946	NY N	110	.236	.292	360	85	9	1	3	0.8	38	31	36	29	9	3	0	130	224	17	22	3.4	.954	3B-73, SS-33
1947		130	.267	.420	531	142	24	3	17	3.2	84	59	51	54	7	1	1	264	358	25	56	5.0	.961	2B-72, 3B-41, SS-24
1948		113	.264	.389	424	112	17	3	10	2.4	72	43	47	54	4	2	0	265	287	20	49	5.1	.965	2B-105, SS-7
1949		122	.278	.404	389	108	19	6	6	1.5	53	47	47	38	3	4	0	185	317	32	46	4.4	.940	SS-81, 2B-26, 3B-14
1950		56	.181	.205	83	15	2	0	0	0.0	8	8	8	13	0	20	3	44	47	3	10	1.7	.968	2B-23, 3B-11
1951		44	.232	.435	69	16	2	1	4	5.8	9	9	8	7	0	16	4	25	39	3	10	1.5	.955	3B-12, SS-9
1952		60	.300	.411	90	27	5	1	1	1.1	15	14	11	6	2	31	10	32	37	6	9	1.3	.920	3B-10, 2B-9, SS-4, 1B-1
1953		19	.250	.250	20	5	0	0	0	0.0	2	1	0	5	0	15	3	5	1	0	0	0.3	1.000	3B-2, 2B-1
8 yrs.		654	.259	.376	1966	510	78	14	41	2.1	281	212	208	206	25	92	21	950	1310	106	202	3.6	.955	2B-245, 3B-163, SS-149, 1B-1

WORLD SERIES

Year	Team	Games	BA	SA	AB	H	2B	3B	HR	HR%	R	RBI	BB	SO	SB	PH AB	PH H	PO	A	E	DP	TC/G	FA	G by Pos
1951	NY N	4	.250	.250	4	1	0	0	0	0.0	0	1	0	1	0	4	1	0	0	0	0	0.0	–	

Topper Rigney

RIGNEY, EMORY ELMO
B. Jan. 7, 1897, Groveton, Tex.   D. June 6, 1972, San Antonio, Tex.
BR TR 5'9" 150 lbs.

Year	Team	Games	BA	SA	AB	H	2B	3B	HR	HR%	R	RBI	BB	SO	SB	PH AB	PH H	PO	A	E	DP	TC/G	FA	G by Pos
1922	DET A	155	.300	.369	536	161	17	7	2	0.4	68	63	68	44	17	0	0	262	493	50	74	5.2	.938	SS-155
1923		129	.315	.419	470	148	24	11	1	0.2	63	74	55	35	7	0	0	209	383	35	46	4.9	.944	SS-129
1924		147	.289	.407	499	144	29	9	4	0.8	81	93	102	39	11	1	0	273	463	25	72	5.2	.967	SS-146
1925		62	.247	.349	146	36	5	2	2	1.4	21	18	21	15	2	6	0	56	95	10	8	2.6	.938	SS-51, 3B-4
1926	BOS A	148	.270	.377	525	142	32	6	4	0.8	71	53	108	31	6	2	0	286	492	25	80	5.4	.969	SS-146
1927 2 teams	BOS A (8G – .111)				WAS A	(45G – .273)																		
" total		53	.253	.347	150	38	6	4	0	0.0	20	13	23	12	1	10	4	77	107	13	24	3.7	.934	SS-33, 3B-10
6 yrs.		694	.288	.387	2326	669	113	39	13	0.6	324	314	377	176	44	19	4	1163	2033	158	304	4.8	.953	SS-660, 3B-14

Year	Team		Games	BA	SA	AB	H	2B	3B	HR	HR%	R	RBI	BB	SO	SB	Pinch Hit AB	H	PO	A	E	DP	TC/G	FA	G by Pos

Cully Rikard

RIKARD, CULLY
B. May 9, 1914, Oxford, Miss.
BL TR 6' 183 lbs.

Year	Team		Games	BA	SA	AB	H	2B	3B	HR	HR%	R	RBI	BB	SO	SB	AB	H	PO	A	E	DP	TC/G	FA	G by Pos
1941	PIT	N	6	.200	.250	20	4	1	0	0	0.0	1	0	1	1	0	1	0	18	0	0	0	3.0	1.000	OF-5
1942			38	.192	.269	52	10	2	1	0	0.0	6	5	7	8	0	15	4	23	0	1	0	0.6	.958	OF-16
1947			109	.287	.398	324	93	16	4	4	1.2	57	32	50	39	1	29	6	177	2	4	0	1.7	.978	OF-79
3 yrs.			153	.270	.374	396	107	19	5	4	1.0	64	37	58	48	1	45	10	218	2	5	0	1.5	.978	OF-100

Ernest Riles

RILES, ERNEST
B. Oct. 2, 1960, Cairo, Ga.
BL TR 6'1" 180 lbs.

Year	Team		Games	BA	SA	AB	H	2B	3B	HR	HR%	R	RBI	BB	SO	SB	AB	H	PO	A	E	DP	TC/G	FA	G by Pos
1985	MIL	A	116	.286	.377	448	128	12	7	5	1.1	54	45	36	54	2	1	0	183	310	22	62	4.4	.957	SS-115, DH-1
1986			145	.252	.357	524	132	24	2	9	1.7	69	47	54	80	7	4	0	212	327	20	76	3.9	.964	SS-142
1987			83	.261	.351	276	72	11	1	4	1.4	38	38	30	47	3	4	0	76	152	13	25	2.9	.946	3B-65, SS-21
1988	2 teams		MIL A (41G – .252)			SF N (79G – .294)																			
"	total		120	.277	.376	314	87	13	3	4	1.3	33	37	17	59	3	26	6	82	197	7	25	2.4	.976	3B-58, SS-25, 2B-17, DH-5
1989	SF	N	122	.278	.404	302	84	13	2	7	2.3	43	40	28	50	0	38	9	69	144	9	16	1.8	.959	3B-83, 2B-18, SS-7, OF-5
5 yrs.			586	.270	.372	1864	503	73	15	29	1.6	237	207	165	290	15	73	15	622	1130	71	204	3.1	.961	SS-310, 3B-206, 2B-35, DH-6, OF-5

LEAGUE CHAMPIONSHIP SERIES

Year	Team		Games	BA	SA	AB	H	2B	3B	HR	HR%	R	RBI	BB	SO	SB	AB	H	PO	A	E	DP	TC/G	FA	G by Pos
1989	SF	N	1	.000	.000	1	0	0	0	0	0.0	0	0	0	0	0	0	0	0	0	0	0	0.0	–	

WORLD SERIES

Year	Team		Games	BA	SA	AB	H	2B	3B	HR	HR%	R	RBI	BB	SO	SB	AB	H	PO	A	E	DP	TC/G	FA	G by Pos
1989	SF	N	4	.000	.000	8	0	0	0	0	0.0	0	0	0	1	0	1	0	0	0	0	0	0.0	–	DH-2

Billy Riley

RILEY, WILLIAM JAMES (Pigtail Billy)
B. 1857, Cincinnati, Ohio   D. Nov. 9, 1887, Cincinnati, Ohio
BR TR 5'10" 160 lbs.

Year	Team		Games	BA	SA	AB	H	2B	3B	HR	HR%	R	RBI	BB	SO	SB	AB	H	PO	A	E	DP	TC/G	FA	G by Pos
1879	CLE	N	44	.145	.158	165	24	2	0	0	0.0	14	9	2	26		0	0	90	12	19	1	2.8	.843	OF-43, 1B-1, C-1

Jim Riley

RILEY, JAMES NORMAN
B. May 25, 1895, Bayfield, N. B., Canada   D. May 25, 1969, Seguin, Tex.
BL TR 5'10½" 185 lbs.

Year	Team		Games	BA	SA	AB	H	2B	3B	HR	HR%	R	RBI	BB	SO	SB	AB	H	PO	A	E	DP	TC/G	FA	G by Pos
1921	STL	A	4	.000	.000	11	0	0	0	0	0.0	1	0	1	3	0	0	0	4	5	2	0	2.8	.818	2B-4
1923	WAS	A	2	.000	.000	3	0	0	0	0	0.0	0	0	2	0	0	0	0	15	0	2	2	8.5	.882	1B-2
2 yrs.			6	.000	.000	14	0	0	0	0	0.0	1	0	3	3	0	0	0	19	5	4	2	4.7	.857	2B-4, 1B-2

Jimmy Riley

RILEY, JAMES JOSEPH
B. Nov. 10, 1886, Buffalo, N. Y.   D. Mar. 25, 1949, Buffalo, N. Y.
BR TR 6' 165 lbs.

Year	Team		Games	BA	SA	AB	H	2B	3B	HR	HR%	R	RBI	BB	SO	SB	AB	H	PO	A	E	DP	TC/G	FA	G by Pos
1910	BOS	N	1	.000	.000	1	0	0	0	0	0.0	0	0	1	1	0	0	0	3	0	2	0	5.0	.600	OF-1

Lee Riley

RILEY, LEON FRANCIS
B. Aug. 20, 1906, Princeton, Neb.   D. Sept. 13, 1970, Schenectady, N. Y.
BL TR 6'1" 185 lbs.

Year	Team		Games	BA	SA	AB	H	2B	3B	HR	HR%	R	RBI	BB	SO	SB	AB	H	PO	A	E	DP	TC/G	FA	G by Pos
1944	PHI	N	4	.083	.167	12	1	1	0	0	0.0	1	1	0	1	0	0	0	2	0	0	0	0.5	1.000	OF-3

Frank Ringo

RINGO, FRANK C.
B. Oct. 12, 1860, Parksville, Mo.   D. Apr. 12, 1889, Kansas City, Mo.
5'11" 175 lbs.

Year	Team		Games	BA	SA	AB	H	2B	3B	HR	HR%	R	RBI	BB	SO	SB	AB	H	PO	A	E	DP	TC/G	FA	G by Pos
1883	PHI	N	60	.190	.244	221	42	10	1	0	0.0	24		6	34		0	0	197	98	64	9	6.0	.822	C-39, OF-11, SS-6, 3B-5, 2B-2
1884	2 teams		PHI N (26G – .132)			PHI AA (2G – .000)																			
"	total		28	.124	.144	97	12	2	0	0	0.0	4		3	19		0	0	120	19	39	2	6.4	.781	C-28
1885	2 teams		DET N (17G – .246)			PIT AA (3G – .182)																			
"	total		20	.237	.276	76	18	3	0	0	0.0	12		0	7		0	0	71	44	18	4	6.7	.865	C-11, 3B-8, OF-1
1886	2 teams		PIT AA (15G – .214)			KC N (16G – .232)																			
"	total		31	.223	.339	112	25	9	2	0	0.0	9	7	6	10		0	0	148	38	19	8	6.6	.907	C-19, 1B-9, OF-2, 3B-1
4 yrs.			139	.192	.251	506	97	24	3	0	0.0	49	9	15	70		0	0	536	199	140	23	6.3	.840	C-97, OF-14, 3B-14, 1B-9, SS-6, 2B-2

Bob Rinker

RINKER, ROBERT JOHN
B. Apr. 21, 1921, Audenried, Pa.
BR TR 6' 190 lbs.

Year	Team		Games	BA	SA	AB	H	2B	3B	HR	HR%	R	RBI	BB	SO	SB	AB	H	PO	A	E	DP	TC/G	FA	G by Pos
1950	PHI	A	3	.333	.333	3	1	0	0	0	0.0	0	0	0	0	0	2	1	0	0	0	0	0.0	–	C-1

Juan Rios

RIOS, JUAN ONOFRE
Born Juan Onofre Velez y Rios.
B. July 14, 1945, Mayaguez, Puerto Rico
BR TR 6'3" 185 lbs.

Year	Team		Games	BA	SA	AB	H	2B	3B	HR	HR%	R	RBI	BB	SO	SB	AB	H	PO	A	E	DP	TC/G	FA	G by Pos
1969	KC	A	87	.224	.276	196	44	5	1	1	0.5	20	5	7	19	1	12	3	103	109	9	23	2.5	.959	2B-46, SS-32, 3B-4

Billy Ripken

RIPKEN, WILLIAM OLIVER
Son of Cal Ripken.   Brother of Cal Ripken.
B. Dec. 16, 1964, Havre de Grace, Md.
BR TR 6'1" 180 lbs.

Year	Team		Games	BA	SA	AB	H	2B	3B	HR	HR%	R	RBI	BB	SO	SB	AB	H	PO	A	E	DP	TC/G	FA	G by Pos
1987	BAL	A	58	.308	.372	234	72	9	0	2	0.9	27	20	21	23	4	0	0	133	162	3	53	5.1	.990	2B-58
1988			150	.207	.258	512	106	18	1	2	0.4	52	34	33	63	8	0	0	310	440	12	110	5.1	.984	2B-149, 3B-2
1989			115	.239	.305	318	76	11	2	2	0.6	31	26	22	53	1	0	0	255	335	9	81	5.2	.985	2B-114, DH-1
3 yrs.			323	.239	.297	1064	254	38	3	6	0.6	110	80	76	139	13	0	0	698	937	24	244	5.1	.986	2B-321, 3B-2, DH-1

Cal Ripken

RIPKEN, CALVIN EDWIN, JR.
Son of Cal Ripken.   Brother of Billy Ripken.
B. Aug. 24, 1960, Havre de Grace, Md.
BR TR 6'4" 200 lbs.

Year	Team		Games	BA	SA	AB	H	2B	3B	HR	HR%	R	RBI	BB	SO	SB	AB	H	PO	A	E	DP	TC/G	FA	G by Pos
1981	BAL	A	23	.128	.128	39	5	0	0	0	0.0	1	0	1	8	0	4	0	13	30	3	6	2.0	.935	SS-12, 3B-6
1982			160	.264	.475	598	158	32	5	28	4.7	90	93	46	95	3	0	0	221	440	19	64	4.3	.972	SS-94, 3B-71
1983			162	.318	.517	663	211	47	2	27	4.1	121	102	58	97	0	0	0	272	534	25	113	5.1	.970	SS-162
1984			162	.304	.510	641	195	37	7	27	4.2	103	86	71	89	2	0	0	297	583	26	122	5.6	.971	SS-162
1985			161	.282	.469	642	181	32	5	26	4.0	116	110	67	68	2	0	0	286	474	26	123	4.9	.967	SS-161
1986			162	.282	.461	627	177	35	1	25	4.0	98	81	70	60	4	0	0	240	482	13	105	4.5	.982	SS-162

Year	Team		Games	BA	SA	AB	H	2B	3B	HR	HR%	R	RBI	BB	SO	SB	Pinch Hit AB	H	PO	A	E	DP	TC/G	FA	G by Pos

Cal Ripken *continued*

Year	Team		Games	BA	SA	AB	H	2B	3B	HR	HR%	R	RBI	BB	SO	SB	Pinch Hit AB	H	PO	A	E	DP	TC/G	FA	G by Pos
1987			162	.252	.436	624	157	28	3	27	4.3	97	98	81	77	3	0	0	240	480	20	103	4.6	.973	SS-162
1988			161	.264	.431	575	152	25	1	23	4.0	87	81	102	69	2	0	0	284	480	21	119	4.9	.973	SS-161
1989			162	.257	.401	646	166	30	0	21	3.3	80	93	57	72	3	0	0	276	531	8	119	5.0	.990	SS-162
9 yrs.			1315	.277	.461	5055	1402	266	24	204	4.0	793	744	553	635	19	4	0	2129	4034	161	874	4.8	.975	SS-1238, 3B-77

LEAGUE CHAMPIONSHIP SERIES

Year	Team		Games	BA	SA	AB	H	2B	3B	HR	HR%	R	RBI	BB	SO	SB	Pinch Hit AB	H	PO	A	E	DP	TC/G	FA	G by Pos
1983	BAL	A	4	.400	.533	15	6	2	0	0	0.0	5	1	2	3	0	0	0	7	11	0	2	4.5	1.000	SS-4

WORLD SERIES

Year	Team		Games	BA	SA	AB	H	2B	3B	HR	HR%	R	RBI	BB	SO	SB	Pinch Hit AB	H	PO	A	E	DP	TC/G	FA	G by Pos
1983	BAL	A	5	.167	.167	18	3	0	0	0	0.0	2	1	3	4	0	0	0	6	14	0	3	4.0	1.000	SS-5

Jimmy Ripple

RIPPLE, JAMES ALBERT
B. Oct. 14, 1909, Export, Pa.
D. July 16, 1959, Greensburg, Pa.

BL TR 5'10" 170 lbs.
BB 1936

Year	Team		Games	BA	SA	AB	H	2B	3B	HR	HR%	R	RBI	BB	SO	SB	Pinch Hit AB	H	PO	A	E	DP	TC/G	FA	G by Pos
1936	NY	N	96	.305	.441	311	95	17	2	7	2.3	42	47	28	15	1	19	9	190	5	4	10	2.1	.980	OF-76
1937			121	.317	.420	426	135	23	3	5	1.2	70	66	29	20	3	11	4	193	6	4	1	1.7	.980	OF-111
1938			134	.261	.375	501	131	21	3	10	2.0	68	60	49	21	2	3	0	236	13	6	2	1.9	.976	OF-131
1939 2 teams	NY	N (66G – .228)				BKN	N	(28G – .330)																	
" total			94	.275	.376	229	63	12	4	1	0.4	28	40	19	15	0	38	9	91	2	0	0	1.0	1.000	OF-51
1940 2 teams	BKN	N (7G – .231)				CIN	N	(32G – .307)																	
" total			39	.298	.491	114	34	10	0	4	3.5	15	20	15	7	1	5	1	55	0	0	0	1.4	1.000	OF-33
1941	CIN	N	38	.216	.324	102	22	6	1	1	1.0	10	9	9	4	0	11	2	36	1	0	0	1.0	1.000	OF-25
1943	PHI	A	32	.238	.278	126	30	3	1	0	0.0	8	15	7	7	0	1	0	55	0	0	0	1.7	1.000	OF-31
7 yrs.			554	.282	.395	1809	510	92	14	28	1.5	241	257	156	89	7	88	25	856	27	14	13	1.6	.984	OF-458

WORLD SERIES

Year	Team		Games	BA	SA	AB	H	2B	3B	HR	HR%	R	RBI	BB	SO	SB	Pinch Hit AB	H	PO	A	E	DP	TC/G	FA	G by Pos
1936	NY	N	5	.333	.583	12	4	0	0	1	8.3	2	3	3	3	0	0	0	8	0	0	0	1.6	1.000	OF-5
1937			5	.294	.294	17	5	0	0	0	0.0	2	0	3	1	0	0	0	11	0	0	0	2.2	1.000	OF-5
1940	CIN	N	7	.333	.571	21	7	2	0	1	4.8	3	6	4	2	0	0	0	14	0	0	0	2.0	1.000	OF-7
3 yrs.			17	.320	.480	50	16	2	0	2	4.0	7	9	10	6	0	0	0	33	0	0	0	1.9	1.000	OF-17

Swede Risberg

RISBERG, CHARLES AUGUST
B. Oct. 13, 1894, San Francisco, Calif.   D. Oct. 13, 1975, Red Bluff, Calif.

BR TR 6'   165 lbs.

Year	Team		Games	BA	SA	AB	H	2B	3B	HR	HR%	R	RBI	BB	SO	SB	Pinch Hit AB	H	PO	A	E	DP	TC/G	FA	G by Pos
1917	CHI	A	149	.203	.285	474	96	20	8	1	0.2	59	45	59	65	16	2	1	291	352	61	57	4.7	.913	SS-146
1918			82	.256	.333	273	70	12	3	1	0.4	36	27	23	32	5	4	1	168	160	21	27	4.3	.940	SS-30, 3B-24, 2B-12, 1B-7, OF-3
1919			119	.256	.345	414	106	19	6	2	0.5	48	38	35	38	19	0	0	379	291	34	49	5.9	.952	SS-97, 1B-22
1920			126	.266	.369	458	122	21	10	2	0.4	53	65	31	45	12	2	0	238	400	45	59	5.4	.934	SS-124
4 yrs.			476	.243	.332	1619	394	72	27	6	0.4	196	175	148	180	52	8	2	1076	1203	161	192	5.1	.934	SS-397, 1B-29, 3B-24, 2B-12, OF-3

WORLD SERIES

Year	Team		Games	BA	SA	AB	H	2B	3B	HR	HR%	R	RBI	BB	SO	SB	Pinch Hit AB	H	PO	A	E	DP	TC/G	FA	G by Pos
1917	CHI	A	2	.500	.500	2	1	0	0	0	0.0	0	1	0	0	0	2	1	0	0	0	0	0.0	–	
1919			8	.080	.160	25	2	0	1	0	0.0	3	0	5	3	1	0	0	23	30	4	6	7.1	.930	SS-8
2 yrs.			10	.111	.185	27	3	0	1	0	0.0	3	1	5	3	1	2	1	23	30	4	6	5.7	.930	SS-8

Pop Rising

RISING, PERCIVAL SUMNER
B. Jan., 1877, Industry, Pa.   D. Jan. 28, 1938, Rochester, Pa.

Year	Team		Games	BA	SA	AB	H	2B	3B	HR	HR%	R	RBI	BB	SO	SB	Pinch Hit AB	H	PO	A	E	DP	TC/G	FA	G by Pos
1905	BOS	A	8	.111	.278	18	2	1	1	0	0.0	2	2	2		0	4	0	4	2	0	0	0.8	1.000	OF-3, 3B-1

Claude Ritchey

RITCHEY, CLAUDE CASSIUS (Little All Right)
B. Oct. 5, 1873, Emlenton, Pa.   D. Nov. 8, 1951, Emlenton, Pa.

BB TR 5'6½" 167 lbs.

Year	Team		Games	BA	SA	AB	H	2B	3B	HR	HR%	R	RBI	BB	SO	SB	Pinch Hit AB	H	PO	A	E	DP	TC/G	FA	G by Pos
1897	CIN	N	101	.282	.341	337	95	12	4	0	0.0	58	41	42		11	0	0	192	229	50	24	4.7	.894	SS-70, OF-22, 2B-8
1898	LOU	N	151	.254	.314	551	140	10	4	5	0.9	65	51	46		19	0	0	402	440	58	62	6.0	.936	SS-80, 2B-71
1899			147	.300	.377	536	161	15	7	4	0.7	65	51	49		21	0	0	375	449	54	56	6.0	.938	2B-137, SS-11
1900	PIT	N	123	.292	.368	476	139	17	8	1	0.2	62	67	29		18	0	0	303	357	33	51	5.6	.952	2B-123
1901			140	.296	.354	540	160	20	4	1	0.2	66	74	47		15	0	0	340	396	46	54	5.6	.941	2B-139, SS-1
1902			115	.277	.328	405	112	13	1	2	0.5	54	55	53		10	0	0	275	341	22	48	5.5	.966	2B-114, OF-1
1903			138	.287	.381	506	145	28	10	0	0.0	66	59	55		15	0	0	281	460	30	45	5.6	.961	2B-137
1904			156	.263	.347	544	143	22	12	0	0.0	79	51	59		12	0	0	332	484	36	48	5.5	.958	2B-156, SS-2
1905			153	.255	.332	533	136	29	6	0	0.0	54	52	51		12	0	0	281	478	31	59	5.2	.961	2B-153, SS-2
1906			152	.269	.339	484	130	21	5	1	0.2	46	62	68		6	1	1	326	439	27	59	5.2	.966	2B-151
1907	BOS	N	144	.255	.317	499	127	17	4	2	0.4	45	51	50		8	0	0	340	460	24	55	5.7	.971	2B-144
1908			121	.273	.325	421	115	10	3	2	0.5	44	36	50		7	1	0	325	368	24	46	5.9	.967	2B-120
1909			30	.172	.184	87	15	1	0	0	0.0	4	3	8		1	4	1	65	52	5	10	4.1	.959	2B-25
13 yrs.			1671	.273	.342	5919	1618	215	68	18	0.3	708	673	607		155	6	2	3837	4953	440	617	5.5	.952	2B-1478, SS-166, OF-23

WORLD SERIES

Year	Team		Games	BA	SA	AB	H	2B	3B	HR	HR%	R	RBI	BB	SO	SB	Pinch Hit AB	H	PO	A	E	DP	TC/G	FA	G by Pos
1903	PIT	N	8	.111	.148	27	3	1	0	0	0.0	2	2	4	7	1	0	0	20	28	0	5	6.0	1.000	2B-8

Charles Ritter

RITTER, CHARLES J.
Deceased.

Year	Team		Games	BA	SA	AB	H	2B	3B	HR	HR%	R	RBI	BB	SO	SB	Pinch Hit AB	H	PO	A	E	DP	TC/G	FA	G by Pos
1885	BUF	N	2	.167	.167	6	1	0	0	0	0.0	0		0		0	0	0	8	5	3	1	8.0	.813	2B-2

Floyd Ritter

RITTER, FLOYD ALEXANDER
B. June 1, 1870, Dorset, Ohio   D. Feb. 7, 1943, Stevenson, Wash.

BR TR 5'8" 155 lbs.

Year	Team		Games	BA	SA	AB	H	2B	3B	HR	HR%	R	RBI	BB	SO	SB	Pinch Hit AB	H	PO	A	E	DP	TC/G	FA	G by Pos
1890	TOL	AA	1	.000	.000	3	0	0	0	0	0.0	0		0		0	0	0	4	3	2	0	9.0	.778	C-1

Lew Ritter

RITTER, LEWIS ELMER (Old Dog)
B. Sept. 7, 1875, Liverpool, England   D. May 27, 1952, Harrisburg, Pa.

BR TR 5'9" 150 lbs.

Year	Team		Games	BA	SA	AB	H	2B	3B	HR	HR%	R	RBI	BB	SO	SB	Pinch Hit AB	H	PO	A	E	DP	TC/G	FA	G by Pos
1902	BKN	N	16	.211	.246	57	12	2	0	0	0.0	5	2	1		2	0	0	91	18	3	2	7.0	.973	C-16
1903			78	.236	.317	259	61	9	6	0	0.0	26	37	19		9	2	1	309	80	25	6	5.3	.940	C-74, OF-2

Year	Team	Games	BA	SA	AB	H	2B	3B	HR	HR%	R	RBI	BB	SO	SB	Pinch Hit AB	H	PO	A	E	DP	TC/G	FA	G by Pos

Lew Ritter *continued*

Year	Team	Games	BA	SA	AB	H	2B	3B	HR	HR%	R	RBI	BB	SO	SB	AB	H	PO	A	E	DP	TC/G	FA	G by Pos
1904		72	.248	.276	214	53	4	1	0	0.0	23	19	20		17	7	2	258	100	13	13	5.2	.965	C-57, 2B-5, 3B-1
1905		92	.219	.293	311	68	10	5	1	0.3	32	28	15		16	2	0	406	109	26	4	5.9	.952	C-84, OF-4, 3B-2
1906		73	.208	.239	226	47	1	3	0	0.0	22	15	16		6	6	1	257	68	10	5	4.6	.970	C-53, OF-9, 1B-3, 3B-2
1907		93	.203	.232	271	55	6	1	0	0.0	15	17	18		5	3	0	391	103	16	11	5.5	.969	C-89
1908		38	.192	.232	99	19	2	1	0	0.0	6	2	7		0	1	0	132	44	7	0	4.8	.962	C-37
7 yrs.		462	.219	.269	1437	315	34	17	1	0.1	129	120	96		55	21	4	1844	522	100	41	5.3	.959	C-410, OF-15, 3B-5, 2B-5, 1B-3

Ed Ritterson

RITTERSON, EDWARD WEST
B. Apr. 26, 1855, Philadelphia, Pa. D. July 28, 1917, Bucks County, Pa.

BR TR 5'8"

Year	Team	Games	BA	SA	AB	H	2B	3B	HR	HR%	R	RBI	BB	SO	SB	AB	H	PO	A	E	DP	TC/G	FA	G by Pos
1876	PHI N	16	.250	.308	52	13	3	0	0	0.0	8	4	0	2		0	0	43	8	23	1	4.6	.689	C-14, OF-4, 3B-1

Jim Ritz

RITZ, JAMES L.
B. 1874, Pittsburgh, Pa. D. Nov. 10, 1896, Pittsburgh, Pa.

Year	Team	Games	BA	SA	AB	H	2B	3B	HR	HR%	R	RBI	BB	SO	SB	AB	H	PO	A	E	DP	TC/G	FA	G by Pos
1894	PIT N	1	.000	.000	4	0	0	0	0	0.0	0	0	1	0		0	0	1	2	1	1	4.0	.750	3B-1

Bombo Rivera

RIVERA, JESUS MANUEL
Born Jesus Manuel Rivera y Torres.
B. Aug. 2, 1952, Ponce, Puerto Rico

BR TR 5'10" 187 lbs.

Year	Team	Games	BA	SA	AB	H	2B	3B	HR	HR%	R	RBI	BB	SO	SB	AB	H	PO	A	E	DP	TC/G	FA	G by Pos
1975	MON N	5	.111	.111	9	1	0	0	0	0.0	1	0	2	3	0	1	0	8	0	1	0	1.8	.889	OF-5
1976		68	.276	.411	185	51	11	4	2	1.1	22	19	13	32	1	15	5	89	7	5	3	1.5	.950	OF-56
1978	MIN A	101	.271	.355	251	68	8	3	3	1.2	35	23	35	47	5	19	4	162	5	3	0	1.7	.982	OF-94, DH-1
1979		112	.281	.392	263	74	13	5	2	0.8	37	31	17	40	5	26	6	169	12	2	0	1.6	.989	OF-105, DH-2
1980		44	.221	.363	113	25	7	0	3	2.7	13	10	4	20	0	6	1	58	1	5	1	1.5	.922	OF-37, DH-1
1982	KC A	5	.100	.100	10	1	0	0	0	0.0	1	0	0	2	0	1	0	4	0	0	0	0.8	1.000	OF-3
6 yrs.		335	.265	.374	831	220	39	11	10	1.2	109	83	71	144	11	68	16	490	25	16	4	1.6	.970	OF-300, DH-4

German Rivera

RIVERA, GERMAN
Born German Rivera y Diaz.
B. July 6, 1960, Santurce, Puerto Rico

BR TR 6'2" 170 lbs.

Year	Team	Games	BA	SA	AB	H	2B	3B	HR	HR%	R	RBI	BB	SO	SB	AB	H	PO	A	E	DP	TC/G	FA	G by Pos
1983	LA N	13	.353	.412	17	6	1	0	0	0.0	1	0	2	2	0	5	1	2	11	1	0	1.1	.929	3B-8
1984		94	.260	.357	227	59	12	2	2	0.9	20	17	21	30	1	5	1	55	167	15	12	2.5	.937	3B-90
1985	HOU N	13	.194	.306	36	7	2	1	0	0.0	3	2	4	8	0	3	0	7	25	3	3	2.6	.941	3B-11
3 yrs.		120	.257	.354	280	72	15	3	2	0.7	24	19	27	40	1	13	2	64	203	18	15	2.4	.937	3B-109

Jim Rivera

RIVERA, MANUEL JOSEPH (Jungle Jim)
B. July 22, 1922, New York, N. Y.

BL TL 6' 196 lbs.

Year	Team	Games	BA	SA	AB	H	2B	3B	HR	HR%	R	RBI	BB	SO	SB	AB	H	PO	A	E	DP	TC/G	FA	G by Pos
1952	2 teams	STL A	(97G – .256)		CHI A	(53G – .249)																		
"	total	150	.253	.363	537	136	20	9	7	1.3	72	48	50	86	21	6	2	430	9	9	2	3.0	.980	OF-141
1953	CHI A	156	.259	.420	567	147	26	16	11	1.9	79	78	53	70	22	0	0	385	15	10	5	2.6	.976	OF-156
1954		145	.286	.431	490	140	16	8	13	2.7	62	61	49	68	18	3	0	255	5	11	0	1.9	.959	OF-143
1955		147	.264	.401	454	120	24	4	10	2.2	71	52	62	59	25	7	2	288	22	6	7	2.1	.981	OF-143
1956		139	.255	.395	491	125	23	5	12	2.4	76	66	49	75	20	9	2	271	9	7	4	2.1	.976	OF-134
1957		125	.256	.443	402	103	21	6	14	3.5	51	52	40	80	18	11	3	374	14	7	22	3.2	.982	OF-82, 1B-31
1958		116	.225	.380	276	62	8	4	9	3.3	37	35	24	49	21	9	0	153	7	1	3	1.4	.994	OF-99
1959		80	.220	.384	177	39	9	4	4	2.3	18	19	11	19	5	4	0	75	5	2	3	1.0	.976	OF-69
1960		48	.294	.471	17	5	0	0	1	5.9	17	1	3	3	4	2	0	16	0	0	0	0.3	1.000	OF-24
1961	2 teams	CHI A	(1G – .000)		KC A	(64G – .241)																		
"	total	65	.241	.340	141	34	8	0	2	1.4	20	10	24	14	6	23	4	51	0	1	0	0.8	.981	OF-43
10 yrs.		1171	.256	.402	3552	911	155	56	83	2.3	503	422	365	523	160	74	13	2298	86	54	46	2.1	.978	OF-1034, 1B-31

WORLD SERIES

Year	Team	Games	BA	SA	AB	H	2B	3B	HR	HR%	R	RBI	BB	SO	SB	AB	H	PO	A	E	DP	TC/G	FA	G by Pos
1959	CHI A	5	.000	.000	11	0	0	0	0	0.0	1	0	3	1	0	0	1	10	1	0	0	2.2	1.000	OF-5

Luis Rivera

RIVERA, LUIS ANTONIO
Born Luis Antonio Rivera y Pedraza.
B. Jan. 3, 1964, Cidra, Puerto Rico

BR TR 5'11" 165 lbs.

Year	Team	Games	BA	SA	AB	H	2B	3B	HR	HR%	R	RBI	BB	SO	SB	AB	H	PO	A	E	DP	TC/G	FA	G by Pos
1986	MON N	55	.205	.283	166	34	11	1	0	0.0	20	13	17	33	1	2	0	64	119	9	24	3.5	.953	SS-55
1987		18	.156	.219	32	5	2	0	0	0.0	0	1	1	8	0	3	1	9	27	3	4	2.2	.923	SS-15
1988		123	.224	.318	371	83	17	3	4	1.1	35	30	24	69	3	8	2	160	301	18	69	3.9	.962	SS-116
1989	BOS A	93	.257	.362	323	83	17	1	5	1.5	35	29	20	60	2	1	0	127	240	16	59	4.1	.958	SS-90, DH-1, 2B-1
4 yrs.		289	.230	.324	892	205	47	5	9	1.0	90	73	62	170	6	14	3	360	687	46	156	3.8	.958	SS-276, DH-1, 2B-1

Mickey Rivers

RIVERS, JOHN MILTON (Mick the Quick)
B. Oct. 31, 1948, Miami, Fla.

BL TL 5'10" 165 lbs.

Year	Team	Games	BA	SA	AB	H	2B	3B	HR	HR%	R	RBI	BB	SO	SB	AB	H	PO	A	E	DP	TC/G	FA	G by Pos
1970	CAL A	17	.320	.400	25	8	2	0	0	0.0	6	3	3	5	1	9	1	10	0	0	0	0.6	1.000	OF-5
1971		78	.265	.336	268	71	12	2	1	0.4	31	12	19	38	13	7	2	159	5	4	2	2.2	.976	OF-75
1972		58	.214	.277	159	34	6	2	0	0.0	18	7	8	26	4	7	2	105	0	2	0	1.8	.981	OF-48
1973		30	.349	.457	129	45	6	4	0	0.0	26	16	8	11	8	2	0	60	0	6	0	2.2	.909	OF-29
1974		118	.285	.393	466	133	19	11	3	0.6	69	31	39	47	30	1	0	309	9	2	3	2.7	.994	OF-116
1975		155	.284	.359	616	175	17	13	1	0.2	70	53	43	42	70	2	0	371	13	9	3	2.5	.977	OF-152, DH-1
1976	NY A	137	.312	.432	590	184	31	8	8	1.4	95	67	13	51	43	1	1	407	6	6	0	3.1	.986	OF-136
1977		138	.326	.439	565	184	18	5	12	2.1	79	69	18	45	22	4	0	380	11	7	1	2.9	.982	OF-136, DH-1
1978		141	.265	.397	559	148	25	8	11	2.0	78	48	29	51	25	3	2	384	8	8	2	2.8	.980	OF-138
1979	2 teams	NY A	(74G – .287)		TEX A	(58G – .300)																		
"	total	132	.293	.424	533	156	27	8	9	1.7	72	50	22	39	10	6	2	300	8	7	1	2.4	.978	OF-126, DH-1
1980	TEX A	147	.333	.437	630	210	32	6	7	1.1	96	60	20	34	18	4	1	342	19	8	4	2.5	.978	OF-141, DH-4
1981		99	.286	.371	399	114	21	2	3	0.8	62	26	24	31	9	5	0	225	12	1	3	2.4	.996	OF-97
1982		19	.235	.324	68	16	1	1	1	1.5	6	4	0	7	0	3	1	0	0	0	0	0.0	–	DH-16
1983		96	.285	.350	309	88	17	0	1	0.3	37	20	11	21	9	20	8	48	1	0	0	0.5	.980	DH-53, OF-23

Year	Team	Games	BA	SA	AB	H	2B	3B	HR	HR%	R	RBI	BB	SO	SB	Pinch Hit AB	Pinch Hit H	PO	A	E	DP	TC/G	FA	G by Pos

Mickey Rivers *continued*

Year	Team	Games	BA	SA	AB	H	2B	3B	HR	HR%	R	RBI	BB	SO	SB	AB	H	PO	A	E	DP	TC/G	FA	G by Pos
1984		102	.300	.387	313	94	13	1	4	1.3	40	33	9	23	5	31	8	49	3	0	2	0.5	1.000	DH-48, OF-30
15 yrs.		1467	.295	.397	5629	1660	247	71	61	1.1	785	499	266	471	267	103	28	3149	95	61	21	2.3	.982	OF-1252, DH-124

LEAGUE CHAMPIONSHIP SERIES

1976	NY A	5	.348	.435	23	8	0	1	0	0.0	5	0	1	1	0	0	0	11	0	0	0	2.2	1.000	OF-5
1977		5	.391	.478	23	9	2	0	0	0.0	5	2	0	2	1	0	0	19	0	0	0	3.8	1.000	OF-5
1978		4	.455	.455	11	5	0	0	0	0.0	0	0	2	0	0	0	0	8	1	0	1	2.3	1.000	OF-4
3 yrs.		14	.386	.456	57	22	2	1	0	0.0	10	2	3	3	1	0	0	38	1	0	1	2.8	1.000	OF-14

WORLD SERIES

1976	NY A	4	.167	.167	18	3	0	0	0	0.0	1	0	1	2	1	0	0	14	0	0	0	3.5	1.000	OF-4
1977		6	.222	.296	27	6	2	0	0	0.0	1	1	0	2	1	0	0	24	1	0	0	4.2	1.000	OF-6
1978		5	.333	.333	18	6	0	0	0	0.0	2	1	0	2	1	1	0	7	0	0	0	1.4	1.000	OF-4
3 yrs.		15	.238	.270	63	15	2	0	0	0.0	4	2	1	6	3	1	0	45	1	0	0	3.1	1.000	OF-14

Johnny Rizzo

RIZZO, JOHN COSTA
B. July 30, 1912, Houston, Tex. D. Dec. 4, 1977, Houston, Tex.   BR TR 6'   190 lbs.

1938	PIT N	143	.301	.514	555	167	31	9	23	4.1	97	111	54	61	1	1	0	284	5	15	1	2.1	.951	OF-140
1939		94	.261	.403	330	86	23	3	6	1.8	49	55	42	27	0	5	1	186	2	5	0	2.1	.974	OF-86
1940	3 teams	143	PIT N (9G – .179)		CIN N (31G – .282)			PHI N (103G – .292)																
"	total	143	.283	.471	505	143	19	2	24	4.8	71	72	56	50	3	6	1	290	38	14	6	2.4	.959	OF-128, 3B-7
1941	PHI N	99	.217	.323	235	51	9	2	4	1.7	20	24	24	34	1	30	5	115	10	6	2	1.3	.954	OF-62, 3B-2
1942	BKN N	78	.230	.323	217	50	8	0	4	1.8	31	27	24	25	2	6	0	124	6	3	1	1.7	.977	OF-70
5 yrs.		557	.270	.435	1842	497	90	16	61	3.3	268	289	200	197	7	48	7	999	61	43	10	2.0	.961	OF-486, 3B-9

Phil Rizzuto

RIZZUTO, PHILIP FRANCIS (Scooter)
B. Sept. 25, 1917, New York, N. Y.   BR TR 5'6"   150 lbs.

1941	NY A	133	.307	.398	515	158	20	9	3	0.6	65	46	27	36	14	3	0	252	399	29	109	5.1	.957	SS-128
1942		144	.284	.374	553	157	24	7	4	0.7	79	68	44	40	22	0	0	324	445	30	114	5.5	.962	SS-144
1946		126	.257	.310	471	121	17	1	2	0.4	53	38	34	39	14	0	0	267	378	26	97	5.3	.961	SS-125
1947		153	.273	.364	549	150	26	9	2	0.4	78	60	57	31	11	1	1	340	450	25	111	5.3	.969	SS-151
1948		128	.252	.328	464	117	13	2	6	1.3	65	50	60	24	6	0	0	259	348	17	85	4.9	.973	SS-128
1949		153	.275	.358	614	169	22	7	5	0.8	110	64	72	34	18	0	0	329	440	23	118	5.2	.971	SS-152
1950		155	.324	.439	617	200	36	7	7	1.1	125	66	92	38	12	0	0	301	452	14	123	4.9	.982	SS-155
1951		144	.274	.346	540	148	21	6	2	0.4	87	43	58	27	18	0	0	317	407	24	113	5.2	.968	SS-144
1952		152	.254	.341	578	147	24	10	2	0.3	89	43	67	42	17	0	0	308	458	19	116	5.2	.976	SS-152
1953		134	.271	.351	413	112	21	3	2	0.5	54	54	71	39	4	0	0	214	409	24	100	4.8	.963	SS-133
1954		127	.195	.251	307	60	11	0	2	0.7	47	15	41	23	3	1	1	185	294	16	84	3.9	.968	SS-126, 2B-1
1955		81	.259	.322	143	37	4	1	1	0.7	19	9	22	18	7	0	0	93	132	10	30	2.9	.957	SS-79, 2B-1
1956		31	.231	.231	52	12	0	0	0	0.0	6	6	6	6	3	0	0	31	54	6	17	2.9	.934	SS-30
13 yrs.		1661	.273	.355	5816	1588	239	62	38	0.7	877	562	651	397	149	5	2	3220	4666	263	1217	4.9	.968	SS-1647, 2B-2

WORLD SERIES

1941	NY A	5	.111	.111	18	2	0	0	0	0.0	0	0	3	1	1	0	0	12	18	1	6	6.2	.968	SS-5
1942		5	.381	.524	21	8	0	0	1	4.8	2	1	2	1	2	0	0	15	14	1	1	6.0	.967	SS-5
1947		7	.308	.346	26	8	1	0	0	0.0	3	2	4	0	2	0	0	19	15	0	3	4.9	1.000	SS-7
1949		5	.167	.167	18	3	0	0	0	0.0	2	1	3	1	1	0	0	5	15	0	3	4.0	1.000	SS-5
1950		4	.143	.143	14	2	0	0	0	0.0	2	0	0	1	0	0	0	5	8	0	2	3.3	1.000	SS-4
1951		6	.320	.440	25	8	0	0	1	4.0	5	3	2	3	0	0	0	15	24	1	9	6.7	.975	SS-6
1952		7	.148	.185	27	4	0	0	0	0.0	2	0	5	2	1	0	0	13	17	1	4	4.4	.968	SS-7
1953		6	.316	.368	19	6	1	0	0	0.0	4	0	3	2	1	0	0	11	19	1	4	5.2	.968	SS-6
1955		7	.267	.267	15	4	0	0	0	0.0	1	2	5	1	2	0	0	13	14	1	1	3.9	1.000	SS-7
9 yrs.		52	.246	.295	183	45	3	0	2	1.1	21	8	30	11	10	0	0	108	144	5	33	4.9	.981	SS-52
		6th			7th	7th							10th		4th		3rd							

Mel Roach

ROACH, MELVIN EARL
B. Jan. 25, 1933, Richmond, Va.   BR TR 6'1"   190 lbs.

1953	MIL N	5	.000	.000	2	0	0	0	0	0.0	0	0	0	0	0	1	0	0	0	0	0	0.0	–	2B-1
1954		3	.000	.000	4	0	0	0	0	0.0	0	0	0	1	0	2	0	3	0	0	2	1.0	1.000	1B-1
1957		7	.167	.167	6	1	0	0	0	0.0	0	1	0	3	0	4	3	4	3	0	0	1.0	1.000	2B-5
1958		44	.309	.426	136	42	7	0	3	2.2	14	10	6	15	0	12	3	65	82	3	13	3.4	.980	2B-27, OF-7, 1B-1
1959		19	.097	.097	31	3	0	0	0	0.0	1	0	2	4	0	5	0	12	16	5	2	1.7	.848	2B-8, OF-4, 3B-1
1960		48	.300	.450	140	42	12	0	3	2.1	12	18	6	19	0	10	3	70	29	4	5	2.1	.961	OF-21, 2B-20, 3B-1, 1B-1
1961	2 teams	36	MIL N (13G – .167)		CHI N (23G – .128)																			
"	total	36	.147	.213	75	11	2	0	1	1.3	4	7	5	13	1	13	3	83	8	2	8	2.6	.978	OF-9, 1B-9, 2B-7
1962	PHI N	65	.190	.229	105	20	4	0	0	0.0	9	8	5	19	0	28	4	42	36	3	5	1.2	.963	3B-26, 2B-9, 1B-4, OF-3
8 yrs.		227	.238	.331	499	119	25	0	7	1.4	42	43	24	75	1	74	13	279	174	17	35	2.1	.964	2B-77, OF-44, 3B-28, 1B-16

Mike Roach

ROACH, JAMES MICHAEL
B. 1876, New York, N. Y. D. Nov. 12, 1916, Binghamton, N. Y.

| 1899 | WAS N | 24 | .218 | .231 | 78 | 17 | 1 | 0 | 0 | 0.0 | 7 | 7 | 3 | | | 3 | 2 | 1 | 82 | 17 | 4 | 3 | 4.3 | .961 | C-20, 1B-3 |

Roxy Roach

ROACH, WILBUR CHARLES
B. Nov. 28, 1882, Anita, Pa. D. Dec. 25, 1947, Bay City, Mich.   BR TR 5'11"   160 lbs.

1910	NY A	70	.214	.273	220	47	9	2	0	0.0	27	20	29		15	3	0	120	173	28	27	4.6	.913	SS-58, OF-9
1911		13	.250	.350	40	10	2	1	0	0.0	4	2	6		0	0	0	26	37	8	5	5.5	.887	SS-8, 2B-5
1912	WAS A	2	.500	2.000	2	1	0	1	1	50.0	1	1	0		0	0	0	0	1	0	0	1.0	.500	SS-2
1915	BUF F	92	.269	.361	346	93	20	3	2	0.6	35	31	17		11	0	0	212	297	22	38	5.8	.959	SS-92
4 yrs.		177	.248	.334	608	151	31	6	3	0.5	67	54	52		26	3	0	358	508	59	70	5.2	.936	SS-160, OF-9, 2B-5

Year Team	Games	BA	SA	AB	H	2B	3B	HR	HR%	R	RBI	BB	SO	SB	Pinch Hit AB	Pinch Hit H	PO	A	E	DP	TC/G	FA	G by Pos

Mike Roarke

ROARKE, MICHAEL THOMAS
B. Nov. 8, 1930, West Warwick, R. I.   BR TR 6'2" 195 lbs.

Year Team	Games	BA	SA	AB	H	2B	3B	HR	HR%	R	RBI	BB	SO	SB	PH AB	PH H	PO	A	E	DP	TC/G	FA	G by Pos
1961 DET A	86	.223	.284	229	51	6	1	2	0.9	21	22	20	31	0	1	0	383	22	5	5	4.8	.988	C-85
1962	56	.213	.346	136	29	4	1	4	2.9	11	14	13	17	0	3	1	247	24	5	1	4.9	.982	C-53
1963	23	.318	.318	44	14	0	0	0	0.0	5	1	2	3	0	1	1	67	5	1	1	3.2	.986	C-16
1964	29	.232	.244	82	19	1	0	0	0.0	4	7	10	10	0	2	1	165	11	1	0	6.1	.994	C-27
4 yrs.	194	.230	.297	491	113	11	2	6	1.2	41	44	45	61	0	13	3	862	62	12	7	4.8	.987	C-181

Fred Roat

ROAT, FREDERICK R.
B. Nov. 10, 1867, Oregon, Ill.   D. Sept. 24, 1913, Oregon, Ill.   TR

Year Team	Games	BA	SA	AB	H	2B	3B	HR	HR%	R	RBI	BB	SO	SB	PH AB	PH H	PO	A	E	DP	TC/G	FA	G by Pos
1890 PIT N	57	.223	.260	215	48	2	0	2	0.9	18	17	16	22	7	0	0	154	102	35	12	5.1	.880	3B-44, 1B-9, OF-4
1892 CHI N	8	.194	.258	31	6	0	1	0	0.0	4	2	2	3	2	0	0	11	24	4	1	4.9	.897	2B-8
2 yrs.	65	.220	.260	246	54	2	1	2	0.8	22	19	18	25	9	0	0	165	126	39	13	5.1	.882	3B-44, 1B-9, 2B-8, OF-4

Tommy Robello

ROBELLO, THOMAS VARDASCO (Tony)
B. Feb. 9, 1913, San Leandro, Calif.   BR TR 5'10½" 175 lbs.

Year Team	Games	BA	SA	AB	H	2B	3B	HR	HR%	R	RBI	BB	SO	SB	PH AB	PH H	PO	A	E	DP	TC/G	FA	G by Pos
1933 CIN N	14	.233	.333	30	7	3	0	0	0.0	1	3	1	5	0	1	0	15	27	2	3	3.1	.955	2B-11, 3B-2
1934	2	.000	.000	2	0	0	0	0	0.0	0	0	0	1	0	2	0	0	0	0	0	0.0	—	
2 yrs.	16	.219	.313	32	7	3	0	0	0.0	1	3	1	6	0	3	0	15	27	2	3	2.8	.955	2B-11, 3B-2

Skippy Roberge

ROBERGE, JOSEPH ALBERT ARMAND
B. May 19, 1917, Lowell, Mass.   BR TR 5'11" 185 lbs.

Year Team	Games	BA	SA	AB	H	2B	3B	HR	HR%	R	RBI	BB	SO	SB	PH AB	PH H	PO	A	E	DP	TC/G	FA	G by Pos
1941 BOS N	55	.216	.251	167	36	6	0	0	0.0	12	15	9	18	0	2	1	98	138	6	32	4.4	.975	2B-46, 3B-5, SS-2
1942	74	.215	.273	172	37	7	0	1	0.6	10	12	9	19	1	2	0	92	129	7	21	3.1	.969	2B-29, 3B-27, SS-6
1946	48	.231	.325	169	39	6	2	2	1.2	13	20	7	12	1	0	0	63	80	4	11	3.1	.973	3B-48
3 yrs.	177	.220	.283	508	112	19	2	3	0.6	35	47	25	49	2	4	1	253	347	17	64	3.5	.972	3B-80, 2B-75, SS-8

Bip Roberts

ROBERTS, LEON JOSEPH
B. Oct. 27, 1963, Berkeley, Calif.   BB TR 5'7" 150 lbs.

Year Team	Games	BA	SA	AB	H	2B	3B	HR	HR%	R	RBI	BB	SO	SB	PH AB	PH H	PO	A	E	DP	TC/G	FA	G by Pos
1986 SD N	101	.253	.303	241	61	5	2	1	0.4	34	12	14	29	14	3	1	166	172	10	33	3.4	.971	2B-87
1988	5	.333	.333	9	3	0	0	0	0.0	1	0	1	2	0	2	0	2	3	1	1	1.2	.833	3B-2, 2B-1
1989	117	.301	.422	329	99	15	8	3	0.9	81	25	49	45	21	17	6	134	113	9	17	2.2	.965	OF-54, 3B-37, SS-14, 2B-9
3 yrs.	223	.282	.371	579	163	20	10	4	0.7	116	37	64	76	35	22	7	302	288	20	51	2.7	.967	2B-97, OF-54, 3B-39, SS-14

Curt Roberts

ROBERTS, CURTIS BENJAMIN
B. Aug. 16, 1929, Pineland, Tex.   D. Nov. 14, 1969, Oakland, Calif.   BR TR 5'8" 165 lbs.

Year Team	Games	BA	SA	AB	H	2B	3B	HR	HR%	R	RBI	BB	SO	SB	PH AB	PH H	PO	A	E	DP	TC/G	FA	G by Pos
1954 PIT N	134	.232	.302	496	115	18	7	1	0.2	47	36	55	49	6	1	0	357	394	24	82	5.8	.969	2B-131
1955	6	.118	.176	17	2	1	0	0	0.0	1	0	2	1	0	0	0	7	14	2	4	3.8	.913	2B-6
1956	31	.177	.323	62	11	5	2	0	0.0	6	4	5	12	1	4	1	39	45	1	12	2.7	.988	2B-27
3 yrs.	171	.223	.301	575	128	24	9	1	0.2	54	40	62	62	7	6	2	403	453	27	98	5.2	.969	2B-164

Dave Roberts

ROBERTS, DAVID LEONARD
B. June 30, 1933, Panama City, Panama   BL TL 6' 172 lbs.

Year Team	Games	BA	SA	AB	H	2B	3B	HR	HR%	R	RBI	BB	SO	SB	PH AB	PH H	PO	A	E	DP	TC/G	FA	G by Pos
1962 HOU N	16	.245	.358	53	13	3	0	1	1.9	3	10	8	8	0	4	1	47	1	0	1	3.0	1.000	OF-12, 1B-6
1964	61	.184	.256	125	23	4	1	1	0.8	9	7	14	28	0	22	4	274	27	6	18	5.0	.980	1B-34, OF-4
1966 PIT N	14	.125	.188	16	2	1	0	0	0.0	3	0	0	7	0	9	2	17	2	1	2	1.4	.950	1B-2
3 yrs.	91	.196	.278	194	38	8	1	2	1.0	15	17	22	43	0	35	7	338	30	7	21	4.1	.981	1B-42, OF-16

Dave Roberts

ROBERTS, DAVID WAYNE
B. Feb. 17, 1951, Lebanon, Ore.   BR TR 6'3" 215 lbs.

Year Team	Games	BA	SA	AB	H	2B	3B	HR	HR%	R	RBI	BB	SO	SB	PH AB	PH H	PO	A	E	DP	TC/G	FA	G by Pos
1972 SD N	100	.244	.321	418	102	17	0	5	1.2	38	33	18	64	7	0	0	92	198	21	27	3.1	.932	3B-84, 2B-20, SS-3, C-1
1973	127	.286	.472	479	137	20	3	21	4.4	56	64	17	83	11	8	1	92	276	24	31	3.1	.939	3B-111, 2B-12
1974	113	.167	.252	318	53	10	1	5	1.6	26	18	32	69	2	4	1	88	180	13	17	2.5	.954	3B-103, SS-3, OF-1
1975	33	.283	.354	113	32	2	0	2	1.8	7	12	13	19	3	0	0	37	68	8	7	3.4	.929	3B-30, 2B-5
1977	82	.220	.323	186	41	14	1	1	0.5	15	23	11	32	2	16	3	256	30	7	4	3.6	.976	C-63, 3B-2, 2B-2, SS-1
1978	54	.216	.309	97	21	4	1	1	1.0	7	7	12	25	0	4	0	150	14	3	0	3.1	.982	C-41, 1B-8, OF-2
1979 TEX A	44	.262	.417	84	22	2	1	3	3.6	12	14	7	17	1	4	2	82	30	1	10	2.6	.991	C-14, OF-11, 2B-8, 1B-6, DH-4, 3B-1
1980	101	.238	.383	235	56	4	0	10	4.3	27	30	13	38	0	13	4	138	100	11	11	2.5	.956	3B-37, SS-33, C-22, OF-5, 2B-4, 1B-4
1981 HOU N	27	.241	.352	54	13	3	0	1	1.9	4	5	3	6	1	11	2	88	16	5	7	4.0	.954	1B-10, 3B-7, 2B-3, C-1
1982 PHI N	28	.182	.212	33	6	1	0	0	0.0	2	2	2	8	0	2	0	23	20	3	4	1.6	.935	3B-11, C-10, 2B-7
10 yrs.	709	.239	.357	2017	483	77	7	49	2.4	194	208	128	361	27	62	13	1046	932	96	118	2.9	.954	3B-386, C-152, 2B-61, SS-40, 1B-28, OF-19, DH-4

DIVISIONAL PLAYOFF SERIES

Year Team	Games	BA	SA	AB	H	2B	3B	HR	HR%	R	RBI	BB	SO	SB	PH AB	PH H	PO	A	E	DP	TC/G	FA	G by Pos
1981 HOU N	1	.000	.000	1	0	0	0	0	0.0	0	0	0	1	0	1	0	0	0	0	0	0.0	—	

Leon Roberts

ROBERTS, LEON KAUFFMAN
B. Jan. 22, 1951, Vicksburg, Mich.   BR TR 6'3" 200 lbs.

Year Team	Games	BA	SA	AB	H	2B	3B	HR	HR%	R	RBI	BB	SO	SB	PH AB	PH H	PO	A	E	DP	TC/G	FA	G by Pos
1974 DET A	17	.270	.381	63	17	3	2	1	1.6	5	7	3	10	0	1	0	25	0	2	0	1.6	.926	OF-17
1975	129	.257	.385	447	115	17	5	10	2.2	51	38	36	94	3	3	1	268	10	5	2	2.2	.982	OF-127, DH-1
1976 HOU N	87	.289	.443	235	68	11	2	7	3.0	31	33	19	43	1	27	7	99	1	2	0	1.2	.980	OF-60
1977	19	.074	.074	27	2	0	0	0	0.0	1	2	1	8	0	10	2	3	2	0	0	0.3	1.000	OF-9
1978 SEA A	134	.301	.515	472	142	21	7	22	4.7	78	92	41	52	6	8	4	296	10	8	4	2.3	.975	OF-128, DH-2
1979	140	.271	.451	450	122	24	6	15	3.3	61	54	56	64	3	4	1	286	6	5	2	2.1	.983	OF-136, DH-1
1980	119	.251	.396	374	94	18	3	10	2.7	48	39	43	59	6	12	2	238	6	4	1	2.1	.984	OF-104, DH-4
1981 TEX A	72	.279	.421	233	65	17	2	4	1.7	26	31	25	38	3	4	0	130	2	1	0	1.8	.992	OF-71

Year Team	Games	BA	SA	AB	H	2B	3B	HR	HR%	R	RBI	BB	SO	SB	Pinch Hit AB	H	PO	A	E	DP	TC/G	FA	G by Pos

Leon Roberts *continued*

Year Team	Games	BA	SA	AB	H	2B	3B	HR	HR%	R	RBI	BB	SO	SB	PH AB	PH H	PO	A	E	DP	TC/G	FA	G by Pos
1982 2 teams	TEX A (31G – .233)			TOR A (40G – .229)																			
" total	71	.230	.303	178	41	7	0	2	1.1	13	11	11	30	1	16	4	66	0	0	0	0.9	1.000	OF-44, DH-22
1983 KC A	84	.258	.404	213	55	7	0	8	3.8	24	24	17	27	1	13	4	139	3	3	0	1.7	.979	OF-76, DH-1
1984	29	.222	.289	45	10	1	1	0	0.0	4	3	4	3	0	13	3	24	0	0	0	0.8	1.000	OF-16, DH-3, P-1
11 yrs.	901	.267	.419	2737	731	126	28	78	2.8	342	328	256	428	26	119	31	1574	40	30	9	1.8	.982	OF-788, DH-34, P-1

Red Roberts

ROBERTS, CHARLES EMORY BR TR 6' 170 lbs.
B. Aug. 8, 1918, Carrollton, Ga.

Year Team	Games	BA	SA	AB	H	2B	3B	HR	HR%	R	RBI	BB	SO	SB	PH AB	PH H	PO	A	E	DP	TC/G	FA	G by Pos
1943 WAS A	9	.261	.435	23	6	1	0	1	4.3	1	3	4	2	0	1	0	8	9	5	1	2.4	.773	SS-6, 3B-1

Skipper Roberts

ROBERTS, CLARENCE ASHLEY BL TR 5'10½" 175 lbs.
B. Jan. 11, 1888, Wardner, Ida. D. Dec. 24, 1963, Long Beach, Calif.

Year Team	Games	BA	SA	AB	H	2B	3B	HR	HR%	R	RBI	BB	SO	SB	PH AB	PH H	PO	A	E	DP	TC/G	FA	G by Pos
1913 STL N	26	.146	.195	41	6	2	0	0	0.0	4	3	3	13	1	7	0	44	11	9	2	2.5	.859	C-16
1914 2 teams	PIT F (52G – .234)			CHI F (4G – .333)																			
" total	56	.237	.351	97	23	4	2	1	1.0	12	9	3		3	29	**8**	77	24	7	3	1.9	.935	C-23, OF-1
2 yrs.	82	.210	.304	138	29	6	2	1	0.7	16	12	6	13	4	36	8	121	35	16	5	2.1	.907	C-39, OF-1

Andre Robertson

ROBERTSON, ANDRE LEVETT BR TR 5'10" 155 lbs.
B. Oct. 2, 1957, Orange, Tex.

Year Team	Games	BA	SA	AB	H	2B	3B	HR	HR%	R	RBI	BB	SO	SB	PH AB	PH H	PO	A	E	DP	TC/G	FA	G by Pos
1981 NY A	10	.263	.316	19	5	1	0	0	0.0	1	0	0	3	1	0	0	9	24	0	3	3.3	1.000	SS-8, 2B-3
1982	44	.220	.314	118	26	5	0	2	1.7	16	9	8	19	0	3	0	84	98	6	27	4.3	.968	SS-27, 2B-15, 3B-2
1983	98	.248	.326	322	80	16	3	1	0.3	37	22	8	54	2	0	0	163	302	15	64	4.9	.969	SS-78, 2B-29
1984	52	.214	.264	140	30	5	1	0	0.0	10	6	4	20	0	0	0	68	142	16	36	4.3	.929	SS-49, 2B-6
1985	50	.328	.416	125	41	5	0	2	1.6	16	17	6	24	1	2	0	32	67	10	16	2.2	.908	3B-33, SS-14, 2B-2
5 yrs.	254	.251	.327	724	182	32	4	5	0.7	80	54	26	120	4	5	0	356	633	47	146	4.1	.955	SS-176, 2B-55, 3B-35

LEAGUE CHAMPIONSHIP SERIES

Year Team	Games	BA	SA	AB	H	2B	3B	HR	HR%	R	RBI	BB	SO	SB	PH AB	PH H	PO	A	E	DP	TC/G	FA	G by Pos
1981 NY A	1	.000	.000	1	0	0	0	0	0.0	0	0	0	0	0	0	0	0	0	0	0	0.0	–	SS-1

WORLD SERIES

Year Team	Games	BA	SA	AB	H	2B	3B	HR	HR%	R	RBI	BB	SO	SB	PH AB	PH H	PO	A	E	DP	TC/G	FA	G by Pos
1981 NY A	1	–	–	0	0	0	0	0	–	0	0	0	0	0	0	0	0	0	0	0	0.0	–	

Bob Robertson

ROBERTSON, ROBERT EUGENE BR TR 6'1" 195 lbs.
B. Oct. 2, 1946, Frostburg, Md.

Year Team	Games	BA	SA	AB	H	2B	3B	HR	HR%	R	RBI	BB	SO	SB	PH AB	PH H	PO	A	E	DP	TC/G	FA	G by Pos
1967 PIT N	9	.171	.343	35	6	0	0	2	5.7	4	4	3	12	0	0	0	91	5	1	9	10.8	.990	1B-9
1969	32	.208	.302	96	20	4	1	1	1.0	7	9	8	30	1	5	2	214	16	1	19	7.2	.996	1B-26
1970	117	.287	.564	390	112	19	4	27	6.9	69	82	51	98	4	8	2	915	81	8	108	8.6	.992	1B-99, 3B-5, OF-3
1971	131	.271	.484	469	127	18	2	26	5.5	65	72	60	101	1	5	0	1089	128	9	107	9.4	.993	1B-126
1972	115	.193	.346	306	59	11	0	12	3.9	25	41	41	84	1	4	0	543	82	7	59	5.5	.993	1B-89, OF-23, 3B-11
1973	119	.239	.385	397	95	16	0	14	3.5	43	40	55	77	0	10	1	957	79	5	91	8.7	.995	1B-107
1974	91	.229	.479	236	54	11	0	16	6.8	25	48	33	48	0	28	8	494	37	5	44	5.9	.991	1B-63
1975	75	.274	.452	124	34	4	0	6	4.8	17	18	23	25	0	40	6	209	18	1	10	3.0	.996	1B-27
1976	61	.217	.318	129	28	5	1	2	1.6	10	25	16	23	0	25	3	257	17	1	28	4.5	.996	1B-29
1978 SEA A	64	.230	.420	174	40	5	2	8	4.6	17	28	24	39	0	16	4	141	8	0	16	2.3	1.000	DH-29, 1B-18
1979 TOR A	15	.103	.207	29	3	0	1	1	3.4	1	1	3	9	0	3	0	54	7	0	6	4.1	1.000	1B-9, DH-4
11 yrs.	829	.242	.434	2385	578	93	10	115	4.8	283	368	317	546	7	144	26	4964	478	38	497	6.6	.993	1B-602, DH-33, OF-26, 3B-16

LEAGUE CHAMPIONSHIP SERIES

Year Team	Games	BA	SA	AB	H	2B	3B	HR	HR%	R	RBI	BB	SO	SB	PH AB	PH H	PO	A	E	DP	TC/G	FA	G by Pos
1970 PIT N	2	.200	.400	5	1	1	0	0	0.0	0	0	0	0	0	1	0	11	1	0	1	6.0	1.000	1B-1
1971	4	.438	1.250	16	7	1	0	4	25.0	5	6	0	2	0	0	0	25	2	0	3	6.8	1.000	1B-4
1972	4	–	–	0	0	0	0	0	–	0	0	1	0	0	0	0	2	1	0	0	0.8	1.000	1B-4
1974	1	.000	.000	5	0	0	0	0	0.0	1	0	0	0	0	0	0	11	0	0	0	11.0	1.000	1B-1
1975	3	.500	.500	2	1	0	0	0	0.0	0	1	1	0	0	2	1	1	0	0	0	0.3	1.000	1B-1
5 yrs.	14	.321	.821	28	9	2	0	4	14.3	6	7	2	2	0	3	1	50	4	0	4	3.9	1.000	1B-11

WORLD SERIES

Year Team	Games	BA	SA	AB	H	2B	3B	HR	HR%	R	RBI	BB	SO	SB	PH AB	PH H	PO	A	E	DP	TC/G	FA	G by Pos
1971 PIT N	7	.240	.480	25	6	0	0	2	8.0	4	5	4	8	0	0	0	64	4	1	5	9.9	.986	1B-7

Daryl Robertson

ROBERTSON, DARYL BERDINE BR TR 6' 184 lbs.
B. Jan. 5, 1936, Cripple Creek, Colo.

Year Team	Games	BA	SA	AB	H	2B	3B	HR	HR%	R	RBI	BB	SO	SB	PH AB	PH H	PO	A	E	DP	TC/G	FA	G by Pos
1962 CHI N	9	.105	.105	19	2	0	0	0	0.0	0	2	2	10	0	2	0	8	14	0	1	2.4	1.000	SS-6, 3B-1

Dave Robertson

ROBERTSON, DAVIS AYDELOTTE BL TL 6' 186 lbs.
B. Sept. 25, 1889, Portsmouth, Va. D. Nov. 5, 1970, Virginia Beach, Va.

Year Team	Games	BA	SA	AB	H	2B	3B	HR	HR%	R	RBI	BB	SO	SB	PH AB	PH H	PO	A	E	DP	TC/G	FA	G by Pos
1912 NY N	3	.500	.500	2	1	0	0	0	0.0	0	0	0	0	0	0	0	2	0	0	0	0.7	1.000	1B-1
1914	82	.266	.359	256	68	12	3	2	0.8	25	32	10	26	9	10	0	101	13	6	2	1.5	.950	OF-71
1915	138	.294	.379	544	160	17	10	3	0.6	72	58	22	52	22	3	0	225	13	11	4	1.8	.956	OF-138
1916	150	.307	.426	587	180	18	8	**12**	2.0	88	69	14	56	21	5	2	248	17	11	5	1.8	.960	OF-144
1917	142	.259	.391	532	138	16	9	**12**	2.3	64	54	10	47	17	1	1	266	12	17	1	2.1	.942	OF-140
1919 2 teams	NY N (1G – .000)			CHI N (27G – .208)																			
" total	28	.208	.260	96	20	2	0	1	1.0	8	10	1	10	3	2	0	53	2	4	0	2.1	.932	OF-25
1920 CHI N	134	.300	.462	500	150	29	11	10	2.0	68	75	40	44	17	0	0	230	10	8	3	1.9	.968	OF-134
1921 2 teams	CHI N (22G – .222)			PIT N (60G – .322)																			
" total	82	.308	.477	266	82	21	3	6	2.3	36	62	13	19	4	15	4	126	2	5	0	1.6	.962	OF-65
1922 NY N	42	.277	.383	47	13	2	0	1	2.1	5	3	3	7	0	30	7	9	1	1	1	0.3	.909	OF-8
9 yrs.	801	.287	.409	2830	812	117	44	47	1.7	366	364	113	262	94	66	14	1260	70	63	14	1.7	.955	OF-725, 1B-1

WORLD SERIES

Year Team	Games	BA	SA	AB	H	2B	3B	HR	HR%	R	RBI	BB	SO	SB	PH AB	PH H	PO	A	E	DP	TC/G	FA	G by Pos
1917 NY N	6	.500	.636	22	11	1	1	0	0.0	3	1	0	0	2	0	0	6	2	1	0	1.5	.889	OF-6

Don Robertson

ROBERTSON, DONALD ALEXANDER BL TL 5'10" 180 lbs.
B. Oct. 15, 1930, Harvey, Ill.

Year	Team	Games	BA	SA	AB	H	2B	3B	HR	HR%	R	RBI	BB	SO	SB	Pinch Hit AB	Pinch Hit H	PO	A	E	DP	TC/G	FA	G by Pos

Don Robertson *continued*

Year	Team	Games	BA	SA	AB	H	2B	3B	HR	HR%	R	RBI	BB	SO	SB	AB	H	PO	A	E	DP	TC/G	FA	G by Pos
1954	CHI N	14	.000	.000	6	0	0	0	0	0.0	2	0	0	2	0	4	0	1	0	0	0	0.1	1.000	OF-6

Gene Robertson

ROBERTSON, EUGENE EDWARD
B. Dec. 25, 1899, St. Louis, Mo. D. Oct. 21, 1981, Fallon, Nev. BL TR 5'7" 152 lbs.

Year	Team	Games	BA	SA	AB	H	2B	3B	HR	HR%	R	RBI	BB	SO	SB	AB	H	PO	A	E	DP	TC/G	FA	G by Pos
1919	STL A	5	.143	.143	7	1	0	0	0	0.0	1	0	0	2	0	2	0	2	1	1	0	0.8	.750	SS-2
1922		18	.296	.444	27	8	2	1	0	0.0	2	1	0	1	1	3	2	8	18	2	1	1.6	.929	3B-7, SS-6, 2B-1
1923		78	.247	.295	251	62	10	1	0	0.0	36	17	21	7	4	0	0	87	118	14	7	2.8	.936	3B-74, 2B-1
1924		121	.319	.421	439	140	25	4	4	0.9	70	52	35	14	3	5	2	114	207	14	22	2.8	.958	3B-110, 2B-2
1925		154	.271	.405	582	158	26	5	14	2.4	97	76	81	30	10	0	0	202	288	32	42	3.4	.939	3B-154, SS-1
1926		78	.251	.360	247	62	12	6	1	0.4	23	19	17	10	5	10	4	75	149	19	13	3.1	.922	3B-55, SS-10, 2B-3
1928	NY A	83	.291	.339	251	73	9	0	1	0.4	29	36	14	9	2	9	0	78	120	15	7	2.6	.930	3B-70, 2B-3
1929	2 teams	NY A (90G – .298)			BOS N	(8G – .286)																		
"	total	98	.297	.377	337	100	15	6	0	0.0	46	41	29	6	4	12	2	87	128	9	6	2.3	.960	3B-83, SS-1
1930	BOS N	21	.186	.203	59	11	1	0	0	0.0	7	7	5	3	0	2	0	15	22	2	3	1.9	.949	3B-17
9 yrs.		656	.280	.373	2200	615	100	23	20	0.9	311	249	203	79	29	43	10	668	1051	108	101	2.8	.941	3B-570, SS-20, 2B-10

WORLD SERIES

Year	Team	Games	BA	SA	AB	H	2B	3B	HR	HR%	R	RBI	BB	SO	SB	AB	H	PO	A	E	DP	TC/G	FA	G by Pos
1928	NY A	3	.125	.125	8	1	0	0	0	0.0	1	2	1	0	1	0	1	1	1	1	0	1.0	.667	3B-3

Jim Robertson

ROBERTSON, ALFRED JAMES
B. Jan. 29, 1928, Chicago, Ill. BR TR 5'9" 183 lbs.

Year	Team	Games	BA	SA	AB	H	2B	3B	HR	HR%	R	RBI	BB	SO	SB	AB	H	PO	A	E	DP	TC/G	FA	G by Pos
1954	PHI A	63	.184	.238	147	27	8	0	0	0.0	9	8	23	25	0	9	1	207	18	6	6	3.7	.974	C-50
1955	KC A	6	.250	.250	8	2	0	0	0	0.0	1	0	1	2	0	2	0	8	2	0	0	1.7	1.000	C-4
2 yrs.		69	.187	.239	155	29	8	0	0	0.0	10	8	24	27	0	11	1	215	20	6	6	3.5	.975	C-54

Sherry Robertson

ROBERTSON, SHERRARD ALEXANDER
B. Jan. 1, 1919, Montreal, Que., Canada D. Oct. 23, 1970, Houghton, S. D. BL TR 6' 180 lbs.

Year	Team	Games	BA	SA	AB	H	2B	3B	HR	HR%	R	RBI	BB	SO	SB	AB	H	PO	A	E	DP	TC/G	FA	G by Pos
1940	WAS A	10	.212	.273	33	7	0	1	0	0.0	4	0	5	6	0	0	0	17	30	3	9	5.0	.940	SS-10
1941		1	.000	.000	3	0	0	0	0	0.0	0	0	0	3	0	0	0	1	2	1	0	4.0	.750	3B-1
1943		59	.217	.342	120	26	4	1	3	2.5	22	14	17	19	0	26	5	27	45	8	1	1.4	.900	3B-27, SS-1
1946		74	.200	.330	230	46	6	3	6	2.6	30	19	30	42	6	13	0	88	132	19	22	3.2	.921	3B-38, 2B-14, SS-12, OF-1
1947		95	.233	.301	266	62	9	3	1	0.4	25	23	32	52	4	23	3	144	27	8	2	1.9	.955	OF-55, 3B-10, 2B-4
1948		71	.246	.369	187	46	11	3	2	1.1	19	22	24	26	8	17	7	105	3	7	0	1.6	.939	OF-51
1949		110	.251	.401	374	94	17	3	11	2.9	59	42	42	35	10	9	2	185	253	25	43	4.2	.946	2B-71, 3B-19, OF-13
1950		71	.260	.382	123	32	3	3	2	1.6	19	16	22	18	1	32	7	49	28	4	5	1.1	.951	OF-14, 2B-12, 3B-1
1951		62	.189	.252	111	21	2	1	1	0.9	14	10	9	22	1	34	6	54	2	3	1	1.0	.949	OF-22
1952	2 teams	WAS A (1G – .000)			PHI A	(43G – .200)																		
"	total	44	.200	.250	60	12	3	0	0	0.0	8	5	21	15	1	19	5	26	12	2	2	0.9	.950	2B-8, OF-7, 3B-2
10 yrs.		597	.230	.342	1507	346	55	18	26	1.7	200	151	202	238	32	173	35	696	534	80	85	2.2	.939	OF-163, 2B-109, 3B-98, SS-23

Billy Jo Robidoux

ROBIDOUX, WILLIAM JOSEPH
B. Jan. 13, 1964, Ware, Mass. BL TR 6'1" 200 lbs.

Year	Team	Games	BA	SA	AB	H	2B	3B	HR	HR%	R	RBI	BB	SO	SB	AB	H	PO	A	E	DP	TC/G	FA	G by Pos
1985	MIL A	18	.176	.392	51	9	2	0	3	5.9	5	8	12	16	0	4	0	64	6	0	6	3.9	1.000	OF-11, 1B-6, DH-1
1986		56	.227	.287	181	41	8	0	1	0.6	15	21	33	36	0	2	0	326	29	5	35	6.4	.986	1B-43, DH-10
1987		23	.194	.194	62	12	0	0	0	0.0	9	4	8	17	0	4	0	53	4	1	9	2.5	.983	DH-10, 1B-10
1988		33	.253	.308	91	23	5	0	0	0.0	9	5	8	14	1	3	1	212	25	4	21	7.3	.983	1B-30, DH-1
1989	CHI A	16	.128	.179	39	5	2	0	0	0.0	2	1	4	9	0	1	0	93	7	1	17	6.3	.990	1B-15, OF-1
5 yrs.		146	.212	.281	424	90	17	0	4	0.9	40	39	65	92	1	14	1	748	71	11	88	5.7	.987	1B-104, DH-22, OF-12

Aaron Robinson

ROBINSON, AARON ANDREW
B. June 23, 1915, Lancaster, S. C. D. Mar. 9, 1966, Lancaster, S. C. BL TR 6'2" 205 lbs.

Year	Team	Games	BA	SA	AB	H	2B	3B	HR	HR%	R	RBI	BB	SO	SB	AB	H	PO	A	E	DP	TC/G	FA	G by Pos
1943	NY A	1	.000	.000	1	0	0	0	0	0.0	0	0	0	1	0	0	0	0	0	0	0	0.0	–	C-45
1945		50	.281	.481	160	45	6	1	8	5.0	19	24	21	23	0	4	3	186	16	0	3	4.0	1.000	C-45
1946		100	.297	.506	330	98	17	2	16	4.8	32	64	48	39	0	4	1	410	50	8	5	4.7	.983	C-95
1947		82	.270	.413	252	68	11	5	5	2.0	23	36	40	26	0	7	1	346	38	1	3	4.7	.997	C-74
1948	CHI A	98	.252	.380	326	82	14	2	8	2.5	47	39	46	30	0	6	1	303	50	4	4	3.6	.989	C-92
1949	DET A	110	.269	.423	331	89	12	0	13	3.9	38	56	73	21	0	2	0	458	44	7	9	4.6	.986	C-108
1950		107	.226	.346	283	64	7	0	9	3.2	37	37	75	35	0	3	3	355	42	3	4	3.7	.993	C-103
1951	2 teams	DET A (36G – .207)			BOS A	(26G – .203)																		
"	total	62	.205	.301	156	32	7	1	2	1.3	12	16	34	19	0	2	1	201	31	2	3	3.8	.991	C-60
8 yrs.		610	.260	.412	1839	478	74	11	61	3.3	208	272	337	194	0	29	10	2259	271	25	31	4.2	.990	C-577

WORLD SERIES

Year	Team	Games	BA	SA	AB	H	2B	3B	HR	HR%	R	RBI	BB	SO	SB	AB	H	PO	A	E	DP	TC/G	FA	G by Pos
1947	NY A	3	.200	.200	10	2	0	0	0	0.0	2	1	2	1	0	0	0	13	2	1	0	5.3	.938	C-3

Bill Robinson

ROBINSON, WILLIAM HENRY
B. June 26, 1943, McKeesport, Pa. BR TR 6'2" 189 lbs.

Year	Team	Games	BA	SA	AB	H	2B	3B	HR	HR%	R	RBI	BB	SO	SB	AB	H	PO	A	E	DP	TC/G	FA	G by Pos
1966	ATL N	6	.273	.455	11	3	0	1	0	0.0	1	3	0	1	0	1	0	4	0	1	0	0.8	.800	OF-5
1967	NY A	116	.196	.281	342	67	6	1	7	2.0	31	29	28	56	2	15	0	169	10	6	1	1.6	.968	OF-102
1968		107	.240	.380	342	82	16	7	6	1.8	34	40	26	54	7	9	1	195	3	3	1	1.9	.985	OF-98
1969	PHI N	87	.171	.279	222	38	11	2	3	1.4	23	21	16	39	3	29	4	103	5	4	0	1.3	.964	OF-62, 1B-1
1972	PHI N	82	.239	.426	188	45	9	1	8	4.3	19	21	5	30	2	9	1	109	2	2	1	1.4	.982	OF-72
1973		124	.288	.529	452	130	32	1	25	5.5	62	65	27	91	5	12	4	234	18	8	1	2.1	.969	OF-113, 3B-14
1974		100	.236	.346	280	66	14	1	5	1.8	32	29	17	61	5	19	5	162	8	5	0	1.8	.971	OF-87
1975	PIT N	92	.280	.450	200	56	12	2	6	3.0	26	33	11	36	3	33	5	107	3	1	0	1.2	.991	OF-57
1976		122	.303	.534	393	119	22	3	21	5.3	55	64	16	73	2	11	5	186	53	8	11	2.0	.968	OF-58, 3B-37, 1B-3
1977		137	.304	.525	507	154	32	1	26	5.1	74	104	25	92	12	8	0	758	59	13	63	6.1	.984	1B-86, OF-43, 3B-17
1978		136	.246	.411	499	123	36	2	14	2.8	70	80	35	105	14	0	0	268	51	8	8	2.4	.976	OF-127, 3B-29, 1B-3
1979		148	.264	.504	421	111	17	6	24	5.7	59	75	24	81	13	12	3	394	19	3	18	2.8	.993	OF-125, 1B-28, 3B-3
1980		100	.287	.463	272	78	10	0	12	4.4	28	36	15	45	1	16	5	427	22	7	30	4.6	.985	1B-49, OF-41

Year	Team		Games	BA	SA	AB	H	2B	3B	HR	HR%	R	RBI	BB	SO	SB	Pinch Hit AB	H	PO	A	E	DP	TC/G	FA	G by Pos

Bill Robinson *continued*

1981			39	.216	.318	88	19	3	0	2	2.3	8	8	5	18	1	15	1	148	10	2	9	4.1	.988	1B-23, OF-7, 3B-1
1982	2 teams	PIT N (31G – .239)		PHI N (35G – .261)																					
"	total		66	.250	.464	140	35	9	0	7	5.0	14	31	12	34	1	26	5	69	4	1	5	1.1	.986	OF-41, 1B-5
1983	PHI N		10	.143	.143	7	1	0	0	0	0.0	0	0	1	4	0	7	1	3	0	1	0	0.4	.750	1B-3, 3B-2, OF-1
16 yrs.			1472	.258	.438	4364	1127	229	29	166	3.8	536	641	263	820	71	222	40	3336	267	73	149	2.5	.980	OF-1059, 1B-201, 3B-103

LEAGUE CHAMPIONSHIP SERIES

1975	PIT N		2	.000	.000	2	0	0	0	0	0.0	0	0	0	1	0	2	0	0	0	0	0	0.0	–	
1979			3	.000	.000	3	0	0	0	0	0.0	0	0	0	0	0	0	0	3	0	0	0	1.0	1.000	OF-3
2 yrs.			5	.000	.000	5	0	0	0	0	0.0	0	0	0	1	0	2	0	3	0	0	0	0.6	1.000	OF-3

WORLD SERIES

| 1979 | PIT N | | 7 | .263 | .316 | 19 | 5 | 1 | 0 | 0 | 0.0 | 2 | 2 | 0 | 4 | 0 | 1 | 1 | 11 | 1 | 0 | 0 | 1.7 | 1.000 | OF-6 |

Brooks Robinson

ROBINSON, BROOKS CALBERT
B. May 18, 1937, Little Rock, Ark.
Hall of Fame 1983.

BR TR 6'1" 180 lbs.

1955	BAL A		6	.091	.091	22	2	0	0	0	0.0	0	1	0	10	0	0	0	2	8	2	1	2.0	.833	3B-6
1956			15	.227	.386	44	10	4	0	1	2.3	5	1	1	5	0	1	0	9	25	2	3	2.4	.944	3B-14, 2B-1
1957			50	.239	.359	117	28	6	1	2	1.7	13	14	7	10	1	5	0	34	66	3	5	2.1	.971	3B-47
1958			145	.238	.305	463	110	16	3	3	0.6	31	32	31	51	1	4	1	157	283	22	32	3.2	.952	3B-140, 2B-16
1959			88	.284	.383	313	89	15	2	4	1.3	29	24	17	37	2	1	1	92	187	13	25	3.3	.955	3B-87, 2B-1
1960			152	.294	.440	595	175	27	9	14	2.4	74	88	35	49	2	0	0	174	330	12	35	3.4	.977	3B-152, 2B-3
1961			163	.287	.397	668	192	38	7	7	1.0	89	61	47	57	1	0	0	155	334	14	34	3.1	.972	3B-163, 2B-2, SS-1
1962			162	.303	.486	634	192	29	9	23	3.6	77	86	42	70	3	0	0	165	340	11	32	3.2	.979	3B-162, 2B-3, SS-2
1963			161	.251	.365	589	148	26	4	11	1.9	67	67	46	84	2	1	0	153	331	12	43	3.1	.976	3B-160, SS-1
1964			163	.317	.521	612	194	35	3	28	4.6	82	118	51	64	1	0	0	153	327	14	40	3.0	.972	3B-163
1965			144	.297	.445	559	166	25	2	18	3.2	81	80	47	47	3	1	1	144	296	15	36	3.2	.967	3B-143
1966			157	.269	.444	620	167	35	2	23	3.7	91	100	56	36	2	0	0	174	313	12	26	3.2	.976	3B-157
1967			158	.269	.434	610	164	25	5	22	3.6	88	77	54	54	1	0	0	147	405	11	37	3.6	.980	3B-158
1968			162	.253	.416	608	154	36	6	17	2.8	65	75	44	55	1	0	0	168	353	16	31	3.3	.970	3B-162
1969			156	.234	.395	598	140	21	3	23	3.8	73	84	56	55	2	0	0	163	370	13	37	3.5	.976	3B-156
1970			158	.276	.429	608	168	31	4	18	3.0	84	94	53	53	1	2	0	157	321	17	30	3.1	.966	3B-156
1971			156	.272	.413	589	160	21	1	20	3.4	67	92	63	50	0	0	0	131	354	16	35	3.2	.968	3B-156
1972			153	.250	.342	556	139	23	2	8	1.4	48	64	43	45	1	3	0	129	333	11	27	3.1	.977	3B-152
1973			155	.257	.344	549	141	17	2	9	1.6	53	72	55	50	2	1	0	129	354	15	25	3.2	.970	3B-154
1974			153	.288	.374	553	159	27	0	7	1.3	46	59	56	47	2	0	0	115	410	18	44	3.5	.967	3B-153
1975			144	.201	.274	482	97	15	1	6	1.2	50	53	44	33	0	2	0	96	326	9	30	3.0	.979	3B-143
1976			71	.211	.307	218	46	8	2	3	1.4	16	11	8	24	0	2	0	59	126	6	11	2.7	.969	3B-71
1977			24	.149	.255	47	7	2	0	1	2.1	3	4	4	4	0	8	1	6	28	0	2	1.4	1.000	3B-15
23 yrs.			2896	.267 8th	.401 7th	10654	2848	482	68	268	2.5	1232	1357	860	990	28	31	4	2712	6220	264	621	3.2	.971	3B-2870, 2B-25, SS-5

LEAGUE CHAMPIONSHIP SERIES

1969	BAL A		3	.500	.571	14	7	1	0	0	0.0	1	0	0	0	0	0	0	5	10	0	0	5.0	1.000	3B-3
1970			3	.583	.750	12	7	2	0	0	0.0	4	1	0	1	0	0	0	3	5	0	0	2.7	1.000	3B-3
1971			3	.364	.727	11	4	1	0	1	9.1	2	3	0	1	0	0	0	4	7	0	0	3.7	1.000	3B-3
1973			5	.250	.350	20	5	2	0	0	0.0	1	2	1	1	0	0	0	2	14	1	0	3.4	.941	3B-5
1974			4	.083	.333	12	1	0	0	1	8.3	1	1	1	0	0	0	0	4	13	0	1	4.3	1.000	3B-4
5 yrs.			18	.348	.522	69	24	6	0	2	2.9	9	7	2	3	0	0	0	18	49	1	1	3.8	.985	3B-18

WORLD SERIES

1966	BAL A		4	.214	.429	14	3	0	0	1	7.1	2	1	1	0	0	0	0	4	6	0	1	2.5	1.000	3B-4
1969			5	.053	.053	19	1	0	0	0	0.0	0	0	2	3	0	0	0	1	16	0	0	3.4	1.000	3B-5
1970			5	.429	.810	21	9	2	0	2	9.5	5	6	0	0	0	0	0	9	14	1	2	4.8	.958	3B-5
1971			7	.318	.318	22	7	0	0	0	0.0	2	5	3	1	0	0	0	6	17	2	1	3.6	.920	3B-7
4 yrs.			21	.263	.408	76	20	2	0	3	3.9	9	14	4	4	0	0	0	20	53	3	4	3.6	.961	3B-21

Bruce Robinson

ROBINSON, BRUCE PHILIP
Brother of Dave Robinson.
B. Apr. 16, 1954, LaJolla, Calif.

BL TR 6'1" 185 lbs.

1978	OAK A		28	.250	.310	84	21	3	1	0	0.0	5	8	3	8	0	1	0	150	16	6	2	6.1	.965	C-28
1979	NY A		6	.167	.167	12	2	0	0	0	0.0	0	2	1	0	0	0	0	33	0	2	1	5.8	.943	C-6
1980			4	.000	.000	5	0	0	0	0	0.0	0	0	0	4	0	1	0	5	0	0	0	1.3	1.000	C-3
3 yrs.			38	.228	.277	101	23	3	1	0	0.0	5	10	4	12	0	2	0	188	16	8	3	5.6	.962	C-37

Charlie Robinson

ROBINSON, CHARLES HENRY
B. July 27, 1856, Westerly, R. I.   D. May 18, 1913, Providence, R. I.

BL TR

1884	IND AA		20	.288	.313	80	23	2	0	0	0.0	11		3			0	0	98	31	5	3	6.7	.963	C-17, SS-3, OF-1
1885	BKN AA		11	.150	.250	40	6	2	1	0	0.0	5		3			0	0	47	16	12	1	6.8	.840	C-11
2 yrs.			31	.242	.292	120	29	4	1	0	0.0	16		6			0	0	145	47	17	4	6.7	.919	C-28, SS-3, OF-1

Craig Robinson

ROBINSON, CRAIG GEORGE
B. Aug. 21, 1948, Abington, Pa.

BR TR 5'10" 165 lbs.

1972	PHI N		5	.200	.267	15	3	1	0	0	0.0	1	2	0	2	0	0	0	4	16	0	4	4.0	1.000	SS-4
1973			46	.226	.274	146	33	7	0	0	0.0	11	7	0	25	1	2	0	70	112	10	26	4.2	.948	SS-42, 2B-4
1974	ATL N		145	.230	.265	452	104	4	1	0	0.0	52	29	30	57	11	1	1	238	395	29	73	4.6	.956	SS-142
1975	2 teams	ATL N (11G – .059)		SF N (29G – .069)																					
"	total		40	.065	.087	46	3	1	0	0	0.0	5	0	2	11	0	2	0	34	37	4	9	1.9	.947	SS-19, 2B-9
1976	2 teams	SF N (15G – .308)		ATL N (15G – .235)																					
"	total		30	.267	.300	30	8	1	0	0	0.0	8	5	8	6	0	3	2	12	36	5	4	1.8	.906	2B-12, SS-3, 3B-3

Year	Team		Games	BA	SA	AB	H	2B	3B	HR	HR%	R	RBI	BB	SO	SB	Pinch Hit AB	H	PO	A	E	DP	TC/G	FA	G by Pos

Craig Robinson *continued*

Year	Team		Games	BA	SA	AB	H	2B	3B	HR	HR%	R	RBI	BB	SO	SB	AB	H	PO	A	E	DP	TC/G	FA	G by Pos
1977	ATL	N	27	.207	.241	29	6	1	0	0	0.0	4	1	1	6	0	4	0	26	27	0	6	2.0	1.000	SS-23
6 yrs.			293	.219	.256	718	157	15	6	0	0.0	80	42	42	107	12	12	3	384	623	48	122	3.6	.955	SS-233, 2B-25, 3B-3

Dave Robinson

ROBINSON, DAVID TANNER
Brother of Bruce Robinson.
B. May 22, 1946, Minneapolis, Minn.

BB TL 6'1" 186 lbs.

Year	Team		Games	BA	SA	AB	H	2B	3B	HR	HR%	R	RBI	BB	SO	SB	AB	H	PO	A	E	DP	TC/G	FA	G by Pos
1970	SD	N	15	.316	.526	38	12	2	0	2	5.3	5	6	5	4	2	2	0	22	1	0	1	1.5	1.000	OF-13
1971			7	.000	.000	6	0	0	0	0	0.0	0	0	1	3	0	6	0	0	0	0	0	0.0	—	OF-13
2 yrs.			22	.273	.455	44	12	2	0	2	4.5	5	6	6	7	2	8	0	22	1	0	1	1.0	1.000	OF-13

Earl Robinson

ROBINSON, EARL JOHN
B. Nov. 3, 1936, New Orleans, La.

BR TR 6'1" 190 lbs.

Year	Team		Games	BA	SA	AB	H	2B	3B	HR	HR%	R	RBI	BB	SO	SB	AB	H	PO	A	E	DP	TC/G	FA	G by Pos
1958	LA	N	8	.200	.200	15	3	0	0	0	0.0	3	0	1	4	0	0	0	4	10	0	0	1.8	1.000	3B-6
1961	BAL	A	96	.266	.455	222	59	12	3	8	3.6	37	30	31	54	4	20	5	136	6	4	3	1.5	.973	OF-82
1962			29	.286	.413	63	18	3	1	1	1.6	12	4	8	10	2	6	3	35	0	0	0	1.2	1.000	OF-17
1964			37	.273	.405	121	33	5	1	3	2.5	11	10	7	24	1	2	1	67	3	1	0	1.9	.986	OF-34
4 yrs.			170	.268	.425	421	113	20	5	12	2.9	63	44	47	92	7	28	9	242	19	5	3	1.6	.981	OF-133, 3B-6

Eddie Robinson

ROBINSON, WILLIAM EDWARD
B. Dec. 15, 1920, Paris, Tex.

BL TR 6'2½" 210 lbs.

Year	Team		Games	BA	SA	AB	H	2B	3B	HR	HR%	R	RBI	BB	SO	SB	AB	H	PO	A	E	DP	TC/G	FA	G by Pos
1942	CLE	A	8	.125	.125	8	1	0	0	0	0.0	1	2	1	0	0	6	1	7	0	0	0	0.9	1.000	1B-1
1946			8	.400	.733	30	12	1	0	3	10.0	6	4	2	4	0	0	0	71	1	1	4	9.1	.986	1B-7
1947			95	.245	.415	318	78	10	1	14	4.4	52	52	30	18	1	5	1	800	55	5	79	9.1	.994	1B-87
1948			134	.254	.408	493	125	18	5	16	3.2	53	83	36	42	1	4	1	1213	79	7	123	9.7	.995	1B-131
1949	WAS	A	143	.294	.459	527	155	27	3	18	3.4	67	78	67	30	3	0	0	1299	100	18	133	9.9	.987	1B-143
1950 2 teams	WAS	A	(36G – .233)		CHI	A	(119G – .314)																		
" total			155	.295	.450	553	163	15	4	21	3.8	83	86	85	32	0	4	0	1300	82	14	141	9.0	.990	1B-155
1951	CHI	A	151	.282	.495	564	159	23	5	29	5.1	85	117	77	54	2	2	0	1296	91	17	143	9.3	.988	1B-147
1952			155	.296	.466	594	176	33	1	22	3.7	79	104	70	49	2	0	0	1329	89	14	145	9.2	.990	1B-155
1953	PHI	A	156	.247	.413	615	152	28	4	22	3.6	64	102	63	56	1	1	0	1366	71	17	135	9.3	.988	1B-155
1954	NY	A	85	.261	.387	142	37	9	0	3	2.1	11	27	19	21	0	49	15	227	19	5	21	3.0	.980	1B-29
1955			88	.208	.491	173	36	1	0	16	9.2	25	42	36	26	0	34	5	390	20	2	35	4.7	.995	1B-46
1956 2 teams	NY	A	(26G – .222)		KC	A	(75G – .198)																		
" total			101	.204	.332	226	46	6	1	7	3.1	20	23	31	23	0	34	6	481	25	9	56	5.1	.983	1B-61
1957 3 teams	DET	A	(13G – .000)		CLE	A	(19G – .222)		BAL	A	(4G – .000)														
" total			36	.154	.256	39	6	1	0	1	2.6	3	4	4	4	0	21	1	44	4	0	3	1.3	1.000	1B-8
13 yrs.			1315	.268	.440	4282	1146	172	24	172	4.0	546	723	521	359	10	156	30	9823	636	109	1018	8.0	.990	1B-1125

WORLD SERIES

Year	Team		Games	BA	SA	AB	H	2B	3B	HR	HR%	R	RBI	BB	SO	SB	AB	H	PO	A	E	DP	TC/G	FA	G by Pos
1948	CLE	A	6	.300	.300	20	6	0	0	0	0.0	0	1	1	0	0	0	0	60	7	0	8	11.2	1.000	1B-6
1955	NY	A	4	.667	.667	3	2	0	0	0	0.0	0	1	2	1	0	1	1	6	0	0	2	1.5	1.000	1B-1
2 yrs.			10	.348	.348	23	8	0	0	0	0.0	0	2	3	1	0	1	1	66	7	0	10	7.3	1.000	1B-7

Floyd Robinson

ROBINSON, FLOYD ANDREW
B. May 9, 1936, Prescott, Ark.

BL TR 5'9" 175 lbs.

Year	Team		Games	BA	SA	AB	H	2B	3B	HR	HR%	R	RBI	BB	SO	SB	AB	H	PO	A	E	DP	TC/G	FA	G by Pos
1960	CHI	A	22	.283	.283	46	13	0	0	0	0.0	7	1	11	8	2	4	0	24	0	1	0	1.1	.960	OF-17
1961			132	.310	.465	432	134	20	7	11	2.5	69	59	52	32	7	23	6	218	7	2	0	1.7	.991	OF-106
1962			156	.312	.475	600	187	**45**	10	11	1.8	89	109	72	47	4	1	0	278	13	8	2	1.9	.973	OF-155
1963			146	.283	.419	527	149	21	6	13	2.5	71	71	62	43	4	9	2	245	8	4	4	1.8	.984	OF-137
1964			141	.301	.408	525	158	17	3	11	2.1	83	59	70	41	9	6	2	225	5	3	0	1.7	.987	OF-138
1965			156	.265	.385	577	153	15	6	14	2.4	70	66	76	51	4	9	2	254	6	4	0	1.7	.985	OF-153
1966	CIN	N	127	.237	.325	342	81	11	2	5	1.5	44	35	44	32	8	17	0	148	2	6	0	1.2	.962	OF-113
1967			55	.238	.338	130	31	1	2	1	0.8	19	10	14	14	3	15	2	53	0	1	0	1.0	.981	OF-39
1968 2 teams	OAK	A	(53G – .247)		BOS	A	(24G – .125)																		
" total			77	.219	.295	105	23	4	0	1	1.0	6	16	7	14	1	42	9	25	1	1	0	0.4	.963	OF-29
9 yrs.			1012	.283	.409	3284	929	140	36	67	2.0	458	426	408	282	42	126	23	1470	42	30	6	1.5	.981	OF-887

Frank Robinson

ROBINSON, FRANK
B. Aug. 31, 1935, Beaumont, Tex.
Manager 1975-77, 1981-84, 1988-89.
Hall of Fame 1982.

BR TR 6'1" 183 lbs.

Year	Team		Games	BA	SA	AB	H	2B	3B	HR	HR%	R	RBI	BB	SO	SB	AB	H	PO	A	E	DP	TC/G	FA	G by Pos
1956	CIN	N	152	.290	.558	572	166	27	6	38	6.6	**122**	83	64	95	8	0	0	323	5	8	1	2.2	.976	OF-152
1957			150	.322	.529	611	197	29	5	29	4.7	97	75	44	92	10	0	0	487	36	6	19	3.5	.989	OF-136, 1B-24
1958			148	.269	.504	554	149	25	6	31	5.6	90	83	62	80	10	5	0	314	24	6	1	2.3	.983	OF-138, 3B-11
1959			146	.311	.583	540	168	31	4	36	6.7	106	125	69	93	18	0	0	1049	78	18	111	7.8	.984	1B-125, OF-40
1960			139	.297	.595	464	138	33	6	31	6.7	86	83	82	67	13	10	5	775	62	10	61	6.1	.988	1B-78, OF-51, 3B-1
1961			153	.323	.611	545	176	32	7	37	6.8	117	124	71	64	22	4	2	284	15	3	3	2.0	.990	OF-150, 3B-1
1962			162	.342	.624	609	208	**51**	2	39	6.4	**134**	136	76	62	18	0	0	315	10	2	2	2.0	.994	OF-161
1963			140	.259	.442	482	125	19	3	21	4.4	79	91	81	69	26	2	1	238	13	4	1	1.8	.984	OF-139, 1B-1
1964			156	.306	.548	568	174	38	6	29	5.1	103	96	79	67	23	0	0	279	7	4	3	1.9	.986	OF-156
1965			156	.296	.540	582	172	33	5	33	5.7	109	113	70	100	13	1	1	282	5	3	1	1.9	.990	OF-155
1966	BAL	A	155	**.316**	**.637**	576	182	34	2	49	8.5	122	122	87	90	8	1	0	282	6	5	3	1.9	.983	OF-151, 1B-3
1967			129	.311	.576	479	149	23	7	30	6.3	83	94	71	84	2	0	0	207	8	2	3	1.7	.991	OF-126, 1B-3
1968			130	.268	.444	421	113	27	1	15	3.6	69	52	73	84	11	12	4	193	5	7	0	1.6	.966	OF-117, 1B-3
1969			148	.308	.540	539	166	19	5	32	5.9	111	100	88	62	9	3	2	367	15	5	18	2.6	.987	OF-134, 1B-9
1970			132	.306	.520	471	144	24	1	25	5.3	88	78	69	70	2	6	3	262	11	4	6	2.1	.986	OF-120, 1B-7
1971			133	.281	.510	455	128	16	2	28	6.2	82	99	72	62	3	8	0	449	20	11	25	3.6	.977	OF-92, 1B-37
1972	LA	N	103	.251	.442	342	86	6	1	19	5.6	41	59	55	76	2	5	0	168	6	6	2	1.7	.967	OF-95
1973	CAL	A	147	.266	.489	534	142	29	0	30	5.6	85	97	82	93	1	2	1	38	3	1	1	0.3	.976	DH-127, OF-17

Year	Team	Games	BA	SA	AB	H	2B	3B	HR	HR%	R	RBI	BB	SO	SB	Pinch Hit AB	Pinch Hit H	PO	A	E	DP	TC/G	FA	G by Pos

Frank Robinson *continued*

Year	Team	Games	BA	SA	AB	H	2B	3B	HR	HR%	R	RBI	BB	SO	SB	PH AB	PH H	PO	A	E	DP	TC/G	FA	G by Pos
1974	2 teams	CAL A (129G – .251)		CLE A (15G – .200)																				
"	total	144	.245	.453	477	117	27	3	22	4.6	81	68	85	95	5	6	0	23	0	1	1	0.2	.958	DH-134, 1B-4, OF-1
1975	CLE A	49	.237	.508	118	28	5	0	9	7.6	19	24	29	15	0	6	2	0	0	0	0	0.0	–	DH-42
1976		36	.224	.358	67	15	0	0	3	4.5	5	10	11	12	0	16	5	11	0	0	1	0.3	1.000	DH-18, 1B-2, OF-1
21 yrs.		2808	.294	.537	10006	2943	528	72	586 4th	5.9	1829	1812 10th	1420	1532	204	87	28	6346	333	106	263	2.4	.984	OF-2132, DH-321, 1B-305, 3B-13

LEAGUE CHAMPIONSHIP SERIES

Year	Team	Games	BA	SA	AB	H	2B	3B	HR	HR%	R	RBI	BB	SO	SB	PH AB	PH H	PO	A	E	DP	TC/G	FA	G by Pos
1969	BAL A	3	.333	.750	12	4	2	0	1	8.3	1	2	3	3	0	0	0	2	0	1	0	1.0	.667	OF-3
1970		3	.200	.500	10	2	0	0	1	10.0	3	2	5	2	0	0	0	2	0	0	0	0.7	1.000	OF-3
1971		3	.083	.167	12	1	1	0	0	0.0	2	1	1	4	0	0	0	7	0	0	0	2.3	1.000	OF-3
3 yrs.		9	.206	.471	34	7	3	0	2	5.9	6	5	9	9	0	0	0	11	0	1	0	1.3	.917	OF-9

WORLD SERIES

Year	Team	Games	BA	SA	AB	H	2B	3B	HR	HR%	R	RBI	BB	SO	SB	PH AB	PH H	PO	A	E	DP	TC/G	FA	G by Pos
1961	CIN N	5	.200	.533	15	3	2	0	1	6.7	3	4	3	4	0	0	0	5	0	0	0	1.0	1.000	OF-5
1966	BAL A	4	.286	.857	14	4	0	1	2	14.3	4	3	2	0	0	0	0	6	0	0	0	1.5	1.000	OF-4
1969		5	.188	.375	16	3	0	0	1	6.3	2	1	4	3	0	0	0	13	0	0	0	2.6	1.000	OF-5
1970		5	.273	.545	22	6	0	0	2	9.1	5	4	0	5	0	0	0	7	0	0	0	1.4	1.000	OF-5
1971		7	.280	.520	25	7	0	0	2	8.0	5	2	2	8	0	0	0	12	0	0	0	1.7	1.000	OF-7
5 yrs.		26	.250	.554	92	23	2	1	8 7th	8.7	19 3rd	14	11	23 10th	0	0	0	43	0	0	0	1.7	1.000	OF-26

Fred Robinson

ROBINSON, FREDERIC HENRY
Brother of Wilbert Robinson.
B. July 6, 1856, South Acton, Mass.   D. Dec. 18, 1933, Hudson, Mass.

BR TR

Year	Team	Games	BA	SA	AB	H	2B	3B	HR	HR%	R	RBI	BB	SO	SB	PH AB	PH H	PO	A	E	DP	TC/G	FA	G by Pos
1884	CIN U	3	.231	.231	13	3	0	0	0	0.0	1		0			0	0	2	6	3	0	3.7	.727	2B-3

Jack Robinson

ROBINSON, JOHN W.
B. July 15, 1880, Portland, Me.   D. July 22, 1921, Macon, Ga.

TR

Year	Team	Games	BA	SA	AB	H	2B	3B	HR	HR%	R	RBI	BB	SO	SB	PH AB	PH H	PO	A	E	DP	TC/G	FA	G by Pos
1902	NY N	4	.000	.000	9	0	0	0	0	0.0	0	0	0		0	1	0	13	3	0	0	4.0	1.000	C-3

Jackie Robinson

ROBINSON, JACK ROOSEVELT
B. Jan. 31, 1919, Cairo, Ga.   D. Oct. 24, 1972, Stamford, Conn.
Hall of Fame 1962.

BR TR 5'11½" 195 lbs.

Year	Team	Games	BA	SA	AB	H	2B	3B	HR	HR%	R	RBI	BB	SO	SB	PH AB	PH H	PO	A	E	DP	TC/G	FA	G by Pos
1947	BKN N	151	.297	.427	590	175	31	5	12	2.0	125	48	74	36	29	0	0	1323	92	16	144	9.5	.989	1B-151
1948		147	.296	.453	574	170	38	8	12	2.1	108	85	57	37	22	2	1	514	342	15	97	5.9	.983	2B-116, 1B-30, 3B-6
1949		156	.342	.528	593	203	38	12	16	2.7	122	124	86	27	37	0	0	395	421	16	119	5.3	.981	2B-156
1950		144	.328	.500	518	170	39	4	14	2.7	99	81	80	24	12	2	1	359	390	11	133	5.3	.986	2B-144
1951		153	.338	.527	548	185	33	7	19	3.5	106	88	79	27	25	3	1	390	435	7	137	5.4	.992	2B-153
1952		149	.308	.465	510	157	17	3	19	3.7	104	75	106	40	24	2	0	353	400	20	113	5.2	.974	2B-146
1953		136	.329	.502	484	159	34	7	12	2.5	109	95	74	30	17	5	1	238	126	6	25	2.7	.984	OF-76, 3B-44, 2B-9, 1B-6, SS-1
1954		124	.311	.505	386	120	22	4	15	3.9	62	59	63	20	7	7	1	166	109	7	6	2.3	.975	OF-64, 3B-50, 2B-4
1955		105	.256	.363	317	81	6	2	8	2.5	51	36	61	18	12	9	1	100	183	10	19	2.8	.966	3B-84, OF-10, 2B-1, 1B-1
1956		117	.275	.412	357	98	15	2	10	2.8	61	43	60	32	12	10	1	169	230	9	37	3.5	.978	3B-72, 2B-22, 1B-9, OF-2
10 yrs.		1382	.311	.474	4877	1518	273	54	137	2.8	947	734	740	291	197	40	7	4007	2728	117	830	5.0	.983	2B-751, 3B-256, 1B-197, OF-152, SS-1

WORLD SERIES

Year	Team	Games	BA	SA	AB	H	2B	3B	HR	HR%	R	RBI	BB	SO	SB	PH AB	PH H	PO	A	E	DP	TC/G	FA	G by Pos
1947	BKN N	7	.259	.333	27	7	2	0	0	0.0	3	3	2	4	2	0	0	49	6	0	8	7.9	1.000	1B-7
1949		5	.188	.250	16	3	1	0	0	0.0	2	2	4	2	0	0	0	12	9	1	1	4.4	.955	2B-5
1952		7	.174	.304	23	4	0	0	1	4.3	4	2	7	5	2	0	0	10	20	0	4	4.3	1.000	2B-7
1953		6	.320	.400	25	8	2	0	0	0.0	3	2	1	1	0	0	0	8	0	0	0	1.3	1.000	OF-6
1955		6	.182	.318	22	4	1	1	0	0.0	5	1	2	1	1	0	0	4	18	2	3	4.0	.917	3B-6
1956		7	.250	.417	24	6	1	0	1	4.2	5	2	5	2	0	0	0	5	12	0	1	2.4	1.000	3B-7
6 yrs.		38	.234	.343	137	32	7 9th	1	2	1.5	22 9th	12	21	14 8th	6	0	0	88	65	3	17	4.1	.981	3B-13, 2B-12, 1B-7, OF-6

Rabbit Robinson

ROBINSON, WILLIAM CLYDE (Tug)
B. Mar. 5, 1882, Wellsburg, W. Va.   D. Apr. 9, 1915, Waterbury, Conn.

BR TR 5'6" 148 lbs.

Year	Team	Games	BA	SA	AB	H	2B	3B	HR	HR%	R	RBI	BB	SO	SB	PH AB	PH H	PO	A	E	DP	TC/G	FA	G by Pos
1903	WAS A	103	.212	.290	373	79	10	8	1	0.3	41	20	33		16	0	0	185	248	43	27	4.6	.910	2B-45, OF-30, SS-24, 3B-5
1904	DET A	101	.241	.319	320	77	13	6	0	0.0	30	37	29		14	5	1	151	216	22	17	3.9	.943	SS-30, 3B-26, OF-20, 2B-19
1910	CIN N	2	.000	.000	7	0	0	0	0	0.0	0	1	1		0	0	0	1	2	0	0	1.5	1.000	3B-2
3 yrs.		206	.223	.300	700	156	23	14	1	0.1	71	58	63	0	30	5	1	337	466	65	44	4.2	.925	2B-64, SS-54, OF-50, 3B-33

Wilbert Robinson

ROBINSON, WILBERT (Uncle Robbie)
Brother of Fred Robinson.
B. June 29, 1863, Bolton, Mass.   D. Aug. 8, 1934, Atlanta, Ga.
Manager 1902, 1914-31.
Hall of Fame 1945.

BR TR 5'8½" 215 lbs.

Year	Team	Games	BA	SA	AB	H	2B	3B	HR	HR%	R	RBI	BB	SO	SB	PH AB	PH H	PO	A	E	DP	TC/G	FA	G by Pos
1886	PHI AA	87	.202	.260	342	69	11	3	1	0.3	57		21		0	0	0	442	118	58	26	7.1	.906	C-61, 1B-22, OF-5
1887		68	.227	.277	264	60	6	2	1	0.4	28		14		15	0	0	291	138	50	9	7.0	.896	C-67, 1B-3, OF-1
1888		66	.244	.299	254	62	7	2	1	0.4	32	31	9		11	0	0	437	143	39	7	9.4	.937	C-65, 1B-1
1889		69	.231	.295	264	61	13	2	0	0.0	31	28	6	34	9	0	0	290	106	24	8	6.1	.943	C-69
1890	2 teams	PHI AA (82G – .237)		BAL AA (14G – .271)																				
"	total	96	.241	.332	377	91	14	4	4	1.1	39		19		21	0	0	515	115	41	14	7.0	.939	C-93, 1B-3
1891	BAL AA	93	.216	.287	334	72	8	5	2	0.6	25	46	16	37	18	0	0	415	80	25	11	5.6	.952	C-92, OF-1
1892	BAL N	90	.267	.352	330	88	14	4	2	0.6	36	57	15	35	5	0	0	349	86	38	11	5.3	.920	C-87, 1B-2, OF-1
1893		95	.334	.435	359	120	21	3	3	0.8	49	57	26	22	17	1	0	350	72	26	8	4.7	.942	C-93, 1B-1
1894		109	.353	.430	414	146	21	4	1	0.2	69	98	46	18	12	0	0	370	84	27	8	4.4	.944	C-109
1895		77	.262	.337	282	74	19	6	0	0.0	38	48	12	19	11	2	1	243	78	7	6	4.3	.979	C-75

Year	Team		Games	BA	SA	AB	H	2B	3B	HR	HR%	R	RBI	BB	SO	SB	Pinch Hit AB	H	PO	A	E	DP	TC/G	FA	G by Pos

Wilbert Robinson *continued*

Year	Team		Games	BA	SA	AB	H	2B	3B	HR	HR%	R	RBI	BB	SO	SB	AB	H	PO	A	E	DP	TC/G	FA	G by Pos
1896			67	.347	.457	245	85	9	6	2	0.8	43	38	14	13	9	0	0	260	48	17	5	4.9	.948	C-67
1897			48	.315	.365	181	57	9	0	0	0.0	25	23	8		0	0	0	184	36	8	2	4.8	.965	C-48
1898			79	.277	.332	289	80	12	2	0	0.0	29	38	16		3	1	1	288	72	13	4	4.7	.965	C-77
1899			108	.284	.337	356	101	15	2	0	0.0	40	47	31		5	3	2	286	83	20	2	3.6	.949	C-105
1900	STL	N	60	.248	.281	210	52	5	1	0	0.0	26	28	11		7	5	1	189	72	7	3	4.5	.974	C-54
1901	BAL	A	68	.301	.377	239	72	12	3	0	0.0	32	26	10		9	1	0	235	61	16	4	4.6	.949	C-67
1902			91	.293	.391	335	98	16	7	1	0.3	39	57	12		11	4	2	262	75	18	4	3.9	.949	C-87
17 yrs.			1371	.273	.346	5075	1388	212	51	18	0.4	638	622	286	178	163	17	7	5406	1467	434	132	5.3	.941	C-1316, 1B-32, OF-8

Yank Robinson

ROBINSON, WILLIAM H.
B. Sept. 19, 1859, Philadelphia, Pa.   D. Aug. 25, 1894, St. Louis, Mo.

BR TR 5'6½" 170 lbs.

Year	Team		Games	BA	SA	AB	H	2B	3B	HR	HR%	R	RBI	BB	SO	SB	AB	H	PO	A	E	DP	TC/G	FA	G by Pos
1882	DET	N	11	.179	.205	39	7	1	0	0	0.0	1	2	1	13		0	0	11	23	8	2	3.8	.810	SS-10, OF-1, P-1
1884	BAL	U	102	.267	.359	415	111	24	4	2	0.5	101		37			0	0	219	238	90	14	5.4	.835	3B-71, SS-14, C-11, P-11, 2B-3
1885	STL	AA	78	.261	.345	287	75	8	8	0	0.0	63		29			0	0	155	76	32	7	3.4	.878	OF-52, 2B-19, C-5, 3B-2, 1B-1
1886			133	.274	.385	481	132	26	9	3	0.6	89		64			0	0	362	418	103	69	6.6	.883	2B-125, 3B-6, OF-1, SS-1, P-1
1887			125	.305	.405	430	131	32	4	1	0.2	102		92		75	0	0	332	368	83	52	6.3	.894	2B-117, 3B-6, OF-2, SS-2, C-1, P-1
1888			134	.231	.314	455	105	17	6	3	0.7	111	53	116		56	0	0	251	350	72	24	5.0	.893	2B-102, SS-34
1889			132	.208	.292	452	94	17	3	5	1.1	97	70	118	55	39	0	0	305	333	81	53	5.4	.887	2B-132
1890	PIT	P	98	.229	.281	306	70	10	3	0	0.0	59	38	101	33	17	0	0	226	286	65	46	5.9	.887	2B-98
1891	2 teams			CIN AA (97G – .178)			STL AA (1G – .000)																			
"	total		98	.177	.235	345	61	9	4	1	0.3	48	37	68	51	23	0	0	225	287	79	33	6.0	.866	2B-98
1892	WAS	N	67	.179	.225	218	39	4	3	0	0.0	26	19	38	28	11	0	0	86	146	42	13	4.1	.847	3B-58, SS-5, 2B-4
10 yrs.			978	.241	.323	3428	825	148	44	15	0.4	697	219	664	180	221	0	0	2172	2525	655	313	5.5	.878	2B-698, 3B-143, SS-66, OF-56, C-17, P-14, 1B-1

Rafael Robles

ROBLES, RAFAEL ORLANDO
Born Rafael Orlando Robles y Natera.
B. Oct. 20, 1947, San Pedro de Macoris, Dominican Republic

BR TR 6' 170 lbs.

Year	Team		Games	BA	SA	AB	H	2B	3B	HR	HR%	R	RBI	BB	SO	SB	AB	H	PO	A	E	DP	TC/G	FA	G by Pos
1969	SD	N	6	.100	.100	20	2	0	0	0	0.0	0	1	3		0	0	7	10	2	1	3.2	.895	SS-6
1970			23	.213	.225	89	19	1	0	0	0.0	5	3	5	11	3	0	0	38	83	4	14	5.4	.968	SS-23
1972			18	.167	.167	24	4	0	0	0	0.0	1	0	0	3	0	8	1	5	16	1	0	1.2	.955	SS-15, 3B-1
3 yrs.			47	.188	.195	133	25	1	0	0	0.0	7	3	6	17	4	8	1	50	109	7	15	3.5	.958	SS-44, 3B-1

Sergio Robles

ROBLES, SERGIO VALENZUELA
B. Apr. 16, 1946, Magdalena, Mexico

BR TR 6'2" 190 lbs.

Year	Team		Games	BA	SA	AB	H	2B	3B	HR	HR%	R	RBI	BB	SO	SB	AB	H	PO	A	E	DP	TC/G	FA	G by Pos
1972	BAL	A	2	.200	.200	5	1	0	0	0	0.0	0	0	0	1	0	1	1	2	0	0	0	1.0	1.000	C-1
1973			8	.077	.077	13	1	0	0	0	0.0	0	0	3	1	0	0	0	32	1	0	0	4.1	1.000	C-8
1976	LA	N	6	.000	.000	3	0	0	0	0	0.0	0	0	0	2	0	0	0	9	0	0	0	1.5	1.000	C-6
3 yrs.			16	.095	.095	21	2	0	0	0	0.0	0	0	3	3	0	1	1	43	1	0	0	2.8	1.000	C-15

Tom Robson

ROBSON, THOMAS JAMES
B. Jan. 15, 1946, Rochester, N. Y.

BR TR 6'3" 215 lbs.

Year	Team		Games	BA	SA	AB	H	2B	3B	HR	HR%	R	RBI	BB	SO	SB	AB	H	PO	A	E	DP	TC/G	FA	G by Pos
1974	TEX	A	6	.231	.308	13	3	1	0	0	0.0	2	2	3	3	0	0	0	2	0	0	1	0.3	1.000	DH-5, 1B-1
1975			17	.200	.200	35	7	0	0	0	0.0	3	2	1	3	0	8	2	38	2	0	6	2.4	1.000	1B-5, DH-4
2 yrs.			23	.208	.229	48	10	1	0	0	0.0	5	4	5	6	0	8	2	40	2	0	7	1.8	1.000	DH-9, 1B-6

Mickey Rocco

ROCCO, MICHAEL DOMINICK
B. Mar. 2, 1916, St. Paul, Minn.

BL TL 5'11" 188 lbs.

Year	Team		Games	BA	SA	AB	H	2B	3B	HR	HR%	R	RBI	BB	SO	SB	AB	H	PO	A	E	DP	TC/G	FA	G by Pos
1943	CLE	A	108	.240	.331	405	97	14	4	5	1.2	43	46	51	40	1	0	0	1012	61	5	111	10.0	.995	1B-108
1944			155	.266	.392	653	174	29	7	13	2.0	87	70	56	51	4	0	0	1467	138	11	158	10.4	.993	1B-155
1945			143	.264	.388	565	149	28	6	10	1.8	81	56	52	40	0	2	0	1203	115	10	112	9.3	.992	1B-141
1946			34	.245	.327	98	24	2	0	2	2.0	8	14	15	15	1	6	1	201	28	1	18	6.8	.996	1B-27
4 yrs.			440	.258	.372	1721	444	73	17	30	1.7	219	186	174	146	6	8	1	3883	342	27	399	9.7	.994	1B-431

Jack Roche

ROCHE, JOHN JOSEPH (Red)
B. Nov. 22, 1890, Los Angeles, Calif.   D. Mar. 30, 1983, Peoria, Ariz.

BR TR 6'1" 178 lbs.

Year	Team		Games	BA	SA	AB	H	2B	3B	HR	HR%	R	RBI	BB	SO	SB	AB	H	PO	A	E	DP	TC/G	FA	G by Pos
1914	STL	N	12	.667	1.111	9	6	1	0	0	0.0	1		1	6	5	0	2	0	1	1	0.3	.667	C-9
1915			46	.205	.256	39	8	0	1	0	0.0	2	6	4	8	1	37	8	1	3	0	1	0.1	1.000	C-4
1917			1	.000	.000	1	0	0	0	0	0.0	0	0	0	0	0	0	0	0	0	1	0	1.0	–	C-1
3 yrs.			59	.286	.408	49	14	2	2	0	0.0	3	9	4	9	2	43	13	3	3	2	2	0.1	.750	C-14

Ben Rochefort

ROCHEFORT, BENNETT HAROLD
Born Bennett Harold Rochefort Gilbert.
B. Aug. 15, 1896, Camden, N. J.   D. Apr. 2, 1981, Red Bank, N. J.

BL TR 6'2" 185 lbs.

Year	Team		Games	BA	SA	AB	H	2B	3B	HR	HR%	R	RBI	BB	SO	SB	AB	H	PO	A	E	DP	TC/G	FA	G by Pos
1914	PHI	A	1	.500	.500	2	1	0	0	0	0.0	0	0	0	0	1	0	0	4	1	0	0	5.0	1.000	1B-1

Lou Rochelli

ROCHELLI, LOUIS JOSEPH
B. Jan. 11, 1919, Williamson, Ill.

BR TR 6'1" 175 lbs.

Year	Team		Games	BA	SA	AB	H	2B	3B	HR	HR%	R	RBI	BB	SO	SB	AB	H	PO	A	E	DP	TC/G	FA	G by Pos
1944	BKN	N	5	.176	.294	17	3	0	1	0	0.0	2	2	2	6	0	0	0	12	15	1	1	5.6	.964	SS-5

Les Rock

ROCK, LESTER HENRY
Born Lester Henry Schwarzrock.
B. Aug. 19, 1912, Springfield, Minn.

BL TR 6'2" 184 lbs.

Year	Team		Games	BA	SA	AB	H	2B	3B	HR	HR%	R	RBI	BB	SO	SB	AB	H	PO	A	E	DP	TC/G	FA	G by Pos
1936	CHI	A	2	.000	.000	1	0	0	0	0	0.0	0	0	1	0	0	0	0	0	0	0	0	0.0	–	1B-2

Year	Team		Games	BA	SA	AB	H	2B	3B	HR	HR%	R	RBI	BB	SO	SB	Pinch Hit AB	Pinch Hit H	PO	A	E	DP	TC/G	FA	G by Pos

Ike Rockenfield

ROCKENFIELD, ISAAC BROC
B. Nov. 3, 1876, Omaha, Neb.   D. Feb. 21, 1927, San Diego, Calif.
BR TR 5'7"   150 lbs.

Year	Team		Games	BA	SA	AB	H	2B	3B	HR	HR%	R	RBI	BB	SO	SB	PH AB	PH H	PO	A	E	DP	TC/G	FA	G by Pos
1905	STL	A	95	.217	.255	322	70	12	0	0	0.0	40	16	46		11	0	0	210	255	37	19	5.3	.926	2B-95
1906			27	.236	.281	89	21	4	0	0	0.0	3	8	1		0	1	1	67	63	6	5	5.0	.956	2B-26
2 yrs.			122	.221	.260	411	91	16	0	0	0.0	43	24	47		11	1	1	277	318	43	24	5.2	.933	2B-121

Pat Rockett

ROCKETT, PATRICK EDWARD
B. Jan. 9, 1955, San Antonio, Tex.
BR TR 5'11"   170 lbs.

Year	Team		Games	BA	SA	AB	H	2B	3B	HR	HR%	R	RBI	BB	SO	SB	PH AB	PH H	PO	A	E	DP	TC/G	FA	G by Pos
1976	ATL	N	4	.200	.200	5	1	0	0	0	0.0	0	0	0	1	0	3	0	0	1	0	0	0.3	1.000	SS-2
1977			93	.254	.303	264	67	10	0	1	0.4	27	24	27	32	1	4	2	152	209	23	38	4.1	.940	SS-84
1978			55	.141	.155	142	20	2	0	0	0.0	6	4	13	12	1	1	0	64	97	5	16	3.0	.970	SS-51
3 yrs.			152	.214	.251	411	88	12	0	1	0.2	33	28	40	45	2	8	2	216	307	28	54	3.6	.949	SS-137

Andre Rodgers

RODGERS, KENNETH ANDRE IAN (Andy)
B. Dec. 2, 1934, Nassau, Bahamas
BR TR 6'3"   200 lbs.

Year	Team		Games	BA	SA	AB	H	2B	3B	HR	HR%	R	RBI	BB	SO	SB	PH AB	PH H	PO	A	E	DP	TC/G	FA	G by Pos
1957	NY	N	32	.244	.395	86	21	2	1	3	3.5	8	9	9	21	0	2	0	44	75	8	14	4.0	.937	SS-20, 3B-8
1958	SF	N	22	.206	.381	63	13	3	1	2	3.2	7	11	4	14	0	4	1	26	43	2	8	3.2	.972	SS-18
1959			71	.250	.390	228	57	12	1	6	2.6	32	24	32	50	2	2	1	110	197	22	35	4.6	.933	SS-66
1960			81	.244	.355	217	53	8	5	2	0.9	22	22	24	44	1	16	7	112	129	12	26	3.1	.953	SS-41, 3B-21, 1B-6, OF-2
1961	CHI	N	73	.266	.430	214	57	17	0	6	2.8	27	23	25	54	1	7	1	408	83	9	44	6.8	.982	1B-42, SS-24, OF-2, 2B-1
1962			138	.278	.388	461	128	20	8	5	1.1	40	44	44	93	5	6	0	250	434	28	92	5.2	.961	SS-133, 1B-1
1963			150	.229	.306	516	118	17	4	5	1.0	51	33	65	90	5	0	0	271	454	35	100	5.1	.954	SS-150
1964			129	.239	.371	448	107	17	3	12	2.7	50	46	53	88	5	3	0	232	428	24	68	5.3	.965	SS-126
1965	PIT	N	75	.287	.388	178	51	12	0	2	1.1	17	25	18	28	2	26	8	88	110	8	27	2.7	.961	SS-33, 3B-15, 1B-6, 2B-1
1966			36	.184	.204	49	9	1	0	0	0.0	6	4	8	7	0	23	6	19	14	2	6	1.0	.943	SS-5, OF-3, 3B-3, 1B-2
1967			47	.230	.377	61	14	3	0	2	3.3	8	4	8	18	1	22	4	47	26	2	5	1.6	.973	1B-9, 3B-5, SS-3, 2B-2
11 yrs.			854	.249	.365	2521	628	112	23	45	1.8	268	245	290	507	22	111	28	1607	1993	152	425	4.4	.959	SS-619, 1B-66, 3B-52, OF-7, 2B-4

Bill Rodgers

RODGERS, WILBUR KINCAID (Raw Meat Bill)
B. Apr. 18, 1887, Pleasant Ridge, Ohio   D. Dec. 24, 1978, Goliad, Tex.
BL TR 5'8½"   170 lbs.

Year	Team		Games	BA	SA	AB	H	2B	3B	HR	HR%	R	RBI	BB	SO	SB	PH AB	PH H	PO	A	E	DP	TC/G	FA	G by Pos
1915	3 teams			CLE	A (16G – .311)		BOS	A (11G – .000)		CIN	N (72G – .239)														
"	total		99	.246	.333	264	65	15	4	0	0.0	30	19	22	38	11	8	2	129	225	20	32	3.8	.947	2B-75, SS-6, OF-1, 3B-1
1916	CIN	N	3	.000	.000	4	0	0	0	0	0.0	0	0	0	2	0	1	0	1	1	0	0	0.7	1.000	SS-1
2 yrs.			102	.243	.328	268	65	15	4	0	0.0	30	19	22	40	11	9	2	130	226	20	32	3.7	.947	2B-75, SS-7, OF-1, 3B-1

Bill Rodgers

RODGERS, WILLIAM SHERMAN
B. Dec. 5, 1922, Harrisburg, Pa.
BL TL 6'   162 lbs.

Year	Team		Games	BA	SA	AB	H	2B	3B	HR	HR%	R	RBI	BB	SO	SB	PH AB	PH H	PO	A	E	DP	TC/G	FA	G by Pos
1944	PIT	N	2	.250	.250	4	1	0	0	0	0.0	1	0	0	0	0	0	0	0	0	0	0	0.0	–	OF-1
1945			1	1.000	1.000	1	1	0	0	0	0.0	0	0	0	1	0	1	1	0	0	0	0	0.0	–	OF-1
2 yrs.			3	.400	.400	5	2	0	0	0	0.0	1	0	0	1	0	1	1	0	0	0	0	0.0	–	OF-1

Buck Rodgers

RODGERS, ROBERT LEROY
B. Aug. 16, 1938, Delaware, Ohio
Manager 1980-82, 1985-89.
BB TR 6'2"   190 lbs.
BR 1968

Year	Team		Games	BA	SA	AB	H	2B	3B	HR	HR%	R	RBI	BB	SO	SB	PH AB	PH H	PO	A	E	DP	TC/G	FA	G by Pos
1961	LA	A	16	.321	.464	56	18	2	0	2	3.6	8	13	1	6	0	3	2	71	11	3	2	5.3	.965	C-14
1962			155	.258	.372	565	146	34	6	6	1.1	65	61	45	68	1	11	1	826	73	10	14	5.9	.989	C-150
1963			100	.233	.293	300	70	6	0	4	1.3	24	23	29	35	2	15	5	416	48	10	5	4.7	.979	C-85
1964			148	.243	.313	514	125	18	3	4	0.8	38	54	40	71	4	5	2	884	87	13	14	6.6	.987	C-146
1965	CAL	A	132	.209	.265	411	86	14	3	1	0.2	33	32	35	61	4	8	2	682	52	7	7	5.6	.991	C-128
1966			133	.236	.339	454	107	20	5	7	1.5	45	48	29	57	1	7	3	662	69	6	7	5.5	.992	C-133
1967			139	.219	.305	429	94	13	3	6	1.4	29	41	34	55	1	6	0	728	73	7	11	5.8	.991	C-134, OF-1
1968			91	.190	.225	258	49	6	0	1	0.4	13	14	16	48	2	7	0	407	50	7	11	5.1	.985	C-87
1969			18	.196	.217	46	9	1	0	0	0.0	4	2	5	8	0	4	0	74	9	0	3	4.6	1.000	C-18
9 yrs.			932	.232	.312	3033	704	114	18	31	1.0	259	288	234	409	17	62	15	4750	472	63	74	5.7	.988	C-895, OF-1

Eric Rodin

RODIN, ERIC CHAPMAN
B. Feb. 5, 1930, Orange, N. J.
BR TR 6'2"   215 lbs.

Year	Team		Games	BA	SA	AB	H	2B	3B	HR	HR%	R	RBI	BB	SO	SB	PH AB	PH H	PO	A	E	DP	TC/G	FA	G by Pos
1954	NY	N	5	.000	.000	6	0	0	0	0	0.0	0	0	0	2	0	3	0	3	0	0	0	0.6	1.000	OF-3

Aurelio Rodriguez

RODRIGUEZ, AURELIO (Leo)
Born Aurelio Rodriguez y Ituarte.
B. Dec. 28, 1947, Cananea, Mexico
BR TR 5'10"   180 lbs.

Year	Team		Games	BA	SA	AB	H	2B	3B	HR	HR%	R	RBI	BB	SO	SB	PH AB	PH H	PO	A	E	DP	TC/G	FA	G by Pos
1967	CAL	A	29	.238	.300	130	31	3	1	1	0.8	14	8	2	21	1	0	0	19	75	1	11	3.3	.989	3B-29
1968			76	.242	.309	223	54	10	1	1	0.4	14	16	17	35	0	3	2	65	116	15	18	2.6	.923	3B-70, 2B-2
1969			159	.232	.307	561	130	17	2	7	1.2	47	49	32	88	5	0	0	145	352	24	42	3.3	.954	3B-159
1970	2 teams			CAL	A (17G – .270)		WAS	A (142G – .247)																		
"	total		159	.249	.420	610	152	33	7	19	3.1	70	83	40	87	15	0	0	127	398	18	42	3.4	.967	3B-153, SS-7
1971	DET	A	154	.253	.401	604	153	30	7	15	2.5	68	39	27	93	4	3	1	128	344	23	35	3.2	.954	3B-153, SS-2
1972			153	.236	.356	601	142	23	5	13	2.2	65	56	28	104	2	1	1	150	350	17	34	3.4	.967	3B-153, SS-2
1973			160	.222	.330	555	123	27	3	9	1.6	46	58	31	85	3	0	0	137	338	14	31	3.1	.971	3B-160
1974			159	.222	.306	571	127	23	5	5	0.9	54	49	26	70	2	0	0	132	389	21	40	3.4	.961	3B-159
1975			151	.245	.385	507	124	20	6	13	2.6	47	60	30	63	1	0	0	136	375	25	33	3.5	.953	3B-151
1976			128	.240	.325	480	115	13	2	8	1.7	40	50	19	61	0	0	0	120	280	9	21	3.2	.978	3B-128
1977			96	.219	.369	306	67	14	1	10	3.3	30	32	16	36	1	10	1	60	222	8	19	3.0	.972	3B-95, SS-1
1978			134	.265	.395	385	102	25	2	8	1.8	40	43	19	37	0	20	7	79	228	4	20	2.3	.987	3B-131
1979			106	.254	.350	343	87	18	0	5	1.5	27	36	11	40	0	3	0	72	211	13	23	2.8	.956	3B-106, 1B-1
1980	2 teams			SD	N (89G – .200)		NY	A (52G – .220)																		
"	total		141	.209	.310	339	71	13	3	5	1.5	21	27	13	61	1	6	1	40	132	6	12	1.3	.966	3B-137, 2B-6, SS-2
1981	NY	A	27	.346	.500	52	18	2	0	2	3.8	4	8	2	10	0	1	1	20	34	2	4	2.1	.964	3B-20, 2B-3, DH-2, 1B-1
1982	CHI	A	118	.241	.342	257	62	15	1	3	1.2	24	31	11	35	0	1	0	79	209	9	20	2.5	.970	3B-112, 2B-3, SS-2

Year	Team	Games	BA	SA	AB	H	2B	3B	HR	HR%	R	RBI	BB	SO	SB	Pinch Hit AB	H	PO	A	E	DP	TC/G	FA	G by Pos

Aurelio Rodriguez *continued*

Year	Team	Games	BA	SA	AB	H	2B	3B	HR	HR%	R	RBI	BB	SO	SB	AB	H	PO	A	E	DP	TC/G	FA	G by Pos
1983	2 teams	BAL A (45G – .119)			CHI A		(22G – .200)																		
"	total	67	.138	.184	87	12	1	0	1	1.1	1	3	0	16	0	0	0	22	67	2	7	1.4	.978	3B-67
	17 yrs.	2017	.237	.351	6611	1570	287	46	124	1.9	612	648	324	942	35	48	12	1531	4120	211	412	2.9	.964	3B-1983, SS-16, 2B-14, DH-2, 1B-2

LEAGUE CHAMPIONSHIP SERIES

Year	Team	Games	BA	SA	AB	H	2B	3B	HR	HR%	R	RBI	BB	SO	SB	AB	H	PO	A	E	DP	TC/G	FA	G by Pos
1972	DET A	5	.000	.000	16	0	0	0	0	0.0	0	0	2	1	0	0	0	2	14	1	2	3.4	.941	3B-5
1980	NY A	2	.333	.500	6	2	1	0	0	0.0	0	0	0	0	0	0	0	2	2	0	0	2.0	1.000	3B-2
1981		1	–	–	0	0	0	0	0	–	0	0	0	0	0	0	0	0	0	0	0	0.0	–	3B-1
1983	CHI A	2	–	–	0	0	0	0	0	–	0	0	0	0	0	0	0	0	0	1	0	0.5	–	3B-2
	4 yrs.	10	.091	.136	22	2	1	0	0	0.0	0	0	2	2	0	0	0	4	16	2	2	2.2	.909	3B-10

WORLD SERIES

Year	Team	Games	BA	SA	AB	H	2B	3B	HR	HR%	R	RBI	BB	SO	SB	AB	H	PO	A	E	DP	TC/G	FA	G by Pos
1981	NY A	4	.417	.417	12	5	0	0	0	0.0	1	0	1	2	0	0	0	3	9	0	0	3.0	1.000	3B-3

Edwin Rodriguez

RODRIGUEZ, EDWIN
Born Edwin Rodriguez y Morales.
B. Aug. 14, 1960, Ponce, Puerto Rico

BR TR 5'11" 172 lbs.

Year	Team	Games	BA	SA	AB	H	2B	3B	HR	HR%	R	RBI	BB	SO	SB	AB	H	PO	A	E	DP	TC/G	FA	G by Pos
1982	NY A	3	.333	.333	9	3	0	0	0	0.0	2	1	1	1	0	0	0	2	12	2	1	5.3	.875	2B-3
1983	SD N	7	.167	.250	12	2	1	0	0	0.0	1	0	1	3	0	0	0	8	8	0	2	2.3	1.000	2B-5, SS-2, 3B-1
1985		1	.000	.000	1	0	0	0	0	0.0	0	0	0	0	0	1	0	0	0	0	0	0.0	–	
	3 yrs.	11	.227	.273	22	5	1	0	0	0.0	3	1	2	4	0	1	0	10	20	2	3	2.9	.938	2B-8, SS-2, 3B-1

Ellie Rodriguez

RODRIGUEZ, ELISEO
Born Eliseo Rodriguez y Delgado.
B. May 24, 1946, Fajardo, Puerto Rico

BR TR 5'11" 185 lbs.

Year	Team	Games	BA	SA	AB	H	2B	3B	HR	HR%	R	RBI	BB	SO	SB	AB	H	PO	A	E	DP	TC/G	FA	G by Pos
1968	NY A	9	.208	.208	24	5	0	0	0	0.0	1	1	3	3	0	0	0	41	3	0	0	4.9	1.000	C-9
1969	KC A	95	.236	.296	267	63	10	0	2	0.7	27	20	31	26	3	6	1	433	39	5	2	5.0	.990	C-90
1970		80	.225	.290	231	52	8	2	1	0.4	25	15	27	35	2	5	2	451	32	6	5	6.1	.988	C-75
1971	MIL A	115	.210	.257	319	67	10	1	1	0.3	28	30	41	51	1	6	1	520	67	5	8	5.1	.992	C-114
1972		116	.285	.352	355	101	14	2	2	0.6	31	35	52	43	1	3	1	542	54	10	6	5.2	.983	C-114
1973		94	.269	.303	290	78	8	1	0	0.0	30	30	41	28	4	6	1	324	40	5	5	3.9	.986	C-75, DH-14
1974	CAL A	140	.253	.357	395	100	20	0	7	1.8	48	36	69	56	4	4	3	782	75	7	7	6.2	.992	C-137, DH-1
1975		90	.235	.301	226	53	6	0	3	1.3	20	27	49	37	2	0	0	492	33	5	2	5.9	.991	C-90
1976	LA N	36	.212	.212	66	14	0	0	0	0.0	10	9	19	12	0	1	1	128	17	2	2	4.1	.986	C-33
	9 yrs.	775	.245	.308	2173	533	76	6	16	0.7	220	203	332	291	17	31	10	3713	360	45	37	5.3	.989	C-737, DH-15

Hec Rodriguez

RODRIGUEZ, HECTOR ANTONIO
Born Hector Antonio Rodriguez y Ordenana.
B. June 13, 1920, Alquizar, Cuba

BR TR 5'8" 165 lbs.

Year	Team	Games	BA	SA	AB	H	2B	3B	HR	HR%	R	RBI	BB	SO	SB	AB	H	PO	A	E	DP	TC/G	FA	G by Pos
1952	CHI A	124	.265	.307	407	108	14	0	1	0.2	55	40	47	22	7	8	2	145	232	16	26	3.2	.959	3B-113

Jose Rodriguez

RODRIGUEZ, JOSE
B. Feb. 23, 1894, Havana, Cuba   D. Jan. 21, 1953, Havana, Cuba

BR TR 6' 170 lbs.

Year	Team	Games	BA	SA	AB	H	2B	3B	HR	HR%	R	RBI	BB	SO	SB	AB	H	PO	A	E	DP	TC/G	FA	G by Pos
1916	NY N	1	–	–	0	0	0	0	0	–	0	0	0	0	0	0	0	0	0	0	0	0.0	–	
1917		7	.200	.300	20	4	0	1	0	0.0	2	2	2	1	2	0	0	45	1	0	2	6.6	1.000	1B-7
1918		50	.160	.192	125	20	0	2	0	0.0	15	15	12	3	6	2	0	122	102	5	16	4.6	.978	2B-40, 1B-8, 3B-2
	3 yrs.	58	.166	.207	145	24	0	3	0	0.0	17	17	14	4	8	2	0	167	103	5	18	4.7	.982	2B-40, 1B-15, 3B-2

Ruben Rodriguez

RODRIGUEZ, RUBEN DARIO
Born Ruben Dario Rodriguez y Martinez.
B. Aug. 4, 1964, Cabrera, Dominican Republic

BR TR 6' 170 lbs.

Year	Team	Games	BA	SA	AB	H	2B	3B	HR	HR%	R	RBI	BB	SO	SB	AB	H	PO	A	E	DP	TC/G	FA	G by Pos
1986	PIT N	2	.000	.000	3	0	0	0	0	0.0	0	0	0	1	0	0	0	6	1	0	0	3.5	1.000	C-2
1988		2	.200	.600	5	1	0	1	0	0.0	1	1	0	2	0	0	0	9	0	0	0	4.5	1.000	C-2
	2 yrs.	4	.125	.375	8	1	0	1	0	0.0	1	1	0	3	0	0	0	15	1	0	0	4.0	1.000	C-4

Vic Rodriguez

RODRIGUEZ, VICTOR MANUEL
Born Victor Manuel Rodriguez y Rivera.
B. July 14, 1961, New York, N. Y.

BR TR 5'11" 160 lbs.

Year	Team	Games	BA	SA	AB	H	2B	3B	HR	HR%	R	RBI	BB	SO	SB	AB	H	PO	A	E	DP	TC/G	FA	G by Pos
1984	BAL A	11	.412	.588	17	7	3	0	0	0.0	4	2	0	2	0	0	0	8	15	1	1	2.2	.958	2B-7, DH-3
1989	MIN A	6	.455	.636	11	5	2	0	0	0.0	2	0	0	1	0	0	0	3	6	1	1	1.7	.900	3B-5, DH-1
	2 yrs.	17	.429	.607	28	12	5	0	0	0.0	6	2	0	3	0	0	0	11	21	2	2	2.0	.941	2B-7, 3B-5, DH-4

Gary Roenicke

ROENICKE, GARY STEVEN
Brother of Ron Roenicke.
B. Dec. 5, 1954, Covina, Calif.

BR TR 6'3" 205 lbs.

Year	Team	Games	BA	SA	AB	H	2B	3B	HR	HR%	R	RBI	BB	SO	SB	AB	H	PO	A	E	DP	TC/G	FA	G by Pos
1976	MON N	29	.222	.344	90	20	3	1	2	2.2	9	5	4	18	0	4	1	39	3	2	0	1.5	.955	OF-25
1978	BAL A	27	.259	.466	58	15	3	0	3	5.2	3	15	8	3	0	6	1	22	1	0	0	0.9	1.000	OF-20
1979		133	.261	.508	376	98	16	1	25	6.6	60	64	61	74	1	2	0	246	10	5	1	2.0	.981	OF-130, DH-2
1980		118	.239	.384	297	71	13	0	10	3.4	40	28	41	49	2	12	6	197	8	0	1	1.7	1.000	OF-113
1981		85	.269	.384	219	59	16	0	3	1.4	31	20	23	29	1	16	3	175	2	3	1	2.1	.983	OF-83
1982		137	.270	.499	393	106	25	1	21	5.3	58	74	70	73	6	18	5	363	13	3	7	2.8	.992	OF-125, 1B-10
1983		115	.260	.477	323	84	13	0	19	5.9	45	64	30	35	2	38	8	219	9	3	5	2.0	.987	OF-100, 1B-7, DH-2, 3B-2
1984		121	.224	.380	326	73	19	1	10	3.1	36	44	58	43	1	21	5	197	6	1	0	1.7	.995	OF-117
1985		113	.218	.458	225	49	9	0	15	6.7	36	43	44	36	2	29	3	134	6	1	0	1.2	.993	OF-88, DH-17
1986	NY A	69	.265	.368	136	36	5	0	3	2.2	11	18	27	30	1	18	6	46	6	0	0	0.8	1.000	OF-37, DH-15, 3B-3, 1B-2
1987	ATL N	67	.219	.464	151	33	8	0	9	6.0	25	28	32	23	0	15	3	110	7	2	8	1.8	.983	OF-44, 1B-9
1988		49	.228	.298	114	26	5	0	1	0.9	11	7	8	15	0	16	1	53	0	0	0	1.1	1.000	OF-35, 1B-1
	12 yrs.	1063	.247	.434	2708	670	135	4	121	4.5	367	410	406	428	16	195	42	1801	71	20	23	1.8	.989	OF-917, DH-36, 1B-29, 3B-5

Year Team	Games	BA	SA	AB	H	2B	3B	HR	HR%	R	RBI	BB	SO	SB	Pinch Hit AB	Pinch Hit H	PO	A	E	DP	TC/G	FA	G by Pos

Gary Roenicke *continued*

LEAGUE CHAMPIONSHIP SERIES

Year Team	Games	BA	SA	AB	H	2B	3B	HR	HR%	R	RBI	BB	SO	SB	AB	H	PO	A	E	DP	TC/G	FA	G by Pos
1979 BAL A	2	.200	.200	5	1	0	0	0	0.0	1	1	0	0	0	1	0	3	1	0	1	2.0	1.000	OF-2
1983	3	.750	1.750	4	3	1	0	1	25.0	4	4	5	0	0	0	0	4	1	0	0	1.7	1.000	OF-3
2 yrs.	5	.444	.889	9	4	1	0	1	11.1	5	5	5	0	0	1	0	7	2	0	1	1.8	1.000	OF-5

WORLD SERIES

Year Team	Games	BA	SA	AB	H	2B	3B	HR	HR%	R	RBI	BB	SO	SB	AB	H	PO	A	E	DP	TC/G	FA	G by Pos
1979 BAL A	6	.125	.188	16	2	1	0	0	0.0	1	0	0	6	0	1	0	14	1	0	0	2.5	1.000	OF-5
1983	3	.000	.000	7	0	0	0	0	0.0	0	0	0	2	0	2	0	2	1	0	0	1.0	1.000	OF-2
2 yrs.	9	.087	.130	23	2	1	0	0	0.0	1	0	0	8	0	3	0	16	2	0	0	2.0	1.000	OF-7

Ron Roenicke

ROENICKE, RONALD JON
Brother of Gary Roenicke.
B. Aug. 19, 1956, Covina, Calif.

BB TL 6'   180 lbs.

Year Team	Games	BA	SA	AB	H	2B	3B	HR	HR%	R	RBI	BB	SO	SB	AB	H	PO	A	E	DP	TC/G	FA	G by Pos
1981 LA N	22	.234	.234	47	11	0	0	0	0.0	6	0	6	8	1	4	0	38	1	0	1	1.8	1.000	OF-20
1982	109	.259	.336	143	37	8	0	1	0.7	18	12	21	32	5	44	13	59	1	1	0	0.6	.984	OF-72
1983 2 teams				LA N (81G – .221)			SEA A (59G – .253)																	
" total	140	.239	.338	343	82	16	0	6	1.7	35	35	47	48	9	24	5	243	14	3	7	1.9	.988	OF-116, 1B-6, DH-1
1984 SD N	12	.300	.500	20	6	1	0	1	5.0	4	2	2	5	0	2	0	10	0	0	0	0.8	1.000	OF-10
1985 SF N	65	.256	.406	133	34	9	1	3	2.3	23	13	35	27	6	23	4	63	0	1	0	1.0	.984	OF-35
1986 PHI N	102	.247	.356	275	68	13	1	5	1.8	42	42	61	52	2	21	4	181	3	2	0	1.8	.989	OF-83
1987	63	.167	.269	78	13	3	1	1	1.3	9	4	14	15	1	38	5	26	1	1	0	0.4	.964	OF-26
1988 CIN N	14	.135	.162	37	5	1	0	0	0.0	4	5	4	8	0	2	1	18	0	0	0	1.3	1.000	OF-14
8 yrs.	527	.238	.338	1076	256	51	3	17	1.6	141	113	190	195	24	158	32	638	20	8	8	1.3	.988	OF-376, 1B-6, DH-1

WORLD SERIES

Year Team	Games	BA	SA	AB	H	2B	3B	HR	HR%	R	RBI	BB	SO	SB	AB	H	PO	A	E	DP	TC/G	FA	G by Pos
1984 SD N	2	–	–	0	0	0	0	0	–	0	0	0	0	0	0	0	0	0	0	0	0.0	–	OF-1

Oscar Roettger

ROETTGER, OSCAR FREDERICK LOUIS
Brother of Wally Roettger.
B. Feb. 19, 1900, St. Louis, Mo.   D. July 4, 1986, St. Louis, Mo.

BR TR 6'   170 lbs.

Year Team	Games	BA	SA	AB	H	2B	3B	HR	HR%	R	RBI	BB	SO	SB	AB	H	PO	A	E	DP	TC/G	FA	G by Pos
1923 NY A	5	.000	.000	2	0	0	0	0	0.0	0	0	0	0	0	0	0	3	2	0	0	1.0	1.000	P-5
1924	1	–		0	0	0	0	0	–	0	0	0	0	0	0	0	0	0	0	0	0.0	–	P-1
1927 BKN N	5	.000	.000	4	0	0	0	0	0.0	0	0	1	1	0	2	0	0	0	0	0	0.0	–	OF-1
1932 PHI A	26	.233	.250	60	14	1	0	0	0.0	7	6	5	4	0	10	0	130	5	3	6	5.3	.978	1B-15
4 yrs.	37	.212	.227	66	14	1	0	0	0.0	7	6	6	5	0	12	0	133	7	3	6	3.9	.979	1B-15, P-6, OF-1

Wally Roettger

ROETTGER, WALTER HENRY
Brother of Oscar Roettger.
B. Aug. 28, 1902, St. Louis, Mo.   D. Sept. 14, 1951, Champaign, Ill.

BR TR 6'1½"   190 lbs.

Year Team	Games	BA	SA	AB	H	2B	3B	HR	HR%	R	RBI	BB	SO	SB	AB	H	PO	A	E	DP	TC/G	FA	G by Pos
1927 STL N	5	.000	.000	1	0	0	0	0	0.0	0	0	1	0	0	0	0	2	0	2	0	0.8	.500	OF-3
1928	68	.341	.506	261	89	17	4	6	2.3	27	44	10	22	2	2	0	152	2	3	1	2.3	.981	OF-66
1929	79	.253	.349	269	68	11	3	3	1.1	27	42	13	27	0	10	1	137	4	1	0	1.8	.993	OF-69
1930 NY N	121	.283	.379	420	119	15	5	5	1.2	51	51	25	29	1	7	3	233	9	2	1	2.0	.992	OF-114
1931 2 teams				CIN N (44G – .351)			STL N (45G – .285)																	
" total	89	.321	.435	336	108	23	6	1	0.3	41	37	16	23	1	3	1	168	4	3	1	2.0	.983	OF-86
1932 CIN N	106	.277	.372	347	96	18	3	3	0.9	26	43	23	10	3	10	3	214	3	2	2	2.1	.991	OF-94
1933	84	.239	.297	209	50	7	1	1	0.5	13	17	8	10	0	28	8	124	4	3	2	1.6	.977	OF-55
1934 PIT N	47	.245	.311	106	26	5	1	0	0.0	7	11	3	8	0	23	7	51	1	0	0	1.1	1.000	OF-23
8 yrs.	599	.285	.387	1949	556	96	23	19	1.0	192	245	99	143	4	83	23	1081	27	16	7	1.9	.986	OF-510

WORLD SERIES

Year Team	Games	BA	SA	AB	H	2B	3B	HR	HR%	R	RBI	BB	SO	SB	AB	H	PO	A	E	DP	TC/G	FA	G by Pos
1931 STL N	3	.286	.357	14	4	1	0	0	0.0	1	0	0	3	0	0	0	4	0	0	0	1.3	1.000	OF-3

Ed Roetz

ROETZ, EDWARD BERNARD
B. Aug. 6, 1905, Philadelphia, Pa.   D. Mar. 16, 1965, Philadelphia, Pa.

BR TR 5'10"   160 lbs.

Year Team	Games	BA	SA	AB	H	2B	3B	HR	HR%	R	RBI	BB	SO	SB	AB	H	PO	A	E	DP	TC/G	FA	G by Pos
1929 STL A	16	.244	.378	45	11	4	1	0	0.0	7	5	4	6	0	0	0	64	25	7	11	6.0	.927	SS-8, 1B-2, 2B-2, 3B-1

Billy Rogell

ROGELL, WILLIAM GEORGE
B. Nov. 24, 1904, Springfield, Ill.

BB TR 5'10½"   163 lbs.

Year Team	Games	BA	SA	AB	H	2B	3B	HR	HR%	R	RBI	BB	SO	SB	AB	H	PO	A	E	DP	TC/G	FA	G by Pos
1925 BOS A	58	.195	.237	169	33	5	1	0	0.0	12	17	11	17	0	2	0	107	161	19	34	4.9	.934	2B-49, SS-6
1927	82	.266	.420	207	55	14	6	2	1.0	35	28	24	28	3	15	3	52	127	6	10	2.3	.968	3B-53, OF-2, 2B-2
1928	102	.233	.294	296	69	10	4	0	0.0	33	29	22	47	2	7	1	158	233	23	34	4.1	.944	SS-67, 2B-22, OF-6, 3B-3
1930 DET A	54	.167	.222	144	24	4	2	0	0.0	20	9	15	23	1	2	0	62	114	10	20	3.4	.946	SS-33, 3B-13, OF-1
1931	48	.303	.432	185	56	12	3	2	1.1	21	24	24	17	8	0	0	91	182	12	26	5.9	.958	SS-48
1932	143	.271	.394	554	150	29	6	9	1.6	88	61	50	38	14	0	0	276	437	42	88	5.3	.944	SS-139, 3B-4
1933	155	.295	.404	587	173	42	11	0	0.0	67	57	79	33	6	0	0	326	526	51	116	5.8	.944	SS-155
1934	154	.296	.392	592	175	32	8	3	0.5	114	100	74	36	13	0	0	259	518	31	99	5.2	.962	SS-154
1935	150	.275	.388	560	154	23	11	6	1.1	88	71	80	29	3	0	0	280	512	24	104	5.4	.971	SS-150
1936	146	.274	.368	585	160	27	5	6	1.0	85	68	73	41	14	1	0	287	464	27	99	5.3	.965	SS-146, 3B-1
1937	146	.276	.403	536	148	30	7	8	1.5	85	64	83	48	5	0	0	323	451	26	103	5.5	.968	SS-146
1938	136	.259	.353	501	130	22	8	3	0.6	76	55	86	37	9	2	0	291	431	31	101	5.5	.959	SS-134
1939	74	.230	.333	174	40	6	3	2	1.1	24	23	26	14	3	3	0	84	135	16	26	3.2	.932	SS-43, 3B-21, 2B-2
1940 CHI N	33	.136	.186	59	8	0	0	1	1.7	7	3	2	8	1	6	1	19	24	6	2	1.5	.878	SS-14, 3B-9, 2B-3
14 yrs.	1481	.267	.370	5149	1375	256	75	42	0.8	755	609	649	416	82	38	5	2615	4315	324	862	4.9	.955	SS-1235, 3B-104, 2B-78, OF-9

WORLD SERIES

Year Team	Games	BA	SA	AB	H	2B	3B	HR	HR%	R	RBI	BB	SO	SB	AB	H	PO	A	E	DP	TC/G	FA	G by Pos
1934 DET A	7	.276	.310	29	8	1	0	0	0.0	3	4	1	4	0	0	0	11	17	3	4	4.4	.903	SS-7
1935	6	.292	.375	24	7	2	0	0	0.0	1	1	2	5	0	0	0	13	12	0	6	4.2	1.000	SS-6
2 yrs.	13	.283	.340	53	15	3	0	0	0.0	4	5	3	9	0	0	0	24	29	3	10	4.3	.946	SS-13

Year	Team	Games	BA	SA	AB	H	2B	3B	HR	HR%	R	RBI	BB	SO	SB	Pinch Hit AB	Pinch Hit H	PO	A	E	DP	TC/G	FA	G by Pos

Emmett Rogers

ROGERS, EMMETT
B. 1865, Rome, N. Y. Deceased.

BB 5'10" 165 lbs.

Year	Team	Games	BA	SA	AB	H	2B	3B	HR	HR%	R	RBI	BB	SO	SB	AB	H	PO	A	E	DP	TC/G	FA	G by Pos
1890	TOL AA	35	.173	.255	110	19	3	3	0	0.0	18		14		2	0	0	190	52	20	3	7.5	.924	C-34, OF-1

Jay Rogers

ROGERS, JAY LEWIS
B. Aug. 3, 1888, Sandusky, N. Y.   D. July 1, 1964, Carlisle, Pa.

BR TR 5'11½" 178 lbs.

Year	Team	Games	BA	SA	AB	H	2B	3B	HR	HR%	R	RBI	BB	SO	SB	AB	H	PO	A	E	DP	TC/G	FA	G by Pos
1914	NY A	5	.000	.000	8	0	0	0	0	0.0	0	0	0	4	0	1	0	10	2	1	0	2.6	.923	C-4

Jim Rogers

ROGERS, JAMES F.
B. Apr. 9, 1872, Hartford, Conn.   D. Jan. 21, 1900, Bridgeport, Conn.
Manager 1897.

5'7½" 180 lbs.

Year	Team	Games	BA	SA	AB	H	2B	3B	HR	HR%	R	RBI	BB	SO	SB	AB	H	PO	A	E	DP	TC/G	FA	G by Pos
1896	2 teams	WAS N	(38G – .279)		LOU N	(72G – .259)																		
"	total	110	.266	.349	444	118	14	10	1	0.2	60	68	25	23	16	0	0	665	154	41	51	7.8	.952	1B-60, 3B-32, SS-12, 2B-6, OF-1
1897	LOU N	41	.147	.233	150	22	3	2	2	1.3	22	22	22		4	0	0	108	121	16	12	6.0	.935	2B-39, 1B-3
2 yrs.		151	.236	.320	594	140	17	12	3	0.5	82	90	47	23	20	0	0	773	275	57	63	7.3	.948	1B-63, 2B-45, 3B-32, SS-12, OF-1

Packy Rogers

ROGERS, STANLEY FRANK
Born Stanley Frank Hazinski.
B. Apr. 26, 1913, Swoyersville, Pa.

BR TR 5'8" 175 lbs.

Year	Team	Games	BA	SA	AB	H	2B	3B	HR	HR%	R	RBI	BB	SO	SB	AB	H	PO	A	E	DP	TC/G	FA	G by Pos
1938	BKN N	23	.189	.270	37	7	1	1	0	0.0	3	5	6	6	0	2	0	25	22	2	3	2.1	.959	SS-9, 3B-8, 2B-3, OF-1

Mike Rogodzinski

ROGODZINSKI, MICHAEL GEORGE
B. Feb. 22, 1948, Evanston, Ill.

BL TR 6' 185 lbs.

Year	Team	Games	BA	SA	AB	H	2B	3B	HR	HR%	R	RBI	BB	SO	SB	AB	H	PO	A	E	DP	TC/G	FA	G by Pos
1973	PHI N	66	.238	.350	80	19	3	0	2	2.5	13	7	12	19	0	47	16	16	2	1	0	0.3	.947	OF-16
1974		17	.067	.067	15	1	0	0	0	0.0	1	1	2	3	0	15	1	0	0	0	0	0.0	–	OF-1
1975		16	.263	.316	19	5	1	0	0	0.0	3	4	3	2	0	11	4	2	0	1	0	0.2	.667	OF-2
3 yrs.		99	.219	.307	114	25	4	0	2	1.8	17	12	17	24	0	73	21	18	2	2	0	0.2	.909	OF-19

George Rohe

ROHE, GEORGE ANTHONY (Whitey)
B. Sept. 15, 1875, Cincinnati, Ohio   D. June 10, 1957, Cincinnati, Ohio

BR TR 5'9" 165 lbs.

Year	Team	Games	BA	SA	AB	H	2B	3B	HR	HR%	R	RBI	BB	SO	SB	AB	H	PO	A	E	DP	TC/G	FA	G by Pos
1901	BAL A	14	.278	.333	36	10	2	0	0	0.0	7	4	5		1	1	0	67	3	7	6	5.5	.909	1B-8, 3B-6
1905	CHI A	34	.212	.248	113	24	1	0	1	0.9	14	12	12		2	1	0	47	72	6	10	3.7	.952	3B-17, 3B-16
1906		75	.258	.289	225	58	5	1	0	0.0	14	25	16		8	12	2	76	137	17	8	3.1	.926	3B-57, 2B-5, OF-1
1907		144	.213	.255	494	105	11	2	2	0.4	46	51	39		16	2	0	183	372	56	38	4.2	.908	3B-76, 2B-39, SS-30
4 yrs.		267	.227	.266	868	197	19	3	3	0.3	81	92	72		27	16	2	373	584	86	62	3.9	.918	3B-156, 2B-60, SS-30, 1B-8, OF-1

WORLD SERIES

Year	Team	Games	BA	SA	AB	H	2B	3B	HR	HR%	R	RBI	BB	SO	SB	AB	H	PO	A	E	DP	TC/G	FA	G by Pos
1906	CHI A	6	.333	.571	21	7	1	2	0	0.0	2	4	3	1	2	0	0	4	16	3	0	3.8	.870	3B-6

Dan Rohn

ROHN, DANIEL JAY
B. Jan. 10, 1956, Alpena, Mich.

BL TR 5'8" 165 lbs.

Year	Team	Games	BA	SA	AB	H	2B	3B	HR	HR%	R	RBI	BB	SO	SB	AB	H	PO	A	E	DP	TC/G	FA	G by Pos
1983	CHI N	23	.387	.613	31	12	3	2	0	0.0	3	6	2	2	1	17	6	12	12	2	2	1.1	.923	2B-6, SS-1
1984		25	.129	.226	31	4	0	0	1	3.2	1	3	1	6	0	13	2	5	15	0	1	0.8	1.000	3B-7, SS-5, 2B-5
1986	CLE A	6	.200	.200	10	2	0	0	0	0.0	1	2	1	1	0	1	0	4	10	2	1	2.7	.875	3B-2, 2B-2, SS-1
3 yrs.		54	.250	.389	72	18	3	2	1	1.4	5	11	4	9	1	31	8	21	37	4	4	1.1	.935	2B-13, 3B-9, SS-7

Ray Rohwer

ROHWER, RAY
B. June 5, 1895, Dixon, Calif.   D. Jan. 24, 1988, Davis, Calif.

BL TL 5'10" 155 lbs.

Year	Team	Games	BA	SA	AB	H	2B	3B	HR	HR%	R	RBI	BB	SO	SB	AB	H	PO	A	E	DP	TC/G	FA	G by Pos
1921	PIT N	30	.250	.425	40	10	3	2	0	0.0	6	9	4	8	0	18	2	14	2	3	0	0.6	.842	OF-10
1922		53	.295	.457	129	38	6	3	3	2.3	19	22	10	17	1	19	5	56	5	4	1	1.2	.938	OF-30
2 yrs.		83	.284	.450	169	48	9	5	3	1.8	25	28	14	25	1	37	7	70	7	7	1	1.0	.917	OF-40

Tony Roig

ROIG, ANTON AMBROSE
B. Dec. 23, 1927, New Orleans, La.

BR TR 6'1" 180 lbs.

Year	Team	Games	BA	SA	AB	H	2B	3B	HR	HR%	R	RBI	BB	SO	SB	AB	H	PO	A	E	DP	TC/G	FA	G by Pos
1953	WAS A	3	.125	.250	8	1	1	0	0	0.0	0	0	0	1	0	1	0	7	7	0	2	4.7	1.000	2B-2
1955		29	.228	.281	57	13	1	1	0	0.0	3	4	2	15	0	3	1	21	52	7	11	2.8	.913	SS-21, 3B-8, 2B-1
1956		44	.210	.286	119	25	5	2	0	0.0	11	7	20	29	2	3	1	83	110	8	30	4.6	.960	2B-27, SS-19
3 yrs.		76	.212	.283	184	39	7	3	0	0.0	14	11	22	45	2	7	3	111	169	15	43	3.9	.949	SS-40, 2B-30, 3B-8

Cookie Rojas

ROJAS, OCTAVIO VICTOR
Born Octavio Victor Rojas y Rivas.
B. Mar. 6, 1939, Havana, Cuba
Manager 1988.

BR TR 5'10" 160 lbs.

Year	Team	Games	BA	SA	AB	H	2B	3B	HR	HR%	R	RBI	BB	SO	SB	AB	H	PO	A	E	DP	TC/G	FA	G by Pos
1962	CIN N	39	.221	.244	86	19	2	0	0	0.0	9	6	9	4	1	2	0	60	52	6	13	3.0	.949	2B-30, 3B-1
1963	PHI N	64	.221	.286	77	17	0	1	1	1.3	18	2	3	8	4	8	3	43	68	1	13	1.8	.991	2B-25, OF-1
1964		109	.291	.394	340	99	19	5	2	0.6	58	31	22	17	1	16	1	164	76	7	11	2.3	.972	OF-70, 2B-20, SS-18, 3B-1, C-1
1965		142	.303	.380	521	158	25	3	3	0.6	78	42	42	33	5	11	2	274	255	9	59	3.8	.983	2B-84, OF-55, SS-11, C-2, 1B-1
1966		156	.268	.329	626	168	18	1	6	1.0	77	55	35	46	4	1	0	319	295	13	69	4.0	.979	2B-106, OF-56, SS-2
1967		147	.259	.330	528	137	21	2	4	0.8	60	45	30	58	8	5	2	297	360	15	92	4.6	.978	2B-137, OF-9, C-3, SS-2, 3B-1, P-1
1968		152	.232	.306	621	144	19	0	9	1.4	53	48	16	55	4	2	0	365	424	10	110	5.3	.987	2B-150, C-1
1969		110	.228	.292	391	89	11	1	4	1.0	35	30	23	28	1	11	1	260	229	11	68	4.5	.978	2B-95, OF-2
1970	2 teams	STL N	(23G – .106)		KC A	(98G – .260)																		
"	total	121	.244	.302	431	105	13	3	2	0.5	38	30	23	33	3	12	2	242	313	9	78	4.7	.984	2B-107, OF-6, SS-2
1971	KC A	115	.300	.406	414	124	22	2	6	1.4	56	59	39	35	8	2	0	254	293	5	76	4.8	.991	2B-111, OF-2, SS-1
1972		137	.261	.331	487	127	25	0	3	0.6	49	53	41	35	2	2	0	265	368	9	83	4.7	.986	2B-133, 3B-6, SS-2
1973		139	.276	.372	551	152	29	3	6	1.1	78	69	37	38	18	3	2	302	424	13	114	5.3	.982	2B-137

Year Team	Games	BA	SA	AB	H	2B	3B	HR	HR%	R	RBI	BB	SO	SB	Pinch Hit AB	Pinch Hit H	PO	A	E	DP	TC/G	FA	G by Pos

Cookie Rojas *continued*

Year Team	Games	BA	SA	AB	H	2B	3B	HR	HR%	R	RBI	BB	SO	SB	PH AB	PH H	PO	A	E	DP	TC/G	FA	G by Pos
1974	144	.271	.339	542	147	17	1	6	1.1	52	60	30	43	8	8	1	292	368	9	94	4.6	.987	2B-141
1975	120	.254	.323	406	103	18	2	2	0.5	34	37	30	24	4	8	3	233	303	11	65	4.6	.980	2B-117, DH-1
1976	63	.242	.288	132	32	6	0	0	0.0	11	16	8	15	2	28	7	53	52	1	13	1.7	.991	2B-40, DH-9, 3B-6, 1B-1
1977	64	.250	.321	156	39	9	1	0	0.0	8	10	8	17	1	17	3	49	80	5	13	2.1	.963	3B-31, 2B-16, DH-6
16 yrs.	1822	.263	.337	6309	1660	254	25	54	0.9	714	593	396	489	74	136	27	3472	3960	134	971	4.2	.982	2B-1449, OF-200, 3B-46, SS-39, DH-16, C-7, 1B-2, P-1

LEAGUE CHAMPIONSHIP SERIES

Year Team	Games	BA	SA	AB	H	2B	3B	HR	HR%	R	RBI	BB	SO	SB	PH AB	PH H	PO	A	E	DP	TC/G	FA	G by Pos
1976 KC A	4	.333	.333	9	3	0	0	0	0.0	2	1	0	1	1	2	0	4	6	0	1	2.5	1.000	2B-4
1977	1	.250	.250	4	1	0	0	0	0.0	0	0	0	1	1	0	0	0	0	0	0	0.0	–	DH-1
2 yrs.	5	.308	.308	13	4	0	0	0	0.0	2	1	0	1	2	2	0	4	6	0	1	2.0	1.000	2B-4, DH-1

Stan Rojek

ROJEK, STANLEY ANDREW
B. Apr. 21, 1919, North Tonawanda, N. Y.

BR TR 5'10" 170 lbs.

Year Team	Games	BA	SA	AB	H	2B	3B	HR	HR%	R	RBI	BB	SO	SB	PH AB	PH H	PO	A	E	DP	TC/G	FA	G by Pos
1942 BKN N	1	–	–	0	0	0	0	0	–	0	0	0	0	0	0	0	0	0	0	0	0.0	–	
1946	45	.277	.362	47	13	2	1	0	0.0	11	2	4	1	1	10	3	20	32	1	4	1.2	.981	SS-15, 2B-6, 3B-4
1947	32	.263	.288	80	21	0	1	0	0.0	7	7	7	3	1	1	0	41	73	2	17	3.6	.983	SS-17, 3B-9, 2B-7
1948 PIT N	156	.290	.367	641	186	27	5	4	0.6	85	51	61	41	24	0	0	262	475	29	91	4.9	.962	SS-156
1949	144	.244	.285	557	136	19	2	0	0.0	72	31	50	31	4	0	0	240	461	25	92	5.0	.966	SS-144
1950	76	.257	.317	230	59	12	1	0	0.0	28	17	18	13	2	4	0	110	161	9	39	3.7	.968	SS-68, 2B-3
1951 2 teams									PIT N (8G – .188)				STL N (51G – .274)										
" total	59	.267	.332	202	54	7	3	0	0.0	21	14	10	11	0	0	0	100	144	8	36	4.3	.968	SS-59
1952 STL A	9	.143	.143	7	1	0	0	0	0.0	0	0	2	0	0	2	0	5	8	0	1	1.4	1.000	SS-4, 2B-1
8 yrs.	522	.266	.326	1764	470	67	13	4	0.2	225	122	152	100	32	17	3	778	1354	74	280	4.2	.966	SS-463, 2B-17, 3B-13

Red Rolfe

ROLFE, ROBERT ABIAL
B. Oct. 17, 1908, Penacook, N. H. D. July 8, 1969, Gifford, N. H.
Manager 1949-52.

BL TR 5'11½" 170 lbs.

Year Team	Games	BA	SA	AB	H	2B	3B	HR	HR%	R	RBI	BB	SO	SB	PH AB	PH H	PO	A	E	DP	TC/G	FA	G by Pos
1931 NY A	1	–	–	0	0	0	0	0	–	0	0	0	0	0	0	0	1	0	0	0	1.0	1.000	SS-1
1934	89	.287	.348	279	80	13	2	0	0.0	54	18	26	16	2	15	5	121	159	19	31	3.4	.936	SS-46, 3B-26
1935	149	.300	.404	639	192	33	9	5	0.8	108	67	57	39	7	0	0	197	283	19	22	3.3	.962	3B-136, SS-17
1936	135	.319	.493	568	181	39	15	10	1.8	116	70	68	38	3	0	0	162	265	19	20	3.3	.957	3B-133
1937	154	.276	.378	648	179	34	10	4	0.6	143	62	90	53	4	0	0	195	309	20	27	3.4	.962	3B-154
1938	151	.311	.441	631	196	36	8	10	1.6	132	80	74	44	13	0	0	151	294	19	26	3.1	.959	3B-151
1939	152	.329	.495	648	213	46	10	14	2.2	139	80	81	41	7	0	0	151	282	19	22	3.0	.958	3B-152
1940	139	.250	.366	588	147	26	6	10	1.7	102	53	50	48	4	1	0	161	288	24	24	3.4	.949	3B-138
1941	136	.264	.364	561	148	22	5	8	1.4	106	42	57	38	3	2	0	140	263	23	28	3.1	.946	3B-134
1942	69	.219	.355	265	58	8	2	8	3.0	42	25	23	18	1	8	1	57	132	8	16	2.9	.959	3B-60
10 yrs.	1175	.289	.413	4827	1394	257	67	69	1.4	942	497	526	335	44	26	6	1336	2275	170	216	3.2	.955	3B-1084, SS-64

WORLD SERIES

Year Team	Games	BA	SA	AB	H	2B	3B	HR	HR%	R	RBI	BB	SO	SB	PH AB	PH H	PO	A	E	DP	TC/G	FA	G by Pos
1936 NY A	6	.400	.400	25	10	0	0	0	0.0	5	4	3	1	0	0	0	14	7	1	0	3.7	.955	3B-6
1937	5	.300	.500	20	6	2	1	0	0.0	3	1	3	2	0	0	0	2	6	0	1	1.6	1.000	3B-5
1938	4	.167	.167	18	3	0	0	0	0.0	0	1	0	3	1	0	0	0	4	2	0	1.5	.667	3B-4
1939	4	.125	.125	16	2	0	0	0	0.0	2	0	0	0	0	0	0	3	8	1	2	3.0	.917	3B-4
1941	5	.300	.300	20	6	0	0	0	0.0	2	0	1	0	0	0	0	7	8	0	1	3.0	1.000	3B-5
1942	4	.353	.471	17	6	2	0	0	0.0	5	0	2	1	0	0	0	3	5	0	1	2.0	1.000	3B-4
6 yrs.	28	.284	.336	116	33	4	1	0	0.0	17	6	9	7	1	0	0	29	38	4	4	2.5	.944	3B-28

Ray Rolling

ROLLING, RAYMOND COPELAND
B. Sept. 8, 1886, Martinsburg, Mo. D. Aug. 25, 1966, St. Paul, Minn.

BR TR 5'10½" 160 lbs.

Year Team	Games	BA	SA	AB	H	2B	3B	HR	HR%	R	RBI	BB	SO	SB	PH AB	PH H	PO	A	E	DP	TC/G	FA	G by Pos
1912 STL N	5	.200	.200	15	3	0	0	0	0.0	0	0	0	5	0	0	0	9	9	1	0	3.8	.947	2B-4

Red Rollings

ROLLINGS, WILLIAM RUSSELL
B. Mar. 31, 1904, Mobile, Ala. D. Dec. 31, 1964, Mobile, Ala.

BL TR 5'11" 167 lbs.

Year Team	Games	BA	SA	AB	H	2B	3B	HR	HR%	R	RBI	BB	SO	SB	PH AB	PH H	PO	A	E	DP	TC/G	FA	G by Pos
1927 BOS A	82	.266	.299	184	49	4	1	0	0.0	19	9	12	10	3	14	6	105	75	7	13	2.3	.963	3B-44, 1B-10, 2B-2
1928	50	.229	.333	48	11	3	1	0	0.0	7	9	6	8	0	29	7	20	1	2	2	0.5	.913	1B-5, OF-4, 2B-4, 3B-1
1930 BOS N	52	.236	.285	123	29	6	0	0	0.0	10	10	9	5	2	12	4	42	73	6	9	2.3	.950	3B-28, 2B-10
3 yrs.	184	.251	.299	355	89	13	2	0	0.0	36	28	27	23	5	55	17	167	149	15	24	1.8	.955	3B-73, 2B-16, 1B-15, OF-4

Rich Rollins

ROLLINS, RICHARD JOHN (Red)
B. Apr. 16, 1938, Mt. Pleasant, Pa.

BR TR 5'10" 185 lbs.

Year Team	Games	BA	SA	AB	H	2B	3B	HR	HR%	R	RBI	BB	SO	SB	PH AB	PH H	PO	A	E	DP	TC/G	FA	G by Pos
1961 MIN A	13	.294	.353	17	5	1	0	0	0.0	3	3	2	2	0	3	2	5	10	0	2	1.2	1.000	2B-5, 3B-4
1962	159	.298	.428	624	186	23	5	16	2.6	96	96	75	62	3	0	0	137	324	28	33	3.1	.943	3B-159, SS-1
1963	136	.307	.444	531	163	23	1	16	3.0	75	61	36	59	2	4	0	122	225	26	22	2.7	.930	3B-132, 2B-1
1964	148	.270	.406	596	161	25	10	12	2.0	87	68	53	80	2	1	0	134	297	24	17	3.1	.947	3B-146
1965	140	.249	.333	469	117	22	1	5	1.1	59	32	37	54	4	13	2	144	264	20	25	3.1	.953	3B-112, 2B-16
1966	90	.245	.390	269	66	7	1	10	3.7	30	40	13	34	0	21	8	57	109	8	13	1.9	.954	3B-65, 2B-2, OF-1
1967	109	.245	.342	339	83	11	2	6	1.8	31	39	27	58	1	14	4	83	153	9	13	2.2	.963	3B-97
1968	93	.241	.355	203	49	5	0	6	3.0	14	30	10	34	3	41	8	28	93	9	4	1.4	.931	3B-56
1969 SEA A	58	.225	.326	187	42	7	0	4	2.1	15	21	7	19	2	14	4	42	104	9	7	2.7	.948	3B-47, SS-1
1970 2 teams									MIL A (14G – .200)				CLE A (42G – .233)										
" total	56	.221	.324	68	15	1	0	2	2.9	9	9	6	9	0	42	8	3	15	2	3	0.4	.900	3B-12
10 yrs.	1002	.269	.388	3303	887	125	20	77	2.3	419	399	266	411	17	153	36	755	1594	134	139	2.5	.946	3B-830, 2B-24, SS-2, OF-1

WORLD SERIES

Year Team	Games	BA	SA	AB	H	2B	3B	HR	HR%	R	RBI	BB	SO	SB	PH AB	PH H	PO	A	E	DP	TC/G	FA	G by Pos
1965 MIN A	3	.000	.000	2	0	0	0	0	0.0	0	0	1	0	0	2	0	0	0	0	0	0.0	–	

Rollinson

ROLLINSON,
Deceased.

Year Team	Games	BA	SA	AB	H	2B	3B	HR	HR%	R	RBI	BB	SO	SB	PH AB	PH H	PO	A	E	DP	TC/G	FA	G by Pos
1884 WAS U	1	.000	.000	3	0	0	0	0	0.0	0	0	0		0	0	0	6	4	4	0	14.0	.714	C-1

Year	Team	Games	BA	SA	AB	H	2B	3B	HR	HR%	R	RBI	BB	SO	SB	Pinch Hit AB	Pinch Hit H	PO	A	E	DP	TC/G	FA	G by Pos

Bill Roman

ROMAN, WILLIAM ANTHONY
B. Oct. 11, 1938, Detroit, Mich.

BL TL 6'4" 190 lbs.

Year	Team	Games	BA	SA	AB	H	2B	3B	HR	HR%	R	RBI	BB	SO	SB	AB	H	PO	A	E	DP	TC/G	FA	G by Pos
1964	DET A	3	.375	.750	8	3	0	0	1	12.5	2	1	0	2	0	2	1	13	1	0	2	4.7	1.000	1B-2
1965		21	.074	.074	27	2	0	0	0	0.0	0	0	2	7	0	13	2	38	1	0	2	1.9	1.000	1B-6
2 yrs.		24	.143	.229	35	5	0	0	1	2.9	2	1	2	9	0	15	3	51	2	0	4	2.2	1.000	1B-8

Johnny Romano

ROMANO, JOHN ANTHONY (Honey)
B. Aug. 23, 1934, Hoboken, N. J.

BR TR 5'11" 205 lbs.

Year	Team	Games	BA	SA	AB	H	2B	3B	HR	HR%	R	RBI	BB	SO	SB	AB	H	PO	A	E	DP	TC/G	FA	G by Pos
1958	CHI A	4	.286	.286	7	2	0	0	0	0.0	1	1	1	0	0	2	0	13	0	0	0	3.3	1.000	C-2
1959		53	.294	.468	126	37	5	1	5	4.0	20	25	23	18	0	13	8	169	16	4	5	3.6	.979	C-38
1960	CLE A	108	.272	.475	316	86	12	2	16	5.1	40	52	37	50	0	11	0	470	30	6	6	4.7	.988	C-99
1961		142	.299	.483	509	152	29	1	21	4.1	76	80	61	60	0	2	0	752	58	9	8	5.8	.989	C-141
1962		135	.261	.479	459	120	19	3	25	5.4	71	81	73	64	0	4	3	657	63	7	6	5.4	.990	C-130
1963		89	.216	.369	255	55	5	2	10	3.9	28	34	38	49	4	16	4	413	28	4	5	5.0	.991	C-71, OF-4
1964		106	.241	.460	352	85	18	1	19	5.4	46	47	51	83	2	10	2	723	38	7	3	7.2	.991	C-96, 1B-1
1965	CHI A	122	.242	.424	356	86	11	0	18	5.1	39	48	59	74	0	8	1	575	62	5	10	5.3	.992	C-111, OF-4, 1B-2
1966		122	.231	.404	329	76	12	0	15	4.6	33	47	58	72	0	16	4	622	46	4	7	5.5	.994	C-102
1967	STL N	24	.121	.138	58	7	1	0	0	0.0	1	2	13	15	1	4	0	111	3	2	1	4.8	.983	C-20
10 yrs.		905	.255	.443	2767	706	112	10	129	4.7	355	417	414	485	7	86	22	4505	344	48	51	5.4	.990	C-810, OF-8, 1B-3

WORLD SERIES

| 1959 | CHI A | 2 | .000 | .000 | 1 | 0 | 0 | 0 | 0 | 0.0 | 0 | 0 | 0 | 0 | 0 | 1 | 0 | 0 | 0 | 0 | 0 | 0.0 | — | |

Tom Romano

ROMANO, THOMAS MICHAEL
B. Oct. 25, 1958, Syracuse, N. Y.

BR TR 5'10" 170 lbs.

Year	Team	Games	BA	SA	AB	H	2B	3B	HR	HR%	R	RBI	BB	SO	SB	AB	H	PO	A	E	DP	TC/G	FA	G by Pos
1987	MON N	7	.000	.000	3	0	0	0	0	0.0	1	0	1	0	2	0	0	0	0	0	0	0.0	—	OF-3

Ed Romero

ROMERO, EDGARDO RALPH
Born Edgardo Ralph Romero y Rivera.
B. Dec. 9, 1957, Santurce, Puerto Rico

BR TR 5'11" 160 lbs.

Year	Team	Games	BA	SA	AB	H	2B	3B	HR	HR%	R	RBI	BB	SO	SB	AB	H	PO	A	E	DP	TC/G	FA	G by Pos
1977	MIL A	10	.280	.320	25	7	1	0	0	0.0	4	2	4	3	0	0	0	9	24	1	3	3.4	.971	SS-10
1980		42	.260	.356	104	27	7	0	1	1.0	20	10	9	11	2	0	0	60	102	12	20	4.1	.931	SS-22, 2B-15, 3B-3
1981		44	.198	.264	91	18	3	0	1	1.1	6	10	4	9	0	0	0	61	102	6	29	3.8	.964	SS-22, 2B-18, 3B-3
1982		52	.250	.326	144	36	8	0	1	0.7	18	7	8	16	0	2	1	103	113	7	34	4.3	.969	2B-39, SS-10, 3B-2, OF-1
1983		59	.317	.386	145	46	7	0	1	0.7	17	18	8	8	1	14	6	59	58	5	14	2.1	.959	SS-22, OF-15, DH-5, 3B-5, 2B-3
1984		116	.252	.294	357	90	12	0	1	0.3	36	31	29	25	3	1	0	141	256	18	35	3.6	.957	3B-59, SS-39, 2B-11, 1B-4, DH-2, OF-1
1985		88	.251	.303	251	63	11	1	0	0.0	24	21	26	20	1	0	0	157	219	8	53	4.4	.979	SS-43, 2B-31, OF-14, 3B-1
1986	BOS A	100	.210	.283	233	49	11	0	2	0.9	41	23	18	16	2	0	0	111	159	12	32	2.8	.957	2B-75, 3B-18, 2B-4, OF-1
1987		88	.272	.294	235	64	5	0	0	0.0	23	14	18	22	0	6	1	122	151	6	28	3.2	.978	2B-29, SS-24, 3B-24, 1B-8
1988		31	.240	.280	75	18	3	0	0	0.0	3	5	3	8	0	2	0	21	42	0	5	2.0	1.000	3B-15, SS-8, 2B-5, DH-1, 1B-1
1989	3 teams	BOS A	(46G – .212)		ATL N	(7G – .263)			MIL A	(15G – .200)															
"	total	68	.214	.275	182	39	4	0	1	0.5	18	10	7	17	0	2	0	89	152	5	32	3.6	.980	2B-37, 3B-19, SS-13, DH-2
11 yrs.		698	.248	.303	1842	457	76	1	8	0.4	210	151	134	155	9	28	8	933	1378	80	285	3.4	.967	SS-288, 2B-192, 3B-149, OF-32, 1B-13, DH-10

DIVISIONAL PLAYOFF SERIES

| 1981 | MIL A | 1 | .500 | .500 | 2 | 1 | 0 | 0 | 0 | 0.0 | 1 | 0 | 0 | 1 | 0 | 0 | 0 | 0 | 0 | 0 | 0 | 0.0 | — | 2B-1 |

LEAGUE CHAMPIONSHIP SERIES

1986	BOS A	1	.000	.000	2	0	0	0	0	0.0	0	0	0	0	0	0	0	0	0	0	0	0.0	—	SS-1
1988		1	–	–	0	0	0	0	0	0.0	0	0	0	0	0	0	0	0	0	0	0	0.0	—	
2 yrs.		2	.000	.000	2	0	0	0	0	0.0	0	0	0	0	0	0	0	0	0	0	0	0.0	—	SS-1

WORLD SERIES

| 1986 | BOS A | 3 | .000 | .000 | 1 | 0 | 0 | 0 | 0 | 0.0 | 0 | 0 | 0 | 0 | 0 | 0 | 0 | 0 | 1 | 0 | 0 | 0.3 | 1.000 | SS-3 |

Kevin Romine

ROMINE, KEVIN ANDREW
B. May 23, 1961, Exeter, N. H.

BR TR 5'11" 185 lbs.

Year	Team	Games	BA	SA	AB	H	2B	3B	HR	HR%	R	RBI	BB	SO	SB	AB	H	PO	A	E	DP	TC/G	FA	G by Pos
1985	BOS A	24	.214	.286	28	6	2	0	0	0.0	3	1	1	4	1	1	1	20	1	0	0	0.9	1.000	OF-23, DH-1
1986		35	.257	.314	35	9	2	0	0	0.0	6	2	3	9	2	1	0	45	1	0	1	1.3	1.000	OF-33
1987		9	.292	.375	24	7	2	0	0	0.0	5	2	2	6	0	1	0	10	1	0	1	1.2	1.000	OF-7, DH-2
1988		57	.192	.282	78	15	2	1	1	1.3	17	6	7	15	2	3	0	44	0	2	0	0.8	.957	OF-45, DH-5
1989		92	.274	.332	274	75	13	0	1	0.4	30	23	21	53	1	8	3	157	9	3	4	1.8	.982	OF-89, DH-2
5 yrs.		217	.255	.321	439	112	21	1	2	0.5	61	34	34	87	6	14	4	276	12	5	6	1.4	.983	OF-197, DH-10

LEAGUE CHAMPIONSHIP SERIES

| 1988 | BOS A | 2 | – | – | 0 | 0 | 0 | 0 | 0 | 0.0 | 1 | 0 | 0 | 0 | 0 | 0 | 0 | 0 | 0 | 0 | 0 | 0.0 | — | |

Henri Rondeau

RONDEAU, HENRI JOSEPH
B. May 5, 1887, Danielson, Conn. D. May 28, 1943, Woonsocket, R. I.

BR TR 5'10½" 175 lbs.

Year	Team	Games	BA	SA	AB	H	2B	3B	HR	HR%	R	RBI	BB	SO	SB	AB	H	PO	A	E	DP	TC/G	FA	G by Pos
1913	DET A	35	.186	.214	70	13	2	0	0	0.0	5	5	14	16	1	13	2	100	26	4	2	3.7	.969	C-14, 1B-6
1915	WAS A	14	.175	.175	40	7	0	0	0	0.0	3	4	3	3	1	3	0	29	2	0	0	2.2	1.000	OF-11
1916		50	.222	.309	162	36	5	3	1	0.6	20	28	18	18	7	0	0	110	4	5	0	2.4	.958	OF-48
3 yrs.		99	.206	.265	272	56	7	3	1	0.4	28	37	36	37	9	16	2	239	32	9	2	2.8	.968	OF-59, C-14, 1B-6

Gene Roof

ROOF, EUGENE LAWRENCE
Brother of Phil Roof.
B. Jan. 13, 1958, Paducah, Ky.

BB TR 6'2" 180 lbs.

Year	Team	Games	BA	SA	AB	H	2B	3B	HR	HR%	R	RBI	BB	SO	SB	AB	H	PO	A	E	DP	TC/G	FA	G by Pos
1981	STL N	23	.300	.400	60	18	6	0	0	0.0	11	3	12	16	5	2	0	38	0	2	0	1.7	.950	OF-20
1982		11	.267	.267	15	4	0	0	0	0.0	3	2	1	4	2	7	2	5	0	0	0	0.5	1.000	OF-5

Year	Team	Games	BA	SA	AB	H	2B	3B	HR	HR%	R	RBI	BB	SO	SB	Pinch Hit AB	H	PO	A	E	DP	TC/G	FA	G by Pos

Gene Roof *continued*

Year	Team	Games	BA	SA	AB	H	2B	3B	HR	HR%	R	RBI	BB	SO	SB	AB	H	PO	A	E	DP	TC/G	FA	G by Pos
1983	2 teams	STL N (6G – .000)			MON N (8G – .167)																			
"	total	14	.133	.267	15	2	0	0	0	0.0	3	1	1	3	0	7	1	3	0	0	0	0.2	1.000	OF-6
	3 yrs.	48	.267	.356	90	24	8	0	0	0.0	17	6	14	23	7	16	3	46	0	2	0	1.0	.958	OF-31

Phil Roof

ROOF, PHILLIP ANTHONY
Brother of Gene Roof.
B. Mar. 5, 1941, Paducah, Ky.

BR TR 6'2" 190 lbs.

Year	Team	Games	BA	SA	AB	H	2B	3B	HR	HR%	R	RBI	BB	SO	SB	AB	H	PO	A	E	DP	TC/G	FA	G by Pos
1961	MIL N	1	–	–	0	0	0	0	0		0	0	0	0	0	0	0	2	0	0	0	2.0	1.000	C-1
1964		1	.000	.000	2	0	0	0	0	0.0	0	0	0	1	0	0	0	8	0	0	0	8.0	1.000	C-1
1965	2 teams	CAL A (9G – .136)			CLE A (43G – .173)																			
"	total	52	.162	.176	74	12	1	0	0	0.0	4	3	5	19	0	4	0	214	23	2	3	4.6	.992	C-50
1966	KC A	127	.209	.320	369	77	14	3	7	1.9	33	44	37	95	2	4	0	684	52	11	8	5.9	.985	C-123, 1B-2
1967		114	.205	.333	327	67	14	5	6	1.8	23	24	23	85	4	1	0	677	55	7	6	6.5	.991	C-113
1968	OAK A	34	.188	.234	64	12	0	0	1	1.6	5	2	2	15	1	2	0	116	6	4	2	3.7	.968	C-32
1969		106	.235	.291	247	58	6	1	2	0.8	19	19	33	55	1	1	0	493	40	9	4	5.1	.983	C-106
1970	MIL A	110	.227	.377	321	73	7	1	13	4.0	39	37	32	72	3	3	1	596	47	8	6	5.9	.988	C-107, 1B-1
1971	2 teams	MIL A (41G – .193)			MIN A (31G – .241)																			
"	total	72	.214	.269	201	43	6	1	1	0.5	12	16	16	46	0	5	0	359	38	8	5	5.6	.980	C-68
1972	MIN A	61	.205	.356	146	30	11	1	3	2.1	16	12	6	27	0	0	0	257	11	6	0	4.5	.978	C-61
1973		47	.197	.274	117	23	4	1	1	0.9	10	15	13	27	0	0	0	218	17	2	4	5.0	.992	C-47
1974		44	.196	.268	97	19	1	0	2	2.1	10	13	6	24	0	0	0	200	24	0	3	5.1	1.000	C-44
1975		63	.302	.484	126	38	2	0	7	5.6	18	21	9	28	0	0	0	245	30	3	4	4.4	.989	C-63
1976	2 teams	MIN A (18G – .217)			CHI A (4G – .111)																			
"	total	22	.200	.255	55	11	3	0	0	0.0	1	4	2	9	0	5	1	76	12	3	3	4.1	.967	C-16, DH-1
1977	TOR A	3	.000	.000	5	0	0	0	0	0.0	0	0	0	1	0	0	0	10	1	0	1	3.7	1.000	C-3
	15 yrs.	857	.215	.319	2151	463	69	13	43	2.0	190	210	184	504	11	25	2	4155	356	63	49	5.3	.986	C-835, 1B-3, DH-1

George Rooks

ROOKS, GEORGE BRINTON McCLELLAN
Born George Brinton McClellan Ruckser.
B. Oct. 21, 1863, Chicago, Ill. D. Mar. 11, 1935, Chicago, Ill.

BR TR 5'11" 170 lbs.

Year	Team	Games	BA	SA	AB	H	2B	3B	HR	HR%	R	RBI	BB	SO	SB	AB	H	PO	A	E	DP	TC/G	FA	G by Pos
1891	BOS N	5	.125	.125	16	2	0	0	0	0.0	1	0	4	1	0	0	0	11	1	0	0	2.4	1.000	OF-5

Rolando Roomes

ROOMES, ROLANDO AUDLEY
B. Feb. 15, 1962, Kingston, Jamaica

BR TR 6'3" 180 lbs.

Year	Team	Games	BA	SA	AB	H	2B	3B	HR	HR%	R	RBI	BB	SO	SB	AB	H	PO	A	E	DP	TC/G	FA	G by Pos
1988	CHI N	17	.188	.188	16	3	0	0	0	0.0	3	0	0	4	0	4	0	5	0	1	0	0.4	.833	OF-5
1989	CIN N	107	.263	.419	315	83	18	5	7	2.2	36	34	13	100	12	11	4	201	4	4	0	2.0	.981	OF-100
	2 yrs.	124	.260	.408	331	86	18	5	7	2.1	39	34	13	104	12	15	4	206	4	5	0	1.7	.977	OF-105

Frank Rooney

ROONEY, FRANK L.
Born Frank Rovny.
B. Oct. 12, 1884, Padebrady, Austria-Hungar, D. Apr. 6, 1977, Bessemer, Mich.

Year	Team	Games	BA	SA	AB	H	2B	3B	HR	HR%	R	RBI	BB	SO	SB	AB	H	PO	A	E	DP	TC/G	FA	G by Pos
1914	IND F	12	.200	.343	35	7	0	1	1	2.9	1	8	1		0	2	3	0	98	2	2	6	8.5	.980	1B-9

Pat Rooney

ROONEY, PATRICK EUGENE
B. Nov. 28, 1957, Chicago, Ill.

BR TR 6'1" 190 lbs.

Year	Team	Games	BA	SA	AB	H	2B	3B	HR	HR%	R	RBI	BB	SO	SB	AB	H	PO	A	E	DP	TC/G	FA	G by Pos
1981	MON N	4	.000	.000	5	0	0	0	0	0.0	0	0	0	3	0	2	0	1	0	0	0	0.3	1.000	OF-2

Jorge Roque

ROQUE, JORGE
Born Jorge Roque y Vargas.
B. Apr. 28, 1950, Ponce, Puerto Rico

BR TR 5'10" 158 lbs.

Year	Team	Games	BA	SA	AB	H	2B	3B	HR	HR%	R	RBI	BB	SO	SB	AB	H	PO	A	E	DP	TC/G	FA	G by Pos
1970	STL N	5	.000	.000	1	0	0	0	0	0.0	2	0	1	0	0	1	0	0	0	0	0	0.0	–	OF-1
1971		3	.300	.300	10	3	0	0	0	0.0	2	1	0	3	1	0	0	6	0	0	0	2.0	1.000	OF-3
1972		32	.104	.209	67	7	2	1	1	1.5	3	5	6	19	1	6	1	50	0	1	0	1.6	.980	OF-24
1973	MON N	25	.148	.230	61	9	2	0	1	1.6	7	6	4	17	2	0	0	41	2	6	0	2.0	.878	OF-24
	4 yrs.	65	.137	.223	139	19	4	1	2	1.4	14	12	10	40	4	7	1	97	2	7	0	1.6	.934	OF-52

Luis Rosado

ROSADO, LUIS (Papo)
Born Luis Rosado y Robles.
B. Dec. 6, 1955, Santurce, Puerto Rico

BR TR 6' 180 lbs.

Year	Team	Games	BA	SA	AB	H	2B	3B	HR	HR%	R	RBI	BB	SO	SB	AB	H	PO	A	E	DP	TC/G	FA	G by Pos
1977	NY N	9	.208	.250	24	5	1	0	0	0.0	1	3	1	3	0	1	0	46	4	2	4	5.8	.962	1B-7, C-1
1980		2	.000	.000	4	0	0	0	0	0.0	0	0	0	1	0	1	0	11	0	0	1	5.5	1.000	1B-1
	2 yrs.	11	.179	.214	28	5	1	0	0	0.0	1	3	1	4	0	2	0	57	4	2	5	5.7	.968	1B-8, C-1

Buddy Rosar

ROSAR, WARREN VINCENT
B. July 3, 1914, Buffalo, N. Y.

BR TR 5'9" 190 lbs.

Year	Team	Games	BA	SA	AB	H	2B	3B	HR	HR%	R	RBI	BB	SO	SB	AB	H	PO	A	E	DP	TC/G	FA	G by Pos
1939	NY A	43	.276	.343	105	29	5	1	0	0.0	18	12	13	10	4	4	3	137	10	3	1	3.5	.980	C-35
1940		73	.298	.425	228	68	11	3	4	1.8	34	37	19	11	7	10	4	258	30	5	8	4.0	.983	C-63
1941		67	.287	.402	209	60	17	2	1	0.5	25	36	22	10	0	6	0	246	24	1	6	4.0	.996	C-60
1942		69	.230	.306	209	48	10	0	2	1.0	18	34	17	20	1	12	3	249	26	1	7	4.0	.996	C-58
1943	CLE A	115	.283	.340	382	108	17	1	1	0.3	53	41	33	12	0	6	1	480	91	10	11	5.1	.983	C-114
1944		99	.263	.308	331	87	9	3	0	0.0	29	30	34	17	1	1	0	409	59	5	13	4.8	.989	C-98
1945	PHI A	92	.210	.267	300	63	12	1	1	0.3	23	25	20	16	2	5	1	338	54	5	6	4.3	.987	C-85
1946		121	.283	.358	424	120	22	2	2	0.5	34	47	36	17	1	1	0	532	73	0	9	5.0	1.000	C-117
1947		102	.259	.334	359	93	20	2	1	0.3	40	33	40	13	1	1	0	406	70	2	12	4.7	.996	C-102
1948		90	.255	.338	302	77	13	0	4	1.3	30	41	39	12	0	0	0	335	39	1	10	4.2	.997	C-90
1949		32	.200	.221	95	19	2	0	0	0.0	7	6	16	5	0	1	0	112	9	1	2	3.8	.992	C-31
1950	BOS A	27	.298	.357	84	25	2	0	1	1.2	13	12	7	4	0	2	1	108	6	1	1	4.3	.991	C-25
1951		58	.229	.288	170	39	7	0	1	0.6	11	13	19	14	0	2	0	235	20	1	6	4.4	.996	C-56
	13 yrs.	988	.261	.334	3198	836	147	15	18	0.6	335	367	315	161	17	54	14	3845	511	36	92	4.4	.992	C-934

Year	Team		Games	BA	SA	AB	H	2B	3B	HR	HR%	R	RBI	BB	SO	SB	Pinch Hit AB	Pinch Hit H	PO	A	E	DP	TC/G	FA	G by Pos

Buddy Rosar *continued*

WORLD SERIES

Year	Team		Games	BA	SA	AB	H	2B	3B	HR	HR%	R	RBI	BB	SO	SB	AB	H	PO	A	E	DP	TC/G	FA	G by Pos
1941	NY	A	1	–	–	0	0	0	0	0	–	0	0	0	0	0	0	0	0	0	0	0	0.0	–	C-1
1942			1	1.000	1.000	1	1	0	0	0	0.0	0	0	0	1	0	0	0	0	0	0	0	0.0	–	C-1
2 yrs.			2	1.000	1.000	1	1	0	0	0	0.0	0	0	0	1	0	0	0	0	0	0	0	0.0	–	C-1

Jimmy Rosario

ROSARIO, ANGEL RAMON
Born Angel Ramon Rosario y Ferrer.
B. May 5, 1945, Bayamon, Puerto Rico

BB TR 5'10'' 155 lbs.

Year	Team		Games	BA	SA	AB	H	2B	3B	HR	HR%	R	RBI	BB	SO	SB	AB	H	PO	A	E	DP	TC/G	FA	G by Pos
1971	SF	N	92	.224	.266	192	43	6	1	0	0.0	26	13	33	35	7	11	1	151	1	0	0	1.7	1.000	OF-67
1972			7	.000	.000	2	0	0	0	0	0.0	1	0	0	0	0	2	0	0	0	0	0	0.0	–	OF-1
1976	MIL	A	15	.189	.270	37	7	0	0	1	2.7	4	5	3	8	1	1	0	20	0	0	0	1.3	1.000	OF-12, DH-2
3 yrs.			114	.216	.264	231	50	6	1	1	0.4	31	18	36	43	8	14	1	171	1	0	0	1.5	1.000	OF-80, DH-2

LEAGUE CHAMPIONSHIP SERIES

Year	Team		Games	BA	SA	AB	H	2B	3B	HR	HR%	R	RBI	BB	SO	SB	AB	H	PO	A	E	DP	TC/G	FA	G by Pos
1971	SF	N	1	–	–	0	0	0	0	0	–	0	0	0	0	0	0	0	0	0	0	0	0.0	–	

Santiago Rosario

ROSARIO, SANTIAGO
B. July 25, 1939, Guayanilla, Puerto Rico

BL TL 5'11'' 165 lbs.

Year	Team		Games	BA	SA	AB	H	2B	3B	HR	HR%	R	RBI	BB	SO	SB	AB	H	PO	A	E	DP	TC/G	FA	G by Pos
1965	KC	A	81	.235	.341	85	20	3	0	2	2.4	8	8	6	16	0	46	11	99	7	1	5	1.3	.991	1B-31, OF-3

Bobby Rose

ROSE, ROBERT RICHARD
B. Mar. 15, 1967, Covina, Calif.

BR TR 5'11'' 170 lbs.

Year	Team		Games	BA	SA	AB	H	2B	3B	HR	HR%	R	RBI	BB	SO	SB	AB	H	PO	A	E	DP	TC/G	FA	G by Pos
1989	CAL	A	14	.211	.421	38	8	1	2	1	2.6	4	3	2	10	0	1	0	10	21	2	1	2.4	.939	3B-10, 2B-3

Pete Rose

ROSE, PETER EDWARD (Charlie Hustle)
B. Apr. 14, 1941, Cincinnati, Ohio
Manager 1984-89.

BB TR 5'11'' 192 lbs.

Year	Team		Games	BA	SA	AB	H	2B	3B	HR	HR%	R	RBI	BB	SO	SB	AB	H	PO	A	E	DP	TC/G	FA	G by Pos
1963	CIN	N	157	.273	.371	623	170	25	9	6	1.0	101	41	55	72	13	0	0	360	366	22	78	4.8	.971	2B-157, OF-1
1964			136	.269	.326	516	139	13	2	4	0.8	64	34	36	51	4	11	2	263	301	12	63	4.2	.979	2B-128
1965			162	.312	.446	670	209	35	11	11	1.6	117	81	69	76	8	0	0	382	403	20	93	5.0	.975	2B-162
1966			156	.313	.460	654	205	38	5	16	2.4	97	70	37	61	4	0	0	409	374	18	83	5.1	.978	2B-140, 3B-16
1967			148	.301	.444	585	176	32	8	12	2.1	86	76	56	66	11	0	0	287	93	11	15	2.6	.972	OF-123, 2B-35
1968			149	.335	.470	626	210	42	6	10	1.6	94	49	56	76	3	0	0	270	20	3	4	2.0	.990	OF-148, 2B-3, 1B-1
1969			156	.348	.512	627	218	33	11	16	2.6	120	82	88	65	7	0	0	317	10	4	3	2.1	.988	OF-156, 2B-2
1970			159	.316	.470	649	205	37	9	15	2.3	120	52	73	64	12	1	0	309	8	1	2	2.0	.997	OF-159
1971			160	.304	.421	632	192	27	4	13	2.1	86	44	68	50	13	2	0	306	13	2	1	2.0	.994	OF-158
1972			154	.307	.417	645	198	31	11	6	0.9	107	57	73	46	10	0	0	330	15	2	2	2.3	.994	OF-154
1973			160	.338	.437	680	230	36	8	5	0.7	115	64	65	42	10	0	0	343	15	3	0	2.3	.992	OF-159
1974			163	.284	.388	652	185	45	7	3	0.5	110	51	106	54	2	0	0	346	11	1	3	2.2	.997	OF-163
1975			162	.317	.432	662	210	47	4	7	1.1	112	74	89	50	0	0	0	161	230	14	21	2.5	.965	3B-137, OF-35
1976			162	.323	.450	665	215	42	6	10	1.5	130	63	86	54	9	3	2	115	293	13	25	2.6	.969	3B-159, OF-1
1977			162	.311	.432	655	204	38	7	9	1.4	95	64	66	42	16	1	0	98	268	16	18	2.4	.958	3B-161
1978			159	.302	.421	655	198	51	3	7	1.1	103	52	62	30	13	0	0	135	256	15	25	2.6	.963	3B-156, OF-7, 1B-2
1979	PHI	N	163	.331	.430	628	208	40	5	4	0.6	90	59	95	32	20	0	0	1429	93	10	124	9.4	.993	1B-159, 3B-5, 2B-1
1980			162	.282	.354	655	185	42	1	1	0.2	95	64	66	33	12	1	0	1427	123	5	113	9.6	.997	1B-162
1981			107	.325	.390	431	140	18	5	0	0.0	73	33	46	26	4	0	0	929	91	4	69	9.6	.996	1B-107
1982			162	.271	.338	634	172	25	4	3	0.5	80	54	66	32	8	0	0	1428	123	8	114	9.6	.995	1B-162
1983			151	.245	.286	493	121	14	3	0	0.0	52	45	52	28	7	22	8	827	74	10	57	6.0	.989	1B-112, OF-35
1984	2 teams			MON	N (95G – .259)			CIN	N	(26G – .365)															
"	total		121	.286	.337	374	107	15	2	0	0.0	43	34	40	27	1	27	7	530	53	8	36	4.9	.986	1B-63, OF-28
1985	CIN	N	119	.264	.319	405	107	12	2	2	0.5	60	46	86	35	8	8	1	870	73	5	80	8.0	.995	1B-110
1986			72	.219	.270	237	52	8	2	0	0.0	15	25	30	31	3	8	1	523	43	6	54	7.9	.990	1B-61
24 yrs.			3562	.303	.409	14053	4256	746	135	160	1.1	2165	1314	1566	1143	198	84	21	12394	3349	213	1083	4.5	.987	OF-1327, 1B-939, 3B-634, 2B-628
				1st		1st	2nd					4th			10th										

DIVISIONAL PLAYOFF SERIES

Year	Team		Games	BA	SA	AB	H	2B	3B	HR	HR%	R	RBI	BB	SO	SB	AB	H	PO	A	E	DP	TC/G	FA	G by Pos
1981	PHI	N	5	.300	.350	20	6	1	0	0	0.0	1	2	2	0	0	0	0	0	0	0	0	0.0	–	1B-5

LEAGUE CHAMPIONSHIP SERIES

Year	Team		Games	BA	SA	AB	H	2B	3B	HR	HR%	R	RBI	BB	SO	SB	AB	H	PO	A	E	DP	TC/G	FA	G by Pos
1970	CIN	N	3	.231	.231	13	3	0	0	0	0.0	1	1	0	0	0	0	0	3	0	0	0	1.0	1.000	OF-3
1972			5	.450	.650	20	9	4	0	0	0.0	1	2	2	2	0	0	0	10	0	0	0	2.0	1.000	OF-5
1973			5	.381	.714	21	8	1	0	2	9.5	3	2	2	2	0	0	0	10	1	0	0	2.2	1.000	OF-5
1975			3	.357	.571	14	5	0	0	1	7.1	3	2	2	0	0	0	0	2	1	0	0	1.0	1.000	3B-3
1976			3	.429	.714	14	6	2	1	0	0.0	3	2	1	0	0	0	0	2	5	1	2	2.7	.875	3B-3
1980	PHI	N	5	.400	.400	20	8	0	0	0	0.0	3	3	5	3	0	0	0	53	7	0	5	12.0	1.000	1B-5
1983			4	.375	.375	16	6	0	0	0	0.0	3	0	1	1	0	0	0	29	2	0	0	7.8	1.000	1B-4
7 yrs.			28	.381	.534	118	45	7	1	3	2.5	17	11	10	10	0	0	0	109	16	1	6	4.5	.992	OF-13, 1B-9, 3B-6

WORLD SERIES

Year	Team		Games	BA	SA	AB	H	2B	3B	HR	HR%	R	RBI	BB	SO	SB	AB	H	PO	A	E	DP	TC/G	FA	G by Pos
1970	CIN	N	5	.250	.450	20	5	0	0	1	5.0	2	2	2	0	0	0	0	14	1	1	0	3.2	.938	OF-5
1972			7	.214	.321	28	6	0	0	1	3.6	3	2	4	4	0	0	0	14	1	0	0	2.1	1.000	OF-7
1975			7	.370	.481	27	10	1	1	0	0.0	3	2	5	1	0	0	0	7	8	0	2	2.1	1.000	3B-7
1976			4	.188	.250	16	3	1	0	0	0.0	2	1	2	0	0	0	0	6	3	0	0	2.3	1.000	3B-4
1980	PHI	N	6	.261	.304	23	6	1	0	0	0.0	2	1	2	2	0	0	0	49	6	0	8	9.2	1.000	1B-6
1983			5	.313	.313	16	5	1	0	0	0.0	0	1	1	0	1	0	0	26	4	0	0	6.0	1.000	1B-5, OF-1
6 yrs.			34	.269	.369	130	35	5	1	2	1.5	12	9	16	12	1	0	0	116	23	1	10	4.1	.993	OF-13, 3B-11, 1B-9

Johnny Roseboro

ROSEBORO, JOHN JUNIOR
B. May 13, 1933, Ashland, Ohio

BL TR 5'11½'' 190 lbs.

Year	Team		Games	BA	SA	AB	H	2B	3B	HR	HR%	R	RBI	BB	SO	SB	AB	H	PO	A	E	DP	TC/G	FA	G by Pos
1957	BKN	N	35	.145	.261	69	10	0	0	2	2.9	6	6	10	20	0	3	0	136	7	3	4	4.2	.979	C-19, 1B-5
1958	LA	N	114	.271	.456	384	104	11	9	14	3.6	52	43	36	56	11	7	1	598	36	8	5	5.6	.988	C-104, OF-5
1959			118	.232	.378	397	92	14	7	10	2.5	39	38	52	69	7	2	0	848	54	8	10	7.7	.991	C-117

Year	Team	Games	BA	SA	AB	H	2B	3B	HR	HR%	R	RBI	BB	SO	SB	Pinch Hit AB	H	PO	A	E	DP	TC/G	FA	G by Pos

Johnny Roseboro *continued*

Year	Team	Games	BA	SA	AB	H	2B	3B	HR	HR%	R	RBI	BB	SO	SB	PH AB	PH H	PO	A	E	DP	TC/G	FA	G by Pos
1960		103	.213	.369	287	61	15	3	8	2.8	22	42	44	53	7	14	4	640	48	5	10	6.7	.993	C-87, 3B-1, 1B-1
1961		128	.251	.459	394	99	16	6	18	4.6	59	59	56	62	6	7	3	877	56	13	16	7.4	.986	C-125
1962		128	.249	.380	389	97	16	7	7	1.8	45	55	50	60	12	4	0	842	57	14	10	7.1	.985	C-128
1963		135	.236	.351	470	111	13	7	9	1.9	50	49	36	50	7	3	1	908	66	8	6	7.3	.992	C-134
1964		134	.287	.372	414	119	24	1	3	0.7	42	45	44	61	3	12	4	809	64	6	8	6.6	.993	C-128
1965		136	.233	.311	437	102	10	0	8	1.8	42	57	34	51	1	9	4	824	55	5	7	6.5	.994	C-131, 3B-1
1966		142	.276	.398	445	123	23	2	9	2.0	47	53	44	51	3	8	1	904	65	7	11	6.9	.993	C-138
1967		116	.272	.374	334	91	18	2	4	1.2	37	24	38	33	2	17	5	550	60	10	6	5.3	.984	C-107
1968	MIN A	135	.216	.311	380	82	12	0	8	2.1	31	39	46	57	2	22	3	689	52	7	5	5.5	.991	C-111
1969		115	.263	.321	361	95	12	0	3	0.8	33	32	39	44	5	3	0	585	52	13	16	5.7	.980	C-111
1970	WAS A	46	.233	.314	86	20	4	0	1	1.2	7	6	18	10	1	17	3	122	6	0	1	2.8	1.000	C-30
14 yrs.		1585	.249	.371	4847	1206	190	44	104	2.1	512	548	547	677	67	128	29	9332	678	107	115	6.4	.989	C-1476, 1B-6, OF-5, 3B-2

LEAGUE CHAMPIONSHIP SERIES

Year	Team	Games	BA	SA	AB	H	2B	3B	HR	HR%	R	RBI	BB	SO	SB	PH AB	PH H	PO	A	E	DP	TC/G	FA	G by Pos
1969	MIN A	2	.200	.200	5	1	0	0	0	0.0	0	0	0	0	0	0	0	6	1	0	0	3.5	1.000	C-2

WORLD SERIES

Year	Team	Games	BA	SA	AB	H	2B	3B	HR	HR%	R	RBI	BB	SO	SB	PH AB	PH H	PO	A	E	DP	TC/G	FA	G by Pos
1959	LA N	6	.095	.095	21	2	0	0	0	0.0	0	1	0	2	0	0	0	35	4	0	1	6.5	1.000	C-6
1963		4	.143	.357	14	2	0	0	1	7.1	1	3	0	4	0	0	0	43	0	0	0	10.8	1.000	C-4
1965		7	.286	.333	21	6	1	0	0	0.0	1	3	5	3	1	0	0	57	4	0	0	8.7	1.000	C-7
1966		4	.071	.071	14	1	0	0	0	0.0	0	0	0	3	0	0	0	22	2	0	1	6.0	1.000	C-4
4 yrs.		21	.157	.214	70	11	1	0	1	1.4	2	7	5	12	1	0	0	157	10	0	2	8.0	1.000	C-21

Bob Roselli

ROSELLI, ROBERT EDWARD
B. Dec. 10, 1931, San Francisco, Calif.

BR TR 5'11" 185 lbs.

Year	Team	Games	BA	SA	AB	H	2B	3B	HR	HR%	R	RBI	BB	SO	SB	PH AB	PH H	PO	A	E	DP	TC/G	FA	G by Pos
1955	MIL N	6	.222	.333	9	2	1	0	0	0.0	1	1	0	4	0	3	0	9	2	1	0	2.0	.917	C-2
1956		4	.500	2.000	2	1	0	1	1	50.0	1	1	0	1	0	1	1	8	1	0	1	2.3	1.000	C-3
1958		1	.000	.000	1	0	0	0	0	0.0	0	0	0	0	0	1	0	0	0	0	0	0.0	—	
1961	CHI A	22	.263	.342	38	10	3	0	0	0.0	2	4	0	11	0	12	4	32	3	0	0	1.6	1.000	C-10
1962		35	.188	.313	64	12	3	1	1	1.6	4	5	11	15	1	15	2	80	5	1	2	2.5	.988	C-20
5 yrs.		68	.219	.351	114	25	7	1	2	1.8	8	10	12	31	1	32	7	129	11	2	3	2.1	.986	C-35

Dave Rosello

ROSELLO, DAVID
Born David Rosello Rodriguez.
B. June 25, 1950, Mayaguez, Puerto Rico

BR TR 5'11" 160 lbs.

Year	Team	Games	BA	SA	AB	H	2B	3B	HR	HR%	R	RBI	BB	SO	SB	PH AB	PH H	PO	A	E	DP	TC/G	FA	G by Pos
1972	CHI N	5	.250	.500	12	3	0	0	1	8.3	3	3	2	2	0	0	0	11	11	4	4	5.2	.846	SS-5
1973		16	.263	.316	38	10	2	0	0	0.0	4	2	2	4	2	1	0	30	29	3	7	3.9	.952	2B-13, SS-1
1974		62	.203	.250	148	30	7	0	0	0.0	9	10	10	28	1	2	1	97	114	8	37	3.5	.963	2B-49, SS-12
1975		19	.259	.345	58	15	2	0	1	1.7	7	8	9	8	0	0	0	27	53	4	7	4.4	.952	SS-19
1976		91	.242	.286	227	55	5	1	1	0.4	27	11	41	33	1	1	0	129	217	12	45	3.9	.966	SS-86, 2B-1
1977		56	.220	.305	82	18	2	1	1	1.2	19	9	12	12	0	22	7	8	42	6	2	1.0	.893	3B-21, SS-10, 2B-3
1979	CLE A	59	.243	.402	107	26	6	1	3	2.8	20	14	15	27	1	3	1	43	98	5	16	2.5	.966	2B-33, 3B-14, SS-11
1980		71	.248	.325	117	29	3	0	2	1.7	16	12	9	19	0	1	0	76	91	4	18	2.4	.977	2B-43, 3B-22, SS-3, DH-1
1981		43	.238	.321	84	20	4	0	1	1.2	11	7	7	12	0	10	1	55	63	3	15	2.8	.975	2B-26, 3B-8, DH-4, SS-4
9 yrs.		422	.236	.313	873	206	31	3	10	1.1	114	76	108	145	5	40	10	476	718	49	151	2.9	.961	2B-168, SS-151, 3B-65, DH-5

Chief Roseman

ROSEMAN, JAMES JOHN
B. July 4, 1856, Brooklyn, N. Y.   D. July 4, 1938, Brooklyn, N. Y.
Manager 1890.

BR TR 5'7" 167 lbs.

Year	Team	Games	BA	SA	AB	H	2B	3B	HR	HR%	R	RBI	BB	SO	SB	PH AB	PH H	PO	A	E	DP	TC/G	FA	G by Pos
1882	TRO N	82	.236	.344	331	78	21	6	1	0.3	41	43	3	41		0	0	107	21	22	6	1.8	.853	OF-82
1883	NY AA	93	.251	.314	398	100	13	6	0	0.0	48		11			0	0	123	19	22	5	1.8	.866	OF-91, 1B-2
1884		107	.298	.413	436	130	16	11	4	0.9	97		21			0	0	157	12	22	0	1.8	.885	OF-107, P-1
1885		101	.278	.405	410	114	13	15	3	0.7	72		25			0	0	177	9	29	1	2.1	.865	OF-101, P-1
1886		134	.227	.324	559	127	19	10	5	0.9	90		24			0	0	203	20	27	6	1.9	.892	OF-134, P-1
1887	3 teams	PHI AA (21G – .219)			NY AA (60G – .228)			BKN AA (1G – .333)																
"	total	82	.227	.278	317	72	12	2	0	0.0	48		19		6	0	0	166	11	27	4	2.5	.868	OF-81, 1B-3, P-2
1890	2 teams	STL AA (80G – .341)			LOU AA (2G – .250)																			
"	total	82	.339	.442	310	105	26	0	2	0.6	47		30		7	0	0	296	17	24	17	4.1	.929	OF-58, 1B-24
7 yrs.		681	.263	.359	2761	726	120	50	15	0.5	443	43	133	41	13	0	0	1229	109	173	39	2.2	.886	OF-654, 1B-29, P-4

Al Rosen

ROSEN, ALBERT LEONARD (Flip)
B. Feb. 29, 1924, Spartanburg, S. C.

BR TR 5'10½" 180 lbs.

Year	Team	Games	BA	SA	AB	H	2B	3B	HR	HR%	R	RBI	BB	SO	SB	PH AB	PH H	PO	A	E	DP	TC/G	FA	G by Pos
1947	CLE A	7	.111	.111	9	1	0	0	0	0.0	1	0	0	3	0	4	1	1	1	0	1	0.3	1.000	3B-2, OF-1
1948		5	.200	.200	5	1	0	0	0	0.0	0	0	0	2	0	3	1	1	1	0	0	0.4	1.000	3B-2
1949		23	.159	.205	44	7	2	0	0	0.0	3	5	7	4	0	13	2	10	16	0	1	1.1	1.000	3B-10
1950		155	.287	.543	554	159	23	4	37	6.7	100	116	100	72	5	1	0	151	322	15	24	3.1	.969	3B-154
1951		154	.265	.447	573	152	30	1	24	4.2	82	102	85	71	7	0	0	157	277	19	20	2.9	.958	3B-154
1952		148	.302	.524	567	171	32	5	28	4.9	101	105	75	54	6	0	0	177	265	20	29	3.1	.957	3B-147, 1B-4, SS-3
1953		155	.336	.613	599	201	27	5	43	7.2	115	145	85	48	8	1	0	178	338	19	39	3.5	.964	3B-154, SS-1, 1B-1
1954		137	.300	.506	466	140	20	2	24	5.2	76	102	85	43	6	5	2	502	188	18	48	5.2	.975	3B-87, 1B-46, SS-1, 2B-1
1955		139	.244	.402	492	120	13	1	21	4.3	61	81	92	44	4	2	0	396	221	18	48	4.6	.972	3B-106, 1B-41
1956		121	.267	.428	416	111	18	2	15	3.6	64	61	58	44	1	4	0	89	219	18	20	2.7	.945	3B-116
10 yrs.		1044	.285	.495	3725	1063	165	20	192	5.2	603	717	587	385	39	33	6	1662	1848	127	230	3.5	.965	3B-932, 1B-92, SS-5, OF-1, 2B-1

WORLD SERIES

Year	Team	Games	BA	SA	AB	H	2B	3B	HR	HR%	R	RBI	BB	SO	SB	PH AB	PH H	PO	A	E	DP	TC/G	FA	G by Pos
1948	CLE A	1	.000	.000	1	0	0	0	0	0.0	0	0	0	0	0	1	0	0	0	0	0	0.0	—	
1954		3	.250	.250	12	3	0	0	0	0.0	1	2	1	0	0	0	0	2	3	0	0	1.7	1.000	3B-3
2 yrs.		4	.231	.231	13	3	0	0	0	0.0	1	2	1	0	0	1	0	2	3	0	0	1.3	1.000	3B-3

Goody Rosen

ROSEN, GOODWIN GEORGE
B. Aug. 28, 1912, Toronto, Ont., Canada

BL TL 5'9½" 160 lbs.

Year	Team	Games	BA	SA	AB	H	2B	3B	HR	HR%	R	RBI	BB	SO	SB	Pinch Hit AB	Pinch Hit H	PO	A	E	DP	TC/G	FA	G by Pos

Goody Rosen continued

Year	Team	Games	BA	SA	AB	H	2B	3B	HR	HR%	R	RBI	BB	SO	SB	PH AB	PH H	PO	A	E	DP	TC/G	FA	G by Pos
1937	BKN N	22	.312	.403	77	24	5	1	0	0.0	10	6	6	6	2	0	0	50	1	1	1	2.4	.981	OF-21
1938		138	.281	.389	473	133	17	11	4	0.8	75	51	65	43	0	19	2	263	19	3	4	2.1	.989	OF-113
1939		54	.251	.344	183	46	6	4	1	0.5	22	12	23	21	4	4	0	106	0	0	0	2.0	1.000	OF-47
1944		89	.261	.314	264	69	8	3	0	0.0	38	23	26	27	0	21	5	199	12	2	0	2.4	.991	OF-65
1945		145	.325	.460	606	197	24	11	12	2.0	126	75	50	36	4	3	0	392	7	3	1	2.8	.993	OF-141
1946	2 teams	BKN	N	(3G – .333)		NY	N	(100G – .281)																
"	total	103	.281	.390	313	88	11	4	5	1.6	39	30	48	33	2	15	3	200	3	5	0	2.0	.976	OF-85
6 yrs.		551	.291	.398	1916	557	71	34	22	1.1	310	197	218	166	12	62	10	1210	42	14	6	2.3	.989	OF-472

Harry Rosenberg

ROSENBERG, HARRY
Brother of Lou Rosenberg.
B. June 22, 1909, San Francisco, Calif.

BR TR 5'10" 180 lbs.

Year	Team	Games	BA	SA	AB	H	2B	3B	HR	HR%	R	RBI	BB	SO	SB	PH AB	PH H	PO	A	E	DP	TC/G	FA	G by Pos
1930	NY N	9	.000	.000	5	0	0	0	0	0.0	1	0	1	4	0	4	0	2	0	0	0	0.2	1.000	OF-3

Lou Rosenberg

ROSENBERG, LOUIS C.
Brother of Harry Rosenberg.
B. Mar. 5, 1903, San Francisco, Calif.

BR TR 5'7" 155 lbs.

Year	Team	Games	BA	SA	AB	H	2B	3B	HR	HR%	R	RBI	BB	SO	SB	PH AB	PH H	PO	A	E	DP	TC/G	FA	G by Pos
1923	CHI A	3	.250	.250	4	1	0	0	0	0.0	0	0	1	0	1	0	1	0	0	0	0	0.3	1.000	2B-2

Max Rosenfeld

ROSENFELD, MAX
B. Dec. 23, 1902, New York, N. Y.   D. Mar. 10, 1969, Miami, Fla.

BR TR 5'8" 175 lbs.

Year	Team	Games	BA	SA	AB	H	2B	3B	HR	HR%	R	RBI	BB	SO	SB	PH AB	PH H	PO	A	E	DP	TC/G	FA	G by Pos
1931	BKN N	3	.222	.333	9	2	1	0	0	0.0	0	0	1	1	0	0	0	6	0	0	0	2.0	1.000	OF-3
1932		34	.359	.590	39	14	3	0	2	5.1	8	7	0	10	2	3	0	31	1	1	1	1.0	.970	OF-30
1933		5	.111	.111	9	1	0	0	0	0.0	0	0	1	1	0	1	0	7	0	0	0	1.4	1.000	OF-2
3 yrs.		42	.298	.474	57	17	4	0	2	3.5	8	7	2	12	2	4	0	44	1	1	1	1.1	.978	OF-35

Larry Rosenthal

ROSENTHAL, LAWRENCE JOHN
B. May 21, 1912, St. Paul, Minn.

BL TL 6'½" 190 lbs.

Year	Team	Games	BA	SA	AB	H	2B	3B	HR	HR%	R	RBI	BB	SO	SB	PH AB	PH H	PO	A	E	DP	TC/G	FA	G by Pos
1936	CHI A	85	.281	.407	317	89	15	8	3	0.9	71	46	59	37	2	4	3	243	7	6	3	3.0	.977	OF-80
1937		58	.289	.402	97	28	5	3	1	1.0	20	9	9	20	1	29	9	46	3	1	1	0.9	.980	OF-25
1938		61	.286	.381	105	30	5	1	1	1.0	14	12	12	13	0	30	6	44	3	2	1	0.8	.959	OF-22
1939		107	.265	.454	324	86	21	5	10	3.1	50	51	53	46	6	12	1	193	5	2	1	1.9	.990	OF-93
1940		107	.301	.453	276	83	14	5	6	2.2	46	42	64	32	2	11	2	208	4	5	0	2.0	.977	OF-91
1941	2 teams	CHI	A	(20G – .237)		CLE	A	(45G – .187)																
"	total	65	.209	.299	134	28	7	1	1	0.7	19	9	21	15	1	30	6	63	4	2	0	1.1	.971	OF-32, 1B-1
1944	2 teams	NY	A	(36G – .198)		PHI	A	(32G – .204)																
"	total	68	.200	.252	155	31	5	0	1	0.6	14	15	24	24	1	19	4	92	2	2	0	1.4	.979	OF-45
1945	PHI A	28	.200	.293	75	15	3	2	0	0.0	6	5	9	8	0	4	0	35	1	0	1	1.3	1.000	OF-21
8 yrs.		579	.263	.392	1483	390	75	25	22	1.5	240	189	251	195	13	139	31	924	29	20	7	1.7	.979	OF-409, 1B-1

Si Rosenthal

ROSENTHAL, SIMON
B. Nov. 13, 1903, Boston, Mass.   D. Apr. 7, 1969, Boston, Mass.

BL TL 5'9" 165 lbs.

Year	Team	Games	BA	SA	AB	H	2B	3B	HR	HR%	R	RBI	BB	SO	SB	PH AB	PH H	PO	A	E	DP	TC/G	FA	G by Pos
1925	BOS A	19	.264	.389	72	19	5	2	0	0.0	6	8	7	3	1	2	0	31	3	3	0	1.9	.919	OF-17
1926		104	.267	.372	285	76	12	3	4	1.4	34	34	19	18	4	35	9	100	0	4	0	1.0	.962	OF-67
2 yrs.		123	.266	.375	357	95	17	5	4	1.1	40	42	26	21	5	37	9	131	3	7	0	1.1	.950	OF-84

Jack Roser

ROSER, JOHN WILLIAM JOSEPH (Bunny)
B. Nov. 15, 1901, St. Louis, Mo.   D. May 6, 1979, Rocky Hill, Conn.

BL TL 5'11" 175 lbs.

Year	Team	Games	BA	SA	AB	H	2B	3B	HR	HR%	R	RBI	BB	SO	SB	PH AB	PH H	PO	A	E	DP	TC/G	FA	G by Pos
1922	BOS N	32	.239	.336	113	27	3	4	0	0.0	13	16	10	19	2	0	0	63	2	6	0	2.2	.915	OF-32

Chet Ross

ROSS, CHESTER JAMES
B. Apr. 1, 1917, Buffalo, N. Y.   D. Feb. 21, 1989, Buffalo, N. Y.

BR TR 6'1" 195 lbs.

Year	Team	Games	BA	SA	AB	H	2B	3B	HR	HR%	R	RBI	BB	SO	SB	PH AB	PH H	PO	A	E	DP	TC/G	FA	G by Pos
1939	BOS N	11	.323	.419	31	10	1	1	0	0.0	2	10	0	3	0	3	0	19	1	0	0	1.8	1.000	OF-8
1940		149	.281	.460	569	160	23	14	17	3.0	84	89	59	127	4	0	0	347	12	14	2	2.5	.962	OF-149
1941		29	.120	.140	50	6	1	0	0	0.0	1	4	9	17	0	17	2	21	1	0	0	0.8	1.000	OF-12
1942		76	.195	.314	220	43	7	2	5	2.3	20	19	16	37	0	18	4	123	2	1	0	1.7	.992	OF-57
1943		94	.218	.347	285	62	12	2	7	2.5	27	32	26	67	1	19	5	165	8	4	1	1.9	.977	OF-78
1944		54	.227	.409	154	35	9	2	5	3.2	20	26	12	23	1	15	2	75	8	0	2	1.5	1.000	OF-38
6 yrs.		413	.241	.392	1309	316	53	21	34	2.6	156	170	124	281	6	72	13	750	32	19	5	1.9	.976	OF-342

Don Ross

ROSS, DONALD RAYMOND
B. July 16, 1914, Pasadena, Calif.

BR TR 6'1" 185 lbs.

Year	Team	Games	BA	SA	AB	H	2B	3B	HR	HR%	R	RBI	BB	SO	SB	PH AB	PH H	PO	A	E	DP	TC/G	FA	G by Pos
1938	DET A	77	.260	.306	265	69	7	1	1	0.4	22	30	28	11	1	2	0	90	157	14	15	3.4	.946	3B-75
1940	BKN N	10	.289	.421	38	11	2	0	1	2.6	4	3	8	3	1	0	0	10	19	4	0	3.3	.879	3B-10
1942	DET A	87	.274	.376	226	62	10	2	3	1.3	29	30	36	16	2	22	8	94	30	7	4	1.5	.947	OF-38, 3B-20
1943		89	.267	.320	247	66	13	0	0	0.0	19	18	20	3	2	24	5	106	65	9	10	2.0	.950	OF-38, SS-18, 2B-7, 1B-1
1944		66	.210	.275	167	35	5	0	2	1.2	14	15	14	9	2	24	8	85	7	3	1	1.4	.968	OF-37, SS-2, 1B-1
1945	2 teams	DET	A	(8G – .379)		CLE	A	(106G – .262)																
"	total	114	.270	.339	392	106	19	1	2	0.5	29	47	47	16	2	1	1	125	193	14	14	2.9	.958	3B-114
1946	CLE A	55	.268	.373	153	41	7	0	3	2.0	12	14	17	12	0	12	1	36	50	5	5	1.7	.945	3B-41, OF-2
7 yrs.		498	.262	.334	1488	390	63	4	12	0.8	129	162	165	70	10	85	23	546	521	56	49	2.3	.950	3B-261, OF-115, SS-20, 2B-7, 1B-1

Joe Rossi

ROSSI, JOSEPH ANTHONY
B. Mar. 13, 1923, Oakland, Calif.

BR TR 6'1" 205 lbs.

Year	Team	Games	BA	SA	AB	H	2B	3B	HR	HR%	R	RBI	BB	SO	SB	PH AB	PH H	PO	A	E	DP	TC/G	FA	G by Pos
1952	CIN N	55	.221	.255	145	32	0	1	1	0.7	14	6	20	20	1	8	2	192	21	4	3	3.9	.982	C-46

Claude Rossman

ROSSMAN, CLAUDE R.
B. June 17, 1881, Philmont, N. Y.   D. Jan. 16, 1928, Poughkeepsie, N. Y.

BL TL 6'

Year	Team	Games	BA	SA	AB	H	2B	3B	HR	HR%	R	RBI	BB	SO	SB	PH AB	PH H	PO	A	E	DP	TC/G	FA	G by Pos
1904	CLE A	18	.210	.290	62	13	5	0	0	0.0	5	6	0		0	0	1	14	0	1	0	0.8	.933	OF-17

Year	Team		Games	BA	SA	AB	H	2B	3B	HR	HR%	R	RBI	BB	SO	SB	Pinch Hit AB	Pinch Hit H	PO	A	E	DP	TC/G	FA	G by Pos

Claude Rossman *continued*

Year	Team		Games	BA	SA	AB	H	2B	3B	HR	HR%	R	RBI	BB	SO	SB	AB	H	PO	A	E	DP	TC/G	FA	G by Pos
1906			118	.308	.359	396	122	13	2	1	0.3	49	53	17		11	11	4	1150	45	19	47	10.3	.984	1B-105, OF-1
1907	DET	A	153	.277	.342	571	158	21	8	0	0.0	60	69	33		20	0	0	1478	62	30	57	10.3	.981	1B-153
1908			138	.294	.418	524	154	33	13	2	0.4	45	71	27		8	0	0	1429	102	29	70	11.3	.981	1B-138
1909	2 teams			DET A (82G – .261)			STL A (2G – .125)																			
"	total		84	.258	.305	295	76	8	3	0	0.0	16	39	13		10	5	0	915	36	18	30	11.5	.981	1B-75, OF-2
5 yrs.			511	.283	.359	1848	523	80	26	3	0.2	175	238	90		49	17	5	4986	245	97	204	10.4	.982	1B-471, OF-20

WORLD SERIES

Year	Team		Games	BA	SA	AB	H	2B	3B	HR	HR%	R	RBI	BB	SO	SB	AB	H	PO	A	E	DP	TC/G	FA	G by Pos
1907	DET	A	5	.400	.500	20	8	0	1	0	0.0	1	2	1	0	2	0	0	52	4	1	0	11.4	.982	1B-5
1908			5	.211	.211	19	4	0	0	0	0.0	3	3	1	4	0	0	0	48	5	2	4	11.0	.964	1B-5
2 yrs.			10	.308	.359	39	12	0	1	0	0.0	4	5	2	4	2	0	0	100	9	3	4	11.2	.973	1B-10

Braggo Roth

ROTH, ROBERT FRANK
Brother of Frank Roth.
B. Aug. 28, 1892, Burlington, Wis. D. Sept. 11, 1936, Chicago, Ill.

BR TR 5'7½" 170 lbs.

Year	Team		Games	BA	SA	AB	H	2B	3B	HR	HR%	R	RBI	BB	SO	SB	AB	H	PO	A	E	DP	TC/G	FA	G by Pos
1914	CHI	A	34	.294	.444	126	37	4	6	1	0.8	14	10	8	25	3	0	0	54	7	5	1	1.9	.924	OF-34
1915	2 teams			CHI A (70G – .250)			CLE A (39G – .299)																			
"	total		109	.268	.438	384	103	10	17	7	1.8	67	55	51	72	26	4	0	139	53	27	2	2.0	.877	OF-69, 3B-35
1916	CLE	A	125	.286	.396	409	117	19	7	4	1.0	50	72	38	48	29	12	6	166	20	9	6	1.6	.954	OF-112
1917			145	.285	.388	495	141	30	9	1	0.2	69	72	52	73	51	10	3	228	18	11	6	1.8	.957	OF-135
1918			106	.283	.411	375	106	21	12	1	0.3	53	59	53	41	35	0	0	175	16	13	3	1.9	.936	OF-106
1919	2 teams			PHI A (48G – .323)			BOS A (63G – .256)																			
"	total		111	.287	.431	422	121	22	12	5	1.2	65	52	39	53	20	5	1	203	8	10	3	2.0	.955	OF-103
1920	WAS	A	138	.291	.432	468	136	23	8	9	1.9	80	92	75	57	24	8	3	184	15	10	0	1.5	.952	OF-128
1921	NY	A	43	.283	.408	152	43	9	2	2	1.3	29	10	19	20	1	6	2	69	3	6	0	1.8	.923	OF-37
8 yrs.			811	.284	.416	2831	804	138	73	30	1.1	427	422	335	389	189	45	15	1218	140	91	21	1.8	.937	OF-724, 3B-35

Frank Roth

ROTH, FRANCIS CHARLES
Brother of Braggo Roth.
B. Oct. 11, 1878, Chicago, Ill. D. Mar. 27, 1955, Burlington, Wis.

BR TR 5'10" 160 lbs.

Year	Team		Games	BA	SA	AB	H	2B	3B	HR	HR%	R	RBI	BB	SO	SB	AB	H	PO	A	E	DP	TC/G	FA	G by Pos
1903	PHI	N	68	.273	.359	220	60	11	4	0	0.0	27	22	9		3	7	3	235	82	25	9	5.0	.935	C-60, 3B-1
1904			81	.258	.314	229	59	8	1	1	0.4	28	20	12		8	12	4	250	76	17	8	4.2	.950	C-67, 2B-1, 1B-1
1905	STL	A	35	.234	.262	107	25	3	0	0	0.0	9	7	6		1	5	0	114	36	6	3	4.5	.962	C-29
1906	CHI	A	16	.196	.255	51	10	1	1	0	0.0	4	7	3		1	1	0	76	19	1	1	6.0	.990	C-15
1909	CIN	N	56	.238	.313	147	35	7	2	0	0.0	12	16	6		5	2	0	188	46	8	4	4.3	.967	C-54
1910			26	.241	.310	29	7	2	0	0	0.0	3	3	0	2	1	19	4	11	4	1	0	0.6	.938	C-4, OF-1
6 yrs.			282	.250	.315	783	196	32	8	1	0.1	83	75	36	2	19	46	11	874	263	55	25	4.2	.954	C-229, OF-1, 3B-1, 2B-1, 1B-1

Bob Rothel

ROTHEL, ROBERT BURTON
B. Sept. 17, 1923, Columbia Station, Ohio D. Mar. 21, 1984, Huron, Ohio

BR TR 5'10½" 170 lbs.

Year	Team		Games	BA	SA	AB	H	2B	3B	HR	HR%	R	RBI	BB	SO	SB	AB	H	PO	A	E	DP	TC/G	FA	G by Pos
1945	CLE	A	4	.200	.200	10	2	0	0	0	0.0	0	0	3	1	0	0	0	2	5	1	0	2.0	.875	3B-4

Bobby Rothermel

ROTHERMEL, EDWARD HILL
B. Dec. 18, 1870, Fleetwood, Pa. D. Feb. 11, 1927, Detroit, Mich.

BR TR 5'10½" 170 lbs.

Year	Team		Games	BA	SA	AB	H	2B	3B	HR	HR%	R	RBI	BB	SO	SB	AB	H	PO	A	E	DP	TC/G	FA	G by Pos
1899	BAL	N	10	.095	.095	21	2	0	0	0	0.0	1	3	1		0	2	1	11	15	4	0	3.0	.867	2B-5, 3B-2, SS-1

Jack Rothfuss

ROTHFUSS, JOHN ALBERT
B. Apr. 18, 1872, Newark, N. J. D. Apr. 20, 1947, Basking Ridge, N. J.

BR TR 5'11½" 195 lbs.

Year	Team		Games	BA	SA	AB	H	2B	3B	HR	HR%	R	RBI	BB	SO	SB	AB	H	PO	A	E	DP	TC/G	FA	G by Pos
1897	PIT	N	35	.313	.409	115	36	3	1	2	1.7	20	18	5		3	2	0	231	12	4	8	7.1	.984	1B-32

Claude Rothgeb

ROTHGEB, CLAUDE JAMES
B. Jan. 1, 1880, Milford, Ill. D. July 6, 1944, Manitowoc, Wis.

BB 6'½" 200 lbs.

Year	Team		Games	BA	SA	AB	H	2B	3B	HR	HR%	R	RBI	BB	SO	SB	AB	H	PO	A	E	DP	TC/G	FA	G by Pos
1905	WAS	A	6	.154	.154	13	2	0	0	0	0.0	2	0	0		1	3	0	4	1	0	0	0.8	1.000	OF-3

Jack Rothrock

ROTHROCK, JOHN HOUSTON
B. Mar. 14, 1905, Long Beach, Calif.
D. Feb. 2, 1980, San Bernardino, Calif.

BB TR 5'11½" 165 lbs.
BR 1925-27

Year	Team		Games	BA	SA	AB	H	2B	3B	HR	HR%	R	RBI	BB	SO	SB	AB	H	PO	A	E	DP	TC/G	FA	G by Pos
1925	BOS	A	22	.345	.509	55	19	3	3	0	0.0	6	7	3	7	0	0	0	37	38	9	6	3.8	.893	SS-22
1926			15	.294	.353	17	5	1	0	0	0.0	3	2	3	2	0	10	4	3	4	4	0	0.9	.692	SS-2
1927			117	.259	.360	428	111	24	8	1	0.2	61	36	24	46	5	6	1	323	284	26	63	5.4	.959	OF-53, 3B-17, 1B-16, SS-13, 2B-2, C-1, P-1
1928			117	.267	.343	344	92	9	4	3	0.9	52	22	33	40	12	9	2	242	61	12	14	2.7	.962	OF-79, 3B-23, 1B-8, 3B-2, SS-1
1929			143	.300	.408	473	142	19	7	6	1.3	70	59	43	47	23	10	2	342	12	11	3	2.6	.970	OF-128
1930			45	.277	.354	65	18	3	1	0	0.0	4	4	2	9	0	32	9	17	3	1	1	0.5	.952	OF-9, 3B-1
1931			133	.278	.383	475	132	32	3	4	0.8	81	42	47	48	13	20	9	294	97	11	15	3.0	.973	OF-79, 2B-23, 1B-8, 3B-2, SS-1
1932	2 teams			BOS A (12G – .208)			CHI A (39G – .188)																			
"	total		51	.196	.241	112	22	3	1	0	0.0	11	6	10	14	4	7	1	58	14	8	1	1.6	.900	OF-31, 3B-8, 1B-1
1934	STL	N	154	.284	.399	647	184	35	3	11	1.7	106	72	49	56	10	0	0	343	12	9	4	2.4	.975	OF-154, 2B-1
1935			129	.273	.347	502	137	18	3	3	0.6	76	56	57	29	7	1	0	283	5	6	1	2.3	.980	OF-127
1937	PHI	A	88	.267	.332	232	62	15	0	0	0.0	28	21	28	15	1	29	8	132	3	1	0	1.5	.993	OF-58, 2B-1
11 yrs.			1014	.276	.370	3350	924	162	35	28	0.8	498	327	299	312	75	124	36	2074	535	98	108	2.7	.964	OF-639, SS-78, 2B-63, 3B-48, 1B-38, C-1, P-1

WORLD SERIES

Year	Team		Games	BA	SA	AB	H	2B	3B	HR	HR%	R	RBI	BB	SO	SB	AB	H	PO	A	E	DP	TC/G	FA	G by Pos
1934	STL	N	7	.233	.400	30	7	3	1	0	0.0	3	6	1	2	0	0	0	19	0	1	0	2.9	.950	OF-7

Edd Roush

ROUSH, EDD J (Eddie)
B. May 8, 1893, Oakland City, Ind. D. Mar. 21, 1988, Bradenton, Fla.
Hall of Fame 1962.

BL TL 5'11" 170 lbs.

Year Team		Games	BA	SA	AB	H	2B	3B	HR	HR%	R	RBI	BB	SO	SB	Pinch Hit AB	H	PO	A	E	DP	TC/G	FA	G by Pos

Edd Roush *continued*

Year Team		Games	BA	SA	AB	H	2B	3B	HR	HR%	R	RBI	BB	SO	SB	AB	H	PO	A	E	DP	TC/G	FA	G by Pos
1913 CHI	A	9	.100	.100	10	1	0	0	0	0.0	2	0	0	2	0	4	1	3	0	0	0	0.3	1.000	OF-2
1914 IND	F	74	.325	.440	166	54	8	4	1	0.6	26	30	6		12	27	7	102	6	2	2	1.5	.982	OF-43, 1B-2
1915 NWK	F	145	.298	.390	551	164	20	11	3	0.5	73	60	38		28	1	1	331	20	10	3	2.5	.972	OF-144
1916 2 teams	NY	N	(39G –	.188)		CIN	N	(69G –	.287)															
" total		108	.267	.375	341	91	7	15	0	0.0	38	20	14	23	19	23	2	210	9	7	2	2.1	.969	OF-84
1917 CIN	N	136	.341	.454	522	178	19	14	4	0.8	82	67	27	24	21	1	0	335	15	14	0	2.7	.962	OF-134
1918		113	.333	.455	435	145	18	10	5	1.1	61	62	22	10	24	0	0	320	13	14	2	3.1	.960	OF-113
1919		133	.321	.431	504	162	19	12	4	0.8	73	71	42	19	20	0	0	335	22	4	5	2.7	.989	OF-133
1920		149	.339	.453	579	196	22	16	4	0.7	81	90	42	22	36	0	0	537	25	13	13	3.9	.977	OF-139, 1B-11, 2B-1
1921		112	.352	.502	418	147	27	12	4	1.0	68	71	31	8	19	2	1	286	9	6	0	2.7	.980	OF-108
1922		49	.352	.461	165	58	7	4	1	0.6	29	24	19	5	5	6	1	96	8	1	0	2.1	.990	OF-43
1923		138	.351	.531	527	185	41	18	6	1.1	88	88	46	16	10	1	0	337	14	11	3	2.6	.970	OF-137
1924		121	.348	.501	483	168	23	21	3	0.6	67	72	22	11	17	2	2	270	10	12	4	2.4	.959	OF-119
1925		134	.339	.494	540	183	28	16	8	1.5	91	83	35	14	22	0	0	343	15	8	3	2.7	.978	OF-134
1926		144	.323	.462	563	182	37	10	7	1.2	95	79	38	17	8	0	0	306	12	15	2	2.3	.955	OF-144, 1B-1
1927 NY	N	140	.304	.402	570	173	27	4	7	1.2	83	58	26	15	18	2	0	327	19	9	4	2.5	.975	OF-138
1928		46	.252	.356	163	41	5	3	2	1.2	20	13	14	8	1	6	3	100	7	5	0	2.4	.955	OF-39
1929		115	.324	.451	450	146	19	7	8	1.8	76	52	45	16	6	6	3	248	18	5	5	2.4	.982	OF-107
1931 CIN	N	101	.271	.338	376	102	12	5	1	0.3	46	41	17	5	2	13	3	197	5	4	1	2.0	.981	OF-88
18 yrs.		1967	.323	.446	7363	2376	339	182	68	0.9	1099	981	484	215	268	94	24	4683	227	140	49	2.6	.972	OF-1849, 1B-14, 2B-1

WORLD SERIES

Year Team		Games	BA	SA	AB	H	2B	3B	HR	HR%	R	RBI	BB	SO	SB	AB	H	PO	A	E	DP	TC/G	FA	G by Pos
1919 CIN	N	8	.214	.357	28	6	2	1	0	0.0	6	7	3	0	2	0	0	30	3	2	2	4.4	.943	OF-8

Phil Routcliffe

ROUTCLIFFE, PHILIP JOHN   BR TR 6'   175 lbs.
B. Oct. 24, 1870, Oswego, N. Y.   D. Oct. 4, 1918, Oswego, N. Y.

Year Team		Games	BA	SA	AB	H	2B	3B	HR	HR%	R	RBI	BB	SO	SB	AB	H	PO	A	E	DP	TC/G	FA	G by Pos
1890 PIT	N	1	.250	.250	4	1	0	0	0	0.0	1	1	0	0	1	0	0	3	0	0	0	3.0	1.000	OF-1

Dave Rowan

ROWAN, DAVID   BL TL 5'11"   175 lbs.
Born David Drohan.
B. Dec. 6, 1882, Elora, Ontario, Canada   D. July 30, 1955, Toronto, Ont., Canada

Year Team		Games	BA	SA	AB	H	2B	3B	HR	HR%	R	RBI	BB	SO	SB	AB	H	PO	A	E	DP	TC/G	FA	G by Pos
1911 STL	A	18	.385	.431	65	25	1	1	0	0.0	7	11	4		0	0	0	161	11	10	5	10.1	.945	1B-18

Wade Rowdon

ROWDON, WADE LEE   BR TR 6'2"   170 lbs.
B. Sept. 7, 1960, Riverhead, N. Y.

Year Team		Games	BA	SA	AB	H	2B	3B	HR	HR%	R	RBI	BB	SO	SB	AB	H	PO	A	E	DP	TC/G	FA	G by Pos
1984 CIN	N	4	.286	.286	7	2	0	0	0	0.0	0	1	0	0	0	0	0	3	5	0	1	2.0	1.000	SS-1, 3B-1
1985		5	.222	.222	9	2	0	0	0	0.0	2	2	2	1	0	0	0	1	3	2	0	1.2	.667	3B-4
1986		38	.250	.338	80	20	5	1	0	0.0	9	10	9	17	2	15	2	22	34	6	7	1.6	.903	3B-8, SS-6, OF-5, 2B-3
1987 CHI	N	11	.226	.419	31	7	1	1	1	3.2	2	4	3	10	0	2	0	3	15	4	0	2.0	.818	3B-9
1988 BAL	A	20	.100	.100	30	3	0	0	0	0.0	1	0	0	6	1	4	2	7	14	1	1	1.1	.955	3B-8, DH-5, OF-5
5 yrs.		78	.217	.299	157	34	6	2	1	0.6	14	16	14	35	3	21	4	36	71	13	9	1.5	.892	3B-29, OF-10, SS-7, DH-5, 2B-3

Dave Rowe

ROWE, DAVID (Eli)   BR TR 5'9"   180 lbs.
Brother of Jack Rowe.
B. Feb., 1856, Jacksonville, Ill.   Deceased.
Manager 1886, 1888.

Year Team		Games	BA	SA	AB	H	2B	3B	HR	HR%	R	RBI	BB	SO	SB	AB	H	PO	A	E	DP	TC/G	FA	G by Pos
1877 CHI	N	2	.286	.286	7	2	0	0	0	0.0	0	0	0	3		0	0	2	0	1	0	1.5	.667	OF-2, P-1
1882 CLE	N	24	.258	.392	97	25	4	3	1	1.0	13	17	4	9		0	0	33	4	7	1	1.8	.841	OF-23, P-1
1883 BAL	AA	59	.313	.402	256	80	11	6	0	0.0	40		2			0	0	98	21	23	2	2.4	.838	OF-50, SS-7, 1B-3, P-1
1884 STL	U	109	.293	.423	485	142	32	11	3	0.6	95		10			0	0	174	62	30	6	2.4	.887	OF-92, SS-14, 2B-2, 1B-2, P-1
1885 STL	N	16	.161	.210	62	10	3	0	0	0.0	8	3	5	8		0	0	28	1	3	1	2.0	.906	OF-16
1886 KC	N	105	.240	.354	429	103	24	8	3	0.7	53	57	15	43		0	0	185	62	44	11	2.8	.849	OF-90, SS-11, 2B-4
1888 KC	AA	32	.172	.262	122	21	3	4	0	0.0	14	13	6		2	0	0	54	10	6	1	2.2	.914	OF-32
7 yrs.		347	.263	.374	1458	383	77	32	7	0.5	223	90	42	63	2	0	0	574	160	114	22	2.4	.866	OF-305, SS-32, 2B-6, 1B-5, P-4

Harland Rowe

ROWE, HARLAND STIMSON (Hypie)   BL TR 6'1"   170 lbs.
B. Apr. 20, 1896, Springvale, Me.   D. May 26, 1969, Springvale, Me.

Year Team		Games	BA	SA	AB	H	2B	3B	HR	HR%	R	RBI	BB	SO	SB	AB	H	PO	A	E	DP	TC/G	FA	G by Pos
1916 PHI	A	17	.139	.167	36	5	1	0	0	0.0	2	3	2	8	0	6	1	5	12	3	0	1.2	.850	3B-7, OF-1

Jack Rowe

ROWE, JOHN CHARLES   BL TR 5'8"   170 lbs.
Brother of Dave Rowe.
B. Dec. 18, 1857, Harrisburg, Pa.   D. Apr. 25, 1911, St. Louis, Mo.
Manager 1890.

Year Team		Games	BA	SA	AB	H	2B	3B	HR	HR%	R	RBI	BB	SO	SB	AB	H	PO	A	E	DP	TC/G	FA	G by Pos
1879 BUF	N	8	.353	.382	34	12	1	0	0	0.0	8	8	0	1		0	0	36	9	6	0	6.4	.882	C-6, OF-2
1880		79	.252	.328	326	82	10	6	1	0.3	43	36	6	17		0	0	267	68	46	3	4.8	.879	C-60, OF-25, 3B-3
1881		64	.333	.480	246	82	11	11	1	0.4	30	43	1	12		0	0	219	73	36	7	5.1	.890	C-46, SS-7, 3B-7, OF-5
1882		75	.266	.354	308	82	14	5	1	0.3	43		12	0		0	0	260	117	31	8	5.4	.924	C-46, SS-22, 3B-7, OF-1
1883		87	.278	.372	374	104	18	7	1	0.3	65		15	14		0	0	280	98	63	6	5.1	.857	C-49, OF-28, SS-18, 3B-3
1884		93	.315	.450	400	126	14	14	4	1.0	85		23	14		0	0	414	75	36	4	5.6	.931	C-65, OF-30, SS-6
1885		98	.290	.409	421	122	28	8	2	0.5	62	51	13	19		0	0	219	216	67	26	5.1	.867	SS-65, C-23, OF-12
1886 DET	N	111	.303	.425	468	142	21	9	6	1.3	97	87	26	27		0	0	97	311	54	26	4.2	.883	SS-110, C-3
1887		124	.318	.445	537	171	30	10	6	1.1	135	96	39	11	22	0	0	119	378	51	36	4.4	.907	SS-124
1888		105	.277	.368	451	125	19	8	2	0.4	62	74	19	28	10	0	0	133	312	72	24	4.9	.861	SS-105
1889 PIT	N	75	.259	.341	317	82	14	3	2	0.6	57	32	22	16	5	0	0	108	228	39	26	5.0	.896	SS-75
1890 BUF	P	125	.250	.333	504	126	22	7	2	0.4	77	76	48	18	10	0	0	228	381	67	56	5.4	.901	SS-125
12 yrs.		1044	.286	.392	4386	1256	202	88	28	0.6	764	503	224	177	47	0	0	2380	2266	568	222	5.0	.891	SS-657, C-298, OF-103, 3B-20

Year	Team		Games	BA	SA	AB	H	2B	3B	HR	HR%	R	RBI	BB	SO	SB	Pinch Hit AB	Pinch Hit H	PO	A	E	DP	TC/G	FA	G by Pos

Schoolboy Rowe

ROWE, LYNWOOD THOMAS
B. Jan. 11, 1910, Waco, Tex.   D. Jan. 8, 1961, El Dorado, Ark.
BR TR 6'4½" 210 lbs.

Year	Team		Games	BA	SA	AB	H	2B	3B	HR	HR%	R	RBI	BB	SO	SB	AB	H	PO	A	E	DP	TC/G	FA	G by Pos
1933	DET	A	21	.220	.240	50	11	1	0	0	0.0	6	6	1	4	0	1	0	1	33	0	1	1.6	1.000	P-19
1934			51	.303	.450	109	33	8	1	2	1.8	15	22	6	20	0	6	1	9	46	0	3	1.1	1.000	P-45
1935			45	.312	.459	109	34	3	2	3	2.8	19	28	12	12	0	3	1	11	42	1	1	1.2	.981	P-42
1936			45	.256	.333	90	23	2	1	1	1.1	16	12	13	15	0	4	2	10	50	1	3	1.4	.984	P-41
1937			10	.200	.200	10	2	0	0	0	0.0	2	1	1	4	0	0	0	6	6	0	0	1.2	1.000	P-10
1938			4	.167	.333	6	1	1	0	0	0.0	1	0	0	1	0	0	0	0	8	1	0	2.3	.889	P-4
1939			31	.246	.328	61	15	0	1	1	1.6	7	12	5	7	1	3	1	9	27	2	5	1.2	.947	P-28
1940			27	.269	.433	67	18	6	1	1	1.5	7	18	5	13	1	0	0	10	28	0	2	1.4	1.000	P-27
1941			32	.273	.436	55	15	0	3	1	1.8	10	12	5	8	0	5	3	9	29	3	2	1.3	.927	P-27
1942 2 teams	DET	A		(2G – .000)		BKN	N	(14G – .211)																	
" total			16	.174	.174	23	4	0	0	0	0.0	2	2	1	4	0	5	1	2	11	0	0	0.8	1.000	P-11
1943	PHI	N	82	.300	.458	120	36	7	0	4	3.3	14	18	15	21	0	49	15	9	42	1	4	0.6	.981	P-27
1946			30	.180	.311	61	11	5	0	1	1.6	4	6	3	16	0	12	2	2	20	0	0	0.7	1.000	P-17
1947			43	.278	.380	79	22	2	0	2	2.5	9	11	13	18	0	12	2	6	32	1	0	0.9	.974	P-31
1948			31	.192	.250	52	10	0	0	1	1.9	3	4	4	10	1	1	0	9	31	1	0	1.3	.976	P-30
1949			23	.235	.471	17	4	1	0	1	5.9	1	1	2	4	0	0	0	4	16	3	1	1.0	.870	P-23
15 yrs.			491	.263	.382	909	239	36	9	18	2.0	116	153	86	157	3	101	28	97	421	14	22	1.1	.974	P-382

WORLD SERIES

Year	Team		Games	BA	SA	AB	H	2B	3B	HR	HR%	R	RBI	BB	SO	SB	AB	H	PO	A	E	DP	TC/G	FA	G by Pos
1934	DET	A	3	.000	.000	7	0	0	0	0	0.0	0	0	0	5	0	0	0	1	1	0	0	0.7	1.000	P-3
1935			3	.250	.375	8	2	1	0	0	0.0	0	0	0	1	0	0	0	3	5	1	0	3.0	.889	P-3
1940			2	.000	.000	1	0	0	0	0	0.0	0	0	0	1	0	0	0	0	1	0	0	0.5	1.000	P-2
3 yrs.			8	.125	.188	16	2	1	0	0	0.0	0	0	0	7	0	0	0	4	7	1	0	1.5	.917	P-8

Bama Rowell

ROWELL, CARVEL WILLIAM
B. Jan. 13, 1916, Citronelle, Ala.
BL TR 5'11" 185 lbs.

Year	Team		Games	BA	SA	AB	H	2B	3B	HR	HR%	R	RBI	BB	SO	SB	AB	H	PO	A	E	DP	TC/G	FA	G by Pos
1939	BOS	N	21	.186	.288	59	11	2	2	0	0.0	5	6	1	4	0	5	0	27	2	5	0	1.6	.853	OF-16
1940			130	.305	.395	486	148	19	8	3	0.6	46	58	18	22	12	8	2	258	360	32	81	5.0	.951	2B-115, OF-7
1941			138	.267	.383	483	129	23	6	7	1.4	49	60	39	36	11	6	1	296	317	41	83	4.7	.937	2B-112, OF-14, 3B-2
1946			95	.280	.392	293	82	12	6	3	1.0	37	31	29	15	5	9	4	168	8	4	2	1.9	.978	OF-85
1947			113	.276	.385	384	106	23	2	5	1.3	48	40	18	14	7	4	1	216	21	15	1	2.2	.940	OF-100, 2B-7, 3B-4
1948	PHI	N	77	.240	.357	196	47	16	2	1	0.5	15	22	8	14	2	28	7	76	42	12	7	1.7	.908	3B-18, OF-17, 2B-12
6 yrs.			574	.275	.382	1901	523	95	26	19	1.0	200	217	113	105	37	60	15	1041	750	109	174	3.3	.943	2B-246, OF-239, 3B-24

Ed Rowen

ROWEN, W. EDWARD
B. Oct. 22, 1857, Bridgeport, Conn.   D. Feb. 22, 1892, Bridgeport, Conn.
6'1" 170 lbs.

Year	Team		Games	BA	SA	AB	H	2B	3B	HR	HR%	R	RBI	BB	SO	SB	AB	H	PO	A	E	DP	TC/G	FA	G by Pos
1882	BOS	N	83	.248	.303	327	81	7	4	1	0.3	36	43	19	18			0	0	258	72	44	5	4.5	.882	OF-48, C-34, SS-6, 3B-1
1883	PHI	AA	49	.219	.281	196	43	10	1	0	0.0	28		10				0	0	276	57	60	2	8.0	.847	C-44, OF-8, 3B-1, 2B-1
1884			4	.400	.467	15	6	1	0	0	0.0	4		1				0	0	21	4	6	1	7.8	.806	C-4
3 yrs.			136	.242	.299	538	130	18	5	1	0.2	68	43	30	18			0	0	555	133	110	8	5.9	.862	C-82, OF-56, SS-6, 3B-2, 2B-1

Chuck Rowland

ROWLAND, CHARLES LELAND
B. July 23, 1899, Warrenton, N. C.
BR TR 6'1" 185 lbs.

Year	Team		Games	BA	SA	AB	H	2B	3B	HR	HR%	R	RBI	BB	SO	SB	AB	H	PO	A	E	DP	TC/G	FA	G by Pos
1923	PHI	A	5	.000	.000	6	0	0	0	0	0.0	0	0	0	2	0	1	0	5	1	0	0	1.2	1.000	C-4

Jim Roxburgh

ROXBURGH, JAMES A.
B. Jan. 17, 1858, San Francisco, Calif.   D. Feb. 21, 1934, San Francisco, Calif.
BR TR

Year	Team		Games	BA	SA	AB	H	2B	3B	HR	HR%	R	RBI	BB	SO	SB	AB	H	PO	A	E	DP	TC/G	FA	G by Pos
1884	BAL	AA	2	.500	.500	4	2	0	0	0	0.0	1		1				0	0	12	2	3	0	8.5	.824	C-2
1887	PHI	AA	2	.125	.125	8	1	0	0	0	0.0	0		0				0	0	6	3	2	0	5.5	.818	C-2, 2B-1
2 yrs.			4	.250	.250	12	3	0	0	0	0.0	1		1				0	0	18	5	5	0	7.0	.821	C-4, 2B-1

Jerry Royster

ROYSTER, JERON KENNIS
B. Oct. 18, 1952, Sacramento, Calif.
BR TR 6' 165 lbs.

Year	Team		Games	BA	SA	AB	H	2B	3B	HR	HR%	R	RBI	BB	SO	SB	AB	H	PO	A	E	DP	TC/G	FA	G by Pos
1973	LA	N	10	.211	.211	19	4	0	0	0	0.0	1	2	0	5	1	0	0	3	14	3	1	2.0	.850	3B-6, 2B-1
1974			6	–	–	0	0	0	0	0	–	2	0	0	0	0	0	0	0	3	0	0	0.5	1.000	OF-1, 3B-1, 2B-1
1975			13	.250	.361	36	9	2	1	0	0.0	2	1	1	3	1	1	0	12	15	2	4	2.2	.931	OF-7, 2B-4, 3B-3, SS-1
1976	ATL	N	149	.248	.304	533	132	13	1	5	0.9	65	45	52	53	24	1	0	158	310	19	35	3.3	.961	3B-148, SS-2
1977			140	.216	.288	445	96	10	2	6	1.3	64	28	38	67	28	4	0	182	267	28	40	3.4	.941	3B-56, SS-51, 2B-38
1978			140	.259	.333	529	137	17	8	2	0.4	67	35	56	49	27	4	2	284	376	23	66	4.9	.966	2B-75, SS-60, 3B-1
1979			154	.273	.349	601	164	25	6	3	0.5	103	51	62	59	35	3	0	261	405	22	62	4.5	.968	3B-80, 2B-77
1980			123	.242	.319	392	95	17	5	1	0.3	42	20	37	48	22	4	1	195	166	18	32	3.1	.953	2B-49, 3B-48, OF-41
1981			64	.204	.269	93	19	4	1	0	0.0	13	9	7	14	7	17	4	35	51	4	9	1.4	.956	3B-24, 2B-13
1982			108	.295	.383	261	77	13	2	2	0.8	43	25	22	36	14	6	1	105	112	11	20	2.1	.952	3B-62, OF-25, 2B-16, SS-10
1983			91	.235	.328	268	63	10	3	3	1.1	32	30	28	35	11	4	1	112	156	10	29	3.1	.964	3B-47, 2B-26, OF-18, SS-13
1984			81	.207	.295	227	47	13	2	1	0.4	22	21	15	41	6	15	1	99	162	9	23	3.3	.967	2B-29, 3B-17, SS-16, OF-11
1985	SD	N	90	.281	.410	249	70	13	2	5	2.0	31	31	32	31	6	10	1	130	214	8	37	3.9	.977	3B-58, SS-29, SS-7, OF-2
1986			118	.257	.362	257	66	12	0	5	1.9	31	26	32	45	3	32	8	87	166	14	23	2.3	.948	3B-59, SS-24, 2B-21, OF-7
1987 2 teams	CHI	A		(55G – .240)		NY	A	(18G – .357)																	
" total			73	.265	.439	196	52	13	0	7	3.6	26	27	23	32	4	9	2	66	75	4	9	2.0	.972	3B-43, OF-14, 2B-6, SS-1
1988	ATL	N	68	.176	.206	102	18	3	0	0	0.0	8	1	6	16	0	31	7	49	11	1	1	0.9	.984	OF-26, 3B-10, SS-2, 2B-2
16 yrs.			1428	.249	.333	4208	1049	165	33	40	1.0	552	352	411	534	189	142	28	1778	2503	176	391	3.1	.961	3B-634, 2B-416, SS-187, OF-152

LEAGUE CHAMPIONSHIP SERIES

Year	Team		Games	BA	SA	AB	H	2B	3B	HR	HR%	R	RBI	BB	SO	SB	AB	H	PO	A	E	DP	TC/G	FA	G by Pos
1982	ATL	N	3	.182	.182	11	2	0	0	0	0.0	0	0	0	2	0	0	0	0	0	0	0	0.0	–	OF-3, 3B-1

Willie Royster

ROYSTER, WILLIE ARTHUR
B. Apr. 11, 1954, Clarksville, Va.
BR TR 5'11" 180 lbs.

Year	Team		Games	BA	SA	AB	H	2B	3B	HR	HR%	R	RBI	BB	SO	SB	Pinch Hit AB	Pinch Hit H	PO	A	E	DP	TC/G	FA	G by Pos

Willie Royster *continued*

Year	Team		Games	BA	SA	AB	H	2B	3B	HR	HR%	R	RBI	BB	SO	SB	PH AB	PH H	PO	A	E	DP	TC/G	FA	G by Pos
1981	BAL	A	4	.000	.000	4	0	0	0	0	0.0	0	0	0	2	0	1	0	5	0	0	0	1.3	1.000	C-4

Vic Roznovsky

ROZNOVSKY, VICTOR JOSEPH
B. Oct. 19, 1938, Shiner, Tex.   BL TR 6' 170 lbs.

Year	Team		Games	BA	SA	AB	H	2B	3B	HR	HR%	R	RBI	BB	SO	SB	PH AB	PH H	PO	A	E	DP	TC/G	FA	G by Pos
1964	CHI	N	35	.197	.211	76	15	1	0	0	0.0	2	5	5	18	0	16	1	67	14	2	2	2.4	.976	C-26
1965			71	.221	.308	172	38	4	1	3	1.7	9	15	16	30	1	11	4	270	30	5	6	4.3	.984	C-63
1966	BAL	A	41	.237	.320	97	23	5	0	1	1.0	4	10	9	11	0	5	2	176	13	1	1	4.6	.995	C-34
1967			45	.206	.258	97	20	5	0	0	0.0	7	10	1	20	0	20	6	133	10	1	2	3.2	.993	C-23
1969	PHI	N	13	.231	.231	13	3	0	0	0	0.0	0	1	1	4	0	12	3	6	0	0	0	0.5	1.000	C-2
5 yrs.			205	.218	.281	455	99	15	1	4	0.9	22	38	32	83	1	64	16	652	67	9	11	3.6	.988	C-148

Al Rubeling

RUBELING, ALBERT WILLIAM
B. May 10, 1913, Baltimore, Md. D. Jan. 28, 1988, Baltimore, Md.   BR TR 6' 185 lbs.

Year	Team		Games	BA	SA	AB	H	2B	3B	HR	HR%	R	RBI	BB	SO	SB	PH AB	PH H	PO	A	E	DP	TC/G	FA	G by Pos
1940	PHI	A	108	.245	.351	376	92	16	6	4	1.1	49	38	48	58	4	0	0	120	211	22	19	3.3	.938	3B-98, 2B-10
1941			6	.263	.263	19	5	0	0	0	0.0	0	2	2	1	0	0	0	7	8	3	1	3.0	.833	3B-6
1943	PIT	N	47	.262	.357	168	44	8	4	0	0.0	23	9	8	17	0	2	1	89	140	6	27	5.0	.974	2B-44, 3B-1
1944			92	.245	.370	184	45	7	2	4	2.2	22	30	19	19	4	41	9	70	56	2	7	1.4	.984	OF-18, 2B-17, 3B-16
4 yrs.			253	.249	.355	747	186	31	12	8	1.1	94	79	77	95	8	43	10	286	415	33	54	2.9	.955	3B-121, 2B-71, OF-18

Sonny Ruberto

RUBERTO, JOHN EDWARD
B. Jan. 2, 1946, Staten Island, N. Y.   BR TR 5'11" 175 lbs.

Year	Team		Games	BA	SA	AB	H	2B	3B	HR	HR%	R	RBI	BB	SO	SB	PH AB	PH H	PO	A	E	DP	TC/G	FA	G by Pos
1969	SD	N	19	.143	.143	21	3	0	0	0	0.0	3	0	1	7	0	1	0	38	6	0	0	2.3	1.000	C-15
1972	CIN	N	2	.000	.000	3	0	0	0	0	0.0	0	0	0	1	0	0	0	5	0	0	0	2.5	1.000	C-2
2 yrs.			21	.125	.125	24	3	0	0	0	0.0	3	0	1	8	0	1	0	43	6	0	0	2.3	1.000	C-17

Art Ruble

RUBLE, WILLIAM ARTHUR (Speedy)
B. Mar. 11, 1903, Knoxville, Tenn. D. Nov. 1, 1983, Marysville, Tenn.   BL TR 5'10½" 168 lbs.

Year	Team		Games	BA	SA	AB	H	2B	3B	HR	HR%	R	RBI	BB	SO	SB	PH AB	PH H	PO	A	E	DP	TC/G	FA	G by Pos
1927	DET	A	56	.165	.253	91	15	4	2	0	0.0	16	11	14	15	2	3	0	62	3	2	2	1.2	.970	OF-43
1934	PHI	N	19	.278	.352	54	15	4	0	0	0.0	7	8	7	3	0	4	0	24	2	5	1	1.6	.839	OF-14
2 yrs.			75	.207	.290	145	30	8	2	0	0.0	23	19	21	18	2	7	0	86	5	7	3	1.3	.929	OF-57

Johnny Rucker

RUCKER, JOHN JOEL (The Crabapple Comet)
B. Jan. 15, 1917, Crabapple, Ga. D. Aug. 7, 1985, Moultrie, Ga.   BL TR 6'2" 175 lbs.

Year	Team		Games	BA	SA	AB	H	2B	3B	HR	HR%	R	RBI	BB	SO	SB	PH AB	PH H	PO	A	E	DP	TC/G	FA	G by Pos
1940	NY	N	86	.296	.401	277	82	7	5	4	1.4	38	23	7	32	4	20	8	121	3	6	0	1.5	.954	OF-57
1941			143	.288	.383	622	179	38	9	1	0.2	95	42	29	61	8	1	1	344	13	12	5	2.6	.967	OF-142
1943			132	.273	.339	505	138	19	4	2	0.4	56	46	22	44	4	13	3	300	9	10	3	2.4	.969	OF-117
1944			144	.244	.325	587	143	14	8	6	1.0	79	39	24	48	8	2	0	310	14	5	0	2.3	.985	OF-139
1945			105	.273	.417	429	117	19	11	7	1.6	58	51	20	36	7	4	1	256	6	6	2	2.6	.978	OF-98
1946			95	.264	.340	197	52	8	2	1	0.5	28	13	7	27	4	12	3	91	1	5	0	1.0	.948	OF-54
6 yrs.			705	.272	.366	2617	711	105	39	21	0.8	354	214	109	248	35	52	16	1422	46	44	10	2.1	.971	OF-607

John Rudderham

RUDDERHAM, JOHN EDMUND
B. Aug. 30, 1863, Quincy, Mass. D. Apr. 3, 1942, Randolph, Mass.   BR TR 5'8" 170 lbs.

Year	Team		Games	BA	SA	AB	H	2B	3B	HR	HR%	R	RBI	BB	SO	SB	PH AB	PH H	PO	A	E	DP	TC/G	FA	G by Pos
1884	BOS	U	1	.250	.250	4	1	0	0	0	0.0	0		0		0		0	0	0	2	0	2.0	—	OF-1

Joe Rudi

RUDI, JOSEPH ODEN
B. Sept. 7, 1946, Modesto, Calif.   BR TR 6'2" 200 lbs.

Year	Team		Games	BA	SA	AB	H	2B	3B	HR	HR%	R	RBI	BB	SO	SB	PH AB	PH H	PO	A	E	DP	TC/G	FA	G by Pos
1967	KC	A	19	.186	.233	43	8	2	0	0	0.0	4	0	3	7	0	4	0	69	1	1	1	3.7	.986	1B-9, OF-6
1968	OAK	A	68	.177	.232	181	32	5	1	1	0.6	10	12	12	32	1	17	2	77	1	1	0	1.2	.987	OF-56
1969			35	.189	.279	122	23	3	1	2	1.6	10	6	5	16	1	5	1	134	9	3	10	4.2	.979	OF-18, 1B-11
1970			106	.309	.480	350	108	23	2	11	3.1	40	42	16	61	3	18	2	302	18	4	17	3.1	.988	OF-63, 1B-28
1971			127	.267	.386	513	137	23	4	10	1.9	62	52	28	62	3	3	0	280	7	2	1	2.3	.993	OF-121, 1B-5
1972			147	.305	.486	593	181	32	9	19	3.2	94	75	37	62	3	0	0	247	5	2	1	1.8	.992	OF-147, 3B-1
1973			120	.270	.414	437	118	25	1	12	2.7	53	66	30	72	0	2	0	231	6	2	2	2.0	.992	OF-117, DH-1, 1B-1
1974			158	.293	.484	593	174	39	4	22	3.7	73	99	34	92	2	1	0	416	18	5	21	2.8	.989	OF-140, 1B-27, DH-2
1975			126	.278	.494	468	130	26	6	21	4.5	66	75	40	56	2	2	1	804	37	7	65	6.7	.992	1B-91, OF-44, DH-2
1976			130	.270	.424	500	135	32	3	13	2.6	54	94	41	71	6	2	1	270	7	3	4	2.2	.989	OF-126, DH-2, 1B-2
1977	CAL	A	64	.264	.496	242	64	13	2	13	5.4	48	53	22	48	1	0	0	131	3	0	1	2.1	1.000	OF-61, DH-3
1978			133	.256	.416	497	127	27	1	17	3.4	58	79	28	82	2	4	1	292	10	2	9	2.3	.993	OF-111, DH-11, 1B-10
1979			90	.242	.394	330	80	11	3	11	3.3	35	61	24	61	0	4	2	207	7	2	5	2.4	.991	OF-80, 1B-5, DH-3
1980			104	.237	.417	372	88	17	1	16	4.3	42	53	17	84	1	7	2	244	5	2	5	2.4	.992	OF-90, 1B-6, DH-3
1981	BOS	A	49	.180	.352	122	22	3	0	6	4.9	14	24	14	29	0	22	5	47	1	0	2	1.0	1.000	DH-21, 1B-5, OF-1
1982	OAK	A	71	.212	.332	193	41	6	1	5	2.6	21	18	24	35	0	10	0	416	20	5	37	6.2	.989	1B-49, OF-14, DH-3
16 yrs.			1547	.264	.427	5556	1468	287	39	179	3.2	684	810	369	870	25	101	17	4167	159	41	180	2.8	.991	OF-1195, 1B-249, DH-51, 3B-1

LEAGUE CHAMPIONSHIP SERIES

Year	Team		Games	BA	SA	AB	H	2B	3B	HR	HR%	R	RBI	BB	SO	SB	PH AB	PH H	PO	A	E	DP	TC/G	FA	G by Pos
1971	OAK	A	2	.143	.286	7	1	1	0	0	0.0	0	0	1	0	0	0	0	4	0	0	0	2.0	1.000	OF-2
1972			5	.250	.300	20	5	1	0	0	0.0	1	2	1	4	0	0	0	11	0	0	0	2.2	1.000	OF-5
1973			5	.222	.389	18	4	0	0	1	5.6	1	3	3	1	0	0	0	11	0	0	0	2.2	1.000	OF-5
1974			4	.154	.308	13	2	0	1	0	0.0	0	0	0	1	0	0	0	5	0	0	0	1.3	1.000	OF-4
1975			3	.250	.417	12	3	2	0	0	0.0	1	1	0	1	0	0	0	22	2	0	0	8.0	1.000	1B-2, OF-1
5 yrs.			19	.214	.343	70	15	4	1	1	1.4	3	6	5	8	0	0	0	53	2	0	0	2.9	1.000	OF-17, 1B-2

WORLD SERIES

Year	Team		Games	BA	SA	AB	H	2B	3B	HR	HR%	R	RBI	BB	SO	SB	PH AB	PH H	PO	A	E	DP	TC/G	FA	G by Pos
1972	OAK	A	7	.240	.360	25	6	0	0	1	4.0	1	1	2	5	0	0	0	20	0	0	0	2.9	1.000	OF-7
1973			7	.333	.407	27	9	2	0	0	0.0	3	4	3	4	0	0	0	20	2	0	1	3.1	1.000	OF-7
1974			5	.333	.500	18	6	0	0	1	5.6	1	4	0	4	0	0	0	28	0	0	1	5.6	1.000	OF-5, 1B-2
3 yrs.			19	.300	.414	70	21	2	0	2	2.9	5	9	5	12	0	0	0	68	2	0	2	3.7	1.000	OF-19, 1B-2

Year	Team	Games	BA	SA	AB	H	2B	3B	HR	HR%	R	RBI	BB	SO	SB	Pinch Hit AB	Pinch Hit H	PO	A	E	DP	TC/G	FA	G by Pos

Dutch Rudolph

RUDOLPH, JOHN HERMAN   BL TL 5'10" 160 lbs.
B. July 10, 1882, Natrona, Pa. D. Apr. 17, 1967, Natrona, Pa.

Year	Team	Games	BA	SA	AB	H	2B	3B	HR	HR%	R	RBI	BB	SO	SB	PH AB	PH H	PO	A	E	DP	TC/G	FA	G by Pos
1903	PHI N	1	.000	.000	1	0	0	0	0	0.0	0	0	0		0	1	0	0	0	0	0	0.0	–	
1904	CHI N	2	.333	.333	3	1	0	0	0	0.0	0	0	0		0	0	0	1	0	0	0	0.5	1.000	OF-2
	2 yrs.	3	.250	.250	4	1	0	0	0	0.0	0	0	0		0	1	0	1	0	0	0	0.3	1.000	OF-2

Ken Rudolph

RUDOLPH, KENNETH VICTOR   BR TR 6'1" 180 lbs.
B. Dec. 29, 1946, Rockford, Ill.

Year	Team	Games	BA	SA	AB	H	2B	3B	HR	HR%	R	RBI	BB	SO	SB	PH AB	PH H	PO	A	E	DP	TC/G	FA	G by Pos
1969	CHI N	27	.206	.324	34	7	1	0	1	2.9	7	6	6	11	0	10	3	41	3	1	0	1.7	.978	C-11, OF-3
1970		20	.100	.125	40	4	1	0	0	0.0	1	2	1	12	0	3	0	67	6	0	1	3.7	1.000	C-16
1971		25	.197	.237	76	15	3	0	0	0.0	5	7	6	20	0	0	0	153	16	0	1	6.8	1.000	C-25
1972		42	.236	.321	106	25	1	1	2	1.9	10	9	6	14	1	1	0	178	23	7	2	5.0	.966	C-41
1973		64	.206	.300	170	35	8	0	2	1.2	12	17	7	25	1	0	0	259	28	9	4	4.6	.970	C-64
1974	SF N	57	.259	.278	158	41	3	0	0	0.0	11	10	21	15	0	0	0	253	25	1	4	4.9	.996	C-56
1975	STL N	44	.200	.263	80	16	2	0	1	1.3	5	6	3	10	0	14	1	93	11	3	1	2.4	.972	C-31
1976		27	.160	.220	50	8	3	0	0	0.0	1	5	1	7	0	13	4	61	2	4	1	2.5	.940	C-14
1977	2 teams		SF N (11G – .200)			BAL A (11G – .286)																		
"	total	22	.241	.276	29	7	1	0	0	0.0	3	2	1	7	0	5	0	66	10	2	4	3.5	.974	C-22
	9 yrs.	328	.213	.273	743	158	23	2	6	0.8	55	64	52	121	2	46	8	1171	124	27	18	4.0	.980	C-280, OF-3

Muddy Ruel

RUEL, HEROLD DOMINIC   BR TR 5'9" 150 lbs.
B. Feb. 20, 1896, St. Louis, Mo. D. Nov. 13, 1963, Palo Alto, Calif.
Manager 1947.

Year	Team	Games	BA	SA	AB	H	2B	3B	HR	HR%	R	RBI	BB	SO	SB	PH AB	PH H	PO	A	E	DP	TC/G	FA	G by Pos
1915	STL A	10	.000	.000	14	0	0	0	0	0.0	0	1	5	5	0	2	0	20	3	1	0	2.4	.958	C-6
1917	NY A	6	.118	.118	17	2	0	0	0	0.0	1	1	2	2	1	0	0	23	6	0	0	4.8	1.000	C-6
1918		3	.333	.333	6	2	0	0	0	0.0	0	0	2	1	1	0	0	8	2	0	0	3.3	1.000	C-2
1919		81	.240	.266	233	56	6	0	0	0.0	18	31	34	26	4	0	0	340	90	11	6	5.4	.975	C-81
1920		82	.268	.341	261	70	14	1	1	0.4	30	15	15	18	4	1	0	317	62	6	2	4.7	.984	C-80
1921	BOS A	113	.277	.349	358	99	21	1	1	0.3	41	43	41	15	2	2	0	375	86	11	7	4.2	.977	C-109
1922		116	.255	.302	361	92	15	1	1	0.3	34	28	41	26	4	4	1	359	96	10	17	4.0	.978	C-112
1923	WAS A	136	.316	.383	449	142	24	3	0	0.0	63	54	55	21	4	3	2	528	144	14	14	5.1	.980	C-133
1924		149	.283	.331	501	142	20	2	0	0.0	50	57	62	20	7	2	1	612	112	15	23	5.0	.980	C-147
1925		127	.310	.344	393	122	9	2	0	0.0	55	54	63	16	4	0	0	493	103	11	19	4.8	.982	C-126, 1B-1
1926		117	.299	.389	368	110	22	4	1	0.3	42	53	61	14	7	0	0	452	81	6	13	4.6	.989	C-117
1927		131	.308	.376	428	132	16	5	1	0.2	61	52	63	18	9	2	0	495	100	7	8	4.6	.988	C-128
1928		108	.257	.320	350	90	18	2	0	0.0	31	55	44	14	12	4	2	416	75	6	6	4.6	.988	C-101, 1B-2
1929		69	.245	.287	188	46	4	2	0	0.0	16	20	31	7	0	6	0	247	52	3	6	4.4	.990	C-63
1930		66	.253	.308	198	50	3	4	0	0.0	18	26	24	13	1	4	2	243	32	4	5	4.2	.986	C-60
1931	2 teams		BOS A (33G – .301)			DET A (14G – .120)																		
"	total	47	.233	.278	133	31	6	0	0	0.0	7	9	14	7	0	2	0	143	38	8	4	4.0	.958	C-44
1932	DET A	50	.235	.294	136	32	4	2	0	0.0	10	18	17	6	1	3	1	150	25	2	3	3.5	.989	C-49
1933	STL A	28	.190	.222	63	12	2	0	0	0.0	13	8	24	4	0	5	0	72	21	0	3	3.3	1.000	C-28
1934	CHI A	22	.211	.263	57	12	3	0	0	0.0	4	7	8	5	0	1	0	75	8	2	1	3.9	.976	C-21
	19 yrs.	1461	.275	.332	4514	1242	187	29	4	0.1	494	532	606	238	61	41	9	5368	1138	117	137	4.5	.982	C-1413, 1B-3

WORLD SERIES

Year	Team	Games	BA	SA	AB	H	2B	3B	HR	HR%	R	RBI	BB	SO	SB	PH AB	PH H	PO	A	E	DP	TC/G	FA	G by Pos
1924	WAS A	7	.095	.143	21	2	1	0	0	0.0	2	0	6	1	0	0	0	51	5	0	1	8.0	1.000	C-7
1925		7	.316	.368	19	6	1	0	0	0.0	0	1	3	2	0	0	0	35	6	0	0	5.9	1.000	C-7
	2 yrs.	14	.200	.250	40	8	2	0	0	0.0	2	1	9	3	0	0	0	86	11	0	1	6.9	1.000	C-14

Dutch Ruether

RUETHER, WALTER HENRY   BL TL 6'1½" 180 lbs.
B. Sept. 13, 1893, Alameda, Calif. D. May 16, 1970, Phoenix, Ariz.

Year	Team	Games	BA	SA	AB	H	2B	3B	HR	HR%	R	RBI	BB	SO	SB	PH AB	PH H	PO	A	E	DP	TC/G	FA	G by Pos
1917	2 teams		CHI N (31G – .273)			CIN N (19G – .208)																		
"	total	50	.250	.382	68	17	3	3	0	0.0	4	12	11	17	1	22	6	43	23	2	3	1.4	.971	P-17, 1B-5
1918	CIN N	2	.000	.000	3	0	0	0	0	0.0	0	0	0	2	0	0	0	0	2	0	0	1.0	1.000	P-2
1919		42	.261	.348	92	24	2	3	0	0.0	8	6	4	18	1	7	2	10	57	2	1	1.6	.971	P-33
1920		45	.192	.231	104	20	4	0	0	0.0	3	10	5	24	0	7	0	10	74	4	6	2.0	.955	P-37, 1B-1
1921	BKN N	49	.351	.505	97	34	5	2	2	2.1	12	13	4	9	1	11	3	6	51	2	3	1.2	.966	P-36
1922		67	.208	.320	125	26	6	1	2	1.6	12	20	12	11	0	27	6	9	56	0	6	1.0	1.000	P-35
1923		49	.274	.282	117	32	1	0	0	0.0	6	10	12	12	0	12	3	9	53	2	7	1.3	.969	P-34, 1B-1
1924		34	.242	.290	62	15	1	1	0	0.0	5	4	5	4	0	4	0	5	46	1	3	1.5	.981	P-30
1925	WAS A	55	.333	.426	108	36	3	2	1	0.9	18	15	10	8	0	19	6	7	46	2	2	1.0	.964	P-30, 1B-1
1926	2 teams		WAS A (47G – .250)			NY A (13G – .095)																		
"	total	60	.221	.265	113	25	2	0	1	0.9	8	11	6	11	0	30	6	2	38	1	2	0.7	.976	P-28
1927	NY A	35	.263	.338	80	21	3	0	1	1.3	7	10	8	15	0	6	2	7	47	0	2	1.5	1.000	P-27
	11 yrs.	488	.258	.335	969	250	30	12	7	0.7	83	111	77	129	3	145	34	108	493	16	35	1.3	.974	P-309, 1B-8

WORLD SERIES

Year	Team	Games	BA	SA	AB	H	2B	3B	HR	HR%	R	RBI	BB	SO	SB	PH AB	PH H	PO	A	E	DP	TC/G	FA	G by Pos
1919	CIN N	3	.667	1.500	6	4	1	2	0	0.0	2	4	1	0	0	1	0	0	2	0	0	0.7	1.000	P-2
1925	WAS A	1	.000	.000	1	0	0	0	0	0.0	0	0	0	0	0	1	0	0	0	0	0	0.0	–	
1926	NY A	3	.000	.000	4	0	0	0	0	0.0	0	0	0	4	0	2	0	0	2	0	0	0.7	1.000	P-3
	3 yrs.	7	.364	.818	11	4	1	2	0	0.0	2	4	1	4	0	4	0	0	4	0	0	0.6	1.000	P-3

Rudy Rufer

RUFER, RUDOLPH JOSEPH   BR TR 6'½" 165 lbs.
B. Oct. 28, 1926, Ridgewood, N. Y.

Year	Team	Games	BA	SA	AB	H	2B	3B	HR	HR%	R	RBI	BB	SO	SB	PH AB	PH H	PO	A	E	DP	TC/G	FA	G by Pos
1949	NY N	7	.067	.067	15	1	0	0	0	0.0	2	2	2	5	0	0	0	9	13	1	2	3.3	.957	SS-7
1950		15	.091	.091	11	1	0	0	0	0.0	1	0	0	1	1	3	0	1	7	1	1	0.6	.889	SS-8
	2 yrs.	22	.077	.077	26	2	0	0	0	0.0	2	2	2	1	1	3	0	10	20	2	3	1.5	.938	SS-15

Red Ruffing

RUFFING, CHARLES HERBERT   BR TR 6'1½" 205 lbs.
B. May 3, 1904, Granville, Ill. D. Feb. 17, 1986, Mayfield Heights, Ohio
Hall of Fame 1967.

Year	Team	Games	BA	SA	AB	H	2B	3B	HR	HR%	R	RBI	BB	SO	SB	PH AB	PH H	PO	A	E	DP	TC/G	FA	G by Pos
1924	BOS A	8	.143	.429	7	1	0	1	0	0.0	0	0	0	1	0	0	0	0	3	0	0	0.4	1.000	P-8

Year	Team	Games	BA	SA	AB	H	2B	3B	HR	HR%	R	RBI	BB	SO	SB	Pinch Hit AB	H	PO	A	E	DP	TC/G	FA	G by Pos

Red Ruffing *continued*

Year	Team	Games	BA	SA	AB	H	2B	3B	HR	HR%	R	RBI	BB	SO	SB	AB	H	PO	A	E	DP	TC/G	FA	G by Pos
1925		37	.215	.316	79	17	4	2	0	0.0	6	11	1	22	0	0	0	7	50	1	3	1.6	.983	P-37
1926		37	.196	.275	51	10	1	0	1	2.0	8	5	2	12	0	0	0	8	42	0	3	1.4	1.000	P-37
1927		29	.255	.345	55	14	3	1	0	0.0	5	4	0	6	0	2	0	8	36	1	1	1.6	.978	P-26
1928		60	.314	.488	121	38	13	1	2	1.7	12	19	3	12	0	17	5	7	51	3	4	1.0	.951	P-42
1929		60	.307	.439	114	35	9	0	2	1.8	9	17	2	13	0	22	6	7	46	3	1	0.9	.946	P-35, OF-2
1930	2 teams	BOS A (6G – .273)			NY A (52G – .374)																			
"	total	58	.364	.582	110	40	8	2	4	3.6	17	22	7	8	0	17	6	3	29	3	0	0.6	.914	P-38
1931	NY A	48	.330	.505	109	36	8	1	3	2.8	14	12	1	13	0	10	3	5	32	0	1	0.8	1.000	P-37, OF-1
1932		55	.306	.444	124	38	6	1	3	2.4	20	19	6	10	0	18	4	4	38	2	4	0.8	.955	P-35
1933		55	.252	.348	115	29	3	1	2	1.7	10	13	7	15	0	19	2	8	45	2	5	1.0	.964	P-35
1934		45	.248	.327	113	28	3	0	2	1.8	11	13	3	17	0	12	2	10	32	3	2	1.0	.933	P-36
1935		50	.339	.486	109	37	10	0	2	1.8	13	18	3	9	0	18	8	17	26	0	3	0.9	1.000	P-30
1936		53	.291	.449	127	37	5	0	5	3.9	14	22	11	12	0	17	6	13	56	1	6	1.3	.986	P-33
1937		54	.202	.248	129	26	3	0	1	0.8	11	10	13	24	0	21	6	9	28	1	2	0.7	.974	P-31
1938		45	.224	.364	107	24	4	1	3	2.8	12	17	17	21	0	12	2	11	34	0	2	1.0	1.000	P-31
1939		44	.307	.342	114	35	1	0	1	0.9	12	20	7	18	1	11	1	8	32	2	2	1.0	.952	P-28
1940		33	.124	.202	89	11	4	0	1	1.1	8	7	3	9	0	1	0	6	30	2	2	1.2	.947	P-30
1941		38	.303	.483	89	27	8	1	2	2.2	10	22	4	12	0	15	6	7	21	0	3	0.7	1.000	P-23
1942		30	.250	.338	80	20	4	0	1	1.3	8	13	5	13	0	6	1	8	30	1	5	1.3	.974	P-24
1945		21	.217	.326	46	10	0	1	1	2.2	4	5	0	8	0	10	1	2	11	1	1	0.7	.929	P-11
1946		25	.120	.160	25	3	1	0	0	0.0	1	1	1	8	0	0	0	2	5	0	0	0.9	1.000	P-8
1947	CHI A	14	.208	.208	24	5	0	0	0	0.0	2	3	1	3	0	4	1	2	7	0	1	0.6	1.000	P-9
22 yrs.		882	.269	.389	1937	521	98	13	36	1.9	207	273	97	266	1	228	58	152	684	26	51	1.0	.970	P-624, OF-3

WORLD SERIES

Year	Team	Games	BA	SA	AB	H	2B	3B	HR	HR%	R	RBI	BB	SO	SB	AB	H	PO	A	E	DP	TC/G	FA	G by Pos
1932	NY A	2	.000	.000	4	0	0	0	0	0.0	0	1	1	1	0	1	0	1	3	0	0	2.0	1.000	P-1
1936		3	.000	.000	5	0	0	0	0	0.0	0	0	1	2	0	1	0	1	3	0	0	1.3	1.000	P-2
1937		1	.500	.750	4	2	1	0	0	0.0	0	3	0	0	0	0	0	0	0	0	0	0.0	–	P-1
1938		2	.167	.167	6	1	0	0	0	0.0	1	1	1	0	0	0	0	2	4	0	1	3.0	1.000	P-2
1939		1	.333	.333	3	1	0	0	0	0.0	0	0	0	1	0	0	0	0	3	0	1	3.0	1.000	P-1
1941		1	.000	.000	3	0	0	0	0	0.0	0	0	0	0	0	0	0	0	0	0	0	0.0	–	P-1
1942		4	.222	.222	9	2	0	0	0	0.0	0	0	0	2	0	2	0	0	1	0	0	0.3	1.000	P-2
7 yrs.		14	.176	.206	34	6	1	0	0	0.0	1	4	3	6	0	3	0	4	14	0	1	1.3	1.000	P-10

Chico Ruiz

RUIZ, HIRALDO
Born Hiraldo Ruiz y Sablon.
B. Dec. 5, 1938, Santo Domingo, Cuba   D. Feb. 9, 1972, San Diego, Calif.

BB TR 6'   169 lbs.

Year	Team	Games	BA	SA	AB	H	2B	3B	HR	HR%	R	RBI	BB	SO	SB	AB	H	PO	A	E	DP	TC/G	FA	G by Pos
1964	CIN N	77	.244	.318	311	76	13	2	2	0.6	33	16	7	41	11	2	0	95	149	11	28	3.3	.957	3B-49, 2B-30
1965		29	.111	.167	18	2	1	0	0	0.0	7	1	0	5	1	7	2	3	5	1	0	0.3	.889	3B-4, SS-3
1966		82	.255	.291	110	28	2	1	0	0.0	13	5	5	14	1	35	13	23	35	4	3	0.8	.935	3B-27, OF-8, SS-6
1967		105	.220	.300	250	55	12	4	0	0.0	32	13	11	35	9	17	3	131	168	10	33	2.9	.968	2B-56, 3B-13, SS-11, OF-5
1968		85	.259	.288	139	36	2	0	0	0.0	15	9	12	18	4	31	7	96	99	5	21	2.4	.975	2B-34, 1B-16, 3B-5, SS-3
1969		88	.245	.276	196	48	4	1	0	0.0	19	13	14	28	4	11	2	120	147	12	36	3.2	.957	2B-39, SS-29, 3B-7, 1B-2, OF-1
1970	CAL A	68	.243	.290	107	26	3	1	0	0.0	10	12	7	16	3	30	3	26	46	2	4	1.1	.973	3B-27, SS-3, 2B-3, 1B-2, C-1
1971		31	.263	.263	19	5	0	0	0	0.0	4	0	2	7	1	11	3	2	4	0	0	0.2	1.000	3B-3, 2B-2
8 yrs.		565	.240	.295	1150	276	37	10	2	0.2	133	69	58	164	34	145	33	496	653	45	125	2.1	.962	2B-164, 3B-135, SS-55, 1B-20, OF-14, C-1

Chico Ruiz

RUIZ, MANUEL (Manny)
Born Manuel Ruiz y Cruz.
B. Nov. 1, 1951, Santurce, Puerto Rico

BR TR 5'11½" 170 lbs.

Year	Team	Games	BA	SA	AB	H	2B	3B	HR	HR%	R	RBI	BB	SO	SB	AB	H	PO	A	E	DP	TC/G	FA	G by Pos
1978	ATL N	18	.283	.348	46	13	3	0	0	0.0	3	2	2	4	0	1	0	31	32	1	5	3.6	.984	2B-14, 3B-1
1980		25	.308	.462	26	8	2	1	0	0.0	3	2	3	7	0	5	0	9	17	3	1	1.2	.897	3B-16, SS-4, 2B-2
2 yrs.		43	.292	.389	72	21	5	1	0	0.0	6	4	5	11	0	6	0	40	49	4	6	2.2	.957	3B-17, 2B-16, SS-4

Joe Rullo

RULLO, JOSEPH VINCENT
B. June 16, 1916, New York, N. Y.   D. Oct. 28, 1969, Philadelphia, Pa.

BR TR 5'11" 168 lbs.

Year	Team	Games	BA	SA	AB	H	2B	3B	HR	HR%	R	RBI	BB	SO	SB	AB	H	PO	A	E	DP	TC/G	FA	G by Pos
1943	PHI A	16	.291	.345	55	16	3	0	0	0.0	2	6	8	7	0	0	0	27	51	3	10	5.1	.963	2B-16
1944		35	.167	.167	96	16	0	0	0	0.0	5	5	6	19	1	0	0	78	88	9	22	5.0	.949	2B-33, 1B-1
2 yrs.		51	.212	.232	151	32	3	0	0	0.0	7	11	14	26	1	0	0	105	139	12	32	5.0	.953	2B-49, 1B-1

Bill Rumler

RUMLER, WILLIAM GEORGE
B. Mar. 27, 1891, Milford, Neb.   D. May 26, 1966, Lincoln, Neb.

BR TR 6'1" 190 lbs.

Year	Team	Games	BA	SA	AB	H	2B	3B	HR	HR%	R	RBI	BB	SO	SB	AB	H	PO	A	E	DP	TC/G	FA	G by Pos
1914	STL A	33	.174	.196	46	8	1	0	0	0.0	2	6	3	12	2	13	2	26	12	1	1	1.2	.974	C-9, OF-6
1916		27	.324	.405	37	12	3	0	0	0.0	6	10	3	7	0	15	6	23	11	1	1	1.3	.971	C-9
1917		78	.261	.420	88	23	3	4	1	1.1	7	16	8	9	2	71	16	13	2	1	0	0.2	.938	OF-9
3 yrs.		138	.251	.357	171	43	7	4	1	0.6	15	32	14	28	4	99	24	62	25	3	2	0.7	.967	C-18, OF-15

Paul Runge

RUNGE, PAUL WILLIAM
B. May 21, 1958, Kingston, N. Y.

BR TR 6'   165 lbs.

Year	Team	Games	BA	SA	AB	H	2B	3B	HR	HR%	R	RBI	BB	SO	SB	AB	H	PO	A	E	DP	TC/G	FA	G by Pos
1981	ATL N	10	.259	.296	27	7	1	0	0	0.0	2	4	4	4	0	0	0	14	27	4	5	4.5	.911	SS-10
1982		4	.000	.000	2	0	0	0	0	0.0	0	0	0	0	0	0	0	2	0	0	0	0.0	–	
1983		5	.250	.250	8	2	0	0	0	0.0	0	1	1	4	0	1	0	4	3	0	1	1.4	1.000	2B-2
1984		28	.267	.322	90	24	3	1	0	0.0	5	3	10	14	5	0	0	53	101	5	18	5.7	.969	2B-22, SS-7, 3B-3
1985		50	.218	.287	87	19	3	0	1	1.1	15	5	18	18	0	12	2	15	66	7	5	1.8	.920	3B-28, SS-5, 2B-2
1986		7	.250	.250	8	2	0	0	0	0.0	1	0	2	4	0	0	0	5	12	0	0	2.4	1.000	2B-5
1987		27	.213	.426	47	10	1	0	3	6.4	9	8	5	10	0	0	0	15	27	2	5	1.6	.955	3B-10, SS-9, 2B-2
1988		52	.211	.276	76	16	5	0	0	0.0	11	7	14	21	0	21	4	22	32	1	3	1.1	.982	3B-19, 2B-7, SS-6
8 yrs.		183	.232	.310	345	80	13	1	4	1.2	43	26	54	75	5	39	6	128	268	19	37	2.3	.954	3B-60, 2B-40, SS-37

Year	Team	Games	BA	SA	AB	H	2B	3B	HR	HR%	R	RBI	BB	SO	SB	Pinch Hit AB	Pinch Hit H	PO	A	E	DP	TC/G	FA	G by Pos

Tom Runnells

RUNNELLS, THOMAS WILLIAM
B. Apr. 17, 1955, Greeley, Colo.

BB TR 6' 175 lbs.

Year	Team	Games	BA	SA	AB	H	2B	3B	HR	HR%	R	RBI	BB	SO	SB	PH AB	PH H	PO	A	E	DP	TC/G	FA	G by Pos
1985	CIN N	28	.200	.229	35	7	1	0	0	0.0	3	0	3	4	0	9	3	10	22	0	4	1.1	1.000	SS-11, 2B-1
1986		12	.091	.182	11	1	1	0	0	0.0	1	0	0	2	0	5	0	4	5	0	1	0.8	1.000	2B-4, 3B-3
2 yrs.		40	.174	.217	46	8	2	0	0	0.0	4	0	3	6	0	14	3	14	27	0	5	1.0	1.000	SS-11, 2B-5, 3B-3

Pete Runnels

RUNNELS, JAMES EDWARD
Born James Edward Runnells.
B. Jan. 28, 1928, Lufkin, Tex.
Manager 1966.

BL TR 6' 170 lbs.

Year	Team	Games	BA	SA	AB	H	2B	3B	HR	HR%	R	RBI	BB	SO	SB	PH AB	PH H	PO	A	E	DP	TC/G	FA	G by Pos
1951	WAS A	78	.278	.337	273	76	12	2	0	0.0	31	25	31	24	0	5	0	159	176	18	41	4.5	.949	SS-73
1952		152	.285	.333	555	158	18	3	1	0.2	70	64	72	55	0	4	1	319	410	25	99	5.0	.967	SS-147, 2B-1
1953		137	.257	.321	486	125	15	5	2	0.4	64	50	64	36	3	8	3	219	351	26	94	4.4	.956	SS-121, 2B-11
1954		139	.268	.383	488	131	17	15	3	0.6	75	56	78	60	2	5	2	264	372	29	94	4.8	.956	SS-107, 2B-27, OF-1
1955		134	.284	.346	503	143	17	4	2	0.4	66	49	55	51	3	4	0	349	340	18	107	5.3	.975	2B-132, SS-2
1956		147	.310	.433	578	179	29	9	8	1.4	72	76	58	64	5	2	1	875	229	14	131	7.6	.987	1B-81, 2B-69, SS-3
1957		134	.230	.298	473	109	18	4	2	0.4	53	35	55	51	2	12	2	699	160	8	84	6.5	.991	1B-72, 3B-32, 2B-23
1958	BOS A	147	.322	.438	568	183	32	5	8	1.4	103	59	87	49	1	0	0	631	335	11	129	6.6	.989	2B-106, 1B-42
1959		147	.314	.427	560	176	33	6	6	1.1	95	57	95	48	6	2	1	663	307	10	131	6.7	.990	2B-101, 1B-44, SS-9
1960		143	**.320**	.394	528	169	29	2	2	0.4	80	35	71	51	5	2	1	420	377	11	114	5.7	.986	2B-129, 1B-57, 3B-3
1961		143	.317	.414	360	114	20	3	3	0.8	49	38	46	32	5	23	5	715	90	6	97	5.7	.993	1B-113, 3B-11, 2B-7, SS-1
1962		152	**.326**	.456	562	183	33	5	10	1.8	80	60	79	57	3	1	0	1309	104	10	125	9.4	.993	1B-151
1963	HOU N	124	.253	.296	388	98	9	1	2	0.5	35	23	45	42	2	16	4	593	111	6	50	5.7	.992	1B-70, 2B-36, 3B-3
1964		22	.196	.216	51	10	1	0	0	0.0	3	3	8	7	0	6	0	138	5	2	8	6.6	.986	1B-14
14 yrs.		1799	.291	.378	6373	1854	283	64	49	0.8	876	630	844	627	37	90	20	7353	3367	194	1302	6.1	.982	1B-644, 2B-642, SS-463, 3B-49, OF-1

Amos Rusie

RUSIE, AMOS WILSON (The Hoosier Thunderbolt)
B. May 30, 1871, Mooresville, Ind.   D. Dec. 6, 1942, Seattle, Wash.
Hall of Fame 1977.

BR TR 6'1" 210 lbs.

Year	Team	Games	BA	SA	AB	H	2B	3B	HR	HR%	R	RBI	BB	SO	SB	PH AB	PH H	PO	A	E	DP	TC/G	FA	G by Pos
1889	IND N	33	.175	.223	103	18	3	1	0	0.0	15	4	2	19	3	0	0	9	32	6	2	1.4	.872	P-33
1890	NY N	73	.278	.366	284	79	13	6	0	0.0	31	28	7	26	6	0	0	39	131	23	5	2.6	.881	P-67, OF-14
1891		62	.245	.286	220	54	5	2	0	0.0	30	15	3	25	2	1	0	10	106	14	4	2.1	.892	P-61, OF-1
1892		69	.210	.278	252	53	6	4	1	0.4	18	26	3	29	4	1	0	30	133	22	5	2.7	.881	P-64, OF-4
1893		56	.269	.363	212	57	3	4	3	1.4	32	27	3	19	0	0	0	23	114	15	5	2.7	.901	P-56
1894		56	.280	.398	186	52	5	4	3	1.6	20	24	5	26	5	2	1	28	113	14	4	2.8	.910	P-54
1895		53	.246	.291	179	44	3	1	1	0.6	14	19	0	28	2	3	0	22	93	11	4	2.4	.913	P-49, OF-1
1897		40	.278	.326	144	40	1	3	0	0.0	25	22	3		1	2	0	19	77	8	3	2.6	.923	P-38
1898		41	.210	.283	138	29	2	4	0	0.0	23	8	1		2	2	1	20	68	12	3	2.4	.880	P-37, OF-1, 1B-1
1901	CIN N	3	.125	.125	8	1	0	0	0	0.0	0	1	0		0	0	0	1	8	1	0	3.3	.900	P-3
10 yrs.		486	.247	.319	1726	427	41	29	8	0.5	208	176	27	170	25	11	2	201	875	126	35	2.5	.895	P-462, OF-21, 1B-1

Bill Russell

RUSSELL, WILLIAM ELLIS
B. Oct. 21, 1948, Pittsburg, Kans.

BR TR 6' 175 lbs.

Year	Team	Games	BA	SA	AB	H	2B	3B	HR	HR%	R	RBI	BB	SO	SB	PH AB	PH H	PO	A	E	DP	TC/G	FA	G by Pos
1969	LA N	98	.226	.344	212	48	6	2	5	2.4	35	15	22	45	4	22	6	132	4	3	1	1.4	.978	OF-86
1970		81	.259	.363	278	72	11	9	2	0.7	30	28	16	28	9	7	1	167	10	3	1	2.2	.983	OF-79, SS-1
1971		91	.227	.327	211	48	7	4	2	0.9	29	15	11	39	6	3	0	131	114	8	23	2.8	.968	2B-41, OF-40, SS-6
1972		129	.272	.366	434	118	19	5	4	0.9	47	34	34	64	14	5	2	202	439	34	69	5.1	.950	SS-121, OF-6
1973		162	.265	.337	615	163	26	3	4	0.7	55	56	34	63	15	0	0	243	560	31	106	5.1	.963	SS-162
1974		160	.269	.351	553	149	18	6	5	0.9	61	65	53	53	14	1	0	194	491	39	68	4.5	.946	SS-160, OF-1
1975		84	.206	.258	252	52	9	2	0	0.0	24	14	23	28	5	0	0	94	230	11	27	4.0	.967	SS-83
1976		149	.274	.343	554	152	17	3	5	0.9	53	65	21	46	15	0	0	251	476	28	90	5.2	.963	SS-149
1977		153	.278	.360	634	176	28	6	4	0.6	84	51	24	43	16	0	0	234	523	29	102	5.1	.963	SS-153
1978		155	.286	.365	625	179	32	4	3	0.5	72	46	30	34	10	1	0	245	533	31	91	5.2	.962	SS-155
1979		153	.271	.359	627	170	26	4	7	1.1	72	56	24	44	6	3	1	218	452	30	70	4.6	.957	SS-150
1980		130	.264	.341	466	123	23	2	3	0.6	38	34	18	44	13	1	0	179	387	19	57	4.5	.968	SS-129
1981		82	.233	.282	262	61	9	2	0	0.0	20	22	19	20	2	0	0	128	261	14	49	4.9	.965	SS-80
1982		153	.274	.340	497	136	20	2	3	0.6	64	46	33	31	10	2	2	216	502	29	64	4.9	.961	SS-150
1983		131	.246	.286	451	111	13	1	1	0.2	47	30	33	31	13	5	0	192	392	22	61	4.6	.964	SS-127
1984		89	.267	.321	262	70	12	1	0	0.0	25	19	25	24	4	6	1	115	173	9	29	3.3	.970	SS-65, OF-18, 2B-5
1985		76	.260	.308	169	44	6	1	0	0.0	19	13	18	9	4	20	5	60	82	10	11	2.0	.934	SS-23, OF-21, 2B-8, 3B-5
1986		105	.250	.301	216	54	11	0	0	0.0	21	18	15	23	7	31	10	103	84	5	17	1.8	.974	OF-48, SS-32, 2B-8, 3B-1
18 yrs.		2181	.263	.338	7318	1926	293	57	46	0.6	796	627	483	667	167	107	28	3104	5713	355	936	4.2	.961	SS-1746, OF-299, 2B-62, 3B-6

DIVISIONAL PLAYOFF SERIES

Year	Team	Games	BA	SA	AB	H	2B	3B	HR	HR%	R	RBI	BB	SO	SB	PH AB	PH H	PO	A	E	DP	TC/G	FA	G by Pos
1981	LA N	5	.250	.313	16	4	1	0	0	0.0	1	2	3	1	0	0	0	0	0	2	0	0.4	–	SS-5

LEAGUE CHAMPIONSHIP SERIES

Year	Team	Games	BA	SA	AB	H	2B	3B	HR	HR%	R	RBI	BB	SO	SB	PH AB	PH H	PO	A	E	DP	TC/G	FA	G by Pos
1974	LA N	4	.389	.389	18	7	0	0	0	0.0	1	3	1	0	0	0	0	13	16	0	4	7.3	1.000	SS-4
1977		4	.278	.333	18	5	1	0	0	0.0	3	2	0	0	0	0	0	11	12	2	3	6.3	.920	SS-4
1978		4	.412	.471	17	7	1	0	0	0.0	1	1	1	0	0	0	0	4	14	0	3	4.5	1.000	SS-4
1981		5	.313	.438	16	5	0	1	0	0.0	2	1	1	1	0	0	0	0	0	0	0	–	–	SS-5
1983		4	.286	.286	14	4	0	0	0	0.0	1	0	2	4	1	0	0	4	10	1	2	3.8	.933	SS-4
5 yrs.		21	.337	.386	83	28	2	1	0	0.0	8	8	5	6	1	0	0	32	52	3	12	4.1	.966	SS-21

WORLD SERIES

Year	Team	Games	BA	SA	AB	H	2B	3B	HR	HR%	R	RBI	BB	SO	SB	PH AB	PH H	PO	A	E	DP	TC/G	FA	G by Pos
1974	LA N	5	.222	.333	18	4	0	1	0	0.0	0	2	0	0	0	0	0	4	11	0	2	3.2	.938	SS-5
1977		6	.154	.231	26	4	0	1	0	0.0	3	2	1	3	0	0	0	9	21	0	4	5.0	1.000	SS-6
1978		6	.423	.500	26	11	2	0	0	0.0	1	1	1	2	1	0	0	11	20	3	3	5.7	.912	SS-6
1981		6	.240	.240	25	6	0	0	0	0.0	1	2	1	1	1	0	0	4	26	1	3	5.2	.968	SS-6
4 yrs.		23	.263	.326	95	25	2	2	0	0.0	5	8	3	8	2	0	0	28	78	5	12	4.8	.955	SS-23

Year Team	Games	BA	SA	AB	H	2B	3B	HR	HR%	R	RBI	BB	SO	SB	Pinch Hit AB	Pinch Hit H	PO	A	E	DP	TC/G	FA	G by Pos

Harvey Russell
RUSSELL, HARVEY HOLMES
B. Jan. 10, 1887, Marshall, Va. D. Jan. 8, 1980, Alexandria, Va.
BL TR 5'9½" 163 lbs.

Year Team	Games	BA	SA	AB	H	2B	3B	HR	HR%	R	RBI	BB	SO	SB	PH AB	PH H	PO	A	E	DP	TC/G	FA	G by Pos
1914 BAL F	81	.232	.274	168	39	3	2	0	0.0	18	13	18		2	29	7	193	46	13	2	3.1	.948	C-47, OF-1, SS-1
1915	53	.260	.329	73	19	1	2	0	0.0	5	11	14		1	24	5	72	20	1	4	1.8	.989	C-21
2 yrs.	134	.241	.290	241	58	4	4	0	0.0	23	24	32		3	53	12	265	66	14	6	2.6	.959	C-68, OF-1, SS-1

Jim Russell
RUSSELL, JAMES WILLIAM
B. Oct. 1, 1918, Fayette City, Pa. D. Nov. 24, 1987, Pittsburgh, Pa.
BB TR 6'1" 181 lbs.

Year Team	Games	BA	SA	AB	H	2B	3B	HR	HR%	R	RBI	BB	SO	SB	PH AB	PH H	PO	A	E	DP	TC/G	FA	G by Pos
1942 PIT N	3	.071	.071	14	1	0	0	0	0.0	2	0	1	4	0	1	0	12	0	0	0	4.0	1.000	OF-3
1943	146	.259	.358	533	138	19	11	4	0.8	79	44	77	67	12	7	2	323	16	3	6	2.3	.991	OF-134, 1B-6
1944	152	.312	.460	580	181	34	14	8	1.4	109	66	79	63	6	2	0	345	20	5	7	2.4	.986	OF-149
1945	146	.284	.433	510	145	24	8	12	2.4	88	77	71	40	15	6	0	313	9	9	1	2.3	.973	OF-140
1946	146	.277	.403	516	143	29	6	8	1.6	68	50	67	54	11	5	1	351	9	12	7	2.5	.968	OF-134, 1B-5
1947	128	.253	.381	478	121	21	8	8	1.7	68	51	63	58	7	9	3	343	6	7	3	2.8	.980	OF-119
1948 BOS N	89	.264	.410	322	85	18	1	9	2.8	44	54	46	31	4	4	0	246	3	2	0	2.8	.992	OF-84
1949	130	.231	.347	415	96	22	1	8	1.9	57	54	64	68	3	6	0	269	3	7	3	2.1	.975	OF-120
1950 BKN N	78	.229	.425	214	49	8	2	10	4.7	37	32	31	36	1	18	3	131	3	1	0	1.7	.993	OF-55
1951	16	.000	.000	13	0	0	0	0	0.0	2	0	4	6	0	10	0	3	0	0	0	0.2	1.000	OF-4
10 yrs.	1034	.267	.400	3595	959	175	51	67	1.9	554	428	503	427	59	68	9	2336	69	46	27	2.4	.981	OF-942, 1B-11

John Russell
RUSSELL, JOHN WILLIAM
B. Jan. 5, 1961, Oklahoma City, Okla.
BR TR 6' 195 lbs.

Year Team	Games	BA	SA	AB	H	2B	3B	HR	HR%	R	RBI	BB	SO	SB	PH AB	PH H	PO	A	E	DP	TC/G	FA	G by Pos
1984 PHI N	39	.283	.444	99	28	8	1	2	2.0	11	11	12	33	0	9	4	51	1	0	0	1.3	1.000	OF-29, C-2
1985	81	.218	.398	216	47	10	0	9	4.2	22	23	18	72	2	15	4	170	9	4	7	2.3	.978	OF-49, 1B-18
1986	93	.241	.444	315	76	21	0	13	4.1	35	60	25	103	0	4	1	498	39	13	10	5.9	.976	C-89
1987	24	.145	.306	62	9	1	0	3	4.8	5	8	3	17	0	6	2	48	1	1	0	2.1	.980	OF-10, C-7
1988	22	.245	.388	49	12	1	0	2	4.1	5	4	3	15	0	7	0	77	9	5	3	4.1	.945	C-15
1989 ATL N	74	.182	.233	159	29	2	0	2	1.3	14	9	8	53	0	17	1	196	28	4	1	3.1	.982	C-45, OF-14, 3B-2, 1B-2, P-1
6 yrs.	333	.223	.383	900	201	45	3	31	3.4	92	115	69	293	2	58	12	1040	87	27	21	3.5	.977	C-158, OF-102, 1B-20, 3B-2, P-1

Lloyd Russell
RUSSELL, LLOYD OPAL (Tex)
B. Apr. 10, 1913, Atoka, Okla. D. May 24, 1968, Waco, Tex.
BR TR 5'11" 166 lbs.

Year Team	Games	BA	SA	AB	H	2B	3B	HR	HR%	R	RBI	BB	SO	SB	PH AB	PH H	PO	A	E	DP	TC/G	FA	G by Pos
1938 CLE A	2	–	–	0	0	0	0	0	–	0	0	0	0	0	0	0	0	0	0	0	0.0	–	

Paul Russell
RUSSELL, PAUL A.
B. 1870, Reading, Pa. D. Pottstown, Pa.

Year Team	Games	BA	SA	AB	H	2B	3B	HR	HR%	R	RBI	BB	SO	SB	PH AB	PH H	PO	A	E	DP	TC/G	FA	G by Pos
1894 STL N	3	.100	.100	10	1	0	0	0	0.0	1	0	0	2	0	0	0	5	6	2	0	4.3	.846	OF-1, 3B-1, 2B-1

Reb Russell
RUSSELL, EWELL ALBERT
B. Apr. 12, 1889, Jackson, Miss. D. Sept. 30, 1973, Indianapolis, Ind.
BL TL 5'11" 185 lbs.

Year Team	Games	BA	SA	AB	H	2B	3B	HR	HR%	R	RBI	BB	SO	SB	PH AB	PH H	PO	A	E	DP	TC/G	FA	G by Pos
1913 CHI A	52	.189	.292	106	20	5	3	0	0.0	9	7	1	29	0	1	1	10	71	4	3	1.6	.953	P-51
1914	43	.266	.313	64	17	1	1	0	0.0	6	7	1	14	0	5	2	3	50	3	0	1.3	.946	P-38
1915	45	.244	.337	86	21	2	3	0	0.0	11	7	4	14	1	3	0	11	56	2	1	1.5	.971	P-41
1916	56	.143	.165	91	13	2	0	0	0.0	9	6	0	18	1	0	0	4	71	2	2	1.4	.974	P-56
1917	39	.279	.412	68	19	3	3	0	0.0	5	9	2	10	0	3	0	14	51	1	2	1.7	.985	P-35, OF-1
1918	27	.140	.200	50	7	3	0	0	0.0	2	3	0	6	0	6	0	4	28	0	1	1.2	1.000	P-19, OF-1
1919	1	–	–	0	0	0	0	0	–	0	0	0	0	0	0	0	0	0	0	0	0.0	–	P-1
1922 PIT N	60	.368	.668	220	81	14	8	12	5.5	51	75	14	18	4	0	0	115	5	4	2	2.1	.968	OF-60
1923	94	.289	.491	291	84	18	7	9	3.1	49	58	20	21	3	17	5	156	4	5	0	1.8	.970	OF-76
9 yrs.	417	.268	.433	976	262	48	25	21	2.2	142	172	42	130	9	35	8	317	336	21	11	1.6	.969	P-241, OF-138

WORLD SERIES

Year Team	Games	BA	SA	AB	H	2B	3B	HR	HR%	R	RBI	BB	SO	SB	PH AB	PH H	PO	A	E	DP	TC/G	FA	G by Pos
1917 CHI A	1	–	–	0	0	0	0	0	–	0	0	0	0	0	0	0	0	0	0	0	0.0	–	P-1

Rip Russell
RUSSELL, GLEN DAVID
B. Jan. 26, 1915, Los Angeles, Calif. D. Sept. 26, 1976, Los Alamitos, Calif.
BR TR 6'1" 180 lbs.

Year Team	Games	BA	SA	AB	H	2B	3B	HR	HR%	R	RBI	BB	SO	SB	PH AB	PH H	PO	A	E	DP	TC/G	FA	G by Pos
1939 CHI N	143	.273	.386	542	148	24	5	9	1.7	55	79	36	56	2	0	0	1383	83	18	109	10.4	.988	1B-143
1940	68	.247	.367	215	53	7	2	5	2.3	15	33	8	23	1	15	5	519	22	10	22	8.1	.982	1B-51, 3B-3
1941	6	.294	.353	17	5	1	0	0	0.0	1	1	1	5	0	0	0	36	3	1	4	6.7	.975	1B-5
1942	102	.242	.351	302	73	9	0	8	2.6	32	41	17	21	0	31	5	392	90	14	40	4.9	.972	1B-35, 2B-24, 3B-10, OF-3
1946 BOS A	80	.208	.318	274	57	10	1	6	2.2	22	35	13	30	1	9	2	61	140	12	25	2.7	.944	3B-70, 2B-3
1947	26	.154	.231	52	8	1	0	1	1.9	8	3	8	7	0	12	1	7	29	3	2	1.5	.923	3B-13
6 yrs.	425	.245	.356	1402	344	52	8	29	2.1	133	192	83	142	4	67	13	2398	367	58	202	6.6	.979	1B-234, 3B-96, 2B-27, OF-3

WORLD SERIES

Year Team	Games	BA	SA	AB	H	2B	3B	HR	HR%	R	RBI	BB	SO	SB	PH AB	PH H	PO	A	E	DP	TC/G	FA	G by Pos
1946 BOS A	2	1.000	1.000	2	2	0	0	0	0.0	1	0	0	0	0	2	2	0	0	0	0	0.0	–	3B-1

Hank Ruszkowski
RUSZKOWSKI, HENRY ALEXANDER
B. Nov. 10, 1925, Cleveland, Ohio
BR TR 6' 190 lbs.

Year Team	Games	BA	SA	AB	H	2B	3B	HR	HR%	R	RBI	BB	SO	SB	PH AB	PH H	PO	A	E	DP	TC/G	FA	G by Pos
1944 CLE A	3	.375	.375	8	3	0	0	0	0.0	1	1	0	1	0	1	0	5	2	0	0	2.3	1.000	C-2
1945	14	.204	.204	49	10	0	0	0	0.0	2	5	4	9	0	0	0	63	14	2	2	5.6	.975	C-14
1947	23	.259	.667	27	7	2	0	3	11.1	5	4	2	6	0	7	2	14	6	0	0	0.9	1.000	C-16
3 yrs.	40	.238	.369	84	20	2	0	3	3.6	8	10	6	16	0	8	2	82	22	2	2	2.7	.981	C-32

Babe Ruth
RUTH, GEORGE HERMAN (The Sultan of Swat, The Bambino)
B. Feb. 6, 1895, Baltimore, Md.
D. Aug. 16, 1948, New York, N. Y.
Hall of Fame 1936.
BL TL 6'2" 215 lbs.
BB 1923

Year Team	Games	BA	SA	AB	H	2B	3B	HR	HR%	R	RBI	BB	SO	SB	PH AB	PH H	PO	A	E	DP	TC/G	FA	G by Pos
1914 BOS A	5	.200	.300	10	2	1	0	0	0.0	1	0	0	4	0	1	0	0	7	0	0	1.4	1.000	P-4

Babe Ruth *continued*

Year	Team	Games	BA	SA	AB	H	2B	3B	HR	HR%	R	RBI	BB	SO	SB	Pinch Hit AB	Pinch Hit H	PO	A	E	DP	TC/G	FA	G by Pos
1915		42	.315	.576	92	29	10	1	4	4.3	16	21	9	23	0	10	1	17	63	2	3	2.0	.976	P-32
1916		67	.272	.419	136	37	5	3	3	2.2	18	16	10	23	0	19	4	24	83	3	6	1.6	.973	P-44
1917		52	.325	.472	123	40	6	3	2	1.6	14	12	12	18	0	7	1	19	101	2	4	2.3	.987	P-41
1918		95	.300	.555	317	95	26	11	11	3.5	50	66	57	58	6	3	1	270	72	18	16	3.8	.950	OF-59, P-20, 1B-13
1919		130	.322	.657	432	139	34	12	29	6.7	103	114	101	58	7	1	0	270	53	4	11	2.5	.988	OF-111, P-17, 1B-4
1920	NY A	142	.376	.847¹	458	172	36	9	54	11.8¹	158	137	148	80	14	1	0	270	21	20	4	2.2	.936	OF-139, 1B-2, P-1
1921		152	.378	.846	540	204	44	16	59	10.9	177	171	144	81	17	0	0	357	19	13	6	2.6	.967	OF-152, 1B-2, P-2
1922		110	.315	.672	406	128	24	8	35	8.6	94	99	84	80	2	0	0	226	14	9	4	2.3	.964	OF-110, 1B-1
1923		152	.393	.764	522	205	45	13	41	7.9	151	131	170¹	93	17	0	0	419	21	12	4	3.0	.973	OF-148, 1B-4
1924		153	.378	.739	529	200	39	7	46	8.7	143	121	142	81	9	1	1	340	18	14	4	2.4	.962	OF-152
1925		98	.290	.543	359	104	12	2	25	7.0	61	66	59	68	2	0	0	207	15	6	3	2.3	.974	OF-98
1926		152	.372	.737	495	184	30	5	47	9.5	139	145	144	76	11	3	0	318	11	7	7	2.2	.979	OF-149, 1B-2
1927		151	.356	.772	540	192	29	8	60	11.1	158	164	138	89	7	0	0	328	14	13	4	2.4	.963	OF-151
1928		154	.323	.709	536	173	29	8	54	10.1	163	142	135	87	4	0	0	304	9	8	0	2.1	.975	OF-154
1929		135	.345	.697	499	172	26	6	46	9.2	121	154	72	60	5	2	1	240	5	4	2	1.8	.984	OF-133
1930		145	.359	.732	518	186	28	9	49	9.5	150	153	136	61	10	0	0	266	14	10	0	2.0	.966	OF-144, P-1
1931		145	.373	.700	534	199	31	3	46	8.6	149	163	128	51	5	2	0	242	5	7	2	1.8	.972	OF-142, 1B-1
1932		133	.341	.661	457	156	13	5	41	9.0	120	137	130	62	2	1	1	212	10	9	1	1.7	.961	OF-127, 1B-1
1933		137	.301	.582	459	138	21	3	34	7.4	97	103	114	90	4	4	1	222	10	8	4	1.8	.967	OF-132, 1B-1, P-1
1934		125	.288	.537	365	105	17	4	22	6.0	78	84	103	63	1	11	2	197	3	8	0	1.7	.962	OF-111
1935	BOS N	28	.181	.431	72	13	0	0	6	8.3	13	12	20	24	0	1	0	39	1	2	0	1.5	.952	OF-26
22 yrs.		2503	.342	.690	8399	2873	506	136	714	8.5	2174	2211	2056	1330	123	67	13	4787	569	179	85	2.2	.968	OF-2238, P-163, 1B-31
				1st						2nd	1st	2nd	2nd	1st										

WORLD SERIES

Year	Team	Games	BA	SA	AB	H	2B	3B	HR	HR%	R	RBI	BB	SO	SB	Pinch Hit AB	Pinch Hit H	PO	A	E	DP	TC/G	FA	G by Pos
1915	BOS A	1	.000	.000	1	0	0	0	0	0.0	0	0	0	0	0	1	0	0	0	0	0	0.0	–	
1916		1	.000	.000	5	0	0	0	0	0.0	0	1	0	2	0	0	0	2	4	0	0	6.0	1.000	P-1
1918		3	.200	.600	5	1	0	1	0	0.0	0	2	0	2	0	0	0	1	5	0	1	2.0	1.000	OF-2, P-2
1921	NY A	6	.313	.500	16	5	0	0	1	6.3	3	4	5	8	2	1	0	9	0	0	0	1.5	1.000	OF-5
1922		5	.118	.176	17	2	1	0	0	0.0	1	1	2	3	0	0	0	9	0	0	0	1.8	1.000	OF-5
1923		6	.368	1.000	19	7	1	1	3	15.8	8	3	8	6	0	0	0	17	0	1	0	3.0	.944	OF-6, 1B-1
1926		7	.300	.900	20	6	0	0	4	20.0	6	5	11	2	1	0	0	8	2	0	0	1.4	1.000	OF-7
1927		4	.400	.800	15	6	0	0	2	13.3	4	7	2	2	1	0	0	10	0	0	0	2.5	1.000	OF-4
1928		4	.625	1.375	16	10	3	0	3	18.8	9	4	1	2	0	0	0	9	1	0	0	2.5	1.000	OF-4
1932		4	.333	.733	15	5	0	0	2	13.3	6	6	4	3	0	0	0	8	0	1	0	2.3	.889	OF-4
10 yrs.		41	.326	.744	129	42	5	2	15	11.6	37	33	33	30	4	2	0	73	12	2	1	2.1	.977	OF-37, P-3, 1B-1
			10th	2nd		10th					2nd	1st	3rd	4th	2nd									

Jim Rutherford

RUTHERFORD, JAMES HOLLIS
B. Sept. 26, 1886, Stillwater, Minn. D. Sept. 18, 1956, Cleveland, Ohio

BL TR 6'1" 180 lbs.

Year	Team	Games	BA	SA	AB	H	2B	3B	HR	HR%	R	RBI	BB	SO	SB	Pinch Hit AB	Pinch Hit H	PO	A	E	DP	TC/G	FA	G by Pos
1910	CLE A	1	.500	.500	2	1	0	0	0	0.0	0	0	0		0	0	0	1	0	0	0	1.0	1.000	OF-1

Mickey Rutner

RUTNER, MILTON
B. Mar. 18, 1920, Hempstead, N. Y.

BR TR 5'11" 190 lbs.

Year	Team	Games	BA	SA	AB	H	2B	3B	HR	HR%	R	RBI	BB	SO	SB	Pinch Hit AB	Pinch Hit H	PO	A	E	DP	TC/G	FA	G by Pos
1947	PHI A	12	.250	.333	48	12	1	0	1	2.1	4	4	3	2	0	1	0	5	18	3	2	2.2	.885	3B-11

Mark Ryal

RYAL, MARK DWAYNE
B. Apr. 28, 1960, Henryetta, Okla.

BL TL 6'1" 180 lbs.

Year	Team	Games	BA	SA	AB	H	2B	3B	HR	HR%	R	RBI	BB	SO	SB	Pinch Hit AB	Pinch Hit H	PO	A	E	DP	TC/G	FA	G by Pos
1982	KC A	6	.077	.077	13	1	0	0	0	0.0	0	0	1	3	0	1	0	9	0	0	0	1.7	.900	OF-5
1985	CHI A	12	.152	.242	33	5	3	0	0	0.0	4	3	3	3	0	0	0	21	0	0	0	1.8	1.000	OF-12
1986	CAL A	13	.375	.563	32	12	0	0	2	6.3	6	5	2	4	1	5	2	32	2	1	1	2.7	.971	OF-6, 1B-4, DH-2
1987		58	.200	.410	100	20	6	0	5	5.0	7	18	3	15	0	31	10	50	1	3	1	0.9	.944	OF-21, DH-5, 1B-4
1989	PHI N	29	.242	.303	33	8	2	0	0	0.0	2	5	1	6	0	19	4	17	0	0	0	0.6	1.000	OF-4, 1B-4, DH-7
5 yrs.		118	.218	.370	211	46	11	0	7	3.3	19	31	10	31	1	56	16	129	3	5	2	1.2	.964	OF-48, 1B-12, DH-7

Blondy Ryan

RYAN, JOHN COLLINS
B. Jan. 4, 1906, Lynn, Mass. D. Nov. 28, 1959, Swampscott, Mass.

BR TR 6'1" 178 lbs.

Year	Team	Games	BA	SA	AB	H	2B	3B	HR	HR%	R	RBI	BB	SO	SB	Pinch Hit AB	Pinch Hit H	PO	A	E	DP	TC/G	FA	G by Pos
1930	CHI A	28	.207	.333	87	18	0	4	1	1.1	9	10	6	13	2	0	0	30	44	10	6	3.0	.881	3B-23, SS-2, 2B-1
1933	NY N	146	.238	.293	525	125	10	5	3	0.6	47	48	15	62	0	0	0	296	494	42	95	5.7	.950	SS-146
1934		110	.242	.306	385	93	19	0	2	0.5	35	41	19	68	3	1	0	159	283	26	33	4.3	.944	3B-65, SS-30, 2B-25
1935	2 teams	PHI N (39G – .264)			NY A	(30G – .238)																		
"	total	69	.252	.308	234	59	4	3	1	0.4	25	21	10	30	1	2	1	135	191	32	36	5.2	.911	SS-65, 3B-1, 2B-1
1937	NY N	21	.240	.347	75	18	3	1	1	1.3	10	13	6	8	0	1	1	41	57	6	13	5.0	.942	SS-19, 3B-1, 2B-1
1938		12	.208	.208	24	5	0	0	0	0.0	1	0	1	3	0	2	1	6	16	2	2	2.0	.917	2B-5, 3B-3, SS-2
6 yrs.		386	.239	.304	1330	318	36	13	8	0.6	127	133	57	184	6	6	3	667	1085	118	185	4.8	.937	SS-264, 3B-93, 2B-33

WORLD SERIES

Year	Team	Games	BA	SA	AB	H	2B	3B	HR	HR%	R	RBI	BB	SO	SB	Pinch Hit AB	Pinch Hit H	PO	A	E	DP	TC/G	FA	G by Pos
1933	NY N	5	.278	.278	18	5	0	0	0	0.0	0	1	1	5	0	0	0	10	20	1	2	6.2	.968	SS-5
1937		1	.000	.000	1	0	0	0	0	0.0	0	0	0	1	0	1	0	0	0	0	0	0.0	–	
2 yrs.		6	.263	.263	19	5	0	0	0	0.0	0	1	1	6	0	1	0	10	20	1	2	5.2	.968	SS-5

Bud Ryan

RYAN, JOHN BUDD
B. Oct. 6, 1885, Denver, Colo. D. July 9, 1956, Sacramento, Calif.

BL TR 5'9½" 172 lbs.

Year	Team	Games	BA	SA	AB	H	2B	3B	HR	HR%	R	RBI	BB	SO	SB	Pinch Hit AB	Pinch Hit H	PO	A	E	DP	TC/G	FA	G by Pos
1912	CLE A	93	.271	.372	328	89	12	9	1	0.3	53	31	30		12	3	1	167	11	7	2	2.0	.962	OF-90
1913		73	.296	.329	243	72	6	1	0	0.0	26	32	11	13	9	4	2	144	8	2	2	2.1	.987	OF-67, 1B-1
2 yrs.		166	.282	.354	571	161	18	10	1	0.2	79	63	41	13	21	7	3	311	19	9	4	2.0	.973	OF-157, 1B-1

Connie Ryan

RYAN, CORNELIUS JOSEPH
B. Feb. 27, 1920, New Orleans, La.
Manager 1975, 1977.

BR TR 5'11" 175 lbs.

Year	Team	Games	BA	SA	AB	H	2B	3B	HR	HR%	R	RBI	BB	SO	SB	Pinch Hit AB	Pinch Hit H	PO	A	E	DP	TC/G	FA	G by Pos
1942	NY N	11	.185	.185	27	5	0	0	0	0.0	4	2	4	3	1	0	1	31	36	4	6	6.5	.944	2B-11
1943	BOS N	132	.212	.249	457	97	10	2	1	0.2	52	24	58	56	7	1	0	257	374	24	47	5.0	.963	2B-100, 3B-30

Year	Team	Games	BA	SA	AB	H	2B	3B	HR	HR%	R	RBI	BB	SO	SB	Pinch Hit AB	Pinch Hit H	PO	A	E	DP	TC/G	FA	G by Pos

Connie Ryan *continued*

Year	Team	Games	BA	SA	AB	H	2B	3B	HR	HR%	R	RBI	BB	SO	SB	PH AB	PH H	PO	A	E	DP	TC/G	FA	G by Pos
1944		88	.295	.416	332	98	18	5	4	1.2	56	25	36	40	13	0	0	233	296	14	58	6.2	.974	2B-80, 3B-14
1946		143	.241	.335	502	121	28	8	1	0.2	55	48	55	63	7	1	0	300	367	22	58	4.8	.968	2B-120, 3B-24
1947		150	.265	.371	544	144	33	5	5	0.9	60	69	71	60	5	0	0	394	433	23	88	5.7	.973	2B-150, SS-1
1948		51	.213	.238	122	26	3	0	0	0.0	14	10	21	16	0	7	1	91	114	7	19	4.2	.967	2B-40, 3B-4
1949		85	.250	.409	208	52	13	1	6	2.9	28	20	21	30	1	23	5	118	131	8	24	3.0	.969	3B-25, SS-18, 2B-16, 1B-3
1950 2 teams	BOS N (20G - .194)				CIN N (106G - .259)																			
" total		126	.248	.358	439	109	20	5	6	1.4	57	49	64	55	4	1	0	361	342	16	29	5.7	.978	2B-123
1951	CIN N	136	.237	.391	473	112	17	4	16	3.4	75	53	79	72	11	7	3	348	353	22	75	5.3	.970	2B-121, 3B-3, 1B-2, OF-1
1952	PHI N	154	.241	.366	577	139	24	6	12	2.1	81	49	69	72	13	0	0	348	462	23	95	5.4	.972	2B-154
1953 2 teams	PHI N (90G - .296)				CHI A (17G - .222)																			
" total		107	.282	.422	301	85	15	6	5	1.7	53	32	39	47	7	22	8	158	199	17	40	3.5	.955	2B-65, 3B-16, 1B-2
1954	CIN N	1	–	–	0	0	0	0	0	–	0	0	0	0	1	0	0	0	0	0	0	0.0	–	
12 yrs.		1184	.248	.357	3982	988	181	42	56	1.4	535	381	518	514	69	62	17	2639	3107	180	539	5.0	.970	2B-980, 3B-116, SS-19, 1B-7, OF-1

WORLD SERIES

Year	Team	Games	BA	SA	AB	H	2B	3B	HR	HR%	R	RBI	BB	SO	SB	PH AB	PH H	PO	A	E	DP	TC/G	FA	G by Pos
1948	BOS N	2	.000	.000	1	0	0	0	0	0.0	0	0	0	1	0	1	0	0	0	0	0	0.0	–	

Cyclone Ryan

RYAN, DANIEL R.
B. 1866, Capperwhite, Ireland D. Jan. 30, 1917, Medfield, Mass.   TR 6'

Year	Team	Games	BA	SA	AB	H	2B	3B	HR	HR%	R	RBI	BB	SO	SB	PH AB	PH H	PO	A	E	DP	TC/G	FA	G by Pos
1887	NY AA	8	.219	.250	32	7	1	0	0	0.0	4		3		1	0	0	72	4	5	7	10.1	.938	1B-8, P-2
1891	BOS N	1	.000	.000	1	0	0	0	0	0.0	0		0		0	0	0	0	1	0	0	1.0	1.000	P-1
2 yrs.		9	.212	.242	33	7	1	0	0	0.0	4	0	3	0	1	0	0	72	5	5	7	9.1	.939	1B-8, P-3

Jack Ryan

RYAN, JOHN FRANCIS
B. May 5, 1905, West Mineral, Kans. D. Sept. 2, 1967, Rochester, Minn.   BR TR 6'   185 lbs.

Year	Team	Games	BA	SA	AB	H	2B	3B	HR	HR%	R	RBI	BB	SO	SB	PH AB	PH H	PO	A	E	DP	TC/G	FA	G by Pos
1929	BOS A	2	.000	.000	3	0	0	0	0	0.0	0	0	0	0	0	1	0	1	0	0	0	0.5	1.000	OF-2

Jimmy Ryan

RYAN, JAMES EDWARD (Pony)
B. Feb. 11, 1863, Clinton, Mass. D. Oct. 26, 1923, Chicago, Ill.   BR TL 5'9"   162 lbs.

Year	Team	Games	BA	SA	AB	H	2B	3B	HR	HR%	R	RBI	BB	SO	SB	PH AB	PH H	PO	A	E	DP	TC/G	FA	G by Pos
1885	CHI N	3	.462	.538	13	6	1	0	0	0.0	2	1	1	1	0	0	0	6	11	7	0	8.0	.708	SS-2, OF-1
1886		84	.306	.431	327	100	17	6	4	1.2	58	53	12	28		0	0	115	55	30	4	2.4	.850	OF-70, SS-6, 3B-6, 2B-5, P-5
1887		126	.285	.435	508	145	23	10	11	2.2	117	74	53	19	50	0	0	172	54	39	8	2.1	.853	OF-122, P-8, 2B-3
1888		129	.332	.515	549	182	33	10	16	2.9	115	64	35	50	60	0	0	219	43	38	6	2.3	.873	OF-128, P-8
1889		135	.307	.498	576	177	31	14	17	3.0	140	72	70	62	45	0	0	286	133	57	19	3.5	.880	OF-106, SS-29
1890	CHI P	118	.340	.463	486	165	32	5	6	1.2	99	89	60	36	30	0	0	257	25	25	5	2.6	.919	OF-118
1891	CHI N	118	.277	.434	505	140	22	15	9	1.8	110	66	53	38	27	0	0	235	29	28	3	2.5	.904	OF-117, SS-2, P-2
1892		128	.293	.438	505	148	21	11	10	2.0	105	65	61	41	27	0	0	258	50	30	7	2.6	.911	OF-120, SS-9
1893		83	.299	.428	341	102	21	7	3	0.9	82	30	59	25	8	0	0	182	41	25	4	3.0	.899	OF-73, SS-10, P-1
1894		108	.360	.484	481	173	37	7	3	0.6	133	62	50	23	11	0	0	221	22	24	3	2.5	.910	OF-108
1895		108	.317	.445	438	139	22	8	6	1.4	83	49	48	22	18	0	0	161	18	12	6	1.8	.937	OF-108
1896		128	.313	.421	489	153	24	10	3	0.6	83	86	46	16	29	0	0	207	21	22	4	2.0	.912	OF-128
1897		136	.300	.458	520	156	33	17	5	1.0	103	85	50		27	0	0	211	28	14	7	1.9	.945	OF-136
1898		144	.323	.446	572	185	32	13	4	0.7	122	79	73		29	0	0	267	20	27	2	2.2	.914	OF-144
1899		125	.301	.394	525	158	20	10	3	0.6	91	68	43		9	0	0	266	18	13	6	2.4	.956	OF-125
1900		105	.277	.393	415	115	25	4	5	1.2	66	59	29		19	0	0	177	12	18	3	2.0	.913	OF-105
1902	WAS A	120	.320	.448	484	155	32	6	6	1.2	92	44	43		10	0	0	280	16	16	0	2.6	.949	OF-120
1903		114	.245	.368	437	107	25	4	7	1.6	42	46	17		9	0	0	288	7	9	1	2.7	.970	OF-114
18 yrs.		2012	.307	.444	8171	2506	451	157	118	1.4	1643	1093	803	361	408	0	0	3808	603	434	88	2.4	.910	OF-1943, SS-58, P-24, 2B-8, 3B-6

John Ryan

RYAN, JOHN A.
Born Daniel Sheehan.
B. Birmingham, Mich. Deceased.

Year	Team	Games	BA	SA	AB	H	2B	3B	HR	HR%	R	RBI	BB	SO	SB	PH AB	PH H	PO	A	E	DP	TC/G	FA	G by Pos
1884 2 teams	WAS U (7G - .143)				WIL U (2G - .167)																			
" total		9	.147	.206	34	5	0	1	0	0.0	2		2			0	0	11	1	5	0	1.9	.706	OF-9, 3B-1

John Ryan

RYAN, JOHN BERNARD (Jack)
B. Nov. 12, 1868, Haverhill, Mass. D. Aug. 21, 1952, Boston, Mass.   BR TR 5'10½" 165 lbs.

Year	Team	Games	BA	SA	AB	H	2B	3B	HR	HR%	R	RBI	BB	SO	SB	PH AB	PH H	PO	A	E	DP	TC/G	FA	G by Pos
1889	LOU AA	21	.177	.190	79	14	1	0	0	0.0	8	2	3	17	2	0	0	63	26	14	1	4.9	.864	C-15, OF-4, 3B-2
1890		93	.217	.288	337	73	16	4	0	0.0	43		12		6	0	0	420	148	43	5	6.6	.930	C-89, OF-3, SS-1, 1B-1
1891		75	.225	.300	253	57	5	4	2	0.8	24	25	15	40	3	0	0	333	99	38	15	6.3	.919	C-56, 1B-11, 3B-6, OF-4, 2B-3
1894	BOS N	53	.269	.413	201	54	12	7	1	0.5	39	29	13	16	3	0	0	173	47	21	8	4.5	.913	C-51, 1B-2
1895		49	.291	.328	189	55	7	0	0	0.0	22	18	6	6	3	0	0	183	63	14	6	5.3	.946	C-43, 2B-5, OF-1
1896		8	.094	.125	32	3	1	0	0	0.0	2	0	1	1	0	0	0	32	9	4	1	5.6	.911	C-8
1898	BKN N	87	.189	.252	301	57	11	4	0	0.0	39	24	15		5	0	0	297	97	17	14	4.7	.959	C-84, 3B-4, 1B-1
1899	BAL N	2	.500	.750	4	2	1	0	0	0.0	0	1	0		1	0	0	4	4	0	1	4.0	1.000	C-2
1901	STL N	83	.197	.250	300	59	6	5	0	0.0	27	31	7		5	1	0	362	118	14	17	6.0	.972	C-65, 2B-9, 1B-5, OF-3
1902		76	.180	.225	267	48	4	4	0	0.0	23	14	4		2	0	0	304	103	12	12	5.5	.971	C-66, 3B-4, 1B-4, 2B-2, SS-1, P-1
1903		67	.238	.282	227	54	5	1	0	0.4	18	10	10		2	0	0	343	81	10	21	6.5	.977	C-47, 1B-18, SS-2
1912	WAS A	1	.000	.000	1	0	0	0	0	0.0	0	0	0	0	0	0	0	1	1	0	0	2.0	1.000	3B-1
1913		1	.000	.000	1	0	0	0	0	0.0	0	0	0	0	0	0	0	1	1	0	0	2.0	1.000	C-1
13 yrs.		616	.217	.281	2192	476	69	29	4	0.2	245	154	85	80	32	1	0	2516	797	187	101	5.7	.947	C-527, 1B-42, 2B-19, 3B-17, OF-15, SS-4, P-1

John Ryan

RYAN, JOHN J.
B. St. Louis, Mo. Deceased.

Year	Team	Games	BA	SA	AB	H	2B	3B	HR	HR%	R	RBI	BB	SO	SB	PH AB	PH H	PO	A	E	DP	TC/G	FA	G by Pos
1895	STL N	2	.000	.000	2	0	0	0	0	0.0	0	0	0	0	0	0	0	0	0	1	0	0.5	–	3B-2

Year Team	Games	BA	SA	AB	H	2B	3B	HR	HR%	R	RBI	BB	SO	SB	Pinch Hit AB	Pinch Hit H	PO	A	E	DP	TC/G	FA	G by Pos

Johnny Ryan

RYAN, JOHN JOSEPH
B. Oct., 1853, Philadelphia, Pa.   D. Mar. 22, 1902, Philadelphia, Pa.

5'7½"   150 lbs.

Year Team	Games	BA	SA	AB	H	2B	3B	HR	HR%	R	RBI	BB	SO	SB	AB	H	PO	A	E	DP	TC/G	FA	G by Pos
1876 LOU N	64	.253	.295	241	61	5	1	1	0.4	32	18	6	23		0	0	132	2	17	1	2.4	.887	OF-64, P-1
1877 CIN N	6	.154	.231	26	4	0	1	0	0.0	2	2	1	5		0	0	10	0	3	0	2.2	.769	OF-6
2 yrs.	70	.243	.288	267	65	5	2	1	0.4	34	20	7	28		0	0	142	2	20	1	2.3	.878	OF-70, P-1

Lew Ryan

Playing record listed under Lew Malone

Mike Ryan

RYAN, MICHAEL JAMES
B. Nov. 25, 1941, Haverhill, Mass.

BR TR 6'2"   205 lbs.

Year Team	Games	BA	SA	AB	H	2B	3B	HR	HR%	R	RBI	BB	SO	SB	AB	H	PO	A	E	DP	TC/G	FA	G by Pos
1964 BOS A	1	.333	.333	3	1	0	0	0	0.0	0	2	1	0	0	0	0	5	0	0	0	5.0	1.000	C-1
1965	33	.159	.262	107	17	0	1	3	2.8	7	9	5	19	0	0	0	194	18	4	0	6.5	.981	C-33
1966	116	.214	.287	369	79	15	3	2	0.5	27	32	29	68	1	3	1	685	50	6	7	6.4	.992	C-114
1967	79	.199	.261	226	45	4	2	2	0.9	21	27	26	42	0	0	0	473	34	6	11	6.5	.988	C-79
1968 PHI N	96	.179	.216	296	53	6	1	1	0.3	12	15	15	59	0	1	0	501	62	5	7	5.9	.991	C-96
1969	133	.204	.332	446	91	17	2	12	2.7	41	44	30	66	1	1	0	769	79	8	13	6.4	.991	C-132
1970	46	.179	.284	134	24	8	0	2	1.5	14	11	16	24	0	0	0	238	15	2	1	5.5	.992	C-46
1971	43	.164	.284	134	22	5	1	3	2.2	9	6	10	32	0	0	0	222	30	0	2	5.9	1.000	C-43
1972	46	.179	.274	106	19	4	0	2	1.9	6	10	10	25	0	0	0	216	21	2	3	5.2	.992	C-46
1973	28	.232	.348	69	16	1	2	1	1.4	7	5	6	19	0	1	0	121	9	1	0	4.7	.992	C-27
1974 PIT N	15	.100	.100	30	3	0	0	0	0.0	2	0	4	16	0	0	0	49	7	0	1	3.7	1.000	C-15
11 yrs.	636	.193	.280	1920	370	60	12	28	1.5	146	161	152	370	4	6	1	3473	325	34	45	6.0	.991	C-632

WORLD SERIES

| 1967 BOS A | 1 | .000 | .000 | 2 | 0 | 0 | 0 | 0 | 0.0 | 0 | 0 | 0 | 1 | 0 | 0 | 0 | 4 | 0 | 0 | 0 | 4.0 | 1.000 | C-1 |

Tom Ryder

RYDER, THOMAS
Deceased.

BL

| 1884 STL U | 8 | .250 | .286 | 28 | 7 | 1 | 0 | 0 | 0.0 | 4 | | 2 | | | 0 | 0 | 10 | 3 | 7 | 0 | 2.5 | .650 | OF-8 |

Gene Rye

RYE, EUGENE RUDOLPH (Half-Pint)
Born Eugene Rudolph Mercantelli.
B. Nov. 15, 1906, Chicago, Ill.   D. Jan. 21, 1980, Park Ridge, Ill.

BL TR 5'6"   165 lbs.

| 1931 BOS A | 17 | .179 | .179 | 39 | 7 | 0 | 0 | 0 | 0.0 | 3 | 1 | 2 | 5 | 0 | 7 | 1 | 17 | 0 | 1 | 0 | 1.1 | .944 | OF-10 |

Alex Sabo

SABO, ALEXANDER (Giz)
Born Alexander Szabo.
B. Feb. 14, 1910, New Brunswick, N. J.

BR TR 6'   192 lbs.

1936 WAS A	4	.375	.375	8	3	0	0	0	0.0	1	1	0	2	0	1	1	10	2	1	0	3.3	.923	C-4
1937	1	–	–	0	0	0	0	0	–	0	0	0	0	0	0	0	1	0	0	0	1.0	1.000	C-1
2 yrs.	5	.375	.375	8	3	0	0	0	0.0	1	1	0	2	0	1	1	11	2	1	0	2.8	.929	C-5

Chris Sabo

SABO, CHRISTOPHER ANDREW (Spuds)
B. Jan. 19, 1962, Detroit, Mich.

BR TR 5'11"   185 lbs.

1988 CIN N	137	.271	.414	538	146	40	2	11	2.0	74	44	29	52	46	2	0	75	318	14	31	3.0	.966	3B-135, SS-2
1989	82	.260	.395	304	79	21	1	6	2.0	40	29	25	33	14	5	0	36	145	11	12	2.3	.943	3B-76
2 yrs.	219	.267	.407	842	225	61	3	17	2.0	114	73	54	85	60	7	0	111	463	25	43	2.7	.958	3B-211, SS-2

Frank Sacka

SACKA, FRANK
B. Aug. 30, 1924, Romulus, Mich.

BR TR 6'   195 lbs.

1951 WAS A	7	.250	.250	16	4	0	0	0	0.0	1	3	0	5	0	1	0	21	4	1	0	3.7	.962	C-6
1953	7	.278	.278	18	5	0	0	0	0.0	2	3	3	1	0	1	0	25	5	0	0	4.3	1.000	C-6
2 yrs.	14	.265	.265	34	9	0	0	0	0.0	3	6	3	6	0	2	0	46	9	1	0	4.0	.982	C-12

Mike Sadek

SADEK, MICHAEL GEORGE
B. May 30, 1946, Minneapolis, Minn.

BR TR 5'9"   165 lbs.

1973 SF N	39	.167	.212	66	11	1	1	0	0.0	6	4	11	8	1	0	0	146	7	3	1	4.0	.981	C-35
1975	42	.236	.321	106	25	5	2	0	0.0	14	9	14	14	1	4	3	207	10	1	3	5.2	.995	C-38
1976	55	.204	.226	93	19	2	0	0	0.0	8	7	11	10	0	2	1	191	11	3	0	3.7	.985	C-51
1977	61	.230	.310	126	29	7	0	1	0.8	12	15	12	5	2	4	2	227	32	2	3	4.3	.992	C-57
1978	40	.239	.321	109	26	3	0	2	1.8	15	9	10	11	1	0	0	182	15	5	2	5.1	.975	C-37
1979	63	.238	.302	126	30	5	0	1	0.8	14	11	15	24	1	3	0	246	21	2	2	4.3	.993	C-60, OF-1
1980	64	.252	.311	151	38	4	1	1	0.7	14	16	27	18	0	3	0	266	29	8	1	4.7	.974	C-59
1981	19	.167	.250	36	6	3	0	0	0.0	5	3	8	7	0	0	0	79	15	2	2	5.1	.979	C-19
8 yrs.	383	.226	.292	813	184	30	4	5	0.6	88	74	108	97	6	16	6	1544	140	26	14	4.5	.985	C-356, OF-1

Bob Sadowski

SADOWSKI, ROBERT FRANK (Sid)
B. Jan. 15, 1937, St. Louis, Mo.

BL TR 6'   175 lbs.

1960 STL N	1	.000	.000	1	0	0	0	0	0.0	0	1	0	0	0	0	0	0	0	1	0	1.0	–	2B-1
1961 PHI N	16	.130	.130	54	7	0	0	0	0.0	4	0	4	7	1	3	0	10	23	1	3	2.1	.971	3B-14
1962 CHI A	79	.231	.438	130	30	3	3	6	4.6	22	24	13	22	0	44	10	33	62	2	9	1.2	.979	3B-16, 2B-12
1963 LA A	88	.250	.313	144	36	6	0	1	0.7	12	22	15	34	2	50	12	49	13	2	1	0.7	.969	OF-25, 3B-6, 2B-4
4 yrs.	184	.222	.331	329	73	9	3	7	2.1	38	46	33	63	3	97	22	92	98	6	13	1.1	.969	3B-36, OF-25, 2B-17

Eddie Sadowski

SADOWSKI, EDWARD ROMAN
Brother of Ted Sadowski.   Brother of Bob Sadowski.
B. Jan. 19, 1932, Pittsburgh, Pa.

BR TR 5'11"   175 lbs.

| 1960 BOS A | 38 | .215 | .333 | 93 | 20 | 2 | 0 | 3 | 3.2 | 10 | 8 | 8 | 13 | 0 | 0 | 0 | 178 | 11 | 1 | 0 | 5.0 | .995 | C-36 |
| 1961 LA A | 69 | .232 | .384 | 164 | 38 | 13 | 0 | 4 | 2.4 | 16 | 12 | 11 | 33 | 2 | 9 | 1 | 295 | 17 | 4 | 4 | 4.6 | .987 | C-56 |

Year	Team		Games	BA	SA	AB	H	2B	3B	HR	HR%	R	RBI	BB	SO	SB	Pinch Hit AB	Pinch Hit H	PO	A	E	DP	TC/G	FA	G by Pos

Eddie Sadowski *continued*

Year	Team		Games	BA	SA	AB	H	2B	3B	HR	HR%	R	RBI	BB	SO	SB	AB	H	PO	A	E	DP	TC/G	FA	G by Pos
1962			27	.200	.327	55	11	4	0	1	1.8	4	3	2	14	1	7	1	86	4	3	0	3.4	.968	C-18
1963			80	.172	.259	174	30	1	1	4	2.3	24	15	17	33	2	6	1	340	38	1	7	4.7	.997	C-68
1966	ATL	N	3	.111	.111	9	1	0	0	0	0.0	1	1	1	1	0	0	0	15	2	0	0	5.7	1.000	C-3
5 yrs.			217	.202	.319	495	100	20	1	12	2.4	55	39	39	94	5	22	3	914	72	9	11	4.6	.991	C-181

Tom Saffell

SAFFELL, THOMAS JUDSON
B. July 26, 1921, Etowah, Tenn.

BL TR 5'11" 170 lbs.

Year	Team		Games	BA	SA	AB	H	2B	3B	HR	HR%	R	RBI	BB	SO	SB	AB	H	PO	A	E	DP	TC/G	FA	G by Pos
1949	PIT	N	73	.322	.395	205	66	7	1	2	1.0	36	25	21	27	5	18	6	122	2	1	1	1.7	.992	OF-53
1950			67	.203	.275	182	37	7	0	2	1.1	18	6	14	34	1	21	4	128	5	1	0	2.0	.993	OF-43
1951			49	.200	.246	65	13	0	0	1	1.5	11	5	5	18	1	24	3	25	1	2	0	0.6	.929	OF-17
1955	2 teams		PIT N (73G – .168)			KC A (9G – .216)																			
"	total		82	.180	.207	150	27	1	0	1	0.7	26	4	19	29	2	17	4	103	2	4	0	1.3	.963	OF-56
4 yrs.			271	.238	.296	602	143	15	1	6	1.0	91	40	59	108	9	80	17	378	10	8	1	1.5	.980	OF-169

Harry Sage

SAGE, HARRY (Doc)
B. Mar. 16, 1864, Rock Island, Ill. D. May 27, 1947, Rock Island, Ill.

BR TR 5'10" 185 lbs.

Year	Team		Games	BA	SA	AB	H	2B	3B	HR	HR%	R	RBI	BB	SO	SB	AB	H	PO	A	E	DP	TC/G	FA	G by Pos
1890	TOL	AA	81	.149	.229	275	41	8	4	2	0.7	40		29		10	0	0	336	154	27	3	6.4	.948	C-80, OF-1

Vic Saier

SAIER, VICTOR SYLVESTER
B. May 4, 1891, Lansing, Mich. D. May 14, 1967, East Lansing, Mich.

BL TR 5'11" 185 lbs.

Year	Team		Games	BA	SA	AB	H	2B	3B	HR	HR%	R	RBI	BB	SO	SB	AB	H	PO	A	E	DP	TC/G	FA	G by Pos
1911	CHI	N	86	.259	.336	259	67	15	1	1	0.4	42	37	25	37	11	12	4	715	33	15	44	8.9	.980	1B-73
1912			122	.288	.419	451	130	25	14	2	0.4	74	61	34	65	11	1	0	1165	52	10	67	10.1	.992	1B-120
1913			148	.288	.477	518	149	14	21	14	2.7	93	92	62	62	26	1	0	1469	71	26	79	10.6	.983	1B-148
1914			153	.240	.415	537	129	24	8	18	3.4	87	72	94	61	19	0	0	1521	59	22	62	10.5	.986	1B-153
1915			144	.264	.445	497	131	35	11	11	2.2	74	64	64	62	29	4	1	1348	65	21	71	10.0	.985	1B-139
1916			147	.253	.357	498	126	25	3	7	1.4	60	50	79	68	20	0	0	1622	74	27	78	11.7	.984	1B-147
1917			6	.238	.286	21	5	1	0	0	0.0	5	2	2	1	0	0	0	56	7	0	3	10.5	1.000	1B-6
1919	PIT	N	58	.223	.313	166	37	3	3	2	1.2	19	17	18	13	5	7	3	493	17	8	18	8.9	.985	1B-51
8 yrs.			864	.263	.408	2947	774	142	61	55	1.9	454	395	378	369	121	25	8	8389	378	129	422	10.3	.985	1B-837

Ebba St. Claire

ST. CLAIRE, EDWARD JOSEPH
Father of Randy St. Claire.
B. Aug. 5, 1921, Whitehall, N. Y. D. Aug. 22, 1982, Whitehall, N. Y.

BB TR 6'1" 219 lbs.

Year	Team		Games	BA	SA	AB	H	2B	3B	HR	HR%	R	RBI	BB	SO	SB	AB	H	PO	A	E	DP	TC/G	FA	G by Pos
1951	BOS	N	72	.282	.391	220	62	17	1	1	0.5	22	25	12	24	0	10	3	267	29	7	5	4.2	.977	C-62
1952			39	.213	.287	108	23	2	0	2	1.9	5	4	8	12	0	5	1	151	21	5	4	4.5	.972	C-34
1953	MIL	N	33	.200	.313	80	16	3	0	2	2.5	7	5	7	9	0	7	1	106	11	1	3	3.6	.992	C-27
1954	NY	N	20	.262	.429	42	11	1	0	2	4.8	5	6	12	7	0	4	1	72	7	2	3	4.1	.975	C-16
4 yrs.			164	.249	.356	450	112	23	2	7	1.6	39	40	35	52	0	26	6	596	68	15	15	4.1	.978	C-139

Lenn Sakata

SAKATA, LENN HARUKI
B. June 8, 1954, Honolulu, Hawaii

BR TR 5'9" 160 lbs.

Year	Team		Games	BA	SA	AB	H	2B	3B	HR	HR%	R	RBI	BB	SO	SB	AB	H	PO	A	E	DP	TC/G	FA	G by Pos
1977	MIL	A	53	.162	.214	154	25	2	0	2	1.3	13	12	9	22	1	0	0	102	159	4	43	5.0	.985	2B-53
1978			30	.192	.244	78	15	4	0	0	0.0	8	3	8	11	1	0	0	50	66	3	12	4.0	.975	2B-29
1979			4	.500	.643	14	7	2	0	0	0.0	1	1	0	1	0	0	0	10	13	0	5	5.8	1.000	2B-4
1980	BAL	A	43	.193	.313	83	16	3	2	1	1.2	12	9	6	10	2	5	4	55	73	2	18	3.0	.985	2B-34, SS-4, DH-1
1981			61	.227	.353	150	34	4	0	3	3.3	19	15	11	18	4	1	0	82	148	7	33	3.9	.970	SS-42, 2B-20
1982			136	.259	.370	343	89	18	1	6	1.7	40	31	30	39	7	9	3	182	299	16	61	3.7	.968	2B-83, SS-56
1983			66	.254	.373	134	34	7	0	3	2.2	23	12	16	17	8	3	0	84	117	2	36	3.1	.990	2B-60, DH-1, C-1
1984			81	.191	.255	157	30	1	0	3	1.9	23	11	6	15	4	5	1	80	161	3	33	3.0	.988	2B-76, OF-1
1985			55	.227	.351	97	22	3	0	3	3.1	15	6	6	15	3	1	0	58	87	6	18	2.7	.960	2B-50, DH-1
1986	OAK	A	17	.353	.412	34	12	2	0	0	0.0	4	5	3	6	0	0	0	21	39	1	4	3.6	.984	2B-16, DH-1
1987	NY	A	19	.267	.444	45	12	0	1	2	4.4	5	4	2	4	0	0	0	8	30	2	4	2.1	.950	2B-12, 2B-6
11 yrs.			565	.230	.330	1289	296	46	4	25	1.9	163	109	97	158	30	24	8	732	1192	46	267	3.5	.977	2B-431, SS-102, 3B-12, DH-4, OF-1, C-1

WORLD SERIES

Year	Team		Games	BA	SA	AB	H	2B	3B	HR	HR%	R	RBI	BB	SO	SB	AB	H	PO	A	E	DP	TC/G	FA	G by Pos
1983	BAL	A	1	.000	.000	1	0	0	0	0	0.0	0	0	0	0	0	0	0	2	2	0	1	4.0	1.000	2B-1

Mark Salas

SALAS, MARK BRUCE
B. Mar. 8, 1961, Montebello, Calif.

BL TR 6' 180 lbs.

Year	Team		Games	BA	SA	AB	H	2B	3B	HR	HR%	R	RBI	BB	SO	SB	AB	H	PO	A	E	DP	TC/G	FA	G by Pos
1984	STL	N	14	.100	.150	20	2	1	0	0	0.0	1	1	0	8	1	0	0	13	2	0	0	1.1	1.000	C-4, OF-3
1985	MIN	A	120	.300	.458	360	108	20	5	9	2.5	51	41	18	37	0	12	1	529	39	5	10	4.8	.991	C-115, DH-3
1986			91	.233	.384	258	60	7	4	8	3.1	28	33	18	32	3	25	5	358	32	8	5	4.4	.980	C-69, DH-8
1987	2 teams		MIN A (22G – .378)			NY A (50G – .200)																			
"	total		72	.250	.400	160	40	0	6	3.8	21	21	15	23	0	19	4	258	16	1	0	3.8	.996	C-55, DH-4, OF-1
1988	CHI	A	75	.250	.332	196	49	7	0	3	1.5	17	9	12	17	0	7	1	251	35	6	5	3.9	.979	C-69, DH-1
1989	CLE	A	30	.221	.377	77	17	4	1	2	2.6	4	7	5	13	0	11	0	3	1	0	0	0.1	1.000	DH-20, C-5
6 yrs.			402	.258	.397	1071	276	45	10	28	2.6	122	112	68	125	3	82	12	1412	125	20	20	3.9	.987	C-317, DH-36, OF-4

Angel Salazar

SALAZAR, ARGENIS ANTONIO
Born Argenis Antonio Salazar y Yepez.
B. Nov. 4, 1961, Anaco-Anzoategui, Venezue,

BR TR 5'11" 180 lbs.

Year	Team		Games	BA	SA	AB	H	2B	3B	HR	HR%	R	RBI	BB	SO	SB	AB	H	PO	A	E	DP	TC/G	FA	G by Pos
1983	MON	N	36	.216	.297	37	8	3	4	0	0.0	5	1	1	8	0	2	0	28	28	2	9	1.6	.966	SS-34
1984			80	.155	.201	174	27	4	2	0	0.0	12	12	4	38	1	0	0	88	155	10	35	3.2	.960	SS-80
1986	KC	A	117	.245	.326	298	73	20	0	0	0.0	24	24	7	47	1	1	0	121	284	9	50	3.5	.978	SS-115, 2B-1
1987			116	.205	.246	317	65	7	0	2	0.6	24	21	6	46	4	0	0	134	332	9	56	4.1	.981	SS-116
1988	CHI	N	34	.250	.300	60	15	1	0	0	0.0	4	1	1	11	0	3	0	38	53	3	11	2.8	.968	SS-29, 2B-2, 3B-1
5 yrs.			383	.212	.270	886	188	33	6	2	0.2	69	59	19	150	6	6	0	409	852	33	161	3.4	.974	SS-374, 2B-3, 3B-1

Luis Salazar

SALAZAR, LUIS ERNESTO
Born Luis Ernesto Salazar y Garacia.
B. May 19, 1956, Barcelona, Venezuela

BR TR 6' 185 lbs.

Year	Team		Games	BA	SA	AB	H	2B	3B	HR	HR%	R	RBI	BB	SO	SB	Pinch Hit AB	Pinch Hit H	PO	A	E	DP	TC/G	FA	G by Pos

Luis Salazar *continued*

Year	Team		Games	BA	SA	AB	H	2B	3B	HR	HR%	R	RBI	BB	SO	SB	AB	H	PO	A	E	DP	TC/G	FA	G by Pos
1980	SD	N	44	.337	.462	169	57	4	7	1	0.6	28	25	9	25	11	0	0	39	88	7	7	3.0	.948	3B-42, OF-4
1981			109	.303	.403	400	121	19	6	3	0.8	37	38	16	72	11	2	0	108	191	14	17	2.9	.955	3B-94, OF-23
1982			145	.242	.336	524	127	15	5	8	1.5	55	62	23	80	32	2	0	133	326	29	32	3.4	.941	3B-129, SS-18, OF-1
1983			134	.258	.387	481	124	16	2	14	2.9	52	45	17	80	24	6	2	122	274	21	22	3.1	.950	3B-118, SS-19
1984			93	.241	.329	228	55	7	2	3	1.3	20	17	6	38	11	14	4	87	97	6	5	2.0	.968	3B-58, OF-24, SS-4
1985	CHI	A	122	.245	.404	327	80	18	2	10	3.1	39	45	12	60	14	15	6	180	57	10	13	2.0	.960	OF-84, OF-39, DH-8, 1B-6
1986			4	.143	.143	7	1	0	0	0	0.0	0	0	1	3	0	2	0	0	0	0	0	0.0	–	DH-2
1987	SD	N	84	.254	.328	189	48	5	0	3	1.6	13	17	14	30	3	18	3	56	95	9	11	1.9	.944	3B-38, SS-22, OF-10, P-2, 1B-1
1988	DET	A	130	.270	.385	452	122	14	1	12	2.7	61	62	21	70	6	9	5	199	151	10	22	2.8	.972	OF-68, SS-37, 3B-31, 2B-5, 1B-4
1989	2 teams			SD N (95G – .268)		CHI N		(26G – .325)																	
"	total		121	.282	.414	326	92	12	2	9	2.8	34	34	15	57	1	15	6	74	131	8	18	1.8	.962	3B-97, OF-16, SS-9, 1B-2
10 yrs.			986	.267	.380	3103	827	110	27	63	2.0	340	345	134	515	113	83	26	998	1410	114	147	2.6	.955	3B-646, OF-230, SS-109, 1B-13, DH-10, 2B-5, P-2

LEAGUE CHAMPIONSHIP SERIES

Year	Team		Games	BA	SA	AB	H	2B	3B	HR	HR%	R	RBI	BB	SO	SB	AB	H	PO	A	E	DP	TC/G	FA	G by Pos
1984	SD	N	3	.200	.600	5	1	0	1	0	0.0	0	0	0	1	0	1	0	0	3	0	0	1.0	1.000	OF-2, 3B-1
1989	CHI	N	5	.368	.632	19	7	0	1	1	5.3	2	2	0	0	0	0	0	4	5	1	0	2.0	.900	3B-5
2 yrs.			8	.333	.625	24	8	0	2	1	4.2	2	2	0	1	0	1	0	4	8	1	0	1.6	.923	3B-6, OF-2

WORLD SERIES

Year	Team		Games	BA	SA	AB	H	2B	3B	HR	HR%	R	RBI	BB	SO	SB	AB	H	PO	A	E	DP	TC/G	FA	G by Pos
1984	SD	N	4	.333	.333	3	1	0	0	0	0.0	0	0	0	0	0	1	1	1	0	0	0	0.3	1.000	OF-2, 3B-1

Ed Sales

SALES, EDWARD A.
B. 1861, Harrisburg, Pa.   D. Aug. 10, 1912, New Haven, Conn.   TR

Year	Team		Games	BA	SA	AB	H	2B	3B	HR	HR%	R	RBI	BB	SO	SB	AB	H	PO	A	E	DP	TC/G	FA	G by Pos
1890	PIT	N	51	.228	.312	189	43	7	3	1	0.5	19	23	16	15	3	0	0	85	151	35	10	5.3	.871	SS-51

Bill Salkeld

SALKELD, WILLIAM FRANKLIN   BL TR 5'10"   190 lbs.
B. Mar. 8, 1917, Pocatello, Ida.   D. Apr. 22, 1967, Los Angeles, Calif.

Year	Team		Games	BA	SA	AB	H	2B	3B	HR	HR%	R	RBI	BB	SO	SB	AB	H	PO	A	E	DP	TC/G	FA	G by Pos
1945	PIT	N	95	.311	.547	267	83	16	1	15	5.6	45	52	50	16	2	8	2	279	40	9	8	3.5	.973	C-86
1946			69	.294	.400	160	47	8	0	3	1.9	18	19	39	16	2	17	3	176	31	6	3	3.1	.972	C-51
1947			47	.213	.246	61	13	2	0	0	0.0	5	8	6	8	0	29	9	29	4	1	0	0.7	.971	C-15
1948	BOS	N	78	.242	.414	198	48	8	1	8	4.0	26	28	42	37	1	12	1	254	32	3	5	3.7	.990	C-59
1949			66	.255	.379	161	41	5	0	5	3.1	17	25	44	24	1	4	0	230	21	5	3	3.9	.980	C-63
1950	CHI	A	1	.000	.000	3	0	0	0	0	0.0	0	0	1	0	0	0	0	4	0	0	0	4.0	1.000	C-1
6 yrs.			356	.273	.433	850	232	39	2	31	3.6	111	132	182	101	6	70	15	972	128	24	19	3.2	.979	C-275

WORLD SERIES

Year	Team		Games	BA	SA	AB	H	2B	3B	HR	HR%	R	RBI	BB	SO	SB	AB	H	PO	A	E	DP	TC/G	FA	G by Pos
1948	BOS	N	5	.222	.556	9	2	0	0	1	11.1	2	1	5	1	0	1	0	19	2	0	0	4.2	1.000	C-5

Chico Salmon

SALMON, RUTHFORD EDUARDO   BR TR 5'10"   160 lbs.
B. Dec. 3, 1940, Colon, Panama

Year	Team		Games	BA	SA	AB	H	2B	3B	HR	HR%	R	RBI	BB	SO	SB	AB	H	PO	A	E	DP	TC/G	FA	G by Pos
1964	CLE	A	86	.307	.424	283	87	17	2	4	1.4	43	25	13	37	10	6	2	191	67	2	14	3.0	.992	OF-53, 2B-36, 1B-13
1965			79	.242	.383	120	29	8	1	3	2.5	20	12	5	19	7	19	5	151	16	3	14	2.2	.982	1B-28, OF-17, 3B-5, 2B-5
1966			126	.256	.346	422	108	13	2	7	1.7	46	40	21	41	10	10	2	315	225	19	53	4.4	.966	SS-61, 2B-28, 1B-24, OF-10, 3B-6
1967			90	.227	.330	203	46	13	1	2	1.0	19	19	17	29	10	5	3	199	103	5	26	3.4	.984	OF-28, 2B-24, 1B-24, SS-14, 3B-4
1968			103	.214	.283	276	59	8	1	3	1.1	24	12	12	30	7	9	0	152	145	8	29	3.0	.974	2B-45, 3B-18, SS-15, OF-13, 1B-11
1969	BAL	A	52	.297	.451	91	27	5	0	3	3.3	18	12	10	22	0	14	3	90	42	8	9	2.7	.943	1B-17, SS-9, 2B-9, 3B-3, OF-1
1970			63	.250	.395	172	43	4	0	7	4.1	19	22	8	30	2	13	2	61	87	9	12	2.5	.943	SS-33, 2B-12, 3B-11, 1B-2
1971			42	.179	.262	84	15	1	0	2	2.4	11	7	3	21	0	19	3	75	30	6	12	2.6	.946	2B-9, 1B-9, 3B-6, SS-5
1972			17	.063	.125	16	1	1	0	0	0.0	2	0	0	4	0	14	1	1	2	0	1	0.2	1.000	1B-2, 3B-1
9 yrs.			658	.249	.354	1667	415	70	6	31	1.9	202	149	89	233	46	109	21	1235	717	60	170	3.1	.970	2B-164, SS-137, 1B-130, OF-122, 3B-54

LEAGUE CHAMPIONSHIP SERIES

Year	Team		Games	BA	SA	AB	H	2B	3B	HR	HR%	R	RBI	BB	SO	SB	AB	H	PO	A	E	DP	TC/G	FA	G by Pos
1969	BAL	A	1	.000	.000	1	0	0	0	0	0.0	0	0	0	0	0	1	0	0	0	0	0	0.0	–	

WORLD SERIES

Year	Team		Games	BA	SA	AB	H	2B	3B	HR	HR%	R	RBI	BB	SO	SB	AB	H	PO	A	E	DP	TC/G	FA	G by Pos
1969	BAL	A	2	–	–	0	0	0	0	0		0	0	0	0	0	0	0	0	0	0	0	0.0	–	
1970			1	1.000	1.000	1	1	0	0	0	0.0	1	0	0	0	0	1	1	0	0	0	0	0.0	–	
2 yrs.			3	1.000	1.000	1	1	0	0	0	0.0	1	0	0	0	0	1	1	0	0	0	0	0.0	–	

Jack Saltzgaver

SALTZGAVER, OTTO HAMLIN   BL TR 5'11"   165 lbs.
B. Jan. 23, 1903, Croton, Iowa   D. Feb. 1, 1978, Keokuk, Iowa

Year	Team		Games	BA	SA	AB	H	2B	3B	HR	HR%	R	RBI	BB	SO	SB	AB	H	PO	A	E	DP	TC/G	FA	G by Pos
1932	NY	A	20	.128	.213	47	6	2	1	0	0.0	10	5	10	10	1	2	0	38	30	3	5	3.6	.958	2B-16
1934			94	.271	.351	350	95	8	1	6	1.7	64	36	48	28	8	6	2	93	132	12	13	2.5	.949	3B-84, 1B-4
1935			61	.262	.362	149	39	6	0	3	2.0	17	18	23	12	0	12	2	70	82	8	11	2.6	.950	2B-25, 3B-18, 1B-6
1936			34	.211	.300	90	19	5	0	1	1.1	14	13	13	18	0	2	0	44	34	2	5	2.4	.975	3B-16, 2B-6, 1B-4
1937			17	.182	.182	11	2	0	0	0	0.0	3	4	0	2	1	3	1	34	1	0	4	2.1	1.000	1B-4
1945	PIT	N	52	.325	.419	117	38	5	3	0	0.0	20	10	8	10	0	20	3	63	66	5	11	2.6	.963	2B-31, 3B-1
6 yrs.			278	.260	.347	764	199	26	5	10	1.3	131	82	105	80	9	44	8	342	345	30	49	2.6	.958	3B-119, 2B-78, 1B-18

Ed Samcoff

SAMCOFF, EDWARD WILLIAM   BR TR 5'10"   165 lbs.
B. Sept. 1, 1924, Sacramento, Calif.

Year	Team		Games	BA	SA	AB	H	2B	3B	HR	HR%	R	RBI	BB	SO	SB	AB	H	PO	A	E	DP	TC/G	FA	G by Pos
1951	PHI	A	4	.000	.000	11	0	0	0	0	0.0	0	0	1	2	0	1	0	5	5	0	3	2.5	1.000	2B-3

Ron Samford

SAMFORD, RONALD EDWARD   BR TR 5'11"   156 lbs.
B. Feb. 28, 1930, Dallas, Tex.

Year	Team		Games	BA	SA	AB	H	2B	3B	HR	HR%	R	RBI	BB	SO	SB	Pinch Hit AB	Pinch Hit H	PO	A	E	DP	TC/G	FA	G by Pos

Ron Samford *continued*

Year	Team		Games	BA	SA	AB	H	2B	3B	HR	HR%	R	RBI	BB	SO	SB	AB	H	PO	A	E	DP	TC/G	FA	G by Pos
1954	NY	N	12	.000	.000	5	0	0	0	0	0.0	2	0	0	1	0	1	0	3	2	0	0	0.4	1.000	2B-3
1955	DET	A	1	.000	.000	1	0	0	0	0	0.0	0	0	0	1	0	0	0	0	2	0	0	2.0	1.000	SS-1
1957			54	.220	.275	91	20	1	2	0	0.0	6	5	6	15	1	0	0	53	95	6	23	2.9	.961	SS-35, 2B-11, 3B-4
1959	WAS	A	91	.224	.342	237	53	13	0	5	2.1	23	22	11	29	1	3	0	130	214	18	39	4.0	.950	SS-64, 2B-23
4 yrs.			158	.219	.317	334	73	14	2	5	1.5	31	27	17	46	2	4	0	186	313	24	62	3.3	.954	SS-100, 2B-37, 3B-4

Billy Sample

SAMPLE, WILLIAM AMOS
B. May 2, 1955, Roanoke, Va.

BR TR 5'9" 175 lbs.

Year	Team		Games	BA	SA	AB	H	2B	3B	HR	HR%	R	RBI	BB	SO	SB	AB	H	PO	A	E	DP	TC/G	FA	G by Pos
1978	TEX	A	8	.467	.600	15	7	2	0	0	0.0	2	3	0	3	0	2	1	0	0	0	0	0.0	—	DH-3, OF-2
1979			128	.292	.415	325	95	21	2	5	1.5	60	35	37	28	8	18	5	173	7	0	1	1.4	1.000	OF-103, DH-9
1980			99	.260	.368	204	53	10	0	4	2.0	29	19	18	15	8	23	5	105	2	3	0	1.1	.973	OF-72, DH-4
1981			66	.283	.391	230	65	16	0	3	1.3	36	25	17	21	4	3	0	132	4	1	1	2.1	.993	OF-64
1982			97	.261	.394	360	94	14	2	10	2.8	56	29	27	35	10	1	0	196	6	4	1	2.1	.981	OF-91, DH-1
1983			147	.274	.401	554	152	28	3	12	2.2	80	57	44	46	44	2	0	329	8	4	0	2.3	.988	OF-146
1984			130	.247	.327	489	121	20	2	5	1.0	67	33	29	46	18	11	4	285	3	4	2	2.2	.986	OF-122, DH-2
1985	NY	A	59	.288	.345	139	40	5	0	1	0.7	18	15	9	10	2	5	2	89	1	1	0	1.5	.989	OF-55
1986	ATL	N	92	.285	.430	200	57	11	0	6	3.0	23	14	14	26	4	33	9	69	1	1	1	0.8	.986	OF-56, 2B-1
9 yrs.			826	.272	.384	2516	684	127	9	46	1.8	371	230	195	230	98	98	26	1378	32	18	6	1.7	.987	OF-711, DH-19, 2B-1

Amado Samuel

SAMUEL, AMADO RUPERTO
B. Dec. 6, 1938, San Pedro de Macoris, Dominican Republic

BR TR 6'1" 170 lbs.

Year	Team		Games	BA	SA	AB	H	2B	3B	HR	HR%	R	RBI	BB	SO	SB	AB	H	PO	A	E	DP	TC/G	FA	G by Pos
1962	MIL	N	76	.206	.297	209	43	10	0	3	1.4	16	20	12	54	0	5	1	85	160	11	29	3.4	.957	SS-36, 2B-28, 3B-3
1963			15	.176	.235	17	3	1	0	0	0.0	0	0	0	4	0	0	0	12	14	4	3	2.0	.867	SS-7, 2B-4
1964	NY	N	53	.232	.282	142	33	7	0	0	0.0	7	5	4	24	0	2	1	52	124	11	24	3.5	.941	SS-34, 3B-17, 2B-3
3 yrs.			144	.215	.288	368	79	18	0	3	0.8	23	25	16	82	0	7	2	149	298	26	56	3.3	.945	SS-77, 2B-35, 3B-20

Juan Samuel

SAMUEL, JUAN MILTON ROMERO (Sammy)
Born Juan Milton Romero y Samuel.
B. Dec. 9, 1960, San Pedro de Macoris, Dominican Republic

BR TR 5'11" 170 lbs.

Year	Team		Games	BA	SA	AB	H	2B	3B	HR	HR%	R	RBI	BB	SO	SB	AB	H	PO	A	E	DP	TC/G	FA	G by Pos
1983	PHI	N	18	.277	.446	65	18	1	2	2	3.1	14	5	4	16	3	0	0	44	54	9	9	5.9	.916	2B-18
1984			160	.272	.442	701	191	36	19	15	2.1	105	69	28	168	72	2	1	388	438	33	77	5.4	.962	2B-160
1985			161	.264	.436	663	175	31	13	19	2.9	101	74	33	141	53	1	0	389	463	15	88	5.4	.983	2B-159
1986			145	.266	.448	591	157	36	12	16	2.7	90	78	26	142	42	2	2	290	440	25	83	5.2	.967	2B-143
1987			160	.272	.502	655	178	37	15	28	4.3	113	100	60	162	35	0	0	374	434	18	99	5.2	.978	2B-160
1988			157	.243	.380	629	153	32	9	12	1.9	68	67	39	151	33	1	1	351	387	16	92	4.8	.979	2B-152, OF-3, 3B-1
1989	2 teams		PHI N (51G — .246)					NY N	(86G — .228)																
"	total		137	.235	.335	532	125	6	2	11	2.1	69	48	42	120	42	2	1	339	6	4	3	2.5	.989	OF-134
7 yrs.			938	.260	.427	3836	997	189	72	103	2.7	560	441	232	900	280	8	5	2175	2222	120	451	4.8	.973	2B-792, OF-137, 3B-1

LEAGUE CHAMPIONSHIP SERIES

Year	Team		Games	BA	SA	AB	H	2B	3B	HR	HR%	R	RBI	BB	SO	SB	AB	H	PO	A	E	DP	TC/G	FA	G by Pos
1983	PHI	N	1	—	—	0	0	0	0	0	0.0	0	0	0	0	0	0	0	0	0	0	0	0.0	—	

WORLD SERIES

Year	Team		Games	BA	SA	AB	H	2B	3B	HR	HR%	R	RBI	BB	SO	SB	AB	H	PO	A	E	DP	TC/G	FA	G by Pos
1983	PHI	N	3	.000	.000	1	0	0	0	0	0.0	0	0	0	0	0	1	0	0	0	0	0	0.0	—	

Ike Samuls

SAMULS, SAMUEL EARL
B. Feb. 20, 1876, Austria-Hungary D. Jan. 1, 1942, Los Angeles, Calif.

BR TR

Year	Team		Games	BA	SA	AB	H	2B	3B	HR	HR%	R	RBI	BB	SO	SB	AB	H	PO	A	E	DP	TC/G	FA	G by Pos
1895	STL	N	24	.230	.257	74	17	2	0	0	0.0	5	5	5	7	5	0	0	22	45	24	1	3.8	.736	3B-21, SS-3

Gus Sanberg

SANBERG, GUSTAVE E.
B. Feb. 23, 1896, Long Island City, N. Y. D. Feb. 3, 1930, Los Angeles, Calif.

BR TR 6'1" 189 lbs.

Year	Team		Games	BA	SA	AB	H	2B	3B	HR	HR%	R	RBI	BB	SO	SB	AB	H	PO	A	E	DP	TC/G	FA	G by Pos
1923	CIN	N	7	.176	.235	17	3	1	0	0	0.0	1	1	1	1	0	2	1	11	3	0	0	2.0	1.000	C-5
1924			24	.173	.173	52	9	0	0	0	0.0	1	3	2	7	0	0	0	56	11	0	1	2.8	1.000	C-24
2 yrs.			31	.174	.188	69	12	1	0	0	0.0	2	4	3	8	0	2	1	67	14	0	1	2.6	1.000	C-29

Alejandro Sanchez

SANCHEZ, ALEJANDRO
Born Alejandro Sanchez y Pimentel.
B. Feb. 14, 1959, San Pedro de Macoris, Dominican Republic

BR TR 6' 175 lbs.

Year	Team		Games	BA	SA	AB	H	2B	3B	HR	HR%	R	RBI	BB	SO	SB	AB	H	PO	A	E	DP	TC/G	FA	G by Pos
1982	PHI	N	7	.286	.786	14	4	1	0	2	14.3	3	4	0	4	0	1	1	7	0	0	0	1.0	1.000	OF-4
1983			8	.286	.286	7	2	0	0	0	0.0	2	2	0	2	0	4	2	1	0	1	0	0.3	.500	OF-2
1984	SF	N	13	.195	.244	41	8	0	0	1	0.0	3	3	0	12	2	2	0	18	2	1	0	1.6	.952	OF-11
1985	DET	A	71	.248	.459	133	33	6	2	6	4.5	19	12	6	39	2	18	6	35	1	3	0	0.5	.923	OF-31, DH-28
1986	MIN	A	8	.125	.125	16	2	0	0	0	0.0	1	1	1	8	0	4	0	0	0	0	0	0.0	—	DH-3, OF-1
1987	OAK	A	2	.000	.000	3	0	0	0	0	0.0	0	0	0	1	0	1	0	1	0	0	0	0.5	1.000	DH-1, OF-1
6 yrs.			109	.229	.402	214	49	7	3	8	3.7	28	21	1	66	4	30	9	62	3	5	0	0.6	.929	OF-50, DH-32

Celerino Sanchez

SANCHEZ, CELERINO PEREZ
B. Feb. 3, 1944, Veracruz, Mexico

BR TR 5'11" 160 lbs.

Year	Team		Games	BA	SA	AB	H	2B	3B	HR	HR%	R	RBI	BB	SO	SB	AB	H	PO	A	E	DP	TC/G	FA	G by Pos
1972	NY	A	71	.248	.304	250	62	8	3	0	0.0	18	22	12	30	0	1	0	47	167	14	13	3.2	.939	3B-68
1973			34	.219	.313	64	14	3	0	1	1.6	12	9	2	12	1	7	0	8	16	1	2	0.7	.960	DH-11, 3B-11, OF-2, SS-2
2 yrs.			105	.242	.306	314	76	11	3	1	0.3	30	31	14	42	1	8	0	55	183	15	15	2.4	.941	3B-79, DH-11, OF-2, SS-2

Orlando Sanchez

SANCHEZ, ORLANDO
Born Orlando Sanchez y Marquez.
B. Sept. 7, 1956, Canovanas, Puerto Rico

BL TR 6'1" 195 lbs.

Year	Team		Games	BA	SA	AB	H	2B	3B	HR	HR%	R	RBI	BB	SO	SB	AB	H	PO	A	E	DP	TC/G	FA	G by Pos
1981	STL	N	27	.286	.367	49	14	1	0	0	0.0	5	6	2	6	1	11	3	50	0	4	1	2.0	.926	C-18
1982			26	.189	.243	37	7	0	1	0	0.0	6	3	5	5	0	9	2	34	4	0	1	1.5	1.000	C-15
1983			6	.000	.000	6	0	0	0	0	0.0	0	0	0	4	0	5	0	1	0	0	0	0.2	1.000	C-1

Year	Team		Games	BA	SA	AB	H	2B	3B	HR	HR%	R	RBI	BB	SO	SB	Pinch Hit AB	Pinch Hit H	PO	A	E	DP	TC/G	FA	G by Pos

Orlando Sanchez *continued*

Year	Team		Games	BA	SA	AB	H	2B	3B	HR	HR%	R	RBI	BB	SO	SB	PH AB	PH H	PO	A	E	DP	TC/G	FA	G by Pos
1984	2 teams	KC A (10G – .100) BAL A (4G – .250)																							
"	total		14	.167	.222	18	3	1	0	0	0.0	0	3	0	4	0	10	2	10	1	0	0	0.8	1.000	C-5
4 yrs.			73	.218	.282	110	24	3	2	0	0.0	11	12	7	19	1	35	7	95	5	4	2	1.4	.962	C-39

Heinie Sand

SAND, JOHN HENRY
B. July 3, 1897, San Francisco, Calif. D. Nov. 3, 1958, San Francisco, Calif.
BR TR 5'8" 160 lbs.

Year	Team		Games	BA	SA	AB	H	2B	3B	HR	HR%	R	RBI	BB	SO	SB	PH AB	PH H	PO	A	E	DP	TC/G	FA	G by Pos
1923	PHI	N	132	.228	.309	470	107	16	5	4	0.9	85	32	82	56	7	1	0	296	424	50	92	5.8	.935	SS-120, 3B-11
1924			137	.245	.340	539	132	21	6	6	1.1	79	40	52	57	5	0	0	333	460	34	95	6.0	.959	SS-137
1925			148	.278	.385	496	138	30	7	3	0.6	69	55	64	65	1	4	0	352	420	60	91	5.6	.928	SS-143
1926			149	.272	.363	567	154	30	5	4	0.7	99	37	66	56	2	0	0	358	495	55	88	6.1	.939	SS-149
1927			141	.299	.376	535	160	22	8	1	0.2	87	49	58	59	5	2	1	244	352	29	46	4.4	.954	SS-86, 3B-58
1928			141	.211	.277	426	90	26	1	0	0.0	38	38	60	47	1	4	1	290	410	36	94	5.2	.951	SS-137
6 yrs.			848	.258	.344	3033	781	145	32	18	0.6	457	251	382	340	21	11	2	1873	2561	264	506	5.5	.944	SS-772, 3B-69

Ryne Sandberg

SANDBERG, RYNE DEE (Ryno)
B. Sept. 18, 1959, Spokane, Wash.
BR TR 6'1" 175 lbs.

Year	Team		Games	BA	SA	AB	H	2B	3B	HR	HR%	R	RBI	BB	SO	SB	PH AB	PH H	PO	A	E	DP	TC/G	FA	G by Pos
1981	PHI	N	13	.167	.167	6	1	0	0	0	0.0	2	0	0	1	0	0	0	7	7	0	1	1.1	1.000	SS-5, 2B-1
1982	CHI	N	156	.271	.372	635	172	33	5	7	1.1	103	54	36	90	32	1	0	136	373	12	28	3.3	.977	3B-133, 2B-24
1983			158	.261	.351	633	165	25	4	8	1.3	94	48	51	79	37	4	2	330	571	13	126	5.8	.986	2B-157, SS-1
1984			156	.314	.520	636	200	36	19	19	3.0	114	84	52	101	32	0	0	314	550	6	102	5.6	.993	2B-156
1985			153	.305	.504	609	186	31	6	26	4.3	113	83	57	97	54	1	0	353	501	12	99	5.7	.986	2B-153, SS-1
1986			154	.284	.411	627	178	28	5	14	2.2	68	76	46	79	34	1	1	309	492	5	86	5.2	.994	2B-153
1987			132	.294	.442	523	154	25	2	16	3.1	81	59	59	79	21	2	1	294	375	10	84	5.1	.985	2B-131
1988			155	.264	.419	618	163	23	8	19	3.1	77	69	54	91	25	2	0	291	522	11	79	5.3	.987	2B-153
1989			157	.290	.497	606	176	25	5	30	5.0	104	76	59	85	15	2	0	294	466	6	80	4.9	.992	2B-155
9 yrs.			1234	.285	.439	4893	1395	226	54	139	2.8	756	549	414	702	250	13	4	2328	3857	75	685	5.1	.988	2B-1083, 3B-133, SS-7

LEAGUE CHAMPIONSHIP SERIES

Year	Team		Games	BA	SA	AB	H	2B	3B	HR	HR%	R	RBI	BB	SO	SB	PH AB	PH H	PO	A	E	DP	TC/G	FA	G by Pos
1984	CHI	N	5	.368	.474	19	7	2	0	0	0.0	3	2	3	2	3	0	0	12	18	1	6	6.2	.968	2B-5
1989			5	.400	.800	20	8	3	1	1	5.0	6	4	3	4	0	0	0	7	11	0	1	3.6	1.000	2B-5
2 yrs.			10	.385	.641	39	15	5	1	1	2.6	9	6	6	6	3	0	0	19	29	1	7	4.9	.980	2B-10

Ben Sanders

SANDERS, ALEXANDER BENNETT
B. Feb. 16, 1865, Catharpin, Va. D. Aug. 29, 1930, Memphis, Tenn.
BR TR 6' 210 lbs.

Year	Team		Games	BA	SA	AB	H	2B	3B	HR	HR%	R	RBI	BB	SO	SB	PH AB	PH H	PO	A	E	DP	TC/G	FA	G by Pos
1888	PHI	N	57	.246	.322	236	58	11	2	1	0.4	26	25	8	12	13	1	0	55	79	10	1	2.5	.931	P-31, OF-25, 3B-1
1889			44	.278	.349	169	47	8	2	0	0.0	21	21	6	11	4	0	0	24	58	11	1	2.1	.882	P-44, OF-3
1890	PHI	P	52	.312	.407	189	59	6	6	0	0.0	31	30	10	10	2	0	0	30	95	11	6	2.6	.919	P-43, OF-10
1891	PHI	AA	40	.250	.359	156	39	6	4	1	0.6	24	19	7	12	2	1	0	32	31	8	1	1.8	.887	OF-22, P-19
1892	LOU	N	54	.273	.399	198	54	12	2	3	1.5	30	18	16	17	6	0	0	172	61	12	7	4.5	.951	P-31, 1B-15, OF-9
5 yrs.			247	.271	.366	948	257	43	16	5	0.5	132	113	47	62	27	1	0	313	324	52	16	2.8	.925	P-168, OF-69, 1B-15, 3B-1

Deion Sanders

SANDERS, DEION LUWYNN (Neon, Prime Time)
B. Aug. 9, 1967, Fort Myers, Fla.
BL TL 6'1" 195 lbs.

Year	Team		Games	BA	SA	AB	H	2B	3B	HR	HR%	R	RBI	BB	SO	SB	PH AB	PH H	PO	A	E	DP	TC/G	FA	G by Pos
1989	NY	A	14	.234	.404	47	11	2	0	2	4.3	7	7	3	8	1	1	0	30	1	1	0	2.3	.969	OF-14

John Sanders

SANDERS, JOHN FRANK
B. Nov. 20, 1945, Grand Island, Neb.
BR TR 6'2" 200 lbs.

Year	Team		Games	BA	SA	AB	H	2B	3B	HR	HR%	R	RBI	BB	SO	SB	PH AB	PH H	PO	A	E	DP	TC/G	FA	G by Pos
1965	KC	A	1	–	–	0	0	0	0	0	–	0	0	0	0	0	0	0	0	0	0	0	0.0	–	

Ray Sanders

SANDERS, RAYMOND FLOYD
B. Dec. 4, 1916, Bonne Terre, Mo. D. Oct. 28, 1983, Washington, Mo.
BL TR 6'2" 185 lbs.

Year	Team		Games	BA	SA	AB	H	2B	3B	HR	HR%	R	RBI	BB	SO	SB	PH AB	PH H	PO	A	E	DP	TC/G	FA	G by Pos
1942	STL	N	95	.252	.379	282	71	17	2	5	1.8	37	39	42	31	2	15	2	626	35	6	54	7.0	.991	1B-77
1943			144	.280	.414	478	134	21	5	11	2.3	69	73	77	33	1	3	0	1302	71	7	142	9.6	.995	1B-141
1944			154	.295	.441	601	177	34	9	12	2.0	87	102	71	50	2	3	1	1370	64	8	142	9.4	.994	1B-152
1945			143	.276	.385	537	148	29	3	8	1.5	85	78	83	55	3	1	0	1259	90	19	113	9.6	.986	1B-142
1946	BOS	N	80	.243	.359	259	63	12	0	6	2.3	43	35	50	38	0	2	1	659	61	9	57	9.1	.988	1B-77
1948			5	.250	.250	4	1	0	0	0	0.0	0	2	1	0	0	4	1	0	0	0	0	0.0	–	
1949			9	.143	.190	21	3	1	0	0	0.0	0	0	4	9	0	1	0	52	9	1	2	6.9	.984	1B-7
7 yrs.			630	.274	.401	2182	597	114	19	42	1.9	321	329	328	216	8	29	5	5268	330	50	510	9.0	.991	1B-596

WORLD SERIES

Year	Team		Games	BA	SA	AB	H	2B	3B	HR	HR%	R	RBI	BB	SO	SB	PH AB	PH H	PO	A	E	DP	TC/G	FA	G by Pos
1942	STL	N	2	.000	.000	1	0	0	0	0	0.0	1	0	1	0	0	1	0	0	0	0	0	0.0	–	
1943			5	.294	.471	17	5	0	0	1	5.9	3	2	3	4	0	0	0	41	5	0	4	9.2	1.000	1B-5
1944			6	.286	.429	21	6	0	0	1	4.8	5	1	5	8	0	0	0	52	2	0	3	9.0	1.000	1B-6
1948	BOS	N	1	.000	.000	1	0	0	0	0	0.0	0	0	0	0	0	1	0	0	0	0	0	0.0	–	
4 yrs.			14	.275	.425	40	11	0	0	2	5.0	9	3	9	12	0	2	0	93	7	0	7	7.1	1.000	1B-11

Reggie Sanders

SANDERS, REGINALD JEROME
B. Sept. 9, 1949, Birmingham, Ala.
BR TR 6'2" 205 lbs.

Year	Team		Games	BA	SA	AB	H	2B	3B	HR	HR%	R	RBI	BB	SO	SB	PH AB	PH H	PO	A	E	DP	TC/G	FA	G by Pos
1974	DET	A	26	.273	.434	99	27	7	0	3	3.0	12	10	5	20	1	0	0	218	17	3	19	9.2	.987	1B-25, DH-1

Mike Sandlock

SANDLOCK, MICHAEL JOSEPH
B. Oct. 17, 1915, Old Greenwich, Conn.
BB TR 6'1" 180 lbs.
BL 1944

Year	Team		Games	BA	SA	AB	H	2B	3B	HR	HR%	R	RBI	BB	SO	SB	PH AB	PH H	PO	A	E	DP	TC/G	FA	G by Pos
1942	BOS	N	2	1.000	1.000	1	1	0	0	0	0.0	0	0	0	0	0	0	0	0	0	0	0	0.0	–	SS-2
1944			30	.100	.100	30	3	0	0	0	0.0	1	2	5	3	0	0	0	17	35	3	3	1.8	.945	3B-22, SS-7
1945	BKN	N	80	.282	.405	195	55	14	2	2	1.0	21	17	18	19	2	4	2	224	53	6	5	3.5	.979	C-47, SS-22, 2B-4, 3B-2
1946			19	.147	.147	34	5	0	0	0	0.0	1	0	3	4	0	1	1	61	13	2	1	4.0	.974	C-17, 3B-1
1953	PIT	N	64	.231	.258	186	43	5	0	0	0.0	10	12	12	19	0	0	0	290	49	3	4	5.3	.991	C-64
5 yrs.			195	.240	.305	446	107	19	2	2	0.4	34	31	38	45	2	5	3	592	150	14	13	3.9	.981	C-128, SS-31, 3B-25, 2B-4

Year	Team		Games	BA	SA	AB	H	2B	3B	HR	HR%	R	RBI	BB	SO	SB	Pinch Hit AB	H	PO	A	E	DP	TC/G	FA	G by Pos

Charlie Sands

SANDS, CHARLES DUANE
B. Dec. 17, 1947, Newport News, Va.
BL TR 6'2" 200 lbs.

Year	Team		Games	BA	SA	AB	H	2B	3B	HR	HR%	R	RBI	BB	SO	SB	AB	H	PO	A	E	DP	TC/G	FA	G by Pos
1967	NY	A	1	.000	.000	1	0	0	0	0	0.0	0	0	0	1	0	1	0	0	0	0	0	0.0	–	
1971	PIT	N	28	.200	.400	25	5	2	0	1	4.0	4	5	7	6	0	18	5	9	1	0	1	0.4	1.000	C-3
1972			1	.000	.000	1	0	0	0	0	0.0	0	0	0	0	0	1	0	0	0	0	0	0.0	–	
1973	CAL	A	17	.273	.485	33	9	2	1	1	3.0	5	5	5	10	0	6	0	32	1	3	2	2.1	.917	C-10
1974			43	.193	.361	83	16	2	0	4	4.8	6	13	23	17	0	12	1	20	0	0	0	0.5	1.000	DH-21, C-5
1975	OAK	A	3	.500	.500	2	1	0	0	0	0.0	0	0	1	1	0	2	1	0	0	0	0	0.0	–	DH-1
	6 yrs.		93	.214	.393	145	31	6	1	6	4.1	15	23	36	35	0	40	7	61	2	3	3	0.7	.955	DH-22, C-18

WORLD SERIES

| 1971 | PIT | N | 1 | .000 | .000 | 1 | 0 | 0 | 0 | 0 | 0.0 | 0 | 0 | 0 | 1 | 0 | 1 | 0 | 0 | 0 | 0 | 0 | 0.0 | – | |

Tom Sandt

SANDT, THOMAS JAMES
B. Dec. 22, 1950, Brooklyn, N. Y.
BR TR 5'11" 175 lbs.

1975	OAK	A	1	–	–	0	0	0	0	0	0.0	0	0	0	0	0	0	0	0	0	0	0	0.0	–	2B-1
1976			41	.209	.224	67	14	1	0	0	0.0	6	3	7	9	0	2	0	44	60	3	11	2.6	.972	SS-29, 2B-9, 3B-2
	2 yrs.		42	.209	.224	67	14	1	0	0	0.0	6	3	7	9	0	2	0	44	60	3	11	2.5	.972	SS-29, 2B-10, 3B-2

Jack Sanford

SANFORD, JOHN HOWARD
B. June 23, 1917, Chatham, Va.
BR TR 6'3" 195 lbs.

1940	WAS	A	34	.197	.262	122	24	4	2	0	0.0	5	10	6	17	0	6	0	282	15	2	38	8.8	.993	1B-34
1941			3	.400	.800	5	2	0	1	0	0.0	1	0	1	1	0	1	1	12	0	0	1	4.0	1.000	1B-1
1946			10	.231	.308	26	6	0	1	0	0.0	7	1	2	6	0	4	0	66	1	2	7	6.9	.971	1B-6
	3 yrs.		47	.209	.288	153	32	4	4	0	0.0	13	11	9	24	0	5	1	360	16	4	46	8.1	.989	1B-41

Manny Sanguillen

SANGUILLEN, MANUEL de JESUS
Born Manuel de Jesus Sanguillen y Magan.
B. Mar. 21, 1944, Colon, Panama
BR TR 6' 193 lbs.

1967	PIT	N	30	.271	.313	96	26	4	0	0	0.0	6	8	4	12	0	1	0	133	11	2	4	4.9	.986	C-28
1969			129	.303	.407	459	139	21	6	5	1.1	62	57	12	48	8	18	7	825	71	17	11	7.1	.981	C-113
1970			128	.325	.444	486	158	19	9	7	1.4	63	61	17	45	2	3	1	775	66	10	12	6.6	.988	C-125
1971			138	.319	.426	533	170	26	5	7	1.3	60	81	19	32	6	4	2	712	72	5	12	5.7	.994	C-135
1972			136	.298	.404	520	155	18	8	7	1.3	55	71	21	38	1	10	4	724	50	9	4	5.8	.989	C-127, OF-2
1973			149	.282	.411	589	166	26	7	12	2.0	64	65	17	29	2	4	1	632	41	17	11	4.6	.975	C-89, OF-59
1974			151	.287	.371	596	171	21	4	7	1.2	77	68	21	27	2	4	1	713	76	12	8	5.3	.985	C-151
1975			133	.328	.451	481	158	24	4	9	1.9	60	58	48	31	5	2	0	650	53	9	4	5.4	.987	C-132
1976			114	.290	.378	389	113	16	6	2	0.5	52	36	28	18	2	5	2	518	52	13	7	5.1	.978	C-111
1977	OAK	A	152	.275	.354	571	157	17	5	6	1.1	42	58	22	35	2	3	2	419	54	7	7	3.2	.985	C-77, DH-58, OF-9, 1B-7
1978	PIT	N	85	.264	.336	220	58	5	1	3	1.4	15	16	9	10	2	27	5	438	20	0	26	5.4	1.000	1B-40, C-18
1979			56	.230	.351	74	17	5	2	0	0.0	8	4	2	5	0	42	9	67	6	2	3	1.3	.973	C-8, 1B-5
1980			47	.250	.313	48	12	3	0	0	0.0	2	2	3	1	3	37	12	40	3	2	3	1.0	.956	1B-5
	13 yrs.		1448	.296	.398	5062	1500	205	57	65	1.3	566	585	223	331	35	160	46	6646	575	105	112	5.1	.986	C-1114, OF-70, DH-58, 1B-57

LEAGUE CHAMPIONSHIP SERIES

1970	PIT	N	3	.167	.167	12	2	0	0	0	0.0	0	0	0	1	0	0	0	13	1	1	0	5.0	.933	C-3
1971			4	.267	.267	15	4	0	0	0	0.0	0	1	1	1	1	0	0	30	1	1	0	7.8	1.000	C-4
1972			5	.313	.563	16	5	1	0	1	6.3	4	2	0	0	0	1	1	22	0	1	1	4.6	.957	C-5
1974			4	.250	.313	16	4	1	0	0	0.0	0	0	0	0	0	2	2	19	2	2	1	5.8	.913	C-4
1975			3	.167	.167	12	2	0	0	0	0.0	1	0	0	0	0	1	1	29	1	1	1	10.3	.968	C-3
	5 yrs.		19	.239	.310	71	17	2	0	1	1.4	5	3	1	2	1	1	1	113	5	5	3	6.5	.959	C-19

WORLD SERIES

1971	PIT	N	7	.379	.414	29	11	1	0	0	0.0	3	0	0	3	2	0	0	37	0	0	1	5.3	1.000	C-7
1979			3	.333	.333	3	1	0	0	0	0.0	0	1	0	0	0	3	1	0	0	0	0	0.0	–	
	2 yrs.		10	.375	.406	32	12	1	0	0	0.0	3	1	0	3	2	3	1	37	0	0	1	3.7	1.000	C-7

Ed Sanicki

SANICKI, EDWARD ROBERT (Butch)
B. July 7, 1924, Wallington, N. J.
BR TR 5'9½" 175 lbs.

1949	PHI	N	7	.231	.923	13	3	0	0	3	23.1	4	7	1	4	0	1	0	12	0	0	0	1.7	1.000	OF-6
1951			13	.500	.750	4	2	1	0	0	0.0	1	1	1	1	1	1	0	1	0	0	0	0.1	1.000	OF-10
	2 yrs.		20	.294	.882	17	5	1	0	3	17.6	5	8	2	5	1	2	0	13	0	0	0	0.7	1.000	OF-16

Ben Sankey

SANKEY, BENJAMIN TURNER
B. Sept. 2, 1907, Nauvoo, Ala.
BR TR 5'10" 155 lbs.

1929	PIT	N	2	.143	.143	7	1	0	0	0	0.0	1	0	0	0	0	0	0	3	7	1	1	5.5	.909	SS-2
1930			13	.167	.167	30	5	0	0	0	0.0	6	0	2	3	0	0	0	17	26	5	3	3.7	.896	SS-6, 2B-4
1931			57	.227	.318	132	30	2	5	0	0.0	14	14	14	10	0	4	0	73	127	18	24	3.8	.917	SS-49, 3B-2, 2B-2
	3 yrs.		72	.213	.284	169	36	2	5	0	0.0	21	14	16	14	0	4	0	93	160	24	28	3.8	.913	SS-57, 2B-6, 3B-2

Rafael Santana

SANTANA, RAFAEL FRANCISCO (Ralph)
Born Rafael Francisco Santana y de la Cruz.
B. Jan. 31, 1958, La Romana, Dominican Republic
BR TR 6'1" 156 lbs.

1983	STL	N	30	.214	.214	14	3	0	0	0	0.0	1	2	2	2	0	4	0	3	8	4	3	0.5	.733	2B-9, SS-6, 3B-4
1984	NY	N	51	.276	.382	152	42	11	1	1	0.7	14	12	9	17	0	1	0	92	104	6	34	4.0	.970	SS-50
1985			154	.257	.302	529	136	19	1	1	0.2	41	29	29	54	1	1	0	301	396	25	81	4.7	.965	SS-153
1986			139	.218	.254	394	86	11	0	1	0.3	38	28	36	43	0	2	0	203	369	16	68	4.2	.973	SS-137, 2B-1
1987			139	.255	.346	439	112	21	2	5	1.1	41	44	29	57	1	1	0	213	396	17	82	4.5	.973	SS-138
1988	NY	A	148	.240	.294	480	115	12	1	4	0.8	50	38	33	61	1	0	0	202	421	22	96	4.4	.966	SS-148
	6 yrs.		661	.246	.306	2008	494	74	5	12	0.6	185	153	138	234	3	9	0	1014	1694	90	364	4.2	.968	SS-632, 2B-10, 3B-4

LEAGUE CHAMPIONSHIP SERIES

| 1986 | NY | N | 6 | .176 | .176 | 17 | 3 | 0 | 0 | 0 | 0.0 | 0 | 0 | 0 | 3 | 0 | 0 | 0 | 13 | 18 | 0 | 5 | 5.2 | 1.000 | SS-6 |

Year	Team	Games	BA	SA	AB	H	2B	3B	HR	HR%	R	RBI	BB	SO	SB	Pinch Hit AB	Pinch Hit H	PO	A	E	DP	TC/G	FA	G by Pos

Rafael Santana *continued*

WORLD SERIES

Year	Team	Games	BA	SA	AB	H	2B	3B	HR	HR%	R	RBI	BB	SO	SB	AB	H	PO	A	E	DP	TC/G	FA	G by Pos
1986	NY N	7	.250	.250	20	5	0	0	0	0.0	3	2	2	5	0	0	0	11	17	1	4	4.1	.966	SS-7

Benito Santiago

SANTIAGO, BENITO
Born Benito Santiago y Rivera.
B. Mar. 9, 1965, Ponce, Puerto Rico

BR TR 6'1" 180 lbs.

Year	Team	Games	BA	SA	AB	H	2B	3B	HR	HR%	R	RBI	BB	SO	SB	AB	H	PO	A	E	DP	TC/G	FA	G by Pos
1986	SD N	17	.290	.468	62	18	2	0	3	4.8	10	6	2	12	0	0	0	80	7	5	2	5.4	.946	C-17
1987		146	.300	.467	546	164	33	2	18	3.3	64	79	16	112	21	0	0	817	80	22	12	6.3	.976	C-146
1988		139	.248	.362	492	122	22	2	10	2.0	49	46	24	82	15	7	2	725	75	12	11	5.8	.985	C-136
1989		129	.236	.387	462	109	16	3	16	3.5	50	62	26	89	11	2	0	685	81	20	10	6.1	.975	C-127
4 yrs.		431	.264	.410	1562	413	73	7	47	3.0	173	193	68	295	47	9	2	2307	243	59	35	6.1	.977	C-426

Ron Santo

SANTO, RONALD EDWARD
B. Feb. 25, 1940, Seattle, Wash.

BR TR 6' 190 lbs.

Year	Team	Games	BA	SA	AB	H	2B	3B	HR	HR%	R	RBI	BB	SO	SB	AB	H	PO	A	E	DP	TC/G	FA	G by Pos
1960	CHI N	95	.251	.409	347	87	24	2	9	2.6	44	44	31	44	0	1	0	78	144	13	6	2.5	.945	3B-94
1961		154	.284	.479	578	164	32	6	23	4.0	84	83	73	77	2	1	1	157	307	31	41	3.2	.937	3B-153
1962		162	.227	.358	604	137	20	4	17	2.8	44	83	65	94	4	2	0	167	343	24	35	3.3	.955	3B-157, SS-8
1963		162	.297	.481	630	187	29	6	25	4.0	79	99	42	92	6	0	0	136	374	26	25	3.3	.951	3B-162
1964		161	.313	.564	592	185	33	13	30	5.1	94	114	86	96	3	0	0	156	367	20	31	3.4	.963	3B-161
1965		164	.285	.510	608	173	30	4	33	5.4	88	101	88	109	3	0	0	155	373	24	27	3.4	.957	3B-164
1966		155	.312	.538	561	175	21	8	30	5.3	93	94	95	78	4	0	0	157	408	26	41	3.8	.956	3B-152, SS-8
1967		161	.300	.512	586	176	23	4	31	5.3	107	98	96	103	1	0	0	187	393	26	33	3.8	.957	3B-161
1968		162	.246	.421	577	142	17	3	26	4.5	86	98	96	106	3	0	0	130	378	15	33	3.2	.971	3B-162
1969		160	.289	.485	575	166	18	4	29	5.0	97	123	96	97	1	1	0	144	334	27	23	3.2	.947	3B-160
1970		154	.267	.476	555	148	30	4	26	4.7	83	114	92	108	2	2	1	144	320	27	36	3.2	.945	3B-152, OF-1
1971		154	.267	.423	555	148	22	1	21	3.8	77	88	79	95	1	0	0	128	275	18	29	2.7	.957	3B-149, OF-6
1972		133	.302	.487	464	140	25	5	17	3.7	68	74	69	75	1	1	1	119	282	22	23	3.2	.948	3B-129, 2B-3, OF-1, SS-1
1973		149	.267	.440	536	143	29	2	20	3.7	65	77	63	97	1	2	0	107	271	20	17	2.7	.950	3B-146
1974	CHI A	117	.221	.299	375	83	12	1	5	1.3	29	41	37	72	0	5	3	135	148	8	49	2.5	.973	DH-47, 2B-39, 3B-28, 1B-3, SS-1
15 yrs.		2243	.277	.464	8143	2254	365	67	342	4.2	1138	1331	1108	1343	35	16	6	2100	4717	327	449	3.2	.954	3B-2130, DH-47, 2B-42, SS-18, OF-8, 1B-3

Rafael Santo Domingo

SANTO DOMINGO, RAFAEL
Born Rafael Santo Domingo y Molina.
B. Nov. 24, 1955, Orocovis, Puerto Rico

BB TR 6' 160 lbs.

Year	Team	Games	BA	SA	AB	H	2B	3B	HR	HR%	R	RBI	BB	SO	SB	AB	H	PO	A	E	DP	TC/G	FA	G by Pos
1979	CIN N	7	.167	.167	6	1	0	0	0	0.0	1	0	0	1	3	0	6	1	0	0	0	0	0.0	—	

Nelson Santovenia

SANTOVENIA, NELSON GIL
Born Nelson Gil Santovenia y Mayol.
B. July 27, 1961, Pinar del Rio, Cuba

BR TR 6'3" 195 lbs.

Year	Team	Games	BA	SA	AB	H	2B	3B	HR	HR%	R	RBI	BB	SO	SB	AB	H	PO	A	E	DP	TC/G	FA	G by Pos
1987	MON N	2	.000	.000	1	0	0	0	0	0.0	0	0	0	0	0	1	0	1	0	0	0	0.5	1.000	C-1
1988		92	.236	.392	309	73	20	2	8	2.6	26	41	24	77	2	1	1	465	63	9	7	5.8	.983	C-86, 1B-1
1989		97	.250	.352	304	76	14	1	5	1.6	30	31	24	37	2	7	1	564	66	12	8	6.6	.981	C-89, 1B-1
3 yrs.		191	.243	.371	614	149	34	3	13	2.1	56	72	48	114	4	9	2	1030	129	21	15	6.2	.982	C-176, 1B-2

Ed Santry

SANTRY, EDWARD
B. 1861, Chicago, Ill. D. Mar. 6, 1899, Chicago, Ill.

Year	Team	Games	BA	SA	AB	H	2B	3B	HR	HR%	R	RBI	BB	SO	SB	AB	H	PO	A	E	DP	TC/G	FA	G by Pos
1884	DET N	6	.182	.182	22	4	0	0	0	0.0	1		1	2		0	0	14	16	5	1	5.8	.857	SS-5, 2B-1

Joe Sargent

SARGENT, JOSEPH ALEXANDER (Horse Belly)
B. Sept. 24, 1893, Rochester, N. Y. D. July 5, 1950, Rochester, N. Y.

BR TR 5'10" 165 lbs.

Year	Team	Games	BA	SA	AB	H	2B	3B	HR	HR%	R	RBI	BB	SO	SB	AB	H	PO	A	E	DP	TC/G	FA	G by Pos
1921	DET A	66	.253	.388	178	45	8	5	2	1.1	21	22	24	26	2	1	0	112	134	21	21	4.0	.921	2B-24, 3B-23, SS-19

Bill Sarni

SARNI, WILLIAM FLORINE
B. Sept. 19, 1927, Los Angeles, Calif. D. Apr. 15, 1983, Creve Coeur, Mo.

BR TR 5'11" 180 lbs.

Year	Team	Games	BA	SA	AB	H	2B	3B	HR	HR%	R	RBI	BB	SO	SB	AB	H	PO	A	E	DP	TC/G	FA	G by Pos
1951	STL N	36	.174	.186	86	15	1	0	0	0.0	7	2	9	13	1	1	0	107	13	2	3	3.4	.984	C-35
1952		3	.200	.200	5	1	0	0	0	0.0	0	0	0	1	0	0	0	19	0	0	0	6.3	1.000	C-3
1954		123	.300	.439	380	114	18	4	9	2.4	40	70	25	42	3	6	3	486	41	2	12	4.3	.996	C-118
1955		107	.255	.342	325	83	15	2	3	0.9	32	34	27	33	1	11	3	482	39	7	8	4.9	.987	C-99
1956	2 teams	STL N	(43G – .291)		NY	N	(78G – .231)																		
"	total	121	.254	.399	386	98	16	5	10	2.6	28	45	28	46	1	6	1	586	61	5	10	5.4	.992	C-116
5 yrs.		390	.263	.380	1182	311	50	11	22	1.9	107	151	89	135	6	24	7	1680	154	16	33	4.7	.991	C-371

Mackey Sasser

SASSER, MACK DANIEL
B. Aug. 3, 1962, Fort Gaines, Ga.

BL TR 6'1" 190 lbs.

Year	Team	Games	BA	SA	AB	H	2B	3B	HR	HR%	R	RBI	BB	SO	SB	AB	H	PO	A	E	DP	TC/G	FA	G by Pos
1987	2 teams	SF N	(2G – .000)		PIT	N	(12G – .217)																		
"	total	14	.185	.185	27	5	0	0	0	0.0	2	2	0	2	0	9	4	29	0	0	0	2.1	1.000	C-6
1988	NY N	60	.285	.407	123	35	10	1	1	0.8	9	17	6	9	0	19	3	235	17	6	2	4.3	.977	C-42, OF-1, 3B-1
1989		72	.291	.407	182	53	14	2	1	0.5	17	22	7	15	0	17	5	335	19	3	3	5.0	.992	C-62, 3B-1
3 yrs.		146	.280	.389	332	93	24	3	2	0.6	28	41	13	26	0	45	12	599	36	9	5	4.4	.986	C-110, 3B-2, OF-1

LEAGUE CHAMPIONSHIP SERIES

Year	Team	Games	BA	SA	AB	H	2B	3B	HR	HR%	R	RBI	BB	SO	SB	AB	H	PO	A	E	DP	TC/G	FA	G by Pos
1988	NY N	4	.200	.200	5	1	0	0	0	0.0	0	0	0	1	0	2	0	2	0	0	0	0.5	1.000	C-2

Tom Satriano

SATRIANO, THOMAS VICTOR NICHOLAS (Satch)
B. Aug. 28, 1940, Pittsburgh, Pa.

BL TR 6'1" 185 lbs.

Year	Team	Games	BA	SA	AB	H	2B	3B	HR	HR%	R	RBI	BB	SO	SB	AB	H	PO	A	E	DP	TC/G	FA	G by Pos
1961	LA A	35	.198	.302	96	19	5	1	1	1.0	15	8	12	16	2	3	0	29	61	8	7	2.8	.918	3B-23, 2B-10, SS-1
1962		10	.421	.842	19	8	2	0	2	10.5	4	6	0	1	0	7	3	2	8	2	1	1.2	.833	3B-5
1963		23	.180	.200	50	9	1	0	0	0.0	1	2	9	10	0	9	0	17	33	3	2	2.3	.943	3B-13, C-2, 1B-1

Year Team	Games	BA	SA	AB	H	2B	3B	HR	HR%	R	RBI	BB	SO	SB	Pinch Hit AB	Pinch Hit H	PO	A	E	DP	TC/G	FA	G by Pos

Tom Satriano *continued*

Year Team	Games	BA	SA	AB	H	2B	3B	HR	HR%	R	RBI	BB	SO	SB	AB	H	PO	A	E	DP	TC/G	FA	G by Pos
1964	108	.200	.247	255	51	9	0	1	0.4	18	17	30	37	0	19	4	383	72	8	32	4.3	.983	3B-38, 1B-32, C-25, SS-2, 2B-1
1965 CAL A	47	.165	.228	79	13	2	0	1	1.3	8	4	10	10	1	11	1	83	33	1	4	2.5	.991	3B-15, 2B-12, C-12, 1B-3
1966	103	.239	.288	226	54	5	3	0	0.0	16	24	27	32	3	8	1	283	58	6	13	3.4	.983	C-43, 1B-36, 3B-25, 2B-4
1967	90	.224	.318	201	45	7	0	4	2.0	13	21	28	25	1	22	4	150	85	7	10	2.7	.971	3B-38, C-23, 2B-15, 1B-5
1968	111	.253	.364	297	75	9	0	8	2.7	20	35	37	44	0	17	4	433	67	8	11	4.6	.984	C-85, 2B-14, 3B-11, 1B-1
1969 2 teams	CAL A (41G – .259)			BOS A	(47G – .189)																		
" total	88	.221	.251	235	52	4	0	1	0.4	14	27	40	27	0	9	3	463	36	6	8	5.7	.988	C-80, 1B-5, 2B-2
1970 BOS A	59	.236	.358	165	39	9	1	3	1.8	21	13	21	23	0	7	1	318	19	5	5	5.8	.985	C-51
10 yrs.	674	.225	.303	1623	365	53	5	21	1.3	130	157	214	225	7	112	21	2161	472	54	93	4.0	.980	C-321, 3B-168, 1B-83, 2B-58, SS-3

Frank Saucier

SAUCIER, FRANCIS FIELD
B. May 28, 1926, Leslie, Mo.

BL TR 6'1" 180 lbs.

Year Team	Games	BA	SA	AB	H	2B	3B	HR	HR%	R	RBI	BB	SO	SB	AB	H	PO	A	E	DP	TC/G	FA	G by Pos
1951 STL A	18	.071	.143	14	1	1	0	0	0.0	4	1	3	4	0	7	1	5	0	2	0	0.4	.714	OF-3

Ed Sauer

SAUER, EDWARD (Horn)
Brother of Hank Sauer.
B. Jan. 3, 1920, Pittsburgh, Pa. D. July 1, 1988, Thousand Oaks, Calif.

BR TR 6'1" 188 lbs.

Year Team	Games	BA	SA	AB	H	2B	3B	HR	HR%	R	RBI	BB	SO	SB	AB	H	PO	A	E	DP	TC/G	FA	G by Pos
1943 CHI N	14	.273	.327	55	15	3	0	0	0.0	3	9	3	6	1	0	0	40	1	1	0	3.0	.976	OF-13, 3B-1
1944	23	.220	.300	50	11	4	0	0	0.0	3	5	2	6	0	9	2	23	1	1	0	1.1	.960	OF-12
1945	49	.258	.387	93	24	4	1	2	2.2	8	11	8	23	2	15	3	44	1	0	1	0.9	1.000	OF-26
1949 2 teams	STL N	(24G – .222)		BOS N	(79G – .266)																		
" total	103	.259	.355	259	67	14	1	3	1.2	31	32	20	42	0	19	4	146	5	4	1	1.5	.974	OF-81, 3B-2
4 yrs.	189	.256	.352	457	117	25	2	5	1.1	45	57	33	77	3	43	9	253	8	6	2	1.4	.978	OF-132, 3B-3

WORLD SERIES

Year Team	Games	BA	SA	AB	H	2B	3B	HR	HR%	R	RBI	BB	SO	SB	AB	H	PO	A	E	DP	TC/G	FA	G by Pos
1945 CHI N	2	.000	.000	2	0	0	0	0	0.0	0	0	0	2	0	2	0	0	0	0	0	0.0	–	

Hank Sauer

SAUER, HENRY JOHN
Brother of Ed Sauer.
B. Mar. 17, 1917, Pittsburgh, Pa.

BR TR 6'3" 198 lbs.

Year Team	Games	BA	SA	AB	H	2B	3B	HR	HR%	R	RBI	BB	SO	SB	AB	H	PO	A	E	DP	TC/G	FA	G by Pos
1941 CIN N	9	.303	.424	33	10	4	0	0	0.0	4	5	1	4	0	1	1	21	1	1	1	2.6	.957	OF-8
1942	7	.250	.550	20	5	0	0	2	10.0	4	4	2	2	0	1	0	37	4	1	8	6.0	.976	1B-4
1945	31	.293	.431	116	34	1	0	5	4.3	18	20	6	16	2	1	0	100	5	3	4	3.5	.972	OF-28, 1B-3
1948	145	.260	.504	530	138	22	1	35	6.6	78	97	60	85	2	2	0	359	22	9	10	2.7	.977	OF-132, 1B-12
1949 2 teams	CIN N	(42G – .237)		CHI N	(96G – .291)																		
" total	138	.275	.507	509	140	23	1	31	6.1	81	99	55	66	0	3	0	302	16	9	2	2.4	.972	OF-135, 1B-1
1950 CHI N	145	.274	.519	540	148	32	2	32	5.9	85	103	60	67	0	3	2	381	29	13	12	2.9	.969	OF-125, 1B-18
1951	141	.263	.486	525	138	19	4	30	5.7	77	89	45	77	2	8	1	286	19	6	2	2.2	.981	OF-132
1952	151	.270	.531	567	153	31	3	37	6.5	89	121	77	92	1	0	0	327	17	6	3	2.3	.983	OF-151
1953	108	.263	.473	395	104	16	5	19	4.8	61	60	50	56	0	5	1	221	5	7	1	2.2	.970	OF-105
1954	142	.288	.563	520	150	18	1	41	7.9	98	103	70	68	2	1	0	282	8	11	2	2.1	.963	OF-141
1955	79	.211	.387	261	55	8	1	12	4.6	29	28	26	47	0	10	0	122	4	2	1	1.6	.984	OF-68
1956 STL N	75	.298	.424	151	45	4	0	5	3.3	11	24	25	31	0	31	6	55	2	0	1	0.8	1.000	OF-37
1957 NY N	127	.259	.508	378	98	14	1	26	6.9	46	76	49	59	1	24	7	125	4	1	0	1.0	.992	OF-98
1958 SF N	88	.250	.436	236	59	8	0	12	5.1	27	46	35	37	0	19	2	93	3	5	1	1.1	.950	OF-67
1959	13	.067	.267	15	1	0	0	1	6.7	1	1	9	7	0	12	1	0	0	0	0	0.0	–	OF-1
15 yrs.	1399	.266	.496	4796	1278	200	19	288	6.0	709	876	561	714	11	123	22	2711	139	74	48	2.1	.975	OF-1228, 1B-38

Rusty Saunders

SAUNDERS, RUSSELL COLLIER
B. Mar. 12, 1906, Trenton, N. J. D. Nov. 24, 1967, Trenton, N. J.

BR TR 6'2" 205 lbs.

Year Team	Games	BA	SA	AB	H	2B	3B	HR	HR%	R	RBI	BB	SO	SB	AB	H	PO	A	E	DP	TC/G	FA	G by Pos
1927 PHI A	5	.133	.200	15	2	1	0	0	0.0	2	2	3	2	0	1	0	8	1	2	0	2.2	.818	OF-4

Al Sauters

SAUTERS, AL
B. Philadelphia, Pa. Deceased.

Year Team	Games	BA	SA	AB	H	2B	3B	HR	HR%	R	RBI	BB	SO	SB	AB	H	PO	A	E	DP	TC/G	FA	G by Pos
1890 PHI AA	14	.098	.098	41	4	0	0	0	0.0	1		11		0	0	0	17	20	8	0	3.2	.822	3B-11, OF-2, 2B-2

Don Savage

SAVAGE, DONALD ANTHONY
B. Mar. 5, 1919, Bloomfield, N. J. D. Dec. 25, 1961, Montclair, N. J.

BR TR 6' 180 lbs.

Year Team	Games	BA	SA	AB	H	2B	3B	HR	HR%	R	RBI	BB	SO	SB	AB	H	PO	A	E	DP	TC/G	FA	G by Pos
1944 NY A	71	.264	.385	239	63	7	4	5	1.7	31	24	20	41	1	10	1	66	109	10	11	2.6	.946	3B-60
1945	34	.224	.241	58	13	1	0	0	0.0	5	3	3	14	1	9	2	19	25	5	3	1.4	.898	3B-14, OF-2
2 yrs.	105	.256	.357	297	76	8	4	5	1.3	36	27	23	55	2	19	3	85	134	15	14	2.2	.936	3B-74, OF-2

Jim Savage

SAVAGE, JAMES HAROLD
B. Aug. 29, 1883, Southington, Conn. D. June 26, 1940, New Castle, Pa.

BB TR 5'5" 150 lbs.

Year Team	Games	BA	SA	AB	H	2B	3B	HR	HR%	R	RBI	BB	SO	SB	AB	H	PO	A	E	DP	TC/G	FA	G by Pos
1912 PHI N	2	.000	.000	3	0	0	0	0	0.0	1	0	0	1	0	0	0	1	2	1	0	2.0	.750	2B-1
1914 PIT F	132	.284	.347	479	136	9	9	1	0.2	81	26	67		17	3	0	193	101	19	10	2.4	.939	OF-93, 3B-29, SS-11, 2B-3
1915	14	.143	.143	21	3	0	0	0	0.0	0	0	1		0	7	2	4	0	1	0	0.4	.800	OF-3, 3B-1
3 yrs.	148	.276	.336	503	139	9	9	1	0.2	82	26	69		17	10	2	198	103	21	10	2.2	.935	OF-96, 3B-30, SS-11, 2B-4

Ted Savage

SAVAGE, THEODORE EDMUND
Born Ephesian Savage.
B. Feb. 21, 1937, Venice, Ill.

BR TR 6'1" 185 lbs.

Year Team	Games	BA	SA	AB	H	2B	3B	HR	HR%	R	RBI	BB	SO	SB	AB	H	PO	A	E	DP	TC/G	FA	G by Pos
1962 PHI N	127	.266	.373	335	89	11	2	7	2.1	54	39	40	66	16	21	3	185	4	5	1	1.5	.974	OF-109
1963 PIT N	85	.195	.322	149	29	2	1	5	3.4	22	14	14	31	4	33	5	47	3	3	1	0.6	.943	OF-47
1965 STL N	30	.159	.254	63	10	3	0	1	1.6	7	4	6	9	1	7	2	29	1	2	0	1.1	.938	OF-20
1966	16	.172	.310	29	5	2	1	0	0.0	4	3	4	7	4	9	2	6	0	0	0	0.6	1.000	OF-7

Ted Savage *continued*

Year	Team	Games	BA	SA	AB	H	2B	3B	HR	HR%	R	RBI	BB	SO	SB	PH AB	PH H	PO	A	E	DP	TC/G	FA	G by Pos
1967	2 teams	STL N (9G – .125)									CHI N (96G – .218)													
"	total	105	.215	.330	233	50	10	1	5	2.1	41	33	41	57	7	17	4	133	7	3	2	1.4	.979	OF-86, 3B-1
1968	2 teams	CHI N (3G – .250)									LA N (61G – .206)													
"	total	64	.209	.313	134	28	6	1	2	1.5	7	7	10	21	1	21	3	64	4	1	1	1.1	.986	OF-41
1969	CIN N	68	.227	.345	110	25	7	0	2	1.8	20	11	20	27	3	27	5	57	0	1	0	0.9	.983	OF-17, 2B-1
1970	MIL A	114	.279	.482	276	77	10	5	12	4.3	43	50	57	44	10	31	6	124	3	6	0	1.2	.955	OF-82, 1B-1
1971	2 teams	MIL A (14G – .176)									KC A (19G – .172)													
"	total	33	.174	.174	46	8	0	0	0	0.0	4	2	8	10	3	18	2	8	2	0	0	0.3	1.000	OF-15
9 yrs.		642	.233	.361	1375	321	51	11	34	2.5	202	163	200	272	49	184	32	656	24	21	5	1.1	.970	OF-424, 3B-1, 2B-1, 1B-1

Bob Saverine

SAVERINE, ROBERT PAUL (Rabbit)
B. June 2, 1941, Norwalk, Conn.

BB TR 5'10" 160 lbs.

Year	Team	Games	BA	SA	AB	H	2B	3B	HR	HR%	R	RBI	BB	SO	SB	PH AB	PH H	PO	A	E	DP	TC/G	FA	G by Pos
1959	BAL A	1	–	–	0	0	0	0	0	.	1	0	0	0	0	0	0	0	0	0	0	0.0	–	
1962		8	.238	.333	21	5	2	0	0	0.0	2	3	1	3	0	1	0	11	19	0	3	3.8	1.000	2B-7
1963		115	.234	.281	167	39	1	2	1	0.6	21	12	25	44	8	16	6	99	89	2	19	1.7	.989	OF-59, 2B-19, SS-13
1964		46	.147	.176	34	5	1	0	0	0.0	14	0	3	6	3	3	0	12	16	0	1	0.6	1.000	SS-15, OF-2
1966	WAS A	120	.251	.333	406	102	10	4	5	1.2	54	24	27	62	4	19	5	186	228	11	44	3.5	.974	2B-70, 3B-26, SS-11, OF-9
1967		89	.236	.292	233	55	13	0	0	0.0	22	8	17	34	8	25	4	90	127	12	24	2.6	.948	2B-48, SS-10, 3B-8, OF-2
6 yrs.		379	.239	.305	861	206	27	6	6	0.7	114	47	73	149	23	64	15	398	479	25	91	2.4	.972	2B-144, OF-72, SS-49, 3B-34

Carl Sawatski

SAWATSKI, CARL ERNEST (Swats)
B. Nov. 4, 1927, Shickshinny, Pa.

BL TR 5'10" 210 lbs.

Year	Team	Games	BA	SA	AB	H	2B	3B	HR	HR%	R	RBI	BB	SO	SB	PH AB	PH H	PO	A	E	DP	TC/G	FA	G by Pos
1948	CHI N	2	.000	.000	2	0	0	0	0	0.0	0	0	0	0	0	2	0	0	0	0	0	0.0	–	
1950		38	.175	.214	103	18	1	0	1	1.0	4	7	11	19	0	7	0	100	19	2	6	3.2	.983	C-32
1953		43	.220	.322	59	13	3	0	1	1.7	5	5	7	7	0	2	0	45	5	3	0	1.2	.943	C-15
1954	CHI A	43	.183	.294	109	20	3	3	1	0.9	6	12	15	20	0	8	1	133	14	2	4	3.5	.987	C-33
1957	MIL N	58	.238	.448	105	25	4	0	6	5.7	13	17	10	15	0	31	6	121	20	2	2	2.5	.986	C-28
1958	2 teams	MIL N (10G – .100)									PHI N (60G – .230)													
"	total	70	.223	.332	193	43	4	1	5	2.6	13	13	18	47	0	13	4	279	20	4	2	4.3	.987	C-56
1959	PHI N	74	.293	.480	198	58	10	0	9	4.5	15	43	32	36	0	7	1	306	23	7	4	4.5	.979	C-69
1960	STL N	78	.229	.352	179	41	4	0	6	3.4	16	27	22	24	0	27	7	279	25	2	5	3.9	.993	C-67
1961		86	.299	.517	174	52	8	0	10	5.7	23	33	25	17	0	39	10	218	19	1	3	2.8	.996	C-60, OF-1
1962		85	.252	.477	222	56	9	1	13	5.9	26	42	36	38	0	15	2	354	24	1	4	4.5	.987	C-70
1963		56	.238	.410	105	25	0	0	6	5.7	12	14	15	28	2	31	4	125	11	2	0	2.5	.986	C-27
11 yrs.		633	.242	.401	1449	351	46	5	58	4.0	133	213	191	251	2	209	41	1960	180	26	30	3.4	.988	C-457, OF-1

WORLD SERIES

Year	Team	Games	BA	SA	AB	H	2B	3B	HR	HR%	R	RBI	BB	SO	SB	PH AB	PH H	PO	A	E	DP	TC/G	FA	G by Pos
1957	MIL N	2	.000	.000	2	0	0	0	0	0.0	0	0	0	2	0	2	0	0	0	0	0	0.0	–	–

Carl Sawyer

SAWYER, CARL EVERETT (Huck)
B. Oct. 19, 1890, Seattle, Wash. D. Jan. 17, 1957, Los Angeles, Calif.

BR TR 5'11" 160 lbs.

Year	Team	Games	BA	SA	AB	H	2B	3B	HR	HR%	R	RBI	BB	SO	SB	PH AB	PH H	PO	A	E	DP	TC/G	FA	G by Pos
1915	WAS A	10	.250	.281	32	8	1	0	0	0.0	8	3	4	5	2	0	0	26	22	2	0	5.0	.960	2B-6, SS-4
1916		16	.194	.226	31	6	1	0	0	0.0	3	2	4	4	3	0	0	27	25	4	5	3.5	.929	2B-6, SS-5, 3B-1
2 yrs.		26	.222	.254	63	14	2	0	0	0.0	11	5	8	9	5	0	0	53	47	6	5	4.1	.943	2B-12, SS-9, 3B-1

Dave Sax

SAX, DAVID JOHN
Brother of Steve Sax.
B. Sept. 22, 1958, Sacramento, Calif.

BR TR 6' 185 lbs.

Year	Team	Games	BA	SA	AB	H	2B	3B	HR	HR%	R	RBI	BB	SO	SB	PH AB	PH H	PO	A	E	DP	TC/G	FA	G by Pos
1982	LA N	2	.000	.000	2	0	0	0	0	0.0	0	0	0	0	0	1	0	1	0	0	0	0.5	1.000	OF-1
1983		7	.000	.000	8	0	0	0	0	0.0	0	1	0	0	0	4	0	11	0	1	0	1.7	.917	C-4
1985	BOS A	22	.306	.389	36	11	3	0	0	0.0	2	6	3	3	0	0	0	66	0	1	0	3.0	.985	C-16, OF-4
1986		4	.455	.818	11	5	1	0	1	9.1	1	1	0	0	0	1	0	14	1	0	0	3.8	1.000	C-2, 1B-1
1987		2	.000	.000	3	0	0	0	0	0.0	0	0	0	1	0	1	0	9	0	0	0	4.5	1.000	C-2
5 yrs.		37	.267	.383	60	16	4	0	1	1.7	3	8	3	5	0	7	0	101	1	2	0	2.8	.981	C-24, OF-5, 1B-1

Ollie Sax

SAX, ERIK OLIVER
B. Nov. 5, 1904, Branford, Conn. D. Mar. 21, 1982, Newark, N. J.

BR TR 5'8" 164 lbs.

Year	Team	Games	BA	SA	AB	H	2B	3B	HR	HR%	R	RBI	BB	SO	SB	PH AB	PH H	PO	A	E	DP	TC/G	FA	G by Pos
1928	STL A	16	.176	.176	17	3	0	0	0	0.0	4	0	5	3	0	1	0	6	15	1	2	1.4	.955	3B-9

Steve Sax

SAX, STEPHEN LOUIS
Brother of Dave Sax.
B. Jan. 29, 1960, Sacramento, Calif.

BR TR 5'11" 185 lbs.

Year	Team	Games	BA	SA	AB	H	2B	3B	HR	HR%	R	RBI	BB	SO	SB	PH AB	PH H	PO	A	E	DP	TC/G	FA	G by Pos
1981	LA N	31	.277	.345	119	33	2	0	2	1.7	15	9	7	14	5	2	1	64	93	4	22	5.2	.975	2B-29
1982		150	.282	.359	638	180	23	7	4	0.6	88	47	49	53	49	1	1	347	452	19	83	5.5	.977	2B-149
1983		155	.281	.350	623	175	18	5	5	0.8	94	41	58	73	56	4	1	331	399	30	74	4.9	.961	2B-152
1984		145	.243	.304	569	138	24	4	1	0.2	70	35	47	53	34	3	0	318	450	21	99	5.4	.973	2B-141
1985		136	.279	.318	488	136	8	4	1	0.2	62	42	54	43	27	1	0	330	358	22	84	5.2	.969	2B-135, 3B-1
1986		157	.332	.441	633	210	43	4	6	0.9	91	56	59	58	40	3	1	367	432	16	71	5.2	.980	2B-154
1987		157	.280	.369	610	171	22	7	6	1.0	84	46	44	61	37	5	0	343	420	14	92	4.9	.982	2B-152, OF-1, 3B-1
1988	NY A	160	.277	.343	**632**	175	19	4	5	0.8	70	57	45	51	42	2	2	276	429	14	69	4.5	.981	2B-158
1989		158	.315	.387	**651**	205	26	3	5	0.8	88	52	52	44	43	0	0	312	460	10	117	4.9	.987	2B-158
9 yrs.		1249	.287	.360	4963	1423	185	38	35	0.7	662	396	415	450	333	21	6	2688	3493	150	711	5.1	.976	2B-1228, 3B-2, OF-1

DIVISIONAL PLAYOFF SERIES

Year	Team	Games	BA	SA	AB	H	2B	3B	HR	HR%	R	RBI	BB	SO	SB	PH AB	PH H	PO	A	E	DP	TC/G	FA	G by Pos
1981	LA N	1	–	–	0	0	0	0	0	–	0	0	0	0	0	0	0	0	0	0	0	0.0	–	2B-1

LEAGUE CHAMPIONSHIP SERIES

Year	Team	Games	BA	SA	AB	H	2B	3B	HR	HR%	R	RBI	BB	SO	SB	PH AB	PH H	PO	A	E	DP	TC/G	FA	G by Pos
1981	LA N	1	–	–	0	0	0	0	0	–	0	0	0	0	0	0	0	0	0	0	0	0.0	–	2B-1
1983		4	.250	.250	16	4	0	0	0	0.0	1	0	1	1	0	0	0	11	12	0	3	5.8	1.000	2B-4
1985		6	.300	.450	20	6	1	0	1	5.0	1	1	1	1	0	0	0	12	20	0	0	5.3	1.000	2B-6

Steve Sax *continued*

Year Team	Games	BA	SA	AB	H	2B	3B	HR	HR%	R	RBI	BB	SO	SB	PH AB	PH H	PO	A	E	DP	TC/G	FA	G by Pos
1988	7	.267	.267	30	8	0	0	0	0.0	7	3	3	3	5	0	0	12	22	0	6	4.9	1.000	2B-7
4 yrs.	18	.273	.318	66	18	3	0	0	0.0	8	4	5	8	6	0	0	35	54	0	9	4.9	1.000	2B-18

WORLD SERIES

Year Team	Games	BA	SA	AB	H	2B	3B	HR	HR%	R	RBI	BB	SO	SB	PH AB	PH H	PO	A	E	DP	TC/G	FA	G by Pos
1981 LA N	2	.000	.000	1	0	0	0	0	0.0	0	0	0	0	0	1	0	0	0	0	0	0.0	—	2B-1
1988	5	.300	.300	20	6	0	0	0	0.0	3	0	1	1	0	0	0	11	11	0	2	4.4	1.000	2B-5
2 yrs.	7	.286	.286	21	6	0	0	0	0.0	3	0	1	1	1	1	0	11	11	0	2	3.1	1.000	2B-6

Jimmy Say

SAY, JAMES I.
Brother of Lew Say.
B. 1862, Baltimore, Md. D. June 23, 1894, Baltimore, Md.

Year Team	Games	BA	SA	AB	H	2B	3B	HR	HR%	R	RBI	BB	SO	SB	PH AB	PH H	PO	A	E	DP	TC/G	FA	G by Pos
1882 2 teams	LOU AA (1G – .250)					PHI AA (22G – .207)																	
" total	23	.209	.233	86	18	2	0	0	0.0	13		1			0	0	32	76	16	10	5.4	.871	SS-22, 3B-1
1884 2 teams	WIL U (16G – .220)					KC U (2G – .250)																	
" total	18	.224	.299	67	15	1	2	0	0.0	3		1			0	0	12	22	16	2	2.8	.680	3B-18
1887 CLE AA	16	.375	.547	64	24	5	3	0	0.0	9		1		0	0	0	19	26	18	3	3.9	.714	3B-16
3 yrs.	57	.263	.346	217	57	8	5	0	0.0	25		3		0	0	0	63	124	50	15	4.2	.789	3B-35, SS-22

Lew Say

SAY, LOUIS I.
Brother of Jimmy Say.
B. Feb. 4, 1854, Baltimore, Md. D. June 5, 1930, Fallston, Md.
BR TR 5'7" 145 lbs.

Year Team	Games	BA	SA	AB	H	2B	3B	HR	HR%	R	RBI	BB	SO	SB	PH AB	PH H	PO	A	E	DP	TC/G	FA	G by Pos
1880 CIN N	48	.199	.251	191	38	8	1	0	0.0	14	15	4	31		0	0	54	164	44	11	5.5	.832	SS-48
1882 PHI AA	49	.226	.291	199	45	4	3	1	0.5	35		8			0	0	69	192	40	7	6.1	.867	SS-49
1883 BAL AA	74	.256	.318	324	83	13	2	1	0.3	52		10			0	0	76	241	82	13	5.4	.794	SS-74
1884 2 teams	BAL U (78G – .239)					KC U (17G – .200)																	
" total	95	.232	.303	409	95	16	2	3	0.7	71		13			0	0	131	302	102	19	5.6	.809	SS-94, 2B-1
4 yrs.	266	.232	.297	1123	261	41	8	5	0.4	172	15	35	31		0	0	330	899	268	50	5.6	.821	SS-265, 2B-1

Jerry Scala

SCALA, GERALD DANIEL
B. Sept. 27, 1926, Bayonne, N. J.
BL TR 5'11" 178 lbs.

Year Team	Games	BA	SA	AB	H	2B	3B	HR	HR%	R	RBI	BB	SO	SB	PH AB	PH H	PO	A	E	DP	TC/G	FA	G by Pos
1948 CHI A	3	.000	.000	6	0	0	0	0	0.0	1	0	0	3	0	0	0	5	0	0	0	1.7	1.000	OF-2
1949	37	.250	.350	120	30	7	1	1	0.8	17	13	17	19	3	5	1	83	1	1	0	2.3	.988	OF-37
1950	40	.194	.254	67	13	2	1	0	0.0	8	6	10	10	0	5	3	43	1	0	0	1.1	1.000	OF-23
3 yrs.	80	.223	.306	193	43	9	2	1	0.5	26	19	27	32	3	10	4	131	2	1	0	1.7	.993	OF-62

Frank Scalzi

SCALZI, FRANK JOHN (Skeeter)
B. June 16, 1913, Lafferty, Ohio D. Aug. 25, 1984, Pittsburgh, Pa.
BR TR 5'6" 160 lbs.

Year Team	Games	BA	SA	AB	H	2B	3B	HR	HR%	R	RBI	BB	SO	SB	PH AB	PH H	PO	A	E	DP	TC/G	FA	G by Pos
1939 NY N	11	.333	.333	18	6	0	0	0	0.0	3	0	3	2	1	2	0	10	18	4	3	2.9	.875	SS-5, 3B-1

Johnny Scalzi

SCALZI, JOHN ANTHONY
B. Mar. 22, 1907, Stamford, Conn. D. Sept. 27, 1962, Port Chester, N. Y.
BR TR 5'7" 170 lbs.

Year Team	Games	BA	SA	AB	H	2B	3B	HR	HR%	R	RBI	BB	SO	SB	PH AB	PH H	PO	A	E	DP	TC/G	FA	G by Pos
1931 BOS N	2	.000	.000	1	0	0	0	0	0.0	0	0	0	1	0	1	0	0	0	0	0	0.0	—	

Mort Scanlan

SCANLAN, MORTIMER J.
B. Mar. 18, 1861, Chicago, Ill. D. Dec. 29, 1928, Chicago, Ill.
6'1" 186 lbs.

Year Team	Games	BA	SA	AB	H	2B	3B	HR	HR%	R	RBI	BB	SO	SB	PH AB	PH H	PO	A	E	DP	TC/G	FA	G by Pos
1890 NY N	3	.000	.000	10	0	0	0	0	0.0	0	0	2	5	1	0	0	28	0	0	2	9.3	1.000	1B-3

Pat Scanlon

SCANLON, JAMES PATRICK
B. Sept. 23, 1952, Minneapolis, Minn.
BL TR 6' 180 lbs.

Year Team	Games	BA	SA	AB	H	2B	3B	HR	HR%	R	RBI	BB	SO	SB	PH AB	PH H	PO	A	E	DP	TC/G	FA	G by Pos
1974 MON N	2	.250	.250	4	1	0	0	0	0.0	0	1			0	1	0	0	3	0	0	1.5	1.000	3B-1
1975	60	.183	.284	109	20	3	1	2	1.8	5	15	17	25	0	26	3	12	57	3	4	1.2	.958	3B-28, 1B-1
1976	11	.185	.333	27	5	1	0	1	3.7	2	2	2	5	0	4	1	11	12	3	0	2.4	.885	3B-7, 1B-1
1977 SD N	47	.190	.266	79	15	3	0	1	1.3	9	11	12	20	0	21	2	22	41	3	5	1.4	.955	2B-15, 3B-11, OF-1
4 yrs.	120	.187	.283	219	41	7	1	4	1.8	17	28	31	51	0	52	6	45	113	9	9	1.4	.946	3B-47, 2B-15, 1B-2, OF-1

John Scannell

SCANNELL, JOHN J.
Deceased.

Year Team	Games	BA	SA	AB	H	2B	3B	HR	HR%	R	RBI	BB	SO	SB	PH AB	PH H	PO	A	E	DP	TC/G	FA	G by Pos
1884 BOS U	6	.292	.333	24	7	1	0	0	0.0	2		0			0	0	6	2	2	0	1.7	.800	OF-6

Russ Scarritt

SCARRITT, RUSSELL MALLORY
B. Jan. 14, 1903, Pensacola, Fla.
BL TR 5'10½" 165 lbs.

Year Team	Games	BA	SA	AB	H	2B	3B	HR	HR%	R	RBI	BB	SO	SB	PH AB	PH H	PO	A	E	DP	TC/G	FA	G by Pos
1929 BOS A	151	.294	.411	540	159	26	17	1	0.2	69	71	34	38	13	4	1	302	16	19	6	2.2	.944	OF-145
1930	113	.289	.376	447	129	17	8	2	0.4	48	48	12	49	4	3	0	256	5	9	0	2.4	.967	OF-110
1931	10	.154	.179	39	6	1	0	0	0.0	2	1	2	2	0	2	0	20	1	0	0	2.1	1.000	OF-9
1932 PHI N	11	.182	.182	11	2	0	0	0	0.0	0	0	1	2	0	6	1	2	0	0	0	0.2	1.000	OF-1
4 yrs.	285	.285	.385	1037	296	44	25	3	0.3	119	120	49	91	17	14	2	580	22	28	6	2.2	.956	OF-265

Les Scarsella

SCARSELLA, LESLIE GEORGE
B. Nov. 23, 1913, Santa Cruz, Calif. D. Dec. 17, 1958, San Francisco, Calif.
BL TL 5'11" 185 lbs.

Year Team	Games	BA	SA	AB	H	2B	3B	HR	HR%	R	RBI	BB	SO	SB	PH AB	PH H	PO	A	E	DP	TC/G	FA	G by Pos
1935 CIN N	6	.200	.300	10	2	1	0	0	0.0	4	0	3	1	0	2	0	17	3	0	2	3.3	1.000	1B-2
1936	115	.313	.412	485	152	21	9	3	0.6	63	65	14	36	6	0	0	1109	84	13	90	10.5	.989	1B-115
1937	110	.246	.331	329	81	11	4	3	0.9	35	34	17	26	5	27	9	607	38	11	55	6.0	.983	1B-65, OF-14
1939	16	.143	.143	14	2	0	0	0	0.0	0	2	0	2	0	14	2	0	0	0	0	0.0	—	
1940 BOS N	15	.300	.417	60	18	1	3	0	0.0	7	8	3	3	1	3	1	137	7	2	17	9.7	.986	1B-12
5 yrs.	262	.284	.378	898	255	34	16	6	0.7	109	109	37	70	13	46	12	1870	132	26	164	7.7	.987	1B-194, OF-14

Paul Schaal

SCHAAL, PAUL
B. Mar. 3, 1943, Pittsburgh, Pa.
BR TR 5'11" 165 lbs.

Year Team	Games	BA	SA	AB	H	2B	3B	HR	HR%	R	RBI	BB	SO	SB	PH AB	PH H	PO	A	E	DP	TC/G	FA	G by Pos
1964 LA A	17	.125	.125	32	4	0	0	0	0.0	3	0	2	5	0	0	0	5	22	2	2	1.7	.931	3B-9, 2B-9

Year	Team	Games	BA	SA	AB	H	2B	3B	HR	HR%	R	RBI	BB	SO	SB	Pinch Hit AB	Pinch Hit H	PO	A	E	DP	TC/G	FA	G by Pos

Paul Schaal *continued*

Year	Team	Games	BA	SA	AB	H	2B	3B	HR	HR%	R	RBI	BB	SO	SB	AB	H	PO	A	E	DP	TC/G	FA	G by Pos
1965	CAL A	155	.224	.313	483	108	12	2	9	1.9	48	45	61	88	6	1	1	101	321	13	20	2.8	.970	3B-153, 2B-1
1966		138	.244	.365	386	94	15	7	6	1.6	59	24	68	56	6	4	0	97	249	19	21	2.6	.948	3B-131
1967		99	.188	.294	272	51	9	1	6	2.2	31	20	38	39	2	7	0	79	158	7	11	2.5	.971	3B-88, SS-2, 2B-1
1968		60	.210	.279	219	46	7	1	2	0.9	22	16	29	25	5	2	0	61	142	9	13	3.5	.958	3B-58
1969	KC A	61	.263	.307	205	54	6	0	1	0.5	22	13	25	27	2	3	0	41	103	15	5	2.6	.906	3B-49, SS-6, 2B-6
1970		124	.268	.355	380	102	12	3	5	1.3	50	35	43	39	7	17	3	95	196	19	19	2.5	.939	3B-97, SS-10, 2B-6
1971		161	.274	.412	548	150	31	6	11	2.0	80	63	103	51	7	0	0	107	335	28	31	2.9	.940	3B-161
1972		127	.228	.326	435	99	19	3	6	1.4	47	41	61	59	1	3	1	77	245	18	16	2.7	.947	3B-123, SS-1
1973		121	.288	.399	396	114	14	3	8	2.0	61	42	63	45	5	1	0	77	237	30	14	2.8	.913	3B-121
1974	2 teams	KC A	(12G – .176)		CAL A	(53G – .248)																		
"	total	65	.236	.317	199	47	7	0	3	1.5	13	24	23	32	2	3	0	35	104	13	13	2.3	.914	3B-63
11 yrs.		1128	.244	.344	3555	869	132	26	57	1.6	436	323	516	466	43	41	5	775	2112	173	165	2.7	.943	3B-1053, 2B-23, SS-19

Germany Schaefer

SCHAEFER, HERMAN A.
B. Feb. 4, 1877, Chicago, Ill. D. May 16, 1919, Saranac Lake, N. Y.

BR TR 5'9" 175 lbs.

Year	Team	Games	BA	SA	AB	H	2B	3B	HR	HR%	R	RBI	BB	SO	SB	AB	H	PO	A	E	DP	TC/G	FA	G by Pos
1901	CHI N	2	.600	.800	5	3	1	0	0	0.0	0	0	0	2		0	0	6	4	0	1	5.0	1.000	3B-1, 2B-1
1902		81	.196	.223	291	57	2	3	0	0.0	32	14	19		12	0	0	143	156	43	14	4.2	.874	3B-75, 1B-3, OF-2, SS-1
1905	DET A	153	.244	.318	554	135	17	9	2	0.4	64	47	45		19	0	0	410	394	37	35	5.5	.956	2B-151, SS-3
1906		124	.238	.296	446	106	14	3	2	0.4	48	42	32		31	2	1	368	352	43	45	6.2	.944	2B-114, SS-7
1907		109	.258	.315	372	96	12	3	1	0.3	45	32	30		21	2	0	239	286	23	23	5.0	.958	2B-74, SS-18, 3B-14, OF-1
1908		153	.259	.342	584	151	20	10	3	0.5	96	52	37		40	0	0	319	479	57	58	5.6	.933	SS-68, 2B-58, 3B-29
1909	2 teams	DET A	(87G – .250)		WAS A	(37G – .242)																		
"	total	124	.248	.301	408	101	17	1	1	0.2	39	26	20		14	4	0	235	356	26	42	5.0	.958	2B-118, OF-1, 3B-1
1910	WAS A	74	.275	.345	229	63	6	5	0	0.0	27	14	25		17	10	2	90	113	11	16	2.9	.949	2B-35, OF-26, 3B-2
1911		125	.334	.398	440	147	14	7	0	0.0	74	45	57		22	9	3	1048	71	23	57	9.1	.980	1B-108, OF-7
1912		60	.247	.325	166	41	7	3	0	0.0	21	19	23		11	11	2	169	30	8	7	3.5	.961	OF-19, 2B-15, 1B-15, P-1
1913		52	.320	.350	100	32	1	1	0	0.0	17	7	15	12	6	21	11	91	40	7	6	2.7	.949	2B-17, 1B-5, 3B-2, OF-1, P-1
1914		25	.241	.276	29	7	1	0	0	0.0	6	2	3	5	4	14	3	6	4	1	0	0.4	.909	OF-3, 2B-3
1915	NWK F	59	.214	.286	154	33	5	3	0	0.0	26	8	25		3	15	2	146	31	7	12	3.1	.962	OF-17, 1B-13, 3B-9, 2B-2
1916	NY A	1	–	–	0	0	0	0	0	–	0	0	0	0	0	0	0	0	0	0	0	0.0	–	OF-1
1918	CLE A	1	.000	.000	5	0	0	0	0	0.0	2	0	0	0	1	0	0	3	3	0	0	6.0	1.000	2B-1
15 yrs.		1143	.257	.320	3783	972	117	48	9	0.2	497	308	333	17	201	88	24	3273	2319	286	316	5.1	.951	2B-589, 1B-144, 3B-133, SS-97, OF-78, P-2

WORLD SERIES

Year	Team	Games	BA	SA	AB	H	2B	3B	HR	HR%	R	RBI	BB	SO	SB	AB	H	PO	A	E	DP	TC/G	FA	G by Pos
1907	DET A	5	.143	.143	21	3	0	0	0	0.0	1	0	0	3	1	0	0	12	21	0	2	6.6	1.000	2B-5
1908		5	.125	.125	16	2	0	0	0	0.0	0	0	1	4	0	0	0	10	11	1	3	4.4	.955	2B-3, 3B-2
2 yrs.		10	.135	.135	37	5	0	0	0	0.0	1	0	1	7	1	0	0	22	32	1	5	5.5	.982	2B-8, 3B-2

Jeff Schaefer

SCHAEFER, JEFFREY SCOTT
B. May 31, 1960, Patchogue, N. Y.

BR TR 5'10" 170 lbs.

Year	Team	Games	BA	SA	AB	H	2B	3B	HR	HR%	R	RBI	BB	SO	SB	AB	H	PO	A	E	DP	TC/G	FA	G by Pos
1989	CHI A	15	.100	.100	10	1	0	0	0	0.0	2	0	0	2	1	0	0	5	7	2	4	0.9	.857	SS-5, 3B-4, 2B-4, DH-1

Harry Schafer

SCHAFER, HARRY C. (Silk Stocking)
B. Aug. 14, 1846, Philadelphia, Pa. D. Feb. 28, 1935, Philadelphia, Pa.

BR TR 5'9½" 143 lbs.

Year	Team	Games	BA	SA	AB	H	2B	3B	HR	HR%	R	RBI	BB	SO	SB	AB	H	PO	A	E	DP	TC/G	FA	G by Pos
1876	BOS N	70	.252	.290	286	72	11	0	0	0.0	47	35	4	11		0	0	122	146	63	8	4.7	.810	3B-70
1877		33	.277	.340	141	39	5	2	0	0.0	20	13	0	7		0	0	34	8	17	1	1.8	.712	OF-23, 3B-9, SS-1
1878		2	.125	.125	8	1	0	0	0	0.0	0	0	0	1		0	0	2	0	0	0	1.0	1.000	OF-2
3 yrs.		105	.257	.303	435	112	16	2	0	0.0	67	48	4	19		0	0	158	154	80	9	3.7	.796	3B-79, OF-25, SS-1

Jimmie Schaffer

SCHAFFER, JIMMIE RONALD
B. Apr. 5, 1936, Limeport, Pa.

BR TR 5'9" 170 lbs.

Year	Team	Games	BA	SA	AB	H	2B	3B	HR	HR%	R	RBI	BB	SO	SB	AB	H	PO	A	E	DP	TC/G	FA	G by Pos
1961	STL N	68	.255	.320	153	39	7	0	1	0.7	15	16	9	29	0	1	1	244	23	1	6	3.9	.996	C-68
1962		70	.242	.303	66	16	2	1	0	0.0	7	6	6	16	1	1	0	134	10	1	1	2.1	.993	C-69
1963	CHI N	57	.239	.437	142	34	7	0	7	4.9	17	19	11	35	0	1	0	231	23	1	3	4.5	.996	C-54
1964		54	.205	.320	122	25	6	1	2	1.6	9	9	17	17	2	9	3	143	19	5	1	3.1	.970	C-43
1965	2 teams	CHI A	(17G – .194)		NY N	(24G – .135)																		
"	total	41	.162	.265	68	11	5	1	0	0.0	2	1	4	19	0	7	0	110	8	2	2	2.9	.983	C-35
1966	PHI N	18	.133	.400	15	2	1	0	1	6.7	2	4	1	7	0	0	0	17	3	1	1	1.2	.952	C-6
1967		2	.000	.000	2	0	0	0	0	0.0	1	0	1	0	0	0	0	5	0	0	0	2.5	1.000	C-1
1968	CIN N	4	.167	.167	6	1	0	0	0	0.0	0	1	0	3	0	2	0	4	0	0	0	1.0	1.000	C-2
8 yrs.		314	.223	.340	574	128	28	3	11	1.9	53	56	49	127	3	23	4	888	86	11	14	3.1	.989	C-278

Johnny Schaive

SCHAIVE, JOHN EDWARD
B. Feb. 25, 1934, Springfield, Ill.

BR TR 5'8" 175 lbs.

Year	Team	Games	BA	SA	AB	H	2B	3B	HR	HR%	R	RBI	BB	SO	SB	AB	H	PO	A	E	DP	TC/G	FA	G by Pos
1958	WAS A	7	.250	.250	24	6	0	0	0	0.0	1	1	1	4	0	1	0	18	13	0	4	4.4	1.000	2B-6
1959		16	.153	.186	59	9	2	0	0	0.0	3	2	0	7	0	0	0	32	52	2	10	5.4	.977	2B-16
1960		6	.250	.333	12	3	1	0	0	0.0	1	0	0	3	0	3	1	5	6	1	2	2.0	.917	2B-4
1962		82	.253	.409	225	57	15	1	6	2.7	20	29	6	25	0	27	5	53	117	5	8	2.1	.971	3B-49, 2B-6
1963		3	.000	.000	3	0	0	0	0	0.0	0	0	0	1	0	3	0	0	0	0	0	0.0	–	
5 yrs.		114	.232	.350	323	75	18	1	6	1.9	25	32	7	40	0	34	6	108	188	8	24	2.7	.974	3B-49, 2B-32

Ray Schalk

SCHALK, RAYMOND WILLIAM (Cracker)
B. Aug. 12, 1892, Harvel, Ill. D. May 19, 1970, Chicago, Ill.
Manager 1927-28.
Hall of Fame 1955.

BR TR 5'9" 165 lbs.

Year	Team	Games	BA	SA	AB	H	2B	3B	HR	HR%	R	RBI	BB	SO	SB	AB	H	PO	A	E	DP	TC/G	FA	G by Pos
1912	CHI A	23	.286	.317	63	18	2	0	0	0.0	7	8	3		2	0	0	115	40	14	4	7.3	.917	C-23
1913		128	.244	.314	401	98	15	5	1	0.2	38	38	27	36	14	3	0	599	154	15	18	6.0	.980	C-125
1914		135	.270	.314	392	106	13	2	0	0.0	30	36	38	24	24	9	3	613	183	21	20	6.1	.974	C-124
1915		135	.266	.327	413	110	14	4	1	0.2	46	54	62	21	15	1	1	655	159	13	8	6.1	.984	C-134
1916		129	.232	.305	410	95	12	6	0	0.0	36	41	41	31	30	0	0	653	166	10	25	6.4	.988	C-124

Year	Team	Games	BA	SA	AB	H	2B	3B	HR	HR%	R	RBI	BB	SO	SB	Pinch Hit AB	Pinch Hit H	PO	A	E	DP	TC/G	FA	G by Pos

Ray Schalk *continued*

Year	Team	Games	BA	SA	AB	H	2B	3B	HR	HR%	R	RBI	BB	SO	SB	PH AB	PH H	PO	A	E	DP	TC/G	FA	G by Pos
1917		140	.226	.295	424	96	12	4	3	0.7	48	51	59	27	19	1	0	624	148	15	13	5.6	.981	C-139
1918		108	.219	.255	333	73	6	3	0	0.0	35	22	36	22	12	2	1	422	114	12	15	5.1	.978	C-106
1919		131	.282	.320	394	111	9	3	0	0.0	57	34	51	25	11	2	0	551	130	13	14	5.3	.981	C-129
1920		151	.270	.348	485	131	25	5	1	0.2	64	61	68	19	10	0	0	581	138	10	19	4.8	.986	C-151
1921		128	.252	.329	416	105	24	4	0	0.0	32	47	40	36	3	2	0	453	129	9	18	4.6	.985	C-125
1922		142	.281	.371	442	124	22	3	4	0.9	57	60	67	36	12	0	0	591	150	8	16	5.3	.989	C-142
1923		123	.228	.277	382	87	12	2	1	0.3	42	44	39	28	6	2	0	481	93	10	20	4.7	.983	C-121
1924		57	.196	.268	153	30	4	2	1	0.7	15	11	21	10	1	1	0	179	55	10	8	4.3	.959	C-56
1925		125	.274	.332	343	94	18	1	0	0.0	44	52	57	27	11	0	0	368	99	8	15	3.8	.983	C-125
1926		82	.265	.314	226	60	9	1	0	0.0	26	32	27	11	5	1	0	251	45	7	6	3.7	.977	C-80
1927		16	.231	.308	26	6	2	0	0	0.0	2	2	2	1	0	1	0	24	8	0	1	2.0	1.000	C-15
1928		2	1.000	1.000	1	1	0	0	0	0.0	0	0	0	0	0	0	0	4	0	0	0	2.0	1.000	C-1
1929	NY N	5	.000	.000	2	0	0	0	0	0.0	0	0	0	1	0	0	0	7	0	0	0	1.4	1.000	C-5
18 yrs.		1760	.253	.316	5306	1345	199	48	12	0.2	579	594	638	355	176	28	5	7171	1811	175	221	5.2	.981	C-1726

WORLD SERIES

Year	Team	Games	BA	SA	AB	H	2B	3B	HR	HR%	R	RBI	BB	SO	SB	PH AB	PH H	PO	A	E	DP	TC/G	FA	G by Pos
1917	CHI A	6	.263	.263	19	5	0	0	0	0.0	1	0	2	1	1	0	0	32	6	1	1	6.7	.950	C-6
1919		8	.304	.304	23	7	0	0	0	0.0	1	2	4	2	1	0	0	29	15	1	1	5.6	.978	C-8
2 yrs.		14	.286	.286	42	12	0	0	0	0.0	2	2	6	3	2	0	0	61	21	3	2	6.1	.965	C-14

Roy Schalk

SCHALK, LeROY JOHN
B. Nov. 9, 1908, Chicago, Ill.

BR TR 5'10" 168 lbs.

Year	Team	Games	BA	SA	AB	H	2B	3B	HR	HR%	R	RBI	BB	SO	SB	PH AB	PH H	PO	A	E	DP	TC/G	FA	G by Pos
1932	NY A	3	.250	.333	12	3	1	0	0	0.0	3	0	2	0	0	0	0	4	9	2	1	5.0	.867	2B-3
1944	CHI A	146	.220	.262	587	129	14	4	1	0.2	47	44	45	52	5	0	0	366	413	29	112	5.5	.964	2B-142, SS-5
1945		133	.248	.302	513	127	23	1	1	0.2	50	65	32	41	3	0	0	380	389	18	90	5.9	.977	2B-133
3 yrs.		282	.233	.281	1112	259	38	5	2	0.2	100	109	79	93	8	0	0	750	811	49	203	5.7	.970	2B-278, SS-5

Biff Schaller

SCHALLER, WALTER
B. Sept. 23, 1889, Chicago, Ill. D. Oct. 9, 1939, Emeryville, Calif.

BL TR 5'11" 168 lbs.

Year	Team	Games	BA	SA	AB	H	2B	3B	HR	HR%	R	RBI	BB	SO	SB	PH AB	PH H	PO	A	E	DP	TC/G	FA	G by Pos
1911	DET A	40	.133	.217	60	8	0	1	1	1.7	8	7	4		1	17	6	27	2	0	1	0.7	1.000	OF-16, 1B-1
1913	CHI A	34	.219	.250	96	21	3	0	0	0.0	12	4	20	16	5	2	0	45	0	4	0	1.4	.918	OF-32
2 yrs.		74	.186	.237	156	29	3	1	1	0.6	20	11	24	16	6	19	6	72	2	4	1	1.1	.949	OF-48, 1B-1

Bobby Schang

SCHANG, ROBERT MARTIN
Brother of Wally Schang.
B. Dec. 7, 1886, Wales Center, N. Y. D. Aug. 29, 1966, Sacramento, Calif.

BR TR 5'7" 165 lbs.

Year	Team	Games	BA	SA	AB	H	2B	3B	HR	HR%	R	RBI	BB	SO	SB	PH AB	PH H	PO	A	E	DP	TC/G	FA	G by Pos
1914	PIT N	11	.229	.314	35	8	1	0	0	0.0	0	1	0	10	0	1	0	42	12	2	1	5.1	.964	C-10
1915	2 teams		PIT N	(56G – .184)		NY N	(12G – .143)																		
"	total	68	.178	.260	146	26	6	3	0	0.0	14	5	18	37	3	9	0	167	50	9	4	3.3	.960	C-50
1927	STL N	3	.200	.200	5	1	0	0	0	0.0	0	0	0	0	0	0	0	3	1	0	0	1.3	1.000	C-3
3 yrs.		82	.188	.269	186	35	7	4	0	0.0	14	6	18	47	3	10	0	212	63	11	5	3.5	.962	C-63

Wally Schang

SCHANG, WALTER HENRY
Brother of Bobby Schang.
B. Aug. 22, 1889, South Wales, N. Y. D. Mar. 6, 1965, St. Louis, Mo.

BB TR 5'10" 180 lbs.
BR 1927-28

Year	Team	Games	BA	SA	AB	H	2B	3B	HR	HR%	R	RBI	BB	SO	SB	PH AB	PH H	PO	A	E	DP	TC/G	FA	G by Pos
1913	PHI A	77	.266	.415	207	55	16	3	3	1.4	32	30	34	44	4	4	1	317	97	14	9	5.6	.967	C-71
1914		107	.287	.404	307	88	11	8	3	1.0	44	45	32	33	7	5	1	498	154	30	11	6.4	.956	C-100
1915		116	.248	.343	359	89	9	11	1	0.3	64	44	66	47	18	5	1	240	139	40	12	3.6	.905	3B-43, OF-41, C-26
1916		110	.266	.420	338	90	15	8	7	2.1	41	38	38	44	14	11	0	266	77	19	6	3.3	.948	OF-61, C-36
1917		118	.285	.415	316	90	14	9	3	0.9	41	36	29	24	6	18	2	293	127	20	13	3.7	.955	C-79, 3B-12, OF-7
1918	BOS A	88	.244	.284	225	55	7	1	0	0.0	36	20	46	35	4	8	3	207	58	14	5	3.2	.950	C-57, OF-16, 3B-5, SS-1
1919		113	.306	.373	330	101	16	3	0	0.0	43	55	71	42	15	5	0	359	131	14	15	4.5	.972	C-103
1920		122	.305	.450	387	118	30	7	4	1.0	58	51	64	37	7	8	1	377	83	18	8	3.9	.962	C-73, OF-40
1921	NY A	134	.316	.453	424	134	30	5	6	1.4	77	55	78	35	7	2	0	500	101	19	13	4.6	.969	C-132
1922		124	.319	.412	408	130	21	7	1	0.2	46	53	53	36	12	5	1	456	102	14	12	4.6	.976	C-124
1923		84	.276	.342	272	75	8	2	2	0.7	39	29	27	17	5	2	0	292	60	11	6	4.3	.970	C-81
1924		114	.292	.427	356	104	19	7	5	1.4	46	52	48	43	2	4	0	423	89	15	9	4.6	.972	C-109
1925		73	.240	.335	167	40	8	1	2	1.2	17	24	17	9	3	11	2	172	55	6	8	3.2	.974	C-58
1926	STL A	103	.330	.516	285	94	19	5	8	2.8	36	50	32	20	5	17	7	232	75	10	7	3.1	.968	C-82, OF-3
1927		97	.319	.449	263	84	15	2	5	1.9	40	42	41	33	3	18	6	213	73	7	10	3.0	.976	C-75
1928		91	.286	.404	245	70	10	5	3	1.2	41	39	68	26	8	7	3	263	46	5	6	3.5	.984	C-82
1929		94	.237	.378	249	59	10	5	5	2.0	43	36	74	22	1	7	1	268	56	4	6	3.5	.988	C-85
1930	PHI A	45	.174	.272	92	16	4	1	1	1.1	16	9	17	15	0	6	1	126	18	4	2	3.3	.973	C-36
1931	DET A	30	.184	.211	76	14	2	0	0	0.0	9	11	14	11	1	0	0	91	20	4	6	3.8	.965	C-30
19 yrs.		1840	.284	.401	5306	1506	264	90	59	1.1	769	710	849	573	122	143	30	5593	1561	268	163	4.0	.964	C-1439, OF-168, 3B-60, SS-1

WORLD SERIES

Year	Team	Games	BA	SA	AB	H	2B	3B	HR	HR%	R	RBI	BB	SO	SB	PH AB	PH H	PO	A	E	DP	TC/G	FA	G by Pos
1913	PHI A	4	.357	.714	14	5	0	1	1	7.1	2	6	2	4	0	0	0	16	4	1	1	5.3	.952	C-4
1914		4	.167	.250	12	2	1	0	0	0.0	0	0	1	4	0	0	0	17	3	1	0	5.3	.952	C-4
1918	BOS A	5	.444	.444	9	4	0	0	0	0.0	1	1	2	3	1	2	1	9	4	0	0	2.6	1.000	C-5
1921	NY A	8	.286	.429	21	6	1	1	0	0.0	1	1	5	4	0	0	0	39	11	0	3	6.3	1.000	C-8
1922		5	.188	.250	16	3	1	0	0	0.0	1	0	1	2	0	0	0	19	4	0	0	4.6	1.000	C-5
1923		6	.318	.364	22	7	1	0	0	0.0	3	0	1	3	0	0	0	21	2	1	0	4.0	.958	C-6
6 yrs.		32	.287	.404	94	27	4	2	1	1.1	8	8	11	20	1	2	1	121	28	3	4	4.8	.980	C-32

Art Scharein

SCHAREIN, ARTHUR OTTO (Scoop)
Brother of George Scharein.
B. June 30, 1905, Decatur, Ill. D. July 2, 1969, San Antonio, Tex.

BR TR 6' 175 lbs.

Year	Team	Games	BA	SA	AB	H	2B	3B	HR	HR%	R	RBI	BB	SO	SB	PH AB	PH H	PO	A	E	DP	TC/G	FA	G by Pos
1932	STL A	81	.304	.380	303	92	19	2	0	0.0	43	42	25	10	4	0	0	107	189	12	26	3.8	.961	3B-77, SS-3, 2B-2
1933		123	.204	.244	471	96	13	3	0	0.0	49	26	41	21	7	2	0	158	286	22	43	3.8	.953	3B-95, SS-24, 2B-7

Year	Team	Games	BA	SA	AB	H	2B	3B	HR	HR%	R	RBI	BB	SO	SB	Pinch Hit AB	Pinch Hit H	PO	A	E	DP	TC/G	FA	G by Pos

Art Scharein *continued*

Year	Team	Games	BA	SA	AB	H	2B	3B	HR	HR%	R	RBI	BB	SO	SB	AB	H	PO	A	E	DP	TC/G	FA	G by Pos
1934		1	.500	.500	2	1	0	0	0	0.0	0	2	0	0	0	2	1	0	0	0	0	0.0	—	3B-1
3 yrs.		205	.244	.298	776	189	32	5	0	0.0	92	70	66	31	11	4	1	265	475	34	69	3.8	.956	3B-172, SS-27, 2B-9

George Scharein

SCHAREIN, GEORGE ALBERT (Tom)
Brother of Art Scharein.
B. Nov. 21, 1914, Decatur, Ill. D. Dec. 23, 1981, Decatur, Ill.

BR TR 6'1" 174 lbs.

Year	Team	Games	BA	SA	AB	H	2B	3B	HR	HR%	R	RBI	BB	SO	SB	AB	H	PO	A	E	DP	TC/G	FA	G by Pos
1937	PHI N	146	.241	.284	511	123	20	1	0	0.0	44	57	36	47	13	0	0	335	456	44	98	5.7	.947	SS-146
1938		117	.238	.308	390	93	16	4	1	0.3	47	29	16	33	11	1	0	246	327	37	57	5.2	.939	SS-77, 2B-39, 3B-1
1939		118	.238	.293	399	95	17	1	1	0.3	35	33	13	40	4	0	0	258	331	26	69	5.2	.958	SS-117
1940		7	.294	.294	17	5	0	0	0	0.0	0	0	0	3	0	0	0	13	13	5	2	4.4	.839	SS-7
4 yrs.		388	.240	.294	1317	316	53	6	2	0.2	126	119	65	123	28	1	0	852	1127	112	226	5.4	.946	SS-347, 2B-39, 3B-1

Nick Scharf

SCHARF, EDWARD T.
B. 1859, Baltimore, Md. D. May 12, 1937, Baltimore, Md.

TR

Year	Team	Games	BA	SA	AB	H	2B	3B	HR	HR%	R	RBI	BB	SO	SB	AB	H	PO	A	E	DP	TC/G	FA	G by Pos
1882	BAL AA	10	.205	.359	39	8	1	1	1	2.6	4		0			0	0	16	1	6	0	2.3	.739	OF-9, 3B-1
1883		3	.154	.231	13	2	1	0	0	0.0	1		1			0	0	3	6	5	1	4.7	.643	SS-3
2 yrs.		13	.192	.327	52	10	2	1	1	1.9	5		1			0	0	19	7	11	1	2.8	.703	OF-9, SS-3, 3B-1

Al Scheer

SCHEER, ALLEN G.
B. Oct. 21, 1888, Dayton, Ohio D. May 6, 1959, Logansport, Ind.

BL TR 5'9" 165 lbs.

Year	Team	Games	BA	SA	AB	H	2B	3B	HR	HR%	R	RBI	BB	SO	SB	AB	H	PO	A	E	DP	TC/G	FA	G by Pos
1913	BKN N	6	.227	.227	22	5	0	0	0	0.0	3	0	2	4	1	0	0	3	1	1	0	0.8	.800	OF-6
1914	IND F	120	.306	.427	363	111	23	6	3	0.8	63	45	49		9	13	5	152	21	13	2	1.6	.930	OF-102, 2B-4, SS-1
1915	NWK F	155	.267	.375	546	146	25	14	2	0.4	75	60	65		31	0	0	287	16	9	5	2.0	.971	OF-155
3 yrs.		281	.281	.392	931	262	48	20	5	0.5	141	105	116	4	41	13	5	442	38	23	7	1.8	.954	OF-263, 2B-4, SS-1

Heinie Scheer

SCHEER, HENRY WILLIAM
B. July 31, 1900, New York, N. Y. D. Mar. 21, 1976, New Haven, Conn.

BR TR 5'8" 146 lbs.

Year	Team	Games	BA	SA	AB	H	2B	3B	HR	HR%	R	RBI	BB	SO	SB	AB	H	PO	A	E	DP	TC/G	FA	G by Pos
1922	PHI A	51	.170	.281	135	23	3	0	4	3.0	10	12	3	25	1	10	2	71	124	7	9	4.0	.965	2B-29, 3B-10
1923		69	.238	.314	210	50	8	1	2	1.0	26	21	17	41	3	4	0	147	156	9	30	4.5	.971	2B-61
2 yrs.		120	.212	.301	345	73	11	1	6	1.7	36	33	20	66	4	14	2	218	280	16	39	4.3	.969	2B-90, 3B-10

Fritz Scheeren

SCHEEREN, FREDERICK (Dutch)
B. Sept. 8, 1891, Kokomo, Ind. D. June 17, 1973, Oil City, Pa.

BR TR 6' 180 lbs.

Year	Team	Games	BA	SA	AB	H	2B	3B	HR	HR%	R	RBI	BB	SO	SB	AB	H	PO	A	E	DP	TC/G	FA	G by Pos
1914	PIT N	11	.290	.452	31	9	0	1	1	3.2	4	2	1	6	1	1	0	14	0	3	0	1.5	.824	OF-10
1915		4	.000	.000	3	0	0	0	0	0.0	0	0	0	0	0	3	0	0	0	0	0	0.0	—	OF-1
2 yrs.		15	.265	.412	34	9	0	1	1	2.9	4	2	1	6	1	4	0	14	0	3	0	1.1	.824	OF-11

Bob Scheffing

SCHEFFING, ROBERT BODEN
B. Aug. 11, 1913, Overland, Mo. D. Oct. 26, 1985, Phoenix, Ariz.
Manager 1957-59, 1961-63.

BR TR 6'2" 180 lbs.

Year	Team	Games	BA	SA	AB	H	2B	3B	HR	HR%	R	RBI	BB	SO	SB	AB	H	PO	A	E	DP	TC/G	FA	G by Pos
1941	CHI N	51	.242	.326	132	32	8	0	1	0.8	9	20	5	19	2	17	3	126	17	5	1	2.9	.966	C-34
1942		44	.196	.284	102	20	8	0	2	2.0	7	12	7	11	2	12	1	122	16	2	6	3.2	.986	C-32
1946		63	.278	.330	115	32	4	1	0	0.0	8	18	12	18	0	19	7	97	10	0	3	1.7	1.000	C-43
1947		110	.264	.364	363	96	11	5	5	1.4	33	50	25	25	0	13	5	379	52	7	4	4.0	.984	C-97
1948		102	.300	.427	293	88	18	2	5	1.7	23	45	22	27	0	23	6	332	36	4	5	3.6	.989	C-78
1949		55	.268	.383	149	40	14	0	3	2.0	12	19	9	9	0	14	3	152	18	4	3	3.2	.977	C-40
1950	2 teams	CHI N (12G – .188)			CIN N (21G – .277)																			
"	total	33	.254	.365	63	16	0	0	2	3.2	4	7	4	4	0	19	5	54	2	1	2	1.7	.982	C-14
1951	2 teams	CIN N (47G – .254)			STL N (12G – .111)																			
"	total	59	.236	.293	140	33	2	0	2	1.4	9	16	19	14	0	7	3	182	15	4	1	3.4	.980	C-52
8 yrs.		517	.263	.360	1357	357	53	9	20	1.5	105	187	103	127	6	124	33	1444	166	27	25	3.2	.984	C-390

Ted Scheffler

SCHEFFLER, THEODORE J.
B. Apr. 5, 1864, New York, N. Y. D. Feb. 24, 1949, Jamaica, N. Y.

BR TR 5'10" 160 lbs.

Year	Team	Games	BA	SA	AB	H	2B	3B	HR	HR%	R	RBI	BB	SO	SB	AB	H	PO	A	E	DP	TC/G	FA	G by Pos
1888	DET N	27	.202	.255	94	19	3	1	0	0.0	17	4	9	9	4	0	0	49	1	9	1	2.2	.847	OF-27
1890	ROC AA	119	.245	.319	445	109	12	6	3	0.7	111		78		77	0	0	197	29	22	6	2.1	.911	OF-119, C-1
2 yrs.		146	.237	.308	539	128	15	7	3	0.6	128	4	87	9	81	0	0	246	30	31	7	2.1	.899	OF-146, C-1

Carl Scheib

SCHEIB, CARL ALVIN
B. Jan. 1, 1927, Gratz, Pa.

BR TR 6'1" 192 lbs.

Year	Team	Games	BA	SA	AB	H	2B	3B	HR	HR%	R	RBI	BB	SO	SB	AB	H	PO	A	E	DP	TC/G	FA	G by Pos
1943	PHI A	6	.000	.000	5	0	0	0	0	0.0	0	0	0	3	0	0	0	1	1	0	0	0.3	1.000	P-6
1944		15	.300	.500	10	3	0	0	0	0.0	1	0	0	2	0	0	0	0	13	0	0	0.9	1.000	P-15
1945		4	.000	.000	2	0	0	0	0	0.0	0	0	0	0	0	0	0	1	2	0	0	0.8	1.000	P-4
1947		22	.133	.133	45	6	0	0	0	0.0	4	3	1	3	0	1	0	3	13	1	2	0.8	.941	P-21
1948		52	.298	.490	104	31	8	3	2	1.9	14	21	8	17	0	16	7	16	36	1	5	1.0	.981	P-32, OF-2
1949		47	.236	.264	72	17	2	0	0	0.0	9	10	8	10	0	9	2	6	24	3	3	0.7	.909	P-38
1950		50	.250	.346	52	13	0	1	1	1.9	6	6	1	9	0	7	1	3	16	0	2	0.4	1.000	P-43
1951		48	.396	.623	53	21	2	2	2	3.8	9	8	1	5	0	2	1	14	43	1	3	1.2	.983	P-46
1952		44	.220	.220	82	18	0	0	0	0.0	4	7	0	4	1	14	2	19	26	2	3	1.1	.957	P-30
1953		35	.195	.195	41	8	0	0	0	0.0	4	4	2	1	0	8	2	4	16	1	1	0.6	.952	P-28
1954	2 teams	PHI A (1G – .000)			STL N (3G – .000)																			
"	total	4	.000	.000	2	0	0	0	0	0.0	0	0	0	0	0	0	0	1	1	0	0	0.5	1.000	P-4
11 yrs.		327	.250	.338	468	117	14	6	5	1.1	51	59	21	59	1	57	15	68	191	9	19	0.8	.966	P-267, OF-2

Frank Scheibeck

SCHEIBECK, FRANK S. (Archer)
B. June 28, 1865, Detroit, Mich. D. Oct. 22, 1956, Detroit, Mich.

BR TR 5'7" 145 lbs.

Year	Team	Games	BA	SA	AB	H	2B	3B	HR	HR%	R	RBI	BB	SO	SB	AB	H	PO	A	E	DP	TC/G	FA	G by Pos
1887	CLE AA	3	.222	.222	9	2	0	0	0	0.0	2		2		0	0	0	1	3	4	0	2.7	.500	SS-1, 3B-1, P-1
1888	DET N	1	.000	.000	4	0	0	0	0	0.0	0	0	0	0	0	0	0	2	0	2	0	4.0	.500	SS-1
1890	TOL AA	134	.241	.295	485	117	13	5	1	0.2	72		76		57	0	0	282	412	92	35	5.9	.883	SS-134

Year	Team	Games	BA	SA	AB	H	2B	3B	HR	HR%	R	RBI	BB	SO	SB	Pinch Hit AB	Pinch Hit H	PO	A	E	DP	TC/G	FA	G by Pos

Frank Scheibeck *continued*

Year	Team	Games	BA	SA	AB	H	2B	3B	HR	HR%	R	RBI	BB	SO	SB	PH AB	PH H	PO	A	E	DP	TC/G	FA	G by Pos
1894	2 teams		PIT	N	(28G –	.353)			WAS	N	(52G – .230)													
"	total	80	.272	.342	298	81	4	7	1	0.3	69	27	56	33	18	4	1	152	242	55	21	5.6	.878	SS-63, OF-9, 3B-3, 2B-2
1895	WAS	N	48	.186	.240	167	31	5	2	0	0.0	17	25	17	21	5	0	0	105	149	35	18	6.0	.879	SS-44, 3B-2, 2B-2
1899		27	.287	.351	94	27	4	1	0	0.0	19	9	11		5	0	0	46	75	17	3	5.1	.877	SS-27
1901	CLE	A	93	.213	.264	329	70	11	3	0	0.0	33	38	18		3	1	0	176	268	51	26	5.3	.897	SS-92
1906	DET	A	3	.100	.100	10	1	0	0	0	0.0	1	0	2		0	0	0	8	8	2	2	6.0	.889	2B-3
8 yrs.		389	.236	.292	1396	329	37	18	2	0.1	213	99	182	54	88	5	1	772	1157	258	105	5.6	.882	SS-362, OF-9, 2B-7, 3B-6, P-1

Richie Scheinblum

SCHEINBLUM, RICHARD ALAN
B. Nov. 5, 1942, New York, N. Y. — BB TR 6'1" 180 lbs.

Year	Team	Games	BA	SA	AB	H	2B	3B	HR	HR%	R	RBI	BB	SO	SB	PH AB	PH H	PO	A	E	DP	TC/G	FA	G by Pos
1965	CLE	A	4	.000	.000	1	0	0	0	0	0.0	1	0	0	0	0	0	0	0	0	0	0	0.0	–	
1967		18	.318	.439	66	21	4	2	0	0.0	8	6	5	10	0	0	0	33	0	2	0	1.9	.943	OF-18
1968		19	.218	.309	55	12	5	0	0	0.0	3	5	8	8	0	2	0	34	0	0	0	1.8	1.000	OF-16
1969		102	.186	.236	199	37	5	1	1	0.5	13	13	19	30	1	54	14	71	4	2	1	0.8	.974	OF-50
1971	WAS	A	27	.143	.204	49	7	3	0	0	0.0	5	4	8	5	0	13	3	23	5	2	1	1.1	.933	OF-13
1972	KC	A	134	.300	.418	450	135	21	4	8	1.8	60	66	58	40	0	16	7	215	6	8	2	1.7	.965	OF-119
1973	2 teams		CIN	N	(29G –	.222)			CAL	A	(77G – .328)													
"	total	106	.307	.406	283	87	12	2	4	1.4	33	29	45	31	0	21	6	114	5	4	1	1.2	.967	OF-73, DH-7
1974	3 teams		CAL	A	(10G – .154)			KC	A	(36G – .181)			STL	N	(6G – .333)								
"	total	52	.183	.200	115	21	2	0	0	0.0	8	4	9	11	0	27	5	13	0	1	0	0.3	.929	DH-18, OF-10
8 yrs.		462	.263	.352	1218	320	52	9	13	1.1	131	127	149	135	0	134	35	503	20	19	5	1.2	.965	OF-299, DH-25

Danny Schell

SCHELL, CLYDE DANIEL
B. Dec. 26, 1927, Fostoria, Mich. D. May 11, 1972, Mayville, Mich. — BR TR 6'1" 195 lbs.

Year	Team	Games	BA	SA	AB	H	2B	3B	HR	HR%	R	RBI	BB	SO	SB	PH AB	PH H	PO	A	E	DP	TC/G	FA	G by Pos
1954	PHI	N	92	.283	.434	272	77	14	3	7	2.6	25	33	17	31	0	24	5	143	4	4	0	1.6	.974	OF-69
1955		2	.000	.000	2	0	0	0	0	0.0	0	0	0	1	0	2	0	0	0	0	0	0.0	–	
2 yrs.		94	.281	.431	274	77	14	3	7	2.6	25	33	17	32	0	26	5	143	4	4	0	1.6	.974	OF-69

Al Schellhase

SCHELLHASE, ALBERT HERMAN (Schelley)
B. Sept. 13, 1864, Evansville, Ind. D. Jan. 3, 1919, Evansville, Ind. — TR

Year	Team	Games	BA	SA	AB	H	2B	3B	HR	HR%	R	RBI	BB	SO	SB	PH AB	PH H	PO	A	E	DP	TC/G	FA	G by Pos
1890	BOS	N	9	.138	.138	29	4	0	0	0	0.0	1	1	1	10	0	0	0	18	5	5	0	3.1	.821	OF-5, C-2, SS-1, 3B-1
1891	LOU	AA	7	.150	.150	20	3	0	0	0	0.0	4	1	1	2	3	0	0	23	10	2	0	5.0	.943	C-7
2 yrs.		16	.143	.143	49	7	0	0	0	0.0	5	2	2	12	3	0	0	41	15	7	0	3.9	.889	C-9, OF-5, SS-1, 3B-1

Fred Schemanske

SCHEMANSKE, FREDERICK GEORGE (Buck)
B. Apr. 28, 1903, Detroit, Mich. D. Feb. 18, 1960, Detroit, Mich. — BR TR 6'2" 190 lbs.

Year	Team	Games	BA	SA	AB	H	2B	3B	HR	HR%	R	RBI	BB	SO	SB	PH AB	PH H	PO	A	E	DP	TC/G	FA	G by Pos
1923	WAS	A	2	1.000	1.000	2	2	0	0	0	0.0	2	1	0	0	2	2	0	0	0	0	0.0	–	P-1

Mike Schemer

SCHEMER, MICHAEL (Lefty)
B. Nov. 20, 1917, Baltimore, Md. D. Apr. 22, 1983, Miami, Fla. — BL TL 6' 180 lbs.

Year	Team	Games	BA	SA	AB	H	2B	3B	HR	HR%	R	RBI	BB	SO	SB	PH AB	PH H	PO	A	E	DP	TC/G	FA	G by Pos
1945	NY	N	31	.333	.407	108	36	3	1	1	0.9	10	10	6	1	2	4	0	268	28	2	21	9.6	.993	1B-27
1946		1	.000	.000	1	0	0	0	0	0.0	0	0	0	1	0	1	0	0	0	0	0	0.0	–	
2 yrs.		32	.330	.404	109	36	3	1	1	0.9	10	10	6	1	2	5	0	268	28	2	21	9.3	.993	1B-27

Bill Schenck

SCHENCK, WILLIAM G.
B. Brooklyn, N. Y. Deceased. — 5'7" 171 lbs.

Year	Team	Games	BA	SA	AB	H	2B	3B	HR	HR%	R	RBI	BB	SO	SB	PH AB	PH H	PO	A	E	DP	TC/G	FA	G by Pos
1882	LOU	AA	60	.260	.333	231	60	11	3	0	0.0	37		8			0	0	70	114	45	5	3.8	.803	3B-58, SS-2, P-2
1884	RIC	AA	42	.205	.291	151	31	4	0	3	2.0	14		1			0	0	40	122	34	8	4.7	.827	SS-40, 2B-2
1885	BKN	AA	1	.000	.000	4	0	0	0	0	0.0	0		0			0	0	2	1	0	0	3.0	1.000	3B-1
3 yrs.		103	.236	.313	386	91	15	3	3	0.8	51		9			0	0	112	237	79	13	4.2	.815	3B-59, SS-42, 2B-2, P-2

Hank Schenz

SCHENZ, HENRY LEONARD
B. Apr. 11, 1919, New Richmond, Ohio D. May 12, 1988, Cincinnati, Ohio — BR TR 5'9½" 175 lbs.

Year	Team	Games	BA	SA	AB	H	2B	3B	HR	HR%	R	RBI	BB	SO	SB	PH AB	PH H	PO	A	E	DP	TC/G	FA	G by Pos
1946	CHI	N	6	.182	.182	11	2	0	0	0	0.0	0	1	0	0	1	0	0	2	4	0	1	1.0	1.000	3B-5
1947		7	.071	.071	14	1	0	0	0	0.0	2	0	2	1	0	0	0	2	9	1	0	1.7	.917	3B-5
1948		96	.261	.326	337	88	17	1	1	0.3	43	14	18	15	3	10	1	187	196	10	45	4.1	.975	2B-78, 3B-5
1949		7	.429	.429	14	6	0	0	0	0.0	2	1	1	0	0	0	0	9	9	0	3	1.4	1.000	3B-5
1950	PIT	N	58	.228	.337	101	23	4	2	1	1.0	17	5	6	7	0	14	5	47	59	1	20	1.8	.991	2B-21, 3B-12, SS-4
1951	2 teams		PIT	N	(25G – .213)			NY	N	(8G – .000)														
"	total	33	.213	.230	61	13	1	0	0	0.0	6	3	0	2	0	1	0	40	36	3	17	2.4	.962	2B-19, 3B-2
6 yrs.		207	.247	.310	538	133	22	3	2	0.4	70	24	27	25	6	25	6	279	313	15	86	2.9	.975	2B-118, 3B-34, SS-4

WORLD SERIES

Year	Team	Games	BA	SA	AB	H	2B	3B	HR	HR%	R	RBI	BB	SO	SB	PH AB	PH H	PO	A	E	DP	TC/G	FA	G by Pos
1951	NY	N	1	–	–	0	0	0	0	0	–	0	0	0	0	0	0	0	0	0	0	0	0.0	–	

Joe Schepner

SCHEPNER, JOSEPH MAURICE (Gentleman Joe)
B. Aug. 10, 1895, Aliquippa, Pa. D. July 25, 1959, Mobile, Ala. — BR TR 5'10" 160 lbs.

Year	Team	Games	BA	SA	AB	H	2B	3B	HR	HR%	R	RBI	BB	SO	SB	PH AB	PH H	PO	A	E	DP	TC/G	FA	G by Pos
1919	STL	A	14	.208	.292	48	10	4	0	0	0.0	2	6	1	5	0	1	0	18	18	2	2	2.7	.947	3B-13

Bob Scherbarth

SCHERBARTH, ROBERT ELMER
B. Jan. 18, 1926, Milwaukee, Wis. — BR TR 6' 180 lbs.

Year	Team	Games	BA	SA	AB	H	2B	3B	HR	HR%	R	RBI	BB	SO	SB	PH AB	PH H	PO	A	E	DP	TC/G	FA	G by Pos
1950	BOS	A	1	–	–	0	0	0	0	0	–	0	0	0	0	0	0	0	0	0	0	0	0.0	–	C-1

Harry Scherer

SCHERER, HARRY
B. Baltimore, Md. Deceased.

Year	Team	Games	BA	SA	AB	H	2B	3B	HR	HR%	R	RBI	BB	SO	SB	PH AB	PH H	PO	A	E	DP	TC/G	FA	G by Pos
1889	LOU	AA	1	.333	.333	3	1	0	0	0	0.0	0		0	0	0	0	0	2	0	2	0	4.0	.500	OF-1

Year	Team	Games	BA	SA	AB	H	2B	3B	HR	HR%	R	RBI	BB	SO	SB	Pinch Hit AB	Pinch Hit H	PO	A	E	DP	TC/G	FA	G by Pos

Lou Schiappacasse
SCHIAPPACASSE, LOUIS JOSEPH (Skippy)
B. Mar. 29, 1881, Ann Arbor, Mich. D. Sept. 20, 1910, Ann Arbor, Mich. BR TR

| 1902 DET A | 2 | .000 | .000 | 5 | 0 | 0 | 0 | 0 | 0.0 | 0 | 1 | 1 | | 0 | 0 | 0 | 0 | 0 | 1 | 0 | 0.5 | – | OF-2 |

Morrie Schick
SCHICK, MAURICE FRANCIS
B. Apr. 17, 1892, Chicago, Ill. D. Oct. 25, 1979, Hazel Crest, Ill. BR TR 5'11" 170 lbs.

| 1917 CHI N | 14 | .147 | .147 | 34 | 5 | 0 | 0 | 0 | 0.0 | 3 | 3 | 3 | 10 | 0 | 0 | 0 | 21 | 3 | 1 | 0 | 1.8 | .960 | OF-12 |

Chuck Schilling
SCHILLING, CHARLES THOMAS
B. Oct. 25, 1937, Brooklyn, N.Y. BR TR 5'10" 160 lbs.

1961 BOS A	158	.259	.327	646	167	25	2	5	0.8	87	62	78	77	7	1	0	397	449	8	121	5.4	.991	2B-158
1962	119	.230	.327	413	95	17	1	7	1.7	48	35	29	48	1	0	0	267	331	9	85	5.1	.985	2B-118
1963	146	.234	.319	576	135	25	0	8	1.4	63	33	41	72	3	4	0	276	369	10	74	4.5	.985	2B-143
1964	47	.196	.233	163	32	6	0	0	0.0	18	7	15	22	0	5	3	89	101	5	20	4.1	.974	2B-42
1965	71	.240	.333	171	41	3	2	3	1.8	14	9	13	17	0	28	6	90	116	5	22	3.0	.976	2B-41
5 yrs.	541	.239	.317	1969	470	76	5	23	1.2	230	146	176	236	11	38	9	1119	1366	37	322	4.7	.985	2B-502

Bill Schindler
SCHINDLER, WILLIAM GIBBONS
B. July 10, 1896, Perryville, Mo. D. Feb. 6, 1979, Perryville, Mo. BR TR 5'11" 160 lbs.

| 1920 STL N | 1 | .000 | .000 | 2 | 0 | 0 | 0 | 0 | 0.0 | 0 | 0 | 0 | 1 | 0 | 0 | 0 | 3 | 0 | 0 | 0 | 3.0 | 1.000 | C-1 |

Dutch Schirick
SCHIRICK, HARRY ERNEST
B. June 15, 1890, Ruby, N.Y. D. Nov. 12, 1968, Kingston, N.Y. BR TR 5'8" 160 lbs.

| 1914 STL A | 1 | – | – | 0 | 0 | 0 | 0 | 0 | – | 0 | 0 | 1 | 0 | 2 | 0 | 0 | 0 | 0 | 0 | 0 | 0.0 | – | |

Harry Schlafly
SCHLAFLY, HARRY LINTON
B. Sept. 20, 1878, Port Washington, Ohio D. June 27, 1919, Canton, Ohio BR TR 5'11" 182 lbs.
Manager 1914-15.

1902 CHI N	10	.323	.516	31	10	0	3	0	0.0	5	5	6		2	0	0	14	15	3	1	3.2	.906	OF-5, 2B-4, 3B-2
1906 WAS A	123	.246	.329	426	105	13	8	2	0.5	60	30	50		29	0	0	341	358	28	42	5.9	.961	2B-123
1907	24	.135	.216	74	10	0	0	2	2.7	10	4	22		7	0	0	67	49	9	5	5.2	.928	2B-24
1914 BUF F	51	.260	.378	127	33	7	1	2	1.6	16	19	12		3	14	5	116	73	6	9	3.8	.969	2B-23, 1B-7, OF-1, 3B-1, C-1
4 yrs.	208	.240	.334	658	158	20	12	6	0.9	91	58	90		41	14	5	538	495	46	57	5.2	.957	2B-174, 1B-7, OF-6, 3B-3, C-1

Admiral Schlei
SCHLEI, GEORGE HENRY
B. Jan. 12, 1878, Cincinnati, Ohio D. Jan. 24, 1958, Huntington, W. Va. BR TR 5'8½" 179 lbs.

1904 CIN N	97	.237	.285	291	69	8	3	0	0.0	25	32	17		7	7	1	384	123	12	5	5.4	.977	C-88
1905	99	.226	.280	314	71	8	3	1	0.3	32	36	22		9	4	2	455	156	23	17	6.4	.964	C-89, 1B-6
1906	116	.245	.351	388	95	13	8	4	1.0	44	54	29		7	4	1	671	156	28	21	7.4	.967	C-91, 1B-21
1907	84	.272	.301	246	67	3	2	0	0.0	28	27	28		5	11	3	287	111	10	6	4.9	.975	C-67, 1B-3, OF-2
1908	92	.220	.277	300	66	6	4	1	0.3	31	22	22		2	4	1	355	96	18	10	5.1	.962	C-88
1909 NY N	92	.244	.287	279	68	12	0	0	0.0	25	30	40		4	3	0	493	127	24	9	7.0	.963	C-89
1910	55	.192	.232	99	19	2	1	0	0.0	10	8	14	10	4	6	1	165	43	3	4	3.8	.986	C-49
1911	1	.000	.000	1	0	0	0	0	0.0	0	0	0		0	1	0	0	0	0	0	0.0	–	
8 yrs.	636	.237	.296	1918	455	52	21	6	0.3	195	209	172	11	38	40	9	2810	812	118	72	5.9	.968	C-561, 1B-30, OF-2

Rudy Schlesinger
SCHLESINGER, WILLIAM CORDES
B. Nov. 5, 1941, Cincinnati, Ohio BR TR 6'2" 175 lbs.

| 1965 BOS A | 1 | .000 | .000 | 1 | 0 | 0 | 0 | 0 | 0.0 | 0 | 0 | 0 | 0 | 0 | 1 | 0 | 0 | 0 | 0 | 0 | 0.0 | – | |

Dutch Schliebner
SCHLIEBNER, FREDERICK PAUL
B. May 19, 1891, Charlottenburg, Germany D. Apr. 15, 1975, Toledo, Ohio BR TR 5'10" 180 lbs.

| 1923 2 teams | BKN N (19G – .250) | | | STL A (127G – .275) | | | | | | | | | | | | | | | | | | | |
| " total | 146 | .271 | .362 | 520 | 141 | 23 | 6 | 4 | 0.8 | 61 | 56 | 44 | 67 | 4 | 0 | 0 | 1331 | 96 | 17 | 121 | 9.9 | .988 | 1B-146 |

Jay Schlueter
SCHLUETER, JAY D.
B. July 31, 1949, Phoenix, Ariz. BR TR 6' 182 lbs.

| 1971 HOU N | 7 | .333 | .333 | 3 | 1 | 0 | 0 | 0 | 0.0 | 1 | 0 | 0 | 1 | 0 | 2 | 1 | 3 | 0 | 0 | 0 | 0.4 | 1.000 | OF-2 |

Norm Schlueter
SCHLUETER, NORMAN JOHN
B. Sept. 25, 1916, Belleville, Ill. BR TR 5'10" 175 lbs.

1938 CHI A	35	.229	.288	118	27	5	1	0	0.0	11	7	4	15	1	1	0	107	13	6	3	3.6	.952	C-34
1939	34	.232	.304	56	13	2	1	0	0.0	5	8	1	11	2	2	0	81	2	1	0	2.5	.988	C-32
1944 CLE A	49	.123	.156	122	15	4	0	0	0.0	2	11	12	22	0	6	0	122	9	2	4	2.7	.985	C-43
3 yrs.	118	.186	.236	296	55	11	2	0	0.0	18	26	17	48	3	9	0	310	24	9	7	2.9	.974	C-109

Ray Schmandt
SCHMANDT, RAYMOND HENRY
B. Jan. 25, 1896, St. Louis, Mo. D. Feb. 2, 1969, St. Louis, Mo. BR TR 6'1" 175 lbs.

1915 STL A	3	.000	.000	4	0	0	0	0	0.0	0	0	0	1	0	2	0	8	0	0	0	2.7	1.000	1B-1
1918 BKN N	34	.307	.421	114	35	5	4	0	0.0	11	18	7	7	1	0	0	79	90	12	8	5.3	.934	2B-34
1919	47	.165	.197	127	21	4	0	0	0.0	8	10	4	13	0	10	2	138	66	11	13	4.6	.949	2B-18, 1B-12, 3B-6
1920	28	.238	.302	63	15	2	1	0	0.0	7	7	3	4	1	6	3	165	17	1	16	6.5	.995	1B-20
1921	95	.306	.366	350	107	8	5	1	0.3	42	43	11	22	3	2	0	941	52	11	74	10.6	.989	1B-92
1922	110	.268	.341	396	106	17	3	2	0.5	54	44	21	28	6	0	0	1017	65	12	83	9.9	.989	1B-110
6 yrs.	317	.269	.337	1054	284	36	13	3	0.3	122	122	46	75	11	20	5	2348	290	47	194	8.5	.982	1B-235, 2B-52, 3B-6

WORLD SERIES

| 1920 BKN N | 1 | .000 | .000 | 1 | 0 | 0 | 0 | 0 | 0.0 | 0 | 0 | 0 | 1 | 0 | 0 | 0 | 0 | 0 | 0 | 0 | 0.0 | – | |

Year Team	Games	BA	SA	AB	H	2B	3B	HR	HR%	R	RBI	BB	SO	SB	Pinch Hit AB	Pinch Hit H	PO	A	E	DP	TC/G	FA	G by Pos

George Schmees

SCHMEES, GEORGE EDWARD (Rocky)
B. Sept. 6, 1924, Cincinnati, Ohio — BL TL 6' 190 lbs.

Year Team	Games	BA	SA	AB	H	2B	3B	HR	HR%	R	RBI	BB	SO	SB	AB	H	PO	A	E	DP	TC/G	FA	G by Pos
1952 2 teams		STL A	(34G – .131)		BOS A	(42G – .203)																	
" total	76	.168	.216	125	21	4	1	0	0.0	17	6	12	29	0	12	0	91	7	4	1	1.3	.961	OF-48, 1B-4, P-2

Bob Schmidt

SCHMIDT, ROBERT BENJAMIN
B. Apr. 22, 1933, St. Louis, Mo. — BR TR 6'2" 205 lbs.

Year Team	Games	BA	SA	AB	H	2B	3B	HR	HR%	R	RBI	BB	SO	SB	AB	H	PO	A	E	DP	TC/G	FA	G by Pos
1958 SF N	127	.244	.412	393	96	20	2	14	3.6	46	54	33	59	0	6	2	616	54	12	10	5.4	.982	C-123
1959	71	.243	.376	181	44	7	1	5	2.8	17	20	13	24	0	3	0	307	30	0	1	4.7	1.000	C-70
1960	110	.267	.378	344	92	12	1	8	2.3	31	37	26	51	0	3	0	631	31	13	6	6.1	.981	C-108
1961 2 teams		SF N	(2G – .167)		CIN N	(27G – .129)																	
" total	29	.132	.171	76	10	0	0	1	1.3	4	5	8	15	0	0	0	154	7	1	1	5.6	.994	C-29
1962 WAS A	88	.242	.414	256	62	14	0	10	3.9	28	31	14	37	0	4	1	342	40	1	3	4.4	.997	C-88
1963	9	.200	.267	15	3	1	0	0	0.0	0	3	0	3	5	0	5	0	18	0	0	0	2.0	1.000	C-6
1965 NY A	20	.250	.350	40	10	1	0	1	2.5	4	3	3	8	0	0	0	93	4	1	0	4.9	.990	C-20
7 yrs.	454	.243	.381	1305	317	55	4	39	3.0	133	150	100	199	0	21	3	2161	166	28	21	5.2	.988	C-444

Boss Schmidt

SCHMIDT, CHARLES
Brother of Walter Schmidt.
B. Sept. 12, 1880, Coal Hill, Ark. D. Nov. 14, 1932, Clarksville, Ark. — BB TR 5'11" 200 lbs.

Year Team	Games	BA	SA	AB	H	2B	3B	HR	HR%	R	RBI	BB	SO	SB	AB	H	PO	A	E	DP	TC/G	FA	G by Pos
1906 DET A	68	.218	.264	216	47	4	3	0	0.0	13	10	6		1		1	0	257	104	16	4	5.5	.958	C-67
1907	104	.244	.295	349	85	6	6	0	0.0	32	23	5		8		1	0	446	132	34	14	5.9	.944	C-104
1908	122	.265	.320	419	111	14	3	1	0.2	45	38	16		5		1	1	541	184	37	12	6.2	.951	C-121
1909	84	.209	.269	253	53	8	2	1	0.4	21	28	7		7		2	1	315	107	20	7	5.3	.955	C-81, OF-1
1910	71	.259	.381	197	51	7	7	1	0.5	22	23	2		2		5	2	239	80	9	1	4.6	.973	C-66
1911	28	.283	.370	46	13	2	1	0	0.0	4	2	0		0		17	6	29	10	0	0	1.4	1.000	C-9, OF-1
6 yrs.	477	.243	.307	1480	360	41	22	3	0.2	137	124	36		23		27	10	1827	617	116	38	5.4	.955	C-448, OF-2

WORLD SERIES

Year Team	Games	BA	SA	AB	H	2B	3B	HR	HR%	R	RBI	BB	SO	SB	AB	H	PO	A	E	DP	TC/G	FA	G by Pos
1907 DET A	4	.167	.167	12	2	0	0	0	0.0	0	0	2		1		1	0	16	9	2	0	6.8	.926	C-3
1908	4	.071	.071	14	1	0	0	0	0.0	0	0	0		2		0	0	22	7	0	1	7.3	1.000	C-4
1909	6	.222	.333	18	4	2	0	0	0.0	4	0	2		0		0	0	31	11	5	3	7.8	.894	C-6
3 yrs.	14	.159	.205	44	7	2	0	0	0.0	0	5	4		3		1	0	69	27	7	4	7.4	.932	C-13

Butch Schmidt

SCHMIDT, CHARLES JOHN
B. July 19, 1886, Baltimore, Md. D. Sept. 4, 1952, Baltimore, Md. — BL TL 6'1½" 200 lbs.

Year Team	Games	BA	SA	AB	H	2B	3B	HR	HR%	R	RBI	BB	SO	SB	AB	H	PO	A	E	DP	TC/G	FA	G by Pos
1909 NY A	1	.000	.000	2	0	0	0	0	0.0	0	0	0		0		0	0	0	1	1	0	2.0	.500	P-1
1913 BOS N	22	.308	.423	78	24	2	2	1	1.3	6	14	2	5	1	0	0	166	12	3	5	8.2	.983	1B-22
1914	147	.285	.356	537	153	17	9	1	0.2	67	71	43	55	14	0	0	1485	88	16	109	10.8	.990	1B-147
1915	127	.251	.352	458	115	26	7	2	0.4	46	60	36	59	3	0	0	1221	60	17	80	10.2	.987	1B-127
4 yrs.	297	.272	.358	1075	292	45	18	4	0.4	119	145	81	119	18	0	0	2872	161	37	194	10.3	.988	1B-296, P-1

WORLD SERIES

Year Team	Games	BA	SA	AB	H	2B	3B	HR	HR%	R	RBI	BB	SO	SB	AB	H	PO	A	E	DP	TC/G	FA	G by Pos
1914 BOS N	4	.294	.294	17	5	0	0	0	0.0	2	2	0	2	1	0	0	52	3	0	3	13.8	1.000	1B-4

Dave Schmidt

SCHMIDT, DAVID FREDERICK
B. Dec. 22, 1956, Mesa, Ariz. — BR TR 6'1" 190 lbs.

Year Team	Games	BA	SA	AB	H	2B	3B	HR	HR%	R	RBI	BB	SO	SB	AB	H	PO	A	E	DP	TC/G	FA	G by Pos
1981 BOS A	15	.238	.405	42	10	1	0	2	4.8	6	3	7	17	0	1	1	53	4	0	0	3.8	1.000	C-15

Mike Schmidt

SCHMIDT, MICHAEL JACK
B. Sept. 27, 1949, Dayton, Ohio — BR TR 6'2" 195 lbs.

Year Team	Games	BA	SA	AB	H	2B	3B	HR	HR%	R	RBI	BB	SO	SB	AB	H	PO	A	E	DP	TC/G	FA	G by Pos
1972 PHI N	13	.206	.294	34	7	0	0	1	2.9	2	3	5	15	0	1	0	10	25	2	3	2.8	.946	3B-11, 2B-1
1973	132	.196	.373	367	72	11	0	18	4.9	43	52	62	136	8	9	2	119	256	18	32	3.0	.954	3B-125, 2B-4, SS-2, 1B-2
1974	162	.282	**.546**	568	160	28	7	36	6.3	108	116	106	**138**	23	0	0	134	404	26	40	3.5	.954	3B-162
1975	158	.249	.523	562	140	34	3	38	6.8	93	95	101	**180**	29	1	0	139	390	26	32	3.5	.953	3B-149, SS-10
1976	160	.262	.524	584	153	31	4	38	6.5	112	107	100	149	14	0	0	139	377	21	29	3.4	.961	3B-160
1977	154	.274	.574	544	149	27	11	38	7.0	114	101	104	122	15	2	0	109	401	20	34	3.4	.962	3B-149, SS-2, 2B-1
1978	145	.251	.435	513	129	27	2	21	4.1	93	78	91	103	19	4	1	98	325	16	34	3.0	.964	3B-139, SS-1
1979	160	.253	.564	541	137	25	4	45	8.3	109	114	120	115	9	2	0	115	363	23	38	3.1	.954	3B-157, SS-2
1980	150	.286	**.624**	548	157	25	8	48	8.8	104	121	89	119	12	1	0	98	372	27	31	3.3	.946	3B-149
1981	102	.316	**.644**	354	112	19	2	31	8.8	78	91	73	71	12	1	1	74	249	15	20	3.3	.956	3B-101
1982	148	.280	**.547**	514	144	26	3	35	6.8	108	87	107	131	14	0	0	110	324	23	28	3.1	.950	3B-148
1983	154	.255	.524	534	136	16	4	40	7.5	104	109	128	148	7	0	0	108	333	19	29	3.0	.959	3B-153, SS-2
1984	151	.277	.536	528	146	23	3	36	6.8	93	106	92	116	5	4	3	93	330	26	20	3.0	.942	3B-145, 1B-2, SS-1
1985	158	.277	.532	549	152	31	5	33	6.0	89	93	87	117	1	4	1	911	193	18	97	7.1	.984	1B-104, SS-54, 3B-54
1986	160	.290	**.547**	552	160	29	1	37	6.7	97	119	89	84	1	8	2	347	238	8	53	3.7	.987	3B-124, 1B-35
1987	147	.293	.548	522	153	28	0	35	6.7	88	113	83	80	2	6	1	138	319	13	35	3.2	.972	3B-138, 1B-9, SS-3
1988	108	.249	.405	390	97	21	2	12	3.1	52	62	49	42	3	5	0	76	223	19	17	2.9	.940	3B-104, 1B-3
1989	42	.203	.372	148	30	7	0	6	4.1	19	28	21	17	0	0	0	18	71	8	8	2.3	.918	3B-42
18 yrs.	2404	.267	.527	8352	2234	408	59	548	6.6	1506	1595	1507	1883	174	48	11	2836	5193	328	580	3.5	.961	3B-2212, 1B-157, SS-24, 2B-6
								7th	8th				3rd										

DIVISIONAL PLAYOFF SERIES

Year Team	Games	BA	SA	AB	H	2B	3B	HR	HR%	R	RBI	BB	SO	SB	AB	H	PO	A	E	DP	TC/G	FA	G by Pos
1981 PHI N	5	.250	.500	16	4	1	0	1	6.3	3	2	4	2	0	0	0	0	0	1	0	0.2	–	3B-5

LEAGUE CHAMPIONSHIP SERIES

Year Team	Games	BA	SA	AB	H	2B	3B	HR	HR%	R	RBI	BB	SO	SB	AB	H	PO	A	E	DP	TC/G	FA	G by Pos
1976 PHI N	3	.308	.462	13	4	2	0	0	0.0	1	2	0	1	0	0	0	4	9	1	2	4.7	.929	3B-3
1977	4	.063	.063	16	1	0	0	0	0.0	2	1	2	3	0	0	0	4	15	0	0	4.8	1.000	3B-4
1978	4	.200	.333	15	3	2	0	0	0.0	1	1	1	1	0	0	0	3	18	2	1	5.8	.913	3B-4
1980	5	.208	.250	24	5	1	0	0	0.0	1	1	1	6	0	0	0	3	17	1	2	4.2	.952	3B-5
1983	4	.467	.800	15	7	2	0	1	6.7	5	2	2	3	0	0	0	6	8	1	0	3.8	.933	3B-4
5 yrs.	20	.241	.361	83	20	7	0	1	1.2	10	7	7	15	0	0	0	20	67	5	4	4.6	.946	3B-20

WORLD SERIES

Year Team	Games	BA	SA	AB	H	2B	3B	HR	HR%	R	RBI	BB	SO	SB	AB	H	PO	A	E	DP	TC/G	FA	G by Pos
1980 PHI N	6	.381	.714	21	8	1	0	2	9.5	6	7	4	3	0	0	0	9	8	0	1	2.8	1.000	3B-6

Year	Team		Games	BA	SA	AB	H	2B	3B	HR	HR%	R	RBI	BB	SO	SB	Pinch Hit AB	Pinch Hit H	PO	A	E	DP	TC/G	FA	G by Pos

Mike Schmidt *continued*

Year	Team		Games	BA	SA	AB	H	2B	3B	HR	HR%	R	RBI	BB	SO	SB	PH AB	PH H	PO	A	E	DP	TC/G	FA	G by Pos
1983			5	.050	.050	20	1	0	0	0	0.0	0	0	0	6	0	0	0	1	10	1	1	2.4	.917	3B-5
2 yrs.			11	.220	.390	41	9	1	0	2	4.9	6	7	4	9	0	0	0	10	18	1	2	2.6	.966	3B-11

Walter Schmidt

SCHMIDT, WALTER JOSEPH
Brother of Boss Schmidt.
B. Mar. 20, 1887, Coal Hill, Ark. D. July 4, 1973, Modesto, Calif.

BR TR 5'9" 159 lbs.

Year	Team		Games	BA	SA	AB	H	2B	3B	HR	HR%	R	RBI	BB	SO	SB	PH AB	PH H	PO	A	E	DP	TC/G	FA	G by Pos
1916	PIT	N	64	.190	.250	184	35	1	2	2	1.1	16	15	10	13	3	3	1	232	88	8	6	5.1	.976	C-57
1917			75	.246	.284	183	45	7	0	0	0.0	9	17	11	11	4	7	1	229	84	7	9	4.3	.978	C-61
1918			105	.238	.276	323	77	6	3	0	0.0	31	27	17	19	7	1	1	373	153	10	19	5.1	.981	C-104
1919			85	.251	.300	267	67	9	2	0	0.0	23	29	23	9	5	0	0	315	110	8	8	5.1	.982	C-85
1920			94	.277	.329	310	86	8	4	0	0.0	22	20	24	15	9	1	0	323	109	13	10	4.7	.971	C-92
1921			114	.282	.321	393	111	9	3	0	0.0	30	38	12	13	10	3	0	438	120	8	15	5.0	.986	C-111
1922			40	.329	.414	152	50	11	1	0	0.0	21	22	1	5	2	0	0	159	22	1	1	4.6	.995	C-40
1923			97	.248	.281	335	83	7	2	0	0.0	39	37	22	12	10	1	1	279	88	7	10	3.9	.981	C-96
1924			58	.243	.299	177	43	3	2	1	0.6	16	20	13	5	6	0	0	166	51	3	6	3.8	.986	C-57
1925	STL	N	37	.253	.299	87	22	2	1	0	0.0	9	9	4	3	1	4	1	84	33	4	2	3.3	.967	C-31
10 yrs.			769	.257	.303	2411	619	63	20	3	0.1	216	234	137	105	57	20	5	2598	858	69	86	4.6	.980	C-734

Hank Schmulbach

SCHMULBACH, HENRY ALRIVES
B. Jan. 17, 1925, East St. Louis, Ill.

BL TR 5'11" 165 lbs.

Year	Team		Games	BA	SA	AB	H	2B	3B	HR	HR%	R	RBI	BB	SO	SB	PH AB	PH H	PO	A	E	DP	TC/G	FA	G by Pos
1943	STL	A	1	–	–	0	0	0	0	0	–	1	0	0	0	0	0	0	0	0	0	0	0.0	–	

Dave Schneck

SCHNECK, DAVID LEE
B. June 18, 1949, Allentown, Pa.

BL TL 5'10" 200 lbs.

Year	Team		Games	BA	SA	AB	H	2B	3B	HR	HR%	R	RBI	BB	SO	SB	PH AB	PH H	PO	A	E	DP	TC/G	FA	G by Pos
1972	NY	N	37	.187	.317	123	23	3	2	3	2.4	7	10	10	26	0	4	0	63	1	1	0	1.8	.985	OF-33
1973			13	.194	.250	36	7	0	1	0	0.0	2	0	1	4	0	1	0	28	0	0	0	2.2	1.000	OF-12
1974			93	.205	.315	254	52	11	1	5	2.0	23	25	16	43	4	6	1	179	7	5	2	2.1	.974	OF-84
3 yrs.			143	.199	.310	413	82	14	4	8	1.9	32	35	27	73	4	11	1	270	8	6	2	2.0	.979	OF-129

Red Schoendienst

SCHOENDIENST, ALBERT FRED
B. Feb. 2, 1923, Germantown, Ill.
Manager 1965-76, 1980.
Hall of Fame 1989.

BB TR 6' 170 lbs.

Year	Team		Games	BA	SA	AB	H	2B	3B	HR	HR%	R	RBI	BB	SO	SB	PH AB	PH H	PO	A	E	DP	TC/G	FA	G by Pos
1945	STL	N	137	.278	.343	565	157	22	6	1	0.2	89	47	21	17	26	7	2	302	30	10	11	2.5	.971	OF-118, SS-10, 2B-1
1946			142	.281	.343	606	170	28	5	0	0.0	94	34	37	27	12	1	0	363	379	13	96	5.3	.983	2B-128, 3B-12, SS-4
1947			151	.253	.332	659	167	25	9	3	0.5	91	48	48	27	6	3	1	364	417	19	111	5.3	.976	2B-142, 3B-5, OF-1
1948			119	.272	.373	408	111	21	4	4	1.0	64	36	28	16	1	17	4	230	269	10	57	4.3	.980	2B-96
1949			151	.297	.356	640	190	25	2	3	0.5	102	54	51	18	8	1	1	428	471	16	110	6.1	.983	2B-138, SS-14, 3B-6, OF-2
1950			153	.276	.403	642	177	43	9	7	1.1	81	63	33	32	3	0	0	425	437	14	134	5.7	.984	2B-143, SS-10, 3B-1
1951			135	.289	.405	553	160	32	7	6	1.1	88	54	35	23	0	1	1	354	419	10	120	5.8	.987	2B-124, SS-8
1952			152	.303	.424	620	188	40	7	7	1.1	91	67	42	30	9	0	0	417	460	20	111	5.9	.978	2B-142, 3B-11, SS-3
1953			146	.342	.502	564	193	35	5	15	2.7	107	79	60	23	3	6	4	365	430	14	109	5.5	.983	2B-140
1954			148	.315	.428	610	192	38	8	5	0.8	98	79	54	22	4	4	1	394	477	18	137	6.0	.980	2B-144
1955			145	.268	.376	553	148	21	3	11	2.0	68	51	54	28	7	2	0	296	381	10	96	4.7	.985	2B-142
1956 2 teams	STL	N	(40G – .314)			NY	N	(92G	–	.296)															
" total			132	.302	.370	487	147	21	3	2	0.4	61	29	41	15	1	10	4	298	308	4	74	4.6	.993	2B-121
1957 2 teams	NY	N	(57G – .307)			MIL	N	(93G	–	.310)															
" total			150	.309	.451	648	200	31	8	15	2.3	91	65	33	15	4	1	0	146	176	5	45	2.2	.985	2B-149, OF-2
1958	MIL	N	106	.262	.328	427	112	23	1	1	0.2	47	24	31	21	3	2	0	233	301	7	77	5.1	.987	2B-105
1959			5	.000	.000	3	0	0	0	0	0.0	0	0	0	0	0	1	0	1	1	1	0	0.6	.667	2B-4
1960			68	.257	.319	226	58	9	1	1	0.4	21	19	17	13	1	4	0	120	148	10	34	4.1	.964	2B-62
1961	STL	N	72	.300	.400	120	36	9	0	1	0.8	9	12	12	6	1	48	16	43	42	4	10	1.2	.955	2B-32
1962			98	.301	.371	143	43	4	0	2	1.4	21	12	9	12	0	72	22	33	48	1	10	0.8	.988	2B-21, 3B-4
1963			6	.000	.000	5	0	0	0	0	0.0	0	0	0	1	0	5	0	0	0	0	0	0.0	–	
19 yrs.			2216	.289	.387	8479	2449	427	78	84	1.0	1223	773	606	346	89	185	56	4812	5194	186	1342	4.6	.982	2B-1834, OF-123, SS-49, 3B-39

WORLD SERIES

Year	Team		Games	BA	SA	AB	H	2B	3B	HR	HR%	R	RBI	BB	SO	SB	PH AB	PH H	PO	A	E	DP	TC/G	FA	G by Pos
1946	STL	N	7	.233	.267	30	7	1	0	0	0.0	3	1	0	2	1	0	0	17	21	1	5	5.6	.974	2B-7
1957	MIL	N	5	.278	.333	18	5	1	0	0	0.0	0	2	0	1	0	0	0	5	10	0	4	3.0	1.000	2B-5
1958			7	.300	.467	30	9	3	1	0	0.0	5	0	2	1	0	0	0	18	19	1	3	5.4	.974	2B-7
3 yrs.			19	.269	.359	78	21	5	1	0	0.0	8	3	2	4	1	0	0	40	50	2	12	4.8	.978	2B-19

Jumbo Schoeneck

SCHOENECK, LEWIS W. (Lon)
B. Mar. 3, 1862, Chicago, Ill. D. Jan. 20, 1930, Chicago, Ill.

BR TR 6'2" 223 lbs.

Year	Team		Games	BA	SA	AB	H	2B	3B	HR	HR%	R	RBI	BB	SO	SB	PH AB	PH H	PO	A	E	DP	TC/G	FA	G by Pos
1884 3 teams	CHI	U	(72G – .325)			PIT	U	(18G	–	.286)		BAL	U	(16G	–	.250)									
" total			106	.308	.387	426	131	24	2	0	0.5	61		8			0	0	1063	31	49	30	10.8	.957	1B-105, SS-1
1888	IND	N	48	.237	.260	169	40	4	0	0	0.0	15	20	9	24	11	0	0	501	16	14	19	11.1	.974	1B-48, P-2
1889			16	.242	.339	62	15	2	2	0	0.0	3	8	3	3	1	0	0	164	12	4	7	11.3	.978	1B-16
3 yrs.			170	.283	.350	657	186	30	4	2	0.3	79	28	20	27	12	0	0	1728	59	67	56	10.9	.964	1B-169, P-2, SS-1

Dick Schofield

SCHOFIELD, JOHN RICHARD (Ducky)
Father of Dick Schofield.
B. Jan. 7, 1935, Springfield, Ill.

BB TR 5'9" 163 lbs.

Year	Team		Games	BA	SA	AB	H	2B	3B	HR	HR%	R	RBI	BB	SO	SB	PH AB	PH H	PO	A	E	DP	TC/G	FA	G by Pos
1953	STL	N	33	.179	.333	39	7	0	0	2	5.1	9	4	2	11	0	1	0	19	36	5	8	1.8	.917	SS-15
1954			43	.143	.429	7	1	0	1	0	0.0	17	1	0	3	1	3	1	4	3	0	1	0.2	1.000	SS-11
1955			12	.000	.000	4	0	0	0	0	0.0	0	0	1	0	0	1	0	1	0	0	0	0.2	1.000	SS-9
1956			16	.100	.167	30	3	0	1	0	0.0	3	1	0	6	0	4	0	11	13	2	4	1.6	.923	SS-9
1957			65	.161	.161	56	9	0	0	0	0.0	10	1	7	13	1	11	1	21	34	3	8	0.9	.948	SS-23

Year	Team		Games	BA	SA	AB	H	2B	3B	HR	HR%	R	RBI	BB	SO	SB	Pinch Hit AB	Pinch Hit H	PO	A	E	DP	TC/G	FA	G by Pos

Dick Schofield *continued*

1958	2 teams	STL N (39G – .213)				PIT N (26G – .148)																			
"	total		65	.200	.267	135	27	4	1	1	0.7	20	10	26	21	0	14	3	54	96	9	18	2.4	.943	SS-32, 3B-2
1959	PIT N		81	.234	.338	145	34	10	1	1	0.7	21	9	16	22	1	14	3	90	105	7	25	2.5	.965	2B-28, SS-8, OF-3
1960			65	.333	.392	102	34	4	1	0	0.0	9	10	16	20	0	19	5	58	78	6	18	2.2	.958	SS-23, 2B-10, 3B-1
1961			60	.192	.244	78	15	2	1	0	0.0	16	2	10	19	0	18	3	30	54	4	10	1.5	.955	3B-11, SS-9, 2B-5, OF-3
1962			54	.288	.375	104	30	3	0	2	1.9	19	10	17	22	0	26	8	18	37	3	4	1.1	.948	3B-20, 2B-5, SS-1
1963			138	.246	.303	541	133	18	2	3	0.6	54	32	69	83	2	10	0	279	422	23	107	5.2	.968	SS-117, 2B-20, 3B-1
1964			121	.246	.349	398	98	22	5	3	0.8	50	36	54	60	1	10	0	184	349	28	78	4.6	.950	SS-111
1965	2 teams	PIT N (31G – .229)				SF N (101G – .203)																			
"	total		132	.209	.256	488	102	15	1	2	0.4	52	25	48	69	3	11	1	194	373	11	78	4.4	.981	SS-121
1966	3 teams	SF N (11G – .063)				NY A (25G – .155)				LA N (20G – .257)															
"	total		56	.194	.208	144	28	2	0	0	0.0	19	6	19	18	1	4	1	47	121	13	14	3.2	.928	SS-30, 3B-19
1967	LA N		84	.216	.293	232	50	10	1	2	0.9	23	15	31	40	1	6	0	109	218	8	37	4.0	.976	SS-69, 2B-4, 3B-2
1968	STL N		69	.220	.315	127	28	7	1	1	0.8	14	8	13	31	1	11	0	109	116	6	22	3.3	.974	SS-43, 2B-28
1969	BOS A		94	.257	.350	226	58	9	3	2	0.9	30	20	29	44	0	33	11	97	150	7	30	2.7	.972	2B-37, SS-11, 3B-9, OF-5
1970			76	.187	.245	139	26	1	2	1	0.7	16	14	21	26	0	43	7	37	64	6	8	1.4	.944	3B-15, 2B-15, SS-3
1971	2 teams	STL N (34G – .217)				MIL A (23G – .107)																			
"	total		57	.182	.261	88	16	4	0	1	1.1	9	7	12	17	0	17	5	35	71	3	14	1.9	.972	SS-21, 3B-15, 2B-15
	19 yrs.		1321	.227	.297	3083	699	113	20	21	0.7	394	211	390	526	12	247	49	1397	2341	144	484	2.9	.963	SS-660, 2B-159, 3B-95, OF-11

WORLD SERIES

1960	PIT N		3	.333	.333	3	1	0	0	0	0.0	0	0	1	0	0	3	1	2	0	0	0	0.7	1.000	SS-2
1968	STL N		2	–	–	0	0	0	0	0	–	0	0	0	0	0	0	0	0	0	0	0	0.0	–	
	2 yrs.		5	.333	.333	3	1	0	0	0	0.0	0	0	1	0	0	3	1	2	0	0	0	0.4	1.000	SS-2

Dick Schofield

SCHOFIELD, RICHARD CRAIG   BR TR 5'10" 175 lbs.
Son of Dick Schofield.
B. Nov. 21, 1962, Springfield, Ill.

1983	CAL A		21	.204	.407	54	11	2	0	3	5.6	4	4	6	8	0	0	0	24	67	7	10	4.7	.929	SS-21
1984			140	.193	.263	400	77	10	3	4	1.0	39	21	33	79	4	0	0	218	420	12	95	4.6	.982	SS-140
1985			147	.219	.331	438	96	19	3	8	1.8	50	41	35	70	11	1	0	261	397	25	108	4.6	.963	SS-147
1986			139	.249	.397	458	114	17	6	13	2.8	67	57	48	55	23	0	0	246	389	18	103	4.7	.972	SS-137
1987			134	.251	.355	479	120	17	3	9	1.9	52	46	37	63	19	0	0	205	351	9	76	4.2	.984	SS-131, 2B-2, DH-1
1988			155	.239	.317	527	126	11	6	6	1.1	61	34	40	57	20	0	0	278	492	13	125	5.1	.983	SS-155
1989			91	.228	.318	302	69	11	2	4	1.3	42	26	28	47	9	1	1	118	276	7	56	4.4	.983	SS-90
	7 yrs.		827	.231	.334	2658	613	87	23	47	1.8	315	229	227	379	86	2	1	1350	2392	91	573	4.6	.976	SS-821, 2B-2, DH-1

LEAGUE CHAMPIONSHIP SERIES

| 1986 | CAL A | | 7 | .300 | .433 | 30 | 9 | 1 | 0 | 1 | 3.3 | 4 | 2 | 1 | 5 | 1 | 0 | 0 | 12 | 23 | 2 | 3 | 5.3 | .946 | SS-7 |

Otto Schomberg

SCHOMBERG, OTTO H.   BL TL
Born Otto H. Shambrick.
B. Nov. 14, 1864, Milwaukee, Wis.   D. May 3, 1927, Ottawa, Kans.

1886	PIT AA		72	.272	.358	246	67	6	6	1	0.4	53		57			0	0	702	6	25	34	10.2	.966	1B-72
1887	IND N		112	.308	.463	419	129	18	16	5	1.2	91	83	56	32	21	0	0	1216	28	55	76	11.6	.958	1B-112, OF-1
1888			30	.214	.304	112	24	5	1	1	0.9	11	10	10	12	6	0	0	151	3	8	8	5.4	.951	OF-15, 1B-15
	3 yrs.		214	.283	.407	777	220	29	23	7	0.9	155	93	123	44	27	0	0	2069	37	88	118	10.3	.960	1B-199, OF-16

Jerry Schoonmaker

SCHOONMAKER, JERALD LEE   BR TR 5'11" 190 lbs.
B. Dec. 14, 1933, Seymour, Mo.

1955	WAS A		20	.152	.261	46	7	0	1	1	2.2	5	4	5	11	1	3	0	22	2	1	0	1.3	.960	OF-15
1957			30	.087	.130	23	2	1	0	0	0.0	5	0	2	11	0	7	0	15	0	0	0	0.5	1.000	OF-13
	2 yrs.		50	.130	.217	69	9	1	1	1	1.4	10	4	7	22	1	10	0	37	2	1	0	0.8	.975	OF-28

Paul Schramka

SCHRAMKA, PAUL EDWARD   BL TL 6' 185 lbs.
B. Mar. 22, 1928, Milwaukee, Wis.

| 1953 | CHI N | | 2 | – | – | 0 | 0 | 0 | 0 | 0 | – | 0 | 0 | 0 | 0 | 0 | 0 | 0 | 0 | 0 | 0 | 0 | 0.0 | – | OF-1 |

Ossee Schreckengost

SCHRECKENGOST, OSSEE FREEMAN   BR TR 5'10" 180 lbs.
B. Apr. 11, 1875, New Bethlehem, Pa.   D. July 9, 1914, Philadelphia, Pa.

1897	LOU N		1	.000	.000	3	0	0	0	0	0.0	0	0	0			0	0	2	1	0	0	3.0	1.000	C-1
1898	CLE N		10	.314	.543	35	11	2	3	0	0.0	5	10	0		1	1	0	33	10	7	1	5.0	.860	C-9
1899	2 teams	STL N (72G – .278)				CLE N (43G – .313)																			
"	total		115	.290	.375	427	124	20	5	2	0.5	57	47	21		18	6	0	637	110	40	41	6.8	.949	C-64, 1B-43, OF-2, SS-1, 2B-1
1901	BOS A		86	.304	.386	280	85	13	5	0	0.0	37	38	19		6	9	3	301	102	30	9	5.0	.931	C-72, 1B-4
1902	2 teams	CLE A (18G – .338)				PHI A (79G – .324)																			
"	total		97	.327	.402	358	117	17	2	2	0.6	50	52	9		5	5	0	619	117	28	11	7.9	.963	C-71, 1B-24, OF-1
1903	PHI A		92	.255	.353	306	78	13	4	3	1.0	26	30	11		0	5	1	597	110	18	8	7.9	.975	C-77, 1B-9
1904			95	.186	.232	311	58	9	1	1	0.3	23	21	5		3	3	1	666	77	14	5	8.0	.982	C-84, 1B-9
1905			121	.272	.358	416	113	19	6	0	0.0	30	45	3		9	7	1	800	114	15	11	7.7	.984	C-112, 1B-2
1906			98	.284	.358	338	96	20	1	0	0.0	29	41	10		5	5	0	568	112	19	8	7.1	.973	C-96, 1B-4
1907			101	.272	.334	356	97	16	3	0	0.0	30	38	17		4	2	0	643	145	12	4	7.9	.985	C-99, 1B-2
1908	2 teams	PHI A (71G – .222)				CHI A (6G – .188)																			
"	total		77	.220	.260	223	49	7	1	0	0.0	17	16	7		1	5	0	404	96	11	5	6.6	.978	C-72, 1B-1
	11 yrs.		893	.271	.345	3053	828	136	31	9	0.3	304	338	102		52	45	9	5270	994	194	103	7.2	.970	C-750, 1B-99, OF-3, SS-1, 2B-1

WORLD SERIES

| 1905 | PHI A | | 3 | .222 | .333 | 9 | 2 | 1 | 0 | 0 | 0.0 | 2 | 0 | 0 | | 0 | 0 | 0 | 17 | 4 | 0 | 1 | 7.0 | 1.000 | C-3 |

Year Team	Games	BA	SA	AB	H	2B	3B	HR	HR%	R	RBI	BB	SO	SB	PH AB	PH H	PO	A	E	DP	TC/G	FA	G by Pos

Hank Schreiber

SCHREIBER, HENRY WALTER
B. July 12, 1891, Cleveland, Ohio. D. Feb. 23, 1968, Indianapolis, Ind.   BR TR 5'11" 165 lbs.

Year Team	Games	BA	SA	AB	H	2B	3B	HR	HR%	R	RBI	BB	SO	SB	PH AB	PH H	PO	A	E	DP	TC/G	FA	G by Pos
1914 CHI A	1	.000	.000	2	0	0	0	0	0.0	0	0	0	1	0	0	0	0	0	0	0	0.0	–	OF-1
1917 BOS N	2	.286	.286	7	2	0	0	0	0.0	1	0	0	1	0	0	0	3	1	0	0	2.0	1.000	SS-1, 3B-1
1919 CIN N	19	.224	.293	58	13	4	0	0	0.0	5	4	0	12	0	0	0	14	50	1	6	3.4	.985	3B-17, SS-2
1921 NY N	4	.333	.333	6	2	0	0	0	0.0	2	2	1	1	0	0	0	5	6	2	0	3.3	.846	SS-2, 2B-2, 3B-1
1926 CHI N	10	.056	.111	18	1	1	0	0	0.0	2	0	0	1	0	0	0	7	11	0	0	1.8	1.000	SS-3, 3B-3, 2B-1
5 yrs.	36	.198	.253	91	18	5	0	0	0.0	10	6	1	16	0	0	0	29	68	3	6	2.8	.970	3B-22, SS-8, 2B-3, OF-1

Ted Schreiber

SCHREIBER, THEODORE HENRY
B. July 11, 1938, Brooklyn, N. Y.   BR TR 5'11" 175 lbs.

Year Team	Games	BA	SA	AB	H	2B	3B	HR	HR%	R	RBI	BB	SO	SB	PH AB	PH H	PO	A	E	DP	TC/G	FA	G by Pos
1963 NY N	39	.160	.160	50	8	0	0	0	0.0	1	2	4	14	0	10	0	15	44	1	3	1.5	.983	3B-17, SS-9, 2B-3

Pop Schriver

SCHRIVER, WILLIAM FREDERICK
B. June 11, 1865, Brooklyn, N. Y.   D. Dec. 27, 1932, Brooklyn, N. Y.   BR TR 5'10" 185 lbs.

Year Team	Games	BA	SA	AB	H	2B	3B	HR	HR%	R	RBI	BB	SO	SB	PH AB	PH H	PO	A	E	DP	TC/G	FA	G by Pos
1886 BKN AA	8	.048	.048	21	1	0	0	0	0.0	2		2			0	0	12	6	3	0	2.6	.857	OF-5, C-3
1888 PHI N	40	.194	.284	134	26	5	2	1	0.0	15	23	7	21	2	0	0	156	63	36	3	6.4	.859	C-27, SS-6, 3B-6, OF-1
1889	55	.265	.327	211	56	10	0	1	0.5	24	19	16	8	5	0	0	241	99	36	6	6.8	.904	C-48, 2B-6, 3B-1
1890	57	.274	.368	223	61	9	6	0	0.0	37	35	22	15	9	0	0	272	63	33	12	6.5	.910	C-34, 1B-10, 3B-8, 2B-3, OF-2
1891 CHI N	27	.333	.467	90	30	1	4	1	1.1	15	21	10	9	1	0	0	135	27	6	3	6.2	.964	C-27, 1B-2
1892	92	.224	.301	326	73	10	6	1	0.3	40	34	27	25	4	0	0	379	103	37	5	5.6	.929	C-82, OF-10
1893	64	.284	.397	229	65	8	3	4	1.7	49	34	14	9	4	3	0	224	63	23	8	4.8	.926	C-56, OF-5
1894	96	.275	.352	349	96	12	3	3	0.9	55	47	29	21	9	1	0	310	106	36	13	4.7	.920	C-88, SS-3, 3B-3, 1B-2
1895 NY N	24	.315	.391	92	29	2	1	1	1.1	16	16	9	10	3	0	0	127	24	16	6	7.0	.904	C-18, 1B-6
1897 CIN N	61	.303	.433	178	54	12	4	1	0.6	29	30	19		3	5	1	147	42	8	3	3.2	.959	C-53
1898 PIT N	95	.229	.295	315	72	15	3	0	0.0	25	32	23		2	0	0	307	95	18	6	4.4	.957	C-92, 1B-1
1899	91	.282	.389	301	85	19	5	1	0.3	31	49	23		4	5	1	356	95	16	9	5.1	.966	C-78, 1B-8
1900	37	.293	.402	92	27	7	0	1	1.1	11	12	10		0	9	3	95	21	5	1	3.3	.959	C-24, 1B-1
1901 STL N	53	.271	.367	166	45	7	3	1	0.6	17	23	12		2	9	**3**	273	61	10	13	6.5	.971	C-24, 1B-19
14 yrs.	800	.264	.354	2727	720	117	40	16	0.6	366	375	223	118	46	34	8	3034	868	283	88	5.2	.932	C-654, 1B-49, OF-23, 3B-18, SS-9, 2B-9

Bob Schroder

SCHRODER, ROBERT JAMES
B. Dec. 30, 1944, Ridgefield, N. J.   BL TR 6' 175 lbs.

Year Team	Games	BA	SA	AB	H	2B	3B	HR	HR%	R	RBI	BB	SO	SB	PH AB	PH H	PO	A	E	DP	TC/G	FA	G by Pos
1965 SF N	31	.222	.222	9	2	0	0	0	0.0	4	1	1	1	0	6	2	4	6	0	1	0.3	1.000	2B-4, 3B-1
1966	10	.242	.242	33	8	0	0	0	0.0	0	2	0	2	0	1	0	9	17	1	2	2.7	.963	SS-9
1967	62	.230	.259	135	31	4	0	0	0.0	20	7	15	15	1	17	3	60	88	1	12	2.4	.993	2B-45, 3B-4
1968	35	.159	.227	44	7	1	1	0	0.0	5	2	7	3	0	11	1	11	20	2	2	0.9	.939	2B-12, SS-4, 3B-2
4 yrs.	138	.217	.249	221	48	5	1	0	0.0	29	12	23	21	1	35	6	84	131	4	17	1.6	.982	2B-61, SS-13, 3B-7

Bill Schroeder

SCHROEDER, ALFRED WILLIAM III
B. Sept. 7, 1958, Baltimore, Md.   BR TR 6'2" 210 lbs.

Year Team	Games	BA	SA	AB	H	2B	3B	HR	HR%	R	RBI	BB	SO	SB	PH AB	PH H	PO	A	E	DP	TC/G	FA	G by Pos
1983 MIL A	23	.178	.356	73	13	2	1	3	4.1	7	7	3	23	0	0	0	92	5	2	1	4.3	.980	C-23
1984	61	.257	.486	210	54	6	1	14	6.7	29	25	8	54	0	1	0	277	24	4	2	5.0	.987	C-58, DH-3, 1B-1
1985	53	.242	.407	194	47	8	0	8	4.1	18	25	12	61	0	0	0	216	23	3	5	4.6	.988	C-48, DH-4, 1B-1
1986	64	.212	.373	217	46	14	0	7	3.2	32	19	9	59	1	0	0	307	25	1	13	5.2	.997	C-35, 1B-19, DH-10
1987	75	.332	.548	250	83	12	0	14	5.6	35	42	16	56	5	4	0	373	27	2	8	5.4	.995	C-67, 1B-4, DH-2
1988	41	.156	.295	122	19	2	0	5	4.1	9	10	6	36	0	0	0	197	21	0	3	5.3	1.000	C-30, 1B-10, DH-1
1989 CAL A	41	.203	.348	138	28	2	0	6	4.3	16	15	3	44	0	0	0	252	32	3	10	7.0	.990	C-33, 1B-8
7 yrs.	358	.241	.423	1204	290	46	1	57	4.7	146	143	57	333	6	5	0	1714	157	15	42	5.3	.992	C-294, 1B-43, DH-20

Rick Schu

SCHU, RICHARD SPENCER
B. Jan. 26, 1962, Philadelphia, Pa.   BR TR 6' 170 lbs.

Year Team	Games	BA	SA	AB	H	2B	3B	HR	HR%	R	RBI	BB	SO	SB	PH AB	PH H	PO	A	E	DP	TC/G	FA	G by Pos
1984 PHI N	17	.276	.621	29	8	2	1	2	6.9	12	5	6	6	0	2	0	7	13	1	3	1.2	.952	3B-15
1985	112	.252	.373	416	105	21	4	7	1.7	54	24	38	78	8	1	0	86	191	20	19	2.7	.933	3B-111
1986	92	.274	.447	208	57	10	1	8	3.8	32	25	18	44	2	29	7	42	94	13	6	1.6	.913	3B-58
1987	92	.235	.403	196	46	6	3	7	3.6	24	23	20	36	0	24	2	193	71	10	11	3.0	.964	3B-45, 1B-28
1988 BAL A	89	.256	.363	270	69	9	4	4	1.5	22	20	21	49	6	5	1	94	110	11	8	2.4	.949	3B-72, DH-9, 1B-4
1989 2 teams		BAL A (1G – .000)		DET A (98G – .214)																			
" total	99	.214	.335	266	57	11	0	7	2.6	25	21	24	37	1	10	2	59	126	12	14	2.0	.939	3B-83, DH-9, 2B-6, SS-3, 1B-3
6 yrs.	501	.247	.384	1385	342	59	13	35	2.5	169	118	127	250	17	71	12	481	605	67	61	2.3	.942	3B-384, 1B-35, DH-18, 2B-6, SS-3

Heinie Schuble

SCHUBLE, HENRY GEORGE
B. Nov. 1, 1906, Houston, Tex.   BR TR 5'9" 152 lbs.

Year Team	Games	BA	SA	AB	H	2B	3B	HR	HR%	R	RBI	BB	SO	SB	PH AB	PH H	PO	A	E	DP	TC/G	FA	G by Pos
1927 STL N	65	.257	.358	218	56	6	2	4	1.8	29	28	7	27	0	0	0	120	192	29	36	5.2	.915	SS-65
1929 DET A	92	.233	.353	258	60	11	7	2	0.8	35	28	19	23	3	1	0	142	217	47	43	4.4	.884	SS-86, 3B-2
1932	101	.271	.409	340	92	20	6	5	1.5	57	52	24	37	14	2	0	112	204	19	24	3.3	.943	3B-76, SS-15
1933	49	.219	.281	96	21	4	1	0	0.0	12	6	5	17	2	9	4	19	46	4	1	1.4	.942	3B-23, SS-2, 2B-1
1934	11	.267	.400	15	4	2	0	0	0.0	2	2	1	0	0	4	0	1	9	0	1	1.0	1.000	SS-3, 3B-2, 2B-1
1935	11	.250	.250	8	2	0	0	0	0.0	3	0	1	0	0	2	1	1	4	2	0	0.6	.714	3B-2, 2B-1
1936 STL N	2	–	–	0	0	0	0	0	–	0	0	0	0	0	0	0	0	0	0	0	–	–	3B-1
7 yrs.	331	.251	.367	935	235	43	16	11	1.2	138	116	57	108	19	18	5	398	672	101	107	3.5	.914	SS-171, 3B-106, 2B-3

Wes Schulmerich

SCHULMERICH, EDWARD WESLEY
B. Aug. 21, 1901, Hillsboro, Ore.   D. June 26, 1985, Corvallis, Ore.   BR TR 5'11" 210 lbs.

Year Team	Games	BA	SA	AB	H	2B	3B	HR	HR%	R	RBI	BB	SO	SB	PH AB	PH H	PO	A	E	DP	TC/G	FA	G by Pos
1931 BOS N	95	.309	.422	327	101	17	7	2	0.6	36	43	28	30	0	6	3	190	6	7	0	2.1	.966	OF-87
1932	119	.260	.421	404	105	22	5	11	2.7	47	57	27	61	5	18	4	232	11	8	5	2.1	.968	OF-101

Year	Team	Games	BA	SA	AB	H	2B	3B	HR	HR%	R	RBI	BB	SO	SB	Pinch Hit AB	Pinch Hit H	PO	A	E	DP	TC/G	FA	G by Pos

Wes Schulmerich *continued*

1933	2 teams	BOS N (29G – .247)				PHI N (97G – .334)																		
"	total	126	.318	.456	450	143	25	5	9	2.0	63	72	37	55	1	7	2	256	9	6	0	2.2	.978	OF-118
1934	2 teams	PHI N (15G – .250)				CIN N (74G – .263)																		
"	total	89	.261	.375	261	68	9	3	5	1.9	23	20	26	51	1	19	8	146	2	4	1	1.7	.974	OF-69
4 yrs.		429	.289	.424	1442	417	73	20	27	1.9	169	192	118	197	7	50	17	824	28	25	6	2.0	.971	OF-375

Art Schult

SCHULT, ARTHUR WILLIAM (Dutch) BR TR 6'3" 210 lbs.
B. June 20, 1928, Brooklyn, N. Y.

1953	NY	A	7	–	–	0	0	0	0	0	0.0	3	0	0	0	0	0	0	0	0	0	0	0.0	–	
1956	CIN	N	5	.429	.429	7	3	0	0	0	0.0	3	2	1	1	0	3	2	0	0	0	0	0.0	–	OF-1
1957	2 teams	CIN N (21G – .265)				WAS A (77G – .263)																		
"	total	98	.263	.363	281	74	16	0	4	1.4	34	39	14	32	0	26	5	379	15	6	35	4.1	.985	OF-36, 1B-35
1959	CHI	N	42	.271	.381	118	32	7	0	2	1.7	17	14	7	14	0	9	2	152	6	2	15	3.8	.988	1B-23, OF-15
1960			12	.133	.200	15	2	1	0	0	0.0	1	1	1	3	0	7	1	4	0	0	0	0.3	1.000	OF-4, 1B-1
5 yrs.		164	.264	.363	421	111	24	0	6	1.4	58	56	23	50	0	45	10	535	21	8	50	3.4	.986	1B-59, OF-56

Fred Schulte

SCHULTE, FRED WILLIAM (Fritz) BR TR 6'1" 183 lbs.
Born Fred William Schult.
B. Jan. 13, 1901, Belvidere, Ill.   D. May 20, 1983, Belvidere, Ill.

1927	STL	A	60	.317	.503	189	60	16	5	3	1.6	32	34	20	14	5	8	4	117	3	11	0	2.2	.916	OF-49
1928			146	.286	.424	556	159	44	6	7	1.3	90	85	51	60	6	1	1	419	21	12	6	3.1	.973	OF-143
1929			121	.307	.404	446	137	24	5	3	0.7	63	71	59	44	8	5	1	361	12	4	2	3.1	.989	OF-116
1930			113	.278	.401	392	109	23	5	5	1.3	59	62	41	44	12	7	1	297	7	11	6	2.8	.965	OF-98, 1B-5
1931			134	.304	.436	553	168	32	7	9	1.6	100	65	56	49	6	0	0	361	13	11	4	2.9	.971	OF-134
1932			146	.294	.425	565	166	35	6	9	1.6	106	73	71	44	5	8	5	370	12	8	4	2.7	.979	OF-129, 1B-5
1933	WAS	A	144	.295	.402	550	162	30	7	5	0.9	98	87	61	27	10	1	0	433	10	9	4	3.1	.980	OF-142
1934			136	.298	.399	524	156	32	6	3	0.6	72	73	53	34	3	2	1	351	5	5	0	2.7	.986	OF-134
1935			75	.268	.357	224	60	6	4	2	0.9	33	23	22	22	0	22	5	96	2	2	0	1.3	.980	OF-55
1936	PIT	N	74	.261	.328	238	62	7	3	1	0.4	28	17	20	20	1	17	7	129	1	3	1	1.8	.977	OF-55
1937			29	.100	.100	20	2	0	0	0	0.0	5	3	4	3	0	12	1	4	0	1	0	0.2	.800	OF-4
11 yrs.		1178	.292	.409	4257	1241	249	54	47	1.1	686	593	462	361	56	83	26	2938	86	77	27	2.6	.975	OF-1059, 1B-10

WORLD SERIES

| 1933 | WAS | A | 5 | .333 | .524 | 21 | 7 | 1 | 0 | 1 | 4.8 | 1 | 4 | 1 | 1 | 0 | 0 | 0 | 9 | 0 | 0 | 0 | 1.8 | 1.000 | OF-5 |

Ham Schulte

SCHULTE, HERMAN JOSEPH BR TR 5'8½" 158 lbs.
Born Herman Joseph Schultehenrich.   Brother of Len Schulte.
B. Sept. 1, 1912, St. Charles, Mo.

| 1940 | PHI | N | 120 | .236 | .294 | 436 | 103 | 18 | 2 | 1 | 0.2 | 44 | 21 | 32 | 30 | 3 | 1 | 0 | 283 | 320 | 13 | 72 | 5.1 | .979 | 2B-119, SS-1 |

Jack Schulte

SCHULTE, JOHN HERMAN FRANK BR TR 5'9" 180 lbs.
B. Nov. 15, 1881, Cincinnati, Ohio   D. Aug. 17, 1975, Roseville, Mich.

| 1906 | BOS | N | 2 | .000 | .000 | 7 | 0 | 0 | 0 | 0 | 0.0 | 0 | 0 | 0 | | 0 | 0 | 0 | 3 | 3 | 0 | 0 | 3.0 | 1.000 | SS-2 |

Johnny Schulte

SCHULTE, JOHN CLEMENT BL TR 5'11" 190 lbs.
B. Sept. 8, 1896, Fredericktown, Mo.   D. June 28, 1978, St. Louis, Mo.

1923	STL	A	7	.000	.000	3	0	0	0	0	0.0	1	1	4	0	0	2	0	5	1	0	1	0.9	1.000	1B-1, C-1
1927	STL	N	64	.288	.538	156	45	8	2	9	5.8	35	32	47	19	1	3	1	172	45	10	6	3.5	.956	C-59
1928	PHI	N	65	.248	.407	113	28	2	2	4	3.5	14	17	15	12	0	26	6	70	23	5	4	1.5	.949	C-34
1929	CHI	N	31	.261	.304	69	18	3	0	0	0.0	6	9	7	11	0	1	1	74	16	2	3	3.0	.978	C-30
1932	2 teams	STL A (15G – .208)				BOS N (10G – .222)																		
"	total	25	.212	.364	33	7	2	0	1	3.0	3	5	3	7	0	8	1	35	2	3	1	1.6	.925	C-16
5 yrs.		192	.262	.436	374	98	15	4	14	3.7	59	64	76	49	1	40	9	356	87	20	15	2.4	.957	C-140, 1B-1

Len Schulte

SCHULTE, LEONARD BERNARD BR TR 5'10" 160 lbs.
Born Leonard Bernard Schultehenrich.   Brother of Ham Schulte.
B. Dec. 5, 1916, St. Charles, Mo.   D. May 6, 1986, Orlando, Fla.

1944	STL	A	1	–	–	0	0	0	0	0	0.0	0	0	0	0	0	0	0	0	0	0	0	0.0	–	
1945			119	.247	.288	430	106	16	1	0	0.0	37	36	24	35	0	3	0	167	245	23	24	3.7	.947	3B-71, 2B-37, SS-14
1946			4	.400	.400	5	2	0	0	0	0.0	1	2	0	0	0	3	1	2	3	0	0	1.3	1.000	3B-1, 2B-1
3 yrs.		124	.248	.290	435	108	16	1	0	0.0	38	38	24	35	0	6	1	169	248	23	24	3.5	.948	3B-72, 2B-38, SS-14

Wildfire Schulte

SCHULTE, FRANK M. BL TR 5'11" 170 lbs.
B. Sept. 17, 1882, Cohocton, N. Y.   D. Oct. 2, 1949, Oakland, Calif.

1904	CHI	N	20	.286	.476	84	24	4	3	2	2.4	16	13	2		1	0	0	34	3	2	0	2.0	.949	OF-20
1905			123	.274	.367	493	135	15	14	1	0.2	67	47	32		25	0	0	189	14	4	0	1.7	.981	OF-123
1906			146	.281	.396	563	158	18	13	7	1.2	77	60	31		25	0	0	218	18	6	7	1.7	.975	OF-146
1907			97	.287	.386	342	98	14	7	2	0.6	44	32	22		7	5	1	130	11	4	1	1.5	.972	OF-91
1908			102	.236	.306	386	91	20	2	1	0.3	42	43	29		15	0	0	148	11	1	3	1.6	.994	OF-102
1909			140	.264	.357	538	142	16	11	4	0.7	57	60	24		23	0	0	169	14	6	1	1.4	.968	OF-140
1910			151	.301	.460	559	168	29	15	10	1.8	93	68	39	57	22	1	0	221	18	8	5	1.6	.968	OF-150
1911			154	.300	.534	577	173	30	21	21	3.6	105	121	76	68	23	0	0	246	19	8	8	1.8	.971	OF-154
1912			139	.264	.423	553	146	27	11	13	2.4	90	70	53	70	17	0	0	219	19	12	6	1.8	.952	OF-139
1913			132	.279	.414	495	138	28	6	9	1.8	85	72	39	68	21	2	1	180	13	9	2	1.5	.955	OF-129
1914			137	.241	.351	465	112	22	7	5	1.1	54	61	39	55	16	3	1	217	9	11	4	1.7	.954	OF-134
1915			151	.249	.373	550	137	20	6	12	2.2	66	69	49	68	19	3	1	280	24	12	3	2.1	.962	OF-147
1916	2 teams	CHI N (72G – .296)				PIT N (55G – .254)																		
"	total	127	.278	.373	407	113	16	4	5	1.2	43	41	37	54	14	9	1	197	10	9	0	1.7	.958	OF-113

Year	Team	Games	BA	SA	AB	H	2B	3B	HR	HR%	R	RBI	BB	SO	SB	Pinch Hit AB	Pinch Hit H	PO	A	E	DP	TC/G	FA	G by Pos

Wildfire Schulte *continued*

Year	Team	Games	BA	SA	AB	H	2B	3B	HR	HR%	R	RBI	BB	SO	SB	AB	H	PO	A	E	DP	TC/G	FA	G by Pos
1917	2 teams		PIT N	(30G – .214)		PHI N	(64G – .215)																	
"	total	94	.214	.294	252	54	15	1	1	0.4	32	22	26	36	9	21	5	96	4	6	0	1.1	.943	OF-70
1918	WAS A	93	.288	.363	267	77	14	3	0	0.0	35	44	47	36	5	16	5	145	10	5	4	1.7	.969	OF-75
15 yrs.		1806	.270	.395	6531	1766	288	124	93	1.4	906	823	545	512	233	60	15	2689	197	103	42	1.7	.966	OF-1733

WORLD SERIES

Year	Team	Games	BA	SA	AB	H	2B	3B	HR	HR%	R	RBI	BB	SO	SB	AB	H	PO	A	E	DP	TC/G	FA	G by Pos
1906	CHI N	6	.269	.385	26	7	3	0	0	0.0	1	3	1	3	0	0	0	6	1	0	1	1.2	1.000	OF-6
1907		5	.250	.250	20	5	0	0	0	0.0	3	2	1	2	1	0	0	6	2	2	0	2.0	.800	OF-5
1908		5	.389	.500	18	7	0	1	0	0.0	4	2	2	1	2	0	0	3	0	0	0	0.6	1.000	OF-5
1910		5	.353	.529	17	6	3	0	0	0.0	3	2	2	3	0	0	0	4	0	1	0	1.0	.800	OF-5
4 yrs.		21	.309	.407	81	25	6	1	0	0.0	11	9	6	9	3	0	0	19	3	3	1	1.2	.880	OF-21

Howie Schultz

SCHULTZ, HOWARD HENRY (Steeple, Stretch)
B. July 3, 1922, St. Paul, Minn.

BR TR 6'6" 200 lbs.

Year	Team	Games	BA	SA	AB	H	2B	3B	HR	HR%	R	RBI	BB	SO	SB	AB	H	PO	A	E	DP	TC/G	FA	G by Pos
1943	BKN N	45	.269	.352	182	49	12	0	1	0.5	20	34	6	24	3	0	0	386	33	6	27	9.4	.986	1B-45
1944		138	.255	.390	526	134	32	3	11	2.1	59	83	24	67	6	6	5	1091	85	14	90	8.6	.988	1B-136
1945		39	.239	.345	142	34	8	2	1	0.7	18	19	10	14	2	1	0	334	32	6	35	9.5	.984	1B-38
1946		90	.253	.353	249	63	14	1	3	1.2	27	27	16	34	2	3	0	576	58	7	65	7.1	.989	1B-87
1947	2 teams	BKN	N	(2G – .000)		PHI	N	(114G – .223)																
"	total	116	.223	.319	404	90	19	1	6	1.5	30	35	21	70	0	1	0	987	67	7	92	9.1	.993	1B-115
1948	2 teams	PHI	N	(6G – .077)		CIN	N	(36G – .167)																
"	total	42	.153	.224	85	13	0	0	2	2.4	9	10	5	9	2	10	2	177	7	3	17	4.5	.984	1B-29
6 yrs.		470	.241	.349	1588	383	85	7	24	1.5	163	208	82	218	15	21	7	3551	282	43	326	8.2	.989	1B-450

Joe Schultz

SCHULTZ, JOSEPH CHARLES, JR. (Dode)
Son of Joe Schultz.
B. Aug. 29, 1918, Chicago, Ill.
Manager 1969, 1973.

BL TR 5'11" 180 lbs.

Year	Team	Games	BA	SA	AB	H	2B	3B	HR	HR%	R	RBI	BB	SO	SB	AB	H	PO	A	E	DP	TC/G	FA	G by Pos
1939	PIT N	4	.286	.429	14	4	2	0	0	0.0	3	2	2	0	0	0	0	24	1	0	0	6.3	1.000	C-4
1940		16	.194	.250	36	7	0	1	0	0.0	2	4	2	1	0	3	2	29	4	3	0	2.3	.917	C-13
1941		2	.500	.500	2	1	0	0	0	0.0	1	0	0	0	0	0	0	0	0	0	0	0.0	–	
1943	STL A	46	.239	.293	92	22	5	0	0	0.0	6	8	9	8	0	23	6	83	9	2	1	2.0	.979	C-26
1944		3	.250	.250	8	2	0	0	0	0.0	1	0	0	1	0	1	0	8	1	2	0	3.7	.818	C-3
1945		41	.295	.341	44	13	2	0	0	0.0	1	8	3	1	0	35	11	15	1	1	0	0.4	.941	C-4
1946		42	.386	.456	57	22	4	0	0	0.0	1	14	11	2	0	23	10	42	0	0	2	1.0	1.000	C-17
1947		43	.184	.263	38	7	0	0	1	2.6	3	1	4	5	0	38	7	0	0	0	0	0.0	–	
1948		43	.189	.189	37	7	0	0	0	0.0	0	9	6	3	0	37	7	0	0	0	0	0.0	–	
9 yrs.		240	.259	.314	328	85	13	1	1	0.3	18	46	37	21	0	160	43	201	16	8	3	0.9	.964	C-67

Joe Schultz

SCHULTZ, JOSEPH CHARLES SR. (Germany)
Father of Joe Schultz.
B. July 24, 1893, Pittsburgh, Pa. D. Apr. 13, 1941, Columbia, S. C.

BR TR 5'11½" 172 lbs.

Year	Team	Games	BA	SA	AB	H	2B	3B	HR	HR%	R	RBI	BB	SO	SB	AB	H	PO	A	E	DP	TC/G	FA	G by Pos
1912	BOS N	4	.250	.333	12	3	1	0	0	0.0	1	4	0	2	0	0	0	6	8	3	1	4.3	.824	2B-4
1913		9	.222	.222	18	4	0	0	0	0.0	2	1	2	7	0	1	0	11	1	0	0	1.3	1.000	OF-5, 2B-1
1915	2 teams	BKN	N	(56G – .292)		CHI	N	(7G – .250)																
"	total	63	.289	.344	128	37	3	2	0	0.0	14	7	10	20	3	29	8	46	46	11	3	1.6	.893	3B-55, 2B-2, SS-1
1916	PIT N	77	.260	.319	204	53	8	2	0	0.0	18	22	7	14	6	20	5	75	86	22	3	2.4	.880	3B-24, 2B-24, OF-6, SS-1
1919	STL N	88	.253	.328	229	58	9	1	2	0.9	24	21	11	7	4	31	8	87	15	4	2	1.2	.962	OF-49, 2B-5
1920		99	.263	.309	320	84	5	5	0	0.0	38	32	21	11	5	14	2	147	7	9	3	1.6	.945	OF-80
1921		92	.309	.469	275	85	20	3	6	2.2	37	45	15	11	4	18	6	137	14	6	4	1.7	.962	OF-67, 3B-3, 1B-2
1922		112	.314	.392	344	108	13	4	2	0.6	50	64	19	10	3	22	8	195	7	5	1	1.8	.976	OF-89
1923		2	.286	.286	7	2	0	0	0	0.0	0	1	0	0	0	0	0	5	0	0	0	2.5	1.000	OF-2
1924	2 teams	STL	N	(12G – .167)		PHI	N	(88G – .282)																
"	total	100	.277	.385	296	82	15	1	5	1.7	35	31	23	18	6	17	4	138	7	6	0	1.5	.960	OF-78
1925	2 teams	PHI	N	(24G – .344)		CIN	N	(33G – .323)																
"	total	57	.333	.421	126	42	9	1	0	0.0	16	21	7	2	4	18	3	51	4	4	1	1.0	.932	OF-35, 2B-1
11 yrs.		703	.285	.370	1959	558	83	19	15	0.8	235	249	116	102	35	170	46	898	195	70	18	1.7	.940	OF-411, 3B-82, 2B-37, SS-2, 1B-2

John Schultz

SCHULTZ, JOHN
B. St. Louis, Mo. Deceased.

Year	Team	Games	BA	SA	AB	H	2B	3B	HR	HR%	R	RBI	BB	SO	SB	AB	H	PO	A	E	DP	TC/G	FA	G by Pos
1891	STL AA	1	.000	.000	2	0	0	0	0	0.0	0	0	0	0	0	0	0	1	1	0	0	2.0	1.000	C-1

Jeff Schulz

SCHULZ, JEFFREY ALAN
B. June 2, 1961, Evansville, Ind.

BL TR 6'1" 190 lbs.

Year	Team	Games	BA	SA	AB	H	2B	3B	HR	HR%	R	RBI	BB	SO	SB	AB	H	PO	A	E	DP	TC/G	FA	G by Pos
1989	KC A	7	.222	.222	9	2	0	0	0	0.0	0	1	0	2	0	2	2	6	0	0	0	0.9	1.000	OF-5

Bill Schuster

SCHUSTER, WILLIAM CHARLES (Broadway)
B. Aug. 4, 1912, Buffalo, N. Y. D. June 28, 1987, El Monte, Calif.

BR TR 5'9" 164 lbs.

Year	Team	Games	BA	SA	AB	H	2B	3B	HR	HR%	R	RBI	BB	SO	SB	AB	H	PO	A	E	DP	TC/G	FA	G by Pos
1937	PIT N	3	.500	.500	6	3	0	0	0	0.0	2	1	0	1	0	0	0	3	6	0	2	3.0	1.000	SS-2
1939	BOS N	2	.000	.000	3	0	0	0	0	0.0	0	0	0	1	0	0	0	2	3	1	0	3.0	.833	SS-1, 3B-1
1943	CHI N	13	.294	.373	51	15	2	1	0	0.0	3	0	3	2	0	0	0	34	52	2	14	6.8	.977	SS-13
1944		60	.221	.299	154	34	7	1	1	0.6	14	14	12	16	4	11	3	71	109	9	21	3.2	.952	SS-38, 2B-6
1945		45	.191	.277	47	9	2	1	0	0.0	8	2	7	4	2	2	0	38	40	4	8	1.8	.951	SS-22, 2B-3, 3B-1
5 yrs.		123	.234	.310	261	61	11	3	1	0.4	27	17	23	23	6	13	3	148	210	16	45	3.0	.957	SS-76, 2B-9, 3B-2

WORLD SERIES

Year	Team	Games	BA	SA	AB	H	2B	3B	HR	HR%	R	RBI	BB	SO	SB	AB	H	PO	A	E	DP	TC/G	FA	G by Pos
1945	CHI N	2	.000	.000	1	0	0	0	0	0.0	1	0	0	0	0	0	0	1	2	0	0	1.5	1.000	SS-1

Bill Schwartz

SCHWARTZ, WILLIAM CHARLES (Blab)
B. Apr. 22, 1884, Cleveland, Ohio D. Aug. 29, 1961, Nashville, Tenn.

BR TR 6'2" 185 lbs.

Year	Team	Games	BA	SA	AB	H	2B	3B	HR	HR%	R	RBI	BB	SO	SB	Pinch Hit AB	Pinch Hit H	PO	A	E	DP	TC/G	FA	G by Pos

Bill Schwartz *continued*

Year	Team	Games	BA	SA	AB	H	2B	3B	HR	HR%	R	RBI	BB	SO	SB	AB	H	PO	A	E	DP	TC/G	FA	G by Pos
1904	CLE A	24	.151	.174	86	13	2	0	0	0.0	5	0	0		4	1	0	244	6	6	4	10.7	.977	1B-22, 3B-1

Pop Schwartz

SCHWARTZ, WILLIAM AUGUST (Scooper Bill)
B. Apr. 3, 1864, Jamestown, Ky. D. Dec. 22, 1940, Newport, Ky.   BR TR 6'1" 195 lbs.

Year	Team	Games	BA	SA	AB	H	2B	3B	HR	HR%	R	RBI	BB	SO	SB	AB	H	PO	A	E	DP	TC/G	FA	G by Pos
1883	COL AA	2	.250	.250	4	1	0	0	0	0.0	0		0			0	0	6	0	5	0	5.5	.545	1B-1, C-1
1884	CIN U	29	.236	.302	106	25	4	0	1	0.9	14		3			0	0	163	35	40	1	8.2	.832	C-25, OF-3, 3B-1
2 yrs.		31	.236	.300	110	26	4	0	1	0.9	14		3			0	0	169	35	45	1	8.0	.819	C-26, OF-3, 3B-1, 1B-1

Randy Schwartz

SCHWARTZ, DOUGLAS RANDALL
B. Feb. 9, 1944, Los Angeles, Calif.   BL TL 6'3" 230 lbs.

Year	Team	Games	BA	SA	AB	H	2B	3B	HR	HR%	R	RBI	BB	SO	SB	AB	H	PO	A	E	DP	TC/G	FA	G by Pos
1965	KC A	6	.286	.286	7	2	0	0	0	0.0	0	1	0	4	0	3	1	9	2	0	0	1.8	1.000	1B-2
1966		10	.091	.091	11	1	0	0	0	0.0	0	1	1	3	0	9	1	8	0	0	1	0.8	1.000	1B-2
2 yrs.		16	.167	.167	18	3	0	0	0	0.0	0	2	1	7	0	12	2	17	2	0	1	1.2	1.000	1B-4

Bill Schwarz

SCHWARZ, WILLIAM DeWITT
B. Jan. 30, 1891, Birmingham, Ala. D. June 24, 1949, Jacksonville, Fla.   TR

Year	Team	Games	BA	SA	AB	H	2B	3B	HR	HR%	R	RBI	BB	SO	SB	AB	H	PO	A	E	DP	TC/G	FA	G by Pos
1914	NY A	1	.000	.000	1	0	0	0	0	0.0	0	0	0	1	0	0	0	1	1	0	0	2.0	1.000	C-1

Al Schweitzer

SCHWEITZER, ALBERT CASPER (Cheese)
B. Dec. 23, 1882, Cleveland, Ohio D. Jan. 27, 1969, Newark, Ohio   BR TR 5'7½" 170 lbs.

Year	Team	Games	BA	SA	AB	H	2B	3B	HR	HR%	R	RBI	BB	SO	SB	AB	H	PO	A	E	DP	TC/G	FA	G by Pos
1908	STL A	64	.291	.352	182	53	4	2	1	0.5	22	14	20		6	9	1	86	14	5	3	1.6	.952	OF-55
1909		27	.224	.250	76	17	2	0	0	0.0	7	2	5		3	5	0	26	2	2	0	1.1	.933	OF-22
1910		113	.230	.285	379	87	11	2	2	0.5	37	37	36		26	3	1	149	15	11	3	1.5	.937	OF-109
1911		76	.215	.295	237	51	11	4	0	0.0	31	34	43		12	8	0	100	13	8	4	1.6	.934	OF-68
4 yrs.		280	.238	.299	874	208	28	8	3	0.3	97	87	104		47	25	2	361	44	26	10	1.5	.940	OF-254

Pius Schwert

SCHWERT, PIUS LOUIS
B. Nov. 22, 1892, Angola, N. Y. D. Mar. 11, 1941, Washington, D. C.   BR TR 5'10½" 160 lbs.

Year	Team	Games	BA	SA	AB	H	2B	3B	HR	HR%	R	RBI	BB	SO	SB	AB	H	PO	A	E	DP	TC/G	FA	G by Pos
1914	NY A	2	.000	.000	5	0	0	0	0	0.0	0	0	2	2	0	0	0	3	7	1	0	5.5	.909	C-2
1915		9	.278	.444	18	5	3	0	0	0.0	6	6	1	6	0	0	0	27	8	1	0	4.0	.972	C-9
2 yrs.		11	.217	.348	23	5	3	0	0	0.0	6	6	3	8	0	0	0	30	15	2	0	4.3	.957	C-11

Art Schwind

SCHWIND, ARTHUR EDWIN
B. Nov. 4, 1889, Fort Wayne, Ind. D. Jan. 13, 1968, Sullivan, Ill.   BB TR 5'8" 150 lbs.

Year	Team	Games	BA	SA	AB	H	2B	3B	HR	HR%	R	RBI	BB	SO	SB	AB	H	PO	A	E	DP	TC/G	FA	G by Pos
1912	BOS N	1	.500	.500	2	1	0	0	0	0.0	0	0	0	0	0	0	0	0	0	0	0	0.0	–	3B-1

Jerry Schypinski

SCHYPINSKI, GERALD ALBERT
B. Sept. 16, 1931, Detroit, Mich.   BL TR 5'10" 170 lbs.

Year	Team	Games	BA	SA	AB	H	2B	3B	HR	HR%	R	RBI	BB	SO	SB	AB	H	PO	A	E	DP	TC/G	FA	G by Pos
1955	KC A	22	.217	.246	69	15	2	0	0	0.0	7	5	1	6	0	0	0	27	52	5	12	3.8	.940	SS-21, 2B-2

Mike Scioscia

SCIOSCIA, MICHAEL LORRI
B. Nov. 27, 1958, Upper Darby, Pa.   BL TR 6'2" 200 lbs.

Year	Team	Games	BA	SA	AB	H	2B	3B	HR	HR%	R	RBI	BB	SO	SB	AB	H	PO	A	E	DP	TC/G	FA	G by Pos
1980	LA N	54	.254	.328	134	34	5	1	1	0.7	8	8	12	9	1	1	0	226	26	2	5	4.7	.992	C-54
1981		93	.276	.331	290	80	10	0	2	0.7	27	29	36	18	0	2	1	493	48	7	4	5.9	.987	C-91
1982		129	.219	.296	365	80	11	1	5	1.4	31	38	44	31	2	8	0	631	57	10	10	5.4	.986	C-123
1983		12	.314	.486	35	11	3	0	1	2.9	3	7	5	2	0	1	0	55	4	0	0	4.9	1.000	C-11
1984		114	.273	.370	341	93	18	0	5	1.5	29	38	52	26	2	7	0	701	64	12	8	6.8	.985	C-112
1985		141	.296	.420	429	127	26	3	7	1.6	47	53	77	21	3	7	1	818	66	13	8	6.4	.986	C-139
1986		122	.251	.345	374	94	18	1	5	1.3	36	26	62	23	3	10	1	756	64	15	4	6.8	.982	C-119
1987		142	.265	.364	461	122	26	1	6	1.3	44	38	55	23	7	11	4	925	80	11	11	7.2	.989	C-138
1988		130	.257	.324	408	105	18	0	3	0.7	29	35	38	31	0	7	1	748	63	7	10	6.3	.991	C-123
1989		133	.250	.363	408	102	16	0	10	2.5	40	44	52	29	0	6	2	822	82	11	12	6.9	.988	C-130
10 yrs.		1070	.261	.354	3245	848	151	7	45	1.4	294	316	433	213	18	60	10	6175	554	88	72	6.4	.987	C-1040

DIVISIONAL PLAYOFF SERIES

Year	Team	Games	BA	SA	AB	H	2B	3B	HR	HR%	R	RBI	BB	SO	SB	AB	H	PO	A	E	DP	TC/G	FA	G by Pos
1981	LA N	4	.154	.154	13	2	0	0	0	0.0	0	1	0	1	0	2	0	0	0	0	0	0.0	–	C-4

LEAGUE CHAMPIONSHIP SERIES

Year	Team	Games	BA	SA	AB	H	2B	3B	HR	HR%	R	RBI	BB	SO	SB	AB	H	PO	A	E	DP	TC/G	FA	G by Pos
1981	LA N	5	.133	.333	15	2	0	0	1	6.7	1	1	2	1	0	0	0	0	0	0	0	0.0	–	C-5
1985		6	.250	.250	16	4	0	0	0	0.0	2	1	4	0	0	0	0	31	4	1	0	6.0	.972	C-6
1988		7	.364	.545	22	8	1	0	1	4.5	3	2	1	2	0	0	0	37	4	0	1	5.9	1.000	C-7
3 yrs.		18	.264	.396	53	14	1	0	2	3.8	6	4	7	3	0	0	0	68	8	1	1	4.3	.987	C-18

WORLD SERIES

Year	Team	Games	BA	SA	AB	H	2B	3B	HR	HR%	R	RBI	BB	SO	SB	AB	H	PO	A	E	DP	TC/G	FA	G by Pos
1981	LA N	3	.250	.250	4	1	0	0	0	0.0	1	0	1	0	0	1	0	7	1	0	0	2.7	1.000	C-3
1988		4	.214	.214	14	3	0	0	0	0.0	0	1	0	1	0	0	0	28	0	1	0	7.3	.966	C-4
2 yrs.		7	.222	.222	18	4	0	0	0	0.0	1	1	1	1	0	1	0	35	1	1	0	5.3	.973	C-7

Lou Scoffic

SCOFFIC, LOUIS (Weaser)
B. May 20, 1913, Herrin, Ill.   BR TR 5'10" 182 lbs.

Year	Team	Games	BA	SA	AB	H	2B	3B	HR	HR%	R	RBI	BB	SO	SB	AB	H	PO	A	E	DP	TC/G	FA	G by Pos
1936	STL N	4	.429	.429	7	3	0	0	0	0.0	2	2	1	2	0	0	0	7	0	1	0	2.0	.875	OF-3

Daryl Sconiers

SCONIERS, DARYL ANTHONY
B. Oct. 3, 1958, San Bernardino, Calif.   BL TL 6'2" 185 lbs.

Year	Team	Games	BA	SA	AB	H	2B	3B	HR	HR%	R	RBI	BB	SO	SB	AB	H	PO	A	E	DP	TC/G	FA	G by Pos
1981	CAL A	15	.269	.385	52	14	1	1	1	1.9	6	7	1	10	0	1	0	95	8	0	11	6.9	1.000	1B-12, DH-3
1982		12	.154	.154	13	2	0	0	0	0.0	0	2	2	1	0	7	1	23	1	0	5	2.0	1.000	1B-3, DH-1
1983		106	.274	.430	314	86	19	3	8	2.5	49	46	17	41	4	28	8	473	23	8	46	4.8	.984	1B-57, DH-27, OF-1
1984		57	.244	.344	160	39	4	0	4	2.5	14	17	13	16	1	10	6	355	26	4	27	6.8	.990	1B-41, DH-3

Year	Team		Games	BA	SA	AB	H	2B	3B	HR	HR%	R	RBI	BB	SO	SB	Pinch Hit AB	Pinch Hit H	PO	A	E	DP	TC/G	FA	G by Pos

Daryl Sconiers *continued*

| 1985 | | | 44 | .286 | .429 | 98 | 28 | 6 | 1 | 2 | 2.0 | 14 | 12 | 15 | 18 | 2 | 14 | 3 | 35 | 1 | 1 | 2 | 0.8 | .973 | DH-20, 1B-6 |
| 5 yrs. | | | 234 | .265 | .399 | 637 | 169 | 30 | 5 | 15 | 2.4 | 83 | 84 | 48 | 86 | 7 | 60 | 18 | 981 | 59 | 13 | 91 | 4.5 | .988 | 1B-119, DH-52, OF-1 |

Scott

SCOTT,
Deceased.

| 1884 | BAL | U | 13 | .226 | .340 | 53 | 12 | 1 | 1 | 1 | 1.9 | 10 | | 2 | | | 0 | 0 | 9 | 2 | 1 | 1 | 0.9 | .917 | OF-13, 3B-1 |

Dick Scott

SCOTT, RICHARD EDWARD   BR TR 6'1"   170 lbs.
B. July 19, 1962, Ellsworth, Me.

| 1989 | OAK | A | 3 | .000 | .000 | 2 | 0 | 0 | 0 | 0 | 0.0 | 0 | 1 | 0 | 0 | 0 | 0 | 0 | 0 | 0 | 0 | 0 | 0.0 | – | SS-3 |

Donnie Scott

SCOTT, DONALD MALCOLM   BB TR 5'11"   185 lbs.
B. Aug. 16, 1961, Dunedin, Fla.

1983	TEX	A	2	.000	.000	4	0	0	0	0	0.0	0	0	0	0	0	0	0	8	2	0	0	5.0	1.000	C-2
1984			81	.221	.298	235	52	9	0	3	1.3	16	20	20	44	0	0	0	400	41	12	9	5.6	.974	C-80
1985	SEA	A	80	.222	.357	185	41	13	0	4	2.2	18	23	15	41	1	20	2	277	31	6	1	3.9	.981	C-74
3 yrs.			163	.219	.321	424	93	22	0	7	1.7	34	43	35	85	1	20	2	685	74	18	10	4.8	.977	C-156

Everett Scott

SCOTT, LEWIS EVERETT (Deacon)   BR TR 5'8"   148 lbs.
B. Nov. 19, 1892, Bluffton, Ind.   D. Nov. 2, 1960, Fort Wayne, Ind.

1914	BOS	A	144	.239	.301	539	129	15	6	2	0.4	66	37	32	43	9	1	1	324	408	39	50	5.4	.949	SS-143
1915			100	.201	.231	359	72	11	0	0	0.0	25	28	17	21	4	0	0	198	298	20	31	5.2	.961	SS-100
1916			123	.232	.295	366	85	19	2	0	0.0	37	27	23	24	8	0	0	217	342	19	36	4.7	.967	SS-121, 3B-1, 2B-1
1917			157	.241	.313	528	127	24	7	0	0.0	40	50	20	46	12	0	0	315	483	39	64	5.3	.953	SS-157
1918			126	.221	.269	443	98	11	5	0	0.0	40	43	12	16	11	0	0	270	419	17	38	5.6	.976	SS-126
1919			138	.278	.316	507	141	19	0	0	0.0	41	38	19	26	8	0	0	276	423	17	63	5.2	.976	SS-138
1920			154	.269	.369	569	153	21	12	4	0.7	41	61	21	15	4	0	0	330	496	23	64	5.5	.973	SS-154
1921			154	.262	.335	576	151	21	9	1	0.2	65	60	27	21	5	0	0	380	528	26	94	6.1	.972	SS-154
1922	NY	A	154	.269	.345	557	150	23	5	3	0.5	64	45	23	22	2	0	0	302	538	31	74	5.7	.964	SS-154
1923			152	.246	.325	533	131	16	4	6	1.1	48	60	13	19	1	0	0	245	414	27	65	4.5	.961	SS-152
1924			153	.250	.316	548	137	12	6	4	0.7	56	64	21	15	3	0	0	322	455	27	80	5.3	.966	SS-153
1925	2 teams		NY	A	(22G – .217)		WAS	A	(33G – .272)																
"	total		55	.252	.301	163	41	6	1	0	0.0	13	22	6	6	1	4	2	96	130	11	35	4.3	.954	SS-48, 3B-2
1926	2 teams		CHI	A	(40G – .252)		CIN	N	(4G – .667)																
"	total		44	.268	.349	149	40	10	1	0	0.0	16	14	9	8	1	1	0	78	126	11	20	4.9	.949	SS-43
13 yrs.			1654	.249	.315	5837	1455	208	58	20	0.3	552	549	243	282	69	6	3	3353	5060	307	714	5.3	.965	SS-1643, 3B-3, 2B-1

WORLD SERIES

1915	BOS	A	5	.056	.056	18	1	0	0	0	0.0	0	0	0	3	0	0	0	8	12	0	1	4.0	1.000	SS-5
1916			5	.125	.250	16	2	0	1	0	0.0	1	1	1	1	0	0	0	9	25	2	3	7.2	.944	SS-5
1918			6	.100	.100	20	2	0	0	0	0.0	0	0	1	1	0	0	0	11	25	0	3	6.0	1.000	SS-6
1922	NY	A	5	.143	.143	14	2	0	0	0	0.0	0	1	1	0	0	0	0	14	15	0	6	5.8	1.000	SS-5
1923			6	.318	.318	22	7	0	0	0	0.0	2	3	0	1	0	0	0	8	20	1	4	4.8	.966	SS-6
5 yrs.			27	.156	.178	90	14	0	1	0	0.0	3	5	3	6	0	0	0	50	97	3	17	5.6	.980	SS-27

George Scott

SCOTT, GEORGE CHARLES, JR. (Boomer)   BR TR 6'2"   200 lbs.
B. Mar. 23, 1944, Greenville, Miss.

1966	BOS	A	162	.245	.433	601	147	18	7	27	4.5	73	90	65	**152**	4	1	1	1362	121	16	131	9.3	.989	1B-158, 3B-5
1967			159	.303	.465	565	171	21	7	19	3.4	74	82	63	119	10	5	3	1321	94	19	115	9.0	.987	1B-152, 3B-2
1968			124	.171	.237	350	60	14	0	3	0.9	23	25	26	88	3	12	1	810	65	11	69	7.1	.988	1B-112, 3B-6
1969			152	.253	.384	549	139	14	5	16	2.9	63	52	61	74	4	0	0	542	226	18	78	5.2	.977	3B-109, 1B-53
1970			127	.296	.467	480	142	24	5	16	3.3	50	63	44	95	4	0	0	551	149	18	55	5.7	.975	3B-68, 1B-59
1971			146	.263	.441	537	141	16	4	24	4.5	72	78	41	102	0	3	1	1256	75	11	122	9.2	.992	1B-143
1972	MIL	A	152	.266	.426	578	154	24	4	20	3.5	71	88	43	130	16	1	1	1223	119	15	108	8.9	.989	1B-139, 3B-23
1973			158	.306	.488	604	185	30	4	24	4.0	98	107	61	94	9	1	1	1388	118	9	144	9.6	.994	1B-157, DH-1
1974			158	.281	.432	604	170	36	2	17	2.8	74	82	59	90	9	1	0	1345	114	12	137	9.3	.992	1B-148, DH-9
1975			158	.285	.515	617	176	26	4	**36**	5.8	86	**109**	51	97	6	1	0	1205	116	15	119	8.5	.989	1B-144, DH-12, 3B-5
1976			156	.274	.414	606	166	21	5	18	3.0	73	77	53	118	0	1	0	1393	107	13	133	9.7	.991	1B-155
1977	BOS	A	157	.269	.500	584	157	26	5	33	5.7	103	95	57	112	1	0	0	1446	115	24	150	10.1	.985	1B-157
1978			120	.233	.379	412	96	16	4	12	2.9	51	54	44	86	1	2	0	1052	55	10	99	9.3	.991	1B-113, DH-7
1979	3 teams		BOS	A	(45G – .224)		KC	A	(44G – .267)		NY	A	(16G – .318)											
"	total		105	.254	.387	346	88	20	4	6	1.7	46	49	31	61	2	10	2	737	46	10	67	7.6	.987	1B-83, DH-17, 3B-1
14 yrs.			2034	.268	.435	7433	1992	306	60	271	3.6	957	1051	699	1418	69	40	10	15631	1520	201	1527	8.5	.988	1B-1773, 3B-219, DH-46

WORLD SERIES

| 1967 | BOS | A | 7 | .231 | .346 | 26 | 6 | 1 | 1 | 0 | 0.0 | 3 | 0 | 3 | 6 | 0 | 0 | 0 | 70 | 3 | 0 | 3 | 10.4 | 1.000 | 1B-7 |

Jack Scott

SCOTT, JOHN WILLIAM   BL TR 6'2½"   199 lbs.
B. Apr. 18, 1892, Ridgeway, N. C.   D. Nov. 30, 1959, Durham, N. C.

1916	PIT	N	3	.000	.000	2	0	0	0	0	0.0	0	0	1	1	0	0	0	1	1	0	0	0.7	1.000	P-1
1917	BOS	N	7	.125	.125	16	2	0	0	0	0.0	0	0	1	4	0	0	0	1	8	1	0	1.4	.900	P-7
1919			24	.175	.200	40	7	1	0	0	0.0	4	4	1	8	0	3	0	4	16	1	0	0.9	.952	P-19, OF-1
1920			44	.212	.242	99	21	3	0	0	0.0	5	4	5	16	0	0	0	8	65	6	1	1.8	.924	P-44
1921			51	.341	.455	88	30	5	1	1	1.1	14	12	5	7	0	3	0	4	56	3	2	1.2	.952	P-47
1922	2 teams		CIN	N	(1G – .000)		NY	N	(17G – .267)																
"	total		18	.258	.258	31	8	0	0	0	0.0	2	4	1	0	0	0	0	0	14	0	0	0.8	.933	P-18
1923	NY	N	40	.316	.405	79	25	4	0	1	1.3	12	10	3	5	1	0	0	6	43	2	1	1.3	.961	P-40
1925			41	.241	.345	87	21	4	1	1	1.1	7	6	8	15	0	5	1	11	63	1	3	1.8	.987	P-36
1926			51	.337	.470	83	28	4	2	1	1.2	9	8	6	13	0	1	0	12	49	2	4	1.2	.968	P-50
1927	PHI	N	83	.289	.368	114	33	6	0	1	0.9	6	17	9	9	0	28	7	7	51	3	1	0.7	.951	P-48
1928	NY	N	16	.267	.333	15	4	1	0	0	0.0	3	2	1	2	0	0	0	3	11	1	2	0.9	.933	P-16

Year Team	Games	BA	SA	AB	H	2B	3B	HR	HR%	R	RBI	BB	SO	SB	Pinch Hit AB	Pinch Hit H	PO	A	E	DP	TC/G	FA	G by Pos

Jack Scott *continued*

Year Team	Games	BA	SA	AB	H	2B	3B	HR	HR%	R	RBI	BB	SO	SB	PH AB	PH H	PO	A	E	DP	TC/G	FA	G by Pos
1929	30	.308	.423	26	8	3	0	0	0.0	6	1	2	0	0	0	0	6	22	0	1	0.9	1.000	P-30
12 yrs.	408	.275	.354	680	187	31	4	5	0.7	67	73	39	76	1	41	8	63	399	21	15	1.2	.957	P-356, OF-1

WORLD SERIES

Year Team	Games	BA	SA	AB	H	2B	3B	HR	HR%	R	RBI	BB	SO	SB	PH AB	PH H	PO	A	E	DP	TC/G	FA	G by Pos
1922 NY N	1	.250	.250	4	1	0	0	0	0.0	0	0	0	0	0	0	0	1	1	0	0	2.0	1.000	P-1
1923	2	.000	.000	1	0	0	0	0	0.0	0	0	0	1	0	0	0	0	1	0	0	0.5	1.000	P-1
2 yrs.	3	.200	.200	5	1	0	0	0	0.0	0	0	0	1	0	0	0	1	2	0	0	1.0	1.000	P-2

Jim Scott

SCOTT, JAMES WALTER
B. Sept. 22, 1888, Shenandoah, Pa.   D. May 12, 1972, So. Pasadena, Fla.   BR TR 5'9½" 165 lbs.

Year Team	Games	BA	SA	AB	H	2B	3B	HR	HR%	R	RBI	BB	SO	SB	PH AB	PH H	PO	A	E	DP	TC/G	FA	G by Pos
1914 PIT F	8	.250	.292	24	6	1	0	0	0.0	2	1	5		1	0	0	13	19	8	4	5.0	.800	SS-8

John Scott

SCOTT, JOHN HENRY
B. Jan. 24, 1952, Jackson, Miss.   BR TR 6'2" 165 lbs.

Year Team	Games	BA	SA	AB	H	2B	3B	HR	HR%	R	RBI	BB	SO	SB	PH AB	PH H	PO	A	E	DP	TC/G	FA	G by Pos
1974 SD N	14	.067	.067	15	1	0	0	0	0.0	3	0	0	4	1	0	0	8	1	0	0	0.6	1.000	OF-8
1975	25	.000	.000	9	0	0	0	0	0.0	6	0	0	2	2	9	0	0	0	0	0	0.0	—	OF-1
1977 TOR A	79	.240	.305	233	56	9	0	2	0.9	26	15	8	39	10	4	0	127	3	5	2	1.7	.963	OF-67, DH-2
3 yrs.	118	.222	.280	257	57	9	0	2	0.8	35	15	8	45	13	13	0	135	4	5	2	1.2	.965	OF-76, DH-2

LeGrant Scott

SCOTT, LeGRANT EDWARD
B. July 25, 1910, Cleveland, Ohio   BL TL 5'8½" 170 lbs.

Year Team	Games	BA	SA	AB	H	2B	3B	HR	HR%	R	RBI	BB	SO	SB	PH AB	PH H	PO	A	E	DP	TC/G	FA	G by Pos
1939 PHI N	76	.280	.366	232	65	15	1	1	0.4	31	26	22	14	5	18	5	109	7	5	1	1.6	.959	OF-55

Milt Scott

SCOTT, MILTON PARKER (Mikado Milt)
B. Jan. 17, 1866, Chicago, Ill.   D. Nov. 3, 1938, Baltimore, Md.   5'9" 160 lbs.

Year Team	Games	BA	SA	AB	H	2B	3B	HR	HR%	R	RBI	BB	SO	SB	PH AB	PH H	PO	A	E	DP	TC/G	FA	G by Pos
1882 CHI N	1	.400	.400	5	2	0	0	0	0.0	1	0			0	0	0	3	0	0	0	3.0	1.000	1B-1
1884 DET N	110	.247	.329	438	108	17	5	3	0.7	29		9	62		0	0	1120	26	38	37	10.8	.968	1B-110
1885 2 teams	DET N (38G – .264)			PIT AA (55G – .248)																			
" total	93	.254	.299	358	91	14	1	0	0.0	29	12	9	16		0	0	1017	34	23	45	11.5	.979	1B-93
1886 BAL AA	137	.190	.242	484	92	11	4	2	0.4	48		22			0	0	1347	59	38	38	10.5	.974	1B-137, P-1
4 yrs.	341	.228	.288	1285	293	42	10	5	0.4	107	12	40	78		0	0	3487	119	99	120	10.9	.973	1B-341, P-1

Pete Scott

SCOTT, FLOYD JOHN
B. Dec. 21, 1898, Woodland, Calif.   D. May 3, 1953, Daly City, Calif.   BR TR 5'11½" 175 lbs.

Year Team	Games	BA	SA	AB	H	2B	3B	HR	HR%	R	RBI	BB	SO	SB	PH AB	PH H	PO	A	E	DP	TC/G	FA	G by Pos
1926 CHI N	77	.286	.413	189	54	13	1	3	1.6	34	34	22	31	3	4	1	116	9	5	3	1.7	.962	OF-59, 3B-1
1927	71	.314	.442	156	49	18	1	0	0.0	28	21	19	18	1	31	7	70	3	1	1	1.0	.986	OF-36
1928 PIT N	60	.311	.497	177	55	10	4	5	2.8	33	33	18	14	1	6	2	186	8	4	6	3.3	.980	OF-42, 1B-8
3 yrs.	208	.303	.450	522	158	41	6	8	1.5	95	88	59	63	5	41	10	372	20	10	10	1.9	.975	OF-137, 1B-8, 3B-1

Rodney Scott

SCOTT, RODNEY DARRELL
B. Oct. 16, 1953, Indianapolis, Ind.   BR TR 6' 160 lbs.

Year Team	Games	BA	SA	AB	H	2B	3B	HR	HR%	R	RBI	BB	SO	SB	PH AB	PH H	PO	A	E	DP	TC/G	FA	G by Pos
1975 KC A	48	.067	.067	15	1	0	0	0	0.0	13	0	1	3	4	1	0	8	12	2	2	0.5	.909	DH-22, 2B-9, SS-8
1976 MON N	7	.400	.400	10	4	0	0	0	0.0	3	0	1	1	2	0	0	6	8	0	2	2.0	1.000	2B-6, SS-3
1977 OAK A	133	.261	.294	364	95	4	4	0	0.0	56	20	43	50	33	8	3	200	273	21	49	3.7	.957	2B-71, SS-70, 3B-5, DH-1, OF-1
1978 CHI N	78	.282	.313	227	64	5	1	0	0.0	41	15	43	41	27	3	0	77	119	14	17	2.7	.933	3B-60, OF-10, SS-6, 2B-6
1979 MON N	151	.238	.294	562	134	12	5	3	0.5	69	42	66	82	39	1	1	362	421	21	82	5.3	.974	2B-113, SS-39
1980	154	.224	.293	567	127	13	13	0	0.0	84	46	70	75	63	3	2	339	432	18	88	5.1	.977	2B-129, SS-21
1981	95	.205	.250	336	69	9	3	0	0.0	43	26	50	35	30	0	0	187	278	8	41	5.0	.983	2B-93
1982 2 teams	MON N (14G – .200)			NY A (10G – .192)																			
" total	24	.196	.196	51	10	0	0	0	0.0	7	1	7	4	7	2	0	31	42	2	8	3.1	.973	2B-16, SS-6
8 yrs.	690	.236	.285	2132	504	43	26	3	0.1	316	150	281	291	205	18	6	1210	1585	86	289	4.2	.970	2B-443, SS-153, 3B-65, DH-23, OF-11

LEAGUE CHAMPIONSHIP SERIES

Year Team	Games	BA	SA	AB	H	2B	3B	HR	HR%	R	RBI	BB	SO	SB	PH AB	PH H	PO	A	E	DP	TC/G	FA	G by Pos
1981 MON N	5	.167	.167	18	3	0	0	0	0.0	0	0	1	3	1	0	0	0	0	1	0	0.2	—	2B-5

Tony Scott

SCOTT, ANTHONY
B. Sept. 18, 1951, Cincinnati, Ohio   BB TR 6' 164 lbs.

Year Team	Games	BA	SA	AB	H	2B	3B	HR	HR%	R	RBI	BB	SO	SB	PH AB	PH H	PO	A	E	DP	TC/G	FA	G by Pos
1973 MON N	11	.000	.000	1	0	0	0	0	0.0	0	0	0	1	0	1	0	0	0	0	1	0	0.1	—	OF-3
1974	19	.286	.286	7	2	0	0	0	0.0	2	1	1	3	1	1	1	7	0	0	0	0.4	1.000	OF-16
1975	92	.182	.238	143	26	4	2	0	0.0	19	11	12	38	5	8	1	94	6	4	0	1.1	.962	OF-71
1977 STL N	95	.291	.397	292	85	16	3	3	1.0	38	41	33	48	13	10	1	223	5	1	0	2.4	.996	OF-89
1978	96	.228	.283	219	50	5	2	1	0.5	28	14	14	41	5	30	6	100	6	6	0	1.2	.946	OF-77
1979	153	.259	.361	587	152	22	10	6	1.0	69	68	34	92	37	3	1	427	14	7	5	2.9	.984	OF-151
1980	143	.251	.311	415	104	19	3	1	0.2	51	28	35	68	22	8	2	324	5	1	2	2.3	.997	OF-134
1981 2 teams	STL N (45G – .227)			HOU N (55G – .293)																			
" total	100	.264	.359	401	106	18	4	1	0.2	49	39	20	54	18	0	0	120	2	0	0	1.2	1.000	OF-99
1982 HOU N	132	.239	.293	460	110	16	3	1	0.2	43	29	15	56	18	10	2	262	7	5	0	2.1	.982	OF-129
1983	80	.226	.301	186	42	6	1	2	1.1	20	17	11	39	5	27	5	89	2	0	1	1.1	1.000	OF-61
1984 2 teams	HOU N (25G – .190)			MON N (45G – .254)																			
" total	70	.239	.293	92	22	5	0	0	0.0	10	5	11	24	1	38	10	30	1	0	0	0.4	1.000	OF-23
11 yrs.	991	.249	.327	2803	699	111	28	17	0.6	331	253	186	464	125	136	29	1676	48	25	8	1.8	.986	OF-853

DIVISIONAL PLAYOFF SERIES

Year Team	Games	BA	SA	AB	H	2B	3B	HR	HR%	R	RBI	BB	SO	SB	PH AB	PH H	PO	A	E	DP	TC/G	FA	G by Pos
1981 HOU N	5	.150	.150	20	3	0	0	0	0.0	0	2	1	6	0	0	0	0	0	0	0	0.0	—	OF-5

Jim Scranton

SCRANTON, JAMES DEAN
B. Apr. 5, 1960, Torrence, Calif.   BR TR 6' 180 lbs.

Year Team	Games	BA	SA	AB	H	2B	3B	HR	HR%	R	RBI	BB	SO	SB	PH AB	PH H	PO	A	E	DP	TC/G	FA	G by Pos
1984 KC A	2	.000	.000	2	0	0	0	0	0.0	0	0	0	0	0	1	0	0	1	0	1	0.5	1.000	SS-1, 3B-1

Year	Team		Games	BA	SA	AB	H	2B	3B	HR	HR%	R	RBI	BB	SO	SB	Pinch Hit AB	H	PO	A	E	DP	TC/G	FA	G by Pos

Jim Scranton *continued*

Year	Team		Games	BA	SA	AB	H	2B	3B	HR	HR%	R	RBI	BB	SO	SB	PH AB	H	PO	A	E	DP	TC/G	FA	G by Pos
1985			6	.000	.000	4	0	0	0	0	0.0	1	0	0	0	0	0	0	1	8	0	1	1.5	1.000	SS-5
2 yrs.			8	.000	.000	6	0	0	0	0	0.0	1	0	0	0	0	1	0	1	9	0	2	1.3	1.000	SS-6, 3B-1

Chuck Scrivener

SCRIVENER, WAYNE ALLISON
B. Oct. 3, 1947, Alexandria, Va.   BR TR 5'9'' 170 lbs.

Year	Team		Games	BA	SA	AB	H	2B	3B	HR	HR%	R	RBI	BB	SO	SB	PH AB	H	PO	A	E	DP	TC/G	FA	G by Pos
1975	DET	A	4	.250	.313	16	4	1	0	0	0.0	0	0	0	1	1	0	0	2	8	0	0	2.5	1.000	3B-3, SS-2
1976			80	.221	.288	222	49	7	1	2	0.9	28	16	19	34	1	2	0	137	230	12	47	4.7	.968	2B-43, SS-37, 3B-5
1977			61	.083	.083	72	6	0	0	0	0.0	10	2	5	9	0	0	0	50	89	3	16	2.3	.979	SS-50, 2B-8, 3B-3
3 yrs.			145	.190	.242	310	59	8	1	2	0.6	38	18	24	44	2	2	0	189	327	15	63	3.7	.972	SS-89, 2B-51, 3B-11

Ken Sears

SEARS, KENNETH EUGENE (Ziggy)
B. July 6, 1917, Streator, Ill.   D. July 17, 1968, Bridgeport, Tex.   BL TR 6'1'' 200 lbs.

Year	Team		Games	BA	SA	AB	H	2B	3B	HR	HR%	R	RBI	BB	SO	SB	PH AB	H	PO	A	E	DP	TC/G	FA	G by Pos
1943	NY	A	60	.278	.348	187	52	7	0	2	1.1	22	22	11	18	1	10	3	233	31	7	5	4.5	.974	C-50
1946	STL	A	7	.333	.333	15	5	0	0	0	0.0	1	1	3	0	0	3	1	10	0	0	0	1.4	1.000	C-4
2 yrs.			67	.282	.347	202	57	7	0	2	1.0	23	23	14	18	1	13	4	243	31	7	5	4.2	.975	C-54

Jimmy Sebring

SEBRING, JAMES DENNISON
B. Mar. 22, 1882, Liberty, Pa.   D. Dec. 22, 1909, Williamsport, Pa.   BL TR 6' 180 lbs.

Year	Team		Games	BA	SA	AB	H	2B	3B	HR	HR%	R	RBI	BB	SO	SB	PH AB	H	PO	A	E	DP	TC/G	FA	G by Pos
1902	PIT	N	19	.325	.475	80	26	4	4	0	0.0	15	15	5		2	0	0	33	5	1	2	2.1	.974	OF-19
1903			124	.277	.383	506	140	16	13	4	0.8	71	64	32		20	0	0	208	20	18	11	2.0	.927	OF-124
1904	2 teams			PIT	N	(80G – .269)		CIN	N	(56G – .225)															
"	total		136	.250	.323	527	132	20	9	0	0.0	50	56	31		16	0	0	234	27	7	8	2.0	.974	OF-136
1905	CIN	N	58	.286	.406	217	62	10	5	2	0.9	31	28	14		11	2	0	63	6	9	2	1.3	.885	OF-56
1909	2 teams			BKN	N	(25G – .099)		WAS	A	(1G – .000)															
"	total		26	.099	.136	81	8	1	1	0	0.0	11	5	11		3	0	0	35	4	2	1	1.6	.951	OF-26
5 yrs.			363	.261	.355	1411	368	51	32	6	0.4	178	168	93		52	2	0	573	62	37	24	1.9	.945	OF-361

WORLD SERIES

Year	Team		Games	BA	SA	AB	H	2B	3B	HR	HR%	R	RBI	BB	SO	SB	PH AB	H	PO	A	E	DP	TC/G	FA	G by Pos
1903	PIT	N	8	.367	.533	30	11	0	1	1	3.3	3	5	1	4	0	0	0	13	1	0	0	1.8	1.000	OF-8

Frank Secory

SECORY, FRANK EDWARD
B. Aug. 24, 1912, Mason City, Iowa   BR TR 6'1'' 200 lbs.

Year	Team		Games	BA	SA	AB	H	2B	3B	HR	HR%	R	RBI	BB	SO	SB	PH AB	H	PO	A	E	DP	TC/G	FA	G by Pos
1940	DET	A	1	.000	.000	1	0	0	0	0	0.0	0	0	0	1	0	1	0	0	0	0	0	0.0	–	
1942	CIN	N	2	.000	.000	5	0	0	0	0	0.0	1	1	3	2	0	0	0	6	0	1	0	3.5	.857	OF-2
1944	CHI	N	22	.321	.554	56	18	1	0	4	7.1	10	17	6	8	1	4	0	44	0	0	0	2.0	1.000	OF-17
1945			35	.158	.175	57	9	1	0	0	0.0	4	6	2	7	0	21	2	20	0	0	0	0.6	1.000	OF-12
1946			33	.233	.512	43	10	3	0	3	7.0	6	12	6	6	0	22	4	10	0	2	0	0.4	.833	OF-9
5 yrs.			93	.228	.389	162	37	5	0	7	4.3	21	36	17	24	1	48	6	80	0	3	0	0.9	.964	OF-40

WORLD SERIES

Year	Team		Games	BA	SA	AB	H	2B	3B	HR	HR%	R	RBI	BB	SO	SB	PH AB	H	PO	A	E	DP	TC/G	FA	G by Pos
1945	CHI	N	5	.400	.400	5	2	0	0	0	0.0	0	0	0	0	0	5	2	0	0	0	0	0.0	–	

Charlie See

SEE, CHARLES HENRY (Chad)
B. Oct. 13, 1896, Pleasantville, N. Y.   D. July 19, 1948, Bridgeport, Conn.   BL TR 5'10½'' 175 lbs.

Year	Team		Games	BA	SA	AB	H	2B	3B	HR	HR%	R	RBI	BB	SO	SB	PH AB	H	PO	A	E	DP	TC/G	FA	G by Pos
1919	CIN	N	8	.286	.286	14	4	0	0	0	0.0	1	1	1	0	0	2	0	5	0	1	0	0.8	.833	OF-4
1920			47	.305	.354	82	25	4	0	0	0.0	9	15	1	7	2	24	8	49	5	2	2	1.2	.964	OF-17, P-1
1921			37	.245	.340	106	26	5	1	1	0.9	11	7	7	5	3	7	2	58	4	3	1	1.8	.954	OF-29
3 yrs.			92	.272	.342	202	55	9	1	1	0.5	21	23	9	12	5	33	10	112	9	6	3	1.4	.953	OF-50, P-1

Larry See

SEE, RALPH LAURENCE
B. June 20, 1960, Norwalk, Calif.   BR TR 6'1'' 195 lbs.

Year	Team		Games	BA	SA	AB	H	2B	3B	HR	HR%	R	RBI	BB	SO	SB	PH AB	H	PO	A	E	DP	TC/G	FA	G by Pos
1986	LA	N	13	.250	.350	20	5	2	0	0	0.0	1	2	2	7	0	4	1	41	6	1	3	3.7	.979	1B-9
1988	TEX	A	13	.130	.130	23	3	0	0	0	0.0	0	0	1	8	0	0	0	13	1	1	2	1.2	.933	1B-2, C-2, 3B-1
2 yrs.			26	.186	.233	43	8	2	0	0	0.0	1	2	3	15	0	4	1	54	7	2	5	2.4	.968	1B-11, C-2, 3B-1

Bob Seeds

SEEDS, ROBERT IRA (Suitcase Bob)
B. Feb. 24, 1907, Ringgold, Tex.   BR TR 6' 180 lbs.

Year	Team		Games	BA	SA	AB	H	2B	3B	HR	HR%	R	RBI	BB	SO	SB	PH AB	H	PO	A	E	DP	TC/G	FA	G by Pos
1930	CLE	A	85	.285	.379	277	79	11	3	3	1.1	37	32	12	22	1	15	4	156	6	8	0	2.0	.953	OF-70
1931			48	.306	.373	134	41	4	1	1	0.7	26	10	11	11	1	9	1	63	4	2	0	1.4	.971	OF-33, 1B-2
1932	2 teams			CLE	A	(2G – .000)		CHI	A	(116G – .290)															
"	total		118	.288	.370	438	126	18	6	2	0.5	53	45	31	37	5	4	0	234	7	9	1	2.1	.964	OF-113
1933	BOS	A	82	.243	.335	230	56	13	4	0	0.0	26	23	21	20	1	7	2	422	22	8	33	5.5	.982	1B-41, OF-32
1934	2 teams			BOS	A	(8G – .167)		CLE	A	(61G – .247)															
"	total		69	.245	.297	192	47	8	1	0	0.0	28	19	21	14	2	15	3	83	2	2	0	1.3	.977	OF-49
1936	NY	A	13	.262	.571	42	11	1	0	4	9.5	12	10	5	3	3	1	0	24	5	1	1	2.3	.967	OF-9, 3B-3
1938	NY	N	81	.291	.443	296	86	12	3	9	3.0	35	52	20	33	1	0	2	147	6	2	2	1.9	.987	OF-76
1939			63	.266	.393	173	46	5	1	5	2.9	33	26	22	31	1	12	2	77	2	2	0	1.3	.975	OF-50
1940			56	.290	.426	155	45	5	2	4	2.6	18	16	17	19	0	15	4	64	3	1	0	1.2	.985	OF-40
9 yrs.			615	.277	.382	1937	537	77	21	28	1.4	268	233	160	190	14	80	16	1270	57	35	37	2.2	.974	OF-472, 1B-43, 3B-3

WORLD SERIES

Year	Team		Games	BA	SA	AB	H	2B	3B	HR	HR%	R	RBI	BB	SO	SB	PH AB	H	PO	A	E	DP	TC/G	FA	G by Pos
1936	NY	A	1	–	–	0	0	0	0	0	–	0	0	0	0	0	0	0	0	0	0	0	0.0	–	

Pat Seerey

SEEREY, JAMES PATRICK
B. Mar. 17, 1923, Wilburton, Okla.   D. Apr. 28, 1986, Jennings, Mo.   BR TR 5'10'' 200 lbs.

Year	Team		Games	BA	SA	AB	H	2B	3B	HR	HR%	R	RBI	BB	SO	SB	PH AB	H	PO	A	E	DP	TC/G	FA	G by Pos
1943	CLE	A	26	.222	.306	72	16	3	0	1	1.4	8	5	4	19	0	9	2	35	3	1	0	1.5	.974	OF-16
1944			101	.234	.412	342	80	16	0	15	4.4	39	39	19	99	0	18	3	196	8	3	1	2.0	.986	OF-86
1945			126	.237	.401	414	98	22	2	14	3.4	56	56	66	97	1	8	0	227	7	6	3	1.9	.975	OF-117
1946			117	.225	.470	404	91	17	2	26	6.4	57	62	65	101	2	2	0	248	4	5	2	2.2	.981	OF-115
1947			82	.171	.352	216	37	4	1	11	5.1	24	29	34	66	0	12	1	105	7	5	1	1.4	.957	OF-68

Year	Team		Games	BA	SA	AB	H	2B	3B	HR	HR%	R	RBI	BB	SO	SB	Pinch Hit AB	Pinch Hit H	PO	A	E	DP	TC/G	FA	G by Pos

Pat Seerey *continued*

Year	Team		Games	BA	SA	AB	H	2B	3B	HR	HR%	R	RBI	BB	SO	SB	PH AB	PH H	PO	A	E	DP	TC/G	FA	G by Pos
1948	2 teams		CLE A (10G – .261)			CHI A (95G – .229)																			
"	total		105	.231	.419	363	84	11	0	19	5.2	51	70	90	102	0	3	0	204	9	4	5	2.1	.982	OF-100
1949	CHI	A	4	.000	.000	4	0	0	0	0	0.0	0	1	3	1	0	2	0	1	0	0	0	0.3	1.000	OF-2
7 yrs.			561	.224	.412	1815	406	73	6	87	4.7	236	261	281	485	3	54	6	1016	38	24	11	1.9	.978	OF-504

Emmett Seery

SEERY, JOHN EMMETT
B. Feb. 13, 1861, Princeville, Ill. Deceased.   BL TR

Year	Team		Games	BA	SA	AB	H	2B	3B	HR	HR%	R	RBI	BB	SO	SB	PH AB	PH H	PO	A	E	DP	TC/G	FA	G by Pos
1884	2 teams		BAL U (105G – .311)			KC U (1G – .500)																			
"	total		106	.313	.411	467	146	26	7	2	0.4	115		21			0	0	166	30	39	4	2.2	.834	OF-105, C-3, 3B-2
1885	STL	N	59	.162	.208	216	35	7	0	1	0.5	20	14	16	37		0	0	96	18	17	1	2.2	.870	OF-59, 3B-1
1886			126	.238	.327	453	108	22	6	2	0.4	73	48	57	82		0	0	176	21	27	2	1.8	.879	OF-126, P-2
1887	IND	N	122	.224	.353	465	104	18	15	4	0.9	104	28	71	68	48	0	0	220	25	30	2	2.3	.891	OF-122, SS-1
1888			133	.220	.330	500	110	20	10	5	1.0	87	50	64	73	80	0	0	260	21	19	6	2.3	.937	OF-133, SS-1
1889			127	.314	.454	526	165	26	12	8	1.5	123	59	67	59	19	0	0	220	20	24	4	2.1	.909	OF-127
1890	BKN	P	104	.223	.297	394	88	12	7	1	0.3	78	50	70	36	44	0	0	216	21	28	3	2.5	.894	OF-104
1891	CIN	AA	97	.285	.411	372	106	15	10	4	1.1	77	36	81	52	19	0	0	160	17	20	3	2.0	.898	OF-97
1892	LOU	N	42	.201	.253	154	31	6	1	0	0.0	18	15	24	19	6	0	0	65	10	3	1	1.9	.962	OF-42
9 yrs.			916	.252	.356	3547	893	152	68	27	0.8	695	300	471	426	216	0	0	1579	183	207	26	2.1	.895	OF-915, 3B-3, C-3, SS-2, P-2

Kal Segrist

SEGRIST, KAL HILL
B. Apr. 14, 1931, Greenville, Tex.   BR TR 6' 180 lbs.

Year	Team		Games	BA	SA	AB	H	2B	3B	HR	HR%	R	RBI	BB	SO	SB	PH AB	PH H	PO	A	E	DP	TC/G	FA	G by Pos
1952	NY	A	13	.043	.043	23	1	0	0	0	0.0	3	1	3	1	0	1	0	15	19	1	5	2.7	.971	2B-11, 3B-1
1955	BAL	A	7	.333	.333	9	3	0	0	0	0.0	1	0	2	0	0	2	1	1	7	0	0	1.1	1.000	3B-3, 2B-1, 1B-1
2 yrs.			20	.125	.125	32	4	0	0	0	0.0	4	1	5	1	0	3	1	16	26	1	5	2.2	.977	2B-12, 3B-4, 1B-1

Kurt Seibert

SEIBERT, KURT ELLIOTT
B. Oct. 16, 1955, Cheverly, Md.   BB TR 6' 165 lbs.

Year	Team		Games	BA	SA	AB	H	2B	3B	HR	HR%	R	RBI	BB	SO	SB	PH AB	PH H	PO	A	E	DP	TC/G	FA	G by Pos
1979	CHI	N	7	.000	.000	2	0	0	0	0	0.0	2	0	1	0	1	0	1	0	2	0	0	0.3	1.000	3B-1

Rick Seilheimer

SEILHEIMER, RICKY ALLEN
B. Aug. 30, 1960, Brenham, Tex.   BL TR 5'11" 185 lbs.

Year	Team		Games	BA	SA	AB	H	2B	3B	HR	HR%	R	RBI	BB	SO	SB	PH AB	PH H	PO	A	E	DP	TC/G	FA	G by Pos
1980	CHI	A	21	.212	.365	52	11	3	1	1	1.9	4	3	4	15	1	0	0	62	8	4	2	3.5	.946	C-21

Kevin Seitzer

SEITZER, KEVIN LEE
B. Mar. 26, 1962, Springfield, Ill.   BR TR 5'11" 180 lbs.

Year	Team		Games	BA	SA	AB	H	2B	3B	HR	HR%	R	RBI	BB	SO	SB	PH AB	PH H	PO	A	E	DP	TC/G	FA	G by Pos
1986	KC	A	28	.323	.448	96	31	4	1	2	2.1	16	11	19	14	0	1	1	224	19	3	17	8.8	.988	1B-22, OF-5, 3B-3
1987			161	.323	.470	641	207	33	8	15	2.3	105	83	80	85	12	0	0	290	315	24	51	3.9	.962	3B-141, 1B-25, OF-3
1988			149	.304	.406	559	170	32	5	5	0.9	90	60	72	64	10	1	0	93	297	26	33	2.8	.938	3B-147, DH-1, OF-1
1989			160	.281	.337	597	168	17	2	4	0.7	78	48	102	76	17	0	0	118	277	20	30	2.6	.952	3B-159, SS-6, OF-3, 1B-2
4 yrs.			498	.304	.408	1893	576	86	16	26	1.4	289	202	273	239	39	2	1	725	908	73	131	3.4	.957	3B-450, 1B-49, OF-12, SS-6, DH-1

Kip Selbach

SELBACH, ALBERT KARL
B. Mar. 24, 1872, Columbus, Ohio   D. Feb. 17, 1956, Columbus, Ohio   BR TR 5'7" 190 lbs.

Year	Team		Games	BA	SA	AB	H	2B	3B	HR	HR%	R	RBI	BB	SO	SB	PH AB	PH H	PO	A	E	DP	TC/G	FA	G by Pos
1894	WAS	N	97	.306	.511	372	114	21	17	7	1.9	69	71	51	20	21	0	0	205	62	38	7	3.1	.875	OF-80, SS-19
1895			129	.322	.483	516	166	21	22	6	1.2	115	55	69	28	31	0	0	320	64	39	6	3.3	.908	OF-118, SS-6, 2B-5
1896			127	.304	.423	487	148	17	13	5	1.0	100	100	76	28	49	2	2	303	13	18	3	2.6	.946	OF-126
1897			124	.313	.461	486	152	25	16	5	1.0	113	59	80		46	0	0	305	14	15	2	2.7	.955	OF-124
1898			132	.303	.417	515	156	28	11	3	0.6	88	60	64		25	0	0	320	30	19	6	2.8	.949	OF-131, SS-1
1899	CIN	N	140	.296	.407	521	154	27	11	3	0.6	104	87	70		38	0	0	355	27	19	10	2.9	.953	OF-140
1900	NY	N	141	.337	.461	523	176	29	12	4	0.8	99	68	72		36	0	0	327	25	18	8	2.6	.951	OF-141
1901			125	.289	.376	502	145	29	6	1	0.2	89	56	45		8	0	0	215	11	14	2	1.9	.942	OF-125
1902	BAL	A	123	.320	.427	503	161	27	9	3	0.6	86	60	58		22	1	1	286	17	19	3	2.5	.941	OF-127
1903	WAS	A	141	.250	.354	536	134	23	12	3	0.6	68	49	41		20	0	0	251	11	12	2	1.9	.956	OF-140, 3B-1
1904	2 teams		WAS A (48G – .275)			BOS A (98G – .258)																			
"	total		146	.264	.356	554	146	27	12	0	0.0	65	44	72		19	0	0	293	13	16	3	2.2	.950	OF-146
1905	BOS	A	124	.246	.342	418	103	16	6	4	1.0	54	47	67		12	5	1	186	8	15	1	1.7	.928	OF-116
1906			60	.211	.268	228	48	9	2	0	0.0	15	23	18		7	2	0	109	6	4	2	2.0	.966	OF-58
13 yrs.			1614	.293	.411	6161	1803	299	149	44	0.7	1065	779	783	76	334	10	4	3475	301	246	55	2.5	.939	OF-1572, SS-26, 2B-5, 3B-1

George Selkirk

SELKIRK, GEORGE ALEXANDER (Twinkletoes)
B. Jan. 4, 1908, Huntsville, Ont., Canada   D. Jan. 19, 1987, Ft. Lauderdale, Fla.   BL TR 6'1" 182 lbs.

Year	Team		Games	BA	SA	AB	H	2B	3B	HR	HR%	R	RBI	BB	SO	SB	PH AB	PH H	PO	A	E	DP	TC/G	FA	G by Pos
1934	NY	A	46	.313	.449	176	55	7	1	5	2.8	23	38	15	17	1	0	0	90	3	1	1	2.0	.989	OF-46
1935			128	.312	.487	491	153	29	12	11	2.2	64	94	44	36	2	2	1	269	9	7	1	2.2	.975	OF-127
1936			137	.308	.511	493	152	28	9	18	3.7	93	107	94	60	13	0	0	290	10	8	3	2.2	.974	OF-135
1937			78	.328	.629	256	84	13	5	18	7.0	49	68	34	24	8	5	1	140	9	2	1	1.9	.987	OF-69
1938			99	.254	.409	335	85	12	5	10	3.0	58	62	68	52	9	2	0	176	7	5	3	1.9	.973	OF-95
1939			128	.306	.517	418	128	17	4	21	5.0	103	101	103	49	12	5	0	254	4	3	1	2.0	.989	OF-124
1940			118	.269	.491	379	102	17	5	19	5.0	68	71	84	43	3	7	2	220	9	9	6	2.0	.962	OF-111
1941			70	.220	.360	164	36	5	0	6	3.7	30	25	28	30	1	19	4	84	4	3	2	1.3	.967	OF-47
1942			42	.192	.231	78	15	3	0	0	0.0	15	10	16	8	0	19	4	36	0	0	0	0.9	1.000	OF-19
9 yrs.			846	.290	.483	2790	810	131	41	108	3.9	503	576	486	319	49	59	12	1559	55	38	18	2.0	.977	OF-773

WORLD SERIES

Year	Team		Games	BA	SA	AB	H	2B	3B	HR	HR%	R	RBI	BB	SO	SB	PH AB	PH H	PO	A	E	DP	TC/G	FA	G by Pos
1936	NY	A	6	.333	.667	24	8	0	1	2	8.3	6	3	4	4	0	0	0	9	0	1	0	1.7	.900	OF-6
1937			5	.263	.316	19	5	1	0	0	0.0	5	6	2	0	0	0	0	7	0	0	0	1.4	1.000	OF-5
1938			3	.200	.200	10	2	0	0	0	0.0	0	1	2	1	0	0	0	3	0	0	0	1.0	1.000	OF-3
1939			4	.167	.250	12	2	1	0	0	0.0	3	2	3	1	0	0	0	9	0	0	0	2.3	1.000	OF-4
1941			2	.500	.500	2	1	0	0	0	0.0	0	0	0	0	0	2	1	0	0	0	0	0.0	—	

Year	Team	Games	BA	SA	AB	H	2B	3B	HR	HR%	R	RBI	BB	SO	SB	Pinch Hit AB	H	PO	A	E	DP	TC/G	FA	G by Pos

George Selkirk *continued*

Year	Team	Games	BA	SA	AB	H	2B	3B	HR	HR%	R	RBI	BB	SO	SB	AB	H	PO	A	E	DP	TC/G	FA	G by Pos
1942		1	.000	.000	1	0	0	0	0	0.0	0	0	0	0	0	1	0	0	0	0	0	0.0	–	
6 yrs.		21	.265	.412	68	18	2	1	2	2.9	11	10	11	7	0	3	1	28	0	1	0	1.4	.966	OF-18

Rube Sellers

SELLERS, OLIVER
B. Mar. 7, 1881, Duquesne, Pa. D. Jan. 14, 1952, Pittsburgh, Pa.   BR TR 5'10" 180 lbs.

Year	Team	Games	BA	SA	AB	H	2B	3B	HR	HR%	R	RBI	BB	SO	SB	AB	H	PO	A	E	DP	TC/G	FA	G by Pos
1910	BOS N	12	.156	.156	32	5	0	0	0	0.0	3	2	6	5	1	3	0	12	0	0	0	1.0	1.000	OF-9

Carey Selph

SELPH, CAREY ISOM
B. Dec. 5, 1901, Donaldson, Ark. D. Feb. 24, 1976, Houston, Tex.   BR TR 5'9½" 175 lbs.

Year	Team	Games	BA	SA	AB	H	2B	3B	HR	HR%	R	RBI	BB	SO	SB	AB	H	PO	A	E	DP	TC/G	FA	G by Pos
1929	STL N	25	.235	.294	51	12	1	0	0	0.0	8	7	6	4	1	5	1	23	29	1	3	2.1	.981	2B-16
1932	CHI A	116	.283	.371	396	112	19	8	0	0.0	50	51	31	9	7	18	2	128	215	28	28	3.2	.925	3B-71, 2B-26
2 yrs.		141	.277	.362	447	124	20	9	0	0.0	58	58	37	13	8	23	3	151	244	29	31	3.0	.932	3B-71, 2B-42

Mike Sember

SEMBER, MICHAEL DAVID
B. Feb. 24, 1953, Hammond, Ind.   BR TR 6' 185 lbs.

Year	Team	Games	BA	SA	AB	H	2B	3B	HR	HR%	R	RBI	BB	SO	SB	AB	H	PO	A	E	DP	TC/G	FA	G by Pos
1977	CHI N	3	.250	.250	4	1	0	0	0	0.0	0	0	0	2	0	2	0	2	2	0	1	1.3	1.000	2B-1
1978		9	.333	.333	3	1	0	0	0	0.0	2	0	1	1	0	2	1	1	3	1	1	0.6	.800	3B-7, SS-1
2 yrs.		12	.286	.286	7	2	0	0	0	0.0	2	0	1	3	0	4	1	3	5	1	2	0.8	.889	3B-7, SS-1, 2B-1

Andy Seminick

SEMINICK, ANDREW WASIL
B. Sept. 12, 1920, Pierce, W. Va.   BR TR 5'11" 187 lbs.

Year	Team	Games	BA	SA	AB	H	2B	3B	HR	HR%	R	RBI	BB	SO	SB	AB	H	PO	A	E	DP	TC/G	FA	G by Pos
1943	PHI N	22	.181	.292	72	13	2	0	2	2.8	9	5	7	22	0	0	0	83	14	7	2	4.7	.933	C-22, OF-1
1944		22	.222	.286	63	14	2	1	0	0.0	9	4	6	17	2	4	0	58	8	2	1	3.1	.971	C-11, OF-7
1945		80	.239	.394	188	45	7	2	6	3.2	18	26	18	38	3	6	0	202	39	9	3	3.1	.964	C-70, 3B-4, OF-1
1946		124	.264	.414	406	107	15	5	12	3.0	55	52	39	86	2	6	0	461	61	14	12	4.3	.974	C-118
1947		111	.252	.427	337	85	16	2	13	3.9	48	50	58	69	4	3	0	438	53	11	6	4.5	.978	C-107
1948		125	.225	.368	391	88	11	3	13	3.3	49	44	58	68	4	1	0	541	74	22	8	5.1	.965	C-124
1949		109	.243	.503	334	81	11	2	24	7.2	52	68	69	74	0	8	1	411	54	12	6	4.4	.975	C-98
1950		130	.288	.524	393	113	15	3	24	6.1	55	68	68	50	0	7	2	551	54	15	9	4.8	.976	C-124
1951		101	.227	.375	291	66	8	1	11	3.8	42	37	63	67	1	9	0	378	47	9	6	4.3	.979	C-91
1952	CIN N	108	.256	.435	336	86	16	1	14	4.2	38	50	35	65	1	9	1	416	47	13	7	4.4	.973	C-99
1953		119	.235	.413	387	91	12	0	19	4.9	46	64	49	82	2	7	1	436	44	9	2	4.1	.982	C-112
1954		86	.235	.389	247	58	9	4	7	2.8	25	30	48	39	0	5	3	327	44	4	11	4.4	.989	C-82
1955	2 teams	CIN N (6G – .133)			PHI N (93G – .246)																			
"	total	99	.240	.405	304	73	12	1	12	3.9	33	35	32	62	1	6	0	461	45	3	6	5.1	.994	C-93
1956	PHI N	60	.199	.360	161	32	3	1	7	4.3	16	23	31	38	3	6	0	266	23	7	2	4.9	.976	C-54
1957		8	.091	.091	11	1	0	0	0	0.0	0	0	1	3	0	0	0	22	1	0	0	2.9	1.000	C-8
15 yrs.		1304	.243	.417	3921	953	139	26	164	4.2	495	556	582	780	23	77	8	5051	608	137	81	4.4	.976	C-1213, OF-9, 3B-4

WORLD SERIES

Year	Team	Games	BA	SA	AB	H	2B	3B	HR	HR%	R	RBI	BB	SO	SB	AB	H	PO	A	E	DP	TC/G	FA	G by Pos
1950	PHI N	4	.182	.182	11	2	0	0	0	0.0	0	0	1	3	0	0	0	14	2	1	0	4.3	.941	C-4

Sonny Senerchia

SENERCHIA, EMANUEL ROBERT
B. Apr. 6, 1931, Newark, N. J.   BR TR 6'1" 195 lbs.

Year	Team	Games	BA	SA	AB	H	2B	3B	HR	HR%	R	RBI	BB	SO	SB	AB	H	PO	A	E	DP	TC/G	FA	G by Pos
1952	PIT N	29	.220	.360	100	22	5	0	3	3.0	5	11	4	21	0	1	0	30	31	3	3	2.2	.953	3B-28

Paul Sentell

SENTELL, LEOPOLD THEODORE
B. Aug. 27, 1879, New Orleans, La. D. Apr. 27, 1923, Cincinnati, Ohio   BR TR 5'9" 176 lbs.

Year	Team	Games	BA	SA	AB	H	2B	3B	HR	HR%	R	RBI	BB	SO	SB	AB	H	PO	A	E	DP	TC/G	FA	G by Pos
1906	PHI N	63	.229	.281	192	44	5	1	1	0.5	19	14	14		15	8	0	72	105	19	4	3.1	.903	3B-33, 2B-19, OF-2, SS-1
1907		3	.000	.000	3	0	0	0	0	0.0	0	0	1		0	0	0	0	1	0	0	0.3	1.000	SS-2, OF-1
2 yrs.		66	.226	.277	195	44	5	1	1	0.5	19	14	15		15	8	0	72	106	19	4	3.0	.904	3B-33, 2B-19, OF-3, SS-3

Ted Sepkowski

SEPKOWSKI, THEODORE WALTER
Born Theodore Walter Sczepkowski.
B. Nov. 9, 1923, Baltimore, Md.   BL TR 5'11" 190 lbs.

Year	Team	Games	BA	SA	AB	H	2B	3B	HR	HR%	R	RBI	BB	SO	SB	AB	H	PO	A	E	DP	TC/G	FA	G by Pos
1942	CLE A	5	.100	.100	10	1	0	0	0	0.0	0	0	0	3	0	2	0	6	8	3	0	3.4	.824	2B-2
1946		2	.500	.625	8	4	1	0	0	0.0	2	1	0	0	0	0	0	3	2	1	1	3.0	.833	3B-2
1947	2 teams	CLE A (10G – .125)			NY A (2G – .000)																			
"	total	12	.125	.250	8	1	1	0	0	0.0	1	0	1	1	0	8	1	0	0	0	0	0.0	–	OF-1
3 yrs.		19	.231	.308	26	6	2	0	0	0.0	3	1	1	4	0	10	1	9	10	4	1	1.2	.826	3B-2, 2B-2, OF-1

Bill Serena

SERENA, WILLIAM ROBERT
B. Oct. 2, 1924, Alameda, Calif.   BR TR 5'9½" 175 lbs.

Year	Team	Games	BA	SA	AB	H	2B	3B	HR	HR%	R	RBI	BB	SO	SB	AB	H	PO	A	E	DP	TC/G	FA	G by Pos
1949	CHI N	12	.216	.378	37	8	3	0	1	2.7	3	7	7	9	0	1	0	9	15	2	0	2.2	.923	3B-11
1950		127	.239	.421	435	104	20	4	17	3.9	56	61	65	75	1	2	1	122	274	23	24	3.3	.945	3B-125
1951		13	.333	.538	39	13	3	1	1	2.6	8	4	11	4	0	0	0	15	17	2	1	2.6	.941	3B-12
1952		122	.274	.469	390	107	21	5	15	3.8	49	61	39	83	1	14	4	198	234	8	30	3.8	.982	3B-58, 2B-49
1953		93	.251	.433	275	69	10	5	10	3.6	30	52	41	46	0	13	4	135	160	7	31	3.2	.977	2B-49, 3B-28
1954		41	.159	.381	63	10	0	1	4	6.3	4	13	14	18	0	22	0	5	26	2	0	0.8	.939	3B-12, 2B-2
6 yrs.		408	.251	.439	1239	311	57	16	48	3.9	154	198	177	235	2	52	13	484	726	44	86	3.1	.965	3B-246, 2B-100

Paul Serna

SERNA, PAUL DAVID
B. Nov. 16, 1958, El Centro, Calif.   BR TR 5'8" 170 lbs.

Year	Team	Games	BA	SA	AB	H	2B	3B	HR	HR%	R	RBI	BB	SO	SB	AB	H	PO	A	E	DP	TC/G	FA	G by Pos
1981	SEA A	30	.255	.404	94	24	6	0	4	4.3	11	9	3	11	2	0	0	42	92	6	12	4.7	.957	SS-23, 2B-7
1982		65	.225	.296	169	38	3	0	3	1.8	15	8	4	13	0	3	0	63	126	9	23	3.0	.955	SS-31, 2B-18, 3B-15, DH-2
2 yrs.		95	.236	.335	263	62	5	0	7	2.7	26	17	7	24	2	3	0	105	218	15	35	3.6	.956	SS-54, 2B-25, 3B-15, DH-2

Walter Sessi

SESSI, WALTER ANTHONY (Watsie)
B. July 23, 1918, Finleyville, Pa.   BL TL 6'3" 225 lbs.

Year	Team	Games	BA	SA	AB	H	2B	3B	HR	HR%	R	RBI	BB	SO	SB	Pinch Hit AB	Pinch Hit H	PO	A	E	DP	TC/G	FA	G by Pos

Walter Sessi *continued*

Year	Team	Games	BA	SA	AB	H	2B	3B	HR	HR%	R	RBI	BB	SO	SB	PH AB	PH H	PO	A	E	DP	TC/G	FA	G by Pos
1941	STL N	5	.000	.000	13	0	0	0	0	0.0	2	0	1	2	0	2	0	3	0	1	0	0.8	.750	OF-3
1946		15	.143	.357	14	2	0	0	1	7.1	2	2	1	4	0	14	2	0	0	0	0	0.0	—	
2 yrs.		20	.074	.185	27	2	0	0	1	3.7	4	2	2	6	0	16	2	3	0	1	0	0.2	.750	OF-3

John Sevcik

SEVCIK, JOHN JOSEPH   BR TR 6'2"   205 lbs.
B. July 11, 1942, Oak Park, Ill.

Year	Team	Games	BA	SA	AB	H	2B	3B	HR	HR%	R	RBI	BB	SO	SB	PH AB	PH H	PO	A	E	DP	TC/G	FA	G by Pos
1965	MIN A	12	.063	.125	16	1	1	0	0	0.0	1	0	1	5	0	2	0	32	5	0	1	3.1	1.000	C-11

Hank Severeid

SEVEREID, HENRY LEVAI   BR TR 6'   175 lbs.
B. June 1, 1891, Story City, Iowa   D. Dec. 17, 1968, San Antonio, Tex.

Year	Team	Games	BA	SA	AB	H	2B	3B	HR	HR%	R	RBI	BB	SO	SB	PH AB	PH H	PO	A	E	DP	TC/G	FA	G by Pos
1911	CIN N	37	.304	.446	56	17	6	1	0	0.0	5	10	3	6	0	17	4	51	12	6	2	1.9	.913	C-22
1912		50	.237	.289	114	27	6	3	0	0.0	10	13	8	11	0	15	3	132	16	8	3	3.1	.949	C-20, 1B-7, OF-6
1913		8	.000	.000	6	0	0	0	0	0.0	0	0	1	1	0	5	0	2	0	0	0	0.3	1.000	C-2, OF-1
1915	STL A	80	.222	.276	203	45	6	1	1	0.5	12	22	16	25	2	15	1	247	66	11	2	4.1	.966	C-64
1916		100	.273	.314	293	80	8	2	0	0.0	23	34	26	17	3	8	1	320	99	10	6	4.3	.977	C-89, 3B-1, 1B-1
1917		143	.265	.333	501	133	23	4	1	0.2	45	57	28	20	6	2	0	532	157	24	10	5.0	.966	C-139, 1B-1
1918		51	.256	.286	133	34	4	0	0	0.0	8	11	18	4	4	7	3	148	44	11	4	4.0	.946	C-42
1919		112	.248	.293	351	87	12	2	0	0.0	16	36	21	13	2	9	1	401	106	9	12	4.6	.983	C-103
1920		123	.277	.348	422	117	14	5	2	0.5	46	49	33	11	5	6	1	480	111	10	11	4.9	.983	C-117
1921		143	.324	.415	472	153	23	7	2	0.4	66	78	42	9	7	14	2	481	117	17	11	4.3	.972	C-126
1922		137	.321	.427	517	166	32	7	3	0.6	49	78	28	12	1	3	0	552	123	11	10	5.0	.984	C-134
1923		122	.308	.419	432	133	27	6	3	0.7	50	51	31	11	3	6	4	513	88	4	9	5.0	.993	C-116
1924		137	.308	.398	432	133	23	2	4	0.9	37	48	36	15	1	6	1	436	104	6	12	4.0	.989	C-129
1925	2 teams		STL A (34G – .367)				WAS A (50G – .355)																		
"	total	84	.361	.461	219	79	17	1	1	0.5	26	35	22	8	0	14	3	243	40	3	6	3.4	.990	C-66
1926	2 teams		WAS A (22G – .206)				NY A (41G – .268)																		
"	total	63	.255	.323	161	41	9	1	0	0.0	15	17	16	6	1	6	1	73	13	1	1	1.4	.989	C-56
15 yrs.		1390	.289	.367	4312	1245	204	42	17	0.4	408	539	329	169	35	133	25	4611	1096	131	99	4.2	.978	C-1225, 1B-9, OF-7, 3B-1

WORLD SERIES

Year	Team	Games	BA	SA	AB	H	2B	3B	HR	HR%	R	RBI	BB	SO	SB	PH AB	PH H	PO	A	E	DP	TC/G	FA	G by Pos
1925	WAS A	1	.333	.333	3	1	0	0	0	0.0	0	0	0	0	0	0	0	6	0	1	0	7.0	.857	C-1
1926	NY A	7	.273	.318	22	6	1	0	0	0.0	1	1	1	2	0	0	0	37	7	0	0	6.3	1.000	C-7
2 yrs.		8	.280	.320	25	7	1	0	0	0.0	1	1	1	2	0	0	0	43	7	1	0	6.4	.980	C-8

Rich Severson

SEVERSON, RICHARD ALLEN   BR TR 6'   174 lbs.
B. Jan. 18, 1945, Artesia, Calif.

Year	Team	Games	BA	SA	AB	H	2B	3B	HR	HR%	R	RBI	BB	SO	SB	PH AB	PH H	PO	A	E	DP	TC/G	FA	G by Pos
1970	KC A	77	.250	.317	240	60	11	1	1	0.4	22	22	16	33	0	6	1	127	202	12	45	4.4	.965	SS-50, 2B-25
1971		16	.300	.433	30	9	0	2	0	0.0	4	1	3	5	0	3	1	15	35	2	11	3.3	.962	SS-6, 2B-6, 3B-1
2 yrs.		93	.256	.330	270	69	11	3	1	0.4	26	23	19	38	0	9	2	142	237	14	56	4.2	.964	SS-56, 2B-31, 3B-1

Ed Seward

SEWARD, EDWARD WILLIAM   TR 5'7"   175 lbs.
Born Edward William Sourhardt.
B. June 29, 1867, Cleveland, Ohio   D. July 30, 1947, Cleveland, Ohio

Year	Team	Games	BA	SA	AB	H	2B	3B	HR	HR%	R	RBI	BB	SO	SB	PH AB	PH H	PO	A	E	DP	TC/G	FA	G by Pos
1885	PRO N	1	.000	.000	3	0	0	0	0	0.0	0	0	0	2		0	0	0	4	0	0	4.0	1.000	P-1
1887	PHI AA	74	.188	.282	266	50	10	0	5	1.9	31	16		14	0	0	0	63	83	18	2	2.2	.890	P-55, OF-21
1888		64	.142	.209	225	32	3	3	2	0.9	27	14	18	12	0	0	0	32	127	19	5	2.8	.893	P-57, OF-7
1889		46	.217	.336	143	31	5	3	2	1.4	22	17	22	19	6	0	0	25	67	9	1	2.2	.911	P-39, OF-8, 2B-1
1890		26	.139	.194	72	10	4	0	0	0.0	7		8		3	0	0	19	27	10	2	2.2	.821	P-21, OF-6
1891	CLE N	7	.211	.316	19	4	2	0	0	0.0	2	1	3	4	0	0	0	8	1	1	0	1.4	.900	OF-3, P-3, 1B-1
6 yrs.		218	.174	.261	728	127	24	6	9	1.2	89	32	67	25	35	0	0	147	309	57	10	2.4	.889	P-176, OF-45, 2B-1, 1B-1

George Seward

SEWARD, GEORGE E.   5'7½"   145 lbs.
B. St. Louis, Mo.   Deceased.

Year	Team	Games	BA	SA	AB	H	2B	3B	HR	HR%	R	RBI	BB	SO	SB	PH AB	PH H	PO	A	E	DP	TC/G	FA	G by Pos
1876	NY N	1	.000	.000	3	0	0	0	0	0.0	0	0	0	0	0	0	0	2	3	0	0	5.0	1.000	2B-1
1882	STL AA	38	.215	.236	144	31	1	1	0	0.0	23		12			0	0	58	17	19	2	2.5	.798	OF-35, C-5
2 yrs.		39	.211	.231	147	31	1	1	0	0.0	23		12			0	0	60	20	19	2	2.5	.808	OF-35, C-5, 2B-1

Joe Sewell

SEWELL, JOSEPH WHEELER   BL TR 5'6½"   155 lbs.
Brother of Luke Sewell.   Brother of Tommy Sewell.
B. Oct. 9, 1898, Titus, Ala.
Hall of Fame 1977.

Year	Team	Games	BA	SA	AB	H	2B	3B	HR	HR%	R	RBI	BB	SO	SB	PH AB	PH H	PO	A	E	DP	TC/G	FA	G by Pos
1920	CLE A	22	.329	.414	70	23	4	1	0	0.0	14	12	9	4	1	0	0	44	70	15	11	5.9	.884	SS-22
1921		154	.318	.444	572	182	36	12	4	0.7	101	91	80	17	7	0	0	319	480	47	75	5.5	.944	SS-154
1922		153	.299	.385	558	167	28	7	2	0.4	80	83	73	20	10	1	0	322	497	52	79	5.7	.940	SS-139, 2B-12
1923		153	.353	.479	553	195	41	10	3	0.5	98	109	98	12	9	1	0	286	497	59	82	5.5	.930	SS-151
1924		153	.316	.429	594	188	**45**	5	4	0.7	99	104	67	13	3	0	0	349	514	36	76	5.9	.960	SS-153
1925		155	.336	.424	608	204	37	7	1	0.2	78	98	64	4	7	0	0	324	535	29	80	5.7	.967	SS-153, 2B-3
1926		154	.324	.433	578	187	41	5	4	0.7	91	85	65	6	17	0	0	326	463	37	86	5.4	.955	SS-154
1927		153	.316	.424	569	180	48	5	1	0.2	83	92	51	7	3	0	0	361	480	33	80	5.7	.962	SS-153
1928		155	.323	.418	588	190	40	2	4	0.7	79	70	58	9	7	0	0	319	499	33	106	5.5	.961	SS-137, 3B-19
1929		152	.315	.392	578	182	38	3	7	1.2	90	73	48	4	6	0	0	163	336	13	28	3.4	.975	3B-152
1930		109	.289	.371	353	102	17	6	0	0.0	44	48	42	3	1	1	0	83	184	14	16	2.6	.950	3B-97
1931	NY A	130	.302	.388	484	146	22	1	6	1.2	102	64	62	8	1	1	0	132	230	18	15	2.9	.953	3B-121, 2B-1
1932		124	.272	.392	503	137	21	3	11	2.2	95	68	56	3	0	1	0	122	221	9	15	2.8	.974	3B-122
1933		135	.273	.323	524	143	18	1	2	0.4	87	54	71	4	5	3	1	123	224	13	27	2.7	.964	3B-131
14 yrs.		1902	.312	.413	7132	2226	436	68	49	0.7	1141	1051	844	114	74	25	5	3273	5230	408	776	4.7	.954	SS-1216, 3B-642, 2B-16

WORLD SERIES

Year	Team	Games	BA	SA	AB	H	2B	3B	HR	HR%	R	RBI	BB	SO	SB	PH AB	PH H	PO	A	E	DP	TC/G	FA	G by Pos
1920	CLE A	7	.174	.174	23	4	0	0	0	0.0	0	0	2	1	0	0	0	11	28	6	3	6.4	.867	SS-7

Year	Team		Games	BA	SA	AB	H	2B	3B	HR	HR%	R	RBI	BB	SO	SB	Pinch Hit AB	H	PO	A	E	DP	TC/G	FA	G by Pos

Joe Sewell *continued*

Year	Team		Games	BA	SA	AB	H	2B	3B	HR	HR%	R	RBI	BB	SO	SB	AB	H	PO	A	E	DP	TC/G	FA	G by Pos
1932	NY	A	4	.333	.400	15	5	1	0	0	0.0	4	3	4	0	0	0	0	4	6	1	1	2.8	.909	3B-4
2 yrs.			11	.237	.263	38	9	1	0	0	0.0	4	3	6	1	0	0	0	15	34	7	4	5.1	.875	SS-7, 3B-4

Luke Sewell

SEWELL, JAMES LUTHER   BR TR 5'9'' 160 lbs.
Brother of Tommy Sewell. Brother of Joe Sewell.
B. Jan. 5, 1901, Titus, Ala. D. May 14, 1987, Akron, Ohio
Manager 1941-46, 1949-52.

Year	Team		Games	BA	SA	AB	H	2B	3B	HR	HR%	R	RBI	BB	SO	SB	AB	H	PO	A	E	DP	TC/G	FA	G by Pos
1921	CLE	A	3	.000	.000	6	0	0	0	0	0.0	0	1	0	3	0	0	0	7	4	0	0	3.7	1.000	C-3
1922			41	.264	.322	87	23	5	0	0	0.0	14	10	5	8	1	1	0	108	21	5	2	3.3	.963	C-38
1923			10	.200	.400	10	2	0	1	0	0.0	2	1	1	0	0	2	0	5	5	2	0	1.2	.833	C-7
1924			63	.291	.358	165	48	9	1	0	0.0	27	17	22	13	1	3	1	171	42	9	5	3.5	.959	C-56
1925			74	.232	.295	220	51	10	2	0	0.0	30	18	33	18	6	4	1	222	54	8	13	3.8	.972	C-66, OF-2
1926			126	.238	.293	433	103	16	4	0	0.0	41	46	36	27	9	1	0	437	91	9	3	4.3	.983	C-125
1927			128	.294	.377	470	138	27	6	0	0.0	52	53	20	23	4	2	0	402	119	20	14	4.2	.963	C-126
1928			122	.270	.375	411	111	16	9	3	0.7	52	52	26	27	3	4	1	430	117	16	13	4.6	.972	C-118
1929			124	.236	.300	406	96	17	3	1	0.2	41	39	29	26	6	0	0	433	81	18	11	4.3	.966	C-124
1930			76	.257	.353	292	75	21	2	1	0.3	40	43	14	9	5	0	0	283	49	9	5	4.5	.974	C-76
1931			108	.275	.384	375	103	30	4	1	0.3	45	53	36	17	1	3	1	384	61	9	5	4.2	.980	C-105
1932			87	.253	.353	300	76	20	2	2	0.7	36	52	38	24	4	2	0	306	50	8	8	4.2	.978	C-84
1933	WAS	A	141	.264	.357	474	125	30	4	2	0.4	65	61	48	24	7	0	0	516	61	6	12	4.1	.990	C-141
1934			72	.237	.329	207	49	7	3	2	1.0	21	21	22	10	0	7	2	215	30	2	11	3.4	.992	C-50, OF-7, 1B-6, 3B-1, 2B-1
1935	CHI	A	118	.285	.359	421	120	19	3	2	0.5	52	67	32	18	3	5	0	399	83	6	10	4.1	.988	C-112
1936			128	.251	.350	451	113	20	5	5	1.1	59	73	54	16	11	2	0	461	87	9	12	4.4	.984	C-126
1937			122	.269	.357	412	111	21	6	1	0.2	51	61	46	18	4	3	2	502	72	9	11	4.8	.985	C-118
1938			65	.213	.242	211	45	4	1	0	0.0	23	27	20	20	0	0	0	205	55	4	7	4.1	.985	C-65
1939	CLE	A	16	.150	.200	20	3	1	0	0	0.0	1	1	3	1	0	0	0	24	4	1	0	1.8	.966	C-15, 1B-1
1942	STL	A	6	.083	.083	12	1	0	0	0	0.0	1	0	1	5	0	0	0	12	5	1	1	3.0	.944	C-6
20 yrs.			1630	.259	.341	5383	1393	273	56	20	0.4	653	696	486	307	65	39	8	5522	1091	151	143	4.1	.978	C-1561, OF-9, 1B-7, 3B-1, 2B-1

WORLD SERIES

Year	Team		Games	BA	SA	AB	H	2B	3B	HR	HR%	R	RBI	BB	SO	SB	AB	H	PO	A	E	DP	TC/G	FA	G by Pos
1933	WAS	A	5	.176	.176	17	3	0	0	0	0.0	1	1	2	0	1	0	0	23	2	0	0	5.0	1.000	C-5

Tommy Sewell

SEWELL, THOMAS WESLEY   BL TR 5'7½'' 155 lbs.
Brother of Joe Sewell. Brother of Luke Sewell.
B. Apr. 16, 1906, Titus, Ala. D. July 30, 1956, Montgomery, Ala.

Year	Team		Games	BA	SA	AB	H	2B	3B	HR	HR%	R	RBI	BB	SO	SB	AB	H	PO	A	E	DP	TC/G	FA	G by Pos
1927	CHI	N	1	.000	.000	1	0	0	0	0	0.0	0	0	0	0	0	1	0	0	0	0	0	0.0	–	

Jimmy Sexton

SEXTON, JIMMY DALE   BR TR 5'10'' 175 lbs.
B. Dec. 15, 1951, Mobile, Ala.

Year	Team		Games	BA	SA	AB	H	2B	3B	HR	HR%	R	RBI	BB	SO	SB	AB	H	PO	A	E	DP	TC/G	FA	G by Pos
1977	SEA	A	14	.216	.378	37	8	1	1	1	2.7	5	3	2	6	1	0	0	12	40	4	10	4.0	.929	SS-12
1978	HOU	N	88	.206	.298	141	29	3	2	2	1.4	17	6	13	28	16	6	1	62	104	5	19	1.9	.971	SS-58, 3B-8, 2B-3
1979			52	.209	.209	43	9	0	0	0	0.0	8	1	7	7	1	17	3	11	24	2	6	0.7	.946	SS-11, 3B-4, 2B-2
1981	OAK	A	7	.000	.000	3	0	0	0	0	0.0	3	0	0	2	2	0	0	0	3	0	0	0.4	1.000	DH-1, 3B-1
1982			69	.245	.317	139	34	4	0	2	1.4	19	14	9	24	16	0	0	63	118	9	19	2.8	.953	SS-47, 3B-8, DH-5
1983	STL	N	6	.111	.222	9	1	1	0	0	0.0	1	0	1	4	0	1	0	4	8	0	2	2.0	1.000	SS-4, 3B-2
6 yrs.			236	.218	.298	372	81	9	3	5	1.3	53	24	32	71	36	24	4	152	297	20	56	2.0	.957	SS-132, 3B-23, DH-6, 2B-5

Tom Sexton

SEXTON, THOMAS WILLIAM
B. Mar. 14, 1865, Rock Island, Ill. D. Feb. 8, 1934, Rock Island, Ill.

Year	Team		Games	BA	SA	AB	H	2B	3B	HR	HR%	R	RBI	BB	SO	SB	AB	H	PO	A	E	DP	TC/G	FA	G by Pos
1884	MIL	U	12	.234	.277	47	11	2	0	0	0.0	9		4			0	0	8	21	5	1	2.8	.853	SS-12

Socks Seybold

SEYBOLD, RALPH ORLANDO   BR TR 5'11'' 175 lbs.
B. Nov. 23, 1870, Washingtonville, Ohio D. Dec. 22, 1921, Greensburg, Pa.

Year	Team		Games	BA	SA	AB	H	2B	3B	HR	HR%	R	RBI	BB	SO	SB	AB	H	PO	A	E	DP	TC/G	FA	G by Pos
1899	CIN	N	22	.224	.306	85	19	5	1	0	0.0	13	8	6		2	0	0	40	4	4	0	2.2	.917	OF-22
1901	PHI	A	114	.333	.499	457	152	24	14	8	1.8	74	90	40		15	0	0	301	17	10	9	2.9	.970	OF-100, 1B-14
1902			137	.316	.506	522	165	27	12	16	3.1	91	97	43		6	0	0	246	11	10	3	1.9	.963	OF-136
1903			137	.299	.462	522	156	45	8	8	1.5	78	84	38		5	0	0	340	17	13	10	2.7	.965	OF-120, 1B-18
1904			143	.292	.396	510	149	26	9	3	0.6	56	64	42		12	3	0	272	16	9	9	2.1	.970	OF-129, 1B-13
1905			132	.270	.400	488	132	37	4	6	1.2	65	59	42		5	0	0	213	13	4	5	1.7	.983	OF-132
1906			116	.316	.418	411	130	23	2	5	1.2	41	59	30		9	2	0	150	10	13	3	1.5	.925	OF-114
1907			147	.271	.362	564	153	28	4	5	0.9	58	92	40		10	0	0	201	19	6	7	1.5	.973	OF-147
1908			48	.215	.231	130	28	2	0	0	0.0	5	3	12		2	12	1	32	3	3	0	0.8	.921	OF-34
9 yrs.			996	.294	.423	3689	1084	217	54	51	1.4	481	556	293		66	17	2	1795	110	72	46	2.0	.964	OF-934, 1B-45

WORLD SERIES

Year	Team		Games	BA	SA	AB	H	2B	3B	HR	HR%	R	RBI	BB	SO	SB	AB	H	PO	A	E	DP	TC/G	FA	G by Pos
1905	PHI	A	5	.125	.125	16	2	0	0	0	0.0	0	0	2	3	0	0	0	5	1	0	1	1.2	1.000	OF-5

Cy Seymour

SEYMOUR, JAMES BENTLEY   BL TL 6' 200 lbs.
B. Dec. 9, 1872, Albany, N. Y. D. Sept. 20, 1919, New York, N. Y.

Year	Team		Games	BA	SA	AB	H	2B	3B	HR	HR%	R	RBI	BB	SO	SB	AB	H	PO	A	E	DP	TC/G	FA	G by Pos
1896	NY	N	12	.219	.219	32	7	0	0	0	0.0	2	0	0	7	0	1	0	5	19	4	1	2.3	.857	P-11, OF-1
1897			44	.241	.336	137	33	5	1	2	1.5	13	14	4		3	0	1	24	98	20	5	3.2	.859	P-38, OF-6
1898			80	.276	.347	297	82	5	2	4	1.3	41	23	9		8	0	0	72	120	25	9	2.7	.885	P-45, OF-35, 2B-1
1899			50	.327	.409	159	52	3	2	2	1.3	25	27	4		2	6	1	50	92	30	3	3.4	.826	P-32, OF-8, 1B-3, 3B-1
1900			23	.300	.300	40	12	0	0	0	0.0	9	2	3		0	6	1	9	20	7	0	1.6	.806	P-13, OF-3, 1B-1
1901	BAL	A	134	.303	.373	547	166	19	8	1	0.2	84	77	28		38	0	0	278	24	18	5	2.4	.944	OF-133, 1B-1
1902	2 teams					BAL A (72G – .268)			CIN N (62G – .349)																	
"	total		134	.305	.404	515	157	16	10	5	1.0	66	78	30		20	0	0	260	23	19	5	2.3	.937	OF-133, 3B-1, P-1
1903	CIN	N	135	.342	.478	558	191	25	15	7	1.3	85	72	33		25	0	0	318	14	36	2	2.7	.902	OF-135
1904			131	.313	.439	531	166	26	13	5	0.9	71	58	29		11	1	1	308	20	17	4	2.6	.951	OF-130

Year	Team	Games	BA	SA	AB	H	2B	3B	HR	HR%	R	RBI	BB	SO	SB	Pinch Hit AB	H	PO	A	E	DP	TC/G	FA	G by Pos

Cy Seymour *continued*

Year	Team	Games	BA	SA	AB	H	2B	3B	HR	HR%	R	RBI	BB	SO	SB	AB	H	PO	A	E	DP	TC/G	FA	G by Pos
1905		149	**.377**	**.559**	581	**219**	**40**	**21**	8	1.4	95	**121**	51		21	0	0	347	25	21	12	2.6	.947	OF-149
1906	2 teams	CIN N (79G – .257)			NY N (72G – .320)																			
"	total	151	.286	.378	576	165	19	5	8	1.4	70	80	42		29	0	0	331	17	10	6	2.4	.972	OF-151
1907	NY N	131	.294	.400	473	139	25	8	3	0.6	46	75	36		21	5	0	300	8	8	4	2.4	.975	OF-126
1908		156	.267	.339	587	157	23	2	5	0.9	60	92	30		18	1	0	340	29	20	9	2.5	.949	OF-155
1909		80	.311	.400	280	87	12	5	1	0.4	37	30	25		14	6	1	138	11	5	3	1.9	.968	OF-74
1910		79	.265	.334	287	76	9	4	1	0.3	32	40	23	18	10	2	0	137	9	10	1	2.0	.936	OF-76
1913	BOS N	39	.178	.205	73	13	2	0	0	0.0	2	10	7	7	2	15	3	34	4	2	0	1.0	.950	OF-18
16 yrs.		1528	.304	.405	5673	1722	229	96	52	0.9	738	799	354	32	222	43	6	2951	533	252	69	2.4	.933	OF-1333, P-140, 1B-5, 3B-2, 2B-1

Ralph Shafer

SHAFER, RALPH NEWTON
B. Mar. 17, 1894, Cincinnati, Ohio   D. Feb. 5, 1950, Akron, Ohio

5'11"

Year	Team	Games	BA	SA	AB	H	2B	3B	HR	HR%	R	RBI	BB	SO	SB	AB	H	PO	A	E	DP	TC/G	FA	G by Pos
1914	PIT N	1	–	–	0	0	0	0	0	–	0	0	0		0	0	0	0	0	0	0	0.0	–	

Tillie Shafer

SHAFER, ARTHUR JOSEPH
B. Mar. 22, 1889, Los Angeles, Calif.   D. Jan. 10, 1962, Los Angeles, Calif.

BB TR 5'10"   165 lbs.

Year	Team	Games	BA	SA	AB	H	2B	3B	HR	HR%	R	RBI	BB	SO	SB	AB	H	PO	A	E	DP	TC/G	FA	G by Pos
1909	NY N	38	.179	.226	84	15	2	1	0	0.0	11	7	14		6	5	0	33	56	15	2	2.7	.856	3B-16, 2B-13, OF-2
1910		29	.190	.238	21	4	1	0	0	0.0	5	1	0	6	6	6	1	5	13	2	2	0.7	.900	3B-8, SS-2, 2B-2
1912		78	.288	.325	163	47	4	1	0	0.0	48	23	30	19	22	7	1	80	119	22	10	2.8	.900	SS-31, 2B-20, 3B-7
1913		138	.287	.398	508	146	17	12	5	1.0	74	52	61	55	32	1	0	220	254	43	26	3.7	.917	3B-79, 2B-25, SS-17, OF-15
4 yrs.		283	.273	.360	776	212	24	14	5	0.6	138	83	105	80	60	19	2	338	442	82	40	3.0	.905	3B-110, 2B-60, SS-50, OF-17

WORLD SERIES

Year	Team	Games	BA	SA	AB	H	2B	3B	HR	HR%	R	RBI	BB	SO	SB	AB	H	PO	A	E	DP	TC/G	FA	G by Pos
1912	NY N	3	–	–	0	0	0	0	0	–	0	0	0		0	0	0	1	4	0	0	1.7	1.000	SS-3
1913		5	.158	.316	19	3	1	1	0	0.0	2	1	2	3	0	0	0	8	0	0	0	1.6	1.000	OF-5, 3B-1
2 yrs.		8	.158	.316	19	3	1	1	0	0.0	2	1	2	3	0	0	0	9	4	0	0	1.6	1.000	OF-5, SS-3, 3B-1

Frank Shaffer

SHAFFER, FRANK
Deceased.

Year	Team	Games	BA	SA	AB	H	2B	3B	HR	HR%	R	RBI	BB	SO	SB	AB	H	PO	A	E	DP	TC/G	FA	G by Pos
1884	3 teams	ALT U (19G – .284)			KC U (44G – .171)				BAL U (3G – .077)															
"	total	66	.199	.235	251	50	5	2	0	0.0	30		18			0	0	95	22	29	0	2.2	.801	OF-61, C-4, 3B-2, SS-1, 2B-1

Orator Shaffer

SHAFFER, GEORGE
Brother of Taylor Shaffer.
B. 1852, Philadelphia, Pa.   Deceased.

BL TR 5'9"   165 lbs.

Year	Team	Games	BA	SA	AB	H	2B	3B	HR	HR%	R	RBI	BB	SO	SB	AB	H	PO	A	E	DP	TC/G	FA	G by Pos
1877	LOU N	61	.285	.392	260	74	9	5	3	1.2	38	34	9			0	0	133	21	28	1	3.0	.846	OF-60, 1B-1
1878	IND N	63	.338	.455	266	90	19	6	0	0.0	48	30	13	20		0	0	105	28	25	2	2.5	.842	OF-63
1879	CHI N	73	.304	.345	316	96	13	0	0	0.0	53	35	6	28		0	0	99	51	38	3	2.6	.798	OF-72, 3B-1
1880	CLE N	83	.266	.361	338	90	14	9	0	0.0	62	21	17	36		0	0	128	35	18	5	2.2	.901	OF-83
1881		85	.257	.338	343	88	13	6	1	0.3	48	34	23	20		0	0	122	24	20	4	2.0	.880	OF-85
1882		84	.214	.300	313	67	14	2	3	1.0	37	28	27	27		0	0	111	17	31	2	1.9	.805	OF-84
1883	BUF N	95	.292	.334	401	117	11	3	0	0.0	67		27	39		0	0	182	41	36	3	2.7	.861	OF-95
1884	STL U	106	.360	.501	467	168	**40**	10	2	0.4	130		30			0	0	132	40	26	4	1.9	.869	OF-100, 2B-7, 1B-1
1885	2 teams	STL N (69G – .195)			PHI AA (2G – .222)																			
"	total	71	.195	.259	266	52	11	3	0	0.0	31	18	20	31		0	0	107	28	12	0	2.1	.918	OF-71
1886	PHI AA	21	.268	.378	82	22	3	3	0	0.0	15		8			0	0	40	4	10	2	2.6	.815	OF-21
1890		100	.282	.354	390	110	15	5	1	0.3	55		47		29	0	0	169	19	8	7	2.0	.959	OF-98, 1B-3
11 yrs.		842	.283	.369	3442	974	162	52	10	0.3	584	200	227	218	29	0	0	1328	308	252	33	2.2	.867	OF-832, 2B-7, 1B-5, 3B-1

Taylor Shaffer

SHAFFER, TAYLOR
Brother of Orator Shaffer.
B. July, 1870, Philadelphia, Pa.   Deceased.

Year	Team	Games	BA	SA	AB	H	2B	3B	HR	HR%	R	RBI	BB	SO	SB	AB	H	PO	A	E	DP	TC/G	FA	G by Pos
1890	PHI AA	69	.172	.215	261	45	3	4	0	0.0	28		28		19	0	0	214	195	35	39	6.4	.921	2B-69

Art Shamsky

SHAMSKY, ARTHUR LOUIS
B. Oct. 14, 1941, St. Louis, Mo.

BL TL 6'1"   168 lbs.

Year	Team	Games	BA	SA	AB	H	2B	3B	HR	HR%	R	RBI	BB	SO	SB	AB	H	PO	A	E	DP	TC/G	FA	G by Pos
1965	CIN N	64	.260	.427	96	25	4	3	2	2.1	13	10	10	29	1	45	13	31	2	1	0	0.5	.971	OF-18, 1B-1
1966		96	.231	.521	234	54	5	0	21	9.0	41	47	32	45	0	24	5	104	3	3	1	1.1	.973	OF-74
1967		76	.197	.293	147	29	3	1	3	2.0	6	13	15	34	0	34	10	59	2	1	1	0.8	.984	OF-40
1968	NY N	116	.238	.406	345	82	14	4	12	3.5	30	48	21	58	1	23	1	239	13	3	8	2.2	.988	OF-82, 1B-17
1969		100	.300	.488	303	91	9	3	14	4.6	42	47	36	32	1	13	5	192	2	2	7	2.0	.990	OF-78, 1B-9
1970		122	.293	.432	403	118	19	2	11	2.7	48	49	49	33	1	11	2	482	37	2	30	4.3	.996	OF-58, 1B-56
1971		68	.185	.370	135	25	5	3	7	5.2	13	18	21	18	1	24	3	59	6	1	2	1.0	.985	OF-38, 1B-1
1972	2 teams	CHI N (15G – .125)			OAK A (8G – .000)																			
"	total	23	.087	.087	23	2	0	0	0	0.0	1	1	4	5	0	15	2	30	1	0	1	1.3	1.000	1B-4
8 yrs.		665	.253	.427	1686	426	60	15	68	4.0	194	233	188	254	5	189	41	1196	65	13	50	1.9	.990	OF-388, 1B-88

LEAGUE CHAMPIONSHIP SERIES

Year	Team	Games	BA	SA	AB	H	2B	3B	HR	HR%	R	RBI	BB	SO	SB	AB	H	PO	A	E	DP	TC/G	FA	G by Pos
1969	NY N	3	.538	.538	13	7	0	0	0	0.0	0	0	0	0	0	0	0	4	0	0	0	1.0	1.000	OF-3

WORLD SERIES

Year	Team	Games	BA	SA	AB	H	2B	3B	HR	HR%	R	RBI	BB	SO	SB	AB	H	PO	A	E	DP	TC/G	FA	G by Pos
1969	NY N	3	.000	.000	6	0	0	0	0	0.0	0	0	0	0	0	2	0	1	0	0	0	0.3	1.000	OF-1

Wally Shaner

SHANER, WALTER DEDAKER (Skinny)
B. May 24, 1900, Lynchburg, Va.

BR TR 6'2"   195 lbs.

Year	Team	Games	BA	SA	AB	H	2B	3B	HR	HR%	R	RBI	BB	SO	SB	AB	H	PO	A	E	DP	TC/G	FA	G by Pos
1923	CLE A	3	.250	.250	4	1	0	0	0	0.0	1	0	1	1	0	0	0	2	0	0	0	0.7	1.000	OF-2, 3B-1
1926	BOS A	69	.283	.366	191	54	12	2	0	0.0	20	21	17	13	1	18	2	106	3	4	2	1.6	.965	OF-48
1927		122	.273	.406	406	111	33	6	3	0.7	54	49	21	35	11	11	1	231	16	12	3	2.1	.954	OF-108, 1B-1

Year	Team		Games	BA	SA	AB	H	2B	3B	HR	HR%	R	RBI	BB	SO	SB	Pinch Hit AB	Pinch Hit H	PO	A	E	DP	TC/G	FA	G by Pos

Wally Shaner *continued*

Year	Team		Games	BA	SA	AB	H	2B	3B	HR	HR%	R	RBI	BB	SO	SB	AB	H	PO	A	E	DP	TC/G	FA	G by Pos
1929	CIN	N	13	.321	.429	28	9	0	0	1	3.6	5	4	4	5	1	2	1	80	1	0	9	6.2	1.000	1B-8, OF-2
4 yrs.			207	.278	.394	629	175	45	8	4	0.6	80	74	43	54	13	31	4	419	20	16	14	2.2	.965	OF-160, 1B-9, 3B-1

Howard Shanks

SHANKS, HOWARD SAMUEL (Hank)
B. July 21, 1890, Chicago, Ill. D. July 30, 1941, Monaca, Pa. — BR TR 5'11" 170 lbs.

Year	Team		Games	BA	SA	AB	H	2B	3B	HR	HR%	R	RBI	BB	SO	SB	AB	H	PO	A	E	DP	TC/G	FA	G by Pos
1912	WAS	A	115	.231	.308	399	92	14	7	1	0.3	52	47	40		21	2	0	189	14	8	2	1.8	.962	OF-113
1913			109	.254	.315	390	99	11	5	1	0.3	38	37	15	40	24	0	0	207	13	5	3	2.1	.978	OF-109
1914			143	.224	.332	500	112	22	10	4	0.8	44	64	29	51	18	3	0	276	14	14	3	2.1	.954	OF-139
1915			141	.250	.321	492	123	19	8	0	0.0	52	47	30	42	12	2	1	226	128	18	15	2.6	.952	OF-80, 3B-49, 2B-10
1916			140	.253	.321	471	119	15	7	1	0.2	51	48	41	34	23	4	2	313	92	17	15	3.0	.960	OF-88, 3B-31, SS-8, 1B-7
1917			126	.202	.260	430	87	15	5	0	0.0	45	28	33	37	15	6	0	296	267	38	49	4.8	.937	SS-90, OF-26, 1B-2
1918			120	.257	.326	436	112	19	4	1	0.2	42	56	31	21	23	6	2	284	154	22	22	3.8	.952	OF-64, 2B-47, 3B-3
1919			135	.248	.299	491	122	8	7	1	0.2	33	54	25	48	13	1	1	329	359	57	11	5.5	.923	SS-94, 2B-34, OF-6
1920			128	.268	.363	444	119	16	7	4	0.9	56	37	29	43	11	6	0	294	154	17	12	3.6	.963	3B-63, OF-35, 1B-14, 2B-5, SS-1
1921			154	.302	.452	562	170	25	19	7	1.2	81	69	57	38	11	0	0	218	330	23	35	3.7	.960	3B-154
1922			84	.283	.397	272	77	10	9	1	0.4	35	32	25	25	6	3	0	125	112	16	16	3.0	.937	3B-54, OF-27
1923	BOS	A	131	.254	.336	464	118	19	5	3	0.6	38	57	19	37	6	5	0	188	261	25	34	3.6	.947	3B-85, 2B-36, OF-6, SS-2
1924			72	.259	.373	193	50	16	3	0	0.0	22	25	20	11	1	5	0	118	129	9	23	3.6	.965	SS-37, 3B-22, OF-4, 2B-2, 1B-2
1925	NY	A	66	.258	.310	155	40	3	1	1	0.6	15	18	20	15	1	13	4	68	87	6	13	2.4	.963	3B-26, 2B-21, OF-4
14 yrs.			1664	.253	.337	5699	1440	212	97	25	0.4	604	619	414	442	185	56	10	3131	2114	275	253	3.3	.950	OF-701, 3B-487, SS-232, 2B-155, 1B-25

Doc Shanley

SHANLEY, HARRY ROOT
B. Jan. 30, 1889, Grandbury, Tex. D. Dec. 13, 1934, St. Petersburg, Fla. — BR TR 5'11" 174 lbs.

Year	Team		Games	BA	SA	AB	H	2B	3B	HR	HR%	R	RBI	BB	SO	SB	AB	H	PO	A	E	DP	TC/G	FA	G by Pos
1912	STL	A	5	.000	.000	8	0	0	0	0	0.0	1	1	2		0	0	0	7	3	2	1	2.4	.833	SS-4

Jim Shanley

SHANLEY, JAMES H.
B. May 4, 1854, Brooklyn, N. Y. D. Nov. 4, 1904, Brooklyn, N. Y.

Year	Team		Games	BA	SA	AB	H	2B	3B	HR	HR%	R	RBI	BB	SO	SB	AB	H	PO	A	E	DP	TC/G	FA	G by Pos
1876	NY	N	2	.125	.125	8	1	0	0	0	0.0	0		0	0	0	0	0	3	0	2	0	2.5	.600	OF-2

Warren Shannabrook

SHANNABROOK, WARREN H.
B. Nov. 30, 1880, Massillon, Ohio D. Mar. 10, 1964, North Canton, Ohio — BR TR 6' 170 lbs.

Year	Team		Games	BA	SA	AB	H	2B	3B	HR	HR%	R	RBI	BB	SO	SB	AB	H	PO	A	E	DP	TC/G	FA	G by Pos
1906	WAS	A	1	.000	.000	2	0	0	0	0	0.0	0	0	0		0	0	0	0	1	0	0	1.0	1.000	3B-1

Dan Shannon

SHANNON, DANIEL W.
B. Mar. 23, 1865, Bridgeport, Conn. D. Oct. 25, 1913, Bridgeport, Conn.
Manager 1889, 1891. — 175 lbs.

Year	Team		Games	BA	SA	AB	H	2B	3B	HR	HR%	R	RBI	BB	SO	SB	AB	H	PO	A	E	DP	TC/G	FA	G by Pos
1889	LOU	AA	121	.257	.373	498	128	22	12	4	0.8	90	48	42	52	26	0	0	307	391	69	59	6.3	.910	2B-121
1890	2 teams			PHI	P	(19G – .240)		NY	P	(83G – .216)															
"	total		102	.221	.326	399	88	12	9	4	1.0	74	60	29	46	25	0	0	208	328	54	39	5.8	.908	2B-96, SS-6
1891	WAS	AA	19	.134	.164	67	9	2	0	0	0.0	7	3	6	9	3	0	0	45	51	11	6	5.6	.897	SS-14, 2B-5
3 yrs.			242	.233	.339	964	225	36	21	8	0.8	171	111	77	107	54	0	0	560	770	134	104	6.0	.908	2B-222, SS-20

Frank Shannon

SHANNON, JOHN FRANCIS (Tod)
B. Dec. 3, 1873, San Francisco, Calif. D. Feb. 27, 1934, Boston, Mass. — 5'3" 155 lbs.

Year	Team		Games	BA	SA	AB	H	2B	3B	HR	HR%	R	RBI	BB	SO	SB	AB	H	PO	A	E	DP	TC/G	FA	G by Pos
1892	WAS	N	1	.250	.250	4	1	0	0	0	0.0	0	2	0		0	0	0	3	2	3	0	8.0	.625	SS-1
1896	LOU	N	31	.157	.209	115	18	1	1	1	0.9	14	15	13	15	3	0	0	66	78	29	9	5.6	.832	SS-28, 3B-3
2 yrs.			32	.160	.210	119	19	1	1	1	0.8	14	17	13	17	3	0	0	69	80	32	9	5.7	.823	SS-29, 3B-3

Joe Shannon

SHANNON, JOSEPH ALOYSIUS
Brother of Red Shannon.
B. Feb. 11, 1897, Jersey City, N. J. D. July 28, 1955, Jersey City, N. J. — BR TR 5'11" 170 lbs.

Year	Team		Games	BA	SA	AB	H	2B	3B	HR	HR%	R	RBI	BB	SO	SB	AB	H	PO	A	E	DP	TC/G	FA	G by Pos
1915	BOS	N	5	.200	.200	10	2	0	0	0	0.0	3	1	0	3	0	2	1	4	3	1	0	1.6	.875	OF-4, 2B-1

Mike Shannon

SHANNON, THOMAS MICHAEL (Moonman)
B. July 15, 1939, St. Louis, Mo. — BR TR 6'3" 195 lbs.

Year	Team		Games	BA	SA	AB	H	2B	3B	HR	HR%	R	RBI	BB	SO	SB	AB	H	PO	A	E	DP	TC/G	FA	G by Pos
1962	STL	N	10	.133	.133	15	2	0	0	0	0.0	3	0	1	3	0	0	0	7	1	0	0	0.8	1.000	OF-7
1963			32	.308	.423	26	8	0	0	1	3.8	2	0	6	4	1	4	1	15	2	1	0	0.6	.944	OF-26
1964			88	.261	.415	253	66	8	2	9	3.6	30	43	19	54	4	2	0	110	7	2	2	1.4	.983	OF-88
1965			124	.221	.352	244	54	17	3	3	1.2	32	25	28	46	2	19	2	193	6	1	2	1.6	.995	OF-101, C-4
1966			137	.288	.462	459	132	20	6	16	3.5	61	64	37	106	8	9	2	248	10	4	4	1.9	.985	OF-129, C-1
1967			130	.245	.369	482	118	18	3	12	2.5	53	77	37	89	2	2	1	98	241	29	18	2.8	.921	3B-122, OF-6
1968			156	.266	.401	576	153	29	2	15	2.6	62	79	37	114	1	0	0	110	310	21	25	2.8	.952	3B-156
1969			150	.254	.365	551	140	15	5	12	2.2	51	55	49	87	1	2	0	123	258	22	22	2.7	.945	3B-149
1970			52	.213	.287	174	37	9	2	0	0.0	18	22	16	20	1	5	1	32	59	8	4	1.9	.919	3B-51
9 yrs.			879	.255	.387	2780	710	116	23	68	2.4	313	367	224	525	19	43	8	936	894	88	77	2.2	.954	3B-478, OF-357, C-5

WORLD SERIES

Year	Team		Games	BA	SA	AB	H	2B	3B	HR	HR%	R	RBI	BB	SO	SB	AB	H	PO	A	E	DP	TC/G	FA	G by Pos
1964	STL	N	7	.214	.321	28	6	0	0	1	3.6	6	2	0	9	1	0	0	13	2	0	1	2.1	1.000	OF-7
1967			7	.208	.375	24	5	1	0	1	4.2	3	2	1	4	0	0	0	5	13	1	1	2.9	.947	3B-7
1968			7	.276	.414	29	8	1	0	1	3.4	3	4	1	5	0	0	0	5	10	1	1	2.3	.938	3B-7
3 yrs.			21	.235	.370	81	19	2	0	3	3.7	12	8	2	18	1	0	0	23	25	3	3	2.4	.941	3B-14, OF-7

Owen Shannon

SHANNON, OWEN DENNIS IGNATIUS
B. Dec. 22, 1885, Omaha, Neb. D. Apr. 10, 1918, Omaha, Neb. — BR TR

Year	Team		Games	BA	SA	AB	H	2B	3B	HR	HR%	R	RBI	BB	SO	SB	AB	H	PO	A	E	DP	TC/G	FA	G by Pos
1903	STL	A	9	.214	.286	28	6	2	0	0	0.0	1	3	1		0	0	0	43	6	2	0	5.7	.961	C-8, 1B-1

Year Team	Games	BA	SA	AB	H	2B	3B	HR	HR%	R	RBI	BB	SO	SB	Pinch Hit AB	Pinch Hit H	PO	A	E	DP	TC/G	FA	G by Pos

Owen Shannon *continued*

Year Team	Games	BA	SA	AB	H	2B	3B	HR	HR%	R	RBI	BB	SO	SB	AB	H	PO	A	E	DP	TC/G	FA	G by Pos
1907 WAS A	4	.143	.143	7	1	0	0	0	0.0	0	0	0		0	0	0	13	7	0	0	5.0	1.000	C-4
2 yrs.	13	.200	.257	35	7	2	0	0	0.0	1	3	1		0	0	0	56	13	2	0	5.5	.972	C-12, 1B-1

Red Shannon

SHANNON, MAURICE JOSEPH
Brother of Joe Shannon.
B. Feb. 11, 1897, Jersey City, N. J. D. Apr. 12, 1970, Jersey City, N. J.

BB TR 5'11" 170 lbs.

Year Team	Games	BA	SA	AB	H	2B	3B	HR	HR%	R	RBI	BB	SO	SB	AB	H	PO	A	E	DP	TC/G	FA	G by Pos
1915 BOS N	1	.000	.000	3	0	0	0	0	0.0	0	0	0	0	0	0	0	3	3	1	1	7.0	.857	2B-1
1917 PHI A	11	.286	.286	35	10	0	0	0	0.0	8	7	6	9	2	1	0	18	31	7	2	5.1	.875	SS-10
1918	72	.240	.311	225	54	6	5	0	0.0	23	16	42	52	5	0	0	155	223	39	40	5.8	.906	SS-45, 2B-26
1919 2 teams		PHI A	(39G – .271)		BOS A	(80G – .259)																	
" total	119	.263	.344	445	117	18	9	0	0.0	50	31	29	**70**	11	3	1	237	344	21	50	5.1	.965	2B-116
1920 2 teams		WAS A	(62G – .288)		PHI A	(25G – .170)																	
" total	87	.255	.335	310	79	8	8	0	0.0	34	33	26	44	3	1	0	132	225	25	23	4.4	.935	SS-55, 2B-16, 3B-15
1921 PHI A	1	.000	.000	1	0	0	0	0	0.0	0	0	0	0	0	1	0	0	0	0	0	0.0	–	
1926 CHI N	19	.333	.431	51	17	5	0	0	0.0	9	4	6	3	0	5	2	25	42	3	6	3.7	.957	SS-13
7 yrs.	310	.259	.336	1070	277	38	22	0	0.0	124	91	109	178	21	11	3	570	868	96	122	4.9	.937	2B-159, SS-123, 3B-15

Spike Shannon

SHANNON, WILLIAM PORTER
B. Feb. 7, 1878, Pittsburgh, Pa. D. May 16, 1940, Minneapolis, Minn.

BB TR 5'11" 180 lbs.

Year Team	Games	BA	SA	AB	H	2B	3B	HR	HR%	R	RBI	BB	SO	SB	AB	H	PO	A	E	DP	TC/G	FA	G by Pos
1904 STL N	134	.280	.318	500	140	10	3	1	0.2	84	26	50		34	1	0	246	18	6	10	2.0	.978	OF-133
1905	140	.268	.309	544	146	16	3	0	0.0	73	41	47		27	0	0	299	7	5	3	2.2	.984	OF-140
1906 2 teams		STL N	(80G – .258)		NY N	(76G – .254)																	
" total	156	.256	.275	589	151	9	1	0	0.0	78	50	70		33	0	0	274	13	10	5	1.9	.966	OF-156
1907 NY N	155	.265	.308	**585**	155	12	5	1	0.2	104	33	82		33	0	0	282	18	7	3	2.0	.977	OF-155
1908 2 teams		NY N	(77G – .224)		PIT N	(32G – .197)																	
" total	109	.215	.243	395	85	2	3	1	0.3	44	33	37		18	2	0	202	10	8	3	2.0	.964	OF-106
5 yrs.	694	.259	.293	2613	677	49	15	3	0.1	383	183	286		145	3	0	1303	66	36	24	2.0	.974	OF-690

Wally Shannon

SHANNON, WALTER CHARLES
B. Jan. 23, 1934, Cleveland, Ohio

BL TR 6' 178 lbs.

Year Team	Games	BA	SA	AB	H	2B	3B	HR	HR%	R	RBI	BB	SO	SB	AB	H	PO	A	E	DP	TC/G	FA	G by Pos
1959 STL N	47	.284	.337	95	27	5	0	0	0.0	5	5	0	12	0	28	9	40	35	3	9	1.7	.962	SS-21, 2B-10
1960	18	.174	.174	23	4	0	0	0	0.0	2	1	3	6	0	9	1	10	23	0	4	1.8	1.000	2B-15, SS-1
2 yrs.	65	.263	.305	118	31	5	0	0	0.0	7	6	3	18	0	37	10	50	58	3	13	1.7	.973	2B-25, SS-22

Billy Shantz

SHANTZ, WILMER EBERT
Brother of Bobby Shantz.
B. July 31, 1927, Pottstown, Pa.

BR TR 6'1" 160 lbs.

Year Team	Games	BA	SA	AB	H	2B	3B	HR	HR%	R	RBI	BB	SO	SB	AB	H	PO	A	E	DP	TC/G	FA	G by Pos
1954 PHI A	51	.256	.366	164	42	9	3	1	0.6	13	17	17	23	0	0	0	170	28	5	1	4.0	.975	C-51
1955 KC A	79	.258	.300	217	56	4	1	1	0.5	18	12	11	14	0	1	0	261	27	3	8	3.7	.990	C-78
1960 NY A	1	–	–	0	0	0	0	0	–	0	0	0	0	0	0	0	1	0	0	0	1.0	1.000	C-1
3 yrs.	131	.257	.328	381	98	13	4	2	0.5	31	29	28	37	0	1	0	432	55	8	9	3.8	.984	C-130

Ralph Sharman

SHARMAN, RALPH EDWARD (Bally)
B. Apr. 11, 1895, Cleveland, Ohio D. May 24, 1918, Camp Sheridan, Ala.

BR TR 5'11" 176 lbs.

Year Team	Games	BA	SA	AB	H	2B	3B	HR	HR%	R	RBI	BB	SO	SB	AB	H	PO	A	E	DP	TC/G	FA	G by Pos
1917 PHI A	13	.297	.405	37	11	2	1	0	0.0	3	2	3	2	1	2	0	16	7	1	0	1.8	.958	OF-10

Dick Sharon

SHARON, RICHARD LOUIS
B. Apr. 15, 1950, San Mateo, Calif.

BR TR 6'2" 195 lbs.

Year Team	Games	BA	SA	AB	H	2B	3B	HR	HR%	R	RBI	BB	SO	SB	AB	H	PO	A	E	DP	TC/G	FA	G by Pos
1973 DET A	91	.242	.410	178	43	9	0	7	3.9	20	16	10	31	2	3	1	124	5	4	1	1.5	.970	OF-91
1974	60	.217	.295	129	28	4	0	2	1.6	12	10	14	29	4	5	0	84	3	1	1	1.5	.989	OF-56
1975 SD N	91	.194	.313	160	31	7	0	4	2.5	14	20	26	35	0	33	8	91	1	5	0	1.1	.948	OF-57
3 yrs.	242	.218	.345	467	102	20	0	13	2.8	46	46	50	95	6	41	9	299	9	10	2	1.3	.969	OF-204

Bill Sharp

SHARP, WILLIAM HOWARD
B. Jan. 18, 1950, Lima, Ohio

BL TL 5'10" 178 lbs.

Year Team	Games	BA	SA	AB	H	2B	3B	HR	HR%	R	RBI	BB	SO	SB	AB	H	PO	A	E	DP	TC/G	FA	G by Pos
1973 CHI A	77	.276	.408	196	54	8	3	4	2.0	23	22	19	28	2	5	2	146	10	3	2	2.1	.981	OF-70, DH-1
1974	100	.253	.344	320	81	13	2	4	1.3	45	24	25	37	0	3	1	210	3	3	0	2.2	.986	OF-99
1975 2 teams		CHI A	(18G – .200)		MIL A	(125G – .255)																	
" total	143	.250	.338	408	102	27	3	1	0.2	38	38	21	29	0	10	3	310	12	3	4	2.3	.991	OF-138
1976 MIL A	78	.244	.267	180	44	4	0	0	0.0	16	11	10	15	1	17	5	108	7	3	2	1.5	.975	OF-56, DH-7
4 yrs.	398	.255	.341	1104	281	52	8	9	0.8	122	95	75	109	3	35	9	774	32	12	8	2.1	.985	OF-363, DH-8

Bud Sharpe

SHARPE, BAYARD HESTON
B. Aug. 6, 1881, West Chester, Pa. D. May 31, 1916, Haddock, Ga.

BL TR

Year Team	Games	BA	SA	AB	H	2B	3B	HR	HR%	R	RBI	BB	SO	SB	AB	H	PO	A	E	DP	TC/G	FA	G by Pos
1905 BOS N	46	.182	.224	170	31	3	2	0	0.0	8	11	7		0	1	0	73	20	7	3	2.2	.930	OF-42, C-3, 1B-1
1910 2 teams		BOS N	(115G – .239)		PIT N	(4G – .188)																	
" total	119	.237	.286	455	108	14	4	0	0.0	32	30	14	33	4	2	1	1159	84	17	72	10.6	.987	1B-117
2 yrs.	165	.222	.269	625	139	17	6	0	0.0	40	41	21	33	4	3	1	1232	104	24	75	8.2	.982	1B-118, OF-42, C-3

Mike Sharperson

SHARPERSON, MICHAEL TYRONE
B. Oct. 4, 1961, Orangeburg, S. C.

BR TR 6'1" 175 lbs.

Year Team	Games	BA	SA	AB	H	2B	3B	HR	HR%	R	RBI	BB	SO	SB	AB	H	PO	A	E	DP	TC/G	FA	G by Pos
1987 2 teams		TOR A	(32G – .208)		LA N	(10G – .273)																	
" total	42	.225	.287	129	29	6	1	0	0.0	11	10	11	20	2	0	0	68	97	5	18	4.0	.971	2B-38, 3B-7
1988 LA N	46	.271	.288	59	16	1	0	0	0.0	8	4	1	12	0	22	3	19	31	2	5	1.1	.962	2B-20, 3B-6, SS-4
1989	27	.250	.357	28	7	3	0	0	0.0	2	5	4	15	0	15	3	11	8	0	2	0.7	1.000	2B-4, 3B-2, 1B-2, SS-1
3 yrs.	115	.241	.296	216	52	10	1	0	0.0	21	19	16	39	2	37	6	98	136	7	25	2.1	.971	2B-62, 3B-15, SS-5, 1B-2

LEAGUE CHAMPIONSHIP SERIES

Year Team	Games	BA	SA	AB	H	2B	3B	HR	HR%	R	RBI	BB	SO	SB	AB	H	PO	A	E	DP	TC/G	FA	G by Pos
1988 LA N	2	.000	.000	1	0	0	0	0	0.0	0	1	1	0	0	1	0	0	0	0	0	0.5	1.000	SS-1, 3B-1

Year	Team		Games	BA	SA	AB	H	2B	3B	HR	HR%	R	RBI	BB	SO	SB	Pinch Hit AB	Pinch Hit H	PO	A	E	DP	TC/G	FA	G by Pos

John Sharrott

SHARROTT, JOHN HENRY
B. Aug. 13, 1869, Bangor, Me. D. Dec. 31, 1927, Los Angeles, Calif.
BL TL 5'9" 165 lbs.

Year	Team		Games	BA	SA	AB	H	2B	3B	HR	HR%	R	RBI	BB	SO	SB	PH AB	PH H	PO	A	E	DP	TC/G	FA	G by Pos
1890	NY	N	32	.202	.266	109	22	3	2	0	0.0	16	14	0	14	6	0	0	11	46	15	0	2.3	.792	P-25, OF-9
1891			10	.333	.500	30	10	2	0	1	3.3	5	7	1	2	3	0	0	4	15	1	0	2.0	.950	P-10
1892			4	.125	.125	8	1	0	0	0	0.0	1	0	0	1	0	0	0	1	0	2	0	0.8	.333	OF-3, P-1
1893	PHI	N	50	.250	.336	152	38	4	3	1	0.7	25	22	8	14	6	4	2	52	19	14	0	1.7	.835	OF-33, P-12
4 yrs.			96	.237	.321	299	71	9	5	2	0.7	47	43	9	31	15	4	2	68	80	32	0	1.9	.822	P-48, OF-45

Shag Shaughnessy

SHAUGHNESSY, FRANCIS JOSEPH
B. Apr. 8, 1883, Amboy, Ill. D. May 15, 1969, Montreal, Que., Canada
BR TR 6'1½" 185 lbs.

Year	Team		Games	BA	SA	AB	H	2B	3B	HR	HR%	R	RBI	BB	SO	SB	PH AB	PH H	PO	A	E	DP	TC/G	FA	G by Pos
1905	WAS	A	1	.000	.000	3	0	0	0	0	0.0	0	0	0			0	0	2	0	1	0	3.0	.667	OF-1
1908	PHI	A	8	.310	.310	29	9	0	0	0	0.0	2	1	2			3	0	13	0	0	0	1.6	1.000	OF-8
2 yrs.			9	.281	.281	32	9	0	0	0	0.0	2	1	2			3	0	15	0	1	0	1.8	.938	OF-9

Al Shaw

SHAW, ALBERT SIMPSON
B. Mar. 1, 1881, Toledo, Ill. D. Dec. 30, 1974, Danville, Ill.
BL TR 5'8½" 165 lbs.

Year	Team		Games	BA	SA	AB	H	2B	3B	HR	HR%	R	RBI	BB	SO	SB	PH AB	PH H	PO	A	E	DP	TC/G	FA	G by Pos
1907	STL	N	8	.304	.304	23	7	0	0	0	0.0	2	1	3			1	0	17	1	1	0	2.4	.947	OF-8
1908			107	.264	.330	367	97	13	4	1	0.3	40	19	25			9	10	5	186	28	19	8	2.2	.918	OF-91, SS-4, 3B-1
1909			114	.248	.344	331	82	12	7	2	0.6	45	34	55			15	15	3	189	14	13	1	1.9	.940	OF-92
1914	BKN	F	112	.324	.473	376	122	27	7	5	1.3	81	49	44			24	7	5	198	14	10	4	2.0	.955	OF-102
1915	KC	F	132	.281	.415	448	126	22	10	6	1.3	67	67	46			15	6	1	184	11	12	0	1.6	.942	OF-124
5 yrs.			473	.281	.392	1545	434	74	28	14	0.9	235	170	173			64	38	14	774	68	55	13	1.9	.939	OF-417, SS-4, 3B-1

Al Shaw

SHAW, ALFRED
B. Oct. 3, 1874, Burslem, England D. Mar. 25, 1958, Uhrichsville, Ohio
BR TR 5'8" 170 lbs.

Year	Team		Games	BA	SA	AB	H	2B	3B	HR	HR%	R	RBI	BB	SO	SB	PH AB	PH H	PO	A	E	DP	TC/G	FA	G by Pos
1901	DET	A	55	.269	.327	171	46	7	0	1	0.6	20	23	10			2	4	0	217	50	17	12	5.2	.940	C-42, 1B-9, 3B-2, SS-1
1907	BOS	A	76	.192	.227	198	38	1	3	0	0.0	10	7	18			1	1	0	296	106	13	11	5.5	.969	C-73, 1B-1
1908	CHI	A	32	.082	.102	49	4	1	0	0	0.0	0	2	2			0	3	0	87	15	5	1	3.3	.953	C-29
1909	BOS	N	17	.098	.098	41	4	0	0	0	0.0	1	0	5			0	2	0	58	21	2	0	4.8	.975	C-13
4 yrs.			180	.200	.240	459	92	9	3	1	0.2	31	32	35			6	10	0	658	192	37	24	4.9	.958	C-157, 1B-10, 3B-2, SS-1

Ben Shaw

SHAW, BENJAMIN NATHANIEL
B. June 18, 1893, La Center, Ky. D. Mar. 16, 1959, Aurora, Ohio
BR TR 5'11½" 190 lbs.

Year	Team		Games	BA	SA	AB	H	2B	3B	HR	HR%	R	RBI	BB	SO	SB	PH AB	PH H	PO	A	E	DP	TC/G	FA	G by Pos
1917	PIT	N	2	.000	.000	2	0	0	0	0	0.0	0	0	0	0	0	0	2	0	0	0	0	0.0	–	
1918			21	.194	.222	36	7	1	0	0	0.0	5	2	2	2	0	1	0	67	2	1	3	3.3	.986	1B-9, C-5
2 yrs.			23	.184	.211	38	7	1	0	0	0.0	5	2	2	2	0	3	0	67	2	1	3	3.0	.986	1B-9, C-5

Dupee Shaw

SHAW, FREDERICK LANDER
B. May 31, 1859, Charlestown, Mass. D. June 11, 1938, Everett, Mass.
BL TL 5'8" 165 lbs.

Year	Team		Games	BA	SA	AB	H	2B	3B	HR	HR%	R	RBI	BB	SO	SB	PH AB	PH H	PO	A	E	DP	TC/G	FA	G by Pos
1883	DET	N	38	.206	.227	141	29	3	0	0	0.0	13		3	36		0	0	21	50	7	5	2.1	.910	P-26, OF-15
1884	2 teams		80	DET	N (36G – .191)			BOS	U (44G – .242)																
"	total		80	.218	.277	289	63	12	1	1	0.3	29		9	21		0	0	39	116	34	3	2.4	.820	P-67, OF-19
1885	PRO	N	49	.133	.145	165	22	2	0	0	0.0	17	9	4	38		0	0	11	76	8	2	1.9	.916	P-49, OF-1
1886	WAS	N	45	.088	.101	148	13	2	0	0	0.0	13	6	14	44		0	0	13	70	3	1	1.9	.945	P-45, OF-1
1887			21	.186	.214	70	13	2	0	0	0.0	7	3	8	14	1	0	0	4	24	2	0	1.4	.933	P-21
1888			3	.000	.000	10	0	0	0	0	0.0	0	0	0	3	0	0	0	0	2	0	0	0.7	1.000	P-3
6 yrs.			236	.170	.202	823	140	21	1	1	0.1	79	18	38	156	1	0	0	88	338	54	11	2.0	.888	P-211, OF-37

Hunky Shaw

SHAW, ROYAL N.
B. Sept. 29, 1884, Yakima, Wash. D. July 3, 1969, Yakima, Wash.
BB TR 5'8" 165 lbs.

Year	Team		Games	BA	SA	AB	H	2B	3B	HR	HR%	R	RBI	BB	SO	SB	PH AB	PH H	PO	A	E	DP	TC/G	FA	G by Pos
1908	PIT	N	1	.000	.000	1	0	0	0	0	0.0	0	0	0			0	1	0	0	0	0	0	0.0	–	

Danny Shay

SHAY, DANIEL C.
Born Daniel C. Shea.
B. Nov. 8, 1876, Springfield, Ohio D. Dec. 1, 1927, Kansas City, Mo.
TR 5'10"

Year	Team		Games	BA	SA	AB	H	2B	3B	HR	HR%	R	RBI	BB	SO	SB	PH AB	PH H	PO	A	E	DP	TC/G	FA	G by Pos
1901	CLE	A	19	.227	.307	75	17	2	2	0	0.0	4	10	2			0	0	38	53	10	3	5.3	.901	SS-19
1904	STL	N	99	.256	.303	340	87	11	1	1	0.3	45	18	39			36	1	0	153	324	46	30	5.3	.912	SS-97, 2B-2
1905			78	.238	.288	281	67	12	1	0	0.0	30	28	35			11	0	0	172	230	35	22	5.6	.920	SS-39, 2B-39
1907	NY	N	35	.190	.266	79	15	1	1	1	1.3	10	6	12			5	11	2	40	53	10	3	2.9	.903	2B-13, SS-9, OF-2
4 yrs.			231	.240	.294	775	186	26	5	2	0.3	89	62	88			52	12	2	403	660	101	58	5.0	.913	SS-164, 2B-54, OF-2

Marty Shay

SHAY, ARTHUR JOSEPH
B. Apr. 25, 1896, Boston, Mass. D. Feb. 20, 1951, Worcester, Mass.
BR TR 5'7½" 148 lbs.

Year	Team		Games	BA	SA	AB	H	2B	3B	HR	HR%	R	RBI	BB	SO	SB	PH AB	PH H	PO	A	E	DP	TC/G	FA	G by Pos
1916	CHI	N	2	.286	.286	7	2	0	0	0	0.0	0	0	0			0	0	6	5	1	2	6.0	.917	SS-2
1924	BOS	N	19	.235	.309	68	16	3	1	0	0.0	4	2	5	5	2	0	0	38	40	4	10	4.3	.951	2B-19, SS-1
2 yrs.			21	.240	.307	75	18	3	1	0	0.0	4	2	5	6	2	0	0	44	45	5	12	4.5	.947	2B-19, SS-3

Gerry Shea

SHEA, GERALD J.
B. July 26, 1881, St. Louis, Mo. D. May 3, 1964, Berkeley, Mo.
TR 5'7" 160 lbs.

Year	Team		Games	BA	SA	AB	H	2B	3B	HR	HR%	R	RBI	BB	SO	SB	PH AB	PH H	PO	A	E	DP	TC/G	FA	G by Pos
1905	STL	N	2	.333	.333	6	2	0	0	0	0.0	0	0	0			0	0	0	7	4	1	1	6.0	.917	C-2

Merv Shea

SHEA, MERVYN DAVID JOHN
B. Sept. 5, 1900, San Francisco, Calif. D. Jan. 27, 1953, Sacramento, Calif.
BR TR 5'11" 175 lbs.

Year	Team		Games	BA	SA	AB	H	2B	3B	HR	HR%	R	RBI	BB	SO	SB	PH AB	PH H	PO	A	E	DP	TC/G	FA	G by Pos
1927	DET	A	34	.176	.318	85	15	6	3	0	0.0	5	9	7	15	0	3	0	94	17	6	1	3.4	.949	C-31
1928			39	.235	.329	85	20	2	3	0	0.0	8	9	9	11	2	7	0	93	24	6	2	3.2	.951	C-30
1929			50	.290	.383	162	47	6	0	3	1.9	23	24	19	18	2	5	0	157	32	7	4	3.9	.964	C-50
1933	2 teams		110	BOS	A (16G – .143)			STL	A (94G – .262)																
"	total		110	.242	.299	335	81	14	1	1	0.3	27	35	47	33	2	8	2	376	71	2	17	4.1	.996	C-101
1934	CHI	A	62	.159	.176	176	28	3	0	0	0.0	8	5	24	19	0	2	0	240	35	8	4	4.6	.972	C-60
1935			46	.230	.246	122	28	2	0	0	0.0	8	13	30	9	0	2	0	161	30	2	4	4.2	.990	C-43
1936			14	.125	.125	24	3	0	0	0	0.0	3	2	6	5	0	0	0	32	3	0	0	2.5	1.000	C-14

Year	Team		Games	BA	SA	AB	H	2B	3B	HR	HR%	R	RBI	BB	SO	SB	Pinch Hit AB	Pinch Hit H	PO	A	E	DP	TC/G	FA	G by Pos

Merv Shea *continued*

1937			25	.211	.225	71	15	1	0	0	0.0	7	5	15	10	1	0	0	91	21	4	1	4.6	.966	C-25
1938	BKN	N	48	.183	.225	120	22	5	0	0	0.0	14	12	28	20	1	0	0	149	19	4	2	3.6	.977	C-47
1939	DET	A	4	.000	.000	2	0	0	0	0	0.0	0	0	0	1	0	0	0	1	0	1	0	0.5	.500	C-4
1944	PHI	N	7	.267	.467	15	4	0	0	1	6.7	2	1	4	4	0	1	0	18	2	1	0	3.0	.952	C-6
11 yrs.			439	.220	.277	1197	263	39	7	5	0.4	105	115	189	145	8	26	2	1412	254	41	33	3.9	.976	C-411

Nap Shea

SHEA, JOHN EDWARD BR TR 5'5" 155 lbs.
B. May 23, 1874, Ware, Mass. D. July 8, 1968, Bloomfield Hills, Mich.

| 1902 | PHI | N | 3 | .125 | .125 | 8 | 1 | 0 | 0 | 0 | 0.0 | 1 | 0 | 1 | | 0 | 0 | 0 | 13 | 2 | 0 | 0 | 5.0 | 1.000 | C-3 |

Danny Sheaffer

SHEAFFER, DANNY TODD BR TR 6' 185 lbs.
B. Aug. 2, 1961, Jacksonville, Fla.

1987	BOS	A	25	.121	.182	66	8	1	0	1	1.5	5	5	0	14	0	1	1	121	5	3	1	5.2	.977	C-25
1989	CLE	A	7	.063	.063	16	1	0	0	0	0.0	1	0	2	2	0	1	0	4	0	0	0	0.6	1.000	DH-3, 3B-2, OF-1
2 yrs.			32	.110	.159	82	9	1	0	1	1.2	6	5	2	16	0	2	1	125	5	3	1	4.2	.977	C-25, DH-3, 3B-2, OF-1

Dave Shean

SHEAN, DAVID WILLIAM BR TR 5'11" 175 lbs.
B. July 9, 1883, Arlington, Mass. D. May 22, 1963, Boston, Mass.

1906	PHI	A	22	.213	.307	75	16	3	2	0	0.0	7	3	5		6	0	0	41	58	2	5	4.6	.980	2B-22
1908	PHI	N	14	.146	.188	48	7	2	0	0	0.0	4	2	1		1	0	0	27	34	9	2	5.0	.871	SS-14
1909	2 teams		111	.243	.317	PHI N (36G – .232)				BOS N (75G – .247)															
"	total		111	.243	.317	379	92	13	6	1	0.3	46	33	31		17	10	3	295	245	19	40	5.0	.966	2B-86, 1B-11, OF-3, SS-1
1910	BOS	N	150	.239	.304	543	130	12	7	3	0.6	52	36	42	45	16	2	1	408	493	44	92	6.3	.953	2B-148
1911	CHI	N	54	.193	.221	145	28	4	0	0	0.0	17	15	8	15	4	9	1	81	107	12	17	3.7	.940	2B-23, SS-19, 3B-1
1912	BOS	N	4	.300	.300	10	3	0	0	0	0.0	1	0	1	2	0	1	0	2	9	1	2	3.0	.917	SS-4
1917	CIN	N	131	.210	.267	442	93	9	5	2	0.5	36	35	22	39	10	0	0	332	412	30	69	5.9	.961	2B-131
1918	BOS	A	115	.264	.315	425	112	16	3	0	0.0	58	34	40	25	11	0	0	241	341	20	38	5.2	.967	2B-115
1919			29	.140	.140	100	14	0	0	0	0.0	4	8	5	7	1	0	0	70	85	3	18	5.4	.981	2B-29
9 yrs.			630	.228	.285	2167	495	59	23	6	0.3	225	166	155	133	66	22	5	1497	1784	140	283	5.4	.959	2B-554, SS-38, 1B-11, OF-3, 3B-1

WORLD SERIES

| 1918 | BOS | A | 6 | .211 | .263 | 19 | 4 | 1 | 0 | 0 | 0.0 | 2 | 0 | 4 | 3 | 1 | 0 | 0 | 15 | 17 | 0 | 3 | 5.3 | 1.000 | 2B-6 |

Ray Shearer

SHEARER, RAY SOLOMON BR TR 6' 200 lbs.
B. Sept. 19, 1929, Jacobus, Pa. D. Feb. 21, 1982, York, Pa.

| 1957 | MIL | N | 2 | .500 | .500 | 2 | 1 | 0 | 0 | 0 | 0.0 | 1 | 0 | 1 | 1 | 0 | 1 | 1 | 0 | 0 | 0 | 0 | 0.0 | – | OF-1 |

John Shearon

SHEARON, JOHN M.
B. 1870, Pittsburgh, Pa. D. Feb. 1, 1923, Bradford, Pa.

1891	CLE	N	30	.242	.266	124	30	1	1	0	0.0	10	13	1	15	6	0	0	32	13	8	1	1.8	.849	OF-28, P-6
1896			16	.172	.203	64	11	0	1	0	0.0	6	3	4	6	3	0	0	18	0	4	0	1.4	.818	OF-16
2 yrs.			46	.218	.245	188	41	1	2	0	0.0	16	16	5	21	9	0	0	50	13	12	1	1.6	.840	OF-44, P-6

Jimmy Sheckard

SHECKARD, SAMUEL JAMES TILDEN BL TR 5'9" 175 lbs.
B. Nov. 23, 1878, Upper Chanceford, Pa. D. Jan. 15, 1947, Lancaster, Pa.

1897	BKN	N	13	.245	.571	49	12	3	2	3	6.1	12	14	6		5	0	0	21	41	20	5	6.3	.756	SS-11, OF-2
1898			105	.277	.392	408	113	17	9	4	1.0	51	64	37		8	0	0	213	13	19	2	2.3	.922	OF-105, 3B-1
1899	BAL	N	147	.295	.382	536	158	18	10	3	0.6	104	75	56		**77**	0	0	306	33	20	14	2.4	.944	OF-146, 1B-1
1900	BKN	N	85	.300	.454	273	82	19	10	1	0.4	74	39	42		30	6	1	171	13	15	3	2.3	.925	OF-78
1901			133	.353	**.536**	558	197	31	**19**	11	2.0	116	104	47		35	0	0	296	37	30	6	2.7	.917	OF-121, 3B-12
1902	2 teams		127	.269	.375	BAL A (4G – .267)				BKN N (123G – .270)															
"	total		127	.269	.375	501	135	21	10	4	0.8	89	37	58		25	0	0	289	12	11	8	2.5	.965	OF-127
1903	BKN	N	139	.332	.476	515	171	29	9	9	1.7	99	75	75		**67**	0	0	314	36	18	7	2.6	.951	OF-139
1904			143	.239	.314	507	121	23	6	1	0.2	70	46	56		21	0	0	296	16	15	5	2.3	.954	OF-141, 2B-2
1905			130	.292	.398	480	140	20	11	3	0.6	58	46	61		23	0	0	266	24	10	6	2.3	.967	OF-129
1906	CHI	N	149	.262	.353	549	144	27	10	1	0.2	90	45	67		30	0	0	264	13	4	1	1.9	.986	OF-149
1907			142	.267	.324	484	129	23	1	1	0.2	76	36	76		31	1	0	223	13	6	2	1.7	.975	OF-142
1908			115	.231	.305	403	93	18	3	2	0.5	54	22	62		18	0	0	201	13	10	3	1.9	.955	OF-115
1909			148	.255	.335	525	134	29	5	1	0.2	81	43	72		15	0	0	277	18	10	5	2.1	.967	OF-148
1910			144	.256	.363	507	130	27	6	5	1.0	82	51	83		22	1	1	308	21	8	3	2.3	.976	OF-143
1911			156	.276	.388	539	149	26	11	4	0.7	**121**	50	**147**	58	32	0	0	332	32	14	12	2.4	.963	OF-156
1912			146	.245	.342	523	128	27	10	3	0.6	85	47	**122**	81	15	0	0	332	26	14	4	2.5	.962	OF-146
1913	2 teams		99	.194	.238	STL N (52G – .199)				CIN N (47G – .190)															
"	total		99	.194	.238	252	49	3	4	0	0.0	34	24	68	41	11	12	2	134	10	6	3	1.5	.960	OF-84
17 yrs.			2121	.274	.379	7609	2085	356	136	56	0.7	1296	813	1135	233	465	20	4	4243	371	230	87	2.3	.953	OF-2071, 3B-13, SS-11, 2B-2, 1B-1

WORLD SERIES

1906	CHI	N	6	.000	.000	21	0	0	0	0	0.0	0	1	2	1	1	0	0	10	1	0	1	1.8	1.000	OF-6
1907			5	.238	.333	21	5	2	0	0	0.0	0	2	0	1	1	0	0	10	0	0	0	2.0	1.000	OF-5
1908			5	.238	.333	21	5	2	0	0	0.0	2	1	2	3	0	0	0	7	1	0	0	1.6	1.000	OF-5
1910			5	.286	.429	14	4	2	0	0	0.0	5	1	7	2	1	0	0	8	2	1	0	2.2	.909	OF-5
4 yrs.			21	.182	.260	77	14	6	0	0	0.0	7	5	11	10	4	0	0	35	4	1	1	1.9	.975	OF-21

Biff Sheehan

SHEEHAN, TIMOTHY JAMES TR 5'9" 165 lbs.
B. Feb. 13, 1868, Hartford, Conn. D. Oct. 21, 1923, Hartford, Conn.

1895	STL	N	52	.317	.417	180	57	3	6	1	0.6	24	18	20	6	7	0	0	151	10	9	7	3.3	.947	OF-41, 1B-11
1896			6	.158	.158	19	3	0	0	0	0.0	0	1	4	0	0	0	0	10	0	0	0	1.7	1.000	OF-6
2 yrs.			58	.302	.392	199	60	3	6	1	0.5	24	19	24	6	7	0	0	161	10	9	7	3.1	.950	OF-47, 1B-11

Year	Team	Games	BA	SA	AB	H	2B	3B	HR	HR%	R	RBI	BB	SO	SB	Pinch Hit AB	H	PO	A	E	DP	TC/G	FA	G by Pos

Dan Sheehan

SHEEHAN, DANIEL
B. Dec. 18, 1872, Cleveland, Ohio Deceased. 5'6" 142 lbs.

Year	Team	Games	BA	SA	AB	H	2B	3B	HR	HR%	R	RBI	BB	SO	SB	AB	H	PO	A	E	DP	TC/G	FA	G by Pos
1900	NY N	1	.000	.000	2	0	0	0	0	0.0	0	0	0		0	0	0	0	0	0	0	0.0	–	SS-1

Jack Sheehan

SHEEHAN, JOHN THOMAS
B. Apr. 15, 1893, Chicago, Ill. D. May 29, 1987, West Palm Beach, Fla. BL TR 5'8½" 165 lbs.

Year	Team	Games	BA	SA	AB	H	2B	3B	HR	HR%	R	RBI	BB	SO	SB	AB	H	PO	A	E	DP	TC/G	FA	G by Pos
1920	BKN N	3	.400	.600	5	2	1	0	0	0.0	0	0	1	0	0	0	0	2	6	2	0	3.3	.800	SS-2, 3B-1
1921		5	.000	.000	12	0	0	0	0	0.0	2	0	0	1	0	0	0	6	8	1	1	3.0	.933	2B-2, SS-1, 3B-1
2 yrs.		8	.118	.176	17	2	1	0	0	0.0	2	0	1	1	0	0	0	8	14	3	1	3.1	.880	SS-3, 3B-2, 2B-2

WORLD SERIES

Year	Team	Games	BA	SA	AB	H	2B	3B	HR	HR%	R	RBI	BB	SO	SB	AB	H	PO	A	E	DP	TC/G	FA	G by Pos
1920	BKN N	3	.182	.182	11	2	0	0	0	0.0	0	1	0	0	0	0	0	3	5	2	0	3.3	.800	3B-3

Jim Sheehan

SHEEHAN, JAMES THOMAS (Big Jim)
B. July 3, 1913, New Haven, Conn. BR TR 6'2" 196 lbs.

Year	Team	Games	BA	SA	AB	H	2B	3B	HR	HR%	R	RBI	BB	SO	SB	AB	H	PO	A	E	DP	TC/G	FA	G by Pos
1936	NY N	1	.000	.000	4	0	0	0	0	0.0	0	0	0	2	0	0	0	5	0	1	0	6.0	.833	C-1

Tommy Sheehan

SHEEHAN, THOMAS H.
B. Nov. 6, 1877, Sacramento, Calif. D. May 22, 1959, Panama City, Panama BR TR 5'8" 160 lbs.

Year	Team	Games	BA	SA	AB	H	2B	3B	HR	HR%	R	RBI	BB	SO	SB	AB	H	PO	A	E	DP	TC/G	FA	G by Pos
1906	PIT N	95	.241	.289	315	76	6	3	1	0.3	28	34	18		13	5	1	104	166	15	11	3.0	.947	3B-90
1907		75	.274	.310	226	62	2	3	0	0.0	23	25	23		10	6	2	74	161	19	3	3.4	.925	3B-57, SS-10
1908	BKN N	146	.214	.261	468	100	18	2	0	0.0	45	29	53		9	1	1	174	280	34	13	3.3	.930	3B-145
3 yrs.		316	.236	.280	1009	238	26	8	1	0.1	96	88	94		32	12	4	352	607	68	27	3.3	.934	3B-292, SS-10

Bud Sheely

SHEELY, HOLLIS KIMBALL
Son of Earl Sheely.
B. Nov. 26, 1920, Spokane, Wash. D. Oct. 17, 1985, Sacramento, Calif. BL TR 6'1" 200 lbs.

Year	Team	Games	BA	SA	AB	H	2B	3B	HR	HR%	R	RBI	BB	SO	SB	AB	H	PO	A	E	DP	TC/G	FA	G by Pos
1951	CHI A	34	.180	.202	89	16	2	0	0	0.0	2	7	6	7	0	6	1	127	11	2	3	4.1	.986	C-33
1952		36	.240	.267	75	18	2	0	0	0.0	1	3	12	7	0	6	2	105	12	1	1	3.3	.992	C-31
1953		31	.217	.239	46	10	1	0	0	0.0	4	2	9	8	0	10	4	60	2	0	1	2.0	1.000	C-17
3 yrs.		101	.210	.233	210	44	5	0	0	0.0	7	12	27	22	0	17	6	292	25	3	5	3.2	.991	C-81

Earl Sheely

SHEELY, EARL HOMER (Whitey)
Father of Bud Sheely.
B. Feb. 12, 1893, Bushnell, Ill. D. Sept. 16, 1952, Seattle, Wash. BR TR 6'3½" 195 lbs.

Year	Team	Games	BA	SA	AB	H	2B	3B	HR	HR%	R	RBI	BB	SO	SB	AB	H	PO	A	E	DP	TC/G	FA	G by Pos
1921	CHI A	154	.304	.428	563	171	25	6	11	2.0	68	95	57	34	4	0	0	1637	119	22	121	11.5	.988	1B-154
1922		149	.317	.437	526	167	37	4	6	1.1	72	80	60	27	4	0	0	1512	103	12	101	10.9	.993	1B-149
1923		156	.296	.372	570	169	25	3	4	0.7	74	88	79	30	5	0	0	1563	96	14	113	10.7	.992	1B-156
1924		146	.320	.411	535	171	34	3	3	0.6	84	103	95	28	7	0	0	1423	79	14	97	10.4	.991	1B-146
1925		153	.315	.442	600	189	43	3	9	1.5	93	111	68	23	3	0	0	1565	95	20	136	11.0	.988	1B-153
1926		145	.299	.417	525	157	40	2	6	1.1	77	89	75	13	3	0	0	1380	84	8	87	10.2	.994	1B-144
1927		45	.209	.279	129	27	3	0	2	1.6	11	16	20	5	1	8	1	315	15	6	25	7.5	.982	1B-36
1929	PIT N	139	.293	.392	485	142	22	4	6	1.2	63	88	75	24	6	0	0	1292	83	5	102	9.9	.996	1B-139
1931	BOS N	147	.273	.314	538	147	15	2	1	0.2	30	77	34	21	0	3	0	1374	70	12	108	9.9	.992	1B-143
9 yrs.		1234	.300	.399	4471	1340	244	27	48	1.1	572	747	563	205	33	11	1	12061	744	113	890	10.5	.991	1B-1220

Charlie Sheerin

SHEERIN, CHARLES JOSEPH
B. Apr. 17, 1909, Brooklyn, N. Y. D. Sept. 27, 1986, Valley Stream, N. Y. BR TR 5'11½" 198 lbs.

Year	Team	Games	BA	SA	AB	H	2B	3B	HR	HR%	R	RBI	BB	SO	SB	AB	H	PO	A	E	DP	TC/G	FA	G by Pos
1936	PHI N	39	.264	.319	72	19	4	0	0	0.0	4	4	7	18	0	2	1	22	54	5	3	2.1	.938	2B-17, 3B-13, SS-5

Larry Sheets

SHEETS, LARRY KENT
B. Dec. 6, 1959, Staunton, Va. BL TR 6'4" 210 lbs.

Year	Team	Games	BA	SA	AB	H	2B	3B	HR	HR%	R	RBI	BB	SO	SB	AB	H	PO	A	E	DP	TC/G	FA	G by Pos
1984	BAL A	8	.438	.688	16	7	1	0	1	6.3	3	2	1	3	0	1	0	12	1	0	0	1.6	1.000	OF-7
1985		113	.262	.442	328	86	8	0	17	5.2	43	50	28	52	0	16	4	12	1	1	1	0.1	.929	DH-93, OF-9, 1B-1
1986		112	.272	.488	338	92	17	1	18	5.3	42	60	21	56	2	13	2	90	8	3	4	0.9	.970	DH-58, OF-32, C-6, 1B-4, 3B-2
1987		135	.316	.563	469	148	23	0	31	6.6	74	94	31	67	1	6	3	243	7	7	3	1.9	.973	OF-124, DH-7, 1B-3
1988		136	.230	.343	452	104	19	1	10	2.2	38	47	42	72	1	12	5	159	12	4	3	1.3	.977	OF-76, DH-50, 1B-3
1989		102	.243	.359	304	74	12	0	7	2.3	33	33	26	58	1	18	6	0	0	0	0	0.0	–	DH-88
6 yrs.		606	.268	.445	1907	511	80	3	84	4.4	233	286	149	308	5	66	20	516	29	15	11	0.9	.973	DH-296, OF-248, 1B-11, C-6, 3B-2

Gary Sheffield

SHEFFIELD, GARY ANTONIAN
B. Nov. 18, 1968, Tampa, Fla. BR TR 5'11" 190 lbs.

Year	Team	Games	BA	SA	AB	H	2B	3B	HR	HR%	R	RBI	BB	SO	SB	AB	H	PO	A	E	DP	TC/G	FA	G by Pos
1988	MIL A	24	.238	.400	80	19	1	0	4	5.0	12	12	7	7	3	0	0	39	48	3	9	3.8	.967	SS-24
1989		95	.247	.337	368	91	18	0	5	1.4	34	32	27	33	10	0	0	100	238	16	44	3.7	.955	SS-70, 3B-21, DH-4
2 yrs.		119	.246	.348	448	110	19	0	9	2.0	46	44	34	40	13	0	0	139	286	19	53	3.7	.957	SS-94, 3B-21, DH-4

John Shelby

SHELBY, JOHN T. (T-Bone)
B. Feb. 23, 1958, Lexington, Ky. BB TR 6'1" 175 lbs.

Year	Team	Games	BA	SA	AB	H	2B	3B	HR	HR%	R	RBI	BB	SO	SB	AB	H	PO	A	E	DP	TC/G	FA	G by Pos
1981	BAL A	7	.000	.000	2	0	0	0	0	0.0	2	0	0	1	2	0	0	1	0	0	0	0.1	1.000	OF-4
1982		26	.314	.486	35	11	3	0	1	2.9	8	2	0	5	3	1	0	20	1	0	1	0.8	1.000	OF-24
1983		126	.258	.363	325	84	15	2	5	1.5	52	27	18	64	15	27	7	200	9	4	3	1.7	.981	OF-115, DH-1
1984		128	.209	.313	383	80	12	5	6	1.6	44	30	20	71	12	12	4	261	9	2	1	2.1	.993	OF-124
1985		69	.283	.434	205	58	6	2	7	3.4	28	27	7	44	5	12	3	148	4	3	0	2.2	.981	OF-59, DH-3, 2B-1
1986		135	.228	.364	404	92	14	4	11	2.7	54	49	18	75	18	19	6	222	5	5	2	1.7	.978	OF-121, DH-2
1987	2 teams	BAL A (21G – .188)		LA N (120G – .277)																				
"	total	141	.272	.453	508	138	26	0	22	4.3	65	72	32	110	16	3	1	294	9	8	3	2.2	.974	OF-136, DH-1
1988	LA N	140	.263	.395	494	130	23	6	10	2.0	65	64	44	128	16	0	0	329	7	6	1	2.4	.982	OF-140

John Shelby *continued*

Year	Team		Games	BA	SA	AB	H	2B	3B	HR	HR%	R	RBI	BB	SO	SB	AB	H	PO	A	E	DP	TC/G	FA	G by Pos
1989			108	.183	.229	345	63	11	1	1	0.3	28	12	25	92	10	11	0	220	3	2	1	2.1	.991	OF-98
9 yrs.			880	.243	.368	2701	656	110	20	63	2.3	346	283	164	590	94	87	22	1695	47	30	12	2.0	.983	OF-821, DH-7, 2B-1

LEAGUE CHAMPIONSHIP SERIES

Year	Team		Games	BA	SA	AB	H	2B	3B	HR	HR%	R	RBI	BB	SO	SB	AB	H	PO	A	E	DP	TC/G	FA	G by Pos
1983	BAL	A	3	.222	.222	9	2	0	0	0	0.0	1	0	1	3	1	0	0	3	0	0	0	1.0	1.000	OF-2
1988	LA	N	7	.167	.167	24	4	0	0	0	0.0	3	3	5	12	2	0	0	19	0	0	0	2.7	1.000	OF-7
2 yrs.			10	.182	.182	33	6	0	0	0	0.0	4	3	6	15	3	0	0	22	0	0	0	2.2	1.000	OF-9

WORLD SERIES

Year	Team		Games	BA	SA	AB	H	2B	3B	HR	HR%	R	RBI	BB	SO	SB	AB	H	PO	A	E	DP	TC/G	FA	G by Pos
1983	BAL	A	5	.444	.444	9	4	0	0	0	0.0	1	0	0	4	1	3	0	10	0	0	0	2.0	1.000	OF-5
1988	LA	N	5	.222	.278	18	4	1	0	0	0.0	0	1	2	7	1	0	0	14	0	0	0	2.8	1.000	OF-5
2 yrs.			10	.296	.333	27	8	1	0	0	0.0	1	2	2	11	1	3	0	24	0	0	0	2.4	1.000	OF-10

Bob Sheldon

SHELDON, BOB MITCHELL
B. Nov. 27, 1950, Montebello, Calif.　　BL TR 6′　170 lbs.

Year	Team		Games	BA	SA	AB	H	2B	3B	HR	HR%	R	RBI	BB	SO	SB	AB	H	PO	A	E	DP	TC/G	FA	G by Pos
1974	MIL	A	10	.118	.294	17	2	1	1	0	0.0	4	0	4	2	0	1	0	1	4	0	0	0.5	1.000	DH-4, 2B-3
1975			53	.287	.337	181	52	3	3	0	0.0	17	14	13	14	0	6	3	87	122	5	33	4.0	.977	2B-44, DH-6
1977			31	.203	.297	64	13	4	1	0	0.0	9	3	6	9	0	8	2	7	9	0	2	0.5	1.000	DH-17, 2B-5
3 yrs.			94	.256	.324	262	67	8	5	0	0.0	30	17	23	25	0	15	5	95	135	5	35	2.5	.979	2B-52, DH-27

Hugh Shelley

SHELLEY, HUBERT LENEIRRE
B. Oct. 26, 1910, Rogers, Tex.　D. June 16, 1978, Beaumont, Tex.　　BR TR 6′　170 lbs.

Year	Team		Games	BA	SA	AB	H	2B	3B	HR	HR%	R	RBI	BB	SO	SB	AB	H	PO	A	E	DP	TC/G	FA	G by Pos
1935	DET	A	7	.250	.250	8	2	0	0	0	0.0	1	1	2	1	0	2	1	5	0	0	0	0.7	1.000	OF-5

Skeeter Shelton

SHELTON, ANDREW KEMPER
B. June 29, 1888, Huntington, W. Va.　D. Jan. 9, 1954, Huntington, W. Va.　　BR TR 5′11″　175 lbs.

Year	Team		Games	BA	SA	AB	H	2B	3B	HR	HR%	R	RBI	BB	SO	SB	AB	H	PO	A	E	DP	TC/G	FA	G by Pos
1915	NY	A	10	.025	.025	40	1	0	0	0	0.0	1	0	2	10	0	0	0	20	2	0	0	2.2	1.000	OF-10

Stan Shemo

SHEMO, STEPHEN MICHAEL
B. Apr. 9, 1915, Swoyersville, Pa.　　BR TR 5′11″　175 lbs.

Year	Team		Games	BA	SA	AB	H	2B	3B	HR	HR%	R	RBI	BB	SO	SB	AB	H	PO	A	E	DP	TC/G	FA	G by Pos
1944	BOS	N	18	.290	.355	31	9	2	0	0	0.0	3	1	1	3	0	0	0	26	34	2	4	3.4	.968	2B-16, 3B-2
1945			17	.239	.261	46	11	1	0	0	0.0	4	7	1	3	0	0	0	23	21	3	1	2.8	.936	2B-12, 3B-3, SS-1
2 yrs.			35	.260	.299	77	20	3	0	0	0.0	7	8	2	6	0	0	0	49	55	5	5	3.1	.954	2B-28, 3B-5, SS-1

Jack Shepard

SHEPARD, JACK LEROY
B. May 13, 1932, Clovis, Calif.　　BR TR 6′2″　195 lbs.

Year	Team		Games	BA	SA	AB	H	2B	3B	HR	HR%	R	RBI	BB	SO	SB	AB	H	PO	A	E	DP	TC/G	FA	G by Pos
1953	PIT	N	2	.250	.250	4	1	0	0	0	0.0	0	0	0	0	0	0	0	6	0	0	0	4.0	.750	C-2
1954			82	.304	.396	227	69	8	2	3	1.3	24	22	26	33	0	14	4	257	46	7	5	3.8	.977	C-67
1955			94	.239	.314	264	63	10	2	2	0.8	24	23	33	25	1	18	5	288	34	6	6	3.5	.982	C-77
1956			100	.242	.383	256	62	11	2	7	2.7	24	30	25	37	1	15	4	359	36	4	4	4.0	.990	C-86, 1B-2
4 yrs.			278	.260	.362	751	195	29	6	12	1.6	72	75	84	97	2	47	13	910	116	19	15	3.8	.982	C-232, 1B-2

Ray Shepardson

SHEPARDSON, RAYMOND FRANCIS
B. May 3, 1897, Little Falls, N. Y.　D. Nov. 8, 1975, Little Falls, N. Y.　　BR TR 5′11½″　170 lbs.

Year	Team		Games	BA	SA	AB	H	2B	3B	HR	HR%	R	RBI	BB	SO	SB	AB	H	PO	A	E	DP	TC/G	FA	G by Pos
1924	STL	N	3	.000	.000	6	0	0	0	0	0.0	1	0	0	3	0	1	0	5	2	0	0	2.3	1.000	C-3

Ron Shepherd

SHEPHERD, RONALD WAYNE
B. Oct. 27, 1960, Longview, Tex.　　BR TR 6′4″　180 lbs.

Year	Team		Games	BA	SA	AB	H	2B	3B	HR	HR%	R	RBI	BB	SO	SB	AB	H	PO	A	E	DP	TC/G	FA	G by Pos
1984	TOR	A	12	.000	.000	4	0	0	0	0	0.0	0	0	0	3	0	0	0	2	1	0	0	0.3	1.000	OF-5, DH-4
1985			38	.114	.171	35	4	2	0	0	0.0	7	1	2	12	3	8	0	24	0	0	0	0.6	1.000	OF-16, DH-15
1986			65	.203	.348	69	14	4	0	2	2.9	16	4	3	22	0	8	1	30	0	0	0	0.5	1.000	OF-32, DH-16
3 yrs.			115	.167	.278	108	18	6	0	2	1.9	23	5	5	37	3	16	1	56	1	0	0	0.5	1.000	OF-53, DH-35

Neill Sheridan

SHERIDAN, NEILL RAWLINS (Wild Horse)
B. Nov. 20, 1921, Sacramento, Calif.　　BR TR 6′1½″　195 lbs.

Year	Team		Games	BA	SA	AB	H	2B	3B	HR	HR%	R	RBI	BB	SO	SB	AB	H	PO	A	E	DP	TC/G	FA	G by Pos
1948	BOS	A	2	.000	.000	1	0	0	0	0	0.0	0	0	0	1	0	1	0	0	0	0	0	0.0	—	

Pat Sheridan

SHERIDAN, PATRICK ARTHUR
B. Dec. 4, 1957, Ann Arbor, Mich.　　BL TR 6′3″　175 lbs.

Year	Team		Games	BA	SA	AB	H	2B	3B	HR	HR%	R	RBI	BB	SO	SB	AB	H	PO	A	E	DP	TC/G	FA	G by Pos
1981	KC	A	3	.000	.000	1	0	0	0	0	0.0	0	0	0	1	0	0	0	2	0	0	0	0.7	1.000	OF-3
1983			109	.270	.381	333	90	12	2	7	2.1	43	36	20	64	12	19	5	237	6	3	2	2.3	.988	OF-100
1984			138	.283	.399	481	136	24	4	8	1.7	64	53	41	91	19	8	4	273	8	4	1	2.1	.986	OF-134
1985			78	.228	.335	206	47	9	2	3	1.5	18	17	23	38	11	10	1	116	3	2	0	1.6	.983	OF-69, DH-1
1986	DET	A	98	.237	.360	236	56	9	1	6	2.5	41	19	21	57	9	5	0	172	1	4	0	1.8	.977	OF-90, DH-5
1987			141	.259	.361	421	109	19	3	6	1.4	57	49	44	90	18	16	2	236	6	6	1	1.8	.976	OF-137
1988			127	.254	.403	347	88	9	5	11	3.2	47	47	44	64	8	16	2	203	2	4	0	1.6	.981	OF-111, DH-3
1989 **2 teams**		DET A (50G – .242)																							SF N (70G – .205)
" total			120	.221	.335	281	62	6	4	6	2.1	36	29	30	66	4	20	2	163	4	3	1	1.4	.982	OF-101, DH-8
8 yrs.			814	.255	.373	2306	588	88	21	47	2.0	306	250	223	471	85	94	16	1402	30	26	5	1.8	.982	OF-745, DH-17

LEAGUE CHAMPIONSHIP SERIES

Year	Team		Games	BA	SA	AB	H	2B	3B	HR	HR%	R	RBI	BB	SO	SB	AB	H	PO	A	E	DP	TC/G	FA	G by Pos
1984	KC	A	3	.000	.000	6	0	0	0	0	0.0	1	0	3	3	0	0	0	9	0	1	0	3.3	.900	OF-3
1985			7	.150	.450	20	3	0	0	2	10.0	4	3	2	3	0	2	1	13	0	0	0	1.9	1.000	OF-6
1987	DET	A	4	.300	.700	10	3	1	0	1	10.0	2	2	0	2	0	0	0	7	1	0	0	1.6	1.000	OF-4
1989	SF	N	5	.154	.308	13	2	0	1	0	0.0	1	0	0	4	1	0	0	9	1	0	0	2.0	1.000	OF-5
4 yrs.			20	.163	.408	49	8	1	1	3	6.1	8	5	5	12	1	2	1	38	2	1	0	2.1	.976	OF-18

WORLD SERIES

Year	Team		Games	BA	SA	AB	H	2B	3B	HR	HR%	R	RBI	BB	SO	SB	AB	H	PO	A	E	DP	TC/G	FA	G by Pos
1985	KC	A	5	.222	.333	18	4	2	0	0	0.0	1	1	0	7	0	1	1	6	0	0	0	1.2	1.000	OF-5

Year	Team		Games	BA	SA	AB	H	2B	3B	HR	HR%	R	RBI	BB	SO	SB	Pinch Hit AB	Pinch Hit H	PO	A	E	DP	TC/G	FA	G by Pos

Pat Sheridan *continued*

| 1989 | SF | N | 1 | .000 | .000 | 2 | 0 | 0 | 0 | 0 | 0.0 | 0 | 0 | 0 | 0 | 0 | 0 | 0 | 0 | 0 | 0 | 0 | 0.0 | – | OF-1 |
| 2 yrs. | | | 6 | .200 | .300 | 20 | 4 | 2 | 0 | 0 | 0.0 | 0 | 1 | 0 | 7 | 0 | 1 | 1 | 6 | 0 | 0 | 0 | 1.0 | 1.000 | OF-6 |

Red Sheridan

SHERIDAN, EUGENE ANTHONY (Gene)
B. Nov. 14, 1896, Brooklyn, N. Y. D. Nov. 25, 1975, Queens Village, N. Y.
BR TR 5'10½" 160 lbs.

1918	BKN	N	2	.250	.250	4	1	0	0	0	0.0	0	0	1	0	1	0	0	3	2	0	0	2.5	1.000	2B-2
1920			3	.000	.000	2	0	0	0	0	0.0	0	0	0	1	0	0	0	3	3	0	2	2.0	1.000	SS-3
2 yrs.			5	.167	.167	6	1	0	0	0	0.0	0	0	1	1	1	0	0	6	5	0	2	2.2	1.000	SS-3, 2B-2

Ed Sherling

SHERLING, EDWARD CREECH (Shine)
B. July 17, 1897, Coalburg, Ala. D. Nov. 16, 1965, Enterprise, Ala.
BR TR 6'1" 185 lbs.

| 1924 | PHI | A | 4 | .500 | 1.000 | 2 | 1 | 1 | 0 | 0 | 0.0 | 2 | 0 | 0 | 0 | 0 | 2 | 1 | 0 | 0 | 0 | 0 | 0.0 | – | |

Monk Sherlock

SHERLOCK, JOHN CLINTON
Brother of Vince Sherlock.
B. Oct. 26, 1904, Buffalo, N. Y. D. Nov. 26, 1985, Buffalo, N. Y.
BR TR 5'10" 175 lbs.

| 1930 | PHI | N | 92 | .324 | .398 | 299 | 97 | 18 | 2 | 0 | 0.0 | 51 | 38 | 27 | 28 | 0 | 15 | 6 | 639 | 66 | 8 | 59 | 7.8 | .989 | 1B-70, 2B-5, OF-1 |

Vince Sherlock

SHERLOCK, VINCENT THOMAS
Brother of Monk Sherlock.
B. Mar. 27, 1909, Buffalo, N. Y.
BR TR 6' 180 lbs.

| 1935 | BKN | N | 9 | .462 | .500 | 26 | 12 | 1 | 0 | 0 | 0.0 | 4 | 6 | 1 | 2 | 1 | 0 | 0 | 23 | 16 | 4 | 1 | 4.8 | .907 | 2B-8 |

Dennis Sherrill

SHERRILL, DENNIS LEE
B. May 3, 1956, Miami, Fla.
BR TR 6' 165 lbs.

1978	NY	A	2	.000	.000	1	0	0	0	0	0.0	1	0	1	0	0	0	0	0	0	0	0	0.0	–	DH-1, 3B-1
1980			3	.250	.250	4	1	0	0	0	0.0	0	0	0	1	0	0	0	5	1	0	0	2.0	1.000	SS-2, 2B-1
2 yrs.			5	.200	.200	5	1	0	0	0	0.0	1	0	0	2	0	0	0	5	1	0	0	1.2	1.000	SS-2, DH-1, 3B-1, 2B-1

Norm Sherry

SHERRY, NORMAN BURT
Brother of Larry Sherry.
B. July 16, 1931, New York, N. Y.
Manager 1976-77.
BR TR 5'11" 180 lbs.

1959	LA	N	2	.333	.333	3	1	0	0	0	0.0	0	2	0	0	0	0	0	4	0	0	0	2.0	1.000	C-2
1960			47	.283	.500	138	39	4	1	8	5.8	22	19	12	29	0	5	1	282	15	2	3	6.4	.993	C-44
1961			47	.256	.397	121	31	2	0	5	4.1	10	21	9	30	0	10	1	253	16	2	3	5.8	.993	C-45
1962			35	.182	.307	88	16	2	0	3	3.4	7	16	6	17	0	1	1	221	13	2	2	6.7	.992	C-34
1963	NY	N	63	.136	.184	147	20	1	0	2	1.4	6	11	10	26	1	2	1	265	26	6	6	4.7	.980	C-61
5 yrs.			194	.215	.346	497	107	9	1	18	3.6	45	69	37	102	1	18	4	1025	70	12	14	5.7	.989	C-186

Barry Shetrone

SHETRONE, BARRY STEVEN
B. July 6, 1938, Baltimore, Md.
BL TR 6'2" 190 lbs.

1959	BAL	A	33	.203	.241	79	16	1	1	0	0.0	8	5	5	9	3	6	0	36	0	2	0	1.2	.947	OF-23
1960			1	–	–	0	0	0	0	0	–	1	0	0	0	0	0	0	0	0	0	0	0.0	–	
1961			3	.143	.143	7	1	0	0	0	0.0	0	1	0	2	0	1	0	3	0	0	0	1.0	1.000	OF-2
1962			21	.250	.417	24	6	1	0	1	4.2	3	1	0	5	0	12	4	11	0	0	0	0.5	1.000	OF-6
1963	WAS	A	2	.000	.000	2	0	0	0	0	0.0	0	0	0	0	0	2	0	0	0	0	0	0.0	–	
5 yrs.			60	.205	.268	112	23	2	1	1	0.9	12	7	5	16	3	21	4	50	0	2	0	0.9	.962	OF-31

John Shetzline

SHETZLINE, JOHN HENRY
B. 1850, Philadelphia, Pa. D. Dec. 15, 1892, Philadelphia, Pa.
5'11½" 190 lbs.

| 1882 | BAL | AA | 73 | .220 | .270 | 282 | 62 | 8 | 3 | 0 | 0.0 | 23 | | 5 | | | 0 | 0 | 151 | 189 | 73 | 16 | 5.7 | .823 | 3B-52, 2B-20, OF-1, SS-1 |

Jimmy Shevlin

SHEVLIN, JAMES CORNELIUS
B. July 9, 1909, Cincinnati, Ohio D. Oct. 30, 1974, Ft. Lauderdale, Fla.
BL TL 5'10½" 155 lbs.

1930	DET	A	28	.143	.143	14	2	0	0	0	0.0	4	2	2	3	0	2	0	55	3	0	0	2.1	1.000	1B-25
1932	CIN	N	7	.208	.292	24	5	2	0	0	0.0	3	4	4	0	4	0	0	63	4	1	3	9.7	.985	1B-7
1934			18	.308	.359	39	12	2	0	0	0.0	6	6	6	5	0	8	3	69	6	0	8	4.2	1.000	1B-10
3 yrs.			53	.247	.299	77	19	4	0	0	0.0	13	12	12	8	4	10	3	187	13	1	11	3.8	.995	1B-42

Pete Shields

SHIELDS, FRANCIS LeROY
B. Sept. 21, 1891, Swiftwater, Miss. D. Feb. 11, 1961, Jackson, Miss.
BR TR 6' 175 lbs.

| 1915 | CLE | A | 23 | .208 | .292 | 72 | 15 | 6 | 0 | 0 | 0.0 | 4 | 6 | 4 | 14 | 3 | 0 | 0 | 208 | 13 | 6 | 5 | 9.9 | .974 | 1B-23 |

Jim Shilling

SHILLING, JAMES ROBERT
B. May 14, 1914, Tulsa, Okla. D. Sept. 12, 1986, Tulsa, Okla.
BR TR 5'11" 175 lbs.

| 1939 | 2 teams | | | CLE A | (31G – .276) | | PHI N | (11G – .303) | | | | | | | | | | | | | | | | | |
| " | total | | 42 | .282 | .420 | 131 | 37 | 8 | 5 | 0 | 0.0 | 11 | 16 | 8 | 13 | 1 | 1 | 0 | 82 | 102 | 14 | 24 | 4.7 | .929 | 2B-32, SS-6, 3B-3, OF-1 |

Ginger Shinault

SHINAULT, ENOCH ERSKINE
B. Sept. 7, 1892, Benton, Ark. D. Dec. 29, 1930, Denver, Colo.
BR TR 5'11" 170 lbs.

1921	CLE	A	22	.379	.414	29	11	1	0	0	0.0	5	3	6	5	1	1	0	27	17	4	1	2.2	.917	C-22
1922			13	.133	.200	15	2	1	0	0	0.0	1	0	0	2	0	2	0	11	1	3	1	1.2	.800	C-11
2 yrs.			35	.295	.341	44	13	2	0	0	0.0	6	3	6	7	1	3	0	38	18	7	2	1.8	.889	C-33

Bill Shindle

SHINDLE, WILLIAM
B. Dec. 5, 1863, Gloucester, N. J. D. June 3, 1936, Lakeland, N. J.
BR TR 5'8½" 155 lbs.

| 1886 | DET | N | 7 | .269 | .269 | 26 | 7 | 0 | 0 | 0 | 0.0 | 4 | 4 | 0 | 5 | | 1 | 0 | 3 | 24 | 3 | 1 | 4.3 | .900 | SS-7 |

Year	Team		Games	BA	SA	AB	H	2B	3B	HR	HR%	R	RBI	BB	SO	SB	Pinch Hit AB	Pinch Hit H	PO	A	E	DP	TC/G	FA	G by Pos

Bill Shindle *continued*

Year	Team		Games	BA	SA	AB	H	2B	3B	HR	HR%	R	RBI	BB	SO	SB	AB	H	PO	A	E	DP	TC/G	FA	G by Pos
1887			22	.286	.369	84	24	3	2	0	0.0	17	12	7	10	13	0	0	25	30	13	5	3.1	.809	3B-21, OF-1
1888	BAL	AA	135	.208	.272	514	107	14	8	1	0.2	61	53	20		52	0	0	218	340	47	26	4.5	.922	3B-135
1889			138	.314	.397	567	178	24	7	3	0.5	122	64	42	37	56	0	0	225	323	88	25	4.6	.862	3B-138
1890	PHI	P	132	.322	.481	584	188	21	21	10	1.7	127	90	40	30	51	0	0	268	444	122	67	6.3	.854	SS-130, 3B-2
1891	PHI	N	103	.210	.246	415	87	13	1	0	0.0	68	38	33	39	17	0	0	157	260	58	25	4.6	.878	SS-3
1892	BAL	N	143	.252	.357	619	156	20	18	3	0.5	100	50	35	34	24	0	0	225	406	90	28	5.0	.875	3B-134, SS-9
1893			125	.261	.351	521	136	22	11	1	0.2	100	75	66	17	17	0	0	176	308	63	24	4.4	.885	3B-125
1894	BKN	N	116	.296	.405	476	141	22	9	4	0.8	94	96	29	20	19	0	0	192	226	48	12	4.0	.897	3B-116
1895			118	.279	.350	477	133	21	2	3	0.6	92	69	47	28	17	0	0	142	257	46	16	3.8	.897	3B-116
1896			131	.279	.366	516	144	24	9	1	0.2	75	61	24	20	24	0	0	144	251	38	20	3.3	.912	3B-131
1897			134	.284	.382	542	154	32	6	3	0.6	83	105	35		23	0	0	185	241	45	13	3.5	.904	3B-134
1898			120	.225	.266	466	105	10	3	1	0.2	50	41	10		3	0	0	154	278	42	23	4.0	.911	3B-120
13 yrs.			1424	.269	.356	5807	1560	226	97	30	0.5	993	758	388	240	316	0	0	2114	3388	703	285	4.4	.887	3B-1272, SS-149, OF-1

Razor Shines

SHINES, ANTHONY RAYMOND
B. July 18, 1956, Durham, N. C.
BB TR 6'1" 210 lbs.

Year	Team		Games	BA	SA	AB	H	2B	3B	HR	HR%	R	RBI	BB	SO	SB	AB	H	PO	A	E	DP	TC/G	FA	G by Pos
1983	MON	N	3	.500	.500	2	1	0	0	0	0.0	0	0	0	0	0	1	1	0	0	0	0	0.0	—	OF-1
1984			12	.300	.350	20	6	1	0	0	0.0	0	2	0	3	0	9	2	26	0	0	2	2.2	1.000	1B-3, 3B-1
1985			47	.120	.120	50	6	0	0	0	0.0	0	3	4	9	0	36	5	34	4	2	1	0.9	.950	1B-5, P-1
1987			6	.222	.222	9	2	0	0	0	0.0	0	0	1	0	1	4	0	13	1	0	2	2.3	1.000	1B-2
4 yrs.			68	.185	.198	81	15	1	0	0	0.0	0	5	5	12	1	50	8	73	5	2	5	1.2	.975	1B-10, OF-1, 3B-1, P-1

Ralph Shinners

SHINNERS, RALPH PETER
B. Oct. 4, 1895, Monches, Wis. D. July 23, 1962, Milwaukee, Wis.
BR TR 6' 180 lbs.

Year	Team		Games	BA	SA	AB	H	2B	3B	HR	HR%	R	RBI	BB	SO	SB	AB	H	PO	A	E	DP	TC/G	FA	G by Pos
1922	NY	N	56	.252	.311	135	34	4	2	0	0.0	16	15	5	22	3	12	2	84	2	8	2	1.7	.915	OF-37
1923			33	.154	.231	13	2	1	0	0	0.0	5	0	2	1	0	9	1	8	0	0	0	0.2	1.000	OF-6
1925	STL	N	74	.295	.430	251	74	9	2	7	2.8	39	36	12	19	8	7	3	161	2	3	1	2.2	.982	OF-66
3 yrs.			163	.276	.383	399	110	14	4	7	1.8	60	51	19	42	11	28	6	253	4	11	3	1.6	.959	OF-109

Tim Shinnick

SHINNICK, TIMOTHY JAMES (Good Eye)
B. Nov. 6, 1867, Exeter, N. H. D. May 18, 1944, Exeter, N. H.
BB TR 6' 150 lbs.

Year	Team		Games	BA	SA	AB	H	2B	3B	HR	HR%	R	RBI	BB	SO	SB	AB	H	PO	A	E	DP	TC/G	FA	G by Pos
1890	LOU	AA	133	.256	.339	493	126	16	11	1	0.2	87		62		62	0	0	297	353	53	45	5.3	.925	2B-130, 3B-3
1891			128	.221	.300	443	98	10	11	1	0.2	79	54	54	47	36	0	0	236	345	58	47	5.0	.909	2B-120, 3B-7, SS-1
2 yrs.			261	.239	.321	936	224	26	22	2	0.2	166	54	116	47	98	0	0	533	698	111	92	5.1	.917	2B-250, 3B-10, SS-1

Bill Shipke

SHIPKE, WILLIAM MARTIN (Muskrat Bill)
Born William Martin Shipkrethaver.
B. Nov. 18, 1882, St. Louis, Mo. D. Sept. 10, 1940, Omaha, Neb.
BR TR 5'7" 145 lbs.

Year	Team		Games	BA	SA	AB	H	2B	3B	HR	HR%	R	RBI	BB	SO	SB	AB	H	PO	A	E	DP	TC/G	FA	G by Pos
1906	CLE	A	2	.000	.000	6	0	0	0	0	0.0	0	0	0	0	0	0	0	6	8	1	2	7.5	.933	2B-2
1907	WAS	A	64	.196	.249	189	37	3	2	1	0.5	17	9	15		6	1	0	57	127	11	2	3.0	.944	3B-63
1908			111	.208	.276	341	71	7	8	0	0.0	40	20	38		15	0	0	111	190	23	11	2.9	.929	3B-110, 2B-1
1909			9	.125	.188	16	2	1	0	0	0.0	2	0	2		0	0	0	6	14	2	1	2.4	.909	3B-5, SS-1
4 yrs.			186	.199	.261	552	110	11	10	1	0.2	59	29	55		21	1	0	180	339	37	16	3.0	.933	3B-178, 2B-3, SS-1

Craig Shipley

SHIPLEY, CRAIG BARRY
B. Jan. 7, 1963, Parramatta, Australia
BB TR 6'1" 175 lbs.

Year	Team		Games	BA	SA	AB	H	2B	3B	HR	HR%	R	RBI	BB	SO	SB	AB	H	PO	A	E	DP	TC/G	FA	G by Pos
1986	LA	N	12	.111	.148	27	3	1	0	0	0.0	3	4	2	5	0	0	0	16	18	3	4	3.1	.919	SS-10, 3B-1, 2B-1
1987			26	.257	.286	35	9	1	0	0	0.0	4	0	2	6	0	2	0	15	28	3	2	1.8	.935	SS-18, 3B-6
1989	NY	N	4	.143	.143	7	1	0	0	0	0.0	3	0	0	1	0	0	0	0	4	0	0	1.0	1.000	SS-3, 3B-2
3 yrs.			42	.188	.217	69	13	2	0	0	0.0	9	6	2	12	0	2	0	31	50	6	6	2.1	.931	SS-31, 3B-9, 2B-1

Art Shires

SHIRES, CHARLES ARTHUR (Art the Great)
B. Aug. 13, 1907, Italy, Tex. D. July 13, 1967, Italy, Tex.
BL TR 6'1" 195 lbs.

Year	Team		Games	BA	SA	AB	H	2B	3B	HR	HR%	R	RBI	BB	SO	SB	AB	H	PO	A	E	DP	TC/G	FA	G by Pos
1928	CHI	A	33	.341	.431	123	42	6	1	1	0.8	20	11	13	10	0	1	1	282	28	3	22	9.5	.990	1B-32
1929			100	.312	.433	353	110	20	7	3	0.8	41	41	32	20	4	9	1	816	58	9	78	8.8	.990	1B-88, 2B-2
1930	2 teams		75	CHI A	(37G – .258)		WAS A	(38G – .369)																		
"	total		75	.302	.387	212	64	10	1	2	0.9	25	37	11	11	3	19	6	468	26	10	37	6.7	.980	1B-54
1932	BOS	N	82	.238	.339	298	71	9	3	5	1.7	32	30	25	21	1	2	0	715	48	9	61	9.4	.988	1B-82
4 yrs.			290	.291	.395	986	287	45	12	11	1.1	118	119	81	62	8	31	8	2281	160	31	198	8.5	.987	1B-256, 2B-2

Bart Shirley

SHIRLEY, BARTON ARVIN
B. Jan. 4, 1940, Corpus Christi, Tex.
BR TR 5'10" 183 lbs.

Year	Team		Games	BA	SA	AB	H	2B	3B	HR	HR%	R	RBI	BB	SO	SB	AB	H	PO	A	E	DP	TC/G	FA	G by Pos
1964	LA	N	18	.274	.323	62	17	1	1	0	0.0	6	7	4	8	0	0	0	19	41	3	5	3.5	.952	3B-10, SS-8
1966			12	.200	.200	5	1	0	0	0	0.0	2	0	0	2	0	4	1	3	2	0	0	0.4	1.000	SS-5
1967	NY	N	6	.000	.000	12	0	0	0	0	0.0	0	0	1	5	0	2	0	2	9	1	1	2.0	.917	2B-3
1968	LA	N	39	.181	.217	83	15	3	0	0	0.0	6	4	10	13	0	1	0	44	80	7	20	3.4	.947	SS-21, 2B-18
4 yrs.			75	.204	.241	162	33	4	1	0	0.0	15	11	14	28	0	7	1	68	132	11	26	2.8	.948	SS-34, 2B-21, 3B-10

Mule Shirley

SHIRLEY, ERNEST RAEFORD
B. May 24, 1901, Snow Hill, N. C. D. Aug. 4, 1955, Goldsboro, N. C.
BL TL 5'11" 180 lbs.

Year	Team		Games	BA	SA	AB	H	2B	3B	HR	HR%	R	RBI	BB	SO	SB	AB	H	PO	A	E	DP	TC/G	FA	G by Pos
1924	WAS	A	30	.234	.312	77	18	2	2	0	0.0	12	16	3	7	0	4	2	176	14	3	17	6.4	.984	1B-25, C-1
1925			14	.130	.174	23	3	1	0	0	0.0	2	2	1	7	0	5	1	49	3	0	4	3.7	1.000	1B-9
2 yrs.			44	.210	.280	100	21	3	2	0	0.0	14	18	4	14	0	9	3	225	17	3	21	5.6	.988	1B-34, C-1

WORLD SERIES

Year	Team		Games	BA	SA	AB	H	2B	3B	HR	HR%	R	RBI	BB	SO	SB	AB	H	PO	A	E	DP	TC/G	FA	G by Pos
1924	WAS	A	3	.500	.500	2	1	0	0	0	0.0	1	1	0	2	0	2	1	0	0	0	0	0.0	—	

Ivey Shiver

SHIVER, IVEY MERWIN (Chick)
B. Jan. 22, 1907, Sylvester, Ga. D. Aug. 31, 1972, Savannah, Ga.
BR TR 6'1½" 190 lbs.

Year	Team		Games	BA	SA	AB	H	2B	3B	HR	HR%	R	RBI	BB	SO	SB	AB	H	PO	A	E	DP	TC/G	FA	G by Pos
1931	DET	A	2	.111	.111	9	1	0	0	0	0.0	2	0	0	3	0	0	0	3	0	0	0	1.5	1.000	OF-2

Year	Team		Games	BA	SA	AB	H	2B	3B	HR	HR%	R	RBI	BB	SO	SB	Pinch Hit AB	H	PO	A	E	DP	TC/G	FA	G by Pos

Ivey Shiver *continued*

| 1934 | CIN | N | 19 | .203 | .322 | 59 | 12 | 1 | 0 | 2 | 3.4 | 6 | 6 | 3 | 15 | 1 | 4 | 1 | 26 | 0 | 0 | 0 | 1.4 | 1.000 | OF-15 |
| 2 yrs. | | | 21 | .191 | .294 | 68 | 13 | 1 | 0 | 2 | 2.9 | 8 | 6 | 3 | 18 | 1 | 4 | 1 | 29 | 0 | 0 | 0 | 1.4 | 1.000 | OF-17 |

George Shoch

SHOCH, GEORGE QUINTUS
B. Jan. 6, 1859, Philadelphia, Pa. D. Sept. 30, 1937, Philadelphia, Pa. BR TR

1886	WAS	N	26	.295	.368	95	28	2	1	1	1.1	11	18	2	13		0	0	29	3	5		1.4	.865	OF-25, SS-1
1887			70	.239	.292	264	63	9	1	1	0.4	47	18	21	16	29	0	0	125	43	25	5	2.8	.870	OF-63, 2B-6, 2B-1
1888			90	.183	.240	317	58	6	3	2	0.6	46	24	25	22	23	0	0	143	175	38	7	4.0	.893	SS-52, OF-35, 2B-1, P-1
1889			30	.239	.257	109	26	2	0	0	0.0	12	11	20	5	9	0	0	52	9	6	1	2.2	.910	OF-29, SS-1
1891	MIL	AA	34	.315	.409	127	40	7	1	1	0.8	29	16	18	5	12	0	0	64	103	15	4	5.4	.918	SS-25, 3B-9
1892	BAL	N	76	.276	.354	308	85	15	3	1	0.3	42	50	24	19	14	0	0	133	216	51	17	5.3	.873	SS-57, OF-12, 3B-7
1893	BKN	N	94	.263	.339	327	86	17	1	2	0.6	53	54	48	13	9	0	0	159	118	27	9	3.2	.911	OF-46, 3B-37, SS-11, 2B-3
1894			64	.322	.402	239	77	6	5	1	0.4	47	37	26	6	16	0	0	130	77	17	6	3.5	.924	OF-35, 3B-9, 2B-9, SS-6
1895			61	.259	.366	216	56	9	7	0	0.0	49	29	32	6	7	0	0	98	63	14	6	2.9	.920	OF-39, 2B-13, SS-6, 3B-3
1896			76	.292	.364	250	73	7	4	1	0.4	36	28	33	10	11	1	0	124	192	19	17	4.4	.943	2B-62, OF-10, 3B-3, SS-1
1897			85	.278	.324	284	79	9	2	0	0.0	42	38	49		6	0	0	231	281	39	30	6.5	.929	2B-68, SS-13, OF-4
11 yrs.			706	.265	.334	2536	671	89	28	10	0.4	414	323	298	115	136	1	0	1288	1280	256	102	4.0	.909	OF-298, SS-179, 2B-157, 3B-73, P-1

Costen Shockley

SHOCKLEY, JOHN COSTEN
B. Feb. 8, 1942, Georgetown, Del. BL TL 6'2" 200 lbs.

1964	PHI	N	11	.229	.314	35	8	0	0	1	2.9	4	2	2	8	0	2	0	57	4	2	7	5.7	.968	1B-9
1965	CAL	A	40	.187	.262	107	20	2	0	2	1.9	5	17	9	16	0	6	1	245	17	1	25	6.6	.996	1B-31, OF-1
2 yrs.			51	.197	.275	142	28	2	0	3	2.1	9	19	11	24	0	8	1	302	21	3	32	6.4	.991	1B-40, OF-1

Charlie Shoemaker

SHOEMAKER, CHARLES LANDIS
B. Aug. 10, 1939, Los Angeles, Calif. BL TR 5'10" 155 lbs.

1961	KC	A	7	.385	.462	26	10	2	0	0	0.0	5	0	2	0	0	1	0	17	18	0	3	5.0	1.000	2B-6
1962			5	.182	.182	11	2	0	0	0	0.0	1	0	0	2	0	1	0	5	9	0	1	2.8	1.000	2B-4
1964			16	.212	.327	52	11	2	2	0	0.0	6	3	0	9	0	1	0	29	25	2	4	3.5	.964	2B-14
3 yrs.			28	.258	.348	89	23	4	2	0	0.0	12	4	2	13	0	3	0	51	52	2	8	3.8	.981	2B-24

Strick Shofner

SHOFNER, FRANK STRICKLAND
B. July 23, 1919, Crawford, Tex. BL TR 5'10½" 187 lbs.

| 1947 | BOS | A | 5 | .154 | .308 | 13 | 2 | 1 | 1 | 0 | 0.0 | 1 | 0 | 0 | 3 | 0 | 1 | 0 | 3 | 7 | 0 | 1 | 2.0 | 1.000 | 3B-4 |

Eddie Shokes

SHOKES, EDWARD CHRISTOPHER
B. Jan. 27, 1920, Charleston, S. C. BL TL 6' 170 lbs.

1941	CIN	N	1	.000	.000	1	0	0	0	0	0.0	0	0	0	1	0	1	0	0	0	0	0	0.0	–	
1946			31	.120	.133	83	10	1	0	0	0.0	3	5	18	21	1	1	0	262	14	1	26	8.9	.996	1B-29
2 yrs.			32	.119	.131	84	10	1	0	0	0.0	3	5	18	22	1	2	0	262	14	1	26	8.7	.996	1B-29

Ray Shook

SHOOK, RAYMOND CURTIS
B. Nov. 18, 1889, Perry, Ohio D. Sept. 16, 1970, South Bend, Ind. BR TR 5'7½" 155 lbs.

| 1916 | CHI | A | 1 | – | – | 0 | 0 | 0 | 0 | 0 | – | 0 | 0 | 0 | 0 | 0 | 0 | 0 | 0 | 0 | 0 | 0 | 0.0 | – | |

Ron Shoop

SHOOP, RONALD LEE
B. Sept. 19, 1931, Rural Valley, Pa. BR TR 5'11" 180 lbs.

| 1959 | DET | A | 3 | .143 | .143 | 7 | 1 | 0 | 0 | 0 | 0.0 | 1 | 1 | 0 | 1 | 0 | 0 | 0 | 8 | 0 | 0 | 0 | 2.7 | 1.000 | C-3 |

Tom Shopay

SHOPAY, THOMAS MICHAEL
B. Feb. 21, 1945, Bristol, Conn. BL TR 5'9½" 160 lbs.

1967	NY	A	8	.296	.556	27	8	1	0	2	7.4	2	6	1	5	2	1	0	9	2	1	0	1.5	.917	OF-7
1969			28	.083	.125	48	4	0	1	0	0.0	2	0	2	10	0	13	2	26	0	0	0	0.9	1.000	OF-11
1971	BAL	A	47	.257	.284	74	19	2	0	0	0.0	10	5	3	7	2	30	8	18	1	0	0	0.4	1.000	OF-13
1972			49	.225	.225	40	9	0	0	0	0.0	3	2	5	12	0	32	7	4	0	0	0	0.1	1.000	OF-3
1975			40	.161	.194	31	5	1	0	0	0.0	4	2	4	7	3	11	2	17	3	0	0	0.5	1.000	OF-13, DH-3, C-1
1976			14	.200	.200	20	4	0	0	0	0.0	4	1	3	3	1	4	1	14	1	0	0	1.1	1.000	OF-11, C-1
1977			67	.188	.275	69	13	3	0	1	1.4	15	4	8	7	3	10	2	53	2	0	1	0.8	1.000	OF-52, DH-2
7 yrs.			253	.201	.259	309	62	7	1	3	1.0	40	20	26	51	11	101	22	141	9	1	1	0.6	.993	OF-110, DH-5, C-2

WORLD SERIES

| 1971 | BAL | A | 5 | .000 | .000 | 4 | 0 | 0 | 0 | 0 | 0.0 | 0 | 0 | 0 | 0 | 0 | 4 | 0 | 0 | 0 | 0 | 0 | 0.0 | – | |

Dave Short

SHORT, DAVID ORVIS
B. May 11, 1917, Magnolia, Ark. D. Nov. 22, 1983, Shreveport, La. BL TR 5'11½" 162 lbs.

1940	CHI	A	4	.333	.333	3	1	0	0	0	0.0	1	0	1	2	0	3	1	0	0	0	0	0.0		OF-2
1941			3	.000	.000	8	0	0	0	0	0.0	0	0	2	1	0	1	0	4	0	1	0	1.7	.800	OF-2
2 yrs.			7	.091	.091	11	1	0	0	0	0.0	1	0	3	3	0	4	1	4	0	1	0	0.7	.800	OF-2

Chick Shorten

SHORTEN, CHARLES HENRY
B. Apr. 19, 1892, Scranton, Pa. D. Oct. 23, 1965, Scranton, Pa. BL TL 6' 175 lbs.

1915	BOS	A	6	.214	.286	14	3	1	0	0	0.0	1	0	1	0	0			6	1	0	0	1.2	1.000	OF-5
1916			53	.295	.330	112	33	2	1	0	0.0	14	11	10	8	1	17	3	46	0	0	0	0.9	1.000	OF-33
1917			69	.179	.226	168	30	4	2	0	0.0	12	16	10	10	2	24	5	82	2	2	0	1.2	.977	OF-43
1919	DET	A	95	.315	.370	270	85	9	3	0	0.0	37	22	22	13	5	19	5	143	2	4	2	1.6	.973	OF-75
1920			116	.288	.354	364	105	9	6	1	0.3	35	40	28	14	2	15	5	168	14	2	3	1.6	.989	OF-99
1921			92	.272	.350	217	59	11	3	0	0.0	33	23	20	11	2	**37**	**9**	101	3	2	1	1.2	.981	OF-52, C-1
1922	STL	A	55	.275	.489	131	36	15	2	1	1.5	22	16	16	8	0	20	5	58	2	0	1	1.1	1.000	OF-32

Chick Shorten *continued*

Year	Team		Games	BA	SA	AB	H	2B	3B	HR	HR%	R	RBI	BB	SO	SB	PH AB	PH H	PO	A	E	DP	TC/G	FA	G by Pos
1924	CIN	N	41	.275	.319	69	19	3	0	0	0.0	7	6	4	2	0	21	6	13	1	0	0	0.3	1.000	OF-15
8 yrs.			527	.275	.349	1345	370	51	20	3	0.2	161	134	110	68	12	154	38	617	25	10	8	1.2	.985	OF-354, C-1

WORLD SERIES

Year	Team		Games	BA	SA	AB	H	2B	3B	HR	HR%	R	RBI	BB	SO	SB	PH AB	PH H	PO	A	E	DP	TC/G	FA	G by Pos
1916	BOS	A	2	.571	.571	7	4	0	0	0	0.0	0	2	0	1	0	0	0	3	0	0	0	1.5	1.000	OF-2

Burt Shotton

SHOTTON, BURTON EDWIN (Barney)
B. Oct. 18, 1884, Brownhelm, Ohio   D. July 29, 1962, Lake Wales, Fla.
Manager 1928-34, 1947-50.
BL TR 5'11" 175 lbs.

Year	Team		Games	BA	SA	AB	H	2B	3B	HR	HR%	R	RBI	BB	SO	SB	PH AB	PH H	PO	A	E	DP	TC/G	FA	G by Pos
1909	STL	A	17	.262	.295	61	16	0	1	0	0.0	5	0	5		3	0	0	41	2	4	0	2.8	.915	OF-17
1911			139	.255	.302	572	146	11	8	0	0.0	85	36	51		26	0	0	356	21	20	2	2.9	.950	OF-139
1912			154	.290	.353	580	168	15	8	2	0.3	87	40	86		35	0	0	381	20	25	7	2.8	.941	OF-154
1913			147	.297	.373	549	163	23	8	1	0.2	105	28	99	63	43	1	0	357	29	20	11	2.8	.951	OF-146
1914			154	.269	.333	579	156	19	9	0	0.0	82	38	64	66	40	2	0	359	15	24	4	2.6	.940	OF-152
1915			156	.283	.360	559	158	18	11	1	0.2	93	30	118	62	43	2	0	295	15	23	4	2.1	.931	OF-154
1916			157	.282	.343	618	174	23	6	1	0.2	97	36	111	67	41	0	0	357	25	20	6	2.6	.950	OF-157
1917			118	.224	.259	398	89	9	1	1	0.3	47	20	62	47	16	5	0	182	10	16	6	1.8	.923	OF-107
1918	WAS	A	126	.261	.321	505	132	16	7	0	0.0	68	21	67	28	25	3	1	277	15	18	6	2.5	.942	OF-122
1919	STL	N	85	.285	.381	270	77	13	5	1	0.4	35	20	22	25	17	14	1	104	10	9	2	1.4	.927	OF-67
1920			62	.228	.272	180	41	5	0	1	0.6	28	12	18	14	5	7	1	85	9	4	2	1.6	.959	OF-51
1921			38	.250	.375	48	12	1	1	1	2.1	9	7	7	4	0	22	7	21	2	1	1	0.6	.958	OF-11
1922			34	.200	.233	30	6	1	0	0	0.0	5	2	4	6	0	26	5	1	0	0	0	0.0	1.000	OF-3
1923			1	.—	.—	0	0	0	0	0	0.0		1	0	0	0	0	0	0	0	0	0	0.0	—	
14 yrs.			1388	.270	.333	4949	1338	154	65	9	0.2	747	290	714	382	294	82	15	2816	173	184	51	2.3	.942	OF-1280

John Shoupe

SHOUPE, JOHN F.
B. Sept. 30, 1851, Cincinnati, Ohio   D. Feb. 13, 1920, Cincinnati, Ohio
BL TL 5'7" 140 lbs.

Year	Team		Games	BA	SA	AB	H	2B	3B	HR	HR%	R	RBI	BB	SO	SB	PH AB	PH H	PO	A	E	DP	TC/G	FA	G by Pos
1879	TRO	N	11	.091	.091	44	4	0	0	0	0.0	5	0		3	0			13	33	12	0	5.3	.793	SS-10, 2B-1
1882	STL	AA	2	.000	.000	7	0	0	0	0	0.0	1	0			0			5	8	0	0	6.5	1.000	2B-2
1884	WAS	U	1	.750	.750	4	3	0	0	0	0.0	1	0			0			4	2	1	1	7.0	.857	OF-1
3 yrs.			14	.127	.127	55	7	0	0	0	0.0	7	1	0	3	0			22	43	13	1	5.6	.833	SS-10, 2B-3, OF-1

John Shovlin

SHOVLIN, JOHN JOSEPH (Brode)
B. Jan. 14, 1891, Drifton, Pa.   D. Feb. 16, 1976, Bethesda, Md.
BR TR 5'7" 163 lbs.

Year	Team		Games	BA	SA	AB	H	2B	3B	HR	HR%	R	RBI	BB	SO	SB	PH AB	PH H	PO	A	E	DP	TC/G	FA	G by Pos
1911	PIT	N	2	.000	.000	1	0	0	0	0	0.0	0	0	0	1	0	1	0	0	0	0	0	0.0	—	
1919	STL	A	9	.200	.200	35	7	0	0	0	0.0	4	1	5	2	0	0		19	25	3	5	5.2	.936	2B-9
1920			7	.286	.286	7	2	0	0	0	0.0	2	2	0	0	0	2	0	3	5	0	0	1.1	1.000	SS-5
3 yrs.			18	.209	.209	43	9	0	0	0	0.0	7	3	5	3	0	3	0	22	30	3	5	3.1	.945	2B-9, SS-5

George Shuba

SHUBA, GEORGE THOMAS (Shotgun)
B. Dec. 13, 1924, Youngstown, Ohio
BL TR 5'11" 180 lbs.

Year	Team		Games	BA	SA	AB	H	2B	3B	HR	HR%	R	RBI	BB	SO	SB	PH AB	PH H	PO	A	E	DP	TC/G	FA	G by Pos
1948	BKN	N	63	.267	.379	161	43	6	0	4	2.5	21	32	34	31	1	6	2	87	1	6	1	1.5	.936	OF-56
1949			1	.000	.000	1	0	0	0	0	0.0	0	0	0	0	0	1	0	0	0	0	0	0.0	—	
1950			34	.207	.396	111	23	8	2	3	2.7	15	12	13	22	2	5	1	56	4	1	2	1.8	.984	OF-27
1952			94	.305	.465	256	78	12	1	9	3.5	40	40	38	29	1	25	8	116	2	1	0	1.3	.992	OF-67
1953			74	.254	.426	169	43	12	1	5	3.0	19	23	17	20	1	29	7	59	1	1	1	0.8	.984	OF-44
1954			45	.154	.323	65	10	5	0	2	3.1	3	10	7	10	0	30	4	21	0	2	0	0.5	.913	OF-13
1955			44	.275	.373	51	14	2	0	1	2.0	8	8	11	10	0	29	11	10	0	1	0	0.3	.909	OF-9
7 yrs.			355	.259	.413	814	211	45	4	24	2.9	106	125	120	122	5	125	33	349	8	12	4	1.0	.967	OF-216

WORLD SERIES

Year	Team		Games	BA	SA	AB	H	2B	3B	HR	HR%	R	RBI	BB	SO	SB	PH AB	PH H	PO	A	E	DP	TC/G	FA	G by Pos
1952	BKN	N	4	.300	.400	10	3	1	0	0	0.0	0	0	0	4	0	1	0	7	0	0	0	1.8	1.000	OF-3
1953			2	1.000	4.000	1	1	0	0	1	0.0	1	2	0	0	0	1	1	0	0	0	0	0.0	—	
1955			1	.000	.000	1	0	0	0	0	0.0	0	0	0	0	0	1	0	0	0	0	0	0.0	—	
3 yrs.			7	.333	.667	12	4	1	0	1	8.3	2	0	0	4	0	3	1	7	0	0	0	1.0	1.000	OF-3

Frank Shugart

SHUGART, FRANK HARRY
Born Frank Harry Shugarts.
B. Dec. 10, 1866, Lutersburg, Pa.   D. Sept. 9, 1944, Clearfield, Pa.
BR TR 5'8" 170 lbs.

Year	Team		Games	BA	SA	AB	H	2B	3B	HR	HR%	R	RBI	BB	SO	SB	PH AB	PH H	PO	A	E	DP	TC/G	FA	G by Pos
1890	CHI	P	29	.189	.330	106	20	5	5	0	0.0	8	15	5	13	5			38	71	14	11	4.2	.886	SS-25, OF-5
1891	PIT	N	75	.275	.403	320	88	19	8	2	0.6	57	33	20	26	21			172	235	44	34	6.0	.902	SS-75
1892			137	.267	.352	554	148	19	14	0	0.0	94	62	47	48	28			309	475	100	43	6.5	.887	SS-134, C-2, OF-1
1893	2 teams			PIT	N	(52G	–	.262)		STL	N	(59G	–	.280)											
"	total		111	.272	.346	456	124	17	7	1	0.2	78	60	41	25	25			207	279	72	26	5.0	.871	SS-74, OF-29, 3B-9
1894	STL	N	133	.292	.436	527	154	19	18	7	1.3	103	72	38	37	21			309	53	42	6	3.0	.896	OF-122, SS-7, 3B-7
1895	LOU	N	113	.264	.374	473	125	14	13	4	0.8	61	70	31	25	14			243	263	71	42	5.1	.877	SS-88, OF-27
1897	PHI	N	40	.252	.417	163	41	8	2	5	3.1	20	25	8		5			104	128	34	15	6.7	.872	SS-40
1901	CHI	A	107	.251	.345	415	104	9	12	2	0.5	62	47	28		12			223	338	73	32	5.9	.885	SS-107
8 yrs.			745	.267	.377	3014	804	110	79	21	0.7	483	384	218	174	131			1605	1842	450	209	5.2	.885	SS-550, OF-184, 3B-16, C-2

Vince Shupe

SHUPE, VINCENT WILLIAM
B. Sept. 5, 1921, East Canton, Ohio   D. Apr. 5, 1962, Canton, Ohio
BL TL 5'11" 180 lbs.

Year	Team		Games	BA	SA	AB	H	2B	3B	HR	HR%	R	RBI	BB	SO	SB	PH AB	PH H	PO	A	E	DP	TC/G	FA	G by Pos
1945	BOS	N	78	.269	.297	283	76	8	0	0	0.0	22	15	17	16	3	1	1	650	53	8	81	9.1	.989	1B-77

Eddie Sicking

SICKING, EDWARD JOSEPH
B. Mar. 30, 1897, St. Bernard, Ohio   D. Aug. 30, 1978, Cincinnati, Ohio
BB TR 5'9½" 165 lbs.

Year	Team		Games	BA	SA	AB	H	2B	3B	HR	HR%	R	RBI	BB	SO	SB	PH AB	PH H	PO	A	E	DP	TC/G	FA	G by Pos
1916	CHI	N	1	.000	.000	0	0	0	0	0	0.0	0	0	0	0	0	0	0	0	0	0	0	0.0	—	
1918	NY	N	46	.250	.280	132	33	4	0	0	0.0	9	12	6	11	2	3	0	63	75	9	2	3.2	.939	3B-24, 2B-18, SS-2

Year	Team		Games	BA	SA	AB	H	2B	3B	HR	HR%	R	RBI	BB	SO	SB	Pinch Hit AB	Pinch Hit H	PO	A	E	DP	TC/G	FA	G by Pos

Eddie Sicking *continued*

1919	2 teams	NY N (6G – .333)				PHI N (61G – .216)																			
"	total		67	.225	.245	200	45	2	1	0	0.0	18	18	9	17	4	3	0	127	180	16	40	4.8	.950	SS-41, 2B-21
1920	2 teams	NY N (46G – .172)				CIN N (37G – .268)																			
"	total		83	.218	.249	257	56	6	1	0	0.0	23	26	23	15	8	1	0	140	204	23	26	4.4	.937	2B-40, 3B-30, SS-12
1927	PIT	N	6	.143	.286	7	1	1	0	0	0.0	1	3	1	0	0	0	0	6	8	0	1	2.3	1.000	2B-5
5 yrs.			203	.226	.255	597	135	13	2	0	0.0	51	59	39	43	14	8	0	336	467	48	69	4.2	.944	2B-84, SS-55, 3B-54

Norm Siebern

SIEBERN, NORMAN LEROY
B. July 26, 1933, St. Louis, Mo.

BL TR 6'2" 200 lbs.

1956	NY	A	54	.204	.333	162	33	1	4	4	2.5	27	21	19	38	1	6	0	100	1	3	0	1.9	.971	OF-51
1958			136	.300	.454	460	138	19	5	14	3.0	79	55	66	87	5	2	1	259	8	5	2	2.0	.982	OF-133
1959			120	.271	.403	380	103	17	0	11	2.9	52	53	41	71	3	20	9	190	3	2	1	1.6	.990	OF-93, 1B-2
1960	KC	A	144	.279	.471	520	145	31	6	19	3.7	69	69	72	68	0	4	1	777	43	10	58	5.8	.988	OF-75, 1B-69
1961			153	.296	.475	560	166	36	5	18	3.2	68	98	82	92	2	2	0	990	79	12	89	7.1	.989	1B-109, OF-47
1962			162	.308	.495	600	185	25	6	25	4.2	114	117	110	88	3	0	0	1405	127	10	122	9.5	.994	1B-162
1963			152	.272	.410	556	151	25	2	16	2.9	80	83	79	82	1	5	2	1223	103	12	95	8.8	.991	1B-131, OF-16
1964	BAL	A	150	.245	.379	478	117	24	2	12	2.5	92	56	**106**	87	2	6	0	1171	101	6	121	8.5	.995	1B-149
1965			106	.256	.407	297	76	13	4	8	2.7	44	32	50	49	1	28	4	631	48	6	64	6.5	.991	1B-76
1966	CAL	A	125	.247	.339	336	83	14	1	5	1.5	29	41	63	61	0	23	6	1014	65	7	96	8.7	.994	1B-99
1967	2 teams	SF N (46G – .155)				BOS A (33G – .205)																			
"	total		79	.176	.245	102	18	1	3	0	0.0	8	11	20	21	0	45	7	91	5	0	7	1.2	1.000	1B-28, OF-3
1968	BOS	A	27	.067	.067	30	2	0	0	0	0.0	0	0	0	5	0	24	1	8	1	0	1	0.3	1.000	OF-2, 1B-2
12 yrs.			1408	.272	.423	4481	1217	206	38	132	2.9	662	636	708	749	18	165	29	7859	584	73	656	6.0	.991	1B-827, OF-420

WORLD SERIES

1956	NY	A	1	.000	.000	1	0	0	0	0	0.0	0	0	0	0	0	1	0	0	0	0	0	0.0	–	
1958			3	.125	.125	8	1	0	0	0	0.0	0	0	3	2	0	0	0	5	0	0	0	1.7	1.000	OF-3
1967	BOS	A	3	.333	.333	3	1	0	0	0	0.0	0	1	0	0	0	2	0	0	0	0	0	–	–	OF-1
3 yrs.			7	.167	.167	12	2	0	0	0	0.0	1	1	3	2	0	3	0	5	0	0	0	0.7	1.000	OF-4

Dick Siebert

SIEBERT, RICHARD WALTHER
Father of Paul Siebert.
B. Feb. 19, 1912, Fall River, Mass.   D. Dec. 9, 1978, Minneapolis, Minn.

BL TL 6' 170 lbs.

1932	BKN	N	6	.286	.286	7	2	0	0	0	0.0	1	0	2	0	0	3	1	13	0	0	0	2.2	1.000	1B-6
1936			2	.000	.000	2	0	0	0	0	0.0	0	0	0	0	0	1	0	0	1	0	0	0.5	1.000	OF-1
1937	STL	N	22	.184	.237	38	7	2	0	0	0.0	3	2	4	8	1	13	3	44	3	1	2	2.2	.979	1B-7
1938	2 teams	STL N (1G – 1.000)				PHI A (48G – .284)																			
"	total		49	.287	.359	195	56	8	3	0	0.0	24	28	10	9	2	3	2	403	41	0	35	9.1	1.000	1B-46
1939	PHI	A	101	.294	.423	402	118	28	3	6	1.5	58	47	21	22	4	2	0	874	74	9	73	9.5	.991	1B-99
1940			154	.286	.383	595	170	31	6	5	0.8	69	77	33	34	8	0	0	1322	119	22	112	9.5	.985	1B-154
1941			123	.334	.460	467	156	28	8	5	1.1	63	79	37	22	1	0	0	1102	106	12	95	9.9	.990	1B-123
1942			153	.260	.333	612	159	25	7	2	0.3	57	74	24	17	4	0	0	1345	104	16	109	9.6	.989	1B-152
1943			146	.251	.328	558	140	26	7	1	0.2	50	72	33	21	6	1	0	1332	111	15	117	10.0	.990	1B-145
1944			132	.306	.423	468	143	27	5	6	1.3	52	52	62	17	2	0	0	759	53	10	60	6.2	.988	1B-74, OF-58
1945			147	.267	.358	573	153	29	5	7	1.2	62	51	50	33	2	0	0	1427	135	14	129	10.7	.991	1B-147
11 yrs.			1035	.282	.379	3917	1104	204	40	32	0.8	439	482	276	185	30	23	6	8621	747	99	732	9.1	.990	1B-953, OF-59

Fred Siefke

SIEFKE, FREDERICK EDWIN
B. Mar. 5, 1870, New York, N. Y.   D. Apr. 18, 1893, New York, N. Y.

| 1890 | BKN | AA | 16 | .138 | .172 | 58 | 8 | 2 | 0 | 0 | 0.0 | 1 | | 5 | | 2 | 0 | 0 | 16 | 44 | 14 | 2 | 4.6 | .811 | 3B-16 |

John Siegel

SIEGEL, JOHN
B. York, Pa.   Deceased.

| 1884 | PHI | U | 8 | .226 | .290 | 31 | 7 | 2 | 0 | 0 | 0.0 | 4 | | 1 | | 2 | 0 | 0 | 8 | 8 | 14 | 0 | 3.8 | .533 | 3B-8 |

Johnny Siegle

SIEGLE, JOHN HERBERT
B. July 8, 1874, Urbana, Ohio   D. Feb. 12, 1968, Urbana, Ohio

BR TR 5'10" 165 lbs.

1905	CIN	N	17	.304	.446	56	17	1	2	1	1.8	9	8	7		0	1	1	23	1	1	0	1.5	.960	OF-16
1906			22	.118	.206	68	8	2	2	0	0.0	4	7	3		0	1	0	46	1	2	1	2.2	.959	OF-21
2 yrs.			39	.202	.315	124	25	3	4	1	0.8	13	15	10		0	2	1	69	2	3	1	1.9	.959	OF-37

Oscar Siemer

SIEMER, OSCAR SYLVESTER (Cotton)
B. Aug. 14, 1901, St. Louis, Mo.   D. Dec. 5, 1959, St. Louis, Mo.

BR TR 5'9" 162 lbs.

1925	BOS	N	16	.304	.413	46	14	1	1	1	2.2	5	6	1	0	0	1	0	35	10	5	1	3.1	.900	C-16
1926			31	.205	.219	73	15	0	0	0	0.0	3	5	2	7	0	1	0	81	11	8	2	3.2	.920	C-30
2 yrs.			47	.244	.294	119	29	1	1	1	0.8	8	11	3	7	0	1	0	116	21	13	3	3.2	.913	C-46

Ruben Sierra

SIERRA, RUBEN ANGEL
Born Ruben Angel Sierra y Garcia.
B. Oct. 6, 1965, Rio Piedras, Puerto Rico

BB TR 6'1" 175 lbs.

1986	TEX	A	113	.264	.476	382	101	13	10	16	4.2	50	55	22	65	7	6	1	200	7	6	1	1.9	.972	OF-107, DH-3
1987			158	.263	.470	**643**	169	35	4	30	4.7	97	109	39	114	16	2	0	272	17	11	6	1.9	.963	OF-157
1988			156	.254	.424	615	156	32	2	23	3.7	77	91	44	91	18	3	1	310	11	7	3	2.1	.979	OF-153, DH-1
1989			162	.306	**.543**	634	194	35	**14**	29	4.6	101	**119**	43	82	8	0	0	313	13	9	2	2.1	.973	OF-162
4 yrs.			589	.273	.479	2274	620	115	30	98	4.3	325	374	148	352	49	11	2	1095	48	33	12	2.0	.972	OF-579, DH-4

Roy Sievers

SIEVERS, ROY EDWARD (Squirrel)
B. Nov. 18, 1926, St. Louis, Mo.

BR TR 6'1" 195 lbs.

1949	STL	A	140	.306	.471	471	144	28	1	16	3.4	84	91	70	75	1	7	2	317	25	10	2	2.5	.972	OF-125, 3B-7
1950			113	.238	.395	370	88	20	4	10	2.7	46	57	34	42	1	15	2	248	48	8	6	2.7	.974	OF-78, 3B-21
1951			31	.225	.303	89	20	2	1	1	1.1	10	11	9	21	0	8	1	63	1	1	0	2.1	.985	OF-25

Year	Team	Games	BA	SA	AB	H	2B	3B	HR	HR%	R	RBI	BB	SO	SB	Pinch Hit AB	Pinch Hit H	PO	A	E	DP	TC/G	FA	G by Pos

Roy Sievers *continued*

Year	Team		Games	BA	SA	AB	H	2B	3B	HR	HR%	R	RBI	BB	SO	SB	AB	H	PO	A	E	DP	TC/G	FA	G by Pos
1952			11	.200	.300	30	6	3	0	0	0.0	3	5	1	4	0	5	0	58	3	2	8	5.7	.968	1B-7
1953			92	.270	.407	285	77	15	0	8	2.8	37	35	32	47	0	17	3	604	31	5	64	7.0	.992	1B-76
1954	WAS	A	145	.232	.446	514	119	26	6	24	4.7	75	102	80	77	2	5	0	350	15	9	8	2.6	.976	OF-133, 1B-8
1955			144	.271	.489	509	138	20	8	25	4.9	74	106	73	66	1	2	0	363	17	4	16	2.7	.990	OF-129, 1B-17, 3B-2
1956			152	.253	.467	550	139	27	2	29	5.3	92	95	100	88	0	0	0	784	54	9	76	5.6	.989	OF-78, 1B-76
1957			152	.301	.579	572	172	23	5	42	7.3	99	114	76	55	1	2	2	413	15	6	23	2.9	.986	OF-130, 1B-21
1958			148	.295	.544	550	162	18	1	39	7.1	85	108	53	63	3	4	1	476	26	5	36	3.4	.990	OF-114, 1B-33
1959			115	.242	.455	385	93	19	0	21	5.5	55	49	53	62	1	7	1	870	72	11	72	8.3	.988	1B-93, OF-13
1960	CHI	A	127	.295	.534	444	131	22	0	28	6.3	87	93	74	69	1	9	1	1085	63	8	117	9.1	.993	1B-114, OF-6
1961			141	.295	.537	492	145	26	6	27	5.5	76	92	61	62	1	10	4	1096	94	8	93	8.5	.993	1B-132
1962	PHI	N	144	.262	.455	477	125	19	5	21	4.4	61	80	56	80	2	12	1	977	93	10	102	7.5	.991	1B-130, OF-7
1963			138	.240	.418	450	108	19	2	19	4.2	46	82	43	72	0	18	6	981	77	12	93	7.8	.989	1B-126
1964	2 teams			PHI	N	(49G – .183)		WAS	A	(33G – .172)															
"	total		82	.180	.348	178	32	4	1	8	4.5	12	27	22	34	0	29	6	328	26	2	37	4.3	.994	1B-48
1965	WAS	A	12	.190	.238	21	4	1	0	0	0.0	3	0	4	3	0	4	1	51	1	0	6	4.3	1.000	1B-7
17 yrs.			1887	.267	.475	6387	1703	292	42	318	5.0	945	1147	841	920	14	154	31	9064	661	110	759	5.2	.989	1B-888, OF-838, 3B-30

Frank Siffell

SIFFELL, FRANK
B. 1861, Germany D. Oct. 26, 1909, Philadelphia, Pa.

Year	Team		Games	BA	SA	AB	H	2B	3B	HR	HR%	R	RBI	BB	SO	SB	AB	H	PO	A	E	DP	TC/G	FA	G by Pos
1884	PHI	AA	7	.176	.235	17	3	1	0	0	0.0	3		0			0	0	22	6	4	0	4.6	.875	C-7
1885			3	.100	.100	10	1	0	0	0	0.0	0		0			0	0	9	0	3	1	4.0	.750	C-2, OF-1
2 yrs.			10	.148	.185	27	4	1	0	0	0.0	3		0			0	0	31	6	7	1	4.4	.841	C-9, OF-1

Frank Sigafoos

SIGAFOOS, FRANCIS LEONARD BR TR 5'9" 170 lbs.
B. Mar. 21, 1904, Easton, Pa. D. Apr. 12, 1968, Indianapolis, Ind.

Year	Team		Games	BA	SA	AB	H	2B	3B	HR	HR%	R	RBI	BB	SO	SB	AB	H	PO	A	E	DP	TC/G	FA	G by Pos
1926	PHI	A	13	.256	.256	43	11	0	0	0	0.0	4	2	0	3	0	1	0	12	31	4	5	3.6	.915	SS-12
1929	2 teams			DET	A	(14G – .174)		CHI	A	(7G – .333)															
"	total		21	.192	.231	26	5	1	0	0	0.0	4	3	7	5	0	5	1	17	18	3	3	1.8	.921	3B-6, 2B-6, SS-5
1931	CIN	N	21	.169	.200	65	11	2	0	0	0.0	6	8	0	6	0	4	1	14	24	5	2	2.0	.884	3B-15, SS-2
3 yrs.			55	.201	.224	134	27	3	0	0	0.0	14	13	7	14	0	6	1	43	73	12	10	2.3	.906	3B-21, SS-19, 2B-6

Paddy Siglin

SIGLIN, WESLEY PETER BR TR 5'10" 160 lbs.
B. Sept. 24, 1891, Aurelia, Iowa D. Aug. 5, 1956, Oakland, Calif.

Year	Team		Games	BA	SA	AB	H	2B	3B	HR	HR%	R	RBI	BB	SO	SB	AB	H	PO	A	E	DP	TC/G	FA	G by Pos
1914	PIT	N	14	.154	.154	39	6	0	0	0	0.0	4	2	6	1	1	3	1	24	17	4	1	3.2	.911	2B-11
1915			6	.286	.286	7	2	0	0	0	0.0	1	0	1	2	1	3	0	1	3	1	0	0.8	.800	2B-1
1916			3	.250	.250	4	1	0	0	0	0.0	0	0	0	2	0	0	0	4	2	1	3	2.3	.857	2B-3
3 yrs.			23	.180	.180	50	9	0	0	0	0.0	5	2	5	10	2	6	1	29	22	6	4	2.5	.895	2B-15

Tripp Sigman

SIGMAN, WESLEY TRIPLETT BL TR 6' 180 lbs.
B. Jan. 17, 1899, Mooresville, N. C. D. Mar. 8, 1971, Augusta, Ga.

Year	Team		Games	BA	SA	AB	H	2B	3B	HR	HR%	R	RBI	BB	SO	SB	AB	H	PO	A	E	DP	TC/G	FA	G by Pos
1929	PHI	N	10	.517	.759	29	15	1	2	2	6.9	8	9	3	1	0	0	0	17	0	1	0	1.8	.944	OF-10
1930			52	.270	.450	100	27	4	1	4	4.0	15	6	6	9	1	32	8	39	2	3	0	0.8	.932	OF-19
2 yrs.			62	.326	.519	129	42	5	1	6	4.7	23	15	9	10	1	32	8	56	2	4	0	1.0	.935	OF-29

Eddie Silber

SILBER, EDWARD JAMES BR TR 5'11" 170 lbs.
B. June 6, 1914, Philadelphia, Pa. D. Oct. 26, 1976, Dunedin, Fla.

Year	Team		Games	BA	SA	AB	H	2B	3B	HR	HR%	R	RBI	BB	SO	SB	AB	H	PO	A	E	DP	TC/G	FA	G by Pos
1937	STL	A	22	.313	.337	83	26	0	0	0	0.0	10	4	5	13	0	1	1	27	0	4	0	1.4	.871	OF-21
1939			1	.000	.000	1	0	0	0	0	0.0	0	0	0	1	0	1	0	0	0	0	0	0.0	–	
2 yrs.			23	.310	.333	84	26	0	0	0	0.0	10	4	5	14	0	2	1	27	0	4	0	1.3	.871	OF-21

Ed Silch

SILCH, EDWARD (Baldy) TR
B. Feb. 22, 1865, St. Louis, Mo. D. Jan. 15, 1895, St. Louis, Mo.

Year	Team		Games	BA	SA	AB	H	2B	3B	HR	HR%	R	RBI	BB	SO	SB	AB	H	PO	A	E	DP	TC/G	FA	G by Pos
1888	BKN	AA	14	.271	.354	48	13	4	0	0	0.0	5	3	4		4	0	0	19	1	3	0	1.6	.870	OF-14

Danny Silva

SILVA, DANIEL JAMES BR TR 6' 170 lbs.
B. Oct. 5, 1896, Everett, Mass. D. Apr. 4, 1974, Hyannis, Mass.

Year	Team		Games	BA	SA	AB	H	2B	3B	HR	HR%	R	RBI	BB	SO	SB	AB	H	PO	A	E	DP	TC/G	FA	G by Pos
1919	WAS	A	1	.250	.250	4	1	0	0	0	0.0	0	0	0	0	0	0	0	1	4	0	0	5.0	1.000	3B-1

Al Silvera

SILVERA, AARON ALBERT BR TR 6' 180 lbs.
B. Aug. 26, 1935, San Diego, Calif.

Year	Team		Games	BA	SA	AB	H	2B	3B	HR	HR%	R	RBI	BB	SO	SB	AB	H	PO	A	E	DP	TC/G	FA	G by Pos
1955	CIN	N	13	.143	.143	7	1	0	0	0	0.0	3	2	1	0	0	6	1	0	0	0	0	0.0	–	OF-1
1956			1	–	–	0	0	0	0	0	–	0	0	0	1	0	0	0	0	0	0	0	0.0	–	
2 yrs.			14	.143	.143	7	1	0	0	0	0.0	3	2	1	1	0	6	1	0	0	0	0	0.0	–	OF-1

Charlie Silvera

SILVERA, CHARLES ANTHONY RYAN (Swede) BR TR 5'10" 175 lbs.
B. Oct. 13, 1924, San Francisco, Calif.

Year	Team		Games	BA	SA	AB	H	2B	3B	HR	HR%	R	RBI	BB	SO	SB	AB	H	PO	A	E	DP	TC/G	FA	G by Pos
1948	NY	A	4	.571	.714	14	8	0	0	0	0.0	1	1	0	0	0	0	0	17	1	0	0	4.5	1.000	C-4
1949			58	.315	.331	130	41	2	0	0	0.0	8	13	18	5	2	6	3	177	22	3	5	3.5	.985	C-51
1950			18	.160	.160	25	4	0	0	0	0.0	2	1	1	2	0	3	1	46	1	2	1	2.7	.959	C-15
1951			18	.275	.392	51	14	3	0	1	2.0	5	7	5	3	0	0	0	66	6	0	2	4.0	1.000	C-18
1952			20	.327	.382	55	18	3	0	0	0.0	4	11	5	2	0	0	0	54	8	0	1	3.1	1.000	C-20
1953			42	.280	.341	82	23	3	1	0	0.0	11	12	9	5	0	2	1	114	15	1	1	3.1	.992	C-39, 3B-1
1954			20	.270	.297	37	10	1	0	0	0.0	1	4	3	2	0	2	0	72	5	3	1	4.0	.963	C-18
1955			14	.192	.192	26	5	0	0	0	0.0	1	1	6	4	0	2	0	47	4	0	1	3.6	1.000	C-11
1956			7	.222	.222	9	2	0	0	0	0.0	0	0	0	2	0	1	1	9	1	1	0	1.6	.909	C-7
1957	CHI	N	26	.208	.264	53	11	3	0	0	0.0	1	2	4	5	0	0	0	97	11	2	2	4.2	.982	C-26
10 yrs.			227	.282	.328	482	136	15	2	1	0.2	34	52	53	32	2	15	5	699	74	12	14	3.5	.985	C-209, 3B-1

WORLD SERIES

Year	Team		Games	BA	SA	AB	H	2B	3B	HR	HR%	R	RBI	BB	SO	SB	AB	H	PO	A	E	DP	TC/G	FA	G by Pos
1949	NY	A	1	.000	.000	2	0	0	0	0	0.0	0	0	0	0	0	0	0	6	0	0	0	6.0	1.000	C-1

Year	Team		Games	BA	SA	AB	H	2B	3B	HR	HR%	R	RBI	BB	SO	SB	Pinch Hit AB	Pinch Hit H	PO	A	E	DP	TC/G	FA	G by Pos

Luis Silverio

SILVERIO, LUIS PASCUAL
Born Luis Pascual Silverio y Delmonte.
B. Oct. 23, 1956, Villa Gonzalez, Dominican Republic

BR TR 5'11" 165 lbs.

Year	Team		Games	BA	SA	AB	H	2B	3B	HR	HR%	R	RBI	BB	SO	SB	PH AB	PH H	PO	A	E	DP	TC/G	FA	G by Pos
1978	KC	A	8	.545	.909	11	6	2	1	0	0.0	7	3	2	3	1	0	0	5	0	1	0	0.8	.833	OF-6, DH-2

Tom Silverio

SILVERIO, TOMAS ROBERTO
Born Tomas Roberto Silverio y Veloz.
B. Oct. 14, 1945, Santiago, Dominican Republic

BL TL 5'10" 170 lbs.

Year	Team		Games	BA	SA	AB	H	2B	3B	HR	HR%	R	RBI	BB	SO	SB	PH AB	PH H	PO	A	E	DP	TC/G	FA	G by Pos
1970	CAL	A	15	.000	.000	15	0	0	0	0	0.0	1	0	2	4	0	10	0	8	0	0	0	0.5	1.000	OF-5, 1B-1
1971			3	.333	.333	3	1	0	0	0	0.0	0	0	0	0	0	3	1	0	0	0	0	0.0	–	OF-1
1972			13	.167	.167	12	2	0	0	0	0.0	1	0	0	5	0	7	1	1	0	0	0	0.1	1.000	OF-4
3 yrs.			31	.100	.100	30	3	0	0	0	0.0	2	0	2	9	0	20	2	9	0	0	0	0.3	1.000	OF-10, 1B-1

Ken Silvestri

SILVESTRI, KENNETH JOSEPH (Hawk)
B. May 3, 1916, Chicago, Ill.
Manager 1967.

BB TR 6'1" 200 lbs.

Year	Team		Games	BA	SA	AB	H	2B	3B	HR	HR%	R	RBI	BB	SO	SB	PH AB	PH H	PO	A	E	DP	TC/G	FA	G by Pos
1939	CHI	A	22	.173	.293	75	13	3	0	2	2.7	6	5	6	13	0	2	1	74	15	5	3	4.3	.947	C-20
1940			28	.250	.583	24	6	2	0	2	8.3	5	10	4	7	0	24	6	1	0	0	0	0.0	1.000	C-1
1941	NY	A	17	.250	.450	40	10	5	0	1	2.5	6	4	7	6	0	3	0	43	6	0	2	2.9	1.000	C-13
1946			13	.286	.333	21	6	1	0	0	0.0	4	1	3	7	0	1	0	40	3	1	1	3.4	.977	C-12
1947			3	.200	.200	10	2	0	0	0	0.0	0	0	2	2	0	0	0	7	1	0	0	2.7	1.000	C-3
1949	PHI	N	4	.000	.000	4	0	0	0	0	0.0	1	0	2	1	0	2	0	8	2	0	0	2.5	1.000	SS-1, 2B-1, C-1
1950			11	.250	.350	20	5	0	1	0	0.0	2	4	4	3	0	2	1	25	1	0	0	2.4	1.000	C-9
1951			4	.222	.222	9	2	0	0	0	0.0	2	1	3	2	0	0	0	3	1	0	0	1.0	1.000	C-3
8 yrs.			102	.217	.355	203	44	11	1	5	2.5	26	25	31	41	0	34	8	201	29	6	6	2.3	.975	C-62, SS-1, 2B-1

WORLD SERIES

Year	Team		Games	BA	SA	AB	H	2B	3B	HR	HR%	R	RBI	BB	SO	SB	PH AB	PH H	PO	A	E	DP	TC/G	FA	G by Pos
1950	PHI	N	1	–	–	0	0	0	0	0	–	0	0	0	0	0	0	0	1	0	0	0	1.0	1.000	C-1

Al Simmons

SIMMONS, ALOYSIUS HARRY (Bucketfoot Al)
Born Aloys Szymanski.
B. May 22, 1902, Milwaukee, Wis.   D. May 26, 1956, Milwaukee, Wis.
Hall of Fame 1953.

BR TR 5'11" 190 lbs.

Year	Team		Games	BA	SA	AB	H	2B	3B	HR	HR%	R	RBI	BB	SO	SB	PH AB	PH H	PO	A	E	DP	TC/G	FA	G by Pos
1924	PHI	A	152	.308	.431	594	183	31	9	8	1.3	69	102	30	60	16	0	0	390	17	10	4	2.7	.976	OF-152
1925			153	.384	.596	658	253	43	12	24	3.6	122	129	35	41	7	0	0	447	8	16	2	3.1	.966	OF-153
1926			147	.343	.566	581	199	53	10	19	3.3	90	109	48	49	10	0	0	333	11	9	5	2.4	.975	OF-147
1927			106	.392	.645	406	159	36	11	15	3.7	86	108	31	30	10	0	0	247	10	4	2	2.5	.985	OF-105
1928			119	.351	.558	464	163	33	9	15	3.2	78	107	31	30	1	3	2	231	10	3	2	2.1	.988	OF-114
1929			143	.365	.642	581	212	41	9	34	5.9	114	157	31	38	4	0	0	349	19	4	2	2.6	.989	OF-142
1930			138	.381	.708	554	211	41	16	36	6.5	152	165	39	34	9	2	1	275	10	3	1	2.1	.990	OF-136
1931			128	.390	.641	513	200	37	13	22	4.3	105	128	47	45	3	0	0	287	10	4	0	2.4	.987	OF-128
1932			154	.322	.548	670	216	28	9	35	5.2	144	151	47	76	4	0	0	290	9	6	4	2.0	.980	OF-154
1933	CHI	A	146	.331	.481	605	200	29	10	14	2.3	85	119	39	39	5	1	0	372	15	4	1	2.7	.990	OF-145
1934			138	.344	.530	558	192	36	7	18	3.2	102	104	53	58	3	0	0	286	14	4	3	2.2	.987	OF-138
1935			128	.267	.427	525	140	22	7	16	3.0	68	79	33	43	4	3	0	349	5	7	1	2.8	.981	OF-126
1936	DET	A	143	.327	.484	568	186	38	6	13	2.3	96	112	49	35	6	4	1	364	8	5	2	2.6	.987	OF-138, 1B-1
1937	WAS	A	103	.279	.434	419	117	21	10	8	1.9	60	84	27	35	3	1	0	240	7	4	5	2.4	.984	OF-102
1938			125	.302	.511	470	142	23	6	21	4.5	79	95	38	40	2	9	2	232	4	4	1	1.9	.983	OF-117
1939	2 teams		BOS N	(93G – .282)		CIN N	(9G – .143)																		
"	total		102	.274	.410	351	96	17	5	7	2.0	39	44	24	43	0	14	2	172	8	4	2	1.8	.978	OF-87
1940	PHI	A	37	.309	.395	81	25	4	0	1	1.2	7	19	4	8	0	16	8	51	1	2	0	1.5	.963	OF-18
1941			9	.125	.167	24	3	1	0	0	0.0	1	1	1	2	0	4	0	16	0	0	0	1.8	1.000	OF-5
1943	BOS	A	40	.203	.263	133	27	5	0	1	0.8	9	12	8	21	0	7	0	66	3	1	1	1.8	.986	OF-33
1944	PHI	A	4	.500	.500	6	3	0	0	0	0.0	0	0	0	1	0	2	1	3	0	0	0	0.8	1.000	OF-2
20 yrs.			2215	.334	.535	8761	2927	539	149	307	3.5	1507	1827	615	737	87	66	17	5000	169	94	38	2.4	.982	OF-2142, 1B-1
				5th									6th													

WORLD SERIES

Year	Team		Games	BA	SA	AB	H	2B	3B	HR	HR%	R	RBI	BB	SO	SB	PH AB	PH H	PO	A	E	DP	TC/G	FA	G by Pos
1929	PHI	A	5	.300	.650	20	6	1	0	2	10.0	6	5	1	4	0	0	0	4	0	0	0	0.8	1.000	OF-5
1930			6	.364	.727	22	8	2	0	2	9.1	4	4	2	2	0	0	0	12	1	0	0	2.2	1.000	OF-6
1931			7	.333	.630	27	9	2	0	2	7.4	4	8	3	3	0	0	0	19	0	0	0	2.7	1.000	OF-7
1939	CIN	N	1	.250	.500	4	1	0	0	0	0.0	1	0	0	0	0	0	0	3	0	0	0	3.0	1.000	OF-1
4 yrs.			19	.329	.658	73	24	6	0	6	8.2	15	17	6	9	0	0	0	38	1	0	0	2.1	1.000	OF-19

Hack Simmons

SIMMONS, GEORGE WASHINGTON
B. Jan. 29, 1885, Brooklyn, N. Y.   D. Apr. 26, 1942, Arverne, N. Y.

BR TR 5'8" 179 lbs.

Year	Team		Games	BA	SA	AB	H	2B	3B	HR	HR%	R	RBI	BB	SO	SB	PH AB	PH H	PO	A	E	DP	TC/G	FA	G by Pos
1910	DET	A	42	.227	.273	110	25	3	1	0	0.0	12	9	10		1	10	3	240	28	6	10	6.5	.978	1B-22, 3B-7, OF-2
1912	NY	A	110	.239	.292	401	96	17	2	0	0.0	45	41	33		19	4	0	299	219	24	30	4.9	.956	2B-88, 3B-13, SS-4
1914	BAL	F	114	.270	.352	352	95	16	5	1	0.3	50	38	32		7	13	7	154	75	17	9	2.2	.931	OF-73, 2B-26, 1B-4, SS-2, 3B-1
1915			39	.205	.341	88	18	7	1	1	1.1	8	14	10		1	13	5	32	21	3	0	1.4	.946	OF-13, 2B-13
4 yrs.			305	.246	.317	951	234	43	9	2	0.2	115	102	85		28	40	15	725	343	50	49	3.7	.955	2B-127, OF-88, 1B-39, 3B-8, SS-6

John Simmons

SIMMONS, JOHN EARL
B. July 7, 1924, Birmingham, Ala.

BR TR 6'1½" 192 lbs.

Year	Team		Games	BA	SA	AB	H	2B	3B	HR	HR%	R	RBI	BB	SO	SB	PH AB	PH H	PO	A	E	DP	TC/G	FA	G by Pos
1949	WAS	A	62	.215	.215	93	20	0	0	0	0.0	12	5	11	6	0	23	5	34	1	0	0	0.6	1.000	OF-26

Nelson Simmons

SIMMONS, NELSON BERNARD III
B. June 27, 1963, Washington, D. C.

BB TR 6'1" 195 lbs.

Year	Team		Games	BA	SA	AB	H	2B	3B	HR	HR%	R	RBI	BB	SO	SB	PH AB	PH H	PO	A	E	DP	TC/G	FA	G by Pos
1984	DET	A	9	.433	.500	30	13	2	0	0	0.0	4	3	2	5	1	1	0	8	0	0	0	0.9	1.000	OF-5, DH-4
1985			75	.239	.402	251	60	11	0	10	4.0	31	33	26	41	1	8	2	67	2	4	1	1.0	.945	OF-38, DH-31

Year	Team		Games	BA	SA	AB	H	2B	3B	HR	HR%	R	RBI	BB	SO	SB	Pinch Hit AB	Pinch Hit H	PO	A	E	DP	TC/G	FA	G by Pos

Nelson Simmons *continued*

| 1987 | BAL | A | 16 | .265 | .388 | 49 | 13 | 1 | 1 | 1 | 2.0 | 3 | 4 | 3 | 8 | 0 | 3 | 1 | 24 | 2 | 0 | 1 | 1.6 | 1.000 | OF-13, DH-1 |
| 3 yrs. | | | 100 | .261 | .409 | 330 | 86 | 14 | 1 | 11 | 3.3 | 38 | 40 | 31 | 54 | 2 | 12 | 3 | 99 | 4 | 4 | 2 | 1.1 | .963 | OF-56, DH-36 |

Ted Simmons

SIMMONS, TED LYLE
B. Aug. 9, 1949, Highland Park, Mich.   BB TR 5'11" 193 lbs.

1968	STL	N	2	.333	.333	3	1	0	0	0	0.0	0	0	1	1	0	0	0	3	1	0	0	2.0	1.000	C-2
1969			5	.214	.357	14	3	0	1	0	0.0	0	3	1	1	0	1	0	22	0	1	0	4.6	.957	C-4
1970			82	.243	.317	284	69	8	2	3	1.1	29	24	37	37	2	4	1	466	37	5	2	6.2	.990	C-79
1971			133	.304	.424	510	155	32	4	7	1.4	64	77	36	50	1	6	1	747	52	9	11	6.1	.989	C-130
1972			152	.303	.465	594	180	36	6	16	2.7	70	96	29	57	1	2	0	967	93	13	15	7.1	.988	C-135, 1B-15
1973			161	.310	.438	619	192	36	2	13	2.1	62	91	61	47	2	1	0	932	78	14	14	6.4	.986	C-153, 1B-6, OF-2
1974			152	.272	.447	599	163	33	6	20	3.3	66	103	47	35	0	2	1	813	87	15	18	6.0	.984	C-141, 1B-12
1975			157	.332	.491	581	193	32	3	18	3.1	80	100	63	35	1	5	1	818	64	15	5	5.7	.983	C-154, OF-2, 1B-2
1976			150	.291	.394	546	159	35	3	5	0.9	60	75	73	35	0	7	4	726	88	10	25	5.5	.988	C-113, 1B-30, OF-7, 3B-2
1977			150	.318	.500	516	164	25	3	21	4.1	82	95	79	37	2	17	2	683	75	10	5	5.1	.987	C-144, OF-1
1978			152	.287	.512	516	148	40	5	22	4.3	71	80	77	39	1	10	3	703	88	10	6	5.3	.988	C-134, OF-23
1979			123	.283	.507	448	127	22	0	26	5.8	68	87	61	34	0	4	0	606	69	10	10	5.6	.985	C-122
1980			145	.303	.505	495	150	33	2	21	4.2	84	98	59	45	1	15	3	528	71	10	12	4.2	.984	C-129, OF-5
1981	MIL	A	100	.216	.376	380	82	13	3	14	3.7	45	61	23	32	0	3	1	333	41	8	7	3.8	.979	C-75, DH-22, 1B-4
1982			137	.269	.451	539	145	29	2	23	4.3	73	97	32	40	0	2	1	570	62	3	8	4.6	.995	C-121, DH-15
1983			153	.308	.448	600	185	39	3	13	2.2	76	108	41	51	4	4	0	395	41	11	4	2.9	.975	C-86, DH-66
1984			132	.221	.300	497	110	23	2	4	0.8	44	52	30	40	3	6	1	352	52	8	37	3.1	.981	DH-77, 1B-37, 3B-14
1985	ATL	N	143	.273	.402	528	144	28	2	12	2.3	60	76	57	32	1	3	1	291	26	3	23	2.2	.991	DH-99, 1B-28, C-15, 3B-2
1986	ATL	N	76	.252	.386	127	32	5	0	4	3.1	14	25	12	14	1	47	11	167	18	6	13	2.5	.969	1B-14, C-10, 3B-9
1987			73	.277	.390	177	49	8	0	4	2.3	20	30	21	23	1	29	9	282	35	5	25	4.4	.984	1B-28, C-15, 3B-2
1988			78	.196	.308	107	21	6	0	2	1.9	6	11	15	9	0	47	5	140	14	3	8	2.0	.981	1B-19, C-10
21 yrs.			2456	.285	.437	8680	2472	483	47	248	2.9	1074	1389	855	694	21	215	45	10544	1092	169	248	4.8	.986	C-1772, DH-279, 1B-195, OF-40, 3B-29

DIVISIONAL PLAYOFF SERIES

| 1981 | MIL | A | 5 | .211 | .421 | 19 | 4 | 1 | 0 | 1 | 5.3 | 1 | 4 | 2 | 2 | 0 | 0 | 0 | 0 | 0 | 1 | 0 | 0.2 | – | C-5 |

LEAGUE CHAMPIONSHIP SERIES

| 1982 | MIL | A | 5 | .167 | .167 | 18 | 3 | 0 | 0 | 0 | 0.0 | 3 | 1 | 0 | 4 | 0 | 0 | 0 | 0 | 0 | 0 | 0 | 0.0 | – | C-5 |

WORLD SERIES

| 1982 | MIL | A | 7 | .174 | .435 | 23 | 4 | 0 | 0 | 2 | 8.7 | 2 | 3 | 5 | 5 | 0 | 0 | 0 | 28 | 2 | 0 | 0 | 4.4 | .968 | C-7 |

Henry Simon

SIMON, HENRY JOSEPH
B. Aug. 25, 1862, Hawkinsville, N. Y.   D. Jan. 1, 1925, Albany, N. Y.   BR TR

1887	CLE	AA	3	.100	.100	10	1	0	0	0	0.0	1		0			0	0	0	3	0	0	0	1.0	1.000	OF-3
1890	2 teams		BKN AA (89G – .257)				SYR AA (38G – .301)																		
"	total		127	.270	.376	529	143	22	14	2	0.4	99		51		35	0	0	238	19	14	5	2.1	.948	OF-127
2 yrs.			130	.267	.371	539	144	22	14	2	0.4	100		51		35	0	0	241	19	14	5	2.1	.949	OF-130

Mike Simon

SIMON, MICHAEL EDWARD
B. Apr. 13, 1883, Hayden, Ind.   D. June 10, 1963, Los Angeles, Calif.   BR TR 5'11" 188 lbs.

1909	PIT	N	11	.167	.167	18	3	0	0	0	0.0	2	2	0		1	1	0	28	5	3	1	3.3	.917	C-9
1910			22	.200	.240	50	10	0	1	0	0.0	3	5	1	2	1	7	0	40	12	0	0	2.4	1.000	C-14
1911			71	.228	.274	215	49	4	3	0	0.0	19	22	10	14	1	3	0	320	75	13	6	5.7	.968	C-68
1912			42	.301	.336	113	34	2	1	0	0.0	10	11	5	9	1	2	0	172	43	2	5	5.2	.991	C-40
1913			92	.247	.298	255	63	6	2	1	0.4	23	17	10	15	3	0	0	393	151	14	6	6.1	.975	C-92
1914	STL	F	93	.207	.261	276	57	11	2	0	0.0	21	21	18		2	13	2	433	132	9	9	6.2	.984	C-78
1915	BKN	F	47	.176	.225	142	25	5	1	0	0.0	7	12	9		1	0	0	175	60	2	4	5.0	.992	C-45
7 yrs.			378	.225	.273	1069	241	28	10	1	0.1	85	90	54	40	9	28	3	1561	478	43	31	5.5	.979	C-346

Syl Simon

SIMON, SYLVESTER ADAM
B. Dec. 14, 1897, Evansville, Ind.   D. Feb. 28, 1973, Chandler, Ind.   BR TR 5'10½" 170 lbs.

1923	STL	A	1	.000	.000	1	0	0	0	0	0.0	0	0	0	0	0	0	0	0	0	0	0	0.0	–	
1924			22	.250	.344	32	8	1	1	0	0.0	5	6	2	5	0	10	2	8	17	4	1	1.3	.862	3B-6, SS-5
2 yrs.			23	.242	.333	33	8	1	1	0	0.0	5	6	2	5	0	11	2	8	17	4	1	1.3	.862	3B-6, SS-5

Mel Simons

SIMONS, MELBERN ELLIS (Butch)
B. July 1, 1900, Carlyle, Ill.   D. Nov. 10, 1974, Paducah, Ky.   BL TR 5'10" 175 lbs.

1931	CHI	A	68	.275	.323	189	52	9	0	0	0.0	24	12	12	17	1	6	1	112	3	6	0	1.8	.950	OF-59
1932			7	.000	.000	5	0	0	0	0	0.0	0	0	0	1	0	1	0	2	0	0	0	0.3	1.000	OF-6
2 yrs.			75	.268	.314	194	52	9	0	0	0.0	24	12	12	18	1	7	1	114	3	6	0	1.6	.951	OF-65

Dick Simpson

SIMPSON, RICHARD CHARLES
B. July 28, 1943, Washington, D. C.   BR TR 6'4" 176 lbs.

1962	LA	A	6	.250	.375	8	2	1	0	0	0.0	1	1	2	3	0	2	0	7	0	0	0	1.2	1.000	OF-4
1964			21	.140	.280	50	7	1	0	2	4.0	11	4	8	15	2	1	0	27	0	0	0	1.3	1.000	OF-16
1965	CAL	A	8	.222	.259	27	6	1	0	0	0.0	2	3	2	8	1	0	0	14	0	2	0	2.0	.875	OF-8
1966	CIN	N	92	.238	.405	84	20	2	0	4	4.8	26	14	10	32	0	18	2	35	0	3	0	0.4	.921	OF-64
1967			44	.259	.370	54	14	3	0	1	1.9	8	6	7	11	0	9	4	34	2	1	0	0.8	.973	OF-26
1968	2 teams		STL N (26G – .232)			HOU N (59G – .186)																			
"	total		85	.197	.322	233	46	7	2	6	2.6	36	19	28	82	4	3	0	89	3	2	1	1.1	.979	OF-71
1969	2 teams		NY A (6G – .273)			SEA A (26G – .176)																			
"	total		32	.194	.355	62	12	4	0	2	3.2	10	9	7	23	3	8	0	26	1	0	0	0.8	1.000	OF-22
7 yrs.			288	.207	.338	518	107	19	2	15	2.9	94	56	64	174	10	40	6	232	6	8	1	0.9	.967	OF-211

Year	Team		Games	BA	SA	AB	H	2B	3B	HR	HR%	R	RBI	BB	SO	SB	Pinch Hit AB	Pinch Hit H	PO	A	E	DP	TC/G	FA	G by Pos

Harry Simpson

SIMPSON, HARRY LEON (Suitcase)
B. Dec. 3, 1925, Atlanta, Ga. D. Apr. 3, 1979, Akron, Ohio   BL TR 6'1" 180 lbs.

Year	Team		Games	BA	SA	AB	H	2B	3B	HR	HR%	R	RBI	BB	SO	SB	AB	H	PO	A	E	DP	TC/G	FA	G by Pos
1951	CLE	A	122	.229	.313	332	76	7	0	7	2.1	51	24	45	48	6	10	2	458	20	8	29	4.0	.984	OF-68, 1B-50
1952			146	.266	.396	545	145	21	10	10	1.8	66	65	56	82	5	1	1	502	19	5	25	3.6	.990	OF-127, 1B-28
1953			82	.227	.335	242	55	3	1	7	2.9	25	22	18	27	0	10	1	130	4	4	1	1.7	.971	OF-69, 1B-2
1955	2 teams			CLE	A	(3G –	.000)		KC	A	(112G –	.301)													
"	total		115	.300	.413	397	119	16	7	5	1.3	43	52	36	61	3	11	4	272	7	6	4	2.5	.979	OF-100, 1B-3
1956	KC	A	141	.293	.490	543	159	22	11	21	3.9	76	105	47	82	2	3	0	457	18	11	34	3.4	.977	OF-111, 1B-32
1957	2 teams			KC	A	(50G –	.296)		NY	A	(75G –	.250)													
"	total		125	.270	.452	403	109	16	9	13	3.2	51	63	31	64	1	20	4	470	37	5	40	4.1	.990	OF-63, 1B-48
1958	2 teams			NY	A	(24G –	.216)		KC	A	(78G –	.264)													
"	total		102	.255	.384	263	67	9	2	7	2.7	22	33	32	45	0	30	5	429	19	5	44	4.4	.989	1B-43, OF-26
1959	3 teams			KC	A	(8G –	.286)		CHI	A	(38G –	.187)		PIT	N	(9G –	.267)								
"	total		55	.212	.385	104	22	7	1	3	2.9	9	17	6	20	0	34	6	62	2	2	2	1.2	.970	OF-15, 1B-5
8 yrs.			888	.266	.408	2829	752	101	41	73	2.6	343	381	271	429	17	119	23	2780	126	46	179	3.3	.984	OF-579, 1B-211

WORLD SERIES

1957	NY	A	5	.083	.083	12	1	0	0	0	0.0	0	1	0	4	0	1	0	24	1	0	2	5.0	1.000	1B-4

Joe Simpson

SIMPSON, JOE ALLEN
B. Dec. 31, 1951, Purcell, Okla.   BL TL 6'3" 175 lbs.

Year	Team		Games	BA	SA	AB	H	2B	3B	HR	HR%	R	RBI	BB	SO	SB	AB	H	PO	A	E	DP	TC/G	FA	G by Pos
1975	LA	N	9	.333	.333	6	2	0	0	0	0.0	3	0	0	2	0	1	0	5	0	0	0	0.6	1.000	OF-6
1976			23	.133	.167	30	4	1	0	0	0.0	2	0	1	6	0	0	0	24	0	0	0	1.0	1.000	OF-20
1977			29	.174	.174	23	4	0	0	0	0.0	2	1	2	6	1	0	0	24	2	1	1	0.9	.963	OF-28, 1B-1
1978			10	.400	.400	5	2	0	0	0	0.0	1	1	0	2	0	0	0	8	0	0	0	0.8	1.000	OF-10
1979	SEA	A	120	.283	.347	265	75	11	0	2	0.8	29	27	11	21	6	9	2	162	10	6	4	1.5	.966	OF-105, DH-3
1980			129	.249	.332	365	91	15	3	3	0.8	42	34	28	43	17	11	1	220	12	7	3	1.9	.971	OF-119, 1B-3
1981			91	.222	.302	288	64	11	3	2	0.7	32	30	15	41	12	7	1	219	5	5	1	2.5	.978	OF-88
1982			105	.257	.351	296	76	14	4	2	0.7	39	23	22	48	8	7	3	177	7	3	0	1.8	.984	OF-97
1983	KC	A	91	.168	.218	119	20	2	2	0	0.0	16	8	11	21	1	2	0	242	18	2	20	2.9	.992	1B-54, OF-38, DH-2, P-2
9 yrs.			607	.242	.317	1397	338	54	12	9	0.6	166	124	90	190	45	37	7	1081	54	24	29	1.9	.979	OF-511, 1B-58, DH-5, P-2

Duke Sims

SIMS, DUANE B
B. June 5, 1941, Salt Lake City, Utah   BL TR 6'2" 197 lbs.

Year	Team		Games	BA	SA	AB	H	2B	3B	HR	HR%	R	RBI	BB	SO	SB	AB	H	PO	A	E	DP	TC/G	FA	G by Pos
1964	CLE	A	2	.000	.000	6	0	0	0	0	0.0	0	0	0	2	0	1	0	13	0	0	0	6.5	1.000	C-1
1965			48	.178	.331	118	21	0	0	6	5.1	9	15	15	33	0	12	2	228	22	5	2	5.3	.980	C-40
1966			52	.263	.444	133	35	2	2	6	4.5	12	19	11	31	0	9	0	260	15	7	2	5.4	.975	C-48
1967			88	.202	.379	272	55	8	2	12	4.4	25	37	30	64	3	5	2	561	56	7	7	7.1	.989	C-85
1968			122	.249	.399	361	90	21	0	11	3.0	48	44	62	68	1	9	2	722	60	16	23	6.5	.980	C-84, 1B-31, OF-4
1969			114	.236	.426	326	77	8	0	18	5.5	40	45	66	80	1	13	1	639	52	6	8	6.1	.991	C-102, OF-3, 1B-1
1970			110	.264	.499	345	91	12	0	23	6.7	46	56	46	59	0	9	1	505	34	8	18	5.0	.985	C-39, OF-36, 1B-29
1971	LA	N	90	.274	.400	230	63	7	2	6	2.6	23	25	30	39	0	18	2	345	33	3	5	4.2	.992	C-74
1972	2 teams			LA	N	(51G –	.192)		DET	A	(38G –	.316)													
"	total		89	.241	.357	249	60	11	0	6	2.4	18	30	36	41	0	12	3	247	17	4	4	3.0	.985	C-73, OF-4
1973	2 teams			DET	A	(80G –	.242)		NY	A	(4G –	.333)													
"	total		84	.245	.387	261	64	10	0	9	3.4	34	31	33	37	1	9	1	389	40	9	7	5.2	.979	C-69, OF-6, DH-2
1974	2 teams			NY	A	(5G –	.133)		TEX	A	(39G –	.208)													
"	total		44	.198	.281	121	24	1	0	3	2.5	8	8	9	29	0	7	3	149	21	5	4	4.0	.971	C-31, DH-5, OF-1
11 yrs.			843	.239	.401	2422	580	80	6	100	4.1	263	310	338	483	6	104	17	4058	350	70	80	5.3	.984	C-646, 1B-61, OF-54, DH-7

LEAGUE CHAMPIONSHIP SERIES

1972	DET	A	4	.214	.500	14	3	2	1	0	0.0	0	0	1	0	0	0	0	3	0	1	0	1.0	.750	OF-2, C-2

Greg Sims

SIMS, GREGORY EMMETT
B. June 28, 1946, San Francisco, Calif.   BB TR 6' 190 lbs.

Year	Team		Games	BA	SA	AB	H	2B	3B	HR	HR%	R	RBI	BB	SO	SB	AB	H	PO	A	E	DP	TC/G	FA	G by Pos
1966	HOU	N	7	.167	.167	6	1	0	0	0	0.0	1	0	1	3	0	5	1	1	0	1	0	0.3	.500	OF-1

Matt Sinatro

SINATRO, MATTHEW STEPHEN
B. Mar. 22, 1960, Hartford, Conn.   BR TR 5'9" 174 lbs.

Year	Team		Games	BA	SA	AB	H	2B	3B	HR	HR%	R	RBI	BB	SO	SB	AB	H	PO	A	E	DP	TC/G	FA	G by Pos
1981	ATL	N	12	.281	.375	32	9	1	1	0	0.0	4	4	5	4	1	0	0	56	10	0	1	5.5	1.000	C-12
1982			37	.136	.198	81	11	2	0	1	1.2	10	4	4	9	0	0	0	112	25	0	1	3.7	1.000	C-35
1983			7	.167	.167	12	2	0	0	0	0.0	2	0	2	1	0	0	0	24	5	1	1	4.3	.967	C-7
1984			2	.000	.000	4	0	0	0	0	0.0	0	0	0	0	0	0	0	4	0	0	0	2.0	1.000	C-2
1987	OAK	A	6	.000	.000	3	0	0	0	0	0.0	0	0	0	1	0	2	0	4	0	0	0	0.7	1.000	C-6
1988			10	.333	.556	9	3	2	0	0	0.0	1	5	0	1	0	0	0	21	2	0	1	2.3	1.000	C-9
1989	DET	A	13	.120	.120	25	3	0	0	0	0.0	2	1	1	3	0	0	0	42	2	0	0	3.4	1.000	C-13
7 yrs.			87	.169	.229	166	28	5	1	1	0.6	17	16	12	19	1	2	0	263	44	1	4	3.5	.997	C-84

Hosea Siner

SINER, HOSEA JOHN
B. Mar. 20, 1885, Shelburn, Ind. D. June 10, 1948, Sullivan, Ind.   BR TR 5'10½" 185 lbs.

Year	Team		Games	BA	SA	AB	H	2B	3B	HR	HR%	R	RBI	BB	SO	SB	AB	H	PO	A	E	DP	TC/G	FA	G by Pos
1909	BOS	N	10	.130	.130	23	3	0	0	0	0.0	1	1	2		0	2	0	10	10	2	1	2.2	.909	3B-5, SS-1, 2B-1

Ken Singleton

SINGLETON, KENNETH WAYNE
B. June 10, 1947, New York, N. Y.   BB TR 6'4" 210 lbs.

Year	Team		Games	BA	SA	AB	H	2B	3B	HR	HR%	R	RBI	BB	SO	SB	AB	H	PO	A	E	DP	TC/G	FA	G by Pos
1970	NY	N	69	.263	.379	198	52	8	0	5	2.5	22	26	30	48	1	18	4	90	1	3	0	1.4	.968	OF-51
1971			115	.245	.393	298	73	5	0	13	4.4	34	46	61	64	0	23	6	143	5	4	0	1.3	.974	OF-96
1972	MON	N	142	.274	.410	507	139	23	2	14	2.8	77	50	70	99	5	5	1	236	9	7	3	1.8	.972	OF-137
1973			162	.302	.479	560	169	26	2	23	4.1	100	103	123	91	2	3	0	278	20	5	3	1.9	.983	OF-161
1974			148	.276	.376	511	141	20	2	9	1.8	68	74	93	84	5	5	1	224	7	11	0	1.6	.955	OF-143
1975	BAL	A	155	.300	.454	586	176	37	4	15	2.6	88	55	118	82	3	1	0	283	9	3	2	1.9	.990	OF-155
1976			154	.278	.403	544	151	25	2	13	2.4	62	70	79	76	2	1	0	278	9	5	2	1.9	.983	OF-134, DH-19
1977			152	.328	.507	536	176	24	0	24	4.5	90	99	107	101	0	1	0	278	8	4	2	1.9	.986	OF-150, DH-1
1978			149	.293	.462	502	147	21	2	20	4.0	67	81	98	94	0	1	0	244	1	6	0	1.7	.976	OF-140, DH-5

Year	Team	Games	BA	SA	AB	H	2B	3B	HR	HR%	R	RBI	BB	SO	SB	Pinch Hit AB	Pinch Hit H	PO	A	E	DP	TC/G	FA	G by Pos

Ken Singleton *continued*

Year	Team	Games	BA	SA	AB	H	2B	3B	HR	HR%	R	RBI	BB	SO	SB	AB	H	PO	A	E	DP	TC/G	FA	G by Pos
1979		159	.295	.533	570	168	29	1	35	6.1	93	111	109	118	3	0	0	247	8	5	2	1.6	.981	OF-143, DH-16
1980		156	.304	.485	583	177	28	3	24	4.1	85	104	92	94	0	0	0	248	3	4	1	1.6	.984	OF-151, DH-5
1981		103	.278	.435	363	101	16	1	13	3.6	48	49	61	59	0	1	0	125	2	0	2	1.2	1.000	OF-72, DH-30
1982		156	.251	.381	561	141	27	2	14	2.5	71	77	86	93	0	4	1	10	0	0	0	0.1	1.000	DH-148, OF-5
1983		151	.276	.436	507	140	21	3	18	3.6	52	84	99	83	0	6	4	0	0	0	0	0.0	–	DH-150
1984		111	.215	.289	363	78	7	1	6	1.7	28	36	37	60	0	0	0	0	0	0	0	0.0	–	DH-103
15 yrs.		2082	.282	.436	7189	2029	317	25	246	3.4	985	1065	1263	1246	21	87	19	2684	82	57	17	1.4	.980	OF-1538, DH-477

LEAGUE CHAMPIONSHIP SERIES

Year	Team	Games	BA	SA	AB	H	2B	3B	HR	HR%	R	RBI	BB	SO	SB	AB	H	PO	A	E	DP	TC/G	FA	G by Pos
1979	BAL A	4	.375	.500	16	6	2	0	0	0.0	4	2	1	2	0	0	0	5	1	0	0	1.5	1.000	OF-4
1983		4	.250	.417	12	3	2	0	0	0.0	0	1	2	2	0	0	0	0	0	0	0	0.0	–	DH-4
2 yrs.		8	.321	.464	28	9	4	0	0	0.0	4	3	3	4	0	0	0	5	1	0	0	0.8	1.000	DH-4, OF-4

WORLD SERIES

Year	Team	Games	BA	SA	AB	H	2B	3B	HR	HR%	R	RBI	BB	SO	SB	AB	H	PO	A	E	DP	TC/G	FA	G by Pos
1979	BAL A	7	.357	.393	28	10	1	0	0	0.0	1	2	2	5	0	0	0	9	0	0	0	1.3	1.000	OF-7
1983		2	.000	.000	1	0	0	0	0	0.0	0	1	1	1	0	1	0	0	0	0	0	0.0	–	
2 yrs.		9	.345	.379	29	10	1	0	0	0.0	1	3	3	6	0	1	0	9	0	0	0	1.0	1.000	OF-7

Fred Sington

SINGTON, FREDERICK WILLIAM
B. Feb. 24, 1910, Birmingham, Ala.
BR TR 6'2" 215 lbs.

Year	Team	Games	BA	SA	AB	H	2B	3B	HR	HR%	R	RBI	BB	SO	SB	AB	H	PO	A	E	DP	TC/G	FA	G by Pos
1934	WAS A	9	.286	.343	35	10	2	0	0	0.0	2	6	4	3	0	0	0	13	1	1	0	1.7	.933	OF-9
1935		20	.182	.182	22	4	0	0	0	0.0	1	3	5	1	0	11	2	7	1	1	0	0.5	.889	OF-4
1936		25	.319	.436	94	30	8	0	1	1.1	13	28	15	9	0	0	0	52	1	3	0	2.2	.946	OF-25
1937		78	.237	.377	228	54	15	4	3	1.3	27	36	37	33	1	14	0	120	4	5	0	1.7	.961	OF-64
1938	BKN N	17	.358	.623	53	19	6	1	2	3.8	10	5	13	5	0	1	0	29	0	0	0	1.7	1.000	OF-17
1939		32	.274	.369	84	23	5	0	1	1.2	13	7	15	15	0	6	2	44	1	1	1	1.4	.978	OF-22
6 yrs.		181	.271	.401	516	140	36	5	7	1.4	66	85	89	66	2	31	4	265	8	11	1	1.6	.961	OF-141

Dick Sipek

SIPEK, RICHARD FRANCIS
B. Jan. 16, 1923, Chicago, Ill.
BL TR 5'9" 170 lbs.

Year	Team	Games	BA	SA	AB	H	2B	3B	HR	HR%	R	RBI	BB	SO	SB	AB	H	PO	A	E	DP	TC/G	FA	G by Pos
1945	CIN N	82	.244	.308	156	38	6	2	0	0.0	14	13	9	15	0	45	10	68	2	2	0	0.9	.972	OF-31

John Sipin

SIPIN, JOHN WHITE
B. Aug. 29, 1946, Watsonville, Calif.
BR TR 6'1½" 175 lbs.

Year	Team	Games	BA	SA	AB	H	2B	3B	HR	HR%	R	RBI	BB	SO	SB	AB	H	PO	A	E	DP	TC/G	FA	G by Pos
1969	SD N	68	.223	.319	229	51	12	2	2	0.9	22	9	8	44	2	5	2	106	173	7	41	4.2	.976	2B-60

Dick Sisler

SISLER, RICHARD ALLAN
Son of George Sisler. Brother of Dave Sisler.
B. Nov. 2, 1920, St. Louis, Mo.
Manager 1964-65.
BL TR 6'2" 205 lbs.

Year	Team	Games	BA	SA	AB	H	2B	3B	HR	HR%	R	RBI	BB	SO	SB	AB	H	PO	A	E	DP	TC/G	FA	G by Pos
1946	STL N	83	.260	.362	235	61	11	2	3	1.3	17	42	14	28	0	13	4	334	31	6	31	4.5	.984	1B-37, OF-29
1947		46	.203	.257	74	15	2	1	0	0.0	4	9	3	8	0	30	4	84	6	2	3	2.0	.978	1B-10, OF-5
1948	PHI N	121	.274	.408	446	122	21	3	11	2.5	60	56	47	46	1	2	0	986	73	18	88	8.9	.983	1B-120
1949		121	.289	.415	412	119	19	6	7	1.7	42	50	25	38	0	23	6	815	40	11	93	7.2	.987	1B-96
1950		141	.296	.442	523	155	29	4	13	2.5	79	83	64	50	1	2	1	293	9	4	0	2.2	.987	OF-137
1951		125	.287	.414	428	123	20	5	8	1.9	46	52	40	39	1	11	4	233	8	8	3	2.0	.968	OF-111
1952	2 teams		CIN N (11G – .185)		STL N (119G – .261)																			
"	total	130	.256	.404	445	114	15	6	13	2.9	51	64	32	40	3	6	1	1033	84	17	116	8.7	.985	1B-114, OF-7
1953	STL N	32	.256	.326	43	11	1	1	0	0.0	3	4	1	4	0	22	5	42	6	0	5	1.5	1.000	1B-10
8 yrs.		799	.276	.406	2606	720	118	28	55	2.1	302	360	226	253	6	109	25	3820	257	66	339	5.2	.984	1B-387, OF-289

WORLD SERIES

Year	Team	Games	BA	SA	AB	H	2B	3B	HR	HR%	R	RBI	BB	SO	SB	AB	H	PO	A	E	DP	TC/G	FA	G by Pos
1946	STL N	2	.000	.000	2	0	0	0	0	0.0	0	0	0	0	0	2	0	0	0	0	0	0.0	–	
1950	PHI N	4	.059	.059	17	1	0	0	0	0.0	0	1	0	5	0	0	0	10	1	0	0	2.8	1.000	OF-4
2 yrs.		6	.053	.053	19	1	0	0	0	0.0	0	1	0	5	0	2	0	10	1	0	0	1.8	1.000	OF-4

George Sisler

SISLER, GEORGE HAROLD (Gorgeous George)
Father of Dick Sisler. Father of Dave Sisler.
B. Mar. 24, 1893, Manchester, Ohio   D. Mar. 26, 1973, Richmond Heights, Mo.
Manager 1924-26.
Hall of Fame 1939.
BL TL 5'11" 170 lbs.

Year	Team	Games	BA	SA	AB	H	2B	3B	HR	HR%	R	RBI	BB	SO	SB	AB	H	PO	A	E	DP	TC/G	FA	G by Pos
1915	STL A	81	.285	.369	274	78	10	2	3	1.1	28	29	7	27	10	0	0	413	38	7	21	5.7	.985	1B-37, OF-29, P-15
1916		151	.305	.400	580	177	21	11	4	0.7	83	76	40	37	34	2	0	1523	97	24	87	10.9	.985	1B-139, OF-3, P-3, 3B-2
1917		135	.353	.453	539	190	30	9	2	0.4	60	52	30	19	37	0	0	1386	106	24	97	11.2	.984	1B-133, 2B-2
1918		114	.341	.440	452	154	21	9	2	0.4	69	41	40	17	45	0	0	1244	97	13	65	11.9	.990	1B-114, P-2
1919		132	.352	.530	511	180	31	15	10	2.0	96	83	27	20	28	1	1	1249	120	13	62	10.5	.991	1B-131
1920		154	**.407**	.632	631	257[1]	49	18	19	3.0	137	122	46	19	42	0	0	1477	140	16	87	10.6	.990	1B-154, P-1
1921		138	.371	.555	582	216	38	18	11	1.9	125	104	34	27	**35**	0	0	1267	108	10	86	10.0	.993	1B-138
1922		142	**.420**	.594	586	246	42	18	8	1.4	**134**	105	49	14	**51**	1	0	1293	125	17	116	10.1	.988	1B-141
1924		151	.305	.421	636	194	27	10	9	1.4	94	74	31	29	19	0	0	1319	111	23	114	9.6	.984	1B-151
1925		150	.345	.479	649	224	21	15	12	1.8	100	105	27	24	11	0	0	1330	133	26	120	9.9	.983	1B-150, P-1
1926		150	.290	.398	613	178	21	12	7	1.1	78	71	30	30	12	0	0	1467	88	21	141	10.6	.987	1B-149, P-1
1927		149	.327	.430	614	201	32	8	5	0.8	87	97	24	15	**27**	0	0	1374	131	24	138	10.3	.984	1B-149
1928	2 teams		WAS A (20G – .245)		BOS N (118G – .340)																			
"	total	138	.331	.419	540	179	27	4	4	0.7	72	70	31	24	11	10	3	1241	86	15	103	9.7	.989	1B-123, OF-5, P-1
1929	BOS N	154	.326	.423	629	205	40	9	1	0.2	67	79	33	17	6	0	0	1398	111	28	131	10.0	.982	1B-154
1930		116	.309	.397	431	133	15	7	3	0.7	54	67	23	15	7	8	2	915	81	13	103	8.7	.987	1B-107
15 yrs.		2055	.340	.468	8267	2812	425	165	100	1.2	1284	1175	472	327	375	22	6	18896	1572	274	1471	10.1	.987	1B-1970, OF-37, P-24, 3B-2, 2B-2

Sibby Sisti

SISTI, SEBASTIAN DANIEL
B. July 26, 1920, Buffalo, N. Y.
BR TR 5'11" 175 lbs.

Year	Team		Games	BA	SA	AB	H	2B	3B	HR	HR%	R	RBI	BB	SO	SB	Pinch Hit AB	H	PO	A	E	DP	TC/G	FA	G by Pos

Sibby Sisti *continued*

1939	BOS	N	63	.228	.284	215	49	7	1	1	0.5	19	11	12	38	4	1	0	136	152	8	8	4.7	.973	2B-34, 3B-17, SS-10
1940			123	.251	.353	459	115	19	5	6	1.3	73	34	36	64	4	2	0	142	225	22	28	3.2	.943	3B-102, 2B-16
1941			140	.259	.320	541	140	24	3	1	0.2	72	45	38	76	7	1	0	169	291	44	29	3.6	.913	3B-137, SS-2, 2B-2
1942			129	.211	.287	407	86	11	4	4	1.0	50	35	45	55	5	2	0	306	351	20	66	5.2	.970	2B-124, OF-1
1946			1	–	–	0	0	0	0	0	–	0	0	0	0	0	0	0	0	0	0	0	0.0	–	3B-1
1947			56	.281	.373	153	43	8	0	2	1.3	22	15	20	17	2	3	1	93	122	12	24	4.1	.947	SS-51, 2B-1
1948			83	.244	.290	221	54	6	2	0	0.0	30	21	31	34	0	2	1	140	173	14	32	3.9	.957	2B-44, SS-26
1949			101	.257	.358	268	69	12	0	5	1.9	39	22	34	42	1	6	3	156	80	7	11	2.4	.971	OF-48, 2B-21, SS-18, 3B-1
1950			69	.171	.276	105	18	3	1	2	1.9	21	11	16	19	1	7	3	72	69	9	11	2.2	.940	SS-23, 2B-19, 3B-13, OF-1, 1B-1
1951			114	.279	.362	362	101	20	2	2	0.6	46	38	32	50	4	4	2	239	230	18	47	4.3	.963	2B-52, SS-25, 3B-6, OF-1, 1B-1
1952			90	.212	.310	245	52	10	1	4	1.6	19	24	14	43	2	13	1	142	129	16	22	3.2	.944	2B-33, OF-23, SS-18, 3B-9
1953	MIL	N	38	.217	.261	23	5	1	0	0	0.0	8	4	5	2	0	1	0	13	18	2	3	0.9	.939	2B-13, SS-6, 3B-4
1954			9	–	–	0	0	0	0	0	–	0	2	0	0	0	0	0	0	0	0	0	0.0	–	
13 yrs.			1016	.244	.324	2999	732	121	19	27	0.9	401	260	283	440	30	42	11	1608	1840	172	281	3.6	.952	2B-359, 3B-290, SS-179, OF-74, 1B-2

WORLD SERIES

| 1948 | BOS | N | 2 | .000 | .000 | 1 | 0 | 0 | 0 | 0 | 0.0 | 0 | 0 | 0 | 0 | 0 | 1 | 0 | 0 | 0 | 0 | 0 | 0.0 | – | 2B-2 |

Ed Sixsmith

SIXSMITH, EDWARD
B. Feb. 26, 1863, Philadelphia, Pa.   D. Dec. 12, 1926, Philadelphia, Pa.   BR TR

| 1884 | PHI | N | 1 | .000 | .000 | 2 | 0 | 0 | 0 | 0 | 0.0 | 0 | | 0 | 0 | | 0 | 0 | 1 | 0 | 0 | 0 | 1.0 | 1.000 | C-1 |

Ted Sizemore

SIZEMORE, THEODORE CRAWFORD
B. Apr. 15, 1945, Gadsden, Ala.   BR TR 5'10" 165 lbs.

1969	LA	N	159	.271	.342	590	160	20	5	4	0.7	69	46	45	40	5	0	0	347	469	24	93	5.3	.971	2B-118, SS-46, OF-1
1970			96	.306	.350	340	104	10	1	1	0.3	40	34	34	19	5	3	2	209	239	9	50	4.8	.980	2B-86, OF-9, SS-2
1971	STL	N	135	.264	.333	478	126	14	5	3	0.6	53	42	42	26	4	6	3	277	379	18	79	5.0	.973	2B-93, SS-39, OF-15, 3B-1
1972			120	.264	.335	439	116	17	4	2	0.5	53	38	37	36	8	13	1	222	342	14	68	4.8	.976	2B-111
1973			142	.282	.334	521	147	22	1	1	0.2	69	54	68	34	6	1	0	313	463	15	84	5.6	.981	2B-139, 3B-3
1974			129	.250	.296	504	126	17	0	2	0.4	68	47	70	37	8	2	0	336	412	16	109	5.9	.979	2B-128, OF-1, SS-1
1975			153	.240	.301	562	135	23	1	3	0.5	56	49	45	37	1	1	1	329	405	21	82	4.9	.972	2B-153
1976	LA	N	84	.241	.278	266	64	8	1	0	0.0	18	18	15	22	2	13	5	178	191	7	51	4.5	.981	2B-71, 3B-3, C-2
1977	PHI	N	152	.281	.355	519	146	20	3	4	0.8	64	47	52	40	8	1	0	348	427	11	104	5.2	.986	2B-152
1978			108	.219	.254	351	77	12	0	0	0.0	38	25	25	29	8	1	0	232	302	12	61	5.1	.978	2B-107
1979 2 teams	CHI	N	(98G – .248)				BOS	A	(26G – .261)																	
" total			124	.251	.330	418	105	24	0	3	0.7	48	30	36	30	4	3	0	285	397	16	92	5.6	.977	2B-122, C-2
1980	BOS	A	9	.217	.261	23	5	1	0	0	0.0	1	0	0	0	0	1	0	16	22	3	7	4.6	.927	2B-8
12 yrs.			1411	.262	.321	5011	1311	188	21	23	0.5	577	430	469	350	59	45	12	3092	4048	166	880	5.2	.977	2B-1288, SS-88, OF-26, 3B-7, C-4

LEAGUE CHAMPIONSHIP SERIES

1977	PHI	N	4	.231	.231	13	3	0	0	0	0.0	1	0	2	0	0	0	0	10	8	2	2	5.0	.900	2B-4
1978			4	.385	.538	13	5	0	1	0	0.0	3	1	1	0	0	0	0	7	8	0	4	3.8	1.000	2B-4
2 yrs.			8	.308	.385	26	8	0	1	0	0.0	4	1	3	0	0	0	0	17	16	2	6	4.4	.943	2B-8

Frank Skaff

SKAFF, FRANCIS MICHAEL
B. Sept. 30, 1913, LaCrosse, Wis.   D. Apr. 12, 1988, Towson, Md.   BR TR 5'10" 185 lbs.
Manager 1966.

1935	BKN	N	6	.545	.818	11	6	1	0	0	0.0	4	3	0	2	0	3	1	4	2	1	0	1.2	.857	3B-3
1943	PHI	A	32	.281	.391	64	18	2	1	1	1.6	8	8	6	11	0	7	1	116	20	4	12	4.4	.971	1B-18, 3B-3, SS-1
2 yrs.			38	.320	.453	75	24	3	2	1	1.3	12	11	6	13	0	10	2	120	22	5	12	3.9	.966	1B-18, 3B-6, SS-1

Dave Skaggs

SKAGGS, DAVID LINDSEY
B. June 12, 1951, Santa Monica, Calif.   BR TR 6'2" 200 lbs.

1977	BAL	A	80	.287	.352	216	62	9	1	1	0.5	22	24	20	34	0	0	0	344	34	2	4	4.8	.995	C-80
1978			36	.151	.186	86	13	1	1	0	0.0	6	2	9	14	0	1	0	149	17	2	2	4.7	.988	C-35
1979			63	.248	.328	137	34	8	0	1	0.7	9	14	13	14	0	0	0	222	24	4	1	4.0	.984	C-63
1980 2 teams	BAL	A	(2G – .200)				CAL	A	(24G – .197)																	
" total			26	.197	.239	71	14	0	1	1	1.4	7	9	9	14	0	0	0	94	6	3	3	4.0	.971	C-26
4 yrs.			205	.241	.302	510	123	18	2	3	0.6	44	49	51	76	0	1	0	809	81	11	10	4.4	.988	C-204

LEAGUE CHAMPIONSHIP SERIES

| 1979 | BAL | A | 1 | .000 | .000 | 4 | 0 | 0 | 0 | 0 | 0.0 | 0 | 0 | 0 | 0 | 0 | 0 | 0 | 3 | 1 | 0 | 0 | 4.0 | 1.000 | C-1 |

WORLD SERIES

| 1979 | BAL | A | 1 | .333 | .333 | 3 | 1 | 0 | 0 | 0 | 0.0 | 1 | 0 | 0 | 0 | 0 | 0 | 0 | 2 | 2 | 0 | 0 | 4.0 | 1.000 | C-1 |

Bud Sketchley

SKETCHLEY, HARRY CLEMENT
B. Mar. 30, 1919, Virden, Man., Canada   D. Dec. 19, 1979, Los Angeles, Calif.   BL TL 5'10½" 180 lbs.

| 1942 | CHI | A | 13 | .194 | .222 | 36 | 7 | 1 | 0 | 0 | 0.0 | 1 | 3 | 7 | 4 | 0 | 0 | 0 | 19 | 1 | 1 | 0 | 1.6 | .952 | OF-12 |

Roe Skidmore

SKIDMORE, ROBERT ROE
B. Oct. 30, 1945, Decatur, Ill.   BR TR 6'3" 188 lbs.

| 1970 | CHI | N | 1 | 1.000 | 1.000 | 1 | 1 | 0 | 0 | 0 | 0.0 | 0 | 1 | 0 | 0 | 0 | 1 | 1 | 0 | 0 | 0 | 0 | 0.0 | – | |

Bill Skiff

SKIFF, WILLIAM FRANKLIN
B. Oct. 16, 1895, New Rochelle, N. Y.   D. Dec. 25, 1976, Bronxville, N. Y.   BR TR 5'10" 170 lbs.

| 1921 | PIT | N | 16 | .289 | .333 | 45 | 13 | 2 | 0 | 0 | 0.0 | 7 | 11 | 0 | 4 | 1 | 2 | 1 | 46 | 8 | 1 | 1 | 3.4 | .982 | C-13 |

Year	Team	Games	BA	SA	AB	H	2B	3B	HR	HR%	R	RBI	BB	SO	SB	Pinch Hit AB	Pinch Hit H	PO	A	E	DP	TC/G	FA	G by Pos

Bill Skiff *continued*

| 1926 | NY | A | 6 | .091 | .091 | 11 | 1 | 0 | 0 | 0 | 0.0 | 0 | 0 | 0 | 1 | 0 | 0 | 0 | 8 | 1 | 0 | 1 | 1.5 | 1.000 | C-6 |
| 2 yrs. | | 22 | .250 | .286 | 56 | 14 | 2 | 0 | 0 | 0.0 | 7 | 11 | 0 | 5 | 1 | 2 | 1 | 54 | 9 | 1 | 2 | 2.9 | .984 | C-19 |

Al Skinner

SKINNER, CHARLES LOUIS
Deceased.

| 1884 | 2 teams | BAL | U (1G – .333) | CHI | U (1G – .333) | | | | | | | | | | | | | | | | | | | |
| " | total | 2 | .333 | .333 | 6 | 2 | 0 | 0 | 0 | 0.0 | 1 | | 0 | | | 0 | 0 | 2 | 0 | 0 | 0 | 1.0 | 1.000 | OF-2 |

Bob Skinner

SKINNER, ROBERT RALPH   BL TR 6'4"   190 lbs.
Father of Joel Skinner.
B. Oct. 3, 1931, La Jolla, Calif.
Manager 1968-69, 1977.

1954	PIT	N	132	.249	.370	470	117	15	9	8	1.7	67	46	47	59	4	11	6	1026	84	16	87	8.5	.986	1B-118, OF-2
1956		113	.202	.326	233	47	8	3	5	2.1	29	29	26	50	1	54	9	217	8	2	21	2.0	.991	OF-36, 1B-24, 3B-1
1957		126	.305	.468	387	118	12	6	13	3.4	58	45	38	50	10	27	8	232	17	8	9	2.0	.969	OF-93, 1B-9, 3B-1
1958		144	.321	.491	529	170	33	9	13	2.5	93	70	58	55	12	3	1	232	19	6	2	1.8	.977	OF-141
1959		143	.280	.399	547	153	18	4	13	2.4	78	61	67	65	10	1	0	285	9	11	1	2.1	.964	OF-142, 1B-1
1960		145	.273	.431	571	156	33	6	15	2.6	83	86	59	86	11	5	2	250	13	5	2	1.8	.981	OF-141
1961		119	.268	.360	381	102	20	3	3	0.8	61	42	51	49	3	18	4	175	5	5	1	1.6	.973	OF-97
1962		144	.302	.504	510	154	29	7	20	3.9	87	75	76	89	10	4	3	210	6	9	0	1.6	.960	OF-139
1963	2 teams	PIT	N (34G – .270)	CIN	N (72G – .253)																			
"	total	106	.259	.380	316	82	15	7	3	0.9	43	25	34	64	5	22	6	131	4	1	1	1.3	.993	OF-83
1964	2 teams	CIN	N (25G – .220)	STL	N (55G – .271)																			
"	total	80	.254	.367	177	45	8	0	4	2.3	16	21	15	32	0	37	8	62	4	5	0	0.9	.930	OF-43
1965	STL	N	80	.309	.493	152	47	5	4	5	3.3	25	26	12	30	1	47	15	43	0	3	0	0.6	.935	OF-33
1966		49	.156	.244	45	7	1	0	1	2.2	2	5	2	17	0	45	7	0	0	0	0	0.0	—	
12 yrs.		1381	.277	.421	4318	1198	197	58	103	2.4	642	531	485	646	67	274	69	2863	169	71	124	2.2	.977	OF-950, 1B-152, 3B-2

WORLD SERIES

1960	PIT	N	2	.200	.200	5	1	0	0	0	0.0	2	1	1	0	0	1	0	4	1	0	1	2.5	1.000	OF-2
1964	STL	N	4	.667	1.000	3	2	1	0	0	0.0	0	1	1	0	0	3	2	0	0	0	0	0.0		OF-2
2 yrs.		6	.375	.500	8	3	1	0	0	0.0	2	2	2	0	1	3	2	4	1	0	1	0.8	1.000	OF-2

Camp Skinner

SKINNER, ELISHA HARRISON   BL TR 5'11"   165 lbs.
B. June 25, 1897, Douglasville, Ga.   D. Aug. 4, 1944, Douglasville, Ga.

1922	NY	A	27	.182	.182	33	6	0	0	0	0.0	1	2	0	4	1	24	4	9	0	0	0	0.3	1.000	OF-4
1923	BOS	A	7	.231	.385	13	3	2	0	0	0.0	1	1	0	0	0	5	2	0	0	0	0	0.3	—	OF-2
2 yrs.		34	.196	.239	46	9	2	0	0	0.0	2	3	0	4	1	29	6	9	0	0	0	0.3	1.000	OF-6

Joel Skinner

SKINNER, JOEL PATRICK   BR TR 6'4"   195 lbs.
Son of Bob Skinner.
B. Feb. 21, 1961, La Jolla, Calif.

1983	CHI	A	6	.273	.273	11	3	0	0	0	0.0	2	1	0	1	0	0	0	20	4	1	1	4.2	.960	C-6
1984		43	.213	.238	80	17	2	0	0	0.0	4	3	7	19	1	0	0	171	11	2	1	4.3	.989	C-43
1985		22	.341	.545	44	15	4	1	1	2.3	9	5	5	13	0	2	0	94	8	3	0	4.8	.971	C-21
1986	2 teams	CHI	A (60G – .201)	NY	A (54G – .259)																			
"	total	114	.232	.314	315	73	9	1	5	1.6	23	37	16	83	1	0	0	507	37	9	9	4.9	.984	C-114
1987	NY	A	64	.137	.230	139	19	4	0	3	2.2	9	14	8	46	0	1	0	232	18	4	2	4.0	.984	C-64
1988		88	.227	.335	251	57	15	0	4	1.6	23	23	14	72	0	0	0	396	16	4	5	4.7	.990	C-85, OF-2, 1B-1
1989	CLE	A	79	.230	.303	178	41	10	0	1	0.6	10	13	9	42	1	0	0	280	22	3	1	4.4	.990	C-79
7 yrs.		416	.221	.309	1018	225	44	2	14	1.4	80	96	59	276	3	3	0	1700	116	26	19	4.4	.986	C-412, OF-2, 1B-1

Lou Skizas

SKIZAS, LOUIS PETER (The Nervous Greek)   BR TR 5'11"   175 lbs.
B. June 2, 1932, Chicago, Ill.

1956	2 teams	NY	A (6G – .167)	KC	A (83G – .316)																			
"	total	89	.314	.479	303	95	11	3	11	3.6	39	40	15	19	3	15	3	148	9	4	0	1.8	.975	OF-74
1957	KC	A	119	.245	.431	376	92	14	1	18	4.8	34	44	27	15	5	24	2	148	62	8	5	1.8	.963	OF-76, 3B-32
1958	DET	A	23	.242	.394	33	8	2	0	1	3.0	4	2	5	1	0	13	2	4	7	3	0	0.6	.786	OF-5, 3B-4
1959	CHI	A	8	.077	.077	13	1	0	0	0	0.0	3	0	3	2	0	2	0	6	1	0	0	0.9	1.000	OF-6
4 yrs.		239	.270	.443	725	196	27	4	30	4.1	80	86	50	37	8	54	7	306	79	15	5	1.7	.963	OF-161, 3B-36

Bill Skowron

SKOWRON, WILLIAM JOSEPH (Moose)   BR TR 5'11"   195 lbs.
B. Dec. 18, 1930, Chicago, Ill.

1954	NY	A	87	.340	.577	215	73	12	9	7	3.3	37	41	19	18	2	22	7	399	45	7	48	5.2	.984	1B-61, 3B-5, 2B-2
1955		108	.319	.524	288	92	17	3	12	4.2	46	61	21	32	1	35	6	520	40	7	63	5.3	.988	1B-74, 3B-3
1956		134	.308	.528	464	143	21	6	23	5.0	78	90	50	60	4	12	2	969	86	8	138	7.9	.992	1B-120, 3B-2
1957		122	.304	.470	457	139	15	5	17	3.7	54	88	31	60	3	9	3	1026	86	9	116	9.2	.992	1B-115
1958		126	.273	.424	465	127	22	3	14	3.0	61	73	28	69	1	7	3	1041	72	13	112	8.9	.988	1B-118, 3B-2
1959		74	.298	.539	282	84	13	5	15	5.3	39	59	20	47	1	3	1	626	43	6	68	9.1	.991	1B-72
1960		146	.309	.528	538	166	34	3	26	4.8	63	91	38	95	2	6	1	1202	115	12	130	9.1	.991	1B-142
1961		150	.267	.472	561	150	23	4	28	5.0	76	89	35	108	0	1	0	1228	102	10	146	8.9	.993	1B-149
1962		140	.270	.473	478	129	16	6	23	4.8	63	80	36	99	0	12	4	1054	77	10	101	8.2	.991	1B-135
1963	LA	N	89	.203	.287	237	48	8	0	4	1.7	19	19	13	49	0	24	6	518	34	5	44	6.3	.991	1B-66, 3B-1
1964	2 teams	WAS	A (73G – .271)	CHI	A (73G – .293)																			
"	total	146	.282	.428	535	151	21	3	17	3.2	47	79	30	92	0	13	1	1212	80	5	94	8.9	.996	1B-136
1965	CHI	A	146	.274	.424	559	153	24	3	18	3.2	63	78	32	77	1	1	1	1297	74	8	116	9.4	.994	1B-145
1966		120	.249	.359	337	84	15	2	6	1.8	27	29	26	45	1	23	3	722	60	7	75	6.6	.991	1B-98
1967	2 teams	CHI	A (8G – .000)	CAL	A (62G – .220)																			
"	total	70	.206	.260	131	27	2	1	1	0.8	8	11	4	19	0	37	7	338	16	3	15	5.1	.992	1B-32
14 yrs.		1658	.282	.459	5547	1566	243	53	211	3.8	681	888	383	870	16	205	47	12152	930	110	1266	8.0	.992	1B-1463, 3B-13, 2B-2

WORLD SERIES

| 1955 | NY | A | 5 | .333 | .750 | 12 | 4 | 2 | 0 | 1 | 8.3 | 2 | 3 | 0 | 1 | 0 | 2 | 0 | 22 | 3 | 1 | 1 | 5.2 | .962 | 1B-3 |

Year	Team	Games	BA	SA	AB	H	2B	3B	HR	HR%	R	RBI	BB	SO	SB	Pinch Hit AB	Pinch Hit H	PO	A	E	DP	TC/G	FA	G by Pos

Bill Skowron continued

Year	Team	Games	BA	SA	AB	H	2B	3B	HR	HR%	R	RBI	BB	SO	SB	PH AB	PH H	PO	A	E	DP	TC/G	FA	G by Pos
1956		3	.100	.400	10	1	0	0	1	10.0	1	4	0	3	0	1	0	21	4	1	3	8.7	.962	1B-2
1957		2	.000	.000	4	0	0	0	0	0.0	0	0	0	0	0	1	0	5	2	0	1	3.5	1.000	1B-2
1958		7	.259	.481	27	7	0	0	2	7.4	3	7	1	4	0	0	0	55	4	0	4	8.4	1.000	1B-7
1960		7	.375	.625	32	12	2	0	2	6.3	7	6	0	6	0	0	0	70	6	0	9	10.9	1.000	1B-7
1961		5	.353	.529	17	6	0	0	1	5.9	3	5	3	4	0	0	0	46	5	0	1	10.2	1.000	1B-5
1962		6	.222	.333	18	4	0	1	0	0.0	1	1	1	5	0	0	0	52	1	0	3	8.8	1.000	1B-6
1963	LA N	4	.385	.615	13	5	0	0	1	7.7	2	3	1	3	0	0	0	30	4	0	1	8.5	1.000	1B-4
8 yrs.		39	.293	.519	133	39	4	1	8	6.0	19	29	6	26	0	4	0	301	29	2	23	8.5	.994	1B-36
									7th			6th		6th										

Bob Skube

SKUBE, ROBERT JACOB
B. Oct. 8, 1957, Northridge, Calif.
BL TL 6' 182 lbs.

Year	Team	Games	BA	SA	AB	H	2B	3B	HR	HR%	R	RBI	BB	SO	SB	PH AB	PH H	PO	A	E	DP	TC/G	FA	G by Pos
1982	MIL A	4	.667	.667	3	2	0	0	0	0.0	0	0	0	0	0	3	2	0	0	0	0	0.0	–	DH-1, OF-1
1983		12	.200	.320	25	5	1	1	0	0.0	2	9	4	7	0	2	0	22	0	0	0	1.8	1.000	OF-8, DH-2, 1B-1
2 yrs.		16	.250	.357	28	7	1	1	0	0.0	2	9	4	7	0	5	2	22	0	0	0	1.4	1.000	OF-9, DH-3, 1B-1

Gordon Slade

SLADE, GORDON LEIGH (Oskie)
B. Oct. 9, 1904, Salt Lake City, Utah   D. Jan. 2, 1974, Long Beach, Calif.
BR TR 5'10½" 160 lbs.

Year	Team	Games	BA	SA	AB	H	2B	3B	HR	HR%	R	RBI	BB	SO	SB	PH AB	PH H	PO	A	E	DP	TC/G	FA	G by Pos
1930	BKN N	25	.216	.351	37	8	3	4	1	2.7	8	3	3	5	0	0	0	22	53	5	13	3.2	.938	SS-21
1931		85	.239	.313	272	65	13	2	1	0.4	27	29	23	28	2	0	0	174	276	26	54	5.6	.945	SS-82, 3B-2
1932		79	.240	.320	250	60	15	1	1	0.4	23	23	11	26	3	1	1	119	201	17	36	4.3	.949	SS-55, 3B-23
1933	STL N	39	.113	.129	62	7	1	0	0	0.0	6	3	6	7	1	3	0	34	61	6	11	2.6	.941	SS-31, 2B-1
1934	CIN N	138	.285	.369	555	158	19	8	4	0.7	61	52	25	34	6	1	0	302	443	28	83	5.6	.964	SS-97, 2B-39
1935		71	.281	.347	196	55	10	0	1	0.5	22	14	16	16	0	7	2	91	115	11	20	3.1	.949	SS-30, 2B-19, OF-8, 3B-7
6 yrs.		437	.257	.335	1372	353	60	11	8	0.6	147	123	84	116	12	12	3	742	1149	93	217	4.5	.953	SS-316, 2B-59, 3B-32, OF-8

Art Sladen

SLADEN, ARTHUR W.
B. Oct. 28, 1860, Lowell, Mass.   D. Feb. 28, 1914, Dracut, Mass.

Year	Team	Games	BA	SA	AB	H	2B	3B	HR	HR%	R	RBI	BB	SO	SB	PH AB	PH H	PO	A	E	DP	TC/G	FA	G by Pos
1884	BOS U	2	.000	.000	7	0	0	0	0	0.0	0		0			0	0	1	0	0	0	0.5	1.000	OF-2

Jimmy Slagle

SLAGLE, JAMES FRANKLIN (Rabbit, Shorty, The Human Mosquito)
B. July 11, 1873, Worthville, Pa.   D. May 10, 1956, Chicago, Ill.
BL TR 5'7" 144 lbs.

Year	Team	Games	BA	SA	AB	H	2B	3B	HR	HR%	R	RBI	BB	SO	SB	PH AB	PH H	PO	A	E	DP	TC/G	FA	G by Pos
1899	WAS N	147	.272	.324	599	163	15	8	0	0.0	92	41	55		22	1	0	407	20	21	8	3.0	.953	OF-146
1900	PHI N	141	.287	.347	574	165	16	9	0	0.0	115	45	60		34	0	0	320	22	29	5	2.6	.922	OF-141
1901	2 teams			PHI N (48G – .202)						BOS N (66G – .271)														
"	total	114	.242	.288	438	106	13	2	1	0.2	55	27	50		19	0	0	197	23	16	6	2.1	.932	OF-114
1902	CHI N	115	.315	.357	454	143	11	4	0	0.0	64	28	53		40	2	1	262	15	10	5	2.5	.965	OF-113
1903		139	.298	.357	543	162	20	6	0	0.0	104	44	81		33	0	0	292	16	21	8	2.4	.936	OF-139
1904		120	.260	.333	481	125	12	10	1	0.2	73	31	41		28	0	0	194	15	18	4	1.9	.921	OF-120
1905		155	.269	.317	568	153	19	4	0	0.0	96	37	97		27	0	0	306	27	13	6	2.2	.962	OF-155
1906		127	.239	.279	498	119	8	6	0	0.0	71	33	63		25	0	0	276	9	7	5	2.3	.976	OF-127
1907		136	.258	.294	489	126	6	6	0	0.0	71	32	76		28	0	0	239	15	10	5	1.9	.962	OF-135
1908		104	.222	.239	352	78	4	1	0	0.0	38	26	43		17	2	0	199	6	5	2	2.0	.976	OF-101
10 yrs.		1298	.268	.317	4996	1340	124	56	2	0.0	779	344	619		273	5	1	2692	168	150	57	2.3	.950	OF-1291

WORLD SERIES

Year	Team	Games	BA	SA	AB	H	2B	3B	HR	HR%	R	RBI	BB	SO	SB	PH AB	PH H	PO	A	E	DP	TC/G	FA	G by Pos
1907	CHI N	5	.273	.273	22	6	0	0	0	0.0	3	4	2	5	0	0	0	13	0	1	0	2.8	.929	OF-5

Jack Slattery

SLATTERY, JOHN TERRENCE
B. Jan. 6, 1878, South Boston, Mass.   D. July 17, 1949, Boston, Mass.
Manager 1928.
BR TR 6'2" 191 lbs.

Year	Team	Games	BA	SA	AB	H	2B	3B	HR	HR%	R	RBI	BB	SO	SB	PH AB	PH H	PO	A	E	DP	TC/G	FA	G by Pos
1901	BOS A	1	.333	.333	3	1	0	0	0	0.0	1	1	1		0	0	0	3	2	0	0	5.0	1.000	C-1
1903	2 teams			CLE A (4G – .000)						CHI A (63G – .218)														
"	total	67	.207	.239	222	46	3	2	0	0.0	9	20	2		2	4	0	270	52	12	6	5.0	.964	C-56, 1B-7
1906	STL A	3	.286	.286	7	2	0	0	0	0.0	0	0	1		0	1	0	12	1	0	0	4.3	1.000	C-2
1909	WAS A	32	.214	.250	56	12	2	0	0	0.0	4	6	2		1	15	4	93	11	5	3	3.4	.954	1B-11, C-5
4 yrs.		103	.212	.243	288	61	5	2	0	0.0	14	27	6		3	20	4	378	66	17	9	4.5	.963	C-64, 1B-18

Mike Slattery

SLATTERY, MICHAEL J.
B. Nov. 26, 1866, Boston, Mass.   D. Oct. 16, 1904, Boston, Mass.
BL TL 6'2" 210 lbs.

Year	Team	Games	BA	SA	AB	H	2B	3B	HR	HR%	R	RBI	BB	SO	SB	PH AB	PH H	PO	A	E	DP	TC/G	FA	G by Pos
1884	BOS U	106	.208	.232	413	86	6	2	0	0.0	60		4			0	0	231	31	47	7	2.9	.848	OF-96, 1B-11
1888	NY N	103	.246	.315	391	96	12	6	1	0.3	50	35	13	28	26	0	0	187	16	18	3	2.1	.919	OF-103
1889		12	.292	.396	48	14	2	0	1	2.1	7	12	4	3	2	0	0	21	2	4	1	2.1	.852	OF-12
1890	NY P	97	.307	.445	411	126	20	11	5	1.2	80	67	27	25	18	0	0	175	5	19	1	2.1	.905	OF-97
1891	2 teams			CIN N (41G – .209)						WAS AA (15G – .283)														
"	total	56	.229	.280	218	50	4	2	1	0.5	32	21	14	15	7	0	0	115	5	10	2	2.3	.923	OF-56
5 yrs.		374	.251	.325	1481	372	44	21	8	0.5	229	135	62	71	53	0	0	729	59	98	14	2.4	.889	OF-364, 1B-11

Don Slaught

SLAUGHT, DONALD MARTIN (Sluggo)
B. Sept. 11, 1958, Long Beach, Calif.
BR TR 6'1" 190 lbs.

Year	Team	Games	BA	SA	AB	H	2B	3B	HR	HR%	R	RBI	BB	SO	SB	PH AB	PH H	PO	A	E	DP	TC/G	FA	G by Pos
1982	KC A	43	.278	.409	115	32	6	0	3	2.6	14	8	9	12	0	0	0	156	7	1	1	3.8	.994	C-43
1983		83	.312	.388	276	86	13	4	0	0.0	21	28	11	27	3	5	2	299	18	12	7	4.0	.964	C-79, DH-1
1984		124	.264	.379	409	108	27	4	4	1.0	48	42	20	55	0	5	2	547	44	11	8	4.9	.982	C-123, DH-1
1985	TEX A	102	.280	.423	343	96	17	4	8	2.3	34	35	20	41	5	1	0	550	33	6	4	5.8	.990	C-102
1986		95	.264	.449	314	83	17	1	13	4.1	39	46	16	59	3	3	3	533	40	4	1	6.1	.993	C-91, DH-2
1987		95	.224	.405	237	53	15	2	8	3.4	25	16	24	51	0	22	5	429	39	7	5	5.5	.985	C-85, DH-5
1988	NY A	97	.283	.450	322	91	25	1	9	2.8	33	43	24	54	1	6	0	496	24	11	4	5.5	.979	C-94, DH-1
1989		117	.251	.371	350	88	21	3	5	1.4	34	38	30	57	1	12	0	493	44	5	8	4.6	.991	C-105, DH-3
8 yrs.		756	.269	.408	2366	637	141	19	50	2.1	248	256	154	356	13	54	17	3503	249	57	38	5.0	.985	C-722, DH-13

Year	Team		Games	BA	SA	AB	H	2B	3B	HR	HR%	R	RBI	BB	SO	SB	Pinch Hit AB	Pinch Hit H	PO	A	E	DP	TC/G	FA	G by Pos

Don Slaught *continued*
LEAGUE CHAMPIONSHIP SERIES

| 1984 | KC | A | 3 | .364 | .364 | 11 | 4 | 0 | 0 | 0 | 0.0 | 0 | 0 | 0 | 0 | 0 | 0 | 0 | 17 | 0 | 3 | 0 | 6.7 | .850 | C-3 |

Enos Slaughter

SLAUGHTER, ENOS BRADSHER (Country)
B. Apr. 27, 1916, Roxboro, N. C.
Hall of Fame 1985.

BL TR 5'9½" 180 lbs.

1938	STL	N	112	.276	.438	395	109	20	10	8	2.0	59	58	32	38	1	20	2	189	7	6	0	1.8	.970	OF-92
1939			149	.320	.482	604	193	52	5	12	2.0	95	86	44	53	2	0	0	348	18	12	5	2.5	.968	OF-149
1940			140	.306	.504	516	158	25	13	17	3.3	96	73	50	35	8	7	2	267	8	3	5	2.0	.989	OF-132
1941			113	.311	.496	425	132	22	9	13	3.1	71	76	53	28	4	2	0	173	5	10	1	1.7	.947	OF-108
1942			152	.318	.494	591	188	31	17	13	2.2	100	98	88	30	9	1	0	287	15	4	2	2.0	.987	OF-151
1946			156	.300	.465	609	183	30	8	18	3.0	100	130	69	41	9	0	0	284	23	6	6	2.0	.981	OF-156
1947			147	.294	.452	551	162	31	13	10	1.8	100	86	59	27	4	4	0	306	15	6	5	2.2	.982	OF-142
1948			146	.321	.470	549	176	27	11	11	2.0	91	90	81	29	4	0	0	330	9	10	1	2.4	.971	OF-146
1949			151	.336	.511	568	191	34	13	13	2.3	92	96	79	37	3	1	0	330	10	6	1	2.3	.983	OF-150
1950			148	.290	.415	556	161	26	7	10	1.8	82	101	66	33	3	3	2	260	9	6	1	1.9	.978	OF-145
1951			123	.281	.391	409	115	17	8	4	1.0	48	64	68	25	7	11	2	198	10	1	3	1.7	.995	OF-106
1952			140	.300	.445	510	153	17	12	11	2.2	73	101	70	25	6	3	1	250	11	3	3	1.9	.989	OF-137
1953			143	.291	.433	492	143	34	9	6	1.2	64	89	80	28	4	7	2	235	2	1	0	1.7	.996	OF-137
1954	NY	A	69	.248	.336	125	31	4	2	1	0.8	19	19	28	21	0	31	11	37	0	1	0	0.6	.974	OF-30
1955	2 teams		NY	A	(10G – .111)		KC	A	(108G – .322)																
"	total		118	.315	.442	276	87	12	4	5	1.8	50	35	41	18	2	42	16	126	5	2	2	1.1	.985	OF-77
1956	2 teams		KC	A	(91G – .278)		NY	A	(24G – .289)																
"	total		115	.281	.392	306	86	18	5	2	0.7	52	27	34	26	2	45	11	133	2	2	0	1.2	.985	OF-76
1957	NY	A	96	.254	.368	209	53	7	1	5	2.4	24	34	40	19	0	33	8	97	2	0	0	1.0	1.000	OF-64
1958			77	.304	.435	138	42	4	1	4	2.9	21	19	21	16	2	48	13	43	1	2	0	0.6	.957	OF-35
1959	2 teams		NY	A	(74G – .172)		MIL	N	(11G – .167)																
"	total		85	.171	.342	117	20	2	0	6	5.1	10	22	16	22	1	48	7	32	0	1	0	0.4	.970	OF-32
19 yrs.			2380	.300	.453	7946	2383	413	148	169	2.1	1247	1304	1019	538	71	306	77	3925	152	82	35	1.7	.980	OF-2065

WORLD SERIES

1942	STL	N	5	.263	.474	19	5	1	0	1	5.3	3	2	3	2	0	0	0	9	1	1	0	2.2	.909	OF-5
1946			7	.320	.560	25	8	1	1	1	4.0	5	2	4	3	1	0	0	20	1	0	1	3.0	1.000	OF-7
1956	NY	A	6	.350	.500	20	7	0	0	1	5.0	6	4	4	0	0	0	0	8	1	0	0	1.5	1.000	OF-6
1957			5	.250	.333	12	3	1	0	0	0.0	1	0	3	2	0	0	0	7	0	0	0	1.4	1.000	OF-5
1958			4	.000	.000	3	0	0	0	0	0.0	2	0	1	1	0	3	0	0	0	0	0	0.0	–	
5 yrs.			27	.291	.468	79	23	3	1	3	3.8	17	8	15	8	1	3	0	44	3	1	1	1.8	.979	OF-23

Scottie Slayback

SLAYBACK, ELBERT
B. Oct. 5, 1901, Paducah, Ky. D. Nov. 30, 1979, Cincinnati, Ohio

BR TR 5'8" 165 lbs.

| 1926 | NY | N | 2 | .000 | .000 | 8 | 0 | 0 | 0 | 0 | 0.0 | 0 | 0 | 0 | 0 | 0 | 0 | 0 | 4 | 4 | 1 | 0 | 4.5 | .889 | 2B-2 |

Bruce Sloan

SLOAN, BRUCE ADAMS (Fatso)
B. Oct. 4, 1914, McAlester, Okla. D. Sept. 24, 1973, Oklahoma City, Okla.

BL TL 5'9" 195 lbs.

| 1944 | NY | N | 59 | .269 | .356 | 104 | 28 | 4 | 1 | 1 | 1.0 | 7 | 9 | 13 | 8 | 0 | 34 | 8 | 29 | 0 | 2 | 0 | 0.5 | .935 | OF-21 |

Tod Sloan

SLOAN, YALE YEASTMAN
B. Dec. 24, 1890, Madisonville, Tenn. D. Sept. 12, 1956, Akron, Ohio

BL TR 6' 175 lbs.

1913	STL	A	7	.269	.308	26	7	1	0	0	0.0	2	2	1	9	1	0	0	17	2	1	1	2.9	.950	OF-7
1917			109	.230	.281	313	72	6	2	2	0.6	32	25	28	34	8	27	5	120	10	5	4	1.2	.963	OF-77
1919			27	.238	.349	63	15	1	3	0	0.0	9	6	12	3	0	4	2	23	5	1	1	1.1	.933	OF-20
3 yrs.			143	.234	.294	402	94	8	5	2	0.5	43	33	41	46	9	31	7	160	17	8	6	1.3	.957	OF-104

Ron Slocum

SLOCUM, RONALD REECE
B. July 2, 1945, Modesto, Calif.

BR TR 6'2" 185 lbs.

1969	SD	N	13	.292	.458	24	7	1	0	1	4.2	6	5	0	5	0	1	0	3	16	1	1	1.5	.950	3B-4, 2B-4, SS-1
1970			60	.141	.268	71	10	2	2	1	1.4	8	11	8	24	0	0	0	72	58	7	9	2.3	.949	C-19, SS-17, 3B-11, 2B-9
1971			7	.000	.000	18	0	0	0	0	0.0	1	0	0	8	0	0	0	7	12	2	0	3.0	.905	3B-6
3 yrs.			80	.150	.265	113	17	3	2	2	1.8	15	16	8	37	0	1	0	82	86	10	10	2.2	.944	3B-21, C-19, SS-18, 2B-13

Craig Smajstrla

SMAJSTRLA, CRAIG LEE (Smash)
B. June 19, 1962, Houston, Tex.

BB TR 5'9" 165 lbs.

| 1988 | HOU | N | 8 | .000 | .000 | 3 | 0 | 0 | 0 | 0 | 0.0 | 2 | 0 | 0 | 1 | 0 | 1 | 0 | 0 | 0 | 0 | 0 | 0.1 | 1.000 | 2B-2 |

Charlie Small

SMALL, CHARLES ALBERT
B. Oct. 24, 1905, Auburn, Me. D. Jan. 14, 1953, Auburn, Me.

BL TR 5'11" 186 lbs.

| 1930 | BOS | A | 25 | .167 | .222 | 18 | 3 | 1 | 0 | 0 | 0.0 | 1 | 0 | 2 | 5 | 1 | 17 | 3 | 6 | 0 | 0 | 0 | 0.3 | 1.000 | OF-1 |

Hank Small

SMALL, GEORGE HENRY
B. July 31, 1953, Atlanta, Ga.

BR TR 6'3" 205 lbs.

| 1978 | ATL | N | 1 | .000 | .000 | 4 | 0 | 0 | 0 | 0 | 0.0 | 0 | 0 | 0 | 0 | 0 | 0 | 0 | 12 | 1 | 0 | 1 | 13.0 | 1.000 | 1B-1 |

Jim Small

SMALL, JAMES ARTHUR
B. Mar. 8, 1937, Portland, Ore.

BL TL 6'1½" 180 lbs.

1955	DET	A	12	.000	.000	4	0	0	0	0	0.0	2	0	1	1	0	2	0	2	1	0	0	0.3	1.000	OF-4
1956			58	.319	.407	91	29	4	2	0	0.0	13	10	6	10	0	15	7	47	0	3	0	0.9	.940	OF-26
1957			36	.214	.262	42	9	2	0	0	0.0	7	0	2	11	0	13	2	15	0	0	0	0.4	1.000	OF-14
1958	KC	A	2	.000	.000	4	0	0	0	0	0.0	0	0	1	0	0	1	0	2	0	0	0	1.0	1.000	OF-1
4 yrs.			108	.270	.340	141	38	6	2	0	0.0	22	10	10	22	0	31	9	66	1	3	0	0.6	.957	OF-45

Year	Team	Games	BA	SA	AB	H	2B	3B	HR	HR%	R	RBI	BB	SO	SB	Pinch Hit AB	H	PO	A	E	DP	TC/G	FA	G by Pos

Roy Smalley

SMALLEY, ROY FREDERICK III
Son of Roy Smalley.
B. Oct. 25, 1952, Los Angeles, Calif.

BB TR 6'1" 185 lbs.

Year	Team	Games	BA	SA	AB	H	2B	3B	HR	HR%	R	RBI	BB	SO	SB	AB	H	PO	A	E	DP	TC/G	FA	G by Pos
1975	TEX A	78	.228	.296	250	57	8	0	3	1.2	22	33	30	42	4	2	1	108	232	20	44	4.6	.944	SS-59, 2B-19, C-1
1976	2 teams		TEX A	(41G – .225)		MIN A	(103G – .271)																	
"	total	144	.259	.324	513	133	18	3	3	0.6	61	44	76	106	2	0	0	274	447	26	90	5.2	.965	SS-108, 2B-38
1977	MIN A	150	.231	.315	584	135	21	5	6	1.0	93	56	74	89	5	1	0	255	504	33	116	5.3	.958	SS-150
1978		158	.273	.433	586	160	31	3	19	3.2	80	77	85	70	2	1	1	287	527	25	121	5.3	.970	SS-157
1979		162	.271	.441	621	168	28	3	24	3.9	94	95	80	80	2	0	0	305	572	29	146	5.6	.968	SS-161, 1B-1
1980		133	.278	.405	486	135	24	1	12	2.5	64	63	65	63	3	4	1	226	448	17	103	5.2	.975	SS-125, DH-3, 1B-3
1981		56	.263	.443	167	44	7	1	7	4.2	24	22	31	24	0	5	1	62	89	8	14	2.8	.950	SS-37, DH-15, 1B-1
1982	2 teams		MIN A	(4G – .154)		NY A	(142G – .257)																	
"	total	146	.255	.413	499	127	15	2	20	4.0	57	67	71	104	0	7	0	142	367	15	55	3.6	.971	SS-93, 3B-53, DH-4, 2B-1
1983	NY A	130	.275	.452	451	124	24	1	18	4.0	70	62	58	68	3	4	1	289	295	21	58	4.7	.965	SS-91, 3B-26, 1B-22
1984	2 teams		NY A	(67G – .239)		CHI A	(47G – .170)																	
"	total	114	.212	.349	344	73	12	1	11	3.2	32	39	37	65	3	21	6	90	158	16	24	2.3	.939	3B-73, SS-16, DH-7, 1B-6
1985	MIN A	129	.258	.402	388	100	20	0	12	3.1	57	45	60	65	0	26	7	70	133	3	18	1.6	.985	DH-56, SS-49, 3B-14, 1B-1
1986		143	.246	.438	459	113	20	4	20	4.4	59	57	68	80	1	19	6	14	34	1	5	0.3	.980	DH-114, SS-19, 3B-8
1987		110	.275	.411	309	85	16	1	8	2.6	32	34	36	52	1	31	6	9	11	3	0	0.2	.870	DH-73, 3B-14, SS-4
13 yrs.		1653	.257	.395	5657	1454	244	25	163	2.9	745	694	771	908	27	121	30	2131	3817	217	794	3.7	.965	SS-1069, DH-272, 3B-188, 2B-58, 1B-34, C-1

WORLD SERIES

| 1987 | MIN A | 4 | .500 | 1.000 | 2 | 1 | 1 | 0 | 0 | 0 | 0 | 0 | 2 | 0 | 0 | 2 | 1 | 0 | 0 | 0 | 0 | 0.0 | – | |

Roy Smalley

SMALLEY, ROY FREDERICK, JR.
Father of Roy Smalley.
B. June 9, 1926, Springfield, Mo.

BR TR 6'3" 190 lbs.

1948	CHI N	124	.216	.302	361	78	11	4	4	1.1	25	36	23	76	0	0	0	189	351	34	70	4.6	.941	SS-124
1949		135	.245	.382	477	117	21	10	8	1.7	57	35	36	77	2	3	1	265	438	39	91	5.5	.947	SS-132
1950		154	.230	.413	557	128	21	9	21	3.8	58	85	49	114	2	0	0	332	541	51	115	6.0	.945	SS-154
1951		79	.231	.395	238	55	7	4	8	3.4	24	31	25	53	0	4	2	117	190	15	42	4.1	.953	SS-74
1952		87	.222	.341	261	58	14	1	5	1.9	36	30	29	58	0	5	1	139	200	17	33	4.1	.952	SS-82
1953		82	.249	.356	253	63	9	0	6	2.4	20	25	28	57	0	5	1	153	191	25	39	4.5	.932	SS-77
1954	MIL N	25	.222	.306	36	8	0	0	1	2.8	5	7	4	9	0	8	2	36	26	1	11	2.5	.984	SS-9, 2B-7, 1B-2
1955	PHI N	92	.196	.327	260	51	11	1	7	2.7	33	39	39	58	0	3	1	138	206	9	32	3.8	.975	SS-87, 3B-1, 2B-1
1956		65	.226	.315	168	38	9	3	0	0.0	14	16	23	29	0	4	0	81	142	12	32	3.6	.949	SS-60
1957		28	.161	.323	31	5	0	1	1	3.2	1	1	9	0	0	6	0	11	21	2	5	1.2	.941	SS-20
1958		1	.000	.000	2	0	0	0	0	0.0	0	0	0	1	0	0	0	3	2	2	1	7.0	.714	SS-1
11 yrs.		872	.227	.360	2644	601	103	33	61	2.3	277	305	257	541	4	38	8	1464	2308	207	471	4.6	.948	SS-820, 2B-8, 1B-2, 3B-1

Will Smalley

SMALLEY, WILLIAM DARWIN
B. June 27, 1871, Oakland, Calif. D. Oct. 11, 1891, Bay City, Mich.

BR TR

1890	CLE N	136	.213	.239	502	107	11	1	0	0.0	62	42	60	44	10	0	0	221	327	64	27	4.5	.895	3B-136
1891	WAS AA	11	.158	.211	38	6	0	1	0	0.0	5	3	5	2	0	0	0	14	23	11	2	4.4	.771	3B-9, 2B-2
2 yrs.		147	.209	.237	540	113	11	2	0	0.0	67	45	65	46	10	0	0	235	350	75	29	4.5	.886	3B-145, 2B-2

Joe Smaza

SMAZA, JOSEPH PAUL
B. July 7, 1923, Detroit, Mich. D. May 30, 1979, Royal Oak, Mich.

BL TL 5'11" 175 lbs.

| 1946 | CHI A | 2 | .200 | .200 | 5 | 1 | 0 | 0 | 0 | 0.0 | 2 | 0 | 0 | 0 | 0 | 0 | 0 | 0 | 0 | 0 | 0 | 0.0 | – | OF-1 |

Bill Smiley

SMILEY, WILLIAM B.
B. 1856, Baltimore, Md. D. July 11, 1884, Baltimore, Md.

| 1882 | 2 teams | | STL AA | (59G – .213) | | BAL AA | (16G – .148) | | | | | | | | | | | | | | | | | |
| " | total | 75 | .199 | .226 | 301 | 60 | 4 | 2 | 0 | 0.0 | 33 | | 6 | | | 0 | 0 | 193 | 212 | 60 | 28 | 6.2 | .871 | 2B-73, OF-2, SS-2 |

Al Smith

SMITH, ALPHONSE EUGENE (Fuzzy)
B. Feb. 7, 1928, Kirkwood, Mo.

BR TR 6'½" 189 lbs.

1953	CLE A	47	.240	.360	150	36	9	0	3	2.0	28	14	20	25	2	2	1	67	2	6	0	1.6	.920	OF-39, 3B-2
1954		131	.281	.435	481	135	29	6	11	2.3	101	50	88	65	2	0	0	265	34	10	4	2.4	.968	OF-109, 3B-21, SS-4
1955		154	.306	.473	607	186	27	4	22	3.6	123	77	93	77	11	0	0	242	67	12	6	2.1	.963	OF-120, 3B-45, SS-5, 2B-1
1956		141	.274	.433	526	144	26	5	16	3.0	87	71	84	72	6	1	0	270	44	10	3	2.3	.969	OF-122, 3B-28, 2B-1
1957		135	.247	.377	507	125	23	5	11	2.2	78	49	79	70	12	1	0	195	159	26	17	2.8	.932	3B-84, OF-50
1958	CHI A	139	.252	.396	480	121	23	5	12	2.5	61	58	48	77	3	3	1	249	9	8	2	1.9	.970	OF-138, 3B-1
1959		129	.237	.396	472	112	16	4	17	3.6	65	55	46	74	7	1	0	303	8	6	2	2.5	.981	OF-128, 3B-1
1960		142	.315	.451	536	169	31	3	12	2.2	80	72	50	65	8	1	0	252	5	9	2	1.9	.966	OF-141
1961		147	.278	.506	532	148	29	4	28	5.3	88	93	56	67	4	5	2	181	164	15	12	2.4	.958	3B-80, OF-71
1962		142	.292	.462	511	149	23	8	16	3.1	62	82	57	60	3	4	2	123	191	20	8	2.4	.940	3B-105, OF-39
1963	BAL A	120	.272	.405	368	100	17	1	10	2.7	45	39	32	74	9	21	6	160	6	5	0	1.4	.971	OF-97
1964	2 teams		CLE A	(61G – .162)		BOS A	(29G – .216)																	
"	total	90	.176	.310	187	33	5	1	6	3.2	25	16	21	42	0	30	4	84	16	3	1	1.1	.971	OF-56, 3B-12
12 yrs.		1517	.272	.429	5357	1458	258	46	164	3.1	843	676	674	768	67	71	15	2391	705	130	57	2.1	.960	OF-1110, 3B-379, SS-9, 2B-2

WORLD SERIES

1954	CLE A	4	.214	.429	14	3	0	0	1	7.1	2	2	2	2	0	0	0	4	0	0	0	1.0	1.000	OF-4
1959	CHI A	6	.250	.400	20	5	3	0	0	0.0	1	1	4	4	0	0	0	10	0	0	0	1.7	1.000	OF-6
2 yrs.		10	.235	.412	34	8	3	0	1	2.9	3	3	6	6	0	0	0	14	0	0	0	1.4	1.000	OF-10

Bernie Smith

SMITH, CALVIN BERNARD
B. Sept. 4, 1941, Ponchatoula, La.

BR TR 5'9" 164 lbs.

| 1970 | MIL A | 44 | .276 | .382 | 76 | 21 | 3 | 1 | 1 | 1.3 | 8 | 6 | 11 | 12 | 1 | 17 | 5 | 46 | 0 | 1 | 0 | 1.1 | .979 | OF-39 |

Year	Team		Games	BA	SA	AB	H	2B	3B	HR	HR%	R	RBI	BB	SO	SB	Pinch Hit AB	H	PO	A	E	DP	TC/G	FA	G by Pos

Bernie Smith *continued*

| 1971 | | | 15 | .139 | .250 | 36 | 5 | 1 | 0 | 1 | 2.8 | 1 | 3 | 0 | 5 | 0 | 5 | 0 | 11 | 1 | 1 | 0 | 0.9 | .923 | OF-12 |
| 2 yrs. | | | 59 | .232 | .339 | 112 | 26 | 4 | 1 | 2 | 1.8 | 9 | 9 | 11 | 17 | 1 | 22 | 5 | 57 | 1 | 2 | 0 | 1.0 | .967 | OF-51 |

Bill Smith

SMITH, WILLIAM S.
B. 1853, Guelph Ont., Canada   Deceased.   6'   168 lbs.

| 1884 | CLE | N | 1 | .000 | .000 | 3 | 0 | 0 | 0 | 0 | 0.0 | 0 | 0 | 0 | 2 | | 0 | 0 | 0 | 0 | 0 | 0 | 0.0 | – | OF-1 |

Billy Smith

SMITH, BILLY EDWARD
B. July 14, 1953, Hodge, La.   BB TR 6'2½" 185 lbs.

1975	CAL	A	59	.203	.252	143	29	5	1	0	0.0	10	14	12	27	1	0	0	95	99	14	19	3.5	.933	SS-50, 1B-6, DH-4, 3B-2
1976			13	.375	.375	8	3	0	0	0	0.0	0	0	0	2	0	3	1	0	5	3	1	0.6	.625	SS-10, DH-1
1977	BAL	A	109	.215	.300	367	79	12	2	5	1.4	44	29	33	71	3	4	1	268	278	7	80	5.1	.987	2B-104, SS-5, 1B-2, 3B-1
1978			85	.260	.384	250	65	12	2	5	2.0	29	30	27	40	3	3	0	147	210	5	43	4.3	.986	2B-83, SS-2
1979			68	.249	.434	189	47	9	4	6	3.2	18	33	15	33	1	3	0	108	151	7	35	3.9	.974	2B-63, SS-5
1981	SF	N	36	.180	.230	61	11	0	0	1	1.6	6	5	9	16	0	12	4	32	50	2	11	2.3	.976	SS-21, 2B-5, 3B-3
6 yrs.			370	.230	.335	1018	234	38	9	17	1.7	107	111	96	189	8	25	6	650	793	38	189	4.0	.974	2B-255, SS-93, 1B-8, 3B-6, DH-5

LEAGUE CHAMPIONSHIP SERIES

| 1979 | BAL | A | 1 | .000 | .000 | 4 | 0 | 0 | 0 | 0 | 0.0 | 0 | 0 | 0 | 1 | 0 | 0 | 0 | 1 | 2 | 0 | 2 | 3.0 | 1.000 | 2B-1 |

WORLD SERIES

| 1979 | BAL | A | 4 | .286 | .286 | 7 | 2 | 0 | 0 | 0 | 0.0 | 1 | 0 | 2 | 1 | 0 | 0 | 0 | 4 | 3 | 0 | 1 | 1.8 | 1.000 | 2B-2 |

Bob Smith

SMITH, ROBERT ELDRIDGE
B. Apr. 22, 1895, Rogersville, Tenn.   D. July 19, 1987, Waycross, Ga.   BR TR 5'10" 175 lbs.

1923	BOS	N	115	.251	.309	375	94	16	3	0	0.0	30	40	17	35	4	3	1	256	388	35	78	5.9	.948	SS-101, 2B-8
1924			106	.228	.297	347	79	12	3	2	0.6	32	38	15	26	5	2	0	198	313	23	59	5.0	.957	SS-80, 3B-23
1925			58	.282	.379	174	49	9	4	0	0.0	17	23	5	6	2	8	0	78	145	17	20	4.1	.929	SS-21, 2B-15, P-13, OF-1
1926			40	.298	.417	84	25	6	2	0	0.0	10	13	2	4	0	7	4	9	60	2	6	1.8	.972	P-33
1927			54	.248	.321	109	27	3	1	1	0.9	10	10	2	4	0	13	2	22	63	3	3	1.6	.966	P-41
1928			39	.250	.304	92	23	2	0	1	1.1	11	8	1	6	1	0	0	16	66	3	5	2.2	.965	P-38
1929			39	.172	.283	99	17	4	2	1	1.0	12	8	2	8	1	0	0	21	75	2	7	2.5	.980	P-34, SS-5
1930			39	.235	.259	81	19	2	0	0	0.0	7	4	0	5	0	1	0	16	47	1	3	1.6	.984	P-38
1931	CHI	N	36	.218	.241	87	19	2	0	0	0.0	7	4	5	2	0	1	0	8	55	0	4	1.8	1.000	P-36
1932			36	.238	.381	42	10	4	1	0	0.0	5	4	0	2	1	0	0	8	36	0	4	1.2	1.000	P-34, 2B-2
1933	2 teams	CIN N (23G – .200)				BOS N (14G – .200)																			P-30, SS-1
"	total		37	.200	.267	45	9	1	1	0	0.0	3	3	1	1	1	1	1	1	34	2	4	1.0	.946	P-30, SS-1
1934	BOS	N	42	.250	.278	36	9	1	0	0	0.0	5	3	0	1	0	0	0	7	30	0	2	0.9	1.000	P-39
1935			47	.270	.270	63	17	0	0	0	0.0	3	4	1	5	0	1	1	10	39	1	1	1.1	.980	P-46
1936			35	.222	.267	45	10	2	0	0	0.0	1	4	0	4	0	0	0	8	34	0	2	1.2	1.000	P-35
1937			19	.200	.200	10	2	0	0	0	0.0	1	0	1	1	0	0	0	1	6	0	0	0.4	1.000	P-18
15 yrs.			742	.242	.309	1689	409	64	17	5	0.3	154	166	52	110	16	37	9	659	1391	89	198	2.9	.958	P-435, SS-208, 2B-25, 3B-23, OF-1

WORLD SERIES

| 1932 | CHI | N | 1 | – | – | 0 | 0 | 0 | 0 | 0 | – | 0 | 0 | 0 | 0 | 0 | 0 | 0 | 0 | 0 | 0 | 0 | 0.0 | – | P-1 |

Bobby Gene Smith

SMITH, BOBBY GENE
B. May 28, 1934, Hood River, Ore.   BR TR 5'11" 180 lbs.

1957	STL	N	93	.211	.308	185	39	7	1	3	1.6	24	18	13	35	1	11	1	138	6	4	4	1.6	.973	OF-79
1958			28	.284	.386	88	25	3	0	2	2.3	8	5	2	18	1	1	0	57	2	0	0	2.1	1.000	OF-27
1959			43	.217	.317	60	13	1	1	1	1.7	11	7	1	9	0	7	2	31	3	1	1	0.8	.971	OF-32
1960	PHI	N	98	.286	.382	217	62	5	2	4	1.8	24	27	10	28	2	35	11	126	5	0	1	1.3	1.000	OF-70, 3B-1
1961			79	.253	.328	174	44	7	0	2	1.1	16	18	15	32	1	31	6	91	8	3	1	1.3	.971	OF-47
1962	3 teams	NY N (8G – .136)				CHI N (13G – .172)						STL N (91G – .231)													OF-93
"	total		112	.210	.287	181	38	9	1	1	0.6	17	16	12	22	1	18	2	86	5	0	1	0.8	1.000	OF-93
1965	CAL	A	23	.228	.281	57	13	3	0	0	0.0	1	5	2	10	0	7	2	22	1	0	0	1.0	1.000	OF-15
7 yrs.			476	.243	.331	962	234	35	5	13	1.4	101	96	55	154	5	110	24	551	30	8	8	1.2	.986	OF-363, 3B-1

Brick Smith

SMITH, BRICK DUDLEY
B. May 2, 1959, Charlotte, N. C.   BR TR 6'4" 225 lbs.

1987	SEA	A	5	.125	.125	8	1	0	0	0	0.0	1	0	2	4	0	1	1	24	2	1	1	5.4	.963	1B-3, DH-1
1988			4	.100	.100	10	1	0	0	0	0.0	1	1	0	1	0	0	0	27	4	0	3	7.8	1.000	1B-4
2 yrs.			9	.111	.111	18	2	0	0	0	0.0	2	1	2	5	0	1	1	51	6	1	4	6.4	.983	1B-7, DH-1

Broadway Aleck Smith

SMITH, ALEXANDER BENJAMIN
B. 1871, New York, N. Y.   D. July 9, 1919, New York, N. Y.   TR

1897	BKN	N	66	.300	.376	237	71	13	1	1	0.4	36	39	4		12	0	0	188	54	20	10	4.0	.924	C-43, OF-18, 1B-6
1898			52	.261	.342	199	52	6	5	0	0.0	25	23	3		7	2	0	106	33	18	5	3.0	.885	OF-26, C-20, 3B-2, 2B-2, 1B-1
1899	2 teams	BKN N (17G – .180)				BAL N (41G – .383)																			C-53, OF-2, 1B-1
"	total		58	.315	.403	181	57	6	5	0	0.0	23	31	6		7	1	0	166	40	13	4	3.8	.941	C-53, OF-2, 1B-1
1900	BKN	N	7	.240	.240	25	6	0	0	0	0.0	2	3	1		2	0	0	9	10	3	0	3.1	.864	3B-6, C-1
1901	NY	N	26	.141	.167	78	11	0	1	0	0.0	5	6	1		3	1	0	107	22	7	0	5.2	.949	C-25
1902	BAL	A	41	.234	.255	145	34	3	0	0	0.0	10	21	8		5	0	0	135	34	7	5	4.3	.960	C-27, 1B-7, OF-4, 2B-3, 3B-1
1903	BOS	A	11	.303	.333	33	10	0	0	0	0.0	4	4	0		0	1	0	44	11	4	0	5.4	.932	C-10
1904	CHI	N	10	.207	.241	29	6	1	0	0	0.0	2	1	3		1	2	0	8	3	2	1	1.3	.846	OF-6, 3B-1, C-1
1906	NY	N	16	.179	.179	28	5	0	0	0	0.0	2	1	2		1	1	0	41	7	0	4	3.0	1.000	C-8, 1B-3, OF-1
9 yrs.			287	.264	.324	955	252	30	12	1	0.1	107	130	26		38	11	0	804	214	74	30	3.8	.932	C-188, OF-57, 1B-18, 3B-10, 2B-5

Year	Team		Games	BA	SA	AB	H	2B	3B	HR	HR%	R	RBI	BB	SO	SB	Pinch Hit AB	Pinch Hit H	PO	A	E	DP	TC/G	FA	G by Pos

Bull Smith

SMITH, LEWIS OSCAR
B. Aug. 20, 1880, Plum, W. Va.   D. May 1, 1928, Charleston, W. Va.
BR TR 6'   180 lbs.

Year	Team		Games	BA	SA	AB	H	2B	3B	HR	HR%	R	RBI	BB	SO	SB	PH AB	PH H	PO	A	E	DP	TC/G	FA	G by Pos
1904	PIT	N	13	.143	.190	42	6	0	1	0	0.0	2	0			1	0	0	22	2	4	0	2.2	.857	OF-13
1906	CHI	N	1	.000	.000	1	0	0	0	0	0.0	0	0	0	0	0	1	0	0	0	0	0	0.0	–	
1911	WAS	A	1	–	–	0	0	0	0	0	–	0	0	0	0	0	0	0	0	0	0	0	0.0	–	
3 yrs.			15	.140	.186	43	6	0	1	0	0.0	2	0			1	0	1	0	22	2	4	0	1.9	.857	OF-13

Carr Smith

SMITH, EMANUEL CARR
B. Apr. 8, 1901, Kernersville, N. C.   D. Apr. 14, 1989, Miami, Fla.
BR TR 6'1"   175 lbs.

Year	Team		Games	BA	SA	AB	H	2B	3B	HR	HR%	R	RBI	BB	SO	SB	PH AB	PH H	PO	A	E	DP	TC/G	FA	G by Pos
1923	WAS	A	5	.111	.222	9	1	1	0	0	0.0	0	1	0	0	0	1	0	4	0	0	0	0.8	1.000	OF-4
1924			5	.200	.200	10	2	0	0	0	0.0	1	0	0	3	0	1	0	3	0	0	0	0.6	1.000	OF-4
2 yrs.			10	.158	.211	19	3	1	0	0	0.0	1	1	0	3	0	2	0	7	0	0	0	0.7	1.000	OF-8

Charley Smith

SMITH, CHARLES WILLIAM
B. Sept. 15, 1937, Charleston, S. C.
BR TR 6'1"   170 lbs.

Year	Team		Games	BA	SA	AB	H	2B	3B	HR	HR%	R	RBI	BB	SO	SB	PH AB	PH H	PO	A	E	DP	TC/G	FA	G by Pos
1960	LA	N	18	.167	.217	60	10	1	1	0	0.0	2	5	1	15	0	0	0	14	27	2	2	2.4	.953	3B-18
1961	2 teams		121	LA N (9G – .250)		PHI N (112G – .248)																			
"	total		121	.248	.375	435	108	14	4	11	2.5	47	50	24	82	3	5	1	107	233	28	28	3.0	.924	3B-98, SS-17
1962	CHI	A	65	.207	.276	145	30	4	0	2	1.4	11	17	9	32	0	13	2	26	76	6	12	1.7	.944	3B-54
1963			4	.286	.571	7	2	0	1	0	0.0	0	1	0	2	0	3	1	3	5	0	4	2.0	1.000	SS-1
1964	2 teams		129	CHI A (2G – .143)		NY N (127G – .239)																			
"	total		129	.238	.402	450	107	12	1	20	4.4	45	58	20	102	2	7	1	159	231	31	28	3.3	.926	3B-87, SS-36, OF-13
1965	NY	N	135	.244	.393	499	122	20	3	16	3.2	49	62	17	123	2	3	0	123	288	18	29	3.2	.958	3B-131, SS-6, 2B-1
1966	STL	N	116	.266	.396	391	104	13	4	10	2.6	34	43	22	81	0	8	3	89	216	11	27	2.7	.965	3B-107, SS-1
1967	NY	A	135	.224	.336	425	95	15	3	9	2.1	38	38	32	110	0	20	6	92	283	21	22	2.9	.947	3B-115
1968			46	.229	.357	70	16	4	1	1	1.4	2	7	5	18	0	31	10	19	30	2	3	1.1	.961	3B-13
1969	CHI	N	2	.000	.000	2	0	0	0	0	0.0	0	0	0	2	0	0	0	0	0	0	0	0.0	–	
10 yrs.			771	.239	.370	2484	594	83	18	69	2.8	228	281	130	565	7	92	25	632	1389	119	155	2.8	.944	3B-623, SS-61, OF-13, 2B-1

Chris Smith

SMITH, CHRISTOPHER WILLIAM
B. July 18, 1957, Torrance, Calif.
BB TR 6'   185 lbs.

Year	Team		Games	BA	SA	AB	H	2B	3B	HR	HR%	R	RBI	BB	SO	SB	PH AB	PH H	PO	A	E	DP	TC/G	FA	G by Pos
1981	MON	N	7	.000	.000	7	0	0	0	0	0.0	0	0	0	2	0	7	0	0	1	0	0	0.1	1.000	2B-1
1982			2	.000	.000	2	0	0	0	0	0.0	0	0	0	1	0	2	0	0	0	0	0	0.0	–	
1983	SF	N	22	.328	.493	67	22	6	1	1	1.5	13	11	7	12	0	3	3	118	8	3	6	5.9	.977	1B-15, OF-4, 3B-1
3 yrs.			31	.289	.434	76	22	6	1	1	1.3	13	11	7	15	0	12	3	118	9	3	6	4.2	.977	1B-15, OF-4, 3B-1, 2B-1

Dick Smith

SMITH, RICHARD ARTHUR
B. May 17, 1939, Lebanon, Ore.
BR TR 6'2"   205 lbs.

Year	Team		Games	BA	SA	AB	H	2B	3B	HR	HR%	R	RBI	BB	SO	SB	PH AB	PH H	PO	A	E	DP	TC/G	FA	G by Pos
1963	NY	N	20	.238	.286	42	10	0	1	0	0.0	4	3	5	10	3	5	1	26	0	0	0	1.3	1.000	OF-10, 1B-2
1964			46	.223	.309	94	21	6	1	0	0.0	14	3	1	29	6	8	1	151	11	2	11	3.6	.988	1B-18, OF-13
1965	LA	N	10	.000	.000	6	0	0	0	0	0.0	0	1	0	3	0	0	0	1	0	0	0	0.1	1.000	OF-9
3 yrs.			76	.218	.289	142	31	6	2	0	0.0	18	7	6	42	9	13	2	178	11	2	11	2.5	.990	OF-32, 1B-20

Dick Smith

SMITH, RICHARD HARRISON
B. July 21, 1927, Blandburg, Pa.
BR TR 5'8"   160 lbs.

Year	Team		Games	BA	SA	AB	H	2B	3B	HR	HR%	R	RBI	BB	SO	SB	PH AB	PH H	PO	A	E	DP	TC/G	FA	G by Pos
1951	PIT	N	12	.174	.174	46	8	0	0	0	0.0	2	4	8	8	0	0	0	14	30	3	6	3.9	.936	3B-12
1952			29	.106	.121	66	7	1	0	0	0.0	8	5	9	3	0	2	0	24	50	3	8	2.7	.961	3B-16, SS-4, 2B-4
1953			13	.163	.209	43	7	0	1	0	0.0	4	2	6	6	0	0	0	18	56	3	10	5.9	.961	SS-13
1954			12	.097	.194	31	3	1	1	0	0.0	2	0	6	5	0	3	0	7	21	2	3	2.5	.933	3B-9
1955			4	–	–	0	0	0	0	0	–	1	0	1	0	0	0	0	0	0	0	0	–	–	SS-1
5 yrs.			70	.134	.167	186	25	2	2	0	0.0	17	11	30	22	0	5	0	63	157	11	27	3.3	.952	3B-37, SS-18, 2B-4

Dick Smith

SMITH, RICHARD KELLY
B. Aug. 25, 1944, Lincolnton, N. C.
BR TR 6'5"   200 lbs.

Year	Team		Games	BA	SA	AB	H	2B	3B	HR	HR%	R	RBI	BB	SO	SB	PH AB	PH H	PO	A	E	DP	TC/G	FA	G by Pos
1969	WAS	A	21	.107	.107	28	3	0	0	0	0.0	2	0	4	7	0	8	0	10	0	1	0	0.5	.909	OF-9

Dwight Smith

SMITH, JOHN DWIGHT
B. Nov. 8, 1963, Tallahassee, Fla.
BL TR 5'11"   175 lbs.

Year	Team		Games	BA	SA	AB	H	2B	3B	HR	HR%	R	RBI	BB	SO	SB	PH AB	PH H	PO	A	E	DP	TC/G	FA	G by Pos
1989	CHI	N	109	.324	.493	343	111	19	6	9	2.6	52	52	31	51	9	15	8	188	7	5	3	1.8	.975	OF-102

LEAGUE CHAMPIONSHIP SERIES

Year	Team		Games	BA	SA	AB	H	2B	3B	HR	HR%	R	RBI	BB	SO	SB	PH AB	PH H	PO	A	E	DP	TC/G	FA	G by Pos
1989	CHI	N	4	.200	.267	15	3	1	0	0	0.0	2	0	2	2	1	0	0	10	0	0	0	2.5	1.000	OF-4

Earl Smith

SMITH, EARL CALVIN
B. Mar. 14, 1928, Sunnyside, Wash.
BR TR 6'   185 lbs.

Year	Team		Games	BA	SA	AB	H	2B	3B	HR	HR%	R	RBI	BB	SO	SB	PH AB	PH H	PO	A	E	DP	TC/G	FA	G by Pos
1955	PIT	N	5	.063	.063	16	1	0	0	0	0.0	1	0	4	2	0	0	0	11	0	0	0	2.2	1.000	OF-5

Earl Smith

SMITH, EARL LEONARD
B. Jan. 20, 1891, Oak Hill, Ohio   D. Mar. 14, 1943, Portsmouth, Ohio
BB TR 5'11"   170 lbs.

Year	Team		Games	BA	SA	AB	H	2B	3B	HR	HR%	R	RBI	BB	SO	SB	PH AB	PH H	PO	A	E	DP	TC/G	FA	G by Pos
1916	CHI	N	14	.259	.370	27	7	1	0	0	0.0	2	4	2	5	1	7	1	4	0	1	0	0.4	.800	OF-7
1917	STL	A	52	.281	.387	199	56	7	7	0	0.0	31	10	15	21	5	1	1	114	12	3	5	2.5	.977	OF-51
1918			89	.269	.339	286	77	10	5	0	0.0	28	32	13	16	13	8	4	164	14	9	4	2.1	.952	OF-81
1919			88	.250	.349	252	63	12	5	1	0.4	21	36	18	27	1	14	5	155	13	5	4	2.0	.971	OF-68
1920			103	.306	.436	353	108	21	8	3	0.8	45	55	13	18	11	16	2	107	150	23	3	2.7	.918	3B-70, OF-15
1921	2 teams		84	STL A (25G – .333)		WAS A (59G – .217)																			
"	total		84	.252	.364	258	65	9	4	4	1.6	27	26	13	23	1	20	6	113	34	13	2	1.9	.919	OF-47, 3B-14
1922	WAS	A	65	.259	.351	205	53	12	4	1	0.5	22	23	8	17	4	10	2	92	16	9	3	1.8	.923	OF-49, 3B-1
7 yrs.			495	.272	.375	1580	429	72	32	9	0.6	176	186	82	127	36	76	21	749	239	63	21	2.1	.940	OF-318, 3B-85

Earl Smith

SMITH, EARL SUTTON (Oil)
B. Feb. 14, 1897, Hot Springs, Ark.   D. June 8, 1963, Little Rock, Ark.
BL TR 5'10½"   180 lbs.

Year	Team		Games	BA	SA	AB	H	2B	3B	HR	HR%	R	RBI	BB	SO	SB	Pinch Hit AB	Pinch Hit H	PO	A	E	DP	TC/G	FA	G by Pos

Earl Smith *continued*

Year	Team		Games	BA	SA	AB	H	2B	3B	HR	HR%	R	RBI	BB	SO	SB	PH AB	PH H	PO	A	E	DP	TC/G	FA	G by Pos
1919	NY	N	21	.250	.361	36	9	2	1	0	0.0	5	8	3	3	1	6	0	26	10	1	0	1.8	.973	C-14, 2B-1
1920			91	.294	.340	262	77	7	1	1	0.4	20	30	18	16	5	8	4	252	73	8	12	3.7	.976	C-82
1921			89	.336	.537	229	77	8	4	10	4.4	35	51	27	8	4	8	3	195	56	9	4	2.9	.965	C-78
1922			90	.278	.474	234	65	11	4	9	3.8	29	39	37	12	1	12	3	214	56	6	3	3.1	.978	C-75
1923	2 teams		NY N (24G – .206)			BOS N (72G – .288)																			
"	total		96	.276	.418	225	62	16	2	4	1.8	24	23	26	11	0	35	6	173	58	6	9	2.5	.975	C-46
1924	2 teams		BOS N (33G – .271)			PIT N (39G – .369)																			
"	total		72	.335	.494	170	57	13	1	4	2.4	13	29	19	7	2	21	10	167	36	7	4	2.9	.967	C-48
1925	PIT	N	109	.313	.471	329	103	22	3	8	2.4	34	64	31	13	4	12	5	317	77	13	15	3.7	.968	C-96
1926			105	.346	.438	292	101	17	2	2	0.7	29	46	28	7	1	7	5	307	63	14	10	3.7	.964	C-98
1927			66	.270	.376	189	51	3	1	5	2.6	16	25	21	11	0	5	3	187	32	3	2	3.4	.986	C-61
1928	2 teams		PIT N (32G – .247)			STL N (24G – .224)																			
"	total		56	.238	.336	143	34	8	0	2	1.4	11	18	16	11	0	8	0	130	17	3	4	2.7	.980	C-46
1929	STL	N	57	.345	.421	145	50	8	0	1	0.7	9	22	18	6	0	7	2	131	21	6	1	2.8	.962	C-50
1930			8	.000	.000	10	0	0	0	0	0.0	0	0	3	1	0	0	0	18	3	2	0	2.9	.913	C-6
12 yrs.			860	.303	.432	2264	686	115	19	46	2.0	225	355	247	106	18	129	41	2117	502	78	64	3.1	.971	C-700, 2B-1

WORLD SERIES

Year	Team		Games	BA	SA	AB	H	2B	3B	HR	HR%	R	RBI	BB	SO	SB	PH AB	PH H	PO	A	E	DP	TC/G	FA	G by Pos
1921	NY	N	3	.000	.000	7	0	0	0	0	0.0	0	0	1	0	0	1	0	7	2	1	1	3.3	.900	C-2
1922			4	.143	.143	7	1	0	0	0	0.0	0	0	0	0	0	3	0	2	1	0	0	0.8	1.000	C-1
1925	PIT	N	6	.350	.400	20	7	1	0	0	0.0	0	1	0	2	0	0	0	28	7	1	1	6.0	.972	C-6
1927			3	.000	.000	8	0	0	0	0	0.0	0	0	0	0	0	1	0	10	1	1	0	4.0	.917	C-2
1928	STL	N	1	.750	.750	4	3	0	0	0	0.0	0	0	1	0	0	0	0	3	1	0	0	4.0	1.000	C-1
5 yrs.			17	.239	.261	46	11	1	0	0	0.0	0	0	2	4	0	5	0	50	12	3	2	3.8	.954	C-12

Edgar Smith

SMITH, ALBERT EDGAR
B. Oct. 15, 1860, North Haven, Conn. Deceased.   TR 6'   200 lbs.

Year	Team		Games	BA	SA	AB	H	2B	3B	HR	HR%	R	RBI	BB	SO	SB	PH AB	PH H	PO	A	E	DP	TC/G	FA	G by Pos
1883	BOS	N	30	.217	.313	115	25	5	3	0	0.0	10	16	5	11		0	0	56	3	6	3	2.2	.908	OF-30, C-1

Edgar Smith

SMITH, EDGAR EUGENE
B. June 12, 1862, Providence, R. I. D. Nov. 3, 1892, Providence, R. I.   BR TR 5'10" 160 lbs.

Year	Team		Games	BA	SA	AB	H	2B	3B	HR	HR%	R	RBI	BB	SO	SB	PH AB	PH H	PO	A	E	DP	TC/G	FA	G by Pos
1883	2 teams		PRO N (2G – .222)			PHI N (1G – .750)																			
"	total		3	.385	.462	13	5	1	0	0	0.0	3		0	2		0	0	3	0	1	0	1.3	.750	OF-3, 1B-2, P-1
1884	WAS	AA	14	.088	.123	57	5	0	1	0	0.0	5		1			0	0	19	14	9	4	3.0	.786	OF-12, P-3
1885	PRO	N	1	.250	.250	4	1	0	0	0	0.0	0		0			0	0	0	3	1	0	4.0	.750	P-1
1890	CLE	N	8	.292	.375	24	7	0	1	0	0.0	2	4	4	1	0	0	0	3	14	2	1	2.4	.895	P-6, OF-2
4 yrs.			26	.184	.235	98	18	1	2	0	0.0	10	4	5	3	0	0	0	25	31	13	5	2.7	.812	OF-17, P-11, 1B-2

Elmer Smith

SMITH, ELMER ELLSWORTH
B. Mar. 23, 1868, Pittsburgh, Pa. D. Nov. 3, 1945, Pittsburgh, Pa.   BL TL 5'11" 178 lbs.

Year	Team		Games	BA	SA	AB	H	2B	3B	HR	HR%	R	RBI	BB	SO	SB	PH AB	PH H	PO	A	E	DP	TC/G	FA	G by Pos
1886	CIN	AA	10	.281	.375	32	9	1	1	0	0.0	7		9			0	0	1	4	2	0	0.7	.714	P-10, OF-1
1887			52	.253	.371	186	47	10	6	0	0.0	26		11		5	0	0	9	67	13	2	1.7	.854	P-52, OF-2
1888			40	.225	.271	129	29	4	1	0	0.0	15	9	20		2	0	0	4	58	12	0	1.9	.838	P-40, OF-2
1889			29	.277	.410	83	23	3	1	2	2.4	12	17	7	18	1	0	0	2	21	5	0	1.0	.821	P-29
1892	PIT	N	138	.274	.387	511	140	18	14	4	0.8	86	63	82	43	22	0	0	232	38	37	0	2.2	.879	OF-124, P-17
1893			128	.346	.525	518	179	26	23	7	1.4	121	103	77	23	26	0	0	271	20	25	7	2.5	.921	OF-128
1894			125	.356	.538	489	174	33	19	6	1.2	128	72	65	12	33	0	0	275	18	21	8	2.5	.933	OF-125, P-1
1895			124	.302	.388	480	145	14	12	1	0.2	88	81	55	25	35	1	0	250	16	31	2	2.4	.896	OF-123
1896			122	.362	.500	484	175	21	14	6	1.2	121	94	74	18	33	0	0	302	14	18	6	2.7	.946	OF-122
1897			123	.310	.463	467	145	19	17	6	1.3	99	54	70		25	0	0	245	19	28	1	2.4	.904	OF-123
1898	CIN	N	123	.342	.432	486	166	21	10	1	0.2	79	66	69		20	0	0	280	15	16	5	2.5	.949	OF-123, P-1
1899			87	.298	.381	339	101	13	6	1	0.3	65	24	47		10	0	0	178	12	16	3	2.4	.922	OF-87
1900	2 teams		CIN N (29G – .279)			NY N (87G – .260)																			
"	total		116	.265	.369	423	112	13	11	3	0.7	62	52	42		19	4	0	154	13	10	3	1.5	.944	OF-110
1901	2 teams		PIT N (4G – .000)			BOS N (18G – .175)																			
"	total		22	.159	.222	63	10	2	1	0	0.0	5	3	8		2	4	0	21	1	4	0	1.2	.846	OF-16
14 yrs.			1239	.310	.434	4690	1455	198	136	37	0.8	914	638	636	139	233	9	0	2224	316	238	37	2.2	.914	OF-1086, P-150

Elmer Smith

SMITH, ELMER JOHN
B. Sept. 21, 1892, Sandusky, Ohio D. Aug. 3, 1984, Columbia, Ky.   BL TR 5'10" 165 lbs.

Year	Team		Games	BA	SA	AB	H	2B	3B	HR	HR%	R	RBI	BB	SO	SB	PH AB	PH H	PO	A	E	DP	TC/G	FA	G by Pos
1914	CLE	A	13	.321	.377	53	17	3	0	0	0.0	8	11	1	11	1	0	0	29	2	0	0	2.4	1.000	OF-13
1915			144	.248	.366	476	118	23	12	3	0.6	37	67	36	75	10	19	6	202	15	18	4	1.6	.923	OF-123
1916	2 teams		CLE A (79G – .277)			WAS A (45G – .214)																			
"	total		124	.249	.386	381	95	25	6	5	1.3	37	67	36	63	7	18	7	152	12	4	4	1.4	.976	OF-102
1917	2 teams		WAS A (35G – .222)			CLE A (64G – .261)																			
"	total		99	.245	.338	278	68	9	4	3	1.1	29	39	18	32	7	26	4	124	9	8	2	1.4	.943	OF-69
1919	CLE	A	114	.278	.438	395	110	24	6	9	2.3	60	54	41	30	15	3	0	167	12	8	8	1.6	.957	OF-111
1920			129	.316	.520	456	144	37	10	12	2.6	82	103	53	35	5	0	0	217	8	7	1	1.8	.970	OF-129
1921			129	.290	.508	431	125	28	9	16	3.7	98	84	56	46	0	0	0	183	16	6	1	1.6	.971	OF-127
1922	2 teams		BOS A (73G – .286)			NY A (21G – .185)																			
"	total		94	.275	.453	258	71	13	6	7	2.7	44	37	28	26	1	21	6	130	8	4	4	1.6	.945	OF-69
1923	NY	A	70	.306	.475	183	56	6	2	7	3.8	30	35	21	21	3	21	11	86	5	5	2	1.4	.948	OF-47
1925	CIN	N	96	.271	.451	284	77	13	7	8	2.8	47	46	28	20	6	13	5	139	8	5	5	1.6	.967	OF-80
10 yrs.			1012	.276	.437	3195	881	181	62	70	2.2	469	540	319	359	54	123	39	1429	95	69	31	1.6	.957	OF-870

WORLD SERIES

Year	Team		Games	BA	SA	AB	H	2B	3B	HR	HR%	R	RBI	BB	SO	SB	PH AB	PH H	PO	A	E	DP	TC/G	FA	G by Pos
1920	CLE	A	5	.308	.692	13	4	0	0	1	7.7	1	6	1	1	0	1	0	7	1	0	0	1.6	1.000	OF-5
1922	NY	A	2	.000	.000	2	0	0	0	0	0.0	0	0	0	2	0	2	0	0	0	0	0	0.0	–	
2 yrs.			7	.267	.600	15	4	0	0	1	6.7	1	6	1	3	0	3	0	7	1	0	0	1.1	1.000	OF-5

Ernie Smith

SMITH, ERNEST HENRY
B. Oct. 11, 1899, Totowa, N. J. D. Apr. 6, 1973, Brooklyn, N. Y.   BR TR 5'8" 155 lbs.

Year	Team		Games	BA	SA	AB	H	2B	3B	HR	HR%	R	RBI	BB	SO	SB	PH AB	PH H	PO	A	E	DP	TC/G	FA	G by Pos
1930	CHI	A	24	.241	.278	79	19	3	0	0	0.0	5	3	5	6	2	3	1	45	58	9	8	4.7	.920	SS-21

Year	Team	Games	BA	SA	AB	H	2B	3B	HR	HR%	R	RBI	BB	SO	SB	Pinch Hit AB	Pinch Hit H	PO	A	E	DP	TC/G	FA	G by Pos

Frank Smith

SMITH, FRANK L.
B. Nov. 24, 1857, Canada D. Oct. 11, 1928, Canandaigua, N. Y.

Year	Team	Games	BA	SA	AB	H	2B	3B	HR	HR%	R	RBI	BB	SO	SB	AB	H	PO	A	E	DP	TC/G	FA	G by Pos
1884	PIT AA	10	.250	.306	36	9	0	1	0	0.0	3		0			0	0	39	7	4	1	5.0	.920	C-7, OF-3

Fred Smith

SMITH, FRED VINCENT   BR TR 5'11½" 185 lbs.
Brother of Charlie Smith.
B. July 29, 1891, Cleveland, Ohio D. May 28, 1961, Cleveland, Ohio

Year	Team	Games	BA	SA	AB	H	2B	3B	HR	HR%	R	RBI	BB	SO	SB	AB	H	PO	A	E	DP	TC/G	FA	G by Pos
1913	BOS N	92	.228	.281	285	65	9	3	0	0.0	35	27	29	55	7	2	1	104	150	27	11	3.1	.904	3B-59, 2B-14, SS-11, OF-4
1914	BUF F	145	.220	.300	473	104	12	10	2	0.4	48	45	49		24	0	0	216	282	36	23	3.7	.933	3B-127, SS-19, 1B-1
1915	2 teams	BUF	F (35G – .237)				BKN	F	(110G – .247)															
"	total	145	.244	.351	499	122	18	10	5	1.0	49	69	38		23	2	0	301	419	62	43	5.4	.921	SS-126, 3B-16
1917	STL N	56	.182	.224	165	30	0	2	1	0.6	11	17	17	22	4	1	0	63	113	9	6	3.3	.951	3B-51, 2B-2, SS-1
4 yrs.		438	.226	.305	1422	321	39	25	8	0.6	143	158	133	77	58	5	1	684	964	134	83	4.1	.925	3B-253, SS-157, 2B-16, OF-4, 1B-1

George Smith

SMITH, GEORGE CORNELIUS   BR TR 5'10" 170 lbs.
B. July 7, 1937, St. Petersburg, Fla. D. June 15, 1987, St. Petersburg, Fla.

Year	Team	Games	BA	SA	AB	H	2B	3B	HR	HR%	R	RBI	BB	SO	SB	AB	H	PO	A	E	DP	TC/G	FA	G by Pos
1963	DET A	52	.216	.287	171	37	8	2	0	0.0	16	17	18	34	4	0	0	120	157	5	28	5.4	.982	2B-52
1964		5	.286	.286	7	2	0	0	0	0.0	0	2	1	4	1	1	1	2	5	0	2	1.4	1.000	2B-3
1965		32	.094	.151	53	5	0	0	1	1.9	6	1	3	18	1	0	5	33	33	1	10	2.1	.985	2B-22, SS-3, 3B-3
1966	BOS A	128	.213	.340	403	86	19	4	8	2.0	41	37	37	86	4	4	0	268	331	24	85	4.9	.961	2B-109, SS-19
4 yrs.		217	.205	.309	634	130	27	6	9	1.4	64	57	59	142	9	10	1	423	526	30	125	4.5	.969	2B-186, SS-22, 3B-3

Germany Smith

SMITH, GEORGE J.   BR TR 6' 175 lbs.
B. Apr. 21, 1863, Pittsburgh, Pa. D. Dec. 1, 1927, Altoona, Pa.

Year	Team	Games	BA	SA	AB	H	2B	3B	HR	HR%	R	RBI	BB	SO	SB	AB	H	PO	A	E	DP	TC/G	FA	G by Pos
1884	2 teams	ALT	U (25G – .315)				CLE	N	(72G – .254)															
"	total	97	.271	.381	399	108	22	5	4	1.0	40	26	3	45		0	0	195	331	69	27	6.1	.884	SS-55, 2B-42, P-1
1885	BKN AA	108	.258	.379	419	108	17	11	4	1.0	63		10			0	0	161	455	81	23	6.5	.884	SS-108
1886		105	.246	.329	426	105	17	6	2	0.5	66		19			0	0	142	381	85	30	5.8	.860	SS-105, OF-1, C-1
1887		103	.294	.439	435	128	19	16	4	0.9	79		13		26	0	0	161	389	72	23	6.0	.884	SS-101, 3B-2
1888		103	.214	.296	402	86	10	7	3	0.7	47	61	22		27	0	0	155	352	94	29	5.8	.844	SS-103, 2B-1
1889		121	.231	.314	446	103	22	3	3	0.7	89	53	40	42	35	0	0	182	417	67	37	5.5	.899	SS-120, OF-1
1890	BKN N	129	.191	.231	481	92	6	5	1	0.2	76	47	42	23	24	0	0	232	468	74	49	6.0	.904	SS-129
1891	CIN N	138	.201	.260	512	103	11	5	3	0.6	50	53	38	32	16	0	0	240	507	75	40	6.0	.909	SS-138
1892		139	.239	.336	506	121	13	6	8	1.6	58	63	42	52	19	0	0	239	561	70	55	6.3	.920	SS-139
1893		130	.236	.314	500	118	18	6	3	0.6	63	56	38	20	14	0	0	250	500	53	67	6.2	.934	SS-130
1894		127	.263	.371	482	127	33	5	3	0.6	73	76	41	28	15	0	0	233	501	72	75	6.3	.911	SS-127
1895		127	.300	.394	503	151	23	6	4	0.8	75	74	34	24	13	0	0	251	457	59	58	6.0	.923	SS-127
1896		120	.287	.388	456	131	22	9	2	0.4	65	71	28	22	22	0	0	207	407	49	47	5.5	.926	SS-120
1897	BKN N	112	.201	.255	428	86	17	3	0	0.0	47	29	14		1	0	0	201	399	61	36	5.9	.908	SS-112
1898	STL N	51	.159	.204	157	25	2	1	1	0.6	16	9	24		1	0	0	79	167	26	14	5.3	.904	SS-51
15 yrs.		1710	.243	.331	6552	1592	252	94	45	0.7	907	618	408	288	213	0	0	2928	6292	7	610	5.4	.999	SS-1665, 2B-43, OF-2, 3B-2, C-1, P-1

Greg Smith

SMITH, GREGORY ALAN   BB TR 5'11" 170 lbs.
B. Apr. 5, 1967, Baltimore, Md.

Year	Team	Games	BA	SA	AB	H	2B	3B	HR	HR%	R	RBI	BB	SO	SB	AB	H	PO	A	E	DP	TC/G	FA	G by Pos
1989	CHI N	4	.400	.400	5	2	0	0	0	0.0	1	2	0	0	0	1	0	4	3	2	1	2.3	.778	2B-2

Hal Smith

SMITH, HAROLD RAYMOND (Cura)   BR TR 5'10½" 186 lbs.
B. June 1, 1931, Barling, Ark.

Year	Team	Games	BA	SA	AB	H	2B	3B	HR	HR%	R	RBI	BB	SO	SB	AB	H	PO	A	E	DP	TC/G	FA	G by Pos
1956	STL N	75	.282	.401	227	64	12	0	5	2.2	27	23	15	22	1	9	3	300	34	6	3	4.5	.982	C-66
1957		100	.279	.351	333	93	12	3	2	0.6	25	37	18	18	2	4	0	468	42	5	8	5.2	.990	C-97
1958		77	.227	.268	220	50	4	1	1	0.5	13	24	14	14	0	5	0	346	22	4	4	4.8	.989	C-71
1959		142	.270	.403	452	122	15	3	13	2.9	35	50	15	28	2	1	0	758	60	9	13	5.8	.989	C-141
1960		127	.228	.294	337	77	16	0	2	0.6	20	28	29	33	1	5	1	664	61	7	9	5.8	.990	C-124
1961		45	.248	.296	125	31	4	1	0	0.0	6	10	11	12	0	1	0	261	28	2	6	6.5	.993	C-45
1965	PIT N	4	.000	.000	3	0	0	0	0	0.0	0	0	0	1	0	0	0	13	0	0	0	3.3	1.000	C-4
7 yrs.		570	.258	.345	1697	437	63	8	23	1.4	126	172	102	128	6	25	6	2810	247	33	43	5.4	.989	C-548

Hal Smith

SMITH, HAROLD WAYNE   BR TR 6' 195 lbs.
B. Dec. 7, 1930, West Frankfort, Ill.

Year	Team	Games	BA	SA	AB	H	2B	3B	HR	HR%	R	RBI	BB	SO	SB	AB	H	PO	A	E	DP	TC/G	FA	G by Pos
1955	BAL A	135	.271	.373	424	115	23	4	4	0.9	41	52	30	21	1	11	4	497	58	8	9	4.2	.986	C-125
1956	2 teams	BAL	A (78G – .262)				KC	A	(36G – .275)															
"	total	114	.267	.380	371	99	23	2	5	1.3	31	42	20	34	2	8	0	496	55	5	14	4.9	.991	C-107
1957	KC A	107	.303	.483	360	109	26	0	13	3.6	41	41	14	44	2	8	1	463	55	9	8	4.9	.983	C-103
1958		99	.273	.394	315	86	19	2	5	1.6	32	46	25	47	0	10	5	313	112	8	19	4.4	.982	3B-43, C-31, 1B-14
1959		108	.288	.380	292	84	12	0	5	1.7	36	31	34	39	0	12	4	210	129	15	15	3.3	.958	3B-77, C-22
1960	PIT N	77	.295	.508	258	76	18	2	11	4.3	37	45	22	48	1	6	2	356	30	6	5	5.1	.985	C-71
1961		67	.223	.321	193	43	10	0	3	1.6	12	26	11	38	0	2	1	290	18	3	1	4.6	.990	C-65
1962	HOU N	109	.235	.380	345	81	14	0	12	3.5	32	35	24	55	0	14	3	580	72	10	10	6.1	.985	C-92, 3B-6, 1B-2
1963		31	.241	.276	58	14	2	0	0	0.0	1	2	4	15	0	19	3	65	2	1	1	2.2	.985	C-11
1964	CIN N	32	.121	.136	66	8	1	0	0	0.0	6	3	12	20	1	12	2	105	8	2	1	3.6	.983	C-20
10 yrs.		879	.267	.394	2682	715	148	10	58	2.2	269	323	196	361	7	102	25	3375	539	67	83	4.5	.983	C-647, 3B-126, 1B-16

WORLD SERIES

Year	Team	Games	BA	SA	AB	H	2B	3B	HR	HR%	R	RBI	BB	SO	SB	AB	H	PO	A	E	DP	TC/G	FA	G by Pos
1960	PIT N	3	.375	.750	8	3	0	0	1	12.5	1	3	0	0	0	0	0	14	1	0	0	5.0	1.000	C-3

Hap Smith

SMITH, HENRY JOSEPH   BL TR 6' 185 lbs.
B. July 14, 1883, Coquille, Ore. D. Feb. 26, 1961, San Jose, Calif.

Year	Team	Games	BA	SA	AB	H	2B	3B	HR	HR%	R	RBI	BB	SO	SB	AB	H	PO	A	E	DP	TC/G	FA	G by Pos
1910	BKN N	35	.237	.263	76	18	2	0	0	0.0	6	5	4	14	4	17	3	33	4	1	2	1.1	.974	OF-16

Year	Team		Games	BA	SA	AB	H	2B	3B	HR	HR%	R	RBI	BB	SO	SB	Pinch Hit AB	H	PO	A	E	DP	TC/G	FA	G by Pos

Harry Smith

SMITH, HARRY THOMAS   BR TR
B. Oct. 31, 1874, Yorkshire, England   D. Feb. 17, 1933, Salem, N. J.
Manager 1909.

Year	Team		Games	BA	SA	AB	H	2B	3B	HR	HR%	R	RBI	BB	SO	SB	AB	H	PO	A	E	DP	TC/G	FA	G by Pos
1901	PHI	A	11	.324	.353	34	11	1	0	0	0.0	3	3	2		1	1	1	21	10	3	0	3.1	.912	C-9, OF-1
1902	PIT	N	50	.189	.222	185	35	4	1	0	0.0	14	12	4		4	0	0	265	49	9	3	6.5	.972	C-50
1903			61	.175	.208	212	37	3	2	0	0.0	15	19	12		2	0	0	259	75	9	2	5.6	.974	C-60, OF-1
1904			47	.248	.284	141	35	3	1	0	0.0	17	18	16		5	0	0	155	61	8	7	4.8	.964	C-44, OF-3
1905			1	.000	.000	3	0	0	0	0	0.0	0	1	0		1	0	0	4	1	0	1	5.0	1.000	C-1
1906			1	.000	.000	1	0	0	0	0	0.0	0	0	0		0	0	0	4	0	1	0	5.0	.800	C-1
1907			18	.263	.289	38	10	1	0	0	0.0	4	1	4		0	0	0	46	16	4	2	3.7	.939	C-18
1908	BOS	N	41	.246	.315	130	32	2	2	1	0.8	13	16	7		2	3	0	143	52	5	2	4.9	.975	C-38
1909			43	.168	.221	113	19	4	1	0	0.0	9	4	5		3	12	1	133	39	5	5	4.1	.972	C-31
1910			70	.238	.286	147	35	4	0	1	0.7	8	15	5	14	5	32	6	138	66	11	3	3.1	.949	C-38
10 yrs.			343	.213	.255	1004	214	22	7	2	0.2	83	89	55	14	23	48	9	1168	369	55	25	4.6	.965	C-290, OF-5

WORLD SERIES

Year	Team		Games	BA	SA	AB	H	2B	3B	HR	HR%	R	RBI	BB	SO	SB	AB	H	PO	A	E	DP	TC/G	FA	G by Pos
1903	PIT	N	1	.000	.000	3	0	0	0	0	0.0	0	0	0		0	0	0	2	1	1	0	4.0	.750	C-1

Harry Smith

SMITH, HARRY W.   BR TR 6' 175 lbs.
B. Feb. 5, 1856, N. Vernon, Ind.   D. June 4, 1898, N. Vernon, Ind.

Year	Team		Games	BA	SA	AB	H	2B	3B	HR	HR%	R	RBI	BB	SO	SB	AB	H	PO	A	E	DP	TC/G	FA	G by Pos
1877	2 teams		CHI N	(24G –	.202)		CIN N	(10G –	.250)																
"	total		34	.215	.254	130	28	3	1	0	0.0	11	6	5	11	0	0	100	48	29	3	5.2	.836	2B-17, OF-13, C-8
1889	LOU	AA	1	.500	.500	2	1	0	0	0	0.0	0	1	0	1	0	0	2	0	1	0	3.0	.667	OF-1, C-1
2 yrs.			35	.220	.258	132	29	3	1	0	0.0	11	7	5	12	0	0	102	48	30	3	5.1	.833	2B-17, OF-14, C-9

Harry Smith

SMITH, JAMES HARRY   BR TR 5'10" 180 lbs.
B. May 15, 1890, Baltimore, Md.   D. Apr. 1, 1922, Charlotte, N. C.

Year	Team		Games	BA	SA	AB	H	2B	3B	HR	HR%	R	RBI	BB	SO	SB	AB	H	PO	A	E	DP	TC/G	FA	G by Pos
1914	NY	N	5	.429	.429	7	3	0	0	0	0.0	0	2	3	1	1	1	0	18	4	0	0	4.4	1.000	C-4
1915	2 teams		NY N	(21G –	.125)		BKN F	(28G –	.200)																
"	total		49	.175	.227	97	17	0	1	1	1.0	6	7	13	12	2	7	2	117	29	5	0	3.1	.967	C-37, OF-1
1917	CIN	N	8	.118	.118	17	2	0	0	0	0.0	0	1	2	7	0	1	0	34	11	1	0	5.8	.978	C-7
1918			13	.185	.370	27	5	1	2	0	0.0	4	4	3	6	1	5	1	22	3	0	1	1.9	1.000	C-6, OF-1
4 yrs.			75	.182	.250	148	27	1	3	1	0.7	10	14	21	26	4	14	3	191	47	6	1	3.3	.975	C-54, OF-2

Harvey Smith

SMITH, HARVEY FETTERHOFF   BL TR 5'8" 160 lbs.
B. July 24, 1871, Union Depot, Pa.   D. Nov. 12, 1962, Harrisburg, Pa.

Year	Team		Games	BA	SA	AB	H	2B	3B	HR	HR%	R	RBI	BB	SO	SB	AB	H	PO	A	E	DP	TC/G	FA	G by Pos
1896	WAS	N	36	.275	.359	131	36	7	2	0	0.0	21	17	12	7	9	0	0	31	87	19	5	3.8	.861	3B-36

Heinie Smith

SMITH, GEORGE HENRY   BR TR 5'9½" 160 lbs.
B. Oct. 24, 1871, Pittsburgh, Pa.   D. June 25, 1939, Buffalo, N. Y.
Manager 1902.

Year	Team		Games	BA	SA	AB	H	2B	3B	HR	HR%	R	RBI	BB	SO	SB	AB	H	PO	A	E	DP	TC/G	FA	G by Pos
1897	LOU	N	21	.263	.342	76	20	3	0	1	1.3	7	7	3		1	0	0	46	57	8	8	5.3	.928	2B-21
1898			35	.190	.223	121	23	4	0	0	0.0	14	13	6		6	2	1	74	87	16	8	5.1	.910	2B-33
1899	PIT	N	15	.283	.377	53	15	3	1	0	0.0	9	12	5		2	0	0	34	46	14	3	6.3	.851	2B-15, SS-1
1901	NY	N	9	.207	.448	29	6	2	1	1	3.4	5	4	1		1	0	0	13	20	1	0	3.8	.971	2B-7, P-2
1902			138	.252	.297	511	129	19	2	0	0.0	46	33	17		32	0	0	347	403	37	58	5.7	.953	2B-138
1903	DET	A	93	.223	.283	336	75	11	3	1	0.3	36	22	19		12	0	0	200	267	36	30	5.4	.928	2B-93
6 yrs.			311	.238	.296	1126	268	42	7	3	0.3	117	91	51		54	2	1	714	880	112	107	5.5	.934	2B-307, P-2, SS-1

Jack Smith

SMITH, JACK   BL TL 5'8" 165 lbs.
B. June 23, 1895, Chicago, Ill.   D. May 2, 1972, Westchester, Ill.

Year	Team		Games	BA	SA	AB	H	2B	3B	HR	HR%	R	RBI	BB	SO	SB	AB	H	PO	A	E	DP	TC/G	FA	G by Pos
1915	STL	N	4	.188	.313	16	3	0	1	0	0.0	2	0	1	5	0	0	0	5	0	0	0	1.3	1.000	OF-4
1916			130	.244	.339	357	87	6	5	6	1.7	43	34	20	50	24	7	1	212	12	12	4	1.8	.949	OF-120
1917			137	.297	.398	462	137	16	11	3	0.6	64	34	38	65	25	8	4	233	12	10	6	1.9	.961	OF-128
1918			42	.211	.235	166	35	2	1	0	0.0	24	4	7	21	5	0	0	87	9	6	6	2.4	.941	OF-42
1919			119	.223	.277	408	91	16	3	0	0.0	47	15	26	29	30	0	0	197	19	9	6	1.9	.960	OF-111
1920			91	.332	.444	313	104	22	5	1	0.3	53	28	25	23	14	4	1	144	12	6	1	1.8	.963	OF-83
1921			116	.328	.477	411	135	22	9	7	1.7	86	33	21	24	11	4	1	179	11	9	3	1.7	.955	OF-103
1922			143	.310	.449	510	158	23	12	8	1.6	117	46	50	30	18	4	1	282	11	15	3	2.2	.951	OF-136
1923			124	.310	.415	407	126	16	6	5	1.2	98	41	27	20	32	3	0	247	11	7	3	2.1	.974	OF-107
1924			124	.283	.362	459	130	18	6	2	0.4	91	33	33	27	24	6	1	251	18	9	8	2.2	.968	OF-114
1925			80	.251	.379	243	61	11	4	4	1.6	53	31	19	13	20	10	4	152	7	7	2	2.1	.958	OF-64
1926	2 teams		STL N	(1G –	.000)		BOS N	(96G –	.311)																
"	total		97	.310	.387	323	100	15	2	2	0.6	46	25	28	13	11	9	0	206	8	6	0	2.3	.973	OF-83
1927	BOS	N	84	.317	.410	183	58	6	4	1	0.5	27	24	16	12	8	30	8	106	7	6	1	1.4	.950	OF-48
1928			96	.280	.343	254	71	9	2	1	0.4	30	32	21	14	6	25	9	165	4	2	0	1.8	.988	OF-65
1929			19	.250	.250	20	5	0	0	0	0.0	2	2	2	2	0	3	0	10	0	2	0	0.6	.833	OF-9
15 yrs.			1406	.287	.385	4532	1301	182	71	40	0.9	783	382	334	348	228	113	29	2476	141	106	43	1.9	.961	OF-1217

Jack Smith

SMITH, JOHN JOSEPH   TR 5'9"
Born John Joseph Coffee.
B. Aug. 8, 1893, Oswayo, Pa.   D. Dec. 4, 1962, New York, N. Y.

Year	Team		Games	BA	SA	AB	H	2B	3B	HR	HR%	R	RBI	BB	SO	SB	AB	H	PO	A	E	DP	TC/G	FA	G by Pos
1912	DET	A	1	–	–	0	0	0	0	0	0.0	0	0	0	0	0	0	0	2	1	0	1	3.0	1.000	3B-1

Jimmy Smith

SMITH, JAMES LAWRENCE   BB TR 5'9" 158 lbs.
Born James Lawrence Greenfield.
B. May 15, 1895, Pittsburgh, Pa.   D. Jan. 1, 1974, Pittsburgh, Pa.

Year	Team		Games	BA	SA	AB	H	2B	3B	HR	HR%	R	RBI	BB	SO	SB	AB	H	PO	A	E	DP	TC/G	FA	G by Pos
1914	CHI	F	3	.500	.667	6	3	1	0	0	0.0	1	1	0		1	0	0	3	5	0	2	2.7	1.000	SS-3
1915	2 teams		CHI F	(95G –	.217)		BAL F	(33G –	.176)																
"	total		128	.207	.293	426	88	12	5	3	0.7	41	41	25		7	0	0	273	333	70	37	5.3	.896	SS-125, 2B-1
1916	PIT	N	36	.188	.219	96	18	1	1	0	0.0	4	5	6	22	0	0	0	58	78	12	6	4.1	.919	SS-27, 3B-6
1917	NY	N	36	.229	.302	96	22	5	1	0	0.0	12	2	9	18	6	0	0	53	83	4	5	3.9	.971	2B-29, SS-7

Year	Team		Games	BA	SA	AB	H	2B	3B	HR	HR%	R	RBI	BB	SO	SB	Pinch Hit AB	Pinch Hit H	PO	A	E	DP	TC/G	FA	G by Pos

Jimmy Smith *continued*

Year	Team		Games	BA	SA	AB	H	2B	3B	HR	HR%	R	RBI	BB	SO	SB	Pinch Hit AB	Pinch Hit H	PO	A	E	DP	TC/G	FA	G by Pos
1918	BOS	N	34	.225	.363	102	23	3	4	1	1.0	8	14	3	13	1	0	0	65	51	12	7	3.8	.906	SS-9, 2B-7, OF-6, 3B-5
1919	CIN	N	28	.275	.525	40	11	1	3	1	2.5	9	10	4	8	1	0	0	18	26	3	5	1.7	.936	3B-6, SS-5, OF-4, 2B-4
1921	PHI	N	67	.231	.320	247	57	8	1	4	1.6	31	22	11	28	2	0	0	125	239	11	19	5.6	.971	2B-66
1922			38	.219	.254	114	25	1	0	1	0.9	13	6	5	9	1	2	0	67	94	8	17	4.4	.953	SS-23, 2B-13, 3B-1
8 yrs.			370	.219	.306	1127	247	32	15	12	1.1	119	101	63	98	18	2	0	662	909	120	98	4.6	.929	SS-199, 2B-120, 3B-18, OF-10

WORLD SERIES

1919	CIN	N	1	—	—	0	0	0	0	0	—	0	0	0	0	0	0	0	0	0	0	0	0.0	—	

Jimmy Smith

SMITH, JAMES LORNE
B. Sept. 8, 1954, Santa Monica, Calif.   BR TR 6'3" 180 lbs.

1982	PIT	N	42	.238	.333	42	10	2	1	0	0.0	5	4	5	7	0	1	0	34	50	7	10	2.2	.923	SS-29, 2B-3, 3B-1

Joe Smith

SMITH, JOSEPH
Born Salvatore Giuseppe Persico.
B. Dec. 29, 1893, New York, N. Y.   D. June 12, 1974, Yonkers, N. Y.   BR TR 5'8" 190 lbs.

1913	NY	A	13	.156	.156	32	5	0	0	0	0.0	1	2	1	14	0	0	0	43	17	3	1	4.8	.952	C-13

John Smith

SMITH, JOHN J.   5'11" 210 lbs.

1882	2 teams			TRO	N (35G – .242)		WOR	N (19G – .243)																	
"	total		54	.242	.320	219	53	7	5	0	0.0	37	19	8	34		0	0	543	19	29	31	10.9	.951	1B-54

John Smith

SMITH, JOHN MARSHALL (Jack)
B. Sept. 27, 1906, Washington, D. C.   D. May 9, 1982, Silver Spring, Md.   BB TR 6'1" 165 lbs.

1931	BOS	A	4	.133	.133	15	2	0	0	0	0.0	2	1	2	1	1	0	0	46	0	0	1	11.5	1.000	1B-4

Jud Smith

SMITH, JUDSON GRANT
B. Jan. 13, 1869, Green Oak, Mich.   D. Dec. 7, 1947, Los Angeles, Calif.   BR TR

1893	2 teams		21	CIN	N (17G – .233)		STL	N (4G – .077)																	
"	total		21	.196	.268	56	11	1	0	1	1.8	8	5	10	7	1	0	0	19	23	10	5	2.5	.808	3B-10, OF-9, SS-1
1896	PIT	N	10	.343	.457	35	12	2	1	0	0.0	6	4	2	2	3	0	0	19	21	4	3	4.4	.909	3B-10
1898	WAS	N	66	.303	.415	234	71	7	5	3	1.3	33	28	22		11	0	0	140	112	28	10	4.2	.900	3B-47, SS-10, 1B-7, 2B-1
1901	PIT	N	6	.143	.190	21	3	1	0	0	0.0	1	0	3		0	0	0	7	11	1	0	3.2	.947	3B-6
4 yrs.			103	.280	.382	346	97	11	6	4	1.2	48	37	37	9	15	0	0	185	167	43	18	3.8	.891	3B-73, SS-11, OF-9, 1B-7, 2B-1

Keith Smith

SMITH, KEITH LAVARNE
B. May 3, 1953, Palmetto, Fla.   BR TR 5'9" 178 lbs.

1977	TEX	A	23	.239	.388	67	16	4	0	2	3.0	13	6	4	7	2	3	1	38	1	1	0	1.7	.975	OF-22
1979	STL	N	6	.231	.231	13	3	0	0	0	0.0	1	0	1	1	0	0	0	14	1	0	0	2.5	1.000	OF-5
1980			24	.129	.161	31	4	1	0	0	0.0	3	2	2	2	0	17	3	10	0	0	0	0.4	1.000	OF-7
3 yrs.			53	.207	.306	111	23	5	0	2	1.8	17	8	6	10	2	20	4	62	2	1	0	1.2	.985	OF-34

Keith Smith

SMITH, PATRICK KEITH
B. Oct. 20, 1961, Los Angeles, Calif.   BB TR 6'1" 175 lbs.

1984	NY	A	2	.000	.000	4	0	0	0	0	0.0	0	0	0	2	0	0	0	2	10	1	1	6.5	.923	SS-2
1985			4			0	0	0	0	0	—	1	0	0	0	0	0	0	0	1	0	0	0.3	1.000	SS-3
2 yrs.			6	.000	.000	4	0	0	0	0	0.0	1	0	0	2	0	0	0	2	11	1	1	2.3	.929	SS-5

Ken Smith

SMITH, KENNETH EARL
B. Feb. 12, 1958, Youngstown, Ohio   BL TR 6'1" 195 lbs.

1981	ATL	N	5	.333	.667	3	1	0	0	0	0.0	0	0	0	1	0	0	0	6	1	0	0	1.4	1.000	1B-4
1982			48	.293	.317	41	12	1	0	0	0.0	6	3	6	13	0	35	8	15	1	0	0	0.3	1.000	1B-6, OF-3
1983			30	.167	.417	12	2	0	0	1	8.3	2	2	1	5	1	8	1	27	6	0	3	1.1	1.000	1B-13
3 yrs.			83	.268	.357	56	15	2	0	1	1.8	8	5	7	19	1	43	9	48	8	0	3	0.7	1.000	1B-23, OF-3

Klondike Smith

SMITH, ARMSTRONG FREDERICK
B. Jan. 4, 1887, London, England   D. Nov. 15, 1959, Springfield, Mass.   BL TL 5'9" 160 lbs.

1912	NY	A	7	.185	.222	27	5	1	0	0	0.0	0		0	1	0	0	0	10	0	0	0	1.4	1.000	OF-7

Leo Smith

SMITH, LIONEL H.
B. May 13, 1859, Brooklyn, N. Y.   D. Aug. 30, 1935, Brooklyn, N. Y.   5'6" 142 lbs.

1890	ROC	AA	35	.188	.250	112	21	1	3	0	0.0	11		14		1	0	0	66	115	10	15	5.5	.948	SS-35

Lonnie Smith

SMITH, LONNIE
B. Dec. 22, 1955, Chicago, Ill.   BR TR 5'9" 170 lbs.

1978	PHI	N	17	.000	.000	4	0	0	0	0	0.0	6	0	4	3	4	1	0	5	1	0	0	0.4	1.000	OF-11
1979			17	.167	.233	30	5	2	0	0	0.0	4	3	1	7	2	4	0	19	1	0	0	1.2	1.000	OF-11
1980			100	.339	.443	298	101	14	4	3	1.0	69	20	26	48	33	8	2	121	2	4	0	1.3	.969	OF-82
1981			62	.324	.472	176	57	14	3	2	1.1	40	11	18	14	21	5	3	89	10	3	2	1.6	.971	OF-51
1982	STL	N	156	.307	.434	592	182	35	8	8	1.4	120	69	64	74	68	9	1	303	16	10	3	2.1	.970	OF-149
1983			130	.321	.453	492	158	31	5	8	1.6	83	45	41	55	43	5	1	225	14	15	4	2.0	.941	OF-126
1984			145	.250	.341	504	126	20	4	6	1.2	77	49	70	90	50	2	1	184	18	11	0	1.5	.948	OF-140
1985	2 teams		148	STL	N (28G – .260)		KC	A (120G – .257)																	
"	total		148	.257	.358	544	140	25	6	6	1.1	92	48	56	89	52	2	0	51	4	1	1	0.4	.982	OF-147
1986	KC	A	134	.287	.411	508	146	25	7	8	1.6	80	44	46	78	26	4	2	245	5	9	1	1.9	.965	OF-118, DH-10
1987			48	.251	.359	167	42	7	1	3	1.8	26	19	24	31	9	1	0	52	5	2	0	1.2	.915	OF-32, DH-15
1988	ATL	N	43	.237	.342	114	27	3	0	3	2.6	14	9	10	25	4	14	3	59	2	2	0	1.5	.968	OF-35

Year	Team	Games	BA	SA	AB	H	2B	3B	HR	HR%	R	RBI	BB	SO	SB	Pinch Hit AB	Pinch Hit H	PO	A	E	DP	TC/G	FA	G by Pos

Lonnie Smith *continued*

Year	Team	Games	BA	SA	AB	H	2B	3B	HR	HR%	R	RBI	BB	SO	SB	AB	H	PO	A	E	DP	TC/G	FA	G by Pos
1989		134	.315	.533	482	152	34	4	21	4.4	89	79	76	95	25	3	0	289	3	2	0	2.2	.993	OF-132
12 yrs.		1134	.290	.418	3911	1136	210	42	68	1.7	700	385	436	609	337	59	13	1642	78	62	11	1.6	.965	OF-1034, DH-25

DIVISIONAL PLAYOFF SERIES

Year	Team	Games	BA	SA	AB	H	2B	3B	HR	HR%	R	RBI	BB	SO	SB	AB	H	PO	A	E	DP	TC/G	FA	G by Pos
1981	PHI N	5	.263	.316	19	5	1	0	0	0.0	1	0	0	4	0	0	0	0	0	0	0	0.0	—	OF-5

LEAGUE CHAMPIONSHIP SERIES

Year	Team	Games	BA	SA	AB	H	2B	3B	HR	HR%	R	RBI	BB	SO	SB	AB	H	PO	A	E	DP	TC/G	FA	G by Pos
1980	PHI N	3	.600	.600	5	3	0	0	0	0.0	2	0	0	1	0	0	0	2	1	0	1	1.0	1.000	OF-2
1982	STL N	3	.273	.273	11	3	0	0	0	0.0	1	1	0	1	0	0	0	0	0	0	0	0.0	—	OF-3
1985	KC A	7	.250	.321	28	7	2	0	0	0.0	2	1	3	6	1	0	0	8	3	1	0	1.7	.917	OF-7
3 yrs.		13	.295	.341	44	13	2	0	0	0.0	5	2	3	7	2	0	0	10	4	1	1	1.2	.933	OF-12

WORLD SERIES

Year	Team	Games	BA	SA	AB	H	2B	3B	HR	HR%	R	RBI	BB	SO	SB	AB	H	PO	A	E	DP	TC/G	FA	G by Pos
1980	PHI N	6	.263	.316	19	5	1	0	0	0.0	2	1	1	1	0	0	0	4	1	0	0	0.8	1.000	OF-4, DH-1
1982	STL N	7	.321	.536	28	9	4	1	0	0.0	6	1	1	5	2	0	0	11	0	0	0	1.6	1.000	OF-6, DH-1
1985	KC A	7	.333	.444	27	9	3	0	0	0.0	4	4	3	8	2	0	0	7	2	0	0	1.3	1.000	OF-7
3 yrs.		20	.311	.446	74	23	8	1	0	0.0	12	6	5	14	4	0	0	22	3	0	0	1.3	1.000	OF-17, DH-2
							6th																	

Mayo Smith

SMITH, EDWARD MAYO
B. Jan. 17, 1915, New London, Mo. D. Nov. 24, 1977, Boynton Beach, Fla.
Manager 1955-59, 1967-70.

BL TR 6' 183 lbs.

Year	Team	Games	BA	SA	AB	H	2B	3B	HR	HR%	R	RBI	BB	SO	SB	AB	H	PO	A	E	DP	TC/G	FA	G by Pos
1945	PHI A	73	.212	.236	203	43	5	0	0	0.0	18	11	36	13	0	6	4	120	4	3	0	1.7	.976	OF-65

Mike Smith

SMITH, ELWOOD HOPE
B. Nov. 16, 1904, Norfolk, Va. D. May 31, 1981, Chesapeake, Va.

BL TR 5'11½" 170 lbs.

Year	Team	Games	BA	SA	AB	H	2B	3B	HR	HR%	R	RBI	BB	SO	SB	AB	H	PO	A	E	DP	TC/G	FA	G by Pos
1926	NY N	4	.143	.143	7	1	0	0	0	0.0	0	0	0	2	0	3	0	3	0	0	0	0.8	1.000	OF-1

Milt Smith

SMITH, MILTON
B. Mar. 27, 1929, Columbus, Ga.

BR TR 5'10" 165 lbs.

Year	Team	Games	BA	SA	AB	H	2B	3B	HR	HR%	R	RBI	BB	SO	SB	AB	H	PO	A	E	DP	TC/G	FA	G by Pos
1955	CIN N	36	.196	.333	102	20	3	1	3	2.9	15	8	13	24	2	2	1	30	61	7	4	2.7	.929	3B-28, 2B-5

Nate Smith

SMITH, NATHANIEL BEVERLY
B. Apr. 26, 1935, Chicago, Ill.

BR TR 5'11" 170 lbs.

Year	Team	Games	BA	SA	AB	H	2B	3B	HR	HR%	R	RBI	BB	SO	SB	AB	H	PO	A	E	DP	TC/G	FA	G by Pos
1962	BAL A	5	.222	.333	9	2	1	0	0	0.0	3	0	1	4	0	2	1	17	1	0	1	3.6	1.000	C-3

Ollie Smith

SMITH, OLIVER H.
B. 1868, Mt. Vernon, Ohio Deceased.

BL TL

Year	Team	Games	BA	SA	AB	H	2B	3B	HR	HR%	R	RBI	BB	SO	SB	AB	H	PO	A	E	DP	TC/G	FA	G by Pos
1894	LOU N	38	.299	.425	134	40	6	1	3	2.2	26	20	27	15	13	0	0	63	5	9	0	2.0	.883	OF-38

Ozzie Smith

SMITH, OSBORNE EARL (The Wizard)
B. Dec. 26, 1954, Mobile, Ala.

BB TR 5'11" 150 lbs.

Year	Team	Games	BA	SA	AB	H	2B	3B	HR	HR%	R	RBI	BB	SO	SB	AB	H	PO	A	E	DP	TC/G	FA	G by Pos
1978	SD N	159	.258	.312	590	152	17	6	1	0.2	69	46	47	43	40	1	0	264	548	25	98	5.3	.970	SS-159
1979		156	.211	.262	587	124	18	6	0	0.0	77	27	37	37	28	0	0	256	555	20	86	5.3	.976	SS-155
1980		158	.230	.276	609	140	18	5	0	0.0	67	35	71	49	57	0	0	288	621	24	113	5.9	.974	SS-158
1981		110	.222	.256	450	100	11	2	0	0.0	53	21	41	37	22	0	0	220	422	16	72	6.0	.976	SS-110
1982	STL N	140	.248	.314	488	121	24	1	2	0.4	58	43	68	32	25	1	0	279	535	13	101	5.9	.984	SS-139
1983		159	.243	.335	552	134	30	6	3	0.5	69	50	64	36	34	2	0	304	519	21	100	5.3	.975	SS-158
1984		124	.257	.337	412	106	20	5	1	0.2	53	44	56	17	35	0	0	233	437	12	94	5.5	.982	SS-124
1985		158	.276	.361	537	148	22	3	6	1.1	70	54	65	27	31	0	0	264	549	14	111	5.2	.983	SS-158
1986		153	.280	.333	514	144	19	4	0	0.0	67	54	79	27	31	8	2	229	453	15	96	4.6	.978	SS-144
1987		158	.303	.383	600	182	40	4	0	0.0	104	75	89	36	43	2	1	245	516	10	111	4.9	.987	SS-158
1988		153	.270	.336	575	155	27	1	3	0.5	80	51	74	43	57	2	0	234	519	22	79	5.1	.972	SS-150
1989		155	.273	.361	593	162	30	8	2	0.3	82	50	55	37	29	2	1	209	483	17	73	4.6	.976	SS-153
12 yrs.		1783	.256	.323	6507	1668	276	51	18	0.3	849	550	746	421	432	18	4	3025	6157	209	1134	5.3	.978	SS-1766

LEAGUE CHAMPIONSHIP SERIES

Year	Team	Games	BA	SA	AB	H	2B	3B	HR	HR%	R	RBI	BB	SO	SB	AB	H	PO	A	E	DP	TC/G	FA	G by Pos
1982	STL N	3	.556	.556	9	5	0	0	0	0.0	0	3	3	0	1	0	0	0	0	0	0	0.0	—	SS-3
1985		6	.435	.696	23	10	1	1	1	4.3	4	3	3	1	0	0	0	6	16	0	2	3.7	1.000	SS-6
1987		7	.200	.280	25	5	0	1	0	0.0	2	1	3	4	1	0	0	10	19	1	4	4.3	.967	SS-7
3 yrs.		16	.351	.491	57	20	1	2	1	1.8	6	7	9	5	2	0	0	16	35	1	6	3.3	.981	SS-16

WORLD SERIES

Year	Team	Games	BA	SA	AB	H	2B	3B	HR	HR%	R	RBI	BB	SO	SB	AB	H	PO	A	E	DP	TC/G	FA	G by Pos
1982	STL N	7	.208	.208	24	5	0	0	0	0.0	1	0	3	0	0	0	0	22	17	0	5	5.6	1.000	SS-7
1985		7	.087	.087	23	2	0	0	0	0.0	2	0	4	0	1	0	0	10	16	1	5	3.9	.963	SS-7
1987		7	.214	.214	28	6	0	0	0	0.0	3	2	2	3	2	0	0	7	19	0	1	3.7	1.000	SS-7
3 yrs.		21	.173	.173	75	13	0	0	0	0.0	6	2	9	3	3	0	0	39	52	1	11	4.4	.989	SS-21

Paddy Smith

SMITH, LAWRENCE PATRICK
B. May 16, 1894, Pelham, N. Y.

BL TR 6' 195 lbs.

Year	Team	Games	BA	SA	AB	H	2B	3B	HR	HR%	R	RBI	BB	SO	SB	AB	H	PO	A	E	DP	TC/G	FA	G by Pos
1920	BOS A	2	.000	.000	2	0	0	0	0	0.0	0	0	0	1	0	1	0	0	0	0	0	0.0	—	C-1

Paul Smith

SMITH, PAUL LESLIE
B. Mar. 19, 1931, New Castle, Pa.

BL TL 5'8" 165 lbs.

Year	Team	Games	BA	SA	AB	H	2B	3B	HR	HR%	R	RBI	BB	SO	SB	AB	H	PO	A	E	DP	TC/G	FA	G by Pos
1953	PIT N	118	.283	.380	389	110	12	7	4	1.0	41	44	24	23	3	23	8	653	54	11	53	6.1	.985	1B-74, OF-19
1957		81	.253	.340	150	38	4	0	3	2.0	12	11	12	17	0	45	9	53	2	0	0	0.7	1.000	OF-33, 1B-1
1958	2 teams		PIT N	(6G – .333)		CHI N	(18G – .150)																		
"	total	24	.174	.174	23	4	0	0	0	0.0	1	1	6	4	0	13	3	14	2	1	0	0.7	.941	1B-4
3 yrs.		223	.270	.361	562	152	16	7	7	1.2	54	56	42	44	3	81	20	720	58	12	53	3.5	.985	1B-79, OF-52

Year	Team		Games	BA	SA	AB	H	2B	3B	HR	HR%	R	RBI	BB	SO	SB	Pinch Hit AB	Pinch Hit H	PO	A	E	DP	TC/G	FA	G by Pos

Paul Smith
SMITH, PAUL STONER   B. May 7, 1888, Mt. Zion, Ill.   D. July 3, 1958, Decatur, Ill.   BL TR 6'1" 190 lbs.

| 1916 | CIN | N | 10 | .227 | .273 | 44 | 10 | 1 | 0 | 0 | 0.0 | 5 | 1 | 1 | 8 | 3 | 0 | 0 | 13 | 1 | 0 | 0 | 1.4 | 1.000 | OF-10 |

Pop Smith
SMITH, CHARLES MARVIN   B. Oct. 12, 1856, Digby, N. S., Canada   D. Apr. 18, 1927, Boston, Mass.   BR TR 5'11" 170 lbs.

1880	CIN	N	83	.207	.290	334	69	10	9	0	0.0	35		6	36		0	0	282	243	89	32	7.4	.855	2B-83
1881	3 teams					CLE N (10G – .118)			WOR N (11G – .073)			BUF N (3G – .000)													
"	total		24	.081	.081	86	7	0	0	0	0.0	5	6	6	18		0	0	55	34	12	5	4.2	.881	3B-10, OF-8, 2B-6
1882	2 teams					BAL AA (1G – .000)			LOU AA (3G – .182)																	
"	total		4	.143	.143	14	2	0	0	0	0.0	1		0			0	0	5	10	5	0	5.0	.750	SS-3, OF-1
1883	COL	AA	97	.262	.410	405	106	14	17	4	1.0	82		22			0	0	286	296	74	40	6.8	.887	2B-73, 3B-24, P-3
1884			108	.238	.364	445	106	18	10	6	1.3	78		20			0	0	324	394	75	55	7.3	.905	2B-108
1885	PIT	AA	106	.249	.331	453	113	11	13	0	0.0	85		25			0	0	372	384	64	53	7.7	.922	2B-106
1886			126	.217	.308	483	105	20	9	2	0.4	75		42			0	0	221	456	75	36	6.0	.900	SS-98, 2B-28, C-1
1887	PIT	N	122	.215	.285	456	98	12	7	2	0.4	69	54	30	48	30	0	0	296	417	65	39	6.4	.916	SS-89, 2B-33
1888			131	.206	.270	481	99	15	2	4	0.8	61	52	22	78	37	0	0	222	431	70	42	5.5	.903	SS-75, 2B-56
1889	2 teams					PIT N (72G – .209)			BOS N (59G – .260)																	
"	total		131	.232	.339	466	108	23	6	5	1.1	47	59	47	68	23	0	0	253	392	72	51	5.5	.900	SS-117, 2B-9, OF-3, 3B-3
1890	BOS	N	134	.229	.322	463	106	16	12	1	0.2	82	53	80	81	39	0	0	236	403	58	41	5.2	.917	2B-134, SS-1
1891	WAS	AA	27	.178	.244	90	16	2	2	0	0.0	13	13	13	16	2	0	0	63	87	18	12	6.2	.893	2B-19, SS-5, 3B-4
12 yrs.			1093	.224	.317	4176	935	141	87	24	0.6	633	264	313	345	131	0	0	2615	3547	677	406	6.3	.901	2B-711, SS-332, 3B-41, OF-12, P-3, C-1

Ray Smith
SMITH, RAYMOND EDWARD   B. Sept. 18, 1955, Glendale, Calif.   BR TR 6'1" 185 lbs.

1981	MIN	A	15	.200	.300	40	8	1	0	1	2.5	4	1	0	3	0	0	0	65	3	0	0	4.5	1.000	C-15
1982			9	.217	.304	23	5	0	0	0	0.0	1	1	1	3	0	0	0	44	2	0	0	5.1	1.000	C-9
1983			59	.224	.257	152	34	5	0	0	0.0	11	8	10	12	1	0	0	272	27	5	3	5.2	.984	C-59
3 yrs.			83	.219	.270	215	47	6	1	1	0.5	16	10	11	18	1	0	0	381	32	5	3	5.0	.988	C-83

Red Smith
SMITH, JAMES CARLISLE   B. Apr. 6, 1890, Greenville, S. C.   D. Oct. 11, 1966, Atlanta, Ga.   BR TR 5'11" 165 lbs.

1911	BKN	N	28	.261	.333	111	29	6	1	0	0.0	10	19	5	13	5	0	0	30	51	9	7	3.2	.900	3B-28
1912			128	.286	.393	486	139	28	6	4	0.8	75	57	54	51	22	3	1	156	251	27	16	3.4	.938	3B-125
1913			151	.296	.441	540	160	40	10	6	1.1	70	76	45	67	22	0	0	175	295	34	13	3.3	.933	3B-151
1914	2 teams		150			BKN N (90G – .245)			BOS N (60G – .314)																	
"	total		150	.272	.395	537	146	27	9	7	1.3	69	85	58	50	15	0	0	220	332	37	28	3.9	.937	3B-150
1915	BOS	N	157	.264	.352	549	145	34	4	2	0.4	66	65	67	49	10	0	0	170	292	26	26	3.1	.947	3B-157
1916			150	.259	.348	509	132	16	10	3	0.6	48	60	53	55	13	0	0	166	299	36	15	3.3	.928	3B-150
1917			147	.295	.392	505	149	31	6	2	0.4	60	62	53	61	16	1	0	141	264	33	27	3.0	.925	3B-147
1918			119	.298	.373	429	128	20	3	2	0.5	55	65	45	47	8	0	0	123	291	35	16	3.8	.922	3B-119
1919			87	.245	.282	241	59	6	0	1	0.4	24	25	40	22	6	15	4	128	64	9	5	2.3	.955	OF-48, 3B-23
9 yrs.			1117	.278	.377	3907	1087	208	49	27	0.7	477	514	420	415	117	19	5	1309	2139	246	153	3.3	.933	3B-1050, OF-48

Red Smith
SMITH, MARVIN HAROLD   B. July 17, 1900, Ashley, Ill.   D. Feb. 19, 1961, Los Angeles, Calif.   BL TR 5'7" 165 lbs.

| 1925 | PHI | A | 20 | .286 | .286 | 14 | 4 | 0 | 0 | 0 | 0.0 | 1 | 1 | 2 | 5 | 0 | 0 | 0 | 7 | 15 | 4 | 1 | 1.3 | .846 | SS-16, 3B-2 |

Red Smith
SMITH, RICHARD PAUL   B. May 18, 1904, Brokaw, Wis.   D. Mar. 8, 1978, Toledo, Ohio   BR TR 5'10" 185 lbs.

| 1927 | NY | N | 1 | – | – | 0 | 0 | 0 | 0 | 0 | – | 0 | 0 | 0 | 0 | 0 | 0 | 0 | 1 | 0 | 0 | 0 | 1.0 | 1.000 | C-1 |

Red Smith
SMITH, WILLARD JEHU   B. Apr. 11, 1892, Logansport, Ind.   D. July 17, 1972, Noblesville, Ind.   BR TR 5'8" 165 lbs.

1917	PIT	N	11	.143	.190	21	3	1	0	0	0.0	1	2	3	4	1	4	1	20	11	0	1	2.8	1.000	C-6
1918			15	.167	.208	24	4	1	0	0	0.0	1	3	3	0	0	4	0	27	4	2	2	2.2	.939	C-10
2 yrs.			26	.156	.200	45	7	2	0	0	0.0	2	5	6	4	1	8	1	47	15	2	3	2.5	.969	C-16

Reggie Smith
SMITH, CARL REGINALD   B. Apr. 2, 1945, Shreveport, La.   BB TR 6' 180 lbs.

1966	BOS	A	6	.154	.192	26	4	1	0	0	0.0	1	0	0	5	0	0	0	17	0	1	0	3.0	.944	OF-6
1967			158	.246	.389	565	139	24	6	15	2.7	78	61	57	95	16	10	1	353	32	7	11	2.5	.982	OF-144, 2B-6
1968			155	.265	.430	558	148	37	5	15	2.7	78	69	64	77	22	0	0	390	8	6	1	2.6	.985	OF-155
1969			143	.309	.527	543	168	29	7	25	4.6	87	93	54	67	7	4	1	321	8	14	1	2.4	.959	OF-139
1970			147	.303	.497	580	176	32	7	22	3.8	109	74	51	60	10	2	0	361	15	9	1	2.6	.977	OF-145
1971			159	.283	.489	618	175	33	2	30	4.9	85	96	63	82	11	0	0	386	15	14	2	2.6	.966	OF-159
1972			131	.270	.475	467	126	25	4	21	4.5	75	74	66	63	15	2	0	247	8	5	2	2.0	.981	OF-129
1973			115	.303	.515	423	128	23	2	21	5.0	79	69	68	49	3	1	0	282	8	5	2	2.6	.983	OF-104, DH-8, 1B-1
1974	STL	N	143	.309	.528	517	160	26	9	23	4.4	79	100	71	70	4	10	4	286	9	7	3	2.1	.977	OF-132, 1B-1
1975			135	.302	.488	477	144	26	3	19	4.0	67	76	63	59	9	7	3	650	39	15	51	5.2	.979	OF-69, 1B-66, 3B-1
1976	2 teams					STL N (47G – .218)			LA N (65G – .280)																	
"	total		112	.253	.453	395	100	15	2	18	4.6	55	49	32	70	3	8	4	314	48	4	20	3.3	.989	OF-74, 1B-17, 3B-14
1977	LA	N	148	.307	.576	488	150	27	4	32	6.6	104	87	104	76	7	6	1	240	7	5	0	1.7	.980	OF-140
1978			128	.295	.559	447	132	27	2	29	6.5	82	93	70	90	12	2	0	220	8	12	4	1.9	.950	OF-126
1979			68	.274	.466	234	64	13	1	10	4.3	41	32	31	50	6	5	2	159	5	2	0	2.4	.988	OF-62
1980			92	.322	.508	311	100	13	0	15	4.8	47	55	41	63	5	6	4	153	15	1	5	1.8	.994	OF-84
1981			41	.200	.314	35	7	1	0	1	2.9	5	8	7	8	0	31	6	15	1	0	1	0.4	1.000	1B-2
1982	SF	N	106	.284	.470	349	99	11	0	18	5.2	51	56	46	46	7	6	1	792	78	16	61	8.4	.982	1B-99
17 yrs.			1987	.287	.489	7033	2020	363	57	314	4.5	1123	1092	890	1030	137	100	26	5186	304	123	165	2.8	.978	OF-1668, 1B-186, 3B-15, DH-8, 2B-6

DIVISIONAL PLAYOFF SERIES

| 1981 | LA | N | 2 | .000 | .000 | 1 | 0 | 0 | 0 | 0 | 0.0 | 0 | 1 | 0 | 1 | 0 | 1 | 0 | 0 | 0 | 0 | 0 | 0.0 | – | |

Year	Team		Games	BA	SA	AB	H	2B	3B	HR	HR%	R	RBI	BB	SO	SB	Pinch Hit AB	H	PO	A	E	DP	TC/G	FA	G by Pos

Reggie Smith *continued*
LEAGUE CHAMPIONSHIP SERIES

Year	Team		Games	BA	SA	AB	H	2B	3B	HR	HR%	R	RBI	BB	SO	SB	AB	H	PO	A	E	DP	TC/G	FA	G by Pos
1977	LA	N	4	.188	.313	16	3	0	1	0	0.0	2	1	2	5	1	0	0	7	0	1	0	2.0	.875	OF-4
1978			4	.188	.250	16	3	1	0	0	0.0	2	1	2	0	0	0	0	5	0	1	0	1.5	.833	OF-4
1981			1	1.000	1.000	1	1	0	0	0	0.0	0	1	0	0	0	1	1	0	0	0	0	0.0	—	
3 yrs.			9	.212	.303	33	7	1	1	0	0.0	4	3	2	7	1	1	1	12	0	2	0	1.6	.857	OF-8

WORLD SERIES

Year	Team		Games	BA	SA	AB	H	2B	3B	HR	HR%	R	RBI	BB	SO	SB	AB	H	PO	A	E	DP	TC/G	FA	G by Pos
1967	BOS	A	7	.250	.542	24	6	1	0	2	8.3	3	3	2	2	0	0	0	14	0	0	0	2.0	1.000	OF-7
1977	LA	N	6	.273	.727	22	6	1	0	3	13.6	7	5	4	3	0	0	0	14	1	0	0	2.5	1.000	OF-6
1978			6	.200	.320	25	5	0	0	1	4.0	3	5	2	6	0	0	0	11	1	1	0	2.2	.923	OF-6
1981			2	.500	.500	2	1	0	0	0	0.0	0	0	0	1	0	2	1	0	0	0	0	0.0	—	
4 yrs.			21	.247	.521	73	18	2	0	6	8.2 (6th)	13	13	8	12	0	2	1	39	2	1	0	2.0	.976	OF-19

Skyrocket Smith
SMITH, SAMUEL J.
B. Mar. 19, 1868, Baltimore, Md.   D. Apr. 26, 1916, St. Louis, Mo.   BR

Year	Team		Games	BA	SA	AB	H	2B	3B	HR	HR%	R	RBI	BB	SO	SB	AB	H	PO	A	E	DP	TC/G	FA	G by Pos
1888	LOU	AA	58	.238	.335	206	49	9	4	1	0.5	27	31	24		5	0	0	568	22	18	15	10.5	.970	1B-58

Stub Smith
SMITH, JAMES A.
B. Nov. 26, 1876, Elmwood, Ill.   Deceased.   BL TR   145 lbs.

Year	Team		Games	BA	SA	AB	H	2B	3B	HR	HR%	R	RBI	BB	SO	SB	AB	H	PO	A	E	DP	TC/G	FA	G by Pos
1898	BOS	N	3	.100	.100	10	1	0	0	0	0.0	1	0	0		0	0	0	5	9	1	0	5.0	.933	SS-3

Syd Smith
SMITH, SYDNEY E.
B. Aug. 31, 1883, Smithville, S. C.   D. June 5, 1961, Orangeburg, S. C.   BR TR   5'10"   190 lbs.

Year	Team		Games	BA	SA	AB	H	2B	3B	HR	HR%	R	RBI	BB	SO	SB	AB	H	PO	A	E	DP	TC/G	FA	G by Pos
1908	2 teams			PHI A (46G – .203)			STL A (27G – .184)																			
"	total		73	.196	.309	204	40	12	4	1	0.5	14	15	8		2	10	1	352	75	11	7	6.0	.975	C-61, 1B-6, OF-2
1910	CLE	A	9	.333	.370	27	9	1	0	0	0.0	1	3	3		0	0	0	33	13	2	3	5.3	.958	C-9
1911			58	.299	.383	154	46	8	1	1	0.6	8	21	11		0	7	3	270	62	7	10	5.8	.979	C-48, 3B-1, 1B-1
1914	PIT	N	5	.273	.273	11	3	0	0	0	0.0	1	1	0	1	0	2	0	12	3	0	0	3.0	1.000	C-3
1915			1	.000	.000	1	0	0	0	0	0.0	0	0	0	0	0	1	0	0	0	0	0	0.0	—	
5 yrs.			146	.247	.340	397	98	21	5	2	0.5	24	40	22	1	2	20	4	667	153	20	20	5.8	.976	C-121, 1B-7, OF-2, 3B-1

Tom Smith
SMITH, THOMAS N.
B. 1851, Guelph, Ontario, Canada   D. Mar. 28, 1889, Detroit, Mich.

Year	Team		Games	BA	SA	AB	H	2B	3B	HR	HR%	R	RBI	BB	SO	SB	AB	H	PO	A	E	DP	TC/G	FA	G by Pos
1882	PHI	AA	20	.092	.092	65	6	0	0	0	0.0	10		12			0	0	28	57	23	0	5.4	.787	3B-11, SS-4, OF-3, 2B-2

Tommy Smith
SMITH, TOMMY ALEXANDER
B. Aug. 1, 1948, Albemarle, N. C.   BL TR   6'4"   210 lbs.

Year	Team		Games	BA	SA	AB	H	2B	3B	HR	HR%	R	RBI	BB	SO	SB	AB	H	PO	A	E	DP	TC/G	FA	G by Pos
1973	CLE	A	14	.244	.439	41	10	2	1	2	4.9	6	3	1	2	1	0	0	27	0	0	0	1.9	1.000	OF-13
1974			23	.097	.129	31	3	1	0	0	0.0	4	0	2	7	0	2	0	29	1	2	0	1.4	.938	OF-17, DH-1
1975			8	.125	.125	8	1	0	0	0	0.0	0	2	0	1	0	1	0	4	0	0	0	0.5	1.000	DH-3, OF-3
1976			55	.256	.323	164	42	3	1	2	1.2	17	12	8	8	8	2	0	90	4	2	0	1.7	.979	OF-50, DH-2
1977	SEA	A	21	.259	.370	27	7	1	0	0	0.0	1	4	0	6	0	8	2	10	3	0	0	0.6	1.000	OF-14
5 yrs.			121	.232	.317	271	63	7	2	4	1.5	28	21	11	24	9	13	2	160	8	4	0	1.4	.977	OF-97, DH-6

Tony Smith
SMITH, ANTHONY
B. May 14, 1884, Chicago, Ill.   D. Feb. 27, 1964, Galveston, Tex.   BR TR   5'9"   150 lbs.

Year	Team		Games	BA	SA	AB	H	2B	3B	HR	HR%	R	RBI	BB	SO	SB	AB	H	PO	A	E	DP	TC/G	FA	G by Pos
1907	WAS	A	51	.187	.209	139	26	1	1	0	0.0	12	8	18		3	0	0	99	141	21	11	5.1	.920	SS-51
1910	BKN	N	106	.181	.227	321	58	10	1	1	0.3	31	16	69	53	9	0	0	262	329	37	57	5.9	.941	SS-101, 3B-6
1911			13	.150	.175	40	6	1	0	0	0.0	3	2	8	7	1	0	0	21	38	8	7	5.2	.881	SS-10, 2B-3
3 yrs.			170	.180	.218	500	90	12	2	1	0.2	46	26	95	60	13	0	0	382	508	66	75	5.6	.931	SS-162, 3B-6, 2B-3

Vinnie Smith
SMITH, VINCENT AMBROSE
B. Dec. 7, 1915, Richmond, Va.   D. Dec. 14, 1979, Virginia Beach, Va.   BR TR   6'1"   176 lbs.

Year	Team		Games	BA	SA	AB	H	2B	3B	HR	HR%	R	RBI	BB	SO	SB	AB	H	PO	A	E	DP	TC/G	FA	G by Pos
1941	PIT	N	9	.303	.333	33	10	1	0	0	0.0	3	5	1	5	0	0	0	27	5	2	0	3.8	.941	C-9
1946			7	.190	.190	21	4	0	0	0	0.0	2	0	1	5	0	0	0	25	4	1	0	4.3	.967	C-7
2 yrs.			16	.259	.278	54	14	1	0	0	0.0	5	5	2	10	0	0	0	52	9	3	0	4.0	.953	C-16

Wally Smith
SMITH, WALLACE H.
B. Mar. 13, 1889, Philadelphia, Pa.   D. June 10, 1930, Florence, Ariz.   BR TR   5'11½"   180 lbs.

Year	Team		Games	BA	SA	AB	H	2B	3B	HR	HR%	R	RBI	BB	SO	SB	AB	H	PO	A	E	DP	TC/G	FA	G by Pos
1911	STL	N	81	.216	.330	194	42	6	5	2	1.0	23	19	21	33	5	16	2	63	139	14	7	2.7	.935	3B-26, SS-25, 2B-8, OF-1
1912			75	.256	.324	219	56	5	5	0	0.0	22	26	29	27	4	12	0	136	130	10	11	3.7	.964	3B-32, SS-22, 1B-6
1914	WAS	A	45	.196	.258	97	19	4	1	0	0.0	11	8	3	12	3	11	1	99	35	4	7	3.1	.971	2B-12, SS-7, 1B-7, 3B-5, OF-1
3 yrs.			201	.229	.314	510	117	15	11	2	0.4	56	53	53	72	12	39	3	298	304	28	25	3.1	.956	3B-63, SS-54, 2B-20, 1B-13, OF-2

Wib Smith
SMITH, WILBUR FLOYD
B. Aug. 30, 1886, Evart, Mich.   D. Nov. 18, 1959, Fargo, N. D.   BL TR   5'10½"   165 lbs.

Year	Team		Games	BA	SA	AB	H	2B	3B	HR	HR%	R	RBI	BB	SO	SB	AB	H	PO	A	E	DP	TC/G	FA	G by Pos
1909	STL	A	17	.190	.190	42	8	0	0	0	0.0	3	2	0		0	3	1	36	11	9	0	3.3	.839	C-13, 1B-1

Willie Smith
SMITH, WILLIE (Wonderful Willie)
B. Feb. 11, 1939, Anniston, Ala.   BL TL   6'   182 lbs.

Year	Team		Games	BA	SA	AB	H	2B	3B	HR	HR%	R	RBI	BB	SO	SB	AB	H	PO	A	E	DP	TC/G	FA	G by Pos
1963	DET	A	17	.125	.125	8	1	0	0	0	0.0	2	0	0	1	0	2	0	1	4	0	0	0.3	1.000	P-11
1964	LA	A	118	.301	.465	359	108	14	6	11	3.1	46	51	8	39	7	23	10	129	8	3	1	1.2	.979	OF-87, P-15
1965	CAL	A	136	.261	.423	459	120	14	9	14	3.1	52	57	32	60	9	21	4	196	12	5	2	1.6	.977	OF-123, 1B-2
1966			90	.185	.236	195	36	3	2	1	0.5	18	20	12	37	1	41	5	71	4	2	1	0.9	.974	OF-52
1967	CLE	A	21	.219	.281	32	7	0	1	0	0.0	0	2	1	10	0	16	4	12	0	1	0	0.6	.923	OF-4, 1B-3

Year	Team	Games	BA	SA	AB	H	2B	3B	HR	HR%	R	RBI	BB	SO	SB	Pinch Hit AB	Pinch Hit H	PO	A	E	DP	TC/G	FA	G by Pos

Willie Smith *continued*

Year	Team	Games	BA	SA	AB	H	2B	3B	HR	HR%	R	RBI	BB	SO	SB	PH AB	PH H	PO	A	E	DP	TC/G	FA	G by Pos
1968	2 teams	CLE A (33G – .143)			CHI N (55G – .275)																			
"	total	88	.245	.402	184	45	10	2	5	2.7	14	28	15	47	0	36	10	113	6	0	6	1.4	1.000	OF-39, 1B-11, P-3
1969	CHI N	103	.246	.441	195	48	9	1	9	4.6	21	25	25	49	1	40	12	185	9	3	14	1.9	.985	OF-33, 1B-24
1970		87	.216	.371	167	36	9	1	5	3.0	15	24	11	32	2	40	9	318	11	2	32	3.8	.994	1B-43, OF-1
1971	CIN N	31	.164	.255	55	9	2	0	1	1.8	3	4	3	9	0	20	0	80	9	0	10	2.9	1.000	1B-10
9 yrs.		691	.248	.395	1654	410	63	21	46	2.8	171	211	107	284	20	239	54	1105	63	16	66	1.7	.986	OF-339, 1B-93, P-29

Homer Smoot

SMOOT, HOMER VERNON
B. Mar. 26, 1878, Galestown, Md. D. Mar. 25, 1928, Salisbury, Md.

BL TR 5'10" 190 lbs.

Year	Team	Games	BA	SA	AB	H	2B	3B	HR	HR%	R	RBI	BB	SO	SB	PH AB	PH H	PO	A	E	DP	TC/G	FA	G by Pos
1902	STL N	129	.311	.380	518	161	19	4	3	0.6	58	48	23		20	0	0	284	14	22	5	2.5	.931	OF-129
1903		129	.296	.396	500	148	22	8	4	0.8	67	49	32		17	0	0	231	14	15	3	2.0	.942	OF-129
1904		137	.281	.365	520	146	23	6	3	0.6	58	66	37		23	0	0	270	17	10	6	2.2	.966	OF-137
1905		139	.311	.433	534	166	21	16	4	0.7	73	58	33		21	1	0	295	18	8	6	2.3	.975	OF-138
1906	2 teams	STL N (86G – .248)			CIN N (60G – .259)																			
"	total	146	.252	.327	563	142	17	11	1	0.2	52	48	24		3	1	0	283	18	16	4	2.2	.950	OF-145
5 yrs.		680	.290	.380	2635	763	102	45	15	0.6	308	269	149		84	2	0	1363	81	71	24	2.2	.953	OF-678

Henry Smoyer

SMOYER, HENRY NEITZ (Hennie)
Born Henry Neitz Smowery.
B. Apr. 24, 1890, Fredericksburg, Pa. D. Feb. 28, 1958, Dubois, Pa.

BR TR 5'6"

Year	Team	Games	BA	SA	AB	H	2B	3B	HR	HR%	R	RBI	BB	SO	SB	PH AB	PH H	PO	A	E	DP	TC/G	FA	G by Pos
1912	STL A	6	.214	.214	14	3	0	0	0	0.0	1	0	2		0	0	0	5	12	0	1	2.8	1.000	SS-4, 3B-2

Frank Smykal

SMYKAL, FRANK JOHN
Born Frank John Smejkal.
B. Oct. 13, 1889, Chicago, Ill. D. Aug. 11, 1950, Chicago, Ill.

BR TR 5'7" 150 lbs.

Year	Team	Games	BA	SA	AB	H	2B	3B	HR	HR%	R	RBI	BB	SO	SB	PH AB	PH H	PO	A	E	DP	TC/G	FA	G by Pos
1916	PIT N	6	.300	.300	10	3	0	0	0	0.0	2	3	1		1	0	0	3	14	3	1	3.3	.850	SS-5, 3B-1

Clancy Smyres

SMYRES, CLARENCE MELVIN
B. May 24, 1922, Culver City, Calif.

BB TR 5'11½" 175 lbs.

Year	Team	Games	BA	SA	AB	H	2B	3B	HR	HR%	R	RBI	BB	SO	SB	PH AB	PH H	PO	A	E	DP	TC/G	FA	G by Pos
1944	BKN N	5	.000	.000	2	0	0	0	0	0.0	1	0	0	0	0	2	0	0	0	0	0	0.0	–	

Red Smyth

SMYTH, JAMES DANIEL
B. Jan. 30, 1893, Holly Springs, Miss. D. Apr. 14, 1958, Inglewood, Calif.

BL TR 5'9" 152 lbs.

Year	Team	Games	BA	SA	AB	H	2B	3B	HR	HR%	R	RBI	BB	SO	SB	PH AB	PH H	PO	A	E	DP	TC/G	FA	G by Pos
1915	BKN N	19	.136	.182	22	3	1	0	0	0.0	3	3	4	1	4	0	0	14	1	0	0	0.8	1.000	OF-9
1916		2	.000	.000	5	0	0	0	0	0.0	0	0	0	3	0	1	0	3	2	0	1	2.5	1.000	2B-2
1917	2 teams	BKN N (29G – .125)			STL N (28G – .208)																			
"	total	57	.188	.229	96	18	0	0	0	0.0	10	5	8	15	3	24	5	30	3	7	1	0.7	.825	OF-25, 3B-4
1918	STL N	40	.212	.257	113	24	1	4	0	0.0	19	4	16	11	3	1	0	56	31	5	2	2.3	.946	OF-25, 2B-11
4 yrs.		118	.191	.233	236	45	2	4	0	0.0	32	12	28	31	7	30	5	103	37	12	4	1.3	.921	OF-59, 2B-13, 3B-4

Jon Sneed

SNEED, JONATHAN L.
B. Columbus, Ohio D. Jan. 4, 1899, Memphis, Tenn.

Year	Team	Games	BA	SA	AB	H	2B	3B	HR	HR%	R	RBI	BB	SO	SB	PH AB	PH H	PO	A	E	DP	TC/G	FA	G by Pos
1884	IND AA	27	.216	.284	102	22	4	0	1	1.0	14		6			0	0	45	4	11	0	2.2	.817	OF-27
1890	2 teams	TOL AA (9G – .200)			COL AA (128G – .291)																			
"	total	137	.286	.381	514	147	13	15	2	0.4	117		71		44	0	0	177	27	29	6	1.7	.876	OF-135, SS-2
1891	COL AA	99	.257	.322	366	94	9	6	1	0.3	66	61	55	29	24	0	0	142	10	18	4	1.7	.894	OF-99
3 yrs.		263	.268	.349	982	263	26	21	4	0.4	197	61	132	29	68	0	0	364	41	58	10	1.8	.875	OF-261, SS-2

Charlie Snell

SNELL, CHARLES ANTHONY
Born Charles Anthony Schnell.
B. Nov. 29, 1893, Hampstead, Md. D. Apr. 4, 1988, Reading, Pa.

BR TR 5'11" 160 lbs.

Year	Team	Games	BA	SA	AB	H	2B	3B	HR	HR%	R	RBI	BB	SO	SB	PH AB	PH H	PO	A	E	DP	TC/G	FA	G by Pos
1912	STL A	8	.211	.263	19	4	1	0	0	0.0	0	0	3		0	0	0	35	13	3	1	6.4	.941	C-8

Wally Snell

SNELL, WALTER HENRY (Doc)
B. Apr. 19, 1889, West Bridgewater, Mass. D. July 23, 1980, Providence, R. I.

BR TR 5'10" 170 lbs.

Year	Team	Games	BA	SA	AB	H	2B	3B	HR	HR%	R	RBI	BB	SO	SB	PH AB	PH H	PO	A	E	DP	TC/G	FA	G by Pos
1913	BOS A	5	.375	.375	8	3	0	0	0	0.0	1	0	0	0	1	4	2	6	2	0	1	1.6	1.000	C-1

Duke Snider

SNIDER, EDWIN DONALD (The Silver Fox)
B. Sept. 19, 1926, Los Angeles, Calif.
Hall of Fame 1980.

BL TR 6'½" 198 lbs.

Year	Team	Games	BA	SA	AB	H	2B	3B	HR	HR%	R	RBI	BB	SO	SB	PH AB	PH H	PO	A	E	DP	TC/G	FA	G by Pos
1947	BKN N	40	.241	.301	83	20	3	1	0	0.0	6	5	3	24	2	15	4	48	0	1	0	1.2	.980	OF-25
1948		53	.244	.450	160	39	6	6	5	3.1	22	21	12	27	4	6	2	87	5	1	0	1.8	.989	OF-47
1949		146	.292	.493	552	161	28	7	23	4.2	100	92	56	92	12	1	1	355	12	6	2	2.6	.984	OF-145
1950		152	.321	.553	620	199	31	10	31	5.0	109	107	58	79	16	1	1	378	15	7	1	2.6	.983	OF-151
1951		150	.277	.483	606	168	26	6	29	4.8	96	101	62	97	14	0	0	382	12	5	1	2.7	.987	OF-150
1952		144	.303	.494	534	162	25	7	21	3.9	80	92	55	77	7	2	1	341	13	3	3	2.5	.992	OF-141
1953		153	.336	**.627**	590	198	38	4	42	7.1	**132**	126	82	90	16	4	3	370	7	5	3	2.5	.987	OF-151
1954		149	.341	.647	584	199	39	10	40	6.8	**120**	130	84	**96**	6	1	1	360	8	7	0	2.5	.981	OF-148
1955		148	.309	.628	538	166	34	6	42	7.8	**126**	**136**	104	87	9	1	0	348	9	4	0	2.4	.989	OF-146
1956		151	.292	**.598**	542	158	33	2	**43**	7.9	112	101	**99**	101	3	1	1	358	11	6	1	2.5	.984	OF-150
1957		139	.274	.587	508	139	25	7	40	**7.9**	91	92	77	**104**	3	3	2	304	6	3	1	2.3	.990	OF-136
1958	LA N	106	.312	.505	327	102	12	3	15	4.6	45	58	32	49	2	15	4	151	4	2	1	1.5	.987	OF-92
1959		126	.308	.535	370	114	11	2	23	6.2	59	88	58	71	1	21	7	157	2	4	1	1.3	.975	OF-107
1960		101	.243	.519	235	57	13	6	14	6.0	38	36	46	54	1	25	6	108	3	4	1	1.1	.965	OF-75
1961		85	.296	.562	233	69	8	3	16	6.9	35	56	29	43	1	18	4	113	6	3	3	1.4	.975	OF-66
1962		80	.278	.481	158	44	11	3	5	3.2	28	30	36	32	2	33	6	56	3	2	0	0.8	.967	OF-39
1963	NY N	129	.243	.401	354	86	8	3	14	4.0	44	45	56	74	0	29	6	139	5	2	0	1.1	.986	OF-106

Year Team	Games	BA	SA	AB	H	2B	3B	HR	HR%	R	RBI	BB	SO	SB	Pinch Hit AB	Pinch Hit H	PO	A	E	DP	TC/G	FA	G by Pos

Duke Snider *continued*

Year Team	Games	BA	SA	AB	H	2B	3B	HR	HR%	R	RBI	BB	SO	SB	AB	H	PO	A	E	DP	TC/G	FA	G by Pos
1964 SF N	91	.210	.323	167	35	7	0	4	2.4	16	17	22	40	0	47	10	44	2	1	0	0.5	.979	OF-43
18 yrs.	2143	.295	.540	7161	2116	358	85	407	5.7	1259	1333	971	1237	99	223	59	4099	123	66	18	2.0	.985	OF-1918

WORLD SERIES

Year Team	Games	BA	SA	AB	H	2B	3B	HR	HR%	R	RBI	BB	SO	SB	AB	H	PO	A	E	DP	TC/G	FA	G by Pos
1949 BKN N	5	.143	.190	21	3	1	0	0	0.0	2	0	0	8	0	0	0	18	1	0	0	3.8	1.000	OF-5
1952	7	.345	.828	29	10	2	0	4	13.8	5	8	1	5	1	0	0	23	0	0	0	3.3	1.000	OF-7
1953	6	.320	.560	25	8	3	0	1	4.0	3	5	2	6	0	0	0	17	1	0	1	3.0	1.000	OF-7
1955	7	.320	.840	25	8	1	0	4	16.0	5	7	2	6	0	0	0	13	0	0	0	1.9	1.000	OF-7
1956	7	.304	.478	23	7	1	0	1	4.3	5	4	6	8	0	0	0	20	0	0	0	2.9	1.000	OF-7
1959 LA N	4	.200	.500	10	2	0	0	1	10.0	1	2	2	0	0	1	0	5	0	2	0	1.8	.714	OF-3
6 yrs.	36	.286	.594	133	38	8	0	11	8.3	21	26	13	33	1	1	0	96	2	2	1	2.8	.980	OF-35
						6th		4th	5th	10th	7th		3rd										

Van Snider

SNIDER, VAN VOORHEES
B. Aug. 11, 1963, Birmingham, Ala. BL TR 6'3" 185 lbs.

Year Team	Games	BA	SA	AB	H	2B	3B	HR	HR%	R	RBI	BB	SO	SB	AB	H	PO	A	E	DP	TC/G	FA	G by Pos
1988 CIN N	11	.214	.357	28	6	1	0	1	3.6	4	6	0	13	0	4	0	15	0	0	0	1.4	1.000	OF-8
1989	8	.143	.143	7	1	0	0	0	0.0	1	0	0	5	0	2	0	6	0	0	0	0.8	1.000	OF-6
2 yrs.	19	.200	.314	35	7	1	0	1	2.9	5	6	0	18	0	6	0	21	0	0	0	1.1	1.000	OF-14

Roxy Snipes

SNIPES, WYATT EURE (Rock)
B. Oct. 28, 1896, Marion, S. C. D. May 1, 1941, Fayetteville, N. C. BL TR 6' 185 lbs.

Year Team	Games	BA	SA	AB	H	2B	3B	HR	HR%	R	RBI	BB	SO	SB	AB	H	PO	A	E	DP	TC/G	FA	G by Pos
1923 CHI A	1	.000	.000	1	0	0	0	0	0.0	0	0	0	0	0	1	0	0	0	0	0	0.0	—	

Chappie Snodgrass

SNODGRASS, AMZIE BEAL
B. Mar. 18, 1870, Springfield, Ohio D. Sept. 9, 1951, New York, N. Y. BR TR 5'10" 165 lbs.

Year Team	Games	BA	SA	AB	H	2B	3B	HR	HR%	R	RBI	BB	SO	SB	AB	H	PO	A	E	DP	TC/G	FA	G by Pos
1901 BAL A	3	.100	.100	10	1	0	0	0	0.0	0	1	0		0	0	0	3	0	3	0	2.0	.500	OF-2

Fred Snodgrass

SNODGRASS, FREDERICK CHARLES (Snow)
B. Oct. 19, 1887, Ventura, Calif. D. Apr. 5, 1974, Ventura, Calif. BR TR 5'11½" 175 lbs.

Year Team	Games	BA	SA	AB	H	2B	3B	HR	HR%	R	RBI	BB	SO	SB	AB	H	PO	A	E	DP	TC/G	FA	G by Pos
1908 NY N	6	.250	.250	4	1	0	0	0	0.0	2	1	0		1	1	0	4	1	0	0	0.8	1.000	C-3
1909	28	.300	.414	70	21	5	0	1	1.4	10	6	7		10	6	1	36	4	3	1	1.5	.930	OF-19, C-2, 1B-1
1910	123	.321	.432	396	127	22	8	2	0.5	69	44	71	52	33	10	3	300	22	10	6	2.7	.970	OF-101, 1B-9, 3B-1, C-1
1911	151	.294	.388	534	157	27	10	1	0.2	83	77	72	59	51	0	0	305	37	9	8	2.3	.974	OF-149, 2B-1, 1B-1
1912	146	.269	.364	535	144	24	9	3	0.6	91	69	70	65	43	2	0	472	36	21	16	3.6	.960	OF-116, 1B-28, 2B-1
1913	141	.291	.383	457	133	21	6	3	0.7	65	49	53	44	27	3	0	317	19	11	1	2.5	.968	OF-133, 1B-3, 2B-1
1914	113	.263	.334	392	103	20	4	0	0.0	54	44	37	43	25	6	1	313	21	7	10	3.0	.979	OF-96, 1B-14, 3B-1, 2B-1
1915 2 teams		NY N (103G – .194)		BOS N (23G – .278)																			
" total	126	.215	.248	331	71	11	0	0	0.0	46	29	42	42	11	4	1	239	14	16	4	2.1	.941	OF-121, 1B-5
1916 BOS N	112	.249	.317	382	95	13	5	1	0.3	33	32	34	54	14	1	0	274	19	5	5	2.7	.983	OF-110
9 yrs.	946	.275	.359	3101	852	143	42	11	0.4	453	351	386	359	215	33	6	2260	173	82	51	2.7	.967	OF-845, 1B-61, C-6, 2B-4, 3B-2

WORLD SERIES

Year Team	Games	BA	SA	AB	H	2B	3B	HR	HR%	R	RBI	BB	SO	SB	AB	H	PO	A	E	DP	TC/G	FA	G by Pos
1911 NY N	6	.105	.105	19	2	0	0	0	0.0	1	1	2	7	0	0	0	9	0	0	0	1.5	1.000	OF-6
1912	8	.212	.273	33	7	2	0	0	0.0	2	2	2	5	1	0	0	17	1	1	0	2.4	.947	OF-8
1913	2	.333	.333	3	1	0	0	0	0.0	0	0	0	0	0	0	0	3	1	0	0	2.0	1.000	OF-1, 1B-1
3 yrs.	16	.182	.218	55	10	2	0	0	0.0	3	3	4	12	1	0	0	29	2	1	0	2.0	.969	OF-15, 1B-1

Bernie Snyder

SNYDER, BERNARD AUSTIN
B. Aug. 25, 1913, Philadelphia, Pa. BR TR 6' 165 lbs.

Year Team	Games	BA	SA	AB	H	2B	3B	HR	HR%	R	RBI	BB	SO	SB	AB	H	PO	A	E	DP	TC/G	FA	G by Pos
1935 PHI A	10	.344	.375	32	11	1	0	0	0.0	5	3	1	2	0	2	0	24	19	5	4	4.8	.896	2B-5, SS-4

Charlie Snyder

SNYDER, CHARLES
B. Camden, N. J. D. Mar. 10, 1901, Philadelphia, Pa. TR

Year Team	Games	BA	SA	AB	H	2B	3B	HR	HR%	R	RBI	BB	SO	SB	AB	H	PO	A	E	DP	TC/G	FA	G by Pos
1890 PHI AA	9	.273	.303	33	9	1	0	0	0.0	5		2			0	0	21	5	11	0	4.1	.703	OF-5, C-5

Cooney Snyder

SNYDER, FRANK C.
B. Toronto, Ont., Canada D. Mar. 9, 1917, Toronto, Ont., Canada

Year Team	Games	BA	SA	AB	H	2B	3B	HR	HR%	R	RBI	BB	SO	SB	AB	H	PO	A	E	DP	TC/G	FA	G by Pos
1898 LOU N	17	.164	.164	61	10	0	0	0	0.0	4	6	3		0	0	0	43	15	4	1	3.6	.935	C-17

Cory Snyder

SNYDER, JAMES CORY
B. Nov. 11, 1962, Inglewood, Calif. BR TR 6'4" 175 lbs.

Year Team	Games	BA	SA	AB	H	2B	3B	HR	HR%	R	RBI	BB	SO	SB	AB	H	PO	A	E	DP	TC/G	FA	G by Pos
1986 CLE A	103	.272	.500	416	113	21	1	24	5.8	58	69	16	123	2	0	0	213	84	10	22	3.0	.967	OF-74, SS-34, 3B-11, DH-1
1987	157	.236	.456	577	136	24	2	33	5.7	74	82	31	166	5	5	2	313	53	15	9	2.4	.961	OF-139, SS-18
1988	142	.272	.483	511	139	24	3	26	5.1	71	75	42	101	5	1	0	314	16	5	0	2.4	.985	OF-141
1989	132	.215	.360	489	105	17	0	18	3.7	49	59	23	134	6	8	0	297	32	1	7	2.5	.997	OF-125, SS-7, DH-2
4 yrs.	534	.247	.449	1993	493	86	6	101	5.1	252	285	112	524	18	16	2	1137	185	31	38	2.5	.977	OF-479, SS-59, 3B-11, DH-3

Frank Snyder

SNYDER, FRANK ELTON (Pancho)
B. May 27, 1893, San Antonio, Tex. D. Jan. 5, 1962, San Antonio, Tex. BR TR 6'2" 185 lbs.

Year Team	Games	BA	SA	AB	H	2B	3B	HR	HR%	R	RBI	BB	SO	SB	AB	H	PO	A	E	DP	TC/G	FA	G by Pos
1912 STL N	11	.111	.111	18	2	0	0	0	0.0	2	0	2	7	1	0	0	25	9	3	0	3.4	.919	C-11
1913	7	.190	.286	21	4	0	1	0	0.0	1	2	0	4	0	0	0	31	12	2	0	6.4	.956	C-7
1914	100	.230	.310	326	75	15	4	1	0.3	19	25	13	28	1	2	0	419	130	12	12	5.6	.979	C-98
1915	144	.298	.387	473	141	22	7	2	0.4	41	55	39	49	3	1	0	592	204	14	9	5.6	.983	C-144
1916	132	.259	.308	406	105	12	4	0	0.0	23	39	18	31	7	13	5	731	138	19	35	6.7	.979	C-72, 1B-46, SS-1
1917	115	.236	.288	313	74	9	2	1	0.3	18	33	27	43	4	18	6	341	134	12	10	4.2	.975	C-94
1918	39	.250	.330	112	28	7	1	0	0.0	5	10	6	13	1	4	2	127	40	6	4	4.4	.965	C-27, 1B-3

Year	Team		Games	BA	SA	AB	H	2B	3B	HR	HR%	R	RBI	BB	SO	SB	Pinch Hit AB	Pinch Hit H	PO	A	E	DP	TC/G	FA	G by Pos

Frank Snyder *continued*

Year	Team		Games	BA	SA	AB	H	2B	3B	HR	HR%	R	RBI	BB	SO	SB	AB	H	PO	A	E	DP	TC/G	FA	G by Pos
1919	2 teams	STL N (50G – .182)				NY	N	(32G – .228)																	
"	total		82	.199	.256	246	49	10	2	0	0.0	14	25	13	22	3	2	1	244	113	6	6	4.4	.983	C-79, 1B-1
1920	NY	N	87	.250	.364	264	66	13	4	3	1.1	26	27	17	18	2	3	0	269	92	8	6	4.2	.978	C-84
1921			108	.320	.453	309	99	13	2	8	2.6	36	45	27	24	3	5	2	299	98	6	7	3.7	.985	C-101
1922			104	.343	.487	318	109	21	5	5	1.6	34	51	23	25	1	5	2	272	74	7	10	3.4	.980	C-97
1923			120	.256	.356	402	103	13	6	5	1.2	37	63	24	29	5	8	5	428	90	5	12	4.4	.990	C-112
1924			118	.302	.412	354	107	18	3	5	1.4	37	53	30	43	3	8	3	308	79	5	8	3.3	.987	C-110
1925			107	.240	.375	325	78	9	1	11	3.4	21	51	20	49	0	11	5	336	71	6	7	3.9	.985	C-96
1926			55	.216	.365	148	32	3	2	5	3.4	10	16	13	13	0	0	0	168	38	4	3	3.8	.981	C-55
1927	STL	N	63	.258	.299	194	50	5	0	1	0.5	7	30	9	18	0	1	1	174	37	4	5	3.4	.981	C-62
16 yrs.			1392	.265	.360	4229	1122	170	44	47	1.1	331	525	281	416	37	86	32	4764	1359	119	134	4.5	.981	C-1249, 1B-50, SS-1

WORLD SERIES

Year	Team		Games	BA	SA	AB	H	2B	3B	HR	HR%	R	RBI	BB	SO	SB	AB	H	PO	A	E	DP	TC/G	FA	G by Pos
1921	NY	N	7	.364	.545	22	8	1	0	1	4.5	4	3	0	2	0	1	0	43	5	0	0	6.9	1.000	C-6
1922			4	.333	.333	15	5	0	0	0	0.0	1	0	0	1	0	0	0	23	5	1	1	7.3	.966	C-4
1923			5	.118	.294	17	2	0	0	1	5.9	1	2	0	2	0	0	0	24	3	0	1	5.4	1.000	C-5
1924			1	.000	.000	1	0	0	0	0	0.0	0	0	0	0	0	1	0	0	0	0	0	0.0	–	
4 yrs.			17	.273	.400	55	15	1	0	2	3.6	6	5	0	5	0	2	0	90	13	1	2	6.1	.990	C-15

Jack Snyder

SNYDER, JOHN WILLIAM
B. Oct. 6, 1886, Allegheny County, Pa. D. Dec. 13, 1981, Brownsville, Pa.

BR TR 5'9" 168 lbs.

Year	Team		Games	BA	SA	AB	H	2B	3B	HR	HR%	R	RBI	BB	SO	SB	AB	H	PO	A	E	DP	TC/G	FA	G by Pos
1914	BUF	F	1	–	–	0	0	0	0	0	–	0	0	1	0	0	0	0	0	0	0	0	0.0	–	C-1
1917	BKN	N	7	.273	.273	11	3	0	0	0	0.0	1	1	0	2	0	1	0	11	4	0	0	2.1	1.000	C-5
2 yrs.			8	.273	.273	11	3	0	0	0	0.0	1	1	1	2	0	1	0	11	4	0	0	1.9	1.000	C-6

Jerry Snyder

SNYDER, GERALD GEORGE
B. July 21, 1929, Jenks, Okla.

BR TR 6' 170 lbs.

Year	Team		Games	BA	SA	AB	H	2B	3B	HR	HR%	R	RBI	BB	SO	SB	AB	H	PO	A	E	DP	TC/G	FA	G by Pos
1952	WAS	A	36	.158	.193	57	9	2	0	0	0.0	5	2	5	8	1	7	0	37	55	5	12	2.7	.948	2B-19, SS-4
1953			29	.339	.403	62	21	4	0	0	0.0	10	4	5	8	1	1	0	33	58	3	10	3.2	.968	SS-17, 2B-4
1954			64	.234	.266	154	36	3	1	0	0.0	17	17	15	18	3	1	0	88	148	7	32	3.8	.971	SS-48, 2B-3
1955			46	.224	.271	107	24	5	0	0	0.0	7	5	6	6	1	6	1	78	68	4	24	3.3	.973	2B-22, SS-20
1956			43	.270	.345	148	40	3	1	2	1.4	14	14	10	9	1	1	0	64	124	9	28	4.6	.954	SS-35, 2B-7
1957			42	.151	.194	93	14	1	0	1	1.1	6	4	4	9	0	12	3	43	59	3	16	2.5	.971	SS-15, 2B-13, 3B-1
1958			6	.111	.111	9	1	0	0	0	0.0	1	1	1	1	0	2	0	8	2	0	1	1.7	1.000	2B-2, SS-1
7 yrs.			266	.230	.279	630	145	18	2	3	0.5	60	47	46	59	7	29	4	351	514	31	123	3.4	.965	SS-140, 2B-70, 3B-1

Jimmy Snyder

SNYDER, JAMES ROBERT
B. Aug. 15, 1932, Dearborn, Mich.
Manager 1988.

BR TR 6'1" 185 lbs.

Year	Team		Games	BA	SA	AB	H	2B	3B	HR	HR%	R	RBI	BB	SO	SB	AB	H	PO	A	E	DP	TC/G	FA	G by Pos
1961	MIN	A	3	.000	.000	5	0	0	0	0	0.0	0	0	0	1	0	0	0	4	3	0	1	2.3	1.000	2B-3
1962			12	.100	.100	10	1	0	0	0	0.0	1	1	0	0	0	0	0	8	8	1	3	1.4	.941	2B-5, 1B-1
1964			26	.155	.225	71	11	2	0	1	1.4	3	9	4	11	0	0	0	49	51	1	16	3.9	.990	2B-25
3 yrs.			41	.140	.198	86	12	2	0	1	1.2	4	10	4	12	0	0	0	61	62	2	20	3.0	.984	2B-33, 1B-1

Pop Snyder

SNYDER, CHARLES N.
B. Oct. 6, 1854, Washington, D. C. D. Oct. 29, 1924, Washington, D. C.
Manager 1882-84, 1891.

BR TR 5'11½" 184 lbs.

Year	Team		Games	BA	SA	AB	H	2B	3B	HR	HR%	R	RBI	BB	SO	SB	AB	H	PO	A	E	DP	TC/G	FA	G by Pos
1876	LOU	N	56	.196	.237	224	44	4	0	1	0.4	21	9	2	7			0	0	252	87	68	3	7.3	.833	C-55, OF-4
1877			61	.258	.327	248	64	7	2	2	0.8	23	28	3	14			0	0	292	103	40	8	7.1	.908	C-61, OF-1, SS-1
1878	BOS	N	60	.212	.235	226	48	5	0	0	0.0	21	14	1	19			0	0	344	92	42	2	8.0	.912	C-58, OF-2
1879			81	.237	.322	329	78	16	3	2	0.6	42	35	5	31			0	0	398	142	44	10	7.2	.925	C-80, OF-2
1881			62	.228	.265	219	50	8	0	0	0.0	14	16	3	23			0	0	261	110	44	0	6.7	.894	C-60, OF-1, SS-1, 2B-1
1882	CIN	AA	72	.291	.353	309	90	12	2	1	0.3	49		9				0	0	368	95	44	6	7.0	.913	C-70, 1B-2, OF-1
1883			58	.256	.360	250	64	14	6	0	0.0	38		8				0	0	286	78	36	4	6.9	.910	C-57, SS-2
1884			67	.257	.358	268	69	9	9	0	0.0	32		7				0	0	363	137	41	6	8.1	.924	C-65, 1B-2, OF-1
1885			39	.237	.322	152	36	4	3	1	0.7	13		6				0	0	192	64	35	3	7.5	.880	C-38, 1B-1
1886			60	.186	.250	220	41	8	3	0	0.0	33		13				0	0	329	80	44	11	7.6	.903	C-41, 1B-19, OF-1
1887	CLE	AA	74	.255	.340	282	72	12	6	0	0.0	33		9		5		0	0	404	148	56	12	8.2	.908	C-63, 1B-13
1888			64	.215	.270	237	51	7	3	0	0.0	22	14	6		9		0	0	335	131	48	12	8.0	.907	C-58, 1B-4, OF-3
1889	CLE	N	22	.193	.229	83	16	3	0	0	0.0	5	12	2	12	4		0	0	88	39	13	5	6.4	.907	C-22
1890	CLE	P	13	.188	.208	48	9	1	0	0	0.0	5	12	1	9	1		0	0	52	16	3	1	5.5	.958	C-13
1891	WAS	AA	8	.185	.259	27	5	0	1	0	0.0	4	2	0	3	0		0	0	51	6	0	0	7.1	1.000	1B-4, C-3, OF-1
15 yrs.			797	.236	.303	3122	737	110	39	7	0.2	355	142	75	118	19		0	0	4015	1328	558	80	7.4	.905	C-744, 1B-45, OF-17, SS-4, 2B-1

Redleg Snyder

SNYDER, EMANUEL SEBASTIAN
Born Emanuel Sebastian Schneider.
B. Dec. 12, 1854, Camden, N. J. D. Nov. 11, 1933, Camden, N. J.

BR TR 5'10" 175 lbs.

Year	Team		Games	BA	SA	AB	H	2B	3B	HR	HR%	R	RBI	BB	SO	SB	AB	H	PO	A	E	DP	TC/G	FA	G by Pos
1876	CIN	N	55	.151	.176	205	31	3	1	0	0.0	10	12	1	19			0	0	168	6	37	1	3.8	.825	OF-55
1884	WIL	U	17	.192	.192	52	10	0	0	0	0.0	4		1				0	0	155	5	4	8	9.6	.976	1B-16, OF-1
2 yrs.			72	.160	.179	257	41	3	1	0	0.0	14	12	2	19			0	0	323	11	41	9	5.2	.891	OF-56, 1B-16

Russ Snyder

SNYDER, RUSSELL HENRY
B. June 22, 1934, Oak., Neb.

BL TR 6'1" 190 lbs.

Year	Team		Games	BA	SA	AB	H	2B	3B	HR	HR%	R	RBI	BB	SO	SB	AB	H	PO	A	E	DP	TC/G	FA	G by Pos
1959	KC	A	73	.313	.420	243	76	13	2	3	1.2	41	21	19	29	6	8	2	127	9	2	2	1.9	.986	OF-64
1960			125	.260	.365	304	79	10	5	4	1.3	45	26	20	28	7	32	5	135	4	2	2	1.1	.986	OF-91
1961	BAL	A	115	.292	.375	312	91	13	5	1	0.3	46	13	20	32	5	8	0	168	3	6	0	1.5	.966	OF-108
1962			139	.305	.435	416	127	19	4	9	2.2	47	40	17	46	7	21	6	218	8	6	2	1.7	.974	OF-121
1963			148	.256	.364	429	110	21	2	7	1.6	51	36	40	48	18	22	4	238	5	3	1	1.7	.988	OF-130
1964			56	.290	.355	93	27	3	0	1	1.1	11	7	11	22	0	18	3	34	0	1	0	0.6	.971	OF-40
1965			132	.270	.322	345	93	11	2	1	0.3	49	29	27	38	3	23	4	188	4	0	1	1.5	1.000	OF-106

Year	Team	Games	BA	SA	AB	H	2B	3B	HR	HR%	R	RBI	BB	SO	SB	Pinch Hit AB	Pinch Hit H	PO	A	E	DP	TC/G	FA	G by Pos

Russ Snyder *continued*

Year	Team	Games	BA	SA	AB	H	2B	3B	HR	HR%	R	RBI	BB	SO	SB	AB	H	PO	A	E	DP	TC/G	FA	G by Pos
1966		117	.306	.413	373	114	21	5	3	0.8	66	41	38	37	2	15	2	209	6	3	2	1.9	.986	OF-104
1967		108	.236	.324	275	65	8	2	4	1.5	40	23	32	48	5	33	4	127	3	2	0	1.2	.985	OF-69
1968 2 teams	CHI A (38G – .134)				CLE A (68G – .281)																			
" total		106	.241	.318	299	72	10	2	3	1.0	32	28	29	37	1	29	6	133	4	1	3	1.3	.993	OF-76, 1B-1
1969	CLE A	122	.248	.308	266	66	10	0	2	0.8	26	24	25	33	3	41	7	144	2	6	1	1.2	.961	OF-84
1970	MIL A	124	.232	.315	276	64	11	0	4	1.4	34	31	16	40	1	28	6	140	1	5	0	1.2	.966	OF-106
12 yrs.		1365	.271	.363	3631	984	150	29	42	1.2	488	319	294	438	58	278	49	1861	49	37	13	1.4	.981	OF-1099, 1B-1

WORLD SERIES

Year	Team	Games	BA	SA	AB	H	2B	3B	HR	HR%	R	RBI	BB	SO	SB	AB	H	PO	A	E	DP	TC/G	FA	G by Pos
1966	BAL A	3	.167	.167	6	1	0	0	0	0.0	1	1	2	0	0	0	0	2	0	0	0	0.7	1.000	OF-3

Louis Sockalexis

SOCKALEXIS, LOUIS M. (Chief)
B. Oct. 24, 1871, Old Town, Me. D. Dec. 24, 1913, Burlington, Me. BL TR 5'11" 185 lbs.

Year	Team	Games	BA	SA	AB	H	2B	3B	HR	HR%	R	RBI	BB	SO	SB	AB	H	PO	A	E	DP	TC/G	FA	G by Pos
1897	CLE N	66	.338	.460	278	94	9	8	3	1.1	43	42	18		16	0	0	117	10	16	3	2.2	.888	OF-66
1898		21	.224	.254	67	15	2	0	0	0.0	11	10	1		0	4	1	21	6	1	3	1.3	.964	OF-16
1899		7	.273	.318	22	6	1	0	0	0.0	0	3	1		0	2	0	7	2	2	1	1.6	.818	OF-5
3 yrs.		94	.313	.414	367	115	12	8	3	0.8	54	55	20		16	6	1	145	18	19	7	1.9	.896	OF-87

Bill Sodd

SODD, WILLIAM
B. Sept. 18, 1914, Fort Worth, Tex. BR TR 6'2" 210 lbs.

Year	Team	Games	BA	SA	AB	H	2B	3B	HR	HR%	R	RBI	BB	SO	SB	AB	H	PO	A	E	DP	TC/G	FA	G by Pos
1937	CLE A	1	.000	.000	1	0	0	0	0	0.0	0	0	0	1	0	1	0	0	0	0	0	0.0	–	

Eric Soderholm

SODERHOLM, ERIC THANE
B. Sept. 24, 1948, Cortland, N. Y. BR TR 5'11" 187 lbs.

Year	Team	Games	BA	SA	AB	H	2B	3B	HR	HR%	R	RBI	BB	SO	SB	AB	H	PO	A	E	DP	TC/G	FA	G by Pos
1971	MIN A	21	.156	.266	64	10	4	0	1	1.6	9	9	10	17	0	0	0	17	48	4	2	3.3	.942	3B-20
1972		93	.188	.359	287	54	10	0	13	4.5	28	39	19	48	3	11	3	66	163	14	17	2.6	.942	3B-79
1973		35	.297	.423	111	33	7	2	1	0.9	22	9	21	16	1	3	1	26	67	8	5	2.9	.921	3B-33, SS-1
1974		141	.276	.392	464	128	18	3	10	2.2	63	51	48	68	7	6	0	101	273	17	19	2.8	.957	3B-130, SS-1
1975		117	.286	.415	419	120	17	2	11	2.6	62	58	53	66	3	1	0	94	277	12	14	3.3	.969	3B-113, DH-3
1977	CHI A	130	.280	.500	460	129	20	3	25	5.4	77	67	47	47	2	0	0	99	249	8	18	2.7	.978	3B-126, DH-3
1978		143	.258	.431	457	118	17	1	20	4.4	57	67	39	44	2	7	4	128	249	14	17	2.7	.964	3B-128, DH-11, 2B-1
1979 2 teams	CHI A (56G – .252)				TEX A (63G – .272)																			
" total		119	.261	.395	357	93	14	2	10	2.8	46	53	31	28	0	14	3	84	203	8	17	2.5	.973	3B-93, DH-14, 1B-2
1980	NY A	95	.287	.462	275	79	13	1	11	4.0	38	35	27	25	0	11	3	15	65	4	4	0.9	.952	DH-51, 3B-37
9 yrs.		894	.264	.421	2894	764	120	14	102	3.5	402	383	295	359	18	53	14	630	1594	89	113	2.6	.962	3B-759, DH-82, SS-2, 1B-2, 2B-1

LEAGUE CHAMPIONSHIP SERIES

Year	Team	Games	BA	SA	AB	H	2B	3B	HR	HR%	R	RBI	BB	SO	SB	AB	H	PO	A	E	DP	TC/G	FA	G by Pos
1980	NY A	2	.167	.167	6	1	0	0	0	0.0	0	0	0	0	0	0	0	0	0	0	0	0.0	–	DH-2

Rick Sofield

SOFIELD, RICHARD MICHAEL
B. Dec. 16, 1956, Cheyenne, Wyo. BL TR 6'1" 195 lbs.

Year	Team	Games	BA	SA	AB	H	2B	3B	HR	HR%	R	RBI	BB	SO	SB	AB	H	PO	A	E	DP	TC/G	FA	G by Pos
1979	MIN A	35	.301	.355	93	28	5	0	0	0.0	8	12	12	27	2	3	1	61	1	3	1	1.9	.954	OF-35
1980		131	.247	.374	417	103	18	4	9	2.2	52	49	24	92	4	13	4	267	7	6	0	2.1	.979	OF-126, DH-2
1981		41	.176	.196	102	18	2	0	0	0.0	9	5	8	22	3	7	1	54	5	1	0	1.5	.983	OF-34
3 yrs.		207	.243	.342	612	149	25	4	9	1.5	69	66	44	141	9	23	6	382	13	10	1	2.0	.975	OF-195, DH-2

Tony Solaita

SOLAITA, TOLIA
B. Jan. 15, 1947, Nuuyli, American Samoa BL TL 6' 210 lbs.

Year	Team	Games	BA	SA	AB	H	2B	3B	HR	HR%	R	RBI	BB	SO	SB	AB	H	PO	A	E	DP	TC/G	FA	G by Pos
1968	NY A	1	.000	.000	1	0	0	0	0	0.0	0	0	0	0	0	0	0	5	0	0	1	5.0	1.000	1B-1
1974	KC A	96	.268	.406	239	64	12	0	7	2.9	31	30	35	70	0	13	4	508	40	5	36	5.8	.991	1B-65, DH-14, OF-1
1975		93	.260	.515	231	60	11	0	16	6.9	35	44	39	79	0	15	3	282	28	2	24	3.4	.994	DH-37, 1B-35
1976 2 teams	KC A (31G – .235)				CAL A (63G – .270)																			
" total		94	.261	.403	283	74	13	0	9	3.2	29	42	40	61	0	13	4	485	57	2	33	5.8	.996	1B-59, DH-21
1977	CAL A	116	.241	.417	324	78	15	0	14	4.3	40	53	56	77	1	23	8	641	57	4	50	6.1	.990	1B-91, DH-6
1978		60	.223	.287	94	21	1	0	1	1.1	10	14	16	25	0	34	9	85	7	0	7	1.5	1.000	DH-18, 1B-11
1979 2 teams	MON N (29G – .286)				TOR A (36G – .265)																			
" total		65	.271	.431	144	39	12	1	3	2.1	19	20	28	32	0	14	2	124	10	1	15	2.1	.993	DH-26, 1B-19
7 yrs.		525	.255	.421	1316	336	66	1	50	3.8	164	203	214	345	2	112	30	2130	199	17	166	4.5	.993	1B-281, DH-122, OF-1

Moe Solomon

SOLOMON, MORRIS HIRSCH (The Rabbi of Swat)
B. Dec. 8, 1900, New York, N. Y. D. June 25, 1966, Miami, Fla. BL TL 5'9½" 180 lbs.

Year	Team	Games	BA	SA	AB	H	2B	3B	HR	HR%	R	RBI	BB	SO	SB	AB	H	PO	A	E	DP	TC/G	FA	G by Pos
1923	NY N	2	.375	.500	8	3	1	0	0	0.0	0	1	0	1	0	0	0	5	0	1	0	3.0	.833	OF-2

Moose Solters

SOLTERS, JULIUS JOSEPH
Born Julius Joseph Soltesz.
B. Mar. 22, 1906, Pittsburgh, Pa. D. Sept. 28, 1975, Pittsburgh, Pa. BR TR 6' 190 lbs.

Year	Team	Games	BA	SA	AB	H	2B	3B	HR	HR%	R	RBI	BB	SO	SB	AB	H	PO	A	E	DP	TC/G	FA	G by Pos
1934	BOS A	101	.299	.447	365	109	25	4	7	1.9	61	58	18	50	9	13	4	197	11	15	1	2.2	.933	OF-89
1935 2 teams	BOS A (24G – .241)				STL A (127G – .330)																			
" total		151	.319	.498	631	201	45	7	18	2.9	94	112	36	42	11	3	1	382	20	6	2	2.7	.985	OF-148
1936	STL A	152	.291	.467	628	183	45	7	17	2.7	100	134	41	76	3	3	0	356	16	17	5	2.6	.956	OF-147
1937	CLE A	152	.323	.533	589	190	42	11	20	3.4	90	109	42	56	6	3	0	283	19	15	3	2.1	.953	OF-149
1938		67	.201	.291	199	40	6	3	2	1.0	30	22	18	28	4	23	4	91	4	3	1	1.5	.969	OF-46
1939 2 teams	CLE A (41G – .275)				STL A (40G – .206)																			
" total		81	.236	.343	233	55	13	3	2	0.9	33	33	19	35	3	27	7	112	3	9	0	1.5	.927	OF-55
1940	CHI A	116	.308	.472	428	132	28	3	12	2.8	65	80	27	54	3	9	1	266	6	8	2	2.4	.971	OF-107
1941		76	.259	.375	251	65	9	4	4	1.6	24	43	18	31	3	13	5	135	7	5	1	1.9	.966	OF-63
1943		42	.155	.186	97	15	0	0	1	1.0	6	6	7	5	0	19	2	30	2	2	0	0.8	.941	OF-21
9 yrs.		938	.289	.449	3421	990	213	42	83	2.4	503	599	221	377	42	112	22	1852	88	80	17	2.2	.960	OF-825

Jock Somerlott

SOMERLOTT, JOHN WESLEY
B. Oct. 26, 1882, Flint, Ind. D. Apr. 21, 1965, Butler, Ind. BR TR 6' 160 lbs.

Year	Team	Games	BA	SA	AB	H	2B	3B	HR	HR%	R	RBI	BB	SO	SB	Pinch Hit AB	Pinch Hit H	PO	A	E	DP	TC/G	FA	G by Pos

Jock Somerlott *continued*

1910	WAS A	16	.222	.222	63	14	0	0	0	0.0	6	2	3		2	0	0	161	8	1	4	10.6	.994	1B-16
1911		13	.175	.175	40	7	0	0	0	0.0	2	2	0		2	1	1	117	10	1	7	9.8	.992	1B-12
2 yrs.		29	.204	.204	103	21	0	0	0	0.0	8	4	3		4	1	1	278	18	2	11	10.3	.993	1B-28

Kid Somers

SOMERS, WILLIAM
B. Toronto, Ont., Canada D. Oct. 16, 1895, Toronto, Ont., Canada   TR

| 1893 | STL N | 2 | .000 | .000 | 1 | 0 | 0 | 0 | 0 | 0.0 | 0 | | 0 | 0 | 0 | 0 | 0 | 1 | 1 | 2 | 0 | 2.0 | .500 | OF-1, C-1 |

Ed Somerville

SOMERVILLE, EDWARD
B. Philadelphia, Pa. D. Sept. 30, 1877, Hamilton, Ont., Canada   BR TR

| 1876 | LOU N | 64 | .188 | .215 | 256 | 48 | 5 | 1 | 0 | 0.0 | 29 | 14 | 1 | 6 | | 0 | 0 | 210 | 251 | 69 | 22 | 8.3 | .870 | 2B-64 |

Joe Sommer

SOMMER, JOSEPH JOHN
B. Nov. 20, 1858, Covington, Ky. D. Jan. 16, 1938, Cincinnati, Ohio   BR TR

1880	CIN N	24	.182	.193	88	16	1	0	0	0.0	10	6	0	2		0	0	42	4	5	1	2.1	.902	OF-22, SS-1, 3B-1, C-1
1882	CIN AA	80	.288	.364	354	102	12	6	1	0.3	82		24			0	0	188	9	16	2	2.7	.925	OF-80
1883		97	.278	.346	413	115	5	7	3	0.7	79		20			0	0	175	17	33	1	2.3	.853	OF-94, 3B-3, P-1
1884	BAL AA	107	.269	.359	479	129	11	10	4	0.8	96		8			0	0	138	176	58	11	3.5	.844	3B-97, OF-9, 2B-1
1885		110	.251	.331	471	118	23	6	1	0.2	84		24			0	0	245	21	24	2	2.6	.917	OF-107, SS-2, 3B-2, 1B-1
1886		139	.209	.261	560	117	18	4	1	0.2	79		24			0	0	290	124	45	14	3.3	.902	OF-95, 2B-32, 3B-11, SS-3, P-1
1887		131	.266	.311	463	123	11	5	0	0.0	88		63		29	0	0	237	84	44	10	2.8	.879	OF-110, 2B-13, 3B-10, SS-2, P-1
1888		79	.219	.253	297	65	10	0	0	0.0	31	35	18		13	0	0	115	109	30	13	3.2	.882	OF-44, SS-34, 2B-2, 1B-1
1889		106	.220	.272	386	85	13	2	1	0.3	51	36	42	49	18	0	0	173	26	15	7	2.0	.930	OF-105, SS-1
1890 2 teams	CLE N (9G – .229)				BAL AA (38G – .256)																			
" total		47	.250	.305	164	41	5	2	0	0.0	17		15	3	10	0	0	84	5	14	3	2.2	.864	OF-47, P-1
10 yrs.		920	.248	.309	3675	911	109	42	11	0.3	617	77	238	54	70	0	0	1687	575	284	64	2.8	.888	OF-713, 3B-124, 2B-48, SS-43, P-6, 1B-2, C-1

Bill Sommers

SOMMERS, WILLIAM DUNN
B. Feb. 17, 1923, Brooklyn, N. Y.   BR TR 6' 170 lbs.

| 1950 | STL A | 65 | .255 | .307 | 137 | 35 | 5 | 1 | 0 | 0.0 | 24 | 14 | 25 | 14 | 0 | 11 | 1 | 53 | 83 | 9 | 10 | 2.2 | .938 | 3B-37, 2B-21 |

Pete Sommers

SOMMERS, JOSEPH ANDREWS
B. Oct. 26, 1866, Cleveland, Ohio D. July 22, 1908, Cleveland, Ohio   BR 5'11½" 181 lbs.

1887	NY AA	33	.181	.233	116	21	3	0	1	0.9	9		7		6	0	0	124	44	35	5	6.2	.828	C-31, OF-1, 1B-1
1888	BOS N	4	.231	.308	13	3	1	0	0	0.0	1		0	3	0	0	0	20	2	3	0	6.3	.880	C-4
1889 2 teams	CHI N (12G – .222)				IND N (23G – .250)																			
" total		35	.240	.372	129	31	7	2	2	1.6	17	22	3	24		0	0	150	32	25	3	5.9	.879	C-32, OF-3
1890 2 teams	NY N (17G – .106)				CLE N (9G – .206)																			
" total		26	.148	.222	81	12	2	2	0	0.0	8	2	6	15		0	0	127	30	19	3	6.8	.892	C-19, 1B-5, OF-3
4 yrs.		98	.198	.286	339	67	13	4	3	0.9	35	24	16	42	8	0	0	421	108	82	11	6.2	.866	C-86, OF-7, 1B-6

Bill Sorrell

SORRELL, WILLIAM
B. Oct. 14, 1940, Morehead, Ky.   BL TR 6' 190 lbs.

1965	PHI N	10	.385	.615	13	5	0	0	1	7.7	2	2	2	1	0	7	3	0	0	0	0	0.0	–	3B-1
1967	SF N	18	.176	.235	17	3	1	0	0	0.0	1	1	3	2	0	10	2	1	0	0	0	0.1	1.000	OF-5
1970	KC A	57	.267	.370	135	36	2	0	4	3.0	12	14	10	13	1	23	6	37	48	9	3	1.6	.904	3B-29, OF-4, 1B-3
3 yrs.		85	.267	.376	165	44	3	0	5	3.0	15	17	15	16	1	40	11	38	48	9	3	1.1	.905	3B-30, OF-9, 1B-3

Chick Sorrells

SORRELLS, RAYMOND EDWIN (Red)
B. July 31, 1896, Stringtown, Okla. D. July 20, 1983, Terrell, Tex.   BR TR 5'9" 155 lbs.

| 1922 | CLE A | 2 | .000 | .000 | 1 | 0 | 0 | 0 | 0 | 0.0 | 0 | 0 | 0 | 0 | 0 | 0 | 0 | 3 | 0 | 0 | 0 | 1.5 | 1.000 | SS-1 |

Paul Sorrento

SORRENTO, PAUL ANTHONY
B. Nov. 17, 1965, Somerville, Mass.   BL TR 6'2" 195 lbs.

| 1989 | MIN A | 14 | .238 | .238 | 21 | 5 | 0 | 0 | 0 | 0.0 | 2 | 1 | 5 | 4 | 0 | 3 | 0 | 13 | 0 | 0 | 1 | 0.9 | 1.000 | DH-5, 1B-5 |

Sammy Sosa

SOSA, SAMUEL PERALTA
B. Nov. 10, 1968, San Pedro de Macoris, Dominican Republic   BR TR 6' 165 lbs.

| 1989 2 teams | TEX A (25G – .238) | | | | CHI A (33G – .273) | | | | | | | | | | | | | | | | | | | |
| " total | | 58 | .257 | .366 | 183 | 47 | 8 | 0 | 4 | 2.2 | 27 | 13 | 11 | 47 | 7 | 4 | 0 | 94 | 2 | 4 | 0 | 1.7 | .960 | OF-52, DH-6 |

Denny Sothern

SOTHERN, DENNIS ELWOOD
B. Jan. 20, 1904, Washington, D. C. D. Dec. 7, 1977, Durham, N. C.   BR TR 5'11" 175 lbs.

1926	PHI N	14	.245	.434	53	13	1	0	3	5.7	5	5	4	10	0	4	1	38	1	1	0	2.9	.975	OF-13
1928		141	.285	.375	579	165	27	5	5	0.9	82	38	34	53	17	2	2	358	19	14	7	2.8	.964	OF-136
1929		76	.306	.449	294	90	21	3	5	1.7	52	27	16	24	13	1	0	193	9	7	2	2.8	.967	OF-71
1930 2 teams	PHI N (90G – .280)				PIT N (17G – .176)																			
" total		107	.266	.392	398	106	30	1	6	1.5	70	40	25	41	8	8	4	251	15	9	6	2.6	.967	OF-97
1931	BKN N	19	.161	.194	31	5	1	0	0	0.0	10		4	8	0	3	1	23	0	1	0	1.3	.958	OF-10
5 yrs.		357	.280	.394	1355	379	80	9	19	1.4	219	115	83	136	38	15	8	863	44	32	15	2.6	.966	OF-327

Steve Souchock

SOUCHOCK, STEPHEN (Bud)
B. Mar. 3, 1919, Yatesboro, Pa.   BR TR 6'2½" 203 lbs.

1946	NY A	47	.302	.477	86	26	3	3	2	2.3	15	10	7	13	0	17	5	180	9	7	19	4.2	.964	1B-20
1948		44	.203	.322	118	24	3	4	3	2.5	11	11	7	13	3	11	2	231	13	3	25	5.6	.988	1B-32
1949	CHI A	84	.234	.409	252	59	13	5	7	2.8	29	37	25	38	5	17	4	346	21	6	30	4.4	.984	OF-39, 1B-30

Year	Team	Games	BA	SA	AB	H	2B	3B	HR	HR%	R	RBI	BB	SO	SB	Pinch Hit AB	Pinch Hit H	PO	A	E	DP	TC/G	FA	G by Pos

Steve Souchock *continued*

Year	Team	Games	BA	SA	AB	H	2B	3B	HR	HR%	R	RBI	BB	SO	SB	AB	H	PO	A	E	DP	TC/G	FA	G by Pos
1951	DET A	91	.245	.505	188	46	10	3	11	5.9	33	28	18	27	0	34	7	94	4	6	1	1.1	.942	OF-59, 2B-1, 1B-1
1952		92	.249	.487	265	66	16	4	13	4.9	40	45	21	28	1	17	4	195	31	8	7	2.5	.966	OF-56, 3B-13, 1B-9
1953		89	.302	.489	278	84	13	3	11	4.0	29	46	8	35	5	10	3	147	7	6	3	1.8	.963	OF-80, 1B-1
1954		25	.179	.462	39	7	0	1	3	7.7	6	8	2	10	1	14	2	15	4	0	0	0.8	1.000	OF-9, 3B-2
1955		1	1.000	1.000	1	1	0	0	0	0.0	0	0	0	0	0	1	1	0	0	0	0	0.0	–	
8 yrs.		473	.255	.457	1227	313	58	20	50	4.1	163	186	88	164	15	121	28	1208	89	36	85	2.8	.973	OF-243, 1B-93, 3B-15, 2B-1

Clyde Southwick

SOUTHWICK, CLYDE AUBRA
B. Nov. 3, 1886, Maxwell, Iowa D. Oct. 14, 1961, Freeport, Ill.

BL TR 6' 180 lbs.

Year	Team	Games	BA	SA	AB	H	2B	3B	HR	HR%	R	RBI	BB	SO	SB	AB	H	PO	A	E	DP	TC/G	FA	G by Pos
1911	STL A	4	.250	.250	12	3	0	0	0	0.0	3	0	1			0	0	11	4	1	0	4.0	.938	C-4

Bill Southworth

SOUTHWORTH, WILLIAM FREDERICK
B. Nov. 10, 1945, Madison, Wis.

BR TR 6'2" 205 lbs.

Year	Team	Games	BA	SA	AB	H	2B	3B	HR	HR%	R	RBI	BB	SO	SB	AB	H	PO	A	E	DP	TC/G	FA	G by Pos
1964	MIL N	3	.286	.714	7	2	0	0	1	14.3	2	2	0	3	0	1	0	0	2	0	0	0.7	1.000	3B-2

Billy Southworth

SOUTHWORTH, WILLIAM HARRISON
B. Mar. 9, 1893, Harvard, Neb. D. Nov. 15, 1969, Columbus, Ohio
Manager 1929, 1940-51.

BL TR 5'9" 170 lbs.

Year	Team	Games	BA	SA	AB	H	2B	3B	HR	HR%	R	RBI	BB	SO	SB	AB	H	PO	A	E	DP	TC/G	FA	G by Pos
1913	CLE A	1	–	–	0	0	0	0	0	–	0	0	0	0	0	0	0	0	0	0	0	0.0	–	OF-1
1915		60	.220	.288	177	39	2	5	0	0.0	25	8	36	12	2	8	0	90	7	6	3	1.7	.942	OF-44
1918	PIT N	64	.341	.443	246	84	5	7	2	0.8	37	43	26	9	19	0	0	137	12	3	4	2.4	.980	OF-64
1919		121	.280	.400	453	127	14	14	4	0.9	56	61	32	23	23	0	0	253	17	9	5	2.3	.968	OF-121
1920		146	.284	.374	546	155	17	13	2	0.4	64	53	52	20	23	2	0	337	12	3	3	2.4	.991	OF-142
1921	BOS N	141	.308	.441	569	175	25	15	7	1.2	86	79	36	13	22	0	0	288	25	8	6	2.3	.975	OF-141
1922		43	.323	.475	158	51	4	4	4	2.5	27	18	18	1	4	2	0	100	7	5	0	2.6	.955	OF-41
1923		153	.319	.448	611	195	29	16	6	1.0	95	76	61	23	14	0	0	329	26	22	6	2.5	.942	OF-151, 2B-2
1924	NY N	94	.256	.335	281	72	13	0	3	1.1	40	36	32	16	1	16	2	167	5	12	2	2.0	.935	OF-75
1925		123	.292	.391	473	138	19	5	6	1.3	79	44	51	11	6	1	0	289	7	11	1	2.5	.964	OF-120
1926	2 teams	NY	N	(36G – .328)		STL	N	(99G – .317)																
"	total	135	.320	.497	507	162	28	7	16	3.2	99	99	33	10	14	5	4	290	7	9	1	2.3	.971	OF-127
1927	STL N	92	.301	.402	306	92	15	5	2	0.7	52	39	23	7	10	9	2	153	6	5	2	1.8	.970	OF-83
1929		19	.188	.250	32	6	2	0	0	0.0	6	5	3	2	4	13	1	12	0	0	0	0.6	1.000	OF-5
13 yrs.		1192	.297	.415	4359	1296	173	91	52	1.2	661	561	402	148	138	56	9	2445	131	93	33	2.2	.965	OF-1115, 2B-2

WORLD SERIES

Year	Team	Games	BA	SA	AB	H	2B	3B	HR	HR%	R	RBI	BB	SO	SB	AB	H	PO	A	E	DP	TC/G	FA	G by Pos
1924	NY N	5	.000	.000	1	0	0	0	0	0.0	0	0	0	0	0	1	0	1	1	0	0	0.4	1.000	OF-2
1926	STL N	7	.345	.552	29	10	1	1	1	3.4	6	4	0	0	0	0	0	8	3	0	1	1.6	1.000	OF-7
2 yrs.		12	.333	.533	30	10	1	1	1	3.3	7	4	0	0	0	1	0	9	4	0	1	1.1	1.000	OF-9

Len Sowders

SOWDERS, LEONARD
Brother of John Sowders. Brother of Bill Sowders.
B. June 29, 1861, Louisville, Ky. D. Nov. 19, 1888, Indianapolis, Ind.

Year	Team	Games	BA	SA	AB	H	2B	3B	HR	HR%	R	RBI	BB	SO	SB	AB	H	PO	A	E	DP	TC/G	FA	G by Pos
1886	BAL AA	23	.263	.329	76	20	3	1	0	0.0	10		12			0	0	33	4	4	0	1.8	.902	OF-23, 1B-1

Al Spalding

SPALDING, ALBERT GOODWILL
B. Sept. 2, 1850, Byron, Ill. D. Sept. 9, 1915, San Diego, Calif.
Manager 1876-77.
Hall of Fame 1939.

BR TR 6'1" 170 lbs.

Year	Team	Games	BA	SA	AB	H	2B	3B	HR	HR%	R	RBI	BB	SO	SB	AB	H	PO	A	E	DP	TC/G	FA	G by Pos
1876	CHI N	66	.312	.373	292	91	14	2	0	0.0	54	44	6	3		0	0	58	94	10	7	2.5	.938	P-61, OF-10, 1B-3
1877		60	.256	.331	254	65	7	6	0	0.0	29	35	3	16		0	0	511	82	33	29	10.4	.947	1B-45, 2B-13, P-4, 3B-2
1878		1	.500	.500	4	2	0	0	0	0.0	0	0	0	0		0	0	3	0	4	0	7.0	.429	2B-1
3 yrs.		127	.287	.355	550	158	21	8	0	0.0	83	79	9	19		0	0	572	176	47	36	6.3	.941	P-65, 1B-48, 2B-14, OF-10, 3B-2

Dick Spalding

SPALDING, CHARLES HARRY
B. Oct. 13, 1893, Philadelphia, Pa. D. Feb. 3, 1950, Philadelphia, Pa.

BL TL 5'11" 185 lbs.

Year	Team	Games	BA	SA	AB	H	2B	3B	HR	HR%	R	RBI	BB	SO	SB	AB	H	PO	A	E	DP	TC/G	FA	G by Pos
1927	PHI N	115	.296	.346	442	131	16	3	0	0.0	68	25	38	40	5	1	0	250	7	2	1	2.3	.992	OF-113
1928	WAS A	16	.348	.348	23	8	0	0	0	0.0	1	0	0	4	0	2	0	9	0	0	0	0.6	1.000	OF-11
2 yrs.		131	.299	.346	465	139	16	3	0	0.0	69	25	38	44	5	3	0	259	7	2	1	2.0	.993	OF-124

Al Spangler

SPANGLER, ALBERT DONALD
B. July 8, 1933, Philadelphia, Pa.

BL TL 6' 175 lbs.

Year	Team	Games	BA	SA	AB	H	2B	3B	HR	HR%	R	RBI	BB	SO	SB	AB	H	PO	A	E	DP	TC/G	FA	G by Pos
1959	MIL N	6	.417	.583	12	5	0	1	0	0.0	3	0	1	1	1	1	1	6	0	0	0	1.0	1.000	OF-4
1960		101	.267	.352	105	28	5	2	0	0.0	26	6	14	17	6	4	0	88	4	1	1	0.9	.989	OF-92
1961		68	.268	.289	97	26	2	0	0	0.0	23	6	28	9	4	16	3	56	2	0	0	0.9	1.000	OF-44
1962	HOU N	129	.285	.388	418	119	10	9	5	1.2	51	35	70	46	7	8	1	183	7	8	2	1.5	.960	OF-121
1963		120	.281	.386	430	121	25	4	4	0.9	52	27	50	38	5	7	3	215	5	3	1	1.9	.987	OF-113
1964		135	.245	.334	449	110	18	5	4	0.9	51	38	41	43	7	10	2	185	3	7	1	1.4	.964	OF-127
1965	2 teams	HOU	N	(38G – .214)		CAL	A	(51G – .260)																
"	total	89	.236	.269	208	49	2	1	1	0.5	35	8	22	17	5	26	4	76	3	3	0	0.9	.963	OF-57
1966	CAL A	6	.667	.667	9	6	0	0	0	0.0	2	0	2	2	0	3	3	3	0	0	0	0.5	1.000	OF-3
1967	CHI N	62	.254	.308	130	33	7	0	0	0.0	18	13	23	17	2	23	4	71	0	1	0	1.2	.986	OF-41
1968		88	.271	.390	177	48	9	3	2	1.1	21	18	20	24	0	41	10	71	2	2	1	0.9	.973	OF-48
1969		82	.211	.315	213	45	8	1	4	1.9	23	23	21	16	0	26	1	75	1	4	0	1.0	.950	OF-58
1970		21	.143	.429	14	2	1	0	1	7.1	2	1	3	3	0	11	2	5	0	0	0	0.2	1.000	OF-6
1971		5	.400	.400	5	2	0	0	0	0.0	0	0	0	1	0	5	2	0	0	0	0	0.0	–	
13 yrs.		912	.262	.351	2267	594	87	26	21	0.9	307	175	295	234	37	181	36	1034	27	29	6	1.2	.973	OF-714

Year	Team		Games	BA	SA	AB	H	2B	3B	HR	HR%	R	RBI	BB	SO	SB	Pinch Hit AB	Pinch Hit H	PO	A	E	DP	TC/G	FA	G by Pos

Bob Speake

SPEAKE, ROBERT CHARLES (Spook)
B. Aug. 22, 1930, Springfield, Mo.
BL TL 6'1" 178 lbs.

Year	Team		Games	BA	SA	AB	H	2B	3B	HR	HR%	R	RBI	BB	SO	SB	PH AB	PH H	PO	A	E	DP	TC/G	FA	G by Pos
1955	CHI	N	95	.218	.429	261	57	9	5	12	4.6	36	43	28	71	3	24	5	159	11	6	8	1.9	.966	OF-55, 1B-8
1957			129	.232	.404	418	97	14	5	16	3.8	65	50	38	68	5	23	9	480	41	7	21	4.1	.987	OF-60, 1B-39
1958	SF	N	66	.211	.380	71	15	3	0	3	4.2	9	10	13	15	0	41	7	13	2	1	0	0.2	.938	OF-10
1959			15	.091	.091	11	1	0	0	0	0.0	0	1	1	4	0	11	1	0	0	0	0	0.0	—	
4 yrs.			305	.223	.406	761	170	26	10	31	4.1	110	104	80	158	8	99	22	652	54	14	29	2.4	.981	OF-125, 1B-47

Tris Speaker

SPEAKER, TRISTRAM E (The Grey Eagle, Spoke)
B. Apr. 4, 1888, Hubbard, Tex.   D. Dec. 8, 1958, Lake Whitney, Tex.
Manager 1919-26.
Hall of Fame 1937.
BL TL 5'11½" 193 lbs.

Year	Team		Games	BA	SA	AB	H	2B	3B	HR	HR%	R	RBI	BB	SO	SB	PH AB	PH H	PO	A	E	DP	TC/G	FA	G by Pos
1907	BOS	A	7	.158	.158	19	3	0	0	0	0.0	0	1	1		0	3	0	4	2	0	1	0.9	1.000	OF-4
1908			31	.220	.288	118	26	2	3	0	0.0	12	9	4		2	0	0	57	8	0	3	2.1	1.000	OF-31
1909			143	.309	.443	544	168	26	13	7	1.3	73	77	38		35	1	0	319	35	10	12	2.5	.973	OF-142
1910			141	.340	.468	538	183	20	14	7	1.3	92	65	52		35	0	0	337	20	16	7	2.6	.957	OF-140
1911			141	.327	.492	510	167	34	13	8	1.6	88	80	59		25	3	2	297	26	15	5	2.4	.956	OF-138
1912			153	.383	.567	580	222	53	12	10	1.7	136	98	82		52	0	0	372	35	18	9	2.8	.958	OF-153
1913			141	.365	.535	520	190	35	22	3	0.6	94	81	65	22	46	2	0	374	30	25	7	3.0	.942	OF-139
1914			158	.338	.503	571	193	46	18	4	0.7	100	90	77	25	42	1	0	425	30	15	14	3.0	.968	OF-156, 1B-1, P-1
1915			150	.322	.411	547	176	25	12	0	0.0	108	69	81	14	29	0	0	378	21	10	8	2.7	.976	OF-150
1916	CLE	A	151	.386	.502	546	211	41	8	2	0.4	102	83	82	20	35	0	0	359	25	10	10	2.6	.975	OF-151
1917			142	.352	.486	523	184	42	11	2	0.4	90	60	67	14	30	0	0	365	23	8	5	2.8	.980	OF-142
1918			127	.318	.435	471	150	33	11	0	0.0	73	61	64	9	27	0	0	352	15	10	6	3.0	.973	OF-127
1919			134	.296	.433	494	146	38	12	2	0.4	83	63	73	12	15	0	0	375	25	7	6	3.0	.983	OF-134
1920			150	.388	.562	552	214	50	11	8	1.4	137	107	97	13	10	1	0	363	24	9	8	2.6	.977	OF-149
1921			132	.362	.538	506	183	52	14	3	0.6	107	74	68	12	2	4	2	345	15	6	2	2.8	.984	OF-128
1922			131	.378	.606	426	161	48	8	11	2.6	85	71	77	11	8	17	9	285	13	5	6	2.3	.983	OF-110
1923			150	.380	.610	574	218	59	11	17	3.0	133	130	93	15	10	0	0	369	26	13	7	2.7	.968	OF-150
1924			135	.344	.510	486	167	36	9	9	1.9	94	65	72	13	5	7	3	323	20	13	3	2.6	.963	OF-128
1925			117	.389	.578	429	167	35	5	12	2.8	79	87	70	12	5	4	1	311	16	11	9	2.9	.967	OF-109
1926			150	.304	.469	540	164	52	8	7	1.3	96	86	94	15	6	1	0	394	20	8	7	2.8	.981	OF-149
1927	WAS	A	141	.327	.444	523	171	43	6	2	0.4	71	73	55	8	9	4	0	423	24	12	23	3.3	.974	OF-120, 1B-17
1928	PHI	A	64	.267	.450	191	51	22	2	3	1.6	28	29	10	5	5	12	3	111	8	3	1	1.9	.975	OF-50
22 yrs.			2789	.344 (7th)	.500	10208	3515 (5th)	792 (1st)	223 (6th)	117	1.1	1881 (8th)	1559	1381	220	433	60	20	6938	461	224	159	2.7	.971	OF-2700, 1B-18, P-1

WORLD SERIES

Year	Team		Games	BA	SA	AB	H	2B	3B	HR	HR%	R	RBI	BB	SO	SB	PH AB	PH H	PO	A	E	DP	TC/G	FA	G by Pos
1912	BOS	A	8	.300	.467	30	9	1	2	0	0.0	4	2	4	2	1	0	0	21	2	2	2	3.1	.920	OF-8
1915			5	.294	.412	17	5	0	1	0	0.0	2	0	4	1	0	0	0	10	0	0	0	2.0	1.000	OF-5
1920	CLE	A	7	.320	.480	25	8	2	1	0	0.0	6	1	3	1	0	0	0	18	0	0	0	2.6	1.000	OF-7
3 yrs.			20	.306	.458	72	22	3	4 (1st)	0	0.0	12	3	11	4	1	0	0	49	2	2	2	2.7	.962	OF-20

Horace Speed

SPEED, HORACE ARTHUR
B. Oct. 4, 1951, Los Angeles, Calif.
BR TR 6'1" 180 lbs.

Year	Team		Games	BA	SA	AB	H	2B	3B	HR	HR%	R	RBI	BB	SO	SB	PH AB	PH H	PO	A	E	DP	TC/G	FA	G by Pos
1975	SF	N	17	.133	.200	15	2	1	0	0	0.0	2	1	1	8	0	1	0	9	0	1	0	0.6	.900	OF-9
1978	CLE	A	70	.226	.283	106	24	4	1	0	0.0	13	4	14	31	2	4	0	85	1	2	0	1.3	.977	OF-61, DH-3
1979			26	.143	.143	14	2	0	0	0	0.0	6	1	5	7	2	0	0	14	0	2	0	0.6	.875	OF-16, DH-4
3 yrs.			113	.207	.259	135	28	5	1	0	0.0	21	6	20	46	4	5	0	108	1	5	0	1.0	.956	OF-86, DH-7

Chris Speier

SPEIER, CHRIS EDWARD
B. June 28, 1950, Alameda, Calif.
BR TR 6'1" 175 lbs.

Year	Team		Games	BA	SA	AB	H	2B	3B	HR	HR%	R	RBI	BB	SO	SB	PH AB	PH H	PO	A	E	DP	TC/G	FA	G by Pos
1971	SF	N	157	.235	.323	601	141	17	6	8	1.3	74	46	56	90	4	2	1	239	517	33	95	5.0	.958	SS-156
1972			150	.269	.400	562	151	25	2	15	2.7	74	71	82	92	9	0	0	243	517	20	69	5.2	.974	SS-150
1973			153	.249	.356	542	135	17	4	11	2.0	58	71	66	69	4	3	2	255	471	33	92	5.0	.957	SS-150, 2B-1
1974			141	.250	.361	501	125	19	5	9	1.8	55	53	62	64	3	4	2	215	453	21	84	4.9	.970	SS-135, 2B-4
1975			141	.271	.415	487	132	30	5	10	2.1	60	69	70	50	4	4	0	247	421	12	81	4.8	.982	SS-136, 3B-1
1976			145	.226	.297	495	112	18	4	3	0.6	51	40	60	52	2	5	1	241	464	19	85	5.0	.974	SS-135, 2B-7, 3B-5, 1B-1
1977	2 teams		145	.234	.339	SF N (6G – .176)	MON N (139G – .235)																		
" total			145	.234	.339	548	128	31	6	5	0.9	59	38	67	81	1	2	0	239	455	23	77	4.9	.968	SS-143
1978	MON	N	150	.251	.329	501	126	18	3	5	1.0	47	51	60	75	1	2	0	245	467	18	93	4.9	.975	SS-148
1979			113	.227	.331	344	78	13	1	7	2.0	31	26	43	45	0	0	0	194	355	17	52	5.0	.970	SS-112
1980			128	.265	.330	388	103	14	4	1	0.3	35	32	52	38	0	0	0	187	397	21	62	4.7	.965	SS-127, 2B-1
1981			96	.225	.290	307	69	10	2	2	0.7	33	25	38	29	1	0	0	175	280	17	57	4.9	.964	SS-96
1982			156	.257	.360	530	136	26	4	7	1.3	41	60	47	67	1	1	0	291	405	13	76	4.5	.982	SS-155
1983			88	.257	.341	261	67	12	2	2	0.8	31	22	29	37	2	5	1	117	203	14	32	3.8	.958	SS-74, 3B-12, 2B-2
1984	3 teams		MON N (25G – .150)			STL N (38G – .178)		MIN A (12G – .212)																	
" total			75	.178	.272	191	34	7	1	3	1.6	13	12	10	34	0	16	3	70	180	5	35	3.4	.980	SS-59, 3B-6
1985	CHI	N	106	.243	.349	218	53	11	0	4	1.8	16	24	17	34	1	12	5	87	177	11	43	2.6	.960	SS-58, 3B-31, 2B-13
1986			95	.284	.452	155	44	8	0	6	3.9	21	23	15	32	2	17	7	62	106	3	15	1.8	.982	3B-53, SS-23, 2B-7
1987	SF	N	111	.249	.394	317	79	13	0	11	3.5	39	39	42	51	4	14	5	118	229	4	41	3.2	.989	2B-55, 3B-44, SS-22
1988			82	.216	.333	171	37	9	1	3	1.8	26	18	23	39	3	10	1	70	142	3	26	2.6	.986	2B-45, 3B-22, SS-12
1989			28	.243	.351	37	9	4	0	0	0.0	7	2	5	9	0	10	3	19	20	1	6	1.4	.975	SS-9, 3B-9, 2B-4, 1B-1
19 yrs.			2260	.246	.349	7156	1759	302	50	112	1.6	770	720	847	988	42	107	31	3314	6259	288	1121	4.4	.971	SS-1900, 3B-183, 2B-139, 1B-2

DIVISIONAL PLAYOFF SERIES

Year	Team		Games	BA	SA	AB	H	2B	3B	HR	HR%	R	RBI	BB	SO	SB	PH AB	PH H	PO	A	E	DP	TC/G	FA	G by Pos
1981	MON	N	5	.400	.533	15	6	2	0	0	0.0	4	3	4	2	0	0	0	0	0	0	0	0.0	—	SS-5

LEAGUE CHAMPIONSHIP SERIES

Year	Team		Games	BA	SA	AB	H	2B	3B	HR	HR%	R	RBI	BB	SO	SB	PH AB	PH H	PO	A	E	DP	TC/G	FA	G by Pos
1971	SF	N	4	.357	.643	14	5	1	0	1	7.1	4	1	1	0	0	0	0	3	14	1	0	4.5	.944	SS-4
1981	MON	N	5	.188	.188	16	3	0	0	0	0.0	0	0	2	0	0	0	0	5	2	0	0	0.4	—	SS-5

Year	Team	Games	BA	SA	AB	H	2B	3B	HR	HR%	R	RBI	BB	SO	SB	Pinch Hit AB	Pinch Hit H	PO	A	E	DP	TC/G	FA	G by Pos

Chris Speier *continued*

| 1987 | SF | N | 3 | .000 | .000 | 5 | 0 | 0 | 0 | 0 | 0.0 | 0 | 0 | 0 | 2 | 0 | 2 | 0 | 1 | 3 | 0 | 0 | 1.3 | 1.000 | 2B-1 |
| | 3 yrs. | | 12 | .229 | .343 | 35 | 8 | 1 | 0 | 1 | 2.9 | 4 | 1 | 3 | 2 | 0 | 2 | 0 | 4 | 17 | 3 | 0 | 2.0 | .875 | SS-9, 2B-1 |

Bob Spence

SPENCE, JOHN ROBERT
B. Feb. 10, 1946, San Diego, Calif.   BL TR 6'4" 215 lbs.

1969	CHI	A	12	.154	.192	26	4	1	0	0	0.0	0	3	0	9	0	7	0	40	2	0	5	3.5	1.000	1B-6
1970			46	.223	.362	130	29	4	1	4	3.1	11	15	11	32	0	9	1	305	28	2	36	7.3	.994	1B-37
1971			14	.148	.148	27	4	0	0	0	0.0	2	1	5	6	0	5	0	69	2	1	6	5.1	.986	1B-7
	3 yrs.		72	.202	.306	183	37	5	1	4	2.2	13	19	16	47	0	21	1	414	32	3	47	6.2	.993	1B-50

Stan Spence

SPENCE, STANLEY ORVILLE
B. Mar. 20, 1915, South Portsmouth, Ky.   D. Jan. 9, 1983, Kinston, N. C.   BL TL 5'10½" 180 lbs.

1940	BOS	A	51	.279	.426	68	19	2	1	2	2.9	5	13	4	9	0	33	11	15	0	0	0	0.3	1.000	OF-15
1941			86	.232	.340	203	47	10	3	2	1.0	22	28	18	14	1	33	6	99	6	0	2	1.2	1.000	OF-52, 1B-1
1942	WAS	A	149	.323	.432	629	203	27	15	4	0.6	94	79	62	16	5	0	0	395	7	11	0	2.8	.973	OF-149
1943			149	.267	.405	570	152	23	10	12	2.1	72	88	84	39	8	1	0	396	12	7	1	2.8	.983	OF-148
1944			153	.316	.486	592	187	31	8	18	3.0	83	100	69	28	3	0	0	454	29	6	9	3.2	.988	OF-150, 1B-3
1946			152	.292	.497	578	169	50	10	16	2.8	83	87	62	31	1	1	0	412	15	8	3	2.9	.982	OF-150
1947			147	.279	.441	506	141	22	6	16	3.2	62	73	81	41	0	5	0	408	12	7	3	2.9	.984	OF-142
1948	BOS	A	114	.235	.391	391	92	17	4	12	3.1	71	61	82	33	0	9	3	316	10	6	7	2.9	.982	OF-92, 1B-14
1949	2 teams		BOS A (7G – .150)			STL A (104G – .245)																			
"	total		111	.240	.416	334	80	14	3	13	3.9	49	46	58	37	1	16	2	219	11	1	2	2.1	.996	OF-90, 1B-1
	9 yrs.		1112	.282	.437	3871	1090	196	60	95	2.5	541	575	520	248	21	98	22	2714	102	46	27	2.6	.984	OF-988, 1B-19

Ben Spencer

SPENCER, LLOYD BENJAMIN
B. May 15, 1890, Patapsco, Md.   D. Sept. 1, 1970, Finksburg, Md.   BL TL 5'8" 160 lbs.

| 1913 | WAS | A | 8 | .286 | .429 | 21 | 6 | 1 | 1 | 0 | 0.0 | 2 | 2 | 4 | 4 | 0 | 0 | 0 | 10 | 1 | 1 | 0 | 1.5 | .917 | OF-8 |

Chet Spencer

SPENCER, CHESTER ARTHUR
B. Mar. 4, 1883, South Webster, Ohio   D. Nov. 10, 1938, Portsmouth, Ohio   BL TR 6' 180 lbs.

| 1906 | BOS | N | 8 | .148 | .185 | 27 | 4 | 1 | 0 | 0 | 0.0 | 0 | | 0 | 0 | | 0 | 0 | 6 | 1 | 1 | 0 | 1.0 | .875 | OF-8 |

Daryl Spencer

SPENCER, DARYL DEAN (Big Dee)
B. July 13, 1929, Wichita, Kans.   BR TR 6'2½" 185 lbs.

1952	NY	N	7	.294	.412	17	5	0	1	0	0.0	0	3	1	4	0	1	0	7	14	0	2	3.0	1.000	SS-3, 3B-3
1953			118	.208	.424	408	85	18	5	20	4.9	55	56	42	74	0	3	0	179	269	32	52	4.1	.933	SS-53, 3B-36, 2B-32
1956			146	.221	.342	489	108	13	5	14	2.9	46	42	35	65	1	2	0	288	377	18	74	4.7	.974	2B-70, SS-66, 3B-12
1957			148	.249	.376	534	133	31	2	11	2.1	65	50	50	50	3	2	0	301	468	37	118	5.4	.954	SS-110, 2B-36, 3B-6
1958	SF	N	148	.256	.406	539	138	20	5	17	3.2	71	74	73	60	1	0	0	262	472	34	102	5.2	.956	SS-134, 2B-17
1959			152	.265	.369	555	147	20	4	12	2.2	59	62	58	67	5	1	0	350	417	24	84	5.2	.970	2B-151, SS-4
1960	STL	N	148	.258	.404	507	131	20	3	16	3.2	70	58	81	74	1	2	1	242	359	32	74	4.3	.949	SS-138, 2B-16
1961	2 teams		STL N (37G – .254)			LA N (60G – .243)																			
"	total		97	.248	.395	319	79	11	0	12	3.8	46	48	43	52	1	1	0	114	208	13	42	3.5	.961	3B-57, SS-40
1962	LA	N	77	.236	.318	157	37	5	1	2	1.3	24	12	32	31	1	13	1	38	101	10	7	1.9	.933	3B-57, SS-10
1963	2 teams		LA N (7G – .111)			CIN N (50G – .239)																			
"	total		57	.232	.293	164	38	7	0	1	0.6	21	23	34	39	1	7	0	47	95	3	9	2.5	.979	3B-51
	10 yrs.		1098	.244	.380	3689	901	145	20	105	2.8	457	428	449	516	13	32	2	1828	2780	203	564	4.4	.958	SS-558, 2B-322, 3B-222

Jim Spencer

SPENCER, JAMES LLOYD
B. July 30, 1946, Hanover, Pa.   BL TL 6'2" 195 lbs.

1968	CAL	A	19	.191	.206	68	13	1	0	0	0.0	2	5	3	10	0	0	0	152	18	0	15	9.0	.994	1B-19
1969			113	.254	.383	386	98	14	3	10	2.6	39	51	26	53	1	8	2	926	66	9	81	8.9	.991	1B-107
1970			146	.274	.399	511	140	20	4	12	2.3	61	68	28	61	0	6	2	1212	85	7	131	8.9	.995	1B-142
1971			148	.237	.392	510	121	21	2	18	3.5	50	59	48	63	0	7	1	1296	93	5	117	9.4	.996	1B-145
1972			82	.222	.259	257	47	5	0	1	0.5	13	14	12	25	0	22	4	289	23	3	25	3.8	.990	1B-35, OF-24
1973	2 teams		CAL A (29G – .241)			TEX A (102G – .267)																			
"	total		131	.262	.362	439	115	16	5	6	1.4	45	44	43	50	1	8	0	994	74	1	134	8.2	.999	1B-125, DH-3
1974	TEX	A	118	.278	.384	352	98	11	4	7	2.0	36	44	22	27	1	8	3	389	27	1	36	3.5	.998	1B-60, DH-54
1975			132	.266	.397	403	107	18	1	11	2.7	50	47	35	43	6	4	0	844	70	5	92	7.0	.995	1B-99, DH-25
1976	CHI	A	150	.253	.367	518	131	13	2	14	2.7	53	70	49	52	6	4	0	1206	112	2	116	8.8	.998	1B-150, DH-2
1977			128	.247	.400	470	116	16	1	18	3.8	56	69	36	50	1	2	1	977	90	10	76	8.4	.991	1B-125
1978	NY	A	71	.227	.440	150	34	9	1	7	4.7	12	24	15	24	0	24	7	90	7	0	4	1.4	1.000	DH-35, 1B-15
1979			106	.288	.593	295	85	15	3	23	7.8	60	53	38	25	0	16	3	232	17	2	35	2.4	.992	DH-71, 1B-26
1980			97	.236	.442	259	61	9	0	13	5.0	38	43	30	44	1	22	8	567	41	6	51	6.3	.990	1B-75, DH-15
1981	2 teams		NY A (25G – .143)			OAK A (54G – .205)																			
"	total		79	.188	.274	234	44	8	0	4	1.7	20	13	19	27	1	13	4	516	53	1	47	7.2	.998	1B-73
1982	OAK	A	33	.168	.277	101	17	3	1	2	2.0	6	5	3	20	0	9	1	230	22	2	30	7.7	.992	1B-32
	15 yrs.		1553	.250	.387	4908	1227	179	27	146	3.0	541	599	407	582	11	151	40	9920	798	55	990	6.9	.995	1B-1221, DH-205, OF-24

DIVISIONAL PLAYOFF SERIES

| 1981 | OAK | A | 1 | .250 | .500 | 4 | 1 | 1 | 0 | 0 | 0.0 | 0 | 0 | 0 | 0 | 0 | 0 | 0 | 0 | 0 | 0 | 0 | 0.0 | – | 1B-1 |

LEAGUE CHAMPIONSHIP SERIES

1980	NY	A	1	.000	.000	1	0	0	0	0	0.0	0	0	0	1	0	1	0	0	0	0	0	0.0	–	1B-2
1981	OAK	A	2	.000	.000	2	0	0	0	0	0.0	0	0	0	2	0	2	0	0	0	0	0	0.0	–	1B-2
	2 yrs.		3	.000	.000	3	0	0	0	0	0.0	0	0	0	3	0	3	0	0	0	0	0	0.0	–	1B-2

WORLD SERIES

| 1978 | NY | A | 4 | .167 | .167 | 12 | 2 | 0 | 0 | 0 | 0.0 | 3 | 0 | 2 | 4 | 0 | 1 | 0 | 23 | 2 | 0 | 4 | 6.3 | 1.000 | 1B-3 |

Roy Spencer

SPENCER, ROY HAMPTON
B. Feb. 22, 1900, Scranton, N. C.   D. Feb. 8, 1973, Port Charlotte, Fla.   BR TR 5'10" 168 lbs.

Year	Team		Games	BA	SA	AB	H	2B	3B	HR	HR%	R	RBI	BB	SO	SB	Pinch Hit AB	Pinch Hit H	PO	A	E	DP	TC/G	FA	G by Pos

Roy Spencer *continued*

1925	PIT	N	14	.214	.250	28	6	1	0	0	0.0	1	2	1	3	1	3	0	18	1	2	2	1.5	.905	C-11
1926			28	.395	.465	43	17	3	0	0	0.0	5	4	1	0	0	10	6	29	3	1	0	1.2	.970	C-16
1927			38	.283	.337	92	26	3	1	0	0.0	9	13	3	3	0	4	2	98	15	3	2	3.1	.974	C-34
1929	WAS	A	50	.155	.216	116	18	4	0	1	0.9	18	9	8	15	0	5	1	128	20	5	2	3.1	.967	C-41
1930			93	.255	.315	321	82	11	4	0	0.0	32	36	18	27	3	0	0	395	44	5	3	4.8	.989	C-93
1931			145	.275	.327	483	133	16	3	1	0.2	48	60	35	21	0	0	0	642	69	11	5	5.0	.985	C-145
1932			102	.246	.284	317	78	9	0	1	0.3	28	41	24	17	0	3	1	313	44	8	9	3.6	.978	C-98
1933	CLE	A	75	.203	.242	227	46	5	2	0	0.0	26	23	23	17	0	3	1	258	42	3	4	4.0	.990	C-72
1934			5	.143	.286	7	1	1	0	0	0.0	0	2	0	1	0	1	1	7	2	0	0	1.8	1.000	C-4
1936	NY	N	19	.278	.333	18	5	1	0	0	0.0	3	3	2	3	0	2	1	18	3	0	1	1.1	1.000	C-14
1937	BKN	N	51	.205	.256	117	24	2	2	0	0.0	5	4	8	17	0	5	0	177	27	0	2	4.0	1.000	C-45
1938			16	.267	.333	45	12	1	1	0	0.0	2	6	5	6	0	0	0	55	5	2	0	3.9	.968	C-16
12 yrs.			636	.247	.298	1814	448	57	13	3	0.2	177	203	128	130	4	36	13	2138	275	40	33	3.9	.984	C-589

WORLD SERIES

| 1927 | PIT | N | 1 | .000 | .000 | 1 | 0 | 0 | 0 | 0 | 0.0 | 0 | 0 | 0 | 0 | 0 | 0 | 0 | 0 | 0 | 0 | 0 | 0.0 | – | C-1 |

Tom Spencer

SPENCER, HUBERT THOMAS
B. Feb. 28, 1951, Gallipolis, Ohio

BR TR 6' 170 lbs.

| 1978 | CHI | A | 29 | .185 | .200 | 65 | 12 | 1 | 0 | 0 | 0.0 | 3 | 4 | 2 | 9 | 0 | 7 | 0 | 52 | 2 | 0 | 0 | 1.9 | 1.000 | OF-27, DH-2 |

Tubby Spencer

SPENCER, EDWARD RUSSELL
B. Jan. 26, 1884, Oil City, Pa.   D. Feb. 1, 1945, San Francisco, Calif.

BR TR 5'10" 215 lbs.

1905	STL	A	35	.235	.278	115	27	1	1	0	0.0	6	11	7		1	1	1	134	41	7	1	5.2	.962	C-34
1906			58	.176	.218	188	33	6	1	0	0.0	15	17	7		4	3	0	226	60	20	3	5.3	.935	C-54
1907			71	.265	.322	230	61	1	1	0	0.0	27	24	7		1	8	2	250	80	15	6	4.9	.957	C-63
1908			91	.210	.238	286	60	6	1	0	0.0	19	28	17		1	2	1	398	109	9	9	5.7	.983	C-89
1909	BOS	A	28	.162	.176	74	12	1	0	0	0.0	6	9	6		2	2	1	94	24	1	0	4.3	.992	C-26
1911	PHI	N	11	.156	.281	32	5	1	0	1	3.1	2	3	3	7	0	0	0	47	15	5	2	6.1	.925	C-11
1916	DET	A	19	.370	.481	54	20	1	1	1	1.9	7	10	6	6	2	0	0	58	21	1	1	4.2	.988	C-19
1917			70	.240	.313	192	46	8	3	0	0.0	13	22	15	15	0	8	0	250	57	7	10	4.5	.978	C-62
1918			66	.219	.284	155	34	8	1	0	0.0	11	8	19	18	1	17	3	153	46	7	3	3.1	.966	C-48, 1B-1
9 yrs.			449	.225	.277	1326	298	43	10	2	0.2	106	132	87	46	13	41	7	1610	453	72	35	4.8	.966	C-406, 1B-1

Vern Spencer

SPENCER, VERNON MURRAY
B. Feb. 24, 1896, Wixom, Mich.   D. June 3, 1971, Wixom, Mich.

BL TR 5'7" 165 lbs.

| 1920 | NY | N | 45 | .200 | .257 | 140 | 28 | 2 | 3 | 0 | 0.0 | 15 | 19 | 11 | 17 | 4 | 3 | 0 | 76 | 6 | 6 | 1 | 2.0 | .932 | OF-40 |

Paul Speraw

SPERAW, PAUL BACHMAN (Polly, Birdie)
B. Oct. 5, 1893, Annville, Pa.   D. Feb. 22, 1962, Cedar Rapids, Iowa

BR TR 5'8½" 145 lbs.

| 1920 | STL | A | 1 | .000 | .000 | 2 | 0 | 0 | 0 | 0 | 0.0 | 0 | 0 | 0 | 0 | 0 | 0 | 0 | 1 | 1 | 0 | 0 | 2.0 | 1.000 | 3B-1 |

Ed Sperber

SPERBER, EDWIN GEORGE
B. Jan. 21, 1895, Cincinnati, Ohio   D. Jan. 5, 1976, Cincinnati, Ohio

BL TL 5'11" 175 lbs.

1924	BOS	N	24	.288	.373	59	17	2	0	1	1.7	8	12	10	9	3	2	0	25	1	3	0	1.2	.897	OF-17
1925			2	.000	.000	2	0	0	0	0	0.0	0	0	0	0	0	2	0	0	0	0	0	0.0		
2 yrs.			26	.279	.361	61	17	2	0	1	1.6	8	12	10	9	3	4	0	25	1	3	0	1.1	.897	OF-17

Rob Sperring

SPERRING, ROBERT WALTER
B. Oct. 10, 1949, San Francisco, Calif.

BR TR 6'1" 185 lbs.

1974	CHI	N	42	.206	.262	107	22	3	0	1	0.9	9	5	9	28	1	1	0	64	101	10	16	4.2	.943	2B-35, SS-8
1975			65	.208	.271	144	30	4	1	1	0.7	25	9	16	31	0	1	0	70	115	12	18	3.0	.939	3B-22, 2B-17, SS-16, OF-8
1976			43	.258	.290	93	24	3	0	0	0.0	8	7	9	25	0	1	0	36	40	1	5	1.8	.987	3B-20, SS-15, 2B-4, OF-3
1977	HOU	N	58	.186	.233	129	24	3	0	1	0.8	6	9	12	23	0	10	3	57	98	6	15	2.8	.963	SS-22, 2B-20, 3B-11
4 yrs.			208	.211	.262	473	100	13	1	3	0.6	48	30	46	107	1	13	3	227	354	29	54	2.9	.952	2B-76, SS-61, 3B-53, OF-11

Stan Sperry

SPERRY, STANLEY KENNETH
B. Feb. 19, 1914, Evansville, Wis.   D. Sept. 27, 1962, Evansville, Wis.

BL TR 5'10½" 164 lbs.

1936	PHI	N	20	.135	.216	37	5	3	0	0	0.0	2	4	3	5	0	3	1	23	22	5	4	2.5	.900	2B-15
1938	PHI	A	60	.273	.320	253	69	6	3	0	0.0	28	27	15	9	1	0	0	121	185	13	26	5.3	.959	2B-60
2 yrs.			80	.255	.307	290	74	9	3	0	0.0	30	31	18	14	1	3	1	144	207	18	30	4.6	.951	2B-75

Bill Spiers

SPIERS, WILLIAM JAMES
B. June 5, 1966, Orangeburg, S. C.

BL TR 6'2" 190 lbs.

| 1989 | MIL | A | 114 | .255 | .333 | 345 | 88 | 9 | 3 | 4 | 1.2 | 44 | 33 | 21 | 63 | 10 | 4 | 3 | 164 | 295 | 21 | 62 | 4.2 | .956 | SS-89, 3B-12, DH-4, 2B-4, 1B-2 |

Harry Spies

SPIES, HENRY
B. June 12, 1866, New Orleans, La.   D. July 8, 1942, Los Angeles, Calif.

BR TR 5'11½" 170 lbs.

| 1895 | 2 teams | | | CIN | N | (14G – .220) | | | LOU | N | (72G – .268) | | | | | | | | | | | | | | |
| " | total | | 86 | .261 | .371 | 326 | 85 | 14 | 8 | 2 | 0.6 | 44 | 40 | 14 | 21 | 4 | 0 | 0 | 573 | 71 | 33 | 38 | 7.9 | .951 | 1B-49, C-38, SS-1 |

Ed Spiezio

SPIEZIO, EDWARD WAYNE
B. Oct. 31, 1941, Joliet, Ill.

BR TR 5'11" 180 lbs.

1964	STL	N	12	.333	.333	12	4	0	0	0	0.0	0	1	0	12	4	0	0	0	0	0	0.0	–	
1965			10	.167	.167	18	3	0	0	0	0.0	0	5	1	4	0	7	2	1	7	0	0	0.8	1.000	3B-3
1966			26	.219	.397	73	16	5	1	2	2.7	4	10	5	11	1	6	0	14	32	6	3	2.0	.885	3B-19
1967			55	.210	.314	105	22	2	0	3	2.9	9	10	7	18	2	27	8	24	35	2	4	1.1	.967	3B-19, OF-7

Year	Team		Games	BA	SA	AB	H	2B	3B	HR	HR%	R	RBI	BB	SO	SB	Pinch Hit AB	H	PO	A	E	DP	TC/G	FA	G by Pos

General Stafford *continued*

1895			124	.279	.346	463	129	12	5	3	0.6	79	73	40	32	42	0	0	265	336	61	44	5.3	.908	2B-110, OF-12, 3B-2
1896			59	.287	.335	230	66	9	1	0	0.0	28	40	13	18	15	0	0	93	26	12	5	2.2	.908	OF-53, SS-6
1897	2 teams	NY N (7G – .087)												LOU N (111G – .278)											
"	total		118	.268	.371	455	122	16	5	7	1.5	68	56	34		14	1	0	222	360	75	34	5.6	.886	SS-105, OF-12, 3B-1
1898	2 teams	LOU N (49G – .298)												BOS N (37G – .260)											
"	total		86	.283	.319	304	86	5	0	2	0.7	47	33	23		10	1	0	162	88	23	9	3.2	.916	OF-57, 2B-28, 3B-1, 1B-1
1899	2 teams	BOS N (55G – .302)												WAS N (31G – .246)											
"	total		86	.280	.370	300	84	9	3	4	1.3	40	54	12		13	5	1	168	98	30	13	3.4	.899	OF-41, 2B-22, SS-18, 3B-2
	8 yrs.		569	.274	.350	2128	583	60	19	21	1.0	341	290	164	96	117	8	1	1077	948	230	114	4.0	.898	OF-251, 2B-161, SS-129, 3B-12, P-12, 1B-2

Heinie Stafford

STAFFORD, HENRY ALEXANDER   BR TR 5'7" 160 lbs.
B. Nov. 1, 1891, Orleans, Vt.   D. Jan. 29, 1972, Lake Worth, Fla.

1916	NY	N	1	.000	.000	1	0	0	0	0	0.0	0	0	0	0	0	1	0	0	0	0	0	0.0	–	

Steve Staggs

STAGGS, STEPHEN ROBERT   BR TR 5'9" 150 lbs.
B. May 6, 1951, Anchorage, Alaska

1977	TOR	A	72	.258	.357	291	75	11	6	2	0.7	37	28	36	38	5	1	0	169	194	13	35	5.2	.965	2B-72
1978	OAK	A	47	.244	.321	78	19	2	2	0	0.0	10	0	19	17	2	4	2	59	68	3	10	2.8	.977	2B-40, DH-2, SS-2, 3B-2
	2 yrs.		119	.255	.350	369	94	13	8	2	0.5	47	28	55	55	7	5	2	228	262	16	45	4.3	.968	2B-112, DH-2, SS-2, 3B-2

Chick Stahl

STAHL, CHARLES SYLVESTER   BL TL 5'10" 160 lbs.
B. Jan. 10, 1873, Avila, Ind.   D. Mar. 28, 1907, West Baden, Ind.
Manager 1906.

1897	BOS	N	114	.354	.499	469	166	30	13	4	0.9	111	97	38		18	1	0	164	17	14	4	1.7	.928	OF-111
1898			125	.308	.407	467	144	21	8	3	0.6	72	52	46		6	0	0	199	14	7	4	1.8	.968	OF-125
1899			148	.351	.495	576	202	23	18	8	1.4	122	53	72		33	0	0	253	27	10	6	2.0	.966	OF-148, P-1
1900			136	.295	.421	553	163	23	16	5	0.9	88	82	34		27	1	1	277	22	10	4	2.3	.968	OF-135
1901	BOS	A	131	.309	.445	515	159	20	16	6	1.2	106	72	54		29	0	0	277	12	13	3	2.3	.957	OF-131
1902			127	.323	.421	508	164	22	11	2	0.4	92	58	37		24	2	2	244	15	12	2	2.1	.956	OF-125
1903			77	.274	.375	299	82	12	6	2	0.7	60	44	28		10	3	0	135	11	6	2	2.0	.961	OF-74
1904			157	.295	.421	587	173	27	19	3	0.5	84	67	64		11	0	0	293	6	12	6	2.0	.961	OF-157
1905			134	.258	.308	500	129	17	4	0	0.0	61	47	50		18	0	0	249	11	6	4	2.0	.977	OF-134
1906			155	.286	.366	595	170	24	6	4	0.7	62	51	47		13	0	0	344	24	15	9	2.5	.961	OF-155
	10 yrs.		1304	.306	.417	5069	1552	219	117	37	0.7	858	623	470		189	7	3	2435	159	105	38	2.1	.961	OF-1295, P-1

WORLD SERIES

1903	BOS	A	8	.303	.515	33	10	1	3	0	0.0	6	3	1	2	2	0	0	14	1	0	0	1.9	1.000	OF-8
								4th																		

Jake Stahl

STAHL, JACOB GARLAND   BR TR 6'2" 195 lbs.
B. Apr. 13, 1879, Elkhart, Ill.   D. Sept. 18, 1922, Monrovia, Calif.
Manager 1905-06, 1912-13.

1903	BOS	A	40	.239	.446	92	22	3	5	2	2.2	14	8	4		1	11	5	105	27	6	0	3.5	.957	C-28, OF-1
1904	WAS	A	142	.262	.381	520	136	29	12	3	0.6	54	50	21		25	0	0	1259	89	33	53	9.7	.976	1B-119, OF-23
1905			141	.244	.365	501	122	22	12	5	1.0	66	66	28		41	1	0	1593	94	21	51	12.1	.988	1B-140
1906			137	.222	.274	482	107	9	8	0	0.0	38	51	21		30	1	0	1322	78	24	51	10.4	.983	1B-136
1908	2 teams	NY A (74G – .255)												BOS A (79G – .248)											
"	total		153	.252	.374	532	134	27	16	2	0.4	63	65	31		30	1	0	1008	62	22	37	7.1	.980	1B-85, OF-67
1909	BOS	A	127	.294	.434	435	128	19	12	6	1.4	62	60	43		16	1	0	1353	50	20	57	11.2	.986	1B-126
1910			144	.271	.424	531	144	19	16	10	1.9	68	77	42		22	2	0	1488	60	23	46	10.9	.985	1B-142
1912			95	.301	.429	326	98	21	6	3	0.9	40	60	31		13	3	1	853	49	18	37	9.7	.980	1B-92
1913			2	.000	.000	2	0	0	0	0	0.0	0	0	0	1	0	2	0	0	0	0	0	0.0	–	
	9 yrs.		981	.260	.382	3421	891	149	87	31	0.9	405	437	221	1	178	22	6	8981	509	167	332	9.8	.983	1B-840, OF-91, C-28

WORLD SERIES

1912	BOS	A	8	.281	.344	32	9	2	0	0	0.0	3	2	0	6	1	0	0	77	3	1	4	10.1	.988	1B-8

Larry Stahl

STAHL, LARRY FLOYD   BL TL 6' 175 lbs.
B. June 29, 1941, Belleville, Ill.

1964	KC	A	15	.261	.478	46	12	1	0	3	6.5	7	6	1	10	0	5	1	20	1	1	1	1.5	.955	OF-10
1965			28	.198	.395	81	16	2	1	4	4.9	9	14	5	16	1	7	1	47	1	0	0	1.7	1.000	OF-21
1966			119	.250	.365	312	78	11	5	5	1.6	37	34	17	63	5	31	7	142	6	3	1	1.3	.980	OF-94
1967	NY	N	71	.239	.290	155	37	5	0	1	0.6	9	18	8	25	2	30	5	90	4	3	0	1.4	.969	OF-43
1968			53	.235	.344	183	43	7	2	3	1.6	15	10	21	38	3	3	1	155	8	2	4	3.1	.988	OF-47, 1B-9
1969	SD	N	95	.198	.315	162	32	6	2	3	1.9	10	10	17	31	3	44	6	136	16	2	8	1.6	.987	OF-37, 1B-13
1970			52	.182	.212	66	12	2	0	0	0.0	5	3	2	14	2	33	7	16	1	0	0	0.3	1.000	OF-20
1971			114	.253	.399	308	78	13	4	8	2.6	27	36	26	59	4	26	8	201	12	2	7	1.9	.991	OF-75, 1B-7
1972			107	.226	.347	297	67	9	3	7	2.4	31	20	31	67	1	28	5	141	4	2	1	1.4	.986	OF-76, 1B-1
1973	CIN	N	76	.225	.333	111	25	2	2	2	1.8	17	12	14	34	1	45	11	44	3	0	3	0.6	1.000	OF-29, 1B-2
	10 yrs.		730	.232	.351	1721	400	58	19	36	2.1	167	163	142	357	22	252	52	992	56	15	25	1.5	.986	OF-452, 1B-32

LEAGUE CHAMPIONSHIP SERIES

1973	CIN	N	4	.500	.500	4	2	0	0	0	0.0	1	0	1	0	0	4	2	0	0	0	0	0.0	–	

Roy Staiger

STAIGER, ROY JOSEPH (Linus)   BR TR 6' 200 lbs.
B. Jan. 6, 1950, Tulsa, Okla.

1975	NY	N	13	.158	.211	19	3	1	0	0	0.0	0	4	0	0	0	0	0	5	11	0	0	1.2	1.000	3B-13
1976			95	.220	.273	304	67	8	1	2	0.7	23	26	25	35	3	1	0	55	209	9	18	2.9	.967	3B-93, SS-1
1977			40	.252	.374	123	31	9	0	2	1.6	16	11	4	20	1	0	0	23	76	7	4	2.7	.934	3B-36, SS-1

Year	Team		Games	BA	SA	AB	H	2B	3B	HR	HR%	R	RBI	BB	SO	SB	Pinch Hit AB	Pinch Hit H	PO	A	E	DP	TC/G	FA	G by Pos

Roy Staiger *continued*

| 1979 | NY | A | 4 | .273 | .364 | 11 | 3 | 1 | 0 | 0 | 0.0 | 1 | 1 | 1 | 0 | 0 | 0 | 0 | 2 | 7 | 0 | 1 | 2.3 | 1.000 | 3B-4 |
| 4 yrs. | | | 152 | .228 | .300 | 457 | 104 | 19 | 1 | 4 | 0.9 | 42 | 38 | 30 | 59 | 4 | 1 | 0 | 85 | 303 | 16 | 23 | 2.7 | .960 | 3B-146, SS-2 |

Tuck Stainback

STAINBACK, GEORGE TUCKER   BR TR 5'11½" 175 lbs.
B. Aug. 4, 1910, Los Angeles, Calif.

1934	CHI	N	104	.306	.379	359	110	14	3	2	0.6	47	46	8	42	7	8	3	186	5	9	1	1.9	.955	OF-96, 3B-1
1935			47	.255	.394	94	24	4	0	3	3.2	16	11	0	13	1	10	3	40	1	3	0	0.9	.932	OF-28
1936			44	.173	.253	75	13	3	0	1	1.3	13	5	6	14	1	9	1	38	1	0	0	0.9	1.000	OF-26
1937			72	.231	.288	160	37	7	1	0	0.0	18	14	7	16	2	9	1	99	4	2	1	1.5	.981	OF-49
1938 3 teams	STL	N (6G – .000)				PHI	N (30G – .259)					BKN	N	(35G – .327)											
" total			71	.282	.374	195	55	9	3	1	0.5	26	31	5	10	2	17	4	107	2	2	0	1.6	.982	OF-50
1939	BKN	N	68	.269	.348	201	54	7	0	3	1.5	22	19	4	23	0	10	2	121	0	8	0	1.9	.938	OF-55
1940	DET	A	15	.225	.275	40	9	2	0	0	0.0	4	1	1	9	0	5	1	26	4	1	0	2.1	.968	OF-9
1941			94	.245	.325	200	49	8	1	2	1.0	19	10	3	21	6	8	1	107	3	6	0	1.2	.948	OF-80
1942	NY	A	15	.200	.200	10	2	0	0	0	0.0	0	0	0	2	0	1	0	6	0	0	0	0.4	1.000	OF-3
1943			71	.260	.325	231	60	11	2	0	0.0	31	10	7	16	3	5	3	141	3	1	2	2.0	.993	OF-61
1944			30	.218	.256	78	17	3	0	0	0.0	13	5	3	7	1	5	1	44	1	2	0	1.6	.957	OF-24
1945			95	.257	.352	327	84	12	2	5	1.5	40	32	13	20	0	9	2	233	10	8	6	2.6	.968	OF-83
1946	PHI	N	91	.244	.292	291	71	10	2	0	0.0	35	20	7	20	3	23	5	153	5	6	1	1.8	.963	OF-66
13 yrs.			817	.259	.333	2261	585	90	14	17	0.8	284	204	64	213	27	120	28	1301	39	48	11	1.7	.965	OF-630, 3B-1

WORLD SERIES

1942	NY	A	2			0	0	0	0	0	–	0	0	0	0	0	0	0	0	0	0	0	0.0	–	
1943			5	.176	.176	17	3	0	0	0	0.0	0	0	0	2	0	0	0	7	1	0	0	1.6	1.000	OF-5
2 yrs.			7	.176	.176	17	3	0	0	0	0.0	0	0	0	2	0	0	0	7	1	0	0	1.1	1.000	OF-5

Gale Staley

STALEY, GEORGE GAYLORD   BL TR 5'8½" 167 lbs.
B. May 2, 1899, De Pere, Wis.

| 1925 | CHI | N | 7 | .423 | .500 | 26 | 11 | 2 | 0 | 0 | 0.0 | 2 | 3 | 2 | 1 | 0 | 0 | 0 | 19 | 28 | 1 | 7 | 6.9 | .979 | 2B-7 |

Virgil Stallcup

STALLCUP, THOMAS VIRGIL (Red)   BR TR 6'3" 185 lbs.
B. Jan. 3, 1922, Ravensford, N. C. D. May 2, 1989, Greenville, S. C.

1947	CIN	N	8	.000	.000	1	0	0	0	0	0.0	1	0	0	0	0	0	0	0	0	0	0	0.0		SS-1
1948			149	.228	.315	539	123	30	4	3	0.6	40	65	18	52	2	1	1	264	433	32	84	4.9	.956	SS-148
1949			141	.254	.336	575	146	28	5	3	0.5	49	45	9	44	1	0	0	256	437	27	87	5.1	.963	SS-141
1950			136	.251	.356	483	121	23	2	8	1.7	44	54	17	39	4	0	0	253	389	18	79	4.9	.973	SS-136
1951			121	.241	.346	428	103	17	2	8	1.9	33	49	6	40	2	4	0	190	333	17	61	4.5	.969	SS-117
1952 2 teams	CIN	N (2G – .000)				STL	N (29G – .129)																		
" total			31	.125	.156	32	4	1	0	0	0.0	4	1	1	5	0	14	3	5	16	0	4	0.7	1.000	SS-13
1953	STL	N	1	.000	.000	1	0	0	0	0	0.0	0	0	0	0	0	1	0	0	0	0	0	0.0		SS-1
7 yrs.			587	.241	.334	2059	497	99	13	22	1.1	171	214	51	181	9	20	4	968	1608	94	315	4.5	.965	SS-556

George Staller

STALLER, GEORGE WALBORN (Stopper)   BL TL 5'11" 190 lbs.
B. Apr. 1, 1916, Rutherford Heights, Pa.

| 1943 | PHI | A | 21 | .271 | .459 | 85 | 23 | 1 | 3 | 3 | 3.5 | 14 | 12 | 5 | 6 | 1 | 0 | 0 | 42 | 1 | 1 | 0 | 2.1 | .977 | OF-20 |

George Stallings

STALLINGS, GEORGE TWEEDY (The Miracle Man)   BR TR 6'1" 187 lbs.
B. Nov. 17, 1867, Augusta, Ga. D. May 13, 1929, Haddock, Ga.
Manager 1897-98, 1901, 1909-10, 1913-20.

1890	BKN	N	4	.000	.000	11	0	0	0	0	0.0	1	0	1	3	0	0	0	13	1	1	0	3.8	.933	C-4
1897	PHI	N	2	.222	.333	9	2	1	0	0	0.0	1	0	0	0	0	0	0	18	1	1	1	10.0	.950	OF-1, 1B-1
1898			1	–	–	0	0	0	0	0	–	1	0	0	0	0	0	0	0	0	0	0	0.0	–	
3 yrs.			7	.100	.150	20	2	1	0	0	0.0	3	0	1	3	0	0	0	31	2	2	1	5.0	.943	C-4, OF-1, 1B-1

Oscar Stanage

STANAGE, OSCAR HARLAND   BR TR 5'11" 190 lbs.
B. Mar. 17, 1883, Tulare, Calif. D. Nov. 11, 1964, Detroit, Mich.

1906	CIN	N	1	.000	.000	1	0	0	0	0	0.0	0		0		0	0	0	1	0	0	0	1.0	1.000	C-1
1909	DET	A	77	.262	.341	252	66	8	6	0	0.0	17	21	11		2	0	0	324	80	15	12	5.4	.964	C-77
1910			88	.207	.284	275	57	7	4	2	0.7	24	25	20		1	4	0	344	148	25	6	5.9	.952	C-84
1911			141	.264	.336	503	133	13	7	3	0.6	45	51	20		3	0	0	599	212	41	13	6.0	.952	C-141
1912			119	.261	.305	394	103	9	4	0	0.0	35	41	34		3	0	0	440	168	32	14	5.4	.950	C-119
1913			80	.224	.295	241	54	13	2	0	0.0	19	21	21	35	5	2	2	277	106	16	6	5.0	.960	C-77
1914			122	.193	.233	400	77	8	4	0	0.0	16	25	24	58	2	0	0	532	190	30	11	6.2	.960	C-122
1915			100	.223	.277	300	67	9	2	1	0.3	20	31	20	41	5	0	0	395	111	19	0	5.3	.964	C-100
1916			94	.237	.316	291	69	17	3	0	0.0	16	30	17	48	3	0	0	387	108	15	11	5.4	.971	C-94
1917			99	.205	.259	297	61	14	1	0	0.0	19	30	20	35	3	4	1	385	88	11	13	4.9	.977	C-95
1918			54	.253	.290	186	47	4	0	1	0.5	9	14	11	18	2	2	0	234	56	8	10	5.5	.973	C-47, 1B-5
1919			38	.242	.317	120	29	4	1	1	0.8	9	15	7	12	1	1	0	150	39	5	8	5.1	.974	C-36, 1B-1
1920			78	.231	.303	238	55	17	0	0	0.0	12	17	14	21	0	1	0	248	75	14	4	4.3	.958	C-78
1925			3	.200	.200	5	1	0	0	0	0.0	0	0	0	0	0	0	0	2	0	0	0	0.7	1.000	C-3
14 yrs.			1094	.234	.295	3503	819	123	34	8	0.2	248	321	219	268	30	14	3	4318	1381	231	108	5.4	.961	C-1074, 1B-6

WORLD SERIES

| 1909 | DET | A | 2 | .200 | .200 | 5 | 1 | 0 | 0 | 0 | 0.0 | 0 | 2 | 0 | 2 | 0 | 0 | 0 | 12 | 2 | 0 | 0 | 7.0 | 1.000 | C-2 |

Jerry Standaert

STANDAERT, JEROME JOHN   BR TR 5'10" 168 lbs.
B. Nov. 2, 1901, Chicago, Ill. D. Aug. 4, 1964, Chicago, Ill.

| 1925 | BKN | N | 1 | .000 | .000 | 1 | 0 | 0 | 0 | 0 | 0.0 | 0 | 0 | 0 | 1 | 0 | 1 | 0 | 0 | 0 | 0 | 0 | 0.0 | | |
| 1926 | | | 66 | .345 | .451 | 113 | 39 | 8 | 2 | 0 | 0.0 | 13 | 14 | 5 | 7 | 0 | 22 | 6 | 40 | 46 | 8 | 5 | 1.4 | .915 | 2B-21, 3B-14, SS-6 |

Year	Team		Games	BA	SA	AB	H	2B	3B	HR	HR%	R	RBI	BB	SO	SB	Pinch Hit AB	Pinch Hit H	PO	A	E	DP	TC/G	FA	G by Pos

Jerry Standaert *continued*

Year	Team		Games	BA	SA	AB	H	2B	3B	HR	HR%	R	RBI	BB	SO	SB	AB	H	PO	A	E	DP	TC/G	FA	G by Pos
1929	BOS	A	19	.167	.278	18	3	2	0	0	0.0	1	4	3	2	0	8	1	21	2	1	2	1.3	.958	1B-10
3 yrs.			86	.318	.424	132	42	10	2	0	0.0	14	18	8	10	0	31	7	61	48	9	7	1.4	.924	2B-21, 3B-14, 1B-10, SS-6

Pete Stanicek

STANICEK, PETER LOUIS
Brother of Steve Stanicek.
B. Apr. 16, 1963, Harvey, Ill.

BB TR 5'11" 175 lbs.

Year	Team		Games	BA	SA	AB	H	2B	3B	HR	HR%	R	RBI	BB	SO	SB	AB	H	PO	A	E	DP	TC/G	FA	G by Pos
1987	BAL	A	30	.274	.301	113	31	3	0	0	0.0	9	9	8	19	8	0	0	37	46	4	15	2.9	.954	2B-19, DH-10, 3B-2
1988			83	.230	.310	261	60	7	1	4	1.5	29	17	28	45	12	10	2	149	24	4	7	2.1	.977	OF-65, 2B-16, DH-1
2 yrs.			113	.243	.307	374	91	10	1	4	1.1	38	26	36	64	20	10	2	186	70	8	22	2.3	.970	OF-65, 2B-35, DH-11, 3B-2

Steve Stanicek

STANICEK, STEPHEN BLAIR
Brother of Pete Stanicek.
B. June 19, 1961, Lake Forest, Ill.

BR TR 6' 190 lbs.

Year	Team		Games	BA	SA	AB	H	2B	3B	HR	HR%	R	RBI	BB	SO	SB	AB	H	PO	A	E	DP	TC/G	FA	G by Pos
1987	MIL	A	4	.286	.286	7	2	0	0	0	0.0	2	0	0	2	0	3	1	0	0	0	0	0.0	–	DH-1
1989	PHI	N	9	.111	.111	9	1	0	0	0	0.0	0	1	0	3	0	9	1	0	0	0	0	0.0	–	DH-1
2 yrs.			13	.188	.188	16	3	0	0	0	0.0	2	1	0	5	0	12	2	0	0	0	0	0.0	–	DH-1

Tom Stankard

STANKARD, THOMAS FRANCIS
B. Mar. 20, 1882, Waltham, Mass. D. June 13, 1958, Waltham, Mass.

BR TR 6' 190 lbs.

Year	Team		Games	BA	SA	AB	H	2B	3B	HR	HR%	R	RBI	BB	SO	SB	AB	H	PO	A	E	DP	TC/G	FA	G by Pos
1904	PIT	N	2	.000	.000	2	0	0	0	0	0.0	0	0	0		0	0	0	1	1	0	0	1.0	1.000	SS-1, 3B-1

Eddie Stanky

STANKY, EDWARD RAYMOND (The Brat, Muggsy)
B. Sept. 3, 1916, Philadelphia, Pa.
Manager 1952-55, 1966-68, 1977.

BR TR 5'8" 170 lbs.

Year	Team		Games	BA	SA	AB	H	2B	3B	HR	HR%	R	RBI	BB	SO	SB	AB	H	PO	A	E	DP	TC/G	FA	G by Pos
1943	CHI	N	142	.245	.278	510	125	15	1	0	0.0	92	47	92	42	4	0	0	379	441	31	85	6.0	.964	2B-131, SS-12, 3B-2
1944 2 teams	CHI	N	(13G – .240)		BKN	N	(89G – .276)																		
" total			102	.273	.325	286	78	9	3	0	0.0	36	16	46	15	4	5	0	207	224	21	37	4.4	.954	2B-61, SS-38, 3B-4
1945	BKN	N	153	.258	.333	555	143	29	5	1	0.2	128	39	148	42	6	0	0	429	441	34	101	5.9	.962	2B-153, SS-1
1946			144	.273	.352	483	132	24	7	0	0.0	98	36	137	56	8	2	0	356	359	17	88	5.1	.977	2B-141
1947			146	.252	.369	559	141	24	5	3	0.5	97	53	103	39	3	0	0	402	406	12	123	5.6	.985	2B-146
1948	BOS	N	67	.320	.417	247	79	14	2	2	0.8	49	29	61	13	3	1	1	168	202	7	45	5.6	.981	2B-66
1949			138	.285	.358	506	144	24	5	1	0.2	90	42	113	41	3	3	0	357	354	15	92	5.3	.979	2B-135
1950	NY	N	152	.300	.412	527	158	25	5	8	1.5	115	51	144	50	9	0	0	407	418	20	128	5.6	.976	2B-151
1951			145	.247	.369	515	127	17	2	14	2.7	88	43	127	63	8	4	0	356	412	18	117	5.4	.977	2B-140
1952	STL	N	53	.229	.277	83	19	4	0	0	0.0	13	7	19	9	0	26	9	41	44	0	9	1.6	1.000	2B-20
1953			17	.267	.267	30	8	0	0	0	0.0	5	1	6	4	0	5	0	16	22	0	4	2.2	1.000	2B-8
11 yrs.			1259	.268	.348	4301	1154	185	35	29	0.7	811	364	996	374	48	46	10	3118	3323	175	829	5.3	.974	2B-1152, SS-51, 3B-6

WORLD SERIES

Year	Team		Games	BA	SA	AB	H	2B	3B	HR	HR%	R	RBI	BB	SO	SB	AB	H	PO	A	E	DP	TC/G	FA	G by Pos
1947	BKN	N	7	.240	.280	25	6	1	0	0	0.0	4	2	3	2	0	0	0	18	19	1	5	5.4	.974	2B-7
1948	BOS	N	6	.286	.357	14	4	1	0	0	0.0	0	1	7	1	0	0	0	8	12	0	2	3.3	1.000	2B-6
1951	NY	N	6	.136	.136	22	3	0	0	0	0.0	3	1	3	2	0	0	0	14	16	1	3	5.2	.968	2B-6
3 yrs.			19	.213	.246	61	13	2	0	0	0.0	7	4	13	5	0	0	0	40	47	2	10	4.7	.978	2B-19

Fred Stanley

STANLEY, FREDERICK BLAIR (Chicken)
B. Aug. 13, 1947, Farnhamville, Iowa

BR TR 5'10" 165 lbs.

Year	Team		Games	BA	SA	AB	H	2B	3B	HR	HR%	R	RBI	BB	SO	SB	AB	H	PO	A	E	DP	TC/G	FA	G by Pos
1969	SEA	A	17	.279	.372	43	12	1	0	0	0.0	2	4	3	8	1	1	0	22	29	2	8	3.1	.962	SS-15, 2B-1
1970	MIL	A	6			0	0	0	0	0		0	1	0	0	0	0	0	1	1	0	0	0.3	1.000	2B-2
1971	CLE	A	60	.225	.302	129	29	4	0	2	1.6	14	12	27	25	1	0	0	61	145	6	29	3.5	.972	SS-55, 2B-3
1972 2 teams	CLE	A	(6G – .167)		SD	N	(39G – .200)																		
" total			45	.196	.227	97	19	3	0	0	0.0	16	2	14	22	1	4	1	68	75	3	16	3.2	.979	SS-22, 2B-22, 3B-4
1973	NY	A	26	.212	.288	66	14	0	1	1	1.5	6	5	7	16	0	0	0	42	72	2	11	4.5	.983	SS-21, 2B-3
1974			33	.184	.184	38	7	0	0	0	0.0	2	3	3	2	1	0	0	32	59	1	14	2.8	.989	SS-19, 2B-15
1975			117	.222	.250	252	56	5	1	0	0.0	34	15	21	27	3	0	0	161	249	9	53	3.6	.979	SS-83, 2B-33, 3B-1
1976			110	.238	.273	260	62	2	2	1	0.4	32	20	34	29	1	1	0	148	252	8	36	3.7	.980	SS-110, 2B-3
1977			48	.261	.326	46	12	0	0	1	2.2	6	7	8	6	1	0	0	36	48	3	7	1.8	.966	SS-42, 3B-3, 2B-2
1978			81	.219	.281	160	35	7	0	1	0.6	14	9	25	31	0	0	0	88	152	9	26	3.1	.964	SS-71, 2B-11, 3B-4
1979			57	.200	.270	100	20	1	0	2	2.0	9	14	5	17	0	0	0	42	113	8	23	2.9	.951	SS-31, 3B-16, 2B-8, 1B-1
1980			49	.209	.244	86	18	3	0	0	0.0	13	5	5	5	0	0	0	39	86	7	18	2.7	.947	SS-19, 2B-17, 3B-12
1981	OAK	A	66	.193	.221	145	28	4	0	0	0.0	15	7	15	23	2	0	0	96	120	3	25	3.3	.986	SS-62, 2B-6
1982			101	.193	.250	228	44	7	0	2	0.9	33	17	29	32	0	0	0	116	226	13	43	3.5	.963	SS-98, 2B-2
14 yrs.			816	.216	.263	1650	356	38	5	10	0.6	197	120	196	243	11	7	1	952	1627	74	309	3.3	.972	SS-648, 2B-128, 3B-40, 1B-1

DIVISIONAL PLAYOFF SERIES

Year	Team		Games	BA	SA	AB	H	2B	3B	HR	HR%	R	RBI	BB	SO	SB	AB	H	PO	A	E	DP	TC/G	FA	G by Pos
1981	OAK	A	3	.000	.000	6	0	0	0	0	0.0	0	0	1	1	0	0	0	0	0	0	0	0.0	–	SS-3

LEAGUE CHAMPIONSHIP SERIES

Year	Team		Games	BA	SA	AB	H	2B	3B	HR	HR%	R	RBI	BB	SO	SB	AB	H	PO	A	E	DP	TC/G	FA	G by Pos
1976	NY	A	5	.333	.467	15	5	2	0	0	0.0	1	0	2	0	0	0	0	7	15	1	2	4.6	.957	SS-5
1977			2	–	–	0	0	0	0	0	0.0	0	0	0	0	0	0	0	1	0	0	0	0.5	1.000	SS-2
1978			2	.200	.200	5	1	0	0	0	0.0	0	0	0	1	0	0	0	3	3	0	0	3.0	1.000	2B-2
1981	OAK	A	2	.333	.333	3	1	0	0	0	0.0	0	1	0	2	0	0	0	0	0	1	0	0.0	–	SS-2
4 yrs.			11	.304	.391	23	7	2	0	0	0.0	1	1	2	3	0	0	0	11	18	1	2	2.7	.967	SS-9, 2B-2

WORLD SERIES

Year	Team		Games	BA	SA	AB	H	2B	3B	HR	HR%	R	RBI	BB	SO	SB	AB	H	PO	A	E	DP	TC/G	FA	G by Pos
1976	NY	A	4	.167	.333	6	1	1	0	0	0.0	1	1	3	1	0	0	0	4	7	1	3	3.0	.917	SS-4
1977			1	–	–	0	0	0	0	0	0.0	0	0	0	0	0	0	0	1	0	0	0	1.0	1.000	SS-1
1978			3	.200	.400	5	1	1	0	0	0.0	0	0	1	0	0	0	0	5	2	0	1	2.3	1.000	2B-3
3 yrs.			8	.182	.364	11	2	2	0	0	0.0	1	1	4	1	0	0	0	10	9	1	4	2.5	.950	SS-5, 2B-3

Jim Stanley

STANLEY, JAMES FRANCIS
B. 1889, Chicago, Ill.

BB TR 5'6" 148 lbs.

Year Team	Games	BA	SA	AB	H	2B	3B	HR	HR%	R	RBI	BB	SO	SB	Pinch Hit AB	Pinch Hit H	PO	A	E	DP	TC/G	FA	G by Pos

Jim Stanley *continued*

Year Team	Games	BA	SA	AB	H	2B	3B	HR	HR%	R	RBI	BB	SO	SB	AB	H	PO	A	E	DP	TC/G	FA	G by Pos
1914 CHI F	54	.194	.224	98	19	3	0	0	0.0	13	4	19		2	6	0	51	64	16	8	2.4	.878	SS-40, 3B-3, OF-1, 2B-1

Joe Stanley

STANLEY, JOSEPH
B. N. J. Deceased.

Year Team	Games	BA	SA	AB	H	2B	3B	HR	HR%	R	RBI	BB	SO	SB	AB	H	PO	A	E	DP	TC/G	FA	G by Pos
1884 BAL U	6	.238	.286	21	5	1	0	0	0.0	3		0		0	0		3	1	5	0	1.5	.444	OF-6

Joe Stanley

STANLEY, JOSEPH BERNARD   BB TR 5'9½" 150 lbs.
Brother of Buck Stanley.
B. Apr. 2, 1881, Washington, D. C.   D. Sept. 13, 1967, Detroit, Mich.

Year Team	Games	BA	SA	AB	H	2B	3B	HR	HR%	R	RBI	BB	SO	SB	AB	H	PO	A	E	DP	TC/G	FA	G by Pos
1897 WAS N	1	.000	.000	1	0	0	0	0	0.0	0	0	0		0	0	0	0	0	0	0	0.0	–	P-1
1902 WAS N	3	.333	.333	12	4	0	0	0	0.0	2	1	0		0	0	0	5	0	1	0	2.0	.833	OF-3
1903 BOS N	86	.250	.331	308	77	12	5	1	0.3	40	47	18		10	5	0	119	23	19	2	1.9	.882	OF-77, SS-1, P-1
1904	3	.000	.000	8	0	0	0	0	0.0	0	0	0		0	0	0	2	2	1	0	1.7	.800	OF-3
1905 WAS A	28	.261	.337	92	24	2	1	1	1.1	13	17	7		4	1	0	47	4	3	0	1.9	.944	OF-27
1906	73	.163	.199	221	36	0	4	0	0.0	18	9	20		6	10	1	78	7	6	0	1.2	.934	OF-64, P-1
1909 CHI N	22	.135	.154	52	7	1	0	0	0.0	4	2	6		0	6	0	17	1	1	0	0.9	.947	OF-16
7 yrs.	216	.213	.272	694	148	15	10	2	0.3	77	76	51		20	22	1	268	37	31	2	1.6	.908	OF-190, P-3, SS-1

Mickey Stanley

STANLEY, MITCHELL JACK   BR TR 6'1" 185 lbs.
B. July 20, 1942, Grand Rapids, Mich.

Year Team	Games	BA	SA	AB	H	2B	3B	HR	HR%	R	RBI	BB	SO	SB	AB	H	PO	A	E	DP	TC/G	FA	G by Pos
1964 DET A	4	.273	.273	11	3	0	0	0	0.0	3	1	0	1	0	0	0	5	0	0	0	1.3	1.000	OF-4
1965	30	.239	.368	117	28	6	0	3	2.6	14	13	3	12	1	0	0	69	1	1	0	2.4	.986	OF-29
1966	92	.289	.426	235	68	15	4	3	1.3	28	19	17	20	2	9	3	163	6	0	1	1.8	1.000	OF-82
1967	145	.210	.312	333	70	7	3	7	2.1	38	24	29	46	9	13	1	264	7	4	5	1.9	.985	OF-128, 1B-8
1968	153	.259	.364	583	151	16	6	11	1.9	88	60	42	57	4	6	0	405	40	4	13	2.9	.991	OF-130, 1B-15, SS-9, 2B-1
1969	149	.235	.367	592	139	28	1	16	2.7	73	70	52	56	8	7	2	342	138	10	24	3.3	.980	OF-101, SS-59, 1B-4
1970	142	.252	.396	568	143	21	11	13	2.3	83	47	45	56	10	5	2	384	9	11	10	2.8	.997	OF-132, 1B-9
1971	139	.292	.404	401	117	14	5	7	1.7	43	41	24	44	1	6	3	315	10	4	3	2.4	.988	OF-139
1972	142	.234	.395	435	102	16	6	14	3.2	45	55	29	49	1	5	3	309	9	2	1	2.3	.994	OF-139
1973	157	.244	.384	602	147	23	5	17	2.8	81	57	48	65	0	0	0	420	10	3	3	2.8	.993	OF-157
1974	99	.221	.325	394	87	13	2	8	2.0	40	34	26	63	5	1	0	341	14	4	11	3.6	.989	OF-91, 1B-8, 2B-1
1975	52	.256	.390	164	42	7	3	3	1.8	26	19	15	27	1	3	2	183	22	2	9	4.0	.990	OF-28, 1B-14, 3B-7, DH-1
1976	84	.257	.402	214	55	17	1	4	1.9	34	29	14	19	2	19	6	187	47	5	14	2.8	.979	OF-38, 1B-17, 3B-11, SS-3, 2B-2
1977	75	.230	.387	222	51	9	1	8	3.6	30	23	18	30	0	13	3	128	5	4	3	1.8	.971	OF-57, 1B-3, DH-2
1978	53	.265	.384	151	40	9	0	3	2.0	15	8	9	19	0	12	2	173	9	2	16	3.5	.989	OF-34, 1B-12
15 yrs.	1516	.248	.377	5022	1243	201	48	117	2.3	641	500	371	564	44	99	27	3688	327	46	113	2.7	.989	OF-1289, 1B-94, SS-74, 3B-18, 2B-4, DH-3

LEAGUE CHAMPIONSHIP SERIES
Year Team	Games	BA	SA	AB	H	2B	3B	HR	HR%	R	RBI	BB	SO	SB	AB	H	PO	A	E	DP	TC/G	FA	G by Pos
1972 DET A	4	.333	.333	6	2	0	0	0	0.0	0	0	0	0	0	1	0	7	0	0	0	1.8	1.000	OF-3

WORLD SERIES
Year Team	Games	BA	SA	AB	H	2B	3B	HR	HR%	R	RBI	BB	SO	SB	AB	H	PO	A	E	DP	TC/G	FA	G by Pos
1968 DET A	7	.214	.286	28	6	0	1	0	0.0	4	0	2	4	0	0	0	15	16	2	3	4.7	.939	SS-7, OF-4

Mike Stanley

STANLEY, ROBERT MICHAEL   BR TR 6'1" 185 lbs.
B. June 25, 1963, Fort Lauderdale, Fla.

Year Team	Games	BA	SA	AB	H	2B	3B	HR	HR%	R	RBI	BB	SO	SB	AB	H	PO	A	E	DP	TC/G	FA	G by Pos
1986 TEX A	15	.333	.533	30	10	3	0	1	3.3	4	3	7	1	5	2	14	8	1	2	1.5	.957	3B-7, C-4, DH-3, OF-1	
1987	78	.273	.403	216	59	8	1	6	2.8	34	37	31	48	3	6	4	389	26	7	7	5.4	.983	C-61, 1B-12, OF-1
1988	94	.229	.297	249	57	8	0	3	1.2	21	27	37	62	0	15	3	342	17	4	4	3.9	.989	C-64, 1B-7, 3B-2
1989	67	.246	.311	122	30	3	1	1	0.8	9	11	12	29	1	23	6	117	8	3	3	1.9	.977	C-25, DH-21, 1B-7, 3B-3
4 yrs.	254	.253	.348	617	156	22	2	11	1.8	68	76	83	146	5	49	15	862	59	15	16	3.7	.984	C-154, 1B-26, DH-24, 3B-12, OF-2

John Stansbury

STANSBURY, JOHN JAMES   BR TR 5'9" 165 lbs.
B. Dec. 6, 1885, Phillipsburg, N. J.   D. Dec. 26, 1970, Easton, Pa.

Year Team	Games	BA	SA	AB	H	2B	3B	HR	HR%	R	RBI	BB	SO	SB	AB	H	PO	A	E	DP	TC/G	FA	G by Pos
1918 BOS A	20	.128	.149	47	6	1	0	0	0.0	3	2	6	3	0	0	0	16	37	1	5	2.7	.981	3B-18, OF-2

Buck Stanton

STANTON, GEORGE WASHINGTON   BL TL 5'10" 150 lbs.
B. June 19, 1906, Stantonsburg, N. C.

Year Team	Games	BA	SA	AB	H	2B	3B	HR	HR%	R	RBI	BB	SO	SB	AB	H	PO	A	E	DP	TC/G	FA	G by Pos
1931 STL A	13	.200	.333	15	3	2	0	0	0.0	3	0	0	6	0	10	1	3	0	1	0	0.3	.750	OF-1

Harry Stanton

STANTON, HARRY ANDREW   TR
B. St. Louis, Mo.

Year Team	Games	BA	SA	AB	H	2B	3B	HR	HR%	R	RBI	BB	SO	SB	AB	H	PO	A	E	DP	TC/G	FA	G by Pos
1900 STL N	1	–	–	0	0	0	0	0	–	0	0	0		0	0	0	0	0	0	0	0.0	–	C-1

Leroy Stanton

STANTON, LEROY BOBBY (Lee)   BR TR 6'1" 195 lbs.
B. Apr. 10, 1946, Latta, S. C.

Year Team	Games	BA	SA	AB	H	2B	3B	HR	HR%	R	RBI	BB	SO	SB	AB	H	PO	A	E	DP	TC/G	FA	G by Pos
1970 NY N	4	.250	.750	4	1	0	1	0	0.0	0	0	0	0	0	3	0	1	0	0	0	0.3	1.000	OF-1
1971	5	.190	.238	21	4	1	0	0	0.0	2	2	2	4	0	0	0	9	0	0	0	1.8	1.000	OF-5
1972 CAL A	127	.251	.393	402	101	15	3	12	3.0	44	39	22	100	2	7	1	225	6	4	2	1.9	.983	OF-124
1973	119	.235	.356	306	72	9	2	8	2.6	41	34	27	88	3	11	5	160	5	6	2	1.4	.965	OF-107
1974	118	.267	.407	415	111	21	2	11	2.7	48	62	33	107	10	7	1	226	11	6	0	2.1	.975	OF-114
1975	137	.261	.416	440	115	20	3	14	3.2	67	82	52	85	18	10	0	230	16	10	2	1.9	.961	OF-131, DH-1
1976	93	.190	.281	231	44	13	1	2	0.9	12	25	24	57	2	15	3	128	1	2	0	1.4	.985	OF-79, DH-4
1977 SEA A	133	.275	.511	454	125	24	1	27	5.9	56	90	42	115	0	11	4	175	9	9	2	1.5	.953	OF-91, DH-33
1978	93	.182	.248	302	55	11	0	3	1.0	24	24	34	80	1	5	0	59	1	0	0	0.6	1.000	DH-59, OF-30
9 yrs.	829	.244	.388	2575	628	114	13	77	3.0	294	358	236	636	36	69	14	1213	49	37	8	1.6	.972	OF-682, DH-97

Year	Team	Games	BA	SA	AB	H	2B	3B	HR	HR%	R	RBI	BB	SO	SB	Pinch Hit AB	Pinch Hit H	PO	A	E	DP	TC/G	FA	G by Pos

Tom Stanton

STANTON, THOMAS PATRICK
B. Oct. 25, 1874, St. Louis, Mo. D. Jan. 17, 1957, St. Louis, Mo.
BB TR 5'10" 175 lbs.

Year	Team	Games	BA	SA	AB	H	2B	3B	HR	HR%	R	RBI	BB	SO	SB	Pinch Hit AB	Pinch Hit H	PO	A	E	DP	TC/G	FA	G by Pos
1904	CHI N	1	.000	.000	3	0	0	0	0	0.0	0	0	0	0		0	0	4	1	0	0	5.0	1.000	C-1

Joe Staples

STAPLES, JOSEPH F.
B. Buffalo, N. Y. Deceased.

Year	Team	Games	BA	SA	AB	H	2B	3B	HR	HR%	R	RBI	BB	SO	SB	Pinch Hit AB	Pinch Hit H	PO	A	E	DP	TC/G	FA	G by Pos
1885	BUF N	7	.045	.045	22	1	0	0	0	0.0	0	0	0	9		0	0	7	4	7	1	2.6	.611	OF-6, 2B-1

Dave Stapleton

STAPLETON, DAVID LESLIE
B. Jan. 16, 1954, Fairhope, Ala.
BR TR 6'1" 178 lbs.

Year	Team	Games	BA	SA	AB	H	2B	3B	HR	HR%	R	RBI	BB	SO	SB	Pinch Hit AB	Pinch Hit H	PO	A	E	DP	TC/G	FA	G by Pos
1980	BOS A	106	.321	.463	449	144	33	5	7	1.6	61	45	13	32	3	4	1	269	338	12	101	5.8	.981	2B-94, 1B-8, OF-6, DH-3, 3B-2
1981		93	.285	.423	355	101	17	1	10	2.8	45	42	21	22	0	4	0	260	204	17	50	5.2	.965	SS-33, 3B-25, 2B-23, 1B-12, DH-3
1982		150	.264	.398	538	142	28	1	14	2.6	66	65	31	40	2	5	0	1032	179	13	116	8.2	.989	1B-106, SS-27, 2B-9, 3B-5, DH-4, OF-1
1983		151	.247	.363	542	134	31	1	10	1.8	54	66	40	44	1	1	0	1249	105	10	132	9.0	.993	1B-145, 2B-5
1984		13	.231	.282	39	9	2	0	0	0.0	4	1	3	3	0	2	1	86	8	0	5	7.2	1.000	1B-10, DH-1
1985		30	.227	.318	66	15	6	0	0	0.0	4	2	4	11	0	6	1	41	36	1	11	2.6	.987	2B-14, 1B-8, DH-5
1986		39	.128	.154	39	5	1	0	0	0.0	4	3	2	10	0	2	2	85	16	0	13	2.6	1.000	1B-29, 2B-6, 3B-2
7 yrs.		582	.271	.398	2028	550	118	8	41	2.0	238	224	114	162	6	24	5	3022	886	53	428	6.8	.987	1B-318, 2B-151, SS-60, 3B-34, DH-16, OF-7

LEAGUE CHAMPIONSHIP SERIES

Year	Team	Games	BA	SA	AB	H	2B	3B	HR	HR%	R	RBI	BB	SO	SB	Pinch Hit AB	Pinch Hit H	PO	A	E	DP	TC/G	FA	G by Pos
1986	BOS A	4	.667	.667	3	2	0	0	0	0.0	2	0	1	0	0	0	0	10	0	0	1	2.5	1.000	1B-4

WORLD SERIES

Year	Team	Games	BA	SA	AB	H	2B	3B	HR	HR%	R	RBI	BB	SO	SB	Pinch Hit AB	Pinch Hit H	PO	A	E	DP	TC/G	FA	G by Pos
1986	BOS A	3	.000	.000	1	0	0	0	0	0.0	0	0	0	0	0	0	0	3	2	0	0	1.7	1.000	1B-3

Willie Stargell

STARGELL, WILVER DORNEL
B. Mar. 6, 1940, Earlsboro, Okla.
Hall of Fame 1987.
BL TL 6'2" 188 lbs.

Year	Team	Games	BA	SA	AB	H	2B	3B	HR	HR%	R	RBI	BB	SO	SB	Pinch Hit AB	Pinch Hit H	PO	A	E	DP	TC/G	FA	G by Pos
1962	PIT N	10	.290	.452	31	9	3	1	0	0.0	1	4	3	10	0	2	0	12	1	1	0	1.4	.929	OF-9
1963		108	.243	.428	304	74	11	6	11	3.6	34	47	19	85	0	25	2	226	12	9	18	2.3	.964	OF-65, 1B-16
1964		117	.273	.501	421	115	19	7	21	5.0	53	78	17	92	1	12	2	565	24	10	50	5.1	.983	OF-59, 1B-50
1965		144	.272	.501	533	145	25	8	27	5.1	68	107	39	127	1	5	1	268	14	8	8	2.0	.972	OF-137, 1B-7
1966		140	.315	.581	485	153	30	0	33	6.8	84	102	48	109	2	9	3	300	13	11	17	2.3	.966	OF-127, 1B-15
1967		134	.271	.465	462	125	18	6	20	4.3	54	73	67	103	1	6	1	447	27	11	26	3.6	.977	OF-98, 1B-37
1968		128	.237	.441	435	103	15	1	24	5.5	57	67	47	105	5	5	0	254	19	9	12	2.2	.968	OF-113, 1B-13
1969		145	.307	.556	522	160	31	6	29	5.6	89	92	61	120	1	8	1	333	14	7	21	2.4	.980	OF-116, 1B-23
1970		136	.264	.511	474	125	18	3	31	6.5	70	85	44	119	0	9	4	184	17	5	1	1.5	.976	OF-125, 1B-1
1971		141	.295	.628	511	151	26	0	**48**	9.4	104	125	83	**154**	0	3	1	237	8	4	4	1.8	.984	OF-135
1972		138	.293	.558	495	145	28	2	33	6.7	75	112	65	129	1	5	0	931	41	17	96	7.2	.983	1B-101, OF-32
1973		148	.299	**.646**	522	156	**43**	3	**44**	8.4	106	**119**	80	129	0	7	2	261	14	7	1	1.9	.975	OF-142
1974		140	.301	.537	508	153	37	4	25	4.9	90	96	87	106	0	3	0	256	8	9	1	2.0	.967	OF-135, 1B-1
1975		124	.295	.516	461	136	32	2	22	4.8	71	90	58	109	0	2	1	1121	54	10	112	9.6	.992	1B-122
1976		117	.257	.458	428	110	20	3	20	4.7	54	65	50	101	2	7	0	1037	53	13	76	9.4	.988	1B-111
1977		63	.274	.548	186	51	12	0	13	7.0	29	35	31	55	0	10	2	449	27	7	26	7.7	.986	1B-55
1978		122	.295	.567	390	115	18	2	28	7.2	60	97	50	93	3	10	3	875	57	6	76	7.7	.994	1B-112
1979		126	.281	.552	424	119	19	0	32	7.5	60	82	47	105	0	15	7	949	47	3	102	7.9	.997	1B-113
1980		67	.262	.485	202	53	10	1	11	5.4	28	38	26	52	0	11	3	460	33	4	54	7.4	.992	1B-54
1981		38	.283	.350	60	17	4	0	0	0.0	2	9	5	9	0	26	8	70	0	0	10	1.8	1.000	1B-9
1982		74	.233	.411	73	17	4	0	3	4.1	6	17	10	24	0	56	14	43	3	0	3	0.6	1.000	1B-8
21 yrs.		2360	.282	.529	7927	2232	423	55	475	6.0	1195	1540	937	1936	17	236	55	9278	486	151	713	4.2	.985	OF-1293, 1B-848
														2nd										

LEAGUE CHAMPIONSHIP SERIES

Year	Team	Games	BA	SA	AB	H	2B	3B	HR	HR%	R	RBI	BB	SO	SB	Pinch Hit AB	Pinch Hit H	PO	A	E	DP	TC/G	FA	G by Pos
1970	PIT N	3	.500	.583	12	6	1	0	0	0.0	0	1	1	0	0	0	0	4	0	0	0	1.3	1.000	OF-3
1971		4	.000	.000	14	0	0	0	0	0.0	1	0	2	6	0	0	0	6	0	0	0	1.5	1.000	OF-4
1972		5	.063	.125	16	1	1	0	0	0.0	1	1	2	5	0	0	0	0	0	0	0	0.0	—	1B-5, OF-1
1974		4	.400	.800	15	6	0	0	2	13.3	3	4	1	2	0	0	0	13	0	0	0	3.3	1.000	OF-4
1975		3	.182	.273	11	2	1	0	0	0.0	1	0	1	3	0	0	0	15	0	0	2	5.0	1.000	1B-3
1979		3	.455	1.182	11	5	2	0	2	18.2	2	6	3	2	0	0	0	32	2	0	2	11.3	1.000	1B-3
6 yrs.		22	.253	.468	79	20	5	0	4	5.1	8	12	10	19	0	0	0	70	2	0	4	3.3	1.000	OF-12, 1B-11

WORLD SERIES

Year	Team	Games	BA	SA	AB	H	2B	3B	HR	HR%	R	RBI	BB	SO	SB	Pinch Hit AB	Pinch Hit H	PO	A	E	DP	TC/G	FA	G by Pos
1971	PIT N	7	.208	.250	24	5	1	0	0	0.0	3	1	7	9	0	0	0	11	1	0	1	1.7	1.000	OF-7
1979		7	.400	.833	30	12	4	0	3	10.0	7	7	0	6	0	0	0	59	2	2	9	9.0	.968	1B-7
2 yrs.		14	.315	.574	54	17	5	0	3	5.6	10	8	7	15	0	0	0	70	3	2	10	5.4	.973	OF-7, 1B-7

Dolly Stark

STARK, MONROE RANDOLPH
B. Jan. 19, 1885, Ripley, Miss. D. Dec. 1, 1924, Memphis, Tenn.
BR TR 5'9" 160 lbs.

Year	Team	Games	BA	SA	AB	H	2B	3B	HR	HR%	R	RBI	BB	SO	SB	Pinch Hit AB	Pinch Hit H	PO	A	E	DP	TC/G	FA	G by Pos
1909	CLE A	19	.200	.200	60	12	0	0	0	0.0	4	1	6			4	0	36	41	11	3	4.6	.875	SS-19
1910	BKN N	30	.165	.194	103	17	3	0	0	0.0	7	8	7	19	2	0	0	68	90	19	13	5.9	.893	SS-30
1911		70	.295	.326	193	57	4	1	0	0.0	25	19	20	24	6	11	3	115	138	19	20	3.9	.930	SS-34, 2B-18, 3B-3
1912		8	.182	.182	22	4	0	0	0	0.0	2	2	1	3	2	1	0	13	20	4	3	4.6	.892	SS-7
4 yrs.		127	.238	.262	378	90	7	1	0	0.0	38	30	34	46	14	12	3	232	289	53	39	4.5	.908	SS-90, 2B-18, 3B-3

Matt Stark

STARK, MATTHEW SCOTT
B. Jan. 21, 1965, Whittier, Calif.
BR TR 6'4" 225 lbs.

Year	Team	Games	BA	SA	AB	H	2B	3B	HR	HR%	R	RBI	BB	SO	SB	Pinch Hit AB	Pinch Hit H	PO	A	E	DP	TC/G	FA	G by Pos
1987	TOR A	5	.083	.083	12	1	0	0	0	0.0	0	0	0	0	0	2	0	25	1	0	0	5.2	1.000	C-5

George Starnagle

STARNAGLE, GEORGE HENRY
Born George Henry Steuernagel.
B. Oct. 6, 1873, Belleville, Ill. D. Feb. 15, 1946, Belleville, Ill.
BR TR 5'11" 175 lbs.

Year	Team	Games	BA	SA	AB	H	2B	3B	HR	HR%	R	RBI	BB	SO	SB	Pinch Hit AB	Pinch Hit H	PO	A	E	DP	TC/G	FA	G by Pos

George Starnagle *continued*

Year	Team		Games	BA	SA	AB	H	2B	3B	HR	HR%	R	RBI	BB	SO	SB	AB	H	PO	A	E	DP	TC/G	FA	G by Pos
1902	CLE	A	1	.000	.000	3	0	0	0	0	0.0	0	0	0		0	0	0	2	0	1	0	3.0	.667	C-1

Charlie Starr

STARR, CHARLES WATKIN   TR
B. Aug. 30, 1878, Pike County, Ohio D. Oct. 18, 1937, Pasadena, Calif.

Year	Team		Games	BA	SA	AB	H	2B	3B	HR	HR%	R	RBI	BB	SO	SB	AB	H	PO	A	E	DP	TC/G	FA	G by Pos
1905	STL	A	24	.206	.206	97	20	0	0	0	0.0	10	6	7		0	2	0	26	56	5	3	3.6	.943	2B-16, 3B-6
1908	PIT	N	20	.186	.220	59	11	2	0	0	0.0	8	8	13		6	1	0	22	51	7	3	4.0	.913	2B-12, SS-5, 3B-2
1909	2 teams		BOS	N (61G – .222)		PHI	N	(3G – .000)																	
"	total		64	.219	.256	219	48	2	3	0	0.0	16	6	31		7	3	0	116	161	21	20	4.7	.930	2B-54, SS-6, 3B-3
3 yrs.			108	.211	.237	375	79	4	3	0	0.0	34	20	51		13	6	0	164	268	33	26	4.3	.929	2B-82, SS-11, 3B-11

Chick Starr

STARR, WILLIAM   BR TR 6'1" 175 lbs.
B. Feb. 26, 1911, Brooklyn, N. Y.

Year	Team		Games	BA	SA	AB	H	2B	3B	HR	HR%	R	RBI	BB	SO	SB	AB	H	PO	A	E	DP	TC/G	FA	G by Pos
1935	WAS	A	12	.208	.208	24	5	0	0	0	0.0	1	1	0	1	0	0	0	28	6	1	2	2.9	.971	C-12
1936			1	–	–	0	0	0	0	0	–	0	0	0	0	0	0	0	0	0	0	0	0.0	–	C-1
2 yrs.			13	.208	.208	24	5	0	0	0	0.0	1	1	0	1	0	0	0	28	6	1	2	2.7	.971	C-13

Joe Start

START, JOSEPH (Old Reliable)   BL TL 5'9" 165 lbs.
B. Oct. 14, 1842, New York, N. Y. D. Mar. 27, 1927, Providence, R. I.
Manager 1873.

Year	Team		Games	BA	SA	AB	H	2B	3B	HR	HR%	R	RBI	BB	SO	SB	AB	H	PO	A	E	DP	TC/G	FA	G by Pos
1876	NY	N	56	.277	.299	264	73	6	0	0	0.0	40	21	1	2		0	0	547	10	21	11	10.3	.964	1B-56
1877	HAR	N	60	.332	.399	271	90	3	6	1	0.4	55	21	6	2		0	0	704	10	27	25	12.4	.964	1B-60
1878	CHI	N	61	.351	.439	285	100	12	5	1	0.4	58	27	2	3		0	0	719	13	33	28	12.5	.957	1B-61
1879	PRO	N	66	.319	.404	317	101	11	5	2	0.6	70	37	7	4		0	0	779	11	22	24	12.3	.973	1B-65, OF-1
1880			82	.278	.354	345	96	14	6	0	0.0	53	27	13	20		0	0	954	10	29	30	12.1	.971	1B-82
1881			79	.328	.397	348	114	12	6	0	0.0	56	29	9	7		0	0	837	17	33	50	11.2	.963	1B-79
1882			82	.329	.407	356	117	8	10	0	0.0	58		11	7		0	0	905	21	25	54	11.6	.974	1B-82
1883			87	.284	.373	370	105	16	7	1	0.3	63		22	16		0	0	923	29	43	48	11.4	.957	1B-87
1884			93	.276	.344	381	105	10	5	2	0.5	80		35	25		0	0	939	21	20	31	10.5	.980	1B-93
1885			101	.275	.326	374	103	11	4	0	0.0	47	41	39	10		0	0	1036	35	31	42	10.9	.972	1B-101
1886	WAS	N	31	.221	.270	122	27	4	1	0	0.0	10	17	5	13		0	0	348	7	10	16	11.8	.973	1B-31
11 yrs.			798	.300	.370	3433	1031	107	55	7	0.2	590	220	150	109		0	0	8691	184	294	359	11.5	.968	1B-797, OF-1

Joe Staton

STATON, JOSEPH (Slim)   BL TL 6'3" 175 lbs.
B. Mar. 8, 1948, Seattle, Wash.

Year	Team		Games	BA	SA	AB	H	2B	3B	HR	HR%	R	RBI	BB	SO	SB	AB	H	PO	A	E	DP	TC/G	FA	G by Pos
1972	DET	A	6	.000	.000	2	0	0	0	0	0.0	0	1	0	1	0	0	0	5	0	0	0	0.8	1.000	1B-2
1973			9	.235	.235	17	4	0	0	0	0.0	2	3	0	3	1	2	0	25	6	1	1	3.6	.969	1B-5
2 yrs.			15	.211	.211	19	4	0	0	0	0.0	3	3	0	4	1	2	0	30	6	1	1	2.5	.973	1B-7

Jigger Statz

STATZ, ARNOLD JOHN   BR TR 5'7½" 150 lbs.
B. Oct. 20, 1897, Waukegan, Ill.   BB 1922
D. Mar. 16, 1988, Corona Del Mar, Calif.

Year	Team		Games	BA	SA	AB	H	2B	3B	HR	HR%	R	RBI	BB	SO	SB	AB	H	PO	A	E	DP	TC/G	FA	G by Pos
1919	NY	N	21	.300	.367	60	18	2	1	0	0.0	7	6	3	8	2	0	0	45	0	1	0	2.2	.978	OF-18, 2B-5
1920	2 teams		NY	N (16G – .133)		BOS	N	(2G – .000)																	
"	total		18	.121	.182	33	4	0	1	0	0.0	0	5	2	9	0	3	0	17	1	1	1	1.1	.947	OF-14
1922	CHI	N	110	.297	.366	462	137	19	5	1	0.2	77	34	41	31	16	0	0	309	16	14	4	3.1	.959	OF-110
1923			154	.319	.440	655	209	33	8	10	1.5	110	70	56	42	29	0	0	438	26	12	7	3.1	.975	OF-154
1924			135	.277	.352	549	152	22	5	3	0.5	69	49	37	50	13	2	1	377	26	19	5	3.1	.955	OF-131, 2B-1
1925			38	.257	.378	148	38	6	3	2	1.4	21	14	11	16	4	1	0	112	3	7	0	3.2	.943	OF-37
1927	BKN	N	130	.274	.355	507	139	24	7	1	0.2	64	21	26	43	10	4	0	371	15	4	5	3.0	.990	OF-122, 2B-1
1928			77	.234	.292	171	40	8	1	0	0.0	28	16	18	12	3	5	2	108	3	4	2	1.5	.965	OF-77, 2B-1
8 yrs.			683	.285	.373	2585	737	114	31	17	0.7	376	215	194	211	77	15	3	1777	90	62	24	2.8	.968	OF-663, 2B-8

Rusty Staub

STAUB, DANIEL JOSEPH (Le Grande Orange)   BL TR 6'2" 190 lbs.
B. Apr. 1, 1944, New Orleans, La.

Year	Team		Games	BA	SA	AB	H	2B	3B	HR	HR%	R	RBI	BB	SO	SB	AB	H	PO	A	E	DP	TC/G	FA	G by Pos
1963	HOU	N	150	.224	.308	513	115	17	4	6	1.2	43	45	59	58	0	5	0	963	63	11	52	6.9	.989	1B-109, OF-49
1964			89	.216	.346	292	63	10	2	8	2.7	26	35	21	31	1	8	3	512	30	9	34	6.2	.984	1B-49, OF-38
1965			131	.256	.412	410	105	20	1	14	3.4	43	63	52	57	3	16	5	203	12	11	1	1.7	.951	OF-112, 1B-1
1966			153	.280	.412	554	155	28	3	13	2.3	60	81	58	61	2	6	3	291	15	12	3	2.1	.962	OF-148, 1B-1
1967			149	.333	.473	546	182	44	1	10	1.8	71	74	60	47	0	5	1	269	10	11	2	1.9	.962	OF-144
1968			161	.291	.387	591	172	37	1	6	1.0	54	72	73	57	2	0	0	1336	94	13	100	9.0	.991	1B-147, OF-15
1969	MON	N	158	.302	.526	549	166	26	5	29	5.3	89	79	110	61	3	2	1	265	16	10	2	1.8	.966	OF-156
1970			160	.274	.497	569	156	23	7	30	5.3	98	94	112	93	12	3	2	308	14	5	4	2.0	.985	OF-160
1971			162	.311	.482	599	186	34	6	19	3.2	94	97	74	42	9	5	1	290	20	18	5	2.0	.945	OF-162
1972	NY	N	66	.293	.452	239	70	11	0	9	3.8	32	38	31	13	0	1	0	108	4	2	2	1.7	.982	OF-65
1973			152	.279	.421	585	163	36	1	15	2.6	77	76	74	52	1	0	0	297	17	7	5	2.1	.978	OF-152
1974			151	.258	.406	561	145	22	2	19	3.4	65	78	77	39	2	4	2	262	19	5	5	1.9	.983	OF-147
1975			155	.282	.448	574	162	30	4	19	3.3	93	105	77	55	2	2	1	267	15	4	3	1.8	.986	OF-153
1976	DET	A	161	.299	.433	589	176	28	3	15	2.5	73	96	83	49	3	0	0	218	8	7	3	1.4	.970	OF-126, DH-36
1977			158	.278	.448	623	173	34	3	22	3.5	84	101	59	47	1	0	0	0	0	0	0	0.0	–	DH-156
1978			162	.273	.435	642	175	30	1	24	3.7	75	121	76	35	3	0	0	0	0	0	0	0.0	–	DH-162
1979	2 teams		DET	A (68G – .236)		MON	N	(38G – .267)																	
"	total		106	.244	.404	332	81	15	1	12	3.6	41	54	46	28	1	14	2	156	7	1	11	1.5	.994	DH-66, 1B-22, OF-1
1980	TEX	A	109	.300	.459	340	102	23	2	9	2.6	42	55	39	18	1	15	5	262	14	6	28	2.6	.979	1B-57, DH-30, OF-14
1981	NY	N	70	.317	.466	161	51	9	0	5	3.1	9	21	22	12	1	24	9	339	20	4	26	5.2	.989	1B-41
1982			112	.242	.324	219	53	9	0	3	1.4	11	27	24	10	0	57	12	172	19	2	12	1.7	.990	OF-27, 1B-18
1983			104	.296	.426	115	34	6	0	3	2.6	5	28	14	10	0	81	24	40	5	2	0	0.5	.957	1B-5, OF-5
1984			78	.264	.361	72	19	4	0	1	1.4	2	18	4	9	0	66	18	13	0	0	2	0.2	1.000	1B-3
1985			54	.267	.400	45	12	3	0	1	2.2	2	8	10	4	0	42	11	1	0	0	0	0.0	1.000	OF-1
23 yrs.			2951	.279	.431	9720	2716	499	47	292	3.0	1189	1466	1255	888	47	358	100	6572	402	140	306	2.4	.980	OF-1675, DH-477, 1B-426
			7th																						

Year	Team		Games	BA	SA	AB	H	2B	3B	HR	HR%	R	RBI	BB	SO	SB	Pinch Hit AB	H	PO	A	E	DP	TC/G	FA	G by Pos

Rusty Staub *continued*

LEAGUE CHAMPIONSHIP SERIES

| 1973 | NY | N | 4 | .200 | .800 | 15 | 3 | 0 | 0 | 3 | 20.0 | 4 | 5 | 3 | 2 | 0 | 0 | 0 | 10 | 0 | 0 | 0 | 2.5 | 1.000 | OF-4 |

WORLD SERIES

| 1973 | NY | N | 7 | .423 | .615 | 26 | 11 | 2 | 0 | 1 | 3.8 | 1 | 6 | 2 | 1 | 0 | 0 | 0 | 5 | 0 | 0 | 0 | 0.7 | 1.000 | OF-6 |

Dan Stearns

STEARNS, DANIEL ECKFORD
B. Oct. 17, 1861, Buffalo, N. Y.   D. June 28, 1944, Glendale, Calif.   BL TR 6'1"   185 lbs.

1880	BUF	N	28	.183	.260	104	19	6	1	0	0.0	8	13	3	23		0	0	39	24	20	3	3.0	.759	OF-20, C-8, 3B-5, SS-1
1881	DET	N	3	.091	.182	11	1	1	0	0	0.0	0	0	0	2		0	0	1	9	4	1	4.7	.714	SS-3
1882	CIN	AA	49	.257	.322	214	55	10	2	0	0.0	28		6			0	0	337	16	30	16	7.8	.922	1B-35, OF-12, 2B-2, SS-1
1883	BAL	AA	93	.246	.327	382	94	10	9	1	0.3	54		34			0	0	985	38	58	38	11.6	.964	1B-92, OF-1
1884			100	.237	.306	396	94	12	3	3	0.8	61		28			0	0	959	48	54	36	10.6	.949	1B-100, 2B-1
1885	2 teams		BAL	AA	(67G – .186)		BUF	N	(30G – .200)																
"	total		97	.190	.274	358	68	9	9	1	0.3	47	9	46	23		0	0	746	73	42	42	8.9	.951	1B-75, SS-19, C-4, OF-3
1889	KC	AA	139	.286	.386	560	160	24	13	2	0.4	96	87	56	69	67	0	0	1400	60	52	75	10.9	.966	1B-135, 3B-4
7 yrs.			509	.242	.325	2025	491	72	37	7	0.3	295	109	173	117	67	0	0	4467	268	260	211	9.8	.948	1B-437, OF-36, SS-24, C-12, 3B-9, 2B-3

John Stearns

STEARNS, JOHN HARDIN (Dude)
B. Aug. 21, 1951, Denver, Colo.   BR TR 6'   185 lbs.

1974	PHI	N	1	.500	.500	2	1	0	0	0	0.0	0	0	0	1	1	1	1	1	0	0	0	1.0	1.000	C-1
1975	NY	N	59	.189	.284	169	32	5	1	3	1.8	25	10	17	15	4	8	1	297	40	2	9	5.7	.994	C-54
1976			32	.262	.379	103	27	6	0	2	1.9	13	10	16	11	1	3	0	200	20	3	2	7.0	.987	C-30
1977			139	.251	.397	431	108	25	1	12	2.8	52	55	77	76	9	9	1	772	79	17	15	6.2	.980	C-127, 1B-6
1978			143	.264	.413	477	126	24	1	15	3.1	65	73	70	57	25	4	2	711	84	12	7	5.6	.985	C-141, 3B-1
1979			155	.243	.355	538	131	29	2	9	1.7	58	66	52	57	15	12	1	754	107	16	29	5.7	.982	C-121, 1B-16, 3B-11, OF-6
1980			91	.285	.370	319	91	25	1	0	0.0	42	45	33	24	7	5	2	552	62	8	17	6.8	.987	C-74, 1B-16, 3B-1
1981			80	.271	.333	273	74	12	1	1	0.4	25	24	24	17	12	6	1	360	52	7	11	5.2	.983	C-66, 1B-9, 3B-4
1982			98	.293	.415	352	103	25	3	4	1.1	46	28	30	35	17	6	2	384	74	10	9	4.8	.979	C-81, 3B-12
1983			4	–	–	0	0	0	0	0	0.0	0	2	0	0	0	0	0	0	0	0	0	0.0	–	
1984			8	.176	.235	17	3	1	0	0	0.0	6	1	4	2	1	0	0	28	2	0	4	3.8	1.000	C-4, 1B-2
11 yrs.			810	.260	.375	2681	696	152	10	46	1.7	334	312	323	294	91	56	12	4059	520	75	103	5.7	.984	C-699, 1B-49, 3B-29, OF-6

Stedronsky

STEDRONSKY,
B. Cleveland, Ohio   Deceased.

| 1879 | CHI | N | 4 | .083 | .083 | 12 | 1 | 0 | 0 | 0 | 0.0 | 0 | 0 | 0 | 3 | | 0 | 0 | 4 | 11 | 4 | 1 | 4.8 | .789 | 3B-4 |

Farmer Steelman

STEELMAN, MORRIS JAMES
B. June 29, 1875, Millville, N. J.   D. Sept. 16, 1944, Merchantville, N. J.   TR

1899	LOU	N	4	.067	.200	15	1	1	0	0	0.0	2	2	2			0	0	11	2	1	0	3.5	.929	C-4
1900	BKN	N	1	.000	.000	4	0	0	0	0	0.0	0	0	0			0	0	4	2	0	0	6.0	1.000	C-1
1901	2 teams		BKN	N	(1G – .333)		PHI	A	(27G – .261)																
"	total		28	.264	.286	91	24	0	0	0	0.0	5	10		4		0	0	66	29	1	2	3.4	.990	C-15, OF-12
1902	PHI	A	10	.188	.219	32	6	1	0	0	0.0	1	6	2			2	0	28	6	1	2	3.5	.971	OF-5, C-5
4 yrs.			43	.218	.254	142	31	3	1	0	0.0	8	15	14			6	0	109	39	3	4	3.5	.980	C-25, OF-17

James Steels

STEELS, JAMES EARL
B. May 30, 1961, Jackson, Miss.   BL TL 5'10"   185 lbs.

1987	SD	N	62	.191	.235	68	13	1	1	0	0.0	9	6	11	14	3	31	8	23	1	1	0	0.4	.960	OF-28
1988	TEX	A	36	.189	.208	53	10	1	0	0	0.0	4	5	0	15	2	9	2	41	2	1	2	1.2	.977	OF-17, DH-7, 1B-6
1989	SF	N	13	.083	.083	12	1	0	0	0	0.0	0	0	2	4	0	7	0	15	2	0	0	1.3	1.000	1B-3, OF-1
3 yrs.			111	.180	.211	133	24	2	1	0	0.0	13	11	13	33	5	47	10	79	5	2	2	0.8	.977	OF-46, 1B-9, DH-7

Fred Steere

STEERE, FREDERICK EUGENE
B. Aug. 16, 1872, S. Scituate, R. I.   D. Mar. 13, 1942, San Mateo, Calif.

| 1894 | PIT | N | 10 | .205 | .205 | 39 | 8 | 0 | 0 | 0 | 0.0 | 3 | 4 | 2 | 1 | 2 | 0 | 0 | 15 | 28 | 5 | 4 | 4.8 | .896 | SS-10 |

John Stefero

STEFERO, JOHN ROBERT
B. Sept. 22, 1959, Sumter, S. C.   BL TR 5'8"   185 lbs.

1983	BAL	A	9	.455	.545	11	5	1	0	0	0.0	2	4	3	2	0	2	0	20	3	2	0	2.8	.920	C-9
1986			52	.233	.300	120	28	2	1	2	1.7	14	13	16	25	0	6	2	221	20	4	2	4.7	.984	C-50, 2B-1
1987	MON	N	18	.196	.250	56	11	0	1	1	1.8	4	3	3	17	0	2	0	90	12	2	0	5.8	.981	C-17
3 yrs.			79	.235	.299	187	44	3	2	3	1.6	20	20	22	44	0	10	2	331	35	8	2	4.7	.979	C-76, 2B-1

Dave Stegman

STEGMAN, DAVID WILLIAM
B. Jan. 30, 1954, Inglewood, Calif.   BR TR 5'11"   190 lbs.

1978	DET	A	8	.286	.643	14	4	2	0	1	7.1	3	3	1	2	0	0	0	11	0	0	0	1.4	1.000	OF-7
1979			12	.194	.484	31	6	0	0	3	9.7	6	5	2	3	1	1	0	35	0	0	0	2.9	1.000	OF-12
1980			65	.177	.262	130	23	5	0	2	1.5	12	9	14	23	1	6	1	82	1	1	0	1.3	.988	OF-57, DH-2
1982	NY	A	2	–	–	0	0	0	0	0	0.0	0	0	0	0	0	0	0	0	0	0	0	0.0	–	
1983	CHI	A	30	.170	.208	53	9	2	0	0	0.0	5	4	10	9	0	3	0	31	1	0	0	1.1	1.000	OF-29
1984			55	.261	.380	92	24	1	2	2	2.2	13	11	4	18	3	5	2	65	1	1	0	1.2	.985	OF-46, DH-3
6 yrs.			172	.206	.325	320	66	10	2	8	2.5	39	32	31	55	5	15	3	224	3	2	0	1.3	.991	OF-151, DH-5

Bill Stein

STEIN, WILLIAM ALLEN
B. Jan. 21, 1947, Battle Creek, Mich.   BR TR 5'10"   170 lbs.

1972	STL	N	14	.314	.543	35	11	0	1	2	5.7	2	3	0	7	1	6	3	5	4	0	0	0.6	1.000	OF-4, 3B-4
1973			32	.218	.255	55	12	2	0	0	0.0	4	2	7	18	0	18	3	37	1	0	1	1.2	1.000	OF-10, 1B-2, 3B-1
1974	CHI	A	13	.279	.302	43	12	1	0	0	0.0	5	5	7	8	0	6	0	7	20	4	0	2.4	.871	3B-11, DH-2

Year	Team	Games	BA	SA	AB	H	2B	3B	HR	HR%	R	RBI	BB	SO	SB	Pinch Hit AB	Pinch Hit H	PO	A	E	DP	TC/G	FA	G by Pos

Bill Stein *continued*

Year	Team	Games	BA	SA	AB	H	2B	3B	HR	HR%	R	RBI	BB	SO	SB	PH AB	PH H	PO	A	E	DP	TC/G	FA	G by Pos
1975		76	.270	.350	226	61	7	1	3	1.3	23	21	18	32	2	6	0	87	118	9	21	2.8	.958	2B-28, 3B-24, DH-18, OF-1
1976		117	.268	.347	392	105	15	2	4	1.0	32	36	22	67	4	8	2	161	243	19	39	3.6	.955	3B-58, 2B-58, DH-1, OF-1, SS-1, 1B-1
1977	SEA A	151	.259	.394	556	144	26	5	13	2.3	53	67	29	79	3	1	0	146	255	15	20	2.8	.964	3B-147, DH-3, SS-2
1978		114	.261	.370	403	105	24	4	4	1.0	41	37	37	56	1	2	0	72	244	24	21	3.0	.929	3B-111, DH-1
1979		88	.248	.384	250	62	9	2	7	2.8	28	27	17	28	1	8	0	64	162	7	20	2.6	.970	3B-67, 2B-17, SS-3
1980		67	.268	.379	198	53	5	1	5	2.5	16	27	16	25	1	11	1	119	115	4	21	3.6	.983	3B-34, 2B-14, 1B-8, DH-5
1981	TEX A	53	.330	.435	115	38	6	2	2	1.7	21	22	7	15	1	20	9	166	26	2	10	3.7	.990	1B-20, OF-8, 3B-7, 2B-3, SS-1
1982		85	.239	.299	184	44	8	0	1	0.5	14	16	12	23	0	34	12	72	122	6	28	2.4	.970	2B-34, 3B-28, SS-6, DH-3, 1B-2, OF-1
1983		78	.310	.409	232	72	15	1	2	0.9	21	33	8	31	2	18	6	222	103	5	40	4.2	.985	2B-32, 1B-23, 3B-10, DH-6
1984		27	.279	.302	43	12	1	0	0	0.0	3	3	5	9	0	13	2	16	17	1	4	1.3	.971	3B-11, 1B-3
1985		44	.253	.354	79	20	3	1	1	1.3	5	12	1	15	0	24	10	52	20	2	4	1.7	.973	3B-11, 1B-8, DH-6, OF-3, 2B-3
14 yrs.		959	.267	.370	2811	751	122	18	44	1.6	268	311	186	413	16	175	48	1226	1450	98	229	2.9	.965	3B-516, 2B-200, 1B-67, DH-49, OF-28, SS-13

Justin Stein

STEIN, JUSTIN MARION (Ott)
B. Aug. 9, 1911, St. Louis, Mo.   BR TR 5'11" 180 lbs.

Year	Team	Games	BA	SA	AB	H	2B	3B	HR	HR%	R	RBI	BB	SO	SB	PH AB	PH H	PO	A	E	DP	TC/G	FA	G by Pos
1938	2 teams	PHI N (11G – .256)			CIN N	(11G – .333)																		
"	total	22	.281	.333	57	16	1	1	0	0.0	9	3	2	5	0	2	1	19	36	7	5	2.8	.887	SS-7, 3B-7, 2B-5

Terry Steinbach

STEINBACH, TERRY LEE
B. Mar. 2, 1962, New Ulm, Minn.   BR TR 6'1" 195 lbs.

Year	Team	Games	BA	SA	AB	H	2B	3B	HR	HR%	R	RBI	BB	SO	SB	PH AB	PH H	PO	A	E	DP	TC/G	FA	G by Pos
1986	OAK A	6	.333	.733	15	5	0	0	2	13.3	3	4	1	0	0	2	1	21	4	1	1	4.3	.962	C-5
1987		122	.284	.463	391	111	16	3	16	4.1	66	56	32	66	1	7	4	642	44	10	6	5.7	.986	C-107, 3B-10, 1B-1
1988		104	.265	.402	351	93	19	1	9	2.6	42	51	33	47	3	4	2	536	58	9	10	5.8	.985	C-84, 3B-9, 1B-8, DH-7, OF-1
1989		130	.273	.352	454	124	13	1	7	1.5	37	42	30	66	1	8	2	612	47	11	14	5.2	.984	C-103, OF-14, 1B-10, DH-4, 3B-3
4 yrs.		362	.275	.407	1211	333	48	5	34	2.8	148	153	96	179	5	21	9	1811	153	31	31	5.5	.984	C-299, 3B-22, 1B-19, OF-15, DH-11

LEAGUE CHAMPIONSHIP SERIES

Year	Team	Games	BA	SA	AB	H	2B	3B	HR	HR%	R	RBI	BB	SO	SB	PH AB	PH H	PO	A	E	DP	TC/G	FA	G by Pos
1988	OAK A	2	.250	.250	4	1	0	0	0	0.0	0	0	2	0	0	0	0	12	0	0	0	6.0	1.000	C-2
1989		4	.200	.200	15	3	0	0	0	0.0	0	1	1	5	0	0	0	17	0	0	0	4.3	1.000	C-3, DH-1
2 yrs.		6	.211	.211	19	4	0	0	0	0.0	0	1	3	5	0	0	0	29	0	0	0	4.8	1.000	C-5, DH-1

WORLD SERIES

Year	Team	Games	BA	SA	AB	H	2B	3B	HR	HR%	R	RBI	BB	SO	SB	PH AB	PH H	PO	A	E	DP	TC/G	FA	G by Pos
1988	OAK A	3	.364	.455	11	4	1	0	0	0.0	0	0	0	2	0	0	0	11	3	0	0	4.7	1.000	C-2, DH-1
1989		4	.250	.563	16	4	0	1	1	6.3	3	7	2	1	0	0	0	27	2	0	0	7.3	1.000	C-4
2 yrs.		7	.296	.519	27	8	1	1	1	3.7	3	7	2	3	0	0	0	38	5	0	0	6.1	1.000	C-6, DH-1

Hank Steinbacher

STEINBACHER, HENRY JOHN
B. Mar. 22, 1913, Sacramento, Calif.   D. Apr. 3, 1977, Sacramento, Calif.   BL TR 5'11" 180 lbs.

Year	Team	Games	BA	SA	AB	H	2B	3B	HR	HR%	R	RBI	BB	SO	SB	PH AB	PH H	PO	A	E	DP	TC/G	FA	G by Pos
1937	CHI A	26	.260	.384	73	19	4	1	1	1.4	13	9	4	7	2	11	1	24	0	1	0	1.0	.960	OF-15
1938		106	.331	.459	399	132	23	8	4	1.0	59	61	41	19	1	4	1	202	7	8	2	2.0	.963	OF-101
1939		71	.171	.234	111	19	2	1	1	0.9	16	15	21	8	0	39	8	38	1	0	0	0.5	1.000	OF-22
3 yrs.		203	.292	.407	583	170	29	10	6	1.0	88	85	66	34	3	54	10	264	8	9	2	1.4	.968	OF-138

Gene Steinbrenner

STEINBRENNER, EUGENE GASS
B. Nov. 17, 1892, Pittsburgh, Pa.   D. Apr. 25, 1970, Pittsburgh, Pa.   BR TR 5'8½" 155 lbs.

Year	Team	Games	BA	SA	AB	H	2B	3B	HR	HR%	R	RBI	BB	SO	SB	PH AB	PH H	PO	A	E	DP	TC/G	FA	G by Pos
1912	PHI N	3	.222	.333	9	2	1	0	0	0.0	0	0	0	3	0	0	0	4	5	1	1	3.3	.900	2B-3

Bill Steinecke

STEINECKE, WILLIAM ROBERT
B. Feb. 7, 1907, Cincinnati, Ohio   D. July 20, 1986, St. Augustine, Fla.   BR TR 5'8½" 175 lbs.

Year	Team	Games	BA	SA	AB	H	2B	3B	HR	HR%	R	RBI	BB	SO	SB	PH AB	PH H	PO	A	E	DP	TC/G	FA	G by Pos
1931	PIT N	4	.000	.000	4	0	0	0	0	0.0	0	0	0	1	0	3	0	0	0	0	0	0.0	–	C-1

Ben Steiner

STEINER, BENJAMIN SAUNDERS
B. July 28, 1921, Alexandria, Va.   D. Oct. 27, 1988, Venice, Calif.   BL TR 5'11" 165 lbs.

Year	Team	Games	BA	SA	AB	H	2B	3B	HR	HR%	R	RBI	BB	SO	SB	PH AB	PH H	PO	A	E	DP	TC/G	FA	G by Pos
1945	BOS A	78	.257	.332	304	78	8	3	3	1.0	39	20	31	29	10	1	0	202	213	14	63	5.5	.967	2B-77
1946		3	.250	.250	4	1	0	0	0	0.0	1	0	0	0	0	0	0	2	1	1	0	1.3	.750	3B-1
1947	DET A	1	–	–	0	0	0	0	0	–	0	0	0	0	0	0	0	0	0	0	0	0.0	–	
3 yrs.		82	.256	.331	308	79	8	3	3	1.0	41	20	31	29	10	1	0	204	214	15	63	5.3	.965	2B-77, 3B-1

Red Steiner

STEINER, JAMES HARRY
B. Jan. 7, 1915, Los Angeles, Calif.   BL TR 5'11" 175 lbs.

Year	Team	Games	BA	SA	AB	H	2B	3B	HR	HR%	R	RBI	BB	SO	SB	PH AB	PH H	PO	A	E	DP	TC/G	FA	G by Pos
1945	2 teams	CLE A (12G – .150)			BOS A	(26G – .203)																		
"	total	38	.190	.203	79	15	1	0	0	0.0	6	6	15	6	0	1	1	76	14	1	5	2.4	.989	C-35

Harry Steinfeldt

STEINFELDT, HARRY M.
B. Sept. 29, 1877, St. Louis, Mo.   D. Aug. 17, 1914, Bellevue, Ky.   BR TR 5'9½" 180 lbs.

Year	Team	Games	BA	SA	AB	H	2B	3B	HR	HR%	R	RBI	BB	SO	SB	PH AB	PH H	PO	A	E	DP	TC/G	FA	G by Pos
1898	CIN N	88	.295	.393	308	91	18	6	0	0.0	47	43	27		9	0	0	202	158	41	17	4.6	.898	2B-31, OF-29, 3B-22, SS-5, 1B-4
1899		107	.244	.326	386	94	16	8	0	0.0	62	43	40		19	0	0	189	262	45	19	4.6	.909	3B-59, 2B-40, SS-8, OF-2
1900		136	.248	.343	513	127	29	7	2	0.4	58	66	27		14	0	0	309	403	48	52	5.6	.937	3B-67, 2B-64, OF-2, SS-2
1901		105	.249	.380	382	95	18	6	6	1.6	40	47	28		10	0	0	198	269	42	28	4.8	.917	3B-55, 2B-50
1902		129	.278	.355	479	133	20	7	1	0.2	53	49	24		12	0	0	191	316	50	30	4.3	.910	3B-129, OF-1
1903		118	.312	.481	439	137	32	12	6	1.4	71	83	47		6	0	0	201	261	35	12	4.2	.930	3B-104, SS-14
1904		99	.244	.318	349	85	11	6	1	0.3	35	52	29		16	1	0	153	168	41	13	3.7	.887	3B-98
1905		114	.271	.367	384	104	16	9	1	0.3	49	39	30		15	8	1	154	223	33	16	3.6	.920	3B-103, OF-1, 2B-1, 1B-1

Year	Team		Games	BA	SA	AB	H	2B	3B	HR	HR%	R	RBI	BB	SO	SB	Pinch Hit AB	H	PO	A	E	DP	TC/G	FA	G by Pos

Harry Steinfeldt *continued*

Year	Team		Games	BA	SA	AB	H	2B	3B	HR	HR%	R	RBI	BB	SO	SB	AB	H	PO	A	E	DP	TC/G	FA	G by Pos
1906	CHI	N	151	.327	.430	539	176	27	10	3	0.6	81	83	47		29	0	0	160	254	20	13	2.9	.954	3B-150, 2B-1
1907			152	.266	.336	542	144	25	5	1	0.2	52	70	37		19	1	0	161	307	16	18	3.2	.967	3B-151
1908			150	.241	.306	539	130	20	6	1	0.2	63	62	36		12	1	0	166	275	28	15	3.1	.940	3B-150
1909			151	.252	.337	528	133	27	6	2	0.4	73	59	57		22	0	0	183	299	31	16	3.4	.940	3B-151
1910			129	.252	.317	448	113	21	1	2	0.4	70	58	36	29	10	1	0	137	246	22	16	3.1	.946	3B-128
1911	BOS	N	19	.254	.365	63	16	4	0	1	1.6	5	8	6	3	1	0	0	23	24	11	2	3.1	.810	3B-19
	14 yrs.		1648	.268	.360	5899	1578	284	90	27	0.5	759	762	471	32	194	12	1	2427	3465	463	267	3.9	.927	3B-1386, 2B-187, OF-35, SS-29, 1B-5

WORLD SERIES

Year	Team		Games	BA	SA	AB	H	2B	3B	HR	HR%	R	RBI	BB	SO	SB	AB	H	PO	A	E	DP	TC/G	FA	G by Pos
1906	CHI	N	6	.250	.300	20	5	1	0	0	0.0	2	2	1	0	0	0	0	3	9	1	0	2.2	.923	3B-6
1907			5	.471	.647	17	8	1	1	0	0.0	2	2	1	2	1	0	0	10	7	0	1	3.4	1.000	3B-5
1908			5	.250	.250	16	4	0	0	0	0.0	3	3	2	5	1	0	0	4	11	1	0	3.2	.938	3B-5
1910			5	.100	.150	20	2	1	0	0	0.0	0	1	0	4	0	0	0	2	12	4	0	3.6	.778	3B-5
	4 yrs.		21	.260	.329	73	19	3	1	0	0.0	7	8	4	11	2	0	0	19	39	6	1	3.0	.906	3B-21

Bill Stellbauer

STELLBAUER, WILLIAMS JENNINGS   BR TR 5'10" 175 lbs.
B. Mar. 20, 1894, Bremond, Tex. D. Feb. 16, 1974, New Braunfels, Tex.

Year	Team		Games	BA	SA	AB	H	2B	3B	HR	HR%	R	RBI	BB	SO	SB	AB	H	PO	A	E	DP	TC/G	FA	G by Pos
1916	PHI	A	25	.271	.354	48	13	2	1	0	0.0	2	5	6	7	2	9	2	18	0	3	0	0.8	.857	OF-14

Rick Stelmaszek

STELMASZEK, RICHARD FRANCIS   BL TR 6'1" 195 lbs.
B. Oct. 8, 1948, Chicago, Ill.

Year	Team		Games	BA	SA	AB	H	2B	3B	HR	HR%	R	RBI	BB	SO	SB	AB	H	PO	A	E	DP	TC/G	FA	G by Pos
1971	WAS	A	6	.000	.000	9	0	0	0	0	0.0	0	0	0	3	0	3	0	4	1	0	0	0.8	1.000	C-3
1973	2 teams			TEX A	(7G –	.111)		CAL A	(22G –	.154)																
"	total		29	.143	.171	35	5	1	0	0	0.0	2	3	7	9	0	0	0	71	5	0	1	2.6	1.000	C-29
1974	CHI	N	25	.227	.341	44	10	2	0	1	2.3	2	7	10	6	0	10	2	55	2	1	1	2.3	.983	C-16
	3 yrs.		60	.170	.239	88	15	3	0	1	1.1	4	10	17	18	0	13	2	130	8	1	2	2.3	.993	C-48

Fred Stem

STEM, FREDERICK BOOTHE   BL TR 6'2" 160 lbs.
B. Sept. 22, 1885, Oxford, N. C. D. Sept. 5, 1964, Darlington, S. C.

Year	Team		Games	BA	SA	AB	H	2B	3B	HR	HR%	R	RBI	BB	SO	SB	AB	H	PO	A	E	DP	TC/G	FA	G by Pos
1908	BOS	N	19	.278	.306	72	20	0	1	0	0.0	9	3	2		1	1	0	192	9	1	9	10.6	.995	1B-18
1909			73	.208	.241	245	51	2	3	0	0.0	13	11	12		5	5	0	656	62	8	31	9.9	.989	1B-68
	2 yrs.		92	.224	.256	317	71	2	4	0	0.0	22	14	14		6	6	0	848	71	9	40	10.1	.990	1B-86

Casey Stengel

STENGEL, CHARLES DILLON (The Old Professor)   BL TL 5'11" 175 lbs.
B. July 30, 1890, Kansas City, Mo. D. Sept. 29, 1975, Glendale, Calif.
Manager 1934-36, 1938-43, 1949-60, 1962-65.
Hall of Fame 1966.

Year	Team		Games	BA	SA	AB	H	2B	3B	HR	HR%	R	RBI	BB	SO	SB	AB	H	PO	A	E	DP	TC/G	FA	G by Pos
1912	BKN	N	17	.316	.386	57	18	1	0	1	1.8	9	13	15	9	5	0	0	36	1	4	0	2.4	.902	OF-17
1913			124	.272	.393	438	119	16	8	7	1.6	60	43	56	58	19	5	1	270	16	12	1	2.4	.960	OF-119
1914			126	.316	.425	412	130	13	10	4	1.0	55	60	56	55	19	4	0	173	15	7	3	1.5	.964	OF-121
1915			132	.237	.353	459	109	20	12	3	0.7	52	50	34	46	5	1	0	220	13	10	2	1.8	.959	OF-129
1916			127	.279	.424	462	129	27	8	8	1.7	66	53	33	51	11	6	2	206	14	8	4	1.8	.965	OF-121
1917			150	.257	.375	549	141	23	12	6	1.1	69	73	60	62	18	0	0	256	30	9	9	2.0	.969	OF-150
1918	PIT	N	39	.246	.320	122	30	4	1	1	0.8	18	12	16	14	11	4	2	64	7	2	3	1.9	.973	OF-27
1919			89	.293		321	94	10	10	4	1.2	38	43	35	35	12	2	0	195	7	9	3	2.4	.957	OF-87
1920	PHI	N	129	.292	.436	445	130	25	6	9	2.0	53	50	38	35	7	10	3	212	16	11	1	1.9	.954	OF-118
1921	2 teams		42				PHI	N	(24G –	.305)			NY	N	(18G –	.227)									
"	total		42	.284	.358	81	23	4	1	0	0.0	11	6	7	12	1	13	3	33	5	2	2	1.0	.950	OF-42
1922	NY	N	84	.368	.564	250	92	8	10	7	2.8	48	48	21	17	4	1	1	179	7	6	2	2.3	.969	OF-77
1923			75	.339	.505	218	74	11	5	5	2.3	39	43	20	18	6	15	3	115	4	2	1	1.6	.983	OF-57
1924	BOS	N	131	.280	.382	461	129	20	6	5	1.1	57	39	45	39	13	4	0	211	12	5	4	1.7	.978	OF-126
1925			12	.077	.077	13	1	0	0	0	0.0	0	2	1	2	0	9	0	1	0	0	0	0.1	1.000	OF-1
	14 yrs.		1277	.284	.410	4288	1219	182	89	60	1.4	575	535	437	453	131	73	12	2171	147	87	35	1.9	.964	OF-1192

WORLD SERIES

Year	Team		Games	BA	SA	AB	H	2B	3B	HR	HR%	R	RBI	BB	SO	SB	AB	H	PO	A	E	DP	TC/G	FA	G by Pos
1916	BKN	N	4	.364	.364	11	4	0	0	0	0.0	2	0	0	1	0	0	0	3	1	1	0	1.3	.800	OF-3
1922	NY	N	2	.400	.400	5	2	0	0	0	0.0	0	0	0	1	0	0	0	4	0	0	0	2.0	1.000	OF-2
1923			6	.417	.917	12	5	0	0	2	16.7	3	4	4	0	0	0	0	11	0	0	0	1.8	1.000	OF-6
	3 yrs.		12	.393	.607	28	11	0	0	2	7.1	5	4	4	2	0	0	0	18	1	1	0	1.7	.950	OF-11

Mike Stenhouse

STENHOUSE, MICHAEL STEVEN   BL TR 6'1" 195 lbs.
Son of Dave Stenhouse.
B. May 29, 1958, Pueblo, Colo.

Year	Team		Games	BA	SA	AB	H	2B	3B	HR	HR%	R	RBI	BB	SO	SB	AB	H	PO	A	E	DP	TC/G	FA	G by Pos
1982	MON	N	1	.000	.000	1	0	0	0	0	0.0	0	0	0	1	0	1	0	0	0	0	0	0.0	–	
1983			24	.125	.150	40	5	1	0	0	0.0	2	2	4	10	0	9	0	37	2	0	3	1.6	1.000	OF-9, 1B-5
1984			80	.183	.297	175	32	8	0	4	2.3	14	16	26	32	0	26	5	118	5	2	8	1.6	.984	OF-48, 1B-14
1985	MIN	A	81	.223	.335	179	40	5	0	5	2.8	23	21	29	18	1	23	5	83	10	3	4	1.2	.969	DH-27, OF-16, 1B-8
1986	BOS	A	21	.095	.143	21	2	1	0	0	0.0	1	1	12	5	0	8	1	23	3	0	3	1.2	1.000	OF-4, 1B-3
	5 yrs.		207	.190	.291	416	79	15	0	9	2.2	40	40	71	66	1	67	11	261	20	5	18	1.4	.983	OF-77, 1B-30, DH-27

Rennie Stennett

STENNETT, RENALDO ANTONIO   BR TR 5'11" 160 lbs.
Born Renaldo Antonio Stennett y Porte.
B. Apr. 5, 1951, Colon, Panama

Year	Team		Games	BA	SA	AB	H	2B	3B	HR	HR%	R	RBI	BB	SO	SB	AB	H	PO	A	E	DP	TC/G	FA	G by Pos
1971	PIT	N	50	.353	.458	153	54	5	4	1	0.7	24	15	7	9	1	15	3	82	106	9	22	3.9	.954	2B-36
1972			109	.286	.376	370	106	14	5	3	0.8	43	30	9	43	4	21	5	197	173	10	45	3.5	.974	2B-49, OF-41, SS-6
1973			128	.242	.358	466	113	18	3	10	2.1	45	55	16	63	2	17	4	281	348	14	84	5.0	.978	2B-84, SS-43, OF-5
1974			157	.291	.374	673	196	29	3	7	1.0	84	56	32	51	8	1	0	444	475	19	115	6.0	.980	2B-154, OF-2
1975			148	.286	.383	616	176	25	7	7	1.1	89	62	33	42	5	4	0	379	463	18	98	5.8	.979	2B-144
1976			157	.257	.341	654	168	31	9	2	0.3	59	60	19	32	18	1	1	432	506	19	111	6.1	.980	2B-157, SS-4
1977			116	.336	.430	453	152	20	4	5	1.1	53	51	29	24	28	3	2	269	315	11	70	5.1	.982	2B-113
1978			106	.243	.309	333	81	9	2	3	0.9	30	35	13	22	2	17	3	167	215	13	40	3.7	.967	2B-80, 3B-6

Year	Team		Games	BA	SA	AB	H	2B	3B	HR	HR%	R	RBI	BB	SO	SB	Pinch Hit AB	Pinch Hit H	PO	A	E	DP	TC/G	FA	G by Pos

Rennie Stennett *continued*

Year	Team		Games	BA	SA	AB	H	2B	3B	HR	HR%	R	RBI	BB	SO	SB	PH AB	PH H	PO	A	E	DP	TC/G	FA	G by Pos
1979			108	.238	.292	319	76	13	2	0	0.0	31	24	24	25	1	6	2	172	282	12	63	4.3	.974	2B-102
1980	SF	N	120	.244	.302	397	97	13	2	2	0.5	34	37	22	31	4	13	1	244	293	15	53	4.6	.973	2B-111
1981			38	.230	.264	87	20	0	0	1	1.1	8	7	3	6	2	20	5	48	46	0	9	2.5	1.000	2B-19
11 yrs.			1237	.274	.359	4521	1239	177	41	41	0.9	500	432	207	348	75	118	26	2715	3222	140	710	4.9	.977	2B-1049, SS-53, OF-48, 3B-6

LEAGUE CHAMPIONSHIP SERIES

Year	Team		Games	BA	SA	AB	H	2B	3B	HR	HR%	R	RBI	BB	SO	SB	PH AB	PH H	PO	A	E	DP	TC/G	FA	G by Pos
1972	PIT	N	5	.286	.286	21	6	0	0	0	0.0	2	1	1	0	0	0	0	0	0	0	0	0.0	–	OF-5, 2B-1
1974			4	.063	.063	16	1	0	0	0	0.0	1	0	1	1	0	0	0	10	10	1	1	5.3	.952	2B-4
1975			3	.214	.214	14	3	0	0	0	0.0	0	0	0	1	0	0	0	3	8	0	2	3.7	1.000	2B-3, SS-1
1979			1	–	–	0	0	0	0	0	–	0	0	0	0	0	0	0	0	1	0	0	1.0	1.000	2B-1
4 yrs.			13	.196	.196	51	10	0	0	0	0.0	3	1	2	2	0	0	0	13	19	1	3	2.5	.970	2B-9, OF-5, SS-1

WORLD SERIES

Year	Team		Games	BA	SA	AB	H	2B	3B	HR	HR%	R	RBI	BB	SO	SB	PH AB	PH H	PO	A	E	DP	TC/G	FA	G by Pos
1979	PIT	N	1	1.000	1.000	1	1	0	0	0	0.0	0	0	0	0	0	1	1	0	0	0	0	0.0	–	

Jake Stenzel

STENZEL, JACOB CHARLES
Born Jacob Charles Stelzle.
B. June 24, 1867, Cincinnati, Ohio   D. Jan. 6, 1919, Cincinnati, Ohio

BR TR 5'10" 168 lbs.

Year	Team		Games	BA	SA	AB	H	2B	3B	HR	HR%	R	RBI	BB	SO	SB	PH AB	PH H	PO	A	E	DP	TC/G	FA	G by Pos
1890	CHI	N	11	.268	.293	41	11	1	0	0	0.0	3	3	1	0	0	0	0	31	6	2	0	3.5	.949	OF-6, C-6
1892	PIT	N	3	.000	.000	9	0	0	0	0	0.0	0	0	1	3	1	0	0	3	2	0	0	1.7	1.000	OF-2, C-1
1893			60	.362	.509	224	81	13	4	4	1.8	57	37	24	17	16	6	1	109	18	20	3	2.5	.864	OF-45, C-12, SS-1, 2B-1
1894			131	.354	.580	522	185	39	20	13	2.5	148	121	75	13	61	0	0	311	23	27	6	2.8	.925	OF-131
1895			129	.374	.539	514	192	38	13	7	1.4	114	97	57	25	53	0	0	257	23	27	6	2.4	.912	OF-129
1896			114	.361	.486	479	173	26	14	2	0.4	104	82	32	13	57	0	0	250	13	23	5	2.5	.920	OF-114, 1B-1
1897	BAL	N	131	.353	.487	536	189	43	7	5	0.9	113	116	36		69	0	0	264	12	20	2	2.3	.932	OF-131
1898	2 teams		BAL	N	(35G – .254)		STL	N	(108G – .282)																
"	total		143	.275	.365	542	149	20	13	1	0.2	97	55	53		25	0	0	314	14	21	3	2.4	.940	OF-143
1899	2 teams		STL	N	(35G – .273)		CIN	N	(9G – .310)																
"	total		44	.280	.363	157	44	10	0	1	0.6	26	22	20		10	3	0	85	3	4	1	2.1	.957	OF-40
9 yrs.			766	.339	.481	3024	1024	190	71	33	1.1	662	533	299	71	292	9	1	1624	114	144	26	2.5	.923	OF-741, C-19, SS-1, 2B-1, 1B-1

Gene Stephens

STEPHENS, GLEN EUGENE
B. Jan. 20, 1933, Gravette, Ark.

BL TR 6'3½" 175 lbs.

Year	Team		Games	BA	SA	AB	H	2B	3B	HR	HR%	R	RBI	BB	SO	SB	PH AB	PH H	PO	A	E	DP	TC/G	FA	G by Pos
1952	BOS	A	21	.226	.321	53	12	5	0	0	0.0	10	5	3	8	4	4	1	24	1	1	0	1.2	.962	OF-13
1953			78	.204	.290	221	45	6	2	3	1.4	30	18	29	56	3	1	0	113	2	4	0	1.5	.966	OF-72
1955			109	.293	.459	157	46	9	4	3	1.9	25	18	20	34	0	23	4	82	7	5	1	0.9	.947	OF-75
1956			104	.270	.349	63	17	2	0	1	1.6	22	7	12	12	0	24	7	57	2	1	0	0.6	.983	OF-71
1957			120	.266	.399	173	46	6	4	3	1.7	25	26	26	20	0	29	5	70	4	1	2	0.6	.987	OF-90
1958			134	.219	.363	270	59	10	1	9	3.3	38	25	22	46	1	22	3	149	5	4	1	1.2	.975	OF-110
1959			92	.278	.367	270	75	13	1	3	1.1	34	39	29	33	5	7	3	141	11	3	0	1.7	.981	OF-85
1960	2 teams		BOS	A	(35G – .229)		BAL	A	(84G – .238)																
"	total		119	.235	.354	302	71	15	0	7	2.3	47	22	39	47	9	11	2	180	7	4	0	1.6	.979	OF-108
1961	2 teams		BAL	A	(32G – .190)		KC	A	(62G – .208)																
"	total		94	.203	.290	241	49	8	1	4	1.7	26	28	30	34	4	11	2	148	8	4	5	1.7	.975	OF-84
1962	KC	A	5	.000	.000	4	0	0	0	0	0.0	0	0	1	1	0	4	0	0	0	0	0	0.0	–	
1963	CHI	A	6	.389	.556	18	7	0	0	1	5.6	5	2	1	3	0	0	0	8	2	1	0	1.8	.909	OF-5
1964			82	.234	.355	141	33	4	2	3	2.1	21	17	21	28	1	19	7	91	2	3	1	1.2	.969	OF-59
12 yrs.			964	.240	.355	1913	460	78	15	37	1.9	283	207	233	322	27	155	34	1063	51	31	11	1.2	.973	OF-772

Jim Stephens

STEPHENS, JAMES WALTER (Little Nemo)
B. Dec. 10, 1883, Salineville, Ohio   D. Jan. 2, 1965, Oxford, Ala.

BR TR 5'6½" 157 lbs.

Year	Team		Games	BA	SA	AB	H	2B	3B	HR	HR%	R	RBI	BB	SO	SB	PH AB	PH H	PO	A	E	DP	TC/G	FA	G by Pos
1907	STL	A	58	.202	.272	173	35	6	3	0	0.0	15	11	15		3	2	0	200	63	9	4	4.7	.967	C-56
1908			47	.200	.240	150	30	4	1	0	0.0	14	6	9		0	2	0	193	68	11	4	5.8	.960	C-45
1909			79	.220	.283	223	49	5	0	3	1.3	18	18	13		5	7	0	335	103	9	9	5.7	.980	C-72
1910			99	.241	.298	299	72	3	7	0	0.0	24	23	16		2	3	1	418	156	17	18	6.0	.971	C-96
1911			70	.231	.302	212	49	5	5	0	0.0	11	17	17		1	2	0	223	94	17	7	4.8	.949	C-66
1912			74	.249	.332	205	51	7	5	0	0.0	13	22	7		3	8	0	262	110	18	10	5.3	.954	C-66
6 yrs.			427	.227	.291	1262	286	30	21	3	0.2	95	97	77		14	24	1	1631	594	81	52	5.4	.965	C-401

Vern Stephens

STEPHENS, VERNON DECATUR (Junior, Buster)
B. Oct. 23, 1920, McAlister, N. M.   D. Nov. 3, 1968, Long Beach, Calif.

BR TR 5'10" 185 lbs.

Year	Team		Games	BA	SA	AB	H	2B	3B	HR	HR%	R	RBI	BB	SO	SB	PH AB	PH H	PO	A	E	DP	TC/G	FA	G by Pos
1941	STL	A	3	.500	.500	2	1	0	0	0	0.0	0	1	0	0	0	1	0	1	1	0	0	0.7	.500	SS-1
1942			145	.294	.433	575	169	26	6	14	2.4	84	92	41	53	0	1	1	290	415	42	82	5.2	.944	SS-144
1943			137	.289	.482	512	148	27	3	22	4.3	75	91	54	73	3	3	1	240	342	34	51	4.5	.945	SS-123, OF-11
1944			145	.293	.462	559	164	32	1	20	3.6	91	109	62	54	2	1	0	239	480	35	71	5.2	.954	SS-143
1945			149	.289	.473	571	165	27	1	24	4.2	90	89	55	70	2	1	1	258	450	30	71	5.0	.959	SS-144, 3B-4
1946			115	.307	.460	450	138	19	4	14	3.1	67	64	35	49	0	3	0	224	343	30	71	5.2	.950	SS-112
1947			150	.279	.406	562	157	18	4	15	2.7	74	83	70	61	0	1	0	283	494	24	113	5.3	.970	SS-149
1948	BOS	A	155	.269	.471	635	171	25	8	29	4.6	114	137	77	56	1	0	0	269	540	24	113	5.4	.971	SS-155
1949			155	.290	.539	610	177	31	2	39	6.4	113	159	101	73	2	0	0	257	508	27	128	5.1	.966	SS-155
1950			149	.295	.511	628	185	34	6	30	4.8	125	144	65	43	1	3	0	258	431	13	115	4.7	.981	SS-146
1951			109	.300	.501	377	113	21	2	17	4.5	62	78	38	33	1	17	4	105	209	7	19	2.9	.978	3B-89, SS-2
1952			92	.254	.383	295	75	13	2	7	2.4	35	44	39	31	2	9	2	110	227	16	48	3.8	.955	SS-53, 3B-29
1953	2 teams		CHI	A	(44G – .186)		STL	A	(46G – .321)																
"	total		90	.262	.361	294	77	14	0	5	1.7	30	31	31	42	2	4	0	84	162	8	16	2.8	.969	3B-84, SS-3
1954	BAL	A	101	.285	.403	365	104	17	1	8	2.2	31	46	17	36	0	5	0	102	186	10	19	3.0	.966	3B-96
1955	2 teams		BAL	A	(3G – .167)		CHI	A	(22G – .250)																
"	total		25	.242	.435	62	15	3	0	3	4.8	10	7	7	11	0	6	1	13	39	0	4	2.1	1.000	3B-20
15 yrs.			1720	.286	.460	6497	1859	307	42	247	3.8	1001	1174	692	685	25	54	10	2732	4827	301	921	4.6	.962	SS-1330, 3B-322, OF-11

WORLD SERIES

Year	Team		Games	BA	SA	AB	H	2B	3B	HR	HR%	R	RBI	BB	SO	SB	PH AB	PH H	PO	A	E	DP	TC/G	FA	G by Pos
1944	STL	A	6	.227	.273	22	5	1	0	0	0.0	0	3	3	0	0	0	0	9	19	3	4	5.2	.903	SS-6

Year	Team		Games	BA	SA	AB	H	2B	3B	HR	HR%	R	RBI	BB	SO	SB	Pinch Hit AB	H	PO	A	E	DP	TC/G	FA	G by Pos

Bobby Stephenson
STEPHENSON, ROBERT LLOYD
B. Aug. 11, 1928, Blair, Okla.　　　　　　BR TR 6'　165 lbs.

| 1955 | STL | N | 67 | .243 | .270 | 111 | 27 | 3 | 0 | 0 | 0.0 | 19 | 6 | 5 | 18 | 2 | 6 | 0 | 65 | 80 | 8 | 21 | 2.3 | .948 | SS-48, 2B-7, 3B-1 |

Dummy Stephenson
STEPHENSON, REUBEN CRANDOL
B. Sept. 22, 1869, Petersburg, N. J.　D. Dec. 1, 1924, Trenton, N. J.　　BR TR 5'11½" 180 lbs.

| 1892 | PHI | N | 8 | .270 | .351 | 37 | 10 | 3 | 0 | 0 | 0.0 | 4 | 5 | 0 | 2 | 0 | 0 | 0 | 11 | 1 | 3 | 0 | 1.9 | .800 | OF-8 |

Joe Stephenson
STEPHENSON, JOSEPH CHESTER
Father of Jerry Stephenson.
B. June 30, 1921, Detroit, Mich.　　　　　BR TR 6'2"　185 lbs.

1943	NY	N	9	.250	.292	24	6	1	0	0	0.0	4	1	0	5	0	1	0	30	6	1	1	4.1	.973	C-6
1944	CHI	N	4	.125	.125	8	1	0	0	0	0.0	1	0	1	3	1	1	0	13	2	0	0	3.8	1.000	C-3
1947	CHI	A	16	.143	.143	35	5	0	0	0	0.0	3	3	1	7	0	1	0	42	5	2	0	3.1	.959	C-13
3 yrs.			29	.179	.194	67	12	1	0	0	0.0	8	4	2	15	1	3	0	85	13	3	1	3.5	.970	C-22

Johnny Stephenson
STEPHENSON, JOHN HERMAN
B. Apr. 13, 1941, South Portsmouth, Ky.　　BL TR 5'11"　180 lbs.

1964	NY	N	37	.158	.211	57	9	0	0	1	1.8	2	2	4	18	0	21	2	10	18	6	1	0.9	.824	3B-14, OF-8
1965			62	.215	.355	121	26	5	0	4	3.3	9	15	8	19	0	29	6	147	13	3	1	2.6	.982	C-47, OF-2
1966			63	.196	.238	143	28	1	1	1	0.7	17	11	8	28	0	25	4	187	30	6	4	3.5	.973	C-52, OF-1
1967	CHI	N	18	.224	.327	49	11	3	1	0	0.0	3	5	1	6	0	3	1	67	8	0	2	4.2	1.000	C-13
1968			2	.000	.000	2	0	0	0	0	0.0	0	0	0	0	0	0	0	0	0	0	0	0.0	–	
1969	SF	N	22	.222	.296	27	6	2	0	0	0.0	2	3	0	4	0	15	4	15	1	3	0	0.9	.842	C-9, 3B-1
1970			23	.070	.093	43	3	1	0	0	0.0	3	6	2	7	0	14	3	52	8	0	1	2.6	1.000	C-9, OF-1
1971	CAL	A	98	.219	.312	279	61	17	0	3	1.1	24	25	22	21	0	16	1	434	33	4	3	4.8	.992	C-88
1972			66	.274	.349	146	40	3	1	2	1.4	14	17	11	8	0	21	8	273	12	2	2	4.3	.993	C-56
1973			60	.246	.311	122	30	5	0	1	0.8	9	9	7	7	0	10	4	233	11	5	1	4.2	.980	C-56
10 yrs.			451	.216	.296	989	214	37	3	12	1.2	83	93	63	118	0	156	33	1418	134	29	15	3.5	.982	C-330, 3B-15, OF-12

Phil Stephenson
STEPHENSON, PHILLIP RAYMOND
B. Sept. 19, 1960, Guthrie, Okla.　　　　　BL TL 6'1"　195 lbs.

| 1989 | 2 teams | | CHI N (17G – .143) | | | SD N (10G – .353) | | | | | | | | | | | | | | | | | | | |
| " | total | | 27 | .237 | .395 | 38 | 9 | 0 | 0 | 2 | 5.3 | 4 | 2 | 5 | 5 | 1 | 14 | 2 | 42 | 4 | 1 | 3 | 1.7 | .979 | 1B-8, OF-3 |

Riggs Stephenson
STEPHENSON, JACKSON RIGGS (Old Hoss)
B. Jan. 5, 1898, Akron, Ala.　D. Nov. 15, 1985, Tuscaloosa, Ala.　　BR TR 5'10"　185 lbs.

1921	CLE	A	65	.330	.461	206	68	17	2	2	1.0	45	34	23	15	4	6	0	122	155	17	32	4.5	.942	2B-54, 3B-2
1922			86	.339	.511	233	79	24	5	2	0.9	47	32	27	18	3	24	6	76	135	12	11	2.6	.946	3B-34, 2B-25, OF-3
1923			91	.319	.475	301	96	20	6	5	1.7	48	65	15	25	6	21	4	205	214	13	49	4.7	.970	2B-66, OF-3, 3B-1
1924			71	.371	.504	240	89	20	4	4	1.7	33	44	27	10	1	6	1	126	180	12	20	4.5	.962	2B-58, OF-7
1925			19	.296	.444	54	16	3	1	1	1.9	8	9	7	3	2	3	2	33	2	2	1	1.9	.946	OF-16
1926	CHI	N	82	.338	.456	281	95	18	3	3	1.1	40	44	31	16	2	6	2	126	7	7	0	1.7	.950	OF-74
1927			152	.344	.491	579	199	46	9	7	1.2	101	82	65	28	8	0	0	309	25	10	7	2.3	.971	OF-146, 3B-6
1928			137	.324	.477	512	166	36	9	8	1.6	75	90	68	29	8	2	1	268	10	5	1	2.1	.982	OF-135
1929			136	.362	.562	495	179	36	6	17	3.4	91	110	67	21	10	5	3	245	9	4	4	1.9	.984	OF-130
1930			109	.367	.478	341	125	21	1	5	1.5	56	68	32	20	2	27	11	132	5	6	1	1.3	.958	OF-80
1931			80	.319	.414	263	84	14	4	1	0.4	34	52	37	14	1	14	2	134	1	2	1	1.7	.985	OF-80
1932			147	.324	.443	583	189	49	4	4	0.7	86	85	54	27	3	0	0	298	7	5	2	2.1	.984	OF-147
1933			97	.329	.436	346	114	17	4	4	1.2	45	51	34	16	5	3	0	187	5	3	2	2.0	.985	OF-91
1934			38	.216	.216	74	16	0	0	0	0.0	5	7	7	5	0	22	5	26	3	0	1	0.8	1.000	OF-15
14 yrs.			1310	.336	.473	4508	1515	321	54	63	1.4	714	773	494	247	54	139	37	2287	758	98	132	2.4	.969	OF-927, 2B-203, 3B-43

WORLD SERIES

1929	CHI	N	5	.316	.368	19	6	1	0	0	0.0	3	3	2	2	0	0	0	13	1	0	0	2.8	1.000	OF-5
1932			4	.444	.500	18	8	1	0	0	0.0	2	4	0	0	0	0	0	4	0	0	0	1.0	1.000	OF-4
2 yrs.			9	.378	.432	37	14	2	0	0	0.0	5	7	2	2	0	0	0	17	1	0	0	2.0	1.000	OF-9

Walter Stephenson
STEPHENSON, WALTER McQUEEN (Tarzan)
B. Mar. 27, 1911, Saluda, N. C.　　　　　BR TR 6'　180 lbs.

1935	CHI	N	16	.385	.500	26	10	1	1	0	0.0	1	9	1	9	0	9	1	17	6	0	1	1.4	1.000	C-6
1936			6	.083	.083	12	1	0	0	0	0.0	0	1	0	5	0	2	0	10	1	0	0	1.8	1.000	C-4
1937	PHI	N	10	.261	.261	23	6	0	0	0	0.0	2	3	2	3	0	2	1	24	5	1	1	3.0	.967	C-7
3 yrs.			32	.279	.328	61	17	1	1	0	0.0	3	5	3	13	0	13	2	51	12	1	2	2.0	.984	C-17

WORLD SERIES

| 1935 | CHI | N | 1 | .000 | .000 | 1 | 0 | 0 | 0 | 0 | 0.0 | 0 | 0 | 0 | 1 | 0 | 1 | 0 | 0 | 0 | 0 | 0 | 0.0 | – | |

Dutch Sterrett
STERRETT, CHARLES HURLBUT
B. Oct. 1, 1889, Milroy, Pa.　D. Dec. 9, 1965, Baltimore, Md.　　BR TR 5'11½" 165 lbs.

1912	NY	A	66	.265	.357	230	61	4	7	1	0.4	30	32	11		8	1	0	259	22	5	4	4.3	.983	OF-37, 1B-17, C-10, 2B-1
1913			21	.171	.171	35	6	0	0	0	0.0	0	3	1	5	1	13	0	48	3	1	1	2.5	.981	1B-6, OF-1, C-1
2 yrs.			87	.253	.332	265	67	4	7	1	0.4	30	35	12	5	9	14	0	307	25	6	5	3.9	.982	OF-38, 1B-23, C-11, 2B-1

Bobby Stevens
STEVENS, ROBERT JORDAN
B. Apr. 17, 1907, Chevy Chase, Md.　　　　BL TR 5'8"　149 lbs.

| 1931 | PHI | N | 12 | .343 | .343 | 35 | 12 | 0 | 0 | 0 | 0.0 | 3 | 4 | 2 | 2 | 0 | 2 | 0 | 19 | 21 | 6 | 5 | 3.8 | .870 | SS-10 |

Chuck Stevens
STEVENS, CHARLES AUGUSTUS
B. July 10, 1918, Van Houten, N. M.　　　　BB TL 6'1"　180 lbs.

| 1941 | STL | A | 4 | .154 | .154 | 13 | 2 | 0 | 0 | 0 | 0.0 | 2 | 2 | 0 | 1 | 0 | 0 | 0 | 28 | 0 | 1 | 3 | 7.3 | .966 | 1B-4 |

Year	Team	Games	BA	SA	AB	H	2B	3B	HR	HR%	R	RBI	BB	SO	SB	Pinch Hit AB	Pinch Hit H	PO	A	E	DP	TC/G	FA	G by Pos

Chuck Stevens *continued*

Year	Team	Games	BA	SA	AB	H	2B	3B	HR	HR%	R	RBI	BB	SO	SB	AB	H	PO	A	E	DP	TC/G	FA	G by Pos
1946		122	.248	.326	432	107	17	4	3	0.7	53	27	47	62	4	2	0	1020	86	6	98	9.1	.995	1B-120
1948		85	.261	.341	287	75	12	4	1	0.3	34	26	41	26	2	0	0	737	56	7	89	9.4	.991	1B-85
3 yrs.		211	.251	.329	732	184	29	8	4	0.5	89	55	88	89	6	2	0	1785	142	14	190	9.2	.993	1B-209

Ed Stevens

STEVENS, EDWARD LEE (Big Ed)
B. Jan. 12, 1925, Galveston, Tex. BL TL 6'1" 190 lbs.

Year	Team	Games	BA	SA	AB	H	2B	3B	HR	HR%	R	RBI	BB	SO	SB	AB	H	PO	A	E	DP	TC/G	FA	G by Pos
1945 BKN N		55	.274	.433	201	55	14	3	4	2.0	29	29	32	20	0	0	0	478	38	7	40	9.5	.987	1B-55
1946		103	.242	.426	310	75	13	7	10	3.2	34	60	27	44	2	4	1	716	48	11	59	7.5	.986	1B-99
1947		5	.154	.231	13	2	1	0	0	0.0	0	0	1	5	0	1	0	29	4	1	2	6.8	.971	1B-5
1948 PIT N		128	.254	.396	429	109	19	6	10	2.3	47	69	35	53	4	10	3	1021	83	4	94	8.7	.996	1B-117
1949		67	.262	.371	221	58	10	1	4	1.8	22	32	22	24	1	9	0	533	58	3	65	8.9	.995	1B-58
1950		17	.196	.239	46	9	2	0	0	0.0	2	3	4	5	0	4	2	92	8	0	11	5.9	1.000	1B-12
6 yrs.		375	.252	.398	1220	308	59	17	28	2.3	134	193	121	151	7	28	6	2869	239	26	271	8.4	.992	1B-346

R C Stevens

STEVENS, R C
B. July 22, 1934, Moultrie, Ga. BR TL 6'5" 219 lbs.

Year	Team	Games	BA	SA	AB	H	2B	3B	HR	HR%	R	RBI	BB	SO	SB	AB	H	PO	A	E	DP	TC/G	FA	G by Pos
1958 PIT N		59	.267	.556	90	24	3	1	7	7.8	16	18	5	25	0	6	1	212	21	2	28	4.0	.991	1B-52
1959		3	.286	.714	7	2	0	0	1	14.3	2	1	0	0	0	2	0	11	1	0	1	4.0	1.000	1B-1
1960		9	.000	.000	3	0	0	0	0	0.0	1	0	0	1	0	2	0	10	2	0	2	1.3	1.000	1B-7
1961 WAS A		33	.129	.145	62	8	1	0	0	0.0	2	2	7	15	1	6	1	147	20	0	18	5.1	1.000	1B-25
4 yrs.		104	.210	.395	162	34	4	1	8	4.9	21	21	12	41	1	16	2	380	44	2	49	4.1	.995	1B-85

Ace Stewart

STEWART, ASA
B. Feb. 14, 1869, Terre Haute, Ind. D. Apr. 17, 1912, Terre Haute, Ind. BR TR 5'10" 176 lbs.

Year	Team	Games	BA	SA	AB	H	2B	3B	HR	HR%	R	RBI	BB	SO	SB	AB	H	PO	A	E	DP	TC/G	FA	G by Pos
1895 CHI N		97	.241	.384	365	88	8	10	8	2.2	52	76	39	40	14	0	0	252	281	52	53	6.0	.911	2B-97

Bill Stewart

STEWART, WILLIAM WAYNE
B. Apr. 12, 1928, Bay City, Mich. BR TR 5'11" 200 lbs.

Year	Team	Games	BA	SA	AB	H	2B	3B	HR	HR%	R	RBI	BB	SO	SB	AB	H	PO	A	E	DP	TC/G	FA	G by Pos
1955 KC A		11	.111	.167	18	2	1	0	0	0.0	2	0	1	6	0	4	0	7	1	0	1	0.7	1.000	OF-6

Bud Stewart

STEWART, EDWARD PERRY
B. June 15, 1916, Sacramento, Calif. BL TR 5'11" 160 lbs.

Year	Team	Games	BA	SA	AB	H	2B	3B	HR	HR%	R	RBI	BB	SO	SB	AB	H	PO	A	E	DP	TC/G	FA	G by Pos
1941 PIT N		73	.267	.308	172	46	7	0	0	0.0	27	10	12	17	3	25	10	71	5	3	2	1.1	.962	OF-41
1942		82	.219	.306	183	40	8	4	0	0.0	21	20	22	16	2	28	6	87	23	3	0	1.4	.973	OF-34, 3B-10, 2B-6
1948 2 teams	NY A (6G – .200)				WAS A	(118G – .279)																		
" total		124	.278	.438	406	113	18	13	7	1.7	57	69	49	27	8	9	1	265	5	7	1	2.2	.975	OF-114
1949 WAS A		118	.284	.425	388	110	23	4	8	2.1	58	43	49	33	6	11	4	207	8	4	3	1.9	.982	OF-105
1950		118	.267	.370	378	101	15	6	4	1.1	46	35	46	33	5	18	2	202	10	2	3	1.8	.991	OF-100
1951 CHI A		95	.276	.465	217	60	13	5	6	2.8	40	40	29	9	1	31	9	111	4	2	0	1.2	.983	OF-63
1952		92	.267	.378	225	60	10	0	5	2.2	23	30	28	17	3	34	6	108	1	2	0	1.2	.982	OF-60
1953		53	.271	.407	59	16	2	0	2	3.4	16	13	14	3	1	34	10	12	0	0	0	0.2	1.000	OF-16
1954		18	.077	.077	13	1	0	0	0	0.0	0	0	3	2	0	12	1	3	0	0	0	0.2	1.000	OF-2
9 yrs.		773	.268	.393	2041	547	96	32	32	1.6	288	260	252	157	29	202	49	1066	56	23	9	1.5	.980	OF-535, 3B-10, 2B-6

Glen Stewart

STEWART, GLEN WELDON (Gabby)
B. Sept. 29, 1912, Tullahoma, Tenn. BR TR 6' 175 lbs.

Year	Team	Games	BA	SA	AB	H	2B	3B	HR	HR%	R	RBI	BB	SO	SB	AB	H	PO	A	E	DP	TC/G	FA	G by Pos
1940 NY N		15	.138	.172	29	4	1	0	0	0.0	1	0	1	2	0	4	1	7	21	3	3	2.1	.903	3B-6, SS-5
1943 PHI N		110	.211	.265	336	71	10	1	2	0.6	23	24	32	41	1	8	1	222	286	23	51	4.8	.957	SS-77, 2B-18, 1B-8, C-1
1944		118	.220	.276	377	83	11	5	0	0.0	32	29	28	40	0	4	1	126	263	13	23	3.4	.968	SS-32, 2B-1
3 yrs.		243	.213	.267	742	158	22	6	2	0.3	56	53	61	83	1	16	3	355	570	39	77	4.0	.960	SS-114, 3B-89, 2B-19, 1B-8, C-1

Jimmy Stewart

STEWART, JAMES FRANKLIN
B. June 11, 1939, Opelika, Ala. BB TR 6' 165 lbs.

Year	Team	Games	BA	SA	AB	H	2B	3B	HR	HR%	R	RBI	BB	SO	SB	AB	H	PO	A	E	DP	TC/G	FA	G by Pos
1963 CHI N		13	.297	.351	37	11	2	0	0	0.0	1	1	1	7	0	5	1	13	29	1	8	3.3	.977	SS-9, 2B-1
1964		132	.253	.316	415	105	17	0	3	0.7	59	33	49	61	10	31	9	217	308	13	64	4.1	.976	2B-61, SS-45, OF-4, 3B-1
1965		116	.223	.284	282	63	9	4	0	0.0	26	19	30	53	13	41	6	117	58	8	11	1.6	.956	OF-55, SS-48
1966		57	.178	.244	90	16	4	1	0	0.0	4	4	7	12	1	31	6	36	3	0	0	0.7	1.000	OF-15, 2B-4, SS-2, 3B-2
1967 2 teams	CHI N (6G – .167)				CHI A	(24G – .167)																		
" total		30	.167	.167	24	4	0	0	0	0.0	6	2	1	6	1	13	1	9	8	3	4	0.7	.850	OF-6, 2B-5, SS-2
1969 CIN N		119	.253	.357	221	56	3	4	4	1.8	26	24	19	33	4	38	9	89	42	4	9	1.1	.970	OF-66, 2B-18, 3B-6, SS-1
1970		101	.267	.343	105	28	3	1	1	1.0	19	8	8	13	5	39	13	46	36	3	8	0.8	.965	OF-48, 2B-18, 3B-9, 1B-1, C-1
1971		80	.232	.305	82	19	2	2	0	0.0	7	9	9	12	3	48	11	13	22	2	3	0.5	.946	OF-19, 3B-9, 2B-6
1972 HOU N		68	.219	.313	96	21	5	2	0	0.0	14	9	6	9	2	40	7	83	18	0	5	1.5	1.000	OF-11, 1B-9, 2B-8, 3B-2
1973		61	.191	.191	68	13	0	0	0	0.0	6	3	9	9	0	44	8	5	17	0	2	0.4	1.000	3B-8, OF-3, 2B-1
10 yrs.		777	.237	.305	1420	336	45	14	8	0.6	164	112	139	218	38	330	71	628	541	34	114	1.5	.972	OF-227, 2B-122, SS-107, 3B-37, 1B-10, C-1

LEAGUE CHAMPIONSHIP SERIES

Year	Team	Games	BA	SA	AB	H	2B	3B	HR	HR%	R	RBI	BB	SO	SB	AB	H	PO	A	E	DP	TC/G	FA	G by Pos
1970 CIN N		1	.000	.000	2	0	0	0	0	0.0	0	0	0	0	0	0	0	0	0	0	0	0.0	–	OF-1

WORLD SERIES

Year	Team	Games	BA	SA	AB	H	2B	3B	HR	HR%	R	RBI	BB	SO	SB	AB	H	PO	A	E	DP	TC/G	FA	G by Pos
1970 CIN N		2	.000	.000	2	0	0	0	0	0.0	0	0	0	1	0	2	0	0	0	0	0	0.0	–	

Mark Stewart

STEWART, MARK (Big Slick)
B. Oct. 11, 1889, Whitlock, Tenn. D. Jan. 17, 1932, Memphis, Tenn. BL TR 6'1" 180 lbs.

Year	Team	Games	BA	SA	AB	H	2B	3B	HR	HR%	R	RBI	BB	SO	SB	AB	H	PO	A	E	DP	TC/G	FA	G by Pos
1913 CIN N		1	.000	.000	1	0	0	0	0	0.0	0	0	0	0	0	0	0	0	0	0	0	0.0	–	C-1

Neb Stewart

STEWART, WALTER NESBITT
B. May 21, 1918, South Charleston, Ohio BR TR 6'1" 195 lbs.

Year	Team		Games	BA	SA	AB	H	2B	3B	HR	HR%	R	RBI	BB	SO	SB	Pinch Hit AB	H	PO	A	E	DP	TC/G	FA	G by Pos

Neb Stewart *continued*

| 1940 | PHI | N | 10 | .129 | .129 | 31 | 4 | 0 | 0 | 0 | 0.0 | 3 | 0 | 1 | 5 | 0 | 0 | 0 | 15 | 2 | 1 | 1 | 1.8 | .944 | OF-9 |

Stuffy Stewart

STEWART, JOHN FRANKLIN
B. Jan. 31, 1894, Jasper, Fla. D. Dec. 30, 1980, Lake City, Fla.

BR TR 5'9½" 160 lbs.

1916	STL	N	9	.176	.176	17	3	0	0	0	0.0	3	0	3	0	0	1	0	11	9	4	2	2.7	.833	2B-8
1917			13	.000	.000	9	0	0	0	0	0.0	4	0	0	4	0	1	0	3	1	0	0	0.3	1.000	OF-7, 2B-2
1922	PIT	N	3	.154	.154	13	2	0	0	0	0.0	3	0	1	0	0	0	0	5	9	2	2	5.3	.875	2B-3
1923	BKN	N	4	.364	.727	11	4	1	0	1	9.1	3	1	1	1	0	0	0	4	7	3	1	3.5	.786	2B-3
1925	WAS	A	7	.353	.412	17	6	1	0	0	0.0	3	3	1	2	1	0	0	4	10	1	1	2.1	.933	3B-5, 2B-1
1926			62	.270	.397	63	17	6	1	0	0.0	27	9	6	6	8	3	1	33	48	2	8	1.3	.976	2B-25, 3B-1
1927			56	.240	.318	129	31	6	2	0	0.0	24	4	8	15	12	3	1	61	95	10	15	3.0	.940	2B-37, 3B-2
1929			22	.000	.000	6	0	0	0	0	0.0	10	0	1	0	0	2	0	3	4	0	0	0.3	1.000	2B-3
	8 yrs.		176	.238	.325	265	63	14	3	1	0.4	74	18	17	32	21	9	1	124	183	22	29	1.9	.933	2B-82, 3B-8, OF-7

Tuffy Stewart

STEWART, CHARLES EUGENE
B. July 31, 1883, Chicago, Ill. D. Nov. 18, 1934, Chicago, Ill.

BL TL 5'10" 167 lbs.

1913	CHI	N	9	.125	.250	8	1	1	0	0	0.0	1	2	2	5	1	5	0	2	0	0	0	0.2	1.000	OF-1
1914			2	.000	.000	1	0	0	0	0	0.0	0	0	0	0	0	1	0	0	0	0	0	0.0		OF-1
	2 yrs.		11	.111	.222	9	1	1	0	0	0.0	1	2	2	5	1	6	0	2	0	0	0	0.2	1.000	OF-1

Royle Stillman

STILLMAN, ROYLE ELDON
B. Jan. 2, 1951, Santa Monica, Calif.

BL TL 5'11" 180 lbs.

1975	BAL	A	13	.429	.429	14	6	0	0	0	0.0	1	1	1	3	0	4	1	3	0	0	0	0.2	1.000	OF-2
1976			20	.091	.091	22	2	0	0	0	0.0	0	1	3	4	0	15	1	2	0	0	0	0.1	1.000	DH-5, 1B-2
1977	CHI	A	56	.210	.361	119	25	7	1	3	2.5	18	13	17	21	2	17	3	47	0	1	0	0.9	.979	OF-26, DH-13, 1B-1
	3 yrs.		89	.213	.329	155	33	7	1	3	1.9	19	15	21	28	2	36	5	52	0	1	0	0.6	.981	OF-28, DH-18, 1B-3

Kurt Stillwell

STILLWELL, KURT ANDREW
Son of Ron Stillwell.
B. June 4, 1965, Glendale, Calif.

BB TR 5'11" 165 lbs.

1986	CIN	N	104	.229	.258	279	64	6	1	0	0.0	31	26	30	47	6	20	6	107	205	16	40	3.2	.951	SS-80
1987			131	.258	.375	395	102	20	7	4	1.0	54	33	32	50	4	29	8	144	247	23	38	3.2	.944	SS-51, 2B-37, 3B-20
1988	KC	A	128	.251	.399	459	115	28	5	10	2.2	63	53	47	76	6	4	0	170	349	13	60	4.2	.976	SS-124
1989			130	.261	.380	463	121	20	7	7	1.5	52	54	42	64	9	4	1	179	334	16	65	4.1	.970	SS-130
	4 yrs.		493	.252	.363	1596	402	74	20	21	1.3	200	166	151	237	25	57	15	600	1135	68	203	3.7	.962	SS-385, 2B-37, 3B-20

Ron Stillwell

STILLWELL, RONALD ROY
Father of Kurt Stillwell.
B. Dec. 3, 1939, Los Angeles, Calif.

BR TR 5'11" 165 lbs.

1961	WAS	A	8	.125	.188	16	2	1	0	0	0.0	3	1	1	4	0	1	1	4	9	1	4	1.8	.929	SS-5
1962			6	.273	.273	22	6	0	0	0	0.0	5	2	2	2	0	0	0	16	12	0	3	4.7	1.000	2B-6, SS-1
	2 yrs.		14	.211	.237	38	8	1	0	0	0.0	8	3	3	6	0	1	1	20	21	1	7	3.0	.976	SS-6, 2B-6

Craig Stimac

STIMAC, CRAIG STEVEN
B. Nov. 18, 1954, Oak Park, Ill.

BR TR 6'2" 185 lbs.

1980	SD	N	20	.220	.260	50	11	2	0	0	0.0	5	7	1	6	0	8	2	51	16	2	2	3.5	.971	C-11, 3B-2
1981			9	.111	.111	9	1	0	0	0	0.0	0	0	0	3	0	9	1	0	0	0	0	0.0	—	
	2 yrs.		29	.203	.237	59	12	2	0	0	0.0	5	7	1	9	0	17	3	51	16	2	2	2.4	.971	C-11, 3B-2

Bob Stinson

STINSON, GORRELL ROBERT
B. Oct. 11, 1945, Elkin, N. C.

BB TR 5'11" 180 lbs.

1969	LA	N	4	.375	.375	8	3	0	0	0	0.0	1	2	0	0	0	0	0	20	0	1	0	5.3	.952	C-4
1970			4	.000	.000	3	0	0	0	0	0.0	0	1	0	0	0	1	0	3	0	0	0	0.8	1.000	C-3
1971	STL	N	17	.211	.263	19	4	1	0	0	0.0	3	1	1	7	0	2	1	36	0	1	0	2.2	.973	C-6, OF-3
1972	HOU	N	27	.171	.200	35	6	1	0	0	0.0	3	2	1	9	0	15	1	26	2	1	0	1.1	.966	C-12, OF-3
1973	MON	N	48	.261	.414	111	29	6	1	3	2.7	12	12	17	15	0	10	3	174	9	4	2	3.9	.979	C-35, 3B-1
1974			38	.172	.230	87	15	2	0	1	1.1	4	6	15	16	1	12	3	122	14	0	4	3.6	1.000	C-29
1975	KC	A	63	.265	.361	147	39	9	1	1	0.7	18	9	18	29	1	4	0	257	33	2	4	4.6	.993	C-59, DH-1, OF-1, 2B-1, 1B-1
1976			79	.263	.335	209	55	7	1	2	1.0	26	25	25	29	3	2	0	304	30	7	4	4.3	.979	C-79
1977	SEA	A	105	.269	.394	297	80	11	1	8	2.7	27	32	37	50	0	11	2	494	43	9	11	5.2	.984	C-99, DH-1
1978			124	.258	.404	364	94	14	3	11	3.0	46	55	45	42	2	7	1	472	60	7	7	4.3	.987	C-123, DH-1
1979			95	.243	.348	247	60	8	0	6	2.4	19	28	33	38	1	1	1	376	29	7	2	4.4	.978	C-91
1980			48	.215	.262	107	23	2	0	1	0.9	6	8	9	0	0	12	1	135	8	3	2	3.0	.979	C-45
	12 yrs.		652	.250	.356	1634	408	61	7	33	2.0	166	180	201	254	8	82	13	2419	228	44	36	4.1	.984	C-585, OF-7, DH-3, 3B-1, 2B-1, 1B-1

LEAGUE CHAMPIONSHIP SERIES

| 1976 | KC | A | 2 | .000 | .000 | 1 | 0 | 0 | 0 | 0 | 0.0 | 0 | 0 | 0 | 0 | 0 | 1 | 0 | 0 | 0 | 0 | 0 | 0.0 | — | C-1 |

Snuffy Stirnweiss

STIRNWEISS, GEORGE HENRY
B. Oct. 26, 1918, New York, N. Y. D. Sept. 15, 1958, Newark Bay, N. J.

BR TR 5'8½" 175 lbs.

1943	NY	A	83	.219	.288	274	60	8	4	1	0.4	34	25	47	37	11	3	0	124	200	20	55	4.1	.942	SS-68, 2B-4
1944			154	.319	.460	643	**205**	35	**16**	8	1.2	**125**	43	73	87	**55**	0	0	433	481	17	113	6.0	.982	2B-154
1945			152	**.309**	**.476**	632	195	32	22	10	1.6	107	37	78	62	33	0	0	432	492	29	119	6.3	.970	2B-152
1946			129	.251	.318	487	122	19	7	0	0.0	75	37	66	58	18	3	0	159	299	8	49	3.6	.983	3B-79, 2B-46, SS-4
1947			148	.256	.342	571	146	18	5	5	0.9	102	41	89	47	5	0	0	337	402	13	107	5.1	.983	2B-148
1948			141	.252	.336	515	130	20	7	3	0.6	90	32	86	62	5	0	0	346	364	5	103	5.1	.993	2B-141
1949			70	.261	.338	157	41	8	2	0	0.0	29	11	29	20	3	5	1	124	109	6	34	3.4	.975	2B-51, 3B-4

Year	Team	Games	BA	SA	AB	H	2B	3B	HR	HR%	R	RBI	BB	SO	SB	Pinch Hit AB	Pinch Hit H	PO	A	E	DP	TC/G	FA	G by Pos

Snuffy Stirnweiss *continued*

Year	Team	Games	BA	SA	AB	H	2B	3B	HR	HR%	R	RBI	BB	SO	SB	PH AB	PH H	PO	A	E	DP	TC/G	FA	G by Pos
1950 2 teams	NY A (7G – .000)				STL A (93G – .218)																			
" total		100	.216	.287	328	71	16	2	1	0.3	32	24	51	49	3	2	1	200	215	13	51	4.3	.970	2B-66, 3B-32, SS-5
1951	CLE A	50	.216	.261	88	19	1	0	1	1.1	10	4	22	25	1	9	1	49	77	1	18	2.5	.992	2B-25, 3B-2
1952		1	–	–	0	0	0	0	0	–	0	0	0	0	0	0	0	0	0	0	0	0.0	–	3B-1
10 yrs.		1028	.268	.371	3695	989	157	68	29	0.8	604	281	541	447	134	22	3	2204	2639	112	649	4.8	.977	2B-787, 3B-118, SS-77

WORLD SERIES

Year	Team	Games	BA	SA	AB	H	2B	3B	HR	HR%	R	RBI	BB	SO	SB	PH AB	PH H	PO	A	E	DP	TC/G	FA	G by Pos
1943	NY A	1	.000	.000	1	0	0	0	0	0.0	1	0	0	0	0	1	0	0	0	0	0	0.0	–	
1947		7	.259	.333	27	7	0	1	0	0.0	3	3	8	8	0	0	0	17	21	0	2	5.4	1.000	2B-7
1949		1	–	–	0	0	0	0	0	–	0	0	0	0	0	0	0	0	0	0	0	0.0	–	
3 yrs.		9	.250	.321	28	7	0	1	0	0.0	4	3	8	8	0	1	0	17	21	0	2	4.2	1.000	2B-7

Jack Stivetts

STIVETTS, JOHN ELMER (Happy Jack) BR TR 6'2" 185 lbs.
B. Mar. 31, 1868, Ashland, Pa. D. Apr. 18, 1930, Ashland, Pa.

Year	Team	Games	BA	SA	AB	H	2B	3B	HR	HR%	R	RBI	BB	SO	SB	PH AB	PH H	PO	A	E	DP	TC/G	FA	G by Pos
1889	STL AA	27	.228	.304	79	18	2	2	0	0.0	12	7	3	13		0	0	12	43	6	0	2.3	.902	P-26, OF-1
1890		67	.288	.500	226	65	15	6	7	3.1	36		16		2	0	0	65	89	17	6	2.6	.901	P-54, OF-10, 1B-3
1891		85	.305	.421	302	92	10	2	7	2.3	45	54	10	32	4	2	0	51	113	17	4	2.1	.906	P-64, OF-24
1892	BOS N	70	.296	.408	240	71	14	2	3	1.3	40	36	27	28	8	0	0	53	97	16	8	2.4	.904	P-53, OF-18, 1B-1
1893		49	.297	.448	172	51	5	6	3	1.7	32	25	12	14	6	1	0	31	55	7	3	1.9	.925	P-37, OF-8, 3B-3
1894		68	.328	.533	244	80	12	7	8	3.3	55	64	16	21	3	5	0	79	53	13	5	2.1	.910	P-45, OF-16, 1B-4
1895		46	.190	.278	158	30	6	4	0	0.0	20	24	6	18	1	2	1	76	53	4	5	2.9	.970	P-38, 1B-5, OF-2
1896		67	.344	.480	221	76	9	6	3	1.4	42	49	12	10	4	5	4	90	62	15	4	2.5	.910	P-42, OF-12, 1B-5, 3B-1
1897		37	.367	.533	199	73	9	9	2	1.0	41	37	15		2	10	3	68	45	8	3	2.0	.934	OF-29, P-18, 2B-3, 1B-2
1898		41	.252	.333	111	28	1	1	2	1.8	16	16	10		1	10	2	97	22	10	4	3.1	.922	OF-14, 1B-10, SS-4, 2B-2, P-2
1899	CLE N	18	.205	.282	39	8	1	1	0	0.0	8	2	6		0	3	0	14	20	1	0	1.9	.971	OF-7, P-7, SS-1, 3B-1
11 yrs.		599	.297	.438	1991	592	84	46	35	1.8	347	314	133	136	31	38	10	636	652	114	42	2.3	.919	P-386, OF-141, 1B-30, SS-5, 3B-5, 2B-4

Milt Stock

STOCK, MILTON JOSEPH BR TR 5'8" 154 lbs.
B. July 11, 1893, Chicago, Ill. D. July 16, 1977, Montrose, Ala.

Year	Team	Games	BA	SA	AB	H	2B	3B	HR	HR%	R	RBI	BB	SO	SB	PH AB	PH H	PO	A	E	DP	TC/G	FA	G by Pos
1913	NY N	7	.176	.235	17	3	1	0	0	0.0	2	1	2	1	2	0	0	12	19	6	4	5.3	.838	SS-1
1914		115	.263	.340	365	96	17	1	3	0.8	52	41	34	21	11	0	0	97	266	23	17	3.4	.940	3B-113, SS-1
1915	PHI N	69	.260	.330	227	59	7	3	1	0.4	37	15	22	26	6	10	1	64	108	5	7	2.6	.972	3B-55, SS-4
1916		132	.281	.360	509	143	25	6	1	0.2	61	43	27	33	21	3	1	150	259	23	29	3.3	.947	3B-117, SS-15
1917		150	.264	.349	564	149	27	6	3	0.5	76	53	51	34	25	0	0	176	315	33	20	3.5	.937	3B-133, SS-19
1918		123	.274	.314	481	132	14	1	1	0.2	62	42	35	22	20	1	0	132	273	23	16	3.5	.946	3B-123
1919	STL N	135	.307	.356	492	151	16	4	0	0.0	56	52	49	21	17	0	0	219	393	29	47	4.7	.955	2B-77, 3B-58
1920		155	.319	.382	639	204	28	6	0	0.0	85	76	40	27	15	0	0	158	300	30	23	3.1	.939	3B-155
1921		149	.307	.388	587	180	27	6	3	0.5	96	84	48	26	11	0	0	148	243	25	21	2.8	.940	3B-149
1922		151	.305	.418	581	177	33	9	5	0.9	85	79	42	29	7	1	0	175	247	22	22	2.9	.950	3B-149, SS-1
1923		151	.289	.363	603	174	33	2	2	0.3	63	96	40	21	9	1	0	166	261	20	24	3.0	.955	3B-150, 2B-1
1924	BKN N	142	.242	.292	561	136	14	4	2	0.4	66	52	26	32	3	0	0	139	200	25	14	2.6	.931	3B-142
1925		146	.328	.408	615	202	28	9	1	0.2	98	62	38	28	8	0	0	315	489	19	75	5.6	.977	2B-141, 3B-5
1926		3	.000	.000	8	0	0	0	0	0.0	0	0	1	0	0	0	0	4	8	1	1	4.3	.923	2B-3
14 yrs.		1628	.289	.361	6249	1806	270	58	22	0.4	839	696	455	321	155	16	2	1955	3381	284	320	3.5	.949	3B-1349, 2B-222, SS-41

WORLD SERIES

Year	Team	Games	BA	SA	AB	H	2B	3B	HR	HR%	R	RBI	BB	SO	SB	PH AB	PH H	PO	A	E	DP	TC/G	FA	G by Pos
1915	PHI N	5	.118	.176	17	2	1	0	0	0.0	1	0	1	0	0	0	0	1	8	0	0	1.8	1.000	3B-5

Len Stockwell

STOCKWELL, LEONARD CLARK TR 5'11" 165 lbs.
B. Aug. 25, 1859, Cordova, Ill. D. Jan. 28, 1905, Niles, Calif.

Year	Team	Games	BA	SA	AB	H	2B	3B	HR	HR%	R	RBI	BB	SO	SB	PH AB	PH H	PO	A	E	DP	TC/G	FA	G by Pos
1879	CLE N	2	.000	.000	6	0	0	0	0	0.0	0	0	0			0	0	2	2	0	1	2.0	1.000	OF-2
1884	LOU AA	2	.111	.111	9	1	0	0	0	0.0	0		0			0	0	4	2	2	0	4.0	.750	OF-2, C-1
1890	CLE N	2	.286	.429	7	2	1	0	0	0.0	2	0	0			0	0	10	1	3	0	7.0	.786	OF-1, 1B-1
3 yrs.		6	.136	.182	22	3	1	0	0	0.0	2	0	0			0	0	16	5	5	1	4.3	.808	OF-5, 1B-1, C-1

Al Stokes

STOKES, ALBERT JOHN BR TR 5'9" 175 lbs.
Born Albert John Stocek.
B. Jan. 1, 1900, Chicago, Ill.

Year	Team	Games	BA	SA	AB	H	2B	3B	HR	HR%	R	RBI	BB	SO	SB	PH AB	PH H	PO	A	E	DP	TC/G	FA	G by Pos
1925	BOS A	17	.212	.250	52	11	1	0	0	0.0	7	1	4	8	0	0	0	40	23	2	3	3.8	.969	C-17
1926		30	.163	.267	86	14	3	3	0	0.0	7	6	8	28	0	1	0	70	24	7	3	3.4	.931	C-29
2 yrs.		47	.181	.261	138	25	3	4	0	0.0	14	7	12	36	0	1	0	110	47	9	6	3.5	.946	C-46

Gene Stone

STONE, EUGENE DANIEL BL TL 5'11" 190 lbs.
B. Jan. 16, 1944, Burbank, Calif.

Year	Team	Games	BA	SA	AB	H	2B	3B	HR	HR%	R	RBI	BB	SO	SB	PH AB	PH H	PO	A	E	DP	TC/G	FA	G by Pos
1969	PHI N	18	.214	.286	28	6	0	1	0	0.0	4	0	4	9	0	10	2	43	1	0	3	2.4	1.000	1B-5

George Stone

STONE, GEORGE ROBERT BL TL 5'9" 175 lbs.
B. Sept. 3, 1877, Lost Nation, Iowa D. Jan. 3, 1945, Clinton, Iowa

Year	Team	Games	BA	SA	AB	H	2B	3B	HR	HR%	R	RBI	BB	SO	SB	PH AB	PH H	PO	A	E	DP	TC/G	FA	G by Pos
1903	BOS A	2	.000	.000	2	0	0	0	0	0.0	0	0	0			0	2	0	0	0	0	0.0	–	
1905	STL A	154	.296	.410	632	187	25	13	7	1.1	76	52	44		26	0	0	278	15	14	5	2.0	.954	OF-154
1906		154	.358	.501	581	208	25	20	6	1.0	91	71	52		35	0	0	295	10	10	3	2.0	.968	OF-154
1907		155	.320	.399	596	191	13	11	4	0.7	77	59	59		23	0	0	276	12	9	5	1.9	.970	OF-155
1908		148	.281	.369	588	165	21	8	5	0.9	89	31	55		20	0	0	274	11	16	3	2.0	.947	OF-148
1909		83	.287	.339	310	89	5	4	1	0.3	33	15	24		8	2	0	147	8	12	4	2.0	.928	OF-81
1910		152	.256	.329	562	144	17	12	0	0.0	60	40	48		20	5	1	220	20	7	2	1.6	.972	OF-147
7 yrs.		848	.301	.396	3271	984	106	68	23	0.7	426	268	282		132	9	1	1490	76	68	22	1.9	.958	OF-839

Jeff Stone

STONE, JEFFREY GLEN BL TR 6' 175 lbs.
B. Dec. 26, 1960, Kennett, Mo.

Year	Team	Games	BA	SA	AB	H	2B	3B	HR	HR%	R	RBI	BB	SO	SB	Pinch Hit AB	Pinch Hit H	PO	A	E	DP	TC/G	FA	G by Pos

Jeff Stone *continued*

Year	Team	Games	BA	SA	AB	H	2B	3B	HR	HR%	R	RBI	BB	SO	SB	AB	H	PO	A	E	DP	TC/G	FA	G by Pos
1983	PHI N	9	.750	1.750	4	3	0	2	0	0.0	2	3	0	1	4	1	1	0	0	0	0	0.0	–	OF-1
1984		51	.362	.465	185	67	4	6	1	0.5	27	15	9	26	27	5	0	75	1	7	0	1.6	.916	OF-46
1985		88	.265	.337	264	70	4	3	3	1.1	36	11	15	50	15	18	5	82	4	3	0	1.0	.966	OF-69
1986		82	.277	.406	249	69	6	4	6	2.4	32	19	20	52	19	21	7	103	8	2	1	1.4	.982	OF-58
1987		66	.256	.352	125	32	7	1	1	0.8	19	16	8	38	3	37	9	32	3	0	1	0.5	1.000	OF-25
1988	BAL A	26	.164	.180	61	10	1	0	0	0.0	4	1	4	11	4	7	2	23	3	1	1	1.0	.963	OF-21, DH-1
1989	2 teams		TEX A	(22G – .167)		BOS A	(18G – .200)																		
"	total	40	.176	.275	51	9	1	2	0	0.0	8	6	4	7	3	12	1	8	0	0	0	0.2	1.000	DH-18, OF-14
7 yrs.		362	.277	.375	939	260	23	18	11	1.2	128	71	60	185	75	101	25	323	19	13	3	1.0	.963	OF-234, DH-19

John Stone

STONE, JOHN THOMAS (Rocky)
B. Oct. 10, 1905, Lynchburg, Tenn. D. Nov. 30, 1955, Shelbyville, Tenn.

BL TR 6'1" 178 lbs.

Year	Team	Games	BA	SA	AB	H	2B	3B	HR	HR%	R	RBI	BB	SO	SB	AB	H	PO	A	E	DP	TC/G	FA	G by Pos
1928	DET A	26	.354	.549	113	40	10	3	2	1.8	20	21	5	21	1			49	2	2	0	2.0	.962	OF-26
1929		51	.260	.400	150	39	11	2	2	1.3	23	15	11	13	1	15	4	68	4	1	0	1.4	.986	OF-36
1930		126	.313	.455	422	132	29	11	3	0.7	60	56	32	49	6	18	4	222	5	8	1	1.9	.966	OF-108
1931		147	.327	.464	584	191	28	11	10	1.7	86	76	56	48	13	0	0	319	11	14	6	2.3	.959	OF-147
1932		144	.297	.486	582	173	35	12	17	2.9	106	108	58	64	2	3	0	334	11	14	2	2.5	.961	OF-141
1933		148	.280	.434	574	161	33	11	11	1.9	86	80	54	37	1	3	3	280	11	9	1	2.0	.970	OF-141
1934	WAS A	113	.315	.465	419	132	28	7	7	1.7	77	67	52	26	1	4	2	245	13	9	3	2.4	.966	OF-112
1935		125	.315	.460	454	143	27	18	1	0.2	78	78	39	29	4	14	2	224	12	11	4	2.0	.955	OF-114
1936		123	.341	.545	437	149	22	11	15	3.4	95	90	60	26	8	6	2	249	12	9	5	2.2	.967	OF-114
1937		139	.330	.480	542	179	33	15	6	1.1	84	88	66	36	6	1	0	300	15	5	3	2.3	.984	OF-137
1938		56	.244	.380	213	52	12	4	3	1.4	24	28	30	16	2	1	0	107	5	3	0	2.1	.974	OF-53
11 yrs.		1198	.310	.468	4490	1391	268	105	77	1.7	739	707	463	352	45	67	17	2397	101	85	25	2.2	.967	OF-1129

Ron Stone

STONE, HARRY RONALD
B. Sept. 9, 1942, Corning, Calif.

BL TL 6'2" 185 lbs.

Year	Team	Games	BA	SA	AB	H	2B	3B	HR	HR%	R	RBI	BB	SO	SB	AB	H	PO	A	E	DP	TC/G	FA	G by Pos
1966	KC A	26	.273	.318	22	6	1	0	0	0.0	2	0	2	1	1	15	6	14	2	2	3	0.7	.889	OF-4, 1B-3
1969	PHI N	103	.239	.293	222	53	7	1	1	0.5	22	24	29	28	3	28	2	85	6	2	0	0.9	.978	OF-69
1970		123	.262	.358	321	84	12	5	3	0.9	30	39	38	45	5	23	4	164	5	6	1	1.4	.966	OF-99, 1B-6
1971		95	.227	.314	185	42	8	1	2	1.1	16	23	25	36	2	43	7	93	6	4	2	1.1	.961	OF-51, 1B-3
1972		41	.167	.204	54	9	0	1	0	0.0	3	3	9	11	0	22	3	24	3	0	0	0.7	1.000	OF-15
5 yrs.		388	.241	.318	804	194	28	8	6	0.7	73	89	101	122	11	131	20	380	22	14	6	1.1	.966	OF-238, 1B-12

Tige Stone

STONE, WILLIAM ARTHUR
B. Sept. 18, 1901, Macon, Ga. D. Jan. 1, 1960, Jacksonville, Fla.

BR TR 5'8" 145 lbs.

Year	Team	Games	BA	SA	AB	H	2B	3B	HR	HR%	R	RBI	BB	SO	SB	AB	H	PO	A	E	DP	TC/G	FA	G by Pos
1923	STL N	5	1.000	1.000	1	1	0	0	0	0.0	0	0	0	2	0	0	0	2	0	0	0	0.4	1.000	OF-4, P-1

John Stoneham

STONEHAM, JOHN ANDREW
B. Nov. 8, 1908, Wood River, Ill.

BL TR 5'9½" 168 lbs.

Year	Team	Games	BA	SA	AB	H	2B	3B	HR	HR%	R	RBI	BB	SO	SB	AB	H	PO	A	E	DP	TC/G	FA	G by Pos
1933	CHI A	10	.120	.240	25	3	0	0	1	4.0	4	3	2	2	0	0	0	13	0	0	0	1.3	1.000	OF-9

Howie Storie

STORIE, HOWARD EDWARD
B. May 15, 1911, Pittsfield, Mass. D. July 27, 1968, Pittsfield, Mass.

BR TR 5'10" 175 lbs.

Year	Team	Games	BA	SA	AB	H	2B	3B	HR	HR%	R	RBI	BB	SO	SB	AB	H	PO	A	E	DP	TC/G	FA	G by Pos
1931	BOS A	6	.118	.118	17	2	0	0	0	0.0	3	2	1	0	0	0	0	20	3	0	0	3.8	1.000	C-6
1932		6	.375	.375	8	3	0	0	0	0.0	0	1	2	0	0	1	0	11	0	0	0	1.8	1.000	C-5
2 yrs.		12	.200	.200	25	5	0	0	0	0.0	3	3	3	0	0	1	0	31	3	0	0	2.8	1.000	C-11

Alan Storke

STORKE, ALAN MARSHALL
B. Sept. 27, 1884, Auburn, N. Y. D. Mar. 18, 1910, Newton, Mass.

BR TR

Year	Team	Games	BA	SA	AB	H	2B	3B	HR	HR%	R	RBI	BB	SO	SB	AB	H	PO	A	E	DP	TC/G	FA	G by Pos
1906	PIT N	5	.250	.333	12	3	1	0	0	0.0	1	1	2	1	0	0	0	2	9	1	1	2.4	.917	3B-2, SS-1
1907		112	.258	.317	357	92	6	6	1	0.3	24	39	16		6	10	3	275	160	28	19	4.1	.940	3B-67, 1B-23, 2B-7, SS-5
1908		64	.252	.322	202	51	5	3	1	0.5	20	12	9		4	8	0	487	28	8	19	8.2	.985	1B-49, 3B-6, 2B-1
1909	2 teams		PIT N	(37G – .254)		STL N	(48G – .282)																		
"	total	85	.271	.318	292	79	10	2	0	0.0	23	22	19		6	4	1	280	189	15	26	5.7	.969	SS-44, 1B-19, 3B-14, 2B-4
4 yrs.		266	.261	.319	863	225	22	11	2	0.2	68	74	45		17	24	5	1044	386	52	65	5.6	.965	1B-91, 3B-89, SS-50, 2B-12

Lin Storti

STORTI, LINDO IVAN
B. Dec. 5, 1906, Santa Monica, Calif.
D. July 24, 1982, Ontario, Calif.

BB TR 5'11" 165 lbs.
BR 1930

Year	Team	Games	BA	SA	AB	H	2B	3B	HR	HR%	R	RBI	BB	SO	SB	AB	H	PO	A	E	DP	TC/G	FA	G by Pos
1930	STL A	7	.321	.429	28	9	1	0	0	0.0	6	2	2	6	0	1	0	19	20	1	8	5.7	.975	2B-6
1931		86	.220	.337	273	60	15	4	3	1.1	32	26	15	50	0	9	2	91	149	18	24	3.0	.930	3B-67, 2B-7
1932		53	.259	.383	193	50	11	2	3	1.6	19	26	5	20	1	2	0	50	81	6	8	2.6	.956	3B-51
1933		70	.195	.310	210	41	7	4	3	1.4	26	21	25	31	2	13	3	105	113	8	26	3.2	.965	3B-32, 2B-24
4 yrs.		216	.227	.345	704	160	34	11	9	1.3	83	75	47	107	3	25	5	265	363	33	66	3.1	.950	3B-150, 2B-37

Tom Stouch

STOUCH, THOMAS CARL
B. Dec. 2, 1870, Perryville, Ohio D. Oct. 7, 1956, Lancaster, Pa.

BR TR 6'2" 165 lbs.

Year	Team	Games	BA	SA	AB	H	2B	3B	HR	HR%	R	RBI	BB	SO	SB	AB	H	PO	A	E	DP	TC/G	FA	G by Pos
1898	LOU N	4	.313	.375	16	5	1	0	0	0.0	4	6	1		0	0	0	8	9	3	1	5.0	.850	2B-4

George Stovall

STOVALL, GEORGE THOMAS (Firebrand)
Brother of Jesse Stovall.
B. Nov. 23, 1878, Independence, Mo. D. Nov. 5, 1951, Burlington, Iowa
Manager 1911-15.

BR TR 6'2" 180 lbs.

Year	Team	Games	BA	SA	AB	H	2B	3B	HR	HR%	R	RBI	BB	SO	SB	AB	H	PO	A	E	DP	TC/G	FA	G by Pos
1904	CLE A	52	.297	.379	182	54	10	1	1	0.5	18	31	2		4	1	0	391	44	12	20	8.6	.973	1B-38, 2B-9, OF-3, 3B-1
1905		111	.272	.368	419	114	31	3	1	0.2	41	47	13		13	3	0	751	161	30	35	8.5	.968	1B-59, 2B-46, OF-4
1906		116	.273	.339	443	121	19	5	0	0.0	54	37	8		15	9	3	666	153	21	53	7.2	.975	1B-55, 3B-30, 2B-19
1907		124	.236	.305	466	110	17	6	1	0.2	38	36	18		13	0	0	1382	71	25	90	11.9	.983	1B-122, 3B-2
1908		138	.292	.380	534	156	29	6	2	0.4	71	45	17		14	0	0	1524	89	16	79	11.8	.990	1B-132, OF-5, SS-1
1909		145	.246	.322	565	139	17	10	2	0.4	60	49	6		25	0	0	1478	109	19	80	11.1	.988	1B-145

Year	Team		Games	BA	SA	AB	H	2B	3B	HR	HR%	R	RBI	BB	SO	SB	Pinch Hit AB	Pinch Hit H	PO	A	E	DP	TC/G	FA	G by Pos

George Stovall *continued*

Year	Team		Games	BA	SA	AB	H	2B	3B	HR	HR%	R	RBI	BB	SO	SB	AB	H	PO	A	E	DP	TC/G	FA	G by Pos
1910			142	.261	.313	521	136	19	4	0	0.0	47	52	14		16	7	2	1404	91	18	60	10.7	.988	1B-132, 2B-2
1911			126	.271	.338	458	124	17	7	0	0.0	48	79	21		11	5	1	1076	92	19	56	9.4	.984	1B-118, 2B-2
1912	STL	A	115	.254	.322	398	101	17	5	0	0.0	35	45	14		11	21	4	845	68	16	64	8.1	.983	1B-94
1913			89	.287	.363	303	87	14	3	1	0.3	34	24	7	23	7	13	2	751	65	10	38	9.3	.988	1B-76
1914	KC	F	124	.284	.398	450	128	20	5	7	1.6	51	75	23		6	8	2	1201	70	14	82	10.4	.989	1B-116, 3B-1
1915			130	.231	.288	480	111	21	3	0	0.0	48	44	31		8	1	0	1417	87	20	61	11.7	.987	1B-129
12 yrs.			1412	.265	.340	5219	1381	231	58	15	0.3	545	564	174	23	143	68	14	12886	1100	220	718	10.1	.985	1B-1216, 2B-78, 3B-34, OF-12, SS-1

Harry Stovey

STOVEY, HARRY DUFFIELD
Born Harry Duffield Stowe.
B. Dec. 20, 1856, Philadelphia, Pa.   D. Sept. 20, 1937, New Bedford, Mass.
Manager 1881, 1885.

BR TR 5'11½" 180 lbs.

Year	Team		Games	BA	SA	AB	H	2B	3B	HR	HR%	R	RBI	BB	SO	SB	AB	H	PO	A	E	DP	TC/G	FA	G by Pos
1880	WOR	N	83	.265	.454	355	94	21	**14**	6	1.7	76	28	12	46		0	0	514	18	35	21	6.8	.938	OF-46, 1B-37, P-2
1881			75	.270	.402	341	92	25	7	2	0.6	57	30	12	23		0	0	592	17	32	26	8.5	.950	1B-57, OF-18
1882			84	.289	.422	360	104	13	10	5	1.4	90	26	22	34		0	0	557	25	45	27	7.5	.928	1B-43, OF-41
1883	PHI	AA	94	.302	**.504**	421	**127**	31	6	14	3.3	110		26			0	0	985	23	39	31	11.1	.963	1B-93, OF-3, P-1
1884			104	**.326**	**.545**	448	**146**	22	**23**	10	2.2	124		26			0	0	1061	32	45	46	10.9	.960	1B-104
1885			112	.315	.488	486	153	27	9	13	2.7	130		39			0	0	927	36	44	49	9.0	.956	1B-82, OF-30
1886			123	.294	.440	489	144	28	11	7	1.4	115		64			0	0	798	25	56	30	7.1	.936	OF-63, 1B-62, P-1
1887			124	.286	.421	497	142	31	12	4	0.8	125		56		74	0	0	613	35	36	22	5.5	.947	OF-80, 1B-46
1888			130	.287	.460	530	152	25	**20**	9	1.7	127	65	62		87	0	0	329	16	14	10	2.8	.961	OF-118, 1B-13
1889			137	.308	**.527**	556	171	37	14	19	3.4	**152**	119	77	68	63	0	0	287	38	37	9	2.6	.898	OF-137, 1B-1
1890	BOS	P	118	.297	.468	481	143	25	12	11	2.3	142	83	81	38	**97**	0	0	189	24	19	4	2.0	.918	OF-134, 1B-1
1891	BOS	N	134	.279	.498	544	152	31	**20**	16	2.9	118	95	78	**69**	57	0	0	233	22	25	4	2.1	.911	OF-135, 1B-1
1892	2 teams		BOS	N	(38G –	.164)		BAL	N	(74G –	.272)														
"	total		112	.235	.359	429	101	15	13	4	0.9	79	67	54	51	40	0	0	285	14	27	7	2.9	.917	OF-102, 1B-10
1893	2 teams		BAL	N	(8G –	.154)		BKN	N	(48G –	.251)														
"	total		56	.239	.353	201	48	8	6	1	0.5	47	34	52	14	23	1	0	133	4	16	0	2.7	.895	OF-55
14 yrs.			1486	.288	.460	6138	1769	339	177	121	2.0	1492	547	661	343	441	1	0	7503	329	470	286	5.6	.943	OF-962, 1B-550, P-4

Ray Stoviak

STOVIAK, RAYMOND THOMAS
B. June 6, 1915, Scottdale, Pa.

BL TL 6'1" 195 lbs.

Year	Team		Games	BA	SA	AB	H	2B	3B	HR	HR%	R	RBI	BB	SO	SB	AB	H	PO	A	E	DP	TC/G	FA	G by Pos
1938	PHI	N	10	.000	.000	10	0	0	0	0	0.0	1	0	0	3	0	3	0	1	1	0	0	0.2	1.000	OF-4

Joe Strain

STRAIN, JOSEPH ALLAN, JR.
B. Apr. 30, 1954, Denver, Colo.

BR TR 5'10" 169 lbs.

Year	Team		Games	BA	SA	AB	H	2B	3B	HR	HR%	R	RBI	BB	SO	SB	AB	H	PO	A	E	DP	TC/G	FA	G by Pos
1979	SF	N	67	.241	.292	257	62	8	1	1	0.4	27	12	13	21	8	0	0	147	189	6	32	5.1	.982	2B-67, 3B-1
1980			77	.286	.317	189	54	6	0	0	0.0	26	16	10	10	1	30	8	88	113	4	16	2.7	.980	2B-42, 3B-6, SS-1
1981	CHI	N	25	.189	.203	74	14	1	0	0	0.0	7	1	5	7	0	3	2	38	81	3	10	4.9	.975	2B-20
3 yrs.			169	.250	.288	520	130	15	1	1	0.2	60	29	28	38	9	33	10	273	383	13	58	4.0	.981	2B-129, 3B-7, SS-1

Paul Strand

STRAND, PAUL EDWARD
B. Dec. 19, 1893, Carbonado, Wash.   D. July 2, 1974, Salt Lake City, Utah

BR TL 6'½" 190 lbs.

Year	Team		Games	BA	SA	AB	H	2B	3B	HR	HR%	R	RBI	BB	SO	SB	AB	H	PO	A	E	DP	TC/G	FA	G by Pos
1913	BOS	N	7	.167	.167	6	1	0	0	0	0.0	0	0	0	0	0	1	0	1	6	1	0	1.1	.875	P-7
1914			16	.105	.211	19	2	2	0	0	0.0	2	3	1	5	0	1	0	0	13	3	1	1.0	.813	P-16
1915			45	.091	.091	22	2	0	0	0	0.0	3	2	0	4	0	9	2	4	3	1	0	0.2	.875	P-6, OF-5
1924	PHI	A	47	.228	.329	167	38	9	4	0	0.0	15	13	8	9	3	3	0	80	3	1	0	1.8	.988	OF-44
4 yrs.			115	.201	.290	214	43	11	4	0	0.0	20	18	9	18	3	13	2	85	25	6	1	1.0	.948	OF-49, P-29

Johnny Strands

STRANDS, JOHN LAWRENCE
B. Dec. 5, 1885, Chicago, Ill.   D. Jan. 19, 1957, Forest Park, Ill.

BR TR 5'10½" 165 lbs.

Year	Team		Games	BA	SA	AB	H	2B	3B	HR	HR%	R	RBI	BB	SO	SB	AB	H	PO	A	E	DP	TC/G	FA	G by Pos
1915	NWK	F	35	.187	.293	75	14	3	1	1	1.3	7	11	6		1	12	2	26	29	4	3	1.7	.932	3B-12, 2B-9, OF-2

Sammy Strang

STRANG, SAMUEL NICKLIN (The Dixie Thrush)
Born Samuel Strang Nicklin.
B. Dec. 16, 1876, Chattanooga, Tenn.   D. Mar. 13, 1932, Chattanooga, Tenn.

BB TR 5'8" 160 lbs.

Year	Team		Games	BA	SA	AB	H	2B	3B	HR	HR%	R	RBI	BB	SO	SB	AB	H	PO	A	E	DP	TC/G	FA	G by Pos
1896	LOU	N	14	.261	.261	46	12	0	0	0	0.0	6	7	6		4	0	0	19	30	12	5	4.4	.803	SS-14
1900	CHI	N	27	.284	.314	102	29	3	0	0	0.0	15	9	8		1	0	0	30	62	16	5	4.0	.852	3B-16, SS-9, 2B-2
1901	NY	N	135	.282	.341	493	139	14	6	1	0.2	55	34	59		40	0	0	189	304	60	27	4.1	.892	3B-91, 2B-37, OF-5, SS-4
1902	2 teams		CHI	A	(137G –	.295)		CHI	N	(3G –	.364)														
"	total		140	.296	.364	547	162	18	5	3	0.5	109	46	76		39	0	0	175	338	63	23	4.1	.891	3B-139, 2B-2
1903	BKN	N	135	.272	.333	508	138	21	5	0	0.0	101	46	75		46	0	0	166	251	38	13	3.4	.916	3B-124, OF-8, 2B-3
1904			77	.192	.244	271	52	11	0	1	0.4	28	9	45		16	0	0	114	185	39	15	4.4	.885	2B-63, 3B-12, SS-1
1905	NY	N	111	.259	.347	294	76	4	4	3	1.0	51	29	58		23	14	**8**	123	144	25	11	2.6	.914	2B-47, OF-38, SS-9, 3B-1, 1B-1
1906			113	.319	.435	313	100	6	4	4	1.3	50	49	54		21	9	1	188	194	25	14	3.6	.939	2B-57, OF-39, SS-4, 3B-3, 1B-1
1907			123	.252	.382	306	77	20	4	4	1.3	56	30	60		21	19	4	174	61	12	8	2.0	.951	OF-70, 2B-13, 3B-7, 1B-5, SS-1
1908			28	.094	.094	53	5	0	0	0	0.0	8	2	23		5	4	2	29	47	12	5	3.1	.864	2B-14, OF-5, SS-3
10 yrs.			903	.269	.343	2933	790	112	28	16	0.5	479	253	464	6	216	46	15	1207	1616	302	126	3.5	.903	3B-393, 2B-238, OF-165, SS-45, 1B-7

WORLD SERIES

Year	Team		Games	BA	SA	AB	H	2B	3B	HR	HR%	R	RBI	BB	SO	SB	AB	H	PO	A	E	DP	TC/G	FA	G by Pos
1905	NY	N	1	.000	.000	1	0	0	0	0	0.0	0	0	0	1	0	1	0	0	0	0	0	0.0	–	

Alan Strange

STRANGE, ALAN COCHRANE (Inky)
B. Nov. 7, 1909, Philadelphia, Pa.

BR TR 5'9" 162 lbs.

Year	Team		Games	BA	SA	AB	H	2B	3B	HR	HR%	R	RBI	BB	SO	SB	AB	H	PO	A	E	DP	TC/G	FA	G by Pos
1934	STL	A	127	.233	.288	430	100	17	2	1	0.2	39	45	48	28	3	2	0	260	392	31	84	5.4	.955	SS-125

Year	Team	Games	BA	SA	AB	H	2B	3B	HR	HR%	R	RBI	BB	SO	SB	Pinch Hit AB	Pinch Hit H	PO	A	E	DP	TC/G	FA	G by Pos

Alan Strange *continued*

Year	Team	Games	BA	SA	AB	H	2B	3B	HR	HR%	R	RBI	BB	SO	SB	PH AB	PH H	PO	A	E	DP	TC/G	FA	G by Pos
1935	2 teams	STL A (49G – .231)			WAS A (20G – .185)																			
"	total	69	.219	.279	201	44	8	2	0	0.0	11	22	21	8	0	2	0	131	184	12	39	4.7	.963	SS-65
1940	STL A	54	.186	.269	167	31	8	3	0	0.0	26	6	22	12	2	13	3	73	128	7	28	3.9	.966	SS-35, 2B-4
1941		45	.232	.268	112	26	4	0	0	0.0	14	11	15	5	1	7	1	74	80	4	17	3.5	.975	SS-32, 1B-2, 3B-1
1942		19	.270	.324	37	10	2	0	0	0.0	3	5	3	0	0	3	0	16	28	3	3	2.5	.936	3B-10, SS-3, 2B-1
5 yrs.		314	.223	.282	947	211	39	7	1	0.1	93	89	109	53	6	27	4	554	812	57	171	4.5	.960	SS-260, 3B-11, 2B-5, 1B-2

Doug Strange

STRANGE, JOSEPH DOUGLAS
B. Apr. 13, 1964, Greenville, S. C.
BB TR 6'2" 170 lbs.

Year	Team	Games	BA	SA	AB	H	2B	3B	HR	HR%	R	RBI	BB	SO	SB	PH AB	PH H	PO	A	E	DP	TC/G	FA	G by Pos
1989	DET A	64	.214	.260	196	42	4	1	1	0.5	16	14	17	36	3	3	0	53	118	19	17	3.0	.900	3B-54, SS-9, 2B-9, DH-1

Asa Stratton

STRATTON, ASA EVANS
B. Feb. 10, 1853, Grafton, Mass. D. Aug. 14, 1925, Fitchburg, Mass.

Year	Team	Games	BA	SA	AB	H	2B	3B	HR	HR%	R	RBI	BB	SO	SB	PH AB	PH H	PO	A	E	DP	TC/G	FA	G by Pos
1881	WOR N	1	.250	.250	4	1	0	0	0	0.0	0	0	0	2		0	0	0	1	2	0	3.0	.333	SS-1

Scott Stratton

STRATTON, C. SCOTT
B. Oct. 2, 1869, Campbellsburg, Ky. D. Mar. 8, 1939, Louisville, Ky.
BL TR 6' 180 lbs.

Year	Team	Games	BA	SA	AB	H	2B	3B	HR	HR%	R	RBI	BB	SO	SB	PH AB	PH H	PO	A	E	DP	TC/G	FA	G by Pos
1888	LOU AA	67	.257	.309	249	64	8	1	1	0.4	35	29	12		10	0	0	66	70	17	1	2.3	.889	OF-38, P-33
1889		62	.288	.415	229	66	7	5	4	1.7	30	34	13	36	10	0	0	198	57	21	15	4.5	.924	OF-29, P-19, 1B-17
1890		55	.323	.392	189	61	3	5	0	0.0	29		16		8	0	0	29	111	4	2	2.6	.972	P-50, OF-5
1891	2 teams	PIT N (2G – .125)			LOU AA (34G – .235)																			
"	total	36	.228	.244	123	28	2	0	0	0.0	10	8	11	16	8	0	0	88	70	11	11	4.7	.935	P-22, 1B-8, OF-6
1892	LOU N	63	.256	.347	219	56	2	9	0	0.0	22	23	17	21	9	0	0	83	94	17	8	3.1	.912	P-42, OF-17, 1B-6
1893		61	.226	.308	221	50	8	5	0	0.0	34	16	25	15	6	0	0	66	96	8	4	2.8	.953	P-38, OF-23, 1B-1
1894	2 teams	LOU N (13G – .324)			CHI N (23G – .375)																			
"	total	36	.361	.564	133	48	6	6	3	2.3	38	27	10	3	4	2	0	44	33	4	5	2.3	.951	P-22, OF-10, 1B-2
1895	CHI N	10	.292	.417	24	7	1	1	0	0.0	3	2	4	2	1	1	0	10	10	5	0	2.5	.800	P-5, OF-4
8 yrs.		390	.274	.364	1387	380	37	32	8	0.6	201	139	108	93	56	3	0	584	541	87	46	3.1	.928	P-231, OF-132, 1B-34

Joe Straub

STRAUB, JOSEPH J.
B. Jan. 19, 1858, Milwaukee, Wis. D. Feb. 13, 1929, Pueblo, Colo.
BR TR 5'10" 160 lbs.

Year	Team	Games	BA	SA	AB	H	2B	3B	HR	HR%	R	RBI	BB	SO	SB	PH AB	PH H	PO	A	E	DP	TC/G	FA	G by Pos
1880	TRO N	3	.250	.250	12	3	0	0	0	0.0	1	3	1	3		0	0	13	9	5	0	9.0	.815	C-3
1882	PHI AA	8	.188	.250	32	6	2	0	0	0.0	2		1			0	0	34	11	10	0	6.9	.818	C-7, OF-1
1883	COL AA	27	.130	.130	100	13	0	0	0	0.0	4		4			0	0	182	22	22	8	8.4	.903	C-14, 1B-12, OF-1
3 yrs.		38	.153	.167	144	22	2	0	0	0.0	7	3	6	3		0	0	229	42	37	8	8.1	.880	C-24, 1B-12, OF-2

Joe Strauss

STRAUSS, JOSEF (The Socker)
B. Mar. 17, 1844, Gecse, Hungary D. June 25, 1906, Cincinnati, Ohio
BR TR

Year	Team	Games	BA	SA	AB	H	2B	3B	HR	HR%	R	RBI	BB	SO	SB	PH AB	PH H	PO	A	E	DP	TC/G	FA	G by Pos
1884	KC U	16	.200	.250	60	12	3	0	0	0.0	4		1			0	0	31	17	14	1	3.9	.774	OF-10, C-3, 2B-2, 3B-1
1885	LOU AA	2	.167	.167	6	1	0	0	0	0.0	0		0			0	0	6	0	2	0	4.0	.750	OF-1, C-1
1886	2 teams	LOU AA (74G – .215)			BKN AA (9G – .250)																			
"	total	83	.219	.288	333	73	6	7	1	0.3	42		9			0	0	123	34	25	0	2.2	.863	OF-80, C-3, P-2
3 yrs.		101	.216	.281	399	86	9	7	1	0.3	46		10			0	0	160	51	41	1	2.5	.837	OF-91, C-7, 2B-2, P-2, 3B-1

Darryl Strawberry

STRAWBERRY, DARRYL EUGENE (The Straw Man)
B. Mar. 12, 1962, Los Angeles, Calif.
BL TL 6'6" 190 lbs.

Year	Team	Games	BA	SA	AB	H	2B	3B	HR	HR%	R	RBI	BB	SO	SB	PH AB	PH H	PO	A	E	DP	TC/G	FA	G by Pos
1983	NY N	122	.257	.512	420	108	15	7	26	6.2	63	74	47	128	19	4	2	232	8	4	0	2.0	.984	OF-117
1984		147	.251	.467	522	131	27	4	26	5.0	75	97	75	131	27	4	0	276	11	6	3	2.0	.980	OF-146
1985		111	.277	.557	393	109	15	4	29	7.4	78	79	73	96	26	2	0	211	5	2	2	2.0	.991	OF-110
1986		136	.259	.507	475	123	27	5	27	5.7	76	93	72	141	28	8	0	226	10	6	3	1.8	.975	OF-131
1987		154	.284	.583	532	151	32	5	39	7.3	108	104	97	122	36	3	1	272	6	8	3	1.9	.972	OF-151
1988		153	.269	**.545**	543	146	27	3	**39**	7.2	101	101	85	127	29	2	0	297	4	9	3	2.0	.971	OF-150
1989		134	.225	.466	476	107	26	1	29	6.1	69	77	61	105	11	6	0	272	4	8	2	2.1	.972	OF-131
7 yrs.		957	.260	.520	3361	875	169	29	215	6.4	570	625	510	850	176	29	4	1786	48	43	16	2.0	.977	OF-936

LEAGUE CHAMPIONSHIP SERIES

Year	Team	Games	BA	SA	AB	H	2B	3B	HR	HR%	R	RBI	BB	SO	SB	PH AB	PH H	PO	A	E	DP	TC/G	FA	G by Pos
1986	NY N	6	.227	.545	22	5	1	0	2	9.1	4	5	3	12	1	0	0	9	0	0	0	1.5	1.000	OF-6
1988		7	.300	.467	30	9	2	0	1	3.3	5	6	2	5	0	0	0	11	0	0	0	1.6	1.000	OF-7
2 yrs.		13	.269	.500	52	14	3	0	3	5.8	9	11	5	17	1	0	0	20	0	0	0	1.5	1.000	OF-13

WORLD SERIES

Year	Team	Games	BA	SA	AB	H	2B	3B	HR	HR%	R	RBI	BB	SO	SB	PH AB	PH H	PO	A	E	DP	TC/G	FA	G by Pos
1986	NY N	7	.208	.375	24	5	0	0	1	4.2	4	1	4	6	3	0	0	19	0	0	0	2.7	1.000	OF-7

Gabby Street

STREET, CHARLES EVARD (Old Sarge)
B. Sept. 30, 1882, Huntsville, Ala. D. Feb. 6, 1951, Joplin, Mo.
Manager 1929-33, 1938.
BR TR 5'11" 180 lbs.

Year	Team	Games	BA	SA	AB	H	2B	3B	HR	HR%	R	RBI	BB	SO	SB	PH AB	PH H	PO	A	E	DP	TC/G	FA	G by Pos
1904	CIN N	11	.121	.152	33	4	1	0	0	0.0	1		1			2	0	55	17	2	0	6.7	.973	C-11
1905	3 teams	CIN N (2G – .000)			BOS N (3G – .167)						CIN N (29G – .253)													
"	total	34	.238	.305	105	25	5	1	0	0.0	8	8	8			2	3	123	54	8	1	5.4	.957	C-30
1908	WAS A	131	.206	.279	394	81	12	7	1	0.3	31	32	40		5	3	2	578	167	21	14	5.8	.973	C-128
1909		137	.211	.246	407	86	12	1	0	0.0	25	29	26		2	0	0	714	210	18	18	6.9	.981	C-137
1910		89	.202	.237	257	52	6	0	1	0.4	13	16	23		1	3	1	417	151	13	8	6.5	.978	C-86
1911		72	.222	.264	216	48	7	1	0	0.0	16	14	14		4	1	0	362	102	13	10	6.6	.973	C-71
1912	NY A	28	.182	.216	88	16	1	1	0	0.0	4	6	7		1	0	0	141	43	8	4	6.9	.958	C-28
1931	STL N	1	.000	.000	1	0	0	0	0	0.0	0	0	0		0	0	0	1	1	0	0	2.0	1.000	C-1
8 yrs.		503	.208	.256	1501	312	44	11	2	0.1	98	105	119		17	10	3	2391	745	83	55	6.4	.974	C-492

Walt Streuli

STREULI, WALTER HERBERT
B. Sept. 26, 1935, Memphis, Tenn.
BR TR 6'2" 195 lbs.

Year	Team	Games	BA	SA	AB	H	2B	3B	HR	HR%	R	RBI	BB	SO	SB	PH AB	PH H	PO	A	E	DP	TC/G	FA	G by Pos
1954	DET A	1	–	–	0	0	0	0	0	–	0	0	1	0	0	0	0	1	0	0	0	1.0	1.000	C-1

Year	Team		Games	BA	SA	AB	H	2B	3B	HR	HR%	R	RBI	BB	SO	SB	Pinch Hit AB	H	PO	A	E	DP	TC/G	FA	G by Pos

Walt Streuli *continued*

Year	Team		Games	BA	SA	AB	H	2B	3B	HR	HR%	R	RBI	BB	SO	SB	AB	H	PO	A	E	DP	TC/G	FA	G by Pos
1955			2	.250	.500	4	1	1	0	0	0.0	1	1	0	0	0	0	0	7	0	0	0	3.5	1.000	C-2
1956			3	.250	.375	8	2	1	0	0	0.0	0	1	1	2	0	0	0	13	1	1	1	5.0	.933	C-3
3 yrs.			6	.250	.417	12	3	2	0	0	0.0	1	2	2	2	0	0	0	21	1	1	1	3.8	.957	C-6

Cub Stricker

STRICKER, JOHN A.
Born John A. Streaker.
B. June 8, 1859, Philadelphia, Pa. D. Nov. 19, 1937, Philadelphia, Pa.
Manager 1892.

BR TR 5'3" 133 lbs.

Year	Team		Games	BA	SA	AB	H	2B	3B	HR	HR%	R	RBI	BB	SO	SB	AB	H	PO	A	E	DP	TC/G	FA	G by Pos
1882	PHI	AA	72	.217	.246	272	59	6	1	0	0.0	34		15			0	0	240	252	52	29	7.6	.904	2B-72, P-2, OF-1
1883			89	.273	.306	330	90	8	0	1	0.3	67		19			0	0	260	226	95	23	6.5	.836	2B-88, C-2
1884			107	.231	.333	399	92	16	11	1	0.3	59		19			0	0	281	257	81	40	5.8	.869	2B-107, OF-1, C-1, P-1
1885			106	.234	.279	398	93	9	3	1	0.3	71		21			0	0	284	304	81	41	6.3	.879	2B-106
1887	CLE	AA	131	.264	.326	534	141	19	4	2	0.4	122		53		86	0	0	469	387	92	63	7.2	.903	2B-126, SS-6, P-3
1888			127	.233	.290	493	115	13	6	1	0.2	80	33	50		60	0	0	397	366	58	58	6.5	.929	2B-122, OF-6, P-2
1889	CLE	N	136	.251	.288	566	142	10	4	1	0.2	83	47	58	18	32	0	0	437	437	64	65	6.9	.932	2B-135, SS-1
1890	CLE	P	127	.244	.320	544	133	19	8	2	0.4	93	65	54	16	24	0	0	325	438	90	61	6.7	.894	2B-109, SS-20
1891	BOS	AA	139	.216	.261	514	111	15	4	0	0.0	96	46	63	34	54	0	0	405	418	51	78	6.3	.942	2B-139
1892	2 teams	STL N	(28G – .204)			BAL N		(75G – .264)																	
"	total		103	.248	.316	367	91	6	5	3	0.8	57	48	42	25	18	0	0	279	298	48	39	6.1	.923	2B-102, SS-1
1893	WAS	N	59	.183	.225	218	40	7	1	0	0.0	28	20	20	12	4	0	0	168	146	36	23	5.9	.897	2B-39, OF-12, SS-4, 3B-4
11 yrs.			1196	.239	.294	4635	1107	128	47	12	0.3	790	259	414	105	278	0	0	3545	3529	748	520	6.5	.904	2B-1145, SS-32, OF-20, P-8, 3B-4, C-3

George Strickland

STRICKLAND, GEORGE BEVAN (Bo)
B. Jan. 10, 1926, New Orleans, La.
Manager 1964, 1966.

BR TR 6'1" 175 lbs.

Year	Team		Games	BA	SA	AB	H	2B	3B	HR	HR%	R	RBI	BB	SO	SB	AB	H	PO	A	E	DP	TC/G	FA	G by Pos
1950	PIT	N	23	.111	.111	27	3	0	0	0	0.0	0	2	3	8	0	1	1	22	24	1	7	2.0	.979	SS-19, 3B-1
1951			138	.216	.333	454	98	12	7	9	2.0	59	47	65	83	4	0	0	255	426	37	97	5.2	.948	SS-125, 2B-13
1952	2 teams	PIT N	(76G – .177)			CLE A		(31G – .216)																	
"	total		107	.188	.288	320	60	10	2	6	1.9	25	30	35	60	4	1	0	212	313	25	74	5.1	.955	SS-58, 2B-46, 3B-1, 1B-1
1953	CLE	A	123	.284	.379	419	119	17	4	5	1.2	43	47	51	52	0	1	0	238	400	17	103	5.3	.974	SS-122, 1B-1
1954			112	.213	.313	361	77	12	3	6	1.7	42	37	55	62	2	0	0	193	321	21	61	4.8	.961	SS-112
1955			130	.209	.273	388	81	9	5	2	0.5	34	34	49	60	1	0	0	221	360	14	84	4.6	.976	SS-128
1956			85	.211	.292	171	36	1	2	3	1.8	22	17	22	27	0	2	0	118	145	5	34	3.2	.981	SS-28, 2B-28, 3B-26
1957			89	.234	.308	201	47	8	2	1	0.5	21	19	26	29	0	2	0	146	164	6	38	3.6	.981	2B-48, SS-23, 3B-19
1959			132	.238	.302	441	105	15	2	3	0.7	55	48	52	64	1	1	0	153	281	18	54	3.4	.960	3B-80, SS-50, 2B-4
1960			32	.167	.238	42	7	0	0	1	2.4	4	3	4	8	0	3	0	11	31	1	6	1.3	.977	SS-14, 3B-12, 2B-2
10 yrs.			971	.224	.311	2824	633	84	27	36	1.3	305	284	362	453	12	11	1	1569	2465	145	558	4.3	.965	SS-679, 2B-141, 3B-139, 1B-2

WORLD SERIES

Year	Team		Games	BA	SA	AB	H	2B	3B	HR	HR%	R	RBI	BB	SO	SB	AB	H	PO	A	E	DP	TC/G	FA	G by Pos
1954	CLE	A	3	.000	.000	9	0	0	0	0	0.0	0	0	0	2	0	0	0	6	8	1	1	5.0	.933	SS-3

George Strief

STRIEF, GEORGE ANDREW
B. Oct. 16, 1856, Cincinnati, Ohio D. Apr. 1, 1946, Cleveland, Ohio

BR TR 5'7" 172 lbs.

Year	Team		Games	BA	SA	AB	H	2B	3B	HR	HR%	R	RBI	BB	SO	SB	AB	H	PO	A	E	DP	TC/G	FA	G by Pos
1879	CLE	N	71	.174	.208	264	46	7	1	0	0.0	24	15	10	23		0	0	141	51	26	4	3.1	.881	OF-55, 2B-16
1882	PIT	AA	79	.195	.286	297	58	9	6	2	0.7	45		13			0	0	241	208	41	29	6.2	.916	2B-78, SS-1
1883	STL	AA	82	.225	.265	302	68	9	0	1	0.3	22		12			0	0	220	217	47	28	5.9	.903	2B-67, OF-15
1884	4 teams	STL AA	(48G – .201)			KC U		(15G – .107)			PIT U	(15G – .208)		CLE N	(8G – .241)										
"	total		86	.189	.273	322	61	17	2	2	0.6	35		20	5		0	0	174	104	36	14	3.7	.885	OF-49, 2B-34, 3B-2, 1B-1
1885	PHI	AA	44	.274	.377	175	48	8	5	0	0.0	19		9			0	0	62	82	19	10	3.7	.883	3B-19, SS-10, OF-8, 2B-7
5 yrs.			362	.207	.275	1360	281	50	14	5	0.4	145	15	64	28		0	0	838	662	169	85	4.6	.899	2B-202, OF-127, 3B-21, SS-11, 1B-1

John Strike

STRIKE, JOHN
B. 1865, Philadelphia, Pa. Deceased.

Year	Team		Games	BA	SA	AB	H	2B	3B	HR	HR%	R	RBI	BB	SO	SB	AB	H	PO	A	E	DP	TC/G	FA	G by Pos
1882	LOU	AA	32	.164	.236	110	18	6	1	0	0.0	17		9			0	0	110	45	22	6	5.5	.876	C-21, OF-6, 2B-6, SS-1, 1B-1
1886	PHI	N	2	.000	.000	7	0	0	0	0	0.0	0		0	4		0	0	1	0	0	0	0.5	1.000	P-2, OF-1
2 yrs.			34	.154	.222	117	18	6	1	0	0.0	17	0	9	4		0	0	111	45	22	6	5.2	.876	C-21, OF-7, 2B-6, P-2, SS-1, 1B-1

Lou Stringer

STRINGER, LOUIS BERNARD
B. May 13, 1917, Grand Rapids, Mich.

BR TR 5'11" 173 lbs.

Year	Team		Games	BA	SA	AB	H	2B	3B	HR	HR%	R	RBI	BB	SO	SB	AB	H	PO	A	E	DP	TC/G	FA	G by Pos
1941	CHI	N	145	.246	.352	512	126	31	4	5	1.0	59	53	59	86	3	0	0	359	462	38	85	5.9	.956	2B-137, SS-7
1942			121	.236	.352	406	96	15	5	9	2.2	45	41	31	55	3	1	3	268	343	29	59	5.3	.955	2B-113, 3B-1
1946			80	.244	.311	209	51	3	1	3	1.4	26	19	26	34	0	5	0	135	152	13	17	3.8	.957	2B-62, SS-1, 3B-1
1948	BOS	A	4	.091	.364	11	1	0	0	1	9.1	1	1	0	3	0	1	0	5	13	1	5	4.8	.947	2B-2
1949			35	.268	.439	41	11	4	0	1	2.4	10	6	5	10	0	9	1	24	20	1	12	1.3	.978	2B-9
1950			24	.294	.353	17	5	1	0	0	0.0	7	2	0	4	1	9	2	4	7	2	2	0.5	.846	3B-3, SS-1, 2B-1
6 yrs.			409	.242	.348	1196	290	49	10	19	1.6	148	122	121	192	7	32	6	796	997	84	180	4.6	.955	2B-324, SS-9, 3B-5

Joe Stripp

STRIPP, JOSEPH VALENTINE (Jersey Joe)
B. Feb. 3, 1903, Harrison, N. J. D. June 10, 1989, Orlando, Fla.

BR TR 5'11½" 175 lbs.

Year	Team		Games	BA	SA	AB	H	2B	3B	HR	HR%	R	RBI	BB	SO	SB	AB	H	PO	A	E	DP	TC/G	FA	G by Pos
1928	CIN	N	42	.288	.403	139	40	7	3	1	0.7	18	17	8	8	0	2	1	42	34	7	2	2.0	.916	OF-21, 3B-17, SS-1
1929			64	.214	.299	187	40	3	2	3	1.6	20	24	15	2	2	7	4	49	120	7	4	2.8	.960	3B-55, 2B-2
1930			130	.306	.431	464	142	37	6	3	0.6	74	64	51	37	15	6	0	774	133	7	83	7.0	.992	1B-75, 3B-48
1931	BKN	N	105	.324	.415	426	138	26	2	3	0.7	71	42	21	31	5	1	1	183	197	14	37	3.8	.964	3B-96, 1B-9
1932	BKN	N	138	.303	.438	534	162	36	6	6	1.1	94	64	36	30	14	0	0	485	237	19	61	5.4	.974	1B-81, 3B-43
1933			141	.277	.346	537	149	20	7	1	0.2	69	51	26	23	5	1	0	170	264	15	17	3.2	.967	3B-140
1934			104	.315	.404	384	121	19	6	1	0.3	50	40	22	20	2	1	0	157	152	16	25	3.1	.951	3B-96, 1B-7, SS-1
1935			109	.306	.391	373	114	13	5	3	0.8	44	43	22	15	2	4	2	180	169	10	24	3.3	.972	3B-88, 1B-15, OF-1

Year	Team	Games	BA	SA	AB	H	2B	3B	HR	HR%	R	RBI	BB	SO	SB	Pinch Hit AB	Pinch Hit H	PO	A	E	DP	TC/G	FA	G by Pos

Joe Stripp *continued*

Year	Team	Games	BA	SA	AB	H	2B	3B	HR	HR%	R	RBI	BB	SO	SB	PH AB	PH H	PO	A	E	DP	TC/G	FA	G by Pos
1936		110	.317	.399	439	139	31	1	1	0.2	51	60	22	12	2	3	1	132	174	10	13	2.9	.968	3B-106
1937		90	.243	.300	300	73	10	2	1	0.3	37	26	20	18	1	9	3	208	102	9	13	3.5	.972	3B-66, 1B-14, SS-3
1938 2 teams	STL N (54G – .286)				BOS N	(59G – .275)																		
" total		113	.280	.327	428	120	17	0	1	0.2	43	37	28	17	2	4	2	114	187	9	21	2.7	.971	3B-109
11 yrs.		1146	.294	.384	4211	1238	219	43	24	0.6	575	464	280	226	50	38	13	2494	1769	123	300	3.8	.972	3B-914, 1B-163, OF-22, SS-5, 2B-2

Allie Strobel

STROBEL, ALBERT IRVING
B. June 11, 1884, Boston, Mass. D. Feb. 10, 1955, Hollywood, Calif.   BR TR 6'   160 lbs.

Year	Team	Games	BA	SA	AB	H	2B	3B	HR	HR%	R	RBI	BB	SO	SB	PH AB	PH H	PO	A	E	DP	TC/G	FA	G by Pos
1905	BOS N	5	.105	.105	19	2	0	0	1	0.0	1	2	0			0	0	5	7	0	1	2.4	1.000	3B-4, OF-1
1906		100	.202	.262	317	64	10	3	1	0.3	28	24	29			2	1	0	193	283	30	33	5.1	.941	2B-93, SS-6, OF-1
2 yrs.		105	.196	.253	336	66	10	3	1	0.3	29	26	29			2	1	0	198	290	30	34	4.9	.942	2B-93, SS-6, 3B-4, OF-2

Jim Stroner

STRONER, JAMES M.
B. Sept. 26, 1892, Chicago, Ill. D. Nov. 16, 1971, Chicago, Ill.   BR TR 5'10"   175 lbs.

Year	Team	Games	BA	SA	AB	H	2B	3B	HR	HR%	R	RBI	BB	SO	SB	PH AB	PH H	PO	A	E	DP	TC/G	FA	G by Pos
1929	PIT N	6	.375	.500	8	3	1	0	0	0.0	0	0	1	0	0	3	2	1	3	3	3	1.2	.571	3B-2

Ed Stroud

STROUD, EDWIN MARVIN (The Creeper)
B. Oct. 31, 1939, Lapine, Ala.   BL TR 5'11"   180 lbs.

Year	Team	Games	BA	SA	AB	H	2B	3B	HR	HR%	R	RBI	BB	SO	SB	PH AB	PH H	PO	A	E	DP	TC/G	FA	G by Pos
1966	CHI A	12	.167	.222	36	6	2	0	0	0.0	3	1	2	8	3	0	0	20	0	0	0	1.7	1.000	OF-11
1967 2 teams	CHI A (20G – .296)				WAS A	(87G – .201)																		
" total		107	.212	.281	231	49	5	4	1	0.4	42	13	26	34	15	6	0	131	3	2	1	1.3	.985	OF-91
1968	WAS A	105	.239	.376	306	73	10	10	4	1.3	41	23	20	50	9	22	2	139	2	3	1	1.4	.979	OF-84
1969		123	.252	.393	206	52	5	6	4	1.9	35	29	30	33	12	44	14	109	1	2	0	0.9	.982	OF-85
1970		129	.266	.349	433	115	11	5	5	1.2	69	32	40	79	29	19	6	271	8	2	3	2.2	.993	OF-118
1971	CHI A	53	.177	.248	141	25	4	3	0	0.0	19	2	11	20	4	14	2	51	0	0	0	1.0	1.000	OF-44
6 yrs.		529	.237	.336	1353	320	37	28	14	1.0	209	100	129	224	72	105	24	721	14	9	5	1.4	.988	OF-433

Steve Stroughter

STROUGHTER, STEPHEN LEWIS
B. Mar. 15, 1952, Visalia, Calif.   BL TR 6'2"   190 lbs.

Year	Team	Games	BA	SA	AB	H	2B	3B	HR	HR%	R	RBI	BB	SO	SB	PH AB	PH H	PO	A	E	DP	TC/G	FA	G by Pos
1982	SEA A	26	.170	.255	47	8	1	0	1	2.1	4	3	9	0	0	10	1	7	1	0	0	0.3	1.000	DH-9, OF-3

Amos Strunk

STRUNK, AMOS AARON
B. Nov. 22, 1889, Philadelphia, Pa. D. July 22, 1979, Llanerch, Pa.   BL TL 5'11½"   175 lbs.

Year	Team	Games	BA	SA	AB	H	2B	3B	HR	HR%	R	RBI	BB	SO	SB	PH AB	PH H	PO	A	E	DP	TC/G	FA	G by Pos
1908	PHI A	12	.235	.265	34	8	1	0	0	0.0	4	0	4			0	1	1	27	1	3	1	2.6	.903	OF-11
1909		11	.114	.114	35	4	0	0	0	0.0	1	2	1			2	0	0	10	2	0	0	1.1	1.000	OF-9
1910		16	.333	.375	48	16	0	1	0	0.0	9	2	3			4	0	0	33	1	0	0	2.1	1.000	OF-14
1911		74	.256	.321	215	55	7	2	1	0.5	42	21	35			13	7	2	145	11	6	5	2.2	.963	OF-62, 1B-2
1912		120	.289	.400	412	119	13	12	3	0.7	58	63	47			29	3	2	278	16	3	3	2.5	.990	OF-118
1913		93	.305	.425	292	89	11	12	0	0.0	30	46	29	23	14	11	4	168	9	7	3	2.0	.962	OF-80
1914		122	.275	.342	404	111	15	3	2	0.5	58	45	57	38	25	2	0	280	14	4	3	2.4	.987	OF-120
1915		132	.297	.421	485	144	28	16	1	0.2	76	45	56	45	17	2	0	413	32	9	21	3.4	.980	OF-111, 1B-19
1916		150	.316	.421	544	172	30	9	3	0.6	71	49	66	59	21	2	0	368	24	8	14	2.7	.980	OF-143, 1B-7
1917		148	.281	.361	540	152	26	7	1	0.2	83	45	68	37	16	3	0	346	15	5	5	2.6	.986	OF-146
1918	BOS A	114	.257	.344	413	106	18	9	0	0.0	50	35	36	13	20	1	0	230	13	3	4	2.2	.988	OF-113
1919 2 teams	BOS A (48G – .272)				PHI A	(60G – .211)																		
" total		108	.241	.323	378	91	17	7	0	0.0	42	30	36	28	6	5	2	216	11	6	0	2.2	.974	OF-100
1920 2 teams	PHI A (58G – .297)				CHI A	(51G – .230)																		
" total		109	.265	.335	385	102	16	4	1	0.3	55	34	49	24	1	7	1	193	5	3	0	1.8	.985	OF-103
1921	CHI A	121	.332	.451	401	133	19	10	3	0.7	68	69	38	27	7	8	3	214	10	7	2	1.9	.970	OF-111
1922		92	.289	.350	311	90	11	4	0	0.0	36	33	33	28	9	10	3	246	13	3	6	2.8	.989	OF-75, 1B-9
1923		54	.315	.315	54	17	0	0	0	0.0	7	8	8	5	1	**39**	**12**	18	0	1	0	0.4	.947	OF-4, 1B-3
1924 2 teams	CHI A (1G – .000)				PHI A	(30G – .143)																		
" total		31	.140	.140	43	6	0	0	0	0.0	5	1	7	4	0	20	3	7	0	0	0	0.2	1.000	OF-8
17 yrs.		1507	.283	.373	4994	1415	212	96	15	0.3	695	528	573	331	185	118	33	3192	175	68	67	2.3	.980	OF-1328, 1B-40

WORLD SERIES

Year	Team	Games	BA	SA	AB	H	2B	3B	HR	HR%	R	RBI	BB	SO	SB	PH AB	PH H	PO	A	E	DP	TC/G	FA	G by Pos
1910	PHI A	4	.278	.444	18	5	1	1	0	0.0	2	2	2	5	0	0	0	10	1	1	0	3.0	.917	OF-4
1911		1	–	–	0	0	0	0	0	–	0	0	0	0	0	0	0	0	0	0	0	0.0	–	
1913		5	.118	.118	17	2	0	0	0	0.0	3	0	2	2	0	0	0	13	0	0	0	2.6	1.000	OF-5
1914		2	.286	.286	7	2	0	0	0	0.0	0	0	0	0	0	0	0	4	0	0	0	2.0	1.000	OF-2
1918	BOS A	6	.174	.304	23	4	1	1	0	0.0	1	0	0	7	0	0	0	8	2	0	0	1.7	1.000	OF-6
5 yrs.		18	.200	.292	65	13	2	2	0	0.0	6	2	4	14	0	0	0	35	3	1	0	2.2	.974	OF-17

Al Struve

STRUVE, ALBERT
B. St. Louis, Mo. Deceased.

Year	Team	Games	BA	SA	AB	H	2B	3B	HR	HR%	R	RBI	BB	SO	SB	PH AB	PH H	PO	A	E	DP	TC/G	FA	G by Pos
1884	STL AA	2	.286	.286	7	2	0	0	0	0.0	2		0			0	0	6	6	0	0	6.0	1.000	OF-1, C-1

Bill Stuart

STUART, WILLIAM ALEXANDER (Chauncey)
B. Aug. 28, 1873, Boalsburg, Pa. D. Oct. 14, 1928, Fort Worth, Tex.   5'11"   170 lbs.

Year	Team	Games	BA	SA	AB	H	2B	3B	HR	HR%	R	RBI	BB	SO	SB	PH AB	PH H	PO	A	E	DP	TC/G	FA	G by Pos
1895	PIT N	19	.247	.286	77	19	3	0	0	0.0	5	10	2	6	2	0	0	39	61	10	5	5.8	.909	SS-17, 2B-2
1899	NY N	1	.000	.000	3	0	0	0	0	0.0	0	0	0	0	0	0	0	2	2	0	0	4.0	1.000	2B-1
2 yrs.		20	.238	.275	80	19	3	0	0	0.0	5	10	2	6	2	0	0	41	63	10	5	5.7	.912	SS-17, 2B-3

Dick Stuart

STUART, RICHARD LEE (Dr. Strangeglove)
B. Nov. 7, 1932, San Francisco, Calif.   BR TR 6'4"   212 lbs.

Year	Team	Games	BA	SA	AB	H	2B	3B	HR	HR%	R	RBI	BB	SO	SB	PH AB	PH H	PO	A	E	DP	TC/G	FA	G by Pos
1958	PIT N	67	.268	.543	254	68	12	5	16	6.3	38	48	11	75	0	3	0	529	49	16	69	8.9	.973	1B-64
1959		118	.297	.549	397	118	15	2	27	6.8	64	78	42	86	1	16	5	831	81	22	87	7.9	.976	1B-105, OF-1
1960		122	.260	.479	438	114	17	5	23	5.3	48	83	39	107	0	13	4	920	77	14	90	8.3	.986	1B-108
1961		138	.301	.581	532	160	28	8	35	6.6	83	117	34	**121**	0	3	1	1152	99	21	141	9.2	.983	1B-132, OF-1
1962		114	.228	.398	394	90	11	4	16	4.1	52	64	32	94	0	13	3	868	78	17	98	8.4	.982	1B-101

Year	Team		Games	BA	SA	AB	H	2B	3B	HR	HR%	R	RBI	BB	SO	SB	Pinch Hit AB	H	PO	A	E	DP	TC/G	FA	G by Pos

Dick Stuart *continued*

Year	Team		Games	BA	SA	AB	H	2B	3B	HR	HR%	R	RBI	BB	SO	SB	AB	H	PO	A	E	DP	TC/G	FA	G by Pos
1963	BOS	A	157	.261	.521	612	160	25	4	42	6.9	81	118	44	144	0	2	1	1207	134	29	100	8.7	.979	1B-155
1964			156	.279	.491	603	168	27	1	33	5.5	73	114	37	130	0	1	0	1159	104	24	105	8.3	.981	1B-155
1965	PHI	N	149	.234	.429	538	126	19	1	28	5.2	53	95	39	136	1	8	1	1119	98	17	100	8.3	.986	1B-143, 3B-1
1966	2 teams		69	NY N (31G – .218)		LA N (38G – .264)																			
"	total		69	.242	.365	178	43	1	0	7	3.9	11	22	20	43	0	16	3	216	13	6	20	3.4	.974	1B-48
1969	CAL	A	22	.157	.255	51	8	2	0	1	2.0	3	4	3	21	0	9	1	102	4	1	11	4.9	.991	1B-13
10 yrs.			1112	.264	.489	3997	1055	157	30	228	5.7	506	743	301	957	2	84	19	8103	737	167	821	8.1	.981	1B-1024, OF-2, 3B-1

WORLD SERIES

Year	Team		Games	BA	SA	AB	H	2B	3B	HR	HR%	R	RBI	BB	SO	SB	AB	H	PO	A	E	DP	TC/G	FA	G by Pos
1960	PIT	N	6	.150	.150	20	3	0	0	0	0.0	0	0	0	3	0	0	0	45	0	0	6	7.5	1.000	1B-6
1966	LA	N	2	.000	.000	2	0	0	0	0	0.0	0	0	0	2	0	2	0	0	0	0	0	0.0	–	
2 yrs.			8	.136	.136	22	3	0	0	0	0.0	0	0	0	4	0	2	0	45	0	0	6	5.6	1.000	1B-6

Luke Stuart

STUART, LUTHER LANE
B. May 23, 1892, Alamance County, N. C. D. June 15, 1947, Winston-Salem, N. C.
BR TR 5'8" 165 lbs.

Year	Team		Games	BA	SA	AB	H	2B	3B	HR	HR%	R	RBI	BB	SO	SB	AB	H	PO	A	E	DP	TC/G	FA	G by Pos
1921	STL	A	3	.333	1.333	3	1	0	0	1	33.3	2	2	0	1	0	0	0	1	1	0	0	0.7	1.000	2B-3

Franklin Stubbs

STUBBS, FRANKLIN LEE
B. Oct. 21, 1960, Richland, N. C.
BL TL 6'2" 205 lbs.

Year	Team		Games	BA	SA	AB	H	2B	3B	HR	HR%	R	RBI	BB	SO	SB	AB	H	PO	A	E	DP	TC/G	FA	G by Pos
1984	LA	N	87	.194	.341	217	42	2	3	8	3.7	22	17	24	63	2	22	4	417	37	4	31	5.3	.991	1B-51, OF-20
1985			10	.222	.222	9	2	0	0	0	0.0	2	0	3	0	7	2	11	0	0	1	1.1	1.000	1B-4	
1986			132	.226	.421	420	95	11	1	23	5.5	55	58	37	107	7	12	0	244	14	7	3	2.0	.974	OF-124, 1B-13
1987			129	.233	.415	386	90	16	3	16	4.1	48	52	31	85	8	11	3	830	79	5	65	7.1	.995	1B-111, OF-18
1988			115	.223	.376	242	54	13	0	8	3.3	30	34	23	61	11	26	8	530	57	13	41	5.2	.978	1B-84, OF-13
1989			69	.291	.466	103	30	6	0	4	3.9	11	15	16	27	3	26	6	70	5	3	5	1.1	.962	OF-28, 1B-7
6 yrs.			542	.227	.401	1377	313	48	7	59	4.3	166	178	131	346	31	104	23	2102	192	32	146	4.3	.986	1B-270, OF-203

LEAGUE CHAMPIONSHIP SERIES

Year	Team		Games	BA	SA	AB	H	2B	3B	HR	HR%	R	RBI	BB	SO	SB	AB	H	PO	A	E	DP	TC/G	FA	G by Pos
1988	LA	N	4	.250	.250	8	2	0	0	0	0.0	0	0	0	4	0	2	0	16	2	0	2	4.5	1.000	1B-3

WORLD SERIES

Year	Team		Games	BA	SA	AB	H	2B	3B	HR	HR%	R	RBI	BB	SO	SB	AB	H	PO	A	E	DP	TC/G	FA	G by Pos
1988	LA	N	5	.294	.412	17	5	2	0	0	0.0	3	2	1	3	0	0	0	34	0	0	3	6.8	1.000	1B-5

Larry Stubing

STUBING, LAWRENCE GEORGE (Moose)
B. Mar. 31, 1938, Bronx, N. Y.
Manager 1988.
BL TL 6'3" 220 lbs.

Year	Team		Games	BA	SA	AB	H	2B	3B	HR	HR%	R	RBI	BB	SO	SB	AB	H	PO	A	E	DP	TC/G	FA	G by Pos
1967	CAL	A	5	.000	.000	5	0	0	0	0	0.0	0	0	0	4	0	5	0	0	0	0	0	0.0	–	

Bill Stumpf

STUMPF, WILLIAM FREDERICK
B. Mar. 21, 1892, Baltimore, Md. D. Feb. 14, 1966, Crownsville, Md.
BR TR 6'½" 175 lbs.

Year	Team		Games	BA	SA	AB	H	2B	3B	HR	HR%	R	RBI	BB	SO	SB	AB	H	PO	A	E	DP	TC/G	FA	G by Pos
1912	NY	A	40	.240	.240	129	31	0	0	0	0.0	8	10	6		5	0	0	74	93	21	10	4.7	.888	SS-26, 2B-8, 3B-4, OF-1, 1B-1
1913			12	.207	.241	29	6	1	0	0	0.0	5	1	3	3	0	1	0	14	23	8	2	3.8	.822	SS-6, 2B-4, OF-1
2 yrs.			52	.234	.241	158	37	1	0	0	0.0	13	11	9	3	5	1	0	88	116	29	12	4.5	.876	SS-32, 2B-12, 3B-4, OF-2, 1B-1

George Stumpf

STUMPF, GEORGE FREDERICK
B. Dec. 15, 1910, New Orleans, La.
BL TL 5'8" 155 lbs.

Year	Team		Games	BA	SA	AB	H	2B	3B	HR	HR%	R	RBI	BB	SO	SB	AB	H	PO	A	E	DP	TC/G	FA	G by Pos
1931	BOS	A	7	.250	.357	28	7	1	1	0	0.0	2	4	1	2	0	0	0	14	0	0	0	2.0	1.000	OF-7
1932			79	.201	.254	169	34	2	1	1	0.6	18	18	18	21	1	25	4	78	2	4	0	1.1	.952	OF-51
1933			22	.341	.415	41	14	3	0	0	0.0	8	5	2	4	5	1	22	0	0	0	1.0	1.000	OF-15	
1936	CHI	A	10	.273	.318	22	6	1	0	0	0.0	3	5	2	1	0	5	3	9	1	0	0	1.0	1.000	OF-4
4 yrs.			118	.235	.296	260	61	7	3	1	0.4	31	32	25	26	5	35	8	123	3	4	0	1.1	.969	OF-77

Guy Sturdy

STURDY, GUY R.
B. Aug. 7, 1899, Sherman, Tex. D. May 4, 1965, Marshall, Tex.
BL TL 6'½" 180 lbs.

Year	Team		Games	BA	SA	AB	H	2B	3B	HR	HR%	R	RBI	BB	SO	SB	AB	H	PO	A	E	DP	TC/G	FA	G by Pos
1927	STL	A	5	.429	.476	21	9	1	0	0	0.0	5	5	1	0	1	0	0	35	2	1	2	7.6	.974	1B-5
1928			54	.222	.311	45	10	1	0	1	2.2	3	8	8	4	1	44	10	2	0	0	0	0.0	1.000	1B-1
2 yrs.			59	.288	.364	66	19	2	0	1	1.5	8	13	9	4	2	44	10	37	2	1	2	0.7	.975	1B-6

Bobby Sturgeon

STURGEON, ROBERT HOWARD
B. Aug. 6, 1919, Clinton, Ind.
BR TR 6' 175 lbs.

Year	Team		Games	BA	SA	AB	H	2B	3B	HR	HR%	R	RBI	BB	SO	SB	AB	H	PO	A	E	DP	TC/G	FA	G by Pos
1940	CHI	N	7	.190	.238	21	4	1	0	0	0.0	2	1	0	1	0	0	0	19	20	7	5	6.6	.848	SS-7
1941			129	.245	.293	433	106	15	3	0	0.0	45	25	9	30	5	0	0	215	366	27	68	4.7	.956	SS-126, 3B-1, 2B-1
1942			63	.247	.302	162	40	7	1	0	0.0	8	7	4	13	2	2	0	113	163	4	33	4.4	.986	2B-32, SS-29, 3B-2
1946			100	.296	.361	294	87	12	2	1	0.3	26	21	10	18	0	0	0	160	209	22	44	3.9	.944	SS-72, 2B-21
1947			87	.254	.341	232	59	10	5	0	0.0	16	21	7	12	0	10	3	137	202	6	43	4.0	.983	SS-45, 2B-30, 3B-5
1948	BOS	N	34	.218	.282	78	17	3	1	0	0.0	10	4	4	5	0	4	2	43	46	7	9	2.8	.927	2B-18, SS-4, 3B-4
6 yrs.			420	.257	.318	1220	313	48	12	1	0.1	106	80	34	79	7	23	8	687	1006	73	202	4.2	.959	SS-283, 2B-102, 3B-12

Dean Sturgis

STURGIS, DEAN DONNELL
B. Dec. 1, 1892, Beloit, Wis. D. June 4, 1950, Uniontown, Pa.
BR TR 6'1" 180 lbs.

Year	Team		Games	BA	SA	AB	H	2B	3B	HR	HR%	R	RBI	BB	SO	SB	AB	H	PO	A	E	DP	TC/G	FA	G by Pos
1914	PHI	A	4	.250	.250	4	1	0	0	0	0.0	0	1	1	2	0	2	0	4	1	0	0	1.3	1.000	C-1

Johnny Sturm

STURM, JOHN PETER JOSEPH
B. Jan. 23, 1916, St. Louis, Mo.
BL TL 6'1" 185 lbs.

Year	Team		Games	BA	SA	AB	H	2B	3B	HR	HR%	R	RBI	BB	SO	SB	AB	H	PO	A	E	DP	TC/G	FA	G by Pos
1941	NY	A	124	.239	.300	524	125	17	3	3	0.6	58	36	37	50	3	0	0	1099	85	12	117	9.6	.990	1B-124

WORLD SERIES

Year	Team		Games	BA	SA	AB	H	2B	3B	HR	HR%	R	RBI	BB	SO	SB	AB	H	PO	A	E	DP	TC/G	FA	G by Pos
1941	NY	A	5	.286	.286	21	6	0	0	0	0.0	0	2	0	2	1	0	0	48	1	0	5	9.8	1.000	1B-5

Year	Team		Games	BA	SA	AB	H	2B	3B	HR	HR%	R	RBI	BB	SO	SB	Pinch Hit AB	H	PO	A	E	DP	TC/G	FA	G by Pos

George Stutz — STUTZ, GEORGE (Kid)
B. Feb. 12, 1893, Philadelphia, Pa. D. Dec. 29, 1930, Philadelphia, Pa. — BR TR 5'5" 150 lbs.

| 1926 | PHI | N | 6 | .000 | .000 | 9 | 0 | 0 | 0 | 0 | 0.0 | 0 | 0 | 0 | 2 | 0 | 1 | 0 | 8 | 7 | 1 | 2 | 2.7 | .938 | SS-5 |

Lena Styles — STYLES, WILLIAM GRAVES
B. Nov. 27, 1899, Gurley, Ala. D. Mar. 14, 1956, Gurley, Ala. — BR TR 6'1" 185 lbs.

1919	PHI	A	8	.273	.318	22	6	1	0	0	0.0	0	5	1	6	0	0	0	31	7	1	1	4.9	.974	C-8
1920			24	.260	.360	50	13	3	1	0	0.0	5	5	6	7	1	1	1	94	15	3	5	4.7	.973	C-9, 1B-7
1921			4	.200	.200	5	1	0	0	0	0.0	0	0	0	2	0	2	1	1	1	4	0	1.5	.333	C-2
1930	CIN	N	7	.250	.417	12	3	0	1	0	0.0	2	1	1	2	0	1	0	13	3	2	0	2.6	.889	C-5, 1B-1
1931			34	.241	.276	87	21	3	0	0	0.0	7	5	8	7	0	3	0	68	7	4	0	2.3	.949	C-31
5 yrs.			77	.250	.313	176	44	7	2	0	0.0	14	16	16	24	1	13	2	207	33	14	6	3.3	.945	C-55, 1B-8

Neil Stynes — STYNES, CORNELIUS WILLIAM
B. Dec. 10, 1868, Arlington, Mass. D. Mar. 26, 1944, Somerville, Mass. — BR TR 6' 165 lbs.

| 1890 | CLE | P | 2 | .000 | .000 | 8 | 0 | 0 | 0 | 0 | 0.0 | 0 | 0 | 0 | 0 | 0 | 0 | 0 | 11 | 0 | 3 | 0 | 7.0 | .786 | C-2 |

Ken Suarez — SUAREZ, KENNETH RAYMOND
B. Apr. 12, 1943, Tampa, Fla. — BR TR 5'9" 175 lbs.

1966	KC	A	35	.145	.174	69	10	1	0	0	0.0	5	2	15	26	2	1	0	145	20	8	7	4.9	.954	C-34
1967			39	.238	.413	63	15	5	0	2	3.2	7	9	16	21	1	2	0	170	20	4	2	5.0	.979	C-36
1968	CLE	A	17	.100	.100	10	1	0	0	0	0.0	1	0	1	3	0	3	0	22	2	0	0	1.4	1.000	C-12, OF-1, 3B-1, 2B-1
1969			36	.294	.388	85	25	5	0	1	1.2	7	9	15	12	1	0	0	191	20	2	3	5.9	.991	C-36
1971			50	.203	.285	123	25	7	0	1	0.8	10	9	18	15	0	2	0	268	14	2	3	5.7	.993	C-48
1972	TEX	A	25	.152	.182	33	5	1	0	0	0.0	2	4	1	4	0	11	1	53	2	2	0	2.3	.965	C-17
1973			93	.248	.299	278	69	11	0	1	0.4	25	27	33	16	1	4	1	501	44	6	4	5.9	.989	C-90
7 yrs.			295	.227	.297	661	150	29	1	5	0.8	57	60	99	97	5	23	2	1350	122	24	19	5.1	.984	C-273, OF-1, 3B-1, 2B-1

Luis Suarez — SUAREZ, LUIS ABELARDO
B. Aug. 24, 1916, Alto Songo, Cuba — BR TR 5'11" 170 lbs.

| 1944 | WAS | A | 1 | .000 | .000 | 2 | 0 | 0 | 0 | 0 | 0.0 | 0 | 0 | 0 | 0 | 0 | 0 | 0 | 0 | 2 | 0 | 0 | 2.0 | 1.000 | 3B-1 |

Tony Suck — SUCK, CHARLES ANTHONY
Born Charles Anthony Zuck.
B. June 11, 1858, Chicago, Ill. D. Jan. 29, 1895, Chicago, Ill. — 5'9" 164 lbs.

1883	BUF	N	2	.000	.000	7	0	0	0	0	0.0	1		1	4		0	0	4	0	3	0	3.5	.571	OF-1, C-1
1884	3 teams		CHI U (43G – .144)				PIT U (10G – .171)				BAL U (3G – .300)														
"	total		56	.157	.167	198	31	2	0	0	0.0	20		13			0	0	242	90	50	4	6.8	.869	C-31, SS-15, OF-12, 3B-1
2 yrs.			58	.151	.161	205	31	2	0	0	0.0	21		14	4		0	0	246	90	53	4	6.7	.864	C-32, SS-15, OF-13, 3B-1

Bill Sudakis — SUDAKIS, WILLIAM PAUL (Suds)
B. Mar. 27, 1946, Joliet, Ill. — BB TR 6'1" 190 lbs.

1968	LA	N	24	.276	.471	87	24	4	2	3	3.4	11	12	15	14	1	0	0	25	57	4	3	3.6	.953	3B-24
1969			132	.234	.383	462	108	17	5	14	3.0	50	53	40	94	3	12	1	98	272	21	26	3.0	.946	3B-121
1970			94	.264	.461	269	71	11	0	14	5.2	37	44	35	46	4	21	5	194	100	14	9	3.3	.955	C-38, 3B-37, OF-3, 1B-1
1971	NY	N	41	.193	.337	83	16	3	0	3	3.6	10	7	12	22	0	21	4	90	16	0	1	2.6	1.000	C-19, 3B-3, OF-1, 1B-1
1972	NY	N	18	.143	.204	49	7	0	0	1	2.0	3	7	6	14	0	6	1	88	8	2	3	5.4	.980	1B-7, C-5
1973	TEX	A	82	.255	.494	235	60	11	0	15	6.4	32	43	23	53	0	14	5	216	62	5	21	3.5	.982	3B-29, 1B-24, C-9, DH-8, OF-2
1974	NY	A	89	.232	.344	259	60	8	0	7	2.7	26	39	25	48	0	15	2	280	26	4	31	3.5	.987	DH-39, 1B-33, 3B-3, C-1
1975	2 teams		CAL A (30G – .121)				CLE A (20G – .196)																			
"	total		50	.154	.231	104	16	2	0	2	1.9	8	9	16	22	1	19	1	121	7	1	10	2.6	.992	1B-14, DH-13, C-11
8 yrs.			530	.234	.393	1548	362	56	7	59	3.8	177	214	172	313	9	108	19	1112	548	51	104	3.2	.970	3B-217, C-83, 1B-80, DH-60, OF-6

Pete Suder — SUDER, PETER (Pecky)
B. Apr. 16, 1916, Aliquippa, Pa. — BR TR 6' 175 lbs.

1941	PHI	A	139	.245	.339	531	130	20	4	4	0.8	45	52	19	47	1	0	0	180	279	21	28	3.5	.956	3B-136, SS-3
1942			128	.256	.340	476	122	20	4	4	0.8	46	54	24	39	4	2	0	242	344	22	59	4.8	.964	SS-69, 3B-34, 2B-31
1943			131	.221	.291	475	105	14	5	3	0.6	30	41	14	40	1	1	0	272	323	17	68	4.7	.972	2B-95, 3B-32, SS-5
1946			128	.281	.352	455	128	20	3	2	0.4	38	50	18	37	1	11	2	247	284	22	56	4.3	.960	SS-67, 3B-33, 2B-12, 1B-3, OF-2
1947			145	.241	.337	528	127	28	4	5	0.9	45	60	35	44	0	1	0	310	418	12	96	5.1	.984	2B-140, SS-3, 3B-2
1948			148	.241	.345	519	125	23	5	7	1.3	64	60	60	60	1	0	0	342	461	10	114	5.5	.988	2B-148
1949			118	.267	.416	445	119	24	6	10	2.2	44	75	23	35	0	0	0	240	331	17	94	5.0	.971	2B-89, 3B-36, SS-2
1950			77	.246	.383	248	61	10	0	8	3.2	34	35	23	31	2	4	1	167	181	9	55	4.6	.975	2B-47, 3B-11, SS-10, 1B-4
1951			123	.245	.298	440	108	18	1	1	0.2	46	42	30	42	5	0	0	321	355	11	107	5.6	.984	2B-103, SS-18, 3B-3
1952			74	.241	.303	228	55	7	2	1	0.4	22	20	16	17	1	0	0	136	179	8	40	4.4	.975	2B-43, SS-17, 3B-16
1953			115	.286	.350	454	130	11	3	4	0.9	44	35	17	35	3	0	0	189	290	11	44	4.3	.978	3B-72, 2B-38, SS-7
1954			89	.200	.263	205	41	11	1	0	0.0	18	16	7	16	1	13	1	100	134	9	25	3.5	.963	2B-35, 3B-20, SS-2
1955	KC	A	26	.210	.284	81	17	4	1	0	0.0	3	1	2	13	0	2	0	51	44	1	17	3.7	.990	2B-24
13 yrs.			1421	.249	.337	5085	1268	210	44	49	1.0	469	541	288	456	19	34	6	2797	3623	170	803	4.6	.974	2B-805, 3B-395, SS-203, 1B-7, OF-2

Willie Sudhoff — SUDHOFF, JOHN WILLIAM (Wee Willie)
B. Sept. 17, 1874, St. Louis, Mo. D. May 25, 1917, St. Louis, Mo. — BR TR 5'7" 165 lbs.

1897	STL	N	11	.238	.262	42	10	1	0	0	0.0	0	3	1	0	0	0	0	8	29	3	2	3.6	.925	P-11
1898			41	.158	.192	120	19	2	1	0	0.0	5	4	5	0	0	0	0	15	114	12	5	3.4	.915	P-41
1899	2 teams		CLE N (11G – .065)				STL N (26G – .206)																			
"	total		37	.162	.212	99	16	1	2	0	0.0	11	8	12	0	0	0	0	11	99	11	3	3.3	.909	P-37
1900	STL	N	35	.189	.217	106	20	1	0	0	0.0	15	6	11	0	8	1	0	26	57	12	1	2.7	.874	P-16, OF-12, 3B-7
1901			38	.176	.278	108	19	2	3	1	0.9	11	17	10	0	0	0	0	14	84	5	4	2.7	.951	P-38

Year	Team		Games	BA	SA	AB	H	2B	3B	HR	HR%	R	RBI	BB	SO	SB	Pinch Hit AB	Pinch Hit H	PO	A	E	DP	TC/G	FA	G by Pos

Willie Sudhoff *continued*

Year	Team		Games	BA	SA	AB	H	2B	3B	HR	HR%	R	RBI	BB	SO	SB	AB	H	PO	A	E	DP	TC/G	FA	G by Pos
1902	STL	A	31	.169	.195	77	13	2	0	0	0.0	6	5	4		3	0	0	8	84	10	4	3.3	.902	P-30, OF-1
1903			41	.182	.227	110	20	1	2	0	0.0	11	6	3		1	2	0	15	104	5	0	3.0	.960	P-38
1904			30	.165	.200	85	14	3	0	0	0.0	5	7	6		0	0	0	13	104	3	4	4.0	.975	P-27, OF-3
1905			32	.186	.244	86	16	3	1	0	0.0	6	3	7		1	0	0	20	96	4	0	3.8	.967	P-32
1906	WAS	A	9	.429	.429	7	3	0	0	0	0.0	0	0	0		0	0	0	1	11	1	0	1.4	.923	P-9
10 yrs.			305	.179	.225	840	150	16	10	1	0.1	77	59	59		13	3	0	131	782	66	23	3.2	.933	P-279, OF-16, 3B-7

Joe Sugden

SUGDEN, JOSEPH
B. July 31, 1870, Philadelphia, Pa. D. June 28, 1959, Philadelphia, Pa.

BB TR 5'10" 180 lbs.

Year	Team		Games	BA	SA	AB	H	2B	3B	HR	HR%	R	RBI	BB	SO	SB	AB	H	PO	A	E	DP	TC/G	FA	G by Pos
1893	PIT	N	27	.261	.370	92	24	4	3	0	0.0	20	12	10	11	1	0	0	81	27	5	3	4.2	.956	C-27
1894			39	.331	.496	139	46	13	2	2	1.4	23	23	14	2	3	0	0	120	43	21	5	4.7	.886	C-31, 3B-4, SS-3, OF-1
1895			49	.310	.368	155	48	4	1	1	0.6	28	17	16	12	4	0	0	176	57	25	4	5.3	.903	C-49
1896			80	.296	.359	301	89	5	7	0	0.0	42	36	19	9	5	0	0	337	73	21	16	5.4	.951	C-70, 1B-7, OF-4
1897			84	.222	.271	288	64	6	4	0	0.0	31	38	18		9	0	0	342	83	27	8	5.4	.940	C-81, 1B-3
1898	STL	N	89	.253	.284	289	73	7	1	0	0.0	29	34	23		5	7	2	272	91	21	13	4.3	.945	C-60, OF-15, 1B-8
1899	CLE	N	76	.276	.304	250	69	5	1	0	0.0	19	14	11		2	2	1	213	111	23	14	4.6	.934	C-66, OF-4, 1B-3, 3B-1
1901	CHI	A	48	.275	.333	153	42	7	1	0	0.0	21	19	13		4	2	0	200	49	7	4	5.3	.973	C-42, 1B-5
1902	STL	A	69	.246	.300	203	50	7	2	0	0.0	25	15	20		2	3	1	210	69	13	9	4.2	.955	C-61, 1B-4, P-1
1903			79	.216	.232	241	52	4	0	0	0.0	18	22	25		4	5	0	391	84	8	10	6.1	.983	C-66, 1B-8
1904			105	.262	.297	347	91	6	3	0	0.0	25	30	28		6	1	0	645	102	9	22	7.2	.988	C-79, 1B-28
1905			85	.173	.188	266	46	4	0	0	0.0	21	23	23		3	4	0	496	114	10	7	7.3	.984	C-71, 1B-9
1912	DET	A	1	.250	.250	4	1	0	0	0	0.0	1	0	0		0	0	0	13	3	1	0	17.0	.941	1B-1
13 yrs.			831	.255	.303	2728	695	72	25	3	0.1	303	283	220	34	48	24	4	3496	906	191	115	5.5	.958	C-703, 1B-76, OF-24, 3B-5, SS-3, P-1

Gus Suhr

SUHR, AUGUST RICHARD
B. Jan. 3, 1906, San Francisco, Calif.

BL TR 6' 180 lbs.

Year	Team		Games	BA	SA	AB	H	2B	3B	HR	HR%	R	RBI	BB	SO	SB	AB	H	PO	A	E	DP	TC/G	FA	G by Pos
1930	PIT	N	151	.286	.480	542	155	26	14	17	3.1	93	107	80	56	11	0	0	1445	79	13	142	10.2	.992	1B-151
1931			87	.211	.333	270	57	13	4	4	1.5	26	32	38	25	4	8	4	684	39	5	72	8.4	.993	1B-76
1932			154	.263	.398	581	153	31	16	5	0.9	78	81	63	39	7	0	0	1388	84	18	111	9.7	.988	1B-154
1933			154	.267	.413	566	151	31	11	10	1.8	72	75	72	52	2	0	0	1451	90	14	151	10.1	.991	1B-154
1934			151	.283	.459	573	162	36	13	13	2.3	67	103	66	52	4	0	0	1326	75	9	108	9.3	.994	1B-151
1935			153	.272	.437	529	144	33	12	10	1.9	68	81	70	54	6	2	1	1316	73	15	83	9.2	.989	1B-149, OF-2
1936			156	.312	.467	583	182	33	12	11	1.9	111	118	95	34	8	1	0	1432	93	10	100	9.8	.993	1B-156
1937			151	.278	.402	575	160	28	14	5	0.9	69	97	83	42	2	0	0	1452	91	11	108	10.3	.993	1B-151
1938			145	.294	.430	530	156	35	14	3	0.6	82	64	87	37	4	0	0	1512	81	12	150	11.1	.993	1B-145
1939	2 teams			PIT	N	(63G –	.289)		PHI	N	(60G –	.318)													
"	total		123	.303	.408	402	122	22	4	4	1.0	44	55	59	37	5	8	1	1041	60	7	92	9.0	.994	1B-112
1940	PHI	N	10	.160	.400	25	4	0	0	2	8.0	4	5	5	5	0	3	1	57	1	2	5	6.0	.967	1B-7
11 yrs.			1435	.279	.428	5176	1446	288	114	84	1.6	714	818	718	433	53	21	7	13104	766	116	1122	9.7	.992	1B-1406, OF-2

Clyde Sukeforth

SUKEFORTH, CLYDE LeROY (Sukey)
B. Nov. 30, 1901, Washington, Me.
Manager 1947.

BL TR 5'10" 155 lbs.

Year	Team		Games	BA	SA	AB	H	2B	3B	HR	HR%	R	RBI	BB	SO	SB	AB	H	PO	A	E	DP	TC/G	FA	G by Pos
1926	CIN	N	1	.000	.000	1	0	0	0	0	0.0	0	0	0	1	0	1	0	0	0	0	0	0.0	–	
1927			38	.190	.224	58	11	2	0	0	0.0	12	2	7	2	2	3	1	52	12	2	1	1.7	.970	C-24
1928			33	.132	.208	53	7	2	1	0	0.0	5	3	3	5	0	4	0	48	8	2	1	1.8	.966	C-26
1929			84	.354	.451	237	84	16	2	1	0.4	31	33	17	6	8	3	2	171	40	4	4	2.6	.981	C-76
1930			94	.284	.345	296	84	9	3	1	0.3	30	19	17	12	1	7	1	234	46	7	8	3.1	.976	C-82
1931			112	.256	.322	351	90	15	0	0	0.0	22	25	38	13	1	0	4	300	59	13	9	3.3	.965	C-106
1932	BKN	N	59	.234	.342	111	26	4	4	0	0.0	14	12	6	10	1	22	3	95	13	1	2	1.8	.991	C-36
1933			20	.056	.056	36	2	0	0	0	0.0	1	0	2	1	0	0	0	50	7	1	2	2.9	.983	C-18
1934			27	.163	.186	43	7	1	0	0	0.0	5	1	1	6	0	5	0	38	4	0	2	1.6	1.000	C-18
1945			18	.294	.314	51	15	1	0	0	0.0	2	1	4	1	0	5	0	53	1	3	0	3.2	.947	C-13
10 yrs.			486	.264	.331	1237	326	50	14	2	0.2	122	96	95	57	12	54	8	1041	190	33	29	2.6	.974	C-399

Guy Sularz

SULARZ, GUY PATRICK
B. Nov. 7, 1955, Minneapolis, Minn.

BR TR 5'11" 165 lbs.

Year	Team		Games	BA	SA	AB	H	2B	3B	HR	HR%	R	RBI	BB	SO	SB	AB	H	PO	A	E	DP	TC/G	FA	G by Pos
1980	SF	N	25	.246	.292	65	16	1	1	0	0.0	3	3	9	6	1	0	0	50	79	3	14	5.3	.977	2B-21, 3B-5
1981			10	.200	.200	20	4	0	0	0	0.0	0	2	2	4	0	3	1	9	24	0	3	3.3	1.000	2B-6, 3B-1
1982			63	.228	.287	101	23	3	0	1	1.0	15	7	9	11	3	6	0	57	100	7	23	2.6	.957	SS-37, 3B-14, 2B-9
1983			10	.100	.100	20	2	0	0	0	0.0	3	0	3	2	0	1	0	10	20	2	3	3.2	.938	SS-6, 3B-4
4 yrs.			108	.218	.262	206	45	4	1	1	0.5	21	12	23	23	4	10	1	126	223	12	43	3.3	.967	SS-43, 2B-36, 3B-24

Ernie Sulik

SULIK, ERNEST RICHARD
B. July 7, 1910, San Francisco, Calif. D. May 31, 1963, Oakland, Calif.

BL TL 5'10" 178 lbs.

Year	Team		Games	BA	SA	AB	H	2B	3B	HR	HR%	R	RBI	BB	SO	SB	AB	H	PO	A	E	DP	TC/G	FA	G by Pos
1936	PHI	N	122	.287	.386	404	116	14	4	6	1.5	69	36	40	22	4	14	2	227	6	7	1	2.0	.971	OF-105

Andy Sullivan

SULLIVAN, ANDREW B.
B. Aug. 30, 1884, Southborough, Mass. D. Feb. 14, 1920, Framingham, Mass.

TR

Year	Team		Games	BA	SA	AB	H	2B	3B	HR	HR%	R	RBI	BB	SO	SB	AB	H	PO	A	E	DP	TC/G	FA	G by Pos
1904	BOS	N	1	.000	.000	1	0	0	0	0	0.0	0	0	1		0	0	0	2	0	0	0	2.0	1.000	SS-1

Bill Sullivan

SULLIVAN, WILLIAM F.
B. July 4, 1853, Holyoke, Mass. D. Nov. 13, 1884, Holyoke, Mass.

Year	Team		Games	BA	SA	AB	H	2B	3B	HR	HR%	R	RBI	BB	SO	SB	AB	H	PO	A	E	DP	TC/G	FA	G by Pos
1878	CHI	N	2	.167	.167	6	1	0	0	0	0.0	1	0	0		0	0	0	1	0	0	0	0.5	1.000	OF-2

Billy Sullivan

SULLIVAN, WILLIAM JOSEPH, SR.
Father of Billy Sullivan.
B. Feb. 1, 1875, Oakland, Wis. D. Jan. 28, 1965, Newberg, Ore.
Manager 1909.

BR TR 5'9" 155 lbs.

Year	Team		Games	BA	SA	AB	H	2B	3B	HR	HR%	R	RBI	BB	SO	SB	Pinch Hit AB	Pinch Hit H	PO	A	E	DP	TC/G	FA	G by Pos

Billy Sullivan *continued*

Year	Team		Games	BA	SA	AB	H	2B	3B	HR	HR%	R	RBI	BB	SO	SB	AB	H	PO	A	E	DP	TC/G	FA	G by Pos
1899	BOS	N	22	.270	.378	74	20	2	0	2	2.7	10	12	1		2	0	0	94	26	6	3	5.7	.952	C-22
1900			72	.273	.399	238	65	6	0	8	3.4	36	41	9		4	3	2	232	77	9	11	4.4	.972	C-66, SS-1, 2B-1
1901	CHI	A	98	.245	.351	367	90	15	6	4	1.1	54	56	10		12	0	0	396	104	19	13	5.3	.963	C-97, 3B-1
1902			76	.243	.323	263	64	12	3	1	0.4	36	26	6		11	2	0	254	81	11	10	4.6	.968	C-70, OF-2, 1B-2
1903			32	.189	.252	111	21	4	0	1	0.9	10	7	5		3	1	0	123	35	2	1	5.0	.988	C-31
1904			108	.229	.307	371	85	18	4	1	0.3	29	44	12		11	1	0	463	130	22	10	5.7	.964	C-107
1905			99	.201	.269	323	65	10	3	2	0.6	25	26	13		14	3	0	404	104	13	10	5.3	.975	C-93, 1B-2, 3B-1
1906			118	.214	.297	387	83	18	4	2	0.5	37	33	22		10	0	0	475	134	16	7	5.3	.974	C-118
1907			112	.174	.221	339	59	8	4	0	0.0	30	36	21		6	3	0	479	119	10	13	5.4	.984	C-108, 2B-1
1908			137	.191	.228	430	82	8	4	0	0.0	40	29	22		15	1	0	553	156	11	11	5.3	.985	C-137
1909			97	.162	.174	265	43	3	0	0	0.0	11	16	17		9	0	0	452	119	10	6	6.0	.983	C-97
1910			45	.183	.225	142	26	4	1	0	0.0	10	6	7		0	0	0	290	71	9	5	8.2	.976	C-45
1911			89	.215	.273	256	55	9	3	0	0.0	26	31	16		1	0	0	447	114	8	13	6.4	.986	C-89
1912			39	.209	.253	91	19	2	1	0	0.0	9	15	9		0	0	0	147	52	5	4	5.2	.975	C-39
1914			1	–	–	0	0	0	0	0	–	0	0	0	0	0	0	0	1	0	0	0	1.0	1.000	C-1
1916	DET	A	1	–	–	0	0	0	0	0	–	0	0	0	0	0	0	0	0	0	0	0	0.0	–	C-1
16 yrs.			1146	.212	.280	3657	777	119	33	21	0.6	363	378	170	0	98	14	2	4810	1322	151	117	5.5	.976	C-1121, 1B-4, OF-2, 3B-2, 2B-2, SS-1

WORLD SERIES

Year	Team		Games	BA	SA	AB	H	2B	3B	HR	HR%	R	RBI	BB	SO	SB	AB	H	PO	A	E	DP	TC/G	FA	G by Pos
1906	CHI	A	6	.000	.000	21	0	0	0	0	0.0	0	0	0	9	0	0	0	35	10	1	1	7.7	.978	C-6

Billy Sullivan

SULLIVAN, WILLIAM JOSEPH, JR.
Son of Billy Sullivan.
B. Oct. 23, 1910, Chicago, Ill.
BL TR 6' 170 lbs.

Year	Team		Games	BA	SA	AB	H	2B	3B	HR	HR%	R	RBI	BB	SO	SB	AB	H	PO	A	E	DP	TC/G	FA	G by Pos
1931	CHI	A	92	.275	.364	363	100	16	5	2	0.6	48	33	20	14	4	7	4	104	152	24	9	3.0	.914	3B-83, OF-2, 1B-1
1932			93	.316	.384	307	97	16	1	1	0.3	31	45	20	9	1	19	3	511	66	13	46	6.3	.978	1B-52, 3B-17, C-5
1933			54	.192	.208	125	24	0	1	0	0.0	9	13	10	5	0	22	5	232	15	8	22	4.7	.969	1B-22, C-8
1935	CIN	N	85	.266	.361	241	64	9	4	2	0.8	29	36	19	16	4	21	7	383	78	8	41	5.5	.983	1B-40, 3B-15, 2B-6
1936	CLE	A	93	.351	.508	319	112	32	6	2	0.6	39	48	16	9	5	11	5	355	52	12	13	4.5	.971	C-72, 3B-5, 1B-3, OF-1
1937			72	.286	.446	168	48	12	3	3	1.8	26	22	17	7	1	24	5	199	23	9	4	3.2	.961	C-38, 1B-5, 3B-1
1938	STL	A	111	.277	.381	375	104	16	1	7	1.9	35	49	20	10	8	8	1	484	69	5	17	5.0	.991	C-99, 1B-6
1939			118	.289	.416	332	96	17	5	5	1.5	53	50	34	18	3	33	9	251	17	12	7	2.4	.957	OF-59, C-19, 1B-4
1940	DET	A	78	.309	.450	220	68	14	4	3	1.4	36	41	31	11	2	15	5	296	43	10	5	4.5	.971	C-57, 3B-6
1941			85	.282	.393	234	66	15	1	3	1.3	29	29	35	11	0	21	6	339	33	9	7	4.5	.976	C-63
1942	BKN	N	43	.267	.337	101	27	2	1	1	1.0	11	14	12	6	1	1	0	140	13	6	2	3.7	.962	C-41
1947	PIT	N	38	.255	.309	55	14	3	0	0	0.0	8	6	3	1	1	25	5	42	4	0	1	1.2	1.000	C-12
12 yrs.			962	.289	.395	2840	820	152	32	29	1.0	347	388	240	119	30	207	55	3336	565	116	174	4.2	.971	C-414, 1B-133, 3B-127, OF-62, 2B-6

WORLD SERIES

Year	Team		Games	BA	SA	AB	H	2B	3B	HR	HR%	R	RBI	BB	SO	SB	AB	H	PO	A	E	DP	TC/G	FA	G by Pos
1940	DET	A	5	.154	.154	13	2	0	0	0	0.0	3	0	5	2	0	1	0	24	2	0	0	5.2	1.000	C-4

Chub Sullivan

SULLIVAN, JOHN FRANK
B. Jan. 12, 1856, Boston, Mass. D. Sept. 12, 1881, Boston, Mass.
BR TR 6' 164 lbs.

Year	Team		Games	BA	SA	AB	H	2B	3B	HR	HR%	R	RBI	BB	SO	SB	AB	H	PO	A	E	DP	TC/G	FA	G by Pos
1877	CIN	N	8	.250	.250	32	8	0	0	0	0.0	4	4	1	0		0	0	66	1	4	1	8.9	.944	1B-8
1878			61	.258	.291	244	63	4	2	0	0.0	29	20	2	9		0	0	680	23	18	33	11.8	.975	1B-61
1880	WOR	N	43	.259	.331	166	43	6	3	0	0.0	22	0	4	6		0	0	447	12	8	19	10.9	.983	1B-43
3 yrs.			112	.258	.303	442	114	10	5	0	0.0	55	24	7	15		0	0	1193	36	30	53	11.2	.976	1B-112

Dan Sullivan

SULLIVAN, DANIEL C. (Link)
B. May 9, 1857, Providence, R. I. D. Oct. 26, 1893, Providence, R. I.
TR 5'11" 194 lbs.

Year	Team		Games	BA	SA	AB	H	2B	3B	HR	HR%	R	RBI	BB	SO	SB	AB	H	PO	A	E	DP	TC/G	FA	G by Pos
1882	LOU	AA	67	.273	.315	286	78	8	2	0	0.0	44		9			0	0	311	115	64	4	7.3	.869	C-54, 3B-10, OF-4, SS-1
1883			37	.211	.272	147	31	5	2	0	0.0	8		3			0	0	157	35	27	2	5.9	.877	C-32, OF-2, 3B-2, SS-1
1884			63	.239	.320	247	59	8	6	0	0.0	27		9			0	0	341	61	30	2	6.9	.931	C-63, OF-1
1885	2 teams	LOU	AA (13G – .182)			STL	AA	(17G – .117)																		
"	total		30	.144	.173	104	15	3	0	0	0.0	7		8			0	0	157	38	11	3	6.9	.947	C-26, 1B-4
1886	PIT	AA	1	.000	.000	4	0	0	0	0	0.0	0		0			0	0	2	1	2	0	5.0	.600	C-1
5 yrs.			198	.232	.288	788	183	24	10	0	0.0	86		29			0	0	968	250	134	11	6.8	.901	C-176, 3B-12, OF-7, 1B-4, SS-2

Denny Sullivan

SULLIVAN, DENNIS J.
B. June 26, 1858, Boston, Mass. D. Dec. 31, 1925, Boston, Mass.
TR

Year	Team		Games	BA	SA	AB	H	2B	3B	HR	HR%	R	RBI	BB	SO	SB	AB	H	PO	A	E	DP	TC/G	FA	G by Pos
1879	PRO	N	5	.263	.368	19	5	2	0	0	0.0	5	2	1	1		0	0	1	5	8	0	2.8	.429	3B-4, OF-1
1880	BOS	N	1	.250	.250	4	1	0	0	0	0.0	1	1	0	1		0	0	6	0	1	0	7.0	.857	C-1
2 yrs.			6	.261	.348	23	6	2	0	0	0.0	6	3	1	2		0	0	7	5	9	0	3.5	.571	3B-4, OF-1, C-1

Denny Sullivan

SULLIVAN, DENNIS WILLIAM
B. Sept. 28, 1882, Hillsboro, Wis. D. June 2, 1956, Los Angeles, Calif.
BL TR

Year	Team		Games	BA	SA	AB	H	2B	3B	HR	HR%	R	RBI	BB	SO	SB	AB	H	PO	A	E	DP	TC/G	FA	G by Pos
1905	WAS	A	3	.000	.000	11	0	0	0	0	0.0	0	0	1		0	0	0	3	0	0	0	1.0	1.000	OF-3
1907	BOS	A	144	.245	.283	551	135	18	0	1	0.2	73	26	44		16	0	0	296	16	8	3	2.2	.975	OF-144
1908	2 teams	BOS	A (101G – .241)			CLE	A	(3G – .000)																		
"	total		104	.237	.295	359	85	7	7	0	0.0	33	25	14		15	4	0	195	18	4	4	2.1	.982	OF-101
1909	CLE	A	3	.500	.500	2	1	0	0	0	0.0	0	0	0		0	1	1	0	0	0	0	0.0	–	OF-2
4 yrs.			254	.239	.285	923	221	25	7	1	0.1	106	51	59		31	5	1	494	34	12	7	2.1	.978	OF-250

Eddie Sullivan

Playing record listed under Eddie Collins

Year	Team	Games	BA	SA	AB	H	2B	3B	HR	HR%	R	RBI	BB	SO	SB	Pinch Hit AB	Pinch Hit H	PO	A	E	DP	TC/G	FA	G by Pos

Haywood Sullivan

SULLIVAN, HAYWOOD COOPER
Father of Marc Sullivan.
B. Dec. 15, 1930, Donalsonville, Ga.
Manager 1965.
BR TR 6'4" 210 lbs.

Year	Team	Games	BA	SA	AB	H	2B	3B	HR	HR%	R	RBI	BB	SO	SB	PH AB	PH H	PO	A	E	DP	TC/G	FA	G by Pos
1955	BOS A	2	.000	.000	6	0	0	0	0	0.0	1	0	0	1	0	0	0	11	1	0	0	6.0	1.000	C-2
1957		1	.000	.000	1	0	0	0	0	0.0	0	0	0	1	0	1	0	2	0	0	0	1.0	1.000	C-1
1959		4	.000	.000	2	0	0	0	0	0.0	0	0	1	1	0	1	0	4	0	0	0	1.0	1.000	C-2
1960		52	.161	.242	124	20	1	0	3	2.4	9	10	16	24	0	2	0	237	13	2	5	4.8	.992	C-50
1961	KC A	117	.242	.356	331	80	16	2	6	1.8	42	40	46	45	1	12	4	494	44	10	19	4.7	.982	C-88, 1B-16, OF-5
1962		95	.248	.332	274	68	7	2	4	1.5	33	29	31	54	1	2	1	449	31	10	2	5.2	.980	C-94, 1B-1
1963		40	.212	.283	113	24	6	1	0	0.0	9	8	15	15	0	5	0	226	15	2	3	6.1	.992	C-37
7 yrs.		312	.226	.318	851	192	30	5	13	1.5	94	87	109	140	2	23	5	1423	104	24	29	5.0	.985	C-274, 1B-17, OF-5

Jack Sullivan

SULLIVAN, CARL MANCEL
B. Feb. 22, 1918, Princeton, Tex.
BR TR 5'11" 185 lbs.

Year	Team	Games	BA	SA	AB	H	2B	3B	HR	HR%	R	RBI	BB	SO	SB	PH AB	PH H	PO	A	E	DP	TC/G	FA	G by Pos
1944	DET A	1	.000	.000	1	0	0	0	0	0.0	0	0	0	0	0	0	0	1	0	0	0	1.0	1.000	2B-1

Joe Sullivan

SULLIVAN, JOSEPH DANIEL
B. Jan. 6, 1870, Charlestown, Mass.   D. Nov. 2, 1897, Charlestown, Mass.

Year	Team	Games	BA	SA	AB	H	2B	3B	HR	HR%	R	RBI	BB	SO	SB	PH AB	PH H	PO	A	E	DP	TC/G	FA	G by Pos
1893	WAS N	128	.266	.360	508	135	16	13	2	0.4	72	64	36	24	7	0	0	233	396	102	34	5.7	.860	SS-128
1894	2 teams					WAS N (17G – .250)			PHI N (75G – .352)																
"	total	92	.335	.440	364	122	13	8	3	0.8	70	68	29	12	13	1	0	207	264	60	34	5.8	.887	SS-81, 2B-8, OF-1, 3B-1
1895	PHI N	94	.338	.389	373	126	7	3	2	0.5	75	50	24	20	15	0	0	195	270	63	32	5.6	.881	SS-89, OF-6
1896	2 teams					PHI N (48G – .251)			STL N (51G – .292)																
"	total	99	.273	.350	403	110	9	5	4	1.0	70	45	27	24	14	0	0	196	28	12	2	2.4	.949	OF-90, 2B-7, SS-2, 3B-2
4 yrs.		413	.299	.382	1648	493	45	29	11	0.7	287	227	116	80	49	1	0	831	958	237	102	4.9	.883	SS-300, OF-97, 2B-15, 3B-3

John Sullivan

SULLIVAN, JOHN EUGENE
B. Feb. 16, 1873, Chicago, Ill.   D. June 5, 1924, St. Paul, Minn.
TR

Year	Team	Games	BA	SA	AB	H	2B	3B	HR	HR%	R	RBI	BB	SO	SB	PH AB	PH H	PO	A	E	DP	TC/G	FA	G by Pos
1905	DET A	12	.161	.161	31	5	0	0	0	0.0	4	4	4		0	0	0	56	21	2	0	6.6	.975	C-12
1908	PIT N	1	.000	.000	1	0	0	0	0	0.0	0	0	0		0	0	0	1	1	0	0	2.0	1.000	C-1
2 yrs.		13	.156	.156	32	5	0	0	0	0.0	4	4	4		0	0	0	57	22	2	0	6.2	.975	C-13

John Sullivan

SULLIVAN, JOHN LAWRENCE
B. Mar. 21, 1890, Williamsport, Pa.   D. Apr. 1, 1966, Milton, Pa.
BR TR 5'11" 180 lbs.

Year	Team	Games	BA	SA	AB	H	2B	3B	HR	HR%	R	RBI	BB	SO	SB	PH AB	PH H	PO	A	E	DP	TC/G	FA	G by Pos
1920	BOS N	82	.296	.396	250	74	14	4	1	0.4	36	28	29	29	3	6	3	164	11	4	6	2.2	.978	OF-66, 1B-6
1921	2 teams					BOS N (5G – .000)			CHI N (76G – .329)																
"	total	81	.322	.461	245	79	14	4	4	1.6	28	41	19	26	3	14	3	122	3	5	0	1.6	.962	OF-65
2 yrs.		163	.309	.428	495	153	28	8	5	1.0	64	69	48	55	6	20	6	286	14	9	6	1.9	.971	OF-131, 1B-6

John Sullivan

SULLIVAN, JOHN PAUL
B. Nov. 2, 1920, Chicago, Ill.
BR TR 5'10" 170 lbs.

Year	Team	Games	BA	SA	AB	H	2B	3B	HR	HR%	R	RBI	BB	SO	SB	PH AB	PH H	PO	A	E	DP	TC/G	FA	G by Pos
1942	WAS A	94	.235	.286	357	84	16	1	0	0.0	38	42	25	30	2	1	0	217	235	31	51	5.1	.936	SS-92
1943		134	.208	.250	456	95	12	2	1	0.2	49	55	57	59	6	0	0	276	445	41	89	5.7	.946	SS-133
1944		138	.251	.280	471	118	12	1	0	0.0	49	30	52	43	3	0	0	276	426	50	89	5.4	.934	SS-138
1947		49	.256	.271	133	34	0	1	0	0.0	13	5	22	14	0	1	0	85	131	8	29	4.6	.964	SS-40, 2B-1
1948		85	.208	.243	173	36	4	1	0	0.0	25	12	22	25	2	9	0	100	155	14	34	3.2	.948	SS-57, 2B-4
1949	STL A	105	.226	.284	243	55	8	3	0	0.0	29	18	38	35	5	3	0	151	187	20	42	3.4	.944	SS-71, 3B-23, 2B-6
6 yrs.		605	.230	.270	1833	422	52	9	1	0.1	203	162	216	206	18	14	0	1105	1579	164	334	4.7	.942	SS-531, 3B-23, 2B-11

John Sullivan

SULLIVAN, JOHN PETER
B. Jan. 3, 1941, Somerville, N. J.
BL TR 6' 195 lbs.

Year	Team	Games	BA	SA	AB	H	2B	3B	HR	HR%	R	RBI	BB	SO	SB	PH AB	PH H	PO	A	E	DP	TC/G	FA	G by Pos
1963	DET A	3	.000	.000	5	0	0	0	0	0.0	0	0	2	1	0	1	0	9	1	0	0	3.3	1.000	C-2
1964		2	.000	.000	3	0	0	0	0	0.0	0	0	0	1	0	1	0	2	2	0	0	2.0	1.000	C-2
1965		34	.267	.337	86	23	0	0	2	2.3	5	11	9	13	0	4	1	163	14	1	1	5.2	.994	C-29
1967	NY N	65	.218	.252	147	32	5	0	0	0.0	4	6	6	26	0	26	4	201	17	2	1	3.4	.991	C-57
1968	PHI N	12	.222	.222	18	4	0	0	0	0.0	0	1	2	4	0	7	1	26	3	1	1	2.5	.967	C-8
5 yrs.		116	.228	.270	259	59	5	0	2	0.8	9	18	19	45	0	37	6	401	37	4	4	3.8	.991	C-98

Marc Sullivan

SULLIVAN, MARC COOPER
Son of Haywood Sullivan.
B. July 25, 1958, Quincy, Mass.
BR TR 6'4" 198 lbs.

Year	Team	Games	BA	SA	AB	H	2B	3B	HR	HR%	R	RBI	BB	SO	SB	PH AB	PH H	PO	A	E	DP	TC/G	FA	G by Pos
1982	BOS A	2	.333	.333	6	2	0	0	0	0.0	0	0	0	2	0	0	0	9	2	0	1	5.5	1.000	C-2
1984		2	.500	.500	6	3	0	0	0	0.0	1	1	1	0	0	0	0	19	0	1	0	10.0	.950	C-2
1985		32	.174	.290	69	12	2	0	2	2.9	10	3	6	15	0	0	0	129	8	1	1	4.3	.993	C-32
1986		41	.193	.252	119	23	4	0	1	0.8	15	14	7	32	0	0	0	203	13	3	1	5.3	.986	C-41
1987		60	.169	.238	160	27	5	0	2	1.3	11	10	4	43	0	0	0	303	29	2	6	5.6	.994	C-60
5 yrs.		137	.186	.258	360	67	11	0	5	1.4	37	28	18	92	0	0	0	663	52	7	9	5.3	.990	C-137

Marty Sullivan

SULLIVAN, MARTIN C.
B. Oct. 20, 1862, Lowell, Mass.   D. Jan. 6, 1894, Lowell, Mass.
BR TR

Year	Team	Games	BA	SA	AB	H	2B	3B	HR	HR%	R	RBI	BB	SO	SB	PH AB	PH H	PO	A	E	DP	TC/G	FA	G by Pos
1887	CHI N	115	.284	.424	472	134	13	16	7	1.5	98	77	36	53	35	0	0	189	10	36	0	2.0	.847	OF-115, P-1
1888		75	.236	.379	314	74	12	6	7	2.2	40	39	15	32	9	0	0	114	13	10	7	1.8	.927	OF-75
1889	IND N	69	.285	.398	256	73	11	3	4	1.6	45	35	50	31	15	0	0	191	9	15	8	3.1	.930	OF-64, 1B-5
1890	BOS N	121	.285	.386	505	144	19	7	6	1.2	82	61	56	48	33	0	0	242	16	13	1	2.2	.952	OF-120, 3B-1
1891	2 teams					BOS N (17G – .224)			CLE N (1G – .250)																
"	total	18	.225	.324	71	16	1	0	2	2.8	15	8	5	4	7	0	0	24	1	2	0	1.5	.926	OF-18
5 yrs.		398	.273	.395	1618	441	56	32	26	1.6	280	220	162	168	99	0	0	760	49	76	16	2.2	.914	OF-392, 1B-5, 3B-1, P-1

Mike Sullivan

SULLIVAN, MICHAEL JOSEPH
B. June 10, 1860, Webster, Mass.   D. Mar. 21, 1929, Webster, Mass.
BR TR 5'8½" 165 lbs.

Year	Team	Games	BA	SA	AB	H	2B	3B	HR	HR%	R	RBI	BB	SO	SB	Pinch Hit AB	Pinch Hit H	PO	A	E	DP	TC/G	FA	G by Pos

Mike Sullivan *continued*

| 1888 | PHI | AA | 28 | .277 | .455 | 112 | 31 | 5 | 6 | 1 | 0.9 | 20 | 19 | 3 | | 10 | 0 | 0 | 34 | 19 | 20 | 0 | 2.6 | .726 | OF-18, 3B-10 |

Pat Sullivan

SULLIVAN, PATRICK B.
B. Dec. 22, 1862, Milwaukee, Wis. D. Mar. 29, 1886, West Roxbury, Mass. TR 5'11" 165 lbs.

| 1884 | KC | U | 31 | .193 | .254 | 114 | 22 | 2 | 1 | 1 | 0.9 | 15 | | 4 | | | 0 | 0 | 47 | 40 | 25 | 5 | 3.6 | .777 | 3B-21, OF-9, C-1, P-1 |

Russ Sullivan

SULLIVAN, RUSSELL GUY
B. Feb. 19, 1923, Fredericksburg, Va. BL TR 6' 196 lbs.

1951	DET	A	7	.192	.346	26	5	1	0	1	3.8	2	1	2	1	0	0	0	14	1	1	0	2.3	.938	OF-7
1952			15	.327	.577	52	17	2	1	3	5.8	7	5	3	5	1	1	0	17	2	4	0	1.5	.826	OF-14
1953			23	.250	.389	72	18	5	1	1	1.4	7	6	13	5	0	3	1	42	4	2	1	2.1	.958	OF-20
3 yrs.			45	.267	.447	150	40	8	2	5	3.3	16	12	18	11	1	4	1	73	7	7	1	1.9	.920	OF-41

Sleeper Sullivan

SULLIVAN, THOMAS JEFFERSON
B. St. Louis, Mo. D. Sept. 25, 1899, Camden, N. J. BR TR 175 lbs.

1881	BUF	N	35	.190	.223	121	23	4	0	0	0.0	13	15	1	21		0	0	111	33	27	1	4.9	.842	C-31, OF-5
1882	STL	AA	51	.181	.229	188	34	3	3	0	0.0	24		3			0	0	232	46	53	4	6.5	.840	C-50, P-1
1883			8	.222	.296	27	6	0	1	0	0.0	2		0			0	0	38	12	4	1	6.8	.926	C-6, OF-2
1884	STL	U	2	.111	.111	9	1	0	0	0	0.0	0		0			0	0	6	1	2	0	4.5	.778	OF-1, C-1, P-1
4 yrs.			96	.186	.229	345	64	7	4	0	0.0	39	15	4	21		0	0	387	92	86	6	5.9	.848	C-88, OF-8, P-2

Suter Sullivan

SULLIVAN, SUTER G.
B. Oct. 14, 1872, Baltimore, Md. D. Apr. 19, 1925, Baltimore, Md.

1898	STL	N	42	.222	.243	144	32	3	0	0	0.0	10	12	13		1	2	0	75	78	19	7	4.1	.890	SS-23, OF-10, 2B-6, 1B-1, P-1
1899	CLE	N	127	.245	.292	473	116	16	3	0	0.0	37	55	25		16	0	0	161	248	29	22	3.4	.934	3B-101, OF-20, SS-3, 1B-3, 2B-2
2 yrs.			169	.240	.280	617	148	19	3	0	0.0	47	67	38		17	2	0	236	326	48	29	3.6	.921	3B-101, OF-30, SS-26, 2B-8, 1B-4, P-1

Ted Sullivan

SULLIVAN, THEODORE PAUL
B. 1851, County Clare, Ireland D. July 5, 1929, Washington, D. C.
Manager 1883-84, 1888.

| 1884 | KC | U | 3 | .333 | .333 | 9 | 3 | 0 | 0 | 0 | 0.0 | 0 | | 1 | | | 0 | 0 | 1 | 3 | 4 | 0 | 2.7 | .500 | OF-2, SS-1 |

Tom Sullivan

SULLIVAN, THOMAS BRANDON
B. Dec. 19, 1906, Nome, Alaska D. Aug. 16, 1944, Seattle, Wash. BR TR 6' 190 lbs.

| 1925 | CIN | N | 1 | .000 | .000 | 1 | 0 | 0 | 0 | 0 | 0.0 | 0 | 0 | 0 | 0 | 0 | 0 | 0 | 1 | 0 | 0 | 0 | 1.0 | 1.000 | C-1 |

Homer Summa

SUMMA, HOMER WAYNE
B. Nov. 3, 1898, Gentry, Mo. D. Jan. 29, 1966, Los Angeles, Calif. BL TR 5'10½" 170 lbs.

1920	PIT	N	10	.318	.455	22	7	1	1	0	0.0	1	1	3	1	1	4	1	18	1	1	0	2.0	.950	OF-6
1922	CLE	A	12	.348	.609	46	16	3	3	1	2.2	9	6	1	1	1	0	0	14	3	0	0	1.4	1.000	OF-12
1923			137	.328	.419	525	172	27	6	3	0.6	92	69	33	20	9	1	1	216	15	11	5	1.8	.955	OF-136
1924			111	.290	.390	390	113	21	6	2	0.5	55	38	11	16	4	14	2	167	10	11	2	1.7	.941	OF-95
1925			75	.330	.384	224	74	10	1	0	0.0	28	25	13	6	3	17	2	86	4	5	0	1.3	.947	OF-54, 3B-2
1926			154	.308	.403	581	179	31	6	4	0.7	74	76	47	9	15	0	0	328	18	9	5	2.3	.975	OF-154
1927			145	.286	.402	574	164	41	7	4	0.7	72	74	32	18	6	0	0	242	12	12	3	1.8	.955	OF-145
1928			134	.284	.365	504	143	26	3	3	0.6	60	57	20	15	4	2	0	223	12	7	5	1.8	.971	OF-132
1929	PHI	A	37	.272	.321	81	22	4	0	0	0.0	12	10	2	1	1	12	2	48	1	1	0	1.4	.980	OF-24
1930			25	.278	.407	54	15	2	1	1	1.9	10	5	4	1	0	7	2	29	1	2	0	1.3	.938	OF-15
10 yrs.			840	.302	.398	3001	905	166	34	18	0.6	413	361	166	88	44	57	10	1371	77	59	20	1.8	.961	OF-773, 3B-2

WORLD SERIES

| 1929 | PHI | A | 1 | .000 | .000 | 0 | 0 | 0 | 0 | 0 | | 0 | 0 | 0 | 1 | 0 | 1 | 0 | 0 | 0 | 0 | 0 | 0.0 | — | |

Champ Summers

SUMMERS, JOHN JUNIOR II
B. June 15, 1946, Bremerton, Wash. BL TR 6'2" 205 lbs.

1974	OAK	A	20	.125	.167	24	3	1	0	0	0.0	2	3	1	5	0	7	1	6	0	0	0	0.3	1.000	OF-12, DH-2
1975	CHI	N	76	.231	.341	91	21	5	1	1	1.1	14	16	10	13	0	46	14	16	0	2	0	0.2	.889	OF-18
1976			83	.206	.294	126	26	2	0	3	2.4	11	13	13	31	1	47	12	95	5	1	10	1.2	.990	OF-26, 1B-10, C-1
1977	CIN	N	59	.171	.342	76	13	4	0	3	3.9	11	6	6	16	0	38	6	24	2	0	0	0.4	1.000	OF-16, 3B-1
1978			13	.257	.400	35	9	2	0	1	2.9	4	3	7	4	2	1	0	14	0	1	0	1.2	.933	OF-12
1979	2 teams	CIN N	(27G – .200)		DET A	(90G – .313)																			
"	total		117	.291	.556	306	89	14	2	21	6.9	57	62	53	48	7	23	5	166	10	3	5	1.5	.983	OF-82, DH-10, 1B-10
1980	DET	A	120	.297	.504	347	103	19	1	17	4.9	61	60	52	52	4	26	7	60	1	3	0	0.5	.953	DH-64, OF-47, 1B-1
1981			64	.255	.358	165	42	8	0	3	1.8	16	21	19	35	0	14	3	26	1	1	0	0.4	.964	DH-37, OF-18
1982	SF	N	70	.248	.384	125	31	5	0	4	3.2	15	19	16	17	0	31	10	46	3	4	0	0.8	.925	OF-31, 1B-3
1983			29	.136	.136	22	3	0	0	0	0.0	3	3	7	8	0	20	3	2	0	0	0	0.1	1.000	OF-1
1984	SD	N	47	.185	.296	54	10	3	0	1	1.9	5	12	4	15	0	36	7	53	1	0	8	1.1	1.000	1B-8
11 yrs.			698	.255	.425	1371	350	63	4	54	3.9	199	218	188	244	15	288	68	508	23	15	23	0.8	.973	OF-263, DH-113, 1B-32, 3B-1, C-1

LEAGUE CHAMPIONSHIP SERIES

| 1984 | SD | N | 2 | .000 | .000 | 2 | 0 | 0 | 0 | 0 | 0.0 | 0 | 0 | 0 | 0 | 0 | 0 | 0 | 0 | 0 | 0 | 0 | 0.0 | — | |

WORLD SERIES

| 1984 | SD | N | 1 | .000 | .000 | 1 | 0 | 0 | 0 | 0 | 0.0 | 0 | 0 | 0 | 1 | 0 | 0 | 0 | 0 | 0 | 0 | 0 | 0.0 | — | |

Carl Sumner

SUMNER, CARL RINGDAHL (Lefty)
B. Sept. 28, 1908, Cambridge, Mass. BL TL 5'8" 160 lbs.

Year	Team		Games	BA	SA	AB	H	2B	3B	HR	HR%	R	RBI	BB	SO	SB	Pinch Hit AB	H	PO	A	E	DP	TC/G	FA	G by Pos

Carl Sumner *continued*

| 1928 | BOS | A | 16 | .276 | .379 | 29 | 8 | 1 | 1 | 0 | 0.0 | 6 | 3 | 5 | 6 | 0 | 3 | 1 | 12 | 0 | 1 | 0 | 0.8 | .923 | OF-10 |

Art Sunday

SUNDAY, ARTHUR   BL TL 5'9" 193 lbs.
Born August Wacher.
B. Jan. 21, 1862, Springfield, Ohio   Deceased.

| 1890 | BKN | P | 24 | .265 | .349 | 83 | 22 | 5 | 1 | 0 | 0.0 | 26 | 13 | 15 | 9 | 0 | 0 | 0 | 28 | 2 | 3 | 0 | 1.4 | .909 | OF-24 |

Billy Sunday

SUNDAY, WILLIAM ASHLEY (The Evangelist)   BL TR 5'10" 160 lbs.
B. Nov. 19, 1862, Ames, Iowa   D. Nov. 6, 1935, Chicago, Ill.

1883	CHI	N	14	.241	.315	54	13	4	0	0	0.0	6		1	18		0	0	10	1	6	0	1.2	.647	OF-14
1884			43	.222	.324	176	39	4	1	4	2.3	25		4	36		0	0	45	8	27	1	1.9	.663	OF-43
1885			46	.256	.343	172	44	3	3	1	1.2	36	20	12	33		0	0	46	6	11	2	1.4	.825	OF-46
1886			28	.243	.301	103	25	2	2	0	0.0	16	6	7	26		0	0	50	3	5	0	2.1	.914	OF-28
1887			50	.291	.427	199	58	6	3	3	1.5	41	32	21	20	34	0	0	78	4	25	2	2.1	.766	OF-50
1888	PIT	N	120	.236	.275	505	119	14	3	0	0.0	69	15	12	36	71	0	0	297	27	21	5	2.9	.939	OF-120
1889			81	.240	.327	321	77	10	6	2	0.6	62	25	27	33	47	0	0	157	17	10	2	2.3	.946	OF-81
1890	2 teams						PIT	N	(86G –	.257)		PHI	N	(31G –	.261)										
"	total		117	.258	.302	477	123	12	3	1	0.2	84	39	50	27	84	0	0	250	30	31	11	2.7	.900	OF-117, P-1
8 yrs.			499	.248	.317	2007	498	55	24	12	0.6	339	137	134	229	236	0	0	933	96	136	23	2.3	.883	OF-499, P-1

Jim Sundberg

SUNDBERG, JAMES HOWARD   BR TR 6' 190 lbs.
B. May 18, 1951, Galesburg, Ill.

1974	TEX	A	132	.247	.323	368	91	13	3	3	0.8	45	36	62	61	2	1	0	722	69	8	15	6.1	.990	C-132
1975			155	.199	.256	472	94	9	0	6	1.3	45	36	51	77	3	0	0	791	101	17	11	5.9	.981	C-155
1976			140	.228	.310	448	102	24	2	3	0.7	33	34	37	61	0	1	1	719	96	7	11	5.9	.991	C-140
1977			149	.291	.389	453	132	20	3	6	1.3	61	65	53	77	2	1	1	801	103	5	12	6.1	.994	C-149
1978			149	.278	.380	518	144	23	6	6	1.2	54	58	64	70	2	1	0	769	91	5	14	5.8	.997	C-148, DH-1
1979			150	.275	.368	495	136	23	4	5	1.0	50	64	51	51	3	1	0	754	75	4	13	5.6	.995	C-150
1980			151	.273	.384	505	138	24	1	10	2.0	59	63	64	67	2	3	2	853	76	7	7	6.2	.993	C-151
1981			102	.277	.366	339	94	17	2	3	0.9	42	28	50	48	2	1	1	465	52	2	9	5.1	.996	C-98, OF-2
1982			139	.251	.383	470	118	22	5	10	2.1	37	47	49	57	2	7	0	612	69	6	15	4.9	.991	C-132, OF-1
1983			131	.201	.254	378	76	14	0	2	0.5	30	28	35	64	0	1	0	618	56	5	2	5.2	.993	C-131
1984	MIL	A	110	.261	.399	348	91	19	4	7	2.0	43	43	38	63	1	3	0	556	55	3	6	5.6	.995	C-109
1985	KC	A	115	.245	.381	367	90	12	4	10	2.7	38	35	33	67	0	5	3	572	41	5	10	5.4	.992	C-112
1986			140	.212	.322	429	91	9	1	12	2.8	41	42	57	91	1	8	2	686	46	4	11	5.3	.995	C-134
1987	CHI	N	61	.201	.302	139	28	7	0	4	2.9	9	15	19	40	0	8	1	273	34	2	2	5.1	.994	C-57
1988	2 teams						CHI	N	(24G –	.241)		TEX	A	(38G –	.286)										
"	total		62	.269	.428	145	39	5	0	6	4.1	21	22	13	32	0	9	1	229	16	0	3	4.0	1.000	C-56
1989	TEX	A	76	.197	.299	147	29	7	1	2	1.4	13	8	23	37	0	5	1	353	27	3	3	5.0	.992	C-73, DH-1
16 yrs.			1962	.248	.348	6021	1493	243	36	95	1.6	621	624	699	963	20	56	16	9773	1007	81	144	5.5	.993	C-1927, OF-3, DH-2

LEAGUE CHAMPIONSHIP SERIES

| 1985 | KC | A | 7 | .167 | .417 | 24 | 4 | 1 | 1 | 1 | 4.2 | 3 | 6 | 1 | 7 | 0 | 0 | 0 | 42 | 2 | 1 | 1 | 6.4 | .978 | C-7 |

WORLD SERIES

| 1985 | KC | A | 7 | .250 | .333 | 24 | 6 | 2 | 0 | 0 | 0.0 | 6 | 1 | 6 | 4 | 0 | 0 | 0 | 47 | 3 | 0 | 1 | 7.1 | 1.000 | C-7 |

B. J. Surhoff

SURHOFF, WILLIAM JAMES   BL TR 6'1" 185 lbs.
Brother of Rick Surhoff.
B. Aug. 4, 1964, Bronx, N. Y.

1987	MIL	A	115	.299	.423	395	118	22	3	7	1.8	50	68	36	30	11	10	3	648	56	11	12	6.2	.985	C-98, 3B-10, 1B-1
1988			139	.245	.318	493	121	21	0	5	1.0	47	38	31	49	21	9	2	550	94	8	3	4.7	.988	C-106, 3B-31, 1B-2, OF-1, SS-1
1989			126	.248	.339	436	108	17	4	5	1.1	42	55	25	29	14	5	0	530	58	10	7	4.7	.983	C-106, DH-12, 3B-6
3 yrs.			380	.262	.356	1324	347	60	7	17	1.3	139	161	92	108	46	24	5	1728	208	29	22	5.2	.985	C-310, 3B-47, DH-12, 1B-3, OF-1, SS-1

George Susce

SUSCE, GEORGE CYRIL METHODIUS (Good Kid)   BR TR 5'11½" 200 lbs.
Father of George Susce.
B. Aug. 13, 1908, Pittsburgh, Pa.   D. Feb. 25, 1986, Sarasota, Fla.

1929	PHI	N	17	.294	.647	17	5	3	0	1	5.9	5	1	1	0	0	5	0	9	0	1	0	0.6	.900	C-11
1932	DET	A	2	–	–	0	0	0	0	0	–	0	0	0	0	0	0	0	1	0	0	0	0.5	1.000	C-2
1939	PIT	N	31	.227	.333	75	17	3	1	1	1.3	8	4	12	5	0	0	0	111	14	2	2	4.1	.984	1B-31
1940	STL	A	61	.212	.248	113	24	4	0	0	0.0	6	13	9	9	1	0	0	168	21	3	3	3.1	.984	C-61
1941	CLE	A	1	–	–	0	0	0	0	0	–	0	0	0	0	0	0	0	1	0	0	0	1.0	1.000	C-1
1942			2	1.000	1.000	1	1	0	0	0	0.0	0	1	0	0	0	0	0	0	0	0	0	1.0	1.000	C-2
1943			3	.000	.000	1	0	0	0	0	0.0	0	0	0	0	0	0	0	0	2	0	0	0.7	1.000	C-3
1944			29	.230	.246	61	14	1	0	0	0.0	3	4	2	2	0	5	0	78	13	5	3	3.3	.948	C-29
8 yrs.			146	.228	.299	268	61	11	1	2	0.7	23	22	25	21	1	5	0	370	50	11	8	3.0	.974	C-109, 1B-31

Pete Susko

SUSKO, PETER JONATHAN   BL TL 5'11" 172 lbs.
B. July 2, 1904, Laura, Ohio   D. May 22, 1978, Jacksonville, Fla.

| 1934 | WAS | A | 58 | .286 | .362 | 224 | 64 | 5 | 3 | 2 | 0.9 | 25 | 25 | 18 | 10 | 3 | 0 | 0 | 608 | 40 | 8 | 58 | 11.3 | .988 | 1B-58 |

Butch Sutcliffe

SUTCLIFFE, CHARLES INIGO   BR TR 5'8½" 165 lbs.
B. July 22, 1915, Fall River, Mass.

| 1938 | BOS | N | 4 | .250 | .250 | 4 | 1 | 0 | 0 | 0 | 0.0 | 1 | 2 | 2 | 1 | 0 | 0 | 0 | 8 | 0 | 2 | 0 | 2.5 | .800 | C-3 |

Sy Sutcliffe

SUTCLIFFE, EDWARD ELMER   BL 6'2" 170 lbs.
B. Apr. 15, 1862, Wheaton, Ill.   D. Feb. 13, 1893, Wheaton, Ill.

Year	Team		Games	BA	SA	AB	H	2B	3B	HR	HR%	R	RBI	BB	SO	SB	Pinch Hit AB	H	PO	A	E	DP	TC/G	FA	G by Pos

Sy Sutcliffe *continued*

Year	Team		Games	BA	SA	AB	H	2B	3B	HR	HR%	R	RBI	BB	SO	SB	PH AB	PH H	PO	A	E	DP	TC/G	FA	G by Pos
1884	CHI	N	4	.200	.267	15	3	1	0	0	0.0	4		2	4		0	0	34	6	1	1	10.3	.976	C-4
1885	2 teams		CHI N (11G – .186)					STL N (16G – .122)																	
"	total		27	.152	.196	92	14	2	1	0	0.0	7	8	7	15		0	0	108	28	24	0	5.9	.850	C-25, OF-3
1888	DET	N	49	.257	.314	191	49	5	3	0	0.0	17	23	5	14	6	0	0	172	127	39	13	6.9	.885	SS-24, C-14, 1B-5, OF-4, 2B-2
1889	CLE	N	46	.248	.311	161	40	3	2	1	0.6	17	21	14	6	5	0	0	253	74	31	10	7.8	.913	C-37, 1B-8, OF-1
1890	CLE	P	99	.329	.422	386	127	14	8	2	0.5	62	60	33	16	10	0	0	286	126	58	11	4.7	.877	C-84, OF-15, SS-4, 3B-2
1891	WAS	AA	53	.353	.453	201	71	8	3	2	1.0	29	33	17	17	8	0	0	118	41	21	4	3.4	.883	OF-35, C-22, SS-3, 3B-1
1892	BAL	N	66	.279	.377	276	77	10	7	1	0.4	41	27	14	15	12	0	0	678	24	31	39	11.1	.958	1B-66
7 yrs.			344	.288	.371	1322	381	43	24	6	0.5	177	172	92	87	41	0	0	1649	426	205	78	6.6	.910	C-186, 1B-79, OF-58, SS-31, 3B-3, 2B-2

Gary Sutherland

SUTHERLAND, GARY LYNN
Brother of Darrell Sutherland.
B. Sept. 27, 1944, Glendale, Calif.   BR TR 6' 185 lbs.

Year	Team		Games	BA	SA	AB	H	2B	3B	HR	HR%	R	RBI	BB	SO	SB	PH AB	PH H	PO	A	E	DP	TC/G	FA	G by Pos
1966	PHI	N	3	.000	.000	3	0	0	0	0	0.0	0	0	0	0	0	0	0	1	2	0	1	1.0	1.000	SS-1
1967			103	.247	.320	231	57	12	1	1	0.4	23	19	17	22	0	22	4	110	115	15	33	2.3	.938	SS-66, OF-25
1968			67	.275	.326	138	38	7	0	0	0.0	16	15	8	15	0	31	9	48	73	3	10	1.9	.976	2B-17, SS-10, 3B-10, OF-7
1969	MON	N	141	.239	.307	544	130	26	1	3	0.6	63	35	37	31	5	1	0	328	389	21	112	5.2	.972	2B-139, SS-15, OF-1
1970			116	.206	.259	359	74	10	1	3	0.8	37	26	31	22	2	23	4	182	264	12	73	3.9	.974	2B-97, SS-15, 3B-1
1971			111	.257	.332	304	78	7	2	4	1.3	25	26	18	12	3	19	3	157	253	21	60	3.9	.951	2B-56, SS-46, OF-4, 3B-2
1972	HOU	N	5	.125	.125	8	1	0	0	0	0.0	0	1	0	0	0	4	0	1	2	0	0	0.6	1.000	3B-1, 2B-1
1973			16	.259	.352	54	14	5	0	0	0.0	8	3	3	5	0	2	1	37	31	2	11	4.4	.971	2B-14, SS-1
1974	DET	A	149	.254	.313	619	157	20	1	5	0.8	60	49	26	37	1	2	1	340	380	18	103	5.0	.976	2B-147, SS-10, 3B-4
1975			129	.258	.330	503	130	12	3	6	1.2	51	39	45	41	0	2	1	278	365	21	83	5.1	.968	2B-128
1976	2 teams		DET A (42G – .205)					MIL A (59G – .217)																	
"	total		101	.211	.272	232	49	7	2	1	0.4	19	15	15	12	0	12	2	161	204	11	52	3.7	.971	2B-87, DH-8, 1B-2
1977	SD	N	80	.243	.301	103	25	3	0	1	1.0	5	11	7	15	0	38	12	39	53	5	12	1.2	.948	2B-30, 3B-21, 1B-4
1978	STL	N	10	.167	.167	6	1	0	0	0	0.0	1	0	0	0	0	6	1	0	3	0	0	0.3	1.000	2B-1
13 yrs.			1031	.243	.308	3104	754	109	10	24	0.8	308	239	207	219	11	163	37	1682	2134	129	550	3.8	.967	2B-717, SS-164, 3B-39, OF-37, DH-8, 1B-6

Leo Sutherland

SUTHERLAND, LEONARDO
Born Leonardo Sutherland y Cantin.
B. Apr. 6, 1958, Santiago, Cuba   BL TL 5'10" 165 lbs.

Year	Team		Games	BA	SA	AB	H	2B	3B	HR	HR%	R	RBI	BB	SO	SB	PH AB	PH H	PO	A	E	DP	TC/G	FA	G by Pos
1980	CHI	A	34	.258	.292	89	23	3	0	0	0.0	9	5	1	11	4	10	4	50	0	3	0	1.6	.943	OF-23
1981			11	.167	.167	12	2	0	0	0	0.0	6	0	3	1	2	1	0	6	0	0	0	0.5	1.000	OF-7
2 yrs.			45	.248	.277	101	25	3	0	0	0.0	15	5	4	12	6	11	4	56	0	3	0	1.3	.949	OF-30

Ezra Sutton

SUTTON, EZRA BALLOU
B. Sept. 17, 1850, Palmyra, N.Y.   D. June 20, 1907, Braintree, Mass.   BR TR 5'8½" 153 lbs.

Year	Team		Games	BA	SA	AB	H	2B	3B	HR	HR%	R	RBI	BB	SO	SB	PH AB	PH H	PO	A	E	DP	TC/G	FA	G by Pos
1876	PHI	N	54	.297	.419	236	70	12	7	1	0.4	45	31	3	2	0	0	0	390	52	58	13	9.3	.884	1B-29, 2B-15, 3B-8, OF-4
1877	BOS	N	58	.292	.379	253	74	10	6	0	0.0	43	39	4	10	0	0	0	104	122	36	10	4.5	.863	SS-36, 3B-22
1878			60	.226	.301	239	54	9	3	1	0.4	31	29	2	14	0	0	0	82	121	25	9	3.8	.890	3B-59, SS-1
1879			84	.248	.310	339	84	13	4	0	0.0	54	34	2	18	0	0	0	89	210	47	18	4.1	.864	SS-51, 3B-33
1880			76	.250	.295	288	72	9	2	0	0.0	41	25	7	7	0	0	0	114	188	35	19	4.4	.896	SS-39, 3B-37
1881			83	.291	.351	333	97	12	4	0	0.0	43	31	13	9	0	0	0	114	161	39	10	3.8	.876	3B-81, SS-2
1882			81	.251	.301	319	80	8	1	2	0.6	44	38	24	25	0	0	0	104	151	42	6	3.7	.859	3B-77, SS-4
1883			94	.324	.486	414	134	28	15	3	0.7	101	73	17	12	0	0	0	123	157	42	14	3.4	.870	3B-93, OF-1, SS-1
1884			110	.346	.455	468	162	28	7	3	0.6	102		29	22	0	0		119	186	31	7	3.1	.908	3B-110
1885			110	.313	.425	457	143	23	8	4	0.9	78	47	17	25	0	0	0	157	222	53	26	3.9	.877	3B-91, SS-16, 2B-2, 1B-1
1886			116	.277	.361	499	138	21	6	3	0.6	83	48	26	21	0	0	0	181	204	56	19	3.8	.873	OF-43, SS-28, 3B-28, 2B-18
1887			77	.304	.429	326	99	14	9	3	0.9	58	46	13	6	17	0	0	178	234	58	12	6.1	.877	SS-37, OF-18, 2B-13, 3B-11
1888			28	.218	.291	110	24	3	1	1	0.9	16	16	7	3	10	0	0	33	49	15	4	3.5	.845	3B-27, SS-1
13 yrs.			1031	.288	.381	4281	1231	190	73	21	0.5	739	457	164	174	27	0	0	1788	2057	537	167	4.3	.877	3B-677, SS-216, OF-66, 2B-48, 1B-30

Dale Sveum

SVEUM, DALE CURTIS
B. Nov. 23, 1963, Richmond, Calif.   BB TR 6'2" 185 lbs.

Year	Team		Games	BA	SA	AB	H	2B	3B	HR	HR%	R	RBI	BB	SO	SB	PH AB	PH H	PO	A	E	DP	TC/G	FA	G by Pos
1986	MIL	A	91	.246	.366	317	78	13	2	7	2.2	35	35	32	63	4	2	0	92	179	30	19	3.3	.900	3B-65, SS-13, 2B-13
1987			153	.252	.454	535	135	27	3	25	4.7	86	95	40	133	2	1	1	242	396	23	89	4.3	.965	SS-142, 2B-13
1988			129	.242	.347	467	113	14	4	9	1.9	41	51	21	122	1	0	0	209	375	27	94	4.7	.956	SS-127, DH-1, 2B-1
3 yrs.			373	.247	.395	1319	326	54	9	41	3.1	162	181	93	318	7	3	1	543	950	80	202	4.2	.949	SS-282, 3B-65, 2B-27, DH-1

Harry Swacina

SWACINA, HARRY JOSEPH (Swats)
B. Aug. 22, 1881, St. Louis, Mo.   D. June 21, 1944, Birmingham, Ala.   BR TR 6'2" 190 lbs.

Year	Team		Games	BA	SA	AB	H	2B	3B	HR	HR%	R	RBI	BB	SO	SB	PH AB	PH H	PO	A	E	DP	TC/G	FA	G by Pos
1907	PIT	N	26	.200	.232	95	19	1	1	0	0.0	9	10	4			1	0	246	12	1	9	10.0	.996	1B-26
1908			53	.216	.261	176	38	6	1	0	0.0	7	13	4		4	2	1	0	501	19	9	19	10.0	.983	1B-50
1914	BAL	F	158	.280	.348	617	173	26	8	0	0.0	70	90	14		15	0	0	1616	104	26	74	11.1	.985	1B-158
1915			85	.246	.306	301	74	13	1	1	0.3	24	38	9		9	8	1	1	735	58	11	50	9.5	.986	1B-75, 2B-1
4 yrs.			322	.256	.315	1189	304	46	11	1	0.1	110	151	32		29	10	2	3098	193	47	152	10.4	.986	1B-309, 2B-1

Andy Swan

SWAN, ANDREW J.
B. May 11, 1845, Tewksbury, Mass.   D. Aug. 27, 1885, Lawrence, Mass.

Year	Team		Games	BA	SA	AB	H	2B	3B	HR	HR%	R	RBI	BB	SO	SB	PH AB	PH H	PO	A	E	DP	TC/G	FA	G by Pos
1884	2 teams		WAS AA (5G – .143)					RIC AA (3G – .500)																	
"	total		8	.258	.290	31	8	1	0	0	0.0	5			0		0	0	58	1	7	0	8.3	.894	1B-6, 3B-2

Year	Team	Games	BA	SA	AB	H	2B	3B	HR	HR%	R	RBI	BB	SO	SB	Pinch Hit AB	Pinch Hit H	PO	A	E	DP	TC/G	FA	G by Pos

Pinky Swander

SWANDER, EDWARD O.
B. July 4, 1880, Portsmouth, Ohio   D. Oct. 24, 1944, Springfield, Mass.
BL TR 5'9" 180 lbs.

Year	Team	Games	BA	SA	AB	H	2B	3B	HR	HR%	R	RBI	BB	SO	SB	PH AB	PH H	PO	A	E	DP	TC/G	FA	G by Pos
1903	STL A	14	.275	.392	51	14	2	2	0	0.0	9	6	10		0	0	0	13	2	3	0	1.3	.833	OF-14
1904		1	.000	.000	1	0	0	0	0	0.0	0		0		0	1	0	0	0	0	0	0.0	–	
2 yrs.		15	.269	.385	52	14	2	2	0	0.0	9	6	10		0	1	0	13	2	3	0	1.2	.833	OF-14

Bill Swanson

SWANSON, WILLIAM ANDREW
B. Oct. 12, 1888, New York, N. Y.   D. Oct. 14, 1954, New York, N. Y.
BB TR 5'6" 156 lbs.

| 1914 | BOS A | 11 | .200 | .300 | 20 | 4 | 2 | 0 | 0 | 0.0 | 0 | 1 | 3 | 4 | 0 | 1 | 0 | 10 | 12 | 3 | 0 | 2.3 | .880 | 2B-6, 3B-3, SS-1 |

Evar Swanson

SWANSON, ERNEST EVAR
B. Oct. 15, 1902, DeKalb, Ill.   D. July 17, 1973, Galesburg, Ill.
BR TR 5'9" 170 lbs.

1929	CIN N	145	.300	.423	574	172	35	12	4	0.7	100	43	41	47	33	2	1	317	9	10	2	2.3	.970	OF-142
1930		95	.309	.399	301	93	15	3	2	0.7	43	22	11	17	4	15	1	178	5	7	1	2.0	.963	OF-71
1932	CHI A	14	.308	.404	52	16	3	1	0	0.0	9	8	8	3	3	0	0	24	0	1	0	1.8	.960	OF-14
1933		144	.306	.384	539	165	25	7	1	0.2	102	63	93	35	19	6	2	281	7	8	0	2.1	.973	OF-139
1934		117	.298	.343	426	127	9	5	0	0.0	71	34	59	31	10	9	2	193	4	4	1	1.7	.980	OF-105
5 yrs.		515	.303	.390	1892	573	87	28	7	0.4	325	170	212	133	69	32	6	993	25	30	4	2.0	.971	OF-471

Karl Swanson

SWANSON, KARL EDWARD
B. Dec. 17, 1903, North Henderson, Ill.
BL TR 5'10" 155 lbs.

1928	CHI A	22	.141	.156	64	9	1	0	0	0.0	2	6	4	7	3	0	0	33	66	6	9	4.8	.943	2B-21
1929		2	.000	.000	1	0	0	0	0	0.0	0		0	0	0	1	0	0	0	0	0	0.0	–	
2 yrs.		24	.138	.154	65	9	1	0	0	0.0	2	6	4	7	3	1	0	33	66	6	9	4.4	.943	2B-21

Stan Swanson

SWANSON, STANLEY LAWRENCE
B. May 19, 1944, Yuba City, Calif.
BR TR 5'11" 168 lbs.

| 1971 | MON N | 49 | .245 | .330 | 106 | 26 | 3 | 0 | 2 | 1.9 | 14 | 11 | 10 | 13 | 1 | 10 | 3 | 54 | 0 | 0 | 0 | 1.1 | 1.000 | OF-38 |

Ed Swartwood

SWARTWOOD, CYRUS EDWARD
B. Jan. 12, 1859, Rockford, Ill.   D. May 15, 1924, Pittsburgh, Pa.
BL TR 198 lbs.

1881	BUF N	1	.333	.333	3	1	0	0	0	0.0	0	0		1	0		0	0	1	0	1	0	2.0	.500	OF-1
1882	PIT AA	76	.329	.498	325	107	18	11	5	1.5	86		21			0	0	133	10	32	3	2.3	.817	OF-73, 1B-4
1883		94	.356	.475	413	147	24	8	3	0.7	86		24			0	0	703	32	63	28	8.5	.921	1B-60, OF-37, C-3
1884		102	.288	.366	399	115	19	6	0	0.0	74		33			0	0	349	46	54	20	4.4	.880	OF-79, 1B-22, 3B-1, P-1
1885	BKN AA	99	.266	.331	399	106	8	9	0	0.0	80		36			0	0	179	9	26	1	2.2	.879	OF-95, SS-1, C-1
1886		122	.280	.369	471	132	13	10	3	0.6	95		70			0	0	190	33	29	4	2.1	.885	OF-122, C-1
1887		91	.253	.344	363	92	14	8	1	0.3	72		46		29	0	0	129	23	30	5	2.0	.835	OF-91
1890	TOL AA	126	.327	.444	462	151	23	11	3	0.6	106		80		53	0	0	224	23	20	2	2.1	.926	OF-126, P-1
1892	PIT N	13	.238	.262	42	10	1	0	0	0.0	8	4	13	11	1	0	0	22	6	2	2	2.3	.933	OF-13
9 yrs.		724	.299	.400	2877	861	120	63	15	0.5	607	4	324	11	83	0	0	1930	182	257	65	3.3	.892	OF-637, 1B-90, C-5, P-2, SS-1, 3B-1

Charlie Sweasy

SWEASY, CHARLES JAMES
Also known as Charles James Swasey.
B. Nov. 2, 1847, Newark, N. J.   D. Mar. 30, 1908, Newark, N. J.
Manager 1875.
BR TR 5'9" 172 lbs.

1876	CIN N	56	.204	.244	225	46	5	2	0	0.0	18	10	2	5	0	0	0	169	158	54	30	6.8	.858	2B-55, OF-1
1878	PRO N	55	.175	.189	212	37	3	0	0	0.0	23	8	7	23	0	0	0	141	183	59	20	7.0	.846	2B-55
2 yrs.		111	.190	.217	437	83	8	2	0	0.0	41	18	9	28	0	0	0	310	341	113	50	6.9	.852	2B-110, OF-1

Bill Sweeney

SWEENEY, WILLIAM JOHN
B. Mar. 6, 1886, Covington, Ky.   D. May 26, 1948, Cambridge, Mass.
BR TR 5'11" 175 lbs.

1907	2 teams	CHI	N (3G – .100)		BOS	N (58G – .262)																		
"	total	61	.254	.264	201	51	2	0			25	19	16		9	2	0	88	112	30	9	3.8	.870	3B-23, SS-18, OF-11, 2B-5, 1B-1
1908	BOS N	127	.244	.294	418	102	15	3	0	0.0	44	40	45		17	3	2	175	282	35	14	3.9	.929	3B-123, SS-2, 2B-1
1909		138	.243	.300	493	120	19	3	1	0.2	45	36	37		25	0	0	222	326	52	26	4.3	.913	3B-112, SS-26
1910		150	.267	.357	499	133	22	4	5	1.0	43	46	61	28	25	4	3	439	369	66	73	5.8	.924	SS-110, 3B-21, 1B-17
1911		137	.314	.417	523	164	33	6	3	0.6	92	63	77	26	33	1	1	372	410	46	61	6.0	.944	2B-136
1912		153	.344	.445	593	204	31	13	1	0.2	84	100	68	34	27	0	0	459	475	40	76	6.4	.959	2B-153
1913		139	.257	.315	502	129	17	6	0	0.0	65	47	66	50	18	2	1	301	391	45	42	5.3	.939	2B-137
1914	CHI N	134	.218	.276	463	101	14	5	1	0.2	45	38	53	15	18	0	0	301	426	35	40	5.7	.954	2B-134
8 yrs.		1039	.272	.344	3692	1004	153	40	11	0.3	443	389	423	153	172	12	7	2357	2791	349	341	5.5	.937	2B-566, 3B-279, SS-156, 1B-18, OF-11

Bill Sweeney

SWEENEY, WILLIAM JOSEPH
B. Dec. 29, 1904, Cleveland, Ohio   D. Apr. 18, 1957, San Diego, Calif.
BR TR 5'11" 180 lbs.

1928	DET A	89	.252	.333	309	78	15	5	0	0.0	47	19	15	28	12	8	1	677	55	5	51	8.3	.993	1B-75, OF-3
1930	BOS A	88	.309	.412	243	75	13	0	4	1.6	32	30	9	15	5	25	4	541	30	2	49	6.5	.997	1B-56, 3B-1
1931		131	.295	.373	498	147	30	3	1	0.2	48	58	20	30	5	6	4	1283	92	9	89	10.6	.993	1B-124
3 yrs.		308	.286	.370	1050	300	58	8	5	0.5	127	107	44	73	22	39	9	2501	177	16	189	8.7	.994	1B-255, OF-3, 3B-1

Charlie Sweeney

SWEENEY, CHARLES FRANCIS (Buck)
B. Apr. 15, 1890, Pittsburgh, Pa.   D. Mar. 15, 1955, Pittsburgh, Pa.

| 1914 | PHI A | 1 | .000 | .000 | 1 | 0 | 0 | 0 | 0 | 0.0 | 0 | 0 | | 1 | 0 | 0 | 0 | 1 | 0 | 0 | 0 | 1.0 | 1.000 | OF-1 |

Charlie Sweeney

SWEENEY, CHARLES J.
B. Apr. 13, 1863, San Francisco, Calif.   D. Apr. 4, 1902, San Francisco, Calif.
BR TR 5'10½" 160 lbs.

| 1882 | PRO N | 1 | .000 | .000 | 4 | 0 | 0 | 0 | 0 | 0.0 | 0 | 0 | | 0 | 0 | 0 | 0 | 0 | 1 | 1 | 0 | 2.0 | .500 | OF-1 |

Year	Team		Games	BA	SA	AB	H	2B	3B	HR	HR%	R	RBI	BB	SO	SB	Pinch Hit AB	Pinch Hit H	PO	A	E	DP	TC/G	FA	G by Pos

Charlie Sweeney *continued*

1883			22	.218	.253	87	19	3	0	0	0.0	9		2	10		0	0	29	38	10	1	3.5	.870	P-20, OF-7
1884	2 teams		86	.307	.404	339	104	23	2	2	0.6	55		21	17		0	0	92	127	15	5	2.7	.936	P-60, OF-30, 1B-2
"	total PRO N (41G – .298) STL U (45G – .316)																								
1885	STL	N	71	.206	.240	267	55	7	1	0	0.0	27	24	12	33		0	0	81	67	27	3	2.5	.846	OF-39, P-35
1886			17	.250	.281	64	16	2	0	0	0.0	4	7	3	10		0	0	9	26	5	1	2.4	.875	P-11, OF-4, SS-2
1887	CLE	AA	36	.226	.316	133	30	4	4	0	0.0	22		21		11	0	0	173	17	20	4	5.8	.905	1B-20, OF-10, P-3, SS-2, 3B-2
6 yrs.			233	.251	.317	894	224	39	7	2	0.2	117	31	59	71	11	0	0	384	276	78	14	3.2	.894	P-129, OF-91, 1B-22, SS-4, 3B-2

Dan Sweeney

SWEENEY, DANIEL J.
B. Jan. 28, 1868, Philadelphia, Pa. D. July 13, 1913, Louisville, Ky.   5'5"   160 lbs.

| 1895 | LOU | N | 22 | .267 | .356 | 90 | 24 | 5 | 0 | 1 | 1.1 | 18 | 16 | 17 | 2 | 2 | 0 | 0 | 26 | 2 | 7 | 0 | 1.6 | .800 | OF-22 |

Hank Sweeney

SWEENEY, HENRY LEON
B. Dec. 28, 1915, Franklin, Tenn. D. May 6, 1980, Columbia, Tenn.   BL TL 6'   185 lbs.

| 1944 | PIT | N | 1 | .000 | .000 | 2 | 0 | 0 | 0 | 0 | 0.0 | 0 | 0 | 0 | 1 | 0 | 0 | 0 | 9 | 1 | 0 | 0 | 10.0 | 1.000 | 1B-1 |

Jeff Sweeney

SWEENEY, EDWARD FRANCIS
B. July 19, 1888, Chicago, Ill. D. July 4, 1947, Chicago, Ill.   BR TR 6'1"   200 lbs.

1908	NY	A	32	.146	.171	82	12	2	0	0	0.0	4	2	5		0	5	0	134	26	9	3	5.3	.947	C-25, OF-1, 1B-1
1909			67	.267	.284	176	47	3	0	0	0.0	19	21	16		3	2	0	293	84	21	8	5.9	.947	C-62, 1B-3
1910			78	.200	.256	215	43	4	4	0	0.0	25	13	17		12	1	0	388	106	13	2	6.5	.974	C-78
1911			83	.231	.301	229	53	6	5	0	0.0	17	18	14		8	0	0	394	94	18	8	6.1	.964	C-83
1912			110	.268	.308	351	94	12	1	0	0.0	37	30	27		6	2	1	548	167	34	9	6.8	.955	C-108
1913			117	.265	.322	351	93	10	2	2	0.6	35	40	37	41	11	3	1	512	180	26	9	6.1	.964	C-112, 1B-1
1914			87	.213	.264	258	55	8	1	1	0.4	25	22	35	30	19	8	2	369	120	10	7	5.7	.980	C-78
1915			53	.190	.204	137	26	2	0	0	0.0	12	5	25	12	3	0	0	213	59	7	4	5.3	.975	C-53
1919	PIT	N	17	.095	.119	42	4	1	0	0	0.0	0	0	5	6	1	2	1	34	17	3	2	3.2	.944	C-15
9 yrs.			644	.232	.277	1841	427	48	13	2	0.1	174	151	181	89	63	23	5	2885	853	141	52	6.0	.964	C-614, 1B-5, OF-1

Jerry Sweeney

SWEENEY, JEREMIAH H.
B. 1860, Boston, Mass. D. Aug. 25, 1891, Boston, Mass.   5'9½"   157 lbs.

| 1884 | KC | U | 31 | .264 | .287 | 129 | 34 | 3 | 0 | 0 | 0.0 | 16 | | 4 | | 0 | 0 | 0 | 304 | 14 | 14 | 15 | 10.7 | .958 | 1B-31 |

Pete Sweeney

SWEENEY, PETER JAY
B. Dec. 31, 1863, Calif. D. Aug. 22, 1901, San Francisco, Calif.   BR TR

1888	WAS	N	11	.182	.227	44	8	0	1	0	0.0	3	5	0	4	0	0	0	22	13	9	1	4.0	.795	3B-8, OF-3
1889	2 teams		58	.251	.329	231	58	9	3	1	0.4	21	31	12	31	10	0	0	86	99	50	7	4.1	.787	3B-55, OF-2, 2B-1
"	total WAS N (49G – .228) STL AA (9G – .368)																								
1890	3 teams		65	.175	.220	246	43	5	3	0	0.0	29		25		9	0	0	176	117	45	14	5.2	.867	2B-32, 3B-23, OF-6, 1B-3, SS-2
"	total STL AA (49G – .179) LOU AA (2G – .143) PHI AA (14G – .163)																								
3 yrs.			134	.209	.269	521	109	14	7	1	0.2	53	36	37	35	19	0	0	284	229	104	22	4.6	.831	3B-86, 2B-33, OF-11, 1B-3, SS-2

Rooney Sweeney

SWEENEY, JOHN J.
B. 1860 D. June 1, 1889, New York, N.Y.   5'8"   155 lbs.

1883	BAL	AA	25	.208	.297	101	21	5	2	0	0.0	13		4		0	0	101	42	19	3	6.5	.883	C-23, OF-3
1884	BAL	U	48	.226	.274	186	42	7	1	0	0.0	37		15		0	0	218	61	35	1	6.5	.889	C-33, OF-16, 3B-1
1885	STL	N	3	.091	.091	11	1	0	0	0	0.0	1	0	0	4	0	0	0	8	2	1	0	3.7	.909	OF-2, C-1
3 yrs.			76	.215	.275	298	64	12	3	0	0.0	51	0	19	4	0	0	327	105	55	4	6.4	.887	C-57, OF-21, 3B-1

Rick Sweet

SWEET, RICKY JOE
B. Sept. 7, 1952, Longview, Wash.   BB TR 6'1"   200 lbs.

1978	SD	N	88	.221	.270	226	50	8	0	1	0.4	15	11	27	22	1	12	0	337	33	6	3	4.3	.984	C-76
1982	2 teams		91	.257	.333	261	67	6	1	4	1.5	29	24	20	25	3	21	2	431	26	3	6	5.1	.993	C-83
"	total NY N (3G – .333) SEA A (88G – .256)																								
1983	SEA	A	93	.221	.269	249	55	9	0	1	0.4	18	22	13	26	2	20	8	413	34	6	6	4.9	.987	C-85
3 yrs.			272	.234	.292	736	172	23	1	6	0.8	62	57	60	73	6	53	10	1181	93	15	15	4.7	.988	C-244

Ham Sweigert

SWEIGERT, HAMPTON
Deceased.

| 1890 | PHI | AA | 1 | .000 | .000 | 1 | 0 | 0 | 0 | 0 | 0.0 | 0 | | 1 | | 1 | 0 | 0 | 1 | 1 | 0 | 0 | 2.0 | 1.000 | OF-1 |

Augie Swentor

SWENTOR, AUGUST WILLIAM
B. Nov. 21, 1899, Seymour, Conn. D. Nov. 10, 1969, Waterbury, Conn.   BR TR 6'   185 lbs.

| 1922 | CHI | A | 1 | .000 | .000 | 0 | 0 | 0 | 0 | 0 | | 0 | 0 | 0 | 0 | 0 | 0 | 0 | 0 | 0 | 0 | 0 | 0.0 | – | C-1 |

Pop Swett

SWETT, CHARLES A.
B. Apr. 16, 1868, San Francisco, Calif.

| 1890 | BOS | P | 37 | .191 | .330 | 94 | 18 | 4 | 4 | 1 | 1.1 | 16 | 12 | 16 | 26 | 1 | 0 | 0 | 83 | 12 | 21 | 1 | 3.1 | .819 | C-34, OF-3 |

Bob Swift

SWIFT, ROBERT VIRGIL
B. Mar. 6, 1915, Salina, Kans. D. Oct. 17, 1966, Detroit, Mich.
Manager 1965-66.   BR TR 5'11½" 180 lbs.

| 1940 | STL | A | 130 | .244 | .299 | 398 | 97 | 20 | 1 | 0 | 0.0 | 37 | 39 | 28 | 39 | 1 | 2 | 0 | 389 | 55 | 9 | 8 | 3.5 | .980 | C-128 |
| 1941 | | | 63 | .259 | .300 | 170 | 44 | 7 | 0 | 0 | 0.0 | 13 | 21 | 22 | 11 | 2 | 5 | 1 | 180 | 22 | 3 | 3 | 3.3 | .985 | C-58 |

Year	Team		Games	BA	SA	AB	H	2B	3B	HR	HR%	R	RBI	BB	SO	SB	Pinch Hit AB	H	PO	A	E	DP	TC/G	FA	G by Pos

Bob Swift *continued*

Year	Team		Games	BA	SA	AB	H	2B	3B	HR	HR%	R	RBI	BB	SO	SB	AB	H	PO	A	E	DP	TC/G	FA	G by Pos
1942	2 teams	STL A (29G – .197)		PHI	A (60G – .229)																				
"	total		89	.220	.257	268	59	7	0	1	0.4	12	23	16	22	1	1	0	334	50	9	5	4.4	.977	C-88
1943	PHI	A	77	.192	.237	224	43	5	1	1	0.4	16	11	35	16	0	0	0	278	53	8	9	4.4	.976	C-77
1944	DET	A	80	.255	.320	247	63	11	1	1	0.4	15	19	27	27	2	4	1	288	48	6	4	4.3	.982	C-76
1945			95	.233	.251	279	65	5	0	0	0.0	19	24	25	22	1	1	0	358	60	5	12	4.5	.988	C-94
1946			42	.234	.308	107	25	2	0	2	1.9	13	10	14	7	0	1	0	187	14	4	2	4.9	.980	C-42
1947			97	.251	.301	279	70	11	0	1	0.4	23	21	33	16	2	1	0	401	45	5	6	4.6	.989	C-97
1948			113	.223	.284	292	65	6	0	4	1.4	23	33	51	29	1	1	0	476	55	5	13	4.7	.991	C-112
1949			74	.238	.302	189	45	6	0	2	1.1	16	18	26	20	0	6	1	232	26	3	6	3.5	.989	C-69
1950			67	.227	.303	132	30	4	0	2	1.5	14	9	25	6	0	1	0	201	20	1	3	3.3	.995	C-66
1951			44	.192	.192	104	20	0	0	0	0.0	8	5	12	10	0	1	0	146	17	3	3	3.8	.982	C-43
1952			28	.138	.155	58	8	1	0	0	0.0	3	4	7	7	0	0	0	118	12	3	1	4.8	.977	C-28
1953			2	.333	.667	3	1	1	0	0	0.0	0	1	2	1	0	0	0	13	0	0	0	6.5	1.000	C-2
14 yrs.			1001	.231	.280	2750	635	86	3	14	0.5	212	238	323	233	10	23	3	3601	477	64	75	4.1	.985	C-980

WORLD SERIES

Year	Team		Games	BA	SA	AB	H	2B	3B	HR	HR%	R	RBI	BB	SO	SB	AB	H	PO	A	E	DP	TC/G	FA	G by Pos
1945	DET	A	3	.250	.250	4	1	0	0	0	0.0	1	0	2	0	0	0	0	9	1	0	0	3.3	1.000	C-3

Charlie Swindells

SWINDELLS, CHARLES JAY
B. Oct. 26, 1878, Rockford, Ill.   D. July 22, 1940, Portland, Ore.

BR TR 5'11½" 180 lbs.

Year	Team		Games	BA	SA	AB	H	2B	3B	HR	HR%	R	RBI	BB	SO	SB	AB	H	PO	A	E	DP	TC/G	FA	G by Pos
1904	STL	N	3	.125	.125	8	1	0	0	0	0.0	0	0	0			0	0	14	1	0	0	5.0	1.000	C-3

Steve Swisher

SWISHER, STEVEN EUGENE
B. Aug. 9, 1951, Parkersburg, W. Va.

BR TR 6'2" 205 lbs.

Year	Team		Games	BA	SA	AB	H	2B	3B	HR	HR%	R	RBI	BB	SO	SB	AB	H	PO	A	E	DP	TC/G	FA	G by Pos
1974	CHI	N	90	.214	.286	280	60	5	0	5	1.8	21	27	37	63	0	0	0	493	50	7	8	6.1	.987	C-90
1975			93	.213	.303	254	54	16	2	1	0.4	20	22	30	57	1	0	0	426	36	10	5	5.1	.979	C-93
1976			109	.236	.326	377	89	13	3	5	1.3	25	42	20	82	2	4	1	574	49	11	6	5.8	.983	C-107
1977			74	.190	.298	205	39	7	0	5	2.4	21	15	9	47	0	4	1	327	38	9	3	5.1	.976	C-72
1978	STL	N	45	.278	.365	115	32	5	1	1	0.9	11	10	8	14	1	3	1	202	13	2	0	4.8	.991	C-42
1979			38	.151	.233	73	11	1	1	1	1.4	4	3	6	17	0	5	0	105	6	3	2	3.0	.974	C-33
1980			18	.250	.292	24	6	1	0	0	0.0	2	2	1	7	0	9	2	21	1	1	0	1.3	.957	C-8
1981	SD	N	16	.143	.143	28	4	0	0	0	0.0	2	0	2	11	0	7	1	33	1	1	0	2.2	.971	C-10
1982			26	.172	.293	58	10	1	0	2	3.4	2	3	5	24	0	0	0	93	9	2	0	4.0	.981	C-26
9 yrs.			509	.216	.303	1414	305	49	7	20	1.4	108	124	118	322	4	32	6	2274	203	46	24	5.0	.982	C-481

Ron Swoboda

SWOBODA, RONALD ALAN (Rocky)
B. June 30, 1944, Baltimore, Md.

BR TR 6'2" 195 lbs.

Year	Team		Games	BA	SA	AB	H	2B	3B	HR	HR%	R	RBI	BB	SO	SB	AB	H	PO	A	E	DP	TC/G	FA	G by Pos
1965	NY	N	135	.228	.424	399	91	15	3	19	4.8	52	50	33	102	2	26	7	188	9	11	2	1.5	.947	OF-112
1966			112	.222	.342	342	76	9	4	8	2.3	34	50	31	76	4	19	8	145	7	2	0	1.4	.987	OF-97
1967			134	.281	.419	449	126	17	3	13	2.9	47	53	41	96	3	9	2	333	25	13	7	2.8	.965	OF-108, 1B-20
1968			132	.242	.373	450	109	14	6	11	2.4	46	59	52	113	8	9	4	217	14	6	4	1.8	.975	OF-125
1969			109	.235	.361	327	77	10	2	9	2.8	38	52	43	90	1	9	2	163	5	2	0	1.6	.988	OF-97
1970			115	.233	.392	245	57	8	2	9	3.7	29	40	40	72	2	20	5	117	3	2	1	1.1	.984	OF-100
1971	2 teams	MON N (39G – .253)		NY	A (54G – .261)																				
"	total		93	.258	.352	213	55	6	4	2	0.9	24	26	38	51	0	29	4	119	5	4	0	1.4	.969	OF-73
1972	NY	A	63	.248	.345	113	28	6	0	1	0.9	9	12	17	29	0	26	4	61	2	1	2	1.0	.984	OF-35, 1B-2
1973			35	.116	.186	43	5	0	0	1	2.3	6	2	4	18	0	1	1	23	0	0	0	0.7	1.000	OF-20, DH-4
9 yrs.			928	.242	.379	2581	624	87	24	73	2.8	285	344	299	647	20	148	37	1366	70	41	16	1.6	.972	OF-767, 1B-22, DH-4

WORLD SERIES

Year	Team		Games	BA	SA	AB	H	2B	3B	HR	HR%	R	RBI	BB	SO	SB	AB	H	PO	A	E	DP	TC/G	FA	G by Pos
1969	NY	N	4	.400	.467	15	6	0	0	0	0.0	1	1	1	3	0	0	0	14	0	0	0	3.5	1.000	OF-4

Lou Sylvester

SYLVESTER, LOUIS J.
B. Feb. 14, 1855, Springfield, Ill.   Deceased.

BR TR 5'3" 165 lbs.

Year	Team		Games	BA	SA	AB	H	2B	3B	HR	HR%	R	RBI	BB	SO	SB	AB	H	PO	A	E	DP	TC/G	FA	G by Pos
1884	CIN	U	82	.267	.372	333	89	13	8	2	0.6	67		18			0	0	111	28	39	2	2.2	.781	OF-81, P-6, SS-2
1886	2 teams	LOU AA (45G – .227)		CIN	AA (17G – .182)																				
"	total		62	.215	.311	209	45	3	3	1	1.4	51		36			0	0	80	13	9	5	1.6	.912	OF-62
1887	STL	AA	29	.223	.339	112	25	4	3	1	0.9	20		13		13	0	0	55	8	6	4	2.4	.913	OF-29, 2B-1
3 yrs.			173	.243	.347	654	159	22	14	6	0.9	138		67		13	0	0	246	49	54	11	2.0	.845	OF-172, P-6, SS-2, 2B-1

Joe Szekely

SZEKELY, JOSEPH
B. Feb. 2, 1925, Cleveland, Ohio

BR TR 5'11" 180 lbs.

Year	Team		Games	BA	SA	AB	H	2B	3B	HR	HR%	R	RBI	BB	SO	SB	AB	H	PO	A	E	DP	TC/G	FA	G by Pos
1953	CIN	N	5	.077	.077	13	1	0	0	0	0.0	0	0	0	3	0	1	0	4	2	0	1	1.2	1.000	OF-3

Ken Szotkiewicz

SZOTKIEWICZ, KENNETH JOHN
B. Feb. 25, 1947, Wilmington, Del.

BL TR 6' 165 lbs.

Year	Team		Games	BA	SA	AB	H	2B	3B	HR	HR%	R	RBI	BB	SO	SB	AB	H	PO	A	E	DP	TC/G	FA	G by Pos
1970	DET	A	47	.107	.226	84	9	1	0	3	3.6	9	9	12	29	0	3	0	32	101	4	20	2.9	.971	SS-44

Jerry Tabb

TABB, JERRY LYNN
B. Mar. 17, 1952, Altus, Okla.

BL TR 6'2" 195 lbs.

Year	Team		Games	BA	SA	AB	H	2B	3B	HR	HR%	R	RBI	BB	SO	SB	AB	H	PO	A	E	DP	TC/G	FA	G by Pos
1976	CHI	N	11	.292	.292	24	7	0	0	0	0.0	2	0	3	2	0	6	1	52	2	0	4	4.9	1.000	1B-6
1977	OAK	A	51	.222	.368	144	32	3	0	6	4.2	8	19	10	26	0	10	2	288	16	2	26	6.0	.993	1B-36, DH-5
1978			12	.111	.111	9	1	0	0	0	0.0	0	1	2	5	0	9	1	3	0	0	0	0.3	1.000	DH-2, 1B-2
3 yrs.			74	.226	.345	177	40	3	0	6	3.4	10	20	15	33	0	25	4	343	18	2	30	4.9	.994	1B-44, DH-7

Pat Tabler

TABLER, PATRICK SEAN
B. Feb. 2, 1958, Hamilton, Ohio

BR TR 6'3" 175 lbs.

Year	Team		Games	BA	SA	AB	H	2B	3B	HR	HR%	R	RBI	BB	SO	SB	AB	H	PO	A	E	DP	TC/G	FA	G by Pos
1981	CHI	N	35	.188	.267	101	19	3	1	1	1.0	11	5	13	26	0	0	0	70	93	3	17	4.7	.982	2B-35
1982			25	.235	.365	85	20	4	2	1	1.2	9	7	6	20	0	0	0	23	33	3	3	2.4	.949	3B-25
1983	CLE	A	124	.291	.409	430	125	23	5	6	1.4	56	65	56	63	2	5	2	197	55	11	6	2.1	.958	OF-80, 3B-25, DH-6, 2B-2

Year	Team	Games	BA	SA	AB	H	2B	3B	HR	HR%	R	RBI	BB	SO	SB	Pinch Hit AB	Pinch Hit H	PO	A	E	DP	TC/G	FA	G by Pos

Pat Tabler *continued*

Year	Team	Games	BA	SA	AB	H	2B	3B	HR	HR%	R	RBI	BB	SO	SB	AB	H	PO	A	E	DP	TC/G	FA	G by Pos
1984		144	.290	.410	473	137	21	3	10	2.1	66	68	47	62	3	6	1	532	89	7	54	4.4	.989	1B-67, OF-43, 3B-36, DH-1, 2B-1
1985		117	.275	.371	404	111	18	3	5	1.2	47	59	27	55	0	8	4	744	77	14	78	7.1	.983	1B-92, DH-18, 3B-4, 2B-1
1986		130	.326	.433	473	154	29	2	6	1.3	61	48	29	75	3	9	1	846	84	9	87	7.2	.990	1B-107, DH-18
1987		151	.307	.439	553	170	34	3	11	2.0	66	86	51	84	5	7	2	650	75	12	49	4.9	.984	1B-82, DH-66
1988 2 teams	CLE A (41G – .224)				KC A (89G – .309)																			
" total		130	.282	.358	444	125	22	3	2	0.5	53	66	46	68	3	8	2	182	10	5	11	1.5	.975	OF-37, DH-29, 1B-17, 3B-1
1989 KC A		123	.259	.308	390	101	11	1	2	0.5	36	42	37	42	0	13	2	217	25	4	11	2.0	.984	OF-55, DH-39, 1B-20, 2B-3, 3B-1
9 yrs.		979	.287	.389	3353	962	165	23	44	1.3	405	446	312	495	16	56	14	3461	541	68	316	4.2	.983	1B-385, OF-215, DH-177, 3B-92, 2B-42

Greg Tabor

TABOR, GREGORY STEVEN
B. May 21, 1961, Castro Valley, Calif.
BR TR 6' 165 lbs.

Year	Team	Games	BA	SA	AB	H	2B	3B	HR	HR%	R	RBI	BB	SO	SB	AB	H	PO	A	E	DP	TC/G	FA	G by Pos
1987 TEX A		9	.111	.222	9	1	1	0	0	0.0	4	1	0	4	0	0	0	4	11	1	2	1.8	.938	2B-4, DH-1

Jim Tabor

TABOR, JAMES REUBIN (Rawhide)
B. Nov. 5, 1916, New Hope, Ala.   D. Aug. 22, 1953, Sacramento, Calif.
BR TR 6'2" 175 lbs.

Year	Team	Games	BA	SA	AB	H	2B	3B	HR	HR%	R	RBI	BB	SO	SB	AB	H	PO	A	E	DP	TC/G	FA	G by Pos
1938 BOS A		19	.316	.491	57	18	3	2	1	1.8	8	8	1	1	0	5	2	18	30	8	4	2.9	.857	3B-11, SS-2
1939		149	.289	.447	577	167	33	8	14	2.4	76	95	40	54	16	1	1	144	338	40	32	3.5	.923	3B-148
1940		120	.285	.510	459	131	28	6	21	4.6	73	81	42	58	14	0	0	143	267	33	25	3.7	.926	3B-120
1941		126	.279	.446	498	139	29	3	16	3.2	65	101	36	48	17	2	1	123	277	30	24	3.4	.930	3B-125
1942		139	.252	.366	508	128	18	2	12	2.4	56	75	37	47	6	0	0	168	236	33	24	3.1	.924	3B-138
1943		137	.242	.374	537	130	26	3	12	2.4	57	85	43	54	7	3	1	137	261	26	32	3.1	.939	3B-133, OF-2
1944		126	.285	.445	438	125	25	3	13	3.0	58	72	31	38	4	2	0	125	258	20	14	3.5	.950	3B-114
1946 PHI N		124	.268	.374	463	124	15	2	10	2.2	53	50	36	51	3	0	0	156	221	18	17	3.2	.954	3B-124
1947		75	.235	.339	251	59	14	0	4	1.6	27	31	20	21	2	7	1	68	96	15	8	2.4	.916	3B-67
9 yrs.		1005	.270	.418	3788	1021	191	29	104	2.7	473	598	286	377	69	20	6	1082	1984	223	180	3.3	.932	3B-980, OF-2, SS-2

Doug Taitt

TAITT, DOUGLAS JOHN (Poco)
B. Aug. 3, 1902, Bay City, Mich.   D. Dec. 12, 1970, Portland, Ore.
BL TR 6' 176 lbs.

Year	Team	Games	BA	SA	AB	H	2B	3B	HR	HR%	R	RBI	BB	SO	SB	AB	H	PO	A	E	DP	TC/G	FA	G by Pos
1928 BOS A		143	.299	.434	482	144	28	14	3	0.6	51	61	36	32	13	3	0	252	19	7	8	1.9	.975	OF-139, P-1
1929 2 teams	BOS A (26G – .277)				CHI A (47G – .169)																			
" total		73	.206	.265	189	39	11	0	0	0.0	17	18	16	18	0	21	6	90	7	4	3	1.4	.960	OF-51
1931 PHI N		38	.225	.298	151	34	4	2	1	0.7	13	15	4	10	0	0	0	95	4	1	0	2.6	.990	OF-38
1932		4	.000	.000	2	0	0	0	0	0.0	0	1	2	0	0	2	0	0	0	0	0	0.0	–	
4 yrs.		258	.263	.369	824	217	43	16	4	0.5	81	95	58	64	13	26	6	437	30	12	11	1.9	.975	OF-228, P-1

Dale Talbot

TALBOT, ROBERT DALE
B. June 6, 1927, Visalia, Calif.
BR TR 6' 170 lbs.

Year	Team	Games	BA	SA	AB	H	2B	3B	HR	HR%	R	RBI	BB	SO	SB	AB	H	PO	A	E	DP	TC/G	FA	G by Pos
1953 CHI N		8	.333	.400	30	10	0	1	0	0.0	5	0	0	4	1	0	0	20	3	0	1	2.9	1.000	OF-7
1954		114	.241	.305	403	97	15	4	1	0.2	45	19	16	25	3	1	0	245	10	4	1	2.3	.985	OF-110
2 yrs.		122	.247	.312	433	107	15	5	1	0.2	50	19	16	29	4	1	0	265	13	4	2	2.3	.986	OF-117

Tim Talton

TALTON, MARION LEE
B. Jan. 14, 1939, Pikeville, N. C.
BL TR 6'3" 200 lbs.

Year	Team	Games	BA	SA	AB	H	2B	3B	HR	HR%	R	RBI	BB	SO	SB	AB	H	PO	A	E	DP	TC/G	FA	G by Pos
1966 KC A		37	.340	.547	53	18	3	1	2	3.8	9	6	1	5	0	25	10	73	5	0	7	2.1	1.000	C-14, 1B-9
1967		46	.254	.339	59	15	3	1	0	0.0	7	5	7	13	0	32	9	67	5	2	0	1.6	.973	C-22, 1B-1
2 yrs.		83	.295	.438	112	33	6	2	2	1.8	15	11	8	18	0	57	19	140	10	2	7	1.8	.987	C-36, 1B-10

John Tamargo

TAMARGO, JOHN FELIX
B. Nov. 7, 1951, Tampa, Fla.
BB TR 5'10" 170 lbs.

Year	Team	Games	BA	SA	AB	H	2B	3B	HR	HR%	R	RBI	BB	SO	SB	AB	H	PO	A	E	DP	TC/G	FA	G by Pos
1976 STL N		10	.300	.300	10	3	0	0	0	0.0	2	1	3	0	0	9	3	4	0	0	0	0.4	1.000	C-1
1977		4	.000	.000	4	0	0	0	0	0.0	0	0	2	0	0	3	0	1	0	0	0	0.3	1.000	C-1
1978 2 teams	STL N (6G – .000)				SF N (36G – .239)																			
" total		42	.224	.316	98	22	4	1	1	1.0	6	8	18	9	1	11	1	157	9	6	4	4.1	.965	C-32
1979 2 teams	SF N (30G – .200)				MON N (12G – .381)																			
" total		42	.247	.383	81	20	3	0	2	2.5	7	11	7	11	0	21	6	80	6	1	4	2.1	.989	C-21
1980 MON N		37	.275	.392	51	14	3	0	1	2.0	4	13	6	5	0	23	7	36	3	1	2	1.1	.975	C-12
5 yrs.		135	.242	.348	244	59	12	1	4	1.6	19	33	34	27	1	65	16	278	18	8	10	2.3	.974	C-67

Leo Tankersley

TANKERSLEY, LAWRENCE WILLIAM
B. June 8, 1901, Terrell, Tex.   D. Sept. 18, 1980, Dallas, Tex.
BR TR 6' 176 lbs.

Year	Team	Games	BA	SA	AB	H	2B	3B	HR	HR%	R	RBI	BB	SO	SB	AB	H	PO	A	E	DP	TC/G	FA	G by Pos
1925 CHI A		1	.000	.000	3	0	0	0	0	0.0	0	0	0	0	0	0	0	1	0	0	0	1.0	1.000	C-1

Jesse Tannehill

TANNEHILL, JESSE NILES (Tanny)
Brother of Lee Tannehill.
B. July 14, 1874, Dayton, Ky.   D. Sept. 22, 1956, Dayton, Ky.
BB TL 5'8" 150 lbs.
BL 1903

Year	Team	Games	BA	SA	AB	H	2B	3B	HR	HR%	R	RBI	BB	SO	SB	AB	H	PO	A	E	DP	TC/G	FA	G by Pos
1894 CIN N		5	.000	.000	11	0	0	0	0	0.0	0	1	1	2	0	0	0	1	2	2	0	1.0	.600	P-5
1897 PIT N		56	.266	.332	184	49	8	2	0	0.0	22	22	18		4	2	0	89	53	13	1	2.8	.916	OF-33, P-21
1898		60	.289	.408	152	44	9	3	1	0.7	25	17	7		4	8	3	28	95	5	2	2.1	.961	P-43, OF-7
1899		47	.258	.341	132	34	5	3	0	0.0	17	10	8		2	6	1	9	95	5	7	2.3	.954	P-41, OF-1
1900		34	.336	.400	110	37	7	0	0	0.0	19	17	5		2	1	1	14	65	6	1	2.5	.929	P-29, OF-4
1901		42	.244	.333	135	33	3	3	1	0.7	19	12	6		0	0	0	23	53	7	1	2.0	.916	P-32, OF-10
1902		44	.291	.365	148	43	6	1	1	0.7	27	17	12		3	2	0	25	57	4	3	2.0	.953	P-26, OF-16
1903 NY N		40	.234	.351	111	26	6	2	1	0.9	18	13	8		1	3	0	14	83	3	2	2.5	.970	P-32, OF-5
1904 BOS A		45	.197	.311	122	24	2	6	0	0.0	14	6	9		1	10	2	12	107	1	4	2.7	.992	P-33, OF-2
1905		37	.226	.280	93	21	2	1	1	1.1	11	12	16		1			9	97	6	1	3.0	.946	P-37
1906		31	.278	.354	79	22	2	0	0	0.0	12	6	4		0	3	1	15	58	4	1	2.5	.948	P-27
1907		21	.196	.294	51	10	3	1	0	0.0	2	6	2		0	2	0	9	42	1	3	2.5	.981	P-18

Year	Team		Games	BA	SA	AB	H	2B	3B	HR	HR%	R	RBI	BB	SO	SB	Pinch Hit AB	Pinch Hit H	PO	A	E	DP	TC/G	FA	G by Pos

Jesse Tannehill *continued*

Year	Team		Games	BA	SA	AB	H	2B	3B	HR	HR%	R	RBI	BB	SO	SB	AB	H	PO	A	E	DP	TC/G	FA	G by Pos
1908	2 teams	BOS A (1G – .500)				WAS A (26G – .256)																			
"	total		27	.267	.289	45	12	1	0	0	0.0	1	3	2		0	15	3	5	34	4	2	1.6	.907	P-11
1909	WAS	A	16	.167	.194	36	6	1	0	0	0.0	2	1	5		0	4	0	14	9	0	1	1.4	1.000	OF-9, P-3
1911	CIN	N	1	.000	.000	1	0	0	0	0	0.0	0	0	0		1	0	0	0	1	0	0	1.0	1.000	P-1
15 yrs.			506	.256	.338	1410	361	55	23	5	0.4	189	141	105	3	19	57	11	267	851	61	31	2.3	.948	P-359, OF-87

Lee Tannehill

TANNEHILL, LEE FORD
Brother of Jesse Tannehill.
B. Oct. 26, 1880, Dayton, Ky.   D. Feb. 16, 1938, Live Oak, Fla.

BR TR 5'11"   170 lbs.

Year	Team		Games	BA	SA	AB	H	2B	3B	HR	HR%	R	RBI	BB	SO	SB	AB	H	PO	A	E	DP	TC/G	FA	G by Pos
1903	CHI	A	138	.225	.276	503	113	14	3	2	0.4	48	50	25		10	0	0	291	457	76	58	6.0	.908	SS-138
1904			153	.229	.303	547	125	31	5	0	0.0	50	61	20		14	0	0	180	369	31	22	3.8	.947	3B-153
1905			142	.200	.244	480	96	17	2	0	0.0	38	39	45		8	0	0	168	358	39	17	4.0	.931	3B-142
1906			116	.183	.220	378	69	8	3	0	0.0	26	33	31		7	0	0	173	332	27	13	4.6	.949	3B-99, SS-17
1907			33	.241	.259	108	26	2	0	0	0.0	9	11	8		3	0	0	25	91	11	4	3.8	.913	3B-31, SS-2
1908			141	.216	.259	482	104	15	3	0	0.0	44	35	25		6	0	0	142	354	35	21	3.8	.934	3B-136, SS-5
1909			155	.222	.281	531	118	21	5	0	0.0	39	47	31		12	0	0	229	419	41	32	4.4	.940	3B-91, SS-64
1910			67	.222	.278	230	51	10	0	1	0.4	17	21	11		3	0	0	267	156	13	21	6.5	.970	SS-38, 1B-23, 3B-6
1911			141	.254	.310	516	131	17	6	0	0.0	60	49	32		0	0	0	385	493	38	53	6.5	.959	SS-102, 2B-27, 3B-8, 1B-5
1912			3	.000	.000	3	0	0	0	0	0.0	0	0	1		0	0	0	2	2	2	1	2.0	.667	3B-3
10 yrs.			1089	.220	.273	3778	833	135	27	3	0.1	331	346	229		63	0	0	1862	3031	313	242	4.8	.940	3B-669, SS-366, 1B-28, 2B-27

WORLD SERIES

Year	Team		Games	BA	SA	AB	H	2B	3B	HR	HR%	R	RBI	BB	SO	SB	AB	H	PO	A	E	DP	TC/G	FA	G by Pos
1906	CHI	A	3	.111	.111	9	1	0	0	0	0.0	1	0	0	2	0	0	0	1	12	0	0	4.3	1.000	SS-3

Chuck Tanner

TANNER, CHARLES WILLIAM
Father of Bruce Tanner.
B. July 4, 1929, New Castle, Pa.
Manager 1970-88.

BL TL 6'   185 lbs.

Year	Team		Games	BA	SA	AB	H	2B	3B	HR	HR%	R	RBI	BB	SO	SB	AB	H	PO	A	E	DP	TC/G	FA	G by Pos
1955	MIL	N	97	.247	.383	243	60	9	3	6	2.5	27	27	27	32	0	32	7	101	4	2	0	1.1	.981	OF-62
1956			60	.238	.317	63	15	2	0	1	1.6	6	4	10	10	0	44	10	4	0	1	0	0.1	.800	OF-8
1957	2 teams	MIL N (22G – .246)				CHI N (95G – .286)																			
"	total		117	.279	.408	387	108	19	2	9	2.3	47	48	28	24	0	16	4	191	5	2	2	1.7	.990	OF-100
1958	CHI	N	73	.262	.437	103	27	6	4	4	3.9	10	17	9	10	1	53	12	21	0	1	0	0.3	.955	OF-15
1959	CLE	A	14	.250	.354	48	12	2	0	1	2.1	6	5	2	9	0	4	0	18	0	0	0	1.3	1.000	OF-10
1960			21	.280	.320	25	7	1	0	0	0.0	2	4	4	6	1	15	3	4	0	0	0	0.2	1.000	OF-4
1961	LA	A	7	.125	.125	8	1	0	0	0	0.0	0	0	2	2	0	4	1	0	0	0	0	0.0	–	OF-1
1962			7	.125	.125	8	1	0	0	0	0.0	0	0	0	0	0	6	1	0	0	0	0	0.0	–	OF-2
8 yrs.			396	.261	.388	885	231	39	5	21	2.4	98	105	82	93	2	174	38	340	9	6	2	0.9	.983	OF-202

Walter Tappan

TAPPAN, WALTER VAN DORN (Tap)
B. Oct. 8, 1890, Carlinville, Ill.   D. Dec. 19, 1967, Lynwood, Calif.

BR TR 5'9"   150 lbs.

Year	Team		Games	BA	SA	AB	H	2B	3B	HR	HR%	R	RBI	BB	SO	SB	AB	H	PO	A	E	DP	TC/G	FA	G by Pos
1914	KC	F	18	.205	.308	39	8	1	0	1	2.6	1	3	1		1	0	0	7	28	5	2	2.2	.875	SS-8, 3B-6, 2B-1

El Tappe

TAPPE, ELVIN WALTER
B. May 21, 1927, Quincy, Ill.
Manager 1961-62.

BR TR 5'11"   180 lbs.

Year	Team		Games	BA	SA	AB	H	2B	3B	HR	HR%	R	RBI	BB	SO	SB	AB	H	PO	A	E	DP	TC/G	FA	G by Pos
1954	CHI	N	46	.185	.210	119	22	3	0	0	0.0	5	4	10	9	0	0	0	185	22	3	2	4.6	.986	C-46
1955			2	–	–	0	0	0	0	0	–	0	0	0	0	0	0	0	3	1	0	0	2.0	1.000	C-2
1956			3	.000	.000	1	0	0	0	0	0.0	0	0	1	0	0	0	0	4	0	0	0	1.3	1.000	C-3
1958			17	.214	.214	28	6	0	0	0	0.0	2	4	3	1	0	1	0	46	4	2	0	3.1	.962	C-16
1960			51	.233	.301	103	24	7	0	0	0.0	11	3	11	12	0	2	0	215	27	2	4	4.8	.992	C-49
1962			26	.208	.208	53	11	0	0	0	0.0	3	6	4	3	0	0	0	101	13	0	4	4.4	1.000	C-26
6 yrs.			145	.207	.240	304	63	10	0	0	0.0	21	17	29	25	0	3	0	554	67	7	10	4.3	.989	C-142

Ted Tappe

TAPPE, THEODORE NASH
B. Feb. 2, 1931, Seattle, Wash.

BL TR 6'3"   185 lbs.

Year	Team		Games	BA	SA	AB	H	2B	3B	HR	HR%	R	RBI	BB	SO	SB	AB	H	PO	A	E	DP	TC/G	FA	G by Pos
1950	CIN	N	7	.200	.800	5	1	0	0	1	20.0	1	1	1	1	0	5	1	0	0	0	0	0.0	–	
1951			4	.333	.333	3	1	0	0	0	0.0	0	0	0	0	0	3	1	0	0	0	0	0.0	–	
1955	CHI	N	23	.260	.540	50	13	2	0	4	8.0	12	10	11	11	0	8	2	18	1	0	0	0.8	1.000	OF-15
3 yrs.			34	.259	.552	58	15	2	0	5	8.6	13	11	12	12	0	16	4	18	1	0	0	0.6	1.000	OF-15

Arlie Tarbert

TARBERT, WILBUR ARLINGTON
B. Sept. 10, 1904, Cleveland, Ohio   D. Nov. 27, 1946, Cleveland, Ohio

BR TR 6'   160 lbs.

Year	Team		Games	BA	SA	AB	H	2B	3B	HR	HR%	R	RBI	BB	SO	SB	AB	H	PO	A	E	DP	TC/G	FA	G by Pos
1927	BOS	A	33	.188	.203	69	13	1	0	0	0.0	5	5	3	12	1	0	0	30	4	2	0	1.1	.944	OF-27
1928			6	.176	.235	17	3	1	0	0	0.0	1	2	1	1	0	0	0	8	0	2	0	1.7	.800	OF-6
2 yrs.			39	.186	.209	86	16	2	0	0	0.0	6	7	4	13	1	0	0	38	4	4	0	1.2	.913	OF-33

Danny Tartabull

TARTABULL, DANILO
Born Danilo Tartabull y Mora.   Son of Jose Tartabull.
B. Oct. 30, 1962, San Juan, Puerto Rico

BR TR 6'1"   185 lbs.

Year	Team		Games	BA	SA	AB	H	2B	3B	HR	HR%	R	RBI	BB	SO	SB	AB	H	PO	A	E	DP	TC/G	FA	G by Pos
1984	SEA	A	10	.300	.650	20	6	1	0	2	10.0	3	7	2	3	0	1	0	8	21	2	5	3.1	.935	SS-8, 2B-1
1985			19	.328	.525	61	20	7	1	1	1.6	8	7	8	14	1	3	1	28	43	4	11	3.9	.947	SS-16, 3B-4
1986			137	.270	.489	511	138	25	6	25	4.9	76	96	61	157	4	2	1	233	111	18	28	2.6	.950	OF-101, 2B-31, DH-3, 3B-1
1987	KC	A	158	.309	.541	582	180	27	3	34	5.8	95	101	79	136	9	3	0	228	11	6	1	1.6	.976	OF-149, DH-6
1988			146	.274	.515	507	139	38	3	26	5.1	80	102	76	119	8	4	1	227	8	9	1	1.7	.963	OF-130, DH-13
1989			133	.268	.440	441	118	22	0	18	4.1	54	62	69	123	4	4	1	108	3	2	0	0.8	.982	OF-71, DH-55
6 yrs.			603	.283	.502	2122	601	120	13	106	5.0	316	375	295	552	26	17	4	832	197	41	46	1.8	.962	OF-451, DH-77, 2B-32, SS-24, 3B-5

Year	Team	Games	BA	SA	AB	H	2B	3B	HR	HR%	R	RBI	BB	SO	SB	Pinch Hit AB	Pinch Hit H	PO	A	E	DP	TC/G	FA	G by Pos

Jose Tartabull

TARTABULL, JOSE MILAGES
Born Jose Milages Tartabull y Guzman.   Father of Danny Tartabull.
B. Nov. 27, 1938, Cienfuegos, Cuba

BL TL 5'11"   165 lbs.

Year	Team	Games	BA	SA	AB	H	2B	3B	HR	HR%	R	RBI	BB	SO	SB	PH AB	PH H	PO	A	E	DP	TC/G	FA	G by Pos
1962	KC A	107	.277	.329	310	86	6	5	0	0.0	49	22	20	19	19	19	5	185	6	5	0	1.8	.974	OF-85
1963		79	.240	.326	242	58	8	5	1	0.4	27	19	17	17	16	6	1	135	3	2	1	1.8	.986	OF-71
1964		104	.200	.220	100	20	2	0	0	0.0	9	3	5	12	4	41	5	42	3	1	1	0.4	.978	OF-59
1965		68	.312	.413	218	68	11	4	1	0.5	28	19	18	20	11	13	7	133	5	2	0	2.1	.986	OF-54
1966	2 teams		KC A	(37G – .236)		BOS A	(68G – .277)																	
"	total	105	.261	.332	322	84	9	7	0	0.0	41	15	17	24	19	24	3	160	2	1	0	1.6	.994	OF-79
1967	BOS A	115	.223	.243	247	55	1	2	0	0.0	36	10	23	26	6	32	9	90	3	1	1	0.8	.989	OF-83
1968		72	.281	.324	139	39	6	0	0	0.0	24	6	6	5	2	30	8	59	1	1	0	0.8	.984	OF-43
1969	OAK A	75	.267	.316	266	71	11	1	0	0.0	28	11	9	11	3	11	2	134	2	1	0	1.8	.993	OF-63
1970		24	.231	.385	13	3	2	0	0	0.0	5	2	0	2	1	7	0	3	0	0	0	0.1	1.000	OF-6
9 yrs.		749	.261	.320	1857	484	56	24	3	0.1	247	107	115	136	81	183	40	941	25	14	3	1.3	.986	OF-543

WORLD SERIES

| 1967 | BOS A | 7 | .154 | .154 | 13 | 2 | 0 | 0 | 0 | 0.0 | 1 | 0 | 1 | 2 | 0 | 1 | 0 | 7 | 0 | 0 | 0 | 1.0 | 1.000 | OF-6 |

LaSchelle Tarver

TARVER, LaSCHELLE
B. Jan. 30, 1959, Modesto, Calif.

BL TL 5'11"   165 lbs.

| 1986 | BOS A | 13 | .120 | .120 | 25 | 3 | 0 | 0 | 0 | 0.0 | 3 | 1 | 1 | 4 | 0 | 1 | 0 | 16 | 0 | 0 | 0 | 1.2 | 1.000 | OF-9 |

Willie Tasby

TASBY, WILLIE
B. Jan. 8, 1933, Shreveport, La.

BR TR 5'11"   170 lbs.

1958	BAL A	18	.200	.320	50	10	3	0	1	2.0	6	1	7	15	1	1	0	30	0	0	0	1.7	1.000	OF-16
1959		142	.250	.378	505	126	16	5	13	2.6	69	48	34	80	3	4	1	320	13	11	4	2.4	.968	OF-137
1960	2 teams		BAL A	(39G – .212)		BOS A	(105G – .281)																	
"	total	144	.268	.362	470	126	19	2	7	1.5	77	40	60	66	4	7	3	279	7	6	1	2.0	.979	OF-138
1961	WAS A	141	.251	.389	494	124	13	2	17	3.4	54	63	58	94	4	0	0	332	5	5	0	2.4	.985	OF-139
1962	2 teams		WAS A	(11G – .206)		CLE A	(75G – .241)																	
"	total	86	.236	.318	233	55	7	0	4	1.7	29	17	27	47	0	16	1	119	2	1	0	1.4	.992	OF-76, 3B-1
1963	CLE A	52	.224	.371	116	26	3	1	4	3.4	11	5	15	25	0	14	0	54	0	1	0	1.1	.982	OF-37, 2B-1
6 yrs.		583	.250	.367	1868	467	61	10	46	2.5	246	174	201	327	12	42	5	1134	27	24	5	2.0	.980	OF-543, 3B-1, 2B-1

Bennie Tate

TATE, HENRY BENNETT
B. Dec. 3, 1901, Whitwell, Tenn.   D. Oct. 27, 1973, W. Frankfort, Ill.

BL TR 5'8"   165 lbs.

1924	WAS A	21	.302	.349	43	13	2	0	0	0.0	2	7	1	2	0	6	3	33	4	7	0	2.1	.841	C-14
1925		16	.481	.593	27	13	3	0	0	0.0	2	7	2	2	0	2	1	36	6	2	2	2.8	.955	C-14
1926		59	.268	.352	142	38	5	2	1	0.7	17	13	15	1	0	9	2	109	35	6	3	2.5	.960	C-45
1927		61	.313	.389	131	41	5	1	1	0.8	12	24	8	4	0	16	5	148	24	4	4	2.9	.977	C-39
1928		57	.246	.295	122	30	6	0	0	0.0	10	15	10	4	0	25	4	111	21	2	1	2.4	.985	C-30
1929		81	.294	.362	265	78	12	3	0	0.0	26	30	16	8	2	6	3	291	49	10	10	4.3	.971	C-74
1930	2 teams		WAS A	(14G – .250)		CHI A	(72G – .317)																	
"	total	86	.312	.372	250	78	11	2	0	0.0	27	29	18	11	2	5	2	231	42	6	5	3.2	.978	C-79
1931	CHI A	89	.267	.333	273	73	12	3	0	0.0	27	22	26	10	1	4	1	310	69	5	11	4.3	.987	C-85
1932	2 teams		CHI A	(4G – .100)		BOS A	(81G – .245)																	
"	total	85	.240	.339	283	68	12	5	2	0.7	22	26	21	6	0	5	3	253	53	8	7	3.7	.975	C-80
1934	CHI N	11	.125	.125	24	3	0	0	0	0.0	1	0	1	3	0	3	0	12	3	0	0	1.4	1.000	C-8
10 yrs.		566	.279	.351	1560	435	68	16	4	0.3	144	173	118	51	5	81	29	1534	306	50	43	3.3	.974	C-468

WORLD SERIES

| 1924 | WAS A | 3 | – | – | 0 | 0 | 0 | 0 | 0 | – | 0 | 1 | 3 | 0 | 0 | 0 | 0 | 0 | 0 | 0 | 0 | 0.0 | – | |

Hugh Tate

TATE, HUGH HENRY
B. May 19, 1880, Everett, Pa.   D. Aug. 7, 1956, Greenville, Pa.

BR TR 5'11"   190 lbs.

| 1905 | WAS A | 4 | .300 | .500 | 10 | 3 | 0 | 1 | 0 | 0.0 | 2 | 2 | 0 | | | 1 | 1 | 0 | 4 | 0 | 0 | 0 | 1.0 | 1.000 | OF-3 |

Lee Tate

TATE, LEE WILLIE (Skeeter)
B. Mar. 18, 1932, Black Rock, Ark.

BR TR 5'10"   165 lbs.

1958	STL N	10	.200	.257	35	7	2	0	0	0.0	4	4	3			0	1	16	22	2	5	4.0	.950	SS-9
1959		41	.140	.260	50	7	1	1	1	2.0	5	4	5	7	0	0	0	33	49	6	10	2.1	.932	SS-39, 3B-2, 2B-2
2 yrs.		51	.165	.259	85	14	3	1	1	1.2	9	5	9	10	0	1	0	49	71	8	15	2.5	.938	SS-48, 3B-2, 2B-2

Pop Tate

TATE, EDWARD CHRISTOPHER (Dimples)
B. Dec. 22, 1860, Richmond, Va.   D. June 25, 1932, Richmond, Va.

BR TL

1885	BOS N	4	.154	.154	13	2	0	0	0	0.0	1	2	1			0	3	0	19	13	5	0	9.3	.865	C-4
1886		31	.226	.274	106	24	3	1	0	0.0	13	3	7	17		0	0	163	44	27	2	7.5	.885	C-31
1887		60	.260	.307	231	60	5	3	0	0.0	34	27	8	9	7	0	0	217	111	27	6	5.9	.924	C-53, OF-8
1888		41	.230	.311	148	34	7	1	1	0.7	18	6	8	7	3	0	0	188	64	43	6	7.2	.854	C-41, OF-1
1889	BAL AA	72	.182	.241	253	46	6	3	1	0.4	28	27	13	37	4	0	0	371	77	30	4	6.6	.937	C-62, 1B-10
1890		19	.183	.225	71	13	1	1	0	0.0	7		4	3		0	0	112	18	7	3	7.2	.949	C-11, 1B-8
6 yrs.		227	.218	.274	822	179	22	9	2	0.2	101	65	41	73	17	0	0	1070	327	139	21	6.8	.910	C-202, 1B-18, OF-9

Jarvis Tatum

TATUM, JARVIS
B. Oct. 11, 1946, Fresno, Calif.

BR TR 6'   185 lbs.

1968	CAL A	17	.176	.196	51	9	1	0	0	0.0	7	2	0	9	0	3	0	25	0	0	0	1.5	1.000	OF-11
1969		10	.318	.318	22	7	0	0	0	0.0	2	0	0	6	0	4	0	6	0	1	0	0.7	.857	OF-5
1970		75	.238	.276	181	43	7	0	0	0.0	28	6	17	35	1	13	1	108	2	2	0	1.4	.982	OF-58
3 yrs.		102	.232	.264	254	59	8	0	0	0.0	37	8	17	50	1	20	1	139	2	3	0	1.4	.979	OF-74

Tommy Tatum

TATUM, V. TOMMY
B. July 16, 1919, Decatur, Tex.   D. Nov. 7, 1989, Oklahoma City, Okla.

BR TR 6'   185 lbs.

| 1941 | BKN N | 8 | .167 | .250 | 12 | 2 | 1 | 0 | 0 | 0.0 | 1 | 1 | 1 | 3 | 0 | 4 | 0 | 4 | 0 | 0 | 0 | 0.5 | 1.000 | OF-4 |

Year	Team	Games	BA	SA	AB	H	2B	3B	HR	HR%	R	RBI	BB	SO	SB	Pinch Hit AB	Pinch Hit H	PO	A	E	DP	TC/G	FA	G by Pos

Tommy Tatum *continued*

Year	Team	Games	BA	SA	AB	H	2B	3B	HR	HR%	R	RBI	BB	SO	SB	PH AB	PH H	PO	A	E	DP	TC/G	FA	G by Pos
1947	2 teams	BKN N (4G – .000)			CIN N (69G – .273)																			
"	total	73	.264	.330	182	48	5	2	1	0.5	19	16	16	17	7	7	0	120	6	0	3	1.7	1.000	OF-52, 2B-1
	2 yrs.	81	.258	.325	194	50	6	2	1	0.5	20	17	17	20	7	11	0	124	6	0	3	1.6	1.000	OF-56, 2B-1

Fred Tauby

TAUBY, FRED JOSEPH — Born Fred Joseph Taubensee. B. Mar. 27, 1906, Canton, Ohio D. Nov. 23, 1955, Concordia, Calif. BR TR 5'9½" 168 lbs.

Year	Team	Games	BA	SA	AB	H	2B	3B	HR	HR%	R	RBI	BB	SO	SB	PH AB	PH H	PO	A	E	DP	TC/G	FA	G by Pos
1935	CHI A	13	.125	.156	32	4	1	0	0	0.0	5	2	2	3	0	4	0	15	2	0	1	1.3	1.000	OF-7
1937	PHI N	11	.000	.000	20	0	0	0	0	0.0	2	3	0	5	1	3	0	8	0	0	0	0.7	1.000	OF-7
	2 yrs.	24	.077	.096	52	4	1	0	0	0.0	7	5	2	8	1	7	0	23	2	0	1	1.0	1.000	OF-14

Don Taussig

TAUSSIG, DONALD FRANKLIN — B. Feb. 19, 1932, New York, N. Y. BR TR 6' 180 lbs.

Year	Team	Games	BA	SA	AB	H	2B	3B	HR	HR%	R	RBI	BB	SO	SB	PH AB	PH H	PO	A	E	DP	TC/G	FA	G by Pos
1958	SF N	39	.200	.260	50	10	0	0	1	2.0	10	4	3	8	0	3	1	28	0	0	0	0.7	1.000	OF-36
1961	STL N	98	.287	.447	188	54	14	5	2	1.1	27	25	16	34	2	8	2	123	6	1	2	1.3	.992	OF-87
1962	HOU N	16	.200	.320	25	5	0	0	1	4.0	1	1	2	11	0	11	3	10	0	0	0	0.6	1.000	OF-4
	3 yrs.	153	.262	.399	263	69	14	5	4	1.5	38	30	21	53	2	22	6	161	6	1	2	1.1	.994	OF-127

Jackie Tavener

TAVENER, JOHN ADAM — B. Dec. 27, 1897, Celina, Ohio D. Sept. 14, 1969, Fort Worth, Tex. BL TR 5'5" 138 lbs.

Year	Team	Games	BA	SA	AB	H	2B	3B	HR	HR%	R	RBI	BB	SO	SB	PH AB	PH H	PO	A	E	DP	TC/G	FA	G by Pos
1921	DET A	2	.000	.000	4	0	0	0	0	0.0	0	0	0	1	0	0	0	3	4	0	0	3.5	1.000	SS-2
1925		134	.245	.318	453	111	11	11	0	0.0	45	47	39	60	5	0	0	229	398	24	73	4.9	.963	SS-134
1926		156	.265	.365	532	141	22	14	1	0.2	65	58	52	53	8	0	0	300	470	39	92	5.2	.952	SS-156
1927		116	.274	.406	419	115	22	9	5	1.2	60	59	36	38	20	1	0	246	356	33	79	5.5	.948	SS-114
1928		132	.260	.406	473	123	24	15	5	1.1	59	52	33	51	13	0	0	302	405	42	81	5.7	.944	SS-131
1929	CLE A	92	.212	.304	250	53	9	4	2	0.8	25	27	26	28	1	0	0	158	275	25	59	5.0	.945	SS-89
	6 yrs.	632	.255	.364	2131	543	88	53	13	0.6	254	243	186	231	47	1	0	1238	1908	163	384	5.2	.951	SS-626

Alex Taveras

TAVERAS, ALEJANDRO ANTONIO — Born Alejandro Antonio Taveras y Betances. B. Oct. 9, 1955, Santiago, Dominican Republic BR TR 5'10" 155 lbs.

Year	Team	Games	BA	SA	AB	H	2B	3B	HR	HR%	R	RBI	BB	SO	SB	PH AB	PH H	PO	A	E	DP	TC/G	FA	G by Pos
1976	HOU N	14	.217	.217	46	10	0	0	0	0.0	3	2	2	1	1	0	0	26	44	3	4	5.2	.959	SS-7, 2B-7
1982	LA N	11	.333	.667	3	1	1	0	0	0.0	1	2	0	1	0	0	0	3	10	0	0	1.2	1.000	3B-4, 2B-4, SS-2
1983		10	.000	.000	4	0	0	0	0	0.0	0	0	0	1	0	0	0	3	5	0	1	0.8	1.000	SS-3, 2B-2, 3B-1
	3 yrs.	35	.208	.226	53	11	1	0	0	0.0	4	4	2	3	1	0	0	32	59	3	5	2.7	.968	2B-13, SS-12, 3B-5

Frank Taveras

TAVERAS, FRANKLIN CRISOSTOMO — Born Franklin Crisostomo Taveras y Fabian. B. Dec. 24, 1949, Las Matas deSanta Cruz, Dominican Republic BR TR 6' 155 lbs.

Year	Team	Games	BA	SA	AB	H	2B	3B	HR	HR%	R	RBI	BB	SO	SB	PH AB	PH H	PO	A	E	DP	TC/G	FA	G by Pos
1971	PIT N	1	–	–	0	0	0	0	0	0	0	0	0	0	0	0	0	0	0	0	0	0.0	–	
1972		4	.000	.000	3	0	0	0	0	0.0	0	0	1	1	0	0	0	2	2	0	1	1.0	1.000	SS-4
1974		126	.246	.270	333	82	4	2	0	0.0	33	26	25	41	13	0	0	170	321	31	60	4.1	.941	SS-124
1975		134	.212	.257	378	80	9	4	0	0.0	44	23	37	42	17	0	0	200	369	28	74	4.5	.953	SS-132
1976		144	.258	.297	519	134	8	6	0	0.0	76	24	44	79	58	1	0	210	481	35	74	5.0	.952	SS-141
1977		147	.252	.331	544	137	20	10	1	0.2	72	29	38	71	70	0	0	178	449	25	62	4.4	.962	SS-146
1978		157	.278	.353	654	182	31	9	0	0.0	81	38	29	60	46	0	0	216	448	38	80	4.5	.946	SS-157
1979	2 teams	PIT N (11G – .244)			NY N (153G – .263)																			
"	total	164	.262	.335	680	178	29	9	1	0.1	93	34	33	74	44	1	1	287	464	28	92	4.8	.964	SS-164
1980	NY N	141	.279	.327	562	157	27	0	0	0.0	65	25	23	64	32	5	0	237	347	25	63	4.3	.959	SS-140
1981		84	.230	.290	283	65	11	3	0	0.0	30	11	12	36	16	4	1	120	202	24	44	4.1	.931	SS-79
1982	MON N	48	.161	.241	87	14	5	1	0	0.0	9	4	7	4	6	2	1	58	70	6	18	2.8	.955	SS-26, 2B-19
	11 yrs.	1150	.255	.313	4043	1029	144	44	2	0.0	503	214	249	474	300	13	3	1678	3153	240	568	4.4	.953	SS-1113, 2B-19

LEAGUE CHAMPIONSHIP SERIES

Year	Team	Games	BA	SA	AB	H	2B	3B	HR	HR%	R	RBI	BB	SO	SB	PH AB	PH H	PO	A	E	DP	TC/G	FA	G by Pos
1974	PIT N	2	.000	.000	2	0	0	0	0	0.0	0	0	0	0	1	0	0	2	1	0	0	1.5	1.000	SS-2
1975		3	.143	.143	7	1	0	0	0	0.0	0	1	1	2	0	0	0	4	6	0	2	3.3	1.000	SS-3
	2 yrs.	5	.111	.111	9	1	0	0	0	0.0	0	1	1	2	1	0	0	6	7	0	2	2.6	1.000	SS-5

Bennie Taylor

TAYLOR, BENJAMIN EUGENE — B. Sept. 30, 1927, Metropolis, Ill. BL TL 6' 195 lbs.

Year	Team	Games	BA	SA	AB	H	2B	3B	HR	HR%	R	RBI	BB	SO	SB	PH AB	PH H	PO	A	E	DP	TC/G	FA	G by Pos
1951	STL A	33	.258	.398	93	24	2	1	3	3.2	14	6	9	22	1	7	2	195	14	6	21	6.5	.972	1B-25
1952	DET A	7	.167	.167	18	3	0	0	0	0.0	0	0	0	5	0	3	0	36	2	0	4	5.4	1.000	1B-4
1955	MIL N	12	.100	.100	10	1	0	0	0	0.0	2	0	2	4	0	9	1	1	0	0	0	0.1	1.000	1B-1
	3 yrs.	52	.231	.339	121	28	2	1	3	2.5	16	6	11	31	1	19	3	232	16	6	25	4.9	.976	1B-30

Bill Taylor

TAYLOR, WILLIAM MICHAEL (Moose) — B. Dec. 30, 1929, Alhambra, Calif. BL TL 6'3" 212 lbs.

Year	Team	Games	BA	SA	AB	H	2B	3B	HR	HR%	R	RBI	BB	SO	SB	PH AB	PH H	PO	A	E	DP	TC/G	FA	G by Pos
1954	NY N	55	.185	.292	65	12	1	0	2	3.1	4	10	3	15	0	42	9	6	0	0	0	0.1	1.000	OF-9
1955		65	.266	.516	64	17	4	0	4	6.3	9	12	1	16	0	60	15	0	0	0	0	0.0	–	OF-2
1956		1	.250	.500	4	1	0	0	0	0.0	0	1	0	0	0	0	0	0	0	0	0	0.0	–	OF-1
1957	2 teams	NY N (11G – .000)			DET A (9G – .348)																			
"	total	20	.250	.406	32	8	0	0	1	3.1	4	3	1	5	0	13	2	5	0	0	0	0.3	1.000	OF-5
1958	DET A	8	.375	.375	8	3	0	0	0	0.0	0	0	2	3	0	6	3	1	0	0	0	0.1	1.000	OF-1
	5 yrs.	149	.237	.405	173	41	8	0	7	4.0	17	26	7	39	0	121	29	12	0	0	0	0.1	1.000	OF-18

Billy Taylor

TAYLOR, WILLIAM HENRY (Bollicky) — B. 1855, Washington, D. C. D. May 14, 1900, Jacksonville, Fla. BR TR 5'11½" 204 lbs.

Year	Team	Games	BA	SA	AB	H	2B	3B	HR	HR%	R	RBI	BB	SO	SB	PH AB	PH H	PO	A	E	DP	TC/G	FA	G by Pos
1881	3 teams	WOR N (6G – .107)			DET N (1G – .500)				CLE N (24G – .243)															
"	total	31	.222	.252	135	30	4	0	0	0.0	15		0	10		0	0	67	9	15	1	2.9	.835	OF-28, 3B-2, P-2
1882	PIT AA	70	.281	.455	299	84	16	12	4	1.3	40		7			0	0	377	73	60	7	7.3	.882	C-27, 1B-23, 3B-14, OF-8, P-1

Year	Team	Games	BA	SA	AB	H	2B	3B	HR	HR%	R	RBI	BB	SO	SB	Pinch Hit AB	Pinch Hit H	PO	A	E	DP	TC/G	FA	G by Pos

Billy Taylor *continued*

Year	Team	Games	BA	SA	AB	H	2B	3B	HR	HR%	R	RBI	BB	SO	SB	AB	H	PO	A	E	DP	TC/G	FA	G by Pos
1883		83	.260	.350	369	96	13	7	2	0.5	43		9			0	0	263	66	58	4	4.7	.850	OF-37, C-33, P-19, 1B-9
1884	2 teams	STL U (43G – .366)			PHI AA (30G – .252)																			
"	total	73	.323	.471	297	96	29	3	3	1.0	52		9			0	0	122	118	37	5	3.8	.866	P-63, 1B-10, OF-4
1885	PHI AA	6	.190	.190	21	4	0	0	0	0.0	0		0			0	0	0	5	4	0	1.5	.556	P-6
1886	BAL AA	10	.308	.359	39	12	0	1	0	0.0	4		1			0	0	18	14	3	0	3.5	.914	P-8, 1B-1, C-1
1887	PHI AA	1	.250	.250	4	1	0	0	0	0.0	0		0		0	0	0	0	1	0	0	1.0	1.000	P-1
7 yrs.		274	.277	.393	1164	323	62	23	9	0.8	148	15	26	10	0	0	0	847	286	177	17	4.8	.865	P-100, OF-77, C-61, 1B-43, 3B-16

Bob Taylor

TAYLOR, ROBERT LEE
B. Mar. 20, 1944, Leland, Miss.   BL TR 5'9"   170 lbs.

Year	Team	Games	BA	SA	AB	H	2B	3B	HR	HR%	R	RBI	BB	SO	SB	AB	H	PO	A	E	DP	TC/G	FA	G by Pos
1970	SF N	63	.190	.262	84	16	0	0	2	2.4	12	10	12	13	0	28	6	27	1	0	1	0.4	1.000	OF-26, C-1

Carl Taylor

TAYLOR, CARL MEANS
B. Jan. 20, 1944, Sarasota, Fla.   BR TR 6'2"   200 lbs.

Year	Team	Games	BA	SA	AB	H	2B	3B	HR	HR%	R	RBI	BB	SO	SB	AB	H	PO	A	E	DP	TC/G	FA	G by Pos
1968	PIT N	44	.211	.225	71	15	1	0	0	0.0	5	7	10	10	1	10	1	83	10	2	1	2.2	.979	C-29, OF-2
1969		104	.348	.457	221	77	10	1	4	1.8	30	33	31	36	0	41	17	267	16	8	26	2.8	.973	OF-36, 1B-24
1970	STL N	104	.249	.388	245	61	12	2	6	2.4	39	45	41	30	5	42	11	176	11	3	11	1.8	.984	OF-46, 1B-15, 3B-1
1971	2 teams	KC A (20G – .179)			PIT N (7G – .167)																			
"	total	27	.176	.216	51	9	0	1	0	0.0	4	3	5	18	0	13	2	31	0	1	0	1.2	.969	OF-18
1972	KC A	63	.265	.301	113	30	2	1	0	0.0	17	11	17	16	4	26	8	161	9	7	7	2.8	.960	C-21, OF-7, 1B-6, 3B-5
1973		69	.228	.283	145	33	6	1	0	0.0	18	16	32	20	2	1	0	270	20	6	2	4.3	.980	C-63, 1B-2, DH-1
6 yrs.		411	.266	.352	846	225	31	6	10	1.2	113	115	136	130	12	133	39	988	66	27	47	2.6	.975	C-113, OF-109, 1B-47, 3B-6, DH-1

Chink Taylor

TAYLOR, C. L.
B. Feb. 9, 1898, Burnet, Tex.   D. July 7, 1980, Temple, Tex.   BR TR 5'9"   160 lbs.

Year	Team	Games	BA	SA	AB	H	2B	3B	HR	HR%	R	RBI	BB	SO	SB	AB	H	PO	A	E	DP	TC/G	FA	G by Pos
1925	CHI N	8	.000	.000	6	0	0	0	0	0.0	2	0	0	0	0	2	0	2	0	0	0	0.3	1.000	OF-2

Danny Taylor

TAYLOR, DANIEL TURNEY
B. Dec. 23, 1900, Lash, Pa.   D. Oct. 11, 1972, Latrobe, Pa.   BR TR 5'10"   190 lbs.

Year	Team	Games	BA	SA	AB	H	2B	3B	HR	HR%	R	RBI	BB	SO	SB	AB	H	PO	A	E	DP	TC/G	FA	G by Pos
1926	WAS A	21	.300	.400	50	15	0	1	1	2.0	10	5	5	7	1	5	2	17	1	0	0	0.9	1.000	OF-12
1929	CHI N	2	.000	.000	3	0	0	0	0	0.0	0	0	1	1	0	1	0	1	0	0	0	0.5	1.000	OF-1
1930		74	.283	.402	219	62	14	3	2	0.9	43	37	27	34	6	14	7	97	3	3	0	1.4	.971	OF-52
1931		88	.300	.448	270	81	18	6	5	1.9	48	41	31	46	4	18	6	170	3	2	0	2.0	.989	OF-67
1932	2 teams	CHI N (6G – .227)			BKN N (105G – .324)																			
"	total	111	.319	.489	417	133	24	7	11	2.6	87	51	36	42	14	3	0	289	8	5	1	2.7	.983	OF-102
1933	BKN N	103	.285	.469	358	102	21	9	9	2.5	75	40	47	45	11	11	3	247	4	6	1	2.5	.977	OF-91
1934		120	.299	.440	405	121	24	6	7	1.7	62	57	63	47	12	10	2	188	8	5	1	1.7	.975	OF-108
1935		112	.290	.432	352	102	19	5	7	2.0	51	59	46	32	6	9	4	193	4	6	0	1.8	.970	OF-99
1936		43	.293	.397	116	34	6	0	2	1.7	12	15	11	14	2	8	1	49	2	1	1	1.2	.981	OF-31
9 yrs.		674	.297	.446	2190	650	121	37	44	2.0	388	305	267	268	56	79	25	1251	33	28	4	1.9	.979	OF-563

Dwight Taylor

TAYLOR, DWIGHT BERNARD
B. Mar. 24, 1960, Los Angeles, Calif.   BL TL 5'9"   172 lbs.

Year	Team	Games	BA	SA	AB	H	2B	3B	HR	HR%	R	RBI	BB	SO	SB	AB	H	PO	A	E	DP	TC/G	FA	G by Pos
1986	KC A	4	.000	.000	2	0	0	0	0	0.0	1	0	1	0	1	0	0	0	0	0	0	0.0	–	DH-2, OF-1

Eddie Taylor

TAYLOR, EDWARD JAMES
B. Nov. 17, 1901, Chicago, Ill.   BR TR 5'6½"   160 lbs.

Year	Team	Games	BA	SA	AB	H	2B	3B	HR	HR%	R	RBI	BB	SO	SB	AB	H	PO	A	E	DP	TC/G	FA	G by Pos
1926	BOS N	92	.268	.313	272	73	8	2	0	0.0	37	33	38	26	4	0	0	117	174	13	28	3.3	.957	3B-62, SS-33

Fred Taylor

TAYLOR, FREDERICK RANKIN
B. Dec. 3, 1924, Zanesville, Ohio   BL TR 6'3"   201 lbs.

Year	Team	Games	BA	SA	AB	H	2B	3B	HR	HR%	R	RBI	BB	SO	SB	AB	H	PO	A	E	DP	TC/G	FA	G by Pos
1950	WAS A	6	.125	.125	16	2	0	0	0	0.0	1	0	1	2	0	3	0	27	3	1	5	5.2	.968	1B-3
1951		6	.167	.250	12	2	1	0	0	0.0	1	0	0	4	0	4	0	24	1	1	4	4.3	.962	1B-2
1952		10	.263	.316	19	5	1	0	0	0.0	3	4	3	2	0	5	2	34	6	0	4	4.0	1.000	1B-5
3 yrs.		22	.191	.234	47	9	2	0	0	0.0	5	4	4	8	0	12	2	85	10	2	13	4.4	.979	1B-10

George Taylor

TAYLOR, GEORGE EDWARD
B. Feb. 3, 1855, Belfast, Me.   D. Feb. 19, 1888, San Francisco, Calif.

Year	Team	Games	BA	SA	AB	H	2B	3B	HR	HR%	R	RBI	BB	SO	SB	AB	H	PO	A	E	DP	TC/G	FA	G by Pos
1884	PIT AA	41	.211	.250	152	32	4	1	0	0.0	22		6			0	0	68	7	19	0	2.3	.798	OF-41

Harry Taylor

TAYLOR, HARRY LEONARD
B. Apr. 4, 1866, Halsey Valley, N. Y.   D. July 12, 1955, Buffalo, N. Y.   BL   6'2"   160 lbs.

Year	Team	Games	BA	SA	AB	H	2B	3B	HR	HR%	R	RBI	BB	SO	SB	AB	H	PO	A	E	DP	TC/G	FA	G by Pos
1890	LOU AA	134	.306	.344	553	169	7	7	0	0.0	115		68		45	0	0	1330	112	36	59	11.0	.976	1B-118, SS-12, 2B-4, C-1
1891		93	.295	.354	356	105	7	4	2	0.6	81	37	55	33	15	0	0	929	49	21	57	10.7	.979	1B-92, 3B-1, 2B-1, C-1
1892	LOU N	125	.260	.278	493	128	7	1	0	0.0	66	34	58	23	24	0	0	498	74	29	29	4.8	.952	OF-73, 1B-34, 2B-14, 3B-5, SS-2
1893	BAL N	88	.283	.322	360	102	9	1	1	0.3	50	54	32	11	24	0	0	882	43	23	58	10.8	.976	1B-88
4 yrs.		440	.286	.323	1762	504	30	13	3	0.2	312	125	213	67	108	0	0	3639	278	109	203	9.2	.973	1B-332, OF-73, 2B-19, SS-14, 3B-6, C-2

Harry Taylor

TAYLOR, HARRY WARREN (Handsome Harry)
B. Dec. 26, 1907, McKeesport, Pa.   D. Apr. 27, 1969, Toledo, Ohio   BL TL 6'1½"   185 lbs.

Year	Team	Games	BA	SA	AB	H	2B	3B	HR	HR%	R	RBI	BB	SO	SB	AB	H	PO	A	E	DP	TC/G	FA	G by Pos
1932	CHI N	10	.125	.125	8	1	0	0	0	0.0	1	0	1	1	0	7	1	5	0	0	0	0.5	1.000	1B-1

Hawk Taylor

TAYLOR, ROBERT DALE
B. Apr. 3, 1939, Metropolis, Ill.   BR TR 6'1"   187 lbs.

Year	Team	Games	BA	SA	AB	H	2B	3B	HR	HR%	R	RBI	BB	SO	SB	AB	H	PO	A	E	DP	TC/G	FA	G by Pos
1957	MIL N	7	.000	.000	1	0	0	0	0	0.0	2	0	0	0	0	1	0	0	0	0	0	0.0	–	C-1
1958		4	.125	.250	8	1	1	0	0	0.0	1	0	0	3	0	0	0	5	0	0	0	1.3	1.000	OF-4

Year	Team	Games	BA	SA	AB	H	2B	3B	HR	HR%	R	RBI	BB	SO	SB	Pinch Hit AB	Pinch Hit H	PO	A	E	DP	TC/G	FA	G by Pos

Hawk Taylor *continued*

Year	Team	Games	BA	SA	AB	H	2B	3B	HR	HR%	R	RBI	BB	SO	SB	PH AB	PH H	PO	A	E	DP	TC/G	FA	G by Pos
1961		20	.192	.308	26	5	0	0	1	3.8	1	1	3	11	0	12	2	8	1	0	0	0.5	1.000	OF-5, C-1
1962		20	.255	.255	47	12	0	0	0	0.0	3	2	2	10	0	8	2	23	1	1	0	1.3	.960	OF-11
1963		16	.069	.069	29	2	0	0	0	0.0	1	0	1	12	0	9	0	14	0	0	0	0.9	1.000	OF-8
1964	NY N	92	.240	.329	225	54	8	0	4	1.8	20	23	8	33	0	34	8	210	28	5	5	2.6	.979	C-45, OF-16
1965		25	.152	.413	46	7	0	0	4	8.7	5	10	1	8	0	13	0	51	6	3	0	2.4	.950	C-15, 1B-1
1966		53	.174	.275	109	19	2	0	3	2.8	5	12	3	19	0	28	4	140	18	3	10	3.0	.981	C-29, 1B-13
1967 2 teams	NY N (13G – .243)				CAL A (23G – .308)																			
" total		36	.281	.382	89	25	6	0	1	1.1	8	7	6	16	0	5	1	140	18	3	3	4.5	.981	C-31
1969	KC A	64	.270	.427	89	24	5	0	3	3.4	7	21	6	18	0	49	13	38	2	2	1	0.7	.952	OF-18, C-6
1970		57	.164	.218	55	9	3	0	0	0.0	3	6	6	16	0	46	9	12	2	1	1	0.3	.933	C-3, 1B-1
11 yrs.		394	.218	.319	724	158	25	0	16	2.2	56	82	36	146	0	205	39	641	76	18	20	1.9	.976	C-131, OF-62, 1B-15

Jack Taylor

TAYLOR, JOHN W.
B. Jan. 14, 1874, New Straightsville, Ohio D. Mar. 4, 1938, Columbus, Ohio

BR TR 5'10" 170 lbs.

Year	Team	Games	BA	SA	AB	H	2B	3B	HR	HR%	R	RBI	BB	SO	SB	PH AB	PH H	PO	A	E	DP	TC/G	FA	G by Pos
1898	CHI N	5	.200	.333	15	3	2	0	0	0.0	4	2	3		0	0	0	0	9	0	1	1.8	1.000	P-5
1899		42	.266	.360	139	37	9	2	0	0.0	25	17	16		0	1	1	24	88	8	8	2.9	.933	P-41
1900		28	.235	.333	81	19	3	1	1	1.2	7	6	3		1	0	0	10	42	7	2	2.1	.881	P-28
1901		35	.217	.274	106	23	6	0	0	0.0	12	2	4		0	2	0	24	78	6	3	3.1	.944	P-33
1902		55	.237	.280	186	44	6	1	0	0.0	18	17	8		6	1	0	42	133	9	5	3.3	.951	P-36, 3B-12, OF-3, 1B-2, 2B-1
1903		40	.222	.310	126	28	3	4	0	0.0	13	17	6		3	0	0	16	91	7	2	2.9	.939	P-37, 3B-1, 2B-1
1904	STL N	42	.211	.301	133	28	3	3	1	0.8	9	8	4		3	0	0	14	109	6	1	3.1	.953	P-41
1905		39	.190	.264	121	23	5	2	0	0.0	11	12	8		4	0	0	12	82	3	1	2.5	.969	P-37, 3B-2
1906 2 teams	STL N (17G – .208)				CHI N (17G – .208)																			
" total		34	.208	.236	106	22	3	0	0	0.0	9	5	14		1	0	0	12	95	2	2	3.2	.982	P-34
1907	CHI N	18	.191	.234	47	9	2	0	0	0.0	2	1	0		0	0	0	6	40	0	1	2.6	1.000	P-18
10 yrs.		338	.223	.292	1060	236	42	13	2	0.2	110	87	66		18	4	1	160	767	48	26	2.9	.951	P-310, 3B-15, OF-3, 2B-2, 1B-2

Joe Taylor

TAYLOR, JOE CEPHUS (Cash)
B. Mar. 2, 1926, Chapman, Ala.

BR TR 6'1" 185 lbs.

Year	Team	Games	BA	SA	AB	H	2B	3B	HR	HR%	R	RBI	BB	SO	SB	PH AB	PH H	PO	A	E	DP	TC/G	FA	G by Pos
1954	PHI A	18	.224	.328	58	13	1	1	1	1.7	5	8	2	9	0	3	2	32	1	2	0	1.9	.943	OF-16
1957	CIN N	33	.262	.439	107	28	7	0	4	3.7	14	9	6	24	0	6	2	63	3	2	1	2.1	.971	OF-27
1958 2 teams	STL N (18G – .304)				BAL A (36G – .273)																			
" total		54	.280	.440	100	28	7	0	3	3.0	13	12	9	23	0	25	7	44	1	1	1	0.9	.978	OF-26
1959	BAL A	14	.156	.281	32	5	1	0	1	3.1	2	2	11	15	0	1	0	10	0	0	0	0.7	1.000	OF-12
4 yrs.		119	.249	.401	297	74	16	1	9	3.0	34	31	28	71	0	35	11	149	5	5	2	1.3	.969	OF-81

Leo Taylor

TAYLOR, LEO THOMAS (Chink)
B. May 13, 1901, Walla Walla, Wash. D. May 20, 1982, Seattle, Wash.

BR TR 5'10½" 150 lbs.

Year	Team	Games	BA	SA	AB	H	2B	3B	HR	HR%	R	RBI	BB	SO	SB	PH AB	PH H	PO	A	E	DP	TC/G	FA	G by Pos
1923	CHI A	2	–	–	0	0	0	0	0	–	0	0	0	0	0	0	0	0	0	0	0	0.0	–	

Live Oak Taylor

TAYLOR, EDWARD S.
B. 1850, Belfast, Me. D. Feb. 19, 1888, San Francisco, Calif.

Year	Team	Games	BA	SA	AB	H	2B	3B	HR	HR%	R	RBI	BB	SO	SB	PH AB	PH H	PO	A	E	DP	TC/G	FA	G by Pos
1877	HAR N	2	.375	.375	8	3	0	0	0	0.0	0	0	0	2		0	0	2	0	0	0	1.0	1.000	OF-2

Sammy Taylor

TAYLOR, SAMUEL DOUGLAS
B. Feb. 27, 1933, Woodruff, S. C.

BL TR 6'2" 185 lbs.

Year	Team	Games	BA	SA	AB	H	2B	3B	HR	HR%	R	RBI	BB	SO	SB	PH AB	PH H	PO	A	E	DP	TC/G	FA	G by Pos
1958	CHI N	96	.259	.372	301	78	12	2	6	2.0	30	36	27	46	2	12	4	460	23	6	4	5.1	.988	C-87
1959		110	.269	.428	353	95	13	2	13	3.7	41	43	35	47	1	9	1	497	37	10	1	4.9	.982	C-109
1960		74	.207	.327	150	31	9	0	3	2.0	14	17	6	18	0	36	6	152	24	4	2	2.4	.978	C-43
1961		89	.238	.391	235	56	8	2	8	3.4	26	23	23	39	0	14	0	319	25	4	5	3.9	.989	C-75
1962 2 teams	CHI N (7G – .133)				NY N (68G – .222)																			
" total		75	.214	.318	173	37	5	2	3	1.7	12	21	26	20	0	16	3	225	26	2	3	3.4	.992	C-56
1963 3 teams	NY N (22G – .257)				CIN N (3G – .000)				CLE A (4G – .300)															
" total		29	.235	.275	51	12	0	1	0	0.0	4	7	5	11	0	14	5	68	5	1	2	2.6	.986	C-17
6 yrs.		473	.245	.375	1263	309	47	9	33	2.6	127	147	122	181	3	101	19	1721	140	27	17	4.0	.986	C-387

Sandy Taylor

TAYLOR, JAMES B.
Deceased.

5'10½" 175 lbs.

Year	Team	Games	BA	SA	AB	H	2B	3B	HR	HR%	R	RBI	BB	SO	SB	PH AB	PH H	PO	A	E	DP	TC/G	FA	G by Pos
1879	TRO N	24	.216	.258	97	21	4	0	0	0.0	10	8	1	8		0	0	37	2	12	0	2.1	.765	OF-24

Tommy Taylor

TAYLOR, THOMAS LIVINGSTONE CARLTON
B. Sept. 17, 1892, Mexia, Tex. D. Apr. 5, 1956, Greenville, Miss.

BR TR 5'8½" 160 lbs.

Year	Team	Games	BA	SA	AB	H	2B	3B	HR	HR%	R	RBI	BB	SO	SB	PH AB	PH H	PO	A	E	DP	TC/G	FA	G by Pos
1924	WAS A	26	.260	.329	73	19	3	1	0	0.0	11	10	2	8	2	6	1	23	17	4	4	1.7	.909	3B-16, 2B-2, OF-1

WORLD SERIES

Year	Team	Games	BA	SA	AB	H	2B	3B	HR	HR%	R	RBI	BB	SO	SB	PH AB	PH H	PO	A	E	DP	TC/G	FA	G by Pos
1924	WAS A	3	.000	.000	2	0	0	0	0	0.0	0	0	0	2	0	0	0	0	3	1	0	1.3	.750	3B-2

Tony Taylor

TAYLOR, ANTONIO NEMESIO
Born Antonio Nemesio Taylor y Sanchez.
B. Dec. 19, 1935, Central Alara, Cuba

BR TR 5'9" 170 lbs.

Year	Team	Games	BA	SA	AB	H	2B	3B	HR	HR%	R	RBI	BB	SO	SB	PH AB	PH H	PO	A	E	DP	TC/G	FA	G by Pos
1958	CHI N	140	.235	.314	497	117	15	3	6	1.2	63	27	40	93	21	0	0	311	374	23	103	5.1	.968	2B-137, 3B-1
1959		150	.280	.393	624	175	30	8	8	1.3	96	38	45	86	23	0	0	355	456	25	105	5.6	.970	2B-149, SS-2
1960 2 teams	CHI N (19G – .263)				PHI N (127G – .287)																			
" total		146	.284	.377	581	165	25	5	5	0.9	80	44	41	98	26	2	0	321	411	23	87	5.2	.970	2B-142, 3B-4
1961	PHI N	106	.250	.323	400	100	17	3	2	0.5	47	26	29	59	11	14	3	233	279	10	74	4.9	.981	2B-91, 3B-3
1962		152	.259	.342	625	162	21	5	7	1.1	87	43	68	82	20	2	1	372	385	22	101	5.1	.972	2B-150, SS-2
1963		157	.281	.367	640	180	20	10	5	0.8	102	49	42	99	23	4	0	325	412	10	88	4.8	.987	2B-149, 3B-13
1964		154	.251	.316	570	143	13	6	4	0.7	62	46	46	74	13	3	1	325	358	16	94	4.5	.977	2B-150
1965		106	.229	.319	323	74	14	3	3	0.9	41	27	22	58	5	14	1	169	222	17	52	3.8	.958	2B-86, 3B-5

Year	Team		Games	BA	SA	AB	H	2B	3B	HR	HR%	R	RBI	BB	SO	SB	Pinch Hit AB	H	PO	A	E	DP	TC/G	FA	G by Pos

Gene Tenace *continued*

Year	Team		Games	BA	SA	AB	H	2B	3B	HR	HR%	R	RBI	BB	SO	SB	AB	H	PO	A	E	DP	TC/G	FA	G by Pos
1969	OAK	A	16	.158	.237	38	6	0	0	1	2.6	1	2	1	15	0	5	0	61	6	0	0	4.2	1.000	C-13
1970			38	.305	.562	105	32	6	0	7	6.7	19	20	23	30	0	7	2	180	18	2	7	5.3	.990	C-30
1971			65	.274	.430	179	49	7	0	7	3.9	26	25	29	34	2	13	4	300	20	2	3	5.0	.994	C-52, OF-1
1972			82	.225	.339	227	51	5	3	5	2.2	22	32	24	42	0	17	7	329	23	7	5	4.4	.981	C-49, OF-9, 1B-7, 3B-2, 2B-2
1973			160	.259	.443	510	132	18	2	24	4.7	83	84	101	94	2	2	0	1218	71	14	108	8.1	.989	1B-134, C-33, DH-3, 2B-1
1974			158	.211	.411	484	102	17	1	26	5.4	71	73	110	105	2	0	0	1110	83	10	83	7.6	.992	1B-106, C-79, 2B-3
1975			158	.255	.464	498	127	17	0	29	5.8	83	87	106	127	7	0	0	942	84	11	37	6.6	.989	C-125, 1B-68, DH-1
1976			128	.249	.458	417	104	19	1	22	5.3	64	66	81	91	5	3	0	840	56	8	50	7.1	.991	1B-70, C-65, DH-2
1977	SD	N	147	.233	.410	437	102	24	4	15	3.4	66	61	125	119	5	5	0	820	112	16	33	6.4	.983	C-99, 1B-36, 3B-14
1978			142	.224	.409	401	90	18	4	16	4.0	60	61	101	98	6	7	1	944	79	8	68	7.3	.992	1B-80, C-71, 3B-1
1979			151	.263	.445	463	122	16	0	20	4.3	61	67	105	106	2	7	2	995	83	8	65	7.2	.993	C-94, 1B-72
1980			133	.222	.424	316	70	11	1	17	5.4	46	50	92	63	4	16	2	540	56	11	16	4.6	.982	1B-104, C-19
1981	STL	N	58	.233	.403	129	30	7	0	5	3.9	26	22	38	26	0	12	3	165	22	3	4	3.3	.984	C-38, 1B-7
1982			66	.258	.500	124	32	9	0	7	5.6	18	18	36	31	1	12	3	188	24	1	4	3.2	.995	1B-19, C-3, OF-1
1983	PIT	N	53	.177	.258	62	11	5	0	0	0.0	7	6	12	17	0	29	3	99	6	2	6	2.0	.981	C-19, 1B-36, 3B-14
15 yrs.			1555	.241	.429	4390	1060	179	20	201	4.6	653	674	984	998	36	135	27	8731	743	103	489	6.2	.989	C-892, 1B-625, 3B-17, OF-11, DH-6, 2B-6

LEAGUE CHAMPIONSHIP SERIES

Year	Team		Games	BA	SA	AB	H	2B	3B	HR	HR%	R	RBI	BB	SO	SB	AB	H	PO	A	E	DP	TC/G	FA	G by Pos
1971	OAK	A	1	.000	.000	3	0	0	0	0	0.0	0	0	1	1	0	0	0	8	0	0	0	8.0	1.000	C-1
1972			5	.059	.059	17	1	0	0	0	0.0	1	1	3	5	0	0	0	3	1	0	1	0.8	1.000	C-6, 1B-1
1973			5	.235	.294	17	4	1	0	0	0.0	3	0	2	4	1	0	0	43	3	0	2	9.2	1.000	1B-5, C-3
1974			4	.000	.000	11	0	0	0	0	0.0	1	1	4	4	1	0	0	35	2	0	3	9.3	1.000	1B-4
1975			3	.000	.000	9	0	0	0	0	0.0	0	0	3	2	0	0	0	19	1	0	3	6.7	1.000	C-3, 1B-1
5 yrs.			18	.088	.105	57	5	1	0	0	0.0	5	2	13	16	2	0	0	108	7	0	9	6.4	1.000	C-13, 1B-11

WORLD SERIES

Year	Team		Games	BA	SA	AB	H	2B	3B	HR	HR%	R	RBI	BB	SO	SB	AB	H	PO	A	E	DP	TC/G	FA	G by Pos
1972	OAK	A	7	.348	.913	23	8	1	0	4	17.4	5	9	2	4	0	0	0	48	5	1	0	7.7	.981	C-6, 1B-1
1973			7	.158	.211	19	3	1	0	0	0.0	0	3	11	7	0	0	0	57	2	2	6	8.7	.967	1B-7, C-3
1974			5	.222	.222	9	2	0	0	0	0.0	0	0	3	4	0	0	0	20	1	0	3	4.2	1.000	1B-5
1982	STL	N	5	.000	.000	6	0	0	0	0	0.0	0	0	1	2	0	4	0	0	0	0	0	0.0	–	DH-1
4 yrs.			24	.228	.474	57	13	2	0	4	7.0 9th	5	12	17	17	0	4	0	125	8	3	9	5.7	.978	1B-13, C-9, DH-1

Tom Tennant

TENNANT, THOMAS FRANCIS
B. July 3, 1882, Monroe, Wis. D. Feb. 15, 1955, San Carlos, Calif.

BL TL 5'11" 165 lbs.

Year	Team		Games	BA	SA	AB	H	2B	3B	HR	HR%	R	RBI	BB	SO	SB	AB	H	PO	A	E	DP	TC/G	FA	G by Pos
1912	STL	A	2	.000	.000	2	0	0	0	0	0.0	1	0	0		0	2	0	0	0	0	0	0.0	–	

Fred Tenney

TENNEY, FRED CLAY
B. July 9, 1859, Marlborough, N. H. D. June 15, 1919, Fall River, Mass.

Year	Team		Games	BA	SA	AB	H	2B	3B	HR	HR%	R	RBI	BB	SO	SB	AB	H	PO	A	E	DP	TC/G	FA	G by Pos
1884	3 teams			**WAS U** (32G – .235)			**BOS U** (4G – .118)			**WIL U** (1G – .000)															
"	total		37	.216	.252	139	30	3	1	0	0.0	18	0	6		0	0	0	80	11	16	3	2.9	.850	OF-27, 1B-6, P-5

Fred Tenney

TENNEY, FREDERICK
B. Nov. 26, 1871, Georgetown, Mass. D. July 3, 1952, Boston, Mass.
Manager 1905-07, 1911.

BL TL 5'9" 155 lbs.

Year	Team		Games	BA	SA	AB	H	2B	3B	HR	HR%	R	RBI	BB	SO	SB	AB	H	PO	A	E	DP	TC/G	FA	G by Pos
1894	BOS	N	27	.395	.570	86	34	7	1	2	2.3	23	21	12	9	6	0	0	64	22	11	3	3.6	.887	C-20, OF-6, 1B-1
1895			49	.272	.353	173	47	9	1	1	0.6	35	21	24	5	6	0	0	109	24	7	2	2.9	.950	OF-28, C-21
1896			88	.336	.411	348	117	14	3	2	0.6	64	49	36	12	18	1	0	183	40	14	4	2.7	.941	OF-60, C-27
1897			132	.318	.376	566	180	24	3	1	0.2	125	85	49		34	0	0	1250	82	16	69	10.2	.988	1B-128, OF-4
1898			117	.328	.400	488	160	25	5	0	0.0	106	62	33		23	0	0	1090	66	23	71	10.1	.980	1B-117, C-1
1899			150	.347	.439	603	209	19	17	1	0.2	115	67	63		28	0	0	1474	99	35	107	10.7	.978	1B-150
1900			112	.279	.339	437	122	13	5	1	0.2	77	56	39		17	1	0	1021	82	21	50	10.0	.981	1B-111
1901			115	.278	.317	457	127	13	1	1	0.2	63	22	37		15	0	0	1069	88	29	58	10.3	.976	1B-113, C-2
1902			134	.315	.376	489	154	18	3	2	0.4	88	30	73		21	0	0	1251	105	21	75	10.3	.985	1B-134
1903			122	.313	.396	447	140	23	3	3	0.7	79	41	70		21	0	0	1145	93	33	60	10.4	.974	1B-122
1904			147	.270	.341	533	144	17	9	1	0.2	76	37	57		17	0	0	1457	115	24	66	10.9	.985	1B-144, OF-4
1905			149	.288	.332	549	158	18	3	1	0.2	84	28	67		17	1	0	1557	152	32	68	11.7	.982	1B-148, P-1
1906			143	.283	.340	544	154	12	8	1	0.2	61	28	58		17	0	0	1456	118	28	78	11.2	.983	1B-143
1907			150	.273	.334	554	151	18	8	0	0.0	83	26	82		15	1	0	1587	113	19	86	11.5	.989	1B-149
1908	NY	N	156	.256	.304	583	149	20	1	2	0.3	101	49	72		17	0	0	1634	117	18	68	11.3	.990	1B-156
1909			101	.235	.291	375	88	8	2	3	0.8	43	30	52		8	1	0	1046	72	16	53	11.2	.986	1B-98
1911	BOS	N	102	.263	.328	369	97	13	4	1	0.3	52	36	50	17	5	4	1	901	64	15	47	9.6	.985	1B-93, OF-2
17 yrs.			1994	.294	.358	7601	2231	270	77	22	0.3	1275	688	874	43	285	9	1	18294	1452	362	965	10.1	.982	1B-1807, OF-104, C-71, P-1

Frank Tepedino

TEPEDINO, FRANK RONALD
B. Nov. 23, 1947, Brooklyn, N. Y.

BL TL 5'11" 185 lbs.

Year	Team		Games	BA	SA	AB	H	2B	3B	HR	HR%	R	RBI	BB	SO	SB	AB	H	PO	A	E	DP	TC/G	FA	G by Pos
1967	NY	A	9	.400	.400	5	2	0	0	0	0.0	0	0	1	1	0	5	2	2	0	0	0	0.2	1.000	1B-1
1969			13	.231	.231	39	9	0	0	0	0.0	6	4	4	4	1	1	0	19	0	1	0	1.5	.950	OF-13
1970			16	.316	.421	19	6	2	0	0	0.0	2	2	1	2	0	11	4	10	0	0	0	0.6	1.000	OF-1, 1B-1
1971	2 teams	NY	A (6G – .000)				**MIL A** (53G – .198)																			
"	total		59	.188	.250	112	21	1	0	2	1.8	11	7	4	17	2	28	3	190	22	3	18	3.6	.986	1B-28, OF-1
1972	NY	A	8	.000	.000	8	0	0	0	0	0.0	0	0	0	1	0	8	0	0	0	0	0	0.0	–	
1973	ATL	N	74	.304	.419	148	45	5	0	4	2.7	20	29	13	21	0	24	9	331	28	3	30	4.9	.992	1B-58
1974			78	.231	.272	169	39	5	1	0	0.0	11	16	9	13	1	33	8	307	26	4	35	4.3	.988	1B-46
1975			8	.000	.000	7	0	0	0	0	0.0	0	0	1	2	0	7	0	0	0	0	0	0.0	–	
8 yrs.			265	.241	.306	507	122	13	1	6	1.2	50	58	33	61	4	117	26	859	76	11	83	3.6	.988	1B-134, OF-15

Joe Tepsic

TEPSIC, JOSEPH JOHN
B. Sept. 18, 1923, Slovan, Pa.

BR TR 5'9" 170 lbs.

Year	Team		Games	BA	SA	AB	H	2B	3B	HR	HR%	R	RBI	BB	SO	SB	Pinch Hit AB	Pinch Hit H	PO	A	E	DP	TC/G	FA	G by Pos

Joe Tepsic *continued*

| 1946 | BKN | N | 15 | .000 | .000 | 5 | 0 | 0 | 0 | 0 | 0.0 | 2 | 0 | 1 | 1 | 0 | 3 | 0 | 1 | 0 | 0 | 0 | 0.1 | 1.000 | OF-1 |

Jerry Terrell

TERRELL, JERRY WAYNE
B. July 13, 1946, Waseca, Minn.

BR TR 5'11" 165 lbs.

1973	MIN	A	124	.265	.315	438	116	15	2	1	0.2	43	32	21	56	13	3	1	170	298	18	55	3.9	.963	SS-81, DH-30, 3B-30, 2B-14, OF-1
1974			116	.245	.314	229	56	4	6	0	0.0	43	19	11	27	3	7	1	114	179	9	35	2.6	.970	SS-34, 2B-26, 3B-21, DH-12, OF-3, 1B-2
1975			108	.286	.345	385	110	16	2	1	0.3	48	36	19	27	4	4	1	267	232	14	60	4.8	.973	SS-41, 2B-39, 1B-15, 3B-12, OF-6, DH-2
1976			89	.246	.275	171	42	3	1	0	0.0	29	8	9	15	11	5	1	82	122	8	27	2.4	.962	2B-31, 3B-26, SS-16, DH-12, OF-6
1977			93	.224	.266	214	48	6	1	1	0.5	32	20	11	21	10	13	3	58	129	6	20	2.1	.969	3B-59, 2B-14, DH-9, SS-7, OF-1, 1B-1
1978	KC	A	73	.203	.211	133	27	1	0	0	0.0	14	8	4	13	8	3	2	88	103	4	15	2.7	.979	2B-31, 3B-25, SS-11, 1B-5
1979			31	.300	.450	40	12	3	0	1	2.5	5	2	1	1	1	5	0	10	28	1	4	1.3	.974	3B-19, 2B-7, DH-2, SS-1, P-1
1980			23	.063	.063	16	1	0	0	0	0.0	4	0	0	0	0	1	1	29	7	0	2	1.6	1.000	OF-7, 2B-3, 1B-3, DH-1, P-1
8 yrs.			657	.253	.304	1626	412	48	11	4	0.2	218	125	76	160	50	41	10	818	1098	60	218	3.0	.970	3B-192, SS-191, 2B-165, DH-68, 1B-26, OF-24, P-2

Tom Terrell

TERRELL, JOHN THOMAS
B. 1866, Louisville, Ky. D. July 9, 1893, Louisville, Ky.

| 1886 | LOU | AA | 1 | .250 | .250 | 4 | 1 | 0 | 0 | 0 | 0.0 | 0 | | 0 | | | 0 | 0 | 4 | 0 | 0 | 0 | 4.0 | 1.000 | OF-1, C-1 |

Adonis Terry

TERRY, WILLIAM H
B. Aug. 7, 1864, Westfield, Mass. D. Feb. 24, 1915, Milwaukee, Wis.

BR TR 5'11½" 168 lbs.

1884	BKN	AA	68	.233	.300	240	56	10	3	0	0.0	16		8			0	0	56	85	37	2	2.6	.792	P-57, OF-13
1885			71	.170	.208	264	45	1	3	1	0.4	23		10			0	0	90	46	15	2	2.1	.901	OF-47, P-25, 3B-1
1886			75	.237	.344	299	71	8	9	2	0.7	34		10			0	0	99	117	35	3	3.3	.861	P-34, OF-32, SS-13
1887			86	.293	.392	352	103	6	10	3	0.9	56		16		27	0	0	128	90	26	2	2.8	.893	OF-49, P-40, SS-2
1888			30	.252	.304	115	29	6	0	0	0.0	13	8	5		7	0	0	34	44	6	3	2.8	.929	P-23, OF-7, 1B-2
1889			49	.300	.450	160	48	6	6	2	1.3	29	26	14	14	8	0	0	88	88	10	4	3.8	.946	P-41, 1B-10
1890	BKN	N	99	.278	.408	363	101	17	9	4	1.1	63	59	40	34	32	0	0	127	79	19	6	2.3	.916	OF-54, P-46, 1B-1
1891			30	.209	.308	91	19	7	1	0	0.0	10	6	9	26	4	0	0	12	35	4	1	1.7	.922	P-25, OF-5
1892	2 teams		BAL	N	(1G –	.000)		PIT	N	(31G –	.160)														
"	total		32	.154	.288	104	16	0	4	2	1.9	10	11	10	12	2	0	0	27	51	7	0	2.7	.918	P-31, OF-1
1893	PIT	N	26	.254	.394	71	18	4	3	0	0.0	9	11	3	11	1	0	0	9	37	4	2	1.9	.920	P-26
1894	2 teams		PIT	N	(1G –	.000)		CHI	N	(30G –	.347)														
"	total		31	.347	.432	95	33	4	2	0	0.0	19	17	11	12	3	0	0	21	27	6	1	1.7	.889	P-24, OF-7, 1B-2
1895	CHI	N	40	.219	.292	137	30	3	2	1	0.7	18	10	2	17	1	0	0	17	83	13	3	2.8	.885	P-38, OF-1, SS-1
1896			30	.263	.343	99	26	4	2	0	0.0	14	15	8	12	4	0	0	18	43	2	0	2.1	.968	P-30
1897			1	.000	.000	3	0	0	0	0	0.0	1	0	0	0	0	0	0	0	3	1	0	4.0	.750	P-1
14 yrs.			668	.249	.344	2393	595	76	54	15	0.6	315	163	146	138	89	0	0	726	828	185	29	2.6	.894	P-441, OF-216, SS-16, 1B-15, 3B-1

Bill Terry

TERRY, WILLIAM HAROLD (Memphis Bill)
B. Oct. 30, 1896, Atlanta, Ga. D. Jan. 9, 1989, Jacksonville, Fla.
Manager 1932-41.
Hall of Fame 1954.

BL TL 6'1" 200 lbs.

1923	NY	N	3	.143	.143	7	1	0	0	0	0.0	1	0	2	2	0	1	0	22	1	0	1	7.7	1.000	1B-2
1924			77	.239	.399	163	39	7	2	5	3.1	26	24	17	18	1	**38**	9	325	14	4	30	4.5	.988	1B-42
1925			133	.319	.474	489	156	31	6	11	2.2	75	70	42	52	4	6	2	1270	77	14	83	10.2	.990	1B-126
1926			98	.289	.453	225	65	12	5	5	2.2	26	43	22	17	3	38	12	418	34	9	36	4.7	.980	1B-38, OF-14
1927			150	.326	.529	580	189	32	13	20	3.4	101	121	46	53	1	0	0	1621	105	12	135	11.6	.993	1B-150
1928			149	.326	.518	568	185	36	11	17	3.0	100	101	64	36	0	0	0	1584	78	12	148	11.2	.993	1B-149
1929			150	.372	.522	607	226	39	5	14	2.3	103	117	48	35	10	0	0	1575	111	12	146	11.3	.993	1B-149, OF-1
1930			154	**.401**	.619	633	**254**	39	15	23	3.6	139	129	57	33	8	0	0	1538	128	17	128	10.9	.990	1B-154
1931			153	.349	.529	611	213	43	**20**	9	1.5	**121**	112	47	36	8	0	0	1411	105	16	108	10.0	.990	1B-153
1932			154	.350	.580	643	225	42	11	28	4.4	124	117	32	23	4	0	0	1493	137	14	125	10.7	.991	1B-154
1933			123	.322	.423	475	153	20	5	6	1.3	68	58	40	23	3	4	0	1246	76	11	103	10.8	.992	1B-117
1934			153	.354	.463	602	213	30	6	8	1.3	109	83	60	47	0	0	0	1592	105	10	131	11.2	.994	1B-153
1935			145	.341	.451	596	203	32	8	6	1.0	91	64	41	55	7	2	1	1379	99	6	105	10.2	.996	1B-143
1936			79	.310	.424	229	71	10	5	2	0.9	36	39	19	19	0	22	6	525	41	2	55	7.2	.996	1B-56
14 yrs.			1721	.341	.506	6428	2193	373	112	154	2.4	1120	1078	537	449	56	113	34	15999	1111	139	1334	10.0	.992	1B-1586, OF-15

WORLD SERIES

1924	NY	N	5	.429	.786	14	6	0	1	1	7.1	3	1	3	1	0	1	0	43	2	0	2	9.0	1.000	1B-4
1933			5	.273	.455	22	6	1	0	1	4.5	1	1	0	0	0	0	0	50	1	0	3	10.2	1.000	1B-5
1936			6	.240	.240	25	6	0	0	0	0.0	1	5	1	4	0	0	0	45	8	0	5	8.8	1.000	1B-6
3 yrs.			16	.295	.443	61	18	1	1	2	3.3	7	7	4	5	0	1	0	138	11	0	10	9.3	1.000	1B-15

Zeb Terry

TERRY, ZEBULON ALEXANDER
B. June 17, 1891, Denison, Tex. D. Mar. 14, 1988, Los Angeles, Calif.

BR TR 5'8" 129 lbs.

1916	CHI	A	94	.190	.249	269	51	8	4	0	0.0	20	17	33	36	4	1	0	148	243	27	36	4.4	.935	SS-93
1917			2	.000	.000	1	0	0	0	0	0.0	0	0	2	0	0	0	0	0	1	0	0	0.5	1.000	SS-1
1918	BOS	N	28	.305	.362	105	32	2	2	0	0.0	17	8	8	14	1	0	0	57	114	4	14	6.3	.977	SS-27
1919	PIT	N	129	.227	.278	472	107	12	6	0	0.0	46	27	31	26	12	2	1	207	395	25	41	4.9	.960	SS-127
1920	CHI	N	133	.280	.369	496	139	26	9	0	0.0	56	52	44	22	12	0	0	291	471	25	62	5.9	.968	SS-70, 2B-63
1921			123	.275	.328	488	134	18	1	2	0.4	59	45	27	19	1	1	0	272	413	20	57	5.7	.972	2B-123

Year	Team		Games	BA	SA	AB	H	2B	3B	HR	HR%	R	RBI	BB	SO	SB	Pinch Hit AB	H	PO	A	E	DP	TC/G	FA	G by Pos

Zeb Terry *continued*

| 1922 | | | 131 | .286 | .343 | 496 | 142 | 24 | 2 | 0 | 0.0 | 56 | 67 | 34 | 16 | 2 | 0 | 0 | 310 | 461 | 29 | 77 | 6.1 | .964 | 2B-125, SS-4, 3B-3 |
| 7 yrs. | | | 640 | .260 | .322 | 2327 | 605 | 90 | 24 | 2 | 0.1 | 254 | 216 | 179 | 133 | 32 | 4 | 2 | 1285 | 2098 | 130 | 287 | 5.5 | .963 | SS-322, 2B-311, 3B-3 |

Wayne Terwilliger

TERWILLIGER, WILLARD WAYNE (Twig)
B. June 27, 1925, Clare, Mich.   BR TR 5'11" 165 lbs.

1949	CHI	N	36	.223	.313	112	25	2	1	2	1.8	11	10	16	22	0	1	0	77	103	4	11	5.1	.978	2B-34
1950			133	.242	.363	480	116	22	3	10	2.1	63	32	43	63	13	4	1	314	380	24	80	5.4	.967	2B-126, OF-1, 3B-1, 1B-1
1951	2 teams			CHI	N	(50G – .214)					BKN	N	(37G – .280)												
"	total		87	.227	.256	242	55	7	0	0	0.0	37	14	37	28	4	7	3	167	187	13	47	4.2	.965	2B-73, 3B-1
1953	WAS	A	134	.252	.347	464	117	24	4	4	0.9	62	46	64	65	7	1	1	333	395	13	108	5.5	.982	2B-133
1954			106	.208	.270	337	70	10	1	3	0.9	42	24	32	40	3	1	0	227	274	16	77	4.9	.969	2B-90, 3B-10, SS-3
1955	NY	N	80	.257	.339	257	66	16	1	1	0.4	29	18	36	42	2	0	0	212	240	7	70	5.7	.985	2B-78, SS-1, 3B-1
1956			14	.222	.278	18	4	1	0	0	0.0	0	0	0	5	0	4	0	14	9	1	3	1.7	.958	2B-6
1959	KC	A	74	.267	.361	180	48	11	0	2	1.1	27	18	19	31	2	6	0	144	167	9	42	4.3	.972	2B-63, SS-2, 3B-1
1960			2	.000	.000	1	0	0	0	0	0.0	0	0	0	0	0	0	0	1	1	0	1	1.0	1.000	2B-2
9 yrs.			666	.240	.325	2091	501	93	10	22	1.1	271	162	247	296	31	24	5	1489	1756	87	439	5.0	.974	2B-605, 3B-14, SS-6, OF-1, 1B-1

Al Tesch

TESCH, ALBERT JOHN JR. (Tiny)
B. Jan. 27, 1891, Jersey City, N. J. D. Aug. 3, 1947, Jersey City, N. J.   BB TR 5'10" 155 lbs.

| 1915 | BKN | F | 8 | .286 | .429 | 7 | 2 | 1 | 0 | 0 | 0.0 | 2 | 2 | 0 | | | 0 | 1 | 0 | 5 | 8 | 2 | 1 | 1.9 | .867 | 2B-3 |

Nick Testa

TESTA, NICHOLAS
B. June 29, 1928, New York, N. Y.   BR TR 5'8" 180 lbs.

| 1958 | SF | N | 1 | – | – | 0 | 0 | 0 | 0 | 0 | – | 0 | 0 | 0 | 0 | 0 | 0 | 0 | 0 | 0 | 0 | 1 | 1.0 | – | C-1 |

Dick Tettelbach

TETTELBACH, RICHARD MORLEY (Tut)
B. June 26, 1929, New Haven, Conn.   BR TR 6' 195 lbs.

1955	NY	A	2	.000	.000	5	0	0	0	0	0.0	0	0	0	0	0	0	0	0	1	0	0	0.5	1.000	OF-2
1956	WAS	A	18	.156	.281	64	10	1	2	1	1.6	10	9	14	15	0	0	0	37	2	0	0	2.2	1.000	OF-18
1957			9	.182	.182	11	2	0	0	0	0.0	2	1	4	2	0	3	1	9	0	1	0	1.1	.900	OF-3
3 yrs.			29	.150	.250	80	12	1	2	1	1.3	12	10	18	17	0	3	1	46	3	1	0	1.7	.980	OF-23

Mickey Tettleton

TETTLETON, MICKEY LEE
B. Sept. 16, 1960, Oklahoma City, Okla.   BB TR 6'2" 190 lbs.

1984	OAK	A	33	.263	.355	76	20	2	1	1	1.3	10	5	11	21	0	3	0	112	10	1	1	3.7	.992	C-32
1985			78	.251	.351	211	53	12	0	3	1.4	23	15	28	59	2	3	1	344	24	4	9	4.8	.984	C-76, DH-1
1986			90	.204	.389	211	43	9	0	10	4.7	26	35	39	51	7	2	0	463	32	8	6	5.6	.984	C-89
1987			82	.194	.322	211	41	3	0	8	3.8	19	26	30	65	1	2	0	435	29	6	1	5.7	.987	C-80, DH-1, 1B-1
1988	BAL	A	86	.261	.424	283	74	11	1	11	3.9	31	37	28	70	0	9	0	361	31	3	1	4.6	.992	C-80
1989			117	.258	.509	411	106	21	2	26	6.3	72	65	73	117	3	3	1	297	42	2	1	2.9	.994	C-75, DH-43
6 yrs.			486	.240	.413	1403	337	58	4	59	4.2	181	183	209	383	13	22	2	2012	168	24	19	4.5	.989	C-432, DH-45, 1B-1

Tim Teufel

TEUFEL, TIMOTHY SHAWN (Tuff)
B. July 7, 1958, Greenwich, Conn.   BR TR 6' 175 lbs.

1983	MIN	A	21	.308	.538	78	24	7	1	3	3.8	11	6	2	8	0	2	0	47	58	1	14	5.0	.991	2B-18, DH-1, SS-1
1984			157	.262	.400	568	149	30	3	14	2.5	76	61	76	73	1	0	0	315	485	13	81	5.2	.984	2B-157
1985			138	.260	.399	434	113	24	3	10	2.3	58	50	48	70	4	6	1	237	352	12	67	4.4	.980	2B-137, DH-1
1986	NY	N	93	.247	.369	279	69	20	1	4	1.4	35	31	32	42	1	16	3	143	174	9	28	3.5	.972	2B-84, 1B-3, 3B-1
1987			97	.308	.545	299	92	29	0	14	4.7	55	61	44	53	3	18	8	139	214	11	44	3.8	.970	2B-92, 1B-1
1988			90	.234	.352	273	64	20	0	4	1.5	35	31	29	41	0	14	4	175	213	7	49	4.4	.982	2B-84, 1B-3
1989			83	.256	.333	219	56	7	2	2	0.9	27	15	32	50	1	12	3	261	112	10	30	4.6	.974	2B-40, 1B-33
7 yrs.			679	.264	.408	2150	567	137	10	51	2.4	297	255	263	337	10	68	19	1317	1608	63	313	4.4	.979	2B-612, 1B-40, DH-2, SS-1, 3B-1

LEAGUE CHAMPIONSHIP SERIES

1986	NY	N	2	.167	.167	6	1	0	0	0	0.0	0	0	0	0	0	0	0	2	8	0	1	5.0	1.000	2B-2
1988			1	.000	.000	3	0	0	0	0	0.0	0	0	0	1	0	0	0	1	3	0	0	4.0	1.000	2B-1
2 yrs.			3	.111	.111	9	1	0	0	0	0.0	0	0	0	1	0	0	0	3	11	0	1	4.7	1.000	2B-3

WORLD SERIES

| 1986 | NY | N | 3 | .444 | .889 | 9 | 4 | 1 | 0 | 1 | 11.1 | 1 | 1 | 0 | 2 | 0 | 0 | 0 | 3 | 3 | 1 | 1 | 2.3 | .857 | 2B-3 |

George Textor

TEXTOR, GEORGE BERNHARDT (Tex)
B. Dec. 27, 1888, Newport, Ky. D. Mar. 10, 1954, Massillon, Ohio   BB TR 5'10½" 174 lbs.

1914	IND	F	22	.175	.175	57	10	0	0	0	0.0	2	4	2			0	1	0	72	34	5	7	5.0	.955	C-21
1915	NWK	F	3	.333	.333	6	2	0	0	0	0.0	1	0	0			0	0	0	5	1	0	0	2.0	1.000	C-3
2 yrs.			25	.190	.190	63	12	0	0	0	0.0	3	4	2			0	1	0	77	35	5	7	4.7	.957	C-24

Moe Thacker

THACKER, MORRIS BENTON
B. May 21, 1934, Louisville, Ky.   BR TR 6'3" 205 lbs.

1958	CHI	N	11	.250	.542	24	6	1	0	2	8.3	4	3	1	7	0	2	1	34	6	2	1	3.8	.952	C-9
1960			54	.156	.167	90	14	1	0	0	0.0	5	6	14	20	1	4	1	170	23	4	2	3.6	.980	C-50
1961			25	.171	.171	35	6	0	0	0	0.0	3	2	11	11	0	0	0	67	5	2	0	3.0	.973	C-25
1962			65	.187	.234	107	20	5	0	0	0.0	8	9	14	40	0	1	0	219	34	1	8	3.9	.996	C-65
1963	STL	N	3	.000	.000	4	0	0	0	0	0.0	0	0	0	3	0	0	0	9	1	0	0	3.3	1.000	C-3
5 yrs.			158	.177	.227	260	46	7	0	2	0.8	20	20	40	81	1	7	2	499	69	9	11	3.7	.984	C-152

Ron Theobald

THEOBALD, RONALD MERRILL
B. July 28, 1943, Oakland, Calif.   BR TR 5'8" 165 lbs.

Year	Team		Games	BA	SA	AB	H	2B	3B	HR	HR%	R	RBI	BB	SO	SB	Pinch Hit AB	Pinch Hit H	PO	A	E	DP	TC/G	FA	G by Pos

Ron Theobald *continued*

1971	MIL	A	126	.276	.325	388	107	12	2	1	0.3	50	23	38	39	11	12	5	233	312	15	81	4.4	.973	2B-111, SS-1, 3B-1
1972			125	.220	.256	391	86	11	0	1	0.3	45	19	68	38	0	14	4	193	299	6	68	4.0	.988	2B-113
2 yrs.			251	.248	.290	779	193	23	2	2	0.3	95	42	106	77	11	26	9	426	611	21	149	4.2	.980	2B-224, SS-1, 3B-1

George Theodore

THEODORE, GEORGE BASIL (The Stork)
B. Nov. 13, 1947, Salt Lake City, Utah   BR TR 6'4"   190 lbs.

1973	NY	N	45	.259	.319	116	30	4	0	1	0.9	14	15	10	13	1	11	2	80	5	1	4	1.9	.988	OF-33, 1B-4
1974			60	.158	.211	76	12	1	0	1	1.3	7	1	8	14	0	30	5	97	3	3	7	1.7	.971	1B-14, OF-12
2 yrs.			105	.219	.276	192	42	5	0	2	1.0	21	16	18	27	1	41	7	177	8	4	11	1.8	.979	OF-45, 1B-18

WORLD SERIES

| 1973 | NY | N | 2 | .000 | .000 | 2 | 0 | 0 | 0 | 0 | 0.0 | 0 | 0 | 0 | 0 | 0 | 1 | 0 | 1 | 0 | 0 | 0 | 0.5 | 1.000 | OF-1 |

Tommy Thevenow

THEVENOW, THOMAS JOSEPH
B. Sept. 6, 1903, Madison, Ind.   D. July 29, 1957, Madison, Ind.   BR TR 5'10"   155 lbs.

1924	STL	N	23	.202	.270	89	18	4	1	0	0.0	4	7	1	6	1	0	0	61	95	8	15	7.1	.951	SS-23
1925			50	.269	.331	175	47	7	2	0	0.0	17	17	7	12	3	0	0	98	169	14	18	5.6	.950	SS-50
1926			156	.256	.311	563	144	15	5	2	0.4	64	63	27	26	8	0	0	371	597	45	98	6.5	.956	SS-156
1927			59	.194	.236	191	37	6	1	0	0.0	23	4	14	8	2	0	0	111	199	18	38	5.6	.945	SS-59
1928			69	.205	.287	171	35	8	3	0	0.0	11	13	20	12	0	0	0	104	166	19	29	4.2	.934	SS-64, 3B-3, 1B-1
1929	PHI	N	90	.227	.262	317	72	11	0	0	0.0	30	35	25	25	3	0	0	188	296	24	56	5.6	.953	SS-90
1930			156	.286	.326	573	164	21	1	0	0.0	57	78	23	26	1	0	0	344	554	56	113	6.1	.941	SS-156
1931	PIT	N	120	.213	.248	404	86	12	1	0	0.0	35	38	28	22	0	0	0	245	432	25	92	5.9	.964	SS-120
1932			59	.237	.284	194	46	3	3	0	0.0	12	26	7	12	0	6	0	82	126	14	24	3.8	.937	SS-29, 3B-22
1933			73	.312	.340	253	79	5	1	0	0.0	20	34	3	5	2	9	1	143	180	9	33	4.5	.973	2B-61, SS-3, 3B-1
1934			122	.271	.316	446	121	16	2	0	0.0	37	54	20	20	0	6	2	214	280	19	37	4.2	.963	2B-75, 3B-44, SS-1
1935			110	.238	.304	408	97	9	9	0	0.0	38	47	12	23	1	7	1	142	216	17	18	3.4	.955	3B-82, SS-13, 2B-8
1936	CIN	N	106	.234	.268	321	75	7	2	0	0.0	25	36	15	23	2	1	0	178	248	23	49	4.2	.949	SS-68, 2B-33, 3B-12
1937	BOS	N	21	.118	.176	34	4	0	1	0	0.0	5	2	4	2	0	1	0	14	32	3	3	2.3	.939	SS-12, 3B-6, 2B-2
1938	PIT	N	15	.200	.200	25	5	0	0	0	0.0	2	2	4	0	0	1	0	13	31	2	7	3.1	.957	2B-9, SS-4, 3B-1
15 yrs.			1229	.247	.294	4164	1030	124	32	2	0.0	380	456	210	222	23	31	4	2308	3621	296	630	5.1	.952	SS-848, 2B-188, 3B-171, 1B-1

WORLD SERIES

1926	STL	N	7	.417	.583	24	10	1	0	1	4.2	5	4	0	1	0	0	0	10	26	2	5	5.4	.947	SS-7
1928			1	–	–	0	0	0	0	0	–	0	0	0	0	0	0	0	1	0	0	0	1.0	1.000	SS-1
2 yrs.			8	.417	.583	24	10	1	0	1	4.2	5	4	0	1	0	0	0	11	26	2	5	4.9	.949	SS-8

Andres Thomas

THOMAS, ANDRES PEREZ
Born Andres Perez y Thomas.
B. Nov. 10, 1963, Boca Chica, Dominican Republic   BR TR 6'1"   170 lbs.

1985	ATL	N	15	.278	.278	18	5	0	0	0	0.0	6	2	0	2	0	1	1	6	17	2	2	1.7	.920	SS-10
1986			102	.251	.372	323	81	17	2	6	1.9	26	32	8	49	4	6	3	143	290	19	62	4.4	.958	SS-97
1987			82	.231	.312	324	75	11	0	5	1.5	29	39	14	50	6	1	0	128	276	20	56	5.2	.953	SS-81
1988			153	.252	.360	606	153	22	2	13	2.1	54	68	14	95	7	3	1	230	456	29	90	4.7	.959	SS-150
1989			141	.213	.316	554	118	18	0	13	2.3	41	57	12	62	3	2	0	231	400	29	81	4.7	.956	SS-138
5 yrs.			493	.237	.339	1825	432	68	4	37	2.0	156	198	48	258	20	13	5	738	1439	99	291	4.6	.957	SS-476

Bill Thomas

THOMAS, WILLIAM MISKEY
Brother of Roy Thomas.
B. Dec. 8, 1877, Norristown, Pa.   D. Jan. 14, 1950, Evansburg, Pa.   BR TR 5'10"   190 lbs.

| 1902 | PHI | N | 6 | .118 | .118 | 17 | 2 | 0 | 0 | 0 | 0.0 | 1 | 0 | 1 | | 0 | 1 | 0 | 9 | 3 | 2 | 1 | 2.3 | .857 | OF-3, 2B-1, 1B-1 |

Bud Thomas

THOMAS, JOHN TILLMAN
B. Mar. 10, 1929, Sedalia, Mo.   BR TR 6'   160 lbs.

| 1951 | STL | A | 14 | .350 | .500 | 20 | 7 | 0 | 0 | 1 | 5.0 | 3 | 1 | 0 | 3 | 2 | 0 | 0 | 12 | 18 | 0 | 4 | 2.1 | 1.000 | SS-14 |

Danny Thomas

THOMAS, DANNY LEE
B. May 9, 1951, Birmingham, Ala.   D. July 3, 1980, Mobile, Ala.   BR TR 6'2"   190 lbs.

1976	MIL	A	32	.276	.457	105	29	5	1	4	3.8	13	15	14	28	1	0	0	60	3	3	1	2.1	.955	OF-32
1977			22	.271	.457	70	19	3	2	2	2.9	11	11	8	11	0	3	1	22	0	0	0	1.0	1.000	DH-9, OF-9
2 yrs.			54	.274	.457	175	48	8	3	6	3.4	24	26	22	39	1	3	1	82	3	3	1	1.6	.966	OF-41, DH-9

Derrel Thomas

THOMAS, DERREL OSBORN
B. Jan. 14, 1951, Los Angeles, Calif.   BB TR 6'   160 lbs.

1971	HOU	N	5	.000	.000	5	0	0	0	0	0.0	0	0	0	2	0	0	0	3	2	0	1	1.0	1.000	2B-1
1972	SD	N	130	.230	.310	500	115	15	5	5	1.0	48	36	41	73	9	2	0	290	357	26	77	5.2	.961	2B-83, SS-49, OF-3
1973			113	.238	.260	404	96	7	1	0	0.0	41	22	34	52	15	6	2	211	324	37	66	5.1	.935	SS-74, 2B-47
1974			141	.247	.333	523	129	24	6	3	0.6	48	41	51	58	7	5	3	310	336	18	53	4.7	.973	2B-104, 3B-22, OF-20, SS-5
1975	SF	N	144	.276	.381	540	149	21	9	6	1.1	99	48	57	56	28	2	1	349	372	19	100	5.1	.974	2B-141, OF-1
1976			81	.232	.301	272	63	5	4	2	0.7	38	19	29	26	10	11	2	163	215	15	52	4.9	.962	2B-69, OF-2, SS-1, 3B-1
1977			148	.267	.379	506	135	13	10	8	1.6	75	44	46	70	15	19	5	307	158	14	24	3.2	.971	OF-78, 2B-27, SS-26, 3B-6, 1B-3
1978	SD	N	128	.227	.293	352	80	10	2	3	0.9	36	26	35	37	11	7	1	328	168	12	39	4.0	.976	OF-77, 2B-40, 3B-26, 1B-14
1979	LA	N	141	.256	.350	406	104	15	4	5	1.2	47	44	41	49	18	11	1	298	38	5	8	2.4	.985	OF-119, 3B-18, 2B-5, SS-3, 1B-1
1980			117	.266	.357	297	79	18	3	1	0.3	32	22	26	48	9	8	3	203	175	14	39	3.4	.964	OF-52, SS-49, 2B-18, C-5, 3B-4
1981			80	.248	.321	218	54	4	0	4	1.8	25	24	25	23	7	3	0	133	144	14	30	3.6	.952	2B-30, SS-26, OF-18, 3B-10

Year	Team		Games	BA	SA	AB	H	2B	3B	HR	HR%	R	RBI	BB	SO	SB	Pinch Hit AB	Pinch Hit H	PO	A	E	DP	TC/G	FA	G by Pos

Derrel Thomas *continued*

1982			66	.265	.306	98	26	2	1	0	0.0	13	2	10	12	2	5	0	58	58	4	14	1.8	.967	OF-28, 2B-18, 3B-14, SS-6
1983			118	.250	.375	192	48	6	6	2	1.0	38	8	27	36	9	16	3	134	51	5	11	1.6	.974	OF-82, SS-13, 2B-9, 3B-7
1984	2 teams	MON N (108G – .255)				CAL A (14G – .138)																			
"	total		122	.243	.309	272	66	12	3	0	0.0	29	22	23	37	0	14	0	130	136	11	34	2.3	.960	SS-66, OF-55, 2B-15, 3B-7, 1B-1
1985	PHI	N	63	.207	.359	92	19	2	0	4	4.3	16	12	11	14	0	35	7	31	38	7	4	1.2	.908	SS-21, OF-7, 3B-1, 2B-1, C-1
15 yrs.			1597	.249	.332	4677	1163	154	54	43	0.9	585	370	456	593	140	144	28	2948	2572	201	552	3.6	.965	2B-608, OF-542, SS-339, 3B-116, 1B-19, C-6

DIVISIONAL PLAYOFF SERIES
| 1981 | LA | N | 4 | .000 | .000 | 2 | 0 | 0 | 0 | 0 | 0.0 | 1 | 0 | 0 | 1 | 0 | 1 | 0 | 0 | 0 | 0 | 0 | 0.0 | – | OF-4 |

LEAGUE CHAMPIONSHIP SERIES
1981	LA	N	2	1.000	1.000	1	1	0	0	0	0.0	2	0	0	0	0	1	1	0	0	0	0	0.0	–	OF-1, 3B-1
1983			4	.444	.556	9	4	1	0	0	0.0	0	0	0	3	1	1	0	7	0	0	0	1.8	1.000	OF-4
2 yrs.			6	.500	.600	10	5	1	0	0	0.0	2	0	0	3	1	2	1	7	0	0	0	1.2	1.000	OF-5, 3B-1

WORLD SERIES
| 1981 | LA | N | 5 | .000 | .000 | 7 | 0 | 0 | 0 | 0 | 0.0 | 2 | 1 | 1 | 2 | 0 | 2 | 0 | 4 | 2 | 0 | 2 | 1.2 | 1.000 | OF-3, SS-1, 3B-1 |

Frank Thomas

THOMAS, FRANK JOSEPH
B. June 11, 1929, Pittsburgh, Pa.   BR TR 6'3" 200 lbs.

1951	PIT	N	39	.264	.392	148	39	9	2	2	1.4	21	16	9	15	0	3	1	87	5	0	2	2.4	1.000	OF-37
1952			6	.095	.095	21	2	0	0	0	0.0	1	0	1	1	0	0	0	8	1	0	0	1.5	1.000	OF-5
1953			128	.255	.505	455	116	22	1	30	6.6	68	102	50	93	1	9	1	306	17	8	1	2.6	.976	OF-118
1954			153	.298	.497	577	172	32	7	23	4.0	81	94	51	74	3	1	1	418	14	5	2	2.9	.989	OF-153
1955			142	.245	.431	510	125	16	2	25	4.9	72	72	60	76	2	3	1	307	8	5	3	2.3	.984	OF-139
1956			157	.282	.461	588	166	24	3	25	4.3	69	80	36	61	0	2	0	216	179	18	22	2.6	.956	3B-111, OF-56, 2B-4
1957			151	.290	.460	594	172	30	1	23	3.9	72	89	44	66	3	0	0	729	119	25	60	5.8	.971	1B-71, OF-59, 3B-31
1958			149	.281	.528	562	158	26	4	35	6.2	89	109	42	79	0	1	0	160	243	30	22	2.9	.931	3B-139, OF-8, 1B-2
1959	CIN	N	108	.225	.380	374	84	18	2	12	3.2	41	47	27	56	0	1	0	206	126	19	19	3.3	.946	3B-64, OF-33, 1B-14
1960	CHI	N	135	.238	.399	479	114	12	1	21	4.4	54	64	28	74	1	11	4	528	92	17	40	4.7	.973	1B-50, OF-49, 3B-33
1961	2 teams	CHI N (15G – .260)				MIL N (124G – .284)																			
"	total		139	.281	.497	473	133	15	3	27	5.7	65	73	31	78	2	11	1	300	12	10	8	2.3	.969	OF-119, 1B-17
1962	NY	N	156	.266	.496	571	152	23	3	34	6.0	69	94	48	95	2	11	4	311	36	14	8	2.3	.961	OF-126, 1B-11, 3B-10
1963			126	.260	.393	420	109	9	1	15	3.6	34	60	33	48	0	15	4	304	17	4	10	2.6	.988	OF-96, 1B-15, 3B-1
1964	NY	N (60G – .254)				PHI N (39G – .294)																			
"	total		99	.271	.415	340	92	17	1	10	2.9	39	45	15	41	1	14	4	498	46	9	49	5.6	.984	1B-58, OF-31, 3B-2
1965	3 teams	PHI N (35G – .260)				HOU N (23G – .172)			MIL N (15G – .212)																
"	total		73	.220	.345	168	37	9	0	4	2.4	17	17	9	36	0	29	3	262	15	5	24	3.9	.982	1B-33, OF-16, 3B-3
1966	CHI	N	5	.000	.000	5	0	0	0	0	0.0	0	0	0	1	0	5	0	0	0	0	0	0.0	–	
16 yrs.			1766	.266	.454	6285	1671	262	31	286	4.6	792	962	484	894	15	123	25	4640	930	169	270	3.2	.971	OF-1045, 3B-394, 1B-271, 2B-4

Fred Thomas

THOMAS, FREDERICK HENRY
B. Dec. 19, 1892, Milwaukee, Wis.   D. Jan. 15, 1986, Rice Lake, Wis.   BR TR 5'10" 160 lbs.

1918	BOS	A	44	.257	.306	144	37	2	1	1	0.7	19	11	15	20	4	1	0	54	97	5	4	3.5	.968	3B-41, SS-1
1919	PHI	A	124	.212	.294	453	96	11	10	2	0.4	42	23	43	52	12	0	0	168	242	24	14	3.5	.945	3B-124
1920	2 teams	PHI A (76G – .231)				WAS A (3G – .143)																			
"	total		79	.229	.286	262	60	6	3	1	0.4	27	11	26	18	8	1	0	106	181	12	13	3.8	.960	3B-63, SS-12
3 yrs.			247	.225	.293	859	193	19	14	4	0.5	88	45	84	90	24	2	0	328	520	41	31	3.6	.954	3B-228, SS-13

WORLD SERIES
| 1918 | BOS | A | 6 | .118 | .118 | 17 | 2 | 0 | 0 | 0 | 0.0 | 0 | 1 | 1 | 2 | 0 | 0 | 0 | 6 | 10 | 0 | 0 | 2.7 | 1.000 | 3B-6 |

George Thomas

THOMAS, GEORGE EDWARD
B. Nov. 29, 1937, Minneapolis, Minn.   BR TR 6'3½" 190 lbs.

1957	DET	A	1	.000	.000	1	0	0	0	0	0.0	0	0	0	1	0	1	0	0	0	1	0	1.0	–	3B-1
1958			1	–	–	0	0	0	0	0	0.0	0	0	0	0	0	0	0	0	0	0	0	0.0	–	OF-1
1961	2 teams	DET A (17G – .000)				LA A (79G – .280)																			
"	total		96	.274	.458	288	79	12	1	13	4.5	41	59	21	70	3	5	0	99	64	13	6	1.8	.926	OF-47, 3B-38, SS-1
1962	LA	A	56	.238	.381	181	43	10	2	4	2.2	13	12	21	37	0	5	1	107	4	5	1	2.1	.957	OF-51
1963	LA	A (53G – .210)				DET A (44G – .239)																			
"	total		97	.221	.330	276	61	11	2	5	1.8	27	26	20	54	2	11	0	178	24	7	4	2.2	.967	OF-79, 3B-10, 1B-4, 2B-1
1964	DET	A	105	.286	.464	308	88	15	2	12	3.9	39	44	18	53	4	18	6	165	5	2	1	1.6	.988	OF-90, 3B-1
1965			79	.213	.308	169	36	5	1	3	1.8	19	10	12	39	2	17	2	88	4	5	0	1.2	.948	OF-59, 2B-1
1966	BOS	A	69	.237	.347	173	41	4	0	5	2.9	25	20	23	33	1	13	3	99	12	0	1	1.6	1.000	OF-48, 3B-6, 1B-2, C-2
1967			65	.213	.270	89	19	2	0	1	1.1	10	6	9	23	0	18	2	57	4	2	0	1.0	.968	OF-43, 3B-3, C-1
1968			12	.200	.500	10	2	0	0	1	10.0	3	1	1	3	0	9	0	9	0	0	0	0.8	1.000	OF-9
1969			29	.353	.451	51	18	3	1	1	2.0	9	8	3	11	0	6	3	85	6	7	9	3.2	.978	1B-20, OF-10, 3B-1, C-1
1970			38	.343	.485	99	34	8	0	2	2.0	13	13	11	12	0	6	3	40	4	4	1	1.3	.917	OF-26, 3B-6
1971	2 teams	BOS A (9G – .077)				MIN A (23G – .267)																			
"	total		32	.209	.233	43	9	1	0	0	0.0	4	3	5	7	0	18	5	7	1	1	0	0.3	.889	OF-16, 3B-1, 1B-1
13 yrs.			680	.255	.389	1688	430	71	9	46	2.7	203	202	138	343	13	119	23	934	128	42	23	1.6	.962	OF-481, 3B-64, 1B-20, C-4, 2B-2, SS-1

WORLD SERIES
| 1967 | BOS | A | 2 | .000 | .000 | 2 | 0 | 0 | 0 | 0 | 0.0 | 0 | 0 | 0 | 1 | 0 | 1 | 0 | 1 | 0 | 0 | 0 | 0.5 | 1.000 | OF-1 |

Gorman Thomas

THOMAS, JAMES GORMAN
B. Dec. 12, 1950, Charleston, S. C.   BR TR 6'2" 210 lbs.

| 1973 | MIL | A | 59 | .187 | .284 | 155 | 29 | 7 | 1 | 2 | 1.3 | 16 | 11 | 14 | 61 | 5 | 4 | 1 | 87 | 1 | 4 | 1 | 1.6 | .957 | OF-50, DH-9, 3B-1 |
| 1974 | | | 17 | .261 | .478 | 46 | 12 | 4 | 0 | 2 | 4.3 | 10 | 11 | 8 | 15 | 4 | 3 | 1 | 26 | 0 | 0 | 0 | 1.5 | 1.000 | OF-13, DH-2 |

Gorman Thomas *continued*

Year Team	Games	BA	SA	AB	H	2B	3B	HR	HR%	R	RBI	BB	SO	SB	Pinch Hit AB	Pinch Hit H	PO	A	E	DP	TC/G	FA	G by Pos
1975	121	.179	.371	240	43	12	2	10	4.2	34	28	31	84	4	2	1	215	5	9	1	1.9	.961	OF-113, DH-6
1976	99	.198	.361	227	45	9	2	8	3.5	27	36	31	67	2	12	1	211	4	4	0	2.2	.982	OF-94, DH-1, 3B-1
1978	137	.246	.515	452	111	24	1	32	**7.1**	70	86	73	133	3	0	0	345	5	6	0	2.6	.983	OF-137
1979	156	.244	.539	557	136	29	0	**45**	**8.1**	97	123	98	**175**	1	0	0	435	4	4	0	2.8	.991	OF-152, DH-4
1980	162	.239	.471	628	150	26	3	38	6.1	78	105	58	**170**	8	0	0	455	6	7	1	2.9	.985	OF-160, DH-2
1981	103	.259	.493	363	94	22	0	21	5.8	54	65	50	85	4	0	0	221	8	5	3	2.3	.979	OF-97, DH-6
1982	158	.245	.506	567	139	29	1	**39**	6.9	96	112	84	143	3	1	0	427	11	4	4	2.8	.991	OF-157
1983 2 teams	MIL A (46G – .183)			CLE A (106G – .221)																			
" total	152	.209	.379	535	112	23	1	22	4.1	72	69	80	148	10	0	0	439	7	7	2	3.0	.985	OF-152
1984 SEA A	35	.157	.213	108	17	3	0	1	0.9	6	13	28	27	0	0	0	45	2	0	0	1.3	1.000	OF-34, DH-1
1985	135	.215	.450	484	104	16	1	32	6.6	76	87	84	126	3	2	0	0	0	0	0	0.0	–	DH-133
1986 2 teams	SEA A (57G – .194)			MIL A (44G – .179)																			
" total	101	.187	.371	315	59	8	1	16	5.1	45	36	58	105	3	12	0	47	3	1	3	0.5	.980	DH-88, 1B-6
13 yrs.	1435	.225	.448	4677	1051	212	13	268	5.7	681	782	697	1339	50	36	4	2953	56	51	15	2.1	.983	OF-1159, DH-246, 1B-6, 3B-2

DIVISIONAL PLAYOFF SERIES

Year Team	Games	BA	SA	AB	H	2B	3B	HR	HR%	R	RBI	BB	SO	SB	Pinch Hit AB	Pinch Hit H	PO	A	E	DP	TC/G	FA	G by Pos
1981 MIL A	5	.118	.294	17	2	0	0	1	5.9	2	1	1	9	0	0	0	0	0	0	0	0.0	–	OF-3, DH-2

LEAGUE CHAMPIONSHIP SERIES

Year Team	Games	BA	SA	AB	H	2B	3B	HR	HR%	R	RBI	BB	SO	SB	Pinch Hit AB	Pinch Hit H	PO	A	E	DP	TC/G	FA	G by Pos
1982 MIL A	5	.067	.267	15	1	0	0	1	6.7	1	3	2	7	0	0	0	0	0	0	0	0.0	–	OF-5

WORLD SERIES

Year Team	Games	BA	SA	AB	H	2B	3B	HR	HR%	R	RBI	BB	SO	SB	Pinch Hit AB	Pinch Hit H	PO	A	E	DP	TC/G	FA	G by Pos
1982 MIL A	7	.115	.115	26	3	0	0	0	0.0	0	3	2	7	0	0	0	15	0	0	0	2.1	1.000	OF-7

Herb Thomas

THOMAS, HERBERT MARX BR TR 5'4½" 157 lbs.
B. May 26, 1902, Sampson City, Fla.

Year Team	Games	BA	SA	AB	H	2B	3B	HR	HR%	R	RBI	BB	SO	SB	Pinch Hit AB	Pinch Hit H	PO	A	E	DP	TC/G	FA	G by Pos
1924 BOS N	32	.220	.291	127	28	4	1	1	0.8	12	8	9	8	5	0	0	109	6	2	1	3.7	.983	OF-32
1925	5	.235	.353	17	4	0	1	0	0.0	2	0	2	0	0	0	0	10	16	1	1	5.4	.963	2B-5
1927 2 teams	BOS N (24G – .230)			NY N (13G – .176)																			
" total	37	.220	.341	91	20	7	2	0	0.0	13	7	4	10	2	8	0	36	44	3	7	2.2	.964	2B-17, OF-3, SS-3
3 yrs.	74	.221	.315	235	52	11	4	1	0.4	27	15	15	18	7	8	0	155	66	6	9	3.1	.974	OF-35, 2B-22, SS-3

Ira Thomas

THOMAS, IRA FELIX BR TR 6'2" 200 lbs.
B. Jan. 22, 1881, Ballston Spa, N. Y.   D. Oct. 11, 1958, Philadelphia, Pa.

Year Team	Games	BA	SA	AB	H	2B	3B	HR	HR%	R	RBI	BB	SO	SB	Pinch Hit AB	Pinch Hit H	PO	A	E	DP	TC/G	FA	G by Pos
1906 NY A	44	.200	.243	115	23	1	2	0	0.0	12	15	8		2	2	0	145	38	12	1	4.4	.938	C-42
1907	80	.192	.269	208	40	5	4	1	0.5	20	24	10		5	16	2	264	92	17	8	4.7	.954	C-66, 1B-2
1908 DET A	40	.307	.317	101	31	1	0	0	0.0	6	8	5		0	11	4	124	15	4	3	3.6	.972	C-29
1909 PHI A	84	.223	.281	256	57	9	3	0	0.0	22	31	18		4	0	0	479	112	9	5	7.1	.985	C-84
1910	60	.278	.361	180	50	8	2	1	0.6	14	19	6		2	0	0	324	86	14	8	7.1	.967	C-60
1911	103	.273	.340	297	81	14	3	0	0.0	33	39	23		4	0	0	499	150	17	12	6.5	.974	C-103
1912	46	.216	.295	139	30	4	1	1	0.7	14	13	8		3	0	0	207	58	8	5	5.9	.971	C-46
1913	21	.283	.396	53	15	4	1	0	0.0	3	6	4	8	0	0	0	88	25	2	1	5.5	.983	C-21
1914	2	.000	.000	3	0	0	0	0	0.0	0	0	0	0	0	1	0	6	1	0	0	3.5	1.000	C-1
1915	1	–		0	0	0	0	0	–	0	0	0	0	0	0	0	0	0	0	0	1.0	1.000	C-1
10 yrs.	481	.242	.308	1352	327	46	17	3	0.2	124	155	82	8	20	30	6	2136	578	83	43	5.8	.970	C-453, 1B-2

WORLD SERIES

Year Team	Games	BA	SA	AB	H	2B	3B	HR	HR%	R	RBI	BB	SO	SB	Pinch Hit AB	Pinch Hit H	PO	A	E	DP	TC/G	FA	G by Pos
1908 DET A	2	.500	.750	4	2	1	0	0	0.0	0	1	1		0	1	1	9	2	0	0	5.5	1.000	C-1
1910 PHI A	4	.250	.250	12	3	0	0	0	0.0	2	1	1		0	0	0	27	8	1	0	9.0	.972	C-4
1911	4	.083	.083	12	1	0	0	0	0.0	0	1	1	2	0	0	0	31	5	0	0	9.0	1.000	C-4
3 yrs.	10	.214	.250	28	6	1	0	0	0.0	3	3	6	3	0	1	1	67	15	1	1	8.3	.988	C-9

Kite Thomas

THOMAS, KEITH MARSHALL BR TR 6'1½" 195 lbs.
B. Apr. 27, 1924, Kansas City, Kans.

Year Team	Games	BA	SA	AB	H	2B	3B	HR	HR%	R	RBI	BB	SO	SB	Pinch Hit AB	Pinch Hit H	PO	A	E	DP	TC/G	FA	G by Pos
1952 PHI A	75	.250	.474	116	29	6	1	6	5.2	24	18	20	27	0	35	8	44	1	2	0	0.6	.957	OF-29
1953 2 teams	PHI A (24G – .122)			WAS A (38G – .293)																			
" total	62	.215	.308	107	23	3	2	1	0.9	11	14	14	13	0	30	7	45	1	2	0	0.8	.958	OF-23, C-1
2 yrs.	137	.233	.395	223	52	9	3	7	3.1	35	32	34	40	0	65	15	89	2	4	0	0.7	.958	OF-52, C-1

Lee Thomas

THOMAS, JAMES LEROY BL TL 6'2" 195 lbs.
B. Feb. 5, 1936, Peoria, Ill.

Year Team	Games	BA	SA	AB	H	2B	3B	HR	HR%	R	RBI	BB	SO	SB	Pinch Hit AB	Pinch Hit H	PO	A	E	DP	TC/G	FA	G by Pos
1961 2 teams	NY A (2G – .500)			LA A (130G – .284)																			
" total	132	.285	.491	452	129	11	5	24	5.3	77	70	47	74	0	18	5	426	19	11	27	3.5	.976	OF-86, 1B-34
1962 LA A	160	.290	.467	583	169	21	2	26	4.5	88	104	55	74	6	3	0	868	47	18	67	5.8	.981	1B-90, OF-74
1963	149	.220	.316	528	116	12	6	9	1.7	52	55	53	82	6	6	2	1032	85	5	89	7.5	.996	1B-104, OF-43
1964 2 teams	LA A (47G – .273)			BOS A (107G – .257)																			
" total	154	.262	.398	573	150	27	3	15	2.6	58	66	52	51	3	1	0	252	10	5	2	1.7	.981	OF-154, 1B-2
1965 BOS A	151	.271	.464	521	141	27	4	22	4.2	74	75	72	42	6	9	1	1064	98	19	86	7.8	.984	1B-127, OF-20
1966 2 teams	ATL N (39G – .198)			CHI N (75G – .242)																			
" total	114	.222	.324	275	61	5	1	7	2.5	26	24	24	30	1	33	9	425	35	5	35	4.1	.989	1B-56, OF-17
1967 CHI N	77	.220	.283	191	42	4	1	2	1.0	16	23	15	22	1	22	4	131	7	2	9	1.8	.986	OF-43, 1B-10
1968 HOU N	90	.194	.229	201	39	4	0	1	0.5	14	11	14	22	2	39	7	80	8	2	3	1.0	.978	OF-48, 1B-2
8 yrs.	1027	.255	.397	3324	847	111	22	106	3.2	405	428	332	397	25	131	28	4278	309	67	318	4.5	.986	OF-485, 1B-425

Leo Thomas

THOMAS, LEO RAYMOND (Tommy) BR TR 5'11½" 178 lbs.
B. July 26, 1923, Turlock, Calif.

Year Team	Games	BA	SA	AB	H	2B	3B	HR	HR%	R	RBI	BB	SO	SB	Pinch Hit AB	Pinch Hit H	PO	A	E	DP	TC/G	FA	G by Pos
1950 STL A	35	.198	.273	121	24	6	0	1	0.8	19	9	20	14	0	0	0	35	72	4	7	3.2	.964	3B-35
1952 2 teams	STL A (41G – .234)			CHI A (19G – .167)																			
" total	60	.223	.270	148	33	5	1	0	0.0	13	18	23	11	2	6	1	53	99	10	11	2.7	.938	3B-46, SS-3, 2B-1
2 yrs.	95	.212	.271	269	57	11	1	1	0.4	32	27	43	25	2	6	1	88	171	14	18	2.9	.949	3B-81, SS-3, 2B-1

Year	Team		Games	BA	SA	AB	H	2B	3B	HR	HR%	R	RBI	BB	SO	SB	Pinch Hit AB	Pinch Hit H	PO	A	E	DP	TC/G	FA	G by Pos

Pinch Thomas

THOMAS, CHESTER DAVID   BL TR 5'9½" 173 lbs.
B. Jan. 24, 1888, Camp Point, Ill.   D. Dec. 24, 1953, Modesto, Calif.

Year	Team		Games	BA	SA	AB	H	2B	3B	HR	HR%	R	RBI	BB	SO	SB	PH AB	PH H	PO	A	E	DP	TC/G	FA	G by Pos
1912	BOS	A	12	.200	.200	30	6	0	0	0	0.0	0	5	2			1	0	0	42	14	2	1	4.8	.966	C-12
1913			37	.286	.374	91	26	1	2	1	1.1	6	15	2	11		1	7	2	135	41	3	2	4.8	.983	C-30
1914			63	.192	.200	130	25	1	0	0	0.0	9	5	18	17	1	1	0	236	47	10	6	4.7	.966	C-61, 1B-1
1915			86	.236	.296	203	48	4	4	0	0.0	21	21	13	20	3	3	2	325	81	13	7	4.9	.969	C-82
1916			99	.264	.333	216	57	10	1	1	0.5	21	21	33	13	4	6	2	321	86	8	7	4.2	.981	C-90
1917			83	.238	.272	202	48	7	0	0	0.0	24	24	27	9	2	6	3	296	69	5	8	4.5	.986	C-77
1918	CLE	A	32	.247	.274	73	18	0	1	0	0.0	2	5	6	6	0	8	4	85	24	6	1	3.6	.948	C-24
1919			34	.109	.109	46	5	0	0	0	0.0	2	4	3	0	13	0	39	9	1	0	1.4	.960	C-21
1920			9	.333	.444	9	3	1	0	0	0.0	2	0	3	1	0	1	0	14	3	0	0	1.9	1.000	C-7
1921			21	.257	.343	35	9	3	0	0	0.0	1	4	10	2	0	2	0	27	3	4	0	1.6	.882	C-19
10 yrs.			476	.237	.284	1035	245	27	8	2	0.2	88	102	118	82	12	47	13	1520	377	52	32	4.1	.973	C-423, 1B-1

WORLD SERIES

Year	Team		Games	BA	SA	AB	H	2B	3B	HR	HR%	R	RBI	BB	SO	SB	PH AB	PH H	PO	A	E	DP	TC/G	FA	G by Pos
1915	BOS	A	2	.200	.200	5	1	0	0	0	0.0	0	0	0	0	0	0	0	10	3	0	1	6.5	1.000	C-2
1916			3	.143	.429	7	1	0	1	0	0.0	0	0	0	1	0	0	0	10	4	0	0	4.7	1.000	C-3
1920	CLE	A	1	–	–	0	0	0	0	0	–	0	0	0	0	0	0	0	1	0	0	0	1.0	1.000	C-1
3 yrs.			6	.167	.333	12	2	0	1	0	0.0	0	0	0	1	0	0	0	21	7	0	1	4.7	1.000	C-6

Ray Thomas

THOMAS, RAYMOND JOSEPH   BR TR 5'11" 175 lbs.
B. July 9, 1910, Dover, N. H.

Year	Team		Games	BA	SA	AB	H	2B	3B	HR	HR%	R	RBI	BB	SO	SB	PH AB	PH H	PO	A	E	DP	TC/G	FA	G by Pos
1938	BKN	N	1	.333	.333	3	1	0	0	0	0.0	1	0	0	0	0	0	0	5	0	0	0	5.0	1.000	C-1

Red Thomas

THOMAS, ROBERT WILLIAM   BR TR 5'11" 165 lbs.
B. Apr. 25, 1898, Hargrove, Ala.   D. Mar. 29, 1962, Fremont, Ohio

Year	Team		Games	BA	SA	AB	H	2B	3B	HR	HR%	R	RBI	BB	SO	SB	PH AB	PH H	PO	A	E	DP	TC/G	FA	G by Pos
1921	CHI	N	8	.267	.467	30	8	3	0	1	3.3	5	5	4	5	0	0	0	24	1	0	1	3.3	.962	OF-8

Roy Thomas

THOMAS, ROY ALLEN   BL TL 5'11" 150 lbs.
Brother of Bill Thomas.
B. Mar. 24, 1874, Norristown, Pa.   D. Nov. 20, 1959, Norristown, Pa.

Year	Team		Games	BA	SA	AB	H	2B	3B	HR	HR%	R	RBI	BB	SO	SB	PH AB	PH H	PO	A	E	DP	TC/G	FA	G by Pos
1899	PHI	N	150	.325	.362	547	178	12	4	0	0.0	137	47	115		42	1	0	454	23	20	14	3.3	.960	OF-135, 1B-14
1900			140	.316	.335	531	168	4	3	0	0.0	131	33	115		37	1	0	303	19	14	6	2.4	.958	OF-139, P-1
1901			129	.309	.334	479	148	5	2	1	0.2	102	28	100		27	0	0	283	9	10	2	2.3	.967	OF-129
1902			138	.286	.322	500	143	4	2	0	0.0	89	24	107		17	0	0	277	23	8	3	2.2	.974	OF-138
1903			130	.327	.365	477	156	11	2	1	0.2	88	27	107		17	0	0	318	19	13	3	2.7	.963	OF-130
1904			139	.290	.345	496	144	6	6	3	0.6	92	29	102		28	0	0	321	21	9	4	2.5	.974	OF-139
1905			147	.317	.358	562	178	11	6	0	0.0	118	31	93		23	0	0	373	27	7	6	2.8	.983	OF-147
1906			142	.254	.302	493	125	10	7	0	0.0	81	16	107		22	0	0	340	12	5	5	2.5	.986	OF-142
1907			121	.243	.301	419	102	15	3	1	0.2	70	23	83		11	0	0	274	15	6	4	2.4	.980	OF-121
1908	2 teams		PHI N (6G – .167)			PIT N (102G – .256)																			
"	total		108	.251	.334	410	103	11	10	0	0.2	54	24	51		11	0	0	282	7	7	4	2.7	.976	OF-107
1909	BOS	N	83	.263	.302	281	74	9	1	0	0.0	36	11	47		5	5	2	155	9	4	1	2.0	.976	OF-71
1910	PHI	N	23	.183	.239	71	13	0	2	0	0.0	7	4	7	5	4	3	0	38	2	2	0	1.8	.952	OF-20
1911			21	.167	.233	30	5	2	0	0	0.0	5	2	8	6	0	7	1	14	3	0	0	0.8	1.000	OF-11
13 yrs.			1471	.290	.333	5296	1537	100	53	7	0.1	1010	299	1042	11	244	17	3	3432	189	105	52	2.5	.972	OF-1429, 1B-14, P-1

Valmy Thomas

THOMAS, VALMY   BR TR 5'9" 165 lbs.
B. Oct. 21, 1928, Santurce, Puerto Rico

Year	Team		Games	BA	SA	AB	H	2B	3B	HR	HR%	R	RBI	BB	SO	SB	PH AB	PH H	PO	A	E	DP	TC/G	FA	G by Pos
1957	NY	N	88	.249	.390	241	60	10	3	6	2.5	30	31	16	29	0	1	0	396	31	4	8	4.9	.991	C-88
1958	SF	N	63	.259	.357	143	37	5	0	3	2.1	14	16	13	24	1	2	0	244	17	2	4	4.2	.992	C-61
1959	PHI	N	66	.200	.236	140	28	2	0	1	0.7	5	9	7	19	1	0	0	310	25	7	3	5.2	.980	C-65, 3B-1
1960	BAL	A	8	.063	.063	16	1	0	0	0	0.0	0	0	0	0	0	0	0	27	2	0	1	3.6	1.000	C-8
1961	CLE	A	27	.209	.314	86	18	3	0	2	2.3	7	6	6	7	0	0	0	151	17	2	6	6.3	.988	C-27
5 yrs.			252	.230	.329	626	144	20	3	12	1.9	56	60	45	79	2	3	0	1128	92	15	22	4.9	.988	C-249, 3B-1

Walt Thomas

THOMAS, WILLIAM WALTER   BR TR 5'8"
B. Apr. 28, 1884, Altoona, Pa.   D. June 6, 1950, Altoona, Pa.

Year	Team		Games	BA	SA	AB	H	2B	3B	HR	HR%	R	RBI	BB	SO	SB	PH AB	PH H	PO	A	E	DP	TC/G	FA	G by Pos
1908	BOS	N	5	.154	.154	13	2	0	0	0	0.0	2	1	3		2	0	0	7	12	3	1	4.4	.864	SS-5

Art Thomason

THOMASON, ARTHUR WILSON (Sillie)   BL TL 5'8" 150 lbs.
B. Feb. 12, 1889, Liberty, Mo.   D. May 2, 1944, Kansas City, Mo.

Year	Team		Games	BA	SA	AB	H	2B	3B	HR	HR%	R	RBI	BB	SO	SB	PH AB	PH H	PO	A	E	DP	TC/G	FA	G by Pos
1910	CLE	A	17	.158	.193	57	9	0	1	0	0.0	3	2	5		3	0	0	26	5	2	1	1.9	.939	OF-17

Gary Thomasson

THOMASSON, GARY LEAH   BL TL 6'1" 180 lbs.
B. July 29, 1951, San Diego, Calif.

Year	Team		Games	BA	SA	AB	H	2B	3B	HR	HR%	R	RBI	BB	SO	SB	PH AB	PH H	PO	A	E	DP	TC/G	FA	G by Pos
1972	SF	N	10	.333	.444	27	9	1	0	0	0.0	5	1	1	7	0	2	1	60	1	0	7	6.1	1.000	1B-7, OF-2
1973			112	.285	.413	235	67	10	4	4	1.7	35	30	22	43	2	18	4	312	15	6	15	3.0	.982	1B-47, OF-43
1974			120	.244	.327	315	77	14	3	2	0.6	41	29	38	56	7	30	6	235	17	7	9	2.2	.973	OF-76, 1B-15
1975			114	.227	.347	326	74	12	3	7	2.1	44	32	37	48	9	17	4	293	18	7	14	2.8	.978	OF-74, 1B-17
1976			103	.259	.424	328	85	20	5	8	2.4	45	38	30	45	8	16	4	436	20	12	28	4.5	.974	OF-54, 1B-39
1977			145	.256	.451	446	114	24	6	17	3.8	63	71	75	102	16	16	5	404	11	14	15	3.0	.967	OF-113, 1B-31
1978	2 teams		OAK A (47G – .201)			NY A (55G – .276)																			
"	total		102	.233	.367	270	63	8	2	8	3.0	37	36	28	66	4	7	2	113	7	4	0	1.2	.968	OF-94, 1B-5, DH-1
1979	LA	N	115	.248	.422	315	78	11	1	14	4.4	39	45	43	70	4	18	2	196	4	4	1	1.8	.980	OF-100, 1B-1
1980			80	.216	.270	111	24	3	0	1	0.9	6	12	17	26	0	45	11	38	1	0	0	0.5	.975	OF-31, 1B-1
9 yrs.			901	.249	.391	2373	591	103	25	61	2.6	315	294	291	463	50	169	39	2087	94	55	89	2.5	.975	OF-587, 1B-163, DH-1

LEAGUE CHAMPIONSHIP SERIES

Year	Team		Games	BA	SA	AB	H	2B	3B	HR	HR%	R	RBI	BB	SO	SB	PH AB	PH H	PO	A	E	DP	TC/G	FA	G by Pos
1978	NY	A	3	.000	.000	1	0	0	0	0	0.0	0	0	0	1	0	1	0	2	0	0	0	0.7	1.000	OF-3

WORLD SERIES

Year	Team		Games	BA	SA	AB	H	2B	3B	HR	HR%	R	RBI	BB	SO	SB	PH AB	PH H	PO	A	E	DP	TC/G	FA	G by Pos
1978	NY	A	3	.250	.250	4	1	0	0	0	0.0	0	1	0	1	0	1	0	3	0	0	0	1.0	1.000	OF-3

Year	Team	Games	BA	SA	AB	H	2B	3B	HR	HR%	R	RBI	BB	SO	SB	Pinch Hit AB	Pinch Hit H	PO	A	E	DP	TC/G	FA	G by Pos

Bobby Thompson
THOMPSON, BOBBY LaRUE
B. Nov. 3, 1953, Charlotte, N. C. BB TR 5'11" 175 lbs.

Year	Team	Games	BA	SA	AB	H	2B	3B	HR	HR%	R	RBI	BB	SO	SB	AB	H	PO	A	E	DP	TC/G	FA	G by Pos
1978	TEX A	64	.225	.350	120	27	3	3	2	1.7	23	12	9	26	7	0	0	109	1	2	0	1.8	.982	OF-52, DH-3

Danny Thompson
THOMPSON, DANNY LEON
B. Feb. 1, 1947, Wichita, Kans. D. Dec. 10, 1976, Rochester, Minn. BR TR 6' 183 lbs.

Year	Team	Games	BA	SA	AB	H	2B	3B	HR	HR%	R	RBI	BB	SO	SB	AB	H	PO	A	E	DP	TC/G	FA	G by Pos
1970	MIN A	96	.219	.248	302	66	9	0	0	0.0	25	22	7	39	0	3	1	156	229	6	39	4.1	.985	2B-81, 3B-37, SS-6
1971		48	.263	.298	57	15	2	0	0	0.0	10	7	7	12	0	20	5	13	24	4	2	0.9	.902	3B-17, 2B-3, SS-1
1972		144	.276	.356	573	158	22	6	4	0.7	54	48	34	57	3	0	0	247	468	32	76	5.2	.957	SS-144
1973		99	.225	.282	347	78	13	2	1	0.3	29	36	16	41	1	2	0	131	326	24	50	4.9	.950	SS-95, 3B-1
1974		97	.250	.326	264	66	6	1	4	1.5	25	25	22	29	1	6	0	131	192	13	41	3.5	.961	SS-88, 3B-5, DH-1
1975		112	.270	.355	355	96	11	2	5	1.4	25	37	18	30	1	6	2	147	261	26	41	3.9	.940	SS-100, 3B-7, DH-3, 2B-1
1976	2 teams	MIN A	(34G – .234)		TEX A	(64G – .214)																		
"	total	98	.222	.253	320	71	7	0	1	0.3	21	19	16	27	3	8	2	118	220	6	35	3.5	.983	SS-44, 3B-39, 2B-14, DH-1
7 yrs.		694	.248	.310	2218	550	70	11	15	0.7	189	194	120	235	8	45	10	943	1720	111	284	4.0	.960	SS-478, 3B-106, 2B-99, DH-5

LEAGUE CHAMPIONSHIP SERIES

Year	Team	Games	BA	SA	AB	H	2B	3B	HR	HR%	R	RBI	BB	SO	SB	AB	H	PO	A	E	DP	TC/G	FA	G by Pos
1970	MIN A	3	.125	.250	8	1	1	0	0	0.0	0	0	0	1	0	0	0	2	3	1	1	2.0	.833	2B-3

Don Thompson
THOMPSON, DONALD NEWLIN
B. Dec. 28, 1923, Swepsonville, N. C. BL TL 6' 185 lbs.

Year	Team	Games	BA	SA	AB	H	2B	3B	HR	HR%	R	RBI	BB	SO	SB	AB	H	PO	A	E	DP	TC/G	FA	G by Pos
1949	BOS N	7	.182	.182	11	2	0	0	0	0.0	0	0	0	2	0	5	0	4	0	1	0	0.7	.800	OF-2
1951	BKN N	80	.229	.254	118	27	3	0	0	0.0	25	6	12	12	2	11	3	75	3	1	1	1.0	.987	OF-61
1953		96	.242	.294	153	37	5	0	1	0.7	25	12	14	13	2	13	0	84	5	1	1	0.9	.989	OF-81
1954		34	.040	.040	25	1	0	0	0	0.0	2	1	5	5	0	5	0	14	1	0	0	0.4	1.000	OF-29
4 yrs.		217	.218	.254	307	67	8	0	1	0.3	52	19	31	32	4	34	3	177	9	3	2	0.9	.984	OF-173

WORLD SERIES

Year	Team	Games	BA	SA	AB	H	2B	3B	HR	HR%	R	RBI	BB	SO	SB	AB	H	PO	A	E	DP	TC/G	FA	G by Pos
1953	BKN N	2	–	–	0	0	0	0	0	–	0	0	0	0	0	0	0	1	0	0	0	0.5	1.000	OF-2

Frank Thompson
THOMPSON, FRANK E
B. July 2, 1895, Springfield, Mo. D. June 27, 1940, Jasper County, Mo. BR TR 5'8" 155 lbs.

Year	Team	Games	BA	SA	AB	H	2B	3B	HR	HR%	R	RBI	BB	SO	SB	AB	H	PO	A	E	DP	TC/G	FA	G by Pos
1920	STL A	22	.170	.170	53	9	0	0	0	0.0	7	5	13	10	1	2	0	17	27	8	2	2.4	.846	3B-14, 2B-2

Fresco Thompson
THOMPSON, LAFAYETTE FRESCO (Tommy)
B. June 6, 1902, Centreville, Ala. D. Nov. 20, 1968, Fullerton, Calif. BR TR 5'8" 150 lbs.

Year	Team	Games	BA	SA	AB	H	2B	3B	HR	HR%	R	RBI	BB	SO	SB	AB	H	PO	A	E	DP	TC/G	FA	G by Pos
1925	PIT N	14	.243	.351	37	9	2	1	0	0.0	4	8	4	1	2	2	0	19	24	1	6	3.1	.977	2B-12
1926	NY N	2	.625	.625	8	5	0	0	0	0.0	1	1	2	0	1	0	0	2	8	0	0	5.0	1.000	2B-2
1927	PHI N	153	.303	.409	597	181	32	14	1	0.2	78	70	34	36	19	0	0	424	485	35	97	6.2	.963	2B-153
1928		152	.287	.390	634	182	34	11	3	0.5	99	50	42	27	19	0	0	409	509	32	109	6.3	.966	2B-152
1929		148	.324	.419	623	202	41	3	4	0.6	115	53	75	34	16	0	0	395	512	33	103	6.4	.965	2B-148
1930		122	.282	.395	478	135	34	4	4	0.8	77	46	35	29	7	8	3	287	386	32	95	5.8	.955	2B-112
1931	BKN N	74	.265	.326	181	48	6	1	1	0.6	26	21	23	16	5	4	1	102	135	13	40	3.4	.948	2B-63, SS-10, 3B-5
1932		3	.000	.000	1	0	0	0	0	0.0	0	0	0	0	0	1	0	0	0	0	0	0.0	–	
1934	NY N	1	.000	.000	1	0	0	0	0	0.0	0	0	0	1	0	1	0	0	0	0	0	0.0	–	
9 yrs.		669	.298	.398	2560	762	149	34	13	0.5	400	249	215	143	69	16	4	1638	2059	146	450	5.7	.962	2B-642, SS-10, 3B-5

Hank Thompson
THOMPSON, HENRY CURTIS
B. Dec. 8, 1925, Oklahoma City, Okla. D. Sept. 30, 1969, Fresno, Calif. BL TR 5'9" 174 lbs.

Year	Team	Games	BA	SA	AB	H	2B	3B	HR	HR%	R	RBI	BB	SO	SB	AB	H	PO	A	E	DP	TC/G	FA	G by Pos
1947	STL A	27	.256	.295	78	20	1	1	0	0.0	10	5	10	7	2	8	3	55	55	5	15	4.3	.957	2B-19
1949	NY N	75	.280	.444	275	77	10	4	9	3.3	51	34	42	30	5	4	1	198	180	15	44	5.2	.962	2B-69, 3B-1
1950		148	.289	.463	512	148	17	6	20	3.9	82	91	83	60	8	1	0	154	305	26	44	3.3	.946	3B-138, OF-10
1951		87	.235	.386	264	62	8	4	8	3.0	37	33	43	23	1	14	1	64	120	15	16	2.3	.925	3B-71
1952		128	.260	.454	423	110	13	9	17	4.0	67	67	50	38	4	9	3	236	108	16	11	2.8	.956	OF-72, 3B-46, 2B-4
1953		114	.302	.567	388	117	15	8	24	6.2	80	74	60	39	6	4	1	99	195	13	18	2.7	.958	3B-101, OF-9, 2B-1
1954		136	.263	.482	448	118	18	1	26	5.8	76	86	90	58	3	5	0	126	269	23	27	3.1	.945	3B-130, 2B-2, OF-1
1955		135	.245	.398	432	106	13	1	17	3.9	65	63	84	56	2	9	1	115	276	23	25	3.1	.944	3B-124, 2B-7, SS-1
1956		83	.235	.415	183	43	9	0	8	4.4	24	29	31	26	2	24	8	36	95	14	7	1.7	.903	3B-44, OF-10, SS-1
9 yrs.		933	.267	.453	3003	801	104	34	129	4.3	492	482	493	337	33	78	18	1083	1603	150	207	3.0	.947	3B-655, OF-102, 2B-102, SS-2

WORLD SERIES

Year	Team	Games	BA	SA	AB	H	2B	3B	HR	HR%	R	RBI	BB	SO	SB	AB	H	PO	A	E	DP	TC/G	FA	G by Pos
1951	NY N	5	.143	.143	14	2	0	0	0	0.0	2	0	5	2	0	0	0	5	0	2	0	1.4	.714	OF-5
1954		4	.364	.455	11	4	1	0	0	0.0	6	2	7	1	0	0	0	5	11	0	1	4.0	1.000	3B-4
2 yrs.		9	.240	.280	25	6	1	0	0	0.0	8	2	12	3	0	0	0	10	11	2	1	2.6	.913	OF-5, 3B-4

Homer Thompson
THOMPSON, THOMAS HOMER
Brother of Tommy Thompson.
B. June 1, 1892, Spring City, Tenn. D. Sept. 12, 1957, Atlanta, Ga. BR TR 5'9" 160 lbs.

Year	Team	Games	BA	SA	AB	H	2B	3B	HR	HR%	R	RBI	BB	SO	SB	AB	H	PO	A	E	DP	TC/G	FA	G by Pos
1912	NY A	1	–	–	0	0	0	0	0	–	0	0	0	0	0	0	0	1	0	1	0	2.0	.500	C-1

Jason Thompson
THOMPSON, JASON DOLPH
B. July 6, 1954, Hollywood, Calif. BL TL 6'4" 200 lbs.

Year	Team	Games	BA	SA	AB	H	2B	3B	HR	HR%	R	RBI	BB	SO	SB	AB	H	PO	A	E	DP	TC/G	FA	G by Pos
1976	DET A	123	.218	.376	412	90	12	1	17	4.1	45	54	68	72	2	3	0	1157	88	8	104	10.2	.994	1B-117
1977		158	.270	.487	585	158	24	5	31	5.3	87	105	73	91	0	0	0	1599	97	16	135	10.8	.991	1B-158
1978		153	.287	.472	589	169	25	3	26	4.4	79	96	74	96	0	1	0	1503	92	11	153	10.5	.993	1B-151
1979		145	.246	.404	492	121	16	1	20	4.1	58	79	70	90	2	8	2	1176	91	8	135	8.8	.994	1B-140, DH-2
1980	2 teams	DET A	(36G – .214)		CAL A	(102G – .317)																		
"	total	138	.288	.475	438	126	19	0	21	4.8	69	90	83	86	2	14	4	679	51	0	66	5.3	1.000	1B-83, DH-45
1981	PIT N	86	.242	.502	223	54	13	0	15	6.7	36	42	59	49	0	13	4	590	46	7	65	7.5	.989	1B-78
1982		156	.284	.511	550	156	32	0	31	5.6	87	101	101	107	1	0	0	1395	105	10	114	9.7	.993	1B-155
1983		152	.259	.406	517	134	20	1	18	3.5	70	76	99	128	1	2	0	1266	89	9	131	9.0	.993	1B-151

Year	Team		Games	BA	SA	AB	H	2B	3B	HR	HR%	R	RBI	BB	SO	SB	Pinch Hit AB	Pinch Hit H	PO	A	E	DP	TC/G	FA	G by Pos

Jason Thompson *continued*

Year	Team		Games	BA	SA	AB	H	2B	3B	HR	HR%	R	RBI	BB	SO	SB	AB	H	PO	A	E	DP	TC/G	FA	G by Pos
1984			154	.254	.389	543	138	22	0	17	3.1	61	74	87	73	0	3	1	1337	74	14	111	9.3	.990	1B-152
1985			123	.241	.378	402	97	17	1	12	3.0	42	61	84	58	0	6	1	995	82	9	69	8.8	.992	1B-114
1986	MON	N	30	.196	.275	51	10	4	0	1	0.0	6	4	18	12	0	12	1	121	4	5	7	4.3	.962	1B-15
11 yrs.			1418	.261	.438	4802	1253	204	12	208	4.3	640	782	816	862	8	62	13	11818	819	97	1090	9.0	.992	1B-1314, DH-47

Milt Thompson

THOMPSON, MILTON BERNARD
B. Jan. 5, 1959, Washington, D. C.   BL TR 5'11" 170 lbs.

Year	Team		Games	BA	SA	AB	H	2B	3B	HR	HR%	R	RBI	BB	SO	SB	AB	H	PO	A	E	DP	TC/G	FA	G by Pos
1984	ATL	N	25	.303	.374	99	30	1	2	2	2.0	16	4	11	11	14	2	2	37	6	2	1	1.8	.956	OF-25
1985			73	.302	.363	182	55	7	2	0	0.0	17	6	7	36	9	30	13	78	2	3	0	1.1	.964	OF-49
1986	PHI	N	96	.251	.341	299	75	7	1	6	2.0	38	23	26	62	19	10	1	212	1	2	1	2.2	.991	OF-89
1987			150	.302	.425	527	159	26	9	7	1.3	86	43	42	87	46	15	5	354	4	4	1	2.4	.989	OF-146
1988			122	.288	.357	378	109	16	2	2	0.5	53	33	39	59	17	16	4	278	5	5	1	2.4	.983	OF-112
1989	STL	N	155	.290	.393	545	158	28	8	4	0.7	60	68	39	91	27	10	1	348	5	8	1	2.3	.978	OF-147
6 yrs.			621	.289	.383	2030	586	85	22	21	1.0	270	177	164	346	132	83	26	1307	23	24	5	2.2	.982	OF-568

Robby Thompson

THOMPSON, ROBERT RANDALL
B. May 10, 1962, West Palm Beach, Fla.   BR TR 5'11" 165 lbs.

Year	Team		Games	BA	SA	AB	H	2B	3B	HR	HR%	R	RBI	BB	SO	SB	AB	H	PO	A	E	DP	TC/G	FA	G by Pos
1986	SF	N	149	.271	.370	549	149	27	3	7	1.3	73	47	42	112	12	1	0	255	451	17	97	4.9	.976	2B-149, SS-1
1987			132	.262	.419	420	110	26	5	10	2.4	62	44	40	91	16	4	2	246	341	17	99	4.6	.972	2B-126
1988			138	.264	.384	477	126	24	6	7	1.5	66	48	40	111	14	5	1	255	365	14	88	4.6	.978	2B-134
1989			148	.241	.400	547	132	26	11	13	2.4	91	50	51	133	12	0	0	307	425	8	88	5.0	.989	2B-148
4 yrs.			567	.259	.392	1993	517	103	25	37	1.9	292	189	173	447	54	10	3	1063	1582	56	372	4.8	.979	2B-557, SS-1

LEAGUE CHAMPIONSHIP SERIES

Year	Team		Games	BA	SA	AB	H	2B	3B	HR	HR%	R	RBI	BB	SO	SB	AB	H	PO	A	E	DP	TC/G	FA	G by Pos
1987	SF	N	7	.100	.350	20	2	0	1	1	5.0	4	2	5	7	2	1	0	11	19	1	6	4.4	.968	2B-6
1989			5	.278	.611	18	5	0	0	2	11.1	5	3	3	2	0	0	0	10	13	0	4	4.6	1.000	2B-5
2 yrs.			12	.184	.474	38	7	0	1	3	7.9	9	5	8	9	2	1	0	21	32	1	10	4.5	.981	2B-11

WORLD SERIES

Year	Team		Games	BA	SA	AB	H	2B	3B	HR	HR%	R	RBI	BB	SO	SB	AB	H	PO	A	E	DP	TC/G	FA	G by Pos
1989	SF	N	4	.091	.091	11	1	0	0	0	0.0	0	2	0	4	0	1	1	4	10	0	2	3.5	1.000	2B-4

Sam Thompson

THOMPSON, SAMUEL LUTHER (Big Sam)
B. Mar. 5, 1860, Danville, Ind.   D. Nov. 7, 1922, Detroit, Mich.
Hall of Fame 1974.   BL TL 6'2" 207 lbs.

Year	Team		Games	BA	SA	AB	H	2B	3B	HR	HR%	R	RBI	BB	SO	SB	AB	H	PO	A	E	DP	TC/G	FA	G by Pos
1885	DET	N	63	.303	.500	254	77	11	9	7	2.8	58	44	16	22		0	0	86	24	14	0	2.0	.887	OF-62, 3B-1
1886			122	.310	.445	503	156	18	13	8	1.6	101	89	35	31		0	0	194	29	13	11	1.9	.945	OF-122
1887			127	**.372**	**.571**	**545**	**203**	29	**23**	11	2.0	118	**166**	32	19	22	0	0	217	24	24	7	2.1	.909	OF-127
1888			56	.282	.466	238	67	10	8	6	2.5	51	40	23	10	5	0	0	86	4	12	0	1.8	.882	OF-56
1889	PHI	N	128	.296	.492	533	158	36	4	**20**	3.8	103	111	36	22	24	0	0	173	19	21	7	1.7	.901	OF-128
1890			132	.313	.443	549	**172**	**41**	9	4	0.7	116	102	42	29	25	0	0	170	29	13	5	1.6	.939	OF-132
1891			133	.294	.415	554	163	23	10	8	1.4	108	90	52	20	29	0	0	234	32	18	6	2.1	.937	OF-133
1892			153	.305	.432	609	186	28	11	9	1.5	109	104	59	19	28	0	0	223	28	17	7	1.8	.937	OF-153
1893			131	.370	.530	**600**	**222**	**37**	13	11	1.8	130	126	50	17	18	0	0	178	17	15	3	1.6	.929	OF-131, 1B-1
1894			102	.404	.670	458	185	29	27	13	2.8	115	141	40	13	29	0	0	159	12	4	2	1.7	.977	OF-102
1895			119	.392	**.654**	538	211	45	21	**18**	3.3	131	**165**	31	11	27	1	1	186	31	13	2	1.9	.943	OF-118
1896			119	.298	.449	517	154	28	7	12	2.3	103	100	28	13	12	0	0	231	28	7	11	2.2	.974	OF-119
1897			3	.231	.385	13	3	0	1	0	0.0	2	3	1		0	0	0	4	1	1	0	2.0	.833	OF-3
1898			14	.349	.571	63	22	5	3	1	1.6	14	15	4		2	0	0	19	5	0	0	1.7	1.000	OF-14
1906	DET	A	8	.226	.290	31	7	0	1	0	0.0	4	3	1		0	0	0	14	0	0	0	1.8	1.000	OF-8
15 yrs.			1410	.331	.505	6005	1986	340	160	128	2.1	1263	1299	450	226	221	1	1	2174	283	172	61	1.9	.935	OF-1408, 3B-1, 1B-1

Scot Thompson

THOMPSON, VERNON SCOT
B. Dec. 7, 1955, Grove City, Pa.   BL TL 6'3" 195 lbs.

Year	Team		Games	BA	SA	AB	H	2B	3B	HR	HR%	R	RBI	BB	SO	SB	AB	H	PO	A	E	DP	TC/G	FA	G by Pos
1978	CHI	N	19	.417	.500	36	15	3	0	0	0.0	7	2	2	4	0	12	6	14	1	0	1	0.8	1.000	OF-5, 1B-2
1979			128	.289	.373	346	100	13	5	2	0.6	36	29	17	37	4	33	12	161	7	5	3	1.4	.971	OF-100
1980			102	.212	.292	226	48	10	1	2	0.9	26	13	28	31	6	21	6	149	6	4	0	1.6	.975	OF-66, 1B-12
1981			57	.165	.209	115	19	5	0	0	0.0	8	8	7	8	2	22	2	56	1	2	0	1.0	.966	OF-30, 1B-3
1982			49	.365	.459	74	27	5	1	0	0.0	11	7	5	4	0	27	7	39	3	0	1	0.9	1.000	OF-23, 1B-4
1983			53	.193	.250	88	17	3	1	0	0.0	4	3	14	14	0	22	4	29	0	0	0	0.5	1.000	OF-29, 1B-1
1984	SF	N	120	.306	.355	245	75	7	1	1	0.4	30	31	30	26	5	31	5	562	36	2	48	5.0	.997	1B-87, OF-6
1985	2 teams		SF	N	(64G – .207)		MON	N	(34G – .281)																
"	total		98	.224	.266	143	32	6	0	0	0.0	10	10	5	17	0	**62**	9	180	18	1	14	2.0	.995	1B-27, OF-3
8 yrs.			626	.262	.328	1273	333	52	9	5	0.4	132	110	97	141	17	236	53	1190	72	14	75	2.0	.989	OF-262, 1B-136

Shag Thompson

THOMPSON, JAMES ALFRED
B. Apr. 29, 1893, Haw River, N. C.   BL TR 5'8½" 165 lbs.

Year	Team		Games	BA	SA	AB	H	2B	3B	HR	HR%	R	RBI	BB	SO	SB	AB	H	PO	A	E	DP	TC/G	FA	G by Pos
1914	PHI	A	16	.172	.241	29	5	0	1	0	0.0	3	2	7	8	1	5	1	13	3	1	1	1.1	.941	OF-8
1915			17	.333	.394	33	11	2	0	0	0.0	5	2	4	6	0	7	2	11	2	0	1	0.8	1.000	OF-7
1916			15	.000	.000	17	0	0	0	0	0.0	4	0	7	6	1	3	0	16	0	0	0	1.1	1.000	OF-7
3 yrs.			48	.203	.253	79	16	2	1	0	0.0	12	4	18	20	2	15	3	40	5	1	2	1.0	.978	OF-22

Tim Thompson

THOMPSON, CHARLES LEMOINE
B. Mar. 1, 1924, Coalport, Pa.   BL TR 5'11" 190 lbs.

Year	Team		Games	BA	SA	AB	H	2B	3B	HR	HR%	R	RBI	BB	SO	SB	AB	H	PO	A	E	DP	TC/G	FA	G by Pos
1954	BKN	N	10	.154	.231	13	2	1	0	0	0.0	2	1	1	1	0	5	1	10	0	1	0	1.1	.909	C-2, OF-1
1956	KC	A	92	.272	.347	268	73	13	2	1	0.4	21	27	17	23	2	23	4	328	38	7	7	4.1	.981	C-68
1957			81	.204	.339	230	47	10	0	7	3.0	25	19	18	26	0	19	1	272	29	2	7	3.7	.993	C-62
1958	DET	A	4	.167	.167	6	1	0	0	0	0.0	1	0	3	2	0	1	0	8	1	0	0	2.3	1.000	C-4
4 yrs.			187	.238	.338	517	123	24	2	8	1.5	49	47	39	52	2	48	6	618	68	10	14	3.7	.986	C-136, OF-1

Tommy Thompson

THOMPSON, RUPERT LOCKHART
B. May 19, 1910, Elkhart, Ill.   D. May 24, 1971, Auburn, Calif.   BL TR 5'9½" 155 lbs.

Year	Team	Games	BA	SA	AB	H	2B	3B	HR	HR%	R	RBI	BB	SO	SB	Pinch Hit AB	Pinch Hit H	PO	A	E	DP	TC/G	FA	G by Pos

Tommy Thompson *continued*

Year	Team	Games	BA	SA	AB	H	2B	3B	HR	HR%	R	RBI	BB	SO	SB	AB	H	PO	A	E	DP	TC/G	FA	G by Pos
1933	BOS N	24	.186	.196	97	18	1	0	0	0.0	6	6	4	6	0	0	0	64	3	0	0	2.8	1.000	OF-24
1934		105	.265	.318	343	91	12	3	0	0.0	40	37	13	19	2	23	8	205	12	8	3	2.1	.964	OF-82
1935		112	.273	.343	297	81	7	1	4	1.3	34	30	36	17	2	24	3	184	9	7	3	1.8	.965	OF-85
1936		106	.286	.365	266	76	9	0	4	1.5	37	36	31	12	3	37	10	359	20	5	19	3.6	.987	OF-39, 1B-25
1938	CHI A	19	.111	.111	18	2	0	0	0	0.0	2	2	1	2	0	17	2	2	0	0	1	0.1	1.000	1B-1
1939	2 teams		CHI	A (1G – .000)		STL	A (30G – .302)																	
"	total	31	.302	.395	86	26	5	0	1	1.2	23	8	23	7	0	5	1	40	3	1	0	1.4	.977	OF-23
6 yrs.		397	.266	.328	1107	294	34	4	9	0.8	142	119	108	63	7	106	24	854	47	21	26	2.3	.977	OF-253, 1B-26

Tug Thompson

THOMPSON, JOHN P.   160 lbs.
B. 1865, London, Ontario, Canada Deceased.

Year	Team	Games	BA	SA	AB	H	2B	3B	HR	HR%	R	RBI	BB	SO	SB	AB	H	PO	A	E	DP	TC/G	FA	G by Pos
1882	CIN AA	1	.200	.200	5	1	0	0	0	0.0	0		0			0	0	0	0	1	0	1.0	–	OF-1
1884	IND AA	24	.206	.237	97	20	3	0	0	0.0	10		2			0	0	65	16	24	0	4.4	.771	OF-12, C-12
2 yrs.		25	.206	.235	102	21	3	0	0	0.0	10		2			0	0	65	16	25	0	4.2	.764	OF-13, C-12

Bobby Thomson

THOMSON, ROBERT BROWN (The Staten Island Scot)   BR TR 6'2"   180 lbs.
B. Oct. 25, 1923, Glasgow, Scotland

Year	Team	Games	BA	SA	AB	H	2B	3B	HR	HR%	R	RBI	BB	SO	SB	AB	H	PO	A	E	DP	TC/G	FA	G by Pos
1946	NY N	18	.315	.537	54	17	4	1	2	3.7	8	9	4	5	0	2	0	18	25	3	0	2.6	.935	3B-16
1947		138	.283	.508	545	154	26	5	29	5.3	105	85	40	78	1	3	0	357	32	12	6	2.9	.970	OF-127, 2B-9
1948		138	.248	.401	471	117	20	2	16	3.4	75	63	30	77	2	9	3	313	10	10	2	2.4	.970	OF-125
1949		156	.309	.518	641	198	35	9	27	4.2	99	109	44	45	10	0	0	488	10	9	4	3.3	.982	OF-156
1950		149	.252	.449	563	142	22	7	25	4.4	79	85	55	45	3	0	0	394	15	9	5	2.8	.978	OF-149
1951		148	.293	.562	518	152	27	8	32	6.2	89	101	73	57	5	2	0	258	139	20	14	2.8	.952	OF-77, 3B-69
1952		153	.270	.482	608	164	29	14	24	3.9	89	108	52	74	5	0	0	234	187	18	13	2.9	.959	3B-91, OF-63
1953		154	.288	.472	608	175	22	6	26	4.3	80	106	43	57	4	0	0	391	16	7	0	2.7	.983	OF-154
1954	MIL N	43	.232	.323	99	23	3	0	2	2.0	7	15	12	29	0	14	5	45	3	1	2	1.1	.980	OF-26
1955		101	.257	.414	343	88	12	3	12	3.5	40	56	34	52	2	13	2	182	5	6	0	1.9	.969	OF-91
1956		142	.235	.408	451	106	10	4	20	4.4	59	74	43	75	2	5	0	262	17	10	0	2.0	.965	OF-136, 3B-3
1957	2 teams		MIL	N (41G – .236)		NY	N (81G – .242)																	
"	total	122	.240	.410	363	87	12	7	12	3.3	39	61	27	66	3	13	2	202	7	2	0	1.7	.991	OF-109, 3B-1
1958	CHI N	152	.283	.466	547	155	27	5	21	3.8	67	82	56	76	0	1	1	358	16	5	4	2.5	.987	OF-148, 3B-4
1959		122	.259	.398	374	97	15	2	11	2.9	55	52	35	50	1	9	4	223	9	3	4	1.9	.987	OF-116
1960	2 teams		BOS	A (40G – .263)		BAL	A (3G – .000)																	
"	total	43	.250	.417	120	30	3	1	5	4.2	12	20	11	18	0	13	3	75	1	4	3	1.9	.950	OF-29, 1B-1
15 yrs.		1779	.270	.462	6305	1705	267	74	264	4.2	903	1026	559	804	38	84	20	3800	492	119	57	2.5	.973	OF-1506, 3B-184, 2B-9, 1B-1

WORLD SERIES

Year	Team	Games	BA	SA	AB	H	2B	3B	HR	HR%	R	RBI	BB	SO	SB	AB	H	PO	A	E	DP	TC/G	FA	G by Pos
1951	NY N	6	.238	.286	21	5	1	0	0	0.0	1	2	5	0	0	0	0	12	15	2	0	4.8	.931	3B-6

Dickie Thon

THON, RICHARD WILLIAM   BR TR 5'11"   160 lbs.
B. June 20, 1958, South Bend, Ind.

Year	Team	Games	BA	SA	AB	H	2B	3B	HR	HR%	R	RBI	BB	SO	SB	AB	H	PO	A	E	DP	TC/G	FA	G by Pos
1979	CAL A	35	.339	.393	56	19	3	0	0	0.0	6	8	5	10	1	0	0	38	46	8	13	2.6	.913	2B-24, SS-8, DH-1, 3B-1
1980		80	.255	.315	267	68	12	2	0	0.0	32	15	10	28	7	13	2	70	128	10	28	2.6	.952	SS-22, 2B-21, DH-15, 3B-10, 1B-1
1981	HOU N	49	.274	.337	95	26	6	0	0	0.0	13	3	9	13	6	2	0	53	63	6	13	2.5	.951	2B-28, SS-13, 3B-5
1982		136	.276	.397	496	137	31	10	3	0.6	73	36	37	48	37	9	4	183	412	17	82	4.5	.972	SS-119, 3B-8, 2B-1
1983		154	.286	.457	619	177	28	9	20	3.2	81	79	54	73	34	0	0	258	533	28	114	5.3	.966	SS-154
1984		5	.353	.471	17	6	1	0	0	0.0	3	1	0	4	0	0	0	8	13	0	1	4.2	1.000	SS-5
1985		84	.251	.355	251	63	6	1	6	2.4	26	29	18	50	8	6	1	106	218	11	48	4.0	.967	SS-79
1986		106	.248	.335	278	69	13	1	3	1.1	24	21	29	49	6	20	5	142	210	10	39	3.4	.972	SS-104
1987		32	.212	.273	66	14	1	0	1	1.5	6	3	16	13	3	9	3	21	53	6	7	2.5	.925	SS-31
1988	SD N	95	.264	.337	258	68	12	2	1	0.4	36	18	33	49	19	19	3	84	171	12	29	2.8	.955	SS-70, 2B-2, 3B-1
1989	PHI N	136	.271	.434	435	118	18	4	15	3.4	45	60	33	81	6	7	3	174	380	16	65	4.2	.972	SS-129
11 yrs.		912	.270	.388	2838	765	130	30	49	1.7	345	273	244	418	126	85	21	1137	2227	124	439	3.8	.964	SS-734, 2B-76, 3B-25, DH-16, 1B-1

DIVISIONAL PLAYOFF SERIES

Year	Team	Games	BA	SA	AB	H	2B	3B	HR	HR%	R	RBI	BB	SO	SB	AB	H	PO	A	E	DP	TC/G	FA	G by Pos
1981	HOU N	4	.182	.182	11	2	0	0	0	0.0	0	0	1	0	0	1	0	0	0	1	0	0.3	–	SS-4

LEAGUE CHAMPIONSHIP SERIES

Year	Team	Games	BA	SA	AB	H	2B	3B	HR	HR%	R	RBI	BB	SO	SB	AB	H	PO	A	E	DP	TC/G	FA	G by Pos
1979	CAL A	1	–	–	0	0	0	0	0	–	1	0	1	0	0	0	0	0	0	0	0	0.0	–	SS-1
1986	HOU N	6	.250	.500	12	3	0	0	1	8.3	1	1	0	1	0	1	0	6	9	0	2	2.5	1.000	SS-6
2 yrs.		7	.250	.500	12	3	0	0	1	8.3	2	1	0	1	0	1	0	6	9	0	2	2.1	1.000	SS-7

Jack Thoney

THONEY, JOHN (Bullet Jack)   BR TR 5'10"   175 lbs.
Born John Thoeny.
B. Dec. 8, 1879, Ft. Thomas, Ky. D. Oct. 24, 1948, Covington, Ky.

Year	Team	Games	BA	SA	AB	H	2B	3B	HR	HR%	R	RBI	BB	SO	SB	AB	H	PO	A	E	DP	TC/G	FA	G by Pos
1902	2 teams		CLE	A (28G – .286)		BAL	A (3G – .000)																	
"	total	31	.259	.336	116	30	1	1	0	0.0	15	11	10		5	1	0	51	57	20	4	4.1	.844	2B-14, SS-11, 3B-3, OF-2
1903	CLE A	32	.205	.254	122	25	3	0	1	0.8	10	9	2		7	2	0	65	13	11	3	2.8	.876	OF-24, 2B-5, 3B-2
1904	2 teams		WAS	A (17G – .300)		NY	A (36G – .188)																	
"	total	53	.227	.283	198	45	7	2	0	0.0	23	18	9		11	1	0	87	46	23	4	2.9	.853	OF-27, 3B-26
1908	BOS A	109	.255	.325	416	106	5	9	2	0.5	58	30	13		16	8	3	208	12	12	2	2.1	.948	OF-101
1909		13	.125	.150	40	5	1	0	0	0.0	1	3	2		2	3	0	23	1	1	1	1.9	.960	OF-10
1911		26	.250	.250	20	5	0	0	0	0.0	5	2	0		1	20	5	0	0	0	0	0.0	–	
6 yrs.		264	.237	.298	912	216	23	12	3	0.3	112	73	36		42	35	8	434	129	67	14	2.4	.894	OF-164, 3B-31, 2B-19, SS-11

Andre Thornton

THORNTON, ANDRE   BR TR 6'3"   200 lbs.
B. Aug. 13, 1949, Tuskegee, Ala.

Year	Team	Games	BA	SA	AB	H	2B	3B	HR	HR%	R	RBI	BB	SO	SB	AB	H	PO	A	E	DP	TC/G	FA	G by Pos
1973	CHI N	17	.200	.286	35	7	3	0	0	0.0	3	2	7	9	0	9	3	81	10	1	3	5.4	.989	1B-9
1974		107	.261	.439	303	79	16	4	10	3.3	41	46	48	50	2	19	6	760	70	7	61	7.8	.992	1B-90, 3B-1

Year	Team	Games	BA	SA	AB	H	2B	3B	HR	HR%	R	RBI	BB	SO	SB	Pinch Hit AB	Pinch Hit H	PO	A	E	DP	TC/G	FA	G by Pos

Andre Thornton *continued*

Year	Team	Games	BA	SA	AB	H	2B	3B	HR	HR%	R	RBI	BB	SO	SB	PH AB	PH H	PO	A	E	DP	TC/G	FA	G by Pos
1975		120	.293	.516	372	109	21	4	18	4.8	70	60	88	63	3	9	1	984	77	13	88	9.0	.988	1B-113, 3B-2
1976 2 teams	CHI N (27G – .200)				MON N (69G – .191)																			
" total		96	.194	.373	268	52	11	2	11	4.1	28	38	48	46	4	21	4	542	46	6	60	6.2	.990	1B-68, OF-11
1977	CLE A	131	.263	.527	433	114	20	5	28	6.5	77	70	70	82	3	7	1	1026	71	6	97	8.4	.995	1B-117, DH-9
1978		145	.262	.516	508	133	22	4	33	6.5	97	105	93	72	4	1	1	1327	106	7	106	9.9	.995	1B-145
1979		143	.233	.449	515	120	31	1	26	5.0	89	93	90	93	5	0	0	1089	82	7	100	8.2	.994	1B-130, DH-13
1981		69	.239	.372	226	54	12	0	6	2.7	22	30	23	37	3	6	3	67	5	1	7	1.1	.986	DH-53, 1B-11
1982		161	.273	.484	589	161	26	1	32	5.4	90	116	109	81	6	0	0	76	5	0	5	0.5	1.000	DH-152, 1B-8
1983		141	.281	.439	508	143	27	1	17	3.3	78	77	87	72	4	2	1	201	21	2	20	1.6	.991	DH-114, 1B-27
1984		155	.271	.484	587	159	26	0	33	5.6	91	99	91	79	6	0	0	86	9	2	11	0.6	.979	DH-144, 1B-11
1985		124	.236	.408	461	109	13	0	22	4.8	49	88	47	75	3	2	1	0	0	0	0	0.0	–	DH-122
1986		120	.229	.392	401	92	14	0	17	4.2	49	66	65	67	4	12	5	0	0	0	0	0.0	–	DH-110
1987		36	.118	.141	85	10	2	0	0	0.0	8	5	10	25	1	15	2	0	0	0	0	0.0	–	DH-21
14 yrs.		1565	.254	.452	5291	1342	244	22	253	4.8	792	895	876	851	48	103	28	6239	502	52	558	4.3	.992	DH-738, 1B-729, OF-11, 3B-3

Lou Thornton

THORNTON, LOUIS, JR.
B. Apr. 26, 1963, Montgomery, Ala.

BL TR 6' 170 lbs.

Year	Team	Games	BA	SA	AB	H	2B	3B	HR	HR%	R	RBI	BB	SO	SB	PH AB	PH H	PO	A	E	DP	TC/G	FA	G by Pos
1985	TOR A	56	.236	.319	72	17	1	1	1	1.4	18	8	2	24	1	3	1	44	0	2	0	0.8	.957	OF-35, DH-16
1987		12	.500	.500	2	1	0	0	0	0.0	5	0	1	0	0	0	0	0	0	0	0	–	OF-4
1988		11	.000	.000	2	0	0	0	0	0.0	1	0	0	0	0	0	0	1	0	0	0	0.1	1.000	OF-10
1989	NY N	13	.308	.385	13	4	1	0	0	0.0	5	1	0	1	2	1	0	9	0	0	0	0.7	1.000	OF-6
4 yrs.		92	.247	.326	89	22	2	1	1	1.1	29	9	3	25	3	4	1	54	0	2	0	0.6	.964	OF-55, DH-16

LEAGUE CHAMPIONSHIP SERIES

Year	Team	Games	BA	SA	AB	H	2B	3B	HR	HR%	R	RBI	BB	SO	SB	PH AB	PH H	PO	A	E	DP	TC/G	FA	G by Pos
1985	TOR A	2	–	–	0	0	0	0	0	–	1	0	0	0	0	0	0	0	0	0	0	0.0	–	

Otis Thornton

THORNTON, OTIS BENJAMIN
B. June 30, 1945, Docena, Ala.

BR TR 6'1" 186 lbs.

Year	Team	Games	BA	SA	AB	H	2B	3B	HR	HR%	R	RBI	BB	SO	SB	PH AB	PH H	PO	A	E	DP	TC/G	FA	G by Pos
1973	HOU N	2	.000	.000	3	0	0	0	0	0.0	0	1	0	2	0	1	0	4	0	0	1	2.0	1.000	C-2

Walter Thornton

THORNTON, WALTER MILLER
B. Feb. 18, 1875, Lewiston, Me. D. July 14, 1960, Los Angeles, Calif.

TL 6'1" 180 lbs.

Year	Team	Games	BA	SA	AB	H	2B	3B	HR	HR%	R	RBI	BB	SO	SB	PH AB	PH H	PO	A	E	DP	TC/G	FA	G by Pos
1895	CHI N	8	.318	.500	22	7	1	0	1	4.5	4	7	3	1	0	0	0	7	5	1	0	1.6	.923	P-7, 1B-1
1896		9	.364	.455	22	8	0	1	0	0.0	6	1	5	2	1	0	0	8	3	3	0	1.6	.786	P-5, OF-3
1897		75	.321	.400	265	85	9	6	0	0.0	39	55	30		13	1	0	85	33	24	1	1.9	.831	OF-59, P-16
1898		62	.295	.338	210	62	5	2	0	0.0	34	14	22		8	2	0	74	53	17	5	2.3	.882	OF-34, P-28
4 yrs.		154	.312	.382	519	162	15	9	1	0.2	83	77	60	3	23	4	0	174	94	45	6	2.0	.856	OF-96, P-56, 1B-1

Bob Thorpe

THORPE, BENJAMIN ROBERT
B. Nov. 19, 1926, Caryville, Fla.

BR TR 6'1½" 190 lbs.

Year	Team	Games	BA	SA	AB	H	2B	3B	HR	HR%	R	RBI	BB	SO	SB	PH AB	PH H	PO	A	E	DP	TC/G	FA	G by Pos
1951	BOS N	2	.500	1.500	2	1	0	1	0	0.0	1	1	0	0	0	2	1	0	0	0	0	0.0	–	
1952		81	.260	.332	292	76	8	2	3	1.0	20	26	5	42	3	9	4	132	9	4	3	1.8	.972	OF-72
1953	MIL N	27	.162	.189	37	6	1	0	0	0.0	1	5	1	6	0	9	1	12	0	0	0	0.4	1.000	OF-18
3 yrs.		110	.251	.323	331	83	9	3	3	0.9	22	32	6	48	3	20	6	144	9	4	3	1.4	.975	OF-90

Jim Thorpe

THORPE, JAMES FRANCIS
B. May 28, 1887, Prague, Okla. D. Mar. 28, 1953, Long Beach, Calif.

BR TR 6'1" 185 lbs.

Year	Team	Games	BA	SA	AB	H	2B	3B	HR	HR%	R	RBI	BB	SO	SB	PH AB	PH H	PO	A	E	DP	TC/G	FA	G by Pos
1913	NY N	19	.143	.229	35	5	0	0	1	2.9	6	2	1	9	2	6	2	15	2	1	1	0.9	.944	OF-9
1914		30	.194	.226	31	6	1	0	0	0.0	5	2	0	4	1	22	5	3	0	1	0	0.1	.750	OF-4
1915		17	.231	.327	52	12	3	1	0	0.0	8	1	2	16	4	1	0	28	0	2	0	1.8	.933	OF-15
1917 2 teams	CIN N (77G – .247)				NY N (26G – .193)																			
" total		103	.237	.357	308	73	5	10	4	1.3	41	40	14	45	12	14	3	174	7	8	2	1.8	.958	OF-87
1918	NY N	58	.248	.381	113	28	4	4	1	0.9	15	11	4	18	3	11	3	57	2	1	1	1.0	.983	OF-44
1919 2 teams	NY N (2G – .333)				BOS N (60G – .327)																			
" total		62	.327	.428	159	52	7	3	1	0.6	16	26	6	30	7	11	1	88	2	8	2	1.6	.918	OF-40, 1B-2
6 yrs.		289	.252	.362	698	176	20	18	7	1.0	91	82	27	122	29	65	14	365	13	21	6	1.4	.947	OF-199, 1B-2

WORLD SERIES

Year	Team	Games	BA	SA	AB	H	2B	3B	HR	HR%	R	RBI	BB	SO	SB	PH AB	PH H	PO	A	E	DP	TC/G	FA	G by Pos
1917	NY N	1	–	–	0	0	0	0	0	–	0	0	0	0	0	0	0	0	0	0	0	0.0	–	OF-1

Buck Thrasher

THRASHER, FRANK EDWARD
B. Aug. 6, 1889, Watkinsville, Ga. D. June 12, 1938, Cleveland, Tenn.

BL TR 5'11" 182 lbs.

Year	Team	Games	BA	SA	AB	H	2B	3B	HR	HR%	R	RBI	BB	SO	SB	PH AB	PH H	PO	A	E	DP	TC/G	FA	G by Pos
1916	PHI A	7	.310	.448	29	9	2	1	0	0.0	4	4	2	1	0	0	0	9	0	0	0	1.3	1.000	OF-7
1917		23	.234	.286	77	18	2	1	0	0.0	5	2	3	12	0	1	0	29	1	2	0	1.4	.938	OF-22
2 yrs.		30	.255	.330	106	27	4	2	0	0.0	9	6	5	13	0	1	0	38	1	2	0	1.4	.951	OF-29

Faye Throneberry

THRONEBERRY, MAYNARD FAYE
Brother of Marv Throneberry.
B. June 22, 1931, Memphis, Tenn.

BL TR 5'11" 185 lbs.

Year	Team	Games	BA	SA	AB	H	2B	3B	HR	HR%	R	RBI	BB	SO	SB	PH AB	PH H	PO	A	E	DP	TC/G	FA	G by Pos
1952	BOS A	98	.258	.361	310	80	11	3	5	1.6	38	23	33	67	16	12	1	141	9	7	5	1.6	.955	OF-86
1955		60	.257	.472	144	37	7	3	6	4.2	20	27	14	31	0	24	5	69	3	3	0	1.3	.960	OF-34
1956		24	.220	.320	50	11	2	0	1	2.0	6	3	3	16	0	11	2	20	0	2	0	0.9	.909	OF-13
1957 2 teams	BOS A (1G – .000)				WAS A (68G – .185)																			
" total		69	.184	.276	196	36	8	2	2	1.0	21	12	17	38	1	7	0	116	2	2	0	1.7	.983	OF-58
1958	WAS A	44	.184	.356	87	16	1	1	4	4.6	12	7	4	28	0	17	5	35	1	0	0	0.8	1.000	OF-26
1959		117	.251	.388	327	82	11	2	10	3.1	36	42	33	61	6	28	3	136	7	7	2	1.3	.953	OF-86
1960		85	.248	.325	157	39	7	1	1	0.6	18	23	18	33	1	40	12	52	2	3	0	0.7	.947	OF-34
1961	LA A	24	.194	.226	31	6	1	0	0	0.0	1	0	5	10	0	16	3	8	1	0	0	0.4	1.000	OF-5
8 yrs.		521	.236	.358	1302	307	48	12	29	2.2	152	137	127	284	23	155	31	577	25	24	7	1.2	.962	OF-342

Year	Team	Games	BA	SA	AB	H	2B	3B	HR	HR%	R	RBI	BB	SO	SB	Pinch Hit AB	Pinch Hit H	PO	A	E	DP	TC/G	FA	G by Pos

Marv Throneberry

THRONEBERRY, MARVIN EUGENE (Marvelous Marv)
Brother of Faye Throneberry.
B. Sept. 2, 1933, Collierville, Tenn.   BL TL 6'1"   190 lbs.

Year	Team	Games	BA	SA	AB	H	2B	3B	HR	HR%	R	RBI	BB	SO	SB	PH AB	PH H	PO	A	E	DP	TC/G	FA	G by Pos
1955	NY A	1	1.000	1.500	2	2	1	0	0	0.0	1	3	0	0	0	0	0	3	1	0	0	4.0	1.000	1B-1
1958		60	.227	.427	150	34	5	2	7	4.7	30	19	19	40	1	12	0	322	21	4	42	5.8	.988	1B-40, OF-5
1959		80	.240	.391	192	46	5	0	8	4.2	27	22	18	51	0	15	1	346	29	4	40	4.7	.989	1B-54, OF-13
1960	KC A	104	.250	.445	236	59	9	2	11	4.7	29	41	23	60	0	33	8	508	40	5	56	5.3	.991	1B-71
1961	2 teams				KC A	(40G – .238)			BAL A	(56G – .208)														
"	total	96	.226	.403	226	51	5	1	11	4.9	26	35	31	50	0	26	7	330	35	4	37	3.8	.989	1B-41, OF-25
1962	2 teams				BAL A	(9G – .000)			NY N	(116G – .244)														
"	total	125	.238	.415	366	87	11	3	16	4.4	30	49	38	89	1	26	5	788	77	17	87	7.1	.981	1B-97, OF-2
1963	NY N	14	.143	.214	14	2	1	0	0	0.0	0	1	1	5	0	10	2	9	0	0	1	0.6	1.000	1B-3
7 yrs.		480	.237	.416	1186	281	37	8	53	4.5	143	170	130	295	3	122	23	2306	203	34	263	5.3	.987	1B-307, OF-45

WORLD SERIES

| 1958 | NY A | 1 | .000 | .000 | 1 | 0 | 0 | 0 | 0 | 0.0 | 0 | 0 | 0 | 1 | 0 | 1 | 0 | 0 | 0 | 0 | 0 | 0.0 | – | |

Bob Thurman

THURMAN, ROBERT BURNS
B. May 14, 1917, Wichita, Kans.   BL TL 6'1"   205 lbs.

1955	CIN N	82	.217	.408	152	33	2	3	7	4.6	19	22	0	44	9			54	2	3	0	0.7	.949	OF-36
1956		80	.295	.532	139	41	5	2	8	5.8	25	22	10	14	0	48	9	39	2	2	1	0.5	.953	OF-29
1957		74	.247	.542	190	47	4	2	16	8.4	38	40	15	33	0	34	9	75	3	1	1	1.1	.987	OF-44
1958		94	.230	.382	178	41	7	4	4	2.2	23	20	20	38	1	48	11	80	2	2	1	0.9	.976	OF-41
1959		4	.250	.250	4	1	0	0	0	0.0	1	2	0	1	0	4	1	0	0	0	0	0.0	–	
5 yrs.		334	.246	.465	663	163	18	11	35	5.3	106	106	62	112	1	178	39	248	9	8	3	0.8	.970	OF-150

Gary Thurman

THURMAN, GARY MONTEZ
B. Nov. 12, 1964, Indianapolis, Ind.   BR TR 5'10"   170 lbs.

1987	KC A	27	.296	.321	81	24	2	0	0	0.0	12	5	8	20	7	0	0	61	5	2	1	2.5	.971	OF-27
1988		35	.167	.182	66	11	0	0	0	0.0	6	2	4	20	5	1	0	36	1	2	0	1.1	.949	OF-32, DH-4
1989		72	.195	.241	87	17	2	1	0	0.0	24	5	15	26	16	1	0	54	2	3	0	0.8	.949	OF-60, DH-4
3 yrs.		134	.222	.252	234	52	5	1	0	0.0	42	12	27	66	28	2	0	151	8	7	1	1.2	.958	OF-119, DH-5

Sloppy Thurston

THURSTON, HOLLIS JOHN
B. June 2, 1899, Fremont, Neb.   D. Sept. 14, 1973, Los Angeles, Calif.   BR TR 5'11"   165 lbs.

1923	2 teams				STL A	(2G – .000)			CHI A	(45G – .316)														
"	total	47	.316	.405	79	25	5	1	0	0.0	10	4	2	6	0	1	0	6	50	2	2	1.2	.966	P-46
1924	CHI A	51	.254	.377	122	31	6	3	1	0.8	15	9	5	14	0	10	3	15	75	3	1	1.8	.968	P-38, OF-1
1925		44	.286	.417	84	24	7	2	0	0.0	2	13	5	13	0	6	2	15	55	2	4	1.6	.972	P-36
1926		38	.311	.377	61	19	4	0	0	0.0	5	5	3	6	0	5	0	4	30	1	1	0.9	.971	P-31
1927	WAS A	42	.315	.467	92	29	4	2	2	2.2	11	17	5	10	1	9	1	12	46	4	4	1.5	.935	P-29
1930	BKN N	36	.200	.320	50	10	3	0	1	2.0	3	11	0	16	0	10	2	3	30	0	0	0.9	1.000	P-24
1931		24	.217	.333	60	13	2	1	1	1.7	8	8	2	10	0	1	0	3	30	2	3	1.5	.943	P-24
1932		29	.304	.429	56	17	5	1	0	0.0	7	5	2	9	0	1	0	10	34	0	2	1.5	1.000	P-28
1933		32	.159	.205	44	7	2	0	0	0.0	4	7	0	7	0	0	0	3	40	1	0	1.4	.977	P-32
9 yrs.		343	.270	.383	648	175	38	10	5	0.8	65	79	24	91	1	42	8	71	390	15	17	1.4	.968	P-288, OF-1

Eddie Tiemeyer

TIEMEYER, EDWARD CARL
B. May 9, 1885, Cincinnati, Ohio   D. Sept. 27, 1946, Cincinnati, Ohio   BR TR 5'11½"   185 lbs.

1906	CIN N	5	.182	.182	11	2	0	0	0	0.0	3	0	1		0	1	0	1	6	0	1	1.4	1.000	3B-3, P-1
1907		1	–		0	0	0	0	0	–	0	1	0		0	0	0	0	0	0	0	0.0	–	
1909	NY A	3	.375	.500	8	3	1	0	0	0.0	1	0	1		0	0	0	25	0	1	0	8.7	.962	1B-3
3 yrs.		9	.263	.316	19	5	1	0	0	0.0	5	1	3		0	1	0	26	6	1	1	3.7	.970	3B-3, 1B-3, P-1

Mike Tiernan

TIERNAN, MICHAEL JOSEPH (Silent Mike)
B. Jan. 21, 1867, Trenton, N. J.   D. Nov. 9, 1918, New York, N. Y.   BL TL 5'11"   165 lbs.

1887	NY N	103	.287	.452	407	117	13	12	10	2.5	82	62	32	31	28	0	0	150	13	25	3	1.8	.867	OF-103, P-5
1888		113	.293	.427	443	130	16	8	9	2.0	75	52	42	42	52	0	0	174	16	8	2	1.8	.960	OF-113
1889		122	.335	.501	499	167	22	14	11	2.2	147	73	96	33	33	0	0	179	19	23	2	1.8	.896	OF-122
1890		133	.304	.495	553	168	25	21	13	2.4	132	59	68	53	56	0	0	210	13	26	5	1.9	.896	OF-133
1891		134	.306	.500	542	166	30	12	17	3.1	111	73	69	32	53	0	0	138	16	17	4	1.3	.901	OF-134
1892		116	.287	.400	450	129	16	10	5	1.1	79	66	57	46	20	0	0	155	15	19	2	1.6	.899	OF-116
1893		125	.309	.481	511	158	19	12	15	2.9	114	102	72	24	26	0	0	178	12	15	2	1.6	.927	OF-125
1894		112	.276	.417	424	117	19	13	5	1.2	84	77	54	21	28	1	0	169	9	15	1	1.7	.922	OF-111
1895		120	.347	.527	476	165	23	21	7	1.5	127	70	66	19	36	0	0	184	8	11	2	1.7	.946	OF-119
1896		133	.369	.516	521	192	24	16	7	1.3	132	89	77	35	35	0	0	213	15	7	4	1.7	.970	OF-133
1897		127	.330	.451	528	174	29	10	5	0.9	123	72	61		40	0	0	178	11	14	2	1.6	.931	OF-127
1898		103	.280	.398	415	116	15	11	4	1.0	90	49	43		19	0	0	130	12	4	2	1.4	.973	OF-103
1899		35	.255	.314	137	35	4	2	0	0.0	17	7	10		6	0	0	42	3	3	1	1.4	.938	OF-35
13 yrs.		1476	.311	.463	5906	1834	255	162	108	1.8	1313	851	747	318	428	1	0	2100	162	187	32	1.7	.924	OF-1474, P-5

Bill Tierney

TIERNEY, WILLIAM J.
B. May 14, 1858, Boston, Mass.   D. Sept. 21, 1898, Boston, Mass.

1882	CIN AA	1	.000	.000	5	0	0	0	0	0.0	1		0		0	0	0	10	1	1	0	12.0	.917	1B-1
1884	BAL U	1	.333	.333	3	1	0	0	0	0.0	0		1		0	0	0	1	0	0	0	1.0	1.000	OF-1
2 yrs.		2	.125	.125	8	1	0	0	0	0.0	1		1		0	0	0	11	1	1	0	6.5	.923	OF-1, 1B-1

Cotton Tierney

TIERNEY, JAMES ARTHUR
B. Feb. 10, 1894, Kansas City, Kans.   D. Apr. 18, 1953, Kansas City, Mo.   BR TR 5'8"   175 lbs.

1920	PIT N	12	.239	.348	46	11	5	0	0	0.0	4	8	3	4	1	0	0	20	40	2	4	5.2	.968	2B-10, SS-2
1921		117	.299	.405	442	132	22	8	3	0.7	49	52	24	31	4	3	0	200	243	18	37	3.9	.961	2B-72, 3B-37, OF-4, SS-3
1922		122	.345	.515	441	152	26	14	7	1.6	58	86	22	40	7	13	2	184	305	20	53	4.2	.961	2B-105, OF-2, SS-1, 3B-1

Year	Team	Games	BA	SA	AB	H	2B	3B	HR	HR%	R	RBI	BB	SO	SB	Pinch Hit AB	Pinch Hit H	PO	A	E	DP	TC/G	FA	G by Pos

Cotton Tierney *continued*

1923	2 teams	PIT	N	(29G – .292)			PHI	N	(121G – .317)															
"	total	150	.312	.447	600	187	36	3	13	2.2	90	88	26	52	5	0	0	323	515	27	105	5.8	.969	2B-143, OF-5, 3B-2
1924	BOS N	136	.259	.331	505	131	16	1	6	1.2	38	58	22	37	11	2	1	266	434	26	88	5.3	.964	2B-115, 3B-22
1925	BKN N	93	.257	.362	265	68	14	4	2	0.8	27	39	12	23	0	28	7	60	105	6	8	1.8	.965	3B-61, 2B-1, 1B-1
6 yrs.		630	.296	.415	2299	681	119	30	31	1.3	266	331	109	187	28	46	11	1053	1642	99	295	4.4	.965	2B-446, 3B-123, OF-11, SS-6, 1B-1

John Tilley

TILLEY, JOHN C.
B. 1856, New York, N. Y. Deceased.

1882	CLE N	15	.089	.143	56	5	1	1	0	0.0	2	4	2	11		0	0	32	4	6	1	2.8	.857	OF-15
1884	2 teams	TOL	AA	(17G – .179)			STP	U	(9G – .154)															
"	total	26	.171	.207	82	14	3	0	0	0.0	7		7			0	0	26	1	8	0	1.3	.771	OF-26
2 yrs.		41	.138	.181	138	19	4	1	0	0.0	9	4	9	11		0	0	58	5	14	1	1.9	.818	OF-41

Bob Tillman

TILLMAN, JOHN ROBERT
B. Mar. 24, 1937, Nashville, Tenn.   BR TR 6'4" 205 lbs.

1962	BOS A	81	.229	.454	249	57	6	4	14	5.6	28	38	19	65	0	16	3	389	19	7	1	5.1	.983	C-66
1963		96	.225	.349	307	69	10	2	8	2.6	24	32	34	64	0	2	1	621	26	5	5	6.8	.992	C-95
1964		131	.278	.445	425	118	18	1	17	4.0	43	61	49	74	0	0	0	897	49	11	5	7.3	.989	C-131
1965		111	.215	.307	368	79	10	3	6	1.6	20	35	40	69	0	6	1	676	45	9	6	6.6	.988	C-106
1966		78	.230	.314	204	47	8	0	3	1.5	12	24	22	35	0	9	3	372	24	4	5	5.1	.990	C-72
1967	2 teams	BOS	A	(30G – .188)			NY	A	(22G – .254)															
"	total	52	.220	.307	127	28	2	0	3	2.4	9	13	10	35	0	10	2	203	24	6	4	4.5	.974	C-41
1968	ATL N	86	.220	.301	236	52	4	0	5	2.1	16	20	16	55	1	10	2	359	29	4	7	4.6	.990	C-75
1969		69	.195	.411	190	37	5	0	12	6.3	18	29	18	47	0	1	0	309	15	4	5	4.8	.988	C-69
1970		71	.238	.408	223	53	5	0	11	4.9	19	30	20	66	0	1	0	404	22	5	0	6.1	.988	C-70
9 yrs.		775	.232	.371	2329	540	68	10	79	3.4	189	282	228	510	1	55	12	4230	253	55	40	5.9	.988	C-725

LEAGUE CHAMPIONSHIP SERIES

| 1969 | ATL N | 1 | – | – | 0 | 0 | 0 | 0 | 0 | – | 0 | 0 | 0 | 0 | 0 | 0 | 0 | 2 | 0 | 0 | 0 | 2.0 | 1.000 | C-1 |

Rusty Tillman

TILLMAN, KERRY JEROME
B. Aug. 29, 1960, Jacksonville, Fla.   BR TR 6' 175 lbs.

1982	NY N	12	.154	.231	13	2	1	0	0	0.0	1	0	0	4	1	5	2	2	0	0	0	0.2	1.000	OF-3
1986	OAK A	22	.256	.359	39	10	1	0	1	2.6	6	6	3	11	2	5	0	20	0	1	0	1.0	.952	OF-17
1988	SF N	4	.250	1.000	4	1	0	0	1	25.0	1	3	2	1	0	3	0	1	0	0	0	0.3	1.000	OF-1
3 yrs.		38	.232	.375	56	13	2	0	2	3.6	11	9	5	16	3	13	2	23	0	1	0	0.6	.958	OF-21

Ron Tingley

TINGLEY, RONALD IRVIN
B. May 27, 1959, Presque Isle, Me.   BR TR 6'2" 160 lbs.

1982	SD N	8	.100	.100	20	2	0	0	0	0.0	0	0	0	7	0	0	0	40	4	2	1	5.8	.957	C-8
1988	CLE A	9	.167	.292	24	4	0	0	1	4.2	1	2	2	8	0	1	1	48	6	0	1	6.0	1.000	C-9
1989	CAL A	4	.333	.333	3	1	0	0	0	0.0	0	0	1	0	0	0	0	7	1	1	0	2.3	.889	C-4
3 yrs.		21	.149	.213	47	7	0	0	1	2.1	1	2	3	15	0	1	1	95	11	3	2	5.2	.972	C-21

Joe Tinker

TINKER, JOSEPH BERT
B. July 27, 1880, Muscotah, Kans. D. July 27, 1948, Orlando, Fla.   BR TR 5'9" 175 lbs.
Manager 1913-16.
Hall of Fame 1946.

1902	CHI N	133	.273	.343	501	137	19	5	2	0.4	54	54	26			27	0	253	468	74	48	6.0	.907	SS-124, 3B-8
1903		124	.291	.380	460	134	21	7	2	0.4	67	70	37			27	0	246	400	67	37	5.8	.906	SS-107, 3B-17
1904		141	.221	.318	488	108	12	13	3	0.6	55	41	29			41	0	331	465	64	54	6.1	.926	SS-140, OF-1
1905		149	.247	.320	547	135	18	8	2	0.4	70	66	34			31	0	345	527	56	67	6.2	.940	SS-149
1906		148	.233	.289	523	122	18	4	1	0.2	75	64	43			30	0	289	474	46	55	5.5	.943	SS-147, 3B-1
1907		117	.221	.271	402	89	11	3	1	0.2	36	36	25			20	0	215	390	39	45	5.5	.939	SS-113
1908		157	.266	.392	548	146	23	14	6	1.1	67	68	32			30	0	314	570	39	48	5.9	.958	SS-157
1909		143	.256	.372	516	132	26	11	4	0.8	56	57	17			23	0	320	470	50	49	5.9	.940	SS-143
1910		133	.288	.397	473	136	25	9	3	0.6	48	69	24	35		20	0	277	411	42	54	5.5	.942	SS-131
1911		144	.278	.390	536	149	24	12	4	0.7	61	69	39	31		30	0	333	486	55	56	6.1	.937	SS-143
1912		142	.282	.351	550	155	24	7	0	0.0	80	75	38	21		25	0	354	470	50	73	6.2	.943	SS-142
1913	CIN N	110	.317	.445	382	121	20	13	1	0.3	47	57	20	26		10	1	237	337	19	34	5.4	.968	SS-101, 3B-9
1914	CHI F	126	.256	.349	438	112	21	7	2	0.5	50	46	38			19	1	271	408	38	48	5.7	.947	SS-125
1915		31	.269	.328	67	18	2	1	0	0.0	7	9	13			3	4	1	27	58	8	4	3.0	.914	SS-16, 2B-5, 3B-4
1916	CHI N	7	.100	.100	10	1	0	0	0	0.0	0	1	1			1	1	0	4	9	1	0	2.0	.929	SS-4, 3B-2
15 yrs.		1805	.263	.354	6441	1695	264	114	31	0.5	773	782	416	114	336	12	1	3816	5943	648	672	5.8	.938	SS-1742, 3B-41, 2B-5, OF-1

WORLD SERIES

1906	CHI N	6	.167	.167	18	3	0	0	0	0.0	0	4	1	2	2	0	0	10	20	2	0	5.3	.938	SS-6
1907		5	.154	.154	13	2	0	0	0	0.0	0	4	1	3	3	2	0	15	23	3	5	8.2	.927	SS-5
1908		5	.263	.421	19	5	0	0	1	5.3	2	5	0	2	1	0	0	8	19	0	2	5.4	1.000	SS-5
1910		5	.333	.444	18	6	2	0	0	0.0	2	2	5	2	0	0	0	11	14	2	2	5.4	.926	SS-5
4 yrs.		21	.235	.309	68	16	2	0	1	1.5	12	7	7	9	6	0	0	44	76	7	9	6.0	.945	SS-21

Eric Tipton

TIPTON, ERIC GORDON (Dukie, Blue Devil)
B. Apr. 20, 1915, Petersburg, Va.   BR TR 5'11" 190 lbs.

1939	PHI A	47	.231	.337	104	24	4	2	1	1.0	12	14	13	7	2	11	2	65	0	4	0	1.5	.942	OF-34
1940		2	.125	.375	8	1	0	0	1	12.5	0	2	0	1	0	0	0	3	0	0	0	1.5	1.000	OF-2
1941		1	.500	.500	4	2	0	0	0	0.0	0	0	0	0	0	0	0	2	0	0	0	2.0	1.000	OF-1
1942	CIN N	63	.222	.353	207	46	5	5	4	1.9	22	18	25	14	1	5	2	126	3	3	0	2.1	.977	OF-58
1943		140	.288	.424	493	142	26	9	9	1.8	82	49	85	36	1	0	0	298	8	5	2	2.2	.984	OF-139
1944		140	.301	.390	479	144	28	3	3	0.6	62	36	59	32	5	1	0	329	8	6	1	2.5	.983	OF-139

Year	Team	Games	BA	SA	AB	H	2B	3B	HR	HR%	R	RBI	BB	SO	SB	Pinch Hit AB	Pinch Hit H	PO	A	E	DP	TC/G	FA	G by Pos

Eric Tipton *continued*

Year	Team	Games	BA	SA	AB	H	2B	3B	HR	HR%	R	RBI	BB	SO	SB	PH AB	PH H	PO	A	E	DP	TC/G	FA	G by Pos
1945		108	.242	.344	331	80	17	1	5	1.5	32	34	40	37	11	22	4	192	2	6	1	1.9	.970	OF-83
7 yrs.		501	.270	.383	1626	439	80	19	22	1.4	212	151	223	127	20	39	8	1015	21	24	4	2.1	.977	OF-456

Joe Tipton

TIPTON, JOE HICKS
B. Feb. 18, 1923, McCaysville, Ga. BR TR 5'11" 185 lbs.

Year	Team	Games	BA	SA	AB	H	2B	3B	HR	HR%	R	RBI	BB	SO	SB	PH AB	PH H	PO	A	E	DP	TC/G	FA	G by Pos
1948	CLE A	47	.289	.356	90	26	3	0	1	1.1	11	13	4	10	0	6	0	84	18	3	4	2.2	.971	C-40
1949	CHI A	67	.204	.309	191	39	5	3	3	1.6	20	17	27	17	1	14	1	203	32	2	4	3.5	.992	C-53
1950	PHI A	64	.266	.402	184	49	5	1	6	3.3	15	20	19	16	0	5	1	201	24	3	3	3.6	.987	C-59
1951		72	.239	.324	213	51	9	0	3	1.4	23	20	51	25	1	0	0	230	52	9	12	4.0	.969	C-72
1952	2 teams				PHI A	(23G – .191)			CLE A	(43G – .248)														
"	total	66	.225	.416	173	39	6	0	9	5.2	21	30	36	31	1	5	2	198	36	5	2	3.6	.979	C-58
1953	CLE A	47	.229	.413	109	25	2	0	6	5.5	17	13	19	13	0	5	0	114	18	0	1	2.8	1.000	C-46
1954	WAS A	54	.223	.293	157	35	6	1	1	0.6	9	10	30	30	0	2	0	220	30	2	6	4.7	.992	C-52
7 yrs.		417	.236	.355	1117	264	36	5	29	2.6	116	125	186	142	3	37	4	1250	210	24	32	3.6	.984	C-380

WORLD SERIES

Year	Team	Games	BA	SA	AB	H	2B	3B	HR	HR%	R	RBI	BB	SO	SB	PH AB	PH H	PO	A	E	DP	TC/G	FA	G by Pos
1948	CLE A	1	.000	.000	1	0	0	0	0	0.0	0	0	0	1	0	1	0	0	0	0	0	0.0	–	

Tom Tischinski

TISCHINSKI, THOMAS ARTHUR
B. July 12, 1944, Kansas City, Mo. BR TR 5'10" 190 lbs.

Year	Team	Games	BA	SA	AB	H	2B	3B	HR	HR%	R	RBI	BB	SO	SB	PH AB	PH H	PO	A	E	DP	TC/G	FA	G by Pos
1969	MIN A	37	.191	.191	47	9	0	0	0	0.0	2	2	8	8	0	5	1	77	5	0	2	2.2	1.000	C-32
1970		24	.196	.261	46	9	0	0	1	2.2	6	2	9	6	0	2	0	90	7	1	0	4.1	.990	C-22
1971		21	.130	.217	23	3	2	0	0	0.0	0	2	1	4	0	0	0	49	6	1	3	2.7	.982	C-21
3 yrs.		82	.181	.224	116	21	2	0	1	0.9	8	6	18	18	0	7	1	216	18	2	5	2.9	.992	C-75

John Titus

TITUS, JOHN FRANKLIN (Silent John)
B. Feb. 21, 1876, St. Clair, Pa. D. Jan. 8, 1943, St. Clair, Pa. BL TL 5'9" 156 lbs.

Year	Team	Games	BA	SA	AB	H	2B	3B	HR	HR%	R	RBI	BB	SO	SB	PH AB	PH H	PO	A	E	DP	TC/G	FA	G by Pos
1903	PHI N	72	.286	.404	280	80	15	6	2	0.7	38	34	19		5	0	0	126	13	7	2	2.0	.952	OF-72
1904		146	.294	.387	504	148	25	5	4	0.8	60	55	46		15	5	1	258	21	14	7	2.0	.952	OF-140
1905		147	.308	.436	548	169	36	14	2	0.4	99	89	69		11	0	0	255	24	11	4	2.0	.962	OF-147
1906		145	.267	.339	484	129	22	5	1	0.2	67	57	78		12	3	1	236	23	7	7	1.8	.974	OF-142
1907		145	.275	.382	523	144	23	12	3	0.6	72	63	47		9	3	1	198	21	17	3	1.6	.928	OF-142
1908		149	.286	.360	539	154	24	5	2	0.4	75	48	53		27	0	0	215	22	9	3	1.7	.963	OF-149
1909		151	.270	.350	540	146	22	6	3	0.6	69	46	66		23	2	0	241	23	8	6	1.8	.971	OF-148
1910		143	.241	.325	535	129	26	5	3	0.6	91	35	93	44	20	1	0	226	22	6	4	1.8	.976	OF-142
1911		76	.284	.453	236	67	14	1	8	3.4	35	26	32	16	3	15	4	85	10	2	3	1.3	.979	OF-60
1912	2 teams				PHI N	(45G – .274)			BOS N	(96G – .325)														
"	total	141	.309	.446	502	155	32	11	5	1.0	99	70	82	34	11	3	0	205	14	11	2	1.6	.952	OF-138
1913	BOS N	87	.297	.420	269	80	14	2	5	1.9	33	38	35	22	4	11	2	94	8	9	1	1.3	.919	OF-75
11 yrs.		1402	.282	.385	4960	1401	253	72	38	0.8	738	561	620	116	140	43	9	2139	201	101	42	1.7	.959	OF-1355

Bill Tobin

TOBIN, WILLIAM F.
B. Oct. 10, 1854, Hartford, Conn. D. Oct. 10, 1912, Hartford, Conn. BL

Year	Team	Games	BA	SA	AB	H	2B	3B	HR	HR%	R	RBI	BB	SO	SB	PH AB	PH H	PO	A	E	DP	TC/G	FA	G by Pos
1880	2 teams				WOR N	(5G – .125)			TRO N	(33G – .162)														
"	total	38	.158	.178	152	24	1	1	0	0.0	15	11	4	25		0	0	357	8	16	27	10.0	.958	1B-38

Jack Tobin

TOBIN, JOHN THOMAS
B. May 4, 1892, St. Louis, Mo. D. Dec. 10, 1969, St. Louis, Mo. BL TL 5'8" 142 lbs.

Year	Team	Games	BA	SA	AB	H	2B	3B	HR	HR%	R	RBI	BB	SO	SB	PH AB	PH H	PO	A	E	DP	TC/G	FA	G by Pos
1914	STL F	139	.270	.393	529	143	24	10	7	1.3	81	35	51		20	2	0	185	31	11	3	1.6	.952	OF-132
1915	STL A	158	.294	.406	625	184	26	13	6	1.0	92	51	68		31	0	0	279	21	11	3	2.0	.965	OF-158
1916		77	.213	.253	150	32	4	1	0	0.0	16	10	12	13	7	26	5	46	2	9	0	0.7	.842	OF-41
1918		122	.277	.338	480	133	19	5	0	0.0	59	36	48	26	13	0	0	244	20	8	8	2.2	.971	OF-122
1919		127	.327	.438	486	159	22	7	6	1.2	54	57	36	24	8	3	0	247	16	13	15	2.2	.953	OF-123
1920		147	.341	.452	593	202	34	10	4	0.7	94	62	39	23	21	0	0	293	18	13	1	2.2	.960	OF-147
1921		150	.352	.487	671	236	31	18	8	1.2	132	59	35	22	7	0	0	277	28	14	5	2.1	.956	OF-150
1922		146	.331	.474	625	207	34	8	13	2.1	122	66	56	22	7	0	0	221	15	15	5	1.7	.940	OF-145
1923		151	.317	.476	637	202	32	15	13	2.0	91	73	42	13	8	0	0	269	14	9	3	1.9	.969	OF-151
1924		136	.299	.390	569	170	30	8	2	0.4	87	48	50	12	6	4	0	248	19	12	5	2.1	.957	OF-131
1925		77	.301	.389	193	58	11	0	2	1.0	25	27	9	5	8	29	6	79	1	1	2	1.1	.988	OF-39, 1B-3
1926	2 teams				WAS A	(27G – .212)			BOS A	(51G – .273)														
"	total	78	.264	.322	242	64	9	1	0	0.4	31	17	16	6	14	1	89	7	3	1	1.3	.970	OF-58
1927	BOS A	111	.310	.390	374	116	18	3	2	0.5	52	40	36	5	13	3	152	10	9	4	1.5	.947	OF-93
13 yrs.		1619	.309	.420	6174	1906	294	99	64	1.0	936	581	498	172	147	91	15	2629	202	128	55	1.8	.957	OF-1490, 1B-3

Jim Tobin

TOBIN, JAMES ANTHONY (Abba Dabba)
Brother of Johnny Tobin.
B. Dec. 27, 1912, Oakland, Calif. D. May 19, 1969, Oakland, Calif. BR TR 6' 185 lbs.

Year	Team	Games	BA	SA	AB	H	2B	3B	HR	HR%	R	RBI	BB	SO	SB	PH AB	PH H	PO	A	E	DP	TC/G	FA	G by Pos
1937	PIT N	21	.441	.559	34	15	4	0	0	0.0	7	6	4	3	0	1	0	5	10	1	0	0.8	.938	P-20
1938		56	.243	.320	103	25	6	1	0	0.0	8	11	9	12	0	14	2	11	41	0	1	0.9	1.000	P-40
1939		43	.243	.392	74	18	3	1	2	2.7	9	11	2	12	0	17	1	2	26	0	2	0.7	1.000	P-25
1940	BOS N	20	.279	.349	43	12	3	0	0	0.0	5	3	1	10	0	5	0	6	16	1	1	1.2	.957	P-15
1941		43	.184	.233	103	19	5	0	0	0.0	6	9	10	31	1	10	0	15	71	3	4	2.1	.966	P-33
1942		47	.246	.421	114	28	2	0	6	5.3	14	15	16	23	0	7	1	14	93	6	6	2.4	.947	P-37
1943		46	.280	.374	107	30	4	0	2	1.9	8	12	6	16	0	11	4	17	67	6	7	2.0	.933	P-33, 1B-1
1944		62	.190	.302	116	22	1	0	2	1.7	13	18	16	28	0	14	2	13	93	3	4	1.8	.972	P-43
1945	2 teams				BOS N	(41G – .143)			DET A	(17G – .120)														
"	total	58	.137	.314	102	14	0	0	5	4.9	11	17	20	27	0	10	0	17	48	0	5	1.1	1.000	P-41
9 yrs.		396	.230	.345	796	183	35	3	17	2.1	81	102	84	162	1	89	10	100	465	20	30	1.5	.966	P-287, 1B-1

WORLD SERIES

Year	Team	Games	BA	SA	AB	H	2B	3B	HR	HR%	R	RBI	BB	SO	SB	PH AB	PH H	PO	A	E	DP	TC/G	FA	G by Pos
1945	DET A	1	.000	.000	0	0	0	0	0	0.0	0	0	0	0	0	0	0	0	1	0	0	1.0	1.000	P-1

Year	Team		Games	BA	SA	AB	H	2B	3B	HR	HR%	R	RBI	BB	SO	SB	Pinch Hit AB	Pinch Hit H	PO	A	E	DP	TC/G	FA	G by Pos

Johnny Tobin

TOBIN, JOHN MARTIN (Tip)
B. Sept. 15, 1906, Jamaica Plain, Mass. D. Aug. 6, 1983, Rhinebeck, N. Y.   BR TR 6'3" 187 lbs.

Year	Team		Games	BA	SA	AB	H	2B	3B	HR	HR%	R	RBI	BB	SO	SB	PH AB	PH H	PO	A	E	DP	TC/G	FA	G by Pos
1932	NY	N	1	.000	.000	1	0	0	0	0	0.0	0	0	0	0	0	1	0	0	0	0	0	0.0	—	

Johnny Tobin

TOBIN, JOHN PATRICK (Jackie)
Brother of Jim Tobin.
B. Jan. 8, 1921, Oakland, Calif. D. Jan. 18, 1982, Oakland, Calif.   BL TR 6' 165 lbs.

Year	Team		Games	BA	SA	AB	H	2B	3B	HR	HR%	R	RBI	BB	SO	SB	PH AB	PH H	PO	A	E	DP	TC/G	FA	G by Pos
1945	BOS	A	84	.252	.288	278	70	6	2	0	0.0	25	21	26	24	2	6	3	101	161	13	20	3.3	.953	3B-72, 2B-5, OF-1

Al Todd

TODD, ALFRED CHESTER
B. Jan. 7, 1902, Troy, N. Y. D. Mar. 8, 1985, Elmira, N. Y.   BR TR 6'1" 198 lbs.

Year	Team		Games	BA	SA	AB	H	2B	3B	HR	HR%	R	RBI	BB	SO	SB	PH AB	PH H	PO	A	E	DP	TC/G	FA	G by Pos
1932	PHI	N	33	.229	.300	70	16	5	0	0	0.0	8	9	1	9	1	7	1	58	4	7	2	2.1	.899	C-25
1933			73	.206	.235	136	28	4	0	0	0.0	13	10	4	18	1	34	7	97	21	2	3	1.6	.983	C-34, OF-2
1934			91	.318	.444	302	96	22	4	4	1.3	33	41	10	39	3	8	4	291	32	8	7	3.6	.976	C-82
1935			107	.290	.390	328	95	18	3	3	0.9	40	42	19	35	3	20	5	292	37	11	5	3.2	.968	C-87
1936	PIT	N	76	.273	.371	267	73	10	5	2	0.7	28	28	11	24	4	6	2	332	39	9	2	5.0	.976	C-70
1937			133	.307	.428	514	158	18	10	8	1.6	51	86	16	36	2	5	2	603	89	20	15	5.4	.972	C-128
1938			133	.265	.375	491	130	19	7	7	1.4	52	75	18	31	2	1	0	574	89	10	7	5.1	.985	C-132
1939	BKN	N	86	.278	.380	245	68	10	0	5	2.0	28	32	13	16	1	13	5	284	35	5	5	3.8	.985	C-73
1940	CHI	N	104	.255	.346	381	97	13	2	6	1.6	31	42	11	29	1	0	0	418	59	8	11	4.7	.984	C-104
1941			6	.167	.167	6	1	0	0	0	0.0	1	0	0	1	0	6	1	0	0	0	0	0.0		
1943			21	.133	.133	45	6	0	0	0	0.0	1	1	1	5	0	4	1	62	7	1	2	3.3	.986	C-17
11 yrs.			863	.276	.377	2785	768	119	29	35	1.3	286	366	104	243	18	104	28	3011	412	81	59	4.1	.977	C-752, OF-2

Phil Todt

TODT, PHILIP JULIUS
B. Aug. 9, 1901, St. Louis, Mo. D. Nov. 15, 1973, St. Louis, Mo.   BL TL 6' 175 lbs.

Year	Team		Games	BA	SA	AB	H	2B	3B	HR	HR%	R	RBI	BB	SO	SB	PH AB	PH H	PO	A	E	DP	TC/G	FA	G by Pos
1924	BOS	A	52	.262	.408	103	27	8	2	1	1.0	17	14	6	9	0	30	4	160	11	3	8	3.3	.983	1B-18, OF-4
1925			141	.278	.439	544	151	29	13	11	2.0	62	75	44	29	3	0	0	1408	100	13	126	10.8	.991	1B-140
1926			154	.255	.362	599	153	19	12	7	1.2	56	69	40	38	3	0	0	1755	126	22	114	12.4	.988	1B-154
1927			140	.236	.337	516	122	22	6	6	1.2	55	52	28	23	6	1	0	1401	112	13	121	10.9	.991	1B-139
1928			144	.252	.406	539	136	31	8	12	2.2	61	73	26	47	6	1	0	1486	94	5	96	11.0	.997	1B-144
1929			153	.262	.391	534	140	37	10	4	0.7	49	64	31	28	6	0	0	1467	102	14	128	10.3	.991	1B-153
1930			111	.269	.439	383	103	22	5	11	2.9	49	62	24	33	4	6	1	1001	65	8	84	9.7	.993	1B-104
1931	PHI	A	62	.244	.411	197	48	14	2	5	2.5	23	44	8	22	1	8	2	403	13	2	36	6.7	.995	1B-52
8 yrs.			957	.258	.395	3415	880	182	58	57	1.7	372	453	207	229	29	47	7	9081	623	80	713	10.2	.992	1B-904, OF-4

WORLD SERIES

Year	Team		Games	BA	SA	AB	H	2B	3B	HR	HR%	R	RBI	BB	SO	SB	PH AB	PH H	PO	A	E	DP	TC/G	FA	G by Pos
1931	PHI	A	1	–	–	0	0	0	0	0	0.0	0	0	1	0	0	0	0	0	0	0	0	0.0	—	

Bobby Tolan

TOLAN, ROBERT
B. Nov. 19, 1945, Los Angeles, Calif.   BL TL 5'11" 170 lbs.

Year	Team		Games	BA	SA	AB	H	2B	3B	HR	HR%	R	RBI	BB	SO	SB	PH AB	PH H	PO	A	E	DP	TC/G	FA	G by Pos
1965	STL	N	17	.188	.217	69	13	2	0	0	0.0	8	6	0	4	2	0	0	32	0	1	0	1.9	.970	OF-17
1966			43	.172	.280	93	16	5	1	1	1.1	10	6	6	15	1	12	3	41	1	2	0	1.0	.955	OF-26, 1B-1
1967			110	.253	.370	265	67	7	3	6	2.3	35	32	19	43	12	33	10	225	9	1	8	2.1	.996	OF-80, 1B-13
1968	CIN	N	92	.230	.335	278	64	12	1	5	1.8	28	17	13	42	9	23	2	199	12	4	8	2.3	.981	OF-67, 1B-9
1969			152	.305	.474	637	194	25	10	21	3.3	104	93	27	92	26	2	0	362	6	10	3	2.5	.974	OF-150
1970			152	.316	.475	589	186	34	6	16	2.7	112	80	62	94	57	5	1	349	7	8	0	2.4	.978	OF-150
1972			149	.283	.386	604	171	28	5	8	1.3	88	82	44	88	42	1	0	401	4	9	3	2.8	.990	OF-149
1973			129	.206	.304	457	94	14	2	9	2.0	42	51	27	68	15	12	3	279	9	10	1	2.3	.966	OF-120
1974	SD	N	95	.266	.384	357	95	16	1	8	2.2	45	40	20	41	7	4	0	161	5	5	0	1.8	.971	OF-88
1975			147	.255	.338	506	129	19	4	5	1.0	58	43	28	45	11	14	2	336	20	7	8	2.5	.981	OF-120, 1B-27
1976	PHI	N	110	.261	.342	272	71	9	0	5	1.8	32	35	7	39	10	33	4	395	14	5	36	3.8	.988	1B-50, OF-35
1977	2 teams					PHI N (15G – .125)					PIT N (49G – .203)														
"	total		64	.189	.300	90	17	4	0	2	2.2	8	10	5	14	1	40	8	125	7	1	10	2.1	.992	1B-25, OF-2
1979	SD	N	22	.190	.286	21	4	0	1	0	0.0	2	2	0	2	0	13	3	10	2	0	2	0.5	1.000	1B-5, OF-1
13 yrs.			1282	.265	.382	4238	1121	173	34	86	2.0	572	497	258	587	193	192	36	2915	101	58	79	2.4	.981	OF-1005, 1B-130

LEAGUE CHAMPIONSHIP SERIES

Year	Team		Games	BA	SA	AB	H	2B	3B	HR	HR%	R	RBI	BB	SO	SB	PH AB	PH H	PO	A	E	DP	TC/G	FA	G by Pos
1970	CIN	N	3	.417	.667	12	5	0	0	1	8.3	3	2	1	1	1	0	0	5	0	0	0	1.7	1.000	OF-3
1972			5	.238	.381	21	5	1	0	0	0.0	3	4	0	4	0	0	0	13	0	0	0	2.6	1.000	OF-5
1976	PHI	N	3	.000	.000	2	0	0	0	0	0.0	0	0	1	0	0	2	0	1	0	0	0	0.3	1.000	OF-1, 1B-1
3 yrs.			11	.286	.457	35	10	1	1	1	2.9	6	6	2	5	1	2	0	19	0	0	0	1.7	1.000	OF-9, 1B-1

WORLD SERIES

Year	Team		Games	BA	SA	AB	H	2B	3B	HR	HR%	R	RBI	BB	SO	SB	PH AB	PH H	PO	A	E	DP	TC/G	FA	G by Pos
1967	STL	N	3	.000	.000	2	0	0	0	0	0.0	1	0	1	0	0	2	0	0	0	0	0	0.0	—	
1968			1	.000	.000	1	0	0	0	0	0.0	0	0	0	1	0	1	0	0	0	0	0	0.0	—	
1970	CIN	N	5	.211	.421	19	4	1	0	1	5.3	5	1	3	2	1	0	0	4	0	1	0	1.0	.800	OF-5
1972			7	.269	.308	26	7	1	0	0	0.0	2	6	1	4	5	0	0	11	0	1	0	1.7	.917	OF-7
4 yrs.			16	.229	.333	48	11	2	0	1	2.1	8	7	5	8	6	3	0	15	0	2	0	1.1	.882	OF-12

Wayne Tolleson

TOLLESON, JIMMY WAYNE
B. Nov. 22, 1955, Spartanburg, S. C.   BB TR 5'9" 160 lbs.

Year	Team		Games	BA	SA	AB	H	2B	3B	HR	HR%	R	RBI	BB	SO	SB	PH AB	PH H	PO	A	E	DP	TC/G	FA	G by Pos
1981	TEX	A	14	.167	.167	24	4	0	0	0	0.0	6	1	1	5	2	1	0	5	8	0	0	0.9	1.000	3B-6, SS-2
1982			38	.114	.129	70	8	1	0	0	0.0	6	2	5	14	1	0	0	47	70	5	20	3.2	.959	SS-26, 3B-4, 2B-1
1983			134	.260	.315	470	122	13	2	3	0.6	64	20	40	68	33	0	0	268	372	17	81	4.9	.974	2B-112, SS-26, DH-1
1984			118	.213	.251	338	72	9	2	0	0.0	35	9	27	47	22	0	0	195	287	10	62	4.2	.980	2B-109, SS-7, 3B-5, DH-1, OF-1
1985			123	.313	.381	323	101	9	5	1	0.3	45	18	21	46	21	5	1	149	255	14	48	3.4	.967	SS-81, 2B-29, 3B-12, DH-6
1986	2 teams					CHI A (81G – .250)					NY A (60G – .284)														
"	total		141	.265	.339	475	126	16	5	3	0.6	61	43	52	76	17	3	0	147	327	14	50	3.5	.971	SS-74, 3B-72, 2B-3, DH-2, OF-2
1987	NY	A	121	.221	.241	349	77	4	0	0	0.3	48	22	43	72	5	0	0	162	326	15	66	4.2	.970	SS-119, 3B-3
1988			21	.254	.288	59	15	2	0	0	0.0	9	5	4	12	1	0	0	28	54	3	9	4.0	.965	2B-12, 3B-10, SS-1

Year Team	Games	BA	SA	AB	H	2B	3B	HR	HR%	R	RBI	BB	SO	SB	Pinch Hit AB	Pinch Hit H	PO	A	E	DP	TC/G	FA	G by Pos

Wayne Tolleson *continued*

Year Team	Games	BA	SA	AB	H	2B	3B	HR	HR%	R	RBI	BB	SO	SB	AB	H	PO	A	E	DP	TC/G	FA	G by Pos
1989	80	.164	.250	140	23	5	2	1	0.7	16	9	16	23	5	10	0	45	107	7	20	2.0	.956	SS-28, 3B-28, 2B-12, DH-10
9 yrs.	790	.244	.296	2248	548	59	16	9	0.4	289	129	213	363	107	20	1	1046	1806	85	356	3.7	.971	SS-364, 2B-278, 3B-140, DH-20, OF-3

Tim Tolman

TOLMAN, TIMOTHY LEE
B. Apr. 20, 1956, Santa Monica, Calif.   BR TR 6'   190 lbs.

Year Team	Games	BA	SA	AB	H	2B	3B	HR	HR%	R	RBI	BB	SO	SB	AB	H	PO	A	E	DP	TC/G	FA	G by Pos
1981 HOU N	4	.125	.125	8	1	0	0	0	0.0	0	0	0	0	0	2	0	2	0	0	0	0.5	1.000	OF-3
1982	15	.192	.385	26	5	2	0	1	3.8	4	3	4	3	0	7	1	17	1	0	2	1.2	1.000	OF-5, 1B-1
1983	43	.196	.375	56	11	4	0	2	3.6	4	10	6	9	0	30	4	55	2	0	6	1.3	1.000	1B-7, OF-3
1984	14	.176	.235	17	3	1	0	0	0.0	2	0	0	3	0	10	1	6	0	0	0	0.4	1.000	OF-3, 1B-1
1985	31	.140	.302	43	6	1	0	2	4.7	4	8	1	10	0	17	3	24	2	0	1	0.8	1.000	OF-9, 1B-6
1986 DET A	16	.176	.206	34	6	1	0	0	0.0	4	2	6	4	1	1	0	23	0	0	2	1.4	1.000	DH-9, OF-4, 1B-3
1987	9	.083	.167	12	1	1	0	0	0.0	3	1	7	2	0	1	0	8	0	0	0	0.9	1.000	OF-7, DH-2
7 yrs.	132	.168	.296	196	33	10	0	5	2.6	21	24	24	31	1	68	9	135	5	0	11	1.1	1.000	OF-34, 1B-18, DH-11

Chick Tolson

TOLSON, CHARLES JULIUS (Slug)
B. May 3, 1895, Washington, D. C.   D. Apr. 16, 1965, Washington, D. C.   BR TR 6'   185 lbs.

Year Team	Games	BA	SA	AB	H	2B	3B	HR	HR%	R	RBI	BB	SO	SB	AB	H	PO	A	E	DP	TC/G	FA	G by Pos
1925 CLE A	3	.250	.250	12	3	0	0	0	0.0	0	0	2	0	0	0	0	32	2	0	1	11.3	1.000	1B-3
1926 CHI N	57	.313	.450	80	25	6	1	1	1.3	4	8	5	8	0	40	14	104	7	1	11	2.0	.991	1B-13
1927	39	.296	.481	54	16	4	0	2	3.7	6	17	4	9	0	27	7	74	5	0	3	2.0	1.000	1B-8
1929	32	.257	.330	109	28	5	0	1	0.9	13	19	9	16	0	0	0	289	16	7	21	9.8	.978	1B-32
1930	13	.300	.350	20	6	1	0	0	0.0	0	1	6	5	1	7	2	43	4	1	6	3.7	.979	1B-5
5 yrs.	144	.284	.393	275	78	16	1	4	1.5	23	45	26	39	1	74	23	542	34	9	42	4.1	.985	1B-61

WORLD SERIES

Year Team	Games	BA	SA	AB	H	2B	3B	HR	HR%	R	RBI	BB	SO	SB	AB	H	PO	A	E	DP	TC/G	FA	G by Pos
1929 CHI N	1	.000	.000	1	0	0	0	0	0.0	0	0	0	1	0	1	0	0	0	0	0	0.0	—	

George Tomer

TOMER, GEORGE CLARENCE
B. Nov. 26, 1895, Perry, Iowa   D. Dec. 15, 1984, Perry, Iowa   BL TR 6'   180 lbs.

Year Team	Games	BA	SA	AB	H	2B	3B	HR	HR%	R	RBI	BB	SO	SB	AB	H	PO	A	E	DP	TC/G	FA	G by Pos
1913 STL A	1	.000	.000	1	0	0	0	0	0.0	0	0	0	1	0	1	0	0	0	0	0	0.0	—	

Phil Tomney

TOMNEY, PHILIP H.
B. July 17, 1863, Reading, Pa.   D. Mar. 18, 1892, Reading, Pa.   BR TR 5'7"   155 lbs.

Year Team	Games	BA	SA	AB	H	2B	3B	HR	HR%	R	RBI	BB	SO	SB	AB	H	PO	A	E	DP	TC/G	FA	G by Pos
1888 LOU AA	34	.150	.175	120	18	3	0	0	0.0	15	4	7		11	0	0	40	117	21	7	5.2	.882	SS-34
1889	112	.213	.293	376	80	8	5	4	1.1	61	38	46	47	26	0	0	229	454	114	57	7.1	.857	SS-112
1890	108	.277	.376	386	107	21	7	1	0.3	72		43		27	0	0	180	406	64	31	6.0	.902	SS-108
3 yrs.	254	.232	.313	882	205	32	12	5	0.6	148	42	96	47	64	0	0	449	977	199	95	6.4	.878	SS-254

Tony Tonneman

TONNEMAN, CHARLES RICHARD
B. Sept. 10, 1881, Chicago, Ill.   D. Aug. 7, 1951, Prescott, Ariz.   BR TR 5'10½" 175 lbs.

Year Team	Games	BA	SA	AB	H	2B	3B	HR	HR%	R	RBI	BB	SO	SB	AB	H	PO	A	E	DP	TC/G	FA	G by Pos
1911 BOS A	2	.200	.400	5	1	1	0	0	0.0	0	3	1		0	0	0	16	2	2	0	10.0	.900	C-2

Bert Tooley

TOOLEY, ALBERT R.
B. Aug. 30, 1886, Howell, Mich.   D. Aug. 17, 1976, Marshall, Mich.   BR TR 5'10" 155 lbs.

Year Team	Games	BA	SA	AB	H	2B	3B	HR	HR%	R	RBI	BB	SO	SB	AB	H	PO	A	E	DP	TC/G	FA	G by Pos
1911 BKN N	119	.206	.252	433	89	11	3	1	0.2	55	29	53	63	18	3	1	226	340	46	42	5.1	.925	SS-114
1912	77	.234	.317	265	62	6	5	2	0.8	34	37	19	21	12	0	0	147	214	47	23	5.3	.885	SS-76
2 yrs.	196	.216	.277	698	151	17	8	3	0.4	89	66	72	84	30	3	1	373	554	93	65	5.2	.909	SS-190

Specs Toporcer

TOPORCER, GEORGE
B. Feb. 9, 1899, New York, N. Y.   D. May 17, 1989, Huntington Station, N. Y.   BL TR 5'10½" 165 lbs.

Year Team	Games	BA	SA	AB	H	2B	3B	HR	HR%	R	RBI	BB	SO	SB	AB	H	PO	A	E	DP	TC/G	FA	G by Pos
1921 STL N	22	.264	.283	53	14	1	0	0	0.0	4	2	3	4	1	6	1	25	42	4	6	3.2	.944	2B-12, SS-2
1922	116	.324	.455	352	114	25	6	3	0.9	56	36	24	18	2	15	6	173	255	30	35	3.9	.934	SS-91, 3B-6, OF-1, 2B-1
1923	97	.254	.340	303	77	11	3	3	1.0	45	35	41	14	4	8	3	193	240	24	57	4.7	.947	2B-52, SS-33, 3B-1, 1B-1
1924	70	.313	.409	198	62	10	3	1	0.5	30	24	11	14	2	10	1	56	105	8	8	2.4	.953	3B-33, SS-25, 2B-3
1925	83	.284	.384	268	76	13	4	2	0.7	38	26	36	15	7	8	2	149	231	16	41	4.8	.960	SS-66, 2B-7
1926	64	.250	.330	88	22	3	2	0	0.0	13	9	8	9	1	23	9	24	40	1	3	1.0	.985	2B-27, SS-5, 3B-1
1927	86	.248	.321	290	72	13	4	0	0.0	37	19	27	16	5	8	3	98	160	13	23	3.2	.952	3B-54, SS-27, 2B-2, 1B-1
1928	8	.000	.000	14	0	0	0	0	0.0	0	0	0	3	0	6	0	12	3	0	1	1.9	1.000	2B-1, 1B-1
8 yrs.	546	.279	.373	1566	437	76	22	9	0.6	223	151	150	93	22	84	25	730	1076	96	174	3.5	.950	SS-249, 2B-105, 3B-95, 1B-3, OF-1

WORLD SERIES

Year Team	Games	BA	SA	AB	H	2B	3B	HR	HR%	R	RBI	BB	SO	SB	AB	H	PO	A	E	DP	TC/G	FA	G by Pos
1926 STL N	1	—	—	0	0	0	0	0	—	0	1	0	0	0	0	0	0	0	0	0	0.0	—	

Jeff Torborg

TORBORG, JEFFREY ALLEN
B. Nov. 26, 1941, Plainfield, N. J.   BR TR 6'½" 195 lbs.
Manager 1977-79, 1989.

Year Team	Games	BA	SA	AB	H	2B	3B	HR	HR%	R	RBI	BB	SO	SB	AB	H	PO	A	E	DP	TC/G	FA	G by Pos
1964 LA N	28	.233	.302	43	10	1	1	0	0.0	4	4	3	8	0	1	0	80	4	2	1	3.1	.977	C-27
1965	56	.240	.347	150	36	5	1	3	2.0	8	13	10	26	0	6	1	300	19	3	1	5.8	.991	C-53
1966	46	.225	.275	120	27	3	0	1	0.8	4	13	10	23	0	2	0	269	17	4	2	6.3	.986	C-45
1967	76	.214	.276	196	42	4	1	2	1.0	11	12	13	31	1	1	1	413	30	5	3	5.9	.989	C-75
1968	37	.161	.183	93	15	2	0	0	0.0	2	4	6	10	0	0	0	206	20	2	10	6.2	.991	C-37
1969	51	.185	.218	124	23	4	0	0	0.0	7	7	9	17	1	1	0	251	26	1	5	5.5	.996	C-50
1970	64	.231	.313	134	31	8	0	1	0.7	11	17	14	15	1	2	1	275	16	5	2	4.6	.983	C-63
1971 CAL A	55	.203	.244	123	25	5	0	0	0.0	5	3	6	0	0	6	0	208	17	3	9	4.1	.987	C-49
1972	59	.209	.229	153	32	3	0	0	0.0	5	8	14	21	0	1	0	383	28	1	5	7.0	.998	C-58
1973	102	.220	.259	255	56	7	0	1	0.4	20	18	21	32	0	0	0	611	37	6	2	6.4	.991	C-102
10 yrs.	574	.214	.265	1391	297	42	3	8	0.6	78	101	103	189	3	20	3	2996	214	32	40	5.6	.990	C-559

Year	Team	Games	BA	SA	AB	H	2B	3B	HR	HR%	R	RBI	BB	SO	SB	Pinch Hit AB	Pinch Hit H	PO	A	E	DP	TC/G	FA	G by Pos

Earl Torgeson

TORGESON, CLIFFORD EARL (The Earl of Snohomish)
B. Jan. 1, 1924, Snohomish, Wash.
BL TL 6'3" 180 lbs.

Year	Team	Games	BA	SA	AB	H	2B	3B	HR	HR%	R	RBI	BB	SO	SB	AB	H	PO	A	E	DP	TC/G	FA	G by Pos
1947	BOS N	128	.281	.481	399	112	20	6	16	4.0	73	78	82	59	11	11	1	1033	76	18	83	8.8	.984	1B-117
1948		134	.253	.397	438	111	23	5	10	2.3	70	67	81	54	19	4	2	1069	81	8	85	8.6	.993	1B-129
1949		25	.260	.450	100	26	5	1	4	4.0	17	19	13	4	4	0	0	242	8	3	21	10.1	.988	1B-25
1950		156	.290	.472	576	167	30	3	23	4.0	120	87	119	69	15	0	0	1365	110	21	126	9.6	.986	1B-156
1951		155	.263	.437	581	153	21	4	24	4.1	99	92	102	70	20	0	0	1330	107	17	137	9.4	.988	1B-155
1952		122	.230	.314	382	88	17	0	5	1.3	49	34	81	38	11	12	2	935	74	12	86	8.4	.988	1B-105, OF-5
1953	PHI N	111	.274	.470	379	104	25	8	11	2.9	58	64	53	57	7	6	1	916	65	13	83	9.0	.987	1B-105
1954		135	.271	.371	490	133	22	6	5	1.0	63	54	75	52	7	1	0	1146	74	12	103	9.1	.990	1B-133
1955	2 teams		PHI	N	(47G – .267)		DET	A	(89G – .283)															
"	total	136	.278	.396	450	125	15	4	10	2.2	87	67	93	49	11	9	3	1044	79	8	106	8.3	.993	1B-126
1956	DET A	117	.264	.425	318	84	9	3	12	3.8	61	42	78	47	6	27	10	623	32	5	62	5.6	.992	1B-83
1957	2 teams		DET	A	(30G – .240)		CHI	A	(86G – .295)															
"	total	116	.286	.429	301	86	13	3	8	2.7	58	51	61	54	7	28	9	710	36	1	83	6.4	.999	1B-87, OF-1
1958	CHI A	96	.266	.468	188	50	8	0	10	5.3	37	30	48	29	7	24	9	470	30	11	54	5.3	.978	1B-73
1959		127	.220	.357	277	61	5	3	9	3.2	40	45	62	55	7	24	5	717	37	13	58	6.0	.983	1B-103
1960		68	.263	.404	57	15	2	0	2	3.5	12	9	21	8	1	41	12	54	4	1	3	0.9	.983	1B-10
1961	2 teams		CHI	A	(20G – .067)		NY	A	(22G – .111)															
"	total	42	.091	.091	33	3	0	0	0	0.0	4	1	11	8	0	23	2	30	2	1	7	0.8	.970	1B-9
15 yrs.		1668	.265	.417	4969	1318	215	46	149	3.0	848	740	980	653	133	210	55	11684	815	144	1097	7.6	.989	1B-1416, OF-6

WORLD SERIES

Year	Team	Games	BA	SA	AB	H	2B	3B	HR	HR%	R	RBI	BB	SO	SB	AB	H	PO	A	E	DP	TC/G	FA	G by Pos
1948	BOS N	5	.389	.556	18	7	3	0	0	0.0	2	1	2	1	1	1	0	44	5	0	2	9.8	1.000	1B-5
1959	CHI A	3	.000	.000	1	0	0	0	0	0.0	1	0	1	0	0	1	0	0	0	0	0	0.0	–	1B-1
2 yrs.		8	.368	.526	19	7	3	0	0	0.0	3	1	3	1	1	2	0	44	5	0	2	6.1	1.000	1B-6

Red Torphy

TORPHY, WALTER ANTHONY
B. Nov. 6, 1891, Fall River, Mass. D. Feb. 11, 1980, Fall River, Mass.
BR TR 5'11" 169 lbs.

Year	Team	Games	BA	SA	AB	H	2B	3B	HR	HR%	R	RBI	BB	SO	SB	AB	H	PO	A	E	DP	TC/G	FA	G by Pos
1920	BOS N	3	.200	.333	15	3	2	0	0	0.0	1	2	0	1	0	0	0	31	0	1	2	10.7	.969	1B-3

Frank Torre

TORRE, FRANK JOSEPH
Brother of Joe Torre.
B. Dec. 30, 1931, Brooklyn, N. Y.
BL TL 6'4" 200 lbs.

Year	Team	Games	BA	SA	AB	H	2B	3B	HR	HR%	R	RBI	BB	SO	SB	AB	H	PO	A	E	DP	TC/G	FA	G by Pos
1956	MIL N	111	.258	.296	159	41	6	0	0	0.0	17	16	11	4	1	23	5	390	42	3	34	3.9	.993	1B-89
1957		129	.272	.393	364	99	19	5	5	1.4	46	40	29	19	0	15	5	859	71	4	89	7.2	.996	1B-117
1958		138	.309	.444	372	115	22	6	6	1.6	41	55	42	14	2	17	6	960	80	6	85	7.6	.994	1B-122
1959		115	.228	.304	263	60	15	1	1	0.4	23	33	35	12	0	28	7	622	46	4	63	5.8	.994	1B-87
1960		21	.205	.227	44	9	1	0	0	0.0	2	5	3	2	0	3	1	105	4	0	12	5.2	1.000	1B-17
1962	PHI N	108	.310	.381	168	52	8	2	0	0.0	13	20	24	6	1	33	4	347	37	8	40	3.6	.980	1B-76
1963		92	.250	.375	112	28	7	2	1	0.9	8	10	11	7	0	32	8	253	28	3	26	3.1	.989	1B-56
7 yrs.		714	.273	.372	1482	404	78	15	13	0.9	150	179	155	64	4	151	36	3536	308	28	329	5.4	.993	1B-564

WORLD SERIES

Year	Team	Games	BA	SA	AB	H	2B	3B	HR	HR%	R	RBI	BB	SO	SB	AB	H	PO	A	E	DP	TC/G	FA	G by Pos
1957	MIL N	7	.300	.900	10	3	0	0	2	20.0	2	3	2	0	0	1	0	37	2	0	4	5.6	1.000	1B-7
1958		7	.176	.176	17	3	0	0	0	0.0	2	1	2	0	0	3	0	40	2	2	4	6.3	.955	1B-7
2 yrs.		14	.222	.444	27	6	0	0	2	7.4	4	4	4	0	0	4	0	77	4	2	8	5.9	.976	1B-14

Joe Torre

TORRE, JOSEPH PAUL
Brother of Frank Torre.
B. July 18, 1940, Brooklyn, N. Y.
Manager 1977-84.
BR TR 6'2" 212 lbs.

Year	Team	Games	BA	SA	AB	H	2B	3B	HR	HR%	R	RBI	BB	SO	SB	AB	H	PO	A	E	DP	TC/G	FA	G by Pos
1960	MIL N	2	.500	.500	2	1	0	0	0	0.0	0	0	0	1	0	2	1	0	0	0	0	0.0		C-112
1961		113	.278	.424	406	113	21	4	10	2.5	40	42	28	60	3	3	2	494	50	10	4	4.9	.982	C-112
1962		80	.282	.395	220	62	8	1	5	2.3	23	26	24	24	1	16	6	325	39	5	4	4.6	.986	C-63
1963		142	.293	.431	501	147	19	4	14	2.8	57	71	42	79	1	7	1	919	76	6	5	7.0	.994	C-105, 1B-37, OF-2
1964		154	.321	.498	601	193	36	5	20	3.3	87	109	36	67	2	2	1	1081	94	7	53	7.7	.994	C-96, 1B-70
1965		148	.291	.489	523	152	21	1	27	5.2	68	80	61	79	0	5	2	1022	73	6	43	7.5	.993	C-100, 1B-49
1966	ATL N	148	.315	.560	546	172	20	3	36	6.6	83	101	60	61	0	3	1	874	87	12	33	6.6	.988	C-114, 1B-36
1967		135	.277	.444	477	132	18	1	20	4.2	67	68	49	75	2	6	1	785	81	8	33	6.5	.991	C-114, 1B-23
1968		115	.271	.377	424	115	11	2	10	2.4	45	55	34	72	1	1	0	733	48	2	26	6.8	.997	C-92, 1B-29
1969	STL N	159	.289	.447	602	174	29	6	18	3.0	72	101	66	85	0	1	0	1360	91	7	117	9.2	.995	1B-144, C-17
1970		161	.325	.498	624	203	27	9	21	3.4	89	100	70	91	2	0	0	651	162	19	16	5.2	.977	C-90, 3B-73, 1B-1
1971		161	**.363**	.555	634	**230**	34	8	24	3.8	97	**137**	63	70	4	0	0	136	271	21	22	2.7	.951	3B-161
1972		149	.289	.419	544	157	26	6	11	2.0	71	81	54	64	3	6	4	336	198	15	34	3.7	.973	3B-117, 1B-27
1973		141	.287	.403	519	149	17	2	13	2.5	67	69	65	78	2	0	0	881	128	12	83	7.2	.988	1B-114, 3B-58
1974		147	.282	.401	529	149	28	1	11	2.1	59	70	69	88	1	4	2	1173	121	14	145	8.9	.989	1B-139, 3B-18
1975	NY N	114	.247	.357	361	89	16	3	6	1.7	33	35	35	55	0	22	5	172	157	15	26	3.0	.956	3B-83, 1B-24
1976		114	.306	.406	310	95	10	3	5	1.6	36	31	21	35	1	35	8	593	52	7	42	5.7	.989	1B-78, 3B-4
1977		26	.176	.294	51	9	1	1	2	1.0	2	9	2	10	0	11	2	83	3	1	9	3.3	.989	1B-16, 3B-1
18 yrs.		2209	.297	.452	7874	2342	344	59	252	3.2	996	1185	779	1094	23	124	36	11618	1731	169	735	6.1	.987	C-903, 1B-787, 3B-515, OF-2

Felix Torres

TORRES, FELIX
Born Felix Torres y Sanchez.
B. May 1, 1932, Ponce, Puerto Rico
BR TR 5'11" 165 lbs.

Year	Team	Games	BA	SA	AB	H	2B	3B	HR	HR%	R	RBI	BB	SO	SB	AB	H	PO	A	E	DP	TC/G	FA	G by Pos
1962	LA A	127	.259	.392	451	117	19	4	11	2.4	44	74	28	73	0	6	1	110	250	24	20	3.0	.938	3B-123
1963		138	.261	.361	463	121	32	1	4	0.9	40	51	30	73	1	12	3	110	237	23	30	2.7	.938	3B-122, 1B-2
1964		100	.231	.397	277	64	10	0	12	4.3	25	28	13	56	1	23	3	89	123	7	12	2.2	.968	3B-72, 1B-3
3 yrs.		365	.254	.381	1191	302	61	5	27	2.3	109	153	71	202	2	41	7	309	610	54	62	2.7	.945	3B-317, 1B-5

Gil Torres

TORRES, DON GILBERTO
Born Don Gilberto Torres y Nunez. Son of Ricardo Torres.
B. Aug. 23, 1915, Regla, Cuba D. Jan. 11, 1983, Regla, Cuba
BR TR 6' 155 lbs.

Year	Team		Games	BA	SA	AB	H	2B	3B	HR	HR%	R	RBI	BB	SO	SB	Pinch Hit AB	Pinch Hit H	PO	A	E	DP	TC/G	FA	G by Pos

Gil Torres *continued*

Year	Team		Games	BA	SA	AB	H	2B	3B	HR	HR%	R	RBI	BB	SO	SB	AB	H	PO	A	E	DP	TC/G	FA	G by Pos
1940	WAS	A	2	–	–	0	0	0	0	0	–	0	0	0	0	0	0	0	0	1	0	0	0.5	1.000	P-2
1944			134	.267	.328	524	140	20	6	0	0.0	42	58	21	24	10	0	0	167	322	24	35	3.8	.953	3B-123, 2B-10, 1B-4
1945			147	.237	.276	562	133	12	5	0	0.0	39	48	21	29	7	0	0	274	440	35	65	5.1	.953	SS-145, 3B-2
1946			63	.254	.297	185	47	8	0	0	0.0	18	13	11	12	3	5	0	82	137	11	20	3.7	.952	SS-31, 3B-18, 2B-7, P-3
4 yrs.			346	.252	.301	1271	320	40	11	0	0.0	99	119	53	65	20	5	0	523	900	70	120	4.3	.953	SS-176, 3B-143, 2B-17, P-5, 1B-4

Hector Torres

TORRES, HECTOR EPITACIO
Born Hector Epitacio Torres y Marroquin.
B. Sept. 16, 1945, Monterrey, Mexico

BR TR 6' 175 lbs.

Year	Team		Games	BA	SA	AB	H	2B	3B	HR	HR%	R	RBI	BB	SO	SB	AB	H	PO	A	E	DP	TC/G	FA	G by Pos
1968	HOU	N	128	.223	.258	466	104	11	1	1	0.2	44	24	18	64	2	1	0	159	393	24	55	4.5	.958	SS-127, 2B-1
1969			34	.159	.217	69	11	1	0	1	1.4	5	8	2	12	0	14	3	30	38	4	7	2.1	.944	SS-22
1970			31	.246	.323	65	16	1	2	0	0.0	6	5	6	8	0	4	1	34	51	4	9	2.9	.955	SS-22, 2B-6
1971	CHI	N	31	.224	.276	58	13	3	0	0	0.0	4	2	4	10	0	4	1	12	45	3	7	1.9	.950	SS-18, 2B-4
1972	MON	N	83	.155	.221	181	28	4	1	2	1.1	14	7	13	26	0	7	1	112	167	9	34	3.5	.969	2B-60, SS-16, OF-2, 3B-1, P-1
1973	HOU	N	38	.091	.106	66	6	1	0	0	0.0	3	2	7	13	0	3	0	32	75	5	10	2.9	.955	SS-22, 2B-13
1975	SD	N	112	.259	.335	352	91	12	0	5	1.4	31	26	22	32	2	0	0	128	338	13	55	4.3	.973	SS-75, 3B-42, 2B-16
1976			74	.195	.279	215	42	6	0	4	1.9	18	15	16	31	2	8	0	72	168	12	30	3.4	.952	SS-63, 3B-4, 2B-3
1977	TOR	A	91	.241	.346	266	64	7	3	5	1.9	33	26	16	33	1	2	1	144	240	10	38	4.3	.975	SS-68, 2B-23, 3B-2
9 yrs.			622	.216	.281	1738	375	46	7	18	1.0	148	115	104	229	7	43	7	723	1515	84	245	3.7	.964	SS-433, 2B-126, 3B-49, OF-2, P-1

Ricardo Torres

TORRES, RICARDO J.
Father of Gil Torres.
B. 1894, Cuba   D. Havana, Cuba

BR TR 5'11" 160 lbs.

Year	Team		Games	BA	SA	AB	H	2B	3B	HR	HR%	R	RBI	BB	SO	SB	AB	H	PO	A	E	DP	TC/G	FA	G by Pos
1920	WAS	A	16	.333	.367	30	10	1	0	0	0.0	8	3	1	4	0	2	1	49	2	0	1	3.2	1.000	1B-7, C-5
1921			2	.333	.333	3	1	0	0	0	0.0	1	0	1	1	0	0	0	3	0	1	0	2.0	.750	C-2
1922			4	.000	.000	4	0	0	0	0	0.0	0	0	0	1	0	1	0	2	3	0	0	1.3	1.000	C-3
3 yrs.			22	.297	.324	37	11	1	0	0	0.0	9	3	2	6	0	3	1	54	5	1	1	2.7	.983	C-10, 1B-7

Rusty Torres

TORRES, ROSENDO
Born Rosendo Torres y Hernandez.
B. Sept. 30, 1948, Aguadilla, Puerto Rico

BB TR 5'10" 175 lbs.

Year	Team		Games	BA	SA	AB	H	2B	3B	HR	HR%	R	RBI	BB	SO	SB	AB	H	PO	A	E	DP	TC/G	FA	G by Pos
1971	NY	A	9	.385	.731	26	10	3	0	2	7.7	5	3	0	8	0	4	0	13	0	0	0	1.4	1.000	OF-5
1972			80	.211	.291	199	42	7	0	3	1.5	15	13	18	44	0	22	7	86	4	2	0	1.2	.978	OF-62
1973	CLE	A	122	.205	.304	312	64	8	1	7	2.2	31	28	50	62	6	7	3	191	9	5	1	1.7	.976	OF-114
1974			108	.187	.260	150	28	2	0	3	2.0	19	12	13	24	2	12	1	110	8	5	0	1.1	.959	OF-94, DH-1
1976	CAL	A	120	.205	.356	264	54	16	3	6	2.3	37	27	36	39	4	3	0	195	5	2	0	1.7	.990	OF-105, DH-6, 3B-1
1977			58	.156	.312	77	12	1	1	3	3.9	9	10	10	18	0	2	1	60	1	1	0	1.1	.984	OF-54
1978	CHI	A	16	.318	.591	44	14	3	0	3	6.8	7	6	6	7	0	1	0	27	0	1	0	1.8	.964	OF-14
1979			90	.253	.424	170	43	5	0	8	4.7	26	24	23	37	0	12	1	117	4	3	0	1.4	.976	OF-85
1980	KC	A	51	.167	.167	72	12	0	0	0	0.0	10	3	8	7	1	1	1	67	4	2	1	1.4	.973	OF-40, DH-1
9 yrs.			654	.212	.334	1314	279	45	5	35	2.7	159	126	164	246	13	64	14	866	35	21	2	1.4	.977	OF-573, DH-8, 3B-1

Kelvin Torve

TORVE, KELVIN CURTIS
B. Jan. 10, 1960, Rapid City, S. D.

BL TR 6'3" 205 lbs.

Year	Team		Games	BA	SA	AB	H	2B	3B	HR	HR%	R	RBI	BB	SO	SB	AB	H	PO	A	E	DP	TC/G	FA	G by Pos
1988	MIN	A	12	.188	.375	16	3	0	0	1	6.3	1	2	1	2	0	6	1	14	1	0	1	1.3	1.000	1B-4

Cesar Tovar

TOVAR, CESAR LEONARDO (Pepito)
Born Cesar Leonardo Perez y Tovar.
B. July 3, 1940, Caracas, Venezuela

BR TR 5'9" 155 lbs.

Year	Team		Games	BA	SA	AB	H	2B	3B	HR	HR%	R	RBI	BB	SO	SB	AB	H	PO	A	E	DP	TC/G	FA	G by Pos
1965	MIN	A	18	.200	.240	25	5	1	0	0	0.0	3	2	2	3	2	4	0	5	14	3	2	1.2	.864	2B-4, OF-2, 3B-2, SS-1
1966			134	.260	.335	465	121	19	5	2	0.4	57	41	44	50	16	2	0	254	274	14	44	4.0	.974	2B-76, SS-31, OF-24
1967			164	.267	.365	649	173	32	7	6	0.9	98	47	46	51	19	0	0	307	184	17	23	3.1	.967	OF-74, 3B-70, 2B-36, SS-9
1968			157	.272	.372	613	167	31	6	6	1.0	89	47	34	41	35	3	0	247	235	26	24	3.2	.949	OF-78, 3B-75, SS-35, 2B-18, 1B-1, C-1, P-1
1969			158	.288	.415	535	154	25	5	11	2.1	99	52	37	37	45	12	3	315	134	13	30	2.9	.972	OF-113, 2B-41, 3B-20
1970			161	.300	.442	650	195	36	13	10	1.5	120	54	52	47	30	3	0	389	25	14	6	2.7	.967	OF-151, 2B-8, 3B-4
1971			157	.311	.368	657	204	29	3	1	0.2	94	45	45	39	18	1	0	352	27	7	5	2.5	.982	OF-154, 3B-7, 2B-2
1972			141	.265	.334	548	145	20	6	2	0.4	86	31	39	39	21	3	0	287	10	5	2	2.1	.983	OF-139
1973	PHI	N	97	.268	.357	328	88	18	4	1	0.3	49	21	29	35	6	14	4	113	113	12	32	2.5	.950	3B-46, OF-24, 2B-22
1974	TEX	A	138	.292	.377	562	164	24	6	4	0.7	78	58	47	33	13	1	0	331	13	7	3	2.5	.980	OF-135, DH-3
1975	2 teams				TEX A (102G – .258)		OAK A (19G – .231)																		
"	total		121	.256	.313	453	116	17	0	3	0.7	58	31	30	28	20	12	1	59	5	6	0	0.6	.914	DH-73, OF-31, 2B-5, 3B-3, SS-1
1976	2 teams				OAK A (29G – .178)		NY A (13G – .154)																		
"	total		42	.167	.179	84	14	1	0	0	0.0	8	6	3	7	1	12	2	27	8	1	3	0.9	.972	OF-20, DH-14, 2B-3
12 yrs.			1488	.278	.368	5569	1546	253	55	46	0.8	834	435	413	410	226	67	10	2686	1042	125	174	2.6	.968	OF-945, 3B-227, 2B-215, DH-90, SS-77, 1B-1, C-1, P-1

LEAGUE CHAMPIONSHIP SERIES

Year	Team		Games	BA	SA	AB	H	2B	3B	HR	HR%	R	RBI	BB	SO	SB	AB	H	PO	A	E	DP	TC/G	FA	G by Pos
1969	MIN	A	3	.077	.077	13	1	0	0	0	0.0	0	0	1	2	0	0	0	10	0	0	0	3.3	1.000	OF-3
1970			3	.385	.538	13	5	2	0	0	0.0	2	1	0	0	0	0	0	0	0	0	0	0.0	–	OF-3, 2B-1
1975	OAK	A	2	.500	.500	2	1	0	0	0	0.0	2	0	1	0	0	1	0	2	2	1	0	2.5	.800	2B-1
3 yrs.			8	.250	.321	28	7	0	1	0	0.0	4	1	2	2	0	1	0	12	2	1	0	1.9	.933	OF-6, 2B-2

Babe Towne

TOWNE, JAY KING
B. Mar. 12, 1880, Coon Rapids, Iowa   D. Oct. 29, 1938, Des Moines, Iowa

BL TR 5'10" 180 lbs.

Year	Team		Games	BA	SA	AB	H	2B	3B	HR	HR%	R	RBI	BB	SO	SB	AB	H	PO	A	E	DP	TC/G	FA	G by Pos
1906	CHI	A	13	.278	.278	36	10	0	0	0	0.0	3	6	7		0	1	0	39	9	4	0	4.0	.923	C-12

Year	Team	Games	BA	SA	AB	H	2B	3B	HR	HR%	R	RBI	BB	SO	SB	Pinch Hit AB	Pinch Hit H	PO	A	E	DP	TC/G	FA	G by Pos

Babe Towne continued
WORLD SERIES

Year	Team	Games	BA	SA	AB	H	2B	3B	HR	HR%	R	RBI	BB	SO	SB	AB	H	PO	A	E	DP	TC/G	FA	G by Pos
1906	CHI	A	1	.000	.000	1	0	0	0	0	0.0	0	0	0	0	0	1	0	0	0	0	0	0.0	–	–

George Townsend
TOWNSEND, GEORGE HODGSON
B. June 4, 1867, Hartsdale, N. Y. D. Mar. 15, 1930, New Haven, Conn.   BR TR 5'7½" 180 lbs.

Year	Team	Games	BA	SA	AB	H	2B	3B	HR	HR%	R	RBI	BB	SO	SB	AB	H	PO	A	E	DP	TC/G	FA	G by Pos
1887	PHI	AA	31	.193	.220	109	21	3	0	0	0.0	12		3		8	0	0	102	39	22	1	5.3	.865	C-28, OF-3
1888		42	.155	.193	161	25	6	0	0	0.0	13	12	4		2	0	0	225	76	31	2	7.9	.907	C-42
1890	BAL	AA	18	.239	.328	67	16	4	1	0	0.0	6		4		3	0	0	72	34	8	2	6.3	.930	C-18
1891		61	.191	.255	204	39	5	4	0	0.0	29	18	20	21	3	0	0	192	68	26	5	4.7	.909	C-58, OF-3
4 yrs.		152	.187	.238	541	101	18	5	0	0.0	60	30	31	21	16	0	0	591	217	87	10	5.9	.903	C-146, OF-6

Jim Toy
TOY, JAMES MADISON
B. Feb. 20, 1858, Beaver Falls, Pa. D. Mar. 13, 1919, Beaver Falls, Pa.   BR TR 5'6" 160 lbs.

Year	Team	Games	BA	SA	AB	H	2B	3B	HR	HR%	R	RBI	BB	SO	SB	AB	H	PO	A	E	DP	TC/G	FA	G by Pos
1887	CLE	AA	109	.222	.300	423	94	20	5	1	0.2	56		17		8	0	0	764	65	34	55	7.9	.961	1B-82, OF-11, C-10, 3B-8, SS-3
1890	BKN	AA	44	.181	.200	160	29	3	0	0	0.0	11		11		2	0	0	148	86	36	4	6.1	.867	C-44
2 yrs.		153	.211	.273	583	123	23	5	1	0.2	67		28		10	0	0	912	151	70	59	7.4	.938	1B-82, C-54, OF-11, 3B-8, SS-3

Jim Traber
TRABER, JAMES JOSEPH
B. Dec. 26, 1961, Columbus, Ohio   BL TL 6' 194 lbs.

Year	Team	Games	BA	SA	AB	H	2B	3B	HR	HR%	R	RBI	BB	SO	SB	AB	H	PO	A	E	DP	TC/G	FA	G by Pos
1984	BAL	A	10	.238	.238	21	5	0	0	0	0.0	3	2	4		3	1	0	0	0	0	0	0.0	–	DH-9
1986		65	.255	.472	212	54	7	0	13	6.1	28	44	18	31	0	7	2	243	23	5	28	4.2	.982	1B-29, DH-21, OF-8
1988		103	.222	.324	352	78	6	0	10	2.8	25	45	19	42	1	9	2	481	59	6	51	5.3	.989	1B-57, DH-30, OF-11
1989		86	.209	.295	234	49	8	0	4	1.7	14	26	19	41	4	16	3	514	54	1	59	6.6	.998	1B-69, DH-5
4 yrs.		264	.227	.352	819	186	21	0	27	3.3	70	117	58	118	5	35	8	1238	136	12	138	5.3	.991	1B-155, DH-65, OF-19

Dick Tracewski
TRACEWSKI, RICHARD JOSEPH
B. Feb. 3, 1935, Eynon, Pa.   BR TR 5'11" 160 lbs.

Year	Team	Games	BA	SA	AB	H	2B	3B	HR	HR%	R	RBI	BB	SO	SB	AB	H	PO	A	E	DP	TC/G	FA	G by Pos
1962	LA	N	15	.000	.000	2	0	0	0	0	0.0	3	0	2	0	0	1	0	1	4	0	0	0.3	1.000	SS-4
1963		104	.226	.258	217	49	2	1	1	0.5	23	10	19	39	2	0	0	105	216	14	34	3.2	.958	SS-81, 2B-23
1964		106	.247	.326	304	75	13	4	1	0.3	31	26	31	61	3	4	2	152	218	15	35	3.6	.961	2B-56, 3B-30, SS-19
1965		78	.215	.263	186	40	6	0	1	0.5	17	20	25	30	2	8	1	51	132	12	7	2.5	.938	3B-53, 2B-14, SS-7
1966	DET	A	81	.194	.218	124	24	1	1	0	0.0	15	7	10	32	1	7	0	71	100	10	27	2.2	.945	2B-70, SS-3
1967		74	.280	.383	107	30	4	2	1	0.9	19	9	8	20	1	9	3	54	90	3	17	2.0	.980	SS-44, 2B-12, 3B-10
1968		90	.156	.236	212	33	3	1	4	1.9	30	15	24	51	3	9	1	82	157	5	27	2.7	.980	SS-51, 3B-16, 2B-14
1969		66	.139	.165	79	11	2	0	0	0.0	10	4	15	20	3	3	1	59	87	5	20	2.3	.967	SS-41, 2B-13, 3B-6
8 yrs.		614	.213	.272	1231	262	31	9	8	0.6	148	91	134	253	15	41	8	575	1004	64	167	2.7	.961	SS-250, 2B-202, 3B-115

WORLD SERIES

Year	Team	Games	BA	SA	AB	H	2B	3B	HR	HR%	R	RBI	BB	SO	SB	AB	H	PO	A	E	DP	TC/G	FA	G by Pos
1963	LA	N	4	.154	.154	13	2	0	0	0	0.0	1	0	1	2	0	0	0	7	7	1	1	3.8	.933	2B-4
1965		6	.118	.118	17	2	0	0	0	0.0	0	0	1	5	0	1	0	11	11	1	4	3.8	.957	2B-6
1968	DET	A	2	–	–	0	0	0	0	0	–	1	0	0	0	0	0	0	0	0	0	0	0.0	–	3B-1
3 yrs.		12	.133	.133	30	4	0	0	0	0.0	2	0	2	7	0	1	0	18	18	2	5	3.2	.947	2B-10, 3B-1

Jim Tracy
TRACY, JAMES EDWIN
B. Dec. 31, 1955, Hamilton, Ohio   BL TR 6' 185 lbs.

Year	Team	Games	BA	SA	AB	H	2B	3B	HR	HR%	R	RBI	BB	SO	SB	AB	H	PO	A	E	DP	TC/G	FA	G by Pos
1980	CHI	N	42	.254	.402	122	31	3	3	3	2.5	12	9	13	37	2	12	5	44	0	2	1	1.1	.957	OF-31, 1B-1
1981		45	.238	.302	63	15	2	1	0	0.0	6	5	12	14	1	29	5	16	0	0	0	0.4	1.000	OF-11
2 yrs.		87	.249	.368	185	46	5	4	3	1.6	18	14	25	51	3	41	7	60	0	2	1	0.7	.968	OF-42, 1B-1

Bill Traffley
TRAFFLEY, WILLIAM F.
Brother of John Traffley.
B. Dec. 21, 1859, Staten Island, N. Y. D. June 24, 1908, Denver, Colo.   BR TR 5'11½" 185 lbs.

Year	Team	Games	BA	SA	AB	H	2B	3B	HR	HR%	R	RBI	BB	SO	SB	AB	H	PO	A	E	DP	TC/G	FA	G by Pos
1878	CHI	N	2	.111	.111	9	1	0	0	0	0.0	1	1			0	0	0	7	3	0	0	5.0	1.000	C-2
1883	CIN	AA	30	.200	.248	105	21	5	0	0	0.0	17		4		0	0	0	121	34	28	2	6.1	.847	C-29, SS-2
1884	BAL	AA	53	.176	.252	210	37	4	6	0	0.0	25		3		0	0	0	336	57	30	6	8.0	.929	C-47, OF-6, 1B-1
1885		69	.154	.220	254	39	4	5	1	0.4	27		17		0	0	0	365	112	32	7	7.4	.937	C-61, OF-10, 2B-3
1886		25	.212	.235	85	18	0	1	0	0.0	15		10		0	0	0	163	35	10	4	8.3	.952	C-25
5 yrs.		179	.175	.235	663	116	13	12	1	0.2	85	1	34		0	0	0	992	241	100	19	7.4	.925	C-164, OF-16, 2B-3, SS-2, 1B-1

John Traffley
TRAFFLEY, JOHN
Brother of Bill Traffley.
B. 1862, Chicago, Ill. D. July 17, 1900, Baltimore, Md.   5'9" 180 lbs.

Year	Team	Games	BA	SA	AB	H	2B	3B	HR	HR%	R	RBI	BB	SO	SB	AB	H	PO	A	E	DP	TC/G	FA	G by Pos
1889	LOU	AA	1	.500	.500	2	1	0	0	0	0.0	0	0	0	0	0	0	0	0	0	1	0	1.0	–	OF-1

Walt Tragesser
TRAGESSER, WALTER JOSEPH
B. June 14, 1887, Lafayette, Ind. D. Dec. 14, 1970, Lafayette, Ind.   BR TR 6' 175 lbs.

Year	Team	Games	BA	SA	AB	H	2B	3B	HR	HR%	R	RBI	BB	SO	SB	AB	H	PO	A	E	DP	TC/G	FA	G by Pos
1913	BOS	N	2	–	–	0	0	0	0	0	–	0	0	0	0	0	0	0	1	0	0	0	0.5	1.000	C-2
1915		7	.000	.000	7	0	0	0	0	0.0	1	0	0	2	0	0	0	15	2	1	1	2.6	.944	C-7
1916		41	.204	.222	54	11	1	0	0	0.0	3	4	5	10	0	11	1	73	27	3	2	2.5	.971	C-29
1917		98	.222	.269	297	66	10	2	0	0.0	23	25	15	36	5	4	2	433	105	16	11	5.7	.971	C-98
1918		7	.000	.000	13	0	0	0	0	0.0	0	0	0	0	0	0	0	4	1	1	0	0.9	.833	C-7
1919 2 teams	BOS	N (20G – .175)			PHI	N (35G – .237)																		
" total		55	.221	.279	154	34	9	0	0	0.0	10	11	11	41	5	6	2	182	69	12	7	4.8	.954	C-48
1920	PHI	N	62	.210	.386	176	37	11	4	6	3.4	17	26	4	36	4	8	2	157	46	12	4	3.5	.944	C-52
7 yrs.		272	.215	.295	689	148	31	3	6	0.9	54	66	35	125	14	29	7	865	250	45	25	4.3	.961	C-243

Year	Team	Games	BA	SA	AB	H	2B	3B	HR	HR%	R	RBI	BB	SO	SB	Pinch Hit AB	Pinch Hit H	PO	A	E	DP	TC/G	FA	G by Pos

Red Tramback

TRAMBACK, STEPHEN JOSEPH
B. Oct. 1, 1915, Iselin, Pa.   D. Dec. 28, 1979, Buffalo, N. Y.

BL TL 6'   175 lbs.

Year	Team	Games	BA	SA	AB	H	2B	3B	HR	HR%	R	RBI	BB	SO	SB	PH AB	PH H	PO	A	E	DP	TC/G	FA	G by Pos
1940	NY N	2	.250	.250	4	1	0	0	0	0.0	0	0	1	1	1	1	0	2	0	1	0	1.5	.667	OF-1

Alan Trammell

TRAMMELL, ALAN STUART
B. Feb. 21, 1958, Garden Grove, Calif.

BR TR 6'   165 lbs.

Year	Team	Games	BA	SA	AB	H	2B	3B	HR	HR%	R	RBI	BB	SO	SB	PH AB	PH H	PO	A	E	DP	TC/G	FA	G by Pos
1977	DET A	19	.186	.186	43	8	0	0	0	0.0	6	0	4	12	0	0	0	15	34	2	5	2.7	.961	SS-19
1978		139	.268	.339	448	120	14	6	2	0.4	49	34	45	56	3	0	0	239	421	14	95	4.8	.979	SS-139
1979		142	.276	.357	460	127	11	4	6	1.3	68	50	43	55	17	0	0	245	388	26	99	4.6	.961	SS-142
1980		146	.300	.404	560	168	21	5	9	1.6	107	65	69	63	12	2	0	225	412	13	89	4.5	.980	SS-144
1981		105	.258	.327	392	101	15	3	2	0.5	52	31	49	31	10	1	1	181	347	9	65	5.1	.983	SS-105
1982		157	.258	.395	489	126	34	3	9	1.8	66	57	52	47	19	0	0	259	459	16	97	4.7	.978	SS-157
1983		142	.319	.471	505	161	31	2	14	2.8	83	66	57	64	30	0	0	236	367	13	71	4.3	.979	SS-140
1984		139	.314	.468	555	174	34	5	14	2.5	85	69	60	63	19	3	1	180	314	10	71	3.6	.980	SS-114, DH-22
1985		149	.258	.380	605	156	21	7	13	2.1	79	57	50	71	14	0	0	225	400	15	89	4.3	.977	SS-149
1986		151	.277	.469	574	159	33	7	21	3.7	107	75	59	57	25	1	0	238	445	22	99	4.7	.969	SS-149, DH-2
1987		151	.343	.551	597	205	34	3	28	4.7	109	105	60	47	21	3	0	222	421	19	94	4.4	.971	SS-149
1988		128	.311	.464	466	145	24	1	15	3.2	73	69	46	46	7	2	2	195	355	11	67	4.4	.980	SS-125
1989		121	.243	.334	449	109	20	3	5	1.1	54	43	45	45	10	2	1	188	396	9	71	4.9	.985	SS-117, DH-2
13 yrs.		1689	.286	.417	6143	1759	292	49	138	2.2	938	721	639	657	187	14	5	2648	4759	179	1012	4.5	.976	SS-1649, DH-26

LEAGUE CHAMPIONSHIP SERIES

Year	Team	Games	BA	SA	AB	H	2B	3B	HR	HR%	R	RBI	BB	SO	SB	PH AB	PH H	PO	A	E	DP	TC/G	FA	G by Pos
1984	DET A	3	.364	.818	11	4	0	1	1	9.1	2	3	3	1	0	0	0	1	8	0	0	3.0	1.000	SS-3
1987		5	.200	.250	20	4	1	0	0	0.0	3	2	1	2	0	0	0	6	9	1	1	3.2	.938	SS-5
2 yrs.		8	.258	.452	31	8	1	1	1	3.2	5	5	4	3	0	0	0	7	17	1	1	3.1	.960	SS-8

WORLD SERIES

Year	Team	Games	BA	SA	AB	H	2B	3B	HR	HR%	R	RBI	BB	SO	SB	PH AB	PH H	PO	A	E	DP	TC/G	FA	G by Pos
1984	DET A	5	.450	.800	20	9	1	0	2	10.0	5	6	2	2	1	0	0	8	9	1	0	3.6	.944	SS-5

Cecil Travis

TRAVIS, CECIL HOWELL
B. Aug. 8, 1913, Riverdale, Ga.

BL TR 6'1½"   185 lbs.

Year	Team	Games	BA	SA	AB	H	2B	3B	HR	HR%	R	RBI	BB	SO	SB	PH AB	PH H	PO	A	E	DP	TC/G	FA	G by Pos
1933	WAS A	18	.302	.326	43	13	1	0	0	0.0	7	2	2	5	0	3	0	8	30	1	1	2.2	.974	3B-15
1934		109	.319	.403	392	125	22	4	1	0.3	48	53	24	37	1	10	1	88	210	20	23	2.9	.937	3B-99
1935		138	.318	.397	534	170	28	7	0	0.0	85	61	41	28	4	7	2	164	258	16	30	3.2	.963	3B-114, OF-16
1936		138	.317	.433	517	164	34	10	2	0.4	77	92	39	21	4	10	4	244	231	31	58	3.7	.939	SS-71, OF-53, 2B-4, 3B-2
1937		135	.344	.439	526	181	27	7	3	0.6	72	66	39	34	3	5	3	229	396	23	99	4.8	.965	SS-129
1938		146	.335	.432	567	190	30	5	5	0.9	96	67	58	22	6	2	0	304	457	40	113	5.5	.950	SS-143
1939		130	.292	.403	476	139	20	9	5	1.1	55	63	34	25	0	10	3	194	359	24	74	4.4	.958	SS-118
1940		136	.322	.445	528	170	37	11	2	0.4	60	76	48	23	0	0	0	164	340	38	50	4.0	.930	3B-113, SS-23
1941		152	.359	.520	608	**218**	39	19	7	1.2	106	101	52	25	2	0	0	293	427	27	103	4.9	.964	SS-136, 3B-16
1945		15	.241	.315	54	13	2	1	0	0.0	4	10	4	5	0	1	0	18	28	4	4	3.3	.920	3B-14
1946		137	.252	.318	465	117	22	3	1	0.2	45	56	45	47	2	6	1	187	290	31	60	3.7	.939	SS-75, 3B-56
1947		74	.216	.260	204	44	4	1	0	0.0	5	10	16	19	1	24	3	53	112	9	15	2.4	.948	3B-39, SS-35
12 yrs.		1328	.314	.416	4914	1544	266	77	27	0.5	665	657	402	291	23	78	17	1946	3138	264	630	4.0	.951	SS-710, 3B-468, OF-69, 2B-4

Jim Tray

TRAY, JAMES
B. Feb. 14, 1860, Jackson, Mich.   D. July 28, 1905, Jackson, Mich.

5'8"   144 lbs.

Year	Team	Games	BA	SA	AB	H	2B	3B	HR	HR%	R	RBI	BB	SO	SB	PH AB	PH H	PO	A	E	DP	TC/G	FA	G by Pos
1884	IND AA	6	.286	.286	21	6	0	0	0	0.0	2		2			0	0	45	5	5	0	9.2	.909	C-4, 1B-2

Pie Traynor

TRAYNOR, HAROLD JOSEPH
B. Nov. 11, 1899, Framingham, Mass.   D. Mar. 16, 1972, Pittsburgh, Pa.
Manager 1934-39.
Hall of Fame 1948.

BR TR 6'   170 lbs.

Year	Team	Games	BA	SA	AB	H	2B	3B	HR	HR%	R	RBI	BB	SO	SB	PH AB	PH H	PO	A	E	DP	TC/G	FA	G by Pos
1920	PIT N	17	.212	.308	52	11	3	1	0	0.0	6	2	3	6	1	0	0	35	39	12	4	5.1	.860	SS-17
1921		7	.263	.263	19	5	0	0	0	0.0	0	2	1	2	0	2	1	4	9	1	0	2.0	.929	3B-3, SS-1
1922		142	.282	.375	571	161	17	12	4	0.7	89	81	27	28	17	1	0	186	278	31	26	3.5	.937	3B-124, SS-18
1923		153	.338	.489	616	208	19	19	12	1.9	108	101	34	19	28	0	0	191	310	26	30	3.4	.951	3B-153
1924		142	.294	.417	545	160	26	13	5	0.9	86	82	37	26	24	1	0	179	268	15	31	3.3	.968	3B-141
1925		150	.320	.464	591	189	39	14	6	1.0	114	106	52	19	15	0	0	228	305	24	42	3.7	.957	3B-150, SS-1
1926		152	.317	.436	574	182	25	17	3	0.5	83	92	38	14	8	1	0	191	294	24	40	3.3	.953	3B-148, SS-3
1927		149	.342	.455	573	196	32	9	5	0.9	93	106	22	11	11	0	0	225	293	20	25	3.6	.963	3B-143, SS-9
1928		144	.337	.462	569	192	38	12	3	0.5	91	124	28	10	12	0	0	175	296	27	15	3.5	.946	3B-144
1929		130	.356	.472	540	192	27	12	4	0.7	94	108	30	7	13	0	0	148	238	20	23	3.1	.951	3B-130
1930		130	.366	.509	497	182	22	11	9	1.8	90	119	48	19	7	0	0	130	268	25	18	3.3	.941	3B-130
1931		155	.298	.416	615	183	37	15	2	0.3	81	103	54	28	6	0	0	172	284	37	21	3.2	.925	3B-155
1932		135	.329	.433	513	169	27	10	2	0.4	74	68	32	20	6	7	2	173	222	27	14	3.1	.936	3B-127
1933		154	.304	.372	624	190	27	6	1	0.2	85	82	35	24	5	0	0	176	300	27	16	3.3	.946	3B-154
1934		119	.309	.410	444	137	22	10	1	0.2	62	61	21	27	3	7	4	116	176	14	16	2.6	.954	3B-110
1935		57	.279	.373	204	57	10	3	1	0.5	24	36	10	17	2	5	0	59	84	18	2	2.8	.888	3B-49, 1B-1
1937		5	.167	.167	12	2	0	0	0	0.0	3	0	1	0	0	0	0	2	8	0	0	2.0	1.000	3B-3
17 yrs.		1941	.320	.435	7559	2416	371	164	58	0.8	1183	1273	472	278	158	24	7	2390	3672	348	323	3.3	.946	3B-1864, SS-49, 1B-1

WORLD SERIES

Year	Team	Games	BA	SA	AB	H	2B	3B	HR	HR%	R	RBI	BB	SO	SB	PH AB	PH H	PO	A	E	DP	TC/G	FA	G by Pos
1925	PIT N	7	.346	.615	26	9	0	2	1	3.8	2	4	3	1	0	0	0	6	18	0	2	3.4	1.000	3B-7
1927		4	.200	.267	15	3	1	0	0	0.0	1	0	0	1	0	0	0	5	9	1	1	3.8	.933	3B-4
2 yrs.		11	.293	.488	41	12	1	2	1	2.4	3	4	3	2	0	0	0	11	27	1	3	3.5	.974	3B-11

Fred Treacey

TREACEY, FREDERICK S.
Brother of Pete Treacey.
B. 1847, Brooklyn, N. Y.   Deceased.

TR 5'9½"   145 lbs.

Year	Team	Games	BA	SA	AB	H	2B	3B	HR	HR%	R	RBI	BB	SO	SB	PH AB	PH H	PO	A	E	DP	TC/G	FA	G by Pos
1876	NY N	57	.211	.238	256	54	5	1	0	0.0	47	18	1	5		0	0	202	9	39	1	4.4	.844	OF-57

Year	Team		Games	BA	SA	AB	H	2B	3B	HR	HR%	R	RBI	BB	SO	SB	Pinch Hit AB	Pinch Hit H	PO	A	E	DP	TC/G	FA	G by Pos

Pete Treacey

TREACEY, PETER
Brother of Fred Treacey.
B. 1852, Brooklyn, N. Y.   Deceased.

| 1876 | NY | N | 2 | .000 | .000 | 5 | 0 | 0 | 0 | 0 | 0.0 | 1 | 0 | 1 | 0 | | 0 | 0 | 0 | 3 | 1 | 0 | 2.0 | .750 | SS-2 |

Ray Treadaway

TREADAWAY, EDGAR RAYMOND   BL TR 5'6"   165 lbs.
B. Oct. 31, 1907, Ragland, Ala.   D. Oct. 12, 1935, Chattanooga, Tenn.

| 1930 | WAS | A | 6 | .211 | .316 | 19 | 4 | 2 | 0 | 0 | 0.0 | 1 | 1 | 0 | 3 | 0 | 2 | 1 | 5 | 5 | 2 | 1 | 2.0 | .833 | 3B-4 |

George Treadway

TREADWAY, GEORGE B.   BL
B. Nov. 11, 1866, Greenup County, Ky.   D. Nov. 17, 1928, Riverside, Calif.

1893	BAL	N	115	.260	.376	458	119	16	17	1	0.2	78	67	57	50	24	0	0	192	27	24	4	2.1	.901	OF-115
1894	BKN	N	123	.328	.518	479	157	27	26	4	0.8	124	102	72	43	27	1	0	274	16	35	2	2.6	.892	OF-122, 1B-1
1895			86	.257	.378	339	87	14	3	7	2.1	54	54	33	22	9	0	0	117	7	16	4	1.6	.886	OF-86
1896	LOU	N	2	.143	.143	7	1	0	0	0	0.0	0	1	1	0	0	0	0	16	1	6	0	11.5	.739	OF-1, 1B-1
4 yrs.			326	.284	.428	1283	364	57	46	12	0.9	256	224	163	115	60	1	0	599	51	81	10	2.2	.889	OF-324, 1B-2

Jeff Treadway

TREADWAY, HUGH JEFFERY   BL TR 5'10"   170 lbs.
B. Jan. 22, 1963, Columbus, Ga.

1987	CIN	N	23	.333	.452	84	28	4	0	2	2.4	9	4	2	6	1	2	1	44	48	4	14	4.2	.958	2B-21
1988			103	.252	.362	301	76	19	4	2	0.7	30	23	27	30	2	7	4	189	253	8	50	4.4	.982	2B-97, 3B-2
1989	ATL	N	134	.277	.378	473	131	18	3	8	1.7	58	40	30	38	3	11	3	273	341	12	80	4.7	.981	2B-123, 3B-6
3 yrs.			260	.274	.380	858	235	41	7	12	1.4	97	67	59	74	6	20	8	506	642	24	144	4.5	.980	2B-241, 3B-8

Red Treadway

TREADWAY, LUIS FRANCISCO   BL TR 5'10"   175 lbs.
B. Apr. 28, 1920, Athalone, N. C.

1944	NY	N	50	.300	.353	170	51	5	2	0	0.0	23	5	13	11	2	10	4	87	3	4	0	1.9	.957	OF-38
1945			88	.241	.330	224	54	4	2	4	1.8	31	23	20	13	3	25	5	107	3	7	0	1.3	.940	OF-60
2 yrs.			138	.266	.340	394	105	9	4	4	1.0	54	28	33	24	5	35	9	194	6	11	0	1.5	.948	OF-98

Frank Trechock

TRECHOCK, FRANK ADAM   BR TR 5'10"   175 lbs.
B. Dec. 24, 1915, Windber, Pa.   D. Jan. 16, 1989, Minneapolis, Minn.

| 1937 | WAS | A | 1 | .500 | .500 | 4 | 2 | 0 | 0 | 0 | 0.0 | 0 | 0 | 0 | 1 | 0 | 0 | 0 | 2 | 4 | 2 | 2 | 8.0 | .750 | SS-1 |

Nick Tremark

TREMARK, NICHOLAS JOSEPH   BL TL 5'5"   150 lbs.
B. Oct. 15, 1912, Yonkers, N. Y.

1934	BKN	N	17	.250	.286	28	7	1	0	0	0.0	3	6	2	2	0	7	1	16	0	0	0	0.9	1.000	OF-9
1935			10	.231	.308	13	3	1	0	0	0.0	1	3	1	1	0	5	2	6	0	0	0	0.6	1.000	OF-4
1936			8	.250	.313	32	8	2	0	0	0.0	6	1	3	2	0	0	0	16	2	0	0	2.3	1.000	OF-8
3 yrs.			35	.247	.301	73	18	4	0	0	0.0	10	10	6	5	0	12	3	38	2	0	0	1.1	1.000	OF-21

Overton Tremper

TREMPER, CARLTON OVERTON   BR TR 5'10"   163 lbs.
B. Mar. 22, 1906, Brooklyn, N. Y.

1927	BKN	N	36	.233	.233	60	14	0	0	0	0.0	4	4	0	2	0	1	0	13	2	0	0	0.4	1.000	OF-18
1928			10	.194	.323	31	6	2	1	0	0.0	1	1	0	1	0	1	1	11	2	0	0	1.3	1.000	OF-10
2 yrs.			46	.220	.264	91	20	2	1	0	0.0	5	5	0	3	0	9	2	24	4	0	0	0.6	1.000	OF-28

Mike Tresh

TRESH, MICHAEL   BR TR 5'11"   170 lbs.
Father of Tom Tresh.
B. Feb. 23, 1914, Hazleton, Pa.   D. Oct. 4, 1966, Detroit, Mich.

1938	CHI	A	10	.241	.310	29	7	2	0	0	0.0	3	2	8	4	0	0	0	37	8	1	1	4.6	.978	C-10
1939			119	.259	.284	352	91	5	2	0	0.0	49	38	64	30	3	0	0	480	59	8	7	4.6	.985	C-119
1940			135	.281	.340	480	135	15	5	1	0.2	62	64	49	40	3	0	0	619	69	12	7	5.2	.983	C-135
1941			115	.251	.282	390	98	10	1	0	0.0	38	33	38	27	1	0	0	488	81	11	12	5.0	.981	C-115
1942			72	.232	.275	233	54	8	1	0	0.0	21	15	28	24	2	0	0	258	37	7	2	4.2	.977	C-72
1943			86	.215	.226	279	60	3	0	0	0.0	20	20	37	20	2	0	0	321	62	7	4	4.5	.982	C-85
1944			93	.260	.292	312	81	8	1	0	0.0	22	25	37	15	0	0	0	370	47	8	5	4.6	.981	C-93
1945			150	.249	.273	458	114	11	0	0	0.0	50	47	65	37	6	0	0	575	102	11	7	4.6	.984	C-150
1946			80	.217	.258	217	47	5	2	0	0.0	28	21	36	24	0	1	0	330	48	2	13	4.8	.995	C-79
1947			90	.241	.277	274	66	6	2	0	0.0	19	20	26	26	2	1	0	313	38	9	10	4.0	.975	C-89
1948			39	.250	.287	108	27	1	0	1	0.9	10	11	9	9	0	5	2	99	16	2	1	3.0	.983	C-34
1949	CLE	A	38	.216	.216	37	8	0	0	0	0.0	4	1	5	7	0	0	0	71	8	0	3	2.1	1.000	C-38
12 yrs.			1027	.249	.283	3169	788	74	14	2	0.1	326	297	402	263	19	7	2	3961	575	78	72	4.5	.983	C-1019

Tom Tresh

TRESH, THOMAS MICHAEL   BB TR 6'1"   180 lbs.
Son of Mike Tresh.
B. Sept. 20, 1937, Detroit, Mich.

1961	NY	A	9	.250	.250	8	2	0	0	0	0.0	1	0	0	1	0	3	1	3	7	0	1	1.1	1.000	SS-3
1962			157	.286	.441	622	178	26	5	20	3.2	94	93	67	74	4	2	0	290	315	20	51	4.0	.968	SS-111, OF-43
1963			145	.269	.487	520	140	28	5	25	4.8	91	71	83	79	3	1	0	305	6	6	1	2.2	.981	OF-144
1964			153	.246	.402	533	131	25	4	16	3.0	75	73	73	110	13	7	1	259	7	1	0	1.7	.996	OF-146
1965			156	.279	.477	602	168	29	6	26	4.3	94	74	59	92	5	0	0	283	11	9	1	1.9	.970	OF-154
1966			151	.233	.421	537	125	12	4	27	5.0	76	68	86	89	5	3	1	224	191	12	18	2.8	.972	OF-84, 3B-64
1967			130	.219	.377	448	98	23	4	14	3.1	45	53	50	86	1	10	1	198	9	6	1	1.6	.972	OF-118
1968			152	.195	.308	507	99	18	3	11	2.2	60	52	76	97	10	6	1	244	410	32	70	4.5	.953	SS-119, OF-27
1969	2 teams			NY	A	(45G – .182)		DET	A	(94G – .224)															
"	total		139	.211	.350	474	100	18	3	14	3.0	59	46	56	70	4	10	1	215	313	17	58	3.9	.969	SS-118, OF-11, 3B-1
9 yrs.			1192	.245	.411	4251	1041	179	34	153	3.6	595	530	550	698	45	44	6	2021	1269	103	201	2.8	.970	OF-727, SS-351, 3B-65

WORLD SERIES

| 1962 | NY | A | 7 | .321 | .464 | 28 | 9 | 1 | 0 | 1 | 3.6 | 5 | 4 | 1 | 4 | 2 | 0 | 0 | 14 | 0 | 0 | 0 | 2.0 | 1.000 | OF-7 |

Year	Team		Games	BA	SA	AB	H	2B	3B	HR	HR%	R	RBI	BB	SO	SB	Pinch Hit AB	H	PO	A	E	DP	TC/G	FA	G by Pos

Tom Tresh *continued*

Year	Team		Games	BA	SA	AB	H	2B	3B	HR	HR%	R	RBI	BB	SO	SB	AB	H	PO	A	E	DP	TC/G	FA	G by Pos
1963			4	.200	.400	15	3	0	0	1	6.7	1	2	1	6	0	0	0	3	0	0	0	0.8	1.000	OF-4
1964			7	.273	.636	22	6	2	0	2	9.1	4	7	6	7	0	0	0	11	0	0	0	1.6	1.000	OF-7
3 yrs.			18	.277	.508	65	18	3	0	4	6.2	10	13	8	17	2	0	0	28	0	0	0	1.6	1.000	OF-18

Alex Trevino

TREVINO, ALEJANDRO
Born Alejandro Trevino y Castro.   Brother of Bobby Trevino.
B. Aug. 26, 1957, Monterrey, Mexico

BR TR 5'10"   165 lbs.

Year	Team		Games	BA	SA	AB	H	2B	3B	HR	HR%	R	RBI	BB	SO	SB	AB	H	PO	A	E	DP	TC/G	FA	G by Pos
1978	NY	N	6	.250	.250	12	3	0	0	0	0.0	3	0	1	2	0	1	0	12	4	0	0	2.7	1.000	C-5, 3B-1
1979			79	.271	.333	207	56	11	1	0	0.0	24	20	20	27	2	16	5	229	71	9	14	3.9	.971	C-36, 3B-27, 2B-8
1980			106	.256	.299	355	91	11	2	0	0.0	26	37	13	41	0	12	3	450	76	16	7	5.1	.970	C-86, 3B-14, 2B-1
1981	CIN	N	56	.262	.275	149	39	2	0	0	0.0	17	10	13	19	3	10	3	215	25	9	1	4.4	.964	C-45, 2B-4, OF-2, 3B-1
1982	CIN	N	120	.251	.304	355	89	10	3	1	0.3	24	33	34	34	3	7	1	725	61	17	7	6.7	.979	C-116, 3B-2
1983			74	.216	.293	167	36	8	1	1	0.6	14	13	17	20	0	7	2	359	32	5	2	5.4	.987	C-63, 3B-4, 2B-1
1984	2 teams		85			CIN N (6G – .167)				ATL N (79G – .244)															
"	total		85	.243	.335	272	66	16	0	3	1.1	36	28	16	29	5	7	1	403	61	5	5	5.5	.989	C-83
1985	SF	N	57	.217	.408	157	34	10	1	6	3.8	17	19	20	24	0	2	0	299	19	7	1	5.7	.978	C-55, 3B-1
1986	LA	N	89	.262	.386	202	53	13	0	4	2.0	31	26	27	35	0	31	7	304	46	11	4	4.1	.970	C-63, 1B-1
1987			72	.222	.347	144	32	7	1	3	2.1	16	16	6	28	1	33	7	206	22	3	3	3.2	.987	C-45, OF-2, 3B-1
1988	HOU	N	78	.249	.368	193	48	17	0	2	1.0	19	13	24	29	5	5	1	360	24	9	5	5.0	.977	C-74, OF-1
1989			59	.290	.405	131	38	7	1	2	1.5	15	16	7	18	0	21	1	173	13	2	2	3.2	.989	C-32, 3B-2, 1B-2
12 yrs.			881	.250	.334	2344	585	112	10	22	0.9	242	231	198	306	19	152	31	3735	454	93	51	4.9	.978	C-703, 3B-53, 2B-14, OF-5, 1B-3

Bobby Trevino

TREVINO, CARLOS
Born Carlos Trevino y Castro.   Brother of Alex Trevino.
B. Aug. 15, 1943, Monterrey, Mexico

BR TR 6'2"   185 lbs.

Year	Team		Games	BA	SA	AB	H	2B	3B	HR	HR%	R	RBI	BB	SO	SB	AB	H	PO	A	E	DP	TC/G	FA	G by Pos
1968	CAL	A	17	.225	.250	40	9	1	0	0	0.0	1	1	2	9	0	6	0	24	1	1	0	1.5	.962	OF-11

Gus Triandos

TRIANDOS, GUS CONSTANTINE
B. July 30, 1930, San Francisco, Calif.

BR TR 6'3"   205 lbs.

Year	Team		Games	BA	SA	AB	H	2B	3B	HR	HR%	R	RBI	BB	SO	SB	AB	H	PO	A	E	DP	TC/G	FA	G by Pos
1953	NY	A	18	.157	.255	51	8	2	0	1	2.0	5	6	3	9	0	3	1	117	7	2	8	7.0	.984	1B-12, C-5
1954			2	.000	.000	1	0	0	0	0	0.0	0	0	0	1	0	1	0	0	0	0	0	0.0	–	C-1
1955	BAL	A	140	.277	.399	481	133	17	3	12	2.5	47	65	40	55	0	14	2	966	84	13	95	7.6	.988	1B-103, C-36, 3B-1
1956			131	.279	.462	452	126	18	1	21	4.6	47	88	48	73	0	5	1	790	89	12	39	6.8	.987	C-89, 1B-52
1957			129	.254	.445	418	106	21	1	19	4.5	44	72	38	73	0	17	1	580	64	5	13	5.0	.992	C-120
1958			137	.245	.456	474	116	10	0	30	6.3	59	79	60	65	1	8	2	698	61	10	11	5.6	.987	C-132
1959			126	.216	.430	393	85	7	1	25	6.4	43	73	65	56	0	3	0	597	63	13	5	5.3	.981	C-125
1960			109	.269	.418	364	98	18	0	12	3.3	36	54	41	62	0	4	0	516	45	6	5	5.2	.989	C-105
1961			115	.244	.426	397	97	21	0	17	4.3	35	63	44	60	0	4	0	642	55	8	9	6.1	.989	C-114
1962			66	.159	.280	207	33	7	0	6	2.9	20	23	29	43	0	4	1	355	28	6	2	5.9	.985	C-63
1963	DET	A	106	.239	.407	327	78	13	0	14	4.3	28	41	32	67	0	13	3	535	29	1	4	5.3	.998	C-90
1964	PHI	N	73	.250	.426	188	47	9	0	8	4.3	17	33	26	41	0	16	4	379	25	6	4	5.6	.985	C-64, 1B-1
1965	2 teams					PHI N (30G – .171)				HOU N (24G – .181)															
"	total		54	.175	.240	154	27	4	0	2	1.3	8	11	14	31	0	8	3	268	15	8	2	5.4	.973	C-48
13 yrs.			1206	.244	.413	3907	954	147	6	167	4.3	389	608	440	636	1	100	18	6443	565	90	197	5.9	.987	C-992, 1B-168, 3B-1

Manny Trillo

TRILLO, JESUS MANUEL (Indio)
Born Jesus Manuel Marcano y Trillo.
B. Dec. 25, 1950, Carapito, Venezuela

BR TR 6'1"   150 lbs.

Year	Team		Games	BA	SA	AB	H	2B	3B	HR	HR%	R	RBI	BB	SO	SB	AB	H	PO	A	E	DP	TC/G	FA	G by Pos
1973	OAK	A	17	.250	.417	12	3	2	0	0	0.0	0	3	0	4	0	0	0	15	17	2	5	2.0	.941	2B-16
1974			21	.152	.152	33	5	0	0	0	0.0	3	2	2	8	0	0	0	31	43	4	10	3.7	.949	2B-21
1975	CHI	N	154	.248	.316	545	135	12	2	7	1.3	55	70	45	78	1	1	0	350	509	29	103	5.8	.967	2B-153, SS-1
1976			158	.239	.311	582	139	24	3	4	0.7	42	59	53	70	17	1	0	350	527	17	103	5.7	.981	2B-156, SS-1
1977			152	.280	.377	504	141	18	5	7	1.4	51	57	44	58	3	5	0	330	467	25	81	5.4	.970	2B-149
1978			152	.261	.332	552	144	17	5	4	0.7	53	55	50	67	0	2	2	354	505	19	99	5.8	.978	2B-149
1979	PHI	N	118	.260	.357	431	112	22	1	6	1.4	40	42	20	59	4	0	0	270	368	10	84	5.5	.985	2B-118
1980			141	.292	.412	531	155	25	9	7	1.3	68	43	32	46	8	0	0	360	467	11	91	5.9	.987	2B-140
1981			94	.287	.395	349	100	14	3	6	1.7	37	36	26	37	10	0	0	245	286	7	61	5.7	.987	2B-94
1982			149	.271	.319	549	149	24	1	0	0.0	52	39	33	53	8	0	0	343	441	5	101	5.3	.994	2B-149
1983	2 teams					CLE A (88G – .272)				MON N (31G – .264)															
"	total		119	.270	.342	441	119	21	1	3	0.7	49	45	31	64	1	0	0	229	355	8	81	5.0	.986	2B-118
1984	SF	N	98	.254	.342	401	102	21	1	4	1.0	45	36	25	55	0	1	0	218	294	6	67	5.3	.988	2B-96, 3B-4
1985			125	.224	.288	451	101	16	2	3	0.7	36	25	40	44	2	5	0	263	361	13	73	5.1	.980	2B-120, 3B-1
1986	CHI	N	81	.296	.382	152	45	10	0	1	0.7	22	19	16	21	0	14	3	114	63	5	14	2.2	.973	3B-53, 1B-11, 2B-6
1987			108	.294	.444	214	63	8	0	8	3.7	27	26	25	37	0	23	7	301	53	4	35	3.3	.989	1B-47, 3B-35, 2B-10, SS-6
1988			76	.250	.299	164	41	5	0	1	0.6	15	14	8	32	2	20	2	177	81	3	19	3.4	.989	1B-24, 3B-17, 2B-13, SS-7
1989	CIN	N	17	.205	.205	39	8	0	0	0	0.0	3	0	2	9	0	4	1	27	16	1	3	2.7	.978	2B-10, 1B-3, SS-1
17 yrs.			1780	.263	.345	5950	1562	239	33	61	1.0	598	571	452	742	56	76	15	3977	4855	169	1029	5.1	.981	2B-1518, 3B-110, 1B-85, SS-16

DIVISIONAL PLAYOFF SERIES

Year	Team		Games	BA	SA	AB	H	2B	3B	HR	HR%	R	RBI	BB	SO	SB	AB	H	PO	A	E	DP	TC/G	FA	G by Pos
1981	PHI	N	5	.188	.188	16	3	0	0	0	0.0	1	1	4	0	0	0	0	0	0	0	0	0.0	–	2B-5

LEAGUE CHAMPIONSHIP SERIES

Year	Team		Games	BA	SA	AB	H	2B	3B	HR	HR%	R	RBI	BB	SO	SB	AB	H	PO	A	E	DP	TC/G	FA	G by Pos
1974	OAK	A	1	–	–	0	0	0	0	0	–	1	0	1	0	0	0	0	0	0	0	0	0.0	–	
1980	PHI	N	5	.381	.571	21	8	2	1	0	0.0	1	4	0	2	0	0	0	18	25	1	4	8.8	.977	2B-5
2 yrs.			6	.381	.571	21	8	2	1	0	0.0	2	4	2	2	0	0	0	18	25	1	4	7.3	.977	2B-5

WORLD SERIES

Year	Team		Games	BA	SA	AB	H	2B	3B	HR	HR%	R	RBI	BB	SO	SB	AB	H	PO	A	E	DP	TC/G	FA	G by Pos
1980	PHI	N	6	.217	.304	23	5	2	0	0	0.0	4	2	0	0	0	0	0	14	25	1	6	6.7	.975	2B-6

Year	Team		Games	BA	SA	AB	H	2B	3B	HR	HR%	R	RBI	BB	SO	SB	Pinch Hit AB	H	PO	A	E	DP	TC/G	FA	G by Pos

Coaker Triplett

TRIPLETT, HERMAN COAKER
B. Dec. 18, 1911, Boone, N. C.

BR TR 5'11" 185 lbs.

Year	Team		Games	BA	SA	AB	H	2B	3B	HR	HR%	R	RBI	BB	SO	SB	AB	H	PO	A	E	DP	TC/G	FA	G by Pos
1938	CHI	N	12	.250	.361	36	9	2	1	0	0.0	4	2	0	0	0	3	0	15	1	0	0	1.3	1.000	OF-9
1941	STL	N	76	.286	.400	185	53	6	3	3	1.6	29	21	18	27	0	25	5	78	4	3	0	1.1	.965	OF-46
1942			64	.273	.390	154	42	7	4	1	0.6	18	23	17	15	1	16	2	82	2	3	0	1.4	.966	OF-46
1943	2 teams		STL N (9G – .080)			PHI N (105G – .272)																			
"	total		114	.260	.439	385	100	16	4	15	3.9	46	56	29	34	2	16	4	197	11	6	0	1.9	.972	OF-96
1944	PHI	N	84	.234	.288	184	43	5	1	1	0.5	15	25	19	10	1	36	8	90	3	1	1	1.1	.989	OF-44
1945			120	.240	.333	363	87	11	1	7	1.9	36	46	40	27	6	28	5	202	3	12	1	1.8	.945	OF-92
6 yrs.			470	.256	.375	1307	334	47	14	27	2.1	148	173	123	114	10	124	24	664	24	25	2	1.5	.965	OF-333

Hal Trosky

TROSKY, HAROLD ARTHUR, SR.
Born Harold Arthur Troyavesky Sr.   Father of Hal Trosky.
B. Nov. 11, 1912, Norway, Iowa   D. June 18, 1979, Cedar Rapids, Iowa

BL TR 6'2" 207 lbs.
BB 1946

Year	Team		Games	BA	SA	AB	H	2B	3B	HR	HR%	R	RBI	BB	SO	SB	AB	H	PO	A	E	DP	TC/G	FA	G by Pos
1933	CLE	A	11	.295	.477	44	13	1	2	1	2.3	6	8	2	12	0	0	0	91	4	1	6	8.7	.990	1B-11
1934			154	.330	.598	625	206	45	9	35	5.6	117	142	58	49	2	0	0	1487	86	22	145	10.4	.986	1B-154
1935			154	.271	.468	632	171	33	7	26	4.1	84	113	46	60	1	1	1	1567	88	11	129	10.8	.993	1B-153
1936			151	.343	.644	629	216	45	9	42	6.7	124	**162**	36	58	6	0	0	1368	86	22	126	9.8	.985	1B-151, 2B-1
1937			153	.298	.547	601	179	36	9	32	5.3	104	128	65	60	3	1	0	1403	76	10	131	9.7	.993	1B-152
1938			150	.334	.542	554	185	40	9	19	3.4	106	110	67	40	5	1	1	1232	102	10	124	9.0	.993	1B-148
1939			122	.335	.589	448	150	31	4	25	5.6	89	104	52	28	2	4	0	1004	97	9	97	9.1	.992	1B-118
1940			140	.295	.529	522	154	39	4	25	4.8	85	93	79	45	1	0	0	1207	70	11	129	9.2	.991	1B-139
1941			89	.294	.455	310	91	17	0	11	3.5	43	51	44	21	1	4	2	727	54	9	77	8.9	.989	1B-85
1944	CHI	A	135	.241	.374	497	120	32	2	10	2.0	55	70	62	30	3	4	1	1310	57	9	122	10.2	.993	1B-130
1946			88	.254	.334	299	76	12	3	2	0.7	22	31	34	37	4	6	1	729	33	7	63	8.7	.991	1B-80
11 yrs.			1347	.302	.522	5161	1561	331	58	228	4.4	835	1012	545	440	28	21	6	12125	753	121	1149	9.7	.991	1B-1321, 2B-1

Mike Trost

TROST, MICHAEL J.
B. 1866, Philadelphia, Pa.   D. Mar. 24, 1901, Philadelphia, Pa.

TR 6'½" 180 lbs.

Year	Team		Games	BA	SA	AB	H	2B	3B	HR	HR%	R	RBI	BB	SO	SB	AB	H	PO	A	E	DP	TC/G	FA	G by Pos
1890	STL	AA	17	.255	.353	51	13	2	0	1	2.0	10	6		4	0	0	0	70	13	9	0	5.4	.902	C-13, OF-4
1895	LOU	N	3	.083	.083	12	1	0	0	0	0.0	1	1		1	0	0	0	17	0	0	1	5.7	1.000	1B-3
2 yrs.			20	.222	.302	63	14	2	0	1	1.6	11	1		6	1	5	0	87	13	9	1	5.5	.917	C-13, OF-4, 1B-3

Sam Trott

TROTT, SAMUEL W.
B. 1858, Washington, D. C.   D. June 5, 1925, Cantonsville, Md.
Manager 1891.

BL TL 5'9" 190 lbs.

Year	Team		Games	BA	SA	AB	H	2B	3B	HR	HR%	R	RBI	BB	SO	SB	AB	H	PO	A	E	DP	TC/G	FA	G by Pos
1880	BOS	N	39	.208	.256	125	26	4	1	0	0.0	14	9	3	5		0	0	177	56	28	0	6.7	.893	C-36, OF-4
1881	DET	N	6	.200	.360	25	5	2	1	0	0.0	3	2	1	3		0	0	27	6	5	0	6.3	.868	C-6
1882			32	.240	.310	129	31	7	1	0	0.0	11	12	0	13		0	0	207	53	33	6	9.2	.887	C-23, SS-3, 2B-3, 1B-3, OF-2, 3B-1
1883			75	.244	.298	295	72	14	1	0	0.0	27		10	23		0	0	273	135	58	20	6.2	.876	2B-42, C-34, OF-6, 1B-1
1884	BAL	AA	71	.257	.401	284	73	17	9	2	0.7	36		4			0	0	513	105	46	15	9.4	.931	C-60, 2B-6, OF-5
1885			21	.273	.341	88	24	2	2	0	0.0	12		5			0	0	91	32	21	6	6.9	.854	C-17, OF-4, 2B-2, SS-1
1887			85	.257	.330	300	77	16	3	0	0.0	44		27		8	0	0	428	136	53	11	7.3	.914	C-69, 2B-11, OF-3, 1B-2, SS-1
1888			31	.278	.454	108	30	11	4	0	0.0	19	22	4		1	0	0	164	36	22	4	7.2	.901	C-27, OF-3, 2B-1, 1B-1
8 yrs.			360	.250	.340	1354	338	73	22	2	0.1	166	45	54	44	9	0	0	1880	559	266	62	7.5	.902	C-272, 2B-65, OF-27, 1B-7, SS-5, 3B-1

Quincy Trouppe

TROUPPE, QUINCY THOMAS
B. Dec. 25, 1912, Dublin, Ga.

BB TR 6'2½" 225 lbs.

Year	Team		Games	BA	SA	AB	H	2B	3B	HR	HR%	R	RBI	BB	SO	SB	AB	H	PO	A	E	DP	TC/G	FA	G by Pos
1952	CLE	A	6	.100	.100	10	1	0	0	0	0.0	1	0	1	3	0	0	0	22	3	0	0	4.2	1.000	C-6

Dasher Troy

TROY, JOHN JOSEPH
B. May 8, 1856, New York, N.Y.   D. Mar. 30, 1938, Ozone Park, N.Y.

BR TR

Year	Team		Games	BA	SA	AB	H	2B	3B	HR	HR%	R	RBI	BB	SO	SB	AB	H	PO	A	E	DP	TC/G	FA	G by Pos
1881	DET	N	11	.341	.409	44	15	3	0	0	0.0	2	4	3	8		0	0	13	23	7	4	3.9	.837	3B-7, 2B-4
1882	2 teams		DET N (40G – .243)			PRO N (4G – .235)																			
"	total		44	.243	.308	169	41	7	2	0	0.0	23	14	5	11		0	0	79	111	46	10	5.4	.805	2B-31, SS-15
1883	NY	N	85	.215	.269	316	68	7	5	0	0.0	37		9	33		0	0	202	262	70	26	6.3	.869	2B-73, SS-12
1884	NY	AA	107	.264	.378	421	111	22	10	2	0.5	80		19			0	0	224	314	74	25	5.7	.879	2B-107
1885			45	.220	.305	177	39	3	3	2	1.1	24		5			0	0	128	103	38	17	6.0	.859	2B-42, OF-2, SS-1
5 yrs.			292	.243	.327	1127	274	42	20	4	0.4	166	18	41	52		0	0	646	813	235	82	5.8	.861	2B-257, SS-28, 3B-7, OF-2

Fred Truax

TRUAX, FREDERICK W.
B. 1868   D. Dec. 18, 1899, Omaha, Neb.

Year	Team		Games	BA	SA	AB	H	2B	3B	HR	HR%	R	RBI	BB	SO	SB	AB	H	PO	A	E	DP	TC/G	FA	G by Pos
1890	PIT	N	1	.333	.333	3	1	0	0	0	0.0	0	1	1	1	0	0	0	1	0	0	1	1.0	1.000	OF-1

Harry Truby

TRUBY, HARRY GARVIN (Bird Eye)
B. May 12, 1870, Ironton, Ohio   D. Mar. 21, 1953, Ironton, Ohio

TR 5'11" 185 lbs.

Year	Team		Games	BA	SA	AB	H	2B	3B	HR	HR%	R	RBI	BB	SO	SB	AB	H	PO	A	E	DP	TC/G	FA	G by Pos
1895	CHI	N	33	.336	.361	119	40	3	0	0	0.0	17	16	10	7	7	0	0	98	93	10	21	6.1	.950	2B-33
1896	2 teams		CHI N (29G – .257)			PIT N (8G – .156)																			
"	total		37	.234	.319	141	33	2	2	2	1.4	14	34	8	9	5	0	0	96	99	13	24	5.6	.938	2B-36
2 yrs.			70	.281	.338	260	73	5	2	2	0.8	31	50	18	16	12	0	0	194	192	23	45	5.8	.944	2B-69

Frank Truesdale

TRUESDALE, FRANK DAY
B. Mar. 31, 1884, St. Louis, Mo.   D. Aug. 27, 1943, Albuquerque, N. M.

BB TR 5'8" 145 lbs.

Year	Team		Games	BA	SA	AB	H	2B	3B	HR	HR%	R	RBI	BB	SO	SB	AB	H	PO	A	E	DP	TC/G	FA	G by Pos
1910	STL	A	123	.219	.253	415	91	7	2	1	0.2	39	25	48		29	1	0	279	313	56	41	5.3	.914	2B-123
1911			1	–	–	0	0	0	0	0	0.0	1	0	0		0	0	0	0	0	0	0	0.0	–	
1914	NY	A	77	.212	.230	217	46	4	0	0	0.0	23	13	39	35	11	3	1	123	189	18	20	4.3	.945	2B-67, 3B-4
1918	BOS	A	15	.278	.306	36	10	1	0	0	0.0	6	2	4	5	1	4	1	14	28	4	2	3.1	.913	2B-10
4 yrs.			216	.220	.249	668	147	12	2	1	0.1	69	40	91	40	41	8	2	416	530	78	63	4.7	.924	2B-200, 3B-4

Year	Team		Games	BA	SA	AB	H	2B	3B	HR	HR%	R	RBI	BB	SO	SB	Pinch Hit AB	Pinch Hit H	PO	A	E	DP	TC/G	FA	G by Pos

Ed Trumbull

TRUMBULL, EDWARD J.
Born Edward J. Trembly.
B. Nov. 3, 1860, Chicopee, Mass. Deceased.

Year	Team		Games	BA	SA	AB	H	2B	3B	HR	HR%	R	RBI	BB	SO	SB	PH AB	PH H	PO	A	E	DP	TC/G	FA	G by Pos
1884	WAS	AA	25	.116	.140	86	10	2	0	0	0.0	5		2			0	0	24	24	14	1	2.5	.774	OF-15, P-10

Ollie Tucker

TUCKER, OLIVER DINWIDDIE   BL TR 5'11" 190 lbs.
B. Jan. 27, 1902, Radiant, Va. D. July 13, 1940, Radiant, Va.

Year	Team		Games	BA	SA	AB	H	2B	3B	HR	HR%	R	RBI	BB	SO	SB	PH AB	PH H	PO	A	E	DP	TC/G	FA	G by Pos
1927	WAS	A	20	.208	.292	24	5	2	0	0	0.0	1	8	4	2	0	10	1	9	0	0	0	0.5	1.000	OF-5
1928	CLE	A	14	.128	.191	47	6	0	0	1	2.1	5	2	7	3	0	0	0	18	3	0	0	1.5	1.000	OF-14
2 yrs.			34	.155	.225	71	11	2	0	1	1.4	6	10	11	5	0	10	1	27	3	0	0	0.9	1.000	OF-19

Thurman Tucker

TUCKER, THURMAN LOWELL (Joe E.)   BL TR 5'10½" 165 lbs.
B. Sept. 26, 1917, Gordon, Tex.

Year	Team		Games	BA	SA	AB	H	2B	3B	HR	HR%	R	RBI	BB	SO	SB	PH AB	PH H	PO	A	E	DP	TC/G	FA	G by Pos
1942	CHI	A	7	.125	.208	24	3	0	1	0	0.0	2	1	0	4	0	2	0	8	1	1	0	1.4	.900	OF-5
1943			139	.235	.303	528	124	15	6	3	0.6	81	39	79	72	29	6	1	399	14	5	1	3.0	.988	OF-132
1944			124	.287	.361	446	128	15	6	2	0.4	59	46	57	40	13	1	0	414	12	4	2	3.5	.991	OF-120
1946			121	.288	.354	438	126	20	3	1	0.2	62	36	54	45	9	8	3	276	11	3	1	2.4	.990	OF-110
1947			89	.236	.315	254	60	9	4	1	0.4	28	17	38	25	10	19	4	171	5	4	2	2.0	.978	OF-65
1948	CLE	A	83	.260	.343	242	63	13	2	1	0.4	52	19	31	17	11	10	3	172	5	0	2	2.1	1.000	OF-66
1949			80	.244	.289	197	48	5	2	0	0.0	28	14	18	19	4	22	2	119	2	2	0	1.5	.984	OF-52
1950			57	.178	.228	101	18	2	0	1	1.0	13	7	14	14	1	18	3	58	2	2	1	1.1	.968	OF-34
1951			1	.000	.000	1	0	0	0	0	0.0	0	0	0	1	0	1	0	0	0	0	0	0.0	—	—
9 yrs.			701	.255	.325	2231	570	79	24	9	0.4	325	179	291	237	77	87	16	1617	52	21	9	2.4	.988	OF-584

WORLD SERIES

Year	Team		Games	BA	SA	AB	H	2B	3B	HR	HR%	R	RBI	BB	SO	SB	PH AB	PH H	PO	A	E	DP	TC/G	FA	G by Pos
1948	CLE	A	1	.333	.333	3	1	0	0	0	0.0	1	0	1	0	0	0	0	3	1	0	1	4.0	1.000	OF-1

Tommy Tucker

TUCKER, THOMAS JOSEPH   BB TR 5'11" 165 lbs.
B. Oct. 28, 1863, Holyoke, Mass. D. Oct. 22, 1935, Montague, Mass.

Year	Team		Games	BA	SA	AB	H	2B	3B	HR	HR%	R	RBI	BB	SO	SB	PH AB	PH H	PO	A	E	DP	TC/G	FA	G by Pos
1887	BAL	AA	136	.275	.372	524	144	15	9	6	1.1	114		29		85	0	0	1346	50	35	49	10.5	.976	1B-136
1888			136	.287	.400	520	149	17	12	6	1.2	74	61	16		43	0	0	1365	59	38	64	10.8	.974	1B-129, OF-7, P-1
1889			134	**.372**	.484	527	196	22	11	5	0.9	103	99	42	26	63	0	0	1165	48	48	63	9.4	.962	1B-123, OF-12
1890	BOS	N	132	.295	.362	539	159	17	8	1	0.2	104	62	56	22	43	0	0	1341	39	29	53	10.7	.979	1B-132
1891			140	.270	.328	548	148	16	5	2	0.4	103	69	37	30	26	0	0	1313	55	34	66	10.0	.976	1B-140, P-1
1892			149	.282	.341	542	153	15	7	1	0.2	85	62	45	35	22	0	0	1484	51	45	96	10.6	.972	1B-149
1893			121	.284	.362	486	138	13	2	1	1.4	83	91	27	31	8	0	0	1252	39	27	89	10.9	.980	1B-121
1894			123	.330	.420	500	165	24	6	3	0.6	112	100	53	21	18	0	0	1108	68	18	82	9.7	.985	1B-123, OF-1
1895			125	.249	.335	462	115	19	6	3	0.6	87	73	61	29	15	0	0	1159	82	28	78	10.2	.978	1B-125
1896			122	.304	.395	474	144	27	5	2	0.4	74	72	30	21	6	0	0	1214	72	20	72	10.7	.985	1B-122
1897	2 teams		BOS	N	(4G – .214)		WAS	N	(93G – .338)																
"	total		97	.333	.456	366	122	20	5	1	1.4	52	65	29		18	0	0	897	46	17	58	9.9	.982	1B-97
1898	2 teams		BKN	N	(73G – .279)		STL	N	(72G – .238)																
"	total		145	.260	.318	535	139	16	6	1	0.2	53	54	30		2	0	0	1552	85	30	84	11.5	.982	1B-145
1899	CLE	N	127	.241	.296	456	110	19	3	0	0.0	40	40	24		3	0	0	1229	58	30	71	10.4	.977	1B-127
13 yrs.			1687	.290	.373	6479	1882	240	85	42	0.6	1084	848	479	223	352	0	0	16425	752	399	925	10.4	.977	1B-1669, OF-20, P-2

Jerry Turbidy

TURBIDY, JEREMIAH   BR TR 5'8" 165 lbs.
B. July 4, 1852, Dudley, Mass. D. Sept. 5, 1920, Webster, Mass.

Year	Team		Games	BA	SA	AB	H	2B	3B	HR	HR%	R	RBI	BB	SO	SB	PH AB	PH H	PO	A	E	DP	TC/G	FA	G by Pos
1884	KC	U	13	.224	.306	49	11	4	0	0	0.0	5		3			0	0	24	54	16	4	7.2	.830	SS-13

Eddie Turchin

TURCHIN, EDWARD LAWRENCE (Smiley)   BR TR 5'10" 165 lbs.
B. Feb. 10, 1917, New York, N. Y. D. Feb. 8, 1982, Brookhaven, N. Y.

Year	Team		Games	BA	SA	AB	H	2B	3B	HR	HR%	R	RBI	BB	SO	SB	PH AB	PH H	PO	A	E	DP	TC/G	FA	G by Pos
1943	CLE	A	11	.231	.231	13	3	0	0	0	0.0	4	1	3	1	0	0	0	5	9	1	1	1.4	.933	3B-4, SS-2

Pete Turgeon

TURGEON, EUGENE JOSEPH   BR TR 5'6" 145 lbs.
B. Jan. 3, 1897, Minneapolis, Minn. D. Jan. 24, 1977, Wichita Falls, Tex.

Year	Team		Games	BA	SA	AB	H	2B	3B	HR	HR%	R	RBI	BB	SO	SB	PH AB	PH H	PO	A	E	DP	TC/G	FA	G by Pos
1923	CHI	N	3	.167	.167	6	1	0	0	0	0.0	1	0	0	0	0	0	0	4	3	1	2	2.7	.875	SS-2

Earl Turner

TURNER, EARL EDWIN   BR TR 5'9" 170 lbs.
B. May 6, 1923, Pittsfield, Mass.

Year	Team		Games	BA	SA	AB	H	2B	3B	HR	HR%	R	RBI	BB	SO	SB	PH AB	PH H	PO	A	E	DP	TC/G	FA	G by Pos
1948	PIT	N	2	.000	.000	1	0	0	0	0	0.0	0	0	0	0	0	1	0	0	0	0	0	0.0	—	C-1
1950			40	.243	.365	74	18	0	0	3	4.1	10	5	4	13	1	6	1	101	11	3	3	2.9	.974	C-34
2 yrs.			42	.240	.360	75	18	0	0	3	4.0	10	5	4	13	1	7	1	101	11	3	3	2.7	.974	C-35

Jerry Turner

TURNER, JOHN WEBBER   BL TL 5'9" 180 lbs.
B. Jan. 17, 1954, Texarkana, Ark.

Year	Team		Games	BA	SA	AB	H	2B	3B	HR	HR%	R	RBI	BB	SO	SB	PH AB	PH H	PO	A	E	DP	TC/G	FA	G by Pos
1974	SD	N	17	.292	.313	48	14	1	0	0	0.0	4	2	3	5	2	6	3	14	1	0	0	0.9	1.000	OF-13
1975			11	.273	.273	22	6	0	0	0	0.0	1	0	2	1	0	6	3	10	0	1	0	1.0	.909	OF-4
1976			105	.267	.413	281	75	16	5	5	1.8	41	37	32	38	12	25	5	115	6	5	0	1.2	.960	OF-74
1977			118	.246	.412	289	71	16	1	10	3.5	43	48	31	43	12	45	12	114	10	7	2	1.1	.947	OF-69
1978			106	.280	.436	225	63	9	1	8	3.6	28	37	21	32	6	49	20	91	5	3	0	0.9	.970	OF-58
1979			138	.248	.368	448	111	23	2	9	2.0	55	61	34	58	4	28	5	197	7	9	2	1.5	.958	OF-115
1980			85	.288	.379	153	44	5	0	3	2.0	22	18	10	18	8	47	13	44	2	0	1	0.5	1.000	OF-34
1981	2 teams		SD	N	(33G – .226)		CHI	A	(10G – .167)																
"	total		43	.209	.349	43	9	0	0	2	4.7	6	8	5	5	0	29	5	7	0	1	0	0.2	.875	OF-5
1982	DET	A	85	.248	.376	210	52	3	0	8	3.8	21	27	20	37	1	24	4	10	0	1	0	0.1	.909	DH-50, OF-13
1983	SD	N	25	.130	.130	23	3	0	0	0	0.0	1	0	1	1	0	23	3	0	0	0	0	0.0	—	OF-1
10 yrs.			733	.257	.387	1742	448	73	9	45	2.6	222	238	159	245	45	282	73	602	31	27	5	0.9	.959	OF-386, DH-50

Shane Turner

TURNER, SHANE LEE   BL TR 5'10" 180 lbs.
B. Jan. 8, 1963, Los Angeles, Calif.

Year	Team	Games	BA	SA	AB	H	2B	3B	HR	HR%	R	RBI	BB	SO	SB	Pinch Hit AB	Pinch Hit H	PO	A	E	DP	TC/G	FA	G by Pos

Shane Turner *continued*

| 1988 | PHI | N | 18 | .171 | .171 | 35 | 6 | 0 | 0 | 0 | 0.0 | 1 | 1 | 5 | 9 | 0 | 5 | 1 | 8 | 14 | 1 | 2 | 1.3 | .957 | 3B-8, SS-5 |

Terry Turner

TURNER, TERRENCE LAMONT (Cotton)
B. Feb. 28, 1881, Sandy Lake, Pa. D. July 18, 1960, Cleveland, Ohio   BR TR 5'8" 149 lbs.

1901	PIT	N	2	.429	.429	7	3	0	0	0	0.0	0	1	0		0	0	0	3	7	2	0	6.0	.833	3B-2
1904	CLE	A	111	.235	.295	404	95	9	6	1	0.2	41	45	11		5	0	0	191	376	36	28	5.4	.940	SS-111
1905			154	.263	.359	582	153	16	14	4	0.7	48	72	14		17	0	0	285	430	41	49	4.9	.946	SS-154
1906			147	.291	.372	584	170	27	7	2	0.3	85	62	35		27	0	0	287	570	36	61	6.1	.960	SS-147
1907			148	.242	.307	524	127	20	7	0	0.0	57	46	19		27	1	0	258	477	39	67	5.2	.950	SS-145
1908			60	.239	.303	201	48	11	1	0	0.0	21	19	15		18	7	1	65	68	6	4	2.3	.957	OF-36
1909			53	.250	.322	208	52	7	4	0	0.0	25	16	14		14	1	0	112	176	11	21	5.6	.963	SS-26, 2B-26
1910			150	.230	.275	574	132	14	6	0	0.0	71	33	53		31	1	0	249	449	25	50	4.8	.965	SS-94, 3B-46, 2B-9
1911			117	.252	.333	417	105	16	9	0	0.0	59	28	34		29	0	0	174	245	19	16	3.7	.957	3B-94, 2B-14, SS-10
1912			103	.308	.368	370	114	14	0	0	0.0	54	33	31		19	0	0	129	199	17	21	3.3	.951	3B-103
1913			120	.247	.302	388	96	13	4	0	0.0	61	44	55	35	13	3	1	188	279	18	35	4.0	.963	3B-71, 2B-25, SS-21
1914			120	.245	.327	428	105	14	4	1	0.2	43	33	44	36	17	0	0	168	290	15	23	3.9	.968	3B-103, 2B-17
1915			95	.252	.313	262	66	14	1	0	0.0	35	14	29	13	12	3	0	92	190	10	14	3.1	.966	2B-51, 3B-20
1916			124	.262	.311	428	112	15	3	0	0.0	52	38	40	29	15	5	1	164	308	14	28	3.9	.971	3B-77, 2B-42
1917			69	.206	.244	180	37	7	0	0	0.0	16	15	14	19	4	5	0	86	119	4	7	3.0	.981	3B-40, 2B-23, SS-1
1918			74	.249	.296	233	58	7	2	0	0.0	24	23	22	15	6	1	1	77	170	5	6	3.4	.980	3B-46, 2B-26, SS-1
1919	PHI	A	38	.189	.213	127	24	3	0	0	0.0	7	6	5	9	2	1	0	61	114	8	16	4.8	.956	SS-19, 2B-17, 3B-1
17 yrs.			1685	.253	.318	5917	1497	207	77	8	0.1	699	528	435	156	256	28	4	2589	4467	306	446	4.4	.958	SS-746, 3B-603, 2B-250, OF-36

Tom Turner

TURNER, THOMAS RICHARD
B. Sept. 8, 1916, Custer, Okla. D. May 14, 1986, Kennewick, Wash.   BR TR 6'½" 215 lbs.

1940	CHI	A	37	.208	.260	96	20	1	2	0	0.0	11	6	3	12	1	7	1	110	13	4	0	3.4	.969	C-29
1941			38	.238	.278	126	30	5	0	0	0.0	7	8	9	15	2	3	1	166	21	4	3	5.0	.979	C-35
1942			56	.242	.352	182	44	9	1	3	1.6	18	21	19	15	0	2	1	199	35	7	5	4.3	.971	C-54
1943			51	.240	.338	154	37	7	1	2	1.3	16	11	13	21	1	2	0	186	34	5	5	4.4	.978	C-49
1944	2 teams			CHI	A	(36G – .230)				STL	A	(15G – .320)													
"	total		51	.246	.341	138	34	7	0	2	1.4	11	17	7	21	0	4	0	149	18	7	3	3.4	.960	C-47
5 yrs.			233	.237	.320	696	165	29	4	7	1.0	63	63	51	84	4	18	3	810	121	27	16	4.1	.972	C-214

WORLD SERIES

| 1944 | STL | A | 1 | .000 | .000 | 1 | 0 | 0 | 0 | 0 | 0.0 | 0 | 0 | 0 | 1 | 0 | 0 | 1 | 0 | 0 | 0 | 0 | 0.0 | — | |

Tuck Turner

TURNER, GEORGE A.
B. Feb. 13, 1873, West Brighton, N. Y. D. July 16, 1945, Staten Island, N. Y.   BB TL

1893	PHI	N	36	.323	.406	155	50	4	3	1	0.6	32	13	9	19	7	0	0	79	5	6	2	2.5	.933	OF-36
1894			80	.416	.540	339	141	21	9	1	0.3	91	82	23	13	11	1	0	134	7	13	1	1.9	.916	OF-78, P-1
1895			59	.386	.510	210	81	8	6	2	1.0	51	43	25	11	14	4	2	89	5	17	0	1.9	.847	OF-55
1896	2 teams			PHI	N	(13G – .219)				STL	N	(51G – .246)													
"	total		64	.243	.362	235	57	9	5	1	0.4	42	27	22	26	12	4	0	84	8	5	1	1.5	.948	OF-59
1897	STL	N	103	.291	.404	416	121	17	12	2	0.5	58	41	35		8	1	0	146	10	9	3	1.6	.945	OF-102
1898			35	.199	.255	141	28	8	0	0	0.0	20	7	14		1	1	0	50	2	4	1	1.6	.929	OF-34
6 yrs.			377	.320	.429	1496	478	67	38	7	0.5	294	213	128	69	53	11	2	582	37	54	8	1.8	.920	OF-364, P-1

Bill Tuttle

TUTTLE, WILLIAM ROBERT
B. July 4, 1929, Elwood, Ill.   BR TR 6' 190 lbs.

1952	DET	A	7	.240	.240	25	6	0	0	0	0.0	2	2	0	1	0	1	0	19	0	0	0	2.7	1.000	OF-6
1954			147	.266	.385	530	141	20	11	7	1.3	64	58	62	60	5	3	1	364	18	6	3	2.6	.985	OF-145
1955			154	.279	.400	603	168	23	4	14	2.3	102	78	76	54	6	1	0	442	12	7	2	3.0	.985	OF-154
1956			140	.253	.357	546	138	22	4	9	1.6	61	65	38	48	5	4	2	348	13	9	2	2.6	.976	OF-137
1957			133	.251	.328	451	113	12	4	5	1.1	49	47	44	41	2	3	1	331	5	6	1	2.5	.982	OF-128
1958	KC	A	148	.231	.358	511	118	14	9	11	2.2	77	51	74	58	7	10	1	311	12	4	2	2.2	.988	OF-145
1959			126	.300	.413	463	139	19	6	7	1.5	74	43	48	38	10	4	1	294	17	5	3	2.5	.984	OF-121
1960			151	.256	.347	559	143	21	3	8	1.4	75	40	66	52	1	5	2	381	16	5	3	2.7	.988	OF-148
1961	2 teams			KC	A	(25G – .262)				MIN	A	(113G – .246)													
"	total		138	.249	.335	454	113	14	5	5	1.1	53	46	52	50	1	3	0	199	167	18	16	2.8	.953	OF-89, 3B-85, 2B-2
1962	MIN	A	110	.211	.285	123	26	4	1	1	0.8	21	13	19	14	1	6	1	71	2	2	0	0.7	.973	OF-104
1963			16	.000	.000												2	0	7	1	0	0	0.5	1.000	OF-14
11 yrs.			1270	.259	.363	4268	1105	149	47	67	1.6	578	443	480	416	38	42	10	2767	263	62	32	2.4	.980	OF-1191, 3B-85, 2B-2

Guy Tutwiler

TUTWILER, GUY ISBELL (King Tut)
B. July 17, 1889, Coalburg, Ala. D. Aug. 15, 1930, Birmingham, Ala.   BL TR 6' 175 lbs.

1911	DET	A	13	.188	.250	32	6	2	0	0	0.0	3	2	3		0	3	0	14	11	6	0	2.4	.806	2B-6, OF-3
1913			14	.213	.255	47	10	0	1	0	0.0	4	7	4	12	2	0	0	140	10	2	10	10.9	.987	1B-14
2 yrs.			27	.203	.253	79	16	2	1	0	0.0	7	10	6	12	2	3	0	154	21	8	10	6.8	.956	1B-14, 2B-6, OF-3

Old Hoss Twineham

TWINEHAM, ARTHUR W.
B. Nov. 26, 1866, Galesburg, Ill. Deceased.   BL TL 6'1½" 190 lbs.

1893	STL	N	14	.313	.354	48	15	2	0	0	0.0	8	11	1	2	0	0	0	48	16	5	1	4.9	.928	C-14
1894			38	.315	.386	127	40	4	1	1	0.8	22	16	9	11	2	0	0	147	38	12	1	5.2	.939	C-38
2 yrs.			52	.314	.377	175	55	6	1	1	0.6	30	27	10	13	2	0	0	195	54	17	2	5.1	.936	C-52

Larry Twitchell

TWITCHELL, LAWRENCE GRANT
B. Feb. 18, 1864, Cleveland, Ohio D. Aug. 23, 1930, Cleveland, Ohio   BR TR 6' 185 lbs.

1886	DET	N	4	.063	.063	16	1	0	0	0	0.0	1				0	0	0	2	8	0	1	2.5	1.000	P-4, OF-2
1887			65	.333	.432	264	88	14	6	0	0.0	44	51	8	19	12	0	0	89	16	13	2	1.8	.890	OF-53, P-15
1888			131	.244	.324	524	128	19	4	5	1.0	71	67	28	45	14	0	0	195	15	28	4	1.8	.882	OF-131, P-2

Year	Team		Games	BA	SA	AB	H	2B	3B	HR	HR%	R	RBI	BB	SO	SB	Pinch Hit AB	Pinch Hit H	PO	A	E	DP	TC/G	FA	G by Pos

Larry Twitchell *continued*

Year	Team		Games	BA	SA	AB	H	2B	3B	HR	HR%	R	RBI	BB	SO	SB	PH AB	PH H	PO	A	E	DP	TC/G	FA	G by Pos
1889	CLE	N	134	.275	.366	549	151	16	11	4	0.7	73	95	29	37	17	0	0	220	10	21	0	1.9	.916	OF-134, P-1
1890	2 teams			CLE	P	(56G – .223)		BUF	P	(44G – .221)															
"	total		100	.222	.294	405	90	9	4	4	1.0	57	53	40	29	8	0	0	125	47	22	2	1.9	.887	OF-88, P-12, 1B-3
1891	COL	AA	57	.277	.379	224	62	9	4	2	0.9	32	35	20	28	10	0	0	70	10	9	0	1.6	.899	OF-56, P-6
1892	WAS	N	51	.219	.318	192	42	9	5	0	0.0	20	20	11	31	8	0	0	80	11	13	1	2.0	.875	OF-48, SS-3, 3B-1
1893	LOU	N	45	.310	.422	187	58	12	3	1	0.5	37	31	17	20	7	0	0	91	6	14	0	2.5	.874	OF-45
1894			52	.267	.400	210	56	16	3	2	1.0	28	32	15	20	8	0	0	103	17	12	4	2.5	.909	OF-51, P-1
9 yrs.			639	.263	.356	2571	676	104	40	18	0.7	362	384	168	231	84	0	0	975	140	132	14	2.0	.894	OF-608, P-41, SS-3, 1B-3, 3B-1

Babe Twombly

TWOMBLY, CLARENCE EDWARD
Brother of George Twombly.
B. Jan. 18, 1896, Jamaica Plain, Mass.   D. Nov. 23, 1974, San Clemente, Calif.

BL TR 5'10"   165 lbs.

Year	Team		Games	BA	SA	AB	H	2B	3B	HR	HR%	R	RBI	BB	SO	SB	PH AB	PH H	PO	A	E	DP	TC/G	FA	G by Pos
1920	CHI	N	78	.235	.284	183	43	1	1	2	1.1	25	14	17	20	5	22	4	91	7	3	0	1.3	.970	OF-45, 2B-2
1921			87	.377	.451	175	66	8	1	1	0.6	22	18	11	10	4	**38**	**15**	81	11	3	0	1.1	.968	OF-45
2 yrs.			165	.304	.366	358	109	9	2	3	0.8	47	32	28	30	9	60	19	172	18	6	0	1.2	.969	OF-90, 2B-2

George Twombly

TWOMBLY, GEORGE FREDERICK (Silent George)
Brother of Babe Twombly.
B. June 4, 1892, Boston, Mass.   D. Feb. 17, 1975, Lexington, Mass.

BR TR 5'9"   165 lbs.

Year	Team		Games	BA	SA	AB	H	2B	3B	HR	HR%	R	RBI	BB	SO	SB	PH AB	PH H	PO	A	E	DP	TC/G	FA	G by Pos
1914	CIN	N	68	.233	.275	240	56	0	5	0	0.0	22	19	14	27	12	0	0	111	11	4	2	1.9	.968	OF-68
1915			46	.197	.227	66	13	0	1	0	0.0	5	5	8	8	5	14	4	30	2	0	0	0.7	1.000	OF-46
1916			3	.000	.000	5	0	0	0	0	0.0	0	0	1	1	0	2	0	2	0	0	0	0.7	1.000	OF-1
1917	BOS	N	32	.186	.216	102	19	1	1	0	0.0	8	9	18	5	4	1	0	61	1	4	1	2.1	.939	OF-29, 1B-1
1919	WAS	A	1	.000	.000	4	0	0	0	0	0.0	0	0	0	0	0	0	0	0	0	0	0	0.0	–	OF-1
5 yrs.			150	.211	.247	417	88	1	7	0	0.0	35	33	41	41	21	17	4	204	14	8	3	1.5	.965	OF-145, 1B-1

Jim Tyack

TYACK, JAMES FRED
B. Jan. 9, 1911, Florence, Mont.

BL TR 6'2"   195 lbs.

Year	Team		Games	BA	SA	AB	H	2B	3B	HR	HR%	R	RBI	BB	SO	SB	PH AB	PH H	PO	A	E	DP	TC/G	FA	G by Pos
1943	PHI	A	54	.258	.323	155	40	8	1	0	0.0	11	23	14	9	1	12	2	82	4	2	0	1.6	.977	OF-38

Fred Tyler

TYLER, FREDERICK FRANKLIN
Brother of Lefty Tyler.
B. Dec. 16, 1891, Derry, N. H.   D. Oct. 14, 1945, East Derry, N. H.

BR TR 5'10½" 180 lbs.

Year	Team		Games	BA	SA	AB	H	2B	3B	HR	HR%	R	RBI	BB	SO	SB	PH AB	PH H	PO	A	E	DP	TC/G	FA	G by Pos
1914	BOS	N	18	.333	.333	24	8	0	0	0	0.0	2	2	0	2	0	0	0	21	8	0	1	1.6	1.000	C-6

Johnnie Tyler

TYLER, JOHN ANTHONY (Ty Ty)
Born John Tylka.
B. July 30, 1906, Mount Pleasant, Pa.   D. July 11, 1972, Mount Pleasant, Pa.

BL TR 6'   175 lbs.
BB 1934

Year	Team		Games	BA	SA	AB	H	2B	3B	HR	HR%	R	RBI	BB	SO	SB	PH AB	PH H	PO	A	E	DP	TC/G	FA	G by Pos
1934	BOS	N	3	.167	.167	6	1	0	0	0	0.0	0	1	0	3	0	2	0	3	1	0	0	1.3	1.000	OF-1
1935			13	.340	.553	47	16	2	1	2	4.3	7	11	4	3	0	1	0	24	1	3	0	2.2	.893	OF-11
2 yrs.			16	.321	.509	53	17	2	1	2	3.8	7	12	4	6	0	3	0	27	2	3	0	2.0	.906	OF-12

Lefty Tyler

TYLER, GEORGE ALBERT
Brother of Fred Tyler.
B. Dec. 14, 1889, Derry, N. H.   D. Sept. 29, 1953, Lowell, Mass.

BL TL 6'   175 lbs.

Year	Team		Games	BA	SA	AB	H	2B	3B	HR	HR%	R	RBI	BB	SO	SB	PH AB	PH H	PO	A	E	DP	TC/G	FA	G by Pos
1910	BOS	N	2	.500	.500	4	2	0	0	0	0.0	1	0	0	1	0	0	0	0	2	0	0	1.0	1.000	P-2
1911			28	.164	.197	61	10	2	0	0	0.0	10	2	8	9	0	0	0	8	58	8	2	2.6	.892	P-28
1912			42	.198	.229	96	19	3	0	0	0.0	8	5	4	16	0	0	0	15	75	5	3	2.3	.947	P-42
1913			43	.206	.275	102	21	7	0	0	0.0	13	10	11	16	0	3	1	13	107	9	1	3.0	.930	P-39
1914			38	.202	.213	94	19	1	0	0	0.0	6	4	4	20	0	0	0	16	57	5	3	2.1	.936	P-38
1915			45	.261	.375	88	23	7	0	1	1.1	11	6	4	19	0	10	1	6	50	1	1	1.3	.982	P-32
1916			39	.204	.355	93	19	3	1	3	3.2	10	20	9	15	0	3	0	9	72	3	3	2.2	.964	P-34
1917	CHI	N	55	.231	.261	134	31	4	0	0	0.0	8	11	17	19	0	12	3	105	80	2	10	3.4	.989	P-32, 1B-11
1918	CHI	N	38	.210	.220	100	21	1	0	0	0.0	9	8	9	15	0	2	0	17	88	3	3	2.8	.972	P-33
1919			6	.143	.143	7	1	0	0	0	0.0	0	1	3	2	0	1	0	1	13	0	1	2.3	1.000	P-6
1920			29	.262	.338	65	17	3	1	0	0.0	6	6	9	7	0	2	2	15	64	2	3	2.8	.975	P-27
1921			19	.231	.308	26	6	0	0	0	0.0	4	2	1	5	0	7	2	3	10	0	1	0.7	1.000	P-10
12 yrs.			384	.217	.274	870	189	33	2	4	0.5	85	75	80	143	0	39	9	208	676	38	31	2.4	.959	P-323, 1B-11

WORLD SERIES

Year	Team		Games	BA	SA	AB	H	2B	3B	HR	HR%	R	RBI	BB	SO	SB	PH AB	PH H	PO	A	E	DP	TC/G	FA	G by Pos
1914	BOS	N	1	.000	.000	3	0	0	0	0	0.0	0	0	0	1	0	0	0	1	5	0	0	6.0	1.000	P-1
1918	CHI	N	3	.200	.200	5	1	0	0	0	0.0	0	2	2	0	0	0	0	2	9	1	0	4.0	.917	P-3
2 yrs.			4	.125	.125	8	1	0	0	0	0.0	0	2	2	1	0	0	0	3	14	1	0	4.5	.944	P-4

Earl Tyree

TYREE, EARL CARLTON
B. Mar. 4, 1890, Huntsville, Ill.   D. May 17, 1954, Rushville, Ill.

BR TR 5'8"   160 lbs.

Year	Team		Games	BA	SA	AB	H	2B	3B	HR	HR%	R	RBI	BB	SO	SB	PH AB	PH H	PO	A	E	DP	TC/G	FA	G by Pos
1914	CHI	N	1	.000	.000	4	0	0	0	0	0.0	1	0	0	0	0	0	0	2	1	0	0	3.0	1.000	C-1

Jim Tyrone

TYRONE, JAMES VERNON
Brother of Wayne Tyrone.
B. Jan. 29, 1949, Alice, Tex.

BR TR 6'1"   185 lbs.

Year	Team		Games	BA	SA	AB	H	2B	3B	HR	HR%	R	RBI	BB	SO	SB	PH AB	PH H	PO	A	E	DP	TC/G	FA	G by Pos
1972	CHI	N	13	.000	.000	8	0	0	0	0	0.0	1	0	0	3	1	3	0	6	1	0	0	0.5	1.000	OF-4
1974			57	.185	.321	81	15	0	1	3	3.7	19	9	6	8	1	28	7	26	2	1	0	0.5	.966	OF-32, 3B-1
1975			11	.227	.318	22	5	0	1	0	0.0	3	0	1	4	1	5	1	7	1	0	0	0.7	1.000	OF-8
1977	OAK	A	96	.245	.340	294	72	11	1	5	1.7	32	26	25	62	3	11	5	168	5	9	0	1.9	.951	OF-81, DH-4, SS-1, 1B-1
4 yrs.			177	.227	.328	405	92	11	3	8	2.0	52	32	32	77	6	47	13	207	9	10	0	1.3	.956	OF-125, DH-4, SS-1, 3B-1, 1B-1

Year	Team		Games	BA	SA	AB	H	2B	3B	HR	HR%	R	RBI	BB	SO	SB	Pinch Hit AB	Pinch Hit H	PO	A	E	DP	TC/G	FA	G by Pos

Wayne Tyrone

TYRONE, OSCAR WAYNE
Brother of Jim Tyrone.
B. Aug. 1, 1950, Alice, Tex.

BR TR 6'1" 185 lbs.

Year	Team		Games	BA	SA	AB	H	2B	3B	HR	HR%	R	RBI	BB	SO	SB	AB	H	PO	A	E	DP	TC/G	FA	G by Pos
1976	CHI	N	30	.228	.298	57	13	1	0	1	1.8	3	8	3	21	0	14	4	39	10	0	6	1.6	1.000	OF-7, 3B-5, 1B-5

Mike Tyson

TYSON, MICHAEL RAY
B. Jan. 13, 1950, Rocky Mount, N. C.

BR TR 5'9" 170 lbs.

Year	Team		Games	BA	SA	AB	H	2B	3B	HR	HR%	R	RBI	BB	SO	SB	AB	H	PO	A	E	DP	TC/G	FA	G by Pos
1972	STL	N	13	.189	.216	37	7	1	0	0	0.0	1	0	1	9	0	0	0	26	36	3	4	5.0	.954	2B-11, SS-2
1973			144	.243	.299	469	114	15	4	1	0.2	48	33	23	66	2	0	0	239	401	33	80	4.7	.951	SS-128, 2B-16
1974			151	.223	.287	422	94	14	5	1	0.2	35	37	22	70	4	0	0	247	434	31	115	4.7	.956	SS-143, 2B-12
1975			122	.266	.342	368	98	16	3	2	0.5	45	37	24	39	5	2	0	184	308	15	52	4.2	.970	SS-95, 2B-24, 3B-5
1976			76	.286	.445	245	70	12	9	3	1.2	26	28	16	34	3	1	0	158	237	12	54	5.4	.971	2B-74
1977			138	.246	.342	418	103	15	2	7	1.7	42	57	30	48	3	2	0	267	423	15	99	5.1	.979	2B-135
1978			125	.233	.300	377	88	16	0	3	0.8	26	26	24	41	2	4	1	246	306	13	78	4.5	.977	2B-124
1979			75	.221	.363	190	42	8	2	5	2.6	18	20	13	28	2	9	2	125	184	8	42	4.2	.975	2B-71
1980	CHI	N	123	.238	.337	341	81	19	3	3	0.9	34	23	15	61	1	6	2	222	329	18	69	4.6	.968	2B-117
1981			50	.185	.272	92	17	2	0	2	2.2	6	8	7	15	1	13	4	50	76	8	14	2.7	.940	2B-36, SS-1
10 yrs.			1017	.241	.327	2959	714	118	28	27	0.9	281	269	175	411	23	37	9	1764	2734	156	607	4.6	.966	2B-620, SS-369, 3B-5

Turkey Tyson

TYSON, CECIL WASHINGTON
B. Dec. 6, 1914, Elm City, N. C.

BL TR 6'5½" 225 lbs.

Year	Team		Games	BA	SA	AB	H	2B	3B	HR	HR%	R	RBI	BB	SO	SB	AB	H	PO	A	E	DP	TC/G	FA	G by Pos
1944	PHI	N	1	.000	.000	1	0	0	0	0	0.0	0	0	0	0	0	1	0	0	0	0	0	0.0	—	

Ty Tyson

TYSON, ALBERT THOMAS
B. June 1, 1892, Wilkes-Barre, Pa. D. Aug. 16, 1953, Buffalo, N. Y.

BR TR 5'11" 169 lbs.

Year	Team		Games	BA	SA	AB	H	2B	3B	HR	HR%	R	RBI	BB	SO	SB	AB	H	PO	A	E	DP	TC/G	FA	G by Pos
1926	NY	N	97	.293	.373	335	98	16	1	3	0.9	40	35	15	28	6	4	1	232	9	5	5	2.5	.980	OF-92
1927			43	.264	.352	159	42	7	2	1	0.6	24	17	10	19	5	1	1	73	5	6	1	2.0	.929	OF-41
1928	BKN	N	59	.271	.348	210	57	11	1	1	0.5	25	21	10	14	3	1	0	130	6	5	3	2.4	.965	OF-55
3 yrs.			199	.280	.361	704	197	34	4	5	0.7	89	73	35	61	14	6	2	435	20	16	9	2.4	.966	OF-188

Bob Uecker

UECKER, ROBERT GEORGE
B. Jan. 26, 1935, Milwaukee, Wis.

BR TR 6'1" 190 lbs.

Year	Team		Games	BA	SA	AB	H	2B	3B	HR	HR%	R	RBI	BB	SO	SB	AB	H	PO	A	E	DP	TC/G	FA	G by Pos
1962	MIL	N	33	.250	.328	64	16	2	0	1	1.6	5	8	7	15	0	7	2	101	10	2	4	3.4	.982	C-24
1963			13	.250	.375	16	4	2	0	0	0.0	3	0	2	5	0	2	1	21	2	1	1	1.8	.958	C-6
1964	STL	N	40	.198	.236	106	21	1	0	1	0.9	8	6	17	24	0	0	0	201	20	3	2	5.6	.987	C-40
1965			53	.228	.317	145	33	7	0	2	1.4	17	10	24	27	0	5	0	240	29	4	1	5.2	.985	C-49
1966	PHI	N	78	.208	.338	207	43	6	0	7	3.4	15	30	22	36	0	4	0	368	33	6	7	5.2	.985	C-76
1967	2 teams	PHI	N (18G – .171)			ATL	N	(62G – .146)																		
"	total		80	.150	.218	193	29	4	0	3	1.6	17	20	24	60	0	6	1	348	36	11	3	4.9	.972	C-76
6 yrs.			297	.200	.287	731	146	22	0	14	1.9	65	74	96	167	0	29	5	1279	130	27	18	4.8	.981	C-271

Frenchy Uhalt

UHALT, BERNARD BARTHOLOMEW
B. Apr. 27, 1910, Bakersfield, Calif.

BL TR 5'10" 180 lbs.

Year	Team		Games	BA	SA	AB	H	2B	3B	HR	HR%	R	RBI	BB	SO	SB	AB	H	PO	A	E	DP	TC/G	FA	G by Pos
1934	CHI	A	57	.242	.285	165	40	5	1	0	0.0	28	16	29	12	6	13	4	85	5	6	1	1.6	.935	OF-40

Ted Uhlaender

UHLAENDER, THEODORE OTTO
B. Oct. 21, 1940, Chicago Heights, Ill.

BL TR 6'2" 190 lbs.

Year	Team		Games	BA	SA	AB	H	2B	3B	HR	HR%	R	RBI	BB	SO	SB	AB	H	PO	A	E	DP	TC/G	FA	G by Pos
1965	MIN	A	13	.182	.182	22	4	0	0	0	0.0	1	1	0	2	1	8	2	7	1	0	0	0.6	1.000	OF-4
1966			105	.226	.286	367	83	12	2	2	0.5	39	22	27	33	10	3	0	258	4	4	2	2.5	.985	OF-100
1967			133	.258	.381	415	107	19	7	6	1.4	41	49	13	45	4	11	2	255	6	1	3	2.0	.996	OF-118
1968			140	.283	.389	488	138	21	5	7	1.4	52	52	28	46	16	2	0	283	3	4	1	2.1	.986	OF-129
1969			152	.273	.356	554	151	18	2	8	1.4	93	62	44	52	15	5	3	278	8	1	1	1.9	.997	OF-150
1970	CLE	A	141	.268	.391	473	127	21	2	11	2.3	56	46	39	44	3	11	5	225	5	2	1	1.6	.991	OF-134
1971			141	.288	.352	500	144	20	3	2	0.4	52	47	38	44	3	11	2	245	6	2	0	1.8	.992	OF-131
1972	CIN	N	73	.159	.186	113	18	3	0	0	0.0	9	6	13	11	0	41	3	37	3	1	0	0.6	.976	OF-27
8 yrs.			898	.263	.353	2932	772	114	21	36	1.2	343	285	202	277	52	92	17	1588	36	15	8	1.8	.991	OF-793

LEAGUE CHAMPIONSHIP SERIES

Year	Team		Games	BA	SA	AB	H	2B	3B	HR	HR%	R	RBI	BB	SO	SB	AB	H	PO	A	E	DP	TC/G	FA	G by Pos
1969	MIN	A	2	.167	.167	6	1	0	0	0	0.0	0	0	0	0	0	0	0	4	0	1	0	2.5	.800	OF-2
1972	CIN	N	2	.500	.500	2	1	0	0	0	0.0	0	0	0	0	0	2	1	0	0	0	0	0.0		
2 yrs.			4	.250	.250	8	2	0	0	0	0.0	0	0	0	0	0	2	1	4	0	1	0	1.3	.800	OF-2

WORLD SERIES

Year	Team		Games	BA	SA	AB	H	2B	3B	HR	HR%	R	RBI	BB	SO	SB	AB	H	PO	A	E	DP	TC/G	FA	G by Pos
1972	CIN	N	4	.250	.500	4	1	0	0	0	0.0	0	0	0	1	0	4	1	0	0	0	0	0.0	—	

George Uhle

UHLE, GEORGE ERNEST (The Bull)
B. Sept. 18, 1898, Cleveland, Ohio D. Feb. 26, 1985, Lakewood, Ohio

BR TR 6' 190 lbs.

Year	Team		Games	BA	SA	AB	H	2B	3B	HR	HR%	R	RBI	BB	SO	SB	AB	H	PO	A	E	DP	TC/G	FA	G by Pos
1919	CLE	A	26	.302	.395	43	13	0	0	0	0.0	7	6	1	5	0	0	0	10	33	4	1	1.8	.915	P-26
1920			27	.344	.344	32	11	0	0	0	0.0	4	2	2	2	1	0	0	6	21	0	0	1.0	1.000	P-27
1921			48	.245	.362	94	23	2	3	1	1.1	21	18	6	9	0	0	0	15	46	4	2	1.4	.938	P-41, C-1
1922			56	.266	.376	109	29	8	2	0	0.0	21	14	13	6	1	2	2	16	53	5	5	1.3	.932	P-50
1923			58	.361	.472	144	52	10	3	0	0.0	23	22	7	10	2	3	0	18	89	2	9	1.9	.982	P-54
1924			59	.308	.411	107	33	6	1	1	0.9	10	19	4	8	0	26	11	19	42	0	5	1.0	1.000	P-28
1925			56	.279	.365	104	29	3	3	0	0.0	10	13	7	7	0	22	5	12	39	3	2	1.0	.944	P-29
1926			50	.227	.273	132	30	3	0	0	0.0	16	11	10	12	2	8	1	30	67	7	3	2.1	.933	P-39
1927			43	.266	.380	79	21	7	0	1	1.3	4	14	5	12	0	18	5	6	31	1	3	0.9	.974	P-25
1928			55	.286		98	28	3	1	1	1.0	9	8	20	4	0	20	4	10	59	2	4	1.3	.972	P-31
1929	DET	A	40	.343	.370	108	37	1	1	0	0.0	18	13	6	6	0	7	1	13	39	4	2	1.4	.929	P-32
1930			59	.308	.427	117	36	4	2	2	1.7	15	21	8	13	0	21	5	10	29	1	2	0.7	.975	P-33
1931			53	.244	.378	90	22	6	0	2	2.2	8	7	8	8	0	21	3	3	38	0	1	0.8	1.000	P-29
1932			38	.182	.273	55	10	3	0	2	3.6	6	5	0	4	0	5	1	5	25	0	0	0.8	1.000	P-33

Year	Team	Games	BA	SA	AB	H	2B	3B	HR	HR%	R	RBI	BB	SO	SB	Pinch Hit AB	H	PO	A	E	DP	TC/G	FA	G by Pos

George Uhle *continued*

Year	Team	Games	BA	SA	AB	H	2B	3B	HR	HR%	R	RBI	BB	SO	SB	PH AB	PH H	PO	A	E	DP	TC/G	FA	G by Pos
1933	3 teams	DET A (1G – .000)			NY N (8G – .000)				NY A (12G – .400)															
"	total	21	.320	.360	25	8	1	0	0	0.0	2	1	5	5	0	2	0	1	13	0	1	0.7	1.000	P-19
1934	NY A	10	.600	1.000	5	3	0	1	0	0.0	1	1	0	0	0	0	0	1	1	0	0	0.2	1.000	P-10
1936	CLE A	24	.381	.571	21	8	1	0	1	4.8	1	4	2	0	0	14	6	0	0	0	0	0.0	–	P-7
17 yrs.		723	.288	.383	1363	393	60	21	9	0.7	172	187	98	112	6	169	44	175	625	33	42	1.2	.960	P-513, C-1

WORLD SERIES

| 1920 | CLE A | 2 | – | – | 0 | 0 | 0 | 0 | 0 | – | 0 | 0 | 0 | 0 | 0 | 0 | 0 | 0 | 1 | 0 | 0 | 0.5 | 1.000 | P-1 |

Maury Uhler

UHLER, MAURICE WILLIAM
B. Dec. 14, 1886, Pikesville, Md. D. May 4, 1918, Baltimore, Md.   BR TR 5'11" 165 lbs.

| 1914 | CIN N | 46 | .214 | .250 | 56 | 12 | 2 | 0 | 0 | 0.0 | 12 | 3 | 5 | 11 | 4 | 3 | 0 | 40 | 1 | 3 | 0 | 1.0 | .932 | OF-36 |

Charlie Uhlir

UHLIR, CHARLES KAREL
B. July 30, 1912, Chicago, Ill.   BL TL 5'7½" 150 lbs.

| 1934 | CHI A | 14 | .148 | .148 | 27 | 4 | 0 | 0 | 0 | 0.0 | 3 | 3 | 2 | 6 | 1 | 5 | 0 | 9 | 0 | 0 | 0 | 0.6 | 1.000 | OF-6 |

Mike Ulisney

ULISNEY, MICHAEL EDWARD (Slugs)
B. Sept. 28, 1917, Greenwald, Pa.   BR TR 5'9" 165 lbs.

| 1945 | BOS N | 11 | .389 | .611 | 18 | 7 | 1 | 0 | 1 | 5.6 | 4 | 4 | 1 | 0 | 0 | 5 | 2 | 4 | 1 | 2 | 0 | 0.6 | .714 | C-4 |

Scott Ullger

ULLGER, SCOTT MATTHEW
B. June 10, 1956, New York, N. Y.   BR TR 6'3" 196 lbs.

| 1983 | MIN A | 35 | .190 | .241 | 79 | 15 | 4 | 0 | 0 | 0.0 | 8 | 5 | 5 | 21 | 0 | 3 | 0 | 186 | 11 | 2 | 14 | 5.7 | .990 | 1B-30, 3B-3, DH-1 |

George Ulrich

ULRICH, GEORGE T.
B. 1870, Philadelphia, Pa.

1892	WAS N	6	.292	.333	24	7	1	0	0	0.0	1	0	0	4	2	0	0	9	14	2	1	4.2	.920	3B-3, SS-2, C-2
1893	CIN N	1	.000	.000	3	0	0	0	0	0.0	0	0	0	1	0	0	0	1	0	0	0	1.0	1.000	OF-1
1896	NY N	14	.178	.200	45	8	1	0	0	0.0	4	1	1	0	1	0	0	20	6	5	1	2.2	.839	OF-11, 3B-3
3 yrs.		21	.208	.236	72	15	2	0	0	0.0	5	1	1	5	3	0	0	30	20	7	2	2.7	.877	OF-12, 3B-6, SS-2, C-2

Tommy Umphlett

UMPHLETT, THOMAS MULLEN
B. May 12, 1930, Scotland Neck, N. C.   BR TR 6'2" 180 lbs.

1953	BOS A	137	.283	.376	495	140	27	5	3	0.6	53	59	34	30	4	1	0	382	12	7	1	2.9	.983	OF-136
1954	WAS A	114	.219	.269	342	75	8	3	1	0.3	21	33	17	42	1	15	0	169	13	2	4	1.6	.989	OF-101
1955		110	.217	.266	323	70	10	0	2	0.6	34	19	24	35	2	8	1	237	8	3	1	2.3	.988	OF-103
3 yrs.		361	.246	.314	1160	285	45	8	6	0.5	108	111	75	107	7	24	1	788	33	12	6	2.3	.986	OF-340

Bob Unglaub

UNGLAUB, ROBERT ALEXANDER
B. July 31, 1881, Baltimore, Md. D. Nov. 29, 1916, Baltimore, Md.   BR TR 5'11" 178 lbs.
Manager 1907.

1904	2 teams	NY A (6G – .211)			BOS A (9G – .154)																			
"	total	15	.188	.219	32	6	1	0	0	0.0	3	4	1		0	0	0	12	10	6	1	1.9	.786	3B-6, 2B-3, SS-2
1905	BOS A	43	.223	.281	121	27	5	1	0	0.0	18	11	6		2	12	2	87	55	10	3	3.5	.934	3B-21, 2B-8, 1B-2
1907		139	.254	.338	544	138	17	13	1	0.2	49	62	23		14	0	0	1504	84	22	71	11.6	.986	1B-139
1908	2 teams	BOS A (72G – .263)			WAS A (72G – .308)																			
"	total	144	.286	.360	542	155	21	8	1	0.2	46	54	15		14	1	0	894	232	31	38	8.0	.973	1B-76, 3B-39, 2B-27
1909	WAS A	130	.265	.350	480	127	14	9	3	0.6	43	41	22		15	1	0	669	121	13	39	6.2	.984	1B-57, OF-43, 2B-25, 3B-4
1910		124	.234	.274	431	101	9	4	0	0.0	29	44	21		21	1	0	1230	79	20	51	10.7	.985	1B-124
6 yrs.		595	.258	.328	2150	554	67	35	5	0.2	188	216	88		66	19	2	4396	581	102	203	8.5	.980	1B-398, 3B-70, 2B-63, OF-43, SS-2

Al Unser

UNSER, ALBERT BERNARD
Father of Del Unser.
B. Oct. 12, 1912, Morrisonville, Ill.   BR TR 6'1" 175 lbs.

1942	DET A	4	.375	.375	8	3	0	0	0	0.0	2	0	0	2	0	0	0	11	3	0	0	3.5	1.000	C-4
1943		38	.248	.297	101	25	5	0	0	0.0	14	4	15	15	0	0	0	143	20	3	4	4.4	.982	C-37
1944		11	.120	.320	25	3	0	1	1	4.0	2	5	3	2	0	5	2	12	7	3	2	2.0	.864	2B-5, C-1
1945	CIN N	67	.265	.387	204	54	10	3	3	1.5	23	21	14	24	0	5	2	207	30	11	5	3.7	.956	C-61
4 yrs.		120	.251	.355	338	85	15	4	4	1.2	41	30	32	43	0	10	4	373	60	17	11	3.8	.962	C-103, 2B-5

Del Unser

UNSER, DELBERT BERNARD
Son of Al Unser.
B. Dec. 9, 1944, Decatur, Ill.   BL TL 6'1" 180 lbs.

1968	WAS A	156	.230	.277	635	146	13	7	1	0.2	66	30	46	66	11	1	1	392	22	5	10	2.7	.988	OF-156, 1B-1
1969		153	.286	.382	581	166	19	8	7	1.2	69	57	58	54	8	11	3	339	8	10	3	2.3	.972	OF-149
1970		119	.258	.326	322	83	5	1	5	1.6	37	30	30	29	1	21	2	173	8	3	2	1.5	.984	OF-103
1971		153	.255	.355	581	148	19	6	9	1.5	63	41	59	68	11	2	0	394	10	8	2	2.7	.981	OF-151
1972	CLE A	132	.238	.277	383	91	12	0	1	0.3	29	17	28	46	5	15	4	248	10	3	1	2.0	.989	OF-119
1973	PHI N	136	.289	.427	440	127	20	4	11	2.5	64	52	47	55	5	12	2	329	14	4	4	2.6	.988	OF-132
1974		142	.264	.399	454	120	18	5	11	2.4	72	61	50	62	6	13	2	300	13	6	0	2.2	.981	OF-135
1975	NY N	147	.294	.392	531	156	18	2	10	1.9	65	53	37	76	4	3	1	362	13	5	2	2.6	.987	OF-144
1976	2 teams	NY N (77G – .228)			MON N (69G – .227)																			
"	total	146	.228	.355	496	113	19	4	12	2.4	57	40	29	84	7	7	1	288	10	3	2	2.1	.990	OF-142
1977	MON N	113	.273	.453	289	79	14	1	12	4.2	33	40	33	41	2	21	4	280	13	3	15	2.6	.990	1B-72, 1B-27
1978		130	.196	.257	179	35	5	0	2	1.1	16	15	24	29	2	37	3	232	12	2	16	1.9	.992	1B-64, OF-33
1979	PHI N	95	.298	.482	141	42	8	0	6	4.3	26	29	14	33	2	46	14	118	5	3	6	1.3	.976	OF-30, 1B-22
1980		96	.264	.391	110	29	6	4	0	0.0	15	10	10	21	0	38	12	116	13	0	7	1.3	1.000	1B-31, OF-23
1981		62	.153	.203	59	9	3	0	0	0.0	5	6	13	9	0	26	5	63	5	0	4	1.1	1.000	1B-18, OF-16

Year	Team		Games	BA	SA	AB	H	2B	3B	HR	HR%	R	RBI	BB	SO	SB	Pinch Hit AB	Pinch Hit H	PO	A	E	DP	TC/G	FA	G by Pos

Del Unser *continued*

| 1982 | | | 19 | .000 | .000 | 14 | 0 | 0 | 0 | 0 | 0.0 | 0 | 0 | 3 | 2 | 0 | 11 | 0 | 9 | 1 | 0 | 1 | 0.5 | 1.000 | 1B-5, OF-2 |
| 15 yrs. | | | 1799 | .258 | .358 | 5215 | 1344 | 179 | 42 | 87 | 1.7 | 617 | 481 | 481 | 675 | 64 | 264 | 54 | 3643 | 157 | 55 | 75 | 2.1 | .986 | OF-1407, 1B-168 |

LEAGUE CHAMPIONSHIP SERIES

| 1980 | PHI | N | 5 | .400 | .600 | 5 | 2 | 1 | 0 | 0 | 0.0 | 2 | 1 | 0 | 2 | 0 | 3 | 1 | 2 | 0 | 0 | 0 | 0.4 | 1.000 | OF-2 |

WORLD SERIES

| 1980 | PHI | N | 3 | .500 | .833 | 6 | 3 | 2 | 0 | 0 | 0.0 | 2 | 2 | 0 | 1 | 0 | 2 | 2 | 1 | 0 | 0 | 0 | 0.3 | 1.000 | OF-3 |

John Upham

UPHAM, JOHN LESLIE
B. Dec. 29, 1941, Windsor, Ont., Canada
BL TL 6' 180 lbs.

1967	CHI	N	8	.667	.667	3	2	0	0	0	0.0	1	0	0	0	0	0	0	0	0	0	0	0.0	–	P-5
1968			13	.200	.200	10	2	0	0	0	0.0	0	0	0	3	0	6	1	0	3	0	0	0.2	1.000	OF-2, P-2
2 yrs.			21	.308	.308	13	4	0	0	0	0.0	1	0	0	3	0	9	3	0	3	0	0	0.1	1.000	P-7, OF-2

Dixie Upright

UPRIGHT, ROY T.
Born R T Upright.
B. May 30, 1926, Kannapolis, N. C. D. Nov. 13, 1986, Concord, N. C.
BL TL 6' 175 lbs.

| 1953 | STL | A | 9 | .250 | .625 | 8 | 2 | 0 | 0 | 1 | 12.5 | 3 | 1 | 1 | 3 | 0 | 8 | 2 | 0 | 0 | 0 | 0 | 0.0 | – | |

Willie Upshaw

UPSHAW, WILLIE CLAY
B. Apr. 27, 1957, Blanco, Tex.
BL TL 6' 185 lbs.

1978	TOR	A	95	.237	.304	224	53	8	2	1	0.4	26	17	21	35	4	12	1	131	4	7	5	1.5	.951	OF-52, DH-18, 1B-10
1980			34	.213	.344	61	13	3	1	1	1.6	10	5	6	14	1	9	2	51	7	1	11	1.7	.983	1B-14, DH-12, OF-1
1981			61	.171	.324	111	19	3	1	4	3.6	15	10	11	16	2	17	4	72	6	0	8	1.3	1.000	DH-15, OF-14, 1B-14
1982			160	.267	.443	580	155	25	7	21	3.6	77	75	52	91	8	2	0	1438	101	17	123	9.7	.989	1B-155, DH-5
1983			160	.306	.515	579	177	26	7	27	4.7	99	104	61	98	10	4	1	1294	117	21	131	9.0	.985	1B-159, DH-1
1984			152	.278	.464	569	158	31	9	19	3.3	79	84	55	86	10	0	0	1246	103	14	133	9.0	.990	1B-151, DH-1
1985			148	.275	.447	501	138	31	4	15	3.0	79	65	48	71	8	2	0	1157	104	10	111	8.6	.992	1B-147, DH-1
1986			155	.251	.368	573	144	28	6	9	1.6	85	60	78	87	23	2	0	1314	131	12	118	9.4	.992	1B-154, DH-1
1987			150	.244	.391	512	125	22	4	15	2.9	68	58	58	78	10	7	2	1169	127	9	114	8.7	.993	1B-146
1988	CLE	A	149	.245	.369	493	121	22	8	11	2.2	58	50	62	66	12	7	2	1162	102	12	93	8.6	.991	1B-144
10 yrs.			1264	.262	.419	4203	1103	199	45	123	2.9	596	528	452	642	88	62	12	9034	802	103	847	7.9	.990	1B-1094, OF-67, DH-54

LEAGUE CHAMPIONSHIP SERIES

| 1985 | TOR | A | 7 | .231 | .308 | 26 | 6 | 2 | 0 | 0 | 0.0 | 2 | 1 | 1 | 4 | 0 | 0 | 0 | 53 | 7 | 1 | 3 | 8.7 | .984 | 1B-7 |

Tom Upton

UPTON, THOMAS HERBERT (Muscles)
Brother of Bill Upton.
B. Dec. 29, 1926, Esther, Mo.
BR TR 6' 160 lbs.

1950	STL	A	124	.237	.296	389	92	5	6	2	0.5	50	30	52	45	7	5	0	199	333	30	65	4.5	.947	SS-115, 2B-2, 3B-1
1951			52	.198	.275	131	26	4	3	0	0.0	9	12	12	22	1	0	0	80	105	10	33	3.8	.949	SS-47
1952	WAS	A	5	.000	.000	5	0	0	0	0	0.0	1	0	1	0	0	0	0	3	8	0	1	2.2	1.000	SS-3
3 yrs.			181	.225	.288	525	118	9	9	2	0.4	60	42	65	67	8	5	0	282	446	40	99	4.2	.948	SS-165, 2B-2, 3B-1

Luke Urban

URBAN, LOUIS JOHN
B. Mar. 22, 1898, Fall River, Mass. D. Dec. 7, 1980, Somerset, Mass.
BR TR 5'8" 168 lbs.

1927	BOS	N	35	.288	.333	111	32	5	0	0	0.0	11	10	3	6	1	1	1	59	30	5	1	2.7	.947	C-34
1928			15	.176	.176	17	3	0	0	0	0.0	0	2	0	1	0	5	1	12	5	0	0	1.1	1.000	C-5
2 yrs.			50	.273	.313	128	35	5	0	0	0.0	11	12	3	7	1	6	2	71	35	5	1	2.2	.955	C-39

Billy Urbanski

URBANSKI, WILLIAM MICHAEL
B. June 5, 1903, Linoleumville, N. Y. D. July 12, 1973, Perth Amboy, N. J.
BR TR 5'8" 165 lbs.

1931	BOS	N	82	.238	.307	303	72	13	4	0	0.0	22	17	10	32	3	0	0	103	188	11	23	3.7	.964	3B-68, SS-19
1932			136	.272	.387	563	153	25	8	8	1.4	80	46	28	60	8	0	0	316	461	44	91	6.0	.946	SS-136
1933			144	.251	.302	566	142	21	4	0	0.0	65	35	33	48	4	1	0	299	473	38	91	5.6	.953	SS-143
1934			146	.293	.397	605	177	30	6	7	1.2	104	53	56	37	4	1	0	298	457	31	84	5.4	.961	SS-145
1935			132	.230	.286	514	118	17	0	4	0.8	53	30	40	32	3	0	0	258	356	40	52	5.0	.939	SS-129
1936			122	.261	.316	494	129	17	5	0	0.0	55	26	31	42	2	3	1	224	280	31	63	4.4	.942	SS-80, 3B-38
1937			1	.000	.000	1	0	0	0	0	0.0	0	0	0	1	0	1	0	0	0	0	0	0.0	–	
7 yrs.			763	.260	.337	3046	791	123	27	19	0.6	379	207	198	252	24	6	1	1498	2215	195	404	5.1	.950	SS-652, 3B-106

Jose Uribe

URIBE, JOSE ALTAGRACIA
Born Jose Altagracia Gonzalez y Uribe. Played as Jose Gonzalez in 1984.
B. Jan. 21, 1952, San Cristobal, Dominican Republic
BB TR 5'10" 156 lbs.

1984	STL	N	8	.211	.211	19	4	0	0	0	0.0	4	3	0	2	1	0	0	7	15	1	4	2.9	.957	SS-5, 2B-1
1985	SF	N	147	.237	.315	476	113	20	4	3	0.6	46	26	30	57	8	2	0	209	438	26	77	4.6	.961	SS-145, 2B-1
1986			157	.223	.280	453	101	15	1	3	0.7	46	43	61	76	22	2	1	249	444	16	95	4.5	.977	SS-156
1987			95	.291	.424	309	90	16	5	5	1.6	44	30	24	35	12	3	1	145	286	13	62	4.7	.971	SS-95
1988			141	.252	.318	493	124	10	7	3	0.6	47	35	36	69	14	0	0	212	404	19	77	4.5	.970	SS-140
1989			151	.221	.280	453	100	12	6	1	0.2	34	30	34	74	6	0	0	225	436	18	85	4.5	.973	SS-150
6 yrs.			699	.241	.316	2203	532	73	23	15	0.7	221	167	185	313	63	7	2	1047	2023	93	400	4.5	.971	SS-691, 2B-2

LEAGUE CHAMPIONSHIP SERIES

1987	SF	N	7	.269	.308	26	7	1	0	0	0.0	1	2	0	4	1	0	0	11	21	1	7	4.7	.970	SS-7
1989			5	.235	.294	17	4	1	0	0	0.0	2	1	1	5	1	0	0	6	9	2	2	3.4	.882	SS-5
2 yrs.			12	.256	.302	43	11	2	0	0	0.0	3	3	1	9	2	0	0	17	30	3	9	4.2	.940	SS-12

WORLD SERIES

| 1989 | SF | N | 3 | .200 | .200 | 5 | 1 | 0 | 0 | 0 | 0.0 | 1 | 0 | 0 | 0 | 0 | 0 | 0 | 1 | 3 | 0 | 0 | 1.3 | 1.000 | SS-3 |

Year Team	Games	BA	SA	AB	H	2B	3B	HR	HR%	R	RBI	BB	SO	SB	Pinch Hit AB	Pinch Hit H	PO	A	E	DP	TC/G	FA	G by Pos

Lou Ury
URY, LOUIS NEWTON   TR 6'
B. Apr., 1877, Fort Scott, Kans.   D. Mar. 4, 1918, Kansas City, Mo.

Year Team	Games	BA	SA	AB	H	2B	3B	HR	HR%	R	RBI	BB	SO	SB	AB	H	PO	A	E	DP	TC/G	FA	G by Pos
1903 STL N	2	.143	.143	7	1	0	0	0	0.0	0	0	0	0	0			23	1	0	1	12.0	1.000	1B-2

Bob Usher
USHER, ROBERT ROYCE   BR TR 6'1½" 180 lbs.
B. Mar. 1, 1925, San Diego, Calif.

Year Team	Games	BA	SA	AB	H	2B	3B	HR	HR%	R	RBI	BB	SO	SB	AB	H	PO	A	E	DP	TC/G	FA	G by Pos
1946 CIN N	92	.204	.270	152	31	5	1	1	0.7	16	14	13	27	2	1	0	104	9	2	3	1.3	.983	OF-80, 3B-1
1947	9	.182	.318	22	4	0	0	1	4.5	2	1	2	2	0	0	0	16	1	0	0	1.9	1.000	OF-8
1950	106	.259	.368	321	83	17	0	6	1.9	51	35	27	38	3	10	2	190	7	3	1	1.9	.985	OF-95
1951	114	.208	.310	303	63	12	2	5	1.7	27	25	19	36	4	13	2	218	9	6	4	2.0	.974	OF-98
1952 CHI N	1	–	–	0	0	0	0	0	–	0	0	1	0	0			0	0	0	0		–	
1957 2 teams	CLE A	(10G – .125)			WAS A	(96G – .261)																	
" total	106	.257	.337	303	78	7	1	5	1.7	37	27	28	33	1	4	0	231	7	5	2	2.3	.979	OF-99, 3B-1
6 yrs.	428	.235	.329	1101	259	41	4	18	1.6	133	102	90	136	9	28	4	759	33	16	10	1.9	.980	OF-380, 3B-2

Dutch Ussat
USSAT, WILLIAM AUGUST   BR TR 6'1" 170 lbs.
B. Apr. 11, 1904, Dayton, Ohio   D. May 29, 1959, Dayton, Ohio

Year Team	Games	BA	SA	AB	H	2B	3B	HR	HR%	R	RBI	BB	SO	SB	AB	H	PO	A	E	DP	TC/G	FA	G by Pos
1925 CLE A	1	.000	.000	1	0	0	0	0	0.0	0	0	0	0	0	0	0	0	1	0	0	1.0	1.000	2B-1
1927	4	.188	.313	16	3	0	1	0	0.0	4	2	2	1	0	0	0	5	6	0	1	2.8	1.000	3B-4
2 yrs.	5	.176	.294	17	3	0	1	0	0.0	4	2	2	1	0	0	0	5	7	0	1	2.4	1.000	3B-4, 2B-1

Tex Vache
VACHE, ERNEST LEWIS   BR TR 6'1" 200 lbs.
B. Nov. 17, 1894, Santa Monica, Calif.   D. June 11, 1953, Los Angeles, Calif.

Year Team	Games	BA	SA	AB	H	2B	3B	HR	HR%	R	RBI	BB	SO	SB	AB	H	PO	A	E	DP	TC/G	FA	G by Pos
1925 BOS A	110	.313	.464	252	79	15	7	3	1.2	41	48	21	33	2	49	10	87	2	9	0	0.9	.908	OF-53

Gene Vadeboncoeur
VADEBONCOEUR, EUGENE F.   BR TR 5'6" 150 lbs.
B. Louiseville, Quebec, Canada   D. Oct. 16, 1935, Haverhill, Mass.

Year Team	Games	BA	SA	AB	H	2B	3B	HR	HR%	R	RBI	BB	SO	SB	AB	H	PO	A	E	DP	TC/G	FA	G by Pos
1884 PHI N	4	.214	.214	14	3	0	0	0	0.0	1		1	2		0	0	13	9	4	0	6.5	.846	C-4

Harry Vahrenhorst
VAHRENHORST, HARRY HENRY   BR TR 6'1" 175 lbs.
B. Feb. 13, 1885, St. Louis, Mo.   D. Oct. 10, 1943, St. Louis, Mo.

Year Team	Games	BA	SA	AB	H	2B	3B	HR	HR%	R	RBI	BB	SO	SB	AB	H	PO	A	E	DP	TC/G	FA	G by Pos
1904 STL A	1	.000	.000	1	0	0	0	0	0.0	0	0	0	1	0	0	0	0	0	0	0	0.0	–	

Mike Vail
VAIL, MICHAEL LEWIS   BR TR 6'1" 180 lbs.
B. Nov. 10, 1951, San Francisco, Calif.

Year Team	Games	BA	SA	AB	H	2B	3B	HR	HR%	R	RBI	BB	SO	SB	AB	H	PO	A	E	DP	TC/G	FA	G by Pos
1975 NY N	38	.302	.420	162	49	8	1	3	1.9	17	17	9	37	0	1	1	92	9	3	1	2.7	.971	OF-36
1976	53	.217	.266	143	31	5	1	0	0.0	8	9	6	19	0	17	4	63	1	4	0	1.3	.941	OF-35
1977	108	.262	.398	279	73	12	1	8	2.9	29	35	19	58	0	30	4	159	5	6	2	1.6	.965	OF-85
1978 2 teams	CLE A	(14G – .235)			CHI N	(74G – .333)																	
" total	88	.318	.439	214	68	8	3	4	1.9	17	35	4	33	1	35	13	68	1	1	0	0.8	.986	OF-54, DH-1, 3B-1
1979 CHI N	87	.335	.520	179	60	8	2	7	3.9	28	35	14	27	0	44	12	51	4	2	0	0.7	.965	OF-39, 3B-2
1980	114	.298	.423	312	93	17	2	6	1.9	30	47	14	77	2	45	8	126	5	5	1	1.2	.963	OF-77
1981 CIN N	31	.161	.161	31	5	0	0	0	0.0	1	3	0	9	0	28	5	3	0	0	0	0.1	1.000	OF-3
1982	78	.254	.381	189	48	10	1	4	2.1	9	29	6	33	0	29	7	72	7	1	0	1.0	.988	OF-52
1983 2 teams	SF N	(18G – .154)			MON N	(34G – .283)																	
" total	52	.241	.354	79	19	3	0	2	2.5	6	7	8	17	0	25	5	50	5	1	1	1.1	.982	OF-17, 1B-5, 3B-1
1984 LA N	16	.063	.063	16	1	0	0	0	0.0	4	1	2	1	1	7	0	13	0	0	0	0.0	1.000	OF-1
10 yrs.	665	.279	.400	1604	447	71	11	34	2.1	146	219	81	317	3	267	61	684	37	23	5	1.1	.969	OF-399, 1B-5, 3B-4, DH-1

Roy Valdes
VALDES, ROGELIO LAZARO   BR TR 5'11" 185 lbs.
Born Rogelio Lazaro Valdes y Rojas.
B. Feb. 20, 1920, Havana, Cuba

Year Team	Games	BA	SA	AB	H	2B	3B	HR	HR%	R	RBI	BB	SO	SB	AB	H	PO	A	E	DP	TC/G	FA	G by Pos
1944 WAS A	1	.000	.000	1	0	0	0	0	0.0	0	0	0	0	0	1	0	0	0	0	0	0.0	–	

Sandy Valdespino
VALDESPINO, HILARIO   BL TL 5'8" 170 lbs.
Born Hilario Valdespino y Borroto.
B. Jan. 24, 1939, San Jose de las Lajas, Cuba

Year Team	Games	BA	SA	AB	H	2B	3B	HR	HR%	R	RBI	BB	SO	SB	AB	H	PO	A	E	DP	TC/G	FA	G by Pos
1965 MIN A	108	.261	.322	245	64	8	2	1	0.4	38	22	20	28	7	47	10	94	4	1	1	0.9	.990	OF-57
1966	52	.176	.259	108	19	1	1	2	1.9	11	9	4	24	2	27	2	36	0	0	0	0.7	1.000	OF-23
1967	99	.165	.216	97	16	2	0	1	1.0	9	3	5	22	3	33	7	40	3	1	0	0.4	.977	OF-65
1968 ATL N	36	.233	.279	86	20	1	0	1	1.2	8	4	10	20	0	15	1	40	0	1	0	1.1	.976	OF-20
1969 2 teams	HOU N	(41G – .244)			SEA A	(20G – .211)																	
" total	61	.236	.268	157	37	5	0	0	0.0	20	14	16	26	2	22	3	60	4	4	0	1.1	.941	OF-36
1970 MIL A	8	.000	.000	9	0	0	0	0	0.0	0	0	0	4	0	9	0	0	0	0	0	0.0	–	OF-1
1971 KC A	18	.317	.508	63	20	6	0	2	3.2	10	15	2	5	0	4	2	18	1	1	0	1.1	.950	OF-15
7 yrs.	382	.230	.295	765	176	23	3	7	0.9	96	67	57	129	14	155	25	288	12	8	1	0.8	.974	OF-217

WORLD SERIES

Year Team	Games	BA	SA	AB	H	2B	3B	HR	HR%	R	RBI	BB	SO	SB	AB	H	PO	A	E	DP	TC/G	FA	G by Pos
1965 MIN A	5	.273	.364	11	3	1	0	0	0.0	1	0	1	0	1	0	3	6	0	0	0	1.2	1.000	OF-2

Julio Valdez
VALDEZ, JULIO JULIAN   BB TR 6'2" 160 lbs.
Born Julio Julian Castillo y Valdez.
B. June 3, 1956, San Cristobal, Dominican Republic

Year Team	Games	BA	SA	AB	H	2B	3B	HR	HR%	R	RBI	BB	SO	SB	AB	H	PO	A	E	DP	TC/G	FA	G by Pos
1980 BOS A	8	.263	.474	19	5	1	0	1	5.3	4	4	0	5	2	0	0	17	26	3	10	5.8	.935	SS-8
1981	17	.217	.217	23	5	0	0	0	0.0	1	3	0	2	0	0	0	12	30	2	3	2.6	.955	SS-17
1982	28	.250	.300	20	5	1	0	0	0.0	3	1	0	7	1	2	1	16	24	1	5	1.5	.976	SS-22, DH-3
1983	12	.120	.120	25	3	0	0	0	0.0	3	0	1	4	0	0	0	16	16	2	3	2.8	.941	2B-9, SS-3, DH-1
4 yrs.	65	.207	.264	87	18	2	0	1	1.1	11	8	1	18	3	2	1	61	96	8	21	2.5	.952	SS-49, 2B-9, DH-4

Jose Valdivielso
VALDIVIELSO, JOSE   BR TR 6'1" 175 lbs.
Born Jose Martinez Valdivielso y Lopez.
B. May 22, 1934, Matanzas, Cuba

Year Team	Games	BA	SA	AB	H	2B	3B	HR	HR%	R	RBI	BB	SO	SB	Pinch Hit AB	Pinch Hit H	PO	A	E	DP	TC/G	FA	G by Pos

Jose Valdivielso *continued*

Year Team	Games	BA	SA	AB	H	2B	3B	HR	HR%	R	RBI	BB	SO	SB	AB	H	PO	A	E	DP	TC/G	FA	G by Pos
1955 WAS A	94	.221	.316	294	65	12	5	2	0.7	32	28	21	38	1	0	0	160	317	22	69	5.3	.956	SS-94
1956	90	.236	.333	246	58	8	2	4	1.6	18	29	29	36	3	1	0	144	266	23	58	4.8	.947	SS-90
1959	24	.286	.286	14	4	0	0	0	0.0	1	0	1	3	0	1	1	13	18	0	6	1.3	1.000	SS-21
1960	117	.213	.246	268	57	1	1	2	0.7	23	19	20	36	1	0	0	179	294	23	68	4.2	.954	SS-115, 3B-1
1961 MIN A	76	.195	.248	149	29	5	0	1	0.7	15	9	8	19	1	0	0	67	107	6	20	2.4	.967	SS-43, 2B-15, 3B-14
5 yrs.	401	.219	.290	971	213	26	8	9	0.9	89	85	79	132	6	2	1	563	1002	74	221	4.1	.955	SS-363, 3B-15, 2B-15

Bob Valentine

VALENTINE, ROBERT
Deceased.

Year Team	Games	BA	SA	AB	H	2B	3B	HR	HR%	R	RBI	BB	SO	SB	AB	H	PO	A	E	DP	TC/G	FA	G by Pos
1876 NY N	1	.000	.000	3	0	0	0	0	0.0	0	0	0	0		0	0	2	0	4	0	6.0	.333	C-1

Bobby Valentine

VALENTINE, ROBERT JOHN
B. May 13, 1950, Stamford, Conn.
Manager 1985-89.

BR TR 5'10" 189 lbs.

Year Team	Games	BA	SA	AB	H	2B	3B	HR	HR%	R	RBI	BB	SO	SB	AB	H	PO	A	E	DP	TC/G	FA	G by Pos
1969 LA N	5	–	–	0	0	0	0	0		3	0	0	0	0	0	0	0	0	0	0	0.0	–	
1971	101	.249	.310	281	70	10	2	1	0.4	32	25	15	20	5	14	5	123	176	16	31	3.1	.949	SS-37, 3B-23, 2B-21, OF-11
1972	119	.274	.335	391	107	11	2	3	0.8	42	32	27	33	5	10	1	178	245	23	38	3.7	.948	2B-49, 3B-39, OF-16, SS-10
1973 CAL A	32	.302	.397	126	38	5	2	1	0.8	12	13	5	9	6	0	0	63	75	6	11	4.5	.958	SS-25, OF-8
1974	117	.261	.329	371	97	10	3	3	0.8	39	39	25	25	8	9	3	160	116	17	10	2.5	.942	OF-62, SS-36, 3B-15, DH-4, 2B-1
1975 2 teams	CAL A (26G – .281)			SD N	(7G – .133)																		
" total	33	.250	.319	72	18	2	0	1	1.4	6	6	8	3	1	10	2	31	1	2	2	1.0	.941	OF-6, 1B-3, 3B-2
1976 SD N	15	.367	.449	49	18	4	0	0	0.0	3	4	6	2	0	1	0	55	6	0	2	4.1	1.000	OF-10, 1B-4
1977 2 teams	SD N (44G – .179)			NY N	(42G – .133)																		
" total	86	.153	.220	150	23	4	0	2	1.3	13	13	13	19	0	44	9	119	64	3	16	2.2	.984	SS-24, 1B-16, 3B-14
1978 NY N	69	.269	.331	160	43	7	0	1	0.6	17	18	19	18	1	15	4	78	109	6	13	2.8	.969	SS-45, 3B-9
1979 SEA A	62	.276	.337	98	27	6	0	0	0.0	9	7	22	5	1	20	7	32	38	2	5	1.2	.972	SS-29, OF-15, 3B-4, 2B-4, C-2, DH-1
10 yrs.	639	.260	.326	1698	441	59	9	12	0.7	176	157	140	134	27	123	31	839	830	75	128	2.7	.957	SS-161, OF-128, 2B-120, 3B-106, 1B-23, DH-5, C-2

Ellis Valentine

VALENTINE, ELLIS CLARENCE
B. July 30, 1954, Helena, Ark.

BR TR 6'4" 205 lbs.

Year Team	Games	BA	SA	AB	H	2B	3B	HR	HR%	R	RBI	BB	SO	SB	AB	H	PO	A	E	DP	TC/G	FA	G by Pos
1975 MON N	12	.364	.576	33	12	4	0	1	3.0	2	3	2	4	0	2	0	12	1	2	1	1.3	.867	OF-11
1976	94	.279	.410	305	85	15	2	7	2.3	36	39	30	51	14	4	0	162	12	5	4	1.9	.972	OF-88
1977	127	.293	.504	508	149	28	2	25	4.9	63	76	30	58	13	1	0	232	9	7	1	2.0	.972	OF-126
1978	151	.289	.489	570	165	35	4	25	4.4	75	76	35	88	13	4	3	296	24	10	3	2.2	.970	OF-146
1979	146	.276	.454	548	151	29	3	21	3.8	73	82	22	74	11	2	1	281	10	5	2	2.0	.983	OF-144
1980	86	.315	.524	394	124	22	2	13	4.2	40	67	25	44	5	2	1	154	6	5	1	1.9	.970	OF-83
1981 2 teams	MON N (22G – .211)			NY N	(48G – .207)																		
" total	70	.208	.359	245	51	11	1	8	3.3	23	36	11	49	0	4	2	115	8	4	0	1.8	.969	OF-68
1982 NY N	111	.288	.407	337	97	14	1	8	2.4	33	48	5	38	1	16	3	159	10	3	4	1.5	.983	OF-98
1983 CAL A	86	.240	.435	271	65	10	2	13	4.8	30	43	18	48	2	3	2	152	5	6	1	1.9	.963	OF-85
1985 TEX A	11	.211	.395	38	8	1	0	2	5.3	5	4	2	8	0	2	1	7	0	0	0	0.6	1.000	OF-7, DH-4
10 yrs.	894	.278	.458	3166	881	169	15	123	3.9	380	474	180	462	59	40	13	1570	85	47	17	1.9	.972	OF-856, DH-4

Fred Valentine

VALENTINE, FRED LEE (Squeaky)
B. Jan. 19, 1935, Clarksdale, Miss.

BB TR 6'1" 190 lbs.

Year Team	Games	BA	SA	AB	H	2B	3B	HR	HR%	R	RBI	BB	SO	SB	AB	H	PO	A	E	DP	TC/G	FA	G by Pos
1959 BAL A	12	.316	.316	19	6	0	0	0	0.0	0	3	4	0	0	0	0	7	1	0	0	0.8	.889	OF-8
1963	26	.268	.293	41	11	1	0	0	0.0	5	1	8	5	0	12	4	15	0	0	0	0.6	1.000	OF-10
1964 WAS A	102	.226	.307	212	48	5	0	4	1.9	20	20	21	44	4	37	5	86	2	2	1	0.9	.978	OF-57
1965	12	.241	.241	29	7	0	0	0	0.0	6	1	4	5	3	2	1	23	0	0	0	1.9	1.000	OF-11
1966	146	.276	.455	508	140	29	7	16	3.1	77	59	51	63	22	7	3	304	7	7	3	2.2	.978	OF-138, 1B-2
1967	151	.234	.346	457	107	16	1	11	2.4	52	44	56	76	17	22	6	258	7	3	0	1.8	.989	OF-136
1968 2 teams	WAS A (37G – .238)			BAL A	(47G – .187)																		
" total	84	.214	.339	192	41	5	2	5	2.6	20	12	13	31	1	33	1	67	4	1	2	0.9	.986	OF-53
7 yrs.	533	.247	.373	1458	360	56	10	36	2.5	180	138	156	228	47	113	20	760	21	14	6	1.5	.982	OF-413, 1B-2

Benny Valenzuela

VALENZUELA, BENJAMIN BELTRAN (Papelero)
B. June 2, 1933, Los Mochis, Mexico

BR TR 5'10" 175 lbs.

Year Team	Games	BA	SA	AB	H	2B	3B	HR	HR%	R	RBI	BB	SO	SB	AB	H	PO	A	E	DP	TC/G	FA	G by Pos
1958 STL N	10	.214	.286	14	3	1	0	0	0.0	0	0	1	0	0	5	2	3	4	1	0	0.8	.875	3B-3

Dave Valle

VALLE, DAVID
B. Oct. 30, 1960, Bayside, N. Y.

BR TR 6'2" 200 lbs.

Year Team	Games	BA	SA	AB	H	2B	3B	HR	HR%	R	RBI	BB	SO	SB	AB	H	PO	A	E	DP	TC/G	FA	G by Pos
1984 SEA A	13	.296	.444	27	8	1	0	1	3.7	4	4	1	5	0	0	0	56	5	0	0	4.7	1.000	C-13
1985	31	.157	.171	70	11	1	0	0	0.0	2	4	1	17	0	0	0	117	7	3	0	4.1	.976	C-31
1986	22	.340	.679	53	18	3	0	5	9.4	10	15	7	7	0	8	2	90	3	2	3	4.3	.979	C-12, 1B-4
1987	95	.256	.435	324	83	16	3	12	3.7	40	53	15	46	2	10	1	422	34	5	2	4.9	.989	C-75, 1B-2, OF-1
1988	93	.231	.400	290	67	15	2	10	3.4	29	50	18	38	0	10	5	490	47	6	8	5.8	.989	C-84, DH-3, 1B-1
1989	94	.237	.354	316	75	10	3	7	2.2	32	34	29	32	0	3	2	496	52	4	3	5.9	.993	C-93
6 yrs.	348	.243	.397	1080	262	46	8	35	3.2	117	160	71	145	2	31	10	1671	148	20	16	5.3	.989	C-308, 1B-7, DH-3, OF-1

Hector Valle

VALLE, HECTOR JOSE
B. Oct. 27, 1940, Vega Baja, Puerto Rico

BR TR 5'9" 180 lbs.

Year Team	Games	BA	SA	AB	H	2B	3B	HR	HR%	R	RBI	BB	SO	SB	AB	H	PO	A	E	DP	TC/G	FA	G by Pos
1965 LA N	9	.308	.308	13	4	0	0	0	0.0	1	2	2	3	0	2	1	20	1	0	0	2.3	1.000	C-6

Elmer Valo

VALO, ELMER WILLIAM
B. Mar. 5, 1921, Ribnik, Czechoslovakia

BL TR 5'11" 190 lbs.

Year Team	Games	BA	SA	AB	H	2B	3B	HR	HR%	R	RBI	BB	SO	SB	AB	H	PO	A	E	DP	TC/G	FA	G by Pos
1940 PHI A	6	.348	.348	23	8	0	0	0	0.0	6	0	3	0	2	0	0	18	0	0	0	3.0	1.000	OF-6

Year	Team	Games	BA	SA	AB	H	2B	3B	HR	HR%	R	RBI	BB	SO	SB	Pinch Hit AB	Pinch Hit H	PO	A	E	DP	TC/G	FA	G by Pos

Elmer Valo *continued*

Year	Team	Games	BA	SA	AB	H	2B	3B	HR	HR%	R	RBI	BB	SO	SB	PH AB	PH H	PO	A	E	DP	TC/G	FA	G by Pos
1941		15	.420	.580	50	21	0	1	2	4.0	13	6	4	2	0	4	1	22	0	0	0	1.5	1.000	OF-10
1942		133	.251	.336	459	115	13	10	2	0.4	64	40	70	21	13	9	2	264	5	10	0	2.1	.964	OF-122
1943		77	.221	.297	249	55	6	2	3	1.2	31	18	35	13	2	13	1	134	4	2	0	1.8	.986	OF-63
1946		108	.307	.411	348	107	21	6	1	0.3	59	31	60	18	9	15	5	182	7	5	0	1.8	.974	OF-90
1947		112	.300	.405	370	111	12	6	5	1.4	60	36	64	21	11	5	1	205	9	6	0	2.0	.973	OF-104
1948		113	.305	.394	383	117	17	4	3	0.8	72	46	81	13	10	3	1	231	4	4	1	2.1	.983	OF-109
1949		150	.283	.404	547	155	27	12	5	0.9	86	85	119	32	14	0	0	395	8	8	0	2.7	.981	OF-150
1950		129	.280	.406	446	125	16	5	10	2.2	62	46	83	22	12	6	1	264	9	5	3	2.2	.982	OF-117
1951		123	.302	.446	444	134	27	8	7	1.6	75	55	75	20	11	8	2	247	5	5	0	2.1	.981	OF-116
1952		129	.281	.407	388	109	26	4	5	1.3	69	47	101	16	12	10	1	223	7	9	1	1.9	.962	OF-121
1953		50	.224	.259	85	19	3	0	0	0.0	15	9	22	7	0	19	4	46	1	0	1	0.9	1.000	OF-25
1954		95	.214	.330	224	48	11	6	1	0.4	28	33	51	18	2	22	1	135	3	5	1	1.5	.965	OF-62
1955	KC A	112	.364	.484	283	103	17	4	3	1.1	50	37	52	18	5	31	14	147	5	2	2	1.4	.987	OF-72
1956	2 teams		KC A	(9G – .222)		PHI N	(98G – .289)																		
"	total	107	.287	.400	300	86	13	5	5	1.7	41	39	49	22	7	16	5	167	4	6	0	1.7	.966	OF-88
1957	BKN N	81	.273	.422	161	44	10	1	4	2.5	14	26	25	16	0	34	8	57	0	0	0	0.7	1.000	OF-36
1958	LA N	65	.248	.317	101	25	2	1	1	1.0	9	14	12	11	0	36	9	24	0	0	0	0.4	1.000	OF-26
1959	CLE A	34	.292	.292	24	7	0	0	0	0.0	3	5	7	0	0	24	7	1	0	0	0	0.0	1.000	OF-2
1960	2 teams		NY A	(8G – .000)		WAS A	(76G – .281)																		
"	total	84	.261	.304	69	18	3	0	0	0.0	7	16	19	5	0	59	14	5	1	0	0	0.1	1.000	OF-8
1961	2 teams		MIN A	(33G – .156)		PHI N	(50G – .186)																		
"	total	83	.173	.267	75	13	4	0	1	1.3	4	12	11	9	0	72	13	2	0	0	0	0.0	1.000	OF-2
20 yrs.		1806	.282	.391	5029	1420	228	73	58	1.2	768	601	943	284	110	386	90	2769	72	67	9	1.6	.977	OF-1329

Deacon Van Buren

VAN BUREN, EDWARD EUGENE
B. Dec. 14, 1870, LaSalle County, Ill.   D. June 29, 1957, Portland, Ore.

BL TR 5'10" 175 lbs.

Year	Team	Games	BA	SA	AB	H	2B	3B	HR	HR%	R	RBI	BB	SO	SB	PH AB	PH H	PO	A	E	DP	TC/G	FA	G by Pos
1904	2 teams		BKN N	(1G – 1.000)		PHI N	(12G – .233)																		
"	total	13	.250	.295	44	11	2	0	0	0.0	2	3	3		2	1	1	23	2	1	1	2.0	.962	OF-12

Al Van Camp

VAN CAMP, ALBERT JOSEPH
B. Sept. 7, 1903, Moline, Ill.   D. Feb. 2, 1981, Bensenville, Ill.

BR TR 5'11½" 175 lbs.

Year	Team	Games	BA	SA	AB	H	2B	3B	HR	HR%	R	RBI	BB	SO	SB	PH AB	PH H	PO	A	E	DP	TC/G	FA	G by Pos
1928	CLE A	5	.235	.294	17	4	1	0	0	0.0	0	2	0	1	1	0	0	47	1	1	1	9.8	.980	1B-5
1931	BOS A	102	.275	.346	324	89	15	4	0	0.0	34	33	20	24	3	16	6	324	18	3	17	3.4	.991	OF-59, 1B-25
1932		34	.223	.301	103	23	4	2	0	0.0	10	6	4	17	0	7	0	249	18	4	20	8.0	.985	1B-25
3 yrs.		141	.261	.333	444	116	20	6	0	0.0	44	41	24	42	4	23	6	620	37	8	38	4.7	.988	OF-59, 1B-55

Carl Vandagrift

VANDAGRIFT, CARL WILLIAM
B. Apr. 22, 1883, Cantrall, Ill.   D. Oct. 9, 1920, Fort Wayne, Ind.

BR TR 5'8" 155 lbs.

Year	Team	Games	BA	SA	AB	H	2B	3B	HR	HR%	R	RBI	BB	SO	SB	PH AB	PH H	PO	A	E	DP	TC/G	FA	G by Pos
1914	IND F	43	.250	.279	136	34	4	0	0	0.0	25	9	9		7	0	0	78	89	14	9	4.2	.923	2B-28, 3B-12, SS-5

Fred Van Dusen

VAN DUSEN, FREDERICK WILLIAM
B. July 31, 1937, Jackson Heights, N. Y.

BL TL 6'3" 180 lbs.

Year	Team	Games	BA	SA	AB	H	2B	3B	HR	HR%	R	RBI	BB	SO	SB	PH AB	PH H	PO	A	E	DP	TC/G	FA	G by Pos
1955	PHI N	1	–	–	0	0	0	0	0	–	0	0	0	0	0	1	0	0	0	0	0	0.0	–	

Bill Van Dyke

VAN DYKE, WILLIAM JENNINGS
B. Dec. 15, 1863, Paris, Ill.   D. May 5, 1933, El Paso, Tex.

BR TR 5'8" 170 lbs.

Year	Team	Games	BA	SA	AB	H	2B	3B	HR	HR%	R	RBI	BB	SO	SB	PH AB	PH H	PO	A	E	DP	TC/G	FA	G by Pos
1890	TOL AA	129	.257	.341	502	129	14	11	2	0.4	74		25		73	0	0	211	52	30	3	2.3	.898	OF-110, 3B-18, 2B-2, C-1
1892	STL N	4	.125	.125	16	2	0	0	0	0.0	2	1	0	1	0	0	0	7	0	1	0	2.0	.875	OF-4
1893	BOS N	3	.250	.333	12	3	1	0	0	0.0	2	1	0		1	0	0	4	0	0	0	1.3	1.000	OF-3
3 yrs.		136	.253	.334	530	134	15	11	2	0.4	78	2	25	2	74	0	0	222	52	31	3	2.2	.898	OF-117, 3B-18, 2B-2, C-1

Dave Van Gorder

VAN GORDER, DAVID THOMAS
B. Mar. 27, 1957, Los Angeles, Calif.

BR TR 6'2" 205 lbs.

Year	Team	Games	BA	SA	AB	H	2B	3B	HR	HR%	R	RBI	BB	SO	SB	PH AB	PH H	PO	A	E	DP	TC/G	FA	G by Pos
1982	CIN N	51	.182	.219	137	25	3	1	0	0.0	4	7	14	19	1	1	0	273	18	4	3	5.8	.986	C-51
1984		38	.228	.248	123	28	2	0	0	0.0	10	6	12	17	0	2	0	194	11	0	1	5.4	1.000	C-36, 1B-1
1985		73	.238	.325	151	36	7	0	2	1.3	12	24	9	19	0	4	1	255	11	3	2	3.7	.989	C-70
1986		9	.000	.000	10	0	0	0	0	0.0	0	0	1	1	0	1	0	20	0	0	0	2.2	1.000	C-7
1987	BAL A	12	.238	.381	21	5	0	0	1	4.8	4	1	3	6	0	1	0	44	1	1	0	3.8	.978	C-12
5 yrs.		183	.212	.267	420	89	12	1	3	0.7	30	38	39	63	1	9	1	786	41	8	6	4.6	.990	C-176, 1B-1

George Van Haltren

VAN HALTREN, GEORGE EDWARD MARTIN
B. Mar. 30, 1866, St. Louis, Mo.   D. Sept. 29, 1945, Oakland, Calif.
Manager 1891-92.

BL TL 5'11" 170 lbs.

Year	Team	Games	BA	SA	AB	H	2B	3B	HR	HR%	R	RBI	BB	SO	SB	PH AB	PH H	PO	A	E	DP	TC/G	FA	G by Pos
1887	CHI N	45	.203	.279	172	35	4	0	3	1.7	30	17	15	15	12	0	0	47	26	8	2	1.8	.901	OF-27, P-20
1888		81	.283	.437	318	90	9	14	4	1.3	46	34	22	34	21	0	0	98	62	17	0	2.2	.904	OF-57, P-30
1889		134	.309	.433	543	168	20	10	9	1.7	126	81	82	41	28	0	0	230	35	32	5	2.2	.892	OF-130, SS-3, 2B-1
1890	BKN P	92	.335	.444	376	126	8	9	5	1.3	84	54	41	23	35	0	0	143	90	22	7	2.8	.914	OF-67, P-28, SS-3
1891	BAL AA	139	.318	.443	566	180	14	15	9	1.6	136	83	71	46	75	0	0	275	190	82	22	3.9	.850	OF-81, SS-59, P-6, 2B-2
1892	2 teams		BAL N	(135G – .302)		PIT N	(13G – .200)																		
"	total	148	.293	.409	611	179	22	14	7	1.1	115	62	76	34	55	0	0	270	47	52	9	2.5	.859	OF-142, P-4, 3B-3, SS-2, 1B-2
1893	PIT N	124	.338	.423	529	179	14	11	3	0.6	129	79	75	25	37	1	0	245	69	49	6	2.9	.865	OF-111, SS-12, 2B-2
1894	NY N	137	.331	.435	519	172	25	4	7	1.3	109	104	55	22	43	0	0	299	29	31	5	2.6	.914	OF-137
1895		131	.340	.503	521	177	23	19	8	1.5	113	103	57	29	32	0	0	252	27	27	3	2.3	.912	OF-131, P-1
1896		133	.351	.484	562	197	18	21	5	0.9	136	74	55	36	39	0	0	273	26	15	4	2.4	.952	OF-133, P-2
1897		129	.330	.417	564	186	22	9	3	0.5	117	64	40		50	0	0	267	31	20	4	2.5	.937	OF-129
1898		156	.312	.413	654	204	28	16	2	0.3	129	68	59		36	0	0	299	22	29	5	2.2	.917	OF-156
1899		151	.301	.356	604	182	21	3	1	0.2	117	58	74		31	0	0	284	31	23	8	2.2	.932	OF-151
1900		141	.315	.398	571	180	30	7	1	0.2	114	51	50		**45**	0	0	325	28	23	7	2.7	.939	OF-141, P-1
1901		135	.342	.414	544	186	22	7	1	0.2	82	47	51		24	0	0	263	27	18	5	2.3	.942	OF-135, P-1
1902		24	.261	.318	88	23	19	0	0	0.0	14	7	17		6	0	0	43	6	4	1	2.2	.925	OF-24

Year	Team		Games	BA	SA	AB	H	2B	3B	HR	HR%	R	RBI	BB	SO	SB	Pinch Hit AB	H	PO	A	E	DP	TC/G	FA	G by Pos

George Van Haltren *continued*

| 1903 | | | 84 | .257 | .286 | 280 | 72 | 6 | 1 | 0 | 0.0 | 42 | 28 | 28 | | 14 | 8 | 1 | 136 | 3 | 6 | 1 | 1.7 | .959 | OF-75 |
| 17 yrs. | | | 1984 | .316 | .418 | 8022 | 2536 | 287 | 162 | 69 | 0.9 | 1639 | 1014 | 868 | 305 | 583 | 9 | 1 | 3749 | 749 | 458 | 94 | 2.5 | .908 | OF-1827, P-93, SS-79, 2B-5, 3B-3, 1B-2 |

John Vann

VANN, JOHN SILAS
B. June 7, 1893, Fairland, Okla. D. June 10, 1958, Shreveport, La. BR TR

| 1913 | STL | N | 1 | .000 | .000 | 1 | 0 | 0 | 0 | 0 | 0.0 | 0 | 0 | 0 | 1 | 0 | 1 | 0 | 0 | 0 | 0 | 0 | 0.0 | – | |

Jay Van Noy

VAN NOY, JAY LOWELL
B. Nov. 4, 1928, Garland, Utah BL TR 6'1" 200 lbs.

| 1951 | STL | N | 6 | .000 | .000 | 7 | 0 | 0 | 0 | 0 | 0.0 | 1 | 0 | 1 | 6 | 0 | 4 | 0 | 2 | 0 | 0 | 0 | 0.3 | 1.000 | OF-1 |

Maurice Van Robays

VAN ROBAYS, MAURICE RENE (Bomber)
B. Nov. 15, 1914, Detroit, Mich. D. Mar. 1, 1965, Detroit, Mich. BR TR 6'½" 190 lbs.

1939	PIT	N	27	.314	.457	105	33	9	0	2	1.9	13	16	6	10	0			36	3	3	1	1.6	.929	OF-25, 2B-1
1940			145	.273	.402	572	156	27	7	11	1.9	82	116	33	58	2	2	1	276	10	11	3	2.0	.963	OF-143, 1B-1
1941			129	.282	.381	457	129	23	5	4	0.9	62	78	41	29	0	6	3	292	9	8	3	2.4	.974	OF-121
1942			100	.232	.311	328	76	13	5	1	0.3	29	46	30	24	0	14	3	199	6	3	3	2.1	.986	OF-84
1943			69	.288	.432	236	68	17	7	1	0.4	32	35	18	19	0	9	4	120	5	8	1	1.9	.940	OF-60
1946			59	.212	.308	146	31	5	3	1	0.7	14	12	11	15	0	20	3	70	2	3	0	1.3	.960	OF-37, 1B-2
6 yrs.			529	.267	.380	1844	493	94	27	20	1.1	232	303	139	155	2	52	14	993	35	36	11	2.0	.966	OF-470, 1B-3, 2B-1

Andy Van Slyke

VAN SLYKE, ANDREW JAMES (Slick)
B. Dec. 21, 1960, Utica, N. Y. BL TR 6'1" 190 lbs.

1983	STL	N	101	.262	.421	309	81	15	5	8	2.6	51	38	46	64	21	5	1	203	59	6	16	2.7	.978	OF-69, 3B-30, 1B-9
1984			137	.244	.368	361	88	16	4	7	1.9	45	50	63	71	28	11	4	357	82	8	40	3.3	.982	OF-81, 3B-32, 1B-30
1985			146	.259	.439	424	110	25	6	13	3.1	61	55	47	54	34	19	4	237	13	1	6	1.7	.996	OF-142, 1B-2
1986			137	.270	.452	418	113	23	7	13	3.1	48	61	47	85	21	10	2	415	34	8	25	3.3	.989	OF-110, 1B-38
1987	PIT	N	157	.293	.507	564	165	36	11	21	3.7	93	82	56	122	34	7	1	338	10	4	9	2.2	.989	OF-150, 1B-1
1988			154	.288	.506	587	169	23	15	25	4.3	101	100	57	126	30	5	0	406	12	4	2	2.7	.991	OF-152
1989			130	.237	.370	476	113	18	9	9	1.9	64	53	47	100	16	10	1	344	9	4	6	2.7	.989	OF-123, 1B-2
7 yrs.			962	.267	.445	3139	839	156	57	96	3.1	463	439	363	622	184	67	13	2300	219	35	104	2.7	.986	OF-827, 1B-82, 3B-62

LEAGUE CHAMPIONSHIP SERIES

| 1985 | STL | N | 5 | .091 | .091 | 11 | 1 | 0 | 0 | 0 | 0.0 | 1 | 1 | 2 | 1 | 0 | 0 | 0 | 7 | 0 | 0 | 0 | 1.4 | 1.000 | OF-5 |

WORLD SERIES

| 1985 | STL | N | 6 | .091 | .091 | 11 | 1 | 0 | 0 | 0 | 0.0 | 0 | 0 | 0 | 5 | 0 | 0 | 0 | 8 | 0 | 0 | 0 | 1.3 | 1.000 | OF-6 |

Ike Van Zandt

VAN ZANDT, CHARLES ISAAC
B. 1877, Brooklyn, N. Y. D. Sept. 14, 1908, Nashua, N. H. BL

1901	NY	N	3	.167	.167	6	1	0	0	0	0.0	1	0	0	0	0	0	0	1	0	3	0	1.3	.250	P-2, OF-1
1904	CHI	N	3	.000	.000	11	0	0	0	0	0.0	0	0	0	0	0	0	0	3	0	0	0	1.0	1.000	OF-3
1905	STL	A	94	.233	.295	322	75	15	1	1	0.3	31	20	7		7	18	4	76	9	11	0	1.0	.885	OF-74, 1B-1, P-1
3 yrs.			100	.224	.283	339	76	15	1	1	0.3	32	20	7		7	18	4	80	9	14	0	1.0	.864	OF-78, P-3, 1B-1

Dick Van Zant

VAN ZANT, RICHARD (Foghorn Dick)
B. Nov., 1864, Richmond, Ind. D. Aug. 6, 1912, Richmond, Ind.

| 1888 | CLE | AA | 10 | .258 | .290 | 31 | 8 | 1 | 0 | 0 | 0.0 | 1 | 1 | 1 | | 1 | 0 | 0 | 7 | 22 | 8 | 2 | 3.7 | .784 | 3B-10 |

Hedi Vargas

VARGAS, HEDIBERTO
Born Hediberto Vargas y Rodriguez.
B. Feb. 23, 1959, Guanica, Puerto Rico BR TR 6'4" 205 lbs.

1982	PIT	N	8	.375	.500	8	3	1	0	0	0.0	1	3	0	2	0	3	2	16	1	0	1	2.1	1.000	1B-5
1984			18	.226	.290	31	7	2	0	0	0.0	3	2	3	5	0	6	4	51	4	1	6	3.1	.982	1B-13
2 yrs.			26	.256	.333	39	10	3	0	0	0.0	4	5	3	7	0	9	6	67	5	1	7	2.8	.986	1B-18

Buck Varner

VARNER, GLEN GANN
B. Aug. 17, 1930, Hixson, Tenn. BL TR 5'10" 170 lbs.

| 1952 | WAS | A | 2 | .000 | .000 | 4 | 0 | 0 | 0 | 0 | 0.0 | 0 | 0 | 0 | 1 | 1 | 0 | 1 | 0 | 1 | 0 | 0 | 0 | 0.5 | 1.000 | OF-1 |

Pete Varney

VARNEY, RICHARD FRED
B. Apr. 10, 1949, Roxbury, Mass. BR TR 6'3" 235 lbs.

1973	CHI	A	5	.000	.000	4	0	0	0	0	0.0	0	1	0	0	0	0	0	10	0	0	0	2.0	1.000	C-5
1974			9	.250	.250	28	7	0	0	0	0.0	1	2	1	8	0	0	0	47	5	1	0	5.9	.981	C-9
1975			36	.271	.393	107	29	5	1	2	1.9	12	8	6	28	2	3	0	151	14	2	1	4.6	.988	C-34, DH-2
1976	2 teams			CHI A	(14G – .244)		ATL N	(5G – .100)																		
"	total		19	.216	.431	51	11	2	0	3	5.9	5	5	2	11	0	0	0	85	7	1	1	4.9	.989	C-19
4 yrs.			69	.247	.374	190	47	7	1	5	2.6	18	15	10	47	2	3	0	293	26	4	2	4.7	.988	C-67, DH-2

Gary Varsho

VARSHO, GARY ANDREW
B. June 20, 1961, Marshfield, Wis. BL TR 5'11" 190 lbs.

1988	CHI	N	46	.274	.315	73	20	3	0	0	0.0	6	5	1	6	5	28	11	29	0	3	0	0.7	.906	OF-18
1989			61	.184	.276	87	16	4	2	0	0.0	10	6	4	13	3	36	5	25	1	2	0	0.5	.929	OF-21
2 yrs.			107	.225	.294	160	36	7	2	0	0.0	16	11	5	19	8	64	16	54	1	5	0	0.6	.917	OF-39

Arky Vaughan

VAUGHAN, JOSEPH FLOYD
B. Mar. 9, 1912, Clifty, Ark. D. Aug. 30, 1952, Eagleville, Calif. BL TR 5'10½" 175 lbs.
Hall of Fame 1985.

Year	Team		Games	BA	SA	AB	H	2B	3B	HR	HR%	R	RBI	BB	SO	SB	Pinch Hit AB	Pinch Hit H	PO	A	E	DP	TC/G	FA	G by Pos

Arky Vaughan *continued*

Year	Team		Games	BA	SA	AB	H	2B	3B	HR	HR%	R	RBI	BB	SO	SB	AB	H	PO	A	E	DP	TC/G	FA	G by Pos
1932	PIT	N	129	.318	.412	497	158	15	10	4	0.8	71	61	39	26	10	1	0	247	403	46	74	5.4	.934	SS-128
1933			152	.314	.478	573	180	29	19	9	1.6	85	97	64	23	3	0	0	310	487	46	95	5.5	.945	SS-152
1934			149	.333	.511	558	186	41	11	12	2.2	115	94	94	38	10	0	0	329	480	41	77	5.7	.952	SS-149
1935			137	**.385**	**.607**	499	192	34	10	19	3.8	108	99	97	18	4	0	0	249	422	35	55	5.2	.950	SS-137
1936			156	.335	.474	568	190	30	11	9	1.6	**122**	78	**118**	21	6	0	0	327	477	47	86	5.5	.945	SS-156
1937			126	.322	.463	469	151	17	**17**	5	1.1	71	72	54	22	7	6	2	257	335	27	58	4.9	.956	SS-108, OF-12
1938			148	.322	.444	541	174	35	5	7	1.3	88	68	104	21	14	1	0	306	507	33	107	5.7	.961	SS-147
1939			152	.306	.424	595	182	30	11	6	1.0	94	62	70	20	12	0	0	330	531	34	103	5.9	.962	SS-152
1940			156	.300	.453	594	178	40	15	7	1.2	**113**	95	88	25	12	0	0	309	546	52	94	5.8	.943	SS-155, 3B-2
1941			106	.316	.455	374	118	20	7	6	1.6	69	38	50	13	8	1	0	174	298	21	43	4.7	.957	SS-97, 3B-3
1942	BKN	N	128	.277	.341	495	137	18	4	2	0.4	82	49	51	17	8	3	1	130	225	14	22	2.9	.962	3B-119, SS-5, 2B-1
1943			149	.305	.413	610	186	39	6	5	0.8	**112**	66	60	13	**20**	1	0	237	375	21	57	4.2	.967	SS-99, 3B-55
1947			64	.325	.444	126	41	5	2	2	1.6	24	25	27	11	4	26	10	56	20	0	3	1.2	1.000	OF-22, 3B-10
1948			65	.244	.341	123	30	3	0	3	2.4	19	22	21	8	0	29	8	47	14	0	1	0.9	1.000	OF-26, 3B-8
14 yrs.			1817	.318	.453	6622	2103	356	128	96	1.4	1173	926	937	276	118	71	21	3308	5120	417	875	4.9	.953	SS-1485, 3B-197, OF-60, 2B-1

WORLD SERIES

Year	Team		Games	BA	SA	AB	H	2B	3B	HR	HR%	R	RBI	BB	SO	SB	AB	H	PO	A	E	DP	TC/G	FA	G by Pos
1947	BKN	N	3	.500	1.000	2	1	1	0	0	0.0	0	0	1	0	0	2	1	0	0	0	0	0.0	—	

Glenn Vaughan

VAUGHAN, GLENN EDWARD (Sparky)
B. Feb. 15, 1944, Compton, Calif.

BB TR 5'11" 170 lbs.

Year	Team		Games	BA	SA	AB	H	2B	3B	HR	HR%	R	RBI	BB	SO	SB	AB	H	PO	A	E	DP	TC/G	FA	G by Pos
1963	HOU	N	9	.167	.167	30	5	0	0	0	0.0	1	0	2	5	1	0	0	13	20	3	1	4.0	.917	SS-9, 3B-1

Bobby Vaughn

VAUGHN, ROBERT
B. June 4, 1885, Stamford, N. Y. D. Apr. 11, 1965, Seattle, Wash.

BR TR 5'9" 150 lbs.

Year	Team		Games	BA	SA	AB	H	2B	3B	HR	HR%	R	RBI	BB	SO	SB	AB	H	PO	A	E	DP	TC/G	FA	G by Pos
1909	NY	A	5	.143	.143	14	2	0	0	0	0.0	1	0	1		0	1	0	10	5	2	0	3.4	.882	2B-4, SS-1
1915	STL	F	144	.280	.351	521	146	19	9	0	0.0	69	32	58		24	0	0	274	382	36	48	4.8	.948	2B-127, SS-12, 3B-8
2 yrs.			149	.277	.346	535	148	19	9	0	0.0	70	32	59		25	1	0	284	387	38	48	4.8	.946	2B-131, SS-13, 3B-8

Farmer Vaughn

VAUGHN, HENRY FRANCIS
B. Mar. 1, 1864, Rural Dale, Ohio D. Feb. 21, 1914, Cincinnati, Ohio

BR TR 6'3" 177 lbs.

Year	Team		Games	BA	SA	AB	H	2B	3B	HR	HR%	R	RBI	BB	SO	SB	AB	H	PO	A	E	DP	TC/G	FA	G by Pos
1886	CIN	AA	1	.000	.000	3	0	0	0	0	0.0	0		0		0	0	0	8	3	1	0	12.0	.917	C-1
1888	LOU	AA	51	.196	.254	189	37	4	2	1	0.5	15	21	4		4	0	0	164	49	28	6	4.7	.884	OF-28, C-25
1889			90	.239	.322	360	86	11	5	3	0.8	39	45	7	41	13	0	0	441	121	51	18	6.8	.917	C-54, OF-20, 1B-18, 3B-3
1890	NY	P	44	.265	.325	166	44	7	0	1	0.6	27	22	10	9	6	0	0	113	22	19	3	3.5	.877	C-30, OF-12, 3B-1, 2B-1
1891	2 teams			CIN	AA	(51G – .257)				MIL	AA	(25G – .333)													
"	total		76	.285	.354	274	78	14	1	1	0.4	34	23	18	20	8	0	0	324	82	32	12	5.8	.927	C-64, OF-7, 1B-6, 3B-2, P-1
1892	CIN	N	91	.254	.329	346	88	10	5	2	0.6	45	50	16	13	10	0	0	394	80	33	22	5.6	.935	C-67, 1B-14, OF-11, 3B-6
1893			121	.280	.371	483	135	17	12	1	0.2	68	108	35	17	16	0	0	533	95	26	27	5.4	.960	C-80, 1B-21
1894			72	.310	.479	284	88	15	6	7	2.5	50	64	12	11	5	1	0	362	64	26	19	6.3	.942	C-43, 1B-27, OF-8, SS-3
1895			92	.305	.404	334	102	23	5	0	0.0	60	48	17	10	15	0	0	379	96	30	13	5.5	.941	C-77, 1B-15, 3B-1, 2B-1
1896			114	.293	.395	433	127	20	9	2	0.5	71	66	16	7	7	2	2	740	82	21	41	7.4	.975	1B-57, C-57
1897			54	.291	.407	199	58	13	5	0	0.0	21	30	2		2	4	0	393	31	10	20	8.0	.977	1B-35, C-15
1898			78	.305	.389	275	84	12	4	1	0.4	35	46	11		4	6	4	462	50	17	28	6.8	.968	1B-39, C-33
1899			31	.176	.185	108	19	1	0	0	0.0	9	2	3		2	2	1	239	24	8	12	8.7	.970	1B-21, C-7, OF-1
13 yrs.			915	.274	.364	3454	946	147	54	19	0.6	474	525	151	128	92	15	7	4552	799	302	221	6.2	.947	C-553, 1B-253, OF-110, 3B-13, SS-3, 2B-2, P-1

Fred Vaughn

VAUGHN, FREDERICK THOMAS (Muscles)
B. Oct. 18, 1918, Coalinga, Calif. D. Mar. 2, 1964, Lake Wales, Fla.

BR TR 5'10" 185 lbs.

Year	Team		Games	BA	SA	AB	H	2B	3B	HR	HR%	R	RBI	BB	SO	SB	AB	H	PO	A	E	DP	TC/G	FA	G by Pos
1944	WAS	A	30	.257	.321	109	28	2	1	1	0.9	10	21	9	24	2	1	1	62	78	10	16	5.0	.933	2B-26, 3B-3
1945			80	.235	.302	268	63	7	4	1	0.4	28	25	23	48	0	4	1	177	189	21	35	4.8	.946	2B-76, SS-1
2 yrs.			110	.241	.308	377	91	9	5	2	0.5	38	46	32	72	2	5	2	239	267	31	51	4.9	.942	2B-102, 3B-3, SS-1

Greg Vaughn

VAUGHN, GREGORY LAMONT
B. July 3, 1965, Sacramento, Calif.

BR TR 6' 195 lbs.

Year	Team		Games	BA	SA	AB	H	2B	3B	HR	HR%	R	RBI	BB	SO	SB	AB	H	PO	A	E	DP	TC/G	FA	G by Pos
1989	MIL	A	38	.265	.425	113	30	3	0	5	4.4	18	23	13	23	4	1	0	32	1	2	0	0.9	.943	OF-24, DH-13

Bobby Veach

VEACH, ROBERT HAYES
B. June 29, 1888, Island, Ky. D. Aug. 7, 1945, Detroit, Mich.

BL TR 5'11" 160 lbs.

Year	Team		Games	BA	SA	AB	H	2B	3B	HR	HR%	R	RBI	BB	SO	SB	AB	H	PO	A	E	DP	TC/G	FA	G by Pos
1912	DET	A	23	.342	.430	79	27	5	1	0	0.0	8	15	5		2	1	0	46	5	4	0	2.4	.927	OF-22
1913			138	.269	.354	494	133	22	10	0	0.0	54	64	53	31	21	1	0	250	16	24	3	2.1	.917	OF-137
1914			149	.275	.369	531	146	19	14	1	0.2	56	72	50	29	20	3	3	282	22	11	6	2.1	.965	OF-145
1915			152	.313	.434	569	178	**40**	10	3	0.5	81	**112**	68	43	16	0	0	297	19	8	4	2.1	.975	OF-152
1916			150	.306	.433	566	173	33	15	3	0.5	92	91	52	41	24	0	0	342	14	12	4	2.5	.967	OF-150
1917			154	.319	.457	571	182	31	12	8	1.4	79	**103**	61	44	21	0	0	356	17	17	5	2.5	.956	OF-154
1918			127	.279	.391	499	139	21	13	3	0.6	59	**78**	35	23	21	0	0	277	14	7	3	2.3	.977	OF-127, P-1
1919			139	.355	.519	538	191	**45**	**17**	3	0.6	87	101	33	33	19	1	1	338	14	12	3	2.6	.967	OF-138
1920			154	.307	.474	612	188	39	15	11	1.8	92	113	36	22	11	0	0	357	26	13	4	2.6	.967	OF-154
1921			150	.338	.529	612	207	43	13	16	2.6	110	128	48	31	14	1	0	384	21	11	4	2.8	.974	OF-149
1922			155	.327	.468	618	202	34	13	9	1.5	96	126	42	27	9	0	0	375	16	7	3	2.6	.982	OF-154
1923			114	.321	.406	293	94	13	3	2	0.7	45	39	29	21	10	22	8	127	6	8	0	1.2	.943	OF-85, C-1
1924	BOS	A	142	.295	.426	519	153	35	9	5	1.0	77	99	47	18	5	12	3	268	15	13	2	2.1	.956	OF-130
1925	3 teams			BOS	A	(1G – .200)			NY	A	(56G – .353)			WAS	A	(18G – .243)								
"	total		75	.323	.430	158	51	13	2	0	0.0	17	25	12		4	26	6	53	6	3	1	0.8	.952	OF-45
14 yrs.			1822	.310	.442	6659	2064	393	147	64	1.0	953	1166	571	367	195	67	21	3752	211	150	42	2.3	.964	OF-1742, C-1, P-1

WORLD SERIES

Year	Team		Games	BA	SA	AB	H	2B	3B	HR	HR%	R	RBI	BB	SO	SB	AB	H	PO	A	E	DP	TC/G	FA	G by Pos
1925	WAS	A	2	.000	.000	1	0	0	0	0	0.0	0	1	0		0	1	0	0	0	0	0	0.0	—	

Year	Team		Games	BA	SA	AB	H	2B	3B	HR	HR%	R	RBI	BB	SO	SB	Pinch Hit AB	Pinch Hit H	PO	A	E	DP	TC/G	FA	G by Pos

Peek-A-Boo Veach

VEACH, WILLIAM WALTER
B. June 15, 1862, Indianapolis, Ind.   D. Nov. 12, 1937, Indianapolis, Ind.

Year	Team		Games	BA	SA	AB	H	2B	3B	HR	HR%	R	RBI	BB	SO	SB	AB	H	PO	A	E	DP	TC/G	FA	G by Pos
1884	KC	U	27	.134	.183	82	11	1	0	1	1.2	9		9			0	0	0	33	28	6	4	2.5	.910	OF-14, P-12, 2B-1, 1B-1
1887	LOU	AA	1	.000	.000	3	0	0	0	0	0.0	0		1			0	0	0	2	1	1	0	4.0	.750	P-1
1890	2 teams		CLE	N	(64G – .235)			PIT	N	(8G – .300)															
"	total		72	.243	.351	268	65	11	6	2	0.7	30	37	41	31	9	0	0	721	44	23	38	10.9	.971	1B-72
3 yrs.			100	.215	.309	353	76	12	6	3	0.8	39	37	51	31	9	0	0	756	73	30	42	8.6	.965	1B-73, OF-14, P-13, 2B-1

Coot Veal

VEAL, ORVILLE INMAN   BR TR 6'1"   165 lbs.
B. July 9, 1932, Sandersville, Ga.

Year	Team		Games	BA	SA	AB	H	2B	3B	HR	HR%	R	RBI	BB	SO	SB	AB	H	PO	A	E	DP	TC/G	FA	G by Pos
1958	DET	A	58	.256	.324	207	53	10	2	0	0.0	29	16	14	21	1	0	0	95	160	5	30	4.5	.981	SS-58
1959			77	.202	.247	89	18	1	0	1	1.1	12	15	8	7	0	0	0	57	96	6	16	2.1	.962	SS-72
1960			27	.297	.406	64	19	5	1	0	0.0	8	8	11	7	0	2	1	30	55	1	10	3.2	.988	SS-22, 3B-3, 2B-1
1961	WAS	A	69	.202	.248	218	44	10	0	0	0.0	21	8	19	29	1	4	0	130	172	8	43	4.5	.974	SS-63
1962	PIT	N	1	.000	.000	1	0	0	0	0	0.0	0	0	0	1	0	1	0	0	0	0	0	0.0	–	
1963	DET	A	15	.219	.219	32	7	0	0	0	0.0	5	4	4	4	0	4	2	14	35	1	1	3.3	.980	SS-12
6 yrs.			247	.231	.288	611	141	26	3	1	0.2	75	51	56	69	2	11	3	326	518	21	100	3.5	.976	SS-227, 3B-3, 2B-1

Jesus Vega

VEGA, JESUS ANTONIO   BR TR 6'1"   176 lbs.
Born Jesus Antonio Vega y Morales.
B. Oct. 14, 1955, Bayamon, Puerto Rico

Year	Team		Games	BA	SA	AB	H	2B	3B	HR	HR%	R	RBI	BB	SO	SB	AB	H	PO	A	E	DP	TC/G	FA	G by Pos
1979	MIN	A	4	.000	.000	7	0	0	0	0	0.0	1	0	0	2	0	3	0	0	0	0	0	0.0	–	DH-3
1980			12	.167	.167	30	5	0	0	0	0.0	3	4	3	7	1	3	0	1	1	0	0	0.2	1.000	DH-9, 1B-1
1982			71	.266	.372	199	53	6	0	5	2.5	23	29	8	19	6	20	5	106	8	3	9	1.6	.974	DH-39, 1B-18, OF-1
3 yrs.			87	.246	.335	236	58	6	0	5	2.1	26	33	11	28	7	26	5	107	9	3	9	1.4	.975	DH-51, 1B-20, OF-1

Randy Velarde

VELARDE, RANDY LEE   BR TR 6'   185 lbs.
B. Nov. 24, 1962, Midland, Tex.

Year	Team		Games	BA	SA	AB	H	2B	3B	HR	HR%	R	RBI	BB	SO	SB	AB	H	PO	A	E	DP	TC/G	FA	G by Pos
1987	NY	A	8	.182	.182	22	4	0	0	0	0.0	1	1	0	6	0	0	0	8	20	2	3	3.8	.933	SS-8
1988			48	.174	.357	115	20	6	0	5	4.3	18	12	8	24	1	0	0	72	98	8	26	3.7	.955	2B-24, SS-14, 3B-11
1989			33	.340	.480	100	34	4	2	2	2.0	12	11	7	14	0	2	1	26	61	4	16	2.8	.956	3B-27, SS-9
3 yrs.			89	.245	.392	237	58	10	2	7	3.0	31	24	15	44	1	2	1	106	179	14	45	3.4	.953	3B-38, SS-31, 2B-24

Freddie Velazquez

VELAZQUEZ, FEDERICO ANTONIO   BR TR 6'1"   185 lbs.
Also known as Federico Velazquez y Velasquez.
B. Dec. 6, 1937, Santo Domingo, Dominican Republic

Year	Team		Games	BA	SA	AB	H	2B	3B	HR	HR%	R	RBI	BB	SO	SB	AB	H	PO	A	E	DP	TC/G	FA	G by Pos
1969	SEA	A	6	.125	.250	16	2	2	0	0	0.0	1	2	1	3	0	1	0	27	0	0	0	4.5	1.000	C-5
1973	ATL	N	15	.348	.391	23	8	1	0	0	0.0	2	3	1	6	0	6	1	36	3	1	0	2.7	.975	C-11
2 yrs.			21	.256	.333	39	10	3	0	0	0.0	3	5	2	6	0	7	1	63	3	1	0	3.2	.985	C-16

Otto Velez

VELEZ, OTONIEL   BR TR 6'   185 lbs.
Born Otoniel Velez y Franceschi.
B. Nov. 29, 1950, Ponce, Puerto Rico

Year	Team		Games	BA	SA	AB	H	2B	3B	HR	HR%	R	RBI	BB	SO	SB	AB	H	PO	A	E	DP	TC/G	FA	G by Pos
1973	NY	A	23	.195	.325	77	15	4	0	2	2.6	9	7	15	24	0	0	0	45	2	2	0	2.1	.959	OF-23
1974			27	.209	.343	67	14	1	1	2	3.0	9	10	15	24	0	2	0	140	8	3	8	5.6	.980	1B-21, OF-3, 3B-2
1975			6	.250	.250	8	2	0	0	0	0.0	1	2	0	2	0	3	1	11	0	0	1	1.8	1.000	DH-1, 1B-1
1976			49	.266	.394	94	25	6	0	2	2.1	11	10	23	26	0	14	3	89	2	2	5	1.9	.978	OF-24, 1B-8, DH-5, 3B-1
1977	TOR	A	120	.256	.458	360	92	19	3	16	4.4	50	62	65	87	4	17	2	140	5	4	1	1.2	.973	OF-79, DH-28
1978			91	.266	.448	248	66	14	2	9	3.6	29	38	45	41	1	20	8	161	12	3	4	1.9	.983	OF-74, DH-9, 1B-1
1979			99	.288	.529	274	79	21	0	15	5.5	45	48	46	45	0	19	5	159	5	4	3	1.7	.976	OF-73, DH-9, 1B-6
1980			104	.269	.487	357	96	12	3	20	5.6	54	62	54	86	0	3	1	36	3	1	2	0.4	.975	DH-97, 1B-3
1981			80	.213	.404	240	51	9	2	11	4.6	32	28	55	60	0	5	1	9	0	0	0	0.1	1.000	DH-74, 1B-1
1982			28	.192	.269	52	10	1	0	1	1.9	4	5	13	15	1	7	1	0	0	0	0	0.0	–	DH-24
1983	CLE	A	10	.080	.080	25	2	0	0	0	0.0	1	3	6	6	0	2	0	0	0	0	0	0.0	–	DH-8
11 yrs.			637	.251	.441	1802	452	87	11	78	4.3	244	272	336	414	6	92	22	790	37	19	24	1.3	.978	OF-276, DH-255, 1B-41, 3B-3

LEAGUE CHAMPIONSHIP SERIES

Year	Team		Games	BA	SA	AB	H	2B	3B	HR	HR%	R	RBI	BB	SO	SB	AB	H	PO	A	E	DP	TC/G	FA	G by Pos
1976	NY	A	1	.000	.000	1	0	0	0	0	0.0	0	0	0	0	0	1	0	0	0	0	0	0.0	–	

WORLD SERIES

Year	Team		Games	BA	SA	AB	H	2B	3B	HR	HR%	R	RBI	BB	SO	SB	AB	H	PO	A	E	DP	TC/G	FA	G by Pos
1976	NY	A	3	.000	.000	3	0	0	0	0	0.0	0	0	0	3	0	3	0	0	0	0	0	0.0	–	

Art Veltman

VELTMAN, ARTHUR PATRICK   BR TR 6'   175 lbs.
B. Mar. 24, 1906, Mobile, Ala.   D. Oct. 1, 1980, San Antonio, Tex.

Year	Team		Games	BA	SA	AB	H	2B	3B	HR	HR%	R	RBI	BB	SO	SB	AB	H	PO	A	E	DP	TC/G	FA	G by Pos
1926	CHI	A	5	.250	.250	4	1	0	0	0	0.0	1	0	1	0	0	3	1	0	1	0	0	0.2	1.000	SS-1
1928	NY	N	1	.333	1.000	3	1	0	1	0	0.0	1	0	1	0	0	0	0	3	0	0	0	3.0	1.000	OF-1
1929			2	.000	.000	1	0	0	0	0	0.0	0	0	2	0	0	1	0	1	0	0	0	0.5	1.000	C-1
1931	BOS	N	1	.000	.000	1	0	0	0	0	0.0	0	0	0	1	0	0	0	0	0	0	0	0.0	–	
1932	NY	N	2	.000	.000	1	0	0	0	0	0.0	0	1	0	1	0	1	0	0	0	0	0	0.0	–	
1934	PIT	N	12	.107	.107	28	3	0	0	0	0.0	2	1	0	1	0	2	0	26	2	0	0	2.3	1.000	C-11
6 yrs.			23	.132	.184	38	5	0	1	0	0.0	4	2	4	3	0	6	1	30	3	0	0	1.4	1.000	C-12, OF-1, SS-1

Max Venable

VENABLE, WILLIAM McKINLEY, JR.   BL TR 5'10"   185 lbs.
B. June 6, 1957, Phoenix, Ariz.

Year	Team		Games	BA	SA	AB	H	2B	3B	HR	HR%	R	RBI	BB	SO	SB	AB	H	PO	A	E	DP	TC/G	FA	G by Pos
1979	SF	N	55	.165	.200	85	14	1	0	0	0.0	12	3	10	18	3	17	5	30	2	3	0	0.6	.914	OF-25
1980			64	.268	.304	138	37	5	0	0	0.0	13	10	15	22	8	26	9	61	0	0	0	1.0	1.000	OF-40
1981			18	.188	.313	32	6	0	2	0	0.0	2	1	4	3	3	12	1	12	0	0	0	0.7	1.000	OF-5
1982			71	.224	.280	125	28	2	1	1	0.8	17	7	7	16	9	17	3	66	6	1	2	1.0	.986	OF-53
1983			94	.219	.364	228	50	7	4	6	2.6	28	27	22	34	15	22	6	141	5	1	0	1.6	.993	OF-66
1984	MON	N	38	.239	.352	71	17	2	0	2	2.8	7	7	3	7	1	13	4	33	0	0	0	0.9	1.000	OF-27
1985	CIN	N	77	.289	.422	135	39	12	3	0	0.0	21	10	6	17	11	35	13	60	3	0	0	0.8	1.000	OF-39
1986			108	.211	.313	147	31	7	1	2	1.4	17	15	17	24	7	51	8	63	0	2	0	0.6	.969	OF-57

Year	Team		Games	BA	SA	AB	H	2B	3B	HR	HR%	R	RBI	BB	SO	SB	Pinch Hit AB	Pinch Hit H	PO	A	E	DP	TC/G	FA	G by Pos

Max Venable *continued*

1987			7	.143	.143	7	1	0	0	0	0.0	2	2	0	0	0	2	1	3	0	0	0	0.4	1.000	OF-4
1989	CAL	A	20	.358	.434	53	19	4	0	0	0.0	7	4	1	16	0	6	1	21	0	0	0	1.1	1.000	OF-13
10 yrs.			552	.237	.332	1021	242	40	12	11	1.1	126	86	85	157	57	201	51	490	16	7	2	0.9	.986	OF-329

Robin Ventura

VENTURA, ROBIN MARK
B. July 14, 1967, Santa Maria, Calif. — BL TR 6'1" 185 lbs.

| 1989 | CHI | A | 16 | .178 | .244 | 45 | 8 | 3 | 0 | 0 | 0.0 | 5 | 7 | 8 | 6 | 0 | 1 | 0 | 17 | 33 | 2 | 2 | 3.3 | .962 | 3B-16 |

Vince Ventura

VENTURA, VINCENT
B. Apr. 18, 1917, New York, N. Y. — BR TR 6'1½" 190 lbs.

| 1945 | WAS | A | 18 | .207 | .207 | 58 | 12 | 0 | 0 | 0 | 0.0 | 4 | 2 | 4 | 4 | 0 | 3 | 1 | 30 | 1 | 4 | 0 | 1.9 | .886 | OF-15 |

Emil Verban

VERBAN, EMIL MATTHEW (Dutch, The Antelope)
B. Aug. 27, 1915, Lincoln, Ill. D. June 8, 1989, Quincy, Ill. — BR TR 5'11" 165 lbs.

1944	STL	N	146	.257	.293	498	128	14	2	0	0.0	51	43	19	14	0	0	0	319	380	23	105	4.9	.968	2B-146
1945			155	.278	.342	597	166	22	8	0	0.0	59	72	19	15	4	0	0	398	406	18	95	5.3	.978	2B-155
1946	2 teams		STL N	(1G – .000)		PHI	N	(138G – .275)																	
"	total		139	.274	.331	474	130	17	5	0	0.0	44	34	21	18	5	1	0	353	381	28	83	5.5	.963	2B-138
1947	PHI	N	155	.285	.341	540	154	14	8	0	0.0	50	42	23	8	5	0	0	450	453	17	111	5.9	.982	2B-155
1948	2 teams		PHI N	(55G – .231)		CHI	N	(56G – .294)																	
"	total		111	.269	.333	417	112	20	2	1	0.2	51	27	15	12	4	1	0	238	290	17	72	4.9	.969	2B-110
1949	CHI	N	98	.289	.327	343	99	11	1	0	0.0	38	22	8	2	3	7	1	218	249	17	60	4.9	.965	2B-88
1950	2 teams		CHI N	(45G – .108)		BOS	N	(4G – .000)																	
"	total		49	.095	.119	42	4	1	0	0	0.0	8	1	3	5	0	13	1	20	21	4	8	0.9	.911	2B-10, SS-3, OF-1, 3B-1
7 yrs.			853	.272	.325	2911	793	99	26	1	0.0	301	241	108	74	21	22	2	1996	2180	124	534	5.0	.971	2B-802, SS-3, OF-1, 3B-1

WORLD SERIES

| 1944 | STL | N | 6 | .412 | .412 | 17 | 7 | 0 | 0 | 0 | 0.0 | 1 | 2 | 2 | 0 | 0 | 0 | 0 | 15 | 7 | 0 | 2 | 3.7 | 1.000 | 2B-6 |

Gene Verble

VERBLE, GENE KERMIT (Satchel)
B. June 29, 1928, Concord, N. C. — BR TR 5'10" 163 lbs.

1951	WAS	A	68	.203	.243	177	36	3	0	0	0.0	16	15	18	10	1	16	2	101	124	5	28	3.4	.978	SS-28, 2B-19, 3B-1
1953			13	.190	.190	21	4	0	0	0	0.0	4	2	2	1	0	1	0	10	18	0	4	2.2	1.000	SS-8
2 yrs.			81	.202	.237	198	40	3	2	0	0.0	20	17	20	11	1	17	2	111	142	5	32	3.2	.981	SS-36, 2B-19, 3B-1

Frank Verdi

VERDI, FRANK MICHAEL
B. June 2, 1926, Brooklyn, N. Y. — BR TR 5'10½" 170 lbs.

| 1953 | NY | A | 1 | – | – | 0 | 0 | 0 | 0 | 0 | – | 0 | 0 | 0 | 0 | 0 | 0 | 0 | 0 | 0 | 0 | 0 | 0.0 | – | SS-1 |

Johnny Vergez

VERGEZ, JOHN LOUIS
B. July 9, 1906, Oakland, Calif. — BR TR 5'8" 165 lbs.

1931	NY	N	152	.278	.396	565	157	24	2	13	2.3	67	81	29	65	11	0	0	146	268	30	23	2.9	.932	3B-152
1932			118	.261	.380	376	98	21	3	6	1.6	42	43	25	36	1	3	1	94	212	23	22	2.8	.930	3B-111, SS-1
1933			123	.271	.448	458	124	21	6	16	3.5	57	72	39	66	1	0	0	101	222	25	17	2.8	.928	3B-123
1934			108	.200	.328	320	64	18	1	7	2.2	31	27	28	55	1	3	0	86	195	17	11	2.8	.943	3B-104
1935	PHI	N	148	.249	.363	546	136	27	4	9	1.6	56	63	46	67	8	0	0	188	222	20	25	2.9	.953	3B-148, SS-2
1936	2 teams		PHI N	(15G – .275)		STL	N	(8G – .167)																	
"	total		23	.241	.345	58	14	3	0	1	1.7	5	6	4	14	0	2	1	19	21	2	3	1.8	.952	3B-20
6 yrs.			672	.255	.385	2323	593	114	16	52	2.2	258	292	171	303	22	8	2	634	1140	117	101	2.8	.938	3B-658, SS-3

Mickey Vernon

VERNON, JAMES BARTON
B. Apr. 22, 1918, Marcus Hook, Pa.
Manager 1961-63. — BL TL 6'2" 170 lbs.

1939	WAS	A	76	.257	.351	276	71	15	4	1	0.4	23	30	24	28	1	0	0	690	40	11	75	9.8	.985	1B-75
1940			5	.158	.158	19	3	0	0	0	0.0	0	0	0	3	0	1	0	41	2	0	5	8.6	1.000	1B-4
1941			138	.299	.443	531	159	27	11	9	1.7	73	93	43	51	9	6	2	1186	80	10	122	9.2	.992	1B-132
1942			151	.271	.388	621	168	34	6	9	1.4	76	86	39	63	25	0	0	1360	95	10	109	9.8	.982	1B-151
1943			145	.268	.387	553	148	29	8	7	1.3	89	70	66	55	24	1	1	1351	75	14	125	9.9	.990	1B-143
1946			148	**.353**	.508	587	207	51	8	8	1.4	88	85	49	64	14	1	1	1320	101	15	133	9.7	.990	1B-147
1947			154	.265	.388	600	159	29	12	7	1.2	77	85	49	42	12	0	0	1299	105	19	123	9.4	.987	1B-154
1948			150	.242	.332	558	135	27	7	3	0.5	78	48	54	43	15	1	0	1297	113	15	128	9.5	.989	1B-150
1949	CLE	A	153	.291	.443	584	170	27	4	18	3.1	72	83	58	51	9	0	0	1438	155	14	168	10.5	.991	1B-153
1950	2 teams		CLE A	(28G – .189)		WAS	A	(90G – .306)																	
"	total		118	.281	.400	417	117	17	3	9	2.2	55	75	62	39	8	8	1	959	78	9	121	8.9	.991	1B-110
1951	WAS	A	141	.293	.423	546	160	30	7	9	1.6	69	87	53	45	7	3	3	1157	87	8	121	8.9	.994	1B-137
1952			154	.251	.394	569	143	33	9	10	1.8	71	80	89	66	7	0	0	1291	115	10	139	9.2	.993	1B-153
1953			152	**.337**	.518	608	205	43	11	15	2.5	101	115	63	57	1	0	0	1376	94	12	158	9.8	.992	1B-152
1954			151	.290	.492	597	173	33	14	20	3.4	90	97	61	61	1	3	2	1365	76	11	144	9.6	.992	1B-148
1955			150	.301	.452	538	162	23	8	14	2.6	74	85	74	50	0	7	2	1258	69	8	137	8.9	.994	1B-144
1956	BOS	A	119	.310	.511	403	125	28	4	15	3.7	67	84	57	40	1	10	4	930	58	11	96	8.4	.989	1B-108
1957			102	.241	.393	270	65	18	1	7	2.6	36	38	41	35	0	22	6	662	51	6	47	7.0	.992	1B-70
1958	CLE	A	119	.293	.439	355	104	22	3	8	2.3	49	55	44	56	0	24	7	774	50	11	90	7.0	.987	1B-96
1959	MIL	N	74	.220	.363	91	20	4	0	3	3.3	8	14	7	20	0	59	13	65	4	2	3	1.0	.972	1B-10, OF-4
1960	PIT	N	9	.125	.125	8	1	0	0	0	0.0	0	1	0	1	0	8	1	0	0	0	0	0.0	–	
20 yrs.			2409	.286	.428	8731	2495	490	120	172	2.0	1196	1311	934	869	137	154	43	19819	1448	212	2044	8.9	.990	1B-2237, OF-4

Zoilo Versalles

VERSALLES, ZOILO CASANOVA (Zorro)
Born Zoilo Casanova Versalles y Rodriguez.
B. Dec. 18, 1939, Havana, Cuba — BR TR 5'10" 146 lbs.

| 1959 | WAS | A | 29 | .153 | .203 | 59 | 9 | 0 | 0 | 1 | 1.7 | 4 | 4 | 4 | 15 | 1 | 0 | 0 | 41 | 59 | 6 | 13 | 3.7 | .943 | SS-29 |
| 1960 | | | 15 | .133 | .267 | 45 | 6 | 2 | 2 | 0 | 0.0 | 2 | 4 | 2 | 5 | 0 | 0 | 0 | 30 | 42 | 5 | 6 | 5.1 | .935 | SS-15 |

Year	Team		Games	BA	SA	AB	H	2B	3B	HR	HR%	R	RBI	BB	SO	SB	Pinch Hit AB	Pinch Hit H	PO	A	E	DP	TC/G	FA	G by Pos

Zoilo Versalles *continued*

Year	Team		Games	BA	SA	AB	H	2B	3B	HR	HR%	R	RBI	BB	SO	SB	AB	H	PO	A	E	DP	TC/G	FA	G by Pos
1961	MIN	A	129	.280	.390	510	143	25	5	7	1.4	65	53	25	61	16	0	0	229	371	30	74	4.9	.952	SS-129
1962			160	.241	.373	568	137	18	3	17	3.0	69	67	37	71	5	0	0	335	501	26	127	5.4	.970	SS-160
1963			159	.261	.401	.21	162	31	13	10	1.6	74	54	33	66	7	0	0	301	448	30	87	4.9	.961	SS-159
1964			160	.259	.431	659	171	33	10	20	3.0	94	64	42	88	14	1	1	271	427	31	89	4.6	.957	SS-160
1965			160	.273	.462	666	182	45	12	19	2.9	126	77	41	122	27	0	0	248	487	39	105	4.8	.950	SS-160
1966			137	.249	.346	543	135	20	6	7	1.3	73	36	40	85	10	2	0	195	377	35	69	4.4	.942	SS-135
1967			160	.200	.282	581	116	16	7	6	1.0	63	50	33	113	5	0	0	229	454	30	81	4.5	.958	SS-159
1968	LA	N	122	.196	.266	403	79	16	3	2	0.5	29	24	26	84	6	2	1	204	380	28	62	5.0	.954	SS-119
1969	2 teams			CLE A (72G – .226)			WAS A (31G – .267)																			
"	total		103	.236	.305	292	69	13	2	1	0.3	30	19	24	60	4	13	4	121	185	11	29	3.1	.965	2B-52, 3B-35, SS-16
1971	ATL	N	66	.191	.325	194	37	11	0	5	2.6	21	22	11	40	2	9	1	63	107	13	13	2.8	.929	3B-30, SS-24, 2B-1
	12 yrs.		1400	.242	.367	5141	1246	230	63	95	1.8	650	471	318	810	97	27	7	2267	3838	284	755	4.6	.956	SS-1265, 3B-65, 2B-53

WORLD SERIES

Year	Team		Games	BA	SA	AB	H	2B	3B	HR	HR%	R	RBI	BB	SO	SB	AB	H	PO	A	E	DP	TC/G	FA	G by Pos
1965	MIN	A	7	.286	.500	28	8	1	1	1	3.6	3	4	2	7	1	0	0	13	12	0	3	3.6	1.000	SS-7

Tom Veryzer

VERYZER, THOMAS MARTIN
B. Feb. 11, 1953, Port Jefferson, N. Y.

BR TR 6'1½" 175 lbs.

Year	Team		Games	BA	SA	AB	H	2B	3B	HR	HR%	R	RBI	BB	SO	SB	AB	H	PO	A	E	DP	TC/G	FA	G by Pos
1973	DET	A	18	.300	.400	20	6	0	1	0	0.0	1	2	2	4	0	0	0	6	12	3	1	1.2	.857	SS-18
1974			22	.236	.382	55	13	2	0	2	3.6	4	9	5	8	1	1	0	18	33	4	4	2.5	.927	SS-20
1975			128	.252	.327	404	102	13	1	5	1.2	37	48	23	76	2	0	0	215	358	24	62	4.7	.960	SS-128
1976			97	.234	.287	354	83	8	2	1	0.3	31	25	21	44	1	0	0	164	313	17	53	5.1	.966	SS-97
1977			125	.197	.254	350	69	12	1	2	0.6	31	28	16	44	0	0	0	185	377	18	62	4.6	.969	SS-124
1978	CLE	A	130	.271	.340	421	114	18	4	0	0.2	48	32	13	36	1	0	0	177	375	21	58	4.4	.963	SS-129
1979			149	.220	.254	449	99	9	3	0	0.0	41	34	34	54	2	0	0	238	446	18	90	4.7	.974	SS-148
1980			109	.271	.321	358	97	12	0	2	0.6	28	28	10	25	0	0	0	169	331	15	59	4.7	.971	SS-108
1981			75	.244	.262	221	54	4	0	0	0.0	13	14	10	10	1	0	0	121	207	10	48	4.5	.970	SS-75
1982	NY	N	40	.333	.370	54	18	2	0	0	0.0	6	4	3	4	1	1	0	40	44	7	4	2.3	.923	2B-26, SS-16
1983	CHI	N	59	.205	.273	88	18	3	0	1	1.1	3	3	3	13	0	11	3	27	73	2	17	1.7	.980	SS-28, 3B-17
1984			44	.189	.203	74	14	1	0	0	0.0	5	4	3	11	0	0	0	44	63	5	13	2.5	.955	SS-36, 3B-5, 2B-4
	12 yrs.		996	.241	.294	2848	687	84	12	14	0.5	250	231	143	329	9	12	3	1404	2632	144	471	4.2	.966	SS-927, 2B-30, 3B-22

LEAGUE CHAMPIONSHIP SERIES

Year	Team		Games	BA	SA	AB	H	2B	3B	HR	HR%	R	RBI	BB	SO	SB	AB	H	PO	A	E	DP	TC/G	FA	G by Pos
1984	CHI	N	3	.000	.000	1	0	0	0	0	0.0	0	0	0	0	0	0	0	0	0	0	0	0.0	–	SS-1, 3B-1

Ernie Vick

VICK, HENRY ARTHUR
B. July 2, 1900, Toledo, Ohio   D. July 16, 1980, Ann Arbor, Mich.

BR TR 5'9½" 185 lbs.

Year	Team		Games	BA	SA	AB	H	2B	3B	HR	HR%	R	RBI	BB	SO	SB	AB	H	PO	A	E	DP	TC/G	FA	G by Pos
1922	STL	N	3	.333	.667	6	2	2	0	0	0.0	1	0	0	0	0	0	0	7	0	1	1	2.7	.875	C-3
1924			16	.348	.391	23	8	1	0	0	0.0	2	0	3	3	0	0	0	26	11	1	4	2.4	.974	C-16
1925			14	.188	.313	32	6	2	1	0	0.0	3	3	3	1	0	5	0	34	5	3	0	3.0	.929	C-9
1926			24	.196	.235	51	10	2	0	0	0.0	6	4	3	4	0	1	0	40	11	3	1	2.3	.944	C-23
	4 yrs.		57	.232	.313	112	26	7	1	0	0.0	12	7	9	8	0	6	0	107	27	8	6	2.5	.944	C-51

Sammy Vick

VICK, SAMUEL BRUCE
B. Apr. 12, 1895, Batesville, Miss.   D. Aug. 17, 1986, Memphis, Tenn.

BR TR 5'10½" 163 lbs.

Year	Team		Games	BA	SA	AB	H	2B	3B	HR	HR%	R	RBI	BB	SO	SB	AB	H	PO	A	E	DP	TC/G	FA	G by Pos
1917	NY	A	10	.278	.361	36	10	3	0	0	0.0	4	2	1	6	2	0	0	14	1	2	0	1.7	.882	OF-10
1918			2	.667	.667	3	2	0	0	0	0.0	1	1	0	0	0	1	0	0	0	0	0	0.0	–	OF-1
1919			106	.248	.344	407	101	15	9	2	0.5	59	27	35	55	9	5	1	166	11	9	2	1.8	.952	OF-100
1920			51	.220	.297	118	26	7	1	0	0.0	21	11	14	20	1	17	6	56	0	3	0	1.2	.949	OF-33
1921	BOS	A	44	.260	.325	77	20	3	1	0	0.0	5	9	1	10	0	28	8	21	1	0	0	0.5	1.000	OF-14, C-1
	5 yrs.		213	.248	.335	641	159	28	11	2	0.3	90	50	51	91	12	51	15	257	13	14	2	1.3	.951	OF-158, C-1

George Vico

VICO, GEORGE STEVE (Sam)
B. Aug. 9, 1923, San Fernando, Calif.

BL TR 6'4" 200 lbs.

Year	Team		Games	BA	SA	AB	H	2B	3B	HR	HR%	R	RBI	BB	SO	SB	AB	H	PO	A	E	DP	TC/G	FA	G by Pos
1948	DET	A	144	.267	.392	521	139	23	9	8	1.5	50	58	39	39	2	0	0	1169	85	15	112	8.8	.988	1B-142
1949			67	.190	.338	142	27	5	2	4	2.8	15	18	21	17	0	13	2	372	32	6	36	6.1	.985	1B-53
	2 yrs.		211	.250	.380	663	166	28	11	12	1.8	65	76	60	56	2	15	2	1541	117	21	148	8.0	.987	1B-195

Jose Vidal

VIDAL, JOSE (Papito)
Born Jose Vidal y Nicolas.
B. Apr. 3, 1940, Batey Lechugas, Dominican Republic

BR TR 6' 190 lbs.

Year	Team		Games	BA	SA	AB	H	2B	3B	HR	HR%	R	RBI	BB	SO	SB	AB	H	PO	A	E	DP	TC/G	FA	G by Pos
1966	CLE	A	17	.188	.281	32	6	1	1	0	0.0	4	3	5	11	0	4	0	16	0	0	0	0.9	1.000	OF-11
1967			16	.118	.118	34	4	0	0	0	0.0	4	0	7	12	0	4	1	20	1	0	0	1.3	1.000	OF-10
1968			37	.167	.278	54	9	0	0	2	3.7	5	5	2	15	3	11	1	22	2	0	0	0.6	1.000	OF-26, 1B-1
1969	SEA	A	18	.192	.385	26	5	0	1	1	3.8	7	2	4	8	1	5	0	11	0	1	0	0.7	.917	OF-6
	4 yrs.		88	.164	.260	146	24	1	2	3	2.1	20	10	18	46	4	24	2	69	3	1	0	0.8	.986	OF-53, 1B-1

Charlie Vinson

VINSON, CHARLES ANTHONY
B. Jan. 5, 1944, Washington, D. C.

BL TL 6'3" 207 lbs.

Year	Team		Games	BA	SA	AB	H	2B	3B	HR	HR%	R	RBI	BB	SO	SB	AB	H	PO	A	E	DP	TC/G	FA	G by Pos
1966	CAL	A	13	.182	.409	22	4	2	0	1	4.5	3	6	5	9	0	0	0	72	2	0	8	5.7	1.000	1B-11

Rube Vinson

VINSON, ERNEST AUGUSTUS
B. Mar. 20, 1879, Dover, Del.   D. Oct. 12, 1951, Chester, Pa.

5'9" 168 lbs.

Year	Team		Games	BA	SA	AB	H	2B	3B	HR	HR%	R	RBI	BB	SO	SB	AB	H	PO	A	E	DP	TC/G	FA	G by Pos
1904	CLE	A	15	.306	.327	49	15	1	0	0	0.0	12	6	10		2	0	0	24	6	0	0	2.0	1.000	OF-15
1905			38	.195	.233	133	26	3	1	0	0.0	12	9	7		4	2	0	65	1	5	0	1.9	.930	OF-36
1906	CHI	A	7	.250	.250	24	6	0	0	0	0.0	2	3	2		1	1	0	6	0	4	0	1.4	.600	OF-4
	3 yrs.		60	.228	.257	206	47	4	1	0	0.0	26	14	19		7	3	0	95	7	9	0	1.9	.919	OF-55

Jim Viox

VIOX, JAMES HENRY
B. Dec. 30, 1890, Lockland, Ohio   D. Jan. 6, 1969, Erlanger, Ky.

BR TR 5'7" 150 lbs.

Year	Team		Games	BA	SA	AB	H	2B	3B	HR	HR%	R	RBI	BB	SO	SB	AB	H	PO	A	E	DP	TC/G	FA	G by Pos
1912	PIT	N	33	.186	.343	70	13	2	3	1	1.4	8	7	3	5	2	8	0	21	30	4	2	1.7	.927	3B-10, SS-8, OF-3, 2B-1

Year	Team		Games	BA	SA	AB	H	2B	3B	HR	HR%	R	RBI	BB	SO	SB	Pinch Hit AB	Pinch Hit H	PO	A	E	DP	TC/G	FA	G by Pos

Jim Viox *continued*

Year	Team	Games	BA	SA	AB	H	2B	3B	HR	HR%	R	RBI	BB	SO	SB	AB	H	PO	A	E	DP	TC/G	FA	G by Pos
1913		137	.317	.427	492	156	32	8	2	0.4	86	65	64	28	14	2	1	241	334	30	30	4.4	.950	2B-124, SS-10
1914		143	.265	.326	506	134	18	5	1	0.2	52	57	63	33	9	1	0	256	402	45	43	4.9	.936	2B-138, OF-2, SS-2
1915		150	.256	.334	503	129	17	8	2	0.4	56	45	75	31	12	2	1	252	387	31	35	4.5	.954	2B-135, 3B-13, OF-2
1916		43	.250	.326	132	33	7	0	1	0.8	12	17	17	11	2	6	1	41	75	9	6	2.9	.928	2B-25, 3B-11
5 yrs.		506	.273	.358	1703	465	76	24	7	0.4	214	191	222	108	39	19	3	811	1228	119	116	4.3	.945	2B-423, 3B-34, SS-20, OF-7

Bill Virdon

VIRDON, WILLIAM CHARLES
B. June 9, 1931, Hazel Park, Mich.
Manager 1972-84.

BL TR 6' 175 lbs.

Year	Team		Games	BA	SA	AB	H	2B	3B	HR	HR%	R	RBI	BB	SO	SB	AB	H	PO	A	E	DP	TC/G	FA	G by Pos
1955	STL	N	144	.281	.433	534	150	18	6	17	3.2	58	68	36	64	2	9	1	339	7	12	1	2.5	.966	OF-142
1956	2 teams		STL N (24G – .211)			PIT N (133G – .334)																			
"	total		157	.319	.445	580	185	23	10	10	1.7	77	46	38	71	6	6	0	387	12	5	2	2.6	.988	OF-154
1957	PIT	N	144	.251	.383	561	141	28	11	8	1.4	59	50	33	69	3	5	1	403	13	6	2	2.9	.986	OF-141
1958			144	.267	.387	604	161	24	11	9	1.5	75	46	52	70	5	1	0	401	11	3	0	2.9	.993	OF-143
1959			144	.254	.355	519	132	24	2	8	1.5	67	41	55	65	7	0	0	404	16	9	5	3.0	.979	OF-144
1960			120	.264	.406	409	108	16	9	8	2.0	60	40	40	44	8	9	3	272	10	5	0	2.4	.983	OF-109
1961			146	.260	.369	599	156	22	8	9	1.5	81	58	49	45	5	1	0	384	6	6	4	2.7	.985	OF-145
1962			156	.247	.345	663	164	27	10	6	0.9	82	47	36	65	5	0	0	360	11	9	4	2.4	.976	OF-156
1963			142	.269	.374	554	149	22	6	8	1.4	58	53	43	55	1	1	0	323	6	4	2	2.3	.988	OF-142
1964			145	.243	.298	473	115	11	3	3	0.6	59	27	30	48	1	10	2	243	5	6	1	1.8	.976	OF-134
1965			135	.279	.370	481	134	22	5	4	0.8	58	24	30	49	4	11	1	260	3	8	1	2.0	.970	OF-128
1968			6	.333	1.333	3	1	0	1	1	33.3	1	2	0	2	0	2	1	1	0	0	0	0.2	1.000	OF-4
12 yrs.			1583	.267	.379	5980	1596	237	81	91	1.5	735	502	442	647	47	54	9	3777	100	73	18	2.5	.982	OF-1542

WORLD SERIES

Year	Team		Games	BA	SA	AB	H	2B	3B	HR	HR%	R	RBI	BB	SO	SB	AB	H	PO	A	E	DP	TC/G	FA	G by Pos
1960	PIT	N	7	.241	.345	29	7	3	0	0	0.0	2	5	1	3	1	0	1	18	0	1	0	2.7	.947	OF-7

Ozzie Virgil

VIRGIL, OSVALDO JOSE
Born Osvaldo Jose Virgil y Pichardo. Father of Ozzie Virgil.
B. May 17, 1933, Montecristi, Dominican Republic

BR TR 6'1" 174 lbs.

Year	Team		Games	BA	SA	AB	H	2B	3B	HR	HR%	R	RBI	BB	SO	SB	AB	H	PO	A	E	DP	TC/G	FA	G by Pos
1956	NY	N	3	.417	.667	12	5	1	0	0	0.0	2	2	0	0	1	0	0	3	1	1	1	1.7	.800	3B-3
1957			96	.235	.305	226	53	0	2	4	1.8	26	24	14	27	2	8	2	64	111	12	10	1.9	.936	3B-62, OF-24, SS-1
1958	DET	A	49	.244	.363	193	47	10	2	3	1.6	19	19	8	20	1	1	0	55	101	3	7	3.2	.981	3B-49
1960			62	.227	.356	132	30	4	2	3	2.3	16	13	4	14	1	8	2	52	85	4	13	2.3	.972	3B-42, 2B-8, SS-5, C-1
1961	2 teams		31			DET A (20G – .133)						KC A (11G – .143)														
"	total		31	.137	.196	51	7	0	0	1	2.0	2	1	1	8	0	12	3	23	17	3	3	1.4	.930	3B-13, C-6, SS-1, 2B-1
1962	BAL	A	1	–	–	0	0	0	0	0	0.0	0	0	1	0	0	0	0	0	0	0	0	0.0	–	
1965	PIT	N	39	.265	.367	49	13	2	0	1	2.0	3	5	2	10	0	18	6	36	17	1	4	1.4	.981	C-15, 3B-7, 2B-5
1966	SF	N	42	.213	.303	89	19	2	0	2	2.2	7	9	4	12	1	12	1	110	26	3	5	3.3	.978	3B-13, C-13, 1B-5, OF-2, 2B-2
1969			1	.000	.000	1	0	0	0	0	0.0	0	0	0	0	0	1	0	0	0	0	0	0.0	–	
9 yrs.			324	.231	.331	753	174	19	7	14	1.9	75	73	34	91	6	60	14	343	358	27	43	2.2	.963	3B-189, C-35, OF-26, 2B-16, SS-7, 1B-5

Ozzie Virgil

VIRGIL, OSVALDO JOSE
Born Osvaldo Jose Virgil y Lopez. Son of Ozzie Virgil.
B. Dec. 7, 1956, Mayaguez, Puerto Rico

BR TR 6'1" 205 lbs.

Year	Team		Games	BA	SA	AB	H	2B	3B	HR	HR%	R	RBI	BB	SO	SB	AB	H	PO	A	E	DP	TC/G	FA	G by Pos
1980	PHI	N	1	.200	.400	5	1	1	0	0	0.0	0	0	0	1	0	0	0	4	0	0	0	4.0	1.000	C-1
1981			6	.000	.000	6	0	0	0	0	0.0	0	0	0	2	0	5	0	2	0	0	0	0.3	1.000	C-1
1982			49	.238	.386	101	24	6	0	3	3.0	11	8	10	26	0	14	3	173	14	7	3	4.0	.964	C-35
1983			55	.214	.393	140	30	7	0	6	4.3	11	23	8	34	0	8	2	228	24	9	2	4.7	.966	C-51
1984			141	.261	.434	456	119	21	2	18	3.9	61	68	45	91	1	8	2	722	58	6	6	5.6	.992	C-137
1985			131	.246	.432	426	105	16	3	19	4.5	47	55	49	85	0	12	4	667	52	4	11	5.5	.994	C-120
1986	ATL	N	114	.223	.373	359	80	9	0	15	4.2	45	48	63	73	1	5	0	682	93	13	9	6.9	.984	C-111
1987			123	.247	.471	429	106	13	1	27	6.3	57	72	47	81	0	3	0	654	74	8	12	6.0	.989	C-122
1988			107	.256	.372	320	82	10	0	9	2.8	23	31	22	54	2	15	7	448	45	5	3	4.7	.990	C-96
1989	TOR	A	9	.182	.545	11	2	1	0	1	9.1	2	2	4	3	0	2	1	1	0	0	0	0.1	1.000	DH-6, C-1
10 yrs.			736	.244	.417	2253	549	84	6	98	4.3	258	307	248	450	4	72	19	3581	360	52	46	5.4	.987	C-675, DH-6

LEAGUE CHAMPIONSHIP SERIES

Year	Team		Games	BA	SA	AB	H	2B	3B	HR	HR%	R	RBI	BB	SO	SB	AB	H	PO	A	E	DP	TC/G	FA	G by Pos
1983	PHI	N	1	.000	.000	1	0	0	0	0	0.0	0	0	0	1	0	1	0	0	0	0	0	0.0	–	

WORLD SERIES

Year	Team		Games	BA	SA	AB	H	2B	3B	HR	HR%	R	RBI	BB	SO	SB	AB	H	PO	A	E	DP	TC/G	FA	G by Pos
1983	PHI	N	3	.500	.500	2	1	0	0	0	0.0	0	0	0	2	0	2	1	0	0	0	0	0.3	1.000	C-1

Jake Virtue

VIRTUE, JACOB KITCHLINE
B. Mar. 2, 1865, Philadelphia, Pa. D. Feb. 3, 1943, Camden, N. J.

BB TR 5'9½" 165 lbs.

Year	Team		Games	BA	SA	AB	H	2B	3B	HR	HR%	R	RBI	BB	SO	SB	AB	H	PO	A	E	DP	TC/G	FA	G by Pos
1890	CLE	N	62	.305	.404	223	68	6	5	2	0.9	39	25	49	15	9	0	0	633	21	12	33	10.7	.982	1B-62
1891			139	.261	.364	517	135	19	14	2	0.4	82	72	75	40	15	0	0	1465	44	44	70	11.2	.972	1B-139
1892			147	.282	.391	557	157	15	20	2	0.4	98	89	84	68	14	0	0	1500	61	26	61	10.8	.984	1B-147
1893			97	.265	.368	378	100	16	10	1	0.3	87	60	54	14	11	0	0	820	76	28	50	9.5	.970	1B-73, OF-13, SS-5, 3B-5, P-1
1894			29	.258	.326	89	23	4	1	0	0.0	15	10	13	3	1	4	0	65	8	7	0	2.8	.913	OF-21, 2B-3, 1B-2, P-1
5 yrs.			474	.274	.376	1764	483	60	50	7	0.4	321	256	275	140	50	4	0	4483	210	117	214	10.1	.976	1B-423, OF-34, SS-5, 3B-5, 2B-3, P-2

Joe Visner

VISNER, JOSEPH PAUL
Born Joseph Paul Vezina.
B. Sept. 27, 1859, Minneapolis, Minn. Deceased.

BL TR 5'11" 180 lbs.

Year	Team		Games	BA	SA	AB	H	2B	3B	HR	HR%	R	RBI	BB	SO	SB	AB	H	PO	A	E	DP	TC/G	FA	G by Pos
1885	BAL	AA	4	.231	.231	13	3	0	0	0	0.0	2			2		0	0	6	0	2	0	2.0	.750	OF-4
1889	BKN	AA	80	.258	.447	295	76	12	10	8	2.7	56	68	36	36	13	0	0	237	74	42	8	4.4	.881	C-53, OF-29
1890	PIT	P	127	.265	.395	521	138	15	22	3	0.6	110	71	76	44	18	0	0	198	18	26	4	1.9	.893	OF-127

Year	Team		Games	BA	SA	AB	H	2B	3B	HR	HR%	R	RBI	BB	SO	SB	Pinch Hit AB	H	PO	A	E	DP	TC/G	FA	G by Pos

Joe Visner *continued*

Year	Team		Games	BA	SA	AB	H	2B	3B	HR	HR%	R	RBI	BB	SO	SB	AB	H	PO	A	E	DP	TC/G	FA	G by Pos
1891	2 teams	WAS AA (18G – .279)			STL AA (6G – .148)																				
"	total		24	.242	.379	95	23	2	4	1	1.1	15	8	8	10	2	0	0	33	4	8	0	1.9	.822	OF-23, 3B-1, C-1
4 yrs.			235	.260	.408	924	240	29	36	12	1.3	183	147	122	90	33	0	0	474	96	78	12	2.8	.880	OF-183, C-54, 3B-1

Ossie Vitt

VITT, OSCAR JOSEPH
B. Jan. 4, 1890, San Francisco, Calif.   D. Jan. 31, 1963, Oakland, Calif.
Manager 1938-40.

BR TR 5'10" 150 lbs.

Year	Team		Games	BA	SA	AB	H	2B	3B	HR	HR%	R	RBI	BB	SO	SB	AB	H	PO	A	E	DP	TC/G	FA	G by Pos
1912	DET	A	73	.245	.289	273	67	4	4	0	0.0	39	19	18		17	7	1	109	99	11	8	3.0	.950	OF-27, 3B-24, 2B-15
1913			99	.240	.304	359	86	11	3	2	0.6	45	33	31	18	5	2	0	174	283	23	25	4.8	.952	2B-78, 3B-17, OF-2
1914			66	.251	.287	195	49	7	0	0	0.0	35	8	31	8	10	8	0	68	155	9	13	3.5	.961	2B-36, 3B-16, OF-2, SS-1
1915			152	.250	.334	560	140	18	13	1	0.2	116	48	80	22	26	0	0	191	325	19	19	3.5	.964	3B-151, 2B-2
1916			153	.226	.295	597	135	17	12	0	0.0	88	42	75	28	18	0	0	210	389	22	32	4.1	.965	3B-151, SS-2
1917			140	.254	.303	512	130	13	6	0	0.0	65	47	56	15	18	0	0	164	260	27	18	3.2	.940	3B-140
1918			81	.240	.273	267	64	5	2	0	0.0	29	17	32	6	5	3	0	128	159	14	17	3.7	.953	3B-66, 2B-9, OF-3
1919	BOS	A	133	.243	.277	469	114	10	3	0	0.0	64	40	44	11	9	0	0	129	254	13	24	3.0	.967	3B-133
1920			87	.220	.291	296	65	10	4	1	0.3	50	28	43	10	5	1	0	99	208	8	17	3.6	.975	3B-64, 2B-21
1921			78	.190	.246	232	44	11	1	0	0.0	29	12	45	13	1	2	1	75	138	9	16	2.8	.959	3B-71, OF-3, 1B-2
10 yrs.			1062	.238	.295	3760	894	106	48	4	0.1	560	294	455	131	114	23	2	1347	2270	155	189	3.6	.959	3B-833, 2B-161, OF-37, SS-3, 1B-2

Jose Vizcaino

VIZCAINO, JOSE LUIS
Born Jose Luis Vizcaino y Pimental.
B. Mar. 26, 1968, San Cristobal, Dominican Republic

BB TR 6'1" 150 lbs.

Year	Team		Games	BA	SA	AB	H	2B	3B	HR	HR%	R	RBI	BB	SO	SB	AB	H	PO	A	E	DP	TC/G	FA	G by Pos
1989	LA	N	7	.200	.200	10	2	0	0	0	0.0	2	0	0	1	0	1	1	6	9	2	2	2.4	.882	SS-5

Omar Vizquel

VIZQUEL, OMAR ENRIQUE
Born Omar Enrique Vizquel y Gonzalez.
B. May 15, 1967, Caracas, Venezuela

BB TR 5'9" 155 lbs.

Year	Team		Games	BA	SA	AB	H	2B	3B	HR	HR%	R	RBI	BB	SO	SB	AB	H	PO	A	E	DP	TC/G	FA	G by Pos
1989	SEA	A	143	.220	.261	387	85	7	3	1	0.3	45	20	28	40	1	2	0	208	388	18	102	4.3	.971	SS-143

Otto Vogel

VOGEL, OTTO HENRY
B. Oct. 26, 1899, Mendota, Ill.   D. July 19, 1969, Iowa City, Iowa

BR TR 6' 195 lbs.

Year	Team		Games	BA	SA	AB	H	2B	3B	HR	HR%	R	RBI	BB	SO	SB	AB	H	PO	A	E	DP	TC/G	FA	G by Pos
1923	CHI	N	41	.210	.272	81	17	0	1	1	1.2	10	6	7	11	2	6	1	37	4	3	1	1.1	.932	OF-24, 3B-1
1924			70	.267	.372	172	46	11	2	1	0.6	28	24	10	26	4	9	2	101	10	5	2	1.7	.957	OF-53, 3B-2
2 yrs.			111	.249	.340	253	63	11	3	2	0.8	38	30	17	37	6	15	3	138	14	8	3	1.4	.950	OF-77, 3B-3

Clyde Vollmer

VOLLMER, CLYDE FREDERICK
B. Sept. 24, 1921, Cincinnati, Ohio

BR TR 6'1" 185 lbs.

Year	Team		Games	BA	SA	AB	H	2B	3B	HR	HR%	R	RBI	BB	SO	SB	AB	H	PO	A	E	DP	TC/G	FA	G by Pos
1942	CIN	N	12	.093	.163	43	4	0	0	1	2.3	2	4	1	5	0	1	0	32	0	0	0	2.7	1.000	OF-11
1946			9	.182	.182	22	4	0	0	0	0.0	1	1	1	3	2	1	0	9	0	0	0	1.0	1.000	OF-7
1947			78	.219	.303	155	34	10	0	1	0.6	19	13	9	18	0	11	3	125	2	2	0	1.7	.984	OF-66
1948	2 teams	CIN N (7G – .111)			WAS A (1G – .400)																				
"	total		8	.214	.214	14	3	0	0	0	0.0	1	0	1	2	0	5	1	3	0	0	0	0.4	1.000	OF-3
1949	WAS	A	129	.253	.391	443	112	22	1	14	3.2	58	59	53	62	1	13	5	324	3	6	1	2.6	.982	OF-114
1950	2 teams	WAS A (6G – .286)			BOS A (57G – .284)																				
"	total		63	.284	.454	183	52	10	3	7	3.8	39	38	23	40	2	19	4	85	4	4	0	1.5	.957	OF-42
1951	BOS	A	115	.251	.456	386	97	9	2	22	5.7	66	85	55	66	0	6	1	206	5	3	0	1.9	.986	OF-106
1952			90	.264	.476	250	66	12	4	11	4.4	35	50	39	47	2	20	5	143	3	0	1	1.6	1.000	OF-70
1953	2 teams	BOS A (1G – .000)			WAS A (118G – .260)																				
"	total		119	.260	.392	408	106	15	3	11	2.7	54	74	49	59	0	12	4	227	8	5	1	2.0	.979	OF-106
1954	WAS	A	62	.256	.342	117	30	4	0	2	1.7	8	15	12	28	0	31	6	33	2	0	1	0.6	1.000	OF-26
10 yrs.			685	.251	.402	2021	508	77	10	69	3.4	283	339	243	330	7	119	29	1187	27	20	4	1.8	.984	OF-551

Fritz Von Kolnitz

VON KOLNITZ, ALFRED HOLMES
B. May 20, 1893, Charleston, S. C.   D. Mar. 18, 1948, Mount Pleasant, S. C.

BR TR 5'10½" 175 lbs.

Year	Team		Games	BA	SA	AB	H	2B	3B	HR	HR%	R	RBI	BB	SO	SB	AB	H	PO	A	E	DP	TC/G	FA	G by Pos
1914	CIN	N	41	.221	.240	104	23	2	0	0	0.0	8	6	6	16	4	7	0	31	44	9	2	2.0	.893	3B-20, OF-11, C-2, 1B-1
1915			50	.192	.269	78	15	4	1	0	0.0	6	6	7	11	1	20	6	15	22	3	4	0.8	.925	3B-18, SS-6, 1B-3, C-2, OF-1
1916	CHI	A	24	.227	.295	44	10	3	0	0	0.0	1	7	2	6	0	10	3	9	11	2	1	0.9	.909	3B-13
3 yrs.			115	.212	.261	226	48	9	1	0	0.0	15	19	15	33	5	37	9	55	77	14	7	1.3	.904	3B-51, OF-12, SS-6, 1B-4, C-4

Joe Vosmik

VOSMIK, JOSEPH FRANKLIN
B. Apr. 4, 1910, Cleveland, Ohio   D. Jan. 27, 1962, Cleveland, Ohio

BR TR 6' 185 lbs.

Year	Team		Games	BA	SA	AB	H	2B	3B	HR	HR%	R	RBI	BB	SO	SB	AB	H	PO	A	E	DP	TC/G	FA	G by Pos
1930	CLE	A	9	.231	.308	26	6	2	0	0	0.0	1	4	1	1	0	2	0	13	1	1	1	1.7	.933	OF-5
1931			149	.320	.464	591	189	36	14	7	1.2	80	117	38	30	7	2	1	315	12	10	2	2.3	.970	OF-147
1932			153	.312	.462	621	194	39	12	10	1.6	106	97	58	42	2	0	1	432	12	5	4	2.9	.989	OF-153
1933			119	.263	.381	438	115	20	10	4	0.9	53	56	42	13	0	5	1	242	15	4	3	2.2	.985	OF-113
1934			104	.341	.477	405	138	33	2	6	1.5	71	78	35	10	1	1	1	199	7	5	2	2.0	.976	OF-104
1935			152	.348	.537	620	216	47	20	10	1.6	93	110	59	30	2	1	1	347	5	5	3	2.3	.986	OF-150
1936			138	.287	.413	506	145	29	4	7	1.4	76	94	79	21	5	2	2	258	11	6	1	2.0	.978	OF-136
1937	STL	A	144	.325	.455	594	193	44	7	4	0.7	81	93	49	38	2	1	0	333	12	10	4	2.5	.972	OF-143
1938	BOS	A	146	.324	.446	621	201	37	6	9	1.4	121	86	59	26	0	0	0	302	14	7	4	2.2	.978	OF-146
1939			145	.276	.388	554	153	29	6	7	1.3	89	84	66	33	4	0	0	296	9	8	0	2.2	.974	OF-144
1940	BKN	N	116	.282	.354	404	114	14	6	1	0.2	45	42	22	21	0	17	5	193	9	5	1	1.8	.976	OF-99
1941			25	.196	.196	56	11	0	0	0	0.0	2	4	4	2	0	9	0	12	0	0	0	0.5	1.000	OF-18
1944	WAS	A	14	.194	.250	36	7	2	0	0	0.0	0	9	2	3	0	0	0	16	0	0	0	1.1	1.000	OF-12
13 yrs.			1414	.307	.438	5472	1682	335	92	65	1.2	818	874	514	272	23	41	15	2958	107	66	25	2.2	.979	OF-1370

Year	Team	Games	BA	SA	AB	H	2B	3B	HR	HR%	R	RBI	BB	SO	SB	Pinch Hit AB	Pinch Hit H	PO	A	E	DP	TC/G	FA	G by Pos

Alex Voss

VOSS, ALEXANDER
B. 1855, Atlanta, Ga. D. Aug. 31, 1906, Cincinnati, Ohio

BR TR 6'1" 180 lbs.

Year	Team	Games	BA	SA	AB	H	2B	3B	HR	HR%	R	RBI	BB	SO	SB	PH AB	PH H	PO	A	E	DP	TC/G	FA	G by Pos
1884	2 teams	WAS U (63G – .192)			KC U (14G – .089)																			
"	total	77	.176	.207	290	51	9	0	0	0.0	34		5			0	0	180	113	36	11	4.3	.891	P-34, OF-21, 3B-16, 1B-15, SS-1

Bill Voss

VOSS, WILLIAM EDWARD
B. Oct. 31, 1943, Glendale, Calif.

BL TL 6'2" 160 lbs.

Year	Team	Games	BA	SA	AB	H	2B	3B	HR	HR%	R	RBI	BB	SO	SB	PH AB	PH H	PO	A	E	DP	TC/G	FA	G by Pos
1965	CHI A	11	.182	.333	33	6	0	1	1	3.0	4	3	3	5	0	0	0	12	0	0	0	1.1	1.000	OF-10
1966		2	.000	.000	2	0	0	0	0	0.0	0	0	0	2	0	1	0	1	0	0	0	0.5	1.000	OF-1
1967		13	.091	.091	22	2	0	0	0	0.0	4	0	0	1	1	0	0	14	0	0	0	1.1	1.000	OF-11
1968		61	.156	.216	167	26	2	1	2	1.2	14	15	16	34	5	7	2	73	5	3	3	1.3	.963	OF-55
1969	CAL A	133	.261	.332	349	91	11	4	2	0.6	33	40	35	40	5	16	6	187	11	1	4	1.5	.995	OF-111, 1B-2
1970		80	.243	.348	181	44	4	3	3	1.7	21	20	23	18	2	26	6	86	7	2	1	1.2	.979	OF-55
1971	MIL A	97	.251	.375	275	69	4	0	10	3.6	31	30	24	45	2	20	5	151	1	2	1	1.6	.987	OF-79
1972	3 teams	MIL A (27G – .083)			OAK A (40G – .227)				STL N (11G – .267)															
"	total	78	.196	.284	148	29	8	1	1	0.7	12	9	16	22	0	30	5	78	3	1	0	1.1	.988	OF-47
8 yrs.		475	.227	.317	1177	267	29	10	19	1.6	119	127	117	167	15	100	24	602	27	9	9	1.3	.986	OF-369, 1B-2

Phil Voyles

VOYLES, PHILIP VANCE
B. May 12, 1900, Murphy, N. C. D. Nov. 3, 1972, Marlboro, Mass.

BL TR 5'11½" 175 lbs.

Year	Team	Games	BA	SA	AB	H	2B	3B	HR	HR%	R	RBI	BB	SO	SB	PH AB	PH H	PO	A	E	DP	TC/G	FA	G by Pos
1929	BOS N	20	.235	.294	68	16	0	2	0	0.0	9	14	6	8	0	0	0	45	2	4	0	2.6	.922	OF-20

George Vukovich

VUKOVICH, GEORGE STEPHEN
B. June 24, 1956, Chicago, Ill.

BL TR 6' 198 lbs.

Year	Team	Games	BA	SA	AB	H	2B	3B	HR	HR%	R	RBI	BB	SO	SB	PH AB	PH H	PO	A	E	DP	TC/G	FA	G by Pos
1980	PHI N	78	.224	.276	58	13	1	1	0	0.0	6	8	6	9	0	45	11	14	0	1	0	0.2	.933	OF-28
1981		20	.385	.500	26	10	1	0	1	3.8	5	4	1	0	1	11	5	10	0	0	0	0.5	1.000	OF-9
1982		123	.272	.391	335	91	18	2	6	1.8	41	42	32	47	2	23	5	168	4	4	3	1.4	.977	OF-102
1983	CLE A	124	.247	.330	312	77	13	2	3	1.0	31	44	24	37	3	10	3	203	3	3	0	1.7	.986	OF-122
1984		134	.304	.439	437	133	22	5	9	2.1	38	60	34	61	1	13	2	316	13	2	5	2.5	.994	OF-130
1985		149	.244	.350	434	106	22	0	8	1.8	43	45	30	75	2	20	5	250	4	3	0	1.7	.988	OF-137
6 yrs.		628	.268	.379	1602	430	76	10	27	1.7	164	203	127	229	9	122	31	961	24	13	8	1.6	.987	OF-528

DIVISIONAL PLAYOFF SERIES

Year	Team	Games	BA	SA	AB	H	2B	3B	HR	HR%	R	RBI	BB	SO	SB	PH AB	PH H	PO	A	E	DP	TC/G	FA	G by Pos
1981	PHI N	5	.444	.778	9	4	0	0	1	11.1	1	2	0	3	0	4	3	0	0	0	0	0.0	–	OF-3

LEAGUE CHAMPIONSHIP SERIES

Year	Team	Games	BA	SA	AB	H	2B	3B	HR	HR%	R	RBI	BB	SO	SB	PH AB	PH H	PO	A	E	DP	TC/G	FA	G by Pos
1980	PHI N	4	.000	.000	3	0	0	0	0	0.0	0	0	0	0	0	3	0	0	0	0	0	0.0	–	OF-1

John Vukovich

VUKOVICH, JOHN CHRISTOPHER
B. July 31, 1947, Sacramento, Calif.
Manager 1988.

BR TR 6'1" 187 lbs.

Year	Team	Games	BA	SA	AB	H	2B	3B	HR	HR%	R	RBI	BB	SO	SB	PH AB	PH H	PO	A	E	DP	TC/G	FA	G by Pos
1970	PHI N	3	.125	.125	8	1	0	0	0	0.0	1	0	1	0	0	0	0	4	8	2	1	4.7	.857	SS-2, 3B-1
1971		74	.166	.189	217	36	5	0	0	0.0	11	14	12	34	2	0	0	58	137	9	8	2.8	.956	3B-74
1973	MIL A	55	.125	.195	128	16	3	0	2	1.6	10	9	9	40	0	1	0	86	67	5	7	2.9	.968	3B-40, 1B-13, SS-1
1974		38	.188	.313	80	15	1	0	3	3.8	5	11	1	16	2	1	0	46	68	5	10	3.1	.958	SS-12, 3B-12, 2B-11, 1B-4
1975	CIN N	31	.211	.289	38	8	3	0	0	0.0	4	2	4	5	0	0	0	12	37	4	4	1.7	.925	3B-31
1976	PHI N	4	.125	.500	8	1	0	0	1	12.5	2	2	0	2	0	0	0	6	2	0	0	2.0	1.000	3B-4, 1B-1
1977		2	.000	.000	2	0	0	0	0	0.0	0	0	0	1	0	2	0	0	0	0	0	0.0	–	
1979		10	.200	.267	15	3	1	0	0	0.0	1	0	0	3	0	0	0	2	13	0	1	1.5	1.000	3B-7, 2B-3
1980		49	.161	.210	62	10	1	1	0	0.0	4	5	2	7	0	4	1	18	35	2	0	1.1	.964	3B-34, 2B-9, SS-5, 1B-1
1981		11	.000	.000	1	0	0	0	0	0.0	1	0	0	1	0	0	0	4	4	1	0	0.8	.889	3B-9, 2B-1, 1B-1
10 yrs.		277	.161	.222	559	90	14	1	6	1.1	37	44	29	109	4	8	1	236	371	28	31	2.3	.956	3B-212, 2B-24, SS-20, 1B-20

Frank Waddey

WADDEY, FRANK ORUM
B. Aug. 21, 1905, Memphis, Tenn.

BL TL 5'10½" 185 lbs.

Year	Team	Games	BA	SA	AB	H	2B	3B	HR	HR%	R	RBI	BB	SO	SB	PH AB	PH H	PO	A	E	DP	TC/G	FA	G by Pos
1931	STL A	14	.273	.318	22	6	1	0	0	0.0	3	2	2	3	0	7	2	6	0	0	0	0.4	1.000	OF-7

Gale Wade

WADE, GALEARD LEE
B. Jan. 20, 1929, Hollister, Mo.

BL TR 6'1½" 185 lbs.

Year	Team	Games	BA	SA	AB	H	2B	3B	HR	HR%	R	RBI	BB	SO	SB	PH AB	PH H	PO	A	E	DP	TC/G	FA	G by Pos
1955	CHI N	9	.182	.303	33	6	1	0	1	3.0	5	1	4	3	0	0	0	12	1	2	0	1.7	.867	OF-9
1956		10	.000	.000	12	0	0	0	0	0.0	0	0	1	0	0	3	0	7	0	1	0	0.8	.875	OF-3
2 yrs.		19	.133	.222	45	6	1	0	1	2.2	5	1	5	3	0	3	0	19	1	3	0	1.2	.870	OF-12

Ham Wade

WADE, ABRAHAM LINCOLN
B. Dec. 20, 1880, Spring City, Pa. D. July 21, 1968, Riverside, N. J.

BR TR 5'8" 155 lbs.

Year	Team	Games	BA	SA	AB	H	2B	3B	HR	HR%	R	RBI	BB	SO	SB	PH AB	PH H	PO	A	E	DP	TC/G	FA	G by Pos
1907	NY N	1	–	–	0	0	0	0	0	–	0	0	0		0	0	0	2	0	0	0	2.0	1.000	OF-1

Rip Wade

WADE, RICHARD FRANK
B. Jan. 12, 1898, Duluth, Minn. D. June 16, 1957, Sandstone, Minn.

BL TR 5'11" 174 lbs.

Year	Team	Games	BA	SA	AB	H	2B	3B	HR	HR%	R	RBI	BB	SO	SB	PH AB	PH H	PO	A	E	DP	TC/G	FA	G by Pos
1923	WAS A	33	.232	.406	69	16	2	2	2	2.9	8	14	5	10	0	8	1	26	3	1	1	0.9	.967	OF-19

Woodie Wagenhorst

WAGENHORST, ELWOOD OTTO
B. June 3, 1863, Kutztown, Pa. D. Feb. 12, 1946

Year	Team	Games	BA	SA	AB	H	2B	3B	HR	HR%	R	RBI	BB	SO	SB	PH AB	PH H	PO	A	E	DP	TC/G	FA	G by Pos
1888	PHI N	2	.125	.125	8	1	0	0	0	0.0	2	0	1	0	0	0	0	2	2	1	1	2.5	.800	3B-2

Bill Wagner

WAGNER, WILLIAM JOSEPH
B. Jan. 2, 1894, Jessup, Iowa D. Jan. 11, 1951, Waterloo, Iowa

BR TR 6' 187 lbs.

Year	Team	Games	BA	SA	AB	H	2B	3B	HR	HR%	R	RBI	BB	SO	SB	PH AB	PH H	PO	A	E	DP	TC/G	FA	G by Pos
1914	PIT N	3	.000	.000	1	0	0	0	0	0.0	0	0	0	0	0	0	0	1	1	0	0	0.7	1.000	C-3
1915		5	.000	.000	5	0	0	0	0	0.0	0	0	1	2	0	1	0	6	5	0	0	2.2	1.000	C-3

Year	Team	Games	BA	SA	AB	H	2B	3B	HR	HR%	R	RBI	BB	SO	SB	Pinch Hit AB	Pinch Hit H	PO	A	E	DP	TC/G	FA	G by Pos

Bill Wagner *continued*

Year	Team	Games	BA	SA	AB	H	2B	3B	HR	HR%	R	RBI	BB	SO	SB	AB	H	PO	A	E	DP	TC/G	FA	G by Pos
1916		19	.237	.342	38	9	0	2	0	0.0	2	2	5	8	0	4	1	54	19	5	3	4.1	.936	C-15
1917		53	.205	.278	151	31	7	2	0	0.0	15	9	11	22	1	6	2	239	49	14	7	5.7	.954	C-37, 1B-12
1918	BOS N	13	.213	.277	47	10	0	0	1	2.1	2	7	4	5	0	0	0	43	12	5	0	4.6	.917	C-13
5 yrs.		93	.207	.281	242	50	7	4	1	0.4	19	18	21	37	1	11	3	343	86	24	10	4.9	.947	C-71, 1B-12

Butts Wagner

WAGNER, ALBERT
Brother of Honus Wagner.
B. Sept. 17, 1869, Mansfield, Pa. D. Nov. 26, 1928, Pittsburgh, Pa.

BR TR 5'10'' 170 lbs.

Year	Team	Games	BA	SA	AB	H	2B	3B	HR	HR%	R	RBI	BB	SO	SB	AB	H	PO	A	E	DP	TC/G	FA	G by Pos
1898 2 teams	WAS N	(63G – .224)			BKN N	(11G – .237)																		
" total		74	.226	.307	261	59	12	3	1	0.4	22	34	16		4	1	0	97	126	46	9	3.6	.829	3B-50, OF-10, SS-8, 2B-5

Hal Wagner

WAGNER, HAROLD EDWARD
B. July 2, 1915, East Riverton, N. J. D. Aug. 4, 1979, Riverside, N. J.

BL TR 6' 165 lbs.

Year	Team	Games	BA	SA	AB	H	2B	3B	HR	HR%	R	RBI	BB	SO	SB	AB	H	PO	A	E	DP	TC/G	FA	G by Pos
1937	PHI A	1	–	–	0	0	0	0	0	–	0	0	0	0	0	0	0	1	0	0	1	1.0	1.000	C-1
1938		33	.227	.273	88	20	2	1	0	0.0	10	8	8	9	0	3	1	87	16	3	2	3.2	.972	C-30
1939		5	.125	.125	8	1	0	0	0	0.0	0	0	0	3	0	1	0	11	3	0	0	2.8	1.000	C-5
1940		34	.253	.347	75	19	5	1	0	0.0	9	10	11	6	0	5	2	91	16	4	4	3.3	.964	C-28
1941		46	.221	.336	131	29	8	2	1	0.8	18	15	19	9	1	4	0	144	19	4	4	3.6	.976	C-42
1942		104	.236	.313	288	68	17	1	1	0.3	26	30	24	29	1	12	2	371	47	6	7	4.1	.986	C-94
1943		111	.239	.315	289	69	17	1	1	0.3	22	26	36	17	3	14	3	340	56	8	3	3.6	.980	C-99
1944 2 teams	PHI A	(5G – .250)			BOS A	(66G – .332)																		
" total		71	.330	.436	227	75	13	4	1	0.4	21	38	29	14	1	7	2	300	30	10	4	4.8	.971	C-65
1946	BOS A	117	.230	.322	370	85	12	2	6	1.6	39	52	69	32	3	0	0	553	39	10	3	5.1	.983	C-116
1947 2 teams	BOS A	(21G – .231)			DET A	(71G – .288)																		
" total		92	.273	.383	256	70	13	0	5	2.0	24	39	37	21	0	1	1	357	34	5	4	4.3	.987	C-92
1948 2 teams	DET A	(54G – .202)			PHI A	(3G – .000)																		
" total		57	.195	.221	113	22	3	0	0	0.0	10	10	20	11	1	2	0	165	14	2	4	3.2	.989	C-53
1949	PHI N	1	.000	.000	4	0	0	0	0	0.0	0	0	0	1	0	0	0	3	0	1	0	4.0	.750	C-1
12 yrs.		672	.248	.334	1849	458	90	12	15	0.8	179	228	253	152	10	48	11	2423	274	53	36	4.1	.981	C-626

WORLD SERIES

Year	Team	Games	BA	SA	AB	H	2B	3B	HR	HR%	R	RBI	BB	SO	SB	AB	H	PO	A	E	DP	TC/G	FA	G by Pos
1946	BOS A	5	.000	.000	13	0	0	0	0	0.0	0	0	0	1	0	0	0	20	2	0	0	4.4	1.000	C-5

Heinie Wagner

WAGNER, CHARLES F.
B. Sept. 23, 1880, New York, N. Y. D. Mar. 20, 1943, New Rochelle, N. Y.
Manager 1930.

BR TR 5'9'' 183 lbs.

Year	Team	Games	BA	SA	AB	H	2B	3B	HR	HR%	R	RBI	BB	SO	SB	AB	H	PO	A	E	DP	TC/G	FA	G by Pos
1902	NY N	17	.214	.232	56	12	1	0	0	0.0	4	2		3	0	0		31	44	12	5	5.1	.862	SS-17
1906	BOS A	9	.281	.281	32	9	0	0	0	0.0	1	4	1		2	0	0	16	34	3	2	5.9	.943	2B-9
1907		111	.213	.275	385	82	10	4	2	0.5	29	21	31		20	0	0	284	393	51	31	6.6	.930	SS-109, 3B-1, 2B-1
1908		153	.247	.293	526	130	11	5	1	0.2	62	46	27		20	0	0	373	569	61	51	6.6	.939	SS-153
1909		124	.256	.333	430	110	16	7	1	0.2	51	49	35		18	0	0	283	415	50	40	6.0	.933	SS-123, 2B-1
1910		142	.273	.360	491	134	26	7	1	0.2	61	52	44		26	2	0	303	424	57	40	5.5	.927	SS-140
1911		80	.257	.379	261	67	13	8	1	0.4	34	38	29		15	8	2	181	198	38	25	5.2	.909	2B-40, SS-32
1912		144	.274	.359	504	138	25	6	2	0.4	75	68	62		21	0	0	332	391	61	43	5.4	.922	SS-144
1913		110	.227	.326	365	83	14	8	2	0.5	43	34	40	29	9	1	0	281	318	40	37	5.8	.937	SS-105, 2B-4
1915		84	.240	.296	267	64	11	2	0	0.0	38	29	37	34	8	3	0	164	197	28	18	4.6	.928	2B-79, OF-1, 3B-1
1916		6	.500	.625	8	4	1	0	0	0.0	2	0	3		0	2	0	5	12	0	0	2.8	1.000	3B-4, SS-1, 2B-1
1918		3	.125	.125	8	1	0	0	0	0.0	0	0	1		0	0	0	2	7	1	2	3.3	.900	2B-2, 3B-1
12 yrs.		983	.250	.326	3333	834	128	47	10	0.3	400	343	310	63	144	14	2	2255	3002	402	294	5.8	.929	SS-824, 2B-137, 3B-7, OF-1

WORLD SERIES

Year	Team	Games	BA	SA	AB	H	2B	3B	HR	HR%	R	RBI	BB	SO	SB	AB	H	PO	A	E	DP	TC/G	FA	G by Pos
1912	BOS A	8	.167	.200	30	5	1	0	0	0.0	1	0	3	6	1	0	0	24	24	3	0	6.4	.941	SS-8

Honus Wagner

WAGNER, JOHN PETER (The Flying Dutchman)
Brother of Butts Wagner.
B. Feb. 24, 1874, Mansfield, Pa. D. Dec. 6, 1955, Carnegie, Pa.
Manager 1917.
Hall of Fame 1936.

BR TR 5'11'' 200 lbs.

Year	Team	Games	BA	SA	AB	H	2B	3B	HR	HR%	R	RBI	BB	SO	SB	AB	H	PO	A	E	DP	TC/G	FA	G by Pos
1897	LOU N	61	.338	.468	237	80	17	4	2	0.8	37	39	15		19	0	0	124	37	16	7	2.9	.910	OF-52, 2B-9
1898		151	.299	.410	588	176	29	3	10	1.7	80	105	31		27	2	1	847	192	43	57	7.2	.960	1B-75, 3B-65, 2B-10
1899		147	.336	.494	571	192	43	13	7	1.2	98	113	40		37	1	0	260	201	28	20	3.3	.943	3B-75, OF-61, 2B-7, 1B-4
1900	PIT N	135	**.381**	**.573**	527	201	**45**	22	4	0.8	107	100	41		38	1	0	216	45	13	9	2.0	.953	OF-118, 3B-9, 2B-7, 1B-3, P-1
1901		141	.353	.491	556	196	37	11	6	1.1	100	**126**	53		**49**	0	0	297	280	48	35	4.4	.923	SS-62, OF-54, 3B-24, 2B-1
1902		137	.329	**.467**	538	177	33	16	3	0.6	**105**	91	43		**42**	0	0	532	176	32	33	5.4	.957	OF-61, SS-44, 1B-32, 2B-1, P-1
1903		129	**.355**	.518	512	182	30	**19**	5	1.0	97	101	44		46	0	0	386	401	52	53	6.5	.938	SS-111, OF-12, 1B-6
1904		132	**.349**	**.520**	490	171	**44**	14	4	0.8	97	75	59		**53**	1	0	319	376	51	46	5.7	.932	SS-121, OF-8, 3B-2, 2B-2
1905		147	**.363**	.505	548	199	32	14	6	1.1	114	101	54		**57**	0	0	363	517	60	64	6.4	.936	SS-145, OF-2
1906		142	**.339**	.459	516	175	**38**	9	2	0.4	**103**	71	58		**53**	1	0	338	474	52	57	6.1	.940	SS-137, OF-2, 3B-1
1907		142	**.350**	.513	515	180	**38**	14	6	1.2	98	82	46		**61**	0	0	358	429	49	33	5.9	.941	SS-138, 1B-4
1908		151	**.354**	**.542**	568	**201**	39	**19**	10	1.8	100	**109**	54		**53**	0	0	354	469	51	47	5.8	.943	SS-151
1909		137	**.339**	.489	495	168	39	10	5	1.0	92	**100**	66		35	0	0	344	430	49	58	6.0	.940	SS-136, OF-1
1910		150	.320	.432	556	**178**	34	8	4	0.7	90	81	59	47	24	0	0	442	427	52	67	6.1	.944	SS-138, 1B-11, 2B-2
1911		130	**.334**	.507	473	158	23	16	9	1.9	87	89	67	34	20	0	0	472	321	47	76	6.5	.962	SS-101, 1B-28, OF-1
1912		145	.324	.496	558	181	35	20	7	1.3	91	102	59	38	26	0	0	341	462	32	74	5.8	.962	SS-143
1913		114	.300	.385	413	124	18	4	3	0.7	51	56	26	40	21	7	1	289	323	24	47	5.6	.962	SS-105
1914		150	.252	.317	552	139	15	9	1	0.2	60	50	51	51	23	1	0	344	460	43	46	5.6	.949	SS-132, 3B-17, 1B-1
1915		151	.274	.422	566	155	32	17	6	1.1	68	78	39	64	22	4	1	421	428	38	62	5.9	.952	SS-131, 2B-12, 1B-8
1916		123	.287	.370	432	124	15	9	1	0.2	45	39	34	36	11	6	1	417	282	35	46	6.0	.952	SS-92, 1B-24, 2B-4

Year	Team	Games	BA	SA	AB	H	2B	3B	HR	HR%	R	RBI	BB	SO	SB	Pinch Hit AB	Pinch Hit H	PO	A	E	DP	TC/G	FA	G by Pos

Honus Wagner *continued*

Year	Team	Games	BA	SA	AB	H	2B	3B	HR	HR%	R	RBI	BB	SO	SB	PH AB	PH H	PO	A	E	DP	TC/G	FA	G by Pos
1917		74	.265	.304	230	61	7	1	0	0.0	15	24	24	17	5	7	1	466	51	10	27	7.1	.981	1B-47, 3B-18, 2B-2, SS-1
21 yrs.		2789	.327	.466	10441	3418	643	252	101	1.0	1735	1732	963	327	722	31	5	7930	6781	824	964	5.6	.947	SS-1888, OF-372, 1B-248, 3B-209, 2B-57, P-2
							8th	7th	7th	3rd						6th								

WORLD SERIES

Year	Team	Games	BA	SA	AB	H	2B	3B	HR	HR%	R	RBI	BB	SO	SB	PH AB	PH H	PO	A	E	DP	TC/G	FA	G by Pos
1903	PIT N	8	.222	.259	27	6	1	0	0	0.0	2	3	3	4	3	0	0	13	27	6	4	5.8	.870	SS-8
1909		7	.333	.500	24	8	2	1	0	0.0	4	6	4	2	6	0	0	13	23	2	1	5.4	.947	SS-7
2 yrs.		15	.275	.373	51	14	3	1	0	0.0	6	9	7	6	9	0	0	26	50	8	5	5.6	.905	SS-15
															6th									

Joe Wagner

WAGNER, JOSEPH BERNARD
B. Apr. 24, 1889, New York, N. Y.   D. Nov. 15, 1948, Bronx, N. Y.

BR TR 5'11" 165 lbs.

Year	Team	Games	BA	SA	AB	H	2B	3B	HR	HR%	R	RBI	BB	SO	SB	PH AB	PH H	PO	A	E	DP	TC/G	FA	G by Pos
1915	CIN N	75	.178	.223	197	35	5	2	0	0.0	17	13	8	35	4	7	2	114	149	10	28	3.6	.963	2B-46, SS-12, 3B-2

Leon Wagner

WAGNER, LEON LAMAR (Daddy Wags)
B. May 13, 1934, Chattanooga, Tenn.

BL TR 6'1" 195 lbs.

Year	Team	Games	BA	SA	AB	H	2B	3B	HR	HR%	R	RBI	BB	SO	SB	PH AB	PH H	PO	A	E	DP	TC/G	FA	G by Pos
1958	SF N	74	.317	.534	221	70	9	0	13	5.9	31	35	18	34	1	18	4	89	5	5	0	1.3	.949	OF-57
1959		87	.225	.419	129	29	4	3	5	3.9	20	22	25	24	0	52	10	48	0	3	0	0.6	.941	OF-28
1960	STL	39	.214	.357	98	21	2	0	4	4.1	12	11	17	17	0	7	1	48	4	2	0	1.4	.963	OF-32
1961	LA A	133	.280	.517	453	127	19	2	28	6.2	74	79	48	65	5	16	3	187	12	6	2	1.5	.971	OF-116
1962		160	.268	.500	612	164	21	5	37	6.0	96	107	50	87	7	3	1	269	7	8	1	1.8	.972	OF-156
1963		149	.291	.456	550	160	11	1	26	4.7	73	90	49	73	5	9	2	254	7	11	1	1.8	.960	OF-141
1964	CLE A	163	.253	.434	641	162	19	2	31	4.8	94	100	56	121	14	2	1	254	5	11	1	1.7	.959	OF-163
1965		144	.294	.495	517	152	18	1	28	5.4	91	79	60	52	12	11	3	175	3	8	0	1.3	.957	OF-134
1966		150	.279	.441	549	153	20	0	23	4.2	70	66	46	69	5	10	3	185	4	2	0	1.3	.990	OF-139
1967		135	.242	.386	433	105	15	1	15	3.5	56	54	37	76	3	15	4	142	4	3	1	1.1	.980	OF-117
1968	2 teams		CLE A (38G – .184)		CHI A		(69G – .284)																	
"	total	107	.261	.332	211	55	12	0	0	0.5	19	24	27	37	2	46	11	51	0	6	0	0.5	.895	OF-56
1969	SF N	11	.333	.333	12	4	0	0	0	0.0	0	2	2	1	0	7	3	3	0	0	0	0.3	1.000	OF-1
12 yrs.		1352	.272	.455	4426	1202	150	15	211	4.8	636	669	435	656	54	196	46	1705	51	65	5	1.3	.964	OF-1140

Mark Wagner

WAGNER, MARK DUANE
B. Mar. 4, 1954, Conneaut, Ohio

BR TR 6' 165 lbs.

Year	Team	Games	BA	SA	AB	H	2B	3B	HR	HR%	R	RBI	BB	SO	SB	PH AB	PH H	PO	A	E	DP	TC/G	FA	G by Pos
1976	DET A	39	.261	.330	115	30	2	3	0	0.0	9	12	6	18	0	0	0	60	135	11	25	5.3	.947	SS-39
1977		22	.146	.250	48	7	0	1	1	2.1	4	3	4	12	0	0	0	15	58	6	10	3.6	.924	SS-21, 2B-1
1978		39	.239	.284	109	26	1	2	0	0.0	10	6	3	11	1	1	1	57	81	5	18	3.7	.965	SS-35, 2B-4
1979		75	.274	.315	146	40	3	0	1	0.7	16	13	16	25	3	1	1	88	146	8	28	3.2	.967	SS-41, 2B-29, 3B-2, DH-1
1980		45	.236	.250	72	17	1	0	0	0.0	5	3	7	11	0	2	0	43	61	7	8	2.5	.937	SS-28, 3B-9, 2B-6
1981	TEX A	50	.259	.365	85	22	4	1	1	1.2	15	14	8	13	1	0	0	54	87	5	18	2.9	.966	SS-43, 2B-4, 3B-2
1982		60	.240	.274	179	43	4	1	0	0.0	14	8	10	28	1	0	0	77	197	13	32	4.8	.955	SS-60
1983		2	.000	.000	2	0	0	0	0	0.0	0	0	0	1	0	0	0	2	4	0	0	3.0	1.000	SS-2
1984	OAK A	82	.230	.310	87	20	5	1	0	0.0	8	12	7	11	2	1	0	73	83	6	15	2.0	.963	SS-58, 3B-15, 2B-8, DH-3, P-1
9 yrs.		414	.243	.299	843	205	20	9	3	0.4	81	71	61	130	8	7	2	469	852	61	154	3.3	.956	SS-327, 2B-52, 3B-28, DH-4, P-1

Kermit Wahl

WAHL, KERMIT EMERSON
B. Nov. 18, 1922, Columbia, S. D.   D. Sept. 16, 1987, Tucson, Ariz.

BR TR 5'11" 170 lbs.

Year	Team	Games	BA	SA	AB	H	2B	3B	HR	HR%	R	RBI	BB	SO	SB	PH AB	PH H	PO	A	E	DP	TC/G	FA	G by Pos
1944	CIN N	4	.000	.000	1	0	0	0	0	0.0	0	0	0	0	0	0	0	0	0	0	0	0.0	–	3B-1
1945		71	.201	.263	194	39	8	2	0	0.0	18	10	23	22	2	0	0	139	180	17	22	4.7	.949	2B-32, SS-31, 3B-7
1947		39	.173	.210	81	14	0	0	1	1.2	8	4	6	12	0	5	1	39	50	2	5	2.3	.978	3B-20, SS-9, 2B-2
1950	PHI A	89	.257	.343	280	72	12	3	2	0.7	26	27	30	30	1	7	2	111	197	17	29	3.7	.948	3B-61, SS-18, 2B-2
1951	2 teams		PHI A (20G – .186)		STL A		(8G – .333)																	
"	total	28	.233	.291	86	20	3	1	0	0.0	6	9	9	8	0	4	0	28	49	3	7	2.9	.963	3B-24
5 yrs.		231	.226	.294	642	145	23	6	3	0.5	58	50	68	72	3	16	3	317	476	39	63	3.6	.953	3B-113, SS-58, 2B-36

Eddie Waitkus

WAITKUS, EDWARD STEPHEN
B. Sept. 4, 1919, Cambridge, Mass.   D. Sept. 15, 1972, Jamaica Plain, Mass.

BL TL 6' 170 lbs.

Year	Team	Games	BA	SA	AB	H	2B	3B	HR	HR%	R	RBI	BB	SO	SB	PH AB	PH H	PO	A	E	DP	TC/G	FA	G by Pos
1941	CHI N	12	.179	.179	28	5	0	0	0	0.0	1	0	0	3	0	3	1	71	3	4	8	6.5	.949	1B-9
1946		113	.304	.408	441	134	24	5	4	0.9	50	55	23	14	3	5	2	992	81	4	76	9.5	.996	1B-106
1947		130	.292	.381	514	150	28	6	2	0.4	60	35	32	17	3	2	0	1161	101	8	109	9.8	.994	1B-126
1948		139	.295	.416	562	166	27	10	7	1.2	87	44	43	19	11	2	0	1107	92	10	77	8.7	.992	1B-116, OF-20
1949	PHI N	54	.306	.426	209	64	16	3	1	0.5	41	28	33	12	3	0	0	452	36	3	51	9.1	.994	1B-54
1950		154	.284	.359	641	182	32	5	2	0.3	102	44	55	29	3	1	1	1387	99	10	142	9.7	.993	1B-154
1951		145	.257	.320	610	157	27	4	1	0.2	65	46	53	22	0	2	0	1214	94	10	121	9.1	.992	1B-144
1952		146	.289	.375	499	144	29	4	2	0.4	51	49	64	23	2	3	0	1281	95	12	119	9.5	.991	1B-143
1953		81	.291	.356	247	72	9	2	1	0.4	24	16	13	23	1	20	7	480	37	6	65	6.5	.989	1B-59
1954	BAL A	95	.283	.383	311	88	17	4	2	0.6	35	33	28	25	0	15	4	618	48	0	72	7.0	1.000	1B-78
1955	2 teams		BAL A (38G – .259)		PHI N		(33G – .280)																	
"	total	71	.271	.344	192	52	6	1	2	1.0	12	23	28	17	2	11	4	430	30	6	46	6.6	.987	1B-57
11 yrs.		1140	.285	.374	4254	1214	215	44	24	0.6	528	373	372	204	28	64	19	9193	716	73	886	8.8	.993	1B-1046, OF-20

WORLD SERIES

Year	Team	Games	BA	SA	AB	H	2B	3B	HR	HR%	R	RBI	BB	SO	SB	PH AB	PH H	PO	A	E	DP	TC/G	FA	G by Pos
1950	PHI N	4	.267	.333	15	4	1	0	0	0.0	2	0	0	0	0	0	0	34	3	0	1	9.3	1.000	1B-4

Charlie Waitt

WAITT, CHARLES C.
B. Oct. 14, 1853, Hallowell, Me.   D. Oct. 21, 1912, San Francisco Calif.,

5'11" 165 lbs.

Year	Team	Games	BA	SA	AB	H	2B	3B	HR	HR%	R	RBI	BB	SO	SB	PH AB	PH H	PO	A	E	DP	TC/G	FA	G by Pos
1877	CHI N	10	.098	.098	41	4	0	0	0	0.0	2	2	0	3		0	0	20	3	6	1	2.9	.793	OF-10
1882	BAL AA	72	.156	.172	250	39	4	0	0	0.0	19		13			0	0	142	11	22	2	2.4	.874	OF-72
1883	PHI N	1	.333	.333	3	1	0	0	0	0.0	0		0	1		0	0	1	0	2	0	3.0	.333	OF-1
3 yrs.		83	.150	.163	294	44	4	0	0	0.0	21	2	13	4		0	0	163	14	30	3	2.5	.855	OF-83

Year	Team		Games	BA	SA	AB	H	2B	3B	HR	HR%	R	RBI	BB	SO	SB	Pinch Hit AB	Pinch Hit H	PO	A	E	DP	TC/G	FA	G by Pos

Dick Wakefield

WAKEFIELD, RICHARD CUMMINGS
Son of Howard Wakefield.
B. May 6, 1921, Chicago, Ill.   D. Aug. 26, 1985, Wayne County, Mich.

BL TR 6'4" 210 lbs.

Year	Team		Games	BA	SA	AB	H	2B	3B	HR	HR%	R	RBI	BB	SO	SB	PH AB	PH H	PO	A	E	DP	TC/G	FA	G by Pos
1941	DET	A	7	.143	.143	7	1	0	0	0	0.0	0	0	0	1	0	6	1	1	0	0	0	0.1	1.000	OF-1
1943			155	.316	.434	633	200	38	8	7	1.1	91	79	62	60	4	0	0	314	11	14	1	2.2	.959	OF-155
1944			78	.355	.576	276	98	15	5	12	4.3	53	53	55	29	2	0	0	155	3	6	1	2.1	.963	OF-78
1946			111	.268	.412	396	106	11	5	12	3.0	64	59	59	55	3	4	0	210	6	8	1	2.0	.964	OF-104
1947			112	.283	.416	368	104	15	5	8	2.2	59	51	80	44	1	10	4	197	10	11	2	1.9	.950	OF-101
1948			110	.276	.472	322	89	20	5	11	3.4	50	53	70	55	0	22	7	198	3	11	1	1.9	.948	OF-86
1949			59	.206	.389	126	26	3	1	6	4.8	17	19	32	24	0	18	3	71	3	0	1	1.3	1.000	OF-32
1950	NY	A	3	.500	.500	2	1	0	0	0	0.0	0	1	1	1	0	2	1	0	0	0	0	0.0	–	
1952	NY	N	3	.000	.000	2	0	0	0	0	0.0	0	0	1	0	0	2	0	0	0	0	0	0.0	–	
9 yrs.			638	.293	.447	2132	625	102	29	56	2.6	334	315	360	269	10	64	16	1146	36	50	7	1.9	.959	OF-557

Howard Wakefield

WAKEFIELD, HOWARD JOHN
Father of Dick Wakefield.
B. Apr. 2, 1884, Bucyrus, Ohio   D. Apr. 16, 1941, Chicago, Ill.

BR TR 6'1" 205 lbs.

Year	Team		Games	BA	SA	AB	H	2B	3B	HR	HR%	R	RBI	BB	SO	SB	PH AB	PH H	PO	A	E	DP	TC/G	FA	G by Pos
1905	CLE	A	9	.160	.160	25	4	0	0	0	0.0	3	1	0		0	1	0	18	7	2	0	3.0	.926	C-8
1906	WAS	A	77	.280	.355	211	59	9	2	1	0.5	17	21	7		6	16	9	237	59	17	5	4.1	.946	C-60
1907	CLE	A	26	.135	.189	37	5	2	0	0	0.0	4	3	3		0	15	2	37	3	3	2	1.7	.930	C-11
3 yrs.			112	.249	.315	273	68	11	2	1	0.4	24	25	10		6	32	11	292	69	22	7	3.4	.943	C-79

Ed Walczak

WALCZAK, EDWIN JOSEPH (Husky)
B. Sept. 21, 1918, Arctic, R. I.

BR TR 5'11" 180 lbs.

Year	Team		Games	BA	SA	AB	H	2B	3B	HR	HR%	R	RBI	BB	SO	SB	PH AB	PH H	PO	A	E	DP	TC/G	FA	G by Pos
1945	PHI	N	20	.211	.263	57	12	3	0	0	0.0	6	9	0	0	0	0	0	49	44	4	14	4.9	.959	2B-17, SS-2

Fred Walden

WALDEN, FREDERICK THOMAS
B. June 25, 1890, Fayette, Mo.   D. Sept. 27, 1955, Jefferson Barracks, Mo.

BR TR

Year	Team		Games	BA	SA	AB	H	2B	3B	HR	HR%	R	RBI	BB	SO	SB	PH AB	PH H	PO	A	E	DP	TC/G	FA	G by Pos
1912	STL	A	1	–	–	0	0	0	0	0	–	0	0	0	0	0	0	0	0	0	1	0	1.0	–	C-1

Irv Waldron

WALDRON, IRVING J. (Wally)
B. Jan. 21, 1876, Hillside, N. Y.   D. July 22, 1944, Worcester, Mass.

BR TR

Year	Team		Games	BA	SA	AB	H	2B	3B	HR	HR%	R	RBI	BB	SO	SB	PH AB	PH H	PO	A	E	DP	TC/G	FA	G by Pos
1901	2 teams		MIL A (62G – .297)			WAS A	(79G – .322)																			
"	total		141	.311	.378	598	186	22	9	0	0.0	102	51	38		20	1	1	237	16	21	0	1.9	.923	OF-140

Jim Walewander

WALEWANDER, JAMES
B. May 2, 1962, Chicago, Ill.

BB TR 5'10" 160 lbs.

Year	Team		Games	BA	SA	AB	H	2B	3B	HR	HR%	R	RBI	BB	SO	SB	PH AB	PH H	PO	A	E	DP	TC/G	FA	G by Pos
1987	DET	A	53	.241	.389	54	13	3	1	1	1.9	24	4	7	6	2	2	0	26	58	1	12	1.6	.988	2B-24, 3B-17, SS-3
1988			88	.211	.240	175	37	5	0	0	0.0	23	6	12	26	11	2	0	125	154	6	38	3.2	.979	2B-61, SS-8, 3B-3
2 yrs.			141	.218	.275	229	50	8	1	1	0.4	47	10	19	32	13	4	0	151	212	7	50	2.6	.981	2B-85, 3B-20, SS-11

Chico Walker

WALKER, CLEOTHA
B. Nov. 25, 1957, Jackson, Miss.

BB TR 5'9" 170 lbs.

Year	Team		Games	BA	SA	AB	H	2B	3B	HR	HR%	R	RBI	BB	SO	SB	PH AB	PH H	PO	A	E	DP	TC/G	FA	G by Pos
1980	BOS	A	19	.211	.263	57	12	0	0	1	1.8	3	5	6	10	3	1	1	15	31	2	7	2.5	.958	2B-11, DH-7
1981			6	.353	.353	17	6	0	0	0	0.0	3	2	1	2	0	1	0	4	10	0	1	2.3	1.000	2B-5
1983			4	.400	1.200	5	2	0	2	0	0.0	2	1	0	1	0	1	0	4	1	0	0	1.3	1.000	OF-3
1984			3	.000	.000	2	0	0	0	0	0.0	1	0	1	2	0	0	0	1	0	0	0	0.3	1.000	2B-1
1985	CHI	N	21	.083	.083	12	1	0	0	0	0.0	3	0	0	5	1	8	1	4	0	0	0	0.2	1.000	OF-6, 2B-2
1986			28	.277	.376	101	28	3	2	1	1.0	21	7	10	20	15	2	0	42	1	2	0	1.6	.956	OF-26
1987			47	.200	.238	105	21	4	0	0	0.0	15	7	12	23	11	6	0	37	0	1	0	0.8	.974	OF-33, 3B-2
1988	CAL	A	33	.154	.167	78	12	1	0	0	0.0	8	2	6	15	2	10	0	33	20	2	1	1.7	.964	OF-17, 2B-7, 3B-2
8 yrs.			161	.218	.276	377	82	8	4	2	0.5	55	25	35	76	32	31	2	139	64	7	9	1.3	.967	OF-85, 2B-26, DH-7, 3B-4

Curt Walker

WALKER, WILLIAM CURTIS
B. July 3, 1896, Beeville, Tex.   D. Dec. 9, 1955, Beeville, Tex.

BL TR 5'9½" 170 lbs.

Year	Team		Games	BA	SA	AB	H	2B	3B	HR	HR%	R	RBI	BB	SO	SB	PH AB	PH H	PO	A	E	DP	TC/G	FA	G by Pos
1919	NY	A	1	.000	.000	1	0	0	0	0	0.0	0	0	0		0	1	0	0	0	0	0	0.0	–	
1920	NY	N	8	.071	.071	14	1	0	0	0	0.0	0	0	1	3	0	4	0	5	0	0	0	0.6	1.000	OF-4
1921	2 teams		NY N (64G – .286)			PHI N	(21G – .338)																			
"	total		85	.301	.435	269	81	15	6	3	1.1	41	43	20	13	4	1	1	277	18	7	5	3.6	.977	OF-79
1922	PHI	N	148	.337	.499	581	196	36	11	12	2.1	102	89	56	46	11	1	0	295	24	15	8	2.3	.955	OF-147
1923			140	.281	.378	527	148	26	5	5	0.9	66	66	45	31	12	2	1	284	19	17	5	2.3	.947	OF-140, 1B-1
1924	2 teams		PHI N (24G – .296)			CIN N	(109G – .300)																			
"	total		133	.299	.436	468	140	27	11	5	1.1	66	54	51	19	7	4	1	239	15	8	5	2.0	.969	OF-129
1925	CIN	N	145	.318	.460	509	162	22	16	6	1.2	86	71	57	31	14	3	0	332	12	6	4	2.4	.983	OF-141
1926			155	.306	.450	571	175	24	20	6	1.1	83	78	60	31	3	3	0	325	21	14	8	2.3	.961	OF-152
1927			146	.292	.395	527	154	16	10	6	1.1	60	80	47	19	5	4	0	316	15	15	8	2.4	.957	OF-141
1928			123	.279	.412	427	119	15	12	6	1.4	64	73	49	14	19	1	1	289	9	14	3	2.5	.955	OF-122
1929			141	.313	.474	492	154	28	15	7	1.4	76	83	85	17	17	2	1	298	11	10	2	2.3	.969	OF-138
1930			134	.307	.460	472	145	26	11	8	1.7	74	51	64	30	4	11	6	241	5	9	2	1.9	.965	OF-120
12 yrs.			1359	.304	.440	4858	1475	235	117	64	1.3	718	688	535	254	96	37	11	2901	149	115	50	2.3	.964	OF-1313, 1B-1

Dixie Walker

WALKER, FRED (The People's Cherce)
Son of Dixie Walker. Brother of Harry Walker.
B. Sept. 24, 1910, Villa Rica, Ga.   D. May 17, 1982, Birmingham, Ala.

BL TR 6'1" 175 lbs.

Year	Team		Games	BA	SA	AB	H	2B	3B	HR	HR%	R	RBI	BB	SO	SB	PH AB	PH H	PO	A	E	DP	TC/G	FA	G by Pos
1931	NY	A	2	.300	.500	10	3	2	0	0	0.0	0	0	0	4	0	0	0	3	0	0	0	1.5	1.000	OF-2
1933			98	.274	.500	328	90	15	7	15	4.6	68	51	26	28	2	18	4	194	7	8	1	2.1	.962	OF-77
1934			17	.118	.118	17	2	0	0	0	0.0	2	0	1	3	0	12	1	7	0	0	0	0.1	1.000	OF-1
1935			8	.154	.231	13	2	1	0	0	0.0	1	1	0	5	1	3	0	3	0	1	0	0.5	.750	OF-2

Year	Team		Games	BA	SA	AB	H	2B	3B	HR	HR%	R	RBI	BB	SO	SB	Pinch Hit AB	Pinch Hit H	PO	A	E	DP	TC/G	FA	G by Pos

Dixie Walker *continued*

Year	Team		Games	BA	SA	AB	H	2B	3B	HR	HR%	R	RBI	BB	SO	SB	AB	H	PO	A	E	DP	TC/G	FA	G by Pos
1936	2 teams	NY A (6G – .350)				CHI A (26G – .271)																			
"	total		32	.289	.389	90	26	2	2	1	1.1	15	16	15	9	2	10	2	55	2	0	0	1.8	1.000	OF-22
1937	CHI A		154	.302	.449	593	179	28	16	9	1.5	105	95	78	26	1	0	0	270	10	14	1	1.9	.952	OF-154
1938	DET A		127	.308	.434	454	140	27	6	6	1.3	84	43	65	32	5	10	3	224	8	5	1	1.9	.979	OF-114
1939	2 teams	DET A (43G – .305)				BKN N (61G – .280)																			
"	total		104	.290	.412	379	110	10	9	6	1.6	57	57	35	18	5	6	2	237	9	8	4	2.4	.969	OF-96
1940	BKN N		143	.308	.435	556	171	37	8	6	1.1	75	66	42	21	3	6	4	360	6	10	3	2.6	.973	OF-136
1941			148	.311	.452	531	165	32	8	9	1.7	88	71	70	18	4	2	0	309	19	8	8	2.3	.976	OF-146
1942			118	.290	.412	393	114	28	4	6	1.5	57	54	47	15	1	6	2	207	8	3	2	1.8	.986	OF-110
1943			138	.302	.411	540	163	32	6	5	0.9	83	71	49	24	3	2	1	262	20	9	2	2.1	.969	OF-136
1944			147	.357	.529	535	191	37	8	13	2.4	77	91	72	27	6	7	2	260	17	11	4	2.0	.962	OF-140
1945			154	.300	.438	607	182	42	9	8	1.3	102	124	75	16	6	1	0	346	18	3	4	2.4	.992	OF-153
1946			150	.319	.448	576	184	29	9	9	1.6	80	116	67	28	14	1	0	237	15	8	3	1.7	.969	OF-149
1947			148	.306	.427	529	162	31	3	9	1.7	77	94	97	26	6	1	0	261	9	10	0	1.9	.964	OF-147
1948	PIT N		129	.316	.392	408	129	19	3	2	0.5	39	54	52	18	1	16	3	168	4	4	0	1.4	.977	OF-112
1949			88	.282	.331	181	51	4	1	1	0.6	26	18	26	11	0	40	13	82	5	•4	2	1.0	.956	OF-39, 1B-3
18 yrs.			1905	.306	.437	6740	2064	376	96	105	1.6	1037	1023	817	325	59	143	39	3479	157	106	35	2.0	.972	OF-1736, 1B-3

WORLD SERIES

Year	Team		Games	BA	SA	AB	H	2B	3B	HR	HR%	R	RBI	BB	SO	SB	AB	H	PO	A	E	DP	TC/G	FA	G by Pos
1941	BKN N		5	.222	.333	18	4	2	0	0	0.0	3	0	2	1	0	0	0	14	0	0	0	2.8	1.000	OF-5
1947			7	.222	.370	27	6	1	0	1	3.7	1	4	3	1	1	0	0	9	1	0	0	1.4	1.000	OF-7
2 yrs.			12	.222	.356	45	10	3	0	1	2.2	4	4	5	2	1	0	0	23	1	0	0	2.0	1.000	OF-12

Duane Walker

WALKER, DUANE ALLEN
B. Mar. 13, 1957, Pasadena, Tex.　　　　BL TL 6'　180 lbs.

Year	Team		Games	BA	SA	AB	H	2B	3B	HR	HR%	R	RBI	BB	SO	SB	AB	H	PO	A	E	DP	TC/G	FA	G by Pos
1982	CIN N		86	.218	.322	239	52	10	0	5	2.1	26	22	27	58	9	14	2	110	7	1	1	1.4	.992	OF-69
1983			109	.236	.324	225	53	12	1	2	0.9	14	29	20	43	6	48	16	104	4	5	0	1.0	.956	OF-60
1984			83	.292	.528	195	57	10	3	10	5.1	35	28	33	35	7	14	4	110	3	6	0	1.4	.950	OF-68
1985	2 teams	CIN N (37G – .167)				TEX A (53G – .174)																			
"	total		90	.172	.322	180	31	4	1	7	3.9	19	17	21	47	3	40	7	66	6	2	1	0.8	.973	OF-42, DH-10
1988	STL N		24	.182	.227	22	4	1	0	0	0.0	1	3	2	7	0	19	4	2	0	0	0	0.1	1.000	OF-4, 1B-1
5 yrs.			392	.229	.367	861	197	37	5	24	2.8	95	99	103	190	25	135	33	392	20	14	2	1.1	.967	OF-243, DH-10, 1B-1

Ernie Walker

WALKER, ERNEST ROBERT
Brother of Dixie Walker.
B. Sept. 17, 1890, Blossburg, Ala.　D. Apr. 1, 1965, Pell City, Ala.　　　BL TR 6'　165 lbs.

Year	Team		Games	BA	SA	AB	H	2B	3B	HR	HR%	R	RBI	BB	SO	SB	AB	H	PO	A	E	DP	TC/G	FA	G by Pos
1913	STL A		7	.214	.214	14	3	0	0	0	0.0	0	2	0	5	0	5	2	5	0	0	0	0.7	1.000	OF-2
1914			71	.298	.405	131	39	5	3	1	0.8	19	14	13	26	6	29	10	45	3	2	0	0.7	.960	OF-36
1915			50	.211	.284	109	23	4	2	0	0.0	15	9	23	32	5	14	3	36	1	5	3	0.8	.881	OF-33
3 yrs.			128	.256	.343	254	65	9	5	1	0.4	34	25	36	63	11	48	15	86	4	7	3	0.8	.928	OF-71

Fleet Walker

WALKER, MOSES FLEETWOOD
Brother of Welday Walker.
B. Oct. 7, 1856, Mt. Pleasant, Ohio　D. May 11, 1924, Cleveland, Ohio　　　BR TR

Year	Team		Games	BA	SA	AB	H	2B	3B	HR	HR%	R	RBI	BB	SO	SB	AB	H	PO	A	E	DP	TC/G	FA	G by Pos
1884	TOL AA		42	.263	.316	152	40	2	3	0	0.0	23		8			0	0	221	70	37	4	7.8	.887	C-41, OF-1

Frank Walker

WALKER, CHARLES FRANKLIN
B. Sept. 22, 1894, Enoree, S. C.　D. Sept. 16, 1974, Bristol, Tenn.　　　BR TR 5'11"　165 lbs.

Year	Team		Games	BA	SA	AB	H	2B	3B	HR	HR%	R	RBI	BB	SO	SB	AB	H	PO	A	E	DP	TC/G	FA	G by Pos
1917	DET A		2	.000	.000	2	0	0	0	0	0.0	0	0	0	1	0	0	0	0	0	0	0	0.0	–	
1918			55	.198	.311	167	33	10	3	1	0.6	10	20	7	29	3	7	1	102	5	9	1	2.1	.922	OF-45
1920	PHI A		24	.231	.297	91	21	2	2	0	0.0	10	10	5	14	0	0	0	57	1	1	0	2.5	.983	OF-24
1921			19	.227	.318	66	15	3	0	1	1.5	6	6	8	11	1	0	0	46	3	2	0	2.7	.961	OF-19
1925	NY N		39	.222	.272	81	18	1	0	1	1.2	12	5	9	11	1	7	1	45	3	2	1	1.3	.960	OF-21
5 yrs.			139	.214	.300	407	87	16	5	3	0.7	38	41	29	66	5	14	2	250	12	14	2	2.0	.949	OF-109

Gee Walker

WALKER, GERALD HOLMES
Brother of Hub Walker.
B. Mar. 19, 1908, Gulfport, Miss.　D. Mar. 20, 1981, Jackson, Miss.　　　BR TR 5'11"　188 lbs.

Year	Team		Games	BA	SA	AB	H	2B	3B	HR	HR%	R	RBI	BB	SO	SB	AB	H	PO	A	E	DP	TC/G	FA	G by Pos
1931	DET A		59	.296	.423	189	56	17	2	1	0.5	20	24	14	21	10	9	4	99	2	5	1	1.8	.953	OF-44
1932			126	.323	.465	480	155	32	6	8	1.7	71	78	13	38	30	8	1	309	9	17	1	2.7	.949	OF-116
1933			127	.280	.424	483	135	29	7	9	1.9	68	64	15	49	26	12	2	234	10	15	3	2.0	.942	OF-113
1934			98	.300	.418	347	104	19	2	6	1.7	54	39	19	20	20	17	5	191	5	11	2	2.1	.947	OF-80
1935			98	.301	.453	362	109	22	6	7	1.9	52	53	15	21	6	14	7	204	2	10	1	2.2	.954	OF-85
1936			134	.353	.536	550	194	55	5	12	2.2	105	93	23	30	17	9	1	280	14	16	5	2.3	.948	OF-125
1937			151	.335	.499	635	213	42	4	18	2.8	105	113	41	74	23	0	0	316	9	15	2	2.3	.956	OF-151
1938	CHI A		120	.305	.493	442	135	23	6	16	3.6	69	87	38	32	9	12	4	197	9	9	2	1.8	.958	OF-107
1939			149	.291	.443	598	174	30	11	13	2.2	95	111	28	43	17	2	0	365	11	13	3	2.6	.967	OF-147
1940	WAS A		140	.294	.432	595	175	29	7	13	2.2	87	96	24	30	21	0	0	285	10	10	2	2.2	.967	OF-140
1941	CLE A		121	.283	.431	445	126	26	11	6	1.3	56	48	18	46	12	13	5	257	9	5	0	2.2	.982	OF-105
1942	CIN N		119	.230	.322	422	97	20	2	5	1.2	40	50	31	44	11	8	1	277	7	8	2	2.5	.973	OF-110
1943			114	.245	.329	429	105	23	2	3	0.7	48	54	12	38	6	6	1	231	8	5	3	2.1	.980	OF-106
1944			121	.278	.366	478	133	21	3	5	1.0	56	62	23	48	7	3	1	293	3	10	0	2.5	.967	OF-117
1945			106	.253	.320	316	80	11	2	2	0.6	28	21	16	38	8	35	9	127	7	7	1	1.3	.950	OF-67, 3B-3
15 yrs.			1783	.294	.430	6771	1991	399	76	124	1.8	954	997	330	600	223	148	41	3665	115	156	28	2.2	.960	OF-1613, 3B-3

WORLD SERIES

Year	Team		Games	BA	SA	AB	H	2B	3B	HR	HR%	R	RBI	BB	SO	SB	AB	H	PO	A	E	DP	TC/G	FA	G by Pos
1934	DET A		3	.333	.333	3	1	0	0	0	0.0	0	1	0	1	0	3	1	0	0	0	0	0.0	–	
1935			3	.250	.250	4	1	0	0	0	0.0	1	0	1	0	0	2	0	0	0	0	0	0.0	–	OF-1
2 yrs.			6	.286	.286	7	2	0	0	0	0.0	1	1	1	1	0	5	1	0	0	0	0	0.0	–	OF-1

Greg Walker

WALKER, GREGORY LEE
B. Oct. 6, 1959, Douglas, Ga.　　　BL TR 6'3"　205 lbs.

Year	Team	Games	BA	SA	AB	H	2B	3B	HR	HR%	R	RBI	BB	SO	SB	Pinch Hit AB	Pinch Hit H	PO	A	E	DP	TC/G	FA	G by Pos

Greg Walker *continued*

1982	CHI A	11	.412	1.000	17	7	2	1	2	11.8	3	7	2	3	0	4	2	0	0	0	0	0.0	–	DH-4
1983		118	.270	.440	307	83	16	3	10	3.3	32	55	28	57	2	35	13	426	19	7	40	3.8	.985	1B-59, DH-21
1984		136	.294	.532	442	130	29	2	24	5.4	62	75	35	66	8	16	3	791	51	4	66	6.2	.995	1B-101, DH-21
1985		163	.258	.454	601	155	38	4	24	4.0	77	92	44	100	5	9	3	1217	97	8	116	8.1	.994	1B-151, DH-7
1986		78	.277	.493	282	78	10	6	13	4.6	37	51	29	44	1	3	1	670	57	5	57	9.4	.993	1B-77, DH-1
1987		157	.256	.465	566	145	33	2	27	4.8	85	94	75	112	2	4	0	1402	80	9	135	9.5	.994	1B-154, DH-3
1988		99	.247	.374	377	93	22	1	8	2.1	45	42	29	77	0	1	0	935	41	7	93	9.9	.993	1B-98
1989		77	.210	.335	233	49	14	0	5	2.1	25	26	23	50	0	9	0	373	17	5	38	5.1	.987	1B-48, DH-23
8 yrs.		839	.262	.453	2825	740	164	19	113	4.0	366	442	265	509	18	81	22	5814	362	45	545	7.4	.993	1B-688, DH-80

LEAGUE CHAMPIONSHIP SERIES

| 1983 | CHI A | 2 | .333 | .333 | 3 | 1 | 0 | 0 | 0 | 0.0 | 0 | 0 | 1 | 2 | 0 | 1 | 0 | 8 | 0 | 0 | 2 | 4.0 | 1.000 | 1B-1 |

Harry Walker

WALKER, HARRY WILLIAM (The Hat)
Son of Dixie Walker. Brother of Dixie Walker.
B. Oct. 22, 1916, Pascagoula, Miss.
Manager 1955, 1965-72.

BL TR 6'2" 175 lbs.

1940	STL N	7	.185	.259	27	5	2	0	0	0.0	2	6	0	2	0	0	0	21	0	1	0	3.3	1.000	OF-7
1941		7	.267	.333	15	4	1	0	0	0.0	3	1	2	1	0	0	0	7	0	1	0	1.1	.875	OF-5
1942		74	.314	.398	191	60	12	2	0	0.0	38	16	11	14	2	16	0	116	6	4	0	1.7	.968	OF-56, 2B-2
1943		148	.294	.398	564	166	28	6	2	0.4	76	53	40	24	5	4	1	322	14	13	4	2.4	.963	OF-144, 2B-1
1946		112	.237	.338	346	82	14	6	3	0.9	53	27	30	22	12	11	3	273	15	7	5	2.6	.976	OF-92, 1B-8
1947	2 teams	STL N (10G – .200)		PHI N (130G – .371)																				
"	total	140	**.363**	.487	513	186	29	**16**	1	0.2	81	41	63	39	13	2	0	383	15	14	4	2.9	.966	OF-136, 1B-4
1948	PHI N	112	.292	.355	332	97	11	2	2	0.6	34	23	33	30	4	26	7	220	8	4	2	2.1	.983	OF-81, 1B-4, 3B-1
1949	2 teams	CHI N (42G – .264)		CIN N (86G – .318)																				
"	total	128	.300	.378	473	142	21	5	2	0.4	73	37	45	23	6	11	2	246	10	11	1	2.1	.959	OF-116, 1B-1
1950	STL N	60	.207	.240	150	31	5	0	0	0.0	17	7	18	12	0	6	0	102	3	3	1	1.8	.972	OF-46, 1B-2
1951		8	.308	.346	26	8	1	0	0	0.0	6	2	2	1	0	0	0	20	1	0	2	2.6	1.000	OF-6, 1B-1
1955		11	.357	.500	14	5	2	0	0	0.0	2	1	1	0	0	9	4	2	1	0	1	0.3	1.000	OF-1
11 yrs.		807	.296	.383	2651	786	126	37	10	0.4	385	214	245	175	42	85	17	1712	75	57	20	2.3	.969	OF-690, 1B-20, 2B-3, 3B-1

WORLD SERIES

1942	STL N	1	.000	.000	1	0	0	0	0	0.0	0	0	0	1	0	0	0	0	0	0	0	0.0	–	OF-1
1943		5	.167	.222	18	3	1	0	0	0.0	0	0	0	2	0	1	1	10	0	2	0	2.4	.833	OF-5
1946		7	.412	.529	17	7	2	0	0	0.0	3	6	4	2	0	1	0	14	0	0	0	2.0	1.000	OF-7
3 yrs.		13	.278	.361	36	10	3	0	0	0.0	3	6	4	5	0	3	1	24	0	2	0	2.0	.923	OF-12

Hub Walker

WALKER, HARVEY WILLOS
Brother of Gee Walker.
B. Aug. 17, 1906, Gulfport, Miss. D. Nov. 26, 1982, San Jose, Calif.

BL TR 5'10½" 175 lbs.

1931	DET A	90	.286	.345	252	72	13	1	0	0.0	27	16	23	25	10	12	2	170	4	7	1	2.0	.961	OF-66
1935		9	.160	.280	25	4	3	0	0	0.0	4	1	3	4	0	4	1	19	0	0	0	2.1	1.000	OF-7
1936	CIN N	92	.275	.399	258	71	18	1	4	1.6	49	23	35	32	8	13	1	162	4	5	2	1.9	.971	OF-73, 1B-1, C-1
1937		78	.249	.339	221	55	9	4	1	0.5	33	19	34	24	7	12	3	137	5	1	3	1.8	.993	OF-58, 2B-3
1945	DET A	28	.130	.130	23	3	0	0	0	0.0	4	1	9	4	1	15	1	5	0	0	0	0.2	1.000	OF-7
5 yrs.		297	.263	.353	779	205	43	6	5	0.6	117	60	104	89	26	54	8	493	13	13	6	1.7	.975	OF-211, 2B-3, 1B-1, C-1

WORLD SERIES

| 1945 | DET A | 2 | .500 | 1.000 | 2 | 1 | 1 | 0 | 0 | 0.0 | 0 | 0 | 0 | 0 | 0 | 2 | 1 | 0 | 0 | 0 | 0 | 0.0 | – | |

Joe Walker

WALKER, JOSEPH RICHARD (Speed)
B. Jan. 23, 1898, Munhall, Pa. D. June 20, 1959, West Mifflin, Pa.

BR TR 6' 170 lbs.

| 1923 | STL N | 2 | .286 | .286 | 7 | 2 | 0 | 0 | 0 | 0.0 | 1 | 0 | 1 | 0 | 0 | 0 | 0 | 19 | 0 | 0 | 1 | 9.5 | 1.000 | 1B-2 |

Johnny Walker

WALKER, JOHN MILES
B. Dec. 11, 1896, Toulon, Ill. D. Aug. 19, 1976, Hollywood, Fla.

BR TR 6' 175 lbs.

1919	PHI A	3	.000	.000	9	0	0	0	0	0.0	0	0	0	2	0	1	0	15	1	1	0	5.7	.941	C-3
1920		9	.227	.273	22	5	1	0	0	0.0	0	5	0	1	0	3	1	20	4	1	0	2.8	.960	C-6
1921		113	.258	.329	423	109	14	5	2	0.5	41	45	9	29	5	7	2	1022	56	12	71	9.6	.989	1B-99, C-7
3 yrs.		125	.251	.319	454	114	15	5	2	0.4	41	50	9	32	5	10	3	1057	61	14	71	9.1	.988	1B-99, C-16

Larry Walker

WALKER, LARRY KENNETH ROBERT
B. Dec. 1, 1966, Maple Ridge B. C., Canada

BL TR 6'2" 185 lbs.

| 1989 | MON N | 20 | .170 | .170 | 47 | 8 | 0 | 0 | 0 | 0.0 | 4 | 4 | 5 | 13 | 1 | 7 | 0 | 19 | 2 | 0 | 1 | 1.1 | 1.000 | OF-15 |

Oscar Walker

WALKER, OSCAR
B. Mar. 18, 1854, Brooklyn, N. Y. D. May 20, 1889, Brooklyn, N. Y.

BL TL 5'10" 166 lbs.

1879	BUF N	72	.275	.380	287	79	15	6	1	0.3	35	35	8	38	0	0	0	828	30	49	52	12.6	.946	1B-72
1880		34	.230	.317	126	29	4	2	1	0.8	12	15	6	18	0	0	0	267	10	27	17	8.9	.911	1B-24, OF-11
1882	STL AA	76	.239	.396	318	76	15	7	7	2.2	48		10		0	0	0	172	18	32	5	2.9	.856	OF-75, 2B-1, 1B-1
1884	BKN AA	95	.270	.359	382	103	12	8	2	0.5	59		9		0	0	0	476	20	31	12	5.5	.941	OF-59, 1B-36
4 yrs.		277	.258	.370	1113	287	46	23	11	1.0	154	50	33	56	0	0	0	1743	78	139	86	7.1	.929	OF-145, 1B-133, 2B-1

Rube Walker

WALKER, ALBERT BLUFORD
B. May 16, 1926, Lenoir, N. C.

BL TR 6' 175 lbs.

1948	CHI N	79	.275	.409	171	47	8	0	5	2.9	17	26	24	17	0	32	7	178	22	4	3	2.6	.980	C-44
1949		56	.244	.331	172	42	4	1	3	1.7	11	22	9	18	0	12	3	166	23	7	2	3.5	.964	C-43
1950		74	.230	.357	213	49	7	1	6	2.8	19	16	18	34	0	14	1	240	34	7	6	3.8	.975	C-62

Year	Team		Games	BA	SA	AB	H	2B	3B	HR	HR%	R	RBI	BB	SO	SB	Pinch Hit AB	H	PO	A	E	DP	TC/G	FA	G by Pos

Rube Walker *continued*

Year	Team		Games	BA	SA	AB	H	2B	3B	HR	HR%	R	RBI	BB	SO	SB	AB	H	PO	A	E	DP	TC/G	FA	G by Pos
1951	2 teams	CHI N (37G – .234)				BKN	N	(36G	– .243)																
"	total		73	.238	.348	181	43	8	0	4	2.2	15	14	18	27	0	17	3	173	23	6	4	2.8	.970	C-54
1952	BKN N		46	.259	.338	139	36	8	0	1	0.7	9	19	8	17	0	6	1	217	16	3	2	5.1	.987	C-40
1953			43	.242	.400	95	23	6	0	3	3.2	5	9	7	11	0	14	5	120	12	3	2	3.1	.978	C-28
1954			50	.181	.323	155	28	7	0	5	3.2	12	23	24	17	0	3	0	259	19	1	4	5.6	.996	C-47
1955			48	.252	.359	103	26	5	0	2	1.9	6	13	15	11	1	10	2	147	10	2	3	3.3	.987	C-35
1956			54	.212	.329	146	31	6	1	3	2.1	5	20	7	18	0	9	2	184	20	3	4	3.8	.986	C-43
1957			60	.181	.265	166	30	8	0	2	1.2	12	23	15	33	2	10	3	230	20	2	3	4.2	.992	C-50
1958	LA N		25	.114	.227	44	5	2	0	1	2.3	3	7	5	10	0	5	1	62	5	1	1	2.7	.985	C-20
11 yrs.			608	.227	.341	1585	360	69	3	35	2.2	114	192	150	213	3	132	28	1976	204	39	34	3.6	.982	C-466

WORLD SERIES

| 1956 | BKN N | | 2 | .000 | .000 | 2 | 0 | 0 | 0 | 0 | 0.0 | 0 | 0 | 0 | 0 | 0 | 2 | 0 | 0 | 0 | 0 | 0 | 0.0 | – | |

Tilly Walker

WALKER, CLARENCE WILLIAM
B. Sept. 4, 1887, Telford, Tenn. D. Sept. 21, 1959, Unicol, Tenn.
BR TR 5'11" 165 lbs.

Year	Team		Games	BA	SA	AB	H	2B	3B	HR	HR%	R	RBI	BB	SO	SB	AB	H	PO	A	E	DP	TC/G	FA	G by Pos
1911	WAS A		95	.278	.334	356	99	6	4	2	0.6	44	39	15		12	0	0	163	14	16	1	2.0	.917	OF-94
1912			36	.273	.309	110	30	2	1	0	0.0	22	9	8		11	4	0	37	6	8	3	1.4	.843	OF-31, 2B-1
1913	STL A		23	.294	.365	85	25	4	1	0	0.0	7	11	2	9	5	0	0	36	5	4	0	2.0	.911	OF-23
1914			151	.298	.441	517	154	24	16	6	1.2	67	78	51	72	29	5	2	311	30	10	5	2.3	.972	OF-145
1915			144	.269	.365	510	137	20	7	5	1.0	53	49	36	77	20	4	2	333	27	23	5	2.7	.940	OF-139
1916	BOS A		128	.266	.394	467	124	29	11	3	0.6	68	46	23	45	14	0	0	290	12	13	4	2.5	.959	OF-128
1917			106	.246	.359	337	83	18	7	2	0.6	41	37	25	38	6	9	3	225	20	7	7	2.4	.972	OF-96
1918	PHI A		114	.295	.423	414	122	20	10	11	2.7	56	48	41	44	8	5	2	242	25	13	4	2.5	.954	OF-109
1919			125	.292	.450	456	133	30	6	10	2.2	47	64	26	41	8	7	2	253	13	19	4	2.3	.933	OF-115
1920			149	.268	.419	585	157	23	7	17	2.9	79	82	40	59	9	0	0	318	26	22	5	2.5	.940	OF-149
1921			142	.304	.504	556	169	32	5	23	4.1	89	101	73	41	3	0	0	337	24	17	3	2.7	.955	OF-142
1922			153	.283	.549	565	160	31	4	37	6.5	111	99	61	64	4	3	0	309	19	15	4	2.2	.956	OF-148
1923			52	.275	.413	109	30	5	2	2	1.8	12	16	14	11	1	22	6	52	1	0	1	1.0	1.000	OF-26
13 yrs.			1418	.281	.427	5067	1423	244	71	118	2.3	696	679	415	501	130	59	17	2906	222	167	46	2.3	.949	OF-1345, 2B-1

WORLD SERIES

| 1916 | BOS A | | 3 | .273 | .455 | 11 | 3 | 0 | 1 | 0 | 0.0 | 1 | 1 | 1 | 2 | 0 | 0 | 0 | 4 | 1 | 0 | 0 | 1.7 | 1.000 | OF-3 |

Tony Walker

WALKER, ANTHONY BRUCE
B. July 1, 1959, San Diego, Calif.
BR TR 6'2" 205 lbs.

Year	Team		Games	BA	SA	AB	H	2B	3B	HR	HR%	R	RBI	BB	SO	SB	AB	H	PO	A	E	DP	TC/G	FA	G by Pos
1986	HOU N		84	.222	.367	90	20	7	0	2	2.2	19	10	11	15	11	7	1	73	0	1	0	0.9	.986	OF-68

Walt Walker

WALKER, WALTER S.
B. Ionia, Mich. Deceased.

Year	Team		Games	BA	SA	AB	H	2B	3B	HR	HR%	R	RBI	BB	SO	SB	AB	H	PO	A	E	DP	TC/G	FA	G by Pos
1885	BAL AA		4	.000	.000	13	0	0	0	0	0.0	1		0			0	0	4	0	2	0	1.5	.667	OF-4

Welday Walker

WALKER, WELDAY WILBERFORCE
Brother of Fleet Walker.
B. July 27, 1860, Steubenville, Ohio D. Nov. 23, 1937, Steubenville, Ohio

Year	Team		Games	BA	SA	AB	H	2B	3B	HR	HR%	R	RBI	BB	SO	SB	AB	H	PO	A	E	DP	TC/G	FA	G by Pos
1884	TOL AA		5	.222	.278	18	4	1	0	0	0.0	0		0			0	0	4	0	2	0	1.2	.667	OF-5

Joe Wall

WALL, JOSEPH FRANCIS (Gummy)
B. July 24, 1873, Brooklyn, N. Y. D. July 17, 1936, Brooklyn, N. Y.
BL TL

Year	Team		Games	BA	SA	AB	H	2B	3B	HR	HR%	R	RBI	BB	SO	SB	AB	H	PO	A	E	DP	TC/G	FA	G by Pos
1901	NY N		4	.500	.500	8	4	0	0	0	0.0	0	1	0			0	1	1	3	0	0	0	0.8	1.000	C-2, OF-1
1902	2 teams	NY N (6G – .357)				BKN	N	(5G	– .167)																
"	total		11	.250	.313	32	8	2	0	0	0.0	2	0	5			0	3	1	23	4	3	0	2.7	.900	C-5, OF-3
2 yrs.			15	.300	.350	40	12	2	0	0	0.0	2	1	5			0	4	2	26	4	3	0	2.2	.909	C-7, OF-4

Bobby Wallace

WALLACE, RHODERICK JOHN (Rhody)
B. Nov. 4, 1873, Pittsburg, Pa. D. Nov. 3, 1960, Torrance, Calif.
Manager 1911-12, 1937.
Hall of Fame 1953.
BR TR 5'8" 170 lbs.

Year	Team		Games	BA	SA	AB	H	2B	3B	HR	HR%	R	RBI	BB	SO	SB	AB	H	PO	A	E	DP	TC/G	FA	G by Pos
1894	CLE N		4	.154	.231	13	2	1	0	0	0.0	0	1	0	1	0	0	0	3	9	0	0	3.0	1.000	P-4
1895			30	.214	.296	98	21	2	3	0	0.0	16	10	6	17	0	0	0	15	66	8	2	3.0	.910	P-30
1896			45	.235	.336	149	35	6	3	1	0.7	19	17	11	21	2	0	0	44	35	5	4	1.9	.940	OF-23, P-22, 1B-1
1897			131	.335	.504	516	173	33	21	4	0.8	99	112	48		14	0	0	191	250	35	10	3.6	.926	3B-130, OF-1
1898			154	.270	.371	593	160	25	13	3	0.5	81	99	63		7	0	0	248	365	39	23	4.2	.940	3B-141, 2B-13
1899	STL N		151	.295	.454	577	170	28	14	12	2.1	91	108	54		17	0	0	322	536	73	53	6.2	.922	SS-100, 3B-52
1900			126	.268	.381	485	130	25	9	4	0.8	72	70	40		7	0	0	329	449	55	31	6.6	.934	SS-126, 3B-1
1901			135	.322	.448	556	179	34	15	2	0.4	69	91	20		15	0	0	326	542	66	67	6.9	.929	SS-134
1902	STL A		133	.287	.394	495	142	32	9	1	0.2	71	63	45		18	1	0	301	475	42	64	6.2	.949	SS-131, OF-1, P-1
1903			136	.245	.356	519	127	21	17	1	0.2	63	54	28		10	0	0	282	468	62	53	6.0	.924	SS-135
1904			139	.273	.351	550	150	29	4	2	0.4	57	69	42		20	0	0	303	482	44	37	6.0	.947	SS-139
1905			156	.271	.349	587	159	25	9	1	0.2	67	59	45		13	0	0	385	506	62	40	6.1	.935	SS-156
1906			139	.258	.345	476	123	21	7	2	0.4	64	67	58		24	1	1	309	461	41	47	5.8	.949	SS-138
1907			147	.257	.320	538	138	20	7	0	0.0	56	70	54		16	0	0	338	517	54	54	6.2	.941	SS-147
1908			137	.253	.324	487	123	24	4	1	0.2	59	60	52		5	0	0	286	510	41	45	6.1	.951	SS-137
1909			116	.238	.285	403	96	12	2	1	0.2	36	35	38		7	0	0	242	336	32	39	5.3	.948	SS-87, 3B-29
1910			138	.258	.323	508	131	19	7	0	0.0	47	37	49		12	0	0	316	444	43	43	5.9	.943	SS-98, 3B-40
1911			125	.232	.271	410	95	12	2	0	0.0	35	31	46		8	0	0	282	417	42	49	5.9	.943	SS-124, 2B-1
1912			99	.241	.316	323	78	14	5	0	0.0	39	31	43		3	1	0	210	296	31	35	5.4	.942	SS-86, 3B-10, 2B-2
1913			53	.211	.245	147	31	5	0	0	0.0	11	21	14	16	1	7	0	75	119	12	8	3.9	.942	SS-38, 3B-7
1914			26	.219	.274	73	16	2	1	0	0.0	3	5	5	13	1	5	0	27	49	9	2	3.3	.894	SS-19, 3B-2
1915			9	.231	.385	13	3	0	1	0	0.0	1	4	0	0	0	0	0	11	17	5	4	3.7	.848	SS-9

Year	Team		Games	BA	SA	AB	H	2B	3B	HR	HR%	R	RBI	BB	SO	SB	Pinch Hit AB	Pinch Hit H	PO	A	E	DP	TC/G	FA	G by Pos

Bobby Wallace *continued*

1916			14	.278	.278	18	5	0	0	0	0.0	0	1	2	1	0	0	0	8	27	2	1	2.6	.946	3B-9, SS-5
1917	STL	N	8	.100	.100	10	1	0	0	0	0.0	0	2	0	1	0	3	1	5	6	1	0	1.5	.917	3B-5, SS-2
1918			32	.153	.163	98	15	1	0	0	0.0	3	4	6	9	1	3	2	61	83	10	13	4.8	.935	2B-17, SS-12, 3B-1
25 yrs.			2383	.266	.359	8642	2303	391	153	35	0.4	1059	1121	774	79	201	21	5	4919	7465	814	724	5.5	.938	SS-1823, 3B-427, P-57, 2B-33, OF-25, 1B-1

Doc Wallace

WALLACE, FREDERICK RENSHAW
B. Sept. 30, 1893, Church Hill, Md. D. Dec. 31, 1964, Haverford, Pa.   BR TR 5'6½" 135 lbs.

1919	PHI	N	2	.250	.250	4	1	0	0	0	0.0	0	0	0	0	0	0	0	3	4	1	0	4.0	.875	SS-2

Don Wallace

WALLACE, DONALD ALLEN
B. Aug. 25, 1940, Sapulpa, Okla.   BL TR 5'8" 165 lbs.

1967	CAL	A	23	.000	.000	6	0	0	0	0	0.0	2	0	3	2	0	3	0	4	5	0	1	0.3	1.000	2B-4, 3B-1, 1B-1

Jack Wallace

WALLACE, CLARENCE EUGENE
B. Aug. 6, 1890, Winnfield, La. D. Oct. 15, 1960, Winnfield, La.   BR TR 5'10½" 175 lbs.

1915	CHI	N	2	.286	.286	7	2	0	0	0	0.0	1	1	0	2	0	0	0	13	6	0	0	9.5	1.000	C-2

Jim Wallace

WALLACE, JAMES L.
B. Nov. 14, 1881, Boston, Mass. D. May 16, 1953, Revere, Mass.   BL TL

1905	PIT	N	7	.207	.241	29	6	1	0	0	0.0	3	3	3		2	0	0	10	3	1	0	2.0	.929	OF-7

Tim Wallach

WALLACH, TIMOTHY CHARLES
B. Sept. 14, 1957, Huntington Park, Calif.   BR TR 6'3" 220 lbs.

1980	MON	N	5	.182	.455	11	2	0	0	1	9.1	1	2	1	5	0	2	0	12	0	0	0	2.4	1.000	OF-3, 1B-1
1981			71	.236	.344	212	50	9	4	4	1.9	19	13	15	37	0	6	1	207	31	1	9	3.4	.996	OF-35, 1B-16, 3B-15
1982			158	.268	.471	596	160	31	3	28	4.7	89	97	36	81	6	3	1	132	287	23	23	2.8	.948	3B-156, OF-2, 1B-1
1983			156	.269	.434	581	156	33	3	19	3.3	54	70	55	97	0	0	0	151	265	19	25	2.8	.956	3B-156
1984			160	.246	.395	582	143	25	4	18	3.1	55	72	50	101	3	0	0	162	332	21	29	3.2	.959	3B-160, SS-1
1985			155	.260	.450	569	148	36	3	22	3.9	70	81	38	79	9	2	0	148	383	18	34	3.5	.967	3B-154
1986			134	.233	.396	480	112	22	1	18	3.8	50	71	44	72	8	1	0	94	270	16	26	2.8	.958	3B-132
1987			153	.298	.514	593	177	42	4	26	4.4	89	123	37	98	9	3	0	128	292	21	21	2.9	.952	3B-150, P-1
1988			159	.257	.389	592	152	32	5	12	2.0	52	69	38	88	2	8	2	124	329	18	32	3.0	.962	3B-153, 2B-1
1989			154	.277	.419	573	159	42	0	13	2.3	76	77	58	81	3	1	1	113	302	18	20	2.8	.958	3B-153, P-1
10 yrs.			1305	.263	.431	4789	1259	272	24	161	3.4	555	675	372	739	40	26	5	1271	2491	155	219	3.0	.960	3B-1229, OF-40, 1B-18, P-2, SS-1, 2B-1

DIVISIONAL PLAYOFF SERIES

1981	MON	N	4	.250	.500	4	1	1	0	0	0.0	1	0	4	0	0	0	0	0	0	0	0	0.0	–	OF-3

LEAGUE CHAMPIONSHIP SERIES

1981	MON	N	1	.000	.000	1	0	0	0	0	0.0	0	0	0	0	0	0	0	0	0	0	0	0.0	–	

Jack Wallaesa

WALLAESA, JOHN
B. Aug. 31, 1919, Easton, Pa.
D. Dec. 27, 1986, Easton, Pa.   BB TR 6'3" 191 lbs. BB 1948

1940	PHI	A	6	.150	.150	20	3	0	0	0	0.0	2	0	0	2	0	0	0	9	19	3	3	5.2	.903	SS-6
1942			36	.256	.359	117	30	4	1	2	1.7	13	13	1	26	0	0	0	62	76	12	16	4.2	.920	SS-36
1946			63	.196	.314	194	38	4	2	5	2.6	16	11	14	47	1	3	1	111	130	22	31	4.2	.916	SS-59
1947	CHI	A	81	.195	.351	205	40	9	1	7	3.4	25	32	23	51	2	27	4	130	96	5	22	2.9	.978	SS-27, OF-22, 3B-1
1948			33	.188	.250	48	9	0	0	1	2.1	2	3	1	12	0	27	6	11	17	0	5	0.8	1.000	SS-5, OF-1
5 yrs.			219	.205	.325	584	120	17	4	15	2.6	56	61	39	138	3	57	11	323	338	42	77	3.2	.940	SS-133, OF-23, 3B-1

Norm Wallen

WALLEN, NORMAN EDWARD
Born Norman Edward Walentoski.
B. Feb. 13, 1917, Milwaukee, Wis.   BR TR 5'11½" 175 lbs.

1945	BOS	N	4	.133	.267	15	2	0	1	0	0.0	1	1	1	1	0	0	0	3	5	2	0	2.5	.800	3B-4

Tye Waller

WALLER, ELLIOTT TYRONE
B. Mar. 14, 1957, Fresno, Calif.   BR TR 6' 180 lbs.

1980	STL	N	5	.083	.083	12	1	0	0	0	0.0	3	0	1	5	0	0	0	1	2	0	0	0.6	1.000	3B-5
1981	CHI	N	30	.268	.451	71	19	2	1	3	4.2	10	13	4	18	2	1	1	18	35	1	2	1.8	.981	3B-22, OF-3, 2B-3
1982			17	.238	.238	21	5	0	0	0	0.0	4	1	2	5	0	6	2	10	1	1	0	0.7	.917	OF-7, 3B-1
1987	HOU	N	11	.167	.333	6	1	1	0	0	0.0	1	0	0	3	0	4	1	2	0	0	0	0.2	1.000	OF-3
4 yrs.			63	.236	.364	110	26	3	1	3	2.7	18	14	7	31	2	11	4	31	38	2	2	1.1	.972	3B-28, OF-13, 2B-3

Denny Walling

WALLING, DENNIS MARTIN
B. Apr. 17, 1954, Neptune, N. J.   BL TR 6' 180 lbs.

1975	OAK	A	6	.125	.250	8	1	1	0	0	0.0	0	2	0	4	0	4	1	3	0	0	0	0.5	1.000	OF-3
1976			3	.273	.273	11	3	0	0	0	0.0	1	0	0	3	0	0	0	8	0	1	0	3.0	.889	OF-3
1977	HOU	N	6	.286	.381	21	6	0	1	0	0.0	1	6	2	4	0	1	0	14	0	0	0	2.3	1.000	OF-5
1978			120	.251	.356	247	62	11	3	3	1.2	30	36	30	24	9	39	10	140	4	3	2	1.2	.980	OF-78
1979			82	.327	.497	147	48	8	4	3	2.0	21	31	17	21	3	37	14	65	2	1	0	0.8	.985	OF-42
1980			100	.299	.387	284	85	6	5	3	1.1	30	29	35	26	4	21	4	525	31	6	46	5.6	.989	1B-63, OF-19
1981			65	.234	.367	158	37	6	0	3	1.9	23	23	28	17	2	18	6	226	9	2	18	3.6	.992	OF-27, 1B-27
1982			85	.205	.267	146	30	4	1	1	0.7	22	14	23	19	4	30	6	167	11	1	8	2.1	.994	OF-32, 1B-20
1983			100	.296	.444	135	40	5	3	3	2.2	24	19	15	16	2	37	8	134	29	6	13	1.7	.964	1B-42, OF-13, 3B-13
1984			87	.281	.402	249	70	11	5	3	1.2	37	31	16	28	7	26	7	116	102	7	21	2.6	.969	3B-52, 1B-16, OF-6
1985			119	.270	.394	345	93	20	1	7	2.0	44	45	25	26	5	23	2	326	124	12	31	3.9	.974	3B-51, 1B-46, OF-13
1986			130	.312	.479	382	119	23	1	13	3.4	54	58	36	31	1	31	12	108	161	9	8	2.1	.968	3B-102, OF-11, 1B-4

Year	Team		Games	BA	SA	AB	H	2B	3B	HR	HR%	R	RBI	BB	SO	SB	Pinch Hit AB	Pinch Hit H	PO	A	E	DP	TC/G	FA	G by Pos

Denny Walling *continued*

1987			110	.283	.418	325	92	21	4	5	1.5	45	33	39	37	5	15	8	175	119	10	21	2.8	.967	3B-79, 1B-16, OF-7
1988	2 teams				HOU N (65G – .244)		STL	N	(19G – .224)																
"	total		84	.239	.325	234	56	13	2	1	0.4	22	21	17	25	2	20	3	73	112	9	17	2.3	.954	3B-56, OF-12, 1B-4
1989	STL	N	69	.304	.430	79	24	7	0	1	1.3	9	11	14	12	0	32	11	67	9	4	4	1.2	.950	1B-20, 3B-9, OF-6
15 yrs.			1166	.276	.399	2771	766	136	30	48	1.7	363	359	297	293	44	334	93	2147	713	71	189	2.5	.976	3B-362, OF-277, 1B-258

DIVISIONAL PLAYOFF SERIES

| 1981 | HOU | N | 3 | .333 | .333 | 6 | 2 | 0 | 0 | 0 | 0.0 | 0 | 1 | 0 | 1 | 0 | 1 | 1 | 0 | 0 | 1 | 0 | 0.3 | – | OF-1, 1B-1 |

LEAGUE CHAMPIONSHIP SERIES

1980	HOU	N	3	.111	.111	9	1	0	0	0	0.0	2	2	1	0	0	1	0	6	0	0	0	2.0	1.000	OF-2, 1B-1
1986			5	.158	.211	19	3	1	0	0	0.0	1	2	0	4	0	2	1	3	6	0	0	1.8	1.000	3B-5
2 yrs.			8	.143	.179	28	4	1	0	0	0.0	3	4	1	4	0	3	1	9	6	0	0	1.9	1.000	3B-5, OF-2, 1B-1

Joe Wallis

WALLIS, HAROLD JOSEPH (Tarzan)
B. Jan. 9, 1952, East St. Louis, Ill.   BL TR 5'10" 185 lbs.

1975	CHI	N	16	.286	.446	56	16	2	2	1	1.8	9	4	5	14	2	3	1	31	1	0	0	2.0	1.000	OF-15
1976			121	.254	.361	338	86	11	5	5	1.5	51	21	33	62	3	26	4	193	11	5	3	1.7	.976	OF-90
1977			56	.250	.363	80	20	3	0	2	2.5	14	8	16	25	0	16	2	36	2	1	0	0.7	.974	OF-35
1978	2 teams		113		CHI N (28G – .309)		OAK	A	(85G – .237)																
"	total		113	.249	.377	334	83	18	2	7	2.1	35	32	31	55	1	10	2	223	8	4	5	2.1	.983	OF-105, DH-1
1979	OAK	A	23	.141	.205	78	11	2	0	1	1.3	6	3	10	18	1	0	0	41	1	0	0	1.8	1.000	OF-23
5 yrs.			329	.244	.359	886	216	36	9	16	1.8	115	68	95	174	7	55	9	524	23	10	8	1.7	.982	OF-268, DH-1

Lee Walls

WALLS, RAY LEE
B. Jan. 6, 1933, San Diego, Calif.   BR TR 6'3" 205 lbs.

1952	PIT	N	32	.188	.288	80	15	0	1	2	2.5	6	5	8	22	1	10	1	44	2	0	1	1.4	1.000	OF-19
1956			143	.274	.432	474	130	20	11	11	2.3	72	54	50	83	3	10	1	284	11	11	1	2.1	.964	OF-133, 3B-1
1957	2 teams				PIT N (8G – .182)		CHI	N	(117G – .240)																
"	total		125	.237	.338	388	92	11	5	6	1.5	45	33	29	72	6	22	8	188	7	3	0	1.6	.985	OF-101, 3B-1
1958	CHI	N	136	.304	.493	513	156	19	3	24	4.7	80	72	47	62	4	4	2	241	10	2	1	1.9	.992	OF-132
1959			120	.257	.393	354	91	18	3	8	2.3	43	33	42	73	0	4	0	203	1	7	0	1.8	.967	OF-119
1960	2 teams				CIN N (29G – .274)		PHI	N	(65G – .199)																
"	total		94	.223	.325	265	59	9	3	4	1.5	31	26	31	52	5	20	5	130	51	8	10	2.0	.958	OF-37, 3B-34, 1B-9
1961	PHI	N	91	.280	.425	261	73	6	4	8	3.1	32	30	19	48	2	19	4	247	59	8	33	3.5	.975	1B-28, 3B-26, OF-18
1962	LA	N	60	.266	.312	109	29	3	1	0	0.0	9	17	10	21	1	27	13	98	12	2	4	1.9	.982	OF-17, 1B-11, 3B-4
1963			64	.233	.349	86	20	1	0	3	3.5	12	11	7	25	0	39	7	55	12	1	3	1.1	.985	3B-15, 1B-5, 2B-2
1964			37	.179	.214	28	5	1	0	0	0.0	1	3	2	12	0	28	5	1	0	0	0	0.0	1.000	OF-6, C-1
10 yrs.			902	.262	.398	2558	670	88	31	66	2.6	331	284	245	470	21	183	46	1491	165	42	53	1.9	.975	OF-600, 3B-68, 1B-53, C-1

Austin Walsh

WALSH, AUSTIN EDWARD
B. Sept. 1, 1891, Cambridge, Mass. D. Jan. 26, 1955, Glenridge, Calif.   BL TL 5'11" 175 lbs.

| 1914 | CHI | F | 57 | .240 | .331 | 121 | 29 | 6 | 1 | 1 | 0.8 | 14 | 10 | 4 | | | 22 | 3 | 0 | 0 | 0 | 0 | 0.0 | – | OF-30 |

Dee Walsh

WALSH, LEO THOMAS
B. Mar. 28, 1890, St. Louis, Mo. D. July 14, 1971, St. Louis, Mo.   BB TR 5'9½" 165 lbs.

1913	STL	A	23	.170	.208	53	9	0	1	0	0.0	8	5	6	11	3	0	0	36	63	7	6	4.6	.934	SS-22, 3B-1
1914			7	.087	.087	23	2	0	0	0	0.0	1	1	2	4	1	0	0	14	20	3	5	5.3	.919	SS-7
1915			59	.220	.253	150	33	5	0	0	0.0	13	6	14	25	6	4	1	71	21	5	0	1.6	.948	OF-45, 3B-2, SS-1, 2B-1, P-1
3 yrs.			89	.195	.226	226	44	5	1	0	0.0	22	12	22	40	10	4	1	121	104	15	11	2.7	.938	OF-45, SS-30, 3B-3, 2B-1, P-1

Ed Walsh

WALSH, EDWARD AUGUSTINE (Big Ed)
Father of Ed Walsh.
B. May 14, 1881, Plains, Pa. D. May 26, 1959, Pompano Beach, Fla.
Manager 1924.
Hall of Fame 1946.   BR TR 6'1" 193 lbs.

1904	CHI	A	18	.220	.366	41	9	1	1	1	2.4	5	4	3		1	0	0	8	35	1	2	2.4	.977	P-18
1905			29	.155	.190	58	9	2	0	0	0.0	5	2	4		0	2	0	13	42	2	1	2.0	.965	P-22, OF-5
1906			42	.141	.212	99	14	3	2	0	0.0	12	4	3		0	1	0	30	108	6	2	3.4	.958	P-41
1907			57	.162	.247	154	25	6	1	1	0.6	7	10	0		2	1	0	35	227	4	2	4.7	.985	P-56
1908			66	.172	.248	157	27	7	1	1	0.6	10	10	7		2	0	0	41	190	6	9	3.6	.975	P-66
1909			32	.214	.274	84	18	5	0	0	0.0	5	11	6		4	0	0	23	93	1	2	3.7	.991	P-31, OF-1
1910			52	.217	.283	138	30	3	0	0	0.0	12	4	5		5	7	1	21	154	9	5	3.5	.951	P-45
1911			62	.206	.226	155	32	3	0	0	0.0	22	9	1		0	7	2	27	159	8	5	3.1	.959	P-56
1912			64	.243	.287	136	33	4	1	0	0.0	12	12	14		0	0	0	22	143	15	3	2.8	.917	P-62
1913			17	.156	.188	32	5	1	0	0	0.0	1	2	1	7	0	1	0	6	32	3	1	2.4	.927	P-16
1914			10	.063	.125	16	1	1	0	0	0.0	0	1	0	4	0	1	0	7	15	1	0	2.3	.957	P-8
1915			5	.364	.364	11	4	0	0	0	0.0	0	1	0	1	0	2	1	3	4	0	0	1.4	1.000	P-3
1916			2	–	–	0	0	0	0	0	–	0	0	0	0	0	0	0	1	2	0	0	1.0	1.000	P-2
1917	BOS	N	4	.250	.250	4	1	0	0	0	0.0	0	1	0	2	0	0	0	1	7	1	0	2.3	.889	P-4
14 yrs.			460	.192	.252	1085	208	36	10	3	0.3	92	69	46	14	14	25	5	237	1211	57	32	3.3	.962	P-430, OF-6

WORLD SERIES

| 1906 | CHI | A | 2 | .000 | .000 | 4 | 0 | 0 | 0 | 0 | 0.0 | 1 | 0 | 3 | 3 | 0 | 0 | 0 | 0 | 5 | 1 | 0 | 3.0 | .833 | P-2 |

Jimmy Walsh

WALSH, JAMES CHARLES
B. Sept. 22, 1885, Kallila, Ireland D. July 3, 1962, Syracuse, N. Y.   BL TR 5'10½" 170 lbs.

| 1912 | PHI | A | 31 | .252 | .364 | 107 | 27 | 8 | 2 | 0 | 0.0 | 11 | 15 | 12 | | 7 | 1 | 0 | 70 | 1 | 4 | 1 | 2.4 | .947 | OF-30 |
| 1913 | | | 94 | .254 | .340 | 303 | 77 | 16 | 5 | 0 | 0.0 | 56 | 27 | 38 | 40 | 15 | 4 | 1 | 184 | 11 | 8 | 4 | 2.2 | .961 | OF-88 |

Year	Team		Games	BA	SA	AB	H	2B	3B	HR	HR%	R	RBI	BB	SO	SB	Pinch Hit AB	Pinch Hit H	PO	A	E	DP	TC/G	FA	G by Pos

Jimmy Walsh *continued*

Year	Team		Games	BA	SA	AB	H	2B	3B	HR	HR%	R	RBI	BB	SO	SB	AB	H	PO	A	E	DP	TC/G	FA	G by Pos
1914	2 teams	NY A (43G – .191)				PHI A (67G – .236)																			
"	total		110	.219	.338	352	77	12	9	4	1.1	48	47	59	48	12	6	1	221	20	9	6	2.3	.964	OF-97, 3B-3, 1B-3, SS-1
1915	PHI	A	117	.206	.278	417	86	15	6	1	0.2	48	20	57	64	22	3	0	240	16	6	1	2.2	.977	OF-109, 3B-2, 1B-1
1916	2 teams	PHI A (114G – .233)				BOS A (13G – .125)																			
"	total		127	.229	.298	406	93	13	6	1	0.2	47	29	58	38	30	4	0	179	13	12	4	1.6	.941	OF-119, 3B-2, 1B-1
1917	BOS	A	57	.265	.330	185	49	6	3	0	0.0	25	12	25	14	6	7	2	103	8	2	0	2.0	.982	OF-47
6 yrs.			536	.231	.316	1770	409	70	31	6	0.3	235	150	249	204	92	25	4	997	69	41	16	2.1	.963	OF-490, 3B-7, 1B-5, SS-1

WORLD SERIES

Year	Team		Games	BA	SA	AB	H	2B	3B	HR	HR%	R	RBI	BB	SO	SB	AB	H	PO	A	E	DP	TC/G	FA	G by Pos
1914	PHI	A	3	.333	.500	6	2	1	0	0	0.0	0	1	3	1	0	0	0	2	0	0	0	0.7	1.000	OF-2
1916	BOS	A	1	.000	.000	3	0	0	0	0	0.0	0	0	0	0	0	0	0	1	0	0	0	1.0	1.000	OF-1
2 yrs.			4	.222	.333	9	2	1	0	0	0.0	0	1	3	1	0	0	0	3	0	0	0	0.8	1.000	OF-3

Jimmy Walsh

WALSH, MICHAEL TIMOTHY (Runt)
B. Mar. 25, 1886, Lima, Ohio D. Jan. 21, 1947, Baltimore, Md.

BR TR 5'9" 174 lbs.

Year	Team		Games	BA	SA	AB	H	2B	3B	HR	HR%	R	RBI	BB	SO	SB	AB	H	PO	A	E	DP	TC/G	FA	G by Pos
1910	PHI	N	88	.248	.343	242	60	8	3	3	1.2	28	31	25	38	5	20	3	122	101	23	11	2.8	.907	OF-27, 2B-26, SS-9, 3B-5
1911			94	.270	.370	289	78	20	3	1	0.3	29	31	21	30	5	10	2	148	79	12	14	2.5	.950	OF-48, 2B-14, SS-9, 3B-7, C-4, 1B-1, P-1
1912			51	.267	.387	150	40	6	3	2	1.3	16	19	8	20	3	10	1	69	112	10	12	3.7	.948	2B-31, 3B-12, C-5
1913			26	.333	.467	30	10	4	0	0	0.0	3	5	1	5	1	12	3	9	10	1	3	0.8	.950	2B-6, SS-3, OF-1, 3B-1
1914	BAL	F	120	.308	.456	428	132	25	4	10	2.3	54	65	22		18	3	1	126	220	26	18	3.1	.930	3B-113, OF-1, SS-1, 2B-1
1915	2 teams	BAL F (106G – .302)				STL F (17G – .194)																			
"	total		123	.294	.410	432	127	21	1	9	2.1	48	61	24		13	7	1	138	204	24	15	3.0	.934	3B-115
6 yrs.			502	.285	.404	1571	447	84	14	25	1.6	178	212	101	93	45	62	11	612	726	96	73	2.9	.933	3B-253, 2B-78, OF-77, SS-22, C-9, 1B-1, P-1

Joe Walsh

WALSH, JOSEPH FRANCIS
B. Oct. 14, 1886, Minersville, Pa. D. Jan. 6, 1967, Buffalo, N. Y.

BR TR 6'2" 170 lbs.

Year	Team		Games	BA	SA	AB	H	2B	3B	HR	HR%	R	RBI	BB	SO	SB	AB	H	PO	A	E	DP	TC/G	FA	G by Pos
1910	NY	A	1	.000	.000	3	0	0	0	0	0.0	0	2	0	0	0	0	0	1	2	0	0	3.0	1.000	C-1
1911			4	.222	.333	9	2	1	0	0	0.0	2	0	0	0	0	1	0	4	1	0	0	1.3	1.000	C-3
2 yrs.			5	.167	.250	12	2	1	0	0	0.0	2	2	0	0	1	0	5	3	0	0	1.6	1.000	C-4

Joe Walsh

WALSH, JOSEPH PATRICK (Tweet)
B. Mar. 13, 1917, Roxbury, Mass.

BR TR 5'10" 155 lbs.

Year	Team		Games	BA	SA	AB	H	2B	3B	HR	HR%	R	RBI	BB	SO	SB	AB	H	PO	A	E	DP	TC/G	FA	G by Pos
1938	BOS	N	4	.000	.000	8	0	0	0	0	0.0	0	0	0	2	0	0	0	6	3	1	1	2.5	.900	SS-4

Joe Walsh

WALSH, JOSEPH R.
B. Nov. 5, 1864, Chicago, Ill. D. Aug. 8, 1911, Omaha, Neb.

Year	Team		Games	BA	SA	AB	H	2B	3B	HR	HR%	R	RBI	BB	SO	SB	AB	H	PO	A	E	DP	TC/G	FA	G by Pos
1891	BAL	AA	26	.210	.260	100	21	0	1	1	1.0	14	10	6	18	4	0	0	65	84	19	16	6.5	.887	SS-13, 2B-13

John Walsh

WALSH, JOHN GABRIEL
B. Mar. 25, 1879, Wilkes-Barre, Pa. D. Apr. 25, 1947, Jamaica, N. Y.

BR TR 5'8½" 162 lbs.

Year	Team		Games	BA	SA	AB	H	2B	3B	HR	HR%	R	RBI	BB	SO	SB	AB	H	PO	A	E	DP	TC/G	FA	G by Pos
1903	PHI	N	1	.000	.000	3	0	0	0	0	0.0	0	0	0	0	0	0	0	0	2	0	0	2.0	1.000	3B-1

Tom Walsh

WALSH, THOMAS JOSEPH
B. Feb. 28, 1885, Davenport, Iowa D. Mar. 16, 1963, Naples, Fla.

BR TR 5'11" 170 lbs.

Year	Team		Games	BA	SA	AB	H	2B	3B	HR	HR%	R	RBI	BB	SO	SB	AB	H	PO	A	E	DP	TC/G	FA	G by Pos
1906	CHI	N	2	.000	.000	1	0	0	0	0	0.0	0	0	0	0	0	0	0	1	1	0	0	1.0	1.000	C-2

Walt Walsh

WALSH, WALTER WILLIAM
B. Apr. 30, 1897, Newark, N. J. D. Jan. 15, 1966, Avon-By-The-Sea, N. J.

BR TR 5'11" 170 lbs.

Year	Team		Games	BA	SA	AB	H	2B	3B	HR	HR%	R	RBI	BB	SO	SB	AB	H	PO	A	E	DP	TC/G	FA	G by Pos
1920	PHI	N	2	–	–	0	0	0	0	0	–	0	0	0	0	0	0	0	0	0	0	0	0.0	–	

Bucky Walters

WALTERS, WILLIAM HENRY
B. Apr. 19, 1909, Philadelphia, Pa.
Manager 1948-49.

BR TR 6'1" 180 lbs.

Year	Team		Games	BA	SA	AB	H	2B	3B	HR	HR%	R	RBI	BB	SO	SB	AB	H	PO	A	E	DP	TC/G	FA	G by Pos
1931	BOS	N	9	.211	.263	38	8	2	0	0	0.0	2	0	0	3	0	0	0	7	22	1	0	3.3	.967	3B-6, 2B-3
1932			22	.187	.253	75	14	3	1	0	0.0	8	4	2	18	0	0	0	17	44	6	8	3.0	.910	3B-22
1933	BOS	A	52	.256	.390	195	50	8	3	4	2.1	27	28	19	24	1	2	1	58	107	10	14	3.4	.943	3B-43, 2B-7
1934	2 teams	BOS A (23G – .216)				PHI N (83G – .260)																			
"	total		106	.250	.410	388	97	24	7	8	2.1	46	56	22	66	1	0	0	116	200	21	19	3.2	.938	3B-103, 2B-3, P-2
1935	PHI	N	49	.250	.292	96	24	2	1	0	0.0	14	6	9	12	0	14	4	15	48	1	4	1.3	.984	P-24, OF-5, 2B-2, 3B-1
1936			64	.240	.364	121	29	10	1	1	0.8	12	16	7	15	0	17	4	15	98	3	6	1.8	.974	P-40, 3B-1, 2B-1
1937			56	.277	.343	137	38	0	1	1	0.7	15	16	5	16	1	10	4	12	85	1	8	1.8	.990	P-37, 3B-8
1938	2 teams	PHI N (15G – .286)				CIN N (36G – .141)																			
"	total		51	.192	.253	99	19	3	0	1	1.0	16	8	8	23	1	5	0	6	66	2	5	1.5	.973	P-39
1939	CIN	N	40	.325	.433	120	39	8	1	1	0.8	16	16	5	12	1	1	0	16	77	2	10	2.4	.979	P-39
1940			37	.205	.256	117	24	3	0	1	0.9	11	18	4	14	2	1	0	13	56	4	7	2.0	.945	P-36
1941			39	.189	.245	106	20	6	0	0	0.0	6	9	7	13	0	2	0	18	68	2	6	2.3	.977	P-37
1942			40	.242	.384	99	24	6	1	2	2.0	13	13	9	13	0	3	0	13	60	3	6	1.9	.961	P-34, OF-1
1943			37	.267	.400	90	24	7	1	1	1.1	14	6	15	1	3	0	19	49	2	7	1.9	.971	P-34
1944			37	.280	.318	107	30	4	0	0	0.0	9	13	8	18	0	1	1	15	55	0	7	1.9	1.000	P-34
1945			24	.230	.426	61	14	3	0	3	4.9	11	8	3	14	2	2	0	6	33	1	3	1.7	.975	P-22
1946			24	.127	.200	55	7	2	0	0	0.0	6	5	4	12	2	1	0	10	37	3	7	2.1	.940	P-22
1947			20	.267	.311	45	12	2	0	0	0.0	3	4	2	7	1	1	0	6	19	1	0	1.3	.962	P-20
1948			7	.267	.267	15	4	0	0	0	0.0	1	2	0	2	0	0	0	1	11	0	0	1.7	1.000	P-7
1950	BOS	N	1	.000	.000	2	0	0	0	0	0.0	0	0	0	0	0	0	0	0	1	0	0	1.0	1.000	P-1
19 yrs.			715	.243	.344	1966	477	99	16	23	1.2	227	234	114	303	12	64	14	364	1135	63	117	2.2	.960	P-428, 3B-184, 2B-16, OF-6

WORLD SERIES

Year	Team		Games	BA	SA	AB	H	2B	3B	HR	HR%	R	RBI	BB	SO	SB	AB	H	PO	A	E	DP	TC/G	FA	G by Pos
1939	CIN	N	2	.000	.000	3	0	0	0	0	0.0	0	0	0	0	0	0	0	0	3	0	1	1.5	1.000	P-2

Year	Team	Games	BA	SA	AB	H	2B	3B	HR	HR%	R	RBI	BB	SO	SB	Pinch Hit AB	H	PO	A	E	DP	TC/G	FA	G by Pos

Bucky Walters *continued*

| 1940 | | 2 | .286 | .857 | 7 | 2 | 1 | 0 | 1 | 14.3 | 2 | 2 | 0 | 1 | 0 | 0 | 0 | 0 | 4 | 0 | 0 | 2.0 | 1.000 | P-2 |
| 2 yrs. | | 4 | .200 | .600 | 10 | 2 | 1 | 0 | 1 | 10.0 | 2 | 2 | 0 | 1 | 0 | 0 | 0 | 0 | 7 | 0 | 1 | 1.8 | 1.000 | P-4 |

Fred Walters

WALTERS, FRED JAMES (Whale)
B. Sept. 4, 1912, Laurel, Miss. D. Feb. 1, 1980, Laurel, Miss.　　　BR TR 6'1"　210 lbs.

| 1945 | BOS A | 40 | .172 | .194 | 93 | 16 | 2 | 0 | 0 | 0.0 | 2 | 5 | 10 | 9 | 1 | 2 | 1 | 108 | 35 | 1 | 2 | 3.6 | .993 | C-38 |

Ken Walters

WALTERS, KENNETH ROGERS
B. Nov. 11, 1933, Fresno, Calif.　　　BR TR 6'1"　180 lbs.

1960	PHI N	124	.239	.319	426	102	10	0	8	1.9	42	37	16	50	4	13	1	220	17	3	4	1.9	.988	OF-119
1961		86	.228	.328	180	41	8	2	2	1.1	23	14	5	25	2	19	5	96	7	2	3	1.2	.981	OF-56, 1B-5, 3B-1
1963	CIN N	49	.187	.253	75	14	2	0	1	1.3	6	7	4	14	0	29	5	24	0	2	0	0.5	.923	OF-21, 1B-1
3 yrs.		259	.231	.314	681	157	20	2	11	1.6	71	58	25	89	6	61	11	340	24	7	7	1.4	.981	OF-196, 1B-6, 3B-1

Roxy Walters

WALTERS, ALFRED JOHN
B. Nov. 5, 1892, San Francisco, Calif. D. June 3, 1956, Alameda, Calif.　　　BR TR 5'8½"　160 lbs.

1915	NY A	2	.333	.333	3	1	0	0	0	0.0	0	0	0	0	0	0	0	8	3	0	1	5.5	1.000	C-2
1916		66	.266	.340	203	54	9	3	0	0.0	13	23	14	42	2	1	0	346	102	13	3	7.0	.974	C-65
1917		61	.263	.275	171	45	2	0	0	0.0	16	14	9	22	2	4	1	263	73	11	6	5.7	.968	C-57
1918		64	.199	.236	191	38	5	1	0	0.0	18	12	9	18	3	4	1	211	49	13	7	4.3	.952	C-50, OF-9
1919	BOS A	48	.193	.207	135	26	2	0	0	0.0	7	9	7	15	1	1	1	162	54	4	3	4.6	.982	C-47
1920		88	.198	.248	258	51	11	4	0	0.0	25	28	30	21	2	0	0	354	94	9	15	5.2	.980	C-85, 1B-2
1921		54	.201	.237	169	34	4	1	0	0.0	17	13	10	11	3	0	0	232	53	3	11	5.3	.990	C-54
1922		38	.194	.214	98	19	2	0	0	0.0	4	6	6	8	0	1	1	117	30	5	5	4.0	.967	C-36
1923		40	.250	.288	104	26	4	0	0	0.0	10	9	5	2	6	0	0	111	36	4	2	3.8	.974	C-36, 2B-1
1924	CLE A	32	.257	.284	74	19	2	0	0	0.0	10	5	10	6	0	0	0	75	34	2	4	3.5	.982	C-25, 2B-7
1925		5	.200	.200	20	4	0	0	0	0.0	0	0	0	2	0	0	0	8	7	0	1	3.0	1.000	C-5
11 yrs.		498	.222	.259	1426	317	41	6	0	0.0	119	115	97	151	13	12	5	1887	535	63	68	5.0	.975	C-462, OF-9, 2B-8, 1B-2

Danny Walton

WALTON, DANIEL JAMES (Mickey)
B. July 14, 1947, Los Angeles, Calif.　　　BR TR 6'　195 lbs.

1968	HOU N	2	.000	.000	2	0	0	0	0	0.0	0	0	0	1	0	2	0	0	0	0	0	0.0	—	
1969	SEA A	23	.217	.370	92	20	1	2	3	3.3	12	10	5	26	2	0	0	40	2	1	1	1.9	.977	OF-23
1970	MIL A	117	.257	.441	397	102	20	1	17	4.3	32	66	51	126	2	6	2	162	4	6	0	1.5	.965	OF-114, 3B-1
1971	2 teams	MIL A	(30G – .203)		NY A	(5G – .143)																		
"	total	35	.193	.337	83	16	3	0	3	3.6	6	11	7	29	0	10	2	28	0	2	0	0.9	.933	OF-23, 3B-1
1973	MIN A	37	.177	.333	96	17	1	1	4	4.2	13	8	17	28	0	5	0	18	3	0	0	0.6	1.000	OF-18, DH-11, 3B-1
1975		42	.175	.254	63	11	2	0	1	1.6	4	8	4	18	0	32	7	27	1	1	4	0.7	.966	1B-7, DH-6, C-2
1976	LA N	18	.133	.133	15	2	0	0	0	0.0	0	2	1	2	0	15	2	0	0	0	0	0.0	—	
1977	HOU N	13	.190	.190	21	4	0	0	0	0.0	0	5	0	5	0	8	2	41	2	2	1	3.5	.956	1B-5
1980	TEX A	10	.200	.200	10	2	0	0	0	0.0	2	1	3	5	0	7	2	0	0	0	0	0.0	—	DH-1
9 yrs.		297	.223	.376	779	174	27	4	28	3.6	69	107	88	240	4	85	17	316	12	12	6	1.1	.965	OF-178, DH-18, 1B-12, 3B-3, C-2

Jerome Walton

WALTON, JEROME O'TERRELL
B. July 8, 1965, Newman, Ga.　　　BR TR 6'1"　175 lbs.

| 1989 | CHI N | 116 | .293 | .385 | 475 | 139 | 23 | 3 | 5 | 1.1 | 64 | 46 | 27 | 77 | 24 | 0 | 0 | 289 | 2 | 3 | 1 | 2.5 | .990 | OF-115 |

LEAGUE CHAMPIONSHIP SERIES

| 1989 | CHI N | 5 | .364 | .364 | 22 | 8 | 0 | 0 | 0 | 0.0 | 4 | 2 | 2 | 2 | 0 | 0 | 0 | 11 | 0 | 0 | 0 | 2.2 | 1.000 | OF-5 |

Reggie Walton

WALTON, REGINALD SHERARD
B. Oct. 24, 1952, Kansas City, Mo.　　　BR TR 6'3"　205 lbs.

1980	SEA A	31	.277	.422	83	23	6	0	2	2.4	8	9	3	10	2	5	2	26	0	2	0	0.9	.929	OF-17, DH-11
1981		12	.000	.000	6	0	0	0	0	0.0	1	0	1	2	0	4	0	0	0	0	0	0.0	—	OF-4, DH-1
1982	PIT N	13	.200	.267	15	3	1	0	0	0.0	1	0	1	1	0	10	0	0	0	0	0	0.0	—	OF-2
3 yrs.		56	.250	.375	104	26	7	0	2	1.9	10	9	5	13	2	19	2	26	0	2	0	0.5	.929	OF-23, DH-12

Bill Wambsganss

WAMBSGANSS, WILLIAM ADOLPH
B. Mar. 19, 1894, Cleveland, Ohio D. Dec. 8, 1985, Lakewood, Ohio　　　BR TR 5'11"　175 lbs.

1914	CLE A	43	.217	.287	143	31	6	2	0	0.0	12	12	8	24	2	0	0	72	117	18	16	4.8	.913	SS-36, 2B-4
1915		121	.195	.227	375	73	4	4	0	0.0	30	21	36	50	8	6	0	169	306	35	28	4.2	.931	2B-78, 3B-35
1916		136	.246	.293	475	117	14	4	0	0.0	57	45	41	40	13	1	0	252	410	52	53	5.3	.927	SS-106, 2B-24, 3B-5
1917		141	.255	.313	499	127	17	6	0	0.0	52	43	37	42	16	1	0	332	443	38	70	5.8	.953	2B-138, 1B-2
1918		87	.295	.356	315	93	15	2	0	0.0	34	40	21	21	16	0	0	204	251	23	35	5.5	.952	2B-87
1919		139	.278	.344	526	146	17	6	2	0.4	60	60	32	24	18	0	0	342	436	30	60	5.8	.963	2B-139
1920		153	.244	.317	565	138	16	11	1	0.2	83	55	54	26	9	0	0	414	489	38	75	6.2	.960	2B-153
1921		107	.285	.393	410	117	28	5	2	0.5	80	46	44	27	13	0	0	271	263	20	51	5.2	.964	2B-103, 3B-2
1922		143	.262	.325	538	141	22	6	1	0.2	89	47	60	26	17	1	0	326	418	34	79	5.4	.956	2B-125, SS-16, C-1
1923		101	.290	.380	345	100	20	4	1	0.3	59	59	43	15	12	3	0	255	278	20	47	5.5	.964	2B-88, 3B-4, SS-2
1924	BOS A	156	.274	.354	636	174	41	5	0	0.0	93	49	54	32	14	0	0	459	490	37	98	6.3	.962	2B-155
1925		111	.231	.294	360	83	12	4	1	0.3	50	41	52	21	3	1	0	301	330	27	65	5.9	.959	2B-103, 1B-6
1926	PHI A	54	.352	.407	54	19	3	0	0	0.0	11	1	8	8	1	20	4	14	31	3	5	0.9	.938	SS-15, 2B-1
13 yrs.		1492	.259	.327	5241	1359	215	59	7	0.1	710	519	490	356	142	33	4	3411	4262	375	682	5.4	.953	2B-1205, SS-175, 3B-46, 1B-8, C-1

WORLD SERIES

| 1920 | CLE A | 7 | .154 | .154 | 26 | 4 | 0 | 0 | 0 | 0.0 | 3 | 1 | 2 | 1 | 0 | 0 | 0 | 22 | 17 | 0 | 4 | 5.6 | 1.000 | 2B-7 |

Lloyd Waner

WANER, LLOYD JAMES (Little Poison)
Brother of Paul Waner.
B. Mar. 16, 1906, Harrah, Okla. D. July 22, 1982, Oklahoma City, Okla.
Hall of Fame 1967.

BL TR 5'9" 150 lbs.

Year Team	Games	BA	SA	AB	H	2B	3B	HR	HR%	R	RBI	BB	SO	SB	PH AB	PH H	PO	A	E	DP	TC/G	FA	G by Pos
1927 PIT N	150	.355	.410	629	223	17	6	2	0.3	133	27	37	23	14	0	0	397	9	10	0	2.8	.976	OF-150, 2B-1
1928	152	.335	.434	659	221	22	14	5	0.8	121	61	40	13	8	0	0	418	15	9	4	2.9	.980	OF-152
1929	151	.353	.479	662	234	28	20	5	0.8	134	74	37	20	6	0	0	450	22	6	6	3.2	.987	OF-151
1930	68	.362	.427	260	94	8	3	1	0.4	32	36	5	5	3	2	1	165	6	3	1	2.6	.983	OF-65
1931	154	.314	.407	681	214	25	13	4	0.6	90	57	39	16	7	0	0	485	22	11	5	3.4	.979	OF-153, 2B-1
1932	134	.333	.435	565	188	27	11	3	0.5	90	38	31	11	6	2	1	426	9	6	0	3.3	.986	OF-131
1933	121	.276	.324	500	138	14	5	0	0.0	59	26	22	8	3	6	4	267	9	5	2	2.3	.982	OF-114
1934	140	.283	.352	611	173	27	6	1	0.2	95	48	38	12	6	1	0	405	8	9	1	3.0	.979	OF-139
1935	122	.309	.402	537	166	22	14	0	0.0	83	46	22	10	1	1	1	350	5	4	1	2.9	.989	OF-121
1936	106	.321	.399	414	133	13	8	1	0.2	67	31	31	5	1	11	1	245	2	4	2	2.4	.984	OF-92
1937	129	.330	.393	537	177	23	4	1	0.2	80	45	34	12	3	5	2	312	8	4	0	2.5	.988	OF-123
1938	147	.313	.401	619	194	25	7	5	0.8	79	57	28	11	5	3	0	341	15	5	5	2.5	.986	OF-144
1939	112	.285	.340	379	108	15	3	0	0.0	49	24	17	13	0	17	3	227	13	2	2	2.2	.992	OF-92, 3B-1
1940	72	.259	.277	166	43	3	0	0	0.0	30	3	5	2	5	18	6	90	3	1	1	1.3	.989	OF-42
1941 3 teams	PIT N (3G - .250)			BOS N (19G - .412)			CIN N (55G - .256)																
" total	77	.292	.324	219	64	5	1	0	0.0		26	11	12	0	1	11	4	102	4	2	1	1.4	.981	OF-60
1942 PHI N	100	.261	.307	287	75	7	3	0	0.0	23	10	16	6	1	22	4	170	6	6	0	1.8	.967	OF-75
1944 2 teams	BKN N (15G - .286)			PIT N (19G - .357)																			
" total	34	.321	.321	28	9	0	0	0	0.0	5	3	5	0	0	18	7	12	0	0	0	0.4	1.000	OF-11
1945 PIT N	23	.263	.263	19	5	0	0	0	0.0	5	1	1	3	0	17	5	2	1	0	0	0.1	1.000	OF-3
18 yrs.	1992	.316	.394	7772	2459	281	118	28	0.4	1201	598	420	173	67	134	39	4864	157	87	31	2.6	.983	OF-1818, 2B-2, 3B-1

WORLD SERIES

Year Team	Games	BA	SA	AB	H	2B	3B	HR	HR%	R	RBI	BB	SO	SB	PH AB	PH H	PO	A	E	DP	TC/G	FA	G by Pos
1927 PIT N	4	.400	.600	15	6	1	1	0	0.0	5	0	1	0	0	0	0	9	1	2	0	3.0	.833	OF-4

Paul Waner

WANER, PAUL GLEE (Big Poison)
Brother of Lloyd Waner.
B. Apr. 16, 1903, Harrah, Okla. D. Aug. 29, 1965, Sarasota, Fla.
Hall of Fame 1952.

BL TL 5'8½" 153 lbs.

Year Team	Games	BA	SA	AB	H	2B	3B	HR	HR%	R	RBI	BB	SO	SB	PH AB	PH H	PO	A	E	DP	TC/G	FA	G by Pos
1926 PIT N	144	.336	.528	536	180	35	22	8	1.5	101	79	66	19	11	3	0	307	21	8	3	2.3	.976	OF-139
1927	155	.380	.543	623	237	40	17	9	1.4	113	131	60	14	5	0	0	430	25	10	12	3.0	.978	OF-143, 1B-14
1928	152	.370	.547	602	223	50	19	6	1.0	142	86	77	16	6	0	0	533	22	12	17	3.7	.979	OF-131, 1B-24
1929	151	.336	.534	596	200	43	15	15	2.5	131	100	89	24	15	1	0	398	18	5	7	2.8	.988	OF-143, 1B-7
1930	145	.368	.525	589	217	32	18	8	1.4	117	77	57	18	18	2	0	344	9	5	4	2.5	.959	OF-143
1931	150	.322	.453	559	180	35	10	6	1.1	88	70	73	21	6	2	0	441	31	9	18	3.2	.981	OF-138, 1B-10
1932	154	.341	.505	630	215	62	10	7	1.1	107	82	56	24	13	0	0	367	13	10	3	2.5	.974	OF-154
1933	154	.309	.456	618	191	38	16	7	1.1	101	70	60	20	3	0	0	346	16	7	2	2.4	.981	OF-154
1934	146	.362	.539	599	217	32	16	14	2.3	122	90	68	24	8	1	1	323	15	5	1	2.3	.985	OF-145
1935	139	.321	.477	549	176	29	12	11	2.0	98	78	61	22	2	3	1	283	13	5	2	2.2	.983	OF-136
1936	148	.373	.520	585	218	53	9	5	0.9	107	94	74	29	7	3	1	323	15	14	7	2.4	.960	OF-150, 1B-3
1937	154	.354	.441	619	219	30	9	3	0.5	94	74	63	34	4	2	0	298	19	11	6	2.1	.966	OF-147
1938	148	.280	.378	625	175	31	6	6	1.0	77	69	47	28	2	1	0	284	11	7	0	2.0	.977	OF-147
1939	125	.328	.438	461	151	30	6	3	0.7	62	45	35	18	0	11	3	206	12	5	4	1.8	.978	OF-106
1940	89	.290	.378	238	69	16	1	1	0.4	32	32	23	14	0	34	6	150	9	2	12	1.8	.988	OF-45, 1B-8
1941 2 teams	BKN N (11G - .171)			BOS N (95G - .279)																			
" total	106	.267	.328	329	88	10	2	2	0.6	45	50	55	14	1	18	3	160	8	8	3	1.7	.955	OF-86, 1B-1
1942 BOS N	114	.258	.324	333	86	17	1	1	0.3	43	39	62	20	2	17	2	150	6	5	3	1.4	.969	OF-94
1943 BKN N	82	.311	.396	225	70	16	0	1	0.4	29	26	35	9	0	21	10	116	4	5	1	1.5	.960	OF-57
1944 2 teams	BKN N (83G - .287)			NY A (9G - .143)																			
" total	92	.280	.322	143	40	4	1	0	0.0	17	17	29	8	1	45	13	54	3	1	0	0.6	.983	OF-32
1945 NY A	1	—	—	0	0	0	0	0	0.0	0	0	0	0	0	0	0	0	0	0	0	0.0	—	
20 yrs.	2549	.333	.473	9459	3152	603	190	112	1.2	1626	1309	1091	376	104	164	40	5513	270	144	105	2.3	.976	OF-2288, 1B-67
						9th	10th																

WORLD SERIES

Year Team	Games	BA	SA	AB	H	2B	3B	HR	HR%	R	RBI	BB	SO	SB	PH AB	PH H	PO	A	E	DP	TC/G	FA	G by Pos
1927 PIT N	4	.333	.400	15	5	1	0	0	0.0	3	0	1	0	0	0	0	8	0	0	0	2.0	1.000	OF-4

Jack Wanner

WANNER, CLARENCE CURTIS
B. Nov. 29, 1885, Geneseo, Ill. D. May 28, 1919, Geneseo, Ill.

BR TR 5'11½" 190 lbs.

Year Team	Games	BA	SA	AB	H	2B	3B	HR	HR%	R	RBI	BB	SO	SB	PH AB	PH H	PO	A	E	DP	TC/G	FA	G by Pos
1909 NY A	3	.125	.125	8	1	0	0	0	0.0	0	0	2		1	1	0	1	5	4	1	3.3	.600	SS-2

Pee Wee Wanninger

WANNINGER, PAUL LOUIS
B. Dec. 12, 1902, Birmingham, Ala. D. Mar. 7, 1981, North Augusta, S. C.

BL TR 5'7" 150 lbs.

Year Team	Games	BA	SA	AB	H	2B	3B	HR	HR%	R	RBI	BB	SO	SB	PH AB	PH H	PO	A	E	DP	TC/G	FA	G by Pos
1925 NY A	117	.236	.305	403	95	13	6	1	0.2	35	22	11	34	3	1	1	219	306	31	61	4.8	.944	SS-111, 3B-3, 2B-1
1927 2 teams	BOS A (18G - .200)			CIN N (28G - .247)																			
" total	46	.229	.268	153	35	2	2	0	0.0	18	9	12	9	2	2	0	88	146	17	32	5.5	.932	SS-43
2 yrs.	163	.234	.295	556	130	15	8	1	0.2	53	31	23	43	5	3	1	307	452	48	93	5.0	.941	SS-154, 3B-3, 2B-1

Aaron Ward

WARD, AARON LEE
B. Aug. 28, 1896, Booneville, Ark. D. Jan. 30, 1961, New Orleans, La.

BR TR 5'10½" 160 lbs.

Year Team	Games	BA	SA	AB	H	2B	3B	HR	HR%	R	RBI	BB	SO	SB	PH AB	PH H	PO	A	E	DP	TC/G	FA	G by Pos
1917 NY A	8	.115	.115	26	3	0	0	0	0.0	0	1	1	5	0	1	0	12	13	2	3	3.4	.926	SS-7
1918	20	.125	.156	32	4	1	0	0	0.0	2	7	1	7	1	1	0	23	25	2	5	2.5	.960	SS-11, OF-4, 2B-4
1919	27	.206	.265	34	7	2	0	0	0.0	5	2	5	6	0	14	4	43	14	1	5	2.1	.983	1B-5, 3B-3, SS-2, 2B-1
1920	127	.256	.387	496	127	18	7	11	2.2	62	54	33	84	7	1	0	169	344	18	36	4.2	.966	3B-114, SS-12
1921	153	.306	.423	556	170	30	10	5	0.9	77	75	42	68	6	0	0	306	487	28	68	5.4	.966	2B-133, SS-33
1922	154	.267	.357	558	149	19	5	7	1.3	69	68	45	64	7	0	0	358	490	23	74	5.7	.974	2B-152, 3B-2
1923	152	.284	.422	567	161	26	11	10	1.8	79	82	56	65	8	0	0	387	493	18	86	5.9	.980	2B-152
1924	120	.253	.395	400	101	13	10	8	2.0	42	66	40	45	1	0	0	303	385	19	60	5.9	.973	2B-120, SS-1
1925	125	.246	.337	439	108	22	3	4	0.9	41	38	49	41	1	2	0	264	336	20	59	5.0	.968	2B-113, 3B-10

Year	Team		Games	BA	SA	AB	H	2B	3B	HR	HR%	R	RBI	BB	SO	SB	Pinch Hit AB	H	PO	A	E	DP	TC/G	FA	G by Pos

Aaron Ward *continued*

Year	Team		Games	BA	SA	AB	H	2B	3B	HR	HR%	R	RBI	BB	SO	SB	AB	H	PO	A	E	DP	TC/G	FA	G by Pos
1926			22	.323	.387	31	10	2	0	0	0.0	5	3	2	6	0	15	5	13	7	0	0	0.9	1.000	2B-4, 3B-1
1927	CHI	A	145	.270	.391	463	125	25	8	5	1.1	75	56	63	56	6	1	0	283	450	27	66	5.2	.964	2B-138, 3B-6
1928	CLE	A	6	.111	.111	9	1	0	0	0	0.0	0	0	1	2	0	0	0	4	13	4	5	3.5	.810	3B-3, SS-2, 2B-1
12 yrs.			1059	.268	.383	3611	966	158	54	50	1.4	457	446	339	457	37	35	9	2165	3057	162	467	5.1	.970	2B-808, 3B-172, SS-35, 1B-5, OF-4

WORLD SERIES

Year	Team		Games	BA	SA	AB	H	2B	3B	HR	HR%	R	RBI	BB	SO	SB	AB	H	PO	A	E	DP	TC/G	FA	G by Pos
1921	NY	A	8	.231	.231	26	6	0	0	0	0.0	1	4	2	6	0	0	0	18	34	2	4	6.8	.963	2B-8
1922			5	.154	.615	13	2	0	0	2	15.4	3	3	3	3	0	0	0	13	16	1	4	6.0	.967	2B-5
1923			6	.417	.542	24	10	0	0	1	4.2	4	2	1	3	1	0	0	11	27	0	3	6.3	1.000	2B-6
3 yrs.			19	.286	.429	63	18	0	0	3	4.8	8	9	6	12	1	0	0	42	77	3	11	6.4	.975	2B-19

Chris Ward

WARD, CHRIS GILBERT
B. May 18, 1949, Oakland, Calif.

BL TL 6'   180 lbs.

Year	Team		Games	BA	SA	AB	H	2B	3B	HR	HR%	R	RBI	BB	SO	SB	AB	H	PO	A	E	DP	TC/G	FA	G by Pos
1972	CHI	N	1	.000	.000	1	0	0	0	0	0.0	0	0	0	0	0	1	0	0	0	0	0	0.0	–	
1974			92	.204	.255	137	28	4	0	1	0.7	8	15	18	13	0	49	9	94	6	1	4	1.1	.990	OF-22, 1B-6
2 yrs.			93	.203	.254	138	28	4	0	1	0.7	8	15	18	13	0	50	9	94	6	1	4	1.1	.990	OF-22, 1B-6

Chuck Ward

WARD, CHARLES WILLIAM
B. July 30, 1894, St. Louis, Mo.   D. Apr. 4, 1969, Indian Rocks, Fla.

BR TR 5'11½" 170 lbs.

Year	Team		Games	BA	SA	AB	H	2B	3B	HR	HR%	R	RBI	BB	SO	SB	AB	H	PO	A	E	DP	TC/G	FA	G by Pos
1917	PIT	N	125	.236	.279	423	100	12	3	0	0.0	25	43	32	43	5	1	0	226	347	52	53	5.0	.917	SS-112, 2B-8, 3B-5
1918	BKN	N	6	.333	.333	6	2	0	0	0	0.0	0	3	0	0	0	0	0	0	3	0	0	1.5	1.000	3B-2
1919			45	.233	.267	150	35	1	2	0	0.0	7	8	7	11	0	1	0	47	79	11	0	3.0	.920	3B-45
1920			19	.155	.169	71	11	1	0	0	0.0	7	4	3	3	1	0	0	46	44	7	5	5.1	.928	SS-19
1921			12	.071	.107	28	2	1	0	0	0.0	1	4	2	2	0	0	0	25	34	4	7	5.3	.937	SS-12
1922			33	.275	.352	91	25	5	1	0	0.0	12	14	5	8	1	0	0	54	89	10	13	4.6	.935	SS-31, 3B-2
6 yrs.			236	.228	.269	769	175	20	6	0	0.0	52	72	51	67	7	1	0	398	596	84	78	4.6	.922	SS-174, 3B-54, 2B-8

Gary Ward

WARD, GARY LAMELL
B. Dec. 6, 1953, Los Angeles, Calif.

BR TR 6'2"   195 lbs.

Year	Team		Games	BA	SA	AB	H	2B	3B	HR	HR%	R	RBI	BB	SO	SB	AB	H	PO	A	E	DP	TC/G	FA	G by Pos
1979	MIN	A	10	.286	.286	14	4	0	0	0	0.0	2	1	3	3	0	1	0	8	0	0	0	0.8	1.000	OF-5, DH-3
1980			13	.463	.780	41	19	2	1	2	2.4	11	10	3	6	0	2	0	14	0	0	0	1.1	1.000	OF-12
1981			85	.264	.359	295	78	7	6	3	1.0	42	29	28	48	5	5	1	185	8	5	4	2.3	.975	OF-80, DH-2
1982			152	.289	.519	570	165	33	7	28	4.9	85	91	37	105	13	5	2	343	13	4	3	2.4	.989	OF-150, DH-2
1983			157	.278	.440	623	173	34	5	19	3.0	76	88	44	98	8	4	0	374	24	9	6	2.6	.978	OF-152, DH-2
1984	TEX	A	153	.284	.447	602	171	21	7	21	3.5	97	79	55	95	7	4	0	376	11	5	1	2.6	.987	OF-148, DH-5
1985			154	.287	.433	593	170	28	7	15	2.5	77	70	39	97	26	1	1	304	11	10	2	2.1	.969	OF-153, DH-1
1986			105	.316	.405	380	120	15	2	5	1.3	54	51	31	72	12	0	0	237	8	1	3	2.3	.996	OF-104, DH-1
1987	NY	A	146	.248	.384	529	131	22	1	16	3.0	65	78	33	101	9	12	8	318	10	3	11	2.3	.991	OF-94, DH-36, 1B-15
1988			91	.225	.312	231	52	8	0	4	1.7	26	24	24	41	0	17	5	220	5	2	9	2.5	.991	OF-54, 1B-11, 3B-2
1989	2 teams	NY A (8G – .294)				DET A (105G – .251)																			
"	total		113	.253	.397	292	74	11	2	9	3.1	27	30	24	59	1	32	6	234	16	3	5	2.2	.988	OF-57, DH-27, 1B-26
11 yrs.			1179	.277	.428	4170	1157	185	39	121	2.9	562	551	321	725	81	83	23	2613	106	42	54	2.3	.985	OF-1009, DH-79, 1B-52, 3B-2

Hap Ward

WARD, JOSEPH NICHOLS
B. Nov. 15, 1885, Leesburg, N. J.   D. Sept. 13, 1979, Elmer, N. J.

Year	Team		Games	BA	SA	AB	H	2B	3B	HR	HR%	R	RBI	BB	SO	SB	AB	H	PO	A	E	DP	TC/G	FA	G by Pos
1912	DET	A	1	.000	.000	2	0	0	0	0	0.0	0	0	0		0	0	0	2	0	0	0	2.0	1.000	OF-1

Jay Ward

WARD, JOHN FRANCIS
B. Sept. 9, 1938, Brookfield, Mo.

BR TR 6'1"   185 lbs.

Year	Team		Games	BA	SA	AB	H	2B	3B	HR	HR%	R	RBI	BB	SO	SB	AB	H	PO	A	E	DP	TC/G	FA	G by Pos
1963	MIN	A	9	.067	.133	15	1	1	0	0	0.0	0	2	1	5	0	2	0	3	5	0	0	0.9	1.000	3B-4, OF-1
1964			12	.226	.290	31	7	2	0	0	0.0	4	2	6	13	0	1	0	25	21	1	4	3.9	.979	2B-9, OF-3
1970	CIN	N	6	.000	.000	3	0	0	0	0	0.0	0	0	2	1	0	2	0	4	1	0	1	0.8	1.000	3B-2, 2B-1, 1B-1
3 yrs.			27	.163	.224	49	8	3	0	0	0.0	4	4	9	19	0	5	0	32	27	1	5	2.2	.983	2B-10, 3B-6, OF-4, 1B-1

Jim Ward

WARD, JAMES H.
B. Mar., 1855, Boston, Mass.   D. June 4, 1886, Boston, Mass.

Year	Team		Games	BA	SA	AB	H	2B	3B	HR	HR%	R	RBI	BB	SO	SB	AB	H	PO	A	E	DP	TC/G	FA	G by Pos
1876	PHI	N	1	.500	.500	4	2	0	0	0	0.0	1	1	0	1		0	0	5	1	2	0	8.0	.750	C-1

Joe Ward

WARD, JOSEPH A.
B. Sept. 2, 1884, Philadelphia, Pa.   D. Aug. 11, 1934, Philadelphia, Pa.

TR

Year	Team		Games	BA	SA	AB	H	2B	3B	HR	HR%	R	RBI	BB	SO	SB	AB	H	PO	A	E	DP	TC/G	FA	G by Pos
1906	PHI	N	35	.295	.450	129	38	8	6	0	0.0	12	11	5		2	5	1	41	50	7	2	2.8	.929	3B-27, 2B-3, SS-1
1909	2 teams	NY A (9G – .179)				PHI N (74G – .266)																			
"	total		83	.255	.311	212	54	8	2	0	0.0	24	23	10		9	27	5	139	112	22	17	3.3	.919	2B-55, SS-8, 1B-6, OF-2
1910	PHI	N	48	.145	.177	124	18	2	1	0	0.0	11	13	3	11	1	14	2	296	25	8	11	6.9	.976	1B-32, SS-1, 3B-1
3 yrs.			166	.237	.314	465	110	18	9	0	0.0	47	47	18	11	12	46	8	476	187	37	30	4.2	.947	2B-58, 1B-38, 3B-28, SS-10, OF-2

John Ward

WARD, JOHN E.
B. Washington, D. C.   Deceased.

Year	Team		Games	BA	SA	AB	H	2B	3B	HR	HR%	R	RBI	BB	SO	SB	AB	H	PO	A	E	DP	TC/G	FA	G by Pos
1884	WAS	U	1	.250	.250	4	1	0	0	0	0.0	0	0	0		0	0	0	0	0	1	0	1.0	–	OF-1
1885	PRO	N	1	.000	.000	3	0	0	0	0	0.0	0	0	0	2	0	0	0	0	1	1	0	2.0	.500	P-1
2 yrs.			2	.143	.143	7	1	0	0	0	0.0	0	0	0	2	0	0	0	0	1	2	0	1.5	.333	OF-1, P-1

Monte Ward

WARD, JOHN MONTGOMERY
B. Mar. 3, 1860, Bellefonte, Pa.
D. Mar. 4, 1925, Augusta, Ga.
Manager 1880, 1884, 1890-94.
Hall of Fame 1964.

BL TR 5'9"   165 lbs.
BB 1888

Year	Team		Games	BA	SA	AB	H	2B	3B	HR	HR%	R	RBI	BB	SO	SB	Pinch Hit AB	Pinch Hit H	PO	A	E	DP	TC/G	FA	G by Pos

Monte Ward *continued*

Year	Team		Games	BA	SA	AB	H	2B	3B	HR	HR%	R	RBI	BB	SO	SB	AB	H	PO	A	E	DP	TC/G	FA	G by Pos
1878	PRO	N	37	.196	.312	138	27	5	4	1	0.7	14	15	2	13		0	0	23	74	15	4	3.0	.866	P-37
1879			83	.286	.349	364	104	9	4	2	0.5	71	41	7	14		0	0	55	167	23	4	3.0	.906	P-70, 3B-16, OF-8
1880			86	.228	.272	356	81	12	2	0	0.0	53	27	6	16		0	0	74	203	17	5	3.4	.942	P-70, 3B-25, OF-2
1881			85	.244	.328	357	87	18	6	0	0.0	56	53	5	10		0	0	110	130	29	11	3.2	.892	OF-40, P-39, SS-13
1882			83	.245	.296	355	87	10	4	0	0.0	58		13	22		0	0	105	105	31	8	2.9	.871	OF-50, P-33, SS-4
1883	NY	N	88	.255	.395	380	97	18	7	7	1.8	76		8	25		0	0	154	116	42	4	3.5	.865	OF-56, P-33, 3B-5, SS-2, 2B-1
1884			113	.253	.322	482	122	11	8	2	0.4	98		28	47		0	0	201	206	58	19	4.1	.875	OF-59, 2B-47, P-9
1885			111	.226	.291	446	101	8	9	0	0.0	72		17	39		0	0	167	350	55	36	5.2	.904	SS-111
1886			122	.273	.340	491	134	17	5	2	0.4	82	81	19	46		0	0	91	369	69	36	4.3	.870	SS-122
1887			129	.338	.391	545	184	16	5	1	0.2	114	53	29	12	111	0	0	226	469	61	53	5.9	.919	SS-129
1888			122	.251	.310	510	128	14	5	2	0.4	70	49	9	13	38	0	0	185	331	86	39	4.9	.857	SS-122
1889			114	.299	.349	479	143	13	4	1	0.2	87	67	27	7	62	0	0	245	339	76	38	5.8	.885	SS-108, 2B-7
1890	BKN	P	128	.337	.428	561	189	15	12	4	0.7	134	60	51	22	63	0	0	303	450	105	59	6.7	.878	SS-128
1891	BKN	N	105	.277	.306	441	122	13	5	0	0.0	85	39	36	10	57	0	0	235	352	72	36	6.3	.891	SS-87, 2B-18
1892			148	.265	.306	614	163	13	3	2	0.3	109	47	82	19	88	0	0	377	472	74	48	6.2	.920	2B-148
1893	NY	N	135	.328	.415	588	193	27	9	2	0.3	129	77	47	5	46	1	0	348	464	73	41	6.6	.918	2B-134
1894			136	.265	.306	540	143	12	5	0	0.0	100	77	34	6	39	0	0	331	446	64	52	6.2	.924	2B-136
17 yrs.			1825	.275	.341	7647	2105	231	97	26	0.3	1408	686	420	326	504	1	0	3230	5043	950	493	5.1	.897	SS-826, 2B-491, P-291, OF-215, 3B-46

Pete Ward

WARD, PETER THOMAS
B. July 26, 1939, Montreal, Que., Canada

BL TR 6'1" 185 lbs.

Year	Team		Games	BA	SA	AB	H	2B	3B	HR	HR%	R	RBI	BB	SO	SB	AB	H	PO	A	E	DP	TC/G	FA	G by Pos
1962	BAL	A	8	.143	.238	21	3	2	0	0	0.0	1	2	4	5	0	1	1	10	0	0	0	1.3	1.000	OF-6
1963	CHI	A	157	.295	.482	600	177	34	6	22	3.7	80	84	52	77	7	3	1	158	303	38	28	3.2	.924	3B-154, SS-1, 2B-1
1964			144	.282	.473	539	152	28	3	23	4.3	61	94	56	76	1	5	1	126	309	19	24	3.2	.958	3B-138
1965			138	.247	.367	507	125	25	3	10	2.0	62	57	56	83	2	5	1	97	320	21	22	3.2	.952	3B-134, 2B-1
1966			84	.219	.351	251	55	7	1	3	1.2	22	28	24	49	3	9	0	112	42	3	6	1.9	.981	3B-56, 1B-5
1967			146	.233	.392	467	109	16	2	18	3.9	49	62	61	109	3	6	3	409	55	7	26	3.2	.985	OF-89, 1B-39, 3B-22
1968			125	.216	.366	399	86	15	0	15	3.8	43	50	76	85	4	6	1	325	170	12	25	4.1	.976	3B-77, 1B-31, OF-22
1969			105	.246	.372	199	49	7	0	6	3.0	22	32	33	38	0	46	17	193	48	3	13	2.3	.988	1B-25, 3B-21, OF-9
1970	NY	A	66	.260	.377	77	20	2	2	1	1.3	5	18	9	17	0	44	10	83	3	0	7	1.3	1.000	1B-13
9 yrs.			973	.254	.405	3060	776	136	17	98	3.2	345	427	371	539	20	125	35	1513	1250	103	151	2.9	.964	3B-562, OF-185, 1B-113, 2B-2, SS-1

Piggy Ward

WARD, FRANK GRAY
B. Apr. 16, 1867, Chambersburg, Pa.   D. Oct. 24, 1912, Altoona, Pa.

5'9½" 196 lbs.

Year	Team		Games	BA	SA	AB	H	2B	3B	HR	HR%	R	RBI	BB	SO	SB	AB	H	PO	A	E	DP	TC/G	FA	G by Pos
1883	PHI	N	1	.000	.000	5	0	0	0	0	0.0	0		0	2		0	0	0	2	0	0	2.0	1.000	3B-1
1889			7	.160	.200	25	4	1	0	0	0.0	0	4	0	7	1	0	0	13	16	7	0	5.1	.806	2B-6, OF-1
1891	PIT	N	6	.333	.333	18	6	0	0	0	0.0	3	2	3	3	3	1	0	5	0	1	0	1.0	.833	OF-5
1892	BAL	N	56	.290	.392	186	54	6	5	1	0.5	28	33	31	18	10	0	0	84	44	16	7	2.6	.889	OF-43, 2B-7, SS-5, C-1
1893	2 teams		BAL	N	(11G – .245)		CIN	N	(42G – .280)																	
"	total		53	.271	.337	199	54	8	4	0	0.0	55	15	42	12	31	1	0	100	9	19	4	2.4	.852	OF-49, 1B-3
1894	WAS	N	98	.303	.375	347	105	11	7	0	0.0	86	36	80	31	41	2	1	195	246	52	22	5.0	.895	2B-79, OF-12, SS-3, 3B-1
6 yrs.			221	.286	.360	780	223	23	16	1	0.1	172	90	156	73	86	4	1	397	317	95	33	3.7	.883	OF-110, 2B-92, SS-8, 1B-3, 3B-2, C-1

Preston Ward

WARD, PRESTON MEYER
B. July 24, 1927, Columbia, Mo.

BL TR 6'4" 190 lbs.

Year	Team		Games	BA	SA	AB	H	2B	3B	HR	HR%	R	RBI	BB	SO	SB	AB	H	PO	A	E	DP	TC/G	FA	G by Pos
1948	BKN	N	42	.260	.370	146	38	9	2	1	0.7	9	21	15	23	0	3	0	268	20	3	21	6.9	.990	1B-38
1950	CHI	N	80	.253	.368	285	72	11	2	6	2.1	31	33	27	42	3	14	1	734	73	4	78	10.1	.995	1B-76
1953	2 teams		CHI	N	(33G – .230)		PIT	N	(88G – .210)																	
"	total		121	.215	.346	381	82	12	1	12	3.1	45	39	62	60	4	9	2	791	65	9	74	7.1	.990	1B-85, OF-27
1954	PIT	N	117	.269	.383	360	97	16	2	7	1.9	37	48	39	61	0	18	4	419	69	15	34	4.3	.970	1B-48, OF-42, 3B-11
1955			84	.212	.380	179	38	7	4	5	2.8	16	25	22	28	0	30	6	384	35	1	41	5.0	.998	1B-48, OF-1
1956	2 teams		PIT	N	(16G – .333)		CLE	A	(87G – .253)																	
"	total		103	.267	.450	180	48	10	1	7	3.9	21	32	22	24	0	26	8	260	25	3	20	2.8	.990	1B-60, OF-22, 3B-5
1957	CLE	A	10	.182	.273	11	2	1	0	0	0.0	2	0	0	2	0	9	1	3	0	0	0	0.3	1.000	1B-1
1958	2 teams		CLE	A	(48G – .338)		KC	A	(81G – .254)																	
"	total		129	.284	.392	416	118	13	2	10	2.4	50	45	37	63	0	18	4	523	116	14	46	5.1	.979	1B-60, 3B-58, OF-2
1959	KC	A	58	.248	.358	109	27	4	1	2	1.8	8	19	7	12	0	32	6	161	7	4	14	3.0	.977	1B-22, OF-1
9 yrs.			744	.253	.380	2067	522	83	15	50	2.4	219	262	231	315	7	159	34	3543	410	53	328	5.4	.987	1B-438, OF-95, 3B-74

Rube Ward

WARD, JOHN ANDREW
B. Feb. 6, 1879, New Lexington, Ohio   D. Jan. 17, 1945, Akron, Ohio

Year	Team		Games	BA	SA	AB	H	2B	3B	HR	HR%	R	RBI	BB	SO	SB	AB	H	PO	A	E	DP	TC/G	FA	G by Pos
1902	BKN	N	13	.290	.323	31	9	1	0	0	0.0	4	2	2		0	2	0	16	1	3	0	1.5	.850	OF-11

Buzzy Wares

WARES, CLYDE ELLSWORTH
B. Mar. 23, 1886, Vandalia, Mich.   D. May 26, 1964, South Bend, Ind.

BR TR 5'10" 150 lbs.

Year	Team		Games	BA	SA	AB	H	2B	3B	HR	HR%	R	RBI	BB	SO	SB	AB	H	PO	A	E	DP	TC/G	FA	G by Pos
1913	STL	A	10	.286	.343	35	10	1	0	0	0.0	5	1	1	3	2	1	0	20	16	1	4	3.7	.973	2B-9
1914			81	.209	.265	215	45	10	1	0	0.0	20	23	28	35	10	1	0	146	214	36	26	4.9	.909	SS-68, 2B-8
2 yrs.			91	.220	.276	250	55	12	1	0	0.0	25	24	29	38	12	2	0	166	230	37	30	4.8	.915	SS-68, 2B-17

Fred Warner

WARNER, FREDERICK JOHN RODNEY
B. 1855, Philadelphia, Pa.   D. Feb. 13, 1886, Philadelphia, Pa.

5'7" 155 lbs.

Year	Team		Games	BA	SA	AB	H	2B	3B	HR	HR%	R	RBI	BB	SO	SB	AB	H	PO	A	E	DP	TC/G	FA	G by Pos
1876	PHI	N	1	.000	.000	3	0	0	0	0	0.0	0		0	0		0	0	3	0	2	0	5.0	.600	OF-1
1878	IND	N	43	.248	.273	165	41	4	0	0	0.0	19	10	2	15		0	0	44	124	18	9	4.3	.903	SS-41, OF-2
1879	CLE	N	76	.244	.304	316	77	11	4	0	0.0	32	22	2	20		0	0	127	113	48	5	3.8	.833	3B-54, OF-21, 1B-1
1883	PHI	N	39	.227	.241	141	32	6	1	0	0.0	13		5	21		0	0	49	55	29	4	3.4	.782	3B-38, OF-1
1884	BKN	AA	84	.222	.241	352	78	4	0	1	0.3	40		17			0	0	94	149	52	13	3.5	.824	3B-83, OF-1
5 yrs.			243	.233	.272	977	228	25	5	1	0.1	104	32	26	56		0	0	317	441	149	31	3.7	.836	3B-175, SS-41, OF-26, 1B-1

Year	Team		Games	BA	SA	AB	H	2B	3B	HR	HR%	R	RBI	BB	SO	SB	Pinch Hit AB	Pinch Hit H	PO	A	E	DP	TC/G	FA	G by Pos

Hooks Warner

WARNER, HOKE HAYDEN
B. May 22, 1894, Del Rio, Tex. D. Feb. 19, 1947, San Francisco, Calif.   BL TR 5'10½" 170 lbs.

1916	PIT	N	44	.238	.292	168	40	1	1	2	1.2	12	14	6	19	6	0	0	62	59	13	5	3.0	.903	3B-42, 2B-1
1917			3	.200	.200	5	1	0	0	0	0.0	0	0	0	1	0	1	1	5	2	0	0	2.3	1.000	3B-1
1919			6	.125	.125	8	1	0	0	0	0.0	0	2	3	1	0	1	1	3	6	2	0	1.8	.818	3B-3
1921	CHI	N	14	.211	.237	38	8	1	0	0	0.0	4	3	2	1	1	3	0	4	18	1	1	1.6	.957	3B-10
4 yrs.			67	.228	.274	219	50	2	1	2	0.9	16	19	11	22	7	5	2	74	85	16	6	2.6	.909	3B-56, 2B-1

Jack Warner

WARNER, JOHN JOSEPH
B. Aug. 15, 1872, New York, N. Y. D. Dec. 21, 1943, Queens, N. Y.   BL TR 5'11" 165 lbs.

1895	2 teams			BOS	N	(3G –	.143)			LOU	N	(67G –	.267)												
"	total		70	.264	.310	239	63	4	2	1	0.4	22	21	12	16	10	0	0	219	54	21	5	4.2	.929	C-67, 1B-3, 2B-1
1896	2 teams			LOU	N	(33G –	.227)			NY	N	(19G –	.259)												
"	total		52	.238	.262	164	39	2	1	0	0.0	18	13	13	17	4	0	0	207	54	18	4	5.4	.935	C-51, 1B-1
1897	NY	N	110	.275	.320	397	109	6	3	2	0.5	50	51	26		8	0	0	513	127	32	17	6.1	.952	C-110
1898			110	.257	.322	373	96	14	5	0	0.0	40	42	22		9	0	0	538	139	22	10	6.4	.969	C-109, OF-1
1899			88	.266	.300	293	78	8	1	0	0.0	38	19	15		15	3	0	329	125	22	9	5.4	.954	C-82, 1B-3
1900			34	.250	.287	108	27	4	0	0	0.0	15	13	8		1	3	1	98	49	8	5	4.6	.948	C-31
1901			87	.241	.268	291	70	6	1	0	0.0	19	20	3		3	3	0	361	107	16	11	5.6	.967	C-84
1902	BOS	A	65	.234	.320	222	52	5	7	0	0.0	19	12	13		0	0	0	252	81	7	8	5.2	.979	C-64
1903	NY	N	89	.284	.347	285	81	8	5	0	0.0	38	34	7		5	3	1	450	123	8	9	6.5	.986	C-85
1904			86	.199	.233	287	57	5	1	1	0.3	29	15	14		7	0	0	427	115	10	7	6.4	.982	C-86
1905	2 teams			STL	N	(41G –	.255)			DET	A	(36G –	.202)												
"	total		77	.230	.297	256	59	4	1	1	0.4	21	19	14		4	0	0	350	103	16	6	6.1	.966	C-77
1906	2 teams			DET	A	(50G –	.242)			WAS	A	(32G –	.204)												
"	total		82	.227	.293	256	58	8	3	1	0.4	20	19	14		7	1	0	348	136	13	5	6.1	.974	C-81
1907	WAS	A	72	.256	.280	207	53	5	0	0	0.0	11	17	12		3	8	1	271	64	10	4	4.8	.971	C-64
1908			51	.241	.276	116	28	2	1	0	0.0	8	8	8		7	8	1	181	38	4	2	4.4	.982	C-41, 1B-1
14 yrs.			1073	.249	.297	3494	870	81	35	6	0.2	348	303	181	33	83	29	4	4544	1315	207	102	5.7	.966	C-1032, 1B-8, OF-1, 2B-1

Jack Warner

WARNER, JOHN RALPH
B. Aug. 29, 1903, Evansville, Ind. D. Mar. 13, 1986, Mt. Vernon, Ill.   BR TR 5'9½" 165 lbs.

1925	DET	A	10	.333	.333	39	13	0	0	0	0.0	7	2	3	6	0	0	0	3	15	0	3	1.8	1.000	3B-10
1926			100	.251	.315	311	78	8	6	0	0.0	41	34	38	24	8	2	0	108	177	13	10	3.0	.956	3B-95, SS-3
1927			139	.267	.343	559	149	22	9	1	0.2	78	45	47	45	15	1	0	156	277	24	34	3.3	.947	3B-138
1928			75	.214	.272	206	44	4	4	0	0.0	33	13	16	15	4	1	0	71	120	12	10	2.7	.941	3B-52, SS-7
1929	BKN	N	17	.274	.306	62	17	2	0	0	0.0	3	4	7	6	3	0	0	34	52	5	8	5.4	.945	SS-17
1930			21	.320	.360	25	8	1	0	0	0.0	4	0	2	7	1	3	1	5	12	0	0	0.8	1.000	3B-21
1931			9	.500	.500	4	2	0	0	0	0.0	2	0	1	1	0	0	0	2	5	0	0	0.8	1.000	SS-2, 3B-1
1933	PHI	N	107	.224	.274	340	76	15	1	0	0.0	31	22	28	33	1	5	1	203	291	17	53	4.8	.967	2B-71, 3B-30, SS-1
8 yrs.			478	.250	.312	1546	387	52	20	1	0.1	199	120	142	137	32	12	2	582	949	71	118	3.4	.956	3B-347, 2B-71, SS-30

Jackie Warner

WARNER, JOHN JOSEPH
B. Aug. 1, 1943, Monrovia, Calif.   BR TR 6' 180 lbs.

| 1966 | CAL | A | 45 | .211 | .431 | 123 | 26 | 4 | 1 | 7 | 5.7 | 22 | 16 | 9 | 55 | 0 | 4 | 0 | 59 | 1 | 1 | 0 | 1.4 | .984 | OF-37 |

Hal Warnock

WARNOCK, HAROLD CHARLES
B. Jan. 6, 1912, New York, N. Y.   BL TR 6'2" 180 lbs.

| 1935 | STL | A | 6 | .286 | .571 | 7 | 2 | 2 | 0 | 0 | 0.0 | 1 | 0 | 0 | 3 | 0 | 6 | 1 | 1 | 0 | 0 | 0 | 0.2 | 1.000 | OF-2 |

Bennie Warren

WARREN, BENNIE LOUIS
B. Mar. 2, 1912, Elk City, Okla.   BR TR 6'1" 184 lbs.

1939	PHI	N	18	.232	.286	56	13	0	0	1	1.8	4	7	7	7	0	1	1	60	8	3	2	3.9	.958	C-17
1940			106	.246	.398	289	71	6	1	12	4.2	33	34	40	46	1	7	4	326	63	11	9	3.8	.973	C-97, 1B-1
1941			121	.214	.342	345	74	13	2	9	2.6	34	35	44	66	0	11	4	412	84	14	16	4.2	.973	C-110
1942			90	.209	.356	225	47	6	3	7	3.1	19	20	24	36	0	9	0	267	51	10	4	3.6	.970	C-78, 1B-1
1946	NY	N	39	.159	.377	69	11	1	1	4	5.8	7	8	14	21	0	7	0	103	8	4	0	2.9	.965	C-30
1947			3	.200	.200	5	1	0	0	0	0.0	0	0	0	1	0	0	0	2	0	0	0	0.7	1.000	C-3
6 yrs.			377	.219	.360	989	217	26	7	33	3.3	97	104	129	177	1	35	9	1170	214	42	31	3.8	.971	C-335, 1B-2

Bill Warren

WARREN, WILLIAM HACKNEY (Hack)
B. Feb. 11, 1887, Cairo, Ill. D. Jan. 28, 1960, Whiteville, Tenn.   BL TR 5'8" 165 lbs.

1914	IND	F	26	.240	.280	50	12	2	0	0	0.0	5	5	5		2	3	0	64	17	6	1	3.3	.931	C-23
1915	NWK	F	5	.333	.333	3	1	0	0	0	0.0	1	0	1		0	3	1	2	0	0	0	0.4	1.000	1B-1, C-1
2 yrs.			31	.245	.283	53	13	2	0	0	0.0	6	5	6		2	6	1	66	17	6	1	2.9	.933	C-24, 1B-1

Rabbit Warstler

WARSTLER, HAROLD BURTON
B. Sept. 13, 1903, North Canton, Ohio D. May 31, 1964, North Canton, Ohio   BR TR 5'7½" 150 lbs.

1930	BOS	A	55	.185	.253	162	30	2	3	1	0.6	16	13	20	21	0	0	0	100	149	14	30	4.8	.947	SS-54
1931			66	.243	.304	181	44	5	3	0	0.0	20	10	15	27	2	5	0	102	167	19	26	4.4	.934	2B-42, SS-19
1932			115	.211	.276	388	82	15	5	0	0.0	26	34	22	43	9	3	0	254	373	41	84	5.8	.939	SS-107
1933			92	.217	.273	322	70	13	1	1	0.3	44	17	42	36	2	1	0	150	275	22	40	4.9	.951	SS-87
1934	PHI	A	117	.236	.303	419	99	19	3	1	0.2	56	36	51	30	9	4	0	232	396	22	88	5.6	.966	2B-107, SS-2
1935			138	.250	.337	496	124	20	7	3	0.6	62	59	56	53	8	0	0	309	486	34	94	6.0	.959	2B-136, 3B-2
1936	2 teams			PHI	A	(66G –	.250)			BOS	N	(74G –	.211)												
"	total		140	.228	.281	540	123	14	6	1	0.2	54	41	58	49	5	0	0	296	543	35	104	6.2	.960	SS-74, 2B-66
1937	BOS	N	149	.223	.276	555	124	20	6	3	0.5	57	36	51	62	4	0	0	298	493	49	85	5.6	.942	SS-149
1938			142	.231	.270	467	108	10	4	0	0.0	37	40	48	38	3	0	0	295	445	49	76	5.6	.938	SS-135, 2B-7
1939			114	.243	.292	342	83	11	3	0	0.0	34	24	24	31	2	1	0	194	301	20	75	4.5	.961	SS-49, 2B-43, 3B-21

Rabbit Warstler *continued*

Year Team	Games	BA	SA	AB	H	2B	3B	HR	HR%	R	RBI	BB	SO	SB	Pinch Hit AB	Pinch Hit H	PO	A	E	DP	TC/G	FA	G by Pos
1940 2 teams	BOS N (33G – .211) CHI N (45G – .226)																						
" total	78	.222	.264	216	48	4	1	1	0.5	25	22	18	24	1	6	0	122	184	16	35	4.1	.950	2B-41, SS-29, 3B-2
11 yrs.	1206	.229	.287	4088	935	133	36	11	0.3	431	332	405	414	42	20	0	2352	3812	321	737	5.4	.951	SS-705, 2B-442, 3B-25

Bill Warwick

WARWICK, FIRMAN NEWTON BR TR 6'½" 180 lbs.
B. Nov. 26, 1897, Philadelphia, Pa. D. Dec. 19, 1984, San Antonio, Tex.

Year Team	Games	BA	SA	AB	H	2B	3B	HR	HR%	R	RBI	BB	SO	SB	Pinch Hit AB	Pinch Hit H	PO	A	E	DP	TC/G	FA	G by Pos
1921 PIT N	1	.000	.000	1	0	0	0	0	0.0	0	0	0	0	0	0	0	0	1	1	0	2.0	.500	C-1
1925 STL N	13	.293	.488	41	12	1	2	1	2.4	8	6	5	5	0	0	0	33	4	0	0	2.8	1.000	C-13
1926	9	.357	.357	14	5	0	0	0	0.0	0	2	0	2	0	0	0	19	5	2	0	2.9	.923	C-9
3 yrs.	23	.304	.446	56	17	1	2	1	1.8	8	8	5	7	0	0	0	52	10	3	0	2.8	.954	C-23

Carl Warwick

WARWICK, CARL WAYNE BR TL 5'10" 170 lbs.
B. Feb. 27, 1937, Dallas, Tex.

Year Team	Games	BA	SA	AB	H	2B	3B	HR	HR%	R	RBI	BB	SO	SB	Pinch Hit AB	Pinch Hit H	PO	A	E	DP	TC/G	FA	G by Pos
1961 2 teams	LA N (19G – .091) STL N (55G – .250)																						
" total	74	.239	.374	163	39	6	2	4	2.5	29	17	20	36	3	13	4	96	2	3	1	1.4	.970	OF-60
1962 2 teams	STL N (13G – .348) HOU N (130G – .260)																						
" total	143	.264	.404	500	132	17	1	17	3.4	67	64	40	79	4	13	4	271	13	4	1	2.0	.986	OF-138
1963 HOU N	150	.254	.348	528	134	19	5	7	1.3	49	47	49	70	3	10	2	260	8	3	2	1.8	.989	OF-141, 1B-2
1964 STL N	88	.259	.373	158	41	7	1	3	1.9	14	15	11	30	2	43	11	53	3	4	2	0.7	.933	OF-49
1965 2 teams	STL N (50G – .156) BAL A (9G – .000)																						
" total	59	.132	.176	91	12	2	1	0	0.0	6	6	7	20	1	36	4	49	1	1	4	0.9	.980	OF-24, 1B-4
1966 CHI N	16	.227	.227	22	5	0	0	0	0.0	3	0	0	6	0	7	2	8	1	0	0	0.6	1.000	OF-10
6 yrs.	530	.248	.360	1462	363	51	10	31	2.1	168	149	127	241	13	122	27	737	28	15	10	1.5	.981	OF-422, 1B-6
WORLD SERIES																							
1964 STL N	5	.750	.750	4	3	0	0	0	0.0	2	1	1	0	0	4	3	0	0	0	0	0.0	–	
																1st							

Jimmy Wasdell

WASDELL, JAMES CHARLES BL TL 5'11" 185 lbs.
B. May 15, 1914, Cleveland, Ohio D. Aug. 6, 1983, New Port Richey, Fla.

Year Team	Games	BA	SA	AB	H	2B	3B	HR	HR%	R	RBI	BB	SO	SB	Pinch Hit AB	Pinch Hit H	PO	A	E	DP	TC/G	FA	G by Pos
1937 WAS A	32	.255	.418	110	28	4	4	2	1.8	13	12	7	13	0	4	1	196	11	1	19	6.5	.995	1B-21, OF-7
1938	53	.236	.307	140	33	2	1	2	1.4	19	16	12	12	5	18	4	234	12	1	26	4.7	.996	1B-26, OF-6
1939	29	.303	.367	109	33	5	1	0	0.0	12	13	9	16	3	1	0	255	15	10	24	9.7	.964	1B-28
1940 2 teams	WAS A (10G – .086) BKN N (77G – .278)																						
" total	87	.253	.374	265	67	15	4	3	1.1	38	37	20	31	4	14	5	268	8	7	12	3.3	.975	OF-42, 1B-25
1941 BKN N	94	.298	.419	265	79	14	3	4	1.5	39	48	16	15	2	23	4	185	7	4	5	2.1	.980	OF-54, 1B-15
1942 PIT N	122	.259	.318	409	106	11	2	3	0.7	44	38	47	22	1	16	1	246	12	11	5	2.2	.959	OF-97, 1B-7
1943 2 teams	PIT N (4G – .500) PHI N (141G – .261)																						
" total	145	.261	.344	524	137	19	6	4	0.8	54	68	48	22	6	5	4	857	61	13	62	6.4	.986	1B-82, OF-56
1944 PHI N	133	.277	.355	451	125	20	3	3	0.7	47	40	45	17	0	9	2	286	6	5	6	2.2	.983	OF-121, 1B-4
1945	134	.300	.412	500	150	19	8	7	1.4	65	60	32	11	7	8	5	739	47	12	52	6.0	.985	OF-65, 1B-63
1946 2 teams	PHI N (26G – .255) CLE A (32G – .268)																						
" total	58	.261	.337	92	24	0	2	1	1.1	8	9	7	6	1	36	10	43	4	4	9	0.9	.922	OF-14, 1B-6
1947 CLE A	1	.000	.000	1	0	0	0	0	0.0	0	0	0	0	0	1	0	0	0	0	0	0.0	–	
11 yrs.	888	.273	.365	2866	782	109	34	29	1.0	339	341	243	165	29	135	36	3309	183	68	220	4.0	.981	OF-462, 1B-277
WORLD SERIES																							
1941 BKN N	3	.200	.400	5	1	1	0	0	0.0	0	2	0	0	0	3	1	2	0	0	0	0.7	1.000	OF-1

Link Wasem

WASEM, LINCOLN WILLIAM BR TR 5'9½" 180 lbs.
B. Jan. 30, 1911, Birmingham, Ohio D. Mar. 6, 1979, South Laguna, Calif.

Year Team	Games	BA	SA	AB	H	2B	3B	HR	HR%	R	RBI	BB	SO	SB	Pinch Hit AB	Pinch Hit H	PO	A	E	DP	TC/G	FA	G by Pos
1937 BOS N	2	.000	.000	1	0	0	0	0	0.0	0	0	0	0	0	0	0	2	12	0	0	7.0	1.000	C-2

Libe Washburn

WASHBURN, LIBEUS BB TL 5'10" 180 lbs.
B. June 16, 1874, Lynn, N. H. D. Mar. 22, 1940, Malone, N. Y.

Year Team	Games	BA	SA	AB	H	2B	3B	HR	HR%	R	RBI	BB	SO	SB	Pinch Hit AB	Pinch Hit H	PO	A	E	DP	TC/G	FA	G by Pos
1902 NY N	6	.444	.444	9	4	0	0	0	0.0	1	0	2		1	3	1	4	0	0	0	0.7	1.000	OF-3
1903 PHI N	8	.167	.167	18	3	0	0	0	0.0	1	1	1		0	2	0	3	7	0	0	1.3	1.000	P-4, OF-2
2 yrs.	14	.259	.259	27	7	0	0	0	0.0	2	1	3		1	5	1	7	7	0	0	1.0	1.000	OF-5, P-4

Claudell Washington

WASHINGTON, CLAUDELL BL TL 6' 190 lbs.
B. Aug. 31, 1954, Los Angeles, Calif.

Year Team	Games	BA	SA	AB	H	2B	3B	HR	HR%	R	RBI	BB	SO	SB	Pinch Hit AB	Pinch Hit H	PO	A	E	DP	TC/G	FA	G by Pos
1974 OAK A	73	.285	.376	221	63	10	5	0	0.0	16	19	13	44	7	8	3	63	2	1	0	0.9	.985	DH-38, OF-32
1975	148	.308	.424	590	182	24	7	10	1.7	86	77	32	80	40	2	1	305	8	7	1	2.2	.978	OF-148
1976	134	.257	.353	490	126	20	6	5	1.0	65	53	30	90	37	3	2	276	10	11	2	2.2	.963	OF-126, DH-6
1977 TEX A	129	.284	.420	521	148	31	2	12	2.3	63	68	25	112	21	2	0	255	11	6	3	2.1	.978	OF-127, DH-1
1978 2 teams	TEX A (12G – .167) CHI A (86G – .264)																						
" total	98	.253	.376	356	90	16	5	6	1.7	34	33	13	69	5	6	2	170	6	8	0	1.9	.957	OF-89, DH-5
1979 CHI A	131	.280	.454	471	132	33	5	13	2.8	79	66	28	93	19	13	4	256	7	7	3	2.1	.974	OF-122, DH-3
1980 2 teams	CHI A (32G – .289) NY N (79G – .275)																						
" total	111	.278	.452	374	104	20	6	11	2.9	53	54	25	82	21	17	1	164	13	6	2	1.6	.967	OF-93, DH-2
1981 ATL N	85	.291	.425	320	93	22	3	5	1.6	37	37	15	47	12	5	3	145	5	1	0	1.8	.993	OF-79
1982	150	.266	.416	563	150	24	6	16	2.8	94	80	50	107	33	7	0	221	9	12	3	1.6	.950	OF-139
1983	134	.278	.413	496	138	24	8	9	1.8	75	44	35	103	31	7	2	218	8	6	3	1.7	.974	OF-128
1984	120	.286	.469	416	119	21	2	17	4.1	62	61	59	77	21	12	2	170	4	6	0	1.5	.967	OF-107
1985	122	.276	.455	398	110	14	6	15	3.8	62	43	40	66	14	26	6	122	3	5	1	1.1	.962	OF-99
1986 2 teams	ATL N (40G – .270) NY A (54G – .237)																						
" total	94	.254	.434	272	69	16	0	11	4.0	36	30	21	59	10	28	5	110	1	3	0	1.2	.974	OF-76
1987 NY A	102	.279	.420	312	87	17	0	9	2.9	42	44	27	54	10	21	4	166	3	2	1	1.7	.988	OF-72, DH-13
1988	126	.308	.442	455	140	22	3	11	2.4	62	64	24	74	15	19	4	309	5	5	1	2.5	.984	OF-117
1989 CAL A	110	.273	.428	418	114	18	4	13	3.1	53	42	27	84	13	6	2	187	6	5	2	1.8	.975	OF-100, DH-7
16 yrs.	1867	.279	.423	6673	1865	332	68	163	2.4	919	815	464	1241	309	182	41	3137	101	91	22	1.8	.973	OF-1654, DH-75
LEAGUE CHAMPIONSHIP SERIES																							
1974 OAK A	4	.273	.364	11	3	1	0	0	0.0	1	0	0	0	0	1	1	11	0	0	0	2.8	1.000	OF-3

Year	Team	Games	BA	SA	AB	H	2B	3B	HR	HR%	R	RBI	BB	SO	SB	Pinch Hit AB	Pinch Hit H	PO	A	E	DP	TC/G	FA	G by Pos

Claudell Washington *continued*

Year	Team	Games	BA	SA	AB	H	2B	3B	HR	HR%	R	RBI	BB	SO	SB	PH AB	PH H	PO	A	E	DP	TC/G	FA	G by Pos
1975		3	.250	.333	12	3	1	0	0	0.0	1	1	0	2	0	0	0	1	0	2	0	1.0	.333	OF-2, DH-1
1982	ATL N	3	.333	.333	9	3	0	0	0	0.0	0	0	2	2	0	0	0	0	0	0	0	0.0	–	OF-3
3 yrs.		10	.281	.344	32	9	2	0	0	0.0	2	1	2	4	0	1	1	12	0	2	0	1.4	.857	OF-8, DH-1

WORLD SERIES

Year	Team	Games	BA	SA	AB	H	2B	3B	HR	HR%	R	RBI	BB	SO	SB	PH AB	PH H	PO	A	E	DP	TC/G	FA	G by Pos
1974	OAK A	5	.571	.571	7	4	0	0	0	0.0	1	0	1	1	0	1	1	3	0	0	0	0.6	1.000	OF-5

George Washington

WASHINGTON, SLOAN VERNON
B. June 4, 1907, Linden, Tex. D. Feb. 17, 1985, Linden, Tex.

BL TR 5'11½" 190 lbs.

Year	Team	Games	BA	SA	AB	H	2B	3B	HR	HR%	R	RBI	BB	SO	SB	PH AB	PH H	PO	A	E	DP	TC/G	FA	G by Pos
1935	CHI A	108	.283	.437	339	96	22	3	8	2.4	40	47	10	18	1	29	9	137	10	4	2	1.4	.974	OF-79
1936		20	.163	.265	49	8	2	0	1	2.0	6	5	1	4	0	6	1	13	2	1	0	0.8	.938	OF-12
2 yrs.		128	.268	.415	388	104	24	3	9	2.3	46	52	11	22	1	35	10	150	12	5	2	1.3	.970	OF-91

Herb Washington

WASHINGTON, HERBERT LEE
B. Nov. 16, 1951, Belzonia, Miss.

BR TR 6' 170 lbs.

Year	Team	Games	BA	SA	AB	H	2B	3B	HR	HR%	R	RBI	BB	SO	SB	PH AB	PH H	PO	A	E	DP	TC/G	FA	G by Pos
1974	OAK A	91	–	–	0	0	0	0	0	–	29	0	0	0	28	0	0	0	0	0	0	0.0	–	
1975		13	–	–	0	0	0	0	0	–	4	0	0	0	2	0	0	0	0	0	0	0.0	–	
2 yrs.		104	–	–	0	0	0	0	0	–	33	0	0	0	30	0	0	0	0	0	0	0.0	–	

LEAGUE CHAMPIONSHIP SERIES

Year	Team	Games	BA	SA	AB	H	2B	3B	HR	HR%	R	RBI	BB	SO	SB	PH AB	PH H	PO	A	E	DP	TC/G	FA	G by Pos
1974	OAK A	2	–	–	0	0	0	0	0	–	0	0	0	0	0	0	0	0	0	0	0	0.0	–	

WORLD SERIES

Year	Team	Games	BA	SA	AB	H	2B	3B	HR	HR%	R	RBI	BB	SO	SB	PH AB	PH H	PO	A	E	DP	TC/G	FA	G by Pos
1974	OAK A	3	–	–	0	0	0	0	0	–	0	0	0	0	0	0	0	0	0	0	0	0.0	–	

LaRue Washington

WASHINGTON, LaRUE
B. Sept. 7, 1953, Long Beach, Calif.

BR TR 6' 170 lbs.

Year	Team	Games	BA	SA	AB	H	2B	3B	HR	HR%	R	RBI	BB	SO	SB	PH AB	PH H	PO	A	E	DP	TC/G	FA	G by Pos
1978	TEX A	3	.000	.000	3	0	0	0	0	0.0	0	0	0	1	0	0	0	0	5	0	2	1.7	1.000	2B-2, DH-1
1979		25	.278	.278	18	5	0	0	0	0.0	5	2	4	0	2	0	0	16	1	0	0	0.7	1.000	OF-13, DH-1, 3B-1
2 yrs.		28	.238	.238	21	5	0	0	0	0.0	5	2	4	1	2	0	0	16	6	0	2	1.0	1.000	OF-13, DH-2, 2B-2, 3B-1

Ron Washington

WASHINGTON, RONALD
B. Apr. 29, 1952, New Orleans, La.

BR TR 5'11" 156 lbs.

Year	Team	Games	BA	SA	AB	H	2B	3B	HR	HR%	R	RBI	BB	SO	SB	PH AB	PH H	PO	A	E	DP	TC/G	FA	G by Pos
1977	LA N	10	.368	.368	19	7	0	0	0	0.0	4	1	0	2	1	0	0	4	14	3	2	2.1	.857	SS-10
1981	MIN A	28	.226	.286	84	19	3	1	0	0.0	8	5	4	14	4	0	0	64	80	8	19	5.4	.947	SS-26, OF-2
1982		119	.271	.368	451	122	17	6	5	1.1	48	39	14	79	3	2	0	201	269	13	58	4.1	.973	SS-91, 2B-37, 3B-1
1983		99	.246	.325	317	78	7	3	4	1.3	28	26	22	50	10	4	1	140	246	16	54	4.1	.960	SS-81, 2B-14, DH-1, 3B-1
1984		88	.294	.447	197	58	11	5	3	1.5	25	23	4	31	1	12	4	77	134	4	24	2.4	.981	SS-71, 2B-9, DH-4, 3B-2
1985		69	.274	.400	135	37	6	4	1	0.7	24	14	8	15	5	12	2	55	100	7	14	2.3	.957	SS-31, 2B-24, DH-7, 3B-7, 1B-1
1986		48	.257	.459	74	19	3	0	4	5.4	15	11	3	21	1	10	2	12	20	2	6	0.7	.941	2B-16, DH-15, SS-7, 3B-3
1987	BAL A	26	.203	.304	79	16	3	1	1	1.3	7	6	1	15	0	0	0	19	42	0	8	2.3	1.000	3B-20, 2B-3, DH-2, OF-2, SS-1
1988	CLE A	69	.256	.363	223	57	14	2	2	0.9	30	21	9	35	3	4	3	95	162	17	29	4.0	.938	SS-54, 3B-8, 2B-7
1989	HOU N	7	.143	.286	7	1	1	0	0	0.0	1	0	1	4	0	5	0	1	0	0	0	0.1	1.000	3B-1, 2B-1
10 yrs.		563	.261	.368	1586	414	65	22	20	1.3	190	146	65	266	28	49	10	667	1068	70	209	3.2	.961	SS-372, 2B-111, 3B-43, DH-29, OF-4, 1B-1

U. L. Washington

WASHINGTON, U. L.
B. Oct. 27, 1953, Stringtown, Okla.

BB TR 5'11" 175 lbs.

Year	Team	Games	BA	SA	AB	H	2B	3B	HR	HR%	R	RBI	BB	SO	SB	PH AB	PH H	PO	A	E	DP	TC/G	FA	G by Pos
1977	KC A	10	.200	.350	20	4	1	1	0	0.0	5	4	1	0	1	0	13	21	5	4	3.9	.872	SS-9, DH-1
1978		69	.264	.295	129	34	2	1	0	0.0	10	9	10	20	12	1	1	79	92	9	18	2.6	.950	SS-49, 2B-19, DH-1
1979		101	.254	.358	268	68	12	5	2	0.7	32	25	20	44	10	3	0	174	243	18	68	4.3	.959	SS-50, 2B-46, DH-3, 3B-1
1980		153	.273	.375	549	150	16	11	6	1.1	79	53	53	78	20	2	1	237	467	32	86	4.8	.957	SS-152
1981		98	.227	.307	339	77	19	1	2	0.6	40	29	41	43	10	0	0	135	297	12	58	4.5	.973	SS-98
1982		119	.286	.412	437	125	19	3	10	2.3	64	60	38	48	23	2	0	173	371	22	63	4.8	.961	SS-117, DH-1
1983		144	.236	.320	547	129	19	6	5	0.9	76	41	48	78	40	3	0	201	448	36	91	4.8	.947	SS-140, DH-1
1984		63	.224	.276	170	38	6	0	1	0.6	18	10	14	31	4	0	0	81	166	10	40	4.1	.961	SS-61
1985	MON N	68	.249	.352	193	48	9	4	1	0.5	24	17	15	33	6	20	3	76	130	7	29	3.1	.967	2B-43, SS-9, 3B-3
1986	PIT N	72	.200	.259	135	27	0	4	0	0.0	14	10	15	27	6	29	5	50	97	8	25	2.2	.948	SS-51, 2B-3
1987		10	.300	.300	10	3	0	0	0	0.0	1	0	2	3	0	6	2	1	4	1	0	0.6	.833	SS-1, 3B-1
11 yrs.		907	.251	.343	2797	703	103	36	27	1.0	358	255	261	409	132	66	12	1220	2336	160	482	4.1	.957	SS-737, 2B-111, DH-7, 3B-5

DIVISIONAL PLAYOFF SERIES

Year	Team	Games	BA	SA	AB	H	2B	3B	HR	HR%	R	RBI	BB	SO	SB	PH AB	PH H	PO	A	E	DP	TC/G	FA	G by Pos
1981	KC A	3	.222	.222	9	2	0	0	0	0.0	0	0	0	0	0	0	0	0	0	1	0	0.3	–	SS-3

LEAGUE CHAMPIONSHIP SERIES

Year	Team	Games	BA	SA	AB	H	2B	3B	HR	HR%	R	RBI	BB	SO	SB	PH AB	PH H	PO	A	E	DP	TC/G	FA	G by Pos
1980	KC A	3	.364	.455	11	4	1	0	0	0.0	1	1	2	3	0	0	0	5	7	0	2	4.0	1.000	SS-3
1984		2	.000	.000	1	0	0	0	0	0.0	0	0	0	1	0	1	0	0	0	0	0	0.0	–	
2 yrs.		5	.333	.417	12	4	1	0	0	0.0	1	1	2	4	0	1	0	5	7	0	2	2.4	1.000	SS-3

WORLD SERIES

Year	Team	Games	BA	SA	AB	H	2B	3B	HR	HR%	R	RBI	BB	SO	SB	PH AB	PH H	PO	A	E	DP	TC/G	FA	G by Pos
1980	KC A	6	.273	.273	22	6	0	0	0	0.0	1	2	0	6	0	0	0	8	20	1	4	4.8	.966	SS-6

Mark Wasinger

WASINGER, MARK THOMAS
B. Aug. 4, 1961, Monterey, Calif.

BR TR 6' 165 lbs.

Year	Team	Games	BA	SA	AB	H	2B	3B	HR	HR%	R	RBI	BB	SO	SB	PH AB	PH H	PO	A	E	DP	TC/G	FA	G by Pos
1986	SD N	3	.000	.000	8	0	0	0	0	0.0	0	1	0	2	0	0	0	2	2	3	1	2.3	.571	3B-3, 2B-1
1987	SF N	44	.275	.350	80	22	3	0	1	1.3	16	3	8	14	2	11	1	21	50	1	9	1.6	.986	3B-21, 2B-10, SS-2
1988		3	.000	.000	2	0	0	0	0	0.0	1	0	0	0	0	1	0	0	0	0	0	0.0	–	3B-1
3 yrs.		50	.244	.311	90	22	3	0	1	1.1	17	4	8	16	2	12	1	23	52	4	10	1.6	.949	3B-25, 2B-11, SS-2

Year	Team		Games	BA	SA	AB	H	2B	3B	HR	HR%	R	RBI	BB	SO	SB	Pinch Hit AB	Pinch Hit H	PO	A	E	DP	TC/G	FA	G by Pos

John Wathan

WATHAN, JOHN DAVID (Duke)
B. Oct. 4, 1949, Cedar Rapids, Iowa
Manager 1987-89.
BR TR 6'2" 205 lbs.

Year	Team		Games	BA	SA	AB	H	2B	3B	HR	HR%	R	RBI	BB	SO	SB	PH AB	PH H	PO	A	E	DP	TC/G	FA	G by Pos
1976	KC	A	27	.286	.310	42	12	1	0	0	0.0	5	5	2	5	0	2	1	63	4	1	1	2.5	.985	C-23, 1B-3
1977			55	.328	.471	119	39	5	3	2	1.7	18	21	5	8	2	18	6	156	9	2	2	3.0	.988	C-35, 1B-5, DH-2
1978			67	.300	.395	190	57	10	1	2	1.1	19	28	3	12	2	13	6	385	28	2	20	6.2	.995	1B-47, C-21
1979			90	.206	.302	199	41	7	3	2	1.0	26	28	7	24	2	31	5	336	24	3	30	4.0	.992	1B-49, C-23, DH-11, OF-3
1980			126	.305	.406	453	138	14	7	6	1.3	57	58	50	42	17	10	3	472	33	8	19	4.1	.984	C-77, OF-35, 1B-12
1981			89	.252	.312	301	76	9	3	1	0.3	24	19	19	23	11	4	0	316	28	7	1	3.9	.980	C-73, OF-16, 1B-1
1982			121	.270	.328	448	121	11	3	3	0.7	79	51	48	46	36	2	0	482	40	10	5	4.4	.981	C-120, 1B-3
1983			128	.245	.314	437	107	18	3	2	0.5	49	32	27	56	28	5	2	615	58	9	29	5.3	.987	C-92, 1B-37, OF-9
1984			97	.181	.269	171	31	7	1	2	1.2	17	10	21	34	6	4	1	304	31	6	10	3.5	.982	C-59, 1B-33, DH-4, OF-1
1985			60	.234	.324	145	34	8	1	1	0.7	11	9	17	15	1	0	0	259	29	4	6	4.9	.986	C-49, 1B-6, DH-2
10 yrs.			860	.262	.343	2505	656	90	25	21	0.8	305	261	199	265	105	91	24	3388	284	52	123	4.3	.986	C-572, 1B-196, OF-64, DH-19

DIVISIONAL PLAYOFF SERIES

Year	Team		Games	BA	SA	AB	H	2B	3B	HR	HR%	R	RBI	BB	SO	SB	PH AB	PH H	PO	A	E	DP	TC/G	FA	G by Pos
1981	KC	A	3	.300	.300	10	3	0	0	0	0.0	1	0	1	1	0	0	0	0	0	1	0	0.3	–	C-3

LEAGUE CHAMPIONSHIP SERIES

Year	Team		Games	BA	SA	AB	H	2B	3B	HR	HR%	R	RBI	BB	SO	SB	PH AB	PH H	PO	A	E	DP	TC/G	FA	G by Pos
1976	KC	A	1	–	–	0	0	0	0	0	–	0	0	0	0	0	0	0	0	0	0	0	0.0	–	C-1
1977			4	.000	.000	6	0	0	0	0	0.0	0	0	0	3	0	2	0	19	0	0	0	4.8	1.000	1B-2, DH-1, C-1
1978			1	.000	.000	3	0	0	0	0	0.0	0	0	0	0	0	0	0	7	0	0	0	7.0	1.000	1B-1
1980			3	.000	.000	6	0	0	0	0	0.0	1	0	3	1	0	1	0	7	0	0	0	2.3	1.000	OF-3
1984			1	.000	.000	1	0	0	0	0	0.0	0	0	0	0	0	1	0	0	0	0	0	0.0	–	
5 yrs.			10	.000	.000	16	0	0	0	0	0.0	1	0	3	4	0	4	0	33	0	0	0	3.3	1.000	OF-3, 1B-3, C-2, DH-1

WORLD SERIES

Year	Team		Games	BA	SA	AB	H	2B	3B	HR	HR%	R	RBI	BB	SO	SB	PH AB	PH H	PO	A	E	DP	TC/G	FA	G by Pos
1980	KC	A	3	.286	.286	7	2	0	0	0	0.0	1	1	2	1	0	1	0	7	1	0	0	2.7	1.000	C-2, OF-1
1985			2	.000	.000	1	0	0	0	0	0.0	0	0	0	1	0	1	0	0	0	0	0	0.0	–	
2 yrs.			5	.250	.250	8	2	0	0	0	0.0	1	1	2	2	0	2	0	7	1	0	0	1.6	1.000	C-2, OF-1

Bill Watkins

WATKINS, WILLIAM HENRY
B. May 5, 1858, Brantford, Ont., Canada   D. June 9, 1937, Port Huron, Mich.
Manager 1884-89, 1893, 1898-99.
5'10" 156 lbs.

Year	Team		Games	BA	SA	AB	H	2B	3B	HR	HR%	R	RBI	BB	SO	SB	PH AB	PH H	PO	A	E	DP	TC/G	FA	G by Pos
1884	IND	AA	34	.205	.236	127	26	4	0	0	0.0	16		5			0	0	45	63	15	4	3.6	.878	3B-23, 2B-9, SS-2

Dave Watkins

WATKINS, DAVID ROGER
B. Mar. 15, 1944, Owensboro, Ky.
BR TR 5'10" 185 lbs.

Year	Team		Games	BA	SA	AB	H	2B	3B	HR	HR%	R	RBI	BB	SO	SB	PH AB	PH H	PO	A	E	DP	TC/G	FA	G by Pos
1969	PHI	N	69	.176	.284	148	26	2	1	4	2.7	17	12	22	53	2	11	1	247	20	5	2	3.9	.982	C-54, OF-5, 3B-1

Ed Watkins

WATKINS, JAMES EDWARD
B. June 21, 1877, Philadelphia, Pa.   D. Mar. 29, 1933, Kelvin, Ariz.

Year	Team		Games	BA	SA	AB	H	2B	3B	HR	HR%	R	RBI	BB	SO	SB	PH AB	PH H	PO	A	E	DP	TC/G	FA	G by Pos
1902	PHI	N	1	.000	.000	3	0	0	0	0	0.0	0	0	1		0	0	0	1	0	0	0	1.0	1.000	OF-1

George Watkins

WATKINS, GEORGE ARCHIBALD
B. June 4, 1900, Freestone County, Tex.   D. June 1, 1970, Houston, Tex.
BL TR 6' 175 lbs.

Year	Team		Games	BA	SA	AB	H	2B	3B	HR	HR%	R	RBI	BB	SO	SB	PH AB	PH H	PO	A	E	DP	TC/G	FA	G by Pos
1930	STL	N	119	.373	.621	391	146	32	7	17	4.3	85	87	24	49	5	15	5	279	18	11	16	2.6	.964	OF-89, 1B-13, 2B-1
1931			131	.288	.477	503	145	30	13	13	2.6	93	51	31	66	15	2	0	263	12	12	4	2.2	.958	OF-129
1932			137	.312	.461	458	143	35	3	9	2.0	67	63	45	46	18	6	2	267	11	15	1	2.1	.949	OF-120
1933			138	.278	.371	525	146	24	5	5	1.0	66	62	39	62	11	3	0	295	9	15	3	2.3	.953	OF-135
1934	NY	N	105	.247	.389	296	73	18	3	6	2.0	38	33	24	34	2	16	3	165	3	10	1	1.7	.944	OF-81
1935	PHI	N	150	.270	.413	600	162	25	5	17	2.8	89	76	40	78	3	2	1	325	18	15	4	2.4	.958	OF-148
1936	2 teams		PHI	N	(19G –	.243)			BKN	N	(105G –	.255)														
" total			124	.253	.387	434	110	28	6	6	1.4	61	48	43	47	7	8	2	206	6	9	2	1.8	.959	OF-115
7 yrs.			904	.288	.443	3207	925	192	42	73	2.3	490	420	246	382	61	52	13	1800	77	87	31	2.2	.956	OF-817, 1B-13, 2B-1

WORLD SERIES

Year	Team		Games	BA	SA	AB	H	2B	3B	HR	HR%	R	RBI	BB	SO	SB	PH AB	PH H	PO	A	E	DP	TC/G	FA	G by Pos
1930	STL	N	4	.167	.417	12	2	0	0	1	8.3	2	1	1	3	0	0	0	5	0	1	0	1.5	.833	OF-4
1931			5	.286	.571	14	4	1	0	1	7.1	4	2	2	1	0	0	0	8	0	0	0	1.6	1.000	OF-5
2 yrs.			9	.231	.500	26	6	1	0	2	7.7	6	3	3	4	0	0	0	13	0	1	0	1.6	.929	OF-9

Neal Watlington

WATLINGTON, JULIUS NEAL
B. Dec. 25, 1922, Yanceyville, N. C.
BL TR 6' 195 lbs.

Year	Team		Games	BA	SA	AB	H	2B	3B	HR	HR%	R	RBI	BB	SO	SB	PH AB	PH H	PO	A	E	DP	TC/G	FA	G by Pos
1953	PHI	A	21	.159	.182	44	7	1	0	0	0.0	4	3	3	8	0	12	2	37	7	1	2	2.1	.978	C-9

Art Watson

WATSON, ARTHUR STANHOPE (Watty)
B. Jan. 11, 1884, Jeffersonville, Ind.   D. May 9, 1950, Buffalo, N. Y.
BL TR 5'11" 170 lbs.

Year	Team		Games	BA	SA	AB	H	2B	3B	HR	HR%	R	RBI	BB	SO	SB	PH AB	PH H	PO	A	E	DP	TC/G	FA	G by Pos
1914	BKN	F	22	.283	.478	46	13	4	1	1	2.2	7	3	1		0	2	1	66	20	2	1	4.0	.977	C-18
1915	2 teams		BKN	F	(9G –	.263)			BUF	F	(22G –	.467)														
" total			31	.388	.592	49	19	1	3	1	2.0	10	14	3		0	16	6	27	9	5	2	1.3	.878	C-13, OF-1
2 yrs.			53	.337	.537	95	32	5	4	2	2.1	17	17	4		0	18	7	93	29	7	3	2.4	.946	C-31, OF-1

Bob Watson

WATSON, ROBERT JOSE (Bull)
B. Apr. 10, 1946, Los Angeles, Calif.
BR TR 6'1½" 201 lbs.

Year	Team		Games	BA	SA	AB	H	2B	3B	HR	HR%	R	RBI	BB	SO	SB	PH AB	PH H	PO	A	E	DP	TC/G	FA	G by Pos
1966	HOU	N	1	.000	.000	1	0	0	0	0	0.0	0	0	0	0	0	1	0	0	0	0	0	0.0	–	
1967			6	.214	.429	14	3	0	0	1	7.1	1	2	0	3	0	3	0	21	2	1	0	4.0	.958	1B-3
1968			45	.229	.321	140	32	7	0	2	1.4	13	8	13	32	1	5	0	46	0	6	0	1.2	.885	OF-40
1969			20	.275	.350	40	11	3	0	0	0.0	3	3	6	5	0	5	3	46	3	0	4	2.5	1.000	OF-6, 1B-5, C-1
1970			97	.272	.443	327	89	19	2	11	3.4	48	61	24	59	1	13	5	707	40	6	54	7.8	.992	1B-83, OF-6, C-1
1971			129	.288	.395	468	135	17	3	9	1.9	49	67	41	56	3	1	1	470	18	7	28	3.8	.986	OF-87, 1B-45
1972			147	.312	.464	548	171	27	4	16	2.9	74	86	53	83	1	2	0	231	7	5	3	1.7	.979	OF-143, 1B-2
1973			158	.312	.449	573	179	24	3	16	2.8	97	94	85	73	1	2	0	433	11	12	7	2.9	.974	OF-142, 1B-26, C-3

Year	Team	Games	BA	SA	AB	H	2B	3B	HR	HR%	R	RBI	BB	SO	SB	Pinch Hit AB	Pinch Hit H	PO	A	E	DP	TC/G	FA	G by Pos

Bob Watson *continued*

1974		150	.298	.412	524	156	19	4	11	2.1	69	67	60	61	3	8	2	298	12	4	9	2.1	.987	OF-140, 1B-35
1975		132	.324	.495	485	157	27	1	18	3.7	67	85	40	50	3	8	2	1089	70	8	106	8.8	.993	1B-118, OF-9
1976		157	.313	.458	585	183	31	3	16	2.7	76	102	62	64	3	3	0	1395	96	15	126	9.6	.990	1B-155
1977		151	.289	.498	554	160	38	6	22	4.0	77	110	57	69	5	5	3	1331	118	9	100	9.7	.994	1B-146
1978		139	.289	.451	461	133	25	4	14	3.0	51	79	51	57	3	9	0	974	95	9	63	7.8	.992	1B-128
1979 2 teams	HOU N (49G – .239)				BOS A		(84G – .337)																	
" total		133	.303	.469	475	144	23	4	16	3.4	63	71	45	56	3	6	0	896	80	10	81	7.4	.990	1B-102, DH-26
1980	NY A	130	.307	.456	469	144	23	4	13	2.8	62	68	48	56	2	11	3	851	63	9	87	7.1	.990	1B-104, DH-21
1981		59	.212	.385	156	33	3	3	6	3.8	15	12	24	17	0	13	3	367	25	1	42	6.7	.997	1B-50, DH-6
1982 2 teams	NY A (7G – .235)				ATL N		(57G – .246)																	
" total		64	.244	.420	131	32	6	1	5	3.8	19	25	17	20	1	25	6	248	8	0	23	4.0	1.000	1B-33, OF-2, DH-1
1983	ATL N	65	.309	.490	149	46	9	0	6	4.0	14	37	18	23	0	27	11	280	19	5	23	4.7	.984	1B-34
1984		49	.212	.329	85	18	4	0	2	2.4	4	12	9	12	0	29	6	165	12	3	17	3.7	.983	1B-19
19 yrs.		1832	.295	.447	6185	1826	307	41	184	3.0	802	989	653	796	27	178	45	9848	679	110	773	5.8	.990	1B-1088, OF-570, DH-54, C-10

DIVISIONAL PLAYOFF SERIES

| 1981 | NY A | 5 | .438 | .438 | 16 | 7 | 0 | 0 | 0 | 0.0 | 2 | 1 | 1 | 1 | 0 | 0 | 0 | 0 | 0 | 0 | 1 | 0 | 0.2 | – | 1B-5 |

LEAGUE CHAMPIONSHIP SERIES

1980	NY A	3	.500	.917	12	6	3	1	0	0.0	0	0	0	0	0	0	0	28	5	1	2	11.3	.971	1B-3
1981		3	.250	.250	12	3	0	0	0	0.0	0	1	0	1	0	0	0	0	0	0	0	0.0	–	1B-3
2 yrs.		6	.375	.583	24	9	3	1	0	0.0	0	1	0	1	0	0	0	28	5	1	2	5.7	.971	1B-6

WORLD SERIES

| 1981 | NY A | 6 | .318 | .636 | 22 | 7 | 1 | 0 | 2 | 9.1 | 2 | 7 | 3 | 0 | 0 | 0 | 0 | 51 | 0 | 0 | 2 | 8.5 | 1.000 | 1B-6 |

Johnny Watson

WATSON, JOHN THOMAS
B. Jan. 16, 1908, Tazewell, Va.   D. Apr. 29, 1965, Huntington, W. Va.   BL TR 6' 175 lbs.

| 1930 | DET A | 4 | .250 | .417 | 12 | 3 | 2 | 0 | 0 | 0.0 | 1 | 3 | 1 | 2 | 0 | 0 | 0 | 6 | 10 | 3 | 2 | 4.8 | .842 | SS-4 |

Allie Watt

WATT, ALBERT BAILEY
Brother of Frank Watt.
B. Dec. 12, 1899, Philadelphia, Pa.   D. Mar. 15, 1968, Norfolk, Va.   BR TR 5'8" 154 lbs.

| 1920 | WAS A | 1 | 1.000 | 2.000 | 1 | 1 | 0 | 0 | 0 | 0.0 | 0 | 1 | 0 | 0 | 0 | 0 | 0 | 0 | 1 | 0 | 0 | 1.0 | 1.000 | 2B-1 |

Cliff Watwood

WATWOOD, JOHN CLIFFORD (Lefty)
B. Aug. 17, 1905, Alexander City, Ala.   D. Mar. 1, 1980, Goodwater, Ala.   BL TL 6'1" 186 lbs.

1929	CHI A	85	.302	.410	278	84	12	6	2	0.7	33	18	22	21	6	7	2	188	7	12	2	2.4	.942	OF-77
1930		133	.302	.393	427	129	25	4	2	0.5	75	51	52	35	5	19	4	707	46	11	59	5.7	.986	1B-62, OF-43
1931		128	.283	.368	367	104	16	6	1	0.3	51	47	56	30	5	17	5	277	14	16	3	2.4	.948	OF-102, 1B-4
1932 2 teams	CHI A (13G – .306)				BOS A		(95G – .248)																	
" total		108	.257	.298	315	81	13	0	0	0.0	31	30	21	14	7	27	9	273	20	14	17	2.8	.954	OF-59, 1B-18
1933	BOS A	13	.133	.133	30	4	0	0	0	0.0	2	3	3	3	0	3	0	19	0	1	0	1.5	.950	OF-9
1939	PHI N	2	.167	.167	6	1	0	0	0	0.0	0	0	0	0	0	0	0	14	0	1	0	7.5	.933	1B-2
6 yrs.		469	.283	.363	1423	403	66	16	5	0.4	192	148	154	103	27	73	20	1478	87	55	81	3.5	.966	OF-290, 1B-86

Bob Way

WAY, ROBERT CLINTON
B. Apr. 2, 1906, Emlenton, Pa.   D. June 20, 1974, Pittsburgh, Pa.   BR TR 5'10½" 168 lbs.

| 1927 | CHI A | 5 | .333 | .333 | 3 | 1 | 0 | 0 | 0 | 0.0 | 3 | 1 | 0 | 1 | 0 | 3 | 1 | 1 | 0 | 0 | 0 | 0.2 | 1.000 | 2B-1 |

Roy Weatherly

WEATHERLY, CYRIL ROY (Stormy)
B. Feb. 25, 1915, Warren, Tex.   BL TR 5'6½" 170 lbs.

1936	CLE A	84	.335	.519	349	117	28	6	8	2.3	64	53	16	29	3	0	0	164	15	5	2	2.2	.973	OF-84
1937		53	.201	.343	134	27	4	0	5	3.7	19	13	6	14	1	13	1	48	8	2	1	1.1	.964	OF-38, 3B-1
1938		83	.262	.386	210	55	14	3	2	1.0	32	18	14	14	8	25	5	110	7	3	1	1.4	.975	OF-55
1939		95	.310	.406	323	100	16	6	1	0.3	43	32	19	23	7	17	4	146	3	6	1	1.6	.961	OF-76
1940		135	.303	.464	578	175	35	11	12	2.1	90	59	27	26	9	0	0	370	10	12	3	2.9	.969	OF-135
1941		102	.289	.399	363	105	21	5	3	0.8	59	37	32	20	2	14	5	208	7	1	1	2.1	.968	OF-88
1942		128	.258	.368	473	122	23	4	5	1.1	61	39	35	25	8	13	5	324	7	3	4	2.6	.991	OF-117
1943	NY A	77	.264	.389	280	74	8	3	7	2.5	37	28	18	9	4	8	2	174	2	3	0	2.3	.983	OF-68
1946		2	.500	.500	2	1	0	0	0	0.0	0	0	0	0	0	2	1	0	0	0	0	0.0	–	
1950	NY N	52	.261	.391	69	18	3	3	0	0.0	10	11	13	10	0	32	9	21	2	0	0	0.4	1.000	OF-15
10 yrs.		811	.286	.418	2781	794	152	44	43	1.5	415	290	180	170	42	124	32	1565	53	41	15	2.0	.975	OF-676, 3B-1

WORLD SERIES

| 1943 | NY A | 1 | .000 | .000 | 1 | 0 | 0 | 0 | 0 | 0.0 | 0 | 0 | 0 | 0 | 0 | 1 | 0 | 0 | 0 | 0 | 0 | 0.0 | – | |

Art Weaver

WEAVER, ARTHUR COGGSHALL
B. Apr. 7, 1879, Wichita, Kans.   D. Mar. 23, 1917, Denver, Colo.   TR 6'1"

1902	STL N	11	.182	.242	33	6	2	0	0	0.0	2	3	1		0	0	0	40	17	1	1	5.3	.983	C-11
1903 2 teams	STL N (16G – .245)				PIT N		(16G – .229)																	
" total		32	.237	.258	97	23	0	1	0	0.0	12	8	6		1	0	0	149	44	6	3	6.2	.970	C-27, 1B-5
1905	STL N	28	.120	.163	92	11	2	1	0	0.0	5	3	1		0	0	0	139	38	7	4	6.6	.962	C-28
1908	CHI A	15	.200	.229	35	7	1	0	0	0.0	1	1	1		0	0	0	32	9	2	2	2.9	.953	C-15
4 yrs.		86	.183	.218	257	47	5	2	0	0.0	20	15	9		1	0	0	360	108	16	10	5.6	.967	C-81, 1B-5

Buck Weaver

WEAVER, GEORGE DANIEL
B. Aug. 18, 1890, Pottstown, Pa.   D. Jan. 31, 1956, Chicago, Ill.   BB TR 5'11" 170 lbs.

1912	CHI A	147	.224	.300	523	117	21	8	1	0.2	55	43	9		12	0	0	342	425	71	53	5.7	.915	SS-147
1913		151	.272	.356	533	145	17	8	4	0.8	51	52	15	60	20	0	0	392	520	70	73	6.5	.929	SS-151
1914		136	.246	.327	541	133	20	4	2	0.4	64	28	20	40	14	2	0	367	389	59	50	6.0	.928	SS-134

Year	Team	Games	BA	SA	AB	H	2B	3B	HR	HR%	R	RBI	BB	SO	SB	Pinch Hit AB	Pinch Hit H	PO	A	E	DP	TC/G	FA	G by Pos

Buck Weaver *continued*

Year	Team	Games	BA	SA	AB	H	2B	3B	HR	HR%	R	RBI	BB	SO	SB	AB	H	PO	A	E	DP	TC/G	FA	G by Pos
1915		148	.268	.355	563	151	18	11	3	0.5	83	49	32	58	24	0	0	281	470	49	54	5.4	.939	SS-148
1916		151	.227	.309	582	132	27	6	3	0.5	78	38	30	48	22	0	0	266	385	36	49	4.5	.948	3B-85, SS-66
1917		118	.284	.362	447	127	16	5	3	0.7	64	32	27	29	19	1	0	174	257	21	27	3.8	.954	3B-107, SS-10
1918		112	.300	.352	420	126	12	5	0	0.0	37	29	11	24	20	2	1	201	339	33	51	5.1	.942	SS-98, 3B-11, 2B-1
1919		140	.296	.401	571	169	33	9	3	0.5	89	75	11	21	22	0	0	200	341	20	28	4.0	.964	3B-97, SS-43
1920		151	.333	.424	630	210	35	8	2	0.3	104	75	28	23	19	0	0	209	351	36	33	3.9	.940	3B-126, SS-25
9 yrs.		1254	.272	.356	4810	1310	199	69	21	0.4	625	421	183	303	172	5	1	2432	3477	395	418	5.0	.937	SS-822, 3B-426, 2B-1

WORLD SERIES

Year	Team	Games	BA	SA	AB	H	2B	3B	HR	HR%	R	RBI	BB	SO	SB	AB	H	PO	A	E	DP	TC/G	FA	G by Pos
1917 CHI	A	6	.333	.381	21	7	1	0	0	0.0	3	1	0	2	0	0	0	13	14	4	4	5.2	.871	SS-6
1919		8	.324	.500	34	11	4	1	0	0.0	4	0	0	2	0	0	0	9	18	0	0	3.4	1.000	3B-8
2 yrs.		14	.327	.455	55	18	5	1	0	0.0	7	1	0	4	0	0	0	22	32	4	4	4.1	.931	3B-8, SS-6

Farmer Weaver

WEAVER, WILLIAM B.
B. Mar. 23, 1865, Parkersburg, W. Va.   D. Jan. 25, 1943, Akron, Ohio

Year	Team	Games	BA	SA	AB	H	2B	3B	HR	HR%	R	RBI	BB	SO	SB	AB	H	PO	A	E	DP	TC/G	FA	G by Pos
1888 LOU	AA	26	.250	.277	112	28	1	0	0	0.0	12	8	3		12	0	0	37	6	6	0	1.9	.878	OF-26
1889		124	.291	.349	499	145	17	6	0	0.0	62	60	40	22	21	0	0	257	36	28	4	2.6	.913	OF-123, C-2, 3B-1, 2B-1
1890		130	.289	.386	557	161	27	9	3	0.5	101	29		45	40	0	0	233	25	22	5	2.2	.921	OF-127, SS-2, 3B-1
1891		135	.283	.358	565	160	25	7	1	0.2	76	55	33	23	30	0	0	310	35	16	7	2.7	.956	OF-132, C-4
1892 LOU	N	138	.254	.296	551	140	15	4	0	0.0	58	57	40	17	30	0	0	245	36	36	5	2.3	.886	OF-122, C-15, 1B-10
1893		106	.292	.376	439	128	17	7	2	0.5	79	49	27	12	17	0	0	208	37	19	6	2.5	.928	OF-85, C-21
1894 2 teams			LOU	N	(64G – .221)			PIT	N	(30G – .348)														
" total		94	.262	.343	359	94	12	4	3	0.8	35	48	13	12	7	1	0	264	75	26	15	3.9	.929	OF-36, C-31, SS-12, 1B-10, 3B-5, 2B-1
7 yrs.		753	.278	.348	3082	856	114	38	9	0.3	423	277	185	86	162	1	0	1554	250	153	41	2.6	.922	OF-651, C-73, 1B-20, SS-14, 3B-7, 2B-2

Jim Weaver

WEAVER, JAMES FRANCIS
B. Oct. 10, 1959, Kingston, N. Y.

BL TL 6'4"   190 lbs.

Year	Team	Games	BA	SA	AB	H	2B	3B	HR	HR%	R	RBI	BB	SO	SB	AB	H	PO	A	E	DP	TC/G	FA	G by Pos
1985 DET	A	12	.143	.286	7	1	1	0	0	0.0	2	0	1	4	0	2	0	1	0	0	0	0.1	1.000	DH-4, OF-4
1987 SEA	A	7	.000	.000	4	0	0	0	0	0.0	2	0	2	3	1	1	0	4	1	0	0	0.7	1.000	OF-4
1989 SF	N	12	.200	.350	20	4	3	0	0	0.0	2	2	0	7	1	2	0	7	0	0	0	0.6	1.000	OF-8
3 yrs.		31	.161	.290	31	5	4	0	0	0.0	6	2	3	14	2	5	0	12	1	0	0	0.4	1.000	OF-16, DH-4

Billy Webb

WEBB, WILLIAM JOSEPH
B. June 25, 1895, Chicago, Ill.   D. Jan. 12, 1943, Chicago, Ill.

BR TR 5'10"   161 lbs.

Year	Team	Games	BA	SA	AB	H	2B	3B	HR	HR%	R	RBI	BB	SO	SB	AB	H	PO	A	E	DP	TC/G	FA	G by Pos
1917 PIT	N	5	.200	.200	15	3	0	0	0	0.0	1	0	2	3	0	0	0	9	13	1	1	4.6	.957	2B-4, SS-1

Earl Webb

WEBB, WILLIAM EARL
B. Sept. 17, 1898, Bon Air, Tenn.   D. May 23, 1965, Jamestown, Tenn.

BL TR 6'1"   185 lbs.

Year	Team	Games	BA	SA	AB	H	2B	3B	HR	HR%	R	RBI	BB	SO	SB	AB	H	PO	A	E	DP	TC/G	FA	G by Pos
1925 NY	N	4	.000	.000	3	0	0	0	0	0.0	0	0	0	0	0	0	0	0	0	0	0	0.0	—	
1927 CHI	N	102	.301	.506	332	100	18	4	14	4.2	58	52	48	31	3	15	3	171	14	8	5	1.9	.959	OF-86
1928		62	.250	.407	140	35	7	3	3	2.1	22	23	14	17	0	24	8	65	4	1	0	1.1	.986	OF-31
1930 BOS	A	127	.323	.523	449	145	30	6	16	3.6	61	66	44	56	2	8	2	200	8	9	4	1.7	.959	OF-116
1931		151	.333	.528	589	196	67	3	14	2.4	96	103	70	51	2	0	0	270	21	16	5	2.0	.948	OF-151
1932 2 teams			BOS	A	(52G – .281)			DET	A	(87G – .287)														
" total		139	.285	.417	530	151	28	9	8	1.5	72	78	64	33	1	1	0	251	16	12	4	2.0	.957	OF-134, 1B-2
1933 2 teams			DET	A	(6G – .273)			CHI	A	(58G – .290)														
" total		64	.288	.356	118	34	5	0	1	0.8	17	11	19	13	0	30	8	129	5	7	8	2.2	.950	OF-18, 1B-10
7 yrs.		649	.306	.478	2161	661	155	25	56	2.6	326	333	260	202	8	81	21	1086	68	53	26	1.9	.956	OF-536, 1B-12

Skeeter Webb

WEBB, JAMES LAVERNE
B. Nov. 4, 1909, Meridian, Miss.   D. July 8, 1986, Meridian, Miss.

BR TR 5'9½"   150 lbs.

Year	Team	Games	BA	SA	AB	H	2B	3B	HR	HR%	R	RBI	BB	SO	SB	AB	H	PO	A	E	DP	TC/G	FA	G by Pos
1932 STL	N	1	—	—	0	0	0	0	0		0	0	0	0	0	0	0	0	0	0	0	0.0	—	SS-1
1938 CLE	A	20	.276	.310	58	16	2	0	0	0.0	11	2	8	7	1	0	0	29	32	4	7	3.3	.938	SS-13, 3B-3, 2B-2
1939		81	.264	.346	269	71	14	1	2	0.7	28	26	15	24	1	0	0	165	203	27	40	4.9	.932	SS-81
1940 CHI	A	84	.237	.290	334	79	11	2	1	0.3	33	29	30	33	3	2	0	152	247	13	46	4.9	.968	2B-74, SS-7, 3B-1
1941		29	.190	.214	84	16	2	0	0	0.0	7	6	3	9	1	3	1	55	64	10	13	4.4	.922	2B-18, SS-5, 3B-3
1942		32	.170	.213	94	16	2	1	0	0.0	5	4	4	13	1	0	0	62	87	6	14	4.8	.961	2B-29
1943		58	.235	.277	213	50	5	2	0	0.0	15	22	6	19	5	3	0	118	169	14	35	5.2	.953	2B-54
1944		139	.211	.271	513	108	19	6	0	0.0	44	30	20	39	7	0	0	221	480	39	88	5.3	.947	SS-135, 2B-5
1945 DET	A	118	.199	.238	407	81	12	2	0	0.0	43	21	30	35	8	0	0	245	368	25	79	5.4	.961	SS-104, 2B-11
1946		64	.219	.237	169	37	1	1	0	0.0	12	17	9	18	3	1	0	105	155	7	30	4.2	.974	2B-50, SS-8
1947		50	.203	.241	79	16	3	0	0	0.0	13	6	7	9	2	2	0	52	78	2	10	2.6	.985	2B-30, SS-6
1948 PHI	A	23	.148	.185	54	8	2	0	0	0.0	5	0	0	9	0	0	0	24	42	2	12	3.0	.971	2B-9, SS-8
12 yrs.		699	.219	.268	2274	498	73	15	3	0.1	216	166	132	215	33	11	1	1228	1925	149	374	4.7	.955	SS-368, 2B-282, 3B-7

WORLD SERIES

Year	Team	Games	BA	SA	AB	H	2B	3B	HR	HR%	R	RBI	BB	SO	SB	AB	H	PO	A	E	DP	TC/G	FA	G by Pos
1945 DET	A	7	.185	.185	27	5	0	0	0	0.0	4	1	3	1	0	0	0	9	24	1	3	4.9	.971	SS-7

Joe Webber

WEBBER, JOSEPH EDWARD
B. 1861, Hamilton, Ontario, Canada   D. Dec. 15, 1921, Hamilton, Ont., Canada

Year	Team	Games	BA	SA	AB	H	2B	3B	HR	HR%	R	RBI	BB	SO	SB	AB	H	PO	A	E	DP	TC/G	FA	G by Pos
1884 IND	AA	3	.000	.000	8	0	0	0	0	0.0	0		0		0	0	0	17	10	7	0	11.3	.794	C-3

Harry Weber

WEBER, HARRY
B. Indianapolis, Ind.   Deceased.

Year	Team	Games	BA	SA	AB	H	2B	3B	HR	HR%	R	RBI	BB	SO	SB	AB	H	PO	A	E	DP	TC/G	FA	G by Pos
1884 DET	N	2	.000	.000	8	0	0	0	0	0.0	0		0	2	0	0	0	2	1	0	0	2.0	.750	OF-2

Lenny Webster

WEBSTER, LEONARD IRELL
B. Feb. 10, 1965, New Orleans, La.

BR TR 5'9"   185 lbs.

Year	Team	Games	BA	SA	AB	H	2B	3B	HR	HR%	R	RBI	BB	SO	SB	AB	H	PO	A	E	DP	TC/G	FA	G by Pos
1989 MIN	A	14	.300	.400	20	6	2	0	0	0.0	3	1	3	2	0	1	1	32	0	0	0	2.3	1.000	C-14

Year	Team	Games	BA	SA	AB	H	2B	3B	HR	HR%	R	RBI	BB	SO	SB	Pinch Hit AB	Pinch Hit H	PO	A	E	DP	TC/G	FA	G by Pos

Mitch Webster

WEBSTER, MITCHELL DEAN
B. May 16, 1959, Larned, Kans. — BB TL 6'½" 170 lbs.

Year	Team	Games	BA	SA	AB	H	2B	3B	HR	HR%	R	RBI	BB	SO	SB	PH AB	PH H	PO	A	E	DP	TC/G	FA	G by Pos
1983	TOR A	11	.182	.182	11	2	0	0	0	0.0	2	0	1	1	0	1	0	5	0	0	0	0.5	1.000	OF-7, DH-2
1984		26	.227	.409	22	5	2	1	0	0.0	9	4	1	7	0	7	1	16	0	2	1	0.7	.889	OF-10, DH-9, 1B-1
1985	2 teams				TOR A (4G – .000)				MON N (74G – .274)															
"	total	78	.272	.484	213	58	8	2	11	5.2	32	30	20	33	15	9	1	133	3	1	0	1.8	.993	OF-66, DH-2
1986	MON N	151	.290	.431	576	167	31	13	8	1.4	89	49	57	78	36	4	1	325	12	8	3	2.3	.977	OF-146
1987		156	.281	.435	588	165	30	8	15	2.6	101	63	70	95	33	7	4	266	8	5	0	1.8	.982	OF-153
1988	2 teams				MON N (81G – .255)				CHI N (70G – .265)															
"	total	151	.260	.356	523	136	16	8	6	1.1	69	39	55	87	22	17	3	322	3	6	0	2.2	.982	OF-136
1989	CHI N	98	.257	.364	272	70	12	4	3	1.1	40	19	30	55	14	30	4	161	3	6	0	1.7	.965	OF-74
7 yrs.		671	.273	.410	2205	603	99	36	43	2.0	342	204	234	356	120	75	14	1228	29	28	4	1.9	.978	OF-592, DH-13, 1B-1

LEAGUE CHAMPIONSHIP SERIES

Year	Team	Games	BA	SA	AB	H	2B	3B	HR	HR%	R	RBI	BB	SO	SB	PH AB	PH H	PO	A	E	DP	TC/G	FA	G by Pos
1989	CHI N	3	.333	.333	3	1	0	0	0	0.0	0	0	0	0	0	1	0	0	0	0	0	0.0	–	OF-2

Ramon Webster

WEBSTER, RAMON ALBERTO
B. Aug. 31, 1942, Colon, Panama — BL TL 6' 185 lbs.

Year	Team	Games	BA	SA	AB	H	2B	3B	HR	HR%	R	RBI	BB	SO	SB	PH AB	PH H	PO	A	E	DP	TC/G	FA	G by Pos
1967	KC A	122	.256	.411	360	92	15	4	11	3.1	41	51	32	44	5	26	5	639	43	8	43	5.7	.988	1B-83, OF-15
1968	OAK A	66	.214	.327	196	42	11	1	3	1.5	17	23	12	24	3	11	6	454	27	6	33	7.4	.988	1B-55
1969		64	.260	.325	77	20	0	1	1	1.3	5	13	12	12	1	39	10	89	8	0	6	1.5	1.000	1B-13
1970	SD N	95	.259	.336	116	30	3	0	2	1.7	12	11	11	12	1	70	17	99	7	2	14	1.1	.981	1B-15, OF-1
1971	3 teams				SD N (10G – .125)				CHI N (16G – .313)				OAK A (7G – .000)											
"	total	33	.207	.276	29	6	2	0	0	0.0	1	0	3	6	0	27	4	3	1	0	1	0.1	1.000	1B-2
5 yrs.		380	.244	.365	778	190	31	6	17	2.2	76	98	70	94	9	173	42	1284	86	16	97	3.6	.988	1B-168, OF-16

Ray Webster

WEBSTER, RAYMOND GEORGE
B. Nov. 15, 1937, Grass Valley, Calif. — BR TR 6' 175 lbs.

Year	Team	Games	BA	SA	AB	H	2B	3B	HR	HR%	R	RBI	BB	SO	SB	PH AB	PH H	PO	A	E	DP	TC/G	FA	G by Pos
1959	CLE A	40	.203	.338	74	15	1	2	2	2.7	10	10	5	7	1	8	1	34	45	8	13	2.2	.908	2B-24, 3B-4
1960	BOS A	7	.000	.000	3	0	0	0	0	0.0	1	1	1	0	0	3	0	1	1	0	1	0.3	1.000	2B-1
2 yrs.		47	.195	.325	77	15	2	1	2	2.6	11	11	6	7	1	11	1	35	46	8	14	1.9	.910	2B-25, 3B-4

Pete Weckbecker

WECKBECKER, PETER
B. Aug. 30, 1864, Butler, Pa. D. May 16, 1935, Hampton, Va. — 5'7" 150 lbs.

Year	Team	Games	BA	SA	AB	H	2B	3B	HR	HR%	R	RBI	BB	SO	SB	PH AB	PH H	PO	A	E	DP	TC/G	FA	G by Pos
1889	IND N	1	.000	.000	1	0	0	0	0	0.0	0	0	0	0	0			2	0	0	0	2.0	1.000	C-1
1890	LOU AA	32	.238	.248	101	24	1	0	0	0.0	17	8	7	0	0			158	33	12	2	6.3	.941	C-32
2 yrs.		33	.235	.245	102	24	1	0	0	0.0	17	8	7	0	0			160	33	12	2	6.2	.941	C-33

Charlie Weeden

WEEDEN, CHARLES ALBERT
B. Dec. 21, 1882, Northwood, N. H. D. Jan. 7, 1939, Northwood, N. H. — BL TL 6' 200 lbs.

Year	Team	Games	BA	SA	AB	H	2B	3B	HR	HR%	R	RBI	BB	SO	SB	PH AB	PH H	PO	A	E	DP	TC/G	FA	G by Pos
1911	BOS N	1	.000	.000	1	0	0	0	0	0.0	0	0	0	0	0	1	0	0	0	0	0	0.0	–	

Johnny Weekly

WEEKLY, JOHNNY
B. June 14, 1937, Waterproof, La. D. Nov. 24, 1974, Walnut Creek, Calif. — BR TR 6' 200 lbs.

Year	Team	Games	BA	SA	AB	H	2B	3B	HR	HR%	R	RBI	BB	SO	SB	PH AB	PH H	PO	A	E	DP	TC/G	FA	G by Pos
1962	HOU N	13	.192	.462	26	5	1	0	2	7.7	3	2	7	4	0	6	1	8	0	0	0	0.6	1.000	OF-7
1963		34	.225	.375	80	18	3	0	3	3.8	4	14	7	14	0	12	3	36	2	0	0	1.1	1.000	OF-23
1964		6	.133	.133	15	2	0	0	0	0.0	0	3	1	3	0	1	0	9	1	0	0	1.7	1.000	OF-5
3 yrs.		53	.207	.364	121	25	4	0	5	4.1	7	19	15	21	0	19	4	53	3	0	0	1.1	1.000	OF-35

Stump Weidman

WEIDMAN, GEORGE EDWARD
B. Feb. 17, 1861, Rochester, N. Y. D. Mar. 3, 1905, New York, N. Y. — BR TR

Year	Team	Games	BA	SA	AB	H	2B	3B	HR	HR%	R	RBI	BB	SO	SB	PH AB	PH H	PO	A	E	DP	TC/G	FA	G by Pos
1880	BUF N	23	.103	.115	78	8	1	0	0	0.0	8	3	2	11				21	20	5	0	2.0	.891	P-17, OF-13
1881	DET N	13	.255	.277	47	12	1	0	0	0.0	8	5	2	2				3	15	0	0	1.4	1.000	P-13
1882		50	.218	.264	193	42	7	1	0	0.0	20	20	2	19				39	76	12	2	2.5	.906	P-46, OF-6, SS-1
1883		79	.185	.220	313	58	6	1	0	0.3	34		4	38				81	94	26	4	2.5	.871	P-52, OF-35, 2B-4
1884		81	.163	.183	300	49	6	0	0	0.0	24		13	41				89	62	37	3	2.3	.803	OF-53, P-26, SS-1, 2B-1
1885		44	.157	.203	153	24	2	1	1	0.7	7	14	8	32				19	60	18	1	2.2	.814	OF-38, P-38, 2B-1
1886	KC N	51	.168	.179	179	30	2	0	0	0.0	20	7	5	46				26	106	9	5	2.8	.936	P-51, OF-3
1887	3 teams				DET N (21G – .207)				NY AA (14G – .152)				NY N (1G – .333)											
"	total	36	.191	.229	131	25	3	1	0	0.0	17	11	7	3	8			20	59	13	2	2.6	.859	P-34, OF-5
1888	NY N	2	.000	.000	7	0	0	0	0	0.0	0	0	1	1	2			3	2	2	0	3.5	.714	P-2
9 yrs.		379	.177	.207	1401	248	28	4	2	0.1	132	61	45	193	8			301	494	122	15	2.4	.867	P-279, OF-153, 2B-6, SS-2

Ralph Weigel

WEIGEL, RALPH RICHARD (Wig)
B. Oct. 2, 1921, Coldwater, Ohio — BR TR 6'1" 180 lbs.

Year	Team	Games	BA	SA	AB	H	2B	3B	HR	HR%	R	RBI	BB	SO	SB	PH AB	PH H	PO	A	E	DP	TC/G	FA	G by Pos
1946	CLE A	6	.167	.167	12	2	0	0	0	0.0	0	0	0	1	0			16	0	0	0	2.7	1.000	C-6
1948	CHI A	66	.233	.313	163	38	7	3	0	0.0	8	26	13	18	1	24	6	109	19	4	4	2.0	.970	C-39, OF-2
1949	WAS A	34	.233	.267	60	14	2	0	0	0.0	4	4	8	6	0	12	2	55	9	1	4	1.9	.985	C-21
3 yrs.		106	.230	.294	235	54	9	3	0	0.0	12	30	21	26	2	36	8	180	28	5	8	2.0	.977	C-66, OF-2

Podgie Weihe

WEIHE, JOHN GARIBALDI
B. Nov. 13, 1862, Cincinnati, Ohio D. Apr. 15, 1914, Cincinnati, Ohio — BR TR 5'11" 175 lbs.

Year	Team	Games	BA	SA	AB	H	2B	3B	HR	HR%	R	RBI	BB	SO	SB	PH AB	PH H	PO	A	E	DP	TC/G	FA	G by Pos
1883	CIN AA	1	.250	.250	4	1	0	0	0	0.0	1		0			0	0	4	0	0	0	4.0	1.000	OF-1
1884	IND AA	63	.254	.367	256	65	13	2	4	1.6	29		9			0	0	110	26	24	4	2.5	.850	OF-58, 2B-4, 1B-3
2 yrs.		64	.254	.365	260	66	13	2	4	1.5	30		9			0	0	114	26	24	4	2.6	.854	OF-59, 2B-4, 1B-3

Elmer Weingartner

WEINGARTNER, ELMER WILLIAM (Dutch)
B. Aug. 13, 1918, Cleveland, Ohio — BR TR 5'11" 178 lbs.

Year	Team	Games	BA	SA	AB	H	2B	3B	HR	HR%	R	RBI	BB	SO	SB	PH AB	PH H	PO	A	E	DP	TC/G	FA	G by Pos
1945	CLE A	20	.231	.256	39	9	1	0	0	0.0	5	1	4	11	0	0	0	29	32	9	7	3.5	.871	SS-20

Year	Team	Games	BA	SA	AB	H	2B	3B	HR	HR%	R	RBI	BB	SO	SB	Pinch Hit AB	Pinch Hit H	PO	A	E	DP	TC/G	FA	G by Pos

Phil Weintraub

WEINTRAUB, PHILIP
B. Oct. 12, 1907, Chicago, Ill.   D. June 21, 1987, Palm Springs, Calif.

BL TL 6'1"   195 lbs.

Year	Team	Games	BA	SA	AB	H	2B	3B	HR	HR%	R	RBI	BB	SO	SB	PH AB	PH H	PO	A	E	DP	TC/G	FA	G by Pos
1933	NY N	8	.200	.400	15	3	0	0	1	6.7	3	1	3	2	0	1	1	4	0	2	0	0.8	.667	OF-6
1934		31	.351	.378	74	26	2	0	0	0.0	13	15	15	10	0	10	1	34	0	2	0	1.2	.944	OF-20
1935		64	.241	.348	112	27	3	3	1	0.9	18	6	17	13	0	29	5	152	11	4	9	2.6	.976	1B-19, OF-7
1937	2 teams	CIN N (49G – .271)			NY N (6G – .333)																			
"	total	55	.274	.430	186	51	12	4	3	1.6	30	21	20	26	1	6	1	79	3	2	1	1.5	.976	OF-48
1938	PHI N	100	.311	.422	351	109	23	2	4	1.1	51	45	64	43	1	2	0	913	75	12	70	10.0	.988	1B-98
1944	NY N	104	.316	.524	361	114	18	9	13	3.6	55	77	59	59	0	5	2	928	72	8	72	9.7	.992	1B-99
1945		82	.272	.417	283	77	9	1	10	3.5	45	42	54	29	2	4	1	774	60	6	49	10.2	.993	1B-77
7 yrs.		444	.295	.440	1382	407	67	19	32	2.3	215	207	232	182	4	57	11	2884	221	36	201	7.1	.989	1B-293, OF-81

Al Weis

WEIS, ALBERT JOHN
B. Apr. 2, 1938, Franklin Square, N. Y.

BB TR 6'   160 lbs.
BR 1969-71

Year	Team	Games	BA	SA	AB	H	2B	3B	HR	HR%	R	RBI	BB	SO	SB	PH AB	PH H	PO	A	E	DP	TC/G	FA	G by Pos
1962	CHI A	7	.083	.083	12	1	0	0	0	0.0	2	0	3	1	0	0	0	3	13	3	0	2.7	.842	SS-4, 3B-1, 2B-1
1963		99	.271	.314	210	57	9	0	0	0.0	41	18	18	37	15	9	2	123	168	10	41	3.0	.967	2B-48, SS-27, 3B-1
1964		133	.247	.302	328	81	4	4	2	0.6	36	23	22	41	22	6	1	205	267	21	65	3.7	.957	2B-116, SS-9, OF-2
1965		103	.296	.393	135	40	4	3	1	0.7	29	12	12	22	4	6	2	117	130	6	31	2.5	.976	2B-74, SS-7, OF-2, 3B-2
1966		129	.155	.187	187	29	4	1	0	0.0	20	9	17	50	3	0	0	151	218	10	52	2.9	.974	2B-96, SS-18
1967		50	.245	.283	53	13	2	0	0	0.0	9	4	1	7	3	0	0	30	62	1	5	1.9	.989	SS-33, 2B-13
1968	NY N	90	.172	.204	274	47	6	0	1	0.4	15	14	21	63	11	4	0	138	244	14	43	4.4	.965	SS-59, 2B-29, 3B-2
1969		103	.215	.291	247	53	9	2	2	0.8	20	23	15	51	3	3	0	138	218	13	50	3.6	.965	SS-52, 2B-43, 3B-1
1970		75	.207	.306	121	25	7	1	1	0.8	20	11	7	21	1	2	0	75	81	8	13	2.2	.951	2B-44, SS-15
1971		11	.000	.000	11	0	0	0	0	0.0	3	1	2	4	0	4	0	5	6	0	2	1.0	1.000	2B-5, 3B-2
10 yrs.		800	.219	.275	1578	346	45	11	7	0.4	195	115	117	299	55	33	5	985	1407	86	302	3.1	.965	2B-488, SS-204, 3B-9, OF-4

LEAGUE CHAMPIONSHIP SERIES

Year	Team	Games	BA	SA	AB	H	2B	3B	HR	HR%	R	RBI	BB	SO	SB	PH AB	PH H	PO	A	E	DP	TC/G	FA	G by Pos
1969	NY N	3	.000	.000	1	0	0	0	0	0.0	0	0	0	0	0	0	0	1	3	0	1	1.3	1.000	2B-3

WORLD SERIES

Year	Team	Games	BA	SA	AB	H	2B	3B	HR	HR%	R	RBI	BB	SO	SB	PH AB	PH H	PO	A	E	DP	TC/G	FA	G by Pos
1969	NY N	5	.455	.727	11	5	0	0	1	9.1	1	3	4	2	0	0	0	8	5	1	0	2.8	.929	2B-5

Butch Weis

WEIS, ARTHUR JOHN
B. Mar. 2, 1903, St. Louis, Mo.

BL TL 5'11"   180 lbs.

Year	Team	Games	BA	SA	AB	H	2B	3B	HR	HR%	R	RBI	BB	SO	SB	PH AB	PH H	PO	A	E	DP	TC/G	FA	G by Pos
1922	CHI N	2	.500	.500	2	1	0	0	0	0.0	2	0	0	0	0	2	1	0	0	0	0	0.4	1.000	OF-6
1923		22	.231	.269	26	6	1	0	0	0.0	5	2	5	8	0	13	3	9	0	0	0	0.4	1.000	OF-6
1924		39	.278	.353	133	37	8	1	0	0.0	19	23	15	14	4	1	1	81	8	2	2	2.3	.978	OF-36
1925		67	.267	.361	180	48	5	3	2	1.1	16	25	23	22	2	20	3	78	3	3	0	1.3	.964	OF-46
4 yrs.		130	.270	.352	341	92	14	4	2	0.6	39	50	43	44	4	36	8	168	11	5	2	1.4	.973	OF-88

Bud Weiser

WEISER, HARRY BUDSON
B. Jan. 8, 1891, Shamokin, Pa.   D. July 31, 1961, Shamokin, Pa.

BR TR 5'11"   165 lbs.

Year	Team	Games	BA	SA	AB	H	2B	3B	HR	HR%	R	RBI	BB	SO	SB	PH AB	PH H	PO	A	E	DP	TC/G	FA	G by Pos
1915	PHI N	37	.141	.172	64	9	2	0	0	0.0	6	8	7	12	2	8	3	26	0	3	0	0.8	.897	OF-20
1916		4	.300	.400	10	3	1	0	0	0.0	1	1	0	3	0	0	0	5	0	0	0	1.3	1.000	OF-4
2 yrs.		41	.162	.203	74	12	3	0	0	0.0	7	9	7	15	2	8	3	31	0	3	0	0.8	.912	OF-24

Gary Weiss

WEISS, GARY LEE
B. Dec. 27, 1955, Brenham, Tex.

BB TR 5'10"   170 lbs.

Year	Team	Games	BA	SA	AB	H	2B	3B	HR	HR%	R	RBI	BB	SO	SB	PH AB	PH H	PO	A	E	DP	TC/G	FA	G by Pos
1980	LA N	8	–	–	0	0	0	0	0	–	0	0	0	0	0	0	0	0	0	0	0	0.0	–	
1981		14	.105	.105	19	2	0	0	0	0.0	2	1	1	4	0	1	0	12	11	2	8	1.8	.920	SS-13
2 yrs.		22	.105	.105	19	2	0	0	0	0.0	4	1	1	4	0	1	0	12	11	2	8	1.1	.920	SS-13

Joe Weiss

WEISS, JOSEPH HAROLD
B. Jan. 27, 1894, Chicago, Ill.   D. July 7, 1967, Cedar Rapids, Iowa

BR TR 6'   175 lbs.

Year	Team	Games	BA	SA	AB	H	2B	3B	HR	HR%	R	RBI	BB	SO	SB	PH AB	PH H	PO	A	E	DP	TC/G	FA	G by Pos
1915	CHI F	29	.224	.282	85	19	1	2	0	0.0	6	11	3		0	0	0	239	10	2	7	8.7	.992	1B-29

Walt Weiss

WEISS, WALTER WILLIAM
B. Nov. 28, 1963, Tuxedo, N. Y.

BB TR 6'   175 lbs.

Year	Team	Games	BA	SA	AB	H	2B	3B	HR	HR%	R	RBI	BB	SO	SB	PH AB	PH H	PO	A	E	DP	TC/G	FA	G by Pos
1987	OAK A	16	.462	.615	26	12	4	0	0	0.0	3	1	2	2	1	1	0	8	30	1	4	2.4	.974	SS-11
1988		147	.250	.321	452	113	17	3	3	0.7	44	39	35	56	4	1	0	254	431	15	83	4.8	.979	SS-147
1989		84	.233	.318	236	55	11	0	3	1.3	30	21	21	39	6	0	0	106	195	15	44	3.8	.953	SS-84
3 yrs.		247	.252	.331	714	180	32	3	6	0.8	77	61	58	97	11	2	0	368	656	31	131	4.3	.971	SS-242

LEAGUE CHAMPIONSHIP SERIES

Year	Team	Games	BA	SA	AB	H	2B	3B	HR	HR%	R	RBI	BB	SO	SB	PH AB	PH H	PO	A	E	DP	TC/G	FA	G by Pos
1988	OAK A	4	.333	.467	15	5	2	0	0	0.0	2	2	0	4	0	0	0	7	10	0	3	4.3	1.000	SS-4
1989		4	.111	.222	9	1	1	0	0	0.0	2	0	1	1	0	0	0	5	9	0	2	3.5	1.000	SS-4
2 yrs.		8	.250	.375	24	6	3	0	0	0.0	4	2	1	5	0	0	0	12	19	0	5	3.9	1.000	SS-8

WORLD SERIES

Year	Team	Games	BA	SA	AB	H	2B	3B	HR	HR%	R	RBI	BB	SO	SB	PH AB	PH H	PO	A	E	DP	TC/G	FA	G by Pos
1988	OAK A	5	.063	.063	16	1	0	0	0	0.0	1	0	2	2	1	0	0	5	11	1	1	3.4	.941	SS-5
1989		4	.133	.333	15	2	0	0	1	6.7	3	1	2	2	0	0	0	7	8	0	1	3.8	1.000	SS-4
2 yrs.		9	.097	.194	31	3	0	0	1	3.2	4	1	2	4	1	0	0	12	19	1	2	3.6	.969	SS-9

Johnny Welaj

WELAJ, JOHN LUDWIG
B. May 27, 1914, Moss Creek, Pa.

BR TR 6'   164 lbs.

Year	Team	Games	BA	SA	AB	H	2B	3B	HR	HR%	R	RBI	BB	SO	SB	PH AB	PH H	PO	A	E	DP	TC/G	FA	G by Pos
1939	WAS A	63	.274	.363	201	55	11	2	1	0.5	23	33	13	20	13	7	2	113	2	3	1	1.9	.975	OF-55
1940		88	.256	.340	215	55	9	0	3	1.4	31	21	19	20	8	20	7	132	1	3	0	1.5	.978	OF-53
1941		49	.208	.250	96	20	4	0	0	0.0	16	5	6	16	3	22	7	47	0	1	0	1.0	.979	OF-19
1943	PHI A	93	.242	.306	281	68	16	1	0	0.0	45	15	15	17	12	10	1	187	3	8	0	2.1	.960	OF-72
4 yrs.		293	.250	.323	793	198	40	3	4	0.5	115	74	53	73	36	59	17	479	6	15	1	1.7	.970	OF-199

Year	Team	Games	BA	SA	AB	H	2B	3B	HR	HR%	R	RBI	BB	SO	SB	Pinch Hit AB	Pinch Hit H	PO	A	E	DP	TC/G	FA	G by Pos

Curt Welch

WELCH, CURTIS BENTON
B. Feb. 11, 1862, East Liverpool, Ohio   D. Aug. 29, 1896, East Liverpool, Ohio
BR TR 5'10" 175 lbs.

Year	Team	Games	BA	SA	AB	H	2B	3B	HR	HR%	R	RBI	BB	SO	SB	PH AB	PH H	PO	A	E	DP	TC/G	FA	G by Pos
1884	TOL AA	109	.224	.304	425	95	24	5	0	0.0	61		10			0	0	212	29	31	4	2.5	.886	OF-106, 2B-2, C-2, 1B-1, P-1
1885	STL AA	112	.271	.363	432	117	18	8	2	0.5	84		23			0	0	236	25	15	5	2.5	.946	OF-112
1886		138	.281	.393	563	158	31	13	2	0.4	114		29			0	0	300	19	18	5	2.4	.947	OF-138, 2B-2
1887		131	.278	.379	544	151	32	7	3	0.6	98		25		89	0	0	370	47	35	10	3.5	.923	OF-123, 2B-8, 1B-1
1888	PHI AA	136	.282	.357	549	155	22	8	1	0.2	125	61	33		95	0	0	277	25	19	6	2.4	.941	OF-135, 2B-3
1889		125	.271	.370	516	140	39	6	0	0.0	134	39	67	30	66	0	0	282	29	26	10	2.7	.923	OF-125
1890	2 teams	122	.248	.332	PHI AA (103G – .268) BAL AA (19G – .132)																			
"	total	122	.248	.332	464	115	25	4	2	0.4	116		58		72	0	0	269	28	23	9	2.6	.928	OF-120, 1B-2, P-1
1891	BAL AA	132	.268	.368	514	138	22	10	3	0.6	122	55	77	42	50	0	0	306	103	24	18	3.3	.945	OF-113, 2B-21, SS-2
1892	2 teams	88	.227	.278	BAL N (63G – .236) CIN N (25G – .202)																			
"	total	88	.227	.278	331	75	1	5	2	0.6	56	29	43	17	21	0	0	189	6	19	2	2.4	.911	OF-88
1893	LOU N	14	.170	.191	47	8	1	0	0	0.0	5	2	16	4	1	0	0	29	2	3	0	2.4	.912	OF-14
10 yrs.		1107	.263	.352	4385	1152	215	66	15	0.3	915	186	381	93	394	0	0	2470	313	213	69	2.7	.929	OF-1074, 2B-36, 1B-4, SS-2, C-2, P-2

Frank Welch

WELCH, FRANK TIGUER (Bugger)
B. Aug. 10, 1897, Birmingham, Ala.   D. July 25, 1957, Birmingham, Ala.
BR TR 5'9" 175 lbs.

Year	Team	Games	BA	SA	AB	H	2B	3B	HR	HR%	R	RBI	BB	SO	SB	PH AB	PH H	PO	A	E	DP	TC/G	FA	G by Pos
1919	PHI A	15	.167	.333	54	9	1	1	2	3.7	5	7	7	10	0	0	0	38	2	4	0	2.9	.909	OF-15
1920		100	.258	.367	360	93	17	5	4	1.1	43	40	26	41	2	3	0	194	14	14	4	2.2	.937	OF-97
1921		115	.285	.412	403	115	18	6	7	1.7	48	45	34	43	6	10	4	251	16	16	1	2.5	.943	OF-104
1922		114	.259	.408	375	97	17	3	11	2.9	43	49	40	40	3	9	4	191	12	11	2	1.9	.949	OF-104
1923		125	.297	.413	421	125	19	9	4	1.0	56	55	48	40	1	7	0	253	13	9	4	2.2	.967	OF-117
1924		94	.290	.399	293	85	13	6	5	1.7	47	31	35	27	2	20	7	120	15	2	2	1.5	.985	OF-74
1925		85	.277	.401	202	56	5	4	4	2.0	40	41	29	14	2	24	4	85	6	3	3	1.1	.968	OF-57
1926		75	.282	.408	174	49	8	1	4	2.3	26	23	26	9	2	19	3	75	4	2	1	1.1	.975	OF-49
1927	BOS A	15	.179	.250	28	5	2	0	0	0.0	2	4	5	1	0	8	1	9	3	0	1	0.8	1.000	OF-6
9 yrs.		738	.274	.398	2310	634	100	31	41	1.8	310	295	250	225	18	100	24	1216	85	61	18	1.8	.955	OF-623

Herb Welch

WELCH, HERBERT M. (Dutch)
B. Oct. 19, 1898, RoEllen, Tenn.   D. Apr. 13, 1967, Memphis, Tenn.
BL TR 5'6" 154 lbs.

Year	Team	Games	BA	SA	AB	H	2B	3B	HR	HR%	R	RBI	BB	SO	SB	PH AB	PH H	PO	A	E	DP	TC/G	FA	G by Pos
1925	BOS A	13	.289	.342	38	11	0	1	0	0.0	2	2	0	6	0	0	0	25	42	8	9	5.8	.893	SS-13

Mickey Welch

WELCH, MICHAEL FRANCIS (Smiling Mickey)
B. July 4, 1859, Brooklyn, N. Y.   D. July 30, 1941, Concord, N. H.
Hall of Fame 1973.
BR TR 5'8" 160 lbs.

Year	Team	Games	BA	SA	AB	H	2B	3B	HR	HR%	R	RBI	BB	SO	SB	PH AB	PH H	PO	A	E	DP	TC/G	FA	G by Pos
1880	TRO N	66	.287	.390	251	72	20	3	0	0.0	25	27	5	24	0	0	0	36	86	23	4	2.2	.841	P-65, OF-2
1881		40	.203	.270	148	30	10	0	0	0.0	12	11	1	16	0	0	0	20	39	7	3	1.7	.894	P-40
1882		38	.245	.305	151	37	6	0	1	0.7	26	17	5	16	0	0	0	15	46	11	4	1.9	.847	P-33, OF-8
1883	NY N	84	.234	.331	320	75	12	5	3	0.9	42	10	38	0	0	0	71	63	38	4	2.0	.779	P-54, OF-38
1884		71	.241	.357	249	60	14	3	3	1.2	47	16	49	0	0	0	25	78	14	6	1.6	.880	P-65, OF-7
1885		56	.206	.276	199	41	8	0	2	1.0	28	14	39	0	0	0	16	70	14	0	1.8	.860	P-56
1886		59	.216	.254	213	46	2	0	0	0.0	17	18	47	0	0	0	19	82	5	0	1.8	.953	P-59, OF-3
1887		40	.243	.338	148	36	4	2	2	1.4	16	15	6	1	2	0	0	17	51	12	0	2.0	.850	P-40, OF-1
1888		47	.189	.254	169	32	5	0	2	1.2	16	10	1	33	4	0	0	16	75	17	1	2.3	.843	P-47
1889		45	.192	.237	156	30	5	1	0	0.0	20	12	5	27	0	0	0	13	59	4	2	1.7	.947	P-45
1890		37	.179	.211	123	22	4	0	0	0.0	15	10	9	25	1	0	0	10	43	4	1	1.5	.930	P-37
1891		22	.141	.141	71	10	0	0	0	0.0	4	4	3	13	0	0	0	7	21	4	0	1.5	.875	P-22
1892		1	.333	.333	3	1	0	0	0	0.0	0	0	0	1	0	0	0	0	1	0	0	1.0	1.000	P-1
13 yrs.		606	.224	.298	2201	492	92	16	13	0.6	268	124	82	329	7	0	0	265	714	153	25	1.9	.865	P-564, OF-59

Milt Welch

WELCH, MILTON EDWARD
B. July 26, 1924, Farmersville, Ill.
BR TR 5'10" 175 lbs.

Year	Team	Games	BA	SA	AB	H	2B	3B	HR	HR%	R	RBI	BB	SO	SB	PH AB	PH H	PO	A	E	DP	TC/G	FA	G by Pos
1945	DET A	1	.000	.000	2	0	0	0	0	0.0	0	1	0	1	0	0	0	3	1	0	1	4.0	1.000	C-1

Harry Welchonce

WELCHONCE, HARRY MONROE
B. Nov. 20, 1883, North Point, Pa.   D. Feb. 26, 1977, Arcadia, Caiif.
BL TR 6' 170 lbs.

Year	Team	Games	BA	SA	AB	H	2B	3B	HR	HR%	R	RBI	BB	SO	SB	PH AB	PH H	PO	A	E	DP	TC/G	FA	G by Pos
1911	PHI N	26	.212	.273	66	14	4	0	0	0.0	9	6	7	8	0	9	3	25	1	2	0	1.1	.929	OF-17

Mike Welday

WELDAY, LYNDON EARL
B. Dec. 19, 1879, Conway, Iowa   D. May 28, 1942, Leavenworth, Kans.
BL TL

Year	Team	Games	BA	SA	AB	H	2B	3B	HR	HR%	R	RBI	BB	SO	SB	PH AB	PH H	PO	A	E	DP	TC/G	FA	G by Pos
1907	CHI A	24	.229	.314	35	8	1	1	0	0.0	2	0	6		0	6	1	13	2	1	0	0.7	.938	OF-15
1909		29	.189	.189	74	14	0	0	0	0.0	3	5	4		2	8	2	35	4	5	1	1.5	.886	OF-20
2 yrs.		53	.202	.229	109	22	1	1	0	0.0	5	5	10		2	14	3	48	6	6	1	1.1	.900	OF-35

Ollie Welf

WELF, OLIVER HENRY
B. Jan. 17, 1889, Cleveland, Ohio   D. June 15, 1967, Cleveland, Ohio
BR TL 5'9" 160 lbs.

Year	Team	Games	BA	SA	AB	H	2B	3B	HR	HR%	R	RBI	BB	SO	SB	PH AB	PH H	PO	A	E	DP	TC/G	FA	G by Pos
1916	CLE A	1	–	–	0	0	0	0	0	–	0	0	0	0	0	0	0	0	0	0	0	0.0	–	

Bob Wellman

WELLMAN, ROBERT JOSEPH
B. July 15, 1925, Norwood, Ohio
BR TR 6'4" 210 lbs.

Year	Team	Games	BA	SA	AB	H	2B	3B	HR	HR%	R	RBI	BB	SO	SB	PH AB	PH H	PO	A	E	DP	TC/G	FA	G by Pos
1948	PHI A	4	.200	.400	10	2	0	1	0	0.0	1	0	3	2	0	1	0	26	1	1	2	7.0	.964	1B-2, OF-1
1950		11	.333	.533	15	5	0	0	1	6.7	1	1	0	3	0	8	2	4	0	0	0	0.4	1.000	OF-2
2 yrs.		15	.280	.480	25	7	0	1	1	4.0	2	1	3	5	0	9	2	30	1	1	2	2.1	.969	OF-3, 1B-2

Brad Wellman

WELLMAN, BRAD EUGENE
B. Aug. 17, 1959, Lodi, Calif.
BR TR 6' 165 lbs.

Year	Team	Games	BA	SA	AB	H	2B	3B	HR	HR%	R	RBI	BB	SO	SB	PH AB	PH H	PO	A	E	DP	TC/G	FA	G by Pos
1982	SF N	6	.250	.250	4	1	0	0	0	0.0	1	0	0	1	0	2	0	0	1	0	0	0.2	1.000	2B-2
1983		82	.214	.247	182	39	3	0	1	0.5	15	16	22	39	5	4	0	94	167	9	27	3.3	.967	2B-74, SS-2

Year	Team		Games	BA	SA	AB	H	2B	3B	HR	HR%	R	RBI	BB	SO	SB	Pinch Hit AB	H	PO	A	E	DP	TC/G	FA	G by Pos

Brad Wellman *continued*

Year	Team		Games	BA	SA	AB	H	2B	3B	HR	HR%	R	RBI	BB	SO	SB	AB	H	PO	A	E	DP	TC/G	FA	G by Pos
1984			93	.226	.291	265	60	9	1	2	0.8	23	25	19	41	10	6	3	151	258	11	37	4.5	.974	2B-54, SS-33, 3B-10
1985			71	.236	.310	174	41	11	1	0	0.0	16	16	4	33	5	6	1	66	107	9	15	2.6	.951	2B-36, 3B-25, SS-3
1986			12	.154	.154	13	2	0	0	0	0.0	0	1	1	2	0	2	1	3	10	0	1	1.1	1.000	SS-8, 3B-1, 2B-1
1987	LA	N	3	.250	.250	4	1	0	0	0	0.0	1	1	0	1	0	1	0	3	3	0	1	2.0	1.000	SS-1, 3B-1, 2B-1
1988	KC	A	71	.271	.327	107	29	3	0	1	0.9	11	6	6	23	1	2	1	67	101	6	27	2.5	.966	2B-46, SS-15, 3B-4
1989			103	.230	.287	178	41	4	0	2	1.1	30	12	7	36	5	1	0	104	184	2	42	2.8	.993	2B-64, SS-34, 3B-3, DH-1
8 yrs.			441	.231	.287	927	214	30	2	6	0.6	97	77	59	176	26	23	6	488	831	37	150	3.1	.973	2B-278, SS-96, 3B-44, DH-1

Boomer Wells

WELLS, GREGORY DeWAYNE
B. Apr. 25, 1954, McIntosh, Ala.

BR TR 6'5" 218 lbs.

Year	Team		Games	BA	SA	AB	H	2B	3B	HR	HR%	R	RBI	BB	SO	SB	AB	H	PO	A	E	DP	TC/G	FA	G by Pos
1981	TOR	A	32	.247	.315	73	18	5	0	0	0.0	7	5	5	12	0	8	3	146	10	1	10	4.9	.994	1B-22, DH-3
1982	MIN	A	15	.204	.296	54	11	1	2	0	0.0	5	3	1	8	0	1	1	74	2	3	6	5.3	.962	1B-10, DH-5
2 yrs.			47	.228	.307	127	29	6	2	0	0.0	12	8	6	20	0	9	4	220	12	4	16	5.0	.983	1B-32, DH-8

Jake Wells

WELLS, JACOB
B. Aug. 9, 1863, Memphis, Tenn.   D. Mar. 16, 1927, Hendersonville, N. C.

BR TR

Year	Team		Games	BA	SA	AB	H	2B	3B	HR	HR%	R	RBI	BB	SO	SB	AB	H	PO	A	E	DP	TC/G	FA	G by Pos
1888	DET	N	16	.158	.175	57	9	1	0	0	0.0	5		0	5		0	0	96	25	11	2	8.3	.917	C-16
1890	STL	AA	30	.238	.267	105	25	3	0	0	0.0	17		10		1	0	0	166	43	13	3	7.4	.941	C-28, OF-3
2 yrs.			46	.210	.235	162	34	4	0	0	0.0	22	2	10	5	1	0	0	262	68	24	5	7.7	.932	C-44, OF-3

Leo Wells

WELLS, LEO DONALD
B. July 18, 1917, Kansas City, Kans.

BR TR 5'10" 180 lbs.

Year	Team		Games	BA	SA	AB	H	2B	3B	HR	HR%	R	RBI	BB	SO	SB	AB	H	PO	A	E	DP	TC/G	FA	G by Pos
1942	CHI	A	35	.194	.274	62	12	2	0	1	1.6	8	4	4	5	1	13	5	23	53	2	10	2.2	.974	SS-12, 3B-6
1946			45	.189	.260	127	24	4	1	0	0.8	11	11	12	34	3	2	0	39	92	8	7	3.1	.942	3B-38, SS-2
2 yrs.			80	.190	.265	189	36	6	1	1	1.1	19	15	16	39	4	15	5	62	145	10	17	2.7	.954	3B-44, SS-14

Jimmy Welsh

WELSH, JAMES DANIEL
B. Oct. 9, 1902, Denver, Colo.   D. Oct. 30, 1970, Oakland, Calif.

BL TR 6'1" 174 lbs.

Year	Team		Games	BA	SA	AB	H	2B	3B	HR	HR%	R	RBI	BB	SO	SB	AB	H	PO	A	E	DP	TC/G	FA	G by Pos
1925	BOS	N	122	.312	.440	484	151	25	8	7	1.4	69	63	20	24	7	3	0	241	36	11	7	2.4	.962	OF-116, 2B-3
1926			134	.278	.378	490	136	18	11	3	0.6	69	57	33	28	6	4	0	283	23	11	8	2.4	.965	OF-129
1927			131	.288	.423	497	143	26	7	9	1.8	72	54	23	27	11	1	0	381	24	13	6	3.2	.969	OF-129, 1B-1
1928	NY	N	124	.307	.431	476	146	22	5	9	1.9	77	54	29	30	4	3	1	310	8	6	3	2.6	.981	OF-117
1929	2 teams			NY	N	(38G – .248)		BOS	N	(53G – .290)															
"	total		91	.273	.403	315	86	15	7	4	1.3	49	24	22	26	4	3	0	220	10	7	2	2.6	.970	OF-86
1930	BOS	N	113	.275	.389	422	116	21	9	3	0.7	51	36	29	23	5	2	1	329	8	7	2	3.0	.980	OF-110
6 yrs.			715	.290	.411	2684	778	127	47	35	1.3	387	288	156	144	37	16	2	1764	109	55	28	2.7	.971	OF-687, 2B-3, 1B-1

Tub Welsh

WELSH, JAMES J.
B. July 3, 1866, St. Louis, Mo.   Deceased.

TR 5'11" 230 lbs.

Year	Team		Games	BA	SA	AB	H	2B	3B	HR	HR%	R	RBI	BB	SO	SB	AB	H	PO	A	E	DP	TC/G	FA	G by Pos
1890	TOL	AA	35	.287	.361	108	31	3	1	1	0.9	15		8		7	0	0	188	44	23	4	7.3	.910	C-25, 1B-10
1895	LOU	N	47	.242	.301	153	37	4	1	1	0.7	18	8	13	7	2	0	0	254	41	21	17	6.7	.934	C-28, 1B-20
2 yrs.			82	.261	.326	261	68	7	2	2	0.8	33	8	21	7	9	0	0	442	85	44	21	7.0	.923	C-53, 1B-30

Lew Wendell

WENDELL, LEWIS CHARLES
B. Mar. 22, 1892, New York, N. Y.   D. July 11, 1953, Brooklyn, N. Y.

BR TR 5'11" 178 lbs.

Year	Team		Games	BA	SA	AB	H	2B	3B	HR	HR%	R	RBI	BB	SO	SB	AB	H	PO	A	E	DP	TC/G	FA	G by Pos
1915	NY	N	20	.222	.306	36	8	1	1	0	0.0	0	5	2	7	0	3	0	33	13	4	1	2.5	.920	C-20
1916			2	.000	.000	2	0	0	0	0	0.0	0	0	2	0	0	0	0	0	0	0	0	0.0	–	
1924	PHI	N	21	.250	.281	32	8	1	0	0	0.0	3	2	3	5	0	2	0	25	6	0	1	1.5	1.000	C-17
1925			18	.077	.077	26	2	0	0	0	0.0	0	3	1	3	0	8	0	16	4	2	0	1.2	.909	C-9
1926			1	.000	.000	4	0	0	0	0	0.0	0	0	0	0	0	0	0	0	1	2	0	3.0	.333	C-1
5 yrs.			62	.180	.220	100	18	2	1	0	0.0	3	10	6	17	0	16	1	74	24	8	1	1.7	.925	C-47

Jack Wentz

WENTZ, JOHN GEORGE
Born John George Wernz.
B. Mar. 4, 1863, Louisville, Ky.   D. Sept. 14, 1907, Louisville, Ky.

BR TR 5'10½" 175 lbs.

Year	Team		Games	BA	SA	AB	H	2B	3B	HR	HR%	R	RBI	BB	SO	SB	AB	H	PO	A	E	DP	TC/G	FA	G by Pos
1891	LOU	AA	1	.250	.250	4	1	0	0	0	0.0	0	0	0	0	0	0	0	2	2	2	0	6.0	.667	2B-1

Stan Wentzel

WENTZEL, STANLEY AARON
B. Jan. 13, 1917, Lorane, Pa.

BR TR 6'1" 200 lbs.

Year	Team		Games	BA	SA	AB	H	2B	3B	HR	HR%	R	RBI	BB	SO	SB	AB	H	PO	A	E	DP	TC/G	FA	G by Pos
1945	BOS	N	4	.211	.316	19	4	0	1	0	0.0	3	6	0	3	1	0	0	8	0	0	0	2.0	1.000	OF-4

Julie Wera

WERA, JULIAN VALENTINE
B. Feb. 9, 1902, Winona, Minn.   D. Dec. 12, 1975, Rochester, Minn.

BR TR 5'8" 164 lbs.

Year	Team		Games	BA	SA	AB	H	2B	3B	HR	HR%	R	RBI	BB	SO	SB	AB	H	PO	A	E	DP	TC/G	FA	G by Pos
1927	NY	A	38	.238	.381	42	10	3	0	1	2.4	7	8	5	12	1	0	0	17	15	0	0	0.8	1.000	3B-19
1929			5	.417	.417	12	5	0	0	0	0.0	1	2	1	0	0	1	0	0	5	0	0	1.0	1.000	3B-4
2 yrs.			43	.278	.389	54	15	3	0	1	1.9	8	10	2	6	5	0	0	17	20	0	0	0.9	1.000	3B-23

Bill Werber

WERBER, WILLIAM MURRAY
B. June 20, 1908, Berwyn, Md.

BR TR 5'10" 170 lbs.

Year	Team		Games	BA	SA	AB	H	2B	3B	HR	HR%	R	RBI	BB	SO	SB	AB	H	PO	A	E	DP	TC/G	FA	G by Pos
1930	NY	A	4	.286	.286	14	4	0	0	0	0.0	5	2	3	1	0	0	0	12	9	1	3	5.5	.955	SS-3, 3B-1
1933	2 teams			NY	A	(3G – .000)		BOS	A	(108G – .259)															
"	total		111	.258	.377	427	110	30	6	3	0.7	64	39	33	39	15	4	1	169	259	39	43	4.2	.916	SS-71, 3B-39, 2B-2
1934	BOS	A	152	.321	.472	623	200	41	10	11	1.8	129	67	77	37	40	0	0	179	392	43	39	4.0	.930	3B-130, SS-22
1935			124	.255	.424	462	118	30	3	14	3.0	84	61	69	41	29	1	0	174	264	27	20	3.8	.942	3B-123
1936			145	.275	.407	535	147	29	6	10	1.9	89	67	89	37	23	0	0	202	167	21	16	2.7	.946	3B-101, OF-45, 2B-1
1937	PHI	A	128	.292	.414	493	144	31	4	7	1.4	85	70	74	39	35	2	0	141	260	17	25	3.3	.959	3B-125, OF-3
1938			134	.259	.389	499	129	22	7	11	2.2	92	69	93	37	19	0	0	168	266	30	21	3.5	.935	3B-134
1939	CIN	N	147	.289	.389	599	173	35	5	5	0.8	115	57	91	46	15	0	0	165	308	34	32	3.4	.933	3B-147
1940			143	.277	.416	584	162	35	5	12	2.1	105	48	68	40	16	0	0	139	287	17	24	3.1	.962	3B-143

Year Team	Games	BA	SA	AB	H	2B	3B	HR	HR%	R	RBI	BB	SO	SB	Pinch Hit AB	H	PO	A	E	DP	TC/G	FA	G by Pos

Bill Werber *continued*

Year Team	Games	BA	SA	AB	H	2B	3B	HR	HR%	R	RBI	BB	SO	SB	AB	H	PO	A	E	DP	TC/G	FA	G by Pos
1941	109	.239	.299	418	100	9	2	4	1.0	56	46	53	24	14	1	0	120	256	16	30	3.6	.959	3B-107
1942 NY N	98	.205	.249	370	76	9	2	1	0.3	51	13	51	22	9	3	1	79	227	24	14	3.4	.927	3B-93
11 yrs.	1295	.271	.392	5024	1363	271	50	78	1.6	875	539	701	363	215	11	2	1548	2695	269	267	3.5	.940	3B-1143, SS-96, OF-48, 2B-3

WORLD SERIES

Year Team	Games	BA	SA	AB	H	2B	3B	HR	HR%	R	RBI	BB	SO	SB	AB	H	PO	A	E	DP	TC/G	FA	G by Pos
1939 CIN N	4	.250	.250	16	4	0	0	0	0.0	1	2	2	0	0	0	0	3	5	0	0	2.0	1.000	3B-4
1940	7	.370	.519	27	10	4	0	0	0.0	5	2	4	2	0	0	0	9	16	2	3	3.9	.926	3B-7
2 yrs.	11	.326	.419	43	14	4	0	0	0.0	6	4	6	2	0	0	0	12	21	2	3	3.2	.943	3B-11

Perry Werden

WERDEN, PERCIVAL WHERITT (Moose)
B. July 21, 1865, St. Louis, Mo. D. Jan. 9, 1934, Minneapolis, Minn. BR TR 6'2" 220 lbs.

Year Team	Games	BA	SA	AB	H	2B	3B	HR	HR%	R	RBI	BB	SO	SB	AB	H	PO	A	E	DP	TC/G	FA	G by Pos
1884 STL U	18	.237	.263	76	18	2	0	0	0.0	7		2			0	0	17	36	6	1	3.3	.898	P-16, OF-6
1888 WAS N	3	.300	.300	10	3	0	0	0	0.0	0	2	1	4	0	0	0	6	0	1	0	2.3	.857	OF-3
1890 TOL AA	128	.295	.456	498	147	22	20	6	1.2	113		78		59	0	0	1190	61	35	57	10.0	.973	1B-124, OF-5
1891 BAL AA	139	.290	.424	552	160	20	18	6	1.1	102	104	52	59	46	0	0	1422	58	30	79	10.9	.980	1B-139
1892 STL N	149	.258	.355	598	154	22	6	8	1.3	73	84	59	52	20	0	0	1467	102	28	81	10.7	.982	1B-149
1893	125	.276	.442	500	138	22	29	1	0.2	73	94	49	25	11	0	0	1194	82	43	75	10.6	.967	1B-124, OF-1
1897 LOU N	131	.302	.429	506	153	21	14	5	1.0	76	83	40		14	0	0	1318	116	23	70	11.1	.984	1B-131
7 yrs.	693	.282	.414	2740	773	109	87	26	0.9	444	367	281	140	150	0	0	6614	455	166	363	10.4	.977	1B-667, P-16, OF-15

Johnny Werhas

WERHAS, JOHN CHARLES (Peaches)
B. Feb. 7, 1938, Highland Park, Mich. BR TR 6'2" 200 lbs.

Year Team	Games	BA	SA	AB	H	2B	3B	HR	HR%	R	RBI	BB	SO	SB	AB	H	PO	A	E	DP	TC/G	FA	G by Pos
1964 LA N	29	.193	.241	83	16	1	0	1	0.0	6	8	13	12	0	1	0	30	49	4	4	2.9	.952	3B-28
1965	4	.000	.000	3	0	0	0	0	0.0	0	0	1	2	0	2	0	3	0	0	0	0.8	1.000	1B-1
1967 2 teams		LA N	(7G – .143)		CAL A	(49G – .160)																	
" total	56	.159	.268	82	13	1	2	2	2.4	8	6	10	25	0	23	3	30	37	2	2	1.2	.971	3B-30, 1B-4, OF-1
3 yrs.	89	.173	.250	168	29	3	2	2	1.2	15	14	24	39	0	26	3	63	86	6	6	1.7	.961	3B-58, 1B-5, OF-1

Don Werner

WERNER, DONALD PAUL
B. Mar. 8, 1953, Appleton, Wis. BR TR 6'1" 175 lbs.

Year Team	Games	BA	SA	AB	H	2B	3B	HR	HR%	R	RBI	BB	SO	SB	AB	H	PO	A	E	DP	TC/G	FA	G by Pos
1975 CIN N	7	.125	.125	8	1	0	0	0	0.0	0	0	0	0	0	0	0	10	2	1	0	1.9	.923	C-7
1976	3	.500	.750	4	2	1	0	0	0.0	0	1	1	1	0	0	0	7	2	0	0	3.0	1.000	C-3
1977	10	.174	.435	23	4	0	0	2	8.7	3	4	2	3	0	0	0	40	4	0	2	4.4	1.000	C-10
1978	50	.150	.186	113	17	2	1	0	0.0	7	11	14	30	1	1	1	214	21	3	4	4.8	.987	C-49
1980	24	.172	.203	64	11	2	0	0	0.0	2	5	7	10	1	1	1	119	6	5	1	5.4	.962	C-24
1981 TEX A	2	.250	.250	8	2	0	0	0	0.0	1	0	0	2	0	0	0	0	0	0	0	0.0	–	DH-2
1982	22	.203	.237	59	12	2	0	0	0.0	4	3	3	7	0	0	0	91	5	2	2	4.5	.980	C-22
7 yrs.	118	.176	.229	279	49	7	1	2	0.7	17	24	27	53	2	2	2	481	40	11	9	4.5	.979	C-115, DH-2

Joe Werrick

WERRICK, JOSEPH ABRAHAM
B. Oct. 25, 1861, St. Paul, Minn. D. May 10, 1943, St. Peter, Minn. TR 5'9" 151 lbs.

Year Team	Games	BA	SA	AB	H	2B	3B	HR	HR%	R	RBI	BB	SO	SB	AB	H	PO	A	E	DP	TC/G	FA	G by Pos
1884 STP U	9	.074	.074	27	2	0	0	0	0.0	3		1			0	0	8	26	11	0	5.0	.756	SS-9
1886 LOU AA	136	.250	.351	561	140	20	14	3	0.5	75		33			0	0	162	257	72	9	3.6	.853	3B-136
1887	136	.285	.413	533	152	21	13	7	1.3	90		38		49	0	0	153	286	89	12	3.9	.831	3B-136
1888	111	.215	.278	413	89	12	7	0	0.0	49	51	30		15	0	0	135	226	79	11	4.0	.820	3B-89, SS-11, 2B-8, OF-3
4 yrs.	392	.250	.348	1534	383	53	34	10	0.7	217	51	102		64	0	0	458	795	251	32	3.8	.833	3B-361, SS-20, 2B-8, OF-3

Don Wert

WERT, DONALD RALPH
B. July 29, 1938, Strasburg, Pa. BR TR 5'10" 162 lbs.

Year Team	Games	BA	SA	AB	H	2B	3B	HR	HR%	R	RBI	BB	SO	SB	AB	H	PO	A	E	DP	TC/G	FA	G by Pos
1963 DET A	78	.259	.382	251	65	2	7	2.8		31	25	24	51	3	4	0	85	173	10	20	3.4	.963	3B-47, 2B-21, SS-8
1964	148	.257	.362	525	135	18	5	9	1.7	63	55	50	74	3	3	0	134	293	16	33	3.0	.964	3B-142, SS-4
1965	162	.261	.363	609	159	22	2	12	2.0	81	54	73	71	5	0	0	164	337	12	34	3.2	.977	3B-161, SS-3, 2B-1
1966	150	.268	.370	559	150	20	2	11	2.0	56	70	64	69	6	0	0	128	253	11	20	2.6	.972	3B-150
1967	142	.257	.341	534	137	23	2	6	1.1	60	40	44	59	1	2	0	113	282	9	22	2.8	.978	3B-140, SS-1
1968	150	.200	.299	536	107	15	1	12	2.2	44	37	37	79	0	1	1	144	284	15	22	2.9	.966	3B-150, SS-2
1969	132	.225	.355	423	95	11	1	14	3.3	46	50	49	60	1	2	0	114	259	13	20	2.9	.966	3B-129
1970	128	.218	.303	363	79	13	0	6	1.7	34	33	44	56	1	15	2	95	193	14	20	2.4	.954	3B-117, 2B-2
1971 WAS A	20	.050	.075	40	2	1	0	0	0.0	2	2	4	10	0	7	0	9	23	2	2	1.7	.941	SS-7, 3B-7, 2B-1
9 yrs.	1110	.242	.343	3840	929	129	15	77	2.0	417	366	389	529	22	34	3	986	2097	102	193	2.9	.968	3B-1043, SS-25, 2B-25

WORLD SERIES

Year Team	Games	BA	SA	AB	H	2B	3B	HR	HR%	R	RBI	BB	SO	SB	AB	H	PO	A	E	DP	TC/G	FA	G by Pos
1968 DET A	6	.118	.118	17	2	0	0	0	0.0	1	2	6	5	0	0	0	5	14	0	1	3.2	1.000	3B-6

Dennis Werth

WERTH, DENNIS DEAN
B. Dec. 29, 1952, Lincoln, Ill. BR TR 6'1" 200 lbs.

Year Team	Games	BA	SA	AB	H	2B	3B	HR	HR%	R	RBI	BB	SO	SB	AB	H	PO	A	E	DP	TC/G	FA	G by Pos
1979 NY A	3	.250	.250	4	1	0	0	0	0.0	1	0	0	0	0	2	0	5	1	0	0	2.0	1.000	1B-1
1980	39	.308	.492	65	20	3	0	3	4.6	15	12	12	19	0	9	1	82	3	2	9	2.2	.977	1B-12, DH-8, OF-8, 3B-1, C-1
1981	34	.109	.127	55	6	1	0	0	0.0	7	1	12	12	1	5	0	104	11	0	7	3.4	1.000	1B-19, OF-8, DH-4, C-3
1982 KC A	41	.133	.133	15	2	0	0	0	0.0	5	2	4	2	0	1	0	94	9	1	10	2.5	.990	1B-35, C-2
4 yrs.	117	.209	.302	139	29	4	0	3	2.2	28	15	28	33	1	17	1	285	24	3	26	2.7	.990	1B-67, OF-16, DH-12, C-6, 3B-1

Del Wertz

WERTZ, DWIGHT LYMAN MOODY
B. Oct. 11, 1888, Canton, Ohio D. May 26, 1958, Sarasota, Fla. BR TR 5'10" 160 lbs.

Year Team	Games	BA	SA	AB	H	2B	3B	HR	HR%	R	RBI	BB	SO	SB	AB	H	PO	A	E	DP	TC/G	FA	G by Pos
1914 BUF F	3	–	–	0	0	0	0	0	–	1	0	0		0	0	0	1	0	0	0	0.3	1.000	SS-1

Vic Wertz

WERTZ, VICTOR WOODROW
B. Feb. 9, 1925, York, Pa. D. July 7, 1983, Detroit, Mich. BL TR 6' 186 lbs.

Year Team	Games	BA	SA	AB	H	2B	3B	HR	HR%	R	RBI	BB	SO	SB	AB	H	PO	A	E	DP	TC/G	FA	G by Pos
1947 DET A	102	.288	.432	333	96	22	4	6	1.8	60	44	47	66	2	18	5	160	6	6	0	1.7	.965	OF-82

Year	Team	Games	BA	SA	AB	H	2B	3B	HR	HR%	R	RBI	BB	SO	SB	Pinch Hit AB	Pinch Hit H	PO	A	E	DP	TC/G	FA	G by Pos

Vic Wertz *continued*

Year	Team	Games	BA	SA	AB	H	2B	3B	HR	HR%	R	RBI	BB	SO	SB	Pinch Hit AB	Pinch Hit H	PO	A	E	DP	TC/G	FA	G by Pos
1948		119	.248	.396	391	97	19	9	7	1.8	49	67	48	70	0	19	4	196	11	10	3	1.8	.954	OF-98
1949		155	.304	.465	608	185	26	6	20	3.3	96	133	80	61	2	0	0	302	14	6	4	2.1	.981	OF-155
1950		149	.308	.533	559	172	37	4	27	4.8	99	123	91	55	0	4	2	286	5	10	3	2.0	.967	OF-145
1951		138	.285	.511	501	143	24	4	27	5.4	86	94	78	61	0	6	0	254	7	3	1	1.9	.989	OF-131
1952 2 teams	DET A (85G – .246)			STL	A	(37G – .346)																		
" total		122	.277	.506	415	115	20	3	23	5.5	68	70	69	64	1	8	2	198	8	5	3	1.7	.976	OF-115
1953	STL A	128	.268	.466	440	118	18	6	19	4.3	61	70	72	44	1	8	2	243	15	7	4	2.1	.974	OF-121
1954 2 teams	BAL A (29G – .202)			CLE	A	(94G – .275)																		
" total		123	.257	.422	389	100	15	2	15	3.9	38	61	45	57	0	7	1	614	57	9	58	5.5	.987	1B-83, OF-32
1955	CLE A	74	.253	.475	257	65	11	2	14	5.4	30	55	32	33	1	5	2	462	34	8	50	6.8	.984	1B-63, OF-9
1956		136	.264	.509	481	127	22	0	32	6.7	65	106	75	87	0	1	0	971	77	9	99	7.8	.991	1B-133
1957		144	.282	.485	515	145	21	0	28	5.4	84	105	78	87	2	4	0	1025	83	14	122	7.8	.988	1B-139
1958		25	.279	.512	43	12	1	0	3	7.0	5	12	5	7	0	16	3	44	5	1	5	2.0	.980	1B-8
1959	BOS A	94	.275	.413	247	68	13	0	7	2.8	38	49	22	32	0	33	7	440	38	4	44	5.1	.992	1B-64
1960		131	.282	.460	443	125	22	0	19	4.3	45	103	37	54	0	18	10	841	78	12	89	7.1	.987	1B-117
1961 2 teams	BOS A (99G – .262)			DET	A	(8G – .167)																		
" total		107	.260	.424	323	84	16	2	11	3.4	33	61	38	44	0	18	3	664	67	7	65	6.9	.991	1B-86
1962	DET A	74	.324	.486	105	34	2	0	5	4.8	7	18	5	13	0	53	17	75	9	1	5	1.1	.988	1B-16
1963 2 teams	DET A (6G – .000)			MIN	A	(35G – .136)																		
" total		41	.122	.306	49	6	0	0	3	6.1	3	7	6	6	0	30	4	32	5	0	2	0.9	1.000	1B-6
17 yrs.		1862	.277	.469	6099	1692	289	42	266	4.4	867	1178	828	841	9	248	62	6807	519	112	557	4.0	.985	OF-888, 1B-715

WORLD SERIES

Year	Team	Games	BA	SA	AB	H	2B	3B	HR	HR%	R	RBI	BB	SO	SB	Pinch Hit AB	Pinch Hit H	PO	A	E	DP	TC/G	FA	G by Pos
1954	CLE A	4	.500	.938	16	8	1	1	1	6.3	2	3	2	3	0	0	0	33	6	1	2	10.0	.975	1B-4

Jim Wessinger

WESSINGER, JAMES MICHAEL
B. Sept. 25, 1955, Utica, N. Y.
BR TR 5'10" 165 lbs.

Year	Team	Games	BA	SA	AB	H	2B	3B	HR	HR%	R	RBI	BB	SO	SB	Pinch Hit AB	Pinch Hit H	PO	A	E	DP	TC/G	FA	G by Pos
1979	ATL N	10	.000	.000	7	0	0	0	0	0.0	2	0	1	4	0	2	0	2	3	1	0	0.6	.833	2B-2

Billy West

WEST, WILLIAM NELSON
B. Aug. 21, 1840, Philadelphia, Pa.   D. Aug. 18, 1891, Radnor, Pa.

Year	Team	Games	BA	SA	AB	H	2B	3B	HR	HR%	R	RBI	BB	SO	SB	Pinch Hit AB	Pinch Hit H	PO	A	E	DP	TC/G	FA	G by Pos
1876	NY N	1	.000	.000	4	0	0	0	0	0.0	0		0	0	0			1	3	0	1	4.0	1.000	2B-1

Buck West

WEST, MILTON DOUGLAS
B. Aug. 29, 1860, Spring Hill, Ohio   D. Jan. 13, 1929, Mansfield, Ohio
BL TR 5'10" 200 lbs.

Year	Team	Games	BA	SA	AB	H	2B	3B	HR	HR%	R	RBI	BB	SO	SB	Pinch Hit AB	Pinch Hit H	PO	A	E	DP	TC/G	FA	G by Pos
1884	CIN AA	33	.244	.397	131	32	2	9	0	0.0	20		2			0	0	46	1	10	0	1.7	.825	OF-33
1890	CLE N	37	.245	.338	151	37	6	1	2	1.3	20	29	7	11	4	0	0	50	9	12	1	1.9	.831	OF-37
2 yrs.		70	.245	.365	282	69	8	10	2	0.7	40	29	9	11	4	0	0	96	10	22	1	1.8	.828	OF-70

Dick West

WEST, RICHARD THOMAS
B. Nov. 24, 1915, Louisville, Ky.
BR TR 6'2" 180 lbs.

Year	Team	Games	BA	SA	AB	H	2B	3B	HR	HR%	R	RBI	BB	SO	SB	Pinch Hit AB	Pinch Hit H	PO	A	E	DP	TC/G	FA	G by Pos
1938	CIN N	1	.000	.000	1	0	0	0	0	0.0	0	0	0	0	0	1	0	0	0	0	0	0.0		
1939		6	.211	.211	19	4	0	0	0	0.0	0	1	1	4	0	1	0	11	0	0	0	1.8	1.000	OF-5, C-1
1940		7	.393	.571	28	11	2	0	1	3.6	4	6	0	2	0	0	0	19	2	0	0	3.0	1.000	C-7
1941		67	.215	.285	172	37	5	2	1	0.6	15	17	6	23	4	1	0	209	21	7	3	3.5	.970	C-64
1942		33	.177	.253	79	14	3	0	1	1.3	9	8	5	13	1	6	0	86	13	1	1	3.0	.990	C-17, OF-6
1943		3	—		0	0	0	0	0	0.0	0		0	0	0	0	0	0	0	0	0			
6 yrs.		117	.221	.298	299	66	10	2	3	1.0	30	35	12	42	6	9	1	325	36	8	4	3.2	.978	C-89, OF-11

Max West

WEST, MAX EDWARD
B. Nov. 28, 1916, Dexter, Mo.
BL TR 6'1½" 182 lbs.

Year	Team	Games	BA	SA	AB	H	2B	3B	HR	HR%	R	RBI	BB	SO	SB	Pinch Hit AB	Pinch Hit H	PO	A	E	DP	TC/G	FA	G by Pos
1938	BOS N	123	.234	.368	418	98	16	5	10	2.4	47	63	38	38	5	3	0	268	8	4	4	2.3	.986	OF-109, 1B-7
1939		130	.285	.497	449	128	26	6	19	4.2	67	82	51	55	1	5	3	287	8	8	2	2.3	.974	OF-124
1940		141	.261	.372	524	137	27	5	7	1.3	72	72	65	54	2	3	1	558	40	11	34	4.3	.982	OF-102, 1B-36
1941		138	.277	.426	484	134	28	4	12	2.5	63	68	72	68	5	6	3	302	13	6	5	2.3	.981	OF-132
1942		134	.254	.409	452	115	22	0	16	3.5	54	56	68	59	4	3	2	913	51	12	67	7.3	.988	1B-85, OF-50
1946 2 teams	BOS N (1G – .000)			CIN	N	(72G – .213)																		
" total		73	.212	.350	203	43	13	0	5	2.5	16	18	32	37	1	12	1	115	6	6	3	1.7	.953	OF-58, 1B-1
1948	PIT N	87	.178	.370	146	26	4	0	8	5.5	19	21	27	29	1	32	5	209	20	2	14	2.7	.991	1B-32, OF-16
7 yrs.		826	.254	.407	2676	681	136	20	77	2.9	338	380	353	340	19	64	15	2652	146	49	129	3.4	.983	OF-591, 1B-161

Max West

WEST, WALTER MAXWELL
B. July 14, 1904, Sunset, Tex.   D. Apr. 25, 1971, Houston, Tex.
BR TR 5'11" 165 lbs.

Year	Team	Games	BA	SA	AB	H	2B	3B	HR	HR%	R	RBI	BB	SO	SB	Pinch Hit AB	Pinch Hit H	PO	A	E	DP	TC/G	FA	G by Pos
1928	BKN N	7	.286	.429	21	6	1	1	0	0.0	4	1	4	1	0	1	0	12	3	2	1	2.4	.882	OF-7
1929		5	.250	.375	8	2	1	0	0	0.0	1	1	1	0	0	2	1	2	0	0	0	0.4	1.000	OF-2
2 yrs.		12	.276	.414	29	8	2	1	0	0.0	5	2	5	1	0	3	1	14	3	2	1	1.6	.895	OF-9

Sammy West

WEST, SAMUEL FILMORE
B. Oct. 5, 1904, Longview, Tex.   D. Nov. 23, 1985, Lubbock, Tex.
BL TL 5'11" 165 lbs.

Year	Team	Games	BA	SA	AB	H	2B	3B	HR	HR%	R	RBI	BB	SO	SB	Pinch Hit AB	Pinch Hit H	PO	A	E	DP	TC/G	FA	G by Pos
1927	WAS A	38	.239	.328	67	16	4	1	0	0.0	9	6	8	8	1	19	4	28	3	2	0	0.9	.939	OF-18
1928		125	.302	.442	378	114	30	7	3	0.8	59	40	20	23	5	7	0	210	13	1	0	1.8	.996	OF-116
1929		142	.267	.347	510	136	16	8	3	0.6	60	75	45	41	9	3	1	376	25	9	8	2.9	.978	OF-139
1930		120	.328	.474	411	135	22	10	6	1.5	75	67	37	34	5	0	0	310	8	9	1	2.7	.972	OF-118
1931		132	.333	.481	526	175	43	13	3	0.6	77	91	30	37	6	0	0	402	13	4	3	3.2	.990	OF-127
1932		146	.287	.412	554	159	27	12	6	1.1	88	83	48	57	4	0	0	450	15	10	7	3.3	.979	OF-143
1933	STL A	133	.300	.458	517	155	25	12	11	2.1	93	48	59	49	10	6	1	329	14	4	3	2.6	.988	OF-127
1934		122	.326	.469	482	157	22	10	9	1.9	90	55	62	55	3	2	0	303	14	9	3	2.7	.972	OF-120
1935		138	.300	.442	527	158	37	4	10	1.9	93	70	75	46	1	3	3	449	7	5	2	3.3	.989	OF-135
1936		152	.278	.381	533	148	26	4	7	1.3	78	70	94	70	2	3	0	442	10	8	2	3.0	.983	OF-148
1937		122	.328	.473	457	150	37	4	7	1.5	68	58	46	28	1	14	3	298	17	4	6	2.6	.987	OF-105

Year	Team	Games	BA	SA	AB	H	2B	3B	HR	HR%	R	RBI	BB	SO	SB	Pinch Hit AB	H	PO	A	E	DP	TC/G	FA	G by Pos

Sammy West *continued*

Year	Team	Games	BA	SA	AB	H	2B	3B	HR	HR%	R	RBI	BB	SO	SB	PH AB	PH H	PO	A	E	DP	TC/G	FA	G by Pos
1938	2 teams	STL A	(44G – .309)		WAS A	(92G – .302)																		
"	total	136	.305	.420	509	155	27	7	6	1.2	68	74	47	30	2	9	2	322	4	7	3	2.4	.979	OF-126
1939	WAS A	115	.282	.397	390	110	20	8	3	0.8	52	52	67	29	1	6	0	365	13	6	12	3.3	.984	OF-89, 1B-17
1940		57	.253	.364	99	25	6	1	1	1.0	7	18	16	13	0	26	8	113	7	1	13	2.1	.992	1B-12, OF-9
1941		26	.270	.270	37	10	0	0	0	0.0	3	6	11	2	1	12	4	19	0	0	0	0.7	1.000	OF-8
1942	CHI A	49	.232	.265	151	35	5	0	0	0.0	14	25	31	18	2	2	0	112	1	2	1	2.3	.983	OF-45
16 yrs.		1753	.299	.425	6148	1838	347	101	75	1.2	934	838	696	540	53	115	26	4528	164	81	64	2.7	.983	OF-1573, 1B-29

Oscar Westerberg

WESTERBERG, OSCAR WILLIAM
B. July 8, 1882, Alameda, Calif. D. Apr. 17, 1909, Alameda, Calif.   BB TR

Year	Team	Games	BA	SA	AB	H	2B	3B	HR	HR%	R	RBI	BB	SO	SB	PH AB	PH H	PO	A	E	DP	TC/G	FA	G by Pos
1907	BOS N	2	.333	.333	6	2	0	0	0	0.0	0	1	1		0	0	0	3	3	0	1	3.0	1.000	SS-2

Jim Westlake

WESTLAKE, JAMES PATRICK
Brother of Wally Westlake.
B. July 3, 1930, Sacramento, Calif.   BL TL 6'1" 190 lbs.

Year	Team	Games	BA	SA	AB	H	2B	3B	HR	HR%	R	RBI	BB	SO	SB	PH AB	PH H	PO	A	E	DP	TC/G	FA	G by Pos
1955	PHI N	1	.000	.000	1	0	0	0	0	0.0	0	0	0	1	0	1	0	0	0	0	0	0.0	–	

Wally Westlake

WESTLAKE, WALDON THOMAS
Brother of Jim Westlake.
B. Nov. 8, 1920, Gridley, Calif.   BR TR 6' 186 lbs.

Year	Team	Games	BA	SA	AB	H	2B	3B	HR	HR%	R	RBI	BB	SO	SB	PH AB	PH H	PO	A	E	DP	TC/G	FA	G by Pos
1947	PIT N	112	.273	.459	407	111	17	4	17	4.2	59	69	27	63	5	2	0	239	8	3	0	2.2	.988	OF-109
1948		132	.285	.456	428	122	10	6	17	4.0	78	65	46	40	2	8	2	274	8	7	2	2.2	.976	OF-125
1949		147	.282	.490	525	148	24	6	23	4.4	77	104	45	69	6	4	0	319	12	6	4	2.3	.982	OF-143
1950		139	.285	.493	477	136	15	6	24	5.0	69	95	48	78	1	15	3	329	4	3	3	2.4	.991	OF-123
1951	2 teams	PIT N	(50G – .282)		STL N	(73G – .255)																		
"	total	123	.266	.462	448	119	12	5	22	4.9	64	84	33	68	1	9	1	203	96	15	14	2.6	.952	OF-79, 3B-34
1952	3 teams	STL N	(21G – .216)		CIN N	(59G – .202)		CLE A	(29G – .232)															
"	total	109	.212	.288	326	69	11	1	4	1.2	47	33	47	56	2	6	0	231	12	1	2	2.2	.996	OF-104
1953	CLE A	82	.330	.495	218	72	7	1	9	4.1	42	46	35	29	2	7	0	128	3	5	2	1.7	.963	OF-72
1954		85	.263	.454	240	63	9	2	11	4.6	36	42	26	37	0	11	2	131	1	5	0	1.6	.964	OF-70
1955	2 teams	CLE A	(16G – .250)		BAL A	(8G – .125)																		
"	total	24	.182	.227	44	8	2	0	0	0.0	2	1	9	10	0	5	1	18	1	0	0	0.8	1.000	OF-14
1956	PHI N	5	.000	.000	4	0	0	0	0	0.0	0	0	0	3	0	4	0	0	0	0	0	0.0	–	
10 yrs.		958	.272	.450	3117	848	107	33	127	4.1	474	539	317	453	19	71	9	1872	145	45	27	2.2	.978	OF-839, 3B-34

WORLD SERIES

Year	Team	Games	BA	SA	AB	H	2B	3B	HR	HR%	R	RBI	BB	SO	SB	PH AB	PH H	PO	A	E	DP	TC/G	FA	G by Pos
1954	CLE A	2	.143	.143	7	1	0	0	0	0.0	0	0	1	3	0	0	0	6	0	1	0	3.5	.857	OF-2

Al Weston

WESTON, ALFRED JOHN
B. Dec. 11, 1905, Lynn, Mass.   BR TR 6' 195 lbs.

Year	Team	Games	BA	SA	AB	H	2B	3B	HR	HR%	R	RBI	BB	SO	SB	PH AB	PH H	PO	A	E	DP	TC/G	FA	G by Pos
1929	BOS N	3	.000	.000	3	0	0	0	0	0.0	0	0	0	2	0	3	0	0	0	0	0	0.0	–	

Wes Westrum

WESTRUM, WESLEY NOREEN
B. Nov. 28, 1922, Clearbrook, Minn.
Manager 1965-67, 1974-75.   BR TR 5'11" 185 lbs.

Year	Team	Games	BA	SA	AB	H	2B	3B	HR	HR%	R	RBI	BB	SO	SB	PH AB	PH H	PO	A	E	DP	TC/G	FA	G by Pos
1947	NY N	6	.417	.500	12	5	1	0	0	0.0	1	2	0	2	0	4	1	8	2	0	0	1.7	1.000	C-2
1948		66	.160	.296	125	20	3	1	4	3.2	14	16	20	36	3	2	0	179	25	4	4	3.2	.981	C-63
1949		64	.243	.402	169	41	4	1	7	4.1	23	28	37	39	1	2	0	224	18	5	4	3.9	.980	C-62
1950		140	.236	.437	437	103	13	3	23	5.3	68	71	92	73	2	0	0	608	71	4	21	4.9	.999	C-139
1951		124	.219	.418	361	79	12	0	20	5.5	59	70	104	93	1	2	0	554	62	8	9	5.0	.987	C-122
1952		114	.220	.385	322	71	11	0	14	4.3	47	43	76	68	1	2	0	481	64	12	11	4.9	.978	C-112
1953		107	.224	.366	290	65	5	0	12	4.1	40	30	56	73	2	1	0	441	56	9	9	4.7	.982	C-106, 3B-1
1954		98	.187	.305	246	46	3	1	8	3.3	25	27	45	60	0	0	0	419	45	7	8	4.8	.985	C-98
1955		69	.212	.307	137	29	1	0	4	2.9	11	18	24	18	0	1	0	280	27	4	5	4.5	.987	C-68
1956		68	.220	.356	132	29	5	2	3	2.3	10	8	25	28	0	1	1	297	26	7	7	4.9	.982	C-67
1957		63	.165	.209	91	15	1	0	1	1.1	4	2	10	14	0	0	0	148	21	6	4	2.8	.966	C-63
11 yrs.		919	.217	.373	2322	503	59	8	96	4.1	302	315	489	514	10	15	2	3639	418	62	82	4.5	.985	C-902, 3B-1

WORLD SERIES

Year	Team	Games	BA	SA	AB	H	2B	3B	HR	HR%	R	RBI	BB	SO	SB	PH AB	PH H	PO	A	E	DP	TC/G	FA	G by Pos
1951	NY N	6	.235	.294	17	4	1	0	0	0.0	1	0	5	3	0	0	0	29	2	1	0	5.3	.969	C-6
1954		4	.273	.273	11	3	0	0	0	0.0	0	3	1	3	0	0	0	23	0	0	0	5.8	1.000	C-4
2 yrs.		10	.250	.286	28	7	1	0	0	0.0	1	3	6	6	0	0	0	52	2	1	0	5.5	.982	C-10

Jeff Wetherby

WETHERBY, JEFFREY BARRET
B. Oct. 18, 1963, Granada Hills, Calif.   BL TL 6'2" 195 lbs.

Year	Team	Games	BA	SA	AB	H	2B	3B	HR	HR%	R	RBI	BB	SO	SB	PH AB	PH H	PO	A	E	DP	TC/G	FA	G by Pos
1989	ATL N	52	.208	.354	48	10	2	1	1	2.1	5	7	4	6	1	36	8	8	0	0	0	0.2	1.000	OF-9

Buzz Wetzel

WETZEL, FRANKLIN BURTON
B. July 7, 1893, Columbus, Ind. D. Mar. 5, 1942, Hollywood, Calif.   BR TR 5'9½" 177 lbs.

Year	Team	Games	BA	SA	AB	H	2B	3B	HR	HR%	R	RBI	BB	SO	SB	PH AB	PH H	PO	A	E	DP	TC/G	FA	G by Pos
1920	STL A	6	.474	.632	19	9	1	1	0	0.0	5	5	4	1	0	1	1	12	1	2	0	2.5	.867	OF-5
1921		61	.210	.277	119	25	2	0	2	1.7	16	10	9	20	0	32	5	52	1	1	0	0.9	.981	OF-27
2 yrs.		67	.246	.326	138	34	3	1	2	1.4	21	15	13	21	0	33	6	64	2	3	0	1.0	.957	OF-32

Bill Whaley

WHALEY, WILLIAM CARL
B. Feb. 10, 1899, Indianapolis, Ind. D. Mar. 3, 1943, Indianapolis, Ind.   BR TR 5'11" 178 lbs.

Year	Team	Games	BA	SA	AB	H	2B	3B	HR	HR%	R	RBI	BB	SO	SB	PH AB	PH H	PO	A	E	DP	TC/G	FA	G by Pos
1923	STL A	23	.240	.320	50	12	2	1	0	0.0	5	5	4	7	0	8	1	25	0	0	0	1.2	1.000	OF-13

Bert Whaling

WHALING, ALBERT JAMES
B. June 22, 1888, Los Angeles, Calif. D. Jan. 21, 1965, Sawtelle, Calif.   BR TR 6' 185 lbs.

Year	Team	Games	BA	SA	AB	H	2B	3B	HR	HR%	R	RBI	BB	SO	SB	PH AB	PH H	PO	A	E	DP	TC/G	FA	G by Pos
1913	BOS N	79	.242	.299	211	51	8	2	0	0.0	22	25	10	32	3	2	1	328	84	4	4	5.3	.990	C-77

Year	Team		Games	BA	SA	AB	H	2B	3B	HR	HR%	R	RBI	BB	SO	SB	Pinch Hit AB	H	PO	A	E	DP	TC/G	FA	G by Pos

Bert Whaling *continued*

Year	Team		Games	BA	SA	AB	H	2B	3B	HR	HR%	R	RBI	BB	SO	SB	AB	H	PO	A	E	DP	TC/G	FA	G by Pos
1914			60	.209	.250	172	36	7	0	0	0.0	18	12	21	28	2	0	0	272	91	7	7	6.2	.981	C-59
1915			72	.221	.274	190	42	6	2	0	0.0	10	13	8	38	0	2	0	292	68	5	2	5.1	.986	C-72
3 yrs.			211	.225	.276	573	129	21	4	0	0.0	50	50	39	98	5	4	1	892	243	16	13	5.5	.986	C-208

Mack Wheat

WHEAT, McKINLEY DAVIS
Brother of Zack Wheat.
B. June 9, 1893, Polo, Mo. D. Aug. 14, 1979, Los Banos, Calif.

BR TR 5'11½" 167 lbs.

Year	Team		Games	BA	SA	AB	H	2B	3B	HR	HR%	R	RBI	BB	SO	SB	AB	H	PO	A	E	DP	TC/G	FA	G by Pos
1915	BKN	N	8	.071	.071	14	1	0	0	0	0.0	0	0	0	5	0	0	0	19	3	1	1	2.9	.957	C-8
1916			2	.000	.000	2	0	0	0	0	0.0	0	0	0	1	0	0	0	5	0	0	0	2.5	1.000	C-2
1917			29	.133	.150	60	8	1	0	0	0.0	2	0	1	12	1	0	0	77	23	3	0	3.6	.971	C-18, OF-9
1918			57	.217	.293	157	34	7	1	1	0.6	11	3	8	24	2	8	2	162	50	8	1	3.9	.964	C-38, OF-7
1919			47	.205	.232	112	23	3	0	0	0.0	5	8	2	22	1	1	0	131	39	10	3	3.8	.944	C-38
1920	PHI	N	78	.226	.335	230	52	10	3	3	1.3	15	20	8	35	3	2	0	262	105	15	8	4.9	.961	C-74
1921			10	.185	.333	27	5	2	1	0	0.0	1	4	0	3	0	1	1	39	11	1	1	5.1	.980	C-9
7 yrs.			231	.204	.279	602	123	23	6	4	0.7	34	35	19	102	7	12	5	695	231	38	14	4.2	.961	C-187, OF-16

Zack Wheat

WHEAT, ZACHARY DAVIS (Buck)
Brother of Mack Wheat.
B. May 23, 1888, Hamilton, Mo. D. Mar. 11, 1972, Sedalia, Mo.
Hall of Fame 1959.

BL TR 5'10" 170 lbs.

Year	Team		Games	BA	SA	AB	H	2B	3B	HR	HR%	R	RBI	BB	SO	SB	AB	H	PO	A	E	DP	TC/G	FA	G by Pos
1909	BKN	N	26	.304	.431	102	31	7	3	0	0.0	15	4	6		1	0	0	54	5	3	1	2.4	.952	OF-26
1910			156	.284	.403	606	172	36	15	2	0.3	78	55	47	80	16	0	0	354	21	15	6	2.5	.962	OF-156
1911			140	.287	.412	534	153	26	13	5	0.9	55	76	29	58	21	4	2	287	12	14	0	2.2	.955	OF-136
1912			123	.305	.450	453	138	28	7	8	1.8	70	65	39	40	16	3	0	285	13	10	2	2.5	.968	OF-122
1913			138	.301	.430	535	161	28	10	7	1.3	64	71	25	45	19	2	0	338	13	8	7	2.6	.978	OF-135
1914			145	.319	.452	533	170	26	9	9	1.7	66	89	47	50	20	1	0	331	21	14	5	2.5	.962	OF-144
1915			146	.258	.360	528	136	15	12	5	0.9	64	66	52	42	21	2	1	345	18	18	4	2.6	.953	OF-144
1916			149	.312	**.461**	568	177	32	13	9	1.6	76	73	43	49	19	0	0	333	14	9	0	2.4	.975	OF-149
1917			109	.312	.423	362	113	15	11	1	0.3	38	41	20	18	5	10	2	216	12	5	5	2.1	.979	OF-109
1918			105	**.335**	.386	409	137	15	3	0	0.0	39	51	16	17	9	0	0	219	11	5	2	2.2	.979	OF-105
1919			137	.297	.409	536	159	23	11	5	0.9	70	62	33	27	15	0	0	297	9	9	2	2.3	.971	OF-137
1920			148	.328	.463	583	191	26	13	9	1.5	89	73	48	21	8	0	0	287	10	9	5	2.1	.971	OF-148
1921			148	.320	.484	568	182	31	10	14	2.5	91	85	44	19	11	0	0	283	18	11	3	2.1	.965	OF-152
1922			152	.335	.503	600	201	29	12	16	2.7	92	112	45	22	9	0	0	317	14	3	1	2.2	.991	OF-87
1923			98	.375	.510	349	131	13	5	8	2.3	63	65	25	12	3	11	4	135	4	14	1	1.6	.908	OF-87
1924			141	.375	.549	566	212	41	8	14	2.5	92	97	49	18	3	1	0	288	13	11	4	2.2	.965	OF-139
1925			150	.359	.541	616	221	42	14	14	2.3	125	103	45	22	3	1	0	320	7	13	2	2.3	.962	OF-149
1926			111	.290	.411	411	119	31	2	5	1.2	68	35	21	14	4	9	2	202	9	10	3	2.0	.955	OF-102
1927	PHI	A	88	.324	.393	247	80	12	1	1	0.4	34	38	18	5	2	24	6	105	8	2	1	1.3	.983	OF-62
19 yrs.			2410	.317	.450	9106	2884	476	172	132	1.4	1289	1261	650	559	205	68	17	4996	232	183	54	2.2	.966	OF-2350

WORLD SERIES

Year	Team		Games	BA	SA	AB	H	2B	3B	HR	HR%	R	RBI	BB	SO	SB	AB	H	PO	A	E	DP	TC/G	FA	G by Pos
1916	BKN	N	5	.211	.316	19	4	0	1	0	0.0	2	1	2	2	1	0	0	14	0	1	0	3.0	.933	OF-5
1920			7	.333	.407	27	9	2	0	0	0.0	2	2	1	2	0	0	0	16	0	2	0	2.6	.889	OF-7
2 yrs.			12	.283	.370	46	13	2	1	0	0.0	4	3	3	4	1	0	0	30	0	3	0	2.8	.909	OF-12

Woody Wheaton

WHEATON, ELWOOD PIERCE
B. Oct. 3, 1914, Philadelphia, Pa.

BL TL 5'8½" 160 lbs.

Year	Team		Games	BA	SA	AB	H	2B	3B	HR	HR%	R	RBI	BB	SO	SB	AB	H	PO	A	E	DP	TC/G	FA	G by Pos
1943	PHI	A	7	.200	.267	30	6	2	0	0	0.0	2	3	3	3	0	0	0	20	1	0	0	3.0	1.000	OF-7
1944			30	.186	.220	59	11	2	0	0	0.0	1	5	5	3	1	11	2	29	6	1	0	1.2	.972	P-11, OF-8
2 yrs.			37	.191	.236	89	17	4	0	0	0.0	3	7	8	5	1	11	2	49	7	1	0	1.5	.982	OF-15, P-11

Dick Wheeler

WHEELER, RICHARD
Born Richard Wheeler Maynard.
B. Jan. 14, 1898, Keene, N. H. D. Feb. 12, 1962, Lexington, Mass.

BR TR 5'11" 185 lbs.

Year	Team		Games	BA	SA	AB	H	2B	3B	HR	HR%	R	RBI	BB	SO	SB	AB	H	PO	A	E	DP	TC/G	FA	G by Pos
1918	STL	N	3	.000	.000	6	0	0	0	0	0.0	0	0	0	3	0	1	0	0	0	0	0	0.0	—	OF-2

Don Wheeler

WHEELER, DONALD WESLEY (Scotty)
B. Sept. 29, 1922, Minneapolis, Minn.

BR TR 5'10" 175 lbs.

Year	Team		Games	BA	SA	AB	H	2B	3B	HR	HR%	R	RBI	BB	SO	SB	AB	H	PO	A	E	DP	TC/G	FA	G by Pos
1949	CHI	A	67	.240	.323	192	46	9	2	1	0.5	17	22	27	19	2	8	1	210	36	6	4	3.8	.976	C-58

Ed Wheeler

WHEELER, EDWARD
B. June 15, 1878, Sherman, Mich. D. Aug. 15, 1960, Ft. Worth, Tex.

BB TR 5'10" 160 lbs.

Year	Team		Games	BA	SA	AB	H	2B	3B	HR	HR%	R	RBI	BB	SO	SB	AB	H	PO	A	E	DP	TC/G	FA	G by Pos
1902	BKN	N	30	.125	.125	96	12	0	0	0	0.0	4	5	3		1	3	0	55	54	19	4	4.3	.852	3B-11, 2B-10, SS-5

Ed Wheeler

WHEELER, EDWARD RAYMOND
B. May 24, 1917, Los Angeles, Calif. D. Aug. 15, 1960, Ft. Worth, Tex.

BR TR 5'9" 160 lbs.

Year	Team		Games	BA	SA	AB	H	2B	3B	HR	HR%	R	RBI	BB	SO	SB	AB	H	PO	A	E	DP	TC/G	FA	G by Pos
1945	CLE	A	46	.194	.222	72	14	2	0	0	0.0	12	2	8	13	1	7	3	29	23	5	1	1.2	.912	3B-14, SS-11, 2B-3

George Wheeler

WHEELER, GEORGE HARRISON (Heavy)
B. Nov. 10, 1881, Shelburn, Ind. D. June 14, 1918, Clinton, Ind.

BL TR 5'9½" 180 lbs.

Year	Team		Games	BA	SA	AB	H	2B	3B	HR	HR%	R	RBI	BB	SO	SB	AB	H	PO	A	E	DP	TC/G	FA	G by Pos
1910	CIN	N	3	.000	.000	3	0	0	0	0	0.0	0	0	0	0	0	0	0	0	0	0	0	0.0	—	

Harry Wheeler

WHEELER, HARRY EUGENE
B. Mar. 3, 1858, Versailles, Ind. D. Oct. 9, 1900, Cincinnati, Ohio
Manager 1884.

BR TR 5'11" 165 lbs.

Year	Team		Games	BA	SA	AB	H	2B	3B	HR	HR%	R	RBI	BB	SO	SB	AB	H	PO	A	E	DP	TC/G	FA	G by Pos
1878	PRO	N	7	.148	.148	27	4	0	0	0	0.0	7	1	2	15		0	0	2	5	1	0	1.1	.875	P-7
1879	CIN	N	1	.000	.000	3	0	0	0	0	0.0	0	0	0	2		0	0	2	0	0	0	2.0	1.000	OF-1, P-1

Year	Team	Games	BA	SA	AB	H	2B	3B	HR	HR%	R	RBI	BB	SO	SB	Pinch Hit AB	Pinch Hit H	PO	A	E	DP	TC/G	FA	G by Pos

Harry Wheeler *continued*

Year	Team	Games	BA	SA	AB	H	2B	3B	HR	HR%	R	RBI	BB	SO	SB	AB	H	PO	A	E	DP	TC/G	FA	G by Pos
1880	2 teams	CLE N (1G – .250)			CIN N (17G – .092)																			
"	total	18	.101	.130	69	7	2	0	0	0.0	1	2	0	15		0	0	39	5	14	1	3.2	.759	OF-18
1882	CIN AA	76	.250	.355	344	86	11	11	1	0.3	59		7			0	0	175	19	35	11	3.0	.847	OF-64, 1B-12, P-4
1883	COL AA	82	.226	.283	371	84	6	6	1	0.3	42		6			0	0	131	17	38	2	2.3	.796	OF-82, 2B-1, P-1
1884	5 teams	STL AA (5G – .263)			KC U (14G – .258)				CHI U (20G – .224)			PIT U (17G – .233)		BAL U (17G – .261)										
"	total	73	.244	.305	308	75	10	3	1	0.3	43		22			0	0	99	10	32	0	1.9	.773	OF-72, P-1
6 yrs.		257	.228	.298	1122	256	29	20	3	0.3	152	3	37	32		0	0	448	56	120	14	2.4	.808	OF-237, P-14, 1B-12, 2B-1

Bobby Wheelock

WHEELOCK, WARREN H.
B. Aug. 6, 1864, Charlestown, Mass.   D. Mar. 13, 1928, Boston, Mass.   BR TR 5'8" 150 lbs.

Year	Team	Games	BA	SA	AB	H	2B	3B	HR	HR%	R	RBI	BB	SO	SB	AB	H	PO	A	E	DP	TC/G	FA	G by Pos
1887	BOS N	48	.253	.337	166	42	4	2	1	1.2	32	15	15	15	20	0	0	73	72	22	5	3.5	.868	OF-28, SS-20, 2B-4
1890	COL AA	52	.237	.295	190	45	6	1	1	0.5	24		25		34	0	0	92	162	33	12	5.5	.885	SS-52
1891		136	.229	.263	498	114	15	1	0	0.0	82	39	78	55	52	0	0	248	474	81	65	5.9	.899	SS-136
3 yrs.		236	.235	.285	854	201	25	4	3	0.4	138	54	118	70	106	0	0	413	708	136	82	5.3	.892	SS-208, OF-28, 2B-4

Jim Whelan

WHELAN, JAMES FRANCIS
B. May 11, 1890, Kansas City, Mo.   D. Nov. 29, 1929, Dayton, Ohio   BR TR 5'8½" 165 lbs.

Year	Team	Games	BA	SA	AB	H	2B	3B	HR	HR%	R	RBI	BB	SO	SB	AB	H	PO	A	E	DP	TC/G	FA	G by Pos
1913	STL N	1	.000	.000	1	0	0	0	0	0.0	0	0	0	0	0	1	0	0	0	0	0	0.0	–	

Tom Whelan

WHELAN, THOMAS JOSEPH
B. Jan. 3, 1894, Lynn, Mass.   D. June 26, 1957, Boston, Mass.   BR TR 5'11" 175 lbs.

Year	Team	Games	BA	SA	AB	H	2B	3B	HR	HR%	R	RBI	BB	SO	SB	AB	H	PO	A	E	DP	TC/G	FA	G by Pos
1920	BOS N	1	.000	.000	1	0	0	0	0	0.0	0	1	1	0	0	0	0	4	0	0	0	4.0	1.000	1B-1

Pete Whisenant

WHISENANT, PETER
B. Dec. 14, 1929, Asheville, N. C.   BR TR 6'2" 190 lbs.

Year	Team	Games	BA	SA	AB	H	2B	3B	HR	HR%	R	RBI	BB	SO	SB	AB	H	PO	A	E	DP	TC/G	FA	G by Pos
1952	BOS N	24	.192	.231	52	10	2	0	0	0.0	4	13	1	9	1	0	0	34	2	1	2	1.5	.973	OF-14
1955	STL N	58	.191	.304	115	22	5	1	2	1.7	10	9	5	29	2	20	5	76	4	3	1	1.4	.964	OF-40
1956	CHI N	103	.239	.414	314	75	16	3	11	3.5	37	46	24	53	8	8	2	242	6	2	0	2.4	.992	OF-93
1957	CIN N	67	.211	.456	90	19	3	2	5	5.6	18	11	5	24	0	20	8	54	0	1	0	0.8	.982	OF-43
1958		85	.236	.463	203	48	9	2	11	5.4	33	40	18	37	3	25	6	122	3	0	1	1.5	1.000	OF-66, 2B-1
1959		36	.239	.479	71	17	2	0	5	7.0	13	11	8	18	0	14	1	27	1	1	0	0.8	.966	OF-21
1960	3 teams	CIN N (1G – .000)			CLE A (7G – .167)				WAS A (58G – .226)															
"	total	66	.221	.369	122	27	9	0	3	2.5	19	9	19	16	2	15	2	69	2	0	0	1.1	1.000	OF-49
1961	2 teams	MIN A (10G – .000)			CIN N (26G – .200)																			
"	total	36	.143	.143	21	3	0	0	0	0.0	7	1	3	6	1	13	1	6	2	1	0	0.3	.889	OF-17, 3B-1, C-1
8 yrs.		475	.224	.399	988	221	46	8	37	3.7	140	134	86	196	17	124	26	630	20	9	5	1.4	.986	OF-343, 3B-1, 2B-1, C-1

Larry Whisenton

WHISENTON, LARRY
B. July 3, 1956, St. Louis, Mo.   BL TL 6'1" 190 lbs.

Year	Team	Games	BA	SA	AB	H	2B	3B	HR	HR%	R	RBI	BB	SO	SB	AB	H	PO	A	E	DP	TC/G	FA	G by Pos
1977	ATL N	4	.250	.250	4	1	0	0	0	0.0	1	0	0	3	0	4	1	0	0	0	0	0.0		
1978		6	.188	.250	16	3	1	0	0	0.0	1	2	1	2	0	1	0	5	0	0	0	0.8	1.000	OF-4
1979		13	.243	.351	37	9	2	1	0	0.0	3	3	3	3	1	0	0	28	3	0	0	2.4	1.000	OF-13
1981		9	.200	.200	5	1	0	0	0	0.0	1	0	2	1	0	5	1	0	0	0	0	0.1	–	OF-2
1982		84	.238	.399	143	34	7	2	4	2.8	21	17	23	33	2	45	8	53	1	2	0	0.7	.964	OF-34
5 yrs.		116	.234	.371	205	48	10	3	4	2.0	27	21	29	42	3	55	10	86	4	3	0	0.8	.968	OF-53

LEAGUE CHAMPIONSHIP SERIES

Year	Team	Games	BA	SA	AB	H	2B	3B	HR	HR%	R	RBI	BB	SO	SB	AB	H	PO	A	E	DP	TC/G	FA	G by Pos
1982	ATL N	2	.000	.000	2	0	0	0	0	0.0	0	0	0	1	0	2	0	0	0	0	0	0.0	–	

Lew Whistler

WHISTLER, LEWIS
Born Lewis Wissler.
B. Mar. 10, 1868, St. Louis, Mo.   D. Dec. 30, 1959, St. Louis, Mo.   TR

Year	Team	Games	BA	SA	AB	H	2B	3B	HR	HR%	R	RBI	BB	SO	SB	AB	H	PO	A	E	DP	TC/G	FA	G by Pos
1890	NY N	45	.288	.459	170	49	9	7	2	1.2	27	29	20	37	8	0	0	490	10	9	28	11.3	.982	1B-45
1891		72	.245	.374	265	65	8	7	4	1.5	39	38	24	45	4	0	0	143	128	49	11	4.4	.847	SS-33, OF-22, 1B-7, 2B-6, 3B-5
1892	2 teams	BAL N (52G – .225)			LOU N (80G – .235)																			
"	total	132	.231	.346	494	114	10	13	7	1.4	74	55	48	67	26	0	0	1329	88	36	75	11.0	.975	1B-123, 2B-10, OF-1
1893	2 teams	LOU N (13G – .213)			STL N (10G – .237)																			
"	total	23	.224	.271	85	19	2	1	0	0.0	10	11	8	7	1	0	0	153	9	9	9	7.4	.947	1B-14, OF-9
4 yrs.		272	.244	.366	1014	247	29	28	13	1.3	150	133	100	156	39	0	0	2115	235	103	123	9.0	.958	1B-189, SS-33, OF-32, 2B-16, 3B-5

Lou Whitaker

WHITAKER, LOUIS RODMAN (Sweet Lou)
B. May 12, 1957, Brooklyn, N. Y.   BL TR 5'11" 160 lbs.

Year	Team	Games	BA	SA	AB	H	2B	3B	HR	HR%	R	RBI	BB	SO	SB	AB	H	PO	A	E	DP	TC/G	FA	G by Pos
1977	DET A	11	.250	.281	32	8	1	0	0	0.0	5	2	4	6	2	0	0	17	18	0	2	3.2	1.000	2B-9
1978		139	.285	.357	484	138	12	7	3	0.6	71	58	61	65	7	6	3	301	458	17	95	5.6	.978	2B-136, DH-2
1979		127	.286	.378	423	121	14	8	3	0.7	75	42	78	66	20	5	0	280	369	9	103	5.2	.986	2B-126
1980		145	.233	.283	477	111	19	1	1	0.2	68	45	73	79	8	8	2	340	428	12	93	5.4	.985	2B-143
1981		109	.263	.373	335	88	14	4	5	1.5	48	36	40	42	5	2	1	227	354	9	77	5.4	.985	2B-108
1982		152	.286	.434	560	160	22	8	15	2.7	76	65	48	58	11	4	1	331	470	10	120	5.3	.988	2B-149, DH-1
1983		161	.320	.457	643	206	40	6	12	1.9	94	72	67	70	17	7	3	299	447	13	92	4.7	.983	2B-160
1984		143	.289	.407	558	161	25	1	13	2.3	90	56	62	63	6	4	1	290	405	15	83	5.0	.979	2B-142
1985		152	.280	.457	608	170	29	8	21	3.5	102	73	80	56	6	4	0	314	414	11	101	4.9	.985	2B-150
1986		144	.269	.437	584	157	26	6	20	3.4	95	73	63	70	13	6	1	276	421	11	98	4.9	.984	2B-141
1987		149	.265	.427	604	160	38	6	16	2.6	110	59	71	108	13	3	1	275	416	17	99	4.8	.976	2B-148
1988		115	.275	.419	403	111	18	2	12	3.0	54	55	66	61	2	9	3	218	284	8	53	4.4	.984	2B-110
1989		148	.251	.462	509	128	21	1	28	5.5	77	85	89	59	6	6	0	327	393	11	99	4.9	.985	2B-146, DH-2
13 yrs.		1695	.276	.412	6220	1719	279	58	149	2.4	965	721	802	803	116	66	19	3495	4877	143	1115	5.0	.983	2B-1668, DH-5

LEAGUE CHAMPIONSHIP SERIES

Year	Team	Games	BA	SA	AB	H	2B	3B	HR	HR%	R	RBI	BB	SO	SB	AB	H	PO	A	E	DP	TC/G	FA	G by Pos
1984	DET A	3	.143	.143	14	2	0	0	0	0.0	3	0	0	3	0	0	0	5	6	0	0	3.7	1.000	2B-3

Year	Team		Games	BA	SA	AB	H	2B	3B	HR	HR%	R	RBI	BB	SO	SB	Pinch Hit AB	Pinch Hit H	PO	A	E	DP	TC/G	FA	G by Pos

Lou Whitaker *continued*

| 1987 | | | 5 | .176 | .353 | 17 | 3 | 0 | 0 | 1 | 5.9 | 4 | 1 | 7 | 3 | 1 | 0 | 0 | 11 | 14 | 0 | 1 | 5.0 | 1.000 | 2B-5 |
| 2 yrs. | | | 8 | .161 | .258 | 31 | 5 | 0 | 0 | 1 | 3.2 | 7 | 1 | 7 | 6 | 1 | 0 | 0 | 16 | 20 | 0 | 1 | 4.5 | 1.000 | 2B-8 |

WORLD SERIES

| 1984 | DET | A | 5 | .278 | .389 | 18 | 5 | 2 | 0 | 0 | 0.0 | 6 | 0 | 4 | 4 | 0 | 0 | 0 | 15 | 18 | 0 | 2 | 6.6 | 1.000 | 2B-5 |

Steve Whitaker

WHITAKER, STEPHEN EDWARD
B. May 7, 1943, Tacoma, Wash.

BL TR 6' 180 lbs.

1966	NY	A	31	.246	.491	114	28	3	2	7	6.1	15	15	9	24	0	0	0	61	3	3	0	2.2	.955	OF-31
1967			122	.243	.358	441	107	12	3	11	2.5	37	50	23	89	2	10	4	202	12	4	6	1.8	.982	OF-114
1968			28	.117	.150	60	7	2	0	0	0.0	3	3	8	18	0	13	2	20	2	2	0	0.9	.917	OF-14
1969	SEA	A	69	.250	.440	116	29	2	1	6	5.2	15	13	12	29	2	25	5	45	5	2	0	0.8	.962	OF-39
1970	SF	N	16	.111	.148	27	3	1	0	0	0.0	3	4	2	14	0	6	2	6	0	1	0	0.4	.857	OF-9
5 yrs.			266	.230	.367	758	174	20	6	24	3.2	73	85	54	174	4	54	13	334	22	12	6	1.4	.967	OF-207

Bill White

WHITE, WILLIAM BARNEY
B. June 25, 1923, Paris, Tex.

BR TR 5'11" 186 lbs.

| 1945 | BKN | N | 4 | .000 | .000 | 1 | 0 | 0 | 0 | 0 | 0.0 | 2 | 0 | 1 | 1 | 0 | 0 | 0 | 1 | 0 | 0 | 0 | 0.5 | 1.000 | SS-1 |

Bill White

WHITE, WILLIAM DeKOVA
B. Jan. 28, 1934, Lakewood, Fla.

BL TL 6' 185 lbs.

1956	NY	N	138	.256	.459	508	130	23	7	22	4.3	63	59	47	72	15	0	0	1256	111	15	106	10.0	.989	1B-138, OF-2
1958	SF	N	26	.241	.379	29	7	1	0	1	3.4	5	4	7	5	1	16	4	19	1	0	2	0.8	1.000	1B-3, OF-2
1959	STL	N	138	.302	.470	517	156	33	9	12	2.3	77	72	34	61	15	5	1	579	27	9	33	4.5	.985	OF-92, 1B-71
1960			144	.283	.455	554	157	27	10	16	2.9	81	79	42	83	12	3	0	1058	66	13	109	7.9	.989	1B-123, OF-29
1961			153	.286	.472	591	169	28	11	20	3.4	89	90	64	84	8	3	0	1373	104	17	125	9.8	.989	1B-151
1962			159	.324	.482	614	199	31	3	20	3.3	93	102	58	69	9	1	0	1260	97	10	116	8.6	.993	1B-159, OF-27
1963			162	.304	.491	658	200	26	8	27	4.1	106	109	59	100	10	0	0	1389	105	13	126	9.3	.991	1B-162
1964			160	.303	.474	631	191	37	4	21	3.3	92	102	52	103	7	0	0	1513	101	6	125	10.1	.996	1B-160
1965			148	.289	.481	543	157	26	3	24	4.4	82	73	63	86	3	4	1	1308	109	11	114	9.6	.992	1B-144
1966	PHI	N	159	.276	.451	577	159	23	6	22	3.8	85	103	68	109	16	4	0	1422	109	9	118	9.7	.994	1B-158
1967			110	.250	.360	308	77	6	2	8	2.6	29	33	52	61	6	14	0	775	52	6	85	7.6	.993	1B-95
1968			127	.239	.361	385	92	16	2	9	2.3	34	40	39	79	0	20	5	982	77	6	94	8.4	.994	1B-111
1969	STL	N	49	.211	.228	57	12	1	0	0	0.0	7	4	11	15	1	31	5	81	7	0	7	1.8	1.000	1B-15
13 yrs.			1673	.286	.455	5972	1706	278	65	202	3.4	843	870	596	927	103	101	16	13015	966	115	1160	8.4	.992	1B-1477, OF-152

WORLD SERIES

| 1964 | STL | N | 7 | .111 | .148 | 27 | 3 | 1 | 0 | 0 | 0.0 | 2 | 2 | 2 | 6 | 1 | 0 | 0 | 62 | 3 | 0 | 4 | 9.3 | 1.000 | 1B-7 |

Bill White

WHITE, WILLIAM DIGHTON
B. May 1, 1860, Bridgeport, Ohio D. Dec. 31, 1924, Bellaire, Ohio

1884	PIT	AA	74	.227	.320	291	66	7	10	0	0.0	25		13			0	0	75	206	69	14	4.7	.803	SS-60, 3B-10, OF-4
1886	LOU	AA	135	.257	.329	557	143	17	10	1	0.2	96		37			0	0	212	431	96	48	5.5	.870	SS-135, P-1
1887			132	.252	.313	512	129	7	9	2	0.4	85		47		41	0	0	204	431	96	45	5.5	.869	SS-132
1888 2 teams					LOU AA (49G – .278)			STL AA (76G – .175)																	
" total			125	.218	.288	473	103	8	8	3	0.6	66	60	28		21	0	0	199	368	86	16	5.2	.868	SS-112, 3B-11, 2B-2
4 yrs.			466	.241	.312	1833	441	39	37	6	0.3	272	60	125		62	0	0	690	1436	347	123	5.3	.860	SS-439, 3B-21, OF-4, 2B-2, P-1

Bill White

WHITE, WILLIAM EDWARD
B. Milner, Ga. Deceased.

| 1879 | PRO | N | 1 | .250 | .250 | 4 | 1 | 0 | 0 | 0 | 0.0 | 1 | 0 | 0 | 1 | | 0 | 0 | 12 | 0 | 0 | 1 | 12.0 | 1.000 | 1B-1 |

C. B. White

WHITE, C. B.
B. Wakeman, Ohio Deceased.

| 1883 | PHI | N | 1 | .000 | .000 | 1 | 0 | 0 | 0 | 0 | 0.0 | 0 | | 0 | 0 | | 0 | 0 | 3 | 1 | 1 | 0 | 5.0 | .800 | SS-1, 3B-1 |

Charlie White

WHITE, CHARLES
B. Aug. 12, 1928, Kinston, N. C.

BL TR 5'11" 192 lbs.

1954	MIL	N	50	.237	.312	93	22	4	0	1	1.1	14	8	9	8	0	24	4	101	4	2	0	2.1	.981	C-28
1955			12	.233	.267	30	7	1	0	0	0.0	3	4	5	7	0	1	0	39	2	0	0	3.4	1.000	C-10
2 yrs.			62	.236	.301	123	29	5	0	1	0.8	17	12	14	15	0	25	4	140	6	2	0	2.4	.986	C-38

Deacon White

WHITE, JAMES LAURIE
Brother of Will White.
B. Dec. 7, 1847, Caton, N. Y. D. July 7, 1939, Aurora, Ill.
Manager 1872, 1879.

BL TR 5'11" 175 lbs.

1876	CHI	N	66	.343	.419	303	104	18	1	0	0.3	66	60	7	3		0	0	318	51	69	3	6.6	.842	C-63, OF-3, 1B-3, 3B-1, P-1
1877	BOS	N	59	**.387**	**.545**	266	**103**	14	11	2	0.8	51	**49**	8	3		0	0	384	22	24	16	7.3	.944	1B-35, OF-19, C-7
1878	CIN	N	61	.314	.337	258	81	4	1	0	0.0	41	29	10	5		0	0	277	71	39	4	6.3	.899	C-48, OF-16, 3B-1
1879			78	.330	.423	333	110	16	6	1	0.3	55	52	6	9		0	0	349	96	55	3	6.4	.890	C-59, OF-21, 1B-2
1880			35	.298	.355	141	42	4	2	0	0.0	21	7	9	7		0	0	59	9	17	3	2.4	.800	OF-33, 1B-3, 2B-1
1881	BUF	N	78	.310	.411	319	99	24	4	0	0.0	58	53	9	8		0	0	371	119	70	24	7.2	.875	1B-26, 2B-25, OF-17, 3B-7, C-4
1882			83	.282	.341	337	95	17	0	1	0.3	51		15	16		0	0	173	150	55	8	4.6	.854	3B-63, C-20
1883			94	.292	.353	391	114	14	5	0	0.0	62		23	18		0	0	183	165	67	11	4.4	.839	3B-77, C-22
1884			110	.325	.442	452	147	16	11	5	1.1	82		32	13		0	0	130	203	66	13	3.6	.835	3B-108, C-3
1885			98	.292	.337	404	118	6	4	0	0.0	54	57	12	11		0	0	118	198	40	12	3.6	.888	3B-98
1886	DET	N	124	.289	.354	491	142	19	5	1	0.2	65	76	31	35		0	0	131	245	68	18	3.6	.847	3B-124
1887			111	.303	.416	449	136	20	11	3	0.7	71	75	26	15	20	0	0	152	227	65	19	4.0	.854	3B-106, OF-3, 1B-2

Year	Team		Games	BA	SA	AB	H	2B	3B	HR	HR%	R	RBI	BB	SO	SB	Pinch Hit AB	Pinch Hit H	PO	A	E	DP	TC/G	FA	G by Pos

Deacon White *continued*

1888			125	.298	.381	527	157	22	5	4	0.8	75	71	21	24	12	0	0	146	244	65	19	3.6	.857	3B-125
1889	PIT	N	55	.253	.307	225	57	10	1	0	0.0	35	26	16	18	2	0	0	98	97	26	10	4.0	.882	3B-52, 1B-3
1890	BUF	P	122	.260	.308	439	114	13	4	0	0.0	62	47	67	30	3	0	0	670	202	47	52	7.5	.949	3B-64, 1B-57, SS-1, P-1
15 yrs.			1299	.303	.382	5335	1619	217	73	18	0.3	849	602	292	215	37	0	0	3559	2099	773	215	5.0	.880	3B-826, C-226, 1B-131, OF-112, 2B-26, P-2, SS-1

Devon White

WHITE, DEVON MARKES
B. Dec. 29, 1962, Kingston, Jamaica

BB TR 6'1" 170 lbs.

1985	CAL	A	21	.143	.143	7	1	0	0	0	0.0	7	0	1	3	3	0	0	10	1	0	0	0.5	1.000	OF-16
1986			28	.235	.353	51	12	1	1	1	2.0	8	3	6	8	6	0	0	49	0	2	0	1.8	.961	OF-28
1987			159	.263	.443	639	168	33	5	24	3.8	103	87	39	135	32	0	0	424	16	9	3	2.8	.980	OF-159
1988			122	.259	.389	455	118	22	2	11	2.4	76	51	23	84	17	5	2	364	7	9	2	3.1	.976	OF-116
1989			156	.245	.371	636	156	18	13	12	1.9	86	56	31	129	44	1	0	430	10	5	3	2.9	.989	OF-154, DH-1
5 yrs.			486	.254	.400	1788	455	74	21	48	2.7	280	197	100	359	102	6	2	1277	34	25	8	2.7	.981	OF-473, DH-1

LEAGUE CHAMPIONSHIP SERIES

| 1986 | CAL | A | 3 | .500 | .500 | 2 | 1 | 0 | 0 | 0 | 0.0 | 2 | 0 | 0 | 1 | 0 | 0 | 0 | 2 | 0 | 0 | 0 | 0.7 | 1.000 | OF-3 |

Doc White

WHITE, GUY HARRIS
B. Apr. 9, 1879, Washington, D. C. D. Feb. 19, 1969, Silver Springs, Md.

BL TL 6'1" 165 lbs.

1901	PHI	N	31	.274	.358	95	26	3	1	1	1.1	15	10	7			0	0	7	72	4	0	2.7	.952	P-31, OF-1
1902			61	.263	.307	179	47	3	1	1	0.6	17	15	11	5	5	1	0	35	84	12	0	2.1	.908	P-36, OF-19
1903	CHI	A	38	.202	.232	99	20	3	0	0	0.0	10	5	19	1	0	0	27	98	4	5	3.4	.969	P-37, OF-1
1904			33	.158	.184	76	12	2	0	0	0.0	7	2	10	3	0	0	33	68	5	2	3.2	.953	P-30, OF-2
1905			37	.163	.233	86	14	4	1	0	0.0	7	7	4	3	0	0	20	77	4	2	2.7	.960	P-36, OF-1
1906			28	.185	.231	65	12	1	1	0	0.0	11	3	13	3	0	0	17	77	8	1	3.6	.922	P-28, OF-1
1907			48	.222	.233	90	20	1	0	0	0.0	12	12	12	2	0	0	33	103	2	1	2.9	.986	P-46, OF-2
1908			51	.229	.239	109	25	1	0	0	0.0	12	10	12	4	6	1	30	116	2	7	2.9	.986	P-41, OF-3
1909			72	.234	.292	192	45	1	5	0	0.0	24	7	33	7	8	1	71	54	8	1	1.8	.940	OF-40, P-24
1910			56	.198	.238	126	25	1	2	0	0.0	14	8	14	2	8	0	44	79	3	4	2.3	.976	P-33, OF-14
1911			39	.256	.295	78	20	1	1	0	0.0	12	6	7	1	0	0	20	57	6	2	2.1	.928	P-34, 1B-2, OF-1
1912			33	.125	.179	56	7	1	0	0	0.0	5	0	7	1	0	0	5	46	0	1	1.5	1.000	P-32
1913			20	.120	.120	25	3	0	0	0	0.0	1	0	3	1	0	0	4	44	2	0	2.5	.960	P-19, 1B-1
13 yrs.			547	.216	.259	1276	276	22	13	2	0.2	147	75	147	1	32	28	3	346	975	60	26	2.5	.957	P-427, OF-85, 1B-3

WORLD SERIES

| 1906 | CHI | A | 3 | .000 | .000 | 3 | 0 | 0 | 0 | 0 | 0.0 | 0 | 0 | 1 | | 0 | 0 | 0 | 1 | 3 | 0 | 0 | 1.3 | 1.000 | P-3 |

Don White

WHITE, DONALD WILLIAM
B. Jan. 8, 1919, Everett, Wash. D. June 15, 1987, Carlsbad, Calif.

BR TR 6'1" 195 lbs.

1948	PHI	A	86	.245	.328	253	62	14	2	1	0.4	29	28	19	16	0	13	2	122	37	9	6	2.0	.946	OF-54, 3B-17
1949			57	.213	.249	169	36	6	0	0	0.0	12	10	14	12	0	8	3	91	9	2	2	1.8	.980	OF-47, 3B-4
2 yrs.			143	.232	.296	422	98	20	2	1	0.2	41	38	33	28	0	21	5	213	46	11	8	1.9	.959	OF-101, 3B-21

Ed White

WHITE, EDWARD PERRY
B. Apr. 6, 1926, Anniston, Ala. D. Sept. 28, 1982, Lakeland, Fla.

BR TR 6'2" 200 lbs.

| 1955 | CHI | A | 3 | .500 | .500 | 4 | 2 | 0 | 0 | 0 | 0.0 | 0 | 0 | 1 | 1 | 0 | 1 | 0 | 2 | 0 | 0 | 0 | 0.7 | 1.000 | OF-2 |

Elder White

WHITE, ELDER LAFAYETTE
B. Dec. 23, 1934, Colerain, N. C.

BR TR 5'11" 165 lbs.

| 1962 | CHI | N | 23 | .151 | .189 | 53 | 8 | 2 | 0 | 0 | 0.0 | 4 | 1 | 8 | 11 | 3 | 6 | 1 | 25 | 47 | 1 | 6 | 3.2 | .986 | SS-15, 2B-1 |

Frank White

WHITE, FRANK JR.
B. Sept. 4, 1950, Greenville, Miss.

BR TR 5'11" 165 lbs.

1973	KC	A	51	.223	.281	139	31	6	1	0	0.0	20	5	8	23	3	1	0	71	121	12	36	4.0	.941	SS-37, 2B-11
1974			99	.221	.294	204	45	6	3	1	0.5	19	18	5	33	3	3	0	119	189	12	40	3.2	.963	2B-50, SS-29, 3B-16, DH-3
1975			111	.250	.365	304	76	10	2	7	2.3	43	36	20	39	11	0	0	180	272	11	56	4.2	.976	2B-67, SS-42, 3B-4, DH-2
1976			152	.229	.307	446	102	17	6	2	0.4	39	46	19	42	20	0	0	296	479	23	89	5.3	.971	2B-130, SS-37
1977			152	.245	.342	474	116	21	5	5	1.1	59	50	25	67	23	0	0	310	437	8	86	5.0	.989	2B-152, SS-4
1978			143	.275	.399	461	127	24	6	7	1.5	66	50	26	59	13	3	0	325	385	16	96	5.1	.978	2B-140
1979			127	.266	.403	467	124	26	4	10	2.1	73	48	25	54	28	1	0	317	332	12	78	5.2	.982	2B-125
1980			154	.264	.357	560	148	23	4	7	1.3	70	60	19	69	19	3	0	395	448	10	103	5.5	.988	2B-153
1981			94	.250	.376	364	91	17	1	9	2.5	35	38	19	50	4	1	1	226	263	6	70	5.3	.988	2B-93
1982			145	.298	.469	524	156	45	6	11	2.1	71	56	16	65	10	1	0	361	389	17	99	5.3	.978	2B-144
1983			146	.260	.406	549	143	35	6	11	2.0	52	77	20	51	13	3	2	390	442	8	123	5.8	.990	2B-145
1984			129	.271	.445	479	130	22	5	17	3.5	58	56	27	72	5	1	0	299	425	11	97	5.7	.985	2B-129
1985			149	.249	.414	563	140	25	1	22	3.9	62	69	28	86	10	0	0	342	490	17	101	5.7	.980	2B-149
1986			151	.272	.465	566	154	37	3	22	3.9	76	84	43	88	4	6	1	317	441	10	92	5.1	.987	2B-151, SS-1, 3B-1
1987			154	.245	.400	563	138	32	2	17	3.0	67	78	51	86	1	1	0	320	458	10	89	5.1	.987	2B-152, DH-1
1988			150	.235	.330	537	126	25	1	8	1.5	48	58	21	67	7	6	2	293	426	4	88	4.8	.994	2B-148, DH-3
1989			135	.256	.328	418	107	22	1	2	0.5	34	36	30	52	3	4	0	238	407	10	64	4.9	.985	2B-132, OF-1
17 yrs.			2242	.256	.385	7618	1954	393	57	158	2.1	892	865	402	1003	177	34	6	4799	6404	197	1407	5.1	.983	2B-2071, SS-150, 3B-21, DH-9, OF-1

DIVISIONAL PLAYOFF SERIES

| 1981 | KC | A | 3 | .182 | .182 | 11 | 2 | 0 | 0 | 0 | 0.0 | 1 | 0 | 1 | 1 | 0 | 0 | 0 | 0 | 0 | 1 | 0 | 0.3 | – | 2B-3 |

LEAGUE CHAMPIONSHIP SERIES

1976	KC	A	4	.125	.125	8	1	0	0	0	0.0	2	0	0	0	0	0	0	6	11	0	3	4.3	1.000	2B-4
1977			5	.278	.333	18	5	1	0	0	0.0	1	2	0	1	0	0	0	13	16	0	1	5.8	1.000	2B-5
1978			4	.231	.231	13	3	0	0	0	0.0	1	2	0	4	0	0	0	9	12	0	1	5.3	1.000	2B-4
1980			3	.545	.909	11	6	1	0	1	9.1	3	3	1	0	0	0	0	9	10	1	3	6.7	.950	2B-3

Year	Team		Games	BA	SA	AB	H	2B	3B	HR	HR%	R	RBI	BB	SO	SB	Pinch Hit AB	Pinch Hit H	PO	A	E	DP	TC/G	FA	G by Pos

Frank White *continued*

Year	Team		Games	BA	SA	AB	H	2B	3B	HR	HR%	R	RBI	BB	SO	SB	AB	H	PO	A	E	DP	TC/G	FA	G by Pos
1984			3	.083	.083	12	1	0	0	0	0.0	1	0	0	3	0	0	0	7	3	0	2	3.3	1.000	2B-3
1985			7	.200	.200	25	5	0	0	0	0.0	1	3	1	2	0	0	0	9	28	0	4	5.3	1.000	2B-7
6 yrs.			26	.241	.299	87	21	2	0	1	1.1	9	10	1	10	2	0	0	53	80	1	16	5.2	.993	2B-26

WORLD SERIES

Year	Team		Games	BA	SA	AB	H	2B	3B	HR	HR%	R	RBI	BB	SO	SB	AB	H	PO	A	E	DP	TC/G	FA	G by Pos
1980	KC	A	6	.080	.080	25	2	0	0	0	0.0	0	0	1	5	1	0	0	13	21	2	6	6.0	.944	2B-6
1985			7	.250	.464	28	7	3	0	1	3.6	4	6	3	4	1	0	0	10	20	0	2	4.3	1.000	2B-7
2 yrs.			13	.170	.283	53	9	3	0	1	1.9	4	6	4	9	2	0	0	23	41	2	8	5.1	.970	2B-13

Fuzz White

WHITE, ALBERT EUGENE
B. June 27, 1918, Springfield, Mo.

BL TR 6' 175 lbs.

Year	Team		Games	BA	SA	AB	H	2B	3B	HR	HR%	R	RBI	BB	SO	SB	AB	H	PO	A	E	DP	TC/G	FA	G by Pos
1940	STL	A	2	.000	.000	2	0	0	0	0	0.0	0	0	0	0	0	2	0	0	0	0	0	0.0	–	
1947	NY	N	7	.231	.231	13	3	0	0	0	0.0	3	0	0	0	0	1	0	11	0	0	0	1.6	1.000	OF-5
2 yrs.			9	.200	.200	15	3	0	0	0	0.0	3	0	0	0	0	3	0	11	0	0	0	1.2	1.000	OF-5

Jack White

WHITE, JOHN PETER
B. Aug. 31, 1905, New York, N. Y.   D. June 19, 1971, Flushing, N. Y.

BB TR 5'7½" 150 lbs.

Year	Team		Games	BA	SA	AB	H	2B	3B	HR	HR%	R	RBI	BB	SO	SB	AB	H	PO	A	E	DP	TC/G	FA	G by Pos
1927	CIN	N	5	.000	.000	4	0	0	0	0	0.0	1	0	0	0	0	0	0	3	5	0	0	1.6	1.000	2B-3, SS-2
1928			1	.000	.000	3	0	0	0	0	0.0	0	0	0	1	0	0	0	5	0	1	0	6.0	.833	2B-1
2 yrs.			6	.000	.000	7	0	0	0	0	0.0	1	0	0	1	0	0	0	8	5	1	1	2.3	.929	2B-4, SS-2

Jack White

WHITE, JOHN WALLACE
B. Jan. 19, 1878, Indianapolis, Ind.   D. Sept. 30, 1963, Indianapolis, Ind.

BR TR 5'6"

Year	Team		Games	BA	SA	AB	H	2B	3B	HR	HR%	R	RBI	BB	SO	SB	AB	H	PO	A	E	DP	TC/G	FA	G by Pos
1904	BOS	N	1	.000	.000	5	0	0	0	0	0.0	1	0	0		0	0	0	2	1	0	0	3.0	1.000	OF-1

Jerry White

WHITE, JEROME CARDELL
B. Aug. 23, 1952, Shirley, Mass.

BB TR 5'10" 164 lbs.

Year	Team		Games	BA	SA	AB	H	2B	3B	HR	HR%	R	RBI	BB	SO	SB	AB	H	PO	A	E	DP	TC/G	FA	G by Pos
1974	MON	N	9	.400	.700	10	4	1	1	0	0.0	0	2	0	0	3	0	0	6	0	0	0	0.7	1.000	OF-7
1975			39	.299	.423	97	29	4	1	2	2.1	14	7	10	7	5	3	0	81	1	2	1	2.2	.976	OF-30
1976			114	.245	.313	278	68	11	1	2	0.7	32	21	27	31	15	17	2	157	4	3	0	1.4	.982	OF-92
1977			16	.190	.190	21	4	0	0	0	0.0	4	1	1	3	1	10	2	5	0	0	0	0.3	1.000	OF-8
1978 2 teams	MON	N (18G – .200)					CHI	N	(59G – .272)																	
" total			77	.267	.329	146	39	6	0	1	0.7	24	10	24	19	5	12	3	102	4	2	1	1.4	.981	OF-57
1979	MON	N	88	.297	.428	138	41	7	1	3	2.2	30	18	21	23	8	38	12	55	2	1	1	0.7	.983	OF-43
1980			110	.262	.430	214	56	9	3	7	3.3	30	22	23	37	8	29	6	101	5	6	1	1.0	.946	OF-84
1981			59	.218	.353	119	26	5	1	3	2.5	11	11	13	17	5	18	5	58	2	3	1	1.1	.952	OF-39
1982			69	.243	.365	115	28	6	1	2	1.7	13	13	8	26	3	39	10	40	1	0	0	0.6	1.000	OF-30
1983			40	.147	.176	34	5	1	0	0	0.0	4	0	12	23	4	23	2	13	0	0	0	0.3	1.000	OF-13
1986	STL	N	25	.125	.250	24	3	0	0	1	4.2	3	3	2	3	0	19	2	5	0	0	0	0.2	1.000	OF-6
11 yrs.			646	.253	.363	1196	303	50	9	21	1.8	155	109	148	174	57	208	44	623	19	17	5	1.0	.974	OF-409

DIVISIONAL PLAYOFF SERIES

Year	Team		Games	BA	SA	AB	H	2B	3B	HR	HR%	R	RBI	BB	SO	SB	AB	H	PO	A	E	DP	TC/G	FA	G by Pos
1981	MON	N	5	.167	.222	18	3	1	0	0	0.0	3	1	2	2	3	0	0	0	0	0	0	0.0	–	OF-5

LEAGUE CHAMPIONSHIP SERIES

Year	Team		Games	BA	SA	AB	H	2B	3B	HR	HR%	R	RBI	BB	SO	SB	AB	H	PO	A	E	DP	TC/G	FA	G by Pos
1981	MON	N	5	.313	.563	16	5	1	0	1	6.3	2	3	3	1	1	0	0	0	0	0	0	0.0	–	OF-5

Jo-Jo White

WHITE, JOYNER CLIFFORD
Father of Mike White.
B. June 1, 1909, Red Oak, Ga.   D. Oct. 9, 1986, Tacoma, Wash.
Manager 1960.

BL TR 5'11" 165 lbs.

Year	Team		Games	BA	SA	AB	H	2B	3B	HR	HR%	R	RBI	BB	SO	SB	AB	H	PO	A	E	DP	TC/G	FA	G by Pos
1932	DET	A	79	.260	.346	208	54	6	3	2	1.0	25	21	22	19	6	25	9	96	6	4	2	1.3	.962	OF-47
1933			91	.252	.359	234	59	9	5	2	0.9	43	34	27	26	5	26	10	122	4	3	1	1.4	.977	OF-54
1934			115	.313	.385	384	120	18	5	0	0.0	97	44	69	39	28	12	2	225	9	10	2	2.1	.959	OF-98
1935			114	.240	.345	412	99	13	12	2	0.5	82	32	68	42	19	13	4	247	7	10	1	2.3	.962	OF-100
1936			58	.275	.333	51	14	3	0	0	0.0	11	6	9	10	2	30	10	14	1	1	0	0.3	.938	OF-18
1937			94	.246	.308	305	75	5	7	0	0.0	50	21	50	40	12	5	2	216	4	6	0	2.4	.973	OF-82
1938			78	.262	.301	206	54	6	1	0	0.0	40	15	28	15	3	18	3	141	4	5	0	1.9	.967	OF-55
1943	PHI	A	139	.248	.316	500	124	17	7	1	0.2	69	30	61	51	12	5	1	335	8	12	2	2.6	.966	OF-133
1944 2 teams	PHI	A (85G – .221)					CIN	N	(24G – .235)																	
" total			109	.224	.261	352	79	6	2	1	0.3	39	26	50	34	5	7	1	217	9	9	2	2.2	.962	OF-97, SS-1
9 yrs.			877	.256	.328	2652	678	83	42	8	0.3	456	229	384	276	92	141	42	1613	52	60	10	2.0	.965	OF-684, SS-1

WORLD SERIES

Year	Team		Games	BA	SA	AB	H	2B	3B	HR	HR%	R	RBI	BB	SO	SB	AB	H	PO	A	E	DP	TC/G	FA	G by Pos
1934	DET	A	7	.130	.130	23	3	0	0	0	0.0	6	0	8	4	1	0	0	22	0	1	0	3.3	.957	OF-7
1935			5	.263	.263	19	5	0	0	0	0.0	3	1	5	7	0	0	0	14	0	0	0	2.8	1.000	OF-5
2 yrs.			12	.190	.190	42	8	0	0	0	0.0	9	1	13	11	1	0	0	36	0	1	0	3.1	.973	OF-12

Mike White

WHITE, JOYNER MICHAEL
Son of Jo-Jo White.
B. Dec. 18, 1938, Detroit, Mich.

BR TR 5'8" 160 lbs.

Year	Team		Games	BA	SA	AB	H	2B	3B	HR	HR%	R	RBI	BB	SO	SB	AB	H	PO	A	E	DP	TC/G	FA	G by Pos
1963	HOU	N	3	.286	.286	7	2	0	0	0	0.0	0	0	0	0	0	1	0	10	3	0	0	4.3	1.000	2B-2
1964			89	.271	.332	280	76	11	3	0	0.0	30	27	20	47	1	13	2	151	41	5	12	2.2	.975	OF-72, 2B-10, 3B-3
1965			8	.000	.000	9	0	0	0	0	0.0	0	0	1	2	0	7	0	0	1	0	0	0.1	1.000	3B-1
3 yrs.			100	.264	.321	296	78	11	3	0	0.0	30	27	21	49	1	21	2	161	45	5	12	2.1	.976	OF-72, 2B-12, 3B-4

Myron White

WHITE, MYRON ALAN
B. Aug. 1, 1957, Long Beach, Calif.

BL TL 5'11" 180 lbs.

Year	Team		Games	BA	SA	AB	H	2B	3B	HR	HR%	R	RBI	BB	SO	SB	AB	H	PO	A	E	DP	TC/G	FA	G by Pos
1978	LA	N	7	.500	.500	4	2	0	0	0	0.0	1	1	0	1	0	0	0	2	0	0	0	0.3	1.000	OF-4

Year	Team		Games	BA	SA	AB	H	2B	3B	HR	HR%	R	RBI	BB	SO	SB	Pinch Hit AB	H	PO	A	E	DP	TC/G	FA	G by Pos

Roy White

WHITE, ROY HILTON
B. Dec. 27, 1943, Los Angeles, Calif.

BB TR 5'10" 160 lbs.
BR 1965

Year	Team		Games	BA	SA	AB	H	2B	3B	HR	HR%	R	RBI	BB	SO	SB	PH AB	H	PO	A	E	DP	TC/G	FA	G by Pos
1965	NY	A	14	.333	.381	42	14	2	0	0	0.0	7	3	4	7	2	2	2	16	4	0	0	1.4	1.000	OF-10, 2B-1
1966			115	.225	.345	316	71	13	2	7	2.2	39	20	37	43	14	22	7	159	6	7	2	1.5	.959	OF-82, 2B-2
1967			70	.224	.290	214	48	8	0	2	0.9	22	18	19	25	10	16	1	79	29	10	1	1.7	.915	OF-36, 3B-17
1968			159	.267	.414	577	154	20	7	17	2.9	89	62	73	50	20	4	1	283	14	1	4	1.9	.997	OF-154
1969			130	.290	.426	448	130	30	5	7	1.6	55	74	81	51	18	5	0	267	9	3	1	2.1	.989	OF-126
1970			162	.296	.473	609	180	30	6	22	3.6	109	94	95	66	24	1	0	315	6	2	0	2.0	.994	OF-161
1971			147	.292	.469	524	153	22	7	19	3.6	86	84	86	66	14	2	0	306	8	0	1	2.1	1.000	OF-145
1972			155	.270	.376	556	150	29	0	10	1.8	76	54	**99**	59	23	0	0	323	8	2	1	2.1	.994	OF-155
1973			162	.246	.374	**639**	157	22	3	18	2.8	88	60	78	81	16	0	0	339	4	8	0	2.2	.977	OF-162
1974			136	.275	.393	473	130	19	8	7	1.5	68	43	67	44	15	18	3	141	2	1	1	1.1	.993	OF-67, DH-53
1975			148	.290	.430	556	161	32	5	12	2.2	81	59	72	50	16	4	1	361	12	6	3	2.6	.984	OF-135, 1B-7, DH-2
1976			156	.286	.409	626	179	29	3	14	2.2	**104**	65	83	52	31	0	0	380	9	5	1	2.5	.987	OF-156
1977			143	.268	.405	519	139	25	2	14	2.7	72	52	75	58	18	4	0	301	7	6	4	2.2	.981	OF-135, DH-4
1978			103	.269	.393	346	93	13	3	8	2.3	44	43	42	35	10	9	0	128	1	1	0	1.3	.992	OF-74, DH-23
1979			81	.215	.288	205	44	6	0	3	1.5	24	27	23	21	2	19	5	45	3	0	0	0.6	1.000	DH-29, OF-27
15 yrs.			1881	.271	.404	6650	1803	300	51	160	2.4	964	758	934	708	233	106	20	3443	122	52	19	1.9	.986	OF-1625, DH-111, 3B-17, 1B-7, 2B-3

LEAGUE CHAMPIONSHIP SERIES

Year	Team		Games	BA	SA	AB	H	2B	3B	HR	HR%	R	RBI	BB	SO	SB	PH AB	H	PO	A	E	DP	TC/G	FA	G by Pos
1976	NY	A	5	.294	.471	17	5	3	0	0	0.0	4	3	5	1	1	0	0	17	0	0	0	3.4	1.000	OF-5
1977			5	.400	.800	5	2	2	0	0	0.0	2	0	1	0	0	1	0	2	0	1	0	0.6	.667	DH-1, OF-1
1978			4	.313	.563	16	5	1	0	1	6.3	5	1	1	2	0	0	0	3	0	0	0	0.8	1.000	OF-3, DH-1
3 yrs.			14	.316	.553	38	12	6	0	1	2.6	11	4	7	3	1	1	0	22	0	1	0	1.6	.957	OF-9, DH-2

WORLD SERIES

Year	Team		Games	BA	SA	AB	H	2B	3B	HR	HR%	R	RBI	BB	SO	SB	PH AB	H	PO	A	E	DP	TC/G	FA	G by Pos
1976	NY	A	4	.133	.133	15	2	0	0	0	0.0	0	0	3	0	0	0	0	13	0	0	0	3.3	1.000	OF-4
1977			2	.000	.000	2	0	0	0	0	0.0	0	0	0	0	0	2	0	0	0	0	0	0.0	—	
1978			6	.333	.458	24	8	0	0	1	4.2	9	4	4	5	2	0	0	15	0	0	0	2.5	1.000	OF-6
3 yrs.			12	.244	.317	41	10	0	0	1	2.4	9	4	7	5	2	2	0	28	0	0	0	2.3	1.000	OF-10

Sam White

WHITE, SAMUEL LAMBETH
B. Aug. 23, 1892, Preston, England   D. Nov. 11, 1929, Philadelphia, Pa.

BL TR 6'   185 lbs.

Year	Team		Games	BA	SA	AB	H	2B	3B	HR	HR%	R	RBI	BB	SO	SB	PH AB	H	PO	A	E	DP	TC/G	FA	G by Pos
1919	BOS	N	1	.000	.000	1	0	0	0	0	0.0	0	0	0	0	0	0	0	0	5	0	0	5.0	1.000	C-1

Sammy White

WHITE, SAMUEL CHARLES
B. July 7, 1928, Wenatchee, Wash.

BR TR 6'3"   195 lbs.

Year	Team		Games	BA	SA	AB	H	2B	3B	HR	HR%	R	RBI	BB	SO	SB	PH AB	H	PO	A	E	DP	TC/G	FA	G by Pos
1951	BOS	A	4	.182	.182	11	2	0	0	0	0.0	0	0	0	3	0	0	0	15	1	0	2	4.0	1.000	C-4
1952			115	.281	.423	381	107	20	2	10	2.6	35	49	16	43	2	5	0	464	59	7	7	4.6	.983	C-110
1953			136	.273	.435	476	130	34	2	13	2.7	59	64	29	48	3	7	2	588	68	9	9	4.9	.986	C-131
1954			137	.282	.426	493	139	25	2	14	2.8	46	75	21	50	1	4	0	677	80	16	11	5.6	.979	C-133
1955			143	.261	.392	544	142	30	4	11	2.0	65	64	44	58	1	0	0	671	71	12	8	5.3	.984	C-143
1956			114	.245	.332	392	96	15	2	5	1.3	28	44	35	40	2	0	0	547	60	10	13	5.4	.984	C-114
1957			111	.215	.276	340	73	10	1	3	0.9	24	31	25	38	0	0	0	489	49	8	13	4.9	.985	C-111
1958			102	.259	.378	328	85	15	3	6	1.8	35	35	21	37	1	0	0	450	38	6	8	4.8	.988	C-102
1959			119	.284	.347	377	107	13	4	1	0.3	34	42	23	39	4	1	0	557	56	6	8	5.2	.990	C-119
1961	MIL	N	21	.222	.286	63	14	1	0	1	1.6	1	5	2	9	0	0	0	107	5	3	0	5.5	.974	C-20
1962	PHI	N	41	.216	.320	97	21	4	0	2	2.1	7	12	2	16	0	2	0	173	19	5	4	4.8	.975	C-40
11 yrs.			1043	.262	.377	3502	916	167	20	66	1.9	324	421	218	381	14	19	2	4738	506	84	83	5.1	.984	C-1027

Warren White

WHITE, WILLIAM WARREN
D. Mar. 3, 1898
Manager 1872, 1874.

Year	Team		Games	BA	SA	AB	H	2B	3B	HR	HR%	R	RBI	BB	SO	SB	PH AB	H	PO	A	E	DP	TC/G	FA	G by Pos
1884	WAS	U	4	.056	.056	18	1	0	0	0	0.0	2		0		0		0	9	7	7	0	5.8	.696	3B-2, SS-1, 2B-1

Ed Whited

WHITED, EDWARD MORRIS
B. Feb. 9, 1964, Bristol, Pa.

BR TR 6'3"   195 lbs.

Year	Team		Games	BA	SA	AB	H	2B	3B	HR	HR%	R	RBI	BB	SO	SB	PH AB	H	PO	A	E	DP	TC/G	FA	G by Pos
1989	ATL	N	36	.162	.243	74	12	3	0	1	1.4	5	4	6	15	1	4	0	23	33	5	3	1.7	.918	3B-29, 1B-3

Burgess Whitehead

WHITEHEAD, BURGESS URQUHART (Whitey)
B. June 29, 1910, Tarboro, N. C.

BR TR 5'10½" 160 lbs.

Year	Team		Games	BA	SA	AB	H	2B	3B	HR	HR%	R	RBI	BB	SO	SB	PH AB	H	PO	A	E	DP	TC/G	FA	G by Pos
1933	STL	N	12	.286	.286	7	2	0	0	0	0.0	2	0	0	1	0	0	0	4	7	0	1	0.9	1.000	SS-9, 2B-3
1934			100	.277	.355	332	92	13	5	1	0.3	55	24	12	19	5	1	0	158	220	16	38	3.9	.959	2B-48, SS-29, 3B-28
1935			107	.263	.305	338	89	10	2	0	0.0	45	33	11	14	5	12	2	188	240	10	47	4.1	.977	2B-80, 3B-8, SS-6
1936	NY	N	154	.278	.356	632	176	31	3	4	0.6	99	47	29	32	14	0	0	442	552	32	107	6.7	.969	2B-153
1937			152	.286	.359	574	164	15	6	5	0.9	64	52	28	20	7	0	0	394	514	24	106	6.1	.974	2B-152
1939			95	.239	.293	335	80	6	3	2	0.6	31	24	24	19	1	0	0	240	336	17	63	6.2	.971	2B-91, SS-4, 3B-1
1940			133	.282	.340	568	160	9	6	4	0.7	68	36	26	17	9	0	0	238	336	16	50	4.4	.973	2B-74, 3B-57, SS-4
1941			116	.228	.293	403	92	15	4	1	0.2	41	23	14	10	7	0	0	288	285	18	60	5.1	.970	2B-104, 3B-1
1946	PIT	N	55	.220	.260	127	28	1	2	0	0.0	10	5	6	6	3	12	0	66	66	5	14	2.5	.964	2B-30, 3B-4, SS-1
9 yrs.			924	.266	.331	3316	883	100	31	17	0.5	415	245	150	138	51	25	4	2018	2556	138	486	5.1	.971	2B-718, 3B-116, SS-53

WORLD SERIES

Year	Team		Games	BA	SA	AB	H	2B	3B	HR	HR%	R	RBI	BB	SO	SB	PH AB	H	PO	A	E	DP	TC/G	FA	G by Pos
1934	STL	N	1	—	—	0	0	0	0	0	—	0	0	0	0	0	0	0	1	0	0	0	1.0	1.000	SS-1
1936	NY	N	6	.048	.048	21	1	0	0	0	0.0	1	2	1	3	0	0	0	14	20	0	5	5.7	1.000	2B-6
1937			5	.250	.375	16	4	2	0	0	0.0	1	0	2	0	1	0	0	8	17	1	5	5.2	.962	2B-5
3 yrs.			12	.135	.189	37	5	2	0	0	0.0	2	2	3	3	1	0	0	23	37	1	10	5.1	.984	2B-11, SS-1

Milt Whitehead

WHITEHEAD, MILTON P.
B. 1862, Canada   D. Aug. 15, 1901, Highland, Calif.

Year	Team	Games	BA	SA	AB	H	2B	3B	HR	HR%	R	RBI	BB	SO	SB	PH AB	PH H	PO	A	E	DP	TC/G	FA	G by Pos

Milt Whitehead *continued*

1884 2 teams: STL U (99G – .211) KC U (5G – .136)

Year	Team	Games	BA	SA	AB	H	2B	3B	HR	HR%	R	RBI	BB	SO	SB	PH AB	PH H	PO	A	E	DP	TC/G	FA	G by Pos
" total		104	.207	.255	415	86	15	1	1	0.2	63		8			0	0	101	291	93	19	4.7	.808	SS-95, 2B-4, OF-2, 3B-2, C-1, P-1

Gil Whitehouse

WHITEHOUSE, GILBERT ARTHUR
B. Oct. 15, 1893, Somerville, Mass. D. Feb. 14, 1926, Brewer, Me.
BB TR 5'10½" 170 lbs.

Year	Team	Games	BA	SA	AB	H	2B	3B	HR	HR%	R	RBI	BB	SO	SB	PH AB	PH H	PO	A	E	DP	TC/G	FA	G by Pos
1912	BOS N	2	.000	.000	6	0	0	0	0	0.0	0	0	0	3	0	0	0	4	0	2	0	3.0	.667	C-2
1915	NWK F	35	.225	.308	120	27	6	2	0	0.0	16	9	6	3	6	1		36	8	2	1	1.3	.957	OF-28, C-1, P-1
2 yrs.		37	.214	.294	126	27	6	2	0	0.0	16	9	6	3	6	1		40	8	4	1	1.4	.923	OF-28, C-3, P-1

Gurdon Whiteley

WHITELEY, GURDON W.
B. Oct. 5, 1859, Ashaway, R. I. D. Nov. 24, 1924, Cranston, R. I.
5'11" 190 lbs.

Year	Team	Games	BA	SA	AB	H	2B	3B	HR	HR%	R	RBI	BB	SO	SB	PH AB	PH H	PO	A	E	DP	TC/G	FA	G by Pos
1884	CLE N	8	.147	.147	34	5	0	0	0	0.0	4	0	1	8	0	0		9	3	3	2	1.9	.800	OF-8
1885	BOS N	33	.185	.252	135	25	2	2	1	0.7	14	7	1	25	0	0		48	9	17	2	2.2	.770	OF-32, C-1
2 yrs.		41	.178	.231	169	30	2	2	1	0.6	18	7	2	33	0	0		57	12	20	4	2.2	.775	OF-40, C-1

George Whiteman

WHITEMAN, GEORGE
B. Dec. 23, 1882, Peoria, Ill. D. Feb. 10, 1947, Houston, Tex.
BR TR 5'7" 160 lbs.

Year	Team	Games	BA	SA	AB	H	2B	3B	HR	HR%	R	RBI	BB	SO	SB	PH AB	PH H	PO	A	E	DP	TC/G	FA	G by Pos
1907	BOS A	3	.182	.182	11	2	0	0	0	0.0	1	0	0	1	0	1	0	2	0	0	0	0.7	1.000	OF-2
1913	NY A	11	.344	.500	32	11	3	1	0	0.0	8	2	7	2	2	0		29	1	2	1	2.9	.938	OF-11
1918	BOS A	71	.266	.346	214	57	14	0	1	0.5	24	28	20	9	9	2		95	5	7	1	1.5	.935	OF-69
3 yrs.		85	.272	.358	257	70	17	1	1	0.4	32	31	27	11	11	3	0	126	6	9	2	1.7	.936	OF-82

WORLD SERIES

Year	Team	Games	BA	SA	AB	H	2B	3B	HR	HR%	R	RBI	BB	SO	SB	PH AB	PH H	PO	A	E	DP	TC/G	FA	G by Pos
1918	BOS A	6	.250	.350	20	5	0	1	0	0.0	2	1	2	1	1	0		15	2	1	1	3.0	.944	OF-6

Fred Whitfield

WHITFIELD, FRED DWIGHT
B. Jan. 7, 1938, Vandiver, Ala.
BL TL 6'1" 190 lbs.

Year	Team	Games	BA	SA	AB	H	2B	3B	HR	HR%	R	RBI	BB	SO	SB	PH AB	PH H	PO	A	E	DP	TC/G	FA	G by Pos
1962	STL N	73	.266	.475	158	42	7	1	8	5.1	20	34	7	30	1	33	11	282	25	4	32	4.3	.987	1B-38
1963	CLE A	109	.251	.500	346	87	17	3	21	6.1	44	54	24	61	0	17	4	690	51	10	64	6.9	.987	1B-92
1964		101	.270	.423	293	79	13	1	10	3.4	29	29	12	58	0	24	4	596	36	5	63	6.3	.992	1B-79
1965		132	.293	.513	468	137	23	1	26	5.6	49	90	16	42	2	18	9	932	80	7	79	7.7	.993	1B-122
1966		137	.241	.440	502	121	15	2	27	5.4	59	78	27	76	1	4	0	1104	76	11	96	8.7	.991	1B-132
1967		100	.218	.362	257	56	10	0	9	3.5	24	31	25	45	3	32	9	494	40	4	51	5.4	.993	1B-66
1968	CIN N	87	.257	.409	171	44	8	0	6	3.5	15	32	9	29	0	46	11	285	21	6	28	3.6	.981	1B-41
1969		74	.149	.189	74	11	0	0	1	1.4	2	8	18	27	0	51	8	57	8	1	5	0.9	.985	1B-14
1970	MON N	4	.067	.067	15	1	0	0	0	0.0	0	0	1	3	0	0	0	34	7	1	3	10.5	.976	1B-4
9 yrs.		817	.253	.443	2284	578	93	8	108	4.7	242	356	139	371	7	225	56	4474	344	49	421	6.0	.990	1B-588

Terry Whitfield

WHITFIELD, TERRY BERTLAND
B. Jan. 12, 1953, Blythe, Calif.
BL TR 6'1½" 197 lbs.

Year	Team	Games	BA	SA	AB	H	2B	3B	HR	HR%	R	RBI	BB	SO	SB	PH AB	PH H	PO	A	E	DP	TC/G	FA	G by Pos
1974	NY A	2	.200	.200	5	1	0	0	0	0.0	0	0	0	1	0	1	0	0	0	0	0	0.0	–	OF-1
1975		28	.272	.309	81	22	1	1	0	0.0	9	7	1	17	1	2	2	42	3	1	0	1.6	.978	OF-25, DH-1
1976		1	–	–	0	0	0	0	0	0.0	0	0	0	0	0	0	0	0	0	0	0	0.0	–	OF-1
1977	SF N	114	.285	.433	326	93	21	3	7	2.1	41	36	20	46	2	32	11	167	4	5	0	1.5	.972	OF-84
1978		149	.289	.400	488	141	20	2	10	2.0	70	32	33	69	5	10	3	249	7	3	2	1.7	.988	OF-141
1979		133	.287	.396	394	113	20	4	5	1.3	52	44	36	47	5	31	7	167	10	8	3	1.4	.957	OF-106
1980		118	.296	.396	321	95	16	2	4	1.2	38	20	20	44	4	25	5	140	11	2	1	1.3	.987	OF-95
1984	LA N	87	.244	.356	180	44	8	0	4	2.2	15	18	17	35	1	29	8	76	4	1	0	0.9	.988	OF-58
1985		79	.260	.413	104	27	7	0	3	2.9	8	16	6	27	0	50	14	23	2	2	0	0.3	.926	OF-28
1986		19	.071	.071	14	1	0	0	0	0.0	0	0	0	5	0	2	0	1	0	0	0	0.1	1.000	OF-1
10 yrs.		730	.281	.394	1913	537	93	12	33	1.7	233	179	138	288	18	192	51	865	41	22	6	1.3	.976	OF-540, DH-1

LEAGUE CHAMPIONSHIP SERIES

Year	Team	Games	BA	SA	AB	H	2B	3B	HR	HR%	R	RBI	BB	SO	SB	PH AB	PH H	PO	A	E	DP	TC/G	FA	G by Pos
1985	LA N	1	–	–	0	0	0	0	0	–	0	0	0	0	0	0	0	0	0	0	0	0.0	–	

Ed Whiting

WHITING, EDWARD C.
Played as Ed Zieber in 1886.
B. 1860, Philadelphia, Pa. Deceased.
BL TR 188 lbs.

Year	Team	Games	BA	SA	AB	H	2B	3B	HR	HR%	R	RBI	BB	SO	SB	PH AB	PH H	PO	A	E	DP	TC/G	FA	G by Pos
1882	BAL AA	74	.260	.338	308	80	14	5	0	0.0	43	7				0	0	320	109	85	9	6.9	.835	C-72, 1B-3, OF-2
1883	LOU AA	58	.292	.417	240	70	16	4	2	0.8	35	9				0	0	269	68	46	6	6.6	.880	C-50, OF-6, 2B-2, 3B-1, 1B-1
1884		42	.223	.306	157	35	7	3	0	0.0	16	9				0	0	225	56	34	10	7.5	.892	C-40, OF-2, 1B-2
1886	WAS N	6	.000	.000	21	0	0	0	0	0.0	0	1		12		0	0	22	12	3	0	6.2	.919	C-6
4 yrs.		180	.255	.347	726	185	37	12	2	0.3	94	26		12		0	0	836	245	168	25	6.9	.865	C-168, OF-10, 1B-6, 2B-2, 3B-1

Dick Whitman

WHITMAN, DICK CORWIN
B. Nov. 9, 1920, Woodburn, Ore.
BL TR 5'11" 170 lbs.

Year	Team	Games	BA	SA	AB	H	2B	3B	HR	HR%	R	RBI	BB	SO	SB	PH AB	PH H	PO	A	E	DP	TC/G	FA	G by Pos
1946	BKN N	104	.260	.362	265	69	15	3	2	0.8	39	31	22	19	5	14	4	178	5	0	0	1.8	1.000	OF-85
1947		4	.400	.400	10	4	0	0	0	0.0	1	2	1	0	0	1	1	7	0	0	0	1.8	1.000	OF-3
1948		60	.291	.370	165	48	13	0	0	0.0	24	20	14	12	4	12	5	93	3	1	0	1.6	.990	OF-48
1949		23	.184	.224	49	9	2	0	0	0.0	8	2	4	4	0	12	2	20	0	1	0	0.9	.952	OF-11
1950	PHI N	75	.250	.303	132	33	7	0	0	0.0	21	12	16	12	1	39	12	56	2	1	0	0.8	.983	OF-32
1951		19	.118	.118	17	2	0	0	0	0.0	0	0	0	1	0	13	2	1	0	0	0	–		OF-6
6 yrs.		285	.259	.335	638	165	37	3	2	0.3	93	67	51	46	10	91	26	354	10	3	0	1.3	.992	OF-185

WORLD SERIES

Year	Team	Games	BA	SA	AB	H	2B	3B	HR	HR%	R	RBI	BB	SO	SB	PH AB	PH H	PO	A	E	DP	TC/G	FA	G by Pos
1949	BKN N	1	.000	.000	1	0	0	0	0	0.0	0	0	0	0	0	1	0	0	0	0	0	0.0	–	
1950	PHI N	3	.000	.000	2	0	0	0	0	0.0	0	0	1	1	0	2	0	0	0	0	0	0.0	–	
2 yrs.		4	.000	.000	3	0	0	0	0	0.0	0	0	1	1	0	3	0	0	0	0	0	0.0	–	

Year Team	Games	BA	SA	AB	H	2B	3B	HR	HR%	R	RBI	BB	SO	SB	Pinch Hit AB	H	PO	A	E	DP	TC/G	FA	G by Pos

Frank Whitman

WHITMAN, WALTER FRANKLIN (Hooker)
B. Aug. 15, 1924, Marengo, Ind.
BR TR 6'2" 175 lbs.

Year Team	Games	BA	SA	AB	H	2B	3B	HR	HR%	R	RBI	BB	SO	SB	PH AB	H	PO	A	E	DP	TC/G	FA	G by Pos
1946 CHI A	17	.063	.063	16	1	0	0	0	0.0	7	1	2	6	0	0	0	20	14	2	2	2.1	.944	SS-6, 2B-1, 1B-1
1948	3	.000	.000	6	0	0	0	0	0.0	0	0	0	3	0	2	0	1	2	3	1	2.0	.500	SS-1
2 yrs.	20	.045	.045	22	1	0	0	0	0.0	7	1	2	9	0	2	0	21	16	5	3	2.1	.881	SS-7, 2B-1, 1B-1

Dan Whitmer

WHITMER, DANIEL CHARLES
B. Nov. 23, 1955, Redlands, Calif.
BR TR 6'3" 195 lbs.

Year Team	Games	BA	SA	AB	H	2B	3B	HR	HR%	R	RBI	BB	SO	SB	PH AB	H	PO	A	E	DP	TC/G	FA	G by Pos
1980 CAL A	48	.241	.276	87	21	3	0	0	0.0	8	7	4	21	1	0	0	190	12	0	2	4.2	1.000	C-48
1981 TOR A	7	.111	.222	9	1	1	0	0	0.0	0	0	1	2	0	0	0	12	3	0	2	2.1	1.000	C-7
2 yrs.	55	.229	.271	96	22	4	0	0	0.0	8	7	5	23	1	0	0	202	15	0	4	3.9	1.000	C-55

Art Whitney

WHITNEY, ARTHUR WILSON
Brother of Frank Whitney.
B. Jan. 16, 1858, Brockton, Mass. D. Aug. 15, 1943, Lowell, Mass.
BR TR 5'8" 155 lbs.

Year Team	Games	BA	SA	AB	H	2B	3B	HR	HR%	R	RBI	BB	SO	SB	PH AB	H	PO	A	E	DP	TC/G	FA	G by Pos
1880 WOR N	76	.222	.308	302	67	13	5	1	0.3	38	36	9	15		0	0	83	162	40	6	3.8	.860	3B-76
1881 DET N	58	.182	.262	214	39	7	5	0	0.0	23	9	7	15		0	0	73	141	38	10	4.3	.849	3B-58
1882 2 teams	PRO N (11G – .075)			DET N			(31G – .183)																
" total	42	.155	.155	155	24	0	0	0	0.0	12	4	3	23		0	0	65	100	32	9	4.7	.838	3B-22, SS-19, P-3
1884 PIT AA	23	.298	.340	94	28	4	0	0	0.0	10		1			0	0	33	49	8	1	3.9	.911	3B-21, OF-1, SS-1
1885	90	.233	.282	373	87	10	4	0	0.0	53		16			0	0	116	244	33	23	4.4	.916	SS-75, 3B-8, 2B-4, OF-3
1886	136	.239	.280	511	122	13	4	0	0.0	70		51			0	0	168	345	61	30	4.2	.894	3B-95, SS-42, P-1
1887 PIT N	119	.260	.304	431	112	11	4	0	0.0	57	51	55	18	10	0	0	166	237	33	13	3.7	.924	3B-119
1888 NY N	90	.220	.256	328	72	1	4	1	0.3	28	28	8	22	7	0	0	90	184	35	11	3.4	.887	3B-90
1889	129	.218	.258	473	103	12	2	1	0.2	71	59	56	39	19	0	0	160	265	57	27	3.7	.882	3B-129, P-1
1890 NY P	119	.219	.260	442	97	12	3	0	0.0	71	45	64	19	8	0	0	176	257	74	23	4.3	.854	3B-88, SS-31
1891 2 teams	CIN AA (93G – .199)			STL AA			(3G – .000)																
" total	96	.193	.240	358	69	6	1	3	0.8	42	33	32	22	8	0	0	129	211	37	12	3.9	.902	3B-96
11 yrs.	978	.223	.269	3681	820	89	32	6	0.2	475	265	302	173	52	0	0	1259	2195	448	165	4.0	.885	3B-802, SS-168, P-5, OF-4, 2B-4

Frank Whitney

WHITNEY, FRANK THOMAS (Jumbo)
Brother of Art Whitney.
B. Feb. 18, 1856, Brockton, Mass. D. Oct. 30, 1943, Baltimore, Md.
BR TR 5'7½" 152 lbs.

Year Team	Games	BA	SA	AB	H	2B	3B	HR	HR%	R	RBI	BB	SO	SB	PH AB	H	PO	A	E	DP	TC/G	FA	G by Pos
1876 BOS N	34	.237	.302	139	33	7	1	0	0.0	27	15	1	3		0	0	75	8	20	4	3.0	.806	OF-34, 2B-1

Jim Whitney

WHITNEY, JAMES EVANS (Grasshopper Jim)
B. Nov. 10, 1857, Conklin, N. Y. D. May 21, 1891, Binghamton, N. Y.
BL TR 6'2" 172 lbs.

Year Team	Games	BA	SA	AB	H	2B	3B	HR	HR%	R	RBI	BB	SO	SB	PH AB	H	PO	A	E	DP	TC/G	FA	G by Pos
1881 BOS N	75	.255	.337	282	72	17	3	0	0.0	37	32	19	18		0	0	40	100	32	3	2.3	.814	P-66, OF-15, 1B-2
1882	61	.323	.510	251	81	18	7	5	2.0	49	48	24	13		0	0	57	88	19	3	2.7	.884	P-49, OF-9, 1B-6
1883	96	.281	.433	409	115	27	10	5	1.2	78	57	25	29		0	0	89	100	27	4	2.3	.875	P-62, OF-40, 1B-2
1884	66	.259	.393	270	70	17	5	3	1.1	41		16	38		0	0	135	80	10	3	3.4	.956	P-41, OF-15, 1B-15, 3B-1
1885	72	.234	.290	290	68	8	4	0	0.0	35	36	17	24		0	0	86	133	26	4	3.4	.894	P-51, OF-17, 1B-5
1886 KC N	67	.239	.340	247	59	13	3	2	0.8	25	23	29	39		0	0	39	119	18	6	2.6	.898	P-46, OF-22, 3B-1
1887 WAS N	54	.264	.398	201	53	9	6	2	1.0	29	22	18	24	10	0	0	16	93	13	5	2.3	.893	P-47, OF-7
1888	42	.170	.191	141	24	0	1	0	0.7	13	17	7	20	3	0	0	24	67	12	2	2.5	.883	P-39, OF-3, 1B-1
1889 IND N	10	.375	.563	32	12	4	1	0	0.0	6	4	5	6	2	0	0	5	9	0	1	1.4	1.000	P-9, OF-1
1890 PHI AA	7	.238	.238	21	5	0	0	0	0.0	3		1			0	0	1	8	1	1	1.4	.900	P-6, OF-1
10 yrs.	550	.261	.375	2144	559	113	39	18	0.8	316	239	161	211	15	0	0	492	797	158	31	2.6	.891	P-416, OF-130, 1B-31, 3B-2

Pinky Whitney

WHITNEY, ARTHUR CARTER
B. Jan. 2, 1905, San Antonio, Tex. D. Sept. 1, 1987, Center, Tex.
BR TR 5'10" 165 lbs.

Year Team	Games	BA	SA	AB	H	2B	3B	HR	HR%	R	RBI	BB	SO	SB	PH AB	H	PO	A	E	DP	TC/G	FA	G by Pos
1928 PHI N	151	.301	.426	585	176	35	4	10	1.7	73	103	36	30	3	2	0	171	293	22	27	3.2	.955	3B-149
1929	154	.327	.482	612	200	43	14	8	1.3	89	115	61	35	7	0	0	168	333	17	29	3.4	.967	3B-154
1930	149	.342	.465	606	207	41	5	8	1.3	87	117	40	41	3	1	0	186	313	18	29	3.5	.965	3B-148
1931	130	.287	.433	501	144	36	4	9	1.8	64	74	30	38	6	2	0	131	217	19	1	2.8	.948	3B-128
1932	154	.298	.449	624	186	33	11	13	2.1	93	124	35	66	6	0	0	194	293	21	36	3.3	.959	3B-151, 2B-5
1933 2 teams	PHI N (31G – .264)			BOS N			(100G – .246)																
" total	131	.250	.366	503	126	21	2	11	2.2	54	68	33	31	3	1	0	146	288	11	29	3.4	.975	3B-115, 2B-18
1934 BOS N	146	.259	.377	563	146	26	2	12	2.1	58	79	25	54	7	0	0	172	345	17	31	3.7	.968	3B-111, 2B-36, SS-2
1935	126	.273	.367	458	125	23	4	4	0.9	41	60	24	36	2	1	0	196	305	17	25	4.1	.967	3B-74, 2B-49
1936 2 teams	BOS N (10G – .175)			PHI N			(114G – .294)																
" total	124	.284	.375	451	128	17	3	6	1.3	45	64	39	37	2	2	1	121	230	16	17	3.0	.956	3B-121, 2B-1
1937 PHI N	138	.341	.446	487	166	19	4	8	1.6	56	79	43	44	6	8	1	136	238	7	17	2.8	.982	3B-130
1938	102	.277	.343	300	83	9	1	3	1.0	27	38	27	22	0	20	4	101	134	14	14	2.4	.944	3B-75, 1B-4, 2B-2
1939	34	.187	.253	75	14	0	1	1	1.3	9	6	7	4	0	13	2	106	30	1	13	4.0	.993	1B-12, 2B-8, 3B-2
12 yrs.	1539	.295	.415	5765	1701	303	56	93	1.6	696	927	400	438	45	50	8	1828	3019	180	268	3.3	.964	3B-1358, 2B-119, 1B-16, SS-2

Ernie Whitt

WHITT, LEO ERNEST
B. June 13, 1952, Detroit, Mich.
BL TR 6'2" 200 lbs.

Year Team	Games	BA	SA	AB	H	2B	3B	HR	HR%	R	RBI	BB	SO	SB	PH AB	H	PO	A	E	DP	TC/G	FA	G by Pos
1976 BOS A	8	.222	.500	18	4	0	0	1	5.6	4	3	2	2	0	1	0	24	0	0	0	3.0	1.000	C-8
1977 TOR A	23	.171	.244	41	7	3	0	0	0.0	4	6	2	12	0	9	1	62	4	0	0	2.9	1.000	C-14
1978	2	.000	.000	4	0	0	0	0	0.0	0	0	1	1	0	1	0	7	1	0	0	4.0	1.000	C-1
1980	106	.237	.353	295	70	12	2	6	2.0	23	34	22	30	1	1	0	436	56	7	11	4.7	.986	C-105
1981	74	.236	.297	195	46	9	0	1	0.5	16	16	20	30	1	5	0	297	46	3	5	4.7	.991	C-72
1982	105	.261	.440	284	74	14	2	11	3.9	28	42	26	34	3	21	7	406	30	8	4	4.2	.982	C-98, DH-1
1983	123	.256	.459	344	88	15	2	17	4.9	53	56	50	55	1	17	5	554	50	5	4	5.0	.992	C-119
1984	124	.238	.425	315	75	12	1	15	4.8	35	46	43	49	0	16	5	583	40	4	8	5.1	.994	C-118
1985	139	.245	.444	412	101	21	2	19	4.6	55	64	47	59	3	16	3	649	38	8	6	5.0	.988	C-134
1986	131	.268	.448	395	106	19	2	16	4.1	48	56	35	39	0	11	3	709	41	7	7	5.8	.991	C-129
1987	135	.269	.455	446	120	24	1	19	4.3	57	75	44	50	0	12	1	803	55	5	10	6.4	.994	C-131

Year	Team		Games	BA	SA	AB	H	2B	3B	HR	HR%	R	RBI	BB	SO	SB	Pinch Hit AB	Pinch Hit H	PO	A	E	DP	TC/G	FA	G by Pos

Ernie Whitt *continued*

Year	Team		Games	BA	SA	AB	H	2B	3B	HR	HR%	R	RBI	BB	SO	SB	AB	H	PO	A	E	DP	TC/G	FA	G by Pos
1988			127	.251	.410	398	100	11	2	16	4.0	63	70	61	38	4	11	0	643	43	4	10	5.4	.994	C-123
1989			129	.262	.416	385	101	24	1	11	2.9	42	53	52	53	5	16	3	550	43	5	5	4.6	.992	C-115, DH-8
13 yrs.			1226	.253	.420	3532	892	166	15	132	3.7	428	521	405	452	22	136	27	5723	447	56	66	5.1	.991	C-1167, DH-9

LEAGUE CHAMPIONSHIP SERIES

Year	Team		Games	BA	SA	AB	H	2B	3B	HR	HR%	R	RBI	BB	SO	SB	AB	H	PO	A	E	DP	TC/G	FA	G by Pos
1985	TOR	A	7	.190	.238	21	4	1	0	0	0.0	1	2	2	4	0	0	0	50	3	0	1	7.6	1.000	C-7
1989			5	.125	.313	16	2	0	0	1	6.3	1	3	2	3	0	0	0	32	2	0	0	6.8	1.000	C-5
2 yrs.			12	.162	.270	37	6	1	0	1	2.7	2	5	4	7	0	0	0	82	5	0	1	7.3	1.000	C-12

Possum Whitted

WHITTED, GEORGE BOSTIC
B. Feb. 4, 1890, Durham, N. C.   D. Oct. 16, 1962, Wilmington, N. C.

BR TR 5'8½" 168 lbs.

Year	Team		Games	BA	SA	AB	H	2B	3B	HR	HR%	R	RBI	BB	SO	SB	AB	H	PO	A	E	DP	TC/G	FA	G by Pos
1912	STL	N	12	.261	.326	46	12	3	0	0	0.0	7	7	3	5	1	0	0	19	17	6	1	3.5	.857	3B-12
1913			122	.221	.271	402	89	10	5	0	0.0	44	38	31	44	9	15	3	225	207	27	27	3.8	.941	OF-40, SS-37, 3B-21, 2B-7, 1B-2
1914	2 teams				STL N	(20G – .129)		BOS N	(66G – .261)																
"	total		86	.245	.349	249	61	12	4	2	0.8	39	32	18	21	11	6	1	11	10	3	1	0.3	.875	OF-41, 3B-16, 2B-16, 1B-4, SS-3
1915	PHI	N	125	.281	.339	448	126	17	3	1	0.2	46	43	29	47	24	1	0	339	21	10	5	3.0	.973	OF-109, 1B-7
1916			147	.281	.399	526	148	20	12	6	1.1	68	68	19	46	29	1	0	383	16	14	8	2.8	.966	OF-136, 1B-16
1917			149	.280	.373	553	155	24	9	3	0.5	69	70	30	56	10	0	0	306	35	9	2	2.3	.974	OF-141, 1B-10, 3B-6, 2B-1
1918			24	.244	.291	86	21	4	0	0	0.0	7	3	4	10	4	2	1	52	3	1	1	2.3	.982	OF-22, 1B-1
1919	2 teams				PHI N	(78G – .249)		PIT N	(35G – .389)																
"	total		113	.293	.402	420	123	21	8	3	0.7	47	53	20	24	12	2	1	491	102	13	29	5.4	.979	OF-48, 1B-35, 2B-20, 3B-2
1920	PIT	N	134	.261	.338	494	129	11	12	1	0.2	53	74	35	36	11	0	0	263	234	16	24	3.8	.969	3B-125, 1B-10, OF-1
1921			108	.283	.427	403	114	23	7	7	1.7	60	63	26	21	5	1	0	276	13	3	10	2.7	.990	OF-107, 1B-7
1922	BKN	N	1	.000	.000	1	0	0	0	0	0.0	0	0	0	0	0	1	0	0	0	0	0	0.0	–	
11 yrs.			1021	.270	.362	3628	978	145	60	23	0.6	440	451	215	310	116	29	6	2365	658	102	108	3.1	.967	OF-640, 3B-182, 1B-92, 2B-44, SS-40

WORLD SERIES

Year	Team		Games	BA	SA	AB	H	2B	3B	HR	HR%	R	RBI	BB	SO	SB	AB	H	PO	A	E	DP	TC/G	FA	G by Pos
1914	BOS	N	4	.214	.357	14	3	0	1	0	0.0	2	2	3	1	1	0	0	5	0	0	0	1.3	1.000	OF-4
1915	PHI	N	5	.067	.067	15	1	0	0	0	0.0	0	1	1	0	1	0	0	12	0	0	0	2.4	1.000	OF-5, 1B-1
2 yrs.			9	.138	.207	29	4	0	1	0	0.0	2	3	4	1	2	0	0	17	0	0	0	1.9	1.000	OF-9, 1B-1

Bob Wicker

WICKER, ROBERT KITRIDGE
B. May 24, 1878, Bedford, Ind.   D. Jan. 22, 1955, Evanston, Ill.

BR TR 6'2" 180 lbs.

Year	Team		Games	BA	SA	AB	H	2B	3B	HR	HR%	R	RBI	BB	SO	SB	AB	H	PO	A	E	DP	TC/G	FA	G by Pos
1901	STL	N	3	.333	.333	3	1	0	0	0	0.0	1	0	0			0	1	0	0	0	0	0	0.0	–	P-1
1902			31	.234	.260	77	18	2	0	0	0.0	6	3	3			2	6	1	22	47	10	3	2.5	.873	P-22, OF-3
1903	2 teams				STL N	(1G – .000)		CHI N	(32G – .245)																
"	total		33	.240	.330	100	24	5	2	0	0.0	19	8	4			1	0	0	13	45	9	2	2.0	.866	P-33
1904	CHI	N	50	.219	.226	155	34	1	0	0	0.0	17	9	4			4	0	0	48	34	7	1	1.8	.921	P-30, OF-20
1905			25	.139	.139	72	10	0	0	0	0.0	5	3	4			1	0	0	8	36	2	3	1.8	.957	P-22, OF-3
1906	2 teams				CHI N	(10G – .100)		CIN N	(20G – .180)																
"	total		30	.157	.229	70	11	2	0	0	0.0	6	4	7			2	0	0	13	38	6	2	1.9	.895	P-30
6 yrs.			172	.205	.241	477	98	9	4	0	0.0	54	27	22			10	7	1	104	200	34	11	2.0	.899	P-138, OF-26

Floyd Wicker

WICKER, FLOYD EULISS
B. Sept. 12, 1943, Burlington, N. C.

BL TR 6'2" 175 lbs.

Year	Team		Games	BA	SA	AB	H	2B	3B	HR	HR%	R	RBI	BB	SO	SB	AB	H	PO	A	E	DP	TC/G	FA	G by Pos
1968	STL	N	5	.500	.500	4	2	0	0	0	0.0	2	0	0	0	0	4	2	0	0	0	0	0.0		
1969	MON	N	41	.103	.103	39	4	0	0	0	0.0	2	2	2	20	0	29	3	11	0	0	0	0.3	1.000	OF-11
1970	MIL	A	15	.195	.293	41	8	1	0	1	2.4	3	3	1	8	0	6	1	16	0	0	0	1.1	1.000	OF-12
1971	2 teams				MIL A	(11G – .125)		SF N	(9G – .143)																
"	total		20	.138	.138	29	4	0	0	0	0.0	3	1	4	5	0	10	1	12	1	0	0	0.7	1.000	OF-7
4 yrs.			81	.159	.195	113	18	1	0	1	0.9	10	6	7	33	0	49	7	39	1	0	0	0.5	1.000	OF-30

Al Wickland

WICKLAND, ALBERT
B. Jan. 27, 1888, Chicago, Ill.   D. Mar. 14, 1980, Port Washington, Wis.

BL TL 5'7" 155 lbs.

Year	Team		Games	BA	SA	AB	H	2B	3B	HR	HR%	R	RBI	BB	SO	SB	AB	H	PO	A	E	DP	TC/G	FA	G by Pos
1913	CIN	N	26	.215	.405	79	17	5	5	0	0.0	7	8	6	19	3	2	0	57	2	1	1	2.3	.983	OF-24
1914	CHI	F	157	.276	.405	536	148	31	10	6	1.1	74	68	81		17	0	0	252	23	11	3	1.8	.962	OF-157
1915	2 teams				CHI F	(30G – .244)		PIT F	(110G – .301)																
"	total		140	.291	.375	475	138	14	10	2	0.4	74	35	65		26	7	1	266	14	10	2	2.1	.966	OF-133
1918	BOS	N	95	.262	.398	332	87	7	13	4	1.2	55	32	53	39	12	0	0	183	11	5	2	2.1	.975	OF-95
1919	NY	A	26	.152	.174	46	7	1	0	0	0.0	2	1	2	10	0	1	1	14	0	0	0	0.5	1.000	OF-15
5 yrs.			444	.270	.386	1468	397	58	38	12	0.8	212	144	207	68	58	19	2	772	50	27	8	1.9	.968	OF-424

Tom Wiedenbauer

WIEDENBAUER, THOMAS JOHN
B. Nov. 5, 1958, Menomonie, Wis.

BR TR 6'1" 180 lbs.

Year	Team		Games	BA	SA	AB	H	2B	3B	HR	HR%	R	RBI	BB	SO	SB	AB	H	PO	A	E	DP	TC/G	FA	G by Pos
1979	HOU	N	4	.667	.833	6	4	1	0	0	0.0	2	0	0	2	0	0	0	3	0	0	0	0.8	1.000	OF-3

Tom Wieghaus

WIEGHAUS, THOMAS ROBERT
B. Feb. 1, 1957, Chicago Heights, Ill.

BR TR 6' 195 lbs.

Year	Team		Games	BA	SA	AB	H	2B	3B	HR	HR%	R	RBI	BB	SO	SB	AB	H	PO	A	E	DP	TC/G	FA	G by Pos
1981	MON	N	1	.000	.000	1	0	0	0	0	0.0	0	0	0	0	0	0	0	5	0	0	0	5.0	1.000	C-1
1983			1	–	–	0	0	0	0	0	–	0	0	0	0	0	0	0	1	0	0	0	1.0	1.000	C-1
1984	HOU	N	6	.000	.000	10	0	0	0	0	0.0	0	1	1	3	0	0	0	30	3	0	0	5.5	1.000	C-6
3 yrs.			8	.000	.000	11	0	0	0	0	0.0	0	1	1	3	0	0	0	36	3	0	0	4.9	1.000	C-8

Whitey Wietelmann

WIETELMANN, WILLIAM FREDERICK
B. Mar. 15, 1919, Zanesville, Ohio

BB TR 6' 170 lbs.
BR 1939-40,1942,
BL 1943,1945

Year	Team		Games	BA	SA	AB	H	2B	3B	HR	HR%	R	RBI	BB	SO	SB	AB	H	PO	A	E	DP	TC/G	FA	G by Pos
1939	BOS	N	23	.203	.217	69	14	1	0	0	0.0	2	5	2	9	1	0	0	38	69	5	12	4.9	.955	SS-22, 2B-1
1940			35	.195	.220	41	8	1	0	0	0.0	3	1	5	5	0	4	0	20	27	2	9	1.4	.959	2B-15, 3B-9, SS-3
1941			16	.091	.091	33	3	0	0	0	0.0	1	0	1	2	0	0	0	26	29	0	3	3.4	1.000	2B-10, SS-5, 3B-2
1942			13	.206	.265	34	7	2	0	0	0.0	4	0	4	4	0	0	0	19	29	3	6	3.9	.941	SS-11, 2B-1

Year	Team	Games	BA	SA	AB	H	2B	3B	HR	HR%	R	RBI	BB	SO	SB	Pinch Hit AB	Pinch Hit H	PO	A	E	DP	TC/G	FA	G by Pos

Whitey Wietelmann *continued*

Year	Team	Games	BA	SA	AB	H	2B	3B	HR	HR%	R	RBI	BB	SO	SB	AB	H	PO	A	E	DP	TC/G	FA	G by Pos
1943		153	.215	.245	534	115	14	1	0	0.0	33	39	46	40	9	0	0	307	581	40	91	6.1	.957	SS-153
1944		125	.240	.302	417	100	18	1	2	0.5	46	32	33	25	0	0	0	269	351	30	75	5.2	.954	SS-103, 2B-23, 3B-1
1945		123	.271	.348	428	116	15	3	4	0.9	53	33	39	27	4	0	0	303	338	21	76	5.4	.968	2B-87, SS-39, 3B-2, P-1
1946		44	.205	.205	78	16	0	0	0	0.0	7	5	14	8	0	12	2	40	39	7	6	2.0	.919	SS-16, 3B-8, 2B-4, P-3
1947	PIT N	48	.234	.305	128	30	4	1	1	0.8	21	7	12	10	0	7	0	69	68	13	14	3.1	.913	SS-22, 2B-14, 3B-6, 1B-1
9 yrs.		580	.232	.282	1762	409	55	6	7	0.4	170	122	156	131	14	24	2	1091	1531	121	292	4.7	.956	SS-374, 2B-155, 3B-28, P-4, 1B-1

Alan Wiggins

WIGGINS, ALAN ANTHONY
B. Feb. 17, 1958, Los Angeles, Calif.

BB TR 6'2" 160 lbs.

Year	Team	Games	BA	SA	AB	H	2B	3B	HR	HR%	R	RBI	BB	SO	SB	AB	H	PO	A	E	DP	TC/G	FA	G by Pos
1981	SD N	15	.357	.357	14	5	0	0	0	0.0	4	0	1	0	2	4	2	6	0	2	0	0.5	.750	OF-4
1982		72	.256	.303	254	65	3	3	1	0.4	40	15	13	19	33	3	0	140	8	5	2	2.1	.967	OF-68, 2B-1
1983		144	.276	.324	503	139	20	2	0	0.0	83	22	65	43	66	2	0	572	35	8	31	4.3	.987	OF-105, 1B-45
1984		158	.258	.329	596	154	19	7	3	0.5	106	34	75	57	70	0	0	391	410	32	95	5.3	.962	2B-157
1985	2 teams	SD N (10G – .054)		BAL A (76G – .285)																				
"	total	86	.260	.319	335	87	12	4	0	0.0	46	21	31	20	30	0	0	170	207	14	62	4.5	.964	2B-85
1986	BAL A	71	.251	.272	239	60	3	1	0	0.0	30	11	22	20	21	1	0	121	151	6	40	3.9	.978	2B-66, DH-1
1987		85	.232	.268	306	71	4	2	1	0.3	37	15	28	34	10	3	0	86	98	4	21	2.2	.979	DH-44, 2B-33, OF-5
7 yrs.		631	.259	.309	2247	581	61	19	5	0.2	346	118	235	193	242	20	5	1486	909	71	251	3.9	.971	2B-342, OF-182, DH-45, 1B-45

LEAGUE CHAMPIONSHIP SERIES

Year	Team	Games	BA	SA	AB	H	2B	3B	HR	HR%	R	RBI	BB	SO	SB	AB	H	PO	A	E	DP	TC/G	FA	G by Pos
1984	SD N	5	.316	.316	19	6	0	0	0	0.0	4	1	2	2	0	0	0	11	11	0	1	4.4	1.000	2B-5

WORLD SERIES

Year	Team	Games	BA	SA	AB	H	2B	3B	HR	HR%	R	RBI	BB	SO	SB	AB	H	PO	A	E	DP	TC/G	FA	G by Pos
1984	SD N	5	.364	.409	22	8	1	0	0	0.0	2	1	0	2	1	0	0	13	6	2	1	4.2	.905	2B-5

Del Wilber

WILBER, DELBERT QUENTIN (Babe)
B. Feb. 24, 1919, Lincoln Park, Mich.
Manager 1973.

BR TR 6'3" 200 lbs.

Year	Team	Games	BA	SA	AB	H	2B	3B	HR	HR%	R	RBI	BB	SO	SB	AB	H	PO	A	E	DP	TC/G	FA	G by Pos
1946	STL N	4	.000	.000	4	0	0	0	0	0.0	0	0	1	0	0	0	0	0	0	0	0	0.0	–	C-4
1947		51	.232	.333	99	23	8	1	0	0.0	7	12	5	13	0	15	5	108	10	2	2	2.4	.983	C-34
1948		27	.190	.224	58	11	2	0	0	0.0	5	10	4	9	0	1	0	67	7	4	1	2.9	.949	C-26
1949		2	.250	.250	4	1	0	0	0	0.0	0	0	0	0	0	0	0	5	1	0	0	3.0	1.000	C-2
1951	PHI N	84	.278	.429	245	68	7	3	8	3.3	30	34	17	26	0	10	1	326	26	8	5	4.3	.978	C-73
1952	2 teams	PHI N (2G – .000)		BOS A (47G – .267)																				
"	total	49	.263	.416	137	36	10	1	3	2.2	7	23	7	21	0	10	4	160	22	1	5	3.7	.995	C-39
1953	BOS A	58	.241	.500	112	27	6	1	7	6.3	16	29	6	21	0	28	4	108	7	2	2	2.0	.983	C-28, 1B-2
1954		24	.131	.246	61	8	2	1	1	1.6	2	7	4	6	0	6	1	49	8	3	2	2.5	.950	C-18
8 yrs.		299	.242	.389	720	174	35	7	19	2.6	67	115	44	96	1	70	15	823	81	20	17	3.1	.978	C-224, 1B-2

Claude Wilborn

WILBORN, CLAUDE EDWARD
B. Sept. 1, 1912, Woodsdale, N. C.

BL TR 6'1" 180 lbs.

Year	Team	Games	BA	SA	AB	H	2B	3B	HR	HR%	R	RBI	BB	SO	SB	AB	H	PO	A	E	DP	TC/G	FA	G by Pos
1940	BOS N	5	.000	.000	7	0	0	0	0	0.0	0	0	1	0	2	0	1	0	1	0	0.4	.500	OF-3

Ted Wilborn

WILBORN, THADDEAUS INGLEHART
B. Dec. 16, 1958, Waco, Tex.

BB TR 6' 165 lbs.

Year	Team	Games	BA	SA	AB	H	2B	3B	HR	HR%	R	RBI	BB	SO	SB	AB	H	PO	A	E	DP	TC/G	FA	G by Pos
1979	TOR A	22	.000	.000	12	0	0	0	0	0.0	3	0	1	7	0	1	0	7	0	1	0	0.4	.875	OF-7, DH-4
1980	NY A	8	.250	.250	8	2	0	0	0	0.0	2	1	0	1	0	0	1	6	1	0	1	0.9	1.000	OF-3
2 yrs.		30	.100	.100	20	2	0	0	0	0.0	5	1	1	8	0	1	1	13	1	1	1	0.5	.933	OF-10, DH-4

Wiley

WILEY,
Deceased.

Year	Team	Games	BA	SA	AB	H	2B	3B	HR	HR%	R	RBI	BB	SO	SB	AB	H	PO	A	E	DP	TC/G	FA	G by Pos
1884	WAS U	1	.000	.000	4	0	0	0	0	0.0	0		0			0	0	0	1	2	0	3.0	.333	3B-1

Rob Wilfong

WILFONG, ROBERT DANIEL
B. Sept. 1, 1953, Pasadena, Calif.

BL TR 6'1" 180 lbs.

Year	Team	Games	BA	SA	AB	H	2B	3B	HR	HR%	R	RBI	BB	SO	SB	AB	H	PO	A	E	DP	TC/G	FA	G by Pos
1977	MIN A	73	.246	.281	171	42	1	1	1	0.6	22	13	17	26	10	2	0	114	164	12	40	4.0	.959	2B-66, DH-1
1978		92	.266	.322	199	53	8	0	1	0.5	23	11	19	27	8	1	0	152	196	5	37	3.8	.986	2B-80, DH-5
1979		140	.313	.458	419	131	22	6	9	2.1	71	59	29	54	11	16	5	287	379	14	92	4.9	.979	2B-133, OF-3
1980		131	.248	.368	416	103	16	5	8	1.9	55	45	34	61	10	14	5	245	338	4	85	4.5	.993	2B-120, OF-6
1981		93	.246	.331	305	75	11	3	1	1.0	32	19	29	43	2	8	0	183	268	9	52	4.9	.980	2B-93
1982	2 teams	MIN A (25G – .160)		CAL A (55G – .245)																				
"	total	80	.208	.273	183	38	5	2	1	0.5	24	16	14	30	4	19	2	31	67	2	19	1.3	.980	2B-50, 3B-5, OF-3, SS-2, DH-1
1983	CAL A	65	.254	.339	177	45	7	1	2	1.1	17	17	10	25	0	6	3	107	144	2	33	3.9	.992	2B-39, 3B-13, SS-6, DH-1
1984		108	.248	.362	307	76	13	2	6	2.0	31	33	20	53	3	18	5	162	268	12	48	4.3	.973	2B-97, SS-4, DH-1
1985		83	.189	.258	217	41	3	0	4	1.8	16	13	16	32	4	11	2	124	216	5	45	4.2	.986	2B-69, DH-2
1986		92	.219	.309	288	63	11	3	3	1.0	25	33	16	34	1	8	2	135	257	7	48	4.3	.982	2B-90
1987	SF N	9	.125	.500	8	1	0	0	1	12.5	2	2	1	2	0	0	0	2	3	1	2	3.0	.833	2B-2
11 yrs.		959	.248	.345	2690	668	97	23	39	1.4	318	261	205	387	54	105	24	1542	2300	73	501	4.1	.981	2B-839, 3B-18, OF-12, SS-12, DH-11

LEAGUE CHAMPIONSHIP SERIES

Year	Team	Games	BA	SA	AB	H	2B	3B	HR	HR%	R	RBI	BB	SO	SB	AB	H	PO	A	E	DP	TC/G	FA	G by Pos
1982	CAL A	2	.000	.000	1	0	0	0	0	0.0	0	0	0	1	0	1	0	0	0	0	0	0.0	–	
1986		4	.308	.385	13	4	1	0	0	0.0	1	2	0	2	0	1	1	9	10	0	4	4.8	1.000	2B-4
2 yrs.		6	.286	.357	14	4	1	0	0	0.0	1	2	0	3	0	2	1	9	10	0	4	3.2	1.000	2B-4

Jim Wilhelm

WILHELM, JAMES WEBSTER
B. Sept. 20, 1952, Greenbrae, Calif.

BR TR 6'3" 190 lbs.

Year	Team	Games	BA	SA	AB	H	2B	3B	HR	HR%	R	RBI	BB	SO	SB	AB	H	PO	A	E	DP	TC/G	FA	G by Pos
1978	SD N	10	.368	.474	19	7	2	0	0	0.0	2	4	0	2	1	0	0	9	0	0	0	0.9	1.000	OF-10

Year	Team		Games	BA	SA	AB	H	2B	3B	HR	HR%	R	RBI	BB	SO	SB	Pinch Hit AB	H	PO	A	E	DP	TC/G	FA	G by Pos

Jim Wilhelm *continued*

| 1979 | | | 39 | .243 | .340 | 103 | 25 | 4 | 3 | 0 | 0.0 | 8 | 8 | 2 | 12 | 1 | 10 | 2 | 61 | 4 | 1 | 0 | 1.7 | .985 | OF-30 |
| 2 yrs. | | | 49 | .262 | .361 | 122 | 32 | 6 | 3 | 0 | 0.0 | 10 | 12 | 2 | 14 | 2 | 10 | 2 | 70 | 4 | 1 | 0 | 1.5 | .987 | OF-40 |

Spider Wilhelm

WILHELM, CHARLES ERNEST
B. May 23, 1929, Baltimore, Md.   BR TR 5'9" 170 lbs.

| 1953 | PHI | A | 7 | .286 | .429 | 7 | 2 | 1 | 0 | 0 | 0.0 | 1 | 0 | 0 | 3 | 0 | 1 | 1 | 2 | 5 | 1 | 0 | 1.1 | .875 | SS-6 |

Joe Wilhoit

WILHOIT, JOSEPH WILLIAM
B. Dec. 20, 1891, Hiawatha, Kans.   D. Sept. 25, 1930, Santa Barbara, Calif.   BL TR 6'2" 175 lbs.

1916	BOS	N	116	.230	.300	383	88	13	4	2	0.5	44	38	18	6	1			177	12	4	3	1.7	.979	OF-108
1917	3 teams		BOS N (54G – .274)			PIT N (9G – .200)			NY N (34G – .340)																
"	total		97	.285	.341	246	70	7	2	1	0.4	29	18	26	21	5	25	5	3	1	0	0	0.0	1.000	OF-66, 1B-1
1918	NY	N	64	.274	.341	135	37	3	3	0	0.0	13	15	17	14	4	6	1	71	7	2	2	1.3	.975	OF-55
1919	BOS	A	6	.333	.333	18	6	0	0	0	0.0	7	2	5	2	1	1	0	8	0	0	0	1.3	1.000	OF-5
4 yrs.			283	.257	.321	782	201	23	9	3	0.4	93	73	75	82	28	38	7	259	20	6	5	1.0	.979	OF-234, 1B-1

WORLD SERIES

| 1917 | NY | N | 2 | .000 | .000 | 1 | 0 | 0 | 0 | 0 | 0.0 | 0 | 0 | 1 | 0 | 0 | 1 | 0 | 0 | 0 | 0 | 0 | 0.0 | – | |

Denney Wilie

WILIE, DENNIS ERNEST
B. Sept. 22, 1890, Mt. Calm, Tex.   D. June 20, 1966, Hayward, Calif.   BL TL 5'8" 155 lbs.

1911	STL	N	28	.235	.333	51	12	3	1	0	0.0	10	3	8	11	3	10	1	18	2	0	0	0.7	1.000	OF-15
1912			30	.229	.271	48	11	0	1	0	0.0	2	6	7	9	0	8	2	21	1	2	0	0.8	.917	OF-16
1915	CLE	A	45	.252	.344	131	33	4	1	2	1.5	14	10	26	18	2	8	0	80	1	8	0	2.0	.910	OF-35
3 yrs.			103	.243	.326	230	56	7	3	2	0.9	26	19	41	38	5	26	3	119	4	10	0	1.3	.925	OF-66

Harry Wilke

WILKE, HENRY JOSEPH
B. Dec. 14, 1900, Cincinnati, Ohio   BR TR 5'10½" 171 lbs.

| 1927 | CHI | N | 3 | .000 | .000 | 9 | 0 | 0 | 0 | 0 | 0.0 | 0 | 0 | 0 | 1 | 0 | 0 | 0 | 2 | 5 | 0 | 0 | 2.3 | 1.000 | 3B-3 |

Curtis Wilkerson

WILKERSON, CURTIS VERNON
B. Apr. 26, 1961, Petersburg, Va.   BB TR 5'9" 158 lbs.

1983	TEX	A	16	.171	.229	35	6	0	1	0	0.0	7	1	2	5	3	1	0	18	31	1	5	3.1	.980	SS-9, 3B-2, 2B-2
1984			153	.248	.279	484	120	12	6	1	0.2	47	26	22	72	12	0	0	227	391	36	73	4.2	.945	SS-116, 2B-47
1985			129	.244	.308	360	88	11	6	0	0.0	35	22	22	63	14	2	1	165	328	21	65	4.0	.959	SS-110, 2B-19, DH-2
1986			110	.237	.305	236	56	10	3	0	0.0	27	15	11	42	9	3	0	125	199	13	56	3.1	.961	2B-60, SS-56, DH-2
1987			85	.268	.391	138	37	5	3	2	1.4	28	14	6	16	6	3	1	79	98	6	18	2.2	.967	SS-33, 2B-28, 3B-18
1988			117	.293	.358	338	99	12	5	0	0.0	41	28	26	43	9	6	0	186	299	16	58	4.3	.970	2B-87, SS-24, 3B-11
1989	CHI	N	77	.244	.313	160	39	4	2	1	0.6	18	10	8	33	4	28	11	42	91	8	10	1.8	.943	3B-26, 2B-15, SS-7, OF-1
7 yrs.			687	.254	.315	1751	445	54	20	4	0.2	203	116	97	274	57	43	13	842	1437	94	285	3.5	.960	SS-355, 2B-258, 3B-57, DH-4, OF-1

LEAGUE CHAMPIONSHIP SERIES

| 1989 | CHI | N | 3 | .500 | .500 | 2 | 1 | 0 | 0 | 0 | 0.0 | 1 | 0 | 0 | 0 | 0 | 2 | 1 | 0 | 0 | 0 | 0 | 0.0 | – | 3B-1 |

Bobby Wilkins

WILKINS, ROBERT LINWOOD
B. Aug. 11, 1922, Denton, N. C.   BR TR 5'9" 165 lbs.

1944	PHI	A	24	.240	.240	25	6	0	0	0	0.0	7	4	1	4	0	2	0	12	21	2	3	1.5	.943	SS-9
1945			62	.260	.299	154	40	6	0	0	0.0	22	4	10	17	2	1	0	79	118	16	23	3.4	.925	SS-40, OF-4
2 yrs.			86	.257	.291	179	46	6	0	0	0.0	29	7	11	21	2	3	0	91	139	18	26	2.9	.927	SS-49, OF-4

Ed Wilkinson

WILKINSON, EDWARD HENRY
B. June 20, 1890, Jacksonville, Ore.   D. Apr. 9, 1918, Tucson, Ariz.   BR TR 6' 170 lbs.

| 1911 | NY | A | 10 | .231 | .231 | 13 | 3 | 0 | 0 | 0 | 0.0 | 2 | 1 | 0 | | 0 | 2 | 0 | 4 | 1 | 1 | 0 | 0.6 | .833 | OF-3, 2B-1 |

Bob Will

WILL, ROBERT LEE (Butch)
B. July 15, 1931, Berwyn, Ill.   BL TL 5'10½" 175 lbs.

1957	CHI	N	70	.223	.277	112	25	3	0	1	0.9	13	10	5	21	1	36	8	51	1	2	0	0.8	.963	OF-30
1958			6	.250	.250	4	1	0	0	0	0.0	1	0	2	0	0	4	1	0	0	0	0	0.0		OF-1
1960			138	.255	.373	475	121	20	9	6	1.3	58	53	47	54	1	20	5	224	10	2	2	1.7	.992	OF-121
1961			86	.257	.336	113	29	9	0	0	0.0	9	8	15	19	0	52	11	36	0	1	0	0.4	.973	OF-30, 1B-1
1962			87	.239	.337	92	22	3	0	2	2.2	6	15	13	22	0	67	17	14	0	0	0	0.2	1.000	OF-9
1963			23	.174	.174	23	4	0	0	0	0.0	0	1	1	3	0	20	4	10	0	0	0	0.4	1.000	1B-1
6 yrs.			410	.247	.344	819	202	35	9	9	1.1	87	87	83	119	2	199	46	335	11	5	4	0.9	.986	OF-191, 1B-2

Jerry Willard

WILLARD, GERALD DUANE, JR.
B. Mar. 14, 1960, Oxnard, Calif.   BL TR 6'2" 200 lbs.

1984	CLE	A	87	.224	.386	246	55	8	1	10	4.1	21	37	26	55	1	12	1	335	35	7	7	4.3	.981	C-76, DH-1
1985			104	.270	.383	300	81	13	0	7	2.3	39	36	28	59	0	10	2	427	52	5	11	4.7	.990	C-96, DH-1
1986	OAK	A	75	.267	.385	161	43	7	0	4	2.5	17	26	22	28	0	7	4	300	12	2	1	4.2	.994	C-71, DH-7
1987			7	.167	.167	6	1	0	0	0	0.0	1	0	2	1	0	1	0	1	0	0	1	0.1	1.000	DH-3, 3B-1, 1B-1
4 yrs.			273	.252	.383	713	180	28	1	21	2.9	78	99	78	143	1	30	7	1063	99	14	20	4.3	.988	C-243, DH-12, 3B-1, 1B-1

Art Williams

WILLIAMS, ARTHUR FRANKLIN
B. Aug. 26, 1877, Somerville, Mass.   D. May 16, 1941, Arlington, Va.   TR

| 1902 | CHI | N | 47 | .231 | .250 | 160 | 37 | 3 | 0 | 0 | 0.0 | 17 | 14 | 15 | | 9 | 4 | 0 | 226 | 15 | 11 | 10 | 5.4 | .956 | OF-24, 1B-19 |

Bernie Williams

WILLIAMS, BERNARD
B. Oct. 8, 1948, Alameda, Calif.   BR TR 6'1" 175 lbs.

Year	Team		Games	BA	SA	AB	H	2B	3B	HR	HR%	R	RBI	BB	SO	SB	Pinch Hit AB	H	PO	A	E	DP	TC/G	FA	G by Pos

Bernie Williams *continued*

Year	Team		Games	BA	SA	AB	H	2B	3B	HR	HR%	R	RBI	BB	SO	SB	AB	H	PO	A	E	DP	TC/G	FA	G by Pos
1970	SF	N	7	.313	.438	16	5	2	0	0	0.0	2	1	2	1	1	1	0	9	1	0	1	1.4	1.000	OF-6
1971			35	.178	.233	73	13	1	0	1	1.4	8	5	12	24	1	9	1	28	0	2	0	0.9	.933	OF-27
1972			46	.191	.397	68	13	3	1	3	4.4	12	9	7	22	0	17	4	34	1	0	0	0.8	1.000	OF-15
1974	SD	N	14	.133	.133	15	2	0	0	0	0.0	1	0	0	6	0	9	1	2	0	0	0	0.1	1.000	OF-3
4 yrs.			102	.192	.308	172	33	6	1	4	2.3	23	15	21	53	2	36	6	73	2	2	1	0.8	.974	OF-51

Billy Williams

WILLIAMS, BILLY LEO   BL TR 6'1"   175 lbs.
B. June 15, 1938, Whistler, Ala.
Hall of Fame 1987.

Year	Team		Games	BA	SA	AB	H	2B	3B	HR	HR%	R	RBI	BB	SO	SB	AB	H	PO	A	E	DP	TC/G	FA	G by Pos
1959	CHI	N	18	.152	.212	33	5	0	1	0	0.0	0	2	1	7	0	6	0	18	0	0	0	1.0	1.000	OF-10
1960			12	.277	.489	47	13	0	2	2	4.3	4	7	5	12	0	0	0	25	0	1	0	2.2	.962	OF-12
1961			146	.278	.484	529	147	20	7	25	4.7	75	86	45	70	6	13	6	220	9	11	3	1.6	.954	OF-135
1962			159	.298	.466	618	184	22	8	22	3.6	94	91	70	72	9	0	0	273	18	10	4	1.9	.967	OF-159
1963			161	.286	.497	612	175	36	9	25	4.1	87	95	68	78	7	1	0	298	13	4	2	2.0	.987	OF-160
1964			162	.312	.532	645	201	39	2	33	5.1	100	98	59	84	10	1	0	233	14	13	0	1.6	.950	OF-162
1965			164	.315	.552	645	203	39	6	34	5.3	115	108	65	76	10	0	0	296	10	10	2	1.9	.968	OF-164
1966			162	.276	.461	648	179	23	5	29	4.5	100	91	69	61	6	0	0	319	9	8	3	2.1	.976	OF-162
1967			162	.278	.481	634	176	21	12	28	4.4	92	84	68	67	6	0	0	271	3	3	1	1.7	.989	OF-162
1968			163	.288	.500	642	185	30	8	30	4.7	91	98	48	53	4	0	0	261	4	9	0	1.7	.967	OF-163
1969			163	.293	.474	642	188	33	10	21	3.3	103	95	59	70	3	2	0	250	15	12	2	1.7	.957	OF-159
1970			161	.322	.586	636	205	34	4	42	6.6	137	129	72	65	7	0	0	259	13	3	1	1.7	.989	OF-160
1971			157	.301	.505	594	179	27	5	28	4.7	86	93	77	44	7	5	1	284	8	7	3	1.9	.977	OF-154
1972			150	**.333**	**.606**	574	191	34	6	37	6.4	95	122	62	59	3	2	1	275	13	4	5	1.9	.986	OF-144, 1B-5
1973			156	.288	.438	576	166	22	2	20	3.5	72	86	76	72	4	3	1	420	34	6	15	2.9	.987	OF-138, 1B-19
1974			117	.280	.453	404	113	22	0	16	4.0	55	68	67	44	4	10	2	635	53	11	50	6.0	.984	1B-65, OF-43
1975	OAK	A	155	.244	.419	520	127	20	1	23	4.4	68	81	76	68	0	3	1	30	3	1	5	0.2	.971	DH-145, 1B-7
1976			120	.211	.339	351	74	12	0	11	3.1	36	41	58	44	4	13	3	0	0	0	0	0.0	–	DH-106, OF-1
18 yrs.			2488	.290	.492	9350	2711	434	88	426	4.6	1410	1475	1045	1046	90	59	15	4367	219	113	96	1.9	.976	OF-2088, DH-251, 1B-96

LEAGUE CHAMPIONSHIP SERIES

Year	Team		Games	BA	SA	AB	H	2B	3B	HR	HR%	R	RBI	BB	SO	SB	AB	H	PO	A	E	DP	TC/G	FA	G by Pos
1975	OAK	A	3	.000	.000	8	0	0	0	0	0.0	0	0	1	1	0	1	0	0	0	0	0	0.0	–	DH-2

Billy Williams

WILLIAMS, WILLIAM   BL TR 6'3"   195 lbs.
B. June 13, 1933, Newberry, S. C.

Year	Team		Games	BA	SA	AB	H	2B	3B	HR	HR%	R	RBI	BB	SO	SB	AB	H	PO	A	E	DP	TC/G	FA	G by Pos
1969	SEA	A	4	.000	.000	10	0	0	0	0	0.0	1	0	0	3	0	0	0	1	2	0	0	0.8	1.000	OF-3

Bob Williams

WILLIAMS, ROBERT ELIAS   BR TR 6'   190 lbs.
B. Apr. 27, 1884, Monday, Ohio   D. Aug. 6, 1962, Nelsonville, Ohio

Year	Team		Games	BA	SA	AB	H	2B	3B	HR	HR%	R	RBI	BB	SO	SB	AB	H	PO	A	E	DP	TC/G	FA	G by Pos
1911	NY	A	20	.191	.234	47	9	2	0	0	0.0	3	8	5		1	0	0	73	24	6	1	5.2	.942	C-20
1912			20	.136	.159	44	6	1	0	0	0.0	7	3	9		0	0	0	91	16	8	0	5.8	.930	C-20
1913			6	.158	.158	19	3	0	0	0	0.0	0	0	1	3	0	0	0	25	9	1	0	5.8	.971	C-6
3 yrs.			46	.164	.191	110	18	3	0	0	0.0	10	11	15	3	1	0	0	189	49	15	1	5.5	.941	C-46

Buff Williams

WILLIAMS, ALVA MITCHEL   BR TR 5'11½" 187 lbs.
B. Jan. 31, 1882, Carthage, Ill.   D. July 23, 1933, Keokuk, Iowa

Year	Team		Games	BA	SA	AB	H	2B	3B	HR	HR%	R	RBI	BB	SO	SB	AB	H	PO	A	E	DP	TC/G	FA	G by Pos
1911	BOS	A	95	.239	.303	284	68	8	5	0	0.0	36	31	24		9	0	0	727	73	20	28	8.6	.976	1B-57, C-38
1912	WAS	A	57	.318	.439	157	50	11	4	0	0.0	14	22	7		2	10	2	234	74	7	6	5.5	.978	C-45
1913			65	.283	.406	106	30	6	2	1	0.9	9	12	9	16	3	29	6	117	21	2	6	2.2	.986	C-18, 1B-8, OF-5
1914			81	.278	.379	169	47	6	4	1	0.6	17	22	13	19	2	25	6	252	58	6	0	3.9	.981	C-44, 1B-8, OF-1
1915			91	.244	.325	197	48	8	4	0	0.0	14	31	18	20	4	30	3	363	67	10	10	4.8	.977	C-40, 1B-15, 3B-1
1916			76	.267	.337	202	54	10	2	0	0.0	16	20	15	19	5	14	2	390	30	6	21	5.6	.986	1B-34, C-23, 3B-1
1918	CLE	A	28	.239	.324	71	17	2	2	0	0.0	5	7	9	6	2	6	1	190	10	4	11	7.3	.980	1B-21, C-1
7 yrs.			493	.265	.352	1186	314	51	23	2	0.2	111	145	95	80	27	114	20	2273	333	55	82	5.4	.979	C-209, 1B-143, OF-6, 3B-2

Cy Williams

WILLIAMS, FRED   BL TL 6'2"   180 lbs.
B. Dec. 21, 1887, Wadena, Ind.   D. Apr. 23, 1974, Eagle River, Wis.

Year	Team		Games	BA	SA	AB	H	2B	3B	HR	HR%	R	RBI	BB	SO	SB	AB	H	PO	A	E	DP	TC/G	FA	G by Pos
1912	CHI	N	28	.242	.290	62	15	1	1	0	0.0	3	1	6	14	2	5	0	36	3	0	0	1.4	1.000	OF-22
1913			49	.224	.359	156	35	3	3	4	2.6	17	32	5	26	5	5	2	77	4	2	0	1.7	.976	OF-44
1914			55	.202	.266	94	19	2	2	0	0.0	12	5	13	13	2	22	4	46	2	3	0	0.9	.941	OF-27
1915			151	.257	.398	518	133	22	6	13	2.5	59	64	26	49	15	1	1	347	14	12	2	2.5	.968	OF-151
1916			118	.279	.459	405	113	19	9	12	3.0	55	66	51	64	6	2	0	260	7	3	0	2.3	.989	OF-116
1917			138	.241	.338	468	113	22	4	5	1.1	53	42	38	78	8	1	1	340	23	15	4	2.7	.960	OF-136
1918	PHI	N	94	.276	.373	351	97	14	1	6	1.7	49	39	27	30	10	1	0	229	10	8	4	2.6	.968	OF-91
1919			109	.278	.393	435	121	21	1	9	2.1	54	39	30	43	9	1	0	278	13	9	2	2.8	.970	OF-108
1920			148	.325	.497	590	192	36	10	15	2.5	88	72	32	45	18	1	0	388	22	12	4	2.9	.972	OF-147
1921			146	.320	.488	562	180	28	6	18	3.2	67	75	30	32	5	0	0	382	29	9	5	2.9	.979	OF-146
1922			151	.308	.514	584	180	30	6	26	4.5	98	92	74	49	11	1	0	376	19	11	2	2.7	.973	OF-150
1923			136	.293	.576	535	157	22	3	41	7.7	98	114	59	57	11	1	0	350	9	7	3	2.7	.981	OF-135
1924			148	.328	.552	558	183	31	11	24	4.3	101	93	67	49	7	3	0	368	13	15	0	2.7	.962	OF-145
1925			107	.331	.522	314	104	11	5	13	4.1	78	60	53	34	4	10	5	173	12	2	3	1.7	.989	OF-96
1926			107	.345	**.568**	336	116	13	4	18	5.4	63	53	38	35	2	13	4	143	14	6	3	1.5	.963	OF-93
1927			131	.274	.502	492	135	18	2	30	6.1	86	98	61	57	0	1	0	241	22	8	8	2.1	.970	OF-130
1928			99	.256	.445	238	61	9	0	12	5.0	31	37	54	34	0	20	7	118	9	0	0	1.3	1.000	OF-69
1929			66	.292	.554	65	19	2	0	5	7.7	11	21	9	22	0	38	9	7	1	0	0	0.4	.966	OF-11
1930			21	.471	.588	17	8	2	0	0	0.0	1	2	4	3	0	16	8	1	0	0	0	0.0	1.000	OF-3
19 yrs.			2002	.292	.470	6780	1981	306	74	251	3.7	1024	1005	690	721	115	142	41	4180	226	123	40	2.3	.973	OF-1820

Dallas Williams

WILLIAMS, DALLAS McKINLEY, JR.   BL TL 5'11" 165 lbs.
B. Feb. 28, 1958, Brooklyn, N. Y.

Year	Team		Games	BA	SA	AB	H	2B	3B	HR	HR%	R	RBI	BB	SO	SB	AB	H	PO	A	E	DP	TC/G	FA	G by Pos
1981	BAL	A	2	.500	.500	2	1	0	0	0	0.0	0	0	0	0	0	2	1	1	0	0	0	0.5	1.000	OF-1

Year	Team	Games	BA	SA	AB	H	2B	3B	HR	HR%	R	RBI	BB	SO	SB	Pinch Hit AB	Pinch Hit H	PO	A	E	DP	TC/G	FA	G by Pos

Dallas Williams *continued*

Year	Team	Games	BA	SA	AB	H	2B	3B	HR	HR%	R	RBI	BB	SO	SB	AB	H	PO	A	E	DP	TC/G	FA	G by Pos
1983	CIN N	18	.056	.056	36	2	0	0	0	0.0	2	1	3	6	0	8	0	18	0	0	0	1.0	1.000	OF-12
2 yrs.		20	.079	.079	38	3	0	0	0	0.0	2	1	3	6	0	10	1	19	0	0	0	1.0	1.000	OF-13

Dana Williams

WILLIAMS, DANA LAMOUNT
B. Mar. 20, 1963, Weirton, W. Va. BR TR 5'10" 170 lbs.

Year	Team	Games	BA	SA	AB	H	2B	3B	HR	HR%	R	RBI	BB	SO	SB	AB	H	PO	A	E	DP	TC/G	FA	G by Pos
1989	BOS A	8	.200	.400	5	1	1	0	0	0.0	1	0	0	1	0	1	0	0	1	0	0	0.1	1.000	DH-2, OF-1

Davey Williams

WILLIAMS, DAVID CARLOUS
B. Nov. 2, 1927, Dallas, Tex. BR TR 5'10" 160 lbs.

Year	Team	Games	BA	SA	AB	H	2B	3B	HR	HR%	R	RBI	BB	SO	SB	AB	H	PO	A	E	DP	TC/G	FA	G by Pos
1949	NY N	13	.240	.360	50	12	1	1	1	2.0	7	5	7	4	0	0	0	19	22	2	5	3.3	.953	2B-13
1951		30	.266	.375	64	17	1	0	2	3.1	17	8	5	8	1	2	0	38	43	0	7	2.7	1.000	2B-22
1952		138	.254	.385	540	137	26	3	13	2.4	70	55	48	63	2	0	0	279	375	18	102	4.9	.973	2B-138
1953		112	.297	.368	340	101	11	2	3	0.9	51	34	44	19	2	10	3	191	254	8	54	4.0	.982	2B-95
1954		142	.222	.316	544	121	18	3	9	1.7	65	46	43	33	1	1	0	353	396	14	112	5.4	.982	2B-142
1955		82	.251	.324	247	62	4	1	4	1.6	25	15	17	17	0	12	4	139	162	10	39	3.8	.968	2B-71
6 yrs.		517	.252	.351	1785	450	61	10	32	1.8	235	163	164	144	6	25	7	1019	1252	52	319	4.5	.978	2B-481

WORLD SERIES

Year	Team	Games	BA	SA	AB	H	2B	3B	HR	HR%	R	RBI	BB	SO	SB	AB	H	PO	A	E	DP	TC/G	FA	G by Pos
1951	NY N	2	.000	.000	1	0	0	0	0	0.0	0	0	0	0	0	1	0	0	0	0	0	0.0	–	
1954		4	.000	.000	11	0	0	0	0	0.0	0	1	2	2	0	0	0	10	9	1	2	5.0	.950	2B-4
2 yrs.		6	.000	.000	12	0	0	0	0	0.0	0	1	2	2	0	1	0	10	9	1	2	3.3	.950	2B-4

Denny Williams

WILLIAMS, EVON DANIEL
B. Dec. 13, 1899, Portland, Ore. D. Mar. 23, 1929, San Clemente, Calif. BL TR 5'8½" 150 lbs.

Year	Team	Games	BA	SA	AB	H	2B	3B	HR	HR%	R	RBI	BB	SO	SB	AB	H	PO	A	E	DP	TC/G	FA	G by Pos
1921	CIN N	10	.000	.000	7	0	0	0	0	0.0	0	0	0	2	0	6	0	1	0	0	0	0.1	1.000	OF-1
1924	BOS A	25	.365	.400	85	31	3	0	0	0.0	17	4	10	5	3	5	0	34	1	1	0	1.4	.972	OF-19
1925		68	.229	.261	218	50	1	3	0	0.0	28	13	17	11	2	13	3	117	4	6	1	1.9	.953	OF-52
1928		16	.222	.222	18	4	0	0	0	0.0	1	1	1	1	0	9	1	5	0	0	0	0.3	1.000	OF-6
4 yrs.		119	.259	.290	328	85	4	3	0	0.0	46	18	28	19	5	33	4	157	5	7	1	1.4	.959	OF-78

Dewey Williams

WILLIAMS, DEWEY EDGAR (Dee)
B. Feb. 5, 1916, Durham, N. C. BR TR 6' 160 lbs.

Year	Team	Games	BA	SA	AB	H	2B	3B	HR	HR%	R	RBI	BB	SO	SB	AB	H	PO	A	E	DP	TC/G	FA	G by Pos
1944	CHI N	79	.240	.282	262	63	7	2	0	0.0	23	27	23	18	2	1	0	317	50	7	7	4.7	.981	C-77
1945		59	.280	.400	100	28	2	2	2	2.0	16	5	13	13	0	4	1	114	20	3	1	2.3	.978	C-54
1946		4	.200	.200	5	1	0	0	0	0.0	0	0	0	2	0	2	1	3	1	0	0	1.0	1.000	C-2
1947		3	.000	.000	2	0	0	0	0	0.0	0	0	0	1	0	2	0	0	0	0	0	0.0	–	C-1
1948	CIN N	48	.168	.221	95	16	2	0	1	1.1	9	5	10	18	0	1	0	137	11	6	1	3.2	.961	C-47
5 yrs.		193	.233	.293	464	108	11	4	3	0.6	48	37	46	52	2	10	2	571	82	16	9	3.5	.976	C-181

WORLD SERIES

Year	Team	Games	BA	SA	AB	H	2B	3B	HR	HR%	R	RBI	BB	SO	SB	AB	H	PO	A	E	DP	TC/G	FA	G by Pos
1945	CHI N	2	.000	.000	2	0	0	0	0	0.0	0	0	0	1	0	1	0	1	1	0	0	1.0	1.000	C-1

Dib Williams

WILLIAMS, EDWIN DIBRELL
B. Jan. 19, 1910, Greenbrier, Ark. BR TR 5'11½" 175 lbs.

Year	Team	Games	BA	SA	AB	H	2B	3B	HR	HR%	R	RBI	BB	SO	SB	AB	H	PO	A	E	DP	TC/G	FA	G by Pos
1930	PHI A	67	.262	.393	191	50	10	3	3	1.6	24	22	15	19	2	5	0	109	151	12	23	4.1	.956	2B-39, SS-19, 3B-1
1931		86	.269	.384	294	79	12	2	6	2.0	41	40	19	21	2	3	1	168	237	27	63	5.0	.938	SS-72, 2B-10, OF-1
1932		62	.251	.363	215	54	10	1	4	1.9	30	24	22	23	0	6	0	124	181	17	32	5.2	.947	2B-53, SS-3
1933		115	.289	.444	408	118	20	5	11	2.7	52	73	32	35	1	0	0	265	320	47	51	5.5	.926	SS-84, 2B-29, 1B-2
1934		66	.273	.361	205	56	10	1	2	1.0	25	17	21	18	0	12	3	111	174	13	31	4.5	.956	2B-53, SS-2
1935	2 teams		PHI A	(4G – .100)						BOS A	(75G – .251)														
"	total	79	.245	.326	261	64	12	0	3	1.1	26	25	24	24	3	0	0	127	159	12	21	3.8	.960	2B-31, 3B-30, SS-15, 1B-1
6 yrs.		475	.267	.385	1574	421	74	12	29	1.8	198	201	133	140	7	29	4	904	1222	128	221	4.7	.943	2B-215, SS-195, 3B-31, 1B-3, OF-1

WORLD SERIES

Year	Team	Games	BA	SA	AB	H	2B	3B	HR	HR%	R	RBI	BB	SO	SB	AB	H	PO	A	E	DP	TC/G	FA	G by Pos
1931	PHI A	7	.320	.360	25	8	1	0	0	0.0	2	1	2	9	0	0	0	7	24	0	2	4.4	1.000	SS-7

Dick Williams

WILLIAMS, RICHARD HIRSCHFELD
B. May 7, 1928, St. Louis, Mo.
Manager 1967-69, 1971-88. BR TR 6' 190 lbs.

Year	Team	Games	BA	SA	AB	H	2B	3B	HR	HR%	R	RBI	BB	SO	SB	AB	H	PO	A	E	DP	TC/G	FA	G by Pos
1951	BKN N	23	.200	.333	60	12	3	1	1	1.7	5	5	4	10	0	8	2	21	1	0	0	1.0	1.000	OF-15
1952		36	.309	.397	68	21	4	1	0	0.0	13	11	2	10	0	6	1	51	3	0	2	1.5	1.000	OF-25, 3B-1, 1B-1
1953		30	.218	.364	55	12	2	0	2	3.6	4	5	3	10	0	5	0	24	0	2	0	0.9	.923	OF-24
1954		16	.147	.235	34	5	0	0	1	2.9	5	2	2	7	0	3	0	12	0	0	0	0.8	1.000	OF-14
1956	2 teams	BKN N	(7G – .286)		BAL A	(87G – .286)																			
"	total	94	.286	.450	360	103	18	4	11	3.1	45	37	30	41	5	8	2	249	17	4	4	2.9	.985	OF-81, 2B-10, 1B-10, 3B-4
1957	2 teams	BAL A	(47G – .234)		CLE A	(67G – .283)																			
"	total	114	.261	.374	372	97	17	2	7	1.9	49	34	26	40	3	11	2	244	72	8	20	2.8	.975	OF-63, 3B-34, 1B-12
1958	BAL A	128	.276	.347	409	113	17	0	4	1.0	36	32	37	47	0	13	0	359	61	8	27	3.3	.981	OF-70, 3B-45, 1B-26, 2B-7
1959	KC A	130	.266	.436	488	130	33	1	16	3.3	72	75	28	60	4	8	1	349	181	13	42	4.2	.976	3B-80, 1B-32, OF-23, 2B-3
1960		127	.288	.448	420	121	31	0	12	2.9	47	65	39	68	0	15	5	376	131	11	28	4.1	.979	3B-57, 1B-34, OF-25
1961	BAL A	103	.206	.345	310	64	15	2	8	2.6	37	24	20	38	0	16	6	209	16	3	11	2.2	.987	OF-75, 1B-20, 3B-2
1962		82	.247	.315	178	44	7	1	1	0.6	20	18	14	26	0	31	13	180	13	0	13	2.4	1.000	OF-29, 1B-21, 3B-4
1963	BOS A	79	.257	.360	136	35	8	0	2	1.5	15	12	15	25	0	48	16	64	28	1	4	1.2	.989	3B-17, 1B-11, OF-7
1964		61	.159	.406	69	11	2	0	5	7.2	10	11	7	10	0	25	3	50	21	1	6	1.2	.986	1B-21, 3B-13, OF-5
13 yrs.		1023	.260	.392	2959	768	157	12	70	2.4	358	331	227	392	12	197	51	2188	544	51	157	2.7	.982	OF-456, 3B-257, 1B-188, 2B-20

WORLD SERIES

Year	Team	Games	BA	SA	AB	H	2B	3B	HR	HR%	R	RBI	BB	SO	SB	AB	H	PO	A	E	DP	TC/G	FA	G by Pos
1953	BKN N	3	.500	.500	2	1	0	0	0	0.0	0	0	1	1	0	2	1	0	0	0	0	0.0	–	

Earl Williams

WILLIAMS, EARL BAXTER
B. Jan. 27, 1903, Cumberland Gap, Tenn. D. Mar. 10, 1958, Knoxville, Tenn. BR TR 6'½" 185 lbs.

Year	Team		Games	BA	SA	AB	H	2B	3B	HR	HR%	R	RBI	BB	SO	SB	Pinch Hit AB	H	PO	A	E	DP	TC/G	FA	G by Pos

Earl Williams *continued*

Year	Team		Games	BA	SA	AB	H	2B	3B	HR	HR%	R	RBI	BB	SO	SB	AB	H	PO	A	E	DP	TC/G	FA	G by Pos
1928	BOS	N	3	.000	.000	2	0	0	0	0	0.0	0	0	0	1	0	2	0	1	0	0	0	0.3	1.000	C-1

Earl Williams

WILLIAMS, EARL CRAIG JR.   BR TR 6'3" 215 lbs.
B. July 14, 1948, Newark, N. J.

Year	Team		Games	BA	SA	AB	H	2B	3B	HR	HR%	R	RBI	BB	SO	SB	AB	H	PO	A	E	DP	TC/G	FA	G by Pos
1970	ATL	N	10	.368	.579	19	7	4	0	0	0.0	4	5	3	4	0	4	2	23	8	0	4	3.1	1.000	1B-4, 3B-3
1971			145	.260	.491	497	129	14	1	33	6.6	64	87	42	80	0	12	3	596	117	18	38	5.0	.975	C-72, 3B-42, 1B-31
1972			151	.258	.457	565	146	24	2	28	5.0	72	87	62	118	0	1	0	740	87	23	18	5.6	.973	C-116, 3B-21, 1B-20
1973	BAL	A	132	.237	.425	459	109	18	1	22	4.8	58	83	66	107	0	4	0	733	52	8	41	6.0	.990	C-95, 1B-42
1974			118	.254	.395	413	105	16	0	14	3.4	47	52	40	79	0	4	0	707	50	8	44	6.5	.990	C-75, 1B-47, DH-1
1975	ATL	N	111	.240	.360	383	92	13	0	11	2.9	42	50	34	63	0	12	1	896	56	12	80	8.7	.988	1B-90, C-11
1976	2 teams		ATL	N	(61G – .212)			MON	N	(61G – .237)															
"	total		122	.225	.406	374	84	13	2	17	4.5	35	55	33	65	0	17	5	715	64	9	50	6.5	.989	1B-64, C-51
1977	OAK	A	100	.241	.391	348	84	13	0	13	3.7	39	38	18	58	2	5	1	305	26	3	14	3.3	.991	DH-45, C-36, 1B-29
8 yrs.			889	.247	.424	3058	756	115	6	138	4.5	361	457	298	574	2	59	12	4715	460	81	289	5.9	.985	C-456, 1B-327, 3B-66, DH-46

LEAGUE CHAMPIONSHIP SERIES

Year	Team		Games	BA	SA	AB	H	2B	3B	HR	HR%	R	RBI	BB	SO	SB	AB	H	PO	A	E	DP	TC/G	FA	G by Pos
1973	BAL	A	5	.278	.556	18	5	2	0	1	5.6	2	4	2	2	0	0	0	43	2	0	2	9.0	1.000	1B-4, C-1
1974			2	.000	.000	6	0	0	0	0	0.0	0	0	0	2	0	0	0	16	1	1	3	9.0	.944	1B-2
2 yrs.			7	.208	.417	24	5	2	0	1	4.2	2	4	2	4	0	0	0	59	3	1	5	9.0	.984	1B-6, C-1

Eddie Williams

WILLIAMS, EDWARD LAQUAN   BR TR 6' 175 lbs.
B. Nov. 1, 1964, Shreveport, La.

Year	Team		Games	BA	SA	AB	H	2B	3B	HR	HR%	R	RBI	BB	SO	SB	AB	H	PO	A	E	DP	TC/G	FA	G by Pos
1986	CLE	A	5	.143	.143	7	1	0	0	0	0.0	2	1	0	3	0	2	0	0	0	0	0	0.0	–	OF-4
1987			22	.172	.281	64	11	4	0	1	1.6	9	4	9	19	0	0	0	17	37	1	6	2.5	.982	3B-22
1988			10	.190	.190	21	4	0	0	0	0.0	3	1	0	3	0	0	0	3	18	0	0	2.1	1.000	3B-10
1989	CHI	A	66	.274	.358	201	55	8	0	3	1.5	25	10	18	31	1	1	0	37	123	16	21	2.7	.909	3B-65
4 yrs.			103	.242	.324	293	71	12	0	4	1.4	39	16	27	56	1	3	0	57	178	17	27	2.4	.933	3B-97, OF-4

George Williams

WILLIAMS, GEORGE   BR TR 5'11" 165 lbs.
B. Oct. 23, 1939, Detroit, Mich.

Year	Team		Games	BA	SA	AB	H	2B	3B	HR	HR%	R	RBI	BB	SO	SB	AB	H	PO	A	E	DP	TC/G	FA	G by Pos
1961	PHI	N	17	.250	.250	36	9	0	0	0	0.0	4	1	4	4	0	1	0	23	36	2	9	3.6	.967	2B-15
1962	HOU	N	5	.375	.500	8	3	1	0	0	0.0	1	2	0	1	0	2	0	1	5	0	1	1.2	1.000	2B-3
1964	KC	A	37	.209	.275	91	19	6	0	0	0.0	10	2	6	12	0	6	0	41	58	4	18	2.8	.961	2B-20, OF-2, SS-2, 3B-2
3 yrs.			59	.230	.281	135	31	7	0	0	0.0	15	5	10	17	0	9	0	65	99	6	28	2.9	.965	2B-38, OF-2, SS-2, 3B-2

Gus Williams

WILLIAMS, AUGUST JOSEPH (Gloomy Gus)   BL TL 6' 185 lbs.
Brother of Harry Williams.
B. May 7, 1888, Omaha, Neb. D. Apr. 16, 1964, Sterling, Ill.

Year	Team		Games	BA	SA	AB	H	2B	3B	HR	HR%	R	RBI	BB	SO	SB	AB	H	PO	A	E	DP	TC/G	FA	G by Pos
1911	STL	A	9	.269	.385	26	7	3	0	0	0.0	1	0	0		0	2	1	13	0	2	0	1.7	.867	OF-7
1912			64	.292	.444	216	63	13	7	2	0.9	32	32	27		18	2	0	94	12	8	3	1.8	.930	OF-62
1913			147	.273	.400	538	147	21	16	5	0.9	72	53	57	87	31	3	0	225	26	13	7	1.8	.951	OF-143
1914			143	.253	.339	499	126	19	6	4	0.8	51	47	36	120	35	1	0	200	24	16	2	1.7	.933	OF-141
1915			45	.202	.277	119	24	2	2	1	0.8	15	11	6	16	11	6	0	35	2	2	1	0.9	.949	OF-35
5 yrs.			408	.263	.374	1398	367	58	31	12	0.9	171	143	126	223	95	14	1	567	64	41	13	1.6	.939	OF-388

Harry Williams

WILLIAMS, HARRY PETER   BR TR 6'1½" 200 lbs.
Brother of Gus Williams.
B. June 23, 1890, Omaha, Neb. D. Dec. 21, 1963, Huntington Park, Calif.

Year	Team		Games	BA	SA	AB	H	2B	3B	HR	HR%	R	RBI	BB	SO	SB	AB	H	PO	A	E	DP	TC/G	FA	G by Pos
1913	NY	A	27	.256	.354	82	21	3	1	1	1.2	18	12	15	10	6	0	0	244	12	5	7	9.7	.981	1B-27
1914			59	.163	.230	178	29	5	2	1	0.6	9	17	26	26	3	1	0	577	25	15	19	10.5	.976	1B-58
2 yrs.			86	.192	.269	260	50	8	3	2	0.8	27	29	41	36	9	1	0	821	37	20	26	10.2	.977	1B-85

Jim Williams

WILLIAMS, JAMES ALFRED   BR TR 6'2" 190 lbs.
B. Apr. 29, 1947, Zachary, La.

Year	Team		Games	BA	SA	AB	H	2B	3B	HR	HR%	R	RBI	BB	SO	SB	AB	H	PO	A	E	DP	TC/G	FA	G by Pos
1969	SD	N	13	.280	.320	25	7	1	0	0	0.0	4	11	0	6	3	9	0	1	0	0.8	.900	OF-6		
1970			11	.286	.286	14	4	0	0	0	0.0	4	0	1	3	1	4	1	6	0	0	0	0.5	1.000	OF-6
2 yrs.			24	.282	.308	39	11	1	0	0	0.0	8	2	4	14	1	10	4	15	0	1	0	0.7	.938	OF-12

Jimmy Williams

WILLIAMS, JAMES THOMAS (Buttons)   BR TR 5'9" 175 lbs.
B. Dec. 20, 1876, St. Louis, Mo. D. Jan. 16, 1965, St. Petersburg, Fla.

Year	Team		Games	BA	SA	AB	H	2B	3B	HR	HR%	R	RBI	BB	SO	SB	AB	H	PO	A	E	DP	TC/G	FA	G by Pos
1899	PIT	N	152	.355	.532	617	219	28	27	9	1.5	126	116	60		26	0	0	251	354	66	14	4.4	.902	3B-152
1900			106	.264	.389	416	110	15	11	5	1.2	72	68	32		18	0	0	156	265	54	22	4.5	.886	3B-103, SS-4
1901	BAL	A	130	.317	.495	501	159	26	21	7	1.4	113	96	56		21	0	0	339	412	52	47	6.2	.935	2B-130
1902			125	.313	.500	498	156	27	21	8	1.6	83	83	36		14	0	0	275	369	48	47	5.5	.931	2B-104, 3B-19, 1B-1
1903	NY	A	132	.267	.392	502	134	30	12	3	0.6	60	82	39		9	0	0	266	438	32	59	5.6	.957	2B-132
1904			146	.263	.354	559	147	31	7	2	0.4	62	74	38		14	0	0	315	465	40	52	5.6	.951	2B-146
1905			129	.228	.343	470	107	20	8	6	1.3	54	60	50		14	0	0	335	332	25	51	5.4	.964	2B-129
1906			139	.277	.373	501	139	25	7	3	0.6	62	77	44		8	0	0	336	412	32	34	5.6	.959	2B-139
1907			139	.270	.359	504	136	17	11	2	0.4	53	60	35		14	0	0	357	393	26	45	5.6	.966	2B-139
1908	STL	A	148	.236	.321	539	127	20	7	4	0.7	63	53	55		7	0	0	352	445	31	50	5.6	.963	2B-148
1909			110	.195	.235	374	73	3	6	0	0.0	32	22	29		6	1	0	221	280	20	42	4.7	.962	2B-109
11 yrs.			1456	.275	.396	5481	1507	242	138	49	0.9	780	794	474		151	3	0	3203	4165	426	463	5.4	.945	2B-1176, 3B-274, SS-4, 1B-1

Jimy Williams

WILLIAMS, JAMES FRANCIS   BR TR 5'10" 170 lbs.
B. Oct. 4, 1943, Santa Maria, Calif.
Manager 1986-89.

Year	Team		Games	BA	SA	AB	H	2B	3B	HR	HR%	R	RBI	BB	SO	SB	AB	H	PO	A	E	DP	TC/G	FA	G by Pos
1966	STL	N	13	.273	.273	11	3	0	0	0	0.0	1	1	1	5	0	1	0	2	5	0	1	0.5	1.000	SS-7, 2B-3

Year	Team		Games	BA	SA	AB	H	2B	3B	HR	HR%	R	RBI	BB	SO	SB	Pinch Hit AB	Pinch Hit H	PO	A	E	DP	TC/G	FA	G by Pos

Jimy Williams *continued*

Year	Team		Games	BA	SA	AB	H	2B	3B	HR	HR%	R	RBI	BB	SO	SB	AB	H	PO	A	E	DP	TC/G	FA	G by Pos
1967			1	.000	.000	2	0	0	0	0	0.0	0	0	0	1	0	0	0	6	1	0	0	7.0	1.000	SS-1
2 yrs.			14	.231	.231	13	3	0	0	0	0.0	1	1	1	6	0	1	0	8	6	0	1	1.0	1.000	SS-8, 2B-3

Ken Williams

WILLIAMS, KENNETH ROY
B. June 28, 1890, Grant's Pass, Ore. D. Jan. 22, 1959, Grant's Pass, Ore.

BL TR 6' 170 lbs.

Year	Team		Games	BA	SA	AB	H	2B	3B	HR	HR%	R	RBI	BB	SO	SB	AB	H	PO	A	E	DP	TC/G	FA	G by Pos
1915	CIN	N	71	.242	.324	219	53	10	4	0	0.0	22	16	15	20	4	9	3	117	11	7	4	1.9	.948	OF-62
1916			10	.111	.111	27	3	0	0	0	0.0	1	1	2	5	1	1	0	19	2	1	1	2.2	.955	OF-10
1918	STL	A	2	.000	.000	1	0	0	0	0	0.0	0	1	1	0	0	0	0	0	0	0	0	0.0	—	
1919			65	.300	.467	227	68	10	5	6	2.6	32	35	26	25	7	2	0	168	10	12	3	2.9	.937	OF-63
1920			141	.307	.480	521	160	34	13	10	1.9	90	72	41	26	18	1	1	331	17	14	6	2.6	.961	OF-138
1921			146	.347	.561	547	190	31	7	24	4.4	115	117	74	42	20	0	0	331	24	26	3	2.6	.932	OF-145
1922			153	.332	.627	585	194	34	11	39	6.7	128	155	74	31	37	0	0	372	16	12	4	2.6	.970	OF-153
1923			147	.357	.623	555	198	37	12	29	5.2	106	91	79	32	18	1	0	333	23	12	5	2.5	.967	OF-145
1924			114	.324	.533	398	129	21	4	18	4.5	78	84	69	17	20	5	1	257	13	9	2	2.4	.968	OF-109
1925			102	.331	**.613**	411	136	31	5	25	6.1	83	105	37	14	10	0	0	242	11	12	4	2.6	.955	OF-102
1926			108	.280	.510	347	97	15	7	17	4.9	55	74	39	23	5	12	3	189	12	11	2	2.0	.948	OF-91, 2B-1
1927			131	.323	.527	421	136	23	6	17	4.0	70	74	57	30	9	14	3	260	15	10	4	2.2	.965	OF-113
1928	BOS	A	133	.303	.413	462	140	25	1	8	1.7	59	67	37	15	4	6	1	253	10	8	0	2.0	.970	OF-127
1929			74	.345	.540	139	48	14	2	3	2.2	21	21	15	7	1	30	10	83	3	3	3	1.2	.966	OF-36, 1B-2
14 yrs.			1397	.319	.531	4860	1552	285	77	196	4.0	860	913	566	287	154	81	22	2955	167	137	41	2.3	.958	OF-1294, 1B-2, 2B-1

Ken Williams

WILLIAMS, KENNETH ROYAL
B. Apr. 6, 1964, Berkeley, Calif.

BR TR 6'2" 187 lbs.

Year	Team		Games	BA	SA	AB	H	2B	3B	HR	HR%	R	RBI	BB	SO	SB	AB	H	PO	A	E	DP	TC/G	FA	G by Pos
1986	CHI	A	15	.129	.226	31	4	0	1	1	3.2	2	1	1	11	1	0	0	18	1	0	1	1.3	1.000	OF-10, DH-1
1987			116	.281	.422	391	110	18	2	11	2.8	48	50	10	83	21	1	0	303	5	6	2	2.7	.981	OF-115
1988			73	.159	.305	220	35	4	2	8	3.6	18	28	10	64	6	2	1	87	69	17	4	2.4	.902	OF-38, 3B-32, DH-3
1989	DET	A	94	.205	.302	258	53	5	1	6	2.3	29	23	18	63	9	10	1	180	11	4	3	2.1	.979	OF-87, DH-1, 1B-1
4 yrs.			298	.224	.352	900	202	27	5	26	2.9	97	102	39	221	37	13	2	588	86	27	10	2.4	.961	OF-250, 3B-32, DH-5, 1B-1

Mark Williams

WILLIAMS, MARK WESTLEY
B. July 28, 1953, Elmira, N.Y.

BL TL 6' 180 lbs.

Year	Team		Games	BA	SA	AB	H	2B	3B	HR	HR%	R	RBI	BB	SO	SB	AB	H	PO	A	E	DP	TC/G	FA	G by Pos
1977	OAK	A	3	.000	.000	2	0	0	0	0	0.0	0	0	1	1	0	2	0	1	0	0	0	0.3	1.000	OF-1

Matt Williams

WILLIAMS, MATTHEW DERRICK
B. Nov. 28, 1965, Bishop, Calif.

BR TR 6'2" 205 lbs.

Year	Team		Games	BA	SA	AB	H	2B	3B	HR	HR%	R	RBI	BB	SO	SB	AB	H	PO	A	E	DP	TC/G	FA	G by Pos
1987	SF	N	84	.188	.339	245	46	9	2	8	3.3	28	21	16	68	4	3	2	110	234	9	52	4.2	.975	SS-70, 3B-17
1988			52	.205	.410	156	32	6	1	8	5.1	17	19	8	41	0	2	0	48	108	7	9	3.1	.957	3B-43, SS-14
1989			84	.202	.455	292	59	18	1	18	6.2	31	50	14	72	1	3	0	90	168	10	15	3.2	.963	3B-73, SS-30
3 yrs.			220	.198	.404	693	137	33	4	34	4.9	76	90	38	181	5	8	2	248	510	26	76	3.6	.967	3B-133, SS-114

LEAGUE CHAMPIONSHIP SERIES

Year	Team		Games	BA	SA	AB	H	2B	3B	HR	HR%	R	RBI	BB	SO	SB	AB	H	PO	A	E	DP	TC/G	FA	G by Pos
1989	SF	N	5	.300	.650	20	6	1	0	2	10.0	2	9	0	2	0	0	0	5	12	0	2	3.4	1.000	3B-5, SS-1

WORLD SERIES

Year	Team		Games	BA	SA	AB	H	2B	3B	HR	HR%	R	RBI	BB	SO	SB	AB	H	PO	A	E	DP	TC/G	FA	G by Pos
1989	SF	N	4	.125	.313	16	2	0	0	1	6.3	1	1	0	6	0	0	0	4	12	0	2	4.0	1.000	SS-4, 3B-3

Otto Williams

WILLIAMS, OTTO GEORGE
B. Nov. 2, 1877, Newark, N.J. D. Mar. 19, 1937, Omaha, Neb.

BR TR 5'6"

Year	Team		Games	BA	SA	AB	H	2B	3B	HR	HR%	R	RBI	BB	SO	SB	AB	H	PO	A	E	DP	TC/G	FA	G by Pos
1902	STL	N	2	.400	.400	5	2	0	0	0	0.0	0	2	1		1	0	0	5	8	3	0	8.0	.813	SS-2
1903	2 teams	STL N (53G – .203)				CHI N (38G – .223)																			
"	total		91	.211	.252	317	67	9	2	0	0.0	24	22	13		14	0	0	189	275	48	26	5.6	.906	SS-78, 2B-8, 1B-3, 3B-1
1904	CHI	N	57	.200	.232	185	37	4	1	0	0.0	21	8	13		9	2	1	161	67	9	3	4.2	.962	OF-21, 1B-11, SS-10, 3B-6, 2B-6
1906	WAS	A	20	.137	.137	51	7	0	0	0	0.0	3	2	2		0	3	0	36	41	6	2	4.2	.928	SS-8, 2B-6, 1B-2, 3B-1
4 yrs.			170	.203	.237	558	113	13	3	0	0.0	48	34	29		24	5	1	391	391	66	31	5.0	.922	SS-98, OF-21, 2B-20, 1B-16, 3B-8

Pap Williams

WILLIAMS, FRED
B. July 17, 1913, Meridian, Miss.

BR TR 6'1" 200 lbs.

Year	Team		Games	BA	SA	AB	H	2B	3B	HR	HR%	R	RBI	BB	SO	SB	AB	H	PO	A	E	DP	TC/G	FA	G by Pos
1945	CLE	A	16	.211	.211	19	4	0	0	0	0.0	1	2	0	1	0	12	2	13	0	0	2	0.9	1.000	1B-3

Reggie Williams

WILLIAMS, REGINALD DEWAYNE
B. Aug. 29, 1960, Memphis, Tenn.

BR TR 5'11" 185 lbs.

Year	Team		Games	BA	SA	AB	H	2B	3B	HR	HR%	R	RBI	BB	SO	SB	AB	H	PO	A	E	DP	TC/G	FA	G by Pos
1985	LA	N	22	.333	.333	9	3	0	0	0	0.0	4	0	0	4	1	3	1	8	1	1	0	0.5	.900	OF-15
1986			128	.277	.376	303	84	14	2	4	1.3	35	32	23	57	9	11	1	179	5	3	2	1.5	.984	OF-124
1987			39	.111	.111	36	4	0	0	0	0.0	6	4	5	9	1	9	0	21	0	2	0	0.6	.913	OF-30
1988	CLE	A	11	.226	.387	31	7	2	0	1	3.2	7	3	0	6	0	1	1	13	1	0	0	1.3	1.000	OF-11
4 yrs.			200	.259	.351	379	98	16	2	5	1.3	52	39	28	76	11	24	3	221	7	6	2	1.2	.974	OF-180

Rinaldo Williams

WILLIAMS, RINALDO LEWIS
B. Dec. 18, 1893, Santa Cruz, Calif. D. Apr. 24, 1966, Cottonwood, Ariz.

BL TR

Year	Team		Games	BA	SA	AB	H	2B	3B	HR	HR%	R	RBI	BB	SO	SB	AB	H	PO	A	E	DP	TC/G	FA	G by Pos
1914	BKN	F	4	.267	.400	15	4	2	0	0	0.0	1	0	0		0	0	0	4	8	1	0	3.3	.923	3B-4

Ted Williams

WILLIAMS, THEODORE SAMUEL (The Splendid Splinter, The Thumper)
B. Aug. 30, 1918, San Diego, Calif.
Manager 1969-72.
Hall of Fame 1966.

BL TR 6'3" 205 lbs.

Year	Team		Games	BA	SA	AB	H	2B	3B	HR	HR%	R	RBI	BB	SO	SB	AB	H	PO	A	E	DP	TC/G	FA	G by Pos
1939	BOS	A	149	.327	.609	565	185	44	11	31	5.5	131	**145**	107	64	2	0	0	318	11	19	3	2.3	.945	OF-149
1940			144	.344	.594	561	193	43	14	23	4.1	**134**	113	96	54	4	0	0	302	15	13	2	2.3	.961	OF-143, P-1
1941			143	**.406**	**.735**	456	185	33	3	37	8.1	**135**	120	**145**	27	2	9	3	262	11	11	2	2.0	.961	OF-133

Year	Team	Games	BA	SA	AB	H	2B	3B	HR	HR%	R	RBI	BB	SO	SB	Pinch Hit AB	Pinch Hit H	PO	A	E	DP	TC/G	FA	G by Pos

Ted Williams *continued*

Year	Team	Games	BA	SA	AB	H	2B	3B	HR	HR%	R	RBI	BB	SO	SB	AB	H	PO	A	E	DP	TC/G	FA	G by Pos
1942		150	**.356**	**.648**	522	186	34	5	**36**	6.9	141	137	145	51	3	0	0	313	15	4	4	2.2	.988	OF-150
1946		150	.342	**.667**	514	176	37	8	38	7.4	142	123	156	44	0	0	0	325	7	10	2	2.3	.971	OF-150
1947		156	.343	**.634**	528	181	40	9	**32**	6.1	125	114	162	47	0	0	0	347	10	9	2	2.3	.975	OF-156
1948		137	**.369**	.615	509	188	**44**	3	25	4.9	124	127	**126**	41	4	2	0	289	9	5	2	2.2	.983	OF-134
1949		155	.343	**.650**	566	194	39	3	**43**	7.6	150	159	162	48	1	0	0	337	12	6	3	2.3	.983	OF-155
1950		89	.317	.647	334	106	24	1	28	8.4	82	97	82	21	3	1	1	165	7	8	0	2.0	.956	OF-86
1951		148	.318	**.556**	531	169	28	4	30	5.6	109	126	**144**	45	1	0	0	315	12	4	6	2.2	.988	OF-147
1952		6	.400	.900	10	4	0	1	1	10.0	2	3	2	2	0	4	1	4	0	0	0	0.7	1.000	OF-2
1953		37	.407	.901	91	37	6	0	13	14.3	17	34	19	10	0	10	2	31	1	1	1	0.9	.970	OF-26
1954		117	.345	**.635**	386	133	23	1	29	7.5	93	89	**136**	32	0	4	2	213	5	4	0	1.9	.982	OF-115
1955		98	.356	.703	320	114	21	3	28	8.8	77	83	91	24	2	2	1	170	5	2	0	1.8	.989	OF-93
1956		136	.345	.605	400	138	28	2	24	6.0	71	82	102	39	0	20	5	174	7	5	2	1.4	.973	OF-110
1957		132	**.388**	**.731**	420	163	28	1	38	**9.0**	96	87	119	43	0	5	3	215	2	1	0	1.7	.995	OF-125
1958		129	**.328**	.584	411	135	23	2	26	6.3	81	85	98	49	1	11	3	154	3	7	0	1.3	.957	OF-114
1959		103	.254	.419	272	69	15	0	10	3.7	32	43	52	27	0	24	11	94	4	3	0	1.0	.970	OF-76
1960		113	.316	.645	310	98	15	0	29	9.4	56	72	75	41	1	19	1	131	6	1	1	1.2	.993	OF-87
19 yrs.		2292	.344	.634	7706	2654	525	71	521	6.8	1798	1839	2019	709	24	111	33	4159	142	113	30	1.9	.974	OF-2151, P-1
			6th	2nd					10th	4th			10th	2nd										

WORLD SERIES

Year	Team	Games	BA	SA	AB	H	2B	3B	HR	HR%	R	RBI	BB	SO	SB	AB	H	PO	A	E	DP	TC/G	FA	G by Pos
1946	BOS A	7	.200	.200	25	5	0	0	0	0.0	2	1	5	5	0	0	0	16	2	0	2	2.6	1.000	OF-7

Walt Williams

WILLIAMS, WALTER ALLEN (No-Neck)
B. Dec. 19, 1943, Brownwood, Tex.   BR TR 5'6"   165 lbs.

Year	Team	Games	BA	SA	AB	H	2B	3B	HR	HR%	R	RBI	BB	SO	SB	AB	H	PO	A	E	DP	TC/G	FA	G by Pos
1964	HOU N	10	.000	.000	9	0	0	0	0	0.0	1	0	0	2	1	2	0	4	0	0	0	0.4	1.000	OF-5
1967	CHI A	104	.240	.353	275	66	16	3	3	1.1	35	15	17	20	3	30	4	112	6	2	2	1.2	.983	OF-73
1968		63	.241	.308	133	32	6	0	1	0.8	6	8	4	17	0	28	5	47	2	0	1	0.8	1.000	OF-34
1969		135	.304	.374	471	143	22	1	3	0.6	59	32	26	33	6	24	7	183	13	3	4	1.5	.985	OF-111
1970		110	.251	.343	315	79	18	1	3	1.0	43	15	19	30	3	29	8	119	12	7	1	1.3	.949	OF-79
1971		114	.294	.424	361	106	17	3	8	2.2	43	35	24	27	5	27	9	157	5	0	2	1.4	1.000	OF-90, 3B-1
1972		77	.249	.317	221	55	7	1	2	0.9	22	11	13	20	6	23	4	93	6	1	2	1.3	.990	OF-57, 3B-1
1973	CLE A	104	.289	.406	350	101	15	1	8	2.3	43	38	14	29	9	17	4	123	7	4	0	1.3	.970	OF-61, DH-26
1974	NY A	43	.113	.113	53	6	0	0	0	0.0	5	3	1	10	1	15	1	20	1	1	0	0.5	.955	OF-24, DH-3
1975		82	.281	.400	185	52	5	1	5	2.7	27	16	8	23	0	31	**10**	57	4	1	0	0.8	.984	OF-31, DH-17, 2B-6
10 yrs.		842	.270	.365	2373	640	106	11	33	1.4	284	173	126	211	34	226	52	915	56	19	12	1.2	.981	OF-565, DH-46, 2B-6, 3B-2

Wash Williams

WILLIAMS, WASHINGTON J.
B. Philadelphia, Pa.   D. Aug. 9, 1892, Philadelphia, Pa.   5'11"   180 lbs.

Year	Team	Games	BA	SA	AB	H	2B	3B	HR	HR%	R	RBI	BB	SO	SB	AB	H	PO	A	E	DP	TC/G	FA	G by Pos
1884	RIC AA	2	.250	.250	8	2	0	0	0	0.0	0		0	0	0	0	0	1	0	1	0	1.0	.500	OF-2
1885	CHI N	1	.250	.250	4	1	0	0	0	0.0	0	0	0	0	0	0	0	1	1	1	0	3.0	.667	OF-1, P-1
2 yrs.		3	.250	.250	12	3	0	0	0	0.0	0	0	0	0	0	0	0	2	1	2	0	1.7	.600	OF-3, P-1

Woody Williams

WILLIAMS, WOODROW WILSON
B. Aug. 22, 1912, Pamplin, Va.   BR TR 5'11"   175 lbs.

Year	Team	Games	BA	SA	AB	H	2B	3B	HR	HR%	R	RBI	BB	SO	SB	AB	H	PO	A	E	DP	TC/G	FA	G by Pos
1938	BKN N	20	.333	.392	51	17	1	1	0	0.0	6	6	4	1	1	1	0	28	28	4	4	3.0	.933	SS-18, 3B-1
1943	CIN N	30	.377	.435	69	26	2	1	0	0.0	8	11	1	3	0	5	1	37	47	6	7	3.0	.933	2B-12, 3B-7, SS-5
1944		155	.240	.289	**653**	157	23	3	1	0.2	73	35	44	24	7	0	0	377	542	27	97	6.1	.971	2B-155
1945		133	.237	.266	482	114	14	0	0	0.0	46	27	39	24	6	0	0	295	393	22	61	5.3	.969	2B-133
4 yrs.		338	.250	.292	1255	314	40	5	1	0.1	133	79	88	52	14	5	1	737	1010	59	169	5.3	.967	2B-300, SS-23, 3B-8

Howie Williamson

WILLIAMSON, NATHANIEL HOWARD (Cow)
B. Dec. 23, 1904, Little Rock, Ark.   D. Aug. 15, 1969, Texarkana, Ark.   BL TL 6'1"   170 lbs.

Year	Team	Games	BA	SA	AB	H	2B	3B	HR	HR%	R	RBI	BB	SO	SB	AB	H	PO	A	E	DP	TC/G	FA	G by Pos
1928	STL N	10	.222	.222	9	2	0	0	0	0.0	0	0	1	4	0	9	2	0	0	0	0	0.0	—	

Ned Williamson

WILLIAMSON, EDWARD NAGLE
B. Oct. 24, 1857, Philadelphia, Pa.   D. Mar. 3, 1894, Willow Springs, Ark.   BR TR 5'11"   170 lbs.

Year	Team	Games	BA	SA	AB	H	2B	3B	HR	HR%	R	RBI	BB	SO	SB	AB	H	PO	A	E	DP	TC/G	FA	G by Pos
1878	IND N	63	.232	.300	250	58	10	2	1	0.4	31	19	5	15		0	0	88	128	33	6	4.0	.867	3B-63
1879	CHI N	80	.294	.447	320	94	20	13	1	0.3	66	36	24	31		0	0	183	199	49	15	5.4	.886	3B-70, 1B-6, C-4
1880		75	.251	.328	311	78	20	2	0	0.0	65	31	15	26		0	0	147	176	34	9	4.8	.905	3B-63, C-11, 2B-3
1881		82	.268	.347	343	92	12	6	1	0.3	56	49	19	19		0	0	135	220	36	13	4.8	.908	3B-76, 2B-4, P-3, SS-2, C-1
1882		83	.282	.408	348	98	27	4	3	0.9	66	60	27	21		0	0	108	211	43	16	4.4	.881	3B-83, P-1
1883		98	.276	.438	402	111	**49**	5	2	0.5	83		22	48		0	0	115	257	88	20	4.7	.809	3B-97, C-3, P-1
1884		107	.278	.554	417	116	18	8	**27**	6.5	84		42	56		0	0	155	271	67	26	4.6	.864	3B-99, C-10, P-2
1885		113	.238	.324	407	97	16	5	3	0.7	87	64	**75**	60		0	0	120	261	45	18	3.8	.894	3B-113, P-2, C-1
1886		121	.216	.335	430	93	17	8	6	1.4	69	58	80	71		0	0	162	356	79	36	4.9	.868	SS-121, C-4, P-2
1887		127	.267	.437	439	117	20	14	9	2.1	77	78	73	57	45	0	0	133	362	61	31	4.4	.890	SS-127, P-1
1888		132	.250	.385	452	113	9	14	8	1.8	75	73	65	71	25	0	0	120	375	65	48	4.2	.884	SS-132
1889		47	.237	.283	173	41	3	1	1	0.6	16	30	23	22	2	0	0	48	130	33	7	4.5	.844	SS-47
1890	CHI P	73	.195	.264	261	51	7	4	1	0.4	34	26	36	35	3	0	0	75	149	51	12	3.8	.815	3B-52, SS-21
13 yrs.		1201	.255	.384	4553	1159	228	86	63	1.4	809	523	506	532	75	0	0	1589	3095	684	257	4.5	.873	3B-716, SS-450, C-34, P-12, 2B-7, 1B-6

Julius Willigrod

WILLIGROD, JULIUS
B. Calif.   D. Sept. 27, 1906, San Francisco, Calif.   BL

Year	Team	Games	BA	SA	AB	H	2B	3B	HR	HR%	R	RBI	BB	SO	SB	AB	H	PO	A	E	DP	TC/G	FA	G by Pos
1882	2 teams		DET N (1G – .333)		CLE N (9G – .139)																			
"	total	10	.154	.231	39	6	1	0	0	0.0	5	2	3	8		0	0	13	2	3	0	1.8	.833	OF-9, SS-1

Hugh Willingham

WILLINGHAM, THOMAS HUGH
B. May 30, 1906, Dalhart, Tex.   D. June 15, 1988, El Reno, Okla.   BR TR 6'   180 lbs.

Year	Team	Games	BA	SA	AB	H	2B	3B	HR	HR%	R	RBI	BB	SO	SB	AB	H	PO	A	E	DP	TC/G	FA	G by Pos
1930	CHI A	3	.250	.250	4	1	0	0	0	0.0	2	0	2	1	0	2	1	1	3	0	0	1.3	1.000	2B-1

Year	Team		Games	BA	SA	AB	H	2B	3B	HR	HR%	R	RBI	BB	SO	SB	Pinch Hit AB	Pinch Hit H	PO	A	E	DP	TC/G	FA	G by Pos

Hugh Willingham *continued*

Year	Team		Games	BA	SA	AB	H	2B	3B	HR	HR%	R	RBI	BB	SO	SB	AB	H	PO	A	E	DP	TC/G	FA	G by Pos
1931	PHI	N	23	.257	.457	35	9	2	1	1	2.9	5	3	2	9	0	5	1	24	18	6	5	2.1	.875	SS-8, 3B-2, OF-1
1932			4	.000	.000	2	0	0	0	0	0.0	0	0	0	0	0	2	0	0	0	0	0	0.0	—	
1933			1	.000	.000	1	0	0	0	0	0.0	0	0	0	0	0	1	0	0	0	0	0	0.0	—	
	4 yrs.		31	.238	.405	42	10	2	1	1	2.4	7	3	4	10	0	10	2	25	21	6	5	1.7	.885	SS-8, 3B-2, OF-1, 2B-1

Wills

WILLS,
Deceased.

Year	Team		Games	BA	SA	AB	H	2B	3B	HR	HR%	R	RBI	BB	SO	SB	AB	H	PO	A	E	DP	TC/G	FA	G by Pos
1884	2 teams		WAS AA (4G – .133)			KC U (5G – .143)																			
"	total		9	.139	.222	36	5	3	0	0	0.0	3		0			0	0	10	5	1	0	1.8	.938	OF-9

Bump Wills

WILLS, ELLIOTT TAYLOR
Son of Maury Wills.
B. July 27, 1952, Washington, D. C.

BB TR 5'9" 172 lbs.

Year	Team		Games	BA	SA	AB	H	2B	3B	HR	HR%	R	RBI	BB	SO	SB	AB	H	PO	A	E	DP	TC/G	FA	G by Pos
1977	TEX	A	152	.287	.410	541	155	28	6	9	1.7	87	62	65	96	28	1	0	321	492	15	89	5.4	.982	2B-150, SS-2, DH-1, 1B-1
1978			157	.250	.347	539	135	17	4	9	1.7	78	57	63	91	52	3	0	350	526	17	84	5.7	.981	2B-156
1979			146	.273	.350	543	148	21	3	5	0.9	90	46	53	58	35	2	1	337	468	20	95	5.7	.976	2B-146
1980			146	.263	.360	578	152	31	5	5	0.9	102	58	51	71	34	0	0	340	473	13	112	5.7	.984	2B-144
1981			102	.251	.307	410	103	13	2	2	0.5	51	41	32	49	12	0	0	268	326	10	70	5.9	.983	2B-101, DH-1
1982	CHI	N	128	.272	.377	419	114	18	4	6	1.4	64	38	46	76	35	21	6	199	297	19	45	4.0	.963	2B-103
	6 yrs.		831	.266	.360	3030	807	128	24	36	1.2	472	302	310	441	196	27	7	1815	2582	94	495	5.4	.979	2B-800, DH-2, SS-2, 1B-1

Dave Wills

WILLS, DAVIS BOWLES
B. Jan. 26, 1877, Charlottesville, Va.   D. Oct. 12, 1959, Washington, D. C.

BL TL

Year	Team		Games	BA	SA	AB	H	2B	3B	HR	HR%	R	RBI	BB	SO	SB	AB	H	PO	A	E	DP	TC/G	FA	G by Pos
1899	LOU	N	24	.223	.277	94	21	3	1	0	0.0	15	12	2		1	0	0	259	8	12	9	11.6	.957	1B-24

Maury Wills

WILLS, MAURICE MORNING
Father of Bump Wills.
B. Oct. 2, 1932, Washington, D. C.
Manager 1980-81.

BB TR 5'11" 170 lbs.

Year	Team		Games	BA	SA	AB	H	2B	3B	HR	HR%	R	RBI	BB	SO	SB	AB	H	PO	A	E	DP	TC/G	FA	G by Pos
1959	LA	N	83	.260	.298	242	63	5	2	0	0.0	27	7	13	27	7	0	0	121	220	12	39	4.3	.966	SS-82
1960			148	.295	.331	516	152	15	2	0	0.0	75	27	35	47	50	0	0	260	431	40	78	4.9	.945	SS-145
1961			148	.282	.339	613	173	12	10	1	0.2	105	31	59	50	35	1	0	253	428	29	104	4.8	.959	SS-148
1962			165	.299	.373	695	208	13	10	6	0.9	130	48	51	57	104	0	0	295	493	36	86	5.0	.956	SS-165
1963			134	.302	.349	527	159	19	3	0	0.0	83	34	44	48	40	0	0	197	381	26	54	4.5	.957	SS-109, 3B-33
1964			158	.275	.324	630	173	15	5	2	0.3	81	34	41	73	53	4	0	275	428	27	77	4.6	.963	SS-149, 3B-6
1965			158	.286	.329	650	186	14	7	0	0.0	92	33	40	64	94	2	0	267	535	25	89	5.2	.970	SS-155
1966			143	.273	.308	594	162	14	2	1	0.2	60	39	34	60	38	1	0	231	460	23	80	5.0	.968	SS-139, 3B-4
1967	PIT	N	149	.302	.365	616	186	12	9	3	0.5	92	45	31	44	29	3	1	102	346	24	32	3.2	.949	3B-144, SS-2
1968			153	.278	.316	627	174	12	6	0	0.0	76	31	45	57	52	3	0	115	308	18	32	2.9	.959	3B-141, SS-10
1969	2 teams		MON N (47G – .222)			LA N (104G – .297)																			
"	total		151	.274	.335	623	171	10	8	4	0.6	80	47	59	61	40	1	1	240	496	28	92	5.1	.963	SS-150, 2B-1
1970	LA	N	132	.270	.318	522	141	19	3	0	0.0	77	34	50	34	28	5	1	171	397	24	58	4.5	.959	SS-126, 3B-4
1971			149	.281	.329	601	169	14	3	3	0.5	73	44	40	44	15	6	1	220	486	17	87	4.9	.976	SS-144, 3B-4
1972			71	.129	.167	132	17	3	1	0	0.0	16	4	10	18	1	5	1	39	103	2	20	2.0	.986	SS-31, 3B-26
	14 yrs.		1942	.281	.331	7588	2134	177	71	20	0.3	1067	458	552	684	586 10th	31	5	2786	5512	331	928	4.4	.962	SS-1555, 3B-362, 2B-1

WORLD SERIES

Year	Team		Games	BA	SA	AB	H	2B	3B	HR	HR%	R	RBI	BB	SO	SB	AB	H	PO	A	E	DP	TC/G	FA	G by Pos
1959	LA	N	6	.250	.250	20	5	0	0	0	0.0	2	1	0	3	1	0	0	10	21	1	3	5.3	.969	SS-6
1963			4	.133	.133	15	2	0	0	0	0.0	1	0	1	3	1	0	0	5	10	1	0	4.0	.938	SS-4
1965			7	.367	.467	30	11	3	0	0	0.0	3	3	1	3	3	0	0	14	26	0	6	5.7	1.000	SS-7
1966			4	.077	.077	13	1	0	0	0	0.0	0	0	3	3	1	0	0	12	15	0	3	6.8	1.000	SS-4
	4 yrs.		21	.244	.282	78	19	3	0	0	0.0	6	4	5	12	6	0	0	41	72	2	12	5.5	.983	SS-21

Kid Willson

WILLSON, FRANK HOXIE
B. Nov. 3, 1895, Bloomington, Neb.   D. Apr. 17, 1964, Union Gap, Wash.

BL TL 6'1" 190 lbs.

Year	Team		Games	BA	SA	AB	H	2B	3B	HR	HR%	R	RBI	BB	SO	SB	AB	H	PO	A	E	DP	TC/G	FA	G by Pos
1918	CHI	A	4	.000	.000	1	0	0	0	0	0.0	2	0	1	1	0	1	0	0	0	0	0	0.0	1.000	OF-2
1927			7	.100	.100	10	1	0	0	0	0.0	1	1	0	2	0	4	0	6	0	0	0	0.9	1.000	OF-2
	2 yrs.		11	.091	.091	11	1	0	0	0	0.0	3	1	1	3	0	5	0	6	0	0	0	0.5	1.000	OF-2

Walt Wilmot

WILMOT, WALTER ROBERT
B. Oct. 18, 1863, Plover, Wis.   D. Feb. 1, 1929, Chicago, Ill.

BB TR

Year	Team		Games	BA	SA	AB	H	2B	3B	HR	HR%	R	RBI	BB	SO	SB	AB	H	PO	A	E	DP	TC/G	FA	G by Pos
1888	WAS	N	119	.224	.321	473	106	16	9	4	0.8	61	43	23	55	46	0	0	260	19	41	4	2.7	.872	OF-119
1889			108	.289	.484	432	125	19	19	9	2.1	88	57	51	32	40	0	0	232	22	20	4	2.5	.927	OF-108
1890	CHI	N	139	.278	.420	571	159	15	12	14	2.5	114	99	64	44	76	0	0	320	26	23	4	2.7	.938	OF-139
1891			121	.279	.414	498	139	14	10	11	2.2	102	71	55	21	42	0	0	223	15	20	0	2.1	.922	OF-121
1892			92	.216	.287	380	82	7	7	2	0.5	47	35	40	20	31	0	0	197	8	22	0	2.5	.903	OF-92
1893			94	.301	.431	392	118	14	14	3	0.8	69	61	40	8	39	0	0	198	16	31	1	2.6	.873	OF-93
1894			133	.330	.471	597	197	45	12	5	0.8	134	130	35	23	74	0	0	264	16	41	5	2.4	.872	OF-133
1895			108	.283	.395	466	132	16	6	8	1.7	86	72	30	19	28	0	0	226	19	23	5	2.5	.914	OF-108
1897	NY	N	11	.265	.412	34	9	2	0	1	2.9	8	4	2		1	1	0	13	2	1	0	1.5	.938	OF-9
1898			35	.239	.341	138	33	4	2	1	0.7	16	22	9		4	0	0	35	4	5	0	1.3	.886	OF-34
	10 yrs.		960	.276	.405	3981	1100	152	91	59	1.5	725	594	349	222	381	3	0	1968	147	227	23	2.4	.903	OF-956

Archie Wilson

WILSON, ARCHIE CLIFTON
B. Nov. 25, 1923, Los Angeles, Calif.

BR TR 5'11" 175 lbs.

Year	Team		Games	BA	SA	AB	H	2B	3B	HR	HR%	R	RBI	BB	SO	SB	AB	H	PO	A	E	DP	TC/G	FA	G by Pos
1951	NY	A	4	.000	.000	4	0	0	0	0	0.0	0	0	0	2	0	3	0	3	0	0	0	0.8	1.000	OF-2
1952	3 teams		NY A (3G – .500)			WAS A (26G – .208)					BOS A (18G – .263)														
"	total		47	.228	.309	136	31	5	3	0	0.0	9	17	7	14	0	9	3	84	1	3	1	1.9	.966	OF-37
	2 yrs.		51	.221	.300	140	31	5	3	0	0.0	9	17	7	14	0	11	3	87	1	3	1	1.8	.967	OF-39

Year	Team		Games	BA	SA	AB	H	2B	3B	HR	HR%	R	RBI	BB	SO	SB	Pinch Hit AB	H	PO	A	E	DP	TC/G	FA	G by Pos

Art Wilson

WILSON, ARTHUR EARL (Dutch)
B. Dec. 11, 1885, Macon, Ill.   D. June 12, 1960, Chicago, Ill.   BR TR 5'8" 170 lbs.

Year	Team		Games	BA	SA	AB	H	2B	3B	HR	HR%	R	RBI	BB	SO	SB	AB	H	PO	A	E	DP	TC/G	FA	G by Pos
1908	NY	N	1	–	–	0	0	0	0	0	–	0	0	0		0	0	0	0	0	0	0	0.0	–	
1909			19	.238	.333	42	10	2	1	0	0.0	4	5	4		0	0	1	50	11	1	1	3.3	.984	C-18
1910			26	.269	.385	52	14	4	1	0	0.0	10	5	9	6	2	0	0	95	22	3	4	4.6	.975	C-25, 1B-1
1911			66	.303	.431	109	33	9	1	1	0.9	17	17	19	12	6	2	0	200	34	9	2	3.7	.963	C-64
1912			65	.289	.413	121	35	6	0	3	2.5	17	19	13	14	2	3	1	213	30	10	5	3.9	.960	C-61
1913			54	.190	.215	79	15	0	1	0	0.0	5	8	11	11	1	2	1	144	38	6	5	3.5	.968	C-49, 1B-2
1914	CHI	F	137	.291	.466	440	128	31	8	10	2.3	78	64	70		13	4	2	674	212	24	19	6.6	.974	C-132
1915			96	.305	.439	269	82	11	2	7	2.6	44	31	65		8	7	2	391	96	10	6	5.2	.980	C-87
1916	2 teams		89	PIT	N	(53G –	.258)		CHI	N	(36G –	.193)													
"	total		89	.227	.298	242	55	8	3	1	0.4	16	17	19	41	5	14	2	307	80	13	6	4.5	.968	C-73
1917	CHI	N	81	.213	.303	211	45	9	2	2	0.9	17	25	32	36	6	4	2	361	92	15	5	5.8	.968	C-75
1918	BOS	N	89	.246	.289	280	69	8	2	0	0.0	15	19	24	31	5	2	0	292	96	9	7	4.5	.977	C-85
1919			71	.257	.309	191	49	8	1	0	0.0	14	16	25	19	2	5	1	214	82	7	4	4.3	.977	C-64, 1B-1
1920			16	.053	.053	19	1	0	0	0	0.0	0	0	1	1	0	7	0	4	5	1	0	0.6	.900	3B-6, C-2
1921	CLE	A	2	.000	.000	1	0	0	0	0	0.0	0	0	0	0	0	0	0	1	1	0	0	1.0	1.000	C-2
14 yrs.			812	.261	.364	2056	536	96	22	24	1.2	237	226	292	171	50	51	11	2946	799	108	64	4.7	.972	C-737, 3B-6, 1B-4

WORLD SERIES

Year	Team		Games	BA	SA	AB	H	2B	3B	HR	HR%	R	RBI	BB	SO	SB	AB	H	PO	A	E	DP	TC/G	FA	G by Pos
1911	NY	N	1	.000	.000	1	0	0	0	0	0.0	0	0	0	0	0	0	0	1	0	0	0	1.0	1.000	C-1
1912			2	1.000	1.000	1	1	0	0	0	0.0	0	0	0	0	0	0	0	2	1	1	0	2.0	.750	C-2
1913			3	.000	.000	3	0	0	0	0	0.0	0	0	0	2	0	0	0	4	1	0	0	1.7	1.000	C-3
3 yrs.			6	.200	.200	5	1	0	0	0	0.0	0	0	0	2	0	0	0	7	2	1	0	1.7	.900	C-6

Artie Wilson

WILSON, ARTHUR LEE
B. Oct. 28, 1920, Springfield, Ala.   BL TR 5'11" 162 lbs.

Year	Team		Games	BA	SA	AB	H	2B	3B	HR	HR%	R	RBI	BB	SO	SB	AB	H	PO	A	E	DP	TC/G	FA	G by Pos
1951	NY	N	19	.182	.182	22	4	0	0	0	0.0	2	1	2	1	2	11	2	14	11	1	5	1.4	.962	SS-3, 2B-3, 1B-2

Bill Wilson

WILSON, WILLIAM DONALD
B. Nov. 6, 1928, Central City, Neb.   BR TR 6'2" 200 lbs.

Year	Team		Games	BA	SA	AB	H	2B	3B	HR	HR%	R	RBI	BB	SO	SB	AB	H	PO	A	E	DP	TC/G	FA	G by Pos
1950	CHI	A	3	.000	.000	6	0	0	0	0	0.0	0	0	2	2	0	0	0	3	0	0	0	1.0	1.000	OF-2
1953			9	.059	.059	17	1	0	0	0	0.0	0	1	0	7	0	4	0	9	0	0	0	1.0	1.000	OF-3
1954	2 teams		114	CHI	A	(20G –	.171)		PHI	A	(94G –	.238)													
"	total		114	.232	.411	358	83	11	1	17	4.7	47	38	46	64	1	5	0	303	7	5	4	2.8	.984	OF-110
1955	KC	A	98	.223	.432	273	61	12	0	15	5.5	39	38	24	63	1	14	3	186	4	6	0	2.0	.969	OF-82, P-1
4 yrs.			224	.222	.407	654	145	23	1	32	4.9	87	77	72	136	2	23	3	501	11	11	4	2.3	.979	OF-197, P-1

Bill Wilson

WILSON, WILLIAM G.
B. Oct. 28, 1867, Hannibal, Mo.   D. May 9, 1924, St. Paul, Minn.   TR

Year	Team		Games	BA	SA	AB	H	2B	3B	HR	HR%	R	RBI	BB	SO	SB	AB	H	PO	A	E	DP	TC/G	FA	G by Pos
1890	PIT	N	83	.214	.270	304	65	11	3	0	0.0	30	21	22	50	5	0	0	409	90	60	22	6.7	.893	C-38, OF-25, 1B-18, SS-1
1897	LOU	N	105	.213	.273	381	81	12	4	1	0.3	43	41	18		9	1	0	339	114	30	7	4.6	.938	C-103, 3B-1
1898			29	.167	.245	102	17	1	2	1	1.0	5	13	5		3	0	0	97	34	16	2	5.1	.891	C-28, 1B-1
3 yrs.			217	.207	.268	787	163	24	9	2	0.3	78	75	45	50	17	1	0	845	238	106	31	5.5	.911	C-169, OF-25, 1B-19, SS-1, 3B-1

Bob Wilson

WILSON, ROBERT
B. Feb. 22, 1928, Dallas, Tex.   BR TR 5'11" 197 lbs.

Year	Team		Games	BA	SA	AB	H	2B	3B	HR	HR%	R	RBI	BB	SO	SB	AB	H	PO	A	E	DP	TC/G	FA	G by Pos
1958	LA	N	3	.200	.200	5	1	0	0	0	0.0	0	0	0	1	0	2	1	1	0	0	0	0.3	1.000	OF-1

Charlie Wilson

WILSON, CHARLES WOODROW (Swamp Baby)
B. Jan. 13, 1905, Clinton, S. C.   D. Dec. 19, 1970, Rochester, N. Y.   BB TR 5'10½" 178 lbs.

Year	Team		Games	BA	SA	AB	H	2B	3B	HR	HR%	R	RBI	BB	SO	SB	AB	H	PO	A	E	DP	TC/G	FA	G by Pos
1931	BOS	N	16	.190	.310	58	11	4	0	1	1.7	7	11	3	5	0	0	0	9	24	3	0	2.3	.917	3B-14
1932	STL	N	24	.198	.323	96	19	3	3	1	1.0	7	2	3	8	0	0	0	28	73	7	14	4.5	.935	SS-24
1933			1	.000	.000	1	0	0	0	0	0.0	0	0	0	1	0	0	0	0	0	0	0	0.0	–	SS-1
1935			16	.323	.323	31	10	0	0	0	0.0	1	1	2	2	0	7	4	6	8	1	1	0.9	.933	3B-8
4 yrs.			57	.215	.317	186	40	7	3	2	1.1	15	14	8	16	0	7	4	43	105	11	15	2.8	.931	SS-25, 3B-22

Craig Wilson

WILSON, CRAIG
B. Nov. 28, 1964, Annapolis, Md.   BR TR 5'11" 175 lbs.

Year	Team		Games	BA	SA	AB	H	2B	3B	HR	HR%	R	RBI	BB	SO	SB	AB	H	PO	A	E	DP	TC/G	FA	G by Pos
1989	STL	N	6	.250	.250	4	1	0	0	0	0.0	1	1	1	2	0	4	1	1	0	1	0	0.3	.500	3B-2

Eddie Wilson

WILSON, EDWARD FRANCIS
B. Sept. 7, 1909, Hamden, Conn.   D. Apr. 11, 1979, Hamden, Conn.   BL TL 5'11" 165 lbs.

Year	Team		Games	BA	SA	AB	H	2B	3B	HR	HR%	R	RBI	BB	SO	SB	AB	H	PO	A	E	DP	TC/G	FA	G by Pos
1936	BKN	N	52	.347	.457	173	60	8	1	3	1.7	28	25	14	25	1	5	0	72	3	6	0	1.6	.926	OF-47
1937			36	.222	.389	54	12	4	1	1	1.9	11	8	17	14	1	9	1	27	1	1	0	0.8	.966	OF-21
2 yrs.			88	.317	.441	227	72	12	2	4	1.8	39	33	31	39	4	14	1	99	4	7	0	1.3	.936	OF-68

Frank Wilson

WILSON, FRANCIS EDWARD (Squash)
B. Apr. 20, 1901, Malden, Mass.   D. Nov. 25, 1974, Leicester, Mass.   BL TR 6' 185 lbs.

Year	Team		Games	BA	SA	AB	H	2B	3B	HR	HR%	R	RBI	BB	SO	SB	AB	H	PO	A	E	DP	TC/G	FA	G by Pos
1924	BOS	N	61	.237	.284	215	51	7	0	1	0.5	20	15	23	22	3	5	2	140	5	4	1	2.4	.973	OF-55
1925			12	.419	.516	31	13	1	0	0	0.0	3	0	4	1	2	1	0	23	1	0	0	2.0	1.000	OF-10
1926			87	.237	.309	236	56	11	3	0	0.0	22	23	20	21	3	28	7	121	6	9	1	1.6	.934	OF-56
1928	2 teams		8	CLE	A	(2G –	.000)		STL	A	(6G –	.000)													
"	total		8	.000	.000	6	0	0	0	0	0.0	1	0	1	0	0	5	0	0	0	0	0	0.0	–	OF-1
4 yrs.			168	.246	.307	488	120	19	4	1	0.2	46	38	48	44	8	39	9	284	12	13	2	1.8	.958	OF-122

Gary Wilson

WILSON, JAMES GARRETT
B. Jan. 12, 1877, Baltimore, Md.   D. May 1, 1969, Randallstown, Md.   BR TR 5'7" 168 lbs.

Year	Team		Games	BA	SA	AB	H	2B	3B	HR	HR%	R	RBI	BB	SO	SB	AB	H	PO	A	E	DP	TC/G	FA	G by Pos
1902	BOS	A	2	.125	.125	8	1	0	0	0	0.0	0	1	0		0	0	0	6	6	3	2	7.5	.800	2B-2

Year	Team		Games	BA	SA	AB	H	2B	3B	HR	HR%	R	RBI	BB	SO	SB	Pinch Hit AB	Pinch Hit H	PO	A	E	DP	TC/G	FA	G by Pos

Glenn Wilson

WILSON, GLENN DWIGHT
B. Dec. 22, 1958, Baytown, Tex.
BR TR 6'1" 190 lbs.

Year	Team		Games	BA	SA	AB	H	2B	3B	HR	HR%	R	RBI	BB	SO	SB	AB	H	PO	A	E	DP	TC/G	FA	G by Pos
1982	DET	A	84	.292	.457	322	94	15	1	12	3.7	39	34	15	51	2	2	0	215	8	3	1	2.7	.987	OF-80, DH-4
1983			144	.268	.408	503	135	25	6	11	2.2	55	65	25	79	1	7	3	225	12	3	2	1.7	.988	OF-143
1984	PHI	N	132	.240	.372	341	82	21	3	6	1.8	28	31	17	56	7	19	2	153	7	7	0	1.3	.958	OF-109, 3B-4
1985			161	.275	.424	608	167	39	5	14	2.3	73	102	35	117	7	5	2	343	18	12	4	2.3	.968	OF-158
1986			155	.271	.413	584	158	30	4	15	2.6	70	84	42	91	5	3	0	331	20	4	5	2.3	.989	OF-154
1987			154	.264	.381	569	150	21	2	14	2.5	55	54	38	82	3	2	1	315	19	11	2	2.2	.968	OF-154, P-1
1988	2 teams	SEA A (78G – .250)			PIT N (37G – .270)																				
"	total		115	.256	.341	410	105	18	1	5	1.2	39	32	18	70	1	3	1	206	5	4	2	1.9	.981	OF-110, DH-2
1989	2 teams	PIT N (100G – .282)			HOU N (28G – .216)																				
"	total		128	.266	.421	432	115	26	4	11	2.5	50	64	37	53	1	15	4	249	13	6	2	2.1	.978	OF-110, 1B-10
8 yrs.			1073	.267	.402	3769	1006	195	26	88	2.3	409	466	227	599	27	56	13	2037	102	50	18	2.0	.977	OF-1018, 1B-10, DH-6, 3B-4, P-1

Grady Wilson

WILSON, GRADY HERBERT
B. Nov. 23, 1922, Columbus, Ga.
BR TR 6½" 170 lbs.

Year	Team		Games	BA	SA	AB	H	2B	3B	HR	HR%	R	RBI	BB	SO	SB	AB	H	PO	A	E	DP	TC/G	FA	G by Pos
1948	PIT	N	12	.100	.200	10	1	1	0	0	0.0	1	1	0	3	0	0	0	7	4	2	2	1.1	.846	SS-7

Hack Wilson

WILSON, LEWIS ROBERT
B. Apr. 26, 1900, Ellwood City, Pa. D. Nov. 23, 1948, Baltimore, Md.
Hall of Fame 1979.
BR TR 5'6" 190 lbs.

Year	Team		Games	BA	SA	AB	H	2B	3B	HR	HR%	R	RBI	BB	SO	SB	AB	H	PO	A	E	DP	TC/G	FA	G by Pos
1923	NY	N	3	.200	.200	10	2	0	0	0	0.0	0	0	0	1	0	0	0	6	0	1	0	2.3	.857	OF-3
1924			107	.295	.486	383	113	19	12	10	2.6	62	57	44	46	4	4	0	230	8	8	2	2.3	.967	OF-103
1925			62	.239	.422	180	43	7	4	6	3.3	28	30	21	33	5	5	2	75	3	2	2	1.3	.975	OF-50
1926	CHI	N	142	.321	.539	529	170	36	8	21	4.0	97	109	69	61	10	2	1	348	11	10	5	2.6	.973	OF-140
1927			146	.318	.579	551	175	30	12	30	5.4	119	129	71	70	13	0	0	400	13	14	3	2.9	.967	OF-146
1928			145	.313	.588	520	163	32	9	31	6.0	89	120	77	94	4	2	0	321	11	14	2	2.4	.960	OF-143
1929			150	.345	.618	574	198	30	5	39	6.8	135	159	78	83	3	0	0	380	14	12	4	2.7	.970	OF-150
1930			155	.356	.723	585	208	35	6	56	9.6	146	190¹	105	84	3	0	0	357	9	19	2	2.5	.951	OF-155
1931			112	.261	.435	395	103	22	4	13	3.3	66	61	63	69	1	8	2	210	9	5	1	2.0	.978	OF-103
1932	BKN	N	135	.297	.538	481	143	37	5	23	4.8	77	123	51	85	2	7	1	220	14	11	4	1.8	.955	OF-125
1933			117	.267	.389	360	96	13	2	9	2.5	41	54	52	50	7	16	5	192	21	10	3	1.9	.955	OF-90, 2B-5
1934	2 teams	BKN N (67G – .262)			PHI N (7G – .100)																				
"	total		74	.245	.365	192	47	5	0	6	3.1	24	30	43	37	0	20	6	82	3	2	6	1.2	.977	OF-49
12 yrs.			1348	.307	.545	4760	1461	266	67	244	5.1	884	1062	674	713	52	64	16	2821	116	108	34	2.3	.965	OF-1257, 2B-5

WORLD SERIES

Year	Team		Games	BA	SA	AB	H	2B	3B	HR	HR%	R	RBI	BB	SO	SB	AB	H	PO	A	E	DP	TC/G	FA	G by Pos
1924	NY	N	7	.233	.267	30	7	1	0	0	0.0	1	3	1	9	0	0	0	19	1	0	0	2.9	1.000	OF-7
1929	CHI	N	5	.471	.588	17	8	0	1	0	0.0	2	0	4	3	0	0	0	14	0	1	0	3.0	.933	OF-5
2 yrs.			12	.319	.383	47	15	1	1	0	0.0	3	3	5	12	0	0	0	33	1	1	0	2.9	.971	OF-12

Henry Wilson

WILSON, HENRY C.
B. Baltimore, Md. Deceased.

Year	Team		Games	BA	SA	AB	H	2B	3B	HR	HR%	R	RBI	BB	SO	SB	AB	H	PO	A	E	DP	TC/G	FA	G by Pos
1898	BAL	N	1	.000	.000	2	0	0	0	0	0.0	0	0	1		0	0	0	3	2	0	0	5.0	1.000	C-1

Hickie Wilson

WILSON, GEORGE ARCHIBALD
B. Brooklyn, N. Y. D. Nov. 28, 1914, Brooklyn, N. Y.

Year	Team		Games	BA	SA	AB	H	2B	3B	HR	HR%	R	RBI	BB	SO	SB	AB	H	PO	A	E	DP	TC/G	FA	G by Pos
1884	BKN	AA	24	.232	.280	82	19	4	0	0	0.0	13		5		0	0	0	80	16	12	5	4.5	.889	OF-12, C-10, 1B-3, 2B-1

Icehouse Wilson

WILSON, GEORGE PEACOCK
B. Sept. 14, 1912, Maricopa, Calif. D. Oct. 13, 1973, Moraga, Calif.
BR TR 6' 186 lbs.

Year	Team		Games	BA	SA	AB	H	2B	3B	HR	HR%	R	RBI	BB	SO	SB	AB	H	PO	A	E	DP	TC/G	FA	G by Pos
1934	DET	A	1	.000	.000	1	0	0	0	0	0.0	0	0	0	0	0	1	0	0	0	0	0	0.0	–	

Jim Wilson

WILSON, JAMES GEORGE
B. Dec. 29, 1960, Corvallis, Ore.
BR TR 6'3" 230 lbs.

Year	Team		Games	BA	SA	AB	H	2B	3B	HR	HR%	R	RBI	BB	SO	SB	AB	H	PO	A	E	DP	TC/G	FA	G by Pos
1985	CLE	A	4	.357	.357	14	5	0	0	0	0.0	2	4	1	3	0	0	0	23	0	0	1	5.8	1.000	DH-2, 1B-2
1989	SEA	A	5	.000	.000	8	0	0	0	0	0.0	0	0	0	3	0	4	0	0	0	0	0	0.0	–	DH-5
2 yrs.			9	.227	.227	22	5	0	0	0	0.0	2	4	1	6	0	4	0	23	0	0	1	2.6	1.000	DH-7, 1B-2

Jimmie Wilson

WILSON, JAMES (Ace)
B. July 23, 1900, Philadelphia, Pa. D. May 31, 1947, Bradenton, Fla.
Manager 1934-38, 1941-44.
BR TR 6'1½" 200 lbs.

Year	Team		Games	BA	SA	AB	H	2B	3B	HR	HR%	R	RBI	BB	SO	SB	AB	H	PO	A	E	DP	TC/G	FA	G by Pos
1923	PHI	N	85	.262	.310	252	66	9	4	1	0.4	27	25	4	17	4	10	3	238	50	15	10	3.6	.950	C-69, OF-2
1924			95	.279	.421	280	78	16	3	6	2.1	32	39	17	12	5	11	2	249	93	12	16	3.7	.966	C-82, 1B-2, OF-1
1925			108	.328	.430	335	110	19	3	3	0.9	42	54	32	25	5	16	4	275	50	6	9	3.1	.982	C-89, OF-1
1926			90	.305	.398	279	85	10	2	4	1.4	40	32	25	20	3	11	3	228	78	16	5	3.6	.950	C-79
1927			128	.275	.332	443	122	15	2	2	0.5	50	45	34	15	13	4	1	377	82	12	12	3.7	.975	C-124
1928	2 teams	PHI N (21G – .300)			STL N (120G – .258)																				
"	total		141	.264	.351	481	127	30	2	1	0.4	56	63	54	32	12	0	0	469	103	9	17	4.1	.985	C-140
1929	STL	N	120	.325	.464	394	128	27	4	4	1.0	59	71	43	19	4	1	1	410	80	14	16	4.2	.972	C-119
1930			107	.318	.434	362	115	25	7	1	0.3	54	58	28	17	8	8	3	456	67	7	11	5.0	.987	C-107
1931			115	.274	.337	383	105	20	2	1	0.3	45	51	28	15	5	5	0	498	75	9	15	5.1	.985	C-110
1932			92	.248	.343	274	68	16	2	2	0.7	36	28	15	18	9	10	3	344	58	8	11	4.5	.980	C-75, 1B-3, 2B-1
1933			113	.255	.309	369	94	11	0	1	0.3	34	45	23	33	6	5	1	498	58	10	13	5.0	.982	C-107
1934	PHI	N	91	.292	.365	277	81	11	0	3	1.1	25	35	14	10	1	13	4	265	42	4	7	3.4	.987	C-77, 2B-1, 1B-1
1935			93	.279	.359	290	81	20	0	1	0.3	38	37	19	19	4	14	4	329	44	7	9	4.1	.982	C-78, 2B-1
1936			85	.278	.343	230	64	12	0	1	0.4	25	27	12	21	5	20	8	196	31	9	5	2.8	.962	C-63, 1B-1
1937			39	.276	.345	87	24	3	0	1	1.1	15	8	6	4	1	16	0	93	13	3	2	2.8	.972	C-22, 1B-2
1938			3	.000	.000	2	0	0	0	0	0.0	0	0	1	0	0	2	0	1	0	0	0	0.7	1.000	C-1
1939	CIN	N	4	.333	.333	3	1	0	0	0	0.0	0	0	0	1	0	2	1	0	0	0	0	0.0	–	C-1

Year Team	Games	BA	SA	AB	H	2B	3B	HR	HR%	R	RBI	BB	SO	SB	Pinch Hit AB	Pinch Hit H	PO	A	E	DP	TC/G	FA	G by Pos

Jimmie Wilson *continued*

Year Team	Games	BA	SA	AB	H	2B	3B	HR	HR%	R	RBI	BB	SO	SB	PH AB	PH H	PO	A	E	DP	TC/G	FA	G by Pos
1940	16	.243	.297	37	9	2	0	0	0.0	2	3	2	1	1	0	0	46	10	1	0	3.6	.982	C-16
18 yrs.	1525	.284	.370	4778	1358	252	32	32	0.7	580	621	356	280	86	148	38	4972	935	142	158	4.0	.977	C-1359, 1B-9, OF-4, 2B-3
WORLD SERIES																							
1928 STL N	3	.091	.182	11	1	1	0	0	0.0	1	1	0	3	0	0	0	14	2	2	0	6.0	.889	C-3
1930	4	.267	.333	15	4	1	0	0	0.0	0	2	0	1	0	0	0	23	0	0	0	5.8	1.000	C-4
1931	7	.217	.217	23	5	0	0	0	0.0	0	2	1	1	0	0	0	50	3	1	1	7.7	.981	C-7
1940 CIN N	6	.353	.353	17	6	0	0	0	0.0	2	0	1	2	1	0	0	26	2	0	1	4.7	1.000	C-6
4 yrs.	20	.242	.273	66	16	2	0	0	0.0	3	5	2	7	1	0	0	113	7	3	2	6.2	.976	C-20

Les Wilson

WILSON, LESTER WILBUR (Tug)
B. July 15, 1885, Gratiot County, Mich.   D. Apr. 4, 1969, Edmonds, Wash.   BL TR 5'11" 170 lbs.

Year Team	Games	BA	SA	AB	H	2B	3B	HR	HR%	R	RBI	BB	SO	SB	PH AB	PH H	PO	A	E	DP	TC/G	FA	G by Pos
1911 BOS A	5	.000	.000	7	0	0	0	0	0.0	0	0	2		0	1	0	4	0	0	0	0.8	1.000	OF-3

Mike Wilson

WILSON, SAMUEL MARSHALL
B. Dec. 2, 1896, Edge Hill, Pa.   D. May 16, 1978, Boynton Beach, Fla.   BR TR 5'10½" 160 lbs.

Year Team	Games	BA	SA	AB	H	2B	3B	HR	HR%	R	RBI	BB	SO	SB	PH AB	PH H	PO	A	E	DP	TC/G	FA	G by Pos
1921 PIT N	5	.000	.000	4	0	0	0	0	0.0	0	0	0	0	0	0	0	3	2	1	0	1.2	.833	C-5

Mookie Wilson

WILSON, WILLIAM HAYWARD
B. Feb. 9, 1956, Bamberg, S. C.   BR TR 5'10" 170 lbs.

Year Team	Games	BA	SA	AB	H	2B	3B	HR	HR%	R	RBI	BB	SO	SB	PH AB	PH H	PO	A	E	DP	TC/G	FA	G by Pos
1980 NY N	27	.248	.352	105	26	5	3	0	0.0	16	4	12	19	7	0	0	72	1	2	0	2.8	.973	OF-26
1981	92	.271	.372	328	89	8	8	3	0.9	49	14	20	59	24	10	1	226	3	4	2	2.5	.983	OF-80
1982	159	.279	.369	639	178	25	9	5	0.8	90	55	32	102	58	7	2	415	12	5	4	2.7	.988	OF-156
1983	152	.276	.367	**638**	176	25	6	7	1.1	91	51	18	103	54	7	0	422	5	7	1	2.9	.984	OF-148
1984	154	.276	.409	587	162	28	10	10	1.7	88	54	26	90	46	8	5	396	8	4	6	2.6	.990	OF-146
1985	93	.276	.424	337	93	16	8	6	1.8	56	26	28	52	24	8	1	216	0	8	0	2.4	.964	OF-83
1986	123	.289	.430	381	110	17	5	9	2.4	61	45	32	72	25	20	7	228	7	5	2	2.0	.979	OF-114
1987	124	.299	.455	385	115	19	7	9	2.3	58	34	35	85	21	32	10	205	3	8	2	1.7	.963	OF-109
1988	112	.296	.431	378	112	17	5	8	2.1	61	41	27	63	15	22	7	200	4	5	1	1.9	.976	OF-104
1989 2 teams	NY N (80G – .205)		TOR A	(54G – .298)																			
" total	134	.251	.329	487	122	19	2	5	1.0	54	35	13	84	19	22	4	162	2	4	0	1.3	.976	OF-125
10 yrs.	1170	.277	.392	4265	1183	179	63	62	1.5	624	359	243	729	293	136	37	2542	45	52	18	2.3	.980	OF-1091
LEAGUE CHAMPIONSHIP SERIES																							
1986 NY N	6	.115	.115	26	3	0	0	0	0.0	2	1	1	7	1	0	0	16	1	0	1	2.8	1.000	OF-6
1988	4	.154	.154	13	2	0	0	0	0.0	2	1	2	2	0	1	0	6	0	0	0	1.5	1.000	OF-3
1989 TOR A	5	.263	.263	19	5	0	0	0	0.0	2	2	2	2	1	0	0	10	0	0	0	2.0	1.000	OF-5
3 yrs.	15	.172	.172	58	10	0	0	0	0.0	6	4	5	11	2	1	0	32	1	0	1	2.2	1.000	OF-14
WORLD SERIES																							
1986 NY N	7	.269	.308	26	7	1	0	0	0.0	3	0	1	6	3	0	0	15	2	0	0	2.4	1.000	OF-7

Neil Wilson

WILSON, SAMUEL O'NEILL
B. June 14, 1935, Lexington, Tenn.   BL TR 6'1" 175 lbs.

Year Team	Games	BA	SA	AB	H	2B	3B	HR	HR%	R	RBI	BB	SO	SB	PH AB	PH H	PO	A	E	DP	TC/G	FA	G by Pos
1960 SF N	6	.000	.000	10	0	0	0	0	0.0	0	1	2	0	0	0	0	23	0	1	0	4.0	.958	C-6

Owen Wilson

WILSON, JOHN OWEN (Chief)
B. Aug. 21, 1883, Austin, Tex.   D. Feb. 22, 1954, Bertram, Tex.   BL TR 6'2" 185 lbs.

Year Team	Games	BA	SA	AB	H	2B	3B	HR	HR%	R	RBI	BB	SO	SB	PH AB	PH H	PO	A	E	DP	TC/G	FA	G by Pos
1908 PIT N	144	.227	.285	529	120	8	7	3	0.6	47	43	22		12	0	0	258	20	13	3	2.0	.955	OF-144
1909	154	.272	.374	569	155	22	12	4	0.7	64	59	19		17	0	0	292	19	14	7	2.1	.957	OF-154
1910	146	.276	.373	536	148	14	13	4	0.7	59	50	21	68	8	0	0	255	23	8	5	2.0	.972	OF-146
1911	148	.300	.472	544	163	34	12	12	2.2	72	107	41	55	10	1	1	273	20	7	10	2.0	.977	OF-146
1912	152	.300	.513	583	175	19	36¹	11	1.9	80	95	35	67	16	0	0	324	20	14	5	2.4	.961	OF-152
1913	155	.266	.386	580	154	12	14	10	1.7	71	73	32	62	9	0	0	301	14	10	3	2.1	.969	OF-155
1914 STL N	154	.259	.393	580	150	27	12	9	1.6	64	73	32	66	14	0	0	312	34	6	11	2.3	.983	OF-154
1915	107	.276	.374	348	96	13	6	3	0.9	33	39	19	43	8	2	0	234	20	4	3	2.4	.984	OF-107
1916	120	.239	.299	355	85	8	2	3	0.8	30	32	20	46	4	6	0	181	11	9	3	1.7	.955	OF-113
9 yrs.	1280	.269	.391	4624	1246	157	114	59	1.3	520	571	241	407	98	9	1	2430	181	85	50	2.1	.968	OF-1271
WORLD SERIES																							
1909 PIT N	7	.154	.192	26	4	1	0	0	0.0	1	0	1		0	0	0	1	1	1	0	0.4	.667	OF-7

Parke Wilson

WILSON, PARKE ASEL
B. Oct. 26, 1867, Keithsburg, Ill.   D. Dec. 20, 1934, Hermosa Beach, Calif.   BR TR 5'11" 166 lbs.

Year Team	Games	BA	SA	AB	H	2B	3B	HR	HR%	R	RBI	BB	SO	SB	PH AB	PH H	PO	A	E	DP	TC/G	FA	G by Pos
1893 NY N	31	.246	.351	114	28	4	1	2	1.8	16	21	7	9	5	0	0	106	20	4	1	4.2	.969	C-31
1894	49	.331	.434	175	58	5	5	1	0.6	35	32	14	5	8	0	0	246	28	31	9	6.2	.898	C-34, 1B-15
1895	67	.235	.273	238	56	9	0	0	0.0	32	30	14	16	11	0	0	313	68	29	20	6.1	.929	C-53, 1B-11, 3B-3
1896	75	.237	.245	253	60	2	0	0	0.0	33	23	13	14	9	2	0	278	64	23	4	4.9	.937	C-71, 1B-2
1897	46	.299	.396	154	46	9	3	0	0.0	29	22	15		5	1	0	222	26	13	9	5.7	.950	C-30, 1B-10, OF-4, 2B-1
1898	1	.000	.000	4	0	0	0	0	0.0	0	0	0		0	0	0	0	0	0	0	0.0	–	OF-1
1899	97	.268	.329	328	88	8	6	0	0.0	49	42	43		16	2	0	416	140	49	34	6.2	.919	C-31, 1B-29, SS-19, 3B-15, OF-6
7 yrs.	366	.265	.325	1266	336	37	15	3	0.2	194	170	106	44	54	5	0	1581	346	149	77	5.7	.928	C-250, 1B-67, SS-19, 3B-18, OF-11, 2B-1

Red Wilson

WILSON, ROBERT JAMES
B. Mar. 7, 1929, Milwaukee, Wis.   BR TR 5'10" 160 lbs.

Year Team	Games	BA	SA	AB	H	2B	3B	HR	HR%	R	RBI	BB	SO	SB	PH AB	PH H	PO	A	E	DP	TC/G	FA	G by Pos
1951 CHI A	4	.273	.364	11	3	1	0	0	0.0	1	0	1	2	0	0	0	9	2	0	0	2.8	1.000	C-4
1952	2	.000	.000	3	0	0	0	0	0.0	0	0	0	1	0	0	0	8	1	0	0	4.5	1.000	C-2
1953	71	.250	.299	164	41	6	1	0	0.0	21	10	26	12	2	7	1	282	24	6	1	4.4	.981	C-63

Year	Team	Games	BA	SA	AB	H	2B	3B	HR	HR%	R	RBI	BB	SO	SB	Pinch Hit AB	Pinch Hit H	PO	A	E	DP	TC/G	FA	G by Pos

Red Wilson *continued*

Year	Team	Games	BA	SA	AB	H	2B	3B	HR	HR%	R	RBI	BB	SO	SB	AB	H	PO	A	E	DP	TC/G	FA	G by Pos
1954	2 teams	CHI A	(8G – .200)		DET A	(54G – .282)																		
"	total	62	.274	.389	190	52	11	1	3	1.6	24	23	28	14	3	1	0	289	28	1	8	5.1	.997	C-61
1955	DET A	78	.220	.282	241	53	9	0	2	0.8	26	17	26	23	1	8	1	292	25	5	5	4.1	.984	C-72
1956		78	.289	.452	228	66	12	2	7	3.1	32	38	42	18	2	1	0	393	34	4	7	5.5	.991	C-78
1957		59	.242	.348	178	43	8	1	3	1.7	21	13	24	19	2	0	0	277	29	0	5	5.2	1.000	C-59
1958		103	.299	.379	298	89	13	1	3	1.0	31	29	35	30	10	3	0	565	34	5	6	5.9	.992	C-101
1959		67	.263	.408	228	60	17	2	4	1.8	28	35	10	23	2	3	0	374	25	5	8	6.0	.988	C-64
1960	2 teams	DET A	(45G – .216)		CLE A	(32G – .216)																		
"	total	77	.216	.275	222	48	7	0	2	0.9	22	24	22	21	3	2	1	392	34	7	1	5.6	.984	C-75
	10 yrs.	601	.258	.356	1763	455	84	8	24	1.4	206	189	214	163	25	25	3	2881	236	33	41	5.2	.990	C-579

Squanto Wilson

WILSON, GEORGE FRANCIS   BB TR 5'9½" 170 lbs.
B. Mar. 29, 1889, Old Town, Me.   D. Mar. 26, 1967, Winthrop, Me.

Year	Team	Games	BA	SA	AB	H	2B	3B	HR	HR%	R	RBI	BB	SO	SB	AB	H	PO	A	E	DP	TC/G	FA	G by Pos
1911	DET A	5	.188	.188	16	3	0	0	0	0.0	2	0	2		0	0	0	20	7	3	0	6.0	.900	C-5
1914	BOS A	1	–	–	0	0	0	0	0	–	0	0	0	0	0	0	0	0	0	0	0	0.0	–	1B-1
	2 yrs.	6	.188	.188	16	3	0	0	0	0.0	2	0	2	0	0	0	0	20	7	3	0	5.0	.900	C-5, 1B-1

Tack Wilson

WILSON, MICHAEL   BR TR 5'10" 186 lbs.
B. May 16, 1956, Shreveport, La.

Year	Team	Games	BA	SA	AB	H	2B	3B	HR	HR%	R	RBI	BB	SO	SB	AB	H	PO	A	E	DP	TC/G	FA	G by Pos
1983	MIN A	5	.250	.500	4	1	1	0	0	0.0	4	1	0	0	0	0	0	1	0	0	0	0.2	1.000	DH-2, OF-1
1987	CAL A	7	.500	.500	2	1	0	0	0	0.0	5	0	1	0	0	0	0	1	0	0	0	0.1	1.000	OF-4, DH-2
	2 yrs.	12	.333	.500	6	2	1	0	0	0.0	9	1	1	0	0	0	0	2	0	0	0	0.2	1.000	OF-5, DH-4

Ted Wilson

WILSON, GEORGE WASHINGTON (Teddy)   BL TR 6'1½" 185 lbs.
B. Aug. 30, 1925, Cherryville, N. C.   D. Oct. 29, 1974, Gastonia, N. C.

Year	Team	Games	BA	SA	AB	H	2B	3B	HR	HR%	R	RBI	BB	SO	SB	AB	H	PO	A	E	DP	TC/G	FA	G by Pos
1952	2 teams	CHI A	(8G – .111)		NY N	(62G – .241)																		
"	total	70	.231	.339	121	28	7	0	2	1.7	9	17	4	16	0	48	12	62	0	3	2	0.9	.954	OF-22, 1B-2
1953	NY N	11	.125	.125	8	1	0	0	0	0.0	0	0	2	2	0	8	1	0	0	0	0	0.0		
1956	2 teams	NY N	(53G – .132)		NY A	(11G – .167)																		
"	total	64	.138	.188	80	11	1	0	1	1.3	6	2	8	14	0	48	8	13	1	0	0	0.2	1.000	OF-14
	3 yrs.	145	.191	.273	209	40	8	0	3	1.4	15	19	14	32	0	104	21	75	1	3	2	0.5	.962	OF-36, 1B-2

WORLD SERIES

Year	Team	Games	BA	SA	AB	H	2B	3B	HR	HR%	R	RBI	BB	SO	SB	AB	H	PO	A	E	DP	TC/G	FA	G by Pos
1956	NY A	1	.000	.000	1	0	0	0	0	0.0	0	0	0	1	0	1	0	0	0	0	0	0.0	–	

Tom Wilson

WILSON, THOMAS G. (Slats)   BB TR 6'1½" 160 lbs.
B. June 3, 1890, Fleming, Kans.   D. Mar. 7, 1953, San Pedro, Calif.

Year	Team	Games	BA	SA	AB	H	2B	3B	HR	HR%	R	RBI	BB	SO	SB	AB	H	PO	A	E	DP	TC/G	FA	G by Pos
1914	WAS A	1	.000	.000	1	0	0	0	0	0.0	0	0	0	0	0	0	0	0	0	0	0	0.0	–	C-1

Willie Wilson

WILSON, WILLIE JAMES   BB TR 6'3" 190 lbs.
B. July 9, 1955, Montgomery, Ala.

Year	Team	Games	BA	SA	AB	H	2B	3B	HR	HR%	R	RBI	BB	SO	SB	AB	H	PO	A	E	DP	TC/G	FA	G by Pos
1976	KC A	12	.167	.167	6	1	0	0	0	0.0	0	0	2	2	2	0	0	6	1	1	0	0.7	.875	OF-6
1977		13	.324	.382	34	11	2	0	0	0.0	10	1	1	8	6	0	0	24	0	1	0	1.9	.960	OF-9, DH-2
1978		127	.217	.278	198	43	8	2	0	1.0	43	16	16	33	46	0	0	171	6	4	2	1.4	.978	OF-112, DH-6
1979		154	.315	.420	588	185	18	13	6	1.0	113	49	28	92	83	0	0	384	13	6	0	2.6	.985	OF-152, DH-2
1980		161	.326	.421	705[1]	230	28	15	3	0.4	133	49	28	81	79	3	0	482	9	6	1	3.1	.988	OF-159
1981		102	.303	.364	439	133	10	7	1	0.2	54	32	18	42	34	0	0	299	14	4	3	3.1	.987	OF-101
1982		136	.332	.431	585	194	19	15	3	0.5	87	46	26	81	37	1	0	376	4	5	0	2.8	.987	OF-135
1983		137	.276	.352	576	159	22	8	2	0.3	90	33	33	75	59	3	1	354	3	9	0	2.7	.975	OF-136
1984		128	.301	.390	541	163	24	9	2	0.4	81	44	39	56	47	0	0	383	6	4	2	3.1	.990	OF-128
1985		141	.278	.408	605	168	25	21	4	0.7	87	43	29	94	43	0	0	378	4	2	1	2.7	.995	OF-140
1986		156	.269	.366	631	170	20	7	9	1.4	77	44	31	97	34	6	0	408	4	3	2	2.7	.993	OF-155
1987		146	.279	.377	610	170	18	15	4	0.7	97	30	32	88	59	1	0	342	3	1	0	2.4	.997	OF-143, DH-2
1988		147	.262	.333	591	155	17	11	1	0.2	81	37	22	106	35	4	1	365	1	4	0	2.5	.989	OF-142
1989		112	.253	.333	383	97	17	7	3	0.8	58	43	27	78	24	2	2	252	2	6	0	2.3	.977	OF-108, DH-1
	14 yrs.	1672	.289	.382	6492	1879	228	130	38	0.6	1011	467	330	933	588 9th	20	4	4224	70	56	12	2.6	.987	OF-1626, DH-13

DIVISIONAL PLAYOFF SERIES

Year	Team	Games	BA	SA	AB	H	2B	3B	HR	HR%	R	RBI	BB	SO	SB	AB	H	PO	A	E	DP	TC/G	FA	G by Pos
1981	KC A	3	.308	.308	13	4	0	0	0	0.0	0	1	0	0	0	0	0	0	0	0	0	0.0	–	OF-3

LEAGUE CHAMPIONSHIP SERIES

Year	Team	Games	BA	SA	AB	H	2B	3B	HR	HR%	R	RBI	BB	SO	SB	AB	H	PO	A	E	DP	TC/G	FA	G by Pos
1978	KC A	3	.250	.250	4	1	0	0	0	0.0	0	0	0	2	0	0	0	2	0	0	0	0.7	1.000	OF-3
1980		3	.308	.615	13	4	2	1	0	0.0	2	4	1	2	0	0	0	6	1	0	0	2.3	1.000	OF-3
1984		3	.154	.154	13	2	0	0	0	0.0	0	0	1	2	0	0	0	10	0	0	0	3.3	1.000	OF-3
1985		7	.310	.414	29	9	0	1	1	3.4	5	2	1	5	1	0	0	12	0	0	0	1.7	1.000	OF-7
	4 yrs.	16	.271	.390	59	16	2	1	1	1.7	7	6	3	11	1	0	0	30	1	0	0	1.9	1.000	OF-16

WORLD SERIES

Year	Team	Games	BA	SA	AB	H	2B	3B	HR	HR%	R	RBI	BB	SO	SB	AB	H	PO	A	E	DP	TC/G	FA	G by Pos
1980	KC A	6	.154	.192	26	4	1	0	0	0.0	3	0	4	12	2	0	0	15	1	0	0	2.7	1.000	OF-6
1985		7	.367	.433	30	11	0	1	0	0.0	2	3	1	4	3	0	0	19	1	0	0	2.9	1.000	OF-7
	2 yrs.	13	.268	.321	56	15	1	1	0	0.0	5	3	5	16	5	0	0	34	2	0	0	2.8	1.000	OF-13

Ed Winceniak

WINCENIAK, EDWARD JOSEPH   BR TR 5'9" 165 lbs.
B. Apr. 16, 1929, Chicago, Ill.

Year	Team	Games	BA	SA	AB	H	2B	3B	HR	HR%	R	RBI	BB	SO	SB	AB	H	PO	A	E	DP	TC/G	FA	G by Pos
1956	CHI N	15	.118	.118	17	2	0	0	0	0.0	1	0	1	3	0	7	0	6	3	1	0	0.7	.900	3B-4, 2B-1
1957		17	.240	.360	50	12	3	0	1	2.0	5	8	2	9	0	5	1	20	20	2	5	2.5	.952	SS-5, 3B-4, 2B-3
	2 yrs.	32	.209	.299	67	14	3	0	1	1.5	6	8	3	12	0	12	1	26	23	3	5	1.6	.942	3B-8, SS-5, 2B-4

Gordie Windhorn

WINDHORN, GORDON RAY   BR TR 6'1" 185 lbs.
B. Dec. 19, 1933, Watseka, Ill.

Year	Team	Games	BA	SA	AB	H	2B	3B	HR	HR%	R	RBI	BB	SO	SB	AB	H	PO	A	E	DP	TC/G	FA	G by Pos
1959	NY A	7	.000	.000	11	0	0	0	0	0.0	0	0	0	3	0	3	0	4	0	0	0	0.6	1.000	OF-4

Year	Team		Games	BA	SA	AB	H	2B	3B	HR	HR%	R	RBI	BB	SO	SB	Pinch Hit AB	Pinch Hit H	PO	A	E	DP	TC/G	FA	G by Pos

Gordie Windhorn *continued*

1961	LA	N	34	.242	.545	33	8	2	1	2	6.1	10	6	4	3	0	8	1	16	1	1	0	0.5	.944	OF-17
1962	2 teams		54	.172	.281	KC A (14G – .158)						LA A (40G – .178)														
"	total		54	.172	.281	64	11	7	0	0	0.0	10	2	7	13	1	12	0	30	0	0	0	0.6	1.000	OF-41
3 yrs.			95	.176	.333	108	19	9	1	2	1.9	20	8	11	19	1	23	1	50	1	1	0	0.5	.981	OF-62

Bill Windle

WINDLE, WILLIS BREWER
B. Dec. 13, 1904, Galena, Kans. D. Dec. 8, 1981, Corpus Christi, Tex.

BL TL 5'11½" 170 lbs.

1928	PIT	N	1	1.000	2.000	1	1	0	0	0	0.0	0	0	0	0	0	0	0	1	0	0	0	1.0	1.000	1B-1
1929			2	.000	.000	1	0	0	0	0	0.0	0	0	0	1	0	0	0	3	0	0	0	1.5	1.000	1B-2
2 yrs.			3	.500	1.000	2	1	1	0	0	0.0	1	0	0	1	0	0	0	4	0	0	0	1.3	1.000	1B-3

Bobby Wine

WINE, ROBERT PAUL, SR.
Father of Robbie Wine.
B. Sept. 17, 1938, New York, N. Y.
Manager 1985.

BR TR 6'1" 187 lbs.

1960	PHI	N	4	.143	.143	14	2	0	0	0	0.0	1	0	0	2	0	0	0	9	10	0	4	4.8	1.000	SS-4
1962			112	.244	.331	311	76	15	0	4	1.3	30	25	11	49	2	2	0	149	263	8	54	3.8	.981	SS-89, 3B-20
1963			142	.215	.306	418	90	14	3	6	1.4	29	44	14	83	1	2	0	224	369	17	73	4.3	.972	SS-132, 3B-8
1964			126	.212	.304	283	60	8	3	4	1.4	28	34	25	37	1	6	3	159	266	15	57	3.5	.966	SS-108, 3B-16
1965			139	.228	.292	394	90	8	1	5	1.3	31	33	31	69	0	1	0	223	387	21	85	4.5	.967	SS-135, 1B-4
1966			46	.236	.292	89	21	5	0	0	0.0	8	5	6	13	0	3	0	57	91	4	19	3.3	.974	SS-40, OF-2
1967			135	.190	.267	363	69	12	5	2	0.6	27	28	29	77	3	0	0	206	392	12	91	4.5	.980	SS-134, 1B-2
1968			27	.169	.296	71	12	3	0	2	2.8	5	7	6	17	0	1	0	37	68	3	12	4.0	.972	SS-25, 3B-1
1969	MON	N	121	.200	.251	370	74	8	1	3	0.8	23	25	28	49	0	2	0	214	367	31	98	5.1	.949	SS-118, 3B-1, 1B-1
1970			159	.232	.303	501	116	21	3	3	0.6	40	51	39	94	0	1	1	284	481	19	137	4.9	.976	SS-159
1971			119	.200	.235	340	68	9	1	1	0.3	25	16	25	46	0	0	0	221	321	10	76	4.6	.982	SS-119
1972			34	.222	.278	18	4	1	0	0	0.0	2	0	0	2	0	8	1	12	15	1	2	0.8	.964	3B-21, SS-4, 2B-1
12 yrs.			1164	.215	.286	3172	682	104	16	30	0.9	249	268	214	538	7	26	5	1795	3030	141	708	4.3	.972	SS-1067, 3B-67, 1B-7, OF-2, 2B-1

Robbie Wine

WINE, ROBERT PAUL, JR.
Son of Bobby Wine.
B. July 13, 1962, Norristown, Pa.

BR TR 6'2" 190 lbs.

1986	HOU	N	9	.250	.333	12	3	1	0	0	0.0	2	0	1	4	0	1	0	28	5	0	0	3.7	1.000	C-8
1987			14	.103	.138	29	3	1	0	0	0.0	1	0	1	10	0	3	0	40	7	1	2	3.4	.979	C-12
2 yrs.			23	.146	.195	41	6	2	0	0	0.0	3	0	2	14	0	4	0	68	12	1	2	3.5	.988	C-20

Ralph Winegarner

WINEGARNER, RALPH LEE
B. Oct. 29, 1909, Benton, Kans. D. Apr. 14, 1988, Wichita, Kans.

BR TR 6' 182 lbs.

1930	CLE	A	5	.455	.500	22	10	1	0	0	0.0	5	2	1	7	0	0	0	5	13	3	2	4.2	.857	3B-5
1932			7	.143	.143	7	1	0	0	0	0.0	1	0	0	5	0	2	0	0	3	1	1	0.6	.750	P-5
1934			32	.196	.294	51	10	2	0	1	2.0	9	5	3	11	0	10	1	2	17	0	0	0.6	1.000	P-22, OF-1
1935			65	.310	.488	84	26	4	1	3	3.6	11	17	9	12	1	29	11	21	21	3	3	0.7	.933	P-25, OF-4, 3B-3, 1B-1
1936			18	.125	.125	16	2	0	0	0	0.0	0	2	1	6	0	10	1	0	2	0	0	0.1	1.000	P-9
1949	STL	A	9	.400	1.000	5	2	0	0	1	20.0	2	2	1	2	0	0	0	1	0	0	0	0.2	1.000	P-9
6 yrs.			136	.276	.405	185	51	7	1	5	2.7	28	28	15	43	1	51	14	29	56	7	6	0.7	.924	P-70, 3B-8, OF-5, 1B-1

Dave Winfield

WINFIELD, DAVID MARK (Winny)
B. Oct. 3, 1951, St. Paul, Minn.

BR TR 6'6" 220 lbs.

1973	SD	N	56	.277	.383	141	39	4	1	3	2.1	9	12	12	19	0	17	8	65	1	3	0	1.2	.957	OF-36, 1B-1
1974			145	.265	.438	498	132	18	4	20	4.0	57	75	40	96	9	15	4	276	11	12	2	2.1	.960	OF-131
1975			143	.267	.403	509	136	20	2	15	2.9	74	76	69	82	23	2	0	302	9	9	1	2.2	.972	OF-138
1976			137	.283	.431	492	139	26	4	13	2.6	81	69	65	78	26	2	1	304	15	6	4	2.4	.982	OF-134
1977			157	.275	.467	615	169	29	7	25	4.1	104	92	58	75	16	2	1	368	15	11	3	2.5	.972	OF-156
1978			158	.308	.499	587	181	30	5	24	4.1	88	97	55	81	21	5	1	328	8	7	1	2.2	.980	OF-154, 1B-2
1979			159	.308	.558	597	184	27	10	34	5.7	97	118	85	71	15	2	0	344	14	5	3	2.3	.986	OF-157
1980			162	.276	.450	558	154	25	6	20	3.6	89	87	79	83	23	9	3	273	20	4	4	1.8	.987	OF-159
1981	NY	A	105	.294	.464	388	114	25	1	13	3.4	52	68	43	41	11	4	3	196	1	3	0	1.9	.985	OF-102, DH-1
1982			140	.280	.560	539	151	24	8	37	6.9	84	106	45	64	5	1	0	279	17	8	2	2.2	.974	OF-135, DH-4
1983			152	.283	.513	598	169	26	8	32	5.4	99	116	58	77	15	3	2	313	5	7	2	2.1	.978	OF-151
1984			141	.340	.515	567	193	34	4	19	3.4	106	100	53	71	6	0	0	306	3	2	1	2.2	.994	OF-140
1985			155	.275	.471	633	174	34	6	26	4.1	105	114	52	96	19	1	1	316	13	3	3	2.1	.991	OF-152, DH-2
1986			154	.262	.462	565	148	31	5	24	4.2	90	104	77	106	6	7	1	292	9	5	5	2.0	.984	OF-145, DH-6, 3B-2
1987			156	.275	.457	575	158	22	1	27	4.7	83	97	76	96	5	4	2	253	6	3	1	1.7	.989	OF-145, DH-8
1988			149	.322	.530	559	180	37	2	25	4.5	96	107	69	88	9	4	0	276	3	3	1	1.9	.989	OF-141, DH-4
16 yrs.			2269	.287	.481	8421	2421	412	74	357	4.2	1314	1438	936	1224	209	78	27	4491	150	91	33	2.1	.981	OF-2176, DH-25, 1B-3, 3B-2

DIVISIONAL PLAYOFF SERIES

| 1981 | NY | A | 5 | .350 | .500 | 20 | 7 | 3 | 0 | 0 | 0.0 | 2 | 0 | 1 | 5 | 0 | 0 | 0 | 0 | 0 | 0 | 0 | 0.0 | – | OF-5 |

LEAGUE CHAMPIONSHIP SERIES

| 1981 | NY | A | 3 | .154 | .231 | 13 | 2 | 1 | 0 | 0 | 0.0 | 2 | 2 | 2 | 2 | 1 | 0 | 0 | 0 | 0 | 0 | 0 | 0.0 | – | OF-3 |

WORLD SERIES

| 1981 | NY | A | 6 | .045 | .045 | 22 | 1 | 0 | 0 | 0 | 0.0 | 0 | 1 | 5 | 4 | 0 | 0 | 0 | 13 | 1 | 0 | 0 | 2.3 | 1.000 | OF-6 |

Al Wingo

WINGO, ABSALOM HOLBROOK (Red)
Brother of Ivy Wingo.
B. May 6, 1898, Norcross, Ga. D. Oct. 9, 1964, Detroit, Mich.

BL TR 5'11" 180 lbs.

| 1919 | PHI | A | 15 | .305 | .424 | 59 | 18 | 1 | 3 | 0 | 0.0 | 9 | 2 | 4 | 12 | 0 | 0 | 0 | 21 | 1 | 5 | 0 | 1.8 | .815 | OF-15 |

1607

Year	Team		Games	BA	SA	AB	H	2B	3B	HR	HR%	R	RBI	BB	SO	SB	Pinch Hit AB	Pinch Hit H	PO	A	E	DP	TC/G	FA	G by Pos

Al Wingo *continued*

Year	Team		Games	BA	SA	AB	H	2B	3B	HR	HR%	R	RBI	BB	SO	SB	AB	H	PO	A	E	DP	TC/G	FA	G by Pos
1924	DET	A	78	.287	.413	150	43	12	2	1	0.7	21	26	21	13	2	29	10	59	3	5	2	0.9	.925	OF-43
1925			130	.370	.527	440	163	34	10	5	1.1	104	68	69	31	14	7	1	282	16	9	6	2.4	.971	OF-122
1926			108	.282	.356	298	84	19	0	1	0.3	45	45	52	32	4	24	6	155	13	14	2	1.7	.923	OF-74, 3B-2
1927			75	.234	.321	137	32	8	2	0	0.0	15	20	25	14	1	33	6	43	6	6	2	0.7	.891	OF-34
1928			87	.285	.380	242	69	13	2	2	0.8	30	30	40	17	2	12	0	144	5	5	1	1.8	.968	OF-71
6 yrs.			493	.308	.423	1326	409	87	19	9	0.7	224	191	211	119	23	105	23	704	44	44	13	1.6	.944	OF-359, 3B-2

Ed Wingo

WINGO, EDMUND ARMAND
Born Edmund Armand LaRiviere.
B. Oct. 8, 1895, Ste. Anne De Bellevue, Canada   D. Dec. 5, 1964, Lachine, Que., Canada

BR TR 5'5" 145 lbs.

Year	Team		Games	BA	SA	AB	H	2B	3B	HR	HR%	R	RBI	BB	SO	SB	AB	H	PO	A	E	DP	TC/G	FA	G by Pos
1920	PHI	A	1	.250	.250	4	1	0	0	0	0.0	0	1	0	0	0	0	0	8	1	0	0	9.0	1.000	C-1

Ivy Wingo

WINGO, IVEY BROWN
Brother of Al Wingo.
B. July 8, 1890, Gainesville, Ga.   D. Mar. 1, 1941, Norcross, Ga.
Manager 1916.

BL TR 5'10" 160 lbs.

Year	Team		Games	BA	SA	AB	H	2B	3B	HR	HR%	R	RBI	BB	SO	SB	AB	H	PO	A	E	DP	TC/G	FA	G by Pos
1911	STL	N	25	.211	.246	57	12	2	0	0	0.0	4	3	3	7	0	6	0	65	22	8	3	3.8	.916	C-18
1912			100	.265	.394	310	82	18	8	2	0.6	38	44	23	45	8	9	1	360	148	23	11	5.3	.957	C-92
1913			111	.256	.344	305	78	5	8	2	0.7	25	35	17	41	18	10	4	393	139	31	14	5.1	.945	C-97, 1B-5, OF-1
1914			80	.300	.426	237	71	8	5	4	1.7	24	26	18	17	15	4	2	276	93	16	7	4.8	.958	C-70
1915	CIN	N	119	.221	.316	339	75	11	6	2	0.6	26	29	13	33	10	17	2	415	124	20	15	4.7	.964	C-97, OF-1
1916			119	.245	.349	347	85	8	11	2	0.6	30	40	25	27	4	10	5	463	170	28	15	5.6	.958	C-107
1917			121	.266	.376	399	106	16	11	2	0.5	37	39	25	13	9	1	0	459	151	21	12	5.2	.967	C-120
1918			100	.254	.337	323	82	15	6	0	0.0	36	31	19	18	6	2	1	321	111	13	13	4.5	.971	C-93, OF-5
1919			76	.273	.371	245	67	12	6	0	0.0	30	27	23	19	4	1	0	266	106	12	6	5.1	.969	C-75
1920			108	.264	.338	364	96	11	5	2	0.5	32	38	19	13	6	0	0	370	117	21	14	4.7	.959	C-107, 2B-2
1921			97	.268	.363	295	79	7	6	3	1.0	20	38	21	14	3	4	1	318	101	19	11	4.5	.957	C-92, OF-1
1922			80	.285	.392	260	74	13	3	3	1.2	24	45	23	11	1	2	0	211	81	11	6	3.8	.964	C-78
1923			61	.263	.357	171	45	9	2	1	0.6	10	24	9	11	1	4	1	172	44	7	2	3.7	.969	C-57
1924			66	.286	.370	192	55	5	4	1	0.5	21	23	14	8	1	1	0	220	50	3	7	4.1	.989	C-65, 1B-1
1925			55	.205	.253	146	30	7	0	0	0.0	6	12	11	8	1	0	0	154	38	7	7	3.6	.965	C-55
1926			7	.200	.200	10	2	0	0	0	0.0	0	1	1	0	0	0	0	12	1	0	0	1.9	1.000	C-7
1929			1	.000	.000	1	0	0	0	0	0.0	0	0	0	0	0	0	0	0	0	0	0	0.0	–	C-1
17 yrs.			1326	.260	.356	4001	1039	147	81	25	0.6	363	455	264	285	87	71	17	4475	1496	240	143	4.7	.961	C-1231, OF-8, 1B-6, 2B-2

WORLD SERIES

| 1919 | CIN | N | 3 | .571 | .571 | 7 | 4 | 0 | 0 | 0 | 0.0 | 1 | 1 | 3 | 1 | 0 | 0 | 0 | 8 | 3 | 0 | 0 | 3.7 | 1.000 | C-3 |

George Winkelman

WINKELMAN, GEORGE EDWARD
B. June 14, 1861, Philadelphia, Pa.   D. May 19, 1960, Washington, D. C.

BL TL

Year	Team		Games	BA	SA	AB	H	2B	3B	HR	HR%	R	RBI	BB	SO	SB	AB	H	PO	A	E	DP	TC/G	FA	G by Pos
1883	LOU	AA	4	.000	.000	13	0	0	0	0	0.0	2		1		0	0	0	8	2	6	0	4.0	.625	OF-4
1886	WAS	N	1	.200	.200	5	1	0	0	0	0.0	0		0	1	0	0	0	0	0	0	0	0.0	–	OF-1, P-1
2 yrs.			5	.056	.056	18	1	0	0	0	0.0	2		1	1	0	0	0	8	2	6	0	3.2	.625	OF-5, P-1

Herm Winningham

WINNINGHAM, HERMAN SON
B. Dec. 1, 1961, Orangeburg, S. C.

BL TR 6'1" 170 lbs.

Year	Team		Games	BA	SA	AB	H	2B	3B	HR	HR%	R	RBI	BB	SO	SB	AB	H	PO	A	E	DP	TC/G	FA	G by Pos
1984	NY	N	14	.407	.519	27	11	1	1	0	0.0	5	5	1	7	2	4	1	7	0	0	0	0.5	1.000	OF-10
1985	MON	N	125	.237	.317	312	74	6	5	3	1.0	30	21	28	72	20	13	6	229	6	4	2	1.9	.983	OF-116
1986			90	.216	.346	185	40	6	3	4	2.2	23	11	18	51	12	23	3	97	2	2	1	1.2	.980	OF-66, SS-1
1987			137	.239	.349	347	83	20	3	4	1.2	34	41	34	68	29	20	5	225	5	6	1	1.7	.975	OF-131
1988	2 teams				MON	N	(47G –	.233)		CIN	N	(53G –	.230)												
"	total		100	.232	.286	203	47	3	6	0	0.0	16	21	17	45	12	21	4	128	1	1	0	1.3	.992	OF-72
1989	CIN	N	115	.251	.355	251	63	11	3	3	1.2	40	13	24	50	14	29	7	146	3	3	0	1.3	.980	OF-85
6 yrs.			581	.240	.336	1325	318	47	19	14	1.1	148	112	122	293	89	110	26	832	17	16	4	1.5	.982	OF-480, SS-1

Tom Winsett

WINSETT, JOHN THOMAS (Long Tom)
B. Nov. 24, 1909, McKenzie, Tenn.

BL TR 6'2" 190 lbs.

Year	Team		Games	BA	SA	AB	H	2B	3B	HR	HR%	R	RBI	BB	SO	SB	AB	H	PO	A	E	DP	TC/G	FA	G by Pos
1930	BOS	A	1	.000	.000	1	0	0	0	0	0.0	0	0	0	0	0	0	0	0	0	0	0	0.0	–	
1931			64	.197	.250	76	15	1	0	1	1.3	6	7	4	21	0	52	11	13	1	0	0	0.2	1.000	OF-8
1933			6	.083	.083	12	1	0	0	0	0.0	1	0	1	6	0	2	0	1	0	0	0	0.2	1.000	OF-4
1935	STL	N	7	.500	.583	12	6	1	0	0	0.0	2	2	2	3	0	5	2	0	0	0	0	0.0	–	OF-2
1936	BKN	N	22	.235	.353	85	20	7	0	1	1.2	13	18	11	14	0	1	1	42	3	0	0	2.0	1.000	OF-21
1937			118	.237	.351	350	83	15	5	5	1.4	32	42	45	64	3	15	5	209	6	9	1	1.9	.960	OF-101, P-1
1938			12	.300	.433	30	9	1	0	1	3.3	6	7	6	4	0	2	0	15	0	2	0	1.4	.882	OF-9
7 yrs.			230	.237	.341	566	134	25	5	8	1.4	60	76	69	113	3	77	19	280	10	11	1	1.3	.963	OF-145, P-1

Matt Winters

WINTERS, MATTHEW LITTLETON
B. Mar. 18, 1960, Buffalo, N. Y.

BL TR 6'3" 215 lbs.

Year	Team		Games	BA	SA	AB	H	2B	3B	HR	HR%	R	RBI	BB	SO	SB	AB	H	PO	A	E	DP	TC/G	FA	G by Pos
1989	KC	A	42	.234	.346	107	25	6	0	2	1.9	14	9	14	23	0	7	1	45	1	3	0	1.2	.939	OF-31, DH-3

Kettle Wirts

WIRTS, ELWOOD VERNON
B. Oct. 31, 1897, Consumnes, Calif.   D. July 12, 1968, Sacramento, Calif.

BR TR 5'11" 170 lbs.

Year	Team		Games	BA	SA	AB	H	2B	3B	HR	HR%	R	RBI	BB	SO	SB	AB	H	PO	A	E	DP	TC/G	FA	G by Pos
1921	CHI	N	7	.182	.182	11	2	0	0	0	0.0	0	0	0	3	0	2	2	13	3	0	1	2.3	1.000	C-5
1922			31	.172	.259	58	10	2	0	1	1.7	7	6	12	15	0	3	0	55	6	2	1	2.0	.968	C-27
1923			5	.200	.200	5	1	0	0	0	0.0	2	1	2	0	0	0	0	10	0	0	0	2.0	1.000	C-3
1924	CHI	A	6	.083	.083	12	1	0	0	0	0.0	0	0	2	2	1	0	0	9	7	0	0	2.7	1.000	C-5
4 yrs.			49	.163	.221	86	14	2	0	1	1.2	9	8	16	20	1	5	2	87	16	2	2	2.1	.981	C-40

Bill Wise

WISE, WILLIAM E.
B. Mar. 15, 1861, Washington, D. C.   D. May 5, 1940, Washington, D. C.

Year	Team		Games	BA	SA	AB	H	2B	3B	HR	HR%	R	RBI	BB	SO	SB	Pinch Hit AB	H	PO	A	E	DP	TC/G	FA	G by Pos

Bill Wise *continued*

Year	Team		Games	BA	SA	AB	H	2B	3B	HR	HR%	R	RBI	BB	SO	SB	PH AB	PH H	PO	A	E	DP	TC/G	FA	G by Pos
1882	BAL	AA	5	.100	.150	20	2	1	0	0	0.0	2		0			0	0	4	7	2	1	2.6	.846	P-3, OF-2
1884	WAS	U	85	.233	.307	339	79	17	1	2	0.6	51		12			0	0	80	137	49	7	3.1	.816	P-50, OF-43, 3B-8, SS-2, 1B-1
1886	WAS	N	1	.000	.000	3	0	0	0	0	0.0	0	0	0	1		0	0	0	0	0	0	0.0	–	P-1
3 yrs.			91	.224	.296	362	81	18	1	2	0.6	53	0	12	1		0	0	84	144	51	8	3.1	.817	P-54, OF-45, 3B-8, SS-2, 1B-1

Casey Wise

WISE, KENDALL COLE
Son of Hughie Wise.
B. Sept. 8, 1932, Lafayette, Ind.
BB TR 6' 170 lbs.

Year	Team		Games	BA	SA	AB	H	2B	3B	HR	HR%	R	RBI	BB	SO	SB	PH AB	PH H	PO	A	E	DP	TC/G	FA	G by Pos
1957	CHI	N	43	.179	.226	106	19	3	1	0	0.0	12	7	11	14	0	4	0	69	84	10	21	3.8	.939	2B-31, SS-5
1958	MIL	N	31	.197	.211	71	14	1	0	0	0.0	8	0	4	8	1	8	0	27	50	1	7	2.5	.987	2B-10, SS-7, 3B-1
1959			22	.171	.237	76	13	2	0	1	1.3	11	5	10	5	0	1	0	48	44	3	15	4.3	.968	2B-20, SS-5
1960	DET	A	30	.147	.294	68	10	0	2	2	2.9	6	5	4	9	1	3	0	33	59	1	12	3.1	.989	2B-17, SS-10, 3B-1
4 yrs.			126	.174	.240	321	56	6	3	3	0.9	37	17	29	36	2	16	0	177	237	15	55	3.4	.965	2B-78, SS-27, 3B-2

WORLD SERIES

Year	Team		Games	BA	SA	AB	H	2B	3B	HR	HR%	R	RBI	BB	SO	SB	PH AB	PH H	PO	A	E	DP	TC/G	FA	G by Pos
1958	MIL	N	2	.000	.000	1	0	0	0	0	0.0	0	0	0	1	0	1	0	0	0	0	0	0.0	–	

Hughie Wise

WISE, HUGH EDWARD
Father of Casey Wise.
B. Mar. 9, 1906, Campbellsville, Ky.   D. July 21, 1987, Plantation, Fla.
BB TR 6' 178 lbs.

Year	Team		Games	BA	SA	AB	H	2B	3B	HR	HR%	R	RBI	BB	SO	SB	PH AB	PH H	PO	A	E	DP	TC/G	FA	G by Pos
1930	DET	A	2	.333	.333	6	2	0	0	0	0.0	0	0	0	0	0	0	0	9	2	0	0	5.5	1.000	C-2

Nick Wise

WISE, NICHOLAS JOSEPH
B. June 15, 1866, Boston, Mass. D. Jan. 15, 1923, Boston, Mass.
BR TR 5'11" 194 lbs.

Year	Team		Games	BA	SA	AB	H	2B	3B	HR	HR%	R	RBI	BB	SO	SB	PH AB	PH H	PO	A	E	DP	TC/G	FA	G by Pos
1888	BOS	N	1	.000	.000	3	0	0	0	0	0.0	0	0	0	0	0	0	0	0	0	0	0	0.0	–	OF-1, C-1

Sam Wise

WISE, SAMUEL WASHINGTON
B. Aug. 18, 1857, Akron, Ohio   D. Jan. 22, 1910, Akron, Ohio
BL TR 5'10½" 170 lbs.

Year	Team		Games	BA	SA	AB	H	2B	3B	HR	HR%	R	RBI	BB	SO	SB	PH AB	PH H	PO	A	E	DP	TC/G	FA	G by Pos
1881	DET	N	1	.500	.500	4	2	0	0	0	0.0	0	0	0	2		0	0	1	3	3	0	7.0	.571	3B-1
1882	BOS	N	78	.221	.326	298	66	11	4	4	1.3	44	34	15	45		0	0	90	199	54	13	4.4	.843	SS-72, 3B-6
1883			96	.271	.397	406	110	25	7	4	1.0	73	58	13	74		0	0	134	274	88	21	5.2	.823	SS-96
1884			114	.214	.319	426	91	15	9	4	0.9	60		25	**104**		0	0	175	330	70	21	5.0	.878	SS-107, 2B-7
1885			107	.283	.406	424	120	20	10	4	0.9	71	46	25	61		0	0	196	338	86	35	5.8	.861	SS-79, 2B-22, OF-6
1886			96	.289	.432	387	112	19	12	4	1.0	71	72	33	61		0	0	592	100	55	27	7.8	.926	1B-57, SS-20, SS-18
1887			113	.334	.522	467	156	27	17	9	1.9	103	92	36	44	43	0	0	231	289	81	29	5.3	.865	SS-72, OF-27, 2B-16
1888			105	.240	.372	417	100	19	12	4	1.0	66	40	34	66	33	0	0	242	281	62	37	5.6	.894	SS-89, 3B-6, 1B-5, OF-4, 2B-2
1889	WAS	N	121	.250	.341	472	118	15	8	4	0.8	79	62	61	62	24	0	0	245	323	76	36	5.3	.882	2B-72, SS-26, 3B-13, OF-10
1890	BUF	P	119	.293	.430	505	148	29	11	6	1.2	95	102	46	45	19	0	0	328	375	73	58	6.5	.906	2B-119
1891	BAL	AA	103	.247	.317	388	96	14	5	1	0.3	70	48	62	52	33	0	0	229	308	68	32	5.9	.888	2B-99, SS-4
1893	WAS	N	122	.311	.457	521	162	27	17	5	1.0	102	77	49	27	20	0	0	345	380	79	53	6.6	.902	2B-91, 3B-31
12 yrs.			1175	.272	.397	4715	1281	221	112	49	1.0	834	631	389	643	172	0	0	2808	3200	795	362	5.8	.883	SS-563, 2B-448, 1B-62, 3B-57, OF-47

Phil Wisner

WISNER, PHILIP N.
B. July, 1869, Washington, D. C.   D. July 5, 1936, Washington, D. C.
TR

Year	Team		Games	BA	SA	AB	H	2B	3B	HR	HR%	R	RBI	BB	SO	SB	PH AB	PH H	PO	A	E	DP	TC/G	FA	G by Pos
1895	WAS	N	1	–	–	0	0	0	0	0	–	0	0	0	0	0	0	0	0	1	3	0	4.0	.250	SS-1

Dave Wissman

WISSMAN, DAVID ALVIN
B. Feb. 17, 1941, Greenfield, Mass.
BL TR 6'2" 178 lbs.

Year	Team		Games	BA	SA	AB	H	2B	3B	HR	HR%	R	RBI	BB	SO	SB	PH AB	PH H	PO	A	E	DP	TC/G	FA	G by Pos
1964	PIT	N	16	.148	.148	27	4	0	0	0	0.0	2	0	1	9	0	6	2	11	0	0	0	0.7	1.000	OF-10

Tex Wisterzil

WISTERZIL, GEORGE JOHN
B. Mar. 7, 1891, Detroit, Mich.   D. June 27, 1964, San Antonio, Tex.
BR TR 5'9½" 150 lbs.

Year	Team		Games	BA	SA	AB	H	2B	3B	HR	HR%	R	RBI	BB	SO	SB	PH AB	PH H	PO	A	E	DP	TC/G	FA	G by Pos
1914	BKN	F	149	.257	.328	534	137	18	10	0	0.0	54	66	34		17	0	0	207	294	23	24	3.5	.956	3B-149, 2B-1
1915	3 teams		93	BKN	F (36G – .311)		CHI	F (49G – .244)			STL	F (8G – .208)													
"	total		93	.265	.320	294	78	8	4	0	0.0	29	39	31		12	5	0	123	194	14	13	3.6	.958	3B-87
2 yrs.			242	.260	.325	828	215	26	14	0	0.0	83	105	65		29	5	0	330	488	37	37	3.5	.957	3B-236, 2B-1

Mickey Witek

WITEK, NICHOLAS JOSEPH
B. Dec. 19, 1915, Luzerne, Pa.
BR TR 5'10" 170 lbs.

Year	Team		Games	BA	SA	AB	H	2B	3B	HR	HR%	R	RBI	BB	SO	SB	PH AB	PH H	PO	A	E	DP	TC/G	FA	G by Pos
1940	NY	N	119	.256	.293	433	111	7	0	3	0.7	34	31	24	17	2	1	1	257	412	29	62	5.9	.958	SS-89, 2B-32
1941			26	.362	.447	94	34	5	0	1	1.1	11	16	4	2	0	1	0	70	70	10	17	5.8	.933	2B-23
1942			148	.260	.344	553	144	19	6	5	0.9	72	48	36	20	2	1	0	371	441	18	72	5.6	.978	2B-147
1943			153	.314	.370	622	195	17	0	6	1.0	68	55	41	23	1	0	0	401	505	31	96	6.1	.967	2B-153
1946			82	.264	.366	284	75	13	2	4	1.4	32	29	28	10	1	7	2	138	150	20	23	3.8	.935	2B-42, 3B-35
1947			51	.219	.313	160	35	4	1	3	1.9	22	17	15	12	1	8	0	105	128	6	28	4.7	.975	2B-40, 3B-3
1949	NY	A	1	1.000	1.000	1	1	0	0	0	0.0	0	0	0	0	0	1	1	0	0	0	0	0.0	–	
7 yrs.			580	.277	.347	2147	595	65	9	22	1.0	239	196	148	84	7	18	4	1342	1706	114	292	5.5	.964	2B-437, SS-89, 3B-38

Corky Withrow

WITHROW, RAYMOND WALLACE
B. Nov. 28, 1937, High Coal, W. Va.
BR TR 6'3½" 197 lbs.

Year	Team		Games	BA	SA	AB	H	2B	3B	HR	HR%	R	RBI	BB	SO	SB	PH AB	PH H	PO	A	E	DP	TC/G	FA	G by Pos
1963	STL	N	6	.000	.000	9	0	0	0	0	0.0	0	1	0	2	0	4	0	3	0	0	0	0.5	1.000	OF-2

Frank Withrow

WITHROW, FRANK BLAINE (Kid)
B. June 14, 1891, Greenwood, Mo.   D. Sept. 5, 1966, Omaha, Neb.
BR TR 5'11½" 187 lbs.

Frank Withrow *continued*

Year	Team	Lg	Games	BA	SA	AB	H	2B	3B	HR	HR%	R	RBI	BB	SO	SB	PH AB	PH H	PO	A	E	DP	TC/G	FA	G by Pos
1920	PHI	N	48	.182	.227	132	24	4	1	0	0.0	8	12	8	26	0	0	0	164	51	6	10	4.6	.973	C-48
1922			10	.333	.429	21	7	2	0	0	0.0	3	3	3	5	0	2	0	24	6	3	1	3.3	.909	C-8
2 yrs.			58	.203	.255	153	31	6	1	0	0.0	11	15	11	31	0	2	0	188	57	9	11	4.4	.965	C-56

Whitey Witt

WITT, LAWTON WALTER
Born Ladislaw Waldemar Wittkowski.
B. Sept. 28, 1895, Orange, Mass. D. July 14, 1988, Salem County, N. J.   BL TR 5'7" 150 lbs.

Year	Team	Lg	Games	BA	SA	AB	H	2B	3B	HR	HR%	R	RBI	BB	SO	SB	PH AB	PH H	PO	A	E	DP	TC/G	FA	G by Pos
1916	PHI	A	143	.245	.337	563	138	16	15	2	0.4	64	36	55	71	19	1	0	299	423	78	59	5.6	.903	SS-142
1917			128	.252	.299	452	114	13	4	0	0.0	62	28	65	45	12	4	0	209	370	40	41	4.8	.935	SS-111, OF-7, 3B-6
1919			122	.267	.326	460	123	15	6	0	0.0	56	33	46	26	11	4	1	267	166	19	25	3.7	.958	OF-59, 2B-56, 3B-2
1920			65	.321	.413	218	70	11	3	1	0.5	29	25	27	16	2	2	0	99	30	5	5	2.1	.963	OF-49, 2B-11, SS-2
1921			154	.315	.418	629	198	31	11	4	0.6	100	45	77	52	16	0	0	288	15	13	3	2.1	.959	OF-154
1922	NY	A	140	.297	.364	528	157	11	6	4	0.8	98	40	**89**	29	5	1	1	312	9	8	1	2.4	.976	OF-139
1923			146	.314	.408	596	187	18	10	6	1.0	113	56	67	42	2	2	0	357	14	8	4	2.6	.979	OF-144
1924			147	.297	.362	600	178	26	5	1	0.2	88	36	45	20	9	3	0	362	11	9	1	2.6	.976	OF-143
1925			31	.200	.300	40	8	2	1	0	0.0	9	0	6	2	1	9	3	19	1	0	0	0.6	1.000	OF-10
1926	BKN	N	63	.259	.294	85	22	1	1	0	0.0	13	3	12	6	1	28	6	44	2	4	1	0.8	.920	OF-22
10 yrs.			1139	.287	.364	4171	1195	144	62	18	0.4	632	302	489	309	78	54	11	2256	1041	184	140	3.1	.947	OF-727, SS-255, 2B-67, 3B-8

WORLD SERIES

Year	Team	Lg	Games	BA	SA	AB	H	2B	3B	HR	HR%	R	RBI	BB	SO	SB	PH AB	PH H	PO	A	E	DP	TC/G	FA	G by Pos
1922	NY	A	5	.222	.389	18	4	1	1	0	0.0	1	0	1	2	0	0	0	7	1	0	0	1.6	1.000	OF-5
1923			6	.240	.320	25	6	2	0	0	0.0	1	1	1	1	0	0	0	18	1	0	0	3.2	1.000	OF-6
2 yrs.			11	.233	.349	43	10	3	1	0	0.0	2	4	2	3	0	0	0	25	2	0	0	2.5	1.000	OF-11

Jerry Witte

WITTE, JEROME CHARLES
B. July 30, 1915, St. Louis, Mo.   BR TR 6'1" 190 lbs.

Year	Team	Lg	Games	BA	SA	AB	H	2B	3B	HR	HR%	R	RBI	BB	SO	SB	PH AB	PH H	PO	A	E	DP	TC/G	FA	G by Pos
1946	STL	A	18	.192	.301	73	14	2	0	2	2.7	7	4	0	18	0	0	0	140	8	5	15	8.5	.967	1B-18
1947			34	.141	.242	99	14	2	1	2	2.0	4	12	11	22	0	8	0	218	16	4	21	7.0	.983	1B-27
2 yrs.			52	.163	.267	172	28	4	1	4	2.3	11	16	11	40	0	8	0	358	24	9	36	7.5	.977	1B-45

John Wockenfuss

WOCKENFUSS, JOHNNY BILTON
B. Feb. 27, 1949, Welch, W. Va.   BR TR 6' 190 lbs.

Year	Team	Lg	Games	BA	SA	AB	H	2B	3B	HR	HR%	R	RBI	BB	SO	SB	PH AB	PH H	PO	A	E	DP	TC/G	FA	G by Pos
1974	DET	A	13	.138	.172	29	4	1	0	0	0.0	1	2	3	2	0	0	0	45	10	4	2	4.5	.932	C-13
1975			35	.229	.432	118	27	6	3	4	3.4	15	13	10	15	0	1	0	195	23	4	4	6.3	.982	C-34
1976			60	.222	.361	144	32	7	2	3	2.1	18	10	17	14	0	1	0	221	19	15	5	4.3	.941	C-59
1977			53	.274	.500	164	45	8	1	9	5.5	26	25	14	18	0	9	2	181	20	3	2	3.8	.985	C-37, OF-9, DH-3
1978			71	.283	.422	187	53	5	0	7	3.7	23	22	21	14	0	17	6	89	2	2	0	1.3	.978	OF-60, DH-2
1979			87	.264	.506	231	61	9	1	15	6.5	27	46	18	40	2	20	6	318	26	3	22	4.0	.991	1B-31, C-20, DH-18, OF-6
1980			126	.274	.449	372	102	13	2	16	4.3	56	65	68	64	1	17	4	575	47	11	44	5.0	.983	1B-52, DH-28, C-25, OF-23
1981			70	.215	.395	172	37	4	0	9	5.2	20	25	28	22	0	13	1	197	6	3	27	2.9	.985	DH-39, 1B-25, C-5, OF-1
1982			70	.301	.472	193	58	9	0	8	4.1	28	32	29	21	0	11	4	228	14	2	9	3.5	.992	C-24, DH-17, 1B-17, OF-10, 3B-1
1983			92	.269	.420	245	66	8	1	9	3.7	32	44	31	37	1	24	7	225	21	2	10	2.7	.992	DH-39, C-29, 1B-13, OF-1, 3B-1
1984	PHI	N	86	.289	.417	180	52	3	1	6	3.3	20	24	30	24	1	27	6	323	20	7	21	4.1	.980	1B-39, C-21, 3B-2
1985			32	.162	.162	37	6	0	0	0	0.0	0	2	8	7	0	24	5	44	1	0	5	1.4	.989	1B-7, C-2
12 yrs.			795	.262	.432	2072	543	73	11	86	4.2	267	310	277	278	5	164	40	2641	209	56	151	3.7	.981	C-269, 1B-184, DH-146, OF-110, 3B-4

Andy Woehr

WOEHR, ANDREW EMIL
B. Feb. 4, 1896, Fort Wayne, Ind.   BR TR 5'11" 165 lbs.

Year	Team	Lg	Games	BA	SA	AB	H	2B	3B	HR	HR%	R	RBI	BB	SO	SB	PH AB	PH H	PO	A	E	DP	TC/G	FA	G by Pos
1923	PHI	N	13	.341	.390	41	14	2	0	0	0.0	3	3	1	1	0	0	0	15	24	1	4	3.1	.975	3B-13
1924			50	.217	.309	152	33	4	5	0	0.0	11	17	5	8	2	3	0	46	58	9	8	2.3	.920	3B-44, 2B-1
2 yrs.			63	.244	.326	193	47	6	5	0	0.0	14	20	6	9	2	3	0	61	82	10	12	2.4	.935	3B-57, 2B-1

Joe Woerlin

WOERLIN, JOSEPH
B. Oct. 9, 1864, France   D. June 22, 1919, St. Louis, Mo.

Year	Team	Lg	Games	BA	SA	AB	H	2B	3B	HR	HR%	R	RBI	BB	SO	SB	PH AB	PH H	PO	A	E	DP	TC/G	FA	G by Pos
1895	WAS	N	1	.333	.333	3	1	0	0	0	0.0	0	0	0	0	0	0	0	0	3	0	0	3.0	1.000	SS-1

Jim Wohlford

WOHLFORD, JAMES EUGENE (Wolfie)
B. Feb. 28, 1951, Visalia, Calif.   BR TR 5'11" 175 lbs.

Year	Team	Lg	Games	BA	SA	AB	H	2B	3B	HR	HR%	R	RBI	BB	SO	SB	PH AB	PH H	PO	A	E	DP	TC/G	FA	G by Pos
1972	KC	A	15	.240	.280	25	6	1	0	0	0.0	3	0	2	6	0	4	0	7	12	1	1	1.3	.950	2B-8
1973			45	.266	.385	109	29	1	3	2	1.8	21	10	11	12	1	5	1	31	2	0	1	0.7	1.000	DH-19, OF-13
1974			143	.271	.343	501	136	16	7	2	0.4	55	44	39	74	16	9	2	273	7	5	4	2.0	.982	OF-138, DH-1
1975			116	.255	.312	353	90	10	5	0	0.0	45	30	34	37	12	14	2	175	9	9	1	1.9	.953	OF-102, DH-4
1976			107	.249	.307	293	73	10	2	1	0.3	47	24	29	24	22	16	2	190	8	5	1	1.9	.975	OF-93, DH-3, 2B-1
1977	MIL	A	129	.248	.320	391	97	16	3	2	0.5	41	36	21	49	17	4	1	246	7	5	1	2.0	.981	OF-125, DH-1, 2B-1
1978			46	.297	.415	118	35	7	2	1	0.8	16	19	6	10	3	8	2	52	2	1	0	1.2	.982	OF-35, DH-4
1979			63	.263	.366	175	46	13	1	1	0.6	19	17	8	28	6	2	1	126	0	4	0	2.1	.969	OF-55, DH-5
1980	SF	N	91	.280	.368	193	54	6	4	1	0.5	17	24	13	23	1	48	12	89	3	2	0	1.0	.979	OF-49, 3B-1
1981			50	.162	.250	68	11	3	0	1	1.5	4	7	4	9	1	40	5	31	1	0	0	0.1	1.000	OF-10
1982			97	.256	.336	250	64	12	1	2	0.8	37	25	30	36	8	27	5	122	4	1	0	1.3	.992	OF-72
1983	MON	N	83	.277	.355	141	39	8	0	1	0.7	7	14	5	14	0	31	11	80	2	1	0	1.0	.988	OF-61
1984			95	.300	.451	213	64	13	2	5	2.3	20	29	14	19	3	39	8	85	4	1	0	0.9	.989	OF-59, 3B-2
1985			70	.192	.272	125	24	5	1	1	0.8	7	15	16	18	0	21	5	58	1	0	0	1.0	1.000	OF-43
1986			70	.266	.383	94	25	4	2	1	1.1	10	11	9	17	0	41	8	22	6	0	0	0.4	1.000	OF-22, 3B-6
15 yrs.			1220	.260	.343	3049	793	125	33	21	0.7	349	305	241	376	89	309	65	1559	68	35	11	1.4	.979	OF-877, DH-37, 2B-10, 3B-9

LEAGUE CHAMPIONSHIP SERIES

Year	Team	Lg	Games	BA	SA	AB	H	2B	3B	HR	HR%	R	RBI	BB	SO	SB	PH AB	PH H	PO	A	E	DP	TC/G	FA	G by Pos
1976	KC	A	5	.182	.182	11	2	0	0	0	0.0	3	0	3	1	2	1	1	7	0	0	0	1.4	1.000	OF-5

Year	Team	Games	BA	SA	AB	H	2B	3B	HR	HR%	R	RBI	BB	SO	SB	Pinch Hit AB	Pinch Hit H	PO	A	E	DP	TC/G	FA	G by Pos

John Wojcik

WOJCIK, JOHN JOSEPH
B. Apr. 6, 1942, Olean, N. Y.

BL TR 6' 175 lbs.

Year	Team	Games	BA	SA	AB	H	2B	3B	HR	HR%	R	RBI	BB	SO	SB	PH AB	PH H	PO	A	E	DP	TC/G	FA	G by Pos
1962	KC A	16	.302	.395	43	13	4	0	0	0.0	8	9	13	4	3	4	2	21	1	0	0	1.4	1.000	OF-12
1963		19	.186	.186	59	11	0	0	0	0.0	7	2	8	8	2	2	0	34	1	0	0	1.8	1.000	OF-17
1964		6	.136	.136	22	3	0	0	0	0.0	1	0	2	8	0	0	0	10	0	0	0	1.7	1.000	OF-6
3 yrs.		41	.218	.250	124	27	4	0	0	0.0	16	11	23	20	5	6	2	65	2	0	0	1.6	1.000	OF-35

Chicken Wolf

WOLF, WILLIAM VAN WINKLE
B. May 12, 1862, Louisville, Ky.   D. May 16, 1903, Louisville, Ky.
Manager 1889.

BR TR 5'9" 190 lbs.

Year	Team	Games	BA	SA	AB	H	2B	3B	HR	HR%	R	RBI	BB	SO	SB	PH AB	PH H	PO	A	E	DP	TC/G	FA	G by Pos
1882	LOU AA	78	.299	.384	318	95	11	8	0	0.0	46		9			0	0	98	45	21	3	2.1	.872	OF-70, SS-9, 1B-1, P-1
1883		98	.262	.360	389	102	17	9	1	0.3	59		5			0	0	244	66	42	9	3.6	.881	OF-78, C-20, SS-5, 2B-1
1884		110	.300	.414	486	146	24	11	3	0.6	79		4			0	0	227	43	35	4	2.8	.885	OF-101, C-11, SS-1, 3B-1, 1B-1
1885		112	.292	.416	483	141	23	17	1	0.2	79		11			0	0	184	23	20	5	2.0	.912	OF-111, C-2, 3B-1, P-1
1886		130	.272	.363	545	148	17	12	3	0.6	93		27			0	0	267	40	27	13	2.6	.919	OF-122, 1B-8, C-3, 2B-1, P-1
1887		137	.281	.381	569	160	28	13	1	0.2	103		34		45	0	0	302	31	24	11	2.6	.933	OF-128, 1B-11
1888		128	.286	.379	538	154	28	11	0	0.0	80	67	25		41	0	0	189	168	63	13	3.3	.850	OF-85, SS-39, 3B-4, C-3, 1B-1
1889		130	.291	.377	546	159	20	9	3	0.5	72	57	29	34	18	0	0	362	96	35	23	3.8	.929	OF-88, 1B-16, 2B-13, SS-10, 3B-7
1890		134	.363	.479	543	197	29	11	4	0.7	100		43		46	0	0	210	38	18	6	2.0	.932	OF-123, 3B-12
1891		138	.253	.320	537	136	17	8	1	0.2	67	82	42	36	13	0	0	222	31	20	10	2.0	.927	OF-133, 1B-5, 3B-1
1892	STL N	3	.143	.143	14	2	0	0	0	0.0	1	1	0	1	0	0	0	1	0	0	0	0.3	1.000	OF-3
11 yrs.		1198	.290	.387	4968	1440	214	109	17	0.3	779	207	229	71	163	0	0	2306	581	305	97	2.7	.904	OF-1042, SS-64, 1B-43, C-39, 3B-26, 2B-15, P-3

Ray Wolf

WOLF, RAYMOND BERNARD
B. July 15, 1904, Chicago, Ill.   D. Oct. 6, 1979, Fort Worth, Tex.

BR TR 5'11" 175 lbs.

Year	Team	Games	BA	SA	AB	H	2B	3B	HR	HR%	R	RBI	BB	SO	SB	PH AB	PH H	PO	A	E	DP	TC/G	FA	G by Pos
1927	CIN N	1	.000	.000	1	0	0	0	0	0.0	0	0	0	0	0	0	0	3	0	0	0	3.0	1.000	1B-1

Harry Wolfe

WOLFE, HAROLD (Whitey)
B. Nov. 24, 1890, Worcester, Mass.   D. July 28, 1971, Ft. Wayne, Ind.

BR TR 5'8" 160 lbs.

Year	Team	Games	BA	SA	AB	H	2B	3B	HR	HR%	R	RBI	BB	SO	SB	PH AB	PH H	PO	A	E	DP	TC/G	FA	G by Pos
1917	2 teams				CHI N (9G – .400)			PIT N (3G – .000)																
"	total	12	.200	.200	10	2	0	0	0	0.0	1	1	2	5	0	3	0	7	6	1	2	1.2	.929	OF-2, SS-2, 2B-1

Larry Wolfe

WOLFE, LAURENCE MARCY
B. Mar. 2, 1953, Melbourne, Fla.

BR TR 5'11" 170 lbs.

Year	Team	Games	BA	SA	AB	H	2B	3B	HR	HR%	R	RBI	BB	SO	SB	PH AB	PH H	PO	A	E	DP	TC/G	FA	G by Pos
1977	MIN A	8	.240	.280	25	6	1	0	0	0.0	3	6	1	0	0	3	2	9	13	0	1	2.8	1.000	3B-8
1978		88	.234	.323	235	55	10	1	3	1.3	25	25	36	27	0	7	2	66	163	12	11	2.7	.950	3B-81, SS-7
1979	BOS A	47	.244	.410	78	19	4	0	3	3.8	12	15	17	21	0	8	4	48	70	5	15	2.6	.959	2B-27, 3B-9, SS-2, DH-1, 1B-1, C-1
1980		18	.130	.304	23	3	1	0	1	4.3	3	4	0	5	0	3	1	3	8	0	2	0.6	1.000	3B-14, DH-4
4 yrs.		161	.230	.338	361	83	16	1	7	1.9	43	50	54	53	0	21	9	126	254	17	29	2.5	.957	3B-112, 2B-27, SS-9, DH-5, 1B-1, C-1

Polly Wolfe

WOLFE, ROY CHAMBERLAIN
B. Sept. 1, 1888, Knoxville, Ill.   D. Nov. 21, 1938, Morris, Ill.

BL TR 5'10" 170 lbs.

Year	Team	Games	BA	SA	AB	H	2B	3B	HR	HR%	R	RBI	BB	SO	SB	PH AB	PH H	PO	A	E	DP	TC/G	FA	G by Pos
1912	CHI A	1	.000	.000	1	0	0	0	0	0.0	0		0			0	0	0	0	0	0	0.0	–	
1914		9	.214	.214	28	6	0	0	0	0.0	0		3	6	1	1	0	7	0	1	0	0.9	.875	OF-8
2 yrs.		10	.207	.207	29	6	0	0	0	0.0	0		3	6	1	2	0	7	0	1	0	0.8	.875	OF-8

Abe Wolstenholme

WOLSTENHOLME, ABRAHAM LINCOLN
B. Mar. 4, 1861, Philadelphia, Pa.   D. Mar. 4, 1916, Philadelphia, Pa.

Year	Team	Games	BA	SA	AB	H	2B	3B	HR	HR%	R	RBI	BB	SO	SB	PH AB	PH H	PO	A	E	DP	TC/G	FA	G by Pos
1883	PHI N	3	.091	.182	11	1	1	0	0	0.0	0		0	0		0	0	4	4	3	0	3.7	.727	C-2, OF-1

Harry Wolter

WOLTER, HARRY MEIGS
B. July 11, 1884, Monterey, Calif.   D. July 7, 1970, Palo Alto, Calif.

BL TL 5'10" 175 lbs.

Year	Team	Games	BA	SA	AB	H	2B	3B	HR	HR%	R	RBI	BB	SO	SB	PH AB	PH H	PO	A	E	DP	TC/G	FA	G by Pos
1907	3 teams				CIN N (4G – .133)			PIT N (1G – .000)			STL N (16G – .340)													
"	total	21	.286	.286	63	18	0	0	0	0.0	5	7	3			1	4	0	20	5	1	1	1.2	.962	OF-13, P-4
1909	BOS N	54	.244	.378	119	29	2	4	2	1.7	14	10	9		2	13	1	189	26	9	6	4.1	.960	1B-17, P-10, OF-9
1910	NY A	135	.267	.361	479	128	15	9	4	0.8	84	42	66		39	2	0	192	11	13	3	1.6	.940	OF-130
1911		122	.304	.440	434	132	17	15	4	0.9	78	36	62		28	3	2	192	20	12	9	1.8	.946	OF-113, 1B-2
1912		12	.344	.469	32	11	2	1	0	0.0	8	1	10		5	3	0	11	1	1	0	1.1	.923	OF-9
1913		126	.254	.339	425	108	18	6	2	0.5	53	43	80	50	13	3	1	228	15	14	1	2.0	.946	OF-121
1917	CHI N	117	.249	.331	353	88	15	7	0	0.0	44	28	38	40	7	16	7	134	14	9	5	1.3	.943	OF-97, 1B-1
7 yrs.		587	.270	.369	1905	514	69	42	12	0.6	286	167	268	90	95	44	11	966	92	59	25	1.9	.947	OF-492, 1B-20, P-14

Harry Wolverton

WOLVERTON, HARRY STERLING
B. Dec. 6, 1873, Mt. Vernon, Ohio   D. Feb. 4, 1937, Oakland, Calif.
Manager 1912.

BL TR 5'11" 205 lbs.

Year	Team	Games	BA	SA	AB	H	2B	3B	HR	HR%	R	RBI	BB	SO	SB	PH AB	PH H	PO	A	E	DP	TC/G	FA	G by Pos
1898	CHI N	13	.327	.347	49	16	1	0	0	0.0	4	2	1			1	0	21	35	10	1	5.1	.848	3B-13
1899		99	.285	.386	389	111	14	11	1	0.3	50	49	30		14	0	0	124	228	58	12	4.1	.859	3B-98, SS-1
1900	2 teams				CHI N (3G – .182)			PHI N (101G – .282)																
"	total	104	.279	.368	394	110	10	8	3	0.8	44	58	22		5	0	0	124	239	49	16	4.0	.881	3B-104
1901	PHI N	93	.309	.369	379	117	15	4	0	0.0	42	43	22		13	0	0	114	190	26	9	3.5	.921	3B-93
1902	2 teams				WAS A (59G – .249)			PHI N (34G – .294)																
"	total	93	.265	.327	385	102	11	5	1	0.3	47	39	22		11	0	0	130	230	34	19	4.2	.914	3B-93
1903	PHI N	123	.308	.383	494	152	13	12	0	0.0	72	53	18		10	0	0	182	247	27	8	3.7	.941	3B-123
1904		102	.266	.329	398	106	15	5	0	0.0	43	49	26		18	0	0	143	191	27	15	3.5	.925	3B-102
1905	BOS N	122	.225	.300	463	104	15	7	2	0.4	38	55	23		10	0	0	139	256	28	12	3.5	.934	3B-122

Year	Team	Games	BA	SA	AB	H	2B	3B	HR	HR%	R	RBI	BB	SO	SB	Pinch Hit AB	Pinch Hit H	PO	A	E	DP	TC/G	FA	G by Pos

Harry Wolverton *continued*

Year	Team	Games	BA	SA	AB	H	2B	3B	HR	HR%	R	RBI	BB	SO	SB	AB	H	PO	A	E	DP	TC/G	FA	G by Pos
1912	NY	A	33	.300	.360	50	15	1	1	0	0.0	6	4	2		1	26	10	13	10	5	1	0.8	.821	3B-7
9 yrs.		782	.278	.352	3001	833	95	53	7	0.2	346	352	166		83	26	10	990	1626	264	93	3.7	.908	3B-755, SS-1

Sid Womack

WOMACK, SIDNEY KIRK (Tex)
B. Oct. 2, 1896, Greensburg, La.   D. Aug. 28, 1958, Jackson, Miss.   BR TR 5'10½" 185 lbs.

Year	Team	Games	BA	SA	AB	H	2B	3B	HR	HR%	R	RBI	BB	SO	SB	AB	H	PO	A	E	DP	TC/G	FA	G by Pos
1926	BOS	N	1	.000	.000	3	0	0	0	0	0.0	0	1	0	0		0	0	3	1	0	0	4.0	1.000	C-1

Bob Wood

WOOD, ROBERT LYNN
B. July 28, 1865, Thorn Hill, Ohio   D. May 22, 1943, Churchill, Ohio   BR TR

Year	Team	Games	BA	SA	AB	H	2B	3B	HR	HR%	R	RBI	BB	SO	SB	AB	H	PO	A	E	DP	TC/G	FA	G by Pos
1898	CIN	N	39	.275	.330	109	30	6	0	0	0.0	14	16	9		1	8	3	109	29	8	1	3.7	.945	C-29, OF-1, 1B-1
1899		62	.314	.443	194	61	11	7	0	0.0	34	24	25		3	2	1	174	52	14	5	3.9	.942	C-53, OF-2, 3B-2, 1B-1
1900		45	.266	.338	139	37	8	1	0	0.0	17	22	10		3	11	1	69	56	12	5	3.0	.912	C-18, 3B-15, OF-1
1901	CLE	A	98	.292	.384	346	101	23	3	1	0.3	45	49	12		6	4	1	328	121	25	12	4.8	.947	C-84, 3B-4, OF-3, SS-1, 2B-1, 1B-1
1902		81	.295	.380	258	76	18	2	0	0.0	23	40	27		1	9	2	347	70	19	11	5.4	.956	C-52, 1B-16, OF-2, 3B-1, 2B-1
1904	DET	A	49	.246	.320	175	43	6	2	1	0.6	15	17	5		1	2	0	232	69	8	5	6.3	.974	C-47
1905		8	.083	.125	24	2	1	0	0	0.0	1	0	1		0	1	0	26	13	5	0	5.5	.886	C-7
7 yrs.		382	.281	.369	1245	350	73	15	2	0.2	149	168	89		15	37	8	1285	410	91	39	4.7	.949	C-290, 3B-22, 1B-19, OF-9, 2B-2, SS-1

Doc Wood

WOOD, CHARLES SPENCER
B. Feb. 28, 1900, Batesville, Miss.   D. Nov. 3, 1974, New Orleans, La.   BR TR 5'10" 150 lbs.

Year	Team	Games	BA	SA	AB	H	2B	3B	HR	HR%	R	RBI	BB	SO	SB	AB	H	PO	A	E	DP	TC/G	FA	G by Pos
1923	PHI	A	3	.333	.333	3	1	0	0	0	0.0	0	0	0		0	0	0	0	5	1	1	2.0	.833	SS-3

Fred Wood

WOOD, FRED S.
Brother of Pete Wood.
B. 1863, Hamilton, Ont., Canada   D. Aug. 23, 1933, New York, N. Y.   5'5" 160 lbs.

Year	Team	Games	BA	SA	AB	H	2B	3B	HR	HR%	R	RBI	BB	SO	SB	AB	H	PO	A	E	DP	TC/G	FA	G by Pos
1884	DET	N	12	.048	.048	42	2	0	0	0	0.0	4		3	18		0	0	41	14	13	1	5.7	.809	C-7, OF-6, SS-1
1885	BUF	N	1	.250	.250	4	1	0	0	0	0.0	0	0	0	0		0	0	4	1	1	1	6.0	.833	C-1
2 yrs.		13	.065	.065	46	3	0	0	0	0.0	4	0	3	18		0	0	45	15	14	2	5.7	.811	C-8, OF-6, SS-1

George Wood

WOOD, GEORGE A. (Dandy)
B. Nov. 9, 1858, Boston, Mass.   D. Apr. 4, 1924, Harrisburg, Pa.   BL TR 5'10½" 175 lbs.
Manager 1891.

Year	Team	Games	BA	SA	AB	H	2B	3B	HR	HR%	R	RBI	BB	SO	SB	AB	H	PO	A	E	DP	TC/G	FA	G by Pos
1880	WOR	N	81	.245	.324	327	80	16	5	0	0.0	37	28	10	37		0	0	128	11	17	1	1.9	.891	OF-80, 3B-2, 1B-1
1881	DET	N	80	.297	.421	337	100	18	9	2	0.6	54	32	19	32		0	0	132	18	24	4	2.2	.862	OF-80
1882		84	.269	.421	375	101	12	12	7	1.9	69	29	14	30		0	0	161	14	23	8	2.4	.884	OF-84
1883		99	.302	.444	441	133	26	11	5	1.1	81		25	37		0	0	226	18	34	3	2.8	.878	OF-99, P-1
1884		114	.252	.378	473	119	16	10	8	1.7	79		39	75		0	0	190	18	24	1	2.0	.897	OF-114, 3B-1
1885		82	.290	.428	362	105	19	8	5	1.4	62	28	13	19		0	0	125	40	21	3	2.3	.887	OF-70, 3B-12, SS-1, P-1
1886	PHI	N	106	.273	.407	450	123	18	15	4	0.9	81	50	23	75		0	0	156	33	22	3	2.0	.896	OF-97, SS-6, 3B-3
1887		113	.289	.497	491	142	22	19	14	2.9	118	66	40	51	19	0	0	164	34	28	4	2.0	.876	OF-104, SS-3, 3B-3, 2B-3
1888		106	.229	.342	433	99	19	6	6	1.4	67	15	39	44	20	0	0	176	19	22	3	2.0	.899	OF-104, 3B-2, P-2
1889	2 teams			PHI	N	(97G – .251)			BAL	AA	(3G – .200)														
"	total	100	.250	.352	432	108	21	4	5	1.2	78	54	53	35	18	0	0	175	27	19	1	2.2	.914	OF-95, SS-6, P-1
1890	PHI	P	132	.289	.429	539	156	20	14	9	1.7	115	102	51	35	20	0	0	255	35	34	10	2.5	.895	OF-132, 3B-1
1891	PHI	AA	132	.309	.413	528	163	18	14	3	0.6	105	61	72	52	22	0	0	236	43	26	13	2.3	.915	OF-122, 3B-6, SS-5
1892	2 teams			BAL	N	(21G – .224)			CIN	N	(30G – .196)														
"	total	51	.208	.279	183	38	3	5	0	0.0	19	24	20	25	5	0	0	74	11	11	2	1.9	.885	OF-51
13 yrs.		1280	.273	.403	5371	1467	228	132	68	1.3	965	489	418	547	104	0	0	2198	321	305	56	2.2	.892	OF-1232, 3B-30, SS-21, P-5, 2B-3, 1B-1

Harry Wood

WOOD, HAROLD AUSTIN
B. Feb. 10, 1885, Waterville, Me.   D. May 18, 1955, Bethesda, Md.   BL TR 5'10" 155 lbs.

Year	Team	Games	BA	SA	AB	H	2B	3B	HR	HR%	R	RBI	BB	SO	SB	AB	H	PO	A	E	DP	TC/G	FA	G by Pos
1903	CIN	N	2	.000	.000	3	0	0	0	0	0.0	0	0	1		0	1	0	0	0	0	0	0.0	–	OF-2

Jake Wood

WOOD, JACOB
B. June 22, 1937, Elizabeth, N. J.   BR TR 6'1" 163 lbs.

Year	Team	Games	BA	SA	AB	H	2B	3B	HR	HR%	R	RBI	BB	SO	SB	AB	H	PO	A	E	DP	TC/G	FA	G by Pos
1961	DET	A	162	.258	.376	663	171	17	14	11	1.7	96	69	58	141	30	1	0	380	396	25	83	4.9	.969	2B-162
1962		111	.226	.346	367	83	10	5	8	2.2	68	30	33	59	24	11	2	185	197	20	33	3.6	.950	2B-90
1963		85	.271	.407	351	95	11	2	11	3.1	50	27	24	61	18	1	0	190	202	17	47	4.8	.958	2B-81, 3B-1
1964		64	.232	.304	125	29	2	2	1	0.8	11	7	4	24	0	29	7	105	30	5	13	2.2	.964	1B-11, 2B-10, 3B-6, OF-1
1965		58	.288	.375	104	30	3	0	2	1.9	12	7	10	19	3	25	9	57	38	2	12	1.7	.979	2B-20, SS-1, 3B-1, 1B-1
1966		98	.252	.343	230	58	9	3	2	0.9	39	27	28	48	4	40	6	124	100	9	26	2.4	.961	2B-52, 3B-4, 1B-2
1967	2 teams			DET	A	(14G – .050)			CIN	N	(16G – .118)														
"	total	30	.081	.108	37	3	1	0	0	0.0	3	1	2	10	0	19	2	15	5	1	3	0.7	.952	OF-2, 2B-2, 1B-2
7 yrs.		608	.250	.362	1877	469	53	26	35	1.9	279	168	159	362	79	126	26	1056	968	79	217	3.5	.962	2B-417, 1B-16, 3B-12, OF-3, SS-1

Joe Wood

WOOD, JOSEPH PERRY (Little General)
B. Oct. 3, 1919, Houston, Tex.   D. Mar. 25, 1985, Houston, Tex.   BR TR 5'9½" 160 lbs.

Year	Team	Games	BA	SA	AB	H	2B	3B	HR	HR%	R	RBI	BB	SO	SB	AB	H	PO	A	E	DP	TC/G	FA	G by Pos
1943	DET	A	60	.323	.415	164	53	4	4	1	0.6	22	17	6	13	2	10	3	70	64	12	6	2.4	.918	2B-22, 3B-18

Ken Wood

WOOD, KENNETH LANIER
B. July 1, 1924, Lincolnton, N. C.   BR TR 6' 200 lbs.

Year	Team	Games	BA	SA	AB	H	2B	3B	HR	HR%	R	RBI	BB	SO	SB	AB	H	PO	A	E	DP	TC/G	FA	G by Pos
1948	STL	A	10	.083	.167	24	2	1	0	0	0.0	2	1	1	4	0	5	0	10	1	0	0	1.1	1.000	OF-5
1949		7	.000	.000	6	0	0	0	0	0.0	0	0	1	2	0	3	0	0	0	0	0	0.0	–	OF-3
1950		128	.225	.396	369	83	24	0	13	3.5	42	62	38	58	0	32	4	162	16	9	2	1.5	.952	OF-94
1951		109	.237	.429	333	79	19	0	15	4.5	40	44	27	49	1	10	1	179	7	8	0	1.8	.959	OF-100

Year	Team		Games	BA	SA	AB	H	2B	3B	HR	HR%	R	RBI	BB	SO	SB	Pinch Hit AB	Pinch Hit H	PO	A	E	DP	TC/G	FA	G by Pos

Ken Wood *continued*

1952	2 teams	BOS A (15G – .100)				WAS	A	(61G – .238)																		
"	total		76	.226	.391	230	52	8	6	6	2.6	26	32	33	25	0	8	0	169	6	9	1	2.4	.951	OF-69
1953	WAS	A	12	.212	.242	33	7	1	0	0	0.0	0	3	2	3	0	5	1	13	1	0	1	1.2	1.000	OF-7
6 yrs.			342	.224	.393	995	223	52	7	34	3.4	110	143	102	141	1	63	6	533	31	26	4	1.7	.956	OF-278

Roy Wood

WOOD, ROY WINTON (Woody)
B. Aug. 29, 1892, Monticello, Ark.   D. Apr. 6, 1974, Fayetteville, Ark.   BR TR 6'   175 lbs.

1913	PIT	N	14	.286	.400	35	10	4	0	0	0.0	4	2	1	8	0	3	0	18	4	2	1	1.7	.917	OF-8, 1B-1
1914	CLE	A	72	.236	.305	220	52	6	3	1	0.5	24	15	13	26	6	10	2	209	16	7	13	3.2	.970	OF-41, 1B-20
1915			33	.192	.244	78	15	2	1	0	0.0	5	3	2	13	1	8	1	183	8	2	7	5.8	.990	1B-21, OF-2
3 yrs.			119	.231	.300	333	77	12	4	1	0.3	33	20	16	47	7	21	3	410	28	11	21	3.8	.976	OF-51, 1B-42

Smoky Joe Wood

WOOD, JOE (Smoky Joe)
Born Howard Ellsworth Wood.   Father of Joe Wood.
B. Oct. 25, 1889, Kansas City, Mo.   D. July 27, 1985, West Haven, Conn.   BR TR 5'11"   180 lbs.

1908	BOS	A	6	.000	.000	7	0	0	0	0	0.0	1	0			0	0	0	3	5	1	1	1.5	.889	P-6
1909			24	.164	.200	55	9	0	1	0	0.0	4	3	2		0	0	0	7	27	1	0	1.5	.971	P-24
1910			35	.261	.362	69	18	2	1	1	1.4	9	5	5		0	0	0	17	62	2	3	2.3	.975	P-35
1911			44	.261	.420	88	23	4	2	2	2.3	15	11	10		1	0	0	23	67	5	3	2.2	.947	P-44
1912			43	.290	.435	124	36	13	1	1	0.8	17	13	11		0	0	0	41	110	4	2	3.6	.974	P-43
1913			24	.268	.357	56	15	5	0	0	0.0	10	10	4	7	1	1	0	9	55	3	1	2.8	.955	P-23
1914			20	.140	.163	43	6	1	0	0	0.0	2	1	3	14	1	2	0	13	28	0	0	2.1	1.000	P-18
1915			29	.259	.370	54	14	1	1	1	1.9	6	7	5	10	1	0	0	8	48	1	6	2.0	.982	P-25
1917	CLE	A	10	.000	.000	6	0	0	0	0	0.0	1	0	0	3	0	2	0	2	5	0	0	0.7	1.000	P-5
1918			119	.296	.403	422	125	22	4	5	1.2	41	66	36	38	8	1	0	273	77	17	7	3.1	.954	OF-95, 2B-19, 1B-4
1919			72	.255	.375	192	49	10	5	1	0.5	30	27	32	21	3	6	0	90	7	7	1	1.4	.933	OF-64, P-1
1920			61	.270	.401	137	37	11	2	1	0.7	25	30	25	16	1	0	0	71	6	1	0	1.3	.987	OF-54, P-1
1921			66	.366	.562	194	71	16	5	4	2.1	32	60	25	17	2	0	0	105	3	3	1	1.7	.973	OF-64
1922			142	.297	.442	505	150	33	8	8	1.6	74	92	50	63	5	1	0	249	18	11	5	2.0	.960	OF-140, 1B-1
14 yrs.			695	.283	.411	1952	553	118	30	24	1.2	267	325	208	189	23	13	0	911	518	56	30	2.1	.962	OF-417, P-225, 2B-19, 1B-5

WORLD SERIES

1912	BOS	A	4	.286	.286	7	2	0	0	0	0.0	1	1	1	0	0	0	0	1	6	0	1	1.8	1.000	P-4
1920	CLE	A	4	.200	.300	10	2	1	0	0	0.0	2	0	1	2	0	1	0	7	0	0	0	1.8	1.000	OF-4
2 yrs.			8	.235	.294	17	4	1	0	0	0.0	3	1	2	2	0	1	0	8	6	0	1	1.8	1.000	OF-4, P-4

Larry Woodall

WOODALL, CHARLES LAWRENCE
B. July 26, 1894, Staunton, Va.   D. May 16, 1963, Cambridge, Mass.   BR TR 5'9"   165 lbs.

1920	DET	A	18	.245	.265	49	12	1	0	0	0.0	4	5	2	6	0	2	0	59	20	1	0	4.4	.988	C-15
1921			46	.363	.438	80	29	4	1	0	0.0	10	14	6	7	1	18	5	48	8	2	1	1.3	.966	C-24
1922			50	.344	.392	125	43	2	2	0	0.0	19	18	8	11	0	11	4	117	11	3	1	2.6	.977	C-39
1923			71	.277	.405	148	41	12	2	1	0.7	20	19	22	9	2	9	4	140	32	3	2	2.5	.983	C-60
1924			67	.309	.388	165	51	9	2	0	0.0	23	24	21	5	0	4	0	174	41	3	5	3.3	.986	C-62
1925			75	.205	.240	171	35	4	1	0	0.0	20	13	24	8	1	0	0	165	38	7	4	2.8	.967	C-75
1926			67	.233	.267	146	34	5	0	0	0.0	18	15	15	2	0	5	1	149	37	4	3	2.8	.979	C-59
1927			88	.280	.362	246	69	8	6	0	0.0	28	39	37	9	9	2	0	265	72	1	6	3.8	.997	C-86
1928			65	.210	.247	186	39	5	1	0	0.0	19	13	24	10	3	3	0	218	44	2	3	4.1	.992	C-62
1929			1	.000	.000	1	0	0	0	0	0.0	0	0	0	0	0	1	0	0	0	0	0	0.0	–	
10 yrs.			548	.268	.331	1317	353	50	15	1	0.1	161	160	159	67	16	55	14	1335	303	26	25	3.0	.984	C-482

Darrell Woodard

WOODARD, DARRELL LEE
B. Dec. 10, 1956, Wilma, Ark.   BR TR 5'11"   160 lbs.

| 1978 | OAK | A | 33 | .000 | .000 | 9 | 0 | 0 | 0 | 0 | 0.0 | 10 | 0 | 1 | 1 | 3 | 0 | 0 | 14 | 14 | 1 | 3 | 0.9 | .966 | 2B-14, DH-1, 3B-1 |

Mike Woodard

WOODARD, MICHAEL CARY
B. Mar. 2, 1960, Melrose Park, Ill.   BL TR 5'9"   155 lbs.

1985	SF	N	24	.244	.256	82	20	1	0	0	0.0	12	9	5	3	6	1	1	49	46	1	14	4.0	.990	2B-23
1986			48	.253	.342	79	20	2	1	1	1.3	14	5	10	9	7	21	4	28	43	2	13	1.5	.973	2B-23, SS-2, 3B-2
1987			10	.211	.263	19	4	1	0	0	0.0	0	1	0	1	0	2	0	13	15	0	4	2.8	1.000	2B-8
1988	CHI	A	18	.133	.178	45	6	0	1	0	0.0	3	4	1	5	1	1	0	41	37	2	8	4.4	.975	2B-14
4 yrs.			100	.222	.271	225	50	4	2	1	0.4	29	19	16	18	14	25	5	131	141	5	39	2.8	.982	2B-68, SS-2, 3B-2

Red Woodhead

WOODHEAD, JAMES
B. July, 1851, Chelsea, Mass.   D. Sept. 7, 1881, Boston, Mass.   5'6"   160 lbs.

| 1879 | SYR | N | 34 | .160 | .168 | 131 | 21 | 1 | 0 | 0 | 0.0 | 4 | 2 | 0 | 23 | | 0 | 0 | 52 | 51 | 27 | 4 | 3.8 | .792 | 3B-34 |

Gene Woodling

WOODLING, EUGENE RICHARD
B. Aug. 16, 1922, Akron, Ohio   BL TR 5'9½"   195 lbs.

1943	CLE	A	8	.320	.600	25	8	2	1	1	4.0	5	5	1	3	0	2	1	8	1	0	0	1.1	1.000	OF-6
1946			61	.188	.256	133	25	1	4	0	0.0	8	9	16	13	1	21	3	81	0	0	0	1.3	1.000	OF-37
1947	PIT	N	22	.266	.342	79	21	2	2	0	0.0	7	10	7	5	0	1	0	59	1	2	0	2.8	.968	OF-21
1949	NY	A	112	.270	.412	296	80	13	7	5	1.7	60	44	52	21	2	13	2	163	5	3	1	1.5	.982	OF-98
1950			122	.283	.412	449	127	20	10	6	1.3	81	60	70	31	5	4	0	263	16	2	3	2.3	.993	OF-118
1951			120	.281	.462	420	118	15	8	15	3.6	65	71	62	37	1	0	5	265	5	2	0	2.3	.993	OF-116
1952			122	.309	.473	408	126	19	6	12	2.9	58	63	59	31	1	5	2	241	12	1	4	2.1	.996	OF-118
1953			125	.306	.468	395	121	26	4	10	2.5	64	58	82	29	2	11	5	240	6	1	2	2.0	.996	OF-119
1954			97	.250	.352	304	76	12	5	3	1.0	33	40	53	35	3	10	3	164	5	3	1	1.8	.983	OF-89

Year	Team	Games	BA	SA	AB	H	2B	3B	HR	HR%	R	RBI	BB	SO	SB	Pinch Hit AB	Pinch Hit H	PO	A	E	DP	TC/G	FA	G by Pos

Gene Woodling *continued*

Year	Team	Games	BA	SA	AB	H	2B	3B	HR	HR%	R	RBI	BB	SO	SB	AB	H	PO	A	E	DP	TC/G	FA	G by Pos
1955	2 teams	BAL A	(47G – .221)		CLE A	(79G – .278)																		
"	total	126	.257	.384	404	104	21	3	8	2.0	55	53	60	33	3	13	2	205	5	1	1	1.7	.995	OF-117
1956	CLE A	100	.262	.391	317	83	17	0	8	2.5	56	38	69	29	2	13	3	154	3	3	0	1.6	.981	OF-85
1957		133	.321	.521	430	138	25	2	19	4.4	74	78	64	35	0	22	5	225	10	2	0	1.8	.992	OF-113
1958	BAL A	133	.276	.429	413	114	16	1	15	3.6	57	65	66	49	4	19	5	181	7	5	1	1.5	.974	OF-116
1959		140	.300	.455	440	132	22	2	14	3.2	63	77	78	35	1	18	10	210	2	4	0	1.5	.981	OF-124
1960		140	.283	.414	435	123	18	3	11	2.5	68	62	84	40	3	18	8	202	7	1	0	1.5	.995	OF-124
1961	WAS A	110	.313	.471	342	107	16	4	10	2.9	39	57	50	24	1	20	7	154	8	2	0	1.5	.988	OF-90
1962	2 teams	WAS A	(44G – .280)		NY N	(81G – .274)																		
"	total	125	.276	.424	297	82	12	1	10	3.4	37	40	48	27	1	39	8	109	0	3	0	0.9	.973	OF-78
	17 yrs.	1796	.284	.431	5587	1585	257	63	147	2.6	830	830	921	477	29	234	65	2924	93	35	13	1.7	.989	OF-1569

WORLD SERIES

Year	Team	Games	BA	SA	AB	H	2B	3B	HR	HR%	R	RBI	BB	SO	SB	AB	H	PO	A	E	DP	TC/G	FA	G by Pos
1949	NY A	3	.400	.700	10	4	3	0	0	0.0	4	0	3	0	0	0	0	7	0	0	0	2.3	1.000	OF-3
1950		4	.429	.429	14	6	0	0	0	0.0	2	1	2	0	0	1	0	7	0	1	0	2.0	.875	OF-4
1951		6	.167	.500	18	3	1	1	1	5.6	6	1	5	3	0	1	0	18	0	1	0	3.2	.947	OF-5
1952		7	.348	.609	23	8	1	1	1	4.3	4	1	3	3	0	1	1	18	0	1	0	2.7	.947	OF-6
1953		6	.300	.450	20	6	0	0	1	5.0	5	3	6	2	0	1	0	9	1	0	1	1.7	1.000	OF-6
	5 yrs.	26	.318	.529	85	27	5	2	3	3.5	21	6	19	8	0	4	1	59	1	3	1	2.4	.952	OF-24
										10th		10th												

Orville Woodruff

WOODRUFF, ORVILLE FRANCIS (Sam)
B. Dec. 27, 1876, Chilo, Ohio   D. July 22, 1937, Cincinnati, Ohio

BR TR 5'9"   160 lbs.

Year	Team	Games	BA	SA	AB	H	2B	3B	HR	HR%	R	RBI	BB	SO	SB	AB	H	PO	A	E	DP	TC/G	FA	G by Pos
1904	CIN N	87	.190	.255	306	58	14	3	0	0.0	20	20	19		9	0	0	126	190	30	16	4.0	.913	3B-61, 2B-17, SS-8, OF-1
1910		21	.148	.164	61	9	1	0	0	0.0	6	2	7	8	2	0	0	32	32	7	3	3.4	.901	3B-17, 2B-4
	2 yrs.	108	.183	.240	367	67	15	3	0	0.0	26	22	26	8	11	0	0	158	222	37	19	3.9	.911	3B-78, 2B-21, SS-8, OF-1

Pete Woodruff

WOODRUFF, PETER FRANK
B. Richmond, Va.

BR TR

Year	Team	Games	BA	SA	AB	H	2B	3B	HR	HR%	R	RBI	BB	SO	SB	AB	H	PO	A	E	DP	TC/G	FA	G by Pos
1899	NY N	20	.246	.393	61	15	1	1	2	3.3	11	7	9		3	0	0	34	3	1	1	1.9	.974	OF-19, 1B-1

Al Woods

WOODS, ALVIS
B. Aug. 8, 1953, Oakland, Calif.

BL TL 6'3"   190 lbs.

Year	Team	Games	BA	SA	AB	H	2B	3B	HR	HR%	R	RBI	BB	SO	SB	AB	H	PO	A	E	DP	TC/G	FA	G by Pos
1977	TOR A	122	.284	.382	440	125	17	4	6	1.4	58	35	36	38	8	4	2	215	6	7	1	1.9	.969	OF-115, DH-4
1978		62	.241	.364	220	53	12	3	4	1.4	19	25	11	23	1	3	1	131	2	3	0	2.2	.978	OF-60
1979		132	.278	.385	436	121	24	4	5	1.1	57	36	40	28	6	2	0	251	10	9	2	2.0	.967	OF-127, DH-2
1980		100	.300	.480	373	112	18	2	15	4.0	54	47	37	35	4	10	2	205	5	2	1	2.1	.991	OF-88, DH-13
1981		85	.247	.309	288	71	15	0	1	0.3	20	21	19	31	3	8	2	179	4	5	0	2.2	.973	OF-77, DH-2
1982		85	.234	.343	201	47	11	1	3	1.5	20	24	21	20	1	20	3	96	2	3	1	1.2	.970	OF-64, DH-10
1986	MIN A	23	.321	.571	28	9	1	0	2	7.1	5	8	3	5	0	16	8	0	0	0	0	0.0	–	DH-7
	7 yrs.	609	.271	.387	1986	538	98	14	35	1.8	233	196	167	180	23	63	18	1077	29	29	5	1.9	.974	OF-531, DH-38

Gary Woods

WOODS, GARY LEE
B. July 20, 1954, Santa Barbara, Calif.

BR TR 6'2"   185 lbs.

Year	Team	Games	BA	SA	AB	H	2B	3B	HR	HR%	R	RBI	BB	SO	SB	AB	H	PO	A	E	DP	TC/G	FA	G by Pos
1976	OAK A	6	.125	.125	8	1	0	0	0	0.0	0	0	0	3	0	2	0	7	0	0	0	1.2	1.000	OF-4, DH-1
1977	TOR A	60	.216	.264	227	49	9	1	0	0.0	21	17	7	38	5	1	1	154	4	1	0	2.7	.994	OF-60
1978		8	.158	.211	19	3	1	0	0	0.0	1	1	1	1	1	1	0	12	0	0	0	1.5	1.000	OF-6
1980	HOU N	19	.377	.585	53	20	5	0	2	3.8	8	15	7	9	1	5	3	19	1	0	0	1.1	1.000	OF-14
1981		54	.209	.264	110	23	4	1	0	0.0	10	12	11	22	2	15	3	61	1	1	0	1.2	.984	OF-40
1982	CHI N	117	.269	.388	245	66	15	1	4	1.6	28	30	21	48	3	22	4	161	6	0	1	1.4	1.000	OF-103
1983		93	.242	.353	190	46	9	0	4	2.1	25	22	15	27	5	31	6	97	4	3	0	1.1	.971	OF-73, 2B-1
1984		87	.235	.388	98	23	4	1	3	3.1	13	10	15	21	2	31	7	54	3	0	1	0.7	1.000	OF-62, 2B-3
1985		81	.244	.280	82	20	3	0	0	0.0	11	4	14	18	0	27	7	42	1	0	0	0.5	1.000	OF-56
	9 yrs.	525	.243	.337	1032	251	50	4	13	1.3	117	110	86	187	19	135	31	607	20	5	2	1.2	.992	OF-418, 2B-4, DH-1

DIVISIONAL PLAYOFF SERIES

Year	Team	Games	BA	SA	AB	H	2B	3B	HR	HR%	R	RBI	BB	SO	SB	AB	H	PO	A	E	DP	TC/G	FA	G by Pos
1981	HOU N	2	.000	.000	2	0	0	0	0	0.0	0	0	1	0	2	0	0	0	0	0	0	0.0	–	

LEAGUE CHAMPIONSHIP SERIES

Year	Team	Games	BA	SA	AB	H	2B	3B	HR	HR%	R	RBI	BB	SO	SB	AB	H	PO	A	E	DP	TC/G	FA	G by Pos
1980	HOU N	4	.250	.250	8	2	0	0	0	0.0	0	1	1	3	1	0	0	1	0	0	0	0.3	1.000	OF-3
1984	CHI N	1	.000	.000	1	0	0	0	0	0.0	0	0	0	1	0	1	0	1	0	0	0	1.0	1.000	OF-1
	2 yrs.	5	.222	.222	9	2	0	0	0	0.0	0	1	1	4	1	3	0	2	0	0	0	0.4	1.000	OF-4

Jim Woods

WOODS, JAMES JEROME (Woody)
B. Sept. 17, 1939, Chicago, Ill.

BR TR 6'   175 lbs.

Year	Team	Games	BA	SA	AB	H	2B	3B	HR	HR%	R	RBI	BB	SO	SB	AB	H	PO	A	E	DP	TC/G	FA	G by Pos
1957	CHI N	2	–	–	0	0	0	0	0	–	1	0	0	0	0	0	0	0	0	0	0	0.0	–	
1960	PHI N	11	.176	.265	34	6	0	0	1	2.9	4	3	3	13	0	0	0	9	22	2	1	3.0	.939	3B-11
1961		23	.229	.417	48	11	3	0	2	4.2	6	9	4	15	0	10	3	12	18	1	3	1.3	.968	3B-15
	3 yrs.	36	.207	.354	82	17	3	0	3	3.7	11	12	7	28	0	10	3	21	40	3	4	1.8	.953	3B-26

Ron Woods

WOODS, RONALD LAWRENCE
B. Feb. 1, 1943, Hamilton, Ohio

BR TR 5'10"   168 lbs.

Year	Team	Games	BA	SA	AB	H	2B	3B	HR	HR%	R	RBI	BB	SO	SB	AB	H	PO	A	E	DP	TC/G	FA	G by Pos
1969	2 teams	DET A	(17G – .267)		NY A	(72G – .175)																		
"	total	89	.183	.263	186	34	5	2	2	1.1	21	10	24	32	2	11	0	135	2	0	0	1.5	1.000	OF-74
1970	NY A	95	.227	.382	225	51	5	3	8	3.6	30	24	33	35	4	19	3	108	6	3	1	1.2	.974	OF-78
1971	2 teams	NY A	(25G – .250)		MON N	(51G – .297)																		
"	total	76	.288	.406	170	49	8	3	2	1.2	30	19	23	20	0	28	5	100	5	2	1	1.4	.981	OF-54
1972	MON N	97	.258	.462	221	57	5	1	10	4.5	21	31	22	33	3	36	7	110	2	1	0	1.2	.991	OF-73
1973		135	.230	.311	318	73	11	3	3	0.9	45	31	56	34	12	28	6	208	7	5	1	1.6	.977	OF-114
1974		90	.205	.228	127	26	0	0	1	0.8	15	12	17	17	6	31	4	75	0	1	0	0.8	.987	OF-61
	6 yrs.	582	.233	.342	1247	290	34	12	26	2.1	162	130	175	171	27	153	25	736	22	12	3	1.3	.984	OF-454

Year	Team	Games	BA	SA	AB	H	2B	3B	HR	HR%	R	RBI	BB	SO	SB	Pinch Hit AB	Pinch Hit H	PO	A	E	DP	TC/G	FA	G by Pos

Walt Woods

WOODS, WALTER SYDNEY   BR TR 5'9½" 165 lbs.
B. Apr. 28, 1875, Rye, N. H. D. Oct. 30, 1951, Portsmouth, N. H.

Year	Team	Games	BA	SA	AB	H	2B	3B	HR	HR%	R	RBI	BB	SO	SB	PH AB	PH H	PO	A	E	DP	TC/G	FA	G by Pos
1898	CHI N	48	.175	.182	154	27	1	0	0	0.0	16	8	4		3	0	0	42	87	15	3	3.0	.896	P-27, OF-11, 2B-6, SS-3, 3B-3
1899	LOU N	42	.151	.198	126	19	1	1	1	0.8	15	14	10		5	0	0	38	108	12	2	3.8	.924	P-26, 2B-11, SS-3, OF-2
1900	PIT N	1	.000	.000	1	0	0	0	0	0.0	0	0	0		0	0	0	0	0	0	0	0.0	–	P-1
3 yrs.		91	.164	.189	281	46	2	1	1	0.4	31	22	14		8	0	0	80	195	27	5	3.3	.911	P-54, 2B-17, OF-13, SS-6, 3B-3

Tracy Woodson

WOODSON, TRACY MICHAEL   BR TR 6'3" 215 lbs.
B. Oct. 5, 1962, Richmond, Va.

Year	Team	Games	BA	SA	AB	H	2B	3B	HR	HR%	R	RBI	BB	SO	SB	PH AB	PH H	PO	A	E	DP	TC/G	FA	G by Pos
1987	LA N	53	.228	.324	136	31	8	1	1	0.7	14	11	9	21	1	4	1	58	58	4	7	2.3	.967	3B-45, 1B-7
1988		65	.249	.335	173	43	4	1	3	1.7	15	15	7	32	1	9	3	160	60	6	13	3.5	.973	3B-41, 1B-25
1989		4	.000	.000	6	0	0	0	0	0.0	0	0	0	1	0	3	0	1	1	0	0	0.5	1.000	3B-1
3 yrs.		122	.235	.324	315	74	12	2	4	1.3	29	26	16	54	2	16	4	219	119	10	20	2.9	.971	3B-87, 1B-32

LEAGUE CHAMPIONSHIP SERIES

Year	Team	Games	BA	SA	AB	H	2B	3B	HR	HR%	R	RBI	BB	SO	SB	PH AB	PH H	PO	A	E	DP	TC/G	FA	G by Pos
1988	LA N	3	.250	.250	4	1	0	0	0	0.0	0	0	0	1	0	2	1	3	0	0	0	1.0	1.000	1B-3

WORLD SERIES

Year	Team	Games	BA	SA	AB	H	2B	3B	HR	HR%	R	RBI	BB	SO	SB	PH AB	PH H	PO	A	E	DP	TC/G	FA	G by Pos
1988	LA N	4	.000	.000	4	0	0	0	0	0.0	0	1	0	0	0	4	0	6	1	0	0	1.8	1.000	1B-3

Woody Woodward

WOODWARD, WILLIAM FREDERICK   BR TR 6'2" 180 lbs.
B. Sept. 23, 1942, Miami, Fla.

Year	Team	Games	BA	SA	AB	H	2B	3B	HR	HR%	R	RBI	BB	SO	SB	PH AB	PH H	PO	A	E	DP	TC/G	FA	G by Pos
1963	MIL N	10	.000	.000	2	0	0	0	0	0.0	1	0	0	0	0	1	0	1	6	0	0	0.7	1.000	SS-5
1964		77	.209	.243	115	24	2	1	0	0.0	18	11	6	28	0	2	0	75	102	5	27	2.4	.973	2B-40, SS-18, 3B-7, 1B-1
1965		112	.208	.264	265	55	7	4	0	0.0	17	11	10	50	2	2	0	150	252	9	62	3.7	.978	SS-107, 2B-8
1966	ATL N	144	.264	.327	455	120	23	3	0	0.0	46	43	37	54	2	1	0	262	399	23	78	4.8	.966	2B-79, SS-73
1967		136	.226	.270	429	97	15	2	0	0.0	30	25	37	51	0	1	0	300	385	11	86	5.1	.984	2B-120, SS-16
1968	2 teams			ATL N	(12G – .167)			CIN N	(56G – .244)															
"	total	68	.231	.252	143	33	3	0	0	0.0	15	11	8	29	2	5	0	71	123	6	20	2.9	.970	SS-47, 2B-10, 3B-2, 1B-1
1969	CIN N	97	.261	.311	241	63	12	0	0	0.0	36	15	24	40	3	0	0	148	249	14	36	4.2	.966	SS-93, 2B-2
1970		100	.223	.288	264	59	8	3	1	0.4	23	14	20	21	1	2	1	131	250	9	55	3.9	.977	SS-77, 3B-20, 2B-10, 1B-2
1971		136	.242	.282	273	66	9	1	0	0.0	22	18	27	28	4	3	1	129	253	7	49	2.9	.982	SS-85, 3B-63, 2B-9
9 yrs.		880	.236	.287	2187	517	79	14	1	0.0	208	148	169	301	14	17	2	1267	2019	84	413	3.8	.975	SS-521, 2B-278, 3B-92, 1B-4

LEAGUE CHAMPIONSHIP SERIES

Year	Team	Games	BA	SA	AB	H	2B	3B	HR	HR%	R	RBI	BB	SO	SB	PH AB	PH H	PO	A	E	DP	TC/G	FA	G by Pos
1970	CIN N	3	.100	.100	10	1	0	0	0	0.0	0	0	1	0	0	0	0	0	0	0	0	0.0	–	SS-3, 3B-3

WORLD SERIES

Year	Team	Games	BA	SA	AB	H	2B	3B	HR	HR%	R	RBI	BB	SO	SB	PH AB	PH H	PO	A	E	DP	TC/G	FA	G by Pos
1970	CIN N	4	.200	.200	5	1	0	0	0	0.0	0	0	0	0	0	1	1	4	5	0	2	2.3	1.000	SS-3

Earl Wooten

WOOTEN, EARL HAZWELL (Junior)   BR TL 5'11" 160 lbs.
B. Jan. 16, 1924, Pelzer, S. C.

Year	Team	Games	BA	SA	AB	H	2B	3B	HR	HR%	R	RBI	BB	SO	SB	PH AB	PH H	PO	A	E	DP	TC/G	FA	G by Pos
1947	WAS A	6	.083	.083	24	2	0	0	0	0.0	1	0	1	4	1	0	0	19	0	2	0	3.5	.905	OF-6
1948		88	.256	.322	258	66	8	3	1	0.4	34	23	24	21	2	8	2	230	18	4	6	2.9	.984	OF-73, 1B-6, P-1
2 yrs.		94	.241	.301	282	68	8	3	1	0.4	34	24	24	25	3	8	2	249	18	6	6	2.9	.978	OF-79, 1B-6, P-1

Chuck Workman

WORKMAN, CHARLES THOMAS   BL TR 6' 175 lbs.
B. Jan. 6, 1915, Leeton, Mo. D. Jan. 3, 1953, Kansas City, Mo.

Year	Team	Games	BA	SA	AB	H	2B	3B	HR	HR%	R	RBI	BB	SO	SB	PH AB	PH H	PO	A	E	DP	TC/G	FA	G by Pos
1938	CLE A	2	.400	.400	5	2	0	0	0	0.0	1	0	0	0	0	1	0	1	0	1	0	1.0	.500	OF-1
1941		9	.000	.000	4	0	0	0	0	0.0	1	0	1	1	0	4	0	0	0	0	0	0.0	–	
1943	BOS N	153	.249	.328	615	153	17	1	10	1.6	71	67	53	72	12	0	0	343	28	6	9	2.5	.984	OF-149, 1B-3, 3B-1
1944		140	.208	.344	418	87	18	3	11	2.6	46	53	42	41	1	16	4	186	60	6	7	1.8	.976	OF-103, 3B-19
1945		139	.274	.459	514	141	16	2	25	4.9	77	87	51	58	9	6	0	150	205	31	18	2.8	.920	3B-107, OF-24
1946	2 teams			BOS N	(25G – .167)			PIT N	(58G – .221)															
"	total	83	.207	.311	193	40	6	1	4	2.1	16	23	14	30	2	24	7	132	5	3	1	1.7	.979	OF-52, 3B-1
6 yrs.		526	.242	.368	1749	423	57	7	50	2.9	213	230	161	202	24	51	11	812	298	47	35	2.2	.959	OF-329, 3B-128, 1B-3

Hank Workman

WORKMAN, HENRY KILGARIFF   BL TR 6'1" 185 lbs.
B. Feb. 5, 1926, Los Angeles, Calif.

Year	Team	Games	BA	SA	AB	H	2B	3B	HR	HR%	R	RBI	BB	SO	SB	PH AB	PH H	PO	A	E	DP	TC/G	FA	G by Pos
1950	NY A	2	.200	.200	5	1	0	0	0	0.0	1	0	0	1	0	1	0	6	0	0	1	3.0	1.000	1B-1

Craig Worthington

WORTHINGTON, CRAIG RICHARD   BR TR 6' 160 lbs.
B. Apr. 17, 1965, Los Angeles, Calif.

Year	Team	Games	BA	SA	AB	H	2B	3B	HR	HR%	R	RBI	BB	SO	SB	PH AB	PH H	PO	A	E	DP	TC/G	FA	G by Pos
1988	BAL A	26	.185	.284	81	15	2	0	2	2.5	5	4	9	24	1	0	0	20	53	3	4	2.9	.961	3B-26
1989		145	.247	.384	497	123	23	0	15	3.0	57	70	61	114	1	0	0	113	277	20	22	2.8	.951	3B-145
2 yrs.		171	.239	.370	578	138	25	0	17	2.9	62	74	70	138	2	0	0	133	330	23	26	2.8	.953	3B-171

Red Worthington

WORTHINGTON, ROBERT LEE (Bob)   BR TR 5'11" 170 lbs.
B. Apr. 24, 1906, Alhambra, Calif. D. Dec. 8, 1963, Sepulveda, Calif.

Year	Team	Games	BA	SA	AB	H	2B	3B	HR	HR%	R	RBI	BB	SO	SB	PH AB	PH H	PO	A	E	DP	TC/G	FA	G by Pos
1931	BOS N	128	.291	.407	491	143	25	10	4	0.8	47	44	26	38	1	4	0	242	8	3	1	2.0	.988	OF-124
1932		105	.303	.476	435	132	35	8	8	1.8	62	61	15	24	1	1	0	216	8	3	2	2.2	.987	OF-104
1933		17	.156	.244	45	7	4	0	0	0.0	3	0	1	3	0	7	0	17	1	2	0	1.2	.900	OF-10
1934	2 teams			BOS N	(41G – .246)			STL N	(1G – .000)															
"	total	42	.242	.318	66	16	5	0	0	0.0	6	6	6	6	0	27	8	23	0	2	0	0.6	.920	OF-11
4 yrs.		292	.287	.423	1037	298	69	18	12	1.2	118	111	48	71	2	39	8	498	17	10	3	1.8	.981	OF-249

Chuck Wortman

WORTMAN, WILLIAM LEWIS   BR TR 5'7" 150 lbs.
B. Jan. 5, 1892, Baltimore, Md. D. Aug. 19, 1977, Las Vegas, Nev.

Year	Team	Games	BA	SA	AB	H	2B	3B	HR	HR%	R	RBI	BB	SO	SB	PH AB	PH H	PO	A	E	DP	TC/G	FA	G by Pos
1916	CHI N	69	.201	.261	234	47	4	2	2	0.9	17	16	18	22	4	0	0	124	191	32	24	5.0	.908	SS-69
1917		75	.174	.205	190	33	4	1	0	0.0	24	9	18	23	6	0	0	85	164	22	26	3.6	.919	SS-65, 3B-1, 2B-1

Year	Team	Games	BA	SA	AB	H	2B	3B	HR	HR%	R	RBI	BB	SO	SB	Pinch Hit AB	Pinch Hit H	PO	A	E	DP	TC/G	FA	G by Pos

Chuck Wortman *continued*

Year	Team	Games	BA	SA	AB	H	2B	3B	HR	HR%	R	RBI	BB	SO	SB	AB	H	PO	A	E	DP	TC/G	FA	G by Pos
1918		17	.118	.294	17	2	0	0	1	5.9	4	3	1	2	3	0	0	13	13	3	1	1.7	.897	2B-8, SS-4
3 yrs.		161	.186	.238	441	82	8	3	3	0.7	45	28	37	47	13	0	0	222	368	57	51	4.0	.912	SS-138, 2B-9, 3B-1

WORLD SERIES

| 1918 | CHI N | 1 | .000 | .000 | 1 | 0 | 0 | 0 | 0 | 0.0 | 0 | 0 | 0 | 0 | 0 | 0 | 0 | 1 | 0 | 0 | 0 | 1.0 | 1.000 | 2B-1 |

Ron Wotus

WOTUS, RONALD ALLAN   BR TR 6'1"   165 lbs.
B. Mar. 3, 1961, Hartford, Conn.

1983	PIT N	5	.000	.000	3	0	0	0	0	0.0	0	0	0	1	0	2	0	2	2	0	1	0.8	1.000	SS-2, 2B-1
1984		27	.218	.327	55	12	6	0	0	0.0	4	2	6	8	0	2	1	28	72	2	12	3.8	.980	SS-17, 2B-7
2 yrs.		32	.207	.310	58	12	6	0	0	0.0	4	2	6	9	0	4	1	30	74	2	13	3.3	.981	SS-19, 2B-8

Jimmy Woulfe

WOULFE, JAMES JOSEPH   TR 5'11"
B. Nov. 25, 1859, New Orleans, La.   D. Dec. 20, 1924, New Orleans, La.

| 1884 | 2 teams | | CIN AA (8G – .147) | | PIT AA (15G – .113) | | | | | | | | | | | | | | | | | | | |
| " | total | 23 | .126 | .161 | 87 | 11 | 1 | 0 | 0 | 0.0 | 10 | | 1 | | | 0 | 0 | 32 | 4 | 10 | 2 | 2.0 | .783 | OF-22, 3B-1 |

Ab Wright

WRIGHT, ALBERT OWEN   BR TR 6'1½"   190 lbs.
B. Nov. 16, 1905, Terlton, Okla.

1935	CLE A	67	.238	.356	160	38	11	1	2	1.3	17	18	10	17	2	20	3	56	4	1	0	0.9	.984	OF-47
1944	BOS N	71	.256	.410	195	50	9	0	7	3.6	20	35	18	31	0	23	5	88	2	3	1	1.3	.968	OF-47
2 yrs.		138	.248	.386	355	88	20	1	9	2.5	37	53	28	48	2	43	8	144	6	4	1	1.1	.974	OF-94

Al Wright

WRIGHT, ALBERT EDGAR   BR TR 6'2"   168 lbs.
B. Nov. 11, 1912, San Francisco, Calif.

| 1933 | BOS N | 4 | 1.000 | 1.000 | 1 | 1 | 0 | 0 | 0 | 0.0 | 0 | 0 | 0 | 0 | 0 | 0 | 0 | 1 | 0 | 1 | 0 | 0.5 | .500 | 2B-3 |

Bill Wright

WRIGHT, WILLIAM H.
Deceased.

| 1887 | WAS N | 1 | .667 | .667 | 3 | 2 | 0 | 0 | 0 | 0.0 | 0 | | 0 | | | 0 | 0 | 7 | 0 | 2 | 0 | 9.0 | .778 | C-1 |

Ceylon Wright

WRIGHT, CEYLON   BL TR 5'9"   150 lbs.
B. Aug. 16, 1893, Minneapolis, Minn.   D. Nov. 7, 1947, Hines, Ill.

| 1916 | CHI A | 8 | .000 | .000 | 18 | 0 | 0 | 0 | 0 | 0.0 | 0 | 0 | 1 | 7 | 0 | 0 | 0 | 8 | 19 | 5 | 2 | 4.0 | .844 | SS-8 |

Dick Wright

WRIGHT, WILLARD JAMES   BR TR 5'10"   170 lbs.
B. May 5, 1890, Worcester, N. Y.   D. Jan. 24, 1952, Bethlehem, Pa.

| 1915 | BKN F | 4 | .000 | .000 | 5 | 0 | 0 | 0 | 0 | 0.0 | 0 | | 0 | 1 | 0 | 0 | 0 | 5 | 0 | 1 | 0 | 1.5 | .833 | C-3 |

George Wright

WRIGHT, GEORGE   BR TR 5'9½"   150 lbs.
Brother of Harry Wright.   Brother of Sam Wright.
B. Jan. 28, 1847, Yonkers, N. Y.   D. Aug. 21, 1937, Boston, Mass.
Manager 1879.
Hall of Fame 1937.

1876	BOS N	70	.299	.397	335	100	18	6	1	0.3	72	34	8	9		0	0	96	253	44	16	5.6	.888	SS-68, 2B-2, P-1
1877		61	.276	.334	290	80	15	1	0	0.0	58	35	9	15		0	0	175	217	55	29	7.3	.877	2B-58, SS-3
1878		59	.225	.251	267	60	5	1	0	0.0	35	12	6	22		0	0	72	197	15	24	4.8	.947	SS-59
1879	PRO N	85	.276	.374	388	107	15	10	1	0.3	79	42	13	20		0	0	96	319	34	17	5.3	.924	SS-85
1880	BOS N	1	.250	.250	4	1	0	0	0	0.0	2	0	0	0		0	0	0	3	0	0	3.0	1.000	SS-1
1881		7	.200	.200	25	5	0	0	0	0.0	4		3	1		0	0	7	19	1	3	3.9	.963	SS-7
1882	PRO N	46	.162	.189	185	30	1	2	0	0.0	14		4	36		0	0	46	133	26	16	4.5	.873	SS-46
7 yrs.		329	.256	.323	1494	383	54	20	2	0.1	264	123	43	103		0	0	492	1141	175	105	5.5	.903	SS-269, 2B-60, P-1

George Wright

WRIGHT, GEORGE DEWITT   BB TR 5'11"   180 lbs.
B. Dec. 22, 1958, Oklahoma City, Okla.

1982	TEX A	150	.264	.377	557	147	20	5	11	2.0	69	50	30	78	3	0	0	398	14	8	3	2.8	.981	OF-149
1983		162	.276	.424	634	175	28	6	18	2.8	79	80	41	82	8	2	0	460	6	7	1	2.9	.985	OF-161
1984		101	.243	.384	383	93	19	4	9	2.3	40	48	15	54	0	2	0	175	3	3	0	1.8	.983	OF-80, DH-18
1985		109	.190	.242	363	69	13	0	2	0.6	21	18	25	49	4	4	0	213	8	2	2	2.0	.991	OF-102, DH-4
1986	2 teams		TEX A (49G – .217)		MON N (56G – .188)																			
"	total	105	.202	.291	223	45	8	3	2	0.9	22	12	15	51	4	35	2	109	4	2	0	1.1	.983	OF-74, DH-1
5 yrs.		627	.245	.361	2160	529	88	18	42	1.9	231	208	126	314	19	43	2	1355	35	22	6	2.3	.984	OF-566, DH-23

Glenn Wright

WRIGHT, FORREST GLENN (Buckshot)   BR TR 5'11"   170 lbs.
B. Feb. 6, 1901, Archie, Mo.   D. Apr. 6, 1984, Olathe, Kans.

1924	PIT N	153	.287	.425	616	177	28	18	7	1.1	80	111	27	52	14	0	0	310	601	52	102	6.3	.946	SS-153
1925		153	.308	.480	614	189	32	10	18	2.9	97	121	31	32	3	0	0	338	530	56	109	6.0	.939	SS-153, 3B-1
1926		119	.308	.459	458	141	15	15	8	1.7	73	77	19	26	6	3	0	242	382	49	82	5.7	.927	SS-116
1927		143	.281	.388	570	160	26	4	9	1.6	78	105	39	46	4	0	0	296	430	45	82	5.4	.942	SS-143
1928		108	.310	.457	407	126	20	8	8	2.0	63	66	21	53	3	6	1	195	301	39	59	5.0	.927	SS-101, OF-1, 1B-1
1929	BKN N	24	.200	.320	25	5	0	0	1	4.0	4	6	3	6	0	17	2	2	2	2	0	0.3	.667	SS-3
1930		135	.321	.543	532	171	28	12	22	4.1	83	126	32	70	2	1	0	297	462	28	97	5.8	.964	SS-134
1931		77	.284	.448	268	76	9	4	9	3.4	36	32	14	35	1	2	0	151	255	25	52	5.6	.942	SS-75
1932		127	.274	.433	446	122	31	5	10	2.2	50	60	12	57	4	4	0	235	387	40	84	5.2	.940	SS-122, 1B-2
1933		71	.255	.339	192	49	13	0	1	0.5	19	18	11	24	1	9	2	161	134	19	35	4.4	.939	SS-51, 1B-9, 3B-2
1935	CHI A	9	.120	.160	25	3	1	0	0	0.0	1	1	0	2	0	2	0	13	20	2	3	3.9	.943	2B-7
11 yrs.		1119	.294	.446	4153	1219	203	76	93	2.2	584	723	209	407	38	44	5	2240	3504	357	705	5.5	.941	SS-1051, 1B-12, 2B-7, 3B-3, OF-1

Year	Team	Games	BA	SA	AB	H	2B	3B	HR	HR%	R	RBI	BB	SO	SB	Pinch Hit AB	Pinch Hit H	PO	A	E	DP	TC/G	FA	G by Pos

Glenn Wright *continued*

WORLD SERIES

Year	Team	Games	BA	SA	AB	H	2B	3B	HR	HR%	R	RBI	BB	SO	SB	AB	H	PO	A	E	DP	TC/G	FA	G by Pos
1925	PIT N	7	.185	.333	27	5	1	0	1	3.7	3	3	1	4	0	0	0	11	24	2	0	5.3	.946	SS-7
1927		4	.154	.154	13	2	0	0	0	0.0	1	2	0	0	0	0	0	5	13	1	2	4.8	.947	SS-4
2 yrs.		11	.175	.275	40	7	1	0	1	2.5	4	5	1	4	0	0	0	16	37	3	2	5.1	.946	SS-11

Harry Wright

WRIGHT, WILLIAM HENRY BR TR 5'9½" 157 lbs.
Brother of Sam Wright. Brother of George Wright.
B. Jan. 10, 1835, Sheffield, England D. Oct. 3, 1895, Atlantic City, N. J.
Manager 1871-93.
Hall of Fame 1953.

Year	Team	Games	BA	SA	AB	H	2B	3B	HR	HR%	R	RBI	BB	SO	SB	AB	H	PO	A	E	DP	TC/G	FA	G by Pos
1876	BOS N	1	.000	.000	3	0	0	0	0	0.0	0	0	0	1		0	0	0	0	0	0	0.0	–	OF-1
1877		1	.000	.000	4	0	0	0	0	0.0	0	0	0	1		0	0	1	1	1	1	3.0	.667	OF-1
2 yrs.		2	.000	.000	7	0	0	0	0	0.0	0	0	0	2		0	0	1	1	1	1	1.5	.667	OF-2

Joe Wright

WRIGHT, JOSEPH BL TL 5'8" 175 lbs.
B. 1873, Pittsburgh, Pa. Deceased.

Year	Team	Games	BA	SA	AB	H	2B	3B	HR	HR%	R	RBI	BB	SO	SB	AB	H	PO	A	E	DP	TC/G	FA	G by Pos
1895	LOU N	60	.276	.368	228	63	10	4	1	0.4	30	30	12	28	7	0	0	127	4	5	1	2.3	.963	OF-59, C-1
1896 2 teams	LOU N (2G – .286)		PIT N (15G – .308)																					
" total		17	.305	.373	59	18	2	1	0	0.0	5	6	1	3	1	2	1	26	0	1	0	1.6	.963	OF-14, 3B-1
2 yrs.		77	.282	.369	287	81	12	5	1	0.3	35	36	13	31	8	2	1	153	4	6	1	2.1	.963	OF-73, 3B-1, C-1

Pat Wright

WRIGHT, PATRICK W. BB TR 6'2" 190 lbs.
B. July 5, 1868, Pottsville, Pa. D. May 29, 1943, Springfield, Ill.

Year	Team	Games	BA	SA	AB	H	2B	3B	HR	HR%	R	RBI	BB	SO	SB	AB	H	PO	A	E	DP	TC/G	FA	G by Pos
1890	CHI N	1	.000	.000	2	0	0	0	0	0.0	0	0	1	0	0	0	0	1	3	0	0	4.0	1.000	2B-1

Rasty Wright

WRIGHT, WILLIAM SMITH 6'1" 258 lbs.
B. Jan. 31, 1863, Birmingham, Mich. D. Oct. 14, 1922, Duluth, Minn.

Year	Team	Games	BA	SA	AB	H	2B	3B	HR	HR%	R	RBI	BB	SO	SB	AB	H	PO	A	E	DP	TC/G	FA	G by Pos
1890 2 teams	SYR AA (88G – .305)		CLE N (13G – .111)																					
" total		101	.282	.341	393	111	11	6	0	0.0	89	2	81	4	33	0	0	191	16	21	7	2.3	.908	OF-101

Sam Wright

WRIGHT, SAMUEL BR TR 5'7½" 146 lbs.
Brother of Harry Wright. Brother of George Wright.
B. Nov. 25, 1848, New York, N. Y. D. May 6, 1928, Boston, Mass.

Year	Team	Games	BA	SA	AB	H	2B	3B	HR	HR%	R	RBI	BB	SO	SB	AB	H	PO	A	E	DP	TC/G	FA	G by Pos
1876	BOS N	2	.125	.125	8	1	0	0	0	0.0	0	0	0	0		0	0	1	6	2	0	4.5	.778	SS-2
1880	CIN N	9	.088	.088	34	3	0	0	0	0.0	0	0	0	5		0	0	5	27	4	0	4.0	.889	SS-9
1881	BOS N	1	.250	.250	4	1	0	0	0	0.0	0	0	0	0		0	0	1	3	2	0	6.0	.667	SS-1
3 yrs.		12	.109	.109	46	5	0	0	0	0.0	0	0	0	5		0	0	7	36	8	0	4.3	.843	SS-12

Taffy Wright

WRIGHT, TAFT SHEDRON BL TR 5'10" 180 lbs.
B. Aug. 10, 1911, Tabor City, N. C. D. Oct. 22, 1981, Orlando, Fla.

Year	Team	Games	BA	SA	AB	H	2B	3B	HR	HR%	R	RBI	BB	SO	SB	AB	H	PO	A	E	DP	TC/G	FA	G by Pos
1938	WAS A	100	.350	.517	263	92	18	10	2	0.8	37	36	13	17	1	**39**	**13**	107	3	2	3	1.1	.982	OF-60
1939		129	.309	.435	499	154	29	11	4	0.8	77	93	38	19	1	6	3	236	10	13	4	2.0	.950	OF-123
1940	CHI A	147	.337	.448	581	196	31	9	5	0.9	79	86	43	25	4	2	1	278	11	11	2	2.0	.963	OF-144
1941		136	.322	.468	513	165	35	5	10	1.9	71	97	60	27	5	1	0	279	8	8	3	2.2	.973	OF-134
1942		85	.333	.410	300	100	13	5	0	0.0	43	47	48	9	1	4	1	176	6	6	1	2.2	.968	OF-81
1946		115	.275	.389	422	116	19	4	7	1.7	46	52	42	17	10	7	2	217	5	2	0	1.9	.991	OF-107
1947		124	.324	.387	401	130	13	0	4	1.0	54	48	48	17	8	18	3	198	6	6	1	1.7	.971	OF-100
1948		134	.279	.365	455	127	15	6	4	0.9	50	61	39	18	2	19	6	227	9	3	3	1.8	.987	OF-114
1949	PHI A	59	.235	.356	149	35	2	5	2	1.3	14	25	16	6	0	19	3	60	5	2	0	1.1	.970	OF-35
9 yrs.		1029	.311	.423	3583	1115	175	55	38	1.1	465	553	347	155	32	115	32	1778	63	53	17	1.8	.972	OF-898

Tom Wright

WRIGHT, THOMAS EVERETTE BL TR 5'11½" 180 lbs.
B. Sept. 22, 1923, Shelby, N. C.

Year	Team	Games	BA	SA	AB	H	2B	3B	HR	HR%	R	RBI	BB	SO	SB	AB	H	PO	A	E	DP	TC/G	FA	G by Pos
1948	BOS A	3	.500	1.500	2	1	0	1	0	0.0	1	0	0	0	0	2	1	0	0	0	0	0.0	–	
1949		5	.250	.500	4	1	1	0	0	0.0	0	1	1	1	0	4	1	0	0	0	0	0.0	–	
1950		54	.318	.383	107	34	7	0	0	0.0	17	20	6	18	0	28	7	40	1	2	1	0.8	.953	OF-24
1951		28	.222	.317	63	14	1	1	1	1.6	8	9	11	8	0	10	1	19	0	1	0	0.7	.950	OF-18
1952 2 teams	STL A (29G – .242)		CHI A (60G – .258)																					
" total		89	.253	.354	198	50	10	2	2	1.0	21	27	28	36	2	34	**10**	98	4	3	0	1.2	.971	OF-52
1953	CHI A	77	.250	.379	132	33	5	3	2	1.5	14	25	12	21	0	42	13	44	1	1	0	0.6	.978	OF-33
1954	WAS A	76	.246	.333	171	42	4	4	1	0.6	13	17	18	38	0	32	8	84	0	0	0	1.1	1.000	OF-43
1955		7	.000	.000	7	0	0	0	0	0.0	0	0	0	1	0	7	0	0	0	0	0	0.0	–	
1956		2	.000	.000	1	0	0	0	0	0.0	0	0	0	0	0	1	0	0	0	0	0	0.0	–	
9 yrs.		341	.255	.355	685	175	28	11	6	0.9	75	99	76	123	2	160	41	285	6	7	1	0.9	.977	OF-170

Russ Wrightstone

WRIGHTSTONE, RUSSELL GUY BL TR 5'10½" 176 lbs.
B. Mar. 18, 1893, Bowmansdale, Pa. D. Feb. 25, 1969, Harrisburg, Pa.

Year	Team	Games	BA	SA	AB	H	2B	3B	HR	HR%	R	RBI	BB	SO	SB	AB	H	PO	A	E	DP	TC/G	FA	G by Pos
1920	PHI N	76	.262	.345	206	54	6	1	3	1.5	23	17	10	25	3	16	4	76	109	13	7	2.6	.934	3B-56, SS-2, 2B-1
1921		109	.296	.425	372	110	13	4	9	2.4	59	51	18	20	4	12	2	135	134	19	6	2.6	.934	3B-54, OF-37, 2B-4
1922		99	.305	.441	331	101	18	6	5	1.5	56	33	28	17	4	20	3	118	227	11	29	3.6	.969	3B-40, SS-35, 1B-2
1923		119	.273	.416	392	107	21	7	7	1.8	59	57	21	19	5	16	5	132	216	15	30	3.1	.959	3B-72, SS-21, 2B-9
1924		118	.307	.443	388	119	24	4	7	1.8	55	58	27	15	5	9	2	139	197	21	23	3.0	.941	3B-97, 2B-9, SS-5, OF-1
1925		72	.346	.591	286	99	18	5	14	4.9	48	61	19	18	0	7	6	152	62	16	11	3.2	.930	OF-45, SS-12, 3B-11, 2B-10, 1B-6
1926		112	.307	.432	368	113	23	4	7	1.9	55	57	27	11	5	0	0	549	125	19	64	6.2	.973	1B-53, 3B-37, 2B-13, OF-5
1927		141	.306	.403	533	163	24	5	6	1.1	62	75	48	20	9	3	0	1268	90	15	114	9.7	.989	1B-136, 3B-1, 2B-1
1928 2 teams	PHI N (33G – .209)		NY N (30G – .160)																					
" total		63	.198	.310	116	23	5	1	2	1.7	10	16	17	7	0	28	4	53	8	5	1	1.0	.918	
9 yrs.		909	.297	.431	2992	889	152	34	60	2.0	427	425	215	152	35	115	28	2622	1163	134	285	4.3	.966	3B-368, 1B-203, OF-114, SS-75, 2B-47

Year	Team		Games	BA	SA	AB	H	2B	3B	HR	HR%	R	RBI	BB	SO	SB	Pinch Hit AB	Pinch Hit H	PO	A	E	DP	TC/G	FA	G by Pos

Zeke Wrigley

WRIGLEY, GEORGE WATSON   B. Jan. 18, 1874, Philadelphia, Pa.   D. Sept. 28, 1952, Philadelphia, Pa.   5'8½"   150 lbs.

Year	Team		Games	BA	SA	AB	H	2B	3B	HR	HR%	R	RBI	BB	SO	SB	PH AB	PH H	PO	A	E	DP	TC/G	FA	G by Pos
1896	WAS	N	5	.111	.111	9	1	0	0	0	0.0	0	2	1		1	0	1	4	15	1	0	4.0	.950	2B-3, SS-1
1897			104	.284	.384	388	110	14	8	3	0.8	65	64	21		5	0	0	175	209	50	18	4.2	.885	OF-36, SS-33, 3B-30, 2B-9
1898			111	.245	.333	400	98	9	10	2	0.5	50	39	20		10	0	0	284	358	72	45	6.4	.899	SS-97, 2B-11, OF-3, 3B-1
1899	NY	N	(4G – .200)			BKN	N	(15G – .204)																	
"	total		19	.203	.297	64	13	2	2	0	0.0	5	12	4		3	0	0	35	42	12	4	4.7	.865	SS-14, 3B-5
4 yrs.			239	.258	.351	861	222	25	20	5	0.6	121	117	46	1	18	1	0	498	624	135	67	5.3	.893	SS-145, OF-39, 3B-36, 2B-23

Rick Wrona

WRONA, RICHARD JAMES   B. Dec. 10, 1963, Tulsa, Okla.   BR TR 6'1"   185 lbs.

Year	Team		Games	BA	SA	AB	H	2B	3B	HR	HR%	R	RBI	BB	SO	SB	PH AB	PH H	PO	A	E	DP	TC/G	FA	G by Pos
1988	CHI	N	4	.000	.000	6	0	0	0	0	0.0	0	0	0	0	0	1	0	11	1	0	0	3.0	1.000	C-2
1989			38	.283	.391	92	26	2	1	2	2.2	11	14	2	21	0	3	2	158	15	3	1	4.6	.983	C-37
2 yrs.			42	.265	.367	98	26	2	1	2	2.0	11	14	2	22	0	4	2	169	16	3	1	4.5	.984	C-39

LEAGUE CHAMPIONSHIP SERIES

| 1989 | CHI | N | 2 | .000 | .000 | 5 | 0 | 0 | 0 | 0 | 0.0 | 0 | 0 | 0 | 3 | 0 | 0 | 0 | 9 | 1 | 0 | 0 | 5.0 | 1.000 | C-2 |

Yats Wuestling

WUESTLING, GEORGE   B. Oct. 18, 1903, St. Louis, Mo.   D. Apr. 26, 1970, St. Louis, Mo.   BR TR 5'11"   167 lbs.

Year	Team		Games	BA	SA	AB	H	2B	3B	HR	HR%	R	RBI	BB	SO	SB	PH AB	PH H	PO	A	E	DP	TC/G	FA	G by Pos
1929	DET	A	54	.200	.240	150	30	4	1	0	0.0	13	16	9	24	0	0	0	78	140	13	19	4.3	.944	SS-52, 3B-1, 2B-1
1930	2 teams		DET	A	(4G – .000)	NY	A	(25G – .190)																	
"	total		29	.164	.194	67	11	0	1	0	0.0	5	3	6	17	0	0	0	41	54	8	12	3.6	.922	SS-25, 3B-3
2 yrs.			83	.189	.226	217	41	4	2	0	0.0	18	19	15	41	0	0	0	119	194	21	31	4.0	.937	SS-77, 3B-4, 2B-1

Joe Wyatt

WYATT, LORAL JOHN   B. Apr. 6, 1900, Petersburg, Ind.   D. Dec. 5, 1970, Oblong, Ill.   BR TR 6'1"   175 lbs.

Year	Team		Games	BA	SA	AB	H	2B	3B	HR	HR%	R	RBI	BB	SO	SB	PH AB	PH H	PO	A	E	DP	TC/G	FA	G by Pos
1924	CLE	A	4	.182	.182	11	2	0	0	0	0.0	1	1	2	1	0	0	0	5	0	1	0	1.5	.833	OF-4

Ren Wylie

WYLIE, JAMES RENWICK   B. Dec. 14, 1861, Elizabeth, Pa.   D. Aug. 17, 1951, Wilkinsburg, Pa.   BR TR 5'11"   155 lbs.

Year	Team		Games	BA	SA	AB	H	2B	3B	HR	HR%	R	RBI	BB	SO	SB	PH AB	PH H	PO	A	E	DP	TC/G	FA	G by Pos
1882	PIT	AA	1	.000	.000	3	0	0	0	0	0.0	0		0			0	0	1	0	1	0	1.0	1.000	OF-1

Frank Wyman

WYMAN, FRANK C.   B. May 10, 1862, Haverhill, Mass.   D. Feb. 4, 1916, Everett, Mass.

Year	Team		Games	BA	SA	AB	H	2B	3B	HR	HR%	R	RBI	BB	SO	SB	PH AB	PH H	PO	A	E	DP	TC/G	FA	G by Pos
1884	2 teams		KC	U	(30G – .218)	CHI	U	(2G – .375)																	
"	total		32	.227	.258	132	30	4	0	0	0.0	17		3			0	0	90	19	26	4	4.2	.807	OF-25, 1B-5, 3B-3, P-3

Butch Wynegar

WYNEGAR, HAROLD DELANO   B. Mar. 14, 1956, York, Pa.   BB TR 6'1"   190 lbs.

Year	Team		Games	BA	SA	AB	H	2B	3B	HR	HR%	R	RBI	BB	SO	SB	PH AB	PH H	PO	A	E	DP	TC/G	FA	G by Pos
1976	MIN	A	149	.260	.363	534	139	21	2	10	1.9	58	69	79	63	0	3	1	650	78	16	6	5.0	.978	C-137, DH-15
1977			144	.261	.370	532	139	22	3	10	1.9	76	79	68	61	2	5	2	676	84	5	8	5.3	.993	C-142, 3B-1
1978			135	.229	.308	454	104	22	1	4	0.9	36	45	47	42	1	8	1	582	70	8	12	4.8	.988	C-131, 3B-1
1979			149	.270	.351	504	136	20	0	7	1.4	74	57	74	36	2	2	0	653	65	6	10	4.9	.992	C-146, DH-2
1980			146	.255	.335	486	124	18	3	5	1.0	61	57	63	36	3	8	2	670	72	9	13	5.1	.988	C-142, DH-1
1981			47	.247	.280	150	37	5	0	0	0.0	11	10	17	9	0	2	0	162	24	1	4	4.0	.995	C-37, DH-9
1982	2 teams		MIN	A	(24G – .209)	NY	A	(63G – .293)																	
"	total		87	.267	.361	277	74	12	1	4	1.4	36	28	50	33	0	2	0	523	26	5	10	6.4	.991	C-86
1983	NY	A	94	.296	.429	301	89	18	2	6	2.0	40	42	52	29	1	4	0	480	29	8	4	5.5	.985	C-93
1984			129	.267	.342	442	118	13	1	6	1.4	48	45	64	36	1	7	1	757	59	6	9	6.4	.993	C-126
1985			102	.223	.320	309	69	15	0	5	1.6	27	32	64	43	0	8	3	547	34	6	7	5.8	.990	C-96
1986			61	.206	.345	194	40	4	1	7	3.6	19	29	30	21	0	8	3	325	22	2	1	5.7	.994	C-57
1987	CAL	A	31	.207	.228	92	19	2	0	0	0.0	4	5	9	13	0	3	0	162	12	1	3	5.6	.994	C-28, DH-1
1988			27	.255	.418	55	14	4	1	1	1.8	8	8	8	7	0	4	1	94	8	2	1	3.9	.981	C-26
13 yrs.			1301	.255	.347	4330	1102	176	15	65	1.5	498	506	625	429	10	64	14	6281	583	75	88	5.3	.989	C-1247, DH-28, 3B-2

Early Wynn

WYNN, EARLY (Gus)   B. Jan. 6, 1920, Hartford, Ala.   Hall of Fame 1972.   BB TR 6'   190 lbs.   BR 1939-44

Year	Team		Games	BA	SA	AB	H	2B	3B	HR	HR%	R	RBI	BB	SO	SB	PH AB	PH H	PO	A	E	DP	TC/G	FA	G by Pos
1939	WAS	A	3	.167	.167	6	1	0	0	0	0.0	0	1	1	1	0	0	0	1	0	0	0	0.3	1.000	P-3
1941			5	.133	.200	15	2	1	0	0	0.0	1	0	0	5	0	0	0	2	9	1	1	2.4	.917	P-5
1942			30	.217	.246	69	15	2	0	0	0.0	4	7	3	13	0	0	0	5	36	2	3	1.4	.953	P-30
1943			38	.296	.378	98	29	3	1	1	1.0	6	11	1	11	0	1	0	5	49	3	3	1.5	.947	P-37
1944			43	.207	.261	92	19	2	0	1	1.1	4	6	3	21	0	11	1	4	31	1	4	0.8	.972	P-33
1946			25	.319	.426	47	15	2	0	1	2.1	4	9	5	7	0	6	3	7	18	1	2	1.0	.962	P-17
1947			54	.275	.375	120	33	6	0	2	1.7	6	13	1	19	0	20	6	15	33	1	3	0.9	.980	P-33
1948			73	.217	.264	106	23	3	1	0	0.0	9	16	14	22	0	32	3	6	32	2	1	0.5	.950	P-33
1949	CLE	A	35	.143	.200	70	10	1	0	1	1.4	3	7	4	10	0	7	0	16	31	0	3	1.3	1.000	P-26
1950			39	.234	.403	77	18	5	1	2	2.6	12	10	10	12	0	5	1	5	36	3	5	1.1	.932	P-32
1951			41	.185	.306	108	20	8	1	1	0.9	8	13	7	17	0	3	0	13	42	1	2	1.4	.982	P-37
1952			44	.222	.242	99	22	2	0	0	0.0	5	10	9	15	0	2	1	20	46	4	2	1.6	.943	P-42
1953			37	.275	.396	91	25	2	0	3	3.3	11	10	7	17	0	1	0	11	36	0	2	1.3	1.000	P-36
1954			40	.183	.215	93	17	3	0	0	0.0	10	4	7	13	0	0	0	17	27	2	1	1.2	.957	P-40
1955			34	.179	.250	84	15	3	0	1	1.2	8	7	6	17	0	2	0	7	27	2	0	1.1	.944	P-32
1956			38	.228	.307	101	23	5	0	1	1.0	5	15	7	22	1	0	0	15	48	3	1	1.7	.955	P-38
1957			40	.116	.116	86	10	0	0	0	0.0	4	4	11	23	0	0	0	10	38	0	6	1.2	1.000	P-40
1958	CHI	A	40	.200	.213	75	15	1	0	0	0.0	7	11	10	25	0	0	0	12	25	0	2	0.9	1.000	P-40
1959			37	.244	.389	90	22	3	2	2	2.2	11	8	9	18	0	0	0	6	39	2	1	1.3	.957	P-37
1960			36	.200	.293	75	15	2	1	1	1.3	8	7	14	17	0	0	0	7	28	1	1	1.0	.972	P-36
1961			17	.162	.162	37	6	0	0	0	0.0	4	2	3	11	0	0	0	4	11	0	0	0.9	1.000	P-17

Year	Team		Games	BA	SA	AB	H	2B	3B	HR	HR%	R	RBI	BB	SO	SB	Pinch Hit AB	Pinch Hit H	PO	A	E	DP	TC/G	FA	G by Pos

Early Wynn *continued*

Year	Team		Games	BA	SA	AB	H	2B	3B	HR	HR%	R	RBI	BB	SO	SB	AB	H	PO	A	E	DP	TC/G	FA	G by Pos
1962			27	.130	.148	54	7	1	0	0	0.0	5	2	7	17	0	0	0	3	20	0	2	0.9	1.000	P-27
1963	CLE	A	20	.273	.273	11	3	0	0	0	0.0	1	0	2	5	0	0	0	2	8	0	0	0.5	1.000	P-20
23 yrs.			796	.214	.285	1704	365	59	5	17	1.0	136	173	141	330	1	90	15	193	670	29	47	1.1	.967	P-691

WORLD SERIES

Year	Team		Games	BA	SA	AB	H	2B	3B	HR	HR%	R	RBI	BB	SO	SB	AB	H	PO	A	E	DP	TC/G	FA	G by Pos
1954	CLE	A	1	.500	1.000	2	1	1	0	0	0.0	0	0	0	1	0	0	0	1	1	0	0	2.0	1.000	P-1
1959	CHI	A	3	.200	.400	5	1	1	0	0	0.0	0	1	0	2	0	0	0	1	3	0	0	1.3	1.000	P-3
2 yrs.			4	.286	.571	7	2	2	0	0	0.0	0	1	0	3	0	0	0	2	4	0	0	1.5	1.000	P-4

Jimmy Wynn

WYNN, JAMES SHERMAN (The Toy Cannon)
B. Mar. 12, 1942, Hamilton, Ohio — BR TR 5'10" 160 lbs.

Year	Team		Games	BA	SA	AB	H	2B	3B	HR	HR%	R	RBI	BB	SO	SB	AB	H	PO	A	E	DP	TC/G	FA	G by Pos
1963	HOU	N	70	.244	.372	250	61	10	5	4	1.6	31	27	30	53	4	1	0	124	33	8	3	2.4	.952	OF-53, SS-21, 3B-2
1964			67	.224	.324	219	49	7	0	5	2.3	19	18	24	58	5	3	0	129	8	6	3	2.1	.958	OF-64
1965			157	.275	.470	564	155	30	7	22	3.9	90	73	84	126	43	3	0	382	13	9	1	2.6	.978	OF-155
1966			105	.256	.440	418	107	21	1	18	4.3	62	62	41	81	13	0	0	259	6	6	4	2.6	.978	OF-104
1967			158	.249	.495	594	148	29	3	37	6.2	102	107	74	137	16	1	0	364	4	12	1	2.4	.968	OF-157
1968			156	.269	.474	542	146	23	5	26	4.8	85	67	90	131	11	3	0	298	20	4	8	2.1	.988	OF-153
1969			149	.269	.507	495	133	17	1	33	6.7	113	87	148	142	23	0	0	318	9	5	3	2.2	.985	OF-149
1970			157	.282	.493	554	156	32	2	27	4.9	82	88	106	96	24	2	1	293	14	4	4	2.0	.987	OF-151
1971			123	.203	.295	404	82	16	0	7	1.7	38	45	56	63	10	9	1	232	9	3	5	2.0	.988	OF-116
1972			145	.273	.470	542	148	29	3	24	4.4	117	90	103	99	17	1	0	284	8	5	2	2.0	.983	OF-144
1973			139	.220	.395	481	106	14	5	20	4.2	90	55	91	102	14	4	0	270	9	4	1	2.0	.986	OF-133
1974	LA	N	150	.271	.497	535	145	17	4	32	6.0	104	108	108	104	18	3	0	365	10	3	3	2.5	.992	OF-148
1975			130	.248	.417	412	102	16	0	18	4.4	80	58	110	77	7	10	0	282	6	5	2	2.3	.983	OF-120
1976	ATL	N	148	.207	.367	449	93	19	1	17	3.8	75	66	127	111	16	8	2	287	17	9	2	2.1	.971	OF-138
1977	2 teams	NY A (30G – .143)				MIL A	(36G – .197)																		
"	total		66	.175	.237	194	34	5	2	1	0.5	17	13	32	47	4	13	1	50	1	1	0	0.8	.981	OF-25, DH-18
15 yrs.			1920	.250	.436	6653	1665	285	39	291	4.4	1105	964	1224	1427	225	61	5	3937	167	84	42	2.2	.980	OF-1810, SS-21, DH-18, 3B-2

LEAGUE CHAMPIONSHIP SERIES

Year	Team		Games	BA	SA	AB	H	2B	3B	HR	HR%	R	RBI	BB	SO	SB	AB	H	PO	A	E	DP	TC/G	FA	G by Pos
1974	LA	N	4	.200	.400	10	2	2	0	0	0.0	4	2	9	1	1	0	0	11	0	0	0	2.8	1.000	OF-4

WORLD SERIES

Year	Team		Games	BA	SA	AB	H	2B	3B	HR	HR%	R	RBI	BB	SO	SB	AB	H	PO	A	E	DP	TC/G	FA	G by Pos
1974	LA	N	5	.188	.438	16	3	1	0	1	6.3	1	2	4	4	0	0	0	5	0	0	0	1.0	1.000	OF-5

Marvell Wynne

WYNNE, MARVELL
B. Dec. 17, 1959, Chicago, Ill. — BL TL 5'11" 176 lbs.

Year	Team		Games	BA	SA	AB	H	2B	3B	HR	HR%	R	RBI	BB	SO	SB	AB	H	PO	A	E	DP	TC/G	FA	G by Pos
1983	PIT	N	103	.243	.355	366	89	16	2	7	1.9	66	26	38	52	12	1	0	223	3	4	2	2.2	.983	OF-102
1984			154	.266	.337	653	174	24	11	0	0.0	77	39	42	81	24	0	0	373	8	4	1	2.5	.990	OF-154
1985			103	.205	.258	337	69	6	3	2	0.6	21	18	18	48	10	3	0	229	7	3	1	2.3	.987	OF-99
1986	SD	N	137	.264	.417	288	76	19	2	7	2.4	34	37	15	45	11	12	3	203	3	3	2	1.5	.986	OF-125
1987			98	.250	.346	188	47	8	2	2	1.1	17	24	20	37	11	30	6	100	2	2	0	1.1	.981	OF-71
1988			128	.264	.426	333	88	13	4	11	3.3	37	42	31	62	3	23	2	216	5	3	2	1.8	.987	OF-113
1989	2 teams	SD N (105G – .252)				CHI N	(20G – .188)																		
"	total		125	.243	.354	342	83	13	2	7	2.0	27	39	13	48	6	17	2	163	7	5	2	1.4	.971	OF-109
7 yrs.			848	.250	.353	2507	626	99	26	36	1.4	279	225	177	373	77	86	13	1507	35	24	10	1.8	.985	OF-773

LEAGUE CHAMPIONSHIP SERIES

Year	Team		Games	BA	SA	AB	H	2B	3B	HR	HR%	R	RBI	BB	SO	SB	AB	H	PO	A	E	DP	TC/G	FA	G by Pos
1989	CHI	N	4	.167	.167	6	1	0	0	0	0.0	0	0	0	0	0	2	0	3	0	0	0	0.8	1.000	OF-2

Johnny Wyrostek

WYROSTEK, JOHN BARNEY
B. July 12, 1919, Fairmont City, Ill. D. Dec. 12, 1986, St. Louis, Mo. — BL TR 6'2" 180 lbs.

Year	Team		Games	BA	SA	AB	H	2B	3B	HR	HR%	R	RBI	BB	SO	SB	AB	H	PO	A	E	DP	TC/G	FA	G by Pos
1942	PIT	N	9	.114	.171	35	4	0	1	0	0.0	0	3	3	2	0	1	0	18	1	0	1	2.1	1.000	OF-8
1943			51	.152	.190	79	12	3	0	0	0.0	7	1	3	15	0	24	4	34	1	5	0	0.8	.875	OF-20, 3B-2, 2B-1, 1B-1
1946	PHI	N	145	.281	.383	545	153	30	4	6	1.1	73	45	70	42	7	3	0	388	18	8	4	2.9	.981	OF-142
1947			128	.273	.390	454	124	24	7	5	1.1	68	51	61	45	7	1	0	261	11	8	2	2.2	.971	OF-126
1948	CIN	N	136	.273	.455	512	140	24	9	17	3.3	74	76	52	63	7	5	0	331	8	8	1	2.6	.977	OF-130
1949			134	.249	.365	474	118	20	4	9	1.9	54	46	58	63	7	5	0	293	10	9	1	2.3	.971	OF-129
1950			131	.285	.418	509	145	34	5	8	1.6	70	76	52	38	1	1	1	258	10	5	4	2.1	.982	OF-129, 1B-4
1951			142	.311	.391	537	167	31	3	2	0.4	52	61	54	54	2	3	2	255	8	8	2	1.9	.970	OF-139
1952	2 teams	CIN N (30G – .236)				PHI N	(98G – .274)																		
"	total		128	.265	.347	427	113	17	6	2	0.5	57	47	62	33	2	11	2	280	16	6	2	2.4	.980	OF-117, 1B-1
1953	PHI	N	125	.271	.359	409	111	14	2	6	1.5	42	47	38	43	0	15	2	192	11	8	2	1.7	.962	OF-110
1954			92	.239	.351	259	62	12	4	3	1.2	28	28	29	39	0	17	5	277	14	4	21	3.2	.986	OF-55, 1B-22
11 yrs.			1221	.271	.383	4240	1149	209	45	58	1.4	525	481	482	437	33	86	16	2587	108	69	40	2.3	.975	OF-1105, 1B-28, 3B-2, 2B-1

Henry Yaik

YAIK, HENRY
B. Mar. 1, 1864, Detroit, Mich. D. Sept. 21, 1935, Detroit, Mich. — 5'11" 185 lbs.

Year	Team		Games	BA	SA	AB	H	2B	3B	HR	HR%	R	RBI	BB	SO	SB	AB	H	PO	A	E	DP	TC/G	FA	G by Pos
1888	PIT	N	2	.333	.333	6	2	0	0	0	0.0	0	1	1	0	0	0	0	9	3	6	1	9.0	.667	OF-1, C-1

Ad Yale

YALE, WILLIAM M.
B. Apr. 17, 1870, Bristol, Conn. D. Apr. 27, 1948, Bridgeport, Conn.

Year	Team		Games	BA	SA	AB	H	2B	3B	HR	HR%	R	RBI	BB	SO	SB	AB	H	PO	A	E	DP	TC/G	FA	G by Pos
1905	BKN	N	4	.077	.077	13	1	0	0	0	0.0	1	1	1		0	0	0	38	1	0	4	9.8	1.000	1B-4

Hugh Yancy

YANCY, HUGH
B. Oct. 16, 1950, Sarasota, Fla. — BR TR 5'11" 170 lbs.

Year	Team		Games	BA	SA	AB	H	2B	3B	HR	HR%	R	RBI	BB	SO	SB	AB	H	PO	A	E	DP	TC/G	FA	G by Pos
1972	CHI	A	3	.111	.111	9	1	0	0	0	0.0	0	0	0	0	0	0	0	2	6	0	0	2.7	1.000	3B-3
1974			1	–	–	0	0	0	0	0	–	0	0	0	0	0	0	0	0	0	0	0	0.0	–	DH-1

Year Team	Games	BA	SA	AB	H	2B	3B	HR	HR%	R	RBI	BB	SO	SB	Pinch Hit AB	Pinch Hit H	PO	A	E	DP	TC/G	FA	G by Pos

Hugh Yancy *continued*

Year Team	Games	BA	SA	AB	H	2B	3B	HR	HR%	R	RBI	BB	SO	SB	PH AB	PH H	PO	A	E	DP	TC/G	FA	G by Pos
1976	3	.100	.200	10	1	1	0	0	0.0	0	0	0	3	0	0	0	8	4	0	3	4.0	1.000	2B-3
3 yrs.	7	.105	.158	19	2	1	0	0	0.0	0	0	0	3	0	0	0	10	10	0	3	2.9	1.000	3B-3, 2B-3, DH-1

George Yankowski

YANKOWSKI, GEORGE EDWARD
B. Nov. 19, 1922, Cambridge, Mass.

BR TR 6' 180 lbs.

Year Team	Games	BA	SA	AB	H	2B	3B	HR	HR%	R	RBI	BB	SO	SB	PH AB	PH H	PO	A	E	DP	TC/G	FA	G by Pos
1942 PHI A	6	.154	.231	13	2	1	0	0	0.0	0	2	0	2	0	0	0	14	3	0	0	2.8	1.000	C-6
1949 CHI A	12	.167	.222	18	3	1	0	0	0.0	0	2	0	6	0	0	0	15	3	0	0	1.5	1.000	C-6
2 yrs.	18	.161	.226	31	5	2	0	0	0.0	0	4	0	4	0	0	0	29	6	0	0	1.9	1.000	C-12

George Yantz

YANTZ, GEORGE WEBB
B. July 27, 1886, Louisville, Ky. D. Feb. 26, 1967, Louisville, Ky.

BR TR 5'6½" 168 lbs.

Year Team	Games	BA	SA	AB	H	2B	3B	HR	HR%	R	RBI	BB	SO	SB	PH AB	PH H	PO	A	E	DP	TC/G	FA	G by Pos
1912 CHI N	1	1.000	1.000	1	1	0	0	0	0.0	0	0	0	0	0	0	0	0	0	0	0	0.0	–	C-1

Yam Yaryan

YARYAN, CLARENCE EVERETT
B. Nov. 5, 1892, Knowlton, Iowa D. Nov. 16, 1964, Birmingham, Ala.

BR TR 5'10½" 180 lbs.

Year Team	Games	BA	SA	AB	H	2B	3B	HR	HR%	R	RBI	BB	SO	SB	PH AB	PH H	PO	A	E	DP	TC/G	FA	G by Pos
1921 CHI A	45	.304	.422	102	31	8	2	0	0.0	11	15	9	16	0	10	1	72	26	7	1	2.3	.933	C-34
1922	36	.197	.310	71	14	2	0	2	2.8	9	9	6	10	1	8	0	71	14	3	1	2.4	.966	C-25
2 yrs.	81	.260	.376	173	45	10	2	2	1.2	20	24	15	26	1	18	1	143	40	10	2	2.4	.948	C-59

Carl Yastrzemski

YASTRZEMSKI, CARL MICHAEL (Yaz)
B. Aug. 22, 1939, Southampton, N. Y.
Hall of Fame 1989.

BL TR 5'11" 175 lbs.

Year Team	Games	BA	SA	AB	H	2B	3B	HR	HR%	R	RBI	BB	SO	SB	PH AB	PH H	PO	A	E	DP	TC/G	FA	G by Pos
1961 BOS A	148	.266	.396	583	155	31	6	11	1.9	71	80	50	96	6	1	0	248	12	10	1	1.8	.963	OF-147
1962	160	.296	.469	646	191	43	6	19	2.9	99	94	66	82	7	0	0	329	15	11	3	2.2	.969	OF-160
1963	151	.321	.475	570	183	40	3	14	2.5	91	68	95	72	8	0	0	283	18	6	3	2.0	.980	OF-151
1964	151	.289	.451	567	164	29	9	15	2.6	77	67	75	90	6	0	0	372	24	11	4	2.7	.973	OF-148, 3B-2
1965	133	.312	.536	494	154	45	3	20	4.0	78	72	70	58	7	3	0	222	11	3	2	1.8	.987	OF-130
1966	160	.278	.431	594	165	39	2	16	2.7	81	80	84	60	8	3	1	310	15	5	2	2.1	.985	OF-158
1967	161	.326	.622	579	189	31	4	44	7.6	112	121	91	69	10	0	0	297	13	7	1	2.0	.978	OF-161
1968	157	.301	.495	539	162	32	2	23	4.3	90	74	119	90	13	0	0	315	13	3	4	2.1	.991	OF-155, 1B-3
1969	162	.255	.507	603	154	28	2	40	6.6	96	111	101	91	15	0	0	427	38	6	31	2.9	.987	OF-143, 1B-22
1970	161	.329	.592	566	186	29	0	40	7.1	125	102	128	66	23	1	0	816	64	14	62	5.6	.984	1B-94, OF-69
1971	148	.254	.392	508	129	21	2	15	3.0	75	70	106	60	8	2	2	281	16	2	4	2.0	.993	OF-146
1972	125	.264	.391	455	120	18	2	12	2.6	70	68	67	44	5	1	0	498	43	8	35	4.4	.985	OF-83, 1B-42
1973	152	.296	.463	540	160	25	4	19	3.5	82	95	105	58	9	1	0	979	119	18	87	7.3	.984	1B-107, 3B-31, OF-14
1974	148	.301	.445	515	155	25	2	15	2.9	93	79	104	48	12	0	0	806	46	6	68	5.8	.993	1B-84, OF-63, DH-4
1975	149	.269	.405	543	146	30	1	14	2.6	91	60	87	67	8	1	0	1217	88	5	103	8.8	.996	1B-140, OF-8, DH-2
1976	155	.267	.432	546	146	23	2	21	3.8	71	102	80	67	5	1	0	922	55	4	78	6.3	.996	1B-94, OF-51, DH-10
1977	150	.296	.505	558	165	27	3	28	5.0	99	102	73	40	11	0	0	344	22	0	5	2.4	1.000	OF-140, 1B-7, DH-6
1978	144	.277	.423	523	145	21	2	17	3.3	70	81	76	44	4	1	0	523	49	5	49	4.0	.991	OF-71, 1B-50, DH-27
1979	147	.270	.450	518	140	28	1	21	4.1	69	87	62	46	3	3	2	529	56	4	42	4.0	.993	DH-56, 1B-51, OF-36
1980	105	.275	.462	364	100	21	1	15	4.1	49	50	44	38	0	6	0	225	13	4	20	2.3	.983	DH-49, OF-39, 1B-16
1981	91	.246	.355	338	83	14	1	7	2.1	36	53	49	28	0	3	0	353	34	3	26	4.3	.992	DH-48, 1B-39
1982	131	.275	.431	459	126	22	1	16	3.5	53	72	59	50	0	15	1	119	10	0	12	1.0	1.000	DH-102, 1B-14, OF-2
1983	119	.266	.408	380	101	24	0	10	2.6	38	56	54	29	0	10	2	22	1	0	1	0.2	1.000	DH-107, 1B-2, OF-1
23 yrs.	3308 / 2nd	.285	.462	11988 / 3rd	3419 / 6th	646 / 6th	59	452	3.8	1816	1844 / 9th	1845 / 4th	1393	168	52	8	10437	775	135	643	3.4	.988	OF-2076, 1B-765, DH-411, 3B-33

LEAGUE CHAMPIONSHIP SERIES

Year Team	Games	BA	SA	AB	H	2B	3B	HR	HR%	R	RBI	BB	SO	SB	PH AB	PH H	PO	A	E	DP	TC/G	FA	G by Pos
1975 BOS A	3	.455	.818	11	5	1	0	1	9.1	4	2	1	1	0	0	0	7	2	0	0	3.0	1.000	OF-3

WORLD SERIES

Year Team	Games	BA	SA	AB	H	2B	3B	HR	HR%	R	RBI	BB	SO	SB	PH AB	PH H	PO	A	E	DP	TC/G	FA	G by Pos
1967 BOS A	7	.400	.840	25	10	2	0	3	12.0	4	5	4	1	0	0	0	16	2	0	0	2.6	1.000	OF-7
1975	7	.310	.310	29	9	0	0	0	0.0	7	4	4	1	0	0	0	36	1	0	4	5.3	1.000	OF-4, 1B-4
2 yrs.	14	.352 / 10th	.556	54	19	2	0	3	5.6	11	9	8	2	0	0	0	52	3	0	4	3.9	1.000	OF-11, 1B-4

Al Yates

YATES, ALBERT ARTHUR (Bunny)
B. May 26, 1945, Jersey City, N. J.

BR TR 6'2" 210 lbs.

Year Team	Games	BA	SA	AB	H	2B	3B	HR	HR%	R	RBI	BB	SO	SB	PH AB	PH H	PO	A	E	DP	TC/G	FA	G by Pos
1971 MIL A	24	.277	.383	47	13	2	0	1	2.1	5	4	3	7	1	11	3	19	2	0	0	0.9	1.000	OF-12

Emil Yde

YDE, EMIL OGDEN
B. Jan. 28, 1900, Great Lakes, Ill.
D. Dec. 4, 1968, Leesburg, Fla.

BB TL 5'11" 165 lbs.
BL 1925

Year Team	Games	BA	SA	AB	H	2B	3B	HR	HR%	R	RBI	BB	SO	SB	PH AB	PH H	PO	A	E	DP	TC/G	FA	G by Pos
1924 PIT N	50	.239	.352	88	21	1	3	1	1.1	8	9	0	13	0	13	3	5	57	6	4	1.4	.912	P-33
1925	47	.191	.258	89	17	4	1	0	0.0	11	11	2	13	1	4	0	8	46	4	8	1.2	.931	P-33
1926	43	.230	.351	74	17	5	2	0	0.0	11	4	5	7	0	0	0	10	47	4	3	1.4	.934	P-37
1927	23	.167	.278	18	3	0	1	0	0.0	8	1	0	4	1	0	2	11	1	0	0.6	.929	P-9
1929 DET A	46	.333	.396	48	16	1	1	0	0.0	8	3	3	6	0	13	5	5	16	2	0	0.5	.913	P-29
5 yrs.	209	.233	.328	317	74	11	8	1	0.3	46	28	10	40	1	34	9	30	177	17	15	1.1	.924	P-141

WORLD SERIES

Year Team	Games	BA	SA	AB	H	2B	3B	HR	HR%	R	RBI	BB	SO	SB	PH AB	PH H	PO	A	E	DP	TC/G	FA	G by Pos
1925 PIT N	2	.000	.000	1	0	0	0	0	0.0	0	0	0	0	0	0	0	0	0	0	0	0.0	–	P-1
1927	1	–	–	0	0	0	0	0	–	0	0	0	0	0	0	0	0	0	0	0	0.0	–	P-1
2 yrs.	3	.000	.000	1	0	0	0	0	0.0	2	0	0	0	0	0	0	0	0	0	0	0.0	–	P-1

Bert Yeabsley

YEABSLEY, ROBERT WATKINS
B. Dec. 17, 1893, Philadelphia, Pa. D. Feb. 8, 1961, Philadelphia, Pa.

BR TR 5'9½" 175 lbs.

Year Team	Games	BA	SA	AB	H	2B	3B	HR	HR%	R	RBI	BB	SO	SB	PH AB	PH H	PO	A	E	DP	TC/G	FA	G by Pos
1919 PHI N	3	–	–	0	0	0	0	0	–	0	0	1	0	0	0	0	0	0	0	0	0.0	–	

Year	Team	Games	BA	SA	AB	H	2B	3B	HR	HR%	R	RBI	BB	SO	SB	Pinch Hit AB	Pinch Hit H	PO	A	E	DP	TC/G	FA	G by Pos

George Yeager

YEAGER, GEORGE J. (Doc) B. June 4, 1873, Cincinnati, Ohio. D. June 5, 1940, Cincinnati, Ohio. BR TR 5'10" 190 lbs.

Year	Team	Games	BA	SA	AB	H	2B	3B	HR	HR%	R	RBI	BB	SO	SB	AB	H	PO	A	E	DP	TC/G	FA	G by Pos
1896	BOS N	2	.200	.200	5	1	0	0	0	0.0	1	0			1	0	0	13	0	0	3	6.5	1.000	1B-2
1897		30	.242	.389	95	23	2	3	2	2.1	20	15	7			2	2	77	31	11	1	4.0	.908	C-13, OF-10, 2B-4, 3B-1
1898		68	.267	.376	221	59	13	1	3	1.4	37	24	16			1	3	303	40	19	6	5.3	.948	C-37, 1B-17, OF-9, SS-2
1899		8	.125	.125	8	1	0	0	0	0.0	1	0	1			0	0	11	1	2	0	4.7	.857	OF-2, C-1
1901	2 teams		CLE A (39G – .223)		PIT N (26G – .264)																			
"	total	65	.239	.278	230	55	7	1	0	0.0	22	24	8			3	5	243	81	20	7	5.3	.942	C-45, 1B-6, 3B-4, OF-3, 2B-2
1902	2 teams		NY N (38G – .204)		BAL A (11G – .184)																			
"	total	49	.199	.233	146	29	3	1	0	0.0	9	10	13			1	7	190	52	14	6	5.2	.945	C-38, 1B-3, OF-1
	6 yrs.	217	.238	.312	705	168	25	6	5	0.7	90	73	45		1	7	17	837	205	66	23	5.1	.940	C-134, 1B-28, OF-25, 2B-6, 3B-5, SS-2

Joe Yeager

YEAGER, JOSEPH F. (Little Joe) B. Aug. 28, 1875, Philadelphia, Pa. D. July 2, 1937, Detroit, Mich. TR

Year	Team	Games	BA	SA	AB	H	2B	3B	HR	HR%	R	RBI	BB	SO	SB	AB	H	PO	A	E	DP	TC/G	FA	G by Pos
1898	BKN N	43	.172	.224	134	23	5	1	0	0.0	12	15	7		1	0	0	21	107	11	3	3.2	.921	P-36, OF-4, SS-2, 2B-1
1899		23	.191	.234	47	9	0	1	0	0.0	12	4	6		0	0	0	21	50	5	10	3.3	.934	SS-11, P-10, OF-1, 3B-1
1900		3	.333	.333	9	3	0	0	0	0.0	0	0	0		0	0	0	0	3	0	0	1.0	1.000	P-2, 3B-1
1901	DET A	41	.296	.416	125	37	7	1	2	1.6	18	17	4		3	2	0	33	104	13	12	3.7	.913	P-26, SS-12, 2B-1
1902		50	.242	.360	161	39	6	5	1	0.6	17	23	5		0	1	0	59	94	9	3	3.2	.944	P-19, OF-13, 2B-12, SS-3, 3B-1
1903		109	.256	.323	402	103	15	6	0	0.0	36	43	18		9	0	0	130	186	27	10	3.1	.921	3B-107, SS-1, P-1
1905	NY A	115	.267	.342	401	107	16	7	0	0.0	53	42	25		8	3	2	148	242	31	14	3.7	.926	3B-90, SS-21
1906		57	.301	.366	123	37	6	1	0	0.0	20	12	13		3	18	3	69	86	10	9	2.9	.939	SS-22, 2B-13, 3B-3
1907	STL A	123	.239	.326	436	104	21	7	1	0.2	32	44	31		11	4	1	172	287	31	23	4.0	.937	3B-92, 2B-17, SS-10
1908		10	.333	.400	15	5	1	0	0	0.0	3	1	1		2	5	1	4	12	0	0	1.6	1.000	2B-4, SS-1
	10 yrs.	574	.252	.331	1853	467	77	29	4	0.2	203	201	110		37	33	7	657	1171	137	84	3.4	.930	3B-295, P-94, SS-83, 2B-48, OF-18

Steve Yeager

YEAGER, STEPHEN WAYNE B. Nov. 24, 1948, Huntington, W. Va. BR TR 6' 190 lbs.

Year	Team	Games	BA	SA	AB	H	2B	3B	HR	HR%	R	RBI	BB	SO	SB	AB	H	PO	A	E	DP	TC/G	FA	G by Pos
1972	LA N	35	.274	.406	106	29	0	1	4	3.8	18	15	16	26	0	0	0	220	19	4	2	6.9	.984	C-35
1973		54	.254	.336	134	34	5	0	2	1.5	18	10	15	33	1	4	1	230	24	5	2	4.8	.981	C-50
1974		94	.266	.437	316	84	16	1	12	3.8	41	41	32	77	2	0	0	552	58	5	4	6.5	.992	C-93
1975		135	.228	.347	452	103	16	1	12	2.7	34	54	40	75	2	0	0	806	62	7	4	6.5	.992	C-135
1976		117	.214	.354	359	77	11	3	11	3.1	42	35	30	84	3	1	1	522	77	9	9	5.2	.985	C-115
1977		125	.256	.444	387	99	21	2	16	4.1	53	55	43	84	1	3	0	690	89	18	12	6.4	.977	C-123
1978		94	.193	.276	228	44	7	0	4	1.8	19	23	36	41	0	4	1	373	55	5	3	4.6	.988	C-91
1979		105	.216	.384	310	67	9	2	13	4.2	33	41	29	68	1	2	2	513	56	9	7	5.5	.984	C-103
1980		96	.211	.273	227	48	8	0	2	0.9	20	20	20	54	2	4	1	382	36	7	5	4.4	.984	C-95
1981		42	.209	.337	86	18	2	0	3	3.5	5	7	6	14	0	1	2	142	13	1	1	3.7	.994	C-40
1982		82	.245	.321	196	48	5	2	2	1.0	13	18	13	28	0	9	2	338	42	4	8	4.7	.990	C-76
1983		113	.203	.379	335	68	8	3	15	4.5	31	41	23	57	1	2	0	579	63	10	10	5.8	.985	C-112
1984		74	.228	.310	197	45	4	0	4	2.0	16	29	20	38	1	17	4	317	30	2	1	4.7	.994	C-65
1985		53	.207	.256	121	25	4	1	0	0.0	4	9	7	24	0	7	1	212	28	2	2	4.6	.992	C-48
1986	SEA A	50	.208	.269	130	27	2	0	2	1.5	10	12	12	23	0	1	0	234	22	0	5	5.1	1.000	C-49
	15 yrs.	1269	.228	.355	3584	816	118	16	102	2.8	357	410	342	726	14	59	15	6110	674	88	75	5.4	.987	C-1230

DIVISIONAL PLAYOFF SERIES

Year	Team	Games	BA	SA	AB	H	2B	3B	HR	HR%	R	RBI	BB	SO	SB	AB	H	PO	A	E	DP	TC/G	FA	G by Pos
1981	LA N	2	.400	.600	5	2	1	0	0	0.0	1	0	0	1	0	1	1	0	0	0	0	0.0	–	C-2

LEAGUE CHAMPIONSHIP SERIES

Year	Team	Games	BA	SA	AB	H	2B	3B	HR	HR%	R	RBI	BB	SO	SB	AB	H	PO	A	E	DP	TC/G	FA	G by Pos
1974	LA N	3	.000	.000	9	0	0	0	0	0.0	1	0	3	3	1	0	0	14	1	0	0	5.0	1.000	C-3
1977		4	.231	.231	13	3	0	0	0	0.0	1	2	1	3	0	0	0	22	1	0	0	5.8	1.000	C-4
1978		4	.231	.462	13	3	0	0	1	7.7	2	2	2	2	1	0	0	21	2	0	0	5.8	1.000	C-4
1981		1	.500	.500	2	1	0	0	0	0.0	1	0	0	0	0	1	1	0	0	0	0	0.0	–	C-1
1983		2	.167	.333	6	1	1	0	0	0.0	0	0	1	1	0	0	0	7	1	0	0	4.0	1.000	C-2
1985		1	.000	.000	2	0	0	0	0	0.0	0	0	0	0	0	1	1	4	0	0	0	4.0	1.000	C-1
	6 yrs.	15	.178	.267	45	8	1	0	1	2.2	5	4	7	9	2	1	1	68	5	0	0	4.9	1.000	C-15

WORLD SERIES

Year	Team	Games	BA	SA	AB	H	2B	3B	HR	HR%	R	RBI	BB	SO	SB	AB	H	PO	A	E	DP	TC/G	FA	G by Pos
1974	LA N	4	.364	.455	11	4	1	0	0	0.0	1	0	1	4	0	0	0	32	4	1	1	9.3	.973	C-4
1977		6	.316	.684	19	6	1	0	2	10.5	2	5	1	1	0	0	0	32	6	0	0	6.3	1.000	C-6
1978		5	.231	.308	13	3	1	0	0	0.0	2	0	1	2	0	0	0	23	2	0	0	5.0	1.000	C-5
1981		6	.286	.786	14	4	1	0	2	14.3	1	4	2	2	0	0	0	20	0	0	0	3.3	1.000	C-6
	4 yrs.	21	.298	.579	57	17	4	0	4	7.0	6	10	3	9	0	0	0	107	12	1	1	5.7	.992	C-21
									9th																

Eric Yelding

YELDING, ERIC GIRARD B. Feb. 22, 1965, Montrose, Ala. BR TR 6'1" 170 lbs.

Year	Team	Games	BA	SA	AB	H	2B	3B	HR	HR%	R	RBI	BB	SO	SB	AB	H	PO	A	E	DP	TC/G	FA	G by Pos
1989	HOU N	70	.233	.256	90	21	2	0	0	0.0	19	9	7	19	11	16	4	37	57	3	9	1.4	.969	SS-15, 2B-13, OF-8

Archie Yelle

YELLE, ARCHIE JOSEPH B. June 11, 1892, Saginaw, Mich. D. May 2, 1983, Woodland, Calif. BR TR 5'10½" 170 lbs.

Year	Team	Games	BA	SA	AB	H	2B	3B	HR	HR%	R	RBI	BB	SO	SB	AB	H	PO	A	E	DP	TC/G	FA	G by Pos
1917	DET A	25	.137	.157	51	7	0	0	0	0.0	4	0	5	4	2	1	0	62	16	2	1	3.2	.975	C-24
1918		56	.174	.194	144	25	3	0	0	0.0	7	7	9	15	0	4	1	172	81	14	5	4.8	.948	C-52
1919		5	.000	.000	4	0	0	0	0	0.0	1	0	1	0	0	0	0	3	1	1	0	1.0	.800	C-5
	3 yrs.	86	.161	.181	199	32	4	0	0	0.0	12	7	15	19	2	5	1	237	98	17	6	4.1	.952	C-81

Steve Yerkes

YERKES, STEPHEN DOUGLAS B. May 15, 1888, Hatboro, Pa. D. Jan. 31, 1971, Lansdale, Pa. BR TR 5'9" 165 lbs.

Year	Team	Games	BA	SA	AB	H	2B	3B	HR	HR%	R	RBI	BB	SO	SB	AB	H	PO	A	E	DP	TC/G	FA	G by Pos
1909	BOS A	5	.500	.500	2	1	0	0	0	0.0	0	0	0		0	2	1	0	0	0	0	0.0	–	SS-3
1911		142	.279	.345	502	140	24	3	1	0.2	70	57	52		14	0	0	288	388	54	39	5.1	.926	SS-116, 2B-14, 3B-11
1912		131	.252	.317	523	132	22	6	0	0.0	73	42	41		4	0	0	244	323	34	39	4.6	.943	2B-131

Year	Team	Games	BA	SA	AB	H	2B	3B	HR	HR%	R	RBI	BB	SO	SB	Pinch Hit AB	Pinch Hit H	PO	A	E	DP	TC/G	FA	G by Pos

Steve Yerkes *continued*

Year	Team	Games	BA	SA	AB	H	2B	3B	HR	HR%	R	RBI	BB	SO	SB	PH AB	PH H	PO	A	E	DP	TC/G	FA	G by Pos
1913		137	.267	.359	487	130	30	6	1	0.2	67	48	50	32	11	7	1	220	341	25	31	4.3	.957	2B-129
1914	2 teams		BOS A (92G – .218)		PIT F (39G – .338)																			
"	total	131	.257	.363	435	112	26	7	2	0.5	41	48	25	23	7	0	0	266	380	18	51	5.1	.973	2B-91, SS-39
1915	PIT F	121	.288	.371	434	125	17	8	1	0.2	44	49	30		17	0	0	255	336	24	42	5.1	.961	2B-114, SS-8
1916	CHI N	44	.263	.358	137	36	6	2	1	0.7	12	10	9	7	1	3	1	79	114	17	14	4.8	.919	2B-41
7 yrs.		711	.268	.350	2520	676	125	32	6	0.2	307	254	207		54	12	3	1352	1882	172	216	4.8	.950	2B-520, SS-166, 3B-11

WORLD SERIES

Year	Team	Games	BA	SA	AB	H	2B	3B	HR	HR%	R	RBI	BB	SO	SB	PH AB	PH H	PO	A	E	DP	TC/G	FA	G by Pos
1912	BOS A	8	.250	.375	32	8	0	2	0	0.0	3	4	2	3	0	0	0	15	22	1	1	4.8	.974	2B-8

Tom Yewcic

YEWCIC, THOMAS J. (Kibby)
B. May 9, 1932, Conemaugh, Pa. BR TR 5'11" 180 lbs.

Year	Team	Games	BA	SA	AB	H	2B	3B	HR	HR%	R	RBI	BB	SO	SB	PH AB	PH H	PO	A	E	DP	TC/G	FA	G by Pos
1957	DET A	1	.000	.000	1	0	0	0	0	0.0	0	0	0	0	0	0	0	4	1	1	0	6.0	.833	C-1

Ed Yewell

YEWELL, EDWIN LEONARD
B. Aug. 22, 1862, Washington, D. C. D. Sept. 15, 1940, Washington, D. C.

Year	Team	Games	BA	SA	AB	H	2B	3B	HR	HR%	R	RBI	BB	SO	SB	PH AB	PH H	PO	A	E	DP	TC/G	FA	G by Pos
1884	2 teams		WAS AA (27G – .247)		WAS U (1G – .000)																			
"	total	28	.237	.289	97	23	3	1	0	0.0	14		1			0	0	42	57	20	7	4.3	.832	2B-11, OF-8, 3B-8, SS-2

Earl Yingling

YINGLING, EARL HERSHEY (Chink)
B. Oct. 29, 1888, Chillicothe, Ohio D. Oct. 2, 1962, Columbus, Ohio BL TL 5'11½" 180 lbs.

Year	Team	Games	BA	SA	AB	H	2B	3B	HR	HR%	R	RBI	BB	SO	SB	PH AB	PH H	PO	A	E	DP	TC/G	FA	G by Pos
1911	CLE A	5	.273	.273	11	3	0	0	0	0.0	1	2	1		0	0	0	2	6	0	1	1.6	1.000	P-4
1912	BKN N	25	.250	.313	64	16	2	1	0	0.0	9	3	4	6	0	0	0	7	36	5	0	1.9	.896	P-25
1913		40	.383	.400	60	23	1	0	0	0.0	11	5	9	8	0	11	4	8	34	4	2	1.2	.913	P-26
1914	CIN N	61	.192	.233	120	23	2	0	1	0.8	9	11	9	15	3	13	2	22	45	8	2	1.2	.893	P-34, OF-13
1918	WAS A	8	.467	.467	15	7	0	0	0	0.0	1	2	2	1	0	3	1	4	12	0	3	2.0	1.000	P-5
5 yrs.		139	.267	.304	270	72	5	1	1	0.4	31	23	25	30	3	27	7	43	133	17	8	1.4	.912	P-94, OF-13

Joe Yingling

YINGLING, JOSEPH GRANVILLE
B. July 23, 1866, Baltimore, Md. D. Oct. 24, 1946, Baltimore, Md. BR TL 5'7½" 145 lbs.

Year	Team	Games	BA	SA	AB	H	2B	3B	HR	HR%	R	RBI	BB	SO	SB	PH AB	PH H	PO	A	E	DP	TC/G	FA	G by Pos
1886	WAS N	1	.000	.000	2	0	0	0	0	0.0	0	0	0	1	0	0	0	0	1	1	1	2.0	.500	P-1
1894	PHI N	1	.250	.250	4	1	0	0	0	0.0	0	0	0	1	0	0	0	1	2	0	0	3.0	1.000	SS-1
2 yrs.		2	.167	.167	6	1	0	0	0	0.0	0	0	0	2	0	0	0	1	3	1	1	2.5	.800	SS-1, P-1

Bill Yohe

YOHE, WILLIAM CLYDE
B. Sept. 2, 1878, Mt. Elere, Ill. D. Dec. 24, 1938, Bremerton, Wash. TR 5'8" 180 lbs.

Year	Team	Games	BA	SA	AB	H	2B	3B	HR	HR%	R	RBI	BB	SO	SB	PH AB	PH H	PO	A	E	DP	TC/G	FA	G by Pos
1909	WAS A	21	.208	.236	72	15	2	0	0	0.0	6	4	3		2	2	1	23	47	6	1	3.6	.921	3B-19

Rudy York

YORK, RUDOLPH PRESTON
B. Aug. 17, 1913, Ragland, Ala. D. Feb. 5, 1970, Rome, Ga. BR TR 6'1" 209 lbs.
Manager 1959.

Year	Team	Games	BA	SA	AB	H	2B	3B	HR	HR%	R	RBI	BB	SO	SB	PH AB	PH H	PO	A	E	DP	TC/G	FA	G by Pos
1934	DET A	3	.167	.167	6	1	0	0	0	0.0	0	0	1	3	0	2	1	4	2	0	0	2.0	1.000	C-2
1937		104	.307	.651	375	115	18	3	35	9.3	72	103	41	52	3	7	1	235	93	18	11	3.3	.948	C-54, 3B-41
1938		135	.298	.579	463	138	27	2	33	7.1	85	127	92	74	1	3	0	431	71	10	11	3.8	.980	C-116, OF-14, 1B-1
1939		102	.307	.544	329	101	16	1	20	6.1	66	68	41	50	5	16	2	434	39	5	22	4.7	.990	C-67, 1B-19
1940		155	.316	.583	588	186	46	4	33	5.6	105	134	89	88	3	0	0	1390	107	15	101	9.8	.990	1B-155
1941		155	.259	.456	590	153	29	3	27	4.6	91	111	92	88	3	0	0	1393	110	21	111	9.8	.986	1B-155
1942		153	.260	.428	577	150	24	3	21	3.6	81	90	73	71	3	1	1	1413	146	19	117	10.3	.988	1B-152
1943		155	.271	.527	571	155	22	11	34	6.0	90	118	84	88	5	0	0	1349	149	15	105	9.8	.990	1B-155
1944		151	.276	.439	583	161	27	7	18	3.1	77	98	68	73	5	0	0	1453	107	17	163	10.4	.989	1B-151
1945		155	.264	.413	595	157	25	5	18	3.0	71	87	59	85	6	0	0	1464	113	19	142	10.3	.988	1B-155
1946	BOS A	154	.276	.437	579	160	30	6	17	2.9	78	119	86	93	3	0	0	1327	116	8	154	9.4	.994	1B-154
1947	2 teams		BOS A (48G – .212)		CHI A (102G – .243)																			
"	total	150	.233	.397	584	136	25	4	21	3.6	56	91	58	87	1	0	0	1327	107	7	149	9.6	.995	1B-150
1948	PHI A	31	.157	.157	51	8	0	0	0	0.0	4	6	7	15	0	18	2	77	5	1	10	2.7	.988	1B-14
13 yrs.		1603	.275	.483	5891	1621	291	52	277	4.7	876	1152	791	867	38	47	7	12297	1165	155	1096	8.5	.989	1B-1261, C-239, 3B-41, OF-14

WORLD SERIES

Year	Team	Games	BA	SA	AB	H	2B	3B	HR	HR%	R	RBI	BB	SO	SB	PH AB	PH H	PO	A	E	DP	TC/G	FA	G by Pos
1940	DET A	7	.231	.423	26	6	0	1	1	3.8	3	2	4	7	0	0	0	59	2	0	4	8.7	1.000	1B-7
1945		7	.179	.214	28	5	1	0	0	0.0	1	3	3	4	0	0	0	67	8	1	3	10.9	.987	1B-7
1946	BOS A	7	.261	.652	23	6	1	1	2	8.7	6	5	6	4	0	0	0	59	4	1	0	9.1	.984	1B-7
3 yrs.		21	.221	.416	77	17	2	2	3	3.9	10	10	13	15	0	0	0	185	14	2	7	9.6	.990	1B-21

Tom York

YORK, THOMAS J.
B. July 13, 1851, Brooklyn, N. Y. D. Feb. 17, 1936, New York, N. Y. BL 5'9" 165 lbs.
Manager 1878, 1881.

Year	Team	Games	BA	SA	AB	H	2B	3B	HR	HR%	R	RBI	BB	SO	SB	PH AB	PH H	PO	A	E	DP	TC/G	FA	G by Pos
1876	HAR N	67	.259	.369	263	68	12	7	1	0.4	47	39	10	4		0	0	153	8	18	1	2.7	.899	OF-67
1877		56	.283	.422	237	67	16	7	1	0.4	43	37	3	11		0	0	130	5	21	1	2.8	.865	OF-56
1878	PRO N	62	.309	.465	269	83	19	10	1	0.4	56	26	8	19		0	0	89	14	15	3	1.9	.873	OF-62
1879		81	.310	.421	342	106	25	5	1	0.3	69	50	19	28		0	0	114	9	14	2	1.7	.898	OF-81
1880		53	.212	.276	203	43	9	2	0	0.0	21	18	8	29		0	0	94	5	7	1	2.0	.934	OF-53
1881		85	.304	.427	316	96	23	4	2	0.6	57	47	29	26		0	0	159	17	29	1	2.4	.859	OF-85
1882		81	.268	.393	321	86	23	7	1	0.3	48		19	14		0	0	159	11	24	3	2.4	.876	OF-81
1883	CLE N	100	.260	.378	381	99	29	5	2	0.5	56		37	55		0	0	176	15	30	3	2.2	.864	OF-100
1884	BAL AA	83	.223	.322	314	70	14	7	1	0.3	64		34			0	0	100	7	20	1	1.5	.843	OF-83
1885		22	.264	.356	87	23	4	0	0	0.0	6		8			0	0	41	4	3	1	2.2	.938	OF-22
10 yrs.		690	.271	.387	2733	741	174	57	10	0.4	467	217	175	186		0	0	1215	95	181	17	2.2	.879	OF-690

Tony York

YORK, ANTHONY BATTON
B. Nov. 27, 1912, Irene, Tex. D. Apr. 18, 1970, Hillsboro, Tex. BR TR 5'10" 165 lbs.

Year	Team	Games	BA	SA	AB	H	2B	3B	HR	HR%	R	RBI	BB	SO	SB	Pinch Hit AB	Pinch Hit H	PO	A	E	DP	TC/G	FA	G by Pos

Tony York *continued*

| 1944 | CHI N | 28 | .235 | .247 | 85 | 20 | 1 | 0 | 0 | 0.0 | 4 | 7 | 4 | 11 | 0 | 0 | 0 | 39 | 81 | 5 | 7 | 4.5 | .960 | SS-15, 3B-12 |

Eddie Yost

YOST, EDWARD FREDERICK (The Walking Man)
B. Oct. 13, 1926, Brooklyn, N. Y.
Manager 1963.

BR TR 5'10" 170 lbs.

1944	WAS A	7	.143	.143	14	2	0	0	0	0.0	3	0	1	2	0	0	0	9	6	2	0	2.4	.882	3B-3, SS-2
1946		8	.080	.120	25	2	1	0	0	0.0	2	1	5	5	2	1	0	7	17	0	1	3.0	1.000	3B-7
1947		115	.238	.292	428	102	17	3	0	0.0	52	14	45	57	3	0	0	125	198	14	11	2.9	.958	3B-114
1948		145	.249	.357	555	138	32	11	2	0.4	74	50	82	51	4	0	0	189	240	15	21	3.1	.966	3B-145
1949		124	.253	.391	435	110	19	7	9	2.1	57	45	91	41	3	1	0	158	232	19	23	3.3	.954	3B-122
1950		155	.295	.405	573	169	26	2	11	1.9	114	58	141	63	6	0	0	205	307	30	45	3.5	.945	3B-155
1951		154	.283	.424	568	161	36	4	12	2.1	109	65	126	55	6	0	0	209	234	21	22	3.0	.955	3B-152, OF-3
1952		157	.233	.359	587	137	32	3	12	2.0	92	49	129	73	4	0	0	212	249	18	26	3.1	.962	3B-157
1953		152	.272	.395	577	157	30	7	9	1.6	107	47	123	59	7	0	0	190	300	18	31	3.3	.965	3B-152
1954		155	.256	.380	539	138	26	4	11	2.0	101	47	131	71	7	0	0	170	347	17	29	3.4	.968	3B-155
1955		122	.243	.371	375	91	17	5	7	1.9	64	48	95	54	4	14	3	100	217	19	22	2.8	.943	3B-107
1956		152	.231	.336	515	119	17	2	11	2.1	94	53	151	82	8	9	0	182	303	18	31	3.3	.964	3B-135, OF-8
1957		110	.251	.372	414	104	13	5	9	2.2	47	38	73	49	1	4	0	109	207	16	18	3.0	.952	3B-107
1958		134	.224	.323	406	91	16	0	8	2.0	55	37	81	43	3	15	3	122	187	11	21	2.4	.966	3B-114, OF-4, 1B-2
1959	DET A	148	.278	.436	521	145	19	0	21	4.0	115	61	135	77	9	3	0	168	260	17	21	3.0	.962	3B-146, 2B-1
1960		143	.260	.398	497	129	23	2	14	2.8	78	47	125	69	5	5	1	155	208	26	18	2.7	.933	3B-142
1961	LA A	76	.202	.263	213	43	4	0	3	1.4	29	15	50	48	0	8	1	57	103	6	4	2.2	.964	3B-67
1962		52	.240	.346	104	25	9	1	0	0.0	22	10	30	21	0	16	1	69	48	4	5	2.3	.967	3B-28, 1B-7
18 yrs.		2109	.254	.371	7346	1863	337	56	139	1.9	1215	683	1614 **7th**	920	72	76	9	2436	3663	271	349	3.0	.957	3B-2008, OF-15, 1B-9, SS-2, 2B-1

Ned Yost

YOST, EDGAR FREDERICK
B. Aug. 19, 1955, Eureka, Calif.

BR TR 6'1" 190 lbs.

1980	MIL A	15	.161	.161	31	5	0	0	0	0.0	0	6	0	6	0	0	0	41	5	0	0	3.1	1.000	C-15
1981		18	.222	.556	27	6	0	0	3	11.1	4	3	3	6	0	0	0	37	6	2	2	2.5	.956	C-16
1982		40	.276	.429	98	27	6	3	1	1.0	13	8	7	20	3	1	0	121	6	3	2	3.3	.977	C-39, DH-1
1983		61	.224	.352	196	44	5	1	6	3.1	21	28	5	36	1	1	1	252	16	8	2	4.5	.971	C-61
1984	TEX A	80	.182	.273	242	44	4	0	6	2.5	15	25	6	47	1	3	0	368	20	2	1	4.9	.995	C-78
1985	MON N	5	.182	.182	11	2	0	0	0	0.0	1	0	0	2	0	0	0	24	1	1	0	5.2	.962	C-5
6 yrs.		219	.212	.329	605	128	15	4	16	2.6	54	64	21	117	5	5	1	843	54	16	7	4.2	.982	C-214, DH-1

WORLD SERIES

| 1982 | MIL A | 1 | – | – | 0 | 0 | 0 | 0 | 0 | – | 0 | 0 | 1 | 0 | 0 | 0 | 0 | 1 | 0 | 0 | 0 | 1.0 | 1.000 | C-1 |

Elmer Yoter

YOTER, ELMER ELLSWORTH
B. June 26, 1900, Plainfield, Pa. D. July 26, 1966, Camp Hill, Pa.

BR TR 5'7" 155 lbs.

1921	PHI A	3	.000	.000	3	0	0	0	0	0.0	0	0	0	1	0	3	0	0	0	0	0	0.0	–	
1924	CLE A	19	.273	.318	66	18	1	1	0	0.0	3	7	5	8	0	0	0	18	39	6	1	3.3	.905	3B-19
1927	CHI N	13	.222	.333	27	6	1	1	0	0.0	2	5	4	4	0	1	0	4	14	1	0	1.5	.947	3B-11
1928		1	–	–	0	0	0	0	0	0.0	0	0	0	0	0	0	0	0	0	0	0	0.0	–	3B-1
4 yrs.		36	.250	.313	96	24	2	2	0	0.0	5	12	9	13	0	4	0	22	53	7	1	2.3	.915	3B-31

Babe Young

YOUNG, NORMAN ROBERT
B. July 1, 1915, Astoria, N. Y. D. Dec. 25, 1983, Everett, Mass.

BL TL 6'2½" 185 lbs.

1936	NY N	1	.000	.000	1	0	0	0	0	0.0	0	0	0	0	0	0	0	0	0	0	0	0.0	–	
1939		22	.307	.480	75	23	4	0	3	4.0	8	14	5	6	0	0	0	214	9	4	18	10.3	.982	1B-22
1940		149	.286	.441	556	159	27	4	17	3.1	75	101	69	28	4	2	0	1505	86	13	112	10.8	.992	1B-147
1941		152	.265	.462	574	152	28	5	25	4.4	90	104	66	39	1	1	1	1395	87	21	124	9.9	.986	1B-150
1942		101	.279	.460	287	80	17	1	11	3.8	37	59	34	22	1	27	6	260	16	6	13	2.8	.979	OF-54, 1B-18
1946		104	.278	.388	291	81	11	0	7	2.4	30	33	30	21	3	32	5	492	24	7	25	5.0	.987	1B-49, OF-24
1947	2 teams	NY N (95G – .283)			CIN N (14G – .071)																			
"	total	109	.275	.460	378	104	22	2	14	3.7	55	79	35	27	0	16	2	730	56	8	66	7.3	.990	1B-93
1948	2 teams	CIN N (49G – .231)			STL N (41G – .243)																			
"	total	90	.237	.344	241	57	12	4	2	0.8	25	25	35	18	0	18	3	529	29	3	54	6.2	.995	1B-66, OF-1
8 yrs.		728	.273	.436	2403	656	121	17	79	3.3	320	415	274	161	9	97	17	5125	307	62	412	7.5	.989	1B-545, OF-79

Bobby Young

YOUNG, ROBERT GEORGE
B. Jan. 22, 1925, Granite, Md. D. Jan. 28, 1985, Baltimore, Md.

BL TR 6'1" 175 lbs.

1948	STL N	3	.000	.000	1	0	0	0	0	0.0	0	0	0	1	0	1	0	2	0	0	0	0.7	1.000	3B-1
1951	STL A	147	.260	.316	611	159	13	9	1	0.2	75	31	44	51	8	0	0	361	462	17	118	5.7	.980	2B-147
1952		149	.247	.325	575	142	15	9	4	0.7	59	39	56	48	3	1	1	380	407	13	127	5.4	.984	2B-149
1953		148	.255	.326	537	137	22	2	4	0.7	48	25	41	40	2	0	0	397	363	18	120	5.3	.977	2B-148
1954	BAL A	130	.245	.331	432	106	13	6	4	0.9	43	24	54	42	4	8	1	299	310	15	76	4.8	.976	2B-127
1955	2 teams	BAL A (59G – .199)			CLE A (18G – .311)																			
"	total	77	.221	.260	231	51	4	1	1	0.4	12	14	12	25	1	7	2	145	180	5	56	4.3	.985	2B-69, 3B-1
1956	CLE A	1	–	–	0	0	0	0	0	–	0	0	0	0	0	0	0	0	0	0	0	0.0	–	
1958	PHI N	32	.233	.333	60	14	1	1	1	1.7	7	4	1	5	0	9	2	28	33	2	6	2.0	.968	2B-21
8 yrs.		687	.249	.318	2447	609	68	28	15	0.6	244	137	208	212	18	26	6	1612	1755	70	503	5.0	.980	2B-661, 3B-2

Del Young

YOUNG, DELMER EDWARD
Son of Del Young.
B. May 11, 1912, Cleveland, Ohio D. Dec. 8, 1979, San Francisco, Calif.

BB TR 5'11" 168 lbs.

1937	PHI N	109	.194	.231	360	70	9	2	0	0.0	36	24	18	55	6	0	0	200	333	28	63	5.1	.950	2B-108
1938		108	.229	.279	340	78	13	2	0	0.0	27	31	20	35	0	2	0	196	307	33	52	5.0	.938	SS-87, 2B-17
1939		77	.263	.364	217	57	9	2	3	1.4	22	20	8	24	1	7	1	109	154	16	28	3.6	.943	SS-55, 2B-17

Year	Team		Games	BA	SA	AB	H	2B	3B	HR	HR%	R	RBI	BB	SO	SB	Pinch Hit AB	H	PO	A	E	DP	TC/G	FA	G by Pos

Del Young *continued*

Year	Team		Games	BA	SA	AB	H	2B	3B	HR	HR%	R	RBI	BB	SO	SB	AB	H	PO	A	E	DP	TC/G	FA	G by Pos
1940			15	.242	.303	33	8	0	1	0	0.0	2	1	2	1	0	0	0	23	23	2	4	3.2	.958	SS-6, 2B-5
4 yrs.			309	.224	.281	950	213	31	7	3	0.3	87	76	48	115	7	9	1	528	817	79	147	4.6	.945	SS-148, 2B-147

Del Young

YOUNG, DELMER JOHN BL TR 5'11" 195 lbs.
Father of Del Young.
B. Oct. 24, 1885, Macon, Mo. D. Dec. 17, 1959, Cleveland, Ohio

Year	Team		Games	BA	SA	AB	H	2B	3B	HR	HR%	R	RBI	BB	SO	SB	AB	H	PO	A	E	DP	TC/G	FA	G by Pos
1909	CIN	N	2	.286	.286	7	2	0	0	0	0.0	0	1	1		0	0	0	2	1	0	0	1.5	1.000	OF-2
1914	BUF	F	80	.276	.431	174	48	5	5	4	2.3	17	22	3		0	37	7	49	2	3	2	0.7	.944	OF-41
1915			12	.133	.133	15	2	0	0	0	0.0	0	0	1		1	9	1	2	0	1	0	0.3	.667	OF-3
3 yrs.			94	.265	.403	196	52	5	5	4	2.0	17	23	5		1	46	8	53	3	4	2	0.6	.933	OF-46

Dick Young

YOUNG, RICHARD ENNIS BL TR 5'11" 175 lbs.
B. June 3, 1928, Seattle, Wash. BB 1952

Year	Team		Games	BA	SA	AB	H	2B	3B	HR	HR%	R	RBI	BB	SO	SB	AB	H	PO	A	E	DP	TC/G	FA	G by Pos
1951	PHI	N	15	.235	.309	68	16	5	0	0	0.0	7	2	3	6	0	0	0	26	33	5	8	4.3	.922	2B-15
1952			5	.222	.333	9	2	1	0	0	0.0	3	0	1	3	1	2	0	5	4	1	1	2.0	.900	2B-2
2 yrs.			20	.234	.312	77	18	6	0	0	0.0	10	2	4	9	1	2	0	31	37	6	9	3.7	.919	2B-17

Don Young

YOUNG, DONALD WAYNE BR TR 6'2" 185 lbs.
B. Oct. 18, 1945, Houston, Tex.

Year	Team		Games	BA	SA	AB	H	2B	3B	HR	HR%	R	RBI	BB	SO	SB	AB	H	PO	A	E	DP	TC/G	FA	G by Pos
1965	CHI	N	11	.057	.143	35	2	0	1	0	2.9	1	2	0	11	0	3	1	14	0	1	0	1.4	.933	OF-11
1969			101	.239	.371	272	65	12	3	6	2.2	36	27	38	74	1	0	0	191	4	5	0	2.0	.975	OF-100
2 yrs.			112	.218	.345	307	67	12	3	7	2.3	37	29	38	85	1	3	1	205	4	6	0	1.9	.972	OF-111

George Young

YOUNG, GEORGE JOSEPH BL TR 6' 185 lbs.
B. Apr. 1, 1890, Brooklyn, N. Y. D. Mar. 13, 1950, Brightwaters, N. Y.

Year	Team		Games	BA	SA	AB	H	2B	3B	HR	HR%	R	RBI	BB	SO	SB	AB	H	PO	A	E	DP	TC/G	FA	G by Pos
1913	CLE	A	2	.000	.000	2	0	0	0	0	0.0	0	0	0	0	0	2	0	0	0	0	0	0.0	—	

Gerald Young

YOUNG, GERALD ANTHONY BB TR 6'2" 185 lbs.
B. Oct. 22, 1964, Tele, Honduras

Year	Team		Games	BA	SA	AB	H	2B	3B	HR	HR%	R	RBI	BB	SO	SB	AB	H	PO	A	E	DP	TC/G	FA	G by Pos
1987	HOU	N	71	.321	.380	274	88	9	2	1	0.4	44	15	26	27	26	2	1	143	5	3	1	2.1	.980	OF-67
1988			149	.257	.325	576	148	21	9	0	0.0	79	37	66	66	65	5	2	357	10	3	1	2.5	.992	OF-145
1989			146	.233	.276	533	124	17	3	0	0.0	71	38	74	60	34	2	1	412	15	1	5	2.9	.998	OF-143
3 yrs.			366	.260	.317	1383	360	47	14	1	0.1	194	90	166	153	125	9	4	912	30	7	7	2.6	.993	OF-355

Herman Young

YOUNG, HERMAN JOHN BR TR 5'8" 155 lbs.
B. Apr. 14, 1886, Boston, Mass. D. Dec. 12, 1966, Ipswich, Mass.

Year	Team		Games	BA	SA	AB	H	2B	3B	HR	HR%	R	RBI	BB	SO	SB	AB	H	PO	A	E	DP	TC/G	FA	G by Pos
1911	BOS	N	9	.240	.240	25	6	0	0	0	0.0	2	0	0	3	0	1	0	10	23	3	3	4.0	.917	3B-5, SS-3

John Young

YOUNG, JOHN THOMAS BL TL 6'3" 210 lbs.
B. Feb. 9, 1949, Los Angeles, Calif.

Year	Team		Games	BA	SA	AB	H	2B	3B	HR	HR%	R	RBI	BB	SO	SB	AB	H	PO	A	E	DP	TC/G	FA	G by Pos
1971	DET	A	2	.500	.750	4	2	1	0	0	0.0	1	1	0	0	0	1	0	7	0	0	0	3.5	1.000	1B-1

Mike Young

YOUNG, MICHAEL DARREN BB TR 6'2" 195 lbs.
B. Mar. 20, 1960, Oakland, Calif.

Year	Team		Games	BA	SA	AB	H	2B	3B	HR	HR%	R	RBI	BB	SO	SB	AB	H	PO	A	E	DP	TC/G	FA	G by Pos
1982	BAL	A	6	.000	.000	2	0	0	0	0	0.0	2	0	0	1	0	2	0	1	0	0	0	0.2	1.000	DH-2, OF-1
1983			25	.167	.278	36	6	2	1	0	0.0	5	2	2	8	1	5	0	25	1	2	0	1.1	.929	OF-22, DH-3
1984			123	.252	.431	401	101	17	2	17	4.2	59	52	58	110	6	7	2	216	4	4	0	1.8	.982	OF-115, DH-1
1985			139	.273	.513	450	123	22	1	28	6.2	72	81	48	104	1	18	6	190	6	5	0	1.4	.975	OF-90, DH-37
1986			117	.252	.371	369	93	15	1	9	2.4	43	42	49	90	3	12	3	149	1	6	0	1.3	.962	OF-69, DH-47
1987			110	.240	.405	363	87	10	1	16	4.4	46	39	46	91	10	10	4	117	0	3	0	1.1	.975	OF-60, DH-47
1988	2 teams	PHI N (75G – .226)				MIL A	(8G – .000)																		
"	total		83	.206	.313	160	33	14	0	1	0.6	15	14	28	48	1	40	7	76	0	5	0	1.0	.938	OF-44, DH-5
1989	CLE	A	32	.186	.237	59	11	0	0	1	1.7	2	5	6	13	1	21	5	1	0	0	0	0.0	1.000	DH-15, OF-1
8 yrs.			635	.247	.414	1840	454	80	6	72	3.9	244	235	237	465	22	115	27	775	12	25	0	1.3	.969	OF-402, DH-148

Pep Young

YOUNG, LEMUEL FLOYD BR TR 5'9" 162 lbs.
B. Aug. 29, 1907, Jamestown, N. C. D. Jan. 14, 1962, Jamestown, N. C.

Year	Team		Games	BA	SA	AB	H	2B	3B	HR	HR%	R	RBI	BB	SO	SB	AB	H	PO	A	E	DP	TC/G	FA	G by Pos
1933	PIT	N	25	.300	.450	20	6	1	1	0	0.0	3	0	0	5	0	20	6	2	1	0	0	0.1	1.000	SS-1, 2B-1
1934			19	.235	.235	17	4	0	0	0	0.0	3	2	0	6	0	4	0	4	9	0	2	0.7	1.000	SS-2, 2B-1
1935			128	.265	.399	494	131	25	10	7	1.4	60	82	21	59	2	0	0	315	326	32	47	5.3	.952	2B-107, OF-6, 3B-6, SS-4
1936			125	.248	.377	475	118	23	10	6	1.3	47	77	29	52	3	1	0	318	361	24	39	5.6	.966	2B-123
1937			113	.260	.390	408	106	20	3	9	2.2	43	54	26	63	4	2	1	195	328	24	52	4.8	.956	SS-45, 3B-39, 2B-30
1938			149	.278	.381	562	156	36	4	7	0		58	79	40	64	7	0	0	370	554	26	120	6.4	.973	2B-149
1939			84	.276	.375	293	81	14	3	3	1.0	34	29	23	29	1	0	0	202	270	16	61	5.8	.967	2B-84
1940			54	.250	.382	136	34	8	2	2	1.5	19	20	12	23	1	7	1	61	98	15	16	3.2	.914	2B-33, SS-7, 3B-5
1941	2 teams	CIN N (4G – .167)				STL	N (2G – .000)																		
"	total		6	.143	.143	14	2	0	0	0	0.0	2	0	0	3	0	3	0	5	7	1	1	2.2	.923	3B-3
1945	STL	N	27	.149	.234	47	7	1	0	1	2.1	5	4	1	8	0	5	0	31	30	2	4	2.3	.968	SS-11, 3B-9, 2B-3
10 yrs.			730	.262	.380	2466	645	128	34	32	1.3	274	347	152	312	18	42	7	1503	1984	140	342	5.0	.961	2B-532, SS-70, 3B-62, OF-6

Ralph Young

YOUNG, RALPH STUART BB TR 5'5" 165 lbs.
B. Sept. 19, 1889, Philadelphia, Pa. D. Jan. 24, 1965, Philadelphia, Pa.

Year	Team		Games	BA	SA	AB	H	2B	3B	HR	HR%	R	RBI	BB	SO	SB	AB	H	PO	A	E	DP	TC/G	FA	G by Pos
1913	NY	A	7	.067	.067	15	1	0	0	0	0.0	2	0	0		0	0	0	11	19	5	3	5.0	.857	SS-7
1915	DET	A	123	.243	.286	378	92	6	5	0	0.0	44	31	53	31	12	0	0	233	371	32	44	5.2	.950	2B-119
1916			153	.263	.322	528	139	16	6	1	0.2	60	45	62	43	20	0	0	380	436	29	56	5.5	.966	2B-146, SS-6, 3B-1
1917			141	.231	.280	503	116	18	2	1	0.2	64	35	61	35	8	0	0	300	449	33	46	5.5	.958	2B-141
1918			91	.188	.218	298	56	7	1	0	0.0	31	21	54	17	15	0	0	190	271	30	28	5.4	.939	2B-91
1919			125	.211	.268	456	96	13	5	1	0.2	63	25	53	32	8	0	0	312	405	23	39	5.9	.969	2B-121, SS-4

Year	Team	Games	BA	SA	AB	H	2B	3B	HR	HR%	R	RBI	BB	SO	SB	Pinch Hit AB	Pinch Hit H	PO	A	E	DP	TC/G	FA	G by Pos

Ralph Young *continued*

Year	Team	Games	BA	SA	AB	H	2B	3B	HR	HR%	R	RBI	BB	SO	SB	AB	H	PO	A	E	DP	TC/G	FA	G by Pos
1920		150	.291	.347	594	173	21	6	0	0.0	84	33	85	30	8	0	0	405	436	27	46	5.8	.969	2B-150
1921		107	.299	.334	401	120	8	3	0	0.0	70	29	69	23	11	1	0	285	270	31	44	5.5	.947	2B-106
1922	PHI A	125	.223	.279	470	105	19	2	1	0.2	62	35	55	21	8	5	2	302	350	27	53	5.4	.960	2B-120
9 yrs.		1022	.247	.296	3643	898	108	30	4	0.1	480	254	495	235	92	6	2	2418	3007	237	359	5.5	.958	2B-994, SS-17, 3B-1

Russ Young

YOUNG, RUSSELL CHARLES   BB TR 6'   175 lbs.
B. Sept. 15, 1902, Bryan, Ohio   D. May 13, 1984, Roseville, Calif.

Year	Team	Games	BA	SA	AB	H	2B	3B	HR	HR%	R	RBI	BB	SO	SB	AB	H	PO	A	E	DP	TC/G	FA	G by Pos
1931	STL A	16	.118	.206	34	4	0	0	1	2.9	2	2	2	4	0	0	0	44	7	0	0	3.2	1.000	C-16

Joel Youngblood

YOUNGBLOOD, JOEL RANDOLPH   BR TR 6'   180 lbs.
B. Aug. 28, 1951, Houston, Tex.

Year	Team	Games	BA	SA	AB	H	2B	3B	HR	HR%	R	RBI	BB	SO	SB	AB	H	PO	A	E	DP	TC/G	FA	G by Pos
1976	CIN N	55	.193	.246	57	11	1	1	0	0.0	8	1	2	8	1	33	5	15	3	2	2	0.4	.900	OF-9, 3B-6, 2B-1, C-1
1977 2 teams	STL N (25G – .185)				NY N (70G – .253)																			
" total		95	.244	.316	209	51	13	1	0	0.0	17	12	16	45	1	22	5	107	94	8	21	2.2	.962	OF-33, 2B-33, 3B-16
1978	NY N	113	.252	.436	266	67	12	8	7	2.6	40	30	16	39	4	23	7	160	96	6	21	2.3	.977	OF-50, 2B-39, 3B-9, SS-1
1979		158	.275	.436	590	162	37	5	16	2.7	90	60	60	84	18	4	1	337	57	9	10	2.6	.978	OF-147, 2B-13, 3B-12
1980		146	.276	.381	514	142	26	2	8	1.6	58	69	52	69	14	13	7	318	65	13	11	2.7	.967	OF-121, 3B-21, 2B-6
1981		43	.350	.531	143	50	10	2	4	2.8	16	25	12	19	2	3	0	70	6	3	0	1.8	.962	OF-41
1982 2 teams	NY N (80G – .257)				MON N (40G – .200)																			
" total		120	.240	.318	292	70	14	0	3	1.0	37	29	17	58	2	15	2	149	23	7	3	1.5	.961	OF-98, 2B-8, SS-1, 3B-1
1983	SF N	124	.292	.499	373	109	20	3	17	4.6	59	53	33	59	7	20	4	147	182	19	28	2.8	.945	2B-64, 3B-28, OF-22
1984		134	.254	.358	469	119	17	1	10	2.1	50	51	48	86	5	6	1	102	206	37	12	2.6	.893	3B-117, OF-11, 2B-5
1985		95	.270	.348	230	62	6	0	4	1.7	24	24	30	37	3	32	9	103	6	6	0	1.2	.948	OF-56, 3B-1
1986		97	.255	.402	184	47	12	0	5	2.7	20	28	18	34	1	58	16	68	14	3	4	0.9	.965	OF-45, 1B-7, 3B-5, 2B-4, SS-1
1987		69	.253	.385	91	23	3	0	3	3.3	9	11	5	13	1	44	13	24	3	0	0	0.4	1.000	OF-22, 3B-2
1988		83	.252	.285	123	31	4	0	0	0.0	12	16	10	17	1	49	15	48	0	1	0	0.6	.980	OF-45
1989	CIN N	76	.212	.331	118	25	5	0	3	2.5	13	13	13	21	0	38	8	31	1	1	1	0.4	.970	OF-45
14 yrs.		1408	.265	.392	3659	969	180	23	80	2.2	453	422	332	589	60	360	93	1679	756	115	113	1.8	.955	OF-745, 3B-218, 2B-173, 1B-7, SS-3, C-1

Henry Youngman

YOUNGMAN, HENRY   TR
B. 1865, Indiana, Pa.   D. Jan. 24, 1936, Pittsburgh, Pa.

Year	Team	Games	BA	SA	AB	H	2B	3B	HR	HR%	R	RBI	BB	SO	SB	AB	H	PO	A	E	DP	TC/G	FA	G by Pos
1890	PIT N	13	.128	.191	47	6	1	1	0	0.0	6	4	6	9	1	0	0	29	28	16	4	5.6	.781	3B-7, 2B-6

Ross Youngs

YOUNGS, ROYCE MIDDLEBROOK (Pep)   BL TR 5'8"   162 lbs.
B. Apr. 10, 1897, Shiner, Tex.   D. Oct. 22, 1927, San Antonio, Tex.
Hall of Fame 1972.

Year	Team	Games	BA	SA	AB	H	2B	3B	HR	HR%	R	RBI	BB	SO	SB	AB	H	PO	A	E	DP	TC/G	FA	G by Pos
1917	NY N	7	.346	.654	26	9	2	3	0	0.0	5	1	1	5	1	0	0	16	2	0	1	2.6	1.000	OF-7
1918		121	.302	.376	474	143	16	8	1	0.2	70	25	44	49	10	1	0	197	22	12	3	1.9	.948	OF-120
1919		130	.311	.415	489	152	31	7	2	0.4	73	43	51	47	24	1	0	235	23	16	7	2.1	.942	OF-130
1920		153	.351	.477	581	204	27	14	6	1.0	92	78	75	55	18	0	0	288	26	22	7	2.2	.935	OF-153
1921		141	.327	.456	504	165	24	16	3	0.6	90	102	71	47	21	4	2	122	11	3	3	1.0	.978	OF-137
1922		149	.331	.465	559	185	34	10	7	1.3	105	86	55	50	17	1	0	280	28	19	6	2.2	.942	OF-147
1923		152	.336	.446	596	200	33	12	3	0.5	121	87	73	36	13	0	0	282	22	13	7	2.1	.959	OF-152
1924		133	.356	.521	526	187	33	12	10	1.9	112	74	77	31	11	1	0	237	19	12	3	2.0	.955	OF-132, 2B-2
1925		130	.264	.372	500	132	24	6	6	1.2	82	53	66	51	17	1	0	219	32	15	3	2.0	.944	OF-127, 2B-3
1926		95	.306	.398	372	114	12	5	4	1.1	62	43	37	19	21	1	1	170	18	5	5	2.0	.974	OF-94
10 yrs.		1211	.322	.441	4627	1491	236	93	42	0.9	812	592	550	390	153	9	3	2046	203	117	45	2.0	.951	OF-1199, 2B-5

WORLD SERIES

Year	Team	Games	BA	SA	AB	H	2B	3B	HR	HR%	R	RBI	BB	SO	SB	AB	H	PO	A	E	DP	TC/G	FA	G by Pos
1921	NY N	8	.280	.400	25	7	1	1	0	0.0	3	3	7	2	2	0	0	7	1	0	0	1.0	1.000	OF-8
1922		5	.375	.375	16	6	0	0	0	0.0	2	2	3	1	0	0	0	9	2	2	1	2.6	.846	OF-5
1923		6	.348	.478	23	8	0	0	1	4.3	2	3	2	0	0	0	0	5	1	2	0	1.3	.750	OF-6
1924		7	.185	.222	27	5	1	0	0	0.0	3	1	5	6	1	0	0	8	1	0	0	1.3	1.000	OF-7
4 yrs.		26	.286	.363	91	26	2	1	1	1.1	10	9	17	9	3	0	0	29	5	4	1	1.5	.895	OF-26

Eddie Yount

YOUNT, FLOYD EDWIN   BR TR 6'1"   185 lbs.
B. Dec. 19, 1916, Newton, N. C.   D. Oct. 26, 1973, Newton, N. C.

Year	Team	Games	BA	SA	AB	H	2B	3B	HR	HR%	R	RBI	BB	SO	SB	AB	H	PO	A	E	DP	TC/G	FA	G by Pos
1937	PHI A	4	.286	.286	7	2	0	0	0	0.0	1	1	0	2	0	2	0	3	0	0	0	0.8	1.000	OF-2
1939	PIT N	2	.000	.000	2	0	0	0	0	0.0	0	0	0	2	0	2	0	0	0	0	0	0.0	—	
2 yrs.		6	.222	.222	9	2	0	0	0	0.0	1	1	0	3	0	4	0	3	0	0	0	0.5	1.000	OF-2

Robin Yount

YOUNT, ROBIN R.   BR TR 6'   165 lbs.
Brother of Larry Yount.
B. Sept. 16, 1955, Danville, Ill.

Year	Team	Games	BA	SA	AB	H	2B	3B	HR	HR%	R	RBI	BB	SO	SB	AB	H	PO	A	E	DP	TC/G	FA	G by Pos
1974	MIL A	107	.250	.346	344	86	14	5	3	0.9	48	26	12	46	7	0	0	148	327	19	55	4.6	.962	SS-107
1975		147	.267	.367	558	149	28	2	8	1.4	67	52	33	69	12	2	0	273	402	44	80	4.9	.939	SS-145
1976		161	.252	.301	638	161	19	3	2	0.3	59	54	38	69	16	0	0	290	510	31	104	5.2	.963	SS-161, OF-1
1977		154	.288	.377	605	174	34	4	4	0.7	66	49	41	80	16	3	1	256	449	26	94	4.7	.964	SS-153
1978		127	.293	.428	502	147	23	9	9	1.8	66	71	24	43	16	2	1	246	453	30	78	5.7	.959	SS-125
1979		149	.267	.371	577	154	26	5	8	1.4	72	51	35	52	11	0	0	267	517	25	97	5.4	.969	SS-149
1980		143	.293	.519	611	179	49	10	23	3.8	121	87	26	67	20	2	0	239	455	28	89	5.0	.961	SS-133, DH-9
1981		96	.273	.419	377	103	15	5	10	2.7	50	49	22	37	4	1	1	161	370	8	83	5.6	.985	SS-93, DH-3
1982		156	.331	.578	635	210	46	12	29	4.6	129	114	54	63	14	2	1	253	489	24	95	4.9	.969	SS-154, DH-1
1983		149	.308	.503	578	178	42	10	17	2.9	102	80	72	58	12	2	2	256	420	19	86	4.7	.973	SS-139, DH-8
1984		160	.298	.441	624	186	27	7	16	2.6	105	80	67	67	14	0	0	199	402	18	80	3.9	.971	SS-120, DH-39
1985		122	.277	.442	466	129	26	3	15	3.2	76	68	49	56	10	0	0	267	5	8	2	2.3	.971	OF-108, DH-12, 1B-3
1986		140	.312	.450	522	163	31	7	9	1.7	82	46	62	73	14	1	0	365	9	2	5	2.7	.995	OF-131, DH-6, 1B-3
1987		158	.312	.479	635	198	25	9	21	3.3	99	103	76	94	19	0	0	380	5	5	2	2.5	.987	OF-150, DH-8
1988		162	.306	.465	621	190	38	11	13	2.1	92	91	63	63	22	0	0	444	12	2	2	2.8	.996	OF-158, DH-4

Year	Team		Games	BA	SA	AB	H	2B	3B	HR	HR%	R	RBI	BB	SO	SB	Pinch Hit AB	Pinch Hit H	PO	A	E	DP	TC/G	FA	G by Pos

Robin Yount *continued*

Year	Team		Games	BA	SA	AB	H	2B	3B	HR	HR%	R	RBI	BB	SO	SB	AB	H	PO	A	E	DP	TC/G	FA	G by Pos
1989			160	.318	.511	614	195	38	9	21	3.4	101	103	63	71	19	0	0	361	8	7	2	2.4	.981	OF-143, DH-17
16 yrs.			2291	.292	.441	8907	2602	481	111	208	2.3	1335	1124	737	1008	226	15	6	4405	4833	296	954	4.2	.969	SS-1479, OF-691, DH-107, 1B-6

DIVISIONAL PLAYOFF SERIES

| 1981 | MIL | A | 5 | .316 | .421 | 19 | 6 | 0 | 1 | 0 | 0.0 | 4 | 1 | 2 | 2 | 1 | 0 | 0 | 0 | 0 | 1 | 0 | 0.2 | — | SS-5 |

LEAGUE CHAMPIONSHIP SERIES

| 1982 | MIL | A | 5 | .250 | .250 | 16 | 4 | 0 | 0 | 0 | 0.0 | 1 | 0 | 5 | 0 | 0 | 0 | 0 | 0 | 1 | 0 | 0.2 | — | SS-5 |

WORLD SERIES

| 1982 | MIL | A | 7 | .414 | .621 | 29 | 12 | 3 | 0 | 1 | 3.4 | 6 | 6 | 2 | 2 | 0 | 0 | 0 | 20 | 19 | 3 | 1 | 6.0 | .929 | SS-7 |

Jeff Yurak

YURAK, JEFFREY LYNN
B. Feb. 26, 1954, Pasadena, Calif.

BB TR 6'3'' 195 lbs.

| 1978 | MIL | A | 5 | .000 | .000 | 5 | 0 | 0 | 0 | 0 | 0.0 | 1 | 0 | 0 | 3 | 0 | 0 | 0 | 4 | 0 | 0 | 0 | 0.8 | 1.000 | OF-1 |

Sal Yvars

YVARS, SALVADOR ANTHONY
B. Feb. 20, 1924, New York, N. Y.

BR TR 5'10'' 187 lbs.

1947	NY	N	1	.200	.200	5	1	0	0	0	0.0	0	2	0	0	0	0	0	3	1	0	0	4.0	1.000	C-1
1948			15	.211	.316	38	8	1	0	1	2.6	4	6	3	1	0	0	0	50	8	0	2	3.9	1.000	C-15
1949			3	.000	.000	8	0	0	0	0	0.0	0	0	1	1	0	1	0	11	1	0	0	4.0	1.000	C-2
1950			9	.143	.143	14	2	0	0	0	0.0	0	0	1	2	0	0	0	22	4	1	0	3.0	.963	C-9
1951			25	.317	.512	41	13	2	0	2	4.9	9	3	5	7	0	2	0	46	3	3	1	2.1	.942	C-23
1952			66	.245	.344	151	37	3	0	4	2.6	15	18	10	16	0	7	1	202	40	3	3	3.7	.988	C-59
1953	2 teams	NY N (23G – .277)				STL	N	(30G – .246)																	
"	total		53	.260	.308	104	27	2	0	1	1.0	5	7	11	7	0	9	1	146	20	1	4	3.2	.994	C-46
1954	STL	N	38	.246	.421	57	14	0	0	2	3.5	8	8	6	5	1	18	4	46	9	0	1	1.4	1.000	C-21
8 yrs.			210	.244	.344	418	102	12	0	10	2.4	41	42	37	41	1	37	6	526	86	8	11	3.0	.987	C-176

WORLD SERIES

| 1951 | NY | N | 1 | .000 | .000 | 1 | 0 | 0 | 0 | 0 | 0.0 | 0 | 0 | 0 | 0 | 0 | 1 | 0 | 0 | 0 | 0 | 0 | 0.0 | — | — |

Elmer Zacher

ZACHER, ELMER HENRY (Silver)
B. Sept. 17, 1883, Buffalo, N. Y. D. Dec. 20, 1944, Buffalo, N. Y.

BR TR 5'9'' 190 lbs.

| 1910 | 2 teams | NY N (1G – .000) | | | | STL | N | (47G – .212) | | | | | | | | | | | | | | | | | |
| " | total | | 48 | .212 | .265 | 132 | 28 | 5 | 1 | 0 | 0.0 | 7 | 10 | 10 | 19 | 3 | 9 | 2 | 78 | 7 | 3 | 1 | 1.8 | .966 | OF-37, 2B-1 |

Fred Zahner

ZAHNER, FREDERICK JOSEPH
B. June 5, 1870, Louisville, Ky. D. July 24, 1900, Louisville, Ky.

1894	LOU	N	13	.200	.244	45	9	0	1	0	0.0	7	3	3	5	2	0	0	31	6	8	2	3.5	.822	C-10, OF-2, 1B-1
1895			21	.224	.286	49	11	1	1	0	0.0	7	6	6	4	0	0	0	28	14	9	0	2.4	.824	C-21
2 yrs.			34	.213	.266	94	20	1	2	0	0.0	14	9	9	9	2	0	0	59	20	17	2	2.8	.823	C-31, OF-2, 1B-1

Frankie Zak

ZAK, FRANK THOMAS
B. Feb. 22, 1922, Passaic, N. J. D. Feb. 6, 1972, Passaic, N. J.

BR TR 5'10'' 150 lbs.

1944	PIT	N	87	.300	.331	160	48	3	1	0	0.0	33	11	22	18	6	0	0	93	162	14	24	3.1	.948	SS-67
1945			15	.143	.214	28	4	2	0	0	0.0	2	3	3	0	0	0	0	9	26	1	3	2.4	.972	SS-10, 2B-1
1946			21	.200	.200	20	4	0	0	0	0.0	8	0	1	0	0	0	0	13	26	3	5	2.0	.929	SS-10
3 yrs.			123	.269	.303	208	56	5	1	0	0.0	43	14	26	23	6	0	0	115	214	18	32	2.8	.948	SS-87, 2B-1

Jack Zalusky

ZALUSKY, JOHN FRANCIS
B. June 22, 1879, Minneapolis, Minn. D. Aug. 11, 1935, Minneapolis, Minn.

BR TR 5'11½'' 172 lbs.

| 1903 | NY | A | 7 | .313 | .313 | 16 | 5 | 0 | 0 | 0 | 0.0 | 1 | 1 | 1 | 0 | 0 | 0 | 0 | 18 | 5 | 0 | 0 | 3.0 | 1.000 | C-6, 1B-1 |

Joe Zapustas

ZAPUSTAS, JOSEPH JOHN
B. July 25, 1907, Boston, Mass.

BR TR 6'1'' 185 lbs.

| 1933 | PHI | A | 2 | .200 | .200 | 5 | 1 | 0 | 0 | 0 | 0.0 | 0 | 0 | 0 | 0 | 0 | 0 | 0 | 2 | 0 | 0 | 0 | 1.0 | 1.000 | OF-2 |

Jose Zardon

ZARDON, JOSE ANTONIO
Born Jose Antonio Zardon y Sanchez.
B. May 20, 1923, Havana, Cuba

BR TR 5'11½'' 160 lbs.

| 1945 | WAS | A | 54 | .290 | .374 | 131 | 38 | 5 | 3 | 0 | 0.0 | 13 | 13 | 7 | 11 | 3 | 2 | 0 | 104 | 2 | 3 | 0 | 2.0 | .972 | OF-43 |

Al Zarilla

ZARILLA, ALLEN LEE (Zeke)
B. May 1, 1919, Los Angeles, Calif.

BL TR 5'11'' 180 lbs.

1943	STL	A	70	.254	.320	228	58	7	1	2	0.9	27	17	17	20	1	11	4	123	5	5	2	1.9	.962	OF-60
1944			100	.299	.448	288	86	13	6	6	2.1	43	45	29	33	1	15	2	167	4	4	1	1.8	.977	OF-79
1946			125	.259	.377	371	96	14	9	4	1.1	46	43	27	37	3	15	1	236	13	7	6	2.0	.973	OF-107
1947			127	.224	.318	380	85	15	6	3	0.8	34	38	40	45	3	16	0	209	6	3	0	1.7	.986	OF-110
1948			144	.329	.482	529	174	39	12	12	2.3	77	74	48	48	11	9	3	322	6	13	0	2.4	.962	OF-136
1949	2 teams	STL A (15G – .250)				BOS	A	(124G – .281)																	
"	total		139	.277	.411	530	147	33	4	10	1.9	78	77	56	53	5	2	0	260	6	4	4	1.9	.985	OF-137
1950	BOS	A	130	.325	.493	471	153	32	10	9	1.9	92	74	76	47	2	1	0	230	12	6	1	1.9	.976	OF-128
1951	CHI	A	120	.257	.401	382	98	21	2	10	2.6	56	60	60	57	2	3	0	164	7	3	2	1.5	.983	OF-117
1952	3 teams	CHI A (39G – .232)				STL	A	(48G – .238)			BOS	A	(21G – .183)											
"	total		108	.225	.325	289	65	10	2	5	1.7	43	24	48	29	5	18	1	141	10	5	0	1.4	.968	OF-86
1953	BOS	A	57	.194	.224	67	13	2	0	0	0.0	11	4	14	13	0	30	4	17	1	1	0	0.3	.947	OF-18
10 yrs.			1120	.276	.405	3535	975	186	43	61	1.7	507	456	415	382	33	120	15	1869	69	51	16	1.8	.974	OF-978

WORLD SERIES

| 1944 | STL | A | 4 | .100 | .100 | 10 | 1 | 0 | 0 | 0 | 0.0 | 1 | 1 | 0 | 4 | 0 | 1 | 0 | 2 | 0 | 0 | 0 | 0.5 | 1.000 | OF-3 |

Year	Team		Games	BA	SA	AB	H	2B	3B	HR	HR%	R	RBI	BB	SO	SB	Pinch Hit AB	Pinch Hit H	PO	A	E	DP	TC/G	FA	G by Pos

Norm Zauchin

ZAUCHIN, NORBERT HENRY BR TR 6'4½" 220 lbs.
B. Nov. 17, 1929, Royal Oak, Mich.

Year	Team		Games	BA	SA	AB	H	2B	3B	HR	HR%	R	RBI	BB	SO	SB	PH AB	PH H	PO	A	E	DP	TC/G	FA	G by Pos
1951	BOS	A	5	.167	.250	12	2	1	0	0	0.0	0	0	0	4	0	1	0	20	2	1	8	4.6	.957	1B-4
1955			130	.239	.430	477	114	10	0	27	5.7	65	93	69	105	3	4	2	1137	84	6	106	9.4	.995	1B-126
1956			44	.214	.310	84	18	2	0	2	2.4	12	11	14	22	0	12	1	189	10	2	18	4.6	.990	1B-31
1957			52	.264	.396	91	24	3	0	3	3.3	11	14	9	13	0	21	4	194	15	6	28	4.1	.972	1B-36
1958	WAS	A	96	.228	.416	303	69	8	2	15	5.0	35	37	38	68	0	5	1	749	56	4	74	8.4	.995	1B-91
1959			19	.211	.394	71	15	4	0	3	4.2	11	4	7	14	2	0	0	203	6	1	17	11.1	.995	1B-19
6 yrs.			346	.233	.408	1038	242	28	2	50	4.8	134	159	137	226	5	43	8	2492	173	20	251	7.8	.993	1B-307

Joe Zdeb

ZDEB, JOSEPH EDMUND BR TR 5'11" 185 lbs.
B. June 27, 1953, Compton, Ill.

Year	Team		Games	BA	SA	AB	H	2B	3B	HR	HR%	R	RBI	BB	SO	SB	PH AB	PH H	PO	A	E	DP	TC/G	FA	G by Pos
1977	KC	A	105	.297	.374	195	58	5	2	2	1.0	26	23	16	23	6	22	7	93	4	3	0	1.0	.970	OF-93, DH-4, 3B-1
1978			60	.252	.315	127	32	2	3	0	0.0	18	11	7	18	3	17	3	66	2	3	0	1.2	.958	OF-52, DH-1, 3B-1, 2B-1
1979			15	.174	.304	23	4	1	1	0	0.0	3	0	2	4	1	8	1	13	0	0	0	0.9	1.000	OF-9
3 yrs.			180	.272	.348	345	94	8	6	2	0.6	47	34	25	45	10	47	11	172	6	6	0	1.0	.967	OF-154, DH-5, 3B-2, 2B-1

LEAGUE CHAMPIONSHIP SERIES

| 1977 | KC | A | 4 | .000 | .000 | 9 | 0 | 0 | 0 | 0 | 0.0 | 0 | 0 | 0 | 2 | 1 | 1 | 0 | 4 | 0 | 0 | 0 | 1.0 | 1.000 | OF-4 |

Dave Zearfoss

ZEARFOSS, DAVID WILLIAM TILDEN TR 5'9"
B. Jan. 1, 1868, Schenectady, N. Y. D. Sept. 12, 1945, Wilmington, Del.

Year	Team		Games	BA	SA	AB	H	2B	3B	HR	HR%	R	RBI	BB	SO	SB	PH AB	PH H	PO	A	E	DP	TC/G	FA	G by Pos
1896	NY	N	19	.217	.267	60	13	1	1	0	0.0	5	6	5	5	2	0	0	53	14	8	1	3.9	.893	C-19
1897			5	.300	.500	10	3	0	1	0	0.0	1		1		0	0	0	15	7	3	1	5.0	.880	C-5
1898			1	1.000	1.000	1	1	0	0	0	0.0	0		0		0	0	0	2	1	0	0	3.0	1.000	C-1
1904	STL	N	27	.213	.238	80	17	2	0	0	0.0	7	9	10		0	1	0	107	33	5	1	5.4	.966	C-25
1905			20	.157	.196	51	8	0	1	0	0.0	2	2	4		0	1	0	62	22	3	0	4.4	.966	C-19
5 yrs.			72	.208	.252	202	42	3	3	0	0.0	15	17	19	5	2	2	0	239	77	19	3	4.7	.943	C-69

George Zeber

ZEBER, GEORGE WILLIAM BB TR 5'11" 170 lbs.
B. Aug. 29, 1950, Ellwood City, Pa.

Year	Team		Games	BA	SA	AB	H	2B	3B	HR	HR%	R	RBI	BB	SO	SB	PH AB	PH H	PO	A	E	DP	TC/G	FA	G by Pos
1977	NY	A	25	.323	.508	65	21	3	0	3	4.6	8	10	9	11	0	1	0	42	56	4	11	4.1	.961	2B-21, DH-2, SS-2, 3B-2
1978			3	.000	.000	6	0	0	0	0	0.0	0	0	0	0	0	1	0	1	2	1	0	1.3	.750	2B-1
2 yrs.			28	.296	.465	71	21	3	0	3	4.2	8	10	9	11	0	2	0	43	58	5	11	3.8	.953	2B-22, DH-2, SS-2, 3B-2

WORLD SERIES

| 1977 | NY | A | 2 | .000 | .000 | 2 | 0 | 0 | 0 | 0 | 0.0 | 0 | 0 | 0 | 2 | 0 | 2 | 0 | 0 | 0 | 0 | 0 | 0.0 | — | |

Rollie Zeider

ZEIDER, ROLLIE HUBERT (Bunions) BR TR 5'10" 162 lbs.
B. Nov. 16, 1883, Auburn, Ind. D. Sept. 12, 1967, Garrett, Ind.

Year	Team		Games	BA	SA	AB	H	2B	3B	HR	HR%	R	RBI	BB	SO	SB	PH AB	PH H	PO	A	E	DP	TC/G	FA	G by Pos
1910	CHI	A	136	.217	.243	498	108	9	2	0	0.0	57	31	62		49	0	0	312	372	60	47	5.5	.919	2B-87, SS-45, 3B-4
1911			73	.253	.295	217	55	3	0	2	0.9	39	21	29		28	8	4	358	92	15	16	6.4	.968	1B-29, SS-17, 3B-10, 2B-9
1912			129	.245	.329	420	103	12	10	1	0.2	57	42	50		47	3	1	742	163	27	39	7.2	.971	1B-66, 3B-56, SS-1
1913	2 teams		62	.246	.257	CHI A (13G – .350)						NY	A (49G – .233)												
"	total		62	.246	.257	179	44	2	0	0	0.0	19	14	29	10	6	2	0	153	114	17	13	4.6	.940	SS-23, 2B-20, 3B-8, 1B-7
1914	CHI	F	119	.274	.319	452	124	13	2	1	0.2	60	36	44		35	1	0	151	219	26	27	3.3	.934	3B-117, SS-1
1915			129	.227	.279	494	112	22	2	0	0.0	65	34	43		16	0	0	281	350	37	47	5.2	.945	2B-83, 3B-30, SS-21
1916	CHI	N	98	.235	.287	345	81	11	2	1	0.3	29	22	26	26	9	1	0	140	199	21	19	3.7	.942	3B-55, 2B-33, OF-7, SS-5, 1B-2
1917			108	.243	.294	354	86	14	2	0	0.0	36	27	28	30	17	15	2	151	226	28	35	3.8	.931	SS-48, 3B-26, 2B-24, OF-1, 1B-1
1918			82	.223	.251	251	56	3	2	0	0.0	31	26	23	20	16	7	1	147	209	16	22	4.5	.957	2B-79, 3B-1, 1B-1
9 yrs.			936	.240	.286	3210	769	89	22	5	0.2	393	253	334	86	223	37	8	2435	1944	247	265	4.9	.947	2B-335, 3B-307, SS-161, 1B-106, OF-8

WORLD SERIES

| 1918 | CHI | N | 2 | — | — | 0 | 0 | 0 | 0 | 0 | — | 0 | 0 | 2 | 0 | 0 | 0 | 0 | 1 | 2 | 0 | 0 | 1.5 | 1.000 | 3B-2 |

Todd Zeile

ZEILE, TODD EDWARD BR TR 6'1" 190 lbs.
B. Sept. 9, 1965, Van Nuys, Calif.

Year	Team		Games	BA	SA	AB	H	2B	3B	HR	HR%	R	RBI	BB	SO	SB	PH AB	PH H	PO	A	E	DP	TC/G	FA	G by Pos
1989	STL	N	28	.256	.354	82	21	3	1	1	1.2	7	8	9	14	0	5	0	125	10	4	1	5.0	.971	C-23

Bart Zeller

ZELLER, BARTON WALLACE BR TR 6'1" 185 lbs.
B. July 22, 1941, Chicago Heights, Ill.

Year	Team		Games	BA	SA	AB	H	2B	3B	HR	HR%	R	RBI	BB	SO	SB	PH AB	PH H	PO	A	E	DP	TC/G	FA	G by Pos
1970	STL	N	1	—	—	0	0	0	0	0	—	0	0	0	0	0	0	0	1	0	0	0	1.0	1.000	C-1

Gus Zernial

ZERNIAL, GUS EDWARD (Ozark Ike) BR TR 6'2½" 210 lbs.
B. June 27, 1923, Beaumont, Tex.

Year	Team		Games	BA	SA	AB	H	2B	3B	HR	HR%	R	RBI	BB	SO	SB	PH AB	PH H	PO	A	E	DP	TC/G	FA	G by Pos
1949	CHI	A	73	.318	.500	198	63	17	2	5	2.5	29	38	15	26	0	25	8	73	4	0	0	1.1	1.000	OF-46
1950			143	.280	.484	543	152	16	4	29	5.3	75	93	38	110	0	5	1	306	9	10	2	2.3	.969	OF-137
1951	2 teams		143	.268	.511	CHI A (4G – .105)						PHI	A (139G – .274)												
"	total		143	.268	.511	571	153	30	5	33	5.8	92	129	63	101	2	1	1	334	18	10	3	2.5	.972	OF-142
1952	PHI	A	145	.262	.452	549	144	15	1	29	5.3	76	100	70	87	5	3	1	302	6	9	0	2.2	.972	OF-141
1953			147	.284	.559	556	158	21	3	42	7.6	85	108	57	79	4	4	3	300	17	9	2	2.2	.972	OF-141
1954			97	.250	.411	336	84	8	2	14	4.2	42	62	30	60	0	6	2	185	4	9	1	2.0	.955	OF-90, 1B-2
1955	KC	A	120	.254	.508	413	105	9	3	30	7.3	62	84	30	90	1	17	2	231	9	9	4	2.1	.964	OF-103
1956			109	.224	.445	272	61	12	0	16	5.9	36	44	33	66	2	35	4	111	9	2	1	1.1	.984	OF-69
1957			131	.236	.471	437	103	20	1	27	6.2	56	69	34	84	1	17	4	217	5	12	1	1.8	.949	OF-113, 1B-1
1958	DET	A	66	.323	.516	124	40	7	1	5	4.0	8	23	6	25	0	38	15	30	1	2	0	0.5	.939	OF-24
1959			60	.227	.417	132	30	4	0	7	5.3	11	26	7	27	0	27	6	198	10	6	20	3.6	.972	1B-32, OF-1
11 yrs.			1234	.265	.486	4131	1093	159	22	237	5.7	572	776	383	755	15	178	47	2287	92	78	34	2.0	.968	OF-1007, 1B-35

Year	Team		Games	BA	SA	AB	H	2B	3B	HR	HR%	R	RBI	BB	SO	SB	Pinch Hit AB	Pinch Hit H	PO	A	E	DP	TC/G	FA	G by Pos

Ed Zieber

Playing record listed under Ed Whiting

Charlie Ziegler

ZIEGLER, CHARLES W.
B. Jan. 13, 1875, Canton, Ohio D. Mar. 16, 1904, Canton, Ohio

Year	Team		Games	BA	SA	AB	H	2B	3B	HR	HR%	R	RBI	BB	SO	SB	PH AB	PH H	PO	A	E	DP	TC/G	FA	G by Pos
1899	CLE	N	2	.250	.250	8	2	0	0	0	0.0	2	0	0		0	0	0	2	5	1	0	4.0	.875	SS-1, 2B-1
1900	PHI	N	3	.273	.273	11	3	0	0	0	0.0	0	1	0		0	0	0	4	4	1	0	3.0	.889	3B-3
2 yrs.			5	.263	.263	19	5	0	0	0	0.0	2	1	0		0	0	0	6	9	2	0	3.4	.882	3B-3, SS-1, 2B-1

Benny Zientara

ZIENTARA, BENEDICT JOSEPH BR TR 5'9" 165 lbs.
B. Feb. 14, 1920, Chicago, Ill. D. Apr. 16, 1985, Lake Elsinore, Calif.

Year	Team		Games	BA	SA	AB	H	2B	3B	HR	HR%	R	RBI	BB	SO	SB	PH AB	PH H	PO	A	E	DP	TC/G	FA	G by Pos
1941	CIN	N	9	.286	.286	21	6	0	0	0	0.0	3	2	1	3	0	0	0	14	18	3	3	3.9	.914	2B-6
1946			78	.289	.339	280	81	10	2	0	0.0	26	16	14	11	3	0	0	114	219	11	38	4.4	.968	2B-39, 3B-36
1947			117	.258	.321	418	108	18	1	2	0.5	60	24	23	23	2	9	5	248	258	12	53	4.4	.977	2B-100, 3B-13
1948			74	.187	.214	187	35	1	2	0	0.0	17	7	12	11	0	7	1	146	144	3	32	4.0	.990	2B-60, 3B-3, SS-2
4 yrs.			278	.254	.304	906	230	29	5	2	0.2	106	49	50	48	5	16	6	522	639	29	126	4.3	.976	2B-205, 3B-52, SS-2

Bill Zies

ZIES, WILLIAM BL
Deceased.

Year	Team		Games	BA	SA	AB	H	2B	3B	HR	HR%	R	RBI	BB	SO	SB	PH AB	PH H	PO	A	E	DP	TC/G	FA	G by Pos
1891	STL	AA	2	.333	.333	3	1	0	0	0	0.0	0	0	0	0	0	0	0	5	1	0	0	3.0	1.000	C-2

Chief Zimmer

ZIMMER, CHARLES LOUIS BR TR 6' 190 lbs.
B. Nov. 23, 1860, Marietta, Ohio D. Aug. 22, 1949, Cleveland, Ohio
Manager 1903.

Year	Team		Games	BA	SA	AB	H	2B	3B	HR	HR%	R	RBI	BB	SO	SB	PH AB	PH H	PO	A	E	DP	TC/G	FA	G by Pos
1884	DET	N	8	.069	.103	29	2	1	0	0	0.0	0		1	14			0	0	31	11	8	3	6.3	.840	C-6, OF-2
1886	NY	AA	6	.158	.158	19	3	0	0	0	0.0	1		1				0	0	33	17	6	0	9.3	.893	C-6
1887	CLE	AA	14	.231	.327	52	12	5	0	0	0.0	9		4		1		0	0	64	13	8	2	6.1	.906	C-12, SS-1
1888			65	.241	.330	212	51	11	4	0	0.0	27	22	18		15		0	0	345	115	42	7	7.7	.916	C-59, OF-3, 1B-3, SS-1
1889	CLE	N	84	.259	.375	259	67	9	9	1	0.4	47	21	44	35	14		0	0	336	131	35	11	6.0	.930	C-81, 1B-3
1890			125	.214	.291	444	95	16	6	2	0.5	54	57	46	54	15		0	0	480	188	45	14	5.7	.937	C-125
1891			116	.255	.341	440	112	21	4	3	0.7	55	69	33	49	15		0	0	477	184	45	7	6.1	.936	C-116, 3B-1
1892			111	.262	.402	413	108	29	13	1	0.2	63	64	32	47	18		0	0	514	122	42	11	6.1	.938	C-111
1893			57	.308	.454	227	70	13	7	2	0.9	27	41	16	15	4	1	0	169	73	8	10	4.4	.968	C-56, 3B-1
1894			90	.284	.408	341	97	20	5	4	1.2	55	65	17	31	14	1	0	289	100	15	16	4.5	.963	C-89
1895			88	.340	.467	315	107	21	2	5	1.6	60	56	33	30	14	1	0	339	79	11	5	4.9	.974	C-84, 1B-3
1896			91	.277	.375	336	93	18	3	3	0.9	46	46	31	48	4	0	0	338	81	12	9	4.7	.972	C-91, 3B-1
1897			80	.316	.412	294	93	23	3	0	0.0	50	40	25		8	0	0	278	81	9	10	4.6	.976	C-80
1898			20	.238	.270	63	15	2	0	0	0.0	5	4	5		2	1	0	78	20	3	2	5.1	.970	C-19
1899	2 teams			CLE	N	(20G – .342)		LOU	N	(75G – .298)															
"	total		95	.307	.406	335	103	13	4	4	1.2	52	43	27		10	2	1	358	111	13	13	5.1	.973	C-82, 1B-11
1900	PIT	N	82	.295	.395	271	80	7	10	0	0.0	27	35	17		4	2	0	343	101	17	9	5.6	.963	C-78, 1B-2
1901			69	.220	.275	236	52	7	3	0	0.0	17	21	20		6	1	1	285	69	9	4	5.3	.975	C-68
1902			42	.268	.324	142	38	4	2	0	0.0	13	17	11		4	0	0	202	48	8	6	6.1	.969	C-41, 1B-1
1903	PHI	N	37	.220	.288	118	26	3	1	1	0.8	9	19			3	2	1	162	50	7	4	5.9	.968	C-35
19 yrs.			1280	.269	.369	4546	1224	222	76	26	0.6	617	620	390	323	151	11	3	5121	1594	343	145	5.5	.951	C-1239, 1B-25, OF-5, 3B-3, SS-1

Don Zimmer

ZIMMER, DONALD WILLIAM BR TR 5'9" 165 lbs.
B. Jan. 17, 1931, Cincinnati, Ohio
Manager 1972-73, 1976-82, 1988-89.

Year	Team		Games	BA	SA	AB	H	2B	3B	HR	HR%	R	RBI	BB	SO	SB	PH AB	PH H	PO	A	E	DP	TC/G	FA	G by Pos
1954	BKN	N	24	.182	.242	33	6	0	1	0	0.0	3	3	8	2	2	0	14	32	3	6	2.0	.939	SS-13
1955			88	.239	.443	280	67	10	1	15	5.4	38	50	19	66	5	3	0	184	207	12	63	4.6	.970	2B-62, SS-21, 3B-8
1956			17	.300	.350	20	6	1	0	0	0.0	4	2	0	7	0	0	0	10	11	1	4	1.3	.955	SS-8, 3B-3, 2B-1
1957			84	.219	.327	269	59	9	1	6	2.2	23	19	16	63	1	1	0	114	186	15	24	3.8	.952	3B-39, SS-37, 2B-5
1958	LA	N	127	.262	.415	455	119	15	2	17	3.7	52	60	28	92	14	1	0	281	395	26	102	5.5	.963	SS-114, 3B-12, OF-1, 2B-1
1959			97	.165	.249	249	41	7	1	4	1.6	21	28	37	56	3	4	1	120	240	10	43	3.8	.973	SS-88, 3B-5, 2B-1
1960	CHI	N	132	.258	.389	368	95	16	7	6	1.6	37	35	27	56	8	13	3	211	274	16	31	3.8	.968	2B-75, 3B-45, SS-5, OF-2
1961			128	.252	.403	477	120	25	4	13	2.7	57	40	25	70	5	8	1	284	332	20	100	5.0	.969	2B-116, 3B-5, OF-1
1962	2 teams			NY	N	(14G – .077)		CIN	N	(63G – .250)															
"	total		77	.213	.303	244	52	12	2	2	0.8	19	17	17	40	1	9	4	77	129	11	14	2.8	.949	3B-57, 2B-17, SS-1
1963	2 teams			LA	N	(22G – .217)		WAS	A	(83G – .248)															
"	total		105	.246	.424	321	79	13	1	14	4.4	41	46	21	67	3	14	5	93	191	20	18	2.9	.934	3B-88, 2B-3, SS-1
1964	WAS	A	121	.246	.411	341	84	16	2	12	3.5	38	38	27	94	1	38	10	72	144	10	6	1.9	.956	3B-87, OF-4, C-2, 2B-1
1965			95	.199	.252	226	45	6	0	2	0.9	20	17	26	59	2	27	5	181	81	12	7	2.9	.956	3B-36, C-33, 2B-12
12 yrs.			1095	.235	.372	3283	773	130	22	91	2.8	353	352	246	678	45	120	29	1641	2222	156	418	3.7	.961	3B-385, 2B-294, SS-288, C-35, OF-8

WORLD SERIES

Year	Team		Games	BA	SA	AB	H	2B	3B	HR	HR%	R	RBI	BB	SO	SB	PH AB	PH H	PO	A	E	DP	TC/G	FA	G by Pos
1955	BKN	N	4	.222	.222	9	2	0	0	0	0.0	2	0	2	5	0	0	0	4	8	2	3	3.5	.857	2B-4
1959	LA	N	1	.000	.000	1	0	0	0	0	0.0	0	0	0	0	0	0	0	0	1	0	0	1.0	1.000	SS-1
2 yrs.			5	.200	.200	10	2	0	0	0	0.0	2	0	2	5	0	1	0	4	9	2	3	3.0	.867	2B-4, SS-1

Bill Zimmerman

ZIMMERMAN, WILLIAM H. BR TR 5'8½" 172 lbs.
B. Jan. 20, 1889, Kengen, Germany D. Oct. 4, 1952, Newark, N. J.

Year	Team		Games	BA	SA	AB	H	2B	3B	HR	HR%	R	RBI	BB	SO	SB	PH AB	PH H	PO	A	E	DP	TC/G	FA	G by Pos
1915	BKN	N	22	.281	.316	57	16	2	0	0	0.0	3	7	4	8	1	3	0	19	0	3	0	1.0	.864	OF-18

Eddie Zimmerman

ZIMMERMAN, EDWARD DESMOND (Zimmie) BR TR 5'9" 160 lbs.
B. Jan. 4, 1883, Oceanic, N. J. D. May 6, 1945, Emmaus, Pa.

Year	Team		Games	BA	SA	AB	H	2B	3B	HR	HR%	R	RBI	BB	SO	SB	PH AB	PH H	PO	A	E	DP	TC/G	FA	G by Pos
1906	STL	N	5	.214	.214	14	3	0	0	0	0.0	0	1	0		0	0	0	7	6	1	0	2.8	.929	3B-5
1911	BKN	N	122	.185	.264	417	77	10	7	3	0.7	31	36	34	37	9	0	0	167	229	16	24	3.4	.961	3B-122
2 yrs.			127	.186	.262	431	80	10	7	3	0.7	31	37	34	37	9	0	0	174	235	17	24	3.4	.960	3B-127

Year	Team		Games	BA	SA	AB	H	2B	3B	HR	HR%	R	RBI	BB	SO	SB	Pinch Hit AB	H	PO	A	E	DP	TC/G	FA	G by Pos

Heinie Zimmerman

ZIMMERMAN, HENRY
B. Feb. 9, 1887, New York, N. Y.   D. Mar. 14, 1969, New York, N. Y.
BR TR 5'11½" 176 lbs.

Year	Team		Games	BA	SA	AB	H	2B	3B	HR	HR%	R	RBI	BB	SO	SB	PH AB	PH H	PO	A	E	DP	TC/G	FA	G by Pos
1907	CHI	N	5	.222	.333	9	2	1	0	0	0.0	0	1	0		0	0	0	10	8	4	2	4.4	.818	2B-4, OF-1, SS-1
1908			46	.292	.345	113	33	4	1	0	0.0	17	9	1		2	15	2	48	48	9	2	2.3	.914	2B-20, OF-8, SS-1, 3B-1
1909			65	.273	.344	183	50	9	2	0	0.0	23	21	3		7	18	6	100	93	19	12	3.3	.910	2B-27, 3B-16, SS-12
1910			99	.284	.394	335	95	16	6	3	0.9	35	38	20	36	7	12	3	164	181	33	28	3.8	.913	2B-33, SS-26, 3B-22, OF-4, 1B-1
1911			143	.307	.462	535	164	22	17	9	1.7	80	85	25	50	23	4	1	388	348	42	52	5.4	.946	2B-108, 3B-20, 1B-11
1912			145	**.372**	**.571**	557	**207**	41	14	**14**	2.5	95	**103**	38	60	23	2	0	354	253	39	31	4.5	.940	3B-121, 1B-22
1913			127	.313	.490	447	140	28	12	9	2.0	69	95	41	40	18	1	0	139	232	36	18	3.2	.912	3B-125
1914			146	.296	.424	564	167	36	12	4	0.7	75	87	20	46	17	1	1	196	270	54	19	3.6	.896	3B-119, SS-15, 2B-12
1915			139	.265	.379	520	138	28	11	3	0.6	65	62	21	33	19	1	1	252	344	40	35	4.6	.937	2B-100, 3B-36, SS-4
1916	2 teams		CHI	N	(107G – .291)	NY	N	(40G – .272)																	
"	total		147	.286	.390	549	157	29	5	6	1.1	76	**83**	23	43	24	4	1	155	329	34	23	3.5	.934	3B-115, SS-14, 2B-14
1917	NY	N	150	.297	.391	585	174	22	9	5	0.9	61	102	16	43	13	0	0	154	352	29	24	3.6	.946	3B-149, 2B-5
1918			121	.272	.363	463	126	19	10	1	0.2	43	56	13	23	14	1	1	312	219	17	15	4.5	.969	3B-100, 1B-19
1919			123	.255	.354	444	113	20	6	4	0.9	56	58	21	30	8	0	0	122	268	25	15	3.4	.940	3B-123
13 yrs.			1456	.295	.419	5304	1566	275	105	58	1.1	695	800	242	404	175	59	16	2394	2945	381	276	3.9	.933	3B-947, 2B-323, SS-63, 1B-53, OF-13

WORLD SERIES

1907	CHI	N	1	.000	.000	1	0	0	0	0	0.0	0	0	0	1	0	0	0	0	1	0	0	1.0	1.000	2B-1
1910			5	.235	.294	17	4	1	0	0	0.0	0	2	1	3	1	0	0	10	18	1	1	5.8	.966	2B-5
1917	NY	N	6	.120	.200	25	3	0	1	0	0.0	1	0	0	0	0	0	0	9	14	2	0	4.2	.920	3B-6
3 yrs.			12	.163	.233	43	7	1	1	0	0.0	1	2	1	4	1	0	0	19	33	3	1	4.6	.945	3B-6, 2B-6

Jerry Zimmerman

ZIMMERMAN, GERALD ROBERT
B. Sept. 21, 1934, Omaha, Neb.
BR TR 6'2" 185 lbs.

Year	Team		Games	BA	SA	AB	H	2B	3B	HR	HR%	R	RBI	BB	SO	SB	PH AB	PH H	PO	A	E	DP	TC/G	FA	G by Pos
1961	CIN	N	76	.206	.230	204	42	5	0	0	0.0	8	10	11	21	1	0	0	374	22	10	8	5.3	.975	C-76
1962	MIN	A	34	.274	.339	62	17	4	0	0	0.0	6	7	3	5	0	1	0	111	9	1	0	3.6	.992	C-34
1963			39	.232	.250	56	13	1	0	0	0.0	3	3	2	8	0	1	0	116	8	0	0	3.2	1.000	C-39
1964			63	.200	.225	120	24	3	0	0	0.0	6	12	10	15	0	3	0	264	22	2	1	4.6	.993	C-63
1965			83	.214	.253	154	33	1	1	1	0.6	8	11	12	23	0	1	0	321	22	1	5	4.1	.997	C-82
1966			60	.252	.328	119	30	4	1	1	0.8	11	15	15	23	0	2	0	264	16	1	5	4.7	.996	C-59
1967			104	.167	.192	234	39	3	0	1	0.4	13	12	22	49	0	1	0	572	44	5	7	6.0	.992	C-104
1968			24	.111	.133	45	5	1	0	0	0.0	3	2	3	10	0	0	0	109	7	1	0	4.9	.991	C-24
8 yrs.			483	.204	.239	994	203	22	2	3	0.3	60	72	78	154	1	6	0	2131	150	21	26	4.8	.991	C-481

WORLD SERIES

1961	CIN	N	2	–	–	0	0	0	0	0	–	0	0	0	0	0	0	0	4	0	0	0	2.0	1.000	C-2
1965	MIN	A	2	.000	.000	1	0	0	0	0	0.0	0	0	0	0	0	0	0	2	1	0	1	1.5	1.000	C-2
2 yrs.			4	.000	.000	1	0	0	0	0	0.0	0	0	0	0	0	0	0	6	1	0	1	1.8	1.000	C-4

Roy Zimmerman

ZIMMERMAN, ROY FRANKLIN
B. Sept. 13, 1916, Pine Grove, Pa.
BL TL 6'2" 187 lbs.

1945	NY	N	27	.276	.439	98	27	1	0	5	5.1	14	15	5	16	1	1	0	226	13	3	13	9.0	.988	1B-25, OF-1

Frank Zinn

ZINN, FRANK PATRICK
B. Dec. 21, 1865, Phoenixville, Pa.   D. May 12, 1936, Manayunk, Pa.
5'8" 150 lbs.

1888	PHI	AA	2	.000	.000	7	0	0	0	0	0.0	0		0		1	0	0	13	2	1	0	8.0	.938	C-2

Guy Zinn

ZINN, GUY
B. Feb. 13, 1887, Hallbrook, W. Va.   D. Oct. 6, 1949, Clarksburg, W. Va.
BL TR 5'10½" 170 lbs.

1911	NY	A	9	.148	.296	27	4	0	0	0	0.0	5	1	4		0	0	0	10	2	1	0	1.4	.923	OF-8
1912			106	.262	.394	401	105	15	10	6	1.5	56	55	50		17	0	0	158	9	20	1	1.8	.893	OF-106
1913	BOS	N	36	.297	.406	138	41	8	2	1	0.7	15	15	4	23	3	1	0	83	8	5	1	2.7	.948	OF-35
1914	BAL	F	61	.280	.418	225	63	10	6	3	1.3	30	25	16		6	3	1	82	5	6	1	1.5	.935	OF-57
1915			102	.269	.394	312	84	18	3	5	1.6	30	43	35		2	9	1	139	11	8	4	1.5	.949	OF-88
5 yrs.			314	.269	.398	1103	297	51	23	15	1.4	136	139	109	23	28	14	2	472	35	40	7	1.7	.927	OF-294

Bud Zipfel

ZIPFEL, MARION SYLVESTER
B. Nov. 18, 1938, Belleville, Ill.
BL TR 6'3" 200 lbs.

1961	WAS	A	50	.200	.371	170	34	7	5	4	2.4	17	18	15	49	1	5	0	429	25	8	40	9.2	.983	1B-44
1962			68	.239	.370	184	44	4	1	6	3.3	21	21	17	43	1	18	2	228	17	8	13	3.7	.968	1B-26, OF-23
2 yrs.			118	.220	.370	354	78	11	6	10	2.8	38	39	32	92	2	23	2	657	42	16	53	6.1	.978	1B-70, OF-23

Richie Zisk

ZISK, RICHARD WALTER
B. Feb. 6, 1949, Brooklyn, N. Y.
BR TR 6'1" 200 lbs.

1971	PIT	N	7	.200	.467	15	3	1	0	1	6.7	2	2	4	7	0	1	0	7	0	0	0	1.0	1.000	OF-6
1972			17	.189	.270	37	7	3	0	0	0.0	4	4	7	10	0	5	1	14	1	1	0	0.9	.938	OF-12
1973			103	.324	.526	333	108	23	7	10	3.0	44	54	21	63	0	19	4	139	12	2	4	1.5	.987	OF-84
1974			149	.313	.476	536	168	30	3	17	3.2	75	100	65	91	1	9	4	312	9	5	3	2.2	.985	OF-141
1975			147	.290	.474	504	146	27	3	20	4.0	69	75	68	109	1	6	0	264	7	7	1	1.9	.975	OF-140
1976			155	.289	.465	581	168	35	2	21	3.6	91	89	52	96	1	3	2	300	11	4	2	2.0	.987	OF-152
1977	CHI	A	141	.290	.514	531	154	17	6	30	5.6	78	101	55	98	0	3	0	210	9	4	3	1.6	.982	OF-109, DH-28
1978	TEX	A	140	.262	.432	511	134	19	1	22	4.3	68	85	58	76	3	1	0	155	6	2	1	1.2	.988	OF-90, DH-49
1979			144	.262	.416	503	132	21	1	18	3.6	69	64	57	75	1	7	2	234	10	7	6	1.7	.972	OF-134, DH-3
1980			135	.290	.460	448	130	17	1	19	4.2	48	77	39	72	0	19	3	45	3	1	1	0.4	.980	DH-86, OF-37
1981	SEA	A	94	.311	.485	357	111	12	1	16	4.5	42	43	28	63	0	0	0	0	0	0	0	0.0	–	DH-93
1982			131	.292	.477	503	147	28	1	21	4.2	61	62	49	89	0	0	0	0	0	0	0	0.0	–	DH-130
1983			90	.242	.411	285	69	12	0	12	4.2	30	36	30	61	0	10	2	0	0	0	0	0.0	–	DH-84
13 yrs.			1453	.287	.466	5144	1477	245	26	207	4.0	681	792	533	910	8	84	18	1680	68	33	20	1.2	.981	OF-905, DH-473

LEAGUE CHAMPIONSHIP SERIES

1974	PIT	N	3	.300	.300	10	3	0	0	0	0.0	1	0	0	3	0	1	0	2	0	0	0	0.7	1.000	OF-2

Year	Team	Games	BA	SA	AB	H	2B	3B	HR	HR%	R	RBI	BB	SO	SB	Pinch Hit AB	Pinch Hit H	PO	A	E	DP	TC/G	FA	G by Pos

Richie Zisk *continued*

Year	Team	Games	BA	SA	AB	H	2B	3B	HR	HR%	R	RBI	BB	SO	SB	AB	H	PO	A	E	DP	TC/G	FA	G by Pos
1975		3	.500	.600	10	5	1	0	0	0.0	0	0	2	2	0	0	0	8	0	0	0	2.7	1.000	OF-3
2 yrs.		6	.400	.450	20	8	1	0	0	0.0	1	0	2	5	0	1	1	10	0	0	0	1.7	1.000	OF-5

Billy Zitzmann

ZITZMANN, WILLIAM ARTHUR   BR TR 5'10½" 175 lbs.
B. Nov. 19, 1895, Long Island City, N. Y.   D. May 29, 1985, Passaic, N. J.

Year	Team	Games	BA	SA	AB	H	2B	3B	HR	HR%	R	RBI	BB	SO	SB	AB	H	PO	A	E	DP	TC/G	FA	G by Pos
1919	2 teams	PIT N (11G – .192)			CIN N (2G – .000)																			
"	total	13	.185	.222	27	5	1	0	0	0.0	5	2	0	6	2	3	0	11	0	1	0	0.9	.917	OF-9
1925	CIN N	104	.252	.316	301	76	13	3	0	0.0	53	21	35	22	11	6	1	136	6	6	0	1.4	.959	OF-89, SS-1
1926		53	.245	.287	94	23	2	1	0	0.0	21	3	6	7	3	3	0	55	0	2	0	1.1	.965	OF-31
1927		88	.284	.362	232	66	10	4	0	0.0	47	24	20	18	9	3	0	149	24	11	0	2.1	.940	OF-60, SS-8, 3B-3
1928		101	.297	.387	266	79	9	3	3	1.1	53	33	13	22	13	3	0	155	5	7	2	1.7	.958	OF-78, 3B-1
1929		47	.226	.262	84	19	3	0	0	0.0	18	6	9	10	4	1	1	77	0	5	1	1.7	.939	OF-22, 1B-5
6 yrs.		406	.267	.336	1004	268	38	11	3	0.3	197	89	83	85	42	16	2	583	35	32	3	1.6	.951	OF-289, SS-9, 1B-5, 3B-4

Frank Zupo

ZUPO, FRANK JOSEPH (Noodles)   BL TR 5'11" 182 lbs.
B. Aug. 29, 1939, San Francisco, Calif.

Year	Team	Games	BA	SA	AB	H	2B	3B	HR	HR%	R	RBI	BB	SO	SB	AB	H	PO	A	E	DP	TC/G	FA	G by Pos
1957	BAL A	10	.083	.083	12	1	0	0	0	0.0	2	0	1	4	0	4	0	20	1	2	0	2.3	.913	C-8
1958		1	.000	.000	2	0	0	0	0	0.0	0	0	0	1	0	0	0	4	0	0	0	4.0	1.000	C-1
1961		5	.500	.750	4	2	1	0	0	0.0	1	0	1	1	0	0	0	7	0	0	0	1.4	1.000	C-4
3 yrs.		16	.167	.222	18	3	1	0	0	0.0	3	0	2	6	0	4	0	31	1	2	0	2.1	.941	C-13

Paul Zuvella

ZUVELLA, PAUL   BR TR 6' 173 lbs.
B. Oct. 31, 1958, San Mateo, Calif.

Year	Team	Games	BA	SA	AB	H	2B	3B	HR	HR%	R	RBI	BB	SO	SB	AB	H	PO	A	E	DP	TC/G	FA	G by Pos
1982	ATL N	2	.000	.000	1	0	0	0	0	0.0	0	0	0	0	0	0	0	0	4	1	0	2.5	.800	SS-1
1983		3	.000	.000	5	0	0	0	0	0.0	0	0	2	1	0	1	0	1	2	1	0	1.3	.750	SS-2
1984		11	.200	.240	25	5	1	0	0	0.0	2	1	2	3	0	0	0	13	21	0	6	3.1	1.000	SS-6, 2B-6
1985		81	.253	.305	190	48	8	1	0	0.0	16	4	16	14	2	5	1	112	173	8	39	3.6	.973	2B-42, SS-33, 3B-5
1986	NY A	21	.083	.104	48	4	1	0	0	0.0	2	2	5	4	0	0	0	30	54	3	12	4.1	.966	SS-21
1987		14	.176	.176	34	6	0	0	0	0.0	0	0	4	3	0	5	0	20	25	0	5	3.2	1.000	2B-7, SS-6, 3B-1
1988	CLE A	51	.231	.285	130	30	5	1	0	0.0	9	7	8	13	0	1	0	77	112	8	21	3.9	.959	SS-49
1989		24	.276	.414	58	16	2	0	2	3.4	10	6	1	11	0	3	1	14	24	2	1	1.7	.950	SS-15, 3B-5, DH-3
8 yrs.		207	.222	.277	491	109	17	2	2	0.4	41	20	34	50	2	13	2	267	415	23	84	3.4	.967	SS-133, 2B-55, 3B-11, DH-3

Dutch Zwilling

ZWILLING, EDWARD HARRISON   BL TL 5'6½" 160 lbs.
B. Nov. 2, 1888, St. Louis, Mo.   D. Mar. 27, 1978, La Crescenta, Calif.

Year	Team	Games	BA	SA	AB	H	2B	3B	HR	HR%	R	RBI	BB	SO	SB	AB	H	PO	A	E	DP	TC/G	FA	G by Pos
1910	CHI A	27	.184	.241	87	16	5	0	0	0.0	7	5	11		1	0	0	45	2	3	1	1.9	.940	OF-27
1914	CHI F	154	.313	.480	592	185	38	8	15	2.5	91	95	46		21	0	0	340	15	14	3	2.4	.962	OF-154
1915		150	.286	.442	548	157	32	7	13	2.4	65	94	67		24	1	0	359	20	8	6	2.6	.979	OF-148, 1B-3
1916	CHI N	35	.113	.189	53	6	1	0	1	1.9	4	8	4	6	0	23	4	11	0	0	0	0.3	1.000	OF-10
4 yrs.		366	.284	.435	1280	364	76	15	29	2.3	167	202	128	6	46	24	4	755	37	25	10	2.2	.969	OF-339, 1B-3

PART EIGHT

Pitcher Register

Alphabetical List of Every Man Who Ever
Pitched in the Major Leagues
And His Pitching, Fielding, and Significant
Batting Records

Pitcher Register

The Pitcher Register is an alphabetical list of every man who pitched in the major leagues from 1876 through today. Included are lifetime totals of League Championship Series and World Series.

Much of this information has never been compiled, especially for the period 1876 through 1919. All information and abbreviations that may appear unfamiliar are explained in the sample format presented below. John Doe, the player used in the sample, is fictitious and serves only to illustrate the information.

Year	Team		W	L	PCT	ERA	G	GS	CG	IP	H	BB	SO	ShO	Relief Pitching W	L	SV	Batting AB	H	HR	BA	PO	A	E	DP	TC/G	FA

John Doe

DOE, JOHN LEE (Slim)   TR 6'2" 165 lbs.
Played as John Cherry part of 1900.
Born John Lee Doughnut. Brother of Bill Doe.
B. Jan. 1, 1850, New York, N. Y. D. July 1, 1955, New York, N. Y.
Manager 1908–15.
Hall of Fame 1946.

Year	Team		W	L	PCT	ERA	G	GS	CG	IP	H	BB	SO	ShO	W	L	SV	AB	H	HR	BA	PO	A	E	DP	TC/G	FA
1884	STL	U	4	2	.667	3.40	26	0	0	54.2	41	38	40	0	1	1	0	28	12	0	.226	15	20	3	2	1.5	.921
1885	LOU	AA	14	10	.583	4.12	40	19	10	207.2	193	76	70	0	0	1	0	43	33	0	.289	13	33	2	3	0.9	.958
1886	CLE	N	10	5	.667	4.08	40	8	4	117	110	55	77	0	0	1	1	40	16	1	.165	7	26	3	1	0.9	.917
1887	BOS	N	9	3	.750	3.38	27	5	2	88	90	36	34	0	2	3	2	40	12	0	.141	12	27	1	5	1.5	.975
1888	NY	N	13	4	.765	4.17	39	4	0	110	121	50	236	0	0	1	0	16	6	0	.273	5	10	0	2	0.4	1.000
1889	3 teams		DET N (10G 4-2)			PIT N (2G 0-0)				PHI N (10G 4-0)																	
"	total		8	2	.800	4.25	22	2	2	91.1	90	41	43	0	0	0	0	3	3	0	.333	6	14	2	2	1.0	.909
1890	NY	P	13	6	.684	4.43	38	0	0	61.1	57	28	30	0	1	0	1	34	17	0	.185	9	9	3	1	0.6	.857
1900	CHI	N	18	4	.818	3.71	35	1	0	63.1	58	15	23	0	0	0	2	35	13	1	.146	3	6	1	0	0.3	.900
1901	BAL	A	18	4	.818	1.98	35	0	0	77.1	68	40	29	0	3	0	0	25	16	0	.254	7	16	5	1	0.8	.821
1906	BOS	N	14	10	.583	3.41	31	0	0	58	66	23	24	0	1	3	0	37	16	1	.286	5	8	0	1	0.4	1.000
1907			13	4	.765	2.51	37	0	0	68	44	30	31	0	1	1	0	9	2	0	.182	10	25	2	0	1.0	.946
1908			0	0	—	3.38	1	1	0	8	8	1	1	0	3	1	3	33	7	0	.226	0	0	0	0	—	—
1914	CHI	F	3	1	.750	2.78	6	0	0	54.2	41	28	9	0	2	3	3	19	2	0	.222	0	2	0	0	0.3	1.000
13 yrs.			137	55	.714	3.50	377	40	18	1059.1	987	461	647	0	21	17	15	492	216	3	.212	92	286	13	7	1.0	.967
						8th																					

LEAGUE CHAMPIONSHIP SERIES

Year	Team		W	L	PCT	ERA	G	GS	CG	IP	H	BB	SO	ShO	W	L	SV	AB	H	HR	BA	PO	A	E	DP	TC/G	FA
1906	BOS	N	1	0	1.000	0.00	1	1	0	8	5	3	7	0	0	0	0	2	0	0	.000	0	1	0	0	1.0	1.000
1908			0	0	—	3.00	2	0	0	6	4	2	7	0	0	0	0	1	0	0	.000	1	0	1	0	2.0	.500
2 yrs.			1	0	1.000	1.29	3	1	0	14	9	5	14	0	0	0	0	3	0	0	.000	1	1	1	0	1.5	.667
							9th																					

WORLD SERIES

Year	Team		W	L	PCT	ERA	G	GS	CG	IP	H	BB	SO	ShO	W	L	SV	AB	H	HR	BA	PO	A	E	DP	TC/G	FA
1906	BOS	N	0	0	—	0.00	2	0	0	1.2	0	1	2	0	0	0	0	0	0	0	.000	1	1	0	0	1.0	1.000

Player Information

John Doe
This shortened version of the player's full name is the name most familiar to the fans. All players in this section are alphabetically arranged by the last name part of this name.

DOE, JOHN LEE
Player's full name. The arrangement is last name first, then first and middle name(s).

(Slim)
Player's nickname. Any name appearing in parentheses is a nickname.

TR
The player's throwing style. Doe, for instance, threw right-handed.

6'2"
Player's height.

165 lbs
Player's average playing weight.

Played as John Cherry part of 1900
The player at one time in his major league career played under another name and can be found in box scores or newspaper stories only under that name.

Born John Lee Doughnut
The name the player was given at birth. (For the most part, the player never used this name while playing in the major leagues, but, if he did, it would be listed as "played as," which is explained above under the heading "Played as John Cherry part of 1900.")

Brother of Bill Doe
The player's brother. (Relatives indicated here are fathers, sons, and brothers who played or managed in the major leagues and the National Association.)

B. Jan. 1, 1850, New York, N.Y.
Date and place of birth.

D. July 1, 1955, New York, N.Y.
Date and place of death. (Some players are listed simply as "deceased." Although no certification of death or other information is now available, it is reasonably certain they are dead.)

Manager 1908–15
Doe also served as a major league manager. All men who were managers can also be found in the Manager Register, where their complete managerial record is shown.

Hall of Fame 1946
Doe was elected to the Baseball Hall of Fame in 1946.

Column Headings Information

Year Team	W	L	PCT	ERA	G	GS	CG	IP	H	BB	SO	ShO	Relief Pitching W L SV	Batting AB H HR	BA	PO	A	E	DP	TC/G	FA

Total Pitching (including all starting and relief appearances)

W	Wins
L	Losses
PCT	Winning Percentage
ERA	Earned Run Average
G	Games Pitched In
GS	Games Started
CG	Complete Games
IP	Innings Pitched
H	Hits Allowed
BB	Bases on Balls Allowed
SO	Strikeouts
ShO	Shutouts

Relief Pitching

W	Wins
L	Losses
SV	Saves

Batting

AB	At Bats
H	Hits
HR	Home Runs
BA	Batting Average

Fielding

PO	Putouts
A	Assists
E	Errors
DP	Double Plays
TC/G	Total Chances Per Game
FA	Fielding Average

Team and League Information

Year	Team	Lg	W	L	PCT	ERA	G	GS	CG	IP	H	BB	SO	ShO	RW	RL	SV	AB	H	HR	BA	PO	A	E	DP	TC/G	FA
1884	STL	U																									
1885	LOU	AA																									
1886	CLE	N																									
1887	BOS	N																									
1888	NY	N																									
1889	3 teams	DET N (10G 4-2) PIT N (2G 0-0) PHI N (10G 4-0)																									
"	total		8	2	.800	4.25	22	2	2	91.1	90	41	43	0	0	0	0	3	3	0	.333	6	14	2	2	1.0	.909
1890	NY	P																									
1900	CHI	N																									
1901	BAL	A																									
1906	BOS	N																									
1907																											
1908																											
1914	CHI	F																									
13 yrs.																											

Doe's record has been exaggerated so that his playing career spans all the years of the six different major leagues. Directly alongside the year and team information is the symbol for the league:

N	National League (1876 to date)
A	American League (1901 to date)
F	Federal League (1914–15)

AA American Association (1882–91)

P Players' League (1890)

U Union Association (1884)

STL The abbreviation of the city in which the team played. Doe, for example, played for St. Louis in 1884. All teams in this section are listed by an abbreviation of the city in which the team played. The abbreviations follow:

ALT	Altoona	IND	Indianapolis
ATL	Atlanta	KC	Kansas City
BAL	Baltimore	LA	Los Angeles
BKN	Brooklyn	LOU	Louisville
BOS	Boston	MIL	Milwaukee
BUF	Buffalo	MIN	Minnesota
CAL	California	MON	Montreal
CHI	Chicago	NWK	Newark
CIN	Cincinnati	NY	New York
CLE	Cleveland	OAK	Oakland
COL	Columbus	PHI	Philadelphia
DET	Detroit	PIT	Pittsburgh
HAR	Hartford	PRO	Providence
HOU	Houston	RIC	Richmond
ROC	Rochester	TEX	Texas
SD	San Diego	TOL	Toledo
SEA	Seattle	TOR	Toronto
SF	San Francisco	TRO	Troy
STL	St. Louis	WAS	Washington
STP	St. Paul	WIL	Wilmington
SYR	Syracuse	WOR	Worcester

Blank space appearing beneath a team and league indicates that the team and league are the same. Doe, for example, played for Boston in the National League from 1906 through 1908.

3 Teams Total. Indicates a player played for more than one team in the same year. Doe played for three teams in 1889. The number of games he played and his wins and losses for each team are also shown. Directly beneath this line, following the word "total," is Doe's combined record for all three teams for 1889.

Total Playing Years. This information, which appears as the first item on the pitcher's lifetime total line, indicates the total number of years in which he pitched at least one game. Doe, for example, pitched in at least one game for 13 years.

Statistical Information

Year Team	W	L	PCT	ERA	G	GS	CG	IP	H	BB	SO	ShO	Relief Pitching W	L	SV	Batting AB	H	HR	BA	PO	A	E	DP	TC/G	FA

John Doe

DOE, JOHN LEE (Slim) TR 6'2" 165 lbs.
Played as John Cherry part of 1900.
Born John Lee Doughnut. Brother of Bill Doe.
B. Jan. 1, 1850, New York, N. Y. D. July 1, 1955, New York, N. Y.
Manager 1908–15.
Hall of Fame 1946.

Year	Team	W	L	PCT	ERA	G	GS	CG	IP	H	BB	SO	ShO	RP W	RP L	RP SV	AB	H	HR	BA	PO	A	E	DP	TC/G	FA
1884	STL U	4	2	.667	3.40	26	0	0	54.2	41	38	40	0	1	1	0	28	12	0	.226	15	20	3	2	1.5	.921
1885	LOU AA	14	10	.583	4.12	40	19	10	207.2	193	76	70	0	0	1	0	43	33	0	.289	13	33	2	3	0.9	.958
1886	CLE N	10	5	.667	4.08	40	8	4	117	110	55	77	0	0	1	1	40	16	1	.165	7	26	3	1	0.9	.917
1887	BOS N	9	3	.750	3.38	27	5	2	88	90	36	34	0	2	3	2	40	12	0	.141	12	27	1	5	1.5	.975
1888	NY N	13	4	.765	4.17	39	4	0	110	121	50	236	0	0	1	0	16	6	0	.273	5	10	0	2	0.4	1.000
1889	3 teams DET N (10G 4-2) PIT N (2G 0-0) PHI N (10G 4-0)																									
	total	8	2	.800	4.25	22	2	2	91.1	90	41	43	0	0	0	0	3	3	0	.333	6	14	2	2	1.0	.909
1890	NY P	13	6	.684	4.43	38	0	0	61.1	57	28	30	0	1	0	1	34	17	0	.185	9	9	3	1	0.6	.857
1900	CHI N	18	4	.818	3.71	35	1	0	63.1	57	15	23	0	0	0	2	35	13	1	.146	3	6	1	0	0.3	.900
1901	BAL A	18	4	.818	1.98	35	0	0	77.1	68	40	29	0	3	0	0	25	16	0	.254	7	16	5	1	0.8	.821
1906	BOS N	14	10	.583	3.41	31	0	0	58	66	23	24	0	1	3	0	37	16	1	.286	5	8	0	1	0.4	1.000
1907		13	4	.765	2.51	37	0	0	68	44	30	31	0	1	1	0	9	2	0	.182	10	25	2	0	1.0	.946
1908		0	0	—	3.38	1	1	0	8	8	1	1	0	3	1	3	33	7	0	.226	0	0	0	0	—	—
1914	CHI F	3	1	.750	2.78	6	0	0	54.2	41	28	9	0	2	3	3	19	2	0	.222	0	2	0	0	0.3	1.000
13 yrs.		137	55	.714	3.50 8th	377	40	18	1059.1	987	461	647	0	21	17	15	492	216	3	.212	92	286	13	7	1.0	.967

Partial Innings Pitched. These are shown in the Innings Pitched column, and are indicated by a ".1" or ".2" after the total. Doe, for example, pitched 54⅔ innings in 1884.

League Leaders. Statistics that appear in boldfaced print indicate the pitcher led his league that year in a particular statistical category. Doe, for example, led the National League in earned run average in 1901. When there is a tie for league lead, the figures for all the men who tied are shown in boldface.

All-Time Single Season Leaders. (Starts with 1893, the first year that the pitcher's box was moved to its present distance of 60 feet 6 inches.) Indicated by the small number that appears next to the statistic. Doe, for example, is shown by a small number "1" next to his earned run average in 1901.

This means he is first on the all-time major league list for having the lowest earned run average in a single season. All pitchers who tied for first are shown by the same number.

Lifetime Leaders. Indicated by the figure that appears beneath the line showing the pitcher's lifetime totals. Doe has an "8th" shown below his lifetime Saves total. This means that, lifetime, Doe ranks eighth among major league pitchers in Saves. Once again, only the top ten are indicated, and players who are tied receive the same number.

Meaningless Averages. Indicated by the use of a dash (—). In the case of Doe, a dash is shown for his 1908 winning percentage. This means that although he pitched in one game he never had a decision. A percentage of .000 would mean that he had at least one loss.

Estimated Earned Run Averages. Any time an earned run average appears in italics, it indicates that not all the earned runs allowed by the pitcher are known, and the information had to be estimated. Doe's 1885 earned run average, for example, appears in italics. It is known that Doe's team, Louisville, allowed 560 runs in 112 games. Of these games, it is known that in 90 of them Louisville allowed 420 runs of which 315 or 75% were earned. Doe pitched 207⅔ innings in 40 games and allowed 134 runs. In 35 of these games, it is known that he allowed 118 runs of which 83 were earned. By multiplying the team's known ratio of earned runs to total runs (75%), by Doe's 16 (134 minus 118) remaining runs allowed, a figure of 12 additional estimated earned runs is calculated. This means that Doe allowed an estimated total of 95 earned runs in 207⅔ innings, for an estimated earned run average of 4.12. In all cases at least 50% of the runs allowed by the team were "known" as a basis for estimating earned run averages. (Any time the symbol "infinity" (∞) is shown for a pitcher's earned run average, it means that the pitcher allowed one or more earned runs during a season without retiring a batter.)

League Leader Qualifications. Throughout baseball there have been different rules used to determine the minimum appearances necessary to qualify for league leader in categories concerning averages (Batting Average, Earned Run Average, etc.). For the rules and the years they were in effect, see Appendix C.

Traded League Leaders. An asterisk (*) next to a boldfaced number indicates that the player led the league in a particular category, but since he played in more than one league that year, the number does not indicate his league-leading total or average.

Batting Statistics. Because a pitcher's batting statistics are of relatively minor importance—and the Designated Hitter rule may eliminate pitchers' batting entirely—only the most significant statistics are given: number of hits, home runs, and batting average.

An Asterisk (*) shown in the lifetime batting totals means that the pitcher's complete year-by-year and lifetime batting record is listed in the Player Register.

Year	Team		W	L	PCT	ERA	G	GS	CG	IP	H	BB	SO	ShO	Relief Pitching W	L	SV	Batting AB	H	HR	BA	PO	A	E	DP	TC/G	FA

Don Aase

AASE, DONALD WILLIAM
B. Sept. 8, 1954, Orange, Calif. — BR TR 6'3" 190 lbs.

Year	Team	W	L	PCT	ERA	G	GS	CG	IP	H	BB	SO	ShO	W	L	SV	AB	H	HR	BA	PO	A	E	DP	TC/G	FA
1977	BOS A	6	2	.750	3.12	13	13	4	92.1	85	19	49	2	0	0	0	0	0	0	–	5	13	1	0	1.5	.947
1978	CAL A	11	8	.579	4.03	29	29	6	178.2	185	80	93	1	0	0	0	0	0	0	–	16	26	3	2	1.6	.933
1979		9	10	.474	4.82	37	28	7	185	200	77	96	1	1	1	2	0	0	0	–	8	17	2	3	0.7	.926
1980		8	13	.381	4.06	40	21	5	175	193	66	74	1	3	0	2	0	0	0	–	10	22	4	2	0.9	.889
1981		4	4	.500	2.35	39	0	0	65	56	24	38	0	4	4	11	0	0	0	–	2	10	1	1	0.3	.923
1982		3	3	.500	3.46	24	0	0	52	45	23	40	0	3	3	4	0	0	0	–	3	5	0	0	0.3	1.000
1984		4	1	.800	1.62	23	0	0	39	30	19	28	0	4	1	8	0	0	0	–	1	5	1	0	0.3	.857
1985	BAL A	10	6	.625	3.78	54	0	0	88	83	35	67	0	10	6	14	0	0	0	–	8	10	0	0	0.3	1.000
1986		6	7	.462	2.98	66	0	0	81.2	71	28	67	0	6	7	34	0	0	0	–	5	12	1	1	0.3	.944
1987		1	0	1.000	2.25	7	0	0	8	8	4	3	0	1	0	2	0	0	0	–	0	0	0	0	0.1	1.000
1988		0	0	–	4.05	35	0	0	46.2	40	37	28	0	0	0	0	0	0	0	–	2	3	0	1	0.1	1.000
1989	NY N	1	5	.167	3.94	49	0	0	59.1	56	26	34	0	1	5	2	5	0	0	.000	6	8	0	0	0.3	1.000
12 yrs.		63	59	.516	3.76	416	91	22	1070.2	1052	438	617	5	33	27	79	5	0	0	.000	66	132	13	10	0.5	.938

LEAGUE CHAMPIONSHIP SERIES

| 1979 | CAL A | 1 | 0 | 1.000 | 1.80 | 2 | 0 | 0 | 5 | 4 | 2 | 6 | 0 | 0 | 0 | 0 | 0 | 0 | 0 | – | 0 | 1 | 0 | 0 | 0.5 | 1.000 |

Bert Abbey

ABBEY, BERT WOOD
B. Nov. 29, 1869, Essex, Vt. D. June 11, 1962, Essex Junction, Vt. — BR TR 5'11" 175 lbs.

Year	Team		W	L	PCT	ERA	G	GS	CG	IP	H	BB	SO	ShO	W	L	SV	AB	H	HR	BA	PO	A	E	DP	TC/G	FA
1892	WAS N		5	18	.217	3.45	27	23	19	195.2	207	76	77	0	0	2	1	75	9	0	.120	6	55	11	2	2.7	.847
1893	CHI N		2	4	.333	5.46	7	7	5	56	74	20	6	0	0	0	0	26	6	0	.231	3	14	4	1	3.0	.810
1894			2	7	.222	5.18	11	11	10	92	119	37	24	0	0	0	0	39	5	0	.128	2	13	3	0	1.6	.833
1895	2 teams	CHI N	(1G 0–1)				BKN N	(8G 5–2)																			
"	total		5	3	.625	4.35	9	7	6	60	76	11	17	0	0	0	0	22	6	0	.273	1	18	0	1	2.1	1.000
1896	BKN N		8	8	.500	5.15	25	18	12	164.1	210	48	37	0	1	1	0	63	12	0	.190	5	34	4	0	1.7	.907
5 yrs.			22	40	.355	4.52	79	66	52	568	686	192	161	0	2	3	1	225	38	0	.169	17	134	22	4	2.2	.873

Charlie Abbey

ABBEY, CHARLES S.
B. Oct., 1868, Falls City, Neb. Deceased. — BL 5'8½" 169 lbs.

| 1896 | WAS N | 0 | 0 | – | 4.50 | 1 | 0 | 0 | 2 | 6 | 0 | 0 | 0 | 0 | 0 | 0 | * | | | | 0 | 0 | 0 | 0 | 0.0 | – |

Dan Abbott

ABBOTT, LEANDER FRANKLIN (Big Dan)
B. Mar. 16, 1862, Portage, Ind. D. Feb. 13, 1930, Ottawa Lake, Mich. — BR TR 5'11" 190 lbs.

| 1890 | TOL AA | 0 | 2 | .000 | 6.23 | 3 | 1 | 1 | 13 | 19 | 8 | 1 | 0 | 0 | 1 | 1 | 7 | 1 | 0 | .143 | 3 | 4 | 0 | 0 | 2.3 | 1.000 |

Glenn Abbott

ABBOTT, WILLIAM GLENN
B. Feb. 16, 1951, Little Rock, Ark. — BR TR 6'6" 200 lbs.

Year	Team		W	L	PCT	ERA	G	GS	CG	IP	H	BB	SO	ShO	W	L	SV	AB	H	HR	BA	PO	A	E	DP	TC/G	FA
1973	OAK A		1	0	1.000	3.86	5	3	1	18.2	16	7	6	0	0	0	0	0	0	0	–	1	2	0	0	0.6	1.000
1974			5	7	.417	3.00	19	17	3	96	89	34	38	0	0	0	0	0	0	0	–	6	13	3	2	1.2	.864
1975			5	5	.500	4.25	30	15	3	114.1	109	50	51	1	0	0	0	0	0	0	–	9	15	2	0	0.9	.923
1976			2	4	.333	5.52	19	10	0	62	87	16	27	0	1	1	0	0	0	0	–	3	12	0	0	0.8	1.000
1977	SEA A		12	13	.480	4.46	36	34	7	204	212	56	100	0	0	0	0	0	0	0	–	16	28	2	2	1.3	.957
1978			7	15	.318	5.27	29	28	8	155.1	191	44	67	1	0	0	0	0	0	0	–	15	22	3	1	1.4	.925
1979			4	10	.286	5.15	23	19	3	117	138	38	25	0	0	0	0	0	0	0	–	6	18	0	2	1.0	1.000
1980			12	12	.500	4.10	31	31	7	215	228	49	78	2	0	0	0	0	0	0	–	25	39	1	1	2.1	.985
1981			4	9	.308	3.95	22	20	1	130	127	28	35	0	0	0	0	0	0	0	–	11	21	1	1	1.5	.970
1983	2 teams	SEA A	(14G 5–3)				DET A	(7G 2–1)																			
"	total		7	4	.636	3.63	21	21	3	129	146	22	49	1	0	0	0	0	0	0	–	17	9	3	2	1.4	.897
1984	DET A		3	4	.429	5.93	13	8	1	44	62	8	8	0	1	1	0	0	0	0	–	4	8	2	1	1.1	.857
11 yrs.			62	83	.428	4.39	248	206	37	1285.1	1405	352	484	5	4	2	0	0	0	0	–	113	187	17	12	1.3	.946

LEAGUE CHAMPIONSHIP SERIES

| 1975 | OAK A | 0 | 0 | – | 0.00 | 1 | 0 | 0 | 1 | 0 | 0 | 0 | 0 | 0 | 0 | 0 | 0 | 0 | 0 | – | 0 | 0 | 0 | 0 | 0.0 | – |

Jim Abbott

ABBOTT, JAMES ANTHONY
B. Sept. 19, 1967, Flint, Mich. — BL TL 6'3" 200 lbs.

| 1989 | CAL A | 12 | 12 | .500 | 3.92 | 29 | 29 | 4 | 181.1 | 190 | 74 | 115 | 2 | 0 | 0 | 0 | 0 | 0 | 0 | – | 6 | 26 | 3 | 1 | 1.2 | .914 |

Al Aber

ABER, ALBERT JULIUS (Lefty)
B. July 31, 1927, Cleveland, Ohio — BL TL 6'2" 195 lbs.

Year	Team		W	L	PCT	ERA	G	GS	CG	IP	H	BB	SO	ShO	W	L	SV	AB	H	HR	BA	PO	A	E	DP	TC/G	FA
1950	CLE A		1	0	1.000	2.00	1	1	1	9	5	4	4	0	0	0	0	2	0	0	.000	1	1	0	0	2.0	1.000
1953	2 teams	CLE A	(6G 1–1)				DET A	(17G 4–3)																			
"	total		5	4	.556	4.71	23	10	2	72.2	69	50	38	0	0	0	0	23	3	0	.130	0	17	0	0	0.7	1.000
1954	DET A		5	11	.313	3.97	32	18	4	124.2	121	40	54	0	1	3	3	39	5	0	.128	13	21	2	2	1.1	.944
1955			6	3	.667	3.38	39	1	0	80	86	28	37	0	4	3	3	17	1	0	.059	4	17	3	2	0.6	.875
1956			4	4	.500	3.43	42	0	0	63	65	25	21	0	4	4	7	10	3	0	.300	1	12	1	1	0.3	.929
1957	2 teams	DET A	(28G 3–3)				KC A	(3G 0–0)																			
"	total		3	3	.500	7.20	31	0	0	40	52	13	15	0	3	3	1	9	2	0	.222	4	11	0	0	0.5	1.000
6 yrs.			24	25	.490	4.18	168	30	7	389.1	398	160	169	0	16	12	14	100	14	0	.140	23	79	6	5	0.6	.944

Bill Abernathie

ABERNATHIE, WILLIAM EDWARD
B. Jan. 30, 1929, Torrance, Calif. — BR TR 5'10" 190 lbs.

| 1952 | CLE A | 0 | 0 | – | 13.50 | 1 | 0 | 0 | 2 | 4 | 1 | 0 | 0 | 0 | 0 | 1 | 1 | 0 | 0 | .000 | 0 | 0 | 0 | 0 | 0.0 | – |

Tal Abernathy

ABERNATHY, TALMADGE LAFAYETTE (Tal)
B. Oct. 30, 1921, Bynum, N. C. — BR TL 6'2" 210 lbs.

| 1942 | PHI A | 0 | 0 | – | 10.13 | 1 | 0 | 0 | 2.2 | 2 | 3 | 0 | 0 | 0 | 0 | 0 | 1 | 0 | 0 | – | 1 | 1 | 0 | 0 | 2.0 | 1.000 |
| 1943 | | 0 | 3 | .000 | 12.89 | 5 | 2 | 0 | 14.2 | 24 | 13 | 10 | 0 | 0 | 1 | 0 | 4 | 1 | 0 | .250 | 2 | 3 | 1 | 0 | 1.2 | .833 |

Year	Team	W	L	PCT	ERA	G	GS	CG	IP	H	BB	SO	ShO	Relief Pitching W	L	SV	Batting AB	H	HR	BA	PO	A	E	DP	TC/G	FA

Tal Abernathy *continued*

| 1944 | | 0 | 0 | – | 3.00 | 1 | 0 | 0 | 3 | 5 | 1 | 2 | 0 | 0 | 0 | 0 | 1 | 0 | 0 | .000 | 0 | 0 | 0 | 0 | 0.0 | – |
| 3 yrs. | | 0 | 3 | .000 | 11.07 | 7 | 2 | 1 | 20.1 | 31 | 17 | 13 | 0 | 0 | 1 | 0 | 5 | 1 | 0 | .200 | 3 | 4 | 1 | 0 | 1.1 | .875 |

Ted Abernathy

ABERNATHY, THEODORE WADE
B. Mar. 6, 1933, Stanley, N. C.
BR TR 6'4"   215 lbs.

1955	WAS A	5	9	.357	5.96	40	14	3	119.1	136	67	79	2	1	1	0	26	4	0	.154	8	22	1	2	0.8	.968
1956		1	3	.250	4.15	5	4	2	30.1	35	10	18	0	0	0	0	11	2	0	.182	2	13	0	1	3.0	1.000
1957		2	10	.167	6.78	26	16	2	85	100	65	50	0	1	0	0	24	4	0	.167	4	19	0	3	0.9	1.000
1960		0	0	–	12.00	2	0	0	3	4	4	1	0	0	0	0	1	1	0	1.000	0	2	0	0	1.0	1.000
1963	CLE A	7	2	.778	2.88	43	0	0	59.1	54	29	47	0	7	2	12	5	2	0	.400	4	18	2	2	0.6	.917
1964		2	6	.250	4.33	53	0	0	72.2	66	46	57	0	2	6	11	6	0	0	.000	3	24	1	2	0.5	.964
1965	CHI N	4	6	.400	2.57	84	0	0	136.1	113	56	104	0	4	6	**31**	18	3	0	.167	11	41	0	3	0.6	1.000
1966	2 teams	CHI N	(20G 1–3)		ATL N	(38G 4–4)																				
"	total	5	7	.417	4.55	58	0	0	93	84	53	60	0	5	7	8	12	2	0	.167	11	25	2	0	0.7	.947
1967	CIN N	6	3	.667	1.27	70	0	0	106.1	63	41	88	0	6	3	**28**	17	1	0	.059	8	25	4	0	0.5	.892
1968		10	7	.588	2.46	78	0	0	135.1	111	55	64	0	10	7	13	17	0	0	.000	14	39	3	0	0.6	.946
1969	CHI N	4	3	.571	3.18	56	0	0	85	75	42	55	0	4	3	3	8	2	0	.250	9	23	2	0	0.6	.941
1970	3 teams	CHI N	(11G 0–0)		STL N	(11G 1–0)		KC A	(36G 9–3)																	
"	total	10	3	.769	2.59	58	0	0	83.1	65	55	59	0	10	3	14	17	3	0	.176	4	21	1	1	0.4	.962
1971	KC A	4	6	.400	2.56	63	0	0	81	60	50	55	0	4	6	23	13	1	0	.077	8	20	2	0	0.5	.933
1972		3	4	.429	1.71	45	0	0	58	44	19	28	0	3	4	5	6	0	0	.000	6	12	3	2	0.5	.857
14 yrs.		63	69	.477	3.46	681	34	7	1148	1010	592	765	2	57	48	148	181	25	0	.138	92	304	21	16	0.5	.950

Woody Abernathy

ABERNATHY, VIRGIL WOODROW
B. Feb. 1, 1915, Forest City, N. C.
BL TL 6'   170 lbs.

1946	NY N	1	1	.500	3.38	15	1	0	40	32	10	6	0	1	0	1	8	0	0	.000	1	6	0	0	0.5	1.000
1947		0	0	–	9.00	1	0	0	2	4	1	0	0	0	0	0	0	0	0	–	0	0	0	0	0.0	–
2 yrs.		1	1	.500	3.64	16	1	0	42	36	11	6	0	1	0	1	8	0	0	.000	1	6	0	0	0.4	1.000

Harry Ables

ABLES, HARRY TERRELL (Hal, Hans)
B. Oct. 4, 1884, Terrell, Tex.   D. Feb. 8, 1951, San Antonio, Tex.
BR TL 6'2½"   200 lbs.

1905	STL A	0	3	.000	3.82	6	3	1	30.2	37	13	11	0	0	0	0	10	0	0	.000	1	6	0	0	1.2	1.000
1909	CLE A	1	1	.500	2.12	5	3	3	29.2	26	10	24	0	0	0	0	12	0	0	.000	0	5	2	0	1.4	.714
1911	NY A	0	1	.000	9.82	3	2	0	11	16	7	6	0	0	0	0	4	0	0	.000	0	1	0	0	0.3	1.000
3 yrs.		1	5	.167	4.04	14	8	4	71.1	79	30	41	0	0	0	0	26	0	0	.000	1	12	2	0	1.1	.867

George Abrams

ABRAMS, GEORGE ALLEN
B. Nov. 9, 1899, Seattle, Wash.   D. Dec. 5, 1986, Clearwater, Fla.
BR TR 5'9"   170 lbs.

| 1923 | CIN N | 0 | 0 | – | 9.64 | 3 | 0 | 0 | 4.2 | 10 | 3 | 1 | 0 | 0 | 0 | 0 | 1 | 1 | 0 | 1.000 | 0 | 1 | 0 | 0 | 0.3 | 1.000 |

Johnny Abrego

ABREGO, JOHNNY RAY
B. July 4, 1962, Corpus Christi, Tex.
BR TR 6'   185 lbs.

| 1985 | CHI N | 1 | 1 | .500 | 6.38 | 6 | 5 | 0 | 24 | 32 | 12 | 13 | 0 | 0 | 0 | 0 | 9 | 0 | 0 | .000 | 1 | 6 | 1 | 0 | 1.3 | .875 |

Jim Acker

ACKER, JAMES JUSTIN
B. Sept. 24, 1958, Freer, Tex.
BR TR 6'2"   210 lbs.

1983	TOR A	5	1	.833	4.33	38	5	0	97.2	103	38	44	0	2	1	1	0	0	0	–	12	15	0	4	0.7	1.000
1984		3	5	.375	4.38	32	3	0	72	79	25	33	0	3	4	1	0	0	0	–	7	8	1	0	0.5	.938
1985		7	2	.778	3.23	61	0	0	86.1	86	43	42	0	7	2	10	0	0	0	–	10	16	0	1	0.4	1.000
1986	2 teams	TOR A	(23G 2–4)		ATL N	(21G 3–8)																				
"	total	5	12	.294	4.01	44	19	0	155	163	48	69	0	2	2	0	28	3	0	.107	16	28	0	4	1.0	1.000
1987	ATL N	4	9	.308	4.16	68	0	0	114.2	109	51	68	0	4	9	14	14	3	0	.214	6	23	0	2	0.4	1.000
1988		0	4	.000	4.71	21	1	0	42	45	14	25	ShO	0	3	0	5	2	0	.400	3	7	0	0	0.5	1.000
1989	2 teams	ATL N	(59G 0–6)		TOR A	(14G 2–1)																				
"	total	2	7	.222	2.43	73	0	0	126	108	32	92	0	2	7	2	7	1	0	.143	13	15	0	4	0.4	1.000
7 yrs.		26	40	.394	3.78	337	28	0	693.2	693	251	373	0	20	28	28	54	9	0	.167	67	112	1	11	0.5	.994

LEAGUE CHAMPIONSHIP SERIES

1985	TOR A	0	0	–	0.00	2	0	0	6	4	0	5	0	0	0	0	0	0	0	–	0	1	0	0	0.5	1.000
1989		0	0	–	1.42	5	0	0	6.1	4	1	4	0	0	0	0	0	0	0	–	1	1	0	0	0.4	1.000
2 yrs.		0	0	–	0.73	7	0	0	12.1	6	1	9	0	0	0	0	0	0	0	–	1	2	0	0	0.4	1.000

Tom Acker

ACKER, THOMAS JAMES (Shoulders)
B. Mar. 7, 1930, Paterson, N. J.
BR TR 6'4"   215 lbs.

1956	CIN N	4	3	.571	2.37	29	7	0	83.2	60	29	54	1	1	2	1	19	1	0	.053	9	15	0	0	0.8	1.000
1957		10	5	.667	4.97	49	6	1	108.2	122	41	67	0	7	4	4	19	1	0	.053	7	16	0	1	0.5	1.000
1958		4	3	.571	4.55	38	10	3	124.2	126	43	90	0	1	1	1	30	2	0	.067	2	13	1	0	0.4	.938
1959		1	2	.333	4.12	37	0	0	63.1	57	37	45	0	1	2	2	9	1	0	.111	1	5	0	0	0.2	1.000
4 yrs.		19	13	.594	4.12	153	23	5	380.1	365	150	256	1	9	9	8	77	5	0	.065	19	49	1	1	0.5	.986

Fritz Ackley

ACKLEY, FLORIAN FREDERICK
B. Apr. 10, 1937, Hayward, Wis.
BL TR 6'1½"   202 lbs.

1963	CHI A	1	0	1.000	2.08	2	2	0	13	7	7	11	0	0	0	0	5	1	0	.200	0	4	0	0	2.0	1.000
1964		0	0	–	8.53	3	2	0	6.1	10	4	6	0	0	0	0	1	1	0	1.000	0	2	0	0	0.7	1.000
2 yrs.		1	0	1.000	4.19	5	4	0	19.1	17	11	17	0	0	0	0	6	2	0	.333	0	6	0	0	1.2	1.000

Cy Acosta

ACOSTA, CECILIO
Born Cecilio Acosta y Miranda.
B. Nov. 22, 1946, Sabino, Mexico
BR TR 5'10"   165 lbs.

| 1972 | CHI A | 3 | 0 | 1.000 | 1.56 | 26 | 0 | 0 | 34.2 | 25 | 17 | 28 | 0 | 3 | 0 | 5 | 4 | 0 | 0 | .000 | 2 | 3 | 1 | 0 | 0.2 | .833 |

Year	Team		W	L	PCT	ERA	G	GS	CG	IP	H	BB	SO	ShO	W	L	SV	AB	H	HR	BA	PO	A	E	DP	TC/G	FA
															Relief Pitching			Batting									

Cy Acosta *continued*

Year	Team		W	L	PCT	ERA	G	GS	CG	IP	H	BB	SO	ShO	W	L	SV	AB	H	HR	BA	PO	A	E	DP	TC/G	FA
1973			10	6	.625	2.23	48	0	0	97	66	39	60	0	10	6	18	1	0	0	.000	2	10	2	2	0.3	.857
1974			0	3	.000	3.72	27	0	0	46	43	18	19	0	0	3	3	2	0	0	.000	2	8	1	1	0.4	.909
1975	PHI	N	0	0	–	6.00	6	0	0	9	9	3	2	0	0	0	1	0	0	0	–	0	0	0	0	0.0	–
4 yrs.			13	9	.591	2.65	107	0	0	186.2	143	77	109	0	13	9	27	7	0	0	.000	6	21	4	3	0.3	.871

Ed Acosta

ACOSTA, EDUARDO ELIXBET
Born Eduardo Elixbet Acosta y Lopez.
B. Mar. 9, 1944, Boquete, Panama

BB TR 6'5" 215 lbs.

Year	Team		W	L	PCT	ERA	G	GS	CG	IP	H	BB	SO	ShO	W	L	SV	AB	H	HR	BA	PO	A	E	DP	TC/G	FA
1970	PIT	N	0	0	–	12.00	3	0	0	3	5	2	1	0	0	0	0	0	0	0	–	0	0	0	0	0.0	–
1971	SD	N	3	3	.500	2.74	8	6	3	46	43	7	16	1	0	1	0	17	0	0	.000	7	3	0	0	1.3	1.000
1972			3	6	.333	4.45	46	2	0	89	105	30	53	0	2	5	0	12	1	0	.083	3	10	1	1	0.3	.929
3 yrs.			6	9	.400	4.04	57	8	3	138	153	39	70	1	2	6	1	29	1	0	.034	10	13	1	1	0.4	.958

Jose Acosta

ACOSTA, JOSE
Brother of Merito Acosta.
B. Mar. 4, 1891, San Antonio Rio Blanco, Cuba

BR TR 5'7" 140 lbs.

Year	Team		W	L	PCT	ERA	G	GS	CG	IP	H	BB	SO	ShO	W	L	SV	AB	H	HR	BA	PO	A	E	DP	TC/G	FA
1920	WAS	A	5	4	.556	4.03	17	5	4	82.2	92	26	9	1	2	2	1	25	6	0	.240	2	10	1	0	0.8	.923
1921			5	4	.556	4.36	33	7	2	115.2	148	36	30	0	3	1	3	30	2	0	.067	3	26	0	0	0.9	1.000
1922	CHI	A	0	2	.000	8.40	5	1	0	15	25	6	6	0	0	1	0	5	1	0	.200	0	1	0	0	0.2	1.000
3 yrs.			10	10	.500	4.51	55	13	6	213.1	265	68	45	1	5	4	4	60	9	0	.150	5	37	1	0	0.8	.977

Ace Adams

ADAMS, ACE TOWNSEND
B. Mar. 2, 1912, Willows, Calif.

BR TR 5'10½" 182 lbs.

Year	Team		W	L	PCT	ERA	G	GS	CG	IP	H	BB	SO	ShO	W	L	SV	AB	H	HR	BA	PO	A	E	DP	TC/G	FA
1941	NY	N	4	1	.800	4.82	38	0	0	71	84	35	18	0	4	1	1	12	1	0	.083	0	11	0	0	0.3	1.000
1942			7	4	.636	1.84	61	0	0	88	69	31	33	0	7	4	11	10	1	0	.100	1	21	1	3	0.4	.957
1943			11	7	.611	2.82	70	3	1	140.1	121	55	46	0	9	7	9	32	4	0	.125	3	28	1	1	0.5	.969
1944			8	11	.421	4.25	65	4	1	137.2	149	58	32	0	6	9	13	29	3	0	.103	3	20	0	1	0.4	1.000
1945			11	9	.550	3.42	65	0	0	113	109	44	39	0	11	9	15	16	3	0	.188	7	27	3	2	0.6	.919
1946			0	1	.000	16.88	3	0	0	2.2	9	1	3	0	0	1	0	0	0	0	–	0	1	0	0	0.3	1.000
6 yrs.			41	33	.554	3.47	302	7	2	552.2	541	224	171	0	37	31	49	99	12	0	.121	14	108	5	7	0.4	.961

Babe Adams

ADAMS, CHARLES BENJAMIN
B. May 18, 1882, Tipton, Ind.   D. July 27, 1968, Silver Spring, Md.

BL TR 5'11½" 185 lbs.

Year	Team		W	L	PCT	ERA	G	GS	CG	IP	H	BB	SO	ShO	W	L	SV	AB	H	HR	BA	PO	A	E	DP	TC/G	FA
1906	STL	N	0	1	.000	13.50	1	1	0	4	9	2	0	0	0	0	0	1	0	0	.000	0	3	1	0	4.0	.750
1907	PIT	N	0	2	.000	6.95	4	3	1	22	40	3	11	0	0	0	0	7	2	0	.286	3	7	1	0	2.8	.909
1909			12	3	.800	1.11	25	12	7	130	88	23	65	3	6	0	2	39	2	0	.051	1	33	3	0	1.5	.919
1910			18	9	.667	2.24	34	30	16	245	217	60	101	3	0	1	0	83	16	0	.193	7	44	5	1	1.6	.911
1911			22	12	.647	2.33	40	37	24	293.1	253	42	133	7	0	0	0	103	26	0	.252	3	42	1	2	1.2	.978
1912			11	8	.579	2.91	28	21	11	170.1	169	35	63	2	1	1	0	53	12	0	.226	2	36	0	0	1.4	1.000
1913			21	10	.677	2.15	43	37	24	313.2	271	49	144	4	0	1	0	114	33	0	.289	10	74	1	1	2.0	.988
1914			13	16	.448	2.51	40	35	19	283	253	39	91	3	0	1	1	97	16	1	.165	13	62	0	2	1.9	1.000
1915			14	14	.500	2.87	40	30	17	245	229	34	62	2	2	3	2	85	12	0	.141	3	67	0	5	1.8	1.000
1916			2	9	.182	5.72	16	10	4	72.1	91	12	22	1	0	1	0	22	6	0	.273	2	20	0	0	1.4	1.000
1918			1	1	.500	1.19	3	3	2	22.2	15	4	6	1	0	0	0	9	3	0	.333	0	4	0	1	1.3	1.000
1919			17	10	.630	1.98	34	29	23	263.1	213	23	92	7	1	0	1	92	17	0	.185	4	55	0	1	1.7	1.000
1920			17	13	.567	2.16	35	33	19	263	240	18	84	8	0	0	0	89	13	1	.146	3	66	2	1	2.0	.972
1921			14	5	.737	2.64	25	20	11	160	155	18	55	2	3	0	0	63	16	0	.254	1	34	0	1	1.4	1.000
1922			8	11	.421	3.57	27	19	12	171.1	191	15	39	4	1	3	0	56	16	0	.286	5	43	1	2	1.8	.980
1923			13	7	.650	4.42	26	22	11	158.2	196	25	38	0	1	1	1	55	15	0	.273	0	29	1	0	1.2	.967
1924			3	1	.750	1.13	9	3	2	39.2	31	3	5	0	1	1	0	11	2	0	.182	1	5	0	0	0.7	1.000
1925			6	5	.545	5.42	33	10	3	101.1	129	17	18	0	3	1	3	31	7	0	.226	0	17	0	0	0.5	1.000
1926			2	3	.400	6.14	19	0	0	36.2	51	8	7	0	2	3	3	9	2	0	.222	0	7	1	0	0.4	.875
19 yrs.			194	140	.581	2.76	482	355	206	2995.1	2841	430	1036	47	21	17	15	1019	216	3	.212	58	648	17	17	1.5	.976

WORLD SERIES

Year	Team		W	L	PCT	ERA	G	GS	CG	IP	H	BB	SO	ShO	W	L	SV	AB	H	HR	BA	PO	A	E	DP	TC/G	FA
1909	PIT	N	3	0	1.000	1.33	3	3	3	27	18	6	11	1	0	0	0	9	0	0	.000	0	7	0	0	2.3	1.000
1925			0	0	–	0.00	1	0	0	1	2	0	0	0	0	0	0	0	0	0	–	0	0	0	0	0.0	–
2 yrs.			3	0	1.000	1.29	4	3	3	28	20	6	11	1	0	0	0	9	0	0	.000	0	7	0	0	1.8	1.000
					1st	**9th**																					

Bob Adams

ADAMS, ROBERT ANDREW
B. Jan. 20, 1907, Birmingham, Ala.   D. Mar. 6, 1970, Jacksonville, Fla.

BR TR 6'½" 165 lbs.

Year	Team		W	L	PCT	ERA	G	GS	CG	IP	H	BB	SO	ShO	W	L	SV	AB	H	HR	BA	PO	A	E	DP	TC/G	FA
1931	PHI	N	0	1	.000	9.00	1	1	0	6	14	1	3	0	0	0	0	3	0	0	.000	1	0	0	0	1.0	1.000
1932			0	0	–	1.50	4	0	0	6	7	2	2	0	0	0	0	0	0	0	–	1	2	0	0	0.8	1.000
2 yrs.			0	1	.000	5.25	5	1	0	12	21	3	5	0	0	0	0	3	0	0	.000	2	2	0	0	0.8	1.000

Bob Adams

ADAMS, ROBERT BURDETTE
B. July 24, 1901, Holyoke, Mass.

BR TR 5'11" 168 lbs.

Year	Team		W	L	PCT	ERA	G	GS	CG	IP	H	BB	SO	ShO	W	L	SV	AB	H	HR	BA	PO	A	E	DP	TC/G	FA
1925	BOS	A	0	0	–	7.94	2	0	0	5.2	10	3	1	0	0	0	0	3	1	0	.333	0	5	0	0	2.5	1.000

Dan Adams

ADAMS, DANIEL LESLIE (Rube)
B. June 19, 1889, St. Louis, Mo.   D. Oct. 6, 1964, St. Louis, Mo.

BR TR 5'11½" 165 lbs.

Year	Team		W	L	PCT	ERA	G	GS	CG	IP	H	BB	SO	ShO	W	L	SV	AB	H	HR	BA	PO	A	E	DP	TC/G	FA
1914	KC	F	3	9	.250	3.51	36	14	6	136	141	52	38	0	1	1	3	46	7	1	.152	8	38	3	1	1.4	.939
1915			0	2	.000	4.63	11	2	0	35	41	13	16	0	0	0	0	9	1	0	.111	6	9	0	0	1.4	1.000
2 yrs.			3	11	.214	3.74	47	16	6	171	182	65	54	0	1	1	3	55	8	1	.145	14	47	3	1	1.4	.953

Joe Adams

ADAMS, JOSEPH EDWARD (Wagon Tongue)
B. Oct. 28, 1877, Cowden, Ill.   D. Oct. 8, 1952, Montgomery City, Mo.

BR TL 6' 190 lbs.

Year	Team		W	L	PCT	ERA	G	GS	CG	IP	H	BB	SO	ShO	W	L	SV	AB	H	HR	BA	PO	A	E	DP	TC/G	FA
1902	STL	N	0	0	–	9.00	1	0	0	4	9	2	0	0	0	0	0	2	0	0	.000	1	3	0	2	4.0	1.000

Year	Team		W	L	PCT	ERA	G	GS	CG	IP	H	BB	SO	ShO	Relief Pitching W	L	SV	Batting AB	H	HR	BA	PO	A	E	DP	TC/G	FA

Karl Adams

ADAMS, KARL TUTWILER (Rebel)
B. Aug. 11, 1891, Columbus, Ga. D. Sept. 17, 1967, Everett, Wash. BR TR 6'2" 170 lbs.

Year	Team		W	L	PCT	ERA	G	GS	CG	IP	H	BB	SO	ShO	W	L	SV	AB	H	HR	BA	PO	A	E	DP	TC/G	FA
1914	CIN	N	0	0	–	9.00	4	0	0	8	14	5	5	0	0	0	0	2	1	0	.500	0	4	1	0	1.3	.800
1915	CHI	N	1	9	.100	4.71	26	12	3	107	105	43	57	0	0	1	0	30	0	0	.000	2	29	2	0	1.3	.939
2 yrs.			1	9	.100	5.01	30	12	3	115	119	48	62	0	0	1	0	32	1	0	.031	2	33	3	0	1.3	.921

Red Adams

ADAMS, CHARLES DWIGHT
B. Oct. 7, 1921, Parlier, Calif. BR TR 6' 185 lbs.

Year	Team		W	L	PCT	ERA	G	GS	CG	IP	H	BB	SO	ShO	W	L	SV	AB	H	HR	BA	PO	A	E	DP	TC/G	FA
1946	CHI	N	0	1	.000	8.25	8	0	0	12	18	7	8	0	0	1	0	1	0	0	.000	0	5	1	1	0.8	.833

Rick Adams

ADAMS, REUBEN ALEXANDER
B. Dec. 24, 1878, Paris, Tex. D. Mar. 10, 1955, Paris, Tex. BL TL 6' 165 lbs.

Year	Team		W	L	PCT	ERA	G	GS	CG	IP	H	BB	SO	ShO	W	L	SV	AB	H	HR	BA	PO	A	E	DP	TC/G	FA
1905	WAS	A	2	4	.333	3.59	11	6	3	62.2	63	24	25	1	1	0	0	23	4	0	.174	4	20	2	0	2.4	.923

Willie Adams

ADAMS, WILLIAM JOHN IRVIN
B. Sept. 27, 1890, Clearfield, Pa. D. June 18, 1937, Albany, N. Y. BR TR 6'4" 180 lbs.

Year	Team		W	L	PCT	ERA	G	GS	CG	IP	H	BB	SO	ShO	W	L	SV	AB	H	HR	BA	PO	A	E	DP	TC/G	FA
1912	STL	A	2	3	.400	3.88	13	5	0	46.1	50	19	16	0	1	0	0	13	0	0	.000	0	8	1	0	0.7	.889
1913			0	0	–	10.00	4	0	0	9	12	4	5	0	0	0	0	1	0	0	.000	0	3	0	0	0.3	1.000
1914	PIT	F	3	1	.750	3.74	15	2	1	55.1	70	22	14	0	2	0	0	15	1	0	.067	4	11	1	0	1.1	.938
1918	PHI	A	5	12	.294	4.42	32	14	7	169	164	97	39	0	3	0	0	57	8	0	.140	5	50	1	2	1.8	.982
1919			0	0	–	3.86	1	0	0	4.2	7	2	0	0	0	0	0	2	0	0	.000	0	1	0	0	1.0	1.000
5 yrs.			10	16	.385	4.37	65	21	8	284.1	303	144	74	0	6	0	0	88	9	0	.102	9	71	3	2	1.3	.964

Mike Adamson

ADAMSON, JOHN MICHAEL
B. Sept. 13, 1947, San Diego, Calif. BR TR 6'2" 185 lbs.

Year	Team		W	L	PCT	ERA	G	GS	CG	IP	H	BB	SO	ShO	W	L	SV	AB	H	HR	BA	PO	A	E	DP	TC/G	FA
1967	BAL	A	0	1	.000	8.38	3	2	0	9.2	9	12	8	0	0	0	0	2	1	0	.500	0	0	0	0	0.0	–
1968			0	2	.000	9.39	2	2	0	7.2	9	4	4	0	0	0	0	3	1	0	.333	0	0	0	0	0.0	–
1969			0	1	.000	4.50	6	0	0	8	10	6	2	0	0	1	0	1	0	0	.000	2	3	0	0	0.8	1.000
3 yrs.			0	4	.000	7.46	11	4	0	25.1	28	22	14	0	0	1	0	6	2	0	.333	2	3	0	0	0.5	1.000

Dewey Adkins

ADKINS, JOHN DEWEY
B. May 11, 1918, Norcatur, Kans. BR TR 6'2" 195 lbs.

Year	Team		W	L	PCT	ERA	G	GS	CG	IP	H	BB	SO	ShO	W	L	SV	AB	H	HR	BA	PO	A	E	DP	TC/G	FA
1942	WAS	A	0	0	–	9.95	1	1	0	6.1	7	6	3	0	0	0	0	2	1	0	.500	0	0	0	0	0.0	–
1943			0	0	–	2.61	7	0	0	10.1	9	5	1	0	0	0	0	0	0	0	–	0	0	0	0	0.0	–
1949	CHI	N	2	4	.333	5.68	30	5	1	82.1	98	39	43	0	1	1	0	20	4	1	.200	9	18	2	1	1.0	.931
3 yrs.			2	4	.333	5.64	38	6	1	99	114	50	47	0	1	1	0	22	5	1	.227	9	18	2	1	0.8	.931

Doc Adkins

ADKINS, MERLE THERON (Babe)
B. Aug. 5, 1872, Troy, Wis. D. Feb. 21, 1934, Durham, N. C. BR TR 5'10½" 220 lbs.

Year	Team		W	L	PCT	ERA	G	GS	CG	IP	H	BB	SO	ShO	W	L	SV	AB	H	HR	BA	PO	A	E	DP	TC/G	FA
1902	BOS	A	1	1	.500	4.05	4	2	1	20	30	7	3	0	0	0	0	9	2	0	.222	0	7	0	0	1.8	1.000
1903	NY	A	0	0	–	7.71	2	1	0	7	10	5	0	0	0	0	1	3	0	0	.000	0	0	0	0	0.0	–
2 yrs.			1	1	.500	5.00	6	3	1	27	40	12	3	0	0	0	1	12	2	0	.167	0	7	0	0	1.2	1.000

Grady Adkins

ADKINS, GRADY EMMETT (Butcher Boy)
B. June 29, 1897, Jacksonville, Ark. D. Mar. 31, 1966, Little Rock, Ark. BR TR 5'11" 175 lbs.

Year	Team		W	L	PCT	ERA	G	GS	CG	IP	H	BB	SO	ShO	W	L	SV	AB	H	HR	BA	PO	A	E	DP	TC/G	FA
1928	CHI	A	10	16	.385	3.73	36	27	14	224.2	233	89	54	0	3	1	1	70	10	0	.143	8	51	4	2	1.8	.937
1929			2	11	.154	5.33	31	15	5	138.1	168	67	24	0	0	1	0	46	11	0	.239	11	37	1	0	1.6	.980
2 yrs.			12	27	.308	4.34	67	42	19	363	401	156	78	0	3	2	1	116	21	0	.181	19	88	5	2	1.7	.955

Juan Agosto

AGOSTO, JUAN ROBERTO
Born Juan Roberto Agosto y Gonzalez.
B. Feb. 23, 1958, Rio Pedras, Puerto Rico BL TL 6' 175 lbs.

Year	Team		W	L	PCT	ERA	G	GS	CG	IP	H	BB	SO	ShO	W	L	SV	AB	H	HR	BA	PO	A	E	DP	TC/G	FA
1981	CHI	A	0	0	–	4.50	2	0	0	6	5	0	3	0	0	0	0	0	0	0	–	0	1	0	0	0.5	1.000
1982			0	0	–	18.00	1	0	0	2	7	0	1	0	0	0	0	0	0	0	–	0	1	0	0	1.0	1.000
1983			2	2	.500	4.10	39	0	0	41.2	41	11	29	0	2	2	7	0	0	0	–	2	8	2	1	0.3	.833
1984			2	1	.667	3.09	49	0	0	55.1	54	34	26	0	2	1	7	0	0	0	–	7	16	1	5	0.5	.958
1985			4	3	.571	3.58	54	0	0	60.1	45	23	39	0	4	3	1	0	0	0	–	10	15	1	0	0.5	.962
1986	2 teams	CHI A (9G 0–2)					MIN A (17G 1–2)																				
"	total		1	4	.200	8.64	26	1	0	25	49	18	12	0	1	3	1	0	0	0	–	3	4	2	0	0.3	.778
1987	HOU	N	1	1	.500	2.63	27	0	0	27.1	26	10	6	0	1	1	2	1	0	0	.000	3	10	1	1	0.5	.929
1988			10	2	.833	2.26	75	0	0	91.2	74	30	33	0	10	2	4	1	0	0	.000	12	34	2	0	0.6	.958
1989			4	5	.444	2.93	71	0	0	83	81	32	46	0	4	5	1	5	1	0	.200	4	19	3	2	0.4	.885
9 yrs.			24	18	.571	3.46	344	1	0	392.1	382	158	195	0	24	17	23	11	1	0	.091	41	108	12	9	0.5	.925

LEAGUE CHAMPIONSHIP SERIES

Year	Team		W	L	PCT	ERA	G	GS	CG	IP	H	BB	SO	ShO	W	L	SV	AB	H	HR	BA	PO	A	E	DP	TC/G	FA
1983	CHI	A	0	0	–	0.00	1	0	0	.1	0	0	0	0	0	0	0	0	0	0	–	0	0	0	0	0.0	–

Rick Aguilera

AGUILERA, RICHARD WARREN (Aggie)
B. Dec. 31, 1961, San Gabriel, Calif. BR TR 6'4" 195 lbs.

Year	Team		W	L	PCT	ERA	G	GS	CG	IP	H	BB	SO	ShO	W	L	SV	AB	H	HR	BA	PO	A	E	DP	TC/G	FA
1985	NY	N	10	7	.588	3.24	21	19	2	122.1	118	37	74	0	1	0	0	36	10	0	.278	8	16	0	1	1.1	1.000
1986			10	7	.588	3.88	28	20	2	141.2	145	36	104	0	1	1	0	51	8	2	.157	13	26	0	1	1.4	1.000
1987			11	3	.786	3.60	18	17	1	115	124	33	77	0	0	0	0	40	9	1	.225	7	29	2	1	2.1	.947
1988			0	4	.000	6.93	11	3	0	24.2	29	10	16	0	0	2	0	4	1	0	.250	3	5	0	0	0.7	1.000
1989	2 teams	NY N (36G 6–6)					MIN A (11G 3–5)																				
"	total		9	11	.450	2.79	47	11	3	145	130	38	137	0	6	6	7	7	0	0	.000	6	21	1	2	0.6	.964
5 yrs.			40	32	.556	3.53	125	70	8	548.2	546	154	408	0	8	9	7	138	28	3	.203	37	97	3	5	1.1	.978

LEAGUE CHAMPIONSHIP SERIES

Year	Team		W	L	PCT	ERA	G	GS	CG	IP	H	BB	SO	ShO	W	L	SV	AB	H	HR	BA	PO	A	E	DP	TC/G	FA
1986	NY	N	0	0	–	0.00	2	0	0	5	2	2	2	0	0	0	0	1	0	0	–	1	1	0	0	1.0	1.000
1988			0	0	–	1.29	3	0	0	7	3	2	4	0	0	0	0	1	0	0	.000	0	1	0	0	0.3	1.000
2 yrs.			0	0	–	0.75	5	0	0	12	5	4	6	0	0	0	0	1	0	0	.000	1	2	0	0	0.6	1.000

Year	Team		W	L	PCT	ERA	G	GS	CG	IP	H	BB	SO	ShO	Relief Pitching W	L	SV	Batting AB	H	HR	BA	PO	A	E	DP	TC/G	FA

Rick Aguilera *continued*
WORLD SERIES

Year	Team		W	L	PCT	ERA	G	GS	CG	IP	H	BB	SO	ShO	W	L	SV	AB	H	HR	BA	PO	A	E	DP	TC/G	FA
1986	NY	N	1	0	1.000	12.00	2	0	0	3	8	1	4	0	1	0	0	0	0	0	–	0	0	0	0	0.0	–

Hank Aguirre
AGUIRRE, HENRY JOHN
B. Jan. 31, 1932, Azusa, Calif.
BR TL 6'4" 205 lbs.
BB 1965-68

Year	Team		W	L	PCT	ERA	G	GS	CG	IP	H	BB	SO	ShO	W	L	SV	AB	H	HR	BA	PO	A	E	DP	TC/G	FA
1955	CLE	A	2	0	1.000	1.42	4	1	1	12.2	6	12	6	1	1	0	0	4	0	0	.000	1	3	0	0	0.3	1.000
1956			3	5	.375	3.72	16	9	2	65.1	63	27	31	1	1	0	1	18	2	0	.111	3	8	2	0	0.8	.846
1957			1	1	.500	5.75	10	1	0	20.1	26	13	9	0	0	1	0	4	0	0	.000	2	2	1	1	0.5	.800
1958	DET	A	3	4	.429	3.75	44	3	0	69.2	67	27	38	0	2	2	5	14	3	0	.214	3	14	0	1	0.4	1.000
1959			0	0	–	3.38	3	0	0	2.2	4	3	3	0	0	0	0	0	0	0	–	0	1	0	1	0.3	1.000
1960			5	3	.625	2.85	37	6	1	94.2	75	30	80	0	2	1	10	28	1	0	.036	2	7	1	0	0.3	.900
1961			4	4	.500	3.25	45	0	0	55.1	44	38	32	0	4	4	8	9	0	0	.000	1	7	2	0	0.2	.800
1962			16	8	.667	**2.21**	42	22	11	216	162	65	156	2	4	2	3	75	2	0	.027	7	22	3	0	0.8	.906
1963			14	15	.483	3.67	38	33	14	225.2	222	68	134	3	2	0	0	76	10	0	.132	7	23	1	1	0.8	.968
1964			5	10	.333	3.79	32	27	3	161.2	134	59	88	0	0	0	1	53	3	0	.057	8	12	4	2	0.8	.833
1965			14	10	.583	3.59	32	32	10	208.1	185	60	141	2	0	0	0	70	6	0	.086	8	32	4	1	1.4	.909
1966			3	9	.250	3.82	30	14	2	103.2	104	26	50	0	0	3	0	25	3	0	.120	2	13	4	0	0.6	.789
1967			0	1	.000	2.40	31	1	0	41.1	34	17	33	0	0	1	0	2	1	0	.500	3	7	1	0	0.4	.909
1968	LA	N	1	2	.333	0.69	25	0	0	39	32	13	25	0	1	2	3	3	0	0	.000	1	4	2	0	0.3	.667
1969	CHI	N	1	0	1.000	2.60	41	0	0	45	45	12	19	0	1	0	1	5	2	0	.400	1	13	0	0	0.3	1.000
1970			3	0	1.000	4.50	17	0	0	14	13	9	11	0	3	0	1	2	0	0	.000	1	2	3	0	0.3	.400
16 yrs.			75	72	.510	3.25	447	149	44	1375.1	1216	479	856	9	19	18	33	388	33	0	.085	48	167	28	6	0.5	.885

Eddie Ainsmith
AINSMITH, EDWARD WILBUR
B. Feb. 4, 1892, Cambridge, Mass. D. Sept. 6, 1981, Fort Lauderdale, Fla.
BR TR 5'11" 180 lbs.

Year	Team		W	L	PCT	ERA	G	GS	CG	IP	H	BB	SO	ShO	W	L	SV	AB	H	HR	BA	PO	A	E	DP	TC/G	FA
1913	WAS	A	0	0	–	54.00	1	0	0	.1	2	0	0	0	0	0	0		*			0	0	0	0	0.0	–

Raleigh Aitchison
AITCHISON, RALEIGH LEONIDAS (Redskin)
B. Dec. 5, 1887, Tyndall, S. D. D. Sept. 26, 1958, Columbus, Kans.
BR TL 5'11½" 175 lbs.

Year	Team		W	L	PCT	ERA	G	GS	CG	IP	H	BB	SO	ShO	W	L	SV	AB	H	HR	BA	PO	A	E	DP	TC/G	FA
1911	BKN	N	0	1	.000	0.00	1	0	1	1.1	1	1	0	0	0	0	0	0	0	0	–	0	0	0	0	0.0	–
1914			12	7	.632	2.66	26	17	8	172.1	156	60	87	3	1	2	0	51	10	0	.196	8	30	4	0	1.6	.905
1915			0	4	.000	4.96	7	5	2	32.2	36	6	14	0	0	0	0	8	0	0	.000	1	12	3	0	2.3	.813
3 yrs.			12	12	.500	3.01	34	22	10	206.1	193	67	101	3	1	3	0	59	10	0	.169	9	42	7	0	1.7	.879

Jack Aker
AKER, JACK DELANE (Chief)
B. July 13, 1940, Tulare, Calif.
BR TR 6'2" 190 lbs.

Year	Team		W	L	PCT	ERA	G	GS	CG	IP	H	BB	SO	ShO	W	L	SV	AB	H	HR	BA	PO	A	E	DP	TC/G	FA
1964	KC	A	0	1	.000	8.82	9	0	0	16.1	17	10	7	0	0	1	0	3	0	0	.000	2	5	0	1	0.8	1.000
1965			4	3	.571	3.16	34	0	0	51.1	45	18	26	0	4	3	3	8	0	0	.000	4	11	0	2	0.4	1.000
1966			8	4	.667	1.99	66	0	0	113	81	28	68	0	8	4	32	21	2	0	.095	9	32	0	1	0.6	1.000
1967			3	8	.273	4.30	57	0	0	88	87	32	65	0	3	8	12	8	1	0	.125	7	19	0	3	0.5	1.000
1968	OAK	A	4	4	.500	4.10	54	0	0	74.2	72	33	44	0	4	4	11	7	1	0	.143	2	14	1	1	0.3	.941
1969	2 teams		SEA A	(15G 0–2)		NY A	(38G 8–4)																					
"	total		8	6	.571	3.17	53	0	0	82.1	76	35	47	0	8	6	14	10	1	0	.100	14	18	0	4	0.6	1.000
1970	NY	A	4	2	.667	2.06	41	0	0	70	57	20	36	0	4	2	16	16	1	0	.063	4	11	1	0	0.4	.938
1971			4	4	.500	2.57	41	0	0	56	48	26	24	0	4	4	4	3	0	0	.000	10	12	3	0	0.6	.880
1972	2 teams		NY N	(4G 0–0)		CHI N	(48G 6–6)																					
"	total		6	6	.500	2.96	52	0	0	73	70	26	37	0	6	6	17	6	0	0	.000	5	20	1	3	0.5	.962
1973	CHI	N	4	5	.444	4.08	47	0	0	64	76	23	25	0	4	5	12	7	0	0	.000	6	17	1	3	0.5	.958
1974	2 teams		ATL N	(17G 0–1)		NY N	(24G 2–1)																					
"	total		2	2	.500	3.57	41	0	0	58	50	24	25	0	2	2	2	3	1	0	.333	2	8	1	1	0.3	.909
11 yrs.			47	45	.511	3.28	495	0	0	746.2	679	274	404	0	47	45	123	92	7	0	.076	65	167	8	19	0.5	.967

Darrel Akerfelds
AKERFELDS, DARREL WAYNE
B. June 12, 1962, Denver, Colo.
BR TR 6'2" 210 lbs.

Year	Team		W	L	PCT	ERA	G	GS	CG	IP	H	BB	SO	ShO	W	L	SV	AB	H	HR	BA	PO	A	E	DP	TC/G	FA
1986	OAK	A	0	0	–	6.75	2	0	0	5.1	7	3	5	0	0	0	0	0	0	0	–	1	0	0	0	1.0	1.000
1987	CLE	A	2	6	.250	6.75	16	13	1	74.2	84	38	42	0	0	0	0	0	0	0	–	0	11	1	1	0.8	.917
1989	TEX	A	0	1	.000	3.27	6	0	0	11	11	5	9	0	0	0	0	0	0	0	–	0	2	0	0	0.3	1.000
3 yrs.			2	7	.222	6.33	24	13	1	91	102	46	56	0	0	0	0	0	0	0	–	1	14	1	1	0.7	.938

Jerry Akers
AKERS, ALBERT EARL
B. Nov. 1, 1887, Shelbyville, Ind. D. May 15, 1979, Bay Pines, Fla.
BR TR 5'11" 175 lbs.

Year	Team		W	L	PCT	ERA	G	GS	CG	IP	H	BB	SO	ShO	W	L	SV	AB	H	HR	BA	PO	A	E	DP	TC/G	FA
1912	WAS	A	1	1	.500	4.87	5	1	0	20.1	24	15	11	0	1	0	0	6	2	0	.333	1	1	1	0	0.6	.667

Gibson Alba
ALBA, GIBSON ALBERTO
Born Gibson Alberto Alba y Rosando.
B. Jan. 18, 1960, Santiago, Dominican Republic
BL TL 6'2" 160 lbs.

Year	Team		W	L	PCT	ERA	G	GS	CG	IP	H	BB	SO	ShO	W	L	SV	AB	H	HR	BA	PO	A	E	DP	TC/G	FA
1988	STL	N	0	0	–	2.70	3	0	0	3.1	1	2	3	0	0	0	0	0	0	0	–	0	0	0	0	0.0	–

Joe Albanese
ALBANESE, JOSEPH PETER
B. June 26, 1933, New York, N. Y.
BR TR 6'3" 215 lbs.

Year	Team		W	L	PCT	ERA	G	GS	CG	IP	H	BB	SO	ShO	W	L	SV	AB	H	HR	BA	PO	A	E	DP	TC/G	FA
1958	WAS	A	0	0	–	4.50	6	0	0	8	8	2	3	0	0	0	0	0	0	0	–	0	2	0	0	0.3	1.000

Cy Alberts
ALBERTS, FREDERICK JOSEPH
B. Jan. 14, 1882, Grand Rapids, Mich. D. Aug. 27, 1917, Fort Wayne, Ind.
BR TR 6' 230 lbs.

Year	Team		W	L	PCT	ERA	G	GS	CG	IP	H	BB	SO	ShO	W	L	SV	AB	H	HR	BA	PO	A	E	DP	TC/G	FA
1910	STL	N	1	2	.333	6.18	4	3	2	27.2	35	20	10	0	0	0	0	7	0	0	.000	1	3	0	0	1.0	1.000

Ed Albosta
ALBOSTA, EDWARD JOHN (Rube)
B. Oct. 27, 1918, Saginaw, Mich.
BR TR 6'1" 175 lbs.

Year	Team		W	L	PCT	ERA	G	GS	CG	IP	H	BB	SO	ShO	W	L	SV	AB	H	HR	BA	PO	A	E	DP	TC/G	FA
1941	BKN	N	0	2	.000	6.23	2	2	0	13	11	8	5	0	0	0	0	4	0	0	.000	0	4	0	0	2.0	1.000

Year	Team	W	L	PCT	ERA	G	GS	CG	IP	H	BB	SO	ShO	Relief Pitching W	L	SV	Batting AB	H	HR	BA	PO	A	E	DP	TC/G	FA

Ed Albosta *continued*

| 1946 | PIT N | 0 | 6 | .000 | 6.13 | 17 | 6 | 0 | 39.2 | 41 | 35 | 19 | 0 | 0 | 1 | 0 | 8 | 1 | 0 | .125 | 2 | 7 | 0 | 1 | 0.5 | 1.000 |
| | 2 yrs. | 0 | 8 | .000 | 6.15 | 19 | 8 | 0 | 52.2 | 52 | 43 | 24 | 0 | 0 | 1 | 0 | 12 | 1 | 0 | .083 | 2 | 11 | 0 | 1 | 0.7 | 1.000 |

Ed Albrecht

ALBRECHT, EDWARD ARTHUR
B. Feb. 28, 1929, St. Louis, Mo.   D. Dec. 29, 1979, Centerville, Iowa   BR TR 5'10½" 165 lbs.

1949	STL A	1	0	1.000	5.40	1	1	1	5	5	4	1	0	0	0	0	2	0	0	.000	0	1	0	0	1.0	1.000
1950		0	1	.000	5.40	2	1	0	6.2	6	7	1	0	0	1	0	1	0	0	.000	0	1	0	0	0.5	1.000
	2 yrs.	1	1	.500	5.40	3	2	1	11.2	7	11	2	0	0	1	0	3	0	0	.000	0	2	0	0	0.7	1.000

Vic Albury

ALBURY, VICTOR
B. May 12, 1947, Key West, Fla.   BL TL 6' 190 lbs.

1973	MIN A	1	0	1.000	2.70	14	0	0	23.1	19	13	13	0	1	0	0	0	0	0	—	0	0	0	0	0.0	—
1974		8	9	.471	4.12	32	22	4	164	159	80	85	1	1	0	0	0	0	0	—	5	20	0	4	0.8	1.000
1975		6	7	.462	4.53	32	15	2	135	115	97	72	0	3	0	1	1	0	0	.000	4	24	2	3	0.9	.933
1976		3	1	.750	3.58	23	0	0	50.1	51	24	23	0	3	1	0	0	0	0	—	1	8	0	0	0.4	1.000
	4 yrs.	18	17	.514	4.11	101	37	6	372.2	338	220	193	1	8	1	1	1	0	0	.000	10	52	2	7	0.6	.969

Santo Alcala

ALCALA, SANTO
Born Santo Anibal y Alcala.
B. Dec. 23, 1952, San Pedro de Macoris, Dominican Republic   BR TR 6'5" 195 lbs.

1976	CIN N	11	4	.733	4.70	30	21	3	132	131	67	67	0	1	1	0	43	6	0	.140	8	17	1	0	0.9	.962
1977	2 teams	CIN N	(7G 1–1)		MON N	(31G 2–6)																				
"	total	3	7	.300	4.83	38	12	0	117.1	126	54	73	0	1	0	2	28	2	1	.071	8	11	0	0	0.5	1.000
	2 yrs.	14	11	.560	4.76	68	33	3	249.1	257	121	140	1	2	1	2	71	8	1	.113	16	28	1	0	0.7	.978

Dale Alderson

ALDERSON, DALE LEONARD
B. Mar. 9, 1918, Belden, Neb.   D. Feb. 12, 1982, Garden Grove, Calif.   BR TR 5'10" 190 lbs.

1943	CHI N	0	1	.000	6.43	4	2	0	14	21	3	4	0	0	0	0	3	0	0	.000	0	4	0	0	1.0	1.000
1944		0	0	—	6.65	12	1	0	21.2	31	9	7	0	0	0	0	4	0	0	.000	2	7	0	1	0.8	1.000
	2 yrs.	0	1	.000	6.56	16	3	0	35.2	52	12	11	0	0	0	0	7	0	0	.000	2	11	0	1	0.8	1.000

Jay Aldrich

ALDRICH, JAY ROBERT
B. Apr. 14, 1961, Alexandria, La.   BR TR 6'3" 210 lbs.

1987	MIL A	3	1	.750	4.94	31	0	0	58.1	71	13	22	0	0	0	0	0	0	0	—	6	5	1	0	0.4	.917
1989	2 teams	MIL A	(16G 1–0)		ATL N	(8G 1–2)																				
"	total	2	2	.500	3.29	24	0	0	38.1	31	19	19	0	2	2	1	1	0	0	.000	4	5	1	1	0.4	.900
	2 yrs.	5	3	.625	4.28	55	0	0	96.2	102	32	41	0	2	2	1	1	0	0	.000	10	10	2	1	0.4	.909

Vic Aldridge

ALDRIDGE, VICTOR EDDINGTON
B. Oct. 25, 1893, Indian Springs, Ind.   D. Apr. 17, 1973, Terre Haute, Ind.   BR TR 5'9½" 175 lbs.

1917	CHI N	6	6	.500	3.12	30	5	1	106.2	100	37	44	1	5	1	2	29	4	0	.138	2	44	3	2	1.6	.939
1918		0	1	.000	1.46	3	0	0	12.1	11	6	10	0	0	0	0	3	1	0	.333	0	2	0	0	0.7	1.000
1922		16	15	.516	3.52	36	34	20	258.1	287	56	66	2	1	0	0	100	26	0	.260	3	68	4	2	2.1	.947
1923		16	9	.640	3.48	30	30	15	217	209	67	64	2	0	0	0	71	19	0	.268	6	46	0	3	1.7	1.000
1924		15	12	.556	3.50	32	32	20	244.1	261	80	74	0	0	0	0	85	15	0	.176	4	59	3	3	2.0	.984
1925	PIT N	15	7	.682	3.63	30	26	14	213.1	218	74	88	1	2	0	0	86	20	1	.233	2	34	2	2	1.2	.973
1926		10	13	.435	4.07	30	26	12	190	204	73	61	1	0	1	0	71	16	0	.225	2	42	3	3	1.5	.933
1927		15	10	.600	4.25	35	34	19	239.1	248	74	86	1	0	0	0	96	21	0	.219	5	35	0	2	1.1	1.000
1928	NY N	4	7	.364	4.83	22	17	3	119.1	133	45	33	0	0	0	2	40	11	1	.275	4	24	0	2	1.3	1.000
	9 yrs.	97	80	.548	3.76	248	204	102	1600.2	1671	512	526	8	8	3	6	581	133	2	.229	26	354	12	19	1.6	.969

WORLD SERIES

1925	PIT N	2	0	1.000	3.93	3	3	2	18.1	18	9	9	0	0	0	0	7	0	0	.000	0	4	0	0	1.3	1.000
1927		0	1	.000	7.36	1	1	0	7.1	10	4	4	0	0	0	0	2	0	0	.000	0	2	0	0	2.0	1.000
	2 yrs.	2	1	.667	4.91	4	4	2	25.2	28	13	13	0	0	0	0	9	0	0	.000	0	6	0	0	1.5	1.000

Bob Alexander

ALEXANDER, ROBERT SOMERVILLE
B. Aug. 7, 1922, Vancouver, B. C., Canada   BR TR 6'2½" 205 lbs.

1955	BAL A	1	0	1.000	13.50	4	0	0	4	8	2	1	0	1	0	0	0	0	0	—	0	0	0	0	0.0	—
1957	CLE A	0	1	.000	9.00	5	0	0	7	10	5	1	0	0	1	0	1	0	0	.000	0	0	0	0	0.0	—
	2 yrs.	1	1	.500	10.64	9	0	0	11	18	7	2	0	1	1	0	1	0	0	.000	0	0	0	0	0.0	—

Doyle Alexander

ALEXANDER, DOYLE LAFAYETTE
B. Sept. 4, 1950, Cordova, Ala.   BR TR 6'3" 190 lbs.

1971	LA N	6	6	.500	3.82	17	12	4	92	105	18	30	0	1	0	0	33	9	0	.273	5	12	1	0	1.1	.944
1972	BAL A	6	8	.429	2.45	35	9	2	106.1	78	30	49	2	4	5	2	25	2	0	.080	14	23	2	1	1.1	.949
1973		12	8	.600	3.86	29	26	10	175	169	52	63	0	1	0	0	0	0	0	—	15	30	2	1	1.6	.957
1974		6	9	.400	4.03	30	12	0	114	127	43	40	0	3	2	0	0	0	0	—	13	30	2	5	1.5	.956
1975		8	8	.500	3.04	32	11	3	133.1	127	47	46	1	3	4	1	0	0	0	—	14	29	2	1	1.4	.956
1976	2 teams	BAL A	(11G 3–4)		NY A	(19G 10–5)																				
"	total	13	9	.591	3.36	30	25	7	201	172	63	58	3	2	0	0	0	0	0	—	11	30	0	2	1.4	1.000
1977	TEX A	17	11	.607	3.65	34	34	12	237	221	82	82	1	0	0	0	0	0	0	—	17	46	4	4	2.0	.940
1978		9	10	.474	3.86	31	28	7	191	198	71	81	1	0	0	0	0	0	0	—	17	36	4	1	1.8	.930
1979		5	7	.417	4.46	23	18	0	113	114	69	50	0	0	0	0	0	0	0	—	12	23	0	1	1.5	1.000
1980	ATL N	14	11	.560	4.19	35	35	0	232	227	74	114	1	0	0	0	83	15	0	.181	16	49	4	4	2.0	.942
1981	SF N	11	7	.611	2.90	24	24	1	152	156	44	77	1	0	0	0	51	9	0	.176	9	16	1	0	1.0	1.000
1982	NY A	1	7	.125	6.08	16	11	0	66.2	81	14	26	0	0	0	0	0	0	0	—	3	9	1	1	0.8	.923
1983	2 teams	NY A	(8G 0–2)		TOR A	(17G 7–6)																				
"	total	7	8	.467	4.41	25	20	5	145	157	33	63	0	0	0	0	0	0	0	—	13	19	1	1	1.3	.970
1984	TOR A	17	6	**.739**	3.13	36	35	11	261.2	238	59	139	1	0	0	0	0	0	0	—	18	33	2	4	1.5	.962
1985		17	10	.630	3.45	36	36	6	260.2	268	67	142	1	0	0	0	0	0	0	—	28	32	1	4	1.7	.984

Year	Team	W	L	PCT	ERA	G	GS	CG	IP	H	BB	SO	ShO	Relief Pitching W	L	SV	Batting AB	H	HR	BA	PO	A	E	DP	TC/G	FA

Doyle Alexander *continued*

Year	Team	W	L	PCT	ERA	G	GS	CG	IP	H	BB	SO	ShO	W	L	SV	AB	H	HR	BA	PO	A	E	DP	TC/G	FA
1986	2 teams	TOR A (17G 5–4)						ATL N (17G 6–6)																		
"	total	11	10	.524	4.14	34	34	5	228.1	255	37	139	0	0	0	0	38	8	0	.211	14	25	3	2	1.2	.929
1987	2 teams	ATL N (16G 5–10)						DET A (11G 9–0)																		
"	total	14	10	.583	3.01	27	27	6	206	178	53	108	3	0	0	0	35	1	0	.029	8	11	0	1	0.7	1.000
1988	DET A	14	11	.560	4.32	34	34	5	229	260	46	126	1	0	0	0	0	0	0	–	12	19	2	1	1.0	.939
1989		6	18	.250	4.44	33	33	5	223	245	76	95	1	0	0	0	0	0	0	–	23	32	1	1	1.7	.982
19 yrs.		194	174	.527	3.76	561	464	98	3367	3376	978	1528	18	15	11	3	265	44	0	.166	262	504	32	36	1.4	.960

LEAGUE CHAMPIONSHIP SERIES

Year	Team	W	L	PCT	ERA	G	GS	CG	IP	H	BB	SO	ShO	W	L	SV	AB	H	HR	BA	PO	A	E	DP	TC/G	FA
1973	BAL A	0	1	.000	4.91	1	1	0	3.2	5	0	1	0	0	0	0	0	0	0	–	0	2	0	1	2.0	1.000
1985	TOR A	0	1	.000	8.71	2	2	0	10.1	14	3	9	0	0	0	0	0	0	0	–	1	0	0	0	0.5	1.000
1987	DET A	0	2	.000	10.00	2	2	0	9	14	1	5	0	0	0	0	0	0	0	–	2	1	0	0	1.5	1.000
3 yrs.		0	4	.000	8.61	5	5	0	23	33	4	15	0	0	0	0	0	0	0	–	3	3	0	1	1.2	1.000

WORLD SERIES

Year	Team	W	L	PCT	ERA	G	GS	CG	IP	H	BB	SO	ShO	W	L	SV	AB	H	HR	BA	PO	A	E	DP	TC/G	FA
1976	NY A	0	1	.000	7.50	1	1	0	6	9	2	1	0	0	0	0	0	0	0	–	0	1	0	1	1.0	1.000

Grover Alexander

ALEXANDER, GROVER CLEVELAND (Pete) BR TR 6'1" 185 lbs.
B. Feb. 26, 1887, Elba, Neb. D. Nov. 4, 1950, St. Paul, Neb.
Hall of Fame 1938.

Year	Team	W	L	PCT	ERA	G	GS	CG	IP	H	BB	SO	ShO	W	L	SV	AB	H	HR	BA	PO	A	E	DP	TC/G	FA
1911	PHI N	28	13	.683	2.57	48	37	31	367	285	129	227	7	4	2	3	138	24	0	.174	11	95	4	3	2.3	.964
1912		19	17	.528	2.81	46	34	25	310.1	289	105	195	3	3	2	2	102	19	2	.186	10	75	3	1	1.9	.966
1913		22	8	.733	2.79	47	35	23	306.1	288	75	159	9	4	2	2	103	13	0	.126	10	82	0	3	2.0	1.000
1914		27	15	.643	2.38	46	39	32	355	327	76	214	6	4	1	1	137	32	0	.234	18	102	3	1	2.7	.976
1915		31	10	.756	1.22	49	42	36	376.1	253	64	241	12	1	1	3	130	22	1	.169	22	120	3	4	3.0	.979
1916		33	12	.733	1.55	48	45	38	388.2	323	50	167	16¹	0	0	3	138	33	0	.239	17	102	1	3	2.5	.992
1917		30	13	.698	1.86	45	44	35	387.2	336	58	201	8	0	0	1	139	30	1	.216	24	108	1	3	3.0	.992
1918	CHI N	2	1	.667	1.73	3	3	3	26	19	3	15	0	0	0	0	10	1	0	.100	0	8	0	0	2.7	1.000
1919		16	11	.593	1.72	30	27	20	235	180	38	121	9	0	1	1	70	12	0	.171	6	85	0	2	3.0	1.000
1920		27	14	.659	1.91	46	40	33	363.1	335	69	173	7	1	0	5	118	27	1	.229	8	105	2	2	2.5	.983
1921		15	13	.536	3.39	31	29	21	252	286	33	77	3	0	1	0	95	29	1	.305	11	60	2	4	2.4	.973
1922		16	13	.552	3.63	33	31	20	245.2	283	34	48	1	1	0	1	85	15	0	.176	9	69	0	5	2.4	1.000
1923		22	12	.647	3.19	39	36	26	305	308	30	72	3	0	1	2	111	24	1	.216	11	90	1	6	2.6	.990
1924		12	5	.706	3.03	21	20	12	169.1	183	25	33	0	0	1	0	65	15	1	.231	4	53	2	2	2.8	.966
1925		15	11	.577	3.39	32	30	20	236	270	29	63	1	0	1	0	79	19	2	.241	7	45	0	4	1.6	1.000
1926	2 teams	CHI N (7G 3–3)						STL N (23G 9–7)																		
"	total	12	10	.545	3.05	30	23	15	200.1	191	31	47	2	2	1	2	65	13	0	.200	3	58	2	1	2.1	.968
1927	STL N	21	10	.677	2.52	37	30	22	268	261	38	48	2	2	1	3	94	23	0	.245	8	66	0	1	2.0	1.000
1928		16	9	.640	3.36	34	31	18	243.2	262	37	59	1	0	0	2	86	25	1	.291	4	57	0	3	1.8	1.000
1929		9	8	.529	3.89	22	19	8	132	149	23	33	0	1	1	0	41	2	0	.049	5	38	1	2	2.0	.977
1930	PHI N	0	3	.000	9.14	9	3	0	21.2	40	6	6	0	0	2	0	4	0	0	.000	1	1	0	0	0.2	1.000
20 yrs.		373	208	.642	2.56	696	598	438	5189.1	4868	953	2199	90	23	17	31	1810	378	11	.209	189	1419	25	50	2.3	.985
		3rd									9th			2nd												

WORLD SERIES

Year	Team	W	L	PCT	ERA	G	GS	CG	IP	H	BB	SO	ShO	W	L	SV	AB	H	HR	BA	PO	A	E	DP	TC/G	FA
1915	PHI N	1	1	.500	1.53	2	2	2	17.2	14	4	10	0	0	0	0	5	1	0	.200	2	5	0	0	3.5	1.000
1926	STL N	2	0	1.000	0.89	3	2	2	20.1	12	4	17	0	0	0	1	7	0	0	.000	0	6	1	1	2.3	.857
1928		0	1	.000	19.80	2	1	0	5	10	4	2	0	0	0	0	1	0	0	.000	0	4	0	0	2.0	1.000
3 yrs.		3	2	.600	3.35	7	5	4	43	36	12	29	0	0	0	1	13	1	0	.077	2	15	1	1	2.6	.944

Brian Allard

ALLARD, BRIAN MARSHALL BR TR 6'1" 175 lbs.
B. Jan. 3, 1958, Spring Valley, Ill.

Year	Team	W	L	PCT	ERA	G	GS	CG	IP	H	BB	SO	ShO	W	L	SV	AB	H	HR	BA	PO	A	E	DP	TC/G	FA
1979	TEX A	1	3	.250	4.36	7	4	2	33	36	13	14	0	0	0	0	0	0	0	–	3	5	0	1	1.1	1.000
1980		0	1	.000	5.79	5	2	0	14	13	10	10	0	0	0	0	0	0	0	–	0	1	1	0	0.4	.500
1981	SEA A	3	2	.600	3.75	7	7	1	48	48	8	20	0	0	0	0	0	0	0	–	4	6	1	1	1.6	.909
3 yrs.		4	6	.400	4.26	19	13	3	95	97	31	44	0	0	0	0	0	0	0	–	7	12	2	1	1.1	.905

Bob Allen

ALLEN, ROBERT EARL BR TR 6'1" 165 lbs.
B. July 2, 1914, Smithville, Tenn.

Year	Team	W	L	PCT	ERA	G	GS	CG	IP	H	BB	SO	ShO	W	L	SV	AB	H	HR	BA	PO	A	E	DP	TC/G	FA
1937	PHI N	0	1	.000	6.75	3	1	0	12	18	8	8	0	0	0	0	3	1	0	.333	0	0	2	0	0.7	–

Bob Allen

ALLEN, ROBERT GRAY BL TL 6'2" 175 lbs.
B. Oct. 23, 1937, Tatum, Tex.

Year	Team	W	L	PCT	ERA	G	GS	CG	IP	H	BB	SO	ShO	W	L	SV	AB	H	HR	BA	PO	A	E	DP	TC/G	FA
1961	CLE A	3	2	.600	3.75	48	0	0	81.2	96	40	42	0	3	2	3	12	2	0	.167	4	14	0	0	0.4	1.000
1962		1	1	.500	5.87	30	0	0	30.2	29	25	23	0	1	1	4	5	0	0	.000	4	6	2	1	0.4	.833
1963		1	2	.333	4.66	43	0	0	56	58	29	51	0	1	2	5	5	1	0	.200	2	9	1	2	0.3	.917
1966		2	2	.500	4.21	36	0	0	51.1	56	13	33	0	2	2	5	9	1	0	.111	2	12	1	1	0.4	.933
1967		0	5	.000	2.98	47	0	0	54.1	49	25	50	0	0	5	2	0	0	0	–	4	10	0	0	0.3	1.000
5 yrs.		7	12	.368	4.11	204	0	0	274	288	132	199	0	7	12	19	31	4	0	.129	16	51	4	4	0.3	.944

Frank Allen

ALLEN, FRANK LEON (Thin Man) BR TL 5'9" 175 lbs.
B. Aug. 26, 1889, Newbern, Ala. D. July 30, 1933, Gainesville, Ala.

Year	Team	W	L	PCT	ERA	G	GS	CG	IP	H	BB	SO	ShO	W	L	SV	AB	H	HR	BA	PO	A	E	DP	TC/G	FA
1912	BKN N	3	9	.250	3.63	20	15	5	109	119	57	58	1	0	0	0	36	6	1	.167	2	28	2	0	1.6	.938
1913		4	18	.182	2.83	34	25	11	174.2	144	81	82	0	0	3	2	51	7	1	.137	6	30	4	0	1.2	.900
1914	2 teams	BKN N (36G 8–14)						PIT F (1G 1–0)																		
"	total	9	14	.391	3.18	37	22	11	178.1	174	57	71	1	1	0	0	49	7	0	.143	4	41	3	2	1.3	.938
1915	PIT F	23	12	.657	2.51	41	37	24	283.1	230	100	127	6	1	1	0	89	7	0	.079	16	80	6	1	2.5	.941
1916	BOS N	8	2	.800	2.07	19	14	7	113	102	31	63	2	1	1	1	34	7	0	.206	2	24	2	0	1.5	.929
1917		3	11	.214	3.94	29	14	2	112	124	47	56	0	0	4	0	29	5	0	.172	1	23	1	0	0.9	.960
6 yrs.		50	66	.431	2.93	180	127	60	970.1	893	373	457	10	3	10	3	288	39	2	.135	31	226	18	3	1.5	.935

Year	Team		W	L	PCT	ERA	G	GS	CG	IP	H	BB	SO	ShO	Relief Pitching			Batting			BA	PO	A	E	DP	TC/G	FA
															W	L	SV	AB	H	HR							

John Allen

ALLEN, JOHN MARSHALL
B. Oct. 27, 1890, Berkeley Springs, W. Va. D. Sept. 24, 1967, Hagerstown, Md.
BR TR 6'1" 170 lbs.

Year	Team		W	L	PCT	ERA	G	GS	CG	IP	H	BB	SO	ShO	W	L	SV	AB	H	HR	BA	PO	A	E	DP	TC/G	FA
1914	BAL	F	0	0	–	18.00	1	0	0	2	2	2	2	0	0	0	0	0	0	0	–	0	1	0	0	1.0	1.000

Johnny Allen

ALLEN, JOHN THOMAS
B. Sept. 30, 1905, Lenoir, N. C. D. Mar. 29, 1959, St. Petersburg, Fla.
BR TR 6' 180 lbs.

Year	Team		W	L	PCT	ERA	G	GS	CG	IP	H	BB	SO	ShO	W	L	SV	AB	H	HR	BA	PO	A	E	DP	TC/G	FA
1932	NY	A	17	4	.810	3.70	33	21	13	192	162	76	109	3	4	0	4	73	9	1	.123	8	31	3	2	1.3	.929
1933			15	7	.682	4.39	25	24	10	184.2	171	87	119	1	0	0	1	72	13	0	.181	10	29	1	0	1.6	.975
1934			5	2	.714	2.89	13	10	4	71.2	62	32	54	0	0	0	0	26	5	0	.192	1	12	0	2	1.0	1.000
1935			13	6	.684	3.61	23	23	12	167	149	58	113	2	0	0	0	67	15	1	.224	9	33	1	1	1.9	.977
1936	CLE	A	20	10	.667	3.44	36	31	19	243	234	97	165	4	2	1	1	87	14	0	.161	9	50	2	1	1.7	.967
1937			15	1	.938	2.55	24	20	14	173	157	60	87	0	0	0	0	67	6	0	.090	7	37	1	1	1.9	.978
1938			14	8	.636	4.19	30	27	13	200	189	81	112	0	1	1	0	79	20	1	.253	14	43	2	3	2.0	.966
1939			9	7	.563	4.58	28	26	9	175	199	56	79	2	0	0	0	71	16	0	.225	17	36	5	7	2.1	.914
1940			9	8	.529	3.44	32	17	5	138.2	126	48	62	3	3	1	5	48	10	0	.208	8	21	0	2	0.9	1.000
1941	2 teams				STL A (20G 2–5)					BKN N	(11G 3–0)																
"	total		5	5	.500	4.71	31	13	4	124.1	127	41	48	0	1	3	1	42	4	1	.095	5	23	2	1	1.0	.933
1942	BKN	N	10	6	.625	3.20	27	15	5	118	106	39	50	1	1	3	3	39	7	0	.179	3	25	0	3	1.0	1.000
1943	2 teams				BKN N	(17G 5–1)				NY N	(15G 1–3)																
"	total		6	4	.600	3.65	32	1	0	79	79	39	39	0	4	3	4	21	3	0	.143	7	18	2	0	0.8	.926
1944	NY	N	4	7	.364	4.07	18	13	2	84	88	24	33	1	0	0	0	24	2	0	.083	6	8	0	0	0.8	1.000
	13 yrs.		142	75	.654	3.75	352	241	109	1950.1	1849	738	1070	17	18	13	18	716	124	4	.173	104	366	19	24	1.4	.961

WORLD SERIES

Year	Team		W	L	PCT	ERA	G	GS	CG	IP	H	BB	SO	ShO	W	L	SV	AB	H	HR	BA	PO	A	E	DP	TC/G	FA
1932	NY	A	0	0	–	40.50	1	1	0	.2	5	0	0	0	0	0	0	0	0	0	–	0	0	0	0	0.0	–
1941	BKN	N	0	0	–	0.00	3	0	0	3.2	1	3	0	0	0	0	0	0	0	0	–	0	0	0	0	0.0	–
	2 yrs.		0	0	–	6.23	4	1	0	4.1	6	3	0	0	0	0	0	0	0	0	–	0	0	0	0	0.0	–

Lloyd Allen

ALLEN, LLOYD CECIL
B. May 8, 1950, Merced, Calif.
BR TR 6'1" 185 lbs.

Year	Team		W	L	PCT	ERA	G	GS	CG	IP	H	BB	SO	ShO	W	L	SV	AB	H	HR	BA	PO	A	E	DP	TC/G	FA
1969	CAL	A	0	1	.000	5.40	4	0	0	10	5	10	5	0	0	0	0	2	1	0	.500	1	4	0	0	1.3	1.000
1970			1	1	.500	2.63	8	2	0	24	23	11	12	0	0	0	0	4	0	0	.000	2	2	0	1	0.5	1.000
1971			4	6	.400	2.49	54	1	0	94	75	40	72	0	4	6	15	17	5	1	.294	5	17	1	0	0.4	.957
1972			3	7	.300	3.49	42	6	0	85	76	55	53	0	3	5	3	17	2	0	.118	3	10	0	2	0.3	1.000
1973	2 teams				CAL A	(5G 0–0)				TEX A	(23G 0–6)																
"	total		0	6	.000	9.42	28	1	0	49.2	73	44	29	0	0	2	0	–				3	11	2	1	0.6	.875
1974	2 teams				TEX A	(14G 0–1)				CHI A	(6G 0–1)																
"	total		0	2	.000	7.45	20	2	0	29	31	30	21	0	0	1	0	–				1	1	0	0	0.1	1.000
1975	CHI	A	0	2	.000	11.81	3	2	0	5.1	8	6	2	0	0	0	0	0	0	0	–	0	1	0	1	0.3	1.000
	7 yrs.		8	25	.242	4.70	159	19	0	297	291	196	194	0	7	12	22	40	8	1	.200	15	46	3	5	0.4	.953

Myron Allen

ALLEN, MYRON SMITH
B. Mar. 22, 1854, Kingston, N. Y. D. Mar. 8, 1924, Kingston, N. Y.
BR TR 5'8" 150 lbs.

Year	Team		W	L	PCT	ERA	G	GS	CG	IP	H	BB	SO	ShO	W	L	SV	AB	H	HR	BA	PO	A	E	DP	TC/G	FA
1883	NY	N	0	1	.000	1.13	1	1	1	8	8	3	0	0	0	0	0	4	0	0	.000	1	1	0	0	2.0	1.000
1887	CLE	AA	1	0	1.000	1.86	2	0	0	9.2	9	3	1	0	1	0	0	463	128	4	.276	0	0	0	0	0.0	–
1888	KC	AA	0	2	.000	2.50	2	2	2	18	17	1	2	0	0	0	0	136	29	0	.213	1	8	1	0	5.0	.900
	3 yrs.		1	3	.250	2.02	5	3	3	35.2	34	7	3	0	1	0	0	*				2	9	1	0	2.4	.917

Neil Allen

ALLEN, NEIL PATRICK
B. Jan. 24, 1958, Kansas City, Kans.
BR TR 6'3" 185 lbs.

Year	Team		W	L	PCT	ERA	G	GS	CG	IP	H	BB	SO	ShO	W	L	SV	AB	H	HR	BA	PO	A	E	DP	TC/G	FA
1979	NY	N	6	10	.375	3.55	50	5	0	99	100	47	65	0	6	6	8	14	0	0	.000	9	14	1	1	0.5	.958
1980			7	10	.412	3.71	59	0	0	97	87	40	79	0	7	10	22	14	2	0	.143	4	10	1	0	0.3	.933
1981			7	6	.538	2.96	43	0	0	67	64	26	50	0	7	6	18	5	1	0	.200	4	13	0	1	0.4	1.000
1982			3	7	.300	3.06	50	0	0	64.2	65	30	59	0	3	7	19	6	1	0	.167	1	8	1	1	0.2	.900
1983	2 teams				NY N	(21G 2–7)				STL N	(25G 10–6)																
"	total		12	13	.480	3.94	46	22	5	175.2	179	84	106	3	3	5	2	49	5	0	.102	17	20	0	0	0.8	1.000
1984	STL	N	9	6	.600	3.55	57	1	0	119	105	49	66	0	9	5	3	25	6	0	.240	5	22	0	0	0.5	1.000
1985	2 teams				STL N	(23G 1–4)				NY A	(17G 1–0)																
"	total		2	4	.333	4.17	40	7	0	58.1	58	30	26	0	2	3	3	2	0	0	.000	5	8	0	0	0.3	1.000
1986	CHI	A	7	2	.778	3.82	22	17	2	113	101	38	57	2	0	0	0	–				15	10	0	0	1.1	1.000
1987	2 teams				CHI A	(15G 0–7)				NY A	(8G 0–1)																
"	total		0	8	.000	5.93	23	11	0	74.1	97	36	42	0	0	0	0	–				7	7	1	1	0.7	.933
1988	NY	A	5	3	.625	3.84	41	2	0	117.1	121	37	61	1	5	1	0	0	0	0	–	6	8	0	0	0.3	1.000
1989	CLE	A	0	1	15.00		3	0	0	3	8	0	0	0	0	0	0	0	0	0	–	2	0	0	0	0.7	1.000
	11 yrs.		58	70	.453	3.88	434	59	7	988.1	985	417	611	6	42	44	75	115	15	0	.130	75	120	4	4	0.5	.980

Doug Allison

ALLISON, DOUGLAS L.
Brother of Art Allison.
B. 1846, Philadelphia, Pa. D. Dec. 19, 1916, Washington, D. C.
BR TR 5'10½" 160 lbs.

Year	Team		W	L	PCT	ERA	G	GS	CG	IP	H	BB	SO	ShO	W	L	SV	AB	H	HR	BA	PO	A	E	DP	TC/G	FA
1878	PRO	N	0	0	–	1.80	1	0	0	5	11	1	0	0	0	0	0	*				0	0	0	0	0.0	–

Mack Allison

ALLISON, MACK PENDLETON
B. Jan. 23, 1887, Owensboro, Ky. D. Mar. 13, 1964, St. Joseph, Mo.
BR TR 6'1" 185 lbs.

Year	Team		W	L	PCT	ERA	G	GS	CG	IP	H	BB	SO	ShO	W	L	SV	AB	H	HR	BA	PO	A	E	DP	TC/G	FA
1911	STL	A	2	1	.667	2.05	3	3	3	26.1	24	5	2	0	0	0	0	10	2	0	.200	2	5	1	0	2.7	.875
1912			6	17	.261	3.62	31	20	11	169	171	49	43	1	0	3	1	52	7	0	.135	4	46	6	2	1.8	.893
1913			1	3	.250	2.28	11	4	3	51.1	52	13	12	0	0	0	0	14	0	0	.000	0	9	0	0	0.8	1.000
	3 yrs.		9	21	.300	3.17	45	27	17	246.2	247	67	57	1	0	3	1	76	9	0	.118	6	60	7	2	1.6	.904

Luis Aloma

ALOMA, LUIS (Witto)
Born Luis Aloma y Barba.
B. July 23, 1923, Havana, Cuba
BR TR 6'2" 195 lbs.

Year	Team		W	L	PCT	ERA	G	GS	CG	IP	H	BB	SO	ShO	W	L	SV	AB	H	HR	BA	PO	A	E	DP	TC/G	FA
1950	CHI	A	7	2	.778	3.80	42	0	0	87.2	77	53	49	0	7	2	4	15	1	0	.067	3	13	0	0	0.4	1.000
1951			6	0	1.000	1.82	25	1	1	69.1	52	24	25	1	5	0	3	20	7	0	.350	6	4	0	0	0.4	1.000

Year	Team		W	L	PCT	ERA	G	GS	CG	IP	H	BB	SO	ShO	Relief Pitching W	L	SV	Batting AB	H	HR	BA	PO	A	E	DP	TC/G	FA

Luis Aloma *continued*

1952			3	1	.750	4.28	25	0	0	40	42	11	18	0	3	1	6	7	0	0	.000	3	6	0	0	0.4	1.000
1953			2	0	1.000	4.70	24	0	0	38.1	41	23	23	0	2	0	2	6	0	0	.000	3	5	0	1	0.3	1.000
4 yrs.			18	3	.857	3.44	116	1	1	235.1	212	111	115	1	17	3	15	48	8	0	.167	15	28	0	1	0.4	1.000

Matty Alou

ALOU, MATEO
Born Mateo Rojas y Alou. Brother of Jesus Alou.
Brother of Felipe Alou.
B. Dec. 22, 1938, Haina, Dominican Republic

BL TL 5'9"   160 lbs.

| 1965 | SF | N | 0 | 0 | – | 0.00 | 1 | 0 | 0 | 2 | 3 | 1 | 3 | 0 | 0 | 0 | 0 | * | | | | 0 | 0 | 0 | 0 | 0.0 | – |

Porfi Altamirano

ALTAMIRANO, PORFIRIO
Born Porfirio Altamirano y Ramirez.
B. May 17, 1952, Darillo, Nicaragua

BR TR 6'   175 lbs.

1982	PHI	N	5	1	.833	4.15	29	0	0	39	41	14	26	0	5	1	2	4	1	0	.250	2	8	1	0	0.4	.909
1983			2	3	.400	3.70	31	0	0	41.1	38	15	24	0	2	3	0	2	0	0	.000	2	8	0	0	0.3	1.000
1984	CHI	N	0	0	–	4.76	5	0	0	11.1	8	1	7	0	0	0	0	2	0	0	.000	0	4	0	0	0.8	1.000
3 yrs.			7	4	.636	4.03	65	0	0	91.2	87	30	57	0	7	4	2	8	1	0	.125	4	20	1	0	0.4	.960

Ernie Alten

ALTEN, ERNEST MATTHIAS (Lefty)
B. Dec. 1, 1894, Avon, Ohio D. Sept. 9, 1981, Napa, Calif.

BR TL 6'   175 lbs.

| 1920 | DET | A | 0 | 1 | .000 | 9.00 | 14 | 1 | 0 | 23 | 40 | 9 | 4 | 0 | 0 | 0 | 0 | 3 | 0 | 0 | .000 | 3 | 6 | 0 | 0 | 0.6 | 1.000 |

Nick Altrock

ALTROCK, NICHOLAS
B. Sept. 15, 1876, Cincinnati, Ohio D. Jan. 20, 1965, Washington, D. C.

BB TL 5'10"   197 lbs.

1898	LOU	N	3	3	.500	4.50	11	7	6	70	89	21	13	0	0	0	0	29	7	0	.241	3	26	0	2	2.6	1.000
1902	BOS	A	0	2	.000	2.00	3	2	1	18	19	7	5	0	0	0	1	8	0	0	.000	1	8	2	1	3.7	.818
1903	2 teams		BOS A	(1G 0–1)		CHI A	(12G 4–3)																				
"	total		4	4	.500	2.85	13	9	7	79	72	23	22	0	0	0	0	33	11	0	.333	7	44	3	1	4.2	.944
1904	CHI	A	19	14	.576	2.96	38	36	31	307	274	48	87	6	0	0	1	111	22	1	.198	43	114	5	3	4.3	.969
1905			22	12	.647	1.88	38	34	31	315.2	274	63	97	3	2	1	0	114	14	0	.123	32	132	2	10	4.4	.988
1906			20	13	.606	2.06	38	30	25	287.2	269	42	99	4	5	1	0	100	16	0	.160	26	102	4	5	3.5	.970
1907			7	13	.350	2.57	30	21	15	213.2	210	31	61	1	2	1	2	72	13	0	.181	26	89	5	0	4.0	.958
1908			5	7	.417	2.71	23	13	8	136	127	18	21	1	1	0	2	49	10	0	.204	20	67	3	0	3.9	.967
1909	2 teams		CHI A	(1G 0–1)		WAS A	(9G 1–3)																				
"	total		1	4	.200	5.36	10	6	3	47	71	6	11	0	0	0	0	22	1	0	.045	7	16	2	0	2.5	.920
1912	WAS	A	0	1	.000	13.50	1	0	0	1.1	1	2	0	0	0	1	0	1	0	0	.000	0	0	0	0	0.0	–
1913			0	0	–	4.82	4	0	0	9.1	7	4	2	0	0	0	0	1	0	0	.000	1	4	1	0	1.5	.833
1914			0	0	–	0.00	1	0	0	1	3	0	0	0	0	0	0	0	0	0	–	0	0	0	0	0.0	–
1915			0	0	–	9.00	1	0	0	3	7	1	2	0	0	0	1	1	0	0	.000	0	0	0	0	0.0	–
1918			1	2	.333	2.96	5	3	1	24.1	24	6	5	0	0	0	0	8	1	1	.125	3	8	1	0	2.4	.917
1919			0	0	–	∞	1	0	0		4	0	0	0	0	0	0	0	0	0	–	0	0	0	0	0.0	–
1924			0	0	–	0.00	1	0	0	2	4	0	0	0	0	0	0	1	1	0	1.000	0	2	1	0	3.0	.667
1929			0	0	–	0.00	0	0	0	0	0	0	0	0	0	0	0	1	1	0	1.000	0	0	0	0	0.0	–
1931			0	0	–	0.00	0	0	0	0	0	0	0	0	0	0	0	0	0	0	–	0	0	0	0	0.0	–
1933			0	0	–	0.00	0	0	0	0	0	0	0	0	0	0	0	1	0	0	.000	0	0	0	0	0.0	–
19 yrs.			82	75	.522	2.67	218	161	128	1515	1455	272	425	16	10	4	7	552	97	2	.176	169	612	29	23	3.7	.964

WORLD SERIES

| 1906 | CHI | A | 1 | 1 | .500 | 1.00 | 2 | 2 | 2 | 18 | 11 | 2 | 5 | 0 | 0 | 0 | 0 | 4 | 1 | 0 | .250 | 6 | 11 | 0 | 2 | 8.5 | 1.000 |

Jose Alvarez

ALVAREZ, JOSE LINO
B. Apr. 12, 1956, Tampa, Fla.

BR TR 5'10"   170 lbs.

1981	ATL	N	0	0	–	0.00	1	0	0	2	0	0	2	0	0	0	0	0	0	0	–	0	0	0	0	0.0	–
1982			0	0	–	4.70	7	0	0	7.2	8	2	6	0	0	0	0	0	0	0	–	0	2	0	0	0.3	1.000
1988			5	6	.455	2.99	60	0	0	102.1	88	53	81	0	5	6	3	8	3	0	.375	11	17	0	4	0.5	1.000
1989			3	3	.500	2.86	30	0	0	50.1	44	24	45	0	3	3	2	3	0	0	.000	5	8	0	1	0.4	1.000
4 yrs.			8	9	.471	2.99	98	0	0	162.1	140	79	134	0	8	9	5	11	3	0	.273	16	27	0	5	0.4	1.000

Wilson Alvarez

ALVAREZ, WILSON EDUARDO
B. Mar. 24, 1970, Maracaibo, Venezuela

BL TL 6'1"   175 lbs.

| 1989 | TEX | A | 0 | 1 | .000 | ∞ | 1 | 1 | 0 | | 3 | 2 | 0 | 0 | 0 | 0 | 0 | 0 | 0 | 0 | – | 0 | 0 | 0 | 0 | 0.0 | – |

Red Ames

AMES, LEON KESSLING
B. Aug. 2, 1882, Warren, Ohio D. Oct. 8, 1936, Warren, Ohio

BB TR 5'10½"   185 lbs.

1903	NY	N	2	0	1.000	1.29	2	2	2	14	5	8	14	1	0	0	0	6	0	0	.000	0	0	0	0	0.0	–
1904			4	6	.400	2.27	16	13	11	115	94	38	93	1	0	0	3	40	5	0	.125	5	26	4	1	2.2	.886
1905			22	8	.733	2.74	34	31	21	263	220	105	198	2	1	0	0	97	14	0	.144	12	69	5	1	2.5	.942
1906			12	10	.545	2.66	31	25	15	203.1	166	93	156	1	1	0	1	61	4	0	.066	10	66	5	0	2.6	.938
1907			10	12	.455	2.16	39	26	17	233.1	184	108	146	2	0	3	0	69	12	1	.174	11	76	8	0	2.4	.916
1908			7	4	.636	1.81	18	15	5	114.1	96	27	81	0	1	0	0	36	7	0	.194	5	32	3	4	2.2	.925
1909			15	10	.600	2.70	34	26	20	240	214	81	156	2	1	0	0	81	6	0	.074	11	99	9	1	3.5	.924
1910			12	11	.522	2.22	33	23	13	190.1	161	63	94	3	1	0	3	62	11	1	.177	11	68	8	4	2.6	.908
1911			11	10	.524	2.68	34	23	13	205	170	54	118	1	1	1	1	64	6	0	.094	7	69	7	0	2.4	.916
1912			11	5	.688	2.46	33	22	9	179	194	35	83	2	1	0	2	58	13	0	.224	6	53	1	3	1.8	.983
1913	2 teams		NY N	(8G 2–1)		CIN N	(31G 11–13)																				
"	total		13	14	.481	2.78	39	29	14	227	220	78	110	1	2	1	3	72	8	0	.111	2	67	1	2	1.8	.986
1914	CIN	N	15	23	.395	2.64	47	36	18	297	274	94	128	4	1	4	6	94	12	1	.128	8	99	9	3	2.5	.922
1915	2 teams		CIN N	(17G 2–4)		STL N	(15G 9–3)																				
"	total		11	7	.611	3.23	32	21	12	181.1	175	56	74	3	0	0	2	55	5	0	.091	5	61	2	1	2.1	.971
1916	STL	N	11	16	.407	2.64	45	22	10	228	225	57	98	2	4	5	7	68	12	0	.176	3	56	6	0	1.4	.908
1917			15	10	.600	2.71	43	19	10	209	189	57	62	2	8	2	3	64	12	0	.188	4	83	2	4	2.1	.978

Year	Team		W	L	PCT	ERA	G	GS	CG	IP	H	BB	SO	ShO	W	L	SV	AB	H	HR	BA	PO	A	E	DP	TC/G	FA
															Relief Pitching			Batting									

Red Ames *continued*

Year	Team		W	L	PCT	ERA	G	GS	CG	IP	H	BB	SO	ShO	W	L	SV	AB	H	HR	BA	PO	A	E	DP	TC/G	FA
1918			9	14	.391	2.31	27	25	17	206.2	192	52	68	0	0	0	1	64	10	0	.156	6	57	3	1	2.4	.955
1919	2 teams	STL N (23G 3–5)				PHI N	(3G 0–2)																				
"	total		3	7	.300	5.13	26	9	2	86	114	28	23	0	2	0	2	23	6	0	.261	1	19	1	0	0.8	.952
17 yrs.			183	167	.523	2.63	533	367	209	3192.1	2893	1034	1702	27	24	19	33	1014	143	3	.141	107	1000	74	25	2.2	.937

WORLD SERIES

Year	Team		W	L	PCT	ERA	G	GS	CG	IP	H	BB	SO	ShO	W	L	SV	AB	H	HR	BA	PO	A	E	DP	TC/G	FA
1905	NY	N	0	0	–	0.00	1	0	0	1	1	1	1	0	0	0	0	0	0	0	–	0	1	0	0	1.0	1.000
1911			0	1	.000	2.25	2	1	0	8	6	1	6	0	0	0	0	2	1	0	.500	0	2	1	0	1.5	.667
1912			0	0	–	4.50	1	0	0	2	3	1	0	0	0	0	0	0	0	0	–	0	1	0	0	1.0	1.000
3 yrs.			0	1	.000	2.45	4	1	0	11	10	3	7	0	0	0	0	2	1	0	.500	0	4	1	0	1.3	.800

Doc Amole

AMOLE, MORRIS GEORGE
B. July 5, 1878, Coatesville, Pa.   D. Mar. 7, 1912, Wilmington, Del.

BR TL 5'9"   165 lbs.

Year	Team		W	L	PCT	ERA	G	GS	CG	IP	H	BB	SO	ShO	W	L	SV	AB	H	HR	BA	PO	A	E	DP	TC/G	FA
1897	BAL	N	4	4	.500	2.57	11	7	6	70	67	17	19	0	1	0	0	28	3	0	.107	2	19	3	0	2.2	.875
1898	WAS	N	0	6	.000	7.84	7	5	4	49.1	83	22	11	0	0	1	0	20	2	0	.100	4	16	3	0	3.3	.870
2 yrs.			4	10	.286	4.75	18	12	10	119.1	150	39	30	0	1	1	0	48	5	0	.104	6	35	6	0	2.6	.872

Vincente Amor

AMOR, VINCENTE
Born Vincente Amor y Alvarez.
B. Aug. 8, 1932, Havana, Cuba

BR TR 6'3"   182 lbs.

Year	Team		W	L	PCT	ERA	G	GS	CG	IP	H	BB	SO	ShO	W	L	SV	AB	H	HR	BA	PO	A	E	DP	TC/G	FA
1955	CHI	N	0	1	.000	4.50	4	0	0	6	11	3	3	0	0	1	0	0	0	0	–	0	4	0	0	1.0	1.000
1957	CIN	N	1	2	.333	5.93	9	4	1	27.1	39	10	9	0	0	1	0	6	1	0	.167	2	3	0	0	0.6	1.000
2 yrs.			1	3	.250	5.67	13	4	1	33.1	50	13	12	0	0	2	0	6	1	0	.167	2	7	0	0	0.7	1.000

Walter Ancker

ANCKER, WALTER (Gee, Liver)
B. Apr. 10, 1894, New York, N. Y.   D. Feb. 13, 1954, Englewood, N. J.

BR TR 6'1"   190 lbs.

Year	Team		W	L	PCT	ERA	G	GS	CG	IP	H	BB	SO	ShO	W	L	SV	AB	H	HR	BA	PO	A	E	DP	TC/G	FA
1915	PHI	A	0	0	–	3.57	4	1	0	17.2	19	17	4	0	0	0	0	6	0	0	.000	1	5	0	1	1.5	1.000

Larry Andersen

ANDERSEN, LARRY EUGENE
B. May 6, 1953, Portland, Ore.

BR TR 6'3"   200 lbs.

Year	Team		W	L	PCT	ERA	G	GS	CG	IP	H	BB	SO	ShO	W	L	SV	AB	H	HR	BA	PO	A	E	DP	TC/G	FA
1975	CLE	A	0	0	–	4.76	3	0	0	5.2	4	2	4	0	0	0	0	0	0	0	–	1	1	0	0	0.7	1.000
1977			0	1	.000	3.21	11	0	0	14	10	9	8	0	0	1	0	0	0	0	–	3	6	2	4	1.0	.818
1979			0	0	–	7.41	8	0	0	17	25	4	7	0	0	0	0	0	0	0	–	0	4	0	1	0.5	1.000
1981	SEA	A	3	3	.500	2.65	41	0	0	68	57	18	40	0	3	3	5	0	0	0	–	5	9	0	1	0.3	1.000
1982			0	0	–	5.99	40	1	0	79.2	100	23	32	0	0	0	1	0	0	0	–	8	14	0	2	0.6	1.000
1983	PHI	N	1	0	1.000	2.39	17	0	0	26.1	19	9	14	0	1	0	0	2	0	0	.000	2	6	0	0	0.5	1.000
1984			3	7	.300	2.38	64	0	0	90.2	85	25	54	0	3	7	4	4	0	0	.000	5	16	4	1	0.4	.840
1985			3	3	.500	4.32	57	0	0	73	78	26	50	0	3	3	3	4	0	0	.000	5	21	2	2	0.5	.929
1986	2 teams	PHI N (10G 0–0)				HOU N	(38G 2–1)																				
"	total		2	1	.667	3.03	48	0	0	77.1	83	26	42	0	2	1	1	6	0	0	.000	2	2	1	1	0.1	.800
1987	HOU	N	9	5	.643	3.45	67	0	0	101.2	95	41	94	0	9	5	5	6	1	0	.167	12	10	3	0	0.4	.880
1988			2	4	.333	2.94	53	0	0	82.2	82	20	66	0	2	4	5	6	2	0	.333	9	9	2	1	0.4	.900
1989			4	4	.500	1.54	60	0	0	87.2	63	24	85	0	4	4	3	3	1	0	.333	10	13	4	0	0.5	.852
12 yrs.			27	28	.491	3.33	469	1	0	723.2	701	227	496	0	27	28	27	31	4	0	.129	62	111	18	13	0.4	.906

LEAGUE CHAMPIONSHIP SERIES

Year	Team		W	L	PCT	ERA	G	GS	CG	IP	H	BB	SO	ShO	W	L	SV	AB	H	HR	BA	PO	A	E	DP	TC/G	FA
1986	HOU	N	0	0	–	0.00	2	0	0	5	1	2	3	0	0	0	0	0	0	0	–	0	0	0	0	0.0	–

WORLD SERIES

Year	Team		W	L	PCT	ERA	G	GS	CG	IP	H	BB	SO	ShO	W	L	SV	AB	H	HR	BA	PO	A	E	DP	TC/G	FA
1983	PHI	N	0	0	–	2.25	2	0	0	4	4	0	1	0	0	0	0	0	0	0	–	1	1	0	1	1.0	1.000

Allan Anderson

ANDERSON, ALLAN LEE
B. Jan. 7, 1964, Lancaster, Ohio

BL TL 5'11½"   178 lbs.

Year	Team		W	L	PCT	ERA	G	GS	CG	IP	H	BB	SO	ShO	W	L	SV	AB	H	HR	BA	PO	A	E	DP	TC/G	FA
1986	MIN	A	3	6	.333	5.55	21	10	1	84.1	106	30	51	0	1	1	1	0	0	0	–	4	14	1	1	0.9	.947
1987			1	0	1.000	10.95	4	2	0	12.1	20	10	3	0	0	0	0	0	0	0	–	1	0	0	0	0.3	1.000
1988			16	9	.640	2.45	30	30	3	202.1	199	37	83	1	0	0	0	0	0	0	–	9	34	2	3	1.5	.956
1989			17	10	.630	3.80	33	33	4	196.2	214	53	69	1	0	0	0	0	0	0	.000	12	27	1	5	1.2	.975
4 yrs.			37	25	.597	3.72	88	75	8	495.2	539	130	206	2	1	1	1	1	0	0	.000	26	75	4	9	1.2	.962

Bill Anderson

ANDERSON, WILLIAM EDWARD (Lefty)
B. Nov. 28, 1895, Boston, Mass.   D. Mar. 13, 1983, Medford, Mass.

BR TL 6'1"   165 lbs.

Year	Team		W	L	PCT	ERA	G	GS	CG	IP	H	BB	SO	ShO	W	L	SV	AB	H	HR	BA	PO	A	E	DP	TC/G	FA
1925	BOS	N	0	0	–	10.13	2	0	0	2.2	5	2	1	0	0	0	0	1	0	0	.000	0	0	0	0	0.0	–

Bob Anderson

ANDERSON, ROBERT CARL
B. Sept. 29, 1935, East Chicago, Ind.

BR TR 6'4½"   210 lbs.

Year	Team		W	L	PCT	ERA	G	GS	CG	IP	H	BB	SO	ShO	W	L	SV	AB	H	HR	BA	PO	A	E	DP	TC/G	FA
1957	CHI	N	0	1	.000	7.71	8	0	0	16.1	20	8	7	0	0	1	0	4	0	0	.000	0	5	2	0	0.9	.714
1958			3	3	.500	3.97	17	8	2	65.2	61	29	51	0	0	0	0	17	2	0	.118	3	11	0	0	0.8	1.000
1959			12	13	.480	4.13	37	36	7	235.1	245	77	113	1	0	0	0	80	6	0	.075	13	43	4	4	1.6	.933
1960			9	11	.450	4.11	38	30	5	203.2	201	68	115	0	0	1	1	71	12	0	.169	10	43	0	7	1.5	1.000
1961			7	10	.412	4.26	57	12	1	152	162	56	96	0	4	3	8	42	6	2	.143	14	38	0	7	0.9	1.000
1962			2	7	.222	5.02	57	4	0	107.2	111	60	82	0	1	6	4	23	3	0	.130	4	16	1	1	0.4	.952
1963	DET	A	3	1	.750	3.30	32	3	0	60	58	21	38	0	2	0	0	9	4	0	.444	2	9	2	0	0.4	.846
7 yrs.			36	46	.439	4.26	246	93	15	840.2	858	319	502	1	7	11	13	246	33	2	.134	46	165	13	14	0.9	.942

Bud Anderson

ANDERSON, KARL ADAM
B. May 27, 1956, Westbury, N. Y.

BR TR 6'3"   210 lbs.

Year	Team		W	L	PCT	ERA	G	GS	CG	IP	H	BB	SO	ShO	W	L	SV	AB	H	HR	BA	PO	A	E	DP	TC/G	FA
1982	CLE	A	3	4	.429	3.35	25	5	1	80.2	84	30	44	0	2	1	0	0	0	0	–	10	8	1	0	0.8	.947
1983			1	6	.143	4.08	39	1	0	68.1	64	32	32	0	1	5	7	0	0	0	–	3	6	2	0	0.3	.818
2 yrs.			4	10	.286	3.68	64	6	1	149	148	62	76	0	3	6	7	0	0	0	–	13	14	3	0	0.5	.900

Year	Team		W	L	PCT	ERA	G	GS	CG	IP	H	BB	SO	ShO	Relief Pitching W	L	SV	Batting AB	H	HR	BA	PO	A	E	DP	TC/G	FA

Craig Anderson

ANDERSON, NORMAN CRAIG
B. July 1, 1938, Washington, D. C.
BR TR 6'2" 205 lbs.

Year	Team		W	L	PCT	ERA	G	GS	CG	IP	H	BB	SO	ShO	W	L	SV	AB	H	HR	BA	PO	A	E	DP	TC/G	FA
1961	STL	N	4	3	.571	3.26	25	0	0	38.2	38	12	21	0	4	3	1	9	3	0	.333	3	7	0	0	0.4	1.000
1962	NY	N	3	17	.150	5.35	50	14	2	131.1	150	63	62	0	3	6	4	32	3	0	.094	8	36	2	3	0.9	.957
1963			0	2	.000	8.68	3	2	0	9.1	17	3	6	0	0	0	0	3	1	0	.333	1	2	1	0	1.3	.750
1964			0	1	.000	5.54	4	1	0	13	21	3	5	0	0	0	0	3	0	0	.000	0	3	0	1	0.8	1.000
4 yrs.			7	23	.233	5.10	82	17	2	192.1	226	81	94	0	7	9	5	47	7	0	.149	12	48	3	4	0.8	.952

Dave Anderson

ANDERSON, DAVID S.
B. Oct. 10, 1868, Chester, Pa. D. Mar. 22, 1897, Chester, Pa.
TL

Year	Team		W	L	PCT	ERA	G	GS	CG	IP	H	BB	SO	ShO	W	L	SV	AB	H	HR	BA	PO	A	E	DP	TC/G	FA
1889	PHI	N	0	1	.000	7.43	5	2	1	23	30	14	8	0	0	0	0	11	2	0	.182	0	7	0	0	1.4	1.000
1890	2 teams		PHI N	(3G 1-1)			PIT N	(13G 2-11)																			
"	total		3	12	.200	5.09	16	15	14	127.1	147	60	48	0	0	0	0	51	4	0	.078	4	42	1	0	2.9	.979
2 yrs.			3	13	.188	5.45	21	17	15	150.1	177	74	56	0	0	0	0	62	6	0	.097	4	49	1	0	2.6	.981

Fred Anderson

ANDERSON, JOHN FREDERICK (Spitball)
B. Dec. 11, 1885, Calahan, N. C. D. Nov. 8, 1957, Winston-Salem, N. C.
BR TR 6'2" 180 lbs.

Year	Team		W	L	PCT	ERA	G	GS	CG	IP	H	BB	SO	ShO	W	L	SV	AB	H	HR	BA	PO	A	E	DP	TC/G	FA
1909	BOS	A	0	0	–	1.13	1	1	0	8	3	1	5	0	0	0	0	3	0	0	.000	0	2	0	1	2.0	1.000
1913			0	6	.000	5.97	10	8	4	57.1	84	21	32	0	0	0	0	20	1	0	.050	5	13	1	0	1.9	.947
1914	BUF	F	13	16	.448	3.08	37	28	21	260.1	243	64	144	2	1	1	0	90	17	0	.189	7	69	3	2	2.1	.962
1915			19	13	.594	2.51	36	28	14	240	192	72	142	5	4	0	0	80	12	0	.150	5	65	4	2	2.1	.946
1916	NY	N	9	13	.409	3.40	38	27	13	188	206	38	98	2	0	1	2	58	8	0	.138	2	38	0	0	1.1	1.000
1917			8	8	.500	1.44	38	18	8	162	122	34	69	1	2	3	3	42	3	0	.071	4	46	1	0	1.2	.979
1918			4	2	.667	2.67	18	4	2	70.2	62	17	24	1	2	1	3	19	0	0	.000	4	34	0	0	2.1	1.000
7 yrs.			53	58	.477	2.86	178	114	62	986.1	912	247	514	11	9	5	8	312	41	0	.131	23	267	9	5	1.7	.970

WORLD SERIES

Year	Team		W	L	PCT	ERA	G	GS	CG	IP	H	BB	SO	ShO	W	L	SV	AB	H	HR	BA	PO	A	E	DP	TC/G	FA
1917	NY	N	0	1	.000	18.00	1	0	0	2	5	0	3	0	0	1	0	0	0	0	–	0	1	0	0	1.0	1.000

John Anderson

ANDERSON, JOHN CHARLES
B. Nov. 23, 1932, St. Paul, Minn.
BR TR 6'1" 190 lbs.

Year	Team		W	L	PCT	ERA	G	GS	CG	IP	H	BB	SO	ShO	W	L	SV	AB	H	HR	BA	PO	A	E	DP	TC/G	FA
1958	PHI	N	0	0	–	7.88	5	1	0	16	26	4	9	0	0	0	0	3	0	0	.000	0	2	0	0	0.4	1.000
1960	BAL	A	0	0	–	13.50	4	0	0	4.2	8	4	1	0	0	0	0	0	0	0	–	2	2	0	0	1.0	1.000
1962	2 teams		STL N	(5G 0-0)			HOU N	(10G 0-0)																				
"	total		0	0	–	4.13	15	0	0	24	30	6	9	0	0	0	1	2	0	0	.000	1	6	0	0	0.5	1.000
3 yrs.			0	0	–	6.45	24	1	0	44.2	64	14	19	0	0	0	1	5	0	0	.000	3	10	0	0	0.5	1.000

Larry Anderson

ANDERSON, LAWRENCE DENNIS
B. Dec. 3, 1952, Maywood, Calif.
BR TR 6'3" 190 lbs.

Year	Team		W	L	PCT	ERA	G	GS	CG	IP	H	BB	SO	ShO	W	L	SV	AB	H	HR	BA	PO	A	E	DP	TC/G	FA
1974	MIL	A	0	0	–	0.00	2	0	0	2	3	1	2	0	0	0	0	0	0	0	–	1	0	0	0	0.5	1.000
1975			1	0	1.000	5.04	8	1	1	30.1	36	6	13	1	0	0	0	0	0	0	–	2	5	0	0	0.9	1.000
1977	CHI	A	1	3	.250	9.00	6	0	0	9	10	15	7	0	1	3	0	0	0	0	–	1	0	0	0	0.2	1.000
3 yrs.			2	3	.400	5.66	16	1	1	41.1	48	22	23	1	1	3	0	0	0	0	–	4	5	0	0	0.6	1.000

Mike Anderson

ANDERSON, MICHAEL ALLEN
Brother of Kent Anderson.
B. June 22, 1951, Florence, S. C.
BR TR 6'2" 200 lbs.

Year	Team		W	L	PCT	ERA	G	GS	CG	IP	H	BB	SO	ShO	W	L	SV	AB	H	HR	BA	PO	A	E	DP	TC/G	FA
1979	PHI	N	0	0	–	0.00	1	0	0	1	2	0	2	0	0	0	0	*				0	0	0	0	0.0	

Red Anderson

ANDERSON, ARNOLD REVOLA
B. June 19, 1912, Lawton, Iowa D. Aug. 7, 1972, Sioux City, Iowa
BR TR 6'3" 210 lbs.

Year	Team		W	L	PCT	ERA	G	GS	CG	IP	H	BB	SO	ShO	W	L	SV	AB	H	HR	BA	PO	A	E	DP	TC/G	FA
1937	WAS	A	0	1	.000	6.75	2	1	0	10.2	11	11	3	0	0	0	0	3	0	0	.000	0	3	1	0	2.0	.750
1940			1	1	.500	3.86	2	2	2	14	12	5	3	0	0	0	0	5	3	0	.600	0	3	0	1	1.5	1.000
1941			4	6	.400	4.18	32	6	1	112	127	53	34	0	2	3	0	31	8	0	.258	3	18	0	1	0.7	1.000
3 yrs.			5	8	.385	4.35	36	9	3	136.2	150	69	40	0	2	3	0	39	11	0	.282	3	24	1	2	0.8	.964

Rick Anderson

ANDERSON, RICHARD ARLEN
B. Nov. 29, 1956, Everett, Wash.
BR TR 6' 175 lbs.

Year	Team		W	L	PCT	ERA	G	GS	CG	IP	H	BB	SO	ShO	W	L	SV	AB	H	HR	BA	PO	A	E	DP	TC/G	FA
1986	NY	N	2	1	.667	2.72	15	5	0	49.2	45	11	21	0	0	0	1	11	1	0	.091	8	4	0	0	0.8	1.000
1987	KC	A	0	2	.000	13.85	6	2	0	13	26	9	12	0	0	0	0	0	0	0	–	1	3	0	0	0.7	1.000
1988			2	1	.667	4.24	7	3	0	34	41	9	9	0	2	0	0	0	0	0	–	1	3	0	0	0.6	1.000
3 yrs.			4	4	.500	4.75	28	10	0	96.2	112	29	42	0	2	0	1	11	1	0	.091	10	10	0	0	0.7	1.000

Rick Anderson

ANDERSON, RICHARD LEE
B. Dec. 25, 1953, Inglewood, Calif. D. June 23, 1989, Wilmington, Calif.
BR TR 6'2" 210 lbs.

Year	Team		W	L	PCT	ERA	G	GS	CG	IP	H	BB	SO	ShO	W	L	SV	AB	H	HR	BA	PO	A	E	DP	TC/G	FA
1979	NY	A	0	0	–	4.50	1	0	0	2	1	4	0	0	0	0	0	0	0	0	–	0	3	0	0	3.0	1.000
1980	SEA	A	0	0	–	3.60	5	2	0	10	8	10	7	0	0	0	0	0	0	0	–	0	0	1	0	0.2	
2 yrs.			0	0	–	3.75	6	2	0	12	9	14	7	0	0	0	0	0	0	0	–	0	3	1	0	0.7	.750

Scott Anderson

ANDERSON, SCOTT RICHARD
B. Aug. 1, 1962, Corvallis, Ore.
BR TR 6'6" 190 lbs.

Year	Team		W	L	PCT	ERA	G	GS	CG	IP	H	BB	SO	ShO	W	L	SV	AB	H	HR	BA	PO	A	E	DP	TC/G	FA
1987	TEX	A	0	1	.000	9.53	8	0	0	11.1	17	8	6	0	0	1	0	0	0	0	–	2	3	0	1	0.6	1.000

Varney Anderson

ANDERSON, VARNEY SAMUEL
B. June 18, 1866, Geneva, Ill. D. Nov. 5, 1941, Rockford, Ill.
BR TR 5'10" 165 lbs.

Year	Team		W	L	PCT	ERA	G	GS	CG	IP	H	BB	SO	ShO	W	L	SV	AB	H	HR	BA	PO	A	E	DP	TC/G	FA
1889	IND	N	0	1	.000	4.50	2	1	1	12	13	9	3	0	0	0	0	5	0	0	.000	0	3	1	0	2.0	.750
1894	WAS	N	0	2	.000	7.07	2	2	2	14	15	6	3	0	0	0	0	7	3	0	.429	1	2	1	0	2.0	.750
1895			9	16	.360	5.89	29	25	18	204.2	288	97	35	0	0	0	0	97	28	0	.289	10	49	7	4	2.3	.894
1896			0	1	.000	13.00	2	2	1	9	23	3	0	0	0	0	0	5	3	0	.600	0				0.5	–
4 yrs.			9	20	.310	6.16	35	30	22	239.2	339	115	41	0	0	0	0	114	34	0	.298	11	54	10	4	2.1	.867

Year	Team	W	L	PCT	ERA	G	GS	CG	IP	H	BB	SO	ShO	W	L	SV	AB	H	HR	BA	PO	A	E	DP	TC/G	FA

Walter Anderson

ANDERSON, WALTER CARL (Lefty)
B. Sept. 25, 1897, Grand Rapids, Mich.   BL TL 6'2"   160 lbs.

Year	Team	W	L	PCT	ERA	G	GS	CG	IP	H	BB	SO	ShO	W	L	SV	AB	H	HR	BA	PO	A	E	DP	TC/G	FA
1917	PHI A	0	0	–	3.03	14	2	0	38.2	32	21	10	0	0	0	0	7	3	0	.429	4	9	1	0	1.0	.929
1919		1	0	1.000	3.86	3	0	0	14	13	8	10	0	1	0	0	4	0	0	.000	0	4	0	0	1.3	1.000
2 yrs.		1	0	1.000	3.25	17	2	0	52.2	45	29	20	0	1	0	0	11	3	0	.273	4	13	1	0	1.1	.944

Wingo Anderson

ANDERSON, WINGO CHARLIE
B. Aug. 13, 1886, Alvarado, Tex.   D. Dec. 19, 1950, Fort Worth, Tex.   BR TL 5'10½"   150 lbs.

Year	Team	W	L	PCT	ERA	G	GS	CG	IP	H	BB	SO	ShO	W	L	SV	AB	H	HR	BA	PO	A	E	DP	TC/G	FA
1910	CIN N	0	0	–	4.67	7	2	0	17.1	16	17	11	0	0	0	0	5	1	0	.200	2	0	0	0	0.3	1.000

John Andre

ANDRE, JOHN EDWARD (Long John)
B. Jan. 3, 1923, Brockton, Mass.   D. Nov. 25, 1976, Centerville, Mass.   BL TR 6'4"   200 lbs.

Year	Team	W	L	PCT	ERA	G	GS	CG	IP	H	BB	SO	ShO	W	L	SV	AB	H	HR	BA	PO	A	E	DP	TC/G	FA
1955	CHI N	0	1	.000	5.80	22	3	0	45	45	28	19	0	0	1	1	9	1	0	.111	2	6	0	0	0.4	1.000

Elbert Andrews

ANDREWS, ELBERT DeVORE
B. Dec. 11, 1901, Greenwood, S. C.   D. Nov. 25, 1979, Greenwood, S. C.   BL TR 6'   175 lbs.

Year	Team	W	L	PCT	ERA	G	GS	CG	IP	H	BB	SO	ShO	W	L	SV	AB	H	HR	BA	PO	A	E	DP	TC/G	FA
1925	PHI A	0	0	–	10.13	6	0	0	8	12	11	0	0	0	0	0	0	0	0	–	0	2	0	0	0.3	1.000

Hub Andrews

ANDREWS, HERBERT CARL (Tuny)
B. Aug. 31, 1922, Burbank, Calif.   BR TR 6'   170 lbs.

Year	Team	W	L	PCT	ERA	G	GS	CG	IP	H	BB	SO	ShO	W	L	SV	AB	H	HR	BA	PO	A	E	DP	TC/G	FA
1947	NY N	0	0	–	6.23	7	0	0	8.2	14	4	2	0	0	0	0	0	0	0	–	0	2	0	0	0.3	1.000
1948		0	0	–	0.00	1	0	0	3	3	0	0	0	0	0	0	0	0	0	–	0	2	0	0	2.0	1.000
2 yrs.		0	0	–	4.63	8	0	0	11.2	17	4	2	0	0	0	0	0	0	0	–	0	4	0	0	0.5	1.000

Ivy Andrews

ANDREWS, IVY PAUL (Poison)
B. May 6, 1907, Dora, Ala.   D. Nov. 24, 1970, Birmingham, Ala.   BR TR 6'1"   200 lbs.

Year	Team	W	L	PCT	ERA	G	GS	CG	IP	H	BB	SO	ShO	W	L	SV	AB	H	HR	BA	PO	A	E	DP	TC/G	FA
1931	NY A	2	0	1.000	4.19	7	3	1	34.1	36	8	10	0	1	0	0	11	2	0	.182	1	6	0	2	1.0	1.000
1932	2 teams									NY A	(4G 2–1)		BOS A	(25G 8–6)												
"	total	10	7	.588	3.52	29	20	9	166.1	164	62	37	0	2	1	0	60	9	0	.150	4	34	1	4	1.3	.974
1933	BOS A	7	13	.350	4.95	34	17	5	140	157	61	37	0	1	1	2	42	9	0	.214	5	28	3	0	1.1	.917
1934	STL A	4	11	.267	4.66	43	13	2	139	166	65	51	0	2	4	3	40	14	0	.350	4	17	1	1	0.5	.955
1935		13	7	.650	3.54	50	20	10	213.1	231	53	43	0	3	2	1	68	9	0	.132	7	32	2	4	0.8	.951
1936		7	12	.368	4.84	36	25	11	191.1	221	50	33	0	0	1	0	59	10	0	.169	2	28	1	1	0.9	.968
1937	2 teams									CLE A	(20G 3–4)		NY A	(11G 3–2)												
"	total	6	6	.500	3.81	31	9	4	108.2	125	26	33	2	3	1	1	27	4	0	.148	4	19	1	1	0.8	.958
1938	NY A	1	3	.250	3.00	19	1	1	48	51	17	13	0	1	2	1	12	2	0	.167	3	10	0	0	0.7	1.000
8 yrs.		50	59	.459	4.14	249	108	43	1041	1151	342	257	2	15	13	8	319	59	0	.185	30	174	9	13	0.9	.958

WORLD SERIES

Year	Team	W	L	PCT	ERA	G	GS	CG	IP	H	BB	SO	ShO	W	L	SV	AB	H	HR	BA	PO	A	E	DP	TC/G	FA
1937	NY A	0	0	–	3.18	1	0	0	5.2	6	4	1	0	0	0	0	2	0	0	.000	0	1	0	0	1.0	1.000

John Andrews

ANDREWS, JOHN RICHARD
B. Feb. 9, 1949, Monterey Park, Calif.   BL TL 5'10"   175 lbs.

Year	Team	W	L	PCT	ERA	G	GS	CG	IP	H	BB	SO	ShO	W	L	SV	AB	H	HR	BA	PO	A	E	DP	TC/G	FA
1973	STL N	1	1	.500	4.42	16	0	0	18.1	16	11	5	0	1	1	0	2	1	0	.500	1	1	0	0	0.1	1.000

Nate Andrews

ANDREWS, NATHAN HARDY
B. Sept. 30, 1913, Pembroke, N. C.   BR TR 6'   195 lbs.

Year	Team	W	L	PCT	ERA	G	GS	CG	IP	H	BB	SO	ShO	W	L	SV	AB	H	HR	BA	PO	A	E	DP	TC/G	FA
1937	STL N	0	0	–	4.00	4	0	0	9	12	3	6	0	0	0	0	0	0	0	–	0	4	0	0	1.0	1.000
1939		1	2	.333	6.75	11	1	0	16	24	12	6	0	1	1	0	2	0	0	.000	1	5	0	0	0.5	1.000
1940	CLE A	0	1	.000	6.00	6	0	0	12	16	6	3	0	0	0	0	0	0	0	–	0	5	0	2	0.8	1.000
1941		0	0	–	11.57	2	0	0	2.1	3	2	1	0	0	0	0	1	0	0	.000	0	0	0	0	0.0	–
1943	BOS N	14	20	.412	2.57	36	34	23	283.2	253	75	80	3	0	0	0	90	14	0	.156	11	71	2	2	2.3	.976
1944		16	15	.516	3.22	37	34	16	257.1	263	74	76	3	1	0	2	88	10	0	.114	14	56	2	2	1.9	.972
1945		7	12	.368	4.58	21	19	8	137.2	160	52	26	0	0	1	0	43	9	0	.209	7	28	1	1	1.7	.972
1946	2 teams									CIN N	(7G 2–4)		NY N	(3G 1–0)												
"	total	3	4	.429	4.39	10	9	4	55.1	67	12	18	0	0	0	0	16	2	0	.125	1	10	0	1	1.1	1.000
8 yrs.		41	54	.432	3.46	127	98	51	773.1	798	236	216	6	2	5	2	240	35	0	.146	34	179	5	7	1.7	.977

Fred Andrus

ANDRUS, FREDERICK HOTHAM
B. Aug. 23, 1850, Washington, Mich.   D. Nov. 10, 1937, Detroit, Mich.   BR TR 6'2"   185 lbs.

Year	Team	W	L	PCT	ERA	G	GS	CG	IP	H	BB	SO	ShO	W	L	SV	AB	H	HR	BA	PO	A	E	DP	TC/G	FA
1884	CHI N	1	0	1.000	2.00	1	1	1	9	11	2	2	0	0	0	0	*				0	3	0	0	3.0	1.000

Joaquin Andujar

ANDUJAR, JOAQUIN
B. Dec. 21, 1952, San Pedro de Macoris, Dominican Republic   BR TR 6'   170 lbs.

Year	Team	W	L	PCT	ERA	G	GS	CG	IP	H	BB	SO	ShO	W	L	SV	AB	H	HR	BA	PO	A	E	DP	TC/G	FA
1976	HOU N	9	10	.474	3.61	28	25	9	172	163	75	59	4	0	0	0	57	8	0	.140	12	24	3	1	1.4	.923
1977		11	8	.579	3.68	26	25	4	159	149	64	69	1	0	0	0	53	10	0	.189	14	38	8	1	2.3	.867
1978		5	7	.417	3.41	35	13	2	111	88	58	55	0	2	3	1	23	3	0	.130	11	27	4	1	1.2	.905
1979		12	12	.500	3.43	46	23	8	194	168	88	77	0	3	2	4	57	5	0	.088	16	50	5	2	1.5	.930
1980		3	8	.273	3.91	35	14	0	122	132	43	75	0	2	2	2	29	5	1	.172	7	27	5	2	1.1	.872
1981	2 teams									HOU N	(9G 2–3)		STL N	(11G 6–1)												
"	total	8	4	.667	4.10	20	11	1	79	85	23	37	0	1	1	0	23	0	0	.000	5	12	2	0	1.0	.895
1982	STL N	15	10	.600	2.47	38	37	9	265.2	237	50	137	5	0	0	0	95	15	0	.158	17	51	5	3	1.9	.932
1983		6	16	.273	4.16	39	34	5	225	215	75	125	2	0	0	0	73	6	0	.082	15	62	6	3	2.1	.928
1984		20	14	.588	3.34	36	36	12	261.1	218	70	147	4	0	0	0	84	11	2	.131	15	54	4	2	2.0	.958
1985		21	12	.636	3.40	38	38	10	269.2	265	82	112	2	0	0	0	94	10	0	.106	18	45	6	4	1.6	.898
1986	OAK A	12	7	.632	3.82	28	26	7	155.1	139	56	72	0	0	0	1				–	16	21	3	4	1.4	.925
1987		3	5	.375	6.08	13	13	1	60.2	63	26	32	0	0	0	0				–	1	11	2	1	1.1	.857
1988	HOU N	2	5	.286	4.00	23	10	0	78.2	94	21	35	0	0	0	0	19	4	0	.211	2	15	2	0	1.0	.909
13 yrs.		127	118	.518	3.58	405	305	68	2153.1	2016	731	1032	19	6	10	9	607	77	5	.127	142	437	54	28	1.6	.915

Year	Team		W	L	PCT	ERA	G	GS	CG	IP	H	BB	SO	ShO	Relief Pitching W	L	SV	Batting AB	H	HR	BA	PO	A	E	DP	TC/G	FA

Joaquin Andujar *continued*

LEAGUE CHAMPIONSHIP SERIES

Year	Team		W	L	PCT	ERA	G	GS	CG	IP	H	BB	SO	ShO	W	L	SV	AB	H	HR	BA	PO	A	E	DP	TC/G	FA
1980	HOU	N	0	0	–	0.00	1	0	0	1	0	1	0	0	0	0	1	0	0	0	–	0	0	0	0	0.0	–
1982	STL	N	1	0	1.000	2.70	1	1	0	6.2	6	2	4	0	0	0	0	1	0	0	.000	0	0	0	0	0.0	–
1985			0	1	.000	6.97	2	2	0	10.1	14	4	9	0	0	0	0	4	1	0	.250	0	0	2	0	1.0	–
3 yrs.			1	1	.500	5.00	4	3	0	18	20	7	13	0	0	0	1	5	1	0	.200	0	0	2	0	0.5	–

WORLD SERIES

Year	Team		W	L	PCT	ERA	G	GS	CG	IP	H	BB	SO	ShO	W	L	SV	AB	H	HR	BA	PO	A	E	DP	TC/G	FA
1982	STL	N	2	0	1.000	1.35	2	2	0	13.1	10	1	4	0	0	0	0	0	0	0	–	1	2	1	0	2.0	.750
1985			0	1	.000	9.00	2	1	0	4	10	4	3	0	0	0	0	1	0	0	.000	0	1	0	0	0.5	1.000
2 yrs.			2	1	.667	3.12	4	3	0	17.1	20	5	7	0	0	0	0	1	0	0	.000	1	3	1	0	1.3	.800

Norm Angelini

ANGELINI, NORMAN STANLEY
B. Sept. 24, 1947, San Francisco, Calif.

BL TL 5'11" 175 lbs.

Year	Team		W	L	PCT	ERA	G	GS	CG	IP	H	BB	SO	ShO	W	L	SV	AB	H	HR	BA	PO	A	E	DP	TC/G	FA
1972	KC	A	2	1	.667	2.25	21	0	0	16	13	12	16	0	2	1	2	2	0	0	.000	2	1	0	0	0.1	1.000
1973			0	0	–	4.50	7	0	0	4	2	7	3	0	0	0	1	0	0	0	–	0	0	0	0	0.0	–
2 yrs.			2	1	.667	2.70	28	0	0	20	15	19	19	0	2	1	3	2	0	0	.000	2	1	0	0	0.1	1.000

Cap Anson

ANSON, ADRIAN CONSTANTINE (Old Anse)
B. Apr. 11, 1852, Marshalltown, Iowa   D. Apr. 14, 1922, Chicago, Ill.
Manager 1875, 1879-98.
Hall of Fame 1939.

BR TR 6' 227 lbs.

Year	Team		W	L	PCT	ERA	G	GS	CG	IP	H	BB	SO	ShO	W	L	SV	AB	H	HR	BA	PO	A	E	DP	TC/G	FA
1883	CHI	N	0	0	–	0.00	2	0	0	3	1	1	0	0	0	0	0	413	127	0	.308	0	1	0	0	0.5	1.000
1884			0	1	.000	18.00	1	0	0	1	3	1	1	0	0	1	0	475	159	21	.335	0	1	0	0	1.0	1.000
2 yrs.			0	1	.000	4.50	3	0	0	4	4	2	1	0	0	1	1	*				0	2	0	0	0.7	1.000

Johnny Antonelli

ANTONELLI, JOHN AUGUST
B. Apr. 12, 1930, Rochester, N. Y.

BL TL 6'1½" 185 lbs.

Year	Team		W	L	PCT	ERA	G	GS	CG	IP	H	BB	SO	ShO	W	L	SV	AB	H	HR	BA	PO	A	E	DP	TC/G	FA
1948	BOS	N	0	0	–	2.25	4	0	0	4	2	3	0	0	0	0	1	0	0	0	–	0	3	0	0	0.8	1.000
1949			3	7	.300	3.56	22	10	3	96	99	44	48	1	0	1	0	25	3	0	.120	5	14	4	0	1.0	.826
1950			2	3	.400	5.93	20	6	2	57.2	81	22	33	1	0	0	0	16	2	0	.125	2	13	1	0	0.8	.938
1953	MIL	N	12	12	.500	3.18	31	26	11	175.1	167	71	131	2	2	1	1	62	11	0	.177	6	34	1	3	1.3	.976
1954	NY	N	21	7	.750	2.30	39	37	18	258.2	209	94	152	6	0	0	2	98	16	2	.163	10	54	2	3	1.7	.970
1955			14	16	.467	3.33	38	34	14	235.1	206	82	143	2	0	0	1	82	17	4	.207	7	46	2	2	1.4	.964
1956			20	13	.606	2.86	41	36	15	258.1	225	75	145	6	3	0	1	89	14	3	.157	11	49	1	5	1.5	.984
1957			12	18	.400	3.77	40	30	8	212.1	228	67	114	3	3	1	0	72	11	3	.153	9	27	3	3	1.0	.923
1958	SF	N	16	13	.552	3.28	41	34	13	241.2	216	87	143	0	1	1	3	84	19	1	.226	10	27	4	3	1.0	.902
1959			19	10	.655	3.10	40	38	17	282	247	76	165	4	0	0	1	101	16	2	.158	8	44	2	3	1.4	.963
1960			6	7	.462	3.77	41	10	1	112.1	106	47	57	1	4	2	11	34	8	0	.235	2	19	0	0	0.5	1.000
1961	2 teams		CLE A		(11G 0–4)		MIL N		(9G 1–0)																		
"	total		1	4	.200	6.75	20	7	0	58.2	84	21	31	0	1	0	0	16	4	0	.250	2	12	1	2	0.8	.933
12 yrs.			126	110	.534	3.34	377	268	102	1992.1	1870	687	1162	26	14	6	21	679	121	15	.178	72	342	21	24	1.2	.952

WORLD SERIES

Year	Team		W	L	PCT	ERA	G	GS	CG	IP	H	BB	SO	ShO	W	L	SV	AB	H	HR	BA	PO	A	E	DP	TC/G	FA
1954	NY	N	1	0	1.000	0.84	2	1	1	10.2	8	7	12	0	0	0	1	3	0	0	.000	0	1	0	0	0.5	1.000

Bob Apodaca

APODACA, ROBERT JOHN
B. Jan. 31, 1950, Los Angeles, Calif.

BR TR 5'11" 170 lbs.

Year	Team		W	L	PCT	ERA	G	GS	CG	IP	H	BB	SO	ShO	W	L	SV	AB	H	HR	BA	PO	A	E	DP	TC/G	FA
1973	NY	N	0	0	–	∞	1	0	0	0	0	2	0	0	0	0	0	0	0	0	–	0	0	0	0	0.0	–
1974			6	6	.500	3.50	35	8	1	103	92	42	54	0	1	5	3	25	3	0	.120	7	13	2	2	0.6	.909
1975			3	4	.429	1.48	46	0	0	85	66	28	45	0	3	4	13	11	4	0	.364	8	22	1	1	0.7	.968
1976			3	7	.300	2.80	43	3	0	90	71	29	45	0	3	5	5	16	2	0	.125	8	17	0	1	0.6	1.000
1977			4	8	.333	3.43	59	0	0	84	83	30	53	0	4	8	5	6	1	0	.167	5	17	1	1	0.4	.957
5 yrs.			16	25	.390	2.86	184	11	1	362	312	131	197	0	11	22	26	58	10	0	.172	28	69	4	5	0.5	.960

Luis Aponte

APONTE, LUIS EDUARDO
Born Luis Eduardo Aponte y Yuripe.
B. June 14, 1953, El Tigre, Venezuela

BR TR 6' 180 lbs.

Year	Team		W	L	PCT	ERA	G	GS	CG	IP	H	BB	SO	ShO	W	L	SV	AB	H	HR	BA	PO	A	E	DP	TC/G	FA
1980	BOS	A	0	0	–	1.29	4	0	0	7	6	2	1	0	0	0	0	0	0	0	–	0	2	0	0	0.5	1.000
1981			1	0	1.000	0.56	7	0	0	16	11	3	11	0	1	0	1	0	0	0	–	1	6	0	0	1.0	1.000
1982			2	2	.500	3.18	40	0	0	85	78	25	44	0	2	2	3	0	0	0	–	11	16	0	0	0.7	1.000
1983			5	4	.556	3.63	34	0	0	62	74	23	32	0	5	4	3	0	0	0	–	10	8	0	1	0.5	1.000
1984	CLE	A	1	0	1.000	4.11	25	0	0	50.1	53	15	25	0	1	0	0	0	0	0	–	1	5	0	0	0.2	1.000
5 yrs.			9	6	.600	3.27	110	0	0	220.1	222	68	113	0	9	6	7	0	0	0	–	23	37	0	4	0.5	1.000

Kevin Appier

APPIER, ROBERT KEVIN
B. Dec. 6, 1967, Lancaster, Calif.

BR TR 6'2" 180 lbs.

Year	Team		W	L	PCT	ERA	G	GS	CG	IP	H	BB	SO	ShO	W	L	SV	AB	H	HR	BA	PO	A	E	DP	TC/G	FA
1989	KC	A	1	4	.200	9.14	6	5	0	21.2	34	12	10	0	0	0	0	0	0	0	–	1	0	0	0	0.2	1.000

Fred Applegate

APPLEGATE, FREDERICK ROMAINE (Snitz)
B. May 9, 1879, Williamsport, Pa.   D. Apr. 21, 1968, Williamsport, Pa.

BR TR 6'2" 180 lbs.

Year	Team		W	L	PCT	ERA	G	GS	CG	IP	H	BB	SO	ShO	W	L	SV	AB	H	HR	BA	PO	A	E	DP	TC/G	FA
1904	PHI	A	1	2	.333	6.43	3	3	3	21	29	8	12	0	0	0	0	7	2	0	.286	0	8	0	0	2.7	1.000

Ed Appleton

APPLETON, EDWARD SAMUEL (Whitey)
B. Feb. 29, 1892, Arlington, Tex.   D. Jan. 27, 1932, Arlington, Tex.

BR TR 6'½" 173 lbs.

Year	Team		W	L	PCT	ERA	G	GS	CG	IP	H	BB	SO	ShO	W	L	SV	AB	H	HR	BA	PO	A	E	DP	TC/G	FA
1915	BKN	N	4	10	.286	3.32	34	10	5	138.1	133	66	50	0	1	4	0	44	7	0	.159	5	36	4	1	1.3	.911
1916			1	2	.333	3.06	14	3	1	47	49	18	14	0	1	0	1	12	2	0	.167	4	8	1	0	0.9	.923
2 yrs.			5	12	.294	3.25	48	13	6	185.1	182	84	64	0	2	4	1	56	9	0	.161	9	44	5	1	1.2	.914

Year	Team		W	L	PCT	ERA	G	GS	CG	IP	H	BB	SO	ShO	Relief Pitching W	L	SV	Batting AB	H	HR	BA	PO	A	E	DP	TC/G	FA

Pete Appleton

APPLETON, PETER WILLIAM
Born Peter William Jablonowski.
B. May 20, 1904, Terryville, Conn.   D. Jan. 18, 1974, Trenton, N. J.   BR TR 5'11"   180 lbs.

Year	Team		W	L	PCT	ERA	G	GS	CG	IP	H	BB	SO	ShO	W	L	SV	AB	H	HR	BA	PO	A	E	DP	TC/G	FA
1927	CIN	N	2	1	.667	1.82	6	2	2	29.2	29	17	3	1	0	0	0	11	6	0	.545	4	8	0	2	2.0	1.000
1928			3	4	.429	4.68	31	1	0	82.2	101	22	20	0	3	4	0	31	10	0	.323	3	28	0	3	1.0	1.000
1930	CLE	A	8	7	.533	4.02	39	7	2	118.2	122	53	45	0	6	5	1	40	8	0	.200	6	30	2	4	1.0	.947
1931			4	4	.500	4.63	29	4	3	79.2	100	29	25	0	1	3	0	24	5	0	.208	4	16	2	1	0.8	.909
1932	2 teams					CLE A	(4G 0–0)			BOS A	(11G 0–3)																
"	total		0	3	.000	5.29	15	3	0	51	60	29	16	0	0	0	0	17	3	0	.176	5	20	0	1	1.7	1.000
1933	NY	A	0	0	–	0.00	1	0	0	2	3	1	0	0	0	0	0	0	0	0	–	0	1	0	1	1.0	1.000
1936	WAS	A	14	9	.609	3.53	38	20	12	201.2	199	77	77	1	4	1	3	76	19	0	.250	9	42	1	1	1.4	.980
1937			8	15	.348	4.39	35	18	7	168	167	72	62	0	3	4	2	59	11	0	.186	8	42	1	4	1.5	.980
1938			7	9	.438	4.60	43	10	5	164.1	175	61	62	0	3	4	5	59	15	0	.254	9	29	4	4	1.0	.905
1939			5	10	.333	4.56	40	4	2	102.2	104	48	50	0	4	7	6	25	4	0	.160	4	17	1	2	0.6	.955
1940	CHI	A	4	0	1.000	5.62	25	0	0	57.2	54	28	21	0	4	0	5	17	3	0	.176	4	8	1	1	0.5	.923
1941			0	3	.000	5.27	13	0	0	27.1	27	17	12	0	0	3	1	4	1	0	.250	1	6	0	0	0.5	1.000
1942	2 teams					CHI A	(4G 0–0)			STL A	(14G 1–1)																
"	total		1	1	.500	3.09	18	0	0	32	27	14	14	0	1	1	2	6	1	0	.167	1	13	0	1	0.8	1.000
1945	2 teams					STL A	(2G 0–0)			WAS A	(6G 1–0)																
"	total		1	0	1.000	4.56	8	2	1	23.2	19	18	13	0	0	0	1	5	1	0	.200	0	5	0	1	0.6	1.000
14 yrs.			57	66	.463	4.30	341	71	34	1141	1187	486	420	6	29	32	26	374	87	0	.233	58	265	12	25	1.0	.964

Luis Aquino

AQUINO, LUIS ANTONIO
Born Luis Antonio Aquino y Colon.
B. May 19, 1964, Santurce, Puerto Rico   BR TR 6'   155 lbs.

Year	Team		W	L	PCT	ERA	G	GS	CG	IP	H	BB	SO	ShO	W	L	SV	AB	H	HR	BA	PO	A	E	DP	TC/G	FA
1986	TOR	A	1	1	.500	6.35	7	0	0	11.1	14	3	5	0	1	1	0	0	0	0	–	1	1	0	0	0.3	1.000
1988	KC	A	1	0	1.000	2.79	7	5	1	29	33	17	11	1	0	0	0	0	0	0	–	2	2	1	1	0.7	.800
1989			6	8	.429	3.50	34	16	2	141.1	148	35	68	1	2	0	0	0	0	0	–	11	23	0	3	1.0	1.000
3 yrs.			8	9	.471	3.57	48	21	3	181.2	195	55	84	2	3	1	0	0	0	0	–	14	26	1	4	0.9	.976

Fred Archer

ARCHER, FREDERICK MARVIN (Lefty)
B. Mar. 7, 1910, Johnson City, Tenn.   D. Oct. 31, 1981, Charlotte, N. C.   BL TL 6'   193 lbs.

Year	Team		W	L	PCT	ERA	G	GS	CG	IP	H	BB	SO	ShO	W	L	SV	AB	H	HR	BA	PO	A	E	DP	TC/G	FA
1936	PHI	A	2	3	.400	6.38	6	5	2	36.2	41	15	9	0	0	0	0	15	4	0	.267	1	6	0	1	1.2	1.000
1937			0	0	–	6.00	1	0	0	3	4	0	2	0	0	0	0	0	0	0	–	0	1	0	0	1.0	1.000
2 yrs.			2	3	.400	6.35	7	5	2	39.2	45	15	11	0	0	0	0	15	4	0	.267	1	7	0	1	1.1	1.000

Jim Archer

ARCHER, JAMES WILLIAM
B. May 25, 1932, Max Meadows, Va.   BR TL 6'   190 lbs.

Year	Team		W	L	PCT	ERA	G	GS	CG	IP	H	BB	SO	ShO	W	L	SV	AB	H	HR	BA	PO	A	E	DP	TC/G	FA
1961	KC	A	9	15	.375	3.20	39	27	9	205.1	204	60	110	2	1	1	5	63	4	0	.063	6	36	2	2	1.1	.955
1962			0	1	.000	9.43	18	1	0	27.2	40	10	12	0	0	0	0	1	1	0	1.000	2	3	1	0	0.3	.833
2 yrs.			9	16	.360	3.94	57	28	9	233	244	70	122	2	1	1	5	64	5	0	.078	8	39	3	2	0.9	.940

Rugger Ardizoia

ARDIZOIA, RINALDO JOSEPH
B. Nov. 20, 1919, Oleggio, Italy   BR TR 5'11"   180 lbs.

Year	Team		W	L	PCT	ERA	G	GS	CG	IP	H	BB	SO	ShO	W	L	SV	AB	H	HR	BA	PO	A	E	DP	TC/G	FA
1947	NY	A	0	0	–	9.00	1	0	0	2	4	1	0	0	0	0	0	0	0	0	–	0	1	0	0	1.0	1.000

Frank Arellanes

ARELLANES, FRANK JULIAN
B. Jan. 28, 1882, Santa Cruz, Calif.   D. Dec. 13, 1918, San Jose, Calif.   BR TR 6'   180 lbs.

Year	Team		W	L	PCT	ERA	G	GS	CG	IP	H	BB	SO	ShO	W	L	SV	AB	H	HR	BA	PO	A	E	DP	TC/G	FA
1908	BOS	A	4	3	.571	1.82	11	8	6	79.1	60	18	33	1	0	0	1	30	5	0	.167	2	19	3	1	2.2	.875
1909			16	12	.571	2.18	45	30	17	230.2	192	43	82	1	3	2	8	78	13	0	.167	13	74	7	2	2.1	.926
1910			4	7	.364	2.88	18	13	2	100	106	24	33	0	1	1	0	34	6	1	.176	2	35	2	2	2.2	.949
3 yrs.			24	22	.522	2.28	74	51	25	410	358	85	148	2	4	3	8	142	24	1	.169	17	128	12	5	2.1	.924

Rudy Arias

ARIAS, RUDOLFO
Born Rudolfo Arias y Martinez.
B. June 6, 1931, Las Villas, Cuba   BL TL 5'10"   165 lbs.

Year	Team		W	L	PCT	ERA	G	GS	CG	IP	H	BB	SO	ShO	W	L	SV	AB	H	HR	BA	PO	A	E	DP	TC/G	FA
1959	CHI	A	2	0	1.000	4.09	34	0	0	44	49	20	28	0	2	0	2	4	0	0	.000	3	10	0	0	0.4	1.000

Don Arlich

ARLICH, DONALD LOUIS
B. Feb. 15, 1943, Wayne, Mich.   BL TL 6'2"   185 lbs.

Year	Team		W	L	PCT	ERA	G	GS	CG	IP	H	BB	SO	ShO	W	L	SV	AB	H	HR	BA	PO	A	E	DP	TC/G	FA
1965	HOU	N	0	0	–	3.00	1	1	0	6	5	1	0	0	0	0	0	2	0	0	.000	0	1	0	0	1.0	1.000
1966			0	1	.000	15.75	7	0	0	4	11	4	1	0	0	1	0	1	0	0	.000	0	0	0	0	0.0	–
2 yrs.			0	1	.000	8.10	8	1	0	10	16	5	1	0	0	1	0	3	0	0	.000	0	1	0	0	0.1	1.000

Steve Arlin

ARLIN, STEPHEN RALPH
B. Sept. 25, 1945, Seattle, Wash.   BR TR 6'3½"   195 lbs.

Year	Team		W	L	PCT	ERA	G	GS	CG	IP	H	BB	SO	ShO	W	L	SV	AB	H	HR	BA	PO	A	E	DP	TC/G	FA
1969	SD	N	0	1	.000	9.00	4	1	0	11	13	9	9	0	0	0	0	2	0	0	.000	0	1	0	0	0.3	1.000
1970			1	0	1.000	2.77	2	2	1	13	11	8	3	1	0	0	0	5	0	0	.000	0	4	0	0	2.0	1.000
1971			9	19	.321	3.47	36	34	10	228	211	103	156	4	0	0	0	73	9	0	.123	18	23	1	3	1.2	.976
1972			10	21	.323	3.60	38	37	12	250	217	122	159	3	0	0	0	72	11	0	.153	17	34	3	1	1.4	.944
1973			11	14	.440	5.10	34	27	0	180	196	72	98	3	2	0	0	60	10	0	.167	11	21	0	4	0.9	1.000
1974	2 teams					SD N	(16G 1–7)			CLE A	(11G 2–5)																
"	total		3	12	.200	6.17	27	22	2	108	144	59	38	0	0	0	0	18	2	0	.111	9	13	5	0	1.0	.815
6 yrs.			34	67	.337	4.32	141	123	32	790	792	373	463	11	3	0	1	230	32	0	.139	55	96	9	8	1.1	.944

Orville Armbrust

ARMBRUST, ORVILLE MARTIN
B. Mar. 2, 1910, Beirne, Ark.   D. Oct. 2, 1967, Mobile, Ala.   BR TR 5'10"   195 lbs.

Year	Team		W	L	PCT	ERA	G	GS	CG	IP	H	BB	SO	ShO	W	L	SV	AB	H	HR	BA	PO	A	E	DP	TC/G	FA
1934	WAS	A	1	0	1.000	2.13	3	2	0	12.2	10	3	3	0	0	0	0	4	0	0	.000	1	6	0	0	2.3	1.000

Year	Team		W	L	PCT	ERA	G	GS	CG	IP	H	BB	SO	ShO	Relief Pitching W	L	SV	Batting AB	H	HR	BA	PO	A	E	DP	TC/G	FA

Howard Armstrong

ARMSTRONG, HOWARD ELMER
B. Dec. 2, 1889, East Claridon, Ohio D. Mar. 8, 1926, Canisted, N. Y.
BR TR 5'9" 165 lbs.

Year	Team		W	L	PCT	ERA	G	GS	CG	IP	H	BB	SO	ShO	W	L	SV	AB	H	HR	BA	PO	A	E	DP	TC/G	FA
1911	PHI	A	0	1	.000	0.00	1	0	0	3	3	1	0	0	0	1	0	1	0	0	.000	0	2	0	0	2.0	1.000

Jack Armstrong

ARMSTRONG, JACK WILLIAM
B. Mar. 7, 1965, Englewood, N. J.
BR TR 6'5" 220 lbs.

Year	Team		W	L	PCT	ERA	G	GS	CG	IP	H	BB	SO	ShO	W	L	SV	AB	H	HR	BA	PO	A	E	DP	TC/G	FA
1988	CIN	N	4	7	.364	5.79	14	13	0	65.1	63	38	45	0	0	0	0	21	2	0	.095	3	13	0	0	1.1	1.000
1989			2	3	.400	4.64	9	8	0	42.2	40	21	23	0	0	0	0	8	0	0	.000	1	9	0	0	1.1	1.000
2 yrs.			6	10	.375	5.33	23	21	0	108	103	59	68	0	0	0	0	29	2	0	.069	4	22	0	0	1.1	1.000

Mike Armstrong

ARMSTRONG, MICHAEL DENNIS
B. Mar. 7, 1954, Glen Cove, N. Y.
BR TR 6'3" 193 lbs.

Year	Team		W	L	PCT	ERA	G	GS	CG	IP	H	BB	SO	ShO	W	L	SV	AB	H	HR	BA	PO	A	E	DP	TC/G	FA
1980	SD	N	0	0	–	5.79	11	0	0	14	16	13	14	0	0	0	0	3	0	0	.000	1	0	1	0	0.2	.500
1981			0	2	.000	6.00	10	0	0	12	14	11	9	0	0	2	0	0	0	0	–	0	0	0	0	0.0	–
1982	KC	A	5	5	.500	3.20	52	0	0	112.2	88	43	75	0	5	5	6	0	0	0	–	9	8	0	1	0.3	1.000
1983			10	7	.588	3.86	58	0	0	102.2	86	45	52	0	10	7	3	0	0	0	–	8	12	0	1	0.3	1.000
1984	NY	A	3	2	.600	3.48	36	0	0	54.1	47	26	43	0	3	2	1	0	0	0	–	7	4	1	0	0.3	.917
1985			0	0	–	3.07	9	0	0	14.2	9	2	11	0	0	0	0	0	0	0	–	1	1	0	0	0.2	1.000
1986			0	1	.000	9.35	7	1	0	8.2	13	5	8	0	0	0	0	0	0	0	–	1	1	1	0	0.4	.667
1987	CLE	A	1	0	1.000	8.68	14	0	0	18.2	27	10	9	0	1	0	1	0	0	0	–	1	2	1	0	0.3	.750
8 yrs.			19	17	.528	4.10	197	1	0	337.2	300	155	221	0	19	16	11	3	0	0	.000	28	28	4	2	0.3	.933

Scott Arnold

ARNOLD, SCOTT GENTRY
B. Aug. 18, 1962, Lexington, Ky.
BR TR 6'2" 210 lbs.

Year	Team		W	L	PCT	ERA	G	GS	CG	IP	H	BB	SO	ShO	W	L	SV	AB	H	HR	BA	PO	A	E	DP	TC/G	FA
1988	STL	N	0	0	–	5.40	6	0	0	6.2	9	4	8	0	0	0	0	0	0	0	–	0	1	0	0	0.2	1.000

Tony Arnold

ARNOLD, TONY DALE
B. May 3, 1959, El Paso, Tex.
BR TR 5'11" 170 lbs.

Year	Team		W	L	PCT	ERA	G	GS	CG	IP	H	BB	SO	ShO	W	L	SV	AB	H	HR	BA	PO	A	E	DP	TC/G	FA
1986	BAL	A	0	2	.000	3.55	11	0	0	25.1	25	11	7	0	0	2	0	0	0	0	–	4	9	0	0	1.2	1.000
1987			0	0	–	5.77	27	0	0	53	71	17	18	0	0	0	0	0	0	0	–	5	17	0	2	0.8	1.000
2 yrs.			0	2	.000	5.06	38	0	0	78.1	96	28	25	0	0	2	0	0	0	0	–	9	26	0	2	0.9	1.000

Brad Arnsberg

ARNSBERG, BRADLEY JAMES
B. Aug. 20, 1963, Seattle, Wash.
BR TR 6'4" 205 lbs.

Year	Team		W	L	PCT	ERA	G	GS	CG	IP	H	BB	SO	ShO	W	L	SV	AB	H	HR	BA	PO	A	E	DP	TC/G	FA
1986	NY	A	0	0	–	3.38	2	1	0	8	13	1	3	0	0	0	0	0	0	0	–	0	0	0	0	0.0	–
1987			1	3	.250	5.59	6	2	0	19.1	22	13	14	0	0	2	0	0	0	0	–	1	5	0	0	1.0	1.000
1989	TEX	A	2	1	.667	4.13	16	1	0	48	45	22	26	0	2	0	1	0	0	0	–	5	10	0	2	0.9	1.000
3 yrs.			3	4	.429	4.42	24	4	0	75.1	80	36	43	0	2	2	1	0	0	0	–	6	15	0	2	0.9	1.000

Orie Arntzen

ARNTZEN, ORIE EDGAR (Old Folks)
B. Oct. 18, 1909, Beverly, Ill. D. Jan. 28, 1970, Cedar Rapids, Iowa
BR TR 6'1" 200 lbs.

Year	Team		W	L	PCT	ERA	G	GS	CG	IP	H	BB	SO	ShO	W	L	SV	AB	H	HR	BA	PO	A	E	DP	TC/G	FA
1943	PHI	A	4	13	.235	4.22	32	20	9	164.1	172	69	66	0	0	0	0	50	8	0	.160	7	19	3	4	0.9	.897

Jerry Arrigo

ARRIGO, GERALD WILLIAM
B. June 12, 1941, Chicago, Ill.
BL TL 6'1" 185 lbs.

Year	Team		W	L	PCT	ERA	G	GS	CG	IP	H	BB	SO	ShO	W	L	SV	AB	H	HR	BA	PO	A	E	DP	TC/G	FA
1961	MIN	A	0	1	.000	10.24	7	2	0	9.2	9	10	6	0	0	0	0	2	1	0	.500	0	2	0	0	0.3	1.000
1962			0	0	–	18.00	1	0	0	1	3	1	1	0	0	0	0	0	0	0	–	0	0	0	0	0.0	–
1963			1	2	.333	2.87	5	1	0	15.2	12	4	13	0	1	1	0	4	0	0	.000	2	3	0	0	1.0	1.000
1964			7	4	.636	3.84	41	12	2	105.1	97	45	96	1	3	2	1	29	5	0	.172	3	18	1	0	0.5	.955
1965	CIN	N	4	3	.333	6.17	27	5	0	54	75	30	43	0	1	2	2	12	2	1	.167	1	3	0	0	0.1	1.000
1966	2 teams		CIN N	(3G 0–0)		NY N	(17G 3–3)																				
"	total		3	3	.500	3.91	20	5	0	50.2	54	19	31	0	2	0	0	11	5	0	.455	4	8	1	2	0.7	.923
1967	CIN	N	6	6	.500	3.16	32	5	1	74	61	35	56	1	4	3	1	19	4	0	.211	1	4	0	0	0.2	1.000
1968			12	10	.545	3.33	36	31	5	205.1	181	77	140	1	1	0	0	67	5	0	.075	3	45	1	1	1.4	.980
1969			4	7	.364	4.14	20	16	1	91.1	89	61	35	0	0	0	0	31	5	0	.161	1	8	1	0	0.5	.900
1970	CHI	A	0	3	.000	13.15	5	3	0	13	24	9	12	0	0	0	0	4	0	0	.000	0	1	0	0	0.2	1.000
10 yrs.			35	40	.467	4.14	194	80	9	620	605	291	433	3	12	8	4	179	27	1	.151	15	92	4	3	0.6	.964

Fernando Arroyo

ARROYO, FERNANDO
B. Mar. 21, 1952, Sacramento, Calif.
BR TR 6'2" 180 lbs.

Year	Team		W	L	PCT	ERA	G	GS	CG	IP	H	BB	SO	ShO	W	L	SV	AB	H	HR	BA	PO	A	E	DP	TC/G	FA
1975	DET	A	2	1	.667	4.56	14	2	1	53.1	56	22	25	0	1	0	0	0	0	0	–	6	11	0	2	1.2	1.000
1977			8	18	.308	4.18	38	28	8	209	227	52	60	1	1	2	0	0	0	0	–	15	63	1	4	2.1	.987
1978			0	0	–	8.31	2	0	0	4.1	8	0	1	0	0	0	0	0	0	0	–	0	1	0	0	0.5	1.000
1979			1	1	.500	8.25	6	0	0	12	17	4	7	0	1	1	0	0	0	0	–	1	2	0	0	0.5	1.000
1980	MIN	A	6	6	.500	4.70	21	11	1	92	97	32	27	1	2	0	0	0	0	0	–	9	8	1	0	0.9	.944
1981			7	10	.412	3.94	23	19	2	128	144	34	39	0	2	0	0	0	0	0	–	7	23	0	1	1.3	1.000
1982	2 teams		MIN A	(6G 0–1)		OAK A	(10G 0–0)																				
"	total		0	1	.000	5.25	16	0	0	36	40	13	13	0	0	1	0	0	0	0	–	3	10	1	1	0.9	.929
1986	OAK	A	0	0	–	0.00	1	0	0	0	0	3	0	0	0	0	0	0	0	0	–	0	0	0	0	0.0	–
8 yrs.			24	37	.393	4.44	121	60	12	534.2	589	160	172	2	5	4	0	0	0	0	–	41	118	3	8	1.3	.981

Luis Arroyo

ARROYO, LUIS ENRIQUE (Yo-Yo)
B. Feb. 18, 1927, Penuelas, Puerto Rico
BL TL 5'8½" 178 lbs.

Year	Team		W	L	PCT	ERA	G	GS	CG	IP	H	BB	SO	ShO	W	L	SV	AB	H	HR	BA	PO	A	E	DP	TC/G	FA
1955	STL	N	11	8	.579	4.19	35	24	9	159	162	63	68	1	1	0	1	56	13	1	.232	5	20	2	0	0.8	.926
1956	PIT	N	3	3	.500	4.71	18	2	1	28.2	32	12	17	0	2	2	0	4	2	0	.500	1	5	0	0	0.3	1.000
1957			3	11	.214	4.68	54	10	0	130.2	151	31	101	0	3	5	1	32	5	0	.156	4	12	1	0	0.3	.941
1959	CIN	N	1	0	1.000	3.95	10	0	0	13.2	17	11	8	0	1	0	0	2	0	0	.000	0	5	1	0	0.6	.833
1960	NY	A	5	1	.833	2.88	29	0	0	40.2	30	22	29	0	5	1	7	5	0	0	.000	2	6	1	0	0.3	1.000
1961			15	5	.750	2.19	65	0	0	119	83	49	87	0	15	5	29	25	7	0	.280	2	15	1	0	0.3	.944
1962			1	3	.250	4.81	27	0	0	33.2	33	17	21	0	1	3	7	4	2	0	.500	2	5	2	0	0.3	.714

Year	Team		W	L	PCT	ERA	G	GS	CG	IP	H	BB	SO	ShO	W	L	SV	AB	H	HR	BA	PO	A	E	DP	TC/G	FA
															Relief Pitching			**Batting**									

Doc Ayers *continued*

Year	Team		W	L	PCT	ERA	G	GS	CG	IP	H	BB	SO	ShO	W	L	SV	AB	H	HR	BA	PO	A	E	DP	TC/G	FA
1916			5	9	.357	3.78	43	17	7	157	173	52	69	0	0	2	2	43	6	0	.140	5	27	5	1	0.9	.865
1917			11	10	.524	2.17	40	15	12	207.2	192	59	78	3	5	4	1	63	13	0	.206	13	55	2	3	1.8	.971
1918			10	12	.455	2.83	40	24	11	219.2	215	63	67	4	3	2	3	66	10	0	.152	8	65	5	1	2.0	.936
1919	2 teams	WAS A (11G 1–6)				DET A	(24G 5–3)																				
"	total		6	9	.400	2.75	35	10	3	137.1	140	45	44	1	4	3	0	36	8	0	.222	5	41	6	4	1.5	.885
1920	DET	A	7	14	.333	3.88	46	22	9	208.2	217	62	103	3	0	2	1	59	9	0	.153	4	52	4	1	1.3	.933
1921			0	0	–	9.00	2	1	0	4	9	2	0	0	0	0	0	0	0	0	–	0	0	0	0	0.0	–
9 yrs.			66	79	.455	2.84	299	138	59	1428.2	1357	379	622	17	20	19	14	420	72	0	.171	64	355	39	13	1.5	.915

Bob Babcock

BABCOCK, ROBERT ERNEST
B. Aug. 25, 1949, New Castle, Pa.
BR TR 6'5" 210 lbs.

Year	Team		W	L	PCT	ERA	G	GS	CG	IP	H	BB	SO	ShO	W	L	SV	AB	H	HR	BA	PO	A	E	DP	TC/G	FA
1979	TEX	A	0	0	–	10.80	4	0	0	5	7	7	6	0	0	0	0	0	0	0	–	0	1	0	0	0.3	1.000
1980			1	2	.333	4.70	19	0	0	23	20	8	15	0	1	2	0	0	0	0	–	0	3	0	0	0.2	1.000
1981			1	1	.500	2.17	16	0	0	29	21	16	18	0	1	1	0	0	0	0	–	2	4	0	0	0.4	1.000
3 yrs.			2	3	.400	3.95	39	0	0	57	48	31	39	0	2	3	0	0	0	0	–	2	8	0	0	0.3	1.000

Johnny Babich

BABICH, JOHN CHARLES
B. May 14, 1913, Albion, Calif.
BR TR 6'1½" 185 lbs.

Year	Team		W	L	PCT	ERA	G	GS	CG	IP	H	BB	SO	ShO	W	L	SV	AB	H	HR	BA	PO	A	E	DP	TC/G	FA
1934	BKN	N	7	11	.389	4.20	25	19	7	135	148	51	62	0	0	2	1	50	7	0	.140	6	36	4	1	1.8	.913
1935			7	14	.333	6.66	37	24	7	143.1	191	52	55	2	0	3	0	49	9	0	.184	6	31	4	1	1.1	.902
1936	BOS	N	0	0	–	10.50	3	0	0	6	11	6	1	0	0	0	0	1	0	0	.000	0	2	1	0	1.0	.667
1940	PHI	A	14	13	.519	3.73	31	30	16	229.1	222	80	94	1	0	0	0	86	10	0	.116	14	42	2	0	1.9	.966
1941			2	7	.222	6.09	16	14	4	78.1	85	31	19	0	0	1	0	25	10	0	.400	9	19	0	1	1.8	1.000
5 yrs.			30	45	.400	4.93	112	87	34	592	657	220	231	3	0	6	1	211	36	0	.171	35	130	11	2	1.6	.938

Les Backman

BACKMAN, LESTER JOHN
B. Mar. 20, 1888, Cleves, Ohio   D. Nov. 8, 1975, Cincinnati, Ohio
BR TR 6'½" 195 lbs.

Year	Team		W	L	PCT	ERA	G	GS	CG	IP	H	BB	SO	ShO	W	L	SV	AB	H	HR	BA	PO	A	E	DP	TC/G	FA
1909	STL	N	3	11	.214	4.14	21	14	8	128.1	146	39	35	0	0	0	0	39	4	0	.103	2	36	1	0	1.9	.974
1910			6	7	.462	3.03	26	11	6	116	117	53	41	0	4	2	1	35	4	0	.114	5	30	3	1	1.5	.921
2 yrs.			9	18	.333	3.61	47	25	14	244.1	263	92	76	0	4	2	1	74	8	0	.108	7	66	4	1	1.6	.948

Eddie Bacon

BACON, EDGAR SUTER
B. Apr. 8, 1895, Franklin County, Ky.   D. Oct. 2, 1963, Frankfort, Ky.

Year	Team		W	L	PCT	ERA	G	GS	CG	IP	H	BB	SO	ShO	W	L	SV	AB	H	HR	BA	PO	A	E	DP	TC/G	FA
1917	PHI	A	0	0	–	6.00	1	0	0	6	5	7	0	0	0	0	0	*				1	7	0	0	8.0	1.000

Mike Bacsik

BACSIK, MICHAEL JAMES
B. Apr. 1, 1952, Dallas, Tex.
BR TR 6'2" 180 lbs.

Year	Team		W	L	PCT	ERA	G	GS	CG	IP	H	BB	SO	ShO	W	L	SV	AB	H	HR	BA	PO	A	E	DP	TC/G	FA
1975	TEX	A	1	2	.333	3.71	7	3	0	26.2	28	9	13	0	0	0	0	0	0	0	–	2	3	0	0	0.7	1.000
1976			3	2	.600	4.25	23	0	0	55	66	26	21	0	3	2	0	0	0	0	–	3	6	1	0	0.4	.900
1977			0	0	–	22.50	2	0	0	2	9	0	1	0	0	0	0	0	0	0	–	0	1	0	0	0.5	1.000
1979	MIN	A	4	2	.667	4.36	31	0	0	66	61	29	33	0	4	2	0	0	0	0	–	4	9	0	0	0.4	1.000
1980			0	0	–	4.30	10	0	0	23	26	11	9	0	0	0	0	0	0	0	–	3	3	0	1	0.6	1.000
5 yrs.			8	6	.571	4.43	73	3	0	172.2	190	75	77	0	7	4	0	0	0	0	–	12	22	1	1	0.5	.971

Fred Baczewski

BACZEWSKI, FREDERIC JOHN (Lefty)
B. May 15, 1926, St. Paul, Minn.   D. Nov. 14, 1976, Culver City, Calif.
BL TL 6'2½" 185 lbs.

Year	Team		W	L	PCT	ERA	G	GS	CG	IP	H	BB	SO	ShO	W	L	SV	AB	H	HR	BA	PO	A	E	DP	TC/G	FA
1953	2 teams	CHI N (9G 0–0)				CIN N	(24G 11–4)																				
"	total		11	4	.733	3.64	33	18	10	148.1	145	58	61	1	1	0	1	47	9	1	.191	5	13	4	2	0.7	.818
1954	CIN	N	6	6	.500	5.26	29	22	4	130	159	53	43	1	0	0	0	42	3	0	.071	12	16	1	1	1.0	.966
1955			0	0	–	18.00	1	0	0	1	2	0	0	0	0	0	0	0	0	0	–	0	0	0	0	0.0	–
3 yrs.			17	10	.630	4.45	63	40	14	279.1	306	111	104	2	1	0	1	89	12	1	.135	17	29	5	3	0.8	.902

Lore Bader

BADER, LORE VERNE (King)
B. Apr. 27, 1888, Bader, Ill.   D. June 2, 1973, Leroy, Kans.
BL TR 6' 175 lbs.

Year	Team		W	L	PCT	ERA	G	GS	CG	IP	H	BB	SO	ShO	W	L	SV	AB	H	HR	BA	PO	A	E	DP	TC/G	FA
1912	NY	N	2	0	1.000	0.90	2	1	1	10	9	6	3	0	1	0	0	3	0	0	.000	1	3	0	0	2.0	1.000
1917	BOS	A	2	0	1.000	2.35	15	1	0	38.1	48	18	14	0	1	0	1	10	3	0	.300	1	15	1	1	1.1	.941
1918			1	3	.250	3.33	5	4	2	27	26	12	10	1	0	0	0	9	1	0	.111	1	2	1	0	0.8	.750
3 yrs.			5	3	.625	2.51	22	6	3	75.1	83	36	27	1	2	0	1	22	4	0	.182	3	20	2	1	1.1	.920

Ed Baecht

BAECHT, EDWARD JOSEPH
B. May 15, 1907, Baden, Okla.   D. Aug. 15, 1957, Grafton, Ill.
BR TR 6'3" 195 lbs.

Year	Team		W	L	PCT	ERA	G	GS	CG	IP	H	BB	SO	ShO	W	L	SV	AB	H	HR	BA	PO	A	E	DP	TC/G	FA
1926	PHI	N	2	0	1.000	6.11	28	1	1	56	73	28	14	0	1	0	0	14	2	0	.143	2	23	2	1	1.0	.926
1927			0	1	.000	12.00	1	1	0	6	12	2	0	0	0	0	0	2	0	0	.000	0	2	0	0	2.0	1.000
1928			1	1	.500	6.00	9	1	0	24	37	9	10	0	1	0	0	7	1	0	.143	0	8	0	0	0.9	1.000
1931	CHI	N	2	4	.333	3.76	22	6	2	67	64	32	34	0	1	1	0	18	5	0	.278	3	18	0	1	1.0	1.000
1932			0	0	–	0.00	1	0	0	1	1	1	0	0	0	0	0	0	0	0	–	0	0	0	0	0.0	–
1937	STL	A	0	0	–	12.79	3	0	0	6.1	13	6	3	0	0	0	0	1	0	0	.000	0	1	0	0	0.3	1.000
6 yrs.			5	6	.455	5.56	64	9	3	160.1	200	78	61	0	3	1	0	42	8	0	.190	5	52	2	2	0.9	.966

Jim Bagby

BAGBY, JAMES CHARLES JACOB, SR. (Sarge)
Father of Jim Bagby.
B. Oct. 5, 1889, Barnett, Ga.   D. July 28, 1954, Marietta, Ga.
BB TR 6' 170 lbs.

Year	Team		W	L	PCT	ERA	G	GS	CG	IP	H	BB	SO	ShO	W	L	SV	AB	H	HR	BA	PO	A	E	DP	TC/G	FA
1912	CIN	N	2	0	1.000	3.12	5	1	0	17.1	17	9	10	0	2	0	0	5	0	0	.000	1	4	0	0	1.0	1.000
1916	CLE	A	16	16	.500	2.55	48	27	14	278.2	253	67	88	3	5	6	5	90	15	0	.167	24	62	5	3	1.9	.945
1917			23	13	.639	1.96	49	37	26	320.2	277	73	83	8	1	1	7	108	25	0	.231	26	77	3	5	2.2	.972
1918			17	16	.515	2.69	45	31	23	271.1	274	78	57	2	2	2	6	99	21	0	.212	15	67	4	1	1.9	.953
1919			17	11	.607	2.80	35	32	21	241.1	258	44	61	0	0	3	3	89	23	1	.258	14	64	4	3	2.3	.951
1920			**31**	12	**.721**	2.89	**48**	**39**	**30**	339.2	**338**	79	73	3	**6**	1	0	131	33	1	.252	16	57	2	1	1.6	.973
1921			14	12	.538	4.70	40	26	12	191.2	238	44	37	1	1	0	1	76	15	0	.197	12	42	3	1	1.4	.947
1922			4	5	.444	6.32	25	10	4	98.1	134	39	25	0	1	0	1	42	11	0	.262	6	28	0	0	1.4	1.000

Year	Team	W	L	PCT	ERA	G	GS	CG	IP	H	BB	SO	ShO	Relief Pitching W	L	SV	Batting AB	H	HR	BA	PO	A	E	DP	TC/G	FA

Jim Bagby *continued*

Year	Team	W	L	PCT	ERA	G	GS	CG	IP	H	BB	SO	ShO	W	L	SV	AB	H	HR	BA	PO	A	E	DP	TC/G	FA
1923	PIT N	3	2	.600	5.24	21	6	2	68.2	95	25	16	0	1	1	3	20	1	0	.050	1	10	0	4	0.5	1.000
9 yrs.		127	87	.593	3.10	316	209	132	1827.2	1884	458	450	16	21	13	29	660	144	2	.218	115	411	21	18	1.7	.962

WORLD SERIES

| 1920 | CLE A | 1 | 1 | .500 | 1.80 | 2 | 2 | 1 | 15 | 20 | 1 | 3 | 0 | 0 | 0 | 0 | 6 | 2 | 1 | .333 | 2 | 3 | 1 | 0 | 3.0 | .833 |

Jim Bagby

BAGBY, JAMES CHARLES JACOB, JR.
Son of Jim Bagby.
B. Sept. 8, 1916, Cleveland, Ohio D. Sept. 2, 1988, Marietta, Ga.

BR TR 6'2" 170 lbs.

Year	Team	W	L	PCT	ERA	G	GS	CG	IP	H	BB	SO	ShO	W	L	SV	AB	H	HR	BA	PO	A	E	DP	TC/G	FA
1938	BOS A	15	11	.577	4.21	43	25	10	198.2	218	90	73	1	4	1	2	67	13	0	.194	16	43	3	3	1.4	.952
1939		5	5	.500	7.09	21	11	3	80	119	36	35	0	2	1	0	34	10	1	.294	3	11	1	2	0.7	.933
1940		10	16	.385	4.73	36	21	6	182.2	217	83	57	1	5	5	2	74	15	0	.203	17	38	1	6	1.6	.982
1941	CLE A	9	15	.375	4.04	33	27	12	200.2	214	76	53	0	0	0	2	74	18	0	.243	16	42	1	5	1.8	.983
1942		17	9	.654	2.96	38	35	16	270.2	267	64	54	4	0	0	1	95	18	1	.189	17	58	4	7	2.1	.949
1943		17	14	.548	3.10	36	33	16	273	248	80	70	3	1	0	1	112	30	0	.268	21	67	2	5	2.5	.978
1944		4	5	.444	4.33	13	10	2	79	101	34	12	0	2	0	0	31	7	1	.226	5	16	2	4	1.8	.913
1945		8	11	.421	3.73	25	19	11	159.1	171	59	38	3	0	1	1	58	17	0	.293	13	47	4	3	2.6	.938
1946	BOS A	7	6	.538	3.71	21	11	6	106.2	117	49	16	1	0	1	0	42	5	0	.119	7	19	2	1	1.3	.929
1947	PIT N	5	4	.556	4.67	37	6	2	115.2	143	37	23	0	2	2	0	32	7	0	.219	7	28	2	2	1.0	.946
10 yrs.		97	96	.503	3.96	303	198	84	1666.1	1815	608	431	13	16	11	9	619	140	3	.226	122	369	22	38	1.7	.957

WORLD SERIES

| 1946 | BOS A | 0 | 0 | — | 3.00 | 1 | 0 | 0 | 3 | 6 | 1 | 1 | 0 | 0 | 0 | 0 | 1 | 0 | 0 | .000 | 0 | 1 | 0 | 0 | 1.0 | 1.000 |

Stan Bahnsen

BAHNSEN, STANLEY RAYMOND
B. Dec. 15, 1944, Council Bluffs, Iowa

BR TR 6'2" 185 lbs.

Year	Team	W	L	PCT	ERA	G	GS	CG	IP	H	BB	SO	ShO	W	L	SV	AB	H	HR	BA	PO	A	E	DP	TC/G	FA
1966	NY A	1	1	.500	3.52	4	3	1	23	15	7	16	0	0	1	0	7	1	0	.143	1	3	0	0	1.0	1.000
1968		17	12	.586	2.05	37	34	10	267.1	216	68	162	1	0	1	0	81	4	0	.049	15	32	3	1	1.4	.940
1969		9	16	.360	3.83	40	33	5	220.2	222	90	130	2	1	2	1	60	5	0	.083	13	36	3	4	1.3	.942
1970		14	11	.560	3.32	36	35	6	233	227	75	116	2	0	0	0	74	11	0	.149	17	40	4	3	1.7	.934
1971		14	12	.538	3.35	36	34	14	242	221	72	110	3	0	0	0	79	12	0	.152	18	55	4	5	2.1	.948
1972	CHI A	21	16	.568	3.60	43	41	5	252.1	263	73	157	1	0	0	0	92	14	0	.152	11	50	2	6	1.5	.968
1973		18	21	.462	3.57	42	42	14	282.1	290	117	120	4	0	0	0	0	0	0	—	20	53	4	4	1.8	.948
1974		12	15	.444	4.71	38	35	10	216	230	110	102	1	1	1	0	0	0	0	—	5	39	2	1	1.2	.957
1975	2 teams					CHI A		(12G 4–6)			OAK A		(21G 6–7)													
"	total	10	13	.435	4.36	33	28	4	167.1	166	77	80	1	0	0	0	1	0	0	.000	10	27	2	1	1.2	.949
1976	OAK A	8	7	.533	3.34	35	14	1	143	124	43	82	1	5	1	0	0	0	0	—	13	23	1	0	1.1	.973
1977	2 teams					OAK A		(11G 1–2)			MON N		(23G 8–9)													
"	total	9	11	.450	5.01	34	24	3	149	166	51	79	1	0	1	1	42	5	0	.119	12	19	4	0	1.0	.886
1978	MON N	1	5	.167	3.84	44	1	0	75	74	31	44	0	1	5	7	11	1	0	.091	6	10	2	0	0.4	.889
1979		3	1	.750	3.16	55	0	0	94	80	42	71	0	3	1	1	14	1	1	.071	4	13	2	0	0.3	.895
1980		7	6	.538	3.07	57	0	0	91	80	33	48	0	7	6	4	9	1	0	.111	6	12	0	1	0.3	1.000
1981		2	1	.667	4.96	25	3	0	49	45	24	28	0	2	0	1	9	1	0	.111	2	2	1	0	0.2	.800
1982	2 teams					CAL A		(7G 0–1)			PHI N		(8G 0–0)													
"	total	0	1	—	2.74	15	0	0	23	21	11	14	0	0	1	0	0	0	0	—	1	1	1	0	0.2	.667
16 yrs.		146	149	.495	3.61	574	327	73	2528	2440	924	1359	16	20	19	20	479	56	1	.117	154	415	35	26	1.1	.942

DIVISIONAL PLAYOFF SERIES

| 1981 | MON N | 0 | 0 | — | 0.00 | 1 | 0 | 0 | 1.1 | 1 | 1 | 1 | 0 | 0 | 0 | 0 | 0 | 0 | 0 | — | 0 | 0 | 0 | 0 | 0.0 | — |

Ed Bahr

BAHR, EDSON GARFIELD
B. Oct. 16, 1919, Rouleau, Sask., Canada

BR TR 6'1½" 172 lbs.

Year	Team	W	L	PCT	ERA	G	GS	CG	IP	H	BB	SO	ShO	W	L	SV	AB	H	HR	BA	PO	A	E	DP	TC/G	FA
1946	PIT N	8	6	.571	2.63	27	14	7	136.2	128	52	44	0	0	0	0	45	8	0	.178	8	28	5	2	1.5	.878
1947		3	5	.375	4.59	19	11	1	82.1	82	43	25	0	1	1	0	23	2	0	.087	2	12	1	1	0.8	.933
2 yrs.		11	11	.500	3.37	46	25	8	219	210	95	69	0	1	1	0	68	10	0	.147	10	40	6	3	1.2	.893

Grover Baichley

BAICHLEY, GROVER CLEVELAND
B. Jan. 7, 1890, Toledo, Ill. D. June 30, 1956, San Jose, Calif.

BR TR 5'9½" 165 lbs.

Year	Team	W	L	PCT	ERA	G	GS	CG	IP	H	BB	SO	ShO	W	L	SV	AB	H	HR	BA	PO	A	E	DP	TC/G	FA
1914	STL A	0	0	—	5.14	4	0	0	7	9	3	3	0	0	0	0	1	0	0	.000	0	4	0	0	1.0	1.000

Scott Bailes

BAILES, SCOTT ALAN
B. Dec. 18, 1961, Chillicothe, Ohio

BL TL 6'2" 170 lbs.

Year	Team	W	L	PCT	ERA	G	GS	CG	IP	H	BB	SO	ShO	W	L	SV	AB	H	HR	BA	PO	A	E	DP	TC/G	FA
1986	CLE A	10	10	.500	4.95	62	10	0	112.2	123	43	60	0	8	7	7	0	0	0	—	4	13	1	0	0.3	.944
1987		7	8	.467	4.64	39	17	0	120.1	145	47	65	0	2	1	6	0	0	0	—	6	19	2	0	0.7	.926
1988		9	14	.391	4.90	37	21	5	145	149	46	53	2	2	3	0	0	0	0	—	14	19	1	0	0.9	.971
1989		5	9	.357	4.28	34	11	0	113.2	116	29	47	0	2	3	0	0	0	0	—	4	20	2	2	0.8	.923
4 yrs.		31	41	.431	4.70	172	59	5	491.2	533	165	225	2	14	14	13	0	0	0	—	28	71	6	2	0.6	.943

Bill Bailey

BAILEY, WILLIAM F.
B. Apr. 12, 1889, Fort Smith, Ark. D. Nov. 2, 1926, Houston, Tex.

BL TL 5'11" 165 lbs.

Year	Team	W	L	PCT	ERA	G	GS	CG	IP	H	BB	SO	ShO	W	L	SV	AB	H	HR	BA	PO	A	E	DP	TC/G	FA
1907	STL A	4	1	.800	2.42	6	5	3	48.1	39	15	17	0	0	0	0	20	3	0	.150	2	11	1	0	2.3	.929
1908		3	5	.375	3.04	22	12	7	106.2	85	50	42	0	0	0	0	34	3	0	.088	1	26	3	0	1.3	.897
1909		9	10	.474	2.44	32	20	17	199	174	75	114	1	0	0	0	77	22	0	.286	4	52	2	1	1.8	.966
1910		3	18	.143	3.32	34	20	13	192.1	186	97	90	0	3	1	0	63	13	0	.206	7	57	6	0	2.1	.914
1911		0	3	.000	4.55	7	2	2	31.2	42	16	8	0	0	0	0	11	0	0	.000	2	11	1	1	2.0	.929
1912		0	1	.000	9.28	3	2	0	10.2	15	10	2	0	0	0	0	2	1	0	.500	1	0	0	0	0.3	1.000
1914	BAL F	7	9	.438	3.08	19	18	10	128.2	106	68	131	1	1	0	0	43	7	0	.163	5	45	0	3	2.7	.962
1915	2 teams					BAL F		(36G 5–19)			CHI F		(5G 3–1)													
"	total	8	20	.286	4.27	41	28	14	223.2	202	125	122	5	1	4		74	17	0	.230	9	61	7	2	1.9	.909
1918	DET A	1	2	.333	5.97	8	4	1	37.2	53	26	13	0	0	0	0	13	1	0	.077	1	14	0	0	1.9	1.000
1921	STL N	2	5	.286	4.26	19	6	3	74	95	22	20	1	1	2	0	22	2	0	.091	2	26	3	1	1.6	.903

Year	Team		W	L	PCT	ERA	G	GS	CG	IP	H	BB	SO	ShO	Relief Pitching W	L	SV	Batting AB	H	HR	BA	PO	A	E	DP	TC/G	FA

Bill Bailey *continued*

Year	Team		W	L	PCT	ERA	G	GS	CG	IP	H	BB	SO	ShO	W	L	SV	AB	H	HR	BA	PO	A	E	DP	TC/G	FA
1922			0	2	.000	5.40	12	0	0	31.2	38	23	11	0	0	2	0	7	2	0	.286	2	11	1	0	1.2	.929
11 yrs.			37	76	.327	3.57	203	117	70	1084.1	1035	527	570	8	7	10	0	366	71	0	.194	34	315	26	5	1.8	.931

Harvey Bailey

BAILEY, HARVEY FRANCIS
B. Nov. 24, 1876, Adrian, Mich.   D. July 10, 1922, Toledo, Ohio

TL 6'

Year	Team		W	L	PCT	ERA	G	GS	CG	IP	H	BB	SO	ShO	W	L	SV	AB	H	HR	BA	PO	A	E	DP	TC/G	FA
1899	BOS	N	6	4	.600	3.95	12	11	8	86.2	83	35	26	0	1	0	0	34	8	0	.235	2	17	2	0	1.8	.905
1900			0	0	–	4.95	4	1	0	20	24	11	9	0	0	0	0	9	2	0	.222	1	8	0	0	2.3	1.000
2 yrs.			6	4	.600	4.13	16	12	8	106.2	107	46	35	0	1	0	0	43	10	0	.233	3	25	2	0	1.9	.933

Howard Bailey

BAILEY, HOWARD LEE
B. July 31, 1957, Grand Haven, Mich.

BR TL 6'   195 lbs.

Year	Team		W	L	PCT	ERA	G	GS	CG	IP	H	BB	SO	ShO	W	L	SV	AB	H	HR	BA	PO	A	E	DP	TC/G	FA
1981	DET	A	1	4	.200	7.30	9	5	0	37	45	13	17	0	0	0	0	0	0	0	–	2	11	0	0	1.4	1.000
1982			0	0	–	0.00	8	0	0	10	6	2	3	0	0	0	1	0	0	0	–	1	2	0	0	0.4	1.000
1983			5	5	.500	4.88	33	3	0	72	69	25	21	0	4	3	0	0	0	0	–	9	10	3	1	0.7	.864
3 yrs.			6	9	.400	5.22	50	8	0	119	120	40	41	0	4	3	1	0	0	0	–	12	23	3	1	0.8	.921

Jim Bailey

BAILEY, JAMES HOPKINS
Brother of Ed Bailey.
B. Dec. 16, 1934, Strawberry Plains, Tenn.

BB TL 6'2½"   210 lbs.

Year	Team		W	L	PCT	ERA	G	GS	CG	IP	H	BB	SO	ShO	W	L	SV	AB	H	HR	BA	PO	A	E	DP	TC/G	FA
1959	CIN	N	0	1	.000	6.17	3	1	0	11.2	17	6	7	0	0	0	0	3	0	0	.000	0	0	0	0	0.0	–

King Bailey

BAILEY, LEMUEL
B. Cincinnati, Ohio

BL TL 6'   185 lbs.

Year	Team		W	L	PCT	ERA	G	GS	CG	IP	H	BB	SO	ShO	W	L	SV	AB	H	HR	BA	PO	A	E	DP	TC/G	FA
1895	CIN	N	1	0	1.000	5.63	1	1	1	8	13	0	0	0	0	0	0	4	2	0	.500	1	2	1	0	4.0	.750

Steve Bailey

BAILEY, STEVEN JOHN
B. Feb. 12, 1942, Bronx, N. Y.

BR TR 6'1"   194 lbs.

Year	Team		W	L	PCT	ERA	G	GS	CG	IP	H	BB	SO	ShO	W	L	SV	AB	H	HR	BA	PO	A	E	DP	TC/G	FA
1967	CLE	A	2	5	.286	3.90	32	1	0	64.2	62	42	46	0	2	4	2	10	0	0	.000	10	7	0	1	0.5	1.000
1968			0	1	.000	3.60	2	1	0	5	4	2	1	0	0	0	0	0	0	0	–	0	0	0	0	0.0	–
2 yrs.			2	6	.250	3.88	34	2	0	69.2	66	44	47	0	2	4	2	10	0	0	.000	10	7	0	1	0.5	1.000

Sweetbreads Bailey

BAILEY, ABRAHAM LINCOLN
B. Feb. 12, 1895, Joliet, Ill.   D. Sept. 27, 1939, Joliet, Ill.

BR TR 6'   205 lbs.

Year	Team		W	L	PCT	ERA	G	GS	CG	IP	H	BB	SO	ShO	W	L	SV	AB	H	HR	BA	PO	A	E	DP	TC/G	FA
1919	CHI	N	3	5	.375	3.15	21	5	0	71.1	75	20	19	0	3	2	0	18	7	0	.389	0	29	0	2	1.4	1.000
1920			1	2	.333	7.12	21	1	0	36.2	38	11	8	0	0	1	0	7	1	0	.143	0	14	0	0	0.7	1.000
1921	2 teams		CHI N	(3G 0–0)		BKN N	(7G 0–0)																				
"	total		0	0	–	4.91	10	0	0	29.1	41	9	8	0	0	0	0	5	0	0	.000	1	8	0	0	1.0	.900
3 yrs.			4	7	.364	4.59	52	6	0	137.1	154	40	35	0	3	3	0	30	8	0	.267	1	51	1	2	1.0	.981

Bob Bailor

BAILOR, ROBERT MICHAEL
B. Mar. 10, 1951, Connellsville, Pa.

BR TR 5'11"   170 lbs.

Year	Team		W	L	PCT	ERA	G	GS	CG	IP	H	BB	SO	ShO	W	L	SV	AB	H	HR	BA	PO	A	E	DP	TC/G	FA
1980	TOR	A	0	0	–	9.00	3	0	0	2	4	1	0	0	0	0	0	*				0	0	0	0	0.0	–

Loren Bain

BAIN, HERBERT LOREN
B. July 4, 1922, Staples, Minn.

BR TR 6'   190 lbs.

Year	Team		W	L	PCT	ERA	G	GS	CG	IP	H	BB	SO	ShO	W	L	SV	AB	H	HR	BA	PO	A	E	DP	TC/G	FA
1945	NY	N	0	0	–	7.88	3	0	0	8	10	4	1	0	0	0	0	3	1	0	.333	0	1	0	0	0.3	1.000

Doug Bair

BAIR, CHARLES DOUGLAS
B. Aug. 22, 1949, Defiance, Ohio

BR TR 6'   180 lbs.

Year	Team		W	L	PCT	ERA	G	GS	CG	IP	H	BB	SO	ShO	W	L	SV	AB	H	HR	BA	PO	A	E	DP	TC/G	FA
1976	PIT	N	0	0	–	5.68	4	0	0	6.1	4	5	4	0	0	0	0	0	0	0	–	1	0	0	0	0.3	1.000
1977	OAK	A	4	6	.400	3.47	45	0	0	83	78	57	68	0	4	6	8	0	0	0	–	7	14	1	1	0.5	.955
1978	CIN	N	7	6	.538	1.98	70	0	0	100	87	38	91	0	7	6	28	14	2	0	.143	11	7	1	1	0.3	.947
1979			11	7	.611	4.31	65	0	0	94	93	51	86	0	11	7	16	8	0	0	.000	5	9	1	1	0.2	.933
1980			3	6	.333	4.24	61	0	0	85	91	39	62	0	3	6	6	2	0	0	.000	3	21	0	1	0.4	1.000
1981	2 teams		CIN N	(24G 2–2)		STL N	(11G 2–0)																				
"	total		4	2	.667	5.10	35	0	0	54.2	55	19	30	0	4	2	1	6	1	1	.167	2	6	0	0	0.3	.889
1982	STL	N	5	3	.625	2.55	63	0	0	91.2	69	36	68	0	5	3	8	13	1	0	.077	9	13	1	1	0.4	.957
1983	2 teams		STL N	(26G 1–1)		DET A	(27G 7–3)																				
"	total		8	4	.667	3.59	53	0	0	85.1	75	32	60	0	7	4	5	2	0	0	.000	3	10	1	0	0.3	.929
1984	DET	A	5	3	.625	3.75	47	1	0	93.2	82	36	57	0	5	2	4	0	0	0	–	12	11	0	2	0.5	1.000
1985	2 teams		DET A	(21G 2–0)		STL N	(2G 0–0)																				
"	total		2	0	1.000	5.96	23	3	0	51.1	55	27	30	0	1	0	0	0	0	0	–	4	9	0	1	0.6	1.000
1986	OAK	A	2	3	.400	3.00	31	0	0	45	37	18	40	0	2	3	4	0	0	0	–	2	7	0	1	0.3	1.000
1987	PHI	N	2	0	1.000	5.93	11	0	0	13.2	15	5	10	0	2	0	0	1	0	0	.000	1	2	1	0	0.4	.750
1988	TOR	A	0	0	–	4.05	10	0	0	13.1	14	3	8	0	0	0	0	0	0	0	–	2	1	0	0	0.3	1.000
1989	PIT	N	2	3	.400	2.27	44	0	0	67.1	52	28	56	0	2	3	1	5	1	0	.200	8	10	1	0	0.4	.947
14 yrs.			55	43	.561	3.60	562	5	0	884.1	809	394	670	0	53	42	81	51	5	1	.098	70	120	8	8	0.4	.960

LEAGUE CHAMPIONSHIP SERIES

Year	Team		W	L	PCT	ERA	G	GS	CG	IP	H	BB	SO	ShO	W	L	SV	AB	H	HR	BA	PO	A	E	DP	TC/G	FA
1979	CIN	N	0	1	.000	9.00	1	0	0	1	2	1	0	0	0	1	0	0	0	0	–	0	1	0	0	1.0	1.000
1982	STL	N	0	0	–	0.00	1	0	0	1	2	3	0	0	0	0	0	0	0	0	–	0	0	0	0	0.0	–
2 yrs.			0	1	.000	4.50	2	0	0	2	4	4	0	0	0	1	0	0	0	0	–	0	1	0	0	0.5	1.000

WORLD SERIES

Year	Team		W	L	PCT	ERA	G	GS	CG	IP	H	BB	SO	ShO	W	L	SV	AB	H	HR	BA	PO	A	E	DP	TC/G	FA
1982	STL	N	0	1	.000	9.00	3	0	0	2	2	2	3	0	0	1	0	0	0	0	–	0	0	0	0	0.0	–
1984	DET	A	0	0	–	0.00	1	0	0	.2	0	0	1	0	0	0	0	0	0	0	–	0	0	0	0	0.0	–
2 yrs.			0	1	.000	6.75	4	0	0	2.2	2	2	4	0	0	1	0	0	0	0	–	0	0	0	0	0.0	–

Year	Team		W	L	PCT	ERA	G	GS	CG	IP	H	BB	SO	ShO	Relief Pitching W	L	SV	Batting AB	H	HR	BA	PO	A	E	DP	TC/G	FA

Bob Baird

BAIRD, ROBERT ALLEN
B. Jan. 16, 1940, Knoxville, Tenn.   D. Apr. 11, 1974, Chattanooga, Tenn.
BL TL 6'4"   195 lbs.

Year	Team		W	L	PCT	ERA	G	GS	CG	IP	H	BB	SO	ShO	W	L	SV	AB	H	HR	BA	PO	A	E	DP	TC/G	FA
1962	WAS	A	0	1	.000	6.75	3	3	0	10.2	13	8	3	0	0	0	0	3	0	0	.000	0	2	0	0	0.7	1.000
1963			0	3	.000	7.71	5	3	0	11.2	12	7	7	0	0	0	0	3	1	0	.333	0	1	1	0	0.4	.500
2 yrs.			0	4	.000	7.25	8	6	0	22.1	25	15	10	0	0	0	0	6	1	0	.167	0	3	1	0	0.5	.750

Jersey Bakely

BAKELY, EDWARD ENOCH
Born Edward Enoch Bakeley.
B. Apr. 17, 1864, Blackwood, N. J.   D. Feb. 17, 1915, Philadelphia, Pa.
BR TR

Year	Team		W	L	PCT	ERA	G	GS	CG	IP	H	BB	SO	ShO	W	L	SV	AB	H	HR	BA	PO	A	E	DP	TC/G	FA
1883	PHI	AA	5	3	.625	3.23	8	8	7	61.1	65	12	14	0	0	0	0	26	5	0	.192	2	12	1	0	1.9	.933
1884	3 teams	PHI U (39G 14–25)				WIL U (2G 0–2)				KC U (5G 2–3)																	
"	total		16	30	.348	4.29	46	45	43	394.2	443	81	226	1	0	1	0	192	25	0	.130	15	77	27	4	2.6	.773
1888	CLE	AA	25	33	.431	2.97	61	61	60	532.2	518	128	212	4	0	0	0	194	26	1	.134	21	114	18	3	2.5	.882
1889	CLE	N	12	22	.353	2.96	36	34	33	304.1	296	106	105	2	0	1	0	111	15	1	.135	19	64	5	5	2.4	.943
1890	CLE	P	13	25	.342	4.47	43	38	32	326.1	412	147	67	0	0	0	0	138	28	0	.203	11	72	7	1	2.1	.922
1891	2 teams	WAS AA (13G 2–10)				BAL AA (8G 4–2)																					
"	total		6	12	.333	4.24	21	18	16	163.1	175	90	45	0	1	0	0	66	12	0	.182	6	31	13	1	2.4	.740
6 yrs.			77	125	.381	3.66	215	204	191	1782.2	1909	564	669	7	1	2	0	727	111	2	.153	74	370	71	14	2.4	.862

Dave Bakenhaster

BAKENHASTER, DAVID LEE
B. Mar. 5, 1945, Columbus, Ohio
BR TR 5'10"   168 lbs.

Year	Team		W	L	PCT	ERA	G	GS	CG	IP	H	BB	SO	ShO	W	L	SV	AB	H	HR	BA	PO	A	E	DP	TC/G	FA
1964	STL	N	0	0	—	6.00	2	0	0	3	9	1	0	0	0	0	0	0	0	0	—	0	1	0	0	0.5	1.000

Al Baker

BAKER, ALBERT JONES
B. Feb. 28, 1906, Batesville, Miss.   D. Nov. 6, 1982, Kenedy, Tex.
BR TR 5'11"   170 lbs.

Year	Team		W	L	PCT	ERA	G	GS	CG	IP	H	BB	SO	ShO	W	L	SV	AB	H	HR	BA	PO	A	E	DP	TC/G	FA
1938	BOS	A	0	0	—	9.39	3	0	0	7.2	13	2	2	0	0	0	0	4	0	0	.000	1	1	0	0	0.7	1.000

Bock Baker

BAKER, CHARLES
B. July 17, 1878, Troy, N. Y.

Year	Team		W	L	PCT	ERA	G	GS	CG	IP	H	BB	SO	ShO	W	L	SV	AB	H	HR	BA	PO	A	E	DP	TC/G	FA
1901	2 teams	CLE A (1G 0–1)				PHI A (1G 0–1)																					
"	total		0	2	.000	7.71	2	2	1	14	29	12	1	0	0	0	0	7	1	0	.143	0	2	0	1	1.0	1.000

Ernie Baker

BAKER, EARNEST GOULD
B. Aug. 8, 1875, Concord, Mich.   D. Oct. 25, 1945, Homer, Mich.
BR TR 5'10"   160 lbs.

Year	Team		W	L	PCT	ERA	G	GS	CG	IP	H	BB	SO	ShO	W	L	SV	AB	H	HR	BA	PO	A	E	DP	TC/G	FA
1905	CIN	N	0	0	—	4.50	1	0	0	4	7	0	1	0	0	0	0	2	0	0	.000	0	0	0	0	0.0	—

Jesse Baker

BAKER, JESSE ORMOND
B. June 3, 1888, Anderson Island, Wash.   D. Sept. 26, 1972, Tacoma, Wash.
BL TL 5'11"   188 lbs.

Year	Team		W	L	PCT	ERA	G	GS	CG	IP	H	BB	SO	ShO	W	L	SV	AB	H	HR	BA	PO	A	E	DP	TC/G	FA
1911	CHI	A	2	7	.222	3.93	22	8	3	94	101	30	51	0	1	0	0	29	3	0	.103	2	33	1	0	1.6	.972

Kirtley Baker

BAKER, KIRTLEY (Whitey)
B. June 24, 1869, Aurora, Ind.   D. Apr. 15, 1927, Lawrenceburg, Ind.
BR TR 5'9"   160 lbs.

Year	Team		W	L	PCT	ERA	G	GS	CG	IP	H	BB	SO	ShO	W	L	SV	AB	H	HR	BA	PO	A	E	DP	TC/G	FA
1890	PIT	N	3	19	.136	5.60	25	21	19	178.1	209	86	76	2	1	0	0	68	10	0	.147	11	32	6	2	2.0	.878
1893	BAL	N	3	8	.273	8.44	15	12	8	91.2	138	58	26	0	0	0	0	57	17	0	.298	8	32	3	1	2.9	.930
1894			0	1	.000	∞	1	0	0		1	2	0	0	0	1	0	4	0	0	.000	0	1	0	0	1.0	—
1898	WAS	N	2	3	.400	3.06	6	5	4	47	56	18	7	0	0	0	0	18	5	0	.278	3	8	0	0	1.8	1.000
1899			1	7	.125	6.83	11	6	3	54	79	22	6	0	1	0	0	19	3	0	.158	1	24	4	0	2.6	.862
5 yrs.			9	38	.191	6.28	58	44	34	371	483	186	115	2	2	2	0	166	35	0	.211	23	96	14	3	2.3	.895

Neal Baker

BAKER, NEAL VERNON
B. Apr. 30, 1904, LaPorte, Tex.   D. Jan. 5, 1982, Houston, Tex.
BR TR 6'1"   175 lbs.

Year	Team		W	L	PCT	ERA	G	GS	CG	IP	H	BB	SO	ShO	W	L	SV	AB	H	HR	BA	PO	A	E	DP	TC/G	FA
1927	PHI	A	0	0	—	5.71	5	2	0	17.1	27	7	3	0	0	0	0	6	1	0	.167	0	5	0	2	1.0	1.000

Norm Baker

BAKER, NORMAN LESLIE (Bones)
B. Oct. 14, 1862, Philadelphia, Pa.   D. Feb. 20, 1949, Hurffville, N. J.

Year	Team		W	L	PCT	ERA	G	GS	CG	IP	H	BB	SO	ShO	W	L	SV	AB	H	HR	BA	PO	A	E	DP	TC/G	FA
1883	PIT	AA	0	2	.000	3.32	3	3	2	19	24	11	5	0	0	0	0	12	0	0	.000	0	1	2	0	1.0	.333
1885	LOU	AA	13	12	.520	3.40	25	24	24	217	210	69	79	1	1	0	0	87	18	0	.207	5	33	12	1	2.0	.760
1890	BAL	AA	1	1	.500	3.71	2	2	2	17	16	6	10	0	0	0	0	7	0	0	.000	0	5	0	0	2.5	1.000
3 yrs.			14	15	.483	3.42	30	29	28	253	250	86	94	1	1	0	0	106	18	0	.170	5	39	14	1	1.9	.759

Steve Baker

BAKER, STEVEN BYRNE
B. Aug. 30, 1956, Eugene, Ore.
BR TR 6'   185 lbs.

Year	Team		W	L	PCT	ERA	G	GS	CG	IP	H	BB	SO	ShO	W	L	SV	AB	H	HR	BA	PO	A	E	DP	TC/G	FA
1978	DET	A	2	4	.333	4.55	15	10	0	63.1	66	42	39	0	1	0	0	0	0	0	—	3	5	1	0	0.6	.889
1979			1	7	.125	6.64	21	12	0	84	97	51	54	0	0	1	0	0	0	0	—	3	8	0	1	0.5	1.000
1982	OAK	A	1	1	.500	4.56	5	3	0	25.2	30	4	14	0	0	0	0	0	0	0	—	0	3	1	0	0.8	.750
1983	2 teams	OAK A (35G 3–3)				STL N (8G 0–1)																					
"	total		3	4	.429	3.94	43	1	0	64	69	30	24	0	3	3	5	0	0	0	—	4	7	0	0	0.3	1.000
4 yrs.			7	16	.304	5.13	84	26	0	237	262	127	131	0	4	5	6	0	0	0	—	10	23	2	1	0.4	.943

Tom Baker

BAKER, THOMAS CALVIN (Rattlesnake)
B. June 11, 1913, Nursery, Tex.
BR TR 6'1½"   180 lbs.

Year	Team		W	L	PCT	ERA	G	GS	CG	IP	H	BB	SO	ShO	W	L	SV	AB	H	HR	BA	PO	A	E	DP	TC/G	FA
1935	BKN	N	1	0	1.000	4.29	7	3	1	42	48	20	10	0	0	0	0	19	9	0	.474	0	5	0	0	0.5	1.000
1936			1	8	.111	4.72	35	8	2	87.2	98	48	35	0	1	2	2	30	7	0	.233	2	21	2	2	0.7	.920
1937	2 teams	BKN N (7G 0–1)				NY N (13G 1–0)																					
"	total		1	1	.500	5.03	20	0	0	39.1	44	21	13	0	1	1	0	9	2	0	.222	2	7	1	0	0.5	.900
1938	NY	N	0	0	—	6.75	6	0	0	4	5	3	0	0	1	0	0	0	0	0	—	1	1	0	0	1.0	1.000
4 yrs.			3	9	.250	4.73	68	9	3	173	195	92	58	0	3	3	2	58	18	0	.310	5	34	3	2	0.6	.929

Year	Team		W	L	PCT	ERA	G	GS	CG	IP	H	BB	SO	ShO	Relief Pitching W	L	SV	Batting AB	H	HR	BA	PO	A	E	DP	TC/G	FA

Tom Baker

BAKER, THOMAS HENRY
B. May 6, 1934, Port Townsend, Wash.   D. Mar. 9, 1980, Port Townsend, Wash.

BL TL 6'   195 lbs.

| 1963 | CHI | N | 0 | 1 | .000 | 3.00 | 10 | 1 | 0 | 18 | 20 | 7 | 14 | 0 | 0 | 0 | 0 | 3 | 0 | 0 | .000 | 1 | 3 | 0 | 0 | 0.4 | 1.000 |

Mike Balas

BALAS, MICHAEL FRANCIS
Born Michael Francis Balaski.
B. May 17, 1910, Lowell, Mass.

BR TR 6'   195 lbs.

| 1938 | BOS | N | 0 | 0 | — | 6.75 | 1 | 0 | 0 | 1.1 | 3 | 0 | 0 | 0 | 0 | 0 | 0 | 0 | 0 | 0 | — | 0 | 0 | 0 | 0 | 0.0 | — |

Jack Baldschun

BALDSCHUN, JACK EDWARD
B. Oct. 16, 1936, Greenville, Ohio

BR TR 6'1"   175 lbs.

1961	PHI	N	5	3	.625	3.88	65	0	0	99.2	90	49	59	0	5	3	3	11	0	0	.000	9	18	0	0	0.4	1.000
1962			12	7	.632	2.96	67	0	0	112.2	95	58	95	0	12	7	13	16	1	0	.063	6	19	1	2	0.4	.962
1963			11	7	.611	2.30	65	0	0	113.2	99	42	89	0	11	7	16	20	0	0	.000	8	27	5	0	0.6	.875
1964			6	9	.400	3.12	71	0	0	118.1	111	40	96	0	6	9	21	16	4	0	.250	5	27	4	2	0.5	.889
1965			5	8	.385	3.82	65	0	0	99	102	42	81	0	5	8	6	7	0	0	.000	2	22	2	0	0.4	.923
1966	CIN	N	1	5	.167	5.49	42	0	0	57.1	71	25	44	0	1	5	0	3	1	0	.333	1	11	1	2	0.3	.923
1967			0	0	—	4.15	9	0	0	13	15	9	12	0	0	0	0	1	0	0	.000	2	1	0	0	0.3	1.000
1969	SD	N	7	2	.778	4.79	61	0	0	77	80	29	67	0	7	2	1	4	1	0	.250	6	10	1	0	0.3	.941
1970			1	0	1.000	10.38	12	0	0	13	24	4	12	0	1	0	0	0	0	0	—	0	1	0	0	0.1	1.000
	9 yrs.		48	41	.539	3.70	457	0	0	703.2	687	298	555	0	48	41	60	78	7	0	.090	39	136	14	6	0.4	.926

Dave Baldwin

BALDWIN, DAVID GEORGE
B. Mar. 30, 1938, Tucson, Ariz.

BR TR 6'2"   200 lbs.

1966	WAS	A	0	0	—	3.86	4	0	0	7	8	1	4	0	0	0	0	0	0	0	—	0	0	0	0	0.0	—
1967			2	4	.333	1.70	58	0	0	68.2	53	20	52	0	2	4	12	4	0	0	.000	2	18	0	0	0.3	1.000
1968			0	2	.000	4.07	40	0	0	42	40	12	30	0	0	2	5	2	0	0	.000	2	9	0	0	0.3	1.000
1969			2	4	.333	4.05	43	0	0	66.2	57	34	51	0	2	4	4	7	0	0	.000	4	7	0	0	0.3	1.000
1970	MIL	A	2	1	.667	2.57	28	0	0	35	25	18	26	0	2	1	1	2	1	0	.500	6	14	0	1	0.7	1.000
1973	CHI	A	0	0	—	3.60	3	0	0	5	7	4	1	0	0	0	0	0	0	0	—	1	1	0	0	0.7	1.000
	6 yrs.		6	11	.353	3.09	176	0	0	224.1	190	89	164	0	6	11	22	15	1	0	.067	15	49	0	1	0.4	1.000

Harry Baldwin

BALDWIN, HOWARD EDWARD
B. June 30, 1900, Baltimore, Md.   D. Jan. 23, 1958, Baltimore, Md.

BR TR 5'11"   160 lbs.

1924	NY	N	3	1	.750	4.28	10	1	0	33.2	42	11	5	0	2	0	0	11	4	0	.364	1	8	0	0	0.9	1.000
1925			0	0	—	9.00	1	1	0	1	3	1	0	0	0	0	0	0	0	0	—	0	0	0	0	0.0	—
	2 yrs.		3	1	.750	4.41	11	2	1	34.2	45	12	5	0	2	0	0	11	4	0	.364	1	8	0	0	0.8	1.000

WORLD SERIES

| 1924 | NY | N | 0 | 0 | — | 0.00 | 1 | 0 | 0 | 2 | 1 | 0 | 1 | 0 | 0 | 0 | 0 | 0 | 0 | 0 | — | 0 | 0 | 0 | 0 | 0.0 | — |

Kid Baldwin

BALDWIN, CLARENCE GEOGHAN
B. Nov. 1, 1864, Newport, Ky.   D. July 12, 1897, Cincinnati, Ohio

BR TR 5'6"   147 lbs.

| 1885 | CIN | AA | 0 | 0 | — | 9.00 | 2 | 1 | 0 | 4 | 5 | 6 | 1 | 0 | 0 | 0 | 0 | * | | | | 0 | 1 | 0 | 0 | 0.5 | 1.000 |

Lady Baldwin

BALDWIN, CHARLES BUSTED
B. Apr. 8, 1859, Ormel, N.Y.   D. Mar. 7, 1937, Hastings, Mich.

BL TL 5'11"   170 lbs.

1884	MIL	U	1	1	.500	2.65	2	2	2	17	7	1	21	0	0	0	0	27	6	0	.222	0	2	0	0	1.0	1.000
1885	DET	N	11	9	.550	1.86	21	20	19	179.1	137	28	135	1	0	0	1	124	30	0	.242	8	43	7	1	2.8	.879
1886			42	13	.764	2.24	56	56	55	487	371	100	323	7	0	0	0	204	41	0	.201	18	105	4	7	2.3	.969
1887			13	10	.565	3.84	24	24	24	211	225	61	60	1	0	0	0	85	23	0	.271	7	43	4	1	2.3	.926
1888			3	3	.500	5.43	6	6	5	53	76	15	26	0	0	0	0	23	6	0	.261	0	9	0	0	1.5	1.000
1890	2 teams					BKN N (2G 1–0)				BUF P (7G 2–5)																
"	total		3	5	.375	4.78	9	8	7	69.2	105	28	17	0	0	0	0	31	8	0	.258	1	20	0	0	2.3	1.000
	6 yrs.		73	41	.640	2.85	118	116	112	1017	921	233	582	9	0	0	1	494	114	0	.231	34	222	15	9	2.3	.945

Mark Baldwin

BALDWIN, MARCUS ELMORE (Fido)
B. Oct. 29, 1863, Pittsburgh, Pa.   D. Nov. 10, 1929, Pittsburgh, Pa.

BR TR 6'   190 lbs.

1887	CHI	N	18	17	.514	3.40	40	39	35	334	329	122	164	1	0	0	1	139	26	4	.187	7	45	6	0	1.5	.897
1888			13	15	.464	2.76	30	30	27	251	241	99	157	2	0	0	0	106	16	1	.151	11	58	5	0	2.5	.932
1889	COL	AA	27	34	.443	3.61	63	59	54	513.2	458	274	368	6	1	2	1	208	39	2	.188	33	91	13	1	2.2	.905
1890	CHI	P	32	24	.571	3.31	59	57	54	501	498	249	211	1	2	0	0	215	45	1	.209	26	146	15	2	3.2	.920
1891	PIT	N	22	28	.440	2.76	53	50	48	437.2	385	227	197	2	1	0	0	177	27	1	.153	37	80	13	4	2.5	.900
1892			26	27	.491	3.47	56	53	45	440.1	447	194	157	0	2	0	0	178	18	1	.101	37	86	18	2	2.5	.872
1893	2 teams					PIT N (1G 0–0)				NY N (45G 16–20)																
"	total		16	20	.444	4.15	46	40	33	333.2	341	142	100	0	2	1	2	135	17	0	.126	24	53	7	1	1.8	.917
	7 yrs.		154	165	.483	3.36	347	328	296	2811.1	2699	1307	1354	14	8	3	4	1158	188	10	.162	175	559	77	10	2.3	.905

Ollie Baldwin

BALDWIN, ORSON F.
B. Youngstown, Ohio

| 1908 | STL | N | 1 | 3 | .250 | 6.14 | 4 | 4 | 0 | 14.2 | 16 | 11 | 5 | 0 | 0 | 0 | 0 | 6 | 0 | 0 | .000 | 0 | 4 | 0 | 0 | 1.0 | 1.000 |

Rick Baldwin

BALDWIN, RICKEY ALAN
B. June 1, 1953, Fresno, Calif.

BL TR 6'3"   180 lbs.

1975	NY	N	3	5	.375	3.34	54	0	0	97	97	34	54	0	3	5	6	15	3	0	.200	3	18	2	2	0.4	.913
1976			0	0	—	2.35	11	0	0	23	14	10	9	0	0	0	0	3	1	0	.333	1	4	0	0	0.5	1.000
1977			1	2	.333	4.43	40	0	0	63	62	31	23	0	1	2	1	4	2	0	.500	6	12	0	3	0.5	.900
	3 yrs.		4	7	.364	3.59	105	0	0	183	173	75	86	0	4	7	7	22	6	0	.273	10	34	2	5	0.4	.957

Year	Team		W	L	PCT	ERA	G	GS	CG	IP	H	BB	SO	ShO	Relief Pitching W	L	SV	Batting AB	H	HR	BA	PO	A	E	DP	TC/G	FA

Jeff Ballard

BALLARD, JEFFREY SCOTT
B. Aug. 13, 1963, Billings, Mont.

BL TL 6'3" 210 lbs.

Year	Team		W	L	PCT	ERA	G	GS	CG	IP	H	BB	SO	ShO	W	L	SV	AB	H	HR	BA	PO	A	E	DP	TC/G	FA
1987	BAL	A	2	8	.200	6.59	14	14	0	69.2	100	35	27	0	0	0	0	0	0	0	–	5	10	0	1	1.1	1.000
1988			8	12	.400	4.40	25	25	6	153.1	167	42	41	1	0	0	0	0	0	0	–	9	13	0	3	0.9	1.000
1989			18	8	.692	3.43	35	35	4	215.1	240	57	62	1	0	0	0	0	0	0	–	13	55	2	6	2.0	.971
3 yrs.			28	28	.500	4.27	74	74	10	438.1	507	134	130	2	0	0	0	0	0	0	–	27	78	2	10	1.4	.981

Jay Baller

BALLER, JAY SCOTT
B. Oct. 6, 1960, Stayton, Ore.

BR TR 6'6" 215 lbs.

Year	Team		W	L	PCT	ERA	G	GS	CG	IP	H	BB	SO	ShO	W	L	SV	AB	H	HR	BA	PO	A	E	DP	TC/G	FA
1982	PHI	N	0	0	–	3.38	4	1	0	8	7	2	7	0	0	0	0	0	0	0	–	0	1	0	0	0.3	1.000
1985	CHI	N	2	3	.400	3.46	20	4	0	52	52	17	31	0	2	0	1	8	0	0	.000	4	6	0	0	0.5	1.000
1986			2	4	.333	5.37	36	0	0	53.2	58	28	42	0	2	4	5	5	0	0	.000	2	4	0	0	0.2	1.000
1987			0	1	.000	6.75	23	0	0	29.1	38	20	27	0	0	1	0	1	1	0	1.000	0	3	1	0	0.2	.750
4 yrs.			4	8	.333	4.85	83	5	0	143	155	67	107	0	4	5	6	14	1	0	.071	6	14	1	0	0.3	.952

Mark Ballinger

BALLINGER, MARK ALAN
B. Jan. 31, 1949, Glendale, Calif.

BR TR 6'6" 205 lbs.

Year	Team		W	L	PCT	ERA	G	GS	CG	IP	H	BB	SO	ShO	W	L	SV	AB	H	HR	BA	PO	A	E	DP	TC/G	FA
1971	CLE	A	1	2	.333	4.63	18	0	0	35	30	13	25	0	1	2	0	5	1	0	.200	1	5	0	0	0.3	1.000

Win Ballou

BALLOU, NOBLE WINFIELD (Old Pard)
B. Nov. 30, 1897, Mount Morgan, Ky.   D. Jan. 30, 1963, San Francisco, Calif.

BR TL 5'10½" 170 lbs.

Year	Team		W	L	PCT	ERA	G	GS	CG	IP	H	BB	SO	ShO	W	L	SV	AB	H	HR	BA	PO	A	E	DP	TC/G	FA
1925	WAS	A	1	1	.500	4.55	10	1	1	27.2	38	13	13	0	0	1	0	7	1	0	.143	0	8	2	1	1.0	.800
1926	STL	A	11	10	.524	4.79	43	13	5	154	186	71	59	0	6	3	2	42	2	1	.048	8	50	4	4	1.4	.935
1927			5	6	.455	4.78	21	11	4	90.1	105	46	17	0	2	1	0	28	1	0	.036	7	20	2	1	1.4	.931
1929	BKN	N	2	3	.400	6.71	25	1	0	57.2	69	38	20	0	2	2	0	16	1	0	.063	5	21	1	1	1.1	.963
4 yrs.			19	20	.487	5.11	99	26	10	329.2	398	168	109	0	11	6	2	93	5	1	.054	20	99	9	7	1.3	.930

WORLD SERIES

Year	Team		W	L	PCT	ERA	G	GS	CG	IP	H	BB	SO	ShO	W	L	SV	AB	H	HR	BA	PO	A	E	DP	TC/G	FA
1925	WAS	A	0	0	–	0.00	2	0	0	1.2	0	1	1	0	0	0	0	0	0	0	–	0	0	0	0	0.0	–

Tony Balsamo

BALSAMO, ANTHONY FRED
B. Nov. 21, 1937, Brooklyn, N. Y.

BR TR 6'2" 185 lbs.

Year	Team		W	L	PCT	ERA	G	GS	CG	IP	H	BB	SO	ShO	W	L	SV	AB	H	HR	BA	PO	A	E	DP	TC/G	FA
1962	CHI	N	0	1	.000	6.44	18	0	0	29.1	34	20	27	0	0	1	0	5	1	0	.200	3	6	1	2	0.6	.900

George Bamberger

BAMBERGER, GEORGE IRVIN
B. Aug. 1, 1925, Staten Island, N. Y.
Manager 1978-80, 1982-83, 1985-86.

BR TR 6' 175 lbs.

Year	Team		W	L	PCT	ERA	G	GS	CG	IP	H	BB	SO	ShO	W	L	SV	AB	H	HR	BA	PO	A	E	DP	TC/G	FA
1951	NY	N	0	0	–	18.00	2	0	0	2	4	2	1	0	0	0	0	0	0	0	–	0	0	0	0	0.0	–
1952			0	0	–	9.00	5	0	0	4	6	6	0	0	0	0	0	0	0	0	–	0	1	0	0	0.2	1.000
1959	BAL	A	0	0	–	7.56	3	1	0	8.1	15	2	2	0	0	0	1	2	0	0	.000	0	3	0	0	1.0	1.000
3 yrs.			0	0	–	9.42	10	1	0	14.1	25	10	3	0	0	0	1	2	0	0	.000	0	4	0	0	0.4	1.000

Sal Bando

BANDO, SALVATORE LEONARD
Brother of Chris Bando.
B. Feb. 13, 1944, Cleveland, Ohio.

BR TR 6' 195 lbs.

Year	Team		W	L	PCT	ERA	G	GS	CG	IP	H	BB	SO	ShO	W	L	SV	AB	H	HR	BA	PO	A	E	DP	TC/G	FA
1979	MIL	A	0	0	–	6.00	1	0	0	3	3	0	0	0	0	0	0	*				0	0	0	0	0.0	–

Eddie Bane

BANE, EDWARD NORMAN
B. Mar. 22, 1952, Chicago, Ill.

BR TL 5'9" 160 lbs.

Year	Team		W	L	PCT	ERA	G	GS	CG	IP	H	BB	SO	ShO	W	L	SV	AB	H	HR	BA	PO	A	E	DP	TC/G	FA
1973	MIN	A	0	5	.000	4.92	23	6	0	60.1	62	30	42	0	0	2	2	0	0	0	–	7	14	3	1	1.0	.875
1975			3	1	.750	2.86	4	4	0	28.1	28	15	14	0	0	0	0	0	0	0	–	1	2	2	0	1.3	.600
1976			4	7	.364	5.11	17	15	1	79.1	92	39	24	0	0	0	0	0	0	0	–	5	4	1	0	0.6	.900
3 yrs.			7	13	.350	4.66	44	25	1	168	182	84	80	0	0	2	2	0	0	0	–	13	20	6	1	0.9	.846

Dick Baney

BANEY, RICHARD LEE
B. Nov. 1, 1946, Fullerton, Calif.

BR TR 6' 185 lbs.

Year	Team		W	L	PCT	ERA	G	GS	CG	IP	H	BB	SO	ShO	W	L	SV	AB	H	HR	BA	PO	A	E	DP	TC/G	FA
1969	SEA	A	1	0	1.000	3.86	9	1	0	18.2	21	7	9	0	0	0	0	2	0	0	.000	1	1	1	1	0.3	.667
1973	CIN	N	2	1	.667	2.93	11	1	0	30.2	26	6	17	0	1	1	2	9	2	0	.222	2	0	0	0	0.2	1.000
1974			1	0	1.000	5.49	22	1	0	41	51	17	12	0	1	0	1	5	0	0	.000	0	2	0	0	0.1	1.000
3 yrs.			4	1	.800	4.28	42	3	0	90.1	98	30	38	0	2	1	3	16	2	0	.125	3	3	1	1	0.2	.857

Dan Bankhead

BANKHEAD, DANIEL ROBERT
B. May 3, 1920, Empire, Ala.   D. May 2, 1976, Houston, Tex.

BR TR 6'1" 184 lbs.

Year	Team		W	L	PCT	ERA	G	GS	CG	IP	H	BB	SO	ShO	W	L	SV	AB	H	HR	BA	PO	A	E	DP	TC/G	FA
1947	BKN	N	0	0	–	7.20	4	0	0	10	15	8	6	0	0	0	1	4	1	1	.250	1	0	0	0	0.3	1.000
1950			9	4	.692	5.50	41	12	2	129.1	119	88	96	1	5	1	3	39	9	0	.231	6	19	4	3	0.7	.862
1951			0	1	.000	15.43	7	1	0	14	27	14	9	0	0	0	0	2	0	0	.000	1	3	0	0	0.6	1.000
3 yrs.			9	5	.643	6.52	52	13	2	153.1	161	110	111	1	5	1	4	45	10	1	.222	8	22	4	3	0.7	.882

WORLD SERIES

Year	Team		W	L	PCT	ERA	G	GS	CG	IP	H	BB	SO	ShO	W	L	SV	AB	H	HR	BA	PO	A	E	DP	TC/G	FA
1947	BKN	N	0	0	–	0.00	0	0	0	0	0	0	0	0	0	0	0	0	0	0	–	0	0	0	0	0.0	–

Scott Bankhead

BANKHEAD, MICHAEL SCOTT
B. July 31, 1963, Raleigh, N. C.

BR TR 5'10" 175 lbs.

Year	Team		W	L	PCT	ERA	G	GS	CG	IP	H	BB	SO	ShO	W	L	SV	AB	H	HR	BA	PO	A	E	DP	TC/G	FA
1986	KC	A	8	9	.471	4.61	24	17	0	121	121	37	94	0	0	0	0	0	0	0	–	11	12	1	0	1.0	.958
1987	SEA	A	9	8	.529	5.42	27	25	2	149.1	168	37	95	0	0	0	0	0	0	0	–	9	9	0	1	0.7	1.000
1988			7	9	.438	3.07	21	21	0	135	115	38	102	1	0	0	0	0	0	0	–	7	11	0	0	0.9	1.000
1989			14	6	.700	3.34	33	33	3	210.1	187	63	140	0	0	0	0	0	0	0	–	14	19	0	2	1.0	1.000
4 yrs.			38	32	.543	4.03	105	96	7	615.2	591	175	431	3	2	1	0	0	0	0	–	41	51	1	3	0.9	.989

Year	Team		W	L	PCT	ERA	G	GS	CG	IP	H	BB	SO	ShO	Relief Pitching W	L	SV	Batting AB	H	HR	BA	PO	A	E	DP	TC/G	FA

Bill Banks

BANKS, WILLIAM JOHN
Born William John Yerrick.
B. Feb. 26, 1874, Danville, Pa. D. Sept. 8, 1936, Danville, Pa.

BR TR 5'11" 150 lbs.

Year	Team		W	L	PCT	ERA	G	GS	CG	IP	H	BB	SO	ShO	W	L	SV	AB	H	HR	BA	PO	A	E	DP	TC/G	FA
1895	BOS	N	1	0	1.000	0.00	1	1	0	7	7	4	4	0	0	0	0	3	0	0	.000	0	2	0	0	2.0	1.000
1896			0	3	.000	10.57	4	3	2	23	42	13	6	0	0	0	0	11	3	0	.273	0	3	0	0	0.8	1.000
2 yrs.			1	3	.250	8.10	5	4	2	30	49	17	10	0	0	0	0	14	3	0	.214	0	5	0	0	1.0	1.000

Floyd Bannister

BANNISTER, FLOYD FRANKLIN
B. June 10, 1955, Pierre, S. D.

BL TL 6'1" 190 lbs.

Year	Team		W	L	PCT	ERA	G	GS	CG	IP	H	BB	SO	ShO	W	L	SV	AB	H	HR	BA	PO	A	E	DP	TC/G	FA
1977	HOU	N	8	9	.471	4.03	24	23	4	143	138	68	112	1	0	0	0	48	9	0	.188	6	14	0	1	0.8	1.000
1978			3	9	.250	4.83	28	16	2	110	120	63	94	2	0	0	0	31	5	0	.161	1	6	0	2	0.3	1.000
1979	SEA	A	10	15	.400	4.05	30	30	6	182	185	68	115	2	0	0	0	0	0	0	—	10	15	0	0	0.8	1.000
1980			9	13	.409	3.47	32	32	8	218	200	66	155	0	0	0	0	0	0	0	—	12	26	1	2	1.2	.974
1981			9	9	.500	4.46	21	20	5	121	128	39	85	2	0	0	0	0	0	0	—	6	15	0	1	1.0	1.000
1982			12	13	.480	3.43	35	35	5	247	225	77	209	3	0	0	0	0	0	0	—	8	30	2	1	1.1	.950
1983	CHI	A	16	10	.615	3.35	34	34	5	217.1	191	71	193	2	0	0	0	0	0	0	—	8	23	2	0	1.0	.939
1984			14	11	.560	4.83	34	33	4	218	211	80	152	0	0	0	0	1	0	0	.000	3	23	1	0	0.8	.963
1985			10	14	.417	4.87	34	34	4	210.2	211	100	198	1	0	0	0	0	0	0	—	4	22	1	0	0.8	.963
1986			10	14	.417	3.54	28	27	6	165.1	162	48	92	1	1	0	0	0	0	0	—	3	22	1	0	0.9	.962
1987			16	11	.593	3.58	34	34	11	228.2	216	49	124	2	0	0	0	0	0	0	—	10	22	1	0	1.0	.970
1988	KC	A	12	13	.480	4.33	31	31	2	189.1	182	68	113	0	0	0	0	0	0	0	—	8	25	1	1	1.1	.971
1989			4	1	.800	4.66	14	14	0	75.1	87	18	35	0	0	0	0	0	0	0	—	3	15	0	3	1.3	1.000
13 yrs.			133	142	.484	4.03	379	363	62	2325.2	2256	815	1677	16	1	1	0	80	14	0	.175	82	258	10	12	0.9	.971

LEAGUE CHAMPIONSHIP SERIES

| 1983 | CHI | A | 0 | 1 | .000 | 4.50 | 1 | 1 | 0 | 6 | 5 | 1 | 5 | 0 | 0 | 0 | 0 | 0 | 0 | 0 | — | 0 | 0 | 0 | 0 | 0.0 | — |

Jimmy Bannon

BANNON, JAMES HENRY (Foxy, grandpa)
Brother of Tom Bannon.
B. May 5, 1871, Amesbury, Mass. D. Mar. 24, 1948, Glen Rock, N. J.

BR TR 5'5" 160 lbs.

Year	Team		W	L	PCT	ERA	G	GS	CG	IP	H	BB	SO	ShO	W	L	SV	AB	H	HR	BA	PO	A	E	DP	TC/G	FA
1893	STL	N	0	1	.000	22.50	1	1	0	4	10	5	1	0	0	0	0	107	36	0	.336	0	0	0	0	0.0	—
1894	BOS	N	0	0	—	0.00	1	0	0	2	4	1	0	0	0	0	0	494	166	13	.336	1	0	0	0	1.0	1.000
1895			0	0	—	6.00	1	0	0	3	4	2	1	0	0	0	0	489	171	6	.350	0	1	0	0	1.0	1.000
3 yrs.			0	1	.000	12.00	3	1	0	9	18	8	2	0	0	0	0	*				1	1	0	0	0.7	1.000

Jack Banta

BANTA, JOHN KAY
B. June 24, 1925, Hutchinson, Kans.

BL TR 6'2½" 175 lbs.

Year	Team		W	L	PCT	ERA	G	GS	CG	IP	H	BB	SO	ShO	W	L	SV	AB	H	HR	BA	PO	A	E	DP	TC/G	FA
1947	BKN	N	0	1	.000	7.04	3	1	0	7.2	7	4	3	0	0	0	0	2	0	0	.000	0	5	0	0	1.7	1.000
1948			0	1	.000	8.10	2	1	0	3.1	5	5	1	0	0	0	0	1	0	0	.000	0	0	0	0	0.0	—
1949			10	6	.625	3.37	48	12	2	152.1	125	68	97	1	6	2	3	46	5	0	.109	8	27	3	3	0.8	.921
1950			4	4	.500	4.35	16	5	1	41.1	39	36	15	0	2	3	2	12	2	0	.167	0	4	0	2	0.3	1.000
4 yrs.			14	12	.538	3.78	69	19	3	204.2	176	113	116	1	8	6	5	61	7	0	.115	8	36	3	5	0.7	.936

WORLD SERIES

| 1949 | BKN | N | 0 | 0 | — | 3.18 | 3 | 0 | 0 | 5.2 | 5 | 1 | 4 | 0 | 0 | 0 | 0 | 0 | 0 | 0 | .000 | 0 | 1 | 0 | 0 | 0.3 | 1.000 |

Steve Barber

BARBER, STEPHEN DAVID
B. Feb. 22, 1939, Takoma Park, Md.

BL TL 6' 195 lbs.

Year	Team		W	L	PCT	ERA	G	GS	CG	IP	H	BB	SO	ShO	W	L	SV	AB	H	HR	BA	PO	A	E	DP	TC/G	FA
1960	BAL	A	10	7	.588	3.22	36	27	6	181.2	148	113	112	1	0	1	2	54	3	0	.056	4	30	2	5	1.0	.944
1961			18	12	.600	3.33	37	34	14	248.1	194	130	150	8	0	0	1	80	13	2	.163	13	66	4	8	2.1	.948
1962			9	6	.600	3.46	28	19	5	140.1	145	61	89	2	0	0	0	42	3	0	.071	16	26	2	1	1.6	.955
1963			20	13	.606	2.75	39	36	11	258.2	253	92	180	2	0	1	0	87	12	1	.138	19	43	4	8	1.7	.939
1964			9	13	.409	3.84	36	26	4	157	144	81	118	0	1	1	1	47	7	1	.149	11	37	2	1	1.4	.960
1965			15	10	.600	2.69	37	32	7	220.2	177	81	130	2	1	1	0	65	5	1	.077	12	47	6	1	1.8	.908
1966			10	5	.667	2.30	25	22	5	133.1	104	49	91	3	0	0	0	44	3	0	.068	5	30	2	1	1.5	.946
1967	2 teams	BAL A	(15G 4–9)			NY A	(17G 6–9)																					
"	total		10	18	.357	4.07	32	32	4	172.1	150	115	118	2	0	0	0	51	7	0	.137	11	25	6	2	1.3	.857
1968	NY	A	6	5	.545	3.23	20	19	3	128.1	127	64	87	1	0	0	0	39	2	0	.051	2	24	4	1	1.5	.867
1969	SEA	A	4	7	.364	4.80	25	16	0	86.1	99	48	69	0	1	0	0	25	5	0	.200	3	13	2	2	0.7	.889
1970	2 teams	CHI N	(5G 0–1)			ATL N	(5G 0–1)																					
"	total		0	2	.000	6.20	10	2	0	20.1	27	11	14	0	0	2	0	4	1	0	.250	0	2	0	0	0.2	1.000
1971	ATL	N	3	1	.750	4.80	39	3	0	75	92	25	40	0	3	1	2	13	2	0	.154	4	13	1	0	0.5	.944
1972	2 teams	ATL N	(5G 0–0)			CAL A	(34G 4–4)																					
"	total		4	4	.500	2.80	39	2	0	74	55	36	40	0	3	4	2	12	2	0	.167	3	12	2	0	0.4	.882
1973	CAL	A	3	2	.600	3.53	50	1	0	89.1	90	32	58	0	2	2	4	0	0	0	—	3	10	0	0	0.3	1.000
1974	SF	N	0	1	—	5.14	13	0	0	14	13	12	13	0	0	1	1	0	0	0	—	0	1	0	0	0.1	—
15 yrs.			121	106	.533	3.36	466	272	59	1999.2	1818	950	1309	21	10	12	13	563	65	5	.115	106	372	38	32	1.1	.926

Steve Barber

BARBER, STEVEN LEE
B. Mar. 13, 1948, Grand Rapids, Mich.

BR TR 6'1" 190 lbs.

Year	Team		W	L	PCT	ERA	G	GS	CG	IP	H	BB	SO	ShO	W	L	SV	AB	H	HR	BA	PO	A	E	DP	TC/G	FA
1970	MIN	A	0	0	—	4.67	18	0	0	27	26	18	14	0	0	0	2	2	0	0	.000	1	3	0	0	0.2	1.000
1971			1	0	1.000	6.00	4	2	0	12	8	13	4	0	1	0	0	5	0	0	.000	1	1	0	0	0.5	1.000
2 yrs.			1	0	1.000	5.08	22	2	0	39	34	31	18	0	1	0	2	7	0	0	.000	2	4	0	0	0.3	1.000

Frank Barberich

BARBERICH, FRANK FREDERICK
B. Feb. 3, 1882, New Town, N. Y. D. May 1, 1965, Ocala, Fla.

BB TR 5'10½" 175 lbs.

Year	Team		W	L	PCT	ERA	G	GS	CG	IP	H	BB	SO	ShO	W	L	SV	AB	H	HR	BA	PO	A	E	DP	TC/G	FA
1907	BOS	N	1	1	.500	5.84	2	2	1	12.1	19	5	1	0	0	0	0	4	0	0	.000	2	3	0	0	2.5	1.000
1910	BOS	A	0	0	—	7.20	2	0	0	5	7	2	0	0	0	0	0	1	0	0	.000	1	2	0	0	1.5	1.000
2 yrs.			1	1	.500	6.23	4	2	1	17.1	26	7	1	0	0	0	0	5	0	0	.000	3	5	0	0	2.0	1.000

Year	Team		W	L	PCT	ERA	G	GS	CG	IP	H	BB	SO	ShO	W	L	SV	AB	H	HR	BA	PO	A	E	DP	TC/G	FA

Curt Barclay

BARCLAY, CURTIS CORDELL
B. Aug. 22, 1931, Chicago, Ill. D. Mar. 25, 1985, Missoula, Mont. — BR TR 6'3" 210 lbs.

Year	Team		W	L	PCT	ERA	G	GS	CG	IP	H	BB	SO	ShO	W	L	SV	AB	H	HR	BA	PO	A	E	DP	TC/G	FA
1957	NY	N	9	9	.500	3.44	37	28	5	183	196	48	67	2	2	0	0	58	11	0	.190	6	48	2	4	1.5	.964
1958	SF	N	1	0	1.000	2.81	6	1	0	16	16	5	6	0	1	0	0	6	4	0	.667	3	2	0	0	0.8	1.000
1959			0	0	—	54.00	1	0	0	.1	2	2	0	0	0	0	0	0	0	0	—	0	0	1	0	1.0	—
3 yrs.			10	9	.526	3.48	44	29	5	199.1	214	55	73	2	3	0	0	64	15	0	.234	9	50	3	4	1.4	.952

Ray Bare

BARE, RAYMOND DOUGLAS
B. Apr. 15, 1949, Miami, Fla. — BR TR 6'2" 185 lbs.

Year	Team		W	L	PCT	ERA	G	GS	CG	IP	H	BB	SO	ShO	W	L	SV	AB	H	HR	BA	PO	A	E	DP	TC/G	FA
1972	STL	N	0	1	.000	0.54	14	0	0	16.2	18	6	5	0	0	1	1	0	0	0	—	0	2	1	0	0.2	.667
1974			1	2	.333	6.00	10	3	0	24	25	9	6	0	1	0	0	5	1	0	.200	4	6	0	1	1.0	1.000
1975	DET	A	8	13	.381	4.48	29	21	6	150.2	174	47	71	1	1	1	0	0	0	0	—	6	31	2	3	1.3	.949
1976			7	8	.467	4.63	30	21	3	134	157	51	59	2	0	0	0	0	0	0	—	6	25	0	2	1.0	1.000
1977			0	2	.000	12.86	5	4	0	14	24	7	4	0	0	0	0	0	0	0	—	2	7	0	2	1.8	1.000
5 yrs.			16	26	.381	4.80	88	49	9	339.1	398	120	145	3	2	2	1	5	1	0	.200	18	71	3	8	1.0	.967

John Barfield

BARFIELD, JOHN DAVID
B. Oct. 15, 1964, Pine Bluff, Ark. — BL TL 6'1" 185 lbs.

Year	Team		W	L	PCT	ERA	G	GS	CG	IP	H	BB	SO	ShO	W	L	SV	AB	H	HR	BA	PO	A	E	DP	TC/G	FA
1989	TEX	A	0	1	.000	6.17	4	2	0	11.2	15	4	9	0	0	0	0	0	0	0	—	1	1	0	0	0.5	1.000

Clyde Barfoot

BARFOOT, CLYDE RAYMOND
B. July 8, 1891, Richmond, Va. D. Mar. 11, 1971, Highland Park, Calif. — BR TR 6' 170 lbs.

Year	Team		W	L	PCT	ERA	G	GS	CG	IP	H	BB	SO	ShO	W	L	SV	AB	H	HR	BA	PO	A	E	DP	TC/G	FA
1922	STL	N	4	5	.444	4.21	42	2	1	117.2	139	30	19	0	3	4	2	34	12	0	.353	2	33	1	1	0.9	.972
1923			3	3	.500	3.73	33	2	1	101.1	112	27	23	1	2	3	1	37	7	0	.189	2	26	2	1	0.9	.933
1926	DET	A	1	2	.333	4.88	11	1	0	31.1	42	9	7	0	1	1	2	5	1	0	.200	2	10	0	2	1.1	1.000
3 yrs.			8	10	.444	4.10	86	5	2	250.1	293	66	49	1	6	8	5	76	20	0	.263	6	69	3	4	0.9	.962

Greg Bargar

BARGAR, GREG ROBERT
B. Jan. 27, 1959, Inglewood, Calif. — BR TR 6'2" 185 lbs.

Year	Team		W	L	PCT	ERA	G	GS	CG	IP	H	BB	SO	ShO	W	L	SV	AB	H	HR	BA	PO	A	E	DP	TC/G	FA
1983	MON	N	2	0	1.000	6.75	8	3	0	20	23	8	9	0	0	0	0	6	1	0	.167	1	1	0	0	0.3	1.000
1984			0	1	.000	7.88	3	1	0	8	8	7	2	0	0	0	0	1	0	0	.000	1	2	1	0	1.3	.750
1986	STL	N	0	2	.000	5.60	22	0	0	27.1	36	10	12	0	0	2	0	2	0	0	.000	3	7	0	0	0.5	1.000
3 yrs.			2	3	.400	6.34	33	4	0	55.1	67	25	23	0	0	2	0	9	1	0	.111	5	10	1	0	0.5	.938

Cy Barger

BARGER, EROS BOLIVAR
B. May 18, 1885, Jamestown, Ky. D. Sept. 23, 1964, Columbia, Ky. — BL TR 6' 160 lbs.

Year	Team		W	L	PCT	ERA	G	GS	CG	IP	H	BB	SO	ShO	W	L	SV	AB	H	HR	BA	PO	A	E	DP	TC/G	FA
1906	NY	A	0	0	—	10.13	2	1	0	5.1	7	3	3	0	0	0	0	3	1	0	.333	0	1	0	0	0.5	1.000
1907			0	0	—	3.00	1	0	0	6	10	1	0	0	0	0	0	2	0	0	.000	0	0	1	0	1.0	—
1910	BKN	N	15	15	.500	2.88	35	30	25	271.2	267	107	87	2	1	0	1	104	24	0	.231	9	87	1	2	2.8	.990
1911			11	15	.423	3.52	30	30	21	217.1	224	71	60	1	0	0	0	145	33	0	.228	9	66	2	1	2.6	.974
1912			1	9	.100	5.46	16	11	6	94	120	42	30	0	0	0	0	37	7	0	.189	2	29	2	0	2.1	.939
1914	PIT	F	10	16	.385	4.34	33	26	18	228.1	252	63	70	1	1	1	1	83	17	0	.205	9	60	1	0	2.1	.986
1915			10	7	.588	2.29	34	13	8	153	130	47	47	1	4	1	5	54	15	0	.278	4	42	0	1	1.4	1.000
7 yrs.			47	62	.431	3.56	151	111	78	975.2	1010	334	297	5	6	2	8	*				33	285	7	4	2.2	.978

Len Barker

BARKER, LEONARD HAROLD
B. July 27, 1955, Ft. Knox, Ky. — BR TR 6'5" 225 lbs.

Year	Team		W	L	PCT	ERA	G	GS	CG	IP	H	BB	SO	ShO	W	L	SV	AB	H	HR	BA	PO	A	E	DP	TC/G	FA
1976	TEX	A	1	0	1.000	2.40	2	2	1	15	7	6	7	0	0	0	0	0	0	0	—	0	2	0	0	1.0	1.000
1977			4	1	.800	2.68	15	3	0	47	36	24	51	0	3	0	1	0	0	0	—	4	8	0	1	0.8	1.000
1978			1	5	.167	4.82	29	0	0	52.1	63	29	33	0	1	5	4	0	0	0	—	2	9	1	0	0.4	.917
1979	CLE	A	6	6	.500	4.93	29	19	2	137	146	70	93	0	0	0	0	0	0	0	—	8	13	2	1	0.8	.913
1980			19	12	.613	4.17	36	36	8	246	237	92	187	1	0	0	0	0	0	0	—	11	24	0	2	1.0	1.000
1981			8	7	.533	3.92	22	22	9	154	150	46	127	3	0	0	0	0	0	0	—	9	21	2	1	1.5	.938
1982			15	11	.577	3.90	33	33	10	244.2	211	88	187	1	0	0	0	0	0	0	—	23	27	2	1	1.6	.962
1983	2 teams		CLE A	(24G 8–13)		ATL N	(6G 1–3)																					
"	total		9	16	.360	4.88	30	30	4	182.2	181	66	126	1	0	0	0	8	1	0	.125	9	24	3	3	1.2	.917
1984	ATL	N	7	8	.467	3.85	21	20	1	126.1	120	38	95	0	0	0	0	38	2	0	.053	5	34	2	2	2.0	.951
1985			2	9	.182	6.35	20	18	0	73.2	84	37	47	0	0	0	0	17	0	0	.000	2	9	1	0	0.6	.917
1987	MIL	A	2	1	.667	5.36	11	11	0	43.2	54	17	22	0	0	0	0	0	0	0	—	3	6	0	0	0.8	1.000
11 yrs.			74	76	.493	4.35	248	194	35	1322.1	1289	513	975	6	4	5	5	63	3	0	.048	76	177	13	12	1.1	.951

Jeff Barkley

BARKLEY, JEFFREY CARVER
B. Nov. 21, 1959, Hickory, N. C. — BB TR 6'3" 178 lbs.

Year	Team		W	L	PCT	ERA	G	GS	CG	IP	H	BB	SO	ShO	W	L	SV	AB	H	HR	BA	PO	A	E	DP	TC/G	FA
1984	CLE	A	0	0	—	6.75	3	0	0	4	6	1	4	0	0	0	0	0	0	0	—	0	1	0	0	0.3	1.000
1985			0	3	.000	5.27	21	0	0	41	37	15	30	0	0	3	1	0	0	0	—	4	5	1	0	0.5	.900
2 yrs.			0	3	.000	5.40	24	0	0	45	43	16	34	0	0	3	1	0	0	0	—	4	6	1	0	0.5	.909

Mike Barlow

BARLOW, MICHAEL ROSWELL
B. Apr. 30, 1948, Stamford, N. Y. — BL TR 6'6" 210 lbs.

Year	Team		W	L	PCT	ERA	G	GS	CG	IP	H	BB	SO	ShO	W	L	SV	AB	H	HR	BA	PO	A	E	DP	TC/G	FA
1975	STL	N	0	0	—	4.50	9	0	0	8	11	3	2	0	0	0	0	0	0	0	—	0	1	0	0	0.2	.500
1976	HOU	N	2	2	.500	4.50	16	0	0	22	27	17	11	0	2	2	0	3	0	0	.000	0	7	0	0	0.4	1.000
1977	CAL	A	4	2	.667	4.58	20	1	0	59	53	27	25	0	3	2	1	0	0	0	—	5	10	2	0	0.9	.882
1978			0	0	—	4.50	1	0	0	2	3	0	1	0	0	0	0	0	0	0	—	0	0	0	0	0.0	—
1979			1	1	.500	5.13	35	0	0	86	106	30	33	0	1	1	0	0	0	0	—	4	11	0	2	0.4	1.000
1980	TOR	A	3	1	.750	4.09	40	1	0	55	57	21	19	0	2	1	5	0	0	0	—	2	9	1	0	0.3	.917
1981			0	0	—	4.20	12	0	0	15	22	6	5	0	0	0	0	0	0	0	—	0	4	1	0	0.4	1.000
7 yrs.			10	6	.625	4.63	133	2	0	247	279	104	96	0	8	6	6	3	0	0	.000	11	43	4	2	0.4	.931

LEAGUE CHAMPIONSHIP SERIES

Year	Team		W	L	PCT	ERA	G	GS	CG	IP	H	BB	SO	ShO	W	L	SV	AB	H	HR	BA	PO	A	E	DP	TC/G	FA
1979	CAL	A	0	0	—	0.00	1	0	0	1	0	0	0	0	0	0	0	0	0	0	—	0	0	0	0	0.0	—

Year	Team		W	L	PCT	ERA	G	GS	CG	IP	H	BB	SO	ShO	Relief Pitching W	L	SV	Batting AB	H	HR	BA	PO	A	E	DP	TC/G	FA

Charlie Barnabe

BARNABE, CHARLES EDWARD BL TL 5'11½" 164 lbs.
B. June 12, 1900, Russell Gulch, Colo. D. Aug. 16, 1977, Waco, Tex.

1927	CHI	A	0	5	.000	5.31	17	5	1	61	86	20	5	0	0	2	0	19	3	0	.158	2	20	0	0	1.3	1.000
1928			0	2	.000	6.52	7	2	0	9.2	17	0	3	0	0	0	0	8	4	1	.500	2	5	0	0	1.0	1.000
2 yrs.			0	7	.000	5.48	24	7	1	70.2	103	20	8	0	0	2	0	27	7	1	.259	4	25	0	0	1.2	1.000

Bob Barnes

BARNES, ROBERT AVERY (Lefty) BL TL 5'11½" 150 lbs.
B. Jan. 6, 1902, Washburn, Ill.

| 1924 | CHI | A | 0 | 0 | — | 19.29 | 2 | 0 | 0 | 4.2 | 14 | 1 | 0 | 0 | 0 | 0 | 0 | 2 | 0 | 0 | .000 | 0 | 2 | 0 | 0 | 1.0 | 1.000 |

Frank Barnes

BARNES, FRANK BR TR 6' 170 lbs.
B. Aug. 26, 1928, Longwood, Miss.

1957	STL	N	0	1	.000	4.50	3	1	0	10	13	9	5	0				2	0	0	.000	0	0	0	0	0.0	—
1958			1	1	.500	7.58	8	1	0	19	19	16	17	0	1	1	0	6	1	0	.167	0	3	1	0	0.5	.750
1960			0	1	.000	3.52	4	1	0	7.2	8	9	8	0	0	0	1	2	0	0	.000	0	0	0	0	0.0	—
3 yrs.			1	3	.250	5.89	15	3	0	36.2	40	34	30	0	1	1	1	10	1	0	.100	0	3	1	0	0.3	.750

Frank Barnes

BARNES, FRANK SAMUEL (Lefty) BL TL 6'2½" 195 lbs.
B. Jan. 9, 1900, Dallas, Tex. D. Sept. 27, 1967, Houston, Tex.

1929	DET	A	0	1	.000	7.20	4	1	0	5	10	3	0	0	0	0	0	1	0	0	.000	0	3	1	0	1.0	.750
1930	NY	A	0	1	.000	8.03	2	2	0	12.1	13	13	2	0	0	0	0	6	2	0	.333	0	10	0	0	5.0	1.000
2 yrs.			0	2	.000	7.79	6	3	0	17.1	23	16	2	0	0	0	0	7	2	0	.286	0	13	1	0	2.3	.929

Jesse Barnes

BARNES, JESSE LAWRENCE BL TR 6' 170 lbs.
Brother of Virgil Barnes.
B. Aug. 26, 1892, Perkins, Okla. D. Sept. 9, 1961, Santa Rosa, N. M.

1915	BOS	N	4	0	1.000	1.39	9	3	2	45.1	41	10	16	0	1	0	0	17	3	0	.176	0	10	0	1	1.1	1.000
1916			6	14	.300	2.37	33	18	9	163	154	37	55	3	1	4	1	48	9	0	.188	11	60	2	2	2.2	.973
1917			13	21	.382	2.68	50	33	27	295	261	50	107	2	0	3	1	101	24	0	.238	18	96	1	1	2.3	.991
1918	NY	N	6	1	.857	1.81	9	9	4	54.2	53	13	12	0	0	0	0	18	4	0	.222	5	25	1	0	3.4	.968
1919			**25**	9	.735	2.40	38	34	23	295.2	263	35	92	4	2	1	1	120	32	0	.267	11	97	3	5	2.9	.973
1920			20	15	.571	2.64	43	35	23	292.2	271	56	63	2	3	2	0	108	22	0	.204	16	93	4	9	2.6	.965
1921			15	9	.625	3.10	42	31	15	258.2	298	44	56	1	1	1	6	92	19	0	.207	24	67	0	4	2.2	1.000
1922			13	8	.619	3.51	37	30	14	212.2	236	38	52	2	0	1	0	77	14	0	.182	10	63	4	5	2.1	.948
1923	2 teams	NY N (12G 3–1)					BOS N (31G 10–14)																				
"	total		13	15	.464	3.31	43	27	13	231.1	252	56	53	5	2	**4**	3	79	13	0	.165	9	75	2	6	2.0	.977
1924	BOS	N	15	**20**	.429	3.23	37	32	21	267.2	292	53	49	**4**	1	2	0	90	20	0	.222	15	68	0	3	2.2	1.000
1925			11	16	.407	4.53	32	28	17	216.1	255	63	55	0	1	0	1	81	16	1	.198	11	39	2	1	1.6	.962
1926	BKN	N	10	11	.476	5.24	31	24	10	158	204	35	29	1	0	0	1	59	14	0	.237	7	37	3	1	1.5	.936
1927			2	10	.167	5.72	18	10	2	78.2	106	25	14	0	1	2	0	23	5	0	.217	1	18	0	1	1.1	1.000
13 yrs.			153	149	.507	3.22	422	314	180	2569.2	2686	515	653	26	12	21	13	913	195	1	.214	138	748	22	37	2.2	.976

WORLD SERIES

1921	NY	N	2	0	1.000	1.65	3	0	0	16.1	6	6	18	0	2	0	0	9	4	0	.444	1	1	0	0	0.7	1.000
1922			0	0	—	1.80	1	1	1	10	8	2	6	0	0	0	0	4	0	0	.000	0	4	0	0	4.0	1.000
2 yrs.			2	0	1.000 **1st**	1.71	4	1	1	26.1	14	8	24		**2nd**			13	4	0	.308	1	5	0	0	1.5	1.000

Junie Barnes

BARNES, JUNE SHOAF (Lefty) BL TL 5'11½" 170 lbs.
B. Dec. 1, 1911, Linwood, N. C. D. Dec. 31, 1963, Jacksonville, N. C.

| 1934 | CIN | N | 0 | 0 | — | 0.00 | 2 | 0 | 0 | .1 | 0 | 1 | 0 | 0 | 0 | 0 | 0 | 0 | 0 | 0 | — | 0 | 0 | 0 | 0 | 0.0 | — |

Rich Barnes

BARNES, RICHARD MONROE BB TL 6'4" 180 lbs.
B. July 21, 1959, Palm Beach, Fla.

1982	CHI	A	0	2	.000	4.76	6	2	0	17	21	4	6	0	0	1	0	—				0	4	0	0	0.7	1.000
1983	CLE	A	1	1	.500	6.94	4	2	0	11.2	18	10	2	0	1	0	0	—				1	1	0	0	0.5	1.000
2 yrs.			1	3	.250	5.65	10	4	0	28.2	39	14	8	0	1	1	0	—				1	5	0	0	0.6	1.000

Ross Barnes

BARNES, ROSCOE CHARLES BR TR 5'8½" 145 lbs.
B. May 8, 1850, Mount Morris, N. Y. D. Feb. 5, 1915, Chicago, Ill.

| 1876 | CHI | N | 0 | 0 | — | 20.25 | 1 | 0 | 0 | 1.1 | 7 | 0 | 0 | 0 | 0 | 0 | 0 | * | | | | 0 | 0 | 0 | 0 | 0.0 | — |

Virgil Barnes

BARNES, VIRGIL JENNINGS (Zeke) BR TR 6' 165 lbs.
Brother of Jesse Barnes.
B. Mar. 5, 1897, Ontario, Kans. D. July 24, 1958, Wichita, Kans.

1919	NY	N	0	0	—	18.00	1	1	0	2	6	1	1	0	0	0	0	0	0	0	—	0	0	0	0	0.0	—
1920			0	1	.000	3.86	1	1	0	7	9	1	2	0	0	0	0	1	0	0	.000	0	4	0	1	4.0	1.000
1922			1	0	1.000	3.48	22	3	1	51.2	46	11	16	0	0	0	2	12	2	0	.167	3	13	0	1	0.7	1.000
1923			2	3	.400	3.91	22	2	0	53	59	19	6	0	0	3	1	14	0	0	.000	0	16	0	0	0.7	1.000
1924			16	10	.615	3.06	35	29	15	229.1	239	57	59	1	1	2	3	77	14	0	.182	10	66	1	3	2.2	.987
1925			15	11	.577	3.53	32	27	17	221.2	242	53	53	1	1	1	2	89	9	0	.101	8	54	3	2	2.0	.969
1926			8	13	.381	2.87	31	25	9	185	183	56	54	2	0	0	1	56	3	0	.054	10	42	2	1	1.7	.963
1927			14	11	.560	3.98	35	29	14	228.2	251	51	66	2	2	2	2	83	9	0	.108	6	49	4	1	1.7	.932
1928	2 teams	NY N (10G 3–3)					BOS N (16G 2–7)																				
"	total		5	10	.333	5.45	26	19	2	115.2	157	44	18	1	0	1	0	39	3	0	.077	2	24	3	1	1.1	.897
9 yrs.			61	59	.508	3.66	205	135	58	1094	1192	293	275	7	4	9	11	371	40	0	.108	39	268	12	10	1.6	.962

WORLD SERIES

1923	NY	N	0	0	—	0.00	2	0	0	4.2	4	0	4	0	0	0	0	1	0	0	.000	1	2	0	0	1.5	1.000
1924			0	1	.000	5.68	2	2	0	12.2	15	1	9	0	0	0	0	4	0	0	.000	2	3	0	0	2.5	1.000
2 yrs.			0	1	.000	4.15	4	2	0	17.1	19	1	13	0	0	0	0	5	0	0	.000	3	5	0	0	2.0	1.000

Year	Team		W	L	PCT	ERA	G	GS	CG	IP	H	BB	SO	ShO	Relief Pitching W	L	SV	Batting AB	H	HR	BA	PO	A	E	DP	TC/G	FA

Rex Barney

BARNEY, REX EDWARD
B. Dec. 19, 1924, Omaha, Neb.   BR TR 6'3"   185 lbs.

Year	Team		W	L	PCT	ERA	G	GS	CG	IP	H	BB	SO	ShO	W	L	SV	AB	H	HR	BA	PO	A	E	DP	TC/G	FA
1943	BKN	N	2	2	.500	6.35	9	8	1	45.1	36	41	23	0	0	1	0	18	1	0	.056	1	7	0	1	0.9	1.000
1946			2	5	.286	5.87	16	9	1	53.2	46	51	36	0	0	0	0	17	4	0	.235	7	6	1	1	0.9	.929
1947			5	2	.714	4.98	28	9	0	77.2	66	59	36	0	2	0	0	27	3	0	.111	1	11	0	4	0.4	1.000
1948			15	13	.536	3.10	44	34	12	246.2	193	122	138	4	1	3	0	84	14	0	.167	5	28	4	1	0.8	.892
1949			9	8	.529	4.41	38	20	6	140.2	108	89	80	2	2	3	1	47	10	0	.213	4	10	2	1	0.4	.875
1950			2	1	.667	6.42	20	1	0	33.2	25	48	23	0	2	1	0	8	1	0	.125	2	3	1	0	0.3	.833
6 yrs.			35	31	.530	4.34	155	81	20	597.2	474	410	336	6	7	8	1	201	33	0	.164	20	65	8	8	0.6	.914

WORLD SERIES

1947	BKN	N	0	1	.000	2.70	3	1	0	6.2	4	10	3	0	0	0	0	1	0	0	.000	0	1	0	0	0.3	1.000
1949			0	1	.000	16.88	1	1	0	2.2	3	6	2	0	0	0	0	0	0	0	–	1	1	1	0	3.0	.667
2 yrs.			0	2	.000	6.75	4	2	0	9.1	7	16	5	0	0	0	0	1	0	0	.000	1	2	1	0	1.0	.750

Ed Barnhart

BARNHART, EDGAR VERNON
B. Sept. 16, 1904, Providence, Mo.   D. Sept. 14, 1984, Columbia, Mo.   BL TR 5'10"   160 lbs.

| 1924 | STL | A | 0 | 0 | – | 0.00 | 1 | 0 | 0 | 1 | 0 | 2 | 0 | 0 | 0 | 0 | 0 | 0 | 0 | 0 | – | 0 | 1 | 0 | 0 | 1.0 | 1.000 |

Les Barnhart

BARNHART, LESLIE EARL
B. Feb. 23, 1905, Hoxie, Kans.   D. Oct. 7, 1971, Scottsdale, Ariz.   BR TR 6'   180 lbs.

1928	CLE	A	0	1	.000	7.00	2	1	0	9	13	4	1	0	0	0	0	2	1	0	.500	0	0	0	0	0.0	–
1930			1	0	1.000	6.48	1	1	0	8.1	12	4	1	0	0	0	0	3	0	0	.000	0	3	0	0	3.0	1.000
2 yrs.			1	1	.500	6.75	3	2	0	17.1	25	8	2	0	0	0	0	5	1	0	.200	0	3	0	0	1.0	1.000

George Barnicle

BARNICLE, GEORGE BERNARD
B. Aug. 26, 1917, Fitchburg, Mass.   BR TR 6'2"   175 lbs.

1939	BOS	N	2	2	.500	4.91	6	1	0	18.1	16	8	15	0	2	1	0	5	0	0	.000	1	4	0	0	0.8	1.000
1940			1	0	1.000	7.44	13	2	1	32.2	28	31	11	0	0	0	0	11	0	0	.000	1	9	0	1	0.8	1.000
1941			0	1	.000	6.75	1	1	0	6.2	5	4	2	0	0	0	0	2	0	0	.000	0	2	0	0	2.0	1.000
3 yrs.			3	3	.500	6.55	20	4	1	57.2	49	43	28	0	2	1	0	18	0	0	.000	2	15	0	1	0.9	1.000

Ed Barnowski

BARNOWSKI, EDWARD ANTHONY
B. Aug. 23, 1943, Scranton, Pa.   BR TR 6'2"   195 lbs.

1965	BAL	A	0	0	–	2.08	4	0	0	4.1	3	7	6	0	0	0	0	0	0	0	–	0	0	0	0	0.0	–
1966			0	0	–	3.00	2	0	0	3	4	1	2	0	0	0	0	0	0	0	–	0	1	0	0	0.5	1.000
2 yrs.			0	0	–	2.45	6	0	0	7.1	7	8	8	0	0	0	0	0	0	0	–	0	1	0	0	0.2	1.000

Salome Barojas

BAROJAS, SALOME
Born Salome Barojas y Romero.
B. June 16, 1957, Cordoba, Mexico   BR TR 5'9"   160 lbs.

1982	CHI	A	6	6	.500	3.54	61	0	0	106.2	96	46	56	0	6	6	21	0	0	0	–	10	28	0	2	0.6	1.000
1983			3	3	.500	2.47	52	0	0	87.1	70	32	38	0	3	3	12	0	0	0	–	2	14	0	1	0.3	1.000
1984	2 teams		CHI A (24G 3–2)			SEA A (19G 6–5)																					
"	total		9	7	.563	4.15	43	14	0	134.1	136	60	55	0	3	3	2	0	0	0	–	8	27	0	1	0.8	1.000
1985	SEA	A	0	5	.000	5.98	17	4	0	52.2	65	33	27	0	0	1	0	0	0	0	–	5	7	1	0	0.8	.923
1988	PHI	N	0	0	–	8.31	6	0	0	8.2	7	8	1	0	0	0	0 ·	0	0	0	–	0	2	1	0	0.5	.667
5 yrs.			18	21	.462	3.95	179	18	0	389.2	374	179	177	0	12	13	35	0	0	0	–	25	78	2	4	0.6	.981

LEAGUE CHAMPIONSHIP SERIES

| 1983 | CHI | A | 0 | 0 | – | 18.00 | 2 | 0 | 0 | .1 | 4 | 0 | 0 | 0 | 0 | 0 | 0 | 0 | 0 | 0 | – | 0 | 2 | 0 | 0 | 1.0 | 1.000 |

Bob Barr

BARR, ROBERT ALEXANDER
B. Mar. 12, 1908, Newton, Mass.   BR TR 6'   175 lbs.

| 1935 | BKN | N | 0 | 0 | – | 3.86 | 2 | 0 | 0 | 2.1 | 5 | 2 | 0 | 0 | 0 | 0 | 0 | 0 | 0 | 0 | – | 0 | 0 | 0 | 0 | 0.0 | – |

Bob Barr

BARR, ROBERT McCLELLAND
B. 1856, Washington, D. C.   D. Mar. 11, 1930, Washington, D. C.   BR TR 6'1"   192 lbs.

1883	PIT	AA	6	18	.250	4.38	26	23	19	203.1	263	28	81	0	0	1	1	142	35	0	.246	23	39	11	1	2.8	.849
1884	2 teams		WAS AA (32G 9–23)			IND AA (16G 3–11)																					
"	total		12	34	.261	3.94	48	48	47	413	471	50	207	2	0	0	0	200	32	2	.160	15	80	33	1	2.7	.742
1886	WAS	N	3	18	.143	4.30	22	22	21	190.2	216	54	80	1	0	0	0	79	13	0	.165	6	36	9	1	2.3	.824
1890	ROC	AA	28	24	.538	3.25	57	54	52	493.1	458	219	209	3	1	0	0	201	36	2	.179	20	111	10	2	2.5	.929
1891	NY	N	0	4	.000	5.33	5	4	2	27	47	12	11	0	0	0	0	11	1	0	.091	1	6	1	1	1.6	.875
5 yrs.			49	98	.333	3.83	158	151	141	1327.1	1455	363	588	6	1	1	1	*				65	272	64	6	2.5	.840

Jim Barr

BARR, JAMES LELAND
B. Feb. 10, 1948, Lynwood, Calif.   BR TR 6'3"   205 lbs.

1971	SF	N	1	1	.500	3.60	17	0	0	35	33	5	16	0	1	1	0	4	0	0	.000	3	9	1	0	0.8	.923
1972			8	10	.444	2.87	44	18	8	179	166	41	86	2	0	3	2	49	9	0	.184	8	32	2	2	1.0	.952
1973			11	17	.393	3.82	41	33	8	231	240	49	88	3	1	1	2	66	10	0	.152	19	31	0	4	1.2	1.000
1974			13	9	.591	2.74	44	27	11	240	223	47	84	5	1	1	2	71	18	1	.254	16	41	3	4	1.4	.950
1975			13	14	.481	3.06	35	33	12	244	244	58	77	2	2	0	0	76	9	0	.118	28	48	3	2	2.3	.962
1976			15	12	.556	2.89	37	37	8	252.1	260	60	75	3	0	0	0	74	12	0	.162	22	56	4	0	2.2	.951
1977			12	16	.429	4.77	38	38	6	234	286	56	97	2	0	0	0	76	10	0	.132	13	53	5	2	1.9	.930
1978			8	11	.421	3.53	32	25	5	163	180	35	44	2	0	1	1	50	5	0	.100	7	35	4	1	1.4	.913
1979	CAL	A	10	12	.455	4.20	36	25	5	197	217	55	69	0	2	0	0	0	0	0	–	6	41	0	5	1.3	1.000
1980			1	4	.200	5.56	24	7	0	68	90	23	22	0	0	1	1	0	0	0	–	1	10	2	0	0.5	.846
1982	SF	N	4	3	.571	3.29	53	9	1	128.2	125	20	36	1	1	2	2	32	8	0	.250	15	19	1	2	0.7	.971
1983			5	3	.625	3.98	53	0	0	92.2	106	20	47	0	5	3	2	15	2	0	.133	10	13	1	0	0.5	.958
12 yrs.			101	112	.474	3.56	454	252	64	2064.2	2170	469	741	20	13	12	12	513	83	1	.162	148	388	26	22	1.2	.954

Year	Team		W	L	PCT	ERA	G	GS	CG	IP	H	BB	SO	ShO	Relief Pitching			Batting			BA	PO	A	E	DP	TC/G	FA
															W	L	SV	AB	H	HR							

Jim Barr *continued*
LEAGUE CHAMPIONSHIP SERIES

| 1971 | SF | N | 0 | 0 | – | 9.00 | 1 | 0 | 0 | 1 | 3 | 0 | 2 | 0 | 0 | 0 | 0 | 1 | 0 | 0 | .000 | 0 | 0 | 0 | 0 | 0.0 | – |

Steve Barr
BARR, STEVEN CHARLES
B. Sept. 8, 1951, St. Louis, Mo. BL TL 6'4" 200 lbs.

1974	BOS	A	1	0	1.000	4.00	1	1	1	9	7	6	1	0	0	0	0	0	1	2	0	0	–	1	2	0	0	3.0	1.000
1975			0	1	.000	2.57	3	2	0	7	11	7	2	0	0	0	0	0	0	0	–	0	1	1	1	0.7	.500
1976	TEX	A	2	6	.250	5.56	20	10	3	68	70	44	27	0	1	0	0	0	0	0	–	1	14	3	1	0.9	.833
3 yrs.			3	7	.300	5.14	24	13	4	84	88	57	32	0	1	0	0	0	0	0	–	2	17	4	2	1.0	.826

Bill Barrett
BARRETT, WILLIAM JOSEPH (Whispering Bill)
B. May 28, 1900, Cambridge, Mass. D. Jan. 26, 1951, Cambridge, Mass. BR TR 6' 175 lbs.

| 1921 | PHI | A | 1 | 0 | 1.000 | 7.20 | 4 | 0 | 0 | 5 | 2 | 9 | 2 | 0 | 1 | 0 | 0 | | | | * | | 1 | 3 | 0 | 0 | 1.0 | 1.000 |

Dick Barrett
BARRETT, TRACEY SOUTER (Kewpie)
Played as Dick Oliver in 1934.
B. Sept. 28, 1906, Montoursville, Pa. D. Oct. 30, 1966, Seattle, Wash. BR TR 5'9" 175 lbs.

1933	PHI	A	4	4	.500	5.76	15	7	3	70.1	74	49	26	0	0	0	0	21	6	0	.286	4	16	1	0	1.4	.952
1934	BOS	N	1	3	.250	6.68	15	3	0	32.1	50	12	14	0	1	1	0	7	1	0	.143	1	12	1	0	0.9	.929
1943	2 teams		CHI N	(15G 0–4)		PHI N	(23G 10–9)																				
"	total		10	13	.435	2.90	38	24	10	214.1	189	79	85	2	0	0	1	58	8	0	.138	16	40	1	3	1.5	.949
1944	PHI	N	12	18	.400	3.86	37	28	11	221.1	223	88	74	1	3	2	0	74	16	0	.216	9	54	0	2	1.7	1.000
1945			7	20	.259	5.43	36	30	8	190.2	216	92	72	0	1	2	1	62	9	0	.145	9	38	2	3	1.4	.959
5 yrs.			34	58	.370	4.30	141	92	32	729	752	320	271	3	5	5	2	222	40	0	.180	39	160	5	8	1.4	.975

Frank Barrett
BARRETT, FRANCIS JOSEPH (Red)
B. July 1, 1913, Fort Lauderdale, Fla. BR TR 6'2" 173 lbs.

1939	STL	N	0	1	.000	5.40	1	0	0	1.2	1	1	3	0	0	1	0	0	0	0	–	1	0	0	0	1.0	1.000
1944	BOS	A	8	7	.533	3.69	38	2	0	90.1	93	42	40	0	7	6	8	28	4	0	.143	5	16	2	1	0.6	.913
1945			4	3	.571	2.62	37	0	0	86	77	29	35	0	4	3	3	20	5	0	.250	4	14	1	1	0.5	.947
1946	BOS	N	2	4	.333	5.09	23	0	0	35.1	35	17	12	0	2	4	1	6	0	0	.000	4	12	1	0	0.7	.941
1950	PIT	N	1	2	.333	4.15	5	0	0	4.1	5	1	0	0	1	2	0	0	0	0	–	1	2	0	1	0.6	1.000
5 yrs.			15	17	.469	3.51	104	2	0	217.2	211	90	90	0	14	16	12	54	9	0	.167	15	44	4	3	0.6	.937

Red Barrett
BARRETT, CHARLES HENRY
B. Feb. 14, 1915, Santa Barbara, Calif. BR TR 5'11" 183 lbs.

1937	CIN	N	0	0	–	1.42	1	0	0	6.1	5	2	1	0	0	0	0	3	0	0	.000	0	0	0	0	0.0	–
1938			2	0	1.000	3.14	6	2	2	28.2	28	15	5	0	0	0	0	7	1	0	.143	5	3	0	0	1.3	1.000
1939			0	0	–	1.69	2	0	0	5.1	5	1	1	0	0	0	0	0	0	0	.000	0	1	0	0	0.5	1.000
1940			1	0	1.000	6.75	3	0	0	2.2	5	1	0	0	1	0	0	0	0	0	–	0	2	0	1	0.7	1.000
1943	BOS	N	12	18	.400	3.18	38	31	14	255	240	63	64	3	0	2	0	81	11	0	.136	17	55	2	9	1.9	.973
1944			9	16	.360	4.06	42	30	11	230.1	257	63	54	1	0	3	2	75	13	0	.173	15	51	3	7	1.6	.957
1945	2 teams		BOS N	(9G 2–3)		STL N	(36G 21–9)																				
"	total		23	12	.657	3.00	45	34	24	284.2	287	54	76	3	0	2	2	98	12	0	.122	24	54	1	1	1.8	.987
1946	STL	N	3	2	.600	4.03	23	9	1	67	75	24	22	1	1	0	2	17	1	0	.059	4	17	0	1	0.9	1.000
1947	BOS	N	11	12	.478	3.55	36	30	12	210.2	200	53	53	3	0	1	1	72	8	0	.111	17	38	3	2	1.6	.948
1948			7	8	.467	3.65	34	13	3	128.1	132	26	40	0	2	3	0	39	7	0	.179	13	26	1	1	1.2	.975
1949			1	1	.500	5.68	23	0	0	44.1	58	10	17	0	1	1	0	5	1	0	.200	3	14	1	0	0.8	.944
11 yrs.			69	69	.500	3.53	253	149	67	1263.1	1292	312	333	11	6	13	7	398	54	0	.136	98	261	11	22	1.5	.970

WORLD SERIES

| 1948 | BOS | N | 0 | 0 | – | 0.00 | 2 | 0 | 0 | 3.2 | 1 | 0 | 1 | 0 | 0 | 0 | 0 | 0 | 0 | 0 | – | 0 | 0 | 0 | 0 | 0.0 | – |

Tim Barrett
BARRETT, TIMOTHY WAYNE
B. Jan. 24, 1961, Huntington, Ind. BL TR 6'1" 185 lbs.

| 1988 | MON | N | 0 | 0 | – | 5.79 | 4 | 0 | 0 | 9.1 | 10 | 2 | 5 | 0 | 0 | 0 | 1 | 0 | 0 | 0 | .000 | 3 | 1 | 1 | 1 | 1.3 | .800 |

Francisco Barrios
BARRIOS, FRANCISCO JAVIER
Born Francisco Javier Barrios y Jimenez.
B. June 10, 1953, Hermosillo, Mexico D. Apr. 9, 1982, Hermosillo, Mexico BR TR 5'11" 155 lbs.

1974	CHI	A	0	0	–	27.00	2	0	0	2	7	2	2	0	0	0	0	0	0	0	0.0	0	0	0	0	0.0	–
1976			5	9	.357	4.31	35	14	6	142	136	46	81	0	0	4	3	0	0	0	–	10	14	1	3	0.7	.960
1977			14	7	.667	4.13	33	31	9	231	241	58	119	0	1	0	0	0	0	0	–	20	27	2	2	1.5	.959
1978			9	15	.375	4.05	33	32	9	195.2	180	85	79	2	0	0	0	0	0	0	–	19	38	0	1	1.7	1.000
1979			8	3	.727	3.60	15	15	2	95	88	33	28	0	0	0	0	0	0	0	–	10	8	3	2	1.4	.857
1980			1	1	.500	5.06	3	3	0	16	21	8	2	0	0	0	0	0	0	0	–	0	3	2	0	1.7	.600
1981			1	3	.250	4.00	8	7	1	36	45	14	12	0	0	0	0	0	0	0	–	1	6	1	0	1.0	.875
7 yrs.			38	38	.500	4.15	129	102	27	717.2	718	246	323	2	1	4	3	0	0	0	–	60	96	9	8	1.3	.945

Frank Barron
BARRON, FRANK JOHN
B. Aug. 6, 1890, St. Mary's, W. Va. D. Sept. 18, 1964, St. Mary's, W. Va. BL TL 6'1" 175 lbs.

| 1914 | WAS | A | 0 | 0 | – | 0.00 | 1 | 0 | 0 | 1 | 1 | 0 | 1 | 0 | 0 | 0 | 0 | 0 | 0 | 0 | – | 1 | 0 | 0 | 0 | 1.0 | 1.000 |

Ed Barry
BARRY, EDWARD (Jumbo)
B. Oct. 2, 1882, Madison, Wis. D. June 19, 1920, Montague, Mass. TL 6'3" 185 lbs.

| 1905 | BOS | A | 1 | 2 | .333 | 2.88 | 7 | 5 | 2 | 40.2 | 38 | 15 | 18 | 0 | 0 | 0 | 0 | 11 | 1 | 0 | .091 | 2 | 3 | 0 | 0 | 0.7 | 1.000 |
| 1906 | | | 0 | 3 | .000 | 6.00 | 3 | 3 | 3 | 21 | 23 | 5 | 10 | 0 | 0 | 0 | 0 | 9 | 1 | 0 | .111 | 1 | 8 | 1 | 0 | 3.3 | .900 |

Year	Team		W	L	PCT	ERA	G	GS	CG	IP	H	BB	SO	ShO	W	L	SV	AB	H	HR	BA	PO	A	E	DP	TC/G	FA

Ed Barry *continued*

| 1907 | | | 0 | 1 | .000 | 2.08 | 2 | 2 | 1 | 17.1 | 13 | 5 | 6 | 0 | 0 | 0 | 0 | 3 | 0 | 0 | .000 | 1 | 5 | 1 | 0 | 3.5 | .857 |
| 3 yrs. | | | 1 | 6 | .143 | 3.53 | 12 | 10 | 6 | 79 | 74 | 25 | 34 | 0 | 0 | 0 | 0 | 23 | 2 | 0 | .087 | 4 | 16 | 2 | 0 | 1.8 | .909 |

Hardin Barry

BARRY, HARDIN (Finn)
B. Mar. 26, 1891, Susanville, Calif.   D. Nov. 5, 1969, Carson City, Nev.   BR TR 6'   185 lbs.

| 1912 | PHI | A | 0 | 0 | – | 7.62 | 3 | 0 | 0 | 13 | 18 | 4 | 3 | 0 | 0 | 0 | 0 | 4 | 0 | 0 | .000 | 2 | 2 | 0 | 0 | 1.3 | 1.000 |

Tom Barry

BARRY, THOMAS ARTHUR
B. Apr. 10, 1879, St. Louis, Mo.   D. June 4, 1946, St. Louis, Mo.   TR 5'9"   155 lbs.

| 1904 | PHI | N | 0 | 1 | .000 | 40.50 | 1 | 1 | 0 | .2 | 6 | 1 | 1 | 0 | 0 | 0 | 0 | 0 | 0 | 0 | – | 0 | 0 | 0 | 0 | 0.0 | – |

Bob Barthelson

BARTHELSON, ROBERT EDWARD
B. July 15, 1924, New Haven, Conn.   BR TR 6'   185 lbs.

| 1944 | NY | N | 1 | 1 | .500 | 4.66 | 7 | 1 | 0 | 9.2 | 13 | 5 | 4 | 0 | 1 | 1 | 0 | 0 | 0 | 0 | – | 0 | 1 | 0 | 0 | 0.1 | 1.000 |

John Barthold

BARTHOLD, JOHN FRANCIS (Hans)
B. Apr. 14, 1882, Philadelphia, Pa.   D. Nov. 4, 1946, Fairview Village, Pa.   BB TR 5'11"   180 lbs.

| 1904 | PHI | A | 0 | 0 | – | 5.06 | 4 | 0 | 0 | 10.2 | 12 | 8 | 5 | 0 | 0 | 0 | 0 | 3 | 1 | 0 | .333 | 0 | 5 | 0 | 1 | 1.3 | 1.000 |

Les Bartholomew

BARTHOLOMEW, LESTER JUSTIN
B. Apr. 4, 1903, Madison, Wis.   D. Sept. 19, 1972, Barrington, Ill.   BR TL 5'11½"   195 lbs.

1928	PIT	N	0	0	–	7.15	6	0	0	22.2	31	9	6	0	0	0	0	7	1	0	.143	0	5	1	1	1.0	.833
1932	CHI	A	0	0	–	5.06	3	0	0	5.1	5	6	1	0	0	0	0	1	0	0	.000	0	1	0	0	0.3	1.000
2 yrs.			0	0	–	6.75	9	0	0	28	36	15	7	0	0	0	0	8	1	0	.125	0	6	1	1	0.8	.857

Bill Bartley

BARTLEY, WILLIAM JACKSON
B. Jan. 8, 1885, Cincinnati, Ohio   D. May 17, 1965, Cincinnati, Ohio   BR TR 5'11½"   190 lbs.

1903	NY	N	0	0	–	0.00	1	0	0	3	3	4	2	0	0	0	0	1	0	0	.000	0	1	0	0	1.0	1.000
1906	PHI	A	0	0	–	9.35	3	0	0	8.2	10	6	6	0	0	0	0	3	1	0	.333	2	4	0	0	2.0	1.000
1907			0	1	.000	2.24	15	3	2	56.1	44	19	16	0	0	1	0	21	2	0	.095	9	14	2	2	1.7	.920
3 yrs.			0	1	.000	3.04	19	3	2	68	57	29	24	0	0	1	1	25	3	0	.120	11	19	2	2	1.7	.938

Charlie Bartson

BARTSON, CHARLES FRANKLIN
B. Mar. 13, 1865, Peoria, Ill.   D. June 9, 1936, Peoria, Ill.   6'   170 lbs.

| 1890 | CHI | P | 8 | 10 | .444 | 4.26 | 25 | 19 | 16 | 188 | 222 | 66 | 47 | 0 | 0 | 1 | 0 | 75 | 13 | 0 | .173 | 10 | 70 | 7 | 1 | 3.5 | .920 |

Jim Baskette

BASKETTE, JAMES BLAINE (Big Jim)
B. Dec. 10, 1887, Athens, Tenn.   D. July 30, 1942, Athens, Tenn.   BR TR 6'2"   185 lbs.

1911	CLE	A	1	2	.333	3.38	4	2	2	21.1	21	9	8	0	0	0	0	6	2	0	.333	4	2	0	0	1.5	1.000
1912			8	4	.667	3.18	29	11	7	116	109	46	51	1	2	1	1	40	5	0	.125	4	19	1	0	0.8	.958
1913			0	0	–	5.79	2	1	0	4.2	8	2	0	0	0	0	0	1	1	0	1.000	0	4	0	0	2.0	1.000
3 yrs.			9	6	.600	3.30	35	14	9	142	138	57	59	1	2	2	1	47	8	0	.170	8	25	1	0	1.0	.971

Dick Bass

BASS, RICHARD WILLIAM
B. July 7, 1906, Rogersville, Tenn.   BR TR 6'2"   175 lbs.

| 1939 | WAS | A | 0 | 1 | .000 | 6.75 | 1 | 1 | 0 | 8 | 7 | 6 | 1 | 0 | 0 | 0 | 0 | 2 | 0 | 0 | .000 | 0 | 1 | 0 | 0 | 1.0 | 1.000 |

Norm Bass

BASS, NORMAN DELANEY
B. Jan. 21, 1939, Laurel, Miss.   BR TR 6'3"   205 lbs.

1961	KC	A	11	11	.500	4.69	40	23	6	170.2	164	82	74	2	0	1	0	59	7	1	.119	5	17	2	2	0.6	.917
1962			2	6	.250	6.09	22	10	0	75.1	96	46	33	0	1	1	0	22	1	0	.045	6	19	0	0	1.1	1.000
1963			0	0	–	11.74	3	1	0	7.2	11	9	4	0	0	0	0	1	0	0	.000	0	1	2	0	1.0	.333
3 yrs.			13	17	.433	5.32	65	34	6	253.2	271	137	111	2	1	2	0	82	8	1	.098	11	37	4	2	0.8	.923

Charlie Bastian

BASTIAN, CHARLES J.
B. July 4, 1860, Philadelphia, Pa.   D. Jan. 18, 1932, Pennsauken, N. J.   BR TR 5'6½"   145 lbs.

| 1884 | 2 teams | | WIL | U | (1G 0–0) | | KC | U | (0G 0–0) | | | | | | | | | | | | | | | | | | |
| " | total | | 0 | 0 | – | 3.00 | 1 | 0 | 0 | 6 | 6 | 0 | 2 | 0 | 0 | 0 | 0 | * | | | | 0 | 0 | 0 | 0 | 0.0 | – |

Joe Batchelder

BATCHELDER, JOSEPH EDWARD (Win)
B. July 11, 1898, Wenham, Mass.   D. May 5, 1989, Beverly, Mass.   BR TL 5'7"   165 lbs.

1923	BOS	N	1	0	1.000	7.00	4	1	0	9	12	1	2	0	0	0	0	1	0	0	.000	1	1	0	0	0.5	1.000
1924			0	0	–	3.86	3	0	0	4.2	4	2	2	0	0	0	0	1	0	0	.000	0	2	0	0	0.7	1.000
1925			0	0	–	5.14	4	0	0	7	10	1	2	0	0	0	0	1	0	0	.000	0	4	1	0	1.3	.800
3 yrs.			1	0	1.000	5.66	11	1	0	20.2	26	4	6	0	0	0	0	3	0	0	.000	1	7	1	0	0.8	.889

Bates

BATES,
B. Texas

| 1889 | KC | AA | 0 | 1 | .000 | 13.50 | 1 | 1 | 1 | 8 | 15 | 3 | 3 | 0 | 0 | 0 | 0 | 4 | 0 | 0 | .000 | 0 | 0 | 0 | 0 | 0.0 | – |

Dick Bates

BATES, CHARLES RICHARD
B. Oct. 7, 1945, McArthur, Ohio   BL TR 6'   190 lbs.

| 1969 | SEA | A | 0 | 0 | – | 27.00 | 1 | 0 | 0 | 1.2 | 3 | 3 | 3 | 0 | 0 | 0 | 0 | 0 | 0 | 0 | – | 1 | 0 | 0 | 0 | 1.0 | 1.000 |

Year	Team		W	L	PCT	ERA	G	GS	CG	IP	H	BB	SO	ShO	Relief Pitching W	L	SV	Batting AB	H	HR	BA	PO	A	E	DP	TC/G	FA

Frank Bates

BATES, CREED F.
B. Chattanooga, Tenn. Deceased.

1898	CLE	N	2	1	.667	3.10	4	4	4	29	30	11	5	0	0	0	0	9	1	0	.111	2	6	1	1	2.3	.889
1899	2 teams	STL N	(2G 0-0)			CLE N	(20G 1-18)																				
"	total		1	18	.053	6.90	22	19	17	161.2	246	110	13	0	0	0	0	68	15	0	.221	6	41	8	2	2.5	.855
2 yrs.			3	19	.136	6.33	26	23	21	190.2	276	121	18	0	0	0	0	77	16	0	.208	8	47	9	3	2.5	.859

Joe Battin

BATTIN, JOSEPH V.   BR TR
B. Nov. 11, 1851, Philadelphia, Pa.   D. Dec. 10, 1937, Akron, Ohio
Manager 1883-84.

1877	STL	N	0	0	—	4.91	1	0	0	3.2	3	1	1	0	0	0	0	226	45	1	.199	1	0	0	0	1.0	1.000
1883	PIT	AA	0	0	—	2.25	2	0	0	4	9	1	0	0	0	0	0	388	83	1	.214	0	0	0	0	0.0	—
2 yrs.			0	0	—	3.52	3	0	0	7.2	12	2	1	0	0	0	0	*				1	0	0	0	0.3	1.000

Chris Batton

BATTON, CHRISTOPHER SEAN   BR TR 6'4"   195 lbs.
B. Aug. 24, 1954, Los Angeles, Calif.

| 1976 | OAK | A | 0 | 0 | — | 9.00 | 2 | 1 | 0 | 4 | 5 | 3 | 4 | 0 | 0 | 0 | 0 | 0 | 0 | 0 | — | 0 | 0 | 0 | 0 | 0.0 | — |

Lou Bauer

BAUER, LOUIS WALTER (Kid)   BR TR 6'   175 lbs.
B. Nov. 30, 1898, Egg Harbor City, N. J.   D. Feb. 4, 1979, Pomona, N. J.

| 1918 | PHI | A | 0 | 0 | — | ∞ | 1 | 0 | 0 | 0 | 0 | 0 | 0 | 0 | 0 | 0 | 0 | 0 | 0 | 0 | — | 0 | 0 | 0 | 0 | 0.0 | — |

Al Bauers

BAUERS, ALBERT J.   TL
B. 1850, Columbus, Ohio   D. Sept. 6, 1913, Wilkes-Barre, Pa.

1884	COL	AA	1	2	.333	4.68	3	3	3	25	22	14	13	0	0	0	0	11	3	0	.273	1	5	1	0	2.3	.857
1886	STL	N	0	4	.000	5.97	4	4	3	28.2	31	27	13	0	0	0	0	12	2	0	.167	0	3	1	0	1.0	.750
2 yrs.			1	6	.143	5.37	7	7	6	53.2	53	41	26	0	0	0	0	23	5	0	.217	1	8	2	0	1.6	.818

Russ Bauers

BAUERS, RUSSELL LEE   BL TR 6'3"   195 lbs.
B. May 10, 1914, Townsend, Wis.

1936	PIT	N	0	0	—	33.75	1	1	0	1.1	2	4	0	0	0	0	0	0	0	0	—	0	0	0	0	0.0	—
1937			13	6	.684	2.88	34	19	11	187.2	174	80	118	2	3	1	1	69	15	0	.217	1	58	2	0	1.8	.967
1938			13	14	.481	3.07	40	34	12	243	207	99	117	3	1	2	3	88	21	0	.239	3	38	6	1	1.2	.872
1939			2	4	.333	3.35	15	8	1	53.2	46	25	12	0	1	1	1	19	4	0	.211	0	7	0	3	0.5	1.000
1940			0	2	.000	7.63	15	2	0	30.2	42	18	11	0	0	0	0	7	2	0	.286	1	7	0	1	0.5	1.000
1941			1	3	.250	5.54	8	5	1	37.1	40	25	20	0	0	0	0	14	5	0	.357	0	4	3	1	0.9	.571
1946	CHI	N	2	1	.667	3.53	15	2	0	43.1	45	19	22	0	1	0	1	10	3	0	.300	5	6	1	0	0.8	.917
1950	STL	A	0	0	—	4.50	1	0	0	2	6	1	0	0	0	0	0	0	0	0	—	0	1	0	0	1.0	1.000
8 yrs.			31	30	.508	3.53	129	71	27	599	562	271	300	5	6	4	6	207	50	0	.242	10	121	12	6	1.1	.916

Frank Baumann

BAUMANN, FRANK MATT (The Beau)   BL TL 6'   205 lbs.
B. July 1, 1933, St. Louis, Mo.

1955	BOS	A	2	1	.667	5.82	7	5	0	34	38	17	27	0	1	0	0	13	3	0	.231	0	6	0	0	0.9	1.000
1956			2	1	.667	3.28	7	1	0	24.2	22	14	18	0	1	1	0	9	3	0	.333	1	1	1	0	0.4	.667
1957			1	0	1.000	3.75	4	1	0	12	13	3	7	0	0	0	0	2	1	0	.500	1	1	0	0	0.3	1.000
1958			2	2	.500	4.47	10	7	2	52.1	56	27	31	0	0	0	0	14	3	0	.214	1	6	0	0	0.7	1.000
1959			6	4	.600	4.05	26	10	2	95.2	96	55	48	0	2	0	1	29	6	0	.207	5	20	3	1	1.1	.893
1960	CHI	A	13	6	.684	**2.67**	44	20	7	185.1	169	53	71	2	6	2	3	52	8	0	.154	4	25	1	1	0.7	.967
1961			10	13	.435	5.61	53	23	5	187.2	249	59	75	1	4	4	3	61	16	2	.262	14	37	1	1	1.0	.981
1962			7	6	.538	3.38	40	10	3	119.2	117	36	55	1	4	2	4	30	8	0	.267	5	23	1	3	0.7	.966
1963			2	1	.667	3.04	24	1	0	50.1	52	17	31	0	2	0	1	11	1	0	.091	2	9	0	1	0.5	1.000
1964			0	3	.000	6.19	22	0	0	32	40	16	19	0	0	3	1	4	0	0	.000	0	4	0	0	0.3	1.000
1965	CHI	N	0	1	.000	7.36	4	0	0	3.2	4	3	2	0	0	0	0	0	0	0	—	0	1	0	0	0.3	1.000
11 yrs.			45	38	.542	4.11	241	78	19	797.1	856	300	384	4	20	13	13	225	49	2	.218	33	133	7	7	0.7	.960

George Baumgardner

BAUMGARDNER, GEORGE WASHINGTON   BL TR 5'11"   178 lbs.
B. July 22, 1891, Barboursville, W. Va.   D. Dec. 13, 1970, Barboursville, W. Va.

1912	STL	A	11	14	.440	3.38	30	26	18	218.1	222	79	102	2	0	1	0	76	11	0	.145	4	61	1	2	2.2	.985
1913			10	19	.345	3.13	38	31	23	253.1	**267**	84	78	2	0	0	1	78	13	0	.167	8	72	6	1	2.3	.930
1914			14	13	.519	2.79	45	18	9	183.2	152	84	93	3	6	5	3	53	7	0	.132	4	49	2	0	1.2	.964
1915			0	2	.000	4.43	7	1	1	22.1	29	11	6	0	0	1	0	6	0	0	.000	0	10	1	0	1.6	.909
1916			1	0	1.000	7.88	4	2	0	8	12	5	4	0	0	0	0	2	0	0	.000	0	0	0	0	0.0	—
5 yrs.			36	48	.429	3.22	124	78	51	685.2	682	263	283	7	6	7	4	215	31	0	.144	16	192	10	3	1.8	.954

Ross Baumgarten

BAUMGARTEN, ROSS   BL TL 6'1"   180 lbs.
B. May 27, 1955, Highland Park, Ill.

1978	CHI	A	2	2	.500	5.87	7	4	1	23	29	9	15	1	0	0	0	0	0	0	—	0	2	0	0	0.3	1.000
1979			13	8	.619	3.53	28	28	4	191	175	83	72	3	0	0	0	0	0	0	—	14	28	1	1	1.5	.977
1980			2	12	.143	3.44	24	23	3	136	127	52	66	1	0	0	0	0	0	0	—	5	31	1	3	1.5	.973
1981			5	9	.357	4.06	19	19	2	102	101	40	52	1	0	0	0	0	0	0	—	7	16	0	1	1.2	1.000
1982	PIT	N	0	5	.000	6.55	12	10	0	44	60	27	17	0	0	0	0	12	1	0	.083	2	8	0	1	0.8	1.000
5 yrs.			22	36	.379	3.99	90	84	10	496	492	211	222	6	0	0	0	12	1	0	.083	28	85	2	6	1.3	.983

Harry Baumgartner

BAUMGARTNER, HARRY E   BR TR 5'11"   175 lbs.
B. Oct. 6, 1892, S. Pittsburg, Tenn.   D. Dec. 3, 1930, Augusta, Ga.

| 1920 | DET | A | 0 | 1 | .000 | 4.00 | 9 | 0 | 0 | 18 | 18 | 6 | 7 | 0 | 0 | 1 | 0 | 4 | 1 | 0 | .250 | 1 | 5 | 0 | 0 | 0.7 | 1.000 |

Stan Baumgartner

BAUMGARTNER, STANWOOD FULTON   BL TL 6'   175 lbs.
B. Dec. 14, 1894, Houston, Tex.   D. Oct. 4, 1955, Philadelphia, Pa.

| 1914 | PHI | N | 3 | 2 | .600 | 3.28 | 15 | 3 | 2 | 60.1 | 60 | 16 | 24 | 1 | 3 | 0 | 0 | 19 | 1 | 0 | .053 | 3 | 11 | 0 | 0 | 0.9 | 1.000 |

Year	Team		W	L	PCT	ERA	G	GS	CG	IP	H	BB	SO	ShO	Relief Pitching			Batting			BA	PO	A	E	DP	TC/G	FA
															W	L	SV	AB	H	HR							

Stan Baumgartner *continued*

1915			0	2	.000	2.42	16	1	0	48.1	38	23	27	0	0	1	0	12	1	0	.083	3	17	1	1	1.3	.952
1916			0	0	–	2.25	1	0	0	4	5	1	0	0	0	0	0	1	0	0	.000	0	0	0	0	0.0	–
1921			3	6	.333	7.02	22	7	2	66.2	103	22	13	0	2	0	0	30	6	0	.200	1	15	1	0	0.8	.941
1922			1	1	.500	6.52	6	1	0	9.2	18	5	2	0	1	0	0	3	1	0	.333	1	3	0	0	0.7	1.000
1924	PHI	A	13	6	.684	2.88	36	16	12	181	181	73	45	1	4	1	4	60	13	0	.217	10	33	3	1	1.3	.935
1925			6	3	.667	3.57	37	11	2	113.1	120	35	18	1	2	1	3	30	7	0	.233	10	25	3	1	1.0	.921
1926			1	1	.500	4.03	10	1	0	22.1	28	10	0	0	1	1	0	3	1	0	.333	2	8	0	0	1.0	1.000
8 yrs.			27	21	.563	3.70	143	40	18	505.2	553	185	129	3	13	4	7	158	30	0	.190	30	112	8	3	1.0	.947

George Bausewine

BAUSEWINE, GEORGE W.
B. Mar. 22, 1869, Philadelphia, Pa. D. July 29, 1947, Norristown, Pa. 6'2"

| 1889 | PHI | AA | 1 | 4 | .200 | 3.90 | 7 | 6 | 6 | 55.1 | 64 | 33 | 18 | 0 | 0 | 0 | 0 | 21 | 1 | 0 | .048 | 0 | 12 | 0 | 0 | 1.7 | 1.000 |

Ed Bauta

BAUTA, EDUARDO
Born Eduardo Bauta y Galvez.
B. Jan. 6, 1935, Florida, Cuba BR TR 6'3" 200 lbs.

1960	STL	N	0	0	–	6.32	9	0	0	15.2	14	11	6	0	0	0	1	1	0	0	.000	0	2	0	0	0.2	1.000
1961			0	1	1.000	1.40	13	0	0	19.1	12	5	12	0	2	0	5	4	2	0	.500	0	3	0	0	0.2	1.000
1962			1	0	1.000	5.01	20	0	0	32.1	28	21	25	0	1	0	1	4	1	0	.250	1	6	0	0	0.4	1.000
1963	2 teams		STL N	(38G 3–4)		NY N	(9G 0–0)																				
"	total		3	4	.429	4.27	47	0	0	71.2	77	30	43	0	3	4	3	8	0	0	.000	0	9	0	0	0.2	1.000
1964	NY	N	0	2	.000	5.40	8	0	0	10	17	3	3	0	0	2	1	0	0	0	–	0	5	1	0	0.8	.833
5 yrs.			6	6	.500	4.35	97	0	0	149	148	70	89	0	6	6	11	17	3	0	.176	1	25	1	0	0.3	.963

Jose Bautista

BAUTISTA, JOSE JOAQUIN
Born Jose Joaquin Bautista y Arias.
B. July 25, 1964, Bani, Dominican Republic BR TR 6'1" 177 lbs.

1988	BAL	A	6	15	.286	4.30	33	25	3	171.2	171	45	76	0	0	1	0	0	0	0	–	27	11	1	3	1.2	.974
1989			3	4	.429	5.31	15	10	0	78	84	15	30	0	0	0	0	0	0	0	–	3	10	1	0	0.9	.929
2 yrs.			9	19	.321	4.61	48	35	3	249.2	255	60	106	0	0	1	0	0	0	0	–	30	21	2	3	1.1	.962

Bill Bayne

BAYNE, WILLIAM LEAR (Beverly)
B. Apr. 18, 1899, Pittsburgh, Pa. D. May 22, 1981, St. Louis, Mo. BL TL 5'9" 160 lbs.

1919	STL	A	1	1	.500	5.25	2	1	0	12	16	6	0	0	0	0	0	5	2	0	.400	1	4	0	0	2.5	1.000
1920			5	6	.455	3.70	18	13	6	99.2	102	41	38	1	0	0	0	35	6	0	.171	3	16	1	1	1.1	.950
1921			11	5	.688	4.72	47	14	7	164	167	80	82	1	5	1	3	60	18	1	.300	9	36	6	0	1.1	.882
1922			4	5	.444	4.56	26	9	3	92.2	86	37	38	0	1	2	2	30	7	0	.233	6	12	0	0	0.7	1.000
1923			2	2	.500	4.50	19	2	0	46	49	31	15	0	2	1	0	13	3	0	.231	3	8	1	1	0.6	.917
1924			1	3	.250	4.17	21	3	0	49.2	46	28	20	0	1	2	0	14	6	0	.429	2	8	2	0	0.6	.833
1928	CLE	A	2	5	.286	5.13	37	6	3	108.2	128	43	39	0	0	3	3	30	11	0	.367	5	32	3	3	1.1	.925
1929	BOS	A	5	5	.500	6.72	27	6	2	84.1	111	29	26	0	4	0	0	25	8	0	.320	4	22	0	3	1.0	1.000
1930			0	0	–	4.50	1	0	0	4	5	1	1	0	0	0	0	2	1	0	.500	1	0	0	0	1.0	1.000
9 yrs.			31	32	.492	4.82	198	55	22	661	710	296	259	2	13	9	8	214	62	1	.290	33	139	13	8	0.9	.930

Walter Beall

BEALL, WALTER ESAU
B. July 29, 1899, Washington, D. C. D. Jan. 28, 1959, Suitland, Md. BR TR 5'10" 178 lbs.

1924	NY	A	2	0	1.000	3.52	4	2	0	23	19	17	18	0	1	0	0	7	1	0	.143	0	4	0	0	1.0	1.000
1925			0	1	.000	12.71	8	1	0	11.1	11	19	11	0	0	0	0	3	0	0	.000	0	4	0	0	0.5	1.000
1926			2	4	.333	3.53	20	9	1	81.2	71	68	56	0	0	0	1	22	3	0	.136	0	24	6	1	1.5	.800
1927			0	0	–	9.00	1	0	0	1	1	0	0	0	0	0	0	0	0	0	–	0	0	0	0	0.0	–
1929	WAS	A	1	0	1.000	3.86	3	0	0	7	8	7	3	0	1	0	0	3	0	0	.000	0	3	0	0	1.0	1.000
5 yrs.			5	5	.500	4.43	36	12	1	124	110	111	85	0	2	0	1	35	4	0	.114	0	35	6	1	1.1	.854

Alex Beam

BEAM, ALEXANDER ROGER
B. Nov. 21, 1870, Johnstown, Pa. D. Apr. 17, 1938, Nogales, Ariz.

| 1889 | PIT | N | 1 | 1 | .500 | 6.50 | 2 | 2 | 2 | 18 | 11 | 15 | 1 | 0 | 0 | 0 | 0 | 6 | 1 | 0 | .167 | 0 | 4 | 3 | 0 | 3.5 | .571 |

Ernie Beam

BEAM, ERNEST JOSEPH
B. Mar. 17, 1867, Mansfield, Ohio D. Sept. 13, 1918, Mansfield, Ohio 185 lbs.

| 1895 | PHI | N | 0 | 2 | .000 | 11.31 | 9 | 1 | 1 | 24.2 | 33 | 25 | 3 | 0 | 0 | 1 | 3 | 11 | 2 | 0 | .182 | 0 | 4 | 0 | 0 | 0.4 | 1.000 |

Charlie Beamon

BEAMON, CHARLES ALFONZO, SR.
Father of Charlie Beamon.
B. Dec. 25, 1934, Oakland, Calif. BR TR 5'11" 195 lbs.

1956	BAL	A	2	0	1.000	1.38	2	1	1	13	9	8	14	1	1	0	0	5	0	0	.000	0	3	0	0	1.5	1.000
1957			0	0	–	5.19	4	1	0	8.2	8	7	5	0	0	0	0	2	0	0	.000	0	2	1	0	0.8	.667
1958			1	3	.250	4.35	21	3	0	49.2	47	21	26	0	1	1	0	10	0	0	.000	6	15	0	4	1.0	1.000
3 yrs.			3	3	.500	3.91	27	5	1	71.1	64	36	45	1	2	1	0	17	0	0	.000	6	20	1	4	1.0	.963

Belve Bean

BEAN, BEVERIC BENTON (Bill)
B. Apr. 23, 1905, Mullin, Tex. D. June 1, 1988, Comanche, Tex. BR TR 6'1½" 197 lbs.

1930	CLE	A	3	3	.500	5.45	23	3	2	74.1	99	32	19	0	3	1	2	26	9	0	.346	3	17	1	0	0.9	.952
1931			0	1	.000	6.43	4	0	0	11	11	4	3	0	0	1	0	1	0	0	.000	0	3	0	0	0.8	1.000
1933			1	2	.333	5.25	27	2	0	70.1	80	20	41	0	1	1	0	22	4	0	.182	4	16	0	0	0.7	1.000
1934			5	1	.833	3.86	21	1	0	51.1	53	21	20	0	5	0	0	15	3	0	.200	0	14	1	0	0.7	.933
1935	2 teams		CLE A	(1G 0–0)		WAS A	(10G 2–0)																				
"	total		2	0	1.000	7.31	11	2	0	32	45	19	6	0	2	0	0	8	3	1	.375	0	4	0	0	0.4	1.000
5 yrs.			11	7	.611	5.32	86	8	2	235	288	96	89	0	11	3	2	72	19	1	.264	7	54	2	0	0.7	.968

Year	Team		W	L	PCT	ERA	G	GS	CG	IP	H	BB	SO	ShO	Relief Pitching W	L	SV	Batting AB	H	HR	BA	PO	A	E	DP	TC/G	FA

Dave Beard

BEARD, CHARLES DAVID
B. Oct. 2, 1959, Atlanta, Ga. BL TR 6'5" 190 lbs.

Year	Team		W	L	PCT	ERA	G	GS	CG	IP	H	BB	SO	ShO	W	L	SV	AB	H	HR	BA	PO	A	E	DP	TC/G	FA
1980	OAK	A	0	1	.000	3.38	13	0	0	16	12	7	12	0	0	1	1	0	0	0	–	0	2	0	0	0.2	1.000
1981			1	1	.500	2.77	8	0	0	13	9	4	15	0	1	1	3	0	0	0	–	2	1	0	0	0.4	1.000
1982			10	9	.526	3.44	54	2	0	91.2	85	35	73	0	10	7	11	0	0	0	–	3	11	2	1	0.3	.875
1983			5	5	.500	5.61	43	0	0	61	55	36	40	0	5	5	10	0	0	0	–	1	3	0	0	0.1	1.000
1984	SEA	A	3	2	.600	5.80	43	0	0	76	88	33	40	0	3	2	5	0	0	0	–	2	12	1	0	0.3	.933
1985	CHI	N	0	0	–	6.39	9	0	0	12.2	16	7	4	0	0	0	0	0	0	0	–	0	2	0	0	0.2	1.000
1989	DET	A	0	2	.000	5.06	2	1	0	5.1	9	2	1	0	0	1	0	0	0	0	–	1	0	0	0	1.0	1.000
7 yrs.			19	20	.487	4.70	172	3	0	275.2	274	124	185	0	19	17	30	0	0	0	–	9	32	3	1	0.3	.932

DIVISIONAL PLAYOFF SERIES

| 1981 | OAK | A | 0 | 0 | – | 0.00 | 1 | 0 | 0 | 1.1 | 0 | 0 | 2 | 0 | 0 | 0 | 0 | 0 | 0 | 0 | – | 0 | 0 | 0 | 0 | 0.0 | – |

LEAGUE CHAMPIONSHIP SERIES

| 1981 | OAK | A | 0 | 0 | – | 40.50 | 1 | 0 | 0 | .2 | 5 | 0 | 0 | 0 | 0 | 0 | 0 | 0 | 0 | 0 | – | 0 | 0 | 0 | 0 | 0.0 | – |

Mike Beard

BEARD, MICHAEL RICHARD
B. June 21, 1950, Little Rock, Ark. BL TL 6'1" 185 lbs.

Year	Team		W	L	PCT	ERA	G	GS	CG	IP	H	BB	SO	ShO	W	L	SV	AB	H	HR	BA	PO	A	E	DP	TC/G	FA
1974	ATL	N	0	0	–	3.00	6	0	0	9	5	1	7	0	0	0	0	0	0	0	–	1	2	0	0	0.5	1.000
1975			4	0	1.000	3.21	34	2	0	70	71	28	27	0	4	0	0	9	1	0	.111	2	13	1	1	0.5	.938
1976			0	2	.000	4.24	30	0	0	34	38	14	8	0	0	2	1	1	0	0	.000	3	9	0	1	0.4	1.000
1977			0	0	–	9.00	4	0	0	5	14	2	1	0	0	0	0	0	0	0	–	0	1	0	0	0.3	1.000
4 yrs.			4	2	.667	3.74	74	2	0	118	128	45	43	0	4	2	1	10	1	0	.100	6	25	1	2	0.4	.969

Ralph Beard

BEARD, RALPH WILLIAM
B. Feb. 11, 1929, Cincinnati, Ohio BR TR 6'5" 200 lbs.

Year	Team		W	L	PCT	ERA	G	GS	CG	IP	H	BB	SO	ShO	W	L	SV	AB	H	HR	BA	PO	A	E	DP	TC/G	FA
1954	STL	N	0	4	.000	3.72	13	10	0	58	62	28	17	0	0	0	0	17	1	0	.059	0	8	1	1	0.7	.889

Gene Bearden

BEARDEN, HENRY EUGENE
B. Sept. 5, 1920, Lexa, Ark. BL TL 6'4" 198 lbs.

Year	Team		W	L	PCT	ERA	G	GS	CG	IP	H	BB	SO	ShO	W	L	SV	AB	H	HR	BA	PO	A	E	DP	TC/G	FA
1947	CLE	A	0	0	–	81.00	1	0	0	.1	2	1	0	0	0	0	0	0	0	0	–	0	0	0	0	0.0	–
1948			20	7	.741	2.43	37	29	15	229.2	187	106	80	6	0	2	1	90	23	2	.256	15	52	1	11	1.8	.985
1949			8	8	.500	5.10	32	19	5	127	140	92	41	0	1	1	0	45	5	0	.111	9	42	1	2	1.6	.981
1950	2 teams		CLE A	(14G 1–3)			WAS A	(12G 3–5)																				
"	total		4	8	.333	4.99	26	12	4	113.2	138	65	30	0	1	2	0	35	7	0	.200	6	22	7	0	1.3	.800
1951	2 teams		WAS A	(1G 0–0)			DET A	(37G 3–4)																				
"	total		3	4	.429	4.64	38	5	2	108.2	118	60	39	1	2	2	0	32	6	0	.188	3	21	1	0	0.7	.960
1952	STL	A	7	8	.467	4.30	34	16	3	150.2	158	78	45	0	3	1	0	65	23	0	.354	12	32	2	0	1.4	.957
1953	CHI	A	3	3	.500	2.93	25	3	0	58.1	48	33	24	0	3	1	0	21	4	0	.190	2	11	3	0	0.6	.813
7 yrs.			45	38	.542	3.96	193	84	29	788.1	791	435	259	7	7	10	1	288	68	4	.236	47	180	15	13	1.3	.938

WORLD SERIES

| 1948 | CLE | A | 1 | 0 | 1.000 | 0.00 | 2 | 1 | 1 | 10.2 | 6 | 1 | 4 | 1 | 0 | 0 | 1 | 4 | 2 | 0 | .500 | 0 | 7 | 0 | 1 | 3.5 | 1.000 |

Gary Beare

BEARE, GARY RAY
B. Aug. 22, 1952, San Diego, Calif. BR TR 6'4" 205 lbs.

Year	Team		W	L	PCT	ERA	G	GS	CG	IP	H	BB	SO	ShO	W	L	SV	AB	H	HR	BA	PO	A	E	DP	TC/G	FA
1976	MIL	A	2	3	.400	3.29	6	5	2	41	43	15	32	0	0	0	0	0	0	0	–	2	4	1	1	1.2	.857
1977			3	3	.500	6.41	17	6	0	59	63	38	32	0	2	0	0	0	0	0	–	5	16	0	0	1.2	1.000
2 yrs.			5	6	.455	5.13	23	11	2	100	106	53	64	0	2	0	0	0	0	0	–	7	20	1	1	1.2	.964

Larry Bearnarth

BEARNARTH, LAWRENCE DONALD
B. Sept. 11, 1941, New York, N. Y. BR TR 6'2" 203 lbs.

Year	Team		W	L	PCT	ERA	G	GS	CG	IP	H	BB	SO	ShO	W	L	SV	AB	H	HR	BA	PO	A	E	DP	TC/G	FA
1963	NY	N	3	8	.273	3.42	58	2	0	126.1	127	47	48	0	3	7	4	30	6	0	.200	11	35	3	1	0.8	.939
1964			5	5	.500	4.15	44	1	0	78	79	38	31	0	5	4	3	14	2	0	.143	9	27	0	0	0.8	1.000
1965			3	5	.375	4.60	40	3	0	60.2	75	28	16	0	3	3	1	9	1	0	.111	2	15	2	2	0.5	.895
1966			2	3	.400	4.45	29	1	0	54.2	59	20	27	0	2	2	0	9	1	0	.111	4	14	0	0	0.6	1.000
1971	MIL	A	0	0	–	18.00	2	0	0	3	10	2	2	0	0	0	0	0	0	0	–	1	1	0	0	1.0	1.000
5 yrs.			13	21	.382	4.13	173	7	0	322.2	350	135	124	0	13	16	8	62	10	0	.161	27	92	5	3	0.7	.960

Eb Beatin

BEATIN, EBENEZER AMBROSE
B. Aug. 10, 1866, Baltimore, Md. D. May 9, 1925, Baltimore, Md. BR TR 5'9" 162 lbs.

Year	Team		W	L	PCT	ERA	G	GS	CG	IP	H	BB	SO	ShO	W	L	SV	AB	H	HR	BA	PO	A	E	DP	TC/G	FA
1887	DET	N	1	1	.500	4.00	2	2	2	18	13	8	6	0	0	0	0	7	0	0	.000	0	2	0	0	1.0	1.000
1888			5	7	.417	2.86	12	12	12	107	111	16	44	0	0	0	0	56	14	2	.250	4	24	4	0	2.7	.875
1889	CLE	N	20	15	.571	3.57	36	36	35	317.2	316	141	126	3	0	0	0	121	14	1	.116	15	52	6	1	2.0	.918
1890			22	31	.415	3.83	54	54	53	474.1	518	186	155	1	0	0	0	191	27	1	.141	30	101	8	7	2.6	.942
1891			0	3	.000	5.28	5	4	2	29	39	21	4	0	0	0	0	13	1	0	.077	0	6	0	0	1.2	1.000
5 yrs.			48	57	.457	3.68	109	108	104	946	997	372	335	4	0	0	0	388	56	4	.144	49	185	18	8	2.3	.929

Jim Beattie

BEATTIE, JAMES LOUIS
B. July 4, 1954, Hampton, Va. BR TR 6'5" 210 lbs.

Year	Team		W	L	PCT	ERA	G	GS	CG	IP	H	BB	SO	ShO	W	L	SV	AB	H	HR	BA	PO	A	E	DP	TC/G	FA
1978	NY	A	6	9	.400	3.73	25	22	0	128	123	51	65	0	0	0	0	0	0	0	–	14	21	3	2	1.5	.921
1979			3	6	.333	5.21	15	13	1	76	85	41	32	1	0	0	0	0	0	0	–	9	16	1	1	1.7	.962
1980	SEA	A	5	15	.250	4.86	33	29	3	187	205	98	67	0	0	1	0	0	0	0	–	10	30	0	1	1.2	1.000
1981			3	2	.600	2.96	13	9	0	67	59	18	36	0	0	0	1	0	0	0	–	8	11	1	0	1.5	.950
1982			8	12	.400	3.34	28	26	6	172.1	149	65	140	1	0	0	0	0	0	0	–	16	21	1	2	1.4	.974
1983			10	15	.400	3.84	30	29	8	196.2	197	66	132	2	0	0	0	0	0	0	–	18	37	2	5	1.9	.965
1984			12	16	.429	3.41	32	32	12	211	206	75	119	2	0	0	0	0	0	0	–	13	33	0	2	1.4	1.000
1985			5	6	.455	7.29	18	15	1	70.1	93	33	45	1	0	0	0	0	0	0	–	4	6	1	0	0.6	.909
1986			0	6	.000	6.02	9	7	0	40.1	57	14	24	0	0	0	0	0	0	0	–	4	6	0	2	1.1	1.000
9 yrs.			52	87	.374	4.17	203	182	31	1148.2	1174	461	660	7	0	1	1	0	0	0	–	96	181	9	15	1.4	.969

Year	Team		W	L	PCT	ERA	G	GS	CG	IP	H	BB	SO	ShO	Relief Pitching W	L	SV	Batting AB	H	HR	BA	PO	A	E	DP	TC/G	FA

Jim Beattie *continued*
LEAGUE CHAMPIONSHIP SERIES

| 1978 | NY | A | 1 | 0 | 1.000 | 1.69 | 1 | 1 | 0 | 5.1 | 2 | 5 | 3 | 0 | 0 | 0 | 0 | 0 | 0 | 0 | – | 2 | 0 | 0 | 0 | 2.0 | 1.000 |

WORLD SERIES

| 1978 | NY | A | 1 | 0 | 1.000 | 2.00 | 1 | 1 | 1 | 9 | 9 | 4 | 8 | 0 | 0 | 0 | 0 | 0 | 0 | 0 | – | 0 | 1 | 0 | 0 | 1.0 | 1.000 |

Blaine Beatty
BEATTY, GORDON BLAINE
B. Apr. 25, 1964, Victoria, Tex.
BL TL 6'2" 185 lbs.

| 1989 | NY | N | 0 | 0 | – | 1.50 | 2 | 1 | 0 | 6 | 5 | 2 | 3 | 0 | 0 | 0 | 0 | 2 | 1 | 0 | .500 | 2 | 0 | 0 | 0 | 1.0 | 1.000 |

Johnny Beazley
BEAZLEY, JOHN ANDREW
B. May 25, 1918, Nashville, Tenn.
BR TR 6'1½" 190 lbs.

1941	STL	N	1	0	1.000	1.00	1	1	1	9	10	3	4	0	0	0	0	3	0	0	.000	0	1	0	0	1.0	1.000
1942			21	6	.778	2.13	43	23	13	215.1	181	73	91	3	6	3	3	73	10	0	.137	10	48	1	1	1.4	.983
1946			7	5	.583	4.46	19	18	5	103	109	55	36	0	0	0	0	33	8	0	.242	10	16	1	1	1.4	.963
1947	BOS	N	2	0	1.000	4.40	9	2	2	28.2	30	19	12	0	0	0	0	7	0	0	.000	3	4	0	0	0.8	1.000
1948			0	1	.000	4.50	3	2	0	16	19	7	4	0	0	0	0	4	0	0	.000	1	2	0	0	1.0	1.000
1949			0	0	–	0.00	1	0	0	2	0	0	0	0	0	0	0	0	0	0	–	0	0	0	0	0.0	–
	6 yrs.		31	12	.721	3.01	76	46	21	374	349	157	147	3	6	3	3	120	18	0	.150	24	71	2	2	1.3	.979

WORLD SERIES

1942	STL	N	2	0	1.000	2.50	2	2	2	18	17	3	6	0	0	0	0	7	1	0	.143	2	0	1	0	1.5	.667
1946			0	0	–	0.00	1	0	0	1	1	0	1	0	0	0	0	0	0	0	–	0	1	0	0	1.0	1.000
	2 yrs.		2	0	1.000	2.37	3	2	2	19	18	3	7	0	0	0	0	7	1	0	.143	2	1	1	0	1.3	.750

Buck Becannon
BECANNON, JAMES MELVIN
B. Aug. 22, 1859, New York, N. Y. D. Nov. 5, 1923, New York, N. Y.
5'10" 165 lbs.

1884	NY	AA	1	0	1.000	1.50	1	1	1	6	2	2	2	0	0	0	0	3	0	0	.000	0	2	0	0	2.0	1.000
1885			2	8	.200	6.25	10	10	10	85	108	24	13	0	0	0	0	33	10	0	.303	1	17	0	0	1.8	1.000
1887	NY	N	0	0	–	0.00	0	0	0	0	0	0	0	0	0	0	0	5	0	0	.000	0	0	0	0	0.0	–
	3 yrs.		3	8	.273	5.93	11	11	11	91	110	26	15	0	0	0	0	41	10	0	.244	1	19	0	0	1.8	1.000

Boom-Boom Beck
BECK, WALTER WILLIAM
B. Oct. 16, 1904, Decatur, Ill. D. May 7, 1987, Champaign, Ill.
BR TR 6'2" 200 lbs.

1924	STL	A	0	0	–	0.00	1	0	0	1	2	1	0	0	0	0	0	0	0	0	–	0	1	0	0	1.0	1.000
1927			1	0	1.000	5.56	3	1	1	11.1	15	5	6	0	0	0	0	4	1	0	.250	1	1	0	0	0.7	1.000
1928			2	3	.400	4.41	16	4	2	49	52	20	17	0	1	0	0	14	6	0	.429	0	11	1	2	0.8	.917
1933	BKN	N	12	20	.375	3.54	43	35	15	257	270	69	89	3	1	1	1	95	18	0	.189	12	52	3	4	1.6	.955
1934			2	6	.250	7.42	22	9	2	57	72	32	24	0	1	1	0	17	4	0	.235	2	17	0	2	0.9	1.000
1939	PHI	N	7	14	.333	4.73	34	16	12	182.2	203	64	77	0	3	4	3	68	9	0	.132	8	37	6	1	1.5	.882
1940			4	9	.308	4.31	29	15	4	129.1	147	41	38	0	2	0	0	36	2	0	.056	10	32	3	0	1.6	.933
1941			1	9	.100	4.63	34	7	2	95.1	104	35	34	0	0	3	0	25	3	0	.120	3	6	1	0	0.3	.900
1942			0	1	.000	4.75	26	2	1	53	69	17	10	0	0	0	0	12	4	0	.333	3	9	1	2	0.5	.923
1943			0	0	–	9.88	7	0	0	13.2	24	5	3	0	0	0	0	4	2	0	.500	4	0	0	0	1.0	1.000
1944	DET	A	1	2	.333	3.89	28	2	0	74	67	27	25	0	1	1	1	22	7	0	.318	0	6	1	1	0.3	.857
1945	2 teams		CIN N		(11G 2–4)		PIT N		(14G 6–1)																			
"	total		8	5	.615	2.68	25	11	6	110.2	96	26	29	0	2	1	0	30	5	0	.167	4	21	0	0	1.0	1.000
	12 yrs.		38	69	.355	4.30	265	101	44	1034	1121	342	352	3	11	11	6	327	61	0	.187	47	193	16	12	1.0	.938

Frank Beck
BECK, FRANK J.
B. 1862, Poughkeepsie, N. Y. Deceased.
TR

| 1884 | 2 teams | | PIT AA | | (3G 0–3) | | BAL U | | (2G 0–2) | | | | | | | | | | | | | | | | | | | |
| " | total | | 0 | 5 | .000 | 6.62 | 5 | 5 | 4 | 34 | 50 | 10 | 18 | 0 | 0 | 0 | 0 | 32 | 6 | 0 | .188 | 2 | 7 | 0 | 0 | 1.8 | 1.000 |

George Beck
BECK, ERNEST GEORGE (Eaglebeak)
B. Feb. 21, 1890, South Bend, Ind. D. Oct. 29, 1973, South Bend, Ind.
BR TR 5'11" 165 lbs.

| 1914 | CLE | A | 0 | 0 | – | 0.00 | 1 | 0 | 0 | 1 | 1 | 0 | 0 | 0 | 0 | 0 | 0 | 0 | 0 | 0 | – | 0 | 0 | 0 | 0 | 0.0 | – |

Rich Beck
BECK, RICHARD HENRY
B. Jan. 21, 1941, Pasco, Wash.
BB TR 6'3" 190 lbs.

| 1965 | NY | A | 2 | 1 | .667 | 2.14 | 3 | 3 | 1 | 21 | 22 | 7 | 10 | 1 | 0 | 0 | 0 | 7 | 0 | 0 | .000 | 3 | 4 | 0 | 2 | 2.3 | 1.000 |

Bob Becker
BECKER, ROBERT CHARLES
B. Aug. 15, 1875, Syracuse, N. Y. D. Oct. 11, 1951, Syracuse, N. Y.
TL

1897	PHI	N	0	2	.000	5.63	5	2	2	24	32	7	10	0	0	0	0	9	1	0	.111	2	3	1	0	1.2	.833
1898			0	0	–	10.80	1	0	0	5	6	5	0	0	0	0	0	1	0	0	.000	0	2	0	0	2.0	1.000
	2 yrs.		0	2	.000	6.52	6	2	2	29	38	12	10	0	0	0	0	10	1	0	.100	2	5	1	0	1.3	.875

Charlie Becker
BECKER, CHARLES S. (Buck)
B. Oct. 14, 1888, Washington, D. C. D. July 30, 1928, Washington, D. C.
BL TL 6'2" 180 lbs.

1911	WAS	A	3	5	.375	4.04	11	5	5	71.1	80	23	31	0	0	3	0	22	5	0	.227	1	18	0	0	1.7	1.000
1912			0	0	–	3.00	4	0	0	9	8	6	5	0	0	0	0	2	1	0	.500	0	1	0	0	0.3	1.000
	2 yrs.		3	5	.375	3.92	15	5	5	80.1	88	29	36	1	0	3	0	24	6	0	.250	1	19	0	0	1.3	1.000

Jake Beckley
BECKLEY, JACOB PETER (St. Jacob)
B. Aug. 4, 1867, Hannibal, Mo. D. June 25, 1918, Kansas City, Mo.
Hall of Fame 1971.
BL TL 5'10" 200 lbs.

| 1902 | CIN | N | 0 | 1 | .000 | 6.75 | 1 | 1 | 0 | 4 | 9 | 1 | 2 | 0 | 0 | 0 | 0 | * | | | | 7 | 2 | 0 | 0 | 9.0 | 1.000 |

Year	Team		W	L	PCT	ERA	G	GS	CG	IP	H	BB	SO	ShO	W	L	SV	AB	H	HR	BA	PO	A	E	DP	TC/G	FA
															Relief Pitching			**Batting**									

Jim Beckman

BECKMAN, JAMES JOSEPH
B. Mar. 1, 1905, Cincinnati, Ohio
BR TR 5'10" 172 lbs.

Year	Team		W	L	PCT	ERA	G	GS	CG	IP	H	BB	SO	ShO	W	L	SV	AB	H	HR	BA	PO	A	E	DP	TC/G	FA
1927	CIN	N	0	1	.000	5.84	4	1	0	12.1	18	6	0	0	0	0	0	1	0	0	.000	0	0	1	0	0.3	—
1928			0	1	.000	5.87	6	0	0	15.1	19	9	4	0	0	1	0	3	0	0	.000	0	2	0	1	0.3	1.000
2 yrs.			0	2	.000	5.86	10	1	0	27.2	37	15	4	0	0	1	0	4	0	0	.000	0	2	1	1	0.3	.667

Bill Beckmann

BECKMANN, WILLIAM ALOYSIUS
B. Dec. 8, 1907, Clayton, Mo.
BR TR 6' 175 lbs.

Year	Team		W	L	PCT	ERA	G	GS	CG	IP	H	BB	SO	ShO	W	L	SV	AB	H	HR	BA	PO	A	E	DP	TC/G	FA
1939	PHI	A	7	11	.389	5.39	27	19	7	155.1	198	41	20	2	2	0	0	52	13	0	.250	10	19	0	0	1.1	1.000
1940			8	4	.667	4.17	34	9	6	127.1	132	35	47	2	3	2	1	39	8	0	.205	11	13	3	0	0.8	.889
1941			5	9	.357	4.57	22	15	4	130	141	33	28	0	3	0	1	47	9	0	.191	5	12	2	0	0.9	.895
1942	2 teams			PHI A	(5G 0–1)		STL N	(2G 1–0)																			
"	total		1	1	.500	5.27	7	1	0	27.1	28	10	13	0	1	0	0	5	2	0	.400	0	5	0	0	0.7	1.000
4 yrs.			21	25	.457	4.79	90	44	17	440	499	119	108	4	9	2	2	143	32	0	.224	26	49	5	0	0.9	.938

Joe Beckwith

BECKWITH, THOMAS JOSEPH
B. Jan. 28, 1955, Auburn, Ala.
BL TR 6'3" 180 lbs.

Year	Team		W	L	PCT	ERA	G	GS	CG	IP	H	BB	SO	ShO	W	L	SV	AB	H	HR	BA	PO	A	E	DP	TC/G	FA
1979	LA	N	1	2	.333	4.38	17	0	0	37	42	15	28	0	1	2	0	5	0	0	.000	5	5	2	0	0.7	.833
1980			3	3	.500	1.95	38	0	0	60	60	23	40	0	3	3	0	2	0	0	.000	1	7	2	0	0.3	.800
1982			2	1	.667	2.70	19	1	0	40	38	14	33	0	2	1	1	7	0	0	.000	2	2	0	0	0.5	1.000
1983			3	4	.429	3.55	42	3	0	71	73	35	50	0	3	2	1	5	1	0	.200	8	13	0	1	0.5	1.000
1984	KC	A	8	4	.667	3.40	49	1	0	100.2	92	25	75	0	8	3	2	0	0	0	—	10	12	0	1	0.4	1.000
1985			1	5	.167	4.07	49	0	0	95	99	32	80	0	1	5	1	0	0	0	—	7	12	2	1	0.4	.905
1986	LA	N	0	0	—	6.87	15	0	0	18.1	28	6	13	0	0	0	0	0	0	0	—	1	0	0	0	0.1	1.000
7 yrs.			18	19	.486	3.54	229	5	0	422	432	150	319	0	18	16	7	19	1	0	.053	34	51	6	3	0.4	.934

LEAGUE CHAMPIONSHIP SERIES

Year	Team		W	L	PCT	ERA	G	GS	CG	IP	H	BB	SO	ShO	W	L	SV	AB	H	HR	BA	PO	A	E	DP	TC/G	FA
1983	LA	N	0	0	—	0.00	2	0	0	2.1	1	2	3	0	0	0	0	0	0	0	—	0	0	0	0	0.0	—

WORLD SERIES

Year	Team		W	L	PCT	ERA	G	GS	CG	IP	H	BB	SO	ShO	W	L	SV	AB	H	HR	BA	PO	A	E	DP	TC/G	FA
1985	KC	A	0	0	—	0.00	1	0	0	2	1	0	3	0	0	0	0	0	0	0	—	0	0	0	0	0.0	—

Julio Becquer

BECQUER, JULIO
Born Julio Becquer y Villegas.
B. Dec. 20, 1931, Havana, Cuba
BL TL 5'11½" 178 lbs.

Year	Team		W	L	PCT	ERA	G	GS	CG	IP	H	BB	SO	ShO	W	L	SV	AB	H	HR	BA	PO	A	E	DP	TC/G	FA
1960	WAS	A	0	0	—	9.00	1	0	0	1	1	1	0	0	0	0	0	298	75	4	.252	0	0	0	0	0.0	—
1961	2 teams			LA A	(0G 0–0)		MIN A	(1G 0–0)																				
"	total		0	0	—	20.25	1	0	0	1.1	4	1	0	0	0	0	0	92	20	0	.217	0	0	0	0	0.0	—
2 yrs.			0	0	—	15.43	2	0	0	2.1	5	1	0	0	0	0	0	*				0	0	0	0	0.0	—

Phil Bedgood

BEDGOOD, PHILLIP BURLETTE
B. Mar. 8, 1898, Harrison, Ga. D. Nov. 8, 1927, Fort Pierce, Fla.
BR TR 6'3" 218 lbs.

Year	Team		W	L	PCT	ERA	G	GS	CG	IP	H	BB	SO	ShO	W	L	SV	AB	H	HR	BA	PO	A	E	DP	TC/G	FA
1922	CLE	A	1	0	1.000	4.00	1	1	1	9	7	4	5	0	0	0	0	2	0	0	.000	1	1	0	0	2.0	1.000
1923			0	2	.000	5.30	9	2	0	18.2	16	14	7	0	0	1	0	4	1	0	.250	0	5	0	0	0.6	1.000
2 yrs.			1	2	.333	4.88	10	3	1	27.2	23	18	12	0	0	1	0	6	1	0	.167	1	6	0	0	0.7	1.000

Hugh Bedient

BEDIENT, HUGH CARPENTER
B. Oct. 23, 1889, Gerry, N. Y. D. July 21, 1965, Jamestown, N. Y.
BR TR 6' 185 lbs.

Year	Team		W	L	PCT	ERA	G	GS	CG	IP	H	BB	SO	ShO	W	L	SV	AB	H	HR	BA	PO	A	E	DP	TC/G	FA
1912	BOS	A	20	9	.690	2.92	41	28	19	231	206	55	122	0	6	0	2	73	14	0	.192	6	67	2	1	1.8	.973
1913			15	14	.517	2.78	43	29	19	259	255	67	122	1	3	1	5	80	10	0	.125	9	55	3	0	1.6	.955
1914			8	12	.400	3.60	42	16	7	177.1	185	45	70	1	3	5	2	50	5	0	.100	5	52	5	2	1.5	.919
1915	BUF	F	15	18	.455	3.17	53	30	16	269.1	284	69	106	2	3	1	10	83	9	0	.108	5	74	7	2	1.6	.919
4 yrs.			58	53	.523	3.08	179	103	61	936.2	930	236	420	4	15	7	19	286	38	0	.133	25	248	17	5	1.6	.941

WORLD SERIES

Year	Team		W	L	PCT	ERA	G	GS	CG	IP	H	BB	SO	ShO	W	L	SV	AB	H	HR	BA	PO	A	E	DP	TC/G	FA
1912	BOS	A	1	0	1.000	0.50	4	2	1	18	10	7	7	0	0	0	0	6	0	0	.000	0	1	0	0	0.3	1.000

Andy Bednar

BEDNAR, ANDREW JACKSON
B. Aug. 16, 1908, Streator, Ill. D. Nov. 26, 1937, Graham, Tex.
BR TR 5'10½" 180 lbs.

Year	Team		W	L	PCT	ERA	G	GS	CG	IP	H	BB	SO	ShO	W	L	SV	AB	H	HR	BA	PO	A	E	DP	TC/G	FA
1930	PIT	N	0	0	—	27.00	2	0	0	1.1	4	1	1	0	0	0	0	0	0	0	—	0	1	0	0	0.5	1.000
1931			0	0	—	11.25	3	0	0	4	10	0	2	0	0	0	0	0	0	0	—	0	1	0	0	0.3	1.000
2 yrs.			0	0	—	15.19	5	0	0	5.1	14	1	3	0	0	0	0	0	0	0	—	0	2	0	0	0.4	1.000

Steve Bedrosian

BEDROSIAN, STEPHEN WAYNE (Bedrock)
B. Dec. 6, 1957, Methuen, Mass.
BR TR 6'3" 200 lbs.

Year	Team		W	L	PCT	ERA	G	GS	CG	IP	H	BB	SO	ShO	W	L	SV	AB	H	HR	BA	PO	A	E	DP	TC/G	FA
1981	ATL	N	1	2	.333	4.50	15	1	0	24	15	15	9	0	1	1	0	2	0	0	.000	1	2	0	1	0.2	1.000
1982			8	6	.571	2.42	64	3	0	137.2	102	57	123	0	7	4	11	26	1	0	.038	12	14	1	2	0.4	.963
1983			9	10	.474	3.60	70	1	0	120	100	51	114	0	9	10	19	19	2	0	.105	4	16	0	2	0.3	1.000
1984			9	6	.600	2.37	40	4	0	83.2	65	33	81	0	6	5	11	17	2	0	.118	1	8	1	0	0.2	.900
1985			7	15	.318	3.83	37	37	0	206.2	198	111	134	0	0	0	0	64	5	0	.078	13	23	4	3	1.1	.900
1986	PHI	N	8	6	.571	3.39	68	0	0	90.1	79	34	82	0	8	6	29	5	1	0	.200	2	10	0	1	0.2	1.000
1987			5	3	.625	2.83	65	0	0	89	79	28	74	0	5	3	**40**	0	0	0	—	3	7	0	0	0.2	1.000
1988			6	6	.500	3.75	57	0	0	74.1	75	27	61	0	6	6	28	2	0	0	.000	5	9	0	0	0.2	1.000
1989	2 teams			PHI N	(28G 2–3)		SF N	(40G 1–4)																				
"	total		3	7	.300	2.87	68	0	0	84.2	56	39	58	0	3	7	23	6	1	0	.167	2	5	1	0	0.1	.875
9 yrs.			56	61	.479	3.23	484	46	0	910.1	769	395	736	0	45	42	161	145	12	0	.083	43	94	7	10	0.3	.951

LEAGUE CHAMPIONSHIP SERIES

Year	Team		W	L	PCT	ERA	G	GS	CG	IP	H	BB	SO	ShO	W	L	SV	AB	H	HR	BA	PO	A	E	DP	TC/G	FA
1982	ATL	N	0	0	—	18.00	2	0	0	1	3	1	0	0	0	0	0	0	0	0	—	0	0	0	0	0.0	—
1989	SF	N	0	0	—	2.70	4	0	0	3.1	4	2	2	0	0	0	3	0	0	0	—	0	0	0	0	0.0	—
2 yrs.			0	0	—	6.23	6	0	0	4.1	7	3	4	0	0	0	3	0	0	0	—	0	0	0	0	0.0	—

Year	Team		W	L	PCT	ERA	G	GS	CG	IP	H	BB	SO	ShO	Relief Pitching W	L	SV	Batting AB	H	HR	BA	PO	A	E	DP	TC/G	FA

Steve Bedrosian continued

WORLD SERIES

| 1989 | SF | N | 0 | 0 | – | 0.00 | 2 | 0 | 0 | 2.2 | 0 | 2 | 2 | 0 | 0 | 0 | 0 | 0 | 0 | 0 | – | 0 | 0 | 0 | 0 | 0.0 | – |

Fred Beebe

BEEBE, FREDERICK LEONARD
B. Dec. 31, 1880, Lincoln, Neb. D. Oct. 30, 1957, Elgin, Ill.
BR TR 6'1" 190 lbs.

1906	2 teams	CHI N (14G 7-1)		STL N	(20G 9-9)																						
"	total		16	10	.615	2.93	34	25	20	230.2	171	100	171	1	3	0	1	87	13	0	.149	9	54	9	1	2.1	.875
1907	STL	N	7	19	.269	2.72	31	29	24	238.1	192	109	141	4	1	0	0	86	11	0	.128	18	62	5	3	2.7	.941
1908			5	13	.278	2.63	29	19	12	174.1	134	66	72	0	0	1	0	56	7	0	.125	9	54	2	5	2.2	.969
1909			15	21	.417	2.82	44	34	18	287.2	256	104	105	1	2	3	1	108	18	0	.167	15	81	7	3	2.3	.932
1910	CIN	N	12	15	.444	3.07	35	26	11	214.1	193	94	93	2	3	0	0	73	12	0	.164	9	74	4	1	2.5	.954
1911	PHI	N	3	3	.500	4.47	9	8	3	48.1	52	24	20	0	0	0	0	19	5	0	.263	2	18	0	0	2.0	1.000
1916	CLE	A	5	3	.625	2.41	20	12	5	100.2	92	37	32	1	0	0	2	28	6	0	.214	8	27	4	1	2.0	.897
7 yrs.			63	84	.429	2.86	202	153	93	1294.1	1090	534	634	9	9	4	4	457	72	0	.158	68	370	31	14	2.3	.934

Ed Beecher

BEECHER, EDWARD H.
B. July 2, 1860, Guilford, Conn. D. Sept. 12, 1935, Hartford, Conn.
BL TL 5'10" 185 lbs.

| 1890 | BUF | P | 0 | 0 | – | 12.00 | 1 | 0 | 0 | 6 | 10 | 3 | 0 | 0 | 0 | 0 | 0 | * | | | | 0 | 0 | 0 | 0 | 0.0 | – |

Roy Beecher

BEECHER, LeROY (Colonel)
B. May 10, 1884, Swanton, Ohio D. Oct. 11, 1952, Toledo, Ohio
BL TR 6'2" 180 lbs.

1907	NY	N	0	2	.000	2.57	2	2	2	14	17	6	5	0	0	0	0	5	0	0	.000	0	3	1	0	2.0	.750
1908			0	0	–	7.94	2	0	0	5.2	11	3	0	0	0	0	1	3	1	0	.333	1	3	0	0	2.0	1.000
2 yrs.			0	2	.000	4.12	4	2	2	19.2	28	9	5	0	0	0	1	8	1	0	.125	1	6	1	0	2.0	.875

Andy Beene

BEENE, RAMON ANDREW
B. Oct. 13, 1956, Freeport, Tex.
BR TR 6'3" 205 lbs.

1983	MIL	A	0	0	–	4.50	1	0	0	2	3	1	0	0	0	0	0	0	0	0	–	0	0	0	0	0.0	–
1984			0	2	.000	11.09	5	3	0	18.2	28	9	11	0	0	0	0	0	0	0	–	1	4	0	1	1.0	1.000
2 yrs.			0	2	.000	10.45	6	3	0	20.2	31	10	11	0	0	0	0	0	0	0	–	1	4	0	1	0.8	1.000

Fred Beene

BEENE, FREDDY RAY
B. Nov. 24, 1942, Angleton, Tex.
BB TR 5'9" 155 lbs.

1968	BAL	A	0	0	–	9.00	1	0	0	1	2	1	1	0	0	0	0	0	0	0	–	0	0	0	0	0.0	–
1969			0	0	–	0.00	2	0	0	2.2	2	1	0	0	0	0	0	0	0	0	–	1	0	0	0	0.5	1.000
1970			0	0	–	6.00	4	0	0	6	8	5	4	0	0	0	0	0	0	0	–	0	0	0	0	0.0	–
1972	NY	A	1	3	.250	2.33	29	1	0	58	55	24	37	0	1	3	3	9	0	0	.000	8	6	1	1	0.5	.933
1973			6	0	1.000	1.68	19	4	0	91	67	27	49	0	4	0	1	0	0	0	–	9	15	0	2	1.3	1.000
1974	2 teams	NY A (6G 0-0)		CLE A	(32G 4-4)																						
"	total		4	4	.500	4.66	38	0	0	83	77	28	45	0	4	3	0	0	0	0	–	9	17	0	0	0.7	1.000
1975	CLE	A	1	0	1.000	6.94	19	1	0	46.2	63	25	20	0	1	0	1	0	0	0	–	3	9	0	0	0.6	1.000
7 yrs.			12	7	.632	3.62	112	6	0	288.1	274	111	156	0	10	7	8	9	0	0	.000	30	47	1	3	0.7	.987

Clarence Beers

BEERS, CLARENCE SCOTT
B. Dec. 9, 1918, El Dorado, Kans.
BR TR 6' 175 lbs.

| 1948 | STL | N | 0 | 0 | – | 13.50 | 1 | 0 | 0 | .2 | 3 | 1 | 0 | 0 | 0 | 0 | 0 | 0 | 0 | 0 | – | 0 | 0 | 0 | 0 | 0.0 | – |

Joe Beggs

BEGGS, JOSEPH STANLEY (Fireman)
B. Nov. 4, 1910, Rankin, Pa. D. July 19, 1983, Indianapolis, Ind.
BR TR 6'1" 182 lbs.

1938	NY	A	3	2	.600	5.40	14	9	4	58.1	69	20	8	0	0	0	0	20	5	0	.250	1	19	0	4	1.4	1.000
1940	CIN	N	12	3	.800	2.00	37	1	0	76.2	68	21	25	0	12	3	7	21	4	0	.190	6	20	0	3	0.7	1.000
1941			4	3	.571	3.79	37	0	0	57	57	27	19	0	4	3	5	10	3	0	.300	3	12	1	1	0.4	.938
1942			6	5	.545	2.13	38	0	0	88.2	65	33	24	0	6	5	8	21	0	0	.000	6	31	0	2	1.0	1.000
1943			7	6	.538	2.34	39	4	4	115.1	120	25	28	2	4	5	6	35	5	0	.143	5	30	0	2	0.9	1.000
1944			1	0	1.000	2.00	2	1	1	9	8	2	5	0	0	0	0	4	0	0	.000	1	2	0	1	3.0	1.000
1946			12	10	.545	2.32	28	22	14	190	175	39	38	2	0	1	1	63	14	0	.222	11	45	1	2	2.0	.982
1947	2 teams	CIN N (11G 0-3)		NY N	(32G 3-3)																						
"	total		3	6	.333	4.58	43	4	0	98.1	123	24	34	0	3	3	2	24	2	0	.083	6	20	0	0	0.6	1.000
1948	NY	N	0	0	–	0.00	1	0	0	.1	2	0	0	0	0	0	0	0	0	0	–	0	0	0	0	0.0	–
9 yrs.			48	35	.578	2.96	238	41	23	693.2	687	189	178	4	29	20	29	198	33	0	.167	39	179	2	14	0.9	.991

WORLD SERIES

| 1940 | CIN | N | 0 | 0 | – | 9.00 | 1 | 0 | 0 | 1 | 3 | 0 | 1 | 0 | 0 | 0 | 0 | 0 | 0 | 0 | – | 0 | 0 | 0 | 0 | 0.0 | – |

Ed Begley

BEGLEY, EDWARD N.
Born Edward N. Bagley.
B. 1863, New York, N.Y. D. July 24, 1919, Waterbury, Conn.

1884	NY	N	12	18	.400	4.16	31	30	30	266	296	99	104	0	0	0	0	121	22	0	.182	16	46	9	2	2.3	.873
1885	NY	AA	4	9	.308	4.93	15	14	10	115	131	48	44	0	0	0	0	52	9	1	.173	7	25	6	0	2.5	.842
2 yrs.			16	27	.372	4.39	46	44	40	381	427	147	148	0	0	0	0	173	31	1	.179	23	71	15	2	2.4	.862

Petie Behan

BEHAN, CHARLES FREDERICK
B. Dec. 11, 1887, Dallas City, Pa. D. Jan. 22, 1957, Bradford, Pa.
BR TR 5'10" 160 lbs.

1921	PHI	N	0	1	.000	5.91	2	2	1	10.2	17	1	3	0	0	0	0	4	0	0	.000	2	1	0	0	1.5	1.000
1922			4	2	.667	2.47	7	5	3	47.1	49	14	13	1	1	0	0	20	5	0	.250	2	6	1	0	1.3	.889
1923			3	12	.200	5.50	31	17	5	131	182	57	27	0	0	1	2	43	8	0	.186	7	27	2	1	1.2	.944
3 yrs.			7	15	.318	4.76	40	24	9	189	248	72	43	1	1	1	2	67	13	0	.194	11	34	3	1	1.2	.938

Year	Team	W	L	PCT	ERA	G	GS	CG	IP	H	BB	SO	ShO	W	L	SV	AB	H	HR	BA	PO	A	E	DP	TC/G	FA

(Header spanning: Relief Pitching = W L SV; Batting = AB H HR)

Rick Behenna

BEHENNA, RICHARD KIPP
B. Mar. 6, 1960, Miami, Fla.
BR TR 6'2" 170 lbs.

Year	Team	W	L	PCT	ERA	G	GS	CG	IP	H	BB	SO	ShO	W	L	SV	AB	H	HR	BA	PO	A	E	DP	TC/G	FA
1983	2 teams	ATL N		(14G 3–3)		CLE A		(5G 0–2)																		
"	total	3	5	.375	4.41	19	10	0	63.1	59	26	26	0	0	2	0	12	4	1	.333	5	8	0	1	0.7	1.000
1984	CLE A	0	3	.000	13.97	3	3	0	9.2	17	8	6	0	0	0	0	0	0	0	–	3	0	0	0	1.0	1.000
1985		0	2	.000	7.78	4	4	0	19.2	29	8	4	0	0	0	0	0	0	0	–	0	1	0	0	0.3	1.000
3 yrs.		3	10	.231	6.12	26	17	0	92.2	105	42	36	0	0	2	0	12	4	1	.333	8	9	0	1	0.7	1.000

Mel Behney

BEHNEY, MELVIN BRIAN
B. Sept. 2, 1947, Newark, N. J.
BL TL 6'2" 180 lbs.

Year	Team	W	L	PCT	ERA	G	GS	CG	IP	H	BB	SO	ShO	W	L	SV	AB	H	HR	BA	PO	A	E	DP	TC/G	FA
1970	CIN N	0	2	.000	4.50	5	1	0	10	15	8	2	0	0	1	0	1	0	0	.000	0	1	0	0	0.2	1.000

Hank Behrman

BEHRMAN, HENRY BERNARD
B. June 27, 1921, Brooklyn, N. Y. D. Jan. 20, 1987, New York, N. Y.
BR TR 5'11" 174 lbs.

Year	Team	W	L	PCT	ERA	G	GS	CG	IP	H	BB	SO	ShO	W	L	SV	AB	H	HR	BA	PO	A	E	DP	TC/G	FA
1946	BKN N	11	5	.688	2.93	47	11	2	150.2	138	69	78	0	6	1	4	42	4	0	.095	10	18	2	0	0.6	.933
1947	2 teams	PIT N		(10G 0–2)		BKN N		(40G 5–3)																		
"	total	5	5	.500	6.25	50	8	0	116.2	130	65	44	0	1	4	8	32	6	0	.188	2	4	2	0	0.2	.750
1948	BKN N	5	4	.556	4.05	34	4	2	91	95	42	42	1	3	2	7	28	3	0	.107	3	15	0	1	0.5	1.000
1949	NY N	3	3	.500	4.92	43	4	1	71.1	64	52	25	0	2	2	0	13	1	0	.077	6	11	0	0	0.4	1.000
4 yrs.		24	17	.585	4.40	174	27	5	429.2	427	228	189	1	12	9	19	115	14	0	.122	21	48	4	1	0.4	.945

WORLD SERIES

Year	Team	W	L	PCT	ERA	G	GS	CG	IP	H	BB	SO	ShO	W	L	SV	AB	H	HR	BA	PO	A	E	DP	TC/G	FA
1947	BKN N	0	0	–	7.11	5	0	0	6.1	9	5	3	0	0	0	0	0	0	0	–	1	3	0	0	0.8	1.000

Tim Belcher

BELCHER, TIMOTHY WAYNE
B. Oct. 19, 1961, Mount Gilead, Ohio
BR TR 6'3" 210 lbs.

Year	Team	W	L	PCT	ERA	G	GS	CG	IP	H	BB	SO	ShO	W	L	SV	AB	H	HR	BA	PO	A	E	DP	TC/G	FA
1987	LA N	4	2	.667	2.38	6	5	0	34	30	7	23	0	1	0	0	10	2	0	.200	1	5	0	0	1.0	1.000
1988		12	6	.667	2.91	36	27	4	179.2	143	51	152	1	1	0	4	56	4	1	.071	14	19	0	2	0.9	1.000
1989		15	12	.556	2.82	39	30	10	230	182	80	200	8	1	2	1	70	7	0	.100	21	18	3	3	1.1	.929
3 yrs.		31	20	.608	2.82	81	62	14	443.2	355	138	375	9	3	2	5	136	13	1	.096	36	42	3	5	1.0	.963

LEAGUE CHAMPIONSHIP SERIES

Year	Team	W	L	PCT	ERA	G	GS	CG	IP	H	BB	SO	ShO	W	L	SV	AB	H	HR	BA	PO	A	E	DP	TC/G	FA
1988	LA N	2	0	1.000	4.11	2	2	0	15.1	12	4	16	0	0	0	0	8	1	0	.125	1	0	0	0	0.5	1.000

WORLD SERIES

Year	Team	W	L	PCT	ERA	G	GS	CG	IP	H	BB	SO	ShO	W	L	SV	AB	H	HR	BA	PO	A	E	DP	TC/G	FA
1988	LA N	1	0	1.000	6.23	2	2	0	8.2	10	6	10	0	0	0	0	0	0	0	–	0	0	0	0	0.0	–

Stan Belinda

BELINDA, STANLEY PETER
B. Aug. 6, 1966, Huntingdon, Pa.
BR TR 6'3" 185 lbs.

Year	Team	W	L	PCT	ERA	G	GS	CG	IP	H	BB	SO	ShO	W	L	SV	AB	H	HR	BA	PO	A	E	DP	TC/G	FA
1989	PIT N	0	1	.000	6.10	8	0	0	10.1	13	2	10	0	0	1	0	0	0	0	–	0	0	0	0	0.0	–

Bo Belinsky

BELINSKY, ROBERT
B. Dec. 7, 1936, New York, N. Y.
BL TL 6'2" 191 lbs.

Year	Team	W	L	PCT	ERA	G	GS	CG	IP	H	BB	SO	ShO	W	L	SV	AB	H	HR	BA	PO	A	E	DP	TC/G	FA
1962	LA A	10	11	.476	3.56	33	31	5	187.1	149	122	145	3	0	0	1	60	10	0	.167	6	30	4	2	1.2	.900
1963		2	9	.182	5.75	13	13	2	76.2	78	35	60	0	0	0	0	27	2	0	.074	2	16	0	1	1.4	1.000
1964		9	8	.529	2.86	23	22	4	135.1	120	49	91	1	0	0	0	42	4	0	.095	4	17	1	2	1.0	.955
1965	PHI N	4	9	.308	4.84	30	14	3	109.2	103	48	71	0	1	1	1	32	6	0	.188	5	17	4	1	0.9	.846
1966		0	2	.000	2.93	9	1	0	15.1	14	5	8	0	0	2	0	3	1	0	.333	0	3	0	0	0.3	1.000
1967	HOU N	3	9	.250	4.68	27	18	0	115.1	112	54	80	0	0	1	0	39	3	0	.077	3	11	2	0	0.6	.875
1969	PIT N	0	3	.000	4.50	8	3	0	18	17	14	15	0	0	0	0	2	0	0	.000	1	3	0	0	0.5	1.000
1970	CIN N	0	0	–	4.50	3	0	0	8	10	6	6	0	0	0	0	1	1	0	1.000	0	0	0	0	0.0	–
8 yrs.		28	51	.354	4.10	146	102	14	665.2	603	333	476	4	1	4	2	206	27	0	.131	21	97	11	4	0.9	.915

Bill Bell

BELL, WILLIAM SAMUEL (Ding Dong)
B. Oct. 24, 1933, Goldsboro, N. C. D. Oct. 11, 1962, Durham, N. C.
BR TR 6'3" 200 lbs.

Year	Team	W	L	PCT	ERA	G	GS	CG	IP	H	BB	SO	ShO	W	L	SV	AB	H	HR	BA	PO	A	E	DP	TC/G	FA
1952	PIT N	0	1	.000	4.60	4	1	0	15.2	16	13	4	0	0	0	0	4	0	0	.000	1	4	0	1	1.3	1.000
1955		0	0	–	0.00	1	0	0	1	0	1	0	0	0	0	0	0	0	0	–	0	0	0	0	0.0	–
2 yrs.		0	1	.000	4.32	5	1	0	16.2	16	14	4	0	0	0	0	4	0	0	.000	1	4	0	1	1.0	1.000

Charlie Bell

BELL, CHARLES C.
Brother of Frank Bell.
B. Aug. 12, 1868, Cincinnati, Ohio D. Feb. 7, 1937, Cincinnati, Ohio
TR

Year	Team	W	L	PCT	ERA	G	GS	CG	IP	H	BB	SO	ShO	W	L	SV	AB	H	HR	BA	PO	A	E	DP	TC/G	FA
1889	KC AA	1	0	1.000	1.00	1	1	1	9	4	3	3	0	0	0	0	6	1	0	.167	1	4	0	0	5.0	1.000
1891	2 teams	LOU AA		(10G 2–6)		CIN AA		(1G 1–0)																		
"	total	3	6	.333	4.19	11	10	9	86	95	23	17	0	0	0	0	32	3	0	.094	5	17	5	0	2.5	.815
2 yrs.		4	6	.400	3.88	12	11	10	95	99	26	20	0	0	0	0	38	4	0	.105	6	21	5	0	2.7	.844

Eric Bell

BELL, ERIC ALVIN
B. Oct. 27, 1963, Modesto, Calif.
BL TL 6' 165 lbs.

Year	Team	W	L	PCT	ERA	G	GS	CG	IP	H	BB	SO	ShO	W	L	SV	AB	H	HR	BA	PO	A	E	DP	TC/G	FA
1985	BAL A	0	0	–	4.76	4	0	0	5.2	4	4	4	0	0	0	0	0	0	0	–	2	1	0	0	0.8	1.000
1986		1	2	.333	5.01	4	4	0	23.1	23	14	18	0	0	0	0	0	0	0	–	1	0	0	0	0.3	1.000
1987		10	13	.435	5.45	33	29	2	165	174	78	111	0	0	0	0	0	0	0	–	8	16	0	2	0.7	1.000
3 yrs.		11	15	.423	5.38	41	33	2	194	201	96	133	0	0	0	0	0	0	0	–	11	17	0	2	0.7	1.000

Gary Bell

BELL, GARY
B. Nov. 17, 1936, San Antonio, Tex.
BR TR 6'1" 196 lbs.

Year	Team	W	L	PCT	ERA	G	GS	CG	IP	H	BB	SO	ShO	W	L	SV	AB	H	HR	BA	PO	A	E	DP	TC/G	FA
1958	CLE A	12	10	.545	3.31	33	23	10	182	141	73	110	0	1	2	1	56	11	0	.196	10	15	0	5	0.8	1.000
1959		16	11	.593	4.04	44	28	12	234	208	105	136	1	3	1	5	75	18	0	.240	19	27	2	3	1.1	.958
1960		9	10	.474	4.13	28	23	6	154.2	139	82	109	2	0	0	1	47	7	0	.149	11	26	2	4	1.4	.949
1961		12	16	.429	4.10	34	34	11	228.1	214	100	163	2	0	0	0	81	16	0	.198	26	24	1	1	1.5	.980
1962		10	9	.526	4.26	57	6	1	107.2	104	52	80	0	9	6	12	24	5	0	.208	14	9	1	2	0.4	.958
1963		8	5	.615	2.95	58	7	0	119	91	52	98	0	7	1	5	26	3	0	.115	6	20	1	2	0.5	.963

Year	Team	W	L	PCT	ERA	G	GS	CG	IP	H	BB	SO	ShO	W	L	SV	AB	H	HR	BA	PO	A	E	DP	TC/G	FA

Gary Bell *continued*

Year	Team	W	L	PCT	ERA	G	GS	CG	IP	H	BB	SO	ShO	W	L	SV	AB	H	HR	BA	PO	A	E	DP	TC/G	FA
1964		8	6	.571	4.33	56	2	0	106	106	53	89	0	7	5	4	16	6	0	.375	3	14	1	1	0.3	.944
1965		6	5	.545	3.04	60	0	0	103.2	86	50	86	0	6	5	17	16	1	1	.063	5	12	0	0	0.3	1.000
1966		14	15	.483	3.22	40	37	12	254.1	211	79	194	0	1	0	0	76	10	0	.132	8	50	2	3	1.5	.967
1967	2 teams	CLE A	(9G 1–5)		BOS A	(29G 12–8)																				
"	total	13	13	.500	3.31	38	33	9	226	193	71	154	0	1	0	3	74	12	0	.162	7	15	0	1	0.6	1.000
1968	BOS A	11	11	.500	3.12	35	27	9	199.1	177	68	103	3	1	1	1	59	13	0	.220	16	29	2	4	1.3	.957
1969	2 teams	SEA A	(13G 2–6)		CHI A	(23G 0–0)																				
"	total	2	6	.250	5.31	36	13	1	100	124	57	56	1	0	0	2	19	3	0	.158	6	17	2	2	0.7	.920
12 yrs.		121	117	.508	3.68	519	233	71	2015	1794	842	1378	9	35	21	51	569	105	1	.185	131	258	14	28	0.8	.965

WORLD SERIES

Year	Team	W	L	PCT	ERA	G	GS	CG	IP	H	BB	SO	ShO	W	L	SV	AB	H	HR	BA	PO	A	E	DP	TC/G	FA
1967	BOS A	0	1	.000	5.06	3	1	0	5.1	8	1	1	0	0	0	1	0	0	0	–	0	2	0	1	0.7	1.000

George Bell

BELL, GEORGE GLENN (Farmer)
B. Nov. 2, 1874, Greenwood, N. Y. D. Dec. 25, 1941, New York, N. Y. BR TR 6' 195 lbs.

Year	Team	W	L	PCT	ERA	G	GS	CG	IP	H	BB	SO	ShO	W	L	SV	AB	H	HR	BA	PO	A	E	DP	TC/G	FA
1907	BKN N	8	16	.333	2.25	35	27	20	263.2	222	77	88	3	1	1	1	84	8	0	.095	4	91	6	2	2.9	.941
1908		4	15	.211	3.59	29	21	12	155.1	162	45	63	2	0	1	1	47	8	0	.170	2	51	1	0	1.9	.981
1909		16	15	.516	2.71	33	30	29	256	236	73	95	6	1	0	1	90	15	0	.167	10	81	6	1	2.9	.938
1910		10	27	.270	2.64	44	36	25	310	267	82	102	4	0	3	1	97	13	0	.134	8	74	2	2	1.9	.976
1911		5	6	.455	4.28	19	12	6	101	123	28	28	2	1	0	0	33	4	0	.121	2	40	3	0	2.4	.933
5 yrs.		43	79	.352	2.85	160	126	92	1086	1010	305	376	17	3	5	4	351	48	0	.137	26	337	18	5	2.4	.953

Hi Bell

BELL, HERMAN S
B. July 16, 1897, Mt. Sherman, Ky. D. June 7, 1949, Glendale, Calif. BR TR 6' 185 lbs.

Year	Team	W	L	PCT	ERA	G	GS	CG	IP	H	BB	SO	ShO	W	L	SV	AB	H	HR	BA	PO	A	E	DP	TC/G	FA
1924	STL N	3	8	.273	4.92	28	11	5	113.1	124	29	29	0	1	1	1	31	2	0	.065	1	31	3	1	1.3	.914
1926		6	6	.500	3.18	27	8	3	85	82	17	27	0	3	2	2	25	3	0	.120	2	17	4	0	0.9	.826
1927		1	3	.250	3.92	25	1	0	57.1	71	22	31	0	1	2	0	11	1	0	.091	0	14	2	0	0.6	.875
1929		0	2	.000	6.92	7	0	0	13	19	4	4	0	0	2	0	3	0	0	.000	0	2	0	0	0.6	.500
1930		4	3	.571	3.90	39	9	2	115.1	143	23	42	0	3	1	8	26	2	0	.077	2	28	3	2	0.8	.909
1932	NY N	8	4	.667	3.68	35	10	3	120	132	16	25	0	3	1	2	34	3	0	.088	4	38	1	2	0.8	.964
1933		6	5	.545	2.05	38	7	1	105.1	100	20	24	1	4	2	5	29	4	0	.138	3	19	1	1	0.6	.957
1934		4	3	.571	3.67	22	2	0	54	72	12	9	0	4	2	6	19	2	0	.105	1	8	1	1	0.5	.900
8 yrs.		32	34	.485	3.69	221	48	14	663.1	743	143	191	1	18	13	24	178	17	0	.096	13	142	17	7	0.8	.901

WORLD SERIES

Year	Team	W	L	PCT	ERA	G	GS	CG	IP	H	BB	SO	ShO	W	L	SV	AB	H	HR	BA	PO	A	E	DP	TC/G	FA
1926	STL N	0	0	–	9.00	1	0	0	2	4	1	1	0	0	0	0	0	0	0	–	0	0	0	0	0.0	–
1930		0	0	–	0.00	1	0	0	1	0	0	0	0	0	0	0	0	0	0	–	0	1	0	0	1.0	1.000
1933	NY N	0	0	–	0.00	1	0	0	1	0	0	0	0	0	0	0	0	0	0	–	0	0	0	0	0.0	–
3 yrs.		0	0	–	4.50	3	0	0	4	4	1	1	0	0	0	0	0	0	0	–	0	1	0	0	0.3	1.000

Jerry Bell

BELL, JERRY HOUSTON
B. Oct. 6, 1947, Madison, Tenn. BB TR 6'4" 190 lbs.

Year	Team	W	L	PCT	ERA	G	GS	CG	IP	H	BB	SO	ShO	W	L	SV	AB	H	HR	BA	PO	A	E	DP	TC/G	FA
1971	MIL A	2	1	.667	3.00	8	0	0	15	10	6	8	0	2	1	0	0	0	0		0	1	0	0	0.1	1.000
1972		5	1	.833	1.65	25	3	0	71	50	33	20	0	2	1	0	14	1	0	.071	7	13	0	1	0.8	1.000
1973		9	9	.500	3.97	31	25	8	183.2	185	70	57	0	1	2	1	0	0	0	–	13	34	1	2	1.5	.979
1974		1	0	1.000	2.57	5	0	0	14	17	5	4	0	1	0	0	0	0	0		0	3	2	0	1.0	.600
4 yrs.		17	11	.607	3.27	69	28	8	283.2	262	114	89	0	6	4	1	14	1	0	.071	20	51	3	3	1.1	.959

Ralph Bell

BELL, RALPH ALBERT
B. Nov. 6, 1890, Kohoka, Mo. D. Oct. 18, 1959, Burlington, Iowa BL TL 5'11½" 170 lbs.

Year	Team	W	L	PCT	ERA	G	GS	CG	IP	H	BB	SO	ShO	W	L	SV	AB	H	HR	BA	PO	A	E	DP	TC/G	FA
1912	CHI A	0	0	–	9.00	3	0	0	6	8	8	5	0	0	0	0	2	0	0	.000	0	3	0	0	1.0	1.000

Chief Bender

BENDER, CHARLES ALBERT
B. May 5, 1884, Crow Wing County, Minn. D. May 22, 1954, Philadelphia, Pa. BR TR 6'2" 185 lbs.
Hall of Fame 1953.

Year	Team	W	L	PCT	ERA	G	GS	CG	IP	H	BB	SO	ShO	W	L	SV	AB	H	HR	BA	PO	A	E	DP	TC/G	FA
1903	PHI A	17	15	.531	3.07	36	33	29	270	239	65	127	2	1	1	0	120	22	0	.183	12	79	9	0	2.8	.910
1904		10	11	.476	2.87	29	20	18	203.2	167	59	149	4	2	0	0	79	18	0	.228	13	48	7	0	2.3	.897
1905		16	10	.615	2.83	35	23	17	229	193	90	142	4	7	1	0	92	20	0	.217	14	77	3	2	2.7	.968
1906		15	10	.600	2.53	36	27	24	238.1	208	48	159	0	1	0	3	99	25	3	.253	25	54	8	1	2.4	.908
1907		16	8	.667	2.05	33	24	20	219.1	185	34	112	4	0	2	3	100	23	0	.230	14	57	5	2	2.3	.934
1908		8	9	.471	1.75	18	17	14	138.2	121	21	85	2	0	0	0	50	11	0	.220	12	28	3	0	2.4	.930
1909		18	8	.692	1.66	34	29	24	250	196	45	161	5	0	0	1	93	20	0	.215	13	78	4	1	2.8	.958
1910		23	5	**.821**	1.58	30	28	25	250	182	47	155	3	1	0	0	93	25	0	.269	13	85	3	3	3.4	.970
1911		17	5	**.773**	2.16	31	24	16	216.1	198	58	114	3	2	1	3	79	13	0	.165	11	58	0	4	2.2	1.000
1912		13	8	.619	2.74	27	19	12	171	169	33	90	1	2	3	2	60	9	0	.150	6	36	2	1	1.6	.955
1913		21	10	.677	2.21	48	22	16	236.2	208	59	135	2	6	5	**13**	78	12	0	.154	8	55	2	1	1.4	.969
1914		17	3	**.850**	2.26	28	23	14	179	159	55	107	7	1	1	2	62	9	1	.145	7	47	2	0	2.0	.964
1915	BAL F	4	16	.200	3.99	26	23	15	178.1	198	37	89	0	0	1	1	60	16	1	.267	12	45	4	3	2.3	.934
1916	PHI N	7	7	.500	3.74	27	13	4	122.2	137	34	43	0	2	1	3	43	12	0	.279	8	39	2	1	1.8	.959
1917		8	2	.800	1.67	20	11	8	113	84	26	43	4	0	0	2	39	8	1	.205	5	22	1	4	1.4	.964
1925	CHI A	0	0	–	18.00	1	0	0	1	1	1	0	0	0	0	0	0	0	0	–	0	0	0	0	0.0	–
16 yrs.		210	127	.623	2.46	459	335	256	3017	2645	712	1711	41	25	16	34	*				173	808	55	24	2.3	.947

WORLD SERIES

Year	Team	W	L	PCT	ERA	G	GS	CG	IP	H	BB	SO	ShO	W	L	SV	AB	H	HR	BA	PO	A	E	DP	TC/G	FA
1905	PHI A	1	1	.500	1.06	2	2	2	17	9	6	13	1	0	0	0	5	0	0	.000	1	6	0	0	3.5	1.000
1910		1	1	.500	1.93	2	2	2	18.2	12	4	14	0	0	0	0	6	2	0	.333	1	6	0	1	1.5	1.000
1911		2	1	.667	1.04	3	3	3	26	16	8	20	0	0	0	0	11	1	0	.091	1	6	0	0	2.3	1.000
1913		2	0	1.000	4.00	2	2	2	18	19	1	9	0	0	0	0	8	0	0	.000	1	3	0	0	2.5	1.000
1914		0	1	.000	10.13	1	1	0	5.1	8	2	3	0	0	0	0	2	0	0	.000	1	1	0	2	4.0	1.000
5 yrs.		6	4	.600	2.44	10	10	9	85	64	21	59	1	0	0	0	32	3	0	.094	4	22	0	3	2.6	1.000
		5th	7th				4th	2nd			4th	5th				6th										

Year	Team		W	L	PCT	ERA	G	GS	CG	IP	H	BB	SO	ShO	Relief Pitching W	L	SV	Batting AB	H	HR	BA	PO	A	E	DP	TC/G	FA

Andy Benes

BENES, ANDREW CHARLES
B. Aug. 20, 1967, Evansville, Ind.
BR TR 6'6" 235 lbs.

Year	Team		W	L	PCT	ERA	G	GS	CG	IP	H	BB	SO	ShO	W	L	SV	AB	H	HR	BA	PO	A	E	DP	TC/G	FA
1989	SD	N	6	3	.667	3.51	10	10	0	66.2	51	31	66	0	0	0	0	24	6	1	.250	4	8	0	1	1.2	1.000

Ray Benge

BENGE, RAYMOND ADELPHIA (Silent Cal)
B. Apr. 22, 1902, Jacksonville, Tex.
BR TR 5'9½" 160 lbs.

Year	Team		W	L	PCT	ERA	G	GS	CG	IP	H	BB	SO	ShO	W	L	SV	AB	H	HR	BA	PO	A	E	DP	TC/G	FA
1925	CLE	A	1	0	1.000	1.54	2	2	1	11.2	9	3	3	1	0	0	0	5	2	0	.400	0	1	0	0	0.5	1.000
1926			1	0	1.000	3.86	8	0	0	11.2	15	4	3	0	1	0	0	3	1	0	.333	0	4	1	0	0.6	.800
1928	PHI	N	8	18	.308	4.55	40	28	12	201.2	219	88	68	1	2	0	1	58	12	0	.207	4	39	1	3	1.1	.977
1929			11	15	.423	6.29	38	27	9	199	255	77	78	2	0	3	4	74	15	0	.203	2	34	3	0	1.0	.923
1930			11	15	.423	5.70	38	29	14	225.2	305	81	70	0	0	3	1	88	18	0	.205	9	44	4	1	1.4	.926
1931			14	18	.438	3.17	38	31	16	247	251	61	117	2	1	2	2	88	18	0	.205	12	36	2	4	1.3	.960
1932			13	12	.520	4.05	41	28	13	222.1	247	58	89	2	0	0	6	75	13	0	.173	7	41	1	2	1.2	.980
1933	BKN	N	10	17	.370	3.42	37	30	16	228.2	238	55	74	2	1	0	1	76	14	1	.184	6	37	0	1	1.2	1.000
1934			14	12	.538	4.32	36	32	14	227	252	61	64	1	1	0	0	89	15	0	.169	13	43	1	3	1.6	.982
1935			9	9	.500	4.48	23	17	5	124.2	142	47	39	1	1	1	1	47	9	0	.191	3	19	1	2	1.0	.957
1936	2 teams		BOS	N	(21G 7–9)		PHI	N	(15G 1–4)																			
"	total		8	13	.381	5.49	36	25	2	160.2	231	57	45	0	1	0	0	53	6	0	.113	2	20	2	0	0.7	.917
1938	CIN	N	1	1	.500	4.11	9	0	0	15.1	13	6	5	0	1	1	2	3	1	0	.333	1	2	0	0	0.3	1.000
	12 yrs.		101	130	.437	4.52	346	249	102	1875.1	2177	598	655	12	8	11	19	659	124	1	.188	59	317	16	16	1.1	.959

Henry Benn

BENN, HENRY OMER
B. Jan. 25, 1890, Viola, Wis. D. June 4, 1967, Madison, Wis.
BR TR 6' 190 lbs.

Year	Team		W	L	PCT	ERA	G	GS	CG	IP	H	BB	SO	ShO	W	L	SV	AB	H	HR	BA	PO	A	E	DP	TC/G	FA
1914	CLE	A	0	0	–	0.00	1	0	0	1	0	0	1	0	0	0	0	0	0	0	–	0	0	0	0	0.0	–

Bugs Bennett

BENNETT, JOSEPH HARLEY
Born Joseph Harley Morris.
B. Apr. 19, 1892, Kansas City, Mo. D. Nov. 21, 1957, Noel, Mo.
BR TR 5'9½" 163 lbs.

Year	Team		W	L	PCT	ERA	G	GS	CG	IP	H	BB	SO	ShO	W	L	SV	AB	H	HR	BA	PO	A	E	DP	TC/G	FA
1918	STL	A	0	2	.000	3.48	4	2	0	10.1	12	7	0	0	0	0	0	4	1	0	.250	0	5	0	0	1.3	1.000
1921	2 teams		CHI	A	(3G 0–3)		STL	A	(3G 0–0)																			
"	total		0	3	.000	8.10	6	3	1	23.1	30	22	5	0	0	1	0	7	3	0	.429	2	7	0	0	1.5	1.000
	2 yrs.		0	5	.000	6.68	10	5	1	33.2	42	29	5	0	0	1	0	11	4	0	.364	2	12	0	0	1.4	1.000

Dave Bennett

BENNETT, DAVID HANS
Brother of Dennis Bennett.
B. Nov. 7, 1945, Berkeley, Calif.
BR TR 6'5" 195 lbs.

Year	Team		W	L	PCT	ERA	G	GS	CG	IP	H	BB	SO	ShO	W	L	SV	AB	H	HR	BA	PO	A	E	DP	TC/G	FA
1964	PHI	N	0	0	–	9.00	1	0	0	1	2	0	1	0	0	0	0	0	0	0	–	0	0	0	0	0.0	–

Dennis Bennett

BENNETT, DENNIS JOHN
Brother of Dave Bennett.
B. Oct. 5, 1939, Oakland, Calif.
BL TL 6'3" 192 lbs.

Year	Team		W	L	PCT	ERA	G	GS	CG	IP	H	BB	SO	ShO	W	L	SV	AB	H	HR	BA	PO	A	E	DP	TC/G	FA
1962	PHI	N	9	9	.500	3.81	31	24	2	174.2	144	68	149	2	1	0	3	63	8	1	.127	8	24	1	0	1.1	.970
1963			9	5	.643	2.64	23	16	6	119.1	102	33	82	1	1	0	1	40	9	1	.225	6	21	1	3	1.2	.964
1964			12	14	.462	3.68	41	32	7	208	222	58	125	2	1	0	1	66	13	0	.197	11	37	3	1	1.2	.941
1965	BOS	A	5	7	.417	4.38	34	18	3	141.2	152	53	85	0	1	0	0	39	7	0	.179	11	21	2	1	1.0	.941
1966			3	3	.500	3.24	16	13	0	75	75	23	47	0	0	0	0	23	3	0	.130	0	9	0	0	0.6	1.000
1967	2 teams		BOS	A	(13G 4–3)		NY	N	(8G 1–1)																			
"	total		5	4	.556	4.22	21	17	4	96	109	29	48	1	0	0	0	33	5	1	.152	4	16	2	1	1.0	.909
1968	CAL	A	0	5	.000	3.54	16	7	1	48.1	46	17	36	0	0	1	1	13	1	0	.077	1	10	0	0	0.7	1.000
	7 yrs.		43	47	.478	3.69	182	127	28	863	850	281	572	6	4	1	6	277	46	4	.166	41	138	9	6	1.0	.952

Frank Bennett

BENNETT, FRANCIS ALLEN (Chip)
B. Oct. 27, 1904, Mardela Springs, Md. D. Mar. 18, 1966, New Castle, Del.
BR TR 5'10½" 163 lbs.

Year	Team		W	L	PCT	ERA	G	GS	CG	IP	H	BB	SO	ShO	W	L	SV	AB	H	HR	BA	PO	A	E	DP	TC/G	FA
1927	BOS	A	0	1	.000	2.92	4	1	0	12.1	15	6	1	0	0	0	0	3	0	0	.000	2	1	0	1	1.0	1.000
1928			0	0	–	0.00	1	0	0	1	1	0	0	0	0	0	0	0	0	0	–	0	1	0	0	1.0	1.000
	2 yrs.		0	1	.000	2.70	5	1	0	13.1	16	6	1	0	0	0	0	3	0	0	.000	2	3	0	1	1.0	1.000

Allen Benson

BENSON, ALLEN WILBERT (Bullet Ben)
B. Mar. 28, 1908, Hurley, S. D.
BR TR 6'1" 185 lbs.

Year	Team		W	L	PCT	ERA	G	GS	CG	IP	H	BB	SO	ShO	W	L	SV	AB	H	HR	BA	PO	A	E	DP	TC/G	FA
1934	WAS	A	0	1	.000	12.10	2	2	0	9.2	19	5	4	0	0	0	0	3	0	0	.000	0	0	0	0	0.0	–

Jack Bentley

BENTLEY, JOHN NEEDLES
B. Mar. 8, 1895, Sandy Springs, Md. D. Oct. 24, 1969, Olney, Md.
BL TL 5'11½" 200 lbs.

Year	Team		W	L	PCT	ERA	G	GS	CG	IP	H	BB	SO	ShO	W	L	SV	AB	H	HR	BA	PO	A	E	DP	TC/G	FA
1913	WAS	A	1	0	1.000	0.00	3	1	0	11	5	2	5	0	0	0	1	3	0	0	.000	0	5	0	0	1.7	1.000
1914			5	7	.417	2.37	30	12	3	125.1	110	53	55	2	0	1	4	40	11	0	.275	9	33	3	1	1.5	.933
1915			0	2	.000	0.79	4	2	0	11.1	8	3	0	0	0	0	0	2	0	0	.000	0	3	0	0	0.8	.750
1916			0	0	–	0.00	2	0	0	1.1	1	1	1	0	0	0	0	0	0	0	–	0	1	0	0	0.5	1.000
1923	NY	N	13	8	.619	4.48	31	26	12	183	198	67	80	1	0	1	3	89	38	0	.427	5	38	1	1	1.4	.977
1924			16	5	.762	3.78	28	24	13	188	196	56	60	1	1	0	1	98	26	0	.265	3	43	3	1	1.7	.979
1925			11	9	.550	5.04	28	22	11	157	200	59	47	0	1	0	0	99	30	3	.303	7	33	3	2	1.5	.930
1926	2 teams		PHI	N	(7G 0–2)		NY	N	(1G 0–0)																			
"	total		0	2	.000	7.57	8	3	0	27.1	37	12	8	0	0	0	0	244	63	2	.258	0	5	0	0	0.6	1.000
1927	NY	N	0	0	–	2.79	4	0	0	9.2	7	10	3	0	0	0	0	9	2	1	.222	1	2	1	0	1.0	.750
	9 yrs.		46	33	.582	4.01	138	90	39	714	761	263	259	4	2	2	9	*				26	162	10	7	1.4	.949

WORLD SERIES

Year	Team		W	L	PCT	ERA	G	GS	CG	IP	H	BB	SO	ShO	W	L	SV	AB	H	HR	BA	PO	A	E	DP	TC/G	FA
1923	NY	N	0	1	.000	9.45	2	1	0	6.2	10	4	1	0	0	0	0	5	3	0	.600	0	2	0	0	1.0	1.000
1924			1	2	.333	3.18	3	2	1	17	18	8	10	0	0	1	0	7	2	1	.286	1	3	0	0	1.3	1.000
	2 yrs.		1	3	.250	4.94	5	3	1	23.2	28	12	11	0	0	1	0	12	5	1	.417	1	5	0	0	1.2	1.000

Year	Team	W	L	PCT	ERA	G	GS	CG	IP	H	BB	SO	ShO	Relief Pitching W	L	SV	Batting AB	H	HR	BA	PO	A	E	DP	TC/G	FA

Al Benton

BENTON, JOHN ALTON
B. Mar. 18, 1911, Noble, Okla. D. Apr. 14, 1968, Lynwood, Calif.
BR TR 6'4" 215 lbs.

Year	Team	W	L	PCT	ERA	G	GS	CG	IP	H	BB	SO	ShO	W	L	SV	AB	H	HR	BA	PO	A	E	DP	TC/G	FA
1934	PHI A	7	9	.438	4.88	32	21	7	155	145	88	58	0	1	1	1	55	6	0	.109	11	28	1	3	1.3	.975
1935		3	4	.429	7.67	27	9	0	78.2	110	47	42	0	3	1	0	25	1	0	.040	2	12	1	0	0.6	.933
1938	DET A	5	3	.625	3.30	19	10	6	95.1	93	39	33	0	0	0	0	33	4	0	.121	3	25	1	0	1.5	.966
1939		6	8	.429	4.56	37	16	3	150	182	58	67	0	1	3	5	44	4	0	.091	6	27	2	0	0.9	.943
1940		6	10	.375	4.42	42	0	0	79.1	93	36	50	0	6	10	17	17	0	0	.000	5	11	3	1	0.5	.842
1941		15	6	.714	2.97	38	14	7	157.2	130	65	63	1	6	2	7	50	3	0	.060	9	27	3	4	1.0	.923
1942		7	13	.350	2.90	35	30	9	226.2	210	84	110	1	0	1	2	67	5	0	.075	18	39	5	0	1.8	.919
1945		13	8	.619	2.02	31	27	12	191.2	175	63	76	5	0	1	3	63	4	0	.063	11	44	2	4	1.8	.965
1946		11	7	.611	3.65	28	15	6	140.2	132	58	60	1	1	2	1	49	9	0	.184	16	26	2	0	1.6	.955
1947		6	7	.462	4.40	36	14	4	133	147	61	33	0	1	0	7	39	6	0	.154	6	24	4	1	0.9	.882
1948		2	2	.500	5.68	30	0	0	44.1	45	36	18	0	2	2	3	11	2	0	.182	2	8	1	1	0.4	.909
1949	CLE A	9	6	.600	2.12	40	11	4	135.2	116	51	41	2	4	0	10	38	5	0	.132	4	17	0	2	0.5	1.000
1950		4	2	.667	3.57	36	0	0	63	57	30	26	0	4	2	4	12	1	0	.083	1	8	0	1	0.3	1.000
1952	BOS A	4	3	.571	2.39	24	0	0	37.2	37	17	20	0	4	3	6	9	0	0	.000	3	5	1	0	0.4	.889
14 yrs.		98	88	.527	3.66	455	167	58	1688.2	1672	733	697	10	33	28	66	512	50	0	.098	97	301	26	18	0.9	.939

WORLD SERIES

Year	Team	W	L	PCT	ERA	G	GS	CG	IP	H	BB	SO	ShO	W	L	SV	AB	H	HR	BA	PO	A	E	DP	TC/G	FA
1945	DET A	0	0	–	1.93	3	0	0	4.2	6	0	5	0	0	0	0	0	0	0	–	0	3	0	0	1.0	1.000

Larry Benton

BENTON, LAWRENCE JAMES
B. Nov. 20, 1897, St. Louis, Mo. D. Apr. 3, 1953, Amberly Village, Ohio
BR TR 5'11" 165 lbs.

Year	Team	W	L	PCT	ERA	G	GS	CG	IP	H	BB	SO	ShO	W	L	SV	AB	H	HR	BA	PO	A	E	DP	TC/G	FA
1923	BOS N	5	9	.357	4.99	35	14	6	128	141	57	42	0	4	4	0	31	5	0	.161	5	33	4	2	1.2	.905
1924		5	7	.417	4.15	30	13	4	128	129	64	41	0	1	0	1	33	3	0	.091	3	30	1	2	1.1	.971
1925		14	7	.667	3.09	31	21	16	183.1	170	70	49	2	1	1	1	58	14	0	.241	4	39	3	2	1.5	.938
1926		14	14	.500	3.85	43	27	12	231.2	244	81	103	1	3	2	1	78	12	0	.154	3	43	0	1	1.1	1.000
1927	2 teams	BOS N	(11G 4–2)		NY N	(29G 13–5)																				
"	total	17	7	.708	4.09	40	33	11	233.1	255	81	90	1	3	1	1	68	12	0	.176	13	43	3	3	1.5	.949
1928	NY N	25	9	.735	2.73	42	35	28	310.1	299	71	90	2	0	1	4	112	16	0	.143	15	69	1	5	2.0	.988
1929		11	17	.393	4.14	39	30	14	237	276	61	63	0	1	3	3	86	9	1	.105	11	58	3	7	1.8	.958
1930	2 teams	NY N	(8G 1–3)		CIN N	(35G 7–12)																				
"	total	8	15	.348	5.50	43	26	10	207.2	288	59	63	0	2	2	0	72	14	1	.194	14	23	1	2	0.9	.974
1931	CIN N	10	15	.400	3.35	38	23	12	204.1	240	53	35	2	3	1	2	66	11	0	.167	10	48	2	5	1.6	.967
1932		6	13	.316	4.31	35	21	7	179.2	201	27	35	1	1	2	1	54	11	0	.204	6	38	2	1	1.3	.957
1933		10	11	.476	3.71	34	19	7	152.2	160	36	33	2	1	4	2	53	9	0	.170	5	27	2	1	1.0	.941
1934		0	1	.000	6.52	16	1	0	29	53	7	5	0	0	0	0	7	2	0	.286	4	0	2	0	0.4	1.000
1935	BOS N	2	3	.400	6.88	29	0	0	72	103	24	21	0	2	3	0	20	4	0	.200	2	12	0	1	0.5	1.000
13 yrs.		127	128	.498	4.03	455	258	123	2297	2559	691	670	13	21	19	22	738	122	2	.165	93	469	22	33	1.3	.962

Rube Benton

BENTON, JOHN CLEBON
B. June 27, 1887, Clinton, N. C. D. Dec. 12, 1937, Dothan, Ala.
BR TL 6'1" 190 lbs.

Year	Team	W	L	PCT	ERA	G	GS	CG	IP	H	BB	SO	ShO	W	L	SV	AB	H	HR	BA	PO	A	E	DP	TC/G	FA
1910	CIN N	1	1	.500	4.74	12	2	0	38	44	23	15	0	0	0	0	11	1	0	.091	1	13	0	1	1.2	1.000
1911		3	3	.500	2.01	6	6	5	44.2	44	23	28	0	0	0	0	14	2	0	.143	1	10	0	0	1.8	1.000
1912		18	21	.462	3.10	50	39	22	302	316	118	162	2	3	1	2	104	14	0	.135	13	78	3	2	1.9	.968
1913		11	7	.611	3.49	23	22	9	144.1	140	60	68	1	1	0	0	48	10	0	.208	0	35	4	0	1.7	.897
1914		17	18	.486	2.96	41	31	16	271	223	95	121	5	2	3	2	91	13	0	.143	9	70	5	3	2.0	.940
1915	2 teams	CIN N	(35G 9–13)		NY N	(10G 4–5)																				
"	total	13	18	.419	3.19	45	28	9	237	222	76	109	2	4	3	5	76	16	0	.211	8	72	3	2	1.8	.964
1916	NY N	16	8	.667	2.87	38	30	15	238.2	210	58	115	3	0	0	3	78	7	0	.090	6	57	0	3	1.7	1.000
1917		15	9	.625	2.72	35	25	14	215	190	41	70	3	0	2	3	72	12	0	.167	2	58	3	0	1.8	.952
1918		1	2	.333	1.88	3	3	2	24	17	3	9	0	0	0	0	7	1	0	.143	1	7	0	1	2.7	1.000
1919		17	11	.607	2.63	35	28	11	209	181	52	53	1	3	0	2	67	13	1	.194	3	60	0	0	1.8	1.000
1920		9	16	.360	3.03	33	25	12	193.1	222	31	52	4	1	1	0	65	6	0	.092	13	74	2	3	2.7	.978
1921		5	2	.714	2.88	18	9	3	72	72	17	11	1	0	1	0	21	3	0	.143	2	16	1	1	1.1	.947
1923	CIN N	14	10	.583	3.66	33	26	15	219	243	57	59	0	1	1	1	80	23	0	.288	7	57	2	2	2.0	.970
1924		7	9	.438	2.77	32	15	6	162.2	166	24	42	1	1	1	1	46	12	0	.261	7	46	4	3	1.8	.930
1925		9	10	.474	4.05	33	16	6	146.2	182	34	36	1	2	2	1	45	9	0	.200	3	31	1	0	1.1	.971
15 yrs.		156	145	.518	3.09	437	305	145	2517.1	2472	712	950	24	18	16	21	825	142	1	.172	76	684	28	21	1.8	.964

WORLD SERIES

Year	Team	W	L	PCT	ERA	G	GS	CG	IP	H	BB	SO	ShO	W	L	SV	AB	H	HR	BA	PO	A	E	DP	TC/G	FA
1917	NY N	1	1	.500	0.00	2	1	1	14	9	1	8	1	0	0	0	4	0	0	.000	1	2	0	0	1.5	1.000

Sid Benton

BENTON, SIDNEY WRIGHT
B. Aug. 4, 1895, Buckner, Ark. D. Mar. 8, 1977, Fayetteville, Ark.
BR TR 6'1" 170 lbs.

Year	Team	W	L	PCT	ERA	G	GS	CG	IP	H	BB	SO	ShO	W	L	SV	AB	H	HR	BA	PO	A	E	DP	TC/G	FA
1922	STL N	0	0	–	0.00	1	0	0	0	2	0	0	0	0	0	0	0	0	0	–	0	0	0	0	0.0	–

Joe Benz

BENZ, JOSEPH LOUIS (Blitzen)
B. Jan. 21, 1886, New Alsace, Ind. D. Apr. 22, 1957, Chicago, Ill.
BR TR 6'1½" 196 lbs.

Year	Team	W	L	PCT	ERA	G	GS	CG	IP	H	BB	SO	ShO	W	L	SV	AB	H	HR	BA	PO	A	E	DP	TC/G	FA
1911	CHI A	3	2	.600	2.26	12	6	2	55.2	52	13	28	0	1	0	0	17	1	0	.059	1	22	5	1	2.3	.821
1912		13	17	.433	2.92	41	31	12	237.2	230	70	96	3	2	2	0	76	10	0	.132	10	77	10	2	2.4	.897
1913		7	10	.412	2.74	33	17	6	151	146	59	79	1	3	0	1	50	9	0	.180	4	66	4	1	2.4	.946
1914		14	19	.424	2.26	48	35	16	283.1	245	66	142	4	3	0	2	92	12	0	.130	5	112	11	8	2.7	.914
1915		15	11	.577	2.11	39	28	17	238.1	209	43	81	2	0	2	0	79	10	0	.127	5	86	3	5	2.4	.968
1916		9	5	.643	2.03	28	16	6	142	108	32	57	4	1	1	0	46	3	0	.065	5	46	4	1	2.0	.927
1917		7	3	.700	2.47	19	13	7	94.2	76	23	25	2	0	1	0	30	5	0	.167	3	32	5	1	2.1	.875
1918		8	8	.500	2.51	29	17	10	154	156	28	30	1	1	0	0	51	11	0	.216	4	62	4	2	2.4	.943
1919		0	0	–	0.00	1	0	0	2	2	0	0	0	0	0	0	0	0	0	–	0	1	0	0	1.0	1.000
9 yrs.		76	75	.503	2.42	250	163	76	1358.2	1224	334	538	17	11	6	3	441	61	0	.138	37	504	46	18	2.3	.922

Juan Berenguer

BERENGUER, JUAN BAUTISTA
B. Nov. 30, 1954, Aguadulce, Panama
BR TR 5'11" 186 lbs.

Year	Team	W	L	PCT	ERA	G	GS	CG	IP	H	BB	SO	ShO	W	L	SV	AB	H	HR	BA	PO	A	E	DP	TC/G	FA
1978	NY N	0	2	.000	8.31	5	3	0	13	17	11	8	0	0	0	0	3	0	0	.000	0	2	0	0	0.4	1.000
1979		1	1	.500	2.90	5	5	0	31	28	12	25	0	0	0	0	7	1	0	.143	0	1	1	0	0.4	.500

Year	Team	W	L	PCT	ERA	G	GS	CG	IP	H	BB	SO	ShO	Relief Pitching W	L	SV	Batting AB	H	HR	BA	PO	A	E	DP	TC/G	FA

Juan Berenguer *continued*

Year	Team		W	L	PCT	ERA	G	GS	CG	IP	H	BB	SO	ShO	W	L	SV	AB	H	HR	BA	PO	A	E	DP	TC/G	FA
1980			0	1	.000	6.00	6	0	0	9	9	10	7	0	0	1	0	0	0	0	–	0	2	0	0	0.3	1.000
1981	2 teams	KC A (8G 0–4)					TOR A	(12G 2–9)																			
"	total		2	13	.133	5.24	20	14	1	91	84	51	49	0	0	2	0	0	0	0	–	0	9	0	0	0.5	1.000
1982	DET	A	0	0	–	6.75	2	1	0	6.2	5	9	8	0	0	0	0	0	0	0	–	0	0	0	0	0.0	–
1983			9	5	.643	3.14	37	19	2	157.2	110	71	129	1	2	0	1	0	0	0	–	10	11	3	1	0.6	.875
1984			11	10	.524	3.48	31	27	3	168.1	146	79	118	1	0	0	0	0	0	0	–	11	15	2	0	0.9	.929
1985			5	6	.455	5.59	31	13	0	95	96	48	82	0	1	1	0	0	0	0	–	11	12	2	1	0.8	.920
1986	SF	N	2	3	.400	2.70	46	4	0	73.1	64	44	72	0	2	2	4	7	1	0	.143	2	7	1	0	0.2	.900
1987	MIN	A	8	1	.889	3.94	47	6	0	112	100	47	110	0	6	1	4	0	0	0	–	5	7	1	0	0.3	.923
1988			8	4	.667	3.96	57	1	0	100	74	61	99	0	8	4	2	0	0	0	–	7	10	0	1	0.3	1.000
1989			9	3	.750	3.48	56	0	0	106	96	47	93	0	9	3	3	0	0	0	–	2	11	0	1	0.2	1.000
12 yrs.			55	49	.529	3.93	343	93	5	963	829	490	800	2	28	14	14	17	2	0	.118	49	87	10	4	0.4	.932

LEAGUE CHAMPIONSHIP SERIES

| 1987 | MIN | A | 0 | 0 | – | 1.50 | 4 | 0 | 0 | 6 | 1 | 3 | 6 | 0 | 0 | 0 | 1 | 0 | 0 | 0 | – | 0 | 0 | 0 | 0 | 0.0 | – |

WORLD SERIES

| 1987 | MIN | A | 0 | 1 | .000 | 10.38 | 3 | 0 | 0 | 4.1 | 10 | 0 | 1 | 0 | 0 | 1 | 0 | 0 | 0 | 0 | – | 0 | 0 | 0 | 0 | 0.0 | – |

Bruce Berenyi

BERENYI, BRUCE MICHAEL
B. Aug. 21, 1954, Bryan, Ohio
BR TR 6'3" 205 lbs.

1980	CIN	N	2	2	.500	7.71	6	6	0	28	34	23	19	0	0	0	0	7	0	0	.000	0	3	0	0	0.5	1.000
1981			9	6	.600	3.50	21	20	5	126	97	77	106	3	0	0	0	42	8	0	.190	7	12	0	2	0.9	1.000
1982			9	18	.333	3.36	34	34	4	222.1	208	96	157	1	0	0	0	62	15	0	.242	18	40	2	1	1.8	.967
1983			9	14	.391	3.86	32	31	4	186.1	173	102	151	1	0	0	0	55	12	0	.218	5	41	2	1	1.5	.958
1984	2 teams	CIN N (13G 3–7)					NY N	(19G 9–6)																			
"	total		12	13	.480	4.45	32	32	0	166	163	95	134	0	1	0	0	53	10	0	.189	12	17	0	1	0.9	1.000
1985	NY	N	1	0	1.000	2.63	3	3	0	13.2	8	10	10	0	0	0	0	4	1	0	.250	2	4	0	1	1.7	1.000
1986			2	2	.500	6.35	14	7	0	39.2	47	22	30	0	1	0	0	11	0	0	.000	3	5	0	0	0.6	1.000
7 yrs.			44	55	.444	4.03	142	131	13	782	730	425	607	5	2	0	0	234	46	0	.197	46	122	4	7	1.2	.977

Bill Bergen

BERGEN, WILLIAM ALOYSIUS
Brother of Marty Bergen.
B. June 13, 1878, N. Brookfield, Mass. D. Dec. 19, 1943, Worcester, Mass.
BR TR 6' 184 lbs.

| 1902 | CIN | N | 1 | 1 | .500 | 2.40 | 2 | 2 | 1 | 15 | 11 | 6 | 4 | 0 | 0 | 0 | 0 | * | | | | 0 | 0 | 0 | 0 | 0.0 | – |

Heinie Berger

BERGER, CHARLES
B. Jan. 7, 1882, LaSalle, Ill. D. Feb. 10, 1954, Lakewood, Ohio
TR 5'9½"

1907	CLE	A	3	3	.500	2.99	14	7	5	87.1	74	20	50	1	0	0	0	28	5	0	.179	2	20	2	0	1.7	.917
1908			13	8	.619	2.12	29	24	16	199.1	152	66	101	0	0	0	0	74	8	0	.108	8	58	1	0	2.3	.985
1909			13	14	.481	2.63	34	29	19	257	221	58	162	4	0	0	1	83	11	0	.133	11	66	6	3	2.5	.929
1910			3	4	.429	3.03	13	8	2	65.1	57	32	24	0	1	1	0	21	3	0	.143	4	20	3	0	2.1	.889
4 yrs.			32	29	.525	2.56	90	68	42	609	504	176	337	5	2	1	1	206	27	0	.131	25	166	12	3	2.3	.941

Jack Berly

BERLY, JOHN CHAMBERS
B. May 24, 1903, Natchitoches, La. D. June 26, 1977, Houston, Tex.
BR TR 5'11½" 190 lbs.

1924	STL	N	0	0	–	5.63	4	0	0	8	8	4	2	0	0	0	0	2	0	0	.000	0	4	0	0	1.0	1.000
1931	NY	N	7	8	.467	3.88	27	11	4	111.1	114	51	45	1	2	4	0	35	6	0	.171	5	29	0	0	1.3	1.000
1932	PHI	N	1	2	.333	7.63	21	1	1	46	61	21	15	0	1	1	2	10	0	0	.000	4	13	1	0	0.9	.944
1933			2	3	.400	5.04	13	6	1	50	62	22	4	1	0	0	0	13	4	0	.308	2	14	0	2	1.2	1.000
4 yrs.			10	13	.435	5.02	65	18	6	215.1	245	98	66	2	3	5	2	60	10	0	.167	11	60	1	2	1.1	.986

Vic Bernal

BERNAL, VICTOR HUGO
B. Oct. 6, 1953, Los Angeles, Calif.
BR TR 6'1" 175 lbs.

| 1977 | SD | N | 1 | 1 | .500 | 5.40 | 15 | 0 | 0 | 20 | 23 | 9 | 6 | 0 | 1 | 0 | 1 | 0 | 0 | 0 | .000 | 1 | 2 | 0 | 0 | 0.3 | .750 |

Dwight Bernard

BERNARD, DWIGHT VERN
B. May 31, 1952, Mt. Vernon, Ill.
BR TR 6'2" 170 lbs.

1978	NY	N	1	4	.200	4.31	30	1	0	48	54	27	26	0	1	3	0	5	1	0	.200	2	7	0	2	0.3	1.000
1979			0	3	.000	4.70	32	1	0	44	59	26	20	0	0	2	0	0	0	0	–	2	8	0	1	0.3	1.000
1981	MIL	A	0	0	–	3.60	6	0	0	5	5	6	1	0	0	0	0	0	0	0	–	0	0	0	0	0.0	–
1982			3	1	.750	3.76	47	0	0	79	78	27	45	0	3	1	6	0	0	0	–	3	8	0	0	0.2	1.000
4 yrs.			4	8	.333	4.14	115	2	0	176	196	86	92	0	4	6	6	5	1	0	.200	7	23	0	3	0.3	1.000

DIVISIONAL PLAYOFF SERIES

| 1981 | MIL | A | 0 | 0 | – | 0.00 | 2 | 0 | 0 | 2.1 | 0 | 0 | 0 | 0 | 0 | 0 | 0 | 0 | 0 | 0 | – | 0 | 0 | 0 | 0 | 0.0 | – |

LEAGUE CHAMPIONSHIP SERIES

| 1982 | MIL | A | 0 | 0 | – | 0.00 | 1 | 0 | 0 | 1 | 0 | 0 | 0 | 0 | 0 | 0 | 0 | 0 | 0 | 0 | – | 0 | 0 | 0 | 0 | 0.0 | – |

WORLD SERIES

| 1982 | MIL | A | 0 | 0 | – | 0.00 | 1 | 0 | 0 | 1 | 0 | 0 | 1 | 0 | 0 | 0 | 0 | 0 | 0 | 0 | – | 0 | 0 | 0 | 0 | 0.0 | – |

Joe Bernard

BERNARD, JOSEPH CARL
B. Mar. 24, 1882, Brighton, Ill. D. Sept. 22, 1960, Springfield, Ill.
BR TR 6'1" 175 lbs.

| 1909 | STL | N | 0 | 0 | – | 0.00 | 1 | 0 | 0 | 1 | 1 | 2 | 2 | 0 | 0 | 0 | 0 | 0 | 0 | 0 | – | 0 | 0 | 0 | 0 | 0.0 | – |

Bill Bernhard

BERNHARD, WILLIAM HENRY (Bernie)
B. Mar. 16, 1871, Clarence, N.Y. D. Mar. 30, 1949, San Diego, Calif.
BB TR 6'1" 205 lbs.

1899	PHI	N	6	6	.500	2.65	21	12	10	132.1	120	36	23	1	0	0	0	54	13	0	.241	2	34	4	1	1.9	.900
1900			15	10	.600	4.77	32	27	20	218.2	284	74	49	0	2	0	2	91	14	0	.154	5	60	4	7	2.2	.942
1901	PHI	A	17	10	.630	4.52	31	27	26	257	328	50	58	1	1	0	0	107	20	0	.187	22	85	4	1	3.6	.964

Year	Team	W	L	PCT	ERA	G	GS	CG	IP	H	BB	SO	ShO	Relief Pitching W	L	SV	Batting AB	H	HR	BA	PO	A	E	DP	TC/G	FA

Bill Bernhard *continued*

Year	Team	W	L	PCT	ERA	G	GS	CG	IP	H	BB	SO	ShO	W	L	SV	AB	H	HR	BA	PO	A	E	DP	TC/G	FA
1902	2 teams	PHI A (1G 1-0)				CLE A	(27G 17-5)																				
"	total	18	5	.783	2.15	28	25	23	226	176	37	58	3	1	0	1	94	18	0	.191	5	71	4	2	2.9	.950
1903	CLE A	14	6	.700	2.12	20	19	18	165.2	151	21	60	3	0	1	0	65	12	0	.185	6	56	2	1	3.2	.969
1904		23	13	.639	2.13	38	37	35	320.2	323	55	137	4	1	0	0	124	22	0	.177	8	102	6	2	3.1	.948
1905		7	13	.350	3.36	22	19	17	174.1	185	34	56	0	2	0	0	69	6	0	.087	14	53	3	1	3.2	.957
1906		16	15	.516	2.54	31	30	23	255.1	235	47	85	2	1	0	0	99	21	0	.212	19	83	3	4	3.4	.971
1907		0	4	.000	3.21	8	4	3	42	58	11	19	0	0	0	0	15	3	0	.200	2	16	4	0	2.8	.818
9 yrs.		116	82	.586	3.04	231	200	175	1792	1860	365	545	14	9	2	3	718	129	0	.180	83	560	34	19	2.9	.950

Walter Bernhardt

BERNHARDT, WALTER JACOB (Sarah)
B. May 20, 1893, Pleasant Village, Pa.   D. July 26, 1958, Watertown, N. Y.   BR TR 6'2"   195 lbs.

| 1918 | NY A | 0 | 0 | – | 0.00 | 1 | 0 | 0 | .2 | 0 | 0 | 0 | 0 | 0 | 0 | 0 | 0 | 0 | 0 | – | 0 | 0 | 0 | 0 | 0.0 | – |

Joe Berry

BERRY, JONAS ARTHUR (Jittery Joe)
B. Dec. 16, 1904, Huntsville, Ark.   D. Sept. 27, 1958, Anaheim, Calif.   BL TR 5'10½"   145 lbs.

1942	CHI N	0	0	–	18.00	2	0	0	2	7	2	1	0	0	0	0	–	0	1	0	0	0.5	1.000			
1944	PHI A	10	8	.556	1.94	53	0	0	111.1	78	23	44	0	10	8	12	25	3	0	.120	14	26	2	2	0.8	.952
1945		8	7	.533	2.35	52	0	0	130.1	114	38	51	0	8	7	5	35	5	0	.143	11	30	1	0	0.8	.976
1946	2 teams	PHI A (5G 0-1)				CLE A	(21G 3-6)																				
"	total	3	7	.300	3.22	26	0	0	50.1	47	24	21	0	3	7	1	10	3	0	.300	3	6	0	0	0.3	1.000
4 yrs.		21	22	.488	2.45	133	0	0	294	246	87	117	0	21	22	18	70	11	0	.157	28	63	3	2	0.7	.968

Frank Bertaina

BERTAINA, FRANK LOUIS
B. Apr. 14, 1944, San Francisco, Calif.   BL TL 5'11"   177 lbs.

1964	BAL A	1	0	1.000	2.77	6	4	1	26	18	13	18	1	0	0	0	5	0	0	.000	0	6	0	0	1.0	1.000
1965		0	0	–	6.00	2	1	0	6	9	4	5	0	0	0	0	1	0	0	.000	1	0	0	0	0.5	1.000
1966		2	5	.286	3.13	16	9	0	63.1	52	36	46	0	1	0	0	19	2	0	.105	2	4	4	0	0.6	.600
1967	2 teams	BAL A (5G 1-1)				WAS A	(18G 6-5)																				
"	total	7	6	.538	2.99	23	19	4	117.1	107	51	86	4	0	0	0	44	3	0	.068	4	16	0	2	0.9	1.000
1968	WAS A	7	13	.350	4.66	27	23	1	127.1	133	69	81	0	0	0	0	38	5	0	.132	9	17	0	2	1.0	1.000
1969	2 teams	WAS A (14G 1-3)				BAL A	(3G 0-0)																				
"	total	1	3	.250	5.62	17	5	0	41.2	44	26	30	0	0	3	1	12	5	1	.417	3	7	2	0	0.7	.833
1970	STL N	1	2	.333	3.19	8	5	0	31	36	15	14	0	0	0	0	7	1	0	.143	0	5	0	0	0.6	1.000
7 yrs.		19	29	.396	3.84	99	66	6	412.2	399	214	280	5	1	3	0	126	16	1	.127	18	56	6	4	0.8	.925

Lefty Bertrand

BERTRAND, ROMAN MATHIAS
B. Feb. 28, 1909, Cobden, Minn.   BR TL 6'   180 lbs.

| 1936 | PHI N | 0 | 0 | – | 9.00 | 1 | 0 | 0 | 2 | 3 | 2 | 1 | 0 | 0 | 0 | 0 | 0 | 0 | 0 | – | 0 | 0 | 0 | 0 | 0.0 | – |

Fred Besana

BESANA, FREDERICK CYRIL
B. Apr. 5, 1931, Lincoln, Calif.   BR TL 6'3½"   200 lbs.

| 1956 | BAL A | 1 | 0 | 1.000 | 5.60 | 7 | 2 | 0 | 17.2 | 22 | 14 | 7 | 0 | 0 | 0 | 0 | 4 | 0 | 0 | .000 | 2 | 5 | 0 | 0 | 1.0 | 1.000 |

Herman Besse

BESSE, HERMAN A. (Long Herm)
B. Aug. 16, 1911, St. Louis, Mo.   D. Aug. 13, 1972, Los Angeles, Calif.   BL TL 6'2"   190 lbs.

1940	PHI A	0	3	.000	8.83	17	5	0	53	70	34	19	0	0	0	0	19	5	0	.263	0	5	0	0	0.3	1.000
1941		2	0	1.000	10.07	6	2	1	19.2	28	12	8	0	1	0	0	5	1	0	.200	1	4	0	1	0.8	1.000
1942		2	9	.182	6.50	30	14	4	133	163	69	78	0	0	0	1	53	12	0	.226	0	18	1	0	0.6	.947
1943		1	1	.500	3.31	5	1	0	16.1	18	4	3	0	0	1	0	8	0	0	.000	0	4	0	0	0.8	1.000
1946		0	2	.000	5.23	7	3	0	20.2	19	9	10	0	0	0	1	5	0	0	.000	0	3	0	0	0.4	1.000
5 yrs.		5	15	.250	6.97	65	25	5	242.2	298	128	118	0	1	2	2	90	18	0	.200	1	34	1	1	0.6	.972

Don Bessent

BESSENT, FRED DONALD (The Weasel)
B. Mar. 13, 1931, Jacksonville, Fla.   BR TR 6'   175 lbs.

1955	BKN N	8	1	.889	2.70	24	2	1	63.1	51	21	29	0	6	1	3	20	2	0	.100	1	11	0	0	0.5	1.000
1956		4	3	.571	2.50	38	0	0	79.1	63	31	52	0	4	3	9	18	2	0	.111	3	8	1	1	0.3	.917
1957		1	3	.250	5.73	27	0	0	44	58	19	24	0	1	3	0	4	1	0	.250	6	4	0	0	0.4	1.000
1958	LA N	1	0	1.000	3.33	19	0	0	24.1	24	17	13	0	1	0	0	2	0	0	.000	2	6	0	2	0.4	1.000
4 yrs.		14	7	.667	3.33	108	2	1	211	196	88	118	0	12	7	12	44	5	0	.114	12	29	1	3	0.4	.976

WORLD SERIES

1955	BKN N	0	0	–	0.00	3	0	0	3.1	3	1	1	0	0	0	0	1	0	0	.000	0	2	0	0	0.7	1.000
1956		1	0	1.000	1.80	2	0	0	10	8	3	5	0	1	0	0	2	1	0	.500	0	0	0	0	0.0	–
2 yrs.		1	0	1.000	1.35	5	0	0	13.1	11	4	6	0	1	0	0	3	1	0	.333	0	2	0	0	0.4	1.000

Karl Best

BEST, KARL JON
B. Mar. 6, 1959, Aberdeen, Wash.   BR TR 6'4"   200 lbs.

1983	SEA A	0	1	.000	13.50	4	0	0	5.1	14	5	3	0	0	1	0	0	0	0	–	0	0	0	0	0.0	–
1984		1	1	.500	3.00	5	0	0	6	7	6	6	0	1	1	0	0	0	0	–	0	0	0	0	0.0	–
1985		2	1	.667	1.95	15	0	0	32.1	25	6	32	0	2	1	4	0	0	0	–	0	3	1	0	0.3	.750
1986		2	3	.400	4.04	26	0	0	35.2	35	21	23	0	2	3	1	0	0	0	–	1	3	0	0	0.2	1.000
1988	MIN A	0	0	–	6.00	11	0	0	12	15	7	9	0	0	0	0	0	0	0	–	0	1	0	0	0.1	1.000
5 yrs.		5	6	.455	4.04	61	0	0	91.1	96	39	73	0	5	6	5	0	0	0	–	1	7	1	0	0.1	.889

Jim Bethke

BETHKE, JAMES CHARLES
B. Nov. 5, 1946, Falls City, Neb.   BR TR 6'3"   185 lbs.

| 1965 | NY N | 2 | 0 | 1.000 | 4.28 | 25 | 0 | 0 | 40 | 41 | 22 | 19 | 0 | 2 | 0 | 0 | 4 | 0 | 0 | .000 | 2 | 12 | 0 | 2 | 0.6 | 1.000 |

Year	Team		W	L	PCT	ERA	G	GS	CG	IP	H	BB	SO	ShO	Relief Pitching W	L	SV	Batting AB	H	HR	BA	PO	A	E	DP	TC/G	FA

Jeff Bettendorf
BETTENDORF, JEFFREY ALLEN
B. Dec. 10, 1960, Lompoc, Calif.   BR TR 6'3"   180 lbs.

Year	Team	W	L	PCT	ERA	G	GS	CG	IP	H	BB	SO	ShO	W	L	SV	AB	H	HR	BA	PO	A	E	DP	TC/G	FA
1984	OAK A	0	0	–	4.66	3	0	0	9.2	9	5	5	0	0	0	1	0	0	0	–	0	0	0	0	0.0	–

Hal Betts
BETTS, HAROLD MATTHEW
B. June 19, 1881, Alliance, Ohio   D. May 22, 1946, San Antonio, Tex.   BR TR 5'10"   200 lbs.

Year	Team	W	L	PCT	ERA	G	GS	CG	IP	H	BB	SO	ShO	W	L	SV	AB	H	HR	BA	PO	A	E	DP	TC/G	FA
1903	STL N	0	1	.000	10.00	1	1	1	9	11	5	2	0	0	0	0	3	0	0	.000	1	1	0	1	2.0	1.000
1913	CIN N	0	0	–	2.70	1	0	0	3.1	1	3	0	0	0	0	0	1	0	0	.000	0	0	0	0	0.0	–
2 yrs.		0	1	.000	8.03	2	1	1	12.1	12	8	2	0	0	0	0	4	0	0	.000	1	1	0	1	1.0	1.000

Huck Betts
BETTS, WALTER MARTIN
B. Feb. 18, 1897, Millsboro, Del.   D. June 16, 1987, Millsboro, Del.   BR TR 5'11"   170 lbs.

Year	Team	W	L	PCT	ERA	G	GS	CG	IP	H	BB	SO	ShO	W	L	SV	AB	H	HR	BA	PO	A	E	DP	TC/G	FA
1920	PHI N	1	1	.500	3.57	27	4	1	88.1	86	33	18	0	1	0	0	25	2	0	.080	3	23	1	0	1.0	.963
1921		3	7	.300	4.47	32	2	1	100.2	141	14	28	0	3	5	4	30	8	0	.267	4	27	2	1	1.0	.939
1922		1	0	1.000	9.60	7	0	0	15	23	8	4	0	1	0	0	4	0	0	.000	0	2	0	0	0.3	1.000
1923		2	4	.333	3.09	19	4	3	84.1	100	14	18	0	1	1	1	31	3	0	.097	3	22	1	0	1.4	.962
1924		7	10	.412	4.30	37	9	2	144.1	160	42	46	0	5	5	2	45	7	0	.156	5	29	3	0	1.0	.919
1925		4	5	.444	5.55	35	7	1	97.1	146	38	28	0	3	1	1	34	10	0	.294	1	30	2	0	0.9	.939
1932	BOS N	13	11	.542	2.80	31	27	16	221.2	229	35	32	3	2	0	1	79	19	0	.241	9	40	0	2	1.6	1.000
1933		11	11	.500	2.79	35	26	17	242	225	55	40	1	0	1	4	76	17	0	.224	5	78	1	2	2.4	.988
1934		17	10	.630	4.06	40	27	10	213	258	42	69	2	3	1	3	69	13	0	.188	9	36	2	3	1.2	.957
1935		2	9	.182	5.47	44	19	2	159.2	213	40	40	1	1	2	0	44	7	0	.159	3	40	1	0	1.0	.977
10 yrs.		61	68	.473	3.93	307	125	53	1366.1	1581	321	323	8	18	17	16	437	86	0	.197	42	327	13	8	1.2	.966

Bill Bevens
BEVENS, FLOYD CLIFFORD
B. Oct. 21, 1916, Hubbard, Ore.   BR TR 6'3½"   210 lbs.

Year	Team	W	L	PCT	ERA	G	GS	CG	IP	H	BB	SO	ShO	W	L	SV	AB	H	HR	BA	PO	A	E	DP	TC/G	FA
1944	NY A	4	1	.800	2.68	8	5	3	43.2	44	13	16	0	0	0	0	16	1	0	.063	1	7	0	2	1.0	1.000
1945		13	9	.591	3.67	29	25	14	184	174	68	76	2	0	1	0	63	7	1	.111	10	39	4	5	1.8	.925
1946		16	13	.552	2.23	31	31	18	249.2	213	78	120	3	0	0	0	84	7	2	.083	9	25	5	1	1.3	.872
1947		7	13	.350	3.82	28	23	11	165	167	77	77	1	1	1	0	58	7	0	.121	8	24	0	2	1.1	1.000
4 yrs.		40	36	.526	3.08	96	84	46	642.1	598	236	289	6	1	2	0	221	22	3	.100	28	95	9	10	1.4	.932

WORLD SERIES

Year	Team	W	L	PCT	ERA	G	GS	CG	IP	H	BB	SO	ShO	W	L	SV	AB	H	HR	BA	PO	A	E	DP	TC/G	FA
1947	NY A	0	1	.000	2.38	2	1	1	11.1	3	11	7	0	0	0	0	4	0	0	.000	0	1	0	0	0.5	1.000

Lou Bevil
BEVIL, LOUIS EUGENE
Born Louis Eugene Bevilacqua.
B. Nov. 27, 1922, Nelson, Ill.   D. Feb. 1, 1973, Dixon, Ill.   BB TR 5'11½"   190 lbs.

Year	Team	W	L	PCT	ERA	G	GS	CG	IP	H	BB	SO	ShO	W	L	SV	AB	H	HR	BA	PO	A	E	DP	TC/G	FA
1942	WAS A	0	1	.000	6.52	4	1	0	9.2	9	11	2	0	0	0	0	3	0	0	.000	0	1	0	0	0.3	1.000

Charlie Beville
BEVILLE, CLARENCE BENJAMIN (Candy Ben)
B. Aug. 28, 1877, Colusa, Calif.   D. Jan. 5, 1937, Yountville, Calif.   BR TR 5'9"   190 lbs.

Year	Team	W	L	PCT	ERA	G	GS	CG	IP	H	BB	SO	ShO	W	L	SV	AB	H	HR	BA	PO	A	E	DP	TC/G	FA
1901	BOS A	0	2	.000	4.00	2	2	1	9	8	9	1	0	0	0	0	7	2	0	.286	0	2	0	0	1.0	1.000

Jim Bibby
BIBBY, JAMES BLAIR
B. Oct. 29, 1944, Franklinton, N. C.   BR TR 6'5"   235 lbs.

Year	Team		W	L	PCT	ERA	G	GS	CG	IP	H	BB	SO	ShO	W	L	SV	AB	H	HR	BA	PO	A	E	DP	TC/G	FA
1972	STL N		1	3	.250	3.35	6	6	0	40.1	29	19	28	0	0	0	0	8	1	0	.125	2	6	0	1	1.3	1.000
1973	2 teams	STL N (6G 0–2)										TEX A (26G 9–10)															
"	total		9	12	.429	3.77	32	26	11	196	140	123	167	2	0	0	1	2	0	0	.000	5	22	2	1	0.9	.931
1974	TEX A		19	19	.500	4.74	41	41	11	264	255	113	149	5	0	0	0	0	0	0	–	22	36	3	4	1.5	.951
1975	2 teams	TEX A (12G 2–6)										CLE A (24G 5–9)															
"	total		7	15	.318	3.88	36	24	8	181	172	78	93	1	1	0	0	0	0	0	–	11	27	2	3	1.1	.950
1976	CLE A		13	7	.650	3.20	34	21	4	163	162	56	84	3	3	1	1	0	0	0	–	10	19	2	2	0.9	.935
1977			12	13	.480	3.57	37	30	9	207	197	73	141	2	0	1	2	0	0	0	–	14	21	5	0	1.1	.875
1978	PIT N		8	7	.533	3.53	34	14	3	107	100	39	72	2	3	2	1	31	4	1	.129	3	20	2	0	0.7	.920
1979			12	4	.750	2.80	34	17	4	138	110	47	103	1	2	1	0	45	8	2	.178	5	12	0	1	0.5	1.000
1980			19	6	**.760**	3.33	35	34	6	238	210	88	144	1	1	0	0	77	12	1	.156	9	30	3	1	1.2	.929
1981			6	3	.667	2.49	14	14	2	94	79	26	48	2	0	0	0	28	4	1	.143	2	11	1	3	1.0	.929
1983			5	12	.294	6.69	29	12	0	78	92	51	44	0	3	4	2	18	2	0	.111	4	10	0	0	0.5	1.000
1984	TEX A		0	0	–	4.41	8	0	0	16.1	19	10	6	0	0	0	0	0	0	0	–	1	2	0	0	0.4	1.000
12 yrs.			111	101	.524	3.76	340	239	56	1722.2	1565	723	1079	19	13	12	8	209	31	5	.148	88	216	20	16	1.0	.938

LEAGUE CHAMPIONSHIP SERIES

Year	Team		W	L	PCT	ERA	G	GS	CG	IP	H	BB	SO	ShO	W	L	SV	AB	H	HR	BA	PO	A	E	DP	TC/G	FA
1979	PIT N		0	0	–	1.29	1	1	0	7	4	4	5	0	0	0	0	0	0	0	–	1	0	0	0	1.0	1.000

WORLD SERIES

Year	Team		W	L	PCT	ERA	G	GS	CG	IP	H	BB	SO	ShO	W	L	SV	AB	H	HR	BA	PO	A	E	DP	TC/G	FA
1979	PIT N		0	0	–	2.61	2	2	0	10.1	10	2	10	0	0	0	0	4	0	0	.000	1	0	0	0	0.5	1.000

Vern Bickford
BICKFORD, VERNON EDGELL
B. Aug. 17, 1920, Hellier, Ky.   D. May 6, 1960, Concord, Va.   BR TR 6'   180 lbs.

Year	Team	W	L	PCT	ERA	G	GS	CG	IP	H	BB	SO	ShO	W	L	SV	AB	H	HR	BA	PO	A	E	DP	TC/G	FA
1948	BOS N	11	5	.688	3.27	33	22	10	146	125	63	60	1	0	1	1	49	10	0	.204	6	22	1	0	0.9	.966
1949		16	11	.593	4.25	37	36	15	230.2	246	106	101	2	0	0	0	81	15	0	.185	7	50	1	3	1.6	.983
1950		19	14	.576	3.47	40	**39**	**27**	311.2	293	122	126	3	0	0	0	116	16	0	.138	26	45	2	5	1.8	.973
1951		11	9	.550	3.12	25	20	12	164.2	146	76	76	3	0	2	0	52	6	0	.115	14	38	1	4	2.1	.981
1952		7	12	.368	3.74	26	22	7	161.1	165	64	62	1	0	0	0	51	9	0	.176	12	32	1	4	1.7	.978
1953	MIL N	2	5	.286	5.28	20	9	2	58	60	35	25	0	0	1	0	15	1	0	.067	3	14	0	3	0.9	1.000
1954	BAL A	0	1	.000	9.00	1	1	0	4	5	1	0	0	0	0	0	1	0	0	.000	0	1	0	0	1.0	1.000
7 yrs.		66	57	.537	3.71	182	149	73	1076.1	1040	467	450	9	1	4	2	365	57	0	.156	68	202	6	19	1.5	.978

WORLD SERIES

Year	Team	W	L	PCT	ERA	G	GS	CG	IP	H	BB	SO	ShO	W	L	SV	AB	H	HR	BA	PO	A	E	DP	TC/G	FA
1948	BOS N	0	1	.000	2.70	1	1	0	3.1	1	4	5	1	0	0	0	0	0	0	–	0	0	0	0	0.0	–

Year	Team		W	L	PCT	ERA	G	GS	CG	IP	H	BB	SO	ShO	Relief Pitching W	L	SV	Batting AB	H	HR	BA	PO	A	E	DP	TC/G	FA

Dan Bickham

BICKHAM, DANIEL DENISON
B. Oct. 31, 1864, Dayton, Ohio   D. Mar. 3, 1951, Dayton, Ohio
BR TR 5'10"   160 lbs.

| 1886 | CIN | AA | 1 | 0 | 1.000 | 3.00 | 1 | 1 | 1 | 9 | 13 | 3 | 6 | 0 | 0 | 0 | 0 | 3 | 1 | 0 | .333 | 0 | 3 | 1 | 0 | 4.0 | .750 |

Charlie Bicknell

BICKNELL, CHARLES STEPHEN (Bud)
B. July 27, 1928, Plainfield, N. J.
BR TR 5'11"   170 lbs.

1948	PHI	N	0	1	.000	5.96	17	1	0	25.2	29	17	5	0	0	0	0	5	0	0	.000	2	2	0	1	0.2	1.000
1949			0	0	—	7.62	13	0	0	28.1	32	17	4	0	0	0	0	1	0	0	.000	2	5	1	1	0.6	.875
2 yrs.			0	1	.000	6.83	30	1	0	54	61	34	9	0	0	0	0	6	0	0	.000	4	7	1	2	0.4	.917

Mike Bielecki

BIELECKI, MICHAEL JOSEPH
B. July 31, 1959, Baltimore, Md.
BR TR 6'3"   195 lbs.

1984	PIT	N	0	0	—	0.00	4	0	0	4.1	4	0	1	0	0	0	0	0	0	0	—	0	1	0	0	0.3	1.000
1985			2	3	.400	4.53	12	7	0	45.2	45	31	22	0	0	0	0	10	0	0	.000	5	11	0	1	1.3	1.000
1986			6	11	.353	4.66	31	27	0	148.2	149	83	83	0	0	0	0	48	3	0	.063	17	16	1	1	1.1	.971
1987			2	3	.400	4.73	8	8	2	45.2	43	12	25	0	0	0	0	16	1	0	.063	6	5	1	0	1.5	.917
1988	CHI	N	2	2	.500	3.35	19	5	0	48.1	55	16	33	0	1	0	0	10	1	0	.100	4	5	0	0	0.5	1.000
1989			18	7	.720	3.14	33	33	4	212.1	187	81	147	3	0	0	0	70	3	0	.043	18	21	1	0	1.2	.975
6 yrs.			30	26	.536	3.85	107	80	6	505	483	223	311	3	1	0	0	154	8	0	.052	50	59	3	1	1.0	.973

LEAGUE CHAMPIONSHIP SERIES

| 1989 | CHI | N | 0 | 1 | .000 | 3.65 | 2 | 2 | 0 | 12.1 | 7 | 6 | 11 | 0 | 0 | 0 | 0 | 5 | 1 | 0 | .200 | 1 | 2 | 0 | 0 | 1.5 | 1.000 |

Harry Biemiller

BIEMILLER, HARRY LEE
B. Oct. 9, 1897, Baltimore, Md.   D. May 25, 1965, Orlando, Fla.
BR TR 6'1"   171 lbs.

1920	WAS	A	1	0	1.000	4.76	5	2	1	17	21	13	10	0	0	0	0	4	0	0	.000	1	7	0	0	1.6	1.000
1925	CIN	N	0	1	.000	4.02	23	1	0	47	45	21	9	0	0	0	2	9	0	0	.000	2	19	1	1	1.0	.955
2 yrs.			1	1	.500	4.22	28	3	1	64	66	34	19	0	0	0	2	13	0	0	.000	3	26	1	1	1.1	.967

Lou Bierbauer

BIERBAUER, LOUIS W.
Also appeared in box score as Bauer
B. Sept. 28, 1865, Erie, Pa.   D. Jan. 31, 1926, Erie, Pa.
BL TR 5'8"   140 lbs.

1886	PHI	AA	0	0	—	4.22	2	0	0	10.2	8	5	1	0	0	0	0	522	118	2	.226	0	0	0	0	0.0	—
1887			0	0	—	0.00	1	0	0	1	0	0	1	0	0	0	1	530	144	1	.272	0	0	0	0	0.0	—
1888			0	0	—	0.00	1	0	0	3	5	0	3	0	0	0	0	535	143	0	.267	0	0	0	0	0.0	—
3 yrs.			0	0	—	3.07	4	0	0	14.2	13	5	5	0	0	0	1	*				0	0	0	0	0.0	—

Lyle Bigbee

BIGBEE, LYLE RANDOLPH (Al)
Brother of Carson Bigbee.
B. Aug. 22, 1893, Sweet Home, Ore.   D. Aug. 5, 1942, Portland, Ore.
BL TR 6'   180 lbs.

1920	PHI	A	0	3	.000	8.00	12	0	0	45	66	25	12	0	0	0	3	70	13	1	.186	3	11	0	0	1.2	1.000
1921	PIT	N	0	0	—	1.13	5	0	0	8	4	4	1	0	0	0	0	2	0	0	.000	0	2	0	0	0.4	1.000
2 yrs.			0	3	.000	6.96	17	0	0	53	70	29	13	0	0	0	3	*				3	13	0	0	0.9	1.000

Charlie Biggs

BIGGS, CHARLES ORVAL
B. Sept. 15, 1906, French Lick, Ind.   D. May 24, 1954, French Lick, Ind.
BR TR 6'1"   185 lbs.

| 1932 | CHI | A | 1 | 1 | .500 | 6.93 | 6 | 4 | 0 | 24.2 | 32 | 12 | 1 | 0 | 0 | 0 | 0 | 9 | 1 | 0 | .111 | 2 | 4 | 0 | 2 | 1.0 | 1.000 |

Larry Biittner

BIITTNER, LAWRENCE DAVID
B. July 27, 1945, Pocahontas, Iowa
BL TL 6'2"   205 lbs.

| 1977 | CHI | N | 0 | 0 | — | 54.00 | 1 | 0 | 0 | 1 | 5 | 1 | 3 | 0 | 0 | 0 | 0 | * | | | | 0 | 0 | 0 | 0 | 0.0 | — |

Jim Bilbrey

BILBREY, JAMES MELVIN
B. Apr. 20, 1924, Rickman, Tenn.   D. Dec. 26, 1985, Toledo, Ohio
BR TR 6'2½"   205 lbs.

| 1949 | STL | A | 0 | 0 | — | 18.00 | 1 | 0 | 0 | 1 | 3 | 1 | 3 | 0 | 0 | 0 | 0 | 0 | 0 | 0 | — | 0 | 1 | 0 | 0 | 1.0 | 1.000 |

Emil Bildilli

BILDILLI, EMIL (Hill Billy)
B. Sept. 16, 1912, Diamond, Ind.   D. Sept. 16, 1946, Hartford City, Ind.
BR TL 5'10"   170 lbs.

1937	STL	A	0	1	.000	10.13	4	1	0	8	12	3	1	0	0	0	0	2	0	0	.000	0	4	0	0	1.0	1.000
1938			1	2	.333	7.06	5	3	2	21.2	33	11	11	0	0	0	0	8	2	0	.250	0	4	0	0	0.8	1.000
1939			1	1	.500	3.32	2	2	0	19	21	6	8	0	0	0	0	5	0	0	.000	1	4	0	0	2.5	1.000
1940			2	4	.333	5.57	28	11	3	97	113	52	32	0	0	0	1	30	6	0	.200	7	32	2	2	1.5	.951
1941			0	0	—	11.57	2	0	0	2.1	5	3	2	0	0	0	0	0	0	0	—	0	1	0	0	0.5	1.000
5 yrs.			4	8	.333	5.84	41	17	7	148	184	75	55	0	0	0	1	45	8	0	.178	8	45	2	2	1.3	.964

Harry Billiard

BILLIARD, HARRY PREE
B. Nov. 11, 1883, Monroe, Ind.   D. June 3, 1923, Wooster, Ohio
BR TR 6'   190 lbs.

1908	NY	A	0	0	—	2.57	5	0	0	14	13	13	9	0	0	0	0	5	1	0	.200	1	2	1	0	0.8	.750
1914	IND	F	8	7	.533	3.72	32	16	5	125.2	117	63	45	0	4	2	1	38	7	0	.184	2	33	5	0	1.3	.875
1915	NWK	F	1	0	1.000	5.72	14	2	0	28.1	32	28	7	0	1	0	0	6	2	0	.333	2	12	0	0	1.0	1.000
3 yrs.			9	7	.563	3.96	51	18	5	168	162	104	61	0	5	2	1	49	10	0	.204	5	47	6	0	1.1	.897

Jack Billingham

BILLINGHAM, JOHN EUGENE
B. Feb. 21, 1943, Orlando, Fla.
BR TR 6'4"   195 lbs.

1968	LA	N	3	0	1.000	2.14	50	1	0	71.1	54	30	46	0	3	0	8	3	0	0	.000	5	15	1	1	0.4	.952
1969	HOU	N	6	7	.462	4.23	52	4	1	83	92	29	71	0	0	0	2	14	1	0	.071	3	12	1	0	0.3	.938
1970			13	9	.591	3.97	46	24	8	188	190	63	134	2	2	0	0	58	6	0	.103	13	30	2	1	1.0	.956
1971			10	16	.385	3.39	33	33	8	228	205	68	139	3	0	0	0	73	9	0	.123	20	32	4	3	1.7	.929
1972	CIN	N	12	12	.500	3.18	36	31	8	217.2	197	64	137	4	0	0	1	71	5	0	.070	14	28	1	0	1.2	.977
1973			19	10	.655	3.04	40	**40**	16	**293.1**	257	95	155	**7**	0	0	0	93	6	0	.065	18	53	2	3	1.8	.973

Year	Team		W	L	PCT	ERA	G	GS	CG	IP	H	BB	SO	ShO	Relief Pitching W	L	SV	Batting AB	H	HR	BA	PO	A	E	DP	TC/G	FA

Jack Billingham *continued*

Year	Team		W	L	PCT	ERA	G	GS	CG	IP	H	BB	SO	ShO	W	L	SV	AB	H	HR	BA	PO	A	E	DP	TC/G	FA
1974			19	11	.633	3.95	36	35	8	212	233	64	103	3	1	0	0	67	5	0	.075	14	35	1	1	1.4	.980
1975			15	10	.600	4.11	33	32	5	208	222	76	79	0	0	0	0	65	7	0	.108	8	24	0	5	1.0	1.000
1976			12	10	.545	4.32	34	29	5	177	190	62	76	2	1	1	1	59	14	0	.237	10	25	1	1	1.1	.972
1977			10	10	.500	5.22	36	23	3	162	195	56	76	2	1	2	0	56	9	0	.161	12	34	1	2	1.3	.979
1978	DET	A	15	8	.652	3.88	30	30	10	201.2	218	65	59	4	0	0	0	0	0	0	—	9	30	1	0	1.3	.975
1979			10	7	.588	3.30	35	19	2	158	163	60	59	0	3	3	3	0	0	0	—	6	21	2	3	0.8	.931
1980	2 teams	DET A (8G 0–0)				BOS A (7G 1–3)																					
"	total		1	3	.250	10.45	15	4	0	31	56	18	7	0	0	0	0	0	0	0	—	1	5	0	0	0.4	1.000
13 yrs.			145	113	.562	3.83	476	305	74	2231	2272	750	1141	27	11	5	15	559	62	0	.111	133	344	17	21	1.0	.966

LEAGUE CHAMPIONSHIP SERIES

Year	Team		W	L	PCT	ERA	G	GS	CG	IP	H	BB	SO	ShO	W	L	SV	AB	H	HR	BA	PO	A	E	DP	TC/G	FA
1972	CIN	N	0	0	–	3.86	1	1	0	4.2	5	2	4	0	0	0	0	2	0	0	.000	1	0	0	0	1.0	1.000
1973			0	1	.000	4.50	2	2	0	12	9	4	9	0	0	0	0	3	0	0	.000	0	2	0	0	1.0	1.000
2 yrs.			0	1	.000	4.32	3	3	0	16.2	14	6	13	0	0	0	0	5	0	0	.000	1	2	0	0	1.0	1.000

WORLD SERIES

Year	Team		W	L	PCT	ERA	G	GS	CG	IP	H	BB	SO	ShO	W	L	SV	AB	H	HR	BA	PO	A	E	DP	TC/G	FA
1972	CIN	N	1	0	1.000	0.00	3	2	0	13.2	6	4	11	0	0	0	0	5	0	0	.000	1	0	0	0	0.7	1.000
1975			0	0	–	1.00	3	1	0	9	8	5	7	0	0	0	0	2	0	0	.000	0	2	0	1	0.7	1.000
1976			1	0	1.000	0.00	1	0	0	2.2	0	0	1	0	0	0	0	0	0	0	—	1	0	0	0	1.0	1.000
3 yrs.			2	0	1.000	0.36 1st	7	3	0	25.1 1st	14	9	19	0	0	1	0	7	0	0	.000	2	3	0	1	0.7	1.000

Haskell Billings

BILLINGS, HASKELL CLARK
B. Sept. 27, 1907, New York, N. Y.   D. Dec. 26, 1983, Greenbrae, Calif.

BR TR 5'11" 180 lbs.

Year	Team		W	L	PCT	ERA	G	GS	CG	IP	H	BB	SO	ShO	W	L	SV	AB	H	HR	BA	PO	A	E	DP	TC/G	FA
1927	DET	A	5	4	.556	4.84	10	9	5	67	64	39	18	0	0	0	0	27	7	0	.259	1	15	0	0	1.6	1.000
1928			5	10	.333	5.12	21	16	3	110.2	118	59	48	1	0	0	0	35	10	0	.286	5	22	1	1	1.3	.964
1929			0	1	.000	5.12	8	0	0	19.1	27	9	1	0	0	1	0	6	0	0	.000	2	9	1	0	1.5	.917
3 yrs.			10	15	.400	5.03	39	25	8	197	209	107	67	1	0	2	0	68	17	0	.250	8	46	2	1	1.4	.964

Doug Bird

BIRD, JAMES DOUGLAS
B. Mar. 5, 1950, Corona, Calif.

BR TR 6'4" 180 lbs.

Year	Team		W	L	PCT	ERA	G	GS	CG	IP	H	BB	SO	ShO	W	L	SV	AB	H	HR	BA	PO	A	E	DP	TC/G	FA
1973	KC	A	4	4	.500	3.00	54	0	0	102	81	30	83	0	4	4	20	0	0	0	—	2	5	0	1	0.1	1.000
1974			7	6	.538	2.74	55	1	1	92	100	27	62	0	7	5	10	0	0	0	—	8	12	0	3	0.4	1.000
1975			9	6	.600	3.25	51	4	0	105.1	100	40	81	0	9	5	11	0	0	0	—	12	8	3	2	0.5	.870
1976			12	10	.545	3.36	39	27	2	198	191	31	107	1	3	0	2	0	0	0	—	14	21	2	1	0.9	.946
1977			11	4	.733	3.89	53	5	0	118	120	29	83	0	11	3	14	0	0	0	—	6	13	0	0	0.4	1.000
1978			6	6	.500	5.29	40	6	0	98.2	110	31	48	0	5	3	1	0	0	0	—	6	13	0	0	0.5	1.000
1979	PHI	N	2	0	1.000	5.16	32	1	1	61	73	16	33	0	1	0	0	6	1	0	.167	4	2	0	0	0.2	1.000
1980	NY	A	3	0	1.000	2.65	22	1	0	51	47	14	17	0	2	0	1	0	0	0	—	3	10	0	1	0.6	1.000
1981	2 teams	NY A (17G 5–1)				CHI N (12G 4–5)																					
"	total		9	6	.600	3.23	29	16	2	128	130	32	62	1	2	0	0	20	2	0	.100	13	14	0	2	0.9	1.000
1982	CHI	N	9	14	.391	5.14	35	33	2	191	230	30	71	1	0	0	0	56	8	0	.143	19	19	0	1	1.1	1.000
1983	BOS	A	1	4	.200	6.65	22	6	0	67.2	91	16	33	0	0	1	1	0	0	0	—	7	7	0	1	0.6	1.000
11 yrs.			73	60	.549	3.99	432	100	8	1212.2	1273	296	680	3	44	21	60	82	11	0	.134	94	124	5	11	0.5	.978

LEAGUE CHAMPIONSHIP SERIES

Year	Team		W	L	PCT	ERA	G	GS	CG	IP	H	BB	SO	ShO	W	L	SV	AB	H	HR	BA	PO	A	E	DP	TC/G	FA
1976	KC	A	1	0	1.000	1.93	1	0	0	4.2	4	0	1	0	1	0	0	0	0	0	—	0	1	0	0	2.0	.500
1977			0	0	–	0.00	3	0	0	2	4	0	1	0	0	0	0	0	0	0	—	0	0	0	0	0.0	–
1978			0	1	.000	9.00	2	0	0	1	2	0	1	0	0	1	0	0	0	0	—	0	1	0	0	0.5	1.000
3 yrs.			1	1	.500	2.35	6	0	0	7.2	10	0	3	0	1	1	0	0	0	0	—	0	2	1	0	0.5	.667

Red Bird

BIRD, JAMES EDWARD
B. Apr. 25, 1890, Stephenville, Tex.   D. Mar. 23, 1972, Murfeesboro, Ark.

BL TL 5'11" 170 lbs.

Year	Team		W	L	PCT	ERA	G	GS	CG	IP	H	BB	SO	ShO	W	L	SV	AB	H	HR	BA	PO	A	E	DP	TC/G	FA
1921	WAS	A	0	0	–	5.40	1	0	0	5	5	1	2	0	0	0	0	0	0	0	.000	0	3	0	0	3.0	1.000

Mike Birkbeck

BIRKBECK, MICHAEL LAWRENCE
B. Mar. 10, 1961, Orrville, Ohio

BR TR 6'1" 180 lbs.

Year	Team		W	L	PCT	ERA	G	GS	CG	IP	H	BB	SO	ShO	W	L	SV	AB	H	HR	BA	PO	A	E	DP	TC/G	FA
1986	MIL	A	1	1	.500	4.50	7	4	0	22	24	12	13	0	0	0	0	0	0	0	—	1	2	0	0	0.4	1.000
1987			1	4	.200	6.20	10	10	1	45	63	19	25	0	0	0	0	0	0	0	—	2	13	1	0	1.6	.938
1988			10	8	.556	4.72	23	23	0	124	141	37	64	0	0	0	0	0	0	0	—	21	19	2	2	1.8	.952
1989			0	4	.000	5.44	9	9	1	44.2	57	22	31	0	0	0	0	0	0	0	—	4	5	3	0	1.3	.750
4 yrs.			12	17	.414	5.12	49	46	2	235.2	285	90	133	0	0	0	0	0	0	0	—	28	39	6	2	1.5	.918

Ralph Birkofer

BIRKOFER, RALPH JOSEPH (Lefty)
B. Nov. 5, 1908, Cincinnati, Ohio   D. Mar. 16, 1971, Cincinnati, Ohio

BL TL 5'11" 213 lbs.

Year	Team		W	L	PCT	ERA	G	GS	CG	IP	H	BB	SO	ShO	W	L	SV	AB	H	HR	BA	PO	A	E	DP	TC/G	FA
1933	PIT	N	4	2	.667	2.31	9	8	3	50.2	43	17	20	1	0	0	0	22	7	0	.318	1	10	0	0	1.2	1.000
1934			11	12	.478	4.10	41	24	11	204	227	66	71	0	2	1	0	75	17	0	.227	2	39	3	1	1.1	.932
1935			9	7	.563	4.07	37	18	8	150.1	173	42	80	1	2	0	1	58	14	0	.241	3	18	4	1	0.7	.840
1936			7	5	.583	4.69	34	13	2	109.1	130	41	44	0	6	3	4	41	9	0	.220	1	14	7	0	0.6	.682
1937	BKN	N	0	2	.000	6.67	11	1	0	29.2	45	9	9	0	0	1	0	11	3	0	.273	0	5	0	0	0.5	1.000
5 yrs.			31	28	.525	4.19	132	64	24	544	618	175	224	2	10	4	2	207	50	0	.242	7	86	14	2	0.8	.869

Babe Birrer

BIRRER, WERNER JOSEPH
B. July 4, 1928, Buffalo, N. Y.

BR TR 6' 195 lbs.

Year	Team		W	L	PCT	ERA	G	GS	CG	IP	H	BB	SO	ShO	W	L	SV	AB	H	HR	BA	PO	A	E	DP	TC/G	FA
1955	DET	A	4	3	.571	4.15	36	3	1	80.1	77	29	28	0	3	1	3	19	3	2	.158	8	8	0	1	0.4	1.000
1956	BAL	A	0	0	–	6.75	4	0	0	5.1	9	1	1	0	0	0	0	1	0	0	.000	0	0	0	0	0.0	–
1958	LA	N	0	0	–	4.50	16	0	0	34	43	7	16	0	0	0	1	7	4	0	.571	1	1	0	0	0.1	1.000
3 yrs.			4	3	.571	4.36	56	3	1	119.2	129	37	45	0	3	1	4	27	7	2	.259	9	9	0	1	0.3	1.000

Tim Birtsas

BIRTSAS, TIMOTHY DEAN
B. Sept. 5, 1960, Pontiac, Mich.

BL TL 6'7" 240 lbs.

Year	Team		W	L	PCT	ERA	G	GS	CG	IP	H	BB	SO	ShO	W	L	SV	AB	H	HR	BA	PO	A	E	DP	TC/G	FA
1985	OAK	A	10	6	.625	4.01	29	25	2	141.1	124	91	94	0	0	0	0	0	0	0	—	0	11	1	1	0.4	.917

Tim Birtsas *continued*

Year	Team		W	L	PCT	ERA	G	GS	CG	IP	H	BB	SO	ShO	Relief Pitching W	L	SV	Batting AB	H	HR	BA	PO	A	E	DP	TC/G	FA
1986			0	0	–	22.50	2	0	0	2	2	4	1	0	0	0	0	0	0	0	–	0	0	0	0	0.0	–
1988	CIN	N	1	3	.250	4.20	36	4	0	64.1	61	24	38	0	1	0	0	10	0	0	.000	2	8	2	0	0.3	.833
1989			2	2	.500	3.75	42	1	0	69.2	68	27	57	0	2	1	1	4	1	1	.250	0	9	1	0	0.2	.900
4 yrs.			13	11	.542	4.12	109	30	2	277.1	255	146	190	0	3	1	1	14	1	1	.071	2	28	4	1	0.3	.882

Frank Biscan

BISCAN, FRANK STEPHEN (Porky)
B. Mar. 13, 1920, Mt. Olive, Ill. D. May 22, 1959, St. Louis, Mo.

BL TL 5'11" 190 lbs.

Year	Team		W	L	PCT	ERA	G	GS	CG	IP	H	BB	SO	ShO	W	L	SV	AB	H	HR	BA	PO	A	E	DP	TC/G	FA
1942	STL	A	0	1	.000	2.33	11	0	0	27	13	11	10	0	1	1	1	6	0	0	.000	1	6	0	0	0.6	1.000
1946			1	1	.500	5.16	16	0	0	22.2	28	22	9	0	1	1	1	3	0	0	.000	0	3	0	0	0.2	1.000
1948			6	7	.462	6.11	47	4	1	98.2	129	71	45	0	6	5	2	26	5	0	.192	3	20	3	2	0.6	.885
3 yrs.			7	9	.438	5.28	74	4	1	148.1	170	104	64	0	7	7	4	35	5	0	.143	4	29	3	2	0.5	.917

Bill Bishop

BISHOP, WILLIAM HENRY (Lefty)
B. Oct. 22, 1900, Houtzdale, Pa. D. Feb. 14, 1956, St. Joseph, Mo.

BL TL 5'8" 170 lbs.

Year	Team		W	L	PCT	ERA	G	GS	CG	IP	H	BB	SO	ShO	W	L	SV	AB	H	HR	BA	PO	A	E	DP	TC/G	FA
1921	PHI	A	0	0	–	9.00	2	0	0	7	8	10	4	0	0	0	0	3	0	0	.000	0	3	0	0	1.5	1.000

Bill Bishop

BISHOP, WILLIAM ROBINSON
B. Dec. 27, 1869, Adamsburg, Pa. D. Dec. 15, 1932, Pittsburgh, Pa.

Year	Team		W	L	PCT	ERA	G	GS	CG	IP	H	BB	SO	ShO	W	L	SV	AB	H	HR	BA	PO	A	E	DP	TC/G	FA
1886	PIT	AA	0	1	.000	3.18	2	2	2	17	17	11	4	0	0	0	0	7	1	0	.143	0	3	4	0	3.5	.429
1887	PIT	N	0	3	.000	13.33	3	3	3	27	45	22	4	0	0	0	0	9	0	0	.000	0	5	1	0	2.0	.833
1889	CHI	N	0	0	–	18.00	2	0	0	3	6	6	1	0	0	0	2	1	0	0	.000	0	0	0	0	0.0	–
3 yrs.			0	4	.000	9.96	7	5	5	47	68	39	9	0	0	0	2	17	1	0	.059	0	8	5	0	1.9	.615

Charlie Bishop

BISHOP, CHARLES TULLER
B. Jan. 1, 1924, Atlanta, Ga.

BR TR 6'2" 195 lbs.

Year	Team		W	L	PCT	ERA	G	GS	CG	IP	H	BB	SO	ShO	W	L	SV	AB	H	HR	BA	PO	A	E	DP	TC/G	FA
1952	PHI	A	2	2	.500	6.46	6	5	1	30.2	29	24	17	0	0	0	0	9	1	0	.111	3	7	1	0	1.8	.909
1953			3	14	.176	5.66	39	20	1	160.2	174	86	66	1	2	1	2	56	5	0	.089	5	36	0	3	1.1	1.000
1954			4	6	.400	4.41	20	12	4	96	98	50	34	0	0	0	1	33	4	0	.121	6	9	0	0	0.8	1.000
1955	KC	A	1	0	1.000	5.40	4	0	0	6.2	6	8	4	0	1	0	0	2	1	0	.500	0	1	0	0	0.3	1.000
4 yrs.			10	22	.313	5.33	69	37	6	294	307	168	121	1	3	1	3	100	11	0	.110	14	53	1	3	1.0	.985

Jim Bishop

BISHOP, JAMES MORTON
B. Jan. 28, 1898, Montgomery City, Mo. D. Sept. 20, 1973, Montgomery City, Mo.

BR TR 6' 185 lbs.

Year	Team		W	L	PCT	ERA	G	GS	CG	IP	H	BB	SO	ShO	W	L	SV	AB	H	HR	BA	PO	A	E	DP	TC/G	FA
1923	PHI	N	0	3	.000	6.34	15	0	0	32.2	48	11	5	0	0	3	1	10	0	0	.000	3	11	0	0	0.9	1.000
1924			0	1	.000	6.48	7	1	0	16.2	24	7	3	0	0	0	0	5	1	0	.200	1	6	0	0	1.0	1.000
2 yrs.			0	4	.000	6.39	22	1	0	49.1	72	18	8	0	0	3	1	15	1	0	.067	4	17	0	0	1.0	1.000

Lloyd Bishop

BISHOP, LLOYD CLIFTON
B. Apr. 25, 1890, Conway Springs, Kans. D. June 18, 1968, Wichita, Kans.

BR TR 6' 180 lbs.

Year	Team		W	L	PCT	ERA	G	GS	CG	IP	H	BB	SO	ShO	W	L	SV	AB	H	HR	BA	PO	A	E	DP	TC/G	FA
1914	CLE	A	0	1	.000	5.63	3	1	0	8	14	3	1	0	0	0	0	2	0	0	.000	0	1	0	0	0.3	1.000

Hi Bithorn

BITHORN, HIRAM GABRIEL
Born Hiram Gabriel Bithorn y Sosa.
B. Mar. 18, 1916, Santurce, Puerto Rico D. Jan. 1, 1952, El Mante, Mexico

BR TR 6'1" 200 lbs.

Year	Team		W	L	PCT	ERA	G	GS	CG	IP	H	BB	SO	ShO	W	L	SV	AB	H	HR	BA	PO	A	E	DP	TC/G	FA
1942	CHI	N	9	14	.391	3.68	38	16	9	171.1	191	81	65	0	3	5	2	57	7	0	.123	5	35	2	3	1.1	.952
1943			18	12	.600	2.60	39	30	19	249.2	226	65	86	7	1	1	2	92	16	0	.174	12	57	1	2	1.8	.986
1946			6	5	.545	3.84	26	7	2	86.2	97	25	34	1	4	2	1	28	5	0	.179	1	17	1	2	0.7	.947
1947	CHI	A	1	0	1.000	0.00	2	0	0	2	2	0	0	0	1	0	0	0	0	0	–	0	0	0	0	0.0	–
4 yrs.			34	31	.523	3.16	105	53	30	509.2	516	171	185	8	9	8	5	177	28	0	.158	18	109	4	7	1.2	.969

Jeff Bittiger

BITTIGER, JEFFREY SCOTT
B. Apr. 13, 1962, Jersey City, N. J.

BR TR 5'10" 175 lbs.

Year	Team		W	L	PCT	ERA	G	GS	CG	IP	H	BB	SO	ShO	W	L	SV	AB	H	HR	BA	PO	A	E	DP	TC/G	FA
1986	PHI	N	1	1	.500	5.52	3	3	0	14.2	16	7	8	0	0	0	0	3	1	1	.333	2	2	0	0	1.3	1.000
1987	MIN	A	1	0	1.000	5.40	3	1	0	8.1	11	0	5	0	0	0	0	0	0	0	–	0	2	0	0	0.7	1.000
1988	CHI	A	2	4	.333	4.23	25	7	0	61.2	59	29	33	0	1	0	0	0	0	0	–	1	6	0	0	0.3	1.000
1989			0	1	.000	6.52	2	1	0	9.2	9	6	7	0	0	0	0	0	0	0	–	0	0	0	0	0.0	–
4 yrs.			4	6	.400	4.77	33	12	0	94.1	95	42	53	0	1	0	0	3	1	1	.333	3	10	0	0	0.4	1.000

Jim Bivin

BIVIN, JAMES NATHANIEL
B. Dec. 11, 1909, Jackson, Miss. D. Nov. 7, 1982, Pueblo, Colo.

BR TR 6' 155 lbs.

Year	Team		W	L	PCT	ERA	G	GS	CG	IP	H	BB	SO	ShO	W	L	SV	AB	H	HR	BA	PO	A	E	DP	TC/G	FA
1935	PHI	N	2	9	.182	5.79	47	14	1	161.2	220	65	54	0	2	1	1	48	7	0	.146	4	32	1	1	0.8	.973

Bill Black

BLACK, WILLIAM CARROLL (Bud)
B. July 9, 1932, St. Louis, Mo.

BR TR 6'3" 197 lbs.

Year	Team		W	L	PCT	ERA	G	GS	CG	IP	H	BB	SO	ShO	W	L	SV	AB	H	HR	BA	PO	A	E	DP	TC/G	FA
1952	DET	A	0	1	.000	10.57	2	2	0	7.2	14	5	0	0	0	0	0	3	0	0	.000	0	1	0	0	0.5	1.000
1955			1	1	.500	1.26	3	2	1	14.1	12	8	7	1	0	1	0	4	1	0	.250	1	3	1	0	1.7	.800
1956			1	1	.500	3.60	5	1	0	10	10	5	7	0	1	0	0	2	0	0	.000	1	2	0	0	0.6	1.000
3 yrs.			2	3	.400	4.22	10	5	1	32	36	18	14	1	1	1	0	9	1	0	.111	2	6	1	0	0.9	.889

Bob Black

BLACK, ROBERT BENJAMIM
B. Dec. 10, 1862, Cincinnati, Ohio D. Mar. 21, 1933, Sioux City, Iowa

Year	Team		W	L	PCT	ERA	G	GS	CG	IP	H	BB	SO	ShO	W	L	SV	AB	H	HR	BA	PO	A	E	DP	TC/G	FA
1884	KC	U	4	9	.308	3.22	16	15	13	123	127	17	93	0	0	0	0	*				16	29	4	2	3.1	.918

Bud Black

BLACK, HARRY RALSTON
B. June 30, 1957, San Mateo, Calif.

BL TL 6'2" 180 lbs.

Year	Team		W	L	PCT	ERA	G	GS	CG	IP	H	BB	SO	ShO	W	L	SV	AB	H	HR	BA	PO	A	E	DP	TC/G	FA
1981	SEA	A	0	0	–	0.00	2	0	0	1	2	3	0	0	0	0	0	0	0	0	–	0	1	0	0	0.5	1.000
1982	KC	A	4	6	.400	4.58	22	14	0	88.1	92	34	40	0	0	0	0	0	0	0	–	6	12	1	1	0.9	.947
1983			10	7	.588	3.79	24	24	3	161.1	159	43	58	0	0	0	0	0	0	0	–	7	32	1	5	1.7	.975

Year	Team	W	L	PCT	ERA	G	GS	CG	IP	H	BB	SO	ShO	Relief Pitching W	L	SV	Batting AB	H	HR	BA	PO	A	E	DP	TC/G	FA

Bud Black *continued*

1984		17	12	.586	3.12	35	35	8	257	226	64	140	1	0	0	0	0	0	0	–	13	51	2	2	1.9	.970
1985		10	15	.400	4.33	33	33	5	205.2	216	59	122	2	0	0	0	0	0	0	–	6	30	4	0	1.2	.900
1986		5	10	.333	3.20	56	4	0	121	100	43	68	0	4	7	9	0	0	0	–	3	21	0	1	0.4	1.000
1987		8	6	.571	3.60	29	18	0	122.1	126	35	61	0	1	1	1	0	0	0	–	4	19	0	0	0.8	1.000
1988	2 teams	KC A	(17G 2–1)			CLE A	(16G 2–3)																			
"	total	4	4	.500	5.00	33	7	0	81	82	34	63	0	3	3	1	0	0	0	–	5	12	0	0	0.5	1.000
1989	CLE A	12	11	.522	3.36	33	32	6	222.1	213	52	88	3	1	0	0	0	0	0	–	13	33	2	3	1.5	.958
9 yrs.		70	71	.496	3.72	267	167	22	1260	1216	367	640	6	9	10	11	0	0	0	–	57	211	10	12	1.0	.964

LEAGUE CHAMPIONSHIP SERIES

1984	KC A	0	1	.000	7.20	1	1	0	5	7	1	3	0	0	0	0	0	0	0	–	1	1	0	0	2.0	1.000
1985		0	0	–	1.69	3	1	0	10.2	11	4	8	0	0	0	0	0	0	0	–	1	2	0	1	1.0	1.000
2 yrs.		0	1	.000	3.45	4	2	0	15.2	18	5	11	0	0	0	0	0	0	0	–	2	3	0	1	1.3	1.000

WORLD SERIES

| 1985 | KC A | 0 | 1 | .000 | 5.06 | 2 | 1 | 0 | 5.1 | 4 | 5 | 4 | 0 | 0 | 0 | 0 | 0 | 0 | 0 | .000 | 1 | 2 | 1 | 1 | 2.0 | .750 |

Dave Black

BLACK, DAVID
B. Apr. 19, 1892, Chicago, Ill.   D. Oct. 27, 1936, Pittsburgh, Pa.   BL TR 6'2"   175 lbs.

1914	CHI F	1	0	1.000	6.12	8	1	1	25	28	4	19	0	0	0	0	12	4	0	.333	0	7	0	0	0.9	1.000
1915	2 teams	CHI F	(25G 6–7)			BAL F	(8G 1–3)																			
"	total	7	10	.412	2.72	33	14	3	155.1	136	48	53	0	1	4		49	7	0	.143	5	57	0	4	1.9	1.000
1923	BOS A	0	0	–	0.00	2	0	0	1	2	0	0	0	0	0	0	0	0	0	–	0	0	0	0	0.0	–
3 yrs.		8	10	.444	3.18	43	15	4	181.1	166	52	72	0	1	4	0	61	11	0	.180	5	64	0	4	1.6	1.000

Don Black

BLACK, DONALD PAUL
B. July 20, 1916, Salix, Iowa   D. Apr. 21, 1959, Cuyahoga Falls, Ohio   BR TR 6'   185 lbs.

1943	PHI A	6	16	.273	4.20	33	26	12	208	193	110	65	1	1	0	1	69	13	0	.188	15	41	0	3	1.7	1.000
1944		10	12	.455	4.06	29	27	8	177.1	177	75	78	0	1	0	0	59	11	0	.186	7	32	1	3	1.4	.975
1945		5	11	.313	5.17	26	18	8	125.1	154	69	47	0	2	1	0	37	6	0	.162	8	18	1	0	1.0	.963
1946	CLE A	1	2	.333	4.53	18	4	0	43.2	45	21	15	0	0	0	0	10	2	0	.200	4	10	1	1	0.8	.933
1947		10	12	.455	3.92	30	28	8	190.2	177	85	72	3	0	0	0	66	12	0	.182	15	31	1	2	1.6	.979
1948		2	2	.500	5.37	18	10	1	52	57	40	16	0	0	0	0	15	3	0	.200	3	11	0	1	0.8	1.000
6 yrs.		34	55	.382	4.35	154	113	37	797	803	400	293	4	3	2	1	256	47	0	.184	52	143	4	10	1.3	.980

Joe Black

BLACK, JOSEPH
B. Feb. 8, 1924, Plainfield, N. J.   BR TR 6'2"   220 lbs.

1952	BKN N	15	4	.789	2.15	56	2	1	142.1	102	41	85	0	14	3	15	36	5	0	.139	7	18	4	2	0.5	.862
1953		6	3	.667	5.33	34	3	0	72.2	74	27	42	0	6	2	5	17	4	0	.235	3	11	1	0	0.4	.933
1954		0	0	–	11.57	5	0	0	7	11	5	3	0	0	0	0	0	0	0	–	0	1	0	0	0.2	1.000
1955	2 teams	BKN N	(6G 1–0)			CIN N	(32G 5–2)																			
"	total	6	2	.750	4.05	38	11	1	117.2	121	30	63	0	3	0	0	33	4	0	.121	3	18	2	1	0.6	.913
1956	CIN N	3	2	.600	4.52	32	0	0	61.2	61	25	27	0	3	2	2	10	0	0	.000	5	7	1	2	0.4	.923
1957	WAS A	0	1	.000	7.11	7	0	0	12.2	22	1	2	0	0	1	0	0	0	0	–	1	3	0	0	0.6	1.000
6 yrs.		30	12	.714	3.91	172	16	2	414	391	129	222	0	26	8	25	96	13	0	.135	19	58	8	5	0.5	.906

WORLD SERIES

1952	BKN N	1	2	.333	2.53	3	3	1	21.1	15	8	9	0	0	0	0	6	0	0	.000	1	2	0	1	1.0	1.000
1953		0	0	–	9.00	1	0	0	1	1	0	2	0	0	0	0	0	0	0	–	0	0	0	0	0.0	–
2 yrs.		1	2	.333	2.82	4	3	1	22.1	16	8	11	0	0	0	0	6	0	0	.000	1	2	0	1	0.8	1.000

Babe Blackburn

BLACKBURN, FOSTER EDWIN (Charlie)
B. Jan. 6, 1895, Chicago, Ill.   D. Mar. 9, 1984, New Port Richey, Fla.   BR TR 6'1"   165 lbs.

1915	KC F	0	1	.000	8.62	7	2	0	15.2	19	13	7	0	0	0	0	4	0	0	.000	1	6	0	0	1.0	1.000
1921	CHI A	0	0	–	0.00	1	0	0	1	0	1	0	0	0	0	0	0	0	0	–	0	0	0	0	0.0	–
2 yrs.		0	1	.000	8.10	8	2	0	16.2	19	14	7	0	0	0	0	4	0	0	.000	1	6	0	0	0.9	1.000

George Blackburn

BLACKBURN, GEORGE W.
B. Sept. 21, 1871, Ozark, Mo.   Deceased.   5'11"   184 lbs.

| 1897 | BAL N | 2 | 2 | .500 | 6.82 | 5 | 4 | 3 | 33 | 34 | 12 | 1 | 0 | 0 | 0 | 0 | 13 | 1 | 0 | .077 | 2 | 7 | 0 | 0 | 1.8 | 1.000 |

Jim Blackburn

BLACKBURN, JAMES RAY (Bones)
B. June 19, 1924, Warsaw, Ky.   D. Oct. 26, 1969, Cincinnati, Ohio   BR TR 6'4"   175 lbs.

1948	CIN N	0	2	.000	4.18	16	0	0	32.1	38	14	10	0	0	2	0	6	0	0	.000	0	6	0	0	0.4	1.000
1951		0	0	–	17.18	2	0	0	3.2	8	2	1	0	0	0	0	0	0	0	–	0	1	0	0	0.5	1.000
2 yrs.		0	2	.000	5.50	18	0	0	36	46	16	11	0	0	2	0	6	0	0	.000	0	7	0	0	0.4	1.000

Ron Blackburn

BLACKBURN, RONALD HAMILTON
B. Apr. 23, 1935, Mt. Airy, N. C.   BR TR 6'½"   160 lbs.

1958	PIT N	2	1	.667	3.39	38	0	0	63.2	61	27	31	0	2	0	3	7	2	0	.286	3	14	1	3	0.5	.944
1959		1	1	.500	3.65	26	0	0	44.1	50	15	19	0	1	1	1	5	1	0	.200	2	5	2	0	0.3	.778
2 yrs.		3	2	.600	3.50	64	0	0	108	111	42	50	0	3	1	4	12	3	0	.250	5	19	3	3	0.4	.889

Lena Blackburne

BLACKBURNE, RUSSELL AUBREY (Slats)
B. Oct. 23, 1886, Clifton Heights, Pa.   D. Feb. 29, 1968, Riverside, N. J.   BR TR 5'11"   160 lbs.
Manager 1928-29.

| 1929 | CHI A | 0 | 0 | – | 0.00 | 1 | 0 | 0 | .1 | 1 | 1 | 0 | 0 | 0 | 0 | 0 | * | | | | 0 | 0 | 0 | 0 | 0.0 | – |

Ewell Blackwell

BLACKWELL, EWELL (The Whip)
B. Oct. 23, 1922, Fresno, Calif.   BR TR 6'6"   195 lbs.

| 1942 | CIN N | 0 | 0 | – | 6.00 | 2 | 0 | 0 | 3 | 3 | 3 | 1 | 0 | 0 | 0 | 0 | 1 | 0 | 0 | .000 | 0 | 2 | 0 | 0 | 1.0 | 1.000 |

Year	Team	W	L	PCT	ERA	G	GS	CG	IP	H	BB	SO	ShO	W	L	SV	AB	H	HR	BA	PO	A	E	DP	TC/G	FA

Ewell Blackwell *continued*

Year	Team	W	L	PCT	ERA	G	GS	CG	IP	H	BB	SO	ShO	W	L	SV	AB	H	HR	BA	PO	A	E	DP	TC/G	FA
1946		9	13	.409	2.45	33	25	10	194.1	160	79	100	6	0	0	0	56	6	0	.107	7	58	3	7	2.1	.956
1947		**22**	8	.733	2.47	33	33	**23**	273	227	95	**193**	6	0	0	0	106	13	0	.123	10	70	3	2	2.5	.964
1948		7	9	.438	4.54	22	20	4	138.2	134	52	114	1	0	0	1	48	11	0	.229	7	40	1	2	2.2	.979
1949		5	5	.500	4.23	30	4	0	76.2	80	34	55	0	4	3	1	19	4	0	.211	4	18	1	1	0.8	.957
1950		17	15	.531	2.97	40	32	18	261	203	112	188	1	1	1	4	89	13	0	.146	8	54	5	2	1.7	.925
1951		16	15	.516	3.45	38	32	11	232.1	204	97	120	2	2	1	2	82	24	1	.293	6	46	5	5	1.5	.912
1952	2 teams	CIN N	(23G 3–12)		NY A	(5G 1–0)																				
"	total	4	12	.250	4.73	28	19	3	118	119	72	55	0	0	0	0	37	6	0	.162	2	19	0	1	0.8	1.000
1953	NY A	2	0	1.000	3.66	8	4	0	19.2	17	13	11	0	0	0	1	5	0	0	.000	1	3	1	0	0.6	.800
1955	KC A	0	1	.000	6.75	2	0	0	4	3	5	2	0	0	1	0	0	0	0	–	0	0	0	0	0.0	–
10 yrs.		82	78	.513	3.30	236	169	69	1320.2	1150	562	839	16	7	7	11	443	77	1	.174	45	310	19	20	1.6	.949

WORLD SERIES

Year	Team	W	L	PCT	ERA	G	GS	CG	IP	H	BB	SO	ShO	W	L	SV	AB	H	HR	BA	PO	A	E	DP	TC/G	FA
1952	NY A	0	0	–	7.20	1	1	0	5	4	3	4	0	0	0	0	1	0	0	.000	0	1	0	0	1.0	1.000

George Blaeholder

BLAEHOLDER, GEORGE FRANKLIN
B. Jan. 26, 1904, Orange, Calif.   D. Dec. 29, 1947, Garden Grove, Calif.

BR TR 5'11"   175 lbs.

Year	Team	W	L	PCT	ERA	G	GS	CG	IP	H	BB	SO	ShO	W	L	SV	AB	H	HR	BA	PO	A	E	DP	TC/G	FA
1925	STL A	0	0	–	31.50	2	0	0	2	6	1	0	0	0	0	0	0	0	0	–	0	0	0	0	0.0	–
1927		0	1	.000	5.00	1	1	1	9	8	4	2	0	0	0	0	3	1	0	.333	1	3	0	0	4.0	1.000
1928		10	15	.400	4.37	38	26	9	214.1	235	52	87	1	1	0	3	71	15	2	.211	13	70	6	2	2.3	.933
1929		14	15	.483	4.18	42	24	13	222	237	61	72	**4**	4	3	2	74	9	1	.122	15	74	1	4	2.1	.989
1930		11	13	.458	4.61	37	23	10	191.1	235	46	70	1	1	2	4	65	12	0	.185	19	27	6	4	1.4	.885
1931		11	15	.423	4.53	35	32	13	226.1	280	56	79	1	0	1	0	77	11	0	.143	25	55	4	3	2.4	.952
1932		14	14	.500	4.70	42	36	16	258.1	304	76	80	1	0	1	0	88	12	0	.136	14	53	4	6	1.7	.944
1933		15	19	.441	4.72	38	36	14	255.2	283	69	63	3	2	1	0	77	14	0	.182	15	68	3	4	2.3	.965
1934		14	18	.438	4.22	39	33	14	234.1	**276**	68	66	1	2	1	3	75	7	0	.093	16	34	3	6	1.6	.952
1935	2 teams	STL A	(6G 1–1)		PHI A	(23G 6–10)																				
"	total	7	11	.389	4.32	29	24	10	166.2	198	55	22	0	1	0	0	50	2	0	.040	11	46	7	3	2.2	.891
1936	CLE A	8	4	.667	5.09	35	16	6	134.1	158	47	30	0	2	0	0	46	6	0	.130	12	30	2	1	1.3	.955
11 yrs.		104	125	.454	4.54	338	251	106	1914.1	2220	535	572	13	12	9	12	626	89	3	.142	141	469	36	33	1.9	.944

Bill Blair

BLAIR, WILLIAM ELLSWORTH
B. Sept. 17, 1863, Pittsburgh, Pa.   D. Feb. 22, 1890, Pittsburgh, Pa.

BL TL 5'8½"   172 lbs.

Year	Team	W	L	PCT	ERA	G	GS	CG	IP	H	BB	SO	ShO	W	L	SV	AB	H	HR	BA	PO	A	E	DP	TC/G	FA
1888	PHI AA	1	3	.250	2.61	4	4	3	31	29	8	16	0	0	0	0	13	4	0	.308	2	12	3	1	4.3	.824

Dennis Blair

BLAIR, DENNIS HERMAN
B. June 5, 1954, Middletown, Ohio

BR TR 6'5"   182 lbs.

Year	Team	W	L	PCT	ERA	G	GS	CG	IP	H	BB	SO	ShO	W	L	SV	AB	H	HR	BA	PO	A	E	DP	TC/G	FA
1974	MON N	11	7	.611	3.27	22	22	4	146	113	72	76	1	0	0	0	51	6	0	.118	10	34	4	3	2.2	.917
1975		8	15	.348	3.81	30	27	1	163	150	106	82	0	0	0	0	49	7	0	.143	8	21	1	2	1.0	.967
1976		0	2	.000	4.02	5	4	1	15.2	21	11	9	0	0	0	0	4	0	0	.000	1	2	0	0	0.6	1.000
1980	SD N	0	1	.000	6.43	5	1	0	14	18	3	11	0	0	1	0	5	1	0	.200	0	0	0	0	0.0	–
4 yrs.		19	25	.432	3.69	62	54	6	338.2	302	192	178	1	0	1	0	109	14	0	.128	19	57	5	5	1.3	.938

Dick Blaisdell

BLAISDELL, HOWARD CARLETON
B. June 18, 1862, Bradford, Mass.   D. Aug. 20, 1886, Malden, Mass.

Year	Team	W	L	PCT	ERA	G	GS	CG	IP	H	BB	SO	ShO	W	L	SV	AB	H	HR	BA	PO	A	E	DP	TC/G	FA
1884	KC U	0	3	.000	8.65	3	3	3	26	49	4	8	0	0	0	0	16	5	0	.313	3	5	4	0	4.0	.667

Ed Blake

BLAKE, EDWARD JAMES
B. Dec. 23, 1925, East St. Louis, Ill.

BR TR 5'11"   175 lbs.

Year	Team	W	L	PCT	ERA	G	GS	CG	IP	H	BB	SO	ShO	W	L	SV	AB	H	HR	BA	PO	A	E	DP	TC/G	FA
1951	CIN N	0	0	–	11.25	3	0	0	4	10	4	0	0	0	0	0	0	0	0	–	1	2	1	1	1.3	.750
1952		0	0	–	0.00	2	0	0	3	3	0	0	0	0	0	0	0	0	0	–	0	2	0	0	1.0	1.000
1953		0	0	–	∞	1	0	0		1	0	0	0	0	0	0	0	0	0	–	0	0	0	0	0.0	–
1957	KC A	0	0	–	5.40	2	0	0	1.2	2	0	0	0	0	0	0	0	0	0	–	0	0	0	0	0.0	–
4 yrs.		0	0	–	8.31	8	0	0	8.2	15	4	1	0	0	0	0	0	0	0	–	1	4	1	1	0.8	.833

Sheriff Blake

BLAKE, JOHN FREDERICK
B. Sept. 17, 1899, Ansted, W. Va.
D. Oct. 31, 1982, Beckley, W. Va.

BB TR 6'   180 lbs.
BR 1920,1925-27,
BB 1937

Year	Team	W	L	PCT	ERA	G	GS	CG	IP	H	BB	SO	ShO	W	L	SV	AB	H	HR	BA	PO	A	E	DP	TC/G	FA
1920	PIT N	0	0	–	8.10	6	0	0	13.1	21	6	7	0	0	0	0	4	1	0	.250	1	2	0	1	0.5	1.000
1924	CHI N	6	6	.500	4.57	29	11	4	106.1	123	44	42	0	2	2	1	31	9	0	.290	2	30	0	1	1.1	1.000
1925		10	18	.357	4.86	36	31	14	231.1	260	114	93	0	0	1	2	79	12	0	.152	7	52	2	6	1.6	.967
1926		11	12	.478	3.60	39	27	11	197.2	204	**92**	95	4	1	1	1	65	14	0	.215	9	54	1	1	1.6	.984
1927		13	14	.481	3.29	32	27	13	224.1	238	82	64	2	1	0	0	83	16	0	.193	10	64	4	5	2.4	.949
1928		17	11	.607	2.47	34	29	16	240.2	209	101	78	**4**	3	0	1	88	19	0	.216	4	48	3	3	1.6	.945
1929		14	13	.519	4.29	35	30	13	218.1	244	103	70	1	1	2	0	81	14	0	.173	6	43	2	1	1.5	.961
1930		10	14	.417	4.82	34	24	7	186.2	213	99	80	0	2	0	0	66	15	0	.227	7	50	1	4	1.7	.983
1931	2 teams	CHI N	(16G 0–4)		PHI N	(14G 4–5)																				
"	total	4	9	.308	5.43	30	14	1	121	154	61	60	0	1	0	3	41	14	0	.341	6	38	0	3	1.5	1.000
1937	2 teams	STL A	(15G 2–2)		STL N	(14G 0–3)																				
"	total	2	5	.286	5.49	29	3	2	80.1	100	38	32	0	2	3	1	20	4	0	.200	3	20	0	1	0.8	1.000
10 yrs.		87	102	.460	4.13	304	196	81	1620	1766	740	621	11	10	15	8	558	118	0	.211	55	401	13	24	1.5	.972

WORLD SERIES

Year	Team	W	L	PCT	ERA	G	GS	CG	IP	H	BB	SO	ShO	W	L	SV	AB	H	HR	BA	PO	A	E	DP	TC/G	FA
1929	CHI N	0	1	.000	13.50	2	0	0	1.1	4	0	1	0	0	0	0	1	1	0	1.000	0	2	0	0	1.0	1.000

Al Blanche

BLANCHE, PROSBY ALBERT
Born Prosber Albert Belangio.
B. Sept. 21, 1909, Somerville, Mass.

BR TR 6'   178 lbs.

Year	Team	W	L	PCT	ERA	G	GS	CG	IP	H	BB	SO	ShO	W	L	SV	AB	H	HR	BA	PO	A	E	DP	TC/G	FA
1935	BOS N	0	0	–	1.56	6	0	0	17.1	14	5	4	0	0	0	0	6	1	0	.167	0	4	0	0	0.7	1.000

Year	Team		W	L	PCT	ERA	G	GS	CG	IP	H	BB	SO	ShO	Relief Pitching W	L	SV	Batting AB	H	HR	BA	PO	A	E	DP	TC/G	FA

Al Blanche *continued*

| 1936 | | | 0 | 1 | .000 | 6.19 | 11 | 0 | 0 | 16 | 20 | 8 | 4 | 0 | 0 | 1 | 1 | 4 | 1 | 0 | .250 | 3 | 7 | 2 | 0 | 1.1 | .833 |
| 2 yrs. | | | 0 | 1 | .000 | 3.78 | 17 | 0 | 0 | 33.1 | 34 | 13 | 8 | 0 | 0 | 1 | 1 | 10 | 2 | 0 | .200 | 3 | 11 | 2 | 0 | 0.9 | .875 |

Gil Blanco

BLANCO, GILBERT HENRY
B. Dec. 15, 1945, Phoenix, Ariz.
BL TL 6'5" 205 lbs.

1965	NY	A	1	1	.500	3.98	17	1	0	20.1	16	12	14	0	1	0	0	0	0	0	—	0	1	0	0	0.1	1.000
1966	KC	A	2	4	.333	4.70	11	8	0	38.1	31	36	21	0	0	0	0	12	2	0	.167	0	9	1	0	0.9	.900
2 yrs.			3	5	.375	4.45	28	9	0	58.2	47	48	35	0	1	0	0	12	2	0	.167	0	10	1	0	0.4	.909

Fred Blanding

BLANDING, FREDERICK JAMES (Fritz)
B. Feb. 8, 1888, Redlands, Calif. D. July 16, 1950, Salem, Va.
BR TR 6' 185 lbs.

1910	CLE	A	2	2	.500	2.78	6	5	4	45.1	43	12	25	1	0	0	0	18	2	0	.111	0	12	0	0	2.0	1.000
1911			7	11	.389	3.68	29	16	11	176	190	60	80	0	4	1	2	65	17	0	.262	8	49	4	4	2.1	.934
1912			18	14	.563	2.92	39	31	23	262	259	79	75	1	3	0	1	93	21	1	.226	9	77	4	6	2.3	.956
1913			15	10	.600	2.55	41	22	14	215	234	72	63	3	4	1	0	86	21	0	.244	4	58	5	0	1.6	.925
1914			3	9	.250	3.96	29	12	5	116	133	54	35	0	0	1	1	39	4	0	.103	2	43	5	1	1.7	.900
5 yrs.			45	46	.495	3.13	144	86	57	814.1	859	277	278	5	11	3	4	301	65	1	.216	23	239	18	11	1.9	.936

Fred Blank

BLANK, FREDERICK AUGUST
B. June 18, 1874, DeSoto, Mo. D. Feb. 5, 1936, St. Louis, Mo.
BL TL 6'½" 175 lbs.

| 1894 | CIN | N | 0 | 1 | .000 | 4.50 | 1 | 1 | 1 | 8 | 5 | 9 | 1 | 0 | 0 | 0 | 0 | 3 | 0 | 0 | .000 | 0 | 4 | 0 | 0 | 4.0 | 1.000 |

Homer Blankenship

BLANKENSHIP, HOMER (Si)
Brother of Ted Blankenship.
B. Aug. 4, 1902, Bonham, Tex. D. June 22, 1974, Longview, Tex.
BR TR 6' 185 lbs.

1922	CHI	A	0	0	—	4.85	4	0	0	13	21	5	3	0	0	0	0	4	0	0	.000	1	2	0	0	0.8	1.000
1923			1	1	.500	3.60	4	0	0	5	9	1	1	0	1	1	1	0	0	0	—	0	2	0	0	0.5	1.000
1928	PIT	N	0	2	.000	5.82	5	2	1	21.2	27	9	6	0	0	0	0	8	3	0	.375	1	8	0	1	1.8	1.000
3 yrs.			1	3	.250	5.22	13	2	1	39.2	57	15	10	0	1	1	1	12	3	0	.250	2	12	0	1	1.1	1.000

Kevin Blankenship

BLANKENSHIP, KEVIN DeWAYNE
B. Jan. 26, 1963, Anaheim, Calif.
BR TR 6' 180 lbs.

1988	2 teams	ATL N (2G 0–1)					CHI N	(1G 1–0)																				
"	total		1	1	.500	4.60	3	3	0	15.2	14	8	9	0	0	0	0	6	0	0	.000	1	0	0	0	0.3	1.000
1989	CHI	N	0	0	—	1.69	2	0	0	5.1	4	2	2	0	0	0	0	1	0	0	.000	1	0	0	0	0.5	1.000
2 yrs.			1	1	.500	3.86	5	3	0	21	18	10	11	0	0	0	0	7	0	0	.000	2	0	0	0	0.4	1.000

Ted Blankenship

BLANKENSHIP, THEODORE
Brother of Homer Blankenship.
B. May 10, 1901, Bonham, Tex. D. Jan. 14, 1945, Atoka, Okla.
BR TR 6'1" 170 lbs.

1922	CHI	A	8	10	.444	3.81	24	15	7	127.2	124	47	42	1	3	1	0	41	7	0	.171	3	31	0	4	1.4	1.000
1923			9	14	.391	4.27	44	23	9	208.2	219	100	57	1	3	3	0	76	16	3	.211	10	51	3	1	1.5	.953
1924			7	6	.538	5.17	25	11	7	125.1	167	38	36	0	1	3	1	46	15	1	.326	1	22	1	1	1.0	.958
1925			17	8	.680	3.16	40	23	16	222	218	69	81	3	3	3	1	88	18	2	.205	4	38	2	3	1.1	.955
1926			13	10	.565	3.61	29	26	15	209.1	217	65	66	1	1	0	1	76	10	0	.132	4	42	0	1	1.6	1.000
1927			12	17	.414	5.06	37	34	11	236.2	280	74	51	3	0	0	0	80	15	0	.188	7	48	2	3	1.5	.965
1928			9	11	.450	4.61	27	22	8	158	186	80	36	0	0	0	0	59	10	0	.169	2	31	1	3	1.3	.971
1929			0	2	.000	8.84	8	1	0	18.1	28	9	7	0	0	0	1	4	1	0	.250	1	0	0	0	0.3	1.000
1930			2	1	.667	9.20	7	1	0	14.2	23	7	2	0	2	0	0	5	1	0	.200	0	2	0	0	0.1	1.000
9 yrs.			77	79	.494	4.32	241	156	73	1320.2	1462	489	378	8	13	11	4	475	93	9	.196	32	265	9	16	1.3	.971

Cy Blanton

BLANTON, DARRELL ELIJAH
B. July 6, 1908, Waurika, Okla. D. Sept. 13, 1945, Norman, Okla.
BL TR 5'11½" 180 lbs.

1934	PIT	N	0	1	.000	3.38	1	1	0	8	5	4	5	0	0	0	0	0	0	0	.000	0	2	0	0	2.0	1.000
1935			18	13	.581	2.58	35	31	23	254.1	220	55	142	4	1	2	1	97	13	0	.134	10	60	2	1	2.1	.972
1936			13	15	.464	3.51	44	32	15	235.2	235	55	127	4	0	5	3	84	13	0	.155	16	50	3	0	1.6	.957
1937			14	12	.538	3.30	36	34	14	242.2	250	76	143	4	0	0	0	85	14	0	.165	9	48	5	5	1.7	.919
1938			11	7	.611	3.70	29	26	10	172.2	190	46	80	1	0	0	0	64	13	0	.203	7	42	2	7	1.8	.961
1939			2	3	.400	4.29	10	6	1	42	45	10	11	0	0	0	0	14	4	0	.286	1	9	1	0	1.1	.909
1940	PHI	N	4	3	.571	4.32	13	10	5	77	82	21	24	0	0	0	0	24	2	0	.083	4	16	0	0	1.5	1.000
1941			6	13	.316	4.12	28	25	7	163.2	186	57	64	1	0	0	0	51	6	0	.118	3	22	2	0	1.0	.926
1942			0	4	.000	5.64	6	3	0	22.1	30	13	15	0	0	0	0	8	1	0	.125	1	4	0	0	0.8	1.000
9 yrs.			68	71	.489	3.55	202	168	75	1218.1	1243	337	611	14	1	8	4	428	66	0	.154	51	253	15	13	1.6	.953

Wade Blasingame

BLASINGAME, WADE ALLEN
B. Nov. 22, 1943, Deming, N. M.
BL TL 6'1" 185 lbs.

1963	MIL	N	0	0	—	12.00	2	1	0	3	7	2	6	0	0	0	0	0	0	0	—	0	1	0	0	0.5	1.000
1964			9	5	.643	4.24	28	13	3	116.2	113	51	70	1	1	1	2	40	7	1	.175	5	23	0	2	1.0	1.000
1965			16	10	.615	3.77	38	36	10	224.2	200	116	117	1	1	0	1	81	15	1	.185	21	41	0	3	1.6	1.000
1966	ATL	N	3	7	.300	5.32	16	12	0	67.2	71	25	34	0	0	0	0	23	5	0	.217	4	10	1	1	0.9	.933
1967	2 teams	ATL N (10G 1–0)					HOU N	(15G 4–7)																				
"	total		5	7	.417	5.63	25	18	0	102.1	118	48	66	0	0	0	0	29	5	0	.172	8	16	0	1	1.0	1.000
1968	HOU	N	1	2	.333	4.75	22	2	0	36	45	10	22	0	1	2	1	5	0	0	.000	1	10	0	1	0.5	1.000
1969			0	5	.000	5.37	26	5	0	52	66	33	33	0	0	0	0	12	0	0	.000	5	9	3	0	0.7	.824
1970			3	3	.500	3.46	13	13	1	78	76	23	55	0	0	0	0	24	2	0	.083	2	15	1	0	1.4	.944
1971			9	11	.450	4.61	30	28	2	158	177	45	93	0	2	0	0	49	10	1	.204	8	29	1	1	1.3	.974
1972	2 teams	HOU N (10G 0–0)					NY A	(12G 0–1)																				
"	total		0	1	.000	5.76	22	1	0	25	18	19	16	0	0	0	0	2	0	0	.000	6	6	0	0	0.5	1.000
10 yrs.			46	51	.474	4.52	222	128	16	863.1	891	372	512	2	4	3	5	265	44	3	.166	60	160	6	8	1.0	.973

Year	Team	W	L	PCT	ERA	G	GS	CG	IP	H	BB	SO	ShO	W	L	SV	AB	H	HR	BA	PO	A	E	DP	TC/G	FA
														Relief Pitching			**Batting**									

Steve Blass

BLASS, STEPHEN ROBERT
B. Apr. 18, 1942, Canaan, Conn.   BR TR 6'   165 lbs.

Year	Team	W	L	PCT	ERA	G	GS	CG	IP	H	BB	SO	ShO	W	L	SV	AB	H	HR	BA	PO	A	E	DP	TC/G	FA
1964	PIT N	5	8	.385	4.04	24	13	3	104.2	107	45	67	1	1	1	0	30	2	0	.067	10	18	2	2	1.3	.933
1966		11	7	.611	3.87	34	25	1	155.2	173	46	76	0	2	1	0	52	12	0	.231	6	15	3	1	0.7	.875
1967		6	8	.429	3.55	32	16	2	126.2	126	47	72	0	1	1	0	39	5	0	.128	7	23	1	2	1.0	.968
1968		18	6	.750	2.12	33	31	12	220.1	191	57	132	7	0	0	0	80	11	0	.138	22	27	0	1	1.5	1.000
1969		16	10	.615	4.46	38	32	9	210	207	86	147	0	0	0	2	84	21	1	.250	21	41	2	3	1.7	.969
1970		10	12	.455	3.52	31	31	6	197	187	73	120	1	0	0	0	70	8	0	.114	21	26	2	1	1.6	.959
1971		15	8	.652	2.85	33	33	12	240	226	68	136	5	0	0	0	83	10	0	.120	27	36	4	2	2.0	.940
1972		19	8	.704	2.49	33	32	11	249.2	227	84	117	2	0	0	0	82	15	0	.183	15	46	2	6	1.9	.968
1973		3	9	.250	9.85	23	18	1	88.2	109	84	27	0	0	0	0	24	10	0	.417	8	18	0	1	1.1	1.000
1974		0	0	—	9.00	1	0	0	5	5	7	2	0	0	0	0	2	0	0	.000	0	1	0	0	1.0	1.000
10 yrs.		103	76	.575	3.63	282	231	57	1597.2	1558	597	896	16	4	3	2	546	94	1	.172	137	251	16	19	1.4	.960

LEAGUE CHAMPIONSHIP SERIES

Year	Team	W	L	PCT	ERA	G	GS	CG	IP	H	BB	SO	ShO	W	L	SV	AB	H	HR	BA	PO	A	E	DP	TC/G	FA
1971	PIT N	0	1	.000	11.57	2	2	0	7	14	2	11	0	0	0	0	1	0	0	.000	1	0	0	0	0.5	1.000
1972		1	0	1.000	1.72	2	2	0	15.2	12	6	5	0	0	0	0	6	0	0	.000	1	3	0	0	2.0	1.000
2 yrs.		1	1	.500	4.76	4	4	0	22.2	26	8	16	0	0	0	0	7	0	0	.000	2	3	0	0	1.3	1.000

WORLD SERIES

Year	Team	W	L	PCT	ERA	G	GS	CG	IP	H	BB	SO	ShO	W	L	SV	AB	H	HR	BA	PO	A	E	DP	TC/G	FA
1971	PIT N	2	0	1.000	1.00	2	2	2	18	7	4	13	0	0	0	0	7	0	0	.000	2	4	0	0	3.0	1.000

Steve Blateric

BLATERIC, STEPHEN LAWRENCE
B. Mar. 20, 1944, Denver, Colo.   BR TR 6'3"   200 lbs.

Year	Team	W	L	PCT	ERA	G	GS	CG	IP	H	BB	SO	ShO	W	L	SV	AB	H	HR	BA	PO	A	E	DP	TC/G	FA
1971	CIN N	0	0	—	12.00	2	0	0	3	5	0	4	0	0	0	0	—	0	1	0	0	0.5	1.000
1972	NY A	0	0	—	0.00	2	0	0	4	2	0	4	0	0	0	0	1	0	0	.000	0	1	0	1	1.0	1.000
1975	CAL A	0	0	—	6.23	2	0	0	4.1	9	1	5	0	0	0	0	0	0	0	—	0	0	0	0	0.0	—
3 yrs.		0	0	—	5.56	5	0	0	11.1	16	1	13	0	0	0	0	1	0	0	.000	0	2	0	1	0.4	1.000

Henry Blauvelt

BLAUVELT, HENRY RUSSELL
B. Apr. 8, 1873, Rochester, N. Y.   D. Dec. 28, 1926, Portland, Ore.

Year	Team	W	L	PCT	ERA	G	GS	CG	IP	H	BB	SO	ShO	W	L	SV	AB	H	HR	BA	PO	A	E	DP	TC/G	FA
1890	ROC AA	0	0	—	10.22	2	0	0	12.1	19	8	5	0	0	0	0	6	3	0	.500	1	4	1	1	3.0	.833

Bob Blaylock

BLAYLOCK, ROBERT EDWARD
B. June 28, 1935, Chattanooga, Tenn.   BR TR 6'1"   185 lbs.

Year	Team	W	L	PCT	ERA	G	GS	CG	IP	H	BB	SO	ShO	W	L	SV	AB	H	HR	BA	PO	A	E	DP	TC/G	FA
1956	STL N	1	6	.143	6.37	14	6	0	41	45	24	39	0	0	1	0	11	1	0	.091	1	8	0	0	0.6	1.000
1959		0	1	.000	4.00	3	1	0	9	8	3	3	0	0	1	0	1	0	0	.000	0	2	0	0	0.7	1.000
2 yrs.		1	7	.125	5.94	17	7	0	50	53	27	42	0	0	2	0	12	1	0	.083	1	10	0	0	0.6	1.000

Gary Blaylock

BLAYLOCK, GARY NELSON
B. Oct. 11, 1931, Clarkton, Mo.   BR TR 6'   196 lbs.

Year	Team	W	L	PCT	ERA	G	GS	CG	IP	H	BB	SO	ShO	W	L	SV	AB	H	HR	BA	PO	A	E	DP	TC/G	FA
1959	2 teams	STL N	(26G 4–5)			NY A	(15G 0–1)																			
"	total	4	6	.400	4.80	41	13	3	125.2	147	58	81	0	1	1	0	36	5	2	.139	13	18	2	1	0.8	.939

Ray Blemker

BLEMKER, RAYMOND (Buddy)
B. Aug. 9, 1937, Huntingburg, Ind.   BR TL 5'11"   190 lbs.

Year	Team	W	L	PCT	ERA	G	GS	CG	IP	H	BB	SO	ShO	W	L	SV	AB	H	HR	BA	PO	A	E	DP	TC/G	FA
1960	KC A	0	0	—	27.00	1	0	0	1.2	3	2	0	0	0	0	0	0	0	0	—	0	0	0	0	0.0	—

Clarence Blethen

BLETHEN, CLARENCE WALDO (Climax)
B. July 11, 1893, Dover-Foxcroft, Me.   D. Apr. 11, 1973, Frederick, Md.   BL TR 5'11"   165 lbs.

Year	Team	W	L	PCT	ERA	G	GS	CG	IP	H	BB	SO	ShO	W	L	SV	AB	H	HR	BA	PO	A	E	DP	TC/G	FA
1923	BOS A	0	0	—	7.13	5	0	0	17.2	29	7	2	0	0	0	0	6	0	0	.000	1	1	0	0	0.4	1.000
1929	BKN N	0	0	—	9.00	2	0	0	2	4	3	0	0	0	0	0	0	0	0	—	0	2	0	0	1.0	1.000
2 yrs.		0	0	—	7.32	7	0	0	19.2	33	10	2	0	0	0	0	6	0	0	.000	1	3	0	0	0.6	1.000

Bob Blewett

BLEWETT, ROBERT LAWRENCE
B. June 28, 1877, Fond du Lac, Wis.   D. Mar. 17, 1958, Sedro Wooley, Wash.   BL TL 5'11"   170 lbs.

Year	Team	W	L	PCT	ERA	G	GS	CG	IP	H	BB	SO	ShO	W	L	SV	AB	H	HR	BA	PO	A	E	DP	TC/G	FA
1902	NY N	0	2	.000	4.82	5	3	2	28	39	7	8	0	0	0	0	10	0	0	.000	0	3	3	0	1.2	.500

Elmer Bliss

BLISS, ELMER WARD
B. Mar. 9, 1875, Penfield, Pa.   D. Mar. 18, 1962, Bradford, Pa.   BL TR 6'   180 lbs.

Year	Team	W	L	PCT	ERA	G	GS	CG	IP	H	BB	SO	ShO	W	L	SV	AB	H	HR	BA	PO	A	E	DP	TC/G	FA
1903	NY A	1	0	1.000	0.00	1	0	0	6	4	0	3	0	1	0	0	3	0	0	.000	0	0	0	0	0.0	—

Terry Blocker

BLOCKER, TERRY FENNELL
B. Aug. 18, 1959, Columbia, S. C.   BL TL 6'2"   195 lbs.

Year	Team	W	L	PCT	ERA	G	GS	CG	IP	H	BB	SO	ShO	W	L	SV	AB	H	HR	BA	PO	A	E	DP	TC/G	FA
1989	ATL N	0	0	—	0.00	1	0	0	1	0	2	0	0	0	0	0	*				0	0	0	0	0.0	—

Joe Blong

BLONG, JOSEPH MYLES
B. Sept. 17, 1853, St. Louis, Mo.   D. Sept. 22, 1892, St. Louis, Mo.   BR TR

Year	Team	W	L	PCT	ERA	G	GS	CG	IP	H	BB	SO	ShO	W	L	SV	AB	H	HR	BA	PO	A	E	DP	TC/G	FA
1876	STL N	0	0	—	0.00	1	0	0	4	2	1	0	0	0	0	0	264	62	0	.235	0	2	0	0	2.0	1.000
1877		10	9	.526	2.74	25	21	17	187.1	203	38	51	0	0	0	0	218	47	0	.216	13	24	5	0	1.7	.881
2 yrs.		10	9	.526	2.68	26	21	17	191.1	205	39	51	0	0	0	0	*				13	26	5	0	1.7	.886

Vida Blue

BLUE, VIDA ROCHELLE
B. July 28, 1949, Mansfield, La.   BB TL 6'   189 lbs.

Year	Team	W	L	PCT	ERA	G	GS	CG	IP	H	BB	SO	ShO	W	L	SV	AB	H	HR	BA	PO	A	E	DP	TC/G	FA
1969	OAK A	1	1	.500	6.21	12	4	0	42	49	18	24	0	0	0	1	10	0	0	.000	1	4	0	0	0.4	1.000
1970		2	0	1.000	2.08	6	6	2	39	20	12	35	2	0	0	0	15	3	1	.200	1	7	0	0	1.3	1.000
1971		24	8	.750	1.82	39	39	24	312	209	88	301	8	0	0	0	102	12	0	.118	15	24	0	0	1.0	1.000
1972		6	10	.375	2.80	25	23	5	151.1	117	48	111	4	0	0	0	45	2	0	.044	4	17	2	0	0.9	.913
1973		20	9	.690	3.28	37	37	13	263.2	214	105	158	4	0	0	0	1	0	0	.000	9	30	0	0	1.1	1.000
1974		17	15	.531	3.26	40	40	12	282	246	98	174	1	0	0	0	0	0	0	—	10	16	3	0	0.7	.897

Year	Team		W	L	PCT	ERA	G	GS	CG	IP	H	BB	SO	ShO	Relief Pitching			Batting			BA	PO	A	E	DP	TC/G	FA
															W	L	SV	AB	H	HR							

Vida Blue *continued*

Year	Team		W	L	PCT	ERA	G	GS	CG	IP	H	BB	SO	ShO	W	L	SV	AB	H	HR	BA	PO	A	E	DP	TC/G	FA
1975			22	11	.667	3.01	39	38	13	278	243	99	189	2	0	0	1	0	0	0	–	4	34	1	1	1.0	.974
1976			18	13	.581	2.36	37	37	20	298	268	63	166	6	0	0	0	0	0	0	–	3	34	1	2	1.0	.974
1977			14	19	.424	3.83	38	38	16	280	284	86	157	1	0	0	0	1	0	0	.000	6	42	3	2	1.3	.941
1978	SF	N	18	10	.643	2.79	35	35	9	258	233	70	171	4	0	0	0	79	6	1	.076	12	29	0	4	1.2	1.000
1979			14	14	.500	5.01	34	34	10	237	246	111	138	0	0	0	0	83	10	1	.120	10	42	1	5	1.6	.981
1980			14	10	.583	2.97	31	31	10	224	202	61	129	3	0	0	0	68	5	0	.074	14	42	1	4	1.8	.982
1981			8	6	.571	2.45	18	18	1	125	97	54	63	0	0	0	0	35	7	0	.200	11	29	1	1	2.3	.976
1982	KC	A	13	12	.520	3.78	31	31	6	181	163	80	103	2	0	0	0	0	0	0	–	14	22	2	0	1.2	.947
1983			0	5	.000	6.01	19	14	1	85.1	96	35	53	0	0	0	0	0	0	0	–	3	10	1	0	0.7	1.000
1985	SF	N	8	8	.500	4.47	33	20	1	131	115	80	103	0	2	1	0	30	4	0	.133	7	21	2	1	0.9	.933
1986			10	10	.500	3.27	28	28	0	156.2	137	77	100	0	0	0	0	43	4	1	.093	3	24	2	0	1.0	.931
17 yrs.			209	161	.565	3.26	502	473	143	3344	2939	1185	2175	37	2	2	2	512	53	4	.104	127	427	19	21	1.1	.967

LEAGUE CHAMPIONSHIP SERIES

Year	Team		W	L	PCT	ERA	G	GS	CG	IP	H	BB	SO	ShO	W	L	SV	AB	H	HR	BA	PO	A	E	DP	TC/G	FA
1971	OAK	A	0	1	.000	6.43	1	1	0	7	7	2	8	0	0	0	0	3	0	0	.000	0	1	0	0	1.0	1.000
1972			0	0	–	0.00	4	0	0	5.1	4	1	5	0	0	0	1	1	0	0	.000	0	1	0	0	0.3	1.000
1973			1	0	1.000	10.29	2	2	0	7	8	5	3	0	0	0	0	0	0	0	–	1	0	0	0	0.5	1.000
1974			1	0	1.000	0.00	1	1	0	9	2	0	7	1	0	0	0	0	0	0	–	0	1	0	0	1.0	1.000
1975			0	0	–	9.00	1	1	0	3	6	0	2	0	0	0	0	0	0	0	–	0	0	0	0	0.0	–
5 yrs.			1	2	.333	4.60	9	5	1	31.1	27	8	25	1	0	0	1	4	0	0	.000	1	3	0	0	0.4	1.000

WORLD SERIES

Year	Team		W	L	PCT	ERA	G	GS	CG	IP	H	BB	SO	ShO	W	L	SV	AB	H	HR	BA	PO	A	E	DP	TC/G	FA
1972	OAK	A	0	1	.000	4.15	4	1	0	8.2	8	5	5	0	0	0	0	1	0	0	.000	0	1	0	0	0.3	1.000
1973			0	1	.000	4.91	2	2	0	11	10	3	8	0	0	0	0	4	0	0	.000	2	1	0	1	1.5	1.000
1974			0	1	.000	3.29	2	2	0	13.2	10	7	9	0	0	0	0	4	0	0	.000	0	3	0	0	1.5	1.000
3 yrs.			0	3	.000	4.05	8	5	0	33.1	28	15	22	0	0	0	1	9	0	0	.000	2	5	0	0	0.9	1.000

Jim Bluejacket

BLUEJACKET, JAMES
Born James Smith.
B. July 8, 1887, Adair, Okla.   D. Mar. 26, 1947, Pekin, Ill.

BR TR 6'2½"   200 lbs.

Year	Team		W	L	PCT	ERA	G	GS	CG	IP	H	BB	SO	ShO	W	L	SV	AB	H	HR	BA	PO	A	E	DP	TC/G	FA
1914	BKN	F	4	5	.444	3.76	17	7	3	67	77	19	29	1	1	1	1	22	3	0	.136	3	24	0	0	1.6	1.000
1915			9	11	.450	3.15	24	21	10	162.2	155	75	48	2	1	0	0	61	8	0	.131	7	35	6	2	2.0	.875
1916	CIN	N	0	1	.000	7.71	3	2	0	7	12	3	1	0	0	0	0	2	0	0	.000	0	1	0	0	0.3	1.000
3 yrs.			13	17	.433	3.46	44	30	13	236.2	244	97	78	3	2	1	1	85	11	0	.129	10	60	6	2	1.7	.921

Clint Blume

BLUME, CLINTON WILLIS
B. Oct. 17, 1898, Brooklyn, N. Y.   D. June 12, 1973, Islip, N. Y.

BR TR 5'11"   175 lbs.

Year	Team		W	L	PCT	ERA	G	GS	CG	IP	H	BB	SO	ShO	W	L	SV	AB	H	HR	BA	PO	A	E	DP	TC/G	FA
1922	NY	N	1	0	1.000	1.00	1	1	1	9	7	1	2	0	0	0	0	1	1	0	1.000	0	0	1	0	1.0	–
1923			2	0	1.000	3.75	12	1	0	24	22	20	2	0	2	0	0	5	0	0	.000	0	4	0	0	0.3	1.000
2 yrs.			3	0	1.000	3.00	13	2	1	33	29	21	4	0	2	0	0	6	1	0	.167	0	4	1	0	0.4	.800

Bert Blyleven

BLYLEVEN, RIK AALBERT
B. Apr. 6, 1951, Zeist, Netherlands

BR TR 6'3"   200 lbs.

Year	Team		W	L	PCT	ERA	G	GS	CG	IP	H	BB	SO	ShO	W	L	SV	AB	H	HR	BA	PO	A	E	DP	TC/G	FA
1970	MIN	A	10	9	.526	3.18	27	25	5	164	143	47	135	1	0	1	0	50	7	0	.140	5	16	1	1	0.8	.955
1971			16	15	.516	2.82	38	38	17	278	267	59	224	5	0	0	0	91	12	0	.132	19	38	2	0	1.6	.966
1972			17	17	.500	2.73	39	38	11	287	247	69	228	3	0	1	0	94	15	0	.160	18	45	3	4	1.7	.955
1973			20	17	.541	2.52	40	40	25	325	296	67	258	9	0	0	0	0	0	0	–	21	34	1	0	1.4	.982
1974			17	17	.500	2.66	37	37	19	281	244	77	249	3	0	0	0	0	0	0	–	19	34	3	2	1.5	.946
1975			15	10	.600	3.00	35	35	20	275.2	219	84	233	3	0	0	0	0	0	0	–	16	48	6	5	2.0	.914
1976	2 teams		MIN A	(12G 4–5)			TEX A	(24G 9–11)																			
"	total		13	16	.448	2.87	36	36	18	297.2	283	81	219	6	0	0	0	0	0	0	–	22	44	0	4	1.8	1.000
1977	TEX	A	14	12	.538	2.72	30	30	15	235	181	69	182	5	0	0	0	0	0	0	–	10	35	1	4	1.5	.978
1978	PIT	N	14	10	.583	3.02	34	34	11	244	217	66	182	4	0	0	0	85	11	0	.129	11	41	1	4	1.6	.981
1979			12	5	.706	3.61	37	37	4	237	238	92	172	0	0	0	0	70	9	0	.129	14	20	0	0	0.9	1.000
1980			8	13	.381	3.82	34	32	5	217	219	59	168	2	0	0	0	61	5	0	.082	10	30	2	2	1.2	.952
1981	CLE	A	11	7	.611	2.89	20	20	9	159	145	40	107	1	0	0	0	0	0	0	–	9	16	1	0	1.3	.962
1982			2	2	.500	4.87	4	4	0	20.1	16	11	19	0	0	0	0	0	0	0	–	2	2	0	1	1.0	1.000
1983			7	10	.412	3.91	24	24	5	156.1	160	44	123	0	0	0	0	0	0	0	–	7	26	1	3	1.4	.971
1984			19	7	.731	2.87	33	32	12	245	204	74	170	4	0	0	0	0	0	0	–	21	30	2	2	1.6	.962
1985	2 teams		CLE A	(23G 9–11)			MIN A	(14G 8–5)																			
"	total		17	16	.515	3.16	37	37	24	293.2	264	75	206	5	0	0	0	0	0	0	–	17	32	0	2	1.3	1.000
1986	MIN	A	17	14	.548	4.01	36	36	16	271.2	262	58	215	3	0	0	0	0	0	0	–	15	31	0	0	1.3	1.000
1987			15	12	.556	4.01	37	37	8	267	249	101	196	1	0	0	0	0	0	0	–	17	43	4	3	1.7	.938
1988			10	17	.370	5.43	33	33	7	207.1	240	51	145	0	0	0	0	0	0	0	–	12	22	1	3	1.1	.971
1989	CAL	A	17	5	.773	2.73	33	33	8	241	225	44	131	5	0	0	0	0	0	0	–	14	38	0	6	1.6	1.000
20 yrs.			271	231	.540	3.22	644	638	239	4702.2	4319	1268	3562	60	0	2	0	451	59	0	.131	279	625	29	47	1.4	.969
													5th	8th													

LEAGUE CHAMPIONSHIP SERIES

Year	Team		W	L	PCT	ERA	G	GS	CG	IP	H	BB	SO	ShO	W	L	SV	AB	H	HR	BA	PO	A	E	DP	TC/G	FA
1970	MIN	A	0	0	–	0.00	1	1	0	2	2	0	2	0	0	0	0	0	0	0	–	1	0	0	0	1.0	1.000
1979	PIT	N	1	0	1.000	1.00	1	1	1	9	8	0	9	0	0	0	0	3	1	0	.333	1	1	0	0	2.0	1.000
1987	MIN	A	2	0	1.000	4.05	2	2	0	13.1	12	3	9	0	0	0	0	0	0	0	–	0	1	0	0	0.5	1.000
3 yrs.			3	0	1.000	2.59	4	4	1	24.1	22	3	20	0	0	0	0	3	1	0	.333	2	2	0	0	1.0	1.000

WORLD SERIES

Year	Team		W	L	PCT	ERA	G	GS	CG	IP	H	BB	SO	ShO	W	L	SV	AB	H	HR	BA	PO	A	E	DP	TC/G	FA
1979	PIT	N	1	0	1.000	1.80	2	1	0	10	8	3	4	0	0	0	0	3	0	0	.000	0	0	0	1	0.5	1.000
1987	MIN	A	1	1	.500	2.77	2	2	0	13	13	2	12	0	0	0	0	1	0	0	.000	0	1	0	0	0.5	1.000
2 yrs.			2	1	.667	2.35	4	3	0	23	21	5	16	0	0	0	0	4	0	0	.000	0	1	0	1	0.5	1.000

Mike Blyzka

BLYZKA, MICHAEL JOHN
B. Dec. 25, 1928, Hamtramck, Mich.

BR TR 5'11½" 190 lbs.

Year	Team		W	L	PCT	ERA	G	GS	CG	IP	H	BB	SO	ShO	W	L	SV	AB	H	HR	BA	PO	A	E	DP	TC/G	FA
1953	STL	A	2	6	.250	6.39	33	9	2	94.1	110	56	23	0	1	1	0	23	0	0	.000	6	13	0	1	0.6	1.000

Year	Team		W	L	PCT	ERA	G	GS	CG	IP	H	BB	SO	ShO	Relief Pitching W	L	SV	Batting AB	H	HR	BA	PO	A	E	DP	TC/G	FA

Mike Blyzka *continued*

| 1954 | BAL | A | 1 | 5 | .167 | 4.69 | 37 | 0 | 0 | 86.1 | 83 | 51 | 35 | 0 | 1 | 5 | 1 | 15 | 2 | 0 | .133 | 4 | 17 | 1 | 0 | 0.6 | .955 |
| 2 yrs. | | | 3 | 11 | .214 | 5.58 | 70 | 9 | 2 | 180.2 | 193 | 107 | 58 | 0 | 2 | 6 | 1 | 38 | 2 | 0 | .053 | 10 | 30 | 1 | 1 | 0.6 | .976 |

Charlie Boardman

BOARDMAN, CHARLES LOUIS BL TL 6'2½" 194 lbs.
B. Apr. 27, 1893, Seneca Falls, N. Y. D. Aug. 10, 1968, Sacramento, Calif.

1913	PHI	A	0	2	.000	2.00	2	2	1	9	10	6	4	0	0	0	0	3	0	0	.000	0	1	0	0	0.5	1.000
1914			0	0	–	4.91	2	0	0	7.1	10	4	2	0	0	0	0	2	0	0	.000	0	2	0	0	1.0	1.000
1915	STL	N	1	0	1.000	1.42	3	1	1	19	12	15	7	0	0	0	0	7	2	0	.286	0	4	0	0	1.3	1.000
3 yrs.			1	2	.333	2.29	7	3	2	35.1	32	25	13	0	0	0	0	12	2	0	.167	0	7	0	0	1.0	1.000

Randy Bockus

BOCKUS, RANDY WALTER BL TR 6'2" 190 lbs.
B. Oct. 5, 1960, Canton, Ohio

1986	SF	N	0	0	–	2.57	5	0	0	7	7	6	4	0	0	0	0	1	0	0	.000	0	4	0	0	0.8	1.000
1987			1	0	1.000	3.63	12	0	0	17.1	17	4	9	0	1	0	0	1	0	0	.000	0	3	1	0	0.3	.750
1988			1	1	.500	4.78	20	0	0	32	35	13	18	0	1	1	0	6	1	0	.167	2	7	0	0	0.5	1.000
1989	DET	A	0	0	–	5.06	2	0	0	5.1	7	2	2	0	0	0	0	0	0	0	–	0	0	0	0	0.0	–
4 yrs.			2	1	.667	4.23	39	0	0	61.2	66	25	33	0	2	1	0	8	1	0	.125	2	14	1	0	0.4	.941

Mike Boddicker

BODDICKER, MICHAEL JAMES BR TR 5'11" 172 lbs.
B. Aug. 23, 1957, Cedar Rapids, Iowa

1980	BAL	A	0	1	.000	6.43	1	1	0	7	7	5	4	0	0	0	0	0	0	0	–	0	0	1	0	1.0	–
1981			0	0	–	4.50	2	0	0	6	6	2	2	0	0	0	0	0	0	0	–	1	0	1	0	1.0	.500
1982			1	0	1.000	3.51	7	0	0	25.2	25	12	20	0	1	0	0	0	0	0	–	5	3	1	0	1.3	.889
1983			16	8	.667	2.77	27	26	10	179	141	52	120	5	0	0	0	0	0	0	–	24	32	3	4	2.2	.949
1984			**20**	11	.645	**2.79**	34	34	16	261.1	218	81	128	4	0	0	0	0	0	0	–	49	49	7	6	3.1	.933
1985			12	17	.414	4.07	32	32	9	203.1	227	89	135	2	0	0	0	0	0	0	–	26	46	2	6	2.3	.973
1986			14	12	.538	4.70	33	33	7	218.1	214	74	175	0	0	0	0	0	0	0	–	28	36	3	4	2.0	.955
1987			10	12	.455	4.18	33	33	7	226	212	78	152	2	0	0	0	0	0	0	–	18	46	2	5	2.0	.970
1988	2 teams	BAL A (21G 6–12)				BOS A (15G 7–3)																					
"	total		13	15	.464	3.39	36	35	3	236	234	77	156	1	0	0	0	0	0	0	–	22	33	2	1	1.6	.965
1989	BOS	A	15	11	.577	4.00	34	34	3	211.2	217	71	145	2	0	0	0	0	0	0	–	14	36	3	2	1.6	.943
10 yrs.			101	87	.537	3.70	239	228	57	1574.1	1500	541	1037	16	1	0	0	0	0	0	–	187	281	25	28	2.1	.949

LEAGUE CHAMPIONSHIP SERIES

1983	BAL	A	1	0	1.000	0.00	1	1	1	9	5	3	14	0	0	0	0	0	0	0	–	0	1	0	0	1.0	1.000
1988	BOS	A	0	1	.000	20.25	1	1	0	2.2	8	1	2	0	0	0	0	0	0	0	–	0	0	0	0	0.0	–
2 yrs.			1	1	.500	4.63	2	2	1	11.2	13	4	16	1	0	0	0	0	0	0	–	0	1	0	0	0.5	1.000

WORLD SERIES

| 1983 | BAL | A | 1 | 0 | 1.000 | 0.00 | 1 | 1 | 1 | 9 | 3 | 0 | 6 | 0 | 0 | 0 | 0 | 3 | 0 | 0 | .000 | 1 | 2 | 0 | 1 | 3.0 | 1.000 |

George Boehler

BOEHLER, GEORGE HENRY BR TR 6'2" 180 lbs.
B. Jan. 2, 1892, Lawrenceburg, Ind. D. June 23, 1958, Lawrenceburg, Ind.

1912	DET	A	0	2	.000	6.68	4	4	1	31	49	14	13	0	0	0	0	10	1	0	.100	0	15	0	0	3.8	1.000
1913			0	1	.000	6.75	1	1	1	8	11	6	2	0	0	0	0	3	1	0	.333	0	5	0	0	5.0	1.000
1914			2	3	.400	3.57	18	6	2	63	54	48	37	0	0	0	1	17	3	0	.176	3	18	1	1	1.2	.955
1915			1	1	.500	1.80	8	0	0	15	19	4	7	0	1	1	0	4	3	0	.750	0	3	0	0	0.4	1.000
1916			1	1	.500	4.73	5	2	1	13.1	12	9	8	0	0	0	0	3	0	0	.000	0	6	0	0	1.2	1.000
1920	STL	A	0	1	.000	7.71	3	1	0	7	10	4	2	0	0	0	0	0	0	0	–	0	3	1	0	1.3	.750
1921			0	0	–	0.00	1	0	0	1	1	0	0	0	0	0	0	0	0	0	–	0	0	0	0	0.0	–
1923	PIT	N	1	3	.250	6.04	10	3	1	28.1	33	26	12	0	0	0	0	10	3	0	.300	0	5	0	0	0.5	1.000
1926	BKN	N	1	0	1.000	4.41	10	1	0	34.2	42	23	10	0	0	0	0	12	3	0	.250	0	7	1	0	0.8	.875
9 yrs.			6	12	.333	4.74	60	18	7	201.1	231	134	91	0	1	3	0	60	14	0	.233	3	62	3	3	1.1	.956

Joe Boehling

BOEHLING, JOHN JOSEPH BL TL 5'11" 168 lbs.
B. Mar. 20, 1891, Richmond, Va. D. Sept. 8, 1941, Richmond, Va.

1912	WAS	A	0	0	–	7.20	3	0	0	5	4	6	2	0	0	0	0	0	0	0	–	0	3	0	0	1.0	1.000
1913			17	7	.708	2.14	38	25	18	235.1	197	82	110	3	2	0	4	86	19	0	.221	14	86	10	4	2.9	.909
1914			12	8	.600	3.03	27	24	14	196	180	76	91	2	0	1	1	71	17	0	.239	19	60	2	2	3.0	.975
1915			14	13	.519	3.22	40	32	14	229.1	217	119	108	2	0	3	0	75	13	1	.173	10	77	2	0	2.2	.978
1916	2 teams	WAS A (27G 9–11)				CLE A (12G 2–4)																					
"	total		11	15	.423	2.97	39	28	10	200.1	197	77	70	2	2	2	0	60	12	0	.200	14	77	5	2	2.5	.948
1917	CLE	A	1	6	.143	4.66	12	7	1	46.1	50	16	11	0	0	1	0	16	3	0	.188	3	12	0	1	1.3	1.000
1920			0	1	.000	4.85	3	2	0	13	16	10	4	0	0	0	0	3	2	0	.667	1	3	0	0	1.3	1.000
7 yrs.			55	50	.524	2.97	162	118	57	925.1	861	386	396	9	4	7	5	311	66	1	.212	61	318	19	9	2.5	.952

Larry Boerner

BOERNER, LAWRENCE HYER BR TR 6'4½" 175 lbs.
B. Jan. 21, 1905, Staunton, Va. D. Oct. 16, 1969, Staunton, Va.

| 1932 | BOS | A | 0 | 4 | .000 | 5.02 | 21 | 5 | 0 | 61 | 71 | 37 | 19 | 0 | 0 | 0 | 0 | 17 | 0 | 0 | .000 | 4 | 14 | 0 | 0 | 0.9 | 1.000 |

Joe Boever

BOEVER, JOSEPH MARTIN BR TR 6'1" 200 lbs.
B. Oct. 4, 1960, St. Louis, Mo.

1985	STL	N	0	0	–	4.41	13	0	0	16.1	17	4	20	0	0	0	0	0	0	0	–	0	0	0	0	0.0	–
1986			0	1	.000	1.66	11	0	0	21.2	19	11	8	0	0	1	0	2	1	0	.500	1	2	0	0	0.3	1.000
1987	ATL	N	1	0	1.000	7.36	14	0	0	18.1	29	12	18	0	1	0	0	0	0	0	–	0	2	0	0	0.1	1.000
1988			0	2	.000	1.77	16	0	0	20.1	12	1	7	0	0	2	0	3	0	0	.000	2	3	0	1	0.3	1.000
1989			4	11	.267	3.94	66	0	0	82.1	78	34	68	0	4	11	21	3	1	0	.333	7	15	0	0	0.3	1.000
5 yrs.			5	14	.263	3.79	120	0	0	159	155	62	121	0	5	14	22	8	2	0	.333	10	22	0	1	0.3	1.000

Year	Team		W	L	PCT	ERA	G	GS	CG	IP	H	BB	SO	ShO	Relief Pitching W	L	SV	Batting AB	H	HR	BA	PO	A	E	DP	TC/G	FA

John Bogart

BOGART, JOHN RENZIE (Big John)
B. Sept. 21, 1900, Bloomsburg, Pa. D. Dec. 7, 1986, Clarence, N. Y.   BR TR 6'2" 195 lbs.

| 1920 | DET | A | 2 | 1 | .667 | 3.04 | 4 | 3 | 0 | 23.2 | 16 | 18 | 5 | 0 | 1 | 0 | 0 | 8 | 2 | 0 | .250 | 0 | 2 | 0 | 0 | 0.5 | 1.000 |

Ray Boggs

BOGGS, RAYMOND JOSEPH (Lefty)
B. Dec. 12, 1904, Reamsville, Kans.   BL TL 6'½" 170 lbs.

| 1928 | BOS | N | 0 | 0 | — | 5.40 | 4 | 0 | 0 | 5 | 2 | 7 | 0 | 0 | 0 | 0 | 0 | 0 | 0 | 0 | — | 0 | 1 | 0 | 0 | 0.3 | 1.000 |

Tommy Boggs

BOGGS, THOMAS WINTON
B. Oct. 25, 1955, Poughkeepsie, N. Y.   BR TR 6'2" 195 lbs.

1976	TEX	A	1	7	.125	3.50	13	13	3	90	87	34	36	0	0	0	0	0	0	0	—	7	10	0	1	1.3	1.000
1977			0	3	.000	6.00	6	6	0	27	40	12	15	0	0	0	0	0	0	0	—	2	2	0	0	0.7	1.000
1978	ATL	N	2	8	.200	6.71	16	12	1	59	80	26	21	1	0	0	0	18	3	1	.167	5	3	3	0	0.7	.727
1979			0	2	.000	6.23	3	3	0	13	21	4	1	0	0	0	0	4	1	0	.250	0	3	0	0	1.0	1.000
1980			12	9	.571	3.42	32	26	4	192	180	46	84	3	0	0	0	63	10	0	.159	17	16	0	0	1.0	1.000
1981			3	13	.188	4.09	25	24	2	143	140	54	81	0	0	0	1	46	7	0	.152	13	20	5	0	1.5	.868
1982			2	2	.500	3.30	10	10	0	46.1	43	22	29	0	0	0	0	17	4	0	.235	3	7	2	0	1.2	.833
1983			0	0	—	5.68	5	0	0	6.1	8	1	5	0	0	0	0	0	0	0	—	0	0	0	0	0.0	—
1985	TEX	A	0	0	—	11.57	4	0	0	7	13	2	6	0	0	0	0	0	0	0	—	0	2	0	0	0.5	1.000
9 yrs.			20	44	.313	4.23	114	94	10	583.2	612	201	278	4	0	0	1	148	25	1	.169	47	63	10	1	1.1	.917

Warren Bogle

BOGLE, WARREN FREDERICK
B. Oct. 19, 1946, Passaic, N. J.   BL TL 6'4" 220 lbs.

| 1968 | OAK | A | 0 | 0 | — | 4.30 | 16 | 0 | 0 | 23 | 26 | 8 | 26 | 0 | 0 | 0 | 0 | 5 | 0 | 0 | .000 | 2 | 5 | 0 | 0 | 0.4 | 1.000 |

Pat Bohen

BOHEN, LEO IGNATIUS
B. Sept. 30, 1891, Oakland, Iowa D. Apr. 8, 1942, Napa, Calif.   BR TR 5'10" 155 lbs.

1913	PHI	A	0	1	.000	1.13	1	1	1	8	3	2	5	0	0	0	0	3	0	0	.000	0	2	0	0	2.0	1.000
1914	PIT	N	0	0	—	18.00	1	0	0	1	2	2	0	0	0	0	0	1	0	0	.000	0	0	0	0	0.0	—
2 yrs.			0	1	.000	3.00	2	1	1	9	5	4	5	0	0	0	0	4	0	0	.000	0	2	0	0	1.0	1.000

Charlie Bohn

BOHN, CHARLES
B. 1857, Cleveland, Ohio D. Aug. 1, 1903, Cleveland, Ohio

| 1882 | LOU | AA | 1 | 1 | .500 | 3.00 | 2 | 2 | 2 | 18 | 21 | 3 | 1 | 0 | 0 | 0 | 0 | 13 | 2 | 0 | .154 | 0 | 8 | 1 | 0 | 4.5 | .889 |

John Bohnet

BOHNET, JOHN KELLY
B. Jan. 18, 1961, Pasadena, Calif.   BB TL 6' 180 lbs.

| 1982 | CLE | A | 0 | 0 | — | 6.94 | 3 | 3 | 0 | 11.2 | 11 | 7 | 4 | 0 | 0 | 0 | 0 | 0 | 0 | 0 | — | 1 | 2 | 0 | 0 | 1.0 | 1.000 |

Danny Boitano

BOITANO, DANNY JON
B. Mar. 22, 1953, Sacramento, Calif.   BR TR 6' 185 lbs.

1978	PHI	N	0	0	—	0.00	1	0	0	1	0	1	0	0	0	0	0	0	0	0	—	0	0	0	0	0.0	—
1979	MIL	A	0	0	—	1.50	5	0	0	6	6	3	5	0	0	0	0	0	0	0	—	0	1	0	0	0.2	1.000
1980			0	1	.000	8.00	11	0	0	18	26	6	11	0	0	1	0	0	0	0	—	0	3	0	0	0.3	1.000
1981	NY	N	2	1	.667	5.63	15	0	0	16	21	5	8	0	2	1	0	0	0	0	—	0	3	0	0	0.2	1.000
1982	TEX	A	0	0	—	5.34	19	0	0	30.1	33	13	28	0	0	0	0	0	0	0	—	1	3	0	0	0.2	1.000
5 yrs.			2	2	.500	5.68	51	0	0	71.1	86	28	52	0	2	2	0	0	0	0	—	1	10	0	0	0.2	1.000

Dick Bokelmann

BOKELMANN, RICHARD WERNER
B. Oct. 26, 1926, Arlington Heights, Ill.   BR TR 6'½" 180 lbs.

1951	STL	N	3	3	.500	3.78	20	1	0	52.1	49	31	22	0	3	2	3	14	0	0	.000	2	7	2	0	0.6	.818
1952			0	1	.000	9.24	11	0	0	12.2	20	7	5	0	0	1	0	0	0	0	—	3	5	0	0	0.7	1.000
1953			0	0	—	6.00	3	0	0	3	4	0	0	0	0	0	0	0	0	0	—	1	2	0	0	1.0	1.000
3 yrs.			3	4	.429	4.90	34	1	0	68	73	38	27	0	3	3	3	14	0	0	.000	6	14	2	0	0.6	.909

Joe Bokina

BOKINA, JOSEPH
B. Apr. 4, 1910, Northampton, Mass.   BR TR 6' 184 lbs.

| 1936 | WAS | A | 0 | 2 | .000 | 8.64 | 5 | 1 | 0 | 8.1 | 15 | 6 | 5 | 0 | 0 | 1 | 0 | 0 | 0 | 0 | .000 | 0 | 1 | 0 | 0 | 0.2 | 1.000 |

Bernie Boland

BOLAND, BERNARD ANTHONY
B. Jan. 21, 1892, Rochester, N. Y. D. Sept. 12, 1973, Detroit, Mich.   BR TR 5'8½" 168 lbs.

1915	DET	A	13	7	.650	3.11	45	18	8	202.2	167	75	72	1	4	2	2	63	11	0	.175	12	59	3	5	1.6	.959
1916			10	3	.769	3.94	46	9	5	130.1	111	73	59	1	5	0	3	32	8	0	.250	3	22	1	1	0.6	.962
1917			16	11	.593	2.68	43	28	13	238	192	95	89	3	2	2	6	72	4	0	.056	9	72	2	0	1.9	.976
1918			14	10	.583	2.65	29	25	14	204	176	67	63	4	1	1	0	69	12	0	.174	11	49	2	2	2.1	.968
1919			14	16	.467	3.04	35	30	18	242.2	222	80	71	1	1	1	1	74	8	0	.108	14	57	2	0	2.1	.973
1920			0	2	.000	7.79	4	3	1	17.1	23	14	4	0	0	0	0	7	1	0	.143	5	3	1	0	2.3	.889
1921	STL	A	1	4	.200	8.89	8	6	0	28.1	34	28	6	0	0	0	0	10	1	0	.100	2	6	0	0	1.0	1.000
7 yrs.			68	53	.562	3.24	210	119	59	1063.1	925	432	364	10	13	6	12	327	45	0	.138	56	268	11	10	1.6	.967

Bill Bolden

BOLDEN, WILLIAM HORACE (Big Bill)
B. May 9, 1893, Dandridge, Tenn. D. Dec. 8, 1966, Jefferson City, Tenn.   BR TR 6'4" 200 lbs.

| 1919 | STL | N | 0 | 1 | .000 | 5.25 | 3 | 1 | 0 | 12 | 17 | 4 | 4 | 0 | 0 | 0 | 0 | 3 | 1 | 0 | .333 | 0 | 4 | 0 | 1 | 1.3 | 1.000 |

Stew Bolen

BOLEN, STEWART O'NEILL
B. Oct. 12, 1902, Jackson, Ala. D. Aug. 30, 1969, Mobile, Ala.   BL TL 5'11" 180 lbs.

1926	STL	A	0	0	—	6.14	5	0	0	14.2	21	6	7	0	0	0	0	4	2	0	.500	1	3	1	0	1.0	.800
1927			0	1	.000	8.38	9	1	1	9.2	14	5	7	0	0	0	0	3	1	0	.333	0	2	0	0	0.7	1.000
1931	PHI	N	3	12	.200	6.39	28	16	2	98.2	117	63	55	0	1	2	0	32	5	0	.156	2	23	4	1	1.0	.862

Year	Team	W	L	PCT	ERA	G	GS	CG	IP	H	BB	SO	ShO	Relief Pitching W	L	SV	Batting AB	H	HR	BA	PO	A	E	DP	TC/G	FA

Stew Bolen *continued*

Year	Team	W	L	PCT	ERA	G	GS	CG	IP	H	BB	SO	ShO	W	L	SV	AB	H	HR	BA	PO	A	E	DP	TC/G	FA
1932		0	0	–	2.81	5	0	0	16	18	10	3	0	0	0	0	7	1	0	.143	0	2	0	0	0.4	1.000
4 yrs.		3	13	.188	6.09	41	17	3	139	170	84	72	0	1	2	0	46	9	0	.196	3	30	5	1	0.9	.868

Bobby Bolin

BOLIN, BOBBY DONALD
B. Jan. 29, 1939, Hickory Grove, S. C.   BR TR 6'4"   185 lbs.

Year	Team	W	L	PCT	ERA	G	GS	CG	IP	H	BB	SO	ShO	W	L	SV	AB	H	HR	BA	PO	A	E	DP	TC/G	FA
1961	SF N	2	2	.500	3.19	37	1	0	48	37	37	48	0	2	2	5	7	2	0	.286	0	4	1	0	0.1	.800
1962		7	3	.700	3.62	41	5	2	92	84	35	74	0	3	2	5	23	6	0	.261	3	10	0	0	0.3	1.000
1963		10	6	.625	3.28	47	12	2	137.1	128	57	134	0	7	2	7	35	5	0	.143	4	11	1	0	0.3	.938
1964		6	9	.400	3.25	38	23	5	174.2	143	77	146	3	1	1	0	50	5	0	.100	13	22	1	4	0.9	.972
1965		14	6	.700	2.76	45	13	2	163	125	56	135	0	8	1	2	54	9	1	.167	9	16	0	1	0.6	1.000
1966		11	10	.524	2.89	36	34	10	224.1	174	70	143	4	0	0	1	76	13	2	.171	13	30	5	0	1.3	.896
1967		6	8	.429	4.88	37	15	0	120	120	50	69	0	4	0	0	33	8	0	.242	12	15	1	0	0.8	.964
1968		10	5	.667	1.99	34	19	6	176.2	128	46	126	3	2	0	0	55	5	0	.091	10	23	2	0	1.0	.943
1969		7	7	.500	4.44	30	22	2	146	149	49	102	0	0	0	0	39	6	1	.154	7	19	0	0	0.9	1.000
1970	2 teams		MIL A	(32G 5–11)		BOS A	(6G 2–0)																			
"	total	7	11	.389	4.63	38	20	3	140	133	72	89	0	3	3	3	37	7	1	.189	5	18	1	0	0.6	.958
1971	BOS A	5	3	.625	4.24	52	0	0	70	74	24	51	0	5	3	6	12	3	0	.250	2	7	1	1	0.2	.900
1972		0	1	.000	2.90	21	0	0	31	24	11	27	0	0	1	5	2	0	0	.000	1	4	1	0	0.3	.833
1973		3	4	.429	2.72	39	0	0	53	45	13	31	0	3	4	15	0	0	0	–	8	11	1	0	0.5	.950
13 yrs.		88	75	.540	3.40	495	164	32	1576	1364	597	1175	10	38	17	50	423	69	6	.163	87	190	15	6	0.6	.949

WORLD SERIES

Year	Team	W	L	PCT	ERA	G	GS	CG	IP	H	BB	SO	ShO	W	L	SV	AB	H	HR	BA	PO	A	E	DP	TC/G	FA
1962	SF N	0	0	–	6.75	2	0	0	2.2	4	2	2	0	0	0	0	0	0	0	–	0	0	0	0	0.0	–

Greg Bollo

BOLLO, GREGORY GENE
B. Nov. 16, 1943, Detroit, Mich.   BR TR 6'4"   183 lbs.

Year	Team	W	L	PCT	ERA	G	GS	CG	IP	H	BB	SO	ShO	W	L	SV	AB	H	HR	BA	PO	A	E	DP	TC/G	FA
1965	CHI A	0	0	–	3.57	15	0	0	22.2	12	9	16	0	0	0	0	1	0	0		3	4	0	1	0.5	1.000
1966		0	1	.000	2.57	3	1	0	7	7	3	4	0	0	0	0	0	0	0	.000	0	1	0	0	0.3	1.000
2 yrs.		0	1	.000	3.34	18	1	0	29.2	19	12	20	0	0	0	0	1	0	0	.000	3	5	0	1	0.4	1.000

Tom Bolton

BOLTON, THOMAS EDWARD
B. May 6, 1962, Nashville, Tenn.   BL TL 6'2"   172 lbs.

Year	Team	W	L	PCT	ERA	G	GS	CG	IP	H	BB	SO	ShO	W	L	SV	AB	H	HR	BA	PO	A	E	DP	TC/G	FA
1987	BOS A	1	0	1.000	4.38	29	0	0	61.2	83	27	49	0	1	0	0	0	0	0	–	3	9	0	1	0.4	1.000
1988		1	3	.250	4.75	28	0	0	30.1	35	14	21	0	1	3	1	0	0	0	–	1	10	0	0	0.4	1.000
1989		0	4	.000	8.31	4	4	0	17.1	21	10	9	0	0	0	0	0	0	0	–	1	2	0	0	0.8	1.000
3 yrs.		2	7	.222	5.10	61	4	0	109.1	139	51	79	0	2	3	1	0	0	0	–	5	21	0	1	0.4	1.000

Mark Bomback

BOMBACK, MARK VINCENT
B. Apr. 14, 1953, Portsmouth, Va.   BR TR 5'11"   170 lbs.

Year	Team	W	L	PCT	ERA	G	GS	CG	IP	H	BB	SO	ShO	W	L	SV	AB	H	HR	BA	PO	A	E	DP	TC/G	FA
1978	MIL A	0	0	–	16.20	2	1	0	1.2	5	1	1	0	0	0	0	0	0	0	–	0	0	0	0	0.0	–
1980	NY N	10	8	.556	4.09	36	25	2	163	191	49	68	1	2	0	0	43	10	0	.233	20	32	1	2	1.5	.981
1981	TOR A	5	5	.500	3.90	20	11	0	90	84	35	33	0	0	0	0	0	0	0	–	6	16	0	0	1.1	1.000
1982		1	5	.167	6.03	16	8	0	59.2	87	25	22	0	0	0	0	0	0	0	–	6	9	0	0	0.9	1.000
4 yrs.		16	18	.471	4.47	74	45	2	314.1	367	110	124	1	2	0	0	43	10	0	.233	32	57	1	2	1.2	.989

Tommy Bond

BOND, THOMAS HENRY
B. Apr. 2, 1856, Granard, Ireland   D. Jan. 24, 1941, Boston, Mass.   BR TR 5'7½"   160 lbs.
Manager 1882.

Year	Team	W	L	PCT	ERA	G	GS	CG	IP	H	BB	SO	ShO	W	L	SV	AB	H	HR	BA	PO	A	E	DP	TC/G	FA
1876	HAR N	31	13	.705	1.68	45	45	45	408	355	13	88	6	0	0	0	182	50	0	.275	25	93	15	0	3.0	.887
1877	BOS N	40	17	.702	2.11	58	58	58	521	530	36	170	6	0	0	0	259	59	0	.228	29	104	9	2	2.4	.937
1878		40	19	.678	2.06	59	59	57	532.2	571	33	182	9	0	0	0	236	50	0	.212	27	117	9	4	2.6	.941
1879		43	19	.694	1.96	64	64	59	555.1	543	24	155	12	0	0	0	257	62	0	.241	33	144	8	7	2.9	.957
1880		26	29	.473	2.67	63	57	49	493	559	45	118	2	0	0	2	282	62	0	.220	32	141	11	6	2.9	.940
1881		0	3	.000	4.26	3	3	2	25.1	40	2	2	0	0	0	0	10	2	0	.200	2	7	0	0	3.0	1.000
1882	WOR N	0	1	.000	4.38	2	2	2	12.1	12	7	2	0	0	0	0	30	4	0	.133	1	1	0	0	1.0	1.000
1884	2 teams		BOS U	(23G 13–9)		IND AA	(5G 0–5)																			
"	total	13	14	.481	3.49	28	26	24	232	247	18	143	0	1	0	0	185	51	0	.276	10	60	13	2	3.0	.843
8 yrs.		193	115	.627	2.25 9th	322	314	294	2779.2	2857	178	860	36	1	2	0	*				159	667	65	21	2.8	.927

Julio Bonetti

BONETTI, JULIO GIACOMO
B. July 14, 1911, Genoa, Italy   D. June 17, 1952, Belmont, Calif.   BR TR 6'   180 lbs.

Year	Team	W	L	PCT	ERA	G	GS	CG	IP	H	BB	SO	ShO	W	L	SV	AB	H	HR	BA	PO	A	E	DP	TC/G	FA
1937	STL A	4	11	.267	5.84	28	16	7	143.1	190	60	43	0	2	0	1	47	7	0	.149	6	38	4	1	1.7	.917
1938		2	3	.400	6.35	17	0	0	28.1	41	13	7	0	2	3	0	8	0	0	.000	0	7	0	2	0.4	1.000
1940	CHI N	0	0	–	20.25	1	0	0	1.1	3	4	0	0	0	0	0	0	0	0	–	0	0	0	0	0.0	–
3 yrs.		6	14	.300	6.03	46	16	7	173	234	77	50	0	4	3	1	55	7	0	.127	6	45	4	3	1.2	.927

Hank Boney

BONEY, HENRY TATE
B. Oct. 28, 1903, Wallace, N. C.   BR TR 5'11"   176 lbs.

Year	Team	W	L	PCT	ERA	G	GS	CG	IP	H	BB	SO	ShO	W	L	SV	AB	H	HR	BA	PO	A	E	DP	TC/G	FA
1927	NY N	0	0	–	2.25	3	0	0	4	4	2	0	0	0	0	0	0	0	0	–	0	0	0	0	0.0	–

Bill Bonham

BONHAM, WILLIAM GORDON
B. Oct. 1, 1948, Glendale, Calif.   BR TR 6'3"   190 lbs.

Year	Team	W	L	PCT	ERA	G	GS	CG	IP	H	BB	SO	ShO	W	L	SV	AB	H	HR	BA	PO	A	E	DP	TC/G	FA
1971	CHI N	2	1	.667	4.65	33	6	0	60	63	36	41	0	2	0	0	12	2	0	.167	5	13	0	1	0.5	1.000
1972		1	1	.500	3.10	19	4	0	58	56	25	49	0	0	0	4	14	4	0	.286	3	9	0	0	0.6	1.000
1973		7	5	.583	3.02	44	15	3	152	126	64	121	0	3	0	6	43	4	0	.093	10	40	2	2	1.2	.962
1974		11	22	.333	3.85	44	36	10	243	246	109	191	2	1	2	1	84	12	0	.143	20	54	6	4	1.8	.925
1975		13	15	.464	4.72	38	37	9	229	254	109	165	2	0	0	0	82	15	0	.183	15	37	4	3	1.5	.929
1976		9	13	.409	4.27	32	31	3	196	215	96	110	0	0	0	0	65	13	0	.200	8	32	3	2	1.3	.930
1977		10	13	.435	4.35	34	34	1	215	207	82	134	0	0	0	0	65	15	0	.231	20	43	3	4	1.9	.955

Year	Team		W	L	PCT	ERA	G	GS	CG	IP	H	BB	SO	ShO	Relief Pitching W	L	SV	Batting AB	H	HR	BA	PO	A	E	DP	TC/G	FA

Bill Bonham *continued*

1978	CIN	N	11	5	.688	3.54	23	23	1	140	151	50	83	0	0	0	0	43	8	0	.186	13	35	3	2	2.2	.941
1979			9	7	.563	3.78	29	29	2	176	173	60	78	0	0	0	0	57	8	0	.140	9	31	4	0	1.5	.909
1980			2	1	.667	4.74	4	4	0	19	21	5	13	0	0	0	0	6	0	0	.000	0	3	1	0	1.0	.750
10 yrs.			75	83	.475	4.00	300	214	27	1488	1512	636	985	4	6	3	11	471	81	0	.172	103	297	26	18	1.4	.939

Ernie Bonham

BONHAM, ERNEST EDWARD (Tiny)
B. Aug. 16, 1913, Ione, Calif. D. Sept. 15, 1949, Pittsburgh, Pa.

BR TR 6'2" 215 lbs.

1940	NY	A	9	3	.750	**1.90**	12	12	10	99.1	83	13	37	3	0	0	0	37	7	0	.189	6	8	0	0	1.2	1.000
1941			9	6	.600	2.98	23	14	7	126.2	118	31	43	1	1	0	2	50	8	0	.160	6	12	2	1	0.9	.900
1942			21	5	**.808**	2.27	28	27	**22**	226	199	24	71	**6**	1	0	0	74	9	0	.122	11	28	0	2	1.4	1.000
1943			15	8	.652	2.27	28	26	17	225.2	197	52	71	4	0	0	1	76	15	0	.197	8	26	0	1	1.2	1.000
1944			12	9	.571	2.99	26	25	17	213.2	228	41	54	1	0	0	0	75	10	0	.133	8	26	1	5	1.3	.971
1945			8	11	.421	3.29	23	23	12	180.2	186	22	42	0	0	0	0	63	15	0	.238	6	23	0	2	1.3	1.000
1946			5	8	.385	3.70	18	14	6	104.2	97	23	30	2	0	0	3	31	4	0	.129	2	13	2	1	0.9	.882
1947	PIT	N	11	8	.579	3.85	33	18	7	149.2	167	35	63	3	3	1	3	45	7	0	.156	5	11	2	1	0.6	.900
1948			6	10	.375	4.31	22	20	7	135.1	145	23	42	0	1	0	0	49	8	0	.163	6	9	1	1	0.7	.938
1949			7	4	.636	4.25	18	14	5	89	81	23	25	1	1	0	0	22	1	0	.045	3	9	0	1	0.7	1.000
10 yrs.			103	72	.589	3.06	231	193	110	1551	1501	287	478	21	6	1	9	522	84	0	.161	63	165	8	15	1.0	.966

WORLD SERIES

1941	NY	A	1	0	1.000	1.00	1	1	1	9	4	2	2	0	0	0	0	4	0	0	.000	0	1	0	0	1.0	1.000
1942			0	1	.000	4.09	2	1	1	11	9	3	3	0	0	0	0	2	0	0	.000	0	2	0	0	1.0	1.000
1943			0	1	.000	4.50	1	1	0	8	6	3	9	0	0	0	0	2	0	0	.000	0	0	0	0	0.0	–
3 yrs.			1	2	.333	3.21	4	3	2	28	19	8	14	0	0	0	0	8	0	0	.000	0	3	0	0	0.8	1.000

Joe Bonikowski

BONIKOWSKI, JOSEPH PETER
B. Jan. 16, 1941, Philadelphia, Pa.

BR TR 6' 175 lbs.

| 1962 | MIN | A | 5 | 7 | .417 | 3.88 | 30 | 13 | 3 | 99.2 | 95 | 38 | 45 | 0 | 2 | 1 | 0 | 27 | 4 | 0 | .148 | 7 | 22 | 0 | 1 | 1.0 | 1.000 |

Bill Bonness

BONNESS, WILLIAM JOHN (Lefty)
B. Dec. 15, 1923, Cleveland, Ohio D. Dec. 3, 1977, Detroit, Mich.

BR TL 6'4" 200 lbs.

| 1944 | CLE | A | 0 | 1 | .000 | 7.71 | 2 | 1 | 0 | 7 | 11 | 5 | 1 | 0 | 0 | 0 | 0 | 3 | 0 | 0 | .000 | 0 | 2 | 0 | 0 | 1.0 | 1.000 |

Gus Bono

BONO, ADLAI WENDELL
B. Aug. 29, 1894, Doe Run, Mo. D. Dec. 3, 1948, Dearborn, Mich.

BR TR 5'11" 175 lbs.

| 1920 | WAS | A | 0 | 2 | .000 | 8.76 | 4 | 1 | 0 | 12.1 | 17 | 6 | 4 | 0 | 0 | 1 | 0 | 3 | 0 | 0 | .000 | 0 | 5 | 1 | 0 | 1.5 | .833 |

Greg Booker

BOOKER, GREGORY SCOTT
B. June 22, 1960, Lynchburg, Va.

BR TR 6'6" 230 lbs.

1983	SD	N	0	1	.000	7.71	6	1	0	11.2	18	9	5	0	0	1	0	1	0	0	.000	0	3	0	0	0.5	1.000
1984			1	1	.500	3.30	32	1	0	57.1	67	27	28	0	1	1	0	7	2	0	.286	9	7	1	0	0.5	.941
1985			0	1	.000	6.85	17	0	0	22.1	20	17	7	0	0	1	0	1	0	0	.000	1	3	1	0	0.3	.800
1986			1	0	1.000	1.64	9	0	0	11	10	4	7	0	1	0	0	0	0	0	–	1	1	1	0	0.3	.667
1987			1	1	.500	3.16	44	0	0	68.1	62	30	17	0	1	1	1	6	0	0	.000	8	8	1	1	0.4	.941
1988			2	2	.500	3.39	34	2	0	63.2	68	19	43	0	1	2	0	8	2	0	.250	6	12	0	1	0.5	1.000
1989	2 teams	SD N (11G 0–1)													MIN A	(6G 0–0)											
"	total		0	1	.000	4.23	17	0	0	27.2	26	12	11	0	0	0	0	1	0	0	–	3	7	0	1	0.6	1.000
7 yrs.			5	7	.417	3.81	159	4	0	262	271	118	118	0	4	6	1	23	4	0	.174	28	41	4	3	0.5	.945

LEAGUE CHAMPIONSHIP SERIES

| 1984 | SD | N | 0 | 0 | – | 0.00 | 1 | 0 | 0 | 2 | 2 | 1 | 2 | 0 | 0 | 0 | 0 | 0 | 0 | 0 | – | 0 | 0 | 0 | 0 | 0.0 | – |

WORLD SERIES

| 1984 | SD | N | 0 | 0 | – | 9.00 | 1 | 0 | 0 | 1 | 4 | 0 | 1 | 0 | 0 | 0 | 0 | 0 | 0 | 0 | – | 0 | 1 | 0 | 0 | 1.0 | 1.000 |

Red Booles

BOOLES, SEABRON JESSE
B. July 14, 1880, Bernice, La. D. Mar. 16, 1955, Monroe, La.

BL TL 5'10" 150 lbs.

| 1909 | CLE | A | 0 | 1 | .000 | 1.99 | 4 | 1 | 0 | 22.2 | 20 | 8 | 6 | 0 | 0 | 0 | 0 | 6 | 1 | 0 | .167 | 0 | 7 | 0 | 0 | 1.8 | 1.000 |

Danny Boone

BOONE, DANIEL HUGH
B. Jan. 14, 1954, Long Beach, Calif.

BL TL 5'8" 150 lbs.

1981	SD	N	1	0	1.000	2.86	37	0	0	63	63	21	43	0	1	0	2	4	2	0	.500	7	14	1	1	0.6	.955
1982	2 teams	SD N (10G 1–0)					HOU N	(10G 0–1)																			
"	total		1	1	.500	4.71	20	0	0	28.2	28	7	12	0	1	1	2	6	1	0	.167	0	7	1	0	0.4	.875
2 yrs.			2	1	.667	3.44	57	0	0	91.2	91	28	55	0	2	1	4	10	3	0	.300	7	21	2	1	0.5	.933

Danny Boone

BOONE, JAMES ALBERT
Brother of Ike Boone.
B. Jan. 19, 1895, Samantha, Ala. D. June 11, 1968, Tuscaloosa, Ala.

BR TR 6'2" 190 lbs.

1919	PHI	A	0	1	.000	6.75	3	2	0	14.2	24	10	1	0	0	0	0	4	0	0	.000	2	7	1	0	3.3	.900
1921	DET	A	0	0	–	0.00	1	0	0	2	1	2	0	0	0	0	1	1	0	0	.000	0	1	0	0	1.0	1.000
1922	CLE	A	4	6	.400	4.06	11	10	4	75.1	87	19	9	2	2	1	0	26	5	0	.192	4	25	0	0	2.5	1.000
1923			4	6	.400	6.01	27	4	2	70.1	93	31	15	0	3	3	0	19	4	0	.211	2	30	0	3	1.3	1.000
4 yrs.			8	13	.381	5.10	42	16	6	162.1	205	62	25	2	3	4	1	50	9	0	.180	8	63	1	3	1.7	.986

George Boone

BOONE, GEORGE MORRIS
B. Mar. 1, 1871, Louisville, Ky. D. Sept. 24, 1910, Louisville, Ky.

| 1891 | LOU | AA | 0 | 0 | – | 7.80 | 4 | 1 | 0 | 15 | 15 | 9 | 4 | 0 | 0 | 0 | 1 | 6 | 2 | 0 | .333 | 0 | 3 | 0 | 0 | 0.8 | 1.000 |

Year	Team		W	L	PCT	ERA	G	GS	CG	IP	H	BB	SO	ShO	Relief Pitching			Batting			BA	PO	A	E	DP	TC/G	FA
															W	L	SV	AB	H	HR							

Amos Booth

BOOTH, AMOS SMITH (The Darling)
B. Sept. 4, 1852, Cincinnati, Ohio D. July 1, 1921, Miamisburg, Ohio

BR TR

1876	CIN	N	0	1	.000	9.31	3	1	0	9.2	22	0	0	0	0	0	0	272	71	0	.261	0	1	1	0	0.7	.500
1877			1	7	.125	3.56	12	8	6	86	114	13	18	0	0	0	0	157	27	0	.172	3	11	1	1	1.3	.933
2 yrs.			1	8	.111	4.14	15	9	6	95.2	136	13	18	0	0	0	0	*				3	12	2	1	1.1	.882

Eddie Booth

BOOTH, EDWARD H.
B. Brooklyn, N. Y.

| 1876 | NY | N | 0 | 0 | – | 10.80 | 1 | 0 | 0 | 5 | 16 | 0 | 0 | 0 | 0 | 0 | 0 | * | | | | 0 | 0 | 0 | 0 | 0.0 | – |

John Boozer

BOOZER, JOHN MORGAN
B. July 6, 1938, Columbia, S. C. D. Jan. 24, 1986, Lexington, S. C.

BR TR 6'3" 205 lbs.

1962	PHI	N	0	0	–	5.75	9	0	0	20.1	22	10	13	0	0	0	0	1	0	0	.000	0	3	0	1	0.3	1.000
1963			3	4	.429	2.93	26	8	2	83	67	33	69	0	2	0	1	21	3	0	.143	2	7	1	0	0.4	.900
1964			3	4	.429	5.07	22	3	0	60.1	64	18	51	0	2	2	2	13	1	0	.077	5	12	0	1	0.8	1.000
1966			0	0	–	6.75	2	2	0	5.1	8	3	5	0	0	0	0	2	0	0	.000	0	1	0	0	0.5	1.000
1967			5	4	.556	4.10	28	7	1	74.2	86	24	48	0	2	1	1	19	4	0	.211	4	13	0	1	0.6	1.000
1968			2	2	.500	3.67	38	0	0	68.2	76	15	49	0	2	2	5	9	1	0	.111	2	14	0	0	0.4	1.000
1969			1	2	.333	4.28	46	2	0	82	91	36	47	0	0	0	6	9	3	0	.333	3	9	1	1	0.3	.923
7 yrs.			14	16	.467	4.09	171	22	3	394.1	414	139	282	0	8	5	15	74	12	0	.162	16	59	2	4	0.5	.974

Pedro Borbon

BORBON, PEDRO
Born Pedro Borbon y Rodriguez.
B. Dec. 2, 1946, Valverde De Mao, Dominican Republic

BR TR 6'2" 185 lbs.

1969	CAL	A	2	3	.400	6.15	22	0	0	41	55	11	20	0	2	3	0	3	0	0	.000	5	4	2	0	0.5	.818
1970	CIN	N	0	2	.000	6.88	12	1	0	17	21	6	6	0	0	1	0	3	0	0	.000	2	11	0	1	1.1	1.000
1971			0	0	–	4.50	3	0	0	4	3	1	4	0	0	0	0	0	0	0	–	0	0	0	0	0.0	–
1972			8	3	.727	3.17	62	2	0	122	115	32	48	0	8	3	11	21	1	0	.048	2	20	3	0	0.4	.880
1973			11	4	.733	2.15	80	0	0	121.1	137	35	60	0	11	4	14	15	5	0	.333	9	19	3	1	0.4	.903
1974			10	7	.588	3.24	73	0	0	139	133	32	53	0	10	7	14	26	5	0	.192	7	19	2	2	0.4	.929
1975			9	5	.643	2.95	67	0	0	125	145	21	29	0	9	5	5	24	7	0	.292	6	19	1	1	0.4	.962
1976			4	3	.571	3.35	69	1	0	121	135	31	53	0	4	2	8	18	4	0	.222	6	18	0	0	0.3	1.000
1977			10	5	.667	3.19	73	0	0	127	131	24	48	0	10	5	18	22	4	0	.182	4	14	2	1	0.3	.900
1978			8	2	.800	5.00	62	0	0	99	102	27	35	0	8	2	8	11	2	0	.182	6	15	0	1	0.3	1.000
1979	2 teams		CIN N	(30G 2–2)		SF N	(30G 4–3)																				
"	total		6	5	.545	4.17	60	0	0	90.2	104	21	49	0	6	5	5	9	3	0	.333	7	10	2	1	0.3	.895
1980	STL	N	1	0	1.000	3.79	10	0	0	19	17	10	4	0	1	0	1	4	1	0	.250	0	3	1	0	0.4	.750
12 yrs.			69	39	.639	3.52	593	4	0	1026	1098	251	409	0	69	37	80	156	32	0	.205	54	152	16	8	0.4	.928

LEAGUE CHAMPIONSHIP SERIES

1972	CIN	N	0	0	–	2.08	3	0	0	4.1	2	0	1	0	0	0	0	0	0	0	–	1	0	0	0	0.3	1.000
1973			1	0	1.000	0.00	4	0	0	4.2	3	0	3	0	1	0	1	0	0	0	–	0	2	0	0	0.5	1.000
1975			0	0	–	0.00	1	0	0	1	0	0	0	0	0	0	0	0	0	0	–	0	0	0	0	0.0	–
1976			0	0	–	0.00	2	0	0	4.1	4	1	1	0	0	0	1	2	0	0	.000	0	0	0	0	0.0	–
4 yrs.			1	0	1.000	0.63	10	0	0	14.1	9	1	5	0	1	0	2	2	0	0	.000	1	2	0	0	0.3	1.000

WORLD SERIES

1972	CIN	N	0	1	.000	3.86	6	0	0	7	7	2	4	0	0	1	0	0	0	0	–	0	3	0	0	0.5	1.000
1975			0	0	–	6.00	3	0	0	3	2	1	0	0	0	0	0	1	0	0	.000	0	0	0	0	0.0	–
1976			0	0	–	0.00	1	0	0	1.2	1	1	1	0	0	0	0	0	0	0	–	0	1	0	0	1.0	1.000
3 yrs.			0	1	.000	3.86	10	0	0	11.2	10	4	5	0	0	1	0	1	0	0	.000	0	4	0	0	0.4	1.000

George Borchers

BORCHERS, GEORGE BERNARD
B. Apr. 18, 1869, Sacramento, Calif. D. Oct. 24, 1938, Sacramento, Calif.

BB TR 5'10" 180 lbs.

1888	CHI	N	4	4	.500	3.49	10	10	7	67	67	29	26	1	0	0	0	33	2	0	.061	1	16	4	1	2.1	.810
1895	LOU	N	0	1	.000	27.00	1	1	0	.2	1	3	0	0	0	0	0	0	0	0	–	0	0	0	0	0.0	–
2 yrs.			4	5	.444	3.72	11	11	7	67.2	68	32	26	1	0	0	0	33	2	0	.061	1	16	4	1	1.9	.810

Joe Borden

BORDEN, JOSEPH EMLEY
Also appeared in box score as Josephs
B. May 9, 1854, Jacobstown, N. J. D. Oct. 14, 1929, Yeadon, Pa.

BR TR 5'9" 140 lbs.

| 1876 | BOS | N | 11 | 12 | .478 | 2.89 | 29 | 24 | 16 | 218.1 | 257 | 51 | 34 | 2 | 0 | 1 | 1 | 121 | 25 | 0 | .207 | 15 | 33 | 22 | 0 | 2.4 | .686 |

Rich Bordi

BORDI, RICHARD ALBERT
B. Apr. 18, 1959, San Francisco, Calif.

BR TR 6'7" 210 lbs.

1980	OAK	A	0	0	–	4.50	1	0	0	2	4	0	0	0	0	0	0	0	0	0	–	0	0	0	0	0.0	–
1981			0	0	–	0.00	2	0	0	2	1	0	0	0	0	0	0	0	0	0	–	0	0	0	0	0.0	–
1982	SEA	A	0	2	.000	8.31	7	2	0	13	18	1	10	0	0	0	0	0	0	0	–	1	1	0	0	0.3	1.000
1983	CHI	N	0	2	.000	4.97	11	1	0	25.1	34	12	20	0	0	1	1	4	0	0	.000	3	3	2	1	0.7	.750
1984			5	2	.714	3.46	31	7	0	83.1	78	20	41	0	1	1	4	19	1	0	.053	4	10	2	0	0.5	.875
1985	NY	A	6	8	.429	3.21	51	3	0	98	95	29	64	0	4	7	0	0	0	0	–	2	12	1	1	0.3	.933
1986	BAL	A	6	4	.600	4.46	52	1	0	107	105	41	83	0	6	3	3	0	0	0	–	7	15	1	2	0.4	.957
1987	NY	A	3	1	.750	7.64	16	1	0	33	42	12	23	0	3	1	0	0	0	0	–	2	1	1	0	0.3	.750
1988	OAK	A	0	1	.000	4.70	2	2	0	7.2	6	5	6	0	0	0	0	0	0	0	–	0	0	0	0	0.0	–
9 yrs.			20	20	.500	4.34	173	17	0	371.1	383	121	247	0	14	12	10	23	1	0	.043	19	42	7	4	0.4	.897

Bill Bordley

BORDLEY, WILLIAM CLARK
B. Jan. 9, 1958, Rolling Hills Est., Calif.

BL TL 6'3" 195 lbs.

| 1980 | SF | N | 2 | 3 | .400 | 4.65 | 8 | 6 | 0 | 31 | 34 | 21 | 11 | 0 | 0 | 0 | 0 | 6 | 1 | 0 | .167 | 2 | 9 | 0 | 0 | 1.4 | 1.000 |

Year	Team	W	L	PCT	ERA	G	GS	CG	IP	H	BB	SO	ShO	Relief Pitching W	L	SV	Batting AB	H	HR	BA	PO	A	E	DP	TC/G	FA

Paul Boris
BORIS, PAUL STANLEY B. Dec. 13, 1955, Irvington, N. J.   BR TR 6'2" 200 lbs.

Year	Team	W	L	PCT	ERA	G	GS	CG	IP	H	BB	SO	ShO	W	L	SV	AB	H	HR	BA	PO	A	E	DP	TC/G	FA
1982	MIN A	1	2	.333	3.99	23	0	0	49.2	46	19	30	0	1	2	0	0	0	0	—	2	4	0	0	0.3	1.000

Frank Bork
BORK, FRANK BERNARD B. July 13, 1940, Buffalo, N. Y.   BR TL 6'2" 175 lbs.

Year	Team	W	L	PCT	ERA	G	GS	CG	IP	H	BB	SO	ShO	W	L	SV	AB	H	HR	BA	PO	A	E	DP	TC/G	FA
1964	PIT N	2	2	.500	4.07	33	2	0	42	51	11	31	0	1	1	2	5	1	0	.200	1	10	0	0	0.3	1.000

Tom Borland
BORLAND, THOMAS BRUCE (Spike) B. Feb. 14, 1933, El Dorado, Kans.   BL TL 6'3" 172 lbs.

Year	Team	W	L	PCT	ERA	G	GS	CG	IP	H	BB	SO	ShO	W	L	SV	AB	H	HR	BA	PO	A	E	DP	TC/G	FA
1960	BOS A	0	4	.000	6.53	26	4	0	51	67	23	32	0	0	1	3	13	0	0	.000	5	7	0	0	0.5	1.000
1961		0	0	—	18.00	1	0	0	1	3	0	0	0	0	0	0	0	0	0	—	0	0	0	0	0.0	—
2 yrs.		0	4	.000	6.75	27	4	0	52	70	23	32	0	0	1	3	13	0	0	.000	5	7	0	0	0.4	1.000

Hank Borowy
BOROWY, HENRY LUDWIG B. May 12, 1916, Bloomfield, N. J.   BR TR 6' 175 lbs.

Year	Team	W	L	PCT	ERA	G	GS	CG	IP	H	BB	SO	ShO	W	L	SV	AB	H	HR	BA	PO	A	E	DP	TC/G	FA
1942	NY A	15	4	.789	2.52	25	21	13	178.1	157	66	85	4	1	0	1	70	11	0	.157	12	38	1	3	2.0	.980
1943		14	9	.609	2.82	29	27	14	217.1	195	72	113	3	1	0	0	74	15	0	.203	12	46	1	4	2.0	.983
1944		17	12	.586	2.64	35	30	19	252.2	224	88	107	3	0	0	2	90	12	0	.133	13	47	1	5	1.7	.984
1945	2 teams								NY A (18G 10-5)		CHI N (15G 11-2)																
"	total	21	7	.750	2.65	33	32	18	254.2	212	105	82	2	0	1	0	91	18	0	.198	10	51	0	3	1.8	1.000
1946	CHI N	12	10	.545	3.76	32	28	8	201	220	61	95	1	1	0	0	72	13	0	.181	9	42	3	1	1.7	.944
1947		8	12	.400	4.38	40	25	7	183	190	63	75	1	1	1	2	56	7	0	.125	7	36	2	2	1.1	.956
1948		5	10	.333	4.89	39	17	2	127	156	49	50	1	1	0	1	36	8	0	.222	6	34	1	3	1.1	.976
1949	PHI N	12	12	.500	4.19	28	24	12	193.1	188	63	43	2	0	0	0	61	13	0	.213	6	32	0	0	1.4	1.000
1950	3 teams								PHI N (3G 0-0)		PIT N (11G 1-3)		DET A (13G 1-1)														
"	total	2	4	.333	4.83	27	5	1	63.1	60	29	24	0	2	1	0	13	2	0	.154	8	10	1	0	0.7	.947
1951	DET A	2	2	.500	6.95	26	1	0	45.1	58	27	16	0	2	2	0	8	0	0	.000	2	14	1	1	0.7	.941
10 yrs.		108	82	.568	3.50	314	214	94	1716	1660	623	690	17	9	4	7	571	99	0	.173	85	350	11	22	1.4	.975

WORLD SERIES

Year	Team	W	L	PCT	ERA	G	GS	CG	IP	H	BB	SO	ShO	W	L	SV	AB	H	HR	BA	PO	A	E	DP	TC/G	FA
1942	NY A	0	0	—	18.00	1	1	0	3	6	3	1	0	0	0	0	0	1	0	.000	0	1	0	0	1.0	1.000
1943		1	0	1.000	2.25	1	1	0	8	6	3	4	0	0	0	0	2	1	0	.500	2	0	0	0	2.0	1.000
1945	CHI N	2	2	.500	4.00	4	3	1	18	21	6	8	1	0	0	0	5	1	0	.200	1	2	0	0	0.8	1.000
3 yrs.		3	2	.600	4.97	6	5	1	29	33	12	13	1	1	0	0	8	2	0	.250	3	3	0	0	1.0	1.000

Chris Bosio
BOSIO, CHRISTOPHER LOUIS B. Apr. 3, 1963, Carmichael, Calif.   BR TR 6'3" 220 lbs.

Year	Team	W	L	PCT	ERA	G	GS	CG	IP	H	BB	SO	ShO	W	L	SV	AB	H	HR	BA	PO	A	E	DP	TC/G	FA
1986	MIL A	0	4	.000	7.01	10	4	0	34.2	41	13	29	0	0	1	0	0	0	0	—	4	5	1	1	1.0	.900
1987		11	8	.579	5.24	46	19	2	170	187	50	150	1	3	1	2	0	0	0	—	14	24	4	5	0.9	.905
1988		7	15	.318	3.36	38	22	9	182	190	38	84	1	1	3	6	0	0	0	—	22	33	3	7	1.5	.948
1989		15	10	.600	2.95	33	33	8	234.2	225	48	173	2	0	0	0	0	0	0	—	16	35	2	2	1.6	.962
4 yrs.		33	37	.471	3.93	127	78	19	621.1	643	149	436	4	4	5	8	0	0	0	—	56	97	10	15	1.3	.939

Dick Bosman
BOSMAN, RICHARD ALLEN B. Feb. 17, 1944, Kenosha, Wis.   BR TR 6'2" 195 lbs.

Year	Team	W	L	PCT	ERA	G	GS	CG	IP	H	BB	SO	ShO	W	L	SV	AB	H	HR	BA	PO	A	E	DP	TC/G	FA
1966	WAS A	2	6	.250	7.62	13	7	0	39	60	12	20	0	0	3	0	12	3	0	.250	1	3	0	0	0.3	1.000
1967		3	1	.750	1.75	7	7	2	51.1	38	10	25	1	0	0	0	15	3	0	.200	4	6	1	0	1.6	.909
1968		2	9	.182	3.69	46	10	0	139	139	35	63	0	1	7	1	30	6	0	.200	8	21	1	2	0.7	.967
1969		14	5	.737	2.19	31	26	5	193	156	39	99	2	1	0	1	64	6	0	.094	18	32	1	1	1.6	.980
1970		16	12	.571	3.00	36	34	7	231	212	71	134	3	0	0	0	80	11	0	.138	19	32	0	3	1.4	1.000
1971		12	16	.429	3.72	35	35	7	237	245	71	113	1	0	0	0	75	7	0	.093	21	27	1	1	1.6	.980
1972	TEX A	8	10	.444	3.64	29	29	1	173	183	48	105	1	0	0	0	53	5	0	.094	17	28	1	3	1.6	.978
1973	2 teams								TEX A (7G 2-5)		CLE A (22G 1-8)																
"	total	3	13	.188	5.64	29	24	3	137.1	172	46	55	1	0	0	0	0	0	0	—	8	17	2	0	0.9	.926
1974	CLE A	7	5	.583	4.11	25	18	2	127	126	29	56	0	0	0	0	0	0	0	—	8	8	3	0	0.8	.842
1975	2 teams								CLE A (6G 0-2)		OAK A (22G 11-4)																
"	total	11	6	.647	3.63	28	24	2	151.1	145	32	53	0	0	0	0	0	0	0	—	6	19	0	0	0.9	1.000
1976	OAK A	4	2	.667	4.10	27	15	0	112	118	19	34	0	0	1	0	0	0	0	—	9	19	1	2	1.1	.966
11 yrs.		82	85	.491	3.67	306	229	29	1591	1594	412	757	10	2	11	2	329	41	0	.125	119	212	11	12	1.1	.968

LEAGUE CHAMPIONSHIP SERIES

Year	Team	W	L	PCT	ERA	G	GS	CG	IP	H	BB	SO	ShO	W	L	SV	AB	H	HR	BA	PO	A	E	DP	TC/G	FA
1975	OAK A	0	0	—	0.00	1	0	0	.1	0	0	0	0	0	0	0	0	0	0	—	0	0	0	0	0.0	—

Mel Bosser
BOSSER, MELVIN EDWARD B. Feb. 8, 1920, Johnstown, Pa.   BR TR 6' 173 lbs.

Year	Team	W	L	PCT	ERA	G	GS	CG	IP	H	BB	SO	ShO	W	L	SV	AB	H	HR	BA	PO	A	E	DP	TC/G	FA
1945	CIN N	2	0	1.000	3.31	7	1	0	16.1	9	17	3	0	1	0	0	4	0	0	.000	0	2	0	0	0.3	1.000

Andy Boswell
BOSWELL, ANDREW COTTRELL B. Sept. 5, 1874, New Gretna, N. J.   D. Feb. 3, 1936, Ocean City, N. J.

Year	Team	W	L	PCT	ERA	G	GS	CG	IP	H	BB	SO	ShO	W	L	SV	AB	H	HR	BA	PO	A	E	DP	TC/G	FA
1895	2 teams								NY N (5G 2-2)		WAS N (6G 1-2)																
"	total	3	4	.429	5.91	11	7	6	64	85	41	30	0	0	0	0	30	7	0	.233	8	6	3	0	1.5	.824

Dave Boswell
BOSWELL, DAVID WILSON B. Jan. 20, 1945, Baltimore, Md.   BR TR 6'3" 185 lbs.

Year	Team	W	L	PCT	ERA	G	GS	CG	IP	H	BB	SO	ShO	W	L	SV	AB	H	HR	BA	PO	A	E	DP	TC/G	FA
1964	MIN A	2	0	1.000	4.24	4	4	0	23.1	21	12	25	0	0	0	0	9	2	0	.222	2	5	0	0	1.8	1.000
1965		6	5	.545	3.40	27	12	1	106	77	46	85	0	1	2	0	38	12	1	.316	5	14	1	1	0.7	.950
1966		12	5	.706	3.14	28	21	8	169.1	120	65	173	1	0	0	0	63	9	0	.143	10	29	2	0	1.5	.951
1967		14	12	.538	3.27	37	32	11	222.2	162	107	204	4	0	0	0	73	16	1	.219	11	24	0	2	0.9	1.000
1968		10	13	.435	3.32	34	28	7	190	148	87	143	2	0	0	0	60	14	1	.233	17	15	3	1	1.0	.914
1969		20	12	.625	3.23	39	38	10	256.1	215	99	190	0	0	0	0	94	16	2	.170	9	31	2	2	1.1	.952
1970		3	7	.300	6.39	18	15	0	69	80	44	45	0	0	0	0	25	4	0	.160	6	5	0	1	0.6	1.000

Year	Team	W	L	PCT	ERA	G	GS	CG	IP	H	BB	SO	ShO	W	L	SV	AB	H	HR	BA	PO	A	E	DP	TC/G	FA

Dave Boswell *continued*

Year	Team	W	L	PCT	ERA	G	GS	CG	IP	H	BB	SO	ShO	W	L	SV	AB	H	HR	BA	PO	A	E	DP	TC/G	FA
1971	2 teams	DET A	(3G 0–0)		BAL A	(15G 1–2)																				
"	total	1	2	.333	4.66	18	1	0	29	35	21	17	0	1	1	0	5	1	0	.200	2	6	0	0	0.4	1.000
8 yrs.		68	56	.548	3.52	205	151	37	1065.2	858	481	882	6	2	3	0	367	74	4	.202	62	129	8	7	1.0	.960

LEAGUE CHAMPIONSHIP SERIES

Year	Team	W	L	PCT	ERA	G	GS	CG	IP	H	BB	SO	ShO	W	L	SV	AB	H	HR	BA	PO	A	E	DP	TC/G	FA
1969	MIN A	0	1	.000	0.84	1	1	0	10.2	7	7	4	0	0	0	0	4	0	0	.000	1	4	0	1	5.0	1.000

WORLD SERIES

Year	Team	W	L	PCT	ERA	G	GS	CG	IP	H	BB	SO	ShO	W	L	SV	AB	H	HR	BA	PO	A	E	DP	TC/G	FA
1965	MIN A	0	0	–	3.38	1	0	0	2.2	3	2	3	0	0	0	0	0	0	0	–	0	0	0	0	0.0	–

Derek Botelho

BOTELHO, DEREK WAYNE
B. Aug. 2, 1956, Long Beach, Calif.
BR TR 6'2" 160 lbs.

Year	Team	W	L	PCT	ERA	G	GS	CG	IP	H	BB	SO	ShO	W	L	SV	AB	H	HR	BA	PO	A	E	DP	TC/G	FA
1982	KC A	2	1	.667	4.13	8	4	0	24	25	8	12	0	0	0	0	0	0	0	–	1	2	0	0	0.4	1.000
1985	CHI N	1	3	.250	5.32	11	7	1	44	52	23	23	0	0	0	0	14	2	0	.143	2	5	0	0	0.6	1.000
2 yrs.		3	4	.429	4.90	19	11	1	68	77	31	35	0	0	0	0	14	2	0	.143	3	7	0	0	0.5	1.000

Ralph Botting

BOTTING, RALPH WAYNE
B. May 12, 1955, Houlton, Me.
BL TL 6' 195 lbs.

Year	Team	W	L	PCT	ERA	G	GS	CG	IP	H	BB	SO	ShO	W	L	SV	AB	H	HR	BA	PO	A	E	DP	TC/G	FA
1979	CAL A	2	0	1.000	8.70	12	1	0	30	46	15	22	0	1	0	0	0	0	0	–	1	4	0	0	0.4	1.000
1980		0	3	.000	5.88	6	6	0	26	40	13	12	0	0	0	0	0	0	0	–	1	3	1	0	0.8	.800
2 yrs.		2	3	.400	7.39	18	7	0	56	86	28	34	0	1	0	0	0	0	0	–	2	7	1	0	0.6	.900

Bob Botz

BOTZ, ROBERT ALLEN (Butterball)
B. Apr. 28, 1935, Milwaukee, Wis.
BR TR 5'11" 170 lbs.

Year	Team	W	L	PCT	ERA	G	GS	CG	IP	H	BB	SO	ShO	W	L	SV	AB	H	HR	BA	PO	A	E	DP	TC/G	FA
1962	LA A	2	1	.667	3.43	35	0	0	63	71	11	24	0	2	1	2	9	0	0	.000	1	8	0	0	0.3	1.000

Carl Bouldin

BOULDIN, CARL EDWARD
B. Sept. 17, 1939, Germantown, Ky.
BB TR 6'2" 180 lbs.
BL 1961

Year	Team	W	L	PCT	ERA	G	GS	CG	IP	H	BB	SO	ShO	W	L	SV	AB	H	HR	BA	PO	A	E	DP	TC/G	FA
1961	WAS A	0	1	.000	16.20	2	1	0	3.1	9	2	2	0	0	0	0	1	0	0	.000	1	1	0	0	1.0	1.000
1962		1	2	.333	5.85	6	3	1	20	26	9	12	0	0	1	0	7	0	0	.000	1	3	1	0	0.8	.800
1963		2	2	.500	5.79	10	3	0	23.1	31	8	10	0	2	0	0	7	0	0	.000	2	4	1	1	0.7	.857
1964		0	3	.000	5.40	9	3	0	25	30	11	12	0	0	1	0	6	0	0	.000	2	4	1	0	0.8	.857
4 yrs.		3	8	.273	6.15	27	10	1	71.2	96	30	36	0	2	2	0	21	0	0	.000	6	12	3	1	0.8	.857

Jake Boultes

BOULTES, JACOB JOHN
B. Aug. 6, 1884, St. Louis, Mo. D. Dec. 24, 1955, St. Louis, Mo.
TR 6'3"

Year	Team	W	L	PCT	ERA	G	GS	CG	IP	H	BB	SO	ShO	W	L	SV	AB	H	HR	BA	PO	A	E	DP	TC/G	FA
1907	BOS N	5	9	.357	2.71	24	12	11	139.2	140	50	49	0	2	0	0	68	9	0	.132	15	54	4	4	3.0	.945
1908		3	5	.375	3.01	17	5	1	74.2	80	8	28	0	2	2	0	21	3	0	.143	7	17	0	0	1.4	1.000
1909		0	0	–	6.75	1	0	0	8	9	0	1	0	0	0	0	3	1	0	.333	2	1	0	0	3.0	1.000
3 yrs.		8	14	.364	2.96	42	17	12	222.1	229	58	78	0	4	2	0	92	13	0	.141	24	72	4	4	2.4	.960

Jim Bouton

BOUTON, JAMES ALAN (Bulldog)
B. Mar. 8, 1939, Newark, N. J.
BR TR 6' 170 lbs.

Year	Team	W	L	PCT	ERA	G	GS	CG	IP	H	BB	SO	ShO	W	L	SV	AB	H	HR	BA	PO	A	E	DP	TC/G	FA
1962	NY A	7	7	.500	3.99	36	16	3	133	124	59	71	1	3	1	0	32	2	0	.063	8	23	0	3	0.9	1.000
1963		21	7	.750	2.53	40	30	12	249.1	191	87	148	6	3	1	1	83	6	0	.072	22	32	2	1	1.4	.964
1964		18	13	.581	3.02	38	37	11	271.1	227	60	125	4	0	0	0	100	13	0	.130	31	27	5	1	1.7	.921
1965		4	15	.211	4.82	30	25	2	151.1	158	60	97	0	0	1	0	43	4	0	.093	13	21	0	3	1.1	1.000
1966		3	8	.273	2.69	24	19	3	120.1	117	38	65	0	1	1	1	38	4	0	.105	13	23	2	2	1.6	.921
1967		1	0	1.000	4.67	17	1	0	44.1	47	18	31	0	1	0	0	7	0	0	.000	1	7	0	0	0.5	1.000
1968		1	1	.500	3.68	12	3	1	44	49	9	24	0	1	0	0	7	0	0	.000	7	11	0	1	1.5	1.000
1969	2 teams	SEA A	(57G 2–1)		HOU N	(16G 0–2)																				
"	total	2	3	.400	3.95	73	2	1	123	109	50	100	0	2	1	2	13	0	0	.000	10	20	1	1	0.4	.968
1970	HOU N	4	6	.400	5.42	29	6	1	73	84	33	49	0	2	4	0	17	6	0	.353	4	11	3	0	0.6	.833
1978	ATL N	1	3	.250	4.97	5	5	0	29	25	21	10	0	0	0	0	7	0	0	.000	3	3	1	0	1.4	.857
10 yrs.		62	63	.496	3.57	304	144	34	1238.2	1131	435	720	11	11	9	6	347	35	0	.101	112	177	15	13	1.0	.951

WORLD SERIES

Year	Team	W	L	PCT	ERA	G	GS	CG	IP	H	BB	SO	ShO	W	L	SV	AB	H	HR	BA	PO	A	E	DP	TC/G	FA
1963	NY A	0	1	.000	1.29	1	1	0	7	4	5	4	0	0	0	0	2	0	0	.000	1	2	0	0	3.0	1.000
1964		2	0	1.000	1.56	2	2	1	17.1	15	5	7	0	0	0	0	7	1	0	.143	4	0	0	0	2.0	1.000
2 yrs.		2	1	.667	1.48	3	3	1	24.1	19	10	11	0	0	0	0	9	1	0	.111	5	2	0	0	2.3	1.000

Cy Bowen

BOWEN, SUTHERLAND McCOY
B. Feb. 17, 1871, Kingston, Ind. D. Jan. 25, 1925, Greensburg, Ind.
BR TR 6' 175 lbs.

Year	Team	W	L	PCT	ERA	G	GS	CG	IP	H	BB	SO	ShO	W	L	SV	AB	H	HR	BA	PO	A	E	DP	TC/G	FA
1896	NY N	0	1	.000	6.00	2	1	0	12	12	9	3	0	0	0	0	3	1	0	.333	0	5	2	0	3.5	.714

Frank Bowerman

BOWERMAN, FRANK EUGENE (Mike)
B. Dec. 5, 1868, Romeo, Mich. D. Nov. 30, 1948, Romeo, Mich.
Manager 1909.
BR TR 6'2" 190 lbs.

Year	Team	W	L	PCT	ERA	G	GS	CG	IP	H	BB	SO	ShO	W	L	SV	AB	H	HR	BA	PO	A	E	DP	TC/G	FA
1904	NY N	0	0	–	9.00	1	0	0	1	3	1	0	0	0	0	0	*				0	0	0	0	0.0	–

Stew Bowers

BOWERS, STEWART COLE (Doc)
B. Feb. 26, 1915, New Freedom, Pa.
BB TR 6' 170 lbs.

Year	Team	W	L	PCT	ERA	G	GS	CG	IP	H	BB	SO	ShO	W	L	SV	AB	H	HR	BA	PO	A	E	DP	TC/G	FA
1935	BOS A	2	1	.667	3.42	10	2	1	23.2	26	17	5	0	1	0	0	5	1	0	.200	0	7	1	0	0.8	.875
1936		0	0	–	9.53	5	0	0	5.2	10	2	0	0	0	0	0	0	0	0	–	0	0	0	0	0.0	–
2 yrs.		2	1	.667	4.60	15	2	1	29.1	36	19	5	0	1	0	0	5	1	0	.200	0	7	1	0	0.5	.875

Grant Bowler

BOWLER, GRANT TIERNEY (Moose)
B. Oct. 24, 1907, Denver, Colo. D. June 25, 1968, Denver, Colo.
BR TR 6' 190 lbs.

Year	Team	W	L	PCT	ERA	G	GS	CG	IP	H	BB	SO	ShO	W	L	SV	AB	H	HR	BA	PO	A	E	DP	TC/G	FA
1931	CHI A	0	1	.000	5.35	13	3	1	35.1	40	24	15	0	0	0	0	10	1	0	.100	2	3	1	0	0.5	.833

Year	Team	W	L	PCT	ERA	G	GS	CG	IP	H	BB	SO	ShO	W	L	SV	AB	H	HR	BA	PO	A	E	DP	TC/G	FA

Grant Bowler *continued*

Year	Team	W	L	PCT	ERA	G	GS	CG	IP	H	BB	SO	ShO	W	L	SV	AB	H	HR	BA	PO	A	E	DP	TC/G	FA
1932		0	0	–	15.63	4	0	0	6.1	15	3	2	0	0	0	0	2	0	0	.000	0	2	1	1	0.8	.667
2 yrs.		0	1	.000	6.91	17	3	1	41.2	55	27	17	0	0	0	0	12	1	0	.083	2	5	2	1	0.5	.778

Charlie Bowles

BOWLES, CHARLES JAMES
B. Mar. 15, 1917, Norwood, Mass.   BR TR 6'3"   180 lbs.

Year	Team	W	L	PCT	ERA	G	GS	CG	IP	H	BB	SO	ShO	W	L	SV	AB	H	HR	BA	PO	A	E	DP	TC/G	FA
1943	PHI A	1	1	.500	3.00	2	2	2	18	17	4	6	0	0	0	0	8	1	0	.125	2	3	1	2	3.0	.833
1945		0	3	.000	5.13	8	4	1	33.1	35	23	11	0	0	0	1	21	5	0	.238	5	6	0	0	1.4	1.000
2 yrs.		1	4	.200	4.38	10	6	3	51.1	52	27	17	0	0	0	1	29	6	0	.207	7	9	1	2	1.7	.941

Emmett Bowles

BOWLES, EMMETT JEROME (Chief)
B. Aug. 2, 1898, Wanette, Okla.   D. Sept. 3, 1959, Flagstaff, Ariz.   BR TR 6'   180 lbs.

Year	Team	W	L	PCT	ERA	G	GS	CG	IP	H	BB	SO	ShO	W	L	SV	AB	H	HR	BA	PO	A	E	DP	TC/G	FA
1922	CHI A	0	0	–	27.00	1	0	0	1	2	1	0	0	0	0	0	0	0	0	–	0	0	0	0	0.0	–

Abe Bowman

BOWMAN, ALVAH EDSON
B. Jan. 25, 1893, Greenup, Ill.   D. Oct. 11, 1979, Longview, Tex.   BR TR 6'1"   190 lbs.

Year	Team	W	L	PCT	ERA	G	GS	CG	IP	H	BB	SO	ShO	W	L	SV	AB	H	HR	BA	PO	A	E	DP	TC/G	FA
1914	CLE A	2	7	.222	4.46	22	10	2	72.2	74	45	27	1	1	0	0	21	1	0	.048	5	19	3	1	1.2	.889
1915		0	1	.000	20.25	2	1	0	1.1	1	3	0	0	0	0	0	0	0	0	–	0	3	0	0	1.5	1.000
2 yrs.		2	8	.200	4.74	24	11	2	74	75	48	27	1	1	0	0	21	1	0	.048	5	22	3	1	1.3	.900

Bob Bowman

BOWMAN, ROBERT JAMES
B. Oct. 3, 1910, Keystone, W. Va.   D. Sept. 4, 1972, Bluefield, W. Va.   BR TR 5'10½" 160 lbs.

Year	Team	W	L	PCT	ERA	G	GS	CG	IP	H	BB	SO	ShO	W	L	SV	AB	H	HR	BA	PO	A	E	DP	TC/G	FA
1939	STL N	13	5	.722	2.60	51	15	4	169.1	141	60	78	2	7	0	9	47	4	0	.085	4	30	2	0	0.7	.944
1940		7	5	.583	4.33	28	17	7	114.1	118	43	43	0	0	2	0	33	2	0	.061	2	23	1	0	0.9	.962
1941	NY N	6	7	.462	5.71	29	6	2	80.1	100	36	25	0	4	4	1	21	1	1	.048	4	20	0	0	0.8	1.000
1942	CHI N	0	0	–	0.00	1	0	0	1	1	0	0	0	0	0	0	0	0	0	–	0	0	0	0	0.0	–
4 yrs.		26	17	.605	3.82	109	38	13	365	360	139	146	2	11	6	10	101	7	1	.069	10	73	3	0	0.8	.965

Bob Bowman

BOWMAN, ROBERT LEROY
B. May 10, 1931, Laytonville, Calif.   BR TR 6'1"   195 lbs.

Year	Team	W	L	PCT	ERA	G	GS	CG	IP	H	BB	SO	ShO	W	L	SV	AB	H	HR	BA	PO	A	E	DP	TC/G	FA
1959	PHI N	0	1	.000	6.00	5	0	0	6	5	5	0	0	0	1	0	*				1	1	0	0	0.4	1.000

Joe Bowman

BOWMAN, JOSEPH EMIL
B. June 17, 1910, Argentine, Kans.   BL TR 6'2"   190 lbs.

Year	Team	W	L	PCT	ERA	G	GS	CG	IP	H	BB	SO	ShO	W	L	SV	AB	H	HR	BA	PO	A	E	DP	TC/G	FA
1932	PHI A	0	1	.000	8.18	7	0	0	11	14	6	4	0	0	1	0	1	1	0	1.000	1	6	1	0	1.1	.875
1934	NY N	5	4	.556	3.61	30	10	3	107.1	119	36	36	0	1	1	3	29	5	0	.172	6	20	0	1	0.9	1.000
1935	PHI N	7	10	.412	4.25	33	17	6	148.1	157	56	58	1	2	3	1	67	13	1	.194	8	28	2	2	1.2	.947
1936		9	20	.310	5.04	40	28	12	203.2	243	53	80	0	1	3	1	77	15	0	.195	7	32	5	4	1.1	.886
1937	PIT N	8	8	.500	4.57	30	19	7	128	161	35	38	0	1	1	1	47	10	0	.213	14	24	0	3	1.3	1.000
1938		3	4	.429	4.65	17	1	0	60	68	20	25	0	3	3	1	21	7	0	.333	2	8	1	2	0.6	.909
1939		10	14	.417	4.48	37	27	10	184.2	217	43	58	1	1	0	1	96	33	0	.344	6	39	0	3	1.2	1.000
1940		9	10	.474	4.46	32	24	10	187.2	209	66	57	0	2	0	2	90	22	1	.244	15	36	1	0	1.6	.981
1941		3	2	.600	2.99	18	7	1	69.1	77	28	22	1	1	1	1	31	8	0	.258	5	13	0	1	1.0	1.000
1944	BOS A	12	8	.600	4.81	26	24	10	168.1	175	64	53	1	0	0	0	100	20	0	.200	9	20	2	3	1.2	.935
1945	2 teams	BOS A	(3G 0–2)		CIN N	(25G 11–13)																				
"	total	11	15	.423	3.92	28	27	15	197.1	216	77	71	1	0	0	0	80	7	0	.088	12	28	3	0	1.5	.930
11 yrs.		77	96	.445	4.40	298	184	74	1465.2	1656	484	502	5	12	13	11	*				85	254	15	17	1.2	.958

Roger Bowman

BOWMAN, ROGER CLINTON
B. Aug. 18, 1927, Amsterdam, N. Y.   BR TL 6'   175 lbs.

Year	Team	W	L	PCT	ERA	G	GS	CG	IP	H	BB	SO	ShO	W	L	SV	AB	H	HR	BA	PO	A	E	DP	TC/G	FA
1949	NY N	0	0	–	4.26	2	2	0	6.1	6	7	4	0	0	0	0	2	0	0	.000	1	3	0	0	2.0	1.000
1951		2	4	.333	6.15	9	5	0	26.1	35	22	24	0	1	1	0	6	0	0	.000	2	1	0	0	0.3	1.000
1952		0	0	–	12.00	2	1	0	3	6	3	3	0	0	0	0	1	0	0	.000	0	0	0	0	0.0	–
1953	PIT N	0	4	.000	4.82	30	2	0	65.1	65	29	36	0	0	2	0	7	2	0	.286	6	11	0	0	0.6	1.000
1955		0	3	.000	8.64	7	2	0	16.2	25	10	8	0	0	1	0	2	1	0	.500	1	5	0	0	0.9	1.000
5 yrs.		2	11	.154	5.81	50	12	0	117.2	137	71	75	0	1	4	0	18	3	0	.167	10	20	0	0	0.6	1.000

Sumner Bowman

BOWMAN, SUMNER SALLADE
B. Feb. 9, 1867, Millersburg, Pa.   D. Jan. 11, 1954, Millersburg, Pa.   BL TL 6'   160 lbs.

Year	Team	W	L	PCT	ERA	G	GS	CG	IP	H	BB	SO	ShO	W	L	SV	AB	H	HR	BA	PO	A	E	DP	TC/G	FA
1890	2 teams	PHI N	(1G 0–0)		PIT N	(9G 2–5)																				
"	total	2	5	.286	6.75	10	8	6	78.2	111	52	24	0	0	0	0	40	12	0	.300	4	14	4	0	2.2	.818
1891	PHI AA	2	5	.286	3.44	8	8	8	68	73	37	22	0	0	0	0	54	13	0	.241	3	12	4	1	2.4	.789
2 yrs.		4	10	.286	5.22	18	16	14	146.2	184	89	46	0	0	0	0	94	25	0	.266	7	26	8	1	2.3	.805

Ted Bowsfield

BOWSFIELD, EDWARD OLIVER
B. Jan. 10, 1935, Vernon, B. C., Canada   BR TL 6'1"   190 lbs.

Year	Team	W	L	PCT	ERA	G	GS	CG	IP	H	BB	SO	ShO	W	L	SV	AB	H	HR	BA	PO	A	E	DP	TC/G	FA
1958	BOS A	4	2	.667	3.84	16	10	2	65.2	58	36	38	0	1	0	0	26	4	0	.154	5	16	1	1	1.4	.955
1959		0	1	.000	15.00	5	2	0	9	16	9	4	0	0	0	0	1	0	0	.000	1	0	0	0	0.2	1.000
1960	2 teams	BOS A	(17G 1–2)		CLE A	(11G 3–4)																				
"	total	4	6	.400	5.11	28	8	1	61.2	67	33	32	0	1	2	2	14	2	0	.143	6	15	1	3	0.8	.955
1961	LA A	11	8	.579	3.73	41	21	4	157	154	63	88	1	2	1	0	51	7	0	.137	4	26	5	1	0.9	.857
1962		9	8	.529	4.40	34	25	1	139	154	40	52	0	1	1	0	37	6	0	.162	12	13	5	0	0.9	.833
1963	KC A	5	7	.417	4.45	41	11	2	111.1	115	47	67	1	2	2	3	23	1	0	.043	12	15	1	2	0.7	.974
1964		4	7	.364	4.10	50	9	2	118.2	135	31	45	1	2	2	1	21	2	0	.095	9	20	2	2	0.6	.935
7 yrs.		37	39	.487	4.35	215	86	12	662.1	699	259	326	4	9	8	6	173	22	0	.127	49	115	15	9	0.8	.916

Gary Boyd

BOYD, GARY LEE
B. Aug. 22, 1946, Pasadena, Calif.   BR TR 6'4"   200 lbs.

Year	Team	W	L	PCT	ERA	G	GS	CG	IP	H	BB	SO	ShO	W	L	SV	AB	H	HR	BA	PO	A	E	DP	TC/G	FA
1969	CLE A	0	2	.000	9.00	8	3	0	11	8	14	9	0	0	0	0	1	0	0	.000	2	0	0	0	0.3	1.000

Year	Team		W	L	PCT	ERA	G	GS	CG	IP	H	BB	SO	ShO	W	L	SV	AB	H	HR	BA	PO	A	E	DP	TC/G	FA

Jake Boyd   **BOYD, JACOB HENRY**   B. Jan. 19, 1874, Martinsburg, W. Va.   D. Aug. 12, 1932, Gettysburg, Pa.   TL   160 lbs.

Year	Team		W	L	PCT	ERA	G	GS	CG	IP	H	BB	SO	ShO	W	L	SV	AB	H	HR	BA	PO	A	E	DP	TC/G	FA
1894	WAS	N	0	3	.000	8.53	3	3	3	19	37	14	3	0	0	0	0	21	3	0	.143	1	6	1	0	2.7	.875
1895			2	11	.154	7.07	14	12	8	85.1	126	35	16	0	0	1	0	157	42	1	.268	3	25	4	0	2.3	.875
1896			1	2	.333	6.75	4	2	2	32	45	15	6	0	1	0	0	13	1	0	.077	1	9	1	0	2.8	.909
3 yrs.			3	16	.158	7.20	21	17	13	136.1	208	64	25	0	1	1	0	*				5	40	6	0	2.4	.882

Oil Can Boyd   **BOYD, DENNIS RAY**   B. Oct. 6, 1959, Meridian, Miss.   BR TR 6'1"   155 lbs.

Year	Team		W	L	PCT	ERA	G	GS	CG	IP	H	BB	SO	ShO	W	L	SV	AB	H	HR	BA	PO	A	E	DP	TC/G	FA
1982	BOS	A	0	1	.000	5.40	3	1	0	8.1	11	2	2	0	0	0	0	0	0	0	–	0	1	0	0	0.3	1.000
1983			4	8	.333	3.28	15	13	5	98.2	103	23	43	0	0	0	0	0	0	0	–	5	10	1	1	1.1	.938
1984			12	12	.500	4.37	29	26	10	197.2	207	53	134	3	0	1	0	0	0	0	–	20	31	2	3	1.8	.962
1985			15	13	.536	3.70	35	35	13	272.1	**273**	67	154	3	0	0	0	0	0	0	–	42	41	1	2	2.4	.988
1986			16	10	.615	3.78	30	30	10	214.1	222	45	129	0	0	0	0	0	0	0	–	24	27	2	4	1.8	.962
1987			1	3	.250	5.89	7	7	0	36.2	47	9	12	0	0	0	0	0	0	0	–	4	11	0	0	2.1	1.000
1988			9	7	.563	5.34	23	23	1	129.2	147	41	71	0	0	0	0	0	0	0	–	8	15	2	0	1.1	.920
1989			3	2	.600	4.42	10	10	0	59	57	19	26	0	0	0	0	0	0	0	–	7	10	0	1	1.7	1.000
8 yrs.			60	56	.517	4.15	152	145	39	1016.2	1067	259	571	6	0	1	0	0	0	0		110	146	8	11	1.7	.970

LEAGUE CHAMPIONSHIP SERIES

Year	Team		W	L	PCT	ERA	G	GS	CG	IP	H	BB	SO	ShO	W	L	SV	AB	H	HR	BA	PO	A	E	DP	TC/G	FA
1986	BOS	A	1	1	.500	4.61	2	2	0	13.2	17	3	8	0	0	0	0	0	0	0	–	2	3	0	0	2.5	1.000

WORLD SERIES

Year	Team		W	L	PCT	ERA	G	GS	CG	IP	H	BB	SO	ShO	W	L	SV	AB	H	HR	BA	PO	A	E	DP	TC/G	FA
1986	BOS	A	0	1	.000	7.71	1	1	0	7	9	1	3	0	0	0	0	0	0	0	–	1	0	0	0	1.0	1.000

Ray Boyd   **BOYD, RAYMOND C.**   B. Feb. 11, 1887, Hortonville, Ind.   D. Feb. 11, 1920, Hortonville, Ind.   BR TR 5'10"   160 lbs.

Year	Team		W	L	PCT	ERA	G	GS	CG	IP	H	BB	SO	ShO	W	L	SV	AB	H	HR	BA	PO	A	E	DP	TC/G	FA
1910	STL	A	0	2	.000	4.40	3	2	1	14.1	16	5	6	0	0	0	0	5	1	0	.200	0	2	0	0	0.7	1.000
1911	CIN	N	3	2	.600	2.66	7	4	3	44	34	19	20	0	1	0	1	12	1	0	.083	4	11	3	0	2.6	.833
2 yrs.			3	4	.429	3.09	10	6	4	58.1	50	24	26	0	1	0	1	17	2	0	.118	4	13	3	0	2.0	.850

Cloyd Boyer   **BOYER, CLOYD VICTOR (Junior)**   Brother of Ken Boyer. Brother of Clete Boyer. B. Sept. 1, 1927, Alba, Mo.   BR TR 6'1"   188 lbs.

Year	Team		W	L	PCT	ERA	G	GS	CG	IP	H	BB	SO	ShO	W	L	SV	AB	H	HR	BA	PO	A	E	DP	TC/G	FA
1949	STL	N	0	0	–	10.80	3	1	0	3.1	5	7	0	0	0	0	0	0	0	0	–	1	0	0	1	0.3	1.000
1950			7	7	.500	3.52	36	14	6	120.1	105	49	82	2	1	1	1	33	6	0	.182	5	27	4	1	0.9	.871
1951			2	5	.286	5.26	19	8	1	63.1	68	46	40	1	0	1	2	20	4	0	.200	1	4	1	0	0.3	.833
1952			6	6	.500	4.24	23	14	4	110.1	108	47	44	2	0	0	0	38	8	0	.211	4	12	2	1	0.8	.889
1955	KC	A	5	5	.500	6.22	30	11	2	98.1	107	69	32	0	1	1	0	29	2	0	.069	9	13	2	0	0.8	.917
5 yrs.			20	23	.465	4.73	111	48	13	395.2	393	218	198	4	4	4	2	120	20	0	.167	20	51	9	3	0.7	.888

Henry Boyle   **BOYLE, HENRY J. (Handsome Henry)**   B. Sept. 20, 1860, Philadelphia, Pa.   D. May 25, 1932, Philadelphia, Pa.   TR

Year	Team		W	L	PCT	ERA	G	GS	CG	IP	H	BB	SO	ShO	W	L	SV	AB	H	HR	BA	PO	A	E	DP	TC/G	FA
1884	STL	U	15	3	.833	*1.74*	19	16	16	150	118	10	88	2	1	1	1	262	68	4	.260	7	26	5	2	2.0	.868
1885	STL	N	16	24	.400	*2.75*	42	39	39	366.2	346	100	133	1	1	0	0	258	52	1	.202	26	71	10	4	2.5	.907
1886			9	15	.375	2.24	25	24	23	165	183	46	101	2	1	0	0	108	27	1	.250	8	38	8	1	2.2	.852
1887	IND	N	13	24	.351	3.65	38	38	37	328	356	69	85	0	0	0	0	141	27	0	.191	1	1	5	0	0.2	.286
1888			15	22	.405	3.26	37	37	36	323	315	58	98	3	0	0	0	125	18	1	.144	14	84	7	1	2.8	.933
1889			21	23	.477	3.92	46	45	38	378.2	422	95	97	2	1	0	0	155	38	1	.245	17	51	3	0	1.5	.958
6 yrs.			89	111	.445	3.14	207	199	189	1711.1	1740	378	602	10	4	1	1	*				73	271	38	8	1.8	.901

Harry Boyles   **BOYLES, HARRY (Stretch)**   B. Nov. 29, 1911, Granite City, Ill.   BR TR 6'5"   185 lbs.

Year	Team		W	L	PCT	ERA	G	GS	CG	IP	H	BB	SO	ShO	W	L	SV	AB	H	HR	BA	PO	A	E	DP	TC/G	FA
1938	CHI	A	0	4	.000	5.22	9	2	1	29.1	31	25	18	0	0	2	1	8	1	0	.125	1	12	2	0	1.7	.867
1939			0	0	–	10.80	2	0	0	3.1	4	6	1	0	0	0	0	1	0	0	.000	0	0	0	0	0.0	–
2 yrs.			0	4	.000	5.79	11	2	1	32.2	35	31	19	0	0	2	1	9	1	0	.111	1	12	2	0	1.4	.867

Gene Brabender   **BRABENDER, EUGENE MATHEW**   B. Aug. 16, 1941, Madison, Wis.   BR TR 6'5½"   225 lbs.

Year	Team		W	L	PCT	ERA	G	GS	CG	IP	H	BB	SO	ShO	W	L	SV	AB	H	HR	BA	PO	A	E	DP	TC/G	FA
1966	BAL	A	4	3	.571	3.55	31	1	0	71	57	29	62	0	3	3	2	13	1	0	.077	7	12	2	0	0.7	.905
1967			6	4	.600	3.35	14	13	3	94	77	23	71	1	0	0	0	28	2	0	.071	7	13	3	1	1.6	.870
1968			6	7	.462	3.32	37	15	3	124.2	116	48	92	2	1	1	3	35	3	1	.086	6	15	1	0	0.6	.875
1969	SEA	A	13	14	.481	4.36	40	29	7	202.1	193	103	139	1	0	2	0	70	9	1	.129	13	17	3	1	0.8	.909
1970	MIL	A	6	15	.286	6.00	29	21	2	129	127	79	76	0	1	1	1	41	4	0	.098	13	17	3	1	1.1	.909
5 yrs.			35	43	.449	4.25	151	80	15	621	570	282	440	4	5	7	6	187	19	2	.102	46	74	14	4	0.9	.896

Jack Bracken   **BRACKEN, JOHN JAMES**   B. Apr. 14, 1881, Cleveland, Ohio   D. July 16, 1954, Highland Park, Mich.   BR TR 5'11"   175 lbs.

Year	Team		W	L	PCT	ERA	G	GS	CG	IP	H	BB	SO	ShO	W	L	SV	AB	H	HR	BA	PO	A	E	DP	TC/G	FA
1901	CLE	A	4	8	.333	6.21	12	12	12	100	137	31	18	0	0	0	0	44	10	0	.227	0	25	0	0	2.1	1.000

John Brackenridge   **BRACKENRIDGE, JOHN GIVLER**   B. Dec. 24, 1880, Harrisburg, Pa.   D. Mar. 20, 1953, Harrisburg, Pa.   BR TR 6'

Year	Team		W	L	PCT	ERA	G	GS	CG	IP	H	BB	SO	ShO	W	L	SV	AB	H	HR	BA	PO	A	E	DP	TC/G	FA
1904	PHI	N	0	1	.000	5.56	7	1	0	34	37	16	11	0	0	0	0	13	2	0	.154	2	19	2	1	3.3	.913

Don Bradey   **BRADEY, DONALD EUGENE**   B. Oct. 4, 1934, Charlotte, N. C.   BR TR 5'9"   180 lbs.

Year	Team		W	L	PCT	ERA	G	GS	CG	IP	H	BB	SO	ShO	W	L	SV	AB	H	HR	BA	PO	A	E	DP	TC/G	FA
1964	HOU	N	0	2	.000	19.29	3	1	0	2.1	6	3	2	0	0	0	0	0	0	0	–	0	0	0	0	0.0	–

Bill Bradford   **BRADFORD, WILLIAM D**   B. Aug. 28, 1921, Choctaw, Ark.   BR TR 6'2"   180 lbs.

Year	Team		W	L	PCT	ERA	G	GS	CG	IP	H	BB	SO	ShO	W	L	SV	AB	H	HR	BA	PO	A	E	DP	TC/G	FA
1956	KC	A	0	0	–	9.00	1	0	0	2	2	1	0	0	0	0	0	0	0	0	–	0	1	0	0	1.0	1.000

Year	Team		W	L	PCT	ERA	G	GS	CG	IP	H	BB	SO	ShO	Relief Pitching W	L	SV	Batting AB	H	HR	BA	PO	A	E	DP	TC/G	FA

Larry Bradford

BRADFORD, LARRY
B. Dec. 21, 1949, Chicago, Ill.   BR TL 6'1"   200 lbs.

Year	Team		W	L	PCT	ERA	G	GS	CG	IP	H	BB	SO	ShO	W	L	SV	AB	H	HR	BA	PO	A	E	DP	TC/G	FA
1977	ATL	N	0	0	–	3.00	2	0	0	3	3	0	1	0	0	0	0	0	0	0	–	0	1	0	0	0.5	1.000
1979			1	0	1.000	0.95	21	0	0	19	11	10	11	0	1	0	2	1	0	0	.000	0	5	1	0	0.3	.833
1980			3	4	.429	2.45	56	0	0	55	49	22	32	0	3	4	4	3	0	0	.000	3	8	0	0	0.2	1.000
1981			2	0	1.000	3.67	25	0	0	27	26	12	14	0	2	0	1	1	1	0	1.000	1	6	0	0	0.3	1.000
4 yrs.			6	4	.600	2.51	104	0	0	104	89	44	58	0	6	4	7	5	1	0	.200	4	20	1	0	0.2	.960

Bert Bradley

BRADLEY, STEVEN BERT
B. Dec. 23, 1956, Athens, Ga.   BB TR 6'1"   190 lbs.

Year	Team		W	L	PCT	ERA	G	GS	CG	IP	H	BB	SO	ShO	W	L	SV	AB	H	HR	BA	PO	A	E	DP	TC/G	FA
1983	OAK	A	0	0	–	6.48	6	0	0	8.1	14	4	3	0	0	0	0	0	0	0	–	0	3	0	2	0.5	1.000

Bill Bradley

BRADLEY, WILLIAM JOSEPH
B. Feb. 13, 1878, Cleveland, Ohio   D. Mar. 11, 1954, Cleveland, Ohio
Manager 1905, 1914.   BR TR 6'   185 lbs.

Year	Team		W	L	PCT	ERA	G	GS	CG	IP	H	BB	SO	ShO	W	L	SV	AB	H	HR	BA	PO	A	E	DP	TC/G	FA
1901	CLE	A	0	0	–	0.00	1	0	0	1	4	0	0	0	0	0	0	*				0	0	0	0	0.0	–

Foghorn Bradley

BRADLEY, GEORGE H.
B. July 1, 1855, Medford, Mass.   D. Apr. 3, 1900, Philadelphia, Pa.   BR TR

Year	Team		W	L	PCT	ERA	G	GS	CG	IP	H	BB	SO	ShO	W	L	SV	AB	H	HR	BA	PO	A	E	DP	TC/G	FA
1876	BOS	N	9	10	.474	2.49	22	21	16	173.1	201	16	16	1	0	0	1	82	19	0	.232	10	24	2	0	1.6	.944

Fred Bradley

BRADLEY, FREDERICK LANGDON
B. July 31, 1920, Parsons, Kans.   BR TR 6'1"   180 lbs.

Year	Team		W	L	PCT	ERA	G	GS	CG	IP	H	BB	SO	ShO	W	L	SV	AB	H	HR	BA	PO	A	E	DP	TC/G	FA
1948	CHI	A	0	0	–	4.60	8	0	0	15.2	11	4	2	0	0	0	0	1	0	0	.000	3	3	0	0	0.8	1.000
1949			0	0	–	13.50	1	0	0	2	4	3	0	0	0	0	0	1	0	0	.000	0	1	0	0	1.0	1.000
2 yrs.			0	0	–	5.60	9	0	0	17.2	15	7	2	0	0	0	0	2	0	0	.000	3	4	0	0	0.8	1.000

George Bradley

BRADLEY, GEORGE WASHINGTON (Grin)
B. July 13, 1852, Reading, Pa.   D. Oct. 2, 1931, Philadelphia, Pa.   BR TR 5'10½" 175 lbs.

Year	Team		W	L	PCT	ERA	G	GS	CG	IP	H	BB	SO	ShO	W	L	SV	AB	H	HR	BA	PO	A	E	DP	TC/G	FA
1876	STL	N	45	19	.703	1.23	64	64	63	573	470	38	103	16	0	0	0	265	66	0	.249	50	87	12	4	2.3	.919
1877	CHI	N	18	23	.439	3.31	50	44	35	394	452	39	59	2	1	0	0	214	52	0	.243	25	71	5	1	2.0	.950
1879	TRO	N	13	40	.245	2.85	54	54	53	487	590	26	133	3	0	0	0	251	62	0	.247	24	132	24	0	3.3	.867
1880	PRO	N	12	9	.571	1.38	28	20	16	196	158	6	54	4	3	0	1	309	70	0	.227	9	49	8	0	2.4	.879
1881	CLE	N	2	4	.333	3.88	6	6	5	51	70	3	6	0	0	0	0	245	60	2	.245	2	8	2	0	2.0	.833
1882			6	10	.375	3.73	18	16	15	147	164	22	32	0	0	0	0	115	21	0	.183	10	42	6	5	3.2	.897
1883	2 teams		CLE N (0G 0–0)				PHI AA (26G 16–7)																				
"	total		16	7	.696	3.15	26	23	22	214.1	215	22	56	0	0	0	0	328	78	1	.238	11	39	10	2	2.3	.833
1884	CIN	U	25	15	.625	2.71	41	38	36	342	350	23	168	3	1	1	0	226	43	0	.190	33	81	11	3	3.0	.912
1886	PHI	AA	0	0	–	0.00	0	0	0	0	0	0	0	0	0	0	0	48	4	0	.083	0	0	0	0	0.0	–
1888	BAL	AA	0	0	–	0.00	0	0	0	0	0	0	0	0	0	0	0	3	0	0	.000	0	0	0	0	0.0	–
10 yrs.			137	127	.519	2.50	287	265	245	2404.1	2469	179	611	28	5	2	1	*				164	509	78	15	2.6	.896

Herb Bradley

BRADLEY, HERBERT THEODORE
B. Jan. 3, 1903, Agenda, Kans.   D. Oct. 16, 1959, Clay Center, Kans.   BR TR 6'   170 lbs.

Year	Team		W	L	PCT	ERA	G	GS	CG	IP	H	BB	SO	ShO	W	L	SV	AB	H	HR	BA	PO	A	E	DP	TC/G	FA
1927	BOS	A	1	1	.500	3.13	6	2	2	23	16	7	6	0	0	0	0	7	3	0	.429	0	5	0	0	0.8	1.000
1928			0	3	.000	7.23	15	5	1	47.1	64	16	14	1	0	0	0	13	2	0	.154	2	17	0	0	1.3	1.000
1929			0	0	–	6.75	3	0	0	4	7	2	0	0	0	0	0	1	0	0	.000	0	2	0	0	0.7	1.000
3 yrs.			1	4	.200	5.93	24	7	3	74.1	87	25	20	1	0	0	0	21	5	0	.238	2	24	0	0	1.1	1.000

Tom Bradley

BRADLEY, THOMAS WILLIAM
B. Mar. 16, 1947, Asheville, N. C.   BR TR 6'2½"   180 lbs.

Year	Team		W	L	PCT	ERA	G	GS	CG	IP	H	BB	SO	ShO	W	L	SV	AB	H	HR	BA	PO	A	E	DP	TC/G	FA
1969	CAL	A	0	1	.000	27.00	3	0	0	2	9	4	0	2	0	0	1	0	0	0	0	–	0	1	0	0	0.3	1.000
1970			2	5	.286	4.11	17	11	1	70	71	33	53	1	0	0	0	18	3	0	.167	5	9	1	0	0.9	.933
1971	CHI	A	15	15	.500	2.96	45	39	7	286	273	74	206	6	0	0	1	96	15	1	.156	24	32	2	0	1.3	.966
1972			15	14	.517	2.98	40	40	11	260	225	65	209	2	0	0	0	91	12	0	.132	13	35	2	1	1.3	.960
1973	SF	N	13	12	.520	3.90	35	34	6	223.2	212	69	136	1	0	0	0	77	15	0	.195	12	25	3	0	1.1	.925
1974			8	11	.421	5.17	30	21	2	134	152	52	72	0	0	0	1	40	3	0	.075	10	13	3	2	0.9	.885
1975			2	3	.400	6.21	13	6	0	42	57	18	13	0	0	0	0	10	0	0	.000	1	9	0	0	1.0	1.000
7 yrs.			55	61	.474	3.72	183	151	27	1017.2	999	311	691	10	0	3	2	332	48	1	.145	65	124	11	4	1.1	.945

Joe Bradshaw

BRADSHAW, JOE SIAH
B. Aug. 17, 1897, Roellen, Tenn.   D. Jan. 30, 1985, Tavares, Fla.   BR TR 6'2½"   200 lbs.

Year	Team		W	L	PCT	ERA	G	GS	CG	IP	H	BB	SO	ShO	W	L	SV	AB	H	HR	BA	PO	A	E	DP	TC/G	FA
1929	BKN	N	0	0	–	4.50	2	0	0	4	3	4	1	0	0	0	0	0	0	0	–	0	2	0	1	1.0	1.000

Bill Brady

BRADY, WILLIAM A.
B. 1888   TR

Year	Team		W	L	PCT	ERA	G	GS	CG	IP	H	BB	SO	ShO	W	L	SV	AB	H	HR	BA	PO	A	E	DP	TC/G	FA
1912	BOS	N	0	0	–	0.00	1	0	0	1	2	0	0	0	0	0	0	0	0	0	–	0	0	0	0	0.0	–

Jim Brady

BRADY, JAMES JOSEPH (Diamond Jim)
B. Mar. 2, 1936, Jersey City, N. J.   BL TL 6'2"   185 lbs.

Year	Team		W	L	PCT	ERA	G	GS	CG	IP	H	BB	SO	ShO	W	L	SV	AB	H	HR	BA	PO	A	E	DP	TC/G	FA
1956	DET	A	0	0	–	28.42	6	0	0	6.1	15	11	3	0	0	0	0	0	0	0	–	0	1	0	0	0.2	1.000

King Brady

BRADY, JAMES WARD
B. May 28, 1881, Elmer, N. J.   D. Aug. 21, 1947, Albany, N. Y.   BL TR 6'   190 lbs.

Year	Team		W	L	PCT	ERA	G	GS	CG	IP	H	BB	SO	ShO	W	L	SV	AB	H	HR	BA	PO	A	E	DP	TC/G	FA
1905	PHI	N	1	1	.500	3.46	2	2	2	13	19	2	3	0	0	0	0	5	1	0	.200	1	3	1	1	2.5	.800
1906	PIT	N	1	1	.500	2.35	3	2	1	23	30	4	14	0	0	0	0	10	1	0	.100	1	3	0	0	1.3	1.000
1907			0	0	–	0.00	1	0	0	2	2	1	0	0	0	0	0	0	0	0	–	0	1	0	0	1.0	1.000
1908	BOS	A	1	0	1.000	0.00	1	1	1	9	8	0	3	1	0	0	0	2	0	0	.000	0	1	0	0	1.0	1.000

Year	Team	W	L	PCT	ERA	G	GS	CG	IP	H	BB	SO	ShO	W	L	SV	AB	H	HR	BA	PO	A	E	DP	TC/G	FA
														Relief Pitching			Batting									

King Brady *continued*

Year	Team		W	L	PCT	ERA	G	GS	CG	IP	H	BB	SO	ShO	W	L	SV	AB	H	HR	BA	PO	A	E	DP	TC/G	FA
1912	BOS	N	0	0	–	20.25	1	0	0	2.2	5	3	0	0	0	0	0	1	0	0	.000	0	1	0	0	1.0	1.000
5 yrs.			3	2	.600	3.08	8	5	4	49.2	64	10	20	1	0	1	0	18	2	0	.111	2	8	2	1	1.5	.833

Neal Brady

BRADY, CORNELIUS JOSEPH
B. Mar. 4, 1897, Covington, Ky.   D. June 19, 1947, Fort Mitchell, Ky.

BR TR 6'½"   197 lbs.

Year	Team		W	L	PCT	ERA	G	GS	CG	IP	H	BB	SO	ShO	W	L	SV	AB	H	HR	BA	PO	A	E	DP	TC/G	FA
1915	NY	A	0	0	–	3.12	2	1	0	8.2	9	7	6	0	0	0	0	4	0	0	.000	0	2	0	0	1.0	1.000
1917			1	0	1.000	2.00	2	1	0	9	6	5	4	0	0	0	0	2	1	0	.500	0	5	0	0	2.5	1.000
1925	CIN	N	1	3	.250	4.66	20	3	2	63.2	73	20	12	0	0	1	1	25	6	0	.240	6	16	2	0	1.2	.917
3 yrs.			2	3	.400	4.20	24	5	2	81.1	88	32	22	0	0	1	1	31	7	0	.226	6	23	2	0	1.3	.935

Dick Braggins

BRAGGINS, RICHARD REALF
B. Dec. 25, 1879, Mercer, Pa.   D. Aug. 16, 1963, Lake Wales, Fla.

BR TR 5'11"   170 lbs.

Year	Team		W	L	PCT	ERA	G	GS	CG	IP	H	BB	SO	ShO	W	L	SV	AB	H	HR	BA	PO	A	E	DP	TC/G	FA
1901	CLE	A	1	2	.333	4.78	4	3	2	32	44	15	1	0	0	0	0	13	2	0	.154	0	10	0	1	2.5	1.000

Al Braithwood

BRAITHWOOD, ALFRED
B. Feb. 15, 1892, Braceville, Ill.   D. Nov. 24, 1960, Rowlesburg, W. Va.

BR TL 6'1½"   145 lbs.

Year	Team		W	L	PCT	ERA	G	GS	CG	IP	H	BB	SO	ShO	W	L	SV	AB	H	HR	BA	PO	A	E	DP	TC/G	FA
1915	PIT	F	0	0	–	0.00	2	0	0	3	0	0	2	0	0	0	0	0	0	0	–	0	0	0	0	0.0	–

Erv Brame

BRAME, ERVIN BECKHAM
B. Oct. 12, 1901, Big Rock, Tenn.   D. Nov. 22, 1949, Hopkinsville, Ky.

BL TR 6'2"   190 lbs.

Year	Team		W	L	PCT	ERA	G	GS	CG	IP	H	BB	SO	ShO	W	L	SV	AB	H	HR	BA	PO	A	E	DP	TC/G	FA
1928	PIT	N	7	4	.636	5.08	24	11	6	95.2	110	44	22	0	0	1	0	49	13	1	.265	2	18	1	0	0.9	.952
1929			16	11	.593	4.55	37	28	19	229.2	250	71	68	1	2	0	0	116	36	4	.310	7	36	3	0	1.2	.935
1930			17	8	.680	4.70	32	29	**22**	235.2	291	56	55	0	1	0	1	116	41	3	.353	1	39	2	0	1.3	.952
1931			9	13	.409	4.21	26	21	15	179.2	211	45	33	2	2	1	0	95	26	0	.274	1	34	1	2	1.4	.972
1932			3	1	.750	7.41	23	3	0	51	84	16	10	0	3	0	0	20	5	0	.250	0	9	0	1	0.4	1.000
5 yrs.			52	37	.584	4.76	142	92	62	791.2	946	232	188	3	8	2	1	*				11	136	7	3	1.1	.955

Ralph Branca

BRANCA, RALPH THEODORE JOSEPH (Hawk)
B. Jan. 6, 1926, Mt. Vernon, N.Y.

BR TR 6'3"   220 lbs.

Year	Team		W	L	PCT	ERA	G	GS	CG	IP	H	BB	SO	ShO	W	L	SV	AB	H	HR	BA	PO	A	E	DP	TC/G	FA
1944	BKN	N	0	2	.000	7.05	21	1	0	44.2	46	32	16	0	0	1	0	6	0	0	.000	2	8	0	0	0.5	1.000
1945			5	6	.455	3.04	16	15	7	109.2	73	79	69	0	0	0	1	40	4	0	.100	7	20	2	1	1.8	.931
1946			3	1	.750	3.88	24	10	2	67.1	62	41	42	2	0	1	3	18	2	0	.111	3	6	1	0	0.4	.900
1947			21	12	.636	2.67	43	36	15	280	251	98	148	4	3	1	1	97	12	0	.124	4	35	3	0	1.1	.936
1948			14	9	.609	3.51	36	28	11	215.2	189	80	122	1	1	0	1	74	15	0	.203	10	18	1	0	0.8	.966
1949			13	5	.722	4.39	34	27	9	186.2	181	91	109	2	0	1	1	62	5	0	.081	6	15	2	0	0.7	.913
1950			7	9	.438	4.69	43	15	5	142	152	55	100	0	2	4	7	34	4	2	.118	8	19	0	0	0.6	1.000
1951			13	12	.520	3.26	42	27	13	204	180	85	118	3	1	2	3	63	11	0	.175	12	19	0	1	0.7	1.000
1952			4	2	.667	3.84	16	7	2	61	52	21	26	0	1	0	0	19	3	0	.158	5	7	1	1	0.8	.923
1953	2 teams		BKN N	(7G 0–0)		DET A	(17G 4–7)																				
"	total		4	7	.364	4.70	24	14	7	113	113	36	55	0	0	0	0	34	4	0	.118	7	12	1	0	0.8	.950
1954	2 teams		DET A	(17G 3–3)		NY A	(5G 1–0)																				
"	total		4	3	.571	5.12	22	8	0	58	72	43	22	0	2	3	0	17	6	0	.353	3	9	1	1	0.6	.923
1956	BKN	N	0	0	–	0.00	1	0	0	2	1	2	2	0	0	0	0	0	0	0	–	0	1	0	0	1.0	1.000
12 yrs.			88	68	.564	3.79	322	188	71	1484	1372	663	829	12	10	13	19	464	66	2	.142	72	169	12	5	0.8	.953

WORLD SERIES

Year	Team		W	L	PCT	ERA	G	GS	CG	IP	H	BB	SO	ShO	W	L	SV	AB	H	HR	BA	PO	A	E	DP	TC/G	FA
1947	BKN	N	1	1	.500	8.64	3	1	0	8.1	12	5	8	0	0	0	0	4	0	0	.000	0	1	0	0	0.3	1.000
1949			0	1	.000	4.15	1	1	0	8.2	4	4	6	0	0	0	0	3	0	0	.000	1	0	0	0	1.0	1.000
2 yrs.			1	2	.333	6.35	4	2	0	17	16	9	14	0	0	0	0	7	0	0	.000	1	1	0	0	0.5	1.000

Harvey Branch

BRANCH, HARVEY ALFRED
B. Feb. 8, 1939, Memphis, Tenn.

BR TL 6'   175 lbs.

Year	Team		W	L	PCT	ERA	G	GS	CG	IP	H	BB	SO	ShO	W	L	SV	AB	H	HR	BA	PO	A	E	DP	TC/G	FA
1962	STL	N	0	1	.000	5.40	1	1	0	5	5	5	2	0	0	0	0	1	0	0	.000	1	2	0	0	3.0	1.000

Norm Branch

BRANCH, NORMAN DOWNS (Red)
B. Mar. 22, 1915, Spokane, Wash.   D. Nov. 21, 1971, Novasota, Tex.

BR TR 6'3"   200 lbs.

Year	Team		W	L	PCT	ERA	G	GS	CG	IP	H	BB	SO	ShO	W	L	SV	AB	H	HR	BA	PO	A	E	DP	TC/G	FA
1941	NY	A	5	1	.833	2.87	27	0	0	47	37	26	28	0	5	1	2	10	0	0	.000	0	12	0	0	0.4	1.000
1942			0	1	.000	6.32	10	0	0	15.2	18	16	13	0	0	1	2	3	1	0	.333	0	5	0	0	0.5	1.000
2 yrs.			5	2	.714	3.73	37	0	0	62.2	55	42	41	0	5	2	4	13	1	0	.077	0	17	0	0	0.5	1.000

Roy Branch

BRANCH, ROY
B. July 12, 1953, St. Louis, Mo.

BR TR 6'   175 lbs.

Year	Team		W	L	PCT	ERA	G	GS	CG	IP	H	BB	SO	ShO	W	L	SV	AB	H	HR	BA	PO	A	E	DP	TC/G	FA
1979	SEA	A	0	1	.000	8.18	2	2	0	11	12	7	1	0	0	0	0	0	0	0	–	0	0	0	0	0.0	–

Chick Brandom

BRANDOM, CHESTER MILTON
B. Mar. 31, 1887, Coldwater, Kans.   D. Oct. 7, 1958, Santa Ana, Calif.

BR TR 5'8"   161 lbs.

Year	Team		W	L	PCT	ERA	G	GS	CG	IP	H	BB	SO	ShO	W	L	SV	AB	H	HR	BA	PO	A	E	DP	TC/G	FA
1908	PIT	N	1	0	1.000	0.53	3	1	1	17	13	4	8	0	0	0	0	7	1	0	.143	1	6	0	0	2.3	1.000
1909			1	0	1.000	1.11	13	2	0	40.2	33	10	21	0	1	0	2	10	1	0	.100	1	17	2	0	1.5	.900
1915	NWK	F	1	1	.500	3.40	16	1	1	50.1	55	15	15	0	1	1	0	10	2	0	.200	1	20	2	0	1.4	.913
3 yrs.			3	1	.750	2.08	32	4	2	108	101	29	44	0	2	1	2	27	4	0	.148	3	43	4	0	1.6	.920

Darrell Brandon

BRANDON, DARRELL G (Bucky)
B. July 8, 1940, Nacogdoches, Tex.

BR TR 6'2"   200 lbs.

Year	Team		W	L	PCT	ERA	G	GS	CG	IP	H	BB	SO	ShO	W	L	SV	AB	H	HR	BA	PO	A	E	DP	TC/G	FA
1966	BOS	A	8	8	.500	3.31	40	17	5	157.2	129	70	101	2	1	1	2	44	8	0	.182	13	26	1	0	1.0	.975
1967			5	11	.313	4.17	39	19	2	157.2	147	59	96	0	2	3	3	43	8	0	.186	11	23	2	0	0.9	.944
1968			0	0	–	6.39	8	0	0	12.2	19	9	10	0	0	0	0	1	0	0	.000	0	2	0	0	0.3	1.000
1969	2 teams		SEA A	(8G 0–1)		MIN A	(3G 0–0)																				
"	total		0	1	.000	7.36	11	1	0	18.1	20	19	11	0	0	0	0	0	0	0	.000	0	3	0	0	0.5	.600
1971	PHI	N	6	6	.500	3.90	52	0	0	83	81	47	44	0	6	6	4	13	2	0	.154	6	10	0	0	0.3	1.000
1972			7	7	.500	3.45	42	6	0	104.1	106	46	67	0	7	4	2	15	1	0	.067	6	7	1	0	0.3	.929

Year	Team		W	L	PCT	ERA	G	GS	CG	IP	H	BB	SO	ShO	Relief Pitching W	L	SV	Batting AB	H	HR	BA	PO	A	E	DP	TC/G	FA

Darrell Brandon *continued*

Year	Team		W	L	PCT	ERA	G	GS	CG	IP	H	BB	SO	ShO	W	L	SV	AB	H	HR	BA	PO	A	E	DP	TC/G	FA
1973			2	4	.333	5.43	36	0	0	56.1	54	25	25	0	2	4	2	5	1	0	.200	5	8	1	1	0.4	.929
7 yrs.			28	37	.431	4.04	228	43	7	590	556	275	354	2	18	17	13	122	20	0	.164	41	79	7	3	0.6	.945

Bill Brandt

BRANDT, WILLIAM GEORGE BR TR 5'8½" 170 lbs.
B. Mar. 21, 1915, Aurora, Ind. D. May 16, 1968, Fort Wayne, Ind.

Year	Team		W	L	PCT	ERA	G	GS	CG	IP	H	BB	SO	ShO	W	L	SV	AB	H	HR	BA	PO	A	E	DP	TC/G	FA
1941	PIT	N	0	1	.000	3.86	2	1	0	7	5	3	0	0	0	0	0	1	0	0	.000	0	1	0	0	0.5	1.000
1942			1	1	.500	4.96	3	3	1	16.1	23	5	4	0	0	0	0	7	1	0	.143	0	2	0	0	0.7	1.000
1943			4	1	.800	3.14	29	3	0	57.1	57	19	17	0	3	0	0	7	1	0	.143	1	12	0	0	0.4	1.000
3 yrs.			5	3	.625	3.57	34	7	1	80.2	85	27	21	0	3	0	0	15	2	0	.133	1	15	0	0	0.5	1.000

Ed Brandt

BRANDT, EDWARD ARTHUR BL TL 6'1" 190 lbs.
B. Feb. 17, 1905, Spokane, Wash. D. Nov. 1, 1944, Spokane, Wash.

Year	Team		W	L	PCT	ERA	G	GS	CG	IP	H	BB	SO	ShO	W	L	SV	AB	H	HR	BA	PO	A	E	DP	TC/G	FA
1928	BOS	N	9	21	.300	5.07	38	31	12	225.1	234	109	84	1	1	2	0	70	17	0	.243	3	61	0	3	1.7	1.000
1929			8	13	.381	5.53	26	21	13	167.2	196	83	50	0	1	0	0	64	15	0	.234	8	47	2	4	2.2	.965
1930			4	11	.267	5.01	41	13	4	147.1	168	59	65	1	2	2	1	50	12	0	.240	6	35	0	2	1.0	1.000
1931			18	11	.621	2.92	33	29	23	250	228	77	112	3	0	1	2	82	21	0	.256	10	64	2	1	2.3	.974
1932			16	16	.500	3.97	35	31	19	254	271	57	79	2	1	2	1	92	19	0	.207	8	63	1	1	2.1	.986
1933			18	14	.563	2.60	41	32	23	287.2	256	77	104	3	1	1	4	97	30	0	.309	14	60	1	2	1.8	.987
1934			16	14	.533	3.53	40	28	20	255	249	83	106	4	2	2	5	96	23	0	.240	12	39	2	0	1.3	.962
1935			5	19	.208	5.00	29	25	12	174.2	224	66	61	0	0	2	0	62	13	0	.210	7	42	3	1	1.8	.942
1936	BKN	N	11	13	.458	3.50	38	29	12	234	246	65	104	1	1	1	2	84	16	0	.190	4	40	1	3	1.2	.978
1937	PIT	N	11	10	.524	3.11	33	25	7	176.1	177	67	74	3	1	1	1	59	10	0	.169	4	43	1	1	1.5	.979
1938			5	4	.556	3.46	24	13	5	96.1	93	35	38	1	1	1	1	37	11	0	.297	2	18	1	1	0.9	.952
11 yrs.			121	146	.453	3.86	378	277	150	2268.1	2342	778	877	18	10	16	17	793	187	0	.236	78	512	14	19	1.6	.977

Jeff Brantley

BRANTLEY, JEFFREY HOKE BR TR 5'11" 180 lbs.
B. Sept. 5, 1963, Florence, Ala.

Year	Team		W	L	PCT	ERA	G	GS	CG	IP	H	BB	SO	ShO	W	L	SV	AB	H	HR	BA	PO	A	E	DP	TC/G	FA
1988	SF	N	0	1	.000	5.66	9	1	0	20.2	22	6	11	0	0	1	0	2	1	0	.500	0	7	0	0	0.8	1.000
1989			7	1	.875	4.07	59	1	0	97.1	101	37	69	0	7	0	0	12	1	0	.083	3	16	0	0	0.3	1.000
2 yrs.			7	2	.778	4.35	68	2	0	118	123	43	80	0	7	0	1	14	2	0	.143	3	23	0	0	0.4	1.000

LEAGUE CHAMPIONSHIP SERIES

Year	Team		W	L	PCT	ERA	G	GS	CG	IP	H	BB	SO	ShO	W	L	SV	AB	H	HR	BA	PO	A	E	DP	TC/G	FA
1989	SF	N	0	0	–	0.00	3	0	0	5	1	2	3	0	0	0	0	0	0	0	–	0	0	0	0	0.0	–

WORLD SERIES

Year	Team		W	L	PCT	ERA	G	GS	CG	IP	H	BB	SO	ShO	W	L	SV	AB	H	HR	BA	PO	A	E	DP	TC/G	FA
1989	SF	N	0	0	–	4.15	3	0	0	4.1	5	3	1	0	0	0	0	0	0	0	–	1	0	0	0	0.3	1.000

Roy Brashear

BRASHEAR, ROY PARKS BR TR
Brother of Kitty Brashear.
B. Jan. 3, 1874, Ashtabula, Ohio D. Apr. 20, 1951, Los Angeles, Calif.

Year	Team		W	L	PCT	ERA	G	GS	CG	IP	H	BB	SO	ShO	W	L	SV	AB	H	HR	BA	PO	A	E	DP	TC/G	FA
1899	LOU	N	1	0	1.000	4.50	3	0	0	8	8	2	5	0	1	0	0	*				*					

John Braun

BRAUN, JOHN PAUL BR TR 6'5" 218 lbs.
B. Dec. 26, 1939, Madison, Wis.

Year	Team		W	L	PCT	ERA	G	GS	CG	IP	H	BB	SO	ShO	W	L	SV	AB	H	HR	BA	PO	A	E	DP	TC/G	FA
1964	MIL	N	0	0	–	0.00	1	0	0	2	2	1	1	0	0	0	0	0	0	0	–	0	0	0	0	0.0	–

Garland Braxton

BRAXTON, EDGAR GARLAND BL TL 5'11" 152 lbs.
B. June 10, 1900, Snow Camp, N. C. BR 1921-22,
D. Feb. 26, 1966, Norfolk, Va. BB 1925-26,1933

Year	Team		W	L	PCT	ERA	G	GS	CG	IP	H	BB	SO	ShO	W	L	SV	AB	H	HR	BA	PO	A	E	DP	TC/G	FA
1921	BOS	N	1	3	.250	4.82	17	2	0	37.1	44	17	16	0	1	1	0	7	0	0	.000	1	13	1	1	0.9	.933
1922			1	2	.333	3.38	25	4	2	66.2	75	24	15	0	0	1	0	16	1	0	.063	3	13	1	0	0.7	.941
1925	NY	A	1	1	.500	6.52	3	2	0	19.1	26	5	11	0	0	0	0	6	2	0	.333	0	5	1	0	2.0	.833
1926			5	1	.833	2.67	37	1	0	67.1	71	19	30	0	5	1	2	20	6	0	.300	3	16	1	1	0.5	.950
1927	WAS	A	10	9	.526	2.95	58	2	0	155.1	143	33	95	0	10	7	13	39	9	0	.231	5	23	2	1	0.5	.933
1928			13	11	.542	2.51	38	24	15	218.1	177	44	94	2	1	3	2	72	9	0	.125	9	50	3	2	1.6	.952
1929			12	10	.545	4.85	37	20	9	182	219	51	59	0	4	1	4	54	8	0	.148	8	32	1	2	1.1	.976
1930	2 teams	WAS A (15G 3–2)				CHI A (19G 4–10)																					
"	total		7	12	.368	5.72	34	10	2	118	149	42	51	0	5	4	6	28	2	0	.071	2	15	2	0	0.6	.895
1931	2 teams	CHI A (17G 0–3)				STL A (11G 0–0)																					
"	total		0	3	.000	7.85	28	4	0	65.1	98	33	35	0	0	1	0	14	3	0	.214	4	15	1	0	0.7	.944
1933	STL	A	0	1	.000	9.72	5	1	0	8.1	11	8	5	0	0	0	0	1	0	0	.000	0	1	0	0	0.2	1.000
10 yrs.			50	53	.485	4.13	282	70	28	938	1013	276	411	2	26	19	32	257	40	0	.156	35	181	13	7	0.8	.943

Al Brazle

BRAZLE, ALPHA EUGENE (Cotton) BL TL 6'2" 185 lbs.
B. Oct. 19, 1913, Loyal, Okla. D. Oct. 24, 1973, Grand Junction, Colo.

Year	Team		W	L	PCT	ERA	G	GS	CG	IP	H	BB	SO	ShO	W	L	SV	AB	H	HR	BA	PO	A	E	DP	TC/G	FA
1943	STL	N	8	2	.800	1.53	13	9	8	88	74	29	26	1	0	0	0	32	9	0	.281	3	20	0	1	1.8	1.000
1946			11	10	.524	3.29	37	15	6	153.1	152	55	58	2	4	2	0	52	11	0	.212	5	33	2	1	1.1	.950
1947			14	8	.636	2.84	44	19	7	168	186	48	85	0	4	1	4	64	14	0	.219	4	47	1	1	1.2	.981
1948			10	6	.625	3.80	42	23	6	156.1	171	50	55	3	3	0	1	55	8	0	.145	5	45	0	1	1.2	1.000
1949			14	8	.636	3.18	39	25	9	206.1	208	61	75	3	3	0	0	82	11	0	.134	4	39	2	1	1.2	.956
1950			11	9	.550	4.10	46	12	3	164.2	188	80	47	0	5	4	6	61	13	0	.213	6	31	4	3	0.9	.902
1951			6	5	.545	3.09	56	8	5	154.1	139	64	66	0	2	2	7	46	5	0	.109	4	19	2	1	0.4	.920
1952			12	5	.706	2.72	46	6	0	109.1	75	42	55	0	8	3	16	32	4	0	.125	5	13	1	0	0.4	.947
1953			6	7	.462	4.21	60	2	0	92	101	43	57	0	6	7	18	15	5	0	.333	4	24	0	0	0.5	1.000
1954			5	4	.556	4.16	58	0	0	84.1	93	24	30	0	5	4	8	14	0	0	.000	3	13	1	2	0.3	.944
10 yrs.			97	64	.602	3.31	441	117	47	1376.2	1387	492	554	9	41	23	60	453	80	0	.177	43	284	13	11	0.8	.962

WORLD SERIES

Year	Team		W	L	PCT	ERA	G	GS	CG	IP	H	BB	SO	ShO	W	L	SV	AB	H	HR	BA	PO	A	E	DP	TC/G	FA
1943	STL	N	0	1	.000	3.68	1	1	0	7.1	5	2	4	0	0	0	0	3	0	0	.000	1	2	0	0	3.0	1.000

Year	Team		W	L	PCT	ERA	G	GS	CG	IP	H	BB	SO	ShO	Relief Pitching W	L	SV	Batting AB	H	HR	BA	PO	A	E	DP	TC/G	FA

Al Brazle *continued*

Year	Team		W	L	PCT	ERA	G	GS	CG	IP	H	BB	SO	ShO	W	L	SV	AB	H	HR	BA	PO	A	E	DP	TC/G	FA
1946			0	1	.000	5.40	1	0	0	6.2	7	6	4	0	0	1	0	2	0	0	.000	0	1	0	0	1.0	1.000
2 yrs.			0	2	.000	4.50	2	1	0	14	12	8	8	0	0	1	0	5	0	0	.000	1	3	0	0	2.0	1.000

Harry Brecheen

BRECHEEN, HARRY DAVID (The Cat)
B. Oct. 14, 1914, Broken Bow, Okla.   BL TL 5'10" 160 lbs.

Year	Team		W	L	PCT	ERA	G	GS	CG	IP	H	BB	SO	ShO	W	L	SV	AB	H	HR	BA	PO	A	E	DP	TC/G	FA
1940	STL	N	0	0	–	0.00	3	0	0	3.1	2	2	4	0	0	0	0	0	0	0	–	0	2	0	0	0.7	1.000
1943			9	6	.600	2.26	29	13	8	135.1	98	39	68	1	4	1	4	42	8	0	.190	8	28	0	3	1.2	1.000
1944			16	5	.762	2.85	30	22	13	189.1	174	46	88	3	3	0	0	68	11	0	.162	3	36	0	2	1.3	1.000
1945			14	4	.778	2.52	24	18	13	157.1	136	44	63	3	2	1	2	57	7	0	.123	6	26	1	2	1.4	.970
1946			15	15	.500	2.49	36	30	14	231.1	212	67	117	5	0	0	3	83	11	0	.133	11	50	1	6	1.7	.984
1947			16	11	.593	3.30	29	28	18	223.1	220	66	89	1	0	0	1	83	20	0	.241	11	47	1	0	2.0	.983
1948			20	7	.741	2.24	33	30	21	233.1	193	49	149	7	0	0	1	82	12	0	.146	5	45	0	2	1.5	1.000
1949			14	11	.560	3.35	32	31	14	214.2	207	65	88	2	0	0	1	77	21	0	.273	5	37	3	0	1.4	.933
1950			8	11	.421	3.80	27	23	12	163.1	151	45	80	2	0	2	1	58	14	1	.241	11	25	0	1	1.3	1.000
1951			8	4	.667	3.25	24	16	5	138.2	134	54	57	0	2	0	2	55	12	1	.218	5	25	2	1	1.3	.938
1952			7	5	.583	3.32	25	13	4	100.1	82	28	54	1	2	1	2	29	6	0	.207	8	26	0	3	1.4	1.000
1953	STL	A	5	13	.278	3.07	26	16	3	117.1	122	31	44	0	2	3	1	39	7	0	.179	5	29	2	1	1.3	.938
12 yrs.			132	92	.589	2.92	318	240	125	1907.2	1731	536	901	25	15	8	18	673	129	2	.192	78	376	8	22	1.5	.983

WORLD SERIES

Year	Team		W	L	PCT	ERA	G	GS	CG	IP	H	BB	SO	ShO	W	L	SV	AB	H	HR	BA	PO	A	E	DP	TC/G	FA
1943	STL	N	0	1	.000	2.45	3	0	0	3.2	5	3	3	0	0	1	0	0	0	0	–	0	2	0	0	0.7	1.000
1944			1	0	1.000	1.00	1	1	1	9	9	4	4	0	0	0	0	4	0	0	.000	1	3	0	0	4.0	1.000
1946			3	0	1.000	0.45	3	2	2	20	14	5	11	1	1	0	0	8	1	0	.125	0	2	0	1	0.7	1.000
3 yrs.			4	1	.800	0.83 2nd	7	3	3	32.2	28	12	18	1	1	1	0	12	1	0	.083	1	7	0	1	1.1	1.000

Bill Breckinridge

BRECKINRIDGE, WILLIAM ROBERTSON
B. Oct. 16, 1907, Tulsa, Okla.   D. Aug. 23, 1958, Tulsa, Okla.   BR TR 5'11" 175 lbs.

Year	Team		W	L	PCT	ERA	G	GS	CG	IP	H	BB	SO	ShO	W	L	SV	AB	H	HR	BA	PO	A	E	DP	TC/G	FA
1929	PHI	A	0	0	–	8.10	3	1	0	10	10	16	2	0	0	0	0	4	0	0	.000	0	0	0	0	0.0	–

Fred Breining

BREINING, FRED LAWRENCE
B. Nov. 15, 1955, San Francisco, Calif.   BR TR 6'4" 185 lbs.

Year	Team		W	L	PCT	ERA	G	GS	CG	IP	H	BB	SO	ShO	W	L	SV	AB	H	HR	BA	PO	A	E	DP	TC/G	FA
1980	SF	N	0	0	–	5.14	5	0	0	7	8	4	3	0	0	0	0	0	0	0	–	0	1	0	0	0.2	1.000
1981			5	2	.714	2.54	45	1	0	78	66	38	37	0	5	2	1	11	0	0	.000	3	12	0	0	0.3	1.000
1982			11	6	.647	3.08	54	9	2	143.1	146	52	98	0	6	3	0	29	6	0	.207	12	25	4	2	0.8	.902
1983			11	12	.478	3.82	32	32	6	202.2	202	60	117	0	0	0	0	67	10	0	.149	21	24	2	0	1.5	.957
1984	MON	N	0	0	–	1.35	4	0	0	6.2	4	5	5	0	0	0	0	1	0	0	.000	0	0	0	0	0.0	–
5 yrs.			27	20	.574	3.33	140	42	8	437.2	426	159	260	0	11	5	1	108	16	0	.148	36	62	6	2	0.7	.942

Alonzo Breitenstein

BREITENSTEIN, ALONZO
B. Nov. 9, 1857, Utica, N. Y.   D. June 19, 1932, Utica, N. Y.

Year	Team		W	L	PCT	ERA	G	GS	CG	IP	H	BB	SO	ShO	W	L	SV	AB	H	HR	BA	PO	A	E	DP	TC/G	FA
1883	PHI	N	0	1	.000	9.00	1	1	0	5	8	2	0	0	0	0	0	2	0	0	.000	0	1	1	0	2.0	.500

Ted Breitenstein

BREITENSTEIN, THEODORE P.
B. June 1, 1869, St. Louis, Mo.   D. May 3, 1935, St. Louis, Mo.   BL TL 5'9" 167 lbs.

Year	Team		W	L	PCT	ERA	G	GS	CG	IP	H	BB	SO	ShO	W	L	SV	AB	H	HR	BA	PO	A	E	DP	TC/G	FA
1891	STL	AA	2	0	1.000	2.20	6	1	1	28.2	15	14	13	1	0	0	0	12	0	0	.000	1	2	0	0	0.5	1.000
1892	STL	N	14	20	.412	4.69	39	32	28	282.1	280	148	126	1	0	0	0	131	16	0	.122	22	68	6	2	2.5	.938
1893			19	20	.487	3.18	48	42	38	382.2	359	156	102	1	0	3	1	160	29	1	.181	42	82	8	4	2.8	.939
1894			27	25	.519	4.79	56	50	46	447.1	497[1]	191	140	1	2	0	0	182	40	0	.220	42	83	9	4	2.4	.933
1895			18	30	.375	4.44	54	50	46	429.2	458	178	127	1	0	1	1	218	42	0	.193	45	98	14	1	2.9	.911
1896			18	26	.409	4.48	44	43	37	339.2	376	138	114	1	1	0	0	162	42	0	.259	34	89	7	4	3.0	.946
1897	CIN	N	23	12	.657	3.62	40	39	37	320.1	345	91	98	2	0	0	0	124	33	0	.266	16	65	3	3	2.1	.964
1898			20	14	.588	3.42	39	37	32	315.2	313	123	68	3	1	0	0	121	26	0	.215	17	89	2	3	2.8	.981
1899			13	9	.591	3.59	26	24	21	210.2	219	71	59	0	1	0	0	105	37	1	.352	14	47	4	1	2.5	.938
1900			10	10	.500	3.65	24	20	18	192.1	205	79	39	1	1	0	0	126	24	0	.190	9	60	4	0	3.0	.945
1901	STL	N	0	3	.000	6.60	3	3	1	15	24	14	3	0	0	0	0	6	2	0	.333	2	7	0	2	3.0	1.000
11 yrs.			164	169	.492	4.04	379	341	300	2964.1	3091	1203	889	12	7	5	3	*				244	690	57	24	2.6	.942

Ad Brennan

BRENNAN, ADDISON FOSTER
B. July 18, 1881, LaHarpe, Kans.   D. Jan. 7, 1962, Kansas City, Mo.   BL TL 5'11" 170 lbs.

Year	Team		W	L	PCT	ERA	G	GS	CG	IP	H	BB	SO	ShO	W	L	SV	AB	H	HR	BA	PO	A	E	DP	TC/G	FA
1910	PHI	N	3	0	1.000	2.33	19	5	2	73.1	72	28	28	0	1	0	0	25	7	0	.280	2	13	1	1	0.8	.938
1911			2	1	.667	3.57	5	3	1	22.2	22	12	12	0	1	0	0	9	2	0	.222	1	8	1	0	2.0	.900
1912			11	9	.550	3.57	27	19	13	174	185	49	78	1	2	1	2	59	15	1	.254	7	53	1	1	2.3	.984
1913			14	12	.538	2.39	40	25	12	207	204	46	94	1	4	1	1	67	11	0	.164	12	53	4	1	1.7	.942
1914	CHI	F	5	4	.556	3.57	16	11	5	85.2	84	21	31	1	0	1	0	32	8	0	.250	1	23	3	2	1.7	.889
1915			3	9	.250	3.74	19	13	7	106	117	30	40	2	0	0	0	27	5	0	.185	2	23	1	0	1.4	.962
1918	2 teams		WAS A (2G 0–0)			CLE A (1G 0–0)																						
"	total		0	0	–	4.32	3	1	0	8.1	10	8	0	0	1	0	0	1	0	0	.000	0	2	0	0	0.7	1.000
7 yrs.			38	35	.521	3.11	129	77	40	677	694	194	283	5	8	3	3	220	48	1	.218	25	175	11	5	1.6	.948

Don Brennan

BRENNAN, JAMES DONALD
B. Dec. 2, 1903, Augusta, Me.   D. Apr. 26, 1953, Boston, Mass.   BR TR 6' 210 lbs.

Year	Team		W	L	PCT	ERA	G	GS	CG	IP	H	BB	SO	ShO	W	L	SV	AB	H	HR	BA	PO	A	E	DP	TC/G	FA
1933	NY	A	5	1	.833	4.98	18	10	3	85	92	47	46	0	1	1	3	27	7	0	.259	3	23	2	2	1.6	.929
1934	CIN	N	4	3	.571	3.81	28	7	2	78	89	35	37	0	2	1	2	22	5	0	.227	1	15	1	0	0.6	.941
1935			5	5	.500	3.15	38	5	2	114.1	101	44	48	1	3	3	5	30	3	0	.100	4	14	1	0	0.5	.947
1936			5	2	.714	4.39	41	4	0	94.1	117	35	40	0	5	2	9	25	2	0	.080	1	19	2	1	0.5	.909
1937	2 teams		CIN N (10G 1–1)			NY N (6G 1–0)																						
"	total		2	1	.667	6.75	16	0	0	25.1	37	19	7	0	2	1	0	6	0	0	.000	1	4	0	0	0.3	1.000
5 yrs.			21	12	.636	4.19	141	26	7	397	436	180	172	1	12	8	19	110	17	0	.155	10	75	5	4	0.6	.944

Year	Team		W	L	PCT	ERA	G	GS	CG	IP	H	BB	SO	ShO	W	L	SV	AB	H	HR	BA	PO	A	E	DP	TC/G	FA
															Relief Pitching			**Batting**									

Don Brennan *continued*
WORLD SERIES

Year	Team		W	L	PCT	ERA	G	GS	CG	IP	H	BB	SO	ShO	W	L	SV	AB	H	HR	BA	PO	A	E	DP	TC/G	FA
1937	NY	N	0	0	–	0.00	2	0	0	3	1	1	1	0	0	0	0	0	0	0	–	0	0	0	0	0.0	–

Tom Brennan
BRENNAN, THOMAS MARTIN (The Gray Flamingo)
B. Oct. 30, 1952, Chicago, Ill. BR TR 6'1" 180 lbs.

Year	Team		W	L	PCT	ERA	G	GS	CG	IP	H	BB	SO	ShO	W	L	SV	AB	H	HR	BA	PO	A	E	DP	TC/G	FA
1981	CLE	A	2	2	.500	3.19	7	6	1	48	49	14	15	0	0	0	0	0	0	0	–	5	12	1	2	2.6	.944
1982			4	2	.667	4.27	30	4	0	92.2	112	10	46	0	1	2	2	0	0	0	–	9	13	0	2	0.7	1.000
1983			2	2	.500	3.86	11	5	1	39.2	45	8	21	1	0	0	0	0	0	0	–	4	4	1	0	0.8	.889
1984	CHI	A	0	1	.000	4.05	4	1	0	6.2	8	3	3	0	0	0	0	0	0	0	–	0	3	0	0	0.8	1.000
1985	LA	N	1	3	.250	7.39	12	4	0	31.2	41	11	17	0	1	1	0	8	1	0	.125	3	11	0	1	1.2	1.000
5 yrs.			9	10	.474	4.40	64	20	2	218.2	255	46	102	1	2	3	2	8	1	0	.125	21	43	2	5	1.0	.970

William Brennan
BRENNAN, WILLIAM RAYMOND
B. Jan. 15, 1963, Tampa, Fla. BR TR 6'3" 200 lbs.

Year	Team		W	L	PCT	ERA	G	GS	CG	IP	H	BB	SO	ShO	W	L	SV	AB	H	HR	BA	PO	A	E	DP	TC/G	FA
1988	LA	N	0	1	.000	6.75	4	2	0	9.1	13	6	7	0	0	0	0	2	0	0	.000	2	2	0	0	1.0	1.000

Jim Brenneman
BRENNEMAN, JAMES LeROY
B. Feb. 13, 1941, San Diego, Calif. BR TR 6'2" 180 lbs.

Year	Team		W	L	PCT	ERA	G	GS	CG	IP	H	BB	SO	ShO	W	L	SV	AB	H	HR	BA	PO	A	E	DP	TC/G	FA
1965	NY	A	0	0	–	18.00	3	0	0	2	5	3	2	0	0	0	0	0	0	0	–	0	0	0	0	0.0	–

Bert Brenner
BRENNER, DELBERT HENRY (Dutch)
B. July 18, 1887, Minneapolis, Minn. D. Apr. 11, 1971, St. Louis Park, Minn. BR TR 6' 175 lbs.

Year	Team		W	L	PCT	ERA	G	GS	CG	IP	H	BB	SO	ShO	W	L	SV	AB	H	HR	BA	PO	A	E	DP	TC/G	FA
1912	CLE	A	1	0	1.000	2.77	2	1	1	13	14	4	3	0	0	0	0	5	0	0	.000	1	5	0	0	3.0	1.000

Lynn Brenton
BRENTON, LYNN DAVIS (Buck, Herb)
B. Oct. 7, 1890, Peoria, Ill. D. Oct. 14, 1968, Los Angeles, Calif. BR TR 5'10" 165 lbs.

Year	Team		W	L	PCT	ERA	G	GS	CG	IP	H	BB	SO	ShO	W	L	SV	AB	H	HR	BA	PO	A	E	DP	TC/G	FA
1913	CLE	A	0	0	–	9.00	1	0	0	2	4	0	2	0	0	0	0	–	0	0	0	–	0	0	0	0	0.0	–
1915			2	3	.400	3.35	11	5	1	51	60	20	18	1	0	0	0	17	2	0	.118	2	12	1	0	1.4	.933
1920	CIN	N	2	1	.667	4.91	5	1	1	18.1	17	4	13	0	1	1	1	8	2	0	.250	0	12	0	1	2.4	1.000
1921			1	8	.111	4.05	17	9	2	60	80	17	19	0	0	0	1	15	2	0	.133	4	25	1	0	1.8	.967
4 yrs.			5	12	.294	3.97	34	15	4	131.1	161	41	52	1	1	1	2	40	6	0	.150	6	49	2	1	1.7	.965

Roger Bresnahan
BRESNAHAN, ROGER PHILIP (The Duke of Tralee)
B. June 11, 1879, Toledo, Ohio D. Dec. 4, 1944, Toledo, Ohio
Manager 1909-12, 1915.
Hall of Fame 1945. BR TR 5'9" 200 lbs.

Year	Team		W	L	PCT	ERA	G	GS	CG	IP	H	BB	SO	ShO	W	L	SV	AB	H	HR	BA	PO	A	E	DP	TC/G	FA
1897	WAS	N	4	0	1.000	3.95	6	5	3	41	52	10	12	1	0	0	0	16	6	0	.375	2	7	0	0	1.5	1.000
1901	BAL	N	0	1	.000	6.00	2	1	0	6	10	4	3	0	0	0	0	295	79	1	.268	0	2	1	0	1.5	.667
1910	STL	N	0	0	–	0.00	1	0	0	3.1	6	1	0	0	0	0	0	234	65	0	.278	0	3	0	1	3.0	1.000
3 yrs.			4	1	.800	3.93	9	6	3	50.1	68	15	15	1	0	0	0	*				2	12	1	1	1.7	.933

Rube Bressler
BRESSLER, RAYMOND BLOOM
B. Oct. 23, 1894, Coder, Pa. D. Nov. 7, 1966, Mt. Washington, Ohio BR TL 6' 187 lbs.

Year	Team		W	L	PCT	ERA	G	GS	CG	IP	H	BB	SO	ShO	W	L	SV	AB	H	HR	BA	PO	A	E	DP	TC/G	FA
1914	PHI	A	10	4	.714	1.77	29	10	8	147.2	112	56	96	1	3	2	2	51	11	0	.216	6	26	2	2	1.2	.941
1915			4	17	.190	5.20	32	20	7	178.1	183	118	69	1	0	4	0	55	8	1	.145	7	56	7	0	2.2	.900
1916			0	2	.000	6.60	4	2	0	15	16	14	8	0	0	0	0	5	1	0	.200	1	2	0	0	0.5	1.000
1917	CIN	N	0	0	–	6.00	2	1	0	9	15	5	2	0	0	0	0	5	1	0	.200	1	1	0	0	1.0	1.000
1918			8	5	.615	2.46	17	13	10	128	124	39	37	0	1	0	0	62	17	0	.274	4	51	1	2	3.3	.982
1919			2	4	.333	3.46	13	4	1	41.2	37	8	13	0	2	1	0	165	34	2	.206	2	15	1	0	1.4	.944
1920			2	0	1.000	1.77	10	2	1	20.1	24	2	4	1	1	0	0	30	8	0	.267	1	6	0	1	0.7	1.000
7 yrs.			26	32	.448	3.40	107	52	27	540	511	242	229	3	7	7	2	*				21	157	11	5	1.8	.942

Herb Brett
BRETT, HERBERT JAMES (Sparky)
B. May 23, 1900, Lawrenceville, Va. D. Nov. 25, 1974, St. Petersburg, Fla. BR TR 6' 175 lbs.

Year	Team		W	L	PCT	ERA	G	GS	CG	IP	H	BB	SO	ShO	W	L	SV	AB	H	HR	BA	PO	A	E	DP	TC/G	FA
1924	CHI	N	0	0	–	5.06	1	1	0	5.1	6	7	1	0	0	0	0	2	0	0	.000	0	0	0	0	0.0	–
1925			1	1	.500	3.63	10	1	0	17.1	12	3	6	0	1	0	0	1	0	0	.000	1	6	0	0	0.7	1.000
2 yrs.			1	1	.500	3.97	11	2	0	22.2	18	10	7	0	1	0	0	3	0	0	.000	1	6	0	0	0.6	1.000

Ken Brett
BRETT, KENNETH ALVEN
Brother of George Brett.
B. Sept. 18, 1948, Brooklyn, N. Y. BL TL 6' 190 lbs.

Year	Team		W	L	PCT	ERA	G	GS	CG	IP	H	BB	SO	ShO	W	L	SV	AB	H	HR	BA	PO	A	E	DP	TC/G	FA
1967	BOS	A	0	0	–	4.50	1	0	0	2	3	0	2	0	0	0	0	0	0	0	–	0	0	0	0	0.0	–
1969			2	3	.400	5.26	8	8	0	39.1	41	22	23	0	0	0	0	10	3	1	.300	2	6	0	0	1.0	1.000
1970			8	9	.471	4.08	41	14	1	139	118	79	155	1	3	5	2	41	13	2	.317	9	20	2	0	0.8	.935
1971			0	3	.000	5.34	29	2	0	59	57	35	57	0	0	0	0	10	2	0	.200	1	2	0	0	0.3	1.000
1972	MIL	A	7	12	.368	4.53	26	22	2	133	121	49	74	1	0	0	0	44	10	3	.227	6	15	3	1	0.9	.875
1973	PHI	N	13	9	.591	3.44	31	25	10	211.2	206	74	111	1	1	1	0	80	20	4	.250	13	39	0	4	1.7	1.000
1974	PIT	N	13	9	.591	3.30	27	27	10	191	192	52	96	3	0	0	0	87	27	2	.310	12	28	0	1	1.5	1.000
1975			9	5	.643	3.36	31	16	4	118	110	43	47	1	1	0	0	52	12	0	.231	13	18	1	0	1.4	.969
1976	2 teams		NY A (2G 0–0)						CHI A	(27G 10–12)																	
"	total		10	12	.455	3.28	29	26	16	203	173	76	92	0	0	0	2	12	1	0	.083	11	35	3	0	1.7	.939
1977	2 teams		CHI A (13G 6–4)						CAL A	(21G 7–10)																	
"	total		13	14	.481	4.52	34	34	7	225	258	53	80	0	0	0	0	–				11	48	2	6	1.8	.967
1978	CAL	A	3	5	.375	4.95	31	10	1	100	100	42	43	1	0	0	0	–				12	20	2	4	1.1	.941
1979	2 teams		MIN A (9G 0–0)						LA N	(30G 4–3)																	
"	total		4	3	.571	3.75	39	0	0	60	68	18	16	0	4	3	2	11	3	0	.273	10	17	0	1	0.7	1.000
1980	KC	A	0	0	–	0.00	8	0	0	13	8	5	4	0	0	0	0	0	0	0	–	0	3	0	0	0.4	1.000

Year	Team	W	L	PCT	ERA	G	GS	CG	IP	H	BB	SO	ShO	W	L	SV	AB	H	HR	BA	PO	A	E	DP	TC/G	FA

Header spans: **Relief Pitching** (W L SV), **Batting** (AB H HR)

Ken Brett *continued*

Year	Team	W	L	PCT	ERA	G	GS	CG	IP	H	BB	SO	ShO	W	L	SV	AB	H	HR	BA	PO	A	E	DP	TC/G	FA
1981		1	1	.500	4.22	22	0	0	32	35	14	7	0	1	1	2	0	0	0	—	5	6	0	1	0.5	1.000
14 yrs.		83	85	.494	3.93	349	184	51	1526	1490	562	807	9	11	13	11	*				104	263	13	18	1.1	.966

LEAGUE CHAMPIONSHIP SERIES

Year	Team	W	L	PCT	ERA	G	GS	CG	IP	H	BB	SO	ShO	W	L	SV	AB	H	HR	BA	PO	A	E	DP	TC/G	FA
1974	PIT N	0	0	—	7.71	1	0	0	2.1	3	2	1	0	0	0	0	1	0	0	.000	0	1	0	0	1.0	1.000
1975		0	0	—	0.00	2	0	0	2.1	1	0	1	0	0	0	0	0	0	0	—	0	0	0	0	0.0	—
2 yrs.		0	0	—	3.86	3	0	0	4.2	4	2	2	0	0	0	0	1	0	0	.000	0	1	0	0	0.3	1.000

WORLD SERIES

Year	Team	W	L	PCT	ERA	G	GS	CG	IP	H	BB	SO	ShO	W	L	SV	AB	H	HR	BA	PO	A	E	DP	TC/G	FA
1967	BOS A	0	0	—	0.00	2	0	0	1.1	0	1	1	0	0	0	0	0	0	0	—	0	0	0	0	0.0	—

Marv Breuer

BREUER, MARVIN HOWARD (Baby Face)
B. Apr. 29, 1914, Rolla, Mo.

BR TR 6'2" 185 lbs.

Year	Team	W	L	PCT	ERA	G	GS	CG	IP	H	BB	SO	ShO	W	L	SV	AB	H	HR	BA	PO	A	E	DP	TC/G	FA
1939	NY A	0	0	—	9.00	1	0	0	2	1	2	1	0	0	0	0	0	0	0	—	0	1	0	0	1.0	1.000
1940		8	9	.471	4.55	27	22	10	164	175	61	71	0	1	0	0	54	2	0	.037	5	26	1	2	1.2	.969
1941		9	7	.563	4.09	26	18	7	141	131	49	77	1	2	1	2	46	4	0	.087	2	23	1	0	1.0	.962
1942		8	9	.471	3.07	27	19	6	164.1	157	37	72	0	2	2	1	54	3	0	.056	12	22	4	2	1.4	.895
1943		0	1	.000	8.36	5	1	0	14	22	6	6	0	0	0	0	3	1	0	.333	0	3	0	0	0.6	1.000
5 yrs.		25	26	.490	4.03	86	60	23	484.1	487	154	226	1	5	3	3	157	10	0	.064	19	75	6	4	1.2	.940

WORLD SERIES

Year	Team	W	L	PCT	ERA	G	GS	CG	IP	H	BB	SO	ShO	W	L	SV	AB	H	HR	BA	PO	A	E	DP	TC/G	FA
1941	NY A	0	0	—	0.00	1	0	0	3	3	1	2	0	0	0	0	1	0	0	.000	0	1	0	0	1.0	1.000
1942		0	0	—	0.00	1	0	0	0	2	0	0	0	0	0	0	0	0	0	—	0	0	1	0	1.0	—
2 yrs.		0	0	—	0.00	2	0	0	3	5	1	2	0	0	0	0	1	0	0	.000	0	1	1	0	1.0	.500

Jack Brewer

BREWER, JOHN HERNDON (Buddy)
B. July 21, 1919, Los Angeles, Calif.

BR TR 6'2" 170 lbs.

Year	Team	W	L	PCT	ERA	G	GS	CG	IP	H	BB	SO	ShO	W	L	SV	AB	H	HR	BA	PO	A	E	DP	TC/G	FA
1944	NY N	1	4	.200	5.56	14	7	2	55	66	16	21	0	0	0	0	19	4	0	.211	2	8	2	0	0.9	.833
1945		8	6	.571	3.83	28	21	8	159.2	162	58	49	0	0	1	0	56	10	0	.179	4	21	2	1	1.0	.926
1946		0	0	—	13.50	1	0	0	2	3	2	3	0	0	0	0	0	0	0	—	0	0	0	0	0.0	—
3 yrs.		9	10	.474	4.36	43	28	10	216.2	231	76	73	0	0	1	0	75	14	0	.187	6	29	4	1	0.9	.897

Jim Brewer

BREWER, JAMES THOMAS
B. Nov. 14, 1937, Merced, Calif. D. Nov. 16, 1987, Tyler, Tex.

BL TL 6'1" 186 lbs.

Year	Team	W	L	PCT	ERA	G	GS	CG	IP	H	BB	SO	ShO	W	L	SV	AB	H	HR	BA	PO	A	E	DP	TC/G	FA
1960	CHI N	0	3	.000	5.82	5	4	0	21.2	25	6	7	0	0	0	0	6	1	0	.167	2	5	0	0	1.6	.875
1961		1	7	.125	5.82	36	11	0	86.2	116	21	57	0	0	1	0	22	4	0	.182	4	8	1	0	0.4	.923
1962		0	1	.000	9.53	6	1	0	5.2	10	3	1	0	0	1	0	0	0	0	—	1	1	0	1	0.3	1.000
1963		3	2	.600	4.89	29	1	0	49.2	59	15	35	0	3	1	0	6	0	0	.000	2	3	1	0	0.2	.833
1964	LA N	4	3	.571	3.00	34	5	1	93	79	25	63	1	2	2	1	22	6	0	.273	3	11	0	0	0.4	1.000
1965		3	2	.600	1.82	19	2	0	49.1	33	28	31	0	3	1	2	10	0	0	.000	1	11	0	0	0.6	1.000
1966		0	2	.000	3.68	13	0	0	22	17	11	8	0	0	2	2	0	0	0	—	1	5	0	1	0.5	1.000
1967		5	4	.556	2.68	30	11	0	100.2	78	31	74	0	1	0	1	22	1	0	.045	1	14	0	0	0.5	1.000
1968		8	3	.727	2.49	54	0	0	76	59	33	75	0	8	3	14	9	2	0	.222	4	11	1	1	0.3	.938
1969		7	6	.538	2.56	59	0	0	88	71	41	92	0	7	6	20	11	1	0	.091	6	13	1	1	0.3	.950
1970		7	6	.538	3.13	58	0	0	89	66	33	91	0	7	6	24	12	1	0	.083	0	14	1	0	0.3	.933
1971		6	5	.545	1.89	55	0	0	81	55	24	66	0	6	5	22	9	3	0	.333	2	15	2	1	0.3	.895
1972		8	7	.533	1.26	51	0	0	78.1	41	25	69	0	8	7	17	1	0	0	.000	1	11	1	1	0.3	.923
1973		6	8	.429	3.01	56	0	0	71.2	58	25	56	0	6	8	20	5	2	0	.400	1	11	1	0	0.2	.923
1974		4	4	.500	2.54	24	0	0	39	29	10	26	0	4	4	0	2	0	0	.000	0	4	0	0	0.2	1.000
1975	2 teams	LA N		(21G 3–1)		CAL A		(21G 1–0)																		
"	total	4	1	.800	3.46	42	0	0	67.2	82	23	43	0	4	1	3	3	0	0	.000	0	10	0	2	0.2	1.000
1976	CAL A	3	1	.750	2.70	13	0	0	20	20	6	16	0	3	1	2	0	0	0	—	2	2	0	0	0.3	1.000
17 yrs.		69	65	.515	3.07	584	35	1	1039.1	898	360	810	1	62	49	132	140	21	0	.150	30	150	10	10	0.3	.947

WORLD SERIES

Year	Team	W	L	PCT	ERA	G	GS	CG	IP	H	BB	SO	ShO	W	L	SV	AB	H	HR	BA	PO	A	E	DP	TC/G	FA
1965	LA N	0	0	—	4.50	1	0	0	2	3	0	1	0	0	0	0	0	0	0	—	0	0	0	0	0.0	—
1966		0	0	—	0.00	1	0	0	1	0	0	1	0	0	0	0	0	0	0	—	0	0	0	0	0.0	—
1974		0	0	—	0.00	1	0	0	.1	0	0	1	0	0	0	0	0	0	0	—	0	0	0	0	0.0	—
3 yrs.		0	0	—	2.70	3	0	0	3.1	3	0	3	0	0	0	0	0	0	0	—	0	0	0	0	0.0	—

Tom Brewer

BREWER, THOMAS AUSTIN
B. Sept. 3, 1931, Wadesboro, N. C.

BR TR 6'1" 175 lbs.

Year	Team	W	L	PCT	ERA	G	GS	CG	IP	H	BB	SO	ShO	W	L	SV	AB	H	HR	BA	PO	A	E	DP	TC/G	FA
1954	BOS A	10	9	.526	4.65	33	23	7	162.2	152	95	69	0	0	0	0	60	16	0	.267	9	18	3	1	0.9	.900
1955		11	10	.524	4.20	31	28	9	192.2	198	87	91	2	1	0	0	73	11	0	.151	15	44	1	4	1.9	.983
1956		19	9	.679	3.50	32	32	15	244.1	200	112	127	4	0	0	0	94	28	1	.298	28	52	1	2	2.5	.988
1957		16	13	.552	3.85	32	32	15	238.1	225	93	128	2	0	0	0	94	19	0	.202	20	65	3	3	2.8	.966
1958		12	12	.500	3.72	33	32	10	227.1	227	93	124	1	0	0	0	82	16	0	.195	13	57	4	7	2.2	.946
1959		10	12	.455	3.76	36	32	11	215.1	219	88	121	3	0	0	2	72	8	0	.111	23	49	2	1	2.1	.973
1960		10	15	.400	4.82	34	29	8	186.2	220	72	60	1	0	1	1	62	12	1	.194	15	45	2	3	1.8	.968
1961		3	2	.600	3.43	10	9	0	42	37	29	13	0	0	0	0	14	4	0	.286	2	13	0	1	1.5	1.000
8 yrs.		91	82	.526	4.00	241	217	75	1509.1	1478	669	733	13	2	1	3	551	114	3	.207	125	343	16	22	2.0	.967

Alan Brice

BRICE, ALAN HEALEY
B. Oct. 1, 1937, New York, N. Y.

BR TR 6'5" 215 lbs.

Year	Team	W	L	PCT	ERA	G	GS	CG	IP	H	BB	SO	ShO	W	L	SV	AB	H	HR	BA	PO	A	E	DP	TC/G	FA
1961	CHI A	0	1	.000	0.00	3	0	0	3.1	4	3	3	0	0	1	0	0	0	0	—	0	0	0	0	0.0	—

Ralph Brickner

BRICKNER, RALPH HAROLD (Brick)
B. May 2, 1925, Cincinnati, Ohio

BR TR 6'3½" 215 lbs.

Year	Team	W	L	PCT	ERA	G	GS	CG	IP	H	BB	SO	ShO	W	L	SV	AB	H	HR	BA	PO	A	E	DP	TC/G	FA
1952	BOS A	3	1	.750	2.18	14	1	0	33	32	11	9	0	3	1	1	8	2	0	.250	2	3	0	0	0.4	1.000

Year	Team	W	L	PCT	ERA	G	GS	CG	IP	H	BB	SO	ShO	Relief Pitching W	L	SV	Batting AB	H	HR	BA	PO	A	E	DP	TC/G	FA

Marshall Bridges

BRIDGES, MARSHALL (Sheriff)
B. June 2, 1931, Jackson, Miss.
BR TL 6'1" 165 lbs.
BB 1959-61

Year	Team	W	L	PCT	ERA	G	GS	CG	IP	H	BB	SO	ShO	W	L	SV	AB	H	HR	BA	PO	A	E	DP	TC/G	FA
1959	STL N	6	3	.667	4.26	27	4	1	76	67	37	76	0	4	2	1	23	5	1	.217	2	3	1	0	0.2	.833
1960	2 teams	STL N	(20G 2–2)			CIN N	(14G 4–0)																			
"	total	6	2	.750	2.38	34	1	0	56.2	47	23	53	0	6	1	3	10	1	0	.100	2	5	0	0	0.2	1.000
1961	CIN N	0	1	.000	7.84	13	0	0	20.2	26	11	17	0	0	1	0	2	0	0	.000	0	3	0	0	0.2	1.000
1962	NY A	8	4	.667	3.14	52	0	0	71.2	49	48	66	0	8	4	18	14	0	0	.000	5	18	1	3	0.5	.958
1963		2	0	1.000	3.82	23	0	0	33	27	30	35	0	2	0	1	0	0	0	–	2	11	0	3	0.6	1.000
1964	WAS A	0	3	.000	5.70	17	0	0	30	37	17	16	0	0	3	2	3	0	0	.000	1	5	0	0	0.4	1.000
1965		1	2	.333	2.67	40	0	0	57.1	62	25	39	0	1	2	0	7	1	0	.143	3	9	1	0	0.3	.923
7 yrs.		23	15	.605	3.75	206	5	1	345.1	315	191	302	0	21	13	25	59	7	1	.119	15	54	3	6	0.3	.958

WORLD SERIES

| 1962 | NY A | 0 | 0 | – | 4.91 | 2 | 0 | 0 | 3.2 | 4 | 2 | 3 | 0 | 0 | 0 | 0 | 0 | 0 | 0 | – | 0 | 1 | 0 | 0 | 0.5 | 1.000 |

Tommy Bridges

BRIDGES, THOMAS JEFFERSON DAVIS
B. Dec. 28, 1906, Gordonsville, Tenn.   D. Apr. 19, 1968, Nashville, Tenn.
BR TR 5'10½" 155 lbs.

Year	Team	W	L	PCT	ERA	G	GS	CG	IP	H	BB	SO	ShO	W	L	SV	AB	H	HR	BA	PO	A	E	DP	TC/G	FA
1930	DET A	3	2	.600	4.06	8	5	2	37.2	28	23	17	0	0	0	0	10	3	0	.300	0	7	1	0	1.0	.875
1931		8	16	.333	4.99	35	23	15	173	182	108	105	2	1	2	0	54	8	0	.148	5	27	2	0	1.0	.941
1932		14	12	.538	3.36	34	26	10	201	174	119	108	4	2	1	1	67	11	0	.164	5	34	2	1	1.2	.951
1933		14	12	.538	3.09	33	28	17	233	192	110	120	2	1	0	2	78	16	0	.205	9	49	3	5	1.8	.951
1934		22	11	.667	3.67	36	35	23	275	249	104	151	3	0	1	0	98	12	0	.122	6	42	2	2	1.4	.960
1935		21	10	.677	3.51	36	34	23	274.1	277	113	163	4	0	1	1	109	26	0	.239	15	39	2	4	1.6	.964
1936		23	11	.676	3.60	39	38	26	294.2	289	115	175	5	0	0	0	118	25	0	.212	19	51	2	3	1.8	.972
1937		15	12	.556	4.07	34	31	18	245.1	267	91	138	3	1	0	0	96	23	0	.240	14	46	1	2	1.8	.984
1938		13	9	.591	4.59	25	20	13	151	171	58	101	1	0	1	1	54	7	0	.130	8	19	2	0	1.3	.931
1939		17	7	.708	3.50	29	26	16	198	186	61	129	2	0	0	0	71	14	0	.197	8	28	3	2	1.3	.923
1940		12	9	.571	3.37	29	28	12	197.2	171	88	133	2	1	0	0	68	12	0	.176	4	30	2	0	1.2	.944
1941		9	12	.429	3.41	25	22	10	147.2	128	70	90	1	1	0	0	47	4	0	.085	15	30	1	1	1.8	.978
1942		9	7	.563	2.74	23	22	11	174	164	61	97	2	0	0	1	63	6	0	.095	15	32	1	2	2.1	.979
1943		12	7	.632	2.39	25	22	11	191.2	159	61	124	3	0	1	0	64	14	0	.219	18	28	0	1	1.8	1.000
1945		1	0	1.000	3.27	4	1	0	11	14	2	6	0	0	0	0	3	0	0	.000	2	4	0	0	1.5	1.000
1946		1	1	.500	5.91	9	1	0	21.1	24	8	17	0	0	0	0	3	0	0	.000	1	3	0	0	0.4	1.000
16 yrs.		194	138	.584	3.57	424	362	207	2826.1	2675	1192	1674	33	8	10	10	1003	181	0	.180	144	469	24	23	1.5	.962

WORLD SERIES

1934	DET A	1	1	.500	3.63	3	2	1	17.1	21	4	12	0	0	0	0	7	1	0	.143	0	2	0	0	0.7	1.000
1935		2	0	1.000	2.50	2	2	2	18	18	4	9	0	0	0	0	8	1	0	.125	1	5	0	1	3.0	1.000
1940		1	0	1.000	3.00	1	1	1	9	10	1	5	0	0	0	0	3	0	0	.000	0	1	0	0	1.0	1.000
1945		0	0	–	16.20	1	0	0	1.2	3	3	1	0	0	0	0	0	0	0	–	0	0	0	0	0.0	–
4 yrs.		4	1	.800	3.52	7	5	4	46	52	9	27	0	0	0	0	18	2	0	.111	1	8	0	1	1.3	1.000

Buttons Briggs

BRIGGS, HERBERT THEODORE
B. July 8, 1875, Poughkeepsie, N. Y.   D. Feb. 18, 1911, Cleveland, Ohio
BR TR 6'1" 180 lbs.

Year	Team	W	L	PCT	ERA	G	GS	CG	IP	H	BB	SO	ShO	W	L	SV	AB	H	HR	BA	PO	A	E	DP	TC/G	FA
1896	CHI N	12	8	.600	4.31	26	21	19	194	202	108	84	0	0	0	1	78	10	0	.128	6	29	4	0	1.5	.897
1897		4	17	.190	5.26	22	22	21	186.2	246	85	60	0	0	0	0	81	13	0	.160	8	35	1	0	2.0	.977
1898		1	3	.250	5.70	4	4	3	30	38	10	14	0	0	0	0	14	6	0	.429	1	6	2	0	2.3	.778
1904		19	11	.633	2.05	34	30	28	277	252	77	112	3	1	0	2	94	16	1	.170	16	54	0	2	2.1	1.000
1905		8	8	.500	2.14	20	20	13	168	141	52	68	5	0	0	0	57	3	0	.053	11	36	2	0	2.5	.959
5 yrs.		44	47	.484	3.41	106	97	84	855.2	879	332	338	8	1	1	3	324	48	1	.148	42	160	9	2	2.0	.957

Johnny Briggs

BRIGGS, JONATHAN TIFT
B. Jan. 24, 1934, Natoma, Calif.
BR TR 5'10" 175 lbs.

Year	Team	W	L	PCT	ERA	G	GS	CG	IP	H	BB	SO	ShO	W	L	SV	AB	H	HR	BA	PO	A	E	DP	TC/G	FA
1956	CHI N	0	0	–	1.69	3	0	0	5.1	5	4	1	0	0	0	0	0	0	0	–	0	1	0	0	0.3	1.000
1957		0	1	.000	12.46	3	0	0	4.1	7	3	1	0	0	1	0	0	0	0	–	0	0	0	0	0.0	–
1958		5	5	.500	4.52	20	17	3	95.2	99	45	46	1	0	0	0	35	9	0	.257	7	12	2	0	1.1	.905
1959	CLE A	0	1	.000	2.13	4	1	0	12.2	12	3	5	0	0	1	0	2	0	0	.000	2	1	0	0	0.8	1.000
1960	2 teams	CLE A	(21G 4–2)			KC A	(8G 0–2)																			
"	total	4	4	.500	6.42	29	3	0	47.2	51	27	27	0	1	2	1	11	1	0	.091	2	3	1	0	0.2	.833
5 yrs.		9	11	.450	5.00	59	21	3	165.2	174	82	80	1	1	3	1	48	10	0	.208	11	17	3	0	0.5	.903

Nellie Briles

BRILES, NELSON KELLEY
B. Aug. 5, 1943, Dorris, Calif.
BR TR 5'11" 195 lbs.

Year	Team	W	L	PCT	ERA	G	GS	CG	IP	H	BB	SO	ShO	W	L	SV	AB	H	HR	BA	PO	A	E	DP	TC/G	FA
1965	STL N	3	3	.500	3.50	37	3	0	82.1	79	26	52	0	2	2	4	15	2	0	.133	6	8	0	1	0.4	1.000
1966		4	15	.211	3.21	49	17	0	154	162	54	100	0	1	6	6	38	3	0	.079	9	29	1	3	0.8	.974
1967		14	5	.737	2.43	49	14	4	155.1	139	40	94	2	4	3	6	40	6	0	.150	10	18	2	1	0.6	.933
1968		19	11	.633	2.81	33	33	13	243.2	251	55	141	4	0	0	0	80	11	0	.138	15	31	2	1	1.5	.958
1969		15	13	.536	3.51	36	33	10	228	218	63	126	3	0	0	0	76	8	1	.105	13	34	3	1	1.4	.940
1970		6	7	.462	6.22	30	19	2	107	129	36	59	1	1	2	0	39	7	0	.179	6	7	0	0	0.4	1.000
1971	PIT N	8	4	.667	3.04	37	14	4	136	131	35	76	2	1	1	0	39	10	1	.256	13	13	1	1	0.7	.963
1972		14	11	.560	3.08	28	27	9	195.2	185	43	120	2	0	0	0	70	11	0	.157	11	26	1	1	1.4	.974
1973		14	13	.519	2.84	33	33	7	218.2	201	51	94	3	0	0	0	72	14	0	.194	14	35	1	3	1.5	.980
1974	KC A	5	7	.417	4.02	18	17	3	103	118	21	41	0	0	0	0	0	0	0	–	8	12	1	1	1.2	.952
1975		6	6	.500	4.26	24	16	3	112	127	25	73	1	0	0	0	0	0	0	–	11	15	1	1	1.1	.963
1976	TEX A	11	9	.550	3.26	32	31	7	210	224	47	98	1	0	0	0	0	0	0	–	10	18	0	0	0.9	1.000
1977	2 teams	TEX A	(30G 6–4)			BAL A	(2G 0–0)																			
"	total	6	4	.600	4.17	32	15	2	112.1	119	30	59	1	2	0	0	0	0	0	–	3	13	0	0	0.5	1.000
1978	BAL A	4	4	.500	4.64	16	8	1	54.1	58	21	30	0	3	0	0	0	0	0	–	2	4	1	0	0.4	.857
14 yrs.		129	112	.535	3.43	454	279	64	2112.1	2141	547	1163	17	16	15	22	469	72	3	.154	131	263	14	17	0.9	.966

LEAGUE CHAMPIONSHIP SERIES

| 1972 | PIT N | 0 | 0 | – | 3.00 | 1 | 1 | 0 | 6 | 6 | 1 | 3 | 0 | 0 | 0 | 0 | 2 | 0 | 0 | .000 | 1 | 0 | 0 | 0 | 2.0 | 1.000 |

WORLD SERIES

| 1967 | STL N | 1 | 0 | 1.000 | 1.64 | 2 | 1 | 1 | 11 | 7 | 1 | 4 | 0 | 0 | 0 | 0 | 3 | 0 | 0 | .000 | 0 | 4 | 0 | 0 | 2.0 | 1.000 |

Year	Team		W	L	PCT	ERA	G	GS	CG	IP	H	BB	SO	ShO	W	L	SV	AB	H	HR	BA	PO	A	E	DP	TC/G	FA
															Relief Pitching			**Batting**									

Nellie Briles *continued*

Year	Team		W	L	PCT	ERA	G	GS	CG	IP	H	BB	SO	ShO	W	L	SV	AB	H	HR	BA	PO	A	E	DP	TC/G	FA
1968			0	1	.000	5.56	2	2	0	11.1	13	4	7	0	0	0	0	4	0	0	.000	0	2	0	0	1.0	1.000
1971	PIT	N	1	0	1.000	0.00	1	1	1	9	2	2	2	1	0	0	0	2	1	0	.500	0	1	0	0	1.0	1.000
3 yrs.			2	1	.667	2.59	5	4	2	31.1	22	7	13	1	0	0	0	9	1	0	.111	0	7	0	0	1.4	1.000

Frank Brill

BRILL, FRANCIS HASBROUCK
Born Francis Hasbrouck Briell.
B. Mar. 28, 1864, Astoria, N. Y.   D. Nov. 19, 1944, Flushing, N. Y.

BR TR 5'8"   155 lbs.

Year	Team		W	L	PCT	ERA	G	GS	CG	IP	H	BB	SO	ShO	W	L	SV	AB	H	HR	BA	PO	A	E	DP	TC/G	FA
1884	DET	N	2	10	.167	5.50	12	12	12	103	148	26	18	1	0	0	0	44	6	0	.136	5	14	1	0	1.7	.950

Jim Brillheart

BRILLHEART, JAMES BENSON (Buck)
B. Sept. 28, 1903, Dublin, Va.   D. Sept. 2, 1972, Radford, Va.

BR TL 5'11"   170 lbs.

Year	Team		W	L	PCT	ERA	G	GS	CG	IP	H	BB	SO	ShO	W	L	SV	AB	H	HR	BA	PO	A	E	DP	TC/G	FA
1922	WAS	A	4	6	.400	3.61	31	10	3	119.2	120	72	47	0	0	2	1	36	3	0	.083	3	22	4	0	0.9	.862
1923			0	1	.000	7.00	12	0	0	18	27	12	8	0	0	1	0	2	0	0	.000	2	6	1	0	0.8	.889
1927	CHI	N	4	2	.667	4.13	32	12	4	128.2	140	38	36	0	0	0	0	44	1	0	.023	1	25	0	3	0.8	1.000
1931	BOS	A	0	0	—	5.49	11	1	0	19.2	27	15	7	0	0	0	0	4	2	1	.500	1	7	0	0	0.7	1.000
4 yrs.			8	9	.471	4.19	86	23	7	286	314	137	98	0	0	3	1	86	6	1	.070	7	60	5	3	0.8	.931

Lou Brissie

BRISSIE, LELAND VICTOR
B. June 5, 1924, Anderson, S. C.

BL TL 6'4½"   210 lbs.

Year	Team		W	L	PCT	ERA	G	GS	CG	IP	H	BB	SO	ShO	W	L	SV	AB	H	HR	BA	PO	A	E	DP	TC/G	FA
1947	PHI	A	0	1	.000	6.43	1	1	0	7	9	5	4	0	0	0	0	2	0	0	.000	1	1	0	0	2.0	1.000
1948			14	10	.583	4.13	39	25	11	194	202	95	127	0	4	2	5	76	18	0	.237	8	22	0	1	0.8	1.000
1949			16	11	.593	4.28	34	29	18	229.1	220	118	118	0	1	0	3	90	24	0	.267	6	21	0	3	0.8	1.000
1950			7	19	.269	4.02	46	31	15	246	237	117	101	2	0	1	8	87	15	0	.172	7	41	2	6	1.1	.960
1951	2 teams		PHI A	(2G 0–2)		CLE A	(54G 4–3)																					
"	total		4	5	.444	3.58	56	6	1	125.2	110	69	53	0	3	1	9	28	7	0	.250	4	12	3	3	0.3	.889
1952	CLE	A	3	2	.600	3.48	42	1	0	82.2	68	34	28	0	3	1	2	12	3	0	.250	3	21	0	0	0.6	1.000
1953			0	0	—	7.62	16	0	0	13	21	13	5	0	0	0	2	0	0	0	—	0	2	0	0	0.1	1.000
7 yrs.			44	48	.478	4.07	234	93	45	897.2	867	451	436	2	11	5	29	295	67	0	.227	29	120	4	13	0.7	.974

John Brittin

BRITTIN, JOHN ALBERT
B. Mar. 4, 1924, Athens, Ill.

BR TR 5'11"   175 lbs.

Year	Team		W	L	PCT	ERA	G	GS	CG	IP	H	BB	SO	ShO	W	L	SV	AB	H	HR	BA	PO	A	E	DP	TC/G	FA
1950	PHI	N	0	0	—	4.50	3	0	0	4	2	3	3	0	0	0	0	0	0	0	—	0	1	0	0	0.3	1.000
1951			0	0	—	9.00	3	0	0	4	5	6	3	0	0	0	0	0	0	0	—	0	1	0	0	0.3	1.000
2 yrs.			0	0	—	6.75	6	0	0	8	7	9	6	0	0	0	0	0	0	0	—	0	2	0	0	0.3	1.000

Jim Britton

BRITTON, JAMES ALLAN
B. Mar. 25, 1944, North Tonawanda, N. Y.

BR TR 6'5"   225 lbs.

Year	Team		W	L	PCT	ERA	G	GS	CG	IP	H	BB	SO	ShO	W	L	SV	AB	H	HR	BA	PO	A	E	DP	TC/G	FA
1967	ATL	N	0	2	.000	6.08	2	2	0	13.1	15	2	4	0	0	0	0	4	0	0	.000	2	1	1	0	2.0	.750
1968			4	6	.400	3.09	34	9	2	90.1	81	34	61	2	2	2	3	21	3	0	.143	2	16	0	1	0.5	1.000
1969			7	5	.583	3.78	24	13	2	88	69	49	60	1	0	0	1	21	4	0	.190	1	12	1	0	0.6	.929
1971	MON	N	2	3	.400	5.67	16	6	0	46	49	27	23	0	1	0	0	9	0	0	.000	2	4	0	0	0.4	1.000
4 yrs.			13	16	.448	4.01	76	30	4	237.2	214	112	148	3	3	2	4	55	7	0	.127	7	33	2	1	0.6	.952

LEAGUE CHAMPIONSHIP SERIES

Year	Team		W	L	PCT	ERA	G	GS	CG	IP	H	BB	SO	ShO	W	L	SV	AB	H	HR	BA	PO	A	E	DP	TC/G	FA
1969	ATL	N	0	0	—	0.00	1	0	0	.1	0	1	0	0	0	0	0	0	0	0	—	0	0	0	0	0.0	—

Tony Brizzolara

BRIZZOLARA, ANTHONY JOHN
B. Jan. 14, 1957, Santa Monica, Calif.

BR TR 6'5"   215 lbs.

Year	Team		W	L	PCT	ERA	G	GS	CG	IP	H	BB	SO	ShO	W	L	SV	AB	H	HR	BA	PO	A	E	DP	TC/G	FA
1979	ATL	N	6	9	.400	5.30	20	19	2	107	133	33	64	0	0	0	0	35	1	0	.029	7	15	1	1	1.2	.957
1983			1	0	1.000	3.54	14	0	0	20.1	22	6	17	0	1	0	1	0	0	0	—	2	0	0	0	0.1	1.000
1984			1	2	.333	5.28	10	4	0	29	33	13	17	0	0	1	0	7	0	0	.000	4	3	0	0	0.7	1.000
3 yrs.			8	11	.421	5.07	44	23	2	156.1	188	52	98	0	1	1	1	42	1	0	.024	13	18	1	1	0.7	.969

Johnny Broaca

BROACA, JOHN JOSEPH
B. Oct. 3, 1909, Lawrence, Mass.   D. May 16, 1985, Lawrence, Mass.

BR TR 5'11"   190 lbs.

Year	Team		W	L	PCT	ERA	G	GS	CG	IP	H	BB	SO	ShO	W	L	SV	AB	H	HR	BA	PO	A	E	DP	TC/G	FA
1934	NY	A	12	9	.571	4.16	26	24	13	177.1	203	65	74	1	0	0	0	66	2	0	.030	3	25	1	1	1.1	.966
1935			15	7	.682	3.58	29	27	14	201	199	79	78	2	1	1	0	80	12	0	.150	4	28	2	1	1.2	.941
1936			12	7	.632	4.24	37	27	12	206	235	66	84	1	0	0	3	82	9	0	.110	6	29	0	0	0.9	1.000
1937			1	4	.200	4.70	7	6	3	44	58	17	9	0	0	0	0	14	0	0	.000	1	4	1	0	0.9	.833
1939	CLE	A	4	2	.667	4.70	22	2	0	46	53	28	13	0	4	1	0	12	0	0	.000	0	8	1	2	0.4	.889
5 yrs.			44	29	.603	4.08	121	86	42	674.1	748	255	258	4	5	2	3	254	23	0	.091	14	94	5	4	0.9	.956

Pete Broberg

BROBERG, PETER SVEN
B. Mar. 2, 1950, West Palm Beach, Fla.

BR TR 6'3"   205 lbs.

Year	Team		W	L	PCT	ERA	G	GS	CG	IP	H	BB	SO	ShO	W	L	SV	AB	H	HR	BA	PO	A	E	DP	TC/G	FA
1971	WAS	A	5	9	.357	3.46	18	18	7	125	104	53	89	1	0	0	0	44	5	1	.114	10	12	0	1	1.2	1.000
1972	TEX	A	5	12	.294	4.30	39	25	3	175.2	153	85	133	2	0	1	1	51	4	0	.078	16	27	1	2	1.1	.977
1973			5	9	.357	5.60	22	20	6	119	130	66	57	1	0	0	0	0	0	0	—	5	18	1	1	1.1	.958
1974			0	4	.000	8.07	12	2	0	29	29	13	15	0	0	2	0	0	0	0	—	2	4	1	0	0.6	.857
1975	MIL	A	14	16	.467	4.13	38	32	7	220.1	219	106	100	2	2	0	0	0	0	0	—	7	36	4	4	1.2	.915
1976			1	7	.125	4.97	20	11	1	92.1	99	72	28	0	0	0	0	0	0	0	—	4	11	1	0	0.8	.938
1977	CHI	N	1	2	.333	4.75	22	0	0	36	34	18	20	0	1	2	0	6	0	0	.000	1	7	0	0	0.4	1.000
1978	OAK	A	10	12	.455	4.62	35	26	2	165.2	174	65	94	0	0	0	0	0	0	0	—	8	28	0	0	1.0	1.000
8 yrs.			41	71	.366	4.56	206	134	26	963	942	478	536	6	3	5	2	101	9	1	.089	53	143	8	9	1.0	.961

Lew Brockett

BROCKETT, LEWIS ALBERT (King)
B. July 23, 1880, Brownsville, Ill.   D. Sept. 19, 1960, Norris City, Ill.

BR TR 5'10½"   168 lbs.

Year	Team		W	L	PCT	ERA	G	GS	CG	IP	H	BB	SO	ShO	W	L	SV	AB	H	HR	BA	PO	A	E	DP	TC/G	FA
1907	NY	A	1	2	.333	6.22	8	4	1	46.1	58	26	13	0	0	0	0	22	4	0	.182	1	10	2	1	1.6	.846
1909			10	8	.556	2.37	26	18	10	152	148	59	70	3	2	0	1	60	17	0	.283	10	71	6	4	3.3	.931

Year	Team		W	L	PCT	ERA	G	GS	CG	IP	H	BB	SO	ShO	Relief Pitching W	L	SV	Batting AB	H	HR	BA	PO	A	E	DP	TC/G	FA

Lew Brockett *continued*

| 1911 | | | 2 | 4 | .333 | 4.66 | 16 | 8 | 2 | 75.1 | 73 | 39 | 25 | 0 | 1 | 1 | 0 | 39 | 12 | 0 | .308 | 2 | 25 | 2 | 1 | 1.8 | .931 |
| 3 yrs. | | | 13 | 14 | .481 | 3.65 | 50 | 30 | 13 | 273.2 | 279 | 124 | 108 | 3 | 3 | 1 | 1 | 121 | 33 | 0 | .273 | 13 | 106 | 10 | 6 | 2.6 | .922 |

Dick Brodowski

BRODOWSKI, RICHARD STANLEY
B. July 26, 1932, Bayonne, N. J.

BR TR 6'1" 182 lbs.

1952	BOS	A	5	5	.500	4.40	20	12	4	114.2	111	50	42	0	0	1	0	39	8	1	.205	11	20	1	1	1.6	.969
1955			1	0	1.000	5.63	16	0	0	32	36	25	10	0	1	0	0	10	5	1	.500	5	7	0	0	0.8	1.000
1956	WAS	A	0	3	.000	9.17	7	3	1	17.2	31	12	8	0	0	3	0	5	0	0	.000	2	3	0	0	0.7	1.000
1957			0	1	.000	11.12	6	0	0	11.1	12	10	4	0	0	1	0	1	0	0	.000	1	2	0	0	0.5	1.000
1958	CLE	A	1	0	1.000	0.00	5	0	0	10	3	6	12	0	1	0	0	1	0	0	.000	0	1	0	0	0.2	1.000
1959			2	2	.500	1.80	18	0	0	30	19	21	9	0	2	2	5	6	2	0	.333	4	3	2	0	0.5	.778
6 yrs.			9	11	.450	4.76	72	15	5	215.2	212	124	85	0	4	4	5	62	15	2	.242	23	36	3	1	0.9	.952

Ernie Broglio

BROGLIO, ERNEST GILBERT
B. Aug. 27, 1935, Berkeley, Calif.

BR TR 6'2" 200 lbs.

1959	STL	N	7	12	.368	4.72	35	25	6	181.1	174	89	133	3	0	3	0	61	6	0	.098	11	30	0	2	1.2	1.000
1960			21	9	.700	2.74	52	24	9	226.1	172	100	188	3	7	2	0	68	14	0	.206	17	35	1	5	1.0	.981
1961			9	12	.429	4.12	29	26	7	174.2	166	75	113	2	0	1	0	62	9	0	.145	13	27	1	0	1.4	.976
1962			12	9	.571	3.00	34	30	11	222.1	193	93	132	4	1	1	0	72	10	0	.139	19	39	2	3	1.8	.967
1963			18	8	.692	2.99	39	35	11	250	202	90	145	5	2	1	0	89	10	0	.112	30	37	4	4	1.8	.944
1964	2 teams		STL N		(11G 3–5)		CHI N		(18G 4–7)																		
"	total		7	12	.368	3.82	29	27	6	169.2	176	56	82	1	0	0	1	56	12	0	.214	12	24	1	0	1.3	.973
1965	CHI	N	1	6	.143	6.93	26	6	0	50.2	63	46	22	0	1	3	0	4	0	0	.000	2	5	0	0	0.3	1.000
1966			2	6	.250	6.35	15	11	2	62.1	70	38	34	0	0	0	1	19	7	0	.368	2	18	0	2	1.3	1.000
8 yrs.			77	74	.510	3.74	259	184	52	1337.1	1216	587	849	18	11	11	2	431	68	0	.158	106	215	9	16	1.3	.973

Ken Brondell

BRONDELL, KENNETH LeROY
B. Oct. 17, 1921, Bradshaw, Neb.

BR TR 6'1" 195 lbs.

| 1944 | NY | N | 0 | 1 | .000 | 8.38 | 7 | 2 | 1 | 19.1 | 27 | 8 | 1 | 0 | 0 | 0 | 0 | 4 | 0 | 0 | .000 | 2 | 1 | 0 | 0 | 0.4 | 1.000 |

Jim Bronstad

BRONSTAD, JAMES WARREN
B. June 22, 1936, Fort Worth, Tex.

BR TR 6'3" 196 lbs.

1959	NY	A	0	3	.000	5.22	16	3	0	29.1	34	13	14	0	0	1	2	5	0	0	.000	3	6	0	0	0.6	1.000
1963	WAS	A	1	3	.250	5.65	25	0	0	57.1	66	22	22	0	1	3	1	12	0	0	.000	7	14	0	2	0.8	1.000
1964			0	1	.000	5.14	4	0	0	7	10	2	9	0	0	1	0	0	0	0	—	0	0	0	0	0.0	—
3 yrs.			1	7	.125	5.48	45	3	0	93.2	110	37	45	0	1	5	3	17	0	0	.000	10	20	0	2	0.7	1.000

Ed Brookens

BROOKENS, EDWARD DWAIN (Ike)
B. Jan. 3, 1949, Chambersburg, Pa.

BR TR 6'5" 170 lbs.

| 1975 | DET | A | 0 | 0 | — | 5.40 | 3 | 0 | 0 | 10 | 11 | 5 | 8 | 0 | 0 | 0 | 0 | 0 | 0 | 0 | — | 0 | 2 | 0 | 0 | 0.7 | 1.000 |

Harry Brooks

BROOKS, HARRY FRANK
B. Nov. 30, 1865, Philadelphia, Pa. D. Dec. 5, 1945, Philadelphia, Pa.

| 1886 | NY | AA | 0 | 1 | .000 | 36.00 | 1 | 1 | 0 | 2 | 9 | 2 | 0 | 0 | 0 | 0 | 0 | 1 | 0 | 0 | .000 | 0 | 0 | 0 | 0 | 0.0 | — |

Jim Brosnan

BROSNAN, JAMES PATRICK (Professor)
B. Oct. 24, 1929, Cincinnati, Ohio

BR TR 6'4" 197 lbs.

1954	CHI	N	1	0	1.000	9.45	18	0	0	33.1	44	18	17	0	1	0	0	8	1	0	.125	3	10	1	2	0.8	.929
1956			5	9	.357	3.79	30	10	1	95	95	45	51	1	3	4	1	22	4	0	.182	8	11	0	0	0.6	1.000
1957			5	5	.500	3.38	41	5	1	98.2	79	46	73	0	4	4	0	20	5	0	.250	4	19	1	1	0.6	.958
1958	2 teams		CHI N		(8G 3–4)		STL N		(33G 8–4)																		
"	total		11	8	.579	3.35	41	20	4	166.2	148	79	89	0	1	1	7	50	5	0	.100	12	30	1	3	1.0	.977
1959	2 teams		STL N		(20G 1–3)		CIN N		(26G 8–3)																		
"	total		9	6	.600	3.79	46	10	1	116.1	113	41	74	1	5	3	4	30	3	0	.100	9	23	0	2	0.7	.970
1960	CIN	N	7	2	.778	2.36	57	2	0	99	79	22	62	0	7	2	12	15	3	1	.200	7	14	0	2	0.4	1.000
1961			10	4	.714	3.04	53	0	0	80	77	18	40	0	10	4	16	13	2	0	.154	9	18	3	0	0.6	.900
1962			4	4	.500	3.34	48	0	0	64.2	76	18	51	0	4	4	13	6	0	0	.000	4	8	1	0	0.3	.923
1963	2 teams		CIN N		(6G 0–1)		CHI A		(45G 3–8)																		
"	total		3	9	.250	3.13	51	0	0	77.2	79	25	50	0	3	9	14	13	4	0	.308	3	13	0	1	0.3	1.000
9 yrs.			55	47	.539	3.54	385	47	7	831.1	790	312	507	2	41	31	67	177	27	1	.153	59	146	8	12	0.6	.962

WORLD SERIES

| 1961 | CIN | N | 0 | 0 | — | 7.50 | 3 | 0 | 0 | 6 | 9 | 4 | 5 | 0 | 0 | 0 | 0 | 0 | 0 | 0 | — | 0 | 0 | 0 | 0 | 0.0 | — |

Frank Brosseau

BROSSEAU, FRANKLIN LEE
B. July 31, 1944, Drayton, N. D.

BR TR 6'1" 180 lbs.

1969	PIT	N	0	0	—	9.00	2	0	0	2	2	2	2	0	0	0	0	0	0	0	—	0	0	0	0	0.0	—
1971			0	0	—	0.00	1	0	0	2	1	0	0	0	0	0	0	0	0	0	—	1	1	0	0	2.0	1.000
2 yrs.			0	0	—	4.50	3	0	0	4	3	2	2	0	0	0	0	0	0	0	—	1	1	0	0	0.7	1.000

Dan Brouthers

BROUTHERS, DENNIS JOSEPH (Big Dan)
B. May 8, 1858, Sylvan Lake, N. Y. D. Aug. 2, 1932, East Orange, N. J.
Hall of Fame 1945.

BL TL 6'2" 207 lbs.

1879	TRO	N	0	2	.000	5.57	3	2	2	21	35	8	6	0	0	0	0	168	46	4	.274	0	1	1	0	0.7	.500
1883	BUF	N	0	0	—	31.50	1	0	0	2	9	3	2	0	0	0	0	425	159	3	.374	0	0	0	0	0.0	—
2 yrs.			0	2	.000	7.83	4	2	2	23	44	11	8	0	0	0	0	*				0	1	1	0	0.5	.500

Frank Brower

BROWER, FRANK WILLARD (Turkeyfoot)
B. Mar. 26, 1893, Gainesville, Va. D. Nov. 20, 1960, Baltimore, Md.

BL TR 6'2" 180 lbs.

| 1924 | CLE | A | 0 | 0 | — | 0.93 | 4 | 0 | 0 | 9.2 | 7 | 4 | 0 | 0 | 0 | 0 | 0 | * | | | | 1 | 0 | 1 | 0 | 0.3 | 1.000 |

Year	Team		W	L	PCT	ERA	G	GS	CG	IP	H	BB	SO	ShO	Relief Pitching			Batting				PO	A	E	DP	TC/G	FA
															W	L	SV	AB	H	HR	BA						

Alton Brown
BROWN, ALTON LEO (Deacon)
B. Apr. 16, 1925, Norfolk, Va. BR TR 6'2" 195 lbs.

Year	Team		W	L	PCT	ERA	G	GS	CG	IP	H	BB	SO	ShO	W	L	SV	AB	H	HR	BA	PO	A	E	DP	TC/G	FA
1951	WAS	A	0	0	–	9.26	7	0	0	11.2	14	12	7	0	0	0	0	1	0	0	.000	0	1	0	0	0.1	1.000

Boardwalk Brown
BROWN, CARROLL WILLIAM
B. Feb. 20, 1887, Woodbury, N. J. D. Feb. 8, 1977, Burlington, N. J. BR TR 6'1½" 178 lbs.

Year	Team		W	L	PCT	ERA	G	GS	CG	IP	H	BB	SO	ShO	W	L	SV	AB	H	HR	BA	PO	A	E	DP	TC/G	FA
1911	PHI	A	0	1	.000	4.50	2	1	1	12	12	2	6	0	0	0	0	4	0	0	.000	1	3	0	0	2.0	1.000
1912			13	11	.542	3.66	34	24	16	199	204	87	64	3	2	2	1	76	11	0	.145	10	72	3	2	2.5	.965
1913			17	11	.607	2.94	43	35	11	235.1	200	87	70	3	1	3	1	82	13	1	.159	7	65	5	2	1.8	.935
1914	2 teams	PHI A	(15G 1–6)				NY A		(20G 5–5)																		
"	total		6	11	.353	3.54	35	22	10	188.1	187	68	77	0	1	1	1	64	8	0	.125	10	69	5	1	2.4	.940
1915	NY	A	2	6	.250	4.10	19	10	5	96.2	95	47	34	0	0	0	1	32	6	0	.188	3	28	3	3	1.8	.912
5 yrs.			38	40	.487	3.47	133	92	43	731.1	698	291	251	6	4	6	4	258	38	1	.147	31	237	16	8	2.1	.944

Bob Brown
BROWN, ROBERT M.
B. 1891 BR TR 5'6" 165 lbs.

Year	Team		W	L	PCT	ERA	G	GS	CG	IP	H	BB	SO	ShO	W	L	SV	AB	H	HR	BA	PO	A	E	DP	TC/G	FA
1914	BUF	F	1	0	1.000	3.44	15	1	0	36.2	39	16	13	0	1	0	2	9	2	0	.222	1	14	1	1	1.1	.938

Bob Brown
BROWN, ROBERT MURRAY
B. Apr. 1, 1911, Dorchester, Mass. BR TR 6'1" 190 lbs.

Year	Team		W	L	PCT	ERA	G	GS	CG	IP	H	BB	SO	ShO	W	L	SV	AB	H	HR	BA	PO	A	E	DP	TC/G	FA
1930	BOS	N	0	0	–	10.50	3	0	0	6	10	8	1	0	0	0	0	2	0	0	.000	1	1	0	0	0.7	1.000
1931			0	1	.000	8.53	3	0	0	6.1	9	3	2	0	0	1	0	2	1	0	.500	0	3	0	0	1.0	1.000
1932			14	7	.667	3.30	35	28	9	213	187	104	110	0	3	0	1	67	13	0	.194	6	39	0	2	1.3	1.000
1933			0	0	–	2.70	5	0	0	6.2	6	3	3	0	0	0	0	2	0	0	.000	0	2	0	0	0.2	1.000
1934			1	3	.250	5.71	16	8	2	58.1	59	36	21	1	0	0	0	21	5	0	.238	5	6	1	0	0.8	.917
1935			1	8	.111	6.37	15	10	2	65	79	36	17	1	0	1	0	19	2	0	.105	4	8	1	0	0.9	.923
1936			0	2	.000	5.40	2	2	0	8.1	10	3	5	0	0	0	0	2	0	0	.000	0	3	0	0	1.5	1.000
7 yrs.			16	21	.432	4.48	79	49	13	363.2	360	193	159	2	3	1	1	115	21	0	.183	16	61	2	2	1.0	.975

Buster Brown
BROWN, CHARLES EDWARD
B. Aug. 31, 1881, Boone, Iowa D. Feb. 9, 1914, Sioux City, Iowa BR TR 6' 180 lbs.

Year	Team		W	L	PCT	ERA	G	GS	CG	IP	H	BB	SO	ShO	W	L	SV	AB	H	HR	BA	PO	A	E	DP	TC/G	FA
1905	STL	N	8	11	.421	2.97	23	21	17	179	172	62	57	0	0	0	0	65	6	0	.092	12	61	4	3	3.3	.948
1906			8	16	.333	2.64	32	27	21	238.1	208	112	109	0	0	1	0	85	14	1	.165	17	71	7	4	3.0	.926
1907	2 teams	STL N	(9G 1–6)				PHI N		(21G 9–6)																		
"	total		10	12	.455	2.74	30	24	19	193.2	175	101	55	4	0	0	0	79	17	0	.215	11	60	2	2	2.4	.973
1908	PHI	N	0	0	–	2.57	3	0	0	7	9	5	3	0	0	0	0	5	1	0	.200	2	6	0	0	2.7	1.000
1909	2 teams	PHI N	(7G 0–0)				BOS N		(18G 4–10)																		
"	total		4	10	.286	3.16	25	18	8	148.1	130	72	42	2	0	0	0	57	7	0	.123	11	44	4	1	2.4	.932
1910	BOS	N	9	23	.281	2.67	46	29	16	263	251	94	88	1	3	5	2	81	16	1	.198	10	80	7	3	2.1	.928
1911			8	18	.308	4.29	42	25	13	241	258	116	76	0	2	1	2	84	21	1	.250	8	67	6	6	1.9	.926
1912			4	15	.211	4.01	31	21	13	168.1	146	66	68	0	0	1	0	61	13	0	.213	4	42	0	1	1.5	1.000
1913			0	0	–	4.73	2	0	0	13.1	19	3	3	0	0	0	0	5	0	0	.000	0	3	0	0	1.5	1.000
9 yrs.			51	105	.327	3.20	234	165	107	1452	1368	631	501	10	5	8	4	522	95	3	.182	75	434	30	20	2.3	.944

Charlie Brown
BROWN, CHARLES E. (Buster, Yank)
B. 1878, Baltimore, Md. Deceased. TL 6' 180 lbs.

Year	Team		W	L	PCT	ERA	G	GS	CG	IP	H	BB	SO	ShO	W	L	SV	AB	H	HR	BA	PO	A	E	DP	TC/G	FA
1897	CLE	N	1	2	.333	7.77	4	4	2	24.1	30	17	8	0	0	0	0	11	3	0	.273	0	5	0	0	1.3	1.000

Clint Brown
BROWN, CLINTON HAROLD
B. July 8, 1903, Blackash, Pa. D. Dec. 31, 1955, Rocky River, Ohio BL TR 6'1" 190 lbs.

Year	Team		W	L	PCT	ERA	G	GS	CG	IP	H	BB	SO	ShO	W	L	SV	AB	H	HR	BA	PO	A	E	DP	TC/G	FA
1928	CLE	A	0	1	.000	4.91	2	1	1	11	14	2	2	0	0	0	0	5	1	0	.200	2	3	0	0	2.5	1.000
1929			0	2	.000	3.31	3	1	1	16.1	18	6	1	0	0	1	0	7	0	0	.000	1	9	0	0	3.3	1.000
1930			11	12	.478	4.97	35	31	16	213.2	271	51	54	2	0	0	1	73	18	0	.247	12	54	5	5	2.0	.930
1931			11	15	.423	4.71	39	33	12	233.1	284	55	50	2	0	0	0	87	15	0	.172	9	67	0	3	1.9	1.000
1932			15	12	.556	4.08	37	32	21	262.2	298	50	59	1	0	0	1	100	25	0	.250	15	63	2	2	2.2	.975
1933			11	12	.478	3.41	33	23	10	185	202	34	47	2	1	1	1	62	9	0	.145	11	53	0	3	1.9	1.000
1934			4	3	.571	5.90	17	2	0	50.1	83	14	15	0	4	2	1	17	5	0	.294	0	10	1	0	0.6	.909
1935			4	3	.571	5.14	23	5	1	49	61	14	20	0	3	0	2	10	2	0	.200	5	12	1	1	0.8	.944
1936	CHI	A	6	2	.750	4.99	38	2	0	83	106	24	19	0	6	1	5	25	4	0	.160	8	15	1	0	0.6	.958
1937			7	7	.500	3.42	53	0	0	100	92	36	51	0	7	7	18	18	4	0	.222	4	24	1	1	0.5	.966
1938			1	3	.250	4.61	8	0	0	13.2	16	9	2	0	1	3	2	2	1	0	.500	1	7	0	0	1.0	1.000
1939			11	10	.524	3.88	61	0	0	118.1	127	27	41	0	11	10	18	19	4	0	.211	3	29	1	3	0.5	.970
1940			4	6	.400	3.68	37	0	0	66	75	16	23	0	4	6	10	14	1	0	.071	2	14	0	0	0.4	1.000
1941	CLE	A	3	3	.500	3.27	41	0	0	74.1	77	28	22	0	3	3	5	17	2	0	.118	2	27	0	3	0.7	1.000
1942			1	1	.500	6.00	7	0	0	9	16	2	4	0	1	1	0	1	0	0	.000	0	0	0	0	0.0	–
15 yrs.			89	92	.492	4.26	434	130	62	1485.2	1740	368	410	7	41	35	64	457	91	2	.199	75	387	12	23	1.1	.975

Curly Brown
BROWN, CHARLES ROY (Lefty)
B. Dec. 9, 1888, Spring Hill, Kans. D. June 10, 1968, Spring Hill, Kans. BL TL 5'10½" 165 lbs.

Year	Team		W	L	PCT	ERA	G	GS	CG	IP	H	BB	SO	ShO	W	L	SV	AB	H	HR	BA	PO	A	E	DP	TC/G	FA
1911	STL	A	1	2	.333	2.74	3	3	2	23	22	5	5	0	0	0	0	9	0	0	.000	1	7	2	1	3.3	.800
1912			1	3	.250	4.87	16	5	2	64.2	69	35	28	1	0	1	0	24	5	0	.208	1	7	1	0	0.6	.889
1913			1	1	.500	2.57	2	2	2	14	12	4	6	0	0	0	0	5	2	0	.400	0	4	0	0	2.0	1.000
1915	CIN	N	0	2	.000	4.67	7	3	0	27	26	6	13	0	0	0	0	11	4	0	.364	0	1	1	0	0.3	.500
4 yrs.			3	8	.273	4.20	28	12	6	128.2	129	50	52	1	1	1	0	49	11	0	.224	2	19	4	1	0.9	.840

Curt Brown
BROWN, CURTIS STEVEN
B. Jan. 15, 1960, Ft. Lauderdale, Fla. BR TR 6'5" 200 lbs.

Year	Team		W	L	PCT	ERA	G	GS	CG	IP	H	BB	SO	ShO	W	L	SV	AB	H	HR	BA	PO	A	E	DP	TC/G	FA
1983	CAL	A	1	1	.500	7.31	10	0	0	16	25	4	7	0	1	1	0	0	0	0	–	1	1	0	0	0.2	1.000
1984	NY	A	1	1	.500	2.70	13	0	0	16.2	18	4	10	0	1	1	0	0	0	0	–	2	2	0	0	0.3	1.000
1986	MON	N	0	1	.000	3.00	6	0	0	12	15	2	4	0	0	1	0	1	0	0	.000	1	3	1	0	0.8	.800

Year	Team		W	L	PCT	ERA	G	GS	CG	IP	H	BB	SO	ShO	Relief Pitching W	L	SV	Batting AB	H	HR	BA	PO	A	E	DP	TC/G	FA

Curt Brown *continued*

| 1987 | | | 0 | 1 | .000 | 7.71 | 5 | 0 | 0 | 7 | 10 | 4 | 6 | 0 | 0 | 1 | 0 | 0 | 0 | 0 | – | 0 | 2 | 1 | 0 | 0.6 | .667 |
| 4 yrs. | | | 2 | 4 | .333 | 4.88 | 34 | 0 | 0 | 51.2 | 68 | 14 | 27 | 0 | 2 | 4 | 0 | 1 | 0 | 0 | .000 | 4 | 8 | 2 | 0 | 0.4 | .857 |

Ed Brown

BROWN, EDWARD P.
B. Chicago, Ill.   Deceased.
Manager 1882.

TR

1882	STL	AA	0	0	–	0.00	1	0	0	2	2	0	1	0	0	0	0	60	11	0	.183	0	0	0	0	0.0	–
1884	TOL	AA	0	1	.000	9.00	1	1	1	9	19	4	1	0	0	0	0	153	27	0	.176	0	1	1	0	2.0	.500
2 yrs.			0	1	.000	7.36	2	1	1	11	21	4	2	0	0	0	0	*				0	1	1	0	1.0	.500

Elmer Brown

BROWN, ELMER YOUNG (Shook)
B. Mar. 25, 1883, Southport, Ind.   D. Jan. 23, 1955, Indianapolis, Ind.

BL TR 5'11½" 172 lbs.

1911	STL	A	1	1	.500	6.61	5	3	1	16.1	16	14	5	0	1	0	0	7	1	0	.143	1	7	0	0	1.6	1.000
1912			5	8	.385	2.99	23	11	2	120.1	122	42	45	1	1	2	0	36	6	0	.167	2	31	2	1	1.5	.943
1913	BKN	N	0	0	–	2.08	3	1	0	13	6	10	6	0	0	0	0	4	0	0	.000	0	3	0	0	1.0	1.000
1914			2	2	.500	3.93	11	4	1	36.2	33	23	22	0	2	0	0	12	1	0	.083	2	12	0	0	1.3	1.000
1915			0	0	–	9.00	1	0	0	2	4	3	1	0	0	0	0	0	0	0	–	0	2	0	0	2.0	1.000
5 yrs.			8	11	.421	3.49	43	19	4	188.1	181	92	79	2	3	4	0	59	8	0	.136	5	55	2	1	1.4	.968

Hal Brown

BROWN, HECTOR HAROLD (Skinny)
B. Dec. 11, 1924, Greensboro, N. C.

BR TR 6'2" 180 lbs.

1951	CHI	A	0	0	–	9.35	3	0	0	8.2	15	4	4	0	0	0	0	2	2	0	1.000	1	2	0	0	1.0	1.000
1952			2	3	.400	4.23	24	8	1	72.1	82	21	31	0	0	0	0	19	3	1	.158	5	11	0	1	0.7	1.000
1953	BOS	A	11	6	.647	4.65	30	25	6	166.1	177	57	62	1	0	1	0	58	17	1	.293	8	27	1	2	1.2	.972
1954			1	8	.111	4.12	40	5	1	118	126	41	66	0	0	1	4	24	3	0	.125	4	23	2	4	0.7	.931
1955	2 teams		BOS A	(2G 1–0)		BAL A	(15G 0–4)																				
"	total		1	4	.200	3.98	17	5	1	61	53	28	28	0	1	1	0	17	1	0	.059	3	7	2	1	0.7	.833
1956	BAL	A	9	7	.563	4.04	35	14	4	151.2	142	37	57	1	3	2	2	42	8	0	.190	7	25	1	4	0.9	.970
1957			7	8	.467	3.90	25	20	7	150	132	37	62	2	0	0	1	48	10	0	.208	12	19	0	4	1.2	1.000
1958			7	5	.583	3.07	19	17	4	96.2	96	20	44	2	0	0	1	27	4	0	.148	6	14	0	1	1.1	1.000
1959			11	9	.550	3.79	31	21	3	164	158	32	81	0	1	0	3	42	2	0	.048	9	25	1	2	1.1	.971
1960			12	5	.706	3.06	30	20	6	159	155	22	66	1	4	0	1	44	8	0	.182	9	20	1	2	1.0	.967
1961			10	6	.625	3.19	27	23	6	166.2	153	33	61	3	0	1	0	50	7	0	.140	16	25	0	1	1.5	1.000
1962	2 teams		BAL A	(22G 6–4)		NY A	(2G 0–1)																				
"	total		6	5	.545	4.29	24	12	0	92.1	97	23	27	0	2	2	1	29	8	0	.276	6	10	0	1	0.7	1.000
1963	HOU	N	5	11	.313	3.31	26	20	6	141.1	137	8	68	3	1	0	0	43	4	0	.093	3	15	0	0	0.7	1.000
1964			3	15	.167	3.95	27	21	3	132	154	26	53	0	1	0	1	39	5	0	.128	4	20	0	0	0.9	1.000
14 yrs.			85	92	.480	3.81	358	211	47	1680	1677	389	710	13	14	12	11	484	82	2	.169	93	243	8	23	1.0	.977

Jackie Brown

BROWN, JACKIE GENE
Brother of Paul Brown.
B. May 31, 1943, Holdenville, Okla.

BR TR 6'1" 195 lbs.

1970	WAS	A	2	2	.500	3.95	24	5	1	57	49	37	47	0	1	0	0	13	2	0	.154	4	2	0	0	0.3	1.000
1971			3	4	.429	5.94	14	9	0	47	60	27	21	0	0	0	0	15	2	0	.133	6	9	0	1	1.1	1.000
1973	TEX	A	5	5	.500	3.90	25	3	2	67	82	25	45	1	3	5	2	0	0	0	–	3	4	0	3	0.3	1.000
1974			13	12	.520	3.57	35	26	9	217	219	74	134	2	1	2	0	0	0	0	–	17	24	2	4	1.2	.953
1975	2 teams		TEX A	(17G 5–5)		CLE A	(25G 1–2)																				
"	total		6	7	.462	4.25	42	10	2	139.2	142	64	76	1	3	4	1	0	0	0	–	8	12	3	1	0.5	.870
1976	CLE	A	9	11	.450	4.25	32	27	5	180	193	55	104	2	2	0	0	0	0	0	–	13	21	1	2	1.1	.971
1977	MON	N	9	12	.429	4.50	42	25	6	186	189	71	89	2	1	0	0	56	7	0	.125	9	21	2	2	0.8	.938
7 yrs.			47	53	.470	4.18	214	105	26	893.2	934	353	516	8	11	11	3	84	11	0	.131	60	93	8	12	0.8	.950

Jim Brown

BROWN, JAMES W. H.
B. Dec. 12, 1860, Clinton County, Pa.   D. Apr. 6, 1908, Williamsport, Pa.

1884	3 teams		ALT U	(11G 1–9)		NY N	(1G 0–1)		STP U	(6G 1–4)																
"	total		2	14	.125	4.84	18	18	12	119	152	58	61	1	0	0	0	107	27	1	.252	7	32	14	0	2.9	.736
1886	PHI	AA	0	1	.000	3.24	1	1	1	8.1	9	3	4	0	0	0	0	3	0	0	.000	0	1	0	0	1.0	1.000
2 yrs.			2	15	.118	4.74	19	19	13	127.1	161	61	65	1	0	0	0	110	27	1	.245	7	33	14	0	2.8	.741

Joe Brown

BROWN, JOSEPH E.
B. Apr. 4, 1859, Warren, Pa.   D. June 28, 1888, Warren, Pa.

1884	CHI	N	4	2	.667	4.68	7	6	5	50	56	7	27	0	0	0	0	61	13	0	.213	0	11	2	0	1.9	.846
1885	BAL	AA	0	4	.000	5.68	4	4	4	38	52	4	9	0	0	0	0	19	3	0	.158	1	5	0	0	1.5	1.000
2 yrs.			4	6	.400	5.11	11	10	9	88	108	11	36	0	0	0	0	80	16	0	.200	1	16	2	0	1.7	.895

Joe Brown

BROWN, JOSEPH HENRY (Smokey, bullet)
B. July 3, 1900, Little Rock, Ark.   D. Mar. 7, 1950, Los Angeles, Calif.

BR TR 6' 176 lbs.

| 1927 | CHI | A | 0 | 0 | – | ∞ | 1 | 0 | 0 | 2 | 1 | 0 | 0 | 0 | 0 | 0 | 0 | 0 | 0 | – | 0 | 0 | 0 | 0 | 0.0 | – |

John Brown

BROWN, JOHN J.
B. Trenton, N. J.   Deceased.

| 1897 | BKN | N | 0 | 1 | .000 | 7.20 | 1 | 1 | 1 | 5 | 7 | 4 | 0 | 0 | 0 | 0 | 0 | 2 | 1 | 0 | .500 | 0 | 3 | 0 | 0 | 3.0 | 1.000 |

Jophrey Brown

BROWN, JOPHREY CLIFFORD
B. Jan. 22, 1945, Grambling, La.

BL TR 6'2" 190 lbs.

| 1968 | CHI | N | 0 | 0 | – | 4.50 | 1 | 0 | 0 | 2 | 2 | 1 | 0 | 0 | 0 | 0 | 0 | 0 | 0 | 0 | – | 1 | 1 | 0 | 0 | 2.0 | 1.000 |

Year	Team		W	L	PCT	ERA	G	GS	CG	IP	H	BB	SO	ShO	Relief Pitching W	L	SV	Batting AB	H	HR	BA	PO	A	E	DP	TC/G	FA

Jumbo Brown

BROWN, WALTER GEORGE
B. Apr. 30, 1907, Greene, R. I. D. Oct. 2, 1966, Freeport, N. Y. BR TR 6'4" 295 lbs.

Year	Team		W	L	PCT	ERA	G	GS	CG	IP	H	BB	SO	ShO	W	L	SV	AB	H	HR	BA	PO	A	E	DP	TC/G	FA
1925	CHI	N	0	0	–	3.00	2	0	0	6	5	4	0	0	0	0	0	1	0	0	.000	0	2	0	0	1.0	1.000
1927	CLE	A	0	2	.000	6.27	8	0	0	18.2	19	26	8	0	0	2	0	3	2	0	.667	1	5	1	1	0.9	.857
1928			0	1	.000	6.75	5	0	0	14.2	19	15	12	0	0	1	0	3	2	0	.667	1	1	0	0	0.4	1.000
1932	NY	A	5	2	.714	4.45	19	3	3	56.2	58	30	31	1	2	2	1	23	4	0	.174	5	16	0	1	1.1	1.000
1933			7	5	.583	5.23	21	8	1	74	78	52	55	0	3	3	0	28	5	0	.179	0	14	1	1	0.7	.933
1935			6	5	.545	3.61	20	8	3	87.1	94	37	41	0	2	1	0	32	10	0	.313	8	16	1	1	1.3	.960
1936			1	4	.200	5.91	20	3	0	64	93	29	19	0	1	2	1	19	0	0	.000	1	17	1	1	1.0	.947
1937	2 teams		CIN N	(4G 1–0)		NY N	(4G 1–0)																					
"	total		2	0	1.000	4.91	8	1	0	18.1	21	8	8	0	1	0	0	2	0	0	.000	0	6	0	0	0.8	1.000
1938	NY	N	5	3	.625	1.80	43	0	0	90	65	28	42	0	5	3	5	16	3	0	.188	5	11	2	1	0.4	.889
1939			4	0	1.000	4.15	31	0	0	56.1	69	25	24	0	4	0	7	11	4	0	.364	0	12	0	1	0.4	1.000
1940			2	4	.333	3.42	41	0	0	55.1	49	25	31	0	2	4	7	10	1	0	.100	0	7	0	0	0.2	1.000
1941			1	5	.167	3.32	31	0	0	57	49	21	30	0	1	5	8	9	1	0	.111	0	6	0	0	0.3	1.000
	12 yrs.		33	31	.516	4.06	249	23	7	598.1	619	300	301	1	21	23	29	157	32	0	.204	21	115	6	7	0.6	.958

Keith Brown

BROWN, KEITH EDWARD
B. Feb. 14, 1964, Flagstaff, Ariz. BB TR 6'4" 215 lbs.

Year	Team		W	L	PCT	ERA	G	GS	CG	IP	H	BB	SO	ShO	W	L	SV	AB	H	HR	BA	PO	A	E	DP	TC/G	FA
1988	CIN	N	2	1	.667	2.76	4	3	0	16.1	14	4	6	0	0	0	0	0	0	0	.000	0	3	0	1	0.8	1.000

Kevin Brown

BROWN, JAMES KEVIN
B. Mar. 14, 1965, Milledgeville, Ga. BR TR 6'4" 195 lbs.

Year	Team		W	L	PCT	ERA	G	GS	CG	IP	H	BB	SO	ShO	W	L	SV	AB	H	HR	BA	PO	A	E	DP	TC/G	FA
1986	TEX	A	1	0	1.000	3.60	1	1	0	5	6	0	4	0	0	0	0	0	0	0	–	0	0	0	0	1.0	1.000
1988			1	1	.500	4.24	4	4	1	23.1	33	8	12	0	0	0	0	0	0	0	–	1	2	0	0	0.8	1.000
1989			12	9	.571	3.35	28	28	7	191	167	70	104	0	0	0	0	0	0	0	–	15	41	2	6	2.1	.966
	3 yrs.		14	10	.583	3.45	33	33	8	219.1	206	78	120	0	0	0	0	0	0	0	–	16	44	2	6	1.9	.968

Lew Brown

BROWN, LEWIS J. (Blower)
B. Feb. 1, 1858, Leominster, Mass. D. Jan. 16, 1889, Boston, Mass. BR TR 5'10½" 185 lbs.

Year	Team		W	L	PCT	ERA	G	GS	CG	IP	H	BB	SO	ShO	W	L	SV	AB	H	HR	BA	PO	A	E	DP	TC/G	FA
1878	PRO	N	0	0	–	18.00	1	0	0	1	0	4	0	0	0	0	0	243	74	1	.305	0	1	0	0	1.0	1.000
1884	BOS	U	0	0	–	36.00	1	0	0	1	6	1	0	0	0	0	1	325	75	1	.231	0	0	0	0	0.0	–
	2 yrs.		0	0	–	27.00	2	0	0	2	6	5	0	0	0	0	1	*				0	1	0	0	0.5	1.000

Lloyd Brown

BROWN, LLOYD ANDREW (Gimpy)
B. Dec. 25, 1904, Beeville, Tex. D. Jan. 14, 1974, Opa-Locka, Fla. BL TL 5'9" 170 lbs.

Year	Team		W	L	PCT	ERA	G	GS	CG	IP	H	BB	SO	ShO	W	L	SV	AB	H	HR	BA	PO	A	E	DP	TC/G	FA
1925	BKN	N	0	3	.000	4.12	17	5	1	63.1	79	25	23	0	0	0	0	23	2	0	.087	3	15	0	1	1.1	1.000
1928	WAS	A	4	4	.500	4.04	27	10	2	107	112	40	38	0	2	0	1	31	5	0	.161	10	36	0	2	1.7	1.000
1929			8	7	.533	4.18	40	15	7	168	186	69	48	1	4	4	0	50	11	0	.220	8	43	0	2	1.3	1.000
1930			16	12	.571	4.25	38	22	10	197	220	65	59	1	6	2	0	65	14	1	.215	9	56	3	5	1.8	.956
1931			15	14	.517	3.20	42	32	15	258.2	256	79	79	1	1	2	0	96	22	0	.229	13	59	1	2	1.7	.986
1932			15	12	.556	4.44	46	24	10	202.2	239	55	53	2	4	2	5	70	7	0	.100	10	50	4	1	1.4	.938
1933	2 teams		STL A	(8G 1–6)		BOS A	(33G 8–11)																					
"	total		9	17	.346	4.63	41	27	9	202.1	237	81	44	2	3	2	2	68	19	2	.279	16	66	3	4	2.1	.965
1934	CLE	A	5	10	.333	3.85	38	15	5	117	116	51	39	0	3	1	6	30	7	0	.233	5	32	1	3	1.0	.974
1935			8	7	.533	3.61	42	8	4	122	123	37	45	2	4	0	4	37	4	0	.108	7	28	1	1	0.9	.972
1936			8	10	.444	4.17	24	16	12	140.1	166	45	34	1	1	1	1	45	10	1	.222	6	29	0	2	1.5	1.000
1937			2	6	.250	6.55	31	5	2	77	107	27	32	0	1	2	0	24	4	0	.167	7	15	2	1	0.8	.917
1940	PHI	N	1	3	.250	6.21	18	2	0	37.2	58	16	16	0	0	3	3	13	1	0	.077	5	7	2	0	0.8	.857
	12 yrs.		91	105	.464	4.20	404	181	77	1693	1899	590	510	10	22	22	21	552	106	4	.192	99	436	17	24	1.4	.969

Mace Brown

BROWN, MACE STANLEY
B. May 21, 1909, North English, Iowa BR TR 6'1" 190 lbs.

Year	Team		W	L	PCT	ERA	G	GS	CG	IP	H	BB	SO	ShO	W	L	SV	AB	H	HR	BA	PO	A	E	DP	TC/G	FA
1935	PIT	N	4	1	.800	3.59	18	5	2	72.2	84	22	28	0	1	0	0	24	4	0	.167	4	23	1	1	1.6	.964
1936			10	11	.476	3.87	47	10	3	165	178	55	56	0	6	4	3	60	10	0	.167	4	41	0	4	1.0	1.000
1937			7	2	.778	4.18	50	2	0	107.2	109	45	60	0	6	1	7	30	9	0	.300	5	17	0	0	0.4	1.000
1938			15	9	.625	3.80	51	2	0	132.2	155	44	55	0	15	8	5	38	5	0	.132	3	28	2	1	0.6	.939
1939			9	13	.409	3.37	47	19	8	200.1	232	52	71	1	2	3	7	64	7	0	.109	8	42	1	3	1.1	.980
1940			10	9	.526	3.49	48	17	5	172.2	181	49	73	2	5	2	7	52	6	0	.115	10	40	2	1	1.1	.962
1941	2 teams		PIT N	(1G 0–0)		BKN N	(24G 3–2)																					
"	total		3	2	.600	3.07	25	0	0	44	33	26	22	0	3	2	3	0	0	0	.000	4	14	1	0	0.8	.947
1942	BOS	A	9	3	.750	3.43	34	0	0	60.1	56	28	20	0	9	3	6	15	1	0	.067	0	17	0	1	0.5	1.000
1943			6	6	.500	2.12	49	0	0	93.1	71	51	40	0	6	6	9	17	1	0	.059	4	20	2	3	0.5	.923
1946			3	1	.750	2.05	18	0	0	26.1	26	16	10	0	3	1	1	5	0	0	.000	0	9	1	0	0.6	.900
	10 yrs.		76	57	.571	3.47	387	55	18	1075	1125	388	435	3	56	30	48	313	43	0	.137	42	251	10	15	0.8	.967

WORLD SERIES

Year	Team		W	L	PCT	ERA	G	GS	CG	IP	H	BB	SO	ShO	W	L	SV	AB	H	HR	BA	PO	A	E	DP	TC/G	FA
1946	BOS	A	0	0	–	27.00	1	0	0	1	4	1	0	0	0	0	0	0	0	0	–	0	0	0	0	0.0	–

Mark Brown

BROWN, MARK ANTHONY
B. July 13, 1959, Bellows Falls, Vt. BB TR 6'2" 190 lbs.

Year	Team		W	L	PCT	ERA	G	GS	CG	IP	H	BB	SO	ShO	W	L	SV	AB	H	HR	BA	PO	A	E	DP	TC/G	FA
1984	BAL	A	1	2	.333	3.91	9	0	0	23	22	7	10	0	1	2	0	0	0	0	–	0	2	0	0	0.2	1.000
1985	MIN	A	0	0	–	6.89	6	0	0	15.2	21	7	5	0	0	0	0	0	0	0	–	1	1	0	0	0.3	1.000
	2 yrs.		1	2	.333	5.12	15	0	0	38.2	43	14	15	0	1	2	0	0	0	0	–	1	3	0	0	0.3	1.000

Mike Brown

BROWN, MICHAEL GARY
B. Mar. 24, 1959, Camden County, N. J. BR TR 6'2" 195 lbs.

Year	Team		W	L	PCT	ERA	G	GS	CG	IP	H	BB	SO	ShO	W	L	SV	AB	H	HR	BA	PO	A	E	DP	TC/G	FA
1982	BOS	A	1	0	1.000	0.00	3	0	0	6	7	1	4	0	1	0	0	0	0	0	–	0	0	0	0	0.0	–
1983			6	6	.500	4.67	19	18	3	104	110	43	35	1	0	0	0	0	0	0	–	11	11	2	0	1.3	.917
1984			1	8	.111	6.85	15	11	0	67	104	19	32	0	0	0	0	0	0	0	–	11	8	2	1	1.4	.905
1985			0	0	–	21.60	2	1	0	3.1	9	3	3	0	0	0	0	0	0	0	–	0	0	0	0	0.0	–

Year	Team	W	L	PCT	ERA	G	GS	CG	IP	H	BB	SO	ShO	Relief Pitching W	L	SV	Batting AB	H	HR	BA	PO	A	E	DP	TC/G	FA

Mike Brown *continued*

Year	Team	W	L	PCT	ERA	G	GS	CG	IP	H	BB	SO	ShO	W	L	SV	AB	H	HR	BA	PO	A	E	DP	TC/G	FA
1986	2 teams	BOS A	(15G 4-4)		SEA A	(6G 0-2)																				
"	total	4	6	.400	5.79	21	12	0	73	91	36	41	0	0	0	0	0	0	0	–	7	12	0	0	0.9	1.000
1987	SEA A	0	0	–	54.00	1	0	0	.1	3	0	0	0	0	0	0	0	0	0	–	0	0	0	0	0.0	–
6 yrs.		12	20	.375	5.75	61	42	3	253.2	324	102	115	1	1	0	0	0	0	0	–	29	31	4	1	1.0	.938

Myrl Brown

BROWN, MYRL LINCOLN (Brainie)
B. Oct. 10, 1894, Waynesboro, Pa.   D. Feb. 23, 1981, Harrisburg, Pa.

BR TR 5'11"   172 lbs.

Year	Team	W	L	PCT	ERA	G	GS	CG	IP	H	BB	SO	ShO	W	L	SV	AB	H	HR	BA	PO	A	E	DP	TC/G	FA
1922	PIT N	3	1	.750	5.97	7	5	1	34.2	42	13	9	0	1	0	0	11	3	0	.273	0	11	1	1	1.7	.917

Norm Brown

BROWN, NORMAN
B. Feb. 1, 1919, Evergreen, N. C.

BB TR 6'3"   180 lbs.

Year	Team	W	L	PCT	ERA	G	GS	CG	IP	H	BB	SO	ShO	W	L	SV	AB	H	HR	BA	PO	A	E	DP	TC/G	FA
1943	PHI A	0	0	–	0.00	1	1	0	7	5	0	1	0	0	0	0	3	0	0	.000	0	3	0	0	4.0	1.000
1946		0	1	.000	6.14	4	0	0	7.1	8	6	3	0	0	1	0	0	0	0	–	1	1	0	0	0.3	1.000
2 yrs.		0	1	.000	3.14	5	1	0	14.1	13	6	4	0	0	1	0	3	0	0	.000	1	4	0	0	1.0	1.000

Paul Brown

BROWN, PAUL DWAYNE
Brother of Jackie Brown.
B. June 18, 1941, Fort Smith, Ark.

BR TR 6'1"   190 lbs.

Year	Team	W	L	PCT	ERA	G	GS	CG	IP	H	BB	SO	ShO	W	L	SV	AB	H	HR	BA	PO	A	E	DP	TC/G	FA
1961	PHI N	0	1	.000	8.10	5	1	0	10	13	8	1	0	0	0	0	2	1	0	.500	0	2	0	0	0.4	1.000
1962		0	6	.000	5.94	23	9	0	63.2	74	33	29	0	0	0	1	13	2	0	.154	7	8	2	1	0.7	.882
1963		0	1	.000	4.11	6	2	0	15.1	15	5	11	0	0	0	0	2	1	0	.500	0	5	0	0	0.8	1.000
1968		0	0	–	9.00	2	0	0	4	6	1	4	0	0	0	0	0	0	0	–	0	0	0	0	0.0	–
4 yrs.		0	8	.000	6.00	36	12	0	93	108	47	45	0	0	0	1	17	4	0	.235	7	15	2	1	0.7	.917

Ray Brown

BROWN, PAUL PERCIVAL
B. Jan. 31, 1889, Chicago, Ill.   D. May 29, 1955, Los Angeles, Calif.

Year	Team	W	L	PCT	ERA	G	GS	CG	IP	H	BB	SO	ShO	W	L	SV	AB	H	HR	BA	PO	A	E	DP	TC/G	FA
1909	CHI N	1	0	1.000	2.00	1	1	1	9	5	4	2	0	0	0	0	3	0	0	.000	0	1	0	0	1.0	1.000

Scott Brown

BROWN, SCOTT EDWARD
B. Aug. 30, 1956, DeQuincy, La.

BR TR 6'2"   220 lbs.

Year	Team	W	L	PCT	ERA	G	GS	CG	IP	H	BB	SO	ShO	W	L	SV	AB	H	HR	BA	PO	A	E	DP	TC/G	FA
1981	CIN N	1	0	1.000	2.77	10	0	0	13	16	1	7	0	1	0	0	1	0	0	.000	0	2	0	0	0.2	1.000

Steve Brown

BROWN, STEVEN ELBERT
B. Feb. 12, 1957, San Francisco, Calif.

BR TR 6'5"   200 lbs.

Year	Team	W	L	PCT	ERA	G	GS	CG	IP	H	BB	SO	ShO	W	L	SV	AB	H	HR	BA	PO	A	E	DP	TC/G	FA
1983	CAL A	2	3	.400	3.52	12	4	2	46	45	16	23	1	1	1	0	0	0	0	–	4	5	0	1	0.8	1.000
1984		0	1	.000	9.00	3	3	0	11	16	9	5	0	0	0	0	0	0	0	–	0	1	0	0	0.3	1.000
2 yrs.		2	4	.333	4.58	15	7	2	57	61	25	28	1	1	1	0	0	0	0	–	4	6	0	1	0.7	1.000

Stub Brown

BROWN, RICHARD P.
B. Aug. 3, 1870, Baltimore, Md.   D. Mar. 11, 1948, Baltimore, Md.

TL 6'2"   220 lbs.

Year	Team	W	L	PCT	ERA	G	GS	CG	IP	H	BB	SO	ShO	W	L	SV	AB	H	HR	BA	PO	A	E	DP	TC/G	FA
1893	BAL N	0	0	–	6.00	2	0	0	9	13	5	0	0	0	0	0	5	1	0	.200	0	0	0	0	0.0	–
1894		4	0	1.000	4.89	9	6	3	49.2	59	24	8	0	0	0	0	23	2	0	.087	0	7	1	1	0.9	.875
1897	CIN N	0	1	.000	4.15	2	1	1	13	17	8	2	0	0	0	0	5	0	0	.000	0	3	0	0	1.5	1.000
3 yrs.		4	1	.800	4.90	13	7	4	71.2	89	37	10	0	0	0	0	33	3	0	.091	0	10	1	1	0.8	.909

Three Finger Brown

BROWN, MORDECAI PETER CENTENNIAL (Miner)
B. Oct. 19, 1876, Nyesville, Ind.   D. Feb. 14, 1948, Terre Haute, Ind.
Manager 1914.
Hall of Fame 1949.

BB TR 5'10"   175 lbs.

Year	Team	W	L	PCT	ERA	G	GS	CG	IP	H	BB	SO	ShO	W	L	SV	AB	H	HR	BA	PO	A	E	DP	TC/G	FA
1903	STL N	9	13	.409	2.60	26	24	19	201	231	59	83	1	0	0	0	77	15	0	.195	5	60	3	7	2.6	.956
1904	CHI N	15	10	.600	1.86	26	23	21	212.1	155	50	81	4	2	0	1	89	19	0	.213	20	50	5	2	2.9	.933
1905		18	12	.600	2.17	30	24	24	249	219	44	89	4	2	2	0	93	13	1	.140	18	66	4	3	2.9	.955
1906		26	6	.813	1.04	36	32	27	277.1	198	61	144	10	1	0	3	98	20	0	.204	18	81	2	4	2.8	.980
1907		20	6	.769	1.39	34	27	20	233	180	40	107	6	1	0	3	85	13	1	.153	20	75	1	5	2.8	.990
1908		29	9	.763	1.47	44	31	27	312.1	214	49	123	9	4	1	5	121	25	0	.207	35	73	0	3	2.5	1.000
1909		27	9	.750	1.31	50	34	32	342.2	246	53	172	8	1	1	7	125	22	0	.176	18	83	3	6	2.1	.971
1910		25	13	.658	1.86	46	31	27	295.1	256	64	143	7	2	2	7	103	18	0	.175	10	92	4	3	2.3	.962
1911		21	11	.656	2.80	53	27	21	270	267	55	129	0	5	3	13	91	23	0	.253	8	53	1	0	1.2	.984
1912		5	6	.455	2.64	15	8	5	88.2	92	20	34	2	2	3	0	31	9	0	.290	1	15	1	1	1.1	.941
1913	CIN N	11	12	.478	2.91	39	16	11	173.1	174	44	41	1	4	3	6	54	11	0	.204	5	40	4	3	1.3	.918
1914	2 teams	STL F	(26G 12-6)		BKN F	(9G 2-5)																				
"	total	14	11	.560	3.52	35	26	18	232.2	235	61	113	2	1	2	0	78	19	0	.244	6	56	3	1	1.9	.954
1915	CHI F	17	8	.680	2.09	35	25	17	236.1	189	64	95	3	3	2	3	82	24	0	.293	6	87	5	5	2.8	.949
1916	CHI N	2	3	.400	3.91	12	4	2	48.1	52	9	21	0	1	0	0	16	4	0	.250	1	12	0	0	1.1	1.000
14 yrs.		239	129	.649	2.06	481	332	271	3172.1	2708	673	1375	57	29	19	48	1143	235	2	.206	171	843	36	43	2.2	.966
					3rd								10th													

WORLD SERIES

Year	Team	W	L	PCT	ERA	G	GS	CG	IP	H	BB	SO	ShO	W	L	SV	AB	H	HR	BA	PO	A	E	DP	TC/G	FA
1906	CHI N	1	2	.333	3.66	3	3	2	19.2	14	4	12	1	0	0	0	6	2	0	.333	2	12	1	0	5.0	.933
1907		1	0	1.000	0.00	1	1	1	9	7	1	4	1	0	0	0	3	0	0	.000	1	1	0	0	2.0	1.000
1908		2	0	1.000	0.00	2	1	1	11	6	1	5	1	0	0	0	4	0	0	.000	0	6	0	1	3.0	1.000
1910		1	2	.333	5.00	3	2	1	18	23	7	14	0	1	0	0	7	0	0	.000	0	10	1	0	3.7	.909
4 yrs.		5	4	.556	2.81	9	7	5	57.2	50	13	35	3	2	0	0	20	2	0	.100	3	29	2	1	3.8	.941
		8th	7th						10th					2nd	2nd											

Tom Brown

BROWN, THOMAS DALE
B. Aug. 10, 1949, Lafayette, La.

BR TR 6'1"   170 lbs.

Year	Team	W	L	PCT	ERA	G	GS	CG	IP	H	BB	SO	ShO	W	L	SV	AB	H	HR	BA	PO	A	E	DP	TC/G	FA
1978	SEA A	0	0	–	4.15	6	0	0	13	14	4	8	0	0	0	0	0	0	0	–	2	2	0	0	0.7	1.000

Tom Brown

BROWN, THOMAS T. (Handsome) — BL TR 5'10" 168 lbs.
B. Sept. 21, 1860, Liverpool, England D. Oct. 25, 1927, Washington, D. C.
Manager 1897-98.

Year	Team	Lg	W	L	PCT	ERA	G	GS	CG	IP	H	BB	SO	ShO	Relief W	Relief L	Relief SV	Bat AB	Bat H	Bat HR	BA	PO	A	E	DP	TC/G	FA
1882	BAL	AA	0	0	–	1.08	2	0	0	8.1	13	6	2	0	0	0	0	181	55	1	.304	0	0	0	0	0.0	–
1883	COL	AA	0	1	.000	*5.79*	3	1	1	14	14	10	6	0	0	0	0	420	115	5	.274	2	0	7	0	3.0	.222
1884			2	1	.667	*7.11*	4	0	0	19	27	7	5	0	2	1	0	451	123	5	.273	1	0	2	0	0.8	.333
1885	PIT	AA	0	0	–	*3.00*	2	0	0	6	0	3	2	0	0	0	0	437	134	4	.307	0	0	1	0	0.5	–
1886			0	0	–	*9.00*	1	0	0	2	2	5	1	0	0	0	0	460	131	1	.285	0	2	0	0	2.0	1.000
5 yrs.			2	2	.500	5.29	12	1	1	49.1	56	31	16	0	2	1	0	*				3	2	10	0	1.3	.333

Walter Brown

BROWN, WALTER IRVING — BR TR 5'11" 175 lbs.
B. Apr. 23, 1915, Jamestown, N. Y.

Year	Team	Lg	W	L	PCT	ERA	G	GS	CG	IP	H	BB	SO	ShO	Relief W	Relief L	Relief SV	Bat AB	Bat H	Bat HR	BA	PO	A	E	DP	TC/G	FA
1947	STL	A	1	0	1.000	4.89	19	0	0	46	50	28	10	0	1	0	0	11	0	0	.000	0	9	0	0	0.5	1.000

Cal Browning

BROWNING, CALVIN DUANE — BL TL 5'11" 190 lbs.
B. Mar. 16, 1938, Burns Flat, Okla.

Year	Team	Lg	W	L	PCT	ERA	G	GS	CG	IP	H	BB	SO	ShO	Relief W	Relief L	Relief SV	Bat AB	Bat H	Bat HR	BA	PO	A	E	DP	TC/G	FA
1960	STL	N	0	0	–	40.50	1	0	0	.2	5	1	0	0	0	0	0	0	0	0	–	0	0	0	0	0.0	–

Frank Browning

BROWNING, FRANK — BR TR 5'5" 145 lbs.
B. Oct. 29, 1882, Falmouth, Ky. D. May 19, 1948, San Antonio, Tex.

Year	Team	Lg	W	L	PCT	ERA	G	GS	CG	IP	H	BB	SO	ShO	Relief W	Relief L	Relief SV	Bat AB	Bat H	Bat HR	BA	PO	A	E	DP	TC/G	FA
1910	DET	A	2	2	.500	3.00	11	6	2	42	51	10	16	0	0	1	3	14	0	0	.000	3	21	1	1	2.3	.960

Pete Browning

BROWNING, LOUIS ROGERS (The Gladiator) — BR TR 6' 180 lbs.
B. June 17, 1861, Louisville, Ky. D. Sept. 10, 1905, Louisville, Ky.

Year	Team	Lg	W	L	PCT	ERA	G	GS	CG	IP	H	BB	SO	ShO	Relief W	Relief L	Relief SV	Bat AB	Bat H	Bat HR	BA	PO	A	E	DP	TC/G	FA
1884	LOU	AA	0	1	.000	*54.00*	1	1	0	.1	2	2	0	0	0	0	0	*				1	1	1	0	3.0	.667

Tom Browning

BROWNING, THOMAS LEO — BL TL 6'1" 190 lbs.
B. Apr. 28, 1960, Casper, Wyo.

Year	Team	Lg	W	L	PCT	ERA	G	GS	CG	IP	H	BB	SO	ShO	Relief W	Relief L	Relief SV	Bat AB	Bat H	Bat HR	BA	PO	A	E	DP	TC/G	FA
1984	CIN	N	1	0	1.000	1.54	3	3	0	23.1	27	5	14	0	0	0	0	7	1	0	.143	1	3	0	0	1.3	1.000
1985			20	9	.690	3.55	38	38	6	261.1	242	73	155	4	0	0	0	88	17	0	.193	12	34	2	1	1.3	.958
1986			14	13	.519	3.81	39	**39**	4	243.1	225	70	147	2	0	0	0	86	14	0	.163	11	26	3	5	1.0	.925
1987			10	13	.435	5.02	32	31	2	183	201	61	117	0	0	0	0	52	8	0	.154	5	23	3	1	1.0	.903
1988			18	5	.783	3.41	36	**36**	5	250.2	205	64	124	2	0	0	0	83	12	0	.145	8	30	3	3	1.1	.927
1989			15	12	.556	3.39	37	**37**	9	249.2	241	64	118	2	0	0	0	78	7	0	.090	8	35	0	3	1.2	1.000
6 yrs.			78	52	.600	3.72	185	184	26	1211.1	1141	337	675	10	0	0	0	394	59	0	.150	45	151	11	13	1.1	.947

Bruce Brubaker

BRUBAKER, BRUCE ELLSWORTH — BR TR 6'1" 198 lbs.
B. Dec. 29, 1941, Harrisburg, Pa.

Year	Team	Lg	W	L	PCT	ERA	G	GS	CG	IP	H	BB	SO	ShO	Relief W	Relief L	Relief SV	Bat AB	Bat H	Bat HR	BA	PO	A	E	DP	TC/G	FA
1967	LA	N	0	0	–	20.25	1	0	0	1.1	3	0	2	0	0	0	0	0	0	0	–	0	1	0	0	1.0	1.000
1970	MIL	A	0	0	–	9.00	1	0	0	2	2	1	0	0	0	0	0	0	0	0	–	0	0	0	0	0.0	–
2 yrs.			0	0	–	13.50	2	0	0	3.1	5	1	2	0	0	0	0	0	0	0	–	0	1	0	0	0.5	1.000

Bob Bruce

BRUCE, ROBERT JAMES — BR TR 6'3" 200 lbs.
B. May 16, 1933, Detroit, Mich.

Year	Team	Lg	W	L	PCT	ERA	G	GS	CG	IP	H	BB	SO	ShO	Relief W	Relief L	Relief SV	Bat AB	Bat H	Bat HR	BA	PO	A	E	DP	TC/G	FA
1959	DET	A	0	1	.000	9.00	2	1	0	2	2	3	1	0	0	0	0	0	0	0	–	0	0	0	0	0.0	–
1960			4	7	.364	3.74	34	15	1	130	127	56	76	0	0	2	0	39	7	0	.179	9	23	1	2	1.0	.970
1961			1	2	.333	4.43	14	6	0	44.2	57	24	25	0	0	1	0	9	1	0	.111	5	1	1	0	0.5	.857
1962	HOU	N	10	9	.526	4.06	32	27	6	175	164	82	135	0	1	0	0	55	11	0	.200	14	26	1	2	1.3	.976
1963			5	9	.357	3.59	30	25	1	170.1	162	60	123	1	0	0	0	55	7	0	.127	13	21	1	1	1.2	.971
1964			15	9	.625	2.76	35	29	9	202.1	191	33	135	4	1	0	0	63	12	0	.190	11	35	1	0	1.3	.979
1965			9	18	.333	3.72	35	34	7	229.2	241	38	145	1	0	0	0	74	9	0	.122	25	36	3	1	1.8	.953
1966			3	13	.188	5.34	25	23	1	129.2	160	29	71	0	0	1	0	39	3	0	.077	15	18	0	1	1.3	1.000
1967	ATL	N	2	3	.400	4.89	12	7	1	38.2	42	15	22	0	0	1	1	12	2	0	.167	3	4	0	0	0.6	1.000
9 yrs.			49	71	.408	3.85	219	167	26	1122.1	1146	340	733	6	2	5	1	346	52	0	.150	95	164	8	7	1.2	.970

Lou Bruce

BRUCE, LOUIS R. — BL TR 5'5" 145 lbs.
B. Jan. 16, 1877, St. Regis, N. Y. D. Feb. 9, 1968, Ilion, N. Y.

Year	Team	Lg	W	L	PCT	ERA	G	GS	CG	IP	H	BB	SO	ShO	Relief W	Relief L	Relief SV	Bat AB	Bat H	Bat HR	BA	PO	A	E	DP	TC/G	FA
1904	PHI	A	0	0	–	4.91	2	0	0	11	11	2	2	0	0	0	0	*				0	7	2	0	4.5	.778

Fred Bruckbauer

BRUCKBAUER, FREDERICK JOHN — BR TR 6'1" 185 lbs.
B. May 27, 1938, New Ulm, Minn.

Year	Team	Lg	W	L	PCT	ERA	G	GS	CG	IP	H	BB	SO	ShO	Relief W	Relief L	Relief SV	Bat AB	Bat H	Bat HR	BA	PO	A	E	DP	TC/G	FA
1961	MIN	A	0	0	–	∞	1	0	0		3	1	0	0	0	0	0	0	0	0	–	0	0	0	0	0.0	–

Andy Bruckmiller

BRUCKMILLER, ANDREW — BR TR 5'11" 175 lbs.
B. Jan. 1, 1882, Pittsburgh, Pa. D. Jan. 12, 1970, McKeesport, Pa.

Year	Team	Lg	W	L	PCT	ERA	G	GS	CG	IP	H	BB	SO	ShO	Relief W	Relief L	Relief SV	Bat AB	Bat H	Bat HR	BA	PO	A	E	DP	TC/G	FA
1905	DET	A	0	0	–	27.00	1	0	0	1	4	1	1	0	0	0	0	1	0	0	.000	0	0	0	0	0.0	–

Mike Bruhert

BRUHERT, MICHAEL EDWIN — BR TR 6'6" 220 lbs.
B. June 24, 1951, Jamaica, N. Y.

Year	Team	Lg	W	L	PCT	ERA	G	GS	CG	IP	H	BB	SO	ShO	Relief W	Relief L	Relief SV	Bat AB	Bat H	Bat HR	BA	PO	A	E	DP	TC/G	FA
1978	NY	N	4	11	.267	4.77	27	22	1	134	171	34	56	1	0	0	0	40	3	0	.075	11	22	5	1	1.4	.868

Jack Bruner

BRUNER, JACK RAYMOND (Pappy) — BL TL 6'1" 185 lbs.
B. July 1, 1924, Waterloo, Iowa

Year	Team	Lg	W	L	PCT	ERA	G	GS	CG	IP	H	BB	SO	ShO	Relief W	Relief L	Relief SV	Bat AB	Bat H	Bat HR	BA	PO	A	E	DP	TC/G	FA
1949	CHI	A	1	2	.333	8.22	4	2	0	7.2	10	8	4	0	1	0	0	1	0	0	.000	0	0	0	0	0.0	–
1950	2 teams	CHI A (9G 0–0)			STL A (13G 1–2)																						
"	total		1	2	.333	4.37	22	1	0	47.1	43	37	24	0	1	1	1	10	0	0	.000	2	4	3	0	0.4	.667
2 yrs.			2	4	.333	4.91	26	3	0	55	53	45	28	0	2	1	1	11	0	0	.000	2	4	3	0	0.3	.667

Year	Team		W	L	PCT	ERA	G	GS	CG	IP	H	BB	SO	ShO	Relief Pitching W	L	SV	Batting AB	H	HR	BA	PO	A	E	DP	TC/G	FA

Roy Bruner

BRUNER, WALTER ROY   BR TR 6'   165 lbs.
B. Feb. 10, 1917, Cecilia, Ky. D. Nov. 30, 1986, St. Matthews, Ky.

Year	Team		W	L	PCT	ERA	G	GS	CG	IP	H	BB	SO	ShO	W	L	SV	AB	H	HR	BA	PO	A	E	DP	TC/G	FA
1939	PHI	N	0	4	.000	6.67	4	4	2	27	38	13	11	0	0	0	0	9	1	0	.111	1	3	0	0	1.0	1.000
1940			0	0	—	5.68	2	0	0	6.1	5	6	4	0	0	0	0	2	1	0	.500	0	2	0	0	1.0	1.000
1941			0	3	.000	4.91	13	1	0	29.1	37	25	13	0	0	2	0	6	0	0	.000	0	4	0	0	0.3	1.000
3 yrs.			0	7	.000	5.74	19	5	2	62.2	80	44	28	0	0	2	0	17	2	0	.118	1	9	0	0	0.5	1.000

George Brunet

BRUNET, GEORGE STUART (Lefty)   BR TL 6'1"   195 lbs.
B. June 8, 1935, Houghton, Mich.

Year	Team		W	L	PCT	ERA	G	GS	CG	IP	H	BB	SO	ShO	W	L	SV	AB	H	HR	BA	PO	A	E	DP	TC/G	FA
1956	KC	A	0	0	—	7.00	6	1	0	9	10	11	5	0	0	0	0	2	0	0	.000	0	3	0	0	0.5	1.000
1957			0	1	.000	5.56	2	0	0	11.1	13	4	3	0	0	0	0	2	0	0	.000	0	2	0	0	0.5	1.000
1959			0	0	—	11.57	2	0	0	4.2	10	7	7	0	0	0	0	0	0	0	—	0	4	1	0	2.5	.800
1960	2 teams		KC A	(3G 0–2)		MIL N	(17G 2–0)																					
"	total		2	2	.500	4.95	20	8	0	60	65	32	43	0	1	0	0	14	1	0	.071	2	16	0	0	0.9	1.000
1961	MIL	N	0	0	—	5.40	5	0	0	5	7	2	0	0	0	0	0	0	0	0	—	0	3	0	0	0.6	1.000
1962	HOU	N	2	4	.333	4.50	17	11	0	54	62	21	36	0	0	0	0	17	1	0	.059	4	12	2	2	1.1	.889
1963	2 teams		HOU N	(5G 0–3)		BAL A	(16G 0–1)																					
"	total		0	4	.000	6.06	21	2	0	32.2	49	15	24	0	0	2	1	4	0	0	.000	3	5	2	0	0.4	1.000
1964	LA	A	2	2	.500	3.61	10	7	0	42.1	38	25	36	0	0	1	0	11	2	0	.182	3	5	0	0	0.8	1.000
1965	CAL	A	9	11	.450	2.56	41	26	8	197	149	69	141	3	1	1	2	56	3	0	.054	6	29	2	1	0.9	.946
1966			13	13	.500	3.31	41	32	8	212	183	106	148	2	1	2	0	68	7	1	.103	11	33	1	2	1.1	.978
1967			11	19	.367	3.31	40	37	7	250	203	90	165	2	0	1	1	78	6	0	.077	5	36	1	0	1.1	.976
1968			13	17	.433	2.86	39	36	8	245.1	191	68	132	5	0	1	1	74	6	0	.081	5	31	1	1	0.9	.973
1969	2 teams		CAL A	(23G 6–7)		SEA A	(12G 2–5)																					
"	total		8	12	.400	4.44	35	30	4	164.1	168	67	93	2	0	0	0	47	4	0	.085	5	27	1	1	0.9	.970
1970	2 teams		WAS A	(24G 8–6)		PIT N	(12G 1–1)																					
"	total		9	7	.563	4.20	36	21	2	135	143	57	84	1	2	2	0	42	6	1	.143	2	19	2	2	0.6	.913
1971	STL	N	0	1	.000	6.00	7	0	0	9	12	7	4	0	0	1	0	3	1	0	.333	0	0	0	0	0.0	—
15 yrs.			69	93	.426	3.62	324	213	39	1431.2	1303	581	921	15	5	10	4	418	37	3	.089	46	225	11	11	0.9	.961

Tom Bruno

BRUNO, THOMAS MICHAEL   BR TR 6'5"   210 lbs.
B. Jan. 26, 1953, Chicago, Ill.

Year	Team		W	L	PCT	ERA	G	GS	CG	IP	H	BB	SO	ShO	W	L	SV	AB	H	HR	BA	PO	A	E	DP	TC/G	FA
1976	KC	A	1	0	1.000	6.88	12	0	0	17	20	9	11	0	1	0	0	0	0	0	—	0	1	0	0	0.1	1.000
1977	TOR	A	0	1	.000	8.00	12	0	0	18	30	13	9	0	0	1	0	0	0	0	—	2	3	1	0	0.5	.833
1978	STL	N	4	3	.571	1.98	18	3	0	50	38	17	33	0	3	2	1	12	1	0	.083	2	4	0	1	0.3	1.000
1979			2	3	.400	4.26	27	1	0	38	37	22	27	0	2	2	0	5	1	0	.200	2	5	0	0	0.3	1.000
4 yrs.			7	7	.500	4.24	69	4	0	123	125	61	80	0	6	5	1	17	2	0	.118	6	13	1	1	0.3	.950

Warren Brusstar

BRUSSTAR, WARREN SCOTT   BR TR 6'3"   200 lbs.
B. Feb. 2, 1952, Oakland, Calif.

Year	Team		W	L	PCT	ERA	G	GS	CG	IP	H	BB	SO	ShO	W	L	SV	AB	H	HR	BA	PO	A	E	DP	TC/G	FA
1977	PHI	N	7	2	.778	2.66	46	0	0	71	64	24	46	0	7	2	3	6	0	0	.000	3	16	0	1	0.4	1.000
1978			6	3	.667	2.33	58	0	0	89	74	30	60	0	6	3	0	7	1	0	.143	5	22	0	4	0.5	1.000
1979			1	0	1.000	7.07	13	0	0	14	23	4	7	0	1	0	1	0	0	0	—	2	2	0	0	0.2	1.000
1980			2	2	.500	3.69	26	0	0	39	42	13	21	0	2	2	0	1	0	0	.000	2	7	1	0	0.4	.900
1981			0	1	.000	4.50	12	0	0	12	12	10	8	0	0	1	0	0	0	0	—	2	1	0	0	0.2	1.000
1982	2 teams		PHI N	(22G 2–3)		CHI A	(10G 2–0)																					
"	total		4	3	.571	4.17	32	0	0	41	50	8	19	0	4	3	2	4	0	0	.000	2	9	0	1	0.3	1.000
1983	CHI	N	3	1	.750	2.35	59	0	0	80.1	67	37	46	0	3	1	1	4	0	0	.000	7	12	0	1	0.3	1.000
1984			1	1	.500	3.11	41	0	0	63.2	57	21	36	0	1	1	3	5	1	0	.200	8	7	0	0	0.4	1.000
1985			4	3	.571	6.05	51	0	0	74.1	87	36	34	0	4	3	4	7	1	0	.143	6	3	2	0	0.2	.818
9 yrs.			28	16	.636	3.51	340	0	0	484.1	476	183	273	0	28	16	14	32	3	0	.094	36	79	3	7	0.3	.975

DIVISIONAL PLAYOFF SERIES

Year	Team		W	L	PCT	ERA	G	GS	CG	IP	H	BB	SO	ShO	W	L	SV	AB	H	HR	BA	PO	A	E	DP	TC/G	FA
1981	PHI	N	0	0	—	4.91	2	0	0	3.2	5	1	3	0	0	0	0	0	0	0	—	0	0	0	0	0.0	—

LEAGUE CHAMPIONSHIP SERIES

Year	Team		W	L	PCT	ERA	G	GS	CG	IP	H	BB	SO	ShO	W	L	SV	AB	H	HR	BA	PO	A	E	DP	TC/G	FA
1977	PHI	N	0	0	—	3.38	2	0	0	2.2	1	2	1	0	0	0	0	0	0	0	—	0	0	0	0	0.0	—
1978			0	0	—	0.00	2	0	0	2.2	2	1	0	0	0	0	0	0	0	0	—	0	0	0	0	0.0	—
1980			1	0	1.000	3.38	2	0	0	2.2	1	1	0	0	1	0	0	1	0	0	.000	0	0	0	0	0.0	—
1984	CHI	N	0	0	—	0.00	3	0	0	4.2	6	0	1	0	0	0	0	0	0	0	—	0	1	0	0	0.3	1.000
4 yrs.			1	0	1.000	1.42	10	0	0	12.2	11	3	3	0	1	0	0	2	0	0	.000	0	1	0	0	0.1	1.000

WORLD SERIES

Year	Team		W	L	PCT	ERA	G	GS	CG	IP	H	BB	SO	ShO	W	L	SV	AB	H	HR	BA	PO	A	E	DP	TC/G	FA
1980	PHI	N	0	0	—	0.00	1	0	0	2.1	0	1	0	0	0	0	0	0	0	0	—	0	0	0	0	0.0	—

Clay Bryant

BRYANT, CLAIBORNE HENRY   BR TR 6'2½"   195 lbs.
B. Nov. 26, 1911, Madison Heights, Va.

Year	Team		W	L	PCT	ERA	G	GS	CG	IP	H	BB	SO	ShO	W	L	SV	AB	H	HR	BA	PO	A	E	DP	TC/G	FA
1935	CHI	N	1	2	.333	5.16	9	1	0	22.2	34	7	13	0	1	2	2	6	2	1	.333	2	3	0	0	0.6	1.000
1936			1	2	.333	3.30	26	0	0	57.1	57	24	35	0	1	2	0	12	5	0	.417	6	13	2	0	0.8	.905
1937			9	3	.750	4.26	38	10	4	135.1	117	78	75	1	7	0	3	45	14	1	.311	4	13	2	3	0.5	.895
1938			19	11	.633	3.10	44	30	17	270.1	235	125	135	3	4	1	2	106	24	3	.226	9	38	2	4	1.1	.959
1939			2	1	.667	5.74	4	4	2	31.1	42	14	9	0	0	0	0	14	3	0	.214	4	2	1	0	1.8	.857
1940			0	1	.000	4.78	8	0	0	26.1	26	14	5	0	0	1	0	9	3	0	.333	3	5	0	0	1.0	1.000
6 yrs.			32	20	.615	3.73	129	45	23	543.1	511	262	272	4	13	6	7	192	51	5	.266	28	74	7	7	0.8	.936

WORLD SERIES

Year	Team		W	L	PCT	ERA	G	GS	CG	IP	H	BB	SO	ShO	W	L	SV	AB	H	HR	BA	PO	A	E	DP	TC/G	FA
1938	CHI	N	0	1	.000	6.75	1	1	0	5.1	6	5	3	0	0	0	0	2	0	0	.000	0	0	0	0	0.0	—

Ron Bryant

BRYANT, RONALD RAYMOND (Bear)   BB TL 6'   190 lbs.
B. Nov. 12, 1947, Redlands, Calif.

Year	Team		W	L	PCT	ERA	G	GS	CG	IP	H	BB	SO	ShO	W	L	SV	AB	H	HR	BA	PO	A	E	DP	TC/G	FA
1967	SF	N	0	0	—	4.50	1	0	0	4	3	1	2	0	0	0	0	1	0	0	.000	0	0	0	0	0.0	—
1969			4	3	.571	4.34	16	8	0	58	60	25	30	0	0	0	1	16	3	0	.188	1	11	1	1	0.8	.923
1970			5	8	.385	4.78	34	11	3	96	103	38	66	0	3	2	0	27	3	0	.111	4	20	0	0	0.7	1.000
1971			7	10	.412	3.79	27	22	3	140	146	49	79	2	1	0	1	50	10	0	.200	1	26	2	1	1.1	.931
1972			14	7	.667	2.90	35	28	11	214	176	77	107	4	0	1	0	70	12	3	.171	3	15	3	2	0.6	.857

Year	Team		W	L	PCT	ERA	G	GS	CG	IP	H	BB	SO	ShO	Relief Pitching			Batting			BA	PO	A	E	DP	TC/G	FA
															W	L	SV	AB	H	HR							

Ron Bryant *continued*

1973			24	12	.667	3.54	41	39	8	269.2	240	115	143	0	1	0	0	95	16	0	.168	9	45	1	1	1.3	.982
1974			3	15	.167	5.60	41	23	0	127	142	68	75	0	0	1	0	31	4	0	.129	5	18	1	1	0.6	.958
1975	STL	N	0	1	.000	16.00	10	1	0	9	20	7	7	0	0	0	0	1	0	0	.000	1	2	0	0	0.3	1.000
8 yrs.			57	56	.504	4.02	205	132	23	917.2	890	379	509	6	5	4	1	291	48	0	.165	24	137	8	6	0.8	.953

LEAGUE CHAMPIONSHIP SERIES

| 1971 | SF | N | 0 | 0 | — | 4.50 | 1 | 0 | 0 | 2 | 1 | 1 | 2 | 0 | 0 | 0 | 0 | 0 | 0 | 0 | — | 0 | 0 | 0 | 0 | 0.0 | — |

T. R. Bryden

BRYDEN, THOMAS RAY
B. Jan. 17, 1959, Moses Lake, Wash.

BR TR 6'4" 190 lbs.

| 1986 | CAL | A | 2 | 1 | .667 | 6.55 | 16 | 0 | 0 | 34.1 | 38 | 21 | 25 | 0 | 2 | 1 | 0 | 0 | 0 | 0 | — | 2 | 4 | 0 | 1 | 0.4 | 1.000 |

Charlie Brynan

BRYNAN, CHARLES RULEY (Tod)
B. July, 1863, Philadelphia, Pa. D. May 10, 1925, Philadelphia, Pa.

BR TR

1888	CHI	N	2	1	.667	6.48	3	3	2	25	29	7	11	0	0	0	0	11	2	0	.182	1	3	1	0	1.7	.800
1891	BOS	N	0	1	.000	54.00	1	1	0	1	4	3	0	0	0	0	0	0	0	0	—	0	0	0	0	0.0	—
2 yrs.			2	2	.500	8.31	4	4	2	26	33	10	11	0	0	0	0	11	2	0	.182	1	3	1	0	1.3	.800

Bob Buchanan

BUCHANAN, ROBERT GORDON
B. May 3, 1961, Ridley Park, Pa.

BL TL 6'1" 185 lbs.

1985	CIN	N	1	0	1.000	8.44	14	0	0	16	25	9	3	0	1	0	0	1	0	0	.000	1	3	0	0	0.3	1.000
1989	KC	A	0	0	—	16.20	2	0	0	3.1	5	3	3	0	0	0	0	0	0	0	—	0	0	0	0	0.0	—
2 yrs.			1	0	1.000	9.78	16	0	0	19.1	30	12	6	0	1	0	0	1	0	0	.000	1	3	0	0	0.3	1.000

Jim Buchanan

BUCHANAN, JAMES FORREST (Buck)
B. July 1, 1876, Chatham Hill, Va. D. June 15, 1949, Norfolk, Neb.

BL TR 5'10½" 170 lbs.

| 1905 | STL | A | 5 | 10 | .333 | 3.50 | 22 | 15 | 12 | 141.1 | 149 | 27 | 54 | 1 | 0 | 1 | 2 | 46 | 7 | 0 | .152 | 8 | 47 | 8 | 1 | 2.9 | .873 |

Garland Buckeye

BUCKEYE, GARLAND MAIERS (Gob)
B. Oct. 16, 1897, Heron Lake, Minn.
D. Nov. 14, 1975, Stone Lake, Wis.

BB TL 6' 260 lbs.
BB 1918,1927

1918	WAS	A	0	0	—	18.00	1	0	0	2	3	6	2	0	0	0	0	0	0	0	—	1	1	0	0	2.0	1.000
1925	CLE	A	13	8	.619	3.65	30	18	11	153	161	58	49	1	3	2	0	62	14	3	.226	8	31	0	2	1.3	1.000
1926			6	9	.400	3.10	32	18	5	165.2	160	69	36	1	2	0	0	60	12	0	.200	7	35	3	5	1.4	.933
1927			10	17	.370	3.96	35	25	13	204.2	231	74	38	2	1	3	1	71	19	0	.268	7	50	3	4	1.7	.950
1928	2 teams		CLE A	(9G 1–5)		NY N	(1G 0–0)																					
"	total		1	5	.167	7.32	10	6	0	39.1	67	7	9	0	0	0	0	11	2	0	.182	1	8	0	1	0.9	1.000
5 yrs.			30	39	.435	3.90	108	67	29	564.2	622	214	134	4	6	7	1	204	47	5	.230	24	125	6	12	1.4	.961

Ed Buckingham

BUCKINGHAM, EDWARD TAYLOR
B. May 22, 1874, Metuchen, N. J. D. July 30, 1942, Bridgeport, Conn.

| 1895 | WAS | N | 0 | 0 | — | 6.00 | 1 | 1 | 0 | 3 | 6 | 2 | 1 | 0 | 0 | 0 | 0 | 1 | 0 | 0 | .000 | 0 | 1 | 0 | 0 | 1.0 | 1.000 |

Jess Buckles

BUCKLES, JESSE ROBERT (Jim)
B. May 20, 1890, LaVerne, Calif. D. Aug. 2, 1975, Westminster, Calif.

BL TL 6'2½" 205 lbs.

| 1916 | NY | A | 0 | 0 | — | 2.25 | 2 | 0 | 0 | 4 | 3 | 4 | 1 | 0 | 0 | 0 | 0 | 1 | 0 | 0 | .000 | 0 | 1 | 0 | 1 | 1.0 | .500 |

John Buckley

BUCKLEY, JOHN EDWARD
B. Mar. 20, 1870, Marlboro, Mass. D. May 3, 1942, Westboro, Mass.

BL TR 6'1" 200 lbs.

| 1890 | BUF | P | 1 | 3 | .250 | 7.68 | 4 | 4 | 4 | 34 | 49 | 16 | 4 | 0 | 0 | 0 | 0 | 15 | 0 | 0 | .000 | 1 | 11 | 0 | 0 | 3.0 | 1.000 |

Mike Budnick

BUDNICK, MICHAEL JOE
B. Sept. 15, 1919, Astoria, Ore.

BR TR 6'1" 200 lbs.

1946	NY	N	2	3	.400	3.16	35	7	1	88.1	75	48	36	1	2	3	3	20	6	1	.300	5	21	2	0	0.8	.929
1947			0	0	—	10.50	7	1	0	12	16	10	6	0	0	0	0	4	1	0	.250	3	3	0	0	0.9	1.000
2 yrs.			2	3	.400	4.04	42	8	1	100.1	91	58	42	1	2	3	3	24	7	1	.292	8	24	2	0	0.8	.941

Charlie Buffinton

BUFFINTON, CHARLES G.
B. June 14, 1861, Fall River, Mass. D. Sept. 23, 1907, Fall River, Mass.
Manager 1890.

BR TR 6'1" 180 lbs.

1882	BOS	N	2	3	.400	4.07	5	5	4	42	53	14	17	1	0	0	0	50	13	0	.260	6	2	5	0	2.6	.615
1883			25	14	.641	3.03	43	41	34	333	346	51	188	5	1	0	1	341	81	1	.238	15	58	13	3	2.0	.849
1884			48	16	.750	2.15	67	67	63	587	506	76	417	8	0	0	0	352	94	1	.267	40	118	9	2	2.5	.946
1885			22	27	.449	2.88	51	50	49	434.1	425	112	242	6	0	0	0	338	81	1	.240	16	118	13	5	2.9	.912
1886			7	10	.412	4.59	18	17	16	151	203	39	47	0	0	0	0	176	51	0	.290	5	31	5	1	2.3	.878
1887	PHI	N	21	17	.553	3.66	40	38	35	332.1	352	92	160	1	1	0	0	269	72	1	.268	18	90	8	3	2.9	.931
1888			28	17	.622	1.91	46	46	43	400.1	324	59	199	6	0	0	0	160	29	0	.181	31	122	10	3	3.5	.939
1889			28	16	.636	3.24	47	43	37	380	390	121	153	2	3	0	0	154	32	0	.208	18	80	9	4	2.3	.916
1890	PHI	P	19	14	.576	3.81	36	33	28	283.1	312	126	89	0	1	0	1	150	41	0	.273	12	77	14	5	2.9	.864
1891	BOS	AA	29	9	.763	2.55	48	43	33	363.2	303	120	158	4	2	0	1	181	34	1	.188	10	117	9	3	2.8	.934
1892	BAL	N	3	8	.273	4.92	13	13	9	97	130	46	30	0	0	0	0	43	15	0	.349	3	30	4	1	2.8	.892
11 yrs.			232	151	.606	2.96	414	396	351	3404	3344	856	1700	33	8	0	3	*				174	843	99	30	2.7	.911

Bob Buhl

BUHL, ROBERT RAY
B. Aug. 12, 1928, Saginaw, Mich.

BR TR 6'2" 180 lbs.
BB 1958-60,1966

1953	MIL	N	13	8	.619	2.97	30	18	8	154.1	133	73	83	3	4	2	0	53	6	0	.113	14	25	1	1	1.3	.975
1954			2	7	.222	4.00	31	14	2	110.1	117	65	57	1	0	2	3	31	1	0	.032	5	18	1	1	0.8	.958
1955			13	11	.542	3.21	38	27	11	201.2	168	109	117	1	1	1	1	57	6	0	.105	12	30	2	1	1.2	.955

Year	Team	W	L	PCT	ERA	G	GS	CG	IP	H	BB	SO	ShO	Relief Pitching W	L	SV	Batting AB	H	HR	BA	PO	A	E	DP	TC/G	FA

Bob Buhl *continued*

Year	Team	W	L	PCT	ERA	G	GS	CG	IP	H	BB	SO	ShO	W	L	SV	AB	H	HR	BA	PO	A	E	DP	TC/G	FA
1956		18	8	.692	3.32	38	33	13	216.2	190	105	86	2	1	0	0	73	7	0	.096	19	35	1	2	1.4	.982
1957		18	7	**.720**	2.74	34	31	14	216.2	191	121	117	2	0	0	0	73	6	0	.082	14	25	2	2	1.2	.951
1958		5	2	.714	3.45	11	10	3	73	74	30	27	0	0	0	1	25	5	0	.200	5	19	2	0	2.4	.923
1959		15	9	.625	2.86	31	25	12	198	181	74	105	4	0	1	0	70	4	0	.057	21	43	1	4	2.1	.985
1960		16	9	.640	3.09	36	33	11	238.2	202	**103**	121	2	1	0	0	89	14	0	.157	26	50	1	3	2.1	.987
1961		9	10	.474	4.11	32	28	9	188.1	180	98	77	1	0	0	0	60	4	0	.067	16	37	1	1	1.7	.981
1962	2 teams	MIL N	(1G 0-1)		CHI N	(34G 12-13)																				
"	total	12	14	.462	3.87	35	31	8	214	210	98	110	1	0	0	0	70	0	0	.000	15	29	3	2	1.3	.936
1963	CHI N	11	14	.440	3.38	37	34	6	226	239	62	108	0	0	0	0	74	8	0	.108	12	44	0	5	1.5	1.000
1964		15	14	.517	3.83	36	35	11	227.2	208	68	107	3	0	0	0	73	7	0	.096	22	48	0	4	1.9	1.000
1965		13	11	.542	4.39	32	31	2	184.1	207	57	92	0	0	0	0	67	4	0	.060	14	34	2	0	1.6	.960
1966	2 teams	CHI N	(1G 0-0)		PHI N	(32G 6-8)																				
"	total	6	8	.429	4.96	33	19	1	134.1	160	40	60	0	0	0	0	42	4	0	.095	16	23	1	3	1.2	.975
1967	PHI N	0	0	–	13.50	3	0	0	2.2	6	2	1	0	0	0	0	0	0	0	–	0	1	0	0	0.3	1.000
15 yrs.		166	132	.557	3.55	457	369	111	2586.2	2446	1105	1268	20	9	8	6	857	76	0	.089	211	461	18	32	1.5	.974

WORLD SERIES

Year	Team	W	L	PCT	ERA	G	GS	CG	IP	H	BB	SO	ShO	W	L	SV	AB	H	HR	BA	PO	A	E	DP	TC/G	FA
1957	MIL N	0	1	.000	10.80	2	2	0	3.1	6	6	4	0	0	0	0	1	0	0	.000	0	2	1	0	1.5	.667

DeWayne Buice

BUICE, DeWAYNE ALLISON
B. Aug. 20, 1957, Lynwood, Calif.

BR TR 6' 170 lbs.

Year	Team	W	L	PCT	ERA	G	GS	CG	IP	H	BB	SO	ShO	W	L	SV	AB	H	HR	BA	PO	A	E	DP	TC/G	FA
1987	CAL A	6	7	.462	3.39	57	0	0	114	87	40	109	0	6	7	17	0	0	0	–	3	15	1	2	0.3	.947
1988		2	4	.333	5.88	32	0	0	41.1	45	19	38	0	2	4	3	0	0	0	–	4	6	0	0	0.3	1.000
1989	TOR A	1	0	1.000	5.82	7	0	0	17	13	13	10	0	1	0	0	0	0	0	–	0	3	0	0	0.4	1.000
3 yrs.		9	11	.450	4.23	96	0	0	172.1	145	72	157	0	9	11	20	0	0	0	–	7	24	1	2	0.3	.969

Cy Buker

BUKER, CYRIL OWEN
B. Feb. 5, 1919, Greenwood, Wis.

BL TR 5'11" 190 lbs.

Year	Team	W	L	PCT	ERA	G	GS	CG	IP	H	BB	SO	ShO	W	L	SV	AB	H	HR	BA	PO	A	E	DP	TC/G	FA
1945	BKN N	7	2	.778	3.30	42	4	0	87.1	90	45	48	1	0	2	5	16	3	0	.188	3	11	1	1	0.4	.933

Red Bullock

BULLOCK, MALTON JOSEPH
B. Oct. 12, 1911, Biloxi, Miss. D. June 27, 1988, Pascagoula, Miss.

BL TL 6'1" 192 lbs.

Year	Team	W	L	PCT	ERA	G	GS	CG	IP	H	BB	SO	ShO	W	L	SV	AB	H	HR	BA	PO	A	E	DP	TC/G	FA
1936	PHI A	0	2	.000	14.04	12	2	0	16.2	19	37	7	0	0	1	0	4	0	0	.000	3	3	0	0	0.5	1.000

Wally Bunker

BUNKER, WALLACE EDWARD
B. Jan. 25, 1945, Seattle, Wash.

BR TR 6'2" 197 lbs.

Year	Team	W	L	PCT	ERA	G	GS	CG	IP	H	BB	SO	ShO	W	L	SV	AB	H	HR	BA	PO	A	E	DP	TC/G	FA
1963	BAL A	0	1	.000	13.50	1	1	0	4	10	3	1	0	0	0	0	2	1	0	.500	0	0	0	0	0.0	–
1964		19	5	**.792**	2.69	29	29	12	214	161	62	96	1	0	0	0	72	5	0	.069	20	34	1	3	1.9	.982
1965		10	8	.556	3.38	34	27	4	189	170	58	84	1	0	0	2	55	4	0	.073	8	32	1	0	1.2	.976
1966		10	6	.625	4.29	29	24	3	142.2	151	48	89	0	0	1	0	48	5	0	.104	8	19	0	3	0.9	1.000
1967		3	7	.300	4.09	29	9	1	88	83	31	51	0	1	2	1	26	2	0	.077	4	20	0	1	0.8	1.000
1968		2	0	1.000	2.41	18	10	2	71	59	14	44	1	0	0	1	18	2	0	.111	5	9	1	0	0.8	.933
1969	KC A	12	11	.522	3.23	35	31	10	222.2	198	62	130	1	0	0	2	70	10	0	.143	19	43	2	6	1.8	.969
1970		2	11	.154	4.20	24	15	2	122	109	50	59	1	0	1	0	31	2	0	.065	5	17	3	0	1.0	.880
1971		2	3	.400	5.06	7	6	2	32	35	6	15	0	0	0	0	9	0	0	.000	1	5	0	0	0.9	1.000
9 yrs.		60	52	.536	3.51	206	152	34	1085.1	976	334	569	5	2	4	5	331	31	0	.094	70	179	8	13	1.2	.969

WORLD SERIES

Year	Team	W	L	PCT	ERA	G	GS	CG	IP	H	BB	SO	ShO	W	L	SV	AB	H	HR	BA	PO	A	E	DP	TC/G	FA
1966	BAL A	1	0	1.000	0.00	1	1	1	9	6	1	6	1	0	0	0	2	0	0	.000	0	3	0	0	3.0	1.000

Jim Bunning

BUNNING, JAMES PAUL DAVID
B. Oct. 23, 1931, Southgate, Ky.

BR TR 6'3" 190 lbs.

Year	Team	W	L	PCT	ERA	G	GS	CG	IP	H	BB	SO	ShO	W	L	SV	AB	H	HR	BA	PO	A	E	DP	TC/G	FA
1955	DET A	3	5	.375	6.35	15	3	0	51	59	32	37	0	2	0	1	15	3	0	.200	4	8	1	1	0.9	.923
1956		5	1	.833	3.71	15	3	0	53.1	55	28	34	0	4	0	1	18	6	0	.333	2	6	0	0	0.5	1.000
1957		**20**	8	.714	2.69	45	30	14	267.1	214	72	182	1	2	1	1	94	20	1	.213	12	19	0	0	0.7	1.000
1958		14	12	.538	3.52	35	34	10	219.2	188	79	177	3	0	0	0	75	14	0	.187	9	16	0	0	0.7	1.000
1959		17	13	.567	3.89	40	35	14	249.2	220	75	201	1	0	1	1	89	17	1	.191	11	16	3	1	0.8	.900
1960		11	14	.440	2.79	36	34	10	252	217	64	201	3	0	0	0	81	13	0	.160	11	31	0	1	1.2	1.000
1961		17	11	.607	3.19	38	37	12	268	232	71	194	4	0	0	0	100	13	0	.130	21	29	3	6	1.4	.943
1962		19	10	.655	3.59	41	35	12	258	262	74	184	2	0	0	0	95	23	1	.242	17	13	0	1	0.7	1.000
1963		12	13	.480	3.88	39	35	6	248.1	245	69	196	2	0	0	0	84	13	0	.155	18	25	1	1	1.1	.977
1964	PHI N	19	8	.704	2.63	41	39	13	284.1	248	46	219	5	0	0	2	99	12	0	.121	10	31	3	2	1.1	.932
1965		19	9	.679	2.60	39	39	15	291	253	62	268	7	0	0	0	103	22	1	.214	29	40	3	2	1.8	.958
1966		19	14	.576	2.41	43	**41**	16	314	260	55	252	5	1	0	1	106	19	0	.179	18	30	2	1	1.2	.960
1967		17	15	.531	2.29	40	**40**	16	302.1	241	73	253	6	0	0	0	104	17	2	.163	16	33	1	1	1.3	.980
1968	PIT N	4	14	.222	3.88	27	26	3	160	168	48	95	1	0	0	0	51	5	0	.098	6	17	2	1	0.9	.920
1969	2 teams	PIT N	(25G 10-9)		LA N	(9G 3-1)																				
"	total	13	10	.565	3.69	34	34	5	212.1	212	59	157	0	0	0	0	65	4	0	.062	5	15	1	2	0.6	.952
1970	PHI N	10	15	.400	4.11	34	33	4	219	233	56	147	0	0	0	0	71	9	0	.127	12	27	2	1	1.2	.951
1971		5	12	.294	5.48	29	16	1	110	126	37	58	0	0	0	0	25	3	1	.120	5	16	1	1	0.8	.955
17 yrs.		224	184	.549	3.27	591	519	151	3760.1	3433	1000	2855	40	9	4	16	1275	213	7	.167	206	372	23	20	1.0	.962

Bill Burbach

BURBACH, WILLIAM DAVID
B. Aug. 22, 1947, Dickeyville, Wis.

BR TR 6'4" 215 lbs.

Year	Team	W	L	PCT	ERA	G	GS	CG	IP	H	BB	SO	ShO	W	L	SV	AB	H	HR	BA	PO	A	E	DP	TC/G	FA
1969	NY A	6	8	.429	3.65	31	24	2	140.2	112	102	82	1	1	0	0	40	4	0	.100	10	16	0	1	0.8	1.000
1970		0	2	.000	10.06	4	4	0	17	23	9	10	0	0	0	0	5	0	0	.000	0	2	1	0	0.8	.667
1971		0	1	.000	12.00	2	0	0	3	6	5	3	0	0	1	0	2	0	0	.000	0	0	1	0	0.5	–
3 yrs.		6	11	.353	4.48	37	28	2	160.2	141	116	95	1	1	1	0	47	4	0	.085	10	18	2	1	0.8	.933

Year	Team		W	L	PCT	ERA	G	GS	CG	IP	H	BB	SO	ShO	Relief Pitching W	L	SV	Batting AB	H	HR	BA	PO	A	E	DP	TC/G	FA

Larry Burchart

BURCHART, LARRY WAYNE
B. Feb. 8, 1946, Tulsa, Okla.   BR TR 6'3" 205 lbs.

| 1969 | CLE | A | 0 | 2 | .000 | 4.25 | 29 | 0 | 0 | 42.1 | 42 | 24 | 26 | 0 | 0 | 2 | 0 | 0 | 0 | 0 | – | 1 | 5 | 2 | 0 | 0.3 | .750 |

Fred Burchell

BURCHELL, FREDERICK DUFF
B. July 14, 1879, Perth Amboy, N. J. D. Nov. 20, 1951, Jordan, N. Y.   BL TL 5'11" 190 lbs.

1903	PHI	N	0	3	.000	2.86	6	3	2	44	48	14	12	0	0	0	0	16	3	0	.188	0	13	3	0	2.7	.813
1907	BOS	A	0	1	.000	2.70	2	1	0	10	8	2	6	0	0	0	0	5	1	0	.200	0	2	0	0	1.0	1.000
1908			10	8	.556	2.96	31	19	9	179.2	161	65	94	0	1	1	0	69	17	0	.246	5	48	8	0	2.0	.869
1909			3	3	.500	2.94	10	5	1	52	51	11	12	0	1	0	0	19	3	0	.158	1	21	3	1	2.5	.880
4 yrs.			13	15	.464	2.93	49	28	12	285.2	268	92	124	0	2	1	0	109	24	0	.220	6	84	14	1	2.1	.865

Freddie Burdette

BURDETTE, FREDDIE THOMASON
B. Sept. 15, 1936, Moultrie, Ga.   BR TR 6'1" 170 lbs.

1962	CHI	N	0	0	–	3.72	8	0	0	9.2	5	8	5	0	0	0	1	1	0	0	.000	0	2	1	0	0.4	.667
1963			0	0	–	3.86	4	0	0	4.2	5	2	1	0	0	0	0	0	0	0	–	0	2	0	1	0.5	1.000
1964			1	0	1.000	3.15	18	0	0	20	17	10	4	0	1	0	0	1	1	0	1.000	3	2	0	0	0.3	1.000
3 yrs.			1	0	1.000	3.41	30	0	0	34.1	27	20	10	0	1	0	1	2	1	0	.500	3	6	1	1	0.3	.900

Lew Burdette

BURDETTE, SELVA LEWIS
B. Nov. 22, 1926, Nitro, W. Va.   BR TR 6'2" 180 lbs.

1950	NY	A	0	0	–	6.75	2	0	0	1.1	3	0	0	0	0	0	0	0	0	0	–	0	1	0	1	0.5	1.000
1951	BOS	N	0	0	–	6.23	3	0	0	4.1	6	5	1	0	0	0	0	1	0	0	.000	0	1	0	0	0.3	1.000
1952			6	11	.353	3.61	45	9	5	137	138	47	47	0	2	8	7	35	4	0	.114	9	29	1	3	0.9	.974
1953	MIL	N	15	5	.750	3.24	46	13	6	175	177	56	58	1	8	0	8	53	9	0	.170	11	37	1	6	1.1	.980
1954			15	14	.517	2.76	38	32	13	238	224	62	79	4	1	1	0	79	7	0	.089	17	49	4	6	1.8	.943
1955			13	8	.619	4.03	42	33	11	230	253	73	70	2	2	1	0	86	20	0	.233	18	47	2	6	1.6	.970
1956			19	10	.655	2.70	39	35	16	256.1	234	52	110	6	0	0	1	86	16	0	.186	19	48	1	4	1.7	.985
1957			17	9	.654	3.72	37	33	14	256.2	260	59	78	1	2	1	0	88	13	2	.148	22	53	4	3	2.1	.949
1958			20	10	.667	2.91	40	36	19	275.1	279	50	113	3	2	0	0	99	24	3	.242	27	53	1	4	2.0	.988
1959			21	15	.583	4.07	41	39	20	289.2	312	38	105	4	0	0	1	104	21	0	.202	21	47	1	6	1.7	.986
1960			19	13	.594	3.36	45	32	18	275.2	277	35	83	4	3	2	4	91	16	2	.176	31	68	2	6	2.2	.980
1961			18	11	.621	4.00	40	36	14	272.1	295	33	92	3	2	0	0	103	21	3	.204	27	60	1	2	2.2	.989
1962			10	9	.526	4.89	37	19	6	143.2	172	23	59	1	3	1	2	51	9	0	.176	8	33	2	1	1.2	.953
1963	2 teams	MIL N	(15G 6–5)		STL N		(21G 3–8)																				
"	total		9	13	.409	3.70	36	27	7	182.2	177	40	73	1	1	2	2	57	4	0	.070	11	27	5	3	1.2	.884
1964	2 teams	STL N	(8G 1–0)		CHI N		(28G 9–9)																				
"	total		10	9	.526	4.66	36	17	8	141	162	22	43	2	2	1	0	44	12	2	.273	10	36	0	3	1.3	1.000
1965	2 teams	CHI N	(7G 0–2)		PHI N		(19G 3–3)																				
"	total		3	5	.375	5.44	26	12	1	91	121	21	28	1	0	1	1	26	8	0	.308	6	17	0	3	0.9	1.000
1966	CAL	A	7	2	.778	3.39	54	0	0	79.2	80	12	27	0	7	2	5	8	1	0	.125	8	11	2	0	0.4	.905
1967			1	0	1.000	4.91	19	0	0	18.1	16	0	8	0	1	0	1	0	0	0	–	0	5	0	0	0.3	1.000
18 yrs.			203	144	.585	3.66	626	373	158	3068	3186	628	1074	33	36	19	31	1011	185	12	.183	245	622	27	55	1.4	.970

WORLD SERIES

1957	MIL	N	3	0	1.000	0.67	3	3	3	27	21	4	13	2	0	0	0	8	0	0	.000	0	9	0	0	3.0	1.000
1958			1	2	.333	5.64	3	3	1	22.1	22	4	12	0	0	0	0	9	1	1	.111	2	2	0	0	1.3	1.000
2 yrs.			4	2	.667	2.92	6	6	4	49.1	43	8	25	2	0	0	0	17	1	1	.059	2	11	0	0	2.2	1.000

4th

Bill Burdick

BURDICK, WILLIAM BYRON
B. Oct. 11, 1859, Austin, Minn. D. Oct. 23, 1949, Spokane, Wash.   BR TR

1888	IND	N	10	10	.500	2.81	20	20	20	176	168	43	55	0	0	0	0	68	10	0	.147	14	34	5	0	2.7	.906
1889			2	4	.333	4.53	10	4	2	45.2	58	13	16	0	0	2	1	17	2	0	.118	2	8	0	0	1.0	1.000
2 yrs.			12	14	.462	3.17	30	24	22	221.2	226	56	71	0	0	2	1	85	12	0	.141	16	42	5	0	2.1	.921

Tom Burgmeier

BURGMEIER, THOMAS HENRY (Bugs)
B. Aug. 2, 1943, St. Paul, Minn.   BL TL 5'11" 185 lbs.

1968	CAL	A	1	4	.200	4.33	56	2	0	72.2	65	24	33	0	1	2	5	2	0	0	.000	11	23	1	7	0.6	.971
1969	KC	A	3	1	.750	4.17	31	0	0	54	67	21	23	0	3	1	0	18	3	0	.167	9	15	0	1	0.8	1.000
1970			6	6	.500	3.18	41	0	0	68	59	23	43	0	6	6	1	14	2	0	.143	3	20	2	0	0.6	.920
1971			9	7	.563	1.74	67	0	0	88	71	30	44	0	9	7	17	20	5	0	.250	7	28	1	3	0.5	.972
1972			6	2	.750	4.25	51	0	0	55	67	33	18	0	6	2	9	12	4	0	.333	6	13	1	0	0.4	.950
1973			0	0	–	5.40	6	0	0	10	13	4	4	0	0	0	0	0	0	0	–	1	0	0	0	0.2	1.000
1974	MIN	A	5	3	.625	4.52	50	0	0	91.2	92	26	34	0	5	3	4	0	0	0	–	11	25	1	0	0.7	.973
1975			5	8	.385	3.09	46	0	0	75.2	76	23	41	0	5	8	11	0	0	0	–	6	12	0	1	0.4	1.000
1976			8	1	.889	2.50	57	0	0	115.1	95	29	45	0	8	1	1	0	0	0	–	8	26	0	2	0.6	1.000
1977			6	4	.600	5.10	61	0	0	97	113	33	35	0	6	4	7	0	0	0	–	11	18	1	1	0.5	.967
1978	BOS	A	2	1	.667	4.40	35	1	0	61.1	74	23	24	0	2	1	2	0	0	0	–	5	13	2	0	0.6	.900
1979			3	2	.600	2.73	44	0	0	89	89	16	60	0	3	2	4	0	0	0	–	5	14	3	1	0.4	1.000
1980			5	4	.556	2.00	62	0	0	99	87	20	54	0	5	4	24	0	0	0	–	7	27	0	5	0.5	1.000
1981			4	5	.444	2.85	32	0	0	60	61	17	35	0	4	5	6	0	0	0	–	7	13	0	1	0.6	1.000
1982			7	0	1.000	2.29	40	0	0	102.1	98	22	44	0	7	0	2	0	0	0	–	17	20	1	4	1.0	.974
1983	OAK	A	6	7	.462	2.81	49	0	0	96	89	32	39	0	6	7	4	0	0	0	–	7	23	2	2	0.7	.909
1984			3	0	1.000	2.35	17	0	0	23	15	8	8	0	3	0	2	0	0	0	–	3	3	0	0	0.4	1.000
17 yrs.			79	55	.590	3.23	745	3	0	1258	1231	384	584	0	79	53	102	66	14	0	.212	124	293	13	36	0.6	.970

Sandy Burk

BURK, CHARLES SANFORD
B. Apr. 22, 1887, Columbus, Ohio D. Oct. 11, 1934, Brooklyn, N. Y.   BR TR 5'8" 155 lbs.

| 1910 | BKN | N | 0 | 3 | .000 | 6.05 | 4 | 3 | 1 | 19.1 | 17 | 27 | 14 | 0 | 0 | 0 | 0 | 5 | 0 | 0 | .000 | 1 | 6 | 3 | 0 | 2.5 | .700 |
| 1911 | | | 1 | 3 | .250 | 5.12 | 13 | 7 | 1 | 58 | 54 | 47 | 15 | 0 | 0 | 0 | 0 | 19 | 2 | 0 | .105 | 1 | 19 | 2 | 0 | 1.7 | .909 |

Year	Team		W	L	PCT	ERA	G	GS	CG	IP	H	BB	SO	ShO	Relief Pitching W	L	SV	Batting AB	H	HR	BA	PO	A	E	DP	TC/G	FA

Sandy Burk *continued*

1912	2 teams	BKN N (2G 0–0) STL N (12G 1–3)																									
"	total		1	3	.250	2.55	14	4	2	53	46	15	19	0	0	1	1	15	1	0	.067	2	9	1	0	0.9	.917
1913	STL	N	1	2	.333	5.14	19	5	0	70	81	33	29	0	0	2	1	22	2	0	.091	1	16	0	1	0.9	1.000
1915	PIT	F	2	0	1.000	1.00	2	2	1	18	8	11	9	0	0	0	0	6	1	0	.167	2	2	0	0	2.0	1.000
5 yrs.			5	11	.313	4.25	52	21	5	218.1	206	133	86	0	0	3	2	67	6	0	.090	7	52	6	0	1.3	.908

Elmer Burkart

BURKART, ELMER ROBERT (Swede)
B. Feb. 1, 1917, Torresdale, Pa.   BR TR 6'2" 190 lbs.

1936	PHI	N	0	0	–	3.52	2	1	0	7.2	4	12	2	0	0	0	0	2	0	0	.000	0	2	0	1	1.0	1.000
1937			0	0	–	6.19	7	0	0	16	20	9	4	0	0	0	0	6	0	0	.000	0	4	0	0	0.6	1.000
1938			0	1	.000	4.50	2	1	1	10	12	3	1	0	0	0	0	3	0	0	.000	1	1	1	0	1.5	.667
1939			1	0	1.000	4.32	5	0	0	8.1	11	2	2	0	1	0	0	1	1	0	1.000	0	1	0	0	0.2	1.000
4 yrs.			1	1	.500	4.93	16	3	2	42	47	26	9	0	1	0	0	12	1	0	.083	1	8	1	0	0.6	.900

Billy Burke

BURKE, WILLIAM IGNATIUS
B. July 11, 1889, Clinton, Mass.   D. Feb. 9, 1967, Worcester, Mass.   BL TL 5'10" 165 lbs.

1910	BOS	N	1	0	1.000	4.08	19	1	1	64	68	29	22	0	0	0	0	21	4	0	.190	6	11	2	0	1.0	.895
1911			0	1	.000	18.90	2	1	0	3.1	6	5	1	0	0	0	0	1	1	0	1.000	0	0	1	0	0.5	–
2 yrs.			1	1	.500	4.81	21	2	1	67.1	74	34	23	0	0	0	0	22	5	0	.227	6	11	3	0	1.0	.850

Bobby Burke

BURKE, ROBERT JAMES (Lefty)
B. Jan. 23, 1907, Joliet, Ill.   D. Feb. 8, 1971, Joliet, Ill.   BL TL 6'½" 150 lbs.

1927	WAS	A	3	2	.600	3.96	36	6	1	100	92	32	21	0	1	0	0	24	3	0	.125	6	24	0	1	0.8	1.000
1928			2	4	.333	3.90	26	7	2	85.1	87	18	27	1	0	1	0	20	5	0	.250	5	19	1	1	1.0	.960
1929			6	8	.429	4.79	37	17	4	141	154	55	51	0	1	1	0	43	6	0	.140	4	20	0	1	0.6	1.000
1930			3	4	.429	3.63	24	4	2	74.1	62	29	35	0	1	2	3	23	4	0	.174	6	8	3	0	0.7	.824
1931			8	3	.727	4.27	30	13	2	128.2	124	50	38	1	3	0	2	47	10	0	.213	4	29	1	1	1.1	.971
1932			3	6	.333	5.14	22	10	2	91	98	44	32	0	1	5	0	25	5	0	.200	3	14	0	0	0.8	1.000
1933			4	3	.571	3.23	25	6	4	64	64	31	28	1	0	1	0	17	4	0	.235	4	17	3	1	0.8	.850
1934			8	8	.500	3.21	37	15	7	168	155	72	52	1	2	2	0	57	13	0	.228	8	36	2	1	1.2	.957
1935			1	8	.111	7.46	15	10	2	66.1	90	27	16	0	0	0	0	22	4	0	.182	4	16	0	0	1.3	1.000
1937	PHI	N	0	0	–	∞	2	0	0		1	2	0	0	0	0	0	0	0	0	–	0	0	0	0	0.0	–
10 yrs.			38	46	.452	4.29	254	88	27	918.2	927	360	300	4	9	7	5	278	54	0	.194	40	183	10	6	0.9	.957

John Burke

BURKE, JOHN PATRICK
B. Jan. 27, 1877, Hazleton, Pa.   D. Aug. 4, 1950, Jersey City, N. J.   BR TR

| 1902 | NY | N | 0 | 1 | .000 | 5.79 | 2 | 1 | 1 | 14 | 21 | 3 | 3 | 0 | 0 | 0 | 0 | 13 | 2 | 0 | .154 | 2 | 3 | 0 | 0 | 2.5 | 1.000 |

Steve Burke

BURKE, STEVEN MICHAEL
B. Mar. 5, 1955, Stockton, Calif.   BB TR 6'2" 200 lbs.

1977	SEA	A	0	1	.000	2.81	6	0	0	16	12	7	6	0	0	1	0	0	0	0	–	2	3	1	0	1.0	.833
1978			0	1	.000	3.49	18	0	0	49	46	24	16	0	0	1	0	0	0	0	–	2	8	2	3	0.7	.833
2 yrs.			0	2	.000	3.32	24	0	0	65	58	31	22	0	0	2	0	0	0	0	–	4	11	3	3	0.8	.833

Tim Burke

BURKE, TIMOTHY PHILIP
B. Feb. 19, 1959, Omaha, Neb.   BR TR 6'3" 205 lbs.

1985	MON	N	9	4	.692	2.39	78	0	0	120.1	86	44	87	0	9	4	8	10	1	0	.100	5	21	1	2	0.3	.963
1986			9	7	.563	2.93	68	2	0	101.1	103	46	82	0	8	7	4	7	0	0	.000	4	22	1	1	0.4	.963
1987			7	0	1.000	1.19	55	0	0	91	64	17	58	0	7	0	18	10	0	0	.000	6	17	0	0	0.4	1.000
1988			3	5	.375	3.40	61	0	0	82	84	25	42	0	3	5	18	2	0	0	.000	8	14	0	0	0.4	1.000
1989			9	3	.750	2.55	68	0	0	84.2	68	22	54	0	9	3	28	3	0	0	.000	4	16	0	0	0.3	1.000
5 yrs.			37	19	.661	2.48	330	2	0	479.1	405	154	323	0	36	19	76	32	1	0	.031	27	90	2	3	0.4	.983

Walter Burke

BURKE, WALTER R.
B. Calif.   D. Mar. 3, 1911, Memphis, Tenn.   6' 200 lbs.

1882	BUF	N	0	1	.000	11.25	1	1	0	4	10	0	0	0	0	0	0	4	0	0	.000	1	4	0	0	5.0	1.000
1883			0	0	–	5.63	1	1	0	8	9	3	1	0	0	0	0	5	1	0	.200	0	1	0	0	1.0	1.000
1884	BOS	U	19	15	.559	2.85	38	36	34	322	326	31	255	0	1	0	0	184	41	0	.223	13	45	11	2	1.8	.841
1887	DET	N	0	1	.000	6.00	2	2	1	15	21	5	3	0	0	0	0	8	2	0	.250	0	3	1	0	2.0	.750
4 yrs.			19	17	.528	3.15	42	40	35	349	366	39	259	0	1	0	0	201	44	0	.219	14	53	12	2	1.9	.848

Jesse Burkett

BURKETT, JESSE CAIL (The Crab)
B. Dec. 4, 1868, Wheeling, W. Va.   D. May 27, 1953, Worcester, Mass.
Hall of Fame 1946.   BL TL 5'8" 155 lbs.

1890	NY	N	3	10	.231	5.57	21	12	6	118	134	92	82	0	2	0	0	401	124	4	.309	3	33	8	1	2.1	.818
1894	CLE	N	0	0	–	4.50	1	0	0	4	6	1	0	0	0	0	0	523	187	8	.358	0	0	0	0	0.0	–
1902	STL	A	0	1	.000	9.00	1	0	0	1	4	1	2	0	0	1	0	549	168	5	.306	0	0	0	0	0.0	–
3 yrs.			3	11	.214	5.56	23	12	6	123	144	94	84	0	2	1	0	*				3	33	8	1	1.9	.818

John Burkett

BURKETT, JOHN DAVID
B. Nov. 28, 1964, New Brighton, Pa.   BR TR 6'2" 175 lbs.

| 1987 | SF | N | 0 | 0 | – | 4.50 | 3 | 0 | 0 | 6 | 7 | 3 | 5 | 0 | 0 | 0 | 0 | 1 | 0 | 0 | .000 | 0 | 1 | 0 | 1 | 0.3 | 1.000 |

Ken Burkhart

BURKHART, KENNETH WILLIAM
Born Kenneth William Burkhardt.
B. Nov. 18, 1916, Knoxville, Tenn.   BR TR 6'1" 190 lbs.

1945	STL	N	19	8	.704	2.90	42	22	12	217.1	206	66	67	4	6	3	1	72	13	0	.181	6	41	2	0	1.2	.959
1946			6	3	.667	2.88	25	13	5	100	111	36	32	2	1	1	2	34	5	0	.147	1	15	2	1	0.7	.889
1947			3	6	.333	5.21	34	6	1	95	108	23	44	0	1	3	1	24	3	0	.125	6	20	0	0	0.8	1.000

Year	Team	W	L	PCT	ERA	G	GS	CG	IP	H	BB	SO	ShO	Relief Pitching W	L	SV	Batting AB	H	HR	BA	PO	A	E	DP	TC/G	FA

Ken Burkhart *continued*

Year	Team	W	L	PCT	ERA	G	GS	CG	IP	H	BB	SO	ShO	W	L	SV	AB	H	HR	BA	PO	A	E	DP	TC/G	FA
1948	2 teams	STL N	(20G 0–0)		CIN N	(16G 0–3)																				
"	total	0	3	.000	6.27	36	0	0	79	92	30	30	0	0	3	1	13	4	1	.308	7	14	1	1	0.6	.955
1949	CIN N	0	0	—	3.18	11	0	0	28.1	29	10	8	0	0	0	1	7	2	0	.286	1	6	0	1	0.6	1.000
5 yrs.		28	20	.583	3.84	148	41	18	519.2	546	165	181	6	8	8	7	150	27	1	.180	21	96	5	3	0.8	.959

Wally Burnette

BURNETTE, WALLACE HARPER
B. June 20, 1929, Blairs, Va.   BR TR 6'½" 178 lbs.

Year	Team	W	L	PCT	ERA	G	GS	CG	IP	H	BB	SO	ShO	W	L	SV	AB	H	HR	BA	PO	A	E	DP	TC/G	FA
1956	KC A	6	8	.429	2.89	18	14	4	121.1	115	39	54	1	2	1	0	39	2	0	.051	6	16	1	2	1.3	.957
1957		7	12	.368	4.30	38	9	1	113	115	44	57	0	5	6	1	32	8	0	.250	10	25	0	6	0.9	1.000
1958		1	1	.500	3.49	12	4	0	28.1	29	14	11	0	0	0	0	6	1	0	.167	0	3	0	0	0.3	1.000
3 yrs.		14	21	.400	3.56	68	27	5	262.2	259	97	122	1	7	7	1	77	11	0	.143	16	44	1	8	0.9	.984

Bill Burns

BURNS, WILLIAM THOMAS (Sleepy Bill)
B. Jan. 29, 1880, San Saba, Tex. D. June 6, 1953, Ramona, Calif.   BB TL 6'2" 195 lbs.

Year	Team	W	L	PCT	ERA	G	GS	CG	IP	H	BB	SO	ShO	W	L	SV	AB	H	HR	BA	PO	A	E	DP	TC/G	FA
1908	WAS A	6	11	.353	1.69	23	19	11	165	135	18	55	2	0	1	0	54	8	0	.148	2	69	6	2	3.3	.922
1909	2 teams	WAS A	(6G 1–1)		CHI A	(22G 7–13)																				
"	total	8	14	.364	1.86	28	23	9	203.2	194	42	65	3	1	1	0	69	12	0	.174	6	72	7	0	3.0	.918
1910	2 teams	CHI A	(1G 0–0)		CIN N	(31G 8–13)																				
"	total	8	13	.381	3.47	32	21	13	179	183	50	57	2	0	3	0	61	16	0	.262	3	57	6	2	2.1	.909
1911	2 teams	CIN N	(6G 1–0)		PHI N	(21G 6–10)																				
"	total	7	10	.412	3.38	27	17	8	138.2	149	29	52	2	1	1	0	47	9	0	.191	6	46	3	3	2.0	.945
1912	DET A	1	4	.200	5.35	6	5	2	38.2	52	9	6	0	0	0	0	13	3	0	.231	1	12	2	1	2.5	.867
5 yrs.		30	52	.366	2.69	116	85	43	725	713	148	235	10	2	7	1	244	48	0	.197	18	256	24	8	2.6	.919

Britt Burns

BURNS, ROBERT BRITT
B. June 8, 1959, Houston, Tex.   BL TL 6'5" 215 lbs.

Year	Team	W	L	PCT	ERA	G	GS	CG	IP	H	BB	SO	ShO	W	L	SV	AB	H	HR	BA	PO	A	E	DP	TC/G	FA
1978	CHI A	0	2	.000	12.91	2	2	0	7.2	14	3	3	0	0	0	0	0	0	0	—	0	2	0	0	1.0	1.000
1979		0	0	—	5.40	6	0	0	5	10	1	2	0	0	0	0	0	0	0	—	0	0	0	0	0.0	—
1980		15	13	.536	2.84	34	32	11	238	213	63	133	1	1	0	0	0	0	0	—	6	34	1	0	1.2	.976
1981		10	6	.625	2.64	24	23	5	157	139	49	108	1	1	0	0	0	0	0	—	0	8	1	0	0.4	.889
1982		13	5	.722	4.04	28	28	5	169.1	168	67	116	1	0	0	0	0	0	0	—	2	14	2	0	0.6	.889
1983		10	11	.476	3.58	29	26	8	173.2	165	55	115	4	1	0	0	0	0	0	—	1	15	1	1	0.6	.941
1984		4	12	.250	5.00	34	16	2	117	130	45	85	0	1	2	3	0	0	0	—	2	17	2	0	0.6	.905
1985		18	11	.621	3.96	36	34	8	227	206	79	172	4	1	0	0	0	0	0	—	6	27	2	0	1.0	.943
8 yrs.		70	60	.538	3.66	193	161	39	1094.2	1045	362	734	11	4	2	3	0	0	0	—	17	117	9	1	0.7	.937

LEAGUE CHAMPIONSHIP SERIES

Year	Team	W	L	PCT	ERA	G	GS	CG	IP	H	BB	SO	ShO	W	L	SV	AB	H	HR	BA	PO	A	E	DP	TC/G	FA
1983	CHI A	0	1	.000	0.96	1	1	0	9.1	6	5	8	0	0	0	0	0	0	0	—	0	2	0	0	2.0	1.000

Denny Burns

BURNS, DENNIS
B. May 24, 1898, Tiff City, Mo. D. May 21, 1969, Tulsa, Okla.   BR TR 5'10" 180 lbs.

Year	Team	W	L	PCT	ERA	G	GS	CG	IP	H	BB	SO	ShO	W	L	SV	AB	H	HR	BA	PO	A	E	DP	TC/G	FA
1923	PHI A	2	1	.667	2.00	4	3	2	27	21	7	8	0	0	0	0	9	1	0	.111	0	6	0	0	1.5	1.000
1924		6	8	.429	5.08	37	17	7	154	191	68	26	0	0	1	1	42	6	0	.143	4	37	1	4	1.1	.976
2 yrs.		8	9	.471	4.62	41	20	9	181	212	75	34	0	0	1	1	51	7	0	.137	4	43	1	4	1.2	.979

Dick Burns

BURNS, RICHARD SIMON
B. Dec. 26, 1863, Holyoke, Mass. D. Nov. 11, 1937, Holyoke, Mass.   BL TL 140 lbs.

Year	Team	W	L	PCT	ERA	G	GS	CG	IP	H	BB	SO	ShO	W	L	SV	AB	H	HR	BA	PO	A	E	DP	TC/G	FA
1883	DET N	2	12	.143	4.51	17	13	13	127.2	172	33	30	0	0	0	1	140	26	0	.186	1	28	6	1	2.1	.829
1884	CIN U	23	15	.605	2.46	40	40	34	329.2	298	47	167	1	0	0	0	350	107	4	.306	34	72	13	0	3.0	.891
1885	STL N	0	0	—	9.00	1	0	0	3	3	0	2	0	0	0	0	54	12	0	.222	0	3	0	0	3.0	1.000
3 yrs.		25	27	.481	3.07	58	53	47	460.1	473	80	199	1	0	0	1	*				35	103	19	1	2.7	.879

Farmer Burns

BURNS, JAMES (Slab)
B. Ashtabula, Ohio   TR 5'7" 168 lbs.

Year	Team	W	L	PCT	ERA	G	GS	CG	IP	H	BB	SO	ShO	W	L	SV	AB	H	HR	BA	PO	A	E	DP	TC/G	FA
1901	STL N	0	0	—	9.00	1	0	0	1	2	1	0	0	0	0	0	0	0	0	—	0	0	0	0	0.0	—

Oyster Burns

BURNS, THOMAS P.
B. Sept. 6, 1864, Philadelphia, Pa. D. Nov. 11, 1928, Brooklyn, N. Y.   BR TR 5'8" 183 lbs.

Year	Team	W	L	PCT	ERA	G	GS	CG	IP	H	BB	SO	ShO	W	L	SV	AB	H	HR	BA	PO	A	E	DP	TC/G	FA
1884	BAL AA	0	0	—	3.00	2	0	0	9	12	2	6	0	0	0	1	138	40	6	.290	0	1	0	0	0.5	1.000
1885		7	4	.636	3.58	15	11	10	105.2	112	21	30	1	0	0	3	321	74	5	.231	6	13	1	0	1.3	.950
1887		1	0	1.000	9.53	2	0	0	11.1	16	4	2	0	1	0	0	551	188	9	.341	0	0	0	0	0.0	—
1888		0	1	.000	4.26	5	0	0	12.2	12	3	2	0	0	1	0	529	155	6	.293	0	3	0	0	0.6	1.000
4 yrs.		8	5	.615	4.09	25	11	10	138.2	152	30	40	1	1	1	4	*				6	17	1	0	1.0	.958

Todd Burns

BURNS, TODD EDWARD
B. July 6, 1963, Maywood, Calif.   BR TR 6'2" 186 lbs.

Year	Team	W	L	PCT	ERA	G	GS	CG	IP	H	BB	SO	ShO	W	L	SV	AB	H	HR	BA	PO	A	E	DP	TC/G	FA
1988	OAK A	8	2	.800	3.16	17	14	2	102.2	93	34	57	0	1	0	0	0	0	0	—	3	11	0	0	0.8	1.000
1989		6	5	.545	2.24	50	2	0	96.1	66	28	49	0	5	5	8	0	0	0	—	9	9	3	1	0.4	.857
2 yrs.		14	7	.667	2.71	67	16	2	199	159	62	106	0	6	5	9	0	0	0	—	12	20	3	2	0.5	.914

WORLD SERIES

Year	Team	W	L	PCT	ERA	G	GS	CG	IP	H	BB	SO	ShO	W	L	SV	AB	H	HR	BA	PO	A	E	DP	TC/G	FA
1988	OAK A	0	0	—	0.00	1	0	0	.1	0	0	0	0	0	0	0	0	0	0	—	0	0	0	0	0.0	—
1989		0	0	—	0.00	2	0	0	1.2	1	1	0	0	0	0	0	0	0	0	—	0	0	0	0	0.0	—
2 yrs.		0	0	—	0.00	3	0	0	2	1	1	0	0	0	0	0	0	0	0	—	0	0	0	0	0.0	—

Tom Burns

BURNS, THOMAS EVERETT
B. Mar. 30, 1857, Honesdale, Pa. D. Mar. 19, 1902, Jersey City, N. J.   BR TR 5'7" 152 lbs.
Manager 1892, 1898-99.

Year	Team	W	L	PCT	ERA	G	GS	CG	IP	H	BB	SO	ShO	W	L	SV	AB	H	HR	BA	PO	A	E	DP	TC/G	FA
1880	CHI N	0	0	—	0.00	1	0	0	1.1	2	2	1	0	0	0	0	*				0	0	0	0	0.0	—

Year	Team		W	L	PCT	ERA	G	GS	CG	IP	H	BB	SO	ShO	Relief Pitching W	L	SV	Batting AB	H	HR	BA	PO	A	E	DP	TC/G	FA

Pete Burnside

BURNSIDE, PETER WILLITS
B. July 2, 1930, Evanston, Ill.

BR TL 6'2" 180 lbs.

Year	Team		W	L	PCT	ERA	G	GS	CG	IP	H	BB	SO	ShO	W	L	SV	AB	H	HR	BA	PO	A	E	DP	TC/G	FA
1955	NY	N	1	0	1.000	2.84	2	2	1	12.2	10	9	2	0	0	0	0	5	1	0	.200	0	2	0	1	1.0	1.000
1957			1	4	.200	8.80	10	9	1	30.2	47	13	18	1	0	1	0	9	0	0	.000	1	5	1	0	0.7	.857
1958	SF	N	0	0	—	6.75	6	1	0	10.2	20	5	4	0	0	0	0	0	0	0	—	0	2	0	0	0.3	1.000
1959	DET	A	1	3	.250	3.77	30	0	0	62	55	25	49	0	1	3	1	10	0	0	.000	3	11	0	1	0.5	1.000
1960			7	7	.500	4.28	31	15	2	113.2	122	50	71	0	3	1	2	27	4	0	.148	3	14	1	1	0.6	.944
1961	WAS	A	4	9	.308	4.53	33	16	4	113.1	106	51	56	2	0	1	0	34	2	0	.059	2	17	2	1	0.6	.905
1962			5	11	.313	4.45	40	20	6	149.2	152	51	74	0	0	1	2	35	2	0	.057	11	16	2	0	0.7	.931
1963	2 teams	BAL A (6G 0–1)			WAS A	(38G 0–1)																					
"	total		0	2	.000	6.03	44	1	0	74.2	95	26	29	0	0	1	0	12	1	0	.083	1	7	1	1	0.2	.889
8 yrs.			19	36	.345	4.81	196	64	14	567.1	607	230	303	3	4	7	7	132	10	0	.076	21	74	7	5	0.5	.931

Sheldon Burnside

BURNSIDE, SHELDON JOHN
B. Dec. 22, 1954, South Bend, Ind.

BR TL 6'5" 200 lbs.

Year	Team		W	L	PCT	ERA	G	GS	CG	IP	H	BB	SO	ShO	W	L	SV	AB	H	HR	BA	PO	A	E	DP	TC/G	FA
1978	DET	A	0	0	—	9.00	2	0	0	4	4	2	3	0	0	0	0	0	0	0	—	0	0	0	0	0.0	—
1979			1	1	.500	6.43	10	0	0	21	28	8	13	0	1	1	0	0	0	0	—	0	4	0	1	0.4	1.000
1980	CIN	N	1	0	1.000	1.80	7	0	0	5	6	1	2	0	1	0	0	1	0	0	.000	0	4	0	0	0.6	1.000
3 yrs.			2	1	.667	6.00	19	0	0	30	38	11	18	0	2	1	0	1	0	0	.000	0	8	0	1	0.4	1.000

George Burpo

BURPO, GEORGE HARVIE
B. June 19, 1922, Jenkins, Ky.

BR TL 6' 195 lbs.

Year	Team		W	L	PCT	ERA	G	GS	CG	IP	H	BB	SO	ShO	W	L	SV	AB	H	HR	BA	PO	A	E	DP	TC/G	FA
1946	CIN	N	0	0	—	15.43	2	0	0	2.1	4	5	1	0	0	0	0	0	0	0	—	0	0	0	0	0.0	—

Harry Burrell

BURRELL, HARRY J.
B. 1866, Vermont D. Dec. 11, 1914, Omaha, Neb.

Year	Team		W	L	PCT	ERA	G	GS	CG	IP	H	BB	SO	ShO	W	L	SV	AB	H	HR	BA	PO	A	E	DP	TC/G	FA
1891	STL	AA	5	2	.714	4.81	7	4	3	43	51	21	19	0	3	0	0	22	5	0	.227	2	8	2	0	1.7	.833

Al Burris

BURRIS, ALVA BURTON
B. Jan. 28, 1874, Warwick, Md. D. Mar. 24, 1938, Salisbury, Md.

BR TR

Year	Team		W	L	PCT	ERA	G	GS	CG	IP	H	BB	SO	ShO	W	L	SV	AB	H	HR	BA	PO	A	E	DP	TC/G	FA
1894	PHI	N	0	0	—	18.00	1	0	0	5	14	2	0	0	0	0	0	4	2	0	.500	0	1	0	0	1.0	1.000

Ray Burris

BURRIS, BERTRAM RAY
B. Aug. 22, 1950, Idabel, Okla.

BR TR 6'5" 200 lbs.

Year	Team		W	L	PCT	ERA	G	GS	CG	IP	H	BB	SO	ShO	W	L	SV	AB	H	HR	BA	PO	A	E	DP	TC/G	FA
1973	CHI	N	1	1	.500	2.91	31	1	0	65	65	27	57	0	0	0	0	7	1	0	.143	0	14	1	2	0.5	.933
1974			3	5	.375	6.60	40	5	0	75	91	26	40	0	3	1	1	13	1	0	.077	4	9	0	0	0.3	1.000
1975			15	10	.600	4.12	36	35	8	238	259	73	108	2	0	0	0	82	15	0	.183	16	16	2	0	0.9	.941
1976			15	13	.536	3.11	37	36	10	249	251	70	112	4	0	0	0	81	9	0	.111	15	42	5	3	1.7	.919
1977			14	16	.467	4.72	39	39	5	221	270	67	105	1	0	0	0	69	12	1	.174	16	46	1	1	1.6	.984
1978			7	13	.350	4.75	40	32	4	199	210	79	94	1	1	1	1	61	7	0	.115	23	38	4	2	1.6	.938
1979	3 teams	CHI N (14G 0–0)			NY A	(15G 1–3)		NY N	(4G 0–2)																		
"	total		1	5	.167	5.30	33	4	0	71.1	84	31	43	0	1	3	0	7	1	0	.143	9	10	1	0	0.6	.950
1980	NY	N	7	13	.350	4.02	29	29	1	170	181	54	83	0	0	0	0	51	5	0	.098	13	22	2	1	1.3	.946
1981	MON	N	9	7	.563	3.04	22	21	4	136	117	41	52	0	0	0	0	37	7	0	.189	8	17	3	2	1.3	.893
1982			4	14	.222	4.73	37	15	2	123.2	143	53	55	0	4	3	2	28	5	0	.179	11	16	2	1	0.8	.931
1983			4	7	.364	3.68	40	17	2	154	139	56	100	1	1	2	0	39	9	0	.231	12	23	0	1	0.9	1.000
1984	OAK	A	13	10	.565	3.15	34	28	5	211.2	193	90	93	1	1	0	0	0	0	0	—	6	20	1	0	0.6	1.000
1985	MIL	A	9	13	.409	4.81	29	28	6	170.1	182	53	81	0	0	0	0	0	0	0	—	18	19	2	0	1.3	.949
1986	STL	N	4	5	.444	5.60	23	10	0	82	92	32	34	0	0	0	0	27	4	0	.148	4	9	0	1	0.6	1.000
1987	MIL	A	2	2	.500	5.87	10	2	0	23	33	12	8	0	1	1	0	0	0	0	—	3	0	0	0	0.6	1.000
15 yrs.			108	134	.446	4.17	480	302	47	2189	2310	764	1065	10	12	13	4	502	76	1	.151	157	300	23	16	1.0	.952

DIVISIONAL PLAYOFF SERIES

| 1981 | MON | N | 0 | 1 | .000 | 5.06 | 1 | 1 | 0 | 5.1 | 7 | 4 | 4 | 0 | 0 | 0 | 0 | 2 | 0 | 0 | .000 | 0 | 0 | 0 | 0 | — | |

LEAGUE CHAMPIONSHIP SERIES

| 1981 | MON | N | 1 | 0 | 1.000 | 0.53 | 2 | 2 | 1 | 17 | 10 | 3 | 4 | 1 | 0 | 0 | 0 | 6 | 0 | 0 | .000 | 0 | 0 | 0 | 0 | 0.0 | — |

John Burrows

BURROWS, JOHN
B. Oct. 30, 1913, Winnfield, La. D. Apr. 27, 1987, Coal Run, Ohio

BR TL 5'10" 200 lbs.

Year	Team		W	L	PCT	ERA	G	GS	CG	IP	H	BB	SO	ShO	W	L	SV	AB	H	HR	BA	PO	A	E	DP	TC/G	FA
1943	2 teams	PHI A (4G 0–1)			CHI N	(23G 0–2)																					
"	total		0	3	.000	4.69	27	2	0	40.1	33	25	21	0	0	1	2	4	2	0	.500	0	9	1	2	0.4	.900
1944	CHI	N	0	0	—	18.00	3	0	0	3	7	3	1	0	0	0	0	0	0	0	—	0	1	1	0	0.7	.500
2 yrs.			0	3	.000	5.61	30	2	0	43.1	40	28	22	0	0	1	2	4	2	0	.500	0	10	2	2	0.4	.833

Jim Burton

BURTON, JIM SCOTT
B. Oct. 27, 1949, Royal Oak, Mich.

BR TL 6'3" 195 lbs.

Year	Team		W	L	PCT	ERA	G	GS	CG	IP	H	BB	SO	ShO	W	L	SV	AB	H	HR	BA	PO	A	E	DP	TC/G	FA
1975	BOS	A	1	2	.333	2.89	29	4	0	53	58	19	39	0	1	0	1	0	0	0	—	2	7	0	1	0.3	1.000
1977			0	0	—	0.00	1	0	0	2.2	2	1	3	0	0	0	0	0	0	0	—	0	0	0	0	0.0	—
2 yrs.			1	2	.333	2.75	30	4	0	55.2	60	20	42	0	1	0	1	0	0	0	—	2	7	0	1	0.3	1.000

WORLD SERIES

| 1975 | BOS | A | 0 | 1 | .000 | 9.00 | 2 | 0 | 0 | 1 | 1 | 3 | 0 | 0 | 0 | 1 | 0 | 0 | 0 | 0 | — | 0 | 0 | 0 | 0 | 0.0 | — |

Moe Burtschy

BURTSCHY, EDWARD FRANK
B. Apr. 18, 1922, Cincinnati, Ohio

BR TR 6'3" 208 lbs.

Year	Team		W	L	PCT	ERA	G	GS	CG	IP	H	BB	SO	ShO	W	L	SV	AB	H	HR	BA	PO	A	E	DP	TC/G	FA
1950	PHI	A	0	1	.000	7.11	9	1	0	19	22	21	12	0	0	0	0	5	0	0	.000	3	2	0	0	0.6	1.000
1951			0	0	—	5.29	7	0	0	17	18	12	4	0	0	0	0	3	1	0	.333	3	2	0	0	0.7	1.000
1954			5	4	.556	3.80	46	0	0	94.2	80	53	54	0	5	4	4	17	2	0	.118	7	15	3	2	0.5	.880
1955	KC	A	2	0	1.000	10.32	7	0	0	11.1	17	10	9	0	2	0	0	3	1	0	.333	0	0	0	0	0.0	—

Year	Team	W	L	PCT	ERA	G	GS	CG	IP	H	BB	SO	ShO	Relief Pitching W	L	SV	Batting AB	H	HR	BA	PO	A	E	DP	TC/G	FA

Moe Burtschy *continued*

Year	Team	W	L	PCT	ERA	G	GS	CG	IP	H	BB	SO	ShO	W	L	SV	AB	H	HR	BA	PO	A	E	DP	TC/G	FA
1956		3	1	.750	3.95	21	0	0	43.1	41	30	18	0	3	1	0	8	1	0	.125	2	15	0	2	0.8	1.000
5 yrs.		10	6	.625	4.71	90	1	0	185.1	178	126	97	0	10	5	4	36	5	0	.139	15	34	3	4	0.6	.942

Dennis Burtt

BURTT, DENNIS ALLEN
B. Nov. 29, 1957, San Diego, Calif.　　BB TR 6'　187 lbs.

Year	Team	W	L	PCT	ERA	G	GS	CG	IP	H	BB	SO	ShO	W	L	SV	AB	H	HR	BA	PO	A	E	DP	TC/G	FA
1985	MIN A	2	2	.500	3.81	5	2	0	28.1	20	7	9	0	0	2	0	0	0	0	–	1	5	0	1	1.2	1.000
1986		0	0	–	31.50	3	0	0	2	7	3	1	0	0	0	0	0	0	0	–	0	0	0	0	0.0	–
2 yrs.		2	2	.500	5.64	8	2	0	30.1	27	10	10	0	0	2	0	0	0	0	–	1	5	0	1	0.8	1.000

Bill Burwell

BURWELL, WILLIAM EDWIN
B. Mar. 27, 1895, Jarbalo, Kans.　D. June 11, 1973, Ormond Beach, Fla.
Manager 1947.　　BL TR 5'11"　175 lbs.

Year	Team	W	L	PCT	ERA	G	GS	CG	IP	H	BB	SO	ShO	W	L	SV	AB	H	HR	BA	PO	A	E	DP	TC/G	FA
1920	STL A	6	4	.600	3.65	33	3	0	113.1	133	42	30	0	6	3	4	42	7	0	.167	14	24	2	1	1.2	.950
1921		2	4	.333	5.12	33	3	1	84.1	102	29	17	0	1	3	2	25	6	0	.240	3	20	3	0	0.8	.885
1928	PIT N	1	0	1.000	5.23	4	1	0	20.2	18	8	2	0	1	0	0	9	2	0	.222	1	8	1	0	2.5	.900
3 yrs.		9	8	.529	4.37	70	6	1	218.1	253	79	49	0	8	6	6	76	15	0	.197	18	52	6	1	1.1	.921

Dick Burwell

BURWELL, RICHARD MATTHEW
B. Jan. 23, 1940, Alton, Ill.　　BR TR 6'1"　190 lbs.

Year	Team	W	L	PCT	ERA	G	GS	CG	IP	H	BB	SO	ShO	W	L	SV	AB	H	HR	BA	PO	A	E	DP	TC/G	FA
1960	CHI N	0	0	–	5.59	3	1	0	9.2	11	7	1	0	0	0	0	3	1	0	.333	1	1	0	1	0.7	1.000
1961		0	0	–	9.00	2	0	0	4	6	4	0	0	0	0	0	1	0	0	.000	0	2	0	0	1.0	1.000
2 yrs.		0	0	–	6.59	5	1	0	13.2	17	11	1	0	0	0	0	4	1	0	.250	1	3	0	1	0.8	1.000

Steve Busby

BUSBY, STEVEN LEE
B. Sept. 29, 1949, Burbank, Calif.　　BR TR 6'2"　205 lbs.

Year	Team	W	L	PCT	ERA	G	GS	CG	IP	H	BB	SO	ShO	W	L	SV	AB	H	HR	BA	PO	A	E	DP	TC/G	FA
1972	KC A	3	1	.750	1.58	5	5	3	40	28	8	31	0	0	0	0	15	3	0	.200	1	4	1	0	1.2	.833
1973		16	15	.516	4.24	37	37	7	238	246	105	174	1	0	0	0	0	0	0	–	10	47	6	3	1.7	.905
1974		22	14	.611	3.39	38	38	20	292.1	284	92	198	3	0	0	0	0	0	0	–	24	53	8	2	2.2	.906
1975		18	12	.600	3.08	34	34	18	260.1	233	81	160	3	0	0	0	0	0	0	–	22	52	3	2	2.3	.961
1976		3	3	.500	4.38	13	13	1	72	58	49	29	0	0	0	0	0	0	0	–	10	9	3	0	1.7	.864
1978		1	0	1.000	7.59	7	5	0	21.1	24	15	10	0	0	0	0	0	0	0	–	0	5	1	0	0.9	.833
1979		6	6	.500	3.64	22	12	4	94	71	64	45	0	1	2	0	0	0	0	–	4	24	0	1	1.3	1.000
1980		1	3	.250	6.21	11	6	0	42	59	19	12	0	0	0	0	0	0	0	–	5	4	1	0	0.9	.900
8 yrs.		70	54	.565	3.72	167	150	53	1060	1003	433	659	7	1	2	0	15	3	0	.200	76	198	23	8	1.8	.923

Don Buschhorn

BUSCHHORN, DONALD LEE
B. Apr. 29, 1946, Independence, Mo.　　BL TR 6'　170 lbs.

Year	Team	W	L	PCT	ERA	G	GS	CG	IP	H	BB	SO	ShO	W	L	SV	AB	H	HR	BA	PO	A	E	DP	TC/G	FA
1965	KC A	0	1	.000	4.35	12	3	0	31	36	8	9	0	0	0	0	4	2	0	.500	2	5	0	0	0.6	1.000

Guy Bush

BUSH, GUY TERRELL (The Mississippi Mudcat)
B. Aug. 23, 1901, Aberdeen, Miss.　D. July 2, 1985, Shannon, Miss.　　BR TR 6'　175 lbs.

Year	Team	W	L	PCT	ERA	G	GS	CG	IP	H	BB	SO	ShO	W	L	SV	AB	H	HR	BA	PO	A	E	DP	TC/G	FA
1923	CHI N	0	0	–	0.00	1	0	0	1	1	0	2	0	0	0	0	0	0	0	–	0	0	0	0	0.0	–
1924		2	5	.286	4.02	16	8	4	80.2	91	24	36	0	0	0	1	0	26	4	0	.154	1	9	1	1	0.7	.909
1925		6	13	.316	4.30	42	15	5	182	213	52	76	0	4	2	4	57	11	0	.193	2	61	4	3	1.6	.940
1926		13	9	.591	2.86	35	16	7	157.1	149	42	32	2	6	2	2	48	8	0	.167	4	39	2	1	1.3	.956
1927		10	10	.500	3.03	36	22	9	193.1	177	79	62	1	3	0	2	65	8	0	.123	9	41	1	4	1.4	.980
1928		15	6	.714	3.83	42	24	9	204.1	229	86	61	2	4	0	2	73	6	0	.082	5	46	2	2	1.3	.962
1929		18	7	.720	3.66	50	29	18	270.2	277	107	82	2	2	1	8	91	15	0	.165	10	60	1	6	1.4	.986
1930		15	10	.600	6.20	46	25	11	225	291	86	75	0	3	2	3	78	22	0	.282	21	46	1	3	1.5	.985
1931		16	8	.667	4.49	39	24	14	180.1	190	66	54	1	4	0	2	57	7	0	.123	10	55	4	7	1.8	.942
1932		19	11	.633	3.21	40	30	15	238.2	262	70	73	1	4	2	0	84	15	0	.179	22	50	3	10	1.9	.960
1933		20	12	.625	2.75	41	32	20	258.2	261	68	84	4	1	1	2	88	11	0	.125	18	72	1	2	2.2	.989
1934		18	10	.643	3.83	40	27	15	209.1	213	54	75	1	3	1	2	70	16	0	.229	13	46	1	3	1.5	.983
1935	PIT N	11	11	.500	4.32	41	25	8	204.1	237	40	42	1	5	1	2	63	8	0	.127	9	41	0	2	1.2	1.000
1936	2 teams	PIT N	(16G 1–3)		BOS N	(15G 4–5)																				
"	total	5	8	.385	4.10	31	11	5	125	147	31	38	0	2	3	0	34	6	0	.176	6	32	0	1	1.2	1.000
1937	BOS N	8	15	.348	3.54	32	20	11	180.2	201	48	56	1	2	3	1	54	6	0	.111	8	45	0	1	1.7	1.000
1938	STL N	0	1	.000	5.06	6	0	0	5.1	6	3	1	0	0	1	1	0	0	0	–	0	0	0	0	0.0	–
1945	CIN N	0	0	–	8.31	4	0	0	4.1	5	3	1	0	0	0	0	0	0	0	–	0	0	0	0	0.0	–
17 yrs.		176	136	.564	3.86	542	308	151	2721	2950	859	850	16	43	20	34	888	143	0	.161	138	643	21	47	1.5	.974

WORLD SERIES

Year	Team	W	L	PCT	ERA	G	GS	CG	IP	H	BB	SO	ShO	W	L	SV	AB	H	HR	BA	PO	A	E	DP	TC/G	FA
1929	CHI N	1	0	1.000	0.82	2	1	1	11	12	2	4	0	0	0	0	3	0	0	.000	0	3	0	0	1.5	1.000
1932		0	1	.000	14.29	2	2	0	5.2	5	6	2	0	0	0	0	1	0	0	.000	0	2	0	0	1.0	1.000
2 yrs.		1	1	.500	5.40	4	3	1	16.2	17	8	6	0	0	0	0	4	0	0	.000	0	5	0	0	1.3	1.000

Joe Bush

BUSH, LESLIE AMBROSE (Bullet Joe)
B. Nov. 27, 1892, Brainerd, Minn.　D. Nov. 1, 1974, Ft. Lauderdale, Fla.　　BR TR 5'9"　173 lbs.

Year	Team	W	L	PCT	ERA	G	GS	CG	IP	H	BB	SO	ShO	W	L	SV	AB	H	HR	BA	PO	A	E	DP	TC/G	FA
1912	PHI A	0	0	–	7.88	1	1	0	8	14	4	3	0	0	0	0	4	2	0	.500	1	1	1	1	3.0	.667
1913		14	6	.700	3.82	39	15	5	200.1	199	66	81	1	7	1	3	70	11	0	.157	15	75	2	4	2.4	.978
1914		16	12	.571	3.06	38	22	14	206	184	81	109	2	4	2	3	74	14	1	.189	8	55	3	1	1.7	.955
1915		5	15	.250	4.14	25	18	8	145.2	137	89	89	0	1	3	0	49	7	0	.143	7	39	3	3	2.0	.939
1916		15	24	.385	2.57	40	33	25	286.2	222	130	157	8	1	5	0	100	14	0	.140	19	94	6	8	3.0	.950
1917		11	17	.393	2.47	37	31	17	233.1	207	111	121	4	1	0	2	80	16	0	.200	20	61	6	0	2.4	.931
1918	BOS A	15	15	.500	2.11	36	31	26	272.2	241	91	125	7	0	0	0	98	27	0	.276	16	81	2	5	2.8	.980
1919		0	0	–	5.00	3	2	0	9	11	4	3	0	0	0	0	5	2	0	.400	0	2	0	1	0.7	1.000
1920		15	15	.500	4.25	35	32	18	243.2	287	94	88	0	1	0	1	102	25	0	.245	24	66	4	7	2.7	.957
1921		16	9	.640	3.50	37	31	20	254.1	244	93	96	3	0	0	1	120	39	1	.325	13	64	1	0	2.1	.987
1922	NY A	26	7	.788	3.31	39	30	20	255.1	240	85	92	0	4	1	3	95	31	0	.326	16	61	0	4	2.0	1.000
1923		19	15	.559	3.43	37	30	23	275.2	263	117	125	3	2	2	0	113	31	2	.274	15	74	3	3	2.5	.967

Year	Team	W	L	PCT	ERA	G	GS	CG	IP	H	BB	SO	ShO	Relief Pitching W	L	SV	Batting AB	H	HR	BA	PO	A	E	DP	TC/G	FA

Joe Bush *continued*

Year	Team	W	L	PCT	ERA	G	GS	CG	IP	H	BB	SO	ShO	W	L	SV	AB	H	HR	BA	PO	A	E	DP	TC/G	FA
1924		17	16	.515	3.57	39	31	19	252	262	109	80	3	1	5	1	124	42	1	.339	24	60	1	4	2.2	.988
1925	STL A	14	14	.500	4.97	33	28	15	213.2	239	91	63	2	2	1	0	102	26	2	.255	17	54	0	5	2.2	1.000
1926	2 teams	WAS A	(12G 1–8)		PIT N	(19G 6–6)																				
"	total	7	14	.333	4.45	31	22	12	182	180	70	65	2	0	1	3	79	20	1	.253	8	39	2	3	1.6	.959
1927	2 teams	PIT N	(5G 1–2)		NY N	(3G 1–1)																				
"	total	2	3	.400	9.64	8	5	1	18.2	32	10	7	0	1	0	0	9	5	0	.556	0	4	0	0	0.5	1.000
1928	PHI A	2	1	.667	5.09	11	2	1	35.1	39	18	15	0	1	0	1	15	1	0	.067	4	10	0	1	1.3	1.000
17 yrs.		194	183	.515	3.51	489	364	224	3092.1	3001	1263	1319	35	26	21	20	*				207	840	34	50	2.2	.969

WORLD SERIES

Year	Team	W	L	PCT	ERA	G	GS	CG	IP	H	BB	SO	ShO	W	L	SV	AB	H	HR	BA	PO	A	E	DP	TC/G	FA
1913	PHI A	1	0	1.000	1.00	1	1	1	9	5	4	3	0	0	0	0	4	1	0	.250	0	1	0	1	1.0	1.000
1914		0	1	.000	3.27	1	1	1	11	9	4	4	0	0	0	0	5	0	0	.000	0	5	1	0	6.0	.833
1918	BOS A	0	1	.000	3.00	2	1	1	9	7	3	0	0	0	0	1	2	0	0	.000	0	3	0	0	1.5	1.000
1922	NY A	0	2	.000	4.80	2	2	1	15	21	5	6	0	0	0	0	6	1	0	.167	1	3	0	2	2.0	1.000
1923		1	1	.500	1.08	3	1	1	16.2	7	4	5	0	1	0	0	7	3	0	.429	2	3	0	0	1.7	1.000
5 yrs.		2	5	.286	2.67	9	6	5	60.2	49	20	18	0	0	1	1	24	5	0	.208	3	15	1	3	2.1	.947
				2nd				10th																		

Jack Bushelman

BUSHELMAN, JOHN FRANCIS
B. Aug. 29, 1885, Cincinnati, Ohio D. Oct. 26, 1955, Roanoke, Va. BR TR 6'2'' 175 lbs.

Year	Team	W	L	PCT	ERA	G	GS	CG	IP	H	BB	SO	ShO	W	L	SV	AB	H	HR	BA	PO	A	E	DP	TC/G	FA
1909	CIN N	0	1	.000	2.57	1	1	1	7	7	4	3	0	0	0	0	1	0	0	.000	0	0	0	0	0.0	—
1911	BOS A	0	1	.000	3.00	3	1	1	12	8	10	5	0	0	0	0	3	0	0	.000	1	2	1	0	1.3	.750
1912		1	0	1.000	4.70	3	0	0	7.2	9	5	5	0	1	0	0	3	0	0	.000	0	4	1	0	1.7	.800
3 yrs.		1	2	.333	3.38	7	2	2	26.2	24	19	13	0	1	0	0	7	0	0	.000	1	6	2	0	1.3	.778

Frank Bushey

BUSHEY, FRANCIS CLYDE
B. Aug. 1, 1906, Wheaton, Kans. D. Mar. 18, 1972, Topeka, Kans. BR TR 6' 180 lbs.

Year	Team	W	L	PCT	ERA	G	GS	CG	IP	H	BB	SO	ShO	W	L	SV	AB	H	HR	BA	PO	A	E	DP	TC/G	FA
1927	BOS A	0	0	—	6.75	1	0	0	1.1	2	2	0	0	0	0	0	0	0	0	—	0	0	0	0	0.0	—
1930		0	1	.000	6.30	11	0	0	30	34	15	4	0	0	1	0	9	1	0	.111	4	6	1	1	1.0	.909
2 yrs.		0	1	.000	6.32	12	0	0	31.1	36	17	4	0	0	1	0	9	1	0	.111	4	6	1	1	0.9	.909

Tom Buskey

BUSKEY, THOMAS WILLIAM
B. Feb. 20, 1947, Harrisburg, Pa. BR TR 6'3'' 200 lbs.

Year	Team	W	L	PCT	ERA	G	GS	CG	IP	H	BB	SO	ShO	W	L	SV	AB	H	HR	BA	PO	A	E	DP	TC/G	FA
1973	NY A	0	1	.000	5.40	8	0	0	16.2	18	4	8	0	0	1	0	0	0	0	—	0	2	0	1	0.3	1.000
1974	2 teams	NY A	(4G 0–1)		CLE A	(51G 2–6)																				
"	total	2	7	.222	3.38	55	0	0	98.2	103	36	43	0	2	7	18	0	0	0	—	7	18	1	0	0.5	.962
1975	CLE A	5	3	.625	2.57	50	0	0	77	69	29	29	0	5	3	7	0	0	0	—	9	19	1	2	0.6	.966
1976		5	4	.556	3.64	39	0	0	94	88	34	32	0	5	4	1	0	0	0	—	4	18	0	2	0.6	1.000
1977		0	0	—	5.29	21	0	0	34	45	8	15	0	0	0	0	0	0	0	—	4	3	0	0	0.3	1.000
1978	TOR A	0	1	.000	3.38	8	0	0	13.1	14	4	7	0	0	1	0	0	0	0	—	0	5	0	0	0.6	1.000
1979		6	10	.375	3.42	44	0	0	79	74	25	44	0	6	10	7	0	0	0	—	5	19	1	1	0.6	.960
1980		3	1	.750	4.43	33	0	0	67	68	26	34	0	3	1	0	0	0	0	—	5	10	0	0	0.5	1.000
8 yrs.		21	27	.438	3.66	258	0	0	479.2	479	166	212	0	21	27	34	0	0	0	—	34	94	3	7	0.5	.977

John Butcher

BUTCHER, JOHN DANIEL
B. Mar. 8, 1957, Glendale, Calif. BR TR 6'4'' 185 lbs.

Year	Team	W	L	PCT	ERA	G	GS	CG	IP	H	BB	SO	ShO	W	L	SV	AB	H	HR	BA	PO	A	E	DP	TC/G	FA
1980	TEX A	3	3	.500	4.11	6	6	1	35	34	13	27	0	0	0	0	0	0	0	—	1	6	1	0	1.3	.875
1981		1	2	.333	1.61	5	3	1	28	18	8	19	1	0	0	0	0	0	0	—	3	5	0	0	1.6	1.000
1982		1	5	.167	4.87	18	13	2	94.1	102	34	39	0	0	0	1	0	0	0	—	7	19	0	3	1.4	1.000
1983		6	6	.500	3.51	36	6	1	123	128	41	58	0	3	4	5	0	0	0	—	11	17	0	0	0.8	1.000
1984	MIN A	13	11	.542	3.44	34	34	8	225	242	53	83	1	0	0	0	0	0	0	—	25	20	3	5	1.4	.938
1985		11	14	.440	4.98	34	33	8	207.2	239	43	92	2	0	0	0	0	0	0	—	24	27	2	2	1.6	.962
1986	2 teams	MIN A	(16G 0–3)		CLE A	(13G 1–5)																				
"	total	1	8	.111	6.56	29	18	2	120.2	168	37	45	0	0	0	0	0	0	0	—	9	15	3	2	0.9	.889
7 yrs.		36	49	.424	4.42	162	113	23	833.2	931	229	363	6	3	4	6	0	0	0	—	80	109	9	12	1.2	.955

Max Butcher

BUTCHER, ALBERT MAXWELL
B. Sept. 21, 1910, Holden, W. Va. D. Sept. 15, 1957, Man, W. Va. BR TR 6'2'' 220 lbs.

Year	Team	W	L	PCT	ERA	G	GS	CG	IP	H	BB	SO	ShO	W	L	SV	AB	H	HR	BA	PO	A	E	DP	TC/G	FA
1936	BKN N	6	6	.500	3.96	38	15	8	147.2	154	59	55	0	2	0	2	48	6	0	.125	5	25	2	1	0.8	.938
1937		11	15	.423	4.27	39	24	8	191.2	203	75	57	1	5	0	0	62	10	0	.161	17	53	1	4	1.8	.986
1938	2 teams	BKN N	(24G 5–4)		PHI N	(12G 4–8)																				
"	total	9	12	.429	4.47	36	20	14	171	198	70	50	1	1	2	2	60	13	0	.217	9	40	2	5	1.4	.961
1939	2 teams	PHI N	(19G 2–13)		PIT N	(14G 4–4)																				
"	total	6	17	.261	4.62	33	28	8	191	235	74	48	2	0	1	0	69	10	0	.145	3	41	0	2	1.3	1.000
1940	PIT N	8	9	.471	6.01	35	24	6	136.1	161	46	40	2	0	0	2	50	15	0	.300	5	34	2	2	1.2	.951
1941		17	12	.586	3.05	33	32	19	236	249	66	61	0	0	1	0	82	15	0	.183	17	48	0	2	2.0	1.000
1942		5	8	.385	2.93	24	18	9	150.2	144	44	49	2	0	0	1	49	7	0	.143	11	33	1	0	1.9	.978
1943		10	8	.556	2.60	33	21	10	193.2	191	57	45	2	1	0	1	61	10	0	.164	11	40	2	4	1.6	.962
1944		13	11	.542	3.12	35	27	13	199	216	46	43	5	1	0	1	63	12	0	.190	12	51	2	3	1.9	.969
1945		10	8	.556	3.03	28	20	12	168.1	184	46	37	2	2	0	0	54	12	0	.222	8	37	1	2	1.6	.978
10 yrs.		95	106	.473	3.73	334	229	104	1786.1	1935	583	485	15	12	4	9	598	110	1	.184	98	402	13	25	1.5	.975

Sal Butera

BUTERA, SALVATORE PHILIP
B. Sept. 25, 1952, Richmond Hill, N. Y. BR TR 6' 190 lbs.

Year	Team	W	L	PCT	ERA	G	GS	CG	IP	H	BB	SO	ShO	W	L	SV	AB	H	HR	BA	PO	A	E	DP	TC/G	FA
1985	MON N	0	0	—	0.00	1	0	0	1	0	0	0	0	0	0	0	120	24	3	.200	0	0	0	0	0.0	—
1986	CIN N	0	0	—	0.00	1	0	0	1	1	1	0	0	0	0	0	113	27	2	.239	0	0	0	0	0.0	—
2 yrs.		0	0	—	0.00	2	0	0	2	1	1	0	0	0	0	0	*				0	0	0	0	0.0	—

Bill Butland

BUTLAND, WILBURN RUE
B. Mar. 22, 1918, Terre Haute, Ind. BR TR 6'5'' 185 lbs.

Year	Team	W	L	PCT	ERA	G	GS	CG	IP	H	BB	SO	ShO	W	L	SV	AB	H	HR	BA	PO	A	E	DP	TC/G	FA
1940	BOS A	1	2	.333	5.57	3	3	1	21	27	10	5	0	0	0	0	7	0	0	.000	1	7	0	0	2.7	1.000

Year	Team	W	L	PCT	ERA	G	GS	CG	IP	H	BB	SO	ShO	Relief Pitching W	L	SV	Batting AB	H	HR	BA	PO	A	E	DP	TC/G	FA

Bill Butland *continued*

Year	Team	W	L	PCT	ERA	G	GS	CG	IP	H	BB	SO	ShO	W	L	SV	AB	H	HR	BA	PO	A	E	DP	TC/G	FA
1942		7	1	.875	2.51	23	10	6	111.1	85	33	46	2	0	0	1	28	1	0	.036	14	20	0	0	1.5	1.000
1946		1	0	1.000	11.02	5	2	0	16.1	23	13	10	0	0	0	0	4	1	0	.250	0	4	0	0	0.8	1.000
1947		0	0	–	4.50	1	0	0	2	3	0	1	0	0	0	0	0	0	0	–	0	0	0	0	0.0	–
4 yrs.		9	3	.750	3.88	32	15	7	150.2	138	56	62	2	0	0	1	39	2	0	.051	15	31	0	0	1.4	1.000

Bill Butler

BUTLER, WILLIAM FRANKLIN
B. Mar. 12, 1947, Hyattsville, Md.   BL TL 6'2"   210 lbs.

Year	Team	W	L	PCT	ERA	G	GS	CG	IP	H	BB	SO	ShO	W	L	SV	AB	H	HR	BA	PO	A	E	DP	TC/G	FA
1969	KC A	9	10	.474	3.90	34	29	5	193.2	174	91	156	4	0	0	0	60	3	0	.050	4	16	1	1	0.6	.952
1970		4	12	.250	3.77	25	25	2	141	117	87	75	1	0	0	0	44	2	0	.045	3	13	1	1	0.7	.941
1971	CLE A	1	2	.333	3.48	14	6	0	44	45	18	32	0	0	0	0	12	1	0	.083	0	7	1	0	0.6	.875
1972		0	0	–	1.50	6	2	0	12.9	9	10	6	0	0	0	0	1	0	0	.000	0	4	0	0	0.2	1.000
1974	MIN A	4	6	.400	4.09	26	12	2	99	91	56	79	0	0	1	0	0	0	0	–	1	6	0	0	0.3	1.000
1975		5	4	.556	5.95	23	8	1	81.2	100	35	55	0	2	2	0	0	0	0	–	4	11	2	0	0.7	.882
1977		0	1	.000	6.86	6	4	0	21	19	15	5	0	0	0	0	0	0	0	–	0	1	0	0	0.2	1.000
7 yrs.		23	35	.397	4.21	134	86	10	592.1	555	312	408	5	3	2	1	117	6	0	.051	12	55	5	2	0.5	.931

Cecil Butler

BUTLER, CECIL DEAN (Slewfoot)
B. Oct. 23, 1937, Dallas, Ga.   BR TR 6'4"   195 lbs.

Year	Team	W	L	PCT	ERA	G	GS	CG	IP	H	BB	SO	ShO	W	L	SV	AB	H	HR	BA	PO	A	E	DP	TC/G	FA
1962	MIL N	2	0	1.000	2.61	9	2	1	31	26	9	22	0	1	0	0	8	0	0	.000	0	7	0	0	0.8	1.000
1964		0	0	–	8.31	2	0	0	4.1	7	0	2	0	0	0	0	0	0	0	–	0	1	0	0	0.5	1.000
2 yrs.		2	0	1.000	3.31	11	2	1	35.1	33	9	24	0	1	0	0	8	0	0	.000	0	8	0	0	0.7	1.000

Charlie Butler

BUTLER, CHARLES THOMAS (Lefty)
B. May 12, 1906, Green Cove Springs, Fla.   D. May 10, 1964, Brunswick, Ga.   BR TL 6'1½"   210 lbs.

Year	Team	W	L	PCT	ERA	G	GS	CG	IP	H	BB	SO	ShO	W	L	SV	AB	H	HR	BA	PO	A	E	DP	TC/G	FA
1933	PHI N	0	0	–	9.00	1	0	0	1	1	2	0	0	0	0	0	0	0	0	–	0	0	0	0	0.0	–

Ike Butler

BUTLER, ISAAC BURR
B. Aug. 22, 1873, Langston, Mich.   D. Mar. 17, 1948, Oakland, Calif.   TR 6'   175 lbs.

Year	Team	W	L	PCT	ERA	G	GS	CG	IP	H	BB	SO	ShO	W	L	SV	AB	H	HR	BA	PO	A	E	DP	TC/G	FA
1902	BAL A	1	10	.091	5.34	16	14	12	116.1	168	45	13	0	0	0	0	53	6	0	.113	4	33	3	0	2.5	.925

Tom Butters

BUTTERS, THOMAS ARDEN
B. Apr. 8, 1938, Delaware, Ohio   BR TR 6'2"   195 lbs.

Year	Team	W	L	PCT	ERA	G	GS	CG	IP	H	BB	SO	ShO	W	L	SV	AB	H	HR	BA	PO	A	E	DP	TC/G	FA
1962	PIT N	0	0	–	1.50	4	0	0	6	5	6	10	0	0	0	0	0	0	0	–	0	1	0	0	0.3	1.000
1963		0	0	–	4.41	6	1	0	16.1	15	8	11	0	0	0	0	3	1	0	.333	1	1	0	1	0.3	1.000
1964		2	2	.500	2.38	28	4	0	64.1	52	37	58	0	2	2	0	11	2	0	.182	4	9	1	1	0.4	.900
1965		0	1	.000	7.00	5	0	0	9	9	5	6	0	0	1	0	1	0	0	.000	3	1	0	0	0.8	1.000
4 yrs.		2	3	.400	3.10	43	5	0	95.2	81	56	85	0	0	1	0	15	3	0	.200	4	12	1	2	0.4	.941

Ralph Buxton

BUXTON, RALPH STANLEY (Buck)
B. June 7, 1911, Wayburn, Sask., Canada   BR TR 5'11½" 163 lbs.

Year	Team	W	L	PCT	ERA	G	GS	CG	IP	H	BB	SO	ShO	W	L	SV	AB	H	HR	BA	PO	A	E	DP	TC/G	FA
1938	PHI A	0	1	.000	4.82	5	0	0	9.1	12	5	9	0	0	1	0	1	0	0	.000	0	1	0	0	0.2	1.000
1949	NY A	0	1	.000	4.05	14	0	0	26.2	22	16	14	0	0	1	2	3	0	0	.000	2	3	0	0	0.4	1.000
2 yrs.		0	2	.000	4.25	19	0	0	36	34	21	23	0	0	2	2	4	0	0	.000	2	4	0	0	0.3	1.000

John Buzhardt

BUZHARDT, JOHN WILLIAM
B. Aug. 17, 1936, Prosperity, S. C.   BR TR 6'2½"   195 lbs.

Year	Team	W	L	PCT	ERA	G	GS	CG	IP	H	BB	SO	ShO	W	L	SV	AB	H	HR	BA	PO	A	E	DP	TC/G	FA
1958	CHI N	3	0	1.000	1.85	6	2	1	24.1	16	7	9	0	1	0	0	8	1	0	.125	2	7	0	0	1.5	1.000
1959		4	5	.444	4.97	31	10	1	101.1	107	29	33	1	1	2	0	29	2	0	.069	7	22	3	1	1.0	.906
1960	PHI N	5	16	.238	3.86	30	29	5	200.1	198	68	73	0	0	0	0	62	10	0	.161	19	30	1	4	1.7	.980
1961		6	18	.250	4.49	41	27	6	202.1	200	65	92	1	0	2	0	57	6	0	.105	20	34	3	4	1.4	.947
1962	CHI A	8	12	.400	4.19	28	25	8	152.1	156	59	64	2	1	0	0	51	6	0	.118	12	32	0	3	1.6	1.000
1963		9	4	.692	2.42	19	18	6	126.1	100	31	59	3	0	0	0	48	4	0	.083	12	25	1	1	2.0	.974
1964		10	8	.556	2.98	31	25	8	160	150	35	97	3	0	0	0	54	11	0	.204	10	27	1	2	1.2	.974
1965		13	8	.619	3.01	32	30	4	188.2	167	56	108	1	0	1	0	56	7	0	.125	15	26	2	4	1.3	.953
1966		6	11	.353	3.83	33	22	5	150.1	144	30	66	4	1	2	1	43	5	0	.116	19	34	1	1	1.6	.981
1967	3 teams	CHI A		(28G 3–9)			BAL A		(7G 0–1)			HOU N		(1G 0–0)												
"	total	3	10	.231	4.01	36	8	0	101	114	42	40	1	1	1	1	21	4	0	.190	9	21	1	1	0.9	.968
1968	HOU N	4	4	.500	3.12	39	4	0	83.2	73	35	37	0	3	3	5	16	4	0	.250	8	17	0	1	0.6	1.000
11 yrs.		71	96	.425	3.66	326	200	44	1490.2	1425	457	678	15	8	15	7	445	60	0	.135	133	275	13	22	1.3	.969

Bud Byerly

BYERLY, ELDRED WILLIAM
B. Oct. 26, 1920, Webster Groves, Mo.   BR TR 6'2½"   185 lbs.

Year	Team	W	L	PCT	ERA	G	GS	CG	IP	H	BB	SO	ShO	W	L	SV	AB	H	HR	BA	PO	A	E	DP	TC/G	FA
1943	STL N	1	0	1.000	3.46	2	2	0	13	14	5	6	0	0	0	0	3	0	0	.000	2	0	0	0	1.0	1.000
1944		2	2	.500	3.40	9	4	2	42.1	37	20	13	0	1	0	0	12	2	0	.167	2	11	0	0	1.4	1.000
1945		4	5	.444	4.74	33	8	2	95	111	41	39	0	2	1	0	23	5	0	.217	10	25	0	3	1.1	1.000
1950	CIN N	0	1	.000	2.45	4	1	0	14.2	12	4	5	0	0	1	0	3	0	0	.000	1	1	0	0	0.5	1.000
1951		2	1	.667	3.27	40	0	0	66	69	25	28	0	2	1	0	6	0	0	.000	4	16	2	0	0.6	.909
1952		0	1	.000	5.11	12	2	0	24.2	29	7	14	0	0	0	0	5	1	0	.200	0	5	0	0	0.4	1.000
1956	WAS A	2	4	.333	2.96	25	0	0	51.2	45	14	19	0	2	4	4	11	1	0	.091	3	10	0	0	0.5	1.000
1957		6	6	.500	3.13	47	0	0	95	94	22	39	0	6	6	6	15	1	0	.067	5	22	1	0	0.6	.964
1958	2 teams	WAS A		(17G 2–0)			BOS A		(18G 1–2)																		
"	total	3	2	.600	3.98	35	0	0	54.1	65	18	29	0	3	2	0	6	0	0	.000	8	6	1	0	0.4	.933
1959	SF N	1	0	1.000	1.38	11	0	0	13	11	5	4	0	1	0	0	–	1	5	0	0	0.5	1.000	
1960		1	0	1.000	5.32	19	0	0	22	32	6	13	0	1	0	2	4	0	0	.000	0	8	0	0	0.4	1.000
11 yrs.		22	22	.500	3.70	237	17	4	491.2	519	167	209	0	18	14	14	85	10	0	.118	34	106	4	3	0.6	.972

WORLD SERIES

Year	Team	W	L	PCT	ERA	G	GS	CG	IP	H	BB	SO	ShO	W	L	SV	AB	H	HR	BA	PO	A	E	DP	TC/G	FA
1944	STL N	0	0	–	0.00	1	0	0	1.1	0	0	1	0	0	0	0	0	0	0	–	0	0	0	0	0.0	–

Year	Team		W	L	PCT	ERA	G	GS	CG	IP	H	BB	SO	ShO	W	L	SV	AB	H	HR	BA	PO	A	E	DP	TC/G	FA

Harry Byrd *continued*

Year	Team		W	L	PCT	ERA	G	GS	CG	IP	H	BB	SO	ShO	W	L	SV	AB	H	HR	BA	PO	A	E	DP	TC/G	FA
1950	PHI	A	0	0	–	16.88	6	0	0	10.2	25	9	2	0	0	0	0	2	0	0	.000	0	2	0	0	0.3	1.000
1952			15	15	.500	3.31	37	28	15	228.1	244	98	116	3	0	2	2	75	10	0	.133	26	32	4	5	1.7	.935
1953			11	20	.355	5.51	40	37	11	236.2	279	115	122	2	0	1	0	81	18	0	.222	6	35	2	1	1.1	.953
1954	NY	A	9	7	.563	2.99	25	21	5	132.1	131	43	52	1	0	0	0	46	9	0	.196	5	21	2	2	1.1	.929
1955	2 teams		BAL A	(14G 3–2)		CHI A	(25G 4–6)																				
"	total		7	8	.467	4.61	39	20	2	156.1	149	58	69	2	1	1	2	49	5	0	.102	9	24	1	0	0.9	.971
1956	CHI	A	0	1	.000	10.38	3	1	0	4.1	9	4	0	0	0	0	0	1	0	0	.000	1	0	0	0	0.7	1.000
1957	DET	A	4	3	.571	3.36	37	1	0	59	53	28	20	0	4	3	5	8	0	0	.000	0	10	0	0	0.3	1.000
7 yrs.			46	54	.460	4.35	187	108	33	827.2	890	355	381	8	5	7	9	262	42	0	.160	46	126	9	8	1.0	.950

Jeff Byrd

BYRD, JEFFREY ALAN
B. Nov. 11, 1956, La Mesa, Calif.   BR TR 6'3" 195 lbs.

Year	Team		W	L	PCT	ERA	G	GS	CG	IP	H	BB	SO	ShO	W	L	SV	AB	H	HR	BA	PO	A	E	DP	TC/G	FA
1977	TOR	A	2	13	.133	6.21	17	17	1	87	98	68	40	0	0	0	0	0	0	0	–	9	15	2	1	1.5	.923

Jerry Byrne

BYRNE, GERALD WILFORD
B. Feb. 2, 1907, Parnell, Mich.   D. Aug. 11, 1955, Lansing, Mich.   BR TR 6' 170 lbs.

Year	Team		W	L	PCT	ERA	G	GS	CG	IP	H	BB	SO	ShO	W	L	SV	AB	H	HR	BA	PO	A	E	DP	TC/G	FA
1929	CHI	A	0	1	.000	7.36	3	1	0	7.1	11	6	1	0	0	0	0	2	0	0	.000	0	0	0	0	0.0	–

Tommy Byrne

BYRNE, THOMAS JOSEPH
B. Dec. 31, 1919, Baltimore, Md.   BL TL 6'1" 182 lbs.

Year	Team		W	L	PCT	ERA	G	GS	CG	IP	H	BB	SO	ShO	W	L	SV	AB	H	HR	BA	PO	A	E	DP	TC/G	FA
1943	NY	A	2	1	.667	6.54	11	1	0	31.2	28	35	22	0	2	0	0	11	1	0	.091	2	8	1	0	1.0	.909
1946			0	1	.000	5.79	4	1	0	9.1	7	8	5	0	0	0	0	9	2	0	.222	1	2	0	0	0.8	1.000
1947			0	0	–	4.15	4	1	0	4.1	5	6	2	0	0	0	0	0	0	0	–	0	1	0	0	0.3	1.000
1948			8	5	.615	3.30	31	11	5	133.2	79	101	93	1	2	1	2	46	15	1	.326	2	17	0	2	0.6	1.000
1949			15	7	.682	3.72	32	30	12	196	125	179	129	3	0	1	0	83	16	0	.193	7	19	3	4	0.9	.897
1950			15	9	.625	4.74	31	31	10	203.1	188	160	118	2	0	0	0	81	22	0	.272	9	23	0	2	1.0	1.000
1951	2 teams		NY A	(9G 2–1)		STL A	(19G 4–10)																				
"	total		6	11	.353	4.26	28	20	7	143.2	120	150	71	2	2	0	0	66	18	2	.273	6	20	1	2	1.0	.963
1952	STL	A	7	14	.333	4.68	29	24	14	196	182	112	91	2	1	0	0	84	21	1	.250	10	15	2	1	0.9	.926
1953	2 teams		CHI A	(6G 2–0)		WAS A	(6G 0–5)																				
"	total		2	5	.286	6.16	12	11	2	49.2	53	48	26	0	0	0	1	35	4	0	.114	4	11	2	0	1.4	.882
1954	NY	A	3	2	.600	2.70	5	5	4	40	36	19	24	1	0	0	0	19	7	0	.368	0	8	1	1	1.8	.889
1955			16	5	.762	3.15	27	22	9	160	137	87	76	3	1	0	2	78	16	1	.205	4	22	2	3	1.0	.929
1956			7	3	.700	3.36	37	8	1	109.2	108	72	52	0	6	2	6	52	14	3	.269	8	18	1	4	0.7	.963
1957			4	6	.400	4.36	30	4	1	84.2	70	60	57	0	4	4	2	37	7	3	.189	6	9	1	0	0.5	.938
13 yrs.			85	69	.552	4.11	281	170	65	1362	1138	1037	766	12	18	9	12	*				*						

WORLD SERIES

Year	Team		W	L	PCT	ERA	G	GS	CG	IP	H	BB	SO	ShO	W	L	SV	AB	H	HR	BA	PO	A	E	DP	TC/G	FA
1949	NY	A	0	0	–	2.70	1	1	0	3.1	2	2	1	0	0	0	0	1	1	0	1.000	0	0	0	0	0.0	
1955			1	1	.500	1.88	2	2	1	14.1	8	8	8	0	0	0	0	6	1	0	.167	0	2	0	0	1.0	1.000
1956			0	0	–	0.00	1	0	0	.1	1	1	1	0	0	0	0	1	0	0	.000	0	0	0	0	0.0	
1957			0	0	–	5.40	2	0	0	3.1	1	1	1	0	0	0	0	2	1	0	.500	0	0	0	0	0.0	
4 yrs.			1	1	.500	2.53	6	3	1	21.1	12	12	11	0	0	0	0	10	3	0	.300	0	2	0	0	0.3	1.000

Marty Bystrom

BYSTROM, MARTIN EUGENE
B. July 26, 1958, Coral Gables, Fla.   BR TR 6'5" 200 lbs.

Year	Team		W	L	PCT	ERA	G	GS	CG	IP	H	BB	SO	ShO	W	L	SV	AB	H	HR	BA	PO	A	E	DP	TC/G	FA
1980	PHI	N	5	0	1.000	1.50	6	5	1	36	26	9	21	1	0	0	0	14	1	0	.071	4	10	0	1	2.3	1.000
1981			4	3	.571	3.33	9	9	1	54	55	16	24	0	0	0	0	17	2	0	.118	3	13	2	0	2.0	.889
1982			5	6	.455	4.85	19	16	1	89	93	35	50	0	0	0	0	24	3	0	.125	6	8	2	1	0.8	.875
1983			6	9	.400	4.60	24	23	1	119.1	136	44	87	1	0	0	0	38	9	0	.237	10	10	1	0	0.9	.952
1984	2 teams		PHI N	(11G 4–4)		NY A	(7G 2–2)																				
"	total		6	6	.500	4.22	18	18	0	96	100	35	60	0	0	0	0	19	3	0	.158	8	8	0	0	0.9	1.000
1985	NY	A	3	2	.600	5.71	8	8	0	41	44	19	16	0	0	0	0	0	0	0	–	1	9	1	0	1.4	.909
6 yrs.			29	26	.527	4.26	84	79	4	435.1	454	158	258	2	0	0	0	112	18	0	.161	32	58	6	2	1.1	.938

LEAGUE CHAMPIONSHIP SERIES

Year	Team		W	L	PCT	ERA	G	GS	CG	IP	H	BB	SO	ShO	W	L	SV	AB	H	HR	BA	PO	A	E	DP	TC/G	FA
1980	PHI	N	0	0	–	1.69	1	1	0	5.1	7	2	1	0	0	0	0	2	0	0	.000	0	0	0	0	0.0	

WORLD SERIES

Year	Team		W	L	PCT	ERA	G	GS	CG	IP	H	BB	SO	ShO	W	L	SV	AB	H	HR	BA	PO	A	E	DP	TC/G	FA
1980	PHI	N	0	0	–	5.40	1	1	0	5	5	1	10	0	0	0	0	0	0	0	–	1	1	0	0	2.0	1.000
1983			0	0	–	0.00	1	0	0	2	1	0	5	0	0	0	0	0	0	0	–	0	0	0	0	0.0	
2 yrs.			0	0	–	4.50	2	1	0	7	6	1	15	0	0	0	0	0	0	0	–	1	1	0	0	1.0	1.000

Greg Cadaret

CADARET, GREGORY JAMES
B. Feb. 27, 1962, Detroit, Mich.   BL TL 6'3" 200 lbs.

Year	Team		W	L	PCT	ERA	G	GS	CG	IP	H	BB	SO	ShO	W	L	SV	AB	H	HR	BA	PO	A	E	DP	TC/G	FA
1987	OAK	A	6	2	.750	4.54	29	0	0	39.2	37	24	30	0	6	2	0	0	0	0	–	6	6	0	1	0.4	1.000
1988			5	2	.714	2.89	58	0	0	71.2	60	36	64	0	5	2	3	0	0	0	–	3	9	0	1	0.2	1.000
1989	2 teams		OAK A	(26G 0–0)		NY A	(20G 5–5)																				
"	total		5	5	.500	4.05	46	13	3	120	130	57	80	1	1	0	0	0	0	0	–	9	21	2	2	0.7	.938
3 yrs.			16	9	.640	3.77	133	13	3	231.1	227	117	174	1	12	4	3	0	0	0	–	18	36	2	4	0.4	.964

LEAGUE CHAMPIONSHIP SERIES

Year	Team		W	L	PCT	ERA	G	GS	CG	IP	H	BB	SO	ShO	W	L	SV	AB	H	HR	BA	PO	A	E	DP	TC/G	FA
1988	OAK	A	0	0	–	27.00	1	0	0	.1	1	0	0	0	0	0	0	0	0	0	–	0	0	0	0	0.0	–

WORLD SERIES

Year	Team		W	L	PCT	ERA	G	GS	CG	IP	H	BB	SO	ShO	W	L	SV	AB	H	HR	BA	PO	A	E	DP	TC/G	FA
1988	OAK	A	0	0	–	0.00	3	0	0	2	2	0	3	0	0	0	0	0	0	0	–	0	0	0	0	0.0	–

Leon Cadore

CADORE, LEON JOSEPH
B. Nov. 20, 1890, Chicago, Ill.   D. Mar. 16, 1958, Spokane, Wash.   BR TR 6'1" 190 lbs.

Year	Team		W	L	PCT	ERA	G	GS	CG	IP	H	BB	SO	ShO	W	L	SV	AB	H	HR	BA	PO	A	E	DP	TC/G	FA
1915	BKN	N	0	2	.000	5.57	7	2	1	21	28	8	12	0	0	0	0	6	0	0	.000	0	6	1	0	1.0	.857
1916			0	0	–	4.50	2	0	0	6	10	0	2	0	0	0	0	3	0	0	.000	0	4	0	0	4.0	1.000
1917			13	13	.500	2.45	37	30	21	264	231	63	115	1	0	0	3	92	24	0	.261	16	62	4	3	2.2	.951
1918			2	1	1.000	0.53	2	2	2	17	6	2	5	1	0	0	0	4	0	0	.000	1	5	0	0	3.0	1.000
1919			14	12	.538	2.37	35	27	16	250.2	228	39	94	3	2	0	0	87	14	0	.161	15	53	6	2	2.1	.919

Leon Cadore *continued*

Year	Team		W	L	PCT	ERA	G	GS	CG	IP	H	BB	SO	ShO	W	L	SV	AB	H	HR	BA	PO	A	E	DP	TC/G	FA
															Relief Pitching			Batting									
1920			15	14	.517	2.62	35	30	16	254.1	256	56	79	4	1	1	0	91	20	2	.220	9	77	2	4	2.5	.977
1921			13	14	.481	4.17	35	30	12	211.2	243	46	79	1	1	2	0	75	14	1	.187	7	49	0	0	1.6	1.000
1922			8	15	.348	4.35	29	21	13	190.1	224	57	49	0	4	0	0	71	19	2	.268	8	30	1	3	1.3	.974
1923	2 teams	BKN N (8G 4–1)				CHI A	(1G 0–1)																				
"	total		4	2	.667	4.46	9	5	3	38.1	45	15	8	0	1	0	0	13	1	0	.077	1	5	1	0	0.8	.857
1924	NY	N	0	0	–	0.00	2	0	0	4	2	3	2	0	0	0	0	0	0	0	–	0	1	0	0	0.5	1.000
10 yrs.			68	72	.486	3.14	192	147	83	1257.1	1273	289	445	10	9	3	3	442	92	5	.208	57	292	15	12	1.9	.959

WORLD SERIES

Year	Team		W	L	PCT	ERA	G	GS	CG	IP	H	BB	SO	ShO	W	L	SV	AB	H	HR	BA	PO	A	E	DP	TC/G	FA
1920	BKN	N	0	1	.000	9.00	2	1	0	2	4	1	1	0	0	0	0	0	0	0	–	1	1	0	0	1.0	1.000

Charlie Cady

CADY, CHARLES B.
B. Dec., 1865, Chicago, Ill.   D. June 7, 1909, Kankakee, Ill.   5'11"   180 lbs.

Year	Team		W	L	PCT	ERA	G	GS	CG	IP	H	BB	SO	ShO	W	L	SV	AB	H	HR	BA	PO	A	E	DP	TC/G	FA
1883	CLE	N	0	1	.000	7.88	1	1	1	8	13	4	5	0	0	0	0	11	0	0	.000	1	1	0	0	2.0	1.000
1884	CHI	U	3	1	.750	2.83	4	4	4	35	37	13	15	0	0	0	0	23	2	0	.087	7	8	7	0	5.5	.682
2 yrs.			3	2	.600	3.77	5	5	5	43	50	17	20	0	0	0	0	*				*					

John Cahill

CAHILL, JOHN PATRICK FRANCIS (Patsy)
B. 1864, San Francisco, Calif.   D. Nov. 1, 1901, Pleasanton, Calif.   BR TR 5'7½"   168 lbs.

Year	Team		W	L	PCT	ERA	G	GS	CG	IP	H	BB	SO	ShO	W	L	SV	AB	H	HR	BA	PO	A	E	DP	TC/G	FA
1884	COL	AA	1	0	1.000	5.06	2	1	1	16	15	4	1	0	0	0	0	210	46	1	.219	71	28	19	2	59.0	.839
1886	STL	N	1	0	1.000	3.00	2	0	0	12	11	3	2	0	1	0	0	463	92	1	.199	166	39	35	5	0.0	.851
1887	IND	N	0	2	.000	14.32	6	1	1	22	40	19	5	0	0	1	0	263	54	0	.205	90	28	28	3	24.3	.808
3 yrs.			2	2	.500	8.64	10	2	2	50	66	26	8	0	1	1	0	*				*					

Bob Cain

CAIN, ROBERT MAX (Sugar)
B. Oct. 16, 1924, Longford, Kans.   BL TL 6'   165 lbs.

Year	Team		W	L	PCT	ERA	G	GS	CG	IP	H	BB	SO	ShO	W	L	SV	AB	H	HR	BA	PO	A	E	DP	TC/G	FA
1949	CHI	A	0	0	–	2.45	6	0	0	11	7	5	5	0	0	0	1	3	0	0	.000	1	0	0	0	0.2	1.000
1950			9	12	.429	3.93	34	23	11	171.2	153	109	77	1	1	1	2	61	12	0	.197	7	31	1	1	1.1	.974
1951	2 teams	CHI A (4G 1–2)				DET A	(35G 11–10)																				
"	total		12	12	.500	4.56	39	26	7	175.2	160	95	61	1	2	2	2	62	16	0	.258	9	30	1	2	1.0	.975
1952	STL	A	12	10	.545	4.13	29	27	8	170	169	62	70	1	0	0	2	58	8	0	.138	7	21	1	1	1.0	1.000
1953			4	10	.286	6.23	32	13	1	99.2	129	45	36	0	0	4	1	30	6	0	.200	4	9	0	1	0.4	1.000
1954	CHI	A	0	0	–	0.00	0	0	0	0	0	0	0	0	0	0	0	0	0	0	–	0	0	0	0	0.0	–
6 yrs.			37	44	.457	4.50	140	89	27	628	618	316	249	3	3	7	8	214	42	0	.196	28	91	3	5	0.9	.975

Les Cain

CAIN, LESLIE
B. Jan. 13, 1948, San Luis Obispo, Calif.   BL TL 6'1"   200 lbs.

Year	Team		W	L	PCT	ERA	G	GS	CG	IP	H	BB	SO	ShO	W	L	SV	AB	H	HR	BA	PO	A	E	DP	TC/G	FA
1968	DET	A	1	0	1.000	3.00	8	4	0	24	25	20	13	0	0	0	0	7	1	0	.143	0	6	0	0	0.8	1.000
1970			12	7	.632	3.83	29	29	5	181	167	98	156	0	0	0	0	68	11	1	.162	8	24	2	0	1.2	.941
1971			10	9	.526	4.34	26	26	3	145	121	91	118	1	0	0	0	55	8	1	.145	5	19	1	2	1.0	.960
1972			0	3	.000	3.75	5	5	0	24	18	16	16	0	0	0	0	7	1	0	.143	0	3	2	0	1.0	.600
4 yrs.			23	19	.548	3.97	68	64	8	374	331	225	303	1	0	0	0	137	21	2	.153	13	52	5	2	1.0	.929

Sugar Cain

CAIN, MERRITT PATRICK
B. Apr. 5, 1907, Macon, Ga.
D. Apr. 3, 1975, Atlanta, Ga.   BL TR 5'11"   190 lbs.   BR 1932,   BB 1933

Year	Team		W	L	PCT	ERA	G	GS	CG	IP	H	BB	SO	ShO	W	L	SV	AB	H	HR	BA	PO	A	E	DP	TC/G	FA
1932	PHI	A	3	4	.429	5.00	10	6	3	45	42	28	24	0	1	0	0	12	3	0	.250	1	8	0	0	0.9	1.000
1933			13	12	.520	4.25	38	32	16	218	244	137	43	1	0	1	1	80	16	0	.200	6	45	2	5	1.4	.962
1934			9	17	.346	4.41	36	32	15	230.2	235	128	66	0	1	1	0	82	13	0	.159	5	47	5	2	1.6	.912
1935	2 teams	PHI A (6G 0–5)				STL A	(31G 9–8)																				
"	total		9	13	.409	5.44	37	29	8	193.2	236	123	73	0	0	0	0	65	11	0	.169	2	26	3	4	0.8	.903
1936	2 teams	STL A (4G 1–1)				CHI A	(30G 14–10)																				
"	total		15	11	.577	4.89	34	29	15	211.2	248	84	50	1	1	0	0	75	9	0	.120	3	28	3	3	1.0	.912
1937	CHI	A	4	2	.667	6.16	18	6	1	68.2	88	51	17	0	3	0	0	22	4	0	.182	1	14	0	1	0.8	1.000
1938			0	1	.000	4.58	5	3	0	19.2	26	18	6	0	0	1	0	8	0	0	.000	1	0	1	0	0.4	.500
7 yrs.			53	60	.469	4.83	178	137	58	987.1	1119	569	279	2	6	4	1	344	56	0	.163	18	168	14	15	1.1	.930

Charlie Caldwell

CALDWELL, CHARLES WILLIAM
B. Aug. 2, 1901, Bristol, Va.   D. Nov. 1, 1957, Princeton, N. J.   BR TR 5'10"   180 lbs.

Year	Team		W	L	PCT	ERA	G	GS	CG	IP	H	BB	SO	ShO	W	L	SV	AB	H	HR	BA	PO	A	E	DP	TC/G	FA
1925	NY	A	0	0	–	16.88	3	0	0	2.2	7	3	1	0	0	0	0	1	0	0	.000	0	0	0	0	0.0	–

Earl Caldwell

CALDWELL, EARL WELTON (Teach)
B. Apr. 9, 1905, Sparks, Tex.   D. Sept. 15, 1981, Mission, Tex.   BR TR 6'1"   178 lbs.

Year	Team		W	L	PCT	ERA	G	GS	CG	IP	H	BB	SO	ShO	W	L	SV	AB	H	HR	BA	PO	A	E	DP	TC/G	FA
1928	PHI	N	1	4	.200	5.71	5	5	1	34.2	46	17	6	1	0	0	0	9	1	0	.111	0	10	0	0	2.0	1.000
1935	STL	A	3	2	.600	3.68	6	5	2	36.2	34	17	5	1	0	0	0	11	2	0	.182	3	13	0	0	2.7	1.000
1936			7	16	.304	6.00	41	25	10	189	252	83	59	0	0	2	2	58	11	1	.190	6	32	5	3	1.0	.884
1937			0	0	–	6.83	9	2	0	29	39	13	8	0	0	0	0	9	2	0	.222	0	6	0	0	0.7	1.000
1945	CHI	A	6	7	.462	3.59	27	11	5	105.1	108	37	45	1	1	3	4	37	8	0	.216	8	34	1	1	1.6	.977
1946			13	4	.765	2.08	39	0	0	90.2	60	29	42	0	13	4	8	18	3	0	.167	5	19	0	0	0.6	1.000
1947			1	4	.200	3.64	40	0	0	54.1	53	30	22	0	1	4	8	7	0	0	.000	1	6	1	0	0.2	.875
1948	2 teams	CHI A (25G 1–5)				BOS A	(8G 1–1)																				
"	total		2	6	.250	6.75	33	1	0	48	64	33	15	0	2	5	3	8	1	0	.125	2	5	0	0	0.2	1.000
8 yrs.			33	43	.434	4.69	200	49	18	587.2	656	259	202	5	17	18	25	157	28	1	.178	25	125	7	6	0.85	.955

Mike Caldwell

CALDWELL, RALPH MICHAEL
B. Jan. 22, 1949, Tarboro, N. C.   BR TL 6'   185 lbs.

Year	Team		W	L	PCT	ERA	G	GS	CG	IP	H	BB	SO	ShO	W	L	SV	AB	H	HR	BA	PO	A	E	DP	TC/G	FA
1971	SD	N	1	0	1.000	0.00	6	0	0	9	7	4	3	0	1	0	0	1	1	0	1.000	1	2	0	0	0.5	1.000
1972			7	11	.389	4.01	42	20	4	163.2	183	49	102	2	2	2	2	50	7	0	.140	9	47	2	3	1.4	.966
1973			5	14	.263	3.74	55	13	3	149	146	53	86	1	2	5	10	35	5	0	.143	12	29	2	1	0.8	.953
1974	SF	N	14	5	.737	2.95	31	27	6	189	176	63	83	2	1	0	1	63	9	0	.143	11	48	0	7	1.9	1.000
1975			7	13	.350	4.80	38	21	4	163	194	48	57	0	1	2	1	44	7	0	.159	10	33	1	2	1.2	.977

Year	Team	W	L	PCT	ERA	G	GS	CG	IP	H	BB	SO	ShO	Relief Pitching W	L	SV	Batting AB	H	HR	BA	PO	A	E	DP	TC/G	FA

Mike Caldwell *continued*

Year	Team	W	L	PCT	ERA	G	GS	CG	IP	H	BB	SO	ShO	W	L	SV	AB	H	HR	BA	PO	A	E	DP	TC/G	FA
1974	SF N	14	5	.737	2.95	31	27	6	189	176	63	83	2	1	0	0	63	9	0	.143	11	48	0	7	1.9	1.000
1975		7	13	.350	4.80	38	21	4	163	194	48	57	0	1	2	1	44	7	0	.159	10	33	1	2	1.2	.977
1976		1	7	.125	4.86	50	9	0	107.1	145	20	55	0	1	3	2	19	3	0	.158	8	22	1	2	0.6	.968
1977	2 teams	CIN N	(14G 0–0)		MIL A	(21G 5–8)																				
"	total	5	8	.385	4.46	35	12	2	119	126	44	49	0	2	0	1	4	2	0	.500	7	31	0	3	1.1	1.000
1978	MIL A	22	9	.710	2.36	37	34	23	293.1	258	54	131	6	0	0	1	0	0	0	–	14	50	0	2	1.7	1.000
1979		16	6	*.727*	3.29	30	30	16	235	252	39	89	4	0	0	0	0	0	0	–	7	64	2	3	2.4	.973
1980		13	11	.542	4.04	34	33	11	225	248	56	74	2	0	0	1	0	0	0	–	8	37	1	5	1.4	.978
1981		11	9	.550	3.94	24	23	3	144	151	38	41	0	0	0	0	0	0	0	–	5	26	0	1	1.3	1.000
1982		17	13	.567	3.91	35	34	12	258	269	58	75	3	0	0	0	0	0	0	–	13	48	1	5	1.8	.984
1983		12	11	.522	4.53	32	32	10	228.1	269	51	58	2	0	0	0	0	0	0	–	4	38	2	4	1.4	.955
1984		6	13	.316	4.64	26	19	4	126	160	21	34	1	0	2	0	0	0	0	–	7	24	3	2	1.3	.912
14 yrs.		137	130	.513	3.81	475	307	98	2407.2	2581	597	939	23	10	14	18	216	34	0	.157	116	499	15	39	1.3	.976

DIVISIONAL PLAYOFF SERIES

| 1981 | MIL A | 0 | 1 | .000 | 4.32 | 2 | 1 | 0 | 8.1 | 9 | 0 | 4 | 0 | 0 | 0 | 0 | 0 | 0 | 0 | – | 0 | 0 | 0 | 0 | 0.0 | – |

LEAGUE CHAMPIONSHIP SERIES

| 1982 | MIL A | 0 | 1 | .000 | 15.00 | 1 | 1 | 0 | 3 | 7 | 1 | 2 | 0 | 0 | 0 | 0 | 0 | 0 | 0 | – | 0 | 1 | 0 | 1.0 | – |

WORLD SERIES

| 1982 | MIL A | 2 | 0 | 1.000 | 2.04 | 3 | 2 | 1 | 17.2 | 19 | 3 | 6 | 1 | 0 | 0 | 0 | 0 | 0 | 0 | – | 4 | 2 | 0 | 0 | 2.0 | 1.000 |

Ralph Caldwell

CALDWELL, RALPH GRANT (Lefty)
B. Jan. 18, 1884, Philadelphia, Pa. D. Aug. 5, 1969, West Trenton, N. J. BL TL 5'9" 155 lbs.

1904	PHI N	2	2	.500	4.17	6	5	4	41	40	15	30	0	0	0	0	18	8	0	.444	4	9	0	2	2.2	1.000
1905		1	2	.333	4.24	7	2	1	34	44	7	29	0	0	1	1	15	0	0	.000	1	4	2	0	1.0	.714
2 yrs.		3	4	.429	4.20	13	7	6	75	84	22	59	0	0	1	1	33	8	0	.242	5	13	2	2	1.5	.900

Ray Caldwell

CALDWELL, RAYMOND BENJAMIN (Slim)
B. Apr. 26, 1888, Croydon, Pa. D. Aug. 17, 1967, Salamanca, N. Y. BL TR 6'2" 190 lbs.

1910	NY A	1	0	1.000	3.72	6	2	1	19.1	19	9	17	0	0	0	0	6	0	0	.000	1	4	0	0	0.8	1.000
1911		14	14	.500	3.35	41	27	19	255	240	79	145	1	4	2	1	147	40	0	.272	9	53	4	2	1.6	.939
1912		8	16	.333	4.47	30	26	13	183.1	196	67	95	3	0	1	0	76	18	0	.237	2	59	4	2	2.2	.938
1913		9	8	.529	2.41	27	16	15	164.1	131	60	87	2	0	1	1	97	28	0	.289	4	42	0	1	1.7	1.000
1914		17	9	.654	1.94	31	23	22	213	153	51	92	5	2	1	1	113	22	0	.195	14	45	2	2	2.0	.967
1915		19	16	.543	2.89	36	35	31	305	266	107	130	3	0	1	0	144	35	4	.243	12	72	1	5	2.4	.988
1916		5	12	.294	2.99	21	18	14	165.2	142	65	76	1	0	2	0	93	19	0	.204	4	42	2	2	2.3	.958
1917		13	16	.448	2.86	32	29	21	236	199	76	102	1	3	0	0	124	32	2	.258	11	60	2	1	2.3	.973
1918		9	8	.529	3.06	24	21	14	176.2	173	62	59	1	0	1	1	151	44	1	.291	8	35	1	1	1.8	.977
1919	2 teams	BOS A	(18G 7–4)		CLE A	(6G 5–1)																				
"	total	12	5	.706	2.98	24	18	10	139	121	49	46	2	1	0	0	71	21	0	.296	2	26	2	0	1.3	.933
1920	CLE A	20	10	.667	3.86	34	33	20	237.2	286	63	80	0	0	0	0	89	19	0	.213	6	49	5	0	1.8	.917
1921		6	6	.500	4.90	37	13	5	147	159	49	76	1	2	3	4	53	11	0	.208	5	35	3	1	1.2	.930
12 yrs.		133	120	.526	3.21	343	261	185	2242	2085	737	1005	20	12	12	9	*				78	522	26	17	1.8	.958

WORLD SERIES

| 1920 | CLE A | 0 | 1 | .000 | 27.00 | 1 | 1 | 0 | .1 | 2 | 1 | 0 | 0 | 0 | 0 | 0 | 0 | 0 | 0 | – | 0 | 0 | 0 | 0 | 0.0 | – |

Jeff Calhoun

CALHOUN, JEFFREY WILTON
B. Apr. 11, 1958, LaGrange, Ga. BL TL 6'2" 190 lbs.

1984	HOU N	0	1	.000	1.17	9	0	0	15.1	5	2	11	0	0	0	0	0	0	0	–	1	1	0	0	0.2	1.000
1985		2	5	.286	2.54	44	0	0	63.2	56	24	47	0	2	5	4	5	0	0	.000	5	10	2	2	0.4	.882
1986		1	0	1.000	3.71	20	0	0	26.2	28	12	14	0	1	0	0	0	0	0	–	2	1	0	0	0.2	1.000
1987	PHI N	3	1	.750	1.48	42	0	0	42.2	25	26	31	0	3	1	1	1	0	0	.000	4	8	0	0	0.3	1.000
1988		0	0	–	15.43	3	0	0	2.1	6	1	1	0	0	0	0	0	0	0	–	0	0	0	0	0.0	–
5 yrs.		6	7	.462	2.51	118	0	0	150.2	120	65	104	0	6	7	5	6	0	0	.000	12	20	2	2	0.3	.941

LEAGUE CHAMPIONSHIP SERIES

| 1986 | HOU N | 0 | 0 | – | 9.00 | 1 | 0 | 0 | 1 | 1 | 1 | 1 | 0 | 0 | 0 | 0 | 0 | 0 | 0 | – | 0 | 0 | 0 | 0 | 0.0 | – |

Fred Caligiuri

CALIGIURI, FREDERICK JOHN
B. Oct. 22, 1918, West Hickory, Pa. BR TR 6' 190 lbs.

1941	PHI A	2	2	.500	2.93	5	5	4	43	45	14	7	0	0	0	0	20	4	0	.200	2	8	0	0	2.0	1.000
1942		0	3	.000	6.38	13	2	0	36.2	45	18	20	0	0	1	1	12	1	0	.083	0	8	1	0	0.7	.889
2 yrs.		2	5	.286	4.52	18	7	4	79.2	90	32	27	0	0	1	1	32	5	0	.156	2	16	1	0	1.1	.947

Will Calihan

CALIHAN, WILLIAM T.
B. 1867, Oswego, N. Y. D. Dec. 20, 1917, Rochester, N. Y. 5'8" 150 lbs.

1890	ROC AA	18	15	.545	*3.28*	37	36	31	296.1	276	125	127	0	0	0	0	159	23	1	.145	14	71	9	6	2.5	.904
1891	PHI AA	6	6	.500	6.43	13	11	11	112	151	47	28	0	1	0	0	56	11	0	.196	5	35	2	1	3.2	.952
2 yrs.		24	21	.533	4.14	50	47	42	408.1	427	172	155	0	1	0	0	215	34	1	.158	19	106	11	7	2.7	.919

Ben Callahan

CALLAHAN, BENJAMIN FRANKLIN III
B. May 19, 1957, Mt. Airy, N. C. BR TR 6'7" 230 lbs.

| 1983 | OAK A | 1 | 2 | .333 | 12.54 | 4 | 2 | 0 | 9.1 | 18 | 5 | 2 | 0 | 0 | 1 | 0 | 0 | 0 | 0 | – | 0 | 3 | 0 | 0 | 0.8 | 1.000 |

Jim Callahan

CALLAHAN, JAMES W.
B. Moberly, Mo. Deceased.

| 1898 | STL N | 0 | 2 | .000 | 16.20 | 2 | 2 | 1 | 8.1 | 18 | 7 | 2 | 0 | 0 | 0 | 0 | 4 | 0 | 0 | .000 | 0 | 2 | 0 | 0 | 1.0 | 1.000 |

Year	Team		W	L	PCT	ERA	G	GS	CG	IP	H	BB	SO	ShO	Relief Pitching W	L	SV	Batting AB	H	HR	BA	PO	A	E	DP	TC/G	FA

Joe Callahan

CALLAHAN, JOSEPH THOMAS
B. Oct. 8, 1916, East Boston, Mass.   D. May 24, 1949, South Boston, Mass.
BR TR 6'2"   170 lbs.

Year	Team		W	L	PCT	ERA	G	GS	CG	IP	H	BB	SO	ShO	W	L	SV	AB	H	HR	BA	PO	A	E	DP	TC/G	FA
1939	BOS	N	1	0	1.000	3.12	4	1	1	17.1	17	3	8	0	0	0	0	4	0	0	.000	3	3	0	0	1.5	1.000
1940			0	2	.000	10.20	6	2	0	15	20	13	3	0	0	0	0	5	0	0	.000	0	6	0	1	1.0	1.000
2 yrs.			1	2	.333	6.40	10	3	1	32.1	37	16	11	0	0	0	0	9	0	0	.000	3	9	0	1	1.2	1.000

Nixey Callahan

CALLAHAN, JAMES JOSEPH (Cal)
B. Mar. 18, 1874, Fitchburg, Mass.   D. Oct. 4, 1934, Boston, Mass.
Manager 1903-04, 1912-14, 1916-17.
BR TR 5'10½" 180 lbs.

Year	Team		W	L	PCT	ERA	G	GS	CG	IP	H	BB	SO	ShO	W	L	SV	AB	H	HR	BA	PO	A	E	DP	TC/G	FA
1894	PHI	N	1	2	.333	9.89	9	2	1	33.2	64	17	9	0	1	0	2	21	5	0	.238	4	8	1	0	1.4	.923
1897	CHI	N	12	9	.571	4.03	23	22	21	189.2	221	55	52	1	0	1	0	360	105	3	.292	14	45	7	4	2.9	.894
1898			20	10	.667	2.46	31	31	30	274.1	267	71	73	2	0	0	0	164	43	0	.262	27	63	5	3	3.1	.947
1899			21	12	.636	3.06	35	34	33	294.1	327	76	77	3	1	0	0	150	39	0	.260	18	95	12	2	3.6	.904
1900			13	16	.448	3.82	32	32	32	285.1	347	74	77	2	0	0	0	115	27	0	.235	21	94	3	2	3.7	.975
1901	CHI	A	15	8	.652	2.42	27	22	20	215.1	195	50	70	1	1	2	0	118	39	1	.331	19	83	6	3	4.0	.944
1902			16	14	.533	3.60	35	31	29	282.1	287	89	75	2	1	0	0	218	51	0	.234	21	106	8	7	3.9	.941
1903			1	2	.333	4.50	3	3	3	28	40	5	12	0	0	0	0	439	128	2	.292	3	12	1	0	5.3	.938
8 yrs.			99	73	.576	3.39	195	177	169	1603	1748	437	445	11	4	3	2	*				127	506	43	21	3.5	.936

Ray Callahan

CALLAHAN, RAYMOND JAMES (Pat)
B. Aug. 29, 1891, Ashland, Wis.   D. Jan. 23, 1973, Olympia, Wash.
BL TL 5'10½" 170 lbs.

Year	Team		W	L	PCT	ERA	G	GS	CG	IP	H	BB	SO	ShO	W	L	SV	AB	H	HR	BA	PO	A	E	DP	TC/G	FA
1915	CIN	N	0	0	—	8.53	3	0	0	6.1	12	1	4	0	0	0	0	3	1	0	.333	0	0	0	0	0.0	—

Dick Calmus

CALMUS, RICHARD LEE
B. Jan. 7, 1944, Los Angeles, Calif.
BR TR 6'4"   187 lbs.

Year	Team		W	L	PCT	ERA	G	GS	CG	IP	H	BB	SO	ShO	W	L	SV	AB	H	HR	BA	PO	A	E	DP	TC/G	FA
1963	LA	N	3	1	.750	2.66	21	1	0	44	32	16	25	0	3	0	0	6	0	0	.000	1	6	0	0	0.3	1.000
1967	CHI	N	0	0	—	8.31	1	1	0	4.1	5	0	1	0	0	0	0	2	1	0	.500	0	1	0	0	1.0	1.000
2 yrs.			3	1	.750	3.17	22	2	0	48.1	37	16	26	0	3	0	0	8	1	0	.125	1	7	0	0	0.4	1.000

Mark Calvert

CALVERT, MARK
B. Sept. 29, 1956, Tulsa, Okla.
BR TR 6'1"   195 lbs.

Year	Team		W	L	PCT	ERA	G	GS	CG	IP	H	BB	SO	ShO	W	L	SV	AB	H	HR	BA	PO	A	E	DP	TC/G	FA
1983	SF	N	1	4	.200	6.27	18	4	0	37.1	46	34	14	0	0	2	0	8	0	0	.000	5	7	0	0	0.7	1.000
1984			2	4	.333	5.06	10	5	1	32	40	9	5	0	0	1	0	8	0	0	.000	2	8	0	0	1.0	1.000
2 yrs.			3	8	.273	5.71	28	9	1	69.1	86	43	19	0	0	3	0	16	0	0	.000	7	15	0	0	0.8	1.000

Paul Calvert

CALVERT, PAUL LEO EMILE
B. Oct. 6, 1917, Montreal, Que., Canada
BR TR 6'   175 lbs.

Year	Team		W	L	PCT	ERA	G	GS	CG	IP	H	BB	SO	ShO	W	L	SV	AB	H	HR	BA	PO	A	E	DP	TC/G	FA
1942	CLE	A	0	0	—	0.00	1	0	0	2	0	2	2	0	0	0	0	0	0	0	—	0	0	0	0	0.0	—
1943			0	0	—	4.32	5	0	0	8.1	6	6	2	0	0	0	0	1	0	0	.000	0	2	0	0	0.4	1.000
1944			1	3	.250	4.56	35	4	0	77	89	38	31	0	0	2	0	15	4	0	.267	9	21	3	2	0.9	.909
1945			0	0	—	13.50	1	0	0	1.1	3	1	1	0	0	0	0	0	0	0	—	0	0	0	0	0.0	—
1949	WAS	A	6	17	.261	5.43	34	23	5	160.2	175	86	52	0	1	2	1	51	7	0	.137	15	40	0	2	1.6	1.000
1950	DET	A	2	2	.500	6.31	32	0	0	51.1	71	25	14	0	2	2	4	7	0	0	.000	5	12	1	0	0.6	.944
1951			0	0	—	0.00	1	0	0	1	0	0	0	0	0	0	0	0	0	0	—	0	1	0	0	1.0	1.000
7 yrs.			9	22	.290	5.31	109	27	5	301.2	345	158	102	0	3	6	5	74	11	0	.149	29	76	4	4	1.0	.963

Ernie Camacho

CAMACHO, ERNEST CARLOS
B. Feb. 1, 1955, Salinas, Calif.
BR TR 6'1"   180 lbs.

Year	Team		W	L	PCT	ERA	G	GS	CG	IP	H	BB	SO	ShO	W	L	SV	AB	H	HR	BA	PO	A	E	DP	TC/G	FA
1980	OAK	A	0	0	—	6.75	5	0	0	12	20	5	9	0	0	0	0	0	0	0	—	0	0	0	0	0.0	—
1981	PIT	N	0	1	.000	4.91	7	3	0	22	23	15	11	0	0	0	0	4	0	0	.000	0	3	0	1	0.4	1.000
1983	CLE	A	0	1	.000	5.06	4	0	0	5.1	5	2	2	0	0	1	0	0	0	0	—	0	0	0	0	0.0	—
1984			5	9	.357	2.43	69	0	0	100	83	37	48	0	5	9	23	0	0	0	—	1	15	0	0	0.2	1.000
1985			0	1	.000	8.10	2	0	0	3.1	4	1	2	0	0	1	0	0	0	0	—	0	1	0	0	0.5	1.000
1986			2	4	.333	4.08	51	0	0	57.1	60	31	36	0	2	4	20	0	0	0	—	5	11	1	0	0.3	.941
1987			0	1	.000	9.22	15	0	0	13.2	21	5	9	0	0	1	1	0	0	0	—	1	5	0	0	0.4	1.000
1988	HOU	N	0	3	.000	7.64	13	0	0	17.2	25	12	13	0	0	3	1	1	0	0	.000	1	3	0	0	0.3	1.000
1989	SF	N	3	0	1.000	2.76	13	0	0	16.1	10	11	14	0	3	0	0	1	0	0	.000	2	5	0	0	0.5	1.000
9 yrs.			10	20	.333	4.14	179	3	0	247.2	251	119	144	0	10	19	45	6	0	0	.000	10	43	1	1	0.3	.981

Fred Cambria

CAMBRIA, FREDERICK DENNIS
B. Jan. 22, 1948, Cambria Heights, N. Y.
BR TR 6'2"   195 lbs.

Year	Team		W	L	PCT	ERA	G	GS	CG	IP	H	BB	SO	ShO	W	L	SV	AB	H	HR	BA	PO	A	E	DP	TC/G	FA
1970	PIT	N	1	2	.333	3.55	6	5	0	33	37	12	14	0	0	0	0	10	2	0	.200	1	6	0	1	1.2	1.000

John Cameron

CAMERON, JOHN S. (Happy Jack)
B. 1885, Canada   D. Aug. 17, 1951, Boston, Mass.

Year	Team		W	L	PCT	ERA	G	GS	CG	IP	H	BB	SO	ShO	W	L	SV	AB	H	HR	BA	PO	A	E	DP	TC/G	FA
1906	BOS	N	0	0	—	0.00	2	1	0	6	4	6	2	0	0	0	0	*				0	2	0	0	1.0	1.000

Harry Camnitz

CAMNITZ, HENRY RICHARDSON
Brother of Howie Camnitz.
B. Oct. 26, 1884, McKinney, Ky.   D. Jan. 6, 1951, Louisville, Ky.
BR TR 6'1"   168 lbs.

Year	Team		W	L	PCT	ERA	G	GS	CG	IP	H	BB	SO	ShO	W	L	SV	AB	H	HR	BA	PO	A	E	DP	TC/G	FA
1909	PIT	N	0	0	—	4.50	1	0	0	4	6	1	1	0	0	0	0	2	0	0	.000	0	3	0	0	3.0	1.000
1911	STL	N	1	0	1.000	0.00	2	0	0	2	0	1	2	0	1	0	0	0	0	0	—	0	0	0	0	0.0	—
2 yrs.			1	0	1.000	3.00	3	0	0	6	6	2	3	0	1	0	0	2	0	0	.000	0	3	0	0	1.0	1.000

Howie Camnitz

CAMNITZ, SAMUEL HOWARD (Red)
Brother of Harry Camnitz.
B. Aug. 22, 1881, Covington, Ky.   D. Mar. 2, 1960, Louisville, Ky.
BR TR 5'9"   169 lbs.

Year	Team		W	L	PCT	ERA	G	GS	CG	IP	H	BB	SO	ShO	W	L	SV	AB	H	HR	BA	PO	A	E	DP	TC/G	FA
1904	PIT	N	1	3	.250	4.22	10	2	2	49	48	20	21	0	1	1	0	16	1	0	.063	2	9	0	0	1.1	1.000
1906			1	0	1.000	2.00	2	1	1	9	6	5	5	0	0	0	0	3	0	0	.000	1	1	0	0	1.0	1.000

Year	Team		W	L	PCT	ERA	G	GS	CG	IP	H	BB	SO	ShO	Relief Pitching W	L	SV	Batting AB	H	HR	BA	PO	A	E	DP	TC/G	FA

Howie Camnitz *continued*

Year	Team		W	L	PCT	ERA	G	GS	CG	IP	H	BB	SO	ShO	W	L	SV	AB	H	HR	BA	PO	A	E	DP	TC/G	FA
1907			13	8	.619	2.15	31	19	15	180	135	59	85	4	3	2	1	60	3	0	.050	8	46	1	1	1.8	.982
1908			16	9	.640	1.56	38	26	17	236.2	182	69	118	3	0	0	2	72	6	0	.083	7	64	6	0	2.0	.922
1909			25	6	**.806**	1.62	41	30	20	283	207	68	133	5	7	0	3	87	12	0	.138	9	63	2	3	1.8	.973
1910			12	13	.480	3.22	38	31	16	260	246	61	120	1	2	0	2	88	11	1	.125	14	57	2	1	1.9	.973
1911			20	15	.571	3.13	40	33	18	267.2	245	84	139	1	3	2	0	84	12	0	.143	4	59	5	1	1.7	.926
1912			22	12	.647	2.83	41	32	22	276.2	256	82	121	2	5	0	2	98	23	0	.235	4	59	4	1	1.6	.940
1913	2 teams	PIT N (36G 6–17)				PHI N (9G 3–3)																					
"	total		9	20	.310	3.73	45	27	6	241.1	252	107	85	1	3	5	3	75	10	0	.133	5	64	4	1	1.6	.945
1914	PIT	F	14	18	.438	3.23	36	34	20	262	256	90	82	1	0	1	1	87	14	0	.161	9	61	7	0	2.1	.909
1915			0	2	.000	4.50	4	2	0	20	19	11	6	0	0	1	0	7	0	0	.000	0	3	0	0	0.8	1.000
11 yrs.			133	106	.556	2.75	326	237	137	2085.1	1852	656	915	19	24	12	14	677	92	1	.136	63	486	31	8	1.8	.947

WORLD SERIES

Year	Team		W	L	PCT	ERA	G	GS	CG	IP	H	BB	SO	ShO	W	L	SV	AB	H	HR	BA	PO	A	E	DP	TC/G	FA
1909	PIT		0	1	.000	12.27	2	1	0	3.2	8	2	2	0	0	0	0	1	0	0	.000	0	2	0	0	1.0	1.000

Kid Camp

CAMP, WINFIELD SCOTT   6'   160 lbs.
Brother of Llewellan Camp.
B. 1870, Columbus, Ohio   D. Mar. 2, 1895, Omaha, Neb.

Year	Team		W	L	PCT	ERA	G	GS	CG	IP	H	BB	SO	ShO	W	L	SV	AB	H	HR	BA	PO	A	E	DP	TC/G	FA
1892	PIT	N	0	1	.000	6.26	4	1	1	23	31	9	6	0	0	0	0	11	1	0	.091	0	2	0	0	1.0	.500
1894	CHI	N	0	1	.000	6.55	3	2	2	22	34	12	6	0	0	0	0	11	0	0	.000	2	6	0	0	2.0	1.000
2 yrs.			0	2	.000	6.40	7	3	3	45	65	21	12	0	0	0	0	22	1	0	.045	2	6	2	0	1.4	.800

Rick Camp

CAMP, RICK LAMAR   BR TR 6'1"   195 lbs.
B. June 10, 1953, Trion, Ga.

Year	Team		W	L	PCT	ERA	G	GS	CG	IP	H	BB	SO	ShO	W	L	SV	AB	H	HR	BA	PO	A	E	DP	TC/G	FA
1976	ATL	N	0	1	.000	6.55	5	1	0	11	13	2	6	0	0	0	0	2	0	0	.000	3	5	1	0	1.8	.889
1977			6	3	.667	3.99	54	0	0	79	89	47	51	0	6	3	10	6	0	0	.000	4	10	2	1	0.3	.875
1978			2	4	.333	3.77	42	4	0	74	99	32	23	0	0	4	0	8	0	0	.000	8	13	3	0	0.5	.870
1980			6	4	.600	1.92	77	0	0	108	92	29	33	0	6	4	22	9	1	0	.111	9	34	1	2	0.6	.977
1981			9	3	.750	1.78	48	0	0	76	68	12	47	0	**9**	3	17	12	0	0	.000	11	9	0	1	0.4	1.000
1982			11	13	.458	3.65	51	21	3	177.1	199	52	68	0	4	3	5	41	1	0	.024	18	30	3	2	1.0	.941
1983			10	9	.526	3.79	40	16	1	140	146	38	61	0	4	2	0	39	3	0	.077	14	23	5	1	1.1	.881
1984			8	6	.571	3.27	31	21	1	148.2	134	63	69	0	1	0	0	45	5	0	.111	12	24	1	0	1.2	.973
1985			4	6	.400	3.95	66	2	0	127.2	130	61	49	0	3	5	3	13	3	1	.231	7	13	4	0	0.4	.833
9 yrs.			56	49	.533	3.37	414	65	5	941.2	970	336	407	0	33	24	57	175	13	1	.074	86	160	20	10	0.6	.925

LEAGUE CHAMPIONSHIP SERIES

Year	Team		W	L	PCT	ERA	G	GS	CG	IP	H	BB	SO	ShO	W	L	SV	AB	H	HR	BA	PO	A	E	DP	TC/G	FA
1982	ATL	N	0	1	.000	36.00	1	1	0	1	4	1	0	0	0	0	0	0	0	0	—	0	0	0	0	0.0	—

Bert Campaneris

CAMPANERIS, DAGOBERTO   BR TR 5'10"   160 lbs.
Born Dagoberto Campaneris y Blanco.
B. Mar. 9, 1942, Pueblo Nuevo, Cuba

Year	Team		W	L	PCT	ERA	G	GS	CG	IP	H	BB	SO	ShO	W	L	SV	AB	H	HR	BA	PO	A	E	DP	TC/G	FA
1965	KC	A	0	0	—	9.00	1	0	0	1	1	2	1	0	0	0	0	*				0	0	0	0	0.0	—

Archie Campbell

CAMPBELL, ARCHIBALD STEWART (Iron Man)   BR TR 6'1"   180 lbs.
B. Oct. 20, 1903, Maplewood, N. J.

Year	Team		W	L	PCT	ERA	G	GS	CG	IP	H	BB	SO	ShO	W	L	SV	AB	H	HR	BA	PO	A	E	DP	TC/G	FA
1928	NY	A	0	1	.000	5.25	13	1	0	24	30	11	9	0	0	1	2	4	1	0	.250	1	4	2	0	0.5	.714
1929	WAS	A	0	1	.000	15.75	4	0	0	4	10	5	1	0	0	1	0	0	0	0	—	0	2	0	1	0.5	1.000
1930	CIN	N	2	4	.333	5.43	23	3	1	58	71	31	19	0	1	2	4	15	4	0	.267	4	22	1	1	1.2	.963
3 yrs.			2	6	.250	5.86	40	4	1	86	111	47	29	0	1	4	6	19	5	0	.263	5	28	3	2	0.9	.917

Bill Campbell

CAMPBELL, WILLIAM RICHARD   BR TR 6'3"   185 lbs.
B. Aug. 9, 1948, Highland Park, Mich.

Year	Team		W	L	PCT	ERA	G	GS	CG	IP	H	BB	SO	ShO	W	L	SV	AB	H	HR	BA	PO	A	E	DP	TC/G	FA
1973	MIN	A	3	3	.500	3.14	28	2	0	51.2	44	20	42	0	3	2	7	0	0	0	—	2	8	1	0	0.4	.909
1974			8	7	.533	2.63	63	0	0	120	109	55	89	0	8	7	19	0	0	0	—	10	16	2	3	0.4	.929
1975			4	6	.400	3.79	47	7	2	121	119	46	76	1	1	4	5	1	0	0	.000	12	18	1	2	0.7	.968
1976			17	5	**.773**	3.01	**78**	0	0	167.2	145	62	115	0	17	5	20	0	0	0	—	12	20	1	1	0.4	.970
1977	BOS	A	13	9	.591	2.96	69	0	0	140	112	60	114	0	13	9	**31**	0	0	0	—	19	20	1	2	0.6	.975
1978			7	5	.583	3.91	29	0	0	50.2	62	17	47	0	7	5	4	0	0	0	—	10	6	1	0	0.6	.941
1979			3	4	.429	4.25	41	0	0	55	55	23	25	0	3	4	9	0	0	0	—	10	11	0	1	0.5	1.000
1980			4	0	1.000	4.83	23	0	0	41	44	22	17	0	4	0	0	0	0	0	—	3	2	0	0	0.2	1.000
1981			1	1	.500	3.19	30	0	0	48	45	20	37	0	1	1	7	0	0	0	—	4	7	1	0	0.4	.917
1982	CHI	N	3	6	.333	3.69	62	0	0	100	89	40	71	0	3	6	8	7	1	0	.143	10	23	0	1	0.5	1.000
1983			6	8	.429	4.49	**82**	0	0	122.1	128	49	97	0	6	8	8	10	1	0	.100	15	24	2	0	0.5	.951
1984	PHI	N	6	5	.545	3.43	57	0	0	81.1	68	35	52	0	6	5	1	1	0	0	.000	6	5	0	0	0.2	1.000
1985	STL	N	5	3	.625	3.50	50	0	0	64.1	55	21	41	0	5	3	4	6	2	0	.333	0	6	1	0	0.1	.857
1986	DET	A	3	6	.333	3.88	34	0	0	55.2	46	21	37	0	3	6	3	0	0	0	.000	6	4	2	1	0.4	.833
1987	MON	N	0	0	—	8.10	7	0	0	10	18	4	4	0	0	0	0	1	0	0	.000	0	2	0	0	0.3	1.000
15 yrs.			83	68	.550	3.55	700	9	2	1228.2	1139	495	864	1	80	65	126	26	4	0	.154	119	172	13	11	0.4	.957

LEAGUE CHAMPIONSHIP SERIES

Year	Team		W	L	PCT	ERA	G	GS	CG	IP	H	BB	SO	ShO	W	L	SV	AB	H	HR	BA	PO	A	E	DP	TC/G	FA
1985	STL	N	0	0	—	0.00	3	0	0	2.1	3	0	2	0	0	0	0	0	0	0	—	0	0	0	0	0.0	—

WORLD SERIES

Year	Team		W	L	PCT	ERA	G	GS	CG	IP	H	BB	SO	ShO	W	L	SV	AB	H	HR	BA	PO	A	E	DP	TC/G	FA
1985	STL	N	0	0	—	2.25	3	0	0	4	4	2	5	0	0	0	0	0	0	0	—	1	0	0	0	0.3	1.000

Billy Campbell

CAMPBELL, WILLIAM JAMES   BL TL 5'10"   165 lbs.
B. Nov. 5, 1873, Pittsburgh, Pa.   D. Oct. 6, 1957, Cincinnati, Ohio

Year	Team		W	L	PCT	ERA	G	GS	CG	IP	H	BB	SO	ShO	W	L	SV	AB	H	HR	BA	PO	A	E	DP	TC/G	FA
1905	STL	N	1	1	.500	7.41	2	2	2	17	27	7	2	0	0	0	0	7	1	0	.143	2	9	0	0	5.5	1.000
1907	CIN	N	3	0	1.000	2.14	3	3	3	21	19	3	4	0	0	0	0	8	2	0	.250	4	7	0	0	3.7	1.000
1908			12	13	.480	2.60	35	24	19	221.1	203	44	73	2	2	1	1	72	6	0	.083	10	87	7	1	3.0	.933

Year	Team	W	L	PCT	ERA	G	GS	CG	IP	H	BB	SO	ShO	Relief Pitching W	L	SV	Batting AB	H	HR	BA	PO	A	E	DP	TC/G	FA

Billy Campbell *continued*

Year	Team	W	L	PCT	ERA	G	GS	CG	IP	H	BB	SO	ShO	W	L	SV	AB	H	HR	BA	PO	A	E	DP	TC/G	FA
1909		7	11	.389	2.67	30	15	7	148.1	162	39	37	0	1	4	2	43	6	0	.140	3	55	1	2	2.0	.983
4 yrs.		23	25	.479	2.80	70	44	31	407.2	411	93	116	2	3	5	3	130	15	0	.115	19	158	8	3	2.6	.957

Dave Campbell

CAMPBELL, DAVID ALAN
B. Sept. 3, 1951, Princeton, Ind.　　BR TR 6'3"　210 lbs.

Year	Team	W	L	PCT	ERA	G	GS	CG	IP	H	BB	SO	ShO	W	L	SV	AB	H	HR	BA	PO	A	E	DP	TC/G	FA
1977	ATL N	0	6	.000	3.03	65	0	0	89	78	33	42	0	0	6	13	12	1	0	.083	0	9	1	0	0.2	.900
1978		4	4	.500	4.83	53	0	0	69	67	49	45	0	4	4	1	0	0	0	–	6	9	1	1	0.3	.938
2 yrs.		4	10	.286	3.82	118	0	0	158	145	82	87	0	4	10	14	12	1	0	.083	6	18	2	1	0.2	.923

John Campbell

CAMPBELL, JOHN MILLARD
B. Sept. 13, 1907, Washington, D. C.　　BR TR 6'1½"　184 lbs.

Year	Team	W	L	PCT	ERA	G	GS	CG	IP	H	BB	SO	ShO	W	L	SV	AB	H	HR	BA	PO	A	E	DP	TC/G	FA
1933	WAS A	0	0	–	0.00	1	0	0	1	1	1	0	0	0	0	0	0	0	0	–	0	0	0	0	0.0	–

Mike Campbell

CAMPBELL, MICHAEL THOMAS
B. Feb. 17, 1964, Seattle, Wash.　　BR TR 6'3"　210 lbs.

Year	Team	W	L	PCT	ERA	G	GS	CG	IP	H	BB	SO	ShO	W	L	SV	AB	H	HR	BA	PO	A	E	DP	TC/G	FA
1987	SEA A	1	4	.200	4.74	9	9	1	49.1	41	25	35	0	0	0	0	0	0	0	–	6	5	0	0	1.2	1.000
1988		6	10	.375	5.89	20	20	2	114.2	128	43	63	0	0	0	0	0	0	0	–	7	13	3	1	1.2	.870
1989		1	2	.333	7.29	5	5	0	21	28	10	6	0	0	0	0	0	0	0	–	2	1	0	0	0.6	1.000
3 yrs.		8	16	.333	5.74	34	34	3	185	197	78	104	0	0	0	0	0	0	0	–	15	19	3	1	1.1	.919

Card Camper

CAMPER, CARDELL
B. July 6, 1952, Boley, Okla.　　BR TR 6'3"　208 lbs.

Year	Team	W	L	PCT	ERA	G	GS	CG	IP	H	BB	SO	ShO	W	L	SV	AB	H	HR	BA	PO	A	E	DP	TC/G	FA
1977	CLE A	1	0	1.000	4.00	3	1	0	9	7	4	9	0	0	0	0	0	0	0	–	0	0	0	0	0.0	–

Sal Campfield

CAMPFIELD, WILLIAM HOLTON
B. Feb. 19, 1868, Meadville, Pa.　D. May 16, 1952, Meadville, Pa.　　BR TR 6'½"

Year	Team	W	L	PCT	ERA	G	GS	CG	IP	H	BB	SO	ShO	W	L	SV	AB	H	HR	BA	PO	A	E	DP	TC/G	FA
1896	NY N	1	1	.500	4.00	6	2	2	27	31	6	6	0	0	0	0	12	2	0	.167	0	5	1	0	1.0	.833

Sal Campisi

CAMPISI, SALVATORE JOHN
B. Aug. 11, 1942, Brooklyn, N. Y.　　BR TR 6'2"　210 lbs.

Year	Team	W	L	PCT	ERA	G	GS	CG	IP	H	BB	SO	ShO	W	L	SV	AB	H	HR	BA	PO	A	E	DP	TC/G	FA
1969	STL N	1	0	1.000	0.90	7	0	0	10	4	6	7	0	1	0	0	0	0	0	–	0	4	2	0	0.9	.667
1970		2	2	.500	2.94	37	0	0	49	53	37	26	0	2	2	4	1	0	0	.000	1	8	0	0	0.2	1.000
1971	MIN A	0	0	–	4.50	6	0	0	4	5	4	2	0	0	0	0	0	0	0	–	0	1	0	0	0.2	1.000
3 yrs.		3	2	.600	2.71	50	0	0	63	62	47	35	0	3	2	4	1	0	0	.000	1	13	2	0	0.3	.875

Hugh Canavan

CANAVAN, HUGH EDWARD (Hugo)
B. May 13, 1897, Worcester, Mass.　D. Sept. 4, 1967, Boston, Mass.　　BL TL 5'8"　160 lbs.

Year	Team	W	L	PCT	ERA	G	GS	CG	IP	H	BB	SO	ShO	W	L	SV	AB	H	HR	BA	PO	A	E	DP	TC/G	FA
1918	BOS N	0	4	.000	6.36	11	3	3	46.2	70	15	18	0	0	1	0	21	2	0	.095	0	20	1	0	1.9	.952

John Candelaria

CANDELARIA, JOHN ROBERT (The Candy Man)
B. Nov. 6, 1953, New York, N. Y.　　BL TL 6'7"　205 lbs.

Year	Team	W	L	PCT	ERA	G	GS	CG	IP	H	BB	SO	ShO	W	L	SV	AB	H	HR	BA	PO	A	E	DP	TC/G	FA
1975	PIT N	8	6	.571	2.75	18	18	4	121	95	36	95	1	0	0	0	43	6	0	.140	3	13	4	0	1.1	.800
1976		16	7	.696	3.15	32	31	11	220	173	60	138	4	0	0	1	76	14	0	.184	3	31	0	2	1.1	1.000
1977		20	5	**.800**	**2.34**	33	33	6	231	197	50	133	1	0	0	0	80	18	0	.225	6	30	1	3	1.1	.973
1978		12	11	.522	3.24	30	29	3	189	191	49	94	1	0	0	1	52	9	0	.173	4	25	0	0	1.0	1.000
1979		14	9	.609	3.22	33	30	8	207	201	41	101	0	0	1	0	68	9	0	.132	2	36	0	3	1.2	1.000
1980		11	14	.440	4.02	35	34	7	233	246	50	97	0	0	0	0	77	15	0	.195	8	38	2	3	1.4	.958
1981		2	2	.500	3.51	6	6	0	41	42	11	14	0	0	0	0	13	3	0	.231	1	7	0	1	1.3	1.000
1982		12	7	.632	2.94	31	30	1	174.2	166	37	133	1	0	0	1	54	12	0	.222	1	23	1	1	0.8	.960
1983		15	8	.652	3.23	33	32	3	197.2	191	45	157	0	0	0	0	65	9	0	.138	5	20	0	1	0.8	1.000
1984		12	11	.522	2.72	33	28	3	185.1	179	34	133	1	0	1	2	62	8	1	.129	3	21	0	1	0.7	1.000
1985	2 teams	PIT N	(37G 2–4)		CAL A	(13G 7–3)																				
"	total	9	7	.563	3.73	50	13	1	125.1	127	38	100	1	2	4	9	1	0	0	.000	3	16	2	0	0.4	.905
1986	CAL A	10	2	.833	2.55	16	16	1	91.2	68	26	81	1	0	0	0	0	0	0	–	3	10	0	0	0.8	1.000
1987	2 teams	CAL A	(20G 8–6)		NY N	(3G 2–0)																				
"	total	10	6	.625	4.81	23	23	0	129	144	23	84	0	0	0	0	5	1	0	.200	6	24	0	1	1.3	1.000
1988	NY A	13	7	.650	3.38	25	24	6	157	150	23	121	2	0	0	1	0	0	0	–	4	22	0	1	1.0	1.000
1989	2 teams	NY A	(10G 3–3)		MON N	(12G 0–2)																				
"	total	3	5	.375	4.68	22	6	1	65.1	66	16	51	0	0	3	0	0	0	0	–	2	7	1	0	0.5	.900
15 yrs.		167	107	.609	3.27	420	353	54	2368	2236	539	1532	13	2	9	16	596	104	1	.174	54	323	11	16	0.9	.972

LEAGUE CHAMPIONSHIP SERIES

Year	Team	W	L	PCT	ERA	G	GS	CG	IP	H	BB	SO	ShO	W	L	SV	AB	H	HR	BA	PO	A	E	DP	TC/G	FA
1975	PIT N	0	0	–	3.52	1	1	0	7.2	3	2	14	0	0	0	0	3	0	0	.000	0	0	0	0	0.0	–
1979		0	0	–	2.57	1	1	0	7	5	1	4	0	0	0	0	3	0	0	.000	0	0	0	0	0.0	–
1986	CAL A	1	1	.500	0.84	2	2	0	10.2	11	6	7	0	0	0	0	0	0	0	–	0	1	0	0	0.5	1.000
3 yrs.		1	1	.500	2.13	4	4	0	25.1	19	9	25	0	0	0	0	6	0	0	.000	0	1	0	0	0.3	1.000

WORLD SERIES

Year	Team	W	L	PCT	ERA	G	GS	CG	IP	H	BB	SO	ShO	W	L	SV	AB	H	HR	BA	PO	A	E	DP	TC/G	FA
1979	PIT N	1	1	.500	5.00	2	2	0	9	14	2	4	0	0	0	0	3	1	0	.333	0	1	0	0	0.5	1.000

Milo Candini

CANDINI, MARIO CAIN
B. Aug. 3, 1917, Manteca, Calif.　　BR TR 6'　187 lbs.

Year	Team	W	L	PCT	ERA	G	GS	CG	IP	H	BB	SO	ShO	W	L	SV	AB	H	HR	BA	PO	A	E	DP	TC/G	FA
1943	WAS A	11	7	.611	2.49	28	21	8	166	144	65	67	3	2	0	1	56	9	1	.161	9	36	0	2	1.6	1.000
1944		6	7	.462	4.11	28	10	4	103	110	49	31	2	1	4	1	32	10	0	.313	4	17	0	4	0.8	1.000
1946		2	0	1.000	2.08	9	0	0	21.2	15	4	6	0	2	0	0	6	2	0	.333	0	3	0	0	0.3	1.000
1947		3	4	.429	5.17	38	2	0	87	96	35	31	0	3	2	1	18	3	0	.167	6	15	0	1	0.6	1.000
1948		2	3	.400	5.15	35	4	1	94.1	96	63	23	0	2	1	3	22	8	0	.364	9	16	2	0	0.8	.926
1949		0	0	–	4.76	3	0	0	5.2	6	1	1	0	0	0	1	1	1	0	1.000	1	0	0	0	0.3	1.000
1950	PHI N	1	0	1.000	2.70	18	0	0	30	32	15	10	0	1	0	1	6	1	0	.167	3	7	0	1	0.6	1.000

Year	Team		W	L	PCT	ERA	G	GS	CG	IP	H	BB	SO	ShO	Relief Pitching W	L	SV	Batting AB	H	HR	BA	PO	A	E	DP	TC/G	FA

Milo Candini *continued*

Year	Team		W	L	PCT	ERA	G	GS	CG	IP	H	BB	SO	ShO	W	L	SV	AB	H	HR	BA	PO	A	E	DP	TC/G	FA
1951			1	0	1.000	6.00	15	0	0	30	33	18	14	0	1	0	0	3	1	0	.333	1	7	1	1	0.6	.889
8 yrs.			26	21	.553	3.92	174	37	13	537.2	530	250	183	5	12	7	8	144	35	1	.243	33	101	3	9	0.8	.978

Tom Candiotti

CANDIOTTI, THOMAS CAESAR
B. Aug. 31, 1957, Walnut Creek, Calif.
BR TR 6'3" 205 lbs.

Year	Team		W	L	PCT	ERA	G	GS	CG	IP	H	BB	SO	ShO	W	L	SV	AB	H	HR	BA	PO	A	E	DP	TC/G	FA
1983	MIL	A	4	4	.500	3.23	10	8	2	55.2	62	16	21	1	0	0	0	0	0	0	–	4	5	0	1	0.9	1.000
1984			2	2	.500	5.29	8	6	0	32.1	38	10	23	0	0	0	0	0	0	0	–	3	1	0	0	0.5	1.000
1986	CLE	A	16	12	.571	3.57	36	34	17	252.1	234	106	167	3	0	0	0	0	0	0	–	27	41	3	7	2.0	.958
1987			7	18	.280	4.78	32	32	7	201.2	193	93	111	2	0	0	0	0	0	0	–	17	29	1	1	1.5	.979
1988			14	8	.636	3.28	31	31	11	216.2	225	53	137	1	0	0	0	0	0	0	–	17	36	1	2	1.7	.981
1989			13	10	.565	3.10	31	31	4	206	188	55	124	0	0	0	0	0	0	0	–	28	41	1	1	2.3	.986
6 yrs.			56	54	.509	3.69	148	142	41	964.2	940	333	583	7	0	0	0	0	0	0	–	96	153	6	12	1.7	.976

John Caneira

CANEIRA, JOHN CASCAES
B. Oct. 7, 1952, Waterbury, Conn.
BR TR 6'3" 180 lbs.

Year	Team		W	L	PCT	ERA	G	GS	CG	IP	H	BB	SO	ShO	W	L	SV	AB	H	HR	BA	PO	A	E	DP	TC/G	FA
1977	CAL	A	2	2	.500	4.08	6	4	0	28.2	27	16	17	0	0	0	0	0	0	0	–	1	2	1	0	0.7	.750
1978			0	0	–	7.04	2	2	0	7.2	8	3	0	0	0	0	0	0	0	0	–	0	0	1	0	0.5	–
2 yrs.			2	2	.500	4.71	8	6	0	36.1	35	19	17	0	0	0	0	0	0	0	–	1	2	2	0	0.6	.600

John Cangelosi

CANGELOSI, JOHN ANTHONY
B. Mar. 10, 1963, Brooklyn, N. Y.
BB TL 5'8" 150 lbs.

Year	Team		W	L	PCT	ERA	G	GS	CG	IP	H	BB	SO	ShO	W	L	SV	AB	H	HR	BA	PO	A	E	DP	TC/G	FA
1988	PIT	N	0	0	–	0.00	1	0	0	2	1	0	0	0	0	0	0	*				0	0	0	0	0.0	–

Jose Cano

CANO, JOSELITO
Born Joselito Cano y Soriano.
B. Mar. 7, 1962, Boca de Soco, Dominican Republic
BR TR 6'3" 175 lbs.

Year	Team		W	L	PCT	ERA	G	GS	CG	IP	H	BB	SO	ShO	W	L	SV	AB	H	HR	BA	PO	A	E	DP	TC/G	FA
1989	HOU	N	1	1	.500	5.09	6	3	1	23	24	7	8	0	0	0	0	6	0	0	.000	2	2	1	1	0.8	.800

Guy Cantrell

CANTRELL, DEWEY GUY (Gunner)
B. Apr. 9, 1904, Clarita, Okla. D. Jan. 31, 1961, McAlester, Okla.
BR TR 6' 190 lbs.

Year	Team		W	L	PCT	ERA	G	GS	CG	IP	H	BB	SO	ShO	W	L	SV	AB	H	HR	BA	PO	A	E	DP	TC/G	FA
1925	BKN	N	1	0	1.000	3.00	3	1	1	36	42	14	13	0	0	0	0	9	0	0	.000	3	13	1	1	1.2	.941
1927	2 teams		BKN N	(6G 0–0)		PHI A	(2G 0–2)																					
"	total		0	2	.000	4.18	8	2	2	28	35	13	12	0	0	0	0	9	2	0	.222	1	8	0	0	1.1	1.000
1930	DET	A	1	5	.167	5.66	16	2	1	35	38	20	20	0	1	3	0	9	0	0	.000	1	10	0	0	0.7	1.000
3 yrs.			2	7	.222	4.27	38	7	4	99	115	47	45	0	1	3	0	27	2	0	.074	5	31	1	1	0.9	.973

Ben Cantwell

CANTWELL, BENJAMIN CALDWELL
B. Apr. 13, 1902, Milan, Tenn. D. Dec. 4, 1962, Salem, Mo.
BR TR 6'1" 168 lbs.

Year	Team		W	L	PCT	ERA	G	GS	CG	IP	H	BB	SO	ShO	W	L	SV	AB	H	HR	BA	PO	A	E	DP	TC/G	FA
1927	NY	N	1	1	.500	4.12	5	2	1	19.2	26	2	6	0	1	0	0	8	2	0	.250	2	2	0	0	0.8	1.000
1928	2 teams		NY N	(7G 1–0)		BOS N	(22G 3–3)																					
"	total		4	3	.571	4.98	29	10	3	108.1	132	40	18	0	1	0	1	33	7	0	.212	7	34	3	1	1.5	.932
1929	BOS	N	4	13	.235	4.47	27	20	8	157	171	52	25	0	1	0	2	50	9	0	.180	12	53	4	5	2.6	.942
1930			9	15	.375	4.88	31	21	10	173.1	213	45	43	0	4	1	2	63	19	0	.302	13	50	1	9	2.1	.984
1931			7	9	.438	3.63	33	16	9	156.1	160	34	32	0	2	1	2	57	13	0	.228	7	49	3	2	1.8	.949
1932			13	11	.542	2.96	37	9	3	146	133	33	33	1	**12**	**8**	5	50	14	0	.280	12	43	1	6	1.5	.982
1933			20	10	**.667**	2.62	40	29	18	254.2	242	54	57	2	4	1	2	85	12	1	.141	12	77	1	2	2.3	.989
1934			5	11	.313	4.33	27	19	6	143.1	163	34	45	1	1	0	5	43	12	0	.279	8	40	3	1	1.9	.941
1935			4	**25**	.138	4.61	39	24	13	210.2	235	44	34	0	1	5	5	67	19	0	.284	12	54	1	4	1.7	.985
1936			9	9	.500	3.04	34	12	4	133.1	127	35	42	0	6	3	2	41	8	0	.195	9	44	2	2	1.6	.964
1937	2 teams		NY N	(1G 0–1)		BKN N	(13G 0–0)																					
"	total		0	1	.000	5.17	14	1	0	31.1	38	9	13	0	0	0	0	6	1	0	.167	1	17	0	1	1.3	1.000
11 yrs.			76	108	.413	3.91	316	163	75	1534	1640	382	348	6	31	19	21	503	116	0	.231	95	463	19	32	1.8	.967

Mike Cantwell

CANTWELL, MICHAEL JOSEPH
Brother of Tom Cantwell.
B. Jan. 15, 1896, Washington, D. C. D. Jan. 5, 1953, Oteen, N. C.
BL TL 6' 160 lbs.

Year	Team		W	L	PCT	ERA	G	GS	CG	IP	H	BB	SO	ShO	W	L	SV	AB	H	HR	BA	PO	A	E	DP	TC/G	FA
1916	NY	A	0	0	–	0.00	1	0	0	2	0	2	0	0	0	0	0	0	0	0	–	0	0	0	0	0.0	–
1919	PHI	N	1	3	.250	5.60	5	3	2	27.1	36	9	6	0	0	1	0	9	2	0	.222	1	4	0	0	1.0	1.000
1920			0	3	.000	3.86	5	1	0	23.1	25	15	8	0	0	2	0	7	1	0	.143	1	8	0	0	1.0	1.000
3 yrs.			1	6	.143	4.61	11	4	2	52.2	61	26	14	0	0	3	0	16	3	0	.188	2	12	0	0	1.3	1.000

Tom Cantwell

CANTWELL, THOMAS ALOYSIUS
Brother of Mike Cantwell.
B. Dec. 23, 1888, Washington, D. C. D. Apr. 1, 1968, Washington, D. C.
BR TR 6'1" 175 lbs.

Year	Team		W	L	PCT	ERA	G	GS	CG	IP	H	BB	SO	ShO	W	L	SV	AB	H	HR	BA	PO	A	E	DP	TC/G	FA
1909	CIN	N	1	0	1.000	1.66	6	1	1	21.2	16	7	7	0	1	0	0	5	3	0	.600	1	5	0	0	1.0	1.000
1910			0	0	–	13.50	2	0	0	1.1	2	3	0	0	0	0	0	0	0	0	–	0	0	0	0	0.0	–
2 yrs.			1	0	1.000	2.35	8	1	1	23	18	10	7	0	1	0	0	5	3	0	.600	1	5	0	0	0.8	1.000

Mike Capel

CAPEL, MICHAEL LEE
B. Oct. 13, 1961, Marshall, Tex.
BR TR 6'1" 175 lbs.

Year	Team		W	L	PCT	ERA	G	GS	CG	IP	H	BB	SO	ShO	W	L	SV	AB	H	HR	BA	PO	A	E	DP	TC/G	FA
1988	CHI	N	2	1	.667	4.91	22	0	0	29.1	34	13	19	0	2	1	0	2	0	0	.000	4	3	1	0	0.4	.875

Doug Capilla

CAPILLA, DOUGLAS EDMUND
B. Jan. 7, 1952, Honolulu, Hawaii
BL TL 5'11" 160 lbs.

Year	Team		W	L	PCT	ERA	G	GS	CG	IP	H	BB	SO	ShO	W	L	SV	AB	H	HR	BA	PO	A	E	DP	TC/G	FA
1976	STL	N	1	0	1.000	5.40	7	0	0	8.1	8	4	5	0	0	0	0	0	0	0	–	1	1	0	0	0.3	1.000
1977	2 teams		STL N	(2G 0–0)		CIN N	(22G 7–8)																					
"	total		7	8	.467	4.47	24	16	1	108.2	96	61	75	0	0	0	0	34	2	0	.059	6	13	3	0	0.9	.864
1978	CIN	N	0	1	.000	9.82	6	3	0	11	14	11	9	0	0	0	0	2	0	0	.000	0	1	0	0	0.2	1.000

Year	Team	W	L	PCT	ERA	G	GS	CG	IP	H	BB	SO	ShO	Relief W	Relief L	SV	AB	H	HR	BA	PO	A	E	DP	TC/G	FA

Doug Capilla *continued*

Year	Team	W	L	PCT	ERA	G	GS	CG	IP	H	BB	SO	ShO	W	L	SV	AB	H	HR	BA	PO	A	E	DP	TC/G	FA
1979	2 teams	CIN N	(5G 1–0)			CHI N	(13G 0–1)																				
"	total	1	1	.500	4.18	18	1	0	23.2	21	12	10	0	1	0	0	1	1	0	1.000	0	7	1	0	0.4	.875
1980	CHI N	2	8	.200	4.10	39	11	0	90	82	51	51	0	1	0	0	21	4	0	.190	6	19	3	0	0.7	.893
1981		1	0	1.000	3.18	42	0	0	51	52	34	28	0	1	0	0	3	0	0	.000	0	10	1	0	0.3	.909
6 yrs.		12	18	.400	4.34	136	31	1	292.2	273	173	178	0	4	0	0	61	7	0	.115	13	51	8	0	0.5	.889

George Cappuzzello

CAPPUZZELLO, GEORGE ANGELO
B. Jan. 15, 1954, Youngstown, Ohio

BR TL 6' 175 lbs.

Year	Team	W	L	PCT	ERA	G	GS	CG	IP	H	BB	SO	ShO	W	L	SV	AB	H	HR	BA	PO	A	E	DP	TC/G	FA
1981	DET A	1	1	.500	3.44	18	3	0	34	28	18	19	0	1	0	1	0	0	0	–	0	5	0	1	0.3	1.000
1982	HOU N	0	1	.000	2.79	17	0	0	19.1	16	7	13	0	0	1	0	1	0	0	.000	1	4	0	1	0.3	1.000
2 yrs.		1	2	.333	3.21	35	3	0	53.1	44	25	32	0	1	1	1	1	0	0	.000	1	9	0	2	0.3	1.000

Buzz Capra

CAPRA, LEE WILLIAM
B. Oct. 1, 1947, Chicago, Ill.

BR TR 5'10" 168 lbs.

Year	Team	W	L	PCT	ERA	G	GS	CG	IP	H	BB	SO	ShO	W	L	SV	AB	H	HR	BA	PO	A	E	DP	TC/G	FA
1971	NY N	0	1	.000	9.00	3	0	0	5	3	5	6	0	0	0	0	1	0	0	.000	0	1	0	0	0.3	1.000
1972		3	2	.600	4.58	14	6	0	53	50	27	45	0	0	0	0	12	3	0	.250	5	10	0	2	1.1	1.000
1973		2	7	.222	3.86	24	0	0	42	35	28	35	0	2	7	4	2	0	0	.000	1	7	0	0	0.3	1.000
1974	ATL N	16	8	.667	**2.28**	39	27	11	217	163	84	137	5	1	2	1	67	11	0	.164	13	19	3	2	0.9	.914
1975		4	7	.364	4.27	12	12	5	78	77	28	35	0	0	0	0	23	1	0	.043	6	13	0	1	1.6	1.000
1976		0	1	.000	9.00	5	0	0	9	9	6	4	0	0	0	0	0	0	0	–	0	3	0	0	0.6	1.000
1977		6	11	.353	5.37	45	16	0	139	142	80	100	0	4	3	0	36	4	0	.111	6	18	1	1	0.6	.960
7 yrs.		31	37	.456	3.88	142	61	16	543	479	258	362	5	7	14	5	141	19	0	.135	31	71	4	6	0.7	.962

Pat Caraway

CARAWAY, CECIL BRADFORD PATRICK
B. Sept. 26, 1906, Erath County, Tex.   D. June 9, 1974, El Paso, Tex.

BL TL 6'4" 175 lbs.

Year	Team	W	L	PCT	ERA	G	GS	CG	IP	H	BB	SO	ShO	W	L	SV	AB	H	HR	BA	PO	A	E	DP	TC/G	FA
1930	CHI A	10	10	.500	3.86	38	21	9	193.1	194	57	83	1	2	1	1	64	11	0	.172	7	53	3	2	1.7	.952
1931		10	**24**	.294	6.22	51	32	11	220	268	101	55	1	1	3	2	72	14	0	.194	11	40	1	0	1.0	.981
1932		2	6	.250	6.82	19	9	1	64.2	80	37	13	0	0	1	0	21	3	0	.143	3	15	2	2	1.1	.900
3 yrs.		22	40	.355	5.35	108	62	21	478	542	195	151	2	3	5	3	157	28	0	.178	21	108	6	4	1.3	.956

John Carden

CARDEN, JOHN BRUTON
B. May 19, 1921, Killeen, Tex.   D. Feb. 8, 1949, Mexia, Tex.

BR TR 6'5" 210 lbs.

Year	Team	W	L	PCT	ERA	G	GS	CG	IP	H	BB	SO	ShO	W	L	SV	AB	H	HR	BA	PO	A	E	DP	TC/G	FA
1946	NY N	0	0	–	22.50	1	0	0	2	4	4	1	0	0	0	0	0	0	0	–	0	0	1	0	1.0	–

Conrad Cardinal

CARDINAL, CONRAD SETH
B. Mar. 30, 1942, Brooklyn, N. Y.

BR TR 6'1" 190 lbs.

Year	Team	W	L	PCT	ERA	G	GS	CG	IP	H	BB	SO	ShO	W	L	SV	AB	H	HR	BA	PO	A	E	DP	TC/G	FA
1963	HOU N	0	1	.000	6.08	6	1	0	13.1	15	7	7	0	0	0	0	2	0	0	.000	0	4	0	0	0.7	1.000

Ben Cardoni

CARDONI, ARMAND JOSEPH (Big Ben)
B. Aug. 21, 1920, Jessup, Pa.   D. Apr. 2, 1969, Jessup, Pa.

BR TR 6'3" 195 lbs.

Year	Team	W	L	PCT	ERA	G	GS	CG	IP	H	BB	SO	ShO	W	L	SV	AB	H	HR	BA	PO	A	E	DP	TC/G	FA
1943	BOS N	0	0	–	6.43	11	0	0	28	38	14	5	0	0	0	0	7	0	0	.000	1	7	0	0	0.7	1.000
1944		0	6	.000	3.93	22	5	1	75.2	83	37	24	0	0	2	0	17	4	0	.235	2	12	2	1	0.7	.875
1945		0	0	–	9.00	3	0	0	4	6	3	5	0	0	0	0	0	0	0	–	0	0	0	0	0.0	–
3 yrs.		0	6	.000	4.76	36	5	1	107.2	127	54	34	0	0	2	0	24	4	0	.167	3	19	2	1	0.7	.917

Don Cardwell

CARDWELL, DONALD EUGENE
B. Dec. 7, 1935, Winston-Salem, N. C.

BR TR 6'4" 210 lbs.

Year	Team	W	L	PCT	ERA	G	GS	CG	IP	H	BB	SO	ShO	W	L	SV	AB	H	HR	BA	PO	A	E	DP	TC/G	FA
1957	PHI N	4	8	.333	4.91	30	19	5	128.1	122	42	92	1	0	0	0	35	7	1	.200	12	18	2	0	1.1	.938
1958		3	6	.333	4.51	16	14	3	107.2	99	37	77	0	0	0	0	38	8	0	.211	11	13	0	2	1.5	1.000
1959		9	10	.474	4.06	25	22	9	153	135	65	106	1	0	1	0	55	3	1	.055	4	13	3	2	0.8	.850
1960	2 teams	PHI N	(5G 1–2)			CHI N	(31G 8–14)																				
"	total	9	16	.360	4.38	36	30	6	205.1	194	79	150	1	1	2	0	77	16	5	.208	13	24	2	0	1.1	.949
1961	CHI N	15	14	.517	3.82	39	**38**	13	259.1	243	88	156	3	0	1	0	95	10	3	.105	18	54	2	3	1.9	.973
1962		7	16	.304	4.92	41	29	6	195.2	205	60	104	1	0	1	4	61	9	0	.148	15	37	1	2	1.3	.981
1963	PIT N	13	15	.464	3.07	33	32	7	213.2	195	52	112	2	1	0	0	71	6	0	.085	16	35	5	1	1.7	.911
1964		1	2	.333	2.79	4	4	1	19.1	15	7	10	1	0	0	0	7	1	0	.143	0	6	1	1	1.8	.857
1965		13	10	.565	3.18	37	34	12	240.1	214	59	107	2	0	0	0	74	12	2	.162	23	51	2	6	2.1	.974
1966		6	6	.500	4.60	32	14	1	101.2	112	27	60	0	3	1	1	29	3	0	.103	13	24	2	2	1.2	.949
1967	NY N	5	9	.357	3.57	26	16	3	118.1	112	39	71	1	0	0	0	38	6	1	.158	13	27	0	3	1.5	1.000
1968		7	13	.350	2.95	29	25	5	180	156	50	82	1	0	0	0	61	3	1	.049	16	39	1	1	1.9	.982
1969		8	10	.444	3.01	30	21	4	152.1	145	47	60	1	0	1	0	47	8	1	.170	9	41	3	0	1.8	.943
1970	2 teams	NY N	(16G 0–2)			ATL N	(16G 2–1)																				
"	total	2	3	.400	7.69	32	1	0	48	62	19	24	0	1	1	0	10	2	0	.200	1	12	1	2	0.4	.929
14 yrs.		102	138	.425	3.92	410	301	72	2123	2009	671	1211	17	9	7	7	698	94	15	.135	164	394	25	25	1.4	.957

WORLD SERIES

Year	Team	W	L	PCT	ERA	G	GS	CG	IP	H	BB	SO	ShO	W	L	SV	AB	H	HR	BA	PO	A	E	DP	TC/G	FA
1969	NY N	0	0	–	0.00	1	0	0	1	0	0	0	0	0	0	0	0	0	0	–	0	0	0	0	0.0	–

Tex Carleton

CARLETON, JAMES OTTO
B. Aug. 19, 1906, Comanche, Tex.
D. Jan. 11, 1977, Fort Worth, Tex.

BB TR 6'1½" 180 lbs.
BR 1933-34

Year	Team	W	L	PCT	ERA	G	GS	CG	IP	H	BB	SO	ShO	W	L	SV	AB	H	HR	BA	PO	A	E	DP	TC/G	FA
1932	STL N	10	13	.435	4.08	44	22	9	196.1	198	70	113	3	3	2	0	60	9	1	.150	11	48	3	3	1.4	.952
1933		17	11	.607	3.38	44	33	15	277	263	97	147	4	1	1	3	91	17	1	.187	13	50	2	1	1.5	.969
1934		16	11	.593	4.26	40	31	16	240.2	260	52	103	0	2	2	1	88	17	1	.193	21	44	3	4	1.7	.956
1935	CHI N	11	8	.579	3.89	31	22	8	171	169	60	84	0	2	2	1	62	8	0	.129	14	42	1	2	1.8	.982
1936		14	10	.583	3.65	35	26	12	197.1	204	67	88	**4**	2	1	1	60	14	3	.233	10	47	0	7	1.6	1.000
1937		16	8	.667	3.15	32	27	18	208.1	183	94	105	4	0	1	0	71	12	0	.169	13	49	3	2	2.0	.954
1938		10	9	.526	5.42	33	24	9	167.2	213	74	80	1	2	1	0	65	15	0	.231	8	32	2	2	1.3	.952

Year	Team		W	L	PCT	ERA	G	GS	CG	IP	H	BB	SO	ShO	W	L	SV	AB	H	HR	BA	PO	A	E	DP	TC/G	FA
															Relief Pitching			**Batting**									

Tex Carleton *continued*

Year	Team		W	L	PCT	ERA	G	GS	CG	IP	H	BB	SO	ShO	W	L	SV	AB	H	HR	BA	PO	A	E	DP	TC/G	FA
1940	BKN	N	6	6	.500	3.81	34	17	4	149	140	47	88	1	2	1	2	43	8	0	.186	3	22	0	2	0.7	1.000
8 yrs.			100	76	.568	3.91	293	202	91	1607.1	1630	561	808	16	12	10	9	540	100	6	.185	93	334	14	23	1.5	.968

WORLD SERIES

Year	Team		W	L	PCT	ERA	G	GS	CG	IP	H	BB	SO	ShO	W	L	SV	AB	H	HR	BA	PO	A	E	DP	TC/G	FA
1934	STL	N	0	0	—	7.36	2	1	0	3.2	5	2	2	0	0	0	0	1	0	0	.000	0	0	0	0	0.0	—
1935	CHI	N	0	1	.000	1.29	1	1	0	7	6	7	4	0	0	0	0	1	0	0	.000	0	2	0	0	2.0	1.000
1938			0	0	—	∞	1	0	0		1	2	0	0	0	0	0	0	0	0	—	0	0	0	0	0.0	—
3 yrs.			0	1	.000	5.06				10.2	12	11	6	0	0	0	0	2	0	0	.000	0	2	0	0	0.5	1.000

Cisco Carlos

CARLOS, FRANCISCO MANUEL
B. Sept. 17, 1940, Monrovia, Calif.

BR TR 6'3" 205 lbs.

Year	Team		W	L	PCT	ERA	G	GS	CG	IP	H	BB	SO	ShO	W	L	SV	AB	H	HR	BA	PO	A	E	DP	TC/G	FA
1967	CHI	A	2	0	1.000	0.86	8	7	1	41.2	23	9	27	1	0	0	0	16	1	0	.063	4	8	1	0	1.6	.923
1968			4	14	.222	3.90	29	21	0	122.1	121	37	57	0	0	0	0	31	2	0	.065	15	26	2	3	1.5	.953
1969	2 teams																										
"	total	CHI A (25G 4–3)	5	4	.556	5.37	31	8	0	67	75	29	33	0	3	0	0	15	1	0	.067	4	17	2	0	0.7	.913
1970	WAS	A	0	0	—	1.50	5	0	0	6	3	4	2	0	0	0	0	0	0	0	—	1	1	0	0	0.4	1.000
4 yrs.			11	18	.379	3.72	73	36	1	237	222	79	119	1	3	2	0	62	4	0	.065	24	52	5	3	1.1	.938

Don Carlsen

CARLSEN, DONALD HERBERT
B. Oct. 15, 1926, Chicago, Ill.

BR TR 6'1" 175 lbs.

Year	Team		W	L	PCT	ERA	G	GS	CG	IP	H	BB	SO	ShO	W	L	SV	AB	H	HR	BA	PO	A	E	DP	TC/G	FA
1948	CHI	N	0	0	—	36.00	1	0	0	1	5	2	1	0	0	0	0	0	0	0	—	0	0	0	0	0.0	—
1951	PIT	N	2	3	.400	4.19	7	6	2	43	50	14	20	0	0	0	0	16	4	0	.250	1	6	2	1	1.3	.778
1952			0	1	.000	10.80	5	1	0	10	20	5	2	0	0	0	0	3	1	0	.333	0	6	0	1	1.2	1.000
3 yrs.			2	4	.333	6.00	13	7	2	54	75	21	23	0	0	0	0	19	5	0	.263	1	12	2	2	1.2	.867

Hal Carlson

CARLSON, HAROLD GUST
B. May 17, 1892, Rockford, Ill. D. May 28, 1930, Chicago, Ill.

BR TR 6' 180 lbs.

Year	Team		W	L	PCT	ERA	G	GS	CG	IP	H	BB	SO	ShO	W	L	SV	AB	H	HR	BA	PO	A	E	DP	TC/G	FA
1917	PIT	N	7	11	.389	2.90	34	17	9	161.1	140	49	68	1	3	2	1	49	6	0	.122	6	53	1	3	1.8	.983
1918			0	1	.000	3.75	3	2	0	12	12	5	5	0	0	0	0	5	1	0	.200	1	2	1	0	1.3	.750
1919			8	10	.444	2.23	22	14	7	141	114	39	49	1	3	1	0	43	7	0	.163	8	44	2	0	2.5	.963
1920			14	13	.519	3.36	39	31	16	246.2	262	63	62	3	1	0	3	85	23	0	.271	10	47	4	2	1.6	.934
1921			4	8	.333	4.27	31	10	3	109.2	121	23	37	0	1	1	2	34	10	0	.294	4	32	1	1	1.2	.973
1922			9	12	.429	5.70	39	18	6	145.1	193	58	64	0	2	4	2	56	15	1	.268	5	44	2	1	1.3	.961
1923			0	0	—	4.73	4	0	0	13.1	19	2	4	0	0	0	0	5	0	0	.000	0	5	0	0	1.3	1.000
1924	PHI	N	8	17	.320	4.86	38	24	12	203.2	267	55	66	1	1	3	2	76	21	2	.276	6	52	0	1	1.5	1.000
1925			13	14	.481	4.23	35	32	18	234	281	52	80	4	0	0	1	93	17	2	.183	7	48	1	3	1.6	.982
1926			17	12	.586	3.23	35	34	20	267.1	293	47	55	3	0	0	0	96	23	0	.240	9	49	3	4	1.7	.951
1927	2 teams	PHI N (11G 4–5) CHI N (27G 12–8)																									
"	total		16	13	.552	3.70	38	31	19	248	281	45	40	2	1	0	1	92	17	0	.185	9	54	0	1	1.7	1.000
1928	CHI	N	3	2	.600	5.91	20	5	2	56.1	74	15	11	0	1	0	4	19	5	0	.263	1	16	1	0	0.9	.944
1929			11	5	.688	5.16	31	14	6	111.2	131	31	35	2	2	2	2	39	9	0	.231	6	33	0	1	1.3	1.000
1930			4	2	.667	5.05	8	6	3	51.2	68	14	14	0	1	0	0	20	5	0	.250	2	18	1	1	2.6	.952
14 yrs.			114	120	.487	3.97	377	238	121	2002	2256	498	590	17	16	16	19	712	159	5	.223	74	497	17	18	1.6	.971

WORLD SERIES

Year	Team		W	L	PCT	ERA	G	GS	CG	IP	H	BB	SO	ShO	W	L	SV	AB	H	HR	BA	PO	A	E	DP	TC/G	FA
1929	CHI	N	0	0	—	6.75	2	0	0	4	7	1	3	0	0	0	0	—	0	0	—	0	0	0	0	0.0	—

Leon Carlson

CARLSON, LEON ALTON (Swede)
B. Feb. 17, 1895, Jamestown, N. Y. D. Sept. 15, 1961, Jamestown, N. Y.

BR TR 6'3" 195 lbs.

Year	Team		W	L	PCT	ERA	G	GS	CG	IP	H	BB	SO	ShO	W	L	SV	AB	H	HR	BA	PO	A	E	DP	TC/G	FA
1920	WAS	A	0	0	—	3.65	3	0	0	12.1	14	2	3	0	0	0	0	6	1	0	.167	0	2	0	0	0.7	1.000

Steve Carlton

CARLTON, STEVEN NORMAN (Lefty)
B. Dec. 22, 1944, Miami, Fla.

BL TL 6'4" 210 lbs.

Year	Team		W	L	PCT	ERA	G	GS	CG	IP	H	BB	SO	ShO	W	L	SV	AB	H	HR	BA	PO	A	E	DP	TC/G	FA
1965	STL	N	0	0	—	2.52	15	2	0	25	27	8	21	0	0	0	0	2	0	0	.000	1	6	0	1	0.5	1.000
1966			3	3	.500	3.12	9	9	2	52	56	18	25	1	0	0	0	15	4	0	.267	2	10	0	2	1.3	1.000
1967			14	9	.609	2.98	30	28	11	193	173	62	168	2	0	1	1	72	11	0	.153	8	30	2	3	1.3	.950
1968			13	11	.542	2.99	34	33	10	232	214	61	162	5	0	1	0	73	12	2	.164	4	39	3	1	1.4	.935
1969			17	11	.607	2.17	31	31	12	236	185	93	210	2	0	0	0	80	17	1	.213	1	34	3	1	1.2	.921
1970			10	19	.345	3.72	34	33	13	254	239	109	193	2	0	0	0	80	16	0	.200	6	38	4	1	1.4	.917
1971			20	9	.690	3.56	37	36	18	273	275	98	172	4	0	0	0	96	17	0	.177	11	40	4	3	1.4	.934
1972	PHI	N	27	10	.730	1.97	41	41	30	346.1	257	87	310	8	0	0	0	117	23	1	.197	8	37	2	1	1.1	.957
1973			13	20	.394	3.90	40	40	18	293.1	293	113	223	3	0	0	0	100	16	2	.160	4	42	5	3	1.3	.902
1974			16	13	.552	3.22	39	39	17	291	249	136	240	1	0	0	0	102	25	0	.245	6	42	4	1	1.3	.923
1975			15	14	.517	3.56	37	37	14	255	217	104	192	3	0	0	0	90	14	0	.156	10	32	1	4	1.2	.977
1976			20	7	.741	3.13	35	35	13	252.2	224	72	195	2	0	0	0	92	20	0	.217	4	19	0	2	0.7	1.000
1977			23	10	.697	2.64	36	36	17	283	229	89	198	2	0	0	0	97	26	3	.268	4	52	1	2	1.6	.982
1978			16	13	.552	2.84	34	34	12	247	228	63	161	4	0	0	0	86	25	0	.291	5	46	3	1	1.6	.944
1979			18	11	.621	3.62	35	35	13	251	202	89	213	4	0	0	0	94	21	0	.223	3	32	5	0	1.1	.875
1980			24	9	.727	2.34	38	38	13	304	243	90	286	3	0	0	0	101	19	0	.188	2	42	0	1	1.2	1.000
1981			13	4	.765	2.42	24	24	10	190	152	62	179	1	0	0	0	67	9	0	.134	3	22	0	0	1.0	1.000
1982			23	11	.676	3.10	38	38	19	295.2	253	86	286	6	0	0	0	101	22	2	.218	6	37	4	2	1.2	.915
1983			15	16	.484	3.11	37	37	8	283.2	277	84	275	3	0	0	0	97	19	0	.196	4	37	4	0	1.2	.911
1984			13	7	.650	3.58	33	33	1	229	214	79	163	0	0	0	0	84	16	1	.190	7	22	0	0	0.9	1.000
1985			1	8	.111	3.33	16	16	0	92	84	53	48	0	0	0	0	28	5	0	.179	3	18	0	1	1.3	1.000
1986	3 teams	PHI N (16G 4–8) SF N (6G 1–3) CHI A (10G 4–3)																									
"	total		9	14	.391	5.10	32	32	3	176.1	196	86	120	0	0	0	0	45	9	1	.200	4	23	0	2	0.8	1.000
1987	2 teams	CLE A (23G 5–9) MIN A (9G 1–5)																									
"	total		6	14	.300	5.74	32	21	3	152	165	86	91	0	2	2	1	0	0	0	—	3	23	1	2	0.8	.963
1988	MIN	A	0	1	.000	16.76	4	1	0	9.2	20	5	5	0	0	0	0	0	0	0	—	0	1	0	0	0.3	1.000
24 yrs.			329	244	.574	3.22	741	709	254	5216.2	4672	1833	4136	55	2	4	2	1719	346	13	.201	109	724	42	36	1.2	.952
			9th									8th	2nd	2nd														

Year	Team		W	L	PCT	ERA	G	GS	CG	IP	H	BB	SO	ShO	Relief Pitching W	L	SV	Batting AB	H	HR	BA	PO	A	E	DP	TC/G	FA

Steve Carlton *continued*

DIVISIONAL PLAYOFF SERIES

| 1981 | PHI | N | 0 | 2 | .000 | 3.86 | 2 | 2 | 0 | 14 | 14 | 8 | 13 | 0 | 0 | 0 | 0 | 4 | 1 | 0 | .250 | 0 | 0 | 0 | 0 | 0.0 | — |

LEAGUE CHAMPIONSHIP SERIES

1976	PHI	N	0	1	.000	5.14	1	1	0	7	8	5	6	0	0	0	0	2	0	0	.000	0	0	0	0	0.0	—
1977			0	1	.000	6.94	2	2	0	11.2	13	8	6	0	0	0	0	4	2	0	.500	0	0	0	0	0.0	—
1978			1	0	1.000	4.00	1	1	1	9	8	2	8	0	0	0	0	4	2	1	.500	0	0	0	0	0.0	—
1980			1	0	1.000	2.19	2	2	0	12.1	11	8	6	0	0	0	0	4	0	0	.000	0	1	0	0	0.5	1.000
1983			2	0	1.000	0.66	2	2	0	13.2	13	5	13	0	0	0	0	5	1	0	.200	1	3	0	0	2.0	1.000
5 yrs.			4	2	.667	3.52	8	8	1	53.2	53	28	39	0	0	0	0	19	5	1	.263	1	4	0	0	0.6	1.000

WORLD SERIES

1967	STL	N	0	1	.000	0.00	1	1	0	6	3	2	5	0	0	0	0	1	0	0	.000	0	0	0	0	0.0	—
1968			0	0	—	6.75	2	0	0	4	7	1	3	0	0	0	0	0	0	0	—	1	0	0	0	1.0	1.000
1980	PHI	N	2	0	1.000	2.40	2	2	0	15	14	9	17	0	0	0	0	0	0	0	—	0	3	0	0	1.5	1.000
1983			0	1	.000	2.70	1	1	0	6.2	5	3	7	0	0	0	0	3	0	0	.000	0	0	0	0	0.0	—
4 yrs.			2	2	.500	2.56	6	4	0	31.2	29	15	32	0	0	0	0	4	0	0	.000	1	4	0	0	0.8	1.000

Don Carman

CARMAN, DONALD WAYNE
B. Aug. 14, 1959, Oklahoma City, Okla.   BL TL 6'3"   195 lbs.

1983	PHI	N	0	0	—	0.00	1	0	0	1	0	0	0	0	0	0	1	0	0	0	—	1	0	0	0	1.0	1.000
1984			0	1	.000	5.40	11	0	0	13.1	14	6	16	0	0	1	0	1	0	0	.000	0	0	0	0	0.0	—
1985			9	4	.692	2.08	71	0	0	86.1	52	38	87	0	9	4	7	3	0	0	.000	5	11	2	2	0.3	.889
1986			10	5	.667	3.22	50	14	2	134.1	113	52	98	1	3	2	1	31	0	0	.000	4	30	0	2	0.7	1.000
1987			13	11	.542	4.22	35	35	3	211	194	69	125	2	0	0	0	61	5	0	.082	7	21	0	0	0.8	1.000
1988			10	14	.417	4.29	36	32	2	201.1	211	70	116	0	0	0	0	63	3	0	.048	9	19	0	0	0.8	1.000
1989			5	15	.250	5.24	49	20	0	149.1	152	86	81	0	2	2	0	34	1	0	.029	4	20	1	0	0.5	.960
7 yrs.			47	50	.485	4.04	253	101	7	796.2	736	321	523	3	14	9	9	193	9	0	.047	30	101	3	4	0.5	.978

Chet Carmichael

CARMICHAEL, CHESTER KELLER
B. Jan. 9, 1888, Muncie, Ind.   D. Aug. 22, 1960, Rochester, N. Y.   BR TR 5'11½" 200 lbs.

| 1909 | CIN | N | 0 | 0 | — | 0.00 | 2 | 0 | 0 | 7 | 9 | 3 | 2 | 0 | 0 | 0 | 0 | 2 | 0 | 0 | .000 | 0 | 1 | 2 | 0 | 1.5 | .333 |

Eddie Carnett

CARNETT, EDWIN ELLIOTT (Lefty)
B. Oct. 21, 1916, Springfield, Mo.   BL TL 6'   185 lbs.

1941	BOS	N	0	0	—	20.25	2	0	0	1.1	4	3	2	0	0	0	0	0	0	0	—	0	0	0	0	0.0	—
1944	CHI	A	0	0	—	9.00	2	0	0	2	3	0	1	0	0	0	0	457	126	1	.276	0	1	0	0	0.5	1.000
1945	CLE	A	0	0	—	0.00	2	0	0	2	0	0	1	0	0	0	0	73	16	0	.219	0	0	0	0	0.0	—
3 yrs.			0	0	—	8.44	6	0	0	5.1	7	3	4	0	0	0	0	*				0	1	0	0	0.2	1.000

Pat Carney

CARNEY, PATRICK JOSEPH (Doc)
B. Aug. 7, 1876, Holyoke, Mass.   D. Jan. 9, 1953, Worcester, Mass.   BL TL 6'   200 lbs.

1902	BOS	N	0	1	.000	9.00	2	1	0	5	6	3	3	0	0	1	0	522	141	2	.270	0	0	0	0	0.0	—
1903			4	5	.444	4.04	10	9	9	78	93	31	29	0	1	0	0	392	94	1	.240	4	19	1	0	2.4	.958
1904			0	3	.000	5.81	4	2	1	26.1	40	12	5	0	0	2	0	279	57	0	.204	0	6	0	0	1.5	1.000
3 yrs.			4	9	.308	4.69	16	12	10	109.1	139	46	37	0	1	2	0	*				4	25	1	0	1.9	.967

Bob Carpenter

CARPENTER, ROBERT LOUIS
B. Dec. 12, 1917, Chicago, Ill.   BR TR 6'3"   195 lbs.

1940	NY	N	2	0	1.000	2.73	5	2	2	33	29	14	25	0	0	0	0	10	1	0	.100	2	5	0	0	1.4	1.000
1941			11	6	.647	3.83	29	19	8	131.2	138	42	42	1	1	0	2	45	7	0	.156	3	17	2	2	0.8	.909
1942			11	10	.524	3.15	28	25	12	185.2	192	51	53	2	1	1	0	65	12	0	.185	14	23	0	0	1.3	1.000
1946			1	3	.250	4.85	12	6	1	39	37	18	13	1	0	0	0	10	1	0	.100	2	6	1	0	0.8	.889
1947	2 teams		NY N (2G 0–0)			CHI N (4G 0–1)																						
"	total		0	1	.000	6.97	6	1	0	10.1	15	7	1	0	0	0	0	1	1	0	1.000	0	3	0	0	0.5	1.000
5 yrs.			25	20	.556	3.60	80	54	23	399.2	411	132	134	4	2	1	2	131	22	0	.168	21	54	3	2	1.0	.962

Cris Carpenter

CARPENTER, CRIS HOWELL
B. Apr. 5, 1965, St. Augustine, Fla.   BR TR 6'1"   195 lbs.

1988	STL	N	2	3	.400	4.72	8	8	1	47.2	56	9	24	0	0	0	0	14	2	0	.143	6	4	0	1	1.3	1.000
1989			4	4	.500	3.18	36	5	0	68	70	26	35	0	3	2	0	9	4	0	.444	3	10	0	1	0.4	1.000
2 yrs.			6	7	.462	3.81	44	13	1	115.2	126	35	59	0	3	2	0	23	6	0	.261	9	14	0	2	0.5	1.000

Lew Carpenter

CARPENTER, LEWIS EMMETT
B. Aug. 16, 1913, Woodstock, Ga.   D. Apr. 25, 1979, Marietta, Ga.   BR TR 6'2"   195 lbs.

| 1943 | WAS | A | 0 | 0 | — | 0.00 | 4 | 0 | 0 | 3.1 | 1 | 4 | 1 | 0 | 0 | 0 | 0 | 0 | 0 | 0 | — | 0 | 0 | 0 | 0 | 0.0 | — |

Paul Carpenter

CARPENTER, PAUL CALVIN
B. Aug. 12, 1894, Granville, Ohio   D. Mar. 14, 1968, Newark, Ohio   BR TR 5'11"   165 lbs.

| 1916 | PIT | N | 0 | 0 | — | 1.17 | 5 | 0 | 0 | 7.2 | 8 | 4 | 0 | 0 | 0 | 0 | 0 | 2 | 0 | 0 | .000 | 0 | 2 | 0 | 0 | 0.4 | 1.000 |

Frank Carpin

CARPIN, FRANK DOMINIC
B. Sept. 14, 1938, Brooklyn, N. Y.   BL TL 5'10"   172 lbs.

1965	PIT	N	3	1	.750	3.18	39	0	0	39.2	35	24	27	0	3	1	4	1	0	0	.000	2	13	0	1	0.4	1.000
1966	HOU	N	1	0	1.000	7.50	10	0	0	6	9	6	2	0	1	0	0	0	0	0	—	0	0	1	0	0.1	—
2 yrs.			4	1	.800	3.74	49	0	0	45.2	44	30	29	0	4	1	4	1	0	0	.000	2	13	1	1	0.3	.938

Year	Team	W	L	PCT	ERA	G	GS	CG	IP	H	BB	SO	ShO	Relief Pitching W	L	SV	Batting AB	H	HR	BA	PO	A	E	DP	TC/G	FA

Alex Carrasquel

CARRASQUEL, ALEJANDRO APARICIO
Born Alejandro Aparicio Eloy y Carrasquel.
B. July 24, 1912, Caracas, Venezuela   D. Aug. 19, 1969, Caracas, Venezuela   BR TR 6'1"   182 lbs.

Year	Team		W	L	PCT	ERA	G	GS	CG	IP	H	BB	SO	ShO	W	L	SV	AB	H	HR	BA	PO	A	E	DP	TC/G	FA
1939	WAS	A	5	9	.357	4.69	40	17	7	159.1	165	68	41	0	1	1	2	42	7	1	.167	5	30	1	3	0.9	.972
1940			6	2	.750	4.88	28	0	0	48	42	29	19	0	6	2	0	7	0	0	.000	1	10	0	2	0.4	1.000
1941			6	2	.750	3.44	35	5	4	96.2	103	49	30	0	4	1	2	21	2	0	.095	13	29	0	7	1.2	1.000
1942			7	7	.500	3.43	35	15	7	152.1	161	53	40	1	2	4	1	44	6	0	.136	6	39	2	3	1.3	.957
1943			11	7	.611	3.68	39	13	4	144.1	160	54	48	1	5	3	5	43	8	0	.186	4	36	1	1	1.1	.976
1944			8	7	.533	3.43	43	7	3	134	143	50	35	0	5	3	2	36	7	0	.194	7	32	3	3	1.0	.929
1945			7	5	.583	2.71	35	7	5	122.2	105	40	38	2	4	3	1	36	3	0	.083	6	26	3	1	1.0	.914
1949	CHI	A	0	0	—	14.73	3	0	0	3.2	8	4	1	0	0	0	0	0	0	0	—	0	1	0	0	0.3	1.000
8 yrs.			50	39	.562	3.73	258	64	30	861	887	347	252	4	26	15	16	229	33	1	.144	42	203	10	20	1.0	.961

Bill Carrick

CARRICK, WILLIAM MARTIN (Cantwin)
B. Sept. 5, 1873, Erie, Pa.   D. Mar. 7, 1932, Philadelphia, Pa.   TR

Year	Team		W	L	PCT	ERA	G	GS	CG	IP	H	BB	SO	ShO	W	L	SV	AB	H	HR	BA	PO	A	E	DP	TC/G	FA
1898	NY	N	3	1	.750	3.40	5	4	4	39.2	39	21	10	0	0	0	0	18	3	0	.167	5	10	0	1	3.0	1.000
1899			16	27	.372	4.65	44	43	40	361.2	485	122	60	3	0	1	0	130	18	0	.138	15	99	12	7	2.9	.905
1900			19	21	.475	3.53	45	41	32	341.2	415	92	63	1	2	1	0	115	20	0	.174	16	84	11	2	2.5	.901
1901	WAS	A	14	23	.378	3.75	42	37	34	324	367	93	70	0	1	0	0	126	20	0	.159	9	94	8	3	2.6	.928
1902			11	17	.393	4.86	31	30	28	257.2	344	72	36	0	0	0	0	108	20	0	.185	7	66	9	5	2.6	.890
5 yrs.			63	89	.414	4.14	167	155	138	1324.2	1650	400	239	4	3	2	0	497	81	0	.163	52	353	40	18	2.7	.910

Don Carrithers

CARRITHERS, DONALD GEORGE
B. Sept. 15, 1949, Lynwood, Calif.   BR TR 6'2"   180 lbs.

Year	Team		W	L	PCT	ERA	G	GS	CG	IP	H	BB	SO	ShO	W	L	SV	AB	H	HR	BA	PO	A	E	DP	TC/G	FA
1970	SF	N	2	1	.667	7.36	11	2	0	22	31	14	14	0	2	0	0	6	0	0	.000	1	3	0	0	0.4	1.000
1971			5	3	.625	4.05	22	12	2	80	77	37	41	1	1	0	1	17	3	0	.176	3	12	3	1	0.8	.833
1972			4	8	.333	5.80	25	14	2	90	108	42	42	1	0	1	1	29	6	0	.207	7	13	1	1	0.8	.952
1973			1	2	.333	4.81	25	3	0	58	64	35	36	0	1	0	0	16	4	0	.250	7	13	0	1	0.8	1.000
1974	MON	N	5	2	.714	3.00	22	3	0	60	56	17	31	0	4	0	1	14	4	0	.286	4	14	2	0	0.9	.900
1975			5	3	.625	3.30	19	14	5	101	90	38	37	2	0	0	0	34	6	0	.176	7	24	0	2	1.6	1.000
1976			6	12	.333	4.43	34	19	2	140.1	153	78	71	0	1	1	0	37	4	0	.108	13	23	1	5	1.1	.973
1977	MIN	A	0	1	.000	7.07	7	0	0	14	16	6	3	0	0	1	0	0	0	0	—	3	2	0	0	0.7	1.000
8 yrs.			28	32	.467	4.46	165	67	11	565.1	595	267	275	4	9	3	3	153	27	0	.176	45	104	7	10	0.9	.955

LEAGUE CHAMPIONSHIP SERIES

Year	Team		W	L	PCT	ERA	G	GS	CG	IP	H	BB	SO	ShO	W	L	SV	AB	H	HR	BA	PO	A	E	DP	TC/G	FA
1971	SF	N	0	0	—	∞	1	0	0		3	0	0	0	0	0	0	0	0	0	—	0	0	0	0	0.0	—

Clay Carroll

CARROLL, CLAY PALMER (Hawk)
B. May 2, 1941, Clanton, Ala.   BR TR 6'1"   178 lbs.

Year	Team		W	L	PCT	ERA	G	GS	CG	IP	H	BB	SO	ShO	W	L	SV	AB	H	HR	BA	PO	A	E	DP	TC/G	FA
1964	MIL	N	2	0	1.000	1.77	11	1	0	20.1	15	3	17	0	2	0	1	2	0	0	.000	2	7	0	0	0.8	1.000
1965			0	1	.000	4.41	19	1	0	34.2	35	13	16	0	0	1	1	5	0	0	.000	3	5	1	1	0.5	.889
1966	ATL	N	8	7	.533	2.37	73	3	0	144.1	127	29	67	0	8	6	11	30	3	0	.100	6	31	0	2	0.5	1.000
1967			6	12	.333	5.52	42	7	1	93	111	29	35	0	3	8	0	16	1	0	.063	3	22	0	4	0.6	1.000
1968	2 teams		ATL N	(10G 0–1)		CIN N	(58G 7–7)																				
"	total		7	8	.467	2.69	68	1	0	144	128	38	71	0	7	8	17	29	6	0	.207	4	36	1	1	0.6	.976
1969	CIN	N	12	6	.667	3.52	71	4	0	151	149	78	90	0	11	6	7	29	6	1	.207	6	39	1	3	0.6	.978
1970			9	4	.692	2.60	65	0	0	104	104	27	63	0	9	4	16	14	1	0	.071	8	22	2	1	0.5	.938
1971			10	4	.714	2.49	61	0	0	94	78	42	64	0	10	4	15	10	1	0	.100	8	29	1	3	0.6	.974
1972			6	4	.600	2.25	65	0	0	96	89	32	51	0	6	4	37	11	2	0	.182	4	21	1	1	0.4	.962
1973			8	8	.500	3.69	53	5	0	92.2	111	34	41	0	6	7	14	14	3	0	.214	4	20	1	0	0.5	.960
1974			12	5	.706	2.14	57	3	0	101	96	30	46	0	10	4	6	18	3	0	.167	4	25	2	3	0.5	.935
1975			7	5	.583	2.63	56	2	0	96	93	32	44	0	7	5	7	19	0	0	.000	2	14	0	2	0.3	1.000
1976	CHI	A	4	4	.500	2.57	29	0	0	77	67	24	38	0	4	4	6	0	0	0	—	0	15	0	2	0.5	1.000
1977	2 teams		CHI A	(8G 1–3)		STL N	(51G 4–2)																				
"	total		5	5	.500	2.76	59	1	0	101	91	28	38	0	5	5	5	11	1	0	.091	6	22	1	3	0.5	.966
1978	PIT	N	0	0	—	2.25	2	0	0	4	2	3	0	0	0	0	0	0	0	0	—	2	0	0	0	1.0	1.000
15 yrs.			96	73	.568	2.94	731	28	1	1353	1296	442	681	0	88	66	143	208	27	1	.130	60	310	11	24	0.5	.971

LEAGUE CHAMPIONSHIP SERIES

Year	Team		W	L	PCT	ERA	G	GS	CG	IP	H	BB	SO	ShO	W	L	SV	AB	H	HR	BA	PO	A	E	DP	TC/G	FA
1970	CIN	N	0	0	—	0.00	2	0	0	1.1	2	1	0	0	0	0	1	0	0	0	—	0	0	0	0	0.0	—
1972			1	1	.500	3.38	2	0	0	2.2	3	3	0	0	1	1	0	0	0	0	—	0	2	0	0	0.5	1.000
1973			1	0	1.000	1.29	3	0	0	7	5	1	2	0	1	0	0	0	0	0	—	0	2	0	0	0.7	1.000
1975			0	0	—	0.00	1	0	0	1	0	1	1	0	0	0	0	0	0	0	—	0	0	0	0	1.0	1.000
4 yrs.			2	1	.667	1.50	8	0	0	12	9	5	5	0	2	1	1	0	0	0	—	0	4	0	0	0.5	1.000

WORLD SERIES

Year	Team		W	L	PCT	ERA	G	GS	CG	IP	H	BB	SO	ShO	W	L	SV	AB	H	HR	BA	PO	A	E	DP	TC/G	FA
1970	CIN	N	1	0	1.000	0.00	4	0	0	9	5	2	11	0	1	0	0	1	0	0	.000	0	0	0	0	0.0	—
1972			0	1	.000	1.59	5	0	0	5.2	6	4	3	0	0	1	1	0	0	0	—	1	3	0	0	0.8	1.000
1975			1	0	1.000	3.18	5	0	0	5.2	4	2	3	0	1	0	0	0	0	0	—	2	0	0	0	0.4	1.000
3 yrs.			2	1	.667	1.33	14	0	0	20.1	15	8	17	0	2	1	1	1	0	0	.000	3	3	0	0	0.4	1.000
							5th																				

Dick Carroll

CARROLL, RICHARD THOMAS (Shadow)
B. July 21, 1884, Cleveland, Ohio   D. Nov. 22, 1945, Cleveland, Ohio   BR TR 6'2"

Year	Team		W	L	PCT	ERA	G	GS	CG	IP	H	BB	SO	ShO	W	L	SV	AB	H	HR	BA	PO	A	E	DP	TC/G	FA
1909	NY	A	0	0	—	3.60	2	1	0	5	7	1	1	0	0	0	0	2	1	0	.500	0	1	1	0	1.0	.500

Ed Carroll

CARROLL, EDGAR FLEISCHER
B. July 27, 1907, Baltimore, Md.   D. Oct. 13, 1984, Rossville, Md.   BR TR 6'3"   185 lbs.

Year	Team		W	L	PCT	ERA	G	GS	CG	IP	H	BB	SO	ShO	W	L	SV	AB	H	HR	BA	PO	A	E	DP	TC/G	FA
1929	BOS	A	1	0	1.000	5.61	24	3	0	67.1	77	20	13	0	0	0	0	16	1	0	.063	2	17	0	1	0.8	1.000

Ownie Carroll

CARROLL, OWEN THOMAS
B. Nov. 11, 1902, Kearny, N. J.   D. June 8, 1975, Orange, N. J.   BR TR 5'10½"   165 lbs.

Year	Team		W	L	PCT	ERA	G	GS	CG	IP	H	BB	SO	ShO	W	L	SV	AB	H	HR	BA	PO	A	E	DP	TC/G	FA
1925	DET	A	3	1	.750	3.76	10	4	1	40.2	46	28	12	0	1	0	0	16	6	0	.375	1	3	2	0	0.6	.667

Year	Team		W	L	PCT	ERA	G	GS	CG	IP	H	BB	SO	ShO	Relief Pitching W	L	SV	Batting AB	H	HR	BA	PO	A	E	DP	TC/G	FA

Ownie Carroll *continued*

Year	Team		W	L	PCT	ERA	G	GS	CG	IP	H	BB	SO	ShO	W	L	SV	AB	H	HR	BA	PO	A	E	DP	TC/G	FA
1927			10	6	.625	3.98	31	15	8	172	186	73	41	0	3	0	0	69	12	0	.174	10	49	1	4	1.9	.983
1928			16	12	.571	3.27	34	28	19	231	219	87	51	2	2	2	2	98	19	0	.194	7	58	5	2	2.1	.929
1929			9	17	.346	4.63	34	26	12	202	249	86	54	0	2	3	1	74	17	0	.230	10	56	5	2	2.1	.930
1930	3 teams	DET A (6G 0–5)				NY A	(10G 0–1)			CIN N	(3G 0–1)																
"	total		0	7	.000	7.39	19	6	1	67	96	30	12	0	0	3	0	22	4	0	.182	5	17	1	3	1.2	.957
1931	CIN	N	3	9	.250	5.53	29	12	4	107.1	135	51	24	0	1	2	0	34	7	0	.206	7	26	2	5	1.2	.943
1932			10	19	.345	4.50	32	26	15	210	245	44	55	0	1	0	1	77	16	0	.208	13	39	1	3	1.7	.981
1933	BKN	N	13	15	.464	3.78	33	31	11	226.1	248	54	45	0	0	0	0	74	11	0	.149	13	64	2	4	2.4	.975
1934			1	3	.250	6.42	26	5	0	74.1	108	33	17	0	1	0	1	25	6	0	.240	5	28	1	1	1.3	.971
9 yrs.			65	89	.422	4.43	248	153	71	1330.2	1532	486	311	2	11	10	5	489	98	0	.200	71	340	20	24	1.7	.954

Tom Carroll

CARROLL, THOMAS MICHAEL
B. Nov. 5, 1952, Oriskany, N. Y.

BL TR 6'3" 190 lbs.

Year	Team		W	L	PCT	ERA	G	GS	CG	IP	H	BB	SO	ShO	W	L	SV	AB	H	HR	BA	PO	A	E	DP	TC/G	FA
1974	CIN	N	4	3	.571	3.69	16	13	0	78	68	44	37	0	0	0	0	26	4	0	.154	5	7	1	0	0.8	.923
1975			4	1	.800	4.98	12	7	0	47	52	26	14	0	1	0	0	14	0	0	.000	1	4	0	1	0.4	1.000
2 yrs.			8	4	.667	4.18	28	20	0	125	120	70	51	0	1	0	0	40	4	0	.100	6	11	1	1	0.6	.944

Kid Carsey

CARSEY, WILFRED
B. Oct. 22, 1870, New York, N. Y. D. Mar. 29, 1960, Miami, Fla.

BL TR 5'7" 168 lbs.

Year	Team		W	L	PCT	ERA	G	GS	CG	IP	H	BB	SO	ShO	W	L	SV	AB	H	HR	BA	PO	A	E	DP	TC/G	FA
1891	WAS	AA	14	37	.275	4.99	54	53	46	415	513	161	174	1	1	0	0	187	28	0	.150	22	120	12	5	2.9	.922
1892	PHI	N	19	16	.543	3.12	43	36	30	317.2	320	104	76	1	2	0	1	131	20	1	.153	19	84	13	3	2.7	.888
1893			20	15	.571	4.81	39	35	30	318.1	375	124	50	1	1	2	0	145	27	0	.186	17	81	8	1	2.7	.925
1894			18	12	.600	5.56	35	31	26	277	349	102	41	0	0	1	0	125	34	0	.272	15	59	5	4	2.3	.937
1895			24	16	.600	4.92	44	40	35	342.1	460	118	64	0	1	1	1	141	41	0	.291	9	77	12	2	2.2	.878
1896			11	11	.500	5.62	27	21	18	187.1	273	72	36	1	2	0	1	81	18	0	.222	9	50	6	3	2.4	.908
1897	2 teams	PHI N (4G 2–1)				STL N	(12G 3–8)																				
"	total		5	9	.357	5.81	16	15	13	127	168	47	15	0	1	0	0	56	16	0	.286	8	32	3	0	2.7	.930
1898	STL	N	2	12	.143	6.33	20	13	10	123.2	177	37	10	0	0	1	0	105	21	1	.200	4	39	3	2	2.3	.935
1899	2 teams	CLE N (10G 1–8)				WAS N	(4G 1–2)																				
"	total		2	10	.167	5.15	14	12	10	106.2	136	28	14	0	1	0	0	65	16	0	.246	6	35	5	2	3.3	.891
1901	BKN	N	1	0	1.000	10.29	2	0	0	7	9	3	4	0	1	0	0	2	0	0	.000	0	1	0	0	0.5	1.000
10 yrs.			116	138	.457	4.95	294	256	218	2222	2780	796	484	4	9	5	3	*				109	578	67	22	2.6	.911

Al Carson

CARSON, ALBERT JAMES (Soldier)
B. Aug. 22, 1882, Chicago, Ill. D. Nov. 26, 1962, San Diego, Calif.

TR

Year	Team		W	L	PCT	ERA	G	GS	CG	IP	H	BB	SO	ShO	W	L	SV	AB	H	HR	BA	PO	A	E	DP	TC/G	FA
1910	CHI	N	0	0	–	4.05	2	0	0	6.2	6	1	2	0	0	0	0	1	0	0	.000	0	2	0	0	1.0	1.000

Arnold Carter

CARTER, ARNOLD LEE (Lefty)
B. Mar. 14, 1918, Rainelle, W. Va.

BL TL 5'10" 170 lbs.

Year	Team		W	L	PCT	ERA	G	GS	CG	IP	H	BB	SO	ShO	W	L	SV	AB	H	HR	BA	PO	A	E	DP	TC/G	FA
1944	CIN	N	11	7	.611	2.61	33	18	9	148.1	143	40	33	3	1	1	3	48	12	2	.250	5	37	2	0	1.3	.955
1945			2	4	.333	3.09	13	6	2	46.2	54	13	4	1	1	0	0	17	3	0	.176	6	9	0	1	1.2	1.000
2 yrs.			13	11	.542	2.72	46	24	11	195	197	53	37	4	2	1	3	65	15	2	.231	11	46	2	1	1.3	.966

Nick Carter

CARTER, CONRAD POWELL
B. May 19, 1879, Oatlands, Va. D. Nov. 23, 1961, Grasonville, Md.

BL TR 5'8" 126 lbs.

Year	Team		W	L	PCT	ERA	G	GS	CG	IP	H	BB	SO	ShO	W	L	SV	AB	H	HR	BA	PO	A	E	DP	TC/G	FA
1908	PHI	A	2	5	.286	2.97	14	6	2	60.2	58	17	17	0	2	0	0	20	2	0	.100	7	22	1	1	2.1	.967

Paul Carter

CARTER, PAUL WARREN (Nick)
B. May 1, 1894, Lake Park, Ga. D. Sept. 11, 1984, Lake Park, Ga.

BL TR 6'3" 175 lbs.

Year	Team		W	L	PCT	ERA	G	GS	CG	IP	H	BB	SO	ShO	W	L	SV	AB	H	HR	BA	PO	A	E	DP	TC/G	FA
1914	CLE	A	1	3	.250	2.92	5	4	1	24.2	35	5	9	0	0	0	0	7	0	0	.000	0	7	1	0	1.6	.875
1915			1	1	.500	3.21	11	2	2	42	44	18	14	0	0	0	0	14	3	0	.214	0	16	0	0	1.5	1.000
1916	CHI	N	2	2	.500	2.75	8	5	2	36	26	17	14	0	0	0	0	12	2	0	.167	0	16	0	0	2.0	1.000
1917			5	8	.385	3.26	23	13	6	113.1	115	19	34	0	1	2	2	33	6	0	.182	2	30	2	1	1.5	.941
1918			4	1	.800	2.71	21	4	1	73	78	19	13	0	3	0	1	25	6	0	.240	4	29	0	3	1.6	1.000
1919			5	4	.556	2.65	28	7	2	85	81	28	17	0	1	0	1	26	7	0	.269	2	26	2	1	1.1	.933
1920			3	6	.333	4.67	31	8	2	106	131	36	14	0	1	2	2	35	6	0	.171	0	25	3	1	0.9	.893
7 yrs.			21	25	.457	3.32	127	43	16	480	510	142	115	0	8	4	6	152	30	0	.197	8	149	8	8	1.3	.952

Sol Carter

CARTER, SOLOMON MOBLEY (Buck)
B. Dec. 23, 1908, Picayune, Miss.

BR TR 6' 178 lbs.

Year	Team		W	L	PCT	ERA	G	GS	CG	IP	H	BB	SO	ShO	W	L	SV	AB	H	HR	BA	PO	A	E	DP	TC/G	FA
1931	PHI	A	0	0	–	19.29	2	0	0	2.1	1	4	1	0	0	0	0	0	0	0	–	0	3	0	0	1.5	1.000

Bob Caruthers

CARUTHERS, ROBERT LEE (Parisian Bob)
B. Jan. 5, 1864, Memphis, Tenn. D. Aug. 5, 1911, Peoria, Ill.
Manager 1892.

BL TR 5'7" 138 lbs.

Year	Team		W	L	PCT	ERA	G	GS	CG	IP	H	BB	SO	ShO	W	L	SV	AB	H	HR	BA	PO	A	E	DP	TC/G	FA
1884	STL	AA	7	2	.778	2.61	13	7	7	82.2	61	15	58	0	3	0	0	82	21	2	.256	3	9	1	0	1.0	.923
1885			40	13	.755	2.07	53	53	53	482.1	430	57	190	6	0	0	0	222	50	1	.225	24	84	11	4	2.2	.908
1886			30	14	.682	2.32	44	43	42	387.1	323	86	166	2	1	0	0	317	106	4	.334	25	65	9	2	2.3	.909
1887			29	9	.763	3.30	39	39	39	341	337	61	74	2	0	0	0	364	130	8	.357	40	92	4	0	3.5	.971
1888	BKN	AA	29	15	.659	2.39	44	43	42	391.2	337	53	140	4	1	0	0	335	77	5	.230	34	92	15	2	3.2	.894
1889			40	11	.784	3.13	56	50	46	445	444	104	118	7	4	0	0	172	43	2	.250	29	95	4	4	2.3	.969
1890	BKN	N	23	11	.676	3.09	37	33	30	300	292	87	64	2	1	0	0	238	63	1	.265	20	79	12	1	3.0	.892
1891			18	14	.563	3.12	38	32	29	297	323	107	69	2	1	0	0	171	48	3	.281	13	66	5	2	2.2	.940
1892	STL	N	2	8	.200	5.84	16	10	10	101.2	131	27	21	0	0	2	1	513	142	3	.277	4	24	0	0	1.8	1.000
9 yrs.			218	97	.692 1st	2.83	340	310	298	2828.2	2678	597	900	25	11	2	3	*				192	606	61	15	2.5	.929

Year	Team		W	L	PCT	ERA	G	GS	CG	IP	H	BB	SO	ShO	Relief Pitching W	L	SV	Batting AB	H	HR	BA	PO	A	E	DP	TC/G	FA

Chuck Cary

CARY, CHARLES DOUGLAS
B. Mar. 3, 1960, Whittier, Calif.   BL TL 6'4" 210 lbs.

Year	Team		W	L	PCT	ERA	G	GS	CG	IP	H	BB	SO	ShO	W	L	SV	AB	H	HR	BA	PO	A	E	DP	TC/G	FA
1985	DET	A	0	1	.000	3.42	16	0	0	23.2	16	8	22	0	0	1	2	0	0	0	–	0	2	0	0	0.1	1.000
1986			1	2	.333	3.41	22	0	0	31.2	33	15	21	0	1	2	0	0	0	0	–	4	1	0	0	0.2	1.000
1987	ATL	N	1	1	.500	3.78	13	0	0	16.2	17	4	15	0	1	1	1	1	0	0	.000	1	3	0	0	0.3	1.000
1988			0	0	–	6.48	7	0	0	8.1	8	4	7	0	0	0	0	0	0	0	–	0	1	0	0	0.1	1.000
1989	NY	A	4	4	.500	3.26	22	11	2	99.1	78	29	79	0	0	1	0	0	0	0	–	4	4	2	0	0.5	.800
5 yrs.			6	8	.429	3.51	80	11	2	179.2	152	60	144	0	2	5	3	1	0	0	.000	9	11	2	0	0.3	.909

Scott Cary

CARY, SCOTT RUSSELL (Red)
B. Apr. 11, 1923, Kendallville, Ind.   BL TL 5'11½" 168 lbs.

Year	Team		W	L	PCT	ERA	G	GS	CG	IP	H	BB	SO	ShO	W	L	SV	AB	H	HR	BA	PO	A	E	DP	TC/G	FA
1947	WAS	A	3	1	.750	5.93	23	3	1	54.2	73	20	25	0	1	0	1	13	1	0	.077	2	6	0	0	0.3	1.000

Jerry Casale

CASALE, JERRY JOSEPH
B. Sept. 27, 1933, Brooklyn, N. Y.   BR TR 6'2" 200 lbs.

Year	Team		W	L	PCT	ERA	G	GS	CG	IP	H	BB	SO	ShO	W	L	SV	AB	H	HR	BA	PO	A	E	DP	TC/G	FA
1958	BOS	A	0	0	–	0.00	2	0	0	3	1	2	3	0	0	0	0		1	0	0	–	0	1	0	0	0.5	1.000
1959			13	8	.619	4.31	31	26	9	179.2	162	89	93	3	1	0	0	59	10	3	.169	8	13	3	1	0.7	.870
1960			2	9	.182	6.17	29	14	1	96.1	113	67	54	0	0	0	0	33	9	0	.273	5	13	0	0	0.6	1.000
1961	2 teams	LA A (13G 1–5)				DET A	(3G 0–0)																					
"	total		1	5	.167	6.26	16	8	0	54.2	67	28	41	0	0	0	1	16	6	1	.375	6	6	3	2	0.9	.800
1962	DET	A	1	2	.333	4.66	18	1	0	36.2	33	18	16	0	1	2	0	8	0	0	.000	4	6	0	0	0.6	1.000
5 yrs.			17	24	.415	5.08	96	49	10	370.1	376	204	207	3	2	2	1	116	25	4	.216	24	37	6	3	0.7	.910

Joe Cascarella

CASCARELLA, JOSEPH THOMAS (Crooning Joe)
B. June 28, 1907, Philadelphia, Pa.   BR TR 5'10½" 175 lbs.

Year	Team		W	L	PCT	ERA	G	GS	CG	IP	H	BB	SO	ShO	W	L	SV	AB	H	HR	BA	PO	A	E	DP	TC/G	FA
1934	PHI	A	12	15	.444	4.68	42	22	9	194.1	214	104	71	2	7	3	1	64	6	0	.094	9	46	4	3	1.4	.932
1935	2 teams	PHI A (9G 1–6)				BOS A	(6G 0–3)																					
"	total		1	9	.100	5.84	15	7	1	49.1	54	33	24	0	1	0	0	10	1	0	.100	1	18	1	0	1.3	.950
1936	2 teams	BOS A (10G 0–2)				WAS A	(22G 9–8)																					
"	total		9	10	.474	4.44	32	17	7	160	174	63	41	1	2	3	1	53	7	0	.132	6	19	0	0	0.8	1.000
1937	2 teams	WAS A (10G 0–5)				CIN N	(11G 1–2)																					
"	total		1	7	.125	5.68	21	7	3	76	94	45	26	0	0	2	0	20	3	0	.150	6	16	2	1	1.1	.917
1938	CIN	N	4	7	.364	4.57	33	1	0	61	66	22	30	0	4	6	4	18	3	0	.167	5	9	0	0	0.4	1.000
5 yrs.			27	48	.360	4.84	143	54	20	540.2	602	267	192	3	14	16	8	165	20	0	.121	27	108	7	5	1.0	.951

Charlie Case

CASE, CHARLES EMMETT
B. Sept. 7, 1879, Smith Landing, Ohio D. Apr. 16, 1964, Clermont, Ohio   BR TR 6' 170 lbs.

Year	Team		W	L	PCT	ERA	G	GS	CG	IP	H	BB	SO	ShO	W	L	SV	AB	H	HR	BA	PO	A	E	DP	TC/G	FA
1901	CIN	N	1	2	.333	4.67	3	3	3	27	34	6	5	0	0	0	0	10	1	0	.100	0	9	3	0	4.0	.750
1904	PIT	N	10	5	.667	2.94	18	17	14	141	129	31	49	3	0	0	0	53	9	0	.170	13	39	3	0	3.1	.945
1905			12	10	.545	2.57	31	24	18	217	202	66	57	3	1	0	1	68	7	0	.103	9	48	3	1	1.9	.950
1906			1	1	.500	5.73	2	2	1	11	8	5	3	0	0	0	0	2	1	0	.500	2	4	1	1	3.5	.857
4 yrs.			24	18	.571	2.93	54	46	36	396	373	108	114	6	1	0	1	133	18	0	.135	24	100	10	2	2.5	.925

Bill Casey

CASEY, WILLIAM B.
B. St. Louis, Mo. Deceased.

Year	Team		W	L	PCT	ERA	G	GS	CG	IP	H	BB	SO	ShO	W	L	SV	AB	H	HR	BA	PO	A	E	DP	TC/G	FA
1887	PHI	AA	0	0	–	18.00	1	0	0	1	4	1	0	0	0	0	0	0	0	0	–	0	0	0	0	0.0	–

Dan Casey

CASEY, DANIEL MAURICE
Brother of Dennis Casey.
B. Nov. 20, 1862, Binghamton, N. Y. D. Feb. 8, 1943, Washington, D. C.   BR TL 6' 180 lbs.

Year	Team		W	L	PCT	ERA	G	GS	CG	IP	H	BB	SO	ShO	W	L	SV	AB	H	HR	BA	PO	A	E	DP	TC/G	FA
1884	WIL	U	1	1	.500	1.00	2	2	2	18	23	4	10	0	0	0	0	6	1	0	.167	0	3	0	0	1.5	1.000
1885	DET	N	4	8	.333	3.29	12	12	12	104	105	35	79	1	0	0	0	43	5	0	.116	3	24	1	0	2.3	.964
1886	PHI	N	24	18	.571	2.41	44	44	39	369	326	104	193	4	0	0	0	151	23	0	.152	17	70	8	0	2.2	.916
1887			28	13	.683	2.86	45	45	43	390.1	377	115	119	4	0	0	0	164	27	1	.165	10	66	9	0	1.9	.894
1888			14	18	.438	3.15	33	33	31	285.2	298	48	108	1	0	0	0	118	18	0	.153	10	66	9	2	2.6	.894
1889			6	10	.375	3.77	20	20	15	152.2	170	72	65	1	0	0	0	68	15	0	.221	5	32	6	2	2.2	.860
1890	SYR	AA	19	22	.463	4.14	45	42	40	360.2	365	165	169	2	0	0	0	160	26	0	.163	22	78	14	4	2.5	.877
7 yrs.			96	90	.516	3.18	201	198	182	1680.1	1664	543	743	13	0	0	0	710	115	1	.162	67	339	47	8	2.3	.896

Hugh Casey

CASEY, HUGH THOMAS
B. Oct. 14, 1913, Atlanta, Ga. D. July 3, 1951, Atlanta, Ga.   BR TR 6'1" 207 lbs.

Year	Team		W	L	PCT	ERA	G	GS	CG	IP	H	BB	SO	ShO	W	L	SV	AB	H	HR	BA	PO	A	E	DP	TC/G	FA
1935	CHI	N	0	0	–	3.86	13	0	0	25.2	29	14	10	0	0	0	0	6	1	0	.167	3	5	0	1	0.6	1.000
1939	BKN	N	15	10	.600	2.93	40	25	15	227.1	228	54	79	0	2	1	1	74	15	0	.203	14	53	0	5	1.7	1.000
1940			11	8	.579	3.62	44	10	5	154	136	51	53	2	6	5	2	36	9	0	.250	5	40	1	1	1.0	.978
1941			14	11	.560	3.89	45	18	4	162	155	57	61	1	8	4	7	50	6	0	.120	10	41	1	6	1.2	.894
1942			6	3	.667	2.25	50	2	0	112	91	44	54	0	6	2	13	27	4	0	.148	7	18	2	2	0.5	.926
1946			11	5	.688	1.99	46	1	0	99.2	101	33	31	0	11	4	5	22	3	0	.136	9	32	2	4	0.9	.953
1947			10	4	.714	3.99	46	0	0	76.2	75	29	40	0	10	4	18	18	1	0	.056	4	13	0	2	0.4	1.000
1948			3	0	1.000	8.00	22	0	0	36	59	17	7	0	3	0	4	7	0	0	.000	1	7	0	0	0.4	1.000
1949	2 teams	PIT N (33G 4–1)				NY A	(4G 1–0)																					
"	total		5	1	.833	5.24	37	0	0	46.1	61	22	14	0	5	1	5	4	1	0	.250	1	1	0	0	0.1	1.000
9 yrs.			75	42	.641	3.45	343	56	24	939.2	935	321	349	3	51	21	55	244	40	0	.164	54	210	6	22	0.8	.978

WORLD SERIES

Year	Team		W	L	PCT	ERA	G	GS	CG	IP	H	BB	SO	ShO	W	L	SV	AB	H	HR	BA	PO	A	E	DP	TC/G	FA
1941	BKN	N	0	2	.000	3.38	3	0	0	5.1	9	2	1	0	0	2	0	2	1	0	.500	0	3	0	1	1.0	1.000
1947			2	0	1.000	0.87	6	0	0	10.1	5	1	3	0	2	0	2	1	0	0	.000	2	3	0	1	0.8	1.000
2 yrs.			2	2	.500	1.72	9	0	0	15.2	14	3	4	0	2	2	2	3	1	0	.333	2	6	0	1	0.9	1.000
															2nd	**2nd**											

Jay Cashion

CASHION, JAY CARL
B. June 6, 1891, Mecklenburg, N. C. D. Nov. 17, 1935, Lake Millicent, Wis.   BL TR 6'2" 200 lbs.

Year	Team		W	L	PCT	ERA	G	GS	CG	IP	H	BB	SO	ShO	W	L	SV	AB	H	HR	BA	PO	A	E	DP	TC/G	FA
1911	WAS	A	1	5	.167	4.16	11	9	5	71.1	67	47	26	0	0	0	0	37	12	0	.324	3	22	0	0	2.3	1.000

Year	Team	W	L	PCT	ERA	G	GS	CG	IP	H	BB	SO	ShO	W	L	SV	AB	H	HR	BA	PO	A	E	DP	TC/G	FA

(Relief Pitching: W L SV; Batting: AB H HR BA)

Jay Cashion *continued*

Year	Team	W	L	PCT	ERA	G	GS	CG	IP	H	BB	SO	ShO	W	L	SV	AB	H	HR	BA	PO	A	E	DP	TC/G	FA
1912		10	6	.625	3.17	26	17	13	170.1	150	103	84	1	1	0	1	103	22	2	.214	15	40	1	1	2.2	.982
1913		1	1	.500	6.23	4	3	0	8.2	7	14	3	0	0	0	0	12	3	0	.250	0	5	1	1	1.5	.833
1914		0	1	.000	10.80	2	1	0	5	4	6	1	0	0	0	0	1	0	0	.000	1	3	1	1	2.5	.800
4 yrs.		12	13	.480	3.70	43	30	18	255.1	228	170	114	1	1	0	1	*				19	70	3	3	2.1	.967

Craig Caskey

CASKEY, CRAIG DOUGLAS
B. Dec. 11, 1949, Visalia, Calif. BB TL 5'11" 185 lbs.

Year	Team	W	L	PCT	ERA	G	GS	CG	IP	H	BB	SO	ShO	W	L	SV	AB	H	HR	BA	PO	A	E	DP	TC/G	FA
1973	MON N	0	0	–	5.65	9	1	0	14.1	15	4	6	0	0	0	0	1	0	0	.000	1	3	1	0	0.6	.800

Ed Cassian

CASSIAN, EDWIN
B. Conn. Deceased. 5'8" 160 lbs.

Year	Team	W	L	PCT	ERA	G	GS	CG	IP	H	BB	SO	ShO	W	L	SV	AB	H	HR	BA	PO	A	E	DP	TC/G	FA
1891	2 teams	PHI N (6G 1–3)			WAS AA (7G 2–4)																					
"	total	3	7	.300	4.45	13	9	8	91	113	51	24	0	1	0	0	43	11	0	.256	0	27	4	2	2.4	.871

John Cassidy

CASSIDY, JOHN P.
B. 1855, Brooklyn, N. Y. D. July 2, 1891, Brooklyn, N. Y. BR TL 5'8" 168 lbs.

Year	Team	W	L	PCT	ERA	G	GS	CG	IP	H	BB	SO	ShO	W	L	SV	AB	H	HR	BA	PO	A	E	DP	TC/G	FA
1877	HAR N	1	1	.500	5.00	2	2	2	18	24	1	2	0	0	0	0	*				1	2	1	0	2.0	.750

George Caster

CASTER, GEORGE JASPER
B. Aug. 4, 1907, Colton, Calif. D. Dec. 18, 1955, Lakewood, Calif. BR TR 6'1½" 180 lbs.

Year	Team	W	L	PCT	ERA	G	GS	CG	IP	H	BB	SO	ShO	W	L	SV	AB	H	HR	BA	PO	A	E	DP	TC/G	FA
1934	PHI A	3	2	.600	3.41	5	3	2	37	32	14	15	0	1	0	0	15	4	0	.267	5	9	1	1	3.0	.933
1935		1	4	.200	6.25	25	1	0	63.1	86	37	24	0	1	3	1	22	5	0	.227	4	19	1	1	1.0	.958
1937		12	19	.387	4.43	34	33	19	231.2	227	107	100	3	0	0	0	90	19	0	.211	8	44	4	2	1.6	.929
1938		16	20	.444	4.37	42	40	20	280.1	310	117	112	2	0	0	1	101	20	0	.198	12	44	4	1	1.4	.933
1939		9	9	.500	4.90	28	17	7	136	144	45	59	1	2	0	0	43	9	0	.209	9	21	1	4	1.1	.968
1940		4	19	.174	6.56	36	24	11	178.1	234	69	75	0	1	1	2	62	8	0	.129	10	27	2	2	1.1	.949
1941	STL A	3	7	.300	5.00	32	9	3	104.1	105	37	36	0	0	3	3	29	3	0	.103	11	20	1	3	1.0	.969
1942		8	2	.800	2.81	39	0	0	80	62	39	34	0	8	5	5	15	1	0	.067	8	17	1	1	0.7	.962
1943		6	8	.429	2.12	35	0	0	76.1	69	41	43	0	6	8	8	22	3	0	.136	2	17	0	1	0.5	1.000
1944		6	6	.500	2.44	42	0	0	81	91	33	46	0	6	6	12	20	5	0	.250	2	13	0	1	0.4	1.000
1945	2 teams	STL A (10G 1–2)			DET A (22G 5–1)																					
"	total	6	3	.667	4.57	32	0	0	67	67	34	32	0	6	3	4	14	3	0	.214	1	2	0	1	0.1	1.000
1946	DET A	2	1	.667	5.66	26	0	0	41.1	42	24	19	0	2	1	4	7	1	0	.143	0	11	1	1	0.5	.917
12 yrs.		76	100	.432	4.54	376	127	62	1376.2	1469	597	595	6	33	26	39	440	81	0	.184	72	244	16	18	0.9	.952

WORLD SERIES

Year	Team	W	L	PCT	ERA	G	GS	CG	IP	H	BB	SO	ShO	W	L	SV	AB	H	HR	BA	PO	A	E	DP	TC/G	FA
1945	DET A	0	0	–	0.00	1	0	0	.2	0	0	0	0	0	0	0	0	0	0	–	0	0	0	0	0.0	–

Bobby Castillo

CASTILLO, ROBERT ERNIE
B. Apr. 18, 1955, Los Angeles, Calif. BR TR 5'10" 170 lbs.

Year	Team	W	L	PCT	ERA	G	GS	CG	IP	H	BB	SO	ShO	W	L	SV	AB	H	HR	BA	PO	A	E	DP	TC/G	FA
1977	LA N	1	0	1.000	4.09	6	1	0	11	12	2	7	0	1	0	0	1	0	0	.000	1	3	0	0	0.7	1.000
1978		0	4	.000	3.97	18	0	0	34	28	33	30	0	0	4	1	7	0	0	.000	1	6	1	0	0.4	.875
1979		2	0	1.000	1.13	19	0	0	24	26	13	25	0	2	0	7	3	0	0	.000	1	1	0	0	0.2	1.000
1980		8	6	.571	2.76	61	0	0	98	70	45	60	0	8	6	5	9	1	0	.111	10	16	1	1	0.4	.963
1981		2	4	.333	5.29	34	1	0	51	50	24	35	0	2	4	5	9	4	0	.444	3	4	0	1	0.2	1.000
1982	MIN N	13	11	.542	3.66	40	25	6	218.2	194	85	123	1	2	1	0	0	0	0	–	20	19	3	1	1.1	.929
1983		8	12	.400	4.77	27	25	3	158.1	170	65	90	0	0	0	0	0	0	0	–	13	22	1	1	1.3	.972
1984		2	1	.667	1.78	10	2	0	25.1	14	19	7	0	0	0	0	0	0	0	–	2	2	0	1	0.4	1.000
1985	LA N	2	2	.500	5.43	35	5	0	68	59	41	57	0	1	1	0	10	1	0	.100	5	11	1	1	0.5	.941
9 yrs.		38	40	.487	3.95	250	59	9	688.1	623	327	434	1	16	16	18	39	6	0	.154	56	86	7	6	0.6	.953

LEAGUE CHAMPIONSHIP SERIES

Year	Team	W	L	PCT	ERA	G	GS	CG	IP	H	BB	SO	ShO	W	L	SV	AB	H	HR	BA	PO	A	E	DP	TC/G	FA
1981	LA N	0	0	–	0.00	1	0	0	1	0	0	1	0	0	0	0	0	0	0	–	0	0	0	0	0.0	–
1985	LA N	0	0	–	3.38	1	0	0	5.1	4	2	4	0	0	0	0	0	0	0	–	1	3	0	1	4.0	1.000
2 yrs.		0	0	–	2.84	2	0	0	6.1	4	2	5	0	0	0	0	0	0	0	–	1	3	0	1	2.0	1.000

WORLD SERIES

Year	Team	W	L	PCT	ERA	G	GS	CG	IP	H	BB	SO	ShO	W	L	SV	AB	H	HR	BA	PO	A	E	DP	TC/G	FA
1981	LA N	0	0	–	9.00	1	0	0	1	0	5	0	0	0	0	0	0	0	0	–	0	2	0	0	2.0	1.000

Manny Castillo

CASTILLO, ESTEBAN MANUEL ANTONIO
Born Esteban Manuel Antonio Castillo y Cabrera.
B. Apr. 1, 1957, Santo Domingo, Dominican Republic BB TR 5'9" 160 lbs.

Year	Team	W	L	PCT	ERA	G	GS	CG	IP	H	BB	SO	ShO	W	L	SV	AB	H	HR	BA	PO	A	E	DP	TC/G	FA
1983	SEA A	0	0	–	23.63	1	0	0	2.2	8	3	2	0	0	0	0	*				0	0	0	0	0.0	–

Tony Castillo

CASTILLO, ANTONIO JOSE
B. Mar. 1, 1963, Quibor, Venezuela BL TL 5'10" 177 lbs.

Year	Team	W	L	PCT	ERA	G	GS	CG	IP	H	BB	SO	ShO	W	L	SV	AB	H	HR	BA	PO	A	E	DP	TC/G	FA
1988	TOR A	1	0	1.000	3.00	14	0	0	15	10	2	14	0	1	0	0	0	0	0	–	0	3	0	0	0.2	1.000
1989	2 teams	TOR A (17G 1–1)			ATL N (12G 0–1)																					
"	total	1	2	.333	5.67	29	0	0	27	31	14	15	0	1	2	1	1	0	0	.000	2	3	0	0	0.2	1.000
2 yrs.		2	2	.500	4.71	43	0	0	42	41	16	29	0	2	2	1	1	0	0	.000	2	6	0	0	0.2	1.000

Slick Castleman

CASTLEMAN, CLYDELL
B. Sept. 8, 1913, Donelson, Tenn. BR TR 6' 185 lbs.

Year	Team	W	L	PCT	ERA	G	GS	CG	IP	H	BB	SO	ShO	W	L	SV	AB	H	HR	BA	PO	A	E	DP	TC/G	FA
1934	NY N	1	0	1.000	5.40	7	1	0	16.2	18	10	5	0	1	0	0	4	1	0	.250	1	6	0	0	1.0	1.000
1935		15	6	.714	4.09	29	25	9	173.2	186	64	64	1	2	0	0	67	12	1	.179	12	42	4	3	2.0	.931
1936		4	7	.364	5.64	29	12	2	111.2	148	56	54	1	3	0	1	39	5	1	.128	5	26	2	2	1.1	.939
1937		11	6	.647	3.31	23	23	10	160.1	148	33	78	2	0	0	0	57	4	0	.070	8	20	2	3	1.3	.933
1938		4	5	.444	4.17	21	14	4	90.2	108	37	18	0	0	0	0	31	3	0	.097	4	14	0	2	0.9	1.000
1939		1	2	.333	4.54	12	4	0	33.2	36	23	6	0	1	0	0	9	3	0	.333	2	4	0	0	0.5	1.000
6 yrs.		36	26	.581	4.25	121	79	25	586.2	644	223	225	4	7	0	1	207	28	3	.135	32	112	8	10	1.3	.947

Year	Team	W	L	PCT	ERA	G	GS	CG	IP	H	BB	SO	ShO	W	L	SV	AB	H	HR	BA	PO	A	E	DP	TC/G	FA

Slick Castleman *continued*

WORLD SERIES

| 1936 | NY N | 0 | 0 | – | 2.08 | 1 | 0 | 0 | 4.1 | 3 | 2 | 5 | 0 | 0 | 0 | 0 | 2 | 1 | 0 | .500 | 0 | 0 | 0 | 0 | 0.0 | – |

Roy Castleton

CASTLETON, ROYAL EUGENE BL TL 5'11" 167 lbs.
B. July 26, 1885, Salt Lake City, Utah D. June 24, 1967, Los Angeles, Calif.

1907	NY A	1	1	.500	2.81	3	2	1	16	11	3	3	0	0	0	0	5	0	0	.000	0	5	0	0	1.7	1.000
1909	CIN N	1	1	.500	1.93	4	1	1	14	14	6	5	0	0	1	0	3	2	0	.667	0	5	0	1	1.3	1.000
1910		1	2	.333	3.29	4	2	1	13.2	15	6	5	0	0	2	0	5	0	0	.000	0	4	0	0	1.0	1.000
3 yrs.		3	4	.429	2.68	11	5	3	43.2	40	15	13	0	0	3	0	13	2	0	.154	0	14	0	1	1.3	1.000

Paul Castner

CASTNER, PAUL HENRY (Lefty) BL TL 5'11" 187 lbs.
B. Feb. 16, 1897, St. Paul, Minn. D. Mar. 3, 1986, St. Paul, Minn.

| 1923 | CHI A | 0 | 0 | – | 6.30 | 6 | 0 | 0 | 10 | 14 | 5 | 0 | 0 | 0 | 0 | 0 | 3 | 0 | 0 | .000 | 0 | 4 | 0 | 0 | 0.7 | 1.000 |

Bill Castro

CASTRO, WILLIAM RADHAMES BR TR 5'11" 170 lbs.
Born William Radhames Castro y Checo.
B. Dec. 13, 1953, Santiago, Dominican Republic

1974	MIL A	0	0	–	4.50	8	0	0	18	19	5	10	0	0	0	0	0	0	0	–	4	1	0	0	0.6	1.000
1975		3	2	.600	2.52	18	5	0	75	78	17	25	0	1	0	1	0	0	0	–	9	11	1	1	1.2	.952
1976		4	6	.400	3.45	39	0	0	70.1	70	19	23	0	4	6	8	0	0	0	–	0	11	0	2	0.3	1.000
1977		8	6	.571	4.17	51	0	0	69	76	23	28	0	8	6	13	0	0	0	–	7	16	3	0	0.5	.885
1978		5	4	.556	1.81	42	0	0	49.2	43	14	17	0	5	4	8	0	0	0	–	3	10	1	0	0.3	.929
1979		3	1	.750	2.05	39	0	0	44	40	13	10	0	3	1	6	0	0	0	–	1	7	1	1	0.2	.889
1980		2	4	.333	2.79	56	0	0	84	89	17	32	0	2	4	8	0	0	0	–	7	15	3	3	0.4	.880
1981	NY A	1	1	.500	3.79	11	0	0	19	26	5	4	0	1	1	0	0	0	0	–	0	3	0	0	0.3	1.000
1982	KC A	3	2	.600	3.45	21	4	0	75.2	72	20	37	0	1	1	1	0	0	0	–	6	4	0	0	0.5	1.000
1983		2	0	1.000	6.64	18	0	0	40.2	51	12	17	0	2	0	0	0	0	0	–	5	7	3	0	0.8	.800
10 yrs.		31	26	.544	3.33	303	9	0	545.1	564	145	203	0	27	23	45	0	0	0	–	42	85	12	7	0.5	.914

Eli Cates

CATES, ELI ELDO BR TR 5'9½" 175 lbs.
B. Jan. 26, 1877, Greensfork, Ind. D. May 29, 1964, Richmond, Ind.

| 1908 | WAS A | 4 | 8 | .333 | 2.51 | 19 | 10 | 7 | 114.2 | 112 | 32 | 33 | 0 | 1 | 2 | 0 | | | | * | 4 | 35 | 4 | 1 | 2.3 | .907 |

Ted Cather

CATHER, THODORE P. BR TR 5'10½" 178 lbs.
B. May 20, 1889, Chester, Pa. D. Apr. 9, 1945, Elkton, Md.

| 1913 | STL N | 0 | 0 | – | 54.00 | 1 | 0 | 0 | .1 | 1 | 2 | 0 | 0 | 0 | 0 | 0 | | | | * | 0 | 0 | 0 | 0 | 0.0 | – |

Hardin Cathey

CATHEY, HARDIN (Abner) BR TR 6' 190 lbs.
B. July 6, 1919, Burns, Tenn.

| 1942 | WAS A | 1 | 1 | .500 | 7.42 | 12 | 2 | 0 | 30.1 | 44 | 16 | 8 | 0 | 0 | 1 | 0 | 8 | 3 | 0 | .375 | 0 | 5 | 0 | 0 | 0.4 | 1.000 |

Keefe Cato

CATO, JOHN KEEFE BR TR 6'1" 180 lbs.
B. May 6, 1958, Yonkers, N. Y.

1983	CIN N	1	0	1.000	2.45	4	0	0	3.2	2	1	3	0	1	0	0	0	0	0	–	0	0	0	0	0.0	–
1984		0	1	.000	8.04	8	0	0	15.2	22	4	12	0	0	1	1	4	2	0	.500	2	3	0	1	0.6	1.000
2 yrs.		1	1	.500	6.98	12	0	0	19.1	24	5	15	0	1	1	1	4	2	0	.500	2	3	0	1	0.4	1.000

John Cattanach

CATTANACH, JOHN LECKIE 5'10" 190 lbs.
B. May 10, 1863, Providence, R. I. D. Nov. 10, 1926, Providence, R. I.

| 1884 | 2 teams | PRO N | | | (1G 0–0) | | STL U | | (2G 1–1) | | | | | | | | | | | | | | | | |
| " | total | 1 | 1 | .500 | 3.68 | 3 | 3 | 2 | 22 | 14 | 8 | 15 | 0 | 0 | 0 | 0 | 11 | 0 | 0 | .000 | 0 | 5 | 2 | 0 | 2.3 | .714 |

Bill Caudill

CAUDILL, WILLIAM HOLLAND BR TR 6'1" 190 lbs.
B. July 13, 1956, Santa Monica, Calif.

1979	CHI N	1	7	.125	4.80	29	12	0	90	89	41	104	0	1	0	0	17	1	0	.059	5	11	0	1	0.6	1.000
1980		4	6	.400	2.18	72	2	0	128	100	59	112	0	4	6	1	9	2	0	.222	7	11	0	0	0.3	1.000
1981		1	5	.167	5.83	30	10	0	71	87	31	45	0	0	0	0	14	2	0	.143	4	8	1	0	0.4	.923
1982	SEA A	12	9	.571	2.35	70	0	0	95.2	65	35	111	0	12	9	26	0	0	0	–	3	5	0	1	0.1	1.000
1983		2	8	.200	4.71	63	0	0	72.2	70	38	73	0	2	8	26	0	0	0	–	2	5	2	0	0.1	.778
1984	OAK A	9	7	.563	2.71	68	0	0	96.1	77	31	89	0	9	7	36	1	0	0	.000	4	4	0	0	0.1	1.000
1985	TOR A	4	6	.400	2.99	67	0	0	69.1	53	35	46	0	4	6	14	0	0	0	–	2	6	0	0	0.1	1.000
1986		2	4	.333	6.19	40	0	0	36.1	36	17	32	0	2	4	2	0	0	0	–	1	2	0	0	0.1	1.000
1987	OAK A	0	0	–	9.00	6	0	0	8	10	1	8	0	0	0	1	0	0	0	–	0	0	0	0	0.0	–
9 yrs.		35	52	.402	3.68	445	24	0	667.1	587	288	620	0	34	40	106	41	5	0	.122	28	52	3	2	0.2	.964

Red Causey

CAUSEY, CECIL ALGERTON BR TR 6'1" 160 lbs.
B. Aug. 11, 1893, Georgetown, Fla. D. Nov. 11, 1960, Avon Park, Fla.

1918	NY N	11	6	.647	2.79	29	18	10	158.1	143	42	48	2	2	2	2	48	6	0	.125	3	45	2	0	1.7	.960
1919	2 teams	NY N			(19G 9–3)		BOS N		(10G 4–5)																
"	total	13	8	.619	4.03	29	26	9	174	180	58	39	0	1	0	0	59	7	0	.119	6	50	3	1	2.0	.949
1920	PHI N	7	14	.333	4.32	35	26	11	181.1	203	79	30	1	0	2	3	59	11	0	.186	5	45	2	2	1.5	.962
1921	2 teams	PHI N			(7G 3–3)		NY N		(7G 1–1)																
"	total	4	4	.500	2.76	14	8	4	65.1	71	17	9	0	1	0	0	23	4	0	.174	3	16	2	1	1.5	.905
1922	NY N	4	3	.571	3.18	24	2	1	70.2	69	34	13	0	3	2	1	21	5	0	.238	5	19	2	1	1.1	.923
5 yrs.		39	35	.527	3.59	131	80	35	649.2	666	230	139	3	6	7	6	210	33	0	.157	22	175	11	5	1.6	.947

Year	Team		W	L	PCT	ERA	G	GS	CG	IP	H	BB	SO	ShO	Relief Pitching W	L	SV	Batting AB	H	HR	BA	PO	A	E	DP	TC/G	FA

Pug Cavet

CAVET, TILLER H.
B. Dec. 26, 1889, McGregor, Tex.   D. Aug. 4, 1966, San Luis Obispo, Calif.

BL TL 6'3"   176 lbs.

Year	Team		W	L	PCT	ERA	G	GS	CG	IP	H	BB	SO	ShO	W	L	SV	AB	H	HR	BA	PO	A	E	DP	TC/G	FA
1911	DET	A	0	0	–	4.50	1	1	0	4	6	1	1	0	0	0	0	1	0	0	.000	0	1	0	0	1.0	1.000
1914			7	7	.500	2.44	31	14	6	151.1	129	44	51	1	2	0	2	47	5	0	.106	0	54	6	1	1.9	.900
1915			4	2	.667	4.06	17	7	2	71	83	22	26	0	1	1	1	24	6	0	.250	4	21	3	1	1.6	.893
3 yrs.			11	9	.550	2.98	49	22	8	226.1	218	67	78	1	3	1	3	72	11	0	.153	4	76	9	2	1.8	.899

Art Ceccarelli

CECCARELLI, ARTHUR EDWARD (Chic)
B. Apr. 2, 1930, New Haven, Conn.

BR TL 6'   190 lbs.
BB 1957

Year	Team		W	L	PCT	ERA	G	GS	CG	IP	H	BB	SO	ShO	W	L	SV	AB	H	HR	BA	PO	A	E	DP	TC/G	FA
1955	KC	A	4	7	.364	5.31	31	16	3	123.2	123	71	68	1	1	0	0	38	3	0	.079	3	14	0	1	0.5	1.000
1956			0	1	.000	7.20	3	2	0	10	13	4	2	0	0	0	0	3	0	0	.000	0	5	0	0	1.7	1.000
1957	BAL	A	0	5	.000	4.50	20	8	1	58	62	31	30	0	0	0	0	14	0	0	.000	2	7	1	0	0.5	.900
1959	CHI	N	5	5	.500	4.76	18	15	4	102	95	37	56	2	0	0	0	33	3	0	.091	2	15	1	1	1.0	.944
1960			0	0	–	5.54	7	1	0	13	16	4	10	0	0	0	0	0	0	0	–	0	2	0	0	0.3	1.000
5 yrs.			9	18	.333	5.05	79	42	8	306.2	309	147	166	3	1	0	0	88	6	0	.068	7	43	2	1	0.7	.962

Jose Cecena

CECENA, JOSE ISABEL
Born Jose Isabel Cecena y Lugo.
B. Aug. 20, 1963, Ciudad Obregon, Mexico

BR TR 5'11"   180 lbs.

Year	Team		W	L	PCT	ERA	G	GS	CG	IP	H	BB	SO	ShO	W	L	SV	AB	H	HR	BA	PO	A	E	DP	TC/G	FA
1988	TEX	A	0	0	–	4.78	22	0	0	26.1	20	23	27	0	0	0	1	0	0	0	–	1	2	0	0	0.1	1.000

Rex Cecil

CECIL, REX ROLSTON
B. Oct. 8, 1916, Lindsay, Okla.   D. Oct. 30, 1966, Long Beach, Calif.

BL TR 6'3"   195 lbs.

Year	Team		W	L	PCT	ERA	G	GS	CG	IP	H	BB	SO	ShO	W	L	SV	AB	H	HR	BA	PO	A	E	DP	TC/G	FA
1944	BOS	A	4	5	.444	5.16	11	9	4	61	72	33	33	0	1	0	0	18	5	0	.278	0	11	1	0	1.1	.917
1945			2	5	.286	5.20	7	7	1	45	46	27	30	0	0	0	0	20	6	0	.300	5	12	1	0	2.6	.944
2 yrs.			6	10	.375	5.18	18	16	5	106	118	60	63	0	1	0	0	38	11	0	.289	5	23	2	0	1.7	.933

Pete Center

CENTER, MARVIN EARL
B. Apr. 22, 1912, Hazel Green, Ky.

BR TR 6'4"   190 lbs.

Year	Team		W	L	PCT	ERA	G	GS	CG	IP	H	BB	SO	ShO	W	L	SV	AB	H	HR	BA	PO	A	E	DP	TC/G	FA
1942	CLE	A	0	0	–	16.20	1	0	0	3.1	7	4	0	0	0	0	0	1	0	0	.000	0	0	0	0	0.0	–
1943			1	2	.333	2.76	24	1	0	42.1	29	18	10	0	1	2	1	5	0	0	.000	1	8	1	0	0.4	.900
1945			6	3	.667	3.99	31	8	2	85.2	89	28	34	0	3	2	1	22	2	0	.091	4	7	0	1	0.4	1.000
1946			0	2	.000	4.97	21	0	0	29	29	20	6	0	0	2	1	3	0	0	.000	0	6	1	0	0.3	.857
4 yrs.			7	7	.500	4.10	77	9	2	160.1	154	70	50	0	4	6	3	31	2	0	.065	5	21	2	1	0.4	.929

Rick Cerone

CERONE, RICHARD ALDO
B. May 19, 1954, Newark, N. J.

BR TR 5'11"   192 lbs.

Year	Team		W	L	PCT	ERA	G	GS	CG	IP	H	BB	SO	ShO	W	L	SV	AB	H	HR	BA	PO	A	E	DP	TC/G	FA
1987	NY	A	0	0	–	0.00	2	0	0	2	0	1	1	0	0	0	0	*				0	0	0	0	0.0	–

John Cerutti

CERUTTI, JOHN JOSEPH
B. Apr. 28, 1960, Albany, N. Y.

BL TL 6'2"   190 lbs.

Year	Team		W	L	PCT	ERA	G	GS	CG	IP	H	BB	SO	ShO	W	L	SV	AB	H	HR	BA	PO	A	E	DP	TC/G	FA
1985	TOR	A	0	2	.000	5.40	4	1	0	6.2	10	4	5	0	0	0	0	–	0	0		0	1	0	0	0.3	1.000
1986			9	4	.692	4.15	34	20	2	145.1	150	47	89	1	2	0	1	0	0	0	–	8	21	0	2	0.9	1.000
1987			11	4	.733	4.40	44	21	2	151.1	144	59	92	0	2	0	0	0	0	0	–	5	15	1	1	0.5	.952
1988			6	7	.462	3.13	46	12	0	123.2	120	42	65	0	1	3	1	0	0	0	–	13	27	0	2	0.9	1.000
1989			11	11	.500	3.07	33	31	3	205.1	214	53	69	1	0	0	0	0	0	0	–	16	45	1	3	1.9	.984
5 yrs.			37	28	.569	3.67	161	85	7	632.1	638	205	320	2	5	4	2	0	0	0	–	42	109	2	8	1.0	.987

LEAGUE CHAMPIONSHIP SERIES

Year	Team		W	L	PCT	ERA	G	GS	CG	IP	H	BB	SO	ShO	W	L	SV	AB	H	HR	BA	PO	A	E	DP	TC/G	FA
1989	TOR	A	0	0	–	0.00	2	0	0	2.2	0	3	1	0	0	0	0	–	0	0	–	0	2	0	0	1.0	1.000

Ray Chadwick

CHADWICK, RAY CHARLES
B. Nov. 17, 1962, Durham, N. C.

BB TR 6'2"   180 lbs.

Year	Team		W	L	PCT	ERA	G	GS	CG	IP	H	BB	SO	ShO	W	L	SV	AB	H	HR	BA	PO	A	E	DP	TC/G	FA
1986	CAL	A	0	5	.000	7.24	7	7	0	27.1	39	15	9	0	0	0	0	0	0	0	–	3	4	0	0	1.0	1.000

Leon Chagnon

CHAGNON, LEON WILBUR (Shag)
B. Sept. 28, 1902, Pittsfield, N. H.   D. July 30, 1953, Amesbury, Mass.

BR TR 6'   182 lbs.

Year	Team		W	L	PCT	ERA	G	GS	CG	IP	H	BB	SO	ShO	W	L	SV	AB	H	HR	BA	PO	A	E	DP	TC/G	FA
1929	PIT	N	0	0	–	9.00	1	1	0	7	11	1	4	0	0	0	0	2	0	0	.000	0	3	0	0	3.0	1.000
1930			0	3	.000	6.82	18	4	3	62	92	23	27	0	0	0	0	20	4	0	.200	4	12	0	0	0.9	1.000
1932			9	6	.600	3.94	30	10	4	128	140	34	52	1	5	1	0	40	9	0	.225	3	21	2	0	0.9	.923
1933			6	4	.600	3.69	39	5	1	100	100	17	35	0	5	2	1	21	1	0	.048	6	17	3	1	0.7	.885
1934			4	1	.800	4.81	33	1	0	58	68	24	19	0	4	1	1	13	3	0	.231	3	18	0	0	0.6	1.000
1935	NY	N	0	2	.000	3.52	14	1	0	38.1	32	5	16	0	0	1	0	9	0	0	.000	4	7	0	1	0.8	1.000
6 yrs.			19	16	.543	4.51	135	22	8	393.1	443	104	153	1	14	5	3	105	17	0	.162	20	78	5	2	0.8	.951

Bob Chakales

CHAKALES, ROBERT EDWARD (Chick)
B. Aug. 10, 1927, Asheville, N. C.

BR TR 6'1"   185 lbs.

Year	Team		W	L	PCT	ERA	G	GS	CG	IP	H	BB	SO	ShO	W	L	SV	AB	H	HR	BA	PO	A	E	DP	TC/G	FA
1951	CLE	A	3	4	.429	4.74	17	10	2	68.1	80	43	32	1	0	0	0	20	7	1	.350	1	11	0	0	0.7	1.000
1952			1	2	.333	9.75	5	1	0	12	19	8	7	0	0	2	0	4	2	0	.500	0	0	0	0	0.0	–
1953			0	2	.000	2.67	7	3	1	27	28	10	6	0	0	0	0	7	2	0	.286	2	5	1	1	1.1	.875
1954	2 teams	CLE A (3G 2–0)				BAL A (38G 3–7)																					
"	total		5	7	.417	3.43	41	6	0	99.2	85	55	47	0	5	4	1	25	9	0	.360	5	16	3	1	0.6	.875
1955	2 teams	CHI A (7G 0–0)				WAS A (29G 2–3)																					
"	total		2	3	.400	4.57	36	0	0	67	66	31	34	0	2	3	0	10	0	0	.000	3	14	1	1	0.5	.944
1956	WAS	A	4	4	.500	4.03	43	1	0	96	94	57	33	0	4	4	4	20	3	0	.150	1	25	1	2	0.6	.963
1957	2 teams	WAS A (4G 0–1)				BOS A (18G 0–2)																					
"	total		0	3	.000	7.15	22	2	0	50.1	73	21	28	0	0	3	3	10	3	0	.300	2	8	1	1	0.5	.909
7 yrs.			15	25	.375	4.54	171	23	3	420.1	445	225	187	1	11	16	10	96	26	1	.271	14	79	7	6	0.6	.930

1735

Year	Team	W	L	PCT	ERA	G	GS	CG	IP	H	BB	SO	ShO	Relief Pitching W	L	SV	Batting AB	H	HR	BA	PO	A	E	DP	TC/G	FA

George Chalmers

CHALMERS, GEORGE W. (Dut)
B. June 7, 1888, Edinburgh, Scotland   D. Aug. 5, 1960, Bronx, N. Y.   BR TR 6'1"   189 lbs.

Year	Team	W	L	PCT	ERA	G	GS	CG	IP	H	BB	SO	ShO	W	L	SV	AB	H	HR	BA	PO	A	E	DP	TC/G	FA
1910	PHI N	1	1	.500	5.32	4	3	2	22	21	11	12	0	0	0	0	7	1	0	.143	3	11	1	0	3.8	.933
1911		13	10	.565	3.11	38	22	11	208.2	196	101	101	3	4	1	4	73	13	0	.178	11	50	5	2	1.7	.924
1912		3	4	.429	3.28	12	8	3	57.2	64	37	22	0	0	1	0	16	3	0	.188	2	6	1	0	0.8	.889
1913		3	10	.231	4.81	26	13	4	116	133	51	46	0	0	2	1	33	7	0	.212	3	35	1	0	1.5	.974
1914		0	3	.000	5.50	3	2	1	18	23	15	6	0	0	1	0	6	0	0	.000	1	5	1	0	2.3	.857
1915		8	9	.471	2.48	26	20	13	170.1	159	45	82	1	0	1	1	59	10	0	.169	8	49	1	1	2.2	.983
1916		1	4	.200	3.19	12	8	2	53.2	49	19	21	0	1	0	1	15	0	0	.000	4	15	1	0	1.7	.950
7 yrs.		29	41	.414	3.41	121	76	36	646.1	645	279	290	4	5	6	6	209	34	0	.163	32	171	11	3	1.8	.949

WORLD SERIES

| 1915 | PHI N | 0 | 1 | .000 | 2.25 | 1 | 1 | 1 | 8 | 8 | 3 | 6 | 0 | 0 | 0 | 0 | 3 | 1 | 0 | .333 | 0 | 4 | 0 | 1 | 4.0 | 1.000 |

Bill Chamberlain

CHAMBERLAIN, WILLIAM VINCENT
B. Apr. 21, 1909, Stoughton, Mass.   BR TL 5'10½" 173 lbs.

| 1932 | CHI A | 0 | 5 | .000 | 4.57 | 12 | 5 | 0 | 41.1 | 39 | 25 | 11 | 0 | 0 | 0 | 0 | 10 | 1 | 0 | .100 | 0 | 5 | 0 | 1 | 0.4 | 1.000 |

Craig Chamberlain

CHAMBERLAIN, CRAIG PHILLIP
B. Feb. 2, 1957, Hollywood, Calif.   BR TR 6'1"   190 lbs.

1979	KC A	4	4	.500	3.73	10	10	4	70	68	18	30	0	0	0	0	0	0	0	–	5	2	0	0	0.7	1.000
1980		0	1	.000	7.00	5	0	0	9	10	5	3	0	0	1	0	0	0	0	–	0	2	0	0	0.4	1.000
2 yrs.		4	5	.444	4.10	15	10	4	79	78	23	33	0	0	1	0	0	0	0	–	5	4	0	0	0.6	1.000

Icebox Chamberlain

CHAMBERLAIN, ELTON P.
B. Nov. 5, 1867, Buffalo, N. Y.   D. Sept. 22, 1929, Baltimore, Md.   BR TR 5'9"   168 lbs.

1886	LOU AA	0	3	.000	6.61	4	4	4	31.1	39	17	18	0	0	0	0	19	3	0	.158	4	4	2	0	2.5	.800
1887		18	16	.529	3.79	36	36	35	309	340	117	118	1	0	0	0	131	26	1	.198	12	72	10	2	2.6	.894
1888	2 teams						LOU AA (24G 14–9)			STL AA (14G 11–2)																
"	total	25	11	.694	2.19	38	38	34	308	238	86	176	2	0	0	0	144	23	1	.160	16	62	3	0	2.1	.963
1889	STL AA	32	15	.681	2.97	53	51	44	421.2	376	165	202	2	0	0	1	171	34	2	.199	15	67	7	0	1.7	.921
1890	2 teams						STL AA (5G 3–1)			COL AA (25G 12–6)																
"	total	15	7	.682	2.83	30	26	22	210	175	96	128	6	0	0	0	80	17	0	.213	8	32	5	0	1.5	.889
1891	PHI AA	22	23	.489	4.22	49	46	44	405.2	397	206	204	0	1	0	0	176	33	2	.188	20	89	10	2	2.4	.916
1892	CIN N	19	23	.452	3.39	52	49	43	406.1	391	170	169	2	0	1	0	160	36	2	.225	16	67	9	0	1.8	.902
1893		16	12	.571	3.73	34	27	19	241	248	112	59	1	3	1	0	97	19	0	.196	8	46	5	0	1.7	.915
1894		10	9	.526	5.77	23	22	18	177.2	220	91	57	0	0	0	0	70	22	1	.314	6	28	3	1	1.6	.919
1896	CLE N	0	1	.000	7.36	2	2	1	11	21	5	2	0	0	0	0	3	0	0	.000	0	1	0	0	0.5	1.000
10 yrs.		157	120	.567	3.57	321	301	264	2521.2	2445	1065	1133	15	4	2	1	1051	213	9	.203	105	468	54	5	2.0	.914

Bill Chambers

CHAMBERS, WILLIAM CHRISTOPHER
B. Sept. 13, 1889, Cameron, W. Va.   D. Mar. 27, 1962, Fort Wayne, Ind.   BR TR 5'9"   185 lbs.

| 1910 | STL N | 0 | 0 | – | 0.00 | 1 | 0 | 0 | 1 | 0 | 0 | 0 | 0 | 0 | 0 | 0 | 0 | 0 | 0 | – | 1 | 0 | 1 | 0 | 2.0 | .500 |

Cliff Chambers

CHAMBERS, CLIFFORD DAY (Lefty)
B. Jan. 10, 1922, Portland, Ore.   BL TL 6'3"   208 lbs.

1948	CHI N	2	9	.182	4.43	29	12	3	103.2	100	48	51	1	0	2	0	30	4	0	.133	5	20	0	1	0.9	1.000
1949	PIT N	13	7	.650	3.96	34	21	10	177.1	186	58	93	1	1	0	0	55	13	0	.236	6	33	0	2	1.1	1.000
1950		12	15	.444	4.30	37	33	11	249.1	262	92	93	1	2	1	2	90	26	2	.289	9	37	2	1	1.3	.958
1951	2 teams						PIT N (10G 3–6)			STL N (21G 11–6)																
"	total	14	12	.538	4.38	31	26	11	189	184	87	64	2	1	0	1	70	15	1	.214	5	24	3	0	1.0	.906
1952	STL N	4	4	.500	4.12	26	13	2	98.1	110	33	47	1	0	0	1	32	9	0	.281	3	16	1	3	0.6	.950
1953		3	6	.333	4.86	32	8	0	79.2	82	43	26	0	2	2	0	17	2	0	.118	3	16	1	1	1.0	.963
6 yrs.		48	53	.475	4.29	189	113	37	897.1	924	361	374	7	5	8	1	294	69	3	.235	38	146	7	8	1.0	.963

John Chambers

CHAMBERS, JOHNNIE MONROE
B. Sept. 10, 1911, Copperhill, Tenn.   D. May 11, 1977, Palatka, Fla.   BL TR 6'   185 lbs.

| 1937 | STL N | 0 | 0 | – | 18.00 | 2 | 0 | 0 | 2 | 5 | 2 | 1 | 0 | 0 | 0 | 0 | 0 | 0 | 0 | – | 0 | 0 | 0 | 0 | 0.0 | – |

Rome Chambers

CHAMBERS, JEROME
B. Aug., 1874, Weaverville, N. C.   Deceased.   BL TL 6'2"   173 lbs.

| 1900 | BOS N | 0 | 0 | – | 11.25 | 1 | 0 | 0 | 4 | 5 | 5 | 2 | 0 | 0 | 0 | 0 | 1 | 0 | 0 | .000 | 0 | 0 | 0 | 0 | 0.0 | – |

Billy Champion

CHAMPION, BUFORD BILLY
B. Sept. 18, 1947, Shelby, N. C.   BR TR 6'4"   188 lbs.

1969	PHI N	5	10	.333	5.00	23	20	4	117	130	63	70	0	0	0	1	35	6	0	.171	10	22	1	2	1.4	.970
1970		0	2	.000	9.00	7	1	0	14	21	10	12	0	0	1	0	3	0	0	.000	0	3	0	0	0.4	1.000
1971		3	5	.375	4.38	37	9	0	109	100	48	49	0	3	0	0	27	3	0	.111	12	19	1	1	0.9	.969
1972		4	14	.222	5.09	30	22	2	132.2	155	54	54	0	0	1	0	34	5	1	.147	9	22	1	2	1.1	.969
1973	MIL A	5	8	.385	3.70	37	11	2	136.1	139	62	67	0	4	3	1	0	0	0	–	7	30	1	1	1.0	.974
1974		11	4	.733	3.61	31	23	2	162	168	49	60	0	0	0	0	0	0	0	–	16	16	3	2	1.1	.914
1975		6	6	.500	5.89	27	9	3	110	125	55	40	0	1	0	0	0	0	0	–	8	19	2	2	1.1	.931
1976		0	1	.000	7.13	10	3	0	24	35	13	8	0	0	0	0	0	0	0	–	2	6	0	0	0.8	1.000
8 yrs.		34	50	.405	4.68	202	102	13	805	873	354	360	3	5	6	2	99	14	1	.141	64	137	9	10	1.0	.957

Dean Chance

CHANCE, WILMER DEAN
B. June 1, 1941, Wayne, Ohio   BR TR 6'3"   200 lbs.

1961	LA A	0	2	.000	6.87	5	4	0	18.1	33	5	11	0	0	0	0	5	0	0	.000	1	6	0	1	1.4	1.000
1962		14	10	.583	2.96	50	24	6	206.2	195	66	127	2	5	2	8	65	4	0	.062	12	37	1	2	1.0	.980
1963		13	18	.419	3.19	45	35	6	248	229	90	168	2	2	1	4	80	12	0	.150	15	46	6	2	1.5	.910
1964		20	9	.690	1.65	46	35	15	278.1	194	86	207	11	2	1	4	89	7	0	.079	10	33	1	1	1.0	.977

Year	Team		W	L	PCT	ERA	G	GS	CG	IP	H	BB	SO	ShO	Relief Pitching W	L	SV	Batting AB	H	HR	BA	PO	A	E	DP	TC/G	FA

Dean Chance *continued*

Year	Team		W	L	PCT	ERA	G	GS	CG	IP	H	BB	SO	ShO	W	L	SV	AB	H	HR	BA	PO	A	E	DP	TC/G	FA
1965	CAL	A	15	10	.600	3.15	36	33	10	225.2	197	101	164	4	0	2	0	75	7	0	.093	14	49	1	6	1.8	.984
1966			12	17	.414	3.08	41	37	11	259.2	206	114	180	2	0	2	1	76	2	0	.026	17	48	4	7	1.7	.942
1967	MIN	A	20	14	.588	2.73	41	39	18	283.2	244	68	220	5	0	0	1	92	3	0	.033	15	51	7	6	1.8	.904
1968			16	16	.500	2.53	43	39	15	292	244	63	234	6	0	0	1	93	5	0	.054	15	57	5	3	1.8	.935
1969			5	4	.556	2.95	20	15	1	88.1	76	35	50	0	1	0	0	24	1	0	.042	3	9	0	1	0.6	1.000
1970	2 teams	CLE A	(45G 9–8)			NY N	(3G 0–1)																				
"	total		9	9	.500	4.36	48	19	1	157	175	61	109	1	4	2	5	42	3	0	.071	3	21	2	2	0.5	.923
1971	DET	A	4	6	.400	3.50	31	14	0	90	91	50	64	0	3	0	0	21	0	0	.000	6	16	6	0	0.9	.786
11 yrs.			128	115	.527	2.92	406	294	83	2147.2	1864	739	1534	33	17	10	23	662	44	0	.066	111	373	33	31	1.3	.936

LEAGUE CHAMPIONSHIP SERIES

Year	Team		W	L	PCT	ERA	G	GS	CG	IP	H	BB	SO	ShO	W	L	SV	AB	H	HR	BA	PO	A	E	DP	TC/G	FA
1969	MIN	A	0	0	–	13.50	1	0	0	2	4	0	2	0	0	0	0	0	0	0	–	0	0	0	0	0.0	–

Ed Chandler

CHANDLER, EDWARD OLIVER
B. Feb. 17, 1922, Pinson, Ala. — BR TR 6'2" 190 lbs.

Year	Team		W	L	PCT	ERA	G	GS	CG	IP	H	BB	SO	ShO	W	L	SV	AB	H	HR	BA	PO	A	E	DP	TC/G	FA
1947	BKN	N	0	1	.000	6.37	15	1	0	29.2	31	12	8	0	0	0	1	2	0	0	.000	2	7	1	0	0.7	.900

Spud Chandler

CHANDLER, SPURGEON FERDINAND
B. Sept. 12, 1907, Commerce, Ga. — BR TR 6' 181 lbs.

Year	Team		W	L	PCT	ERA	G	GS	CG	IP	H	BB	SO	ShO	W	L	SV	AB	H	HR	BA	PO	A	E	DP	TC/G	FA
1937	NY	A	7	4	.636	2.84	12	10	6	82.1	79	20	31	2	0	1	0	30	4	0	.133	9	23	0	1	2.7	1.000
1938			14	5	.737	4.03	23	23	14	172	183	47	36	2	0	0	0	69	14	3	.203	18	50	0	3	3.0	1.000
1939			3	0	1.000	2.84	11	0	0	19	26	9	4	0	3	0	0	5	2	0	.400	1	7	0	0	0.7	1.000
1940			8	7	.533	4.60	27	24	6	172	184	60	56	1	0	0	0	60	9	2	.150	4	50	2	3	2.1	.964
1941			10	4	.714	3.19	28	20	11	163.2	146	60	60	4	0	0	4	60	11	0	.183	15	42	1	1	2.1	.983
1942			16	5	.762	2.38	24	24	17	200.2	176	74	74	3	0	0	0	71	15	0	.211	25	46	2	8	3.0	.973
1943			20	4	.833	1.64	30	30	20	253	197	54	134	5	0	0	0	97	25	2	.258	10	63	3	4	2.5	.961
1944			0	0	–	4.50	1	1	0	6	6	1	1	0	0	0	0	1	0	0	.000	0	3	0	0	3.0	1.000
1945			2	1	.667	4.65	4	4	2	31	30	7	12	1	0	0	0	12	4	0	.333	5	5	0	0	2.5	1.000
1946			20	8	.714	2.10	34	32	20	257.1	200	90	138	6	0	0	2	94	14	0	.149	13	60	1	7	2.2	.986
1947			9	5	.643	2.46	17	16	13	128	100	41	68	2	0	0	0	49	12	2	.245	6	36	1	1	2.5	.977
11 yrs.			109	43	.717	2.84	211	184	109	1485	1327	463	614	26	3	1	6	548	110	9	.201	106	385	10	28	2.4	.980

WORLD SERIES

Year	Team		W	L	PCT	ERA	G	GS	CG	IP	H	BB	SO	ShO	W	L	SV	AB	H	HR	BA	PO	A	E	DP	TC/G	FA
1941	NY	A	0	1	.000	3.60	1	1	0	5	4	2	2	0	0	0	0	2	1	0	.500	0	0	0	0	0.0	–
1942			0	1	.000	1.08	2	1	0	8.1	5	1	3	0	0	0	1	2	0	0	.000	2	2	0	0	2.0	1.000
1943			2	0	1.000	0.50	2	2	2	18	17	3	10	1	0	0	0	6	1	0	.167	0	4	0	0	2.0	1.000
1947			0	0	–	9.00	1	0	0	2	2	3	1	0	0	0	0	0	0	0	–	0	0	0	0	0.0	–
4 yrs.			2	2	.500	1.62	6	4	2	33.1	28	9	16	1	0	0	1	10	2	0	.200	2	6	0	0	1.3	1.000

Esty Chaney

CHANEY, ESTY CLYON
B. Jan. 29, 1891, Hadley, Pa. D. Feb. 5, 1952, Cleveland, Ohio — BR TR 5'11" 170 lbs.

Year	Team		W	L	PCT	ERA	G	GS	CG	IP	H	BB	SO	ShO	W	L	SV	AB	H	HR	BA	PO	A	E	DP	TC/G	FA
1913	BOS	A	0	0	–	9.00	1	0	0	1	1	2	0	0	0	0	0	0	0	0	–	0	0	0	0	0.0	–
1914	BKN	F	0	0	–	6.75	1	0	0	4	7	2	1	0	0	0	0	1	0	0	.000	0	1	0	0	1.0	1.000
2 yrs.			0	0	–	7.20	2	0	0	5	8	4	1	0	0	0	0	1	0	0	.000	0	1	0	0	0.5	1.000

Tiny Chaplin

CHAPLIN, JAMES BAILEY
B. July 13, 1905, Los Angeles, Calif. D. Mar. 25, 1939, National City, Calif. — BR TR 6'1" 195 lbs.

Year	Team		W	L	PCT	ERA	G	GS	CG	IP	H	BB	SO	ShO	W	L	SV	AB	H	HR	BA	PO	A	E	DP	TC/G	FA
1928	NY	N	0	2	.000	4.50	12	1	0	24	27	8	5	0	0	2	0	5	0	0	.000	2	3	0	0	0.4	1.000
1930			2	6	.250	5.18	19	8	3	73	89	16	20	0	0	2	1	19	2	1	.105	8	14	0	0	1.2	1.000
1931			2	1	.667	3.19	16	3	1	42.1	39	16	7	0	0	0	1	11	2	0	.182	4	4	0	0	0.5	1.000
1936	BOS	N	10	15	.400	4.12	40	31	14	231.1	273	62	86	0	1	0	2	84	17	0	.202	13	57	3	2	1.8	.959
4 yrs.			14	24	.368	4.25	87	43	18	370.2	428	102	118	0	1	4	4	119	21	1	.176	27	78	3	2	1.2	.972

Ben Chapman

CHAPMAN, WILLIAM BENJAMIN
B. Dec. 25, 1908, Nashville, Tenn.
Manager 1945-48. — BR TR 6' 190 lbs.

Year	Team		W	L	PCT	ERA	G	GS	CG	IP	H	BB	SO	ShO	W	L	SV	AB	H	HR	BA	PO	A	E	DP	TC/G	FA
1944	BKN	N	5	3	.625	3.40	11	9	6	79.1	75	33	37	0	0	0	0	38	14	0	.368	3	6	1	0	0.9	.900
1945	2 teams	BKN N	(10G 3–3)			PHI N	(3G 0–0)																				
"	total		3	3	.500	5.79	13	7	2	60.2	71	38	27	0	1	0	0	73	19	0	.260	2	14	1	2	1.3	.941
1946	PHI	N	0	0	–	0.00	1	0	0	1.1	1	0	1	0	0	0	0	1	0	0	.000	0	0	0	0	0.0	–
3 yrs.			8	6	.571	4.39	25	16	8	141.1	147	71	65	0	1	1	0	*				5	20	2	2	1.1	.926

Ed Chapman

CHAPMAN, EDWIN VOLNEY
B. Nov. 28, 1905, Courtland, Miss. — BB TR 6'1" 185 lbs.

Year	Team		W	L	PCT	ERA	G	GS	CG	IP	H	BB	SO	ShO	W	L	SV	AB	H	HR	BA	PO	A	E	DP	TC/G	FA
1933	WAS	A	0	0	–	8.00	6	1	0	9	7	2	4	0	0	0	0	3	0	0	.000	0	1	0	0	0.2	1.000

Fred Chapman

CHAPMAN, FREDERICK JOSEPH
B. Nov. 24, 1872, Little Cooley, Pa. D. Dec. 14, 1957, Union City, Pa. — BR TR 5'8" 165 lbs.

Year	Team		W	L	PCT	ERA	G	GS	CG	IP	H	BB	SO	ShO	W	L	SV	AB	H	HR	BA	PO	A	E	DP	TC/G	FA
1887	PHI	AA	0	0	–	7.20	1	1	1	5	8	2	4	0	0	0	0	2	0	0	.000	0	0	0	0	0.0	–

Bill Chappelle

CHAPPELLE, WILLIAM HOGAN (Big Bill)
B. Mar. 22, 1884, Waterloo, N. Y. D. Dec. 31, 1944, Mineola, N. Y. — BR TR 6'2" 206 lbs.

Year	Team		W	L	PCT	ERA	G	GS	CG	IP	H	BB	SO	ShO	W	L	SV	AB	H	HR	BA	PO	A	E	DP	TC/G	FA
1908	BOS	N	2	4	.333	1.79	13	7	3	70.1	60	17	23	1	0	0	0	21	1	0	.048	3	25	1	0	2.2	.966
1909	2 teams	BOS N	(5G 1–1)			CIN N	(1G 0–0)																				
"	total		1	1	.500	1.91	6	3	2	33	36	13	8	0	0	0	0	12	4	1	.333	3	15	1	1	3.2	.947
1914	BKN	F	4	2	.667	3.15	16	6	4	74.1	71	29	31	0	1	0	1	23	0	0	.000	2	17	2	1	1.3	.905
3 yrs.			7	7	.500	2.38	35	16	9	177.2	167	59	62	1	1	0	1	56	5	1	.089	8	57	4	2	2.0	.942

Year	Team		W	L	PCT	ERA	G	GS	CG	IP	H	BB	SO	ShO	Relief Pitching			Batting			BA	PO	A	E	DP	TC/G	FA
															W	L	SV	AB	H	HR							

Norm Charlton

CHARLTON, NORMAN WOOD
B. Jan. 6, 1963, Fort Polk, La.　　　　　　　　　　　　　　　　BB TL 6'3" 195 lbs.

Year	Team		W	L	PCT	ERA	G	GS	CG	IP	H	BB	SO	ShO	W	L	SV	AB	H	HR	BA	PO	A	E	DP	TC/G	FA
1988	CIN	N	4	5	.444	3.96	10	10	0	61.1	60	20	39	0	0	0	0	15	0	0	.000	1	9	0	0	1.0	1.000
1989			8	3	.727	2.93	69	0	0	95.1	67	40	98	0	8	3	0	5	0	0	.000	3	13	3	0	0.3	.842
2 yrs.			12	8	.600	3.33	79	10	0	156.2	127	60	137	0	8	3	0	20	0	0	.000	4	22	3	0	0.4	.897

Pete Charton

CHARTON, FRANK LANE
B. Dec. 21, 1942, Jackson, Tenn.　　　　　　　　　　　　　　　BL TR 6'2" 190 lbs.

Year	Team		W	L	PCT	ERA	G	GS	CG	IP	H	BB	SO	ShO	W	L	SV	AB	H	HR	BA	PO	A	E	DP	TC/G	FA
1964	BOS	A	0	2	.000	5.26	25	5	0	65	67	24	37	0	0	1	0	10	1	0	.100	7	16	0	0	0.9	1.000

Ken Chase

CHASE, KENDALL FAY (Lefty)
B. Oct. 6, 1913, Oneonta, N. Y.　D. Jan. 16, 1985, Oneonta, N. Y.　　BL TL 6'2" 210 lbs.

Year	Team		W	L	PCT	ERA	G	GS	CG	IP	H	BB	SO	ShO	W	L	SV	AB	H	HR	BA	PO	A	E	DP	TC/G	FA
1936	WAS	A	0	0	—	11.57	1	0	0	2.1	2	4	1	0	0	0	0	1	1	0	1.000	0	0	0	0	0.0	—
1937			4	3	.571	4.13	14	9	4	76.1	74	60	43	0	0	0	0	29	1	0	.034	1	13	2	1	1.1	.875
1938			9	10	.474	5.58	32	21	7	150	151	113	64	0	2	1	1	48	10	0	.208	4	36	6	0	1.4	.870
1939			10	19	.345	3.80	32	31	15	232	215	114	118	1	1	0	0	89	15	0	.169	11	39	3	2	1.7	.943
1940			15	17	.469	3.23	35	34	20	261.2	260	143	129	1	1	0	0	92	15	1	.163	7	44	3	1	1.5	.944
1941			6	18	.250	5.08	33	30	8	205.2	228	115	98	1	1	0	0	74	11	0	.149	8	43	2	3	1.6	.962
1942	BOS	A	5	1	.833	3.81	13	10	4	80.1	82	41	34	0	0	0	0	33	6	0	.182	4	12	2	1	1.4	.889
1943	2 teams		BOS A	(7G 0–4)		NY N	(21G 4–12)																					
"	total		4	16	.200	4.60	28	25	4	156.2	176	104	95	1	0	0	0	53	10	0	.189	2	31	3	0	1.3	.917
8 yrs.			53	84	.387	4.27	188	160	62	1165	1188	694	582	4	4	2	1	419	69	1	.165	37	218	21	8	1.5	.924

Jim Chatterton

CHATTERTON, JAMES M.
B. Oct. 14, 1864, Brooklyn, N. Y.　D. Dec. 15, 1944, Tewksbury, Mass.

Year	Team		W	L	PCT	ERA	G	GS	CG	IP	H	BB	SO	ShO	W	L	SV	AB	H	HR	BA	PO	A	E	DP	TC/G	FA
1884	KC	U	0	1	.000	3.60	1	1	0	5	11	2	0	0	0	0	0	*				1	1	0	0	2.0	1.000

Nestor Chavez

CHAVEZ, NESTOR ISAIS
Born Nestor Isais Chavez y Silva.
B. July 6, 1947, Chacao, Venezuela　D. Mar. 16, 1969, Maracaibo, Venezuela　BR TR 6' 170 lbs.

Year	Team		W	L	PCT	ERA	G	GS	CG	IP	H	BB	SO	ShO	W	L	SV	AB	H	HR	BA	PO	A	E	DP	TC/G	FA
1967	SF	N	1	0	1.000	0.00	2	0	0	5	4	3	3	0	1	0	0	1	0	0	.000	1	2	1	0	2.0	.750

Dave Cheadle

CHEADLE, DAVID BAIRD
B. Feb. 19, 1952, Greensboro, N. C.　　　　　　　　　　　　　BL TL 6'2" 203 lbs.

Year	Team		W	L	PCT	ERA	G	GS	CG	IP	H	BB	SO	ShO	W	L	SV	AB	H	HR	BA	PO	A	E	DP	TC/G	FA
1973	ATL	N	0	1	.000	18.00	2	0	0	2	2	3	2	0	0	1	0	0	0	0	—	0	0	0	0	0.0	—

Charlie Chech

CHECH, CHARLES WILLIAM
B. Apr. 27, 1878, Madison, Wis.　D. Jan. 31, 1938, Los Angeles, Calif.　　BR TR 5'11½" 190 lbs.

Year	Team		W	L	PCT	ERA	G	GS	CG	IP	H	BB	SO	ShO	W	L	SV	AB	H	HR	BA	PO	A	E	DP	TC/G	FA
1905	CIN	N	14	15	.483	2.89	39	25	20	268	300	77	79	1	2	3	0	89	17	0	.191	11	74	6	7	2.3	.934
1906			1	4	.200	2.32	11	5	5	66	59	24	17	0	0	0	3	25	5	0	.200	2	21	2	0	2.3	.920
1908	CLE	A	11	7	.611	1.74	27	20	14	165.2	136	34	51	4	0	0	0	48	5	0	.104	7	60	1	2	2.5	.985
1909	BOS	A	7	5	.583	2.95	17	13	6	106.2	107	27	40	1	2	1	0	36	3	0	.083	4	33	2	0	2.3	.949
4 yrs.			33	31	.516	2.52	94	63	45	606.1	602	162	187	6	4	4	3	198	30	0	.152	24	188	11	9	2.4	.951

Virgil Cheeves

CHEEVES, VIRGIL EARL (Chief)
B. Feb. 12, 1901, Oklahoma City, Okla.　D. May 5, 1979, Dallas, Tex.　　BR TR 6' 195 lbs.

Year	Team		W	L	PCT	ERA	G	GS	CG	IP	H	BB	SO	ShO	W	L	SV	AB	H	HR	BA	PO	A	E	DP	TC/G	FA
1920	CHI	N	0	0	—	3.50	5	1	0	18	16	7	3	0	0	0	0	4	0	0	.000	0	2	0	0	0.4	1.000
1921			11	12	.478	4.64	37	22	9	163	192	47	39	1	3	1	0	48	8	0	.167	4	33	4	0	1.1	.902
1922			12	11	.522	4.09	39	23	9	182.2	195	76	40	1	3	3	2	62	13	1	.210	3	38	0	3	1.1	1.000
1923			3	4	.429	6.18	19	8	0	71.1	89	37	13	0	3	1	0	23	4	0	.174	2	13	0	1	0.8	1.000
1924	CLE	A	0	0	—	7.79	8	1	0	17.1	26	17	2	0	0	0	0	4	1	0	.250	0	5	0	0	0.6	1.000
1927	NY	N	0	0	—	4.26	3	0	0	6.1	8	4	1	0	0	0	0	0	0	0	—	1	2	0	0	1.0	1.000
6 yrs.			26	27	.491	4.73	111	56	18	458.2	526	188	98	2	9	5	2	141	26	1	.184	10	93	4	4	1.0	.963

Italo Chelini

CHELINI, ITALO VINCENT (Lefty)
B. Oct. 10, 1914, San Francisco, Calif.　D. Aug. 25, 1972, San Francisco, Calif.　　BL TL 5'10½" 175 lbs.

Year	Team		W	L	PCT	ERA	G	GS	CG	IP	H	BB	SO	ShO	W	L	SV	AB	H	HR	BA	PO	A	E	DP	TC/G	FA
1935	CHI	A	0	0	—	12.60	2	0	0	5	7	4	1	0	0	0	0	2	1	0	.500	0	1	0	0	0.5	1.000
1936			4	3	.571	4.95	18	6	5	83.2	100	30	16	0	1	0	0	32	5	0	.156	8	9	1	0	1.0	.944
1937			0	1	.000	10.38	4	0	0	8.2	15	0	3	0	0	1	0	1	0	0	.000	0	1	0	0	0.3	1.000
3 yrs.			4	4	.500	5.83	24	6	5	97.1	122	34	20	0	1	1	0	35	6	0	.171	8	11	1	0	0.8	.950

Larry Cheney

CHENEY, LAURANCE RUSSELL
B. May 2, 1886, Belleville, Kans.　D. Jan. 6, 1969, Daytona Beach, Fla.　　BR TR 6'1½" 185 lbs.

Year	Team		W	L	PCT	ERA	G	GS	CG	IP	H	BB	SO	ShO	W	L	SV	AB	H	HR	BA	PO	A	E	DP	TC/G	FA
1911	CHI	N	1	0	1.000	0.00	3	1	0	10	8	3	11	0	0	0	0	4	1	0	.250	0	5	0	0	1.7	1.000
1912			26	10	.722	2.85	42	37	28	303.1	262	111	140	4	2	0	0	106	24	1	.226	4	67	3	0	1.8	.959
1913			21	14	.600	2.57	54	36	25	305	271	98	136	2	4	3	11	104	20	0	.192	4	82	9	1	1.8	.905
1914			20	18	.526	2.54	50	40	21	311.1	239	140	157	6	3	0	5	100	18	0	.180	7	84	6	4	1.9	.938
1915	2 teams		CHI N	(25G 8–9)		BKN N	(5G 0–2)																					
"	total		8	11	.421	3.24	30	22	7	158.1	136	72	79	2	2	0	0	47	7	0	.149	13	52	8	0	2.4	.890
1916	BKN	N	18	12	.600	1.92	41	32	15	253	178	105	166	5	2	3	0	79	9	0	.114	7	61	7	2	1.8	.907
1917			8	12	.400	2.35	35	24	14	210.1	185	73	102	1	1	0	2	68	14	0	.206	4	56	4	0	1.8	.938
1918			11	13	.458	3.00	32	21	15	200.2	177	74	83	0	2	2	1	66	16	0	.242	8	63	6	0	2.4	.922
1919	3 teams		BKN N	(9G 1–3)		BOS N	(8G 0–2)		PHI N	(9G 2–5)																		
"	total		3	10	.231	4.18	26	12	7	129.1	149	57	52	0	0	0	0	43	6	0	.140	8	31	3	1	1.6	.929
9 yrs.			116	100	.537	2.70	313	225	132	1881.1	1605	733	926	20	18	8	19	617	115	1	.186	55	501	46	8	1.9	.924

WORLD SERIES

Year	Team		W	L	PCT	ERA	G	GS	CG	IP	H	BB	SO	ShO	W	L	SV	AB	H	HR	BA	PO	A	E	DP	TC/G	FA
1916	BKN	N	0	0	—	3.00	1	0	0	3	4	1	5	0	0	0	0	0	0	0	—	0	0	1	0	1.0	—

Year	Team	W	L	PCT	ERA	G	GS	CG	IP	H	BB	SO	ShO	Relief Pitching W	L	SV	Batting AB	H	HR	BA	PO	A	E	DP	TC/G	FA

Tom Cheney

CHENEY, THOMAS EDGAR
B. Oct. 14, 1934, Morgan, Ga.   BR TR 5'11"   170 lbs.

Year	Team	W	L	PCT	ERA	G	GS	CG	IP	H	BB	SO	ShO	W	L	SV	AB	H	HR	BA	PO	A	E	DP	TC/G	FA
1957	STL N	0	1	.000	5.00	4	3	0	9	6	15	10	0	0	0	0	2	0	0	.000	1	2	0	1	0.8	1.000
1959		0	1	.000	6.94	11	2	0	11.2	17	11	8	0	0	1	0	0	0	0	–	0	2	0	0	0.2	1.000
1960	PIT N	2	2	.500	3.98	11	8	1	52	44	33	35	1	0	0	0	17	3	0	.176	2	3	2	0	0.6	.714
1961	2 teams	PIT N	(1G 0–0)			WAS A	(10G 1–3)																			
"	total	1	3	.250	10.01	11	7	0	29.2	33	30	20	0	0	0	0	8	4	0	.500	1	3	1	0	0.5	.800
1962	WAS A	7	9	.438	3.17	37	23	4	173.1	134	97	147	3	0	1	1	48	3	0	.063	9	26	1	1	1.0	.972
1963		8	9	.471	2.71	23	21	7	136.1	99	40	97	4	0	0	0	46	5	0	.109	9	10	3	1	1.0	.864
1964		1	3	.250	3.70	15	6	0	48.2	45	13	25	0	0	0	1	12	3	0	.250	1	7	0	0	0.5	1.000
1966		0	1	.000	5.06	3	1	0	5.1	4	6	3	0	0	0	0	0	0	0	–	0	2	0	1	0.7	1.000
8 yrs.		19	29	.396	3.77	115	71	13	466	382	245	345	8	0	2	2	133	18	0	.135	23	55	7	4	0.7	.918

WORLD SERIES

Year	Team	W	L	PCT	ERA	G	GS	CG	IP	H	BB	SO	ShO	W	L	SV	AB	H	HR	BA	PO	A	E	DP	TC/G	FA
1960	PIT N	0	0	–	4.50	3	0	0	4	4	1	6	0	0	0	0	0	0	0	–	0	1	0	0	0.3	1.000

Jack Chesbro

CHESBRO, JOHN DWIGHT (Happy Jack)
B. June 5, 1874, North Adams, Mass.   D. Nov. 6, 1931, Conway, Mass.   BR TR 5'9"   180 lbs.
Hall of Fame 1946.

Year	Team	W	L	PCT	ERA	G	GS	CG	IP	H	BB	SO	ShO	W	L	SV	AB	H	HR	BA	PO	A	E	DP	TC/G	FA
1899	PIT N	6	9	.400	4.11	19	17	15	149	165	59	28	0	0	0	0	58	9	0	.155	5	26	3	0	1.8	.912
1900		15	13	.536	3.67	32	26	20	215.2	220	79	56	3	1	1	1	85	15	0	.176	4	44	7	3	1.7	.873
1901		21	10	.677	2.38	36	28	26	287.2	261	52	129	6	2	1	1	116	25	1	.216	12	57	5	2	2.1	.932
1902		28	6	.824	2.17	35	33	31	286.1	242	62	136	8	1	0	1	112	20	0	.179	11	60	4	2	2.1	.947
1903	NY A	21	15	.583	2.77	40	36	33	324.2	300	74	147	1	0	1	0	124	23	2	.185	13	103	2	2	3.0	.983
1904		41	12	.774	1.82	55	51	48	454.2	338	88	239	6	3	0	0	174	41	1	.236	24	166	12	7	3.7	.941
1905		19	15	.559	2.20	41	38	24	303.1	262	71	156	3	1	1	0	112	21	0	.188	11	97	7	5	2.8	.939
1906		24	16	.600	2.96	49	42	24	325	314	75	152	4	3	0	1	125	26	1	.208	11	95	5	3	2.3	.955
1907		10	10	.500	2.53	30	25	17	206	192	46	78	1	0	0	0	72	15	0	.208	3	66	5	2	2.5	.932
1908		14	20	.412	2.93	45	31	21	289	271	67	124	3	3	0	1	102	18	0	.176	6	94	6	2	2.4	.943
1909	2 teams	NY A	(9G 0–4)			BOS A	(1G 0–1)																			
"	total	0	5	.000	6.14	10	5	2	55.2	77	17	20	0	0	0	0	19	4	0	.211	2	21	0	0	2.3	1.000
11 yrs.		199	131	.603	2.68	392	332	261	2897	2642	690	1265	35	14	4	5	1099	217	5	.197	102	829	56	28	2.5	.943

Bob Chesnes

CHESNES, ROBERT VINCENT
B. May 6, 1921, Oakland, Calif.   D. May 23, 1979, Everett, Wash.   BB TR 6'   180 lbs.

Year	Team	W	L	PCT	ERA	G	GS	CG	IP	H	BB	SO	ShO	W	L	SV	AB	H	HR	BA	PO	A	E	DP	TC/G	FA
1948	PIT N	14	6	.700	3.57	25	23	15	194.1	180	90	69	0	0	0	0	91	25	1	.275	21	45	3	5	2.8	.957
1949		7	13	.350	5.88	27	25	8	145.1	153	82	49	1	0	0	1	68	17	1	.250	13	35	2	4	1.9	.960
1950		3	3	.500	5.54	9	7	2	39	44	17	12	0	1	0	0	13	2	0	.154	3	15	0	3	2.0	1.000
3 yrs.		24	22	.522	4.66	61	55	25	378.2	377	189	130	1	1	0	1	172	44	2	.256	37	95	5	12	2.2	.964

Mitch Chetkovich

CHETKOVICH, MITCHELL
B. July 21, 1917, Fairpoint, Ohio   D. Aug. 24, 1971, Grass Valley, Calif.   BR TR 6'3½"   208 lbs.

Year	Team	W	L	PCT	ERA	G	GS	CG	IP	H	BB	SO	ShO	W	L	SV	AB	H	HR	BA	PO	A	E	DP	TC/G	FA
1945	PHI N	0	0	–	0.00	4	0	0	3	2	3	0	0	0	0	0	0	0	0	–	0	0	1	0	0.3	–

Tony Chevez

CHEVEZ, SILVIO ANTONIO
Born Silvio Antonio Aquilera y Chevez.
B. June 20, 1954, Telica, Nicaragua   BR TR 5'11"   177 lbs.

Year	Team	W	L	PCT	ERA	G	GS	CG	IP	H	BB	SO	ShO	W	L	SV	AB	H	HR	BA	PO	A	E	DP	TC/G	FA
1977	BAL A	0	0	–	12.38	4	0	0	8	10	8	7	0	0	0	0	0	0	0	–	0	1	1	0	0.5	.500

Floyd Chiffer

CHIFFER, FLOYD JOHN
B. Apr. 20, 1956, Glen Cove, N. Y.   BR TR 6'2"   185 lbs.

Year	Team	W	L	PCT	ERA	G	GS	CG	IP	H	BB	SO	ShO	W	L	SV	AB	H	HR	BA	PO	A	E	DP	TC/G	FA
1982	SD N	4	3	.571	2.95	51	0	0	79.1	73	34	48	0	4	3	4	8	0	0	.000	5	10	0	0	0.3	1.000
1983		0	2	.000	3.18	15	0	0	22.2	17	10	15	0	0	2	1	1	0	0	.000	3	4	0	0	0.5	1.000
1984		1	0	1.000	7.71	15	1	0	28	42	16	20	0	1	0	0	3	0	0	.000	0	2	0	0	0.1	1.000
3 yrs.		5	5	.500	4.02	81	1	0	130	132	60	83	0	5	5	5	12	0	0	.000	8	16	0	0	0.3	1.000

Harry Child

CHILD, HARRY STEPHEN PATRICK
Born Harry Stephen Patrick Chesley.
B. May 23, 1905, Baltimore, Md.   D. Nov. 8, 1972, Alexandria, Va.   BB TR 5'11"   175 lbs.

Year	Team	W	L	PCT	ERA	G	GS	CG	IP	H	BB	SO	ShO	W	L	SV	AB	H	HR	BA	PO	A	E	DP	TC/G	FA
1930	WAS A	0	0	–	6.30	5	0	0	10	10	5	5	0	0	0	0	4	1	0	.250	0	2	0	0	0.4	1.000

Childers

CHILDERS,
B. St. Louis, Mo.   Deceased.

Year	Team	W	L	PCT	ERA	G	GS	CG	IP	H	BB	SO	ShO	W	L	SV	AB	H	HR	BA	PO	A	E	DP	TC/G	FA
1895	LOU N	0	0	–	∞	1	0	0		2	5	0	0	0	0	0	0	0	0	–	0	0	0	0	0.0	–

Rocky Childress

CHILDRESS, RODNEY OSBORNE
B. Feb. 18, 1962, Santa Rosa, Calif.   BR TR 6'2"   185 lbs.

Year	Team	W	L	PCT	ERA	G	GS	CG	IP	H	BB	SO	ShO	W	L	SV	AB	H	HR	BA	PO	A	E	DP	TC/G	FA
1985	PHI N	0	1	.000	6.21	16	1	0	33.1	45	9	14	0	0	0	0	6	1	0	.167	1	4	0	0	0.3	1.000
1986		0	0	–	6.75	2	0	0	2.2	4	1	1	0	0	0	0	0	0	0	–	0	0	0	0	0.0	–
1987	HOU N	1	2	.333	2.98	32	0	0	48.1	46	18	26	0	1	2	0	2	0	0	.000	2	6	0	0	0.3	1.000
1988		1	0	1.000	6.17	11	0	0	23.1	26	9	24	0	1	0	0	4	1	0	.250	0	1	1	1	0.2	.500
4 yrs.		2	3	.400	4.76	61	1	0	107.2	121	37	65	0	2	2	0	12	2	0	.167	3	11	1	1	0.2	.933

Bob Chipman

CHIPMAN, ROBERT HOWARD (Mr. Chips)
B. Oct. 11, 1918, Brooklyn, N. Y.   D. Nov. 8, 1973, Huntington, N. Y.   BL TL 6'2"   190 lbs.

Year	Team	W	L	PCT	ERA	G	GS	CG	IP	H	BB	SO	ShO	W	L	SV	AB	H	HR	BA	PO	A	E	DP	TC/G	FA
1941	BKN N	1	0	1.000	0.00	1	1	0	5	3	1	3	0	1	0	0	3	0	0	.000	1	0	0	0	1.0	1.000
1942		0	0	–	0.00	2	0	0	1.1	1	2	1	0	0	0	0	0	0	0	–	0	0	0	0	0.0	–
1943		0	0	–	0.00	1	0	0	1.2	2	2	0	0	0	0	0	0	0	0	–	0	0	0	0	0.0	–

Year	Team	W	L	PCT	ERA	G	GS	CG	IP	H	BB	SO	ShO	Relief Pitching W	L	SV	Batting AB	H	HR	BA	PO	A	E	DP	TC/G	FA

Bob Chipman *continued*

Year	Team	W	L	PCT	ERA	G	GS	CG	IP	H	BB	SO	ShO	W	L	SV	AB	H	HR	BA	PO	A	E	DP	TC/G	FA
1944	2 teams	BKN N	(11G 3–1)		CHI N	(26G 9–9)																				
"	total	12	10	.545	3.65	37	24	9	165.1	185	64	61	1	2	3	2	59	7	0	.119	5	32	2	2	1.1	.949
1945	CHI N	4	5	.444	3.50	25	10	3	72	63	34	29	1	0	1	0	17	3	0	.176	4	16	1	1	0.8	.952
1946		6	5	.545	3.13	34	10	5	109.1	103	54	42	3	1	0	2	33	2	0	.061	10	15	1	3	0.8	.962
1947		7	6	.538	3.68	32	17	5	134.2	135	66	51	1	1	0	0	44	4	0	.091	5	32	0	2	1.2	1.000
1948		2	1	.667	3.58	34	3	0	60.1	73	24	16	0	2	0	4	16	4	0	.250	2	18	0	0	0.6	1.000
1949		7	8	.467	3.97	38	11	3	113.1	110	63	46	1	3	2	1	24	3	0	.125	9	12	0	1	0.6	1.000
1950	BOS N	7	7	.500	4.43	27	12	4	124	127	37	40	0	2	1	1	39	6	0	.154	5	12	2	0	0.7	.895
1951		4	3	.571	4.85	33	0	0	52	59	19	17	0	4	3	4	10	1	0	.100	9	5	0	1	0.4	1.000
1952		1	1	.500	2.81	29	0	0	41.2	28	20	16	0	1	1	0	5	2	0	.400	3	8	1	1	0.4	.917
12 yrs.		51	46	.526	3.72	293	87	29	880.2	889	386	322	7	17	11	14	250	32	0	.128	53	150	7	11	0.7	.967

WORLD SERIES

Year	Team	W	L	PCT	ERA	G	GS	CG	IP	H	BB	SO	ShO	W	L	SV	AB	H	HR	BA	PO	A	E	DP	TC/G	FA
1945	CHI N	0	0	–	0.00	1	0	0	.1	0	1	0	0	0	0	0	0	0	0	–	0	0	0	0	0.0	–

Nels Chittum

CHITTUM, NELSON BOYD
B. Mar. 25, 1933, Harrisonburg, Va.   BR TR 6'1"   180 lbs.

Year	Team	W	L	PCT	ERA	G	GS	CG	IP	H	BB	SO	ShO	W	L	SV	AB	H	HR	BA	PO	A	E	DP	TC/G	FA
1958	STL N	0	1	.000	6.44	13	2	0	29.1	31	7	13	0	0	0	0	4	1	0	.250	4	4	0	0	0.6	1.000
1959	BOS A	3	0	1.000	1.19	21	0	0	30.1	29	11	12	0	3	0	0	5	1	0	.200	1	9	0	0	0.5	1.000
1960		0	0	–	4.32	6	0	0	8.1	8	6	5	0	0	0	0	1	0	0	.000	1	1	0	0	0.3	1.000
3 yrs.		3	1	.750	3.84	40	2	0	68	68	24	30	0	3	0	0	10	2	0	.200	6	14	0	0	0.5	1.000

Bob Chlupsa

CHLUPSA, ROBERT JOSEPH
B. Sept. 16, 1945, New York, N. Y.   BR TR 6'7"   215 lbs.

Year	Team	W	L	PCT	ERA	G	GS	CG	IP	H	BB	SO	ShO	W	L	SV	AB	H	HR	BA	PO	A	E	DP	TC/G	FA
1970	STL N	0	2	.000	9.00	14	0	0	16	26	9	10	0	0	2	0	0	0	0	–	1	5	0	1	0.4	1.000
1971		0	0	–	9.00	1	0	0	2	3	0	1	0	0	0	0	0	0	0	–	0	1	0	0	1.0	1.000
2 yrs.		0	2	.000	9.00	15	0	0	18	29	9	11	0	0	2	0	0	0	0	–	1	6	0	1	0.5	1.000

Don Choate

CHOATE, DONALD LEON
B. July 2, 1938, Potosi, Mo.   BR TR 6'   185 lbs.

Year	Team	W	L	PCT	ERA	G	GS	CG	IP	H	BB	SO	ShO	W	L	SV	AB	H	HR	BA	PO	A	E	DP	TC/G	FA
1960	SF N	0	0	–	2.25	4	0	0	8	7	4	7	0	0	0	0	0	0	0	–	0	3	0	1	0.8	1.000

Chief Chouneau

CHOUNEAU, WILLIAM
Born William Cadreau.
B. Sept. 2, 1889, Cloquet, Minn.   D. Sept. 17, 1948, Cloquet, Minn.   BR TR 5'9"   150 lbs.

Year	Team	W	L	PCT	ERA	G	GS	CG	IP	H	BB	SO	ShO	W	L	SV	AB	H	HR	BA	PO	A	E	DP	TC/G	FA
1910	CHI A	0	1	.000	3.38	1	1	0	5.1	7	0	1	0	0	0	0	1	0	0	.000	0	0	0	0	0.0	–

Mike Chris

CHRIS, MICHAEL
B. Oct. 8, 1957, Santa Monica, Calif.   BL TL 6'3"   180 lbs.

Year	Team	W	L	PCT	ERA	G	GS	CG	IP	H	BB	SO	ShO	W	L	SV	AB	H	HR	BA	PO	A	E	DP	TC/G	FA
1979	DET A	3	3	.500	6.92	13	8	0	39	46	21	31	0	0	0	0	0	0	0	–	1	8	0	0	0.7	1.000
1982	SF N	0	2	.000	4.85	9	6	0	26	23	26	10	0	0	0	0	7	1	0	.143	2	10	0	0	1.3	1.000
1983		0	0	–	8.10	7	0	0	13.1	16	16	5	0	0	0	0	2	0	0	.000	0	1	1	0	0.3	.500
3 yrs.		3	5	.375	6.43	29	14	0	78.1	85	63	46	0	0	0	0	9	1	0	.111	3	19	1	0	0.8	.957

Gary Christenson

CHRISTENSON, GARY RICHARD
B. May 5, 1953, Mineola, N. Y.   BL TL 6'5"   200 lbs.

Year	Team	W	L	PCT	ERA	G	GS	CG	IP	H	BB	SO	ShO	W	L	SV	AB	H	HR	BA	PO	A	E	DP	TC/G	FA
1979	KC A	0	0	–	3.27	6	0	0	11	10	2	4	0	0	0	0	0	0	0	–	2	1	0	1	0.5	1.000
1980		3	0	1.000	5.23	24	0	0	31	35	18	16	0	3	0	1	0	0	0	–	0	8	0	0	0.3	1.000
2 yrs.		3	0	1.000	4.71	30	0	0	42	45	20	20	0	3	0	1	0	0	0	–	2	9	0	1	0.4	1.000

Larry Christenson

CHRISTENSON, LARRY RICHARD
B. Nov. 10, 1953, Everett, Wash.   BR TR 6'4"   215 lbs.

Year	Team	W	L	PCT	ERA	G	GS	CG	IP	H	BB	SO	ShO	W	L	SV	AB	H	HR	BA	PO	A	E	DP	TC/G	FA
1973	PHI N	1	4	.200	6.55	10	9	1	34.1	53	20	11	0	0	0	0	10	0	0	.000	2	5	0	0	0.7	1.000
1974		1	1	.500	4.30	10	1	0	23	20	15	18	0	1	0	2	4	0	0	.000	1	2	0	0	0.3	1.000
1975		11	6	.647	3.66	29	26	5	172	149	45	88	2	0	0	0	57	14	2	.246	14	12	2	1	1.0	.929
1976		13	8	.619	3.68	32	29	2	168.2	199	42	54	0	0	0	0	51	10	2	.196	9	14	3	1	0.8	.885
1977		19	6	.760	4.07	34	34	5	219	229	69	118	1	0	0	0	74	10	3	.135	14	28	8	1	1.5	.840
1978		13	14	.481	3.24	33	33	9	228	209	47	131	3	0	0	0	67	5	1	.075	8	37	3	1	1.5	.938
1979		5	10	.333	4.50	19	17	2	106	118	30	53	0	0	0	0	31	9	1	.290	4	15	0	0	1.0	1.000
1980		5	1	.833	4.01	14	14	0	74	62	27	49	0	0	0	0	19	7	1	.368	5	16	3	0	1.7	.875
1981		4	7	.364	3.53	20	15	0	107	108	30	70	0	1	1	1	30	3	0	.100	8	13	2	2	1.2	.913
1982		9	10	.474	3.47	33	33	3	223	212	53	145	0	0	0	0	67	5	1	.075	16	26	2	2	1.3	.955
1983		2	4	.333	3.91	9	9	0	48.1	42	17	44	0	0	0	0	17	1	0	.059	4	9	1	0	1.6	.929
11 yrs.		83	71	.539	3.79	243	220	27	1403.1	1401	395	781	6	2	1	4	427	64	11	.150	85	177	24	6	1.2	.916

DIVISIONAL PLAYOFF SERIES

Year	Team	W	L	PCT	ERA	G	GS	CG	IP	H	BB	SO	ShO	W	L	SV	AB	H	HR	BA	PO	A	E	DP	TC/G	FA
1981	PHI N	1	0	1.000	1.50	1	1	0	6	4	1	8	0	0	0	0	2	0	0	.000	0	0	0	0	0.0	–

LEAGUE CHAMPIONSHIP SERIES

Year	Team	W	L	PCT	ERA	G	GS	CG	IP	H	BB	SO	ShO	W	L	SV	AB	H	HR	BA	PO	A	E	DP	TC/G	FA
1977	PHI N	0	0	–	8.10	1	1	0	3.1	7	0	2	0	0	0	0	0	0	0	–	0	0	0	0	0.0	–
1978		0	1	.000	12.46	1	1	0	4.1	7	1	3	0	0	0	0	1	0	0	.000	0	0	0	0	0.0	–
1980		0	0	–	4.05	2	0	0	6.2	5	5	2	0	0	0	0	2	0	0	.000	0	1	1	0	1.0	.500
3 yrs.		0	1	.000	7.53	4	3	0	14.1	19	6	7	0	0	0	0	3	0	0	.000	0	1	1	0	0.5	.500

WORLD SERIES

Year	Team	W	L	PCT	ERA	G	GS	CG	IP	H	BB	SO	ShO	W	L	SV	AB	H	HR	BA	PO	A	E	DP	TC/G	FA
1980	PHI N	0	1	.000	108.00	1	1	0	.1	5	0	0	0	0	0	0	0	0	0	–	0	0	1	0	1.0	–

Clay Christiansen

CHRISTIANSEN, CLAY C.
B. June 28, 1958, Wichita, Kans.   BR TR 6'5"   215 lbs.

Year	Team	W	L	PCT	ERA	G	GS	CG	IP	H	BB	SO	ShO	W	L	SV	AB	H	HR	BA	PO	A	E	DP	TC/G	FA
1984	NY A	2	4	.333	6.05	24	1	0	38.2	50	12	27	0	2	3	2	0	0	0	–	5	3	1	0	0.4	.889

Year	Team	W	L	PCT	ERA	G	GS	CG	IP	H	BB	SO	ShO	Relief Pitching W	L	SV	Batting AB	H	HR	BA	PO	A	E	DP	TC/G	FA

Russ Christopher

CHRISTOPHER, RUSSELL ORMAND
Brother of Lloyd Christopher.
B. Sept. 12, 1917, Richmond, Calif. D. Dec. 5, 1954, Richmond, Calif.

BR TR 6'3½" 170 lbs.

Year	Team	W	L	PCT	ERA	G	GS	CG	IP	H	BB	SO	ShO	W	L	SV	AB	H	HR	BA	PO	A	E	DP	TC/G	FA
1942	PHI A	4	13	.235	3.82	30	18	10	165	154	99	58	0	0	1	1	56	5	0	.089	10	60	2	5	2.4	.972
1943		5	8	.385	3.45	24	15	5	133	120	58	56	0	1	3	2	45	7	0	.156	11	61	1	5	3.0	.986
1944		14	14	.500	2.97	35	24	13	215.1	200	63	84	1	2	2	1	81	18	1	.222	27	58	3	5	2.5	.966
1945		13	13	.500	3.17	33	27	17	227.1	213	75	100	2	1	0	2	76	13	1	.171	26	71	1	4	3.0	.990
1946		5	7	.417	4.30	30	13	1	119.1	119	44	79	0	0	1	0	36	5	0	.139	7	38	1	1	1.5	.978
1947		10	7	.588	2.90	44	0	0	80.2	70	33	33	0	10	7	12	16	2	0	.125	10	13	1	0	0.5	.958
1948	CLE A	3	2	.600	2.90	45	0	0	59	55	27	14	0	3	2	17	6	0	0	.000	2	13	0	0	0.3	1.000
7 yrs.		54	64	.458	3.37	241	97	46	999.2	931	399	424	3	17	16	35	316	50	2	.158	93	314	9	20	1.7	.978

WORLD SERIES

| 1948 | CLE A | 0 | 0 | — | ∞ | 1 | 0 | 0 | | 2 | 0 | 0 | 0 | 0 | 0 | 0 | 0 | 0 | 0 | — | 0 | 0 | 0 | 0 | 0.0 | — |

Bubba Church

CHURCH, EMORY NICHOLAS
B. Sept. 12, 1924, Birmingham, Ala.

BR TR 6' 180 lbs.

Year	Team	W	L	PCT	ERA	G	GS	CG	IP	H	BB	SO	ShO	W	L	SV	AB	H	HR	BA	PO	A	E	DP	TC/G	FA
1950	PHI N	8	6	.571	2.73	31	18	8	142	113	56	50	2	0	0	1	44	8	0	.182	7	24	1	5	1.0	.969
1951		15	11	.577	3.53	38	33	15	247	246	90	104	4	1	1	1	86	22	1	.256	14	34	1	3	1.3	.980
1952	2 teams	PHI N	(2G 0–0)		CIN N	(29G 5–9)																				
"	total	5	9	.357	4.55	31	23	5	158.1	184	49	50	1	0	0	1	51	12	1	.235	14	24	3	1	1.3	.974
1953	2 teams	CIN N	(11G 3–3)		CHI N	(27G 4–5)																				
"	total	7	8	.467	3.25	38	18	3	148	170	68	59	0	2	2	1	48	11	1	.229	6	24	5	2	0.9	.857
1954	CHI N	1	3	.250	9.82	7	3	1	14.2	21	13	8	0	0	1	0	5	0	0	.000	2	2	0	0	0.6	1.000
1955		0	0	—	5.40	2	0	0	3.1	4	1	3	0	0	0	0	1	0	0	.000	0	0	0	0	0.0	—
6 yrs.		36	37	.493	4.10	147	95	32	713.1	738	277	274	7	3	4	4	235	53	3	.226	43	108	8	13	1.1	.950

Len Church

CHURCH, LEONARD
B. Mar. 21, 1942, Chicago, Ill. D. Apr. 22, 1988, Richardson, Tex.

BB TR 6' 190 lbs.

Year	Team	W	L	PCT	ERA	G	GS	CG	IP	H	BB	SO	ShO	W	L	SV	AB	H	HR	BA	PO	A	E	DP	TC/G	FA
1966	CHI N	0	1	.000	7.50	4	0	0	6	10	7	3	0	0	1	0	1	0	0	.000	0	1	0	0	0.3	1.000

Chuck Churn

CHURN, CLARENCE NOTTINGHAM
B. Feb. 1, 1930, Bridgetown, Va.

BR TR 6'3" 205 lbs.

Year	Team	W	L	PCT	ERA	G	GS	CG	IP	H	BB	SO	ShO	W	L	SV	AB	H	HR	BA	PO	A	E	DP	TC/G	FA
1957	PIT N	0	0	—	4.32	5	0	0	8.1	9	4	4	0	0	0	0	0	0	0	.000	2	4	0	1	1.2	1.000
1958	CLE A	0	0	—	6.23	6	0	0	8.2	12	5	4	0	0	0	0	0	0	0	—	1	1	0	0	0.3	1.000
1959	LA N	3	2	.600	4.99	14	0	0	30.2	28	10	24	0	3	2	1	6	1	0	.167	1	7	0	0	0.6	1.000
3 yrs.		3	2	.600	5.10	25	0	0	47.2	49	19	32	0	3	2	1	7	1	0	.143	4	12	0	1	0.6	1.000

WORLD SERIES

| 1959 | LA N | 0 | 0 | — | 27.00 | 1 | 0 | 0 | .2 | 5 | 0 | 0 | 0 | 0 | 0 | 0 | 0 | 0 | 0 | — | 0 | 1 | 0 | 0 | 1.0 | 1.000 |

Mark Ciardi

CIARDI, MARK THOMAS
B. Aug. 19, 1961, New Brunswick, N. J.

BR TR 6' 180 lbs.

Year	Team	W	L	PCT	ERA	G	GS	CG	IP	H	BB	SO	ShO	W	L	SV	AB	H	HR	BA	PO	A	E	DP	TC/G	FA
1987	MIL A	1	1	.500	9.37	4	3	0	16.1	26	9	8	0	0	0	0	0	0	0	—	0	3	0	0	0.8	1.000

Al Cicotte

CICOTTE, ALVA WARREN (Bozo)
B. Dec. 23, 1929, Melvindale, Mich. D. Nov. 29, 1982, Westland, Mich.

BR TR 6'3" 185 lbs.

Year	Team	W	L	PCT	ERA	G	GS	CG	IP	H	BB	SO	ShO	W	L	SV	AB	H	HR	BA	PO	A	E	DP	TC/G	FA
1957	NY A	2	2	.500	3.03	20	2	0	65.1	57	30	36	0	2	0	2	20	3	0	.150	6	10	0	0	0.8	1.000
1958	2 teams	WAS A	(8G 0–3)		DET A	(14G 3–1)																				
"	total	3	4	.429	4.06	22	6	0	71	86	29	35	0	2	1	0	27	5	0	.185	6	15	2	0	1.0	.913
1959	CLE A	3	1	.750	5.32	26	1	0	44	46	25	23	0	3	1	1	3	1	0	.333	3	8	0	0	0.4	1.000
1961	STL N	2	6	.250	5.28	29	7	0	75	83	34	51	0	2	3	1	21	6	0	.286	7	12	0	1	0.7	1.000
1962	HOU N	0	0	—	3.86	5	0	0	4.2	8	1	4	0	0	0	0	0	0	0	—	1	0	0	0	0.2	1.000
5 yrs.		10	13	.435	4.36	102	16	0	260	280	119	149	0	9	5	4	71	15	0	.211	23	45	2	1	0.7	.971

Eddie Cicotte

CICOTTE, EDWARD VICTOR
B. June 19, 1884, Detroit, Mich. D. May 5, 1969, Detroit, Mich.

BB TR 5'9" 175 lbs.

Year	Team	W	L	PCT	ERA	G	GS	CG	IP	H	BB	SO	ShO	W	L	SV	AB	H	HR	BA	PO	A	E	DP	TC/G	FA
1905	DET A	1	1	.500	3.50	3	1	1	18	25	5	6	0	0	1	0	7	3	0	.429	1	2	0	0	1.0	1.000
1908	BOS A	11	12	.478	2.43	39	24	17	207.1	198	59	95	2	1	2	2	72	17	0	.236	12	65	8	0	2.2	.906
1909		13	5	.722	1.97	27	15	10	159.2	117	56	82	1	4	0	2	49	11	0	.224	4	50	8	0	2.3	.871
1910		15	11	.577	2.74	36	30	20	250	213	86	104	4	1	0	0	85	12	0	.141	9	98	6	1	3.1	.947
1911		11	15	.423	2.81	35	25	16	221	236	73	106	1	2	2	0	71	10	0	.141	11	62	7	2	2.3	.913
1912	2 teams	BOS A	(9G 1–3)		CHI A	(20G 9–7)																				
"	total	10	10	.500	3.50	29	24	15	198	217	52	90	1	0	0	1	69	15	0	.217	10	71	6	6	3.0	.931
1913	CHI A	18	12	.600	1.58	41	30	18	268	224	73	121	3	2	0	1	91	13	0	.143	10	109	3	9	3.0	.975
1914		11	16	.407	2.04	45	29	15	269.1	220	72	122	4	1	0	3	86	14	0	.163	8	110	6	4	2.8	.952
1915		13	12	.520	3.02	39	26	15	223.1	216	48	106	1	1	0	3	67	14	0	.209	5	68	3	2	1.9	.961
1916		15	7	.682	1.78	44	19	11	187	138	70	91	2	3	2	5	57	12	0	.211	9	55	6	4	1.6	.914
1917		28	12	.700	1.53	49	35	29	346.2	246	70	150	7	5	1	4	112	20	0	.179	14	94	5	2	2.3	.956
1918		12	19	.387	2.64	38	30	24	266	275	40	104	1	2	1	0	86	14	0	.163	9	71	4	0	2.2	.952
1919		29	7	.806	1.82	40	35	30	306.2	256	49	110	5	2	1	0	99	20	0	.202	13	64	3	1	2.0	.963
1920		21	10	.677	3.26	37	35	28	303.1	316	74	87	4	0	0	2	112	22	0	.196	13	81	5	3	2.7	.949
14 yrs.		208	149	.583	2.37	502	358	249	3224.1	2897	827	1374	36	24	13	25	1063	197	0	.185	128	1000	70	36	2.4	.942

WORLD SERIES

1917	CHI A	1	1	.500	1.96	3	2	2	23	23	2	13	0	0	0	0	7	1	0	.143	0	7	1	0	2.7	.875
1919		1	2	.333	2.91	3	3	2	21.2	19	5	7	0	0	0	0	8	0	0	.000	0	7	2	1	3.0	.778
2 yrs.		2	3	.400	2.42	6	5	4	44.2	42	7	20	0	0	0	0	15	1	0	.067	0	14	3	1	2.8	.824

Pete Cimino

CIMINO, PETER WILLIAM
B. Oct. 17, 1942, Philadelphia, Pa.

BR TR 6'2" 195 lbs.

Year	Team	W	L	PCT	ERA	G	GS	CG	IP	H	BB	SO	ShO	W	L	SV	AB	H	HR	BA	PO	A	E	DP	TC/G	FA
1965	MIN A	0	0	—	0.00	1	0	0	1	0	0	0	0	0	0	0	0	0	0	—	0	0	0	0	0.0	—
1966		2	5	.286	2.92	35	0	0	64.2	53	30	57	0	2	5	4	6	0	0	.000	0	8	1	1	0.3	.889

Year	Team		W	L	PCT	ERA	G	GS	CG	IP	H	BB	SO	ShO	W	L	SV	AB	H	HR	BA	PO	A	E	DP	TC/G	FA
															Relief Pitching			**Batting**									

Pete Cimino *continued*

Year	Team		W	L	PCT	ERA	G	GS	CG	IP	H	BB	SO	ShO	W	L	SV	AB	H	HR	BA	PO	A	E	DP	TC/G	FA
1967	CAL	A	3	3	.500	3.26	46	1	0	88.1	73	31	80	0	3	3	1	12	5	0	.417	4	6	1	0	0.2	.909
1968			0	0	–	2.57	4	0	0	7	7	4	2	0	0	0	0	0	0	0	–	0	0	0	0	0.0	–
4 yrs.			5	8	.385	3.07	86	1	0	161	133	65	139	0	5	8	5	18	5	0	.278	4	14	2	1	0.2	.900

Lou Ciola

CIOLA, LOUIS ALEXANDER
B. Sept. 6, 1922, Norfolk, Va.

BR TR 5'9" 165 lbs.

Year	Team		W	L	PCT	ERA	G	GS	CG	IP	H	BB	SO	ShO	W	L	SV	AB	H	HR	BA	PO	A	E	DP	TC/G	FA
1943	PHI	A	1	3	.250	5.56	12	3	2	43.2	48	22	7	0	0	1	0	18	3	0	.167	2	9	2	0	1.1	.846

Galen Cisco

CISCO, GALEN BERNARD
B. Mar. 7, 1936, St. Mary's, Ohio

BR TR 6' 200 lbs.

Year	Team		W	L	PCT	ERA	G	GS	CG	IP	H	BB	SO	ShO	W	L	SV	AB	H	HR	BA	PO	A	E	DP	TC/G	FA
1961	BOS	A	2	4	.333	6.71	17	8	0	52.1	67	28	26	0	1	0	0	10	1	0	.100	3	7	0	1	0.6	1.000
1962	2 teams		BOS A	(23G 4–7)		NY N	(4G 1–1)																				
"	total		5	8	.385	6.07	27	11	2	102.1	110	61	56	0	1	1	0	32	2	0	.063	6	22	1	3	1.1	.966
1963	NY	N	7	15	.318	4.34	51	17	1	155.2	165	64	81	0	5	3	0	38	5	0	.132	9	26	1	0	0.7	.972
1964			6	19	.240	3.62	36	25	5	191.2	182	54	78	2	0	3	0	54	6	0	.111	15	42	2	6	1.6	.966
1965			4	8	.333	4.49	35	17	1	112.1	119	51	58	1	0	0	0	27	7	0	.259	7	12	2	3	0.6	.905
1967	BOS	A	0	1	.000	3.63	11	0	0	22.1	21	8	8	0	0	1	1	3	0	0	.000	1	4	0	0	0.5	1.000
1969	KC	A	1	1	.500	3.63	15	0	0	22.1	17	15	18	0	1	1	1	0	0	0	–	2	5	1	0	0.5	.875
7 yrs.			25	56	.309	4.56	192	78	9	659	681	281	325	3	8	9	2	164	21	0	.128	43	118	7	13	0.9	.958

Ralph Citarella

CITARELLA, RALPH ALEXANDER
B. Feb. 7, 1958, East Orange, N. J.

BR TR 6' 175 lbs.

Year	Team		W	L	PCT	ERA	G	GS	CG	IP	H	BB	SO	ShO	W	L	SV	AB	H	HR	BA	PO	A	E	DP	TC/G	FA
1983	STL	N	0	0	–	1.64	6	0	0	11	8	3	4	0	0	0	0	1	0	0	.000	1	1	0	0	0.3	1.000
1984			0	1	.000	3.63	10	2	0	22.1	20	7	15	0	0	0	0	4	1	0	.250	0	6	0	0	0.6	1.000
1987	CHI	A	0	0	–	7.36	5	0	0	11	13	4	9	0	0	0	0	0	0	0	–	0	1	0	0	0.2	1.000
3 yrs.			0	1	.000	4.06	21	2	0	44.1	41	14	28	0	0	0	0	5	1	0	.200	1	8	0	0	0.4	1.000

Bobby Clack

CLACK, ROBERT S. (Gentlemanly Bobby)
Born Robert S. Clark.
B. 1851, Brooklyn, N. Y. D. Oct. 22, 1933, Danvers, Mass.

BR TR 5'9" 153 lbs.

Year	Team		W	L	PCT	ERA	G	GS	CG	IP	H	BB	SO	ShO	W	L	SV	AB	H	HR	BA	PO	A	E	DP	TC/G	FA
1876	CIN	N	0	0	–	4.50	1	0	0	2	2	0	0	0	0	0	0	*				0	1	0	0	1.0	1.000

Jim Clancy

CLANCY, JAMES
B. Dec. 18, 1955, Chicago, Ill.

BR TR 6'2" 185 lbs.

Year	Team		W	L	PCT	ERA	G	GS	CG	IP	H	BB	SO	ShO	W	L	SV	AB	H	HR	BA	PO	A	E	DP	TC/G	FA
1977	TOR	A	4	9	.308	5.03	13	13	4	77	80	47	44	1	0	0	0				–	6	14	3	4	1.8	.870
1978			10	12	.455	4.09	31	30	7	193.2	199	91	106	0	0	0	0				–	14	30	2	3	1.5	.957
1979			2	7	.222	5.48	12	11	2	64	65	31	33	0	0	0	0				–	1	11	0	0	1.0	1.000
1980			13	16	.448	3.30	34	34	15	251	217	**128**	152	2	0	0	0				–	14	35	2	1	1.5	.961
1981			6	12	.333	4.90	22	22	2	125	126	64	56	0	0	0	0				–	2	10	0	0	0.5	1.000
1982			16	14	.533	3.71	40	**40**	11	266.2	251	77	139	3	0	0	0				–	14	27	2	2	1.1	.953
1983			15	11	.577	3.91	34	34	11	223	238	61	99	1	0	0	0				–	23	17	1	1	1.2	.976
1984			13	15	.464	5.12	36	**36**	5	219.2	249	88	118	0	0	0	0				–	15	30	1	4	1.3	.978
1985			9	6	.600	3.78	23	23	1	128.2	117	37	66	0	0	0	0				–	6	15	1	1	1.0	.955
1986			14	14	.500	3.94	34	34	6	219.1	202	63	126	3	0	0	0				–	34	23	1	2	1.7	.983
1987			15	11	.577	3.54	37	37	5	241.1	234	80	180	1	0	0	0				–	25	36	2	4	1.7	.968
1988			11	13	.458	4.49	36	31	4	196.1	207	47	118	0	0	0	1				–	15	21	3	4	1.1	.923
1989	HOU	N	7	14	.333	5.08	33	26	1	147	155	66	91	0	1	1	0	41	6	0	.146	9	10	7	2	0.8	.731
13 yrs.			135	154	.467	4.16	385	371	74	2352.2	2340	880	1328	11	1	1	1	41	6	0	.146	178	279	25	29	1.3	.948

LEAGUE CHAMPIONSHIP SERIES

Year	Team		W	L	PCT	ERA	G	GS	CG	IP	H	BB	SO	ShO	W	L	SV	AB	H	HR	BA	PO	A	E	DP	TC/G	FA
1985	TOR	A	0	1	.000	9.00	1	0	0	1	2	1	0	0	0	0	0				–	0	1	0	0	1.0	1.000

Bill Clark

CLARK, WILLIAM WINFIELD (Win)
B. Apr. 11, 1875, Circleville, Ohio D. Apr. 15, 1959, Los Angeles, Calif.

BR TR 5'10" 175 lbs.

Year	Team		W	L	PCT	ERA	G	GS	CG	IP	H	BB	SO	ShO	W	L	SV	AB	H	HR	BA	PO	A	E	DP	TC/G	FA
1897	LOU	N	1	1	.500	4.15	3	2	2	21.2	30	1	1	0	0	0	0	*				3	5	0	0	2.7	1.000

Bob Clark

CLARK, ROBERT WILLIAM
B. Aug. 22, 1897, Newport, Pa. D. May 18, 1944, Carlsbad, N. M.

BR TR 6'3" 188 lbs.

Year	Team		W	L	PCT	ERA	G	GS	CG	IP	H	BB	SO	ShO	W	L	SV	AB	H	HR	BA	PO	A	E	DP	TC/G	FA
1920	CLE	A	1	2	.333	3.43	11	2	2	42	59	13	8	1	0	1	0	10	2	0	.200	0	10	0	0	0.9	1.000
1921			0	0	–	14.46	5	0	0	9.1	23	6	2	0	0	0	0	3	0	0	.000	0	2	0	0	0.4	1.000
2 yrs.			1	2	.333	5.44	16	2	2	51.1	82	19	10	1	0	1	0	13	2	0	.154	0	12	0	0	0.8	1.000

Bryan Clark

CLARK, BRYAN DONALD
B. July 12, 1956, Madera, Calif.

BL TL 6'2" 185 lbs.

Year	Team		W	L	PCT	ERA	G	GS	CG	IP	H	BB	SO	ShO	W	L	SV	AB	H	HR	BA	PO	A	E	DP	TC/G	FA
1981	SEA	A	2	5	.286	4.35	29	9	1	93	92	55	52	0	2	1	0	0	0	0	–	0	22	1	0	0.8	.957
1982			5	2	.714	2.75	37	5	1	114.2	104	58	70	1	2	1	0	0	0	0	–	7	20	0	3	0.7	1.000
1983			7	10	.412	3.94	41	17	2	162.1	160	72	76	0	4	2	0	0	0	0	–	8	38	3	4	1.2	.939
1984	TOR	A	1	2	.333	5.91	20	3	0	45.2	66	22	21	0	1	1	0	0	0	0	–	1	13	0	0	0.7	1.000
1985	CLE	A	3	4	.429	6.32	31	3	0	62.2	78	34	24	0	3	2	2	0	0	0	–	7	13	1	2	0.7	.952
1986	CHI	A	0	0	–	4.50	5	0	0	8	8	2	5	0	0	0	0	0	0	0	–	2	0	0	0	0.4	1.000
1987			0	0	–	2.41	11	0	0	18.2	19	8	8	0	0	0	0	0	0	0	–	0	1	0	0	0.1	1.000
7 yrs.			18	23	.439	4.17	174	37	4	505	527	251	256	1	12	7	4	0	0	0	–	25	107	5	9	0.8	.964

Ed Clark

CLARK, EDWARD C.
B. Cincinnati, Ohio Deceased.

Year	Team		W	L	PCT	ERA	G	GS	CG	IP	H	BB	SO	ShO	W	L	SV	AB	H	HR	BA	PO	A	E	DP	TC/G	FA
1886	PHI	AA	0	1	.000	6.75	1	1	1	8	10	2	1	0	0	0	0	2	0	0	.000	0	0	0	0	0.0	–
1891	COL	AA	0	0	–	0.00	1	0	0	2	2	0	1	0	0	0	0	1	0	0	.000	0	1	0	1	1.0	1.000
2 yrs.			0	1	.000	5.40	2	1	1	10	12	2	3	0	0	0	0	3	0	0	.000	0	1	0	1	0.5	1.000

Year	Team		W	L	PCT	ERA	G	GS	CG	IP	H	BB	SO	ShO	W	L	SV	AB	H	HR	BA	PO	A	E	DP	TC/G	FA
															Relief Pitching			**Batting**									

George Clark

CLARK, GEORGE MYRON
B. May 19, 1891, Smithland, Iowa D. Nov. 14, 1940, Sioux City, Iowa

BR TL 6' 190 lbs.

Year	Team	W	L	PCT	ERA	G	GS	CG	IP	H	BB	SO	ShO	W	L	SV	AB	H	HR	BA	PO	A	E	DP	TC/G	FA
1913	NY A	0	1	.000	9.00	11	1	0	19	22	19	5	0	0	0	0	4	2	0	.500	0	6	1	0	0.6	.857

Ginger Clark

CLARK, HARVEY DANIEL
B. Mar. 7, 1879, Wooster, Ohio D. May 10, 1943, Lake Charles, La.

BR TR 5'11" 165 lbs.

Year	Team	W	L	PCT	ERA	G	GS	CG	IP	H	BB	SO	ShO	W	L	SV	AB	H	HR	BA	PO	A	E	DP	TC/G	FA
1902	CLE A	1	0	1.000	6.00	1	0	0	6	10	3	1	0	1	0	0	4	2	0	.500	0	3	0	0	3.0	1.000

Mike Clark

CLARK, MICHAEL JOHN
B. Feb. 12, 1922, Camden, N. J.

BR TR 6'4" 190 lbs.

Year	Team	W	L	PCT	ERA	G	GS	CG	IP	H	BB	SO	ShO	W	L	SV	AB	H	HR	BA	PO	A	E	DP	TC/G	FA
1952	STL N	2	0	1.000	6.04	12	4	0	25.1	32	14	10	0	2	0	0	5	0	0	.000	3	5	1	1	0.8	.889
1953		1	0	1.000	4.79	23	2	0	35.2	46	21	17	0	0	0	1	6	0	0	.000	3	9	3	1	0.7	.800
2 yrs.		3	0	1.000	5.31	35	6	0	61	78	35	27	0	2	0	1	11	0	0	.000	6	14	4	2	0.7	.833

Otie Clark

CLARK, WILLIAM OTIS
B. May 22, 1918, Boscobel, Wis.

BR TR 6'1½" 190 lbs.

Year	Team	W	L	PCT	ERA	G	GS	CG	IP	H	BB	SO	ShO	W	L	SV	AB	H	HR	BA	PO	A	E	DP	TC/G	FA
1945	BOS A	4	4	.500	3.06	12	9	4	82.1	86	19	20	1	0	0	0	24	5	0	.208	4	7	0	0	0.9	1.000

Phil Clark

CLARK, PHILIP JAMES
B. Oct. 3, 1932, Albany, Ga.

BR TR 6'3" 210 lbs.

Year	Team	W	L	PCT	ERA	G	GS	CG	IP	H	BB	SO	ShO	W	L	SV	AB	H	HR	BA	PO	A	E	DP	TC/G	FA
1958	STL N	0	1	.000	3.52	7	0	0	7.2	11	3	1	0	0	1	1	0	0	0	.000	0	0	0	0	0.0	—
1959		0	1	.000	12.86	7	0	0	7	8	8	5	0	0	1	0	0	0	0	—	0	3	0	0	0.4	1.000
2 yrs.		0	2	.000	7.98	14	0	0	14.2	19	11	6	0	0	2	1	0	0	0	.000	0	3	0	0	0.2	1.000

Rickey Clark

CLARK, RICKEY CHARLES
B. Mar. 21, 1946, Mt. Clemens, Mich.

BR TR 6'2" 170 lbs.

Year	Team	W	L	PCT	ERA	G	GS	CG	IP	H	BB	SO	ShO	W	L	SV	AB	H	HR	BA	PO	A	E	DP	TC/G	FA
1967	CAL A	12	11	.522	2.59	32	30	1	174	144	69	81	1	1	0	0	50	2	0	.040	16	34	6	2	1.8	.893
1968		1	11	.083	3.53	21	17	0	94.1	74	54	60	0	0	0	0	28	3	0	.107	5	18	3	1	1.2	.885
1969		0	0	—	5.59	6	1	0	9.2	12	7	6	0	0	0	0	2	1	0	.500	0	0	1	0	0.2	—
1971		2	1	.667	2.86	11	7	1	44	36	28	28	1	0	0	1	15	4	0	.267	2	5	1	0	0.7	.875
1972		4	9	.308	4.50	26	15	2	110	105	55	61	0	0	1	1	31	3	0	.097	7	20	1	1	1.1	.964
5 yrs.		19	32	.373	3.38	96	70	4	432	371	213	236	2	1	1	2	126	13	0	.103	30	77	12	4	1.2	.899

Spider Clark

CLARK, OWEN F.
B. Sept. 16, 1867, Brooklyn, N. Y. D. Feb. 8, 1892, Brooklyn, N. Y.

TR 5'10" 150 lbs.

Year	Team	W	L	PCT	ERA	G	GS	CG	IP	H	BB	SO	ShO	W	L	SV	AB	H	HR	BA	PO	A	E	DP	TC/G	FA
1890	BUF P	0	0	—	6.75	1	0	0	4	8	2	2	0	0	0	0	*				0	0	0	0	0.0	—

Terry Clark

CLARK, TERRY LEE
B. Oct. 18, 1960, Los Angeles, Calif.

BR TR 6'2" 190 lbs.

Year	Team	W	L	PCT	ERA	G	GS	CG	IP	H	BB	SO	ShO	W	L	SV	AB	H	HR	BA	PO	A	E	DP	TC/G	FA
1988	CAL A	6	6	.500	5.07	15	15	2	94	120	31	39	1	0	0	0	0	0	0	—	8	13	0	0	1.4	1.000
1989		0	2	.000	4.91	4	2	0	11	13	3	7	0	0	0	0	0	0	0	—	0	2	0	0	0.5	1.000
2 yrs.		6	8	.429	5.06	19	17	2	105	133	34	46	1	0	0	0	0	0	0	—	8	15	0	0	1.2	1.000

Watty Clark

CLARK, WILLIAM WATSON
B. May 16, 1902, St. Joseph, La. D. Mar. 4, 1972, Clearwater, Fla.

BL TL 6'½" 175 lbs.

Year	Team		W	L	PCT	ERA	G	GS	CG	IP	H	BB	SO	ShO	W	L	SV	AB	H	HR	BA	PO	A	E	DP	TC/G	FA
1924	CLE A		1	3	.250	7.01	12	1	0	25.2	38	14	6	0	1	2	0	9	2	0	.222	1	4	0	0	0.5	1.000
1927	BKN N		7	2	.778	2.32	27	3	1	73.2	74	19	32	0	5	2	2	21	3	0	.143	3	17	1	0	0.8	.952
1928			12	9	.571	2.68	40	19	10	194.2	193	50	85	2	4	3	3	66	10	0	.152	1	49	1	1	1.3	.980
1929			16	19	.457	3.74	41	36	19	279	295	71	140	3	0	3	1	97	16	0	.165	8	57	2	3	1.6	.970
1930			13	13	.500	4.19	44	24	9	200	209	38	81	1	4	1	6	68	14	1	.206	4	43	1	2	1.1	.979
1931			14	10	.583	3.20	34	28	16	233.1	243	52	96	3	1	0	1	84	21	0	.250	3	37	0	1	1.2	1.000
1932			20	12	.625	3.49	40	36	19	273	282	49	99	2	1	0	0	97	21	0	.216	9	63	3	1	1.9	.960
1933	2 teams	BKN N (11G 2–4)						NY N (16G 3–4)																				
"	total		5	8	.385	4.75	27	13	4	94.2	119	17	25	1	2	1	0	24	5	0	.208	2	24	0	0	1.0	1.000
1934	2 teams	NY N (5G 1–2)				BKN N (17G 2–0)																						
"	total		3	2	.600	5.93	22	5	1	44	63	14	16	0	1	0	0	14	2	0	.143	5	7	0	0	0.5	1.000
1935	BKN N		13	8	.619	3.30	33	25	11	207	215	28	35	1	4	0	0	79	14	0	.177	11	54	2	3	2.0	.970
1936			7	11	.389	4.43	33	16	1	120	162	28	28	1	3	2	2	39	9	0	.231	6	27	1	1	1.0	.971
1937			0	0	—	7.71	2	0	0	2.1	4	3	0	0	0	0	0	0	0	0	—	1	0	0	0	1.0	1.000
12 yrs.			111	97	.534	3.66	355	206	91	1747.1	1897	383	643	14	24	15	16	598	117	1	.196	54	384	11	12	1.3	.976

Alan Clarke

CLARKE, ALAN THOMAS (Lefty)
B. Mar. 8, 1896, Clarksville, Md. D. Mar. 11, 1975, Cheverly, Md.

BL TL 5'11" 180 lbs.

Year	Team	W	L	PCT	ERA	G	GS	CG	IP	H	BB	SO	ShO	W	L	SV	AB	H	HR	BA	PO	A	E	DP	TC/G	FA
1921	CIN N	0	1	.000	5.40	1	1	0	5	7	2	1	0	0	0	0	1	0	0	.000	0	0	0	0	0.0	—

Dad Clarke

CLARKE, WILLIAM H.
B. Jan. 7, 1865, Oswego, N. Y. D. June 3, 1911, Lorain, Ohio

BB TR

Year	Team		W	L	PCT	ERA	G	GS	CG	IP	H	BB	SO	ShO	W	L	SV	AB	H	HR	BA	PO	A	E	DP	TC/G	FA
1888	CHI N		1	0	1.000	5.06	2	2	1	16	23	6	6	0	0	0	0	7	2	1	.286	2	4	2	1	4.0	.750
1891	COL AA		1	2	.333	6.86	4	3	2	21	30	16	2	0	0	0	0	9	1	0	.111	0	5	0	0	1.3	1.000
1894	NY N		3	4	.429	4.93	15	6	5	84	114	26	15	0	0	1	1	37	8	0	.216	6	15	2	1	1.5	.913
1895			18	15	.545	3.39	37	30	27	281.2	336	60	67	1	1	4		121	29	0	.240	13	49	7	6	1.9	.899
1896			17	24	.415	4.26	48	40	33	351	431	60	66	1	2	0	1	147	30	0	.204	12	72	8	1	1.9	.913
1897	2 teams	NY N (6G 2–1)				LOU N (4G 1–3)																						
"	total		3	4	.429	4.92	10	8	6	64	87	20	16	0	0	0	0	30	5	0	.167	6	12	3	0	2.1	.857
1898	LOU N		0	1	.000	5.00	1	1	1	9	10	2	1	0	0	0	0	3	0	0	.000	0	2	0	0	2.0	1.000
7 yrs.			43	50	.462	4.17	117	90	75	826.2	1031	190	173	2	3	5	3	354	75	1	.212	39	159	22	9	1.9	.900

Henry Clarke

CLARKE, HENRY TEFFT
B. Aug. 28, 1875, Bellevue, Neb. D. Mar. 28, 1950, Colorado Springs, Colo.

BR TR

Year	Team	W	L	PCT	ERA	G	GS	CG	IP	H	BB	SO	ShO	W	L	SV	AB	H	HR	BA	PO	A	E	DP	TC/G	FA
1897	CLE N	0	4	.000	5.87	5	4	3	30.2	32	12	3	0	0	0	0	25	7	0	.280	0	5	2	0	1.4	.714

Year	Team		W	L	PCT	ERA	G	GS	CG	IP	H	BB	SO	ShO	Relief Pitching W	L	SV	Batting AB	H	HR	BA	PO	A	E	DP	TC/G	FA

Henry Clarke *continued*

| 1898 | CHI | N | 1 | 0 | 1.000 | 2.00 | 1 | 1 | 1 | 9 | 8 | 5 | 1 | 0 | 0 | 0 | 0 | 4 | 1 | 0 | .250 | 0 | 1 | 0 | 0 | 1.0 | 1.000 |
| | 2 yrs. | | 1 | 4 | .200 | 4.99 | 6 | 5 | 4 | 39.2 | 40 | 17 | 4 | 0 | 0 | 0 | 0 | 29 | 8 | 0 | .276 | 0 | 6 | 2 | 0 | 1.3 | .750 |

Rufe Clarke

CLARKE, RUFUS RIVERS
Brother of Sumpter Clarke.
B. Apr. 13, 1900, Estill, S. C.   D. Feb. 8, 1983, Columbia, S. C.   BR TR 6'1"   203 lbs.

1923	DET	A	1	1	.500	4.50	5	0	0	6	6	6	2	0	1	1	0	0	0	0	—	1	2	0	0	0.6	1.000
1924			0	0	—	3.38	2	0	0	5.1	3	5	1	0	0	0	0	1	0	0	.000	2	0	0	0	1.0	1.000
	2 yrs.		1	1	.500	3.97	7	0	0	11.1	9	11	3	0	1	1	0	1	0	0	.000	3	2	0	0	0.7	1.000

Stan Clarke

CLARKE, STANLEY MARTEN
B. Aug. 9, 1960, Toledo, Ohio   BR TL 6'1"   180 lbs.

1983	TOR	A	1	1	.500	3.27	10	0	0	11	10	5	7	0	0	0	0	0	0	0	—	0	2	0	0	0.2	1.000
1985			0	0	—	4.50	4	0	0	4	3	2	2	0	0	0	0	0	0	0	—	0	1	0	0	0.3	1.000
1986			0	1	.000	9.24	10	0	0	12.2	18	10	9	0	0	0	0	0	0	0	—	0	3	0	0	0.3	1.000
1987	SEA	A	2	2	.500	5.48	22	0	0	23	31	10	13	0	2	2	0	0	0	0	—	1	2	0	0	0.1	1.000
1989	KC	A	0	2	.000	15.43	2	2	0	7	14	4	2	0	0	0	0	0	0	0	—	0	1	0	0	0.5	1.000
	5 yrs.		3	6	.333	7.02	48	0	0	57.2	76	31	33	0	3	4	0	0	0	0	—	1	9	0	0	0.2	1.000

Webbo Clarke

CLARKE, VIBERT ERNESTO
B. June 8, 1928, Colon, Panama   D. June 14, 1970, Cristobal, Canal Zone   BL TL 6'   165 lbs.

| 1955 | WAS | A | 0 | 0 | — | 4.64 | 7 | 2 | 0 | 21.1 | 17 | 14 | 9 | 0 | 0 | 0 | 0 | 6 | 1 | 0 | .167 | 1 | 4 | 0 | 0 | 0.7 | 1.000 |

Bill Clarkson

CLARKSON, WILLIAM HENRY (Blackie)
B. Sept. 27, 1898, Portsmouth, Va.   D. Aug. 27, 1971, Raleigh, N. C.   BR TR 6'   165 lbs.

1927	NY	N	3	9	.250	4.36	26	7	2	86.2	92	52	28	0	3	2	2	20	1	0	.050	2	20	0	0	0.8	1.000
1928	2 teams		NY N (4G 0–0)			BOS N (19G 0–2)																					
"	total		0	2	.000	6.92	23	1	0	40.1	63	23	11	0	0	0	0	3	0	0	.000	2	15	1	1	0.8	.944
1929	BOS	N	0	1	.000	10.29	2	1	0	7	16	4	0	0	0	0	0	2	1	0	.500	1	2	1	0	2.0	.750
	3 yrs.		3	12	.200	5.44	51	9	2	134	171	79	39	0	3	3	2	25	2	0	.080	5	37	2	1	0.9	.955

Dad Clarkson

CLARKSON, ARTHUR HAMILTON
Brother of Walter Clarkson.   Brother of John Clarkson.
B. Aug. 31, 1866, Cambridge, Mass.   D. Feb. 6, 1911, Cambridge, Mass.   BR TR 5'10"   165 lbs.

1891	NY	N	1	2	.333	2.89	5	2	1	28	24	18	11	0	1	0	0	9	4	0	.444	2	6	2	0	2.0	.800
1892	BOS	N	1	0	1.000	1.29	1	1	1	7	5	3	0	0	0	0	0	3	0	0	.000	1	1	0	0	2.0	1.000
1893	STL	N	12	9	.571	3.48	24	21	17	186.1	194	79	37	1	1	0	0	75	10	0	.133	11	47	8	1	2.8	.879
1894			8	17	.320	6.36	32	32	24	233.1	318	117	46	1	0	0	0	88	16	0	.182	11	46	5	5	1.9	.919
1895	2 teams		STL N (7G 1–6)			BAL N (20G 12–3)																					
"	total		13	9	.591	4.92	27	21	17	203	260	90	32	0	2	1	0	80	9	1	.113	6	51	4	1	2.3	.934
1896	BAL	N	4	2	.667	4.98	7	4	3	47	72	18	7	0	2	0	0	18	5	0	.278	0	11	1	0	1.7	.917
	6 yrs.		39	39	.500	4.90	96	81	63	704.2	873	325	133	2	6	1	0	273	44	1	.161	31	162	20	7	2.2	.906

John Clarkson

CLARKSON, JOHN GIBSON
Brother of Dad Clarkson.   Brother of Walter Clarkson.
B. July 1, 1861, Cambridge, Mass.   D. Feb. 4, 1909, Belmont, Mass.
Hall of Fame 1963.   BR TR 5'10"   155 lbs.

1882	WOR	N	1	2	.333	4.50	3	3	2	24	49	2	49	0	0	0	0	11	4	0	.364	1	6	1	0	2.7	.875
1884	CHI	N	10	3	.769	2.14	14	13	12	118	94	25	102	0	0	0	0	84	22	3	.262	6	38	11	5	3.9	.800
1885			53	16	.768	1.85	70	70	68	623	497	97	308	10	0	0	0	283	61	4	.216	26	174	20	8	3.1	.909
1886			35	17	.673	2.41	55	55	50	466.2	419	86	313	3	0	0	0	210	49	3	.233	19	114	19	3	2.8	.875
1887			38	21	.644	3.08	60	59	56	523	513	92	237	1	2	1	0	215	52	6	.242	34	125	7	5	2.8	.958
1888	BOS	N	33	20	.623	2.76	54	54	53	483.1	448	119	223	3	0	0	0	205	40	1	.195	22	117	19	3	2.9	.880
1889			49	19	.721	2.73	73	72	68	620	589	203	284	8	0	0	1	262	54	2	.206	36	172	27	8	3.2	.885
1890			25	18	.581	3.27	44	44	43	383	370	140	138	2	0	0	0	173	43	2	.249	21	72	14	3	2.4	.893
1891			33	19	.635	2.79	55	51	47	460.2	435	154	141	3	0	1	3	187	42	0	.225	27	114	13	2	2.8	.916
1892	2 teams		BOS N (16G 8–6)			CLE N (29G 17–10)																					
"	total		25	16	.610	2.48	45	44	42	389	350	132	139	5	0	0	1	158	27	1	.171	11	87	15	4	2.5	.867
1893	CLE	N	16	17	.485	4.45	36	35	31	295	358	95	62	0	0	1	0	131	27	1	.206	15	82	7	1	2.9	.933
1894			8	9	.471	4.42	22	18	13	150.2	173	46	28	1	0	2	0	55	11	0	.200	3	42	9	2	2.5	.833
	12 yrs.		326	177	.648	2.81	531	518	485	4536.1	4295	1191	1978	37	1	4	5	*				221	1143	162	44	2.9	.894
								8th																			

Walter Clarkson

CLARKSON, WALTER HAMILTON
Brother of John Clarkson.   Brother of Dad Clarkson.
B. Nov. 3, 1878, Cambridge, Mass.   D. Oct. 10, 1946, Cambridge, Mass.   BR TR 5'10"   150 lbs.

1904	NY	A	1	2	.333	5.02	13	4	2	66.1	63	25	43	0	1	0	1	26	7	0	.269	2	14	1	0	1.3	.941
1905			3	3	.500	3.91	9	4	3	46	40	13	35	0	2	1	0	19	1	0	.053	1	11	2	0	1.6	.857
1906			9	4	.692	2.32	32	16	9	151	135	55	64	3	1	0	0	51	8	0	.157	3	39	1	1	1.3	.977
1907	2 teams		NY A (5G 1–1)			CLE A (17G 4–6)																					
"	total		5	7	.417	2.67	22	12	9	108	96	37	35	1	1	0	0	35	3	0	.086	10	30	3	3	2.0	.930
1908	CLE	A	0	0	—	10.80	2	1	0	3.1	6	2	1	0	0	0	0	1	1	0	1.000	0	0	0	0	0.0	—
	5 yrs.		18	16	.529	3.17	78	37	23	374.2	340	132	178	4	5	1	1	132	20	0	.152	16	94	7	4	1.5	.940

Marty Clary

CLARY, MARTIN KEITH
B. Apr. 3, 1962, Detroit, Mich.   BR TR 6'4"   190 lbs.

1987	ATL	N	0	1	.000	6.14	7	1	0	14.2	20	4	7	0	0	0	0	1	0	0	.000	0	2	0	0	0.3	1.000
1989			4	3	.571	3.15	18	17	2	108.2	103	31	30	1	0	0	0	31	5	0	.161	10	18	0	1	1.6	1.000
	2 yrs.		4	4	.500	3.50	25	18	2	123.1	123	35	37	1	0	0	0	32	5	0	.156	10	20	0	1	1.2	1.000

Year	Team		W	L	PCT	ERA	G	GS	CG	IP	H	BB	SO	ShO	Relief Pitching W	L	SV	Batting AB	H	HR	BA	PO	A	E	DP	TC/G	FA

Gowell Claset

CLASET, GOWELL SYLVESTER (Lefty)
B. Nov. 26, 1907, Battle Creek, Mich.   D. Mar. 8, 1981, St. Petersburg, Fla.
BB TL 6'3½" 210 lbs.

| 1933 | PHI | A | 2 | 0 | 1.000 | 9.53 | 8 | 1 | 0 | 11.1 | 23 | 11 | 1 | 0 | 2 | 0 | 0 | 2 | 1 | 0 | .500 | 0 | 4 | 0 | 0 | 0.5 | 1.000 |

Fritz Clausen

CLAUSEN, FREDERICK WILLIAM
B. Apr. 26, 1869, New York, N. Y.   D. Feb. 11, 1960, Memphis, Tenn.
BR TL 5'11" 190 lbs.

1892	LOU	N	9	13	.409	3.06	24	24	24	200	181	87	94	2	0	0	0	84	13	0	.155	11	37	6	0	2.3	.889
1893	2 teams		LOU N	(5G 1–4)		CHI N	(10G 6–2)																				
"	total		7	6	.538	3.96	15	14	11	109	112	61	35	0	0	0	1	47	7	0	.149	5	24	1	1	2.0	.967
1894	CHI	N	0	1	.000	10.38	1	1	0	4.1	5	3	1	0	0	0	0	1	0	0	.000	0	2	0	0	2.0	1.000
1896	LOU	N	0	2	.000	6.55	2	2	1	11	17	6	4	0	0	0	0	4	0	0	.000	1	4	1	0	3.0	.833
4 yrs.			16	22	.421	3.58	42	41	36	324.1	315	157	134	2	0	0	1	136	20	0	.147	17	67	8	1	2.2	.913

Al Clauss

CLAUSS, ALBERT STANLEY (Lefty)
B. June 24, 1891, New Haven, Conn.   D. Sept. 13, 1952, New Haven, Conn.
BR TL 5'10½" 178 lbs.

| 1913 | DET | A | 0 | 1 | .000 | 4.73 | 5 | 1 | 0 | 13.1 | 11 | 12 | 1 | 0 | 0 | 0 | 0 | 4 | 0 | 0 | .000 | 0 | 3 | 0 | 1 | 0.6 | 1.000 |

Danny Clay

CLAY, DANNY BRUCE
B. Oct. 24, 1961, Sun Valley, Calif.
BR TR 6'1" 190 lbs.

| 1988 | PHI | N | 0 | 1 | .000 | 6.00 | 17 | 0 | 0 | 24 | 27 | 21 | 12 | 0 | 0 | 1 | 0 | 2 | 0 | 0 | .000 | 1 | 2 | 0 | 0 | 0.2 | .750 |

Ken Clay

CLAY, KENNETH EARL
B. Apr. 6, 1954, Lynchburg, Va.
BR TR 6'3" 185 lbs.

1977	NY	A	2	3	.400	4.34	21	3	0	56	53	24	20	0	2	1	1	0	0	0	–	8	7	0	0	0.7	1.000
1978			3	4	.429	4.28	28	6	0	75.2	89	21	32	0	3	4	0	0	0	0	–	6	9	2	1	0.6	.882
1979			1	7	.125	5.42	32	5	0	78	88	25	28	0	1	3	2	0	0	0	–	8	12	1	0	0.7	.952
1980	TEX	A	2	3	.400	4.60	8	8	0	43	43	29	17	0	0	0	0	0	0	0	–	3	4	1	0	1.0	.875
1981	SEA	A	2	7	.222	4.63	22	14	0	101	116	42	32	0	0	1	0	0	0	0	–	6	10	1	1	0.8	.941
5 yrs.			10	24	.294	4.68	111	36	0	353.2	389	141	129	0	6	9	3	0	0	0	–	31	42	5	2	0.7	.936

LEAGUE CHAMPIONSHIP SERIES

| 1978 | NY | A | 0 | 0 | – | 0.00 | 1 | 0 | 0 | 3.2 | 0 | 3 | 2 | 0 | 0 | 0 | 0 | 0 | 0 | 0 | – | 0 | 0 | 0 | 0 | 0.0 | – |

WORLD SERIES

1977	NY	A	0	0	–	2.45	2	0	0	3.2	2	1	0	0	0	0	0	0	0	0	–	1	0	0	0	1.0	1.000
1978			0	0	–	11.57	1	0	0	2.1	4	2	2	0	0	0	0	0	0	0	–	0	0	0	0	0.0	–
2 yrs.			0	0	–	6.00	3	0	0	6	6	3	2	0	0	0	0	0	0	0	–	1	1	0	0	0.7	1.000

Mark Clear

CLEAR, MARK ALAN
B. May 27, 1956, Los Angeles, Calif.
BR TR 6'4" 200 lbs.

1979	CAL	A	11	5	.688	3.63	52	0	0	109	87	68	98	0	11	5	14	0	0	0	–	4	10	2	0	0.3	.875
1980			11	11	.500	3.31	58	0	0	106	82	65	105	0	11	11	9	0	0	0	–	3	10	0	0	0.2	1.000
1981	BOS	A	8	3	.727	4.09	34	0	0	77	69	51	82	0	8	3	9	0	0	0	–	5	4	0	0	0.3	1.000
1982			14	9	.609	3.00	55	0	0	105	92	61	109	0	14	9	14	0	0	0	–	7	11	3	0	0.4	.857
1983			4	5	.444	6.28	48	0	0	96	101	68	81	0	4	5	4	0	0	0	–	8	5	1	0	0.3	.929
1984			8	3	.727	4.03	47	0	0	67	47	70	76	0	8	3	8	0	0	0	–	4	8	0	0	0.3	1.000
1985			1	3	.250	3.72	41	0	0	55.2	45	50	55	0	1	3	3	0	0	0	–	4	12	2	0	0.4	.889
1986	MIL	A	5	5	.500	2.20	59	0	0	73.2	53	36	85	0	5	5	16	0	0	0	–	4	6	1	0	0.2	.909
1987			8	5	.615	4.48	58	1	0	78.1	70	55	81	0	8	4	6	0	0	0	–	8	12	1	0	0.4	.952
1988			1	0	1.000	2.79	25	0	0	29	23	21	26	0	1	0	0	0	0	0	–	2	1	0	0	0.1	1.000
10 yrs.			71	49	.592	3.83	477	1	0	796.2	669	545	798	0	71	48	83	0	0	0	–	49	79	10	0	0.3	.928

LEAGUE CHAMPIONSHIP SERIES

| 1979 | CAL | A | 0 | 0 | – | 4.76 | 1 | 0 | 0 | 5.2 | 4 | 2 | 3 | 0 | 0 | 0 | 0 | 0 | 0 | 0 | – | 0 | 0 | 0 | 0 | 0.0 | – |

Joe Cleary

CLEARY, JOSEPH CHRISTOPHER (Fire)
B. Dec. 3, 1919, Cork, Ireland
BR TR 5'9" 145 lbs.

| 1945 | WAS | A | 0 | 0 | – | 189.00 | 1 | 0 | 0 | .1 | 5 | 3 | 1 | 0 | 0 | 0 | 0 | 0 | 0 | 0 | – | 0 | 0 | 0 | 0 | 0.0 | – |

Roger Clemens

CLEMENS, WILLIAM ROGER (Rocket Man)
B. Aug. 4, 1962, Dayton, Ohio
BR TR 6'4" 205 lbs.

1984	BOS	A	9	4	.692	4.32	21	20	5	133.1	146	29	126	1	0	0	0	0	0	0	–	11	14	0	0	1.2	1.000
1985			7	5	.583	3.29	15	15	3	98.1	83	37	74	1	0	0	0	0	0	0	–	12	9	0	1	1.4	1.000
1986			24	4	.857	2.48	33	33	10	254	179	67	238	1	0	0	0	0	0	0	–	27	21	4	0	1.6	.923
1987			20	9	.690	2.97	36	36	18	281.2	248	83	256	7	0	0	0	0	0	0	–	15	25	0	1	1.1	1.000
1988			18	12	.600	2.93	35	35	14	264	217	62	291	8	0	0	0	0	0	0	–	17	17	1	1	1.0	.971
1989			17	11	.607	3.13	35	35	8	253.1	215	93	230	3	0	0	0	0	0	0	–	17	27	0	1	1.3	1.000
6 yrs.			95	45	.679	3.06	175	174	58	1284.2	1088	371	1215	21	0	0	0	0	0	0	–	99	113	5	4	1.2	.977

LEAGUE CHAMPIONSHIP SERIES

1986	BOS	A	1	1	.500	4.37	3	3	0	22.2	22	7	17	0	0	0	0	0	0	0	–	1	2	0	0	1.0	1.000
1988			0	0	–	3.86	1	1	0	7	6	0	8	0	0	0	0	0	0	0	–	0	1	1	0	1.0	–
2 yrs.			1	1	.500	4.25	4	4	0	29.2	28	7	25	0	0	0	0	0	0	0	–	1	2	1	0	1.0	.750

WORLD SERIES

| 1986 | BOS | A | 0 | 0 | – | 3.18 | 2 | 2 | 0 | 11.1 | 9 | 6 | 11 | 0 | 0 | 0 | 0 | 0 | 4 | 0 | .000 | 1 | 2 | 0 | 0 | 1.5 | 1.000 |

Bill Clemensen

CLEMENSEN, WILLIAM MELVILLE
B. June 20, 1919, New Brunswick, N. J.
BR TR 6'1" 193 lbs.

| 1939 | PIT | N | 0 | 1 | .000 | 7.33 | 12 | 1 | 0 | 27 | 32 | 20 | 73 | 0 | 0 | 0 | 0 | 6 | 2 | 0 | .333 | 3 | 11 | 1 | 1 | 1.3 | .933 |
| 1941 | | | 1 | 0 | 1.000 | 2.77 | 2 | 1 | 1 | 13 | 7 | 7 | 4 | 0 | 0 | 0 | 0 | 4 | 0 | 0 | .000 | 1 | 1 | 0 | 0 | 1.5 | .667 |

Year	Team		W	L	PCT	ERA	G	GS	CG	IP	H	BB	SO	ShO	Relief Pitching W	L	SV	Batting AB	H	HR	BA	PO	A	E	DP	TC/G	FA

Bill Clemensen *continued*

| 1946 | | | 0 | 0 | – | 0.00 | 1 | 0 | 0 | 2 | 0 | 0 | 2 | 0 | 0 | 0 | 0 | 0 | 0 | 0 | .200 | 0 | 0 | 0 | 0 | 0.0 | – |
| 3 yrs. | | | 1 | 1 | .500 | 5.57 | 15 | 2 | 1 | 42 | 39 | 27 | 79 | 0 | 0 | 0 | 0 | 10 | 2 | 0 | .200 | 4 | 12 | 2 | 1 | 1.2 | .889 |

Pat Clements

CLEMENTS, PATRICK BRIAN
B. Feb. 2, 1962, McCloud, Calif.

BR TL 6' 175 lbs.

1985	2 teams	CAL A (41G 5–0)	PIT N	(27G 0–2)																							
"	total		5	2	.714	3.46	68	0	0	96.1	86	40	36	0	5	2	3	3	1	0	.333	2	18	1	0	0.3	.952
1986	PIT	N	0	4	.000	2.80	65	0	0	61	53	32	31	0	0	4	2	6	0	0	.000	7	11	0	1	0.3	1.000
1987	NY	A	3	3	.500	4.95	55	0	0	80	91	30	36	0	3	3	7	0	0	0	–	5	15	0	2	0.4	1.000
1988			0	0	–	6.48	6	1	0	8.1	12	4	3	0	0	0	0	0	0	0	–	1	1	0	0	0.3	1.000
1989	SD	N	4	1	.800	3.92	23	1	0	39	39	15	18	0	4	0	0	6	0	0	.000	1	8	0	1	0.4	1.000
5 yrs.			12	10	.545	3.89	217	2	0	284.2	281	121	124	0	12	9	12	15	1	0	.067	16	53	1	6	0.3	.986

Lance Clemons

CLEMONS, LANCE LEVIS
B. July 6, 1947, Philadelphia, Pa.

BL TL 6'2" 205 lbs.

1971	KC	A	1	0	1.000	4.13	10	3	0	24	26	12	20	0	1	0	0	7	2	1	.286	1	4	1	0	0.6	.833
1972	STL	N	0	1	.000	10.13	3	1	0	5.1	8	5	2	0	0	1	0	1	0	0	.000	1	1	0	1	0.3	1.000
1974	BOS	A	1	0	1.000	10.50	6	0	0	6	8	4	1	0	1	0	0	0	0	0	–	1	1	0	0	0.3	1.000
3 yrs.			2	1	.667	6.11	19	4	0	35.1	42	21	23	0	2	0	0	8	2	1	.250	2	6	1	1	0.5	.889

Reggie Cleveland

CLEVELAND, REGINALD LESLIE
B. May 23, 1948, Swift Current, Sask., Canada

BR TR 6'1" 195 lbs.

1969	STL	N	0	0	–	9.00	1	1	0	4	7	1	3	0	0	0	0	1	0	0	.000	0	0	0	0	0.0	–
1970			0	4	.000	7.62	16	1	0	26	31	18	22	0	0	3	0	4	1	0	.250	1	1	1	0	0.2	.667
1971			12	12	.500	4.01	34	34	10	222	238	53	148	2	0	0	0	82	14	0	.171	15	30	1	1	1.4	.978
1972			14	15	.483	3.94	33	33	11	230.2	229	60	153	3	0	0	0	71	17	0	.239	17	25	4	0	1.4	.913
1973			14	10	.583	3.01	32	32	6	224	211	61	122	3	0	0	0	74	17	0	.230	11	24	3	2	1.2	.921
1974	BOS	A	12	14	.462	4.32	41	27	10	221	234	69	103	0	2	1	0	–				12	38	2	0	1.3	.962
1975			13	9	.591	4.43	31	20	8	170.2	173	52	78	1	3	2	0	–				12	25	2	1	1.3	.949
1976			10	9	.526	3.07	41	14	3	170	159	61	76	0	5	3	2	–				10	25	4	4	1.0	.897
1977			11	8	.579	4.26	36	27	9	190.1	211	43	85	1	0	0	2	–				18	20	3	3	1.1	.927
1978	2 teams	BOS A (1G 0–1)	TEX A	(53G 5–7)																							
"	total		5	8	.385	3.08	54	0	0	76	66	23	46	0	5	8	12	–				3	13	1	0	0.3	.941
1979	MIL	A	1	5	.167	6.71	29	1	0	55	77	23	22	0	1	4	4	0	0	0	–	2	5	2	1	0.3	.778
1980			11	9	.550	3.74	45	13	5	154	150	49	54	2	7	4	4	0	0	0	–	17	16	0	1	0.7	1.000
1981			2	3	.400	5.12	35	0	0	65	57	30	18	0	2	3	1	0	0	0	–	3	5	1	1	0.3	.889
13 yrs.			105	106	.498	4.02	428	203	57	1808.2	1843	543	930	12	25	28	25	232	49	0	.211	121	227	24	14	0.9	.935

LEAGUE CHAMPIONSHIP SERIES

| 1975 | BOS | A | 0 | 0 | – | 5.40 | 1 | 1 | 0 | 5 | 7 | 1 | 2 | 0 | 0 | 0 | 0 | 0 | 0 | 0 | – | 0 | 1 | 0 | 0 | 1.0 | 1.000 |

WORLD SERIES

| 1975 | BOS | A | 0 | 1 | .000 | 6.75 | 3 | 1 | 0 | 6.2 | 7 | 3 | 5 | 0 | 0 | 0 | 0 | 2 | 0 | 0 | .000 | 0 | 0 | 0 | 0 | 0.0 | – |

Tex Clevenger

CLEVENGER, TRUMAN EUGENE
B. July 9, 1932, Visalia, Calif.

BR TR 6'1" 180 lbs.

1954	BOS	A	2	4	.333	4.79	23	8	1	67.2	67	29	43	0	1	0	0	14	3	0	.214	6	11	2	0	0.8	.895
1956	WAS	A	0	0	–	5.40	20	1	0	31.2	33	21	17	0	0	0	0	2	0	0	.000	4	4	1	0	0.5	.889
1957			7	6	.538	4.19	52	9	2	139.2	139	47	75	0	5	4	8	33	7	0	.212	10	27	3	6	0.8	.925
1958			9	9	.500	4.35	55	4	0	124	119	50	70	0	3	6	6	22	3	0	.136	8	31	1	4	0.7	.975
1959			8	5	.615	3.91	50	7	2	117.1	114	51	71	2	5	2	8	23	4	0	.174	10	35	1	3	0.9	.978
1960			5	11	.313	4.20	53	11	1	128.2	150	49	49	0	3	4	7	22	2	0	.091	3	21	0	3	0.5	1.000
1961	2 teams	LA A (12G 2–1)	NY A	(21G 1–1)																							
"	total		3	2	.600	3.78	33	0	0	47.2	48	34	25	0	3	2	1	7	1	0	.143	5	12	0	1	0.5	1.000
1962	NY	A	2	0	1.000	2.84	21	0	0	38	36	17	11	0	2	0	0	4	0	0	.000	4	5	0	3	0.4	1.000
8 yrs.			36	37	.493	4.18	307	40	6	694.2	706	298	361	2	19	15	30	127	20	0	.157	50	146	8	20	0.7	.961

Stewart Cliburn

CLIBURN, STEWART WALKER
Brother of Stan Cliburn.
B. Dec. 19, 1956, Jackson, Miss.

BR TR 6' 195 lbs.

1984	CAL	A	0	0	–	13.50	1	0	0	2	3	1	1	0	0	0	0	0	0	0	–	1	1	0	0	2.0	1.000
1985			9	3	.750	2.09	44	0	0	99	87	26	48	0	9	3	6	0	0	0	–	8	17	0	3	0.6	1.000
1988			4	2	.667	4.07	40	1	0	84	83	32	42	0	4	1	0	0	0	0	–	6	12	0	2	0.5	1.000
3 yrs.			13	5	.722	3.11	85	1	0	185	173	59	91	0	13	4	6	0	0	0	–	15	30	0	5	0.5	1.000

Jim Clinton

CLINTON, JAMES LAWRENCE (Big Jim)
B. Aug. 10, 1850, New York, N. Y.   D. Sept. 3, 1921, Brooklyn, N. Y.
Manager 1872.

BR TR 5'8½" 174 lbs.

| 1876 | LOU | N | 0 | 1 | .000 | 6.00 | 1 | 1 | 1 | 9 | 12 | 0 | 1 | 0 | 0 | 0 | 0 | * | | | | 0 | 3 | 2 | 0 | 5.0 | .600 |

Tony Cloninger

CLONINGER, TONY LEE
B. Aug. 13, 1940, Lincoln, N. C.

BR TR 6' 210 lbs.

1961	MIL	N	7	2	.778	5.25	19	10	3	84	84	33	51	0	2	0	0	30	5	0	.167	11	16	0	0	1.4	1.000
1962			8	3	.727	4.30	24	15	4	111	113	46	69	0	1	0	0	39	4	0	.103	8	18	1	3	1.2	.966
1963			9	11	.450	3.78	41	18	4	145.1	131	63	100	2	2	4	1	37	5	0	.135	8	17	1	0	0.6	.962
1964			19	14	.576	3.56	38	34	15	242.2	206	82	163	3	1	0	2	87	21	0	.241	14	41	2	1	1.5	.965
1965			24	11	.686	3.29	40	38	16	279	247	119	211	1	0	0	1	105	17	1	.162	15	41	6	2	1.6	.903
1966	ATL	N	14	11	.560	4.12	39	38	11	257.2	253	116	178	1	0	0	0	111	26	5	.234	14	43	8	1	1.7	.877
1967			4	7	.364	5.17	16	16	1	76.2	85	31	55	0	0	0	0	25	5	0	.200	3	11	0	0	0.9	1.000

Year	Team		W	L	PCT	ERA	G	GS	CG	IP	H	BB	SO	ShO	Relief Pitching W	L	SV	Batting AB	H	HR	BA	PO	A	E	DP	TC/G	FA

Tony Cloninger *continued*

Year	Team		W	L	PCT	ERA	G	GS	CG	IP	H	BB	SO	ShO	W	L	SV	AB	H	HR	BA	PO	A	E	DP	TC/G	FA
1968	2 teams	ATL N (8G 1–3)								CIN N (17G 4–3)																	
"	total		5	6	.455	4.08	25	18	2	110.1	96	59	72	2	1	2	0	38	7	2	.184	12	15	1	0	1.1	.964
1969	CIN	N	11	17	.393	5.02	35	34	6	190	184	103	103	2	0	0	0	72	12	1	.167	9	23	3	3	1.0	.914
1970			9	7	.563	3.83	30	18	0	148	136	78	56	0	1	1	1	47	10	2	.213	13	31	2	5	1.5	.957
1971			3	6	.333	3.90	28	8	1	97	79	49	51	1	0	2	0	27	7	0	.259	4	16	2	3	0.8	.909
1972	STL	N	0	2	.000	5.19	17	0	0	26	29	19	11	0	0	2	0	3	0	0	.000	1	7	0	1	0.5	1.000
12 yrs.			113	97	.538	4.07	352	247	63	1767.2	1643	798	1120	13	7	11	6	621	119	11	.192	114	279	26	20	1.2	.938

LEAGUE CHAMPIONSHIP SERIES

| 1970 | CIN | N | 0 | 0 | – | 3.60 | 1 | 1 | 0 | 5 | 7 | 4 | 1 | 0 | 0 | 0 | 0 | 1 | 0 | 0 | .000 | 0 | 2 | 0 | 0 | 2.0 | 1.000 |

WORLD SERIES

| 1970 | CIN | N | 0 | 1 | .000 | 7.36 | 2 | 1 | 0 | 7.1 | 10 | 5 | 4 | 0 | 0 | 0 | 0 | 2 | 0 | 0 | .000 | 0 | 1 | 0 | 0 | 0.5 | 1.000 |

Al Closter

CLOSTER, ALAN EDWARD
B. June 15, 1943, Creighton, Neb.

BL TL 6'2" 190 lbs.

1966	WAS	A	0	0	–	0.00	1	0	0	.1	1	2	0	0	0	0	0	0	0	0	–	0	0	0	0	0.0	–
1971	NY	A	2	2	.500	5.14	14	1	0	28	33	13	22	0	2	1	0	6	0	0	.000	0	8	1	0	0.6	.889
1972			0	0	–	13.50	2	0	0	2	2	4	2	0	0	0	0	1	0	0	.000	0	1	0	0	0.5	1.000
1973	ATL	N	0	0	–	15.75	4	0	0	4	7	4	2	0	0	0	0	0	0	0	–	1	1	0	0	0.5	1.000
4 yrs.			2	2	.500	6.82	21	1	0	34.1	43	23	26	0	2	1	0	7	0	0	.000	1	10	1	0	0.6	.917

Ed Clough

CLOUGH, EDGAR GEORGE (Spec)
B. Oct. 28, 1906, Wiconisco, Pa. D. Jan. 30, 1944, Harrisburg, Pa.

BL TL 6' 188 lbs.

1925	STL	N	0	1	.000	8.10	3	1	0	10	11	5	3	0	0	0	0	4	1	0	.250	1	1	0	0	0.7	1.000
1926			0	0	–	22.50	1	0	0	2	5	3	0	0	0	0	0	1	0	0	.000	0	0	0	0	0.0	–
2 yrs.			0	1	.000	10.50	4	1	0	12	16	8	3	0	0	0	0	*					1	1	0	0	0.5	1.000

Bill Clowers

CLOWERS, WILLIAM PERRY
B. Aug. 14, 1898, San Marcos, Tex. D. Jan. 13, 1978, Sweeney, Tex.

BL TL 5'11" 175 lbs.

| 1926 | BOS | A | 0 | 0 | – | 0.00 | 2 | 0 | 0 | 1.2 | 2 | 2 | 0 | 0 | 0 | 0 | 0 | 0 | 0 | 0 | – | 1 | 0 | 0 | 0 | 0.5 | 1.000 |

Bryan Clutterbuck

CLUTTERBUCK, BRYAN RICHARD
B. Dec. 17, 1959, Detroit, Mich.

BR TR 6'4" 223 lbs.

1986	MIL	A	0	1	.000	4.29	20	0	0	56.2	68	16	38	0	0	1	0	0	0	0	–	7	5	0	0	0.6	1.000
1989			2	5	.286	4.14	14	11	1	67.1	73	16	29	0	0	0	0	0	0	0	–	2	3	0	0	0.4	1.000
2 yrs.			2	6	.250	4.21	34	11	1	124	141	32	67	0	0	1	0	0	0	0	–	9	8	0	0	0.5	1.000

David Clyde

CLYDE, DAVID EUGENE
B. Apr. 22, 1955, Kansas City, Kans.

BL TL 6'1½" 180 lbs.

1973	TEX	A	4	8	.333	5.03	18	18	0	93	106	54	74	0	0	0	0	0	0	0	–	3	12	2	2	0.9	.882
1974			3	9	.250	4.38	28	21	4	117	129	47	52	0	0	0	0	0	0	0	–	2	12	1	0	0.6	.875
1975			0	1	.000	2.57	1	1	0	7	6	6	2	0	0	0	0	0	0	0	–	0	1	1	0	2.0	.500
1978	CLE	A	8	11	.421	4.28	28	25	5	153.1	166	60	83	0	0	0	0	0	0	0	–	9	18	1	0	1.0	.964
1979			3	4	.429	5.87	9	8	1	46	50	13	17	0	0	0	0	0	0	0	–	2	6	1	0	1.0	.889
5 yrs.			18	33	.353	4.63	84	73	10	416.1	457	180	228	0	0	0	0	0	0	0	–	16	49	7	3	0.9	.903

Tom Clyde

CLYDE, THOMAS KNOX
B. Aug. 17, 1923, Wachapreague, Va.

BR TR 6'3" 195 lbs.

| 1943 | PHI | A | 0 | 0 | – | 9.00 | 4 | 0 | 0 | 6 | 7 | 4 | 0 | 0 | 0 | 0 | 0 | 2 | 0 | 0 | .000 | 0 | 1 | 2 | 0 | 0.8 | .333 |

Andy Coakley

COAKLEY, ANDREW JAMES
Played as Jack McAllister in 1902.
B. Nov. 20, 1882, Providence, R. I. D. Sept. 27, 1963, New York, N. Y.

BL TR 6' 165 lbs.

1902	PHI	A	2	1	.667	2.67	3	3	3	27	25	9	9	0	0	0	0	8	3	0	.375	3	9	2	1	4.7	.857
1903			0	3	.000	5.50	6	3	2	37.2	48	11	20	0	0	0	0	15	3	0	.200	1	11	2	0	2.3	.857
1904			4	4	.500	2.03	8	8	8	62	50	23	33	2	0	0	0	23	2	0	.087	1	18	0	0	2.4	1.000
1905			20	7	.741	1.84	35	31	22	255	227	73	145	3	1	0	0	90	13	0	.144	10	68	8	2	2.5	.907
1906			7	8	.467	3.14	22	16	10	149	144	44	59	0	1	0	0	49	7	0	.143	8	32	3	0	2.0	.930
1907	CIN	N	17	16	.515	2.34	37	30	21	265.1	269	79	89	1	4	1	1	84	6	0	.071	12	58	2	2	1.9	.972
1908	2 teams	CIN N (32G 8–18)								CHI N (4G 2–0)																	
"	total		10	18	.357	1.78	36	31	22	262.2	233	70	68	5	0	1	2	82	7	0	.085	8	56	4	0	1.9	.941
1909	CHI	N	0	1	.000	18.00	1	1	0	2	7	3	1	0	0	0	0	0	0	0	–	0	1	0	0	1.0	1.000
1911	NY	A	0	1	.000	5.40	2	1	1	11.2	20	2	4	0	0	0	0	4	1	0	.250	1	3	0	0	2.0	1.000
9 yrs.			60	59	.504	2.36	150	124	89	1072.1	1023	314	428	11	6	2	3	355	42	0	.118	44	256	21	5	2.1	.935

WORLD SERIES

| 1905 | PHI | A | 0 | 1 | .000 | 2.00 | 1 | 1 | 1 | 9 | 9 | 5 | 2 | 0 | 0 | 0 | 0 | 2 | 0 | 0 | .000 | 0 | 2 | 0 | 1 | 2.0 | 1.000 |

Jim Coates

COATES, JAMES ALTON
B. Aug. 4, 1932, Farnham, Va.

BR TR 6'4" 192 lbs.

1956	NY	A	0	0	–	13.50	2	0	0	2	1	4	0	0	0	0	0	0	0	0	–	0	1	0	0	0.5	1.000
1959			6	1	.857	2.87	37	4	2	100.1	89	36	64	0	4	1	3	21	2	0	.095	7	17	2	0	0.7	.923
1960			13	3	.813	4.28	35	18	6	149.1	139	66	73	2	4	0	1	48	12	0	.250	9	15	4	1	0.8	.857
1961			11	5	.688	3.44	43	11	4	141.1	128	53	80	1	6	2	5	35	1	0	.029	12	19	2	2	0.8	.939
1962			7	6	.538	4.44	50	6	0	117.2	119	50	67	0	7	5	4	32	4	0	.125	6	12	2	2	0.4	.900
1963	2 teams	WAS A (20G 2–4)								CIN N (9G 0–0)																	
"	total		2	4	.333	5.34	29	2	0	60.2	72	28	42	0	2	4	0	9	0	0	.000	2	10	0	0	0.4	1.000
1965	CAL	A	2	0	1.000	3.54	17	0	0	28	23	16	15	0	2	0	3	1	0	0	.000	1	6	2	0	0.5	.778
1966			1	1	.500	3.98	9	4	1	31.2	32	10	16	1	1	0	0	11	1	0	.091	3	3	0	0	0.7	1.000

Year	Team		W	L	PCT	ERA	G	GS	CG	IP	H	BB	SO	ShO	W	L	SV	AB	H	HR	BA	PO	A	E	DP	TC/G	FA

Jim Coates *continued*

Year	Team		W	L	PCT	ERA	G	GS	CG	IP	H	BB	SO	ShO	W	L	SV	AB	H	HR	BA	PO	A	E	DP	TC/G	FA
1967			1	2	.333	4.30	25	1	0	52.1	47	23	39	0	1	1	0	3	1	0	.333	4	8	0	2	0.5	1.000
9 yrs.			43	22	.662	4.00	247	46	13	683.1	650	286	396	4	26	13	18	160	21	0	.131	44	91	12	9	0.6	.918

WORLD SERIES

Year	Team		W	L	PCT	ERA	G	GS	CG	IP	H	BB	SO	ShO	W	L	SV	AB	H	HR	BA	PO	A	E	DP	TC/G	FA
1960	NY	A	0	0	—	5.68	3	0	0	6.1	6	1	3	0	0	0	0	1	0	0	.000	1	1	0	0	0.7	1.000
1961			0	0	—	0.00	1	0	0	4	1	1	2	0	0	0	1	1	0	0	.000	0	0	0	0	0.0	—
1962			0	1	.000	6.75	2	0	0	2.2	1	1	3	0	0	1	0	0	0	0	—	1	0	0	0	0.0	—
3 yrs.			0	1	.000	4.15	6	0	0	13	8	3	8	0	0	1	1	2	0	0	.000	2	1	0	0	0.3	1.000

George Cobb

COBB, GEORGE WASHINGTON
B. San Francisco, Calif.   Deceased.

Year	Team		W	L	PCT	ERA	G	GS	CG	IP	H	BB	SO	ShO	W	L	SV	AB	H	HR	BA	PO	A	E	DP	TC/G	FA
1892	BAL	N	10	37	.213	4.86	53	47	42	394.1	495	140	159	0	1	1	0	172	36	1	.209	12	96	14	0	2.3	.885

Herb Cobb

COBB, HERBERT EDWARD   BR TR 5'11"   150 lbs.
B. Aug. 6, 1904, Pinetops, N. C.   D. Jan. 8, 1980, Tarboro, N. C.

Year	Team		W	L	PCT	ERA	G	GS	CG	IP	H	BB	SO	ShO	W	L	SV	AB	H	HR	BA	PO	A	E	DP	TC/G	FA
1929	STL	A	0	0	—	36.00	1	0	0	1	3	1	0	0	0	0	0	0	0	0	—	0	0	0	0	0.0	—

Ty Cobb

COBB, TYRUS RAYMOND (The Georgia Peach)   BL TR 6'1"   175 lbs.
B. Dec. 18, 1886, Narrows, Ga.   D. July 17, 1961, Atlanta, Ga.
Manager 1921-26.
Hall of Fame 1936.

Year	Team		W	L	PCT	ERA	G	GS	CG	IP	H	BB	SO	ShO	W	L	SV	AB	H	HR	BA	PO	A	E	DP	TC/G	FA
1918	DET	A	0	0	—	4.50	2	0	0	4	6	2	0	0	0	0	0	421	161	3	.382	0	1	0	0	0.5	1.000
1925			0	0	—	0.00	1	0	0	1	0	0	0	0	0	0	1	415	157	12	.378	0	1	0	0	1.0	1.000
2 yrs.			0	0	—	3.60	3	0	0	5	6	2	0	0	0	0	1	*				0	2	0	0	0.7	1.000

Jaime Cocanower

COCANOWER, JAMES STANLEY   BR TR 6'4"   200 lbs.
Born James Stanley Cocanower y Geiser.
B. Feb. 14, 1957, San Juan, Puerto Rico

Year	Team		W	L	PCT	ERA	G	GS	CG	IP	H	BB	SO	ShO	W	L	SV	AB	H	HR	BA	PO	A	E	DP	TC/G	FA
1983	MIL	A	2	0	1.000	1.80	5	3	1	30	21	12	8	0	0	0	0	—				4	6	1	0	2.2	.909
1984			8	16	.333	4.02	33	27	1	174.2	188	78	65	0	0	2	0	—				15	32	6	0	1.6	.887
1985			6	8	.429	4.33	24	15	3	116.1	122	73	44	1	1	0	0	—				7	20	4	1	1.3	.871
1986			0	1	.000	4.43	17	2	0	44.2	40	38	22	0	0	0	0	—				7	11	3	3	1.2	.857
4 yrs.			16	25	.390	3.99	79	47	5	365.2	371	201	139	1	1	2	0	—				33	69	14	4	1.5	.879

Al Cochran

COCHRAN, ALVAH JACKSON (Goat)   BR TR 5'10"   175 lbs.
B. Jan. 31, 1891, Concord, Ga.   D. May 23, 1947, Atlanta, Ga.

Year	Team		W	L	PCT	ERA	G	GS	CG	IP	H	BB	SO	ShO	W	L	SV	AB	H	HR	BA	PO	A	E	DP	TC/G	FA
1915	CIN	N	0	0	—	9.00	1	0	0	2	5	0	1	0	0	0	0	—				0	0	0	0	0.0	—

Gene Cocreham

COCREHAM, EUGENE   BR TR 6'3½"   192 lbs.
B. Nov. 14, 1884, Luling, Tex.   D. Dec. 27, 1945, Luling, Tex.

Year	Team		W	L	PCT	ERA	G	GS	CG	IP	H	BB	SO	ShO	W	L	SV	AB	H	HR	BA	PO	A	E	DP	TC/G	FA
1913	BOS	N	0	1	.000	7.56	1	1	0	8.1	13	4	3	0	0	0	0	4	0	0	.000	2	1	0	0	3.0	1.000
1914			3	4	.429	4.84	15	3	1	44.2	48	27	15	0	2	2	0	10	1	0	.100	1	6	1	0	0.5	.875
1915			0	0	—	5.40	1	0	0	1.2	3	0	0	0	0	0	0	0	0	0	—	0	0	0	0	0.0	—
3 yrs.			3	5	.375	5.27	17	4	1	54.2	64	31	18	0	2	2	0	14	1	0	.071	3	7	1	0	0.6	.909

Chris Codiroli

CODIROLI, CHRISTOPHER ALLEN   BR TR 6'1"   160 lbs.
B. Mar. 26, 1958, Oxnard, Calif.

Year	Team		W	L	PCT	ERA	G	GS	CG	IP	H	BB	SO	ShO	W	L	SV	AB	H	HR	BA	PO	A	E	DP	TC/G	FA
1982	OAK	A	1	2	.333	4.32	3	3	0	16.2	16	4	5	0	0	0	0	—				3	3	0	0	2.0	1.000
1983			12	12	.500	4.46	37	31	7	205.2	208	72	85	2	1	1	1	0	0	0	—	14	21	4	1	1.1	.897
1984			6	4	.600	5.84	28	14	1	89.1	111	34	44	0	1	0	1	0	0	0	—	5	11	1	1	0.6	.941
1985			14	14	.500	4.46	37	37	4	226	228	78	111	0	0	0	0	0	0	0	—	18	27	4	1	1.3	.918
1986			5	8	.385	4.03	16	16	1	91.2	91	38	43	0	0	0	0	0	0	0	—	13	15	5	2	2.1	.848
1987			0	2	.000	8.74	3	3	0	11.1	12	8	4	0	0	0	0	0	0	0	—	1	1	0	0	0.7	1.000
1988	CLE	A	0	4	.000	9.31	14	2	0	19.1	32	10	12	0	0	2	1	0	0	0	—	3	2	0	1	0.4	1.000
7 yrs.			38	46	.452	4.80	138	106	13	660	698	244	304	2	1	3	3	0	0	0	—	57	80	14	6	1.1	.907

Dick Coffman

COFFMAN, SAMUEL RICHARD   BR TR 6'2"   195 lbs.
Brother of Slick Coffman.
B. Dec. 18, 1906, Veto, Ala.   D. Mar. 24, 1972, Athens, Ala.

Year	Team		W	L	PCT	ERA	G	GS	CG	IP	H	BB	SO	ShO	W	L	SV	AB	H	HR	BA	PO	A	E	DP	TC/G	FA
1927	WAS	A	0	1	.000	3.38	5	2	0	16	20	2	5	0	0	0	0	3	1	0	.333	3	4	0	0	1.4	1.000
1928	STL	A	4	5	.444	6.09	29	7	3	85.2	122	37	25	0	0	1	1	23	1	0	.043	4	21	1	1	0.9	.962
1929			1	1	.500	5.98	27	3	1	52.2	61	14	11	0	1	0	1	7	0	0	.000	3	12	0	0	0.6	1.000
1930			8	18	.308	5.14	38	30	12	196	250	69	54	0	1	1	1	66	9	0	.136	6	43	0	0	1.3	1.000
1931			9	13	.409	3.88	32	17	11	169.1	159	51	39	2	2	4	1	51	4	0	.078	15	24	1	1	1.3	.975
1932	2 teams		STL A	(9G 5-3)		WAS A	(22G 1-6)																					
"	total		6	9	.400	4.06	31	15	5	137.1	158	52	31	2	1	1	0	44	3	0	.068	11	19	0	1	1.0	1.000
1933	STL	A	3	7	.300	5.89	21	13	3	81	114	39	19	1	0	1	1	27	1	0	.037	5	19	1	0	1.2	.960
1934			9	10	.474	4.53	40	21	6	173	212	59	55	0	2	0	3	51	11	0	.216	7	36	4	1	1.2	.915
1935			5	11	.313	6.14	41	18	5	143.2	206	46	34	0	1	3	7	41	6	0	.146	5	27	5	0	0.9	.865
1936	NY	N	7	5	.583	3.90	42	2	0	101.2	119	23	26	0	7	3	7	20	4	0	.200	11	26	1	1	0.9	.974
1937			8	3	.727	3.04	42	1	0	80	93	31	30	0	8	3	3	19	7	0	.368	2	20	1	2	0.5	.957
1938			8	4	.667	3.48	51	3	1	111.1	116	21	21	0	7	2	12	28	2	0	.071	3	18	3	1	0.5	.875
1939			1	2	.333	3.08	28	0	0	38	50	6	9	0	1	2	4	4	0	0	.000	2	7	0	0	0.4	.818
1940	BOS	N	1	5	.167	5.40	31	0	0	48.1	63	11	11	0	1	5	3	12	1	0	.083	4	7	0	0	0.4	1.000
1945	PHI	N	2	1	.667	5.13	14	0	0	26.1	39	2	2	0	2	1	0	4	1	0	.250	0	11	0	2	0.8	1.000
15 yrs.			72	95	.431	4.65	472	132	47	1460.1	1782	463	372	9	33	28	38	400	51	0	.128	82	293	19	10	0.8	.952

WORLD SERIES

Year	Team		W	L	PCT	ERA	G	GS	CG	IP	H	BB	SO	ShO	W	L	SV	AB	H	HR	BA	PO	A	E	DP	TC/G	FA
1936	NY	N	0	0	—	32.40	2	0	0	1.2	5	1	1	0	0	0	0	0	0	0	—	0	1	0	0	0.5	1.000

Year	Team		W	L	PCT	ERA	G	GS	CG	IP	H	BB	SO	ShO	W	L	SV	AB	H	HR	BA	PO	A	E	DP	TC/G	FA
															Relief Pitching			**Batting**									

Dick Coffman *continued*

Year	Team		W	L	PCT	ERA	G	GS	CG	IP	H	BB	SO	ShO	W	L	SV	AB	H	HR	BA	PO	A	E	DP	TC/G	FA
1937			0	0	–	4.15	2	0	0	4.1	2	5	1	0	0	0	0	1	0	0	.000	0	1	0	0	0.5	1.000
2 yrs.			0	0	–	12.00	4	0	0	6	7	6	2	0	0	0	0	1	0	0	.000	0	2	0	0	0.5	1.000

Kevin Coffman

COFFMAN, KEVIN REESE
B. Jan. 19, 1965, Austin, Tex.
BR TR 6'2" 175 lbs.

Year	Team		W	L	PCT	ERA	G	GS	CG	IP	H	BB	SO	ShO	W	L	SV	AB	H	HR	BA	PO	A	E	DP	TC/G	FA
1987	ATL	N	2	3	.400	4.62	5	5	0	25.1	31	22	14	0	0	0	0	10	1	0	.100	1	9	0	1	2.0	1.000
1988			2	6	.250	5.78	18	11	0	67	62	54	24	0	0	0	0	22	5	0	.227	9	12	2	1	1.3	.913
2 yrs.			4	9	.308	5.46	23	16	0	92.1	93	76	38	0	0	0	0	32	6	0	.188	10	21	2	2	1.4	.939

Slick Coffman

COFFMAN, GEORGE DAVID
Brother of Dick Coffman.
B. Dec. 11, 1910, Veto, Ala.
BR TR 6' 155 lbs.

Year	Team		W	L	PCT	ERA	G	GS	CG	IP	H	BB	SO	ShO	W	L	SV	AB	H	HR	BA	PO	A	E	DP	TC/G	FA
1937	DET	A	7	5	.583	4.37	28	5	1	101	121	39	22	0	5	3	0	29	5	0	.172	4	16	1	1	0.8	.952
1938			4	4	.500	6.02	39	6	0	95.2	120	48	31	0	3	1	2	24	4	0	.167	1	16	0	0	0.4	1.000
1939			2	1	.667	6.38	23	1	0	42.1	51	22	10	0	2	1	0	5	0	0	.000	1	8	0	0	0.4	1.000
1940	STL	A	2	2	.500	6.27	31	4	1	74.2	108	23	26	0	1	0	1	15	3	0	.200	3	19	0	0	0.7	1.000
4 yrs.			15	12	.556	5.60	121	16	2	313.2	400	132	89	0	11	5	3	73	12	0	.164	9	59	1	1	0.6	.986

Dick Cogan

COGAN, RICHARD HENRY
B. Dec. 5, 1871, Paterson, N. J. D. May 2, 1948, Paterson, N. J.
BR TR 5'7" 150 lbs.

Year	Team		W	L	PCT	ERA	G	GS	CG	IP	H	BB	SO	ShO	W	L	SV	AB	H	HR	BA	PO	A	E	DP	TC/G	FA
1897	BAL	N	0	0	–	13.50	1	0	0	2	4	2	0	0	0	0	0	1	0	0	.000	0	0	0	0	0.0	–
1899	CHI	N	2	3	.400	4.30	5	5	5	44	54	24	9	0	0	0	0	25	5	0	.200	2	8	4	0	2.8	.714
1900	NY	N	0	0	–	6.75	2	0	0	8	10	6	1	0	0	0	0	8	1	0	.125	0	1	0	0	0.5	1.000
3 yrs.			2	3	.400	5.00	8	5	5	54	68	32	10	0	0	0	0	34	6	0	.176	2	9	4	0	1.9	.733

Hy Cohen

COHEN, HYMAN
B. Jan. 29, 1931, Brooklyn, N. Y.
BR TR 6'5" 215 lbs.

Year	Team		W	L	PCT	ERA	G	GS	CG	IP	H	BB	SO	ShO	W	L	SV	AB	H	HR	BA	PO	A	E	DP	TC/G	FA
1955	CHI	N	0	0	–	7.94	7	1	0	17	28	10	4	0	0	0	0	3	0	0	.000	0	2	0	0	0.3	1.000

Syd Cohen

COHEN, SYDNEY HARRY
Brother of Andy Cohen.
B. May 7, 1908, Baltimore, Md. D. Apr. 9, 1988, El Paso, Tex.
BB TL 5'11" 180 lbs.

Year	Team		W	L	PCT	ERA	G	GS	CG	IP	H	BB	SO	ShO	W	L	SV	AB	H	HR	BA	PO	A	E	DP	TC/G	FA
1934	WAS	A	1	1	.500	7.50	3	2	2	18	25	6	6	0	0	0	0	11	3	0	.273	2	8	0	1	3.3	1.000
1936			0	2	.000	5.25	19	1	0	36	44	14	21	0	0	0	1	8	0	0	.000	2	16	0	0	0.9	1.000
1937			2	4	.333	3.11	33	0	0	55	64	17	22	0	2	4	4	14	2	0	.143	3	17	1	2	0.6	.952
3 yrs.			3	7	.300	4.54	55	3	2	109	133	37	49	0	2	5	5	33	5	0	.152	7	41	1	3	0.9	.980

Rocky Colavito

COLAVITO, ROCCO DOMENICO
B. Aug. 10, 1933, New York, N. Y.
BR TR 6'3" 190 lbs.

Year	Team		W	L	PCT	ERA	G	GS	CG	IP	H	BB	SO	ShO	W	L	SV	AB	H	HR	BA	PO	A	E	DP	TC/G	FA
1958	CLE	A	0	0	–	0.00	1	0	0	3	0	3	1	0	0	0	0	489	148	41	.303	0	1	0	0	1.0	1.000
1968	NY	A	1	0	1.000	0.00	1	0	0	2.2	1	2	1	0	1	0	0	204	43	8	.211	0	0	0	0	0.0	–
2 yrs.			1	0	1.000	0.00	2	0	0	5.2	1	5	2	0	1	0	0	*				0	1	0	0	0.5	1.000

Vince Colbert

COLBERT, VINCENT NORMAN
B. Dec. 20, 1945, Washington, D. C.
BR TR 6'4" 200 lbs.

Year	Team		W	L	PCT	ERA	G	GS	CG	IP	H	BB	SO	ShO	W	L	SV	AB	H	HR	BA	PO	A	E	DP	TC/G	FA
1970	CLE	A	1	1	.500	7.26	23	0	0	31	37	16	17	0	1	1	2	2	0	0	.000	2	6	1	0	0.4	.889
1971			7	6	.538	3.97	50	10	2	143	140	71	74	0	2	1	2	29	4	0	.138	11	26	4	0	0.8	.902
1972			1	7	.125	4.56	22	11	1	75	74	38	36	1	0	0	0	20	4	0	.200	1	15	0	2	0.7	1.000
3 yrs.			9	14	.391	4.55	95	21	3	249	251	125	127	1	3	2	4	51	8	0	.157	14	47	5	2	0.7	.924

Jim Colborn

COLBORN, JAMES WILLIAM
B. May 22, 1946, Santa Paula, Calif.
BR TR 6' 185 lbs.

Year	Team		W	L	PCT	ERA	G	GS	CG	IP	H	BB	SO	ShO	W	L	SV	AB	H	HR	BA	PO	A	E	DP	TC/G	FA
1969	CHI	N	1	0	1.000	3.00	6	2	0	15	15	9	4	0	0	0	0	3	0	0	.000	1	4	0	1	0.8	1.000
1970			3	1	.750	3.58	34	5	0	73	88	23	50	0	2	1	4	15	1	0	.067	4	13	1	1	0.5	.944
1971			0	1	.000	7.20	14	0	0	10	18	3	2	0	0	1	0	0	0	0	–	0	4	0	0	0.3	1.000
1972	MIL	A	7	7	.500	3.10	39	12	4	148	135	43	97	1	2	0	0	37	3	0	.081	8	17	1	1	0.7	.962
1973			20	12	.625	3.18	43	36	22	314.1	297	87	135	4	2	0	1	0	0	0	–	19	55	0	4	1.7	1.000
1974			10	13	.435	4.06	33	31	10	224	230	60	83	1	1	0	0	0	0	0	–	19	35	4	0	1.8	.931
1975			11	13	.458	4.27	36	29	8	206.1	215	65	79	1	0	1	2	0	0	0	–	15	36	2	2	1.5	.962
1976			9	15	.375	3.71	32	32	7	225.2	234	54	101	4	0	0	0	0	0	0	–	11	32	1	4	1.4	.977
1977	KC	A	18	14	.563	3.62	36	35	6	239	233	81	103	1	0	0	0	0	0	0	–	27	39	3	3	2.0	.930
1978	2 teams																										
"	total		4	12	.250	5.26	28	24	3	142	156	50	34	0	0	0	0	0	0	0	–	10	39	3	2	1.9	.942
10 yrs.			83	88	.485	3.80	301	204	60	1597.1	1619	475	688	8	7	4	7	55	4	0	.073	114	274	17	18	1.3	.958

1978 2 teams: KC A (8G 1-2) SEA A (20G 3-10)

Tom Colcolough

COLCOLOUGH, THOMAS BERNARD
B. Oct. 8, 1870, Charleston, S. C. D. Dec. 10, 1919, Charleston, S. C.
BR TR 5'10½" 180 lbs.

Year	Team		W	L	PCT	ERA	G	GS	CG	IP	H	BB	SO	ShO	W	L	SV	AB	H	HR	BA	PO	A	E	DP	TC/G	FA
1893	PIT	N	2	0	1.000	4.12	8	3	1	43.2	45	32	7	0	1	0	1	14	2	0	.143	3	7	1	0	1.4	.909
1894			8	5	.615	7.08	22	14	11	148.2	207	70	29	0	1	0	0	70	14	0	.200	7	30	3	1	1.8	.925
1895			1	1	.500	5.60	6	5	2	35.1	38	21	15	0	1	0	0	15	5	0	.333	1	5	1	0	1.2	.857
1899	NY	N	4	5	.444	3.97	11	8	7	81.2	85	41	14	0	0	0	0	37	10	0	.270	6	24	2	0	2.9	.938
4 yrs.			15	11	.577	5.67	47	30	21	309.1	375	164	65	0	3	0	1	136	31	0	.228	17	66	7	1	1.9	.922

Bert Cole

COLE, ALBERT GEORGE
B. July 1, 1896, San Francisco, Calif. D. May 30, 1975, San Mateo, Calif.
BL TL 6'1" 180 lbs.

Year	Team		W	L	PCT	ERA	G	GS	CG	IP	H	BB	SO	ShO	W	L	SV	AB	H	HR	BA	PO	A	E	DP	TC/G	FA
1921	DET	A	7	4	.636	4.27	20	11	7	109.2	134	36	22	1	1	0	1	46	13	0	.283	3	28	0	0	1.6	1.000
1922			1	6	.143	4.88	23	5	2	79.1	105	39	21	1	0	3	0	25	4	0	.160	6	21	2	1	1.3	.931
1923			13	5	.722	4.14	52	13	5	163	183	61	32	1	5	2	5	55	14	1	.255	9	37	1	1	0.9	.979
1924			3	9	.250	4.69	28	11	2	109.1	135	35	16	1	2	2	1	37	10	0	.270	11	28	1	0	1.4	.975

Year	Team	W	L	PCT	ERA	G	GS	CG	IP	H	BB	SO	ShO	Relief Pitching W	L	SV	Batting AB	H	HR	BA	PO	A	E	DP	TC/G	FA

Bert Cole *continued*

Year	Team	W	L	PCT	ERA	G	GS	CG	IP	H	BB	SO	ShO	W	L	SV	AB	H	HR	BA	PO	A	E	DP	TC/G	FA
1925	2 teams	DET A	(14G 2–3)	CLE A	(13G 1–1)																					
"	total	3	4	.429	6.03	27	4	1	77.2	99	40	16	0	2	2	2	24	5	0	.208	6	22	2	0	1.1	.933
1927	CHI A	1	4	.200	4.73	27	2	0	66.2	79	19	12	0	1	3	0	18	3	0	.167	1	27	2	1	1.1	.933
6 yrs.		28	32	.467	4.67	177	46	17	605.2	735	230	119	4	10	12	10	205	49	1	.239	36	163	8	3	1.2	.961

Dave Cole

COLE, DAVID BRUCE
B. Aug. 29, 1930, Williamsport, Pa.

BR TR 6'2" 175 lbs.

Year	Team	W	L	PCT	ERA	G	GS	CG	IP	H	BB	SO	ShO	W	L	SV	AB	H	HR	BA	PO	A	E	DP	TC/G	FA
1950	BOS N	0	1	.000	1.13	4	0	0	8	7	3	8	0	0	1	0	1	0	0	.000	1	0	0	0	0.3	1.000
1951		2	4	.333	4.26	23	7	1	67.2	64	64	33	0	0	2	0	17	6	1	.353	4	13	1	2	0.8	.944
1952		1	1	.500	4.03	22	3	0	44.2	38	42	22	0	0	0	0	8	0	0	.000	1	9	0	1	0.5	1.000
1953	MIL N	0	1	.000	8.59	10	0	0	14.2	17	14	13	0	0	1	0	2	1	1	.500	1	4	0	0	0.5	1.000
1954	CHI N	3	8	.273	5.36	18	14	2	84	74	62	37	1	0	0	0	28	6	1	.214	9	11	1	0	1.2	.952
1955	PHI N	0	3	.000	6.38	7	3	0	18.1	21	14	6	0	0	0	0	5	1	0	.200	0	6	1	1	1.0	.857
6 yrs.		6	18	.250	4.93	84	27	3	237.1	221	199	119	1	0	4	0	61	14	3	.230	16	43	3	4	0.7	.952

Ed Cole

COLE, EDWARD WILLIAM
Born Edward William Kisleauskas.
B. Mar. 22, 1909, Wilkes-Barre, Pa.

BR TR 5'11" 170 lbs.

Year	Team	W	L	PCT	ERA	G	GS	CG	IP	H	BB	SO	ShO	W	L	SV	AB	H	HR	BA	PO	A	E	DP	TC/G	FA
1938	STL A	1	5	.167	5.18	36	6	1	88.2	116	48	26	0	0	2	3	21	3	0	.143	0	15	2	0	0.5	.882
1939		0	2	.000	7.11	6	0	0	6.1	8	6	5	0	0	2	0	1	0	0	.000	0	1	0	0	0.2	1.000
2 yrs.		1	7	.125	5.31	42	6	1	95	124	54	31	0	0	4	3	22	3	0	.136	0	16	2	0	0.4	.889

King Cole

COLE, LEONARD LESLIE
B. Apr. 15, 1886, Toledo, Iowa   D. Jan. 6, 1916, Bay City, Mich.

BR TR 6'1" 170 lbs.

Year	Team	W	L	PCT	ERA	G	GS	CG	IP	H	BB	SO	ShO	W	L	SV	AB	H	HR	BA	PO	A	E	DP	TC/G	FA
1909	CHI N	1	0	1.000	0.00	1	1	1	9	6	3	1	0	0	0	0	4	3	0	.750	0	1	0	0	1.0	1.000
1910		20	4	**.833**	1.80	33	29	21	239.2	174	130	114	4	2	0	0	91	21	0	.231	3	65	7	3	2.3	.907
1911		18	7	.720	3.13	32	27	13	221.1	188	99	101	2	1	0	0	79	12	0	.152	3	52	5	5	1.9	.917
1912	2 teams	CHI N	(8G 1–2)	PIT N	(12G 2–2)																					
"	total	3	4	.429	7.68	20	7	2	68	97	26	20	0	1	1	0	20	4	0	.200	1	21	3	0	1.3	.880
1914	NY A	11	9	.550	3.30	33	15	8	141.2	151	51	43	2	5	2	0	42	2	0	.048	4	29	3	1	1.1	.917
1915		3	3	.500	3.18	10	6	2	51	41	22	19	0	1	0	1	13	1	0	.077	1	16	4	1	2.1	.810
6 yrs.		56	27	.675	3.12	129	85	47	730.2	657	331	298	9	10	4	1	249	43	0	.173	12	184	22	10	1.7	.899

WORLD SERIES

Year	Team	W	L	PCT	ERA	G	GS	CG	IP	H	BB	SO	ShO	W	L	SV	AB	H	HR	BA	PO	A	E	DP	TC/G	FA
1910	CHI N	0	0	–	3.38	1	1	0	8	10	3	5	0	0	0	0	2	0	0	.000	1	3	0	1	4.0	1.000

Joe Coleman

COLEMAN, JOSEPH HOWARD
Son of Joe Coleman.
B. Feb. 3, 1947, Boston, Mass.

BR TR 6'3" 175 lbs.

Year	Team	W	L	PCT	ERA	G	GS	CG	IP	H	BB	SO	ShO	W	L	SV	AB	H	HR	BA	PO	A	E	DP	TC/G	FA
1965	WAS A	2	0	1.000	1.50	2	2	2	18	9	8	7	0	0	0	0	6	0	0	.000	0	6	0	1	3.0	1.000
1966		1	0	1.000	2.00	1	1	1	9	9	2	4	0	0	0	0	3	0	0	.000	2	2	0	1	4.0	1.000
1967		8	9	.471	4.63	28	23	3	134	154	47	77	0	0	1	0	36	2	0	.056	9	14	1	0	0.9	.958
1968		12	16	.429	3.27	33	33	12	223	212	51	139	2	0	0	0	70	9	0	.129	30	20	3	0	1.6	.943
1969		12	13	.480	3.27	40	36	12	247.2	222	100	182	4	0	0	1	84	9	0	.107	21	35	2	3	1.5	.966
1970		8	12	.400	3.58	39	29	6	219	190	89	152	1	0	0	0	67	8	0	.119	16	30	0	3	1.2	1.000
1971	DET A	20	9	.690	3.15	39	38	16	286	241	96	236	3	0	0	0	96	9	0	.094	18	32	3	2	1.4	.943
1972		19	14	.576	2.80	40	39	9	279.2	216	110	222	3	0	0	0	82	9	0	.110	6	39	1	2	1.2	.978
1973		23	15	.605	3.53	40	40	13	288	283	93	202	2	0	0	0	0	0	0	–	23	37	2	1	1.6	.968
1974		14	12	.538	4.31	41	41	11	286	272	158	177	2	0	0	0	0	0	0	–	21	47	3	4	1.7	.958
1975		10	18	.357	5.55	31	31	6	201	234	85	125	1	0	0	0	0	0	0	–	6	32	2	1	1.3	.950
1976	2 teams	DET A	(12G 2–5)	CHI N	(39G 2–8)																					
"	total	4	13	.235	4.44	51	16	1	146	152	69	104	0	2	5	4	13	2	0	.154	8	31	4	2	0.8	.907
1977	OAK A	4	4	.500	2.95	43	12	2	128	114	49	55	0	0	2	2	0	0	0	–	13	17	3	2	0.8	.909
1978	2 teams	OAK A	(10G 3–0)	TOR A	(31G 2–0)																					
"	total	5	0	1.000	3.78	41	0	0	81	79	35	32	0	5	0	0	0	0	0	–	5	9	0	0	0.3	1.000
1979	2 teams	SF N	(5G 0–0)	PIT N	(10G 0–0)																					
"	total	0	0	–	5.18	15	0	0	24.1	32	11	14	0	0	0	0	5	1	0	.200	1	0	1	0	0.1	.500
15 yrs.		142	135	.513	3.69	484	340	94	2570.2	2416	1003	1728	18	7	6	7	462	49	0	.106	179	351	25	22	1.1	.955

LEAGUE CHAMPIONSHIP SERIES

Year	Team	W	L	PCT	ERA	G	GS	CG	IP	H	BB	SO	ShO	W	L	SV	AB	H	HR	BA	PO	A	E	DP	TC/G	FA
1972	DET A	1	0	1.000	0.00	1	1	1	9	7	3	14	1	0	0	0	2	1	0	.500	0	0	0	0	0.0	

Joe Coleman

COLEMAN, JOSEPH PATRICK
Father of Joe Coleman.
B. July 30, 1922, Medford, Mass.

BR TR 6'2½" 200 lbs.

Year	Team	W	L	PCT	ERA	G	GS	CG	IP	H	BB	SO	ShO	W	L	SV	AB	H	HR	BA	PO	A	E	DP	TC/G	FA
1942	PHI A	0	1	.000	3.00	1	0	0	6	8	1	0	0	0	1	0	4	0	0	.000	0	1	0	0	1.0	1.000
1946		0	2	.000	5.54	4	2	0	13	19	8	8	0	0	0	0	5	2	0	.400	0	1	0	0	0.3	1.000
1947		6	12	.333	4.32	32	21	9	160.1	171	62	65	2	1	0	1	48	7	0	.146	5	16	1	0	0.7	.955
1948		14	13	.519	4.09	33	29	13	215.2	224	90	86	3	1	1	0	74	9	0	.122	6	33	3	3	1.3	.929
1949		13	14	.481	3.86	33	30	18	240.1	249	127	109	1	1	1	0	79	14	1	.177	7	23	2	3	1.0	.938
1950		0	5	.000	8.50	15	6	2	54	74	50	12	0	0	0	0	17	1	0	.059	3	0	0	0	0.2	1.000
1951		1	6	.143	5.98	26	9	1	96.1	117	59	34	0	0	2	2	27	7	0	.259	7	9	1	1	0.6	.941
1953		3	4	.429	4.00	21	9	2	90	85	49	18	1	0	1	0	28	8	0	.286	1	10	0	0	0.5	1.000
1954	BAL A	13	17	.433	3.50	33	32	15	221.1	184	96	103	4	0	1	0	74	13	2	.176	15	41	3	5	1.8	.949
1955	2 teams	BAL A	(6G 0–1)	DET A	(17G 2–1)																					
"	total	2	2	.500	5.59	23	2	0	37	41	24	9	0	2	1	3	7	5	0	.714	3	8	0	0	0.5	1.000
10 yrs.		52	76	.406	4.38	223	140	60	1134	1172	566	444	11	4	6	6	363	66	4	.182	44	145	10	12	0.9	.950

John Coleman

COLEMAN, JOHN
B. Bristol, Pa.   Deceased.

TR

Year	Team	W	L	PCT	ERA	G	GS	CG	IP	H	BB	SO	ShO	W	L	SV	AB	H	HR	BA	PO	A	E	DP	TC/G	FA
1890	PHI N	0	1	.000	21.60	1	1	0	1.2	4	3	2	0	0	0	0	0	0	0	–	0	0	0	0	0.0	–

Year	Team		W	L	PCT	ERA	G	GS	CG	IP	H	BB	SO	ShO	Relief Pitching W	L	SV	Batting AB	H	HR	BA	PO	A	E	DP	TC/G	FA

John Coleman

COLEMAN, JOHN
B. 1870, Jefferson City, Mo. Deceased.

TL

| 1895 | STL | N | 0 | 1 | .000 | 13.50 | 1 | 1 | 1 | 8 | 12 | 8 | 5 | 0 | 0 | 0 | 0 | 5 | 1 | 0 | .200 | 0 | 2 | 1 | 0 | 3.0 | .667 |

John Coleman

COLEMAN, JOHN FRANCIS
B. Mar. 6, 1863, Saratoga Springs, N. Y.
D. May 31, 1922, Detroit, Mich.

BL TR 5'9½" 170 lbs.
BB 1887

1883	PHI	N	12	48	.200	4.87	65	61	59	538.1	772	48	159	3	0	1	0	354	83	0	.234	22	118	18	2	2.4	.886
1884	2 teams	PHI N (21G 5–15)				PHI AA (3G 0–2)																					
"	total		5	17	.227	4.72	24	21	16	175.1	244	24	42	1	1	0	0	278	64	2	.230	14	43	3	0	2.5	.950
1885	PHI	AA	2	2	.500	3.43	8	3	3	60.1	82	5	12	0	1	0	0	398	119	2	.299	2	9	0	0	1.4	1.000
1886			1	1	.500	2.61	3	1	1	20.2	18	5	2	0	0	1	0	535	136	0	.254	0	1	0	0	0.3	1.000
1889			3	2	.600	2.91	5	5	4	34	38	14	6	0	0	0	0	19	1	0	.053	3	10	1	0	2.8	.929
1890	PIT	N	0	2	.000	9.64	2	2	1	14	28	6	3	0	0	0	0	11	2	0	.182	1	1	0	0	1.0	1.000
6 yrs.			23	72	.242	4.68	107	93	84	842.2	1182	102	224	4	2	2	0	*				42	182	22	2	2.3	.911

Percy Coleman

COLEMAN, PIERCE D.
B. Oct. 15, 1876, Mason, Ohio D. Feb. 16, 1948, Van Nuys, Calif.

1897	STL	N	1	3	.250	8.16	12	4	2	57.1	99	32	10	0	0	0	0	28	6	0	.214	5	15	2	0	1.8	.909
1898	CIN	N	0	1	.000	3.00	1	1	1	9	13	3	2	0	0	0	0	3	0	0	.000	0	1	1	0	2.0	.500
2 yrs.			1	4	.200	7.46	13	5	3	66.1	112	35	12	0	0	0	0	31	6	0	.194	5	16	3	0	1.8	.875

Rip Coleman

COLEMAN, WALTER GARY
B. July 31, 1931, Troy, N. Y.

BL TL 6'2" 185 lbs.

1955	NY	A	2	1	.667	5.28	10	6	0	29	40	16	15	0	0	0	1	10	2	0	.200	2	5	0	0	0.7	1.000
1956			3	5	.375	3.67	29	9	0	88.1	97	42	42	0	1	3	2	24	1	0	.042	10	14	2	0	0.9	.923
1957	KC	A	0	7	.000	5.93	19	6	1	41	53	25	15	1	0	4	0	9	0	0	.000	1	9	1	1	0.6	.909
1959	2 teams	KC A (29G 2–10)				BAL A (3G 0–0)																					
"	total		2	10	.167	4.34	32	11	0	85	89	36	58	0	0	4	2	25	2	0	.080	1	18	2	3	0.7	.905
1960	BAL	A	0	2	.000	11.25	5	1	0	4	8	5	0	0	0	1	0	1	0	0	.000	1	2	0	0	0.6	1.000
5 yrs.			7	25	.219	4.58	95	33	3	247.1	287	124	130	1	1	12	5	69	5	0	.072	15	48	5	4	0.7	.926

WORLD SERIES

| 1955 | NY | A | 0 | 0 | — | 9.00 | 1 | 0 | 0 | 1 | 5 | 0 | 1 | 0 | 0 | 0 | 0 | 0 | 0 | 0 | — | 0 | 0 | 0 | 0 | 0.0 | — |

Allan Collamore

COLLAMORE, ALLAN EDWARD
B. June 5, 1887, Worcester, Mass. D. Aug. 8, 1980, Battle Creek, Mich.

BR TR 6' 170 lbs.

1911	PHI	A	0	1	.000	36.00	2	0	0	2	6	3	1	0	0	0	0	—	0	0	—	0	0	0	0	0.0	—
1914	CLE	A	3	7	.300	3.25	27	8	3	105.1	100	49	32	0	1	1	0	32	3	0	.094	5	28	3	2	1.3	.917
1915			2	5	.286	2.38	11	6	5	64.1	52	22	15	2	0	1	0	23	4	0	.174	4	22	1	1	2.5	.963
3 yrs.			5	13	.278	3.30	40	14	8	171.2	158	74	48	2	1	3	0	55	7	0	.127	9	50	4	3	1.6	.937

Hap Collard

COLLARD, EARL CLINTON
B. Aug. 29, 1898, Williams, Ariz. D. July 9, 1968, Jamestown, Calif.

BR TR 6' 170 lbs.

1927	CLE	A	0	0	—	5.06	4	0	0	5.1	8	3	2	0	0	0	0	—	0	0	—	0	3	1	0	1.0	.750
1928			0	0	—	2.25	1	0	0	4	4	4	1	0	0	0	0	1	1	0	1.000	0	0	0	0	0.0	—
1930	PHI	N	6	12	.333	6.80	30	15	4	127	188	39	25	0	2	2	0	44	9	0	.205	8	32	1	2	1.4	.976
3 yrs.			6	12	.333	6.60	35	15	4	136.1	200	46	28	0	2	2	0	45	10	0	.222	8	35	2	2	1.3	.956

Orlin Collier

COLLIER, ORLIN EDWARD
B. Feb. 17, 1907, East Prairie, Mo. D. Sept. 9, 1944, Memphis, Tenn.

BR TR 5'11½" 180 lbs.

| 1931 | DET | A | 0 | 1 | .000 | 7.84 | 2 | 2 | 0 | 10.1 | 17 | 7 | 3 | 0 | 0 | 0 | 0 | 3 | 0 | 0 | .000 | 0 | 1 | 0 | 0 | 0.5 | 1.000 |

Harry Colliflower

COLLIFLOWER, JAMES HARRY (Collie)
B. Mar. 11, 1869, Petersville, Md. D. Aug. 12, 1961, Washington, D. C.

BL TL 5'11½" 175 lbs.

| 1899 | CLE | N | 1 | 11 | .083 | 8.17 | 14 | 12 | 11 | 98 | 152 | 41 | 8 | 0 | 0 | 0 | 0 | 76 | 23 | 0 | .303 | 1 | 26 | 4 | 2 | 2.2 | .871 |

Don Collins

COLLINS, DONALD EDWARD
B. Sept. 15, 1952, Lyons, Ga.

BR TL 6'2" 195 lbs.

1977	ATL	N	3	9	.250	5.07	40	6	0	71	82	41	27	0	3	4	2	11	0	0	.000	1	7	0	0	0.2	1.000
1980	CLE	A	0	0	—	7.50	4	0	0	6	9	7	0	0	0	0	0	0	0	0	—	0	1	0	0	0.3	1.000
2 yrs.			3	9	.250	5.26	44	6	0	77	91	48	27	0	3	4	2	11	0	0	.000	1	8	0	0	0.2	1.000

Orth Collins

COLLINS, ORTH STEIN (Buck)
B. Apr. 27, 1880, Lafayette, Ind. D. Dec. 13, 1949, Fort Lauderdale, Fla.

BL TR 6' 150 lbs.

| 1909 | WAS | A | 0 | 0 | — | 0.00 | 1 | 0 | 0 | 1 | 0 | 0 | 1 | 0 | 0 | 0 | 0 | * | | | | 0 | 0 | 0 | 0 | 0.0 | — |

Phil Collins

COLLINS, PHILIP EUGENE (Fidgety Phil)
B. Aug. 27, 1901, Chicago, Ill. D. Aug. 14, 1948, Chicago, Ill.

BR TR 5'11" 175 lbs.

1923	CHI	N	1	0	1.000	3.60	1	1	0	5	8	1	2	0	0	0	0	2	0	0	.000	0	3	0	1	3.0	1.000
1929	PHI	N	9	7	.563	5.75	43	11	3	153.1	172	83	61	0	7	2	5	58	11	1	.190	7	27	1	0	0.8	.971
1930			16	11	.593	4.78	47	25	7	239	287	86	87	1	3	1	3	87	22	3	.253	12	39	5	0	1.2	.911
1931			12	16	.429	3.86	42	27	16	240.1	268	83	73	2	0	2	4	95	16	0	.168	17	51	5	2	1.7	.932
1932			14	12	.538	5.27	43	21	6	184.1	231	65	66	0	5	3	3	68	18	0	.265	7	41	9	3	1.3	.842
1933			8	13	.381	4.11	42	13	5	151	178	57	40	1	3	6	6	53	7	0	.132	8	25	2	3	0.8	.943
1934			13	18	.419	4.18	45	32	15	254	277	87	72	0	4	1	1	88	15	0	.170	7	40	3	2	1.1	.940
1935	2 teams	PHI N (3G 0–2)				STL N (26G 7–6)																					
"	total		7	8	.467	5.64	29	11	2	97.1	120	35	22	0	3	2	2	31	4	0	.129	7	17	1	1	0.9	.960
8 yrs.			80	85	.485	4.66	292	141	64	1324.1	1541	497	423	4	25	17	24	482	93	4	.193	65	243	26	12	1.1	.922

Year	Team		W	L	PCT	ERA	G	GS	CG	IP	H	BB	SO	ShO	Relief Pitching W	L	SV	Batting AB	H	HR	BA	PO	A	E	DP	TC/G	FA

Ray Collins *continued*

Year	Team		W	L	PCT	ERA	G	GS	CG	IP	H	BB	SO	ShO	W	L	SV	AB	H	HR	BA	PO	A	E	DP	TC/G	FA
1915			4	7	.364	4.30	25	9	2	104.2	101	31	43	0	2	2	2	28	8	0	.286	2	16	1	2	0.8	.947
7 yrs.			84	62	.575	2.51	199	150	90	1345	1251	271	513	19	10	4	4	419	69	1	.165	38	299	15	7	1.8	.957

WORLD SERIES

| 1912 | BOS | A | 0 | 0 | — | 1.88 | 2 | 1 | 0 | 14.1 | 14 | 0 | 6 | 0 | 0 | 0 | 0 | 5 | 0 | 0 | .000 | 0 | 3 | 0 | 3 | 1.5 | 1.000 |

Rip Collins

COLLINS, HARRY WARREN
B. Feb. 26, 1896, Weatherford, Tex.
D. May 27, 1968, Bryan, Tex.

BR TR 6'1" 205 lbs.
BL 1920,
BB 1921-23

Year	Team		W	L	PCT	ERA	G	GS	CG	IP	H	BB	SO	ShO	W	L	SV	AB	H	HR	BA	PO	A	E	DP	TC/G	FA
1920	NY	A	14	8	.636	3.17	36	20	12	187.1	171	79	66	3	4	0	1	62	8	0	.129	7	44	2	3	1.5	.962
1921			11	5	.688	5.44	28	16	7	137.1	158	78	64	2	1	2	0	56	11	0	.196	3	29	2	1	1.2	.941
1922	BOS	A	14	11	.560	3.76	32	29	15	210.2	219	103	69	3	0	0	0	76	12	0	.158	16	45	1	2	1.9	.984
1923	DET	A	3	7	.300	4.87	17	13	3	92.1	104	32	25	1	0	0	0	27	3	0	.111	8	24	2	0	2.0	.941
1924			14	7	.667	3.21	34	30	11	216	199	63	75	1	0	0	0	76	11	0	.145	11	50	3	2	1.9	.953
1925			6	11	.353	4.56	26	20	5	140	149	52	33	0	0	0	0	42	5	0	.119	7	53	1	0	2.3	.984
1926			8	8	.500	2.73	30	13	5	122	128	44	44	3	2	3	1	39	6	0	.154	5	37	5	2	1.6	.894
1927			13	7	.650	4.69	30	25	10	172.2	207	59	37	1	1	0	0	54	11	0	.204	11	64	1	6	2.5	.987
1929	STL	A	11	6	.647	4.00	26	20	10	155.1	162	73	47	1	1	1	1	62	17	1	.274	7	34	0	1	1.6	1.000
1930			9	7	.563	4.35	35	20	6	171.2	168	63	75	1	0	0	2	54	7	0	.130	11	29	0	1	1.1	1.000
1931			5	5	.500	3.79	17	14	2	107	130	38	34	0	0	1	0	34	5	0	.147	4	28	1	2	1.9	.970
11 yrs.			108	82	.568	3.99	311	220	86	1712.1	1795	684	569	16	9	7	5	582	96	1	.165	90	437	18	20	1.8	.967

WORLD SERIES

| 1921 | NY | A | 0 | 0 | — | 54.00 | 1 | 0 | 0 | .2 | 4 | 1 | 0 | 0 | 0 | 0 | 0 | 0 | 0 | 0 | — | 0 | 0 | 0 | 0 | 0.0 | — |

Jackie Collum

COLLUM, JACK DEAN
B. June 21, 1927, Victor, Iowa

BL TL 5'7½" 160 lbs.

Year	Team		W	L	PCT	ERA	G	GS	CG	IP	H	BB	SO	ShO	W	L	SV	AB	H	HR	BA	PO	A	E	DP	TC/G	FA
1951	STL	N	2	1	.667	1.59	3	2	1	17	11	10	5	1	0	1	0	7	3	0	.429	2	4	0	0	2.0	1.000
1952			0	0	—	0.00	2	0	0	3	2	1	0	0	0	0	0	0	0	0	—	0	2	0	0	1.0	1.000
1953	2 teams	STL N (7G 0-0)				CIN N		(30G 7-11)																				
"	total		7	11	.389	3.97	37	12	4	136	138	43	56	1	3	3	3	39	10	0	.256	4	33	0	3	1.0	1.000
1954	CIN	N	7	3	.700	3.74	36	2	1	79.1	86	32	28	0	7	2	0	13	3	1	.231	11	24	1	0	1.0	.972
1955			9	8	.529	3.63	32	17	5	134	128	37	49	0	2	1	1	40	10	0	.250	6	24	3	0	1.0	.909
1956	STL	N	6	2	.750	4.20	38	1	0	60	63	27	17	0	6	2	7	14	3	0	.214	4	16	2	1	0.6	.909
1957	2 teams	CHI N (9G 0-0)				BKN N		(3G 0-0)																				
"	total		1	1	.500	7.20	12	0	0	15	15	10	10	0	0	0	0	0	0	0	—	2	1	0	0	0.3	1.000
1958	LA	N	0	0	—	8.10	2	0	0	3.1	4	2	0	0	0	0	0	1	0	0	.000	0	1	0	1	0.5	1.000
1962	2 teams	MIN A (8G 0-2)				CLE A		(1G 0-0)																				
"	total		0	2	.000	11.34	9	3	0	16.2	33	11	6	0	0	0	0	4	0	0	.000	1	4	1	0	0.7	.833
9 yrs.			32	28	.533	4.15	171	37	11	464.1	480	173	171	2	19	10	12	118	29	1	.246	30	109	7	5	0.9	.952

Dick Colpaert

COLPAERT, RICHARD CHARLES
B. Jan. 3, 1944, Freaser, Mich.

BR TR 5'10" 182 lbs.

Year	Team		W	L	PCT	ERA	G	GS	CG	IP	H	BB	SO	ShO	W	L	SV	AB	H	HR	BA	PO	A	E	DP	TC/G	FA
1970	PIT	N	1	0	1.000	5.73	8	0	0	11	9	8	6	0	1	0	0	0	0	0	—	2	0	0	0	0.3	1.000

Loyd Colson

COLSON, LOYD ALBERT
B. Nov. 4, 1947, Wellington, Tex.

BR TR 6'1" 190 lbs.

Year	Team		W	L	PCT	ERA	G	GS	CG	IP	H	BB	SO	ShO	W	L	SV	AB	H	HR	BA	PO	A	E	DP	TC/G	FA
1970	NY	A	0	0	—	4.50	1	0	0	2	3	0	3	0	0	0	0	0	0	0	—	0	0	0	0	0.0	—

Larry Colton

COLTON, LAWRENCE ROBERT
B. June 8, 1942, Los Angeles, Calif.

BL TR 6'3" 200 lbs.

Year	Team		W	L	PCT	ERA	G	GS	CG	IP	H	BB	SO	ShO	W	L	SV	AB	H	HR	BA	PO	A	E	DP	TC/G	FA
1968	PHI	N	0	0	—	4.50	1	0	0	2	0	2	0	0	0	0	0	0	0	0	—	0	0	0	0	0.0	—

Jeff Combe

COMBE, GEOFFREY WADE
B. Feb. 1, 1956, Melrose, Mass.

BR TR 6'2" 185 lbs.

Year	Team		W	L	PCT	ERA	G	GS	CG	IP	H	BB	SO	ShO	W	L	SV	AB	H	HR	BA	PO	A	E	DP	TC/G	FA
1980	CIN	N	0	0	—	10.29	4	0	0	7	9	4	10	0	0	0	0	0	0	0	—	0	1	0	0	0.3	1.000
1981			1	0	1.000	7.50	14	0	0	18	27	10	9	0	1	0	0	0	0	0	—	0	2	0	0	0.1	1.000
2 yrs.			1	0	1.000	8.28	18	0	0	25	36	14	19	0	1	0	0	0	0	0	—	0	3	0	0	0.2	1.000

Pat Combs

COMBS, PATRICK DENNIS
B. Oct. 29, 1966, Newport, R. I.

BL TL 6'3" 200 lbs.

Year	Team		W	L	PCT	ERA	G	GS	CG	IP	H	BB	SO	ShO	W	L	SV	AB	H	HR	BA	PO	A	E	DP	TC/G	FA
1989	PHI	N	4	0	1.000	2.09	6	6	1	38.2	36	6	30	1	0	0	0	12	2	0	.167	1	3	0	0	0.7	1.000

Jorge Comellas

COMELLAS, JORGE (Pancho)
Born Jorge Comellas y Pous.
B. Dec. 7, 1916, Havana, Cuba

BR TR 6' 185 lbs.

Year	Team		W	L	PCT	ERA	G	GS	CG	IP	H	BB	SO	ShO	W	L	SV	AB	H	HR	BA	PO	A	E	DP	TC/G	FA
1945	CHI	N	0	2	.000	4.50	7	1	0	12	11	6	6	0	0	1	0	3	0	0	.000	0	9	0	1	1.3	1.000

Steve Comer

COMER, STEPHEN MICHAEL
B. Jan. 13, 1954, Minneapolis, Minn.

BB TR 6'3" 195 lbs.

Year	Team		W	L	PCT	ERA	G	GS	CG	IP	H	BB	SO	ShO	W	L	SV	AB	H	HR	BA	PO	A	E	DP	TC/G	FA
1978	TEX	A	11	5	.688	2.30	30	11	3	117.1	107	37	65	2	5	5	1	0	0	0	—	8	20	1	0	1.0	.966
1979			17	12	.586	3.68	36	36	6	242	230	84	86	1	0	0	0	0	0	0	—	19	38	4	0	1.7	.934
1980			2	4	.333	7.93	12	11	0	42	65	22	9	0	0	0	0	0	0	0	—	6	5	1	1	1.0	.917
1981			8	2	.800	2.57	36	1	0	77	70	31	22	0	8	1	6	0	0	0	—	5	18	1	2	0.7	.958
1982			1	6	.143	5.10	37	3	1	97	133	36	23	0	0	4	6	0	0	0	—	3	15	1	1	0.5	.947
1983	PHI	N	1	0	1.000	5.19	3	1	0	8.2	11	3	1	0	0	0	0	1	0	0	.000	2	0	0	0	0.7	1.000
1984	CLE	A	4	8	.333	5.68	22	20	1	117.1	146	39	39	0	0	0	0	0	0	0	—	7	20	1	1	1.3	.964
7 yrs.			44	37	.543	4.13	176	83	11	701.1	762	252	245	3	13	7	13	0	0	0	.000	50	116	9	5	1.0	.949

Year	Team		W	L	PCT	ERA	G	GS	CG	IP	H	BB	SO	ShO	Relief Pitching W	L	SV	Batting AB	H	HR	BA	PO	A	E	DP	TC/G	FA

Steve Comer *continued*

1981			8	2	.800	2.57	36	1	0	77	70	31	22	0	8	1	6	0	0	0	—	5	18	1	2	0.7	.958
1982			1	6	.143	5.10	37	3	1	97	133	36	23	0	0	4	6	0	0	0	—	3	15	1	1	0.5	.947
1983	PHI	N	1	0	1.000	5.19	3	1	0	8.2	11	3	1	0	0	0	0	1	0	0	.000	2	0	0	0	0.7	1.000
1984	CLE	A	4	8	.333	5.68	22	20	1	117.1	146	39	39	0	0	0	0	0	0	0	—	7	20	1	1	1.3	.964
7 yrs.			44	37	.543	4.13	176	83	11	701.1	762	252	245	3	13	7	13	1	0	0	.000	50	116	9	5	1.0	.949

Charlie Comiskey

COMISKEY, CHARLES ALBERT (Commy, The Old Roman)   BR TR 6'   180 lbs.
B. Aug. 15, 1859, Chicago, Ill.   D. Oct. 26, 1931, Eagle River, Wis.
Manager 1883-94.
Hall of Fame 1939.

1882	STL	AA	0	1	.000	0.00	2	1	1	8	12	3	2	0	0	0	0	329	80	1	.243	1	2	0	0	1.5	1.000
1884			0	0	—	2.25	1	0	0	4	1	0	4	0	0	0	0	460	110	2	.239	0	0	0	0	0.0	—
1889			0	0	—	0.00	1	0	0	.1	0	0	0	0	0	0	0	587	168	3	.286	0	0	0	0	0.0	—
3 yrs.			0	1	.000	0.73	4	1	1	12.1	13	3	6	0	0	0	0	*				1	2	0	0	0.8	1.000

Clint Compton

COMPTON, ROBERT CLINTON   BL TL 5'11"   185 lbs.
B. Nov. 1, 1950, Montgomery, Ala.

| 1972 | CHI | N | 0 | 0 | — | 9.00 | 1 | 0 | 0 | 2 | 2 | 2 | 0 | 0 | 0 | 0 | 0 | 0 | 0 | 0 | — | 0 | 0 | 0 | 0 | 0.0 | — |

Jack Compton

COMPTON, HARRY LEROY   BR TR 5'9"   157 lbs.
B. Mar. 9, 1882, Lancaster, Ohio   D. July 4, 1974, Lancaster, Ohio

| 1911 | CIN | N | 0 | 1 | .000 | 3.91 | 8 | 3 | 0 | 25.1 | 19 | 15 | 6 | 0 | 0 | 0 | 1 | 6 | 2 | 0 | .333 | 0 | 7 | 1 | 0 | 1.0 | .875 |

Keith Comstock

COMSTOCK, KEITH MARTIN   BL TL 6'   174 lbs.
B. Dec. 23, 1955, San Francisco, Calif.

1984	MIN	A	0	0	—	8.53	4	0	0	6.1	6	4	2	0	0	0	0	0	0	0	—	1	2	0	0	0.8	1.000
1987	2 teams	SF N (15G 2-0)				SD N (26G 0-1)																					
"	total		2	1	.667	4.61	41	0	0	56.2	52	31	59	0	2	1	0	2	0	0	.000	2	4	0	1	0.1	1.000
1988	SD	N	0	0	—	6.75	7	0	0	8	8	3	9	0	0	0	0	0	0	0	—	1	1	0	0	0.3	1.000
1989	SEA	A	1	2	.333	2.81	31	0	0	25.2	26	10	22	0	1	2	0	0	0	0	—	0	4	1	0	0.2	.800
4 yrs.			3	3	.500	4.56	83	0	0	96.2	92	48	92	0	3	3	1	2	0	0	.000	4	11	1	1	0.2	.938

Ralph Comstock

COMSTOCK, RALPH REMICK (Commy)   BR TR 5'10"   168 lbs.
B. Nov. 24, 1890, Sylvania, Ohio   D. Sept. 13, 1966, Toledo, Ohio

1913	DET	A	2	5	.286	5.37	10	7	1	60.1	90	16	37	0	0	0	1	22	5	0	.227	3	17	1	1	2.1	.952
1915	2 teams	BOS A (3G 1-0)				PIT F (12G 3-3)																					
"	total		4	3	.571	3.06	15	7	3	61.2	54	9	19	0	1	0	2	18	0	0	.000	2	18	2	0	1.5	.909
1918	PIT	N	5	6	.455	3.00	15	8	6	81	78	14	44	0	2	1	1	26	5	0	.192	2	22	1	1	1.7	.960
3 yrs.			11	14	.440	3.72	40	22	10	203	222	39	100	0	3	1	4	66	10	0	.152	7	57	4	2	1.7	.941

Dave Concepcion

CONCEPCION, DAVID ISMAEL   BR TR 6'2"   155 lbs.
Born David Ismael Concepcion y Benitez.
B. June 17, 1948, Aragua, Venezuela

| 1988 | CIN | N | 0 | 0 | — | 0.00 | 1 | 0 | 0 | 1.1 | 2 | 0 | 1 | 0 | 0 | 0 | 0 | * | | | | 0 | 0 | 0 | 0 | 0.0 | — |

Bob Cone

CONE, ROBERT EARL (Ike)   BR TR 6'2"   172 lbs.
B. Feb. 27, 1894, Galveston, Tex.   D. May 24, 1955, Galveston, Tex.

| 1915 | PHI | A | 0 | 0 | — | 40.50 | 1 | 1 | 0 | .2 | 5 | 0 | 0 | 0 | 0 | 0 | 0 | 0 | 0 | 0 | — | 0 | 0 | 0 | 0 | 0.0 | — |

David Cone

CONE, DAVID BRIAN   BL TR 6'1"   180 lbs.
B. Jan. 2, 1963, Kansas City, Mo.

1986	KC	A	0	0	—	5.56	11	0	0	22.2	29	13	21	0	0	0	0	0	0	0	—	4	0	0	0	0.4	1.000
1987	NY	N	5	6	.455	3.71	21	13	1	99.1	87	44	68	0	1	1	1	31	2	0	.065	12	10	1	0	1.1	.957
1988			20	3	.870	2.22	35	28	8	231.1	178	80	213	4	2	0	0	80	12	0	.150	17	23	1	0	1.2	.976
1989			14	8	.636	3.52	34	33	7	219.2	183	74	190	2	0	0	0	77	18	0	.234	21	14	1	0	1.1	.972
4 yrs.			39	17	.696	3.11	101	74	16	573	477	211	492	6	3	1	1	188	32	0	.170	54	47	3	0	1.0	.971

LEAGUE CHAMPIONSHIP SERIES

| 1988 | NY | N | 1 | 1 | .500 | 4.50 | 3 | 2 | 1 | 12 | 10 | 5 | 9 | 0 | 0 | 0 | 0 | 4 | 0 | 0 | .000 | 0 | 0 | 0 | 0 | 0.3 | 1.000 |

Dick Conger

CONGER, RICHARD   BR TR 6'   185 lbs.
B. Apr. 3, 1921, Los Angeles, Calif.   D. Feb. 16, 1970, Los Angeles, Calif.

1940	DET	A	1	0	1.000	3.00	2	0	0	3	2	3	1	0	1	0	0	0	0	0	—	0	0	0	0	0.0	—
1941	PIT	N	0	0	—	0.00	2	1	0	4	3	3	2	0	0	0	0	0	0	0	—	0	0	0	0	0.0	—
1942			0	0	—	2.16	2	1	0	8.1	9	5	3	0	0	0	0	3	0	0	.000	0	5	1	0	3.0	.833
1943	PHI	N	2	7	.222	6.09	13	10	2	54.2	72	24	18	0	0	0	0	16	1	0	.063	1	12	1	0	1.1	.929
4 yrs.			3	7	.300	5.14	19	12	2	70	86	35	24	0	1	0	0	19	1	0	.053	1	17	2	0	1.1	.900

Red Conkwright

CONKWRIGHT, ALLEN HOWARD (Red)   BR TR 5'10"   170 lbs.
B. Dec. 4, 1896, Sedalia, Mo.

| 1920 | DET | A | 2 | 1 | .667 | 6.98 | 5 | 2 | 0 | 19.1 | 29 | 16 | 4 | 0 | 2 | 0 | 1 | 4 | 1 | 0 | .250 | 5 | 4 | 0 | 0 | 1.8 | 1.000 |

Bob Conley

CONLEY, ROBERT BURNS   BR TR 6'1"   188 lbs.
B. Feb. 1, 1934, Knott County, Ky.

| 1958 | PHI | N | 0 | 0 | — | 7.56 | 2 | 2 | 0 | 8.1 | 9 | 6 | 0 | 0 | 0 | 0 | 0 | 1 | 0 | 0 | .000 | 0 | 1 | 0 | 0 | 0.5 | 1.000 |

Year	Team		W	L	PCT	ERA	G	GS	CG	IP	H	BB	SO	ShO	Relief Pitching W	L	SV	Batting AB	H	HR	BA	PO	A	E	DP	TC/G	FA

Ed Conley

CONLEY, EDWARD J.
B. July 10, 1864, Sandwich, Mass.   D. Oct. 16, 1894, Cumberland, R. I.   5'11½"

| 1884 | PRO | N | 4 | 4 | .500 | 2.15 | 8 | 8 | 8 | 71 | 63 | 22 | 33 | 1 | 0 | 0 | 0 | 28 | 4 | 0 | .143 | 1 | 9 | 0 | 0 | 1.3 | 1.000 |

Gene Conley

CONLEY, DONALD EUGENE
B. Nov. 10, 1930, Muskogee, Okla.   BR TR 6'8" 225 lbs.

1952	BOS	N	0	3	.000	7.82	4	3	0	12.2	23	9	6	0	0	0	0	5	2	0	.400	1	2	0	0	0.8	1.000
1954	MIL	N	14	9	.609	2.96	28	27	12	194.1	171	79	113	2	1	0	0	77	12	0	.156	10	29	1	3	1.4	.975
1955			11	7	.611	4.16	22	21	10	158	152	52	107	0	0	1	0	54	11	0	.204	7	24	0	1	1.4	1.000
1956			8	9	.471	3.13	31	19	5	158.1	169	52	68	1	1	1	0	45	7	0	.156	8	25	2	3	1.1	.943
1957			9	9	.500	3.16	35	18	6	148	133	64	61	1	4	1	1	46	9	0	.196	5	27	1	3	0.9	.970
1958			0	6	.000	4.88	26	7	0	72	89	17	53	0	0	3	2	16	3	1	.188	1	12	0	0	0.5	1.000
1959	PHI	N	12	7	.632	3.00	25	22	12	180	159	42	102	3	0	0	0	67	16	0	.239	9	29	2	2	1.6	.950
1960			8	14	.364	3.68	29	25	9	183.1	192	42	117	2	1	0	0	63	8	0	.127	6	26	5	2	1.3	.865
1961	BOS	A	11	14	.440	4.91	33	30	6	199.2	229	65	113	2	0	1	1	73	16	2	.219	12	28	2	2	1.3	.952
1962			15	14	.517	3.95	34	33	9	241.2	238	68	134	2	0	0	0	87	18	1	.207	17	35	5	2	1.7	.912
1963			3	4	.429	6.64	9	9	0	40.2	51	21	14	0	0	0	0	15	3	0	.200	2	4	1	0	0.8	.857
11 yrs.			91	96	.487	3.82	276	214	69	1588.2	1606	511	888	13	7	8	9	548	105	5	.192	78	241	19	17	1.2	.944

WORLD SERIES

| 1957 | MIL | N | 0 | 0 | – | 10.80 | 1 | 0 | 0 | 1.2 | 1 | 1 | 0 | 0 | 0 | 0 | 0 | 0 | 0 | 0 | – | 1 | 0 | 0 | 0 | 1.0 | 1.000 |

Snipe Conley

CONLEY, JAMES PATRICK
B. Apr. 25, 1894, Cressona, Pa.   D. Jan. 7, 1978, DeSoto, Tex.   BR TR 5'11½" 179 lbs.

1914	BAL	F	4	6	.400	2.52	35	11	4	125	112	47	86	1	1	3	0	35	4	0	.114	5	28	2	2	1.0	.943
1915			1	4	.200	4.29	25	6	4	86	97	32	40	0	0	1	0	24	6	0	.250	4	22	1	0	1.1	.963
1918	CIN	N	2	0	1.000	5.27	5	0	0	13.2	17	5	2	0	1	0	1	4	1	0	.250	2	4	0	1	1.2	1.000
3 yrs.			7	10	.412	3.36	65	17	8	224.2	226	84	128	2	3	4	1	63	11	0	.175	11	54	3	3	1.0	.956

Bert Conn

CONN, ALBERT THOMAS
B. Sept. 22, 1879, Philadelphia, Pa.   D. Nov. 2, 1944, Philadelphia, Pa.   TR

1898	PHI	N	0	1	.000	6.43	1	1	0	7	13	2	3	0	0	0	0	3	1	0	.333	0	1	0	0	1.0	1.000
1900			0	2	.000	8.31	4	1	1	17.1	29	16	2	0	0	1	0	9	3	0	.333	3	1	2	0	1.5	.667
2 yrs.			0	3	.000	7.77	5	2	1	24.1	42	18	5	0	0	1	0	*					3	2	2	0	1.4	.714

Sarge Connally

CONNALLY, GEORGE WALTER
B. Aug. 31, 1898, McGregor, Tex.   D. Jan. 27, 1978, Temple, Tex.   BR TR 5'11" 170 lbs.

1921	CHI	A	0	1	.000	6.45	5	2	0	22.1	29	10	6	0	0	0	0	8	4	0	.500	1	5	0	0	1.2	1.000
1923			0	0	–	6.23	3	0	0	8.2	7	12	3	0	0	0	0	3	1	0	.333	0	2	0	0	0.7	1.000
1924			7	13	.350	4.05	44	13	6	160	177	68	55	0	5	5	6	50	11	0	.220	10	50	3	4	1.4	.952
1925			6	7	.462	4.64	40	2	0	104.2	122	58	45	0	5	6	8	28	7	0	.250	3	39	1	0	1.1	.977
1926			6	5	.545	3.16	31	8	5	108.1	128	35	47	0	2	4	3	32	5	0	.156	7	32	1	3	1.3	.975
1927			10	15	.400	4.08	43	18	11	198.1	217	83	58	1	5	3	5	67	22	0	.328	10	50	1	5	1.4	.984
1928			2	5	.286	4.84	28	5	1	74.1	89	29	28	0	1	4	2	19	2	0	.105	3	15	2	1	0.7	.900
1929			0	0	–	4.76	11	0	0	11.1	13	8	3	0	0	0	0	0	0	0	–	1	1	1	0	0.3	.667
1931	CLE	A	5	5	.500	4.20	17	9	5	85.2	87	50	37	0	2	0	1	27	5	0	.185	4	17	4	0	1.5	.840
1932			8	6	.571	4.33	35	7	4	112.1	119	42	32	0	4	4	3	40	7	1	.175	5	24	3	2	0.9	.906
1933			5	3	.625	4.89	41	3	1	103	112	44	30	0	4	2	1	26	6	0	.231	5	11	2	0	0.4	.889
1934			0	0	–	5.06	5	0	0	5.1	4	5	1	0	0	0	1	1	0	0	.000	1	2	0	0	0.6	1.000
12 yrs.			49	60	.450	4.30	303	67	33	994.1	1104	449	345	2	28	28	31	301	70	1	.233	50	248	18	19	1.0	.943

Bill Connelly

CONNELLY, WILLIAM WIRT (Wild Bill)
B. June 29, 1925, Alberta, Va.   D. Nov. 27, 1980, Richmond, Va.   BL TR 6' 175 lbs.

1945	PHI	A	1	1	.500	4.50	2	1	0	8	7	8	0	0	1	0	0	1	0	0	.000	1	0	1	0	1.0	.500
1950	2 teams	CHI A	(2G 0–0)			DET A	(2G 0–0)																					
"	total		0	0	–	8.53	4	0	0	6.1	9	3	1	0	0	0	0	1	0	0	.000	0	1	0	0	0.3	1.000
1952	NY	N	5	0	1.000	4.55	11	4	0	31.2	22	25	22	0	2	0	0	11	4	0	.364	3	7	0	0	0.9	1.000
1953			0	1	.000	11.07	8	2	0	20.1	33	17	11	0	0	0	0	6	0	0	.000	0	2	0	0	0.3	1.000
4 yrs.			6	2	.750	6.92	25	7	0	66.1	71	53	34	0	3	0	0	19	4	0	.211	4	10	1	1	0.6	.933

Ed Connolly

CONNOLLY, EDWARD JOSEPH, JR.
Son of Ed Connolly.
B. Dec. 3, 1939, Brooklyn, N. Y.   BL TL 6'1" 190 lbs.

1964	BOS	A	4	11	.267	4.91	27	15	1	80.2	80	64	73	1	0	1	0	18	3	0	.167	4	6	2	0	0.4	.833
1967	CLE	A	2	1	.667	7.48	15	4	0	49.1	63	34	45	0	1	0	0	11	2	0	.182	0	7	0	0	0.5	1.000
2 yrs.			6	12	.333	5.88	42	19	1	130	143	98	118	1	1	1	0	29	5	0	.172	4	13	2	0	0.5	.895

John Connor

CONNOR, JOHN
B. 1853, Scotland   D. Oct. 13, 1932, Boston, Mass.

1884	BOS	N	1	4	.200	3.15	7	7	7	60	70	18	29	0	0	0	0	25	2	0	.080	2	15	3	0	2.9	.850
1885	2 teams	BUF N	(1G 0–1)			LOU AA	(4G 1–3)																					
"	total		1	4	.200	4.70	5	5	5	44	57	14	19	0	0	0	0	17	2	0	.118	1	0	0	0	0.2	1.000
2 yrs.			2	8	.200	3.81	12	12	12	104	127	32	48	0	0	0	0	42	4	0	.095	3	15	3	0	1.8	.857

Bill Connors

CONNORS, WILLIAM JOSEPH
B. Nov. 2, 1941, Schenectady, N. Y.   BR TR 6'1" 180 lbs.

1966	CHI	N	0	1	.000	7.31	11	0	0	16	20	7	3	0	0	1	0	0	0	0	–	0	3	0	0	0.3	1.000
1967	NY	N	0	0	–	6.23	6	1	0	13	8	5	13	0	0	0	0	1	0	0	.000	0	0	0	0	0.0	–
1968			0	1	.000	9.00	9	0	0	14	21	7	8	0	0	1	0	1	1	0	1.000	3	2	0	0	0.6	1.000
3 yrs.			0	2	.000	7.53	26	1	0	43	49	19	24	0	0	2	0	2	1	0	.500	3	5	0	0	0.3	1.000

Year	Team	W	L	PCT	ERA	G	GS	CG	IP	H	BB	SO	ShO	Relief Pitching W	L	SV	Batting AB	H	HR	BA	PO	A	E	DP	TC/G	FA

Joe Connors

CONNORS, JOSEPH P.
B. Paterson, N. J.   Deceased.

| 1884 | 2 teams | ALT U | (1G 0–1) | | KC U | (2G 0–1) | | | | | | | | | | | | | | | | | | | | |
| " | total | 0 | 2 | .000 | 5.57 | 3 | 2 | 2 | 21 | 42 | 5 | 1 | 0 | 0 | 0 | 0 | 22 | 2 | 0 | .091 | 1 | 4 | 0 | 0 | 1.7 | 1.000 |

Ted Conovar

CONOVAR, THEODORE   BR TR 5'10½" 165 lbs.
B. Mar. 10, 1868, Lexington, Ky.   D. July 27, 1910, Paris, Ky.

| 1889 | CIN | AA | 0 | 0 | – | 13.50 | 1 | 0 | 0 | 2 | 4 | 2 | 1 | 0 | 0 | 0 | 1 | 0 | 0 | 0 | – | 0 | 0 | 0 | 0 | 0.0 | – |

Tim Conroy

CONROY, TIMOTHY JAMES   BL TL 6'   178 lbs.
B. Apr. 3, 1960, McKeesport, Pa.

1978	OAK	A	0	0	–	7.71	2	2	0	4.2	3	9	0	0	0	0	0	0	0	0	–	0	0	1	0	0.5	–
1982			2	2	.500	3.55	5	5	1	25.1	20	18	17	0	0	0	0	0	0	0	–	1	3	2	0	1.2	.667
1983			7	10	.412	3.94	39	18	3	162.1	141	98	112	1	2	0	0	0	0	0	–	7	11	2	0	0.5	.900
1984			1	6	.143	5.23	38	14	0	93	82	63	69	0	0	0	0	0	0	0	–	0	7	0	1	0.2	1.000
1985			0	1	.000	4.26	16	2	0	25.1	22	15	8	0	0	0	0	0	0	0	–	0	3	1	0	0.3	.750
1986	STL	N	5	11	.313	5.23	25	21	1	115.1	122	56	79	0	1	0	0	29	4	0	.138	3	16	5	1	1.0	.792
1987			3	2	.600	5.53	10	9	0	40.2	48	25	22	0	0	0	0	15	0	0	.000	3	4	1	1	0.8	.875
7 yrs.			18	32	.360	4.69	135	71	5	466.2	438	284	307	1	3	0	0	44	4	0	.091	14	44	12	2	0.5	.829

Jim Constable

CONSTABLE, JIMMY LEE (Sheriff)   BB TL 6'1"   185 lbs.
B. June 14, 1933, Jonesboro, Tenn.

1956	NY	N	0	0	–	14.54	3	0	0	4.1	9	7	1	0	0	0	0	0	0	0	–	1	0	0	0	0.3	1.000
1957			1	1	.500	2.86	16	0	0	28.1	27	7	13	0	1	1	0	5	0	0	.000	3	2	0	0	0.3	1.000
1958	3 teams	SF	N	(9G 1–0)		CLE A	(6G 0–1)		WAS A	(15G 0–1)																	
"	total	1	2	.333	6.40	30	4	0	45	56	22	32	0	1	1	0	7	4	0	.571	2	7	1	1	0.3	.900
1962	MIL	N	1	1	.500	2.00	3	2	1	18	14	4	12	1	0	0	0	5	0	0	.000	2	0	0	0	0.7	1.000
1963	SF	N	0	0	–	3.86	4	0	0	2.1	3	1	1	0	0	0	0	0	0	0	–	0	1	0	0	0.3	1.000
5 yrs.			3	4	.429	4.87	56	6	1	98	109	41	59	1	2	2	2	17	4	0	.235	8	10	1	1	0.3	.947

Sandy Consuegra

CONSUEGRA, SANDALIO SIMEON   BR TR 5'11"   165 lbs.
Born Sandalio Simeon Consuerga y Castello.
B. Sept. 3, 1920, Potrerillos, Cuba

1950	WAS	A	7	8	.467	4.40	21	18	8	124.2	132	57	38	2	0	0	2	40	7	0	.175	6	24	2	2	1.5	.938
1951			7	8	.467	4.01	40	12	5	146	140	63	31	0	2	5	3	43	10	0	.233	3	31	0	2	0.9	1.000
1952			6	0	1.000	3.05	30	2	0	73.2	80	27	19	0	5	0	5	17	3	0	.176	2	11	0	1	0.4	1.000
1953	2 teams	WAS	A	(4G 0–0)		CHI A	(29G 7–5)																				
"	total	7	5	.583	2.86	33	13	5	129	131	32	30	1	3	0	3	35	2	0	.057	11	36	1	1	1.5	.979
1954	CHI	A	16	3	.842	2.69	39	17	3	154	142	35	31	2	8	0	3	48	11	0	.229	8	34	1	1	1.1	.977
1955			6	5	.545	2.64	44	7	3	126.1	120	18	35	0	3	3	7	29	3	0	.103	5	23	2	1	0.7	.933
1956	2 teams	CHI	A	(28G 1–2)		BAL A	(4G 1–1)																				
"	total	2	3	.400	4.98	32	2	0	47	55	13	8	0	1	1	3	6	1	0	.167	1	9	1	0	0.3	.909
1957	2 teams	BAL	A	(5G 0–0)		NY N	(4G 0–0)																				
"	total	0	0	–	2.08	9	0	0	8.2	11	1	1	0	0	0	0	0	0	0	–	0	2	0	0	0.2	1.000
8 yrs.			51	32	.614	3.37	248	71	24	809.1	811	246	193	5	22	9	26	218	37	0	.170	38	170	7	8	0.9	.967

Nardi Contreras

CONTRERAS, ARNALDO JUAN   BB TR 6'2"   193 lbs.
B. Sept. 19, 1951, Tampa, Fla.

| 1980 | CHI | A | 0 | 0 | – | 5.79 | 8 | 0 | 0 | 14 | 18 | 7 | 8 | 0 | 0 | 0 | 0 | 0 | 0 | 0 | – | 1 | 4 | 2 | 1 | 0.9 | .714 |

Dick Conway

CONWAY, RICHARD BUTLER   BL TR 5'7½" 140 lbs.
Brother of Bill Conway.
B. Apr. 25, 1866, Lowell, Mass.   D. Sept. 9, 1926, Lowell, Mass.

1886	BAL	AA	2	7	.222	6.81	9	9	8	76.2	106	43	64	0	0	0	0	34	7	0	.206	1	21	2	0	2.7	.917
1887	BOS	N	9	15	.375	4.66	26	26	25	222.1	249	86	45	0	0	0	0	145	36	0	.248	4	49	5	0	2.2	.914
1888			4	2	.667	2.38	6	6	6	53	49	8	12	0	0	0	0	25	4	0	.160	3	9	0	0	2.0	1.000
3 yrs.			15	24	.385	4.78	41	41	39	352	404	137	121	0	0	0	0	204	47	0	.230	8	79	7	0	2.3	.926

Jim Conway

CONWAY, JAMES P.   TR
Brother of Pete Conway.
B. Clifton, Pa.   Deceased.

1884	BKN	AA	3	9	.250	4.44	13	13	10	105.1	132	15	25	0	0	0	0	47	6	0	.128	5	18	12	0	2.7	.657
1885	PHI	AA	0	1	.000	7.30	2	2	1	12.1	19	2	0	0	0	0	0	6	0	0	.000	0	2	0	0	1.0	1.000
1889	KC	AA	19	19	.500	3.25	41	37	33	335	334	90	115	0	1	0	0	149	31	0	.208	10	85	7	2	2.5	.931
3 yrs.			22	29	.431	3.64	56	52	44	452.2	485	107	140	0	1	0	0	202	37	0	.183	15	105	19	2	2.5	.863

Pat Conway

CONWAY, JEROME PATRICK   BL TL 6'2"   190 lbs.
B. June 7, 1901, Holyoke, Mass.   D. Apr. 16, 1980, Holyoke, Mass.

| 1920 | WAS | A | 0 | 0 | – | 0.00 | 1 | 0 | 0 | 2 | 1 | 1 | 0 | 0 | 0 | 0 | 0 | 0 | 0 | 0 | – | 0 | 0 | 0 | 0 | 0.0 | – |

Pete Conway

CONWAY, PETER J.   BR TR 5'10½"
Brother of Jim Conway.
B. Oct. 30, 1866, Burmont, Pa.   D. Jan. 14, 1903, Media, Pa.

1885	BUF	N	10	17	.370	4.67	27	27	26	210	256	44	94	0	0	0	0	90	10	1	.111	3	53	7	0	2.3	.889
1886	2 teams	KC	N	(23G 5–15)		DET N	(11G 6–5)																				
"	total	11	20	.355	4.95	34	31	30	271	329	86	116	0	0	0	0	237	55	3	.232	7	50	12	1	2.0	.826
1887	DET	N	8	9	.471	2.90	17	17	16	146	132	47	40	0	0	0	0	95	22	1	.232	11	36	1	0	2.8	.979
1888			30	14	.682	2.26	45	45	43	391	315	57	176	4	0	0	0	167	46	3	.275	10	96	7	4	2.5	.938
1889	PIT	N	2	1	.667	4.91	3	3	2	22	26	16	2	0	0	0	0	10	1	1	.100	1	6	1	0	2.7	.875
5 yrs.			61	61	.500	3.59	126	123	117	1040	1058	250	428	4	0	0	0	*				32	241	28	5	2.4	.907

Year	Team		W	L	PCT	ERA	G	GS	CG	IP	H	BB	SO	ShO	Relief Pitching W	L	SV	Batting AB	H	HR	BA	PO	A	E	DP	TC/G	FA

Joe Conzelman

CONZELMAN, JOSEPH HARRISON
B. July 14, 1885, Bristol, Conn. D. Apr. 17, 1979, Mountain Brook, Ala.
BR TR 6' 170 lbs.

1913	PIT	N	0	1	.000	1.20	3	2	1	15	13	5	9	0	0	0	0	4	0	0	.000	0	4	0	0	1.3	1.000
1914			5	6	.455	2.94	33	9	4	101	88	40	39	1	2	2	1	27	3	0	.111	4	33	0	1	1.1	1.000
1915			1	1	.500	3.42	18	1	0	47.1	41	20	22	0	1	0	0	11	1	0	.091	0	16	1	0	0.9	.941
3 yrs.			6	8	.429	2.92	54	12	5	163.1	142	65	70	1	3	2	1	42	4	0	.095	4	53	1	1	1.1	.983

Dennis Cook

COOK, DENNIS BRYAN
B. Oct. 4, 1962, LaMarque, Tex.
BL TL 6'3" 185 lbs.

1988	SF	N	2	1	.667	2.86	4	4	1	22	9	11	13	1	0	0	0	4	0	0	.000	0	1	0	0	0.3	1.000
1989	2 teams	SF N (2G 1-0)										PHI N (21G 6-8)																
"	total		7	8	.467	3.72	23	18	2	121	110	38	67	1	1	0	0	42	9	0	.214	4	16	3	0	1.0	.870
2 yrs.			9	9	.500	3.59	27	22	3	143	119	49	80	2	1	0	0	46	9	0	.196	4	17	3	0	0.9	.875

Earl Cook

COOK, EARL DAVIS
B. Dec. 10, 1908, Stouffville, Ont., Canada
BR TR 6' 195 lbs.

| 1941 | DET | A | 0 | 0 | — | 4.50 | 1 | 0 | 0 | 2 | 4 | 0 | 1 | 0 | 0 | 0 | 0 | 0 | 0 | 0 | — | 0 | 0 | 0 | 0 | 0.0 | — |

Glen Cook

COOK, GLEN PATRICK
B. Sept. 8, 1959, Buffalo, N. Y.
BR TR 5'11" 180 lbs.

| 1985 | TEX | A | 2 | 3 | .400 | 9.45 | 9 | 7 | 0 | 40 | 53 | 18 | 19 | 0 | 0 | 0 | 0 | 0 | 0 | 0 | — | 3 | 2 | 1 | 1 | 0.7 | .833 |

Mike Cook

COOK, MICHAEL HORACE
B. Aug. 14, 1963, Charleston, S. C.
BR TR 6'3" 200 lbs.

1986	CAL	A	0	2	.000	9.00	5	1	0	9	13	7	6	0	0	0	0	0	0	0	—	0	2	0	0	0.4	1.000
1987			1	2	.333	5.50	16	1	0	34.1	34	18	27	0	1	1	0	0	0	0	—	4	8	0	1	0.8	1.000
1988			0	1	.000	4.91	3	0	0	3.2	4	1	2	0	0	0	0	0	0	0	—	0	0	0	0	0.0	—
1989	MIN	A	0	1	.000	5.06	15	0	0	21.1	22	17	15	0	0	0	0	0	0	0	—	2	0	0	0	0.1	1.000
4 yrs.			1	6	.143	5.80	39	2	0	68.1	73	43	50	0	1	4	0	0	0	0	—	6	10	0	1	0.4	1.000

Rollin Cook

COOK, ROLLIN EDWARD
B. Oct. 5, 1890, Toledo, Ohio D. Aug. 11, 1975, Toledo, Ohio
BR TR 5'9" 160 lbs.

| 1915 | STL | A | 0 | 0 | — | 7.24 | 5 | 0 | 0 | 13.2 | 16 | 9 | 7 | 0 | 0 | 0 | 0 | 4 | 1 | 0 | .250 | 0 | 6 | 0 | 0 | 1.2 | 1.000 |

Ron Cook

COOK, RONALD WAYNE
B. July 11, 1947, Jefferson, Tex.
BL TL 6'1" 175 lbs.

1970	HOU	N	4	4	.500	3.73	41	0	0	82	80	42	50	0	3	4	2	17	4	0	.235	3	13	2	1	0.4	.889
1971			0	4	.000	4.85	5	4	0	26	23	8	10	0	0	0	0	8	2	0	.250	1	5	1	0	1.4	.857
2 yrs.			4	8	.333	4.00	46	11	0	108	103	50	60	0	3	4	2	25	6	0	.240	4	18	3	1	0.5	.880

Bobby Coombs

COOMBS, RAYMOND FRANKLIN
B. Feb. 2, 1908, Goodwins Mills, Me.
BR TR 5'9½" 160 lbs.

1933	PHI	A	0	1	.000	7.47	21	0	0	31.1	47	20	8	0	0	1	2	5	2	0	.400	2	5	0	0	0.3	1.000
1943	NY	N	0	1	.000	12.94	9	0	0	16	33	8	5	0	0	1	0	2	0	0	.000	0	6	1	0	0.8	.857
2 yrs.			0	2	.000	9.32	30	0	0	47.1	80	28	13	0	0	2	2	7	2	0	.286	2	11	1	0	0.5	.929

Danny Coombs

COOMBS, DANIEL BERNARD
B. Mar. 23, 1942, Lincoln, Me.
BR TL 6'4" 200 lbs.
BL 1967

1963	HOU	N	0	0	—	27.00	1	0	0	.1	3	0	0	0	0	0	0	0	0	0	—	0	0	0	0	1.0	1.000
1964			1	1	.500	5.00	7	1	0	18	21	10	14	0	0	1	0	4	0	0	.000	0	2	0	0	0.3	1.000
1965			0	2	.000	4.79	26	3	0	47	54	23	35	0	0	0	0	9	1	0	.111	4	10	1	1	0.6	.933
1966			0	0	—	3.38	2	0	0	2.2	4	0	3	0	0	0	0	1	0	0	.000	0	0	0	0	0.0	—
1967			3	0	1.000	3.33	6	2	0	24.1	21	9	23	0	3	0	0	8	1	0	.125	0	6	0	0	1.0	1.000
1968			4	3	.571	3.28	40	2	0	46.2	52	17	29	0	3	2	1	10	4	0	.400	2	11	1	0	0.4	.929
1969			0	1	.000	6.75	8	0	0	8	12	2	3	0	0	1	0	2	0	0	.000	0	0	0	0	0.0	—
1970	SD	N	10	14	.417	3.30	35	27	5	188	185	76	105	1	2	1	0	52	5	0	.096	4	20	0	1	0.7	1.000
1971			1	6	.143	6.21	19	7	0	58	81	25	37	0	0	2	0	14	3	0	.214	2	15	0	1	0.9	1.000
9 yrs.			19	27	.413	4.08	144	42	5	393	433	162	249	1	8	7	2	100	14	0	.140	12	65	2	4	0.5	.975

Jack Coombs

COOMBS, JOHN WESLEY (Cy)
B. Nov. 18, 1882, LeGrand, Iowa D. Apr. 15, 1957, Palestine, Tex.
Manager 1919.
BB TR 6' 185 lbs.

1906	PHI	A	10	10	.500	2.50	23	18	13	173	144	68	90	1	2	2	0	67	16	0	.239	16	44	2	4	2.7	.968
1907			6	9	.400	3.12	23	17	10	132.2	109	64	73	2	0	0	2	48	8	1	.167	9	37	1	2	2.0	.979
1908			7	5	.583	2.00	26	18	10	153	130	64	80	4	1	0	0	220	56	1	.255	10	42	3	1	2.1	.945
1909			12	11	.522	2.32	31	25	19	205.2	156	73	97	6	0	3	1	83	14	0	.169	12	60	2	2	2.4	.973
1910			31	9	.775	1.30	45	38	35	353	248	115	224	13	4	1	1	132	29	0	.220	19	77	1	2	2.2	.990
1911			28	12	.700	3.53	47	40	26	336.2	360	119	185	1	3	1	2	141	45	2	.319	24	71	9	3	2.2	.913
1912			21	10	.677	3.29	40	32	23	262.1	227	94	120	1	2	2	0	110	28	0	.255	16	66	0	4	2.1	1.000
1913			1	0	1.000	10.13	2	2	0	5.1	5	6	0	0	0	0	0	3	1	0	.333	1	0	0	0	1.0	.500
1914			0	1	.000	4.50	2	2	0	8	8	3	1	0	0	0	0	11	3	0	.273	0	1	0	0	0.5	1.000
1915	BKN	N	15	10	.600	2.58	29	24	17	195.2	166	91	56	2	2	1	0	75	21	0	.280	17	31	1	2	1.7	.980
1916			13	8	.619	2.66	27	21	10	159	136	44	47	3	2	0	0	61	11	0	.180	7	15	0	1	0.8	1.000
1917			7	11	.389	3.96	31	14	9	141	147	49	34	0	3	2	0	44	10	0	.227	8	26	1	1	1.1	.971
1918			8	14	.364	3.81	27	22	16	189	191	49	44	2	1	0	0	113	19	0	.168	9	41	2	0	1.9	.962
1920	DET	A	0	0	—	3.18	2	0	0	5.2	7	2	1	0	0	0	0	2	0	0	.000	0	1	0	0	0.5	1.000
14 yrs.			159	110	.591	2.78	355	273	188	2320	2034	841	1052	35	21	10	8	*				148	512	23	22	1.9	.966

WORLD SERIES

| 1910 | PHI | A | 3 | 0 | 1.000 | 3.33 | 3 | 3 | 3 | 27 | 23 | 14 | 17 | 0 | 0 | 0 | 0 | 13 | 5 | 0 | .385 | 1 | 4 | 2 | 0 | 2.3 | .714 |
| 1911 | | | 1 | 0 | 1.000 | 1.35 | 2 | 2 | 1 | 20 | 11 | 6 | 16 | 0 | 0 | 0 | 0 | 8 | 2 | 0 | .250 | 1 | 2 | 0 | 0 | 1.5 | 1.000 |

Jack Coombs *continued*

Year	Team	Lg	W	L	PCT	ERA	G	GS	CG	IP	H	BB	SO	ShO	Relief W	Relief L	Relief SV	Batting AB	Batting H	Batting HR	BA	PO	A	E	DP	TC/G	FA
1916	BKN	N	1	0	1.000	4.26	1	1	0	6.1	7	1	1	0	0	0	0	3	1	0	.333	0	2	0	0	2.0	1.000
3 yrs.			5	0	1.000	2.70	6	6	4	53.1	41	21	34	0	0	0	0	24	8	0	.333	2	8	2	0	2.0	.833
			8th		1st																						

William Coon

COON, WILLIAM K.
B. Mar. 21, 1855, Philadelphia, Pa. D. Aug. 30, 1915, Burlington, N. J.

Year	Team	Lg	W	L	PCT	ERA	G	GS	CG	IP	H	BB	SO	ShO	Relief W	Relief L	Relief SV	Batting AB	Batting H	Batting HR	BA	PO	A	E	DP	TC/G	FA
1876	PHI	N	0	0	–	5.14	2	0	0	7	9	0	0	0	0	0	0	*				0	0	1	0	0.5	–

Bill Cooney

COONEY, WILLIAM A. TR
B. Apr. 4, 1887, Boston, Mass. D. Nov. 6, 1928, Roxbury, Mass.

Year	Team	Lg	W	L	PCT	ERA	G	GS	CG	IP	H	BB	SO	ShO	Relief W	Relief L	Relief SV	Batting AB	Batting H	Batting HR	BA	PO	A	E	DP	TC/G	FA
1909	BOS	N	0	0	–	1.42	3	0	0	6.1	4	2	3	0	0	0	0	*				0	1	1	0	0.7	.500

Bob Cooney

COONEY, ROBERT DANIEL BR TR 5'11" 160 lbs.
B. July 12, 1907, Glens Falls, N. Y. D. May 4, 1976, Glens Falls, N. Y.

Year	Team	Lg	W	L	PCT	ERA	G	GS	CG	IP	H	BB	SO	ShO	Relief W	Relief L	Relief SV	Batting AB	Batting H	Batting HR	BA	PO	A	E	DP	TC/G	FA
1931	STL	A	0	3	.000	4.12	5	4	1	39.1	46	20	13	0	0	0	0	13	5	0	.385	2	6	0	0	1.6	1.000
1932			1	2	.333	6.97	23	3	1	71	94	36	23	0	0	0	1	22	0	0	.000	3	5	0	1	0.3	1.000
2 yrs.			1	5	.167	5.95	28	7	2	110.1	140	56	36	0	0	0	1	35	5	0	.143	5	11	0	1	0.6	1.000

Johnny Cooney

COONEY, JOHN WALTER BR TL 5'10" 165 lbs.
Son of Jimmy Cooney. Brother of Jimmy Cooney.
B. Mar. 18, 1901, Cranston, R. I. D. July 8, 1986, Sarasota, Fla.
Manager 1949.

Year	Team	Lg	W	L	PCT	ERA	G	GS	CG	IP	H	BB	SO	ShO	Relief W	Relief L	Relief SV	Batting AB	Batting H	Batting HR	BA	PO	A	E	DP	TC/G	FA
1921	BOS	N	0	1	.000	3.92	8	1	0	20.2	19	10	9	0	0	0	0	5	1	0	.200	2	5	0	0	0.9	1.000
1922			1	2	.333	2.16	4	3	1	25	19	6	7	0	0	0	0	8	0	0	.000	1	6	0	1	1.8	1.000
1923			3	5	.375	3.31	23	8	5	98	92	22	23	2	0	0	0	66	25	0	.379	5	14	0	1	0.8	1.000
1924			8	9	.471	3.18	34	19	12	181	176	50	67	2	0	0	2	130	33	0	.254	18	32	2	3	1.5	.962
1925			14	14	.500	3.48	31	29	20	245.2	267	50	65	2	2	0	0	103	33	0	.320	14	60	4	6	2.5	.949
1926			3	3	.500	4.00	19	8	3	83.1	106	29	23	1	1	1	0	126	38	0	.302	7	21	2	1	1.6	.933
1928			3	7	.300	4.32	24	6	2	89.2	106	31	18	0	2	2	1	41	7	0	.171	11	32	0	3	1.8	1.000
1929			2	3	.400	5.00	14	2	1	45	57	22	11	0	1	3	3	72	23	0	.319	4	16	1	1	1.5	.952
1930			0	0	–	18.00	2	0	0	7	16	3	1	0	0	0	0	3	0	0	.000	0	4	0	0	2.0	1.000
9 yrs.			34	44	.436	3.72	159	76	44	795.1	858	223	224	7	6	6	6	*				62	190	9	16	1.6	.966

Cal Cooper

COOPER, CALVIN ASA BR TR 6'2½" 180 lbs.
B. Aug. 11, 1922, Great Falls, S. C.

Year	Team	Lg	W	L	PCT	ERA	G	GS	CG	IP	H	BB	SO	ShO	Relief W	Relief L	Relief SV	Batting AB	Batting H	Batting HR	BA	PO	A	E	DP	TC/G	FA
1948	WAS	A	0	0	–	45.00	1	0	0	1	5	1	0	0	0	0	0	0	0	0	–	0	0	0	0	0.0	–

Don Cooper

COOPER, DONALD JAMES BR TR 6'1" 185 lbs.
B. Feb. 15, 1957, New York, N. Y.

Year	Team	Lg	W	L	PCT	ERA	G	GS	CG	IP	H	BB	SO	ShO	Relief W	Relief L	Relief SV	Batting AB	Batting H	Batting HR	BA	PO	A	E	DP	TC/G	FA
1981	MIN	A	1	5	.167	4.27	27	2	0	59	61	32	33	0	1	3	0	0	0	0	–	1	6	0	0	0.3	1.000
1982			0	1	.000	9.53	6	1	0	11.1	14	11	5	0	0	0	0	0	0	0	–	1	1	0	0	0.3	1.000
1983	TOR	A	0	0	–	6.75	4	0	0	5.1	8	0	5	0	0	0	0	0	0	0	–	0	0	0	0	0.0	–
1985	NY	A	0	0	–	5.40	7	0	0	10	12	3	4	0	0	0	0	0	0	0	–	0	0	0	0	0.0	–
4 yrs.			1	6	.143	5.25	44	3	0	85.2	95	46	47	0	1	3	0	0	0	0	–	2	7	0	0	0.2	1.000

Guy Cooper

COOPER, GUY EVANS (Rebel) BB TR 6'1" 185 lbs.
B. Jan. 28, 1893, Rome, Ga. D. Aug. 2, 1951, Santa Monica, Calif.

Year	Team	Lg	W	L	PCT	ERA	G	GS	CG	IP	H	BB	SO	ShO	Relief W	Relief L	Relief SV	Batting AB	Batting H	Batting HR	BA	PO	A	E	DP	TC/G	FA
1914	2 teams		NY A (1G 0–0)			BOS A (9G 1–1)																					
"	total		1	1	.500	5.76	10	1	0	25	26	11	8	0	0	1	0	8	0	0	.000	0	4	0	0	0.4	1.000
1915	BOS	A	0	0	–	0.00	1	0	0	2	0	2	0	0	0	0	0	0	0	0	–	1	0	0	0	1.0	1.000
2 yrs.			1	1	.500	5.33	11	1	0	27	26	13	8	0	0	1	0	8	0	0	.000	1	4	0	0	0.5	1.000

Mort Cooper

COOPER, MORTON CECIL BR TR 6'2" 210 lbs.
Brother of Walker Cooper.
B. Mar. 2, 1913, Atherton, Mo. D. Nov. 17, 1958, Little Rock, Ark.

Year	Team	Lg	W	L	PCT	ERA	G	GS	CG	IP	H	BB	SO	ShO	Relief W	Relief L	Relief SV	Batting AB	Batting H	Batting HR	BA	PO	A	E	DP	TC/G	FA
1938	STL	N	2	1	.667	3.04	4	3	1	23.2	17	12	11	0	0	0	1	9	2	0	.222	2	8	1	0	2.8	.909
1939			12	6	.667	3.25	45	26	7	210.2	208	97	130	2	2	0	4	69	16	2	.232	7	25	3	0	0.8	.914
1940			11	12	.478	3.63	38	29	16	230.2	225	86	95	3	1	0	3	83	13	0	.157	4	38	2	1	1.2	.955
1941			13	9	.591	3.91	29	25	12	186.2	175	69	118	0	1	0	0	70	13	0	.186	6	32	1	3	1.3	.974
1942			**22**	7	.759	**1.78**	37	35	22	278.2	207	68	152	**10**	0	1	0	103	19	0	.184	6	44	2	3	1.4	.962
1943			**21**	8	**.724**	2.30	37	32	24	274	228	79	141	6	1	1	3	100	17	1	.170	7	46	3	3	1.5	.946
1944			22	7	.759	2.46	34	33	22	252.1	227	60	97	**7**	0	0	1	94	19	0	.202	4	28	0	1	0.9	1.000
1945	2 teams		STL N (4G 2–0)			BOS N (20G 7–4)																					
"	total		9	4	.692	2.92	24	14	5	101.2	97	34	59	1	3	2	1	32	8	1	.250	3	17	2	3	0.9	.909
1946	BOS	N	13	11	.542	3.12	28	27	15	199	181	39	83	4	0	0	1	67	14	1	.209	6	25	2	3	1.2	.939
1947	2 teams		BOS N (10G 2–5)			NY N (8G 1–5)																					
"	total		3	10	.231	5.40	18	15	4	83.1	99	26	27	0	1	0	0	27	6	1	.222	5	7	0	0	0.7	1.000
1949	CHI	N	0	0	–	∞	1	0	0		2	1	0	0	0	0	0	0	0	0	–	0	0	0	0	0.0	–
11 yrs.			128	75	.631	2.97	295	239	128	1840.2	1666	571	913	33	9	4	14	654	127	6	.194	50	270	16	17	1.1	.952
WORLD SERIES																											
1942	STL	N	0	1	.000	5.54	2	2	0	13	17	4	9	0	0	0	0	5	1	0	.200	0	1	0	0	0.5	1.000
1943			1	1	.500	2.81	2	2	1	16	11	3	10	0	0	0	0	5	0	0	.000	0	1	0	0	0.5	1.000
1944			1	1	.500	1.13	2	2	1	16	9	5	16	1	0	0	0	4	0	0	.000	0	6	0	0	3.0	1.000
3 yrs.			2	3	.400	3.00	6	6	2	45	37	12	35	1	0	0	0	14	1	0	.071	0	8	0	0	1.3	1.000

Pat Cooper

COOPER, ORGE PATTERSON BR TR 6'3" 180 lbs.
B. Nov. 26, 1917, Albermarle, N. C.

Year	Team	Lg	W	L	PCT	ERA	G	GS	CG	IP	H	BB	SO	ShO	Relief W	Relief L	Relief SV	Batting AB	Batting H	Batting HR	BA	PO	A	E	DP	TC/G	FA
1946	PHI	A	0	0	–	0.00	1	0	0	1	1	1	0	0	0	0	0	*				0	1	0	0	1.0	1.000

Year	Team		W	L	PCT	ERA	G	GS	CG	IP	H	BB	SO	ShO	Relief Pitching W	L	SV	Batting AB	H	HR	BA	PO	A	E	DP	TC/G	FA

Wilbur Cooper

COOPER, ARLEY WILBUR
B. Feb. 24, 1892, Bearsville, W. Va.   D. Aug. 7, 1973, Encino, Calif.
BR TL 5'11"   175 lbs.

Year	Team		W	L	PCT	ERA	G	GS	CG	IP	H	BB	SO	ShO	W	L	SV	AB	H	HR	BA	PO	A	E	DP	TC/G	FA
1912	PIT	N	3	0	1.000	1.66	6	4	3	38	32	15	30	2	0	0	0	13	2	0	.154	0	8	0	0	1.3	1.000
1913			5	3	.625	3.29	30	9	3	93	98	45	39	1	3	1	0	26	2	0	.077	0	18	2	1	0.7	.900
1914			16	15	.516	2.13	40	34	19	266.2	246	79	102	0	0	1	0	92	19	0	.207	6	72	8	2	2.3	.913
1915			5	16	.238	3.30	38	21	11	185.2	180	52	71	1	1	0	4	60	7	0	.117	6	58	6	0	1.8	.914
1916			12	11	.522	1.87	42	23	16	246	189	74	111	2	4	0	2	79	17	0	.215	15	58	5	2	1.9	.936
1917			17	11	.607	2.36	40	34	23	297.2	276	54	99	7	1	0	1	103	21	0	.204	11	71	3	4	2.1	.965
1918			19	14	.576	2.11	38	29	26	273.1	219	65	117	3	4	1	3	95	23	0	.242	4	68	0	0	1.9	1.000
1919			19	13	.594	2.67	35	32	27	286.2	229	74	106	4	1	0	1	101	29	0	.287	4	63	5	0	2.1	.931
1920			24	15	.615	2.39	44	37	28	327	307	52	114	3	2	1	2	113	25	0	.221	11	75	1	2	2.0	.989
1921			**22**	14	.611	3.25	38	**38**	29	**327**	**341**	80	134	2	0	0	0	122	31	0	.254	10	68	3	4	2.1	.963
1922			23	14	.622	3.18	41	37	**27**	294.2	330	61	129	4	0	1	0	108	29	4	.269	7	55	0	5	1.5	1.000
1923			17	**19**	.472	3.57	39	**38**	26	294.2	331	71	77	1	1	0	0	107	28	2	.262	11	63	2	1	1.9	.974
1924			20	14	.588	3.28	38	35	25	268.2	296	40	62	**4**	1	0	1	104	36	0	.346	6	51	4	4	1.6	.934
1925	CHI	N	12	14	.462	4.28	32	26	13	212.1	249	61	41	0	3	1	0	82	17	2	.207	4	42	1	1	1.5	.979
1926	2 teams		CHI N (8G 2–1)			DET A (8G 0–4)																						
"	total		2	5	.286	5.77	16	11	3	68.2	92	30	20	2	0	1	0	22	7	0	.318	1	15	1	0	1.1	.941
15 yrs.			216	178	.548	2.89	517	408	279	3480	3415	853	1252	36	21	7	14	1227	293	6	.239	102	785	41	27	1.8	.956

Mays Copeland

COPELAND, MAYS
B. Aug. 31, 1913, Mountain View, Ark.   D. Nov. 29, 1982, Indio, Calif.
BR TR 6'   180 lbs.

Year	Team		W	L	PCT	ERA	G	GS	CG	IP	H	BB	SO	ShO	W	L	SV	AB	H	HR	BA	PO	A	E	DP	TC/G	FA
1935	STL	N	0	0	–	13.50	1	0	0	.2	2	0	0	0	0	0	0	0	0	0	–	1	1	0	0	2.0	.500

Henry Coppola

COPPOLA, HENRY PETER
B. Aug. 6, 1912, East Douglas, Mass.
BR TR 5'11"   175 lbs.

Year	Team		W	L	PCT	ERA	G	GS	CG	IP	H	BB	SO	ShO	W	L	SV	AB	H	HR	BA	PO	A	E	DP	TC/G	FA
1935	WAS	A	3	4	.429	5.92	19	5	2	59.1	72	29	19	1	1	2	1	14	1	0	.071	2	11	1	0	0.7	.929
1936			0	0	–	4.50	6	0	0	14	17	12	2	0	0	0	0	3	1	0	.333	1	4	0	0	0.8	1.000
2 yrs.			3	4	.429	5.65	25	5	2	73.1	89	41	21	1	1	2	1	17	2	0	.118	3	15	1	0	0.8	.947

Doug Corbett

CORBETT, DOUGLAS MITCHELL
B. Nov. 4, 1952, Sarasota, Fla.
BR TR 6'1"   185 lbs.

Year	Team		W	L	PCT	ERA	G	GS	CG	IP	H	BB	SO	ShO	W	L	SV	AB	H	HR	BA	PO	A	E	DP	TC/G	FA
1980	MIN	A	8	6	.571	1.99	73	0	0	136	102	42	89	0	8	6	23	0	0	0	–	13	31	1	1	0.6	.978
1981			2	6	.250	2.56	54	0	0	88	80	34	60	0	2	6	17	0	0	0	–	7	22	2	0	0.6	.935
1982	2 teams		MIN A (10G 0–2)			CAL A (33G 1–7)																						
"	total		1	9	.100	5.13	43	0	0	79	73	35	52	0	1	9	11	0	0	0	–	13	12	1	0	0.6	.962
1983	CAL	A	1	1	.500	3.63	11	0	0	17.1	26	4	18	0	1	1	0	0	0	0	–	0	1	0	0	0.1	1.000
1984			5	1	.833	2.12	45	1	0	85	76	30	48	0	4	1	4	0	0	0	–	4	13	0	0	0.4	1.000
1985			3	3	.500	4.89	30	0	0	46	49	20	24	0	3	3	0	0	0	0	–	1	9	1	0	0.4	.909
1986			4	2	.667	3.66	46	0	0	78.2	66	22	36	0	4	2	10	0	0	0	–	8	15	0	3	0.5	1.000
1987	BAL	A	0	2	.000	7.83	11	0	0	23	25	13	16	0	0	2	1	0	0	0	–	2	5	0	2	0.6	1.000
8 yrs.			24	30	.444	3.32	313	1	0	553	497	200	343	0	23	30	66	0	0	0	–	48	108	5	6	0.5	.969

LEAGUE CHAMPIONSHIP SERIES

Year	Team		W	L	PCT	ERA	G	GS	CG	IP	H	BB	SO	ShO	W	L	SV	AB	H	HR	BA	PO	A	E	DP	TC/G	FA
1986	CAL	A	1	0	1.000	5.40	3	0	0	6.2	9	2	2	0	1	0	0	0	0	0	–	0	1	0	0	0.3	1.000

Joe Corbett

CORBETT, JOSEPH A.
B. Dec. 4, 1875, San Francisco, Calif.   D. May 2, 1945, San Francisco, Calif.
BR TR 5'10"

Year	Team		W	L	PCT	ERA	G	GS	CG	IP	H	BB	SO	ShO	W	L	SV	AB	H	HR	BA	PO	A	E	DP	TC/G	FA
1895	WAS	N	0	2	.000	5.68	3	3	3	19	26	9	3	0	0	0	0	15	2	0	.133	3	5	0	0	2.7	1.000
1896	BAL	N	3	1	1.000	2.20	8	3	3	41	31	17	28	0	0	0	1	22	6	0	.273	4	5	1	0	1.3	.900
1897			24	8	.750	3.11	37	37	34	313	330	115	149	1	0	0	0	150	37	0	.247	21	76	16	1	3.1	.858
1904	STL	N	5	9	.357	4.39	14	14	12	108.2	110	51	68	0	0	0	0	43	9	0	.209	9	28	5	2	3.0	.881
4 yrs.			32	19	.627	3.42	62	57	52	481.2	497	192	248	1	0	0	1	230	54	0	.235	37	114	22	3	2.8	.873

Sherman Corbett

CORBETT, SHERMAN STANLEY
B. Nov. 3, 1962, New Braunfels, Tex.
BL TL 6'4"   205 lbs.

Year	Team		W	L	PCT	ERA	G	GS	CG	IP	H	BB	SO	ShO	W	L	SV	AB	H	HR	BA	PO	A	E	DP	TC/G	FA
1988	CAL	A	2	1	.667	4.14	34	0	0	45.2	47	23	28	0	2	1	1	0	0	0	–	1	7	1	0	0.3	.889
1989			0	0	–	3.38	4	0	0	5.1	3	1	3	0	0	0	0	0	0	0	–	0	0	0	0	0.0	–
2 yrs.			2	1	.667	4.06	38	0	0	51	50	24	31	0	2	1	1	0	0	0	–	1	7	1	0	0.2	.889

Ray Corbin

CORBIN, ALTON RAY
B. Feb. 12, 1949, Live Oak, Fla.
BR TR 6'2"   200 lbs.

Year	Team		W	L	PCT	ERA	G	GS	CG	IP	H	BB	SO	ShO	W	L	SV	AB	H	HR	BA	PO	A	E	DP	TC/G	FA
1971	MIN	A	8	11	.421	4.11	52	11	2	140	141	70	83	0	6	4	3	34	7	0	.206	7	30	2	0	0.8	.949
1972			8	9	.471	2.61	31	19	5	162	135	53	83	3	2	0	0	49	4	0	.082	12	16	4	1	1.0	.875
1973			8	5	.615	3.03	51	7	1	148.1	124	60	83	0	4	5	14	0	0	0	–	13	16	2	0	0.6	.935
1974			7	6	.538	5.30	29	15	1	112	133	40	50	0	3	1	0	0	0	0	–	11	21	3	1	1.2	.914
1975			5	7	.417	5.12	18	11	3	89.2	105	38	49	0	2	0	0	0	0	0	–	6	16	2	2	1.3	.917
5 yrs.			36	38	.486	3.84	181	63	12	652	638	261	348	3	17	10	17	83	11	0	.133	49	99	13	4	0.9	.919

John Corcoran

CORCORAN, JOHN H.
B. 1860, Lowell, Mass.   Deceased.

Year	Team		W	L	PCT	ERA	G	GS	CG	IP	H	BB	SO	ShO	W	L	SV	AB	H	HR	BA	PO	A	E	DP	TC/G	FA
1884	BKN	AA	0	0	–	0.00	1	0	0	1	0	1	0	0	0	0	0	*					0	0	0	0	0.0	–

Larry Corcoran

CORCORAN, LAWRENCE J.
Brother of Mike Corcoran.
B. Aug. 10, 1859, Brooklyn, N. Y.   D. Oct. 14, 1891, Newark, N. J.
BL TR

Year	Team		W	L	PCT	ERA	G	GS	CG	IP	H	BB	SO	ShO	W	L	SV	AB	H	HR	BA	PO	A	E	DP	TC/G	FA
1880	CHI	N	43	14	.754	1.95	63	60	57	536.1	404	**99**	**268**	5	0	0	2	286	66	0	.231	34	122	7	2	2.6	.957
1881			**31**	14	.689	2.31	45	44	43	396.2	380	78	150	4	1	0	0	189	42	0	.222	29	63	11	0	2.3	.893
1882			27	13	**.675**	**1.95**	40	40	39	355.2	281	63	170	3	0	0	0	169	35	1	.207	0	0	0	0	0.0	–
1883			34	20	.630	2.49	56	53	51	473.2	483	82	216	3	1	0	0	263	55	0	.209	37	88	13	3	2.5	.906
1884			35	23	.603	2.40	60	59	57	516.2	473	116	272	7	0	1	0	251	61	1	.243	47	132	24	5	3.4	.882

Year	Team		W	L	PCT	ERA	G	GS	CG	IP	H	BB	SO	ShO	Relief Pitching W	L	SV	Batting AB	H	HR	BA	PO	A	E	DP	TC/G	FA

Larry Corcoran *continued*

Year	Team		W	L	PCT	ERA	G	GS	CG	IP	H	BB	SO	ShO	W	L	SV	AB	H	HR	BA	PO	A	E	DP	TC/G	FA
1885	2 teams	CHI N (7G 5–2)								NY	N	(3G	2–1)														
"	total		7	3	.700	3.42	10	10	8	84.1	87	35	20	1	0	0	0	36	11	0	.306	6	23	2	2	3.1	.935
1886	NY	N	0	1	.000	5.79	2	1	1	14	16	4	3	0	0	0	0	85	15	0	.176	2	2	2	0	3.0	.667
1887	IND	N	0	2	.000	12.60	2	1	1	15	23	19	4	0	0	0	0	10	2	0	.200	0	4	0	0	2.0	1.000
8 yrs.			177	90	.663 7th	2.36	278	269	257	2392.1	2147	496	1103	23	2	1	2	*				155	434	59	12	2.3	.909

Mike Corcoran

CORCORAN, MICHAEL
Brother of Larry Corcoran.
B. Brooklyn, N. Y.

Year	Team		W	L	PCT	ERA	G	GS	CG	IP	H	BB	SO	ShO	W	L	SV	AB	H	HR	BA	PO	A	E	DP	TC/G	FA
1884	CHI	N	0	1	.000	4.00	1	1	1	9	16	7	2	0	0	0	0	3	0	0	.000	2	0	0	0	2.0	1.000

Ed Corey

COREY, EDWARD NORMAN
Born Abraham Simon Cohen.
B. July 13, 1899, Chicago, Ill.   D. Sept. 17, 1970, Kenosha, Wis.

BR TR 6'   170 lbs.

Year	Team		W	L	PCT	ERA	G	GS	CG	IP	H	BB	SO	ShO	W	L	SV	AB	H	HR	BA	PO	A	E	DP	TC/G	FA
1918	CHI	A	0	0	–	4.50	1	0	0	2	2	1	0	0	0	0	0	1	0	0	.000	0	1	0	0	1.0	1.000

Fred Corey

COREY, FREDERICK HARRISON
B. 1857, S. Kingston, R. I.   D. Nov. 27, 1912, Providence, R. I.

BR TR

Year	Team		W	L	PCT	ERA	G	GS	CG	IP	H	BB	SO	ShO	W	L	SV	AB	H	HR	BA	PO	A	E	DP	TC/G	FA
1878	PRO	N	1	2	.333	2.35	5	5	2	23	22	7	7	0	0	0	0	21	3	0	.143	1	2	0	0	0.6	1.000
1880	WOR	N	8	9	.471	2.43	25	17	9	148.1	131	16	47	2	0	1	2	138	24	0	.174	6	16	6	1	1.1	.786
1881			6	15	.286	3.72	23	21	20	188.2	231	31	33	1	0	0	0	203	45	0	.222	13	31	2	1	2.0	.957
1882			1	13	.071	3.56	21	14	12	139	180	19	36	0	0	0	1	255	63	0	.247	7	32	6	0	2.1	.867
1883	PHI	AA	10	7	.588	3.40	18	16	15	148.1	182	24	42	0	0	0	1	298	77	1	.258	9	38	10	0	3.2	.825
1885			1	0	1.000	7.00	1	1	1	9	18	1	3	0	0	0	0	384	94	1	.245	2	0	0	0	3.0	1.000
6 yrs.			27	46	.370	3.32	93	74	59	656.1	764	98	168	3	0	3	2	*				37	121	24	2	2.0	.868

Pop Corkhill

CORKHILL, JOHN STEWART
B. Apr. 11, 1858, Parkesburg, Pa.   D. Apr. 4, 1921, Pennsauken, N. J.

BL TR 5'10"   180 lbs.

Year	Team		W	L	PCT	ERA	G	GS	CG	IP	H	BB	SO	ShO	W	L	SV	AB	H	HR	BA	PO	A	E	DP	TC/G	FA
1884	CIN	AA	1	0	1.000	1.80	1	0	0	5	1	2	4	0	0	0	0	452	124	4	.274	0	0	0	0	0.0	–
1885			1	4	.200	3.65	8	1	0	37	36	10	12	0	1	3	1	440	111	1	.252	1	4	1	0	0.8	.833
1886			0	0	–	13.50	1	0	0	.2	1	0	1	0	0	0	0	540	143	4	.265	0	0	0	0	0.0	–
1887			1	0	1.000	5.52	5	0	0	14.2	22	5	3	0	1	0	0	541	168	5	.311	0	2	0	0	0.4	1.000
1888	2 teams	CIN AA (2G 0–0)								BKN	AA	(0G	0–0)														
"	total		0	0	–	10.80	2	0	0	5	8	0	1	0	0	0	1	561	160	2	.285	0	1	0	0	0.5	1.000
5 yrs.			3	4	.429	4.62	17	1	0	62.1	68	17	21	0	3	3	2	*				1	7	1	0	0.5	.889

Mike Corkins

CORKINS, MICHAEL PATRICK
B. May 25, 1946, Riverside, Calif.

BR TR 6'1"   190 lbs.

Year	Team		W	L	PCT	ERA	G	GS	CG	IP	H	BB	SO	ShO	W	L	SV	AB	H	HR	BA	PO	A	E	DP	TC/G	FA
1969	SD	N	1	3	.250	8.47	6	4	0	17	27	8	13	0	0	0	0	3	0	0	.000	1	3	0	0	0.7	1.000
1970			5	6	.455	4.62	24	18	1	111	109	79	75	0	0	0	0	37	8	1	.216	8	10	3	1	0.9	.857
1971			0	0	–	3.46	8	0	0	13	14	6	16	0	0	0	0	0	0	0	–	2	0	0	0	0.3	1.000
1972			6	9	.400	3.54	47	9	2	140	125	62	108	1	4	3	6	38	9	1	.237	8	22	2	0	0.7	.938
1973			5	8	.385	4.50	47	11	2	122	130	61	82	0	2	3	3	33	7	3	.212	8	8	4	0	0.4	.800
1974			2	2	.500	4.82	25	2	0	56	53	32	41	0	2	1	0	8	0	0	.000	1	5	0	0	0.2	1.000
6 yrs.			19	28	.404	4.39	157	44	5	459	458	248	335	1	8	7	9	119	24	5	.202	28	48	9	1	0.5	.894

Mardie Cornejo

CORNEJO, NIEVES MARDIE
B. Aug. 5, 1951, Wellington, Kans.

BR TR 6'3"   200 lbs.

Year	Team		W	L	PCT	ERA	G	GS	CG	IP	H	BB	SO	ShO	W	L	SV	AB	H	HR	BA	PO	A	E	DP	TC/G	FA
1978	NY	N	4	2	.667	2.43	25	0	0	37	37	14	17	0	4	2	3	0	0	0	–	2	4	0	0	0.2	1.000

Jeff Cornell

CORNELL, JEFFREY RAY
B. Feb. 10, 1957, Kansas City, Mo.

BB TR 6'   170 lbs.

Year	Team		W	L	PCT	ERA	G	GS	CG	IP	H	BB	SO	ShO	W	L	SV	AB	H	HR	BA	PO	A	E	DP	TC/G	FA
1984	SF	N	1	3	.250	6.10	23	0	0	38.1	51	22	19	0	1	3	0	4	0	0	.000	0	4	0	1	0.2	1.000

Terry Cornutt

CORNUTT, TERRY STANTON
B. Oct. 2, 1952, Roseburg, Ore.

BR TR 6'2"   195 lbs.

Year	Team		W	L	PCT	ERA	G	GS	CG	IP	H	BB	SO	ShO	W	L	SV	AB	H	HR	BA	PO	A	E	DP	TC/G	FA
1977	SF	N	1	2	.333	3.89	28	1	0	44	38	22	23	0	1	1	0	1	0	0	.000	1	3	2	0	0.2	.667
1978			0	0	–	0.00	1	0	0	3	1	0	0	0	0	0	0	0	0	0	–	0	0	0	0	0.0	–
2 yrs.			1	2	.333	3.64	29	1	0	47	39	22	23	0	1	1	0	1	0	0	.000	1	3	2	0	0.2	.667

Ed Correa

CORREA, EDWIN JOSUE
Born Edwin Josue Correa y Andino.
B. Apr. 29, 1966, Hato Rey, Puerto Rico

BR TR 6'2"   190 lbs.

Year	Team		W	L	PCT	ERA	G	GS	CG	IP	H	BB	SO	ShO	W	L	SV	AB	H	HR	BA	PO	A	E	DP	TC/G	FA
1985	CHI	A	1	0	1.000	6.97	5	5	0	10.1	11	11	10	0	0	0	0	0	0	0	–	0	0	0	0	0.0	–
1986	TEX	A	12	14	.462	4.23	32	32	4	202.1	167	126	189	2	0	0	0	0	0	0	–	20	34	3	0	1.8	.947
1987			3	5	.375	7.59	15	15	0	70	83	52	61	0	0	0	0	0	0	0	–	5	9	3	1	1.1	.824
3 yrs.			16	19	.457	5.16	52	48	4	282.2	261	189	260	2	0	0	0	0	0	0	–	25	43	6	1	1.4	.919

Frank Corridon

CORRIDON, FRANK J. (Fiddler)
B. Nov. 25, 1880, Newport, R. I.   D. Feb. 21, 1941, Syracuse, N. Y.

BR TR 6'   170 lbs.

Year	Team		W	L	PCT	ERA	G	GS	CG	IP	H	BB	SO	ShO	W	L	SV	AB	H	HR	BA	PO	A	E	DP	TC/G	FA
1904	2 teams	CHI N (12G 5–5)								PHI	N	(12G	6–5)														
"	total		11	10	.524	2.64	24	21	20	194.2	176	65	78	1	1	1	0	93	19	0	.204	14	78	4	3	4.0	.958
1905	PHI	N	10	13	.435	3.48	35	26	18	212	203	57	79	1	1	1	1	72	15	1	.208	13	72	8	2	2.7	.914
1907			18	14	.563	2.46	37	32	23	274	228	89	131	3	1	1	0	97	16	0	.165	14	99	9	3	3.3	.926
1908			14	10	.583	2.51	27	24	18	208.1	178	48	50	2	0	0	1	73	9	0	.123	13	78	5	0	3.6	.948
1909			11	7	.611	2.11	27	19	11	171	147	61	69	3	1	1	0	59	11	0	.186	8	70	4	0	3.0	.951

Year	Team		W	L	PCT	ERA	G	GS	CG	IP	H	BB	SO	ShO	Relief Pitching W	L	SV	Batting AB	H	HR	BA	PO	A	E	DP	TC/G	FA

Frank Corridon *continued*

| 1910 | STL | N | 6 | 14 | .300 | 3.81 | 30 | 18 | 9 | 156 | 168 | 55 | 51 | 0 | 1 | 2 | 2 | 51 | 10 | 0 | .196 | 10 | 56 | 3 | 2 | 2.3 | .957 |
| 6 yrs. | | | 70 | 68 | .507 | 2.80 | 180 | 140 | 99 | 1216 | 1100 | 375 | 458 | 10 | 4 | 6 | 5 | 445 | 80 | 1 | .180 | 72 | 453 | 33 | 10 | 3.1 | .941 |

Jim Corsi

CORSI, JAMES BERNARD
B. Sept. 9, 1961, Newton, Mass.   BR TR 6'1" 210 lbs.

1988	OAK	A	0	1	.000	3.80	11	1	0	21.1	20	6	10	0	0	1	0	0	0	0	–	0	3	1	0	0.4	.750
1989			1	2	.333	1.88	22	0	0	38.1	26	10	21	0	1	2	0	0	0	0	–	3	5	0	0	0.4	1.000
2 yrs.			1	3	.250	2.56	33	1	0	59.2	46	16	31	0	1	3	0	0	0	0	–	3	8	1	0	0.4	.917

Barry Cort

CORT, BARRY LEE
B. Apr. 15, 1956, Toronto, Ontario, Canada   BR TR 6'5" 210 lbs.

| 1977 | MIL | A | 1 | 1 | .500 | 3.38 | 7 | 3 | 1 | 24 | 25 | 9 | 17 | 0 | 0 | 0 | 0 | 0 | 0 | 0 | – | 1 | 4 | 0 | 0 | 0.7 | 1.000 |

Al Corwin

CORWIN, ELMER NATHAN
B. Dec. 3, 1926, Newburgh, N. Y.   BR TR 6'1" 170 lbs.

1951	NY	N	5	1	.833	3.66	15	8	3	59	49	21	30	1	1	0	1	20	1	0	.050	0	1	1	0	0.1	.500
1952			6	1	.857	2.66	21	7	1	67.2	58	36	36	0	3	0	1	21	2	0	.095	3	6	0	1	0.4	1.000
1953			6	4	.600	4.98	48	7	2	106.2	122	68	49	1	4	2	2	32	9	2	.281	5	13	0	1	0.4	1.000
1954			1	3	.250	4.02	20	0	0	31.1	35	14	14	0	1	3	0	3	0	0	.000	1	3	0	0	0.2	1.000
1955			0	1	.000	4.01	13	0	0	24.2	25	17	13	0	0	1	0	3	0	0	.000	0	3	1	1	0.3	.750
5 yrs.			18	10	.643	3.98	117	22	6	289.1	289	156	142	2	9	6	5	79	12	2	.152	9	26	2	3	0.3	.946

WORLD SERIES

| 1951 | NY | N | 0 | 0 | – | 0.00 | 1 | 0 | 0 | 1.2 | 1 | 1 | 1 | 0 | 1 | 0 | 0 | 0 | 0 | 0 | – | 1 | 0 | 0 | 0 | 1.0 | 1.000 |

Mike Cosgrove

COSGROVE, MICHAEL JOHN
B. Feb. 17, 1951, Phoenix, Ariz.   BL TL 6'1" 170 lbs.

1972	HOU	N	0	1	.000	4.61	7	1	0	13.2	16	3	7	0	0	1	0	2	0	0	.000	0	0	0	0	0.0	–
1973			1	1	.500	1.80	13	0	0	10	11	8	2	0	1	1	0	0	0	0	–	0	0	0	0	0.0	–
1974			7	3	.700	3.49	45	0	0	90.1	76	39	47	0	7	3	2	18	1	0	.056	1	13	1	2	0.3	.933
1975			1	2	.333	3.04	32	3	1	71	62	37	32	0	0	1	5	13	2	0	.154	3	12	1	1	0.5	.933
1976			3	4	.429	5.50	22	16	1	90	106	58	34	1	0	0	0	23	2	0	.087	1	14	0	2	0.7	1.000
5 yrs.			12	11	.522	4.03	119	20	2	275	271	145	122	1	8	5	8	56	5	0	.089	5	39	2	5	0.4	.957

Jim Cosman

COSMAN, JAMES HENRY
B. Feb. 19, 1943, Brockport, N. Y.   BR TR 6'4½" 211 lbs.

1966	STL	N	1	0	1.000	0.00	1	1	1	9	2	2	5	1	0	0	0	3	0	0	.000	1	0	0	0	1.0	1.000
1967			1	0	1.000	3.16	10	5	0	31.1	21	24	11	0	0	0	0	8	1	0	.125	5	2	0	0	0.7	1.000
1970	CHI	N	0	0	–	27.00	1	0	0	1	3	1	0	0	0	0	0	0	0	0	–	0	0	0	0	0.0	–
3 yrs.			2	0	1.000	3.05	12	6	1	41.1	26	27	16	1	0	0	0	11	1	0	.091	6	2	0	0	0.7	1.000

John Costello

COSTELLO, JOHN REILLY
B. Dec. 24, 1960, Bronx, N. Y.   BR TR 6'1" 190 lbs.

1988	STL	N	5	2	.714	1.81	36	0	0	49.2	44	25	38	0	5	2	1	5	0	0	.000	3	3	0	0	0.2	1.000
1989			5	4	.556	3.32	48	0	0	62.1	48	20	40	0	5	4	3	6	0	0	.000	3	4	0	0	0.1	1.000
2 yrs.			10	6	.625	2.65	84	0	0	112	92	45	78	0	10	6	4	11	0	0	.000	6	7	0	0	0.2	1.000

Dan Cotter

COTTER, DANIEL JOSEPH
B. Apr. 14, 1867, Boston, Mass.   D. Sept. 14, 1935, Dorchester, Mass.   BR TR

| 1890 | BUF | P | 0 | 1 | .000 | 14.00 | 1 | 1 | 1 | 9 | 18 | 7 | 0 | 0 | 0 | 0 | 0 | 4 | 0 | 0 | .000 | 1 | 1 | 1 | 0 | 3.0 | .667 |

Ensign Cottrell

COTTRELL, ENSIGN STOVER
B. Aug. 29, 1888, Hoosick Falls, N. Y.   D. Feb. 27, 1947, Syracuse, N. Y.   BL TL 5'9½" 173 lbs.

1911	PIT	N	0	0	–	9.00	1	0	0	1	1	1	0	0	0	0	0	0	0	0	–	0	0	0	0	0.0	–
1912	CHI	N	0	0	–	9.00	1	0	0	4	8	1	1	0	0	0	0	1	0	0	.000	0	0	0	0	0.0	–
1913	PHI	A	1	0	1.000	5.40	2	1	1	10	15	2	3	0	0	0	0	4	1	0	.250	0	1	0	1	0.5	1.000
1914	BOS	N	0	1	.000	9.00	1	1	0	1	2	3	1	0	0	0	0	0	0	0	–	0	0	0	0	0.0	–
1915	NY	A	0	1	.000	3.38	7	0	0	21.1	29	7	7	0	0	1	0	7	0	0	.000	2	8	1	1	1.6	.909
5 yrs.			1	2	.333	4.82	12	2	1	37.1	58	14	12	0	0	1	0	12	1	0	.083	2	9	1	2	1.0	.917

Johnny Couch

COUCH, JOHN DANIEL
B. Mar. 31, 1891, Vaughn, Mont.   D. Dec. 8, 1975, San Mateo, Calif.   BL TR 6' 180 lbs.

1917	DET	A	0	0	–	2.70	3	0	0	13.1	13	1	1	0	0	0	0	4	0	0	.000	1	6	1	0	2.7	.875
1922	CIN	N	16	9	.640	3.89	43	34	18	264	301	56	45	2	1	0	1	91	12	0	.132	9	65	0	3	1.7	1.000
1923	2 teams		CIN N	(19G 2–7)		PHI N	(11G 2–4)																					
"	total		4	11	.267	5.63	30	15	3	134.1	189	36	32	0	1	0	0	47	10	0	.213	8	26	4	1	1.3	.895
1924	PHI	N	4	8	.333	4.73	37	6	3	137	170	39	23	0	4	3	3	49	10	2	.204	3	40	2	1	1.2	.956
1925			5	6	.455	5.44	34	7	2	94.1	112	39	11	1	4	1	1	31	5	1	.161	3	30	2	2	1.0	.943
5 yrs.			29	34	.460	4.63	147	62	26	643	785	171	112	3	9	4	5	222	37	3	.167	24	167	9	7	1.4	.955

Mike Couchee

COUCHEE, MICHAEL EUGENE
B. Dec. 4, 1957, San Jose, Calif.   BR TR 6' 190 lbs.

| 1983 | SD | N | 0 | 1 | .000 | 5.14 | 8 | 0 | 0 | 14 | 12 | 6 | 5 | 0 | 0 | 1 | 0 | 2 | 1 | 0 | .500 | 1 | 0 | 0 | 0 | 0.3 | 1.000 |

Ed Coughlin

COUGHLIN, EDWARD E.
B. Aug. 5, 1861, Hartford, Conn.   D. Dec. 25, 1952, Hartford, Conn.

| 1884 | BUF | N | 0 | 0 | – | ∞ | 1 | 0 | 0 | | 3 | 0 | 0 | 0 | 0 | 0 | 0 | 4 | 1 | 0 | .250 | 0 | 0 | 0 | 0 | 0.0 | – |

Year	Team		W	L	PCT	ERA	G	GS	CG	IP	H	BB	SO	ShO	Relief Pitching W	L	SV	Batting AB	H	HR	BA	PO	A	E	DP	TC/G	FA

Roscoe Coughlin

COUGHLIN, WILLIAM EDWARD
B. Mar. 15, 1868, Walpole, Mass. D. Mar. 20, 1951, Chelsea, Mass.
TR 5'10" 160 lbs.

Year	Team		W	L	PCT	ERA	G	GS	CG	IP	H	BB	SO	ShO	W	L	SV	AB	H	HR	BA	PO	A	E	DP	TC/G	FA
1890	CHI	N	4	6	.400	4.26	11	10	10	95	102	40	29	0	0	0	0	39	10	0	.256	6	25	2	1	3.0	.939
1891	NY	N	3	4	.429	3.84	8	7	6	61	74	23	22	0	0	0	0	23	3	0	.130	7	14	0	1	2.6	1.000
2 yrs.			7	10	.412	4.10	19	17	16	156	176	63	51	0	0	0	0	62	13	0	.210	13	39	2	2	2.8	.963

Fritz Coumbe

COUMBE, FREDERICK NICHOLAS
B. Dec. 13, 1889, Antrim, Pa. D. Mar. 21, 1978, Paradise, Calif.
BL TL 6' 152 lbs.

Year	Team		W	L	PCT	ERA	G	GS	CG	IP	H	BB	SO	ShO	W	L	SV	AB	H	HR	BA	PO	A	E	DP	TC/G	FA
1914	2 teams	BOS A (17G 1-2)				CLE A (14G 1-5)																					
"	total		2	7	.222	2.29	31	10	3	117.2	108	32	39	0	1	1	1	41	8	0	.195	11	39	6	1	1.8	.893
1915	CLE	A	4	7	.364	3.47	30	12	4	114	123	37	37	1	1	0	2	37	10	0	.270	11	49	9	1	2.3	.870
1916			7	5	.583	2.02	29	13	7	120.1	121	27	39	2	2	0	0	35	2	0	.057	10	55	2	6	2.3	.970
1917			8	6	.571	2.14	34	10	4	134.1	119	35	30	1	3	1	5	39	6	0	.154	6	56	7	2	2.0	.899
1918			13	7	.650	3.00	30	17	9	150	164	52	41	0	3	2	3	56	12	0	.214	9	66	1	1	2.5	.987
1919			1	1	.500	5.32	8	2	0	23.2	32	9	7	0	0	1	1	6	3	0	.500	0	9	2	0	1.4	.818
1920	CIN	N	0	1	.000	4.91	3	0	0	14.2	17	4	7	0	0	1	0	13	3	1	.231	0	6	0	0	2.0	1.000
1921			3	4	.429	3.22	28	6	3	86.2	89	21	12	0	1	1	1	25	8	0	.320	5	35	1	1	1.5	.976
8 yrs.			38	38	.500	2.79	193	70	30	761.1	773	217	212	4	11	7	13	252	52	1	.206	52	315	28	12	2.0	.929

Henry Courtney

COURTNEY, HENRY SEYMOUR
B. Nov. 19, 1898, Asheville, N. C. D. Dec. 11, 1954, Lyme, Calif.
BB TL 6'4" 185 lbs.

Year	Team		W	L	PCT	ERA	G	GS	CG	IP	H	BB	SO	ShO	W	L	SV	AB	H	HR	BA	PO	A	E	DP	TC/G	FA
1919	WAS	A	3	0	1.000	2.73	4	3	3	26.1	25	19	6	1	0	0	0	10	2	0	.200	2	1	0	0	0.8	1.000
1920			8	11	.421	4.74	37	24	10	188	223	77	48	1	0	2	0	69	16	1	.232	3	36	7	3	1.2	.848
1921			6	9	.400	5.63	30	15	3	132.2	159	71	26	0	1	1	1	47	14	0	.298	5	36	3	1	1.5	.932
1922	2 teams	WAS A (5G 0-0)				CHI A (18G 5-6)																					
"	total		5	6	.455	4.81	23	11	5	97.1	111	46	32	0	1	0	0	37	9	0	.243	0	22	0	2	1.0	1.000
4 yrs.			22	26	.458	4.90	94	53	21	444.1	518	213	112	2	2	3	1	163	41	1	.252	10	95	10	6	1.2	.913

Harry Coveleski

COVELESKI, HARRY FRANK (The Giant Killer)
Born Harry Frank Kowalewski. Brother of Stan Coveleski.
B. Apr. 23, 1886, Shamokin, Pa. D. Aug. 4, 1950, Shamokin, Pa.
BB TL 6' 180 lbs.

Year	Team		W	L	PCT	ERA	G	GS	CG	IP	H	BB	SO	ShO	W	L	SV	AB	H	HR	BA	PO	A	E	DP	TC/G	FA
1907	PHI	N	1	0	1.000	0.00	4	0	0	20	10	3	6	0	0	0	0	8	0	0	.000	0	6	1	0	1.8	.857
1908			4	1	.800	1.24	6	5	5	43.2	29	12	22	2	0	0	0	15	2	0	.133	3	15	0	0	3.0	1.000
1909			6	10	.375	2.74	24	17	8	121.2	109	49	56	2	1	0	1	37	4	0	.108	6	39	2	1	2.0	.957
1910	CIN	N	1	1	.500	5.26	7	4	2	39.1	35	42	27	0	0	0	0	16	1	0	.063	1	14	0	0	2.1	1.000
1914	DET	A	22	12	.647	2.49	44	36	23	303.1	251	100	124	5	2	1	2	95	23	0	.242	12	123	5	4	3.2	.964
1915			22	13	.629	2.45	50	38	20	312.2	271	87	150	4	1	4	4	103	18	0	.175	16	109	11	5	2.7	.919
1916			21	11	.656	1.97	44	39	22	324.1	278	63	108	3	1	1	2	118	25	0	.212	4	119	5	5	2.9	.961
1917			4	6	.400	2.61	16	11	2	69	70	14	15	0	1	0	0	22	5	0	.227	3	30	4	1	2.3	.892
1918			0	1	.000	3.86	3	1	1	14	17	6	3	0	0	0	0	4	1	0	.250	1	6	0	0	2.3	1.000
9 yrs.			81	55	.596	2.39	198	151	83	1248	1070	376	511	13	10	4	9	418	79	0	.189	46	461	28	16	2.7	.948

Stan Coveleski

COVELESKI, STANLEY ANTHONY
Born Stanley Anthony Kowalewski. Brother of Harry Coveleski.
B. July 13, 1889, Shamokin, Pa. D. Mar. 20, 1984, South Bend, Ind.
Hall of Fame 1969.
BR TR 5'11" 166 lbs.

Year	Team		W	L	PCT	ERA	G	GS	CG	IP	H	BB	SO	ShO	W	L	SV	AB	H	HR	BA	PO	A	E	DP	TC/G	FA
1912	PHI	A	2	1	.667	3.43	5	2	2	21	18	4	9	1	1	0	0	7	1	0	.143	1	4	1	0	1.2	.833
1916	CLE	A	15	13	.536	3.41	45	27	11	232	247	58	76	1	2	4	3	75	13	1	.173	19	72	1	3	2.0	.989
1917			19	14	.576	1.81	45	36	24	298.1	202	94	133	9	1	2	4	97	13	0	.134	12	66	4	3	1.8	.951
1918			22	13	.629	1.82	38	33	25	311	261	76	87	2	1	1	1	110	21	0	.191	14	83	4	4	2.7	.960
1919			24	12	.667	2.52	43	34	24	296	286	60	118	4	1	4	4	94	20	0	.213	15	88	3	2	2.5	.972
1920			24	14	.632	2.49	41	37	26	315	284	65	133	3	1	0	2	111	25	0	.225	17	90	3	6	2.7	.973
1921			23	13	.639	3.36	43	40	29	315.2	341	84	99	2	0	0	0	116	18	0	.155	23	108	1	3	3.1	.992
1922			17	14	.548	3.32	35	33	21	276.2	292	64	98	3	0	1	0	99	10	0	.101	14	69	3	4	2.5	.965
1923			13	14	.481	2.76	33	31	17	228	251	42	54	5	0	0	2	79	7	0	.089	18	70	1	5	2.7	.989
1924			15	16	.484	4.04	37	33	18	240.1	286	73	58	2	2	1	0	82	11	0	.134	21	49	1	2	1.9	.986
1925	WAS	A	20	5	.800	2.84	32	32	15	241	230	73	58	3	0	0	0	81	9	0	.111	10	61	3	7	2.3	.959
1926			14	11	.560	3.12	36	34	11	245.1	272	81	50	3	0	0	0	82	17	0	.207	8	69	2	6	2.2	.975
1927			2	1	.667	3.14	5	4	0	14.1	13	8	3	0	0	0	0	6	2	0	.333	0	3	1	0	0.8	.750
1928	NY	A	5	1	.833	5.74	12	8	2	58	72	20	5	0	0	0	0	19	1	0	.053	2	19	1	0	1.8	.955
14 yrs.			215	142	.602	2.88	450	384	225	3092.2	3055	802	981	38	9	12	21	1058	168	1	.159	174	851	29	45	2.3	.972

WORLD SERIES

Year	Team		W	L	PCT	ERA	G	GS	CG	IP	H	BB	SO	ShO	W	L	SV	AB	H	HR	BA	PO	A	E	DP	TC/G	FA
1920	CLE	A	3	0	1.000	0.67	3	3	3	27	15	2	8	1	0	0	0	10	1	0	.100	1	5	1	0	2.3	.857
1925	WAS	A	0	2	.000	3.77	2	2	1	14.1	16	5	3	0	0	0	0	3	0	0	.000	0	4	0	1	2.0	1.000
2 yrs.			3	2	.600	1.74	5	5	4	41.1	31	7	11	1	0	0	0	13	1	0	.077	1	9	1	1	2.2	.909

Chet Covington

COVINGTON, CHESTER ROGERS (Chesty)
B. Nov. 6, 1910, Cairo, Ill. D. June 11, 1976, Pembroke Park, Fla.
BB TL 6'2" 225 lbs.

Year	Team		W	L	PCT	ERA	G	GS	CG	IP	H	BB	SO	ShO	W	L	SV	AB	H	HR	BA	PO	A	E	DP	TC/G	FA
1944	PHI	N	1	1	.500	4.66	19	0	0	38.2	46	8	13	0	1	0	1	6	0	0	.000	2	6	0	0	0.4	1.000

Tex Covington

COVINGTON, WILLIAM WILKES
Brother of Sam Covington.
B. Mar. 19, 1887, Henryville, Tenn. D. Dec. 10, 1931, Denison, Tex.
BL TR 6'1" 175 lbs.

Year	Team		W	L	PCT	ERA	G	GS	CG	IP	H	BB	SO	ShO	W	L	SV	AB	H	HR	BA	PO	A	E	DP	TC/G	FA
1911	DET	A	7	1	.875	4.09	17	6	5	83.2	94	33	29	0	2	0	0	32	6	0	.188	3	17	0	2	1.2	1.000
1912			3	4	.429	4.12	14	9	2	63.1	58	30	19	1	0	0	0	15	2	0	.133	0	19	3	0	1.6	.864
2 yrs.			10	5	.667	4.10	31	15	7	147	152	63	48	1	2	0	0	47	8	0	.170	3	36	3	2	1.4	.929

Joe Cowley

COWLEY, JOSEPH ALAN
B. Aug. 15, 1958, Lexington, Ky.
BR TR 6'5" 205 lbs.

Year	Team		W	L	PCT	ERA	G	GS	CG	IP	H	BB	SO	ShO	W	L	SV	AB	H	HR	BA	PO	A	E	DP	TC/G	FA
1982	ATL	N	1	2	.333	4.47	17	8	0	52.1	53	16	27	0	1	0	0	15	3	0	.200	6	6	0	1	0.7	1.000
1984	NY	A	9	2	.818	3.56	16	11	3	83.1	75	31	71	1	2	0	0	0	0	0	—	7	12	2	0	1.3	.905

Year	Team		W	L	PCT	ERA	G	GS	CG	IP	H	BB	SO	ShO	W	L	SV	AB	H	HR	BA	PO	A	E	DP	TC/G	FA

Joe Cowley *continued*

Year	Team		W	L	PCT	ERA	G	GS	CG	IP	H	BB	SO	ShO	W	L	SV	AB	H	HR	BA	PO	A	E	DP	TC/G	FA
1985			12	6	.667	3.95	30	26	1	159.2	132	85	97	0	1	0	0	0	0	0	–	6	22	3	1	1.0	.903
1986	CHI	A	11	11	.500	3.88	27	27	4	162.1	133	83	132	0	0	0	0	0	0	0	–	16	16	4	0	1.3	.889
1987	PHI	N	0	4	.000	15.43	5	4	0	11.2	21	17	5	0	0	0	0	3	1	0	.333	1	0	1	0	0.4	.500
5 yrs.			33	25	.569	4.20	95	76	8	469.1	414	232	332	1	3	2	0	18	4	0	.222	36	56	10	2	1.1	.902

Bill Cox

COX, WILLIAM DONALD
B. June 23, 1913, Ashmore, Ill.
BR TR 6'1" 185 lbs.

Year	Team		W	L	PCT	ERA	G	GS	CG	IP	H	BB	SO	ShO	W	L	SV	AB	H	HR	BA	PO	A	E	DP	TC/G	FA
1936	STL	N	0	0	–	6.75	2	0	0	2.2	4	1	1	0	0	0	0	0	0	0	–	0	0	1	0	0.5	–
1937	CHI	A	1	0	1.000	0.71	3	2	1	12.2	9	5	8	0	0	0	0	4	1	0	.250	0	1	0	0	0.3	1.000
1938	2 teams	CHI A (7G 0–2)				STL A (22G 1–4)																					
"	total		1	6	.143	6.99	29	8	1	74.2	92	48	21	0	0	1	0	19	1	0	.053	4	15	1	1	0.7	.950
1939	STL	A	0	2	.000	9.64	4	2	1	9.1	10	8	8	0	0	0	0	1	0	0	.000	2	4	0	0	1.5	1.000
1940			0	1	.000	7.27	12	0	0	17.1	23	12	7	0	0	1	0	1	0	0	.000	1	4	0	0	0.4	1.000
5 yrs.			2	9	.182	6.56	50	12	3	116.2	138	74	45	0	0	2	0	25	2	0	.080	7	24	2	1	0.7	.939

Casey Cox

COX, JOSEPH CASEY
B. July 3, 1941, Long Beach, Calif.
BR TR 6'5" 200 lbs.

Year	Team		W	L	PCT	ERA	G	GS	CG	IP	H	BB	SO	ShO	W	L	SV	AB	H	HR	BA	PO	A	E	DP	TC/G	FA
1966	WAS	A	4	5	.444	3.50	66	0	0	113	104	35	46	0	4	5	7	8	0	0	.000	2	24	1	1	0.4	.963
1967			7	4	.636	2.96	54	0	0	73	67	21	32	0	7	4	1	3	0	0	.000	4	14	0	0	0.3	1.000
1968			0	1	.000	2.35	4	0	0	7.2	7	0	4	0	0	1	0	0	0	0	–	1	0	0	0	0.3	1.000
1969			12	7	.632	2.78	52	13	4	171.2	161	64	73	0	7	3	0	47	5	0	.106	11	21	0	0	0.6	1.000
1970			8	12	.400	4.45	37	30	1	192	211	44	68	0	0	0	1	58	7	0	.121	13	24	2	0	1.1	.949
1971			5	7	.417	3.99	54	11	0	124	131	40	43	0	5	4	7	26	2	0	.077	5	20	1	2	0.5	.962
1972	2 teams	TEX A (35G 3–5)				NY A (5G 0–1)																					
"	total		3	6	.333	4.44	40	5	0	77	86	29	31	0	2	2	4	9	1	0	.111	5	11	0	0	0.4	1.000
1973	NY	A	0	0	–	6.00	1	0	0	3	5	1	0	0	0	0	0	0	0	0	–	0	1	0	0	1.0	1.000
8 yrs.			39	42	.481	3.70	308	59	5	761.1	772	234	297	0	25	19	20	151	15	0	.099	41	115	4	6	0.5	.975

Danny Cox

COX, DANNY BRADFORD (Coxie)
B. Sept. 21, 1959, Northampton, England
BR TR 6'4" 220 lbs.

Year	Team		W	L	PCT	ERA	G	GS	CG	IP	H	BB	SO	ShO	W	L	SV	AB	H	HR	BA	PO	A	E	DP	TC/G	FA
1983	STL	N	3	6	.333	3.25	12	12	0	83	92	23	36	0	0	0	0	27	2	0	.074	9	16	2	1	2.3	.926
1984			9	11	.450	4.03	29	27	1	156.1	171	54	70	1	1	0	0	53	7	0	.132	11	27	1	4	1.3	.974
1985			18	9	.667	2.88	35	35	10	241	226	64	131	4	0	0	0	79	12	0	.152	22	31	2	1	1.6	.964
1986			12	13	.480	2.90	32	32	8	220	189	60	108	0	0	0	0	65	5	0	.077	22	10	5	0	1.2	.865
1987			11	9	.550	3.88	31	31	2	199.1	224	71	101	0	0	0	0	69	8	0	.116	23	24	1	1	1.5	.979
1988			3	8	.273	3.98	13	13	0	86	89	25	47	0	0	0	0	23	1	0	.043	10	12	0	2	1.7	1.000
6 yrs.			56	56	.500	3.40	152	150	21	985.2	991	297	493	5	1	0	0	316	35	0	.111	97	120	11	9	1.5	.952

LEAGUE CHAMPIONSHIP SERIES

Year	Team		W	L	PCT	ERA	G	GS	CG	IP	H	BB	SO	ShO	W	L	SV	AB	H	HR	BA	PO	A	E	DP	TC/G	FA
1985	STL	N	1	0	1.000	3.00	1	1	0	6	4	5	4	0	0	0	0	2	0	0	.000	0	3	0	0	3.0	1.000
1987			1	1	.500	2.12	2	2	2	17	17	3	11	1	0	0	0	6	2	0	.333	4	5	0	2	4.5	1.000
2 yrs.			2	1	.667	2.35	3	3	2	23	21	8	15	1	0	0	0	8	2	0	.250	4	8	0	2	4.0	1.000

WORLD SERIES

Year	Team		W	L	PCT	ERA	G	GS	CG	IP	H	BB	SO	ShO	W	L	SV	AB	H	HR	BA	PO	A	E	DP	TC/G	FA
1985	STL	N	0	0	–	1.29	2	2	0	14	14	4	13	0	0	0	0	4	0	0	.000	1	2	0	0	1.5	1.000
1987			1	2	.333	7.71	3	2	0	11.2	13	8	9	0	0	0	0	2	0	0	.000	1	1	0	0	0.7	1.000
2 yrs.			1	2	.333	4.21	5	4	0	25.2	27	12	22	0	0	0	0	6	0	0	.000	2	3	0	0	1.0	1.000

Ernie Cox

COX, ERNEST THOMPSON (Elmer)
B. Feb. 19, 1894, Birmingham, Ala. D. Apr. 29, 1974, Birmingham, Ala.
BL TR 6'1" 180 lbs.

Year	Team		W	L	PCT	ERA	G	GS	CG	IP	H	BB	SO	ShO	W	L	SV	AB	H	HR	BA	PO	A	E	DP	TC/G	FA
1922	CHI	A	0	0	–	18.00	1	0	0	1	1	2	0	0	0	0	0	0	0	0	–	0	0	0	0	0.0	–

George Cox

COX, GEORGE MELVIN
B. Nov. 15, 1904, Sherman, Tex.
BR TR 6'1" 170 lbs.

Year	Team		W	L	PCT	ERA	G	GS	CG	IP	H	BB	SO	ShO	W	L	SV	AB	H	HR	BA	PO	A	E	DP	TC/G	FA
1928	CHI	A	1	2	.333	5.26	26	2	0	89	110	39	22	0	1	1	0	26	2	0	.077	0	29	0	2	1.1	1.000

Glenn Cox

COX, GLENN MELVIN (Jingles)
B. Feb. 3, 1931, Montebello, Calif.
BR TR 6'2" 210 lbs.

Year	Team		W	L	PCT	ERA	G	GS	CG	IP	H	BB	SO	ShO	W	L	SV	AB	H	HR	BA	PO	A	E	DP	TC/G	FA
1955	KC	A	0	2	.000	30.86	2	0	0	2.1	11	1	2	0	0	0	0	1	0	0	.000	2	0	0	0	1.0	1.000
1956			0	2	.000	4.24	3	3	1	23.1	15	22	6	0	0	0	0	7	0	0	.000	0	0	0	0	0.0	–
1957			1	0	1.000	5.02	10	0	0	14.1	18	9	8	0	1	0	0	2	0	0	.000	0	3	0	0	0.3	1.000
1958			0	0	–	9.82	2	0	0	3.2	6	3	1	0	0	0	0	0	0	0	–	0	0	0	0	0.0	–
4 yrs.			1	4	.200	6.39	17	5	1	43.2	50	35	17	0	1	0	0	10	0	0	.000	2	5	0	0	0.3	1.000

Les Cox

COX, LESLIE WARREN
B. Aug. 14, 1905, Junction, Tex. D. Oct. 14, 1934, San Angelo, Tex.
BR TR 6' 164 lbs.

Year	Team		W	L	PCT	ERA	G	GS	CG	IP	H	BB	SO	ShO	W	L	SV	AB	H	HR	BA	PO	A	E	DP	TC/G	FA
1926	CHI	A	0	1	.000	5.40	2	0	0	5	6	5	3	0	0	1	0	2	1	0	.500	0	1	0	0	0.5	1.000

Red Cox

COX, PLATEAU REX
B. Feb. 16, 1895, Laurel Springs, N. C. D. Oct. 15, 1984, Roanoke, Va.
BL TR 6'2" 190 lbs.

Year	Team		W	L	PCT	ERA	G	GS	CG	IP	H	BB	SO	ShO	W	L	SV	AB	H	HR	BA	PO	A	E	DP	TC/G	FA
1920	DET	A	0	0	–	5.40	3	0	0	5	9	3	1	0	0	0	0	1	0	0	.000	0	2	2	0	1.3	.500

Terry Cox

COX, TERRY LEE
B. Mar. 30, 1949, Odessa, Tex.
BR TR 6'5" 215 lbs.

Year	Team		W	L	PCT	ERA	G	GS	CG	IP	H	BB	SO	ShO	W	L	SV	AB	H	HR	BA	PO	A	E	DP	TC/G	FA
1970	CAL	A	0	0	–	4.50	3	0	0	2	4	0	3	0	0	0	0	0	0	0	–	0	0	0	0	0.0	–

Bill Coyle

COYLE, WILLIAM CLAUDE
B. Pittsburgh, Pa. Deceased.
TR

Year	Team		W	L	PCT	ERA	G	GS	CG	IP	H	BB	SO	ShO	W	L	SV	AB	H	HR	BA	PO	A	E	DP	TC/G	FA
1893	BOS	N	0	1	.000	9.00	2	1	0	8	14	3	2	0	0	0	0	4	0	0	.000	0	2	0	0	1.0	1.000

Year	Team		W	L	PCT	ERA	G	GS	CG	IP	H	BB	SO	ShO	Relief Pitching W	L	SV	Batting AB	H	HR	BA	PO	A	E	DP	TC/G	FA

Charlie Cozart

COZART, CHARLES RHUBIN
B. Oct. 17, 1919, Lenoir, N. C.

BR TL 6' 190 lbs.

| 1945 | BOS | N | 1 | 0 | 1.000 | 10.13 | 5 | 0 | 0 | 8 | 10 | 15 | 4 | 0 | 1 | 0 | 0 | 2 | 0 | 0 | .000 | 0 | 7 | 0 | 0 | 1.4 | 1.000 |

Jim Crabb

CRABB, JAMES ROY
B. Aug. 23, 1890, Monticello, Iowa D. Mar. 30, 1940, Lewistown, Mont.

BR TR 5'11" 160 lbs.

| 1912 | 2 teams | CHI A (2G 0–1) | | | | | PHI A (7G 2–4) | | | | | | | | | | | | | | | | | | | | |
| " | total | | 2 | 5 | .286 | 3.29 | 9 | 8 | 3 | 52 | 54 | 21 | 15 | 0 | 0 | 0 | 0 | 19 | 0 | 0 | .000 | 3 | 17 | 2 | 1 | 2.4 | .909 |

George Crable

CRABLE, GEORGE E.
B. Dec., 1885, Nebraska

BL TL 6'1" 190 lbs.

| 1910 | BKN | N | 0 | 0 | – | 4.91 | 2 | 1 | 1 | 7.1 | 5 | 5 | 3 | 0 | 0 | 0 | 0 | 2 | 0 | 0 | .000 | 0 | 2 | 0 | 0 | 1.0 | 1.000 |

Walter Craddock

CRADDOCK, WALTER ANDERSON
B. Mar. 25, 1932, Pax, W. Va. D. July 6, 1980, Parma Heights, Ohio

BR TL 5'11½" 176 lbs.

1955	KC	A	0	2	.000	7.80	4	2	0	15	18	10	9	0	0	1	0	5	0	0	.000	0	2	0	0	0.5	1.000
1956			0	2	.000	6.75	2	2	0	9.1	9	10	8	0	0	0	0	2	0	0	.000	0	1	0	0	0.5	1.000
1958			0	3	.000	5.89	23	1	0	36.2	41	20	22	0	0	0	2	2	0	0	.000	1	8	0	1	0.4	1.000
3 yrs.			0	7	.000	6.49	29	5	0	61	68	40	39	0	0	3	0	9	0	0	.000	1	11	0	1	0.4	1.000

Molly Craft

CRAFT, MAURICE MONTAGUE
B. Nov. 28, 1895, Portsmouth, Va. D. Oct. 25, 1978, Los Angeles, Calif.

BR TR 6'2" 165 lbs.

1916	WAS	A	0	1	.000	3.27	2	1	1	11	12	6	9	0	0	0	0	4	0	0	.000	0	4	0	0	2.0	1.000
1917			0	0	–	3.86	8	0	0	14	17	8	2	0	0	0	0	2	1	0	.500	1	5	0	1	0.8	1.000
1918			0	0	–	1.29	3	0	0	7	5	1	5	0	0	0	0	2	0	0	.000	1	2	0	0	1.0	1.000
1919			0	3	.000	3.88	16	2	0	48.2	59	18	17	0	0	0	2	18	2	0	.111	2	13	1	0	1.0	.938
4 yrs.			0	4	.000	3.57	29	3	0	80.2	93	33	33	0	0	0	2	26	3	0	.115	4	24	1	1	1.0	.966

Howard Craghead

CRAGHEAD, HOWARD OLIVER (Judge)
B. May 25, 1908, Selma, Calif. D. July 15, 1962, San Zielde, Calif.

BR TR 6'2" 200 lbs.

1931	CLE	A	0	0	–	6.35	4	0	0	5.2	8	2	2	0	0	0	0	0	0	0	–	0	2	0	0	0.5	1.000
1933			0	0	–	6.23	11	0	0	17.1	19	10	2	0	0	0	0	3	0	0	.000	1	5	1	0	0.6	.857
2 yrs.			0	0	–	6.26	15	0	0	23	27	12	4	0	0	0	0	3	0	0	.000	1	7	1	0	0.6	.889

George Craig

CRAIG, GEORGE McCARTHY (Lefty)
B. Nov. 15, 1887, Philadelphia, Pa. D. Apr. 23, 1911, Indianapolis, Ind.

TL

| 1907 | PHI | A | 0 | 0 | – | 10.80 | 2 | 0 | 0 | 1.2 | 2 | 3 | 0 | 0 | 0 | 0 | 0 | 1 | 0 | 0 | .000 | 0 | 0 | 0 | 0 | 0.0 | – |

Pete Craig

CRAIG, PETER JOEL
B. July 10, 1940, La Salle, Ont., Canada

BL TR 6'5" 220 lbs.

1964	WAS	A	0	0	–	48.60	2	1	0	1.2	8	4	0	0	0	0	0	0	0	0	–	0	0	0	0	0.0	–
1965			0	3	.000	8.16	3	3	0	14.1	18	8	2	0	0	0	0	3	2	0	.667	6	3	0	0	3.0	1.000
1966			0	0	–	4.50	1	0	0	2	2	1	1	0	0	0	0	0	0	0	–	0	0	1	0	1.0	–
3 yrs.			0	3	.000	11.50	6	4	0	18	28	13	3	0	0	0	0	3	2	0	.667	6	3	1	0	1.7	.900

Roger Craig

CRAIG, ROGER LEE
B. Feb. 17, 1930, Durham, N. C.
Manager 1978-79, 1985-89.

BR TR 6'4" 185 lbs.

1955	BKN	N	5	3	.625	2.78	21	10	3	90.2	81	43	48	0	0	1	2	26	2	0	.077	6	11	1	1	0.9	.944
1956			12	11	.522	3.71	35	32	8	199	169	87	109	2	0	2	1	61	1	0	.016	10	22	0	1	0.9	1.000
1957			6	9	.400	4.61	32	13	1	111.1	102	47	69	0	0	4	2	29	4	0	.138	11	19	0	0	0.9	1.000
1958	LA	N	2	1	.667	4.50	9	2	1	32	30	12	16	0	0	1	0	9	0	0	.000	0	3	1	0	0.4	.750
1959			11	5	.688	2.06	29	17	7	152.2	122	45	76	4	2	0	0	52	3	0	.058	19	18	1	2	1.3	.974
1960			8	3	.727	3.27	21	15	6	115.2	99	43	69	1	1	0	0	36	2	0	.056	10	16	0	2	1.2	1.000
1961			5	6	.455	6.15	40	14	2	112.2	130	52	63	0	2	1	2	27	4	0	.148	5	15	1	1	0.5	.952
1962	NY	N	10	24	.294	4.51	42	33	13	233.1	261	70	118	0	4	2	3	76	4	0	.053	23	54	4	4	1.9	.951
1963			5	22	.185	3.78	46	31	14	236	249	58	108	0	0	1	2	69	6	0	.087	18	60	8	4	1.9	.907
1964	STL	N	7	9	.438	3.25	39	19	3	166	180	35	84	0	2	1	5	48	10	0	.208	13	37	1	2	1.3	.980
1965	CIN	N	1	4	.200	3.64	40	0	0	64.1	74	25	30	0	1	4	3	11	2	0	.182	2	13	1	0	0.4	.938
1966	PHI	N	2	1	.667	5.56	14	0	0	22.2	31	5	13	0	2	1	1	4	0	0	.000	1	4	0	0	0.6	1.000
12 yrs.			74	98	.430	3.83	368	186	58	1536.1	1528	522	803	7	18	16	19	448	38	0	.085	120	274	18	21	1.1	.956

WORLD SERIES

1955	BKN	N	1	0	1.000	3.00	1	1	0	6	4	5	4	0	0	0	0	0	0	0	–	0	0	0	0	1.0	1.000
1956			0	1	.000	12.00	2	1	0	6	10	3	4	0	0	0	0	2	1	0	.500	1	1	0	0	1.0	1.000
1959	LA	N	0	1	.000	8.68	2	2	0	9.1	15	5	8	0	0	0	0	3	0	0	.000	0	2	0	1	1.0	1.000
1964	STL	N	1	0	1.000	0.00	2	0	0	5	2	3	9	0	0	1	0	1	0	0	.000	0	2	0	0	1.0	1.000
4 yrs.			2	2	.500	6.49	7	4	0	26.1	31	16	25	0	0	1	0	6	1	0	.167	1	6	0	1	1.0	1.000

Jerry Cram

CRAM, GERALD ALLEN
B. Dec. 9, 1947, Los Angeles, Calif.

BR TR 6' 180 lbs.

1969	KC	A	0	1	.000	3.24	5	2	0	16.2	15	6	10	0	0	0	0	3	0	0	.000	2	1	0	0	0.6	1.000
1974	NY	N	0	1	.000	1.64	10	0	0	22	22	4	8	0	0	0	0	3	1	0	.333	1	4	0	1	0.5	1.000
1975			0	1	.000	5.40	4	0	0	5	7	2	2	0	0	0	1	0	0	0	–	0	1	0	0	0.3	1.000
1976	KC	A	0	0	–	6.75	4	0	0	4	8	1	2	0	0	0	1	0	0	0	–	2	0	0	0	0.5	1.000
4 yrs.			0	3	.000	3.02	23	2	0	47.2	52	13	22	0	0	0	2	6	1	0	.167	5	6	0	1	0.5	1.000

Bill Cramer

CRAMER, WILLIAM WENDELL
B. May 21, 1891, Bedford, Ind. D. Sept. 11, 1966, Fort Wayne, Ind.

BR TR 6' 175 lbs.

| 1912 | CIN | N | 0 | 0 | – | 0.00 | 1 | 0 | 0 | 2.1 | 6 | 0 | 2 | 0 | 0 | 0 | 0 | 1 | 0 | 0 | .000 | 0 | 4 | 0 | 0 | 5.0 | .200 |

Year	Team		W	L	PCT	ERA	G	GS	CG	IP	H	BB	SO	ShO	Relief Pitching W	L	SV	Batting AB	H	HR	BA	PO	A	E	DP	TC/G	FA

Doc Cramer

CRAMER, ROGER MAXWELL (Flit)
B. July 22, 1905, Beach Haven, N. J.　　　　　　　　BL TR 6'2" 185 lbs.

| 1938 | BOS | A | 0 | 0 | – | 4.50 | 1 | 0 | 0 | 4 | 3 | 3 | 1 | 0 | 0 | 0 | 0 | * | | | | 0 | 1 | 0 | 0 | 1.0 | 1.000 |

Doc Crandall

CRANDALL, JAMES OTIS
B. Oct. 8, 1887, Wadena, Ind.　D. Aug. 17, 1951, Bell, Calif.　　BR TR 5'10½" 180 lbs.

1908	NY	N	12	12	.500	2.93	32	24	13	214.2	198	59	77	0	2	1	0	72	16	2	.222	15	52	1	2	2.1	.985
1909			6	4	.600	2.88	30	7	4	122	117	33	55	0	5	1	4	41	10	1	.244	9	39	3	4	1.7	.941
1910			17	4	.810	2.56	42	18	13	207.2	194	43	73	2	7	1	4	73	25	1	.342	12	49	1	3	1.5	.984
1911			15	5	.750	2.63	41	15	9	198.2	199	51	94	2	7	0	5	113	27	2	.239	9	59	3	2	1.7	.958
1912			13	7	.650	3.61	37	10	7	162	181	35	60	0	6	5	2	80	25	0	.313	4	41	2	0	1.3	.957
1913			4	4	.500	2.86	35	3	2	97.2	102	24	42	0	3	3	6	49	15	0	.306	0	2	0	0	0.1	1.000
1914	STL	F	13	9	.591	3.54	27	21	18	196	194	52	84	1	1	0	0	278	86	2	.309	8	52	4	2	2.4	.938
1915			21	15	.583	2.59	51	33	22	312.2	307	77	117	4	6	3	0	141	40	1	.284	15	99	5	3	2.3	.958
1916	STL	A	0	0	–	27.00	2	0	0	1.1	7	1	0	0	0	0	0	12	1	0	.083	0	1	0	0	0.5	–
1918	BOS	N	1	2	.333	2.38	5	3	3	34	39	4	4	0	0	0	0	28	8	0	.286	2	10	0	1	2.4	1.000
10 yrs.			102	62	.622	2.92	302	134	91	1546.2	1538	379	606	9	37	14	21	*				74	403	20	17	1.6	.960

WORLD SERIES

1911	NY	N	1	0	1.000	0.00	2	0	0	4	2	0	1	0	1	0	0	2	1	0	.500	0	1	0	0	1.0	1.000
1912			0	0	–	0.00	1	0	0	2	1	0	3	0	0	0	0	1	0	0	.000	0	1	0	0	1.0	1.000
1913			0	0	–	3.86	2	0	0	4.2	4	0	2	0	0	0	0	4	0	0	.000	0	2	0	0	1.0	1.000
3 yrs.			1	0	1.000	1.69	5	0	0	10.2	7	0	6	0	1	0	0	7	1	0	.143	0	5	0	0	1.0	1.000

Cannonball Crane

CRANE, EDWARD NICHOLAS
B. May, 1862, Boston, Mass.　D. Sept. 19, 1896, Rochester, N. Y.　　BR TR 5'10½" 204 lbs.

1884	BOS	U	0	2	.000	4.00	4	2	1	18	17	6	13	0	0	0	0	428	122	12	.285	1	7	0	0	2.0	1.000
1885	BUF	N	0	0	–	0.00	0	0	0	0	0	0	0	0	0	0	0	53	14	2	.264	0	0	0	0	0.0	–
1886	WAS	N	1	7	.125	7.20	10	8	7	70	91	53	39	1	0	0	0	292	50	0	.171	4	14	0	0	1.8	1.000
1888	NY	N	5	6	.455	2.43	12	11	11	92.2	70	40	58	1	0	0	0	37	6	1	.162	3	23	4	0	2.5	.867
1889			14	10	.583	3.68	29	25	23	230	221	136	130	0	1	1	0	103	21	2	.204	9	23	11	1	1.5	.744
1890	NY	P	16	19	.457	4.63	43	35	28	330.1	323	210	117	0	1	0	0	146	46	0	.315	17	71	16	0	2.4	.846
1891	2 teams		CIN AA (32G 14–14)							CIN N	(15G 4–8)																
"	total		18	22	.450	2.97	47	44	36	366.2	350	203	173	2	0	0	1	156	22	1	.141	8	81	16	2	2.2	.848
1892	NY	N	16	24	.400	3.80	47	43	35	364.1	350	189	174	2	0	1	1	163	40	2	.245	27	69	22	4	2.5	.814
1893	2 teams		NY N	(10G 2–4)						BKN N	(2G 0–2)																
"	total		2	6	.250	6.89	12	9	5	78.1	103	50	16	0	0	0	0	31	14	0	.452	3	14	3	0	1.7	.850
9 yrs.			72	96	.429	3.99	204	177	146	1550.1	1525	887	720	6	2	3	2	*				72	302	72	7	2.2	.839

Jim Crawford

CRAWFORD, JAMES FREDERICK (Catfish)
B. Sept. 29, 1950, Chicago, Ill.　　　　　　　　BL TL 6'3" 200 lbs.

1973	HOU	N	2	4	.333	4.50	48	0	0	70	69	33	56	0	2	4	6	13	3	0	.231	3	14	1	0	0.4	.944
1975			3	5	.375	3.62	44	2	0	87	92	37	37	0	3	3	4	17	5	0	.294	8	13	2	2	0.5	.913
1976	DET	A	1	8	.111	4.53	32	5	1	109.1	115	43	68	0	0	5	2	0	0	0	–	1	40	1	2	1.3	.976
1977			7	8	.467	4.79	37	7	0	126	156	50	91	0	5	4	1	0	0	0	–	1	24	0	0	0.7	1.000
1978			2	3	.400	4.35	20	0	0	39.1	45	19	24	0	2	3	0	0	0	0	–	1	4	0	2	0.3	1.000
5 yrs.			15	28	.349	4.40	181	14	1	431.2	477	182	276	0	12	19	13	30	8	0	.267	14	95	4	6	0.6	.965

Larry Crawford

CRAWFORD, CHARLES LOWRIE
B. Apr. 27, 1914, Swissvale, Pa.　　　　　　　　BL TL 6'1" 165 lbs.

| 1937 | PHI | N | 0 | 0 | – | 15.00 | 6 | 0 | 0 | 6 | 12 | 1 | 2 | 0 | 0 | 0 | 0 | 0 | 0 | 0 | – | 1 | 0 | 0 | 0 | 0.2 | 1.000 |

Steve Crawford

CRAWFORD, STEVEN RAY
B. Apr. 29, 1958, Pryor, Okla.　　　　　　　　BR TR 6'5" 225 lbs.

1980	BOS	A	2	0	1.000	3.66	6	4	2	32	41	8	10	0	0	0	0	0	0	0	–	4	2	0	0	1.0	1.000
1981			0	5	.000	4.97	14	11	0	58	69	18	29	0	0	0	0	0	0	0	–	8	8	0	1	1.1	1.000
1982			1	0	1.000	2.00	5	0	0	9	14	0	2	0	1	0	0	0	0	0	–	0	1	0	0	0.2	1.000
1984			5	0	1.000	3.34	35	0	0	62	69	21	21	0	5	0	1	0	0	0	–	4	8	0	1	0.3	1.000
1985			6	5	.545	3.76	44	1	0	91	103	28	58	0	5	5	12	0	0	0	–	7	15	3	2	0.6	.880
1986			0	2	.000	3.92	40	0	0	57.1	69	19	32	0	0	2	4	0	0	0	–	4	7	1	2	0.3	.917
1987			5	4	.556	5.33	29	0	0	72.2	91	32	43	0	5	4	0	0	0	0	–	8	10	0	2	0.6	1.000
1989	KC	A	3	1	.750	2.83	25	0	0	54	48	19	33	0	3	1	0	0	0	0	–	7	13	0	1	0.8	1.000
8 yrs.			22	17	.564	3.98	198	16	2	436	504	145	228	0	19	12	17	0	0	0	–	42	64	4	9	0.6	.964

LEAGUE CHAMPIONSHIP SERIES

| 1986 | BOS | A | 1 | 0 | 1.000 | 0.00 | 1 | 0 | 0 | 1.2 | 1 | 2 | 1 | 0 | 1 | 0 | 0 | 0 | 0 | 0 | – | 1 | 0 | 0 | 0 | 1.0 | 1.000 |

WORLD SERIES

| 1986 | BOS | A | 1 | 0 | 1.000 | 6.23 | 3 | 0 | 0 | 4.1 | 5 | 0 | 4 | 0 | 1 | 0 | 0 | 0 | 0 | 0 | .000 | 0 | 0 | 0 | 0 | 0.0 | – |

Jack Creel

CREEL, JACK DALTON (Tex)
B. Apr. 23, 1916, Kyle, Tex.　　　　　　　　BR TR 6' 165 lbs.

| 1945 | STL | N | 5 | 4 | .556 | 4.14 | 26 | 8 | 2 | 87 | 78 | 45 | 34 | 0 | 2 | 0 | 2 | 26 | 2 | 0 | .077 | 3 | 19 | 1 | 0 | 0.9 | .957 |

Keith Creel

CREEL, STEVEN KEITH
B. Feb. 4, 1959, Dallas, Tex.　　　　　　　　BR TR 6'2" 180 lbs.

1982	KC	A	1	4	.200	5.40	9	6	0	41.2	43	25	13	0	0	0	0	0	0	0	–	1	8	0	1	1.0	1.000
1983			2	5	.286	6.35	25	10	1	89.1	116	35	31	0	0	1	0	0	0	0	–	6	8	0	0	0.6	1.000
1985	CLE	A	2	5	.286	4.79	15	8	0	62	73	23	31	0	0	1	0	0	0	0	–	4	2	0	1	0.4	1.000
1987	TEX	A	0	0	–	4.66	6	0	0	9.2	12	5	5	0	0	0	0	0	0	0	–	1	3	0	0	0.7	1.000
4 yrs.			5	14	.263	5.60	55	24	1	202.2	244	88	80	0	0	2	0	0	0	0	–	12	21	0	2	0.6	1.000

Year	Team	W	L	PCT	ERA	G	GS	CG	IP	H	BB	SO	ShO	Relief Pitching W	L	SV	Batting AB	H	HR	BA	PO	A	E	DP	TC/G	FA

Bob Cremins

CREMINS, ROBERT ANTHONY (Crooked Arm)
B. Feb. 15, 1906, Pelham Manor, N. Y.   BL TL 5'11" 178 lbs.

Year	Team	W	L	PCT	ERA	G	GS	CG	IP	H	BB	SO	ShO	W	L	SV	AB	H	HR	BA	PO	A	E	DP	TC/G	FA
1927	BOS A	0	0	–	5.06	4	0	0	5.1	5	3	0	0	0	0	0	0	0	0	–	0	2	1	0	0.8	.667

Walker Cress

CRESS, WALKER JAMES (Foots)
B. Mar. 16, 1917, Ben Hur, Va.   BR TR 6'5" 205 lbs.

Year	Team	W	L	PCT	ERA	G	GS	CG	IP	H	BB	SO	ShO	W	L	SV	AB	H	HR	BA	PO	A	E	DP	TC/G	FA
1948	CIN N	0	1	.000	4.50	30	2	1	60	60	42	33	0	0	0	0	8	4	0	.500	0	8	2	0	0.3	.800
1949		0	0	–	0.00	3	0	0	2	2	3	0	0	0	0	0	0	0	0	–	0	0	1	0	0.3	
2 yrs.		0	1	.000	4.35	33	2	1	62	62	45	33	0	0	0	0	8	4	0	.500	0	8	3	0	0.3	.727

Tim Crews

CREWS, STANLEY TIMOTHY
B. Apr. 3, 1961, Tampa, Fla.   BR TR 6' 180 lbs.

Year	Team	W	L	PCT	ERA	G	GS	CG	IP	H	BB	SO	ShO	W	L	SV	AB	H	HR	BA	PO	A	E	DP	TC/G	FA
1987	LA N	1	1	.500	2.48	20	0	0	29	30	8	20	0	1	1	3	2	0	0	.000	2	5	0	0	0.4	1.000
1988		4	0	1.000	3.14	42	0	0	71.2	77	16	45	0	4	0	0	5	1	0	.200	6	4	1	1	0.3	.909
1989		0	1	.000	3.21	44	0	0	61.2	69	23	56	0	0	1	1	0	0	0	–	3	7	0	0	0.2	1.000
3 yrs.		5	2	.714	3.05	106	0	0	162.1	176	47	121	0	5	2	4	7	1	0	.143	11	16	1	1	0.3	.964

Jerry Crider

CRIDER, JERRY STEPHEN
B. Sept. 2, 1941, Sioux Falls, S. D.   BR TR 6'2" 200 lbs.

Year	Team	W	L	PCT	ERA	G	GS	CG	IP	H	BB	SO	ShO	W	L	SV	AB	H	HR	BA	PO	A	E	DP	TC/G	FA
1969	MIN A	1	0	1.000	4.71	21	1	0	28.2	31	15	16	0	1	0	1	9	4	0	.444	2	4	0	0	0.3	1.000
1970	CHI A	4	7	.364	4.45	32	8	0	91	101	34	40	0	2	2	4	24	2	0	.083	3	7	1	0	0.3	.909
2 yrs.		5	7	.417	4.51	53	9	0	119.2	132	49	56	0	3	2	5	33	6	0	.182	5	11	1	1	0.3	.941

Chuck Crim

CRIM, CHARLES ROBERT
B. July 23, 1961, Van Nuys, Calif.   BR TR 6' 175 lbs.

Year	Team	W	L	PCT	ERA	G	GS	CG	IP	H	BB	SO	ShO	W	L	SV	AB	H	HR	BA	PO	A	E	DP	TC/G	FA
1987	MIL A	6	8	.429	3.67	53	5	0	130	133	39	56	0	5	4	12	0	0	0	–	14	17	4	3	0.7	.886
1988		7	6	.538	2.91	70	0	0	105	95	28	58	0	7	6	9	0	0	0	–	12	13	3	1	0.4	.893
1989		9	7	.563	2.83	76	0	0	117.2	114	36	59	0	9	7	7	0	0	0	–	5	13	1	2	0.3	.947
3 yrs.		22	21	.512	3.16	199	5	0	352.2	342	103	173	0	21	17	28	0	0	0	–	31	43	8	6	0.4	.902

Jack Crimian

CRIMIAN, JOHN MELVIN
B. Feb. 17, 1926, Philadelphia, Pa.   BR TR 5'10" 180 lbs.

Year	Team	W	L	PCT	ERA	G	GS	CG	IP	H	BB	SO	ShO	W	L	SV	AB	H	HR	BA	PO	A	E	DP	TC/G	FA
1951	STL N	1	0	1.000	9.00	11	0	0	17	24	8	5	0	1	0	1	3	1	0	.333	1	1	0	0	0.2	1.000
1952		0	0	–	9.72	5	0	0	8.1	15	4	4	0	0	0	0	1	0	0	.000	0	1	0	0	0.2	1.000
1956	KC A	4	8	.333	5.51	54	7	0	129	129	49	59	0	3	3	3	22	5	0	.227	3	22	1	1	0.5	.962
1957	DET A	0	1	.000	12.71	4	0	0	5.2	9	4	1	0	0	1	0	0	0	0	–	0	1	0	0	0.3	1.000
4 yrs.		5	9	.357	6.36	74	7	0	160	177	65	69	0	4	4	4	26	6	0	.231	4	25	1	1	0.4	.967

Dode Criss

CRISS, DODE
B. Mar. 12, 1885, Sherman, Miss.   D. Sept. 8, 1955, Sherman, Miss.   BL TR 6'2" 200 lbs.

Year	Team	W	L	PCT	ERA	G	GS	CG	IP	H	BB	SO	ShO	W	L	SV	AB	H	HR	BA	PO	A	E	DP	TC/G	FA
1908	STL A	0	1	.000	6.50	9	1	0	18	15	13	9	0	0	1	0	82	28	0	.341	1	2	1	0	0.4	.750
1909		1	5	.167	3.42	11	6	3	55.1	53	32	43	0	0	1	0	48	14	0	.292	2	10	0	0	1.1	1.000
1910		2	1	.667	1.40	6	0	0	19.1	12	9	9	0	2	1	0	91	21	1	.231	0	6	0	0	1.0	1.000
1911		0	2	.000	8.35	4	2	0	18.1	24	10	9	0	0	0	0	83	21	2	.253	0	6	0	0	1.5	1.000
4 yrs.		3	9	.250	4.38	30	9	3	111	104	64	70	0	2	3	0	*				3	24	1	0	0.9	.964

Bill Cristall

CRISTALL, WILLIAM ARTHUR (Lefty)
B. Sept. 12, 1878, Odessa, Russia   D. Jan. 28, 1939, Buffalo, N. Y.   BL TL 5'7" 147 lbs.

Year	Team	W	L	PCT	ERA	G	GS	CG	IP	H	BB	SO	ShO	W	L	SV	AB	H	HR	BA	PO	A	E	DP	TC/G	FA
1901	CLE A	1	5	.167	4.84	6	6	5	48.1	54	30	12	1	0	0	0	20	7	0	.350	3	19	1	3	3.8	.957

Chris Cristante

CRISTANTE, DANTE LEO
B. Dec. 10, 1926, Detroit, Mich.   D. Aug. 24, 1977, Dearborn, Mich.   BR TR 6'1" 195 lbs.

Year	Team	W	L	PCT	ERA	G	GS	CG	IP	H	BB	SO	ShO	W	L	SV	AB	H	HR	BA	PO	A	E	DP	TC/G	FA
1951	PHI N	1	1	.500	4.91	10	1	0	22	28	9	6	0	1	0	1	6	1	0	.167	1	5	0	0	0.6	1.000
1955	DET A	0	1	.000	3.19	20	1	0	36.2	37	14	9	0	0	1	0	7	0	0	.000	1	1	1	0	0.2	.667
2 yrs.		1	2	.333	3.84	30	2	0	58.2	65	23	15	0	1	1	0	13	1	0	.077	2	6	1	0	0.3	.889

Morrie Critchley

CRITCHLEY, MORRIS ARTHUR
B. Mar. 26, 1850, New London, Conn.   D. Mar. 6, 1910, Pittsburgh, Pa.   6'1" 190 lbs.

Year	Team	W	L	PCT	ERA	G	GS	CG	IP	H	BB	SO	ShO	W	L	SV	AB	H	HR	BA	PO	A	E	DP	TC/G	FA
1882	2 teams	PIT AA (1G 0–0)				STL AA (4G 0–4)																				
"	total	1	4	.200	3.35	5	5	5	43	50	8	5	1	0	0	0	19	3	0	.158	2	9	1	0	2.4	.917

Claude Crocker

CROCKER, CLAUDE ARTHUR
B. July 20, 1924, Caroleen, N. C.   BR TR 6'2" 185 lbs.

Year	Team	W	L	PCT	ERA	G	GS	CG	IP	H	BB	SO	ShO	W	L	SV	AB	H	HR	BA	PO	A	E	DP	TC/G	FA
1944	BKN N	0	0	–	10.80	2	0	0	3.1	6	5	1	0	0	0	0	1	1	0	1.000	0	1	0	0	0.5	1.000
1945		0	0	–	0.00	1	0	0	2	2	1	1	0	0	0	0	0	0	0	–	0	0	0	0	0.0	–
2 yrs.		0	0	–	6.75	3	0	0	5.1	8	6	2	0	0	0	0	1	1	0	1.000	0	1	0	0	0.3	1.000

Ray Crone

CRONE, RAYMOND HAYES
B. Aug. 7, 1931, Memphis, Tenn.   BR TR 6'2" 165 lbs.

Year	Team	W	L	PCT	ERA	G	GS	CG	IP	H	BB	SO	ShO	W	L	SV	AB	H	HR	BA	PO	A	E	DP	TC/G	FA
1954	MIL N	1	0	1.000	2.02	19	2	0	49	44	19	33	0	0	0	0	10	2	0	.200	1	7	0	0	0.4	1.000
1955		10	9	.526	3.46	33	15	6	140.1	117	42	76	1	5	2	0	44	7	0	.159	11	19	0	5	0.9	1.000
1956		11	10	.524	3.87	35	21	6	169.2	173	44	73	0	1	2	2	49	6	0	.122	15	23	1	2	1.1	.974
1957	2 teams	MIL N		(11G 3–1)		NY N		(25G 4–8)																		
"	total	7	9	.438	4.36	36	22	4	163	185	55	71	0	0	1	1	51	3	0	.059	11	42	0	4	1.5	1.000
1958	SF N	1	2	.333	6.75	14	1	0	24	35	13	7	0	1	2	0	2	0	0	.000	0	4	0	0	0.3	1.000
5 yrs.		30	30	.500	3.87	137	61	17	546	554	173	260	1	7	7	4	156	18	0	.115	38	95	1	11	1.0	.993

Year	Team		W	L	PCT	ERA	G	GS	CG	IP	H	BB	SO	ShO	Relief Pitching W	L	SV	Batting AB	H	HR	BA	PO	A	E	DP	TC/G	FA

John Cronin

CRONIN, JOHN J.
B. May 26, 1874, West New Brighton, N. Y. D. July 13, 1929, Middletown, N. Y.
BR TR 6' 200 lbs.

Year	Team		W	L	PCT	ERA	G	GS	CG	IP	H	BB	SO	ShO	W	L	SV	AB	H	HR	BA	PO	A	E	DP	TC/G	FA
1895	BKN	N	0	0	–	10.80	2	0	0	5	10	3	1	0	0	0	2	2	1	0	.500	0	0	0	0	0.0	–
1898	PIT	N	2	2	.500	3.54	4	4	2	28	35	8	9	1	0	0	0	10	1	0	.100	2	8	1	0	2.8	.909
1899	CIN	N	2	2	.500	5.49	5	5	5	41	56	16	9	0	0	0	0	17	2	0	.118	1	7	3	0	2.2	.727
1901	DET	A	13	15	.464	3.89	30	28	21	219.2	261	42	62	1	1	0	0	85	21	0	.247	11	51	12	3	2.5	.838
1902	3 teams		DET A	(4G 0–0)		BAL A	(10G 3–5)		NY N	(13G 5–6)																		
"	total		8	11	.421	3.09	27	20	19	207	197	50	77	0	0	0	0	99	15	0	.152	14	66	6	1	3.2	.930
1903	NY	N	6	4	.600	3.81	20	11	8	115.2	130	37	50	0	1	0	1	46	9	0	.196	9	29	3	1	2.1	.927
1904	BKN	N	12	23	.343	2.70	40	34	33	307	284	79	110	4	1	1	0	108	17	0	.157	18	84	8	3	2.8	.927
7 yrs.			43	57	.430	3.40	128	102	88	923.1	973	235	318	6	3	1	3	367	66	0	.180	55	245	33	8	2.6	.901

George Crosby

CROSBY, GEORGE WASHINGTON
B. 1860, Iowa D. Jan. 9, 1913, San Francisco, Calif.

Year	Team		W	L	PCT	ERA	G	GS	CG	IP	H	BB	SO	ShO	W	L	SV	AB	H	HR	BA	PO	A	E	DP	TC/G	FA
1884	CHI	N	1	2	.333	3.54	3	3	3	28	27	12	11	0	0	0	0	13	4	1	.308	2	8	0	0	3.3	1.000

Ken Crosby

CROSBY, KENNETH STEWART
B. Dec. 15, 1947, New Denver, B. C., Canada
BR TR 6'2" 179 lbs.

Year	Team		W	L	PCT	ERA	G	GS	CG	IP	H	BB	SO	ShO	W	L	SV	AB	H	HR	BA	PO	A	E	DP	TC/G	FA
1975	CHI	N	1	0	1.000	3.38	9	0	0	8	10	7	6	0	1	0	0	0	0	0	–	0	3	0	0	0.3	1.000
1976			0	0	–	12.00	7	1	0	12	20	8	5	0	0	0	0	2	1	0	.500	1	2	0	0	0.4	1.000
2 yrs.			1	0	1.000	8.55	16	1	0	20	30	15	11	0	1	0	0	2	1	0	.500	1	5	0	0	0.4	1.000

Lem Cross

CROSS, GEORGE LEWIS
B. Jan. 9, 1872, Sanbornton, N. H. D. Oct. 9, 1930, Manchester, N. H.
5'9" 155 lbs.

Year	Team		W	L	PCT	ERA	G	GS	CG	IP	H	BB	SO	ShO	W	L	SV	AB	H	HR	BA	PO	A	E	DP	TC/G	FA
1893	CIN	N	0	2	.000	5.57	3	3	2	21	24	9	7	0	0	0	0	6	2	0	.333	1	6	0	0	2.3	1.000
1894			3	4	.429	8.49	8	7	3	53	94	21	11	0	0	0	0	26	6	0	.231	1	8	1	0	1.3	.900
2 yrs.			3	6	.333	7.66	11	10	5	74	118	30	18	0	0	0	0	32	8	0	.250	2	14	1	0	1.5	.941

Dug Crothers

CROTHERS, DOUGLASS
B. Nov. 16, 1859, Natchez, Miss. D. Mar. 29, 1907, St. Louis, Mo.
BR TR

Year	Team		W	L	PCT	ERA	G	GS	CG	IP	H	BB	SO	ShO	W	L	SV	AB	H	HR	BA	PO	A	E	DP	TC/G	FA
1884	KC	U	1	2	.333	1.80	3	3	3	25	26	6	11	0	0	0	0	15	2	0	.133	0	6	5	0	3.7	.545
1885	NY	AA	7	11	.389	5.08	18	18	18	154	192	49	40	1	0	0	0	51	8	0	.157	5	30	7	1	2.3	.833
2 yrs.			8	13	.381	4.63	21	21	21	179	218	55	51	1	0	0	0	66	10	0	.152	5	36	12	1	2.5	.774

Bill Crouch

CROUCH, WILLIAM HENRY (Skip)
Father of Bill Crouch.
B. Dec. 3, 1886, Marshallton, Del. D. Dec. 22, 1945, Highland Park, Mich.
BL TL 6'1" 210 lbs.

Year	Team		W	L	PCT	ERA	G	GS	CG	IP	H	BB	SO	ShO	W	L	SV	AB	H	HR	BA	PO	A	E	DP	TC/G	FA
1910	STL	A	0	0	–	3.38	1	1	0	8	6	7	2	0	0	0	0	3	0	0	.000	2	1	0	0	3.0	1.000

Bill Crouch

CROUCH, WILMER ELMER
Son of Bill Crouch.
B. Aug. 20, 1910, Wilmington, Del. D. Dec. 26, 1980, Howell, Mich.
BB TR 6'1" 180 lbs.

Year	Team		W	L	PCT	ERA	G	GS	CG	IP	H	BB	SO	ShO	W	L	SV	AB	H	HR	BA	PO	A	E	DP	TC/G	FA
1939	BKN	N	4	0	1.000	2.58	6	3	3	38.1	37	14	10	0	1	0	0	15	2	0	.133	3	4	0	0	1.2	1.000
1941	2 teams		PHI N	(20G 2–3)		STL N	(18G 1–2)																				
"	total		3	5	.375	3.81	38	9	1	104	110	31	41	0	0	2	7	24	1	0	.042	3	26	1	1	0.8	.967
1945	STL	N	1	0	1.000	3.38	6	0	0	13.1	12	7	4	0	1	0	0	2	0	0	.000	1	3	0	0	0.7	1.000
3 yrs.			8	5	.615	3.47	50	12	4	155.2	159	52	55	0	2	2	7	41	3	0	.073	7	33	1	1	0.8	.976

Zach Crouch

CROUCH, ZACHARY QUINN
B. Oct. 26, 1965, Folsom, Calif.
BL TL 6'3" 190 lbs.

Year	Team		W	L	PCT	ERA	G	GS	CG	IP	H	BB	SO	ShO	W	L	SV	AB	H	HR	BA	PO	A	E	DP	TC/G	FA
1988	BOS	A	0	0	–	6.75	3	0	0	1.1	4	2	0	0	0	0	0	0	0	0	–	0	0	0	0	0.0	–

General Crowder

CROWDER, ALVIN FLOYD
B. Jan. 11, 1899, Winston-Salem, N. C. D. Apr. 3, 1972, Winston-Salem, N. C.
BL TR 5'10" 170 lbs.

Year	Team		W	L	PCT	ERA	G	GS	CG	IP	H	BB	SO	ShO	W	L	SV	AB	H	HR	BA	PO	A	E	DP	TC/G	FA
1926	WAS	A	7	4	.636	3.96	19	12	6	100	97	60	26	0	1	0	1	38	9	0	.237	5	13	1	0	1.0	.947
1927	2 teams		WAS A	(15G 4–7)		STL A	(21G 3–5)																				
"	total		7	12	.368	4.79	36	19	6	141	129	84	52	3	2	1	3	45	9	0	.200	4	24	0	1	0.8	1.000
1928	STL	A	21	5	.808	3.69	41	31	19	244	238	91	99	1	0	0	2	80	15	0	.188	4	33	2	3	1.0	.949
1929			17	15	.531	3.92	40	34	19	266.2	272	93	79	4	1	0	4	96	18	0	.188	6	50	1	1	1.4	.982
1930	2 teams		STL A	(13G 3–7)		WAS A	(27G 15–9)																				
"	total		18	16	.529	3.89	40	35	25	279.2	276	96	107	1	0	0	2	101	17	0	.168	8	42	1	3	1.3	.980
1931	WAS	A	18	11	.621	3.88	44	26	13	234.1	255	72	85	1	4	2	2	88	19	0	.216	5	34	1	1	0.9	.975
1932			26	13	.667	3.33	50	39	21	327	319	77	103	3	5	0	1	122	27	0	.221	7	53	1	5	1.2	.984
1933			24	15	.615	3.97	52	35	17	299.1	311	81	110	0	4	4	4	102	19	0	.186	6	53	0	2	1.0	1.000
1934	2 teams		WAS A	(29G 4–10)		DET A	(9G 5–1)																				
"	total		9	11	.450	5.75	38	22	7	167.1	223	58	69	1	1	1	0	62	11	0	.177	3	18	0	0	0.6	1.000
1935	DET	A	16	10	.615	4.26	33	32	16	241	269	67	59	2	0	0	0	93	17	0	.183	10	31	0	5	1.2	1.000
1936			4	3	.571	8.39	9	7	1	44	64	21	10	0	0	0	0	20	3	0	.150	4	6	0	1	1.1	1.000
11 yrs.			167	115	.592	4.12	402	292	150	2344.1	2453	800	799	16	19	11	22	847	164	0	.194	56	357	7	22	1.0	.983

WORLD SERIES

Year	Team		W	L	PCT	ERA	G	GS	CG	IP	H	BB	SO	ShO	W	L	SV	AB	H	HR	BA	PO	A	E	DP	TC/G	FA
1933	WAS	A	0	1	.000	7.36	2	2	0	11	16	5	7	0	0	0	0	4	1	0	.250	0	3	0	0	1.5	1.000
1934	DET	A	0	1	.000	1.50	2	1	0	6	6	1	2	0	0	0	0	1	0	0	.000	0	0	0	0	0.0	–
1935			1	0	1.000	1.00	1	1	1	9	5	3	5	0	0	0	0	3	1	0	.333	2	1	0	0	3.0	1.000
3 yrs.			1	2	.333	3.81	5	4	1	26	27	9	14	0	0	0	0	8	2	0	.250	2	4	0	0	1.2	1.000

Billy Crowell

CROWELL, WILLIAM THEODORE
B. Nov. 6, 1865, Cincinnati, Ohio D. July 24, 1935, Fort Worth, Tex.
BR TR 5'8½" 160 lbs.

Year	Team		W	L	PCT	ERA	G	GS	CG	IP	H	BB	SO	ShO	W	L	SV	AB	H	HR	BA	PO	A	E	DP	TC/G	FA
1887	CLE	AA	14	31	.311	4.88	45	45	45	389.1	541	138	72	1	0	0	0	156	22	0	.141	5	65	5	4	1.7	.933

Year	Team		W	L	PCT	ERA	G	GS	CG	IP	H	BB	SO	ShO	Relief Pitching W	L	SV	Batting AB	H	HR	BA	PO	A	E	DP	TC/G	FA

Billy Crowell *continued*

1888	2 teams	CLE AA (18G 5–13)					LOU AA (1G 0–1)																				
"	total		5	14	.263	5.81	19	19	17	159.2	224	67	66	0	0	0	0	61	5	0	.082	2	35	3	1	2.1	.925
2 yrs.			19	45	.297	5.15	64	64	62	549	765	205	138	1	0	0	0	217	27	0	.124	7	100	8	5	1.8	.930

Cap Crowell

CROWELL, MINOT JOY   BR TR 6'1"   178 lbs.
B. Sept. 5, 1892, Roxbury, Mass.   D. Sept. 30, 1962, Central Falls, R. I.

1915	PHI	A	2	6	.250	5.47	10	8	4	54.1	56	47	15	0	0	0	0	22	5	0	.227	1	15	0	0	1.6	1.000
1916			0	5	.000	4.76	9	6	1	39.2	43	34	15	0	0	0	0	12	0	0	.000	2	8	1	0	1.2	.909
2 yrs.			2	11	.154	5.17	19	14	5	94	99	81	30	0	0	0	0	34	5	0	.147	3	23	1	0	1.4	.963

Woody Crowson

CROWSON, THOMAS WOODROW   BR TR 6'2"   185 lbs.
B. Sept. 9, 1918, Fuquay Springs, N. C.   D. Aug. 14, 1947, Mayodan, N. C.

| 1945 | PHI | A | 0 | 0 | – | 6.00 | 1 | 0 | 0 | 3 | 2 | 3 | 2 | 0 | 0 | 0 | 0 | 1 | 0 | 0 | .000 | 0 | 2 | 0 | 0 | 2.0 | 1.000 |

Cal Crum

CRUM, CALVIN N.   BR TR 6'1"   175 lbs.
B. July 27, 1890, Cooks Mills, Ill.   D. Dec. 7, 1945, Tulsa, Okla.

1917	BOS	N	0	0	–	0.00	1	0	0	1	1	1	0	0	0	0	0	0	0	0	–	0	2	0	0	2.0	1.000
1918			0	1	.000	15.43	1	1	0	2.1	6	3	0	0	0	0	0	1	0	0	.000	0	2	0	0	2.0	1.000
2 yrs.			0	1	.000	10.80	2	1	0	3.1	7	4	0	0	0	0	0	1	0	0	.000	0	4	0	0	2.0	1.000

Roy Crumpler

CRUMPLER, ROY MAXTON   BL TL 6'1"   195 lbs.
B. July 8, 1896, Clinton, N. C.   D. Oct. 6, 1969, Fayetteville, N. C.

1920	DET	A	1	0	1.000	5.54	3	2	1	13	17	11	2	0	0	0	0	9	3	0	.333	1	2	0	0	1.0	.667
1925	PHI	N	0	0	–	7.71	3	1	0	4.2	8	2	1	0	0	0	0	2	0	0	.000	0	3	1	0	1.0	1.000
2 yrs.			1	0	1.000	6.11	6	3	1	17.2	25	13	3	0	0	0	0	11	3	0	.273	1	5	1	0	1.0	.833

Dick Crutcher

CRUTCHER, RICHARD LOUIS   BR TR 5'9"   148 lbs.
B. Nov. 25, 1889, Frankfort, Ky.   D. June 19, 1952, Frankfort, Ky.

1914	BOS	N	5	6	.455	3.46	33	15	5	158.2	169	66	48	1	2	2	0	54	8	0	.148	3	48	1	0	1.6	.981
1915			2	2	.500	4.33	14	4	1	43.2	50	16	17	0	1	0	2	13	3	0	.231	4	14	3	0	1.5	.857
2 yrs.			7	8	.467	3.65	47	19	6	202.1	219	82	65	1	3	2	2	67	11	0	.164	7	62	4	0	1.6	.945

Todd Cruz

CRUZ, TODD RUBEN   BR TR 6'   175 lbs.
B. Nov. 23, 1955, Highland Park, Mich.

| 1984 | BAL | A | 0 | 0 | – | 0.00 | 1 | 0 | 0 | 1 | 0 | 0 | 0 | 0 | 0 | 0 | 0 | * | | | | 1 | 0 | 0 | 0 | 0.0 | – |

Victor Cruz

CRUZ, VICTOR MANUEL   BR TR 5'9"   174 lbs.
Born Victor Manuel De La Cruz y Gil.
B. Dec. 24, 1957, Ranch Viejo la Vega, Dominican Republic

1978	TOR	A	7	3	.700	1.71	32	0	0	47.1	28	36	51	0	7	3	9	0	0	0	–	1	5	0	0	0.2	1.000
1979	CLE	A	3	9	.250	4.22	61	0	0	79	70	44	63	0	3	9	10	0	0	0	–	1	4	2	0	0.1	.714
1980			6	7	.462	3.45	55	0	0	86	71	27	88	0	6	7	12	0	0	0	–	1	5	1	0	0.1	.857
1981	PIT	N	1	1	.500	2.65	22	0	0	34	33	15	28	0	1	1	1	4	0	0	.000	1	5	0	1	0.3	1.000
1983	TEX	A	1	3	.250	1.44	17	0	0	25	16	10	18	0	1	3	5	0	0	0	–	1	2	1	0	0.2	.750
5 yrs.			18	23	.439	3.08	187	0	0	271.1	218	132	248	0	18	23	37	4	0	0	.000	5	21	4	2	0.2	.867

Cookie Cuccurullo

CUCCURULLO, ARTHUR JOSEPH   BL TL 5'10"   168 lbs.
B. Feb. 8, 1918, Asbury Park, N. J.   D. Jan. 23, 1983, West Orange, N. J.

1943	PIT	N	0	1	.000	6.43	1	1	0	7	10	3	3	0	0	0	0	0	0	0	–	1	2	1	1	4.0	.750
1944			2	1	.667	4.06	32	4	0	106.1	110	44	31	0	2	1	4	38	14	0	.368	9	23	2	2	1.1	.941
1945			1	3	.250	5.24	29	4	0	56.2	68	34	17	0	1	1	1	14	3	0	.214	2	12	1	0	0.5	.933
3 yrs.			3	5	.375	4.55	62	9	0	170	188	81	51	0	3	2	5	52	17	0	.327	12	37	4	3	0.9	.925

Jim Cudworth

CUDWORTH, JAMES ALARIC   BR TR 6'   165 lbs.
B. Aug. 22, 1858, Fairhaven, Mass.   D. Dec. 21, 1943, Middleboro, Mass.

| 1884 | KC | U | 0 | 0 | – | 4.24 | 2 | 1 | 1 | 17 | 19 | 3 | 6 | 0 | 0 | 0 | 0 | * | | | | 1 | 1 | 0 | 0 | 1.0 | 1.000 |

Bobby Cuellar

CUELLAR, ROBERT   BR TR 5'11"   188 lbs.
B. Aug. 20, 1952, Alice, Tex.

| 1977 | TEX | A | 0 | 0 | – | 1.29 | 4 | 0 | 0 | 7 | 4 | 2 | 3 | 0 | 0 | 0 | 0 | 0 | 0 | 0 | – | 0 | 0 | 0 | 0 | 0.0 | – |

Charlie Cuellar

CUELLAR, JESUS PATRACIS   BR TR 5'11"   183 lbs.
B. Sept. 24, 1917, Ybor City, Fla.

| 1950 | CHI | A | 0 | 0 | – | 33.75 | 2 | 0 | 0 | 1.1 | 6 | 3 | 1 | 0 | 0 | 0 | 0 | 0 | 0 | 0 | – | 0 | 0 | 0 | 0 | 0.0 | – |

Mike Cuellar

CUELLAR, MIGUEL ANGEL   BL TL 6'   165 lbs.
Born Miguel Angel Cuellar y Santana.
B. May 8, 1937, Las Villas, Cuba

1959	CIN	N	0	0		15.75	2	0	0	4	7	4	5	0	0	0	0	1	0	0	.000	0	0	0	0	0.0	–
1964	STL	N	5	5	.500	4.50	32	7	1	72	80	33	56	0	3	0	4	18	0	0	.000	4	18	3	1	0.8	.880
1965	HOU	N	1	4	.200	3.54	25	4	0	56	55	21	46	0	1	1	2	12	0	0	.000	2	10	1	1	0.5	.923
1966			12	10	.545	2.22	38	28	11	227.1	193	52	175	1	3	1	2	71	8	1	.113	5	38	2	4	1.2	.956
1967			16	11	.593	3.03	36	32	16	246.1	233	63	203	3	1	0	1	93	13	0	.140	15	35	2	1	1.4	.962
1968			8	11	.421	2.74	28	24	11	170.2	152	45	133	2	0	1	0	57	11	0	.193	13	24	4	1	1.5	.902
1969	BAL	A	23	11	.676	2.38	39	39	18	290.2	213	79	182	5	0	0	0	103	12	0	.117	9	45	2	7	1.4	.964
1970			**24**	8	**.750**	3.47	40	**40**	21	298	273	69	190	4	0	0	0	112	10	2	.089	9	34	2	1	1.1	.956
1971			20	9	.690	3.08	38	38	21	292	250	78	124	4	0	0	0	107	11	1	.103	14	53	2	5	1.8	.971

Year	Team		W	L	PCT	ERA	G	GS	CG	IP	H	BB	SO	ShO	Relief Pitching W	L	SV	Batting AB	H	HR	BA	PO	A	E	DP	TC/G	FA

Mike Cuellar *continued*

Year	Team		W	L	PCT	ERA	G	GS	CG	IP	H	BB	SO	ShO	W	L	SV	AB	H	HR	BA	PO	A	E	DP	TC/G	FA
1972			18	12	.600	2.57	35	35	17	248.1	197	71	132	4	0	0	0	87	11	2	.126	10	43	5	5	1.7	.914
1973			18	13	.581	3.27	38	38	17	267	265	84	140	2	0	0	0	0	0	0	–	9	47	3	2	1.6	.949
1974			22	10	**.688**	3.11	38	38	20	269	253	86	106	5	0	0	0	0	0	0	–	5	35	1	1	1.1	.976
1975			14	12	.538	3.66	36	36	17	256	229	84	105	5	0	0	0	0	0	0	–	11	53	2	3	1.8	.970
1976			4	13	.235	4.96	26	19	2	107	129	50	32	1	0	2	1	0	0	0	–	2	18	1	1	0.8	.952
1977	CAL	A	0	1	.000	18.90	2	1	0	3.1	9	3	3	0	0	0	0	0	0	0	–	0	0	0	0	0.0	–
15 yrs.			185	130	.587	3.14	453	379	172	2807.2	2538	822	1632	36	8	5	11	661	76	7	.115	108	453	30	33	1.3	.949

LEAGUE CHAMPIONSHIP SERIES

Year	Team		W	L	PCT	ERA	G	GS	CG	IP	H	BB	SO	ShO	W	L	SV	AB	H	HR	BA	PO	A	E	DP	TC/G	FA
1969	BAL	A	0	0	–	2.25	1	1	0	8	3	1	7	0	0	0	0	2	0	0	.000	0	0	0	0	0.0	–
1970			0	0	–	12.46	1	1	0	4.1	10	1	2	0	0	0	0	2	1	1	.500	1	3	0	0	4.0	1.000
1971			1	0	1.000	1.00	1	1	1	9	6	1	2	0	0	0	0	3	1	0	.333	0	2	0	0	2.0	1.000
1973			0	1	.000	1.80	1	1	0	10	4	3	11	0	0	0	0	0	0	0	–	0	2	0	0	2.0	1.000
1974			1	1	.500	2.84	2	2	0	12.2	9	13	6	0	0	0	0	0	0	0	–	0	5	0	0	2.5	1.000
5 yrs.			2	2	.500	3.07	6	6	2	44	32	19	28	0	0	0	0	7	2	1	.286	1	12	0	0	2.2	1.000

WORLD SERIES

Year	Team		W	L	PCT	ERA	G	GS	CG	IP	H	BB	SO	ShO	W	L	SV	AB	H	HR	BA	PO	A	E	DP	TC/G	FA
1969	BAL	A	1	0	1.000	1.13	2	2	1	16	13	4	13	0	0	0	0	5	2	0	.400	0	1	0	0	0.5	1.000
1970			1	0	1.000	3.18	2	2	1	11.1	10	2	5	0	0	0	0	4	0	0	.000	0	1	0	0	0.5	1.000
1971			0	2	.000	3.86	2	2	0	14	11	6	10	0	0	0	0	3	0	0	.000	0	3	1	0	2.0	.750
3 yrs.			2	2	.500	2.61	6	6	2	41.1	34	12	28	0	0	0	0	12	2	0	.167	0	5	1	1	1.0	.833

Berto Cueto

CUETO, DAGOBERTO
Born Dagoberto Cueto y Concepcion.
B. Aug. 14, 1937, San Luis Pinar, Cuba

BR TR 6'4" 170 lbs.

Year	Team		W	L	PCT	ERA	G	GS	CG	IP	H	BB	SO	ShO	W	L	SV	AB	H	HR	BA	PO	A	E	DP	TC/G	FA
1961	MIN	A	1	3	.250	7.17	7	5	0	21.1	27	10	5	0	1	1	0	5	0	0	.000	2	4	1	0	1.0	.857

Jack Cullen

CULLEN, JOHN PATRICK
B. Oct. 6, 1939, Newark, N. J.

BR TR 5'11" 170 lbs.

Year	Team		W	L	PCT	ERA	G	GS	CG	IP	H	BB	SO	ShO	W	L	SV	AB	H	HR	BA	PO	A	E	DP	TC/G	FA
1962	NY	A	0	0	–	0.00	2	0	0	3	2	2	2	0	0	0	1	0	0	0	–	0	0	0	0	0.0	–
1965			3	4	.429	3.05	12	9	2	59	59	21	25	1	0	0	0	20	3	0	.150	2	16	2	0	1.7	.900
1966			1	0	1.000	3.97	5	0	0	11.1	11	5	7	0	1	0	0	3	0	0	.000	1	0	1	0	0.4	.500
3 yrs.			4	4	.500	3.07	19	9	2	73.1	72	28	34	1	1	0	1	23	3	0	.130	3	16	3	0	1.2	.864

Nick Cullop

CULLOP, HENRY NICHOLAS (Tomato Face)
B. Oct. 16, 1900, St. Louis, Mo. D. Dec. 8, 1978, Gahanna, Ohio

BR TR 6' 200 lbs.

Year	Team		W	L	PCT	ERA	G	GS	CG	IP	H	BB	SO	ShO	W	L	SV	AB	H	HR	BA	PO	A	E	DP	TC/G	FA
1927	CLE	A	0	0	–	9.00	1	0	0	1	3	0	0	0	0	0	0	*				0	0	0	0	0.0	–

Nick Cullop

CULLOP, NORMAN ANDREW
B. Sept. 17, 1887, Chilhowie, Va. D. Apr. 15, 1961, Gahanna, Ohio

BL TL 5'11½" 172 lbs.

Year	Team		W	L	PCT	ERA	G	GS	CG	IP	H	BB	SO	ShO	W	L	SV	AB	H	HR	BA	PO	A	E	DP	TC/G	FA
1913	CLE	A	3	7	.300	4.42	23	8	4	97.2	105	35	30	0	1	3	0	31	4	0	.129	7	32	1	0	1.7	.975
1914	2 teams	CLE A (1G 0–1)					KC	F	(44G 14–17)																		
"	total		14	18	.438	2.35	45	36	22	299	260	88	152	4	1	2	1	100	14	0	.140	9	92	9	3	2.4	.918
1915	KC	F	22	11	.667	2.44	44	36	22	302.1	278	67	111	3	2	0	2	96	18	0	.188	12	121	5	3	3.1	.964
1916	NY	A	13	6	.684	2.05	28	22	9	167	151	32	77	0	2	0	1	55	6	0	.109	8	24	1	0	1.2	.970
1917			5	9	.357	3.32	30	18	5	146.1	161	31	27	2	1	1	1	44	7	0	.159	5	44	1	2	1.7	.980
1921	STL	A	0	2	.000	8.49	4	1	0	11.2	18	6	3	0	0	1	0	3	0	0	.000	3	2	0	0	1.3	1.000
6 yrs.			57	53	.518	2.73	174	121	62	1024	973	259	400	9	7	5	5	329	49	0	.149	44	315	17	8	2.2	.955

Bud Culloton

CULLOTON, BERNARD ALOYSIUS
B. May 19, 1896, Kingston, N. Y. D. Nov. 9, 1976, Kingston, N. Y.

BR TR 5'11" 180 lbs.

Year	Team		W	L	PCT	ERA	G	GS	CG	IP	H	BB	SO	ShO	W	L	SV	AB	H	HR	BA	PO	A	E	DP	TC/G	FA
1925	PIT	N	0	1	.000	2.57	9	1	0	21	19	1	3	0	0	0	0	3	0	0	.000	0	4	0	0	0.4	1.000
1926			0	0	–	7.36	4	0	0	3.2	3	6	1	0	0	0	0	0	0	0	–	0	1	0	0	0.3	1.000
2 yrs.			0	1	.000	3.28	13	1	0	24.2	22	7	4	0	0	0	0	3	0	0	.000	0	5	0	0	0.4	1.000

Bill Culp

CULP, WILLIAM EDWARD
B. June 11, 1887, Bellaire, Ohio D. Sept. 3, 1969, Arnold, Pa.

BB TR 6'1½" 165 lbs.

Year	Team		W	L	PCT	ERA	G	GS	CG	IP	H	BB	SO	ShO	W	L	SV	AB	H	HR	BA	PO	A	E	DP	TC/G	FA
1910	PHI	N	0	0	–	8.10	4	0	0	6.2	8	4	4	0	0	0	0	2	0	0	.000	1	5	0	1	1.5	1.000

Ray Culp

CULP, RAYMOND LEONARD
B. Aug. 6, 1941, Elgin, Tex.

BR TR 6' 200 lbs.

Year	Team		W	L	PCT	ERA	G	GS	CG	IP	H	BB	SO	ShO	W	L	SV	AB	H	HR	BA	PO	A	E	DP	TC/G	FA
1963	PHI	N	14	11	.560	2.97	34	30	10	203.1	148	**102**	176	5	2	1	0	66	9	0	.136	13	27	0	3	1.2	1.000
1964			8	7	.533	4.13	30	19	3	135	139	56	96	1	1	0	0	44	5	0	.114	10	20	2	0	1.1	.938
1965			14	10	.583	3.22	33	30	11	204.1	188	78	134	2	1	1	0	68	6	0	.088	19	24	0	2	1.3	1.000
1966			7	4	.636	5.04	34	12	1	110.2	106	53	100	0	4	0	1	26	2	0	.077	3	14	2	0	0.6	.895
1967	CHI	N	8	11	.421	3.89	30	22	4	152.2	138	59	111	1	1	1	0	51	5	0	.098	7	21	1	2	1.0	.966
1968	BOS	A	16	6	.727	2.91	35	30	11	216.1	166	82	190	6	0	0	0	70	8	0	.114	15	23	1	0	1.1	1.000
1969			17	8	.680	3.81	32	32	9	227	195	79	172	2	0	0	0	79	12	1	.152	20	31	8	1	1.8	.864
1970			17	14	.548	3.05	33	33	15	251	211	91	197	1	0	0	0	97	12	0	.124	22	24	5	4	1.5	.902
1971			14	16	.467	3.61	35	35	12	242	236	67	115	3	0	0	0	68	8	0	.118	8	32	3	1	1.2	.930
1972			5	8	.385	4.46	16	16	4	105	104	53	52	1	0	0	0	33	7	0	.212	12	14	0	1	1.6	1.000
1973			2	6	.250	4.50	10	9	0	50	46	32	32	0	0	0	0	0	0	0	–	6	7	1	0	1.4	.929
11 yrs.			122	101	.547	3.58	322	268	80	1897.1	1677	752	1411	22	9	3	1	602	74	1	.123	135	237	22	15	1.2	.944

George Culver

CULVER, GEORGE RAYMOND
B. July 8, 1943, Salinas, Calif.

BR TR 6'2" 185 lbs.

Year	Team		W	L	PCT	ERA	G	GS	CG	IP	H	BB	SO	ShO	W	L	SV	AB	H	HR	BA	PO	A	E	DP	TC/G	FA
1966	CLE	A	0	2	.000	8.38	5	1	0	9.2	15	7	6	0	0	1	0	2	0	0	.000	1	3	0	1	0.8	1.000
1967			7	3	.700	3.96	53	1	0	75	79	31	41	0	7	2	3	4	1	0	.250	6	11	1	1	0.4	.957
1968	CIN	N	11	16	.407	3.23	42	35	5	226	229	84	114	2	2	0	0	66	8	0	.121	23	45	2	2	1.7	.971
1969			5	7	.417	4.28	32	13	0	101	117	52	58	0	0	0	4	31	3	0	.097	10	23	1	1	1.1	.971

Year	Team	W	L	PCT	ERA	G	GS	CG	IP	H	BB	SO	ShO	W	L	SV	AB	H	HR	BA	PO	A	E	DP	TC/G	FA

George Culver *continued*

Year	Team	W	L	PCT	ERA	G	GS	CG	IP	H	BB	SO	ShO	W	L	SV	AB	H	HR	BA	PO	A	E	DP	TC/G	FA
1970	2 teams	STL N	(11G 3–3)		HOU N	(32G 3–3)																				
"	total	6	6	.500	3.98	43	7	2	101.2	108	45	54	0	3	6	3	21	4	0	.190	8	19	2	2	0.7	.931
1971	HOU N	5	8	.385	2.65	59	0	0	95	89	38	57	0	5	8	7	11	1	0	.091	7	17	3	3	0.5	.889
1972	"	6	2	.750	3.05	45	0	0	97.1	73	43	82	0	6	2	2	19	3	0	.158	6	12	2	1	0.4	.900
1973	2 teams	LA N	(28G 4–4)		PHI N	(14G 3–1)																				
"	total	7	5	.583	3.56	42	0	0	60.2	71	36	30	0	7	5	2	4	0	0	.000	6	18	0	2	0.6	1.000
1974	PHI N	1	0	1.000	6.55	14	0	0	22	20	16	9	0	1	0	0	3	0	0	.000	0	3	2	0	0.4	.600
9 yrs.		48	49	.495	3.62	335	57	7	788.1	793	352	451	2	31	24	23	161	20	0	.124	67	156	13	13	0.7	.945

John Cumberland

CUMBERLAND, JOHN SHELDON
B. May 10, 1947, Westbrook, Me. BR TL 6' 185 lbs.

Year	Team	W	L	PCT	ERA	G	GS	CG	IP	H	BB	SO	ShO	W	L	SV	AB	H	HR	BA	PO	A	E	DP	TC/G	FA
1968	NY A	0	0	–	9.00	1	0	0	2	3	1	1	0	0	0	0	0	0	0	–	1	2	0	0	3.0	1.000
1969	"	0	0	–	4.50	2	0	0	4	3	4	0	0	0	0	0	0	0	0	–	0	1	0	0	0.5	1.000
1970	2 teams	NY A	(15G 3–4)		SF N	(7G 2–0)																				
"	total	5	4	.556	3.48	22	8	1	75	68	19	44	0	3	0	0	18	1	0	.056	2	8	0	0	0.5	1.000
1971	SF N	9	6	.600	2.92	45	21	5	185	153	55	65	2	2	0	2	59	7	0	.119	7	20	3	1	0.7	.900
1972	2 teams	SF N	(9G 0–4)		STL N	(14G 1–1)																				
"	total	1	5	.167	7.71	23	7	0	46.2	61	14	15	0	0	1	0	14	1	0	.071	1	0	2	0	0.1	.333
1974	CAL A	0	1	.000	3.68	17	0	0	22	24	10	12	0	0	0	0	0	0	0	–	0	2	1	0	0.2	.667
6 yrs.		15	16	.484	3.82	110	36	6	334.2	312	103	137	2	6	1	2	91	9	0	.099	11	33	6	1	0.5	.880

LEAGUE CHAMPIONSHIP SERIES

Year	Team	W	L	PCT	ERA	G	GS	CG	IP	H	BB	SO	ShO	W	L	SV	AB	H	HR	BA	PO	A	E	DP	TC/G	FA
1971	SF N	0	1	.000	9.00	1	1	0	3	7	0	4	0	0	0	0	0	0	0	–	0	0	0	0	0.0	–

Candy Cummings

CUMMINGS, WILLIAM ARTHUR
B. Oct. 18, 1848, Ware, Mass. D. May 16, 1924, Toledo, Ohio BR TR 5'9" 120 lbs.
Hall of Fame 1939.

Year	Team	W	L	PCT	ERA	G	GS	CG	IP	H	BB	SO	ShO	W	L	SV	AB	H	HR	BA	PO	A	E	DP	TC/G	FA
1876	HAR N	16	8	.667	1.67	24	24	24	216	215	14	26	5	0	0	0	105	17	0	.162	9	27	2	0	1.6	.947
1877	CIN N	5	14	.263	4.34	19	19	16	155.2	219	13	11	0	0	0	0	70	14	0	.200	6	31	3	0	2.1	.925
2 yrs.		21	22	.488	2.78	43	43	40	371.2	434	27	37	5	0	0	0	175	31	0	.177	15	58	5	0	1.8	.936

Steve Cummings

CUMMINGS, STEVEN BRENT
B. July 15, 1964, Houston, Tex. BB TR 6'2" 200 lbs.

Year	Team	W	L	PCT	ERA	G	GS	CG	IP	H	BB	SO	ShO	W	L	SV	AB	H	HR	BA	PO	A	E	DP	TC/G	FA
1989	TOR A	2	0	1.000	3.00	5	2	0	21	18	11	8	0	0	0	0	0	0	0	–	0	4	1	0	1.0	.800

Bert Cunningham

CUNNINGHAM, ELLSWORTH ELMER
B. Nov. 25, 1865, Wilmington, Del. D. May 14, 1952, Cragmere, Del. BR TR

Year	Team	W	L	PCT	ERA	G	GS	CG	IP	H	BB	SO	ShO	W	L	SV	AB	H	HR	BA	PO	A	E	DP	TC/G	FA
1887	BKN AA	0	2	.000	5.09	3	3	3	23	26	13	8	0	0	0	0	8	0	0	.000	1	4	1	0	2.0	.833
1888	BAL AA	22	29	.431	3.39	51	51	50	453.1	412	157	186	0	0	0	0	177	33	1	.186	20	106	25	3	3.0	.834
1889	"	16	19	.457	4.87	39	33	29	279.1	306	141	140	0	2	0	1	131	27	0	.206	8	60	9	0	2.0	.883
1890	2 teams	PHI P	(14G 3–9)		BUF P	(25G 9–15)																				
"	total	12	24	.333	5.63	39	36	35	319.2	384	201	111	2	0	0	0	153	29	0	.190	14	86	21	5	3.1	.826
1891	BAL AA	11	14	.440	4.01	30	25	21	237.2	241	138	59	0	1	0	0	100	15	1	.150	11	69	7	3	2.9	.920
1895	LOU N	11	16	.407	4.75	31	28	24	231	299	104	49	1	0	0	0	100	30	0	.300	19	56	10	3	2.7	.882
1896	"	7	14	.333	5.09	27	20	17	189.1	242	74	37	0	0	0	1	88	22	2	.250	23	48	9	3	3.0	.888
1897	"	14	13	.519	4.14	29	27	25	234.2	286	72	49	0	0	0	0	93	22	2	.237	27	58	7	0	3.2	.924
1898	"	28	15	.651	3.16	44	42	41	362	387	65	34	0	0	0	0	140	32	1	.229	29	81	13	5	2.8	.894
1899	"	17	17	.500	3.84	39	37	33	323.2	385	75	35	1	0	0	0	154	40	2	.260	35	100	8	2	3.7	.944
1900	CHI N	4	3	.571	4.36	8	7	7	64	84	21	7	0	0	0	0	27	4	0	.148	8	9	1	1	2.3	.944
1901	"	0	1	.000	5.00	1	1	1	9	11	3	2	0	0	0	0	1	0	0	.000	2	5	0	0	7.0	1.000
12 yrs.		142	167	.460	4.22	341	310	286	2726.2	3063	1064	718	4	5	4	2	1172	254	9	.217	197	682	111	25	2.9	.888

Bruce Cunningham

CUNNINGHAM, BRUCE LEE
B. Sept. 29, 1905, San Francisco, Calif. D. Mar. 8, 1984, Hayward, Calif. BR TR 5'10½" 165 lbs.

Year	Team	W	L	PCT	ERA	G	GS	CG	IP	H	BB	SO	ShO	W	L	SV	AB	H	HR	BA	PO	A	E	DP	TC/G	FA
1929	BOS N	4	6	.400	4.52	17	8	4	91.2	100	32	22	0	1	1	1	27	4	0	.148	5	27	1	0	1.9	.970
1930	"	5	6	.455	5.48	36	6	2	106.2	121	41	28	0	3	2	0	31	6	0	.194	4	35	1	3	1.1	1.000
1931	"	3	12	.200	4.48	33	16	6	136.2	157	54	32	1	0	3	1	42	3	0	.071	6	50	1	4	1.7	.982
1932	"	1	0	1.000	3.45	18	3	0	47	50	19	21	0	1	0	0	9	2	0	.222	1	12	0	5	0.7	1.000
4 yrs.		13	24	.351	4.64	104	33	12	382	428	146	103	1	5	6	2	109	15	0	.138	16	124	2	12	1.4	.986

George Cunningham

CUNNINGHAM, GEORGE HAROLD
B. July 13, 1894, Sturgeon Lake, Minn. D. Mar. 10, 1972, Chattanooga, Tenn. BR TR 5'11" 185 lbs.

Year	Team	W	L	PCT	ERA	G	GS	CG	IP	H	BB	SO	ShO	W	L	SV	AB	H	HR	BA	PO	A	E	DP	TC/G	FA
1916	DET A	7	10	.412	2.75	35	14	5	150.1	146	74	68	0	2	1	2	41	11	0	.268	6	46	2	2	1.5	.963
1917	"	2	7	.222	2.91	44	8	4	139	113	51	49	0	2	1	4	34	6	1	.176	4	43	4	3	1.2	.922
1918	"	6	7	.462	3.15	27	14	10	140	131	38	39	0	2	0	1	112	25	0	.223	3	35	4	1	1.6	.905
1919	"	1	1	.500	4.91	17	0	0	47.2	54	15	11	0	1	1	1	23	5	0	.217	2	16	3	1	1.2	.857
1921	"	0	0	–	0.00	0	0	0	0	0	0	0	0	0	0	0	0	0	0	–	0	0	0	0	0.0	–
5 yrs.		16	25	.390	3.13	123	36	19	477	444	178	167	0	7	3	8	*				15	140	13	7	1.4	.923

Mike Cunningham

CUNNINGHAM, MODY
B. June 14, 1882, Lancaster, S. C. D. Dec. 10, 1969, Lancaster, S. C. BR TR 5'10½" 175 lbs.

Year	Team	W	L	PCT	ERA	G	GS	CG	IP	H	BB	SO	ShO	W	L	SV	AB	H	HR	BA	PO	A	E	DP	TC/G	FA
1906	PHI A	1	0	1.000	3.21	5	1	1	28	29	9	15	0	0	0	0	12	4	0	.333	2	6	0	0	1.6	1.000

Nig Cuppy

CUPPY, GEORGE JOSEPH
Born George Maceo Koppe.
B. July 3, 1869, Logansport, Ind. D. July 27, 1922, Elkhart, Ind. BR TR 5'7" 160 lbs.

Year	Team	W	L	PCT	ERA	G	GS	CG	IP	H	BB	SO	ShO	W	L	SV	AB	H	HR	BA	PO	A	E	DP	TC/G	FA
1892	CLE N	28	13	.683	2.51	47	42	38	376	333	121	103	1	0	0	1	168	36	0	.214	10	103	6	3	2.5	.950
1893	"	17	10	.630	4.47	31	30	24	243.2	316	75	39	0	0	0	0	109	27	0	.248	13	48	5	1	2.1	.924
1894	"	24	15	.615	4.56	43	33	29	316	381	128	65	3	8	0	0	135	35	0	.259	17	60	2	5	1.8	.975
1895	"	26	14	.650	3.54	47	40	36	353	384	95	91	1	3	0	2	140	40	0	.286	30	90	4	2	2.6	.968
1896	"	25	14	.641	3.12	46	40	35	358	388	75	86	1	2	0	1	141	38	1	.270	14	106	4	3	2.7	.968

Year	Team		W	L	PCT	ERA	G	GS	CG	IP	H	BB	SO	ShO	Relief Pitching W	L	SV	Batting AB	H	HR	BA	PO	A	E	DP	TC/G	FA

Nig Cuppy *continued*

1897			10	6	.625	3.18	19	17	13	138.2	150	26	23	1	0	0	0	55	8	0	.145	1	32	2	0	1.8	.943
1898			9	8	.529	3.30	18	15	13	128	147	25	27	1	1	2	0	48	5	0	.104	3	24	2	1	1.6	.931
1899	STL	N	11	8	.579	3.15	21	21	18	171.2	203	26	25	1	0	1	0	70	13	0	.186	4	47	5	1	2.7	.911
1900	BOS	N	8	4	.667	3.08	17	13	9	105.1	107	24	23	0	1	0	1	42	11	0	.262	0	22	2	0	1.4	.917
1901	BOS	A	4	6	.400	4.15	13	11	9	93.1	111	14	22	0	0	0	0	49	10	0	.204	2	20	2	0	1.8	.917
10 yrs.			162	98	.623	3.48	302	262	224	2283.2	2520	609	504	9	15	2	5	957	223	1	.233	94	552	34	16	2.3	.950

Sam Curran

CURRAN, SIMON FRANCIS
B. Oct. 30, 1874, Dorchester, Mass. D. May 19, 1936, Dorchester, Mass.

| 1902 | BOS | N | 0 | 0 | – | 1.35 | 1 | 0 | 0 | 6.2 | 6 | 0 | 3 | 0 | 0 | 0 | 0 | 2 | 0 | 0 | .000 | 0 | 0 | 0 | 0 | 0.0 | – |

Lafayette Currence

CURRENCE, DELANCEY LAFAYETTE BB TL 5'11" 175 lbs.
B. Dec. 3, 1951, Rock Hill, S. C.

| 1975 | MIL | A | 0 | 2 | .000 | 7.71 | 8 | 1 | 0 | 18.2 | 25 | 14 | 7 | 0 | 1 | 0 | 0 | 0 | 0 | 0 | – | 0 | 1 | 0 | 0 | 0.1 | 1.000 |

Bill Currie

CURRIE, WILLIAM CLEVELAND BR TR 6' 175 lbs.
B. Nov. 29, 1928, Leary, Ga.

| 1955 | WAS | A | 0 | 0 | – | 12.46 | 3 | 0 | 0 | 4.1 | 7 | 2 | 2 | 0 | 0 | 0 | 0 | 0 | 0 | 0 | – | 0 | 2 | 0 | 0 | 0.7 | 1.000 |

Clarence Currie

CURRIE, CLARENCE FRANKLIN BR TR
B. Dec. 30, 1878, Glencoe, Ont., Canada D. July 15, 1941, Little Chute, Wis.

1902	2 teams		CIN N	(10G 3–4)		STL N	(15G 6–5)																				
"	total		9	9	.500	3.10	25	18	15	183	192	48	49	2	0	0	0	70	11	0	.157	8	64	4	3	3.0	.947
1903	2 teams		STL N	(22G 4–12)		CHI N	(6G 1–2)																				
"	total		5	14	.263	3.82	28	19	15	181.1	190	69	61	1	2	1	2	59	9	0	.153	9	74	8	3	3.3	.912
2 yrs.			14	23	.378	3.46	53	37	30	364.1	382	117	110	3	2	1	2	129	20	0	.155	17	138	12	6	3.2	.928

Murphy Currie

CURRIE, MURPHY ARCHIBALD BR TR 5'11½" 185 lbs.
B. Aug. 31, 1893, Fayetteville, N. C. D. June 22, 1939, Asheboro, N. C.

| 1916 | STL | N | 0 | 0 | – | 1.88 | 6 | 0 | 0 | 14.1 | 7 | 9 | 8 | 0 | 0 | 0 | 0 | 3 | 0 | 0 | .000 | 0 | 1 | 1 | 0 | 0.3 | .500 |

George Curry

CURRY, GEORGE JAMES (Soldier Boy) BR TR 6' 185 lbs.
B. Dec. 21, 1888, Bridgeport, Conn. D. Oct. 5, 1963, Stratford, Conn.

| 1911 | STL | A | 0 | 3 | .000 | 7.47 | 3 | 3 | 0 | 15.2 | 19 | 24 | 2 | 0 | 0 | 0 | 0 | 5 | 0 | 0 | .000 | 0 | 4 | 0 | 0 | 1.3 | 1.000 |

Steve Curry

CURRY, STEPHEN THOMAS BR TR 6'6" 217 lbs.
B. Sept. 13, 1965, Winter Park, Fla.

| 1988 | BOS | A | 0 | 1 | .000 | 8.18 | 3 | 3 | 0 | 11 | 15 | 14 | 4 | 0 | 0 | 0 | 0 | 0 | 0 | 0 | – | 0 | 3 | 0 | 0 | 1.0 | 1.000 |

Wes Curry

CURRY, WESLEY
B. Apr. 1, 1860, Wilmington, Del. D. May 19, 1933, Philadelphia, Pa.

| 1884 | RIC | AA | 0 | 2 | .000 | 5.06 | 2 | 2 | 2 | 16 | 15 | 3 | 1 | 0 | 0 | 0 | 0 | 8 | 2 | 0 | .250 | 0 | 4 | 4 | 0 | 4.0 | .500 |

Cliff Curtis

CURTIS, CLIFTON GARFIELD BR TR 6'2" 180 lbs.
B. July 3, 1883, Delaware, Ohio D. Apr. 23, 1943, Newark, Ohio

1909	BOS	N	4	5	.444	1.41	10	9	8	83	53	30	22	2	0	1	0	29	1	0	.034	3	28	5	1	3.6	.861
1910			6	24	.200	3.55	43	37	12	251	251	124	75	2	0	1	2	82	12	0	.146	9	102	5	1	2.7	.957
1911	3 teams		BOS N	(12G 1–8)		CHI N	(4G 1–2)	PHI N	(8G 2–1)																		
"	total		4	11	.267	3.77	24	15	8	129	131	54	40	1	1	2	1	45	12	0	.267	7	37	5	1	2.0	.898
1912	2 teams		PHI N	(10G 2–5)		BKN N	(19G 4–7)																				
"	total		6	12	.333	3.67	29	17	5	130	127	54	42	0	1	2	0	41	8	0	.195	3	37	2	1	1.4	.952
1913	BKN	N	8	9	.471	3.26	30	16	5	151.2	145	55	57	0	3	1	1	49	6	0	.122	11	44	1	0	1.9	.982
5 yrs.			28	61	.315	3.31	136	94	38	744.2	707	317	236	5	5	7	4	246	39	0	.159	33	248	18	4	2.2	.940

Jack Curtis

CURTIS, JACK PATRICK BL TL 5'10" 175 lbs.
B. Jan. 11, 1937, Rhodhiss, N. C.

1961	CHI	N	10	13	.435	4.89	31	27	6	180.1	220	51	57	0	0	0	0	60	10	2	.167	5	42	3	1	1.6	.940
1962	2 teams		CHI N	(4G 0–2)		MIL N	(30G 4–4)																				
"	total		4	6	.400	4.04	34	8	0	93.2	100	33	48	0	4	3	1	22	5	0	.227	6	11	1	1	0.5	.944
1963	CLE	A	0	0	–	18.00	4	0	0	5	8	5	3	0	0	0	0	0	0	0	–	0	2	0	0	0.5	1.000
3 yrs.			14	19	.424	4.84	69	35	6	279	328	89	108	0	4	3	1	82	15	2	.183	11	55	4	2	1.0	.943

John Curtis

CURTIS, JOHN DUFFIELD II BL TL 6'1" 175 lbs.
B. Mar. 9, 1948, Newton, Mass.

1970	BOS	A	0	0	–	13.50	1	1	0	2	4	1	1	0	0	0	0	0	0	0	–	0	2	0	0	2.0	1.000
1971			2	2	.500	3.12	5	3	1	26	30	6	19	0	1	0	0	9	1	0	.111	0	1	0	0	0.2	1.000
1972			11	8	.579	3.73	26	21	8	154.1	161	50	106	3	1	0	0	53	5	0	.094	4	23	2	4	1.1	.931
1973			13	13	.500	3.58	35	30	10	221	225	83	101	4	0	0	0	0	0	0	–	9	33	2	1	1.3	.955
1974	STL	N	10	14	.417	3.78	33	29	5	195	199	83	89	2	0	1	1	63	10	0	.159	10	31	0	2	1.2	1.000
1975			8	9	.471	3.43	39	18	4	147	151	65	67	0	0	1	1	38	8	0	.211	7	31	1	3	1.0	.974
1976			6	11	.353	4.50	37	15	3	134	139	65	52	1	0	0	1	35	7	0	.200	7	22	0	1	0.8	1.000
1977	SF	N	3	3	.500	5.49	43	9	1	77	95	48	47	1	1	1	1	13	3	0	.231	9	14	0	3	0.5	1.000
1978			4	3	.571	3.71	46	0	0	63	60	29	38	0	4	3	1	2	0	0	.000	6	9	2	1	0.4	.882
1979			10	9	.526	4.17	27	18	3	121	121	42	85	2	1	0	1	34	5	0	.147	4	13	0	1	0.6	1.000
1980	SD	N	10	8	.556	3.51	30	27	6	187	184	67	71	0	0	0	0	62	12	0	.194	5	37	1	2	1.4	.977
1981			2	6	.250	5.10	28	8	0	67	70	30	31	0	2	4	0	13	1	0	.077	0	12	1	0	0.5	.923

Year	Team	W	L	PCT	ERA	G	GS	CG	IP	H	BB	SO	ShO	Relief Pitching W	L	SV	Batting AB	H	HR	BA	PO	A	E	DP	TC/G	FA

John Curtis *continued*

Year	Team	W	L	PCT	ERA	G	GS	CG	IP	H	BB	SO	ShO	W	L	SV	AB	H	HR	BA	PO	A	E	DP	TC/G	FA
1982	2 teams	SD N	(26G 8–6)		CAL A	(8G 0–1)																				
"	total	8	7	.533	4.28	34	18	1	128.1	137	49	64	1	1	2	1	37	11	0	.297	2	18	2	1	0.6	.909
1983	CAL A	1	2	.333	3.80	37	3	0	90	89	40	36	0	1	1	5	0	0	0	–	1	10	1	1	0.3	.917
1984		1	2	.333	4.40	17	0	0	28.2	30	11	18	0	1	2	0	0	0	0	–	2	4	0	0	0.4	1.000
15 yrs.		89	97	.478	3.96	438	199	42	1641.1	1695	669	825	14	13	21	11	359	63	0	.175	66	260	12	21	0.8	.964

Vern Curtis

CURTIS, VERNON EUGENE (Turk)
B. May 24, 1920, Cairo, Ill.   BR TR 6'   170 lbs.

Year	Team	W	L	PCT	ERA	G	GS	CG	IP	H	BB	SO	ShO	W	L	SV	AB	H	HR	BA	PO	A	E	DP	TC/G	FA
1943	WAS A	0	0	–	6.75	2	0	0	4	3	6	1	0	0	0	0	0	0	0	–	1	0	0	0	0.5	1.000
1944		0	1	.000	2.79	3	1	0	9.2	8	3	2	0	0	0	0	2	0	0	.000	2	1	0	0	1.0	1.000
1946		0	0	–	7.16	11	0	0	16.1	19	10	7	0	0	0	0	2	0	0	.000	3	2	0	0	0.5	1.000
3 yrs.		0	1	.000	5.70	16	1	0	30	30	19	10	0	0	0	0	4	0	0	.000	6	3	0	0	0.6	1.000

Ed Cushman

CUSHMAN, EDGAR LEANDER
B. Mar. 27, 1852, Eaglesville, Ohio   D. Sept. 26, 1915, Erie, Pa.   BR TL

Year	Team	W	L	PCT	ERA	G	GS	CG	IP	H	BB	SO	ShO	W	L	SV	AB	H	HR	BA	PO	A	E	DP	TC/G	FA
1883	BUF N	3	3	.500	3.93	7	7	5	50.1	61	17	34	0	0	0	0	23	5	0	.217	1	8	3	0	1.7	.750
1884	MIL U	4	0	1.000	1.00	4	4	4	36	10	3	47	2	0	0	0	11	1	0	.091	0	4	1	0	1.3	.800
1885	2 teams	PHI AA	(10G 3–7)		NY AA	(22G 8–14)																				
"	total	11	21	.344	3.01	32	32	32	278	259	50	170	0	0	0	0	106	17	0	.160	5	32	10	0	1.5	.787
1886	NY AA	17	20	.459	3.12	38	37	37	325.2	278	99	167	2	0	0	0	126	19	0	.151	5	59	9	2	1.9	.877
1887		10	14	.417	5.97	26	26	25	220	310	83	64	0	0	0	0	93	23	0	.247	4	42	7	2	2.0	.868
1890	TOL AA	17	21	.447	4.19	40	38	34	315.2	346	107	125	0	0	1	1	130	13	0	.100	1	46	7	1	1.4	.870
6 yrs.		62	79	.440	3.86	147	144	137	1225.2	1264	359	607	4	0	1	1	489	78	0	.160	16	191	37	5	1.7	.848

Harv Cushman

CUSHMAN, HARVEY BARNES
B. July 10, 1877, Rockland, Me.   D. Dec. 27, 1920, Ensworth, Pa.

Year	Team	W	L	PCT	ERA	G	GS	CG	IP	H	BB	SO	ShO	W	L	SV	AB	H	HR	BA	PO	A	E	DP	TC/G	FA
1902	PIT N	0	4	.000	7.36	4	4	3	25.2	30	31	12	0	0	0	0	10	2	0	.200	1	4	2	0	1.8	.714

Mike Cvengros

CVENGROS, MICHAEL JOHN
B. Dec. 1, 1901, Pana, Ill.   D. Aug. 2, 1970, Hot Springs, Ark.   BL TL 5'8"   159 lbs.

Year	Team	W	L	PCT	ERA	G	GS	CG	IP	H	BB	SO	ShO	W	L	SV	AB	H	HR	BA	PO	A	E	DP	TC/G	FA
1922	NY N	0	1	.000	4.00	1	1	1	9	6	3	3	0	0	0	0	3	0	0	.000	1	2	0	0	3.0	1.000
1923	CHI A	12	13	.480	4.39	41	26	14	215.1	216	107	86	0	2	1	3	74	15	0	.203	9	53	2	4	1.6	.969
1924		3	12	.200	5.88	26	15	2	105.2	119	67	36	0	1	3	0	30	6	0	.200	2	26	1	1	1.1	.966
1925		3	9	.250	4.30	22	11	4	104.2	109	55	32	0	1	2	0	33	5	0	.152	2	27	3	2	1.5	.906
1927	PIT N	2	1	.667	3.35	23	4	0	53.2	55	24	21	0	2	0	1	19	3	0	.158	3	16	0	0	0.8	1.000
1929	CHI N	5	4	.556	4.64	32	2	0	64	82	29	23	0	5	4	2	15	6	0	.400	2	14	0	1	0.5	1.000
6 yrs.		25	40	.385	4.58	145	59	21	552.1	587	285	201	0	11	10	6	174	35	0	.201	19	138	6	8	1.1	.963

WORLD SERIES

Year	Team	W	L	PCT	ERA	G	GS	CG	IP	H	BB	SO	ShO	W	L	SV	AB	H	HR	BA	PO	A	E	DP	TC/G	FA
1927	PIT N	0	0	–	3.86	2	0	0	2.1	3	0	2	0	0	0	0	0	0	0	–	0	0	0	0	0.0	–

John D'Acquisto

D'ACQUISTO, JOHN FRANCIS
B. Dec. 24, 1951, San Diego, Calif.   BR TR 6'2"   205 lbs.

Year	Team	W	L	PCT	ERA	G	GS	CG	IP	H	BB	SO	ShO	W	L	SV	AB	H	HR	BA	PO	A	E	DP	TC/G	FA
1973	SF N	1	1	.500	3.54	7	3	1	28	23	19	29	0	0	0	0	9	0	0	.000	0	2	0	0	0.3	1.000
1974		12	14	.462	3.77	38	36	5	215	182	124	167	1	0	0	0	71	8	1	.113	11	12	2	1	0.7	.920
1975		2	4	.333	10.29	10	6	0	28	29	34	22	0	1	0	0	7	0	0	.000	1	2	2	1	0.5	.600
1976		3	8	.273	5.35	28	19	0	106	93	102	53	0	0	0	0	26	7	0	.269	5	6	1	0	0.9	.917
1977	2 teams	STL N	(3G 0–0)		SD N	(17G 1–2)																				
"	total	1	2	.333	6.54	20	14	0	52.1	54	57	54	0	1	0	0	8	0	0	.000	4	6	2	0	0.6	.833
1978	SD N	4	3	.571	2.13	45	3	0	93	60	56	104	0	3	2	10	21	4	0	.190	3	6	0	0	0.2	1.000
1979		9	13	.409	4.90	51	11	1	134	140	86	97	1	5	7	2	31	4	0	.129	3	9	1	0	0.3	.923
1980	2 teams	SD N	(39G 2–3)		MON N	(11G 0–2)																				
"	total	2	5	.286	3.38	50	0	0	88	81	45	59	0	5	5	3	8	0	0	.000	1	12	0	1	0.3	1.000
1981	CAL A	0	0	–	10.89	6	0	0	19	26	12	8	0	0	0	0	0	0	0	–	1	1	0	0	0.3	1.000
1982	OAK A	0	1	.000	5.29	11	0	0	17	20	9	7	0	0	1	0	0	0	0	–	1	0	0	0	0.2	1.000
10 yrs.		34	51	.400	4.56	266	92	7	780.1	708	544	600	2	12	15	15	181	23	1	.127	29	69	9	8	0.4	.916

John Dagenhard

DAGENHARD, JOHN DOUGLAS
B. Apr. 25, 1917, Magnolia, Ohio   BR TR 6'2"   195 lbs.

Year	Team	W	L	PCT	ERA	G	GS	CG	IP	H	BB	SO	ShO	W	L	SV	AB	H	HR	BA	PO	A	E	DP	TC/G	FA
1943	BOS N	1	0	1.000	0.00	2	1	1	11	9	4	2	0	0	0	0	3	0	0	.000	1	4	0	0	2.5	1.000

Pete Daglia

DAGLIA, PETER GEORGE
B. Feb. 28, 1906, Napa, Calif.   D. Mar. 11, 1952, Willits, Calif.   BR TR 6'1"   200 lbs.

Year	Team	W	L	PCT	ERA	G	GS	CG	IP	H	BB	SO	ShO	W	L	SV	AB	H	HR	BA	PO	A	E	DP	TC/G	FA
1932	CHI A	2	4	.333	5.76	12	5	2	50	67	20	16	0	1	0	0	13	1	0	.077	4	5	0	1	0.8	1.000

Jay Dahl

DAHL, JAY STEVEN
B. Dec. 6, 1945, San Bernardino, Calif.   D. June 20, 1965, Salisbury, N. C.   BB TL 5'10"   183 lbs.

Year	Team	W	L	PCT	ERA	G	GS	CG	IP	H	BB	SO	ShO	W	L	SV	AB	H	HR	BA	PO	A	E	DP	TC/G	FA
1963	HOU N	0	1	.000	16.88	1	1	0	2.2	7	0	0	0	0	0	0	0	0	0	–	0	0	0	0	0.0	–

Jerry Dahlke

DAHLKE, JEROME ALEXANDER (Joe)
B. June 8, 1930, Marathon, Wis.   BR TR 6'   180 lbs.

Year	Team	W	L	PCT	ERA	G	GS	CG	IP	H	BB	SO	ShO	W	L	SV	AB	H	HR	BA	PO	A	E	DP	TC/G	FA
1956	CHI A	0	0	–	19.29	5	0	0	2.1	5	6	1	0	0	0	0	0	0	0	–	0	1	0	0	0.2	1.000

Bill Dailey

DAILEY, WILLIAM GARLAND
B. May 13, 1935, Arlington, Va.   BR TR 6'3"   185 lbs.

Year	Team	W	L	PCT	ERA	G	GS	CG	IP	H	BB	SO	ShO	W	L	SV	AB	H	HR	BA	PO	A	E	DP	TC/G	FA
1961	CLE A	1	0	1.000	0.95	12	0	0	19	16	6	7	0	1	0	0	2	0	0	.000	2	5	0	0	0.6	1.000
1962		2	2	.500	3.59	27	0	0	42.2	43	17	24	0	2	2	1	3	0	0	.000	4	6	1	0	0.4	.909
1963	MIN A	6	3	.667	1.99	66	0	0	108.2	80	19	72	0	3	3	21	21	5	1	.238	4	32	4	0	0.6	.900

Year	Team		W	L	PCT	ERA	G	GS	CG	IP	H	BB	SO	ShO	Relief Pitching W	L	SV	Batting AB	H	HR	BA	PO	A	E	DP	TC/G	FA

Bill Dailey *continued*

| 1964 | | | 1 | 2 | .333 | 8.22 | 14 | 0 | 0 | 15.1 | 23 | 17 | 6 | 0 | 1 | 2 | 0 | 0 | 0 | 0 | – | 0 | 4 | 0 | 1 | 0.3 | 1.000 |
| 4 yrs. | | | 10 | 7 | .588 | 2.76 | 119 | 0 | 0 | 185.2 | 162 | 59 | 109 | 0 | 10 | 7 | 22 | 26 | 5 | 1 | .192 | 10 | 47 | 5 | 1 | 0.5 | .919 |

Sam Dailey

DAILEY, SAMUEL LAWRENCE BL TR 5'11" 168 lbs.
B. Mar. 31, 1904, Oakford, Ill. D. Dec. 2, 1979, Columbia, Mo.

| 1929 | PHI | N | 2 | 2 | .500 | 7.54 | 20 | 5 | 0 | 51.1 | 74 | 23 | 18 | 0 | 2 | 0 | 0 | 17 | 1 | 0 | .059 | 4 | 3 | 0 | 0 | 0.4 | 1.000 |

Vince Dailey

DAILEY, VINCENT PERRY 6' 200 lbs.
B. Dec. 25, 1864, Osceola, Pa. D. Nov. 14, 1919, Hornell, N. Y.

| 1890 | CLE | N | 0 | 1 | .000 | 7.71 | 2 | 1 | 0 | 7 | 12 | 7 | 0 | 0 | 0 | 0 | 0 | * | | | | 0 | 0 | 0 | 0 | 0.0 | – |

Ed Daily

DAILY, EDWARD M. BR TR
Brother of Con Daily.
B. Sept. 7, 1862, Providence, R. I. D. Oct. 21, 1891, Washington, D. C.

1885	PHI	N	26	23	.531	2.21	50	50	49	440	370	90	140	4	0	0	0	184	38	1	.207	11	87	12	2	2.2	.891
1886			16	9	.640	3.06	27	23	22	218	211	59	95	1	3	0	0	309	70	4	.227	10	53	5	1	2.5	.926
1887	2 teams	PHI N (6G 0–4)				WAS N	(1G 0–1)																				
"	total		0	5	.000	7.26	7	6	5	48.1	57	31	10	0	0	0	0	417	108	3	.259	3	15	0	0	2.6	1.000
1888	WAS	N	2	7	.222	4.89	9	8	8	73.2	88	19	20	0	0	0	1	453	102	8	.225	4	18	3	1	2.8	.880
1889	COL	AA	0	0	–	21.60	2	0	0	1.2	1	4	2	0	0	0	1	578	148	3	.256	0					
1890	3 teams	BKN AA (27G 10–15)				NY	N	(2G 2–0)			LOU AA	(12G 6–3)															
"	total		18	18	.500	3.33	41	38	37	343.2	341	129	113	1	2	0	0	489	116	1	.237	27	87	10	3	3.0	.919
1891	LOU	AA	4	8	.333	5.74	15	14	11	111.1	149	48	27	0	0	0	0	143	34	0	.238	10	28	5	0	2.9	.884
7 yrs.			66	70	.485	3.37	151	139	132	1236.2	1217	380	407	6	5	1	1	*				65	288	35	7	2.6	.910

One Arm Daily

DAILY, HUGH IGNATIUS BR TR 6'2" 180 lbs.
Born Harry Criss.
B. 1857, Baltimore, Md. Deceased.

1882	BUF	N	15	14	.517	2.99	29	29	29	255.2	246	70	116	0	0	0	0	110	18	0	.164	1	28	4	0	1.1	.879
1883	CLE	N	23	19	.548	2.42	45	43	43	378.2	360	99	171	4	0	1	1	142	18	0	.127	6	71	5	1	1.8	.939
1884	3 teams	CHI U (46G 22–23)				PIT U	(10G 5–4)			WAS U	(2G 1–1)																
"	total		28	28	.500	2.44	58	58	56	500.2	446	72	483	4	0	0	0	201	43	0	.214	13	106	20	2	2.4	.856
1885	STL	N	3	8	.273	3.94	11	11	10	91.1	92	44	31	1	0	0	0	35	3	0	.086	0	21	1	1	2.0	.955
1886	WAS	N	0	6	.000	7.35	6	6	6	49	69	40	15	0	0	0	0	16	2	0	.125	2	10	1	0	2.2	.923
1887	CLE	AA	4	12	.250	3.67	16	16	16	139.2	181	44	30	0	0	0	0	58	4	0	.069	0	26	3	0	1.8	.897
6 yrs.			73	87	.456	2.93	165	163	157	1415	1394	369	846	9	0	1	1	562	88	0	.157	22	262	34	4	1.9	.893

Bruce Dal Canton

DAL CANTON, JOHN BRUCE BR TR 6'2" 205 lbs.
B. June 15, 1942, California, Pa.

1967	PIT	N	2	1	.667	1.88	8	2	1	24	19	10	13	0	2	0	0	6	2	0	.333	1	2	0	0	0.4	1.000
1968			1	1	.500	2.12	7	0	0	17	7	6	8	0	1	1	2	3	0	0	.000	0	1	0	0	0.1	1.000
1969			8	2	.800	3.35	57	0	0	86	79	49	56	0	8	2	5	10	3	0	.300	7	12	1	1	0.4	.950
1970			9	4	.692	4.55	41	6	1	85	94	39	53	0	6	3	1	16	0	0	.000	3	10	2	0	0.3	1.000
1971	KC	A	8	6	.571	3.45	25	22	2	141	144	44	58	0	0	0	0	46	4	0	.087	11	16	2	0	1.2	.931
1972			6	6	.500	3.40	35	16	1	132.1	135	29	75	0	2	2	2	41	4	0	.098	5	14	1	1	0.6	.950
1973			4	3	.571	4.82	32	3	1	97	108	46	38	0	3	1	3	0	0	0	–	5	17	1	1	0.7	.957
1974			8	10	.444	3.14	31	22	9	175	135	82	96	2	2	2	0	0	0	0	–	14	25	1	2	1.3	.975
1975	2 teams	KC A (4G 0–2)				ATL N	(26G 2–7)																				
"	total		2	9	.182	4.76	30	11	0	75.2	86	31	43	0	2	3	3	19	2	0	.105	7	13	0	1	0.7	1.000
1976	ATL	N	3	5	.375	3.58	42	1	0	73	67	42	36	0	3	4	1	9	2	0	.222	4	17	2	0	0.5	.913
1977	CHI	A	0	2	.000	3.75	8	0	0	24	20	13	9	0	0	0	0	0	0	0	–	1	0	0	0	0.3	1.000
11 yrs.			51	49	.510	3.68	316	83	15	930	894	391	485	2	29	19	19	150	17	0	.113	58	128	8	8	0.6	.959

Gene Dale

DALE, EMMETT EUGENE BR TR 6'3" 179 lbs.
B. June 16, 1889, St. Louis, Mo. D. Mar. 20, 1958, St. Louis, Mo.

1911	STL	N	0	2	.000	6.75	5	2	0	14.2	13	16	13	0	0	0	0	5	2	0	.400	2	2	0	1	0.8	1.000
1912			0	5	.000	6.57	19	3	1	61.2	76	51	37	0	0	2	0	22	6	0	.273	3	10	2	1	0.8	.867
1915	CIN	N	18	17	.514	2.46	49	35	20	296.2	256	107	104	4	3	2	3	91	20	0	.220	8	76	6	4	1.8	.933
1916			3	4	.429	5.17	17	5	2	69.2	80	33	23	0	2	1	0	21	3	0	.143	3	26	0	0	1.7	1.000
4 yrs.			21	28	.429	3.60	90	45	23	442.2	425	207	177	4	5	5	3	139	31	0	.223	16	114	8	6	1.5	.942

Bill Daley

DALEY, WILLIAM TL
B. June 27, 1868, Poughkeepsie, N. Y. D. May 4, 1922, Poughkeepsie, N. Y.

1889	BOS	N	3	3	.500	4.31	9	7	4	48	34	43	40	1	0	0	0	20	3	0	.150	3	20	1	3	2.7	.958
1890	BOS	P	18	7	.720	3.60	34	25	19	235	246	167	110	2	4	0	2	110	17	2	.155	21	46	6	2	2.1	.918
1891	BOS	AA	8	6	.571	2.98	19	11	10	126.2	119	81	68	0	1	2	2	59	10	0	.169	4	32	4	1	2.1	.900
3 yrs.			29	16	.644	3.49	62	43	33	409.2	399	291	218	2	5	2	4	189	30	2	.159	28	98	11	6	2.2	.920

Bud Daley

DALEY, LEAVITT LEO BL TL 6'1" 185 lbs.
B. Oct. 7, 1932, Orange, Calif.

1955	CLE	A	0	1	.000	6.43	2	1	0	7	10	1	2	0	0	0	0	2	0	0	.000	0	3	1	0	2.0	.750
1956			1	0	1.000	6.20	14	0	0	20.1	21	14	13	0	1	0	0	2	0	0	.000	4	6	0	0	0.7	1.000
1957			2	8	.200	4.43	34	10	1	87.1	99	40	54	0	1	4	2	20	4	0	.200	6	22	5	2	1.0	.848
1958	KC	A	3	2	.600	3.31	26	5	1	70.2	67	19	39	0	2	0	0	16	2	0	.125	3	16	1	0	0.8	.950
1959			16	13	.552	3.16	39	29	12	216.1	212	62	125	2	1	1	1	78	23	0	.295	10	35	2	2	1.2	.957
1960			16	16	.500	4.56	37	35	13	231	234	96	126	1	1	1	0	75	12	0	.160	19	36	1	4	1.5	.982
1961	2 teams	KC A (16G 4–8)				NY	A	(23G 8–9)																			
"	total		12	17	.414	4.28	39	27	9	193.1	211	73	119	0	1	3	1	63	8	0	.127	16	28	4	3	1.2	.917
1962	NY	A	7	5	.583	3.59	43	6	0	105.1	105	21	55	0	5	3	4	27	5	0	.185	9	17	2	0	0.7	.929
1963			0	0	–	0.00	1	0	0	1	2	0	0	0	0	0	0	0	0	0	–	0	0	0	0	0.0	–

Year	Team	W	L	PCT	ERA	G	GS	CG	IP	H	BB	SO	ShO	W	L	SV	AB	H	HR	BA	PO	A	E	DP	TC/G	FA

Bud Daley *continued*

Year	Team	W	L	PCT	ERA	G	GS	CG	IP	H	BB	SO	ShO	W	L	SV	AB	H	HR	BA	PO	A	E	DP	TC/G	FA
1964		3	2	.600	4.63	13	3	0	35	37	25	16	0	0	2	1	8	2	0	.250	2	9	0	0	0.8	1.000
10 yrs.		60	64	.484	4.03	248	116	36	967.1	998	351	549	3	11	13	10	291	56	0	.192	69	172	16	13	1.0	.938

WORLD SERIES

Year	Team	W	L	PCT	ERA	G	GS	CG	IP	H	BB	SO	ShO	W	L	SV	AB	H	HR	BA	PO	A	E	DP	TC/G	FA
1961	NY A	1	0	1.000	0.00	2	0	0	7	5	0	3	0	1	0	0	1	0	0	.000	0	0	1	0	0.5	—
1962		0	0	—	0.00	1	0	0	1	1	1	0	0	0	0	0	0	0	0	—	0	0	0	0	0.0	—
2 yrs.		1	0	1.000	0.00	3	0	0	8	6	1	3	0	1	0	0	1	0	0	.000	0	0	1	0	0.3	—

George Daly

DALY, GEORGE JOSEPHS (Pecks)
B. July 28, 1887, Buffalo, N. Y.   D. Dec. 12, 1957, Buffalo, N. Y.   BR TR 5'10½" 175 lbs.

Year	Team	W	L	PCT	ERA	G	GS	CG	IP	H	BB	SO	ShO	W	L	SV	AB	H	HR	BA	PO	A	E	DP	TC/G	FA
1909	NY N	0	3	.000	6.00	3	3	3	21	31	8	8	0	0	0	0	9	1	0	.111	0	0	0	0	0.0	—

Bill Dammann

DAMMANN, WILLIAM HENRY (Wee Willie)
B. Aug. 9, 1872, Chicago, Ill.   D. Dec. 6, 1948, Lynnhaven, Va.   BL TL 5'7" 155 lbs.

Year	Team	W	L	PCT	ERA	G	GS	CG	IP	H	BB	SO	ShO	W	L	SV	AB	H	HR	BA	PO	A	E	DP	TC/G	FA
1897	CIN N	6	4	.600	4.74	16	11	7	95	122	37	21	1	1	1	0	31	5	0	.161	4	26	2	0	2.0	.938
1898		16	10	.615	3.61	35	22	16	224.2	277	67	51	2	4	2	2	82	16	0	.195	9	44	7	1	1.7	.883
1899		2	1	.667	4.88	9	5	3	48	74	11	2	1	0	0	1	18	1	0	.056	3	13	2	1	2.0	.889
3 yrs.		24	15	.615	4.06	60	38	26	367.2	473	115	74	4	5	3	3	131	22	0	.168	16	83	11	2	1.8	.900

Lee Daney

DANEY, ARTHUR LEE
Born Arthur Lee Whitehorn.
B. July 9, 1904, Talihina, Okla.   D. Mar. 11, 1988, Phoenix, Ariz.   BR TR 5'11" 165 lbs.

Year	Team	W	L	PCT	ERA	G	GS	CG	IP	H	BB	SO	ShO	W	L	SV	AB	H	HR	BA	PO	A	E	DP	TC/G	FA
1928	PHI A	0	0	—	0.00	1	0	0	1	1	0	0	0	0	0	0	0	0	0	—	0	1	0	0	1.0	1.000

Dave Danforth

DANFORTH, DAVID CHARLES (Dauntless Dave)
B. Mar. 7, 1890, Granger, Tex.   D. Sept. 19, 1970, Baltimore, Md.   BL TL 6' 167 lbs.

Year	Team	W	L	PCT	ERA	G	GS	CG	IP	H	BB	SO	ShO	W	L	SV	AB	H	HR	BA	PO	A	E	DP	TC/G	FA
1911	PHI A	4	1	.800	3.74	14	2	1	33.2	29	17	21	0	3	0	1	6	1	0	.167	3	7	0	0	0.7	1.000
1912		0	0	—	3.98	3	0	0	20.1	26	12	8	0	0	0	0	8	2	0	.250	1	6	0	1	2.3	1.000
1916	CHI A	6	5	.545	3.27	28	8	1	93.2	87	37	49	0	5	0	2	23	2	0	.087	2	32	3	0	1.3	.919
1917		11	6	.647	2.65	50	9	1	173	155	74	79	1	6	3	9	46	6	0	.130	0	42	4	0	0.9	.913
1918		6	15	.286	3.43	39	13	5	139	148	40	48	0	6	6	2	42	6	0	.143	7	39	2	1	1.2	.958
1919		1	2	.333	7.78	15	1	0	41.2	58	20	17	0	1	1	1	9	1	0	.111	1	10	0	0	0.7	1.000
1922	STL A	5	2	.714	3.28	20	10	3	79.2	93	38	48	0	0	0	1	23	2	0	.087	6	11	0	2	0.9	1.000
1923		16	14	.533	3.94	38	29	16	226.1	221	87	96	1	1	2	1	71	15	0	.211	7	40	0	0	1.2	1.000
1924		15	12	.556	4.51	41	27	12	219.2	246	69	65	1	3	2	4	76	13	0	.171	4	40	2	2	1.1	.957
1925		7	9	.438	4.36	38	15	5	159	172	61	53	0	3	2	2	46	8	0	.174	4	21	2	0	0.7	.926
10 yrs.		71	66	.518	3.89	286	114	44	1186	1235	455	484	3	28	16	23	350	56	0	.160	35	248	13	8	1.0	.956

WORLD SERIES

Year	Team	W	L	PCT	ERA	G	GS	CG	IP	H	BB	SO	ShO	W	L	SV	AB	H	HR	BA	PO	A	E	DP	TC/G	FA
1917	CHI A	0	0	—	18.00	1	0	0	1	3	0	0	0	0	0	0	0	0	0	—	0	1	0	0	1.0	1.000

Chuck Daniel

DANIEL, CHARLES EDWARD
B. Sept. 17, 1933, Bluffton, Ark.   BR TR 6'2" 195 lbs.

Year	Team	W	L	PCT	ERA	G	GS	CG	IP	H	BB	SO	ShO	W	L	SV	AB	H	HR	BA	PO	A	E	DP	TC/G	FA
1957	DET A	0	0	—	7.71	1	0	0	2.1	3	0	2	0	0	0	0	0	0	0	—	0	0	0	0	0.0	—

Bennie Daniels

DANIELS, BENNIE
B. June 17, 1932, Tuscaloosa, Ala.   BL TR 6'1½" 193 lbs.

Year	Team	W	L	PCT	ERA	G	GS	CG	IP	H	BB	SO	ShO	W	L	SV	AB	H	HR	BA	PO	A	E	DP	TC/G	FA
1957	PIT N	0	1	.000	1.29	1	1	0	7	5	3	2	0	0	0	0	2	0	0	.000	1	4	1	0	6.0	.833
1958		0	3	.000	5.53	8	5	1	27.2	31	15	7	0	0	0	0	8	1	0	.125	4	10	2	1	2.0	.875
1959		7	9	.438	5.45	34	12	0	100.2	115	39	67	0	4	3	1	29	9	1	.310	6	14	2	0	0.6	.909
1960		1	3	.250	7.81	10	6	0	40.1	52	17	16	0	0	0	0	16	3	0	.188	4	11	0	0	1.5	1.000
1961	WAS A	12	11	.522	3.44	32	28	12	212	184	80	110	1	0	0	0	76	15	2	.197	18	38	3	1	1.8	.949
1962		7	16	.304	4.85	44	21	8	161.1	172	68	66	1	3	3	2	46	6	1	.130	24	45	3	2	1.6	.958
1963		5	10	.333	4.38	35	24	6	168.2	163	58	88	1	0	0	1	46	7	0	.152	16	41	5	0	1.6	.919
1964		8	10	.444	3.70	33	24	3	163	147	64	73	2	1	0	0	47	6	1	.128	10	39	3	4	1.6	.942
1965		5	13	.278	4.72	33	18	1	116.1	135	39	42	0	2	1	1	30	4	0	.133	3	22	0	1	0.8	1.000
9 yrs.		45	76	.372	4.44	230	139	26	997	1004	383	471	5	10	8	5	300	51	5	.170	86	224	19	9	1.4	.942

Charlie Daniels

DANIELS, CHARLES L.
B. July 1, 1861, Roxbury, Mass.   D. Feb. 9, 1938, Boston, Mass.

Year	Team	W	L	PCT	ERA	G	GS	CG	IP	H	BB	SO	ShO	W	L	SV	AB	H	HR	BA	PO	A	E	DP	TC/G	FA
1884	BOS U	0	2	.000	4.32	2	2	2	16.2	20	2	12	0	0	0	0	11	3	0	.273	0	3	1	0	2.0	.750

Pete Daniels

DANIELS, PETER J.
B. Apr. 8, 1864, County Cavan, Ireland   D. Feb. 13, 1928, Indianapolis, Ind.   BL TL

Year	Team	W	L	PCT	ERA	G	GS	CG	IP	H	BB	SO	ShO	W	L	SV	AB	H	HR	BA	PO	A	E	DP	TC/G	FA
1890	PIT N	1	2	.333	7.07	4	4	3	28	40	12	8	0	0	0	0	12	4	0	.333	1	5	2	0	2.0	.750
1898	STL N	1	6	.143	3.62	10	6	3	54.2	62	14	13	0	1	0	0	17	3	0	.176	2	14	4	1	2.0	.800
2 yrs.		2	8	.200	4.79	14	10	6	82.2	102	26	21	0	1	0	0	29	7	0	.241	3	19	6	1	2.0	.786

George Darby

DARBY, GEORGE WILLIAM (Deek)
B. Feb. 6, 1869, Kansas City, Mo.   D. Feb. 25, 1937, Sacramento, Calif.   BL TR 5'10½" 160 lbs.

Year	Team	W	L	PCT	ERA	G	GS	CG	IP	H	BB	SO	ShO	W	L	SV	AB	H	HR	BA	PO	A	E	DP	TC/G	FA
1893	CIN N	1	1	.500	7.76	4	3	2	29	41	18	6	0	0	0	0	10	3	0	.300	0	13	0	0	3.3	1.000

Pat Darcy

DARCY, PATRICK LEONARD
B. May 12, 1950, Troy, Ohio   BR TR 6'3" 175 lbs.

Year	Team	W	L	PCT	ERA	G	GS	CG	IP	H	BB	SO	ShO	W	L	SV	AB	H	HR	BA	PO	A	E	DP	TC/G	FA
1974	CIN N	1	0	1.000	3.71	6	1	0	17	17	8	14	0	0	0	0	3	1	0	.333	0	2	0	0	0.3	1.000
1975		11	5	.688	3.57	27	22	1	131	134	59	46	0	2	0	1	47	4	0	.085	8	21	2	0	1.1	.935
1976		2	3	.400	6.23	11	4	0	39	41	22	15	0	0	1	2	11	2	0	.182	1	5	1	0	0.6	.857
3 yrs.		14	8	.636	4.14	44	28	1	187	192	89	75	0	2	1	3	61	7	0	.115	9	28	3	0	0.9	.925

Year	Team		W	L	PCT	ERA	G	GS	CG	IP	H	BB	SO	ShO	Relief Pitching W	L	SV	Batting AB	H	HR	BA	PO	A	E	DP	TC/G	FA

Pat Darcy *continued*

WORLD SERIES

Year	Team		W	L	PCT	ERA	G	GS	CG	IP	H	BB	SO	ShO	W	L	SV	AB	H	HR	BA	PO	A	E	DP	TC/G	FA
1975	CIN	N	0	1	.000	4.50	2	0	0	4	3	2	1	0	0	1	0	1	0	0	.000	0	1	0	0	0.5	1.000

Alvin Dark

DARK, ALVIN RALPH (Blackie)
B. Jan. 7, 1922, Comanche, Okla.
Manager 1961-64, 1966-71, 1974-75, 1977.

BR TR 5'11" 185 lbs.

| 1953 | NY | N | 0 | 0 | — | 18.00 | 1 | 1 | 0 | 1 | 1 | 1 | 0 | 0 | 0 | 0 | 0 | * | | | | 0 | 0 | 0 | 0 | 0.0 | — |

Ron Darling

DARLING, RONALD MAURICE JR.
B. Aug. 19, 1960, Honolulu, Hawaii

BR TR 6'3" 205 lbs.

1983	NY	N	1	3	.250	2.80	5	5	1	35.1	31	17	23	0	0	0	0	10	1	0	.100	2	6	0	1	1.6	1.000
1984			12	9	.571	3.81	33	33	2	205.2	179	104	136	2	0	0	0	67	10	0	.149	17	38	3	3	1.8	.948
1985			16	6	.727	2.90	36	35	4	248	214	114	167	2	0	0	0	76	13	0	.171	24	47	2	5	2.0	.973
1986			15	6	.714	2.81	34	34	4	237	203	81	184	2	0	0	0	81	8	0	.099	24	47	7	7	2.3	.910
1987			12	8	.600	4.29	32	32	2	207.2	183	96	167	0	0	0	0	65	8	0	.123	17	43	3	5	2.0	.952
1988			17	9	.654	3.25	34	34	7	240.2	218	60	161	4	0	0	0	82	18	0	.220	17	35	3	4	1.6	.945
1989			14	14	.500	3.52	33	33	4	217.1	214	70	153	0	0	0	2	73	9	2	.123	15	37	4	5	1.7	.929
7 yrs.			87	55	.613	3.38	207	206	24	1391.2	1242	542	991	10	0	0	0	454	67	2	.148	116	253	22	30	1.9	.944

LEAGUE CHAMPIONSHIP SERIES

1986	NY	N	0	0	—	7.20	1	1	0	5	6	2	5	0	0	0	0	1	0	0	.000	1	2	0	0	3.0	1.000
1988			0	1	.000	7.71	2	2	0	7	11	4	7	0	0	0	0	3	0	0	.000	1	3	0	0	2.0	1.000
2 yrs.			0	1	.000	7.50	3	3	0	12	17	6	12	0	0	0	0	4	0	0	.000	2	5	0	0	2.3	1.000

WORLD SERIES

| 1986 | NY | N | 1 | 1 | .500 | 1.53 | 3 | 3 | 0 | 17.2 | 13 | 10 | 12 | 0 | 0 | 0 | 0 | 3 | 0 | 0 | .000 | 0 | 4 | 0 | 0 | 1.3 | 1.000 |

Bob Darnell

DARNELL, ROBERT JACK
B. Nov. 6, 1930, Wewoka, Okla.

BR TR 5'10" 175 lbs.

1954	BKN	N	0	0	—	3.14	6	1	0	14.1	15	7	5	0	0	0	0	2	0	0	.000	0	5	0	0	0.8	1.000
1956			0	0	—	0.00	1	0	0	1.1	1	0	0	0	0	0	0	0	0	0	—	0	0	0	0	0.0	—
2 yrs.			0	0	—	2.87	7	1	0	15.2	16	7	5	0	0	0	0	2	0	0	.000	0	5	0	0	0.7	1.000

Mike Darr

DARR, MICHAEL EDWARD
B. Mar. 23, 1956, Pomona, Calif.

BR TR 6'4" 190 lbs.

| 1977 | TOR | A | 0 | 1 | .000 | 45.00 | 1 | 1 | 0 | 1 | 3 | 4 | 1 | 0 | 0 | 0 | 0 | 0 | 0 | 0 | — | 0 | 0 | 0 | 0 | 0.0 | — |

George Darrow

DARROW, GEORGE OLIVER
B. July 12, 1903, Beloit, Kans. D. Mar. 24, 1983, Sun City, Ariz.

BL TL 6' 180 lbs.

| 1934 | PHI | N | 2 | 6 | .250 | 5.51 | 17 | 8 | 2 | 49 | 57 | 28 | 14 | 0 | 1 | 1 | 1 | 15 | 2 | 0 | .133 | 2 | 12 | 2 | 1 | 0.9 | .875 |

Bobby Darwin

DARWIN, ARTHUR BOBBY LEE
B. Feb. 16, 1943, Los Angeles, Calif.

BR TR 6'2" 190 lbs.

1962	LA	A	0	1	.000	10.80	1	1	0	3.1	8	4	6	0	0	0	0	1	0	0	.000	0	0	1	0	1.0	—
1969	LA	N	0	0	—	9.00	3	0	0	4	4	5	0	0	0	0	0	0	0	0	—	0	0	0	0	0.0	—
2 yrs.			0	1	.000	9.82	4	1	0	7.1	12	9	6	0	0	0	0	*				0	0	1	0	0.3	—

Danny Darwin

DARWIN, DANIEL WAYNE
B. Oct. 25, 1955, Bonham, Tex.

BR TR 6'3" 185 lbs.

1978	TEX	A	1	0	1.000	4.15	3	1	0	8.2	11	1	8	0	1	0	0	0	0	0	—	0	0	0	0	0.0	—
1979			4	4	.500	4.04	20	6	1	78	50	30	58	0	1	3	0	0	0	0	—	2	6	0	0	0.4	1.000
1980			13	4	.765	2.62	53	2	0	110	98	50	104	0	12	3	8	0	0	0	—	7	11	0	1	0.3	1.000
1981			9	9	.500	3.64	22	22	6	146	115	57	98	2	0	0	0	0	0	0	—	8	16	2	3	1.2	.923
1982			10	8	.556	3.44	56	1	0	89	95	37	61	0	10	7	7	0	0	0	—	5	19	0	0	0.4	1.000
1983			8	13	.381	3.49	28	26	9	183	175	62	92	2	0	0	0	0	0	0	—	20	18	3	1	1.5	.927
1984			8	12	.400	3.94	35	32	5	223.2	249	54	123	1	0	0	0	0	0	0	—	13	21	3	2	1.1	.919
1985	MIL	A	8	18	.308	3.80	39	29	11	217.2	212	65	125	1	1	2	2	0	0	0	—	15	16	2	1	0.8	.939
1986	2 teams		MIL A	(27G 6–8)		HOU N	(12G 5–2)																					
"	total		11	10	.524	3.17	39	22	6	184.2	170	44	120	1	3	1	0	16	1	0	.063	10	27	3	2	1.0	.925
1987	HOU	N	9	10	.474	3.59	33	30	3	195.2	184	69	134	1	0	0	0	66	12	0	.182	10	22	2	0	1.0	.941
1988			8	13	.381	3.84	44	20	3	192	189	48	129	0	4	3	3	56	4	1	.071	14	37	1	2	1.2	.981
1989			11	4	.733	2.36	68	0	0	122	92	33	104	0	11	4	7	17	2	0	.118	2	12	2	2	0.2	.875
12 yrs.			100	105	.488	3.51	440	191	44	1750.1	1640	550	1156	8	43	23	27	155	19	1	.123	106	205	18	14	0.7	.945

Lee Dashner

DASHNER, LEE CLAIRE (Lefty)
B. Apr. 25, 1887, Renault, Ill. D. Dec. 16, 1959, El Dorado, Kans.

BB TL 5'11½" 192 lbs.

| 1913 | CLE | A | 0 | 0 | — | 5.40 | 1 | 0 | 0 | 1.2 | 1 | 1 | 2 | 0 | 0 | 0 | 0 | 0 | 0 | 0 | — | 0 | 0 | 0 | 0 | 0.0 | — |

Frank Dasso

DASSO, FRANCIS JOSEPH NICHOLAS
B. Aug. 31, 1917, Chicago, Ill.

BR TR 5'11½" 185 lbs.

1945	CIN	N	4	5	.444	3.67	16	12	6	95.2	89	53	39	0	1	1	0	31	5	0	.161	6	19	0	1	1.6	1.000
1946			0	0	—	27.00	2	0	0	1	2	2	1	0	0	0	0	0	0	0	—	0	0	0	0	0.0	—
2 yrs.			4	5	.444	3.91	18	12	6	96.2	91	55	40	0	1	1	0	31	5	0	.161	6	19	0	1	1.4	1.000

Dan Daub

DAUB, DANIEL WILLIAM (Mickey)
B. Jan. 12, 1868, Middletown, Ohio D. Mar. 25, 1951, Bradenton, Fla.

BR TR 5'10" 160 lbs.

1892	CIN	N	1	2	.333	2.88	4	3	2	25	23	13	7	0	0	0	0	7	0	0	.000	1	6	1	0	2.0	.875
1893	BKN	N	6	6	.500	3.84	12	12	12	103	104	61	25	0	0	0	0	42	8	0	.190	7	35	2	1	3.7	.955
1894			9	12	.429	6.32	33	26	14	215	283	90	45	0	0	0	0	92	16	0	.174	4	42	7	0	1.6	.868

Year	Team	W	L	PCT	ERA	G	GS	CG	IP	H	BB	SO	ShO	W	L	SV	AB	H	HR	BA	PO	A	E	DP	TC/G	FA
														Relief Pitching			Batting									

Dan Daub *continued*

Year	Team	W	L	PCT	ERA	G	GS	CG	IP	H	BB	SO	ShO	W	L	SV	AB	H	HR	BA	PO	A	E	DP	TC/G	FA
1895		10	10	.500	4.29	25	21	16	184.2	212	51	36	0	1	0	0	71	14	0	.197	3	54	3	3	2.4	.950
1896		12	11	.522	3.60	32	24	18	225	255	63	53	0	2	0	0	84	19	0	.226	8	74	2	1	2.6	.976
1897		6	11	.353	6.08	19	16	11	137.2	180	48	19	0	2	1	0	49	11	0	.224	5	32	4	2	2.2	.902
6 yrs.		44	52	.458	4.79	125	102	73	890.1	1057	326	185	0	5	1	0	345	68	0	.197	28	243	19	7	2.3	.934

Hooks Dauss

DAUSS, GEORGE AUGUST
Born George August Daus.
B. Sept. 22, 1889, Indianapolis, Ind.   D. July 27, 1963, St. Louis, Mo.

BR TR 5'10½" 168 lbs.

Year	Team	W	L	PCT	ERA	G	GS	CG	IP	H	BB	SO	ShO	W	L	SV	AB	H	HR	BA	PO	A	E	DP	TC/G	FA
1912	DET A	1	1	.500	3.18	2	2	2	17	11	9	7	0	0	0	0	4	1	0	.250	0	8	0	0	4.0	1.000
1913		13	12	.520	2.68	33	29	22	225	188	82	107	2	0	1	1	79	14	0	.177	8	64	9	2	2.5	.889
1914		18	15	.545	2.86	45	35	22	302	286	87	150	3	1	2	4	97	21	1	.216	9	89	4	1	2.3	.961
1915		24	13	.649	2.50	46	35	27	309.2	261	112	132	1	3	2	2	103	15	0	.146	11	137	5	3	3.3	.967
1916		19	12	.613	3.21	39	29	18	238.2	220	90	95	1	4	0	4	72	16	1	.222	5	85	6	2	2.5	.938
1917		17	14	.548	2.43	37	31	22	270.2	243	87	102	6	0	0	0	87	11	0	.126	10	100	4	2	3.1	.965
1918		12	16	.429	2.99	33	26	21	249.2	243	58	73	1	1	3	3	77	14	0	.182	6	79	4	1	2.7	.955
1919		21	9	.700	3.55	34	32	22	256.1	262	63	73	2	1	0	0	97	14	0	.144	5	101	2	6	3.2	.981
1920		13	21	.382	3.56	38	32	16	270.1	308	84	82	0	1	0	0	83	14	0	.169	7	114	2	0	3.2	.984
1921		10	15	.400	4.33	32	28	16	233	275	81	68	0	1	1	1	88	23	1	.261	10	84	1	2	3.0	.989
1922		13	13	.500	4.20	39	25	12	218.2	251	59	78	1	5	1	4	72	15	1	.208	5	61	2	1	1.7	.971
1923		21	13	.618	3.62	50	39	22	316	331	78	105	4	1	0	3	104	24	0	.231	6	92	1	2	2.0	.990
1924		12	11	.522	4.59	40	10	5	131.1	155	40	44	0	8	5	6	38	5	0	.132	4	32	0	1	0.9	1.000
1925		16	11	.593	3.16	35	30	16	228	238	85	58	1	2	1	1	81	15	1	.185	7	52	1	2	1.7	.983
1926		12	6	.667	4.20	35	5	0	124.1	135	49	27	0	11	4	9	42	10	1	.238	7	30	1	0	1.1	.974
15 yrs.		222	182	.550	3.32	538	388	245	3390.2	3407	1064	1201	22	40	23	40	1124	212	6	.189	100	1128	42	25	2.4	.967

Vic Davalillo

DAVALILLO, VICTOR JOSE
Born Victor Jose Davalillo y Romero.   Brother of Yo-Yo Davalillo.
B. July 31, 1936, Cabimas, Venezuela

BL TL 5'7" 150 lbs.

Year	Team	W	L	PCT	ERA	G	GS	CG	IP	H	BB	SO	ShO	W	L	SV	AB	H	HR	BA	PO	A	E	DP	TC/G	FA
1969	2 teams	CAL A	(0G 0–0)			STL N	(2G 0–0)																			
"	total	0	0	–	∞	2	0	0		2	2	0	0	0	0	0	*				0	0	0	0	0.0	–

Claude Davenport

DAVENPORT, CLAUDE EDWIN
Brother of Dave Davenport.
B. May 28, 1898, Runge, Tex.   D. June 13, 1976, Corpus Christi, Tex.

BR TR 6'6" 193 lbs.

Year	Team	W	L	PCT	ERA	G	GS	CG	IP	H	BB	SO	ShO	W	L	SV	AB	H	HR	BA	PO	A	E	DP	TC/G	FA
1920	NY N	0	0	–	4.50	1	0	0	2	2	1	0	0	0	0	0	1	0	0	.000	0	0	0	0	0.0	–

Dave Davenport

DAVENPORT, DAVID W. (Big Dave)
Brother of Claude Davenport.
B. Feb. 20, 1890, DeRidder, La.   D. Oct. 16, 1954, El Dorado, Ark.

BR TR 6'6" 220 lbs.

Year	Team	W	L	PCT	ERA	G	GS	CG	IP	H	BB	SO	ShO	W	L	SV	AB	H	HR	BA	PO	A	E	DP	TC/G	FA
1914	2 teams	CIN N	(10G 2–2)			STL F	(33G 8–13)																			
"	total	10	15	.400	3.27	43	32	16	269.2	242	110	164	3	0	4	6	86	8	0	.093	10	76	3	3	2.1	.966
1915	STL F	22	18	.550	2.20	55	46	30	392.2	300	96	229	10	0	2	1	130	12	0	.092	1	79	4	2	1.5	.952
1916	STL A	12	11	.522	2.85	59	31	13	290.2	267	100	129	1	2	3	2	73	10	0	.137	2	72	5	2	1.3	.937
1917		17	17	.500	3.08	47	39	19	280.2	273	105	100	2	0	0	2	92	9	0	.098	4	83	6	0	2.0	.935
1918		10	11	.476	3.25	31	22	12	180	182	69	60	2	0	0	1	52	7	1	.135	3	61	7	2	2.3	.901
1919		3	11	.214	3.94	24	16	5	123.1	135	41	37	0	1	1	0	39	3	0	.077	5	36	1	2	1.8	.976
6 yrs.		74	83	.471	2.93	259	186	95	1537	1399	521	719	18	3	10	12	472	49	1	.104	25	407	26	11	1.8	.943

Lum Davenport

DAVENPORT, JOUBERT LUM
B. June 27, 1900, Tucson, Ariz.   D. Apr. 21, 1961, Dallas, Tex.

BL TL 6'1" 165 lbs.

Year	Team	W	L	PCT	ERA	G	GS	CG	IP	H	BB	SO	ShO	W	L	SV	AB	H	HR	BA	PO	A	E	DP	TC/G	FA
1921	CHI A	0	3	.000	6.88	13	2	0	35.1	41	32	9	0	0	0	0	17	7	0	.412	0	9	2	1	0.8	.818
1922		1	1	.500	10.80	9	1	0	16.2	14	13	9	0	0	1	0	3	0	0	.000	0	6	0	0	0.7	1.000
1923		0	0	–	6.23	2	0	0	4.1	7	4	1	0	0	0	0	1	1	0	1.000	0	1	0	0	0.5	1.000
1924		0	0	–	0.00	1	0	0	2	1	2	1	0	0	0	0	0	0	0	–	0	0	1	0	1.0	–
4 yrs.		1	4	.200	7.71	25	3	0	58.1	63	51	20	0	0	3	0	21	8	0	.381	0	16	3	1	0.8	.842

Mike Davey

DAVEY, MICHAEL GERARD
B. June 2, 1952, Spokane, Wash.

BR TL 6'2" 190 lbs.

Year	Team	W	L	PCT	ERA	G	GS	CG	IP	H	BB	SO	ShO	W	L	SV	AB	H	HR	BA	PO	A	E	DP	TC/G	FA
1977	ATL N	0	0	–	5.06	16	0	0	16	19	9	7	0	0	0	2	1	0	0	.000	3	1	0	0	0.3	1.000
1978		0	0	–	0.00	3	0	0	3	1	1	0	0	0	0	0	0	0	0	–	0	0	0	0	0.0	–
2 yrs.		0	0	–	4.26	19	0	0	19	20	10	7	0	0	0	2	1	0	0	.000	3	1	0	0	0.2	1.000

Ray Daviault

DAVIAULT, RAYMOND JOSEPH ROBERT
B. May 27, 1934, Montreal, Que., Canada

BR TR 6'1" 170 lbs.

Year	Team	W	L	PCT	ERA	G	GS	CG	IP	H	BB	SO	ShO	W	L	SV	AB	H	HR	BA	PO	A	E	DP	TC/G	FA
1962	NY N	1	5	.167	6.22	36	3	0	81	92	48	51	0	1	3	0	15	1	0	.067	9	6	0	0	0.4	1.000

Bobby Davidson

DAVIDSON, ROBERT BANKS
B. Jan. 6, 1963, Bad Kurznach, W. Germany

BR TR 6' 185 lbs.

Year	Team	W	L	PCT	ERA	G	GS	CG	IP	H	BB	SO	ShO	W	L	SV	AB	H	HR	BA	PO	A	E	DP	TC/G	FA
1989	NY A	0	0	–	18.00	1	0	0	1	1	0	1	0	0	0	0	0	0	0	–	0	0	0	0	0.0	–

Ted Davidson

DAVIDSON, THOMAS EUGENE
B. Oct. 4, 1939, Las Vegas, Nev.

BR TL 6' 192 lbs.

Year	Team	W	L	PCT	ERA	G	GS	CG	IP	H	BB	SO	ShO	W	L	SV	AB	H	HR	BA	PO	A	E	DP	TC/G	FA
1965	CIN N	4	3	.571	2.23	24	1	0	68.2	57	17	54	0	3	3	1	17	0	0	.000	1	14	1	1	0.7	.938
1966		5	4	.556	3.90	54	0	0	85.1	82	23	54	0	5	4	4	12	0	0	.000	3	14	1	0	0.3	.944
1967		1	0	1.000	4.15	9	0	0	13	13	3	6	0	1	0	0	0	0	0	–	0	4	0	0	0.4	1.000
1968	2 teams	CIN N	(23G 1–0)			ATL N	(4G 0–0)																			
"	total	1	0	1.000	6.35	27	0	0	28.1	37	11	10	0	1	0	0	2	0	0	.000	0	7	0	0	0.3	1.000
4 yrs.		11	7	.611	3.69	114	1	0	195.1	189	54	124	0	10	7	5	31	0	0	.000	4	39	2	1	0.4	.956

Year	Team		W	L	PCT	ERA	G	GS	CG	IP	H	BB	SO	ShO	Relief Pitching W	L	SV	Batting AB	H	HR	BA	PO	A	E	DP	TC/G	FA

Jerry Davie

DAVIE, GERALD LEE
B. Feb. 10, 1933, Detroit, Mich.

BR TR 6' 180 lbs.

Year	Team		W	L	PCT	ERA	G	GS	CG	IP	H	BB	SO	ShO	W	L	SV	AB	H	HR	BA	PO	A	E	DP	TC/G	FA
1959	DET	A	2	2	.500	4.17	11	5	1	36.2	40	17	20	0	0	0	0	10	4	0	.400	4	9	0	0	1.2	1.000

Chick Davies

DAVIES, LLOYD GARRISON
B. Mar. 6, 1892, Peabody, Mass.   D. Sept. 5, 1973, Middletown, Conn.

BL TL 5'8" 145 lbs.

Year	Team		W	L	PCT	ERA	G	GS	CG	IP	H	BB	SO	ShO	W	L	SV	AB	H	HR	BA	PO	A	E	DP	TC/G	FA
1914	PHI	A	1	0	1.000	1.00	1	1	0	9	8	3	4	0	0	0	0	46	11	0	.239	0	3	1	1	4.0	.750
1915			1	2	.333	8.80	4	2	0	15.1	20	12	2	0	1	0	0	132	24	0	.182	3	6	0	0	2.3	1.000
1925	NY	N	0	0	—	6.14	2	1	0	7.1	13	4	5	0	0	0	0	6	0	0	.000	0	3	0	0	1.5	1.000
1926			2	4	.333	3.94	38	1	0	89	96	35	27	0	2	3	6	18	4	0	.222	4	26	2	2	0.8	.938
4 yrs.			4	6	.400	4.48	45	5	1	120.2	137	54	38	0	3	3	6	*				7	38	3	3	1.1	.938

George Davies

DAVIES, GEORGE WASHINGTON
B. Feb. 22, 1868, Portage, Wis.   D. Sept. 22, 1906, Waterloo, Wis.

180 lbs.

Year	Team		W	L	PCT	ERA	G	GS	CG	IP	H	BB	SO	ShO	W	L	SV	AB	H	HR	BA	PO	A	E	DP	TC/G	FA
1891	MIL	AA	7	5	.583	2.66	12	12	12	101.2	94	35	61	1	0	0	0	37	9	0	.243	2	18	2	0	1.8	.909
1892	CLE	N	10	16	.385	2.59	26	26	23	215.2	201	69	95	0	0	0	0	87	12	0	.138	8	61	9	2	3.0	.885
1893	2 teams		CLE N	(3G 0–2)		NY N	(5G 1–1)																					
"	total		1	3	.250	7.71	8	4	2	51.1	69	23	10	0	0	0	0	18	6	0	.333	3	16	3	0	2.8	.864
3 yrs.			18	24	.429	3.32	46	42	37	368.2	364	127	166	1	0	0	0	142	27	0	.190	13	95	14	2	2.7	.885

Bob Davis

DAVIS, ROBERT EDWARD
B. Sept. 11, 1933, New York, N. Y.

BR TR 6' 170 lbs.

Year	Team		W	L	PCT	ERA	G	GS	CG	IP	H	BB	SO	ShO	W	L	SV	AB	H	HR	BA	PO	A	E	DP	TC/G	FA
1958	KC	A	0	4	.000	7.84	8	4	0	31	45	12	22	0	0	0	0	6	1	0	.167	0	7	1	1	1.0	.875
1960			0	0	—	3.66	21	0	0	32	31	22	28	0	0	0	1	4	1	0	.250	7	7	0	1	0.7	1.000
2 yrs.			0	4	.000	5.71	29	4	0	63	76	34	50	0	0	0	1	10	2	0	.200	7	14	1	2	0.8	.955

Bud Davis

DAVIS, JOHN WILBUR (Country)
B. July 7, 1896, Merry Point, Va.   D. May 26, 1967, Williamsburg, Va.

BL TR 6' 207 lbs.

Year	Team		W	L	PCT	ERA	G	GS	CG	IP	H	BB	SO	ShO	W	L	SV	AB	H	HR	BA	PO	A	E	DP	TC/G	FA
1915	PHI	A	0	2	.000	4.05	18	2	2	66.2	65	59	18	0	0	0	0	26	8	0	.308	0	20	4	1	1.3	.833

Curt Davis

DAVIS, CURTIS BENTON (Coonskin)
B. Sept. 7, 1903, Greenfield, Mo.   D. Oct. 13, 1965, Covina, Calif.

BR TR 6'2" 185 lbs.

Year	Team		W	L	PCT	ERA	G	GS	CG	IP	H	BB	SO	ShO	W	L	SV	AB	H	HR	BA	PO	A	E	DP	TC/G	FA
1934	PHI	N	19	17	.528	2.95	51	31	18	274.1	283	60	99	3	6	2	5	95	20	1	.211	21	95	8	12	2.4	.935
1935			16	14	.533	3.66	44	27	19	231	264	47	74	3	2	2	2	75	13	1	.173	21	50	2	4	1.7	.973
1936	2 teams		PHI N	(10G 2–4)		CHI N	(24G 11–9)																					
"	total		13	13	.500	3.46	34	28	13	213.1	217	50	70	0	1	2	1	79	12	0	.152	21	53	3	5	2.3	.961
1937	CHI	N	10	5	.667	4.08	28	14	8	123.2	138	30	32	0	1	1	1	40	12	1	.300	10	34	1	1	1.6	.978
1938	STL	N	12	8	.600	3.63	40	21	8	173.1	187	27	36	2	4	0	3	57	13	3	.228	9	38	0	2	1.2	1.000
1939			22	16	.579	3.63	49	31	13	248	279	48	70	3	5	5	7	105	40	1	.381	7	59	1	2	1.4	.985
1940	2 teams		STL N	(14G 0–4)		BKN N	(22G 8–7)																					
"	total		8	11	.421	4.19	36	25	9	191	208	38	58	0	1	1	3	66	6	1	.091	18	48	2	1	1.9	.971
1941	BKN	N	13	7	.650	2.97	28	16	10	154.1	141	27	50	5	2	3	2	59	11	2	.186	3	55	1	0	2.1	.983
1942			15	6	.714	2.36	32	26	13	206	179	51	60	5	2	0	2	68	12	0	.176	6	61	0	7	2.1	1.000
1943			10	13	.435	3.78	31	21	8	164.1	182	39	47	2	3	1	3	55	9	0	.164	13	43	1	2	1.8	.982
1944			10	11	.476	3.34	31	23	12	194	207	39	49	1	1	0	4	63	10	0	.159	9	47	1	1	1.8	.982
1945			10	10	.500	3.25	24	18	10	149.2	171	21	39	0	0	0	1	51	7	1	.137	8	32	1	0	1.7	.976
1946			0	0	—	13.50	1	0	0	2	3	2	0	0	0	0	0	0	0	0	—	0	1	0	0	1.0	1.000
13 yrs.			158	131	.547	3.42	429	281	141	2325	2459	479	684	24	26	19	33	813	165	11	.203	146	616	21	37	1.8	.973

WORLD SERIES

Year	Team		W	L	PCT	ERA	G	GS	CG	IP	H	BB	SO	ShO	W	L	SV	AB	H	HR	BA	PO	A	E	DP	TC/G	FA
1941	BKN	N	0	1	.000	5.06	1	1	0	5.1	6	3	1	0	0	0	0	2	0	0	.000	1	0	0	0	1.0	1.000

Daisy Davis

DAVIS, JOHN A.
B. May 17, 1858, Boston, Mass.   Deceased.

Year	Team		W	L	PCT	ERA	G	GS	CG	IP	H	BB	SO	ShO	W	L	SV	AB	H	HR	BA	PO	A	E	DP	TC/G	FA
1884	2 teams		STL AA	(25G 10–12)		BOS N	(4G 1–3)																					
"	total		11	15	.423	3.57	29	28	23	229.1	246	43	156	1	0	0	0	103	15	0	.146	10	40	14	1	2.2	.781
1885	BOS	N	5	6	.455	4.29	11	11	10	94.1	110	28	30	1	0	0	0	37	7	0	.189	1	16	1	0	1.6	.944
2 yrs.			16	21	.432	3.78	40	39	33	323.2	356	71	186	2	0	0	0	140	22	0	.157	11	56	15	1	2.1	.817

Dixie Davis

DAVIS, FRANK TALMADGE
B. Oct. 12, 1890, Wilson Mills, N. C.   D. Feb. 4, 1944, Raleigh, N. C.

BR TR 5'11" 155 lbs.

Year	Team		W	L	PCT	ERA	G	GS	CG	IP	H	BB	SO	ShO	W	L	SV	AB	H	HR	BA	PO	A	E	DP	TC/G	FA
1912	CIN	N	0	1	.000	2.70	7	0	0	26.2	25	16	12	0	0	0	1	10	2	0	.200	0	4	0	0	0.6	1.000
1915	CHI	A	0	0	—	0.00	2	0	0	3	2	2	2	0	0	0	0	0	0	0	—	0	1	0	0	0.5	1.000
1916	PHI	N	0	2	.000	3.06	17	2	1	47	43	30	18	0	0	0	0	9	0	0	.000	4	7	2	0	0.8	.846
1920	STL	A	18	12	.600	3.17	38	31	22	269.1	250	149	85	0	1	0	0	94	25	0	.266	13	47	3	3	1.7	.952
1921			16	16	.500	4.44	40	36	20	265.1	279	123	100	2	0	0	0	95	20	0	.211	19	54	1	3	1.9	.986
1922			11	6	.647	4.08	25	25	7	174.1	162	87	65	2	0	0	0	59	8	0	.136	8	40	2	2	2.0	.960
1923			4	6	.400	3.62	19	17	5	109.1	106	63	36	1	0	0	0	40	10	0	.250	5	18	2	2	1.3	.920
1924			11	13	.458	4.10	29	24	11	160.1	159	72	45	5	1	0	0	46	7	0	.152	10	29	2	7	1.4	.951
1925			12	7	.632	4.59	35	23	9	180.1	192	106	58	0	2	1	1	64	11	0	.172	8	49	4	3	1.7	.934
1926			3	8	.273	4.66	27	7	2	83	93	40	39	0	3	3	1	24	4	0	.167	2	19	1	0	0.8	.955
10 yrs.			75	71	.514	3.97	239	165	77	1318.2	1311	688	460	10	7	5	2	441	87	0	.197	69	268	17	20	1.5	.952

George Davis

DAVIS, GEORGE ALLEN (Iron)
B. Mar. 9, 1890, Lancaster, N. Y.   D. June 4, 1961, Buffalo, N. Y.

BB TR 5'10½" 175 lbs.

Year	Team		W	L	PCT	ERA	G	GS	CG	IP	H	BB	SO	ShO	W	L	SV	AB	H	HR	BA	PO	A	E	DP	TC/G	FA
1912	NY	A	1	4	.200	6.50	10	4	2	54	61	28	22	0	0	0	0	18	2	0	.111	0	9	0	0	0.9	1.000
1913	BOS	N	0	0	—	4.50	2	0	0	8	7	5	3	0	0	0	0	2	0	0	.000	0	1	1	0	1.0	.500
1914			3	3	.500	3.40	9	6	4	55.2	42	24	26	1	0	0	0	18	3	0	.167	1	7	0	0	0.9	1.000
1915			3	3	.500	3.80	15	9	4	73.1	85	19	26	0	0	0	0	23	6	0	.261	2	21	1	1	1.6	.958
4 yrs.			7	10	.412	4.48	36	22	13	191	195	78	77	1	0	0	0	61	11	0	.180	3	38	2	1	1.2	.953

Year	Team		W	L	PCT	ERA	G	GS	CG	IP	H	BB	SO	ShO	Relief Pitching W	L	SV	Batting AB	H	HR	BA	PO	A	E	DP	TC/G	FA

George Davis

DAVIS, GEORGE STACEY
B. Aug. 23, 1870, Cohoes, N. Y.   D. Oct. 17, 1940, Philadelphia, Pa.
Manager 1895, 1900-01.

BB TR 5'9"   180 lbs.

| 1891 | CLE | N | 0 | 1 | .000 | 15.75 | 3 | 0 | 0 | 4 | 8 | 3 | 4 | 0 | 0 | 1 | 1 | * | | | | 0 | 0 | 0 | 0 | 0.0 | – |

Jim Davis

DAVIS, JAMES BENNETT
B. Sept. 15, 1924, Red Bluff, Calif.

BB TL 6'   180 lbs.

1954	CHI	N	11	7	.611	3.52	46	12	2	127.2	114	51	58	0	6	2	4	32	2	0	.0^3	13	24	1	0	0.8	.974
1955			7	11	.389	4.44	42	16	0	133.2	122	58	62	0	5	3	3	37	1	0	.027	5	22	1	0	0.7	.964
1956			5	7	.417	3.66	46	11	2	120.1	116	59	66	1	3	2	2	28	5	0	.179	2	23	0	3	0.5	1.000
1957	2 teams	STL N (10G 0–1)				NY N (10G 1–0)																				
"	total		1	1	.500	5.84	20	0	0	24.2	31	11	11	0	1	1	1	2	1	0	.500	0	6	1	1	0.4	.857
4 yrs.			24	26	.480	4.01	154	39	4	406.1	383	179	197	1	15	8	10	99	9	0	.091	20	75	3	4	0.6	.969

Joel Davis

DAVIS, JOEL CLARK
B. Jan. 30, 1965, Jacksonville, Fla.

BL TR 6'5"   205 lbs.

1985	CHI	A	3	3	.500	4.16	12	11	1	71.1	71	26	37	0	0	0	0	0	0	0	–	4	3	1	1	0.7	.875
1986			4	5	.444	4.70	19	19	1	105.1	115	51	54	0	0	0	0	0	0	0	–	7	18	2	1	1.4	.926
1987			1	5	.167	5.73	13	9	1	55	56	29	25	0	0	0	0	0	0	0	–	5	1	1	1	0.5	.857
1988			0	1	.000	6.75	5	2	0	16	21	5	10	0	0	0	1	0	0	0	–	1	1	0	0	0.4	1.000
4 yrs.			8	14	.364	4.91	49	41	3	247.2	263	111	126	0	0	0	1	0	0	0	–	17	23	4	3	0.9	.909

John Davis

DAVIS, JOHN KIRK
B. Jan. 5, 1963, Chicago, Ill.

BR TR 6'7"   215 lbs.

1987	KC	A	5	2	.714	2.27	27	0	0	43.2	29	26	24	0	5	2	2	0	0	0	–	5	7	1	1	0.5	.923
1988	CHI	A	2	5	.286	6.64	34	1	0	63.2	77	50	37	0	2	4	1	0	0	0	–	5	7	1	1	0.4	.923
1989			0	1	.000	4.50	4	0	0	6	5	2	5	0	0	1	1	0	0	0	–	0	1	0	0	0.3	1.000
3 yrs.			7	8	.467	4.84	65	1	0	113.1	111	78	66	0	7	7	4	0	0	0	–	10	15	2	2	0.4	.926

Mark Davis

DAVIS, MARK WILLIAM
B. Oct. 19, 1960, Livermore, Calif.

BL TL 6'3"   180 lbs.

1980	PHI	N	0	0	–	2.57	2	1	0	7	4	5	5	0	0	0	0	2	1	0	.500	0	0	0	0	0.0	–
1981			1	4	.200	7.74	9	9	0	43	49	24	29	0	0	0	0	11	1	0	.091	0	6	0	0	0.7	1.000
1983	SF	N	6	4	.600	3.49	20	20	0	111	93	50	83	2	0	0	0	30	4	0	.133	4	13	0	0	0.9	1.000
1984			5	17	.227	5.36	46	27	1	174.2	201	54	124	0	3	4	0	46	6	0	.130	1	22	3	1	0.6	.885
1985			5	12	.294	3.54	77	1	0	114.1	89	41	131	0	5	11	7	12	3	0	.250	2	12	0	0	0.2	1.000
1986			5	7	.417	2.99	67	2	0	84.1	63	34	90	0	5	6	4	8	1	0	.125	3	11	3	1	0.3	.824
1987	2 teams	SF N (20G 4–5)				SD N (43G 5–3)																				
"	total		9	8	.529	3.99	63	11	1	133	123	59	98	0	5	3	2	30	7	0	.233	4	20	2	3	0.4	.923
1988	SD	N	5	10	.333	2.01	62	0	0	98.1	70	42	102	0	5	10	28	10	2	1	.200	4	21	1	2	0.4	.962
1989			4	3	.571	1.85	70	0	0	92.2	66	31	92	0	4	3	44	13	0	0	.000	1	11	3	0	0.2	.800
9 yrs.			40	65	.381	3.76	416	71	4	858.1	758	340	754	2	27	37	85	162	25	1	.154	19	116	12	7	0.4	.918

Peaches Davis

DAVIS, RAY THOMAS
B. May 31, 1905, Glen Rose, Tex.

BL TR 6'3½"   190 lbs.

1936	CIN	N	8	8	.500	3.58	26	15	5	125.2	139	36	32	0	2	1	5	43	7	0	.163	14	26	3	0	1.7	.930
1937			11	13	.458	3.59	42	24	11	218	252	51	59	1	1	3	3	78	10	0	.128	21	31	5	2	1.4	.912
1938			7	12	.368	3.97	29	19	11	167.2	193	40	28	1	1	2	1	61	15	0	.246	1	23	1	2	0.9	.960
1939			1	0	1.000	6.46	20	0	0	30.2	43	11	4	0	1	0	2	3	1	0	.333	2	8	0	0	0.5	1.000
4 yrs.			27	33	.450	3.87	117	58	27	542	627	138	123	2	5	6	11	185	33	0	.178	38	88	9	4	1.2	.933

Ron Davis

DAVIS, RONALD GENE
B. Aug. 6, 1955, Houston, Tex.

BR TR 6'4"   205 lbs.

1978	NY	A	0	0		11.57	4	0	0	2.1	3	3	0	0	0	0	0	0	0	0	–	1	0	0	0	0.3	1.000
1979			14	2	.875	2.86	44	0	0	85	84	28	43	0	14	2	9	1	0	0	.000	5	15	0	2	0.5	1.000
1980			9	3	.750	2.95	53	0	0	131	121	32	65	0	9	3	7	1	0	0	.000	4	23	1	0	0.5	.964
1981			4	5	.444	2.71	43	0	0	73	47	25	83	0	4	5	6	0	0	0	–	4	5	0	0	0.2	1.000
1982	MIN	A	3	9	.250	4.42	63	0	0	106	106	47	89	0	3	9	22	0	0	0	–	6	10	0	1	0.3	1.000
1983			5	8	.385	3.34	66	0	0	89	89	33	84	0	5	8	30	0	0	0	–	0	4	1	0	0.1	.800
1984			7	11	.389	4.55	64	0	0	83	79	41	74	0	7	11	29	0	0	0	–	4	8	0	0	0.2	1.000
1985			2	6	.250	3.48	57	0	0	64.2	55	35	72	0	2	6	25	0	0	0	–	3	5	0	1	0.1	1.000
1986	2 teams	MIN A (36G 2–6)				CHI N (17G 0–2)																				
"	total		2	8	.200	8.59	53	0	0	58.2	86	32	40	0	2	8	2	2	0	0	.000	6	6	1	0	0.2	.923
1987	2 teams	CHI N (21G 0–0)				LA N (4G 0–0)																				
"	total		0	0		5.94	25	0	0	36.1	50	18	32	0	0	0	0	0	0	0	–	1	3	0	2	0.2	1.000
1988	SF	N	1	1	.500	4.67	9	0	0	17.1	15	6	15	0	1	1	0	2	0	0	.000	1	4	1	0	0.7	.833
11 yrs.			47	53	.470	4.05	481	0	0	746.1	735	300	597	0	47	53	130	6	0	0	.000	35	83	4	6	0.3	.967

DIVISIONAL PLAYOFF SERIES

| 1981 | NY | A | 1 | 0 | 1.000 | 0.00 | 3 | 0 | 0 | 6 | 1 | 2 | 6 | 0 | 1 | 0 | 0 | 0 | 0 | 0 | – | 0 | 0 | 0 | 0 | 0.0 | – |

LEAGUE CHAMPIONSHIP SERIES

1980	NY	A	0	0	–	2.25	1	0	0	4	3	1	3	0	0	0	0	0	0	0	–	0	2	0	0	2.0	1.000
1981			0	0	–	0.00	2	0	0	3.1	0	2	4	0	0	0	0	0	0	0	–	0	0	0	0	0.0	–
2 yrs.			0	0	–	1.23	3	0	0	7.1	3	3	7	0	0	0	0	0	0	0	–	0	2	0	0	0.7	1.000

WORLD SERIES

| 1981 | NY | A | 0 | 0 | – | 23.14 | 4 | 0 | 0 | 2.1 | 4 | 5 | 4 | 0 | 0 | 0 | 0 | 0 | 0 | 0 | – | 0 | 0 | 0 | 0 | 0.0 | – |

Steve Davis

DAVIS, STEVEN KENNON
B. Aug. 4, 1960, San Antonio, Tex.

BL TL 6'1"   183 lbs.

| 1985 | TOR | A | 2 | 1 | .667 | 3.54 | 10 | 5 | 0 | 28 | 23 | 13 | 22 | 0 | 1 | 0 | 0 | 0 | 0 | 0 | – | 0 | 4 | 0 | 0 | 0.4 | 1.000 |
| 1986 | | | 0 | 0 | – | 17.18 | 3 | 0 | 0 | 3.2 | 8 | 5 | 5 | 0 | 0 | 0 | 0 | 0 | 0 | 0 | – | 0 | 0 | 0 | 0 | 0.0 | – |

Year	Team		W	L	PCT	ERA	G	GS	CG	IP	H	BB	SO	ShO	Relief Pitching W	L	SV	Batting AB	H	HR	BA	PO	A	E	DP	TC/G	FA

Steve Davis *continued*

Year	Team		W	L	PCT	ERA	G	GS	CG	IP	H	BB	SO	ShO	W	L	SV	AB	H	HR	BA	PO	A	E	DP	TC/G	FA
1989	CLE	A	1	1	.500	8.06	12	2	0	25.2	34	14	12	0	0	0	0	0	0	0	–	1	3	0	0	0.3	1.000
3 yrs.			3	2	.600	6.44	25	7	0	57.1	65	32	39	0	1	0	0	0	0	0	–	1	7	0	0	0.3	1.000

Storm Davis

DAVIS, GEORGE EARL
B. Dec. 26, 1961, Dallas, Tex.

BR TR 6'4" 210 lbs.

Year	Team		W	L	PCT	ERA	G	GS	CG	IP	H	BB	SO	ShO	W	L	SV	AB	H	HR	BA	PO	A	E	DP	TC/G	FA
1982	BAL	A	8	4	.667	3.49	29	8	1	100.2	96	28	67	0	3	2	0	0	0	0	–	6	12	1	0	0.7	.947
1983			13	7	.650	3.59	34	29	6	200.1	180	64	125	1	0	0	0	0	0	0	–	14	19	3	1	1.1	.917
1984			14	9	.609	3.12	35	31	10	225	205	71	105	2	0	1	1	0	0	0	–	15	18	2	1	1.0	.943
1985			10	8	.556	4.53	31	28	8	175	172	70	93	1	0	0	0	0	0	0	–	15	20	0	1	1.1	1.000
1986			9	12	.429	3.62	25	25	2	154	166	49	96	0	0	0	0	0	0	0	–	22	21	1	3	1.8	.977
1987	2 teams	SD N (21G 2–7)								OAK A	(5G 1–1)																
"	total		3	8	.273	5.23	26	15	0	93	98	47	65	0	0	0	0	16	1	0	.063	8	9	1	0	0.7	.944
1988	OAK	A	16	7	.696	3.70	33	33	1	201.2	211	91	127	0	0	0	0	0	0	0	–	6	21	1	2	0.8	.964
1989			19	7	.731	4.36	31	31	1	169.1	187	68	91	0	0	0	0	0	0	0	–	12	17	2	0	1.0	.935
8 yrs.			92	62	.597	3.86	244	200	29	1319	1315	488	769	4	3	4	1	16	1	0	.063	98	137	11	7	1.0	.955

LEAGUE CHAMPIONSHIP SERIES

Year	Team		W	L	PCT	ERA	G	GS	CG	IP	H	BB	SO	ShO	W	L	SV	AB	H	HR	BA	PO	A	E	DP	TC/G	FA
1983	BAL	A	0	0	–	0.00	1	0	0	6	5	2	2	0	0	0	0	0	0	0	–	0	0	0	0	0.0	–
1988	OAK	A	0	0	–	0.00	1	1	0	6.1	2	5	4	0	0	0	0	0	0	0	–	0	2	0	0	2.0	1.000
1989			0	1	.000	7.11	1	1	0	6.1	5	2	3	0	0	0	0	0	0	0	–	0	0	0	0	0.0	–
3 yrs.			0	1	.000	2.41	3	3	0	18.2	12	9	9	0	0	0	0	0	0	0	–	0	2	0	0	0.7	1.000

WORLD SERIES

Year	Team		W	L	PCT	ERA	G	GS	CG	IP	H	BB	SO	ShO	W	L	SV	AB	H	HR	BA	PO	A	E	DP	TC/G	FA
1983	BAL	A	1	0	1.000	5.40	1	1	0	5	6	1	3	0	0	0	0	2	0	0	.000	0	1	0	0	1.0	1.000
1988	OAK	A	0	2	.000	11.25	2	2	0	8	14	1	7	0	0	0	0	1	0	0	.000	2	1	0	0	1.5	1.000
2 yrs.			1	2	.333	9.00	3	3	0	13	20	2	10	0	0	0	0	3	0	0	.000	2	2	0	0	1.3	1.000

Wiley Davis

DAVIS, WILEY ANDERSON
B. Aug. 1, 1875, Seymour, Tenn.   D. Sept. 22, 1942, Detroit, Mich.

BR TR 5'10" 165 lbs.

Year	Team		W	L	PCT	ERA	G	GS	CG	IP	H	BB	SO	ShO	W	L	SV	AB	H	HR	BA	PO	A	E	DP	TC/G	FA
1896	CIN	N	1	1	.500	8.31	2	0	0	4.1	8	2	1	0	1	1	0	1	0	0	.000	0	4	0	0	2.0	1.000

Woody Davis

DAVIS, WOODROW WILSON (Babe)
B. Apr. 25, 1913, Nicholas, Ga.

BL TR 6'1" 200 lbs.

Year	Team		W	L	PCT	ERA	G	GS	CG	IP	H	BB	SO	ShO	W	L	SV	AB	H	HR	BA	PO	A	E	DP	TC/G	FA
1938	DET	A	0	0	–	1.50	2	0	0	6	3	4	1	0	0	0	0	1	0	0	.000	1	0	1	0	1.0	.500

Mike Davison

DAVISON, MICHAEL LYNN
B. Aug. 4, 1945, Galesburg, Ill.

BL TL 6'1" 170 lbs.

Year	Team		W	L	PCT	ERA	G	GS	CG	IP	H	BB	SO	ShO	W	L	SV	AB	H	HR	BA	PO	A	E	DP	TC/G	FA
1969	SF	N	0	0	–	4.50	1	0	0	2	2	0	2	0	0	0	0	0	0	0	–	0	0	0	0	0.0	–
1970			3	5	.375	6.50	31	0	0	36	46	22	21	0	3	5	1	1	0	0	.000	4	9	0	1	0.4	1.000
2 yrs.			3	5	.375	6.39	32	0	0	38	48	22	23	0	3	5	1	1	0	0	.000	4	9	0	1	0.4	1.000

Bill Dawley

DAWLEY, WILLIAM CHESTER
B. Feb. 6, 1958, Norwich, Conn.

BR TR 6'5" 235 lbs.

Year	Team		W	L	PCT	ERA	G	GS	CG	IP	H	BB	SO	ShO	W	L	SV	AB	H	HR	BA	PO	A	E	DP	TC/G	FA
1983	HOU	N	6	6	.500	2.82	48	0	0	79.2	51	22	60	0	6	6	14	9	2	0	.222	2	5	0	1	0.1	1.000
1984			11	4	.733	1.93	60	0	0	98	82	35	47	0	11	4	5	9	3	0	.333	6	11	1	0	0.3	.944
1985			5	3	.625	3.56	49	0	0	81	76	37	48	0	5	3	2	10	2	0	.200	6	13	1	2	0.4	.950
1986	CHI	N	0	7	.000	3.32	46	0	0	97.2	91	28	66	0	0	7	2	5	0	0	.000	8	1	1	0	0.4	.941
1987	STL	N	5	8	.385	4.47	60	0	0	96.2	93	38	65	0	5	8	2	12	2	0	.167	10	17	0	2	0.5	1.000
1988	PHI	N	0	2	.000	13.50	8	0	0	8.2	16	4	3	0	0	2	0	0	0	0	–	0	1	0	0	0.1	1.000
1989	OAK	A	0	0	–	4.00	4	0	0	9	11	2	3	0	0	0	0	0	0	0	–	0	1	0	0	0.3	1.000
7 yrs.			27	30	.474	3.42	275	0	0	470.2	420	166	292	0	27	30	25	42	9	0	.214	32	56	3	5	0.3	.967

Joe Dawson

DAWSON, RALPH FENTON
B. Mar. 9, 1897, Bow, Wash.   D. Jan. 4, 1978, Longview, Tex.

BR TR 5'11" 182 lbs.

Year	Team		W	L	PCT	ERA	G	GS	CG	IP	H	BB	SO	ShO	W	L	SV	AB	H	HR	BA	PO	A	E	DP	TC/G	FA
1924	CLE	A	1	2	.333	6.64	4	4	0	20.1	24	21	7	0	0	0	0	7	2	0	.286	1	8	0	0	2.3	1.000
1927	PIT	N	3	7	.300	4.46	20	7	4	80.2	80	32	17	0	2	2	0	25	5	0	.200	1	18	2	0	1.1	.905
1928			7	7	.500	3.29	31	7	1	128.2	116	56	36	0	5	3	2	43	12	0	.279	6	15	0	0	0.7	1.000
1929			0	1	.000	8.31	4	0	0	8.2	13	3	2	0	0	1	0	2	1	0	.500	0	2	0	0	0.5	1.000
4 yrs.			11	17	.393	4.15	59	18	5	238.1	233	112	62	0	7	5	3	77	20	0	.260	8	43	2	0	0.9	.962

WORLD SERIES

Year	Team		W	L	PCT	ERA	G	GS	CG	IP	H	BB	SO	ShO	W	L	SV	AB	H	HR	BA	PO	A	E	DP	TC/G	FA
1927	PIT	N	0	0	–	0.00	1	0	0	1	0	0	0	0	0	0	0	0	0	0	–	0	0	0	0	0.0	–

Rex Dawson

DAWSON, REXFORD PAUL
B. Feb. 10, 1889, Skagit County, Wash.   D. Oct. 20, 1958, Indianapolis, Ind.

BL TR 6' 185 lbs.

Year	Team		W	L	PCT	ERA	G	GS	CG	IP	H	BB	SO	ShO	W	L	SV	AB	H	HR	BA	PO	A	E	DP	TC/G	FA
1913	WAS	A	0	0	–	0.00	1	0	0	1	1	0	0	0	0	0	0	0	0	0	–	0	0	0	0	0.0	–

Bill Day

DAY, WILLIAM M.
B. July 28, 1867, Wilmington, Del.   D. Aug. 16, 1923, Wilmington, Del.

TR 5'8" 150 lbs.

Year	Team		W	L	PCT	ERA	G	GS	CG	IP	H	BB	SO	ShO	W	L	SV	AB	H	HR	BA	PO	A	E	DP	TC/G	FA
1889	PHI	N	0	3	.000	5.21	4	3	2	19	16	23	20	0	0	0	0	10	0	0	.000	1	3	2	0	1.5	.667
1890	2 teams	PHI N (4G 1–1)								PIT N	(6G 0–6)																
"	total		1	7	.125	4.52	10	8	8	73.2	92	36	19	0	0	0	0	33	2	0	.061	1	24	2	0	2.7	.926
2 yrs.			1	10	.091	4.66	14	11	10	92.2	108	59	39	0	0	0	0	43	2	0	.047	2	27	4	0	2.4	.879

Pea Ridge Day

DAY, CLYDE HENRY
B. Aug. 26, 1899, Pea Ridge, Ark.   D. Mar. 21, 1934, Kansas City, Mo.

BR TR 6' 190 lbs.

Year	Team		W	L	PCT	ERA	G	GS	CG	IP	H	BB	SO	ShO	W	L	SV	AB	H	HR	BA	PO	A	E	DP	TC/G	FA
1924	STL	N	1	1	.500	4.58	3	3	1	17.2	22	6	3	0	0	0	0	8	1	0	.125	0	3	0	0	1.0	1.000
1925			2	4	.333	6.30	17	4	1	40	53	7	13	0	1	1	1	13	2	0	.154	0	6	0	0	0.4	1.000
1926	CIN	N	0	0	–	7.36	4	0	0	7.1	13	2	2	0	0	0	0	2	0	0	.000	0	0	0	0	0.0	–

Year	Team	W	L	PCT	ERA	G	GS	CG	IP	H	BB	SO	ShO	W	L	SV	AB	H	HR	BA	PO	A	E	DP	TC/G	FA
														Relief Pitching			**Batting**									

Pea Ridge Day *continued*

| 1931 | BKN N | 2 | 2 | .500 | 4.55 | 22 | 2 | 1 | 57.1 | 75 | 13 | 30 | 0 | 2 | 0 | 1 | 18 | 4 | 0 | .222 | 0 | 9 | 2 | 0 | 0.5 | .818 |
| 4 yrs. | | 5 | 7 | .417 | 5.30 | 46 | 9 | 3 | 122.1 | 163 | 28 | 48 | 0 | 3 | 1 | 2 | 41 | 7 | 0 | .171 | 0 | 18 | 2 | 0 | 0.4 | .900 |

Ken Dayley

DAYLEY, KENNETH GRANT
B. Feb. 25, 1959, Jerome, Ida.

BL TL 6' 178 lbs.

1982	ATL N	5	6	.455	4.54	20	11	0	71.1	79	25	34	0	2	0	0	20	5	0	.250	3	5	0	0	0.4	1.000
1983		5	8	.385	4.30	24	16	0	104.2	100	39	70	0	1	2	0	32	7	0	.219	0	7	0	0	0.3	1.000
1984	2 teams	ATL N	(4G 0–3)		STL N	(3G 0–2)																				
"	total	0	5	.000	7.99	7	6	0	23.2	44	11	10	0	0	0	0	4	2	0	.500	1	4	0	0	0.7	1.000
1985	STL N	4	4	.500	2.76	57	0	0	65.1	65	18	62	0	4	4	11	5	2	0	.400	5	15	0	0	0.4	1.000
1986		0	3	.000	3.26	31	0	0	38.2	42	11	33	0	0	3	5	5	1	0	.200	1	7	0	0	0.3	1.000
1987		9	5	.643	2.66	53	0	0	61	52	33	63	0	9	5	4	0	0	0	–	3	4	0	1	0.1	1.000
1988		2	7	.222	2.77	54	0	0	55.1	48	19	38	0	2	7	5	4	0	0	.000	2	7	0	0	0.2	1.000
1989		4	3	.571	2.87	71	0	0	75.1	63	30	40	0	4	3	12	5	0	0	.000	2	5	1	0	0.1	.875
8 yrs.		29	41	.414	3.63	317	33	0	495.1	493	186	350	0	22	24	37	75	17	0	.227	17	54	1	1	0.2	.986

LEAGUE CHAMPIONSHIP SERIES

1985	STL N	0	0	–	0.00	5	0	0	6	2	1	3	0	0	0	2	2	1	0	.500	0	1	0	0	0.2	1.000
1987		0	0	–	0.00	3	0	0	4	1	2	4	0	0	0	2	0	0	0	–	0	0	0	0	0.0	–
2 yrs.		0	0	–	0.00	8	0	0	10	3	3	7	0	0	0	4	2	1	0	.500	0	1	0	0	0.1	1.000

WORLD SERIES

1985	STL N	1	0	1.000	0.00	4	0	0	6	1	3	5	0	1	0	0	–	0	0	0	0	0.0	–
1987		0	0	–	1.93	4	0	0	4.2	2	0	3	0	0	0	1	1	0	0	.000	0	0	0	0	0.0	–
2 yrs.		1	0	1.000	0.84	8	0	0	10.2	3	3	8	0	1	0	1	1	0	0	.000	0	0	0	0	0.0	–

Ren Deagle

DEAGLE, LORENZO BURROUGHS
B. June 26, 1858, New York, N. Y. D. Dec. 24, 1936, Kansas City, Mo.

BR TR 5'9" 190 lbs.

1883	CIN AA	10	8	.556	*2.31*	18	18	17	148	136	34	46	1	0	0	0	70	9	0	.129	4	28	10	0	2.3	.762
1884	2 teams	CIN AA	(4G 3–1)		LOU AA	(12G 4–6)																				
"	total	7	7	.500	*3.26*	16	16	12	121.1	119	22	35	1	0	0	0	58	6	0	.103	5	28	3	0	2.3	.917
2 yrs.		17	15	.531	2.74	34	34	29	269.1	255	56	81	2	0	0	0	128	15	0	.117	9	56	13	0	2.3	.833

Cot Deal

DEAL, ELLIS FERGUSON
B. Jan. 23, 1923, Arapaho, Okla.

BB TR 5'10½" 185 lbs.
BL 1947–48

1947	BOS A	0	1	.000	9.24	5	2	0	12.2	20	7	6	0	0	0	0	4	2	0	.500	1	2	0	0	0.6	1.000
1948		1	0	1.000	0.00	4	0	0	4	3	3	2	0	1	0	0	0	0	0	–	0	1	0	0	0.3	1.000
1950	STL N	0	0	–	18.00	3	0	0	1	3	2	1	0	0	0	0	0	0	0	–	0	0	1	0	0.3	–
1954		2	3	.400	6.28	33	0	0	71.2	85	36	25	0	2	3	1	20	2	0	.100	5	12	0	1	0.5	1.000
4 yrs.		3	4	.429	6.55	45	2	0	89.1	111	48	34	0	3	3	1	24	4	0	.167	6	15	1	1	0.5	.955

Chubby Dean

DEAN, ALFRED LOVELL
B. Aug. 24, 1916, Mt. Airy, N. C. D. Dec. 21, 1970, Riverside, Calif.

BL TL 5'11" 181 lbs.

1937	PHI A	1	0	1.000	4.00	2	1	0	9	7	6	4	0	0	0	0	309	81	2	.262	1	2	0	0	1.5	1.000
1938		2	1	.667	3.52	6	1	0	23	22	15	3	0	2	0	0	20	6	0	.300	0	8	0	0	1.3	1.000
1939		5	8	.385	5.25	54	1	0	116.2	132	80	39	0	5	7	7	77	27	0	.351	3	36	2	4	0.8	.951
1940		6	13	.316	6.61	30	19	8	159.1	220	63	38	1	1	3	1	90	26	0	.289	4	36	1	1	1.4	.976
1941	2 teams	PHI A	(18G 2–4)		CLE A	(8G 1–4)																				
"	total	3	8	.273	5.44	26	15	4	129	147	59	36	0	1	0	0	62	13	0	.210	7	28	0	1	1.3	1.000
1942	CLE A	8	11	.421	3.81	27	22	8	172.2	170	66	46	0	2	0	1	101	27	0	.267	7	24	2	0	1.2	.939
1943		5	5	.500	4.50	17	9	3	76	83	34	29	0	1	2	0	46	9	0	.196	2	11	1	1	0.8	.929
7 yrs.		30	46	.395	5.08	162	68	23	685.2	781	323	195	1	12	12	9	*				24	145	6	7	1.1	.966

Dizzy Dean

DEAN, JAY HANNA
Brother of Paul Dean.
B. Jan. 16, 1911, Lucas, Ark. D. July 17, 1974, Reno, Nev.
Hall of Fame 1953.

BR TR 6'2" 182 lbs.

1930	STL N	1	0	1.000	1.00	1	1	1	9	3	3	5	0	0	0	0	3	1	0	.333	1	4	0	0	5.0	1.000
1932		18	15	.545	3.30	46	33	16	**286**	280	102	**191**	4	0	3	2	97	25	2	.258	9	46	3	7	1.3	.948
1933		20	18	.526	3.04	**48**	34	**26**	293	279	64	199	3	1	3	4	105	19	1	.181	9	35	5	1	1.0	.898
1934		**30**	7	**.811**	2.66	50	33	**24**	311.2	288	75	**195**	7	4	2	7	118	29	2	.246	18	46	2	1	1.3	.970
1935		28	12	.700	3.04	50	**36**	**29**	325.1	324	77	190	3	4	3	5	128	30	2	.234	13	42	2	0	1.1	.965
1936		24	13	.649	3.17	**51**	34	28	**315**	310	53	195	2	2	3	11	121	27	1	.223	10	44	1	3	1.1	.982
1937		13	10	.565	2.69	27	25	17	197.1	206	33	120	4	0	1	1	66	15	1	.227	4	24	1	3	1.1	.966
1938	CHI N	7	1	.875	1.81	13	10	3	74.2	63	8	22	1	0	0	0	26	5	0	.192	2	11	0	0	1.0	1.000
1939		6	4	.600	3.36	19	13	7	96.1	98	17	27	2	0	1	0	34	5	0	.147	5	16	0	0	1.1	1.000
1940		3	3	.500	5.17	10	9	3	54	68	20	18	0	0	0	0	18	4	0	.222	5	15	1	0	2.1	.952
1941		0	0	–	18.00	1	1	0	1	4	1	0	0	0	0	0	0	0	0	–	0	0	0	0	0.0	–
1947	STL A	0	0	–	0.00	1	1	0	4	3	1	0	0	0	0	0	1	1	0	1.000	0	0	0	0	0.0	–
12 yrs.		150	83	.644	3.02	317	230	154	1967.1	1925	453	1163	26	11	16	30	717	161	8	.225	76	283	15	15	1.2	.960

WORLD SERIES

1934	STL N	2	1	.667	1.73	3	3	2	26	20	5	17	1	0	0	0	12	3	0	.250	2	5	0	0	1.3	1.000
1938	CHI N	0	1	.000	6.48	2	1	0	8.1	8	1	2	0	0	0	0	3	2	0	.667	0	2	0	0	1.0	1.000
2 yrs.		2	2	.500	2.88	5	4	2	34.1	28	6	19	1	0	0	0	15	5	0	.333	2	4	0	0	1.2	1.000

Dory Dean

DEAN, CHARLES WILSON
B. Nov. 6, 1852, Cincinnati, Ohio D. May 4, 1935, Nashville, Tenn.

BR TR 5'9" 160 lbs.

| 1876 | CIN N | 4 | 26 | .133 | 3.73 | 30 | 30 | 26 | 262.2 | 397 | 24 | 22 | 0 | 0 | 0 | 0 | 138 | 36 | 0 | .261 | 22 | 38 | 13 | 2 | 2.4 | .822 |

Year	Team		W	L	PCT	ERA	G	GS	CG	IP	H	BB	SO	ShO	Relief Pitching W	L	SV	Batting AB	H	HR	BA	PO	A	E	DP	TC/G	FA

Harry Dean

DEAN, JAMES HARRY
B. May 12, 1915, Rockmart, Ga. D. June 1, 1960, Rockmart, Ga.
BR TR 6'4" 185 lbs.

Year	Team		W	L	PCT	ERA	G	GS	CG	IP	H	BB	SO	ShO	W	L	SV	AB	H	HR	BA	PO	A	E	DP	TC/G	FA
1941	WAS	A	0	0	—	4.50	2	0	0	2	2	3	0	0	0	0	0	0	0	0	—	0	0	1	0	0.5	—

Paul Dean

DEAN, PAUL DEE (Daffy)
Brother of Dizzy Dean.
B. Aug. 14, 1913, Lucas, Ark. D. Mar. 17, 1981, Springdale, Ark.
BR TR 6' 175 lbs.

Year	Team		W	L	PCT	ERA	G	GS	CG	IP	H	BB	SO	ShO	W	L	SV	AB	H	HR	BA	PO	A	E	DP	TC/G	FA
1934	STL	N	19	11	.633	3.43	39	26	16	233.1	225	52	150	5	2	4	2	83	20	0	.241	3	20	4	0	0.7	.852
1935			19	12	.613	3.37	46	33	19	269.2	261	55	143	2	3	1	5	90	12	0	.133	6	27	3	2	0.8	.917
1936			5	5	.500	4.60	17	14	5	92	113	20	28	0	0	1	1	34	2	0	.059	2	7	1	0	0.6	.900
1937			0	0	—	∞	1	0	0		1	2	0	0	0	0	0	0	0	0	—	0	0	0	0	0.0	—
1938			3	1	.750	2.61	5	4	2	31	37	5	14	1	0	0	0	11	2	0	.182	1	3	0	0	0.8	1.000
1939			0	1	.000	6.07	16	2	0	43	54	10	16	0	0	0	0	9	1	0	.111	1	8	2	0	0.7	.818
1940	NY	N	4	4	.500	3.90	27	7	2	99.1	110	29	32	0	2	3	0	26	3	0	.115	3	14	0	0	0.6	1.000
1941			0	0	—	3.18	5	0	0	5.2	8	3	3	0	0	0	0	0	0	0	—	0	1	0	0	0.2	1.000
1943	STL	A	0	0	—	3.38	3	1	0	13.1	16	3	1	0	0	0	0	3	0	0	.000	0	2	0	0	0.7	1.000
9 yrs.			50	34	.595	3.75	159	87	44	787.1	825	179	387	8	7	9	8	256	40	0	.156	16	82	10	2	0.7	.907

WORLD SERIES

| 1934 | STL | N | 2 | 0 | 1.000 | 1.00 | 2 | 2 | 2 | 18 | 15 | 7 | 11 | 0 | 0 | 0 | 0 | 6 | 1 | 0 | .167 | 0 | 0 | 1 | 0 | 0.5 | — |

Wayland Dean

DEAN, WAYLAND OGDEN
B. June 20, 1902, Richmond, Va.
D. Apr. 10, 1930, Huntington, W. Va.
BB TR 6'2" 178 lbs.
BL 1926-27

Year	Team		W	L	PCT	ERA	G	GS	CG	IP	H	BB	SO	ShO	W	L	SV	AB	H	HR	BA	PO	A	E	DP	TC/G	FA
1924	NY	N	6	12	.333	5.01	26	20	6	125.2	139	45	39	0	1	1	2	40	8	2	.200	12	41	3	2	2.2	.946
1925			10	7	.588	4.64	33	14	6	151.1	169	50	53	1	5	1	1	51	12	1	.235	10	36	6	1	1.6	.885
1926	PHI	N	8	16	.333	6.10	33	26	15	163.2	245	89	52	1	0	4	1	102	27	3	.265	6	44	3	3	1.6	.943
1927	2 teams		PHI N	(2G 0–1)		CHI N	(2G 0–0)																					
"	total		0	1	.000	7.20	4	0	0	5	6	4	3	0	0	0	0	3	2	0	.667	0	2	0	1	0.5	1.000
4 yrs.			24	36	.400	5.31	96	60	27	445.2	559	188	147	2	6	6	1	*				28	123	12	7	1.7	.926

WORLD SERIES

| 1924 | NY | N | 0 | 0 | — | 4.50 | 1 | 0 | 0 | 2 | 3 | 0 | 2 | 0 | 0 | 0 | 0 | 0 | 0 | 0 | — | 0 | 0 | 0 | 0 | 0.0 | — |

Denny DeBarr

DeBARR, DENNIS LEE
B. Jan. 16, 1953, Cheyenne, Wyo.
BL TL 6'2" 190 lbs.

Year	Team		W	L	PCT	ERA	G	GS	CG	IP	H	BB	SO	ShO	W	L	SV	AB	H	HR	BA	PO	A	E	DP	TC/G	FA
1977	TOR	A	0	1	.000	6.00	14	0	0	21	29	8	10	0	0	1	0	0	0	0	—	1	3	0	0	0.3	1.000

Joe DeBerry

DeBERRY, JOSEPH GADDY
B. Nov. 29, 1896, Mt. Gilead, N. C. D. Oct. 9, 1944, Southern Pines, N. C.
BL TR 6'1" 175 lbs.

Year	Team		W	L	PCT	ERA	G	GS	CG	IP	H	BB	SO	ShO	W	L	SV	AB	H	HR	BA	PO	A	E	DP	TC/G	FA
1920	STL	A	2	4	.333	4.94	10	7	3	54.2	65	20	12	1	0	0	0	18	3	0	.167	7	14	1	0	2.2	.955
1921			0	1	.000	6.57	10	1	0	12.1	15	10	1	0	0	0	0	2	0	0	.000	1	3	0	0	0.4	1.000
2 yrs.			2	5	.286	5.24	20	8	3	67	80	30	13	1	0	0	0	20	3	0	.150	8	17	1	0	1.3	.962

Dave DeBusschere

DeBUSSCHERE, DAVID ALBERT
B. Oct. 16, 1940, Detroit, Mich.
BR TR 6'6" 225 lbs.

Year	Team		W	L	PCT	ERA	G	GS	CG	IP	H	BB	SO	ShO	W	L	SV	AB	H	HR	BA	PO	A	E	DP	TC/G	FA
1962	CHI	A	0	0	—	2.00	12	0	0	18	5	23	8	0	0	0	0	0	0	0	—	1	3	0	0	0.3	1.000
1963			3	4	.429	3.09	24	10	1	84.1	80	34	53	1	0	0	0	22	1	0	.045	8	13	1	2	0.9	.955
2 yrs.			3	4	.429	2.90	36	10	1	102.1	85	57	61	1	0	0	0	22	1	0	.045	9	16	1	2	0.7	.962

Art Decatur

DECATUR, ARTHUR RUE
B. Jan. 14, 1894, Cleveland, Ohio D. Apr. 25, 1966, Talladega, Ala.
BR TR 6'1" 190 lbs.

Year	Team		W	L	PCT	ERA	G	GS	CG	IP	H	BB	SO	ShO	W	L	SV	AB	H	HR	BA	PO	A	E	DP	TC/G	FA
1922	BKN	N	3	4	.429	2.77	29	2	1	87.2	87	29	31	0	3	3	1	25	2	0	.080	1	14	1	0	0.6	.938
1923			3	3	.500	2.67	36	5	2	104.2	115	34	27	0	2	0	3	21	0	0	.000	3	17	2	0	0.6	.909
1924			10	9	.526	4.07	31	10	4	128.1	158	28	39	0	7	2	1	44	5	0	.114	3	21	2	3	0.8	.923
1925	2 teams		BKN N	(1G 0–0)		PHI N	(25G 4–13)																					
"	total		4	13	.235	5.37	26	15	4	129	173	35	31	0	0	4	2	41	2	0	.049	3	21	0	1	0.9	1.000
1926	PHI	N	0	0	—	6.00	2	1	0	3	6	2	0	0	0	0	0	1	0	0	.000	0	0	0	0	0.0	—
1927			3	5	.375	7.26	29	3	0	96.2	130	20	27	0	3	3	0	27	6	0	.222	2	11	1	0	0.5	.929
6 yrs.			23	34	.404	4.47	153	36	11	549.1	669	148	155	0	15	12	7	159	15	0	.094	12	84	6	4	0.7	.941

Joe Decker

DECKER, GEORGE HENRY
B. June 16, 1947, Storm Lake, Iowa
BR TR 6' 183 lbs.

Year	Team		W	L	PCT	ERA	G	GS	CG	IP	H	BB	SO	ShO	W	L	SV	AB	H	HR	BA	PO	A	E	DP	TC/G	FA
1969	CHI	N	1	0	1.000	3.00	4	1	0	12	10	6	13	0	0	0	0	2	0	0	.000	1	0	0	0	0.3	1.000
1970			2	7	.222	4.62	24	17	1	109	108	56	79	0	0	0	0	34	6	1	.176	4	14	3	0	0.9	.857
1971			3	2	.600	4.70	21	4	0	46	62	25	37	0	2	0	0	8	2	0	.250	0	11	0	0	0.5	1.000
1972			1	0	1.000	2.08	5	1	0	13	9	4	7	0	0	0	0	2	0	0	.000	1	0	0	0	0.2	1.000
1973	MIN	A	10	10	.500	4.17	29	24	6	170.1	167	88	109	3	0	0	0	0	0	0	—	24	20	3	0	1.6	.936
1974			16	14	.533	3.29	37	37	11	249	234	97	158	1	0	0	0	0	0	0	—	19	20	1	2	1.1	.975
1975			1	3	.250	8.54	10	7	1	26.1	25	36	8	0	0	0	0	0	0	0	—	1	3	0	0	0.4	1.000
1976			2	7	.222	5.28	13	12	0	58	60	51	35	0	0	0	0	0	0	0	—	4	13	0	0	1.3	1.000
1979	SEA	A	0	1	.000	4.33	9	2	0	27	27	14	12	0	0	0	0	0	0	0	—	4	6	1	1	1.2	.909
9 yrs.			36	44	.450	4.17	152	105	19	710.2	702	377	458	4	2	0	0	46	8	1	.174	58	87	8	3	1.0	.948

Marty Decker

DECKER, DEE MARTIN
B. June 7, 1957, Upland, Calif.
BR TR 5'11" 170 lbs.

Year	Team		W	L	PCT	ERA	G	GS	CG	IP	H	BB	SO	ShO	W	L	SV	AB	H	HR	BA	PO	A	E	DP	TC/G	FA
1983	SD	N	0	0	—	2.08	4	0	0	8.2	5	3	9	0	0	0	0	0	0	0	—	0	2	1	0	0.8	.667

Jeff Dedmon

DEDMON, JEFFREY LINDEN
B. Mar. 4, 1960, Torrance, Calif.
BL TR 6'3" 185 lbs.

Year	Team		W	L	PCT	ERA	G	GS	CG	IP	H	BB	SO	ShO	W	L	SV	AB	H	HR	BA	PO	A	E	DP	TC/G	FA
1983	ATL	N	0	0	—	13.50	5	0	0	4	10	0	3	0	0	0	0	0	0	0	—	1	1	0	0	0.4	1.000

Year	Team	W	L	PCT	ERA	G	GS	CG	IP	H	BB	SO	ShO	Relief Pitching W	L	SV	Batting AB	H	HR	BA	PO	A	E	DP	TC/G	FA

Jeff Dedmon *continued*

Year	Team	W	L	PCT	ERA	G	GS	CG	IP	H	BB	SO	ShO	W	L	SV	AB	H	HR	BA	PO	A	E	DP	TC/G	FA
1984		4	3	.571	3.78	54	0	0	81	86	35	51	0	4	3	4	6	0	0	.000	2	22	2	1	0.5	.923
1985		6	3	.667	4.08	60	0	0	86	84	49	41	0	6	3	0	9	1	0	.111	9	27	2	4	0.6	.947
1986		6	6	.500	2.98	57	0	0	99.2	90	39	58	0	6	6	3	16	2	0	.125	9	22	2	1	0.6	.939
1987		3	4	.429	3.91	53	3	0	89.2	82	42	40	0	3	3	4	16	4	0	.250	10	17	0	1	0.5	1.000
1988	CLE A	1	0	1.000	4.54	21	0	0	33.2	35	21	17	0	1	0	1	0	0	0	–	4	9	0	2	0.6	1.000
6 yrs.		20	16	.556	3.84	250	3	0	394	387	186	210	0	20	15	12	47	7	0	.149	35	98	6	9	0.6	.957

Dummy Deegan

DEEGAN, WILLIAM JOHN
B. New York, N. Y. Deceased.

Year	Team	W	L	PCT	ERA	G	GS	CG	IP	H	BB	SO	ShO	W	L	SV	AB	H	HR	BA	PO	A	E	DP	TC/G	FA
1901	NY N	0	2	.000	6.35	2	1	1	17	27	6	8	0	0	1	0	5	0	0	.000	0	5	0	0	2.5	1.000

John Deering

DEERING, JOHN THOMAS
B. June 25, 1878, Lynn, Mass. D. Feb. 15, 1943, Beverly, Mass.

TR

Year	Team	W	L	PCT	ERA	G	GS	CG	IP	H	BB	SO	ShO	W	L	SV	AB	H	HR	BA	PO	A	E	DP	TC/G	FA
1903	2 teams	DET A (10G 3–4)				NY A (9G 3–3)																				
"	total	6	7	.462	3.80	19	15	11	120.2	136	42	28	1	0	0	0	47	9	0	.191	6	30	3	0	2.1	.923

Mike DeGerick

DeGERICK, MICHAEL ARTHUR
B. Apr. 1, 1943, New York, N. Y.

BR TR 6'2" 178 lbs.

Year	Team	W	L	PCT	ERA	G	GS	CG	IP	H	BB	SO	ShO	W	L	SV	AB	H	HR	BA	PO	A	E	DP	TC/G	FA
1961	CHI A	0	0	–	5.40	1	0	0	1.2	2	1	0	0	0	0	0	0	0	0	–	0	1	0	0	1.0	1.000
1962		0	0	–	0.00	1	0	0	1	1	1	0	0	0	0	0	0	0	0	–	0	1	0	0	1.0	1.000
2 yrs.		0	0	–	3.38	2	0	0	2.2	3	2	0	0	0	0	0	0	0	0	–	0	2	0	0	1.0	1.000

Pep Deininger

DEININGER, OTTO CHARLES
B. Oct. 10, 1877, Wasseralfingen, Germany D. Sept. 25, 1950, Boston, Mass.

BL TL 5'8½" 180 lbs.

Year	Team	W	L	PCT	ERA	G	GS	CG	IP	H	BB	SO	ShO	W	L	SV	AB	H	HR	BA	PO	A	E	DP	TC/G	FA
1902	BOS A	0	0	–	9.75	2	1	0	12	19	9	2	0	0	0	0	*				1	0	1	0.5	1.000

Jose DeJesus

DeJESUS, JOSE LUIS
B. Jan. 6, 1965, Brooklyn, N. Y.

BR TR 6'5" 175 lbs.

Year	Team	W	L	PCT	ERA	G	GS	CG	IP	H	BB	SO	ShO	W	L	SV	AB	H	HR	BA	PO	A	E	DP	TC/G	FA
1988	KC A	0	1	.000	27.00	2	1	0	2.2	6	5	2	0	0	0	0	0	0	0	–	0	0	0	0	0.0	–
1989		0	0	–	4.50	3	1	0	8	7	8	2	0	0	0	0	0	0	0	–	0	1	0	0	0.3	1.000
2 yrs.		0	1	.000	10.13	5	2	0	10.2	13	13	4	0	0	0	0	0	0	0	–	0	1	0	0	0.2	1.000

Tommy De La Cruz

DE LA CRUZ, TOMAS
Born Tomas De La Cruz y Rivero.
B. Sept. 18, 1914, Marianao, Cuba D. Sept. 6, 1958, Havana, Cuba

BR TR 6'1" 168 lbs.

Year	Team	W	L	PCT	ERA	G	GS	CG	IP	H	BB	SO	ShO	W	L	SV	AB	H	HR	BA	PO	A	E	DP	TC/G	FA
1944	CIN N	9	9	.500	3.25	34	20	9	191.1	170	45	65	0	2	1	1	58	9	0	.155	6	37	1	0	1.3	.977

Jim Delahanty

DELAHANTY, JAMES CHRISTOPHER
Brother of Ed Delahanty. Brother of Frank Delahanty.
Brother of Tom Delahanty. Brother of Joe Delahanty.
B. June 20, 1879, Cleveland, Ohio D. Oct. 17, 1953, Cleveland, Ohio

BR TR 5'10½" 170 lbs.

Year	Team	W	L	PCT	ERA	G	GS	CG	IP	H	BB	SO	ShO	W	L	SV	AB	H	HR	BA	PO	A	E	DP	TC/G	FA
1904	BOS N	0	0	–	0.00	1	0	0	3.1	5	1	0	0	0	0	0	499	142	3	.285	0	2	1	0	3.0	.667
1905		0	0	–	4.50	1	1	0	2	5	0	0	0	0	0	0	461	119	5	.258	0	1	0	0	1.0	1.000
2 yrs.		0	0	–	1.69	2	1	0	5.1	10	1	0	0	0	0	0	*				0	3	1	0	2.0	.750

Art Delaney

DELANEY, ARTHUR DEWEY (Swede)
Born Arthur Dewey Helenius.
B. Jan. 5, 1897, Chicago, Ill. D. May 2, 1970, Hayward, Calif.

BR TR 5'10½" 178 lbs.

Year	Team	W	L	PCT	ERA	G	GS	CG	IP	H	BB	SO	ShO	W	L	SV	AB	H	HR	BA	PO	A	E	DP	TC/G	FA
1924	STL N	1	0	1.000	1.80	8	1	1	20	19	6	2	0	0	0	0	7	2	0	.286	1	7	0	0	1.0	1.000
1928	BOS N	9	17	.346	3.79	39	22	8	192.1	197	56	45	0	4	3	2	63	9	0	.143	13	47	2	3	1.6	.968
1929		3	5	.375	6.12	20	8	3	75	103	35	17	1	1	1	0	21	3	1	.143	3	14	2	0	1.0	.895
3 yrs.		13	22	.371	4.26	67	31	12	287.1	319	97	64	1	5	4	2	91	14	1	.154	17	68	4	3	1.3	.955

Jose DeLeon

DeLEON, JOSE
Born Jose Deleon y Chestaro.
B. Dec. 20, 1960, La Vega, Dominican Republic

BR TR 6'3" 195 lbs.

Year	Team	W	L	PCT	ERA	G	GS	CG	IP	H	BB	SO	ShO	W	L	SV	AB	H	HR	BA	PO	A	E	DP	TC/G	FA
1983	PIT N	7	3	.700	2.83	15	15	3	108	75	47	118	2	0	0	0	34	2	0	.059	6	9	1	0	1.1	.938
1984		7	13	.350	3.74	30	28	5	192.1	147	92	153	1	1	0	0	59	5	0	.085	6	16	2	1	0.8	.917
1985		2	19	.095	4.70	31	25	1	162.2	138	89	149	0	0	1	3	36	2	0	.056	9	16	1	1	0.8	.962
1986	2 teams	PIT N (9G 1–3)				CHI A (13G 4–5)																				
"	total	5	8	.385	3.87	22	14	1	95.1	66	59	79	0	1	2	1	1	0	0	.000	6	14	1	2	1.0	.952
1987	CHI A	11	12	.478	4.02	33	31	2	206	177	97	153	0	0	0	0	0	0	0	–	10	14	3	0	0.8	.889
1988	STL N	13	10	.565	3.67	34	34	3	225.1	198	86	208	1	0	0	0	72	10	0	.139	10	21	0	0	0.9	1.000
1989		16	12	.571	3.05	36	36	5	244.2	173	80	201	3	0	0	0	83	8	0	.096	9	15	5	0	0.8	.833
7 yrs.		61	77	.442	3.70	201	183	20	1234.1	974	550	1061	7	2	3	4	285	27	0	.095	56	106	13	4	0.9	.926

Luis DeLeon

DeLEON, LUIS ANTONIO
Born Luis Antonio DeLeon y Tricoche.
B. Aug. 19, 1958, Ponce, Puerto Rico

BR TR 6'1" 153 lbs.

Year	Team	W	L	PCT	ERA	G	GS	CG	IP	H	BB	SO	ShO	W	L	SV	AB	H	HR	BA	PO	A	E	DP	TC/G	FA
1981	STL N	0	1	.000	2.40	10	0	0	15	11	3	8	0	0	1	0	0	0	0	.000	2	0	0	0	0.2	1.000
1982	SD N	9	5	.643	2.03	61	0	0	102	77	16	60	0	9	5	15	11	1	0	.091	13	18	3	1	0.6	.912
1983		6	6	.500	2.68	63	0	0	111	89	27	90	0	6	6	13	14	2	0	.143	2	9	1	1	0.2	.917
1984		2	2	.500	5.48	32	0	0	42.2	44	12	44	0	2	2	0	4	0	0	.000	1	4	1	1	0.3	.889
1985		0	3	.000	4.19	29	0	0	38.2	39	10	31	0	0	3	3	5	1	0	.200	1	5	0	0	0.2	1.000
1987	BAL A	0	2	.000	4.79	11	0	0	20.2	19	8	13	0	0	2	1	0	0	0	–	2	0	0	0	0.2	1.000
1989	SEA A	0	0	–	2.25	1	1	0	4	5	1	2	0	0	0	0	0	0	0	–	0	0	0	0	0.0	–
7 yrs.		17	19	.472	3.13	207	1	0	334	284	77	248	0	17	19	32	35	4	0	.114	22	38	5	3	0.3	.923

Year	Team		W	L	PCT	ERA	G	GS	CG	IP	H	BB	SO	ShO	Relief Pitching W	L	SV	Batting AB	H	HR	BA	PO	A	E	DP	TC/G	FA

Flame Delhi

DELHI, LEE WILLIAM
B. Nov. 2, 1890, Harqua Hala, Ariz.   D. May 9, 1966, San Rafael, Calif.   BR TR 6'2½" 198 lbs.

Year	Team		W	L	PCT	ERA	G	GS	CG	IP	H	BB	SO	ShO	W	L	SV	AB	H	HR	BA	PO	A	E	DP	TC/G	FA
1912	CHI	A	0	0	–	9.00	1	0	0	3	7	3	2	0	0	0	0	0	0	0	–	1	2	0	0	3.0	1.000

Wheezer Dell

DELL, WILLIAM GEORGE
B. June 11, 1887, Tuscarora, Nev.   D. Aug. 24, 1966, Independence, Calif.   BR TR 6'4" 210 lbs.

Year	Team		W	L	PCT	ERA	G	GS	CG	IP	H	BB	SO	ShO	W	L	SV	AB	H	HR	BA	PO	A	E	DP	TC/G	FA
1912	STL	N	0	0	–	11.57	3	0	0	2.1	3	3	0	0	0	0	0	0	0	0	–	0	0	0	0	0.0	–
1915	BKN	N	11	10	.524	2.34	40	24	12	215	166	100	94	4	2	0	1	66	10	0	.152	3	60	1	2	1.6	.984
1916			8	9	.471	2.26	32	16	9	155	143	43	76	2	2	1	1	44	4	0	.091	6	32	1	2	1.2	.974
1917			0	4	.000	3.72	17	4	0	58	55	25	28	0	0	1	1	16	1	0	.063	1	13	3	0	1.0	.824
4 yrs.			19	23	.452	2.55	92	44	21	430.1	367	171	198	6	4	2	3	126	15	0	.119	10	105	5	4	1.3	.958

WORLD SERIES

Year	Team		W	L	PCT	ERA	G	GS	CG	IP	H	BB	SO	ShO	W	L	SV	AB	H	HR	BA	PO	A	E	DP	TC/G	FA
1916	BKN	N	0	0	–	0.00	1	0	0	1	1	0	0	0	0	0	0	0	0	0	–	0	0	0	0	0.0	–

Ike Delock

DELOCK, IVAN MARTIN
B. Nov. 11, 1929, Highland Park, Mich.   BR TR 5'11" 175 lbs.

Year	Team		W	L	PCT	ERA	G	GS	CG	IP	H	BB	SO	ShO	W	L	SV	AB	H	HR	BA	PO	A	E	DP	TC/G	FA
1952	BOS	A	4	9	.308	4.26	39	7	1	95	88	50	46	1	2	5	5	22	1	0	.045	1	16	0	1	0.4	1.000
1953			3	1	.750	4.44	23	1	0	48.2	60	20	22	0	2	1	1	10	1	0	.100	1	5	0	0	0.3	1.000
1955			9	7	.563	3.76	29	18	6	143.2	136	61	88	0	1	1	3	49	7	0	.143	6	19	1	1	0.9	.962
1956			13	7	.650	4.21	48	8	1	128.1	122	80	105	0	11	2	9	29	3	0	.103	10	18	2	1	0.6	.933
1957			9	8	.529	3.83	49	2	0	94	80	45	62	0	9	6	11	21	1	0	.048	3	12	0	1	0.3	1.000
1958			14	8	.636	3.38	31	19	9	160	155	56	82	1	4	0	2	48	3	0	.063	9	22	1	1	1.0	.969
1959			11	6	.647	2.95	28	17	4	134.1	120	62	55	0	5	0	0	47	3	1	.064	8	15	1	1	0.9	.958
1960			9	10	.474	4.73	24	23	3	129.1	145	52	49	1	0	0	0	43	5	0	.116	10	16	2	3	1.2	.929
1961			6	9	.400	4.90	28	28	3	156	185	52	80	1	0	0	0	48	5	0	.104	13	17	4	1	1.2	.882
1962			4	5	.444	3.75	17	13	4	86.1	89	24	49	0	0	0	0	23	2	0	.087	3	12	0	0	0.9	1.000
1963	2 teams		BOS A	(6G 1-2)		BAL A	(7G 1-3)																					
"	total		2	5	.286	4.76	13	11	1	62.1	56	28	34	0	0	0	0	21	0	0	.000	8	1	0	1	1.3	.941
11 yrs.			84	75	.528	4.03	329	147	32	1238	1236	530	672	6	34	15	31	361	31	1	.086	72	160	12	10	0.7	.951

Ramon De Los Santos

DE LOS SANTOS, RAMON
Born Ramon De Los Santos y Genero.
B. Jan. 19, 1949, Santo Domingo, Dominican Republic   BL TL 6' 175 lbs.

Year	Team		W	L	PCT	ERA	G	GS	CG	IP	H	BB	SO	ShO	W	L	SV	AB	H	HR	BA	PO	A	E	DP	TC/G	FA
1974	HOU	N	1	1	.500	2.25	12	0	0	12	11	9	7	0	1	1	0	0	0	0	–	1	1	0	1	0.2	1.000

Al Demaree

DEMAREE, ALBERT WENTWORTH
B. Sept. 8, 1884, Quincy, Ill.   D. Apr. 30, 1962, Los Angeles, Calif.   BL TR 6' 170 lbs.

Year	Team		W	L	PCT	ERA	G	GS	CG	IP	H	BB	SO	ShO	W	L	SV	AB	H	HR	BA	PO	A	E	DP	TC/G	FA
1912	NY	N	1	0	1.000	1.69	2	2	1	16	17	2	11	0	0	0	0	5	0	0	.000	1	4	0	0	2.5	1.000
1913			13	4	.765	2.21	31	24	11	199.2	176	38	76	3	0	1	2	66	7	0	.106	1	38	1	1	1.3	.975
1914			10	17	.370	3.09	38	30	13	224	219	77	89	2	0	2	0	68	9	0	.132	3	58	2	0	1.7	.968
1915	PHI	N	14	11	.560	3.05	32	26	13	209.2	201	58	69	3	0	1	1	68	12	0	.176	8	35	0	0	1.3	1.000
1916			19	14	.576	2.62	39	35	25	285	252	48	130	4	2	0	1	101	11	0	.109	2	47	3	0	1.3	.942
1917	2 teams		CHI N	(24G 5-9)		NY N	(15G 4-5)																					
"	total		9	14	.391	2.58	39	29	7	219.2	195	54	66	1	2	0	1	59	7	0	.119	4	68	0	1	1.8	1.000
1918	NY	N	8	6	.571	2.47	26	14	8	142	143	25	39	2	0	1	1	47	6	0	.128	4	40	1	1	1.7	.978
1919	BOS	N	6	6	.500	3.80	25	13	6	128	147	35	34	0	2	1	3	42	2	0	.048	5	27	0	2	1.3	1.000
8 yrs.			80	72	.526	2.77	232	173	84	1424	1350	337	514	16	6	6	9	456	54	0	.118	28	317	7	5	1.5	.980

WORLD SERIES

Year	Team		W	L	PCT	ERA	G	GS	CG	IP	H	BB	SO	ShO	W	L	SV	AB	H	HR	BA	PO	A	E	DP	TC/G	FA
1913	NY	N	0	1	.000	4.50	1	1	0	4	7	1	0	0	0	0	0	1	0	0	.000	0	2	0	0	2.0	1.000

Fred Demarris

DEMARRIS, FRED
B. 1865, Nashua, N. H.   Deceased.   TR

Year	Team		W	L	PCT	ERA	G	GS	CG	IP	H	BB	SO	ShO	W	L	SV	AB	H	HR	BA	PO	A	E	DP	TC/G	FA
1890	CHI	N	0	0	–	0.00	1	0	0	2	1	1	1	0	0	0	0	2	0	0	.000	0	0	0	0	0.0	–

Larry Demery

DEMERY, LAWRENCE CALVIN
B. June 4, 1953, Bakersfield, Calif.   BR TR 6' 170 lbs.

Year	Team		W	L	PCT	ERA	G	GS	CG	IP	H	BB	SO	ShO	W	L	SV	AB	H	HR	BA	PO	A	E	DP	TC/G	FA
1974	PIT	N	6	6	.500	4.26	19	15	3	95	95	51	51	0	0	0	0	33	5	0	.152	6	10	1	0	0.9	.941
1975			7	5	.583	2.90	45	8	1	115	95	43	59	0	4	3	4	24	3	0	.125	7	13	1	1	0.5	.952
1976			10	7	.588	3.17	39	15	4	145	123	58	72	1	4	1	2	40	5	0	.125	9	21	2	2	0.9	.938
1977			6	5	.545	5.10	39	8	0	90	100	47	35	0	3	2	1	20	3	0	.150	5	14	2	0	0.5	.905
4 yrs.			29	23	.558	3.72	139	46	7	445	413	199	217	1	11	6	7	117	16	0	.137	27	58	6	3	0.7	.934

LEAGUE CHAMPIONSHIP SERIES

Year	Team		W	L	PCT	ERA	G	GS	CG	IP	H	BB	SO	ShO	W	L	SV	AB	H	HR	BA	PO	A	E	DP	TC/G	FA
1974	PIT	N	0	0	–	27.00	2	0	0	1	3	2	0	0	0	0	0	0	0	0	–	0	0	0	0	0.5	1.000
1975			0	0	–	18.00	1	0	0	2	4	1	1	0	0	0	0	0	0	0	–	0	0	0	0	0.0	–
2 yrs.			0	0	–	21.00	3	0	0	3	7	3	1	0	0	0	0	0	0	0	–	0	0	0	0	0.3	1.000

Harry DeMiller

DeMILLER, HARRY
B. Nov. 12, 1867, Wooster, Ohio   D. Oct. 19, 1928, Santa Ana, Calif.   BR TL

Year	Team		W	L	PCT	ERA	G	GS	CG	IP	H	BB	SO	ShO	W	L	SV	AB	H	HR	BA	PO	A	E	DP	TC/G	FA
1892	CHI	N	1	1	.500	6.38	4	2	2	24	29	16	15	0	0	0	0	10	3	0	.300	1	6	1	0	2.0	.875

Don DeMola

DeMOLA, DONALD JOHN
B. July 5, 1952, Glen Cove, N. Y.   BR TR 6'2" 185 lbs.

Year	Team		W	L	PCT	ERA	G	GS	CG	IP	H	BB	SO	ShO	W	L	SV	AB	H	HR	BA	PO	A	E	DP	TC/G	FA
1974	MON	N	1	0	1.000	3.10	25	1	0	58	46	21	47	0	1	0	0	4	0	0	.000	2	5	0	1	0.3	1.000
1975			4	7	.364	4.13	60	0	0	98	92	42	63	0	4	7	1	8	0	0	.000	1	3	1	0	0.1	.800
2 yrs.			5	7	.417	3.75	85	1	0	156	138	63	110	0	5	7	1	12	0	0	.000	3	8	1	1	0.1	.917

Ben DeMott

DeMOTT, BENYEW HARRISON
B. Apr. 2, 1889, Green Village, N. J.   D. July 5, 1963, Somerville, N. J.   BR TR 6' 192 lbs.

Year	Team		W	L	PCT	ERA	G	GS	CG	IP	H	BB	SO	ShO	W	L	SV	AB	H	HR	BA	PO	A	E	DP	TC/G	FA
1910	CLE	A	0	3	.000	5.40	6	4	1	28.1	90	8	13	0	0	0	0	14	3	0	.214	2	10	0	0	2.0	1.000

Year	Team		W	L	PCT	ERA	G	GS	CG	IP	H	BB	SO	ShO	Relief Pitching W	L	SV	Batting AB	H	HR	BA	PO	A	E	DP	TC/G	FA

Ben DeMott *continued*

| 1911 | | | 0 | 1 | .000 | 12.27 | 1 | 1 | 0 | 3.2 | 10 | 2 | 2 | 0 | 0 | 0 | 0 | 4 | 0 | 0 | .000 | 0 | 3 | 0 | 0 | 3.0 | 1.000 |
| 2 yrs. | | | 0 | 4 | .000 | 6.19 | 7 | 5 | 1 | 32 | 100 | 10 | 15 | 0 | 0 | 0 | 0 | 18 | 3 | 0 | .167 | 2 | 13 | 0 | 0 | 2.1 | 1.000 |

Con Dempsey

DEMPSEY, CORNELIUS FRANCIS
B. Sept. 16, 1923, San Francisco, Calif. BR TR 6'4" 190 lbs.

| 1951 | PIT | N | 0 | 2 | .000 | 9.00 | 3 | 2 | 0 | 7 | 11 | 4 | 3 | 0 | 0 | 0 | 0 | 1 | 0 | 0 | .000 | 0 | 2 | 0 | 0 | 0.7 | 1.000 |

Mark Dempsey

DEMPSEY, MARK STEVEN
B. Dec. 17, 1957, Dayton, Ohio BR TR 6'6" 220 lbs.

| 1982 | SF | N | 0 | 0 | – | 7.94 | 3 | 1 | 0 | 5.2 | 11 | 2 | 4 | 0 | 0 | 0 | 0 | 1 | 0 | 0 | .000 | 0 | 1 | 0 | 0 | 0.3 | 1.000 |

Bill Denehy

DENEHY, WILLIAM FRANCIS
B. Mar. 31, 1946, Middletown, Conn. BB TR 6'3" 200 lbs.

1967	NY	N	1	7	.125	4.70	15	8	0	53.2	51	29	35	0	0	0	0	9	0	0	.000	3	7	1	0	0.7	.909
1968	WAS	A	0	0	–	9.00	3	0	0	2	4	4	1	0	0	0	0	0	0	0	–	1	0	0	0	0.3	1.000
1971	DET	A	0	3	.000	4.22	31	1	0	49	47	28	27	0	0	2	1	2	0	0	.000	4	6	0	0	0.3	1.000
3 yrs.			1	10	.091	4.56	49	9	0	104.2	102	61	63	0	0	2	1	11	0	0	.000	8	13	1	0	0.4	.955

Brian Denman

DENMAN, BRIAN JOHN
B. Feb. 12, 1956, Minneapolis, Minn. BR TR 6'4" 215 lbs.

| 1982 | BOS | A | 3 | 4 | .429 | 4.78 | 9 | 9 | 2 | 49 | 55 | 9 | 9 | 1 | 0 | 0 | 0 | 0 | 0 | 0 | – | 6 | 5 | 0 | 0 | 1.2 | 1.000 |

Don Dennis

DENNIS, DONALD RAY
B. Mar. 3, 1942, Uniontown, Kans. BR TR 6'2" 190 lbs.

1965	STL	N	2	3	.400	2.29	41	0	0	55	47	16	29	0	2	3	6	5	2	0	.400	6	16	0	1	0.5	1.000
1966			4	2	.667	4.98	38	1	0	59.2	73	17	25	0	4	2	2	12	1	0	.083	5	24	1	0	0.8	.967
2 yrs.			6	5	.545	3.69	79	1	0	114.2	120	33	54	0	6	5	8	17	3	0	.176	11	40	1	1	0.7	.981

Jerry Denny

DENNY, JEREMIAH DENNIS
Born Jeremiah Dennis Eldridge.
B. Mar. 16, 1859, New York, N. Y. D. Aug. 16, 1927, Houston, Tex. BR TR 5'11½" 180 lbs.

| 1888 | IND | N | 0 | 0 | – | 9.00 | 1 | 0 | 0 | 4 | 5 | 4 | 1 | 0 | 0 | 0 | 0 | * | | | | 0 | 1 | 0 | 0 | 1.0 | 1.000 |

John Denny

DENNY, JOHN ALLEN
B. Nov. 8, 1952, Prescott, Ariz. BR TR 6'3" 185 lbs.

1974	STL	N	0	0	–	0.00	2	0	0	2	3	0	1	0	0	0	0	0	0	0	–	0	0	0	0	0.0	–
1975			10	7	.588	3.97	25	24	3	136	149	51	72	2	0	0	0	44	10	0	.227	11	30	4	2	1.8	.911
1976			11	9	.550	2.52	30	30	8	207	189	74	74	3	0	0	0	67	15	0	.224	24	34	4	3	2.1	.935
1977			8	8	.500	4.50	26	26	3	150	165	62	60	1	0	0	0	51	5	0	.098	9	37	3	3	1.9	.939
1978			14	11	.560	2.96	33	33	11	234	200	74	103	2	0	0	0	73	13	0	.178	17	73	4	8	2.8	.957
1979			8	11	.421	4.85	31	31	5	206	206	100	99	2	0	0	0	70	9	0	.129	16	36	2	4	1.7	.963
1980	CLE	A	8	6	.571	4.38	16	16	4	109	116	47	59	1	0	0	0	0	0	0	–	8	18	1	2	1.7	.963
1981			10	6	.625	3.14	19	19	6	146	139	66	94	3	0	0	0	0	0	0	–	14	40	3	7	3.0	.947
1982	2 teams					CLE A	(21G 6–11)			PHI N		(4G 0–2)															
"	total		6	13	.316	4.87	25	25	6	160.2	144	83	113	1	0	0	0	6	1	0	.167	13	26	0	3	1.6	1.000
1983	PHI	N	19	6	.760	2.37	36	36	7	242.2	229	53	139	1	0	0	0	77	13	0	.169	16	42	8	6	1.8	.879
1984			7	7	.500	2.45	22	22	8	154.1	122	29	94	0	0	0	0	47	9	0	.191	20	36	1	2	2.6	.982
1985			11	14	.440	3.82	33	33	6	230.2	252	83	123	2	0	0	0	81	10	0	.123	15	39	0	4	1.6	1.000
1986	CIN	N	11	10	.524	4.20	27	27	2	171.1	179	56	115	1	0	0	0	54	12	0	.222	16	40	2	2	2.1	.966
13 yrs.			123	108	.532	3.58	325	322	62	2149.2	2093	778	1146	18	0	0	0	570	97	0	.170	179	451	32	46	2.0	.952

LEAGUE CHAMPIONSHIP SERIES

| 1983 | PHI | N | 0 | 1 | .000 | 0.00 | 1 | 1 | 0 | 6 | 3 | 5 | 3 | 0 | 0 | 0 | 0 | 1 | 0 | 0 | .000 | 0 | 0 | 0 | 0 | 0.0 | – |

WORLD SERIES

| 1983 | PHI | N | 1 | 1 | .500 | 3.46 | 2 | 2 | 0 | 13 | 12 | 3 | 9 | 0 | 0 | 0 | 0 | 5 | 1 | 0 | .200 | 3 | 1 | 0 | 0 | 2.0 | 1.000 |

Eddie Dent

DENT, ELLIOTT ESTILL
B. Dec. 8, 1887, Baltimore, Md. D. Nov. 25, 1974, Birmingham, Ala. BR TR 6'1" 190 lbs.

1909	BKN	N	2	4	.333	4.29	6	5	4	42	47	15	17	0	0	0	1	15	1	0	.067	0	9	0	0	1.5	1.000
1911			2	1	.667	3.69	5	3	0	31.2	30	10	3	0	0	0	0	10	1	0	.100	2	11	0	0	2.6	1.000
1912			0	0	–	36.00	1	0	0	1	4	1	1	0	0	0	0	1	0	0	.000	1	0	0	0	1.0	1.000
3 yrs.			4	5	.444	4.46	12	8	5	74.2	81	26	21	0	0	0	1	26	2	0	.077	3	20	0	0	1.9	1.000

Roger Denzer

DENZER, ROGER (Peaceful Valley)
B. Oct. 5, 1871, LeSueur, Minn. D. Sept. 18, 1949, LeSueur, Minn. BL TR 6' 180 lbs.

1897	CHI	N	2	8	.200	5.13	12	10	8	94.2	125	34	17	0	1	0	0	39	6	0	.154	8	17	0	0	2.1	1.000
1901	NY	N	2	5	.286	3.36	11	9	3	61.2	69	5	22	1	0	0	0	22	2	0	.091	0	9	2	1	1.0	.818
2 yrs.			4	13	.235	4.43	23	19	11	156.1	194	39	39	1	1	0	0	61	8	0	.131	8	26	2	1	1.6	.944

George Derby

DERBY, GEORGE H.
B. July 6, 1857, Webster, Mass. D. July 4, 1925, Philadelphia, Pa. BL TR 6' 175 lbs.

1881	DET	N	29	26	.527	2.20	56	55	55	494.2	505	86	212	9	0	0	0	236	44	0	.186	25	97	9	4	2.3	.931
1882			17	20	.459	3.26	40	39	38	362	386	81	182	3	0	0	0	149	29	0	.195	19	69	4	1	2.3	.957
1883	BUF	N	2	10	.167	5.85	14	13	12	107.2	173	15	34	0	0	0	1	59	14	0	.237	5	26	4	1	2.5	.886
3 yrs.			48	56	.462	3.01	110	107	105	964.1	1064	182	428	12	0	0	1	444	87	0	.196	49	192	17	6	2.3	.934

Year	Team		W	L	PCT	ERA	G	GS	CG	IP	H	BB	SO	ShO	Relief Pitching W	L	SV	Batting AB	H	HR	BA	PO	A	E	DP	TC/G	FA

Paul Derringer

DERRINGER, SAMUEL PAUL (Duke, 'Oom Paul)
B. Oct. 17, 1906, Springfield, Ky. D. Nov. 17, 1987, Sarasota, Fla. BR TR 6'3½" 205 lbs.

Year	Team		W	L	PCT	ERA	G	GS	CG	IP	H	BB	SO	ShO	W	L	SV	AB	H	HR	BA	PO	A	E	DP	TC/G	FA
1931	STL	N	18	8	.692	3.36	35	23	15	211.2	225	65	134	4	4	0	2	72	7	0	.097	9	38	2	3	1.4	.959
1932			11	14	.440	4.05	39	30	14	233.1	296	67	78	1	1	1	0	73	13	0	.178	9	43	3	0	1.4	.945
1933	2 teams		STL N	(3G 0–2)		CIN N	(33G 7–25)																				
"	total		7	27	.206	3.30	36	33	17	248	264	60	89	2	0	1	1	81	14	0	.173	4	61	1	1	1.8	.985
1934	CIN	N	15	21	.417	3.59	47	31	18	261	297	59	122	1	2	4	4	92	18	0	.196	11	44	1	2	1.2	.982
1935			22	13	.629	3.51	45	33	20	276.2	295	49	120	3	3	2	0	93	13	0	.140	9	69	1	5	1.8	.987
1936			19	19	.500	4.02	51	37	13	282.1	331	42	121	2	1	3	5	90	18	0	.200	19	53	2	5	1.5	.973
1937			10	14	.417	4.04	43	26	12	222.2	240	55	94	1	1	4	1	80	16	0	.200	17	50	4	3	1.7	.944
1938			21	14	.600	2.93	41	37	26	307	315	49	132	4	0	0	3	119	21	2	.176	13	51	1	3	1.6	.985
1939			25	7	.781	2.93	38	35	28	301	321	35	128	5	1	0	0	110	23	0	.209	11	48	3	1	1.6	.952
1940			20	12	.625	3.06	37	37	26	296.2	280	48	115	3	0	0	0	108	18	0	.167	8	47	3	0	1.6	.948
1941			12	14	.462	3.31	29	28	17	228.1	233	54	76	2	0	0	1	84	13	0	.155	10	42	1	2	1.8	.981
1942			10	11	.476	3.06	29	27	13	208.2	203	49	68	1	0	0	0	68	9	0	.132	8	28	1	1	1.3	.973
1943	CHI	N	10	14	.417	3.57	32	22	10	174	184	39	75	2	1	2	3	58	13	0	.224	3	20	1	0	0.8	.958
1944			7	13	.350	4.15	42	16	7	180	205	39	69	0	2	5	3	57	9	0	.158	7	30	1	3	0.9	.974
1945			16	11	.593	3.45	35	30	15	213.2	223	51	86	1	1	0	4	75	15	0	.200	9	32	1	0	1.2	.976
15 yrs.			223	212	.513	3.46	579	445	251	3645	3912	761	1507	32	17	22	29	1260	220	2	.175	147	656	26	29	1.4	.969

WORLD SERIES

Year	Team		W	L	PCT	ERA	G	GS	CG	IP	H	BB	SO	ShO	W	L	SV	AB	H	HR	BA	PO	A	E	DP	TC/G	FA
1931	STL	N	0	2	.000	4.26	3	2	0	12.2	14	7	14	0	0	0	0	2	0	0	.000	0	2	0	0	0.7	1.000
1939	CIN	N	0	1	.000	2.35	2	2	1	15.1	9	3	9	0	0	0	0	5	1	0	.200	0	0	0	0	1.0	1.000
1940			2	1	.667	2.79	3	3	2	19.1	17	10	6	0	0	0	0	7	0	0	.000	0	5	0	1	1.7	1.000
1945	CHI	N	0	0	—	6.75	3	0	0	5.1	5	7	1	0	0	0	0	0	0	0	—	0	0	0	0	0.0	—
4 yrs.			2	4	.333	3.42	11	7	3	52.2	45	27	30	0	0	0	0	14	1	0	.071	2	7	0	1	0.8	1.000
					7th		10th						6th														

Jim Derrington

DERRINGTON, CHARLES JAMES (Blackie)
B. Nov. 29, 1939, Compton, Calif. BL TL 6'3" 190 lbs.

Year	Team		W	L	PCT	ERA	G	GS	CG	IP	H	BB	SO	ShO	W	L	SV	AB	H	HR	BA	PO	A	E	DP	TC/G	FA
1956	CHI	A	0	1	.000	7.50	1	1	0	6	9	6	3	0	0	0	0	2	1	0	.500	0	0	0	0	0.0	—
1957			0	1	.000	4.86	20	5	0	37	29	29	14	0	0	0	0	4	0	0	.000	3	1	1	0	0.3	.800
2 yrs.			0	2	.000	5.23	21	6	0	43	38	35	17	0	0	0	0	6	1	0	.167	3	1	1	0	0.2	.800

Jim Deshaies

DESHAIES, JAMES JOSEPH
B. June 23, 1960, Massena, N. Y. BL TL 6'4" 222 lbs.

Year	Team		W	L	PCT	ERA	G	GS	CG	IP	H	BB	SO	ShO	W	L	SV	AB	H	HR	BA	PO	A	E	DP	TC/G	FA
1984	NY	A	0	1	.000	11.57	2	2	0	7	14	7	5	0	0	0	0	0	0	0	—	0	1	0	0	0.5	1.000
1985	HOU	N	0	0	—	5.00	2	0	0	3	1	0	2	0	0	0	0	0	0	0	—	0	0	0	0	0.0	—
1986			12	5	.706	3.25	26	26	1	144	124	59	128	1	0	0	0	43	2	0	.047	9	13	2	0	0.9	.917
1987			11	6	.647	4.62	26	25	1	152	149	57	104	0	0	0	0	53	5	0	.094	5	22	1	0	1.1	.964
1988			11	14	.440	3.00	31	31	3	207	164	72	127	2	0	0	0	63	3	0	.048	7	25	2	1	1.1	.941
1989			15	10	.600	2.91	34	34	6	225.2	180	79	153	3	0	0	0	75	9	0	.120	8	31	3	2	1.2	.929
6 yrs.			49	36	.576	3.42	121	118	11	738.2	632	274	519	6	0	0	0	234	19	0	.081	29	92	8	3	1.1	.938

Jimmie DeShong

DeSHONG, JAMES BROOKLYN
B. Nov. 30, 1909, Harrisburg, Pa. BR TR 5'11" 165 lbs.

Year	Team		W	L	PCT	ERA	G	GS	CG	IP	H	BB	SO	ShO	W	L	SV	AB	H	HR	BA	PO	A	E	DP	TC/G	FA
1932	PHI	A	0	0	—	11.70	6	0	0	10	17	9	5	0	0	0	0	3	0	0	.000	0	3	0	0	0.5	1.000
1934	NY	A	6	7	.462	4.11	31	12	6	133.2	126	56	40	0	0	2	3	42	8	0	.190	4	28	1	0	1.1	.970
1935			4	1	.800	3.26	29	3	0	69	64	33	30	0	3	1	3	14	1	0	.071	4	22	1	0	0.9	.963
1936	WAS	A	18	10	.643	4.63	34	31	16	223.2	255	96	59	2	0	1	2	79	15	0	.190	4	34	2	6	1.2	.950
1937			14	15	.483	4.90	37	34	20	264.1	290	124	86	0	1	0	1	94	19	0	.202	15	52	2	2	1.9	.971
1938			5	8	.385	6.58	31	14	0	131.1	160	83	41	0	1	2	0	46	12	0	.261	8	26	3	4	1.2	.919
1939			0	3	.000	8.63	7	6	1	40.2	56	31	12	0	0	0	0	15	3	0	.200	1	14	1	0	2.3	.938
7 yrs.			47	44	.516	5.08	175	100	44	872.2	968	432	273	2	5	6	9	293	58	0	.198	36	179	10	12	1.3	.956

Shorty DesJardien

DesJARDIEN, PAUL RAYMOND
B. Aug. 24, 1893, Coffeyville, Kans. D. Mar. 7, 1956, Monrovia, Calif. BR TR 6'4½" 205 lbs.

Year	Team		W	L	PCT	ERA	G	GS	CG	IP	H	BB	SO	ShO	W	L	SV	AB	H	HR	BA	PO	A	E	DP	TC/G	FA
1916	CLE	A	0	0	—	18.00	1	0	0	1	1	1	0	0	0	0	0	0	0	0	—	0	0	0	0	0.0	—

Rube Dessau

DESSAU, FRANK ROLLAND
B. Mar. 29, 1883, New Galilee, Pa. D. May 6, 1952, York, Pa. BB TR 5'11" 175 lbs.

Year	Team		W	L	PCT	ERA	G	GS	CG	IP	H	BB	SO	ShO	W	L	SV	AB	H	HR	BA	PO	A	E	DP	TC/G	FA
1907	BOS	N	0	1	.000	10.61	2	2	1	9.1	13	10	1	0	0	0	0	4	0	0	.000	1	2	2	0	2.5	.600
1910	BKN	N	2	3	.400	5.79	19	0	0	51.1	67	29	24	0	2	3	0	15	1	0	.067	0	9	2	0	0.6	.818
2 yrs.			2	4	.333	6.53	21	2	1	60.2	80	39	25	0	2	3	0	19	1	0	.053	1	11	4	0	0.8	.750

Tom Dettore

DETTORE, THOMAS ANTHONY
B. Nov. 17, 1947, Canonsburg, Pa. BL TR 6'4" 200 lbs.

Year	Team		W	L	PCT	ERA	G	GS	CG	IP	H	BB	SO	ShO	W	L	SV	AB	H	HR	BA	PO	A	E	DP	TC/G	FA
1973	PIT	N	0	1	.000	5.96	12	1	0	22.2	33	14	13	0	0	0	0	4	0	0	.000	2	1	0	0	0.3	1.000
1974	CHI	N	3	5	.375	4.15	16	9	0	65	64	31	43	0	1	0	0	20	5	0	.250	10	8	0	1	1.1	1.000
1975			5	4	.556	5.40	36	5	0	85	88	31	46	0	4	2	0	24	6	0	.250	6	14	2	2	0.6	.909
1976			0	1	.000	10.29	4	0	0	7	11	2	4	0	0	1	0	0	0	0	—	2	0	0	0	0.5	1.000
4 yrs.			8	11	.421	5.21	68	15	0	179.2	196	78	106	0	5	3	0	48	11	0	.229	20	23	2	3	0.7	.956

Mel Deutsch

DEUTSCH, MELVIN ELLIOTT
B. July 26, 1915, Caldwell, Tex. BR TR 6'4" 215 lbs.

Year	Team		W	L	PCT	ERA	G	GS	CG	IP	H	BB	SO	ShO	W	L	SV	AB	H	HR	BA	PO	A	E	DP	TC/G	FA
1946	BOS	A	0	0	—	5.68	3	0	0	6.1	7	3	2	0	0	0	0	2	0	0	.000	0	1	1	0	0.7	.500

Charlie Devens

DEVENS, CHARLES
B. Jan. 1, 1910, Milton, Mass. BR TR 6'1" 180 lbs.

Year	Team		W	L	PCT	ERA	G	GS	CG	IP	H	BB	SO	ShO	W	L	SV	AB	H	HR	BA	PO	A	E	DP	TC/G	FA
1932	NY	A	1	0	1.000	2.00	1	1	1	9	6	7	4	0	0	0	0	2	0	0	.000	0	1	0	0	1.0	1.000
1933			3	3	.500	4.35	14	8	2	62	59	50	23	0	1	1	0	21	2	0	.095	3	9	1	1	0.9	.923

Year	Team		W	L	PCT	ERA	G	GS	CG	IP	H	BB	SO	ShO	Relief Pitching W	L	SV	Batting AB	H	HR	BA	PO	A	E	DP	TC/G	FA

Charlie Devens *continued*

| 1934 | | | 1 | 0 | 1.000 | 1.64 | 1 | 1 | 1 | 11 | 9 | 5 | 4 | 0 | 0 | 0 | 0 | 2 | 1 | 0 | .500 | 0 | 3 | 0 | 1 | 3.0 | 1.000 |
| 3 yrs. | | | 5 | 3 | .625 | 3.73 | 16 | 10 | 4 | 82 | 74 | 62 | 31 | 0 | 1 | 1 | 0 | 25 | 3 | 0 | .120 | 3 | 13 | 1 | 2 | 1.1 | .941 |

Adrian Devine

DEVINE, PAUL ADRIAN
B. Dec. 2, 1951, Galveston, Tex.   BR TR 6'4" 185 lbs.

1973	ATL	N	2	3	.400	6.47	24	1	0	32	45	12	15	0	2	2	4	4	1	0	.250	2	2	0	0	0.2	1.000
1975			1	0	1.000	4.50	5	2	0	16	19	7	8	0	0	0	0	5	0	0	.000	1	1	0	0	0.4	1.000
1976			5	6	.455	3.21	48	1	0	73	72	26	48	0	5	6	9	14	0	0	.000	3	8	1	0	0.3	.917
1977	TEX	A	11	6	.647	3.57	56	2	0	106	102	31	67	0	10	6	15	0	0	0	—	12	24	0	1	0.6	1.000
1978	ATL	N	5	4	.556	5.95	31	6	0	65	84	25	26	0	2	2	3	11	1	0	.091	10	9	1	1	0.6	.950
1979			1	2	.333	3.22	40	0	0	67	84	25	22	0	1	2	0	7	0	0	.000	1	12	4	1	0.4	.765
1980	TEX	A	1	1	.500	4.82	13	0	0	28	49	9	8	0	1	1	0	0	0	0	—	2	3	1	0	0.5	.833
7 yrs.			26	22	.542	4.21	217	12	0	387	455	135	194	0	21	19	31	41	2	0	.049	31	59	7	3	0.4	.928

Jim Devine

DEVINE, WALTER JAMES   TL
B. Oct. 5, 1858, Brooklyn, N. Y. D. Jan. 11, 1905, Syracuse, N. Y.

1883	BAL	AA	1	1	.500	7.36	2	2	1	11	15	1	3	0	0	0	0	9	2	0	.222	1	0	1	0	1.0	.500
1886	NY	N	0	0	—	0.00	0	0	0	0	0	0	0	0	0	0	0	3	0	0	.000	0	0	0	0	0.0	—
2 yrs.			1	1	.500	7.36	2	2	1	11	15	1	3	0	0	0	0	12	2	0	.167	1	0	1	0	1.0	.500

Hal Deviney

DEVINEY, HAROLD JOHN   BR TR
B. Apr. 11, 1893, Newton, Mass. D. Jan. 4, 1933, Westwood, Mass.

| 1920 | BOS | A | 0 | 0 | — | 15.00 | 1 | 0 | 0 | 3 | 7 | 2 | 0 | 0 | 0 | 0 | 0 | 2 | 2 | 0 | 1.000 | 0 | 0 | 0 | 0 | 0.0 | — |

Jim Devlin

DEVLIN, JAMES ALEXANDER   BR TR 5'11" 175 lbs.
B. 1849, Philadelphia, Pa. D. Oct. 10, 1883, Philadelphia, Pa.

1876	LOU	N	30	35	.462	1.56	68	68	66	622	566	37	122	5	0	0	0	298	94	0	.315	44	100	9	4	2.3	.941
1877			35	25	.583	2.25	61	61	61	559	617	41	141	4	0	0	0	268	72	1	.269	30	110	10	2	2.5	.933
2 yrs.			65	60	.520	1.89	129	129	127	1181	1183	78	263	9	0	0	0	566	166	1	.293	74	210	19	6	2.3	.937

Jim Devlin

DEVLIN, JAMES H.   TL
B. Apr. 16, 1866, Troy, N. Y. D. Dec. 14, 1900, Troy, N. Y.

1886	NY	N	0	0	—	18.00	1	0	0	2	3	4	2	0	0	0	0	1	0	0	.000	1	1	0	0	2.0	1.000
1887	PHI	N	0	2	.000	6.00	2	2	2	18	20	10	6	0	0	0	0	6	2	0	.333	0	5	0	0	2.5	1.000
1888	STL	AA	6	5	.545	3.19	11	11	10	90.1	82	20	45	0	0	0	0	37	11	0	.297	3	22	4	0	2.6	.862
1889			5	3	.625	2.40	9	8	5	60	56	24	37	0	1	0	0	26	5	0	.192	0	18	3	0	2.3	.857
4 yrs.			11	10	.524	3.38	23	21	17	170.1	161	58	90	0	1	0	1	70	18	0	.257	4	46	7	0	2.5	.877

Charlie Dewald

DEWALD, CHARLES H.   TL
B. 1867, Newark, N. J. D. Aug. 22, 1904, Cleveland, Ohio

| 1890 | CLE | P | 2 | 0 | 1.000 | 0.64 | 2 | 2 | 2 | 14 | 13 | 5 | 6 | 0 | 0 | 0 | 0 | 8 | 3 | 0 | .375 | 0 | 2 | 1 | 0 | 1.5 | .667 |

Carlos Diaz

DIAZ, CARLOS ANTONIO   BR TL 6' 161 lbs.
B. Jan. 7, 1958, Kaneohe, Hawaii

1982	2 teams	ATL N (19G 3–2)				NY N	(4G 0–0)																				
"	total		3	2	.600	4.03	23	0	0	29	37	13	16	0	3	2	1	3	0	0	.000	5	4	0	0	0.4	1.000
1983	NY	N	3	1	.750	2.05	54	0	0	83.1	62	35	64	0	3	1	2	5	0	0	.000	8	13	0	2	0.4	1.000
1984	LA	N	1	0	1.000	5.49	37	0	0	41	47	24	36	0	1	0	1	1	0	0	.000	2	2	0	0	0.1	1.000
1985			6	3	.667	2.61	46	0	0	79.1	70	18	73	0	6	3	0	4	0	0	.000	1	8	0	0	0.2	1.000
1986			0	0	—	4.26	19	0	0	25.1	33	7	18	0	0	0	0	1	0	0	.000	1	6	1	0	0.4	.875
5 yrs.			13	6	.684	3.21	179	0	0	258	249	97	207	0	13	6	4	14	0	0	.000	17	33	1	2	0.3	.980

LEAGUE CHAMPIONSHIP SERIES

| 1985 | LA | N | 0 | 0 | — | 3.00 | 2 | 0 | 0 | 3 | 5 | 1 | 2 | 0 | 0 | 0 | 0 | 0 | 0 | 0 | — | 1 | 0 | 0 | 0 | 0.5 | 1.000 |

Rob Dibble

DIBBLE, ROBERT KEITH   BL TR 6'4" 230 lbs.
B. Jan. 24, 1964, Bridgeport, Conn.

1988	CIN	N	1	1	.500	1.82	37	0	0	59.1	43	21	59	0	1	1	0	2	0	0	.000	1	3	0	0	0.1	1.000
1989			10	5	.667	2.09	74	0	0	99	62	39	141	0	10	5	2	8	0	0	.000	3	5	1	0	0.1	.889
2 yrs.			11	6	.647	1.99	111	0	0	158.1	105	60	200	0	11	6	2	10	0	0	.000	4	8	1	0	0.1	.923

Pedro Dibut

DIBUT, PEDRO   BR TR 5'8" 190 lbs.
Born Pedro Dibut y Villafana.
B. Nov. 18, 1892, Cienfuegos, Cuba D. Dec. 4, 1979, Hialeah, Fla.

1924	CIN	N	3	0	1.000	2.21	7	2	2	36.2	24	12	15	0	1	0	0	11	3	0	.273	2	12	0	0	2.0	1.000
1925			0	0	—	∞	1	0	0	0	3	0	0	0	0	0	0	0	0	0	—	0	0	0	0	0.0	—
2 yrs.			3	0	1.000	2.70	8	2	2	36.2	27	12	15	0	1	0	0	11	3	0	.273	2	12	0	0	1.8	1.000

Leo Dickerman

DICKERMAN, LEO LOUIS   BR TR 6'4" 192 lbs.
B. Oct. 31, 1896, DeSoto, Mo. D. Apr. 30, 1982, Atkins, Ark.

1923	BKN	N	8	12	.400	3.59	35	20	7	165.2	185	71	57	1	2	1	0	52	13	2	.250	2	50	4	3	1.6	.929
1924	2 teams	BKN N (7G 0–0)				STL N	(18G 7–4)																				
"	total		7	4	.636	2.84	25	15	8	139.1	128	67	37	1	0	0	0	45	10	0	.222	5	36	2	4	1.7	.953
1925	STL	N	4	11	.267	5.58	29	20	7	130.2	135	79	40	2	0	0	1	44	5	0	.114	6	47	0	1	1.8	1.000
3 yrs.			19	27	.413	3.95	89	55	22	435.2	448	217	134	4	2	1	1	141	28	2	.199	13	133	6	8	1.7	.961

George Dickerson

DICKERSON, GEORGE CLARK   BR TR 6'1" 170 lbs.
B. Dec. 1, 1892, Renner, Tex. D. July 9, 1938, Los Angeles, Calif.

| 1917 | CLE | A | 0 | 0 | — | 0.00 | 1 | 0 | 0 | 1 | 0 | 0 | 0 | 0 | 0 | 0 | 0 | 0 | 0 | 0 | — | 0 | 0 | 0 | 0 | 0.0 | — |

Emerson Dickman

DICKMAN, GEORGE EMERSON BR TR 6'2" 175 lbs.
B. Nov. 12, 1914, Buffalo, N. Y. D. Apr. 27, 1981, New York, N. Y.

Year	Team		W	L	PCT	ERA	G	GS	CG	IP	H	BB	SO	ShO	Relief Pitching W	Relief Pitching L	Relief Pitching SV	Batting AB	Batting H	Batting HR	BA	PO	A	E	DP	TC/G	FA
1936	BOS	A	0	0	–	9.00	1	0	0	1	2	1	2	0	0	0	0	0	0	0	–	0	0	0	0	0.0	–
1938			5	5	.500	5.28	32	11	3	104	117	54	22	1	2	0	0	35	10	1	.286	4	18	0	2	0.7	1.000
1939			8	3	.727	4.43	48	1	0	113.2	126	43	46	0	8	3	5	36	2	0	.056	4	33	2	3	0.8	.949
1940			8	6	.571	6.03	35	9	2	100	121	38	40	0	5	1	3	28	3	0	.107	5	29	3	5	1.1	.919
1941			1	1	.500	6.39	9	3	1	31	37	17	16	0	0	0	0	11	1	0	.091	1	1	1	0	0.3	.667
5 yrs.			22	15	.595	5.33	125	24	6	349.2	403	153	126	1	15	4	8	110	16	1	.145	14	81	6	10	0.8	.941

Jim Dickson

DICKSON, JAMES EDWARD BL TR 6'1" 185 lbs.
B. Apr. 20, 1938, Portland, Ore.

Year	Team		W	L	PCT	ERA	G	GS	CG	IP	H	BB	SO	ShO	Relief Pitching W	Relief Pitching L	Relief Pitching SV	Batting AB	Batting H	Batting HR	BA	PO	A	E	DP	TC/G	FA
1963	HOU	N	0	1	.000	6.14	13	0	0	14.2	22	2	6	0	0	1	2	1	0	0	.000	0	2	0	0	0.2	1.000
1964	CIN	N	1	0	1.000	7.20	4	0	0	5	8	5	6	0	1	0	0	0	0	0	–	0	1	0	0	0.3	1.000
1965	KC	A	3	2	.600	3.47	68	0	0	85.2	68	47	54	0	3	2	0	2	0	0	.000	2	12	1	0	0.2	.933
1966			1	0	1.000	5.35	24	1	0	37	37	23	20	0	1	0	1	4	1	0	.250	0	7	1	0	0.3	.875
4 yrs.			5	3	.625	4.36	109	1	0	142.1	135	77	86	0	5	3	3	7	1	0	.143	2	22	2	0	0.2	.923

Murry Dickson

DICKSON, MURRY MONROE BR TR 5'10½" 157 lbs.
B. Aug. 21, 1916, Tracy, Mo. D. Sept. 21, 1989, Kansas City, Kans.

Year	Team		W	L	PCT	ERA	G	GS	CG	IP	H	BB	SO	ShO	Relief Pitching W	Relief Pitching L	Relief Pitching SV	Batting AB	Batting H	Batting HR	BA	PO	A	E	DP	TC/G	FA
1939	STL	N	0	0	–	0.00	1	0	0	3.2	1	1	2	0	0	0	0	1	0	0	.000	0	2	0	0	2.0	1.000
1940			0	0	–	16.20	1	1	0	1.2	5	1	0	0	0	0	0	0	0	0	–	0	0	1	0	1.0	–
1942			6	3	.667	2.91	36	7	2	120.2	91	61	66	0	4	1	2	42	8	0	.190	10	27	0	2	1.0	1.000
1943			8	2	.800	3.58	31	7	2	115.2	114	49	44	0	2	2	0	34	9	0	.265	6	21	2	3	0.9	.931
1946			15	6	**.714**	2.88	47	19	12	184.1	160	56	82	2	4	2	1	65	18	0	.277	13	52	1	5	1.4	.985
1947			13	16	.448	3.07	47	25	11	231.2	211	88	111	4	3	2	3	80	17	0	.213	13	47	4	3	1.4	.938
1948			12	16	.429	4.14	42	29	11	252.1	257	85	113	1	2	4	1	96	27	0	.281	12	51	0	0	1.5	1.000
1949	PIT	N	12	14	.462	3.29	44	20	11	224.1	216	80	89	2	3	5	0	84	17	0	.202	26	52	3	8	1.8	.963
1950			10	15	.400	3.80	51	22	8	225	227	83	76	0	5	3	3	82	21	0	.256	20	45	1	6	1.3	.985
1951			20	16	.556	4.02	45	35	19	288.2	**294**	101	112	3	4	2	2	110	30	1	.273	19	70	3	3	2.0	.967
1952			14	**21**	.400	3.57	43	34	21	277.2	278	76	112	2	2	0	2	107	24	0	.224	29	62	4	7	2.2	.958
1953			10	**19**	.345	4.53	45	26	10	200.2	240	58	88	1	2	4	4	61	7	0	.115	14	34	4	2	1.2	.923
1954	PHI	N	10	**20**	.333	3.78	40	31	12	226.1	256	73	64	4	1	1	3	79	15	0	.190	12	55	3	3	1.8	.957
1955			12	11	.522	3.50	36	28	12	216	190	82	92	4	1	1	0	82	18	1	.220	17	39	1	4	1.6	.982
1956	2 teams	PHI N (3G 0–3) STL N (28G 13–8)																									
"	total		13	11	.542	3.28	31	30	12	219.1	195	69	110	3	0	1	0	86	22	0	.256	24	51	1	5	2.5	.987
1957	STL	N	5	3	.625	4.14	14	13	3	74	87	25	29	1	0	0	0	27	6	0	.222	11	20	1	0	2.3	.969
1958	2 teams	KC A (27G 9–5) NY A (6G 1–2)																									
"	total		10	7	.588	3.70	33	11	3	119.1	117	43	55	0	7	3	2	42	11	1	.262	9	27	0	3	1.1	1.000
1959	KC	A	2	1	.667	4.94	38	0	0	71	85	27	36	0	2	1	0	17	3	0	.176	1	13	1	0	0.4	.933
18 yrs.			172	181	.487	3.66	625	338	149	3052.1	3024	1058	1281	27	42	32	23	1095	253	3	.231	236	668	30	54	1.5	.968
WORLD SERIES																											
1943	STL	N	0	0	–	0.00	1	0	0	.2	0	1	0	0	0	0	0	0	0	0	–	1	0	0	0	1.0	1.000
1946			0	1	.000	3.86	2	2	0	14	11	4	7	0	0	0	0	5	2	0	.400	0	3	0	0	1.5	1.000
1958	NY	A	0	0	–	4.50	2	0	0	4	4	0	1	0	0	0	0	0	0	0	–	0	0	0	0	0.0	–
3 yrs.			0	1	.000	3.86	5	2	0	18.2	15	5	8	0	0	0	0	5	2	0	.400	1	3	0	0	0.8	1.000

Walt Dickson

DICKSON, WALTER R. (Hickory) BR TR 5'11½" 175 lbs.
B. Dec. 3, 1878, New Summerfield, Tex. D. Dec. 9, 1918, Ardmore, Okla.

Year	Team		W	L	PCT	ERA	G	GS	CG	IP	H	BB	SO	ShO	Relief Pitching W	Relief Pitching L	Relief Pitching SV	Batting AB	Batting H	Batting HR	BA	PO	A	E	DP	TC/G	FA
1910	NY	N	1	0	1.000	5.46	12	1	0	29.2	31	9	9	0	1	0	0	4	1	0	.250	0	6	1	0	0.6	.857
1912	BOS	N	3	19	.136	3.86	36	20	9	189	233	61	47	1	2	4	0	60	10	0	.167	4	63	6	1	2.0	.918
1913			6	7	.462	3.23	19	15	8	128	118	45	47	0	0	1	0	45	8	0	.178	6	26	1	1	1.7	.970
1914	PIT	F	9	**21**	.300	3.16	40	32	19	256.2	262	74	63	3	0	2	1	83	7	0	.084	8	81	3	3	2.3	.967
1915			6	5	.545	4.19	27	11	4	96.2	115	33	36	0	2	2	0	31	4	0	.129	3	32	1	0	1.3	.972
5 yrs.			25	52	.325	3.60	134	79	40	700	759	222	202	4	5	9	1	223	30	0	.135	21	208	12	5	1.8	.950

George Diehl

DIEHL, GEORGE KRAUSE BR TR 6'2" 196 lbs.
B. Feb. 25, 1918, Emmaus, Pa. D. Aug. 24, 1986, Kingsport, Tenn.

Year	Team		W	L	PCT	ERA	G	GS	CG	IP	H	BB	SO	ShO	Relief Pitching W	Relief Pitching L	Relief Pitching SV	Batting AB	Batting H	Batting HR	BA	PO	A	E	DP	TC/G	FA
1942	BOS	N	0	0	–	2.45	1	0	0	3.2	2	2	0	0	0	0	0	1	0	0	.000	0	1	0	0	1.0	1.000
1943			0	0	–	4.50	1	0	0	4	4	3	1	0	0	0	0	1	0	0	.000	0	5	0	0	5.0	1.000
2 yrs.			0	0	–	3.52	2	0	0	7.2	6	5	1	0	0	0	0	2	0	0	.000	0	6	0	0	3.0	1.000

Larry Dierker

DIERKER, LAWRENCE EDWARD BR TR 6'4" 215 lbs.
B. Sept. 22, 1946, Hollywood, Calif.

Year	Team		W	L	PCT	ERA	G	GS	CG	IP	H	BB	SO	ShO	Relief Pitching W	Relief Pitching L	Relief Pitching SV	Batting AB	Batting H	Batting HR	BA	PO	A	E	DP	TC/G	FA
1964	HOU	N	0	1	.000	2.00	3	1	0	9	7	3	5	0	0	0	0	3	0	0	.000	0	0	1	0	0.3	–
1965			7	8	.467	3.50	26	19	1	146.2	135	37	109	0	1	0	0	50	5	1	.100	10	17	4	0	1.2	.871
1966			10	8	.556	3.18	29	28	8	187	173	45	108	2	0	0	0	67	10	1	.149	13	26	2	1	1.4	.951
1967			6	5	.545	3.36	15	15	4	99	95	25	68	0	0	0	0	31	7	0	.226	7	10	2	0	1.3	.895
1968			12	15	.444	3.31	32	32	10	233.2	206	89	161	1	0	0	0	73	5	0	.068	13	28	1	2	1.3	.976
1969			20	13	.606	2.33	39	37	20	305	240	72	232	4	0	0	0	118	17	1	.144	14	42	3	5	1.5	.949
1970			16	12	.571	3.87	37	36	17	270	263	82	191	2	0	0	1	92	16	0	.174	19	31	3	3	1.4	.943
1971			12	6	.667	2.72	24	23	6	159	150	33	91	2	0	0	0	54	4	0	.074	16	23	1	0	1.7	.975
1972			15	8	.652	3.40	31	31	12	214.2	209	51	115	5	0	0	0	78	13	0	.167	16	19	0	1	1.1	1.000
1973			1	1	.500	4.33	14	3	0	27	27	13	18	0	1	0	0	4	0	0	.000	0	3	0	0	0.2	1.000
1974			11	10	.524	2.89	33	33	7	224	189	82	150	3	0	0	0	71	14	0	.197	10	34	1	1	1.4	.978
1975			14	16	.467	4.00	34	34	14	232	225	91	127	2	0	0	0	76	7	0	.092	15	31	3	1	1.4	.939
1976			13	14	.481	3.69	28	28	7	188	171	72	112	4	0	0	0	64	9	1	.141	17	18	2	2	1.3	.946
1977	STL	N	2	6	.250	4.62	11	9	0	39	40	16	6	0	0	0	0	8	0	0	.000	2	5	0	0	0.6	1.000
14 yrs.			139	123	.531	3.30	356	329	106	2334	2130	711	1493	25	2	0	1	789	107	4	.136	152	287	23	16	1.3	.950

Bill Dietrich

DIETRICH, WILLIAM JOHN (Bullfrog) BR TR 6' 185 lbs.
B. Mar. 29, 1910, Philadelphia, Pa. D. June 20, 1978, Philadelphia, Pa.

Year	Team		W	L	PCT	ERA	G	GS	CG	IP	H	BB	SO	ShO	Relief Pitching W	Relief Pitching L	Relief Pitching SV	Batting AB	Batting H	Batting HR	BA	PO	A	E	DP	TC/G	FA
1933	PHI	A	0	1	.000	5.82	8	1	0	17	13	19	4	0	0	0	0	3	1	0	.333	0	5	0	1	0.6	1.000

Year	Team	W	L	PCT	ERA	G	GS	CG	IP	H	BB	SO	ShO	W	L	SV	AB	H	HR	BA	PO	A	E	DP	TC/G	FA

Bill Dietrich *continued*

Year	Team	W	L	PCT	ERA	G	GS	CG	IP	H	BB	SO	ShO	W	L	SV	AB	H	HR	BA	PO	A	E	DP	TC/G	FA
1934		11	12	.478	4.68	39	23	14	207.2	201	114	88	4	0	2	3	72	15	1	.208	12	31	3	0	1.2	.935
1935		7	13	.350	5.39	43	15	8	185.1	203	101	59	1	4	3	3	60	5	0	.083	10	34	3	0	1.1	.936
1936	3 teams	PHI A	(21G 4-6)		WAS A	(5G 0-1)	CHI A	(14G 4-4)																		
"	total	8	11	.421	5.75	40	15	6	162.2	197	82	77	1	4	3	3	57	11	0	.193	5	34	3	3	1.1	.929
1937	CHI A	8	10	.444	4.90	29	20	7	143.1	162	72	62	1	1	0	1	44	8	0	.182	3	31	1	1	1.2	.971
1938		2	4	.333	5.44	8	7	1	48	49	31	11	0	0	0	0	16	1	0	.063	3	7	0	0	1.3	1.000
1939		7	8	.467	5.22	25	19	2	127.2	134	56	43	0	1	0	0	37	8	1	.216	5	19	2	2	1.0	.923
1940		10	6	.625	4.03	23	17	6	149.2	154	65	43	1	1	0	0	50	12	1	.240	8	20	1	2	1.3	.966
1941		5	8	.385	5.35	19	15	4	109.1	114	50	26	1	0	1	0	34	3	0	.088	10	13	2	1	1.3	.920
1942		6	11	.353	4.89	26	23	6	160	173	70	39	0	0	0	0	48	5	0	.104	7	32	0	2	1.5	1.000
1943		12	10	.545	2.80	26	26	12	186.2	180	53	52	2	0	0	0	56	8	1	.143	10	46	1	3	2.2	.982
1944		16	17	.485	3.62	36	36	15	246	269	68	70	2	0	0	0	77	9	1	.117	10	46	3	0	1.6	.949
1945		7	10	.412	4.19	18	16	6	122.1	136	36	43	4	0	2	0	36	6	0	.167	4	23	1	2	1.8	.970
1946		3	3	.500	2.61	11	9	3	62	63	24	20	0	0	0	1	19	1	0	.053	2	17	0	2	1.7	1.000
1947	PHI A	5	2	.714	3.12	11	9	2	60.2	48	40	18	1	1	0	0	16	1	0	.063	1	8	4	3	1.2	.692
1948		1	2	.333	5.87	4	2	0	15.1	21	9	5	0	0	0	0	2	0	0	.000	0	3	0	0	0.8	1.000
16 yrs.		108	128	.458	4.48	366	253	92	2003.2	2117	890	660	18	13	11	11	627	94	5	.150	95	369	24	22	1.3	.951

Dutch Dietz

DIETZ, LLOYD ARTHUR
B. Feb. 12, 1912, Cincinnati, Ohio D. Oct. 29, 1972, Beaumont, Tex.
BR TR 5'11½" 180 lbs.

Year	Team	W	L	PCT	ERA	G	GS	CG	IP	H	BB	SO	ShO	W	L	SV	AB	H	HR	BA	PO	A	E	DP	TC/G	FA
1940	PIT N	0	1	.000	5.87	4	2	0	15.1	22	4	8	0	0	0	0	7	1	0	.143	0	2	1	0	0.8	.667
1941		7	2	.778	2.33	33	6	4	100.1	88	33	22	1	4	0	1	25	4	0	.160	13	18	1	1	1.0	.969
1942		6	9	.400	3.95	40	13	3	134.1	139	57	35	0	2	3	2	35	7	0	.200	7	21	1	1	0.7	.966
1943	2 teams	PIT N	(8G 0-3)		PHI N	(21G 1-1)																				
"	total	1	4	.200	6.40	29	0	0	45	54	19	14	0	1	4	2	6	1	0	.167	0	12	0	0	0.4	1.000
4 yrs.		14	16	.467	3.87	106	21	7	295	303	113	79	1	7	6	6	73	13	0	.178	20	53	3	3	0.7	.961

Reese Diggs

DIGGS, REESE WILSON (Diggsy)
B. Sept. 22, 1915, Mathews, Va. D. Oct. 30, 1978, Baltimore, Md.
BB TR 6'2" 180 lbs.

Year	Team	W	L	PCT	ERA	G	GS	CG	IP	H	BB	SO	ShO	W	L	SV	AB	H	HR	BA	PO	A	E	DP	TC/G	FA
1934	WAS A	1	2	.333	6.75	4	3	2	21.1	26	15	2	0	0	0	0	8	2	0	.250	0	4	0	0	1.0	1.000

Jack DiLauro

DiLAURO, JACK EDWARD
B. May 3, 1943, Akron, Ohio
BB TL 6'2" 185 lbs.

Year	Team	W	L	PCT	ERA	G	GS	CG	IP	H	BB	SO	ShO	W	L	SV	AB	H	HR	BA	PO	A	E	DP	TC/G	FA
1969	NY N	1	4	.200	2.40	23	4	0	63.2	50	18	27	0	1	1	1	12	0	0	.000	6	10	0	0	0.7	1.000
1970	HOU N	1	3	.250	4.24	42	0	0	34	34	17	23	0	1	3	3	2	0	0	.000	2	4	2	0	0.2	.750
2 yrs.		2	7	.222	3.04	65	4	0	97.2	84	35	50	0	2	4	4	14	0	0	.000	8	14	2	0	0.4	.917

Gordon Dillard

DILLARD, GORDON LEE
B. May 20, 1964, Salinas, Calif.
BL TL 6'1" 180 lbs.

Year	Team	W	L	PCT	ERA	G	GS	CG	IP	H	BB	SO	ShO	W	L	SV	AB	H	HR	BA	PO	A	E	DP	TC/G	FA
1988	BAL A	0	0	–	6.00	2	1	0	3	3	4	2	0	0	0	0	0	0	0	–	0	1	0	0	0.5	1.000
1989	PHI N	0	0	–	6.75	5	0	0	4	7	0	2	0	0	0	0	0	0	0	–	0	1	0	0	0.2	1.000
2 yrs.		0	0	–	6.43	7	1	0	7	10	4	4	0	0	0	0	0	0	0	–	0	2	0	0	0.3	1.000

Harley Dillinger

DILLINGER, HARLEY HUGH (Hoke, Lefty)
B. Oct. 30, 1894, Pomeroy, Ohio D. Jan. 8, 1959, Cleveland, Ohio
BR TL 5'11" 175 lbs.

Year	Team	W	L	PCT	ERA	G	GS	CG	IP	H	BB	SO	ShO	W	L	SV	AB	H	HR	BA	PO	A	E	DP	TC/G	FA
1914	CLE A	0	1	.000	4.54	11	2	1	33.2	41	25	11	0	0	0	0	10	0	0	.000	0	8	1	0	0.8	.889

Bill Dillman

DILLMAN, WILLIAM HOWARD
B. May 25, 1945, Trenton, N. J.
BR TR 6'2" 180 lbs.

Year	Team	W	L	PCT	ERA	G	GS	CG	IP	H	BB	SO	ShO	W	L	SV	AB	H	HR	BA	PO	A	E	DP	TC/G	FA
1967	BAL A	5	9	.357	4.35	32	15	2	124	115	33	69	1	2	0	3	31	5	0	.161	7	15	0	1	0.7	1.000
1970	MON N	2	3	.400	5.23	18	0	0	31	28	18	17	0	2	3	0	2	0	0	.000	3	6	0	0	0.5	1.000
2 yrs.		7	12	.368	4.53	50	15	2	155	143	51	86	1	4	3	3	33	5	0	.152	10	21	0	1	0.6	1.000

Steve Dillon

DILLON, STEPHEN EDWARD
B. Mar. 20, 1943, Yonkers, N. Y.
BL TL 5'10" 160 lbs.

Year	Team	W	L	PCT	ERA	G	GS	CG	IP	H	BB	SO	ShO	W	L	SV	AB	H	HR	BA	PO	A	E	DP	TC/G	FA
1963	NY N	0	0	–	10.80	1	0	0	1.2	3	0	1	0	0	0	0	0	0	0	–	1	0	0	0	1.0	1.000
1964		0	0	–	9.00	2	0	0	3	4	2	2	0	0	0	0	0	0	0	–	0	0	0	0	0.0	–
2 yrs.		0	0	–	9.64	3	0	0	4.2	7	2	3	0	0	0	0	0	0	0	–	1	0	0	0	0.3	1.000

Frank DiMichele

DiMICHELE, FRANK LAWRENCE
B. Feb. 16, 1965, Philadelphia, Pa.
BR TL 6'3" 205 lbs.

Year	Team	W	L	PCT	ERA	G	GS	CG	IP	H	BB	SO	ShO	W	L	SV	AB	H	HR	BA	PO	A	E	DP	TC/G	FA
1988	CAL A	0	0	–	9.64	4	0	0	4.2	5	2	1	0	0	0	0	0	0	0	–	0	0	0	0	0.0	–

Bill Dinneen

DINNEEN, WILLIAM HENRY (Big Bill)
B. Apr. 5, 1876, Syracuse, N. Y. D. Jan. 13, 1955, Syracuse, N. Y.
BR TR 6'1" 190 lbs.

Year	Team	W	L	PCT	ERA	G	GS	CG	IP	H	BB	SO	ShO	W	L	SV	AB	H	HR	BA	PO	A	E	DP	TC/G	FA
1898	WAS N	9	16	.360	4.00	29	27	22	218.1	238	88	83	0	1	0	0	80	8	0	.100	6	50	5	1	2.1	.918
1899		14	18	.438	3.93	37	35	30	291	350	106	91	0	0	2	0	119	36	0	.303	16	85	10	1	3.0	.910
1900	BOS N	20	14	.588	3.12	40	37	33	320.2	304	105	107	1	0	0	0	125	35	0	.280	25	80	6	0	2.8	.946
1901		15	18	.455	2.94	37	34	31	309.1	295	77	141	0	1	0	0	147	31	0	.211	14	72	7	2	2.5	.925
1902	BOS A	21	21	.500	2.93	42	42	39	371.1	348	99	136	2	0	0	0	141	18	0	.128	14	77	4	1	2.1	.955
1903		21	13	.618	2.26	37	34	32	299	255	66	148	6	0	1	2	106	17	0	.160	11	79	2	4	2.5	.978
1904		23	14	.622	2.20	37	37	37	335.2	283	63	153	5	0	0	0	120	25	0	.208	19	98	4	3	3.3	.967
1905		12	15	.444	3.73	31	29	23	243.2	235	50	97	2	1	0	1	88	13	0	.148	11	77	6	3	3.0	.936
1906		8	19	.296	2.92	28	27	22	218.2	209	52	60	1	0	0	0	63	7	0	.111	10	58	7	1	2.7	.907
1907	2 teams	BOS A	(5G 0-4)		STL A	(24G 7-10)																				
"	total	7	14	.333	2.92	29	21	18	188	195	41	46	2	0	0	4	59	10	0	.169	5	46	3	1	1.9	.944
1908	STL A	14	7	.667	2.10	27	16	11	167	133	53	39	2	4	1	0	59	12	0	.203	3	44	1	1	1.8	.979

Year	Team	W	L	PCT	ERA	G	GS	CG	IP	H	BB	SO	ShO	Relief Pitching W	L	SV	Batting AB	H	HR	BA	PO	A	E	DP	TC/G	FA

Bill Dinneen *continued*

| 1909 | | 6 | 7 | .462 | 3.46 | 17 | 13 | 8 | 112 | 112 | 29 | 26 | 3 | 1 | 0 | 0 | 36 | 7 | 0 | .194 | 6 | 34 | 1 | 1 | 2.4 | .976 |
| 12 yrs. | | 170 | 176 | .491 | 3.01 | 391 | 352 | 306 | 3074.2 | 2957 | 829 | 1127 | 24 | 8 | 5 | 7 | 1143 | 219 | 1 | .192 | 133 | 800 | 56 | 19 | 2.5 | .943 |

WORLD SERIES

| 1903 | BOS A | 3 | 1 | .750 | 2.06 | 4 | 4 | 4 | 35 | 29 | 8 | 28 | 2 4th | 0 | 0 | 0 | 12 | 3 | 0 | .250 | 1 | 9 | 0 | 0 | 2.5 | 1.000 |

Ron Diorio

DIORIO, RONALD MICHAEL
B. July 15, 1946, Waterbury, Conn. — BR TR 6'6" 212 lbs.

1973	PHI N	0	0	–	2.33	23	0	0	19.1	18	6	11	0	0	0	1	0	0	0	–	0	2	0	1	0.1	1.000
1974		0	0	–	18.00	2	0	0	1	2	1	0	0	0	0	0	0	0	0	–	0	1	0	0	0.5	1.000
2 yrs.		0	0	–	3.10	25	0	0	20.1	20	7	11	0	0	0	1	0	0	0	–	0	3	0	1	0.1	1.000

Frank DiPino

DiPINO, FRANK MICHAEL
B. Oct. 22, 1956, Syracuse, N. Y. — BL TL 5'10" 175 lbs.

1981	MIL A	0	0	–	0.00	2	0	0	2	0	3	3	0	0	0	0	0	0	0	–	0	0	0	0	0.0	
1982	HOU N	2	2	.500	6.04	6	6	0	28.1	32	11	25	0	0	0	0	8	0	0	.000	0	2	0	0	0.3	1.000
1983		3	4	.429	2.65	53	0	0	71.1	52	20	67	0	3	4	20	6	1	0	.167	5	11	0	1	0.3	1.000
1984		4	9	.308	3.35	57	0	0	75.1	74	36	65	0	4	9	14	10	0	0	.000	3	12	0	0	0.3	1.000
1985		3	7	.300	4.03	54	0	0	76	69	43	49	0	3	7	6	12	2	0	.167	3	5	1	0	0.2	.889
1986	2 teams	HOU N	(31G 1–3)		CHI N	(30G 2–4)																				
"	total	3	7	.300	4.37	61	0	0	80.1	74	30	70	0	3	7	3	6	1	0	.167	8	17	1	1	0.4	.962
1987	CHI N	3	3	.500	3.15	69	0	0	80	75	34	61	0	3	3	4	2	1	0	.500	2	16	1	2	0.3	.947
1988		2	3	.400	4.98	63	0	0	90.1	102	32	69	0	2	3	0	10	1	0	.100	3	12	0	0	0.2	1.000
1989	STL N	9	0	1.000	2.45	67	0	0	88.1	73	20	44	0	9	0	0	13	1	0	.077	6	13	0	0	0.3	1.000
9 yrs.		29	35	.453	3.69	432	6	0	592	551	229	453	0	27	33	53	67	7	0	.104	30	88	3	4	0.3	.975

George Disch

DISCH, GEORGE CHARLES
B. Mar. 15, 1879, Lincoln, Mo.   D. Aug. 25, 1950, Rapid City, S. D. — 5'11"

| 1905 | DET A | 0 | 2 | .000 | 2.64 | 8 | 3 | 1 | 47.2 | 43 | 8 | 14 | 0 | 0 | 1 | 0 | 19 | 2 | 0 | .105 | 2 | 14 | 0 | 2 | 2.0 | 1.000 |

Alec Distaso

DISTASO, ALEC JOHN
B. Dec. 23, 1948, Los Angeles, Calif. — BR TR 6'2" 200 lbs.

| 1969 | CHI N | 0 | 0 | – | 3.60 | 2 | 0 | 0 | 5 | 6 | 1 | 1 | 0 | 0 | 0 | 0 | 0 | 0 | 0 | – | 0 | 2 | 0 | 0 | 1.0 | 1.000 |

Art Ditmar

DITMAR, ARTHUR JOHN
B. Apr. 3, 1929, Winthrop, Mass. — BR TR 6'2" 185 lbs.

1954	PHI A	1	4	.200	6.41	14	5	0	39.1	50	36	14	0	0	2	0	8	1	0	.125	4	5	1	1	0.7	.900
1955	KC A	12	12	.500	5.03	35	22	7	175.1	180	86	79	1	3	2	1	62	13	0	.210	15	29	1	3	1.3	.978
1956		12	22	.353	4.42	44	34	14	254.1	254	108	126	2	3	1	1	91	13	1	.143	20	33	2	3	1.3	.964
1957	NY A	8	3	.727	3.25	46	11	0	127.1	128	35	64	0	6	1	6	35	7	0	.200	8	19	4	0	0.7	.871
1958		9	8	.529	3.42	38	13	4	139.2	124	38	52	0	4	4	4	44	11	0	.250	6	15	0	1	0.6	1.000
1959		13	9	.591	2.90	38	25	7	202	156	52	96	1	1	1	1	76	15	1	.197	21	25	3	2	1.3	.939
1960		15	9	.625	3.06	34	28	8	200	195	56	65	1	1	2	0	69	11	0	.159	18	24	1	3	1.3	.977
1961	2 teams	NY A	(12G 2–3)		KC A	(20G 0–5)																				
"	total	2	8	.200	5.15	32	13	1	108.1	119	37	43	0	0	2	1	31	3	0	.097	9	19	1	0	0.9	.966
1962	KC A	0	2	.000	6.65	6	5	0	21.2	31	13	13	0	0	0	0	6	1	0	.167	2	3	0	0	0.8	1.000
9 yrs.		72	77	.483	3.98	287	156	41	1268	1237	461	552	5	18	15	14	422	75	2	.178	103	172	13	13	1.0	.955

WORLD SERIES

1957	NY A	0	0	–	0.00	2	0	0	6	2	0	2	0	0	0	0	1	0	0	.000	0	0	0	0	0.0	–
1958		0	0	–	0.00	1	0	0	3.2	2	0	2	0	0	0	0	1	0	0	.000	1	0	1	0	2.0	.500
1960		0	2	.000	21.60	2	2	0	1.2	6	1	0	0	0	0	0	0	0	0	–	0	0	0	0	0.0	–
3 yrs.		0	2	.000	3.18	5	2	0	11.1	10	1	4	0	0	0	0	2	0	0	.000	1	0	1	0	0.4	.500

Ken Dixon

DIXON, KENNETH JOHN
B. Oct. 17, 1960, Monroe, Va. — BB TR 5'10" 175 lbs.

1984	BAL A	0	1	.000	4.15	2	2	0	13	14	4	8	0	0	0	0	0	0	0	–	2	2	0	0	2.0	1.000
1985		8	4	.667	3.67	34	18	3	162	144	64	108	1	0	1	1	0	0	0	–	13	17	4	0	1.0	.882
1986		11	13	.458	4.58	35	33	2	202.1	194	83	170	0	0	0	0	0	0	0	–	12	21	2	1	1.0	.943
1987		7	10	.412	6.43	34	15	0	105	128	27	91	0	2	4	5	0	0	0	–	17	7	1	1	0.7	.960
4 yrs.		26	28	.481	4.66	105	68	5	482.1	480	178	377	1	2	5	6	0	0	0	–	44	47	7	2	0.9	.929

Sonny Dixon

DIXON, JOHN CRAIG
B. Nov. 5, 1924, Charlotte, N. C. — BB TR 6'2½" 205 lbs.

1953	WAS A	5	8	.385	3.75	43	6	3	120	123	31	40	0	0	2	3	26	4	0	.154	6	31	0	0	0.9	1.000
1954	2 teams	WAS A	(16G 1–2)		PHI A	(38G 5–7)																				
"	total	6	9	.400	4.47	54	0	1	137	162	39	49	0	4	6	5	34	7	0	.206	11	39	1	1	0.9	.980
1955	KC A	0	0	–	16.20	2	0	0	1.2	6	0	0	0	0	0	0	0	0	0	–	1	0	0	0	0.5	1.000
1956	NY A	0	1	.000	2.08	3	0	0	4.1	5	5	1	0	0	1	1	1	0	0	.000	0	2	0	0	0.7	1.000
4 yrs.		11	18	.379	4.17	102	12	4	263	296	75	90	0	4	9	9	61	11	0	.180	18	72	1	1	0.9	.989

Tom Dixon

DIXON, THOMAS EARL
B. Apr. 23, 1955, Orlando, Fla. — BR TR 5'11" 175 lbs.

1977	HOU N	1	0	1.000	3.30	9	4	1	30	40	7	15	0	0	0	0	7	0	0	.000	2	6	2	0	1.1	.800
1978		7	11	.389	3.99	30	19	3	140	140	40	66	2	2	0	1	40	4	0	.100	12	16	1	1	1.0	.966
1979		1	2	.333	6.58	19	1	0	26	39	15	9	0	1	2	0	1	0	0	1.000	3	6	0	1	0.5	1.000
1983	MON N	0	1	.000	9.82	4	0	0	3.2	6	1	4	0	0	1	0	0	0	0	–	0	0	0	0	0.0	–
4 yrs.		9	14	.391	4.33	62	24	4	199.2	225	63	94	2	3	3	1	48	5	0	.104	17	28	3	2	0.8	.938

Year	Team		W	L	PCT	ERA	G	GS	CG	IP	H	BB	SO	ShO	Relief Pitching W	L	SV	Batting AB	H	HR	BA	PO	A	E	DP	TC/G	FA

Bill Doak
DOAK, WILLIAM LEOPOLD (Spittin' Bill)
B. Jan. 28, 1891, Pittsburgh, Pa. D. Nov. 26, 1954, Bradenton, Fla. BR TR 6'½" 165 lbs.

Year	Team		W	L	PCT	ERA	G	GS	CG	IP	H	BB	SO	ShO	W	L	SV	AB	H	HR	BA	PO	A	E	DP	TC/G	FA
1912	CIN	N	0	0	–	4.50	1	1	0	2	4	1	0	0	0	0	0	0	0	0	–	0	0	0	0	0.0	–
1913	STL	N	2	8	.200	3.10	15	12	5	93	79	39	51	1	0	0	1	31	1	0	.032	7	26	2	1	2.3	.943
1914			20	6	.769	1.72	36	33	16	256	193	87	118	7	1	0	0	85	10	0	.118	9	93	8	1	3.1	.927
1915			16	18	.471	2.64	38	36	19	276	263	85	124	3	0	0	1	86	15	0	.174	10	108	3	3	3.2	.975
1916			12	8	.600	2.63	29	26	11	192	177	55	82	3	0	0	0	62	8	0	.129	6	64	4	1	2.6	.946
1917			16	20	.444	3.10	44	37	16	281.1	257	85	111	3	2	1	2	95	12	0	.126	10	103	3	2	2.6	.974
1918			9	15	.375	2.43	31	23	16	211	191	60	74	1	0	2	1	66	12	0	.182	7	88	2	0	3.1	.979
1919			13	14	.481	3.11	31	29	13	202.2	182	55	69	3	1	0	0	64	7	0	.109	11	78	3	2	3.0	.967
1920			20	12	.625	2.53	39	37	20	270	256	80	90	5	0	0	1	88	10	0	.114	17	71	3	5	2.3	.967
1921			15	6	.714	2.59	32	28	13	208.2	224	37	83	1	1	0	1	70	10	0	.143	7	62	4	4	2.3	.945
1922			11	13	.458	5.54	37	29	8	180.1	222	69	73	2	1	1	2	54	7	0	.130	3	43	2	2	1.3	.958
1923			8	13	.381	3.26	30	26	7	185	199	69	53	3	0	3	0	67	3	0	.045	1	62	3	3	2.2	.955
1924	2 teams	STL N (11G 2-1)				BKN N	(21G 11-5)																				
"	total		13	6	.684	3.10	32	17	8	171.1	155	49	39	2	4	2	3	61	11	0	.180	7	57	2	6	2.1	.970
1927	BKN	N	11	8	.579	3.48	27	20	6	145	153	40	32	1	3	0	0	47	6	0	.128	5	40	1	1	1.7	.978
1928			3	8	.273	3.26	28	12	4	99.1	104	35	12	1	1	2	3	27	3	0	.111	3	38	2	2	1.5	.953
1929	STL	N	1	2	.333	12.00	3	2	0	9	17	5	3	0	0	1	0	2	0	0	.000	0	1	0	0	0.7	.500
16 yrs.			170	157	.520	2.98	453	368	162	2782.2	2676	851	1014	36	14	12	15	905	115	0	.127	103	934	43	33	2.4	.960

Walt Doan
DOAN, WALTER RUDOLPH
B. Mar. 12, 1887, Bellevue, Ida. D. Oct. 19, 1935, West Brandywine, Pa. BL TR 6' 165 lbs.

Year	Team		W	L	PCT	ERA	G	GS	CG	IP	H	BB	SO	ShO	W	L	SV	AB	H	HR	BA	PO	A	E	DP	TC/G	FA
1909	CLE	A	0	1	.000	5.40	1	1	0	5	10	1	2	0	0	0	0	9	1	0	.111	0	1	0	0	1.0	1.000
1910			0	0	–	5.60	6	0	0	17.2	31	8	7	0	0	0	0	7	2	0	.286	1	2	1	0	0.7	.750
2 yrs.			0	1	.000	5.56	7	1	0	22.2	41	9	9	0	0	0	0	16	3	0	.188	1	3	1	0	0.7	.800

John Dobb
DOBB, JOHN KENNETH (Lefty)
B. Nov. 15, 1901, Muskegon, Mich. BR TL 6'2" 180 lbs.

Year	Team		W	L	PCT	ERA	G	GS	CG	IP	H	BB	SO	ShO	W	L	SV	AB	H	HR	BA	PO	A	E	DP	TC/G	FA
1924	CHI	A	0	0	–	9.00	2	0	0	2	4	1	2	0	0	0	0	0	0	0	–	0	0	0	0	0.0	–

Ray Dobens
DOBENS, RAYMOND JOSEPH (Lefty)
B. July 28, 1906, Nashua, N. H. D. Apr. 21, 1980, Stuart, Fla. BL TL 5'8" 175 lbs.

Year	Team		W	L	PCT	ERA	G	GS	CG	IP	H	BB	SO	ShO	W	L	SV	AB	H	HR	BA	PO	A	E	DP	TC/G	FA
1929	BOS	A	0	0	–	3.81	11	2	0	28.1	32	9	4	0	0	0	0	8	3	0	.375	2	2	1	0	0.5	.800

Jess Dobernic
DOBERNIC, ANDREW JOSEPH
B. Nov. 20, 1917, Mt. Olive, Ill. BR TR 5'10" 170 lbs.

Year	Team		W	L	PCT	ERA	G	GS	CG	IP	H	BB	SO	ShO	W	L	SV	AB	H	HR	BA	PO	A	E	DP	TC/G	FA
1939	CHI	A	0	1	.000	13.50	4	0	0	3.1	3	6	1	0	0	1	0	1	0	0	.000	0	1	0	0	0.3	1.000
1948	CHI	N	7	2	.778	3.15	54	0	0	85.2	67	40	48	0	7	2	1	10	2	0	.200	6	6	2	0	0.3	.857
1949	2 teams	CHI N (4G 0-0)				CIN N	(14G 0-0)																				
"	total		0	0	–	11.57	18	0	0	23.1	37	20	6	0	0	0	0	2	0	0	.000	2	3	0	0	0.3	1.000
3 yrs.			7	3	.700	5.21	76	0	0	112.1	107	66	55	0	7	3	1	13	2	0	.154	8	10	2	0	0.3	.900

Chuck Dobson
DOBSON, CHARLES THOMAS
B. Jan. 10, 1944, Kansas City, Mo. BR TR 6'4" 200 lbs.

Year	Team		W	L	PCT	ERA	G	GS	CG	IP	H	BB	SO	ShO	W	L	SV	AB	H	HR	BA	PO	A	E	DP	TC/G	FA
1966	KC	A	4	6	.400	4.09	14	14	1	83.2	71	50	61	0	0	0	0	26	3	0	.115	6	18	0	1	1.7	1.000
1967			10	10	.500	3.69	32	29	4	197.2	172	75	110	1	0	0	0	72	13	0	.181	8	33	0	2	1.3	1.000
1968	OAK	A	12	14	.462	3.00	35	34	11	225.1	197	80	168	3	0	0	0	75	15	0	.200	11	40	1	3	1.5	.981
1969			15	13	.536	3.86	35	35	11	235.1	244	80	137	1	0	0	0	79	8	0	.101	9	28	1	3	1.1	.947
1970			16	15	.516	3.74	41	40	13	267	230	92	149	5	0	1	0	93	11	0	.118	19	28	1	3	1.2	.979
1971			15	5	.750	3.81	30	30	7	189	185	71	100	1	0	0	0	66	13	0	.197	15	30	0	2	1.5	1.000
1973			0	1	.000	7.71	1	1	0	2.1	6	2	3	0	0	0	0	0	0	0	–	0	1	0	0	1.0	1.000
1974	CAL	A	2	3	.400	5.70	5	5	2	30	39	13	16	0	0	0	0	0	0	0	–	4	3	1	0	1.6	.875
1975			0	2	.000	6.75	9	2	0	28	30	13	14	0	0	0	0	0	0	0	–	0	2	0	0	0.2	1.000
9 yrs.			74	69	.517	3.78	202	190	49	1258.1	1174	476	758	11	0	1	0	411	63	0	.153	70	184	5	16	1.3	.981

Joe Dobson
DOBSON, JOSEPH GORDON (Burrhead)
B. Jan. 20, 1917, Durant, Okla. BR TR 6'2" 197 lbs.

Year	Team		W	L	PCT	ERA	G	GS	CG	IP	H	BB	SO	ShO	W	L	SV	AB	H	HR	BA	PO	A	E	DP	TC/G	FA
1939	CLE	A	2	3	.400	5.88	35	3	0	78	87	51	27	0	2	1	1	18	1	0	.056	3	16	0	0	0.5	1.000
1940			3	7	.300	4.95	40	7	2	100	101	48	57	1	2	2	3	24	3	0	.125	6	15	0	1	0.5	1.000
1941	BOS	A	12	5	.706	4.49	27	18	7	134.1	136	67	69	1	2	1	0	47	7	1	.149	10	13	0	0	0.9	1.000
1942			11	9	.550	3.30	30	23	10	182.2	155	68	72	3	1	1	0	69	10	0	.145	17	42	0	2	2.0	1.000
1943			7	11	.389	3.12	25	20	9	164.1	144	57	63	3	0	1	0	52	5	0	.096	9	22	1	2	1.3	.969
1946			13	7	.650	3.24	32	24	9	166.2	148	68	91	1	2	0	0	50	5	0	.100	18	33	1	1	1.6	.981
1947			18	8	.692	2.95	33	31	15	228.2	203	73	110	1	0	0	1	77	16	0	.208	13	25	0	1	1.2	1.000
1948			16	10	.615	3.56	38	32	16	245.1	237	92	116	0	0	0	0	84	17	1	.202	10	36	2	3	1.3	.958
1949			14	12	.538	3.85	33	27	12	212.2	219	97	87	2	2	1	2	68	10	0	.147	12	30	0	3	1.3	1.000
1950			15	10	.600	4.18	39	27	12	206.2	217	81	81	1	2	0	4	70	15	0	.214	8	44	3	4	1.4	.945
1951	CHI	A	7	6	.538	3.62	28	21	6	146.2	136	51	67	0	0	0	1	46	3	0	.065	6	25	1	5	1.1	.969
1952			14	10	.583	2.51	29	25	11	200.2	164	60	101	3	1	1	1	63	12	0	.190	7	26	1	2	1.2	.971
1953			5	5	.500	3.67	23	15	3	100.2	96	37	50	1	0	1	1	29	2	0	.069	6	14	2	0	1.0	.909
1954	BOS	A	0	0	–	6.75	2	0	0	2.2	1	1	1	0	0	0	0	0	0	0	–	1	0	0	0	0.5	1.000
14 yrs.			137	103	.571	3.62	414	273	112	2170	2048	851	992	22	14	10	18	697	106	2	.152	126	341	11	24	1.2	.977

WORLD SERIES

Year	Team		W	L	PCT	ERA	G	GS	CG	IP	H	BB	SO	ShO	W	L	SV	AB	H	HR	BA	PO	A	E	DP	TC/G	FA
1946	BOS	A	1	0	1.000	0.00	3	1	1	12.2	4	3	10	0	0	0	0	3	0	0	.000	0	2	0	0	0.7	1.000

Pat Dobson
DOBSON, PATRICK EDWARD
B. Feb. 12, 1942, Depew, N. Y. BR TR 6'3" 190 lbs.

Year	Team		W	L	PCT	ERA	G	GS	CG	IP	H	BB	SO	ShO	W	L	SV	AB	H	HR	BA	PO	A	E	DP	TC/G	FA
1967	DET	A	1	2	.333	2.92	28	1	0	49.1	38	27	34	0	1	1	0	5	0	0	.000	4	4	0	0	0.3	1.000
1968			5	8	.385	2.66	47	10	2	125	89	48	93	1	3	3	7	28	4	0	.143	12	22	1	0	0.7	.971
1969			5	10	.333	3.60	49	9	1	105	100	39	64	0	3	6	9	22	2	0	.091	8	16	1	1	0.5	.960

Year	Team		W	L	PCT	ERA	G	GS	CG	IP	H	BB	SO	ShO	Relief Pitching W	L	SV	Batting AB	H	HR	BA	PO	A	E	DP	TC/G	FA

Pat Dobson *continued*

Year	Team		W	L	PCT	ERA	G	GS	CG	IP	H	BB	SO	ShO	W	L	SV	AB	H	HR	BA	PO	A	E	DP	TC/G	FA
1970	SD	N	14	15	.483	3.76	40	34	8	251	257	78	185	1	0	0	1	71	10	0	.141	17	31	0	2	1.2	1.000
1971	BAL	A	20	8	.714	2.90	38	37	18	282	248	63	187	4	0	0	1	91	10	0	.110	11	42	2	1	1.4	.964
1972			16	18	.471	2.65	38	36	13	268.1	220	69	161	3	0	0	0	85	12	0	.141	15	33	2	2	1.3	.960
1973	2 teams	ATL N	(12G 3–7)				NY A	(22G 9–8)																			
"	total		12	15	.444	4.40	34	31	7	200.1	223	53	93	2	2	0	0	15	1	0	.067	16	32	4	1	1.5	.923
1974	NY	A	19	15	.559	3.07	39	39	12	281	282	75	157	2	0	0	0	0	0	0	–	22	32	3	4	1.5	.947
1975			11	14	.440	4.07	33	30	7	207.2	205	83	129	1	0	0	0	0	0	0	–	14	27	1	0	1.3	.976
1976	CLE	A	16	12	.571	3.48	35	35	6	217	226	65	117	0	0	0	0	0	0	0	–	14	28	3	3	1.3	.933
1977			3	12	.200	6.16	33	17	0	133	155	65	81	0	1	2	1	0	0	0	–	9	22	2	0	1.0	.939
11 yrs.			122	129	.486	3.54	414	279	74	2119.2	2043	665	1301	14	10	12	19	317	39	0	.123	142	289	19	14	1.1	.958

WORLD SERIES

Year	Team		W	L	PCT	ERA	G	GS	CG	IP	H	BB	SO	ShO	W	L	SV	AB	H	HR	BA	PO	A	E	DP	TC/G	FA
1968	DET	A	0	0	–	3.86	3	0	0	4.2	5	1	0	0	0	0	0	0	0	0	–	1	0	0	0	0.3	1.000
1971	BAL	A	0	0	–	4.05	3	0	0	6.2	13	4	6	0	0	0	0	2	0	0	.000	0	3	0	0	1.0	1.000
2 yrs.			0	0	–	3.97	6	1	0	11.1	18	5	6	0	0	0	0	2	0	0	.000	1	3	0	0	0.7	1.000

George Dockins

DOCKINS, GEORGE WOODROW (Lefty)
B. May 5, 1917, Clyde, Kans.

BL TL 6' 175 lbs.

Year	Team		W	L	PCT	ERA	G	GS	CG	IP	H	BB	SO	ShO	W	L	SV	AB	H	HR	BA	PO	A	E	DP	TC/G	FA
1945	STL	N	8	6	.571	3.21	31	12	5	126.1	132	38	33	2	3	4	0	34	6	0	.176	5	24	1	0	1.0	.967
1947	BKN	N	0	0	–	11.81	4	0	0	5.1	10	2	1	0	0	0	0	1	0	0	.000	0	2	0	0	0.5	1.000
2 yrs.			8	6	.571	3.55	35	12	5	131.2	142	40	34	2	3	4	0	35	6	0	.171	5	26	1	0	0.9	.969

Sam Dodge

DODGE, SAMUEL EDWARD
B. Dec. 19, 1899, Philadelphia, Pa.

BR TR 6'1" 170 lbs.

Year	Team		W	L	PCT	ERA	G	GS	CG	IP	H	BB	SO	ShO	W	L	SV	AB	H	HR	BA	PO	A	E	DP	TC/G	FA
1921	BOS	A	0	0	–	9.00	1	0	0	1	1	1	0	0	0	0	0	–	0	0	0	0	0	0	0	0.0	–
1922			0	0	–	4.50	3	0	0	6	11	3	3	0	0	0	0	2	0	0	.000	0	3	0	0	1.0	1.000
2 yrs.			0	0	–	5.14	4	0	0	7	12	4	3	0	0	0	0	2	0	0	.000	0	3	0	0	0.8	1.000

Al Doe

DOE, ALFRED GEORGE (Count)
B. Apr. 18, 1864, Gloucester, Mass. D. Oct. 4, 1938, Quincy, Mass.

BR TR 5'10" 165 lbs.

Year	Team		W	L	PCT	ERA	G	GS	CG	IP	H	BB	SO	ShO	W	L	SV	AB	H	HR	BA	PO	A	E	DP	TC/G	FA
1890	2 teams	BUF P	(1G 0–1)				PIT P	(1G 0–0)																			
"	total		0	1	.000	9.00	2	1	1	10	14	9	4	0	0	0	0	4	1	0	.250	0	2	0	0	1.0	1.000

Ed Doheny

DOHENY, EDWARD R.
B. Nov. 24, 1874, Northfield, Vt. D. Dec. 29, 1916, Worcester, Mass.

BL TL 5'10½" 165 lbs.

Year	Team		W	L	PCT	ERA	G	GS	CG	IP	H	BB	SO	ShO	W	L	SV	AB	H	HR	BA	PO	A	E	DP	TC/G	FA
1895	NY	N	0	3	.000	6.66	3	3	3	25.2	37	19	9	0	0	0	0	10	1	0	.100	2	4	3	1	3.0	.667
1896			6	7	.462	4.49	17	15	9	108.1	112	59	39	0	0	0	0	40	6	0	.150	5	23	5	2	1.9	.848
1897			4	4	.500	2.12	10	10	10	85	69	45	37	0	0	0	0	35	7	0	.200	4	31	4	3	3.9	.897
1898			7	19	.269	3.68	28	27	23	213	238	101	96	0	0	0	1	86	14	2	.163	14	62	10	2	3.1	.884
1899			14	17	.452	4.51	35	33	30	265.1	282	156	115	1	0	0	0	112	27	0	.241	15	87	16	1	3.4	.864
1900			4	14	.222	5.45	20	18	12	133.2	148	96	44	0	1	0	0	54	12	0	.222	4	43	10	1	2.9	.825
1901	2 teams	NY N	(10G 2–5)				PIT N	(11G 6–2)																			
"	total		8	7	.533	3.23	21	16	12	150.2	156	39	64	1	0	1	0	55	13	0	.236	2	37	8	0	2.2	.830
1902	PIT	N	16	4	.800	2.53	22	21	19	188.1	161	61	88	2	0	0	0	77	12	1	.156	9	43	5	1	2.6	.912
1903			16	8	.667	3.19	27	25	22	222.2	209	89	75	2	0	0	0	91	19	0	.209	17	86	10	0	4.2	.912
9 yrs.			75	83	.475	3.75	183	168	140	1392.2	1412	665	567	6	1	2	2	560	111	3	.198	72	416	71	11	3.1	.873

Cozy Dolan

DOLAN, PATRICK HENRY
B. Dec. 3, 1872, Cambridge, Mass. D. Mar. 29, 1907, Louisville, Ky.

BL TL 5'10" 160 lbs.

Year	Team		W	L	PCT	ERA	G	GS	CG	IP	H	BB	SO	ShO	W	L	SV	AB	H	HR	BA	PO	A	E	DP	TC/G	FA
1892	WAS	N	2	2	.500	4.38	5	4	3	37	39	15	8	0	0	0	1	13	3	0	.231	1	6	0	0	1.4	1.000
1895	BOS	N	11	7	.611	4.27	25	21	18	198.1	215	67	47	3	0	0	1	83	20	0	.241	13	62	4	2	3.2	.949
1896			1	4	.200	4.83	6	5	3	41	55	27	14	0	0	0	0	14	2	0	.143	5	8	4	0	2.8	.765
1905			0	1	.000	9.00	2	0	0	4	7	1	1	0	0	0	0	510	137	3	.269	0	0	0	0	0.0	–
1906			0	1	.000	4.50	2	0	0	12	12	6	7	0	0	0	0	549	136	0	.248	0	0	0	0	0.0	–
5 yrs.			14	15	.483	4.43	40	30	24	292.1	328	116	77	3	0	3	1	*				19	76	8	2	2.6	.922

John Dolan

DOLAN, JOHN
B. Sept. 12, 1867, Newport, Ky. D. May 8, 1948, Springfield, Ohio

TR 5'10" 170 lbs.

Year	Team		W	L	PCT	ERA	G	GS	CG	IP	H	BB	SO	ShO	W	L	SV	AB	H	HR	BA	PO	A	E	DP	TC/G	FA
1890	CIN	N	1	1	.500	4.50	2	2	2	18	17	10	9	0	0	0	0	8	1	0	.125	0	2	0	0	1.0	1.000
1891	COL	AA	12	11	.522	4.16	27	24	19	203.1	216	84	68	0	0	0	0	78	7	1	.090	7	40	5	1	1.9	.904
1893	STL	N	0	2	.000	4.15	3	1	1	17.1	26	7	1	0	0	0	1	7	1	1	.143	4	1	1	0	2.0	.833
1895	CHI	N	0	1	.000	6.55	2	1	1	11	16	6	1	0	0	0	0	3	0	0	.000	1	4	0	0	2.5	1.000
4 yrs.			13	15	.464	4.29	34	29	23	249.2	275	107	79	0	0	0	1	96	9	2	.094	12	47	6	1	1.9	.908

Tom Dolan

DOLAN, THOMAS J.
B. Jan. 10, 1859, New York, N.Y. D. Jan. 16, 1913, St. Louis, Mo.

BR TR

Year	Team		W	L	PCT	ERA	G	GS	CG	IP	H	BB	SO	ShO	W	L	SV	AB	H	HR	BA	PO	A	E	DP	TC/G	FA
1883	STL	AA	0	0	–	4.50	1	0	0	4	4	0	0	0	0	0	0	*				0	1	0	0	1.0	1.000

Art Doll

DOLL, ARTHUR JAMES (Moose)
B. May 7, 1913, Chicago, Ill. D. Apr. 28, 1978, Calumet City, Ill.

BR TR 6'1" 190 lbs.

Year	Team		W	L	PCT	ERA	G	GS	CG	IP	H	BB	SO	ShO	W	L	SV	AB	H	HR	BA	PO	A	E	DP	TC/G	FA
1935	BOS	N	0	0	–	0.00	0	0	0	0	0	0	0	0	0	0	0	10	1	0	.100	0	0	0	0	0.0	–
1936			0	1	.000	3.38	1	1	0	8	11	2	2	0	0	0	0	2	0	0	.000	0	1	0	0	1.0	1.000
1938			0	0	–	2.25	3	0	0	4	4	3	1	0	0	0	0	1	1	0	1.000	0	2	0	0	0.7	1.000
3 yrs.			0	1	.000	3.00	4	1	0	12	15	5	3	0	0	0	0	13	2	0	.154	0	3	0	0	0.8	1.000

Deacon Donahue

DONAHUE, JOHN STEPHEN MICHAEL
B. June 23, 1920, Chicago, Ill.

BR TR 6' 175 lbs.

Year	Team		W	L	PCT	ERA	G	GS	CG	IP	H	BB	SO	ShO	W	L	SV	AB	H	HR	BA	PO	A	E	DP	TC/G	FA
1943	PHI	N	0	0	–	4.50	2	0	0	4	4	1	1	0	0	0	0	0	0	0	–	0	1	0	0	0.5	1.000

Year	Team		W	L	PCT	ERA	G	GS	CG	IP	H	BB	SO	ShO	Relief Pitching W	L	SV	Batting AB	H	HR	BA	PO	A	E	DP	TC/G	FA

Deacon Donahue *continued*

| 1944 | | | 0 | 2 | .000 | 7.71 | 6 | 0 | 0 | 9.1 | 18 | 2 | 2 | 0 | 0 | 2 | 0 | 1 | 0 | 0 | .000 | 0 | 3 | 0 | 1 | 0.5 | 1.000 |
| 2 yrs. | | | 0 | 2 | .000 | 6.75 | 8 | 0 | 0 | 13.1 | 22 | 3 | 3 | 0 | 0 | 2 | 0 | 1 | 0 | 0 | .000 | 0 | 4 | 0 | 1 | 0.5 | 1.000 |

Red Donahue

DONAHUE, FRANCIS ROSTELL
B. Jan. 23, 1873, Waterbury, Conn. D. Aug. 25, 1913, Philadelphia, Pa. — BR TR

1893	NY	N	0	0	–	9.00	2	0	1	5	8	3	1	0	0	0	1	2	0	0	.000	0	1	0	0	0.5	1.000
1895	STL	N	0	1	.000	6.75	1	1	1	8	9	3	2	0	0	0	0	3	0	0	.000	0	2	0	0	2.0	1.000
1896			7	24	.226	5.80	32	32	28	267	376	98	70	0	0	0	0	107	17	0	.159	13	58	7	4	2.4	.910
1897			11	33	.250	6.13	46	42	38	348	484	106	64	1	1	1	1	155	33	0	.213	24	97	3	1	2.7	.976
1898	PHI	N	17	17	.500	3.55	35	35	33	284.1	327	80	57	1	0	0	0	112	16	0	.143	12	87	9	4	3.1	.917
1899			21	8	.724	3.39	35	31	27	279	292	63	51	4	1	1	0	111	20	0	.180	10	82	4	0	2.7	.958
1900			15	10	.600	3.60	32	24	21	240	299	50	41	2	3	1	0	90	20	0	.222	9	58	2	0	2.2	.971
1901			21	13	.618	2.60	35	34	34	304.1	307	60	89	1	1	0	0	117	11	0	.094	8	75	4	0	2.5	.954
1902	STL	A	22	11	.667	2.76	35	34	33	316.1	322	65	63	2	1	0	0	118	11	0	.093	15	130	8	3	4.4	.948
1903	2 teams		STL A	(16G 8–7)		CLE A	(16G 7–9)																					
"	total		15	16	.484	2.59	32	30	28	267.2	287	34	96	4	1	1	0	104	16	0	.154	11	93	9	2	3.5	.920
1904	CLE	A	19	14	.576	2.40	35	32	30	277	281	49	127	6	1	1	0	101	17	0	.168	6	101	2	2	3.1	.982
1905			6	12	.333	3.40	20	18	13	137.2	132	25	45	1	0	0	0	53	4	0	.075	9	48	0	2	2.9	1.000
1906	DET	A	13	14	.481	2.73	28	28	26	241	260	54	82	3	0	0	0	81	10	0	.123	10	73	3	4	3.1	.965
13 yrs.			167	173	.491	3.61	368	341	312	2975.1	3384	690	788	25	9	6	2	1154	175	1	.152	127	905	51	22	2.9	.953

Atley Donald

DONALD, RICHARD ATLEY (Swampy)
B. Aug. 19, 1910, Morton, Miss. — BL TR 6'1" 186 lbs.

1938	NY	A	0	1	.000	5.25	2	2	0	12	7	14	6	0	0	0	0	6	1	0	.167	1	4	0	0	2.5	1.000
1939			13	3	.813	3.71	24	20	11	153	144	60	55	1	1	0	1	60	15	0	.250	3	22	0	2	1.0	1.000
1940			8	3	.727	3.03	24	11	6	118.2	113	59	60	1	2	0	0	41	6	0	.146	2	12	4	0	0.8	.778
1941			9	5	.643	3.57	22	20	10	159	141	69	71	0	0	0	0	62	5	0	.081	8	28	2	1	1.7	.947
1942			11	3	.786	3.11	20	19	10	147.2	133	45	53	1	0	0	0	61	9	0	.148	7	21	2	1	1.5	.933
1943			6	4	.600	4.60	22	15	2	119.1	134	38	57	0	2	0	0	47	6	0	.128	1	15	0	0	0.8	1.000
1944			13	10	.565	3.34	30	19	9	159	173	59	48	0	3	4	0	55	10	0	.182	4	24	0	4	1.0	1.000
1945			5	4	.556	2.97	9	9	6	63.2	62	25	19	2	0	0	0	24	5	1	.208	1	7	3	0	1.2	.727
8 yrs.			65	33	.663	3.52	153	115	54	932.1	907	369	369	5	8	4	1	356	57	1	.160	29	133	11	9	1.1	.936

WORLD SERIES

1941	NY	A	0	0	–	9.00	1	1	0	4	6	3	2	0	0	0	0	2	0	0	.000	0	1	0	0	1.0	1.000
1942			0	1	.000	6.00	1	0	0	3	3	2	1	0	0	1	0	2	0	0	.000	0	0	0	0	0.0	–
2 yrs.			0	1	.000	7.71	2	1	0	7	9	5	3	0	0	1	0	4	0	0	.000	0	1	0	0	0.5	1.000

Ed Donalds

DONALDS, EDWARD ALEXANDER (Skipper)
B. June 22, 1885, Bidwell, Ohio D. July 3, 1950, Columbus, Ohio — BR TR 5'11" 180 lbs.

| 1912 | CIN | N | 1 | 0 | 1.000 | 4.50 | 1 | 0 | 0 | 4 | 7 | 0 | 1 | 0 | 1 | 0 | 0 | 1 | 0 | 0 | .000 | 0 | 1 | 0 | 0 | 1.0 | 1.000 |

Mike Donlin

DONLIN, MICHAEL JOSEPH (Highlonesome)
B. May 30, 1878, Peoria, Ill. D. Sept. 24, 1933, Hollywood, Calif. — BL TL 5'9" 170 lbs.

1899	STL	N	0	1	.000	7.63	3	1	0	15.1	15	14	6	0	0	0	0	266	86	6	.323	1	9	0	1	3.3	1.000
1902	CIN	N	0	0	–	0.00	1	0	0	1	1	0	0	0	0	0	0	143	42	0	.294	0	0	0	0	0.0	–
2 yrs.			0	1	.000	7.16	4	1	0	16.1	16	14	6	0	0	0	0	*				1	9	0	1	2.5	1.000

Blix Donnelly

DONNELLY, SYLVESTER URBAN
B. Jan. 21, 1914, Olivia, Minn. D. June 20, 1976, Olivia, Minn. — BR TR 5'10" 166 lbs.

1944	STL	N	2	1	.667	2.12	27	4	2	76.1	61	34	45	1	0	1	2	16	1	0	.063	3	17	1	0	0.8	.952
1945			8	10	.444	3.52	31	23	9	166.1	157	87	76	4	0	1	2	54	7	0	.130	4	17	2	0	0.7	.913
1946	2 teams		STL N	(13G 1–2)		PHI N	(12G 3–4)																					
"	total		4	6	.400	3.10	25	8	2	90	81	34	49	0	1	2	0	25	7	0	.280	3	11	0	0	0.6	1.000
1947	PHI	N	4	6	.400	2.98	38	10	5	120.2	113	46	31	1	0	3	5	32	2	0	.063	2	24	2	2	0.7	.929
1948			5	7	.417	3.69	26	19	8	131.2	125	49	46	1	0	0	2	45	10	0	.222	2	15	2	0	0.7	.895
1949			2	1	.667	5.06	23	10	1	78.1	84	40	36	0	1	0	0	23	4	0	.174	0	7	1	0	0.3	.875
1950			2	4	.333	4.29	14	1	0	21	30	10	10	0	2	1	0	5	1	0	.200	1	4	0	0	0.4	1.000
1951	BOS	N	0	1	.000	7.36	6	0	0	7.1	8	6	3	0	0	1	0	1	0	0	.000	1	2	0	0	0.5	1.000
8 yrs.			27	36	.429	3.49	190	75	27	691.2	659	306	296	7	4	11	12	201	32	0	.159	15	99	8	2	0.6	.934

WORLD SERIES

| 1944 | STL | N | 1 | 0 | 1.000 | 0.00 | 2 | 0 | 0 | 6 | 1 | 2 | 9 | 1 | 1 | 0 | 0 | 1 | 0 | 0 | .000 | 2 | 0 | 0 | 0 | 1.0 | 1.000 |

Ed Donnelly

DONNELLY, EDWARD
Born Edward O'Donnell.
B. July 29, 1880, Hampton, N. Y. D. Nov. 28, 1957, Rutland, Vt. — BR TR 6'1" 205 lbs.

1911	BOS	N	3	2	.600	2.45	5	4	4	36.2	33	9	16	1	0	1	0	14	1	0	.071	3	9	1	0	2.6	.923
1912			5	10	.333	4.35	37	18	10	184.1	225	72	67	0	0	1	2	69	19	0	.275	7	51	4	1	1.7	.935
2 yrs.			8	12	.400	4.03	42	22	14	221	258	81	83	1	0	2	2	83	20	0	.241	10	60	5	1	1.8	.933

Ed Donnelly

DONNELLY, EDWARD VINCENT
B. Dec. 10, 1934, Allen, Mich. — BR TR 6' 175 lbs.

| 1959 | CHI | N | 1 | 1 | .500 | 3.14 | 9 | 0 | 0 | 14.1 | 18 | 9 | 6 | 0 | 0 | 1 | 0 | 0 | 0 | 0 | – | 0 | 3 | 0 | 0 | 0.3 | 1.000 |

Frank Donnelly

DONNELLY, FRANKLIN MARION
B. Oct. 7, 1869, Tamaroa, Ill. D. Feb. 3, 1953, Canton, Ill. — 180 lbs.

| 1893 | CHI | N | 3 | 1 | .750 | 5.36 | 7 | 5 | 3 | 42 | 51 | 17 | 6 | 0 | 0 | 0 | 2 | 18 | 8 | 0 | .444 | 7 | 8 | 4 | 0 | 2.7 | .789 |

Year	Team	W	L	PCT	ERA	G	GS	CG	IP	H	BB	SO	ShO	W	L	SV	AB	H	HR	BA	PO	A	E	DP	TC/G	FA
														Relief Pitching			**Batting**									

Jim Donohue

DONOHUE, JAMES THOMAS
B. Oct. 31, 1938, St. Louis, Mo.
BR TR 6'4" 190 lbs.

Year	Team	W	L	PCT	ERA	G	GS	CG	IP	H	BB	SO	ShO	W	L	SV	AB	H	HR	BA	PO	A	E	DP	TC/G	FA
1961	2 teams	DET A	(14G 1–1)		LA A	(38G 4–6)																				
"	total	5	7	.417	4.18	52	7	0	120.2	116	65	99	0	5	5	6	28	4	0	.143	8	13	0	1	0.4	1.000
1962	2 teams	LA A	(12G 1–0)		MIN A	(6G 0–1)																				
"	total	1	1	.500	4.67	18	2	0	34.2	36	17	17	0	1	1	1	6	1	0	.167	0	5	1	0	0.3	.833
2 yrs.		6	8	.429	4.29	70	9	0	155.1	152	82	116	0	6	6	7	34	5	0	.147	8	18	1	1	0.4	.963

Pete Donohue

DONOHUE, PETER JOSEPH
B. Nov. 5, 1900, Athens, Tex. D. Feb. 23, 1988, Fort Worth, Tex.
BR TR 6'2" 185 lbs.

Year	Team	W	L	PCT	ERA	G	GS	CG	IP	H	BB	SO	ShO	W	L	SV	AB	H	HR	BA	PO	A	E	DP	TC/G	FA
1921	CIN N	7	6	.538	3.35	21	11	7	118.1	117	26	44	0	1	2	1	38	8	1	.211	4	41	2	0	2.2	.957
1922		18	9	**.667**	3.12	33	30	18	242	257	43	66	2	0	1	1	88	16	0	.182	7	62	3	2	2.2	.958
1923		21	15	.583	3.38	42	36	19	274.1	304	68	84	2	2	0	3	96	24	1	.250	9	70	8	4	2.1	.908
1924		16	9	.640	3.60	35	32	16	222.1	248	36	72	3	0	1	0	73	14	1	.192	8	46	0	3	1.5	1.000
1925		21	14	.600	3.08	42	**38**	**27**	**301**	310	49	78	3	1	0	2	109	32	1	.294	6	62	4	2	1.7	.944
1926		**20**	14	.588	3.37	47	**38**	17	**285.2**	298	39	73	**5**	4	0	2	106	33	0	.311	6	60	4	4	1.5	.943
1927		6	16	.273	4.11	33	24	12	190.2	253	32	48	1	0	1	1	64	16	0	.250	11	42	2	4	1.7	.964
1928		7	11	.389	4.74	23	18	8	150	180	32	37	0	1	0	0	48	7	1	.146	8	42	1	0	2.2	.980
1929		10	13	.435	5.42	32	24	7	177.2	243	51	30	0	2	0	0	60	20	0	.333	7	44	4	4	1.7	.927
1930	2 teams	CIN N	(8G 1–3)		NY N	(18G 7–6)																				
"	total	8	9	.471	6.17	26	16	6	121	188	31	30	0	1	2	0	43	10	1	.233	4	23	1	2	1.1	.964
1931	2 teams	NY N	(4G 0–1)		CLE A	(2G 0–0)																				
"	total	0	1	.000	6.48	6	1	0	16.2	23	9	8	0	0	0	0	4	0	0	.000	0	2	0	0	0.3	1.000
1932	BOS A	0	1	.000	7.82	4	2	0	12.2	18	6	1	0	0	0	0	3	0	0	.000	0	5	0	0	1.5	1.000
12 yrs.		134	118	.532	3.87	344	270	137	2112.1	2439	422	571	16	12	7	12	732	180	6	.246	71	499	29	23	1.7	.952

Lino Donoso

DONOSO, LINO
Born Lino Donoso y Galeta.
B. Sept. 23, 1922, Havana, Cuba
BL TL 5'11" 160 lbs.

Year	Team	W	L	PCT	ERA	G	GS	CG	IP	H	BB	SO	ShO	W	L	SV	AB	H	HR	BA	PO	A	E	DP	TC/G	FA
1955	PIT N	4	6	.400	5.31	25	9	3	95	106	35	38	0	1	2	1	27	5	0	.185	6	18	2	1	1.0	.923
1956		0	0	–	0.00	3	0	0	1.2	2	1	1	0	0	0	0	0	0	0	–	0	1	0	0	0.3	1.000
2 yrs.		4	6	.400	5.21	28	9	3	96.2	108	36	39	0	1	2	1	27	5	0	.185	6	19	2	1	1.0	.926

Bill Donovan

DONOVAN, WILLARD EARL
B. July 6, 1916, Maywood, Ill.
BR TL 6'2" 198 lbs.

Year	Team	W	L	PCT	ERA	G	GS	CG	IP	H	BB	SO	ShO	W	L	SV	AB	H	HR	BA	PO	A	E	DP	TC/G	FA
1942	BOS N	3	6	.333	3.43	31	10	2	89.1	97	32	23	1	1	1	0	25	6	0	.240	5	32	2	0	1.3	.949
1943		1	0	1.000	1.84	7	0	0	14.2	17	9	1	0	1	0	0	3	1	0	.333	0	9	0	0	1.3	1.000
2 yrs.		4	6	.400	3.20	38	10	2	104	114	41	24	1	2	1	0	28	7	0	.250	5	41	2	0	1.3	.958

Dick Donovan

DONOVAN, RICHARD EDWARD
B. Dec. 7, 1927, Boston, Mass.
BL TR 6'3" 190 lbs.

Year	Team	W	L	PCT	ERA	G	GS	CG	IP	H	BB	SO	ShO	W	L	SV	AB	H	HR	BA	PO	A	E	DP	TC/G	FA
1950	BOS N	0	2	.000	8.19	10	3	0	29.2	28	34	9	0	0	0	0	6	1	0	.167	1	5	0	1	0.6	1.000
1951		0	0	–	5.27	8	2	0	13.2	17	11	4	0	0	0	0	3	1	0	.333	1	4	0	0	0.6	1.000
1952		0	2	.000	5.54	7	2	0	13	18	12	6	0	0	0	1	3	0	0	.000	0	6	1	0	1.0	.857
1954	DET A	0	0	–	10.50	2	0	0	6	9	5	2	0	0	0	0	1	0	0	.000	0	1	0	0	0.5	1.000
1955	CHI A	15	9	.625	3.32	29	24	11	187	186	48	88	5	2	1	0	76	17	1	.224	11	33	0	2	1.5	1.000
1956		12	10	.545	3.64	34	31	14	234.2	212	59	120	3	0	0	0	90	20	3	.222	11	46	1	4	1.7	.983
1957		16	6	**.727**	2.77	28	28	**16**	220.2	203	45	88	2	0	0	0	83	12	3	.145	18	37	0	3	2.0	1.000
1958		15	14	.517	3.01	34	34	16	248	240	53	127	4	0	0	0	80	9	0	.113	16	24	1	1	1.3	.962
1959		9	10	.474	3.66	31	29	5	179.2	171	58	71	1	0	0	0	61	8	1	.131	11	26	4	1	1.3	.962
1960		6	1	.857	5.38	33	8	0	78.2	87	25	30	0	5	0	3	23	3	0	.130	6	19	1	0	0.8	.962
1961	WAS A	10	10	.500	**2.40**	23	22	11	168.2	138	35	62	2	0	0	0	56	10	1	.179	15	26	4	1	2.0	.911
1962	CLE A	20	10	.667	3.59	34	34	16	250.2	255	47	94	**5**	0	0	0	89	16	4	.180	23	36	3	6	1.8	.952
1963		11	13	.458	4.24	30	30	7	206	211	28	84	3	0	0	0	69	9	1	.130	20	29	2	1	1.7	.961
1964		7	9	.438	4.55	30	23	5	158.1	181	29	83	0	0	0	0	48	7	1	.146	9	30	1	3	1.3	.975
1965		1	3	.250	5.96	12	3	0	22.2	32	6	12	0	0	1	0	6	0	0	.000	2	4	1	0	0.6	.857
15 yrs.		122	99	.552	3.67	345	273	101	2017.1	1988	495	880	25	7	2	5	694	113	15	.163	144	336	20	25	1.4	.960

WORLD SERIES

Year	Team	W	L	PCT	ERA	G	GS	CG	IP	H	BB	SO	ShO	W	L	SV	AB	H	HR	BA	PO	A	E	DP	TC/G	FA
1959	CHI A	0	1	.000	5.40	3	1	0	8.1	4	3	5	0	0	0	0	3	1	0	.333	1	1	0	0	0.7	1.000

Tom Donovan

DONOVAN, THOMAS JOSEPH
D. Mar. 25, 1933, Deceased
BR TR 6'2" 168 lbs.

Year	Team	W	L	PCT	ERA	G	GS	CG	IP	H	BB	SO	ShO	W	L	SV	AB	H	HR	BA	PO	A	E	DP	TC/G	FA
1901	CLE A	0	0	–	5.14	1	0	0	7	16	3	0	0	0	0	0	*				0	2	0	0	2.0	1.000

Wild Bill Donovan

DONOVAN, WILLIAM EDWARD
B. Oct. 13, 1876, Lawrence, Mass. D. Dec. 9, 1923, Forsyth, N. Y.
Manager 1915-17, 1921.
BR TR 5'11" 190 lbs.

Year	Team	W	L	PCT	ERA	G	GS	CG	IP	H	BB	SO	ShO	W	L	SV	AB	H	HR	BA	PO	A	E	DP	TC/G	FA
1898	WAS N	1	6	.143	4.30	17	7	6	88	88	69	36	0	0	0	0	103	17	1	.165	6	17	3	2	1.5	.885
1899	BKN N	1	2	.333	4.32	5	2	2	25	35	13	11	0	0	0	1	13	3	0	.231	1	5	1	0	1.4	.857
1900		1	2	.333	6.68	5	4	2	31	36	18	13	0	0	0	0	13	0	0	.000	0	12	0	0	2.4	1.000
1901		**25**	15	.625	2.77	**45**	38	36	351	324	152	226	2	4	0	1	135	23	2	.170	14	75	7	5	2.1	.927
1902		17	15	.531	2.78	35	33	30	297.2	250	111	170	4	0	0	1	161	27	1	.168	20	71	5	2	2.7	.948
1903	DET A	17	16	.515	2.29	35	34	**34**	307	247	95	187	4	0	0	0	124	30	0	.242	25	65	4	2	2.7	.938
1904		17	16	.515	2.46	34	34	30	293	251	94	137	3	0	0	0	140	38	1	.271	28	89	4	2	3.6	.967
1905		18	15	.545	2.60	34	32	27	280.2	236	101	135	5	1	1	0	130	25	0	.192	16	67	6	3	2.6	.933
1906		9	15	.375	3.15	25	25	22	211.2	221	72	85	0	0	0	0	91	11	0	.121	11	62	3	1	3.0	.961
1907		25	4	**.862**	2.19	32	28	27	271	222	82	123	3	2	0	0	109	29	0	.266	13	56	4	0	2.3	.945
1908		18	7	.720	2.08	29	28	25	242.2	210	53	141	6	0	0	0	82	13	0	.159	16	39	5	0	2.1	.917
1909		8	7	.533	2.31	21	17	13	140.1	121	60	76	0	0	0	2	45	9	0	.200	9	29	1	1	1.9	.974
1910		17	7	.708	2.42	26	23	20	208.2	184	61	107	3	1	0	0	69	10	0	.145	9	33	2	0	1.7	.955
1911		10	9	.526	3.31	20	19	15	168.1	160	64	81	1	0	0	0	60	12	1	.200	4	25	2	0	1.6	.935

Year	Team		W	L	PCT	ERA	G	GS	CG	IP	H	BB	SO	ShO	W	L	SV	AB	H	HR	BA	PO	A	E	DP	TC/G	FA
															Relief Pitching			Batting									

Wild Bill Donovan *continued*

Year	Team		W	L	PCT	ERA	G	GS	CG	IP	H	BB	SO	ShO	W	L	SV	AB	H	HR	BA	PO	A	E	DP	TC/G	FA
1912			1	0	1.000	0.90	3	1	0	10	5	2	6	0	0	0	0	13	1	0	.077	0	1	0	0	0.3	1.000
1915	NY	A	0	3	.000	4.81	9	1	0	33.2	35	10	17	0	0	2	0	12	1	0	.083	1	7	0	0	0.9	1.000
1916			0	0	—	0.00	1	0	0	1	1	0	1	0	0	0	0	0	0	0	—	0	0	0	0	0.0	—
1918	DET	A	1	0	1.000	1.50	2	1	0	6	5	1	1	0	0	0	0	2	1	0	.500	0	1	0	0	0.5	1.000
18 yrs.			186	139	.572	2.69	378	327	289	2966.2	2631	1059	1552	35	9	4	6	*				173	654	49	20	2.3	.944

WORLD SERIES

Year	Team		W	L	PCT	ERA	G	GS	CG	IP	H	BB	SO	ShO	W	L	SV	AB	H	HR	BA	PO	A	E	DP	TC/G	FA
1907	DET	A	0	1	.000	1.29	2	2	2	21	17	5	16	0	0	0	0	8	0	0	.000	3	3	0	0	3.0	1.000
1908			0	2	.000	4.24	2	2	2	17	17	4	10	0	0	0	0	4	0	0	.000	1	2	1	0	2.0	.750
1909			1	1	.500	3.00	2	2	1	12	7	8	7	0	0	0	0	4	0	0	.000	0	5	1	0	3.0	.833
3 yrs.			1	4	.200	2.70	6	6	5	50	41	17	33	0	0	0	0	16	0	0	.000	4	10	2	0	2.7	.875
					7th				10th																		

John Dopson

DOPSON, JOHN ROBERT JR.
B. July 14, 1963, Baltimore, Md.
BL TR 6'4" 205 lbs.

Year	Team		W	L	PCT	ERA	G	GS	CG	IP	H	BB	SO	ShO	W	L	SV	AB	H	HR	BA	PO	A	E	DP	TC/G	FA
1985	MON	N	0	2	.000	11.08	4	3	0	13	25	4	4	0	0	0	0	4	0	0	.000	0	2	0	0	0.5	1.000
1988			3	11	.214	3.04	26	26	1	168.2	150	58	101	0	0	0	0	51	3	0	.059	10	15	2	1	1.0	.926
1989	BOS	A	12	8	.600	3.99	29	28	2	169.1	166	69	95	0	1	0	0	0	0	0	—	20	34	1	1	1.9	.982
3 yrs.			15	21	.417	3.79	59	57	3	351	341	131	200	0	1	0	0	55	3	0	.055	30	51	3	2	1.4	.964

John Doran

DORAN, JOHN F.
B. 1869, N. J. Deceased.
TL 5'11" 175 lbs.

Year	Team		W	L	PCT	ERA	G	GS	CG	IP	H	BB	SO	ShO	W	L	SV	AB	H	HR	BA	PO	A	E	DP	TC/G	FA
1891	LOU	AA	5	10	.333	5.43	15	14	12	126	160	75	55	1	0	1	0	53	10	0	.189	4	29	6	1	2.6	.846

Mike Dorgan

DORGAN, MICHAEL CORNELIUS
Brother of Jerry Dorgan.
B. Oct. 2, 1853, Middletown, Conn. D. Apr. 26, 1909, Syracuse, N. Y.
Manager 1879-81.
BR TR 5'9" 180 lbs.

Year	Team		W	L	PCT	ERA	G	GS	CG	IP	H	BB	SO	ShO	W	L	SV	AB	H	HR	BA	PO	A	E	DP	TC/G	FA
1879	SYR	N	0	0	—	2.25	2	0	0	12	13	2	8	0	0	0	0	270	72	1	.267	1	3	1	0	2.5	.800
1880	PRO	N	0	0	—	1.13	1	0	0	8	4	2	0	0	0	0	0	321	79	0	.246	1	2	0	0	3.0	1.000
1883	NY	N	0	1	.000	3.86	1	1	1	7	8	6	3	0	0	0	0	261	61	0	.234	0	1	0	0	1.0	1.000
1884			8	6	.571	3.50	14	14	12	113	98	51	90	0	0	0	0	341	94	1	.276	14	25	18	1	4.1	.684
4 yrs.			8	7	.533	3.28	18	15	13	140	123	59	103	0	0	0	0	*				16	31	19	1	3.7	.712

Harry Dorish

DORISH, HARRY (Fritz)
B. July 13, 1921, Swoyersville, Pa.
BR TR 5'11" 204 lbs.

Year	Team		W	L	PCT	ERA	G	GS	CG	IP	H	BB	SO	ShO	W	L	SV	AB	H	HR	BA	PO	A	E	DP	TC/G	FA
1947	BOS	A	7	8	.467	4.70	41	9	2	136	149	54	50	0	4	3	2	35	5	0	.143	10	27	4	0	1.0	.902
1948			0	1	.000	5.65	9	0	0	14.1	18	6	5	0	0	1	0	4	1	0	.250	1	2	0	0	0.3	1.000
1949			0	0	—	2.35	5	0	0	7.2	7	1	5	0	0	0	0	0	0	0	—	1	2	0	0	0.6	1.000
1950	STL	A	4	9	.308	6.44	29	13	4	109	162	36	36	0	1	2	0	31	5	0	.161	5	14	1	3	0.7	.950
1951	CHI	A	5	6	.455	3.54	32	4	2	96.2	101	31	29	1	3	5	0	31	8	0	.258	3	20	1	1	0.8	.958
1952			8	4	.667	2.47	39	1	1	91	66	42	47	0	7	4	11	22	2	0	.091	4	23	0	1	0.7	1.000
1953			10	6	.625	3.40	55	4	2	145.2	140	52	69	0	7	4	18	41	7	0	.171	15	31	0	0	0.8	1.000
1954			6	4	.600	2.72	37	4	2	109	88	29	48	1	2	2	6	27	3	0	.111	6	14	0	1	0.5	1.000
1955	2 teams	CHI A (13G 2–0)						BAL A	(35G 3–3)																		
"	total		5	3	.625	2.83	48	1	0	82.2	74	37	28	0	5	2	7	13	1	0	.077	5	26	0	1	0.6	1.000
1956	2 teams	BAL A (13G 0–0)						BOS A	(15G 0–2)																		
"	total		0	2	.000	3.83	28	0	0	42.1	45	13	15	0	0	2	0	—				6	15	0	1	0.8	1.000
10 yrs.			45	43	.511	3.83	323	40	13	834.1	850	301	332	2	29	25	44	204	32	0	.157	56	174	6	9	0.7	.975

Gus Dorner

DORNER, AUGUSTUS
B. Aug. 18, 1876, Chambersburg, Pa. D. May 4, 1956, Chambersburg, Pa.
BR TR 5'10" 176 lbs.

Year	Team		W	L	PCT	ERA	G	GS	CG	IP	H	BB	SO	ShO	W	L	SV	AB	H	HR	BA	PO	A	E	DP	TC/G	FA
1902	CLE	A	3	1	.750	1.25	4	4	4	36	33	13	5	1	0	0	0	13	5	0	.385	2	10	0	0	3.0	1.000
1903			4	5	.444	3.30	12	8	8	73.2	83	24	28	1	1	0	0	25	2	0	.080	1	25	0	0	2.2	1.000
1906	2 teams	CIN N	(2G 1–1)					BOS N	(34G 8–25)																		
"	total		9	26	.257	3.73	36	33	30	272.1	280	107	109	0	1	0	0	105	14	0	.133	19	92	10	5	3.4	.917
1907	BOS	N	12	16	.429	3.12	36	31	24	271.1	253	92	85	2	1	0	0	92	12	0	.130	17	58	0	3	2.1	1.000
1908			8	19	.296	3.54	38	28	14	216.1	176	77	41	3	2	0	0	67	12	0	.179	8	77	5	2	2.4	.944
1909			1	2	.333	2.55	5	2	0	24.2	17	17	7	0	0	1	1	6	1	0	.167	1	6	2	0	1.8	.778
6 yrs.			37	69	.349	3.33	131	106	76	894.1	842	330	275	8	5	3	1	308	46	0	.149	48	268	17	10	2.5	.949

Bert Dorr

DORR, CHARLES ALBERT
B. Feb. 2, 1862, New York, N. Y. D. June 16, 1914, Dickinson, N. Y.

Year	Team		W	L	PCT	ERA	G	GS	CG	IP	H	BB	SO	ShO	W	L	SV	AB	H	HR	BA	PO	A	E	DP	TC/G	FA
1882	STL	AA	2	6	.250	2.59	8	8	8	66	53	1	34	0	0	0	0	26	4	0	.154	5	22	2	0	3.6	.931

Cal Dorsett

DORSETT, CALVIN LEAVELLE (Preacher)
B. June 10, 1913, Long Oak, Tex. D. Oct. 22, 1970, Elk City, Okla.
BR TR 6' 180 lbs.

Year	Team		W	L	PCT	ERA	G	GS	CG	IP	H	BB	SO	ShO	W	L	SV	AB	H	HR	BA	PO	A	E	DP	TC/G	FA
1940	CLE	A	0	0	—	9.00	1	0	0	1	0	0	0	0	0	0	0	0	0	0	—	0	0	0	0	0.0	—
1941			0	1	.000	10.32	5	2	0	11.1	21	10	5	0	0	0	0	2	0	0	.000	0	0	0	0	0.4	1.000
1947			0	0	—	27.00	2	0	0	1.1	3	3	1	0	0	0	0	0	0	0	—	0	0	0	0	0.0	—
3 yrs.			0	1	.000	11.85	8	2	0	13.2	25	13	6	0	0	0	0	2	0	0	.000	0	0	0	0	0.3	1.000

Jerry Dorsey

DORSEY, MICHAEL JEREMIAH
B. 1854, Canada D. Nov. 3, 1938, Auburn, N. Y.

Year	Team		W	L	PCT	ERA	G	GS	CG	IP	H	BB	SO	ShO	W	L	SV	AB	H	HR	BA	PO	A	E	DP	TC/G	FA
1884	BAL	U	0	1	.000	9.00	1	1	0	4	7	0	3	0	0	0	0	3	0	0	.000	0	1	0	0	1.0	1.000

Jim Dorsey

DORSEY, JAMES EDWARD
B. Aug. 2, 1955, Chicago, Ill.
BR TR 6'7" 190 lbs.

Year	Team		W	L	PCT	ERA	G	GS	CG	IP	H	BB	SO	ShO	W	L	SV	AB	H	HR	BA	PO	A	E	DP	TC/G	FA
1980	CAL	A	1	2	.333	9.00	4	4	0	16	25	8	8	0	0	0	0	—				1	2	0	0	0.8	1.000
1984	BOS	A	0	0	—	10.13	2	0	0	2.2	6	2	4	0	0	0	0	—				0	1	0	0	0.5	1.000

Year	Team	W	L	PCT	ERA	G	GS	CG	IP	H	BB	SO	ShO	Relief Pitching W	L	SV	Batting AB	H	HR	BA	PO	A	E	DP	TC/G	FA

Jim Dorsey *continued*

| 1985 | | 0 | 1 | .000 | 20.25 | 2 | 1 | 0 | 5.1 | 12 | 10 | 2 | 0 | 0 | 0 | 0 | 0 | 0 | 0 | – | 0 | 0 | 1 | 0 | 0.5 | – |
| 3 yrs. | | 1 | 3 | .250 | 11.63 | 8 | 5 | 0 | 24 | 43 | 20 | 14 | 0 | 0 | 0 | 0 | 0 | 0 | 0 | – | 1 | 3 | 1 | 0 | 0.6 | .800 |

Jack Doscher

DOSCHER, JOHN HENRY, JR.
Son of Herm Doscher.
B. July 27, 1880, Troy, N. Y.   D. May 27, 1971, Park Ridge, N. J.

BL TL 6'1"

1903	2 teams	CHI N	(1G 0–1)		BKN N	(3G 0–0)																				
"	total	0	1	.000	9.00	4	1	0	10	14	11	9	0	0	0	0	4	0	0	.000	1	1	0	0	0.5	1.000
1904	BKN N	0	0	–	0.00	2	0	0	6.1	1	1	2	0	0	1	0	2	1	0	.500	0	1	0	0	0.5	1.000
1905		1	5	.167	3.17	12	7	6	71	60	30	33	0	0	0	0	24	2	0	.083	2	13	3	0	1.5	.833
1906		0	1	.000	1.29	2	1	1	14	12	4	10	0	0	0	0	5	0	0	.000	1	2	0	0	1.5	1.000
1908	CIN N	1	3	.250	1.83	7	4	3	44.1	31	22	7	0	0	0	0	15	2	0	.133	1	13	2	0	2.3	.875
5 yrs.		2	11	.154	2.84	27	13	10	145.2	118	68	61	0	0	0	1	50	5	0	.100	5	30	5	0	1.5	.875

Richard Dotson

DOTSON, RICHARD ELLIOTT
B. Jan. 10, 1959, Cincinnati, Ohio

BR TR 6'1"   190 lbs.

1979	CHI A	2	0	1.000	3.75	5	5	0	24	28	6	13	1	0	0	0	0	0	0	–	1	4	0	0	1.0	1.000
1980		12	10	.545	4.27	33	32	8	198	185	87	109	0	0	0	0	0	0	0	–	13	33	1	0	1.4	.979
1981		9	8	.529	3.77	24	24	5	141	145	49	73	0	0	0	0	0	0	0	–	7	20	0	4	1.1	1.000
1982		11	15	.423	3.84	34	31	3	196.2	219	73	109	1	0	0	0	0	0	0	–	13	24	1	1	1.1	.974
1983		22	7	.759	3.23	35	35	8	240	209	106	137	1	0	0	0	0	0	0	–	20	48	1	8	2.0	.986
1984		14	15	.483	3.59	32	32	14	245.2	216	103	120	1	0	0	0	0	0	0	–	8	36	1	3	1.4	.978
1985		3	4	.429	4.47	9	9	0	52.1	53	17	33	0	0	0	0	0	0	0	–	3	5	0	0	0.9	1.000
1986		10	17	.370	5.48	34	34	3	197	226	69	110	1	0	0	0	0	0	0	–	13	23	3	0	1.1	.923
1987		11	12	.478	4.17	31	31	7	211.1	201	86	114	2	0	0	0	0	0	0	–	14	38	2	4	1.7	.963
1988	NY A	12	9	.571	5.00	32	29	4	171	178	72	77	0	0	0	0	0	0	0	–	17	14	0	1	1.0	1.000
1989	2 teams	NY A	(11G 2–5)		CHI A	(17G 3–7)																				
"	total	5	12	.294	4.46	28	26	2	151.1	181	58	69	0	0	0	0	0	0	0	–	5	21	2	3	1.0	.929
11 yrs.		111	109	.505	4.16	297	288	55	1828.1	1841	726	964	11	0	0	0	0	0	0	–	114	266	11	24	1.3	.972

LEAGUE CHAMPIONSHIP SERIES

| 1983 | CHI A | 0 | 1 | .000 | 10.80 | 1 | 1 | 0 | 5 | 6 | 3 | 3 | 0 | 0 | 0 | 0 | 0 | 0 | 0 | – | 1 | 1 | 0 | 0 | 2.0 | 1.000 |

Gary Dotter

DOTTER, GARY RICHARD
B. Aug. 7, 1942, St. Louis, Mo.

BL TL 6'1"   180 lbs.

1961	MIN A	0	0	–	9.00	2	0	0	6	6	4	2	0	0	0	0	1	0	0	.000	1	1	0	0	1.0	1.000
1963		0	0	–	0.00	2	0	0	2	0	0	2	0	0	0	0	0	0	0	–	0	1	0	0	0.5	1.000
1964		0	0	–	2.08	3	0	0	4.1	3	3	6	0	0	0	0	0	0	0	–	0	0	0	0	0.0	–
3 yrs.		0	0	–	5.11	7	0	0	12.1	9	7	10	0	0	0	0	1	0	0	.000	1	2	0	0	0.4	1.000

Babe Doty

DOTY, ELMER L.
B. Dec. 17, 1867, Genoa, Ohio   D. Nov. 20, 1929, Toledo, Ohio

BL TR 6'   160 lbs.

| 1890 | TOL AA | 1 | 0 | 1.000 | 1.00 | 1 | 1 | 1 | 9 | 9 | 1 | 4 | 0 | 0 | 0 | 0 | 3 | 0 | 0 | .000 | 0 | 0 | 0 | 0 | 0.0 | – |

Tom Dougherty

DOUGHERTY, THOMAS JAMES (Sugar Boy)
B. May 30, 1881, Chicago, Ill.   D. Nov. 6, 1953, Milwaukee, Wis.

BL TR

| 1904 | CHI A | 1 | 0 | 1.000 | 0.00 | 1 | 0 | 0 | 2 | 0 | 0 | 0 | 0 | 1 | 0 | 0 | 0 | 0 | 0 | .000 | 1 | 1 | 0 | 0 | 2.0 | 1.000 |

Larry Douglas

DOUGLAS, LAWRENCE HOWARD (Doug)
B. June 5, 1890, Jellico, Tenn.   D. Nov. 4, 1949, Jellico, Tenn.

BR TR 6'3"   175 lbs.

| 1915 | BAL F | 0 | 0 | – | 3.00 | 2 | 0 | 0 | 3 | 3 | 2 | 1 | 0 | 0 | 0 | 0 | 0 | 0 | 0 | – | 0 | 1 | 0 | 0 | 0.5 | 1.000 |

Phil Douglas

DOUGLAS, PHILLIP BROOKS (Shufflin' Phil)
B. June 17, 1890, Cedartown, Ga.   D. Aug. 1, 1952, Sequatchie Valley, Tenn.

BR TR 6'3"   190 lbs.

1912	CHI A	0	1	.000	7.30	3	1	0	12.1	21	6	7	0	0	0	0	2	0	0	.000	0	5	1	0	2.0	.833
1914	CIN N	11	18	.379	2.56	45	25	13	239.1	186	92	121	0	4	4	1	73	10	0	.137	7	54	6	0	1.5	.910
1915	3 teams	CIN N	(8G 1–5)		BKN N	(20G 5–5)		CHI N	(4G 1–1)																	
"	total	7	11	.389	3.25	32	24	7	188.1	174	47	110	2	0	0	0	64	8	0	.125	5	51	4	3	1.9	.933
1917	CHI N	14	20	.412	2.55	51	37	20	293.1	269	50	151	5	3	0	1	89	11	0	.124	9	102	7	3	2.3	.941
1918		9	9	.500	2.13	25	19	11	156.2	145	31	51	2	1	1	2	55	14	0	.255	4	61	2	3	2.7	.970
1919	2 teams	CHI N	(25G 10–6)		NY N	(8G 2–4)																				
"	total	12	10	.545	2.03	33	25	12	213	186	40	84	4	2	0	0	66	8	0	.121	7	83	2	1	2.8	.978
1920	NY N	14	10	.583	2.71	46	21	10	226	225	55	71	3	4	5	2	73	11	0	.151	11	65	3	3	1.7	.962
1921		15	10	.600	4.22	40	27	13	221.2	266	55	55	3	2	1	2	81	16	1	.198	5	64	3	3	1.8	.958
1922		11	4	.733	2.63	24	21	9	157.2	154	35	33	1	1	0	1	58	12	1	.207	13	36	4	2	2.2	.925
9 yrs.		93	93	.500	2.80	299	200	95	1708.1	1626	411	683	20	17	11	8	561	90	2	.160	61	521	32	18	2.1	.948

WORLD SERIES

1918	CHI N	0	1	.000	0.00	1	0	0	1	1	0	0	0	0	0	0	0	0	0	–	0	1	0	0	1.0	–
1921	NY N	2	1	.667	2.08	3	3	2	26	24	5	17	0	0	0	0	7	0	0	.000	2	10	0	0	4.0	1.000
2 yrs.		2	2	.500	2.00	4	3	2	27	25	5	17	0	0	0	0	7	0	0	.000	2	10	0	0	3.3	.923

Whammy Douglas

DOUGLAS, CHARLES WILLIAM
B. Feb. 17, 1935, Carrboro, N. C.

BR TR 6'2"   185 lbs.

| 1957 | PIT N | 3 | 3 | .500 | 3.26 | 11 | 8 | 0 | 47 | 48 | 30 | 28 | 0 | 0 | 0 | 0 | 16 | 1 | 0 | .063 | 4 | 6 | 1 | 0 | 1.0 | .909 |

Skip Dowd

DOWD, JAMES JOSEPH
B. Feb. 16, 1889, Holyoke, Mass.   D. Dec. 20, 1960, Holyoke, Mass.

BR TR 5'10½"   160 lbs.

| 1910 | PIT N | 0 | 0 | – | 0.00 | 1 | 0 | 0 | 2 | 4 | 2 | 1 | 0 | 0 | 0 | 0 | 0 | 0 | 0 | – | 0 | 0 | 0 | 0 | 0.0 | – |

Year	Team	W	L	PCT	ERA	G	GS	CG	IP	H	BB	SO	ShO	Relief Pitching W	L	SV	Batting AB	H	HR	BA	PO	A	E	DP	TC/G	FA

Dave Dowling

DOWLING, DAVID BARCLAY
B. Aug. 23, 1942, Baton Rouge, La. BR TL 6'2" 181 lbs.

Year	Team	W	L	PCT	ERA	G	GS	CG	IP	H	BB	SO	ShO	W	L	SV	AB	H	HR	BA	PO	A	E	DP	TC/G	FA
1964	STL N	0	0	–	0.00	1	0	0	1	2	0	0	0	0	0	0	0	0	0	–	0	0	0	0	0.0	–
1966	CHI N	1	0	1.000	2.00	1	1	1	9	10	0	3	0	0	0	0	2	0	0	.000	1	0	0	0	1.0	1.000
	2 yrs.	1	0	1.000	1.80	2	1	1	10	12	0	3	0	0	0	0	2	0	0	.000	1	0	0	0	0.5	1.000

Pete Dowling

DOWLING, HENRY PETER
B. St. Louis, Mo. D. June 30, 1905, Hot Lake, Ore. TL 5'11"

Year	Team	W	L	PCT	ERA	G	GS	CG	IP	H	BB	SO	ShO	W	L	SV	AB	H	HR	BA	PO	A	E	DP	TC/G	FA
1897	LOU N	1	2	.333	5.88	4	4	2	26	39	8	3	0				10	2	0	.200	4	3	0	1	1.8	1.000
1898		13	20	.394	4.16	36	32	30	285.2	284	120	84	0	1	1	0	107	21	0	.196	11	68	12	2	2.5	.868
1899		13	17	.433	3.11	34	32	29	289.2	321	93	88	0	1	0	0	116	27	0	.233	5	73	11	2	2.6	.876
1901	2 teams	MIL A	(10G 1–4)		CLE A	(33G 11–22)																				
"	total	12	26	.316	4.15	43	34	31	306	340	118	124	2	0	4	1	118	20	1	.169	10	84	7	2	2.3	.931
	4 yrs.	39	65	.375	3.87	117	102	92	907.1	984	339	299	2	2	5	1	351	70	1	.199	30	228	30	7	2.5	.896

Al Downing

DOWNING, ALPHONSO ERWIN
B. June 28, 1941, Trenton, N. J. BR TL 5'11" 175 lbs.

Year	Team	W	L	PCT	ERA	G	GS	CG	IP	H	BB	SO	ShO	W	L	SV	AB	H	HR	BA	PO	A	E	DP	TC/G	FA
1961	NY A	0	1	.000	8.00	5	1	0	9	7	12	12	0	0	0	0	1	0	0	.000	0	2	0	0	0.4	1.000
1962		0	0	–	0.00	1	0	0	1	0	1	0	0	0	0	0	0	0	0	–	0	0	0	0	0.0	–
1963		13	5	.722	2.56	24	22	10	175.2	114	80	171	4	0	0	1	0	58	6	0	.103	7	18	1	1	1.1	.962
1964		13	8	.619	3.47	37	35	11	244	201	120	217	1	0	0	2	85	15	0	.176	6	39	0	0	1.2	1.000
1965		12	14	.462	3.40	35	32	8	212	185	105	179	2	0	0	0	74	8	1	.108	6	36	2	4	1.3	.955
1966		10	11	.476	3.56	30	30	1	200	178	79	152	0	0	0	0	70	7	0	.100	4	16	3	2	0.8	.870
1967		14	10	.583	2.63	31	28	10	201.2	158	61	171	4	2	0	0	66	8	1	.121	4	27	1	2	1.2	.973
1968		3	3	.500	3.52	15	12	1	61.1	54	20	40	0	0	0	0	17	3	0	.176	2	9	0	0	0.7	1.000
1969		7	5	.583	3.38	30	15	5	130.2	117	49	85	1	1	1	0	44	6	0	.136	4	16	1	1	0.6	.944
1970	2 teams	OAK A	(10G 3–3)		MIL A	(17G 2–10)																				
"	total	5	13	.278	3.52	27	22	3	135.1	118	81	79	0	0	0	0	35	4	0	.114	9	30	3	2	1.6	.929
1971	LA N	20	9	.690	2.68	37	36	12	262	245	84	136	5	0	0	0	92	16	0	.174	7	40	1	2	1.3	.979
1972		9	9	.500	2.98	31	30	7	202.2	196	67	117	4	0	0	0	66	8	0	.121	5	54	1	5	1.9	.983
1973		9	9	.500	3.31	30	28	5	193	155	68	124	2	1	0	0	57	5	0	.088	8	34	3	1	1.5	.933
1974		5	6	.455	3.67	21	16	1	98	94	45	63	1	0	0	0	29	5	0	.172	2	20	1	2	1.1	.957
1975		2	1	.667	2.88	22	6	0	75	59	28	39	0	2	1	1	16	0	0	.000	4	17	0	0	1.0	1.000
1976		1	2	.333	3.86	17	3	0	46.2	43	18	30	0	1	1	0	6	0	0	.000	0	9	0	1	0.5	1.000
1977		0	1	.000	6.75	12	1	0	20	22	16	23	0	0	1	0	4	0	0	.000	0	3	1	0	0.3	.750
	17 yrs.	123	107	.535	3.22	405	317	73	2268	1946	933	1639	24	7	5	3	717	91	2	.127	72	368	18	23	1.1	.961

LEAGUE CHAMPIONSHIP SERIES

Year	Team	W	L	PCT	ERA	G	GS	CG	IP	H	BB	SO	ShO	W	L	SV	AB	H	HR	BA	PO	A	E	DP	TC/G	FA
1974	LA N	0	0	–	0.00	1	0	0	4	1	1	0	0	0	0	0	1	0	0	.000	0	0	1	0	1.0	–

WORLD SERIES

Year	Team	W	L	PCT	ERA	G	GS	CG	IP	H	BB	SO	ShO	W	L	SV	AB	H	HR	BA	PO	A	E	DP	TC/G	FA
1963	NY A	0	1	.000	5.40	1	1	0	5	7	1	6	0	0	0	0	1	0	0	.000	0	1	0	0	1.0	1.000
1964		0	1	.000	8.22	3	1	0	7.2	9	2	5	0	0	0	0	2	0	0	.000	0	1	0	0	0.3	1.000
1974	LA N	0	1	.000	2.45	1	1	0	3.2	4	4	3	0	0	0	0	1	0	0	.000	0	3	0	0	3.0	1.000
	3 yrs.	0	3	.000	6.06	5	3	0	16.1	20	7	14	0	0	0	0	4	0	0	.000	0	5	0	0	1.0	1.000

Dave Downs

DOWNS, DAVID RALPH
Brother of Kelly Downs.
B. June 21, 1952, Logan, Utah BR TR 6'5" 220 lbs.

Year	Team	W	L	PCT	ERA	G	GS	CG	IP	H	BB	SO	ShO	W	L	SV	AB	H	HR	BA	PO	A	E	DP	TC/G	FA
1972	PHI N	1	1	.500	2.74	4	4	1	23	25	3	5	1	0	0	0	8	2	0	.250	0	5	0	0	1.3	1.000

Kelly Downs

DOWNS, KELLY ROBERT
Brother of Dave Downs.
B. Oct. 25, 1960, Ogden, Utah BR TR 6'4" 195 lbs.

Year	Team	W	L	PCT	ERA	G	GS	CG	IP	H	BB	SO	ShO	W	L	SV	AB	H	HR	BA	PO	A	E	DP	TC/G	FA
1986	SF N	4	4	.500	2.75	14	14	1	88.1	78	30	64	0	0	0	0	29	5	0	.172	6	13	1	0	1.4	.950
1987		12	9	.571	3.63	41	28	4	186	185	67	137	3	1	1	1	56	8	0	.143	11	10	3	0	0.6	.875
1988		13	9	.591	3.32	27	26	6	168	140	47	118	3	0	0	0	54	9	0	.167	15	22	1	2	1.4	.974
1989		4	8	.333	4.79	18	15	0	82.2	82	26	49	0	0	0	0	22	2	0	.091	7	8	1	1	0.9	.938
	4 yrs.	33	30	.524	3.57	100	83	11	525	485	170	368	6	1	1	1	161	24	0	.149	39	53	6	3	1.0	.939

LEAGUE CHAMPIONSHIP SERIES

Year	Team	W	L	PCT	ERA	G	GS	CG	IP	H	BB	SO	ShO	W	L	SV	AB	H	HR	BA	PO	A	E	DP	TC/G	FA
1987	SF N	0	0	–	0.00	1	0	0	1.1	1	0	0	0	0	0	0	0	0	0	–	0	0	0	0	0.0	–
1989		1	0	1.000	3.12	2	0	0	8.2	8	6	6	0	1	0	0	3	0	0	.000	0	1	1	1	0.5	1.000
	2 yrs.	1	0	1.000	2.70	3	0	0	10	9	6	6	0	1	0	0	3	0	0	.000	0	1	1	1	0.3	1.000

WORLD SERIES

Year	Team	W	L	PCT	ERA	G	GS	CG	IP	H	BB	SO	ShO	W	L	SV	AB	H	HR	BA	PO	A	E	DP	TC/G	FA
1989	SF N	0	0	–	7.71	3	0	0	4.2	3	2	4	0	0	0	0	0	0	0	–	0	0	0	0	0.0	–

Tom Dowse

DOWSE, THOMAS JOSEPH
B. Aug. 12, 1866, Ireland D. Dec. 14, 1946, Riverside, Calif. BR TR 5'11" 175 lbs.

Year	Team	W	L	PCT	ERA	G	GS	CG	IP	H	BB	SO	ShO	W	L	SV	AB	H	HR	BA	PO	A	E	DP	TC/G	FA
1890	CLE N	0	0	–	5.40	1	0	0	5	6	1	0	0	0	0	0	*				0	2	0	0	2.0	1.000

Carl Doyle

DOYLE, WILLIAM CARL
B. July 30, 1912, Knoxville, Tenn. D. Sept. 4, 1951, Knoxville, Tenn. BR TR 6'1" 185 lbs.

Year	Team	W	L	PCT	ERA	G	GS	CG	IP	H	BB	SO	ShO	W	L	SV	AB	H	HR	BA	PO	A	E	DP	TC/G	FA
1935	PHI A	2	7	.222	5.99	14	9	3	79.2	86	72	34	0	0	0	0	30	4	0	.133	5	17	0	3	1.6	1.000
1936		0	3	.000	10.94	8	1	0	38.2	66	29	12	0	0	0	0	15	4	0	.267	1	2	1	0	0.5	.750
1939	BKN N	1	2	.333	1.02	5	1	0	17.2	8	7	7	1	0	2	1	6	1	0	.167	1	4	0	0	1.0	1.000
1940	2 teams	BKN N	(3G 0–0)		STL N	(21G 3–3)																				
"	total	3	3	.500	7.27	24	5	1	86.2	117	47	48	0	2	2	1	31	7	1	.226	5	15	0	2	0.8	1.000
	4 yrs.	6	15	.286	6.95	51	21	4	222.2	277	155	101	1	2	4	2	82	16	1	.195	12	38	1	5	1.0	.980

Year	Team	W	L	PCT	ERA	G	GS	CG	IP	H	BB	SO	ShO	Relief Pitching W	L	SV	Batting AB	H	HR	BA	PO	A	E	DP	TC/G	FA

Ed Doyle

DOYLE, EDWARD H.
B. 1853, Lasalle, Ill. D. Feb. 6, 1929, Havre Mont.,

Year	Team	W	L	PCT	ERA	G	GS	CG	IP	H	BB	SO	ShO	W	L	SV	AB	H	HR	BA	PO	A	E	DP	TC/G	FA
1882	STL AA	0	3	.000	2.63	3	3	3	24	41	3	5	0	0	0	0	11	2	0	.182	1	5	0	0	2.0	1.000

Jess Doyle

DOYLE, JESSE HERBERT BR TR 5'11" 175 lbs.
B. Apr. 14, 1898, Knoxville, Tenn. D. Apr. 15, 1961, Belleville, Ill.

Year	Team	W	L	PCT	ERA	G	GS	CG	IP	H	BB	SO	ShO	W	L	SV	AB	H	HR	BA	PO	A	E	DP	TC/G	FA
1925	DET A	4	7	.364	5.93	45	3	0	118.1	158	50	31	0	4	5	8	33	8	2	.242	4	27	0	0	0.7	1.000
1926		0	0	–	4.15	2	0	0	4.1	6	1	2	0	0	0	1	1	1	0	1.000	0	1	1	0	1.0	.500
1927		0	0	–	8.03	7	0	0	12.1	16	5	5	0	0	0	0	3	1	0	.333	0	3	0	1	0.4	1.000
1931	STL A	0	0	–	27.00	1	0	0	1	3	1	0	0	0	0	0	0	0	0	–	0	0	0	0	0.0	–
4 yrs.		4	7	.364	6.22	55	3	0	136	183	57	38	0	4	5	9	37	10	2	.270	4	31	1	1	0.7	.972

Paul Doyle

DOYLE, PAUL SINNOTT BL TL 5'11" 172 lbs.
B. Oct. 2, 1939, Philadelphia, Pa.

Year	Team	W	L	PCT	ERA	G	GS	CG	IP	H	BB	SO	ShO	W	L	SV	AB	H	HR	BA	PO	A	E	DP	TC/G	FA
1969	ATL N	2	0	1.000	2.08	36	0	0	39	31	16	25	0	2	0	4	3	0	0	.000	2	10	0	0	0.3	1.000
1970	2 teams	CAL A	(40G 3–1)		SD N	(9G 0–2)																				
"	total	3	3	.500	5.33	49	0	0	49	52	27	36	0	3	3	7	4	0	0	.000	1	16	0	2	0.3	1.000
1972	CAL A	0	0	–	0.00	2	0	0	2	2	3	4	0	0	0	0	0	0	0	–	0	1	0	0	0.5	1.000
3 yrs.		5	3	.625	3.80	87	0	0	90	85	46	65	0	5	3	11	7	0	0	.000	3	27	0	2	0.3	1.000

LEAGUE CHAMPIONSHIP SERIES

Year	Team	W	L	PCT	ERA	G	GS	CG	IP	H	BB	SO	ShO	W	L	SV	AB	H	HR	BA	PO	A	E	DP	TC/G	FA
1969	ATL N	0	0	–	0.00	1	0	0	1	1	3	0	0	0	0	0	0	0	0	–	0	0	0	0	0.0	–

Slow Joe Doyle

DOYLE, JUDD BRUCE BL TR 5'8" 150 lbs.
B. Sept. 15, 1881, Clay Center, Kans. D. Nov. 21, 1947, Tannersville, Ky.

Year	Team	W	L	PCT	ERA	G	GS	CG	IP	H	BB	SO	ShO	W	L	SV	AB	H	HR	BA	PO	A	E	DP	TC/G	FA
1906	NY A	2	2	.500	2.38	9	6	3	45.1	34	13	28	2	0	0	0	14	3	0	.214	4	13	0	0	1.9	1.000
1907		11	11	.500	2.65	29	23	15	193.2	169	67	94	1	1	0	1	58	8	0	.138	5	45	3	2	1.8	.943
1908		1	1	.500	2.63	12	4	2	48	42	14	20	1	0	0	0	14	3	0	.214	1	8	2	1	0.9	.818
1909		8	6	.571	2.58	17	15	8	125.2	103	37	57	3	0	0	0	42	7	0	.167	5	23	1	0	1.7	.966
1910	2 teams	NY A	(3G 0–2)		CIN N	(5G 0–0)																				
"	total	0	2	.000	7.23	8	2	1	23.2	35	16	10	0	0	0	0	7	1	0	.143	0	9	3	0	1.5	.750
5 yrs.		22	22	.500	2.85	75	50	29	436.1	383	147	209	7	1	0	1	135	22	0	.163	15	98	9	3	1.6	.926

Buzz Dozier

DOZIER, WILLIAM JOSEPH BR TR 6'3" 185 lbs.
B. Aug. 31, 1927, Waco, Tex.

Year	Team	W	L	PCT	ERA	G	GS	CG	IP	H	BB	SO	ShO	W	L	SV	AB	H	HR	BA	PO	A	E	DP	TC/G	FA
1947	WAS A	0	0	–	0.00	2	0	0	4.2	2	1	2	0	0	0	0	1	0	0	.000	0	1	0	0	0.5	1.000
1949		0	0	–	11.37	2	0	0	6.1	12	6	1	0	0	0	0	2	0	0	.000	0	0	0	0	0.0	–
2 yrs.		0	0	–	6.55	4	0	0	11	14	7	3	0	0	0	0	3	0	0	.000	0	1	0	0	0.3	1.000

Tom Dozier

DOZIER, THOMAS DEAN BR TR 6'2" 190 lbs.
B. Sept. 5, 1961, San Pablo, Calif.

Year	Team	W	L	PCT	ERA	G	GS	CG	IP	H	BB	SO	ShO	W	L	SV	AB	H	HR	BA	PO	A	E	DP	TC/G	FA
1986	OAK A	0	0	–	5.68	4	0	0	6.1	6	5	4	0	0	0	0	0	0	0	–	1	0	0	0	0.3	1.000

Doug Drabek

DRABEK, DOUGLAS DEAN BR TR 6'1" 185 lbs.
B. July 25, 1962, Victoria, Tex.

Year	Team	W	L	PCT	ERA	G	GS	CG	IP	H	BB	SO	ShO	W	L	SV	AB	H	HR	BA	PO	A	E	DP	TC/G	FA
1986	NY A	7	8	.467	4.10	27	21	0	131.2	126	50	76	0	0	0	0	–				5	13	0	0	0.7	1.000
1987	PIT N	11	12	.478	3.88	29	28	1	176.1	165	46	120	1	0	0	0	59	7	0	.119	24	23	2	0	1.7	.959
1988		15	7	.682	3.08	33	32	3	219.1	194	50	127	1	0	0	0	76	13	0	.171	29	21	6	6	1.7	.893
1989		14	12	.538	2.80	35	34	8	244.1	215	69	123	5	1	0	0	77	8	0	.104	24	34	2	0	1.7	.967
4 yrs.		47	39	.547	3.35	124	115	12	771.2	700	215	446	7	1	0	0	212	28	0	.132	82	91	10	6	1.5	.945

Moe Drabowsky

DRABOWSKY, MYRON WALTER BR TR 6'3" 190 lbs.
B. July 21, 1935, Ozanna, Poland

Year	Team	W	L	PCT	ERA	G	GS	CG	IP	H	BB	SO	ShO	W	L	SV	AB	H	HR	BA	PO	A	E	DP	TC/G	FA
1956	CHI N	2	4	.333	2.47	9	7	3	51	37	39	36	0	0	0	0	16	4	0	.250	2	7	0	0	1.0	1.000
1957		13	15	.464	3.53	36	33	12	239.2	214	94	170	2	0	0	0	82	15	1	.183	19	35	0	0	1.5	1.000
1958		9	11	.450	4.51	22	20	4	125.2	118	73	77	1	1	1	0	45	7	0	.156	12	16	1	2	1.3	.966
1959		5	10	.333	4.13	31	23	3	141.2	138	75	70	1	0	0	0	45	5	0	.111	12	21	2	1	1.1	.943
1960		3	1	.750	6.44	32	7	0	50.1	71	23	26	0	2	0	1	6	0	0	.000	1	6	0	0	0.2	1.000
1961	MIL N	0	2	.000	4.62	16	0	0	25.1	26	18	5	0	0	2	2	4	1	0	.250	1	7	1	0	0.6	.889
1962	2 teams	CIN N	(23G 2–6)		KC A	(10G 1–1)																				
"	total	3	7	.300	5.03	33	13	1	111	113	41	75	0	1	1	1	23	1	0	.043	9	12	2	2	0.7	.913
1963	KC A	7	13	.350	3.05	26	22	9	174.1	135	64	109	2	0	0	0	62	10	2	.161	11	19	1	1	1.2	.968
1964		5	13	.278	5.29	53	21	1	168.1	176	72	119	0	1	2	1	43	1	0	.023	11	26	1	4	0.7	.974
1965		1	5	.167	4.42	14	5	0	38.2	44	18	25	0	1	2	0	11	1	0	.091	2	5	0	1	0.5	1.000
1966	BAL A	6	0	1.000	2.81	44	3	0	96	62	29	98	0	5	0	7	22	8	0	.364	1	12	0	0	0.3	1.000
1967			7	5	.583	1.60	43	0	0	95.1	66	25	96	0	7	5	12	20	7	0	.350	4	15	0	1	0.4	1.000
1968			4	4	.500	1.91	45	0	0	61.1	35	25	46	0	4	4	7	7	2	0	.286	2	8	2	1	0.3	.833
1969	KC A	11	9	.550	2.94	52	0	0	98	68	30	76	0	11	9	11	17	4	0	.235	6	19	0	0	0.5	1.000
1970	2 teams	KC A	(24G 1–2)		BAL A	(21G 4–2)																				
"	total	5	4	.556	3.52	45	0	0	69	58	27	59	0	5	4	3	9	1	0	.111	3	4	0	0	0.2	1.000
1971	STL N	6	1	.857	3.45	51	0	0	60	45	33	49	0	6	1	8	6	1	0	.167	2	5	0	0	0.1	1.000
1972	2 teams	STL N	(30G 1–1)		CHI A	(7G 0–0)																				
"	total	1	1	.500	2.57	37	0	0	35	35	16	26	0	1	1	2	2	0	0	.000	1	3	0	0	0.2	.500
17 yrs.		88	105	.456	3.71	589	154	33	1640.2	1441	702	1162	6	45	32	55	420	68	3	.162	100	218	13	14	0.6	.961

WORLD SERIES

Year	Team	W	L	PCT	ERA	G	GS	CG	IP	H	BB	SO	ShO	W	L	SV	AB	H	HR	BA	PO	A	E	DP	TC/G	FA
1966	BAL A	1	0	1.000	0.00	1	0	0	6.2	1	2	11	0	1	0	0	2	0	0	.000	0	0	0	0	0.0	–
1970		0	0	–	2.70	2	0	0	3.1	2	1	1	0	0	0	0	1	0	0	.000	0	0	0	0	0.5	1.000
2 yrs.		1	0	1.000	0.90	3	0	0	10	3	3	12	0	1	0	0	3	0	0	.000	0	0	0	0	0.3	1.000

Year	Team		W	L	PCT	ERA	G	GS	CG	IP	H	BB	SO	ShO	W	L	SV	AB	H	HR	BA	PO	A	E	DP	TC/G	FA
															Relief Pitching			Batting									

Dick Drago

DRAGO, RICHARD ANTHONY B. June 25, 1945, Toledo, Ohio — BR TR 6'1" 190 lbs.

Year	Team		W	L	PCT	ERA	G	GS	CG	IP	H	BB	SO	ShO	W	L	SV	AB	H	HR	BA	PO	A	E	DP	TC/G	FA
1969	KC	A	11	13	.458	3.77	41	26	10	200.2	190	65	108	2	0	1	1	52	3	0	.058	25	32	1	6	1.4	.983
1970			9	15	.375	3.75	35	34	7	240	239	72	127	1	0	0	0	76	4	0	.053	10	33	1	5	1.3	.977
1971			17	11	.607	2.99	35	34	15	241	251	46	109	4	0	0	0	77	10	0	.130	7	42	2	9	1.5	.961
1972			12	17	.414	3.01	34	33	11	239.1	230	51	135	2	0	0	0	68	4	0	.059	4	28	3	3	1.0	.941
1973			12	14	.462	4.23	37	33	10	212.2	252	76	98	1	0	1	0	0	0	0	–	14	38	3	3	1.5	.945
1974	BOS	A	7	10	.412	3.48	33	18	8	176	165	56	90	0	3	0	3	0	0	0	–	3	21	0	1	0.7	1.000
1975			2	2	.500	3.84	40	2	0	72.2	69	31	43	0	2	2	15	0	0	0	–	3	12	0	0	0.4	1.000
1976	CAL	A	7	8	.467	4.42	43	0	0	79.1	80	31	43	0	7	8	6	0	0	0	–	3	4	1	0	0.2	.875
1977	2 teams		CAL A	(13G 0–1)		BAL A	(36G 6–3)																					
"	total		6	4	.600	3.41	49	0	0	60.2	71	18	35	0	6	4	4	0	0	0	–	0	9	1	0	0.2	.900
1978	BOS	A	4	4	.500	3.03	37	1	0	77.1	71	32	42	0	4	4	7	0	0	0	–	2	10	1	0	0.4	.923
1979			10	6	.625	3.03	53	1	0	89	85	21	67	0	10	6	13	0	0	0	–	5	11	1	2	0.3	.941
1980			7	7	.500	4.13	43	7	1	133	127	44	63	0	4	4	3	0	0	0	.000	6	17	0	1	0.5	1.000
1981	SEA	A	4	6	.400	5.50	39	0	0	54	71	15	27	0	4	6	5	0	0	0	–	2	11	0	1	0.3	1.000
13 yrs.			108	117	.480	3.62	519	189	62	1875.2	1901	558	987	10	40	36	58	274	21	0	.077	83	268	13	33	0.7	.964

LEAGUE CHAMPIONSHIP SERIES

Year	Team		W	L	PCT	ERA	G	GS	CG	IP	H	BB	SO	ShO	W	L	SV	AB	H	HR	BA	PO	A	E	DP	TC/G	FA
1975	BOS	A	0	0	–	0.00	2	0	0	4.2	2	1	2	0	0	0	2	0	0	0	–	1	1	0	0	1.0	1.000

WORLD SERIES

Year	Team		W	L	PCT	ERA	G	GS	CG	IP	H	BB	SO	ShO	W	L	SV	AB	H	HR	BA	PO	A	E	DP	TC/G	FA
1975	BOS	A	0	1	.000	2.25	2	0	0	4	3	1	1	0	0	1	0	0	0	0	–	0	0	0	0	0.0	–

Logan Drake

DRAKE, LOGAN GAFFNEY B. Dec. 26, 1900, Spartanburg, S. C. D. June 1, 1940, Columbia, S. C. — BR TR 5'10½" 165 lbs.

Year	Team		W	L	PCT	ERA	G	GS	CG	IP	H	BB	SO	ShO	W	L	SV	AB	H	HR	BA	PO	A	E	DP	TC/G	FA
1922	CLE	A	0	0	–	3.00	1	0	0	3	4	1	2	0	0	0	0		0	0	.000	0	0	0	0	0.0	
1923			0	0	–	4.15	4	0	0	4.1	2	5	2	0	0	0	0	0	0	0	–	0	0	0	0	0.0	
1924			0	1	.000	10.32	5	1	0	11.1	18	10	8	0	0	0	0	1	0	0	.000	0	2	1	0	0.6	.667
3 yrs.			0	1	.000	7.71	10	1	0	18.2	24	17	11	0	0	0	0	2	0	0	.000	0	2	1	0	0.3	.667

Tom Drake

DRAKE, THOMAS KENDALL B. Aug. 7, 1914, Birmingham, Ala. D. July 2, 1988, Birmingham, Ala. — BR TR 6'1" 185 lbs.

Year	Team		W	L	PCT	ERA	G	GS	CG	IP	H	BB	SO	ShO	W	L	SV	AB	H	HR	BA	PO	A	E	DP	TC/G	FA
1939	CLE	A	0	1	.000	9.00	8	1	0	15	23	19	1	0	0	1	0	2	0	0	.000	2	4	1	0	0.9	.857
1941	BKN	N	1	1	.500	4.38	10	2	0	24.2	26	9	12	0	0	0	0	5	2	0	.400	3	3	0	0	0.6	1.000
2 yrs.			1	2	.333	6.13	18	3	0	39.2	49	28	13	0	0	1	0	7	2	0	.286	5	7	1	0	0.7	.923

Dave Dravecky

DRAVECKY, DAVID FRANCIS B. Feb. 14, 1956, Youngstown, Ohio — BR TL 6'1" 195 lbs.

Year	Team		W	L	PCT	ERA	G	GS	CG	IP	H	BB	SO	ShO	W	L	SV	AB	H	HR	BA	PO	A	E	DP	TC/G	FA
1982	SD	N	5	3	.625	2.57	31	10	0	105	86	33	59	0	1	1	2	23	3	0	.130	7	24	0	3	1.0	1.000
1983			14	10	.583	3.58	28	28	9	183.2	181	44	74	1	0	0	0	61	6	0	.098	7	35	1	3	1.5	.977
1984			9	8	.529	2.93	50	14	3	156.2	125	51	71	2	4	4	8	41	4	0	.098	5	19	1	1	0.5	.960
1985			13	11	.542	2.93	34	31	7	214.2	200	57	105	2	0	1	0	69	8	0	.116	13	30	3	2	1.4	.935
1986			9	11	.450	3.07	26	26	3	161.1	149	54	87	1	0	0	0	50	7	1	.140	10	27	1	0	1.5	.974
1987	2 teams		SD N	(30G 3–7)		SF N	(18G 7–5)																					
"	total		10	12	.455	3.43	48	28	5	191.1	186	64	138	3	0	0	0	56	8	0	.143	16	30	2	2	1.0	.958
1988	SF	N	2	2	.500	3.16	7	7	1	37	33	8	19	0	0	0	0	10	1	0	.100	0	8	2	0	1.4	.800
1989			2	0	1.000	3.46	3	2	0	13	8	4	5	0	0	0	0	3	1	0	.333	0	3	0	0	1.5	1.000
8 yrs.			64	57	.529	3.13	226	146	28	1062.2	968	315	558	9	5	10	10	313	38	1	.121	58	176	10	11	1.1	.959

LEAGUE CHAMPIONSHIP SERIES

Year	Team		W	L	PCT	ERA	G	GS	CG	IP	H	BB	SO	ShO	W	L	SV	AB	H	HR	BA	PO	A	E	DP	TC/G	FA
1984	SD	N	0	0	–	0.00	3	0	0	6	2	0	5	0	0	0	0	0	0	0	–	1	1	0	0	0.7	1.000
1987	SF	N	1	1	.500	0.60	2	2	1	15	7	4	14	1	0	0	0	6	1	0	.167	0	2	0	0	1.0	1.000
2 yrs.			1	1	.500	0.43	5	2	1	21	9	4	19	1	0	0	0	6	1	0	.167	1	3	0	0	0.8	1.000

WORLD SERIES

Year	Team		W	L	PCT	ERA	G	GS	CG	IP	H	BB	SO	ShO	W	L	SV	AB	H	HR	BA	PO	A	E	DP	TC/G	FA
1984	SD	N	0	0	–	0.00	2	0	0	4.2	3	1	5	0	0	0	0	0	0	0	–	0	0	0	0	0.0	

Clem Dreisewerd

DREISEWERD, CLEMENT JOHN (Steamboat) B. Jan. 24, 1916, Old Monroe, Mo. — BL TL 6'1½" 195 lbs.

Year	Team		W	L	PCT	ERA	G	GS	CG	IP	H	BB	SO	ShO	W	L	SV	AB	H	HR	BA	PO	A	E	DP	TC/G	FA
1944	BOS	A	2	4	.333	4.07	7	7	3	48.2	52	9	9	0	0	0	0	16	3	0	.188	1	7	1	0	1.3	.889
1945			0	1	.000	4.66	2	2	0	9.2	13	2	3	0	0	0	0	3	0	0	.000	0	0	0	0	0.0	–
1946			4	1	.800	4.18	20	1	0	47.1	50	15	19	0	3	1	0	10	0	0	.000	1	15	1	0	0.9	.941
1948	2 teams		STL A	(13G 0–2)		NY N	(4G 0–0)																					
"	total		0	2	.000	5.66	17	0	0	35	45	13	8	0	0	2	2	9	1	0	.111	1	4	0	1	0.3	1.000
4 yrs.			6	8	.429	4.54	46	10	3	140.2	160	39	39	0	3	3	2	38	4	0	.105	3	26	2	1	0.7	.935

WORLD SERIES

Year	Team		W	L	PCT	ERA	G	GS	CG	IP	H	BB	SO	ShO	W	L	SV	AB	H	HR	BA	PO	A	E	DP	TC/G	FA
1946	BOS	A	0	0	–	0.00	1	0	0	.1	0	0	0	0	0	0	0	0	0	0	–	0	0	0	0	0.0	–

Bob Dresser

DRESSER, ROBERT NICHOLSON B. Oct. 4, 1878, Newton, Mass. D. July 27, 1924, Duxbury, Mass. — BL TL

Year	Team		W	L	PCT	ERA	G	GS	CG	IP	H	BB	SO	ShO	W	L	SV	AB	H	HR	BA	PO	A	E	DP	TC/G	FA
1902	BOS	N	0	1	.000	3.00	1	1	1	9	12	4	8	0	0	0	0	4	1	0	.250	0	1	1	0	2.0	.500

Rob Dressler

DRESSLER, ROBERT ANTHONY B. Feb. 2, 1954, Portland, Ore. — BR TR 6'3" 180 lbs.

Year	Team		W	L	PCT	ERA	G	GS	CG	IP	H	BB	SO	ShO	W	L	SV	AB	H	HR	BA	PO	A	E	DP	TC/G	FA
1975	SF	N	1	0	1.000	1.13	3	2	1	16	17	4	6	0	0	0	0	4	0	0	.000	2	4	0	0	2.0	1.000
1976			3	10	.231	4.43	25	19	0	107.2	125	35	33	0	1	0	0	31	4	0	.129	13	19	4	1	1.4	.889
1978	STL	N	0	1	.000	2.08	13	0	0	13	12	4	4	0	0	0	0	3	0	0	.000	0	2	0	0	0.7	1.000
1979	SEA	A	3	2	.600	4.93	21	11	2	104	134	22	36	0	0	0	0	0	0	0	–	4	16	0	1	1.0	1.000
1980			4	10	.286	3.99	30	14	3	149	161	33	50	0	0	3	0	0	0	0	–	8	30	3	3	1.4	.927
5 yrs.			11	23	.324	4.18	82	48	6	389.2	449	98	129	0	1	3	0	38	4	0	.105	27	71	7	5	1.3	.933

Year	Team		W	L	PCT	ERA	G	GS	CG	IP	H	BB	SO	ShO	Relief Pitching			Batting				PO	A	E	DP	TC/G	FA
															W	L	SV	AB	H	HR	BA						

Dave Drew

DREW, DAVID
Deceased.

| 1884 | PHI | U | 0 | 1 | .000 | 3.86 | 1 | 0 | 0 | 7 | 7 | 0 | 2 | 0 | 0 | 0 | 1 | 0 | * | | | | 0 | 0 | 0 | 0 | 0.0 | |

Karl Drews

DREWS, KARL AUGUST   BR TR 6'4½" 192 lbs.
B. Feb. 22, 1920, Staten Island, N. Y.   D. Aug. 13, 1963, Dania, Fla.

1946	NY	A	0	1	.000	8.53	3	1	0	6.1	6	6	4	0	0	0	0	1	0	0	.000	0	1	1	0	0.7	.500
1947			6	6	.500	4.91	30	10	0	91.2	92	55	45	0	4	0	1	27	1	0	.037	4	17	1	1	0.7	.955
1948	2 teams	NY A	(19G 2–3)			STL A	(20G 3–2)																				
"	total		5	5	.500	5.92	39	4	0	76	78	69	22	0	4	4	3	15	0	0	.000	3	20	0	1	0.6	1.000
1949	STL	A	4	12	.250	6.64	31	23	3	139.2	180	66	35	1	0	1	0	46	0	0	.000	5	23	0	1	0.9	1.000
1951	PHI	N	1	0	1.000	6.26	5	3	1	23	29	7	13	0	0	0	0	8	2	0	.250	3	4	0	0	1.4	1.000
1952			14	15	.483	2.72	33	30	15	228.2	213	52	96	5	1	0	0	82	9	0	.110	15	44	3	1	1.9	.952
1953			9	10	.474	4.52	47	27	6	185.1	218	50	72	0	0	1	3	59	7	0	.119	13	38	1	3	1.1	.981
1954	2 teams	PHI N	(8G 1–0)			CIN N	(22G 4–4)																				
"	total		5	4	.556	5.92	30	9	1	76	97	27	35	1	2	1	0	16	2	0	.125	3	15	0	1	0.6	1.000
	8 yrs.		44	53	.454	4.76	218	107	26	826.2	913	332	322	7	11	7	7	254	21	0	.083	46	162	6	10	1.0	.972

WORLD SERIES

| 1947 | NY | A | 0 | 0 | — | 3.00 | 2 | 0 | 0 | 3 | 2 | 1 | 0 | 0 | 0 | 0 | 0 | 2 | 0 | 0 | .000 | 0 | 3 | 0 | 0 | 1.5 | 1.000 |

Denny Driscoll

DRISCOLL, JOHN F.   BL TL 5'10½" 160 lbs.
B. Nov. 19, 1855, Lowell, Mass.   D. July 11, 1886, Lowell, Mass.

1880	BUF	N	1	3	.250	3.89	6	4	4	41.2	48	9	17	0	0	0	0	65	10	0	.154	3	8	2	0	2.2	.846
1882	PIT	AA	13	9	.591	1.21	23	23	23	201	162	12	59	0	0	0	0	80	11	1	.138	4	50	7	1	2.7	.885
1883			18	21	.462	3.99	41	40	35	336.1	427	39	79	1	0	0	0	148	27	0	.182	14	99	14	2	3.1	.890
1884	LOU	AA	6	6	.500	3.44	13	13	10	102	110	7	16	0	0	0	0	48	9	0	.188	3	37	9	2	3.8	.816
1885	BUF	N	0	0	—	0.00	0	0	0	0	0	0	0	0	0	0	0	19	3	0	.158	0	0	0	0		
	5 yrs.		38	39	.494	3.08	83	80	72	681	747	67	171	1	0	0	0	*				24	194	32	5	3.0	.872

Mike Driscoll

DRISCOLL, MICHAEL COLUMBUS   BR TR 6'1" 160 lbs.
B. Oct. 19, 1892, Rockland, Mass.   D. Mar. 22, 1953, Foxboro, Mass.

| 1916 | PHI | A | 0 | 1 | .000 | 5.40 | 1 | 0 | 0 | 5 | 6 | 2 | 0 | 0 | 0 | 1 | 0 | 2 | 0 | 0 | .000 | 0 | 4 | 0 | 0 | 4.0 | 1.000 |

Tom Drohan

DROHAN, THOMAS F   BR TR 5'10" 175 lbs.
B. Aug. 26, 1887, Fall River, Mass.   D. Sept. 17, 1926, Kewanee, Ill.

| 1913 | WAS | A | 0 | 0 | — | 9.00 | 2 | 0 | 0 | 2 | 5 | 0 | 2 | 0 | 0 | 0 | 0 | 0 | 0 | 0 | — | 0 | 0 | 0 | 0 | 0.5 | 1.000 |

Dick Drott

DROTT, RICHARD FRED (Hummer)   BR TR 6' 185 lbs.
B. July 1, 1936, Cincinnati, Ohio   D. Aug. 16, 1985, Glendale Heights, Ill.

1957	CHI	N	15	11	.577	3.58	38	32	7	229	200	129	170	3	2	0	0	80	8	0	.100	7	33	0	2	1.1	.976
1958			7	11	.389	5.43	39	31	4	167.1	156	99	127	0	0	0	0	55	15	0	.273	9	27	1	0	0.9	.973
1959			1	2	.333	5.93	8	6	1	27.1	25	26	15	1	0	0	0	8	1	0	.125	0	4	1	0	0.6	.800
1960			0	6	.000	7.16	23	9	0	55.1	63	42	32	0	0	0	0	10	1	0	.100	4	7	0	0	0.5	1.000
1961			1	4	.200	4.22	35	8	0	98	75	51	48	0	1	0	0	22	6	0	.273	1	11	1	0	0.4	.923
1962	HOU	N	1	0	1.000	7.62	6	1	0	13	12	9	10	0	0	0	0	4	0	0	.000	1	1	1	0	0.5	.667
1963			2	12	.143	4.98	27	14	2	97.2	95	49	58	1	0	0	2	23	3	0	.130	2	13	1	0	0.6	.938
	7 yrs.		27	46	.370	4.78	176	101	14	687.2	626	405	460	5	3	3	2	202	34	0	.168	24	96	6	2	0.7	.952

Louis Drucke

DRUCKE, LOUIS FRANK   BR TR 6'1" 188 lbs.
B. Dec. 3, 1888, Waco, Tex.   D. Sept. 22, 1955, Waco, Tex.

1909	NY	N	2	1	.667	2.25	3	3	2	24	20	13	8	0	0	0	0	8	1	0	.125	0	5	0	0	1.7	1.000
1910			12	10	.545	2.47	34	27	15	215.1	174	82	151	0	0	0	0	70	15	1	.214	11	59	8	5	2.3	.897
1911			4	4	.500	4.04	15	10	4	75.2	83	41	42	0	0	0	0	23	2	0	.087	4	23	1	1	1.9	.964
1912			0	0	—	13.50	1	0	0	2	5	1	0	0	0	0	1	0	0	0	—	0	0	0	0	0.0	
	4 yrs.		18	15	.545	2.90	53	40	21	317	282	137	201	0	0	0	1	101	18	1	.178	15	87	9	6	2.1	.919

Carl Druhot

DRUHOT, CARL A.   BL TL 5'7" 150 lbs.
B. Sept. 1, 1882, Ohio   D. Feb. 11, 1918, Portland, Ore.

1906	2 teams	CIN N	(4G 2–2)			STL N	(15G 6–7)																				
"	total		8	9	.471	2.90	19	16	13	155.1	144	53	59	1	2	0	0	65	15	0	.231	9	39	1	4	2.6	.980
1907	STL	N	0	1	.000	15.43	1	1	0	2.1	3	4	1	0	0	0	0	0	0	0	—	0	1	0	0	1.0	1.000
	2 yrs.		8	10	.444	3.08	20	17	13	157.2	147	57	60	1	2	0	0	65	15	0	.231	9	40	1	4	2.5	.980

Tim Drummond

DRUMMOND, TIMOTHY DARNELL   BR TR 6'3" 170 lbs.
B. Dec. 24, 1964, La Plata, Md.

1987	PIT	N	0	0	—	4.50	6	0	0	6	5	3	5	0	0	0	0	1	0	0	.000	0	2	0	0	0.3	1.000
1989	MIN	A	0	0	—	3.86	8	0	0	16.1	16	8	9	0	0	0	1	0	0	0	—	0	1	0	0	0.1	1.000
	2 yrs.		0	0	—	4.03	14	0	0	22.1	21	11	14	0	0	0	1	1	0	0	.000	0	3	0	0	0.2	1.000

Don Drysdale

DRYSDALE, DONALD SCOTT (Big D)   BR TR 6'5" 190 lbs.
B. July 23, 1936, Van Nuys, Calif.
Hall of Fame 1984.

1956	BKN	N	5	5	.500	2.64	25	12	2	99	95	31	55	0	1	0	0	26	5	1	.192	8	20	2	1	1.2	.933
1957			17	9	.654	2.69	34	29	9	221	197	61	148	4	2	1	0	73	9	2	.123	15	60	2	4	2.3	.974
1958	LA	N	12	13	.480	4.17	44	29	6	211.2	214	72	131	1	1	1	0	66	15	7	.227	15	45	6	10	1.5	.909
1959			17	13	.567	3.46	44	36	15	270.2	237	93	242	4	0	1	2	91	15	4	.165	18	48	3	4	1.6	.957
1960			15	14	.517	2.84	41	36	15	269	214	72	246	5	0	1	2	83	13	0	.157	18	60	3	3	2.0	.963
1961			13	10	.565	3.69	40	37	10	244	236	83	182	3	0	0	0	83	16	5	.193	13	36	3	3	1.3	.942
1962			25	9	.735	2.83	43	41	19	314.1	272	78	232	2	0	0	1	111	22	0	.198	10	60	7	5	1.8	.909
1963			19	17	.528	2.63	42	42	17	315.1	287	57	251	3	0	0	0	96	16	0	.167	19	62	4	7	2.0	.953

Year	Team		W	L	PCT	ERA	G	GS	CG	IP	H	BB	SO	ShO	W	L	SV	AB	H	HR	BA	PO	A	E	DP	TC/G	FA
															Relief Pitching			Batting									

Don Drysdale *continued*

Year	Team		W	L	PCT	ERA	G	GS	CG	IP	H	BB	SO	ShO	W	L	SV	AB	H	HR	BA	PO	A	E	DP	TC/G	FA
1964			18	16	.529	2.18	40	40	21	321.1	242	68	237	5	0	0	0	110	19	1	.173	13	68	3	5	2.1	.964
1965			23	12	.657	2.77	44	42	20	308.1	270	66	210	7	0	0	1	130	39	7	.300	22	55	9	4	2.0	.895
1966			13	16	.448	3.42	40	40	11	273.2	279	45	177	3	0	0	0	106	20	2	.189	10	45	7	1	1.6	.887
1967			13	16	.448	2.74	38	38	9	282	269	60	196	3	0	0	0	93	12	0	.129	11	64	5	3	2.1	.938
1968			14	12	.538	2.15	31	31	12	239	201	56	155	8	0	0	0	79	14	0	.177	15	50	5	4	2.3	.929
1969			5	4	.556	4.43	12	12	1	63	71	13	24	1	0	0	0	22	3	0	.136	1	13	0	1	1.2	1.000
14 yrs.			209	166	.557	2.95	518	465	167	3432.1	3084	855	2486	49	6	6	6	1169	218	29	.186	188	686	59	55	1.8	.937
WORLD SERIES																											
1956	BKN	N	0	0	–	9.00	1	0	0	2	2	1	1	0	0	0	0	0	0	0	–	0	0	0	0	0.0	–
1959	LA	N	1	0	1.000	1.29	1	1	0	7	11	4	5	0	0	0	0	2	0	0	.000	1	1	0	0	2.0	1.000
1963			1	0	1.000	0.00	1	1	1	9	3	1	9	1	0	0	0	1	0	0	.000	1	3	0	0	4.0	1.000
1965			1	1	.500	3.86	2	2	1	11.2	12	3	15	0	0	0	0	5	0	0	.000	0	2	0	0	1.0	1.000
1966			0	2	.000	4.50	2	2	1	10	8	3	6	0	0	0	0	2	0	0	.000	0	2	0	0	1.0	1.000
5 yrs.			3	3	.500	2.95	7	6	3	39.2	36	12	36	1	0	0	0	10	0	0	.000	2	9	0	0	1.6	1.000

Monk Dubiel

DUBIEL, WALTER JOHN
B. Feb. 12, 1919, Hartford, Conn. D. Oct. 25, 1969, Hartford, Conn.
BR TR 6' 190 lbs.

Year	Team		W	L	PCT	ERA	G	GS	CG	IP	H	BB	SO	ShO	W	L	SV	AB	H	HR	BA	PO	A	E	DP	TC/G	FA
1944	NY	A	13	13	.500	3.38	30	28	19	232	217	86	79	3	0	0	0	83	15	0	.181	13	45	2	2	2.0	.967
1945			10	9	.526	4.64	26	20	9	151.1	157	62	45	1	1	1	0	58	16	1	.276	9	21	1	2	1.2	.968
1948	PHI	N	9	10	.474	3.89	37	17	6	150.1	139	58	42	2	1	1	0	42	7	0	.167	12	18	1	1	0.8	.968
1949	CHI	N	6	9	.400	4.14	32	20	3	147.2	142	54	52	1	1	1	4	35	10	0	.286	13	31	4	3	1.5	.917
1950			6	10	.375	4.16	39	12	4	142.2	152	67	51	2	3	3	2	45	9	0	.200	10	34	1	2	1.2	.978
1951			2	2	.500	2.30	22	0	0	54.2	46	22	19	0	2	2	1	12	0	0	.000	7	8	0	1	0.7	1.000
1952			0	0	–	0.00	1	0	0	.2	1	0	1	0	0	0	0	0	0	0	–	0	0	0	0	0.0	–
7 yrs.			46	53	.465	3.87	187	97	41	879.1	854	349	289	9	9	10	11	275	57	1	.207	64	157	9	11	1.2	.961

Brian Dubois

DUBOIS, BRIAN ANDREW
B. Apr. 18, 1967, Joliet, Ill.
BL TL 5'10" 165 lbs.

Year	Team		W	L	PCT	ERA	G	GS	CG	IP	H	BB	SO	ShO	W	L	SV	AB	H	HR	BA	PO	A	E	DP	TC/G	FA
1989	DET	A	0	4	.000	1.75	6	5	0	36	29	17	13	0	0	0	1	0	0	0	–	2	5	0	0	1.2	1.000

Jean Dubuc

DUBUC, JEAN JOSEPH OCTAVE (Chauncey)
Born Jean Baptiste Arthur Dubuc.
B. Sept. 15, 1888, St. Johnsbury, Vt. D. Aug. 28, 1958, Ft. Myers, Fla.
BR TR 5'10½" 185 lbs.

Year	Team		W	L	PCT	ERA	G	GS	CG	IP	H	BB	SO	ShO	W	L	SV	AB	H	HR	BA	PO	A	E	DP	TC/G	FA
1908	CIN	N	5	6	.455	2.74	15	9	7	85.1	62	41	32	1	2	0	0	29	4	0	.138	6	26	2	0	2.3	.941
1909			3	5	.375	3.66	19	5	2	71.1	72	46	19	0	2	2	2	18	3	0	.167	4	23	5	0	1.7	.844
1912	DET	A	17	10	.630	2.77	37	26	23	250	217	109	97	2	1	1	3	108	29	1	.269	11	93	4	5	2.9	.963
1913			15	14	.517	2.89	36	28	22	242.2	228	91	73	1	0	2	2	135	36	2	.267	15	110	5	7	3.6	.962
1914			13	14	.481	3.46	36	27	15	224	216	76	70	2	2	0	1	124	28	1	.226	14	83	6	3	2.9	.942
1915			17	12	.586	3.21	39	33	22	258	231	88	74	5	2	0	0	112	23	0	.205	9	86	3	5	2.5	.969
1916			10	10	.500	2.96	36	16	8	170.1	134	84	40	1	5	5	1	78	20	0	.256	6	73	4	5	2.3	.952
1918	BOS	N	0	1	.000	4.22	2	1	1	10.2	11	5	1	0	0	0	0	6	1	0	.167	2	2	0	0	2.0	1.000
1919	NY	N	6	4	.600	2.66	36	5	1	132	119	37	32	0	6	4	3	42	6	0	.143	8	46	2	1	1.6	.964
9 yrs.			86	76	.531	3.04	256	150	101	1444.1	1290	577	438	12	18	13	14	*				76	542	31	23	2.5	.952

Jim Duckworth

DUCKWORTH, JAMES RAYMOND
B. May 24, 1939, National City, Calif.
BR TR 6'4" 194 lbs.

Year	Team		W	L	PCT	ERA	G	GS	CG	IP	H	BB	SO	ShO	W	L	SV	AB	H	HR	BA	PO	A	E	DP	TC/G	FA
1963	WAS	A	4	12	.250	6.04	37	15	2	120.2	131	67	66	0	2	3	0	27	0	0	.000	6	18	4	0	0.8	.857
1964			1	6	.143	4.34	30	2	0	56	52	25	56	0	1	4	3	9	2	0	.222	1	9	1	2	0.4	.909
1965			2	2	.500	3.94	17	8	0	64	45	36	74	0	0	0	0	18	0	0	.000	3	5	0	0	0.5	1.000
1966	2 teams		WAS A	(5G 0–3)		KC A	(8G 0–2)																				
"	total		0	5	.000	6.84	13	4	0	26.1	28	20	24	0	1	2	1	5	0	0	.000	1	2	0	0	0.2	1.000
4 yrs.			7	25	.219	5.26	97	29	2	267	256	148	220	0	4	9	4	59	2	0	.034	11	34	5	2	0.5	.900

Clise Dudley

DUDLEY, ELZIE CLISE
B. Aug. 8, 1903, Graham, N. C. D. Jan. 12, 1989, Moncks Corner, S. C.
BL TR 6'1" 195 lbs.

Year	Team		W	L	PCT	ERA	G	GS	CG	IP	H	BB	SO	ShO	W	L	SV	AB	H	HR	BA	PO	A	E	DP	TC/G	FA
1929	BKN	N	6	14	.300	5.69	35	21	8	156.2	202	64	33	1	1	2	0	51	5	2	.098	8	48	4	2	1.7	.933
1930			2	4	.333	6.35	21	7	2	66.2	103	27	18	0	0	0	1	24	5	0	.208	2	17	1	2	1.0	.950
1931	PHI	N	8	14	.364	3.52	30	24	8	179	206	56	50	0	0	0	0	84	18	0	.214	12	41	0	1	1.8	1.000
1932			1	1	.500	7.13	13	0	0	17.2	23	8	5	0	1	1	1	14	4	1	.286	0	6	0	0	0.5	1.000
1933	PIT	N	0	0	–	135.00	1	0	0	.1	6	1	0	0	0	0	0	0	0	0	–	0	0	0	0	0.0	–
5 yrs.			17	33	.340	5.03	100	52	18	420.1	540	156	106	1	2	3	2	173	32	3	.185	22	112	5	5	1.4	.964

Hal Dues

DUES, HAL JOSEPH
B. Sept. 22, 1954, LaMarque, Tex.
BR TR 6'3" 180 lbs.

Year	Team		W	L	PCT	ERA	G	GS	CG	IP	H	BB	SO	ShO	W	L	SV	AB	H	HR	BA	PO	A	E	DP	TC/G	FA
1977	MON	N	1	1	.500	4.30	6	4	0	23	26	9	9	0	0	0	0	5	0	0	.000	2	5	0	0	1.2	1.000
1978			5	6	.455	2.36	25	12	1	99	85	42	36	0	1	1	0	31	6	0	.194	5	16	2	0	0.9	.913
1980			0	1	.000	6.75	6	1	0	12	17	4	2	0	0	1	0	3	0	0	.000	0	4	0	0	0.7	1.000
3 yrs.			6	8	.429	3.09	37	17	1	134	128	55	47	0	1	2	0	39	6	0	.154	7	25	2	0	0.9	.941

Larry Duff

DUFF, CECIL ELBA
B. May 6, 1895, Radersburg, Mont. D. Nov. 10, 1969, Bend, Ore.
BL TR 6'1" 175 lbs.

Year	Team		W	L	PCT	ERA	G	GS	CG	IP	H	BB	SO	ShO	W	L	SV	AB	H	HR	BA	PO	A	E	DP	TC/G	FA
1922	CHI	A	1	1	.500	4.97	3	1	0	12.2	16	3	1	0	0	0	0	5	2	0	.400	0	1	0	0	0.3	1.000

Jim Duffalo

DUFFALO, JAMES FRANCIS
B. Nov. 25, 1935, Helvetia, Pa.
BR TR 6'1" 175 lbs.

Year	Team		W	L	PCT	ERA	G	GS	CG	IP	H	BB	SO	ShO	W	L	SV	AB	H	HR	BA	PO	A	E	DP	TC/G	FA
1961	SF	N	5	1	.833	4.23	24	4	1	61.2	59	32	37	0	3	0	1	17	5	0	.294	2	9	0	0	0.5	1.000
1962			1	2	.333	3.64	24	2	0	42	42	23	29	0	1	1	0	6	0	0	.000	2	5	1	1	0.3	.857
1963			4	2	.667	2.87	34	5	0	75.1	56	37	55	0	3	1	0	18	2	0	.111	7	15	1	0	0.7	.957
1964			5	1	.833	2.92	35	3	1	74	57	31	55	0	4	1	3	14	1	0	.071	4	9	1	0	0.4	.929

Year	Team		W	L	PCT	ERA	G	GS	CG	IP	H	BB	SO	ShO	W	L	SV	AB	H	HR	BA	PO	A	E	DP	TC/G	FA
															Relief Pitching			**Batting**									

Jim Duffalo *continued*

Year	Team		W	L	PCT	ERA	G	GS	CG	IP	H	BB	SO	ShO	W	L	SV	AB	H	HR	BA	PO	A	E	DP	TC/G	FA
1965	2 teams	SF N (2G 0–1)				CIN N	(22G 0–1)																					
"	total		0	2	.000	3.63	24	0	0	44.2	34	32	34	0	0	2	0	8	0	0	.000	5	8	0	1	0.5	1.000
5 yrs.			15	8	.652	3.39	141	14	2	297.2	248	155	210	0	11	4	6	63	8	1	.127	19	46	3	2	0.5	.956

John Duffie

DUFFIE, JOHN BROWN
B. Oct. 4, 1945, Greenwood, S. C.

BR TR 6'7" 210 lbs.

Year	Team		W	L	PCT	ERA	G	GS	CG	IP	H	BB	SO	ShO	W	L	SV	AB	H	HR	BA	PO	A	E	DP	TC/G	FA
1967	LA	N	0	2	.000	2.79	2	2	0	9.2	11	4	6	0	0	0	0	2	0	0	.000	1	2	2	0	2.5	.600

Bernie Duffy

DUFFY, BERNARD ALLEN
B. Aug. 18, 1893, Vinson, Okla. D. Feb. 9, 1962, Abilene, Tex.

BR TR 5'11" 180 lbs.

Year	Team		W	L	PCT	ERA	G	GS	CG	IP	H	BB	SO	ShO	W	L	SV	AB	H	HR	BA	PO	A	E	DP	TC/G	FA
1913	PIT	N	0	0	–	5.56	3	2	0	11.1	18	3	8	0	0	0	0	4	1	0	.250	0	4	0	0	1.3	1.000

Dan Dugan

DUGAN, DANIEL PHILLIP
B. Feb. 22, 1907, Plainfield, N. J. D. June 25, 1968, Greenbrook, N. J.

BL TL 6'1½" 187 lbs.

Year	Team		W	L	PCT	ERA	G	GS	CG	IP	H	BB	SO	ShO	W	L	SV	AB	H	HR	BA	PO	A	E	DP	TC/G	FA
1928	CHI	A	0	0	–	0.00	1	0	0	.1	0	0	0	0	0	0	0	0	0	0	–	0	0	0	0	0.0	–
1929			1	4	.200	6.65	19	2	0	65	77	19	15	0	1	2	1	20	3	0	.150	2	6	0	0	0.4	1.000
2 yrs.			1	4	.200	6.61	20	2	0	65.1	77	19	15	0	1	2	1	20	3	0	.150	2	6	0	0	0.4	1.000

Ed Dugan

DUGAN, EDWARD JOHN
Brother of Bill Dugan.
B. 1864, Brooklyn, N. Y. D. July 19, 1943, Sea Cliff, N. J.

Year	Team		W	L	PCT	ERA	G	GS	CG	IP	H	BB	SO	ShO	W	L	SV	AB	H	HR	BA	PO	A	E	DP	TC/G	FA
1884	RIC	AA	5	14	.263	4.49	20	20	20	166.1	196	15	60	0	0	0	0	70	8	0	.114	13	23	13	0	2.5	.735

Bill Duggleby

DUGGLEBY, WILLIAM JAMES (Frosty Bill)
B. Mar. 16, 1874, Utica, N. Y. D. Aug. 30, 1944, Redfield, N. Y.

TR

Year	Team		W	L	PCT	ERA	G	GS	CG	IP	H	BB	SO	ShO	W	L	SV	AB	H	HR	BA	PO	A	E	DP	TC/G	FA
1898	PHI	N	3	3	.500	5.50	9	5	4	54	70	18	12	0	1	0	0	21	5	1	.238	4	16	1	1	2.3	.952
1901			19	12	.613	2.87	34	28	25	275.2	294	40	94	5	1	1	0	111	19	0	.171	20	94	8	2	3.6	.934
1902	2 teams	PHI A (2G 1–1)				PHI N	(33G 11–17)																					
"	total		12	18	.400	3.36	35	30	27	275.2	301	61	64	0	1	0	0	105	17	0	.162	14	89	7	3	3.1	.936
1903	PHI	N	13	18	.419	3.75	36	30	28	264.1	318	79	57	3	1	0	1	104	24	0	.231	13	80	9	2	2.8	.912
1904			12	13	.480	3.78	32	27	22	223.2	265	53	55	2	1	1	1	82	14	2	.171	9	69	8	1	2.7	.907
1905			18	17	.514	2.46	38	36	29	289	270	83	75	1	1	1	0	101	11	1	.109	14	86	5	1	2.5	.952
1906			13	19	.406	2.25	42	30	22	280.1	241	66	83	5	1	2	2	99	14	2	.141	14	86	5	1	2.5	.952
1907	2 teams	PHI N (5G 0–2)				PIT N	(9G 2–2)																					
"	total		2	4	.333	4.67	14	5	3	69.1	77	23	12	1	1	0	0	22	3	0	.136	4	30	1	1	2.5	.971
8 yrs.			92	104	.469	3.19	240	191	158	1732	1836	423	452	17	8	5	4	645	107	6	.166	86	541	43	15	2.8	.936

Martin Duke

DUKE, MARTIN F.
Born Martin F. Duck.
B. Columbus, Ohio D. Dec. 31, 1898, Minneapolis, Minn.

TL

Year	Team		W	L	PCT	ERA	G	GS	CG	IP	H	BB	SO	ShO	W	L	SV	AB	H	HR	BA	PO	A	E	DP	TC/G	FA
1891	WAS	AA	0	3	.000	7.43	4	3	2	23	36	19	5	0	0	0	0	9	1	0	.111	0	6	2	1	2.0	.750

Jan Dukes

DUKES, NOBLE JAN
B. Aug. 16, 1945, Cheyenne, Wyo.

BL TL 5'11" 175 lbs.

Year	Team		W	L	PCT	ERA	G	GS	CG	IP	H	BB	SO	ShO	W	L	SV	AB	H	HR	BA	PO	A	E	DP	TC/G	FA
1969	WAS	A	0	2	.000	2.45	8	0	0	11	8	4	3	0	0	2	0	1	0	0	.000	0	0	0	0	0.0	
1970			0	0	–	2.57	5	0	0	7	6	1	4	0	0	0	0	1	0	0	.000	1	0	0	0	0.4	1.000
1972	TEX	A	0	0	–	4.50	3	0	0	2	1	5	0	0	0	0	0	0	0	0	–	0	1	0	0	0.3	1.000
3 yrs.			0	2	.000	2.70	16	0	0	20	15	10	7	0	0	2	0	2	0	0	.000	1	1	0	0	0.2	1.000

Tom Dukes

DUKES, THOMAS EARL
B. Aug. 31, 1942, Knoxville, Tenn.

BR TR 6'2" 185 lbs.

Year	Team		W	L	PCT	ERA	G	GS	CG	IP	H	BB	SO	ShO	W	L	SV	AB	H	HR	BA	PO	A	E	DP	TC/G	FA
1967	HOU	N	0	2	.000	5.32	17	0	0	23.2	25	11	23	0	0	2	1	2	1	0	.500	1	2	0	0	0.2	1.000
1968			2	2	.500	4.27	43	0	0	52.2	62	28	37	0	2	2	4	4	0	0	.000	1	11	1	0	0.3	.923
1969	SD	N	1	0	1.000	7.36	13	0	0	22	26	10	15	0	1	0	1	4	0	0	.000	0	4	0	0	0.3	1.000
1970			1	6	.143	4.04	53	0	0	69	62	25	56	0	1	6	10	7	0	0	.000	2	8	1	0	0.2	.909
1971	BAL	A	1	5	.167	3.55	28	0	0	38	40	8	30	0	1	5	4	7	1	0	.143	1	3	0	0	0.1	1.000
1972	CAL	A	0	1	.000	1.64	7	0	0	11	11	0	8	0	0	1	1	0	0	0	–	0	0	1	0	0.1	
6 yrs.			5	16	.238	4.37	161	0	0	216.1	226	82	169	0	5	16	21	21	2	0	.095	5	28	3	1	0.2	.917

WORLD SERIES

Year	Team		W	L	PCT	ERA	G	GS	CG	IP	H	BB	SO	ShO	W	L	SV	AB	H	HR	BA	PO	A	E	DP	TC/G	FA
1971	BAL	A	0	0	–	0.00	2	0	0	2	2	0	1	0	0	0	0	0	0	0	–	0	0	0	0	0.0	–

Bob Duliba

DULIBA, ROBERT JOHN
B. Jan. 9, 1935, Glen Lyon, Pa.

BR TR 5'10" 180 lbs.

Year	Team		W	L	PCT	ERA	G	GS	CG	IP	H	BB	SO	ShO	W	L	SV	AB	H	HR	BA	PO	A	E	DP	TC/G	FA
1959	STL	N	0	1	.000	2.78	11	0	0	22.2	19	12	14	0	0	1	1	4	0	0	.000	4	7	0	1	1.0	1.000
1960			4	4	.500	4.20	27	0	0	40.2	49	16	23	0	4	4	0	5	1	0	.200	3	5	0	0	0.3	1.000
1962			2	0	1.000	2.06	28	0	0	39.1	33	17	22	0	2	0	2	4	0	0	.000	3	7	0	0	0.4	1.000
1963	LA	A	1	1	.500	1.17	6	0	0	7.2	3	6	4	0	1	1	1	1	0	0	.000	0	0	0	0	0.0	
1964			6	4	.600	3.59	58	0	0	72.2	80	22	33	0	6	4	9	5	0	0	.000	5	14	2	1	0.4	.905
1965	BOS	A	4	2	.667	3.78	39	0	0	64.1	60	22	27	0	4	2	1	7	0	0	.000	2	12	2	1	0.4	.875
1967	KC	A	0	0	–	6.52	7	0	0	9.2	13	1	6	0	0	0	0	0	0	0	–	0	1	0	0	0.1	1.000
7 yrs.			17	12	.586	3.47	176	0	0	257	257	96	129	0	17	12	14	26	1	0	.038	17	46	2	3	0.4	.969

George Dumont

DUMONT, GEORGE HENRY (Pea Soup)
B. Nov. 13, 1895, Minneapolis, Minn. D. Oct. 13, 1956, Minneapolis, Minn.

BR TR 5'11" 163 lbs.

Year	Team		W	L	PCT	ERA	G	GS	CG	IP	H	BB	SO	ShO	W	L	SV	AB	H	HR	BA	PO	A	E	DP	TC/G	FA
1915	WAS	A	2	1	.667	2.03	6	4	3	40	23	12	18	2	0	0	0	12	2	0	.167	3	7	1	0	1.8	.909
1916			2	3	.400	3.06	17	5	2	53	37	17	21	0	0	1	1	14	1	0	.071	1	11	2	0	0.8	.857
1917			5	14	.263	2.55	37	23	8	204.2	171	76	65	2	2	1	2	58	2	0	.034	11	46	8	2	1.8	.877
1918			1	1	.500	5.14	4	1	1	14	18	6	12	0	1	0	0	3	1	0	.333	0	4	0	0	1.0	1.000

Year	Team	W	L	PCT	ERA	G	GS	CG	IP	H	BB	SO	ShO	W	L	SV	AB	H	HR	BA	PO	A	E	DP	TC/G	FA

(Header spanning groups: **Relief Pitching** over W/L/SV, **Batting** over AB/H/HR)

George Dumont *continued*

| 1919 | BOS A | 0 | 4 | .000 | 4.33 | 13 | 2 | 0 | 35.1 | 45 | 19 | 12 | 0 | 0 | 3 | 0 | 7 | 0 | 0 | .000 | 4 | 11 | 2 | 0 | 1.3 | .882 |
| 5 yrs. | | 10 | 23 | .303 | 2.85 | 77 | 35 | 14 | 347 | 294 | 130 | 128 | 4 | 3 | 5 | 3 | 94 | 6 | 0 | .064 | 19 | 79 | 13 | 2 | 1.4 | .883 |

Dan Dumoulin

DUMOULIN, DANIEL LYNN   BR TR 6' 175 lbs.
B. Aug. 20, 1953, Kokomo, Ind.

1977	CIN N	0	0	–	14.40	5	0	0	5	12	3	5	0	0	0	0	0	0	0	–	1	1	0	0	0.4	1.000
1978		1	0	1.000	1.80	3	0	0	5	7	3	2	0	1	0	0	0	0	0	–	0	2	0	0	0.7	1.000
2 yrs.		1	0	1.000	8.10	8	0	0	10	19	6	7	0	1	0	0	0	0	0	–	1	3	0	0	0.5	1.000

Nick Dumovich

DUMOVICH, NICHOLAS   BL TL 6' 170 lbs.
B. Jan. 2, 1902, Sacramento, Calif.   D. Dec. 12, 1979, Laguna Hills, Calif.

| 1923 | CHI N | 3 | 5 | .375 | 4.60 | 28 | 8 | 1 | 94 | 118 | 45 | 23 | 0 | 2 | 1 | 1 | 29 | 7 | 0 | .241 | 4 | 27 | 0 | 0 | 1.1 | 1.000 |

Ed Dundon

DUNDON, EDWARD JOSEPH (Dummy)   TR
B. July 10, 1859, Columbus, Ohio   D. Aug. 18, 1893, Columbus, Ohio

1883	COL AA	3	16	.158	4.48	20	19	16	166.2	213	38	31	0	0	0	0	93	15	0	.161	10	35	11	3	2.8	.804
1884		6	4	.600	3.78	11	9	7	81	85	15	37	0	1	0	0	86	12	0	.140	8	18	0	1	2.4	1.000
2 yrs.		9	20	.310	4.25	31	28	23	247.2	298	53	68	0	1	0	0	*				18	53	11	4	2.6	.866

Jim Dunegan

DUNEGAN, JAMES WILLIAM JR   BR TR 6'1" 205 lbs.
B. Aug. 6, 1947, Burlington, Iowa

| 1970 | CHI N | 0 | 2 | .000 | 4.85 | 7 | 0 | 0 | 13 | 13 | 12 | 3 | 0 | 0 | 2 | 0 | 4 | 1 | 0 | .250 | 1 | 4 | 0 | 0 | 0.7 | 1.000 |

Wiley Dunham

DUNHAM, HENRY HUSTON   6'1" 180 lbs.
B. Jan. 30, 1877, Piketon, Ohio   D. Jan. 16, 1934, Cleveland, Ohio

| 1902 | STL N | 2 | 3 | .400 | 5.68 | 7 | 5 | 3 | 38 | 47 | 13 | 15 | 0 | 0 | 0 | 1 | 12 | 1 | 0 | .083 | 1 | 8 | 1 | 0 | 1.4 | .900 |

Davey Dunkle

DUNKLE, EDWARD PERKS   BB TR 6'2" 220 lbs.
B. Aug. 30, 1872, Philipsburg, Pa.   D. Nov. 19, 1941, Lock Haven, Pa.

1897	PHI N	5	2	.714	3.48	7	7	7	62	72	23	9	0	0	0	0	23	4	0	.174	2	14	5	1	3.0	.762
1898		1	4	.200	6.98	12	7	4	68.1	83	38	21	0	0	0	0	28	6	0	.214	1	11	2	0	1.2	.857
1899	WAS N	0	2	.000	10.04	4	2	2	26	46	14	9	0	0	0	0	11	3	0	.273	1	5	2	0	2.0	.750
1903	2 teams				CHI A (12G 4–4)				WAS A	(14G 5–9)																
"	total	9	13	.409	4.16	26	20	16	190.1	207	64	77	0	2	0	1	74	14	0	.189	5	41	7	0	2.0	.868
1904	WAS A	2	9	.182	4.96	12	11	7	74.1	95	23	23	0	0	0	0	28	4	0	.143	3	23	0	1	2.2	1.000
5 yrs.		17	30	.362	5.02	61	47	36	421	503	162	139	0	2	0	1	164	31	0	.189	12	94	16	2	2.0	.869

Fred Dunlap

DUNLAP, FREDERICK C. (Sure Shot)   BR TR 5'8" 165 lbs.
B. May 21, 1859, Philadelphia, Pa.   D. Dec. 1, 1902, Philadelphia, Pa.
Manager 1882, 1884-85, 1889.

1884	STL U	0	0	–	13.50	1	0	0	.2	2	0	1	0	0	0	1	449	185	13	.412	0	0	0	0	0.0	–
1887	DET N	0	0	–	4.50	1	0	0	2	4	0	1	0	0	0	0	272	72	5	.265	0	0	0	0	0.0	–
2 yrs.		0	0	–	6.75	2	0	0	2.2	6	0	2	0	0	0	1	*				0	0	0	0	0.0	–

Jack Dunleavy

DUNLEAVY, JOHN FRANCIS   TL 5'6" 167 lbs.
B. Sept. 14, 1879, Harrison, N. J.   D. Apr. 12, 1944, South Norwalk, Conn.

1903	STL N	6	8	.429	4.06	14	13	9	102	101	57	51	0	1	0	0	193	48	0	.249	0	32	1	0	2.4	.970
1904		1	4	.200	4.42	7	5	5	55	63	23	28	0	0	0	0	172	40	1	.233	9	14	1	0	3.4	.958
2 yrs.		7	12	.368	4.18	21	18	14	157	164	80	79	0	1	0	0	*				9	46	2	0	2.7	.965

Jack Dunn

DUNN, JOHN JOSEPH (Handyman)   BR TR 5'9"
B. Oct. 6, 1872, Meadville, Pa.   D. Oct. 22, 1928, Towson, Md.

1897	BKN N	14	9	.609	4.57	25	21	21	216.2	251	66	26	0	1	1	0	131	29	0	.221	17	55	7	2	3.2	.911
1898		16	21	.432	3.60	41	37	31	322.2	352	82	66	0	2	0	0	167	41	0	.246	22	70	6	2	2.4	.939
1899		23	13	.639	3.70	41	34	29	299.1	323	86	48	2	2	1	2	122	30	0	.246	21	83	4	1	2.6	.963
1900	2 teams				BKN N (10G 3–4)				PHI N	(10G 5–5)																
"	total	8	9	.471	5.16	20	16	14	143	175	57	18	1	1	1	0	59	16	0	.271	7	40	3	0	2.5	.940
1901	2 teams				PHI N (2G 0–1)				BAL A	(9G 3–3)																
"	total	3	4	.429	4.90	11	8	6	64.1	85	28	6	0	0	0	0	363	91	0	.251	4	21	2	1	2.5	.926
1902	NY N	0	3	.000	3.71	3	2	2	26.2	28	12	6	0	0	0	1	342	72	0	.211	4	9	1	0	4.7	.929
1904		0	0	–	4.50	1	0	0	4	3	3	1	0	0	0	1	181	56	0	.309	2	0	0	0	2.0	1.000
7 yrs.		64	59	.520	4.11	142	118	103	1076.2	1217	334	171	3	6	4	3	*				77	278	23	6	2.7	.939

Jim Dunn

DUNN, JAMES WILLIAM (Bill)   BR TR 6'½" 185 lbs.
B. Feb. 25, 1931, Valdosta, Ga.

| 1952 | PIT N | 0 | 0 | – | 3.38 | 3 | 0 | 0 | 5.1 | 4 | 3 | 2 | 0 | 0 | 0 | 0 | 1 | 0 | 0 | .000 | 2 | 0 | 0 | 0 | 0.7 | 1.000 |

Mike Dunne

DUNNE, MICHAEL DENNIS   BR TR 6'4" 190 lbs.
B. Oct. 27, 1962, South Bend, Ind.

1987	PIT N	13	6	.684	3.03	23	23	5	163.1	143	68	72	1	0	0	0	53	5	0	.094	18	32	1	3	2.2	.980
1988		7	11	.389	3.92	30	28	1	170	163	88	70	0	0	0	0	46	5	0	.109	18	27	1	0	1.5	.978
1989	2 teams				PIT N (3G 1–1)				SEA A	(15G 2–9)																
"	total	3	10	.231	5.60	18	18	1	99.2	125	46	42	0	0	0	0	4	1	0	.250	7	17	1	2	1.4	.960
3 yrs.		23	27	.460	3.97	71	69	7	433	431	202	184	1	0	0	0	103	11	0	.107	43	76	3	5	1.7	.975

Andy Dunning

DUNNING, ANDREW JACKSON   BR TR 6' 175 lbs.
B. Aug. 12, 1871, New York, N. Y.   D. June 21, 1952, New York, N. Y.

| 1889 | PIT N | 0 | 2 | .000 | 7.00 | 2 | 2 | 2 | 18 | 20 | 16 | 4 | 0 | 0 | 0 | 0 | 7 | 0 | 0 | .000 | 2 | 4 | 0 | 0 | 3.0 | 1.000 |

1801

Year	Team		W	L	PCT	ERA	G	GS	CG	IP	H	BB	SO	ShO	Relief Pitching W	L	SV	Batting AB	H	HR	BA	PO	A	E	DP	TC/G	FA

Andy Dunning *continued*

| 1891 | NY | N | 0 | 1 | .000 | 4.50 | 1 | 1 | 0 | 2 | 3 | 3 | 2 | 0 | 0 | 0 | 0 | 0 | 0 | 0 | – | 0 | 0 | 0 | 0 | 0.0 | – |
| 2 yrs. | | | 0 | 3 | .000 | 6.75 | 3 | 3 | 2 | 20 | 23 | 19 | 6 | 0 | 0 | 0 | 0 | 7 | 0 | 0 | .000 | 2 | 4 | 0 | 0 | 2.0 | 1.000 |

Steve Dunning

DUNNING, STEVEN JOHN
B. May 15, 1949, Denver, Colo.   BR TR 6'2"   205 lbs.

1970	CLE	A	4	9	.308	4.98	19	17	0	94	93	54	77	0	0	0	0	31	5	0	.161	7	17	2	2	1.4	.923
1971			8	14	.364	4.50	31	29	3	184	173	109	132	1	0	0	1	55	10	1	.182	13	38	2	0	1.7	.962
1972			6	4	.600	3.26	16	16	1	105	98	43	52	0	0	0	0	33	9	3	.273	2	16	2	0	1.3	.900
1973	2 teams		CLE A	(4G 0–2)		TEX A	(23G 2–6)																				
"	total		2	8	.200	5.53	27	15	2	112.1	118	65	48	0	0	0	0	0	0	0	–	9	17	3	0	1.1	.897
1974	TEX	A	0	0	–	22.50	1	0	0	2	3	3	1	0	0	0	0	0	0	0	–	1	0	0	0	1.0	1.000
1976	2 teams		CAL A	(4G 0–0)		MON N	(32G 2–6)																				
"	total		2	6	.250	4.35	36	7	1	97.1	102	39	76	0	0	2	0	15	2	0	.133	8	14	3	0	0.7	.880
1977	OAK	A	1	0	1.000	4.00	6	0	0	18	17	10	4	0	0	0	0	0	0	0	–	1	3	0	1	0.7	1.000
7 yrs.			23	41	.359	4.57	136	84	7	612.2	604	323	390	1	1	2	1	134	26	4	.194	41	105	12	3	1.2	.924

Frank Dupee

DUPEE, FRANK OLIVER
B. Apr. 29, 1877, Monkton, Vt. D. Aug. 14, 1956, Portland, Me.   TL 6'1"   200 lbs.

| 1901 | CHI | A | 0 | 1 | .000 | ∞ | 1 | 1 | 0 | 0 | 3 | 0 | 0 | 0 | 0 | 0 | 0 | 0 | 0 | 0 | – | 0 | 0 | 0 | 0 | 0.0 | – |

Mike Dupree

DUPREE, MICHAEL DENNIS
B. May 29, 1953, Kansas City, Kans.   BR TR 6'1"   185 lbs.

| 1976 | SD | N | 0 | 0 | – | 9.19 | 12 | 0 | 0 | 15.2 | 18 | 7 | 5 | 0 | 0 | 0 | 0 | 1 | 1 | 0 | 1.000 | 1 | 4 | 0 | 0 | 0.4 | 1.000 |

Kid Durbin

DURBIN, BLAINE ALPHONSUS
B. Sept. 10, 1886, Lamar, Kans. D. Sept. 11, 1943, Kirkwood, Mo.   BL TL 5'8"   155 lbs.

| 1907 | CHI | N | 0 | 1 | .000 | 5.40 | 5 | 1 | 1 | 16.2 | 14 | 10 | 6 | 0 | 0 | 0 | 1 | * | | | | 1 | 5 | 0 | 0 | 1.2 | 1.000 |

Ryne Duren

DUREN, RINOLD GEORGE
B. Feb. 22, 1929, Cazenovia, Wis.   BR TR 6'2"   190 lbs.

1954	BAL	A	0	0	–	9.00	1	0	0	2	3	1	2	0	0	0	0	0	0	0	–	0	0	0	0	0.0	–
1957	KC	A	0	3	.000	5.27	14	6	0	42.2	37	30	37	0	0	1	0	14	1	0	.071	3	8	0	0	0.8	1.000
1958	NY	A	6	4	.600	2.02	44	1	0	75.2	40	43	87	0	6	4	20	13	1	0	.077	1	11	1	2	0.3	.923
1959			3	6	.333	1.88	41	0	0	76.2	49	43	96	0	3	6	14	14	0	0	.000	1	9	0	0	0.2	1.000
1960			3	4	.429	4.96	42	1	0	49	27	49	67	0	3	4	9	2	0	0	.000	2	9	0	0	0.3	1.000
1961	2 teams		NY A	(4G 0–1)		LA A	(40G 6–12)																				
"	total		6	13	.316	5.19	44	14	1	104	89	79	115	1	4	9	2	25	1	0	.040	6	6	2	0	0.3	.857
1962	LA	A	2	9	.182	4.42	42	3	0	71.1	53	57	74	0	2	8	8	15	1	0	.067	0	8	1	0	0.3	.889
1963	PHI	N	6	2	.750	3.30	33	7	1	87.1	65	52	84	0	3	1	2	21	3	0	.143	3	7	0	0	0.3	1.000
1964	2 teams		PHI N	(2G 0–0)		CIN N	(26G 0–2)																				
"	total		0	2	.000	3.09	28	0	0	46.2	46	16	44	0	0	2	1	5	0	0	.000	1	4	2	0	0.3	.714
1965	2 teams		PHI N	(6G 0–0)		WAS A	(16G 1–1)																				
"	total		1	1	.500	5.56	22	0	0	34	34	22	24	0	1	1	0	1	0	0	.000	0	6	0	0	0.3	1.000
10 yrs.			27	44	.380	3.83	311	32	2	589.1	443	392	630	1	22	35	57	114	7	0	.061	17	68	6	4	0.3	.934

WORLD SERIES

1958	NY	A	1	1	.500	1.93	3	0	0	9.1	7	6	14	0	1	1	1	3	0	0	.000	0	1	0	0	0.3	1.000
1960			0	0	–	2.25	2	0	0	4	2	1	5	0	0	0	0	0	0	0	–	0	2	0	1	1.0	1.000
2 yrs.			1	1	.500	2.03	5	0	0	13.1	9	7	19	0	1	1	1	3	0	0	.000	0	3	0	1	0.6	1.000

Bull Durham

DURHAM, LOUIS STAUB (Judge, Whitey)
Born Louis Raphael Staub.
B. June 27, 1877, New Oxford, Pa. D. June 28, 1960, Bentley, Kans.   BR TR 5'10"

1904	BKN	N	1	0	1.000	3.27	2	2	1	11	10	5	1	0	0	0	0	4	1	0	.250	0	2	1	0	1.5	.667
1907	WAS	A	0	0	–	12.60	2	0	0	5	10	4	1	0	0	0	0	1	0	0	.000	0	1	0	0	0.5	1.000
1908	NY	N	0	0	–	9.00	1	0	0	2	2	1	2	0	0	0	0	0	0	0	–	0	0	0	0	0.0	–
1909			0	0	–	3.27	4	0	0	11	15	2	2	0	0	0	1	2	0	0	.000	0	3	1	0	1.0	.750
4 yrs.			1	0	1.000	5.28	9	2	1	29	37	12	6	0	0	0	1	7	1	0	.143	0	6	2	0	0.9	.750

Don Durham

DURHAM, DONALD GARY (Bull)
B. Mar. 21, 1949, Yosemite, Ky.   BR TR 6'   170 lbs.

1972	STL	N	2	7	.222	4.34	10	8	1	47.2	42	22	35	0	0	0	1	14	7	2	.500	1	4	0	0	0.5	1.000
1973	TEX	A	0	4	.000	7.65	15	4	0	40	49	23	23	0	0	0	1	0	0	0	–	4	2	0	1	0.4	1.000
2 yrs.			2	11	.154	5.85	25	12	1	87.2	91	45	58	0	0	0	1	14	7	2	.500	5	6	0	1	0.4	1.000

Ed Durham

DURHAM, EDWARD FANT (Bull)
B. Aug. 17, 1908, Chester, S. C. D. Apr. 27, 1976, Chester, S. C.   BL TR 5'11"   170 lbs.

1929	BOS	A	1	0	1.000	9.27	14	1	0	22.1	34	14	6	0	0	0	0	4	0	0	.000	2	4	1	0	0.5	.857
1930			4	15	.211	4.69	33	12	6	140	144	43	28	1	2	5	1	41	4	0	.098	0	30	1	2	0.9	.968
1931			8	10	.444	4.25	38	15	7	165.1	175	50	53	2	2	3	0	54	3	0	.056	7	24	3	0	0.9	.912
1932			6	13	.316	3.80	34	22	4	175.1	187	49	52	0	2	1	0	57	7	0	.123	14	37	1	4	1.5	.981
1933	CHI	A	10	6	.625	4.48	24	21	6	138.2	137	46	65	0	1	0	0	46	10	0	.217	1	25	0	0	1.1	1.000
5 yrs.			29	44	.397	4.45	143	71	23	641.2	677	202	204	3	7	9	1	202	24	0	.119	24	120	6	6	1.0	.960

Jimmy Durham

DURHAM, JAMES GARFIELD
B. Oct. 7, 1881, Douglass, Kans. D. May 7, 1949, Coffeyville, Kans.   BR TR 6'   175 lbs.

| 1902 | CHI | A | 1 | 1 | .500 | 5.85 | 3 | 3 | 3 | 20 | 21 | 16 | 3 | 0 | 0 | 0 | 0 | 15 | 1 | 0 | .067 | 1 | 6 | 0 | 1 | 2.3 | 1.000 |

Year	Team		W	L	PCT	ERA	G	GS	CG	IP	H	BB	SO	ShO	W	L	SV	AB	H	HR	BA	PO	A	E	DP	TC/G	FA

Dick Durning

DURNING, RICHARD KNOTT
B. Oct. 10, 1892, Louisville, Ky. D. Sept. 23, 1948, Castle Point, N. Y.
BL TL 6'2'' 178 lbs.

1917	BKN	N	0	0	–	0.00	1	0	0	1	0	0	0	0	0	0	0	0	0	0	–	0	0	0	0	0.0	–
1918			0	0	–	13.50	1	0	0	2	3	4	0	0	0	0	0	0	0	0	–	0	1	0	0	1.0	1.000
2 yrs.			0	0	–	9.00	2	0	0	3	3	4	0	0	0	0	0	0	0	0	–	0	1	0	0	0.5	1.000

Jesse Duryea

DURYEA, JAMES WHITNEY (Cyclone Jim)
B. Sept. 7, 1862, Osage, Iowa D. Aug. 7, 1942, Algona, Iowa
BR TR 5'10'' 175 lbs.

1889	CIN	AA	32	19	.627	2.56	53	48	38	401	372	127	183	2	2	2	1	162	44	0	.272	15	80	11	1	2.0	.896
1890	CIN	N	16	12	.571	2.92	33	32	29	274	270	60	108	2	0	0	0	99	15	1	.152	7	59	10	4	2.3	.868
1891	2 teams				CIN N (10G 1–9)		STL AA (3G 1–1)																				
"	total		2	10	.167	4.90	13	13	10	101	120	35	36	0	0	0	0	43	5	0	.116	5	21	4	0	2.3	.867
1892	2 teams				CIN N (9G 2–5)		WAS N (18G 3–10)																				
"	total		5	15	.250	2.82	27	22	18	195	157	71	69	1	1	1	2	77	9	0	.117	16	63	7	0	3.2	.919
1893	WAS	N	4	10	.286	7.54	17	15	9	117	182	56	20	0	0	1	0	47	13	0	.277	4	29	2	0	2.1	.943
5 yrs.			59	66	.472	3.45	143	130	104	1088	1101	349	416	5	3	4	3	428	86	1	.201	47	252	34	5	2.3	.898

Erv Dusak

DUSAK, ERVIN FRANK (Four Sack)
B. July 29, 1920, Chicago, Ill.
BR TR 6'2'' 185 lbs.

1948	STL	N	0	0	–	0.00	1	0	0	1	0	1	0	0	0	0	0	311	65	6	.209	0	0	0	0	0.0	–
1950			0	2	.000	3.72	14	2	0	36.1	27	27	16	0	0	0	1	12	1	0	.083	1	7	0	1	0.6	1.000
1951	2 teams				STL N (5G 0–0)		PIT N (3G 0–1)																				
"	total		0	1	.000	9.18	8	1	0	16.2	24	16	10	0	0	0	0	41	13	2	.317	0	3	0	0	0.4	1.000
3 yrs.			0	3	.000	5.33	23	3	0	54	51	44	26	0	0	0	1	*				1	10	0	1	0.5	1.000

Carl Duser

DUSER, CARL ROBERT
B. July 22, 1932, Hazleton, Pa.
BL TL 6'1'' 175 lbs.

1956	KC	A	1	1	.500	9.00	2	2	0	6	14	2	5	0	0	0	0	3	0	0	.000	0	2	0	0	1.0	1.000
1958			0	0	–	4.50	1	0	0	2	5	1	0	0	0	0	0	0	0	0	–	0	0	0	0	0.0	–
2 yrs.			1	1	.500	7.88	3	2	0	8	19	3	5	0	0	0	0	3	0	0	.000	0	2	0	0	0.7	1.000

Bob Dustal

DUSTAL, ROBERT ANDREW
B. Sept. 28, 1935, Sayreville, N. J.
BR TR 6' 172 lbs.

| 1963 | DET | A | 0 | 1 | .000 | 9.00 | 7 | 0 | 0 | 6 | 10 | 5 | 4 | 0 | 0 | 1 | 0 | 0 | 0 | 0 | – | 1 | 4 | 0 | 0 | 0.7 | 1.000 |

Bill Duzen

DUZEN, WILLIAM GEORGE
B. Feb. 21, 1870, Buffalo, N. Y. D. Mar. 11, 1944, Buffalo, N. Y.
BR TR 5'11'' 165 lbs.

| 1890 | BUF | P | 0 | 2 | .000 | 13.85 | 2 | 2 | 2 | 13 | 20 | 14 | 5 | 0 | 0 | 0 | 0 | 4 | 1 | 0 | .250 | 0 | 2 | 0 | 0 | 1.0 | 1.000 |

Frank Dwyer

DWYER, JOHN FRANCIS
B. Mar. 25, 1868, Lee, Mass. D. Feb. 4, 1943, Pittsfield, Mass.
Manager 1902.
BR TR 5'8'' 145 lbs.

1888	CHI	N	4	1	.800	1.07	5	5	5	42	32	9	17	1	0	0	0	21	4	0	.190	2	10	2	0	2.8	.857
1889			16	13	.552	3.59	32	30	27	276	307	72	63	0	1	0	0	135	27	1	.200	20	43	6	2	2.2	.913
1890	CHI	P	3	6	.333	6.23	12	6	6	69.1	98	25	17	0	2	1	1	53	14	0	.264	3	24	3	0	2.5	.900
1891	2 teams				CIN AA (35G 13–19)		MIL AA (10G 6–4)																				
"	total		19	23	.452	3.99	45	41	39	374.2	424	145	128	1	0	1	0	181	49	0	.271	22	94	11	1	2.8	.913
1892	2 teams				STL N (10G 2–8)		CIN N (33G 19–10)																				
"	total		21	18	.538	2.98	43	37	30	323.1	341	73	61	3	2	1	1	154	23	0	.149	20	70	5	3	2.2	.947
1893	CIN	N	18	15	.545	4.13	37	30	28	287.1	332	93	53	1	2	2	2	120	24	1	.200	33	66	2	5	2.7	.980
1894			19	22	.463	5.07	45	40	34	348	471	106	49	1	1	1	1	172	46	2	.267	31	62	5	2	2.2	.949
1895			18	15	.545	4.24	37	31	23	280.1	355	74	46	2	2	3	0	113	30	1	.265	26	54	4	6	2.3	.952
1896			24	11	.686	3.15	36	34	30	288.2	321	60	57	3	1	0	1	110	29	0	.264	24	52	6	5	2.3	.927
1897			18	13	.581	3.78	37	31	22	247.1	315	56	41	0	0	0	0	94	25	0	.266	11	42	4	0	1.5	.930
1898			16	10	.615	3.04	31	28	24	240	257	42	29	0	1	0	0	85	12	0	.141	11	52	6	3	2.2	.913
1899			0	5	.000	5.51	5	5	4	32.2	48	9	2	0	0	0	0	11	4	0	.364	1	8	0	1	1.8	1.000
12 yrs.			176	152	.537	3.85	365	318	270	2809.2	3301	764	563	12	15	10	6	*				204	577	54	28	2.3	.935

Ben Dyer

DYER, BENJAMIN FRANKLIN
B. Feb. 13, 1893, Chicago, Ill. D. Aug. 7, 1959, Kenosha, Wis.
BR TR 5'10'' 170 lbs.

| 1918 | DET | A | 0 | 0 | – | 0.00 | 2 | 0 | 0 | 1.2 | 0 | 0 | 0 | 0 | 0 | 0 | 0 | * | | | | 0 | 1 | 0 | 0 | 0.5 | 1.000 |

Eddie Dyer

DYER, EDWIN HAWLEY
B. Oct. 11, 1900, Morgan City, La. D. Apr. 20, 1964, Houston, Tex.
Manager 1946-50.
BL TL 5'11½'' 168 lbs.

1922	STL	N	0	0	–	2.45	2	0	0	3.2	7	0	3	0	0	0	0	3	1	0	.333	3	0	0	0	1.5	1.000
1923			2	1	.667	4.09	4	3	2	22	30	5	7	1	0	0	0	45	12	2	.267	0	4	0	0	1.0	1.000
1924			8	11	.421	4.61	29	15	7	136.2	174	51	23	1	3	2	0	76	18	0	.237	10	40	5	1	1.9	.909
1925			4	3	.571	4.15	27	5	1	82.1	93	24	25	0	3	2	3	31	3	0	.097	0	22	2	1	0.9	.917
1926			1	0	1.000	11.57	6	0	0	9.1	7	14	4	0	1	0	0	2	1	0	.500	0	3	0	0	0.5	1.000
1927			0	0	–	18.00	1	0	0	2	5	2	1	0	0	0	0	0	0	0	–	0	0	0	0	0.0	–
6 yrs.			15	15	.500	4.75	69	23	10	256	316	96	63	2	7	4	3	*				13	69	7	2	1.3	.921

Mike Dyer

DYER, MICHAEL LAWRENCE
B. Sept. 8, 1966, Upland, Calif.
BR TR 6'3'' 195 lbs.

| 1989 | MIN | A | 4 | 7 | .364 | 4.82 | 16 | 12 | 1 | 71 | 74 | 37 | 37 | 0 | 0 | 1 | 0 | 0 | 0 | 0 | – | 6 | 3 | 0 | 1 | 0.6 | 1.000 |

Jimmy Dygert

DYGERT, JAMES HENRY (Sunny Jim)
B. July 5, 1884, Utica, N. Y. D. Feb. 8, 1936, New Orleans, La.
BR TR 5'10'' 185 lbs.

| 1905 | PHI | A | 1 | 4 | .200 | 4.33 | 6 | 3 | 2 | 35.1 | 41 | 11 | 24 | 0 | 1 | 0 | 0 | 15 | 4 | 0 | .267 | 1 | 18 | 1 | 1 | 3.3 | .950 |

Year	Team		W	L	PCT	ERA	G	GS	CG	IP	H	BB	SO	ShO	Relief Pitching W	L	SV	Batting AB	H	HR	BA	PO	A	E	DP	TC/G	FA

Jimmy Dygert *continued*

Year	Team		W	L	PCT	ERA	G	GS	CG	IP	H	BB	SO	ShO	W	L	SV	AB	H	HR	BA	PO	A	E	DP	TC/G	FA
1906			11	13	.458	2.70	35	25	15	213.2	175	91	106	4	2	2	0	74	13	1	.176	3	68	2	1	2.1	.973
1907			21	8	.724	2.34	42	28	18	261.2	200	85	151	5	3	2	1	94	12	0	.128	13	74	9	2	2.3	.906
1908			11	15	.423	2.87	41	27	15	238.2	184	97	164	5	2	1	1	75	6	0	.080	8	79	2	0	2.2	.978
1909			9	5	.643	2.42	32	12	6	137.1	117	50	79	1	3	1	0	42	9	0	.214	1	34	2	1	1.2	.946
1910			4	4	.500	2.54	19	8	6	99.1	81	49	59	1	0	0	0	36	3	0	.083	1	20	1	1	1.2	.955
6 yrs.			57	49	.538	2.65	175	103	62	986	798	383	583	16	11	7	2	336	47	1	.140	27	293	17	6	1.9	.950

Jimmy Dykes

DYKES, JAMES JOSEPH
B. Nov. 10, 1896, Philadelphia, Pa. D. June 15, 1976, Philadelphia, Pa.
Manager 1934-46, 1951-54, 1958-61.

BR TR 5'9" 185 lbs.

Year	Team		W	L	PCT	ERA	G	GS	CG	IP	H	BB	SO	ShO	W	L	SV	AB	H	HR	BA	PO	A	E	DP	TC/G	FA
1927	PHI	A	0	0	—	4.50	2	0	0	2	2	1	0	0	0	0	0	*				0	0	0	0	0.0	—

Arnie Earley

EARLEY, ARNOLD CARL
B. June 4, 1933, Lincoln Park, Mich.

BL TL 6'1" 195 lbs.

Year	Team		W	L	PCT	ERA	G	GS	CG	IP	H	BB	SO	ShO	W	L	SV	AB	H	HR	BA	PO	A	E	DP	TC/G	FA
1960	BOS	A	0	1	.000	15.75	2	0	0	4	9	4	5	0	0	1	0	1	0	0	.000	0	0	0	0	0.0	—
1961			2	4	.333	3.99	33	0	0	49.2	42	34	44	0	2	4	7	6	0	0	.000	1	9	2	0	0.4	.833
1962			4	5	.444	5.80	38	3	0	68.1	76	46	59	0	3	5	3	10	2	0	.200	4	14	2	0	0.5	.900
1963			3	7	.300	4.75	53	4	0	115.2	124	43	97	0	1	5	1	18	5	0	.278	11	16	3	1	0.6	.900
1964			1	1	.500	2.68	25	3	1	50.1	51	18	45	0	0	0	1	9	1	0	.111	4	9	1	0	0.5	1.000
1965			0	1	.000	3.63	57	0	0	74.1	79	29	47	0	0	1	0	6	0	0	.000	4	13	3	1	0.4	.850
1966	CHI	N	2	1	.667	3.57	13	0	0	17.2	14	9	12	0	2	1	0	1	0	0	.000	0	1	0	0	0.1	—
1967	HOU	N	0	0	—	27.00	2	0	0	1.1	5	1	0	0	0	0	0	0	0	0	—	0	0	0	0	0.5	1.000
8 yrs.			12	20	.375	4.48	223	10	1	381.1	400	184	310	0	8	15	14	51	8	0	.157	24	62	11	3	0.4	.887

Bill Earley

EARLEY, WILLIAM ALBERT
B. Jan. 30, 1956, Cincinnati, Ohio

BR TL 6'4" 200 lbs.

Year	Team		W	L	PCT	ERA	G	GS	CG	IP	H	BB	SO	ShO	W	L	SV	AB	H	HR	BA	PO	A	E	DP	TC/G	FA
1986	STL	N	0	0	—	0.00	3	0	0	3	0	2	2	0	0	0	0	0	0	0	—	0	0	0	0	0.0	—

Tom Earley

EARLEY, THOMAS FRANCIS ALOYSIUS (Chick)
B. Feb. 19, 1917, Roxbury, Mass. D. Apr. 5, 1988, Nantucket, Mass.

BR TR 6' 180 lbs.

Year	Team		W	L	PCT	ERA	G	GS	CG	IP	H	BB	SO	ShO	W	L	SV	AB	H	HR	BA	PO	A	E	DP	TC/G	FA
1938	BOS	N	1	0	1.000	3.27	2	1	1	11	8	1	4	0	0	0	0	4	0	0	.000	0	2	0	0	1.0	1.000
1939			1	4	.200	4.73	14	2	0	40	49	19	9	0	1	0	3	10	3	0	.300	1	11	0	0	0.9	1.000
1940			2	0	1.000	3.86	4	1	1	16.1	16	3	5	1	1	0	0	5	2	0	.400	2	1	0	0	0.8	1.000
1941			6	8	.429	2.53	33	13	6	138.2	120	46	54	1	1	1	3	47	11	0	.234	4	24	2	6	0.9	.935
1942			6	11	.353	4.71	27	18	6	112.2	120	55	28	0	1	1	1	34	4	0	.118	3	29	1	0	1.2	.970
1945			2	1	.667	4.61	11	2	1	41	36	19	4	0	1	1	0	14	3	0	.214	2	9	0	0	1.0	1.000
6 yrs.			18	24	.429	3.78	91	37	15	359.2	349	143	104	2	4	6	5	114	23	0	.202	13	76	3	6	1.0	.967

George Earnshaw

EARNSHAW, GEORGE LIVINGSTON (Moose)
B. Feb. 15, 1900, New York, N. Y. D. Dec. 1, 1976, Little Rock, Ark.

BR TR 6'4" 210 lbs.

Year	Team		W	L	PCT	ERA	G	GS	CG	IP	H	BB	SO	ShO	W	L	SV	AB	H	HR	BA	PO	A	E	DP	TC/G	FA
1928	PHI	A	7	7	.500	3.81	26	22	7	158.1	143	100	117	3	3	0	1	57	14	0	.246	6	27	4	0	1.4	.892
1929			24	8	.750	3.29	44	33	13	254.2	233	125	149	3	3	0	1	87	15	1	.172	12	38	6	1	1.3	.893
1930			22	13	.629	4.44	49	39	20	296	299	139	193	3	2	2	2	114	26	0	.228	8	53	5	2	1.3	.924
1931			21	7	.750	3.67	43	30	23	281.2	255	75	152	3	1	0	6	114	30	2	.263	15	52	5	4	1.7	.931
1932			19	13	.594	4.77	36	33	21	245.1	262	94	109	1	1	1	0	91	26	0	.286	7	54	3	3	1.8	.953
1933			5	10	.333	5.97	21	18	4	117.2	153	58	37	0	1	0	0	44	8	0	.182	6	30	0	2	1.7	1.000
1934	CHI	A	14	11	.560	4.52	33	30	16	227	242	104	97	2	0	1	0	79	16	0	.203	4	45	4	0	1.6	.925
1935	2 teams	CHI A	(3G 1-2)				BKN N	(25G 8-12)																			
"	total		9	14	.391	4.60	28	25	6	184	201	64	80	2	1	1	0	67	15	0	.224	5	38	1	3	1.6	.977
1936	2 teams	BKN N	(19G 4-9)				STL N	(20G 2-1)																			
"	total		6	10	.375	5.73	39	19	5	150.2	193	50	71	1	3	0	1	51	12	0	.235	8	34	2	1	1.1	.955
9 yrs.			127	93	.577	4.38	319	249	115	1915.1	1981	809	1005	18	12	5	12	704	162	3	.230	71	371	30	17	1.5	.936

WORLD SERIES

Year	Team		W	L	PCT	ERA	G	GS	CG	IP	H	BB	SO	ShO	W	L	SV	AB	H	HR	BA	PO	A	E	DP	TC/G	FA
1929	PHI	A	1	1	.500	2.63	2	2	1	13.2	14	6	17	0	0	0	0	5	0	0	.000	0	2	0	0	1.0	1.000
1930			2	0	1.000	0.72	3	3	2	25	13	7	19	0	0	0	0	9	0	0	.000	1	6	0	0	2.3	1.000
1931			1	2	.333	1.88	3	3	2	24	12	4	20	1	0	0	0	8	0	0	.000	1	7	0	0	2.7	1.000
3 yrs.			4	3	.571	1.58	8	8	5	62.2	39	17	56	1	0	0	0	22	0	0	.000	2	15	0	0	2.1	1.000
						10th	10th						7th														

Logan Easley

EASLEY, KENNETH LOGAN
B. Nov. 4, 1961, Salt Lake City, Utah

BR TR 6'1" 185 lbs.

Year	Team		W	L	PCT	ERA	G	GS	CG	IP	H	BB	SO	ShO	W	L	SV	AB	H	HR	BA	PO	A	E	DP	TC/G	FA
1987	PIT	N	1	1	.500	5.47	17	0	0	26.1	23	17	21	0	1	1	1	2	0	0	.000	2	8	0	1	0.6	1.000
1989			1	0	1.000	4.38	10	0	0	12.1	8	7	6	0	1	0	1	1	0	0	.000	0	2	1	0	0.3	.667
2 yrs.			2	1	.667	5.12	27	0	0	38.2	31	24	27	0	2	1	2	3	0	0	.000	2	10	1	1	0.5	.923

Mal Eason

EASON, MALCOLM WAYNE (Kid)
B. Mar. 13, 1879, Brookville, Pa. D. Apr. 16, 1970, Douglas, Ariz.

TR

Year	Team		W	L	PCT	ERA	G	GS	CG	IP	H	BB	SO	ShO	W	L	SV	AB	H	HR	BA	PO	A	E	DP	TC/G	FA
1900	CHI	N	1	0	1.000	1.00	1	1	1	9	9	3	2	0	0	0	0	3	0	0	.000	0	1	0	0	1.0	1.000
1901			8	17	.320	3.59	27	25	23	220.2	246	60	68	1	0	0	0	87	12	0	.138	13	51	6	0	2.6	.914
1902	2 teams	CHI N	(2G 1-1)				BOS N	(27G 9-11)																			
"	total		10	12	.455	2.61	29	28	22	224.1	258	61	54	2	0	0	0	77	7	0	.091	11	60	6	0	2.7	.922
1903	DET	A	2	5	.286	3.36	7	6	6	56.1	60	19	21	1	0	1	0	20	2	0	.100	2	24	1	0	3.9	.963
1905	BKN	N	5	21	.192	4.30	27	27	20	207	230	72	64	3	0	0	0	81	14	0	.173	4	69	5	1	2.9	.936
1906			10	17	.370	3.25	34	26	18	227	212	74	64	3	1	0	1	88	8	0	.091	10	71	1	2	2.4	.988
6 yrs.			36	72	.333	3.39	125	113	90	944.1	1015	289	273	10	1	1	0	356	43	0	.121	40	276	19	3	2.7	.943

Carl East

EAST, CARLTON WILLIAM
B. Aug. 27, 1894, Marietta, Ga. D. Jan. 15, 1953, Whitesburg, Ga.

BL TR 6'2" 178 lbs.

Year	Team		W	L	PCT	ERA	G	GS	CG	IP	H	BB	SO	ShO	W	L	SV	AB	H	HR	BA	PO	A	E	DP	TC/G	FA
1915	STL	A	0	0	—	16.20	1	1	0	3.1	6	2	1	0	0	0	0	*				0	0	0	0	0.0	—

Year	Team		W	L	PCT	ERA	G	GS	CG	IP	H	BB	SO	ShO	Relief Pitching			Batting				PO	A	E	DP	TC/G	FA
															W	L	SV	AB	H	HR	BA						

Hugh East

EAST, GORDON HUGH
B. July 7, 1919, Birmingham, Ala.   D. Nov. 2, 1981, Charleston, S. C.   BR TR 6'2"   185 lbs.

Year	Team		W	L	PCT	ERA	G	GS	CG	IP	H	BB	SO	ShO	W	L	SV	AB	H	HR	BA	PO	A	E	DP	TC/G	FA
1941	NY	N	1	1	.500	3.45	2	2	0	15.2	19	9	4	0	0	0	0	9	2	0	.222	2	3	1	0	3.0	.833
1942			0	2	.000	9.82	4	1	0	7.1	15	7	2	0	0	1	0	2	1	1	.500	0	2	0	0	0.5	1.000
1943			1	3	.250	5.36	13	5	1	40.1	51	25	21	0	0	0	0	13	1	0	.077	0	5	0	0	0.4	1.000
3 yrs.			2	6	.250	5.40	19	8	1	63.1	85	41	27	0	0	1	0	24	4	1	.167	2	10	1	0	0.7	.923

Jamie Easterly

EASTERLY, JAMES MORRIS
B. Feb. 17, 1953, Houston, Tex.   BB TL 5'9"   180 lbs.

Year	Team		W	L	PCT	ERA	G	GS	CG	IP	H	BB	SO	ShO	W	L	SV	AB	H	HR	BA	PO	A	E	DP	TC/G	FA
1974	ATL	N	0	0	–	15.00	3	0	0	3	6	4	0	0	0	0	0	0	0	0	–	0	1	0	0	0.3	1.000
1975			2	9	.182	4.96	21	13	0	69	73	42	34	0	0	0	0	18	1	0	.056	1	9	0	1	0.5	1.000
1976			1	1	.500	4.91	4	4	0	22	23	13	11	0	0	0	0	9	1	0	.111	1	4	0	0	1.3	1.000
1977			2	4	.333	6.10	22	5	0	59	72	30	37	0	0	2	1	15	4	0	.267	2	3	1	0	0.3	.833
1978			3	6	.333	5.65	37	6	0	78	91	45	42	0	2	3	1	19	4	0	.211	2	14	1	1	0.5	.941
1979			0	0	–	12.00	4	0	0	3	7	3	3	0	0	0	0	0	0	0	–	0	1	0	0	0.3	1.000
1981	MIL	A	3	3	.500	3.19	44	0	0	62	46	34	31	0	3	3	4	0	0	0	–	7	10	0	1	0.4	1.000
1982			0	2	.000	4.70	28	0	0	30.2	39	15	16	0	0	2	2	0	0	0	–	3	7	0	0	0.4	1.000
1983	2 teams		MIL A	(12G 0–1)			CLE A	(41G 4–2)																			
"	total		4	3	.571	3.67	53	0	0	68.2	83	32	45	0	4	3	4	1	0	0	.000	5	10	0	0	0.3	1.000
1984	CLE	A	3	1	.750	3.38	26	1	0	69.1	74	23	42	0	3	1	2	0	0	0	–	6	10	0	1	0.6	1.000
1985			4	1	.800	3.92	50	7	0	98.2	96	53	58	0	2	0	0	0	0	0	–	11	10	0	1	0.4	1.000
1986			0	2	.000	7.64	13	0	0	17.2	27	12	9	0	0	2	0	0	0	0	–	2	1	0	0	0.2	1.000
1987			1	1	.500	4.55	16	0	0	31.2	26	13	22	0	1	0	0	0	0	0	–	3	4	0	0	0.4	1.000
13 yrs.			23	33	.411	4.61	321	36	0	612.2	663	319	350	0	15	17	14	62	10	0	.161	43	84	2	3	0.4	.984

DIVISIONAL PLAYOFF SERIES

Year	Team		W	L	PCT	ERA	G	GS	CG	IP	H	BB	SO	ShO	W	L	SV	AB	H	HR	BA	PO	A	E	DP	TC/G	FA
1981	MIL	A	0	0	–	6.75	2	0	0	1.1	2	0	1	0	0	0	0	0	0	0	–	0	0	0	0	0.0	–

John Easton

EASTON, JOHN S.
B. Feb. 28, 1867, Bridgeport, Ohio   D. Nov. 28, 1903, Steubenville, Ohio

Year	Team		W	L	PCT	ERA	G	GS	CG	IP	H	BB	SO	ShO	W	L	SV	AB	H	HR	BA	PO	A	E	DP	TC/G	FA
1889	COL	AA	1	0	1.000	3.50	4	1	1	18	13	21	7	0	0	0	1	7	0	0	.000	1	4	3	0	2.0	.625
1890			15	14	.517	3.52	37	29	23	255.2	213	125	147	0	2	1	1	107	19	0	.178	12	52	12	3	2.1	.842
1891	2 teams		COL AA	(20G 5–12)			STL AA	(7G 3–2)																			
"	total		8	14	.364	4.59	27	24	19	198	208	86	87	0	0	0	0	102	20	0	.196	4	41	5	1	1.9	.900
1892	STL	N	2	0	1.000	6.39	5	2	2	31	38	26	4	0	0	0	0	17	3	0	.176	3	8	1	0	2.4	.917
1894	PIT	N	0	1	.000	4.12	3	1	1	19.2	26	4	1	0	0	0	0	5	0	0	.000	1	1	2	0	1.3	.500
5 yrs.			26	29	.473	4.12	76	57	46	522.1	498	262	246	0	2	1	2	238	42	0	.176	21	106	23	4	2.0	.847

Rawly Eastwick

EASTWICK, RAWLINS JACKSON III
B. Oct. 24, 1950, Camden, N. J.   BR TR 6'3"   180 lbs.

Year	Team		W	L	PCT	ERA	G	GS	CG	IP	H	BB	SO	ShO	W	L	SV	AB	H	HR	BA	PO	A	E	DP	TC/G	FA
1974	CIN	N	0	0	–	2.00	8	0	0	18	12	5	14	0	0	0	2	1	0	0	.000	1	1	0	0	0.3	1.000
1975			5	3	.625	2.60	58	0	0	90	77	25	61	0	5	3	22	15	1	0	.067	5	5	0	1	0.2	1.000
1976			11	5	.688	2.08	71	0	0	108	93	27	70	0	11	5	26	17	0	0	.000	3	9	0	0	0.2	1.000
1977	2 teams		CIN N	(23G 2–2)			STL N	(41G 3–7)																			
"	total		5	9	.357	3.90	64	0	0	97	114	29	47	0	5	8	11	11	3	0	.273	5	6	0	0	0.2	1.000
1978	2 teams		NY A	(8G 2–1)			PHI N	(22G 2–1)																			
"	total		4	2	.667	3.76	30	0	0	64.2	53	22	27	0	4	2	0	3	0	0	.000	3	7	0	0	0.3	1.000
1979	PHI	N	3	6	.333	4.88	51	0	0	83	90	25	47	0	3	6	6	7	0	0	.000	4	4	0	0	0.2	1.000
1980	KC	A	0	1	.000	5.32	14	0	0	22	37	8	5	0	0	1	0	0	0	0	–	3	6	1	0	0.7	.900
1981	CHI	N	0	1	.000	2.30	30	0	0	43	43	15	24	0	0	1	1	2	0	0	.000	4	8	1	0	0.4	.923
8 yrs.			28	27	.509	3.30	326	1	0	525.2	519	156	295	0	28	26	68	56	4	0	.071	28	46	2	1	0.4	.974

LEAGUE CHAMPIONSHIP SERIES

Year	Team		W	L	PCT	ERA	G	GS	CG	IP	H	BB	SO	ShO	W	L	SV	AB	H	HR	BA	PO	A	E	DP	TC/G	FA
1975	CIN	N	1	0	1.000	0.00	2	0	0	3.2	2	2	1	0	1	0	0	0	0	0	–	1	0	0	0	0.5	1.000
1976			1	0	1.000	12.00	2	0	0	3	7	2	1	0	1	0	0	0	0	0	–	0	1	0	0	0.5	1.000
1978	PHI	N	0	0	–	9.00	1	0	0	1	3	0	1	0	0	0	0	0	0	0	–	0	0	0	0	0.0	–
3 yrs.			2	0	1.000	5.87	5	0	0	7.2	12	4	3	0	2	0	0	0	0	0	–	1	1	0	0	0.4	1.000

WORLD SERIES

Year	Team		W	L	PCT	ERA	G	GS	CG	IP	H	BB	SO	ShO	W	L	SV	AB	H	HR	BA	PO	A	E	DP	TC/G	FA
1975	CIN	N	2	0	1.000	2.25	5	0	0	8	6	3	4	0	2	0	1	1	0	0	.000	0	0	0	0	0.0	–

2nd

Craig Eaton

EATON, CRAIG
B. Sept. 7, 1954, Cincinnati, Ohio   BR TR 5'11"   175 lbs.

Year	Team		W	L	PCT	ERA	G	GS	CG	IP	H	BB	SO	ShO	W	L	SV	AB	H	HR	BA	PO	A	E	DP	TC/G	FA
1979	KC	A	0	0	–	2.70	5	0	0	10	8	3	4	0	0	0	0	0	0	0	–	1	1	0	1	0.4	1.000

Zeb Eaton

EATON, ZEBULON VANCE (Red)
B. Feb. 2, 1920, Cooleemee, N. C.   D. Dec. 17, 1989, West Palm Beach, Fla.   BR TR 5'10"   185 lbs.

Year	Team		W	L	PCT	ERA	G	GS	CG	IP	H	BB	SO	ShO	W	L	SV	AB	H	HR	BA	PO	A	E	DP	TC/G	FA
1944	DET	A	0	0	–	5.74	6	0	0	15.2	19	8	4	0	0	0	0	10	1	0	.100	1	2	0	0	0.5	1.000
1945			4	2	.667	4.05	17	3	0	53.1	48	40	15	0	3	0	0	32	8	2	.250	4	11	2	0	1.0	.882
2 yrs.			4	2	.667	4.43	23	3	0	69	67	48	19	0	3	0	0	42	9	2	.214	5	13	2	0	0.9	.900

Gary Eave

EAVE, GARY LOUIS
B. July 22, 1963, Monroe, La.   BR TR 6'4"   200 lbs.

Year	Team		W	L	PCT	ERA	G	GS	CG	IP	H	BB	SO	ShO	W	L	SV	AB	H	HR	BA	PO	A	E	DP	TC/G	FA
1988	ATL	N	0	0	–	9.00	5	0	0	5	7	3	0	0	0	0	0	0	0	0	–	0	0	0	0	0.0	–
1989			2	0	1.000	1.31	3	3	0	20.2	15	12	9	0	0	0	0	6	0	0	.000	1	0	0	0	0.3	1.000
2 yrs.			2	0	1.000	2.81	8	3	0	25.2	22	15	9	0	0	0	0	6	0	0	.000	1	0	0	0	0.1	1.000

Vallie Eaves

EAVES, VALLIE ENNIS (Chief)
B. Sept. 6, 1911, Allen, Okla.   D. Apr. 19, 1960, Norman, Okla.   BR TR 6'2½"   180 lbs.

Year	Team		W	L	PCT	ERA	G	GS	CG	IP	H	BB	SO	ShO	W	L	SV	AB	H	HR	BA	PO	A	E	DP	TC/G	FA
1935	PHI	A	1	2	.333	5.14	3	1	1	14	12	15	6	0	0	0	0	4	0	0	.000	0	2	0	0	0.7	1.000
1939	CHI	A	0	1	.000	4.63	2	1	1	11.2	11	8	5	0	0	0	0	6	2	0	.333	0	2	0	0	1.0	1.000
1940			0	2	.000	6.75	5	3	0	18.2	22	24	11	0	0	0	0	5	0	0	.000	0	0	0	0	0.0	–

Year	Team	W	L	PCT	ERA	G	GS	CG	IP	H	BB	SO	ShO	Relief Pitching W	L	SV	Batting AB	H	HR	BA	PO	A	E	DP	TC/G	FA

Vallie Eaves *continued*

Year	Team	W	L	PCT	ERA	G	GS	CG	IP	H	BB	SO	ShO	W	L	SV	AB	H	HR	BA	PO	A	E	DP	TC/G	FA
1941	CHI N	3	3	.500	3.53	12	7	4	58.2	56	21	24	0	1	0	0	20	2	0	.100	0	6	0	0	0.5	1.000
1942		0	0	—	9.00	2	0	0	3	4	2	0	0	0	0	0	0	0	0	—	0	0	1	0	0.5	—
5 yrs.		4	8	.333	4.58	24	14	6	106	105	70	46	0	1	0	0	35	4	0	.114	0	10	1	0	0.5	.909

Eddie Eayrs

EAYRS, EDWIN
B. Nov. 10, 1890, Blackstone, Mass.   D. Nov. 30, 1969, Warwick, R. I.

BL TL 5'7"   160 lbs.

Year	Team	W	L	PCT	ERA	G	GS	CG	IP	H	BB	SO	ShO	W	L	SV	AB	H	HR	BA	PO	A	E	DP	TC/G	FA
1913	PIT N	0	0	—	2.25	2	0	0	8	8	6	5	0	0	0	0	6	1	0	.167	0	2	1	0	1.5	.667
1920	BOS N	1	2	.333	5.47	7	3	0	26.1	36	12	7	0	0	0	0	244	80	1	.328	1	12	0	1	1.9	1.000
1921	BKN N	0	0	—	17.36	2	0	0	4.2	9	9	1	0	0	0	0	21	2	0	.095	0	0	0	0	0.0	—
3 yrs.		1	2	.333	6.23	11	3	0	39	53	27	13	0	0	0	0	*				1	14	1	0	1.5	.938

Harry Eccles

ECCLES, HARRY JOSIAH (Buggs)
B. July 9, 1893, Kennedy, N. Y.   D. June 2, 1955, Jamestown, N. Y.

BL TL 6'2"   170 lbs.

Year	Team	W	L	PCT	ERA	G	GS	CG	IP	H	BB	SO	ShO	W	L	SV	AB	H	HR	BA	PO	A	E	DP	TC/G	FA
1915	PHI A	0	1	.000	6.86	5	1	0	21	18	6	13	0	0	0	1	6	1	0	.167	1	3	2	0	1.2	.667

Dennis Eckersley

ECKERSLEY, DENNIS LEE
B. Oct. 3, 1954, Oakland, Calif.

BR TR 6'2"   190 lbs.

Year	Team	W	L	PCT	ERA	G	GS	CG	IP	H	BB	SO	ShO	W	L	SV	AB	H	HR	BA	PO	A	E	DP	TC/G	FA
1975	CLE A	13	7	.650	2.60	34	24	6	186.2	147	90	152	2	1	0	2	0	0	0	—	7	12	1	0	0.6	.950
1976		13	12	.520	3.44	36	30	9	199	155	78	200	3	1	0	1	0	0	0	—	9	20	1	1	0.8	.967
1977		14	13	.519	3.53	33	33	12	247	214	54	191	3	0	0	0	0	0	0	—	6	22	2	1	0.9	.933
1978	BOS A	20	8	.714	2.99	35	35	16	268.1	258	71	162	3	0	0	0	0	0	0	—	19	29	0	1	1.4	1.000
1979		17	10	.630	2.99	33	33	17	247	234	59	150	2	0	0	0	0	0	0	—	12	42	6	3	1.8	.900
1980		12	14	.462	4.27	30	30	8	198	188	44	121	0	0	0	0	0	0	0	—	10	24	3	0	1.2	.919
1981		9	8	.529	4.27	23	23	8	154	160	35	79	2	0	0	0	0	0	0	—	12	19	1	1	1.4	.969
1982		13	13	.500	3.73	33	33	11	224.1	228	43	127	3	0	0	0	0	0	0	—	21	21	1	2	1.3	.977
1983		9	13	.409	5.61	28	28	2	176.1	223	39	77	0	0	0	0	0	0	0	—	19	18	1	0	1.4	.974
1984	2 teams		BOS A	(9G 4-4)		CHI N	(24G 10-8)																				
"	total	14	12	.538	3.60	33	33	4	225	223	49	114	0	0	0	0	55	6	0	.109	27	38	5	3	2.1	.929
1985	CHI N	11	7	.611	3.08	25	25	6	169.1	145	19	117	2	0	0	0	56	7	1	.125	10	26	3	1	1.6	.923
1986		6	11	.353	4.57	33	32	1	201	226	43	137	0	0	0	0	69	11	2	.159	16	28	3	3	1.4	.936
1987	OAK A	6	8	.429	3.03	54	2	0	115.2	99	17	113	0	6	6	16	0	0	0	—	4	13	1	0	0.3	.944
1988		4	2	.667	2.35	60	0	0	72.2	52	11	70	0	4	2	45	0	0	0	—	7	3	0	0	0.2	1.000
1989		4	0	1.000	1.56	51	0	0	57.2	32	3	55	0	4	0	33	0	0	0	—	4	4	0	1	0.2	1.000
15 yrs.		165	138	.545	3.56	541	361	100	2742	2584	655	1865	20	16	8	97	180	24	3	.133	183	319	28	17	1.0	.947

LEAGUE CHAMPIONSHIP SERIES

Year	Team	W	L	PCT	ERA	G	GS	CG	IP	H	BB	SO	ShO	W	L	SV	AB	H	HR	BA	PO	A	E	DP	TC/G	FA
1984	CHI N	0	1	.000	8.44	1	1	0	5.1	9	0	6	0	0	0	0	2	0	0	.000	0	0	0	0	0.0	—
1988	OAK A	0	0	—	0.00	4	0	0	6	1	2	5	0	0	0	4	0	0	0	—	2	0	0	0	0.5	1.000
1989		0	0	—	1.59	4	0	0	5.2	4	0	2	0	0	0	2	0	0	0	—	0	1	0	0	0.3	1.000
3 yrs.		0	1	.000	3.18	9	1	0	17	14	2	7	0	0	0	7	2	0	0	.000	2	1	0	0	0.3	1.000

WORLD SERIES

Year	Team	W	L	PCT	ERA	G	GS	CG	IP	H	BB	SO	ShO	W	L	SV	AB	H	HR	BA	PO	A	E	DP	TC/G	FA
1988	OAK A	0	1	.000	10.80	2	0	0	1.2	2	1	2	0	0	1	0	0	0	0	—	0	0	0	0	0.0	—
1989		0	0	—	0.00	2	0	0	1.2	0	0	0	0	0	0	1	0	0	0	—	1	0	0	0	0.5	1.000
2 yrs.		0	1	.000	5.40	4	0	0	3.1	2	1	2	0	0	1	1	0	0	0	—	1	0	0	0	0.3	1.000

Al Eckert

ECKERT, ALBERT GEORGE (Obbie)
B. May 17, 1906, Milwaukee, Wis.   D. Apr. 20, 1974, Milwaukee, Wis.

BL TL 5'10"   174 lbs.

Year	Team	W	L	PCT	ERA	G	GS	CG	IP	H	BB	SO	ShO	W	L	SV	AB	H	HR	BA	PO	A	E	DP	TC/G	FA
1930	CIN N	0	1	.000	7.20	2	1	0	5	7	4	1	0	0	0	0	1	0	0	.000	0	2	0	0	1.0	1.000
1931		0	1	.000	9.16	14	1	0	18.2	26	9	5	0	0	0	0	3	1	0	.333	0	3	0	2	0.2	1.000
1935	STL N	0	0	—	12.00	2	0	0	3	7	1	1	0	0	0	0	0	0	0	—	0	0	0	0	0.0	—
3 yrs.		0	2	.000	9.11	18	2	0	26.2	40	14	7	0	0	0	0	4	1	0	.250	0	5	0	2	0.3	1.000

Charlie Eckert

ECKERT, CHARLES WILLIAM (Buzz)
B. Aug. 8, 1897, Philadelphia, Pa.   D. Aug. 22, 1986, Trevose, Pa.

BR TR 5'10½"   165 lbs.

Year	Team	W	L	PCT	ERA	G	GS	CG	IP	H	BB	SO	ShO	W	L	SV	AB	H	HR	BA	PO	A	E	DP	TC/G	FA
1919	PHI A	0	1	.000	3.94	2	1	1	16	17	3	6	0	0	0	0	6	1	0	.167	2	4	0	0	3.0	1.000
1920		0	0	—	4.76	2	0	0	5.2	8	1	1	0	0	0	0	1	0	0	.000	0	0	1	0	0.5	—
1922		0	2	.000	4.68	21	0	0	50	61	23	15	0	0	2	0	11	1	0	.091	1	20	0	0	1.0	1.000
3 yrs.		0	3	.000	4.52	25	1	1	71.2	86	27	22	0	0	2	0	18	2	0	.111	3	24	1	0	1.1	.964

Don Eddy

EDDY, DONALD EUGENE
B. Oct. 25, 1946, Mason City, Iowa

BR TL 5'11"   170 lbs.

Year	Team	W	L	PCT	ERA	G	GS	CG	IP	H	BB	SO	ShO	W	L	SV	AB	H	HR	BA	PO	A	E	DP	TC/G	FA
1970	CHI A	0	0	—	2.25	7	0	0	12	10	6	9	0	0	0	0	0	0	0	—	2	1	0	0	0.4	1.000
1971		0	2	.000	2.35	22	0	0	23	19	19	14	0	0	2	0	1	1	0	1.000	1	2	1	0	0.2	.750
2 yrs.		0	2	.000	2.31	29	0	0	35	29	25	23	0	0	2	0	1	1	0	1.000	3	3	1	0	0.2	.857

Steve Eddy

EDDY, STEVEN ALLEN
B. Aug. 21, 1957, Sterling, Ill.

BR TR 6'2"   185 lbs.

Year	Team	W	L	PCT	ERA	G	GS	CG	IP	H	BB	SO	ShO	W	L	SV	AB	H	HR	BA	PO	A	E	DP	TC/G	FA
1979	CAL A	1	1	.500	4.78	7	4	0	32	36	20	7	0	0	0	0	0	0	0	—	5	7	2	0	2.0	.857

Ed Edelen

EDELEN, EDWARD JOSEPH (Doc)
B. Mar. 16, 1912, Bryantown, Md.   D. Feb. 1, 1982, La Plata, Md.

BR TR 6'   191 lbs.

Year	Team	W	L	PCT	ERA	G	GS	CG	IP	H	BB	SO	ShO	W	L	SV	AB	H	HR	BA	PO	A	E	DP	TC/G	FA
1932	WAS A	0	0	—	20.25	2	0	0	1.1	0	6	0	0	0	0	0	0	0	0	—	0	0	0	0	0.0	—

Joe Edelen

EDELEN, BENNY JOE
B. Sept. 16, 1955, Durant, Okla.

BR TR 6'   165 lbs.

Year	Team	W	L	PCT	ERA	G	GS	CG	IP	H	BB	SO	ShO	W	L	SV	AB	H	HR	BA	PO	A	E	DP	TC/G	FA
1981	2 teams		STL N	(13G 1-0)		CIN N	(5G 1-0)																				
"	total	2	0	1.000	5.70	18	0	0	30	34	3	15	0	2	0	0	5	1	0	.200	1	2	0	0	0.2	1.000

Year	Team		W	L	PCT	ERA	G	GS	CG	IP	H	BB	SO	ShO	Relief Pitching W	L	SV	Batting AB	H	HR	BA	PO	A	E	DP	TC/G	FA

Joe Edelen *continued*

| 1982 | CIN | N | 0 | 0 | – | 8.80 | 9 | 0 | 0 | 15.1 | 22 | 8 | 11 | 0 | 0 | 0 | 0 | 2 | 1 | 0 | .500 | 2 | 1 | 0 | 0 | 0.3 | 1.000 |
| 2 yrs. | | | 2 | 0 | 1.000 | 6.75 | 27 | 0 | 0 | 45.1 | 56 | 11 | 26 | 0 | 2 | 0 | 0 | 7 | 2 | 0 | .286 | 3 | 3 | 0 | 0 | 0.2 | 1.000 |

John Edelman

EDELMAN, JOHN ROGERS
B. July 27, 1935, Philadelphia, Pa.   BR TR 6'3"   185 lbs.

| 1955 | MIL | N | 0 | 0 | – | 11.12 | 5 | 0 | 0 | 5.2 | 7 | 8 | 3 | 0 | 0 | 0 | 0 | 0 | 0 | 0 | – | 0 | 1 | 0 | 0 | 0.2 | 1.000 |

Charlie Eden

EDEN, CHARLES M.
B. Jan. 18, 1855, Lexington, Ky.   D. Sept. 17, 1920, Cincinnati, Ohio   BR TR

1884	PIT	AA	0	1	.000	6.00	2	1	1	12	12	3	3	0	0	0	0	122	33	1	.270	0	0	0	0	0.0	–
1885			1	2	.333	5.17	4	1	0	15.2	22	3	5	0	1	1	0	405	103	0	.254	0	0	2	0	0.5	–
2 yrs.			1	3	.250	5.53	6	2	1	27.2	34	6	8	0	1	1	0	*				0	0	2	0	0.3	–

Tom Edens

EDENS, THOMAS PATRICK
B. June 9, 1961, Ontario, Ore.   BR TR 6'3"   185 lbs.

| 1987 | NY | N | 0 | 0 | – | 6.75 | 2 | 2 | 0 | 8 | 15 | 4 | 4 | 0 | 0 | 0 | 0 | 3 | 0 | 0 | .000 | 0 | 4 | 1 | 0 | 2.5 | .800 |

Butch Edge

EDGE, CLAUDE LEE, JR.
B. July 18, 1956, Houston, Tex.   BR TR 6'3"   203 lbs.

| 1979 | TOR | A | 3 | 4 | .429 | 5.19 | 9 | 9 | 1 | 52 | 60 | 24 | 19 | 0 | 0 | 0 | 0 | 0 | 0 | 0 | – | 1 | 7 | 0 | 0 | 0.9 | 1.000 |

Bill Edgerton

EDGERTON, WILLIAM ALBERT
B. Aug. 16, 1941, South Bend, Ind.   BL TL 6'2"   185 lbs.

1966	KC	A	0	1	.000	3.24	6	1	0	8.1	10	7	3	0	0	1	0	0	0	0	–	0	3	0	0	0.5	1.000
1967			1	0	1.000	2.16	7	0	0	8.1	11	3	6	0	1	0	0	0	0	0	–	0	2	0	0	0.3	1.000
1969	SEA	A	0	1	.000	13.50	4	0	0	4	10	0	2	0	0	1	0	0	0	0	–	0	1	0	1	0.3	1.000
3 yrs.			1	2	.333	4.79	17	1	0	20.2	31	10	11	0	1	2	0	0	0	0	–	0	6	0	1	0.4	1.000

George Edmondson

EDMONDSON, GEORGE HENDERSON (Big Ed)
B. May 18, 1896, Waxahachie, Tex.   D. July 11, 1973, Waco, Tex.   BR TR 6'1"   179 lbs.

1922	CLE	A	0	0	–	9.00	2	0	0	2	4	0	0	0	0	0	0	0	0	0	–	0	1	0	0	0.5	1.000
1923			0	0	–	11.25	1	0	0	4	8	3	0	0	0	0	0	1	0	0	.000	0	2	0	1	2.0	1.000
1924			0	0	–	9.00	5	1	0	8	10	5	3	0	0	0	0	3	1	0	.333	0	0	0	0	0.0	–
3 yrs.			0	0	–	9.64	8	1	0	14	22	8	3	0	0	0	0	4	1	0	.250	0	3	0	1	0.4	1.000

Paul Edmondson

EDMONDSON, PAUL MICHAEL
B. Feb. 12, 1943, Kansas City, Kans.   D. Feb. 13, 1970, Santa Barbara, Calif.   BR TR 6'5"   195 lbs.

| 1969 | CHI | A | 1 | 6 | .143 | 3.70 | 14 | 13 | 1 | 87.2 | 72 | 39 | 46 | 0 | 0 | 0 | 1 | 0 | 29 | 5 | 0 | .172 | 6 | 27 | 1 | 1 | 2.4 | .971 |

Sam Edmonston

EDMONSTON, SAMUEL SHERWOOD
B. Aug. 30, 1883, Washington, D. C.   D. Apr. 12, 1979, Corpus Christi, Tex.   BL TL 5'11½"   185 lbs.

1906	WAS	A	0	1	.000	4.50	2	1	1	10	10	2	0	0	0	0	0	3	1	0	.333	0	5	0	0	2.5	1.000
1907			0	0	–	9.00	1	0	0	3	8	1	0	0	0	0	0	2	0	0	.000	0	2	0	0	2.0	1.000
2 yrs.			0	1	.000	5.54	3	1	1	13	18	3	0	0	0	0	0	5	1	0	.200	0	7	0	0	2.3	1.000

Foster Edwards

EDWARDS, FOSTER HAMILTON (Eddie)
B. Sept. 1, 1903, Holstein, Iowa   D. Jan. 4, 1980, Orleans, Mass.   BR TR 6'3"   175 lbs.

1925	BOS	N	0	0	–	9.00	1	0	0	2	6	1	1	0	0	0	0	0	0	0	–	0	0	0	0	0.0	–
1926			2	0	1.000	0.72	3	1	0	25	20	13	4	0	0	0	0	9	0	0	.000	2	5	0	1	2.3	1.000
1927			2	8	.200	4.99	29	11	1	92	95	45	37	0	0	1	0	22	1	0	.045	1	17	2	1	0.7	.900
1928			2	1	.667	5.66	21	3	2	49.1	67	23	17	0	0	0	0	11	1	0	.091	3	10	0	1	0.6	1.000
1930	NY	A	0	0	–	21.60	2	0	0	1.2	5	2	1	0	0	0	0	0	0	0	–	0	0	0	0	0.0	–
5 yrs.			6	9	.400	4.76	56	17	4	170	193	84	60	0	1	0	0	42	2	0	.048	6	32	2	3	0.7	.950

Jim Joe Edwards

EDWARDS, JAMES CORBETTE
B. Dec. 14, 1894, Banner, Miss.   D. Jan. 19, 1965, Serepta, Miss.   BR TL 6'2"   185 lbs.

1922	CLE	A	3	8	.273	4.70	25	7	0	88	113	40	44	0	2	3	2	23	2	0	.087	4	19	2	1	1.0	.920
1923			10	10	.500	3.71	38	21	7	179.1	200	75	68	1	0	3	1	59	7	0	.119	8	42	1	1	1.3	.980
1924			4	3	.571	2.84	10	7	5	57	64	34	15	1	0	0	0	20	3	0	.150	2	14	1	0	1.7	.941
1925	2 teams						CLE A (13G 0–3)								CHI A			(9G 1–2)									
"	total		1	5	.167	5.86	22	7	2	81.1	106	46	32	0	0	2	0	26	4	0	.154	2	29	1	0	1.5	.969
1926	CHI	A	6	9	.400	4.18	32	16	8	142	140	63	41	0	2	3	1	46	5	0	.109	6	31	0	0	1.2	1.000
1928	CIN	N	2	2	.500	7.59	18	1	0	32	43	20	11	0	1	2	0	10	3	0	.300	1	4	1	0	0.3	.833
6 yrs.			26	37	.413	4.41	145	59	22	579.2	666	278	211	2	5	13	4	184	24	0	.130	23	139	6	2	1.2	.964

Sherman Edwards

EDWARDS, SHERMAN STANLEY
B. July 25, 1909, Mt. Ida, Ark.   BR TR 6'   165 lbs.

| 1934 | CIN | N | 0 | 0 | – | 3.00 | 1 | 0 | 0 | 3 | 4 | 1 | 1 | 0 | 0 | 0 | 0 | 1 | 0 | 0 | .000 | 0 | 1 | 0 | 0 | 1.0 | 1.000 |

Wayne Edwards

EDWARDS, WAYNE MAURICE
B. Mar. 7, 1964, Burbank, Calif.   BL TL 6'5"   185 lbs.

| 1989 | CHI | A | 0 | 0 | – | 3.68 | 7 | 0 | 0 | 7.1 | 7 | 3 | 9 | 0 | 0 | 0 | 0 | 0 | 0 | 0 | – | 0 | 0 | 0 | 1 | 0.1 | 1.000 |

Harry Eells

EELLS, HARRY ARCHIBALD
B. Feb. 14, 1881, Ida Grove, Iowa   D. Oct. 15, 1940, Los Angeles, Calif.   BR TR 6'1"   195 lbs.

| 1906 | CLE | A | 4 | 5 | .444 | 2.61 | 14 | 8 | 6 | 86.1 | 77 | 48 | 35 | 1 | 0 | 1 | 0 | 32 | 6 | 0 | .188 | 8 | 26 | 1 | 2 | 2.5 | .971 |

Year	Team		W	L	PCT	ERA	G	GS	CG	IP	H	BB	SO	ShO	Relief Pitching			Batting			BA	PO	A	E	DP	TC/G	FA
															W	L	SV	AB	H	HR							

Dick Egan

EGAN, RICHARD WALLIS
B. Mar. 24, 1937, Berkeley, Calif.　　　BL TL 6'4"　193 lbs.

Year	Team		W	L	PCT	ERA	G	GS	CG	IP	H	BB	SO	ShO	W	L	SV	AB	H	HR	BA	PO	A	E	DP	TC/G	FA
1963	DET	A	0	1	.000	5.14	20	0	0	21	25	3	16	0	0	1	0	0	0	0	–	2	3	0	0	0.3	1.000
1964			0	0	–	4.46	23	0	0	34.1	33	17	21	0	0	0	2	3	0	0	.000	2	8	1	1	0.5	.909
1966	CAL	A	0	0	–	4.40	11	0	0	14.1	17	6	11	0	0	0	0	1	0	0	.000	2	1	0	0	0.3	1.000
1967	LA	N	1	1	.500	6.25	20	0	0	31.2	34	15	20	0	1	1	0	1	0	0	.000	3	4	3	0	0.5	.700
4 yrs.			1	2	.333	5.15	74	0	0	101.1	109	41	68	0	1	2	2	5	0	0	.000	9	16	4	1	0.4	.862

Jim Egan

EGAN, JAMES K. (Troy Terrier)
B. 1858, Derby, Conn.　D. Sept. 26, 1884, New Haven, Conn.　　　TL

Year	Team		W	L	PCT	ERA	G	GS	CG	IP	H	BB	SO	ShO	W	L	SV	AB	H	HR	BA	PO	A	E	DP	TC/G	FA
1882	TRO	N	4	6	.400	4.14	12	10	10	100	133	24	20	0	0	0	0	*				5	11	8	2	2.0	.667

Rip Egan

EGAN, JOHN JOSEPH
B. July 9, 1871, Philadelphia, Pa.　D. Dec. 22, 1950, Cranston, R. I.　　　5'11"　168 lbs.

Year	Team		W	L	PCT	ERA	G	GS	CG	IP	H	BB	SO	ShO	W	L	SV	AB	H	HR	BA	PO	A	E	DP	TC/G	FA
1894	WAS	N	0	0	–	10.80	1	0	0	5	8	2	2	0	0	0	0	3	0	0	.000	0	1	0	0	1.0	1.000

Wish Egan

EGAN, ALOYSIUS JEROME
B. June 16, 1881, Evart, Mich.　D. Apr. 13, 1951, Detroit, Mich.　　　BR TR 6'3"　185 lbs.

Year	Team		W	L	PCT	ERA	G	GS	CG	IP	H	BB	SO	ShO	W	L	SV	AB	H	HR	BA	PO	A	E	DP	TC/G	FA
1902	DET	A	0	2	.000	2.86	3	3	2	22	23	6	0	0	0	0	0	8	2	0	.250	1	9	0	2	3.3	1.000
1905	STL	N	6	15	.286	3.58	23	19	18	171	189	39	29	0	0	0	2	59	6	0	.102	15	72	3	1	3.9	.967
1906			2	9	.182	4.59	16	12	7	86.1	97	27	23	0	0	0	1	29	2	0	.069	4	30	1	1	2.2	.971
3 yrs.			8	26	.235	3.83	42	34	27	279.1	309	72	52	0	0	0	3	96	10	0	.104	20	111	4	4	3.2	.970

Howard Ehmke

EHMKE, HOWARD JONATHAN (Bob)
B. Apr. 24, 1894, Silver Creek, N. Y.
D. Mar. 17, 1959, Philadelphia, Pa.　　　BR TR 6'3"　190 lbs.
BB 1923

Year	Team		W	L	PCT	ERA	G	GS	CG	IP	H	BB	SO	ShO	W	L	SV	AB	H	HR	BA	PO	A	E	DP	TC/G	FA
1915	BUF	F	0	2	.000	5.53	18	2	0	53.2	69	25	18	0	0	0	0	12	0	0	.000	2	25	3	2	1.7	.900
1916	DET	A	3	1	.750	3.13	5	4	4	37.1	34	15	15	0	0	0	0	14	2	0	.143	10	15	1	0	5.2	.962
1917			10	15	.400	2.97	35	25	13	206	174	88	90	4	0	1	2	69	17	0	.246	14	68	4	1	2.5	.953
1919			17	10	.630	3.18	33	31	20	248.2	255	107	79	2	1	0	0	91	23	0	.253	9	86	3	3	3.0	.969
1920			15	18	.455	3.29	38	33	33	268.1	250	124	98	2	0	0	3	105	25	0	.238	20	93	4	2	3.1	.966
1921			13	14	.481	4.54	30	22	13	196.1	220	81	68	1	3	2	1	74	21	0	.284	9	55	2	3	2.2	.970
1922			17	17	.500	4.22	45	30	16	279.2	299	101	108	1	7	1	1	102	16	0	.157	11	75	2	2	2.0	.977
1923	BOS	A	20	17	.541	3.78	43	39	28	316.2	318	119	121	2	0	0	3	112	25	0	.223	18	101	3	8	2.8	.975
1924			19	17	.528	3.46	45	36	26	315	324	81	119	4	2	1	4	126	28	0	.222	15	78	3	1	2.1	.969
1925			9	20	.310	3.73	34	31	22	260.2	285	85	95	0	0	1	0	88	13	0	.148	6	88	6	4	2.9	.940
1926	2 teams		BOS A	(14G 3–10)		PHI A	(20G 12–4)																				
"	total		15	14	.517	3.86	34	27	17	244.2	240	95	93	2	1	0	1	80	12	0	.150	10	66	7	5	2.4	.916
1927	PHI	A	12	10	.545	4.22	30	27	10	189.2	200	60	68	1	1	0	0	68	14	0	.206	11	57	4	1	2.5	.946
1928			9	8	.529	3.62	23	18	5	139.1	135	44	34	1	0	0	1	46	11	0	.239	6	35	2	2	1.9	.953
1929			7	2	.778	3.29	11	8	2	54.2	48	15	20	0	2	0	0	19	2	0	.105	7	10	1	0	1.6	.944
1930			0	1	.000	11.70	3	1	0	10	22	2	4	0	0	0	0	3	1	0	.333	0	1	0	0	1.0	1.000
15 yrs.			166	166	.500	3.75	427	339	199	2820.2	2873	1042	1030	20	17	9	14	1009	210	0	.208	150	855	45	35	2.5	.957

WORLD SERIES

Year	Team		W	L	PCT	ERA	G	GS	CG	IP	H	BB	SO	ShO	W	L	SV	AB	H	HR	BA	PO	A	E	DP	TC/G	FA
1929	PHI	A	1	0	1.000	1.42	2	2	1	12.2	14	3	13	0	0	0	0	5	1	0	.200	0	4	0	0	2.0	1.000

Red Ehret

EHRET, PHILIP SYDNEY
B. Aug. 31, 1868, Louisville, Ky.　D. July 28, 1940, Cincinnati, Ohio　　　BR TR 6'　175 lbs.

Year	Team		W	L	PCT	ERA	G	GS	CG	IP	H	BB	SO	ShO	W	L	SV	AB	H	HR	BA	PO	A	E	DP	TC/G	FA
1888	KC	AA	3	2	.600	3.98	7	6	5	52	58	22	12	0	0	0	0	63	12	0	.190	3	15	0	0	2.6	1.000
1889	LOU	AA	10	29	.256	4.80	45	38	35	364	441	115	135	1	0	2	0	258	65	1	.252	9	97	12	3	2.6	.898
1890			25	14	.641	2.53	43	38	35	359	351	79	174	4	1	1	2	146	31	0	.212	9	64	12	2	2.0	.859
1891			13	13	.500	3.47	26	24	23	220.2	225	70	76	2	0	2	0	91	22	0	.242	4	57	9	4	2.7	.871
1892	PIT	N	16	20	.444	2.65	39	36	32	316	290	83	101	0	0	1	0	132	34	0	.258	14	57	12	1	2.1	.855
1893			18	18	.500	3.44	39	35	32	314.1	322	115	70	4	1	2	0	136	24	1	.176	12	80	11	0	2.6	.893
1894			19	21	.475	5.14	46	38	31	346.2	441	128	102	1	5	0	0	135	23	0	.170	12	61	6	2	1.8	.859
1895	STL	N	6	19	.240	6.02	37	32	18	231.2	360	88	55	0	1	0	0	96	21	1	.219	11	56	12	0	2.1	.848
1896	CIN	N	18	14	.563	3.42	34	33	29	276.2	298	74	60	2	1	0	0	102	20	1	.196	15	69	7	3	2.7	.923
1897			8	10	.444	4.78	34	19	11	184.1	256	47	43	0	2	1	2	66	13	0	.197	12	33	2	4	1.4	.957
1898	LOU	N	3	7	.300	5.76	12	10	9	89	130	20	20	0	0	0	0	40	9	0	.225	3	17	5	0	2.1	.800
11 yrs.			139	167	.454	4.02	362	309	260	2754.1	3172	841	848	14	11	9	4	*				104	606	94	19	2.2	.883

Rube Ehrhardt

EHRHARDT, WELTON CLAUDE
B. Nov. 20, 1894, Beecher, Ill.　D. Apr. 27, 1980, Chicago Heights, Ill.　　　BR TR 6'2"　190 lbs.

Year	Team		W	L	PCT	ERA	G	GS	CG	IP	H	BB	SO	ShO	W	L	SV	AB	H	HR	BA	PO	A	E	DP	TC/G	FA
1924	BKN	N	5	3	.625	2.26	15	9	6	83.2	71	17	13	2	0	0	0	29	4	0	.138	3	12	1	0	1.1	.938
1925			10	14	.417	5.03	36	24	12	207.2	239	62	47	0	1	3	1	71	15	1	.211	13	67	4	4	2.3	.952
1926			2	5	.286	3.90	44	1	0	97	101	35	25	0	2	4	4	24	6	0	.250	1	18	1	0	0.5	.950
1927			3	7	.300	3.57	46	3	2	95.2	90	37	22	0	2	6	2	24	6	0	.250	5	36	3	1	1.0	.932
1928			1	3	.250	4.67	28	2	1	54	74	27	12	0	0	2	2	14	4	0	.286	1	18	4	2	0.8	.826
1929	CIN	N	1	2	.333	4.74	24	1	1	49.1	58	22	9	1	0	2	1	11	2	0	.182	0	15	0	1	0.6	1.000
6 yrs.			22	34	.393	4.15	193	40	22	587.1	633	200	128	3	5	17	10	173	37	1	.214	23	166	13	8	1.0	.936

Hack Eibel

EIBEL, HENRY HACK
B. Dec. 6, 1893, Brooklyn, N. Y.　D. Oct. 16, 1945, Macon, Ga.　　　BL TL 5'11"　220 lbs.

Year	Team		W	L	PCT	ERA	G	GS	CG	IP	H	BB	SO	ShO	W	L	SV	AB	H	HR	BA	PO	A	E	DP	TC/G	FA
1920	BOS	A	0	0	–	3.48	3	0	0	10.1	10	3	5	0	0	0	0	*				0	2	0	0	0.7	1.000

Juan Eichelberger

EICHELBERGER, JUAN TYRONE
B. Oct. 21, 1953, St. Louis, Mo.　　　BR TR 6'2"　195 lbs.

Year	Team		W	L	PCT	ERA	G	GS	CG	IP	H	BB	SO	ShO	W	L	SV	AB	H	HR	BA	PO	A	E	DP	TC/G	FA
1978	SD	N	0	0	–	12.00	3	0	0	3	4	2	2	0	0	0	0	0	0	0	–	1	1	0	0	0.3	1.000
1979			1	1	.500	3.43	3	3	1	21	15	11	12	0	0	0	0	5	2	0	.400	2	0	0	0	0.7	1.000
1980			4	2	.667	3.64	15	13	0	89	73	55	43	0	1	0	0	27	3	0	.111	2	10	3	0	1.0	.800
1981			8	8	.500	3.51	25	24	3	141	136	74	81	1	0	0	0	46	4	0	.087	10	28	7	4	1.8	.844

Year	Team		W	L	PCT	ERA	G	GS	CG	IP	H	BB	SO	ShO	W	L	SV	AB	H	HR	BA	PO	A	E	DP	TC/G	FA
															Relief Pitching			Batting									

Juan Eichelberger *continued*

Year	Team		W	L	PCT	ERA	G	GS	CG	IP	H	BB	SO	ShO	W	L	SV	AB	H	HR	BA	PO	A	E	DP	TC/G	FA
1982			7	14	.333	4.20	31	24	8	177.2	171	72	74	0	0	2	0	55	5	0	.091	9	25	1	0	1.1	.971
1983	CLE	A	4	11	.267	4.90	28	15	2	134	132	59	56	0	1	0	0	0	0	0	—	9	14	0	3	0.8	1.000
1988	ATL	N	2	0	1.000	3.86	20	0	0	37.1	44	10	13	0	2	0	0	3	0	0	.000	4	8	1	1	0.7	.923
7 yrs.			26	36	.419	4.10	125	79	14	603	575	283	281	1	4	2	0	136	14	0	.103	35	87	12	8	1.1	.910

Mark Eichhorn

EICHHORN, MARK ANTHONY
B. Nov. 21, 1960, San Jose, Calif.

BR TR 6'4" 200 lbs.

Year	Team		W	L	PCT	ERA	G	GS	CG	IP	H	BB	SO	ShO	W	L	SV	AB	H	HR	BA	PO	A	E	DP	TC/G	FA
1982	TOR	A	0	3	.000	5.45	7	7	0	38	40	14	16	0	0	0	0	0	0	0	—	1	3	0	0	0.6	1.000
1986			14	6	.700	1.72	69	0	0	157	105	45	166	0	14	6	10	0	0	0	—	16	21	0	1	0.5	1.000
1987			10	6	.625	3.17	89	0	0	127.2	110	52	96	0	10	6	4	0	0	0	—	2	30	1	2	0.4	.970
1988			0	3	.000	4.19	37	0	0	66.2	79	27	28	0	0	3	1	0	0	0	—	5	13	0	1	0.5	1.000
1989	ATL	N	5	5	.500	4.35	45	0	0	68.1	70	19	49	0	5	5	0	2	0	0	.000	9	17	0	1	0.6	1.000
5 yrs.			29	23	.558	3.19	247	7	0	457.2	404	157	355	0	29	20	15	2	0	0	.000	33	84	1	5	0.5	.992

Dave Eiland

EILAND, DAVID WILLIAM
B. July 5, 1966, Dade City, Fla.

BR TR 6'3" 210 lbs.

Year	Team		W	L	PCT	ERA	G	GS	CG	IP	H	BB	SO	ShO	W	L	SV	AB	H	HR	BA	PO	A	E	DP	TC/G	FA
1988	NY	A	0	0	—	6.39	3	3	0	12.2	15	4	7	0	0	0	0	0	0	0	—	1	3	0	0	1.3	1.000
1989			1	3	.250	5.77	6	6	0	34.1	44	13	11	0	0	0	0	0	0	0	—	2	2	0	0	0.7	1.000
2 yrs.			1	3	.250	5.94	9	9	0	47	59	17	18	0	0	0	0	0	0	0	—	3	5	0	0	0.9	1.000

Dave Eilers

EILERS, DAVID LOUIS
B. Dec. 3, 1936, Oldenberg, Tex.

BR TR 5'11" 188 lbs.

Year	Team		W	L	PCT	ERA	G	GS	CG	IP	H	BB	SO	ShO	W	L	SV	AB	H	HR	BA	PO	A	E	DP	TC/G	FA
1964	MIL	N	0	0	—	4.70	6	0	0	7.2	11	1	1	0	0	0	0	1	0	0	—	1	0	0	0	0.2	1.000
1965	2 teams		MIL N	(6G 0–0)		NY N	(11G 1–1)																				
"	total		1	1	.500	5.40	17	0	0	21.2	28	4	10	0	1	1	2	1	1	0	1.000	2	3	0	0	0.3	1.000
1966	NY	N	1	1	.500	4.67	23	0	0	34.2	39	7	14	0	1	1	1	1	0	0	.000	2	8	0	1	0.4	1.000
1967	HOU	N	6	4	.600	3.94	35	0	0	59.1	68	17	27	0	6	4	1	7	0	0	.000	3	10	0	1	0.4	1.000
4 yrs.			8	6	.571	4.45	81	0	0	123.1	146	29	52	0	8	6	3	9	1	0	.111	8	21	0	2	0.4	1.000

Jake Eisenhart

EISENHART, JACOB HENRY (Hank)
B. Oct. 3, 1922, Perkasie, Pa. D. Huntingdon, Pa.

BL TL 6'3½" 195 lbs.

Year	Team		W	L	PCT	ERA	G	GS	CG	IP	H	BB	SO	ShO	W	L	SV	AB	H	HR	BA	PO	A	E	DP	TC/G	FA
1944	CIN	N	0	0	—	0.00	1	0	0	1	1	0	0	0	0	0	0	0	0	0	—	0	0	0	0	0.0	—

Harry Eisenstat

EISENSTAT, HARRY
B. Oct. 10, 1915, Brooklyn, N. Y.

BL TL 5'11" 185 lbs.

Year	Team		W	L	PCT	ERA	G	GS	CG	IP	H	BB	SO	ShO	W	L	SV	AB	H	HR	BA	PO	A	E	DP	TC/G	FA
1935	BKN	N	0	1	.000	13.50	2	0	0	4.2	9	2	2	0	0	1	0	1	0	0	.000	0	4	0	0	2.0	1.000
1936			1	2	.333	5.65	5	2	0	14.1	22	6	5	0	0	1	0	3	1	0	.333	1	4	0	0	1.0	1.000
1937			3	3	.500	3.97	13	4	0	47.2	61	11	12	0	2	1	0	11	0	0	.000	2	15	1	0	1.4	.944
1938	DET	A	9	6	.600	3.73	32	9	1	125.1	131	29	37	0	6	5	4	36	5	0	.139	6	27	2	0	1.1	.943
1939	2 teams		DET A	(10G 2–2)		CLE A	(26G 6–7)																				
"	total		8	9	.471	4.12	36	13	5	133.1	148	32	44	1	4	2	2	40	11	0	.275	4	22	0	0	0.7	1.000
1940	CLE	A	1	4	.200	3.14	27	3	0	71.2	78	12	27	0	1	2	4	22	6	0	.273	2	12	0	1	0.5	1.000
1941			1	1	.500	4.24	21	0	0	34	43	16	11	0	1	1	2	6	2	0	.333	0	3	0	0	0.1	1.000
1942			2	1	.667	2.45	29	1	0	47.2	58	6	19	0	2	0	2	4	1	0	.250	2	8	0	1	0.3	1.000
8 yrs.			25	27	.481	3.84	165	32	11	478.2	550	114	157	1	16	13	14	123	26	0	.211	17	95	3	5	0.7	.974

Ed Eiteljorg

EITELJORG, EDWARD HENRY
B. Oct. 14, 1871, Berlin, Germany D. Dec. 7, 1942, Greencastle, Ind.

BR TR 6'2" 190 lbs.

Year	Team		W	L	PCT	ERA	G	GS	CG	IP	H	BB	SO	ShO	W	L	SV	AB	H	HR	BA	PO	A	E	DP	TC/G	FA
1890	CHI	N	0	1	.000	22.50	1	1	0	2	5	1	1	0	0	0	0	1	0	0	.000	0	0	0	0	0.0	—
1891	WAS	AA	1	5	.167	6.16	8	7	6	61.1	79	41	23	0	0	0	0	26	5	0	.192	3	20	1	2	3.0	.958
2 yrs.			1	6	.143	6.68	9	8	6	63.1	84	42	24	0	0	0	0	27	5	0	.185	3	20	1	2	2.7	.958

Heinie Elder

ELDER, HENRY KNOX
B. Aug. 23, 1890, Seattle, Wash. D. Nov. 13, 1958, Long Beach, Calif.

BL TL 6'2" 200 lbs.

Year	Team		W	L	PCT	ERA	G	GS	CG	IP	H	BB	SO	ShO	W	L	SV	AB	H	HR	BA	PO	A	E	DP	TC/G	FA
1913	DET	A	0	0	—	8.10	1	0	0	3.1	4	5	0	0	0	0	0	1	0	0	.000	0	0	0	0	0.0	—

Hod Eller

ELLER, HORACE OWEN
B. July 5, 1894, Muncie, Ind. D. July 18, 1961, Indianapolis, Ind.

BR TR 5'11½" 185 lbs.

Year	Team		W	L	PCT	ERA	G	GS	CG	IP	H	BB	SO	ShO	W	L	SV	AB	H	HR	BA	PO	A	E	DP	TC/G	FA
1917	CIN	N	10	5	.667	2.36	37	11	7	152.1	131	37	77	1	4	1	1	45	6	0	.133	5	33	0	0	1.0	1.000
1918			16	12	.571	2.36	37	22	14	217.2	205	59	84	0	7	1	1	70	11	0	.157	4	39	0	3	1.2	1.000
1919			20	9	.690	2.39	38	30	16	248.1	216	50	137	7	3	0	2	93	26	1	.280	3	52	2	1	1.5	.965
1920			13	12	.520	2.95	35	22	15	210.1	208	52	76	2	2	1	0	87	22	0	.253	8	51	1	1	1.7	.983
1921			2	2	.500	4.98	13	3	0	34.1	46	15	7	0	0	2	1	13	3	0	.231	1	4	1	0	0.5	.833
5 yrs.			61	40	.604	2.62	160	88	52	863	806	213	381	10	16	5	5	308	68	1	.221	21	179	4	6	1.3	.980

WORLD SERIES

Year	Team		W	L	PCT	ERA	G	GS	CG	IP	H	BB	SO	ShO	W	L	SV	AB	H	HR	BA	PO	A	E	DP	TC/G	FA
1919	CIN	N	2	0	1.000	2.00	2	2	2	18	13	2	15	1	0	0	0	7	2	0	.286	0	2	0	0	1.0	1.000

Joe Ellick

ELLICK, JOSEPH J.
B. Apr. 3, 1854, Cincinnati, Ohio D. Apr. 21, 1923, Kansas City, Mo.
Manager 1884.

5'10" 162 lbs.

Year	Team		W	L	PCT	ERA	G	GS	CG	IP	H	BB	SO	ShO	W	L	SV	AB	H	HR	BA	PO	A	E	DP	TC/G	FA
1878	MIL	N	0	1	.000	3.00	1	1	0	3	1	1	0	0	0	1	0	*				0	0	0	0	0.0	—

Bruce Ellingsen

ELLINGSEN, HAROLD BRUCE (Little Pod)
B. Apr. 26, 1949, Pocatello, Ida.

BL TL 6' 180 lbs.

Year	Team		W	L	PCT	ERA	G	GS	CG	IP	H	BB	SO	ShO	W	L	SV	AB	H	HR	BA	PO	A	E	DP	TC/G	FA
1974	CLE	A	1	1	.500	3.21	16	2	0	42	45	17	16	0	1	0	0	0	0	0	—	1	7	1	0	0.6	.889

Year	Team		W	L	PCT	ERA	G	GS	CG	IP	H	BB	SO	ShO	Relief Pitching W	L	SV	Batting AB	H	HR	BA	PO	A	E	DP	TC/G	FA

Claude Elliott

ELLIOTT, CLAUDE JUDSON (Chaucer, Old Pardee)
B. Nov. 17, 1879, Pardeeville, Wis. D. June 21, 1923, Pardeeville, Wis.
BR TR 6' 190 lbs.

Year	Team		W	L	PCT	ERA	G	GS	CG	IP	H	BB	SO	ShO	W	L	SV	AB	H	HR	BA	PO	A	E	DP	TC/G	FA
1904	2 teams	CIN N (9G 3–1)				NY N (3G 0–2)																					
"	total		3	3	.500	2.97	12	7	5	72.2	74	26	27	1	0	0	0	29	6	1	.207	2	19	2	0	1.9	.913
1905	NY	N	1	1	.500	4.03	10	2	2	38	41	12	20	0	0	0	6	16	3	0	.188	3	11	0	1	1.4	1.000
2 yrs.			4	4	.500	3.33	22	9	7	110.2	115	38	47	1	0	0	6	45	9	1	.200	5	30	2	1	1.7	.946

Glenn Elliott

ELLIOTT, HERBERT GLENN (Lefty)
B. Nov. 11, 1919, Sapulpa, Okla. D. July 27, 1969, Portland, Ore.
BB TL 5'11" 175 lbs.

Year	Team		W	L	PCT	ERA	G	GS	CG	IP	H	BB	SO	ShO	W	L	SV	AB	H	HR	BA	PO	A	E	DP	TC/G	FA
1947	BOS	N	0	1	.000	4.74	11	0	0	19	18	11	8	0	0	1	0	2	1	0	.500	0	5	0	1	0.5	1.000
1948			1	0	1.000	3.00	1	1	0	3	5	1	2	0	0	0	0	2	0	0	.000	0	0	0	0	0.0	—
1949			3	4	.429	3.95	22	6	1	68.1	70	27	15	0	2	0	0	17	1	0	.059	2	16	0	1	0.8	1.000
3 yrs.			4	5	.444	4.08	34	7	1	90.1	93	39	25	0	2	1	1	21	2	0	.095	2	21	0	2	0.7	1.000

Hal Elliott

ELLIOTT, HAROLD WILLIAM (Ace)
B. May 29, 1899, Mt. Clemens, Mich. D. Apr. 25, 1963, Honolulu, Hawaii
BR TR 6'1½" 170 lbs.

Year	Team		W	L	PCT	ERA	G	GS	CG	IP	H	BB	SO	ShO	W	L	SV	AB	H	HR	BA	PO	A	E	DP	TC/G	FA
1929	PHI	N	3	7	.300	6.06	40	8	2	114.1	146	59	32	0	2	2	2	30	5	0	.167	9	29	0	2	1.0	1.000
1930			6	11	.353	7.67	48	11	2	117.1	191	58	37	0	5	2	0	32	3	0	.094	2	34	3	0	0.8	.923
1931			0	2	.000	9.55	16	4	0	33	46	19	8	0	0	1	2	9	1	0	.111	2	8	0	0	0.6	1.000
1932			2	4	.333	5.77	16	7	0	57.2	70	38	13	0	1	1	0	18	3	0	.167	1	8	0	0	0.6	1.000
4 yrs.			11	24	.314	6.95	120	30	4	322.1	453	174	90	0	8	6	4	89	12	0	.135	14	79	3	2	0.8	.969

Jumbo Elliott

ELLIOTT, JAMES THOMAS
B. Oct. 22, 1900, St. Louis, Mo. D. Jan. 7, 1970, Terre Haute, Ind.
BR TL 6'3" 235 lbs.

Year	Team		W	L	PCT	ERA	G	GS	CG	IP	H	BB	SO	ShO	W	L	SV	AB	H	HR	BA	PO	A	E	DP	TC/G	FA
1923	STL	A	0	0	—	27.00	1	0	0	1	3	3	0	0	0	0	0	0	0	0	—	0	0	0	0	0.0	—
1925	BKN	N	0	2	.000	8.44	3	1	0	10.2	17	9	3	0	0	1	0	4	0	0	.000	0	1	0	0	0.3	1.000
1927			6	13	.316	3.30	30	21	12	188.1	188	60	99	2	2	1	0	64	9	0	.141	6	19	1	1	0.9	.962
1928			9	14	.391	3.89	41	21	7	192	194	64	74	2	2	4	1	68	12	3	.176	2	34	4	0	1.0	.900
1929			1	2	.333	6.63	6	3	0	19	21	16	7	0	0	0	0	4	1	0	.250	0	2	1	0	0.3	1.000
1930			10	7	.588	3.95	35	21	6	198.1	204	70	59	2	3	0	1	68	10	1	.147	4	29	0	2	0.9	1.000
1931	PHI	N	19	14	.576	4.27	52	30	12	249	288	83	99	2	3	0	5	90	11	0	.122	8	25	1	3	0.7	.971
1932			11	10	.524	5.42	39	22	8	166	210	47	62	0	2	3	0	61	12	0	.197	4	28	5	2	0.9	.865
1933			6	10	.375	3.84	35	21	6	161.2	188	49	43	1	0	1	2	52	12	0	.231	8	19	4	1	0.9	.871
1934	2 teams	PHI N (3G 0–1)				BOS N (7G 1–1)																					
"	total		1	2	.333	6.97	10	4	0	20.2	27	13	7	0	0	0	0	5	1	0	.200	0	3	1	0	0.4	.750
10 yrs.			63	74	.460	4.24	252	144	51	1206.2	1338	414	453	8	11	11	12	416	68	4	.163	32	160	16	10	0.8	.923

Dock Ellis

ELLIS, DOCK PHILLIP
B. Mar. 11, 1945, Los Angeles, Calif.
BB TR 6'3" 205 lbs.

Year	Team		W	L	PCT	ERA	G	GS	CG	IP	H	BB	SO	ShO	W	L	SV	AB	H	HR	BA	PO	A	E	DP	TC/G	FA
1968	PIT	N	6	5	.545	2.50	26	10	2	104.1	82	38	52	0	1	2	0	29	2	0	.069	5	18	0	2	0.9	1.000
1969			11	17	.393	3.58	35	33	8	219	206	76	173	2	0	0	0	68	6	0	.088	15	35	3	2	1.5	.943
1970			13	10	.565	3.21	30	30	9	202	194	87	128	4	0	0	0	70	7	0	.100	21	34	2	1	1.9	.965
1971			19	9	.679	3.05	31	31	11	227	207	63	137	2	0	0	0	79	16	0	.203	22	32	2	1	1.8	.964
1972			15	7	.682	2.70	25	25	4	163.1	156	33	96	1	0	0	0	59	9	0	.153	16	15	0	2	1.2	1.000
1973			12	14	.462	3.05	28	28	3	192	176	55	122	1	0	0	0	65	7	0	.108	16	30	1	3	1.7	.979
1974			12	9	.571	3.15	26	26	9	177	163	41	91	0	0	0	0	56	12	0	.214	14	22	4	2	1.5	.900
1975			8	9	.471	3.79	27	24	5	140	163	43	69	2	0	0	0	36	4	0	.111	8	16	2	4	1.0	.923
1976	NY	A	17	8	.680	3.19	32	32	8	211.2	195	76	65	1	0	0	0	0	0	0		19	20	3	0	1.3	.929
1977	3 teams	NY A (3G 1–1)				OAK A (7G 1–5)			TEX A (23G 10–6)																			
"	total		12	12	.500	3.64	33	32	8	212.2	211	64	106	1	0	0	0	0	0	0		17	21	3	4	1.2	.927
1978	TEX	A	9	7	.563	4.20	22	22	3	141.1	131	46	45	0	0	0	0	0	0	0		11	22	2	2	1.6	.943
1979	3 teams	TEX A (10G 1–5)				NY N (17G 3–7)			PIT N (3G 0–0)																			
"	total		4	12	.250	5.83	30	24	1	139	183	52	52	0	1	0	0	27	2	0	.074	9	22	1	1	1.1	.969
12 yrs.			138	119	.537	3.45	345	317	71	2129.1	2067	674	1136	14	2	2	1	489	65	0	.133	173	287	23	26	1.4	.952

LEAGUE CHAMPIONSHIP SERIES

Year	Team		W	L	PCT	ERA	G	GS	CG	IP	H	BB	SO	ShO	W	L	SV	AB	H	HR	BA	PO	A	E	DP	TC/G	FA
1970	PIT	N	0	1	.000	2.79	1	1	0	9.2	9	4	1	0	0	0	0	2	0	0	.000	0	3	0	0	3.0	1.000
1971			1	0	1.000	3.60	1	1	0	5	6	4	1	0	0	0	0	3	0	0	.000	0	0	0	0	0.0	—
1972			0	1	.000	0.00	1	1	0	5	5	1	3	0	0	0	0	1	0	0	.000	0	0	0	0	0.0	—
1975			0	0	—	0.00	1	0	0	2	2	0	2	0	0	0	0	0	0	0	—	0	0	0	0	0.0	—
1976	NY	A	1	0	1.000	3.38	1	1	0	8	6	2	5	0	0	0	0	0	0	0		0	1	0	0	1.0	1.000
5 yrs.			2	2	.500	2.43	5	4	0	29.2	28	11	12	0	0	0	0	6	0	0	.000	0	4	0	0	0.8	1.000

WORLD SERIES

Year	Team		W	L	PCT	ERA	G	GS	CG	IP	H	BB	SO	ShO	W	L	SV	AB	H	HR	BA	PO	A	E	DP	TC/G	FA
1971	PIT	N	0	1	.000	15.43	1	1	0	2.1	4	1	1	0	0	0	0	1	0	0	.000	1	0	0	0	1.0	1.000
1976	NY	A	0	1	.000	10.80	1	1	0	3.1	7	0	1	0	0	0	0	0	0	0	—	0	0	0	0	0.0	—
2 yrs.			0	2	.000	12.71	2	2	0	5.2	11	1	2	0	0	0	0	1	0	0	.000	1	0	0	0	0.5	1.000

Jim Ellis

ELLIS, JAMES RUSSELL
B. Mar. 25, 1945, Tulare, Calif.
BR TL 6'2" 185 lbs.

Year	Team		W	L	PCT	ERA	G	GS	CG	IP	H	BB	SO	ShO	W	L	SV	AB	H	HR	BA	PO	A	E	DP	TC/G	FA
1967	CHI	N	1	1	.500	3.24	8	1	0	16.2	20	9	8	0	0	1	0	5	1	0	.200	2	1	0	0	0.4	1.000
1969	STL	N	0	0	—	1.80	2	1	0	5	7	3	0	0	0	0	0	0	0	0	—	0	0	0	0	0.0	—
2 yrs.			1	1	.500	2.91	10	2	0	21.2	27	12	8	0	0	1	0	5	1	0	.200	2	1	0	0	0.3	1.000

Sammy Ellis

ELLIS, SAMUEL JOSEPH
B. Feb. 11, 1941, Youngstown, Ohio
BL TR 6'1" 175 lbs.

Year	Team		W	L	PCT	ERA	G	GS	CG	IP	H	BB	SO	ShO	W	L	SV	AB	H	HR	BA	PO	A	E	DP	TC/G	FA
1962	CIN	N	2	2	.500	6.75	8	4	0	28	29	17	24	0	0	0	0	10	2	0	.200	1	3	2	1	0.8	.667
1964			10	3	.769	2.57	52	5	2	122.1	101	28	125	0	7	2	14	24	2	0	.083	8	18	1	3	0.5	.963
1965			22	10	.688	3.79	44	39	15	263.2	222	104	183	2	2	0	2	96	12	0	.125	15	32	5	1	1.2	.904
1966			12	19	.387	5.29	41	36	7	221	226	78	154	1	0	0	0	70	8	0	.114	8	23	1	1	0.8	.969
1967			8	11	.421	3.84	32	27	8	175.2	197	67	80	1	0	0	0	49	4	0	.082	9	27	2	1	1.2	.947
1968	CAL	A	9	10	.474	3.95	42	24	3	164	150	56	93	0	1	1	2	44	2	0	.045	12	14	2	0	0.7	.929

Year	Team		W	L	PCT	ERA	G	GS	CG	IP	H	BB	SO	ShO	Relief Pitching W	L	SV	Batting AB	H	HR	BA	PO	A	E	DP	TC/G	FA

Sammy Ellis *continued*

Year	Team		W	L	PCT	ERA	G	GS	CG	IP	H	BB	SO	ShO	W	L	SV	AB	H	HR	BA	PO	A	E	DP	TC/G	FA
1969	CHI	A	0	3	.000	5.83	10	5	0	29.1	42	16	15	0	0	1	0	6	1	0	.167	3	6	0	0	0.9	1.000
7 yrs.			63	58	.521	4.15	229	140	35	1004	967	378	677	3	11	4	18	299	31	0	.104	56	123	13	7	0.8	.932

George Ellison

ELLISON, GEORGE RUSSELL
B. Jan. 24, 1895, California D. Jan. 20, 1978, San Francisco, Calif.

BR TR 6'3" 185 lbs.

Year	Team		W	L	PCT	ERA	G	GS	CG	IP	H	BB	SO	ShO	W	L	SV	AB	H	HR	BA	PO	A	E	DP	TC/G	FA
1920	CLE	A	0	0	–	0.00	1	0	0	1	0	2	1	0	0	0	0	0	0	0	–	0	1	0	0	1.0	1.000

Dick Ellsworth

ELLSWORTH, RICHARD CLARK
Father of Steve Ellsworth.
B. Mar. 22, 1940, Lusk, Wyo.

BL TL 6'3½" 180 lbs.

Year	Team		W	L	PCT	ERA	G	GS	CG	IP	H	BB	SO	ShO	W	L	SV	AB	H	HR	BA	PO	A	E	DP	TC/G	FA
1958	CHI	N	0	1	.000	15.43	1	1	0	2.1	4	3	0	0	0	0	0	1	0	0	.000	0	0	0	0	0.0	–
1960			7	13	.350	3.72	31	27	6	176.2	170	72	94	0	0	0	0	48	2	0	.042	12	29	0	1	1.3	1.000
1961			10	11	.476	3.86	37	31	7	186.2	213	48	91	1	0	0	0	56	2	0	.036	8	49	2	7	1.6	.966
1962			9	20	.310	5.09	37	33	6	208.2	241	77	113	0	1	1	1	62	7	0	.113	7	41	3	3	1.4	.941
1963			22	10	.688	2.11	37	37	19	290.2	223	75	185	4	0	0	0	94	9	0	.096	15	60	3	3	2.1	.962
1964			14	18	.438	3.75	37	36	16	256.2	**267**	71	148	1	0	1	0	87	4	0	.046	13	58	6	2	2.1	.922
1965			14	15	.483	3.81	36	34	8	222.1	227	57	130	0	1	0	1	73	7	0	.096	8	50	2	3	1.7	.967
1966			8	**22**	.267	3.98	38	37	9	269.1	**321**	51	144	0	0	0	0	90	14	0	.156	19	53	5	3	2.0	.935
1967	PHI	N	6	7	.462	4.38	32	21	3	125.1	152	36	45	1	0	0	0	37	4	0	.108	8	31	2	1	1.3	.951
1968	BOS	A	16	7	.696	3.03	31	28	10	196	196	37	106	1	1	0	0	72	4	0	.056	10	30	1	2	1.3	.976
1969	2 teams		BOS A	(2G 0–0)		CLE A	(34G 6–9)																					
"	total		6	9	.400	4.10	36	24	3	147	178	44	52	1	0	0	0	48	6	0	.125	15	21	1	3	1.0	.973
1970	2 teams		CLE A	(29G 3–3)		MIL A	(14G 0–0)																					
"	total		3	3	.500	3.79	43	1	0	59.1	60	17	22	0	3	2	3	4	0	0	.000	4	14	0	1	0.4	1.000
1971	MIL	A	0	1	.000	4.80	11	0	0	15	22	7	10	0	0	1	0	1	0	0	.000	1	1	0	0	0.2	1.000
13 yrs.			115	137	.456	3.72	407	310	87	2156	2274	595	1140	9	7	5	5	673	59	0	.088	120	437	25	29	1.4	.957

Steve Ellsworth

ELLSWORTH, STEVEN CLARK
Son of Dick Ellsworth.
B. July 30, 1960, Chicago, Ill.

BR TR 6'8" 220 lbs.

Year	Team		W	L	PCT	ERA	G	GS	CG	IP	H	BB	SO	ShO	W	L	SV	AB	H	HR	BA	PO	A	E	DP	TC/G	FA
1988	BOS	A	1	6	.143	6.75	8	7	0	36	47	16	16	0	0	1	0	0	0	0	–	4	2	0	0	0.8	1.000

Don Elston

ELSTON, DONALD RAY
B. Apr. 6, 1929, Campbellstown, Ohio

BR TR 6' 165 lbs.

Year	Team		W	L	PCT	ERA	G	GS	CG	IP	H	BB	SO	ShO	W	L	SV	AB	H	HR	BA	PO	A	E	DP	TC/G	FA
1953	CHI	N	0	1	.000	14.40	2	1	0	5	11	2	2	0	0	0	0	1	0	0	.000	1	0	0	0	0.5	1.000
1957	2 teams		BKN N	(1G 0–0)		CHI N	(39G 6–7)																					
"	total		6	7	.462	3.54	40	14	2	145	140	55	103	0	3	1	8	37	4	0	.108	9	23	2	1	0.9	.941
1958	CHI	N	9	8	.529	2.88	69	0	0	97	75	39	84	0	**9**	8	10	14	5	0	.357	7	19	0	1	0.4	1.000
1959			10	8	.556	3.32	65	0	0	97.2	77	46	82	0	10	8	13	19	4	0	.211	3	14	2	1	0.3	.895
1960			8	9	.471	3.40	60	0	0	127	109	55	85	0	8	**9**	11	24	3	0	.125	10	13	4	1	0.5	.852
1961			6	7	.462	5.59	58	0	0	93.1	108	45	59	0	6	7	8	11	2	0	.182	4	18	0	1	0.4	1.000
1962			4	8	.333	2.44	57	0	0	66.1	57	32	37	0	4	8	8	8	0	0	.000	5	16	0	2	0.4	1.000
1963			4	1	.800	2.83	51	0	0	70	57	21	41	0	4	1	4	4	0	0	.000	4	9	0	1	0.3	1.000
1964			2	5	.286	5.30	48	0	0	54.1	68	34	26	0	2	5	1	6	1	0	.167	3	16	3	4	0.5	.864
9 yrs.			49	54	.476	3.69	450	15	2	755.2	702	327	519	0	46	47	63	124	19	0	.153	46	128	11	12	0.4	.941

Bones Ely

ELY, FREDERICK WILLIAM
B. June 7, 1863, North Girard, Pa. D. Jan. 10, 1952, Imola, Calif.

BR TR 6'1" 155 lbs.

Year	Team		W	L	PCT	ERA	G	GS	CG	IP	H	BB	SO	ShO	W	L	SV	AB	H	HR	BA	PO	A	E	DP	TC/G	FA
1884	BUF	N	0	1	.000	14.40	1	1	0	5	17	5	4	0	0	0	0	4	0	0	.000	0	1	0	0	1.0	1.000
1886	LOU	AA	0	4	.000	*5.32*	6	4	4	44	53	26	28	0	0	0	1	32	5	0	.156	2	8	0	0	1.7	1.000
1890	SYR	AA	0	0	–	22.50	1	0	0	2	7	0	0	0	0	0	0	496	130	0	.262	0	1	0	0	1.0	1.000
1894	STL	N	0	0	–	0.00	1	0	0	1	0	3	0	0	0	0	0	510	156	12	.306	0	0	0	0	0.0	–
4 yrs.			0	5	.000	6.75	9	5	4	52	77	34	32	0	0	0	1	*				2	10	0	0	1.3	1.000

Harry Ely

ELY, HARRY
B. Unknown.

Year	Team		W	L	PCT	ERA	G	GS	CG	IP	H	BB	SO	ShO	W	L	SV	AB	H	HR	BA	PO	A	E	DP	TC/G	FA
1892	BAL	N	0	1	.000	7.71	1	1	1	7	14	7	0	0	0	0	0	3	0	0	.000	1	1	1	0	3.0	.667

Red Embree

EMBREE, CHARLES WILLARD
B. Aug. 30, 1917, El Monte, Calif.

BR TR 6' 165 lbs.

Year	Team		W	L	PCT	ERA	G	GS	CG	IP	H	BB	SO	ShO	W	L	SV	AB	H	HR	BA	PO	A	E	DP	TC/G	FA
1941	CLE	A	0	1	.000	6.75	1	1	0	4	7	3	4	0	0	0	0	1	0	0	.000	0	0	0	0	0.0	–
1942			3	4	.429	3.86	19	6	2	63	58	31	44	0	2	1	0	15	2	0	.133	1	11	1	1	0.7	.923
1944			0	1	.000	13.50	3	1	0	3.1	2	5	4	0	0	0	0	0	0	0	–	1	0	0	0	0.3	1.000
1945			4	4	.500	1.93	8	8	5	70	56	26	42	1	0	0	0	21	3	0	.143	5	15	0	0	2.5	1.000
1946			8	12	.400	3.47	28	26	8	200	170	79	87	0	1	0	0	70	13	0	.186	11	29	3	3	1.5	.930
1947			8	10	.444	3.15	27	21	6	162.2	137	67	56	0	2	0	0	52	9	0	.173	6	30	1	4	1.4	.973
1948	NY	A	5	3	.625	3.76	20	8	4	76.2	77	30	25	0	0	1	0	27	4	0	.148	2	9	0	0	0.6	1.000
1949	STL	A	3	13	.188	5.37	35	19	4	127.1	146	89	24	0	0	2	1	37	6	0	.162	2	24	1	0	0.8	.963
8 yrs.			31	48	.392	3.72	141	90	29	707	653	330	286	1	5	3	1	223	37	0	.166	27	119	6	11	1.1	.961

Slim Embry

EMBRY, CHARLES AKIN
B. Aug. 17, 1901, Columbia, Tenn. D. Oct. 10, 1947, Nashville, Tenn.

BR TR 6'2" 184 lbs.

Year	Team		W	L	PCT	ERA	G	GS	CG	IP	H	BB	SO	ShO	W	L	SV	AB	H	HR	BA	PO	A	E	DP	TC/G	FA
1923	CHI	A	0	0	–	10.13	1	0	0	2.2	7	2	1	0	0	0	0	0	0	0	–	1	1	0	0	2.0	1.000

Charlie Emig

EMIG, CHARLES H.
B. Bellevue, Ky. Deceased.

Year	Team		W	L	PCT	ERA	G	GS	CG	IP	H	BB	SO	ShO	W	L	SV	AB	H	HR	BA	PO	A	E	DP	TC/G	FA
1896	LOU	N	0	1	.000	7.88	1	1	1	8	12	7	1	0	0	0	0	3	0	0	.000	0	5	1	0	6.0	.833

Year	Team		W	L	PCT	ERA	G	GS	CG	IP	H	BB	SO	ShO	W	L	SV	AB	H	HR	BA	PO	A	E	DP	TC/G	FA
															Relief Pitching			**Batting**									

Slim Emmerich

EMMERICH, WILLIAM PETER
B. Sept. 29, 1919, Allentown, Pa.
BR TR 6'1" 170 lbs.

Year	Team		W	L	PCT	ERA	G	GS	CG	IP	H	BB	SO	ShO	W	L	SV	AB	H	HR	BA	PO	A	E	DP	TC/G	FA
1945	NY	N	4	4	.500	4.86	31	7	1	100	111	33	27	0	3	0	0	25	3	0	.120	3	19	0	0	0.7	1.000
1946			0	0	—	4.50	2	0	0	4	6	0	1	0	0	0	0	0	0	0	—	1	1	0	0	1.0	1.000
2 yrs.			4	4	.500	4.85	33	7	1	104	117	33	28	0	3	0	0	25	3	0	.120	4	20	0	0	0.7	1.000

Bob Emslie

EMSLIE, ROBERT DANIEL
B. Jan. 27, 1859, Guelph, Ont., Canada   D. Apr. 26, 1943, St. Thomas, Ont., Canada
BR TR 5'11"

Year	Team		W	L	PCT	ERA	G	GS	CG	IP	H	BB	SO	ShO	W	L	SV	AB	H	HR	BA	PO	A	E	DP	TC/G	FA
1883	BAL	AA	9	13	.409	3.17	24	23	21	201.1	188	41	62	1	0	0	0	97	16	0	.165	10	50	12	1	3.0	.833
1884			32	17	.653	2.75	50	50	50	455.1	419	88	264	4	0	0	0	195	37	0	.190	27	83	22	0	2.6	.833
1885	2 teams						BAL AA (13G 3–10)			PHI AA (4G 0–4)																	
"	total		3	14	.176	4.71	17	17	14	135.2	168	36	36	0	0	0	0	63	13	0	.206	6	23	8	0	2.2	.784
3 yrs.			44	44	.500	3.19	91	90	85	792.1	775	165	362	5	0	0	0	355	66	0	.186	43	156	42	1	2.6	.826

Joe Engel

ENGEL, JOSEPH WILLIAM
B. Mar. 12, 1893, Washington, D. C.   D. June 12, 1969, Chattanooga, Tenn.
BR TL 6'1½" 183 lbs.

Year	Team		W	L	PCT	ERA	G	GS	CG	IP	H	BB	SO	ShO	W	L	SV	AB	H	HR	BA	PO	A	E	DP	TC/G	FA
1912	WAS	A	2	5	.286	3.96	17	10	2	75	70	50	29	0	1	0	1	17	1	0	.059	0	28	1	1	1.7	.966
1913			8	9	.471	3.06	36	23	6	164.2	124	85	70	2	1	0	0	49	3	0	.061	2	52	7	0	1.7	.885
1914			7	5	.583	2.97	35	15	1	124.1	108	75	41	0	2	1	3	28	3	0	.107	4	39	6	0	1.4	.878
1915			0	3	.000	3.21	11	3	0	33.2	30	19	9	0	0	0	0	6	0	0	.000	1	13	1	1	1.4	.933
1917	CIN	N	0	1	.000	5.63	1	1	1	8	12	6	2	0	0	0	0	3	0	0	.000	1	3	1	0	5.0	.800
1919	CLE	A	0	0	—	∞	1	0	0	0	3	3	0	0	0	0	0	0	0	0	—	0	0	0	0	0.0	—
1920	WAS	A	0	0	—	21.60	1	0	0	1.2	4	4	0	0	0	0	0	1	0	0	.000	0	0	0	0	0.0	—
7 yrs.			17	23	.425	3.38	102	52	10	407.1	344	242	151	2	4	1	4	104	7	0	.067	8	135	16	2	1.6	.899

Steve Engel

ENGEL, STEVEN MICHAEL
B. Dec. 31, 1961, Cincinnati, Ohio
BR TL 6'3" 210 lbs.

Year	Team		W	L	PCT	ERA	G	GS	CG	IP	H	BB	SO	ShO	W	L	SV	AB	H	HR	BA	PO	A	E	DP	TC/G	FA
1985	CHI	N	1	5	.167	5.57	11	8	1	51.2	61	26	29	0	0	0	1	16	3	1	.188	2	8	0	0	0.9	1.000

Rick Engle

ENGLE, RICHARD DOUGLAS
B. Apr. 7, 1957, Corbin, Ky.
BR TL 5'11½" 181 lbs.

Year	Team		W	L	PCT	ERA	G	GS	CG	IP	H	BB	SO	ShO	W	L	SV	AB	H	HR	BA	PO	A	E	DP	TC/G	FA
1981	MON	N	0	0	—	18.00	1	0	0	2	6	1	2	0	0	0	0	0	0	0	—	0	0	0	0	0.0	—

Jack Enright

ENRIGHT, JACKSON PERCY
B. Nov. 29, 1895, Fort Worth, Tex.   D. Aug. 17, 1975, Pompano Beach, Fla.
BR TR 5'11" 177 lbs.

Year	Team		W	L	PCT	ERA	G	GS	CG	IP	H	BB	SO	ShO	W	L	SV	AB	H	HR	BA	PO	A	E	DP	TC/G	FA
1917	NY	A	0	1	.000	5.40	1	1	0	5	5	3	1	0	0	0	0	1	0	0	.000	1	5	0	0	6.0	1.000

Terry Enyart

ENYART, TERRY GENE
B. Oct. 10, 1950, Ironton, Ohio
BR TL 6'2" 190 lbs.

Year	Team		W	L	PCT	ERA	G	GS	CG	IP	H	BB	SO	ShO	W	L	SV	AB	H	HR	BA	PO	A	E	DP	TC/G	FA
1974	MON	N	0	0	—	13.50	2	0	0	2	4	4	2	0	0	0	0	0	0	0	—	0	0	1	0	0.5	—

Johnny Enzmann

ENZMANN, JOHN (Gentleman John)
B. Mar. 4, 1890, Brooklyn, N. Y.   D. Mar. 14, 1984, Riverhead, N. Y.
BR TR 5'10" 165 lbs.

Year	Team		W	L	PCT	ERA	G	GS	CG	IP	H	BB	SO	ShO	W	L	SV	AB	H	HR	BA	PO	A	E	DP	TC/G	FA
1914	BKN	N	1	0	1.000	4.74	7	1	0	19	21	8	5	0	0	0	0	6	0	0	.000	0	9	1	1	1.4	.900
1918	CLE	A	5	7	.417	2.37	30	14	8	136.2	130	29	38	0	1	1	2	47	7	0	.149	7	39	1	0	1.6	.979
1919			3	2	.600	2.28	14	4	2	55.1	67	8	13	0	1	0	0	15	2	0	.133	0	14	0	2	1.0	1.000
1920	PHI	N	2	3	.400	3.84	16	1	1	58.2	79	16	35	0	1	2	0	24	4	0	.167	2	14	0	0	1.0	1.000
4 yrs.			11	12	.478	2.84	67	20	11	269.2	297	61	91	0	3	4	2	92	13	0	.141	9	76	2	3	1.3	.977

Al Epperly

EPPERLY, ALBERT PAUL (Pard)
B. May 7, 1918, Glidden, Iowa
BL TR 6'2" 194 lbs.

Year	Team		W	L	PCT	ERA	G	GS	CG	IP	H	BB	SO	ShO	W	L	SV	AB	H	HR	BA	PO	A	E	DP	TC/G	FA
1938	CHI	N	2	1	1.000	3.67	9	4	1	27	28	15	10	0	0	0	0	8	2	0	.250	1	6	0	0	0.8	1.000
1950	BKN	N	0	0	—	5.00	5	0	0	9	14	5	3	0	0	0	0	0	0	0	—	0	1	0	0	0.2	1.000
2 yrs.			2	0	1.000	4.00	14	4	1	36	42	20	13	0	0	0	0	8	2	0	.250	1	7	0	0	0.6	1.000

Joe Erardi

ERARDI, JOSEPH GREGORY
B. May 31, 1954, Syracuse, N. Y.
BR TR 6'1" 190 lbs.

Year	Team		W	L	PCT	ERA	G	GS	CG	IP	H	BB	SO	ShO	W	L	SV	AB	H	HR	BA	PO	A	E	DP	TC/G	FA
1977	SEA	A	0	1	.000	6.00	5	0	0	9	12	6	5	0	0	1	0	0	0	0	—	0	1	0	0	0.2	1.000

Eddie Erautt

ERAUTT, EDWARD LORENZ SEBASTIAN
Brother of Joe Erautt.
B. Sept. 26, 1924, Portland, Ore.
BR TR 5'11½" 185 lbs.

Year	Team		W	L	PCT	ERA	G	GS	CG	IP	H	BB	SO	ShO	W	L	SV	AB	H	HR	BA	PO	A	E	DP	TC/G	FA
1947	CIN	N	4	9	.308	5.07	36	10	2	119	146	53	43	0	3	2	0	29	2	0	.069	7	26	2	2	1.0	.943
1948			0	0	—	6.00	2	0	0	3	3	3	1	0	0	0	0	0	0	0	—	0	0	0	0	0.0	—
1949			4	11	.267	3.36	39	9	1	112.2	99	61	43	0	3	5	1	23	4	0	.174	3	18	1	0	0.6	.955
1950			4	2	.667	5.65	33	2	1	65.1	82	22	35	0	3	1	1	13	2	0	.154	4	9	0	0	0.4	1.000
1951			0	0	—	5.72	30	0	0	39.1	50	23	20	0	0	0	0	3	0	0	.000	2	4	0	1	0.2	1.000
1953	2 teams						CIN N (4G 0–0)			STL N (20G 3–1)																	
"	total		3	1	.750	6.25	24	1	0	40.1	54	19	16	0	0	0	0	7	1	0	.143	1	9	0	2	0.4	1.000
6 yrs.			15	23	.395	4.86	164	22	4	379.2	434	179	157	0	12	8	2	75	9	0	.120	17	66	3	5	0.5	.965

Don Erickson

ERICKSON, DON LEE
B. Dec. 13, 1931, Springfield, Ill.
BR TR 6' 175 lbs.

Year	Team		W	L	PCT	ERA	G	GS	CG	IP	H	BB	SO	ShO	W	L	SV	AB	H	HR	BA	PO	A	E	DP	TC/G	FA
1958	PHI	N	0	1	.000	4.63	9	0	0	11.2	11	9	9	0	0	1	1	0	0	0	.000	0	0	0	0	0.0	—

Eric Erickson

ERICKSON, ERIC GEORGE ADOLPH
B. Mar. 13, 1895, Goteborg, Sweden   D. May 19, 1965, Jamestown, N. Y.
BR TR 6'2" 190 lbs.

Year	Team		W	L	PCT	ERA	G	GS	CG	IP	H	BB	SO	ShO	W	L	SV	AB	H	HR	BA	PO	A	E	DP	TC/G	FA
1914	NY	N	0	1	.000	0.00	1	1	0	5	8	3	3	0	0	0	0	1	0	0	.000	0	0	0	0	0.0	—
1916	DET	A	0	0	—	2.81	8	0	0	16	13	8	7	0	0	0	0	4	0	0	.000	0	3	0	0	0.8	.500

Year	Team	W	L	PCT	ERA	G	GS	CG	IP	H	BB	SO	ShO	Relief Pitching W	L	SV	Batting AB	H	HR	BA	PO	A	E	DP	TC/G	FA

Eric Erickson *continued*

Year	Team	W	L	PCT	ERA	G	GS	CG	IP	H	BB	SO	ShO	W	L	SV	AB	H	HR	BA	PO	A	E	DP	TC/G	FA
1918		4	5	.444	2.48	12	9	8	94.1	81	29	48	0	0	1	1	33	4	0	.121	0	13	1	0	1.2	.929
1919	2 teams	DET A		(3G 0–2)	WAS A			(20G 6–11)																		
"	total	6	13	.316	4.23	23	17	7	146.2	147	73	90	1	1	1	0	53	8	0	.151	3	25	1	0	1.3	.966
1920	WAS A	12	16	.429	3.84	39	28	12	239.1	231	128	87	0	2	3	1	83	23	1	.277	9	44	4	0	1.5	.930
1921		8	10	.444	3.62	32	22	9	179	181	65	71	3	0	1	0	60	9	0	.150	5	32	2	0	1.2	.949
1922		4	12	.250	4.96	30	17	6	141.2	144	73	61	2	0	1	2	45	6	0	.133	6	23	4	2	1.1	.879
7 yrs.		34	57	.374	3.85	145	94	42	822	805	379	367	6	3	7	4	279	50	1	.179	23	140	15	2	1.2	.916

Hal Erickson

ERICKSON, HAROLD JAMES
B. July 17, 1919, Portland, Ore.
BR TR 6'5" 230 lbs.

Year	Team	W	L	PCT	ERA	G	GS	CG	IP	H	BB	SO	ShO	W	L	SV	AB	H	HR	BA	PO	A	E	DP	TC/G	FA
1953	DET A	0	1	.000	4.73	18	0	0	32.1	43	10	19	0	0	1	1	4	0	0	.000	3	3	0	0	0.3	1.000

Paul Erickson

ERICKSON, PAUL WALFORD (Li'l Abner)
B. Dec. 14, 1915, Zion, Ill.
BR TR 6'2½" 200 lbs.

Year	Team	W	L	PCT	ERA	G	GS	CG	IP	H	BB	SO	ShO	W	L	SV	AB	H	HR	BA	PO	A	E	DP	TC/G	FA
1941	CHI N	5	7	.417	3.70	32	15	7	141	126	64	85	1	0	0	1	46	7	1	.152	2	21	1	0	0.8	.958
1942		1	6	.143	5.43	18	7	1	63	70	41	26	0	1	0	0	21	3	0	.143	5	12	0	2	0.9	1.000
1943		1	3	.250	6.12	15	4	0	42.2	47	22	24	0	0	1	0	15	3	0	.200	1	6	0	0	0.5	1.000
1944		5	9	.357	3.55	33	15	5	124.1	113	67	82	3	1	2	1	36	2	1	.056	7	30	2	1	1.2	.949
1945		7	4	.636	3.32	28	9	3	108.1	94	48	53	0	2	2	3	32	5	0	.156	2	19	0	0	0.8	1.000
1946		9	7	.563	2.43	32	14	5	137	119	65	70	1	2	0	0	40	2	0	.050	5	22	0	0	0.8	1.000
1947		7	12	.368	4.34	40	20	6	174	179	93	82	0	3	1	1	60	15	1	.250	8	33	1	3	1.1	.976
1948	3 teams	CHI N		(3G 0–0)	PHI N		(4G 2–0)	NY N		(2G 0–0)																
"	total	2	0	1.000	5.25	9	2	0	24	26	25	10	0	0	0	0	8	1	0	.125	3	5	0	0	0.9	1.000
8 yrs.		37	48	.435	3.86	207	86	27	814.1	774	425	432	5	9	6	6	258	38	3	.147	33	148	4	6	0.9	.978

WORLD SERIES

Year	Team	W	L	PCT	ERA	G	GS	CG	IP	H	BB	SO	ShO	W	L	SV	AB	H	HR	BA	PO	A	E	DP	TC/G	FA
1945	CHI N	0	0	—	3.86	4	0	0	7	8	3	5	0	0	0	0	0	0	0	—	0	1	0	0	0.3	1.000

Ralph Erickson

ERICKSON, RALPH LEIF
B. June 25, 1904, Dubois, Ida.
BL TL 6'1" 175 lbs.

Year	Team	W	L	PCT	ERA	G	GS	CG	IP	H	BB	SO	ShO	W	L	SV	AB	H	HR	BA	PO	A	E	DP	TC/G	FA
1929	PIT N	0	0	—	27.00	1	0	0	1	2	2	0	0	0	0	0	0	0	0	—	0	0	0	0	0.0	—
1930		1	0	1.000	7.07	7	0	0	14	21	10	2	0	1	0	0	4	1	0	.250	1	3	0	0	0.6	1.000
2 yrs.		1	0	1.000	8.40	8	0	0	15	23	12	2	0	1	0	0	4	1	0	.250	1	3	0	0	0.5	1.000

Roger Erickson

ERICKSON, ROGER FARRELL
B. Aug. 30, 1956, Springfield, Ill.
BR TR 6'3" 180 lbs.

Year	Team	W	L	PCT	ERA	G	GS	CG	IP	H	BB	SO	ShO	W	L	SV	AB	H	HR	BA	PO	A	E	DP	TC/G	FA
1978	MIN A	14	13	.519	3.96	37	37	14	265.2	268	79	121	0	0	0	0	0	0	0	—	13	44	5	3	1.7	.919
1979		3	10	.231	5.63	24	21	0	123	154	48	47	0	0	0	0	0	0	0	—	9	17	2	1	1.2	.929
1980		7	13	.350	3.25	32	27	7	191	198	56	97	0	0	0	0	0	0	0	—	8	28	1	4	1.2	.973
1981		3	8	.273	3.86	14	14	1	91	93	31	44	0	0	0	0	0	0	0	—	8	13	2	1	1.6	.913
1982	2 teams	MIN A		(7G 4–3)	NY A		(16G 4–5)																			
"	total	8	8	.500	4.61	23	18	2	111.1	142	29	49	0	0	0	1	0	0	0	—	6	14	1	0	0.9	.952
1983	NY A	0	1	.000	4.32	5	0	0	16.2	13	8	7	0	0	1	0	0	0	0	—	4	2	0	0	1.2	1.000
6 yrs.		35	53	.398	4.14	135	117	24	798.2	868	251	365	0	0	2	1	0	0	0	—	48	118	11	9	1.3	.938

Dick Errickson

ERRICKSON, RICHARD MERRIWELL (Lief)
B. Mar. 4, 1914, Vineland, N. J.
BL TR 6'1" 175 lbs.

Year	Team	W	L	PCT	ERA	G	GS	CG	IP	H	BB	SO	ShO	W	L	SV	AB	H	HR	BA	PO	A	E	DP	TC/G	FA
1938	BOS N	9	7	.563	3.15	34	10	6	122.2	113	56	40	1	3	3	6	35	4	0	.114	6	34	2	0	1.2	.952
1939		6	9	.400	4.00	28	11	3	128.1	143	54	33	0	1	3	1	44	10	0	.227	5	36	2	0	1.5	.953
1940		12	13	.480	3.16	34	29	17	236.1	241	90	34	3	0	0	4	83	13	0	.157	9	58	2	5	2.0	.971
1941		6	12	.333	4.78	38	23	5	165.2	192	62	45	2	1	1	1	45	8	0	.178	7	39	1	0	1.2	.979
1942	2 teams	BOS N		(21G 2–5)	CHI N		(13G 1–1)																			
"	total	3	6	.333	4.75	34	4	0	83.1	115	28	24	0	1	5	1	21	2	0	.095	2	18	0	1	0.6	1.000
5 yrs.		36	47	.434	3.85	168	77	31	736.1	804	290	176	6	6	12	13	228	37	0	.162	29	185	7	6	1.3	.968

Carl Erskine

ERSKINE, CARL DANIEL (Oisk)
B. Dec. 13, 1926, Anderson, Ind.
BR TR 5'10" 165 lbs.

Year	Team	W	L	PCT	ERA	G	GS	CG	IP	H	BB	SO	ShO	W	L	SV	AB	H	HR	BA	PO	A	E	DP	TC/G	FA
1948	BKN N	6	3	.667	3.23	17	9	3	64	51	35	29	0	3	0	1	21	2	0	.095	2	6	1	2	0.5	.889
1949		8	1	.889	4.63	22	3	2	79.2	68	51	49	0	6	1	0	26	3	0	.115	3	13	1	2	0.8	.941
1950		7	6	.538	4.72	22	13	3	103	109	35	50	0	1	0	1	37	9	0	.243	10	12	2	2	1.1	.917
1951		16	12	.571	4.46	46	19	7	189.2	206	78	95	0	9	7	4	61	8	0	.131	13	32	2	1	1.0	.957
1952		14	6	.700	2.70	33	26	10	206.2	167	71	131	4	1	1	2	66	10	0	.152	16	45	3	4	1.9	.953
1953		20	6	**.769**	3.54	39	33	16	246.2	213	95	187	4	1	0	3	93	20	0	.215	15	30	4	0	1.3	.918
1954		18	15	.545	4.15	38	37	12	260.1	239	92	166	2	0	0	1	88	14	0	.159	14	41	2	2	1.5	.965
1955		11	8	.579	3.79	31	29	7	194.2	185	64	84	2	1	0	1	74	15	1	.203	6	26	3	1	1.1	.914
1956		13	11	.542	4.25	31	28	6	186.1	189	57	95	1	2	1	0	66	8	0	.121	4	34	1	2	1.4	.977
1957		5	3	.625	3.55	15	7	1	66	62	20	26	0	1	0	0	22	2	0	.091	9	5	0	0	0.7	1.000
1958	LA N	4	4	.500	5.13	31	9	2	98.1	115	35	54	1	1	1	0	27	1	0	.037	10	15	1	4	0.8	.962
1959		0	3	.000	7.71	10	3	0	23.1	33	13	15	0	0	0	1	7	0	0	.000	1	3	0	0	0.4	1.000
12 yrs.		122	78	.610	4.00	335	216	71	1718.2	1637	646	981	14	26	12	13	588	92	1	.156	105	262	20	20	1.2	.948

WORLD SERIES

Year	Team	W	L	PCT	ERA	G	GS	CG	IP	H	BB	SO	ShO	W	L	SV	AB	H	HR	BA	PO	A	E	DP	TC/G	FA
1949	BKN N	0	0	—	16.20	2	0	0	1.2	3	1	0	0	0	0	0	0	0	0	—	0	0	0	0	0.0	—
1952		1	1	.500	4.50	3	2	1	18	12	10	10	0	0	0	0	6	0	0	.000	0	2	0	0	0.7	1.000
1953		1	0	1.000	5.79	3	3	1	14	14	9	16	0	0	0	0	4	1	0	.250	1	4	0	0	1.7	1.000
1955		0	0	—	9.00	1	1	0	3	3	2	3	0	0	0	0	1	0	0	.000	0	1	0	0	1.0	1.000
1956		0	1	.000	5.40	2	1	0	5	4	2	2	0	0	0	0	1	0	0	.000	1	0	0	0	1.5	1.000
5 yrs.		2	2	.500	5.83	11	7	2	41.2	36	24	31	0	0	0	0	12	1	0	.083	2	7	0	0	0.9	.900

10th

Year	Team		W	L	PCT	ERA	G	GS	CG	IP	H	BB	SO	ShO	W	L	SV	AB	H	HR	BA	PO	A	E	DP	TC/G	FA
															Relief Pitching			**Batting**									

Ernesto Escarrega

ESCARREGA, ERNESTO (Chico)
Born Ernesto Escarrega y Acosta.
B. Dec. 27, 1949, Los Mochis, Mexico

BR TR 5'11" 185 lbs.

Year	Team	W	L	PCT	ERA	G	GS	CG	IP	H	BB	SO	ShO	W	L	SV	AB	H	HR	BA	PO	A	E	DP	TC/G	FA
1982	CHI A	1	3	.250	3.67	38	2	0	73.2	73	16	33	0	1	1	1	0	0	0	–	6	7	0	1	0.3	1.000

Duke Esper

ESPER, CHARLES H.
B. July 28, 1868, Salem, N. J.   D. Aug. 31, 1910, Philadelphia, Pa.

TL 5'11½" 185 lbs.

Year	Team	W	L	PCT	ERA	G	GS	CG	IP	H	BB	SO	ShO	W	L	SV	AB	H	HR	BA	PO	A	E	DP	TC/G	FA
1890	3 teams	PHI AA (18G 8–9)				PIT N (2G 0–2)			PHI N (5G 5–0)																	
"	total	13	11	.542	4.55	25	23	20	201.2	234	93	88	1	1	0	0	87	22	0	.253	12	43	3	3	2.3	.948
1891	PHI N	20	15	.571	3.56	39	36	25	296	302	121	108	1	0	0	0	123	27	0	.220	4	67	4	2	1.9	.947
1892	2 teams	PHI N (21G 11–6)				PIT N (3G 2–0)																				
"	total	13	6	.684	3.63	24	21	15	178.2	189	70	50	0	1	0	1	79	17	1	.215	8	36	1	1	1.9	.978
1893	WAS N	12	28	.300	4.71	42	36	34	334.1	442	156	78	1	2	2	0	143	41	0	.287	14	79	9	0	2.4	.912
1894	2 teams	WAS N (19G 5–10)				BAL N (16G 10–2)																				
"	total	15	12	.556	5.86	35	24	15	224.1	298	76	52	0	3	2	0	102	26	1	.255	14	43	1	2	1.7	.983
1895	BAL N	10	12	.455	3.92	34	25	16	218.1	248	79	39	1	1	4	1	90	16	0	.178	5	43	6	0	1.6	.889
1896		14	5	.737	3.58	20	18	14	155.2	168	39	19	1	2	0	0	66	13	0	.197	4	32	1	0	1.9	.973
1897	STL N	1	6	.143	5.28	8	8	7	61.1	95	12	8	0	0	0	0	25	8	0	.320	5	19	0	0	3.0	1.000
1898		3	5	.375	5.98	10	8	6	64.2	86	22	14	0	0	0	0	27	10	0	.370	2	17	1	0	2.0	.950
9 yrs.		101	100	.502	4.40	237	199	152	1735	2062	668	456	4	11	8	5	742	180	2	.243	68	379	26	8	2.0	.945

Nino Espinosa

ESPINOSA, ARNULFO
Born Arnulfo Acevedo y Espinosa.
B. Aug. 15, 1953, Villa Altagracia, Dominican Republic
D. Dec. 24, 1987, Santo Domingo, Dominican Republic

BR TR 6'1" 165 lbs.

Year	Team	W	L	PCT	ERA	G	GS	CG	IP	H	BB	SO	ShO	W	L	SV	AB	H	HR	BA	PO	A	E	DP	TC/G	FA
1974	NY N	0	0	–	5.00	2	1	0	9	12	0	2	0	0	0	0	2	1	0	.500	0	2	0	0	1.0	1.000
1975		0	1	.000	18.00	2	0	0	3	8	1	2	0	1	0	0	0	0	0	–	0	0	0	0	0.3	–
1976		4	4	.500	3.64	12	5	0	42	41	13	30	0	2	2	0	9	0	0	.000	0	3	0	0	1.3	1.000
1977		10	13	.435	3.42	32	29	7	200	188	55	105	1	1	0	0	62	8	0	.129	16	25	0	4	1.3	1.000
1978		11	15	.423	4.72	32	32	6	204	230	75	76	1	0	0	0	67	14	0	.209	10	47	1	2	1.8	.983
1979	PHI N	14	12	.538	3.65	33	33	8	212	211	65	88	3	0	0	0	72	14	0	.194	11	34	2	2	1.4	.957
1980		3	5	.375	3.79	12	12	1	76	73	19	13	0	0	0	0	26	3	0	.115	8	10	1	0	1.6	.947
1981	2 teams	PHI N (14G 2–5)				TOR A (1G 0–0)																				
"	total	2	5	.286	6.12	15	14	2	75	102	24	22	0	0	0	0	20	4	0	.200	6	8	0	0	0.9	1.000
8 yrs.		44	55	.444	4.17	140	126	24	821	865	252	338	5	3	3	0	258	44	0	.171	51	129	4	8	1.3	.978

Mark Esser

ESSER, MARK GERALD
B. Apr. 1, 1956, Erie, Pa.

BR TL 6'1" 190 lbs.

Year	Team	W	L	PCT	ERA	G	GS	CG	IP	H	BB	SO	ShO	W	L	SV	AB	H	HR	BA	PO	A	E	DP	TC/G	FA
1979	CHI A	0	0	–	13.50	2	0	0	2	4	1	0	0	0	0	0	0	0	0	–	0	0	0	0	0.0	–

Bill Essick

ESSICK, WILLIAM EARL (Vinegar Bill)
B. Dec. 18, 1881, Grand Ridge, Ill.   D. Oct. 12, 1951, Los Angeles, Calif.

TR

Year	Team	W	L	PCT	ERA	G	GS	CG	IP	H	BB	SO	ShO	W	L	SV	AB	H	HR	BA	PO	A	E	DP	TC/G	FA
1906	CIN N	2	1	.667	2.97	6	4	3	39.1	39	16	16	0	0	0	0	13	1	0	.077	2	5	0	0	1.2	1.000
1907		0	2	.000	2.91	3	2	2	21.2	23	8	7	0	0	0	0	8	0	0	.000	0	11	1	0	4.0	.917
2 yrs.		2	3	.400	2.95	9	6	5	61	62	24	23	0	0	0	0	21	1	0	.048	2	16	1	0	2.1	.947

Dick Estelle

ESTELLE, RICHARD HENRY
B. Jan. 18, 1942, Lakewood, N. J.

BB TL 6'2" 170 lbs.

Year	Team	W	L	PCT	ERA	G	GS	CG	IP	H	BB	SO	ShO	W	L	SV	AB	H	HR	BA	PO	A	E	DP	TC/G	FA
1964	SF N	1	2	.333	3.02	6	6	0	41.2	39	23	23	0	0	0	0	15	1	0	.067	2	3	0	0	0.8	1.000
1965		0	0	–	3.97	6	1	0	11.1	12	8	6	0	0	0	0	1	0	0	.000	1	3	1	0	0.8	.800
2 yrs.		1	2	.333	3.23	12	7	0	53	51	31	29	0	0	0	0	16	1	0	.063	3	6	1	0	0.8	.900

George Estock

ESTOCK, GEORGE JOHN
B. Nov. 2, 1924, Stirling, N. J.

BR TR 6' 185 lbs.

Year	Team	W	L	PCT	ERA	G	GS	CG	IP	H	BB	SO	ShO	W	L	SV	AB	H	HR	BA	PO	A	E	DP	TC/G	FA
1951	BOS N	0	1	.000	4.33	37	1	0	60.1	56	37	11	0	0	0	3	7	2	0	.286	4	13	1	1	0.5	.944

Chuck Estrada

ESTRADA, CHARLES LEONARD
B. Feb. 15, 1938, San Luis Obispo, Calif.

BR TR 6'1" 185 lbs.

Year	Team	W	L	PCT	ERA	G	GS	CG	IP	H	BB	SO	ShO	W	L	SV	AB	H	HR	BA	PO	A	E	DP	TC/G	FA
1960	BAL A	18	11	.621	3.58	36	25	12	208.2	162	101	144	1	5	2	2	64	9	0	.141	8	29	0	4	1.0	1.000
1961		15	9	.625	3.69	33	31	6	212	159	132	160	0	0	0	0	70	8	0	.114	19	17	1	1	1.1	.973
1962		9	17	.346	3.83	34	33	6	223.1	199	121	165	0	0	0	0	66	10	1	.152	7	24	2	1	1.0	.939
1963		3	2	.600	4.60	8	7	0	31.1	26	19	16	0	0	0	0	10	1	0	.100	3	2	0	0	0.6	1.000
1964		3	2	.600	5.27	17	6	0	54.2	62	21	32	0	1	2	0	14	2	0	.143	2	3	0	0	0.3	1.000
1966	CHI N	1	1	.500	7.30	9	1	0	12.1	16	5	3	0	0	0	0	3	0	0	.000	0	1	0	0	0.1	1.000
1967	NY N	1	2	.333	9.41	9	2	0	22	28	17	15	0	1	0	0	5	0	0	.000	2	2	0	0	0.4	1.000
7 yrs.		50	44	.532	4.07	146	105	24	764.1	652	416	535	2	7	4	2	232	30	1	.129	41	78	3	6	0.8	.975

Oscar Estrada

ESTRADA, OSCAR
B. Feb. 15, 1904, Havana, Cuba   D. Jan. 2, 1978, Havana, Cuba

BL TL 5'8" 160 lbs.

Year	Team	W	L	PCT	ERA	G	GS	CG	IP	H	BB	SO	ShO	W	L	SV	AB	H	HR	BA	PO	A	E	DP	TC/G	FA
1929	STL A	0	0	–	0.00	1	0	0	1	1	1	0	0	0	0	0	0	0	0	–	0	1	0	0	1.0	1.000

John Eubank

EUBANK, JOHN FRANKLIN (Honest John)
B. Sept. 9, 1872, Servia, Ind.   D. Nov. 3, 1958, Bellevue, Mich.

BR TR 6'2" 215 lbs.

Year	Team	W	L	PCT	ERA	G	GS	CG	IP	H	BB	SO	ShO	W	L	SV	AB	H	HR	BA	PO	A	E	DP	TC/G	FA
1905	DET A	1	0	1.000	2.08	3	2	0	17.1	13	3	3	0	0	0	0	11	4	0	.364	1	3	1	0	1.7	.800
1906		4	10	.286	3.53	24	12	7	135	147	35	38	1	1	1	2	60	12	0	.200	4	49	3	0	2.3	.946
1907		3	3	.500	2.67	15	8	4	81	88	20	17	1	1	1	0	31	4	0	.129	3	32	2	0	2.5	.946
3 yrs.		8	13	.381	3.12	42	22	11	233.1	248	58	56	2	2	2	2	102	20	0	.196	8	84	6	0	2.3	.939

Year	Team		W	L	PCT	ERA	G	GS	CG	IP	H	BB	SO	ShO	Relief Pitching W	L	SV	Batting AB	H	HR	BA	PO	A	E	DP	TC/G	FA

Uel Eubanks

EUBANKS, UEL MELVIN (Poss)
B. Feb. 14, 1903, Quinlan, Tex.   D. Nov. 21, 1954, Dallas, Tex.
BR TR 6'3" 175 lbs.

| 1922 | CHI | N | 0 | 0 | – | 27.00 | 2 | 0 | 0 | 1.2 | 5 | 4 | 1 | 0 | 0 | 0 | 0 | 1 | 1 | 0 | 1.000 | 0 | 1 | 0 | 0 | 0.5 | 1.000 |

Frank Eufemia

EUFEMIA, FRANK ANTHONY
B. Dec. 23, 1959, Bronx, N. Y.
BR TR 5'11" 185 lbs.

| 1985 | MIN | A | 4 | 2 | .667 | 3.79 | 39 | 0 | 0 | 61.2 | 56 | 21 | 30 | 0 | 4 | 2 | 2 | 0 | 0 | 0 | – | 4 | 12 | 0 | 1 | 0.4 | 1.000 |

Art Evans

EVANS, WILLIAM ARTHUR
B. Aug. 3, 1911, Elvins, Mo.   D. Jan. 8, 1952, Wichita, Kans.
BB TL 6'1½" 181 lbs.

| 1932 | CHI | A | 0 | 0 | – | 3.00 | 7 | 0 | 0 | 18 | 19 | 10 | 6 | 0 | 0 | 0 | 0 | 5 | 0 | 0 | .000 | 4 | 4 | 0 | 1 | 1.1 | 1.000 |

Bill Evans

EVANS, WILLIAM JAMES
B. Feb. 10, 1894, Reidsville, N. C.   D. Dec. 21, 1946, Burlington, N. C.
BR TR 6' 175 lbs.

1916	PIT	N	2	5	.286	3.00	13	6	3	63	57	16	21	0	1	0	0	20	3	0	.150	5	23	1	4	2.2	.966
1917			0	4	.000	3.38	8	2	1	26.2	24	14	5	0	0	2	0	9	1	0	.111	1	7	0	0	1.0	1.000
1919			0	4	.000	5.65	7	3	2	36.2	41	18	15	0	0	1	0	11	0	0	.000	6	11	0	0	2.4	1.000
3 yrs.			2	13	.133	3.85	28	11	6	126.1	122	48	41	0	1	3	0	40	4	0	.100	12	41	1	4	1.9	.981

Bill Evans

EVANS, WILLIAM LAWRENCE
B. Mar. 25, 1919, Quanah, Tex.   D. Nov. 30, 1983, Grand Junction, Colo.
BR TR 6'2" 180 lbs.

1949	CHI	A	0	1	.000	7.11	4	0	0	6.1	6	8	1	0	0	1	0	1	0	0	.000	0	0	0	0	0.0	–
1951	BOS	A	0	0	–	4.11	9	0	0	15.1	15	8	3	0	0	0	0	4	0	0	.000	1	2	0	0	0.3	1.000
2 yrs.			0	1	.000	4.98	13	0	0	21.2	21	16	4	0	0	1	0	5	0	0	.000	1	2	0	0	0.2	1.000

Chick Evans

EVANS, CHARLES FRANKLIN
B. Oct. 15, 1889, Arlington, Vt.   D. Sept. 2, 1916, Schenectady, N. Y.
BR TR

1909	BOS	N	0	3	.000	4.57	4	3	1	21.2	25	14	11	0	0	0	0	9	0	0	.000	0	7	3	0	2.5	.700
1910			1	1	.500	5.23	13	1	0	31	28	27	12	0	1	0	0	10	1	0	.100	0	10	0	1	0.8	1.000
2 yrs.			1	4	.200	4.96	17	4	1	52.2	53	41	23	0	1	0	0	19	1	0	.053	0	17	3	1	1.2	.850

Jake Evans

EVANS, JACOB (Bloody Jake)
B. Baltimore, Md.   D. Feb. 3, 1907, Baltimore, Md.
TR 5'8" 154 lbs.

1880	TRO	N	0	0	–	13.50	1	0	0	4	11	0	0	0	0	0	0	180	46	0	.256	1	2	0		3.0	1.000
1882	WOR	N	0	1	.000	5.63	1	1	1	8	13	0	2	0	0	0	0	334	71	0	.213	0	0	0		0.0	–
1883	CLE	N	0	0	–	0.00	1	0	0	3	0	0	1	0	0	0	0	332	79	0	.238	0	4	1	0	5.0	.800
3 yrs.			0	1	.000	6.60	3	1	1	15	24	0	3	0	0	0	0	*				1	6	1	0	2.7	.875

Red Evans

EVANS, RUSSELL EDISON
B. Nov. 12, 1906, Chicago, Ill.   D. June 14, 1982, Lakeview, Ark.
BR TR 5'11" 168 lbs.

1936	CHI	A	0	3	.000	7.61	17	0	0	47.1	70	22	19	0	0	3	1	15	2	0	.133	3	15	1	0	1.1	.947
1939	BKN	N	1	8	.111	5.18	24	6	0	64.1	74	26	28	0	1	2	1	13	4	0	.308	5	18	1	0	1.0	.958
2 yrs.			1	11	.083	6.21	41	6	0	111.2	144	48	47	0	1	5	2	28	6	0	.214	8	33	2	0	1.0	.953

Roy Evans

EVANS, ROY
B. Mar. 19, 1874, Knoxville, Tenn.   D. Aug. 15, 1915, Galveston, Tex.
BR TR 6' 180 lbs.

1897	2 teams		STL	N	(3G 0–0)		LOU	N	(9G 5–4)																			
"	total		5	4	.556	5.10	12	8	6	72.1	99	37	24	0	0	1	0	26	3	0	.115	1	11	2	0	1.2	.857
1898	WAS	N	3	3	.500	3.38	7	6	4	50.2	50	25	11	0	0	0	0	19	1	0	.053	1	8	2	0	1.6	.818
1899			3	4	.429	5.67	7	7	6	54	60	25	27	0	0	0	0	20	4	0	.200	2	12	2	0	2.3	.875
1902	2 teams		NY	N	(23G 8–13)		BKN	N	(13G 5–6)																			
"	total		13	19	.406		36	28	28	273.1	277	91	83	2	2	3	0	88	17	0	.193	16	62	7	3	2.4	.918
1903	2 teams		BKN	N	(15G 4–8)		STL	A	(7G 0–4)																			
"	total		4	12	.250	3.57	22	19	13	164	187	55	66	0	1	1	0	48	7	0	.146	4	40	4	1	2.2	.917
5 yrs.			28	42	.400	3.66	84	68	57	614.1	673	233	211	2	3	5	0	201	32	0	.159	24	133	17	4	2.1	.902

Leon Everitt

EVERITT, EDWARD LEON
B. Jan. 12, 1947, Marshall, Tex.
BL TR 6'1½" 195 lbs.

| 1969 | SD | N | 0 | 1 | .000 | 7.88 | 5 | 0 | 0 | 16 | 18 | 12 | 11 | 0 | 0 | 1 | 0 | 3 | 0 | 0 | .000 | 0 | 5 | 0 | 0 | 1.0 | 1.000 |

Bob Ewing

EWING, GEORGE LEMUEL (Long Bob)
B. Apr. 24, 1873, New Hampshire, Ohio   D. June 20, 1947, Wapakoneta, Ohio
BR TR 6'1½" 170 lbs.

1902	CIN	N	6	6	.500	2.98	15	12	10	117.2	126	47	44	0	0	0	0	71	12	0	.169	4	27	2	0	2.2	.939
1903			14	13	.519	2.77	29	28	27	246.2	254	64	104	1	0	0	1	95	24	0	.253	12	80	4	3	3.3	.958
1904			11	13	.458	2.46	26	24	22	212	198	58	99	0	1	0	0	97	25	0	.258	10	50	2	3	2.4	.968
1905			20	11	.645	2.51	40	34	30	312	284	79	164	4	0	0	0	122	32	0	.262	9	70	5	1	2.1	.940
1906			13	14	.481	2.38	33	32	26	287.2	248	60	145	2	0	1	0	101	14	1	.139	19	76	5	1	2.9	.990
1907			17	19	.472	1.73	41	37	32	332.2	279	85	147	2	1	1	0	123	19	1	.154	14	60	3	2	1.9	.961
1908			17	15	.531	2.21	37	34	23	293.2	247	57	95	4	1	1	3	94	14	0	.149	11	69	3	0	2.2	.964
1909			11	12	.478	2.43	31	29	14	218.1	195	63	86	2	0	1	0	73	8	0	.110	7	42	8	1	1.8	.860
1910	PHI	N	16	14	.533	3.00	34	32	20	255.1	235	86	102	4	0	1	0	90	20	0	.222	5	60	2	2	2.0	.970
1911			0	1	.000	7.88	4	3	1	24	29	14	12	0	0	0	0	6	2	0	.333	1	5	0	0	1.5	1.000
1912	STL	N	0	0	–	0.00	1	0	0	1.1	2	1	0	0	0	0	0	1	0	0	–	1	0	0	0	1.0	1.000
11 yrs.			125	118	.514	2.49	291	264	205	2301.1	2097	614	998	19	6	5	4	872	170	3	.195	93	539	30	15	2.3	.955

Buck Ewing

EWING, WILLIAM
Brother of John Ewing.
B. Oct. 17, 1859, Hoaglands, Ohio   D. Oct. 20, 1906, Cincinnati, Ohio
Manager 1890, 1895-1900.
Hall of Fame 1939.
BR TR 5'10" 188 lbs.

Year	Team	W	L	PCT	ERA	G	GS	CG	IP	H	BB	SO	ShO	Relief Pitching W	L	SV	Batting AB	H	HR	BA	PO	A	E	DP	TC/G	FA

Buck Ewing *continued*

Year	Team	W	L	PCT	ERA	G	GS	CG	IP	H	BB	SO	ShO	W	L	SV	AB	H	HR	BA	PO	A	E	DP	TC/G	FA
1882	TRO N	0	0	—	9.00	1	0	0	1	2	1	0	0	0	0	0	328	89	2	.271	0	1	0	0	1.0	1.000
1884	NY N	0	1	.000	1.13	1	1	1	8	7	4	3	0	0	0	0	382	106	3	.277	0	1	0	0	1.0	1.000
1885		0	1	.000	4.50	1	0	0	2	4	3	0	0	0	0	1	342	104	6	.304	0	0	0	0	0.0	—
1888		0	0	—	2.57	2	0	0	7	8	4	6	0	0	0	0	415	127	6	.306	0	0	0	0	0.0	—
1889		2	0	1.000	4.05	3	2	2	20	23	8	12	0	0	0	0	407	133	4	.327	0	3	2	0	1.7	.600
1890	NY P	0	1	.000	4.00	1	1	1	9	11	3	2	0	0	0	0	352	119	8	.338	0	2	2	1	4.0	.500
6 yrs.		2	3	.400	3.45	9	4	4	47	55	23	23	0	0	0	1	*				0	7	4	1	1.2	.636

John Ewing   TR

EWING, JOHN
Brother of Buck Ewing.
B. June 1, 1863, Cincinnati, Ohio   D. Apr. 23, 1895, Denver, Colo.

Year	Team	W	L	PCT	ERA	G	GS	CG	IP	H	BB	SO	ShO	W	L	SV	AB	H	HR	BA	PO	A	E	DP	TC/G	FA
1883	STL AA	0	0	—	0.00	0	0	0	0	0	0	0	0	0	0	0	5	0	0	.000	0	0	0	0	0.0	—
1884	CIN U	0	0	—	0.00	0	0	0	0	0	0	0	0	0	0	0	9	1	0	.111	0	0	0	0	0.0	—
1888	LOU AA	8	13	.381	2.83	21	21	21	191	175	34	87	2	0	0	0	79	16	0	.203	4	44	5	0	2.5	.906
1889		6	30	.167	4.87	40	39	37	331	407	147	155	1	0	0	0	134	23	0	.172	9	73	4	3	2.2	.953
1890	NY P	18	12	.600	4.24	35	31	27	267.1	293	104	145	1	1	0	2	114	24	1	.211	14	61	4	1	2.3	.949
1891	NY N	21	8	.724	2.27	33	30	28	269.1	237	105	138	5	1	0	0	113	23	0	.204	17	49	6	3	2.2	.917
6 yrs.		53	63	.457	3.68	129	121	113	1058.2	1112	390	525	9	2	0	2	454	87	2	.192	44	227	19	7	2.2	.934

George Eyrich   BR TR 5'11" 175 lbs.

EYRICH, GEORGE LINCOLN
B. Mar. 3, 1925, Reading, Pa.

Year	Team	W	L	PCT	ERA	G	GS	CG	IP	H	BB	SO	ShO	W	L	SV	AB	H	HR	BA	PO	A	E	DP	TC/G	FA
1943	PHI N	0	0	—	3.38	9	0	0	18.2	23	9	5	0	0	0	0	2	0	0	.000	1	3	0	0	0.4	1.000

Red Faber   BB TR 6'2" 180 lbs. / BR 1925

FABER, URBAN CHARLES
B. Sept. 6, 1888, Cascade, Iowa
D. Sept. 25, 1976, Chicago, Ill.
Hall of Fame 1964.

Year	Team	W	L	PCT	ERA	G	GS	CG	IP	H	BB	SO	ShO	W	L	SV	AB	H	HR	BA	PO	A	E	DP	TC/G	FA
1914	CHI A	10	9	.526	2.68	40	20	11	181.1	154	64	88	2	2	2	4	55	8	0	.145	7	58	2	3	1.7	.970
1915		24	14	.632	2.55	50	32	22	299.2	264	99	182	3	5	4	2	84	11	0	.131	7	85	8	4	2.0	.920
1916		17	9	.654	2.02	35	25	15	205.1	167	61	87	3	2	1	1	63	6	0	.095	3	71	5	1	2.3	.937
1917		16	13	.552	1.92	41	29	16	248	224	85	84	3	2	3	3	69	4	0	.058	13	84	8	0	2.6	.924
1918		4	1	.800	1.23	11	9	5	80.2	70	23	26	1	0	1	0	24	1	0	.042	1	29	1	1	2.8	.968
1919		11	9	.550	3.83	25	20	9	162.1	185	45	45	0	3	0	0	54	10	0	.185	6	48	5	1	2.4	.915
1920		23	13	.639	2.99	40	39	28	319	332	88	108	2	0	0	1	104	11	0	.106	15	78	10	5	2.6	.903
1921		25	15	.625	2.48	43	39	32	330.2	293	87	124	4	1	1	1	108	16	0	.148	10	90	5	3	2.4	.952
1922		21	17	.553	2.80	43	38	31	353	334	83	148	4	1	1	2	125	25	0	.200	4	94	4	1	2.4	.961
1923		14	11	.560	3.41	32	31	15	232.1	233	62	91	2	0	1	0	69	15	1	.217	8	70	4	3	2.6	.951
1924		9	11	.450	3.85	21	20	9	161.1	173	58	47	0	0	1	0	54	8	0	.148	4	31	1	1	1.7	.972
1925		12	11	.522	3.78	34	32	16	238	266	59	71	0	0	1	0	77	8	0	.104	13	67	4	1	2.5	.952
1926		15	9	.625	3.56	27	25	13	184.2	203	57	65	1	0	2	0	60	9	0	.150	1	33	2	1	1.3	.944
1927		4	7	.364	4.55	18	15	6	110.2	131	41	39	0	0	0	0	37	10	0	.270	5	37	0	0	2.3	1.000
1928		13	9	.591	3.75	27	27	16	201.1	223	68	43	0	0	0	0	70	8	0	.114	11	52	1	2	2.4	.984
1929		13	13	.500	3.88	31	31	15	234	241	61	68	0	1	0	0	78	10	1	.128	7	61	2	1	2.3	.971
1930		8	13	.381	4.21	29	26	10	169	188	49	62	0	0	0	1	49	2	0	.041	3	47	1	2	1.8	.980
1931		10	14	.417	3.82	44	19	5	184	210	57	49	1	5	2	1	53	4	0	.075	6	33	3	0	1.0	.929
1932		2	11	.154	3.74	42	5	0	106	123	38	26	0	2	6	6	18	4	0	.222	3	21	1	1	0.6	.960
1933		3	4	.429	3.44	36	2	0	86.1	92	28	18	0	3	2	5	18	0	0	.000	3	19	4	1	0.7	.846
20 yrs.		254	213	.544	3.15	669	484	274	4087.2	4106	1213	1471	30	27	27	28	1269	170	3	.134	130	1108	71	33	2.0	.946

WORLD SERIES

Year	Team	W	L	PCT	ERA	G	GS	CG	IP	H	BB	SO	ShO	W	L	SV	AB	H	HR	BA	PO	A	E	DP	TC/G	FA
1917	CHI A	3	1	.750	2.33	4	3	2	27	21	3	9	0	1	0	0	7	1	0	.143	1	9	0	2	2.5	1.000

Roy Face   BB TR 5'8" 155 lbs. / BR 1953-59

FACE, ELROY LEON
B. Feb. 20, 1928, Stephentown, N. Y.

Year	Team	W	L	PCT	ERA	G	GS	CG	IP	H	BB	SO	ShO	W	L	SV	AB	H	HR	BA	PO	A	E	DP	TC/G	FA
1953	PIT N	6	8	.429	6.58	41	13	6	119	145	30	56	0	3	2	0	30	4	0	.133	11	12	0	1	0.6	1.000
1955		5	7	.417	3.58	42	10	4	125.2	128	40	84	0	1	1	5	26	3	0	.115	14	13	1	1	0.7	.964
1956		12	13	.480	3.52	68	3	0	135.1	131	42	96	0	11	12	6	26	5	0	.192	10	25	1	2	0.5	.972
1957		4	6	.400	3.07	59	1	0	93.2	97	24	53	0	4	6	10	16	2	0	.125	4	9	0	0	0.2	1.000
1958		5	2	.714	2.89	57	0	0	84	77	22	47	0	5	2	20	7	0	0	.000	6	18	0	0	0.4	1.000
1959		18	1	.947	2.70	57	0	0	93.1	91	25	69	0	18	1	10	13	3	0	.231	7	12	1	0	0.4	.950
1960		10	8	.556	2.90	68	0	0	114.2	93	29	72	0	10	8	24	17	7	0	.412	12	21	0	1	0.5	1.000
1961		6	12	.333	3.82	62	0	0	92	94	10	55	0	6	12	17	11	3	0	.273	13	22	3	2	0.6	.921
1962		8	7	.533	1.88	63	0	0	91	74	18	45	0	8	7	28	12	1	0	.083	4	12	2	3	0.3	.889
1963		3	9	.250	3.23	56	0	0	69.2	75	19	41	0	3	9	16	8	2	0	.250	6	17	3	1	0.5	.885
1964		3	3	.500	5.20	55	0	0	79.2	82	27	63	0	3	3	4	4	0	0	.000	8	11	0	1	0.3	1.000
1965		5	2	.714	2.66	16	0	0	20.1	20	7	14	0	5	2	4	1	0	0	.000	1	0	0	0	0.1	1.000
1966		6	6	.500	2.70	54	0	0	70	68	24	67	0	6	6	18	11	0	0	.000	2	15	2	1	0.4	.895
1967		7	5	.583	2.42	61	0	0	74.1	62	22	41	0	7	5	17	6	0	0	.000	2	6	0	0	0.2	1.000
1968	2 teams	PIT N	(43G 2-4)		DET A	(2G 0-0)																				
"	total	2	4	.333	2.55	45	0	0	53	48	8	35	0	2	4	13	4	0	0	.000	2	7	1	1	0.2	.900
1969	MON N	4	2	.667	3.94	44	0	0	59.1	62	15	34	0	4	2	5	2	1	0	.500	3	7	0	0	0.2	1.000
16 yrs.		104	95	.523	3.48	848	27	6	1375	1347	362	877	0	96	82	193	194	31	0	.160	104	212	14	15	0.4	.958
															6th	10th										

WORLD SERIES

Year	Team	W	L	PCT	ERA	G	GS	CG	IP	H	BB	SO	ShO	W	L	SV	AB	H	HR	BA	PO	A	E	DP	TC/G	FA
1960	PIT N	0	0	—	5.23	4	0	0	10.1	9	2	4	0	0	0	3	3	0	0	.000	0	2	0	0	0.5	1.000
																4th										

Tony Faeth   BR TR 6' 180 lbs.

FAETH, ANTHONY JOSEPH
B. July 9, 1893, Aberdeen, S. D.   D. Dec. 22, 1982, St. Paul, Minn.

Year	Team	W	L	PCT	ERA	G	GS	CG	IP	H	BB	SO	ShO	W	L	SV	AB	H	HR	BA	PO	A	E	DP	TC/G	FA
1919	CLE A	0	0	—	0.49	6	0	0	18.1	13	10	7	0	0	0	0	4	0	0	.000	0	4	0	0	0.7	1.000

Year	Team		W	L	PCT	ERA	G	GS	CG	IP	H	BB	SO	ShO	Relief Pitching W	L	SV	AB	H	HR	BA	PO	A	E	DP	TC/G	FA

Tony Faeth *continued*

| 1920 | | | 0 | 0 | – | 4.32 | 13 | 0 | 0 | 25 | 31 | 20 | 14 | 0 | 0 | 0 | 0 | 5 | 0 | 0 | .000 | 0 | 6 | 0 | 0 | 0.5 | 1.000 |
| 2 yrs. | | | 0 | 0 | – | 2.70 | 19 | 0 | 0 | 43.1 | 44 | 30 | 21 | 0 | 0 | 0 | 0 | 9 | 0 | 0 | .000 | 0 | 10 | 0 | 0 | 0.5 | 1.000 |

Bill Fagan

FAGAN, WILLIAM A. (Clinkers)
B. Feb. 15, 1869, Troy, N. Y.   D. Mar. 21, 1930, Troy, N. Y.

TL 5'11"   165 lbs.

1887	NY	AA	1	4	.200	4.00	6	6	6	45	55	24	12	0	0	0	0	21	3	0	.143	1	11	2	0	2.3	.857
1888	KC	AA	5	11	.313	5.69	17	17	15	142.1	179	75	49	0	0	0	0	65	14	0	.215	5	37	5	2	2.8	.894
2 yrs.			6	15	.286	5.28	23	23	21	187.1	234	99	61	0	0	0	0	86	17	0	.198	6	48	7	2	2.7	.885

Everett Fagan

FAGAN, EVERETT JOSEPH
B. Jan. 13, 1918, Pottersville, N. J.   D. Feb. 16, 1983, Morristown, N. J.

BR TR 6'   195 lbs.

1943	PHI	A	2	6	.250	6.27	18	2	0	37.1	41	14	9	0	2	4	3	7	0	0	.000	2	10	1	0	0.7	.923
1946			0	1	.000	4.80	20	0	0	45	47	24	12	0	0	1	0	14	4	0	.286	2	7	1	0	0.5	.900
2 yrs.			2	7	.222	5.47	38	2	0	82.1	88	38	21	0	2	5	3	21	4	0	.190	4	17	2	0	0.6	.913

Frank Fahey

FAHEY, FRANCIS RAYMOND
B. Jan. 22, 1896, Milford, Mass.   D. Mar. 19, 1954, Boston, Mass.

BB TR 6'1"   190 lbs.

| 1918 | PHI | A | 0 | 0 | – | 6.00 | 3 | 0 | 0 | 9 | 5 | 14 | 1 | 0 | 0 | 0 | 0 | * | | | | 0 | 0 | 0 | 0 | 0.0 | – |

Red Fahr

FAHR, GERALD WARREN
B. Dec. 9, 1924, Marmaduke, Ark.

BR TR 6'5"   185 lbs.

| 1951 | CLE | A | 0 | 0 | – | 4.76 | 5 | 0 | 0 | 5.2 | 11 | 2 | 0 | 0 | 0 | 0 | 0 | 0 | 0 | 0 | – | 0 | 1 | 0 | 0 | 0.2 | 1.000 |

Pete Fahrer

FAHRER, CLARENCE WILLIE
B. Mar. 10, 1890, Holgate, Ohio   D. June 10, 1967, Fremont, Mich.

BL TR 6'   190 lbs.

| 1914 | CIN | N | 0 | 0 | – | 1.13 | 5 | 0 | 0 | 8 | 4 | 2 | 0 | 0 | 0 | 0 | 0 | 1 | 0 | 0 | .000 | 1 | 3 | 0 | 0 | 0.8 | 1.000 |

Jim Fairbank

FAIRBANK, JAMES LEE (Smoky, Lee)
B. Mar. 17, 1881, Deansboro, N. Y.   D. Dec. 27, 1955, Utica, N. Y.

BR TR 5'10"   185 lbs.

1903	PHI	A	1	1	.500	4.88	4	1	1	24	33	12	10	0	0	0	1	10	1	0	.100	4	10	0	0	3.5	1.000
1904			0	1	.000	6.35	3	1	1	17	19	13	6	0	0	0	0	6	0	0	.000	0	10	0	0	3.3	1.000
2 yrs.			1	2	.333	5.49	7	2	2	41	52	25	16	0	0	0	1	16	1	0	.063	4	20	0	0	3.4	1.000

Rags Faircloth

FAIRCLOTH, JAMES LAMAR
B. Aug. 19, 1892, Kenton, Tenn.   D. Oct. 5, 1953, Tucson, Ariz.

BR TR 5'11"   160 lbs.

| 1919 | PHI | N | 0 | 0 | – | 9.00 | 2 | 0 | 0 | 2 | 5 | 0 | 0 | 0 | 0 | 0 | 0 | 0 | 0 | 0 | – | 0 | 1 | 0 | 0 | 0.5 | 1.000 |

Pete Falcone

FALCONE, PETER
B. Oct. 1, 1953, Brooklyn, N. Y.

BL TL 6'2"   185 lbs.

1975	SF	N	12	11	.522	4.17	34	32	3	190	171	111	131	1	0	0	0	65	4	0	.062	2	29	2	0	1.0	.939
1976	STL	N	12	16	.429	3.23	32	32	9	212	173	93	138	2	0	0	0	62	8	0	.129	3	14	0	0	0.5	1.000
1977			4	8	.333	5.44	27	22	1	124	130	61	75	1	0	1	1	41	10	0	.244	4	15	0	1	0.7	1.000
1978			2	7	.222	5.76	19	14	0	75	94	48	28	0	0	0	0	21	5	0	.238	2	5	0	0	0.5	.778
1979	NY	N	6	14	.300	4.16	33	31	1	184	194	76	113	1	0	0	0	52	9	0	.173	3	14	1	0	0.5	.944
1980			7	10	.412	4.53	37	23	1	157	163	58	109	0	1	1	1	41	6	0	.146	1	12	0	0	0.4	1.000
1981			5	3	.625	2.56	35	9	3	95	84	36	56	1	2	1	1	22	4	1	.182	2	9	1	0	0.3	.917
1982			8	10	.444	3.84	40	23	3	171	159	71	101	0	0	1	2	53	6	0	.113	2	16	0	1	0.5	1.000
1983	ATL	N	9	4	.692	3.63	33	15	2	106.2	102	60	59	0	2	1	0	26	3	0	.115	1	11	0	0	0.4	1.000
1984			5	7	.417	4.13	35	16	2	120	115	57	55	1	1	0	2	33	7	0	.212	0	17	1	0	0.5	.944
10 yrs.			70	90	.438	4.07	325	217	25	1434.2	1385	671	865	7	6	5	7	416	62	1	.149	18	144	7	3	0.5	.959

Chet Falk

FALK, CHESTER EMANUEL (Spot)
Brother of Bibb Falk.
B. May 15, 1905, Austin, Tex.   D. Jan. 7, 1982, Austin, Tex.

BL TL 6'2"   170 lbs.

1925	STL	A	0	0	–	8.28	13	0	0	25	38	17	7	0	0	0	0	8	5	0	.625	0	8	0	0	0.6	1.000
1926			4	4	.500	5.35	18	8	3	74	95	27	7	0	1	0	0	31	6	0	.194	3	16	1	4	1.1	.950
1927			1	0	1.000	5.74	9	0	0	15.2	25	10	2	0	1	0	0	5	1	0	.200	2	5	0	0	0.8	1.000
3 yrs.			5	4	.556	6.04	40	8	3	114.2	158	54	16	0	2	0	0	44	12	0	.273	5	29	1	4	0.9	.971

Cy Falkenberg

FALKENBERG, FREDERICK PETER
B. Dec. 17, 1880, Chicago, Ill.   D. Apr. 14, 1961, San Francisco, Calif.

BR TR 6'5"   180 lbs.

1903	PIT	N	2	4	.333	3.86	10	6	3	56	65	32	24	1	0	0	0	21	4	0	.190	7	21	3	0	3.1	.903
1905	WAS	A	7	1	.875	3.82	12	10	6	75.1	71	31	35	2	1	0	0	32	4	0	.125	6	17	2	1	2.1	.920
1906			14	20	.412	2.86	40	36	30	298.2	277	108	178	2	0	0	0	106	18	1	.170	12	92	8	3	2.9	.929
1907			6	17	.261	2.35	32	24	17	233.2	195	77	108	1	0	2	0	86	12	0	.140	10	82	6	2	3.1	.939
1908	2 teams		WAS A (17G 6-2)			CLE A	(8G 2-4)																					
"	total		8	6	.571	2.65	25	15	7	129	122	31	51	1	1	0	0	44	8	0	.182	3	42	1	0	1.8	.978
1909	CLE	A	10	9	.526	2.40	24	18	13	165	135	50	82	2	1	0	0	52	9	0	.173	12	61	4	1	3.2	.948
1910			14	13	.519	2.95	37	29	18	256.2	246	75	107	3	3	0	1	82	15	0	.183	14	97	4	3	3.1	.965
1911			8	5	.615	3.29	15	13	7	106.2	117	24	46	0	1	0	0	40	7	0	.175	4	33	3	1	2.7	.925
1913			23	10	.697	2.22	39	36	23	276	238	88	166	4	1	0	0	84	10	0	.119	8	69	7	1	2.2	.917
1914	IND	F	25	16	.610	2.22	49	43	33	377.1	332	89	236	9	0	2	3	125	21	0	.168	20	113	5	5	2.8	.964
1915	2 teams		NWK F	(25G 9-11)		BKN F	(7G 3-3)																					
"	total		12	14	.462	2.86	32	28	19	220	206	59	96	1	1	0	0	72	4	0	.056	6	71	4	4	2.5	.951
1917	PHI	A	2	6	.250	3.35	15	8	4	80.2	86	26	35	0	0	1	0	27	5	0	.185	2	30	5	5	2.5	.865
12 yrs.			131	121	.520	2.68	330	266	180	2275	2090	690	1164	27	6	7	7	771	117	1	.152	104	728	52	26	2.7	.941

Year	Team		W	L	PCT	ERA	G	GS	CG	IP	H	BB	SO	ShO	Relief Pitching W	L	SV	Batting AB	H	HR	BA	PO	A	E	DP	TC/G	FA

Ed Fallenstin

FALLENSTIN, EDWARD JOSEPH (Jack)
Born Edward Joseph Valestin.
B. Dec. 22, 1908, Newark, N. J. D. Nov. 24, 1971, Orange, N. J.
BR TR 6'3" 180 lbs.

Year	Team		W	L	PCT	ERA	G	GS	CG	IP	H	BB	SO	ShO	W	L	SV	AB	H	HR	BA	PO	A	E	DP	TC/G	FA
1931	PHI	N	0	0	–	7.13	24	0	0	41.2	56	26	15	0	0	0	0	5	1	0	.200	3	9	1	0	0.5	.923
1933	BOS	N	2	1	.667	3.60	9	4	1	35	43	13	5	1	0	0	0	8	3	0	.375	1	7	1	0	1.0	.889
2 yrs.			2	1	.667	5.52	33	4	1	76.2	99	39	20	1	0	0	0	13	4	0	.308	4	16	2	0	0.7	.909

Bob Fallon

FALLON, ROBERT JOSEPH
B. Feb. 18, 1960, Bronx, N. Y.
BL TL 6'3" 200 lbs.

Year	Team		W	L	PCT	ERA	G	GS	CG	IP	H	BB	SO	ShO	W	L	SV	AB	H	HR	BA	PO	A	E	DP	TC/G	FA
1984	CHI	A	0	0	–	3.68	3	3	0	14.2	12	11	10	0	0	0	0	0	0	0	–	1	3	0	0	1.3	1.000
1985			0	0	–	6.19	10	0	0	16	25	9	17	0	0	0	0	0	0	0	–	2	3	0	1	0.5	1.000
2 yrs.			0	0	–	4.99	13	3	0	30.2	37	20	27	0	0	0	0	0	0	0	–	3	6	0	1	0.7	1.000

Cliff Fannin

FANNIN, CLIFFORD BRYSON (Mule)
B. May 13, 1924, Louisa, Ky. D. Dec. 11, 1966, Sandusky, Ohio
BL TR 6' 170 lbs.

Year	Team		W	L	PCT	ERA	G	GS	CG	IP	H	BB	SO	ShO	W	L	SV	AB	H	HR	BA	PO	A	E	DP	TC/G	FA
1945	STL	A	0	0	–	2.61	5	0	0	10.1	8	5	5	0	0	0	0	1	0	0	.000	0	1	0	0	0.2	1.000
1946			5	2	.714	3.01	27	7	4	86.2	76	42	52	0	0	0	2	31	5	0	.161	3	13	0	1	0.6	1.000
1947			6	8	.429	3.58	26	18	6	145.2	134	77	77	2	0	0	1	46	9	0	.196	10	23	2	1	1.3	.943
1948			10	14	.417	4.17	34	29	10	213.2	198	104	102	3	0	0	1	65	11	0	.169	10	24	2	3	1.1	.944
1949			8	14	.364	6.17	30	25	5	143	177	93	57	0	0	2	1	55	9	0	.164	4	15	0	0	0.6	1.000
1950			5	9	.357	6.53	25	16	3	102	116	58	42	0	2	1	1	34	6	0	.176	3	17	2	2	0.9	.909
1951			0	2	.000	6.46	7	1	0	15.1	20	5	11	0	0	2	0	4	1	0	.250	2	0	0	0	0.6	1.000
1952			0	2	.000	12.67	10	2	0	16.1	34	9	6	0	0	0	0	1	0	0	.000	0	3	0	0	0.1	1.000
8 yrs.			34	51	.400	4.85	164	98	28	733	763	393	352	6	2	5	6	237	41	0	.173	32	96	6	8	0.8	.955

Jack Fanning

FANNING, JOHN JACOB
B. 1863, South Orange, N. J. D. June 10, 1917, Aberdeen, Wash.
5'9" 163 lbs.

Year	Team		W	L	PCT	ERA	G	GS	CG	IP	H	BB	SO	ShO	W	L	SV	AB	H	HR	BA	PO	A	E	DP	TC/G	FA
1889	IND	N	0	1	.000	18.00	1	1	0	1	3	2	0	0	0	0	0	1	0	0	.000	0	1	0	0	1.0	1.000
1894	PHI	N	1	3	.250	8.07	5	4	2	32.1	45	20	7	0	0	0	0	13	2	0	.154	1	6	2	0	1.8	.778
2 yrs.			1	4	.200	8.37	6	5	2	33.1	48	22	7	0	0	0	0	14	2	0	.143	1	7	2	0	1.7	.800

Harry Fanok

FANOK, HARRY MICHAEL (The Flame Thrower)
B. May 11, 1940, Whippany, N. J.
BB TR 6' 180 lbs.

Year	Team		W	L	PCT	ERA	G	GS	CG	IP	H	BB	SO	ShO	W	L	SV	AB	H	HR	BA	PO	A	E	DP	TC/G	FA
1963	STL	N	2	1	.667	5.26	12	0	0	25.2	24	21	25	0	2	1	1	5	2	0	.400	2	3	1	0	0.5	.833
1964			0	0	–	5.87	4	0	0	7.2	5	3	10	0	0	0	0	1	0	0	.000	0	1	1	0	0.5	.500
2 yrs.			2	1	.667	5.40	16	0	0	33.1	29	24	35	0	2	1	1	6	2	0	.333	2	4	2	0	0.5	.750

Frank Fanovich

FANOVICH, FRANK JOSEPH (Lefty)
B. Jan. 11, 1922, New York, N. Y.
BL TL 5'11" 180 lbs.

Year	Team		W	L	PCT	ERA	G	GS	CG	IP	H	BB	SO	ShO	W	L	SV	AB	H	HR	BA	PO	A	E	DP	TC/G	FA
1949	CIN	N	0	2	.000	5.40	29	1	0	43.1	44	28	27	0	0	1	0	4	0	0	.000	1	9	2	1	0.4	.833
1953	PHI	A	0	3	.000	5.55	26	3	0	61.2	62	37	37	0	0	1	0	11	2	0	.182	2	8	2	0	0.5	.833
2 yrs.			0	5	.000	5.49	55	4	0	105	106	65	64	0	0	2	0	15	2	0	.133	3	17	4	1	0.4	.833

Stan Fansler

FANSLER, STANLEY ROBERT
B. Feb. 12, 1965, Elkins, W. Va.
BR TR 5'11" 180 lbs.

Year	Team		W	L	PCT	ERA	G	GS	CG	IP	H	BB	SO	ShO	W	L	SV	AB	H	HR	BA	PO	A	E	DP	TC/G	FA
1986	PIT	N	0	3	.000	3.75	5	5	0	24	20	15	13	0	0	0	0	6	1	0	.167	5	1	0	1	1.2	1.000

Harry Fanwell

FANWELL, HARRY CLAYTON
B. Oct. 16, 1886, Patapsco, Md. D. July 15, 1965, Baltimore, Md.
BB TR 6' 175 lbs.

Year	Team		W	L	PCT	ERA	G	GS	CG	IP	H	BB	SO	ShO	W	L	SV	AB	H	HR	BA	PO	A	E	DP	TC/G	FA
1910	CLE	A	2	9	.182	3.62	17	11	5	92	87	38	30	1	1	0	0	30	1	0	.033	2	36	0	0	2.2	1.000

Ed Farmer

FARMER, EDWARD JOSEPH
B. Oct. 18, 1949, Evergreen Park, Ill.
BR TR 6'5" 200 lbs.

Year	Team		W	L	PCT	ERA	G	GS	CG	IP	H	BB	SO	ShO	W	L	SV	AB	H	HR	BA	PO	A	E	DP	TC/G	FA
1971	CLE	A	5	4	.556	4.33	43	4	0	79	77	41	48	0	5	2	4	14	1	0	.071	2	12	0	2	0.3	1.000
1972			2	5	.286	4.43	46	1	0	61	51	27	33	0	2	4	7	7	1	0	.143	4	12	1	0	0.4	.941
1973	2 teams	CLE A	(16G 0–2)			DET A	(24G 3–0)																					
"	total		3	2	.600	4.91	40	0	0	62.1	77	32	38	0	3	2	3	0	0	0	–	4	3	0	1	0.2	1.000
1974	PHI	N	2	1	.667	8.42	14	3	0	31	41	27	20	0	1	0	0	9	1	0	.111	0	4	1	0	0.4	.800
1977	BAL	A	0	0	–	∞	1	0	0		1	1	0	0	0	0	0	0	0	0	–	0	0	0	0	0.0	–
1978	MIL	A	0	1	.000	0.82	3	0	0	11	7	4	6	0	0	1	0	0	0	0	–	0	2	0	0	0.7	1.000
1979	2 teams	TEX A	(11G 2–0)			CHI A	(42G 3–7)																					
"	total		5	7	.417	3.00	53	5	0	114	96	53	73	0	5	7	14	0	0	0	–	9	15	0	1	0.5	1.000
1980	CHI	A	7	9	.438	3.33	64	0	0	100	92	56	54	0	7	9	30	0	0	0	–	5	17	0	4	0.3	1.000
1981			3	3	.500	4.58	42	0	0	53	53	34	42	0	3	3	10	0	0	0	–	5	9	1	1	0.4	.933
1982	PHI	N	2	6	.250	4.86	47	4	0	76	66	50	58	0	1	4	6	11	0	0	.000	1	12	0	0	0.3	1.000
1983	2 teams	PHI N	(12G 0–6)			OAK A	(5G 0–0)																					
"	total		0	6	.000	5.35	17	4	0	37	50	20	23	0	0	3	0	6	1	0	.167	3	5	0	0	0.5	1.000
11 yrs.			30	43	.411	4.30	370	21	0	624.1	611	345	395	0	28	34	75	47	4	0	.085	34	90	3	10	0.3	.976

Jimmy Farr

FARR, JAMES ALFRED
B. May 18, 1956, Waverly, N. Y.
BR TR 6'1" 195 lbs.

Year	Team		W	L	PCT	ERA	G	GS	CG	IP	H	BB	SO	ShO	W	L	SV	AB	H	HR	BA	PO	A	E	DP	TC/G	FA
1982	TEX	A	0	0	–	2.50	5	0	0	18	20	7	6	0	0	0	0	0	0	0	–	0	2	0	0	0.4	1.000

Steve Farr

FARR, STEVEN MICHAEL
B. Dec. 12, 1956, Cheverly, Md.
BR TR 5'10" 190 lbs.

Year	Team		W	L	PCT	ERA	G	GS	CG	IP	H	BB	SO	ShO	W	L	SV	AB	H	HR	BA	PO	A	E	DP	TC/G	FA
1984	CLE	A	3	11	.214	4.58	31	16	0	116	106	46	83	0	1	2	1	0	0	0	–	7	18	2	1	0.9	.926
1985	KC	A	2	1	.667	3.11	16	3	0	37.2	34	20	36	0	1	0	1	0	0	0	–	3	6	0	0	0.6	1.000
1986			8	4	.667	3.13	56	0	0	109.1	90	39	83	0	8	4	8	0	0	0	–	8	16	0	1	0.4	1.000
1987			4	3	.571	4.15	47	0	0	91	97	44	88	0	4	3	1	0	0	0	–	3	6	2	0	0.2	.818
1988			5	4	.556	2.50	62	1	0	82.2	74	30	72	0	4	4	20	0	0	0	–	3	7	0	0	0.2	1.000

Year	Team	W	L	PCT	ERA	G	GS	CG	IP	H	BB	SO	ShO	Relief Pitching W	L	SV	Batting AB	H	HR	BA	PO	A	E	DP	TC/G	FA

Steve Farr *continued*

| 1989 | | 2 | 5 | .286 | 4.12 | 51 | 2 | 0 | 63.1 | 75 | 22 | 56 | 0 | 1 | 5 | 18 | 0 | 0 | 0 | – | 7 | 4 | 0 | 0 | 0.2 | 1.000 |
| 6 yrs. | | 24 | 28 | .462 | 3.67 | 263 | 22 | 0 | 500 | 476 | 201 | 418 | 0 | 19 | 18 | 49 | 0 | 0 | 0 | – | 31 | 57 | 4 | 2 | 0.3 | .957 |

LEAGUE CHAMPIONSHIP SERIES

| 1985 | KC A | 1 | 0 | 1.000 | 1.42 | 2 | 0 | 0 | 6.1 | 4 | 1 | 3 | 0 | 1 | 0 | 0 | 0 | 0 | 0 | – | 0 | 1 | 0 | 1 | 0.5 | 1.000 |

Dick Farrell

FARRELL, RICHARD JOSEPH (Turk) BR TR 6'4" 215 lbs.
B. Apr. 8, 1934, Boston, Mass. D. June 10, 1977, Great Yarmouth, England

1956	PHI N	0	1	.000	12.46	1	1	0	4.1	6	3	0	0	0	0	0	1	0	0	.000	0	3	0	0	3.0	1.000
1957		10	2	.833	2.38	52	0	0	83.1	74	36	54	0	10	2	10	9	1	1	.111	3	16	1	0	0.4	.950
1958		8	9	.471	3.35	54	0	0	94	84	40	73	0	8	9	11	24	5	0	.208	2	8	2	0	0.2	.833
1959		1	6	.143	4.74	38	0	0	57	61	25	31	0	1	6	6	6	1	0	.167	2	8	0	0	0.3	1.000
1960		10	6	.625	2.70	59	0	0	103.1	88	29	70	0	10	6	11	15	3	0	.200	6	13	2	1	0.4	.905
1961	2 teams		PHI N	(5G 2–1)		LA N	(50G 6–6)																				
"	total	8	7	.533	5.20	55	0	0	98.2	117	49	90	0	8	7	10	20	1	0	.050	2	7	0	0	0.2	1.000
1962	HOU N	10	20	.333	3.02	43	29	11	241.2	210	55	203	2	2	4	4	78	14	2	.179	10	28	2	1	0.9	.950
1963		14	13	.519	3.02	34	26	12	202.1	161	35	141	0	3	1	1	63	9	0	.143	9	27	0	1	1.1	1.000
1964		11	10	.524	3.27	32	27	7	198.1	196	52	117	0	0	0	0	69	5	0	.072	5	31	0	2	1.1	1.000
1965		11	11	.500	3.50	33	29	8	208.1	202	35	122	3	1	0	1	74	10	0	.135	9	30	3	3	1.3	.929
1966		6	10	.375	4.60	32	21	3	152.2	167	28	101	0	2	0	2	48	7	1	.146	11	13	2	1	0.8	.923
1967	2 teams		HOU N	(7G 1–0)		PHI N	(50G 9–6)																				
"	total	10	6	.625	2.34	57	0	0	103.2	87	22	78	0	10	5	12	20	2	0	.100	3	12	1	0	0.3	.938
1968	PHI N	4	6	.400	3.48	54	0	0	82.2	83	32	57	0	4	6	12	6	1	0	.167	0	14	1	0	0.3	.933
1969		3	4	.429	4.01	46	0	0	74	92	27	40	0	3	4	3	3	0	0	.000	2	2	0	0	0.1	1.000
14 yrs.		106	111	.488	3.45	590	134	41	1704.1	1628	468	1177	5	62	51	83	436	59	4	.135	64	212	14	9	0.5	.952

John Farrell

FARRELL, JOHN EDWARD BR TR 6'4" 210 lbs.
B. Aug. 4, 1962, Monmouth Beach, N. J.

1987	CLE A	5	1	.833	3.39	10	9	1	69	68	22	28	0	1	0	0	0	0	0	–	8	7	2	1	1.7	.882
1988		14	10	.583	4.24	31	30	4	210.1	216	67	92	0	0	0	0	0	0	0	–	21	23	0	2	1.4	1.000
1989		9	14	.391	3.63	31	31	7	208	196	71	132	2	0	0	0	0	0	0	–	18	20	2	1	1.3	.950
3 yrs.		28	25	.528	3.86	72	70	12	487.1	480	160	252	2	1	0	0	0	0	0	–	47	50	4	4	1.4	.960

Kerby Farrell

FARRELL, MAJOR KERBY BL TL 5'11" 172 lbs.
B. Sept. 3, 1913, Leapwood, Tenn. D. Dec. 17, 1975, Nashville, Tenn.
Manager 1957.

| 1943 | BOS N | 0 | 1 | .000 | 4.30 | 5 | 0 | 0 | 23 | 24 | 9 | 4 | 0 | 0 | 1 | 0 | * | | | | 0 | 5 | 1 | 1 | 1.2 | .833 |

Fast

FAST,
B. Milwaukee, Wis. Deceased.

| 1887 | IND N | 0 | 1 | .000 | 10.34 | 4 | 2 | 1 | 15.2 | 25 | 8 | 0 | 0 | 0 | 0 | 1 | 11 | 2 | 0 | .182 | 0 | 4 | 0 | 0 | 1.0 | 1.000 |

Darcy Fast

FAST, DARCY RAE BL TL 6'3" 195 lbs.
B. Mar. 10, 1947, Dallas, Ore.

| 1968 | CHI N | 0 | 1 | .000 | 5.40 | 8 | 1 | 0 | 10 | 8 | 8 | 10 | 0 | 0 | 1 | 0 | 3 | 0 | 0 | .000 | 1 | 1 | 0 | 0 | 0.3 | 1.000 |

Jack Faszholz

FASZHOLZ, JOHN EDWARD (Preacher) BR TR 6'3" 205 lbs.
B. Apr. 11, 1927, St. Louis, Mo.

| 1953 | STL N | 0 | 0 | – | 6.94 | 4 | 1 | 0 | 11.2 | 16 | 1 | 7 | 0 | 0 | 0 | 0 | 3 | 0 | 0 | .000 | 0 | 0 | 0 | 0 | 0.0 | – |

Bill Faul

FAUL, WILLIAM ALVAN BR TR 5'10" 184 lbs.
B. Apr. 21, 1940, Cincinnati, Ohio

1962	DET A	0	0	–	32.40	1	0	0	1.2	4	3	2	0	0	0	0	0	0	0	–	0	0	0	0	0.0	–
1963		5	6	.455	4.64	28	10	2	97	93	48	64	0	1	1	1	27	4	0	.148	3	6	0	0	0.3	1.000
1964		0	0	–	10.80	1	1	0	5	5	2	1	0	0	0	0	2	0	0	.000	0	0	0	0	0.0	–
1965	CHI N	6	6	.500	3.54	17	16	5	96.2	83	18	59	3	0	0	0	30	3	0	.100	5	10	3	0	1.1	.833
1966		1	4	.200	5.08	17	6	1	51.1	47	18	32	0	0	0	0	13	0	0	.000	5	4	1	0	0.6	.900
1970	SF N	0	0	–	7.20	7	0	0	10	15	6	6	0	0	0	1	0	0	0	–	0	0	0	0	0.0	–
6 yrs.		12	16	.429	4.71	71	33	8	261.2	247	95	164	3	1	1	2	72	7	0	.097	13	20	4	0	0.5	.892

Jim Faulkner

FAULKNER, JAMES LeROY (Lefty) BB TL 6'3" 190 lbs.
B. July 27, 1899, Beatrice, Neb. BL 1927
D. June 1, 1962, West Palm Beach, Fla.

1927	NY N	1	0	1.000	3.72	3	1	0	9.2	13	5	2	0	0	0	0	2	1	0	.500	1	1	0	0	0.7	1.000
1928		9	8	.529	3.53	38	8	3	117.1	131	41	32	0	7	6	2	39	9	0	.231	3	31	1	3	0.9	.971
1930	BKN N	0	0	–	81.00	2	1	0	.1	2	1	0	0	0	0	1	0	0	0	–	0	1	0	0	0.5	1.000
3 yrs.		10	8	.556	3.75	43	10	3	127.1	146	47	34	0	7	6	3	41	10	0	.244	4	33	1	3	0.9	.974

Buck Fausett

FAUSETT, ROBERT SHAW (Leaky) BL TR 5'10" 170 lbs.
B. Apr. 8, 1908, Sheridan, Ark.

| 1944 | CIN N | 0 | 0 | – | 5.91 | 2 | 0 | 0 | 10.2 | 13 | 7 | 3 | 0 | 0 | 0 | 0 | * | | | | 0 | 3 | 1 | 0 | 2.0 | .750 |

Charlie Faust

FAUST, CHARLES VICTOR (Victory) BR TR 6'2"
B. Oct. 9, 1880, Marion, Kans. D. June 18, 1915, Fort Steilacoom, Wash.

| 1911 | NY N | 0 | 0 | – | 4.50 | 2 | 0 | 0 | 2 | 2 | 0 | 0 | 0 | 0 | 0 | 0 | 0 | 0 | 0 | – | 0 | 2 | 0 | 0 | 1.0 | 1.000 |

Year	Team		W	L	PCT	ERA	G	GS	CG	IP	H	BB	SO	ShO	W	L	SV	AB	H	HR	BA	PO	A	E	DP	TC/G	FA
															Relief Pitching			**Batting**									

Clay Fauver
FAUVER, CLAYTON KING (Pop)
B. Aug. 1, 1872, North Eaton, Ohio   D. Mar. 3, 1942, Chatsworth, Ga.   BB TR 5'10"

Year	Team		W	L	PCT	ERA	G	GS	CG	IP	H	BB	SO	ShO	W	L	SV	AB	H	HR	BA	PO	A	E	DP	TC/G	FA
1899	LOU	N	1	0	1.000	0.00	1	1	1	9	11	2	1	0	0	0	0	4	0	0	.000	0	2	0	0	2.0	1.000

Vern Fear
FEAR, LUVERN CARL
B. Aug. 21, 1924, Everly, Iowa   D. Sept. 6, 1976, Spencer, Iowa   BB TR 6'   170 lbs.

Year	Team		W	L	PCT	ERA	G	GS	CG	IP	H	BB	SO	ShO	W	L	SV	AB	H	HR	BA	PO	A	E	DP	TC/G	FA
1952	CHI	N	0	0	—	7.88	4	0	0	8	9	3	4	0	0	0	0	1	0	0	.000	0	1	0	0	0.3	1.000

Jack Fee
FEE, JOHN
B. 1870, Carbondale, Pa.   D. Mar. 3, 1913, Carbondale, Pa.

Year	Team		W	L	PCT	ERA	G	GS	CG	IP	H	BB	SO	ShO	W	L	SV	AB	H	HR	BA	PO	A	E	DP	TC/G	FA
1889	IND	N	2	2	.500	4.28	7	3	2	40	39	31	10	0	0	0	0	21	3	0	.143	2	11	1	0	2.0	.929

Harry Feldman
FELDMAN, HARRY
B. Nov. 10, 1919, New York, N. Y.   D. Mar. 16, 1962, Ft. Smith, Ark.   BR TR 6'   175 lbs.

Year	Team		W	L	PCT	ERA	G	GS	CG	IP	H	BB	SO	ShO	W	L	SV	AB	H	HR	BA	PO	A	E	DP	TC/G	FA
1941	NY	N	1	1	.500	3.98	3	3	1	20.1	21	6	9	1	0	0	0	6	1	0	.167	0	3	1	0	1.3	.750
1942			7	1	.875	3.16	31	6	2	114	100	73	49	1	5	0	0	39	11	1	.282	4	22	1	3	0.9	.963
1943			4	5	.444	4.30	31	10	1	104.2	114	58	49	0	2	0	0	30	4	0	.133	5	20	1	4	0.8	.962
1944			11	13	.458	4.16	40	27	8	205.1	214	91	70	1	2	2	2	73	15	0	.205	9	29	7	3	1.1	.844
1945			12	13	.480	3.27	35	30	10	217.2	213	69	74	3	0	2	1	72	7	1	.097	12	31	1	0	1.3	.977
1946			0	2	.000	18.00	3	2	0	4	9	3	3	0	0	0	0	1	0	0	.000	0	0	0	0	0.0	
	6 yrs.		35	35	.500	3.80	143	78	22	666	671	300	254	6	9	4	3	221	38	2	.172	30	105	11	10	1.0	.925

Harry Felix
FELIX, HARRY
B. 1870, Brooklyn, N. Y.   D. Oct. 17, 1961, Miami, Fla.   BR TR 5'7½"   160 lbs.

Year	Team		W	L	PCT	ERA	G	GS	CG	IP	H	BB	SO	ShO	W	L	SV	AB	H	HR	BA	PO	A	E	DP	TC/G	FA
1901	NY	N	0	0	—	0.00	1	0	0	2	3	0	0	0	0	0	0	1	0	0	.000	0	0	0	0	0.0	—
1902	PHI	N	1	3	.250	5.60	9	5	3	45	61	11	10	0	0	0	0	37	5	0	.135	2	9	0	0	1.2	1.000
	2 yrs.		1	3	.250	5.36	10	5	3	47	64	11	10	0	0	0	0	38	5	0	.132	2	9	0	0	1.1	1.000

Bob Feller
FELLER, ROBERT WILLIAM ANDREW (Rapid Robert)
B. Nov. 3, 1918, Van Meter, Iowa
Hall of Fame 1962.   BR TR 6'   185 lbs.

Year	Team		W	L	PCT	ERA	G	GS	CG	IP	H	BB	SO	ShO	W	L	SV	AB	H	HR	BA	PO	A	E	DP	TC/G	FA
1936	CLE	A	5	3	.625	3.34	14	8	5	62	52	47	76	0	0	0	1	22	3	0	.136	0	5	0	0	0.4	1.000
1937			9	7	.563	3.39	26	19	9	148.2	116	106	150	0	2	0	1	53	9	0	.170	0	27	2	1	1.1	.931
1938			17	11	.607	4.08	39	36	20	277.2	225	208	240	2	0	1	1	94	17	0	.181	8	37	3	1	1.2	.938
1939			24	9	.727	2.85	39	35	24	296.2	227	142	246	4	1	0	1	99	21	0	.212	8	44	3	2	1.4	.945
1940			27	11	.711	2.61	43	37	31	320.1	245	118	261	4	1	1	4	115	18	2	.157	5	34	2	2	1.0	.951
1941			25	13	.658	3.15	44	40	28	343	284	194	260	6	0	1	2	120	18	1	.150	12	50	1	1	1.4	.984
1945			5	3	.625	2.50	9	9	7	72	50	35	59	1	0	0	0	25	4	0	.160	7	4	0	0	1.2	1.000
1946			26	15	.634	2.18	48	42	36	371.1	277	153	348	10	0	0	4	124	16	0	.129	13	47	1	2	1.3	.984
1947			20	11	.645	2.68	42	37	20	299	230	127	196	5	0	1	3	98	18	0	.184	17	50	1	2	1.6	.985
1948			19	15	.559	3.56	44	38	18	280.1	255	116	164	3	0	1	2	95	9	0	.095	16	39	2	1	1.3	.965
1949			15	14	.517	3.75	36	28	15	211	198	84	108	0	1	0	0	72	17	2	.236	12	19	1	2	0.9	.969
1950			16	11	.593	3.43	35	34	16	247	230	103	119	3	0	1	0	83	10	2	.120	8	23	0	2	0.9	1.000
1951			22	8	.733	3.50	33	32	16	249.2	239	95	111	4	0	0	0	81	10	0	.123	6	32	2	1	1.2	.950
1952			9	13	.409	4.74	30	30	11	191.2	219	83	81	1	0	0	0	60	7	1	.117	13	34	3	1	1.7	.940
1953			10	7	.588	3.59	25	25	10	175.2	163	60	60	1	0	0	0	56	6	0	.107	10	31	0	5	1.6	1.000
1954			13	3	.813	3.09	19	19	9	140	127	39	59	1	0	0	0	48	9	0	.188	7	15	0	2	1.2	1.000
1955			4	4	.500	3.47	25	11	2	83	71	31	25	1	1	0	0	21	1	0	.048	2	11	3	2	0.6	.813
1956			0	4	.000	4.97	19	4	2	58	63	23	18	0	1	1	0	16	0	0	.000	2	8	1	0	0.6	.909
	18 yrs.		266	162	.621	3.25	570	484	279	3827	3271	1764	2581	46	6	8	21	1282	193	8	.151	146	510	25	28	1.2	.963
												5th																

WORLD SERIES

Year	Team		W	L	PCT	ERA	G	GS	CG	IP	H	BB	SO	ShO	W	L	SV	AB	H	HR	BA	PO	A	E	DP	TC/G	FA
1948	CLE	A	0	2	.000	5.02	2	2	1	14.1	10	5	7	0	0	0	0	4	0	0	.000	2	4	0	0	3.0	1.000

Terry Felton
FELTON, TERRY LANE
B. Oct. 29, 1957, Texarkana, Tex.   BR TR 6'1"   180 lbs.

Year	Team		W	L	PCT	ERA	G	GS	CG	IP	H	BB	SO	ShO	W	L	SV	AB	H	HR	BA	PO	A	E	DP	TC/G	FA
1979	MIN	A	0	0	—	0.00	1	0	0	2	0	0	1	0	0	0	0	0	0	0	—	0	0	0	0	0.0	—
1980			0	3	.000	7.00	5	4	0	18	20	9	14	0	0	0	0	0	0	0	—	0	2	1	0	0.6	.667
1981			0	0	—	54.00	1	0	0	1	4	2	1	0	0	0	0	0	0	0	—	0	0	0	0	0.0	—
1982			0	13	.000	4.99	48	6	0	117.1	99	76	92	0	0	9	3	0	0	0	—	5	5	1	0	0.2	.909
	4 yrs.		0	16	.000	5.53	55	10	0	138.1	123	87	108	0	0	9	3	0	0	0	—	5	7	2	0	0.3	.857

Hod Fenner
FENNER, HORACE ALFRED
B. July 12, 1897, Martin, Mich.   D. Nov. 20, 1954, Detroit, Mich.   BR TR 5'10½" 165 lbs.

Year	Team		W	L	PCT	ERA	G	GS	CG	IP	H	BB	SO	ShO	W	L	SV	AB	H	HR	BA	PO	A	E	DP	TC/G	FA
1921	CHI	A	0	0	—	7.71	2	1	0	7	14	3	1	0	0	0	0	2	0	0	.000	0	0	0	0	0.0	—

Stan Ferens
FERENS, STANLEY (Lefty)
B. Mar. 5, 1915, Wendell, Pa.   BB TL 5'11"   170 lbs.

Year	Team		W	L	PCT	ERA	G	GS	CG	IP	H	BB	SO	ShO	W	L	SV	AB	H	HR	BA	PO	A	E	DP	TC/G	FA
1942	STL	A	3	4	.429	3.78	19	3	1	69	76	21	23	1	0	3	0	21	3	0	.143	5	13	1	1	1.0	.947
1946			2	9	.182	4.50	34	6	1	88	100	38	28	0	1	5	0	24	4	0	.167	4	14	3	1	0.6	.857
	2 yrs.		5	13	.278	4.18	53	9	2	157	176	59	51	0	3	8	0	45	7	0	.156	9	27	4	2	0.8	.900

Alex Ferguson
FERGUSON, JAMES ALEXANDER
B. Feb. 16, 1897, Montclair, N. J.   D. Apr. 26, 1976, Sepulveda, Calif.   BR TR 6'   180 lbs.

Year	Team		W	L	PCT	ERA	G	GS	CG	IP	H	BB	SO	ShO	W	L	SV	AB	H	HR	BA	PO	A	E	DP	TC/G	FA
1918	NY	A	0	0	—	0.00	1	0	0	1.2	2	2	1	0	0	0	0	0	0	0	.000	0	0	0	0	0.0	—
1921			3	1	.750	5.91	17	4	1	56.1	64	27	9	0	1	0	1	19	4	0	.211	2	15	1	0	1.1	.944
1922	BOS	A	9	16	.360	4.31	39	27	10	198.1	201	62	44	1	3	0	2	65	6	0	.092	10	43	2	4	1.4	.964
1923			9	13	.409	4.04	34	27	11	198.1	229	67	72	0	1	0	0	62	6	0	.097	5	45	4	5	1.6	.926
1924			14	17	.452	3.79	40	32	15	235	257	107	78	0	3	1	2	85	11	0	.129	12	60	1	1	1.8	.986

Year	Team	W	L	PCT	ERA	G	GS	CG	IP	H	BB	SO	ShO	Relief Pitching W	L	SV	Batting AB	H	HR	BA	PO	A	E	DP	TC/G	FA

Alex Ferguson *continued*

Year	Team	W	L	PCT	ERA	G	GS	CG	IP	H	BB	SO	ShO	W	L	SV	AB	H	HR	BA	PO	A	E	DP	TC/G	FA
1925	3 teams			BOS A	(5G 0–2)			NY A	(21G 4–2)		WAS A	(7G 5–1)														
"	total	9	5	.643	6.18	33	15	3	125.1	157	70	49	0	3	2	2	39	3	0	.077	4	26	1	2	0.9	.968
1926	WAS A	3	4	.429	7.74	19	4	0	47.2	69	18	16	0	2	2	1	11	2	0	.182	2	14	1	1	0.9	.941
1927	PHI N	8	16	.333	4.84	31	31	16	227	280	65	73	0	0	0	0	70	7	0	.100	12	49	5	3	2.1	.924
1928		5	10	.333	5.67	34	19	5	131.2	162	48	50	1	1	0	2	39	1	0	.026	9	35	0	0	1.3	1.000
1929	2 teams			PHI N	(5G 1–2)			BKN N	(3G 0–1)																	
"	total	1	3	.250	13.50	8	7	1	14.2	26	11	4	0	0	0	0	5	1	0	.200	1	6	0	0	1.000	
10 yrs.		61	85	.418	4.91	256	166	62	1236	1447	477	396	2	14	5	10	396	41	0	.104	57	293	15	16	1.4	.959

WORLD SERIES

| 1925 | WAS A | 1 | 1 | .500 | 3.21 | 2 | 2 | 2 | 14 | 13 | 6 | 11 | 0 | 0 | 0 | 0 | 4 | 0 | 0 | .000 | 0 | 0 | 0 | 0 | 0.0 | – |

Bob Ferguson

FERGUSON, ROBERT LESTER
B. Apr. 18, 1919, Birmingham, Ala. BR TR 6'1½" 180 lbs.

| 1944 | CIN N | 0 | 3 | .000 | 9.00 | 9 | 2 | 0 | 16 | 24 | 10 | 9 | 0 | 0 | 3 | 1 | 3 | 1 | 0 | .333 | 1 | 3 | 1 | 0 | 0.6 | .800 |

Bob Ferguson

FERGUSON, ROBERT V. (Death to Flying Things)
B. Jan. 31, 1845, Brooklyn, N. Y. D. May 3, 1894, Brooklyn, N. Y. BB TR 5'9½" 149 lbs.
Manager 1871-84, 1886-87.

1877	HAR N	1	1	.500	3.96	3	2	2	25	38	2	1	0	0	0	0	254	65	0	.256	4	4	1	0	3.0	.889
1883	PHI N	0	0		9.00	1	0	0	1	2	0	0	0	0	0	0	329	85	0	.258	0	1	0	0	1.0	1.000
2 yrs.		1	1	.500	4.15	4	2	2	26	40	2	1	0	0	0	0	*				4	5	1	0	2.5	.900

Charlie Ferguson

FERGUSON, CHARLES AUGUSTUS
B. May 10, 1875, Okemos, Mich. D. May 17, 1931, Sault Ste. Marie, Mich. TR 5'11"

| 1901 | CHI N | 0 | 0 | – | 0.00 | 1 | 0 | 0 | 2 | 1 | 2 | 0 | 0 | 0 | 0 | 0 | 1 | 0 | 0 | .000 | 0 | 0 | 0 | 0 | 0.0 | – |

Charlie Ferguson

FERGUSON, CHARLES J.
B. Apr. 17, 1863, Charlottesville, Va. D. Apr. 29, 1888, Philadelphia, Pa. BB TR 6' 165 lbs.

1884	PHI N	21	25	.457	3.54	50	47	46	416.2	443	93	194	2	0	0	1	203	50	0	.246	23	72	12	4	2.1	.888
1885		26	20	.565	2.22	48	45	45	405	345	81	197	5	1	1	0	235	72	1	.306	27	87	9	3	2.6	.927
1886		30	9	.769	1.98	48	45	43	395.2	317	69	212	4	0	0	2	261	66	2	.253	33	97	9	1	2.9	.935
1887		22	10	.688	3.00	37	33	31	297.1	297	47	125	2	1	0	1	264	89	3	.337	16	54	6	4	2.1	.921
4 yrs.		99	64	.607	2.67	183	170	165	1514.2	1402	290	728	13	2	1	4	*				99	310	36	12	2.4	.919

George Ferguson

FERGUSON, GEORGE CECIL
B. Aug. 19, 1886, Ellsworth, Kans. D. Sept. 5, 1943, Orlando, Fla. BR TR 5'10" 165 lbs.

1906	NY N	2	1	.667	2.58	22	1	1	52.1	43	24	32	1	2	1	6	15	5	0	.333	3	18	1	1	1.0	.955
1907		3	1	.750	2.11	15	5	4	64	63	20	37	0	0	1	1	18	1	0	.056	8	12	1	0	1.4	.952
1908	BOS N	12	11	.522	2.47	37	20	13	208	180	84	98	3	3	2	0	65	11	0	.169	9	45	6	1	1.6	.900
1909		5	23	.179	3.73	36	30	19	226.2	235	83	87	3	0	0	0	73	15	0	.205	10	63	5	1	2.2	.936
1910		8	7	.533	3.80	26	14	10	123	110	58	40	1	2	0	0	40	7	1	.175	6	33	3	1	1.6	.929
1911		1	3	.250	9.75	6	3	0	24	40	12	4	0	1	0	0	7	2	0	.286	0	8	2	0	1.7	.800
6 yrs.		31	46	.403	3.34	142	73	47	698	659	281	298	8	8	6	7	218	41	1	.188	36	179	18	4	1.6	.923

Sid Fernandez

FERNANDEZ, CHARLES SIDNEY (El Sid)
B. Oct. 12, 1962, Honolulu, Hawaii BL TL 6'1" 220 lbs.

1983	LA N	0	1	.000	6.00	2	1	0	6	7	9	9	0	0	0	0	1	1	0	1.000	1	1	0	0	1.0	1.000
1984	NY N	6	6	.500	3.50	15	15	0	90	74	34	62	0	0	0	0	28	5	0	.179	0	6	0	0	0.4	1.000
1985		9	9	.500	2.80	26	26	3	170.1	108	80	180	0	0	0	0	52	11	0	.212	1	23	0	0	0.9	1.000
1986		16	6	.727	3.52	32	31	2	204.1	161	91	200	1	0	0	1	68	11	0	.162	3	18	1	1	0.7	.955
1987		12	8	.600	3.81	28	27	3	156	130	67	134	1	0	0	0	43	7	0	.163	4	12	1	0	0.6	.941
1988		12	10	.545	3.03	31	31	1	187	127	70	189	1	0	0	0	56	14	0	.250	2	13	0	0	0.5	1.000
1989		14	5	.737	2.83	35	32	6	219.1	157	75	198	2	0	0	0	71	15	0	.211	4	13	0	2	0.5	1.000
7 yrs.		69	45	.605	3.22	169	163	15	1033	764	424	972	5	0	0	1	319	64	1	.201	15	86	2	3	0.6	.981

LEAGUE CHAMPIONSHIP SERIES

1986	NY N	0	1	.000	4.50	1	1	0	6	3	1	5	0	0	0	0	1	0	0	.000	0	0	0	0	0.0	–
1988		0	1	.000	13.50	1	1	0	4	7	1	5	0	0	0	0	1	0	0	.000	0	0	0	0	0.0	–
2 yrs.		0	2	.000	8.10	2	2	0	10	10	2	10	0	0	0	0	2	0	0	.000	0	0	0	0	0.0	–

WORLD SERIES

| 1986 | NY N | 0 | 0 | – | 1.35 | 3 | 0 | 0 | 6.2 | 6 | 1 | 10 | 0 | 0 | 0 | 0 | 0 | 0 | 0 | | 0 | 0 | 0 | 0 | 0.0 | – |

Don Ferrarese

FERRARESE, DONALD HUGH (Midget)
B. June 19, 1929, Oakland, Calif. BR TL 5'9" 170 lbs.

1955	BAL A	0	0	–	3.00	6	0	0	9	8	11	5	0	0	0	0	1	0	0	.000	0	1	0	0	0.2	1.000
1956		4	10	.286	5.03	36	14	3	102	86	64	81	1	2	2	2	28	1	0	.036	10	14	1	0	0.7	.960
1957		1	1	.500	4.74	8	2	0	19	14	12	13	0	1	0	0	3	0	0	.000	1	4	0	0	0.6	1.000
1958	CLE A	3	4	.429	3.71	28	10	2	94.2	91	46	62	0	2	1	1	26	3	0	.115	2	13	3	1	0.6	.833
1959		5	3	.625	3.20	15	10	0	76	58	51	45	0	0	0	0	27	7	0	.259	0	15	0	2	1.0	1.000
1960	CHI A	0	1	.000	18.00	5	0	0	4	8	9	4	0	0	1	0	2	1	0	.500	0	0	0	0	0.0	–
1961	PHI N	5	12	.294	3.76	42	14	3	138.2	120	68	89	1	2	3	1	35	6	0	.171	8	12	1	1	0.5	.952
1962	2 teams			PHI N	(5G 0–1)			STL N	(38G 1–4)																	
"	total	1	5	.167	3.27	43	0	0	63.1	64	34	51	0	1	5	0	6	2	0	.333	4	15	0	3	0.4	1.000
8 yrs.		19	36	.345	4.00	183	50	12	506.2	449	295	350	2	8	12	5	128	20	0	.156	25	74	5	9	0.6	.952

Bill Ferrazzi

FERRAZZI, WILLIAM JOSEPH
B. Apr. 19, 1907, West Quincy, Mass. BR TR 6'2½" 200 lbs.

| 1935 | PHI A | 1 | 2 | .333 | 5.14 | 3 | 2 | 0 | 7 | 7 | 5 | 0 | 0 | 1 | 0 | 0 | 1 | 0 | 0 | .000 | 1 | 2 | 0 | 0 | 1.0 | 1.000 |

Year	Team		W	L	PCT	ERA	G	GS	CG	IP	H	BB	SO	ShO	W	L	SV	AB	H	HR	BA	PO	A	E	DP	TC/G	FA
															Relief Pitching			**Batting**									

Tony Ferreira

FERREIRA, ANTHONY ROSS
B. Oct. 4, 1962, Riverside, Calif.

BL TL 6'1" 160 lbs.

Year	Team		W	L	PCT	ERA	G	GS	CG	IP	H	BB	SO	ShO	W	L	SV	AB	H	HR	BA	PO	A	E	DP	TC/G	FA
1985	KC	A	0	0	—	7.94	2	0	0	5.2	6	2	5	0	0	0	0	0	0	0	—	0	2	0	1	1.0	1.000

Wes Ferrell

FERRELL, WESLEY CHEEK
Brother of Rick Ferrell.
B. Feb. 2, 1908, Greensboro, N. C. D. Dec. 9, 1976, Sarasota, Fla.

BR TR 6'2" 195 lbs.

Year	Team		W	L	PCT	ERA	G	GS	CG	IP	H	BB	SO	ShO	W	L	SV	AB	H	HR	BA	PO	A	E	DP	TC/G	FA
1927	CLE	A	0	0	—	27.00	1	0	0	1	3	2	0	0	0	0	0	0	0	0	—	0	0	0	0	0.0	—
1928			0	2	.000	2.25	2	2	1	16	15	5	4	0	0	0	0	4	1	0	.250	1	4	0	0	2.5	1.000
1929			21	10	.677	3.60	43	25	18	242.2	256	109	100	1	4	2	5	93	22	1	.237	10	63	2	3	1.7	.973
1930			25	13	.658	3.31	43	35	25	296.2	303	106	143	1	2	1	3	118	35	0	.297	19	39	2	0	1.4	.967
1931			22	12	.647	3.75	40	35	**27**	276.1	276	**130**	123	2	1	1	3	116	37	9	.319	19	74	3	3	2.4	.969
1932			23	13	.639	3.66	38	34	26	287.2	299	104	105	3	1	2	1	128	31	2	.242	14	59	1	5	1.9	.986
1933			11	12	.478	4.21	28	26	16	201	225	70	41	1	0	0	0	140	38	7	.271	12	48	0	4	2.1	1.000
1934	BOS	A	14	5	.737	3.63	26	23	17	181	205	49	67	3	1	0	1	78	22	4	.282	8	23	1	2	1.2	.969
1935			**25**	14	.641	3.52	41	**38**	**31**	**322.1**	**336**	108	110	3	0	3	0	150	52	7	.347	9	76	2	1	2.1	.977
1936			20	15	.571	4.19	39	**38**	28	301	330	119	106	3	0	0	0	135	36	5	.267	9	42	2	2	1.4	.962
1937	2 teams		BOS A	(12G 3–6)		WAS A	(25G 11–13)																					
"	total		14	19	.424	4.90	37	35	26	281	325	122	123	3	0	0	0	139	39	1	.281	11	55	2	4	1.8	.971
1938	2 teams		WAS A	(23G 13–8)		NY A	(5G 2–2)																					
"	total		15	10	.600	6.28	28	26	10	179	245	86	43	0	1	0	0	61	13	1	.213	10	41	2	6	1.9	.962
1939	NY	A	1	2	.333	4.66	3	3	1	19.1	14	17	6	0	0	0	0	8	1	0	.125	0	4	0	0	1.3	1.000
1940	BKN	N	0	0	—	6.75	1	0	0	4	4	4	4	0	0	0	0	2	0	0	.000	0	0	0	0	0.0	—
1941	BOS	N	2	1	.667	5.14	4	3	1	14	13	9	10	0	1	0	0	4	2	1	.500	1	2	0	0	3.0	1.000
15 yrs.			193	128	.601	4.04	374	323	227	2623	2849	1040	985	17	11	9	13	*				122	532	17	30	1.8	.975

Tom Ferrick

FERRICK, THOMAS JEROME
B. Jan. 6, 1915, New York, N. Y.

BR TR 6'2½" 220 lbs.

Year	Team		W	L	PCT	ERA	G	GS	CG	IP	H	BB	SO	ShO	W	L	SV	AB	H	HR	BA	PO	A	E	DP	TC/G	FA
1941	PHI	A	8	10	.444	3.77	36	4	2	119.1	130	33	30	1	1	2	7	44	9	0	.205	12	31	1	4	1.2	.977
1942	CLE	A	3	2	.600	1.99	31	2	2	81.1	56	32	28	0	2	1	3	19	4	0	.211	7	24	1	4	1.0	.969
1946	2 teams		CLE A	(9G 0–0)		STL A	(25G 4–1)																					
"	total		4	1	.800	3.58	34	1	0	50.1	51	9	22	0	4	1	6	7	2	0	.286	2	12	3	1	0.5	.824
1947	WAS	A	1	7	.125	3.15	31	0	0	60	57	20	23	0	1	**7**	9	10	1	0	.100	7	15	0	1	0.7	1.000
1948			2	5	.286	4.15	37	0	0	73.2	75	38	34	0	2	5	10	15	1	0	.067	8	17	2	1	0.7	.926
1949	STL	A	6	4	.600	3.88	50	0	0	104.1	102	41	34	0	6	4	6	21	3	0	.143	6	26	1	2	0.7	.970
1950	2 teams		STL A	(16G 1–3)		NY A	(30G 8–4)																					
"	total		9	7	.563	3.79	46	0	0	80.2	73	29	26	0	**9**	7	11	18	3	0	.167	3	6	0	1	0.2	1.000
1951	2 teams		NY A	(9G 1–1)		WAS A	(22G 2–0)																					
"	total		3	1	.750	3.52	31	0	0	53.2	57	14	20	0	3	1	3	8	3	0	.375	5	8	1	2	0.5	.929
1952	WAS	A	4	3	.571	3.02	27	0	0	50.1	53	11	28	0	4	3	1	5	1	0	.200	4	13	1	0	0.7	.944
9 yrs.			40	40	.500	3.47	323	7	4	674	654	227	245	1	32	31	56	147	27	0	.184	54	152	10	15	0.7	.954

WORLD SERIES

Year	Team		W	L	PCT	ERA	G	GS	CG	IP	H	BB	SO	ShO	W	L	SV	AB	H	HR	BA	PO	A	E	DP	TC/G	FA
1950	NY	A	1	0	1.000	0.00	1	0	0	1	1	1	0	0	1	0	0	0	0	0	—	0	0	0	0	0.0	—

Bob Ferris

FERRIS, ROBERT EUGENE
B. May 7, 1955, Arlington, Va.

BR TR 6'6" 225 lbs.

Year	Team		W	L	PCT	ERA	G	GS	CG	IP	H	BB	SO	ShO	W	L	SV	AB	H	HR	BA	PO	A	E	DP	TC/G	FA
1979	CAL	A	0	0	—	1.50	2	0	0	6	5	3	2	0	0	0	0	0	0	0	—	0	2	0	0	1.0	1.000
1980			0	2	.000	6.00	5	3	0	15	23	9	4	0	0	0	0	0	0	0	—	0	3	0	0	0.6	1.000
2 yrs.			0	2	.000	4.71	7	3	0	21	28	12	6	0	0	0	0	0	0	0	—	0	5	0	0	1.0	1.000

Boo Ferriss

FERRISS, DAVID MEADOW
B. Dec. 5, 1921, Shaw, Miss.

BL TR 6'2" 208 lbs.

Year	Team		W	L	PCT	ERA	G	GS	CG	IP	H	BB	SO	ShO	W	L	SV	AB	H	HR	BA	PO	A	E	DP	TC/G	FA
1945	BOS	A	21	10	.677	2.96	35	31	26	264.2	**263**	85	94	5	1	0	2	120	32	1	.267	22	67	2	10	2.6	.978
1946			25	6	**.806**	3.25	40	35	26	274	274	71	106	6	1	0	3	115	24	0	.209	25	43	1	5	1.7	.986
1947			12	11	.522	4.04	33	28	14	218.1	241	92	64	1	0	1	0	99	27	0	.273	13	33	2	1	1.5	.958
1948			7	3	.700	5.23	31	9	1	115.1	127	61	30	0	5	1	3	37	9	0	.243	10	21	0	1	1.0	1.000
1949			0	0	—	4.05	4	0	0	6.2	7	4	1	0	0	0	0	1	1	0	1.000	1	0	0	0	0.3	1.000
1950			0	0	—	18.00	1	0	0	1	2	1	1	0	0	0	0	0	0	0	—	0	0	0	0	0.0	—
6 yrs.			65	30	.684	3.64	144	103	67	880	914	314	296	12	7	2	8	*				71	164	5	18	1.7	.979

WORLD SERIES

Year	Team		W	L	PCT	ERA	G	GS	CG	IP	H	BB	SO	ShO	W	L	SV	AB	H	HR	BA	PO	A	E	DP	TC/G	FA
1946	BOS	A	1	0	1.000	2.03	2	2	1	13.1	13	2	4	1	0	0	0	6	0	0	.000	0	3	0	0	1.5	1.000

Cy Ferry

FERRY, ALFRED JOSEPH
Brother of Jack Ferry.
B. Sept. 27, 1878, Hudson, N. Y. D. Sept. 27, 1938, Pittsfield, Mass.

BR TR 6'1" 170 lbs.

Year	Team		W	L	PCT	ERA	G	GS	CG	IP	H	BB	SO	ShO	W	L	SV	AB	H	HR	BA	PO	A	E	DP	TC/G	FA
1904	DET	A	0	1	.000	6.23	3	1	1	13	12	11	4	0	0	0	0	6	2	0	.333	0	4	0	1	1.3	1.000
1905	CLE	A	0	0	—	13.50	1	1	0	2	3	0	2	0	0	0	0	1	0	0	.000	0	1	0	1	1.0	1.000
2 yrs.			0	1	.000	7.20	4	2	1	15	15	11	6	0	0	0	0	7	2	0	.286	0	5	0	1	1.3	1.000

Jack Ferry

FERRY, JOHN FRANCIS
Brother of Cy Ferry.
B. Apr. 7, 1887, Pittsfield, Mass. D. Aug. 29, 1954, Pittsfield, Mass.

BR TR 5'11" 175 lbs.

Year	Team		W	L	PCT	ERA	G	GS	CG	IP	H	BB	SO	ShO	W	L	SV	AB	H	HR	BA	PO	A	E	DP	TC/G	FA
1910	PIT	N	1	2	.333	2.32	6	3	2	31	26	8	12	0	0	0	0	9	3	0	.333	1	9	0	0	1.7	1.000
1911			6	4	.600	3.15	26	8	4	85.2	83	27	32	1	2	4	3	29	9	0	.310	2	17	3	0	0.8	.864
1912			2	0	1.000	3.00	11	3	1	39	33	23	10	1	0	0	1	13	1	0	.077	0	14	1	0	1.4	.933
1913			1	0	1.000	5.40	4	0	0	5	4	2	2	0	1	0	0	0	0	0	—	0	2	0	0	0.5	1.000
4 yrs.			10	6	.625	3.02	47	14	7	160.2	146	60	56	2	3	4	4	51	13	0	.255	3	42	4	0	1.0	.918

Alex Ferson

FERSON, ALEXANDER (Colonel)
B. July 14, 1866, Philadelphia, Pa. D. Dec. 5, 1957, Boston, Mass.

BR TR 5'9" 165 lbs.

Year	Team		W	L	PCT	ERA	G	GS	CG	IP	H	BB	SO	ShO	W	L	SV	AB	H	HR	BA	PO	A	E	DP	TC/G	FA
1889	WAS	N	17	17	.500	3.90	36	34	28	288.1	319	105	85	1	1	0	0	114	13	0	.114	4	50	8	1	1.7	.871

Year	Team		W	L	PCT	ERA	G	GS	CG	IP	H	BB	SO	ShO	Relief Pitching W	L	SV	Batting AB	H	HR	BA	PO	A	E	DP	TC/G	FA

Alex Ferson *continued*

Year	Team		W	L	PCT	ERA	G	GS	CG	IP	H	BB	SO	ShO	W	L	SV	AB	H	HR	BA	PO	A	E	DP	TC/G	FA
1890	BUF	P	1	7	.125	5.45	10	10	7	71	88	40	13	0	0	0	0	32	7	0	.219	1	19	0	0	2.0	1.000
1892	BAL	N	0	1	.000	11.00	2	1	1	9	17	6	8	0	0	0	0	4	0	0	.000	0	0	0	0	0.0	—
3 yrs.			18	25	.419	4.37	48	45	36	368.1	424	151	106	1	1	0	0	150	20	0	.133	5	69	8	1	1.7	.902

Lou Fette

FETTE, LOUIS HENRY WILLIAM   BR TR 6'1½" 200 lbs.
B. Mar. 15, 1907, Alma, Mo.   D. Jan. 3, 1981, Warrensburg, Mo.

Year	Team		W	L	PCT	ERA	G	GS	CG	IP	H	BB	SO	ShO	W	L	SV	AB	H	HR	BA	PO	A	E	DP	TC/G	FA
1937	BOS	N	20	10	.667	2.88	35	33	23	259	243	81	70	**5**	0	0	1	92	22	0	.239	8	63	3	3	2.1	.959
1938			11	13	.458	3.15	33	32	17	239.2	235	79	83	3	0	0	1	85	16	0	.188	10	56	0	4	2.0	1.000
1939			10	10	.500	2.96	27	26	11	146	123	61	35	**6**	0	0	0	49	3	0	.061	5	46	3	0	2.0	.944
1940	2 teams	BOS N (7G 0–5)				BKN N	(2G 0–0)																				
"	total		0	5	.000	5.09	9	5	0	35.1	41	20	2	0	0	0	0	8	3	0	.375	1	4	0	0	0.6	1.000
1945	BOS	N	0	2	.000	5.73	5	1	0	11	16	7	4	0	0	1	0	2	0	0	.000	0	3	0	0	0.6	1.000
5 yrs.			41	40	.506	3.15	109	97	51	691	658	248	194	14	0	0	2	236	44	0	.186	24	172	6	7	1.9	.970

Mike Fetters

FETTERS, MICHAEL LEE   BR TR 6'4" 200 lbs.
B. Dec. 19, 1964, Van Nuys, Calif.

Year	Team		W	L	PCT	ERA	G	GS	CG	IP	H	BB	SO	ShO	W	L	SV	AB	H	HR	BA	PO	A	E	DP	TC/G	FA
1989	CAL	A	0	0	—	8.10	1	0	0	3.1	5	1	4	0	0	0	0	0	0	0	—	0	1	0	0	1.0	1.000

John Fick

FICK, JOHN RALPH   BL TL 5'10" 150 lbs.
B. May 18, 1921, Baltimore, Md.   D. June 9, 1958, Somers Point, N. J.

Year	Team		W	L	PCT	ERA	G	GS	CG	IP	H	BB	SO	ShO	W	L	SV	AB	H	HR	BA	PO	A	E	DP	TC/G	FA
1944	PHI	N	0	0	—	3.38	4	0	0	5.1	3	3	2	0	0	0	0	0	0	0	—	0	1	1	0	0.5	.500

Mark Fidrych

FIDRYCH, MARK STEVEN (The Bird)   BR TR 6'3" 175 lbs.
B. Aug. 14, 1954, Worcester, Mass.

Year	Team		W	L	PCT	ERA	G	GS	CG	IP	H	BB	SO	ShO	W	L	SV	AB	H	HR	BA	PO	A	E	DP	TC/G	FA
1976	DET	A	19	9	.679	**2.34**	31	29	**24**	250	217	53	97	4	0	0	0	0	0	0	—	19	59	0	4	2.5	1.000
1977			6	4	.600	2.89	11	11	7	81	82	12	42	1	0	0	0	0	0	0	—	7	6	1	0	1.3	.929
1978			2	0	1.000	2.45	3	3	2	22	17	5	10	0	0	0	0	0	0	0	—	4	7	0	0	3.7	1.000
1979			0	3	.000	10.20	4	4	0	15	23	9	5	0	0	0	0	0	0	0	—	2	1	0	0	0.8	1.000
1980			2	3	.400	5.73	9	9	1	44	58	20	16	0	0	0	0	0	0	0	—	5	9	0	0	1.6	1.000
5 yrs.			29	19	.604	3.10	58	56	34	412	397	99	170	5	0	0	0	0	0	0	—	37	82	1	4	2.1	.992

Clarence Fieber

FIEBER, CLARENCE THOMAS (Lefty)   BL TL 6'4" 187 lbs.
B. Sept. 4, 1913, San Francisco, Calif.   D. Aug. 20, 1985, Redwood City, Calif.

Year	Team		W	L	PCT	ERA	G	GS	CG	IP	H	BB	SO	ShO	W	L	SV	AB	H	HR	BA	PO	A	E	DP	TC/G	FA
1932	CHI	A	1	0	1.000	1.69	3	0	0	5.1	6	3	1	0	1	0	0	0	0	0	—	0	2	0	0	0.7	1.000

Jim Field

FIELD, JAMES C.
B. Apr. 24, 1863, Philadelphia, Pa.   D. May 13, 1953, Atlantic City, N. J.

Year	Team		W	L	PCT	ERA	G	GS	CG	IP	H	BB	SO	ShO	W	L	SV	AB	H	HR	BA	PO	A	E	DP	TC/G	FA
1890	ROC	AA	1	0	1.000	*2.79*	2	1	1	9.2	7	4	2	0	0	0	1	*				0	1	0	0	0.5	1.000

Jocko Fields

FIELDS, JOHN JOSEPH   BR TR 5'10" 160 lbs.
B. Oct. 20, 1864, Cork, Ireland   D. Oct. 14, 1950, Jersey City, N. J.

Year	Team		W	L	PCT	ERA	G	GS	CG	IP	H	BB	SO	ShO	W	L	SV	AB	H	HR	BA	PO	A	E	DP	TC/G	FA
1887	PIT	N	0	0	—	0.00	1	0	0	2	0	2	0	0	0	0	0	*				0	0	1	0	1.0	—

Lou Fiene

FIENE, LOUIS HENRY (Big Finn)   BR TR 6' 175 lbs.
B. Dec. 29, 1884, Fort Dodge, Iowa   D. Dec. 22, 1964, Chicago, Ill.

Year	Team		W	L	PCT	ERA	G	GS	CG	IP	H	BB	SO	ShO	W	L	SV	AB	H	HR	BA	PO	A	E	DP	TC/G	FA
1906	CHI	A	1	1	.500	2.90	6	2	1	31	35	9	12	0	0	0	0	10	2	0	.200	3	9	1	0	2.2	.923
1907			0	1	.000	4.15	6	1	1	26	30	7	15	0	0	0	1	11	2	0	.182	4	7	0	0	1.8	1.000
1908			0	1	.000	4.00	1	1	1	9	9	1	3	0	0	0	0	3	0	0	.000	0	5	0	0	5.0	1.000
1909			2	5	.286	4.13	13	6	4	72	75	18	24	0	1	0	0	29	2	0	.069	3	30	5	1	2.9	.868
4 yrs.			3	8	.273	3.85	26	10	7	138	149	35	54	0	1	0	1	53	6	0	.113	10	51	6	1	2.6	.910

Dan Fife

FIFE, DANNY WAYNE   BR TR 6'3" 175 lbs.
B. Oct. 5, 1949, Harrisburg, Ill.

Year	Team		W	L	PCT	ERA	G	GS	CG	IP	H	BB	SO	ShO	W	L	SV	AB	H	HR	BA	PO	A	E	DP	TC/G	FA
1973	MIN	A	3	2	.600	4.35	10	7	1	51.2	54	29	18	0	0	1	0	0	0	0	—	4	7	0	0	1.1	1.000
1974			0	0	—	17.36	4	0	0	4.2	10	4	3	0	0	0	0	0	0	0	—	0	0	0	0	0.0	—
2 yrs.			3	2	.600	5.43	14	7	1	56.1	64	33	21	0	0	1	0	0	0	0	—	4	7	0	0	0.8	1.000

Jack Fifield

FIFIELD, JOHN PROCTOR   BR TR 5'11" 160 lbs.
B. Oct. 5, 1871, Enfield, N. H.   D. Nov. 27, 1939, Syracuse, N. Y.

Year	Team		W	L	PCT	ERA	G	GS	CG	IP	H	BB	SO	ShO	W	L	SV	AB	H	HR	BA	PO	A	E	DP	TC/G	FA
1897	PHI	N	5	18	.217	5.51	27	26	21	210.2	263	80	38	0	0	0	0	77	18	2	.234	12	49	2	1	2.3	.968
1898			11	9	.550	3.31	21	21	18	171.1	170	60	31	2	0	0	0	64	7	0	.109	5	29	3	2	1.8	.919
1899	2 teams	PHI N (14G 3–8)				WAS N	(6G 2–4)																				
"	total		5	12	.294	4.77	20	17	15	139.2	183	53	20	1	0	0	1	55	13	0	.236	5	36	5	0	2.3	.891
3 yrs.			21	39	.350	4.59	68	64	54	521.2	616	193	89	3	0	0	1	196	38	2	.194	22	114	10	3	2.1	.932

Frank Figgemeier

FIGGEMEIER, FRANK Y.
B. Apr. 22, 1873, St. Louis, Mo.   D. Apr. 15, 1915, St. Louis, Mo.

Year	Team		W	L	PCT	ERA	G	GS	CG	IP	H	BB	SO	ShO	W	L	SV	AB	H	HR	BA	PO	A	E	DP	TC/G	FA
1894	PHI	N	0	1	.000	11.25	1	1	1	8	12	4	2	0	0	0	0	3	1	0	.333	1	2	0	0	3.0	1.000

Ed Figueroa

FIGUEROA, EDUARDO (Figgy)   BR TR 6'1" 190 lbs.
Born Eduardo Figueroa y Padilla.
B. Oct. 14, 1948, Ciales, Puerto Rico

Year	Team		W	L	PCT	ERA	G	GS	CG	IP	H	BB	SO	ShO	W	L	SV	AB	H	HR	BA	PO	A	E	DP	TC/G	FA
1974	CAL	A	2	8	.200	3.69	25	12	5	105	119	36	49	1	0	0	0	0	0	0	—	4	17	1	1	0.9	.955
1975			16	13	.552	2.91	33	32	16	244.2	213	84	139	2	0	0	0	0	0	0	—	11	42	6	5	1.8	.898
1976	NY	A	19	10	.655	3.02	34	34	14	256.2	237	94	119	4	0	0	0	0	0	0	—	16	23	1	0	1.2	.975
1977			16	11	.593	3.58	32	32	12	239	228	75	104	2	0	0	0	0	0	0	—	18	29	2	1	1.5	.959
1978			20	9	.690	2.99	35	35	12	253	233	77	92	2	0	0	0	0	0	0	—	17	37	1	2	1.6	.982
1979			4	6	.400	4.11	16	16	4	105	109	35	42	0	0	0	0	0	0	0	—	9	16	2	1	1.7	.926

Year	Team	W	L	PCT	ERA	G	GS	CG	IP	H	BB	SO	ShO	Relief Pitching W	L	SV	Batting AB	H	HR	BA	PO	A	E	DP	TC/G	FA

Ed Figueroa *continued*

1980	2 teams	NY A	(15G 3–3)		TEX A	(8G 0–7)																13	17	3	4	1.4	.909
"	total	3	10	.231	6.52	23	17	0	98	152	36	25	0	0	0	1	0	0	0	–	13	17	3	4	1.4	.909
1981	OAK A	0	0	–	5.63	2	1	0	8	8	6	1	0	0	0	0	0	0	0	–	1	1	0	0	1.0	1.000
8 yrs.		80	67	.544	3.51	200	179	63	1309.1	1299	443	571	12	0	0	1	0	0	0	–	89	182	16	15	1.4	.944

LEAGUE CHAMPIONSHIP SERIES

1976	NY A	0	1	.000	5.84	2	2	0	12.1	14	2	5	0	0	0	0	0	0	0	–	0	2	0	0	1.0	1.000
1977		0	0	–	10.80	1	1	0	3.1	5	2	3	0	0	0	0	0	0	0	–	0	0	0	0	0.0	–
1978		0	1	.000	27.00	1	1	0	1	5	0	0	0	0	0	0	0	0	0	–	0	0	0	0	0.0	–
3 yrs.		0	2	.000	8.10	4	4	0	16.2	24	4	8	0	0	0	0	0	0	0	–	0	2	0	0	0.5	1.000

WORLD SERIES

1976	NY A	0	1	.000	5.63	1	1	0	8	6	5	2	0	0	0	0	0	0	0	–	0	1	0	0	0.0	–
1978		0	1	.000	8.10	2	2	0	6.2	9	5	2	0	0	0	0	0	0	0	–	0	0	0	0	0.0	–
2 yrs.		0	2	.000	6.75	3	3	0	14.2	15	10	4	0	0	0	0	0	0	0	–	0	1	0	0	0.3	1.000

Tom Filer

FILER, THOMAS CARSON
B. Dec. 1, 1956, Philadelphia, Pa.   BR TR 6'1"   195 lbs.

1982	CHI N	1	2	.333	5.53	8	8	0	40.2	50	18	15	0	0	0	0	12	1	0	.083	13	10	0	2	2.9	1.000
1985	TOR A	7	0	1.000	3.88	11	9	0	48.2	38	18	24	0	0	0	0	0	0	0	–	1	5	0	1	0.5	1.000
1988	MIL A	5	8	.385	4.43	19	16	2	101.2	108	33	39	1	0	1	0	0	0	0	–	24	17	0	4	2.2	1.000
1989		7	3	.700	3.61	13	13	0	72.1	74	23	20	0	0	0	0	0	0	0	–	4	16	2	4	1.7	.909
4 yrs.		20	13	.606	4.27	51	46	2	263.1	270	92	98	1	0	1	0	12	1	0	.083	42	48	2	11	1.8	.978

Eddie Files

FILES, CHARLES EDWARD
B. May 19, 1883, Portland, Me.   D. May 10, 1954, Cornish, Me.   BR TR

| 1908 | PHI A | 0 | 0 | – | 6.00 | 2 | 0 | 0 | 9 | 8 | 3 | 6 | 0 | 0 | 0 | 0 | 3 | 0 | 0 | .000 | 1 | 0 | 0 | 0 | 0.5 | 1.000 |

Marc Filley

FILLEY, MARCUS LUCIUS
B. Feb. 28, 1912, Troy, N. Y.   BR TR 5'11"   172 lbs.

| 1934 | WAS A | 0 | 0 | – | 27.00 | 1 | 0 | 0 | .1 | 2 | 0 | 0 | 0 | 0 | 0 | 0 | 0 | 0 | 0 | – | 0 | 0 | 0 | 0 | 0.0 | – |

Dana Fillingim

FILLINGIM, DANA
B. Nov. 6, 1893, Columbus, Ga.   D. Feb. 3, 1961, Tuskegee, Ala.   BL TR 5'10"   175 lbs.

1915	PHI A	0	5	.000	3.43	8	4	1	39.1	42	32	17	0	0	0	0	12	2	0	.167	0	10	0	0	1.3	1.000
1918	BOS N	7	6	.538	2.23	14	13	10	113	99	28	29	4	0	0	0	42	9	0	.214	1	34	0	1	2.5	1.000
1919		6	13	.316	3.38	32	19	9	186.1	185	39	50	0	2	0	0	65	16	0	.246	4	67	2	2	2.3	.973
1920		12	21	.364	3.11	37	30	22	272	292	79	66	2	1	2	0	92	16	0	.174	6	104	2	6	3.0	.982
1921		15	10	.600	3.45	44	22	11	239.2	249	56	54	3	4	1	1	85	21	2	.247	2	62	2	1	1.5	.970
1922		5	9	.357	4.54	25	12	5	117	143	37	25	1	1	3	2	38	6	0	.158	2	24	0	1	1.0	1.000
1923		1	9	.100	5.20	35	12	1	100.1	141	36	27	0	1	1	0	31	7	0	.226	0	25	0	0	0.7	1.000
1925	PHI N	1	0	1.000	10.38	5	1	0	8.2	19	6	2	0	1	0	0	3	0	0	.000	1	2	0	1	0.6	1.000
8 yrs.		47	73	.392	3.56	200	113	59	1076.1	1170	313	270	10	10	8	5	368	77	2	.209	16	328	6	13	1.8	.983

Pete Filson

FILSON, WILLIAM PETER
B. Sept. 28, 1958, Darby, Pa.   BB TL 6'2"   195 lbs.

1982	MIN A	0	2	.000	8.76	5	3	0	12.1	17	8	10	0	0	0	0	0	0	0	–	0	0	0	0	0.0	–
1983		4	1	.800	3.40	26	8	0	90	87	29	49	0	1	0	0	0	0	0	–	2	6	1	0	0.3	.889
1984		6	5	.545	4.10	55	7	0	118.2	106	54	59	0	4	3	1	0	0	0	–	2	13	1	0	0.3	.938
1985		4	5	.444	3.67	40	6	1	95.2	93	30	42	0	3	0	2	0	0	0	–	3	13	2	0	0.5	.889
1986	2 teams	MIN A	(4G 0–0)		CHI A	(3G 0–1)																				
"	total	0	1	.000	6.00	7	1	0	18	27	7	8	0	0	0	0	0	0	0	–	0	0	0	0	0.1	1.000
1987	NY A	1	0	1.000	3.27	7	2	0	22	26	9	10	0	0	0	0	0	0	0	–	1	7	0	0	1.1	1.000
6 yrs.		15	14	.517	4.01	140	27	1	356.2	356	137	178	0	8	3	4	0	0	0	–	9	39	4	0	0.4	.923

Joel Finch

FINCH, JOEL D.
B. Aug. 20, 1956, South Bend, Ind.   BR TR 6'2"   175 lbs.

| 1979 | BOS A | 0 | 3 | .000 | 4.89 | 15 | 7 | 0 | 57 | 65 | 25 | 25 | 0 | 0 | 0 | 0 | 1 | 0 | 0 | .000 | 10 | 10 | 1 | 1 | 1.4 | .952 |

Bill Fincher

FINCHER, WILLIAM ALLEN
B. May 26, 1894, Atlanta, Ga.   D. May 7, 1946, Shreveport, La.   BR TR 6'1"   180 lbs.

| 1916 | STL A | 0 | 1 | .000 | 2.14 | 12 | 1 | 0 | 21 | 22 | 7 | 5 | 0 | 0 | 0 | 0 | 4 | 1 | 0 | .250 | 1 | 12 | 0 | 0 | 1.1 | 1.000 |

Tom Fine

FINE, THOMAS MORGAN
B. Oct. 10, 1914, Cleburne, Tex.   BB TR 6'   180 lbs.

1947	BOS A	1	2	.333	5.50	9	7	1	36	41	19	10	0	0	0	0	9	3	0	.333	4	12	0	1	1.8	1.000
1950	STL A	0	1	.000	8.10	14	0	0	36.2	53	25	6	0	0	1	0	12	4	0	.333	1	6	0	2	0.5	1.000
2 yrs.		1	3	.250	6.81	23	7	1	72.2	94	44	16	0	0	1	0	21	7	0	.333	5	18	0	3	1.0	1.000

Rollie Fingers

FINGERS, ROLAND GLEN
B. Aug. 25, 1946, Steubenville, Ohio   BR TR 6'4"   190 lbs.

1968	OAK A	0	0	–	27.00	1	0	0	1.1	4	1	0	0	0	0	0	0	0	0	.200	0	0	0	0	0.0	–
1969		6	7	.462	3.71	60	8	1	119	116	41	61	1	4	3	12	25	5	0	.200	9	30	3	3	0.7	.929
1970		7	9	.438	3.65	45	19	0	148	137	48	79	0	3	1	2	39	4	1	.103	7	26	2	3	0.8	.943
1971		4	6	.400	3.00	48	8	2	129	94	30	98	1	3	3	17	33	7	0	.212	14	24	0	4	0.8	1.000
1972		11	9	.550	2.51	65	2	0	111.1	85	32	113	0	11	9	21	19	6	1	.316	7	11	0	1	0.3	1.000
1973		7	8	.467	1.92	62	2	0	126.2	107	39	110	0	7	6	22	0	0	0	.000	3	14	1	0	0.3	.944
1974		9	5	.643	2.65	76	0	0	119	104	29	95	0	9	5	18	0	0	0	–	9	21	0	4	0.4	1.000
1975		10	6	.625	2.98	75	0	0	126.2	95	33	115	0	10	6	24	1	0	0	.000	8	14	0	2	0.3	1.000
1976		13	11	.542	2.47	70	0	0	135	118	40	113	0	13	11	20	0	0	0	–	4	26	1	0	0.4	.968

Year	Team		W	L	PCT	ERA	G	GS	CG	IP	H	BB	SO	ShO	Relief Pitching W	L	SV	Batting AB	H	HR	BA	PO	A	E	DP	TC/G	FA

Rollie Fingers *continued*

Year	Team		W	L	PCT	ERA	G	GS	CG	IP	H	BB	SO	ShO	W	L	SV	AB	H	HR	BA	PO	A	E	DP	TC/G	FA
1977	SD	N	8	9	.471	3.00	**78**	0	0	132	123	36	113	0	8	9	**35**	20	1	0	.050	5	19	3	1	0.3	.889
1978			6	13	.316	2.52	67	0	0	107	84	29	72	0	6	**13**	37	12	2	0	.167	14	12	1	1	0.4	.963
1979			9	9	.500	4.50	54	0	0	84	91	37	65	0	9	9	13	12	1	0	.083	3	9	1	0	0.2	.923
1980			11	9	.550	2.80	66	0	0	103	101	32	69	0	11	9	23	18	5	0	.278	9	11	1	0	0.3	.952
1981	MIL	A	6	3	.667	1.04	47	0	0	78	55	13	61	0	6	3	**28**	0	0	0	–	2	13	1	1	0.3	.938
1982			5	6	.455	2.60	50	0	0	79.2	63	20	71	0	5	6	29	0	0	0	–	4	10	0	1	0.3	1.000
1984			1	2	.333	1.96	33	0	0	46	38	13	40	0	1	2	23	0	0	0	–	3	3	0	0	0.2	1.000
1985			1	6	.143	5.04	47	0	0	55.1	59	19	24	0	1	6	17	0	0	0	–	7	10	0	1	0.4	1.000
17 yrs.			114	118	.491	2.90	944	37	4	1701	1474	492	1299	2	107	101	341	180	31	2	.172	108	253	14	22	0.4	.963
							4th								3rd		1st										

DIVISIONAL PLAYOFF SERIES

Year	Team		W	L	PCT	ERA	G	GS	CG	IP	H	BB	SO	ShO	W	L	SV	AB	H	HR	BA	PO	A	E	DP	TC/G	FA
1981	MIL	A	1	0	1.000	3.86	3	0	0	4.2	7	1	5	0	1	0	1	0	0	0	–	0	0	0	0	0.0	–

LEAGUE CHAMPIONSHIP SERIES

Year	Team		W	L	PCT	ERA	G	GS	CG	IP	H	BB	SO	ShO	W	L	SV	AB	H	HR	BA	PO	A	E	DP	TC/G	FA
1971	OAK	A	0	0	–	7.71	2	0	0	2.1	2	1	2	0	0	0	0	0	0	0	–	0	0	0	0	0.0	–
1972			1	0	1.000	1.69	3	0	0	5.1	4	1	3	0	1	0	0	1	0	0	.000	0	0	0	0	0.0	–
1973			0	1	.000	1.93	3	0	0	4.2	4	2	4	0	0	1	1	0	0	0	–	0	0	0	0	0.0	–
1974			0	0	–	3.00	2	0	0	3	3	1	3	0	0	0	1	0	0	0	–	0	0	0	0	0.0	–
1975			0	1	.000	6.75	1	0	0	4	5	1	3	0	0	1	0	0	0	0	–	1	0	0	0	1.0	1.000
5 yrs.			1	2	.333	3.72	11	0	0	19.1	18	6	15	0	1	2	2	1	0	0	.000	1	0	0	0	0.1	1.000

WORLD SERIES

Year	Team		W	L	PCT	ERA	G	GS	CG	IP	H	BB	SO	ShO	W	L	SV	AB	H	HR	BA	PO	A	E	DP	TC/G	FA
1972	OAK	A	1	1	.500	1.74	6	0	0	10.1	4	4	11	0	1	1	2	1	0	0	.000	0	3	0	0	0.3	1.000
1973			0	1	.000	0.66	6	0	0	13.2	13	4	8	0	0	1	2	3	1	0	.333	0	2	0	0	0.3	1.000
1974			1	0	1.000	1.93	4	0	0	9.1	8	2	6	0	1	0	2	2	0	0	.000	0	0	0	0	0.3	1.000
3 yrs.			2	2	.500	1.35	16	0	0	33.1	25	10	25	0	2	2	6	6	1	0	.167	0	5	0	0	0.3	1.000
							2nd								2nd	2nd	1st										

Herman Fink

FINK, HERMAN ADAM
B. Aug. 22, 1911, Concord, N. C. D. Aug. 24, 1980, Salisbury, N. C.

BR TR 6'2"   198 lbs.

Year	Team		W	L	PCT	ERA	G	GS	CG	IP	H	BB	SO	ShO	W	L	SV	AB	H	HR	BA	PO	A	E	DP	TC/G	FA
1935	PHI	A	0	3	.000	9.19	5	3	0	15.2	18	10	2	0	0	0	0	5	1	0	.200	2	3	1	1	1.2	.833
1936			8	16	.333	5.39	34	24	9	188.2	222	78	53	0	0	2	3	64	8	0	.125	3	28	3	0	1.0	.912
1937			2	1	.667	4.05	28	3	1	80	82	35	18	0	2	0	1	24	5	0	.208	0	16	0	1	0.6	1.000
3 yrs.			10	20	.333	5.22	67	30	10	284.1	322	123	73	0	2	2	4	93	14	0	.151	5	47	4	2	0.8	.929

Pembroke Finlayson

FINLAYSON, PEMBROKE
B. July 31, 1888, Cheraw, S. C. D. Mar. 6, 1912, Brooklyn, N. Y.

BR TR

Year	Team		W	L	PCT	ERA	G	GS	CG	IP	H	BB	SO	ShO	W	L	SV	AB	H	HR	BA	PO	A	E	DP	TC/G	FA
1908	BKN	N	0	0	–	135.00	1	0	0	.1	0	4	0	0	0	0	0	0	0	0	–	0	0	0	0	0.0	–
1909			0	0	–	5.14	1	0	0	7	7	4	2	0	0	0	0	3	0	0	.000	0	1	0	0	1.0	1.000
2 yrs.			0	0	–	11.05	2	0	0	7.1	7	8	2	0	0	0	0	3	0	0	.000	0	1	0	0	0.5	1.000

Chuck Finley

FINLEY, CHARLES EDWARD
B. Nov. 26, 1962, Monroe, La.

BL TL 6'6"   220 lbs.

Year	Team		W	L	PCT	ERA	G	GS	CG	IP	H	BB	SO	ShO	W	L	SV	AB	H	HR	BA	PO	A	E	DP	TC/G	FA
1986	CAL	A	3	1	.750	3.30	25	0	0	46.1	40	23	37	0	3	1	0	0	0	0	–	8	8	0	1	0.6	1.000
1987			2	7	.222	4.67	35	3	0	90.2	102	43	63	0	2	6	0	0	0	0	–	6	11	1	1	0.5	.944
1988			9	15	.375	4.17	31	31	2	194.1	191	82	111	0	0	0	0	0	0	0	–	5	24	1	1	1.0	.967
1989			16	9	.640	2.57	29	29	9	199.2	171	82	156	1	0	0	0	0	0	0	–	4	16	2	0	0.8	.909
4 yrs.			30	32	.484	3.58	120	63	11	531	504	230	367	1	5	7	0	0	0	0	–	23	59	4	3	0.7	.953

LEAGUE CHAMPIONSHIP SERIES

Year	Team		W	L	PCT	ERA	G	GS	CG	IP	H	BB	SO	ShO	W	L	SV	AB	H	HR	BA	PO	A	E	DP	TC/G	FA
1986	CAL	A	0	0	–	0.00	3	0	0	2	1	0	1	0	0	0	0	0	0	0	–	0	0	0	0	0.0	–

Happy Finneran

FINNERAN, JOSEPH IGNATIUS (Smokey Joe)
B. Oct. 29, 1891, East Orange, N. J. D. Feb. 3, 1942, Orange, N. J.

BB TR 5'10½" 169 lbs.

Year	Team		W	L	PCT	ERA	G	GS	CG	IP	H	BB	SO	ShO	W	L	SV	AB	H	HR	BA	PO	A	E	DP	TC/G	FA
1912	PHI	N	0	2	.000	2.53	14	4	0	46.1	50	10	10	0	0	1	0	10	2	0	.200	3	11	0	0	1.0	1.000
1913			0	0	–	7.20	3	0	0	5	12	2	0	0	0	0	0	3	2	0	.667	0	0	0	0	0.0	–
1914	BKN	F	12	11	.522	3.18	27	23	13	175.1	153	60	54	2	1	0	1	55	7	0	.127	8	48	2	1	2.1	.966
1915			12	13	.480	2.80	37	24	12	215.1	197	87	68	1	3	2	0	74	11	0	.149	15	61	2	1	2.1	.974
1918	2 teams	DET A (5G 0-2)					NY A (23G 3-6)																				
"	total		3	8	.273	4.43	28	15	4	128	156	43	36	0	1	0	1	42	9	0	.214	4	35	0	1	1.4	1.000
5 yrs.			27	34	.443	3.30	109	66	29	570	568	202	168	3	5	3	3	184	31	0	.168	30	155	4	3	1.7	.979

Steve Fireovid

FIREOVID, STEPHEN JOHN
B. June 6, 1957, Bryan, Ohio

BB TR 6'2"   195 lbs.

Year	Team		W	L	PCT	ERA	G	GS	CG	IP	H	BB	SO	ShO	W	L	SV	AB	H	HR	BA	PO	A	E	DP	TC/G	FA
1981	SD	N	0	1	.000	2.77	5	4	0	26	30	7	11	0	0	0	0	7	1	0	.143	0	5	0	0	1.0	1.000
1983			0	0	–	1.80	3	0	0	5	4	2	1	0	0	0	0	0	0	0	–	0	1	0	0	0.3	1.000
1984	PHI	N	0	0	–	1.59	6	0	0	5.2	4	0	3	0	0	0	0	0	0	0	–	3	1	0	1	0.7	1.000
1985	CHI	A	0	0	–	5.14	4	0	0	7	17	2	2	0	0	0	0	0	0	0	–	0	0	0	0	0.0	–
1986	SEA	A	2	0	1.000	4.29	10	1	0	21	28	4	10	0	2	0	0	0	0	0	–	3	2	1	0	0.6	.833
5 yrs.			2	1	.667	3.34	28	5	0	64.2	83	15	27	0	2	0	0	7	1	0	.143	6	9	1	1	0.6	.938

Ted Firth

FIRTH, THEODORE JOHN
B. 1856, Massachusetts D. Apr. 18, 1885, Marshalltown, Iowa

Year	Team		W	L	PCT	ERA	G	GS	CG	IP	H	BB	SO	ShO	W	L	SV	AB	H	HR	BA	PO	A	E	DP	TC/G	FA
1884	RIC	AA	0	1	.000	8.00	1	1	1	9	14	5	0	0	0	0	0	3	1	0	.333	1	1	0	0	2.0	1.000

Bill Fischer

FISCHER, WILLIAM CHARLES
B. Oct. 11, 1930, Wausau, Wis.

BR TR 6'   190 lbs.

Year	Team		W	L	PCT	ERA	G	GS	CG	IP	H	BB	SO	ShO	W	L	SV	AB	H	HR	BA	PO	A	E	DP	TC/G	FA
1956	CHI	A	0	0	–	21.60	3	0	0	1.2	6	1	2	0	0	0	0	0	0	0	–	1	0	0	0	0.3	1.000
1957			7	8	.467	3.48	33	11	3	124	139	35	48	1	3	4	1	40	6	0	.150	6	20	1	0	0.8	.963

Year	Team		W	L	PCT	ERA	G	GS	CG	IP	H	BB	SO	ShO	Relief Pitching W	L	SV	Batting AB	H	HR	BA	PO	A	E	DP	TC/G	FA

Bill Fischer *continued*

1958	3 teams	CHI A (17G 2-3) DET A (22G 2-4) WAS A (3G 0-3)																									
"	total		4	10	.286	6.34	42	6	0	88	113	31	42	0	2	6	2	13	2	0	.154	4	23	0	2	0.6	1.000
1959	WAS A		9	11	.450	4.28	34	29	6	187.1	211	43	62	1	0	0	0	54	7	0	.130	21	48	1	2	2.1	.986
1960	2 teams	WAS A (20G 3-5) DET A (20G 5-3)																									
"	total		8	8	.500	4.30	40	13	2	132	135	35	55	0	2	1	0	30	7	1	.233	8	28	0	4	0.9	1.000
1961	2 teams	DET A (26G 3-2) KC A (15G 1-0)																									
"	total		4	2	.667	4.66	41	1	0	67.2	80	23	30	0	4	1	5	9	0	0	.000	7	9	0	0	0.4	1.000
1962	KC A		4	12	.250	3.95	34	16	5	127.2	150	8	38	0	1	0	2	38	4	0	.105	15	16	0	1	0.9	1.000
1963			9	6	.600	3.57	45	2	0	95.2	86	29	34	0	9	6	3	15	1	0	.067	3	14	1	1	0.4	.944
1964	MIN A		0	1	.000	7.36	9	0	0	7.1	16	5	2	0	0	0	0	0	0	0	—	0	3	0	0	0.3	1.000
9 yrs.			45	58	.437	4.34	281	78	16	831.1	936	210	313	2	21	19	13	199	27	1	.136	65	161	3	10	0.8	.987

Carl Fischer

FISCHER, CHARLES WILLIAM
B. Nov. 5, 1905, Medina, N. Y. D. Dec. 10, 1963, Medina, N. Y. BR TL 6' 180 lbs.

1930	WAS A		1	1	.500	4.86	8	4	1	33.1	37	18	21	0	0	0	0	9	0	0	.000	1	9	1	0	1.4	.909
1931			13	9	.591	4.38	46	23	7	191	207	80	96	0	2	0	3	66	8	0	.121	1	23	2	0	0.6	.923
1932	2 teams	WAS A (12G 3-2) STL A (24G 3-7)																									
"	total		6	9	.400	5.36	36	18	5	147.2	179	76	58	1	1	0	1	49	12	0	.245	5	15	1	1	0.6	.952
1933	DET A		11	15	.423	3.55	35	22	9	182.1	176	84	93	0	5	1	3	62	9	0	.145	1	29	1	1	0.9	.968
1934			6	4	.600	4.37	20	15	4	94.2	107	38	39	1	1	1	1	31	2	0	.065	3	8	0	0	0.6	1.000
1935	2 teams	DET A (3G 0-1) CHI A (24G 5-5)																									
"	total		5	6	.455	6.17	27	12	3	100.2	118	44	38	1	2	0	0	23	4	0	.174	5	13	1	0	0.7	.947
1937	2 teams	CLE A (2G 0-1) WAS A (17G 4-5)																									
"	total		4	6	.400	4.58	19	11	2	72.2	76	32	31	0	0	2	2	22	3	0	.136	1	5	1	0	0.4	.857
7 yrs.			46	50	.479	4.63	191	105	31	822.2	900	372	376	3	11	5	11	262	38	0	.145	17	102	7	2	0.7	.944

Hank Fischer

FISCHER, HENRY WILLIAM (Bulldog)
B. Jan. 11, 1940, Yonkers, N. Y. BR TR 6' 190 lbs.

1962	MIL N		2	3	.400	5.30	29	0	0	37.1	43	20	29	0	2	3	4	4	0	0	.000	3	5	0	0	0.3	1.000
1963			4	3	.571	4.96	31	6	1	74.1	74	28	72	0	1	3	0	19	2	0	.105	4	9	1	0	0.5	.929
1964			11	10	.524	4.01	37	28	9	168.1	177	39	99	5	0	0	2	52	8	0	.154	14	23	2	0	1.1	.949
1965			8	9	.471	3.89	31	22	2	122.2	126	39	79	0	0	1	0	37	4	0	.108	10	11	3	0	0.8	.875
1966	3 teams	ATL N (14G 2-3) CIN N (11G 0-6) BOS A (6G 2-3)																									
"	total		4	12	.250	4.53	31	22	1	117.1	143	40	72	0	1	0	1	33	3	0	.091	2	15	2	0	0.6	.895
1967	BOS A		1	2	.333	2.36	9	2	1	26.2	24	8	18	0	0	1	1	7	1	0	.143	1	4	0	0	0.6	1.000
6 yrs.			30	39	.435	4.23	168	77	14	546.2	587	174	369	5	4	7	7	152	18	0	.118	34	67	8	0	0.6	.927

Jeff Fischer

FISCHER, JEFFREY THOMAS
B. Aug. 17, 1963, West Palm Beach, Fla. BR TR 6'3" 185 lbs.

1987	MON N		0	1	.000	8.56	4	2	0	13.2	21	5	6	0	0	0	0	5	1	0	.200	1	2	0	0	0.8	1.000
1989	LA N		0	0	—	13.50	2	0	0	3.1	7	0	2	0	0	0	0	0	0	0	—	0	0	0	0	0.0	—
2 yrs.			0	1	.000	9.53	6	2	0	17	28	5	8	0	0	0	0	5	1	0	.200	1	2	0	0	0.5	1.000

Rube Fischer

FISCHER, REUBEN WALTER
B. Sept. 19, 1916, Carlock, S. D. BR TR 6'4" 190 lbs.

1941	NY N		1	0	1.000	2.45	2	1	1	11	10	6	9	0	0	0	0	3	1	0	.333	1	1	0	0	1.0	1.000
1943			5	10	.333	4.61	22	17	4	130.2	140	59	47	0	1	0	1	43	11	1	.256	2	18	1	2	1.0	.952
1944			6	14	.300	5.18	38	18	2	128.2	128	87	39	1	3	4	2	40	5	0	.125	2	17	0	0	0.5	1.000
1945			3	8	.273	5.63	31	4	0	76.2	90	49	27	0	2	5	1	19	4	1	.211	5	10	1	1	0.5	.938
1946			1	2	.333	6.31	15	1	0	35.2	48	21	14	0	1	2	0	9	1	0	.111	0	9	3	0	0.8	.750
5 yrs.			16	34	.320	5.10	108	41	7	382.2	416	222	136	1	7	11	4	114	22	2	.193	10	55	5	3	0.6	.929

Todd Fischer

FISCHER, TODD RICHARD
B. Sept. 15, 1960, Columbus, Ohio BR TR 5'10" 170 lbs.

| 1986 | CAL A | | 0 | 0 | — | 4.24 | 9 | 0 | 0 | 17 | 18 | 8 | 7 | 0 | 0 | 0 | 0 | 0 | 0 | 0 | — | 0 | 2 | 0 | 1 | 0.2 | 1.000 |

Leo Fishel

FISHEL, LEO
B. Dec. 13, 1877, Babylon, N. Y. D. May 19, 1960, Hempstead, N. Y. BR TR 6' 175 lbs.

| 1899 | NY N | | 0 | 1 | .000 | 6.00 | 1 | 1 | 1 | 9 | 9 | 6 | 6 | 0 | 0 | 0 | 0 | 4 | 1 | 0 | .250 | 1 | 2 | 0 | 0 | 3.0 | 1.000 |

Fisher

FISHER,
B. Johnstown, Pa. Deceased.

1884	PHI U		1	7	.125	*3.57*	8	8	8	70.2	76	13	42	0	0	0	0	65	10	0	.154	3	15	9	0	3.4	.667
1885	BUF N		0	1	.000	5.00	1	1	1	9	10	2	4	0	0	0	0	4	0	0	.000	1	3	0	0	4.0	1.000
2 yrs.			1	8	.111	3.73	9	9	9	79.2	86	15	46	0	0	0	0	*				4	18	9	0	3.4	.710

Brian Fisher

FISHER, BRIAN KEVIN
B. Mar. 18, 1962, Honolulu, Hawaii BR TR 6'4" 210 lbs.

1985	NY A		4	4	.500	2.38	55	0	0	98.1	77	29	85	0	4	4	14	0	0	0	—	4	13	1	1	0.3	.944
1986			9	5	.643	4.93	62	0	0	96.2	105	37	67	0	9	5	6	0	0	0	—	3	7	1	1	0.2	.909
1987	PIT N		11	9	.550	4.52	37	26	6	185.1	185	72	117	3	0	0	0	58	11	2	.190	13	20	1	1	0.9	.971
1988			8	10	.444	4.61	33	22	1	146.1	157	57	66	1	2	0	1	42	2	0	.048	6	17	3	2	0.8	.885
1989			0	3	.000	7.94	9	3	0	17	25	10	8	0	0	1	1	5	0	0	.000	2	1	0	0	0.3	1.000
5 yrs.			32	31	.508	4.34	196	51	7	543.2	549	205	343	4	15	10	22	105	13	2	.124	28	58	6	5	0.5	.935

Chauncey Fisher

FISHER, CHAUNCEY BURR (Peach)
Brother of Tom Fisher.
B. Jan. 8, 1872, Anderson, Ind. D. Apr. 27, 1939, Los Angeles, Calif. BR TR 5'11" 175 lbs.

| 1893 | CLE N | | 0 | 2 | .000 | 5.50 | 2 | 2 | 2 | 18 | 26 | 9 | 9 | 0 | 0 | 0 | 0 | 8 | 2 | 0 | .250 | 3 | 3 | 0 | 0 | 3.0 | 1.000 |

Year	Team	W	L	PCT	ERA	G	GS	CG	IP	H	BB	SO	ShO	Relief Pitching W	L	SV	Batting AB	H	HR	BA	PO	A	E	DP	TC/G	FA

Chauncey Fisher *continued*

Year	Team	W	L	PCT	ERA	G	GS	CG	IP	H	BB	SO	ShO	W	L	SV	AB	H	HR	BA	PO	A	E	DP	TC/G	FA
1894	2 teams	CLE N	(3G 0–2)		CIN N	(11G 2–8)																				
"	total	2	10	.167	7.76	14	13	10	102	156	49	14	0	0	0	0	47	10	1	.213	3	17	2	1	1.6	.909
1896	CIN N	10	7	.588	4.45	27	15	13	159.2	199	36	25	2	2	2	2	57	14	0	.246	10	37	4	2	1.9	.922
1897	BKN N	9	7	.563	4.23	20	13	11	149	184	43	31	1	2	1	1	59	12	0	.203	4	26	0	2	1.5	1.000
1901	2 teams	NY N	(1G 0–1)		STL N	(1G 0–0)																				
"	total	0	1	.000	15.43	2	1	0	7	18	3	1	0	0	0	0	3	0	0	.000	0	2	0	0	1.0	1.000
5 yrs.		21	27	.438	5.37	65	44	36	435.2	583	140	80	3	4	3	3	174	38	1	.218	20	85	6	5	1.7	.946

Cherokee Fisher

FISHER, WILLIAM CHARLES
B. Dec., 1845, Philadelphia, Pa.   D. Sept. 26, 1912, New York, N. Y.   BR TR 5'9"   164 lbs.

Year	Team	W	L	PCT	ERA	G	GS	CG	IP	H	BB	SO	ShO	W	L	SV	AB	H	HR	BA	PO	A	E	DP	TC/G	FA
1876	CIN N	4	20	.167	3.02	28	24	22	229.1	294	6	29	0	0	0	0	129	32	0	.248	19	27	12	0	2.1	.793
1877	CHI N	0	0	–	0.00	0	0	0	0	0	0	0	0	0	0	0	4	0	0	.000	0	0	0	0	0.0	–
1878	PRO N	0	1	.000	4.00	1	1	1	9	14	0	2	0	0	0	0	3	0	0	.000	2	1	0	0	3.0	1.000
3 yrs.		4	21	.160	3.06	29	25	23	238.1	308	6	31	0	0	0	0	136	32	0	.235	21	28	12	0	2.1	.803

Clarence Fisher

FISHER, CLARENCE HENRY
B. Aug. 27, 1898, Letart, W. Va.   D. Nov. 2, 1965, Point Pleasant, W. Va.   BR TR 6'   174 lbs.

Year	Team	W	L	PCT	ERA	G	GS	CG	IP	H	BB	SO	ShO	W	L	SV	AB	H	HR	BA	PO	A	E	DP	TC/G	FA
1919	WAS A	0	0	–	13.50	2	0	0	4	8	3	1	0	0	0	0	0	0	0	–	0	1	0	0	0.5	1.000
1920		0	1	.000	9.82	2	0	0	3.2	5	5	0	0	0	1	0	1	0	0	.000	0	4	0	0	2.0	1.000
2 yrs.		0	1	.000	11.74	4	0	0	7.2	13	8	1	0	0	1	0	1	0	0	.000	0	5	0	0	1.3	1.000

Don Fisher

FISHER, DONALD RAYMOND
B. Feb. 6, 1916, Cleveland, Ohio   D. July 29, 1973, Mayfield Heights, Ohio   BR TR 6'   210 lbs.

Year	Team	W	L	PCT	ERA	G	GS	CG	IP	H	BB	SO	ShO	W	L	SV	AB	H	HR	BA	PO	A	E	DP	TC/G	FA
1945	NY N	1	0	1.000	2.00	2	1	1	18	12	7	4	0	0	0	0	7	1	0	.143	0	4	1	0	2.5	.800

Ed Fisher

FISHER, EDWARD FREDRICK
B. Oct. 31, 1876, Wayne, Mich.   D. July 24, 1951, Spokane, Wash.   BR TR 6'2"   200 lbs.

Year	Team	W	L	PCT	ERA	G	GS	CG	IP	H	BB	SO	ShO	W	L	SV	AB	H	HR	BA	PO	A	E	DP	TC/G	FA
1902	DET A	0	0	–	0.00	1	0	0	4	4	1	0	0	0	0	0	2	0	0	.000	0	0	0	0	0.0	–

Eddie Fisher

FISHER, EDDIE GENE
B. July 16, 1936, Shreveport, La.   BR TR 6'2½"   200 lbs.

Year	Team	W	L	PCT	ERA	G	GS	CG	IP	H	BB	SO	ShO	W	L	SV	AB	H	HR	BA	PO	A	E	DP	TC/G	FA
1959	SF N	2	6	.250	7.88	17	5	0	40	57	8	15	0	0	4	1	8	0	0	.000	5	3	0	0	0.5	1.000
1960		1	0	1.000	3.55	9	3	1	12.2	11	2	7	0	0	0	0	5	3	0	.600	1	2	0	0	1.0	1.000
1961	CHI A	0	2	.000	5.35	15	1	0	33.2	36	9	16	0	0	2	1	7	1	0	.143	3	6	1	0	0.7	.900
1962		9	5	.643	3.10	57	12	2	182.2	169	45	88	1	4	3	5	46	6	0	.130	16	30	3	3	0.9	.939
1963		9	8	.529	3.95	33	15	2	120.2	114	28	67	1	2	3	0	36	5	0	.139	10	24	2	0	1.1	.944
1964		6	3	.667	3.02	59	2	0	125	86	32	74	0	6	3	9	18	3	0	.167	7	20	0	1	0.5	1.000
1965		15	7	.682	2.40	82	0	0	165.1	118	43	90	0	15	7	24	29	4	0	.138	9	35	1	3	0.5	.978
1966	2 teams	CHI A	(23G 1–3)		BAL A	(44G 5–3)																				
"	total	6	6	.500	2.52	67	0	0	107	87	36	57	0	6	6	19	15	2	0	.133	7	19	3	0	0.4	.897
1967	BAL A	4	3	.571	3.61	46	0	0	89.2	82	26	53	0	4	3	1	5	1	0	.200	4	12	1	1	0.4	.941
1968	CLE A	4	2	.667	2.85	54	0	0	94.2	87	17	42	0	4	2	4	12	0	0	.000	9	18	0	1	0.5	1.000
1969	CAL A	3	2	.600	3.63	52	1	0	96.2	100	28	47	0	2	2	3	13	0	0	.000	6	16	2	3	0.5	.917
1970		4	4	.500	3.05	67	2	0	130	117	35	74	0	4	4	8	11	1	0	.091	11	25	1	1	0.6	.973
1971		10	8	.556	2.72	57	3	0	119	92	50	82	0	9	5	3	16	1	0	.063	6	17	0	0	0.4	1.000
1972	2 teams	CAL A	(43G 4–5)		CHI A	(6G 0–1)																				
"	total	4	6	.400	3.91	49	5	0	103.2	104	40	42	0	4	3	4	24	2	0	.083	6	17	2	1	0.5	.920
1973	2 teams	CHI A	(26G 6–7)		STL N	(6G 2–1)																				
"	total	8	8	.500	4.67	32	16	2	117.2	138	39	58	0	2	1	0	1	1	0	1.000	7	18	1	3	0.8	.962
15 yrs.		85	70	.548	3.41	690	63	7	1538.1	1398	438	812	2	62	49	81	246	30	0	.122	107	262	17	17	0.6	.956

Fritz Fisher

FISHER, FREDERICK BROWN
B. Nov. 28, 1941, Adrian, Mich.   BL TL 6'1"   180 lbs.

Year	Team	W	L	PCT	ERA	G	GS	CG	IP	H	BB	SO	ShO	W	L	SV	AB	H	HR	BA	PO	A	E	DP	TC/G	FA
1964	DET A	0	0	–	108.00	1	0	0	.1	2	2	1	0	0	0	0	0	0	0	–	0	0	0	0	0.0	–

Harry Fisher

FISHER, HARRY DEVERAUX
B. Jan. 3, 1926, Newbury, Ont., Canada   D. Sept. 20, 1981, Waterloo, Ont., Canada   BL TR 6'   180 lbs.

Year	Team	W	L	PCT	ERA	G	GS	CG	IP	H	BB	SO	ShO	W	L	SV	AB	H	HR	BA	PO	A	E	DP	TC/G	FA
1952	PIT N	1	2	.333	6.87	8	3	0	18.1	17	13	5	0	0	0	0	*				1	1	0	0	0.3	1.000

Jack Fisher

FISHER, JOHN HOWARD (Fat Jack)
B. Mar. 4, 1939, Frostburg, Md.   BR TR 6'2"   215 lbs.

Year	Team	W	L	PCT	ERA	G	GS	CG	IP	H	BB	SO	ShO	W	L	SV	AB	H	HR	BA	PO	A	E	DP	TC/G	FA
1959	BAL A	1	6	.143	3.05	27	7	1	88.2	76	38	52	1	0	2	2	23	3	0	.130	2	11	1	0	0.5	.929
1960		12	11	.522	3.41	40	20	8	197.2	174	78	99	3	6	3	2	60	11	1	.183	11	33	1	1	1.1	.978
1961		10	13	.435	3.90	36	25	10	196	205	75	118	1	0	4	1	56	5	0	.089	8	22	2	1	0.9	.938
1962		7	9	.438	5.09	32	25	4	152	173	56	81	0	0	2	1	49	5	0	.102	18	18	0	1	1.1	1.000
1963	SF N	6	10	.375	4.58	36	12	2	116	132	38	57	0	3	2	1	29	3	0	.103	10	19	0	0	0.8	1.000
1964	NY N	10	17	.370	4.23	40	34	8	227.2	256	56	115	1	0	2	0	76	12	0	.158	18	34	3	5	1.4	.945
1965		8	24	.250	3.94	43	36	10	253.2	252	68	116	0	0	2	1	78	12	0	.154	27	49	3	4	1.8	.987
1966		11	14	.440	3.68	38	33	10	230	229	54	127	2	1	0	0	67	6	0	.090	26	45	3	3	1.9	.959
1967		9	18	.333	4.70	39	30	7	220.1	251	64	117	1	1	1	0	70	7	0	.100	15	43	1	1	1.5	.983
1968	CHI A	8	13	.381	2.99	35	28	2	180.2	176	48	80	0	1	1	1	53	6	0	.113	18	24	1	2	1.2	.977
1969	CIN N	4	4	.500	5.50	34	15	0	113	137	30	55	0	1	0	1	33	4	0	.121	4	14	2	0	0.6	.900
11 yrs.		86	139	.382	4.06	400	265	62	1975.2	2061	605	1017	9	12	18	9	594	74	1	.125	157	312	15	18	1.2	.969

Maury Fisher

FISHER, MAURICE WAYNE
B. Feb. 16, 1931, Uniondale, Ind.   BR TR 6'5"   210 lbs.

Year	Team	W	L	PCT	ERA	G	GS	CG	IP	H	BB	SO	ShO	W	L	SV	AB	H	HR	BA	PO	A	E	DP	TC/G	FA
1955	CIN N	0	0	–	6.75	1	0	0	2.2	5	2	1	0	0	0	0	1	0	0	.000	0	0	0	0	0.0	–

Year	Team	W	L	PCT	ERA	G	GS	CG	IP	H	BB	SO	ShO	Relief Pitching W	L	SV	Batting AB	H	HR	BA	PO	A	E	DP	TC/G	FA

Ray Fisher

FISHER, RAYMUND LYLE BR TR 5'11½" 180 lbs.
B. Oct. 4, 1887, Middlebury, Vt. D. Nov. 3, 1982, Ann Arbor, Mich.

Year	Team	W	L	PCT	ERA	G	GS	CG	IP	H	BB	SO	ShO	W	L	SV	AB	H	HR	BA	PO	A	E	DP	TC/G	FA
1910	NY A	5	3	.625	2.92	17	7	3	92.1	95	18	42	0	1	0	1	29	3	0	.103	2	37	3	0	2.5	.929
1911		10	11	.476	3.25	29	22	8	171.2	178	55	99	2	2	1	0	59	7	1	.119	6	67	5	1	2.7	.936
1912		2	8	.200	5.88	17	13	5	90.1	107	32	47	0	1	0	0	31	2	0	.065	3	38	4	0	2.6	.911
1913		12	16	.429	3.18	43	31	14	246.1	244	71	92	1	0	1	1	79	22	0	.278	12	85	7	0	2.4	.933
1914		10	12	.455	2.28	29	26	17	209	177	61	86	2	0	0	1	65	9	0	.138	8	77	4	4	3.1	.955
1915		18	11	.621	2.11	30	28	20	247.2	219	62	97	4	2	0	0	83	9	0	.108	9	76	6	0	3.0	.934
1916		11	8	.579	3.17	31	21	9	179	191	51	56	1	2	1	2	62	11	0	.177	6	51	3	1	1.9	.950
1917		8	9	.471	2.19	23	18	12	144	126	43	64	3	0	0	0	50	9	1	.180	12	42	2	5	2.4	.964
1919	CIN N	14	5	.737	2.17	26	20	12	174.1	141	38	41	5	1	0	1	59	16	0	.271	8	68	2	1	3.0	.974
1920		10	11	.476	2.73	33	22	10	201	189	50	56	1	1	0	1	70	17	0	.243	6	69	3	1	2.4	.962
10 yrs.		100	94	.515	2.82	278	208	110	1755.2	1667	481	680	19	10	3	7	587	105	3	.179	72	610	39	13	2.6	.946

WORLD SERIES

| 1919 | CIN N | 0 | 1 | .000 | 2.35 | 2 | 1 | 0 | 7.2 | 7 | 2 | 2 | 0 | 0 | 0 | 0 | 2 | 1 | 0 | .500 | 0 | 6 | 1 | 0 | 3.5 | .857 |

Tom Fisher

FISHER, THOMAS CHALMERS (Red) BR TR 5'10½" 185 lbs.
Brother of Chauncey Fisher.
B. Nov. 1, 1880, Anderson, Ind. D. Sept. 3, 1972, Anderson, Ind.

| 1904 | BOS N | 6 | 15 | .286 | 4.25 | 31 | 21 | 19 | 214 | 257 | 82 | 84 | 3 | 0 | 1 | 0 | 99 | 21 | 2 | .212 | 26 | 34 | 7 | 0 | 2.2 | .896 |

Tom Fisher

FISHER, THOMAS GENE BR TR 6' 180 lbs.
B. Apr. 4, 1942, Cleveland, Ohio

| 1967 | BAL A | 0 | 0 | – | 0.00 | 2 | 0 | 0 | 3.1 | 2 | 2 | 1 | 0 | 0 | 0 | 0 | 0 | 0 | 0 | – | 0 | 0 | 0 | 0 | 0.0 | – |

Max Fiske

FISKE, MAXIMILIAN PATRICK (Mox Ski) BR TR 5'11" 185 lbs.
B. Oct. 12, 1888, Chicago, Ill. D. May 15, 1928, Chicago, Ill.

| 1914 | CHI F | 12 | 9 | .571 | 3.14 | 38 | 22 | 7 | 198 | 161 | 59 | 87 | 0 | 4 | 1 | 0 | 68 | 16 | 0 | .235 | 0 | 63 | 3 | 1 | 1.7 | .955 |

Paul Fittery

FITTERY, PAUL CLARENCE BB TL 5'8" 168 lbs.
B. Oct. 10, 1887, Lebanon, Pa. D. Jan. 28, 1974, Cartersville, Ga.

1914	CIN N	0	2	.000	3.09	8	4	2	43.2	41	12	21	0	0	0	0	17	1	0	.059	3	13	3	0	2.4	.842
1917	PHI N	1	1	.500	4.53	17	2	1	55.2	69	27	13	0	0	0	0	22	2	0	.091	6	23	0	2	1.7	1.000
2 yrs.		1	3	.250	3.90	25	6	3	99.1	110	39	34	0	0	0	0	39	3	0	.077	9	36	3	2	1.9	.938

John Fitzgerald

FITZGERALD, JOHN FRANCIS BL TL 6'3" 190 lbs.
B. Sept. 15, 1933, Brooklyn, N. Y.

| 1958 | SF N | 0 | 0 | – | 3.00 | 1 | 1 | 0 | 3 | 1 | 1 | 3 | 0 | 0 | 0 | 0 | 1 | 0 | 0 | .000 | 1 | 1 | 0 | 0 | 2.0 | 1.000 |

John Fitzgerald

FITZGERALD, JOHN H. BL TL 6'3" 190 lbs.
B. May 30, 1870, Natick, Mass. D. Mar. 31, 1921, Boston, Mass.

| 1891 | BOS AA | 1 | 1 | .500 | 5.63 | 6 | 3 | 2 | 32 | 49 | 11 | 16 | 0 | 0 | 0 | 1 | 14 | 1 | 0 | .071 | 0 | 8 | 1 | 0 | 1.5 | .889 |

John Fitzgerald

FITZGERALD, JOHN J.

| 1890 | ROC AA | 3 | 8 | .273 | 4.04 | 11 | 11 | 8 | 78 | 77 | 45 | 35 | 1 | 0 | 0 | 0 | 31 | 6 | 0 | .194 | 3 | 21 | 1 | 0 | 2.3 | .960 |

John Fitzgerald

FITZGERALD, JOHN T.
B. Leadville, Colo. Deceased.

1891	LOU AA	14	18	.438	3.59	33	32	29	276	280	95	111	3	0	1	0	112	19	1	.170	13	45	5	2	1.9	.921
1892	LOU N	1	3	.250	4.24	4	4	4	34	45	11	3	0	0	0	0	15	2	0	.133	0	6	0	0	1.5	1.000
2 yrs.		15	21	.417	3.66	37	36	33	310	325	106	114	3	0	1	0	127	21	1	.165	13	51	5	2	1.9	.928

Paul Fitzke

FITZKE, PAUL FREDERICK HERMAN (Bob) BR TR 5'11½" 185 lbs.
B. July 30, 1900, LaCrosse, Wis. D. June 30, 1950, Sacramento, Calif.

| 1924 | CLE A | 0 | 0 | – | 4.50 | 1 | 0 | 0 | 4 | 5 | 3 | 1 | 0 | 0 | 0 | 0 | 1 | 0 | 0 | .000 | 0 | 0 | 0 | 0 | 0.0 | – |

Al Fitzmorris

FITZMORRIS, ALAN JAMES BB TR 6'2" 190 lbs.
B. Mar. 21, 1946, Buffalo, N. Y.

1969	KC A	1	1	.500	4.22	7	0	0	10.2	9	4	3	0	1	1	0	1	0	0	.000	1	1	0	0	0.3	1.000
1970		8	5	.615	4.42	43	11	2	118	112	52	47	0	4	1	1	31	9	0	.290	12	21	1	1	0.8	.971
1971		7	5	.583	4.18	36	15	2	127	112	55	53	1	0	0	0	44	11	0	.250	15	25	2	4	1.2	.952
1972		2	5	.286	3.74	38	2	0	101	99	28	51	0	2	3	3	23	4	0	.174	7	22	0	3	0.8	1.000
1973		8	3	.727	2.83	15	13	3	89	88	25	26	1	1	0	0	0	0	0	–	9	20	0	1	1.9	1.000
1974		13	6	.684	2.79	34	27	9	190	189	63	53	4	0	0	1	0	0	0	–	20	39	0	4	1.7	1.000
1975		16	12	.571	3.57	35	35	11	242	239	76	78	3	0	0	0	0	0	0	–	26	37	1	1	1.8	.984
1976		15	11	.577	3.07	35	33	8	220	227	56	80	2	0	0	0	0	0	0	–	19	49	3	4	2.0	.958
1977	CLE A	6	10	.375	5.41	29	21	1	133	164	53	54	0	1	0	0	0	0	0	–	7	22	1	1	1.0	.967
1978	2 teams	CLE A (7G 0-1)			CAL A	(9G 1-0)																				
"	total	1	1	.500	3.13	16	0	0	46	45	21	13	0	0	0	0	0	0	0	–	3	6	1	0	0.6	.900
10 yrs.		77	59	.566	3.65	288	159	36	1276.2	1284	433	458	11	9	6	7	99	24	0	.242	119	242	9	19	1.3	.976

Freddie Fitzsimmons

FITZSIMMONS, FREDERICK LANDIS (Fat Freddie) BR TR 5'11" 185 lbs.
B. July 26, 1901, Mishawaka, Ind. D. Nov. 18, 1979, Yucca Valley, Calif.
Manager 1943-45.

1925	NY N	6	3	.667	2.65	10	8	6	74.2	70	18	17	1	0	0	0	29	9	0	.310	3	27	0	0	3.0	1.000
1926		14	10	.583	2.88	37	26	12	219	224	58	48	0	1	2	0	86	11	0	.128	20	62	0	5	2.2	1.000
1927		17	10	.630	3.72	42	31	14	244.2	260	67	78	1	2	1	3	87	18	0	.207	19	59	2	3	1.9	.975
1928		20	9	.690	3.68	40	32	16	261.1	264	65	67	1	4	0	1	94	18	0	.191	23	63	0	4	2.2	1.000

Year	Team	W	L	PCT	ERA	G	GS	CG	IP	H	BB	SO	ShO	W	L	SV	AB	H	HR	BA	PO	A	E	DP	TC/G	FA

Freddie Fitzsimmons *continued*

Year	Team	W	L	PCT	ERA	G	GS	CG	IP	H	BB	SO	ShO	W	L	SV	AB	H	HR	BA	PO	A	E	DP	TC/G	FA
1929		15	11	.577	4.10	37	31	14	221.2	242	66	55	4	1	0	1	82	15	0	.183	13	70	4	7	2.4	.954
1930		19	7	.731	4.25	41	29	17	224.1	230	59	76	1	3	0	1	83	22	2	.265	22	70	2	6	2.3	.979
1931		18	11	.621	3.05	35	33	19	253.2	242	62	78	4	0	1	0	92	21	4	.228	13	89	4	9	3.0	.962
1932		11	11	.500	4.43	35	31	11	237.2	287	83	65	0	0	0	0	86	19	2	.221	16	78	2	10	2.7	.979
1933		16	11	.593	2.90	36	35	13	251.2	243	72	65	1	0	0	0	95	19	2	.200	12	83	4	6	2.8	.960
1934		18	14	.563	3.04	38	37	14	263.1	266	51	73	3	0	0	1	95	22	2	.232	24	71	3	10	2.6	.969
1935		4	8	.333	4.02	18	15	6	94	104	22	23	4	0	0	0	31	8	0	.258	8	24	0	1	1.8	1.000
1936		10	7	.588	3.32	28	17	7	141	147	39	35	0	1	2	2	47	7	0	.149	11	31	3	5	1.6	.933
1937	2 teams	NY N	(6G 2–2)		BKN N	(13G 4–8)																				
"	total	6	10	.375	4.35	19	17	5	118	119	40	42	1	1	0	0	40	8	1	.200	5	28	0	1	1.7	1.000
1938	BKN N	11	8	.579	3.02	27	26	12	202.2	205	43	38	3	0	0	0	70	12	0	.171	13	66	1	7	3.0	.988
1939		7	9	.438	3.87	27	20	5	151.1	178	28	44	0	1	1	3	47	11	1	.234	13	52	0	1	2.4	1.000
1940		16	2	.889	2.81	20	18	11	134.1	120	25	35	4	1	0	1	47	5	0	.106	15	28	2	2	2.3	.956
1941		6	1	.857	2.07	13	12	3	82.2	78	26	19	1	1	0	0	28	4	0	.143	3	30	0	1	2.5	1.000
1942		0	0	—	15.00	1	1	0	3	6	1	0	0	0	0	0	2	1	0	.500	0	1	0	0	1.0	1.000
1943		3	4	.429	5.44	9	7	1	44.2	50	21	12	0	0	0	0	14	1	0	.071	4	9	1	1	1.7	.933
19 yrs.		217	146	.598	3.51	513	426	186	3223.2	3335	846	870	29	17	8	13	1155	231	14	.200	237	942	28	79	2.4	.977

WORLD SERIES

Year	Team	W	L	PCT	ERA	G	GS	CG	IP	H	BB	SO	ShO	W	L	SV	AB	H	HR	BA	PO	A	E	DP	TC/G	FA
1933	NY N	0	1	.000	5.14	1	1	0	7	9	0	2	0	0	0	0	2	1	0	.500	0	1	0	0	1.0	1.000
1936		0	2	.000	5.40	2	2	1	11.2	13	2	6	0	0	0	0	4	2	0	.500	1	2	0	0	1.5	1.000
1941	BKN N	0	0		0.00	1	1	0	7	4	3	1	0	0	0	0	2	0	0	.000	0	2	0	0	2.0	1.000
3 yrs.		0	3	.000	3.86	4	4	1	25.2	26	5	9	0	0	0	0	8	3	0	.375	1	5	0	0	1.5	1.000

Patsy Flaherty   FLAHERTY, PATRICK JOSEPH

B. June 29, 1876, Mansfield, Pa. D. Jan. 23, 1968, Alexandria, La.   BL TL 5'8"   165 lbs.

Year	Team	W	L	PCT	ERA	G	GS	CG	IP	H	BB	SO	ShO	W	L	SV	AB	H	HR	BA	PO	A	E	DP	TC/G	FA
1899	LOU N	2	3	.400	2.31	5	4	4	39	41	5	5	0	1	0	0	24	5	0	.208	2	7	4	0	2.6	.692
1900	PIT N	0	0	—	6.14	4	1	0	22	30	9	5	0	0	0	0	9	1	0	.111	0	10	0	0	2.5	1.000
1903	CHI A	11	25	.306	3.74	40	34	29	293.2	338	50	65	2	2	1	1	102	14	0	.137	21	107	12	5	3.5	.914
1904	2 teams	CHI A	(5G 1–2)		PIT N	(29G 19–9)																				
"	total	20	11	.645	2.05	34	33	32	285	246	69	68	5	0	0	0	116	26	2	.224	28	105	7	3	4.1	.950
1905	PIT N	9	10	.474	3.49	27	20	15	188	197	49	44	0	0	1	1	76	15	0	.197	6	70	9	1	3.1	.894
1907	BOS N	12	15	.444	2.70	27	25	23	217	197	59	34	0	1	1	0	115	22	2	.191	12	76	9	7	3.6	.907
1908		12	18	.400	3.25	31	31	21	244	221	81	50	0	0	0	0	86	12	0	.140	20	79	4	3	3.3	.961
1910	PHI N	0	0	—	0.00	1	0	0	.1	1	0	0	0	0	0	0	2	1	0	.500	0	0	0	0	0.0	—
1911	BOS N	0	2	.000	7.07	4	2	1	14	21	8	0	0	0	0	0	94	27	2	.287	0	4	2	0	1.5	.667
9 yrs.		66	84	.440	3.10	173	150	125	1303	1292	331	271	7	4	3	2	*				89	458	47	19	3.4	.921

Mike Flanagan   FLANAGAN, MICHAEL KENDALL

B. Dec. 16, 1951, Manchester, N. H.   BL TL 6'   180 lbs.

Year	Team	W	L	PCT	ERA	G	GS	CG	IP	H	BB	SO	ShO	W	L	SV	AB	H	HR	BA	PO	A	E	DP	TC/G	FA
1975	BAL A	0	1	.000	2.79	2	1	0	9.2	9	6	7	0	0	0	0	0	0	0	—	0	2	0	0	1.0	1.000
1976		3	5	.375	4.13	20	10	4	85	83	33	56	0	0	3	0	0	0	0	—	4	13	0	0	0.9	1.000
1977		15	10	.600	3.64	36	33	15	235	235	70	149	2	0	1	1	0	0	0	—	7	36	0	3	1.2	1.000
1978		19	15	.559	4.03	40	40	11	281.1	271	87	167	2	0	0	0	0	0	0	—	6	38	2	1	1.2	.957
1979		23	9	.719	3.08	39	38	16	266	245	70	190	5	0	0	0	0	0	0	—	4	41	2	2	1.2	.957
1980		16	13	.552	4.12	37	37	12	251	278	71	128	0	0	0	0	0	0	0	—	6	42	1	0	1.3	.980
1981		9	6	.600	4.19	20	20	3	116	108	37	72	1	0	0	0	0	0	0	—	4	24	1	1	1.5	.966
1982		15	11	.577	3.97	36	35	11	236	233	76	103	1	0	0	0	0	0	0	—	7	38	0	1	1.3	1.000
1983		12	4	.750	3.30	20	20	8	125.1	135	31	50	1	0	0	0	0	0	0	—	6	15	2	1	1.2	.913
1984		13	13	.500	3.53	34	34	10	226.2	213	81	115	2	0	0	0	0	0	0	—	3	20	0	0	1.1	1.000
1985		4	5	.444	5.13	15	15	1	86	101	28	42	0	0	0	0	0	0	0	—	4	11	0	0	1.0	1.000
1986		7	11	.389	4.24	29	28	2	172	179	66	96	1	0	0	0	0	0	0	—	4	17	0	1	0.7	1.000
1987	2 teams	BAL A	(16G 3–6)		TOR A	(7G 3–2)																				
"	total	6	8	.429	4.06	23	23	4	144	148	51	93	0	0	0	0	0	0	0	—	8	17	1	2	1.1	.962
1988	TOR A	13	13	.500	4.18	34	34	2	211	220	80	99	1	0	0	0	0	0	0	—	6	35	0	2	1.2	1.000
1989		8	10	.444	3.93	30	30	1	171.2	186	47	47	0	0	0	0	0	0	0	—	8	33	0	4	1.4	1.000
15 yrs.		163	134	.549	3.89	415	398	101	2616.2	2644	834	1414	19	0	4	1	0	0	0	—	77	395	9	22	1.2	.981

LEAGUE CHAMPIONSHIP SERIES

Year	Team	W	L	PCT	ERA	G	GS	CG	IP	H	BB	SO	ShO	W	L	SV	AB	H	HR	BA	PO	A	E	DP	TC/G	FA
1979	BAL A	1	0	1.000	5.14	1	1	0	7	6	1	2	0	0	0	0	0	0	0	—	0	0	0	0	0.0	—
1983		1	0	1.000	1.80	1	1	0	5	5	0	1	0	0	0	0	0	0	0	—	0	0	0	0	0.0	—
1989	TOR A	0	1	.000	10.38	1	1	0	4.1	7	1	3	0	0	0	0	0	0	0	—	2	3	0	2	5.0	1.000
3 yrs.		2	1	.667	5.51	3	3	0	16.1	18	2	6	0	0	0	0	0	0	0	—	2	3	0	2	1.7	1.000

WORLD SERIES

Year	Team	W	L	PCT	ERA	G	GS	CG	IP	H	BB	SO	ShO	W	L	SV	AB	H	HR	BA	PO	A	E	DP	TC/G	FA
1979	BAL A	1	1	.500	3.00	3	2	1	15	18	2	13	0	0	0	0	5	0	0	.000	0	4	0	0	1.3	1.000
1983		0	0	—	4.50	1	1	0	4	6	1	1	0	0	0	0	1	0	0	.000	0	0	0	0	0.0	—
2 yrs.		1	1	.500	3.32	4	3	1	19	24	3	14	0	0	0	0	6	0	0	.000	0	4	0	0	1.0	1.000

Ray Flanigan   FLANIGAN, RAYMOND ARTHUR

B. Jan. 8, 1923, Morgantown, W. Va.   BR TR 6'   190 lbs.

Year	Team	W	L	PCT	ERA	G	GS	CG	IP	H	BB	SO	ShO	W	L	SV	AB	H	HR	BA	PO	A	E	DP	TC/G	FA
1946	CLE A	0	1	.000	11.00	3	1	0	9	11	8	2	0	0	0	0	2	1	0	.500	0	3	0	0	1.0	1.000

Tom Flanigan   FLANIGAN, THOMAS ANTHONY

B. Sept. 6, 1934, Cincinnati, Ohio   BR TL 6'3"   175 lbs.

Year	Team	W	L	PCT	ERA	G	GS	CG	IP	H	BB	SO	ShO	W	L	SV	AB	H	HR	BA	PO	A	E	DP	TC/G	FA
1954	CHI A	0	0	—	0.00	2	0	0	1.2	1	1	0	0	0	0	0	0	0	0	—	0	1	0	0	0.5	1.000
1958	STL N	0	0	—	9.00	1	0	0	1	2	1	0	0	0	0	0	0	0	0	—	0	0	0	0	0.0	—
2 yrs.		0	0	—	3.38	3	0	0	2.2	3	2	0	0	0	0	0	0	0	0	—	0	1	0	0	0.3	1.000

Jack Flater   FLATER, JOHN WILLIAM

B. Sept. 22, 1880, Sandymount, Md. D. Mar. 20, 1970, Westminster, Md.   BR TR 5'10"   175 lbs.

Year	Team	W	L	PCT	ERA	G	GS	CG	IP	H	BB	SO	ShO	W	L	SV	AB	H	HR	BA	PO	A	E	DP	TC/G	FA
1908	PHI A	1	3	.250	2.06	5	3	3	39.1	35	12	8	0	1	0	0	15	2	0	.133	6	19	3	2	5.6	.893

Year	Team		W	L	PCT	ERA	G	GS	CG	IP	H	BB	SO	ShO	Relief Pitching W	L	SV	Batting AB	H	HR	BA	PO	A	E	DP	TC/G	FA

John Flavin

FLAVIN, JOHN THOMAS
B. May 7, 1942, Albany, Calif.

BL TL 6'2" 208 lbs.

Year	Team	W	L	PCT	ERA	G	GS	CG	IP	H	BB	SO	ShO	W	L	SV	AB	H	HR	BA	PO	A	E	DP	TC/G	FA
1964	CHI N	0	1	.000	13.50	5	1	0	4.2	11	3	5	0	0	0	0	1	0	0	.000	0	0	0	0	0.0	—

Bill Fleming

FLEMING, LESLIE FLETCHARD
B. July 31, 1913, Rowland, Calif.

BR TR 6' 190 lbs.

Year	Team	W	L	PCT	ERA	G	GS	CG	IP	H	BB	SO	ShO	W	L	SV	AB	H	HR	BA	PO	A	E	DP	TC/G	FA
1940	BOS A	1	2	.333	4.86	10	6	1	46.1	53	20	24	0	0	1	0	13	0	0	.000	1	5	0	0	0.6	1.000
1941		1	1	.500	3.92	16	1	0	41.1	32	24	20	0	1	1	1	9	2	0	.222	2	10	0	0	0.8	1.000
1942	CHI N	5	6	.455	3.01	33	14	4	134.1	117	63	59	2	1	0	2	39	2	0	.051	5	24	2	2	0.9	.935
1943		0	1	.000	6.40	11	0	0	32.1	40	12	12	0	0	1	0	8	0	0	.000	3	10	0	0	1.2	1.000
1944		9	10	.474	3.13	39	18	9	158.1	163	62	42	1	1	**2**	0	53	9	0	.170	8	39	3	0	1.3	.940
1946		0	1	.000	6.14	14	1	0	29.1	37	12	10	0	0	0	0	3	0	0	.000	0	7	0	0	0.5	1.000
6 yrs.		16	21	.432	3.79	123	40	14	442	442	193	167	3	3	5	3	125	13	0	.104	19	95	5	2	1.0	.958

Sam Fletcher

FLETCHER, SAMUEL S.
B. Altoona, Pa.

TR 6'2" 210 lbs.

Year	Team	W	L	PCT	ERA	G	GS	CG	IP	H	BB	SO	ShO	W	L	SV	AB	H	HR	BA	PO	A	E	DP	TC/G	FA
1909	BKN N	0	1	.000	8.00	1	1	1	9	13	2	5	0	0	0	0	3	0	0	.000	0	2	0	0	2.0	1.000
1912	CIN N	0	0	—	12.10	2	0	0	9.2	15	11	3	0	0	0	0	4	2	0	.500	0	3	0	0	1.5	1.000
2 yrs.		0	1	.000	10.13	3	1	1	18.2	28	13	8	0	0	0	0	7	2	0	.286	0	5	0	0	1.7	1.000

Tom Fletcher

FLETCHER, THOMAS WAYNE
B. June 28, 1942, Elmira, N. Y.

BB TL 6' 170 lbs.

Year	Team	W	L	PCT	ERA	G	GS	CG	IP	H	BB	SO	ShO	W	L	SV	AB	H	HR	BA	PO	A	E	DP	TC/G	FA
1962	DET A	0	0	—	0.00	1	0	0	2	2	2	1	0	0	0	0	0	0	0	—	1	0	0	0	1.0	1.000

Van Fletcher

FLETCHER, ALFRED VANOIDE
B. Aug. 6, 1924, East Bend, N. C.

BR TR 6'2" 185 lbs.

Year	Team	W	L	PCT	ERA	G	GS	CG	IP	H	BB	SO	ShO	W	L	SV	AB	H	HR	BA	PO	A	E	DP	TC/G	FA
1955	DET A	0	0	—	3.00	9	0	0	12	13	2	4	0	0	0	0	0	0	0	—	1	1	1	0	0.3	.667

John Flinn

FLINN, JOHN RICHARD
B. Sept. 2, 1954, Merced, Calif.

BR TR 6' 175 lbs.

Year	Team	W	L	PCT	ERA	G	GS	CG	IP	H	BB	SO	ShO	W	L	SV	AB	H	HR	BA	PO	A	E	DP	TC/G	FA
1978	BAL A	1	1	.500	8.04	13	0	0	15.2	24	13	8	0	1	1	0	0	0	0	—	1	3	0	0	0.4	.800
1979		0	0	—	0.00	4	0	0	3	2	1	0	0	0	0	0	0	0	0	—	1	0	0	0	0.3	1.000
1980	MIL A	2	1	.667	3.89	20	1	0	37	31	20	15	0	2	1	2	0	0	0	—	6	3	0	0	0.5	1.000
1982	BAL A	2	0	1.000	1.32	5	0	0	13.2	13	3	13	0	2	0	0	0	0	0	—	2	0	0	0	0.4	1.000
4 yrs.		5	2	.714	4.15	42	1	0	69.1	70	37	36	0	5	2	2	0	0	0	—	10	6	1	0	0.4	.941

Hilly Flitcraft

FLITCRAFT, HILDRETH MILTON
B. Aug. 21, 1923, Woodstown, N. J.

BL TL 6'2" 180 lbs.

Year	Team	W	L	PCT	ERA	G	GS	CG	IP	H	BB	SO	ShO	W	L	SV	AB	H	HR	BA	PO	A	E	DP	TC/G	FA
1942	PHI N	0	0	—	8.10	3	0	0	3.1	6	4	1	0	0	0	0	0	0	0	—	0	1	0	0	0.3	1.000

Mort Flohr

FLOHR, MORITZ HERMAN (Dutch)
B. Aug. 15, 1911, Canisted, N. Y.

BL TL 6' 173 lbs.

Year	Team	W	L	PCT	ERA	G	GS	CG	IP	H	BB	SO	ShO	W	L	SV	AB	H	HR	BA	PO	A	E	DP	TC/G	FA
1934	PHI A	0	2	.000	5.87	14	3	0	30.2	34	33	6	0	0	0	0	12	4	0	.333	1	12	1	0	1.0	.929

Jesse Flores

FLORES, JESSE SANDOVAL
B. Nov. 2, 1914, Guadalajara, Mexico

BR TR 5'10" 175 lbs.

Year	Team	W	L	PCT	ERA	G	GS	CG	IP	H	BB	SO	ShO	W	L	SV	AB	H	HR	BA	PO	A	E	DP	TC/G	FA
1942	CHI N	0	1	.000	3.38	4	0	0	5.1	5	2	6	0	0	1	0	0	0	0	—	0	2	1	0	0.8	.667
1943	PHI A	12	14	.462	3.11	31	27	13	231.1	208	70	113	0	1	2	0	80	14	0	.175	11	50	3	5	2.1	.953
1944		9	11	.450	3.39	27	25	11	185.2	172	49	65	2	0	0	0	64	11	0	.172	9	33	1	0	1.6	.977
1945		7	10	.412	3.43	29	24	9	191.1	180	63	52	4	0	1	0	61	9	0	.148	14	23	4	3	1.4	.902
1946		9	7	.563	2.32	29	15	8	155	147	38	48	4	0	0	0	44	11	0	.250	8	18	3	1	1.0	.897
1947		4	13	.235	3.39	28	20	1	151.1	139	59	41	0	1	0	0	44	10	0	.227	12	19	3	3	1.2	.912
1950	CLE A	3	3	.500	3.74	28	2	1	53	53	25	27	1	0	4	0	11	0	0	.000	2	2	3	0	0.3	.571
7 yrs.		44	59	.427	3.18	176	113	46	973	904	306	352	11	2	5	6	304	55	0	.181	56	147	18	12	1.3	.919

Ben Flowers

FLOWERS, BENNETT
B. June 15, 1927, Wilson, N. C.

BR TR 6'4" 195 lbs.

Year	Team		W	L	PCT	ERA	G	GS	CG	IP	H	BB	SO	ShO	W	L	SV	AB	H	HR	BA	PO	A	E	DP	TC/G	FA
1951	BOS A		0	0	—	0.00	1	0	0	3	2	1	2	0	0	0	0	1	0	0	.000	0	0	0	0	0.0	—
1953			1	4	.200	3.86	32	6	1	79.1	87	24	36	1	0	0	3	19	3	0	.158	4	15	1	2	0.6	.950
1955	2 teams	DET A (4G 0–0)				STL N (4G 1–0)																					
"	total		1	0	1.000	4.05	8	4	0	33.1	32	14	21	0	0	0	0	11	1	0	.091	2	5	2	1	1.1	.778
1956	2 teams	STL N (3G 1–1)				PHI N (32G 0–2)																					
"	total		1	3	.250	5.98	35	3	0	52.2	69	15	27	0	0	2	0	5	0	0	.000	2	13	1	1	0.5	.938
4 yrs.			3	7	.300	4.49	76	13	1	168.1	190	54	86	1	0	2	3	36	4	0	.111	8	33	4	4	0.6	.911

Wes Flowers

FLOWERS, CHARLES WESLEY
B. Aug. 13, 1913, Vanndale, Ark.

BL TL 6'1½" 190 lbs.

Year	Team	W	L	PCT	ERA	G	GS	CG	IP	H	BB	SO	ShO	W	L	SV	AB	H	HR	BA	PO	A	E	DP	TC/G	FA
1940	BKN N	1	1	.500	3.43	5	2	0	21	23	10	8	0	1	0	0	5	1	0	.200	0	5	0	0	1.0	1.000
1944		1	1	.500	7.79	9	1	0	17.1	26	13	3	0	0	1	0	5	3	0	.600	1	3	0	0	0.4	1.000
2 yrs.		2	2	.500	5.40	14	3	0	38.1	49	23	11	0	1	1	0	10	4	0	.400	1	8	0	0	0.6	1.000

Carney Flynn

FLYNN, CORNELIUS FRANCIS XAVIER
B. Jan. 23, 1875, Cincinnati, Ohio D. Feb. 10, 1947, Cincinnati, Ohio

BL TL 5'11" 165 lbs.

Year	Team		W	L	PCT	ERA	G	GS	CG	IP	H	BB	SO	ShO	W	L	SV	AB	H	HR	BA	PO	A	E	DP	TC/G	FA
1894	CIN N		0	2	.000	17.61	2	1	0	7.2	16	10	4	0	0	1	0	3	0	0	.000	0	0	0	0	0.0	—
1896	2 teams	NY N (3G 0–2)				WAS N (4G 0–1)																					
"	total		0	3	.000	9.68	7	3	2	30.2	61	18	7	0	0	0	0	12	4	1	.333	5	3	2	0	1.4	.800
2 yrs.			0	5	.000	11.27	9	4	2	38.1	77	28	11	0	0	1	0	15	4	1	.267	5	3	2	0	1.1	.800

Year	Team		W	L	PCT	ERA	G	GS	CG	IP	H	BB	SO	ShO	Relief Pitching W	L	SV	Batting AB	H	HR	BA	PO	A	E	DP	TC/G	FA

Jocko Flynn
FLYNN, JOHN A.
B. June 30, 1864, Lawrence, Mass.   D. Dec. 30, 1907, Lawrence, Mass.   5'6½" 143 lbs.

Year	Team		W	L	PCT	ERA	G	GS	CG	IP	H	BB	SO	ShO	W	L	SV	AB	H	HR	BA	PO	A	E	DP	TC/G	FA
1886	CHI	N	24	6	.800	2.24	32	29	28	257	207	63	146	2	1	0	1	205	41	4	.200	19	57	7	1	2.6	.916
1887			0	0	–	0.00	0	0	0	0	0	0	0	0	0	0	0	0	0	0	–	0	0	0	0	0.0	–
2 yrs.			24	6	.800	2.24	32	29	28	257	207	63	146	2	1	0	1	*				19	57	7	1	2.6	.916

Stu Flythe
FLYTHE, STUART McGUIRE
B. Dec. 5, 1911, Conway, N. C.   D. Oct. 18, 1963, Durham, N. C.   BR TR 6'2" 175 lbs.

Year	Team		W	L	PCT	ERA	G	GS	CG	IP	H	BB	SO	ShO	W	L	SV	AB	H	HR	BA	PO	A	E	DP	TC/G	FA
1936	PHI	A	0	0	–	13.04	17	3	0	39.1	49	61	14	0	0	0	0	15	4	0	.267	1	7	0	0	0.5	1.000

Gene Fodge
FODGE, EUGENE ARLAN (Suds)
B. July 9, 1931, South Bend, Ind.   BR TR 6' 175 lbs.

Year	Team		W	L	PCT	ERA	G	GS	CG	IP	H	BB	SO	ShO	W	L	SV	AB	H	HR	BA	PO	A	E	DP	TC/G	FA
1958	CHI	N	1	1	.500	4.76	16	4	1	39.2	47	11	15	0	0	0	0	7	0	0	.000	1	7	0	1	0.5	1.000

Jim Fogarty
FOGARTY, JAMES G.
Brother of Joe Fogarty.
B. Feb. 12, 1864, San Francisco, Calif.   D. May 20, 1891, San Francisco, Calif.   BR TR 5'10½" 180 lbs.
Manager 1890.

Year	Team		W	L	PCT	ERA	G	GS	CG	IP	H	BB	SO	ShO	W	L	SV	AB	H	HR	BA	PO	A	E	DP	TC/G	FA
1884	PHI	N	0	0	–	0.00	1	0	0	1	2	0	1	0	0	0	0	378	80	1	.212	0	0	0	0	0.0	–
1886			0	1	.000	0.00	1	0	0	6	7	0	4	0	0	1	0	280	82	3	.293	0	2	0	0	2.0	1.000
1887			0	0	–	9.00	1	0	0	3	3	1	0	0	0	0	0	495	129	8	.261	0	0	0	0	0.0	–
1889			0	0	–	9.00	4	0	0	4	4	2	0	0	0	0	0	499	129	3	.259	0	1	1	0	0.5	.500
4 yrs.			0	1	.000	4.50	7	0	0	14	16	3	5	0	0	1	0	*				0	3	1	0	0.6	.750

Curry Foley
FOLEY, CHARLES JOSEPH
B. Jan. 14, 1856, Milltown, Ireland   D. Oct. 20, 1898, New York, N. Y.   TL 180 lbs.

Year	Team		W	L	PCT	ERA	G	GS	CG	IP	H	BB	SO	ShO	W	L	SV	AB	H	HR	BA	PO	A	E	DP	TC/G	FA
1879	BOS	N	9	9	.500	2.51	21	16	16	161.2	175	15	57	0	2	0	1	146	46	0	.315	4	26	5	0	1.7	.857
1880			14	14	.500	3.89	36	28	21	238	264	40	68	0	1	1	0	332	97	2	.292	12	49	3	0	1.8	.953
1881	BUF	N	2	4	.333	5.27	10	6	2	41	70	5	2	0	1	0	0	375	96	1	.256	1	8	1	0	1.0	.900
1882			0	0	–	18.00	1	0	0	1	2	0	0	0	0	0	0	341	104	3	.305	0	0	0	0	0.0	–
1883			1	0	1.000	0.00	1	0	0	1	0	4	0	0	1	0	0	111	30	0	.270	0	0	0	0	0.0	–
5 yrs.			26	27	.491	3.54	69	50	39	442.2	511	64	127	0	5	1	1	*				17	83	9	0	1.6	.917

John Foley
FOLEY, JOHN J.
B. Mar., 1860, England   Deceased.   TL

Year	Team		W	L	PCT	ERA	G	GS	CG	IP	H	BB	SO	ShO	W	L	SV	AB	H	HR	BA	PO	A	E	DP	TC/G	FA
1885	PRO	N	0	1	.000	4.50	1	1	1	8	6	5	2	0	0	0	0	2	0	0	.000	0	2	0	0	2.0	1.000

Tom Foley
FOLEY, THOMAS MICHAEL
B. Sept. 9, 1959, Fort Benning, Ga.   BL TR 6'1" 160 lbs.

Year	Team		W	L	PCT	ERA	G	GS	CG	IP	H	BB	SO	ShO	W	L	SV	AB	H	HR	BA	PO	A	E	DP	TC/G	FA
1989	MON	N	0	0	–	27.00	1	0	0	.1	1	0	0	0	0	0	0	*				0	0	0	0	0.0	–

Rich Folkers
FOLKERS, RICHARD NEVIN
B. Oct. 17, 1946, Waterloo, Iowa   BL TL 6'2" 180 lbs.

Year	Team		W	L	PCT	ERA	G	GS	CG	IP	H	BB	SO	ShO	W	L	SV	AB	H	HR	BA	PO	A	E	DP	TC/G	FA
1970	NY	N	0	2	.000	6.52	16	1	0	29	36	25	15	0	0	1	2	6	2	0	.333	0	10	0	2	0.6	1.000
1972	STL	N	1	0	1.000	3.38	9	0	0	13.1	12	5	7	0	1	0	0	1	0	0	.000	0	2	0	0	0.2	1.000
1973			4	4	.500	3.61	34	9	1	82.1	74	34	44	0	1	0	3	20	2	0	.100	4	11	1	0	0.5	.938
1974			6	2	.750	3.00	55	0	0	90	65	38	57	0	6	2	2	10	1	0	.100	3	7	1	2	0.2	.909
1975	SD	N	6	11	.353	4.18	45	15	4	142	155	39	87	0	1	3	0	36	6	0	.167	10	20	3	0	0.7	.909
1976			2	3	.400	5.28	33	3	0	59.2	67	25	26	0	2	0	0	4	0	0	.000	4	8	0	0	0.4	1.000
1977	MIL	A	0	1	.000	4.50	3	0	0	6	7	4	6	0	0	1	0	0	0	0	–	0	1	0	0	0.3	1.000
7 yrs.			19	23	.452	4.11	195	28	5	422.1	416	170	242	0	11	7	7	77	11	0	.143	21	59	5	5	0.4	.941

Lew Fonseca
FONSECA, LEWIS ALBERT
B. Jan. 21, 1899, Oakland, Calif.   D. Nov. 26, 1989, Ely, Iowa   BR TR 5'10½" 180 lbs.
Manager 1932-34.

Year	Team		W	L	PCT	ERA	G	GS	CG	IP	H	BB	SO	ShO	W	L	SV	AB	H	HR	BA	PO	A	E	DP	TC/G	FA
1932	CHI	A	0	0	–	0.00	1	0	0	1	0	0	0	0	0	0	0	*				0	0	0	0	0.0	–

Ray Fontenot
FONTENOT, SILTON RAY
B. Aug. 8, 1957, Lake Charles, La.   BL TL 6' 175 lbs.

Year	Team		W	L	PCT	ERA	G	GS	CG	IP	H	BB	SO	ShO	W	L	SV	AB	H	HR	BA	PO	A	E	DP	TC/G	FA
1983	NY	A	8	2	.800	3.33	15	15	3	97.1	101	25	27	1	0	0	0	0	0	0	–	3	19	1	1	1.5	.957
1984			8	9	.471	3.61	33	24	0	169.1	189	58	85	0	1	0	0	0	0	0	–	6	28	3	1	1.1	.919
1985	CHI	N	6	10	.375	4.36	38	23	0	154.2	177	45	70	0	0	1	0	41	2	0	.049	6	35	1	3	1.1	.976
1986	2 teams		CHI N	(42G 3–5)		MIN A	(15G 0–0)																					
"	total		3	5	.375	5.23	57	0	0	72.1	84	25	34	0	3	5	2	7	1	0	.143	4	13	5	0	0.4	.773
4 yrs.			25	26	.490	4.03	143	62	3	493.2	551	153	216	1	4	6	2	48	3	0	.063	19	95	10	5	0.9	.919

Jim Foor
FOOR, JAMES EMERSON
B. Jan. 13, 1949, St. Louis, Mo.   BL TL 6'2" 170 lbs.

Year	Team		W	L	PCT	ERA	G	GS	CG	IP	H	BB	SO	ShO	W	L	SV	AB	H	HR	BA	PO	A	E	DP	TC/G	FA
1971	DET	A	0	0	–	18.00	3	0	0	1	2	4	2	0	0	0	0	0	0	0	–	0	0	0	0	0.0	–
1972			1	0	1.000	13.50	7	0	0	4	6	6	2	0	1	0	0	0	0	0	–	0	1	0	0	0.1	1.000
1973	PIT	N	0	0	–	0.00	3	0	0	1.1	2	1	1	0	0	0	0	0	0	0	–	0	1	0	0	0.3	1.000
3 yrs.			1	0	1.000	11.37	13	0	0	6.1	10	11	5	0	1	0	0	0	0	0	–	0	2	0	0	0.2	1.000

Dave Ford
FORD, DAVID ALAN
B. Dec. 29, 1956, Cleveland, Ohio   BR TR 6'4" 190 lbs.

Year	Team		W	L	PCT	ERA	G	GS	CG	IP	H	BB	SO	ShO	W	L	SV	AB	H	HR	BA	PO	A	E	DP	TC/G	FA
1978	BAL	A	1	0	1.000	0.00	2	1	0	15	10	2	5	0	0	0	0	0	0	0	–	2	1	0	0	1.5	1.000
1979			2	1	.667	2.10	9	2	0	30	23	7	7	0	1	1	2	0	0	0	–	0	7	0	0	0.8	1.000
1980			1	3	.250	4.24	25	3	1	70	66	13	22	0	0	1	1	0	0	0	–	4	8	0	0	0.5	1.000

Year	Team	W	L	PCT	ERA	G	GS	CG	IP	H	BB	SO	ShO	W	L	SV	AB	H	HR	BA	PO	A	E	DP	TC/G	FA
														Relief Pitching			Batting									

Dave Ford *continued*

Year	Team	W	L	PCT	ERA	G	GS	CG	IP	H	BB	SO	ShO	W	L	SV	AB	H	HR	BA	PO	A	E	DP	TC/G	FA
1981		1	2	.333	6.53	15	2	0	40	61	10	12	0	1	1	0	0	0	0	–	2	5	0	0	0.5	1.000
4 yrs.		5	6	.455	4.01	51	8	1	155	160	32	46	0	2	3	3	0	0	0	–	8	21	0	0	0.6	1.000

Gene Ford

FORD, EUGENE MATTHEW   BR TR 6'2" 195 lbs.
B. June 23, 1912, Fort Dodge, Iowa D. Sept. 7, 1970, Emmetsburg, Iowa

Year	Team	W	L	PCT	ERA	G	GS	CG	IP	H	BB	SO	ShO	W	L	SV	AB	H	HR	BA	PO	A	E	DP	TC/G	FA
1936	BOS N	0	0	–	13.50	2	1	0	2	2	3	0	0	0	0	0	0	0	0	–	0	1	0	0	0.5	1.000
1938	CHI A	0	0	–	10.29	4	0	0	14	21	12	2	0	0	0	0	6	1	0	.167	2	2	0	0	1.0	1.000
2 yrs.		0	0	–	10.69	6	1	0	16	23	15	2	0	0	0	0	6	1	0	.167	2	3	0	0	0.8	1.000

Gene Ford

FORD, EUGENE WYMAN   BR TR 6' 170 lbs.
Brother of Russ Ford.
B. Apr. 16, 1881, Milton, N. S., Canada D. Aug. 23, 1973, Dunedin, Fla.

Year	Team	W	L	PCT	ERA	G	GS	CG	IP	H	BB	SO	ShO	W	L	SV	AB	H	HR	BA	PO	A	E	DP	TC/G	FA
1905	DET A	0	1	.000	5.66	7	1	1	35	51	14	20	0	0	0	0	10	0	0	.000	1	12	3	0	2.3	.813

Russ Ford

FORD, RUSSELL WILLIAM   BR TR 5'11" 175 lbs.
Brother of Gene Ford.
B. Apr. 25, 1883, Brandon, Man., Canada D. Jan. 24, 1960, Rockingham, N. C.

Year	Team	W	L	PCT	ERA	G	GS	CG	IP	H	BB	SO	ShO	W	L	SV	AB	H	HR	BA	PO	A	E	DP	TC/G	FA
1909	NY A	0	0	–	9.00	1	0	0	3	4	4	2	0	0	0	0	1	0	0	.000	1	2	1	1	4.0	.750
1910		26	6	.813	1.65	36	33	29	299.2	194	70	209	8	0	0	1	96	20	0	.208	7	75	7	4	2.5	.921
1911		22	11	.667	2.27	37	33	26	281.1	251	76	158	1	2	1	0	102	20	0	.196	16	70	5	0	2.5	.945
1912		13	21	.382	3.55	36	35	30	291.2	317	79	112	0	0	0	0	112	32	1	.286	13	90	5	6	3.0	.954
1913		12	18	.400	2.66	33	28	15	237	244	58	72	1	3	0	2	74	12	0	.162	11	56	8	1	2.3	.893
1914	BUF F	20	6	.769	1.82	35	26	19	247.1	190	41	123	5	0	2	6	78	10	0	.128	9	72	1	2	2.3	.988
1915		5	9	.357	4.52	21	15	7	127.1	140	48	34	0	0	1	0	43	12	0	.279	2	40	0	1	2.0	1.000
7 yrs.		98	71	.580	2.59	199	170	126	1487.1	1340	376	710	15	5	4	9	506	106	1	.209	59	405	27	15	2.5	.945

Tom Ford

FORD, THOMAS WALTER   5'10½" 155 lbs.
B. 1866, Chattanooga, Tenn. Deceased.

Year	Team	W	L	PCT	ERA	G	GS	CG	IP	H	BB	SO	ShO	W	L	SV	AB	H	HR	BA	PO	A	E	DP	TC/G	FA
1890	2 teams		COL AA (1G 0–0)							BKN AA (7G 0–6)																
"	total	0	6	.000	6.71	8	6	6	51	70	35	12	0	0	0	0	31	1	0	.032	3	13	1	0	2.1	.941

Wenty Ford

FORD, PERCIVAL EDMUND WENTWORTH   BR TR 5'11" 165 lbs.
B. Nov. 25, 1946, Nassau, Bahamas D. July 8, 1980, Nassau, Bahamas

Year	Team	W	L	PCT	ERA	G	GS	CG	IP	H	BB	SO	ShO	W	L	SV	AB	H	HR	BA	PO	A	E	DP	TC/G	FA
1973	ATL N	1	2	.333	5.63	4	2	1	16	17	8	4	0	1	0	0	5	2	0	.400	1	3	0	0	1.0	1.000

Whitey Ford

FORD, EDWARD CHARLES (The Chairman of the Board)   BL TL 5'10" 178 lbs.
B. Oct. 21, 1926, New York, N. Y.
Hall of Fame 1974.

Year	Team	W	L	PCT	ERA	G	GS	CG	IP	H	BB	SO	ShO	W	L	SV	AB	H	HR	BA	PO	A	E	DP	TC/G	FA
1950	NY A	9	1	.900	2.81	20	12	7	112	87	52	59	2	0	1	1	36	7	0	.194	7	17	0	1	1.2	1.000
1953		18	6	.750	3.00	32	30	11	207	187	110	110	3	0	0	0	75	20	1	.267	8	35	1	3	1.4	.977
1954		16	8	.667	2.82	34	28	11	210.2	170	101	125	3	2	2	1	62	10	0	.161	7	39	2	3	1.4	.958
1955		18	7	.720	2.63	39	33	18	253.2	188	113	137	5	0	1	2	86	14	1	.163	10	41	1	1	1.3	.981
1956		19	6	.760	2.47	31	30	18	225.2	187	84	141	2	0	0	1	78	17	0	.218	9	57	1	6	2.2	.985
1957		11	5	.688	2.57	24	17	5	129.1	114	53	84	0	3	0	0	42	6	0	.143	6	28	2	5	1.5	.944
1958		14	7	.667	2.01	30	29	15	219.1	174	62	145	7	0	0	1	73	15	0	.205	7	44	6	2	1.9	.895
1959		16	10	.615	3.04	35	29	9	204	194	89	114	2	2	2	1	65	15	1	.231	15	49	1	5	1.9	.985
1960		12	9	.571	3.08	33	29	8	192.2	168	65	85	4	0	0	0	53	8	0	.151	12	38	1	2	1.5	.980
1961		25	4	.862	3.21	39	39	11	283	242	92	209	3	0	0	0	96	17	0	.177	12	45	5	5	1.6	.919
1962		17	8	.680	2.90	38	37	7	257.2	243	69	160	0	0	0	0	85	10	0	.118	25	58	3	4	2.3	.965
1963		24	7	.774	2.74	38	37	13	269.1	240	56	189	3	0	0	0	92	13	1	.141	20	38	5	3	1.7	.921
1964		17	6	.739	2.13	39	36	12	244.2	212	57	172	8	0	0	0	67	8	0	.119	18	47	1	2	1.7	.985
1965		16	13	.552	3.24	37	36	9	244.1	241	50	162	2	0	1	0	82	15	0	.183	7	53	0	4	1.6	1.000
1966		2	5	.286	2.47	22	9	0	73	79	24	43	0	2	1	0	18	0	0	.000	7	26	4	2	1.7	.892
1967		2	4	.333	1.64	7	7	2	44	40	9	21	1	0	0	0	13	2	0	.154	3	15	0	1	2.6	1.000
16 yrs.		236	106	.690	2.75	498	438	156	3170.1	2766	1086	1956	45	9	7	10	1023	177	3	.173	173	630	33	49	1.7	.961
				3rd																						

WORLD SERIES

Year	Team	W	L	PCT	ERA	G	GS	CG	IP	H	BB	SO	ShO	W	L	SV	AB	H	HR	BA	PO	A	E	DP	TC/G	FA
1950	NY A	1	0	1.000	0.00	1	1	0	8.2	7	1	7	0	0	0	0	3	0	0	.000	1	0	0	0	1.0	1.000
1953		0	1	.000	4.50	2	2	0	8	9	2	7	0	0	0	0	3	1	0	.333	0	1	0	0	0.5	1.000
1955		2	0	1.000	2.12	2	2	1	17	13	8	10	0	0	0	0	6	0	0	.000	1	4	0	0	2.5	1.000
1956		1	1	.500	5.25	2	2	1	12	14	2	8	0	0	0	0	4	0	0	.000	1	0	0	0	0.5	1.000
1957		1	1	.500	1.13	2	2	1	16	11	5	7	0	0	0	0	5	0	0	.000	1	0	0	0	1.0	1.000
1958		0	1	.000	4.11	3	1	0	15.1	19	5	16	0	0	0	0	4	0	0	.000	0	0	0	0	0.7	1.000
1960		2	0	1.000	0.00	2	2	2	18	11	2	8	2	0	0	0	5	0	0	.250	3	5	0	0	4.0	1.000
1961		2	0	1.000	0.00	2	2	1	14	6	1	7	1	0	0	0	5	0	0	.000	0	1	0	0	0.5	1.000
1962		1	1	.500	4.12	3	3	1	19.2	24	4	12	0	0	0	0	7	0	0	.000	0	4	1	0	1.7	.800
1963		0	2	.000	4.50	2	2	0	12	10	3	8	0	0	0	0	3	0	0	.000	2	5	0	0	2.5	1.000
1964		0	1	.000	8.44	1	1	0	5.1	8	1	4	0	0	0	0	1	1	0	1.000	0	0	0	0	1.0	1.000
11 yrs.		10	8	.556	2.71	22	22	7	146	132	34	94	3	0	0	0	49	4	0	.082	11	20	1	1	1.5	.969
		1st	1st																							
						1st	1st	4th	1st	1st	1st	1st	2nd													

Brownie Foreman

FOREMAN, JOHN DAVIS   BL TL 5'8" 150 lbs.
Brother of Frank Foreman.
B. Aug. 6, 1875, Baltimore, Md. D. Oct. 10, 1926, Baltimore, Md.

Year	Team	W	L	PCT	ERA	G	GS	CG	IP	H	BB	SO	ShO	W	L	SV	AB	H	HR	BA	PO	A	E	DP	TC/G	FA
1895	PIT N	8	6	.571	3.22	19	16	12	139.2	131	64	54	0	0	0	2	46	3	0	.065	3	43	5	1	2.7	.902
1896	2 teams		PIT N (9G 3–3)							CIN N (4G 0–4)																
"	total	3	7	.300	8.81	13	12	7	79.2	112	51	22	0	0	1	0	28	4	0	.143	2	22	1	1	1.9	.960
2 yrs.		11	13	.458	5.25	32	28	19	219.1	243	115	76	0	0	1	2	74	7	0	.095	5	65	6	2	2.4	.921

Year	Team		W	L	PCT	ERA	G	GS	CG	IP	H	BB	SO	ShO	Relief Pitching W	L	SV	Batting AB	H	HR	BA	PO	A	E	DP	TC/G	FA

Frank Foreman

FOREMAN, FRANCIS ISAIAH (Monk)
Brother of Brownie Foreman.
B. May 1, 1863, Baltimore, Md.   D. Nov. 19, 1957, Baltimore, Md.

BL TL 6'   160 lbs.

Year	Team		W	L	PCT	ERA	G	GS	CG	IP	H	BB	SO	ShO	W	L	SV	AB	H	HR	BA	PO	A	E	DP	TC/G	FA
1884	2 teams	CHI U (3G 1-2)								KC U (1G 0-1)																	
"	total		1	3	.250	4.50	4	4	2	26	40	4	15	0	0	0	0	14	1	0	.071	9	6	2	0	4.3	.882
1885	BAL	AA	2	1	.667	6.00	3	3	2	27	33	9	11	0	0	0	0	14	4	0	.286	0	4	1	0	1.7	.800
1889			23	21	.523	3.52	51	48	43	414	364	137	180	5	0	0	0	181	26	1	.144	9	72	14	1	1.9	.853
1890	CIN	N	13	10	.565	3.95	25	24	20	198.1	201	89	57	0	0	0	0	75	10	1	.133	10	23	6	0	1.6	.846
1891			18	21	.462	3.73	43	41	39	345.1	381	142	170	1	0	0	0	157	35	4	.223	13	66	4	4	1.9	.952
1892	2 teams	WAS N (11G 2-4)								BAL N (4G 0-3)																	
"	total		2	7	.222	4.34	15	10	6	85	93	48	21	0	0	0	0	51	17	1	.333	3	16	7	0	1.7	.731
1893	NY	N	0	1	.000	27.00	2	1	0	5.2	19	10	0	0	0	0	0	3	0	0	.000	0	1	0	0	0.5	1.000
1895	CIN	N	11	14	.440	4.11	32	27	19	219	253	92	55	0	0	0	1	94	29	2	.309	11	34	6	1	1.6	.882
1896			15	6	.714	3.68	27	23	18	190.2	214	62	38	1	1	1	1	76	19	0	.250	8	45	4	2	2.1	.930
1901	2 teams	BOS A (1G 0-1)								BAL A (24G 13-6)																	
"	total		13	7	.650	3.88	25	23	19	199.1	233	60	42	1	0	0	0	84	26	0	.310	4	45	6	0	2.2	.891
1902	BAL	A	0	2	.000	6.06	2	2	2	16.1	28	6	2	0	0	0	0	7	3	0	.429	0	9	2	0	5.5	.818
	11 yrs.		98	93	.513	3.94	229	206	170	1726.2	1859	659	591	8	1	2	4	756	170	9	.225	67	321	52	8	1.9	.882

Happy Foreman

FOREMAN, AUGUST
B. July 20, 1897, Memphis, Tenn.   D. Feb. 13, 1953, New York, N. Y.

BL TL 5'7"   160 lbs.

Year	Team		W	L	PCT	ERA	G	GS	CG	IP	H	BB	SO	ShO	W	L	SV	AB	H	HR	BA	PO	A	E	DP	TC/G	FA
1924	CHI	A	0	0	–	2.25	3	0	0	4	7	4	1	0	0	0	0	2	0	0	.000	0	0	0	0	0.0	–
1926	BOS	A	0	0	–	3.68	3	0	0	7.1	3	5	3	0	0	0	0	2	0	0	.000	0	5	0	0	1.7	1.000
	2 yrs.		0	0	–	3.18	6	0	0	11.1	10	9	4	0	0	0	0	4	0	0	.000	0	5	0	0	0.8	1.000

Bill Forman

FORMAN, WILLIAM ORANGE
B. Oct. 10, 1886, Venango, Pa.   D. Oct. 3, 1958, Uniontown, Pa.

BB TR 5'11"   180 lbs.

Year	Team		W	L	PCT	ERA	G	GS	CG	IP	H	BB	SO	ShO	W	L	SV	AB	H	HR	BA	PO	A	E	DP	TC/G	FA
1909	WAS	A	0	2	.000	4.91	2	2	1	11	8	7	2	0	0	0	0	3	1	0	.333	0	7	1	1	4.0	.875
1910			0	0	–	13.50	1	0	0	.2	1	0	0	0	0	0	0	0	0	0	–	0	0	0	0	0.0	–
	2 yrs.		0	2	.000	5.40	3	2	1	11.2	9	7	2	0	0	0	0	3	1	0	.333	0	7	1	1	2.7	.875

Mike Fornieles

FORNIELES, JOSE MIGUEL
Born Jose Miguel Fornieles y Torres.
B. Jan. 18, 1932, Havana, Cuba

BR TR 5'11"   155 lbs.

Year	Team		W	L	PCT	ERA	G	GS	CG	IP	H	BB	SO	ShO	W	L	SV	AB	H	HR	BA	PO	A	E	DP	TC/G	FA
1952	WAS	A	2	2	.500	1.37	4	2	2	26.1	13	11	12	1	1	1	0	10	0	0	.000	1	4	0	0	1.3	1.000
1953	CHI	A	8	7	.533	3.59	39	16	5	153	160	61	72	0	4	1	3	41	4	0	.098	16	30	2	2	1.2	.958
1954			1	2	.333	4.29	15	6	0	42	41	14	18	0	1	1	1	11	3	0	.273	1	11	2	1	0.9	.857
1955			6	3	.667	3.86	26	9	2	86.1	84	29	23	0	3	1	1	29	3	0	.103	1	18	1	2	0.8	.950
1956	2 teams	CHI A (6G 0-1)								BAL A (30G 4-7)																	
"	total		4	8	.333	4.05	36	11	1	126.2	131	31	59	1	3	2	1	35	6	0	.171	5	30	0	3	1.0	1.000
1957	2 teams	BAL A (15G 2-6)								BOS A (25G 8-7)																	
"	total		10	13	.435	3.75	40	22	8	182.1	193	55	107	2	3	3	2	62	11	0	.177	14	25	3	2	1.1	.929
1958	BOS	A	4	6	.400	4.96	37	7	1	110.2	123	33	49	0	3	3	1	29	6	0	.207	5	18	1	1	0.6	.958
1959			5	3	.625	3.07	46	0	0	82	77	29	54	0	5	3	11	19	3	0	.158	5	13	1	0	0.4	.947
1960			10	5	.667	2.64	70	0	0	109	86	49	64	0	10	5	14	15	6	0	.400	7	19	3	3	0.4	.897
1961			9	8	.529	4.68	57	2	1	119.1	121	54	70	0	8	7	15	32	5	1	.156	12	25	1	2	0.7	.974
1962			3	6	.333	5.36	42	1	0	82.1	96	37	36	0	3	5	5	16	3	0	.188	5	14	1	1	0.5	.950
1963	2 teams	BOS A (9G 0-0)								MIN A (11G 1-1)																	
"	total		1	1	.500	5.40	20	0	0	36.2	40	18	12	0	1	1	0	9	2	0	.222	3	2	0	0	0.3	1.000
	12 yrs.		63	64	.496	3.96	432	76	20	1156.2	1165	421	576	4	45	33	55	308	52	1	.169	75	209	15	17	0.7	.950

Bob Forsch

FORSCH, ROBERT HERBERT
Brother of Ken Forsch.
B. Jan. 13, 1950, Sacramento, Calif.

BR TR 6'4"   200 lbs.

Year	Team		W	L	PCT	ERA	G	GS	CG	IP	H	BB	SO	ShO	W	L	SV	AB	H	HR	BA	PO	A	E	DP	TC/G	FA
1974	STL	N	7	4	.636	2.97	19	14	5	100	84	34	39	2	0	0	0	29	7	0	.241	10	13	0	0	1.2	1.000
1975			15	10	.600	2.86	34	34	7	230	213	70	108	4	0	0	0	78	24	1	.308	18	37	1	7	1.6	.982
1976			8	10	.444	3.94	33	32	2	194	209	71	76	0	0	1	0	62	11	1	.177	24	28	4	2	1.7	.929
1977			20	7	.741	3.48	35	35	8	217	210	69	95	2	0	0	0	72	12	0	.167	12	29	2	2	1.2	.953
1978			11	17	.393	3.69	34	34	4	234	205	97	114	3	0	0	0	83	15	1	.181	18	37	0	4	1.6	1.000
1979			11	11	.500	3.82	33	32	7	219	215	52	92	1	0	0	0	73	8	0	.110	25	31	1	3	1.7	.982
1980			11	10	.524	3.77	31	31	8	215	225	33	87	0	0	0	0	78	23	3	.295	11	44	2	5	1.8	.965
1981			10	5	.667	3.19	20	20	1	124	106	29	41	0	0	0	0	41	5	0	.122	14	24	0	1	1.9	1.000
1982			15	9	.625	3.48	36	34	6	233	238	54	69	2	0	0	1	73	15	0	.205	21	30	2	1	1.5	.962
1983			10	12	.455	4.28	34	30	6	187	190	54	56	2	1	0	0	54	13	1	.241	14	29	1	1	1.3	.977
1984			2	5	.286	6.02	16	11	1	52.1	64	19	21	0	1	0	0	16	4	0	.250	8	8	0	0	1.0	1.000
1985			9	6	.600	3.90	34	19	3	136	132	47	48	1	1	0	2	45	11	1	.244	12	20	1	0	1.0	.970
1986			14	10	.583	3.25	33	33	3	230	211	68	104	0	0	0	0	76	13	2	.171	17	32	0	5	1.5	1.000
1987			11	7	.611	4.32	33	30	2	179	189	45	89	1	0	0	0	57	17	2	.298	9	25	0	2	1.0	1.000
1988	2 teams	STL N (30G 9-4)								HOU N (6G 1-4)																	
"	total		10	8	.556	4.29	36	18	1	136.1	153	44	54	1	4	2	0	32	8	0	.250	8	13	3	1	0.7	.875
1989	HOU	N	4	5	.444	5.32	37	15	0	108.1	133	46	40	0	1	0	0	24	4	0	.167	9	11	1	1	0.6	.957
	16 yrs.		168	136	.553	3.76	498	422	67	2795	2777	832	1133	19	8	4	3	893	190	12	.213	234	405	18	35	1.3	.973

LEAGUE CHAMPIONSHIP SERIES

Year	Team		W	L	PCT	ERA	G	GS	CG	IP	H	BB	SO	ShO	W	L	SV	AB	H	HR	BA	PO	A	E	DP	TC/G	FA
1982	STL	N	1	0	1.000	0.00	1	1	1	9	3	0	6	1	0	0	0	3	2	0	.667	0	0	0	0	0.0	–
1985			0	0	–	5.40	1	1	0	3.1	3	2	0	0	0	0	0	0	0	0	–	0	1	0	0	1.0	1.000
1987			1	1	.500	12.00	3	0	0	3	4	1	3	0	1	1	0	0	0	0	–	0	1	0	0	0.3	1.000
	3 yrs.		2	1	.667	3.52	5	2	1	15.1	10	3	9	1	1	1	0	3	2	0	.667	0	2	0	0	0.4	1.000

WORLD SERIES

Year	Team		W	L	PCT	ERA	G	GS	CG	IP	H	BB	SO	ShO	W	L	SV	AB	H	HR	BA	PO	A	E	DP	TC/G	FA
1982	STL	N	0	2	.000	4.97	2	2	0	12.2	18	3	4	0	0	0	0	0	0	0	–	1	0	1	0	1.0	.500
1985			0	1	.000	12.00	2	1	0	3	6	1	3	0	0	0	0	0	0	0	–	0	0	0	0	0.0	–
1987			1	0	1.000	9.95	3	0	0	6.1	8	5	3	0	1	0	0	2	0	0	.000	1	0	0	1	0.3	1.000
	3 yrs.		1	3	.250	7.36	7	3	0	22	32	9	10	0	1	0	0	2	0	0	.000	2	0	1	1	0.4	.667

Year	Team		W	L	PCT	ERA	G	GS	CG	IP	H	BB	SO	ShO	Relief Pitching W	L	SV	Batting AB	H	HR	BA	PO	A	E	DP	TC/G	FA

Ken Forsch

FORSCH, KENNETH ROTH
Brother of Bob Forsch.
B. Sept. 8, 1946, Sacramento, Calif.   BR TR 6'4"   195 lbs.

Year	Team		W	L	PCT	ERA	G	GS	CG	IP	H	BB	SO	ShO	W	L	SV	AB	H	HR	BA	PO	A	E	DP	TC/G	FA
1970	HOU	N	1	2	.333	5.63	4	4	1	24	28	5	13	0	0	0	0	6	0	0	.000	2	2	0	1	1.0	1.000
1971			8	8	.500	2.54	33	23	7	188	162	53	131	2	0	0	0	59	8	0	.136	8	19	2	1	0.9	.931
1972			6	8	.429	3.91	30	24	1	156.1	163	62	113	0	0	0	0	41	6	0	.146	9	9	2	1	0.7	.900
1973			9	12	.429	4.20	46	26	5	201.1	197	74	149	0	1	3	4	62	4	0	.065	15	16	0	1	0.7	1.000
1974			8	7	.533	2.80	70	0	0	103	98	37	48	0	8	7	10	7	0	0	.000	9	14	2	1	0.4	.920
1975			4	8	.333	3.22	34	9	2	109	114	30	54	0	2	3	2	22	1	0	.045	6	14	2	3	0.6	.909
1976			4	3	.571	2.15	52	0	0	92	76	26	49	0	4	3	19	11	1	0	.091	4	17	0	0	0.4	1.000
1977			5	8	.385	2.72	42	5	0	86	80	28	45	0	5	5	8	13	1	0	.077	10	15	1	1	0.6	.962
1978			10	6	.625	2.71	52	6	4	133	136	37	71	2	6	4	7	27	5	0	.185	9	24	2	0	0.7	.943
1979			11	6	.647	3.03	26	24	10	178	155	35	58	2	1	0	0	58	8	0	.138	10	37	1	5	1.8	.979
1980			12	13	.480	3.20	32	32	6	222	230	41	84	3	0	0	0	77	18	0	.234	11	45	3	2	1.8	.949
1981	CAL	A	11	7	.611	2.88	20	20	10	153	143	27	55	4	0	0	0	0	0	0	—	18	24	2	2	2.2	.955
1982			13	11	.542	3.87	37	35	12	228	225	57	73	4	2	0	0	0	0	0	—	13	29	5	2	1.3	.894
1983			11	12	.478	4.06	31	31	11	219.1	226	61	81	1	0	0	0	0	0	0	—	9	31	3	1	1.4	.930
1984			1	1	.500	2.20	2	2	1	16.1	14	3	10	0	0	0	0	0	0	0	—	1	6	0	1	3.5	1.000
1986			0	1	.000	9.53	10	0	0	17	24	10	13	0	0	1	0	0	0	0	—	1	2	1	1	0.4	.750
16 yrs.			114	113	.502	3.37	521	241	70	2126.1	2071	586	1047	18	29	26	51	383	52	0	.136	134	305	26	24	0.9	.944

LEAGUE CHAMPIONSHIP SERIES

| 1980 | HOU | N | 0 | 1 | .000 | 4.15 | 2 | 1 | 1 | 8.2 | 10 | 1 | 6 | 0 | 0 | 0 | 0 | 2 | 2 | 0 | 1.000 | 1 | 0 | 0 | 0 | 0.5 | 1.000 |

Terry Forster

FORSTER, TERRY JAY
B. Jan. 14, 1952, Sioux Falls, S. D.   BL TL 6'3"   200 lbs.

Year	Team		W	L	PCT	ERA	G	GS	CG	IP	H	BB	SO	ShO	W	L	SV	AB	H	HR	BA	PO	A	E	DP	TC/G	FA
1971	CHI	A	2	3	.400	3.96	45	3	0	50	46	23	48	0	2	1	1	5	2	0	.400	4	6	0	0	0.2	1.000
1972			6	5	.545	2.25	62	0	0	100	75	44	104	0	6	5	29	19	10	0	.526	1	21	2	0	0.4	.917
1973			6	11	.353	3.23	51	12	4	172.2	174	78	120	0	3	4	16	1	0	0	.000	8	45	2	8	1.1	.964
1974			7	8	.467	3.63	59	1	0	134	120	48	105	0	7	7	24	0	0	0	—	6	33	1	4	0.7	.975
1975			3	3	.500	2.19	17	1	0	37	30	24	32	0	3	3	4	0	0	0	—	2	14	1	1	1.0	.941
1976			2	12	.143	4.38	29	16	1	111	126	41	70	0	0	5	1	0	0	0	—	5	26	2	0	1.1	.939
1977	PIT	N	6	4	.600	4.45	33	6	0	87	90	32	58	0	4	1	1	26	9	0	.346	4	13	1	1	0.5	.944
1978	LA	N	5	4	.556	1.94	47	0	0	65	56	23	46	0	5	4	22	8	4	0	.500	2	10	2	0	0.3	.857
1979			1	2	.333	5.63	17	0	0	16	18	11	8	0	1	2	2	0	0	0	—	1	5	0	0	0.4	1.000
1980			0	0	—	3.00	9	0	0	12	10	4	2	0	0	0	0	0	0	0	—	2	4	1	0	0.8	.857
1981			0	1	.000	4.06	21	0	0	31	37	15	17	0	0	1	0	2	0	0	.000	0	11	0	0	0.5	1.000
1982			5	6	.455	3.04	56	0	0	83	66	31	52	0	5	6	3	2	0	0	.000	4	18	1	0	0.4	.957
1983	ATL	N	3	2	.600	2.16	56	0	0	79.1	60	31	54	0	3	2	13	8	4	0	.500	3	15	1	1	0.3	.947
1984			2	0	1.000	2.70	25	0	0	26.2	30	7	10	0	2	0	5	3	2	0	.667	2	4	0	1	0.2	1.000
1985			2	3	.400	2.28	46	0	0	59.1	49	28	37	0	2	3	1	4	0	0	.000	2	7	1	0	0.2	.900
1986	CAL	A	4	1	.800	3.51	41	0	0	41	47	17	28	0	4	1	5	0	0	0	—	2	11	0	2	0.3	1.000
16 yrs.			54	65	.454	3.23	614	39	5	1105	1034	457	791	0	47	46	127	78	31	0	.397	48	243	15	18	0.5	.951

DIVISIONAL PLAYOFF SERIES

| 1981 | LA | N | 0 | 0 | — | 0.00 | 1 | 0 | 0 | .1 | 0 | 0 | 0 | 0 | 0 | 0 | 0 | 0 | 0 | 0 | — | 0 | 0 | 0 | 0 | 0.0 | — |

LEAGUE CHAMPIONSHIP SERIES

1978	LA	N	1	0	1.000	0.00	1	0	0	1	1	0	2	0	1	0	0	0	0	0	—	0	0	0	0	0.0	—
1981			0	0	—	0.00	1	0	0	.1	0	0	1	0	0	0	0	0	0	0	—	0	0	0	0	0.0	—
2 yrs.			1	0	1.000	0.00	2	0	0	1.1	1	0	3	0	1	0	0	0	0	0	—	0	0	0	0	0.0	—

WORLD SERIES

1978	LA	N	0	0	—	0.00	3	0	0	4	5	1	6	0	0	0	0	0	0	0	—	0	1	0	0	0.3	1.000
1981			0	0	—	0.00	2	0	0	2	1	3	0	0	0	0	0	0	0	0	—	0	1	0	0	0.5	1.000
2 yrs.			0	0	—	0.00	5	0	0	6	6	4	6	0	0	0	0	0	0	0	—	0	2	0	0	0.4	1.000

Gary Fortune

FORTUNE, GARRETT REESE
B. Oct. 11, 1894, High Point, N. C. D. Sept. 23, 1955, Washington, D. C.   BB TR 5'11½" 176 lbs.

Year	Team		W	L	PCT	ERA	G	GS	CG	IP	H	BB	SO	ShO	W	L	SV	AB	H	HR	BA	PO	A	E	DP	TC/G	FA
1916	PHI	N	0	1	.000	3.60	1	1	0	5	2	4	3	0	0	0	0	2	0	0	.000	0	0	0	0	0.0	—
1918			0	2	.000	8.13	5	2	1	31	41	19	10	0	0	0	0	10	2	0	.200	1	8	1	0	2.0	.900
1920	BOS	A	0	2	.000	5.83	14	3	1	41.2	46	23	10	0	0	1	0	12	2	0	.167	1	9	0	0	0.7	1.000
3 yrs.			0	5	.000	6.61	20	6	2	77.2	89	46	23	0	0	1	0	24	4	0	.167	2	17	1	0	1.0	.950

Jerry Fosnow

FOSNOW, GERALD EUGENE
B. Sept. 21, 1940, Deshler, Ohio   BR TL 6'4"   195 lbs.

Year	Team		W	L	PCT	ERA	G	GS	CG	IP	H	BB	SO	ShO	W	L	SV	AB	H	HR	BA	PO	A	E	DP	TC/G	FA
1964	MIN	A	0	1	.000	10.97	7	0	0	10.2	13	8	9	0	0	1	0	0	0	0	—	0	1	1	0	0.3	.500
1965			3	3	.500	4.44	29	0	0	46.2	33	25	35	0	3	3	2	5	0	0	.000	1	12	3	0	0.6	.813
2 yrs.			3	4	.429	5.65	36	0	0	57.1	46	33	44	0	3	4	2	5	0	0	.000	1	13	4	0	0.5	.778

Larry Foss

FOSS, LARRY CURTIS
B. Apr. 18, 1936, Castleton, Kans.   BR TR 6'2"   187 lbs.

Year	Team		W	L	PCT	ERA	G	GS	CG	IP	H	BB	SO	ShO	W	L	SV	AB	H	HR	BA	PO	A	E	DP	TC/G	FA
1961	PIT	N	1	1	.500	5.87	3	3	0	15.1	15	11	9	0	0	0	0	6	1	0	.167	1	2	1	0	1.3	.750
1962	NY	N	0	1	.000	4.63	5	1	0	11.2	17	7	3	0	0	0	0	1	0	0	.000	2	1	0	0	0.6	1.000
2 yrs.			1	2	.333	5.33	8	4	0	27	32	18	12	0	0	0	0	7	1	0	.143	3	3	1	0	0.9	.857

Tony Fossas

FOSSAS, EMILIO ANTONIO
Born Emilio Antonio Fossas y Morejon.
B. Sept. 23, 1957, Havana, Cuba   BL TL 6'   195 lbs.

Year	Team		W	L	PCT	ERA	G	GS	CG	IP	H	BB	SO	ShO	W	L	SV	AB	H	HR	BA	PO	A	E	DP	TC/G	FA
1988	TEX	A	0	0	—	4.76	5	0	0	5.2	11	2	0	0	0	0	0	0	0	0	—	1	1	0	1	0.4	1.000
1989	MIL	A	2	2	.500	3.54	51	0	0	61	57	22	42	0	2	2	1	0	0	0	—	1	12	2	0	0.3	.867
2 yrs.			2	2	.500	3.65	56	0	0	66.2	68	24	42	0	2	2	1	0	0	0	—	2	13	2	1	0.3	.882

Year	Team		W	L	PCT	ERA	G	GS	CG	IP	H	BB	SO	ShO	Relief Pitching W	L	SV	Batting AB	H	HR	BA	PO	A	E	DP	TC/G	FA

Alan Foster

FOSTER, ALAN BENTON
B. Dec. 8, 1946, Pasadena, Calif.　　　　　　　　BR TR 6'　180 lbs.

Year	Team		W	L	PCT	ERA	G	GS	CG	IP	H	BB	SO	ShO	W	L	SV	AB	H	HR	BA	PO	A	E	DP	TC/G	FA
1967	LA	N	0	1	.000	2.16	4	2	1	16.2	10	3	15	0	0	0	0	4	0	0	.000	3	3	0	0	1.5	1.000
1968			1	1	.500	1.72	3	3	0	15.2	11	2	10	0	0	0	0	4	1	0	.250	0	2	0	0	0.7	1.000
1969			3	9	.250	4.37	24	15	2	103	119	29	59	2	0	0	0	27	2	0	.074	2	18	1	0	0.9	.952
1970			10	13	.435	4.25	33	33	7	199	200	81	83	1	0	0	0	64	7	0	.109	17	23	2	4	1.3	.952
1971	CLE	A	8	12	.400	4.15	36	26	3	182	158	82	97	0	1	0	0	51	2	0	.039	10	9	2	0	0.6	.905
1972	CAL	A	0	1	.000	4.85	8	0	0	13	12	6	11	0	0	1	0	0	0	0	—	2	2	0	0	0.5	1.000
1973	STL	N	13	9	.591	3.14	35	29	6	203.2	195	63	106	2	0	0	2	68	13	0	.191	17	21	3	1	1.2	.927
1974			7	10	.412	3.89	31	25	5	162	167	61	78	1	0	0	0	48	8	0	.167	14	20	4	1	1.2	.895
1975	SD	N	3	1	.750	2.40	17	4	1	45	41	21	20	0	1	0	0	11	1	0	.091	4	8	2	0	0.8	.857
1976			3	6	.333	3.22	26	11	2	86.2	75	35	22	0	0	0	0	18	1	0	.056	9	9	0	1	0.7	1.000
10 yrs.			48	63	.432	3.73	217	148	26	1026.2	988	383	501	6	2	3	0	295	35	0	.119	78	115	14	7	1.0	.932

Larry Foster

FOSTER, LARRY LYNN
B. Dec. 24, 1937, Lansing, Mich.　　　　　　　　BL TR 6'　185 lbs.

1963	DET	A	0	0	—	13.50	1	0	0	2	4	1	1	0	0	0	0	0	0	0	—	0	1	0	0	1.0	1.000

Rube Foster

FOSTER, GEORGE
B. Jan. 5, 1888, Lehigh, Okla.　D. Mar. 1, 1976, Bokoshe, Okla.　BR TR 5'7½"　170 lbs.

1913	BOS	A	3	4	.429	3.16	19	8	4	68.1	64	28	36	1	0	0	0	21	2	0	.095	5	21	1	0	1.4	.963
1914			14	8	.636	1.65	32	27	17	212.2	162	52	92	5	0	0	0	63	11	0	.175	18	58	4	1	2.5	.950
1915			19	8	.704	2.11	37	33	22	255.1	217	86	82	5	0	0	1	83	23	1	.277	18	77	2	0	2.6	.979
1916			14	7	.667	3.06	33	19	9	182.1	173	86	53	3	4	0	2	62	11	0	.177	16	57	1	5	2.2	.986
1917			8	7	.533	2.53	17	16	9	124.2	108	53	34	1	0	1	0	41	11	0	.268	14	38	2	1	3.2	.963
5 yrs.			58	34	.630	2.35	138	103	61	843.1	724	305	297	15	4	1	3	270	58	1	.215	71	251	10	7	2.4	.970

WORLD SERIES

1915	BOS	A	2	0	1.000	2.00	2	2	2	18	12	2	13	0	0	0	0	8	4	0	.500	4	3	0	1	3.5	1.000
1916			0	0	—	0.00	1	0	0	3	3	0	1	0	0	0	0	1	0	0	.000	1	2	0	1	3.0	1.000
2 yrs.			2	0	1.000	1.71	3	2	2	21	15	2	14	0	0	0	0	9	4	0	.444	5	5	0	1	3.3	1.000

Slim Foster

FOSTER, EDWARD LEE
B. 1885, Birmingham, Ala.　D. Mar. 1, 1929, Montgomery, Ala.　BR TR 6'1"

1908	CLE	A	1	0	1.000	2.14	6	1	1	21	16	12	11	0	0	0	2	6	0	0	.000	0	2	0	0	0.3	1.000

Steve Foucault

FOUCAULT, STEVEN RAYMOND
B. Oct. 3, 1949, Duluth, Minn.　　　　　　　　BL TR 6'　205 lbs.

1973	TEX	A	2	4	.333	3.86	32	0	0	56	54	31	28	0	2	4	8	0	0	0	—	4	10	0	1	0.4	1.000
1974			8	9	.471	2.25	69	0	0	144	123	40	106	0	8	9	12	0	0	0	—	11	19	2	3	0.5	.938
1975			8	4	.667	4.12	59	0	0	107	96	55	56	0	8	4	10	0	0	0	—	5	13	1	3	0.3	.947
1976			8	8	.500	3.32	46	0	0	76	68	25	41	0	8	8	5	0	0	0	—	4	20	0	3	0.5	1.000
1977	DET	A	7	7	.500	3.16	44	0	0	74	64	17	58	0	7	7	13	0	0	0	—	3	8	0	0	0.3	1.000
1978	2 teams		DET A	(24G 2–4)			KC	A	(3G 0–0)																			
"	total		2	4	.333	3.23	27	0	0	39	53	22	18	0	2	4	4	0	0	0	—	2	5	2	0	0.3	.778
6 yrs.			35	36	.493	3.21	277	0	0	496	458	190	307	0	35	36	52	0	0	0	—	29	75	5	10	0.4	.954

Henry Fournier

FOURNIER, JULIUS HENRY (Frenchy)
B. Aug. 8, 1865, Syracuse, N. Y.　D. Dec. 8, 1945, Eloise, Mich.　TL

1894	CIN	N	1	3	.250	5.40	6	4	4	45	71	20	5	0	0	0	0	19	2	0	.105	0	11	1	1	2.0	.917

Jack Fournier

FOURNIER, JACQUES FRANK
B. Sept. 29, 1892, Au Sable, Mich.　D. Sept. 5, 1973, Tacoma, Wash.　BL TR 6'　195 lbs.

1922	STL	N	0	0	—	0.00	1	0	0	1	0	0	0	0	0	0	0	*				0	1	0	0	1.0	1.000

Dave Foutz

FOUTZ, DAVID LUTHER (Scissors)
Brother of Frank Foutz.
B. Sept. 7, 1856, Carroll County, Md.　D. Mar. 5, 1897, Waverly, Md.
Manager 1893-96.　　　　　　　　BR TR 6'2"　161 lbs.

1884	STL	AA	15	6	.714	2.18	25	25	19	206.2	167	36	95	2	0	0	0	119	27	0	.227	18	45	4	6	2.7	.940
1885			33	14	.702	2.63	47	46	46	407.2	351	92	147	2	1	0	0	238	59	0	.248	24	104	14	3	3.0	.901
1886			41	16	.719	2.11	59	57	55	504	418	144	283	11	1	0	1	414	116	3	.280	57	74	7	2	2.3	.949
1887			25	12	.676	3.87	40	38	36	339.1	369	90	94	1	0	0	0	423	151	4	.357	44	57	10	0	2.8	.910
1888	BKN	AA	12	7	.632	2.51	23	19	19	176	146	35	73	0	0	0	0	563	156	3	.277	18	45	5	4	3.0	.926
1889			3	0	1.000	4.37	12	4	3	59.2	70	19	21	0	0	0	0	553	153	7	.277	5	15	1	1	1.8	.952
1890	BKN	N	2	1	.667	1.86	5	2	2	29	29	6	4	0	1	0	2	509	154	5	.303	2	3	0	0	1.0	1.000
1891			3	2	.600	3.29	6	5	5	52	51	16	14	0	0	0	0	521	134	2	.257	7	7	0	2	2.3	1.000
1892			13	8	.619	3.41	27	20	17	203	210	63	56	0	0	0	2	220	41	1	.186	21	55	8	2	3.1	.905
1893			0	0	—	7.50	2	0	0	18	28	8	3	0	0	0	0	557	137	7	.246	0	0	0	0	1.2	1.000
1894			0	0	—	13.50	1	0	0	2	4	1	0	0	0	0	0	293	90	0	.307	0	0	0	0	0.0	—
11 yrs.			147	66	.690 2nd	2.84	251	216	202	1997.1	1843	510	790	16	3	2	4	*				196	412	49	22	2.6	.925

Art Fowler

FOWLER, JOHN ARTHUR
Brother of Jesse Fowler.
B. July 3, 1922, Converse, S. C.　　　　　　　　BR TR 5'11"　180 lbs.

1954	CIN	N	12	10	.545	3.83	40	29	8	227.2	256	85	93	1	1	2	0	60	6	0	.100	10	35	2	4	1.2	.957
1955			11	10	.524	3.90	46	28	8	207.2	198	63	94	3	1	0	2	60	12	0	.200	12	30	0	1	0.9	1.000
1956			11	11	.500	4.05	45	23	8	177.2	191	35	86	0	3	1	1	48	7	0	.146	12	35	1	0	1.1	.979
1957			3	0	1.000	6.47	33	7	1	87.2	111	24	45	0	1	0	0	17	3	0	.176	5	15	0	0	0.6	1.000
1959	LA	N	3	4	.429	5.31	36	0	0	61	70	23	47	0	3	4	2	12	1	0	.083	2	12	1	0	0.4	.933
1961	LA	A	5	8	.385	3.64	53	3	0	89	68	29	78	0	5	6	11	13	1	0	.077	4	7	0	0	0.2	1.000

Year	Team		W	L	PCT	ERA	G	GS	CG	IP	H	BB	SO	ShO	Relief Pitching W	L	SV	Batting AB	H	HR	BA	PO	A	E	DP	TC/G	FA

Art Fowler *continued*

1962			4	3	.571	2.81	48	0	0	77	67	25	38	0	4	3	5	11	3	0	.273	5	12	0	0	0.4	1.000
1963			5	3	.625	2.42	57	0	0	89.1	70	19	53	0	5	3	10	9	2	0	.222	4	9	1	0	0.2	.929
1964			0	2	.000	10.29	4	0	0	7	8	5	5	0	0	1	0	1	0	0	.000	1	2	0	1	0.8	1.000
9 yrs.			54	51	.514	4.03	362	90	25	1024	1039	308	539	4	23	21	32	231	35	0	.152	55	157	5	6	0.6	.977

Dick Fowler

FOWLER, RICHARD JOHN
B. Mar. 30, 1921, Toronto, Ont., Canada   D. May 22, 1972, Oneonta, N. Y.   BR TR 6'4½" 215 lbs.

1941	PHI	A	1	2	.333	3.38	4	3	1	24	26	8	8	0	0	0	0	9	0	0	.000	0	4	0	1	1.0	1.000
1942			6	11	.353	4.95	31	17	4	140	159	45	38	0	2	2	1	50	8	0	.160	8	18	3	2	0.9	.897
1945			1	2	.333	4.82	7	3	2	37.1	41	18	21	1	0	1	0	18	8	0	.444	1	4	0	0	0.7	1.000
1946			9	16	.360	3.28	32	28	14	205.2	213	75	89	1	0	0	0	71	13	0	.183	13	29	3	2	1.4	.933
1947			12	11	.522	2.81	36	31	16	227.1	210	85	75	3	1	1	0	82	14	0	.171	14	29	2	1	1.3	.956
1948			15	8	.652	3.78	29	26	16	204.2	221	76	50	2	0	0	2	82	14	1	.171	10	30	1	4	1.4	.976
1949			15	11	.577	3.75	31	28	15	213.2	210	115	43	4	1	0	1	77	18	0	.234	15	46	1	5	2.0	.984
1950			1	5	.167	6.48	11	9	2	66.2	75	56	15	0	0	0	0	26	5	0	.192	6	11	1	2	1.6	.944
1951			5	11	.313	5.62	22	22	4	125	141	72	29	0	0	0	0	42	8	0	.190	11	16	2	3	1.3	.931
1952			1	2	.333	6.44	18	3	1	58.2	71	28	14	0	0	0	0	15	0	0	.000	5	14	0	0	1.1	1.000
10 yrs.			66	79	.455	4.11	221	170	75	1303	1367	578	382	11	4	5	4	472	88	1	.186	83	201	13	20	1.3	.956

Jesse Fowler

FOWLER, JESSE PETER
Brother of Art Fowler.
B. Oct. 30, 1898, Spartanburg, S. C.   D. Sept. 23, 1973, Columbia, S. C.   BR TL 5'10½" 158 lbs.

| 1924 | STL | N | 1 | 1 | .500 | 4.41 | 13 | 3 | 0 | 32.2 | 28 | 18 | 5 | 0 | 1 | 0 | 0 | 9 | 2 | 0 | .222 | 0 | 5 | 1 | 0 | 0.5 | .833 |

Alan Fowlkes

FOWLKES, ALAN KIM
B. Aug. 8, 1958, Brawley, Calif.   BR TR 6'2" 190 lbs.

1982	SF	N	4	2	.667	5.19	21	15	1	85	111	24	50	0	0	0	0	26	3	0	.115	4	13	2	0	0.9	.895
1985	CAL	A	0	0	—	9.00	2	0	0	7	8	4	5	0	0	0	0	0	0	0	—	1	1	0	0	1.0	1.000
2 yrs.			4	2	.667	5.48	23	15	1	92	119	28	55	0	0	0	0	26	3	0	.115	5	14	2	0	0.9	.905

Henry Fox

FOX, HENRY
Born Henry Fuchs.
B. Nov. 18, 1874, Scranton, Pa.   D. June 6, 1927, Scranton, Pa.

| 1902 | PHI | N | 0 | 0 | — | 18.00 | 1 | 0 | 0 | 2 | 1 | 1 | 0 | 0 | 0 | 0 | 1 | 0 | 0 | 0 | — | 0 | 0 | 0 | 0 | 0.0 | — |

Howie Fox

FOX, HOWARD FRANCIS
B. Mar. 1, 1921, Coburg, Ore.   D. Oct. 9, 1955, San Antonio, Tex.   BR TR 6'3" 210 lbs.

1944	CIN	N	0	0	—	0.00	2	0	0	2.1	2	0	0	0	0	0	0	1	0	0	.000	0	0	0	0	0.0	—
1945			8	13	.381	4.93	45	15	7	164.1	169	77	54	0	4	2	0	46	13	0	.283	9	52	1	0	1.4	.984
1946			0	0	—	18.00	4	0	0	5	12	5	1	0	0	0	0	0	0	0	—	1	1	0	0	0.5	1.000
1948			6	9	.400	4.53	34	24	5	171	185	62	63	0	0	0	0	60	12	0	.200	14	33	2	15	1.4	.959
1949			6	19	.240	3.98	38	30	9	215	221	77	60	0	1	0	0	72	17	0	.236	14	65	3	7	2.2	.963
1950			11	8	.579	4.33	34	22	10	187	196	85	64	1	0	0	1	63	11	1	.175	8	52	3	1	1.9	.952
1951			9	14	.391	3.83	40	30	9	228	239	69	57	4	0	1	2	70	8	1	.114	8	46	3	6	1.5	.966
1952	PHI	N	2	7	.222	5.08	13	11	2	62	70	26	16	0	0	2	0	21	1	0	.048	6	31	2	1	1.8	.957
1954	BAL	A	1	2	.333	3.67	38	0	0	73.2	80	34	27	0	1	2	2	16	4	0	.250	3	19	0	0	0.6	1.000
9 yrs.			43	72	.374	4.33	248	132	42	1108.1	1174	435	342	5	7	7	6	349	66	2	.189	60	290	12	31	1.5	.967

John Fox

FOX, JOHN JOSEPH
B. Feb. 7, 1859, Roxbury, Mass.   D. Apr. 18, 1893, Boston, Mass.

1881	BOS	N	6	8	.429	3.33	17	16	12	124.1	144	39	30	0	0	0	0	118	21	0	.178	8	25	3	2	2.1	.917
1883	BAL	AA	6	13	.316	4.03	20	19	18	165.1	209	32	49	0	0	0	0	92	14	0	.152	15	32	17	0	3.2	.734
1884	PIT	AA	1	6	.143	5.64	7	7	7	59	76	16	22	0	0	0	0	25	6	0	.240	2	15	2	1	2.7	.895
1886	WAS	N	0	1	.000	9.00	1	1	1	8	11	11	3	0	0	0	0	3	1	0	.333	0	2	0	0	2.0	1.000
4 yrs.			13	28	.317	4.16	45	43	38	356.2	440	98	104	0	0	0	0	238	42	0	.176	25	74	22	3	2.7	.818

Terry Fox

FOX, TERRENCE EDWARD
B. July 31, 1935, Chicago, Ill.   BR TR 6' 175 lbs.

1960	MIL	N	0	0	—	4.32	5	0	0	8.1	6	6	5	0	0	0	0	1	0	0	.000	0	1	0	0	0.2	1.000
1961	DET	A	5	2	.714	1.41	39	0	0	57.1	42	16	32	0	5	2	12	12	2	0	.167	6	12	1	1	0.5	.947
1962			3	1	.750	1.71	44	0	0	58	48	16	23	0	3	1	16	8	2	0	.250	2	13	1	1	0.4	.938
1963			8	6	.571	3.59	46	0	0	80.1	81	20	35	0	8	6	11	11	1	0	.091	7	16	3	0	0.6	.885
1964			4	3	.571	3.39	32	0	0	61	77	16	28	0	4	3	5	12	3	0	.250	5	11	1	3	0.5	.941
1965			6	4	.600	2.78	42	0	0	77.2	59	31	34	0	6	4	10	15	0	0	.000	6	22	1	2	0.7	.966
1966	2 teams	DET A	(4G 0–1)				PHI N	(36G 3–2)																			
"	total		3	3	.500	4.80	40	0	0	54.1	66	19	28	0	3	3	5	6	0	0	.000	1	11	0	0	0.3	1.000
7 yrs.			29	19	.604	2.99	248	0	0	397	379	124	185	0	29	19	59	65	8	0	.123	27	86	7	7	0.5	.942

Bill Foxen

FOXEN, WILLIAM ALOYSIUS
B. May 31, 1884, Tenafly, N. J.   D. Apr. 17, 1937, Brooklyn, N. Y.   BL TL 5'11½" 165 lbs.

1908	PHI	N	7	7	.500	1.95	22	16	10	147.1	126	53	52	2	0	0	0	53	5	0	.094	9	51	3	0	2.9	.952
1909			3	7	.300	3.35	18	7	5	83.1	65	32	37	1	0	3	0	24	5	1	.208	6	42	2	0	2.8	.960
1910	2 teams	PHI N	(16G 5–5)				CHI N	(2G 0–0)																			
"	total		5	5	.500	2.94	18	9	5	82.2	80	43	35	0	2	0	0	25	4	0	.160	1	30	2	3	1.8	.939
1911	CHI	N	1	1	.500	2.08	3	1	0	13	12	12	6	0	0	0	0	4	1	0	.250	2	6	0	0	2.7	1.000
4 yrs.			16	20	.444	2.56	61	33	20	326.1	283	140	130	3	2	3	0	106	15	1	.142	18	129	7	3	2.5	.955

Year	Team		W	L	PCT	ERA	G	GS	CG	IP	H	BB	SO	ShO	Relief Pitching W	L	SV	Batting AB	H	HR	BA	PO	A	E	DP	TC/G	FA

Jimmie Foxx

FOXX, JAMES EMORY (Double X, The Beast)
B. Oct. 22, 1907, Sudlersville, Md. D. July 21, 1967, Miami, Fla.
Hall of Fame 1951.
BR TR 6' 195 lbs.

Year	Team		W	L	PCT	ERA	G	GS	CG	IP	H	BB	SO	ShO	W	L	SV	AB	H	HR	BA	PO	A	E	DP	TC/G	FA
1939	BOS	A	0	0	–	0.00	1	0	0	1	0	0	1	0	0	0	0	467	168	35	.360	0	0	0	0	0.0	–
1945	PHI	N	1	0	1.000	1.59	9	2	0	22.2	13	14	10	0	0	0	0	224	60	7	.268	2	1	0	0	0.3	1.000
2 yrs.			1	0	1.000	1.52	10	2	0	23.2	13	14	11	0	0	0	0	*				2	1	0	0	0.3	1.000

Paul Foytack

FOYTACK, PAUL EUGENE
B. Nov. 16, 1930, Scranton, Pa.
BR TR 5'11" 175 lbs.

Year	Team		W	L	PCT	ERA	G	GS	CG	IP	H	BB	SO	ShO	W	L	SV	AB	H	HR	BA	PO	A	E	DP	TC/G	FA
1953	DET	A	0	0	–	11.17	6	0	0	9.2	15	9	7	0	0	0	0	1	0	0	.000	0	1	0	0	0.2	1.000
1955			0	1	.000	5.26	22	1	0	49.2	48	36	38	0	0	0	0	11	1	0	.091	2	7	0	0	0.4	1.000
1956			15	13	.536	3.59	43	33	16	256	211	142	184	1	1	0	1	90	11	0	.122	11	33	3	5	1.1	.936
1957			14	11	.560	3.14	38	27	8	212	175	104	118	1	3	2	1	63	14	0	.222	3	30	4	1	1.0	.892
1958			15	13	.536	3.44	39	33	16	230	198	77	135	2	0	0	1	75	18	0	.240	12	25	0	3	0.9	1.000
1959			14	14	.500	4.64	39	37	11	240.1	239	64	110	2	0	0	0	81	9	0	.111	9	36	1	0	1.2	.978
1960			2	11	.154	6.14	28	13	1	96.2	108	49	38	0	0	4	2	25	7	0	.280	7	7	0	0	0.5	1.000
1961			11	10	.524	3.93	32	20	6	169.2	152	56	89	0	3	2	0	54	12	1	.222	8	13	0	2	0.7	1.000
1962			10	7	.588	4.39	29	21	5	143.2	145	86	63	1	2	0	0	42	6	0	.143	13	25	0	1	1.3	1.000
1963	2 teams	DET A (9G 0–1)						LA A	(25G 5–5)																		
"	total		5	6	.455	4.70	34	8	0	88	86	37	44	0	2	2	1	19	4	0	.211	6	11	2	0	0.6	.895
1964	LA	A	0	1	.000	15.43	2	0	0	2.1	4	2	1	0	0	1	0	0	0	0	–	0	0	0	0	0.0	–
11 yrs.			86	87	.497	4.14	312	193	63	1498	1381	662	827	7	11	11	7	461	82	1	.178	71	188	10	12	0.9	.963

Ken Frailing

FRAILING, KENNETH DOUGLAS
B. Jan. 19, 1948, Madison, Wis.
BL TL 6' 190 lbs.

Year	Team		W	L	PCT	ERA	G	GS	CG	IP	H	BB	SO	ShO	W	L	SV	AB	H	HR	BA	PO	A	E	DP	TC/G	FA
1972	CHI	A	1	0	1.000	3.00	4	0	0	3	3	1	1	0	1	0	0	–				0	1	0	0	0.3	1.000
1973			0	0	–	1.96	10	0	0	18.1	18	7	15	0	0	0	0	–				2	1	0	0	0.5	.800
1974	CHI	N	6	9	.400	3.89	55	16	1	125	150	43	71	0	1	2	1	31	8	0	.258	8	19	1	0	0.5	.964
1975			2	5	.286	5.43	41	0	0	53	61	26	39	0	2	5	1	7	1	0	.143	7	15	0	0	0.5	1.000
1976			1	2	.333	2.37	6	3	0	19	20	5	10	0	1	0	0	3	0	0	.000	1	3	0	0	0.7	1.000
5 yrs.			10	16	.385	3.96	116	19	1	218.1	252	82	136	0	5	7	2	41	9	0	.220	18	40	2	0	0.5	.967

Ossie France

FRANCE, OSMAN BEVERLY
B. Oct. 4, 1858, Greenburg, Ohio D. May 2, 1947, Greensburg, Ohio
BL TL 5'8" 155 lbs.

Year	Team		W	L	PCT	ERA	G	GS	CG	IP	H	BB	SO	ShO	W	L	SV	AB	H	HR	BA	PO	A	E	DP	TC/G	FA
1890	CHI	N	0	0	–	13.50	1	0	0	2	3	2	0	0	0	0	0	1	0	0	.000	0	0	0	0	0.0	–

Earl Francis

FRANCIS, EARL COLEMAN
B. July 14, 1935, Slab Fork, W. Va.
BR TR 6'2" 210 lbs.

Year	Team		W	L	PCT	ERA	G	GS	CG	IP	H	BB	SO	ShO	W	L	SV	AB	H	HR	BA	PO	A	E	DP	TC/G	FA
1960	PIT	N	1	0	1.000	2.00	7	0	0	18	14	4	8	0	1	0	0	5	0	0	.000	1	2	0	1	0.4	1.000
1961			2	8	.200	4.21	23	15	0	102.2	110	47	53	0	0	1	0	28	3	0	.107	8	20	1	1	1.3	.966
1962			9	8	.529	3.07	36	23	5	176	153	83	121	1	2	0	0	61	10	1	.164	12	33	1	3	1.3	.978
1963			4	6	.400	4.53	33	13	0	97.1	107	43	72	0	2	0	0	26	8	0	.308	4	19	4	3	0.8	.852
1964			0	1	.000	8.53	2	1	0	6.1	7	1	6	0	0	0	0	1	0	0	.000	0	0	0	0	0.0	–
1965	STL	N	0	0	–	5.06	2	0	0	5.1	7	3	3	0	0	0	0	1	0	0	.000	0	0	0	0	0.5	–
6 yrs.			16	23	.410	3.77	103	52	5	405.2	398	181	263	1	5	1	0	122	21	1	.172	25	74	7	8	1.0	.934

Ray Francis

FRANCIS, RAY JAMES
B. Mar. 8, 1893, Sherman, Tex. D. July 6, 1934, Atlanta, Ga.
BL TL 6'1½" 182 lbs.

Year	Team		W	L	PCT	ERA	G	GS	CG	IP	H	BB	SO	ShO	W	L	SV	AB	H	HR	BA	PO	A	E	DP	TC/G	FA
1922	WAS	A	7	18	.280	4.28	39	26	15	225	265	66	64	2	0	3	2	78	13	0	.167	10	54	5	2	1.8	.928
1923	DET	A	5	8	.385	4.42	33	6	0	79.1	95	28	27	0	1	3	1	21	3	0	.143	2	19	0	1	0.6	1.000
1925	2 teams	NY A (4G 0–0)						BOS A	(6G 0–2)																		
"	total		0	2	.000	7.71	10	4	0	32.2	49	16	5	0	0	0	0	8	1	0	.125	2	8	0	1	1.0	1.000
3 yrs.			12	28	.300	4.65	82	36	15	337	409	110	96	2	1	6	3	107	17	0	.159	14	81	5	3	1.2	.950

John Franco

FRANCO, JOHN ANTHONY
B. Sept. 17, 1960, Brooklyn, N. Y.
BL TL 5'10" 175 lbs.

Year	Team		W	L	PCT	ERA	G	GS	CG	IP	H	BB	SO	ShO	W	L	SV	AB	H	HR	BA	PO	A	E	DP	TC/G	FA
1984	CIN	N	6	2	.750	2.61	54	0	0	79.1	74	36	55	0	6	2	4	3	0	0	.000	5	15	0	0	0.4	1.000
1985			12	3	.800	2.18	67	0	0	99	83	40	61	0	12	3	12	6	2	0	.333	9	21	1	1	0.5	.968
1986			6	6	.500	2.94	74	0	0	101	90	44	84	0	6	6	29	4	0	0	.000	6	22	4	2	0.4	.875
1987			8	5	.615	2.52	68	0	0	82	76	27	61	0	8	5	32	2	0	0	.000	4	7	0	0	0.2	1.000
1988			6	6	.500	1.57	70	0	0	86	60	27	46	0	6	6	39	1	0	0	.000	3	18	1	1	0.3	.955
1989			4	8	.333	3.12	60	0	0	80.2	77	36	60	0	4	8	32	3	1	0	.333	2	19	1	1	0.4	.955
6 yrs.			42	30	.583	2.49	393	0	0	528	460	210	367	0	42	30	148	19	3	0	.158	29	102	7	5	0.4	.949

Terry Francona

FRANCONA, TERRY JON
Son of Tito Francona.
B. Apr. 22, 1959, Aberdeen, S. D.
BB TL 6'1" 190 lbs.

Year	Team		W	L	PCT	ERA	G	GS	CG	IP	H	BB	SO	ShO	W	L	SV	AB	H	HR	BA	PO	A	E	DP	TC/G	FA
1989	MIL	A	0	0	–	0.00	1	0	0	1	0	1	0	0	0	0	0	*				0	0	0	0	0.0	–

Charlie Frank

FRANK, CHARLES
B. May 30, 1870, Mobile, Ala. D. May 24, 1922, Memphis, Tenn.

Year	Team		W	L	PCT	ERA	G	GS	CG	IP	H	BB	SO	ShO	W	L	SV	AB	H	HR	BA	PO	A	E	DP	TC/G	FA
1894	STL	N	0	0	–	15.00	2	0	0	3	6	7	1	0	3	0	0	*				0	0	0	0	0.0	–

Fred Frankhouse

FRANKHOUSE, FREDERICK MELOY
B. Apr. 9, 1904, Port Royal, Pa. D. Aug. 17, 1989, Port Royal, Pa.
BR TR 5'11" 175 lbs.

Year	Team		W	L	PCT	ERA	G	GS	CG	IP	H	BB	SO	ShO	W	L	SV	AB	H	HR	BA	PO	A	E	DP	TC/G	FA
1927	STL	N	5	1	.833	2.70	6	6	5	50	41	16	20	1	0	0	0	20	5	0	.250	3	6	2	0	1.8	.818
1928			3	2	.600	3.96	21	10	1	84	91	36	29	0	0	0	1	27	5	0	.185	2	23	1	4	1.2	.962
1929			7	2	.778	4.12	30	12	6	133.1	149	43	37	0	0	0	1	52	15	1	.288	5	41	1	5	1.6	.979

Year	Team	W	L	PCT	ERA	G	GS	CG	IP	H	BB	SO	ShO	Relief Pitching W	L	SV	Batting AB	H	HR	BA	PO	A	E	DP	TC/G	FA

Fred Frankhouse *continued*

Year	Team	W	L	PCT	ERA	G	GS	CG	IP	H	BB	SO	ShO	W	L	SV	AB	H	HR	BA	PO	A	E	DP	TC/G	FA
1930	2 teams	STL N	(8G 2–3)			BOS N	(27G 7–6)																			
"	total	9	9	.500	5.87	35	12	3	130.1	169	54	34	1	5	3	0	44	14	0	.318	8	27	1	1	1.0	.972
1931	BOS N	8	8	.500	4.03	26	15	6	127.1	125	43	50	0	0	1	1	40	6	0	.150	7	29	3	3	1.5	.923
1932		4	6	.400	3.56	37	6	3	108.2	113	45	35	0	2	3	0	30	3	0	.100	7	41	4	1	1.4	.923
1933		16	15	.516	3.16	43	30	14	244.2	249	77	83	2	2	2	2	80	19	0	.238	12	71	1	6	2.0	.988
1934		17	9	.654	3.20	37	31	13	233.2	239	77	78	2	0	0	1	85	17	0	.200	9	48	1	2	1.6	.983
1935		11	15	.423	4.76	40	29	10	230.2	278	81	64	1	0	0	0	76	20	0	.263	15	63	2	2	2.0	.975
1936	BKN N	13	10	.565	3.65	41	31	9	234.1	236	89	84	1	1	1	2	91	13	0	.143	15	52	1	3	1.7	.985
1937		10	13	.435	4.27	33	26	9	179.1	214	78	64	1	2	1	0	58	11	0	.190	20	48	5	2	2.2	.932
1938		3	5	.375	4.04	30	8	2	93.2	92	44	32	1	2	1	0	26	4	0	.154	5	24	2	1	1.0	.935
1939	BOS N	0	2	.000	2.61	23	0	0	38	37	18	12	0	0	2	4	7	0	0	.000	0	4	0	0	0.2	1.000
	13 yrs.	106	97	.522	3.92	402	216	81	1888	2033	701	622	10	15	14	12	636	132	1	.208	108	477	24	30	1.5	.961

Jack Franklin

FRANKLIN, JAMES WILFORD
B. Oct. 20, 1919, Paris, Ill.

BR TR 5'11½" 170 lbs.

Year	Team	W	L	PCT	ERA	G	GS	CG	IP	H	BB	SO	ShO	W	L	SV	AB	H	HR	BA	PO	A	E	DP	TC/G	FA
1944	BKN N	0	0	–	13.50	1	0	0	2	2	4	0	0	0	0	0	0	0	0	–	0	0	0	0	0.0	

Jay Franklin

FRANKLIN, JOHN WILLIAM
B. Mar. 16, 1953, Arlington, Va.

BR TR 6'2" 180 lbs.

Year	Team	W	L	PCT	ERA	G	GS	CG	IP	H	BB	SO	ShO	W	L	SV	AB	H	HR	BA	PO	A	E	DP	TC/G	FA
1971	SD N	0	1	.000	6.00	3	1	0	6	5	4	4	0	0	0	0	1	0	0	.000	0	2	0	0	0.7	1.000

Chick Fraser

FRASER, CHARLES CARROLTON
B. Mar. 17, 1871, Chicago, Ill. D. May 8, 1940, Wendell, Ida.

BR TR 5'10½" 188 lbs.

Year	Team	W	L	PCT	ERA	G	GS	CG	IP	H	BB	SO	ShO	W	L	SV	AB	H	HR	BA	PO	A	E	DP	TC/G	FA
1896	LOU N	12	27	.308	4.87	43	38	36	349.1	396	166	91	0	0	2	1	146	22	0	.151	39	95	25	5	3.7	.843
1897		15	19	.441	4.09	35	34	32	286.1	332	133	70	0	1	0	0	112	18	2	.161	33	84	12	5	3.7	.907
1898	2 teams	LOU N	(26G 7–17)			CLE N	(6G 2–3)																			
"	total	9	20	.310	5.36	32	32	26	245	279	112	77	1	0	0	0	94	17	0	.181	20	73	1	3	3.0	.969
1899	PHI N	21	12	.636	3.36	35	33	29	270.2	278	85	68	4	0	0	1	117	21	0	.179	24	71	9	3	3.0	.913
1900		16	10	.615	3.14	29	26	22	223.1	250	93	58	1	0	0	0	85	22	0	.259	27	63	4	2	3.2	.957
1901	PHI A	22	16	.579	3.81	40	37	35	331	344	132	110	2	1	0	0	139	26	0	.187	35	91	7	4	3.3	.947
1902	PHI N	12	13	.480	3.42	27	26	24	224	238	74	97	3	0	1	0	86	15	0	.174	15	51	4	1	2.6	.943
1903		12	17	.414	4.50	31	29	26	250	260	97	104	1	0	1	1	93	19	1	.204	14	70	3	2	2.8	.966
1904		14	24	.368	3.25	42	36	32	302	287	100	127	2	2	1	0	110	17	0	.155	28	87	10	3	3.0	.920
1905	BOS N	14	21	.400	3.29	39	38	35	334	320	149	130	2	0	0	0	156	35	0	.224	36	80	9	1	3.2	.928
1906	CIN N	10	20	.333	2.67	31	28	25	236	221	80	58	2	1	2	0	82	14	0	.171	23	70	4	3	3.1	.959
1907	CHI N	8	5	.615	2.28	22	15	9	138.1	112	46	41	2	4	0	0	45	3	0	.067	7	42	3	0	2.4	.942
1908		11	9	.550	2.27	26	17	11	162.2	141	61	66	2	3	0	2	50	6	0	.120	14	61	1	2	2.9	.987
1909		0	0	–	0.00	1	0	0	3	2	4	1	0	0	0	0	1	0	0	.000	0	0	0	0	0.0	
	14 yrs.	176	213	.452	3.68	433	389	342	3355.2	3460	1332	1098	22	12	8	5	1316	235	3	.179	315	938	94	32	3.1	.930

Willie Fraser

FRASER, WILLIAM PATRICK
B. May 26, 1964, New York, N.Y.

BR TR 6'3" 200 lbs.

Year	Team	W	L	PCT	ERA	G	GS	CG	IP	H	BB	SO	ShO	W	L	SV	AB	H	HR	BA	PO	A	E	DP	TC/G	FA
1986	CAL A	0	0	–	8.31	1	1	0	4.1	6	1	2	0	0	0	0	0	0	0	–	0	0	0	0	0.0	
1987		10	10	.500	3.92	36	23	5	176.2	160	63	106	1	3	1	1	0	0	0	–	6	15	1	0	0.6	.955
1988		12	13	.480	5.41	34	32	2	194.2	203	80	86	0	1	0	0	0	0	0	–	21	20	3	3	1.3	.932
1989		4	7	.364	3.24	44	0	0	91.2	80	23	46	0	4	7	2	0	0	0	–	6	14	0	1	0.5	1.000
	4 yrs.	26	30	.464	4.45	115	56	7	467.1	449	167	240	1	8	8	3	0	0	0	–	33	49	4	4	0.7	.953

Vic Frasier

FRASIER, VICTOR PATRICK
B. Aug. 5, 1904, Ruston, La. D. Jan. 10, 1977, Jacksonville, Tex.

BR TR 6' 182 lbs.

Year	Team	W	L	PCT	ERA	G	GS	CG	IP	H	BB	SO	ShO	W	L	SV	AB	H	HR	BA	PO	A	E	DP	TC/G	FA
1931	CHI A	13	15	.464	4.46	46	29	13	254	258	127	87	2	1	1	4	86	18	0	.209	6	50	6	2	1.3	.903
1932		3	13	.188	6.23	29	21	4	146	180	70	33	0	1	0	0	44	4	0	.091	5	42	1	1	1.7	.979
1933	2 teams	CHI A	(10G 1–1)			DET A	(20G 5–5)																			
"	total	6	6	.500	7.00	30	15	4	124.2	161	70	30	0	1	0	0	41	7	0	.171	4	35	0	1	1.3	1.000
1934	DET A	1	3	.250	5.96	8	2	0	22.2	30	12	11	0	1	2	0	7	2	0	.286	1	13	2	0	2.0	.875
1937	BOS N	0	0	–	5.63	3	0	0	8	12	1	2	0	0	0	0	1	0	0	.000	0	2	0	0	1.0	1.000
1939	CHI A	0	1	.000	10.27	10	1	0	23.2	45	11	7	0	0	0	0	7	2	0	.286	1	5	0	0	0.5	1.000
	6 yrs.	23	38	.377	5.77	126	68	21	579	686	291	170	2	2	4	4	186	33	0	.177	17	147	9	5	1.4	.948

George Frazier

FRAZIER, GEORGE ALLEN
B. Oct. 13, 1954, Oklahoma City, Okla.

BR TR 6'5" 205 lbs.

Year	Team	W	L	PCT	ERA	G	GS	CG	IP	H	BB	SO	ShO	W	L	SV	AB	H	HR	BA	PO	A	E	DP	TC/G	FA
1978	STL N	0	3	.000	4.09	14	0	0	22	22	6	8	0	0	3	0	3	1	0	.333	0	5	1	0	0.4	.833
1979		2	4	.333	4.50	25	0	0	32	35	12	14	0	2	4	0	1	0	0	.000	4	4	1	0	0.4	.889
1980		1	4	.200	2.74	22	0	0	23	24	7	11	0	1	4	3	0	0	0	–	1	4	0	0	0.2	1.000
1981	NY A	0	1	.000	1.61	16	0	0	28	26	11	17	0	0	1	3	0	0	0	–	1	4	1	0	0.4	.885
1982		4	4	.500	3.47	63	0	0	111.2	103	39	69	0	4	4	1	0	0	0	–	6	17	3	2	0.4	.885
1983		4	4	.500	3.43	61	0	0	115.1	94	45	78	0	4	4	8	0	0	0	–	5	17	2	0	0.4	.917
1984	2 teams	CLE A	(22G 3–2)			CHI N	(37G 6–3)																			
"	total	9	5	.643	3.92	59	0	0	108	98	40	82	0	9	5	4	7	2	0	.286	7	9	3	0	0.3	.842
1985	CHI N	7	8	.467	6.39	51	0	0	76	88	52	46	0	7	8	2	6	0	0	.000	5	9	1	2	0.3	.933
1986	2 teams	CHI N	(35G 2–4)			MIN A	(15G 1–1)																			
"	total	3	5	.375	5.06	50	0	0	78.1	86	50	66	0	3	5	6	0	0	0	–	3	6	0	0	0.2	1.000
1987	MIN A	5	5	.500	4.98	54	0	0	81.1	77	51	58	0	5	5	2	0	0	0	–	2	8	1	0	0.2	.909
	10 yrs.	35	43	.449	4.20	415	0	0	675.2	653	313	449	0	35	43	29	21	3	0	.143	34	83	13	4	0.3	.900

LEAGUE CHAMPIONSHIP SERIES

Year	Team	W	L	PCT	ERA	G	GS	CG	IP	H	BB	SO	ShO	W	L	SV	AB	H	HR	BA	PO	A	E	DP	TC/G	FA
1981	NY A	1	0	1.000	0.00	1	0	0	5.2	5	1	5	0	1	0	0	0	0	0	–	0	0	0	0	0.0	
1984	CHI N	0	0	–	10.80	1	0	0	1.2	2	0	1	0	0	0	0	0	0	0	–	0	0	0	0	0.0	
	2 yrs.	1	0	1.000	2.45	2	0	0	7.1	7	1	6	0	1	0	0	0	0	0	–	0	0	0	0	0.0	

WORLD SERIES

Year	Team	W	L	PCT	ERA	G	GS	CG	IP	H	BB	SO	ShO	W	L	SV	AB	H	HR	BA	PO	A	E	DP	TC/G	FA
1981	NY A	0	3	.000	17.18	3	0	0	3.2	9	3	2	0	0	3	0	2	0	0	.000	0	0	0	0	0.0	

Year	Team		W	L	PCT	ERA	G	GS	CG	IP	H	BB	SO	ShO	Relief Pitching W	L	SV	Batting AB	H	HR	BA	PO	A	E	DP	TC/G	FA

George Frazier *continued*

Year	Team		W	L	PCT	ERA	G	GS	CG	IP	H	BB	SO	ShO	W	L	SV	AB	H	HR	BA	PO	A	E	DP	TC/G	FA
1987	MIN	A	0	0	–	0.00	1	0	0	2	1	0	2	0	0	0	0	0	0	0	–	0	1	0	0	1.0	1.000
2 yrs.			0	3	.000	11.12	4	0	0	5.2	10	3	4	0	0	3	0	2	0	0	.000	0	1	0	0	0.3	1.000
															1st												

Buck Freeman

FREEMAN, ALEXANDER VERNON
B. July 5, 1896, Mart, Tex.
D. Feb. 21, 1953, Fort Sam Houston, Tex.

BB TR 5'10" 167 lbs.
BR 1922

Year	Team		W	L	PCT	ERA	G	GS	CG	IP	H	BB	SO	ShO	W	L	SV	AB	H	HR	BA	PO	A	E	DP	TC/G	FA
1921	CHI	N	9	10	.474	4.11	38	20	6	177.1	189	70	42	0	4	2	3	53	11	0	.208	3	43	3	2	1.3	.939
1922			0	1	.000	8.77	11	1	0	25.2	47	10	10	0	0	0	1	8	1	0	.125	0	11	2	2	1.2	.846
2 yrs.			9	11	.450	4.70	49	21	6	203	236	80	52	0	4	2	4	61	12	0	.197	3	54	5	4	1.3	.919

Buck Freeman

FREEMAN, JOHN FRANK
B. Oct. 30, 1871, Catasauqua, Pa.   D. June 25, 1949, Wilkes-Barre, Pa.

BL TL 5'9" 169 lbs.

Year	Team		W	L	PCT	ERA	G	GS	CG	IP	H	BB	SO	ShO	W	L	SV	AB	H	HR	BA	PO	A	E	DP	TC/G	FA
1891	WAS	AA	3	2	.600	3.89	5	4	4	44	35	33	28	0	1	0	0	18	4	0	.222	0	10	3	0	2.6	.769
1899	WAS	N	0	0	–	7.71	2	0	0	7	15	3	0	0	0	0	0	588	187	25	.318	0	3	1	0	2.0	.750
2 yrs.			3	2	.600	4.41	7	4	4	51	50	36	28	0	1	0	0	*				0	13	4	0	2.4	.765

Harvey Freeman

FREEMAN, HARVEY BAYARD (Buck)
B. Dec. 22, 1897, Mottville, Mich.   D. Jan. 10, 1970, Kalamazoo, Mich.

BR TR 5'10" 145 lbs.

Year	Team		W	L	PCT	ERA	G	GS	CG	IP	H	BB	SO	ShO	W	L	SV	AB	H	HR	BA	PO	A	E	DP	TC/G	FA
1921	PHI	A	1	4	.200	7.24	18	4	2	51	65	35	5	0	0	1	0	12	1	0	.083	0	19	0	0	1.1	1.000

Hersh Freeman

FREEMAN, HERSHELL BASKIN (Buster)
B. July 1, 1928, Gadsden, Ala.

BR TR 6'3" 220 lbs.

Year	Team		W	L	PCT	ERA	G	GS	CG	IP	H	BB	SO	ShO	W	L	SV	AB	H	HR	BA	PO	A	E	DP	TC/G	FA
1952	BOS	A	1	0	1.000	3.29	4	1	1	13.2	13	5	5	0	0	0	0	4	2	0	.500	0	4	0	0	1.0	1.000
1953			1	4	.200	5.54	18	2	0	39	50	17	15	0	1	2	0	11	1	0	.091	0	7	0	0	0.4	1.000
1955	2 teams				BOS A	(2G 0–0)				CIN N	(52G 7–4)																
"	total		7	4	.636	2.12	54	0	0	93.1	95	31	38	0	7	4	11	18	3	1	.167	4	20	0	4	0.4	1.000
1956	CIN	N	14	5	.737	3.40	64	0	0	108.2	112	34	50	0	14	5	18	18	1	0	.056	8	15	0	2	0.4	1.000
1957			7	2	.778	4.52	52	0	0	83.2	90	14	36	0	7	2	8	10	2	0	.200	5	12	0	1	0.3	1.000
1958	2 teams				CIN N	(3G 0–0)				CHI N	(9G 0–1)																
"	total		0	1	.000	6.53	12	0	0	20.2	27	8	14	0	0	1	0	2	0	0	.000	2	5	0	0	0.6	1.000
6 yrs.			30	16	.652	3.74	204	3	1	359	387	109	158	0	29	14	37	63	9	1	.143	19	63	0	7	0.4	1.000

Jimmy Freeman

FREEMAN, JIMMY LEE
B. June 29, 1951, Carlsbad, N. M.

BL TL 6'4" 180 lbs.

Year	Team		W	L	PCT	ERA	G	GS	CG	IP	H	BB	SO	ShO	W	L	SV	AB	H	HR	BA	PO	A	E	DP	TC/G	FA
1972	ATL	N	2	2	.500	6.00	6	6	1	36	40	22	18	0	0	0	0	13	1	0	.077	1	2	1	0	0.7	.750
1973			0	2	.000	7.78	13	5	0	37	50	25	20	0	0	1	1	13	2	0	.154	1	3	0	1	0.3	1.000
2 yrs.			2	4	.333	6.90	19	11	1	73	90	47	38	0	0	1	1	26	3	0	.115	2	5	1	0	0.4	.875

Julie Freeman

FREEMAN, JULIUS BENJAMIN
B. Nov. 7, 1868, Missouri   D. June 10, 1921, St. Louis, Mo.

Year	Team		W	L	PCT	ERA	G	GS	CG	IP	H	BB	SO	ShO	W	L	SV	AB	H	HR	BA	PO	A	E	DP	TC/G	FA
1888	STL	AA	0	1	.000	4.26	1	1	0	6.1	7	4	1	0	0	0	0	3	1	0	.333	0	1	0	0	1.0	1.000

Mark Freeman

FREEMAN, MARK PRICE
B. Dec. 7, 1930, Memphis, Tenn.

BR TR 6'4" 220 lbs.

Year	Team		W	L	PCT	ERA	G	GS	CG	IP	H	BB	SO	ShO	W	L	SV	AB	H	HR	BA	PO	A	E	DP	TC/G	FA
1959	2 teams				NY A	(1G 0–0)				KC A	(3G 0–0)																
"	total		0	0	–	5.06	4	1	0	10.2	12	5	5	0	0	0	0	2	0	0	.000	0	1	0	0	0.3	1.000
1960	CHI	N	3	3	.500	5.63	30	8	1	76.2	70	33	50	0	1	2	1	20	3	0	.150	3	6	1	0	0.3	.900
2 yrs.			3	3	.500	5.56	34	9	1	87.1	82	38	55	0	1	2	1	22	3	0	.136	3	7	1	0	0.3	.909

Marvin Freeman

FREEMAN, MARVIN (Starvin' Marvin)
B. Apr. 10, 1963, Chicago, Ill.

BR TR 6'7" 200 lbs.

Year	Team		W	L	PCT	ERA	G	GS	CG	IP	H	BB	SO	ShO	W	L	SV	AB	H	HR	BA	PO	A	E	DP	TC/G	FA
1986	PHI	N	2	0	1.000	2.25	3	3	0	16	6	10	8	0	0	0	0	6	0	0	.000	0	1	0	0	0.3	1.000
1988			2	3	.400	6.10	11	11	0	51.2	55	43	37	0	0	0	0	14	3	0	.214	2	9	0	0	1.0	1.000
1989			0	0	–	6.00	1	1	0	3	2	5	0	0	0	0	0	2	0	0	.000	0	0	0	0	0.0	–
3 yrs.			4	3	.571	5.22	15	15	0	70.2	63	58	45	0	0	0	0	22	3	0	.136	2	10	0	0	0.8	1.000

Jake Freeze

FREEZE, CARL ALEXANDER
B. Apr. 25, 1900, Huntington, Ark.   D. Apr. 9, 1983, San Angelo, Tex.

BR TR 5'8" 150 lbs.

Year	Team		W	L	PCT	ERA	G	GS	CG	IP	H	BB	SO	ShO	W	L	SV	AB	H	HR	BA	PO	A	E	DP	TC/G	FA
1925	CHI	A	0	0	–	2.45	2	0	0	3.2	5	3	1	0	0	0	0	1	0	0	.000	0	0	0	0	0.0	–

Dave Freisleben

FREISLEBEN, DAVID JAMES
B. Oct. 31, 1951, Coraopolis, Pa.

BR TR 5'11" 195 lbs.

Year	Team		W	L	PCT	ERA	G	GS	CG	IP	H	BB	SO	ShO	W	L	SV	AB	H	HR	BA	PO	A	E	DP	TC/G	FA
1974	SD	N	9	14	.391	3.65	33	31	6	212	194	112	130	2	0	0	0	64	11	0	.172	12	28	1	3	1.2	.976
1975			5	14	.263	4.28	36	27	4	181	206	82	77	1	0	0	0	48	4	0	.083	15	26	1	2	1.2	.976
1976			10	13	.435	3.51	34	24	6	172	163	66	81	3	2	1	1	37	7	0	.189	16	33	2	2	1.5	.961
1977			7	9	.438	4.60	33	23	1	139	140	71	72	0	1	0	0	37	5	0	.135	6	11	1	2	0.5	.944
1978	2 teams				SD N	(12G 0–3)				CLE A	(12G 1–4)																
"	total		1	7	.125	6.69	24	14	0	71.1	93	46	35	0	0	0	0	6	0	0	.000	7	8	2	0	0.7	.882
1979	TOR	A	2	3	.400	4.95	42	2	0	91	101	53	35	0	2	2	3	0	0	0	–	3	13	1	1	0.4	.941
6 yrs.			34	60	.362	4.29	202	121	17	866.1	897	430	430	6	5	5	4	192	27	0	.141	59	119	8	10	0.9	.957

Tony Freitas

FREITAS, ANTONIO
B. May 5, 1908, Mill Valley, Calif.

BR TL 5'8" 161 lbs.

Year	Team		W	L	PCT	ERA	G	GS	CG	IP	H	BB	SO	ShO	W	L	SV	AB	H	HR	BA	PO	A	E	DP	TC/G	FA
1932	PHI	A	12	5	.706	3.83	23	18	10	150.1	150	48	31	1	1	2	0	54	8	0	.148	16	32	0	2	2.1	1.000
1933			2	4	.333	7.27	19	9	2	64.1	90	24	15	0	1	0	1	16	1	0	.063	8	12	2	2	1.2	.909
1934	CIN	N	6	12	.333	4.01	30	18	5	152.2	194	25	37	0	1	2	1	47	9	0	.191	10	42	2	4	1.8	.963
1935			5	10	.333	4.57	31	18	5	143.2	174	38	51	0	0	1	2	46	6	0	.130	15	27	1	5	1.4	.977

Year	Team		W	L	PCT	ERA	G	GS	CG	IP	H	BB	SO	ShO	Relief Pitching W	L	SV	Batting AB	H	HR	BA	PO	A	E	DP	TC/G	FA

Tony Freitas *continued*

| 1936 | | | 0 | 2 | .000 | 1.29 | 4 | 0 | 0 | 7 | 6 | 2 | 1 | 0 | 0 | 2 | 0 | 2 | 0 | 0 | .000 | 1 | 1 | 0 | 0 | 0.5 | 1.000 |
| 5 yrs. | | | 25 | 33 | .431 | 4.48 | 107 | 63 | 22 | 518 | 614 | 137 | 135 | 1 | 2 | 8 | 4 | 165 | 24 | 0 | .145 | 50 | 114 | 5 | 13 | 1.6 | .970 |

Larry French

FRENCH, LAWRENCE HERBERT
B. Nov. 1, 1907, Visalia, Calif.
D. Feb. 9, 1987, San Diego, Calif.

BR TL 6'1" 195 lbs.
BB 1934,1940-42

1929	PIT	N	7	5	.583	4.90	30	13	6	123	130	62	49	0	2	1	1	42	8	0	.190	3	35	2	1	1.3	.950
1930			17	18	.486	4.36	42	35	21	274.2	325	89	90	3	1	1	1	91	22	0	.242	5	53	3	3	1.5	.951
1931			15	13	.536	3.26	39	33	20	275.2	301	70	73	1	1	0	1	95	17	0	.179	7	56	3	6	1.7	.955
1932			18	16	.529	3.02	47	33	20	274.1	301	62	72	3	2	2	4	92	19	0	.207	8	45	7	3	1.3	.883
1933			18	13	.581	2.72	47	35	21	291.1	290	55	88	5	1	2	1	101	15	0	.149	12	45	3	4	1.3	.950
1934			12	18	.400	3.58	49	35	16	263.2	299	59	103	3	1	4	1	84	16	0	.190	10	40	3	4	1.1	.943
1935	CHI	N	17	10	.630	2.96	42	30	16	246.1	279	44	90	4	1	3	2	85	12	0	.141	16	55	2	5	1.7	.973
1936			18	9	.667	3.39	43	28	16	252.1	262	54	104	4	3	2	3	85	18	0	.212	14	37	3	3	1.3	.944
1937			16	10	.615	3.98	42	28	11	208	229	65	100	4	3	1	0	71	9	0	.127	10	55	4	4	1.6	.942
1938			10	19	.345	3.80	43	27	10	201.1	210	62	83	2	2	4	0	62	13	0	.210	19	41	1	1	1.4	.984
1939			15	8	.652	3.29	36	21	10	194	205	50	98	2	4	0	1	73	14	1	.192	5	47	2	3	1.5	.963
1940			14	14	.500	3.29	40	33	18	246	240	64	107	3	1	0	0	85	14	0	.165	7	63	2	2	1.8	.972
1941	2 teams		CHI N	(26G 5–14)			BKN N	(6G 0–0)																			
"	total		5	14	.263	4.51	32	19	6	153.2	177	47	68	1	1	0	0	51	10	0	.196	1	26	2	0	0.9	.931
1942	BKN	N	15	4	.789	1.83	38	14	8	147.2	127	36	62	4	7	1	0	40	12	0	.300	7	27	2	1	0.9	.944
14 yrs.			197	171	.535	3.44	570	384	199	3152	3375	819	1187	40	30	22	17	1057	199	1	.188	124	625	39	40	1.4	.951

WORLD SERIES

1935	CHI	N	0	2	.000	3.38	2	1	1	10.2	15	2	8	0	0	1	0	4	1	0	.250	1	2	0	0	1.5	1.000
1938			0	0	—	2.70	3	0	0	3.1	1	1	2	0	0	0	0	0	0	0	—	0	0	0	0	0.7	1.000
1941	BKN	N	0	0	—	0.00	2	0	0	1	0	0	0	0	0	0	0	0	0	0	—	0	0	0	0	0.0	—
3 yrs.			0	2	.000	3.00	7	1	1	15	16	3	10	0	0	1	0	4	1	0	.250	1	4	0	0	0.7	1.000

Benny Frey

FREY, BENJAMIN RUDOLPH
B. Apr. 6, 1906, Dexter, Mich.   D. Nov. 1, 1937, Jackson, Mich.

BR TR 5'10" 165 lbs.

1929	CIN	N	1	2	.333	4.13	3	3	2	24	29	8	1	0	0	0	0	8	3	0	.375	2	11	3	2	5.3	.813
1930			11	18	.379	4.70	44	28	14	245	295	62	43	2	2	2	1	88	25	0	.284	10	79	1	7	2.0	.989
1931			8	12	.400	4.92	34	17	7	133.2	166	36	19	1	3	0	2	44	14	0	.318	4	48	1	5	1.6	.981
1932	2 teams		STL N	(2G 0–2)			CIN N	(28G 4–10)																			
"	total		4	12	.250	4.49	30	15	5	134.1	165	32	27	1	2	0	0	45	9	0	.200	7	39	0	1	1.5	1.000
1933	CIN	N	6	4	.600	3.82	37	9	1	132	144	21	12	1	4	0	0	42	11	0	.262	11	36	3	3	1.4	.940
1934			11	16	.407	3.52	39	30	12	245.1	288	42	33	2	1	1	2	82	14	0	.171	8	74	1	6	2.1	.988
1935			6	10	.375	6.85	38	13	3	114.1	164	32	24	1	3	2	2	32	11	0	.344	6	34	1	5	1.1	.976
1936			10	8	.556	4.25	31	12	5	131.1	164	30	20	1	4	2	0	44	11	0	.250	6	33	5	2	1.4	.886
8 yrs.			57	82	.410	4.50	256	127	49	1160	1415	263	179	7	18	9	7	385	98	0	.255	54	354	15	33	1.7	.965

Steve Frey

FREY, STEVEN FRANCIS
B. July 29, 1963, Meadowbrook, Pa.

BR TL 5'9" 170 lbs.

| 1989 | MON | N | 3 | 2 | .600 | 5.48 | 20 | 0 | 0 | 21.1 | 29 | 11 | 15 | 0 | 3 | 2 | 0 | 0 | 0 | 0 | — | 1 | 2 | 0 | 0 | 0.2 | 1.000 |

Barney Friberg

FRIBERG, GUSTAF BERNHARD
B. Aug. 18, 1899, Manchester, N. H.   D. Dec. 8, 1958, Lynn, Mass.

BR TR 5'11" 178 lbs.

| 1925 | CHI | N | 0 | 0 | — | 4.50 | 1 | 0 | 0 | 4 | 4 | 3 | 1 | 0 | 0 | 0 | 0 | * | | | | 0 | 0 | 0 | 0 | 0.0 | — |

Marion Fricano

FRICANO, MARION JOHN
B. July 15, 1923, Brant, N. Y.   D. May 18, 1976, Tijuana, Mexico

BR TR 6' 170 lbs.

1952	PHI	A	1	0	1.000	1.80	2	0	0	5	5	1	0	0	1	0	0	0	0	0	—	0	1	0	0	0.5	1.000
1953			9	12	.429	3.88	39	23	10	211	206	90	67	0	1	0	0	69	10	0	.145	8	28	0	2	0.9	1.000
1954			5	11	.313	5.16	37	20	4	151.2	163	64	43	0	1	0	1	41	4	0	.098	9	20	3	2	0.9	.906
1955	KC	A	0	0	—	3.15	10	0	0	20	19	9	5	0	0	0	0	3	2	0	.667	5	4	1	0	1.0	.900
4 yrs.			15	23	.395	4.32	88	43	14	387.2	393	164	115	0	3	0	1	113	16	0	.142	22	53	4	4	0.9	.949

Skipper Friday

FRIDAY, GRIER WILLIAM
B. Oct. 26, 1897, Gastonia, N. C.   D. Aug. 25, 1962, Gastonia, N. C.

BR TR 5'11" 170 lbs.

| 1923 | WAS | A | 0 | 1 | .000 | 6.90 | 7 | 2 | 1 | 30 | 35 | 22 | 9 | 0 | 0 | 0 | 0 | 9 | 2 | 0 | .222 | 1 | 12 | 0 | 1 | 1.9 | 1.000 |

Cy Fried

FRIED, ARTHUR EDWIN
B. July 23, 1897, San Antonio, Tex.   D. Oct. 10, 1970, San Antonio, Tex.

BL TL 5'11½" 150 lbs.

| 1920 | DET | A | 0 | 0 | — | 16.20 | 2 | 0 | 0 | 1.2 | 3 | 4 | 0 | 0 | 0 | 0 | 0 | 0 | 0 | 0 | — | 0 | 1 | 0 | 0 | 0.5 | 1.000 |

Bob Friedrich

FRIEDRICH, ROBERT GEORGE
B. Aug. 30, 1906, Cincinnati, Ohio

BR TR 5'11½" 165 lbs.

| 1932 | WAS | A | 0 | 0 | — | 11.25 | 2 | 0 | 0 | 4 | 7 | 2 | 0 | 0 | 0 | 0 | 0 | 1 | 0 | 0 | .000 | 0 | 0 | 0 | 0 | 0.0 | — |

Bill Friel

FRIEL, WILLIAM EDWARD
Brother of Pat Friel.
B. Apr. 1, 1876, Renovo, Pa.   D. Dec. 24, 1959, St. Louis, Mo.

BL TR 5'10" 215 lbs.

| 1902 | STL | A | 0 | 0 | — | 4.50 | 1 | 0 | 0 | 4 | 4 | 0 | 0 | 0 | 0 | 0 | 0 | * | | | | 0 | 0 | 1 | 0 | 1.0 | — |

Bob Friend

FRIEND, ROBERT BARTMESS (Warrior)
B. Nov. 24, 1930, Lafayette, Ind.

BR TR 6' 190 lbs.

| 1951 | PIT | N | 6 | 10 | .375 | 4.27 | 34 | 22 | 3 | 149.2 | 173 | 68 | 41 | 1 | 0 | 1 | 0 | 44 | 4 | 0 | .091 | 10 | 29 | 1 | 1 | 1.2 | .975 |
| 1952 | | | 7 | 17 | .292 | 4.18 | 35 | 23 | 6 | 185 | 186 | 84 | 75 | 1 | 2 | 2 | 0 | 52 | 3 | 0 | .058 | 10 | 37 | 2 | 3 | 1.4 | .959 |

Year	Team	W	L	PCT	ERA	G	GS	CG	IP	H	BB	SO	ShO	W	L	SV	AB	H	HR	BA	PO	A	E	DP	TC/G	FA

Bob Friend *continued*

Year	Team	W	L	PCT	ERA	G	GS	CG	IP	H	BB	SO	ShO	W	L	SV	AB	H	HR	BA	PO	A	E	DP	TC/G	FA
1953		8	11	.421	4.90	32	24	8	170.2	193	57	66	0	0	1	0	52	7	0	.135	7	36	3	2	1.4	.935
1954		7	12	.368	5.07	35	20	4	170.1	204	58	73	2	1	1	2	51	14	1	.275	7	27	1	1	1.0	.971
1955		14	9	.609	2.83	44	20	9	200.1	178	52	98	2	5	1	2	61	10	0	.164	7	50	2	6	1.3	.966
1956		17	17	.500	3.46	49	42	19	314.1	310	85	166	4	0	0	3	97	16	1	.165	14	49	2	1	1.3	.969
1957		14	18	.438	3.38	40	38	17	277	273	68	143	3	0	0	0	87	16	0	.184	18	38	1	3	1.4	.982
1958		22	14	.611	3.68	38	38	16	274	299	61	135	1	0	0	0	94	10	0	.106	7	47	1	4	1.4	.982
1959		8	19	.296	4.03	35	35	7	234.2	267	52	104	2	0	0	0	73	12	0	.164	24	37	1	2	1.8	.984
1960		18	12	.600	3.00	38	37	16	275.2	266	45	183	4	0	0	1	88	6	0	.068	24	43	1	1	1.8	.985
1961		14	19	.424	3.85	41	35	10	236	271	45	108	1	1	1	1	79	11	0	.139	19	37	3	3	1.4	.949
1962		18	14	.563	3.06	39	36	13	261.2	280	53	144	5	0	0	1	91	11	0	.121	18	43	1	3	1.6	.984
1963		17	16	.515	2.34	39	38	12	268.2	236	44	144	4	1	0	0	86	9	0	.105	23	41	2	2	1.7	.970
1964		13	18	.419	3.33	35	35	13	240.1	253	50	128	3	0	0	0	71	5	0	.070	12	55	2	3	2.0	.971
1965		8	12	.400	3.24	34	34	8	222	221	47	74	2	0	0	0	71	3	0	.042	21	39	1	5	1.8	.984
1966	2 teams	NY A		(12G 1–4)	NY N			(22G 5–8)																		
"	total	6	12	.333	4.55	34	20	2	130.2	162	25	52	1	1	4	1	40	1	0	.025	7	22	3	0	0.9	.906
16 yrs.		197	230	.461	3.58	602	497	163	3611	3772	894	1734	36	11	12	11	1137	138	2	.121	228	630	27	40	1.5	.969

WORLD SERIES

Year	Team	W	L	PCT	ERA	G	GS	CG	IP	H	BB	SO	ShO	W	L	SV	AB	H	HR	BA	PO	A	E	DP	TC/G	FA
1960	PIT N	0	2	.000	13.50	3	2	0	6	13	3	7	0	0	0	0	1	0	0	.000	1	3	0	0	1.3	1.000

Danny Friend   FRIEND, DANIEL SEBASTIAN   TL 5'9" 175 lbs.
B. Apr. 8, 1873, Cincinnati, Ohio D. June 1, 1942, Chillicothe, Ohio

Year	Team	W	L	PCT	ERA	G	GS	CG	IP	H	BB	SO	ShO	W	L	SV	AB	H	HR	BA	PO	A	E	DP	TC/G	FA
1895	CHI N	2	2	.500	5.27	5	5	5	41	50	14	10	0	0	0	0	17	4	0	.235	3	8	0	0	2.2	1.000
1896		18	14	.563	4.74	36	33	28	290.2	298	139	86	1	1	1	0	126	30	1	.238	18	59	10	3	2.4	.885
1897		12	11	.522	4.52	24	24	23	203	244	86	58	0	0	0	0	88	25	0	.284	18	32	7	6	2.4	.877
1898		0	2	.000	5.29	2	2	2	17	20	10	4	0	0	0	0	7	2	0	.286	3	13	0	0	8.0	1.000
4 yrs.		32	29	.525	4.71	67	64	58	551.2	612	249	158	1	1	1	0	238	61	1	.256	42	112	17	9	2.6	.901

Pete Fries   FRIES, PETER MARTIN   BL TL 5'8" 160 lbs.
B. Oct. 30, 1857, Scranton, Pa. D. July 30, 1937, Chicago, Ill.

Year	Team	W	L	PCT	ERA	G	GS	CG	IP	H	BB	SO	ShO	W	L	SV	AB	H	HR	BA	PO	A	E	DP	TC/G	FA
1883	COL AA	0	3	.000	6.48	3	3	3	25	34	14	7	0	0	0	0	10	3	0	.300	1	5	1	0	2.3	.857
1884	IND AA	0	0	–	0.00												3	1	0	.333	0	0	0	0	0.0	–
2 yrs.		0	3	.000	6.48	3	3	3	25	34	14	7	0	0	0	0	13	4	0	.308	1	5	1	0	2.3	.857

John Frill   FRILL, JOHN EDMOND   BR TL 5'10½" 170 lbs.
B. Apr. 3, 1879, Reading, Pa. D. Sept. 28, 1918, Westerly, R. I.

Year	Team	W	L	PCT	ERA	G	GS	CG	IP	H	BB	SO	ShO	W	L	SV	AB	H	HR	BA	PO	A	E	DP	TC/G	FA
1910	NY A	2	2	.500	4.47	10	5	3	48.1	55	5	27	1	0	1	0	18	2	0	.111	2	16	2	0	2.0	.900
1912	2 teams	STL A		(3G 0–1)	CIN N		(3G 1–0)																			
"	total	1	1	.500	9.31	6	5	0	19.1	35	2	6	0	0	0	1	6	2	0	.333	0	6	0	0	1.0	1.000
2 yrs.		3	3	.500	5.85	16	10	3	67.2	90	7	33	1	0	1	1	24	4	0	.167	2	22	2	0	1.6	.923

Danny Frisella   FRISELLA, DANIEL VINCENT (Bear)   BL TR 6' 185 lbs.
B. Mar. 4, 1946, San Francisco, Calif. D. Jan. 1, 1977, Phoenix, Ariz.

Year	Team	W	L	PCT	ERA	G	GS	CG	IP	H	BB	SO	ShO	W	L	SV	AB	H	HR	BA	PO	A	E	DP	TC/G	FA
1967	NY N	1	6	.143	3.41	14	11	0	74	68	33	51	0	0	0	0	23	2	0	.087	3	12	2	0	1.2	.882
1968		2	4	.333	3.91	19	4	0	50.2	53	17	47	0	0	0	2	12	1	0	.083	3	8	0	0	0.6	1.000
1969		0	0	–	7.71	3	0	0	4.2	8	3	5	0	0	0	0	1	0	0	.000	0	0	0	0	0.0	–
1970		8	3	.727	3.00	30	1	0	66	49	34	54	0	7	3	1	13	4	0	.308	3	8	0	1	0.4	1.000
1971		8	5	.615	1.98	53	0	0	91	76	30	93	0	8	5	12	13	3	0	.231	7	13	0	0	0.4	1.000
1972		5	8	.385	3.34	39	0	0	67.1	63	20	46	0	5	8	9	7	2	0	.286	5	15	1	0	0.5	.952
1973	ATL N	1	2	.333	4.20	42	0	0	45	40	23	27	0	1	2	8	2	1	0	.500	4	6	1	0	0.3	.909
1974		3	4	.429	5.14	36	1	0	42	37	28	27	0	3	4	6	1	0	0	.000	5	2	2	0	0.2	1.000
1975	SD N	1	6	.143	3.12	65	0	0	98	86	51	67	0	1	6	9	5	1	0	.200	6	13	2	0	0.3	.905
1976	2 teams	STL N		(18G 0–0)	MIL A		(32G 5–2)																			
"	total	5	2	.714	3.13	50	0	0	72	49	47	54	0	5	2	10		0	0	.000	3	10	0	0	0.3	1.000
10 yrs.		34	40	.459	3.32	351	17	0	610.2	529	286	471	0	30	32	57	78	14	0	.179	39	87	6	3	0.4	.955

Emil Frisk   FRISK, JOHN EMIL   BL TR 6'1" 190 lbs.
B. Oct. 15, 1874, Kalkaska, Mich. D. Jan. 27, 1922, Seattle, Wash.

Year	Team	W	L	PCT	ERA	G	GS	CG	IP	H	BB	SO	ShO	W	L	SV	AB	H	HR	BA	PO	A	E	DP	TC/G	FA
1899	CIN N	3	6	.333	3.95	9	9	9	68.1	81	17	17	0	0	0	0	25	7	0	.280	4	15	1	0	2.2	.950
1901	DET A	5	4	.556	4.34	11	7	6	74.2	94	26	22	0	2	0	0	48	15	1	.313	4	36	7	0	4.3	.851
2 yrs.		8	10	.444	4.15	20	16	15	143	175	43	39	0	2	0	0	*				8	51	8	0	3.4	.881

Charlie Fritz   FRITZ, CHARLES CORNELIUS   TL
B. June 18, 1882, Mobile, Ala. D. July 30, 1943, Mobile, Ala.

Year	Team	W	L	PCT	ERA	G	GS	CG	IP	H	BB	SO	ShO	W	L	SV	AB	H	HR	BA	PO	A	E	DP	TC/G	FA
1907	PHI A	0	0	–	3.38	1	1	0	2.2	0	3	1	0	0	0	0	1	0	0	.000	0	0	0	0	0.0	–

Bill Froats   FROATS, WILLIAM JOHN   BL TL 6' 180 lbs.
B. Oct. 20, 1930, New York, N. Y.

Year	Team	W	L	PCT	ERA	G	GS	CG	IP	H	BB	SO	ShO	W	L	SV	AB	H	HR	BA	PO	A	E	DP	TC/G	FA
1955	DET A	0	0	–	0.00	1	0	0	2	0	2	0	0	0	0	0	0	0	0	–	0	1	0	0	1.0	1.000

Sam Frock   FROCK, SAMUEL WILLIAM   BR TR 6' 168 lbs.
B. Dec. 23, 1882, Baltimore, Md. D. Nov. 3, 1925, Baltimore, Md.

Year	Team	W	L	PCT	ERA	G	GS	CG	IP	H	BB	SO	ShO	W	L	SV	AB	H	HR	BA	PO	A	E	DP	TC/G	FA
1907	BOS N	1	2	.333	2.97	5	3	3	33.1	28	11	12	1	0	0	0	14	1	0	.071	0	2	0	0	0.4	1.000
1909	PIT N	2	1	.667	2.48	8	4	4	36.1	44	4	11	0	1	0	0	14	2	0	.143	0	12	0	0	1.5	1.000
1910	2 teams	PIT N		(1G 0–1)	BOS N		(45G 11–19)																			
"	total	11	20	.355	3.22	46	29	15	257.1	247	93	171	2	5	2	2	84	16	0	.190	7	71	2	3	1.7	.975
1911	BOS N	0	1	.000	5.63	4	1	1	16	29	5	8	0	0	0	0	5	1	0	.200	1	4	0	0	1.3	1.000
4 yrs.		14	24	.368	3.23	63	37	23	343	348	113	202	3	6	2	2	117	20	0	.171	8	89	2	3	1.6	.980

Year	Team		W	L	PCT	ERA	G	GS	CG	IP	H	BB	SO	ShO	W	L	SV	AB	H	HR	BA	PO	A	E	DP	TC/G	FA
															Relief Pitching			**Batting**									

Todd Frohwirth

FROHWIRTH, TODD GERARD
B. Sept. 28, 1962, Milwaukee, Wis. BR TR 6'4" 190 lbs.

Year	Team		W	L	PCT	ERA	G	GS	CG	IP	H	BB	SO	ShO	W	L	SV	AB	H	HR	BA	PO	A	E	DP	TC/G	FA
1987	PHI	N	1	0	1.000	0.00	10	0	0	11	12	2	9	0	1	0	0	1	0	0	.000	1	1	0	1	0.2	1.000
1988			1	2	.333	8.25	12	0	0	12	16	11	11	0	1	2	0	0	0	0	–	0	5	0	0	0.4	1.000
1989			1	0	1.000	3.59	45	0	0	62.2	56	18	39	0	1	0	0	1	0	0	.000	5	8	0	0	0.3	1.000
3 yrs.			3	2	.600	3.78	67	0	0	85.2	84	31	59	0	3	2	0	2	0	0	.000	6	14	0	1	0.3	1.000

Art Fromme

FROMME, ARTHUR HENRY
B. Sept. 3, 1883, Quincy, Ill. D. Aug. 24, 1956, Los Angeles, Calif. BR TR 6' 178 lbs.

Year	Team		W	L	PCT	ERA	G	GS	CG	IP	H	BB	SO	ShO	W	L	SV	AB	H	HR	BA	PO	A	E	DP	TC/G	FA
1906	STL	N	1	2	.333	1.44	3	3	3	25	19	10	11	0	1	0	0	9	2	0	.222	0	12	3	0	5.0	.800
1907			5	13	.278	2.90	23	16	13	145.2	138	67	67	2	1	1	0	55	10	0	.182	9	39	3	1	2.2	.941
1908			5	13	.278	2.72	20	14	9	116	102	50	62	2	1	3	0	36	5	0	.139	3	30	0	1	1.7	1.000
1909	CIN	N	19	13	.594	1.90	37	34	22	279.1	195	101	126	4	1	0	2	94	18	0	.191	7	89	8	1	2.8	.923
1910			3	4	.429	2.92	11	5	1	49.1	44	39	10	0	2	1	0	15	2	0	.133	1	16	1	0	1.6	.944
1911			10	11	.476	3.46	38	26	11	208	190	79	107	1	0	0	0	74	14	0	.189	8	56	3	3	1.8	.955
1912			16	18	.471	2.74	43	37	23	296	285	88	120	3	0	1	0	103	9	0	.087	7	76	9	3	2.1	.902
1913	2 teams	CIN N (9G 1–4)					DET A (26G 11–6)																				
"	total		12	10	.545	4.06	35	19	5	168.1	167	50	74	0	6	0	0	56	9	0	.161	7	44	0	1	1.5	1.000
1914	NY	N	9	5	.643	3.20	38	12	3	138	142	44	57	1	4	0	2	31	7	0	.226	6	53	2	0	1.6	.967
1915			0	1	.000	5.84	4	1	0	12.1	15	2	4	0	0	1	0	3	1	0	.333	0	4	1	0	1.3	.800
10 yrs.			80	90	.471	2.90	252	167	90	1438	1297	530	638	14	15	8	4	476	77	0	.162	48	419	30	10	2.0	.940

Dave Frost

FROST, CARL DAVID
B. Nov. 17, 1952, Long Beach, Calif. BR TR 6'6" 235 lbs.

Year	Team		W	L	PCT	ERA	G	GS	CG	IP	H	BB	SO	ShO	W	L	SV	AB	H	HR	BA	PO	A	E	DP	TC/G	FA
1977	CHI	A	1	1	.500	3.00	4	3	0	24	30	3	15	0	0	0	0	0	0	0	–	2	3	0	0	1.3	1.000
1978	CAL	A	5	4	.556	2.58	11	10	2	80.1	71	24	30	1	0	0	0	0	0	0	–	5	19	1	0	2.3	.960
1979			16	10	.615	3.58	36	33	12	239	226	77	107	2	0	1	1	0	0	0	–	8	34	2	1	1.2	.955
1980			4	8	.333	5.31	15	15	2	78	97	21	28	0	0	0	0	0	0	0	–	2	7	1	1	0.7	.900
1981			1	8	.111	5.55	12	9	0	47	44	19	16	0	0	0	0	0	0	0	–	1	9	0	0	0.8	1.000
1982	KC	A	6	6	.500	5.51	21	14	0	81.2	103	30	26	0	3	0	0	0	0	0	–	5	6	1	1	0.6	.917
6 yrs.			33	37	.471	4.11	99	84	16	550	571	174	222	3	3	2	1	0	0	0	–	23	78	5	4	1.1	.953

LEAGUE CHAMPIONSHIP SERIES

Year	Team		W	L	PCT	ERA	G	GS	CG	IP	H	BB	SO	ShO	W	L	SV	AB	H	HR	BA	PO	A	E	DP	TC/G	FA
1979	CAL	A	0	1	.000	18.69	2	1	0	4.1	8	5	1	0	0	0	0	0	0	0	–	0	0	0	0	0.0	–

Jay Fry

FRY, JOHNSON
B. Nov. 21, 1901, Huntington, W. Va. D. Apr. 7, 1959, Carmi, Ill. BR TR 6'1" 150 lbs.

Year	Team		W	L	PCT	ERA	G	GS	CG	IP	H	BB	SO	ShO	W	L	SV	AB	H	HR	BA	PO	A	E	DP	TC/G	FA
1923	CLE	A	0	0	–	12.27	1	0	0	3.2	6	4	0	0	0	0	0	1	1	0	1.000	0	1	0	0	1.0	1.000

Charlie Frye

FRYE, CHARLES ANDREW
B. July 17, 1914, Hickory, N. C. D. May 25, 1945, Hickory, N. C. BR TR 6'1" 175 lbs.

Year	Team		W	L	PCT	ERA	G	GS	CG	IP	H	BB	SO	ShO	W	L	SV	AB	H	HR	BA	PO	A	E	DP	TC/G	FA
1940	PHI	N	0	6	.000	4.65	15	5	1	50.1	58	26	18	0	0	1	0	19	5	1	.263	0	7	0	1	0.5	1.000

Woodie Fryman

FRYMAN, WOODROW THOMPSON
B. Apr. 12, 1940, Ewing, Ky. BR TL 6'3" 197 lbs.

Year	Team		W	L	PCT	ERA	G	GS	CG	IP	H	BB	SO	ShO	W	L	SV	AB	H	HR	BA	PO	A	E	DP	TC/G	FA
1966	PIT	N	12	9	.571	3.81	36	28	9	181.2	182	47	105	3	1	0	1	63	10	0	.159	6	21	0	1	0.8	1.000
1967			3	8	.273	4.05	28	18	3	113.1	121	44	74	1	0	0	1	34	4	0	.118	6	26	0	3	1.1	1.000
1968	PHI	N	12	14	.462	2.78	34	32	10	213.2	198	64	151	5	0	0	0	71	6	0	.085	3	31	1	2	1.0	.971
1969			12	15	.444	4.42	36	35	10	228	243	89	150	1	0	0	0	76	9	1	.118	3	38	0	1	1.1	1.000
1970			8	6	.571	4.08	27	20	4	128	122	43	97	3	1	0	0	39	5	0	.128	5	17	0	1	0.8	1.000
1971			10	7	.588	3.38	37	17	3	149	133	46	104	2	3	2	2	37	7	0	.189	6	35	1	1	1.1	.976
1972	2 teams	PHI N (23G 4–10)					DET A (16G 10–3)																				
"	total		14	13	.519	3.24	39	31	9	233.2	224	70	141	3	0	0	1	73	10	0	.137	5	25	0	0	0.8	1.000
1973	DET	A	6	13	.316	5.35	34	29	1	170	200	64	119	0	0	0	0	0	0	0	–	11	28	1	2	1.2	.975
1974			6	9	.400	4.31	27	22	4	142	120	67	92	1	0	0	0	0	0	0	–	8	15	0	1	0.9	1.000
1975	MON	N	9	12	.429	3.32	38	20	7	157	141	68	118	3	2	4	3	49	10	0	.204	6	26	0	4	0.8	1.000
1976			13	13	.500	3.37	34	32	4	216.1	218	76	123	2	0	0	2	64	7	0	.109	9	30	0	1	1.1	1.000
1977	CIN	N	5	5	.500	5.40	17	12	0	75	83	45	57	0	0	1	1	22	7	0	.318	3	14	0	1	1.0	1.000
1978	2 teams	CHI N (13G 2–4)					MON N (19G 5–7)																				
"	total		7	11	.389	4.19	32	26	4	150.1	157	74	81	3	1	0	1	50	3	0	.060	8	27	0	1	1.1	1.000
1979	MON	N	3	6	.333	2.79	44	0	0	58	52	22	44	0	3	6	10	7	0	0	.000	3	11	0	1	0.3	1.000
1980			7	4	.636	2.25	61	0	0	80	61	30	59	0	7	4	17	12	2	0	.167	1	10	1	1	0.2	.917
1981			5	3	.625	1.88	35	0	0	43	38	14	25	0	5	3	7	3	2	0	.667	2	8	0	1	0.4	.957
1982			9	4	.692	3.75	60	0	0	69.2	66	26	46	0	9	4	12	9	2	0	.222	6	16	1	2	0.4	.957
1983			0	3	.000	21.00	9	0	0	9	3	8	1	0	0	3	0	0	0	0	–	0	0	0	0	0.3	1.000
18 yrs.			141	155	.476	3.77	625	322	68	2411.2	2367	890	1587	27	32	27	58	609	84	2	.138	91	380	5	25	0.8	.989

DIVISIONAL PLAYOFF SERIES

Year	Team		W	L	PCT	ERA	G	GS	CG	IP	H	BB	SO	ShO	W	L	SV	AB	H	HR	BA	PO	A	E	DP	TC/G	FA
1981	MON	N	0	0	–	6.75	1	0	0	1.1	3	1	0	0	0	0	0	0	0	0	–	0	0	0	0	0.0	–

LEAGUE CHAMPIONSHIP SERIES

Year	Team		W	L	PCT	ERA	G	GS	CG	IP	H	BB	SO	ShO	W	L	SV	AB	H	HR	BA	PO	A	E	DP	TC/G	FA
1972	DET	A	0	2	.000	3.65	2	2	0	12.1	11	2	8	0	0	0	0	3	0	0	.000	0	3	0	0	1.5	1.000
1981	MON	N	0	0	–	36.00	1	0	0	1	3	1	1	0	0	0	0	0	0	0	–	0	0	0	0	0.0	–
2 yrs.			0	2	.000	6.08	3	2	0	13.1	14	3	9	0	0	0	0	3	0	0	.000	0	3	0	0	1.0	1.000

Charlie Fuchs

FUCHS, CHARLES THOMAS
B. Nov. 18, 1913, Union City, N. J. D. June 10, 1969, Weehawken, N. J. BB TR 5'10" 178 lbs.

Year	Team		W	L	PCT	ERA	G	GS	CG	IP	H	BB	SO	ShO	W	L	SV	AB	H	HR	BA	PO	A	E	DP	TC/G	FA
1942	DET	A	3	3	.500	6.63	9	4	1	36.2	43	19	15	1	0	2	0	13	1	0	.077	3	12	0	1	1.7	1.000
1943	2 teams	PHI N (17G 2–7)					STL A (13G 0–0)																				
"	total		2	7	.222	4.21	30	9	4	113.1	118	45	21	1	0	1	1	29	2	0	.069	10	18	2	1	1.0	.933
1944	BKN	N	1	0	1.000	5.74	8	0	0	15.2	25	9	5	0	1	0	0	1	0	0	.000	2	5	0	0	0.9	1.000
3 yrs.			6	10	.375	4.89	47	13	5	165.2	186	73	41	2	1	3	1	43	3	0	.070	15	35	2	1	1.1	.962

Year	Team		W	L	PCT	ERA	G	GS	CG	IP	H	BB	SO	ShO	Relief Pitching W	L	SV	Batting AB	H	HR	BA	PO	A	E	DP	TC/G	FA

Mickey Fuentes

FUENTES, MIGUEL
Born Miguel Fuentes y Pinet.
B. May 10, 1946, Loiza, Puerto Rico   D. Jan. 29, 1970, Loiza, Puerto Rico
BR TR 6'   160 lbs.

| 1969 | SEA | A | 1 | 3 | .250 | 5.19 | 8 | 4 | 1 | 26 | 29 | 16 | 14 | 0 | 0 | 0 | 0 | 6 | 2 | 0 | .333 | 1 | 2 | 1 | 0 | 0.5 | .750 |

Oscar Fuhr

FUHR, OSCAR LAWRENCE
B. Aug. 22, 1893, Defiance, Mo.   D. Mar. 27, 1975, Dallas, Tex.
BR TL 5'10"   170 lbs.

1921	CHI	N	0	0	–	9.00	1	0	0	4	11	0	2	0	0	0	0	1	0	0	.000	0	1	0	0	1.0	1.000
1924	BOS	A	3	6	.333	5.94	23	10	4	80.1	100	39	30	1	0	2	0	22	4	0	.182	4	23	1	0	1.2	.964
1925			0	6	.000	6.60	39	6	0	91.1	138	30	27	0	0	2	0	20	5	0	.250	6	25	1	3	0.8	.969
3 yrs.			3	12	.200	6.35	63	16	4	175.2	249	69	59	1	0	4	0	43	9	0	.209	10	49	2	3	1.0	.967

John Fulgham

FULGHAM, JOHN THOMAS
B. June 9, 1956, St. Louis, Mo.
BR TR 6'2"   205 lbs.

1979	STL	N	10	6	.625	2.53	20	19	10	146	123	26	75	2	0	0	0	42	6	0	.143	7	12	2	1	1.1	.905
1980			4	6	.400	3.39	15	14	4	85	66	32	48	1	0	0	0	27	0	0	.000	7	11	1	1	1.3	.947
2 yrs.			14	12	.538	2.84	35	33	14	231	189	58	123	3	0	0	0	69	6	0	.087	14	23	3	2	1.1	.925

Ed Fuller

FULLER, EDWARD ASTON WHITE
B. Mar. 22, 1869, Washington, D. C.   D. Mar. 15, 1935, Hyattsville, Md.
BR TR 6'   158 lbs.

| 1886 | WAS | N | 0 | 1 | .000 | 6.92 | 2 | 1 | 1 | 13 | 15 | 5 | 3 | 0 | 0 | 0 | 0 | 7 | 1 | 0 | .143 | 0 | 3 | 1 | 0 | 2.0 | .750 |

Curt Fullerton

FULLERTON, CURTIS HOOPER
B. Sept. 13, 1898, Ellsworth, Me.   D. Jan. 2, 1975, Winthrop, Mass.
BL TR 6'   162 lbs.

1921	BOS	A	0	1	.000	8.80	4	1	1	15.1	22	10	4	0	0	0	0	4	0	0	.000	2	1	1	0	1.0	.750
1922			1	4	.200	5.46	31	3	0	64.1	70	35	17	0	1	2	0	8	2	0	.250	3	22	0	0	0.8	1.000
1923			2	15	.118	5.09	37	16	7	143.1	167	71	37	0	1	1	0	37	11	0	.297	5	31	3	1	1.1	.923
1924			7	12	.368	4.32	33	20	9	152	166	73	33	0	1	0	2	42	3	0	.071	1	38	2	1	1.2	.951
1925			0	3	.000	3.18	4	2	0	22.2	22	9	3	0	0	1	0	10	2	0	.200	2	8	1	1	2.8	.909
1933			0	2	.000	8.53	6	2	2	25.1	36	13	10	0	0	0	0	9	2	0	.222	0	2	0	1	0.3	1.000
6 yrs.			10	37	.213	5.11	115	44	19	423	483	211	104	0	3	4	3	110	20	0	.182	13	102	7	4	1.1	.943

Chris Fulmer

FULMER, CHRISTOPHER
B. July 4, 1858, Tamaqua, Pa.   D. Nov. 9, 1931, Tamaqua, Pa.
BR TR 5'8"   165 lbs.

| 1886 | BAL | AA | 0 | 0 | – | 4.50 | 1 | 0 | 0 | 2 | 2 | 1 | 0 | 0 | 0 | 0 | 0 | * | | | | 0 | 0 | 0 | 0 | 0.0 | – |

Bill Fulton

FULTON, WILLIAM DAVID
B. Oct. 22, 1963, Pittsburgh, Pa.
BR TR 6'3"   195 lbs.

| 1987 | NY | A | 1 | 0 | 1.000 | 11.57 | 3 | 0 | 0 | 4.2 | 9 | 1 | 2 | 0 | 1 | 0 | 0 | 0 | 0 | 0 | – | 0 | 1 | 0 | 0 | 0.3 | 1.000 |

Frank Funk

FUNK, FRANKLIN RAY
B. Aug. 30, 1935, Washington, D. C.
BR TR 6'   175 lbs.

1960	CLE	A	4	2	.667	1.99	9	0	0	31.2	27	9	18	0	4	2	1	9	1	0	.111	2	5	0	1	0.8	1.000
1961			11	11	.500	3.31	56	0	0	92.1	79	31	64	0	11	11	11	17	1	0	.059	14	11	2	0	0.5	.926
1962			2	1	.667	3.24	47	0	0	80.2	62	32	49	0	2	1	6	15	1	0	.067	5	11	0	1	0.3	1.000
1963	MIL	N	3	3	.500	2.68	25	0	0	43.2	42	13	19	0	3	3	0	4	0	0	.000	3	3	1	0	0.3	.857
4 yrs.			20	17	.541	3.01	137	0	0	248.1	210	85	150	0	20	17	18	45	3	0	.067	24	30	3	2	0.4	.947

Tom Funk

FUNK, THOMAS JAMES
B. Mar. 13, 1962, Kansas City, Mo.
BL TL 6'2"   210 lbs.

| 1986 | HOU | N | 0 | 0 | – | 6.48 | 8 | 0 | 0 | 8.1 | 10 | 6 | 2 | 0 | 0 | 0 | 0 | 1 | 0 | 0 | .000 | 1 | 1 | 0 | 0 | 0.3 | 1.000 |

Ed Fusselbach

FUSSELBACH, EDWARD L.
B. July 4, 1858, Philadelphia, Pa.   D. Apr. 14, 1926, Philadelphia, Pa.
5'6"   156 lbs.

| 1882 | STL | AA | 1 | 2 | .333 | 4.70 | 4 | 2 | 2 | 23 | 34 | 2 | 3 | 0 | 1 | 0 | 1 | * | | | | 0 | 4 | 1 | 0 | 1.3 | .800 |

Fred Fussell

FUSSELL, FREDERICK MORRIS (Moonlight Ace)
B. Oct. 7, 1895, Sheridan, Mo.   D. Oct. 23, 1966, Syracuse, N. Y.
BL TL 5'10"   155 lbs.

1922	CHI	N	1	1	.500	4.74	3	2	1	19	24	8	4	0	0	0	0	6	0	0	.000	0	6	0	0	2.0	1.000
1923			3	5	.375	5.54	28	2	1	76.1	90	31	38	0	3	3	3	20	4	0	.200	2	19	3	2	0.9	.875
1928	PIT	N	8	9	.471	3.61	28	20	9	159.2	183	41	43	2	1	1	1	58	7	0	.121	4	25	2	1	1.1	.935
1929			2	2	.500	8.62	21	3	0	39.2	68	8	18	0	1	1	1	16	4	2	.250	4	7	0	0	0.5	1.000
4 yrs.			14	17	.452	4.86	80	27	11	294.2	365	88	103	2	5	5	5	100	15	2	.150	10	57	5	3	0.9	.931

Frank Gabler

GABLER, FRANK HAROLD (The Great Gabbo)
B. Nov. 6, 1911, East Highlands, Calif.   D. Nov. 1, 1967, Long Beach, Calif.
BR TR 6'1"   175 lbs.

1935	NY	N	2	1	.667	5.70	26	1	0	60	79	20	24	0	1	0	0	16	2	0	.125	3	13	1	0	0.7	.941
1936			9	8	.529	3.12	43	14	5	161.2	170	34	46	0	3	2	6	48	10	0	.208	5	31	1	4	0.9	.973
1937	2 teams		NY N (6G 0-0)			BOS N	(19G 4-7)																					
"	total		4	7	.364	5.61	25	9	2	85	104	18	22	1	2	2	2	22	4	0	.182	6	17	1	1	1.0	.958
1938	2 teams		BOS N (1G 0-0)			CHI A	(18G 1-7)																					
"	total		1	7	.125	9.43	19	7	3	69.2	104	35	17	0	0	3	0	21	5	0	.238	2	9	0	1	0.6	1.000
4 yrs.			16	23	.410	5.26	113	31	10	376.1	457	107	109	1	7	7	8	107	21	0	.196	16	70	3	6	0.8	.966

WORLD SERIES

| 1936 | NY | N | 0 | 0 | – | 7.20 | 2 | 0 | 0 | 5 | 7 | 4 | 0 | 0 | 0 | 0 | 0 | 0 | 0 | 0 | – | 1 | 0 | 0 | 0 | 0.5 | 1.000 |

Year	Team		W	L	PCT	ERA	G	GS	CG	IP	H	BB	SO	ShO	Relief Pitching W	L	SV	Batting AB	H	HR	BA	PO	A	E	DP	TC/G	FA

John Gabler

GABLER, JOHN RICHARD (Gabe)
B. Oct. 2, 1930, Kansas City, Mo.

BL TR 6'2" 165 lbs.
BB 1960

1959	NY	A	1	1	.500	2.79	3	1	0	19.1	21	10	11	0	1	0	0	6	0	0	.000	1	3	0	1	1.3	1.000
1960			3	3	.500	4.15	21	4	0	52	46	32	19	0	2	1	1	11	1	0	.091	4	9	1	0	0.7	.929
1961	WAS	A	3	8	.273	4.86	29	9	0	92.2	104	37	33	0	2	2	4	25	5	0	.200	11	20	1	1	1.1	.969
3 yrs.			7	12	.368	4.39	53	14	0	164	171	79	63	0	5	3	5	42	6	0	.143	16	32	2	2	0.9	.960

Ken Gables

GABLES, KENNETH HARLIN
B. Jan. 31, 1919, Walnut Grove, Mo. D. Jan. 2, 1960, Walnut Grove, Mo.

BR TR 5'11" 210 lbs.

1945	PIT	N	11	7	.611	4.15	29	16	6	138.2	139	46	49	0	5	1	1	39	4	0	.103	5	17	0	0	0.8	1.000
1946			2	4	.333	5.27	32	7	0	100.2	113	52	39	0	1	0	1	24	6	0	.250	3	12	1	0	0.5	.938
1947			0	0	—	54.00	1	0	0	.1	3	0	0	0	0	0	0	0	0	0	—	0	0	0	0	0.0	—
3 yrs.			13	11	.542	4.69	62	23	6	239.2	255	98	88	0	6	1	2	63	10	0	.159	8	29	1	0	0.6	.974

John Gaddy

GADDY, JOHN WILSON (Sheriff)
B. Feb. 5, 1914, Wadesboro, N. C. D. May 3, 1966, Albermarle, N. C.

BR TR 6'½" 182 lbs.

| 1938 | BKN | N | 2 | 0 | 1.000 | 0.69 | 2 | 2 | 1 | 13 | 13 | 4 | 3 | 0 | 0 | 0 | 0 | 6 | 0 | 0 | .000 | 0 | 2 | 0 | 0 | 1.0 | 1.000 |

Brent Gaff

GAFF, BRENT ALLEN
B. Oct. 5, 1958, Fort Wayne, Ind.

BR TR 6'2" 200 lbs.

1982	NY	N	0	3	.000	4.55	7	5	0	31.2	41	10	14	0	0	0	0	8	0	0	.000	2	5	2	1	1.3	.778
1983			1	0	1.000	6.10	4	0	0	10.1	18	1	4	0	1	0	0	3	0	0	.000	1	2	2	0	1.3	.600
1984			3	2	.600	3.63	47	0	0	84.1	77	36	42	0	3	2	1	6	0	0	.000	11	12	1	0	0.5	.958
3 yrs.			4	5	.444	4.06	58	5	0	126.1	136	47	60	0	4	2	1	17	0	0	.000	14	19	5	1	0.7	.868

Charlie Gagus

GAGUS, CHARLES FREDERICK
B. Mar. 25, 1862, San Francisco, Calif. D. Jan. 16, 1918, San Francisco, Calif.

| 1884 | WAS | U | 10 | 9 | .526 | 2.54 | 23 | 21 | 19 | 177.1 | 143 | 38 | 156 | 0 | 0 | 0 | 0 | 154 | 38 | 0 | .247 | 15 | 40 | 14 | 0 | 3.0 | .797 |

Nemo Gaines

GAINES, WILLARD ROLAND
B. Dec. 23, 1897, Alexandria, Va. D. Jan. 28, 1979, Warrentown, Va.

BL TL 6' 180 lbs.

| 1921 | WAS | A | 0 | 0 | — | 0.00 | 4 | 0 | 0 | 4.2 | 5 | 2 | 1 | 0 | 0 | 0 | 0 | 1 | 0 | 0 | .000 | 0 | 0 | 0 | 0 | 0.0 | — |

Fred Gaiser

GAISER, FREDERICK JACOB
B. Aug. 31, 1885, Stuttgart, Germany D. Oct. 9, 1918, Trenton, N. J.

| 1908 | STL | N | 0 | 0 | — | 7.71 | 1 | 0 | 0 | 2.1 | 4 | 3 | 2 | 0 | 0 | 0 | 0 | 1 | 0 | 0 | .000 | 0 | 1 | 0 | 0 | 1.0 | 1.000 |

Bob Galasso

GALASSO, ROBERT JOSEPH
B. Jan. 13, 1952, Connellsville, Pa.

BL TR 6'1" 205 lbs.

1977	SEA	A	0	6	.000	9.00	11	7	0	35	57	8	21	0	0	1	0	0	0	0	—	1	4	0	0	0.5	1.000
1979	MIL	A	3	1	.750	4.41	31	0	0	51	64	26	28	0	3	1	3	0	0	0	—	0	7	0	0	0.2	1.000
1981	SEA	A	1	1	.500	4.78	13	1	0	32	32	13	14	0	0	0	1	0	0	0	—	3	4	0	0	0.5	1.000
3 yrs.			4	8	.333	5.87	55	8	0	118	153	47	63	0	3	2	4	0	0	0	—	4	15	0	0	0.3	1.000

Milt Galatzer

GALATZER, MILTON
B. May 4, 1907, Chicago, Ill. D. Jan. 29, 1976, San Francisco, Calif.

BL TL 5'10" 168 lbs.

| 1936 | CLE | A | 0 | 0 | — | 4.50 | 1 | 0 | 0 | 6 | 7 | 5 | 3 | 0 | 0 | 0 | 0 | * | | | | 0 | 1 | 0 | 0 | 1.0 | 1.000 |

Rich Gale

GALE, RICHARD BLACKWELL
B. Jan. 19, 1954, Littleton, N. H.

BR TR 6'7" 225 lbs.

1978	KC	A	14	8	.636	3.09	31	30	9	192.1	171	100	88	3	0	0	0	0	0	0	—	3	26	4	1	1.1	.879
1979			9	10	.474	5.64	34	31	2	182	197	99	103	1	0	0	0	0	0	0	—	9	25	4	3	1.1	.895
1980			13	9	.591	3.91	32	28	6	191	169	78	97	1	0	0	2	0	0	0	—	10	26	1	1	1.2	.973
1981			6	6	.500	5.38	19	15	2	102	107	38	47	0	1	0	0	0	0	0	—	6	8	1	1	0.8	.933
1982	SF	N	7	14	.333	4.23	33	29	2	170.1	193	81	102	0	1	2	0	48	6	1	.125	10	31	1	1	1.3	.976
1983	CIN	N	4	6	.400	5.82	33	7	0	89.2	103	43	53	0	2	1	1	20	3	0	.150	7	10	2	0	0.6	.895
1984	BOS	A	2	3	.400	5.56	13	4	0	43.2	57	18	28	0	1	2	0	0	0	0	—	4	3	0	0	0.5	1.000
7 yrs.			55	56	.495	4.53	195	144	21	971	997	457	518	5	5	7	2	68	9	2	.132	49	129	13	7	1.0	.932

WORLD SERIES

| 1980 | KC | A | 0 | 1 | .000 | 4.26 | 2 | 2 | 0 | 6.1 | 11 | 4 | 4 | 0 | 0 | 0 | 0 | 0 | 0 | 0 | — | 0 | 1 | 0 | 0 | 0.5 | 1.000 |

Denny Galehouse

GALEHOUSE, DENNIS WARD
B. Dec. 7, 1911, Marshallville, Ohio

BR TR 6'1" 195 lbs.

1934	CLE	A	0	0	—	18.00	1	0	0	1	2	1	0	0	0	0	0	0	0	0	—	0	0	1	0	1.0	—
1935			1	0	1.000	9.00	5	1	1	13	16	9	8	0	0	0	0	4	1	0	.250	1	3	0	0	0.8	1.000
1936			8	7	.533	4.85	36	15	11	148.1	161	68	71	0	2	1	1	47	8	0	.170	6	15	1	0	0.6	.955
1937			9	14	.391	4.57	36	29	7	200.2	238	83	78	0	2	0	3	72	15	0	.208	6	42	2	3	1.4	.960
1938			7	8	.467	4.34	36	12	5	114	119	65	66	1	4	5	3	39	6	0	.154	4	21	0	2	0.7	1.000
1939	BOS	A	9	10	.474	4.54	30	18	6	146.2	160	52	68	1	3	1	0	47	3	0	.064	11	24	3	2	1.3	.921
1940			6	6	.500	5.18	25	20	5	120	155	41	53	0	1	0	0	39	3	0	.077	11	22	0	1	1.3	1.000
1941	STL	A	9	10	.474	3.64	30	24	11	190.1	183	68	61	2	1	0	0	68	13	0	.191	15	35	0	3	1.7	1.000
1942			12	12	.500	3.62	32	28	12	191.1	193	79	75	3	0	1	1	72	14	0	.194	15	41	2	3	1.8	.966
1943			11	11	.500	2.77	31	28	14	224	217	74	114	2	0	1	1	72	9	0	.125	7	33	2	0	1.4	.952
1944			9	10	.474	3.12	24	19	6	153	162	44	80	2	1	1	0	48	3	0	.063	3	21	3	0	1.1	.889
1946			8	12	.400	3.65	30	24	11	180	194	52	90	2	0	0	0	55	5	0	.091	11	17	1	1	1.0	.966
1947	2 teams		STL A (9G 1–3)			BOS A	(21G 11–7)																					
"	total		12	10	.545	3.82	30	25	11	181.1	192	50	49	3	0	1	0	60	5	0	.083	8	28	1	2	1.2	.973
1948	BOS	A	8	8	.500	4.00	27	15	6	137.1	152	46	38	1	4	1	3	42	7	0	.167	6	17	2	2	0.9	.920

Year	Team		W	L	PCT	ERA	G	GS	CG	IP	H	BB	SO	ShO	W	L	SV	AB	H	HR	BA	PO	A	E	DP	TC/G	FA

Denny Galehouse *continued*

| 1949 | | | 0 | 0 | – | 13.50 | 2 | 0 | 0 | 2 | 4 | 3 | 0 | 0 | 0 | 0 | 0 | 0 | 0 | 0 | – | 0 | 1 | 0 | 0 | 0.5 | 1.000 |
| 15 yrs. | | | 109 | 118 | .480 | 3.98 | 375 | 258 | 106 | 2003 | 2148 | 735 | 851 | 17 | 17 | 10 | 13 | 665 | 92 | 0 | .138 | 104 | 320 | 18 | 20 | 1.2 | .959 |
| WORLD SERIES |
| 1944 | STL | A | 1 | 1 | .500 | 1.50 | 2 | 2 | 2 | 18 | 13 | 5 | 15 | 0 | 0 | 0 | 0 | 5 | 1 | 0 | .200 | 0 | 5 | 0 | 0 | 2.5 | 1.000 |

Bill Gallagher

GALLAGHER, WILLIAM JOHN
B. Philadelphia, Pa. Deceased.   TL

1883	PHI	N	0	5	.000	5.40	7	5	4	51.2	79	6	19	0	0	0	0	69	10	0	.145	4	6	3	0	1.9	.769
1884	PHI	U	1	2	.333	3.24	3	3	3	25	32	4	12	0	0	0	0	11	1	0	.091	2	6	2	0	3.3	.800
2 yrs.			1	7	.125	4.70	10	8	7	76.2	111	10	31	0	0	0	0	*				6	12	5	0	2.3	.783

Doug Gallagher

GALLAGHER, DOUGLAS EUGENE
B. Feb. 21, 1940, Fremont, Ohio   BR TL 6'3½" 195 lbs.

| 1962 | DET | A | 0 | 4 | .000 | 4.68 | 9 | 2 | 0 | 25 | 31 | 15 | 14 | 0 | 0 | 2 | 1 | 6 | 2 | 0 | .333 | 3 | 4 | 1 | 1 | 0.9 | .875 |

Ed Gallagher

GALLAGHER, EDWARD MICHAEL (Lefty)
B. Nov. 28, 1910, Dorchester, Mass. D. Dec. 22, 1981, Hyannis, Mass.   BB TL 6'2" 197 lbs.

| 1932 | BOS | A | 0 | 3 | .000 | 12.55 | 9 | 3 | 0 | 23.2 | 30 | 28 | 6 | 0 | 0 | 0 | 0 | 5 | 0 | 0 | .000 | 2 | 5 | 0 | 0 | 0.9 | .875 |

Bert Gallia

GALLIA, MELVIN ALLYS
B. Oct. 14, 1891, Beeville, Tex. D. Mar. 19, 1976, Devine, Tex.   BR TR 6' 165 lbs.

1912	WAS	A	0	0	–	0.00	2	0	0	2	0	3	0	0	0	0	0	0	0	0	–	0	0	0	0	0.0	–
1913			1	5	.167	4.13	31	4	0	96	85	46	46	0	1	2	3	23	2	0	.087	5	39	3	1	1.5	.936
1914			0	0	–	4.50	2	0	0	6	3	4	4	0	0	0	0	2	0	0	.000	0	1	2	0	1.5	.333
1915			17	11	.607	2.29	43	29	14	259.2	220	64	130	3	4	1	1	85	14	0	.165	11	66	3	2	1.9	.963
1916			17	12	.586	2.76	49	31	13	283.2	278	99	120	1	4	3	2	93	18	0	.194	9	65	3	2	1.6	.961
1917			9	13	.409	2.99	42	23	9	207.2	191	93	84	1	3	4	1	67	14	0	.209	5	54	3	3	1.5	.952
1918	STL	A	8	6	.571	3.48	19	17	10	124	126	61	48	1	0	0	0	46	6	0	.130	1	38	3	0	2.2	.929
1919			11	14	.440	3.60	34	25	14	222.1	220	92	83	1	1	2	2	72	11	0	.153	18	63	2	4	2.4	.976
1920	2 teams		STL A	(2G 0–1)		PHI N	(18G 2–6)																					
"	total		2	7	.222	4.64	20	6	1	75.2	87	32	35	0	2	1	2	24	4	0	.167	5	15	1	0	1.1	.952
9 yrs.			65	68	.489	3.14	242	135	61	1277	1210	494	550	7	15	13	11	412	69	1	.167	54	341	20	11	1.7	.952

Phil Gallivan

GALLIVAN, PHILIP JOSEPH
B. May 29, 1907, Seattle, Wash. D. Nov. 24, 1969, St. Paul, Minn.   BR TR 6' 180 lbs.

1931	BKN	N	0	1	.000	5.28	6	1	0	15.1	23	7	1	0	0	0	0	3	0	0	.000	3	6	0	1	1.5	1.000
1932	CHI	A	1	3	.250	7.56	13	3	1	33.1	49	24	12	0	1	0	0	8	3	0	.375	2	5	0	0	0.5	1.000
1934			4	7	.364	5.61	35	7	3	126.2	155	64	55	0	4	4	1	40	9	0	.225	5	20	2	0	0.8	.926
3 yrs.			5	11	.313	5.95	54	11	4	175.1	227	95	68	0	5	4	1	51	12	0	.235	10	31	2	1	0.8	.953

Balvino Galvez

GALVEZ, BALVINO
Born Balvino Galvez y Jerez.
B. Mar. 31, 1964, San Pedro de Macoris, Dominican Republic   BR TR 6' 170 lbs.

| 1986 | LA | N | 0 | 1 | .000 | 3.92 | 10 | 0 | 0 | 20.2 | 19 | 12 | 11 | 0 | 0 | 1 | 0 | 2 | 0 | 0 | .000 | 3 | 3 | 1 | 1 | 0.7 | .857 |

Lou Galvin

GALVIN, LOUIS J.
B. Apr., 1862, St. Paul, Minn.

| 1884 | STP | U | 0 | 2 | .000 | 2.88 | 3 | 3 | 3 | 25 | 21 | 10 | 17 | 0 | 0 | 0 | 0 | 9 | 2 | 0 | .222 | 1 | 1 | 1 | 0 | 1.0 | .667 |

Pud Galvin

GALVIN, JAMES FRANCIS (Gentle Jeems, The Little Steam Engine)
B. Dec. 25, 1856, St. Louis, Mo. D. Mar. 7, 1902, Pittsburgh, Pa.   BR TR 5'8" 190 lbs.
Manager 1885.
Hall of Fame 1965.

1879	BUF	N	37	27	.578	2.28	66	66	65	593	585	31	136	6	0	0	0	265	66	0	.249	35	141	26	8	3.1	.871
1880			20	35	.364	2.71	58	54	46	458.2	528	32	128	5	0	2	0	241	51	0	.212	24	97	13	1	2.3	.903
1881			29	24	.547	2.37	56	53	48	474	546	46	136	5	0	0	0	236	50	0	.212	36	123	19	7	3.2	.893
1882			28	23	.549	3.17	52	51	48	445.1	476	40	162	3	0	0	0	206	44	0	.214	20	85	8	1	2.2	.929
1883			46	29	.613	2.72	76	75	72	656.1	676	50	279	5	1	0	0	322	71	1	.220	20	127	10	4	2.1	.936
1884			46	22	.676	1.99	72	72	71	636.1	566	63	369	12	0	0	0	274	49	0	.179	32	154	7	3	2.7	.964
1885	2 teams		BUF N	(33G 13–19)		PIT AA	(11G 3–7)																					
"	total		16	26	.381	3.99	44	43	40	372.1	453	44	120	3	0	0	1	160	27	1	.169	21	96	16	3	3.0	.880
1886	PIT	AA	29	21	.580	2.67	50	50	49	434.2	457	75	72	2	0	0	0	194	49	0	.253	22	101	8	3	2.6	.939
1887	PIT	N	28	21	.571	3.29	49	48	47	440.2	490	67	76	3	1	0	0	193	41	2	.212	22	123	11	2	3.2	.929
1888			23	25	.479	2.63	50	50	49	437.1	446	53	107	6	0	0	1	175	25	1	.143	23	113	10	2	2.9	.932
1889			23	16	.590	4.17	41	40	38	341	392	78	77	4	0	0	0	150	28	0	.187	20	72	11	6	2.5	.893
1890	PIT	P	12	13	.480	4.35	26	25	23	217	275	49	35	1	0	0	0	97	20	0	.206	22	71	7	1	3.8	.930
1891	PIT	N	14	13	.519	2.88	33	31	23	246.2	256	62	46	2	0	0	0	109	18	0	.165	20	52	8	1	2.4	.900
1892	2 teams		PIT N	(12G 5–6)		STL N	(12G 5–7)																					
"	total		10	13	.435	2.92	24	24	20	188	206	54	56	0	0	0	0	80	7	0	.088	7	35	7	1	2.0	.857
14 yrs.			361	308	.540	2.87	697	682	639	5941.1	6352	744	1799	57	3	2	1	*				324	1390	161	43	2.7	.914
			6th	2nd					2nd			2nd		10th													

Bob Gamble

GAMBLE, ROBERT J.
B. Feb., 1867, Hazleton, Pa. Deceased.   5'10" 155 lbs.

| 1888 | PHI | AA | 0 | 1 | .000 | 8.00 | 1 | 1 | 1 | 9 | 10 | 3 | 2 | 0 | 0 | 0 | 0 | 3 | 1 | 0 | .333 | 2 | 2 | 2 | 0 | 6.0 | .667 |

Year	Team		W	L	PCT	ERA	G	GS	CG	IP	H	BB	SO	ShO	Relief Pitching W	L	SV	Batting AB	H	HR	BA	PO	A	E	DP	TC/G	FA

Bill Gannon

GANNON, WILLIAM G.
B. 1876, New Haven, Conn.   D. Apr. 26, 1927, Ft. Worth, Tex.

Year	Team		W	L	PCT	ERA	G	GS	CG	IP	H	BB	SO	ShO	W	L	SV	AB	H	HR	BA	PO	A	E	DP	TC/G	FA
1898	STL	N	0	1	.000	11.00	1	1	1	9	13	5	2	0	0	0	0	*				0	2	0	0	2.0	1.000

Gussie Gannon

GANNON, JAMES EDWARD
B. Nov. 26, 1873, Erie, Pa.   D. Apr. 12, 1966, Erie, Pa.

BL TL 5'11"   154 lbs.

Year	Team		W	L	PCT	ERA	G	GS	CG	IP	H	BB	SO	ShO	W	L	SV	AB	H	HR	BA	PO	A	E	DP	TC/G	FA
1895	PIT	N	0	0	–	1.80	1	0	0	5	7	2	0	0	0	0	0	2	0	0	.000	0	0	0	0	0.0	–

Jim Gantner

GANTNER, JAMES ELMER
B. Jan. 5, 1953, Fond du Lac, Wis.

BL TR 6'   180 lbs.

Year	Team		W	L	PCT	ERA	G	GS	CG	IP	H	BB	SO	ShO	W	L	SV	AB	H	HR	BA	PO	A	E	DP	TC/G	FA
1979	MIL	A	0	0	–	0.00	1	0	0	1	2	0	0	0	0	0	0	*				0	1	0	0	1.0	1.000

John Ganzel

GANZEL, JOHN HENRY
Brother of Charlie Ganzel.
B. Apr. 7, 1874, Kalamazoo, Mich.   D. Jan. 14, 1959, Orlando, Fla.
Manager 1908, 1915.

BR TR 6'½"   195 lbs.

Year	Team		W	L	PCT	ERA	G	GS	CG	IP	H	BB	SO	ShO	W	L	SV	AB	H	HR	BA	PO	A	E	DP	TC/G	FA
1898	PIT	N	0	0	–	0.00	1	0	0	0	0	0	0	0	0	0	0	*				0	0	0	0	0.0	–

Bob Garber

GARBER, ROBERT MITCHELL
B. Sept. 10, 1928, Hunker, Pa.

BR TR 6'1"   190 lbs.

Year	Team		W	L	PCT	ERA	G	GS	CG	IP	H	BB	SO	ShO	W	L	SV	AB	H	HR	BA	PO	A	E	DP	TC/G	FA
1956	PIT	N	0	0	–	2.25	2	0	0	4	3	3	3	0	0	0	0	0	0	0	–	0	0	0	0	0.5	–

Gene Garber

GARBER, HENRY EUGENE
B. Nov. 13, 1947, Lancaster, Pa.

BR TR 5'10"   175 lbs.

Year	Team		W	L	PCT	ERA	G	GS	CG	IP	H	BB	SO	ShO	W	L	SV	AB	H	HR	BA	PO	A	E	DP	TC/G	FA
1969	PIT	N	0	0	–	5.40	2	1	0	5	6	1	3	0	0	0	0	1	0	0	.000	0	0	0	0	0.0	–
1970			0	3	.000	5.32	14	0	0	22	22	10	7	0	0	3	0	3	2	0	.667	2	7	0	2	0.6	1.000
1972			0	0	–	7.50	4	0	0	6	7	3	3	0	0	0	0	1	0	0	.000	1	1	0	0	0.5	1.000
1973	KC	A	9	9	.500	4.24	48	8	4	153	164	49	60	0	7	4	11	0	0	0	–	14	26	2	3	0.9	.952
1974	2 teams		KC A (17G 1-2)			PHI N (34G 4-0)																					
"	total		5	2	.714	3.08	51	0	0	76	74	44	41	0	5	2	5	3	0	0	.000	8	12	3	0	0.5	.870
1975	PHI	N	10	12	.455	3.60	71	0	0	110	103	27	69	0	10	12	14	12	2	0	.167	13	12	0	0	0.4	1.000
1976			9	3	.750	2.82	59	0	0	92.2	78	30	92	0	9	3	11	7	2	0	.286	13	14	1	0	0.5	.964
1977			8	6	.571	2.36	64	0	0	103	82	23	78	0	8	6	19	10	0	0	.000	12	20	1	3	0.5	.970
1978	2 teams		PHI N (22G 2-1)			ATL N (43G 4-4)																					
"	total		6	5	.545	2.15	65	0	0	117	84	24	85	0	6	5	25	14	1	0	.071	16	15	0	0	0.5	1.000
1979	ATL	N	6	16	.273	4.33	68	0	0	106	121	24	56	0	6	16	25	10	3	0	.300	14	16	1	1	0.5	.968
1980			5	5	.500	3.84	68	0	0	82	95	24	51	0	5	5	7	2	1	0	.500	8	18	0	1	0.4	1.000
1981			4	6	.400	2.59	35	0	0	59	49	20	34	0	4	6	2	5	0	0	.000	8	17	1	1	0.7	.962
1982			8	10	.444	2.34	69	0	0	119.1	100	32	68	0	8	10	30	15	2	0	.133	13	27	4	5	0.6	.909
1983			4	5	.444	4.60	43	0	0	60.2	72	23	45	0	4	5	9	3	0	0	.000	4	17	0	1	0.5	1.000
1984			3	6	.333	3.06	62	0	0	106	103	24	55	0	3	6	11	14	2	0	.143	6	19	0	1	0.4	1.000
1985			6	6	.500	3.61	59	0	0	97.1	98	25	66	0	6	6	1	5	1	0	.200	11	17	0	1	0.5	1.000
1986			5	5	.500	2.54	61	0	0	78	76	20	56	0	5	5	24	6	1	0	.167	7	14	0	1	0.3	1.000
1987	2 teams		ATL N (49G 8-10)			KC A (13G 0-0)																					
"	total		8	10	.444	4.09	62	0	0	83.2	100	29	51	0	8	10	18	4	0	0	.000	6	22	1	2	0.5	.966
1988	KC	A	0	4	.000	3.58	26	0	0	32.2	29	13	20	0	0	4	6	0	0	0	–	3	6	1	1	0.4	.900
19 yrs.			96	113	.459	3.34	931	9	4	1509.1	1463	445	940	0	94	108	218	115	17	0	.148	159	280	15	23	0.5	.967
						5th									7th	9th											

LEAGUE CHAMPIONSHIP SERIES

Year	Team		W	L	PCT	ERA	G	GS	CG	IP	H	BB	SO	ShO	W	L	SV	AB	H	HR	BA	PO	A	E	DP	TC/G	FA
1976	PHI	N	0	1	.000	13.50	2	0	0	.2	2	1	0	0	0	1	0	0	0	0	–	0	0	0	0	0.0	–
1977			1	1	.500	3.38	3	0	0	5.1	4	0	3	0	1	1	0	0	0	0	–	0	2	1	0	1.0	.667
1982	ATL	N	0	1	.000	8.10	2	0	0	3.1	4	1	3	0	0	1	0	1	0	0	.000	0	0	0	0	0.0	–
3 yrs.			1	3	.250	5.79	7	0	0	9.1	10	2	6	0	1	3	0	1	0	0	.000	0	2	1	0	0.4	.667

Miguel Garcia

GARCIA, MIGUEL ANGEL
Born Miguel Angel Garcia y Sifontes.
B. Apr. 19, 1966, Caracas, Venezuela

BL TL 5'11"   173 lbs.

Year	Team		W	L	PCT	ERA	G	GS	CG	IP	H	BB	SO	ShO	W	L	SV	AB	H	HR	BA	PO	A	E	DP	TC/G	FA
1987	2 teams		CAL A (1G 0-0)			PIT N (1G 0-0)																					
"	total		0	0	–	11.57	2	0	0	2.1	3	3	0	0	0	0	0	0	0	0	–	0	1	0	0	0.5	1.000
1988	PIT	N	0	0	–	4.50	1	0	0	2	3	2	2	0	0	0	0	0	0	0	–	0	0	0	0	0.0	–
1989			0	2	.000	8.44	11	0	0	16	25	7	9	0	0	2	0	1	1	0	1.000	1	3	0	0	0.4	1.000
3 yrs.			0	2	.000	8.41	14	0	0	20.1	31	12	11	0	0	2	0	1	1	0	1.000	1	4	0	0	0.4	1.000

Mike Garcia

GARCIA, EDWARD MIGUEL (The Big Bear)
B. Nov. 17, 1923, San Gabriel, Calif.   D. Jan. 13, 1986, Fairview Park, Ohio

BR TR 6'1"   195 lbs.

Year	Team		W	L	PCT	ERA	G	GS	CG	IP	H	BB	SO	ShO	W	L	SV	AB	H	HR	BA	PO	A	E	DP	TC/G	FA
1948	CLE	A	0	0	–	0.00	1	0	0	2	3	1	0	0	0	0	0	0	0	0	–	0	2	0	0	2.0	1.000
1949			14	5	.737	2.36	41	20	8	175.2	154	60	94	5	3	1	2	51	12	1	.235	11	34	1	4	1.1	.978
1950			11	11	.500	3.86	33	29	11	184	191	74	76	0	0	0	0	65	13	0	.200	10	42	1	2	1.6	.981
1951			20	13	.606	3.15	47	30	15	254	239	82	118	1	3	2	6	85	18	1	.212	18	46	2	4	1.4	.970
1952			22	11	.667	2.37	46	36	19	292.1	284	87	143	6	1	2	4	95	13	0	.137	17	59	3	4	1.7	.962
1953			18	9	.667	3.25	38	35	21	271.2	260	81	134	3	0	1	0	96	24	0	.250	14	39	0	4	1.4	1.000
1954			19	8	.704	2.64	45	34	13	258.2	220	71	129	5	0	0	5	81	11	0	.136	20	41	1	2	1.4	.984
1955			11	13	.458	4.02	38	31	6	210.2	230	56	120	2	0	2	3	69	15	0	.217	12	29	1	0	1.1	.976
1956			11	12	.478	3.78	35	30	8	197.2	213	74	119	4	0	1	0	61	7	0	.115	13	27	1	2	1.1	.976
1957			12	8	.600	3.75	38	27	9	211.1	221	73	110	1	1	0	0	75	12	0	.160	12	22	1	5	0.9	.971
1958			1	1	.500	9.00	6	1	0	8	15	7	2	0	1	0	0	0	0	0	.000	0	2	0	0	0.3	1.000
1959			3	6	.333	4.00	29	8	1	72	72	31	49	0	3	3	1	14	1	0	.071	6	11	1	0	0.6	.944
1960	CHI	A	0	0	–	4.58	15	0	0	17.2	23	10	8	0	0	0	2	3	1	0	.333	1	4	0	0	0.3	1.000

Year	Team	W	L	PCT	ERA	G	GS	CG	IP	H	BB	SO	ShO	Relief Pitching W	L	SV	Batting AB	H	HR	BA	PO	A	E	DP	TC/G	FA

Mike Garcia *continued*

Year	Team	W	L	PCT	ERA	G	GS	CG	IP	H	BB	SO	ShO	W	L	SV	AB	H	HR	BA	PO	A	E	DP	TC/G	FA
1961	WAS A	0	1	.000	4.74	16	0	0	19	23	13	14	0	0	1	0	0	0	0	–	0	1	3	0	0.3	.250
14 yrs		142	97	.594	3.27	428	281	111	2174.2	2148	719	1117	27	12	13	23	696	127	2	.182	134	359	14	27	1.2	.972

WORLD SERIES

| 1954 | CLE A | 0 | 1 | .000 | 5.40 | 2 | 1 | 0 | 5 | 6 | 4 | 4 | 0 | 0 | 0 | 0 | 0 | 0 | 0 | – | 0 | 2 | 1 | 0 | 1.5 | .667 |

Ralph Garcia

GARCIA, RALPH
B. Dec. 14, 1948, Los Angeles, Calif. BR TR 6' 195 lbs.

1972	SD N	0	0	–	1.80	3	0	0	5	4	3	3	0	0	0	0	0	0	0	–	0	2	0	0	0.7	1.000
1974		0	0	–	6.30	8	0	0	10	15	7	9	0	0	0	0	0	0	0	–	1	2	0	0	0.4	1.000
2 yrs		0	0	–	4.80	11	0	0	15	19	10	12	0	0	0	0	0	0	0	–	1	4	0	0	0.5	1.000

Ramon Garcia

GARCIA, RAMON
Born Ramon Garcia y Garcia.
B. Mar. 5, 1924, La Esperanza, Cuba BR TR 5'10" 170 lbs.

| 1948 | WAS A | 0 | 0 | – | 17.18 | 4 | 0 | 0 | 3.2 | 11 | 4 | 2 | 0 | 0 | 0 | 0 | 1 | 1 | 0 | 1.000 | 0 | 1 | 0 | 0 | 0.3 | 1.000 |

Art Gardiner

GARDINER, ARTHUR CECIL
B. Dec. 26, 1899, Brooklyn, N. Y. D. Oct. 21, 1954, Copiage, N. Y. BR TR

| 1923 | PHI N | 0 | 0 | – | 0.00 | 1 | 0 | 0 | 1 | 1 | 0 | 0 | 0 | 0 | 0 | 0 | 0 | 0 | 0 | – | 0 | 0 | 0 | 0 | 0.0 | – |

Fred Gardner

GARDNER, FREDERICK
B. Palmer, Mass. Deceased.

| 1887 | BAL AA | 0 | 1 | .000 | 11.08 | 3 | 2 | 1 | 13 | 23 | 10 | 3 | 0 | 0 | 0 | 0 | 11 | 3 | 0 | .273 | 0 | 1 | 1 | 0 | 0.7 | .500 |

Gid Gardner

GARDNER, FRANKLIN WASHINGTON
B. June 9, 1859, Attleborough, Mass. D. Aug. 1, 1914, Cambridge, Mass.

1879	TRO N	0	2	.000	5.79	2	2	1	14	27	3	0	0	0	0	0	6	1	0	.167	1	2	4	0	3.5	.429
1880	CLE N	1	8	.111	2.57	9	9	9	77	80	20	21	0	0	0	0	32	6	0	.188	0	17	3	0	2.2	.850
1883	BAL AA	1	0	1.000	5.14	2	0	0	7	9	1	2	0	1	0	0	161	44	1	.273	0	2	2	0	2.0	.500
1884	3 teams					BAL AA (0G 0–0)			CHI U (1G 0–1)			BAL U (0G 0–0)															
"	total	0	1	.000	6.00	1	1	0	6	10	1	4	0	0	0	0	326	76	2	.233	1	1	0	0	4.0	1.000
1885	BAL AA	0	1	.000	10.00	1	1	1	9	16	6	3	0	0	0	0	170	37	0	.218	2	1	1	0	4.0	.750
5 yrs		2	12	.143	3.90	15	13	12	113	142	28	33	0	1	0	0	*				4	25	10	0	2.6	.744

Glenn Gardner

GARDNER, MILES GLENN
B. Jan. 25, 1916, Burnsville, N. C. D. July 7, 1964, Rochester, N. Y. BR TR 5'11" 180 lbs.

| 1945 | STL N | 3 | 1 | .750 | 3.29 | 17 | 4 | 2 | 54.2 | 50 | 27 | 20 | 0 | 1 | 1 | 1 | 21 | 7 | 0 | .333 | 2 | 8 | 0 | 0 | 0.6 | 1.000 |

Harry Gardner

GARDNER, HARRY RAY
B. Sept. 20, 1888, Portland, Ore. D. Aug. 2, 1961, Barlow, Ore. BB TR 6'2" 180 lbs.

1911	PIT N	1	1	.500	4.50	13	3	2	42	39	20	24	0	0	0	2	14	3	0	.214	0	7	0	0	0.5	1.000
1912		0	0	–		1	0	0	.1	3	1	0	0	0	0	0	0	0	0	–	1	0	0	0	1.0	1.000
2 yrs		1	1	.500	4.46	14	3	2	42.1	42	21	24	0	0	0	2	14	3	0	.214	1	7	0	0	0.6	1.000

Jim Gardner

GARDNER, JAMES ANDERSON
B. Oct. 4, 1874, Pittsburgh, Pa. D. Apr. 24, 1905, Pittsburgh, Pa. TR

1895	PIT N	8	2	.800	2.64	11	10	8	85.1	99	27	31	0	0	0	0	34	9	0	.265	3	16	2	1	1.9	.905
1897		5	5	.500	5.19	14	11	8	95.1	115	32	35	0	1	0	0	76	12	1	.158	3	20	3	0	1.9	.885
1898		10	13	.435	3.21	25	22	19	185.1	179	48	41	1	0	1	0	91	14	0	.154	10	34	2	1	1.8	.957
1899		1	0	1.000	7.52	6	3	0	32.1	52	13	2	0	0	0	0	13	3	0	.231	3	1	0	0	0.7	.750
1902	CHI N	1	2	.333	2.88	3	3	2	25	23	10	6	0	0	0	0	10	2	0	.200	2	7	0	0	3.0	1.000
5 yrs		25	22	.532	3.85	59	49	37	423.1	468	130	115	1	1	1	0	224	40	1	.179	21	77	8	2	1.8	.925

Mark Gardner

GARDNER, MARK ALLAN
B. Mar. 1, 1962, Los Angeles, Calif. BR TR 6'1" 190 lbs.

| 1989 | MON N | 0 | 3 | .000 | 5.13 | 7 | 4 | 0 | 26.1 | 26 | 11 | 21 | 0 | 0 | 0 | 0 | 6 | 1 | 0 | .167 | 1 | 3 | 0 | 0 | 0.6 | 1.000 |

Rob Gardner

GARDNER, RICHARD FRANK
B. Dec. 19, 1944, Binghamton, N. Y. BR TL 6'1" 176 lbs.

1965	NY N	0	2	.000	3.21	5	4	0	28	23	7	19	0	0	0	0	7	0	0	.000	2	5	0	1	1.4	1.000
1966		4	8	.333	5.12	41	17	3	133.2	147	64	74	0	1	1	1	41	7	0	.171	4	24	1	1	0.7	.966
1967	CHI N	0	2	.000	3.98	18	5	0	31.2	33	6	16	0	1	0	0	6	0	0	.000	1	6	0	0	0.4	1.000
1968	CLE A	0	0	–	6.75	5	0	0	2.2	5	2	6	0	0	0	0	0	0	0	–	0	0	0	0	0.0	–
1970	NY N	1	0	1.000	5.14	1	1	0	7	8	4	6	0	0	0	0	3	1	0	.333	0	1	0	0	1.0	1.000
1971	2 teams					OAK A (4G 0–0)			NY A (2G 0–0)																		
"	total	0	0	–	2.53	6	1	0	10.2	11	5	7	0	0	0	0	2	1	0	.500	1	2	0	0	0.5	1.000
1972	NY A	8	5	.615	3.06	20	14	1	97	91	28	58	0	0	0	1	28	3	0	.107	2	13	0	1	0.8	1.000
1973	2 teams					MIL A (10G 1–1)			OAK A (3G 0–0)																		
"	total	1	1	.500	8.10	13	0	0	20	27	17	7	0	1	1	1					1	3	0	0	0.3	1.000
8 yrs		14	18	.438	4.35	109	42	4	330.2	345	133	193	0	3	2	3	87	12	0	.138	11	54	1	4	0.6	.985

Wes Gardner

GARDNER, WESLEY BRIAN
B. Apr. 29, 1961, Benton, Ark. BR TR 6'4" 195 lbs.

1984	NY N	1	1	.500	6.39	21	0	0	25.1	34	8	19	0	1	1	1	1	0	0	.000	1	3	0	0	0.2	1.000
1985		0	2	.000	5.25	9	0	0	12	18	8	11	0	0	2	0	0	0	0	–	0	4	0	0	0.4	1.000
1986	BOS A	0	0	–	9.00	1	0	0	1	1	0	0	0	0	0	0	0	0	0	–	0	0	0	0	0.0	–
1987		3	6	.333	5.42	49	1	0	89.2	98	42	70	0	3	6	10	0	0	0	–	2	14	0	0	0.3	1.000
1988		8	6	.571	3.50	36	18	1	149	119	64	106	0	1	2	2	0	0	0	–	15	14	0	0	0.8	1.000

Year	Team		W	L	PCT	ERA	G	GS	CG	IP	H	BB	SO	ShO	Relief Pitching W	L	SV	Batting AB	H	HR	BA	PO	A	E	DP	TC/G	FA

Wes Gardner *continued*

Year	Team		W	L	PCT	ERA	G	GS	CG	IP	H	BB	SO	ShO	W	L	SV	AB	H	HR	BA	PO	A	E	DP	TC/G	FA
1989			3	7	.300	5.97	22	16	0	86	97	47	81	0	1	0	0	0	0	0	–	3	8	1	1	0.5	.917
6 yrs.			15	22	.405	4.83	138	35	1	363	367	169	288	0	6	10	13	1	0	0	.000	21	36	1	1	0.4	.983
LEAGUE CHAMPIONSHIP SERIES																											
1988	BOS	A	0	0	–	5.79	1	0	0	4.2	6	2	8	0	0	0	0	0	0	0	–	0	0	0	0	0.0	–

Bill Garfield

GARFIELD, WILLIAM MILTON   BR TR 5'11½" 160 lbs.
B. Oct. 26, 1867, Sheffield, Ohio   D. Dec. 16, 1941, Danville, Ill.

Year	Team		W	L	PCT	ERA	G	GS	CG	IP	H	BB	SO	ShO	W	L	SV	AB	H	HR	BA	PO	A	E	DP	TC/G	FA
1889	PIT	N	0	2	.000	7.76	4	2	2	29	45	17	4	0	0	0	0	13	0	0	.000	2	6	1	1	2.3	.889
1890	CLE	N	1	7	.125	4.89	9	8	7	70	91	35	16	0	0	0	0	26	4	0	.154	4	13	1	0	2.0	.944
2 yrs.			1	9	.100	5.73	13	10	9	99	136	52	20	0	0	0	0	39	4	0	.103	6	19	2	1	2.1	.926

Bob Garibaldi

GARIBALDI, ROBERT ROY   BL TR 6'4" 210 lbs.
B. Mar. 3, 1942, Stockton, Calif.

Year	Team		W	L	PCT	ERA	G	GS	CG	IP	H	BB	SO	ShO	W	L	SV	AB	H	HR	BA	PO	A	E	DP	TC/G	FA
1962	SF	N	0	0	–	5.11	9	0	0	12.1	13	5	9	0	0	0	1	1	0	0	.000	2	3	1	0	0.7	.833
1963			0	1	.000	1.13	4	0	0	8	8	4	4	0	0	1	1	1	0	0	.000	0	2	1	1	0.8	.667
1966			0	0	–	0.00	1	0	0	1	1	0	0	0	0	0	0	0	0	0	–	0	0	0	0	0.0	–
1969			0	1	.000	1.80	1	1	0	5	6	2	1	0	0	0	0	2	0	0	.000	0	1	0	0	1.0	1.000
4 yrs.			0	2	.000	3.08	15	1	0	26.1	28	11	14	0	0	1	2	4	0	0	.000	2	6	2	1	0.7	.800

Lou Garland

GARLAND, LOUIS LYMAN   BR TR 6'2½" 200 lbs.
B. July 16, 1905, Archie, Mo.

Year	Team		W	L	PCT	ERA	G	GS	CG	IP	H	BB	SO	ShO	W	L	SV	AB	H	HR	BA	PO	A	E	DP	TC/G	FA
1931	CHI	A	0	2	.000	10.26	7	2	0	16.2	30	14	4	0	0	2	0	3	0	0	.000	1	7	1	0	1.3	.889

Wayne Garland

GARLAND, MARCUS WAYNE   BR TR 6' 195 lbs.
B. Oct. 26, 1950, Nashville, Tenn.

Year	Team		W	L	PCT	ERA	G	GS	CG	IP	H	BB	SO	ShO	W	L	SV	AB	H	HR	BA	PO	A	E	DP	TC/G	FA
1973	BAL	A	0	1	.000	3.94	4	1	0	16	14	7	10	0	0	0	0	0	0	0	–	1	1	0	0	0.5	1.000
1974			5	5	.500	2.97	20	6	0	91	68	26	40	0	3	1	1	0	0	0	–	5	11	2	1	0.9	.889
1975			2	5	.286	3.71	29	1	0	87.1	80	31	46	0	2	5	4	0	0	0	–	6	11	0	0	0.6	1.000
1976			20	7	.741	2.68	38	25	14	232	224	64	113	4	4	1	1	0	0	0	–	27	37	3	2	1.8	.955
1977	CLE	A	13	19	.406	3.59	38	38	21	283	281	88	118	1	0	0	0	0	0	0	–	24	42	3	3	1.8	.957
1978			2	3	.400	7.89	6	6	0	29.2	43	16	13	0	0	0	0	0	0	0	–	1	5	0	0	1.0	1.000
1979			4	10	.286	5.21	18	14	2	95	120	34	40	0	1	1	0	0	0	0	–	11	8	3	0	1.2	.864
1980			6	9	.400	4.62	25	20	4	150	163	48	55	0	0	0	0	0	0	0	–	14	16	0	0	1.2	1.000
1981			3	7	.300	5.79	12	10	2	56	89	14	15	1	0	0	0	0	0	0	–	4	11	0	0	1.3	1.000
9 yrs.			55	66	.455	3.89	190	121	43	1040	1082	328	450	7	10	7	6	0	0	0	–	93	142	11	6	1.3	.955
LEAGUE CHAMPIONSHIP SERIES																											
1974	BAL	A	0	0	–	0.00	1	0	0	.2	1	1	0	0	0	0	0	0	0	0	–	0	0	0	0	0.0	–

Mike Garman

GARMAN, MICHAEL DOUGLAS   BR TR 6'3" 195 lbs.
B. Sept. 16, 1949, Caldwell, Ida.

Year	Team		W	L	PCT	ERA	G	GS	CG	IP	H	BB	SO	ShO	W	L	SV	AB	H	HR	BA	PO	A	E	DP	TC/G	FA
1969	BOS	A	1	0	1.000	4.38	2	2	0	12.1	13	10	10	0	0	0	0	5	2	0	.400	3	1	0	0	2.0	1.000
1971			1	1	.500	3.79	3	3	0	19	15	9	6	0	0	0	0	6	2	0	.333	0	0	0	0	0.0	–
1972			0	1	.000	12.00	3	1	0	3	4	2	1	0	0	0	0	0	0	0	–	0	0	0	0	0.0	–
1973			0	0	–	5.32	12	0	0	22	32	15	9	0	0	0	0	0	0	0	–	1	3	1	0	0.4	.800
1974	STL	N	7	2	.778	2.63	64	0	0	82	66	27	45	0	7	2	6	10	1	0	.100	2	14	2	4	0.3	.889
1975			3	8	.273	2.39	66	0	0	79	73	48	48	0	3	8	10	2	0	0	.000	3	9	4	0	0.2	.750
1976	CHI	N	2	4	.333	4.97	47	2	0	76	79	35	37	0	2	2	1	7	0	0	.000	3	14	0	1	0.4	1.000
1977	LA	N	4	4	.500	2.71	49	0	0	63	60	22	29	0	4	4	12	7	0	0	.000	3	8	1	1	0.2	.917
1978	2 teams	LA N (10G 0–1)				MON N (47G 4–6)																					
"	total		4	7	.364	4.40	57	0	0	77.2	69	34	28	0	4	7	13	5	0	0	.000	4	10	1	1	0.3	.933
9 yrs.			22	27	.449	3.63	303	8	0	434	411	202	213	0	20	23	42	42	5	0	.119	19	59	9	7	0.3	.897
LEAGUE CHAMPIONSHIP SERIES																											
1977	LA	N	0	0	–	0.00	2	0	0	1.1	0	0	1	0	0	0	1	0	0	0	–	0	0	0	0	0.0	–
WORLD SERIES																											
1977	LA	N	0	0	–	0.00	2	0	0	4	2	1	3	0	0	0	0	0	0	0	–	0	0	0	0	0.0	–

Willie Garoni

GARONI, WILLIAM   BR TR 6'1" 165 lbs.
B. July 28, 1877, Fort Lee, N. J.   D. Sept. 9, 1914, Fort Lee, N. J.

Year	Team		W	L	PCT	ERA	G	GS	CG	IP	H	BB	SO	ShO	W	L	SV	AB	H	HR	BA	PO	A	E	DP	TC/G	FA
1899	NY	N	0	1	.000	4.50	3	1	0	10	12	3	2	0	0	0	0	4	0	0	.000	0	4	1	1	1.7	.800

Scott Garrelts

GARRELTS, SCOTT WILLIAM   BR TR 6'4" 200 lbs.
B. Oct. 30, 1961, Champaign, Ill.

Year	Team		W	L	PCT	ERA	G	GS	CG	IP	H	BB	SO	ShO	W	L	SV	AB	H	HR	BA	PO	A	E	DP	TC/G	FA
1982	SF	N	0	0	–	13.50	1	0	0	2	3	2	4	0	0	0	0	0	0	0	–	0	0	0	0	0.0	–
1983			2	2	.500	2.52	5	5	1	35.2	33	19	16	1	0	0	0	9	2	0	.222	1	7	0	1	1.6	1.000
1984			2	3	.400	5.65	21	3	0	43	45	34	32	0	2	3	0	10	1	0	.100	2	4	0	0	0.3	1.000
1985			9	6	.600	2.30	74	0	0	105.2	76	58	106	0	9	6	13	9	2	0	.222	7	22	2	0	0.4	.935
1986			13	9	.591	3.11	53	18	0	173.2	144	74	125	0	8	10	10	45	8	1	.178	9	37	2	2	0.9	.958
1987			11	7	.611	3.22	64	0	0	106.1	70	55	127	0	11	7	12	10	2	0	.200	5	10	1	1	0.3	.938
1988			5	9	.357	3.58	65	0	0	98	80	46	86	0	5	9	13	13	1	0	.077	5	12	2	0	0.3	.895
1989			14	5	**.737**	**2.28**	30	29	0	193.1	149	46	119	0	0	0	0	66	9	0	.136	18	24	1	0	1.4	.977
8 yrs.			56	41	.577	3.01	313	55	5	757.2	600	334	615	2	35	27	48	162	25	1	.154	47	116	8	4	0.5	.953
LEAGUE CHAMPIONSHIP SERIES																											
1987	SF	N	0	0	–	6.75	2	0	0	2.2	4	2	4	0	0	0	0	0	0	0	–	1	0	0	0	0.5	1.000
1989			1	0	1.000	5.40	2	2	0	11.2	16	2	8	0	0	0	0	4	0	0	.000	0	1	0	0	0.5	1.000
2 yrs.			1	0	1.000	5.65	4	2	0	14.1	18	6	12	0	0	0	0	4	0	0	.000	1	1	0	0	0.5	1.000

Year	Team		W	L	PCT	ERA	G	GS	CG	IP	H	BB	SO	ShO	W	L	SV	AB	H	HR	BA	PO	A	E	DP	TC/G	FA

Scott Garrelts *continued*

WORLD SERIES

Year	Team		W	L	PCT	ERA	G	GS	CG	IP	H	BB	SO	ShO	W	L	SV	AB	H	HR	BA	PO	A	E	DP	TC/G	FA
1989	SF	N	0	2	.000	9.82	2	2	0	7.1	13	1	8	0	0	0	0	1	0	0	.000	0	2	0	0	1.0	1.000

Clarence Garrett

GARRETT, CLARENCE RAYMOND (Laz)
B. Mar. 6, 1891, Reader, W. Va.   D. Feb. 11, 1977, Moundsville, W. Va.   BR TR 6'5½" 185 lbs.

Year	Team		W	L	PCT	ERA	G	GS	CG	IP	H	BB	SO	ShO	W	L	SV	AB	H	HR	BA	PO	A	E	DP	TC/G	FA
1915	CLE	A	2	2	.500	2.31	4	4	2	23.1	19	6	5	0	0	0	0	8	0	0	.000	1	12	1	0	3.5	.929

Greg Garrett

GARRETT, GREGORY
B. Mar. 12, 1948, Atascadero, Calif.   BB TL 6' 200 lbs.

Year	Team		W	L	PCT	ERA	G	GS	CG	IP	H	BB	SO	ShO	W	L	SV	AB	H	HR	BA	PO	A	E	DP	TC/G	FA
1970	CAL	A	5	6	.455	2.64	32	7	0	75	48	44	53	0	4	0	1	15	1	0	.067	0	12	0	0	0.4	1.000
1971	CIN	N	0	1	.000	1.00	2	1	0	9	7	10	2	0	0	1	0	3	1	0	.333	0	1	0	0	0.5	1.000
2 yrs.			5	7	.417	2.46	34	8	0	84	55	54	55	0	4	3	0	18	2	0	.111	0	13	0	0	0.4	1.000

Cliff Garrison

GARRISON, CLIFFORD WILLIAM
B. Aug. 13, 1905, Belmont, Okla.   BR TR 6' 195 lbs.

Year	Team		W	L	PCT	ERA	G	GS	CG	IP	H	BB	SO	ShO	W	L	SV	AB	H	HR	BA	PO	A	E	DP	TC/G	FA
1928	BOS	A	0	0	–	7.88	6	0	0	16	22	6	0	0	0	0	0	3	0	0	.000	1	7	0	0	1.3	1.000

Jim Garry

GARRY, JAMES THOMAS
B. Sept. 21, 1869, Great Barrington, Mass.   D. Jan. 15, 1917, Pittsfield, Mass.

Year	Team		W	L	PCT	ERA	G	GS	CG	IP	H	BB	SO	ShO	W	L	SV	AB	H	HR	BA	PO	A	E	DP	TC/G	FA
1893	BOS	N	0	1	.000	63.00	1	0	0	1	5	4	2	0	0	1	0	1	0	0	.000	0	0	0	0	0.0	–

Ned Garver

GARVER, NED FRANKLIN
B. Dec. 25, 1925, Ney, Ohio   BR TR 5'10½" 180 lbs.

Year	Team		W	L	PCT	ERA	G	GS	CG	IP	H	BB	SO	ShO	W	L	SV	AB	H	HR	BA	PO	A	E	DP	TC/G	FA
1948	STL	A	7	11	.389	3.41	38	24	7	198	200	95	75	0	1	0	5	66	19	1	.288	19	34	1	3	1.4	.981
1949			12	17	.414	3.98	41	32	16	223.2	245	102	70	1	3	0	3	75	14	0	.187	15	42	5	3	1.5	.919
1950			13	18	.419	3.39	37	31	22	260	264	108	85	2	1	2	0	91	26	1	.286	28	51	5	4	2.3	.940
1951			20	12	.625	3.73	33	30	24	246	237	96	84	1	2	1	0	95	29	1	.305	26	42	3	6	2.2	.958
1952	2 teams		STL A	(21G 7–10)		DET A	(1G 1–0)																				
"	total		8	10	.444	3.60	22	22	8	157.2	139	58	63	2	0	0	0	51	9	0	.176	12	26	1	7	1.8	.974
1953	DET	A	11	11	.500	4.45	30	26	13	198.1	228	66	69	0	1	0	1	72	11	1	.153	13	39	1	0	1.8	.981
1954			14	11	.560	2.81	35	32	16	246.1	216	62	93	3	0	0	0	79	13	0	.165	21	48	2	2	2.0	.972
1955			12	16	.429	3.98	33	32	16	230.2	251	67	83	1	0	0	0	76	17	1	.224	17	40	3	4	1.8	.950
1956			0	2	.000	4.08	6	3	1	17.2	15	13	6	0	0	0	0	5	0	0	.000	1	5	0	1	1.0	1.000
1957	KC	A	6	13	.316	3.84	24	23	6	145.1	120	55	61	1	0	0	0	44	8	0	.182	13	21	1	2	1.5	.971
1958			12	11	.522	4.03	31	28	10	201	192	66	72	3	0	0	1	69	12	0	.174	18	57	2	4	2.5	.974
1959			10	13	.435	3.71	32	30	9	201.1	214	42	61	2	0	0	0	71	20	2	.282	10	35	1	3	1.4	.978
1960			4	9	.308	3.83	28	15	5	122.1	110	35	50	2	0	0	0	27	2	0	.074	9	18	2	2	1.0	.931
1961	LA	A	0	3	.000	5.59	12	2	0	29	40	16	9	0	0	1	0	6	0	0	.000	1	11	0	0	1.0	1.000
14 yrs.			129	157	.451	3.73	402	330	153	2477.1	2471	881	881	18	8	4	12	827	180	7	.218	203	469	27	41	1.7	.961

Jerry Garvin

GARVIN, THEODORE JARED
B. Oct. 21, 1955, Oakland, Calif.   BL TL 6'3" 195 lbs.

Year	Team		W	L	PCT	ERA	G	GS	CG	IP	H	BB	SO	ShO	W	L	SV	AB	H	HR	BA	PO	A	E	DP	TC/G	FA
1977	TOR	A	10	18	.357	4.19	34	34	12	245	247	85	127	1	0	0	0	0	0	0	–	12	66	3	1	2.4	.963
1978			4	12	.250	5.54	26	22	3	144.2	189	48	67	0	0	0	0	0	0	0	–	9	28	0	1	1.4	1.000
1979			0	1	.000	2.74	8	1	0	23	15	10	14	0	0	0	1	0	0	0	–	1	1	0	1	0.3	1.000
1980			4	7	.364	2.28	61	0	0	83	70	27	52	0	4	7	8	0	0	0	–	5	14	0	1	0.3	1.000
1981			1	2	.333	3.40	35	4	0	53	46	23	25	0	1	1	0	0	0	0	–	1	9	0	2	0.3	1.000
1982			1	1	.500	7.25	32	4	0	58.1	81	26	35	0	1	1	0	0	0	0	–	5	17	0	0	0.7	1.000
6 yrs.			20	41	.328	4.42	196	65	15	607	648	219	320	1	6	10	8	0	0	0	–	33	135	3	6	0.9	.982

Ned Garvin

GARVIN, VIRGIL LEE
B. Jan. 1, 1874, Navasota, Tex.   D. June 16, 1908, Fresno, Calif.   TR 6'3½" 160 lbs.

Year	Team		W	L	PCT	ERA	G	GS	CG	IP	H	BB	SO	ShO	W	L	SV	AB	H	HR	BA	PO	A	E	DP	TC/G	FA
1896	PHI	N	0	1	.000	7.62	2	1	1	13	19	6	4	0	0	0	0	6	0	0	.000	0	0	0	0	0.5	1.000
1899	CHI	N	9	13	.409	2.85	24	23	22	199	202	42	69	4	0	0	0	71	11	0	.155	7	51	3	1	2.5	.951
1900			10	18	.357	2.41	30	28	25	246.1	225	63	107	1	0	1	0	91	14	0	.154	5	78	6	1	3.0	.933
1901	MIL	A	7	20	.259	3.46	37	27	22	257.1	258	90	122	1	0	0	2	93	10	0	.108	14	83	7	2	2.8	.933
1902	2 teams		CHI A	(23G 10–10)		BKN N	(2G 1–1)																				
"	total		11	11	.500	2.09	25	21	18	193.1	184	47	62	3	1	0	0	66	10	0	.152	4	73	4	3	3.2	.951
1903	BKN	N	15	18	.455	3.08	38	34	30	298	277	84	154	2	0	1	2	106	8	0	.075	7	117	11	3	3.6	.919
1904	2 teams		BKN N	(23G 5–15)		NY A	(2G 0–1)																				
"	total		5	16	.238	1.72	25	24	16	193.2	155	80	94	2	0	0	0	67	8	0	.119	18	73	11	5	4.1	.892
7 yrs.			57	97	.370	2.72	181	158	134	1400.2	1320	413	612	13	1	2	4	500	61	0	.122	55	476	42	15	3.2	.927

Harry Gaspar

GASPAR, HARRY LAMBERT
B. Apr. 28, 1883, Kingsley, Iowa   D. May 14, 1940, Orange, Calif.   BR TR 6' 180 lbs.

Year	Team		W	L	PCT	ERA	G	GS	CG	IP	H	BB	SO	ShO	W	L	SV	AB	H	HR	BA	PO	A	E	DP	TC/G	FA
1909	CIN	N	18	11	.621	2.01	44	29	19	260	228	57	65	4	2	2	2	82	10	0	.122	2	56	3	2	1.4	.951
1910			15	17	.469	2.59	48	31	16	275	257	75	74	4	1	1	5	87	10	0	.115	6	73	6	2	1.8	.929
1911			10	17	.370	3.30	44	32	11	253.2	272	69	76	2	2	2	3	85	13	0	.153	7	66	7	5	1.8	.913
1912			1	3	.250	4.17	7	6	2	36.2	38	16	13	1	0	1	0	12	3	0	.250	1	10	1	0	1.7	.917
4 yrs.			44	48	.478	2.69	143	98	48	825.1	795	217	228	11	5	6	10	266	36	0	.135	16	205	17	9	1.7	.929

Charlie Gassaway

GASSAWAY, CHARLES CASON (Sheriff)
B. Aug. 12, 1918, Gassaway, Tenn.   BL TL 6'2½" 210 lbs.

Year	Team		W	L	PCT	ERA	G	GS	CG	IP	H	BB	SO	ShO	W	L	SV	AB	H	HR	BA	PO	A	E	DP	TC/G	FA
1944	CHI	N	0	1	.000	7.71	2	2	0	11.2	20	10	7	0	0	0	0	4	1	0	.250	0	1	0	0	0.5	1.000
1945	PHI	A	4	7	.364	3.74	24	11	4	118	114	55	50	0	0	0	0	39	6	0	.154	3	20	6	1	1.2	.793
1946	CLE	A	1	1	.500	3.91	13	6	0	50.2	54	26	23	0	0	0	0	15	1	0	.067	5	7	0	1	0.9	1.000
3 yrs.			5	9	.357	4.04	39	19	4	180.1	188	91	80	0	0	0	0	58	8	0	.138	8	28	6	2	1.1	.857

Year	Team		W	L	PCT	ERA	G	GS	CG	IP	H	BB	SO	ShO	Relief Pitching W	L	SV	Batting AB	H	HR	BA	PO	A	E	DP	TC/G	FA

Milt Gaston

GASTON, NATHANIEL MILTON
Brother of Alex Gaston.
B. Jan. 27, 1896, Ridgefield Park, N. J.

BR TR 6'1" 185 lbs.
BB 1933

Year	Team		W	L	PCT	ERA	G	GS	CG	IP	H	BB	SO	ShO	W	L	SV	AB	H	HR	BA	PO	A	E	DP	TC/G	FA
1924	NY	A	5	3	.625	4.50	29	2	1	86	92	44	24	0	5	1	1	27	6	0	.222	2	14	0	1	0.6	1.000
1925	STL	A	15	14	.517	4.41	42	30	16	238.2	284	101	84	0	3	3	1	80	21	1	.263	10	49	0	2	1.4	1.000
1926			10	18	.357	4.33	32	28	14	214.1	227	101	39	1	0	2	0	78	13	1	.167	16	47	2	2	2.0	.969
1927			13	17	.433	5.00	37	30	21	254	275	100	77	0	0	2	1	96	25	3	.260	18	58	4	9	2.2	.950
1928	WAS	A	6	12	.333	5.51	28	22	8	148.2	179	53	45	3	0	1	0	49	7	0	.143	9	38	3	1	1.8	.940
1929	BOS	A	12	19	.387	3.73	39	29	20	243.2	265	81	83	1	2	3	2	78	15	1	.192	13	42	4	4	1.5	.965
1930			13	20	.394	3.92	38	34	20	273	272	98	99	2	0	1	2	98	20	0	.204	15	58	4	4	2.0	.948
1931			2	13	.133	4.46	23	18	4	119	137	41	33	0	0	1	1	38	6	0	.158	4	24	3	3	1.3	.903
1932	CHI	A	7	17	.292	4.00	28	25	7	166.2	183	73	44	1	0	1	1	60	14	0	.233	6	42	4	7	1.9	.923
1933			8	12	.400	4.85	30	25	7	167	177	60	39	1	0	0	0	52	8	0	.154	4	36	3	1	1.4	.930
1934			6	19	.240	5.85	29	28	10	194	247	84	48	1	0	0	0	68	10	0	.147	9	52	1	2	2.1	.984
11 yrs.			97	164	.372	4.55	355	271	127	2105	2338	836	615	10	10	14	8	724	145	6	.200	106	460	26	36	1.7	.956

Welcome Gaston

GASTON, WELCOME THORNBURG
B. Dec. 19, 1872, Guernsey County, Ohio   D. Dec. 13, 1944, Columbus, Ohio

TL

Year	Team		W	L	PCT	ERA	G	GS	CG	IP	H	BB	SO	ShO	W	L	SV	AB	H	HR	BA	PO	A	E	DP	TC/G	FA
1898	BKN	N	1	1	.500	2.81	2	2	2	16	17	9	0	0	0	0	0	8	1	0	.125	1	3	1	1	2.5	.800
1899			0	0	—	3.00	1	0	0	3	3	4	0	0	0	0	0	1	1	0	1.000	0	1	0	0	1.0	1.000
2 yrs.			1	1	.500	2.84	3	2	2	19	20	13	0	0	0	0	0	9	2	0	.222	1	4	1	1	2.0	.833

Hank Gastright

GASTRIGHT, HENRY CARL
Born Henry Carl Gastreich.
B. Mar. 29, 1865, Covington, Ky.   D. Oct. 9, 1937, Cold Springs, Ky.

BR TR 6'2" 190 lbs.

Year	Team		W	L	PCT	ERA	G	GS	CG	IP	H	BB	SO	ShO	W	L	SV	AB	H	HR	BA	PO	A	E	DP	TC/G	FA
1889	COL	AA	10	16	.385	4.57	32	26	21	222.2	255	104	115	0	0	1	0	94	17	0	.181	6	47	5	1	1.8	.914
1890			30	14	.682	2.94	48	45	41	401.1	312	135	199	4	3	0	0	169	36	0	.213	12	55	5	2	1.5	.931
1891			12	19	.387	3.78	35	33	28	283.2	280	136	109	1	0	1	0	117	23	0	.197	11	73	5	2	2.5	.944
1892	WAS	N	3	3	.500	5.08	11	7	6	79.2	94	38	32	0	0	0	0	29	4	0	.138	1	10	1	2	1.1	.917
1893	2 teams		PIT N	(9G 3–1)			BOS N	(19G 12–4)																				
"	total		15	5	.750	5.44	28	23	19	215	253	115	39	0	2	0	0	92	14	0	.152	4	46	3	1	1.9	.943
1894	BKN	N	2	6	.250	6.39	16	8	6	93	135	55	20	0	0	2	2	41	7	0	.171	5	14	2	0	1.3	.905
1896	CIN	N	0	0	—	4.50	1	0	0	6	8	1	0	0	0	0	0	2	0	0	.000	0	1	0	0	1.0	1.000
7 yrs.			72	63	.533	4.20	171	142	121	1301.1	1337	584	514	6	5	4	2	544	101	0	.186	39	246	21	8	1.8	.931

Aubrey Gatewood

GATEWOOD, AUBREY LEE
B. Nov. 17, 1938, Little Rock, Ark.

BR TR 6'1" 170 lbs.

Year	Team		W	L	PCT	ERA	G	GS	CG	IP	H	BB	SO	ShO	W	L	SV	AB	H	HR	BA	PO	A	E	DP	TC/G	FA
1963	LA	A	1	1	.500	1.50	4	3	1	24	12	16	13	0	0	0	0	8	0	0	.000	0	4	0	0	1.0	1.000
1964			3	3	.500	2.24	15	7	0	60.1	59	12	25	0	1	1	0	20	2	0	.100	8	6	0	0	0.9	1.000
1965	CAL	A	4	5	.444	3.42	46	3	0	92	91	37	37	0	4	3	0	14	3	0	.214	6	15	1	0	0.5	.955
1970	ATL	N	0	0	—	4.50	3	0	0	2	4	2	0	0	0	0	0	0	0	0	—	1	1	0	0	0.7	1.000
4 yrs.			8	9	.471	2.78	68	13	1	178.1	166	67	75	0	5	4	0	42	5	0	.119	15	26	1	0	0.6	.976

Chippy Gaw

GAW, GEORGE JOSEPH
B. Mar. 13, 1892, West Newton, Mass.   D. May 26, 1968, Boston, Mass.

BR TR 5'11" 180 lbs.

Year	Team		W	L	PCT	ERA	G	GS	CG	IP	H	BB	SO	ShO	W	L	SV	AB	H	HR	BA	PO	A	E	DP	TC/G	FA
1920	CHI	N	1	1	.500	4.85	6	1	0	13	16	3	4	0	1	0	0	4	1	0	.250	0	3	0	0	0.5	1.000

Dale Gear

GEAR, DALE DUDLEY
B. Feb. 2, 1872, Lone Elm, Kans.   D. Sept. 23, 1951, Topeka, Kans.

BR TR 5'11" 165 lbs.

Year	Team		W	L	PCT	ERA	G	GS	CG	IP	H	BB	SO	ShO	W	L	SV	AB	H	HR	BA	PO	A	E	DP	TC/G	FA
1896	CLE	N	0	2	.000	5.48	3	2	2	23	35	6	6	0	0	0	0	15	6	0	.400	2	4	0	0	2.3	.857
1901	WAS	A	4	11	.267	4.03	24	16	14	163	199	22	35	1	1	1	0	199	47	0	.236	11	53	3	0	2.8	.955
2 yrs.			4	13	.235	4.21	27	18	16	186	234	28	41	1	1	1	0	*				13	57	4	0	2.7	.946

Dinty Gearin

GEARIN, DENNIS JOHN
B. Oct. 15, 1897, Providence, R. I.   D. Mar. 11, 1959, Providence, R. I.

BL TL 5'4" 148 lbs.

Year	Team		W	L	PCT	ERA	G	GS	CG	IP	H	BB	SO	ShO	W	L	SV	AB	H	HR	BA	PO	A	E	DP	TC/G	FA
1923	NY	N	1	1	.500	3.38	6	2	1	24	23	10	9	0	1	0	0	7	2	0	.286	0	5	1	0	1.0	.833
1924	2 teams		NY N	(6G 1–2)			BOS N	(1G 0–1)																				
"	total		1	3	.250	4.03	7	4	2	29	33	18	4	0	0	1	0	9	3	0	.333	0	7	1	0	1.1	.875
2 yrs.			2	4	.333	3.74	13	6	3	53	56	28	13	0	1	1	0	16	5	0	.313	0	12	2	0	1.1	.857

Bob Geary

GEARY, ROBERT NORTON (Speed)
B. May 10, 1891, Cincinnati, Ohio   D. Jan. 3, 1980, Cincinnati, Ohio

BR TR 5'11" 168 lbs.

Year	Team		W	L	PCT	ERA	G	GS	CG	IP	H	BB	SO	ShO	W	L	SV	AB	H	HR	BA	PO	A	E	DP	TC/G	FA
1918	PHI	A	2	5	.286	2.69	16	7	6	87	94	31	22	2	0	0	4	27	4	0	.148	1	21	0	0	1.4	1.000
1919			0	3	.000	4.73	9	2	1	32.1	32	18	9	0	0	1	0	10	5	0	.500	2	11	2	0	1.7	.867
1921	CIN	N	1	1	.500	4.34	10	1	0	29	38	2	10	0	0	0	0	8	2	0	.250	1	6	1	0	0.8	.875
3 yrs.			3	9	.250	3.46	35	10	7	148.1	164	51	41	2	0	1	4	45	11	0	.244	4	38	3	0	1.3	.933

Bob Gebhard

GEBHARD, ROBERT HENRY
B. Jan. 3, 1943, Lamberton, Minn.

BR TR 6'2" 210 lbs.

Year	Team		W	L	PCT	ERA	G	GS	CG	IP	H	BB	SO	ShO	W	L	SV	AB	H	HR	BA	PO	A	E	DP	TC/G	FA
1971	MIN	A	1	2	.333	3.00	17	0	0	18	17	11	13	0	1	2	0	0	0	0	—	0	7	0	0	0.4	1.000
1972			0	1	.000	8.57	13	0	0	21	36	13	13	0	0	1	1	0	0	0	—	2	5	0	1	0.5	1.000
1974	MON	N	0	0	—	4.50	1	0	0	2	5	0	0	0	0	0	0	0	0	0	—	0	1	0	0	1.0	1.000
3 yrs.			1	3	.250	5.93	31	0	0	41	58	24	26	0	1	3	1	0	0	0	—	2	13	0	1	0.5	1.000

Pete Gebrian

GEBRIAN, PETER (Gabe)
B. Aug. 10, 1923, Bayonne, N. J.

BR TR 6' 170 lbs.

Year	Team		W	L	PCT	ERA	G	GS	CG	IP	H	BB	SO	ShO	W	L	SV	AB	H	HR	BA	PO	A	E	DP	TC/G	FA
1947	CHI	A	2	3	.400	4.48	27	4	0	66.1	61	33	17	0	2	3	5	13	0	0	.000	2	9	1	0	0.4	.917

Year	Team	W	L	PCT	ERA	G	GS	CG	IP	H	BB	SO	ShO	W	L	SV	AB	H	HR	BA	PO	A	E	DP	TC/G	FA

Jim Geddes

GEDDES, JAMES LEE
B. Mar. 23, 1949, Columbus, Ohio
BR TR 6'2" 200 lbs.

Year	Team	W	L	PCT	ERA	G	GS	CG	IP	H	BB	SO	ShO	W	L	SV	AB	H	HR	BA	PO	A	E	DP	TC/G	FA
1972	CHI A	0	0	–	6.97	5	1	0	10.1	12	10	3	0	0	0	0	1	0	0	.000	0	1	1	1	0.4	.500
1973		0	0	–	2.87	6	1	0	15.2	14	14	7	0	0	0	0	0	0	0	–	1	3	0	1	0.7	1.000
2 yrs.		0	0	–	4.50	11	2	0	26	26	24	10	0	0	0	0	1	0	0	.000	1	4	1	2	0.5	.833

Joe Gedeon

GEDEON, ELMER JOSEPH
B. Dec. 5, 1893, Sacramento, Calif.   D. May 19, 1941, San Francisco, Calif.
BR TR 6' 167 lbs.

Year	Team	W	L	PCT	ERA	G	GS	CG	IP	H	BB	SO	ShO	W	L	SV	AB	H	HR	BA	PO	A	E	DP	TC/G	FA
1913	WAS A	0	0	–	0.00	1	0	0	0	0	0	0	0	0	0	1	*				0	0	0	0	0.0	–

Johnny Gee

GEE, JOHN ALEXANDER (Whiz)
B. Dec. 7, 1915, Syracuse, N. Y.   D. Jan. 23, 1988, Cortland, N. Y.
BL TL 6'9" 225 lbs.

Year	Team	W	L	PCT	ERA	G	GS	CG	IP	H	BB	SO	ShO	W	L	SV	AB	H	HR	BA	PO	A	E	DP	TC/G	FA
1939	PIT N	1	2	.333	4.12	3	3	1	19.2	20	10	16	0	0	0	0	6	0	0	.000	1	6	1	0	2.7	.875
1941		0	2	.000	6.14	3	2	0	7.1	10	5	2	0	0	0	0	3	1	0	.333	0	1	0	0	0.3	1.000
1943		4	4	.500	4.28	15	10	2	82	89	27	18	0	2	0	0	26	3	0	.115	2	5	1	0	0.5	.875
1944	2 teams	PIT N	(4G 0–0)		NY N	(4G 0–0)																				
"	total	0	0	–	4.96	8	0	0	16.1	25	5	6	0	0	0	0	2	1	0	.500	0	5	0	0	0.6	1.000
1945	NY N	0	0	–	9.00	2	0	0	3	5	2	1	0	0	0	1	1	0	0	.000	1	0	0	0	0.5	1.000
1946		2	4	.333	3.99	13	6	1	47.1	60	15	22	0	0	0	0	13	3	0	.231	1	7	1	0	0.7	.889
6 yrs.		7	12	.368	4.41	44	21	4	175.2	209	64	65	0	2	0	1	51	8	0	.157	5	24	3	0	0.7	.906

Billy Geer

GEER, WILLIAM HENRY HARRISON
Born George Harrison Geer.
B. Aug. 13, 1849, Syracuse, N. Y.   D. Jan. 5, 1922, Syracuse, N. Y.
TR 5'8" 160 lbs.

Year	Team	W	L	PCT	ERA	G	GS	CG	IP	H	BB	SO	ShO	W	L	SV	AB	H	HR	BA	PO	A	E	DP	TC/G	FA
1884	BKN AA	0	0	–	12.60	2	0	0	5	14	3	1	0	0	0	0	*				0	0	0	0	0.0	–

Henry Gehring

GEHRING, HENRY
B. Jan. 24, 1881, St. Paul, Minn.   D. Apr. 18, 1912, Kansas City, Mo.
BR TR

Year	Team	W	L	PCT	ERA	G	GS	CG	IP	H	BB	SO	ShO	W	L	SV	AB	H	HR	BA	PO	A	E	DP	TC/G	FA
1907	WAS A	3	7	.300	3.31	15	9	8	87	92	14	31	2	0	0	0	44	9	1	.205	3	19	1	2	1.5	.957
1908		0	1	.000	14.40	3	1	0	5	9	2	0	0	0	0	0	4	2	0	.500	0	2	0	0	0.7	1.000
2 yrs.		3	8	.273	3.91	18	10	8	92	101	16	31	2	0	1	0	48	11	1	.229	3	21	1	2	1.4	.960

Paul Gehrman

GEHRMAN, PAUL ARTHUR (Dutch)
B. May 3, 1912, Marquam, Ore.   D. Oct. 23, 1986, Bend, Ore.
BR TR 6' 195 lbs.

Year	Team	W	L	PCT	ERA	G	GS	CG	IP	H	BB	SO	ShO	W	L	SV	AB	H	HR	BA	PO	A	E	DP	TC/G	FA
1937	CIN N	0	1	.000	2.89	2	1	0	9.1	11	5	1	0	0	0	0	3	0	0	.000	0	3	1	1	2.0	.750

Gary Geiger

GEIGER, GARY MERLE
B. Apr. 4, 1937, Sand Ridge, Ill.
BL TR 6' 168 lbs.

Year	Team	W	L	PCT	ERA	G	GS	CG	IP	H	BB	SO	ShO	W	L	SV	AB	H	HR	BA	PO	A	E	DP	TC/G	FA
1958	CLE A	0	0	–	9.00	1	0	0	2	2	1	2	0	0	0	0	*				0	1	0	0	1.0	1.000

Emil Geis

GEIS, EMIL MICHAEL
B. Mar., 1861, Villmer, Germany   Deceased.
BR TR 5'11" 170 lbs.

Year	Team	W	L	PCT	ERA	G	GS	CG	IP	H	BB	SO	ShO	W	L	SV	AB	H	HR	BA	PO	A	E	DP	TC/G	FA
1882	BAL AA	4	9	.308	4.80	13	13	10	95.2	84	22	10	1	0	0	0	41	6	0	.146	8	23	11	0	3.2	.738

Dave Geisel

GEISEL, JOHN DAVID
B. Jan. 18, 1955, Windber, Pa.
BL TL 6'3" 210 lbs.

Year	Team	W	L	PCT	ERA	G	GS	CG	IP	H	BB	SO	ShO	W	L	SV	AB	H	HR	BA	PO	A	E	DP	TC/G	FA
1978	CHI N	1	0	1.000	4.30	18	1	0	23	27	11	15	0	0	0	0	3	0	0	.000	1	2	0	0	0.2	1.000
1979		0	0	–	0.60	7	0	0	15	10	4	5	0	0	0	0	1	0	0	.000	2	0	0	0	0.3	1.000
1981		2	0	1.000	0.56	11	2	0	16	11	10	7	0	2	0	0	3	0	0	.000	2	1	0	0	0.3	1.000
1982	TOR A	1	1	.500	3.98	16	2	0	31.2	32	17	22	0	1	0	0	0	0	0	–	0	3	0	0	0.2	1.000
1983		0	3	.000	4.64	47	0	0	52.1	47	31	50	0	0	3	5	0	0	0	–	0	4	0	0	0.1	1.000
1984	SEA A	1	1	.500	4.15	20	3	0	43.1	47	9	28	0	1	0	3	0	0	0	–	2	2	0	0	0.2	1.000
1985		0	0	–	6.33	12	0	0	27	35	15	17	0	0	0	0	0	0	0	–	0	3	0	1	0.3	1.000
7 yrs.		5	5	.500	4.02	131	8	0	208.1	209	97	144	0	4	3	8	7	0	0	.000	7	15	0	1	0.2	1.000

Vern Geishert

GEISHERT, VERNON WILLIAM
B. Jan. 10, 1946, Madison, Wis.
BR TR 6'1" 215 lbs.

Year	Team	W	L	PCT	ERA	G	GS	CG	IP	H	BB	SO	ShO	W	L	SV	AB	H	HR	BA	PO	A	E	DP	TC/G	FA
1969	CAL A	1	1	.500	4.65	11	3	0	31	32	7	18	0	1	0	1	9	0	0	.000	1	6	1	1	0.7	.875

Bill Geiss

GEISS, WILLIAM J
Brother of Emil Geiss.
B. July 15, 1858, Chicago, Ill.   D. Sept. 18, 1924, Chicago, Ill.
5'10" 164 lbs.

Year	Team	W	L	PCT	ERA	G	GS	CG	IP	H	BB	SO	ShO	W	L	SV	AB	H	HR	BA	PO	A	E	DP	TC/G	FA
1884	DET N	0	0	–	14.40	1	0	0	5	14	2	1	0	0	0	0	*				0	1	0	0	1.0	1.000

Emil Geiss

GEISS, EMIL AUGUST
Brother of Bill Geiss.
B. Mar. 20, 1867, Chicago, Ill.   D. Oct. 4, 1911, Chicago, Ill.
BR TR

Year	Team	W	L	PCT	ERA	G	GS	CG	IP	H	BB	SO	ShO	W	L	SV	AB	H	HR	BA	PO	A	E	DP	TC/G	FA
1887	CHI N	0	1	.000	8.00	1	1	1	9	17	3	4	0	0	0	0	*				0	2	0	0	2.0	1.000

Charley Gelbert

GELBERT, CHARLES MAGNUS
B. Jan. 26, 1906, Scranton, Pa.   D. Jan. 13, 1967, Easton, Pa.
BR TR 5'11" 170 lbs.

Year	Team	W	L	PCT	ERA	G	GS	CG	IP	H	BB	SO	ShO	W	L	SV	AB	H	HR	BA	PO	A	E	DP	TC/G	FA
1940	BOS A	0	0	–	9.00	2	0	0	4	5	3	1	0	0	0	0	*				0	0	0	0	0.5	1.000

John Gelnar

GELNAR, JOHN RICHARD
B. June 25, 1943, Granite, Okla.
BR TR 6'2" 185 lbs.

Year	Team	W	L	PCT	ERA	G	GS	CG	IP	H	BB	SO	ShO	W	L	SV	AB	H	HR	BA	PO	A	E	DP	TC/G	FA
1964	PIT N	0	0	–	5.00	7	0	0	9	11	1	4	0	0	0	0	0	0	0	–	1	1	1	0	0.4	.667
1967		0	1	.000	8.05	10	1	0	19	30	11	5	0	0	0	0	6	1	0	.167	0	5	0	0	0.5	1.000
1969	SEA A	3	10	.231	3.31	39	10	0	108.2	103	26	69	0	2	3	3	19	1	0	.053	7	14	0	0	0.5	1.000

Year	Team	W	L	PCT	ERA	G	GS	CG	IP	H	BB	SO	ShO	Relief Pitching			Batting				PO	A	E	DP	TC/G	FA
														W	L	SV	AB	H	HR	BA						

John Gelnar *continued*

Year	Team		W	L	PCT	ERA	G	GS	CG	IP	H	BB	SO	ShO	W	L	SV	AB	H	HR	BA	PO	A	E	DP	TC/G	FA
1970	MIL	A	4	3	.571	4.21	53	0	0	92	98	23	48	0	4	3	4	12	1	0	.083	6	20	1	2	0.5	.963
1971			0	0	–	18.00	2	0	0	1	3	1	0	0	0	0	0	0	0	0	–	0	1	0	0	0.5	1.000
5 yrs.			7	14	.333	4.19	111	11	0	229.2	245	62	126	0	6	6	7	37	3	0	.081	14	41	2	2	0.5	.965

Joe Genewich

GENEWICH, JOSEPH EDWARD BR TR 6' 174 lbs.
B. Jan. 15, 1897, Elmira, N. Y. D. Dec. 21, 1985, Lockport, N. Y.

Year	Team		W	L	PCT	ERA	G	GS	CG	IP	H	BB	SO	ShO	W	L	SV	AB	H	HR	BA	PO	A	E	DP	TC/G	FA
1922	BOS	N	0	2	.000	7.04	6	2	1	23	29	11	4	0	0	0	0	6	1	0	.167	0	5	0	0	0.8	1.000
1923			13	14	.481	3.72	43	24	12	227.1	272	46	54	1	1	4	1	77	19	0	.247	17	58	2	1	1.8	.974
1924			10	19	.345	5.21	34	27	11	200.1	258	65	43	2	2	1	1	60	10	0	.167	3	50	0	4	1.6	1.000
1925			12	10	.545	3.99	34	21	10	169	185	41	34	0	3	2	0	55	15	0	.273	8	36	4	5	1.4	.917
1926			8	16	.333	3.88	37	26	12	216	239	63	59	2	1	1	2	67	11	0	.164	15	53	2	4	1.9	.971
1927			11	8	.579	3.83	40	19	7	181	199	54	38	0	5	0	1	57	11	0	.193	8	40	0	2	1.2	1.000
1928	2 teams		BOS N	(13G 3–7)		NY	N	(26G 11–4)																			
"	total		14	11	.560	3.50	39	29	14	239	224	72	52	2	1	1	3	90	14	0	.156	8	65	1	3	1.9	.986
1929	NY	N	3	7	.300	6.78	21	9	1	85	133	30	19	0	2	3	1	32	12	0	.375	6	19	2	1	1.3	.926
1930			2	5	.286	5.61	18	9	3	61	71	20	13	0	0	3	0	20	3	0	.150	4	23	1	2	1.6	.964
9 yrs.			73	92	.442	4.29	272	166	71	1401.2	1610	402	316	7	15	12	12	464	96	0	.207	69	349	12	22	1.6	.972

Gary Gentry

GENTRY, GARY EDWARD BR TR 6' 170 lbs.
B. Oct. 6, 1946, Phoenix, Ariz.

Year	Team		W	L	PCT	ERA	G	GS	CG	IP	H	BB	SO	ShO	W	L	SV	AB	H	HR	BA	PO	A	E	DP	TC/G	FA
1969	NY	N	13	12	.520	3.43	35	35	6	233.2	192	81	154	3	0	0	0	74	6	0	.081	13	41	0	4	1.5	1.000
1970			9	9	.500	3.69	32	29	5	188	155	86	134	2	0	0	1	59	4	0	.068	15	17	1	1	1.0	.970
1971			12	11	.522	3.24	32	31	8	203	167	82	155	3	0	0	0	68	5	0	.074	10	22	0	3	1.0	1.000
1972			7	10	.412	4.01	32	26	3	164	153	75	120	0	0	0	0	48	5	0	.104	15	27	0	1	1.3	1.000
1973	ATL	N	4	6	.400	3.41	16	14	3	87	74	35	42	0	0	0	1	30	7	0	.233	9	7	0	1	1.0	1.000
1974			0	0	–	1.29	3	1	0	7	4	2	0	0	0	0	0	1	0	0	.000	1	0	0	0	0.3	1.000
1975			1	1	.500	4.95	7	2	0	20	25	8	10	0	0	0	0	5	0	0	.000	0	4	0	0	0.6	1.000
7 yrs.			46	49	.484	3.56	157	138	25	902.2	770	369	615	8	1	1	2	285	27	0	.095	62	119	1	9	1.2	.995

LEAGUE CHAMPIONSHIP SERIES

Year	Team		W	L	PCT	ERA	G	GS	CG	IP	H	BB	SO	ShO	W	L	SV	AB	H	HR	BA	PO	A	E	DP	TC/G	FA
1969	NY	N	0	0	–	9.00	1	1	0	2	5	1	1	0	0	0	0	0	0	0	–	0	0	0	0	0.0	–

WORLD SERIES

Year	Team		W	L	PCT	ERA	G	GS	CG	IP	H	BB	SO	ShO	W	L	SV	AB	H	HR	BA	PO	A	E	DP	TC/G	FA
1969	NY	N	1	0	1.000	0.00	1	1	0	6.2	3	5	4	0	0	0	0	3	1	0	.333	0	0	0	0	0.0	–

Rufe Gentry

GENTRY, JAMES RUFFUS BR TR 6'1" 180 lbs.
B. May 18, 1918, Winston-Salem, N. C.

Year	Team		W	L	PCT	ERA	G	GS	CG	IP	H	BB	SO	ShO	W	L	SV	AB	H	HR	BA	PO	A	E	DP	TC/G	FA
1943	DET	A	1	3	.250	3.68	4	4	2	29.1	30	12	8	0	0	0	0	10	0	0	.000	1	6	0	0	1.8	1.000
1944			12	14	.462	4.24	37	30	10	203.2	211	108	68	4	2	0	0	76	15	0	.197	5	43	1	6	1.3	.980
1946			0	0	–	15.00	2	0	0	3	7	1	0	0	0	0	0	0	0	0	–	0	0	0	0	0.0	–
1947			0	0	–	81.00	1	0	0	.1	1	2	0	0	0	0	0	0	0	0	–	0	0	0	0	0.0	–
1948			0	0	–	2.70	4	0	0	6.2	5	11	2	0	0	0	0	1	1	0	1.000	2	0	0	0	0.5	1.000
5 yrs.			13	17	.433	4.37	48	34	12	243	251	134	78	4	2	0	0	87	16	0	.184	8	49	1	6	1.2	.983

Bill George

GEORGE, WILLIAM M. BR TL 5'8" 165 lbs.
B. Jan. 27, 1865, Bellaire, Ohio D. Aug. 23, 1916, Wheeling, W. Va.

Year	Team		W	L	PCT	ERA	G	GS	CG	IP	H	BB	SO	ShO	W	L	SV	AB	H	HR	BA	PO	A	E	DP	TC/G	FA
1887	NY	N	3	9	.250	5.25	13	13	11	108	126	89	49	0	0	0	0	53	9	0	.170	8	27	6	0	3.2	.854
1888			2	1	.667	1.34	4	3	3	33.2	18	11	26	1	1	0	0	39	9	1	.231	1	5	1	0	1.8	.857
1889			0	0	–	7.88	2	0	0	8	11	3	3	0	0	1	0	32	8	0	.250	1	1	0	1	1.0	1.000
3 yrs.			5	10	.333	4.51	19	16	14	149.2	155	103	78	1	1	1	0	124	26	1	.210	10	33	7	1	2.6	.860

Lefty George

GEORGE, THOMAS EDWARD BL TL 6' 155 lbs.
B. Aug. 13, 1886, Pittsburgh, Pa. D. May 13, 1955, York, Pa.

Year	Team		W	L	PCT	ERA	G	GS	CG	IP	H	BB	SO	ShO	W	L	SV	AB	H	HR	BA	PO	A	E	DP	TC/G	FA
1911	STL	A	4	9	.308	4.18	27	13	6	116.1	136	51	23	1	2	1	0	44	5	0	.114	5	30	5	2	1.5	.875
1912	CLE	A	0	5	.000	4.87	11	5	2	44.1	69	18	18	0	0	0	0	14	3	0	.214	0	15	2	0	1.5	.882
1915	CIN	N	2	2	.500	3.86	5	3	2	28	24	8	11	1	1	0	0	12	4	0	.333	2	11	0	0	2.2	1.000
1918	BOS	N	1	5	.167	2.32	9	5	4	54.1	56	21	22	0	0	1	0	22	2	0	.091	0	23	0	1	2.8	1.000
4 yrs.			7	21	.250	3.85	52	26	14	243	285	98	74	2	3	2	0	92	14	0	.152	7	79	7	3	1.8	.925

Oscar Georgy

GEORGY, OSCAR JOHN BR TR 6'3½" 180 lbs.
B. Nov. 25, 1916, New Orleans, La.

Year	Team		W	L	PCT	ERA	G	GS	CG	IP	H	BB	SO	ShO	W	L	SV	AB	H	HR	BA	PO	A	E	DP	TC/G	FA
1938	NY	N	0	0	–	18.00	1	0	0	1	2	1	0	0	0	0	0	0	0	0	–	0	0	0	0	0.0	–

Dave Gerard

GERARD, DAVID FREDERICK BR TR 6'2" 205 lbs.
B. Aug. 6, 1936, New York, N. Y.

Year	Team		W	L	PCT	ERA	G	GS	CG	IP	H	BB	SO	ShO	W	L	SV	AB	H	HR	BA	PO	A	E	DP	TC/G	FA
1962	CHI	N	2	3	.400	4.91	39	0	0	58.2	67	28	30	0	2	3	3	8	3	0	.375	4	9	2	0	0.4	.867

George Gerberman

GERBERMAN, GEORGE ALOIS BR TR 6' 180 lbs.
B. Mar. 8, 1942, El Campo, Tex.

Year	Team		W	L	PCT	ERA	G	GS	CG	IP	H	BB	SO	ShO	W	L	SV	AB	H	HR	BA	PO	A	E	DP	TC/G	FA
1962	CHI	N	0	0	–	1.69	1	1	0	5.1	3	5	1	0	0	0	0	1	0	0	.000	0	1	0	0	2.0	.500

Allen Gerhardt

GERHARDT, ALLEN RUSSELL (Rusty) BB TL 5'9" 175 lbs.
B. Aug. 13, 1950, Baltimore, Md.

Year	Team		W	L	PCT	ERA	G	GS	CG	IP	H	BB	SO	ShO	W	L	SV	AB	H	HR	BA	PO	A	E	DP	TC/G	FA
1974	SD	N	2	1	.667	7.00	23	1	0	36	44	17	22	0	1	1	1	6	1	0	.167	0	4	1	1	0.2	.800

Al Gerheauser

GERHEAUSER, ALBERT (Lefty) BL TL 6'3" 190 lbs.
B. June 24, 1917, St. Louis, Mo. D. May 28, 1972, Springfield, Mo.

Year	Team		W	L	PCT	ERA	G	GS	CG	IP	H	BB	SO	ShO	W	L	SV	AB	H	HR	BA	PO	A	E	DP	TC/G	FA
1943	PHI	N	10	19	.345	3.60	38	31	11	215	222	70	92	2	1	1	0	71	8	0	.113	9	36	2	3	1.2	.957
1944			8	16	.333	4.58	30	29	10	182.2	210	65	66	2	0	0	0	65	15	1	.231	6	29	1	1	1.2	.972

Year	Team		W	L	PCT	ERA	G	GS	CG	IP	H	BB	SO	ShO	Relief Pitching W	L	SV	Batting AB	H	HR	BA	PO	A	E	DP	TC/G	FA

Al Gerheauser *continued*

Year	Team		W	L	PCT	ERA	G	GS	CG	IP	H	BB	SO	ShO	W	L	SV	AB	H	HR	BA	PO	A	E	DP	TC/G	FA
1945	PIT	N	5	10	.333	3.91	32	14	5	140.1	170	54	55	0	2	3	1	48	12	0	.250	9	33	2	0	1.4	.955
1946			2	2	.500	3.97	35	3	1	81.2	92	25	32	0	2	1	0	21	7	0	.333	3	21	0	2	0.7	1.000
1948	STL	A	0	3	.000	7.33	14	2	0	23.1	32	10	10	0	0	1	0	6	2	0	.333	1	3	0	0	0.3	1.000
5 yrs.			25	50	.333	4.13	149	79	27	643	726	224	255	4	5	6	1	211	44	1	.209	28	122	5	6	1.0	.968

Steve Gerkin

GERKIN, STEPHEN PAUL (Splinter)
B. Nov. 19, 1915, Grafton, W. Va. D. Nov. 8, 1978, Bay Pines, Fla.

BR TR 6'1" 162 lbs.

Year	Team		W	L	PCT	ERA	G	GS	CG	IP	H	BB	SO	ShO	W	L	SV	AB	H	HR	BA	PO	A	E	DP	TC/G	FA
1945	PHI	A	0	12	.000	3.62	21	12	3	102	112	27	25	0	0	3	0	34	2	0	.059	5	24	3	1	1.5	.906

Les German

GERMAN, LESTER STANLEY
B. June 1, 1869, Baltimore, Md. D. June 10, 1934, Germantown, Md.

BR TR 5'8" 165 lbs.

Year	Team		W	L	PCT	ERA	G	GS	CG	IP	H	BB	SO	ShO	W	L	SV	AB	H	HR	BA	PO	A	E	DP	TC/G	FA
1890	BAL	AA	5	11	.313	4.84	17	16	15	132	147	54	37	0	1	0	0	51	6	0	.118	3	21	4	0	1.6	.857
1893	NY	N	8	8	.500	4.14	20	18	14	152	162	70	35	0	1	1	0	74	23	0	.311	8	30	5	0	2.2	.884
1894			9	8	.529	5.78	23	15	10	134	178	66	17	0	2	2	1	57	17	0	.298	9	36	3	1	2.1	.938
1895			7	11	.389	5.96	25	18	16	178.1	243	78	36	0	0	2	0	111	29	2	.261	6	37	2	5	1.8	.956
1896	2 teams		NY N	(1G 0–0)		WAS N	(28G 2–20)																				
"	total		2	20	.091	6.43	29	20	14	169.1	249	75	20	0	1	3		71	16	1	.225	11	46	6	1	2.2	.905
1897	WAS	N	3	5	.375	5.59	15	5	4	83.2	117	33	2	0	2	1	0	44	15	0	.341	6	16	1	0	1.5	.957
6 yrs.			34	63	.351	5.49	129	92	73	849.1	1096	376	147	0	7	9	2	408	106	3	.260	43	186	21	7	1.9	.916

Ed Gerner

GERNER, EDWIN FREDERICK (Lefty)
B. July 22, 1897, Philadelphia, Pa. D. May 15, 1970, Philadelphia, Pa.

BL TL 5'8½" 175 lbs.

Year	Team		W	L	PCT	ERA	G	GS	CG	IP	H	BB	SO	ShO	W	L	SV	AB	H	HR	BA	PO	A	E	DP	TC/G	FA
1919	CIN	N	1	0	1.000	3.18	5	1	0	17	22	3	2	0	0	0	0	6	1	0	.167	1	7	0	1	1.6	1.000

Lefty Gervais

GERVAIS, LUCIEN EDWARD
B. July 6, 1890, Grover, Wis. D. Oct. 19, 1950, Los Angeles, Calif.

BL TL 5'10" 165 lbs.

Year	Team		W	L	PCT	ERA	G	GS	CG	IP	H	BB	SO	ShO	W	L	SV	AB	H	HR	BA	PO	A	E	DP	TC/G	FA
1913	BOS	N	0	1	.000	5.74	5	2	1	15.2	18	4	1	0	0	0	0	5	0	0	.000	0	4	1	0	1.0	.800

Charlie Gessner

GESSNER, CHARLES J.
B. Philadelphia, Pa. Deceased.

Year	Team		W	L	PCT	ERA	G	GS	CG	IP	H	BB	SO	ShO	W	L	SV	AB	H	HR	BA	PO	A	E	DP	TC/G	FA
1886	PHI	AA	0	1	.000	9.00	1	1	1	8	13	5	0	0	0	0	0	4	1	0	.250	0	1	2	0	3.0	.333

Al Gettel

GETTEL, ALLEN JONES
B. Sept. 17, 1917, Norfolk, Va.

BR TR 6'3½" 200 lbs.

Year	Team		W	L	PCT	ERA	G	GS	CG	IP	H	BB	SO	ShO	W	L	SV	AB	H	HR	BA	PO	A	E	DP	TC/G	FA
1945	NY	A	9	8	.529	3.90	27	17	9	154.2	141	53	67	0	0	0	3	57	16	0	.281	4	24	1	3	1.1	.966
1946			6	7	.462	2.97	26	11	5	103	89	40	54	2	3	0	0	32	4	0	.125	5	18	0	2	0.9	1.000
1947	CLE	A	11	10	.524	3.20	31	21	9	149	122	62	64	2	1	2	0	51	15	0	.294	7	28	0	1	1.1	1.000
1948	2 teams		CLE A	(5G 0–1)		CHI A	(22G 8–10)																				
"	total		8	11	.421	4.68	27	21	7	155.2	169	70	53	0	0	2	1	57	13	0	.228	5	23	0	2	1.0	1.000
1949	2 teams		CHI A	(19G 2–5)		WAS A	(16G 0–2)																				
"	total		2	7	.222	6.08	35	8	1	97.2	112	50	29	1	1	4	2	26	3	0	.115	5	18	0	1	0.7	1.000
1951	NY	N	1	2	.333	4.87	30	1	0	57.1	52	25	36	0	1	2	0	12	1	0	.083	4	13	1	0	0.6	.944
1955	STL	N	1	0	1.000	9.00	8	0	0	17	26	10	7	0	1	0	0	6	3	0	.500	1	2	2	0	0.5	.500
7 yrs.			38	45	.458	4.28	184	79	31	734.1	711	310	310	5	7	10	6	241	55	0	.228	31	125	4	9	0.9	.975

Charlie Gettig

GETTIG, CHARLES HENRY
B. 1871, Baltimore, Md. D. Apr. 11, 1935, Baltimore, Md.

5'10" 172 lbs.

Year	Team		W	L	PCT	ERA	G	GS	CG	IP	H	BB	SO	ShO	W	L	SV	AB	H	HR	BA	PO	A	E	DP	TC/G	FA
1896	NY	N	1	0	1.000	9.64	4	1	1	14	20	8	5	0	0	0	0	9	3	0	.333	0	5	0	0	1.3	1.000
1897			1	1	.500	5.21	3	2	2	19	23	9	7	0	0	0	0	75	15	0	.200	0	6	2	0	2.7	.750
1898			6	3	.667	3.83	17	8	7	115	141	39	14	0	1	1	0	196	49	0	.250	5	36	3	1	2.6	.932
1899			7	8	.467	4.43	18	15	12	128	161	54	25	0	0	0	0	97	24	0	.247	3	32	7	0	2.3	.833
4 yrs.			15	12	.556	4.50	42	26	22	276	345	110	51	0	1	1	0	*				8	79	12	1	2.4	.879

Tom Gettinger

GETTINGER, THOMAS L.
B. 1869, Md. Deceased.

BL TL 5'10" 180 lbs.

Year	Team		W	L	PCT	ERA	G	GS	CG	IP	H	BB	SO	ShO	W	L	SV	AB	H	HR	BA	PO	A	E	DP	TC/G	FA
1895	LOU	N	0	0	–	7.11	2	0	0	6.1	13	1	0	0	0	0	0	*				0	2	1	0	1.5	.667

Charlie Getzien

GETZIEN, CHARLES H. (Pretzels)
B. Feb. 14, 1864, Germany D. June 19, 1932, Chicago, Ill.

BR TR 5'10" 172 lbs.

Year	Team		W	L	PCT	ERA	G	GS	CG	IP	H	BB	SO	ShO	W	L	SV	AB	H	HR	BA	PO	A	E	DP	TC/G	FA
1884	DET	N	5	12	.294	1.95	17	17	17	147.1	118	25	107	1	0	0	0	55	6	0	.109	3	22	7	1	1.9	.781
1885			12	25	.324	3.03	37	37	37	330	360	92	110	1	0	0	0	137	29	0	.212	17	66	8	0	2.5	.912
1886			30	11	.732	3.03	43	43	42	386.2	388	85	172	1	0	0	0	165	29	0	.176	16	65	1	3	1.9	.988
1887			29	13	.690	3.73	43	42	41	366.2	373	106	135	2	1	0	0	156	29	0	.186	23	58	3	1	2.0	.964
1888			19	25	.432	3.05	46	46	45	404	411	54	202	2	0	0	0	167	41	1	.246	29	70	16	5	2.5	.861
1889	IND	N	18	22	.450	4.54	45	44	36	349	395	100	139	0	0	0	1	139	25	2	.180	22	53	11	0	1.9	.872
1890	BOS	N	23	17	.575	3.19	40	40	39	350	342	82	140	1	0	0	0	147	34	2	.231	14	63	19	2	2.4	.802
1891	2 teams		BOS N	(11G 4–5)		CLE N	(1G 0–1)																				
"	total		4	6	.400	4.22	12	10	8	98	124	27	33	0	0	0	0	45	7	1	.156	4	22	2	1	2.3	.929
1892	STL	N	5	8	.385	5.67	13	13	12	108	159	31	32	0	0	0	0	45	9	1	.200	7	18	2	0	2.1	.926
9 yrs.			145	139	.511	3.46	296	292	277	2539.2	2670	602	1070	11	1	0	1	1056	209	8	.198	135	437	69	13	2.2	.892

Rube Geyer

GEYER, JACOB BOWMAN
B. Mar. 22, 1884, Allegheny, Pa. D. Oct. 12, 1962, Wahkon, Minn.

BR TR 5'10" 170 lbs.

Year	Team		W	L	PCT	ERA	G	GS	CG	IP	H	BB	SO	ShO	W	L	SV	AB	H	HR	BA	PO	A	E	DP	TC/G	FA
1910	STL	N	0	1	.000	4.50	4	0	0	4	5	3	5	0	0	1	0	0	0	0	.000	0	1	0	1	0.3	–
1911			9	6	.600	3.27	29	11	7	148.2	141	56	46	1	3	2	0	57	13	0	.228	5	35	4	2	1.5	.909
1912			7	14	.333	3.28	41	18	6	181	191	84	61	0	4	3	0	53	11	0	.208	7	49	5	1	1.5	.918
1913			1	5	.167	5.26	30	4	2	78.2	83	38	21	0	0	2	1	22	2	0	.091	2	19	4	3	0.8	.840
4 yrs.			17	26	.395	3.67	104	33	15	412.1	420	181	133	1	7	8	1	133	26	0	.195	14	103	14	6	1.3	.893

Year	Team		W	L	PCT	ERA	G	GS	CG	IP	H	BB	SO	ShO	W	L	SV	AB	H	HR	BA	PO	A	E	DP	TC/G	FA

Tony Ghelfi
GHELFI, ANTHONY PAUL
B. Aug. 23, 1961, La Crosse, Wis.
BR TR 6'3" 185 lbs.

Year	Team	Lg	W	L	PCT	ERA	G	GS	CG	IP	H	BB	SO	ShO	W	L	SV	AB	H	HR	BA	PO	A	E	DP	TC/G	FA
1983	PHI	N	1	1	.500	3.14	3	3	0	14.1	15	6	14	0	0	0	0	4	1	0	.250	0	5	0	0	1.7	1.000

Bob Giallombardo
GIALLOMBARDO, ROBERT PAUL
B. May 20, 1937, Brooklyn, N. Y.
BL TL 6' 175 lbs.

Year	Team	Lg	W	L	PCT	ERA	G	GS	CG	IP	H	BB	SO	ShO	W	L	SV	AB	H	HR	BA	PO	A	E	DP	TC/G	FA
1958	LA	N	1	1	.500	3.76	6	5	0	26.1	29	15	14	0	0	0	0	6	1	0	.167	2	7	3	1	2.0	.750

Joe Giard
GIARD, JOSEPH OSCAR (Peco)
B. Oct. 7, 1898, Ware, Mass. D. July 10, 1956, Worcester, Mass.
BL TL 5'10½" 170 lbs.

Year	Team	Lg	W	L	PCT	ERA	G	GS	CG	IP	H	BB	SO	ShO	W	L	SV	AB	H	HR	BA	PO	A	E	DP	TC/G	FA
1925	STL	A	10	5	.667	5.04	30	21	9	160.2	179	87	43	4	0	0	0	53	3	0	.057	18	44	4	3	2.2	.939
1926			3	10	.231	7.00	22	16	2	90	113	67	18	0	0	1	0	29	8	0	.276	6	18	2	2	1.2	.923
1927	NY	A	0	0	–	8.00	16	0	0	27	38	19	10	0	0	0	0	7	2	0	.286	2	5	1	0	0.5	.875
3 yrs.			13	15	.464	5.96	68	37	11	277.2	330	173	71	4	0	1	0	89	13	0	.146	26	67	7	5	1.5	.930

Joe Gibbon
GIBBON, JOSEPH CHARLES
B. Apr. 10, 1935, Hickory, Miss.
BR TL 6'4" 210 lbs.
BB 1967-68

Year	Team	Lg	W	L	PCT	ERA	G	GS	CG	IP	H	BB	SO	ShO	W	L	SV	AB	H	HR	BA	PO	A	E	DP	TC/G	FA
1960	PIT	N	4	2	.667	4.03	27	9	0	80.1	87	31	60	0	3	0	0	19	4	0	.211	2	15	1	1	0.7	.944
1961			13	10	.565	3.32	30	29	7	195.1	185	57	145	3	0	0	0	59	8	0	.136	3	35	0	2	1.3	1.000
1962			3	4	.429	3.63	19	8	0	57	53	24	26	0	1	1	0	17	3	0	.176	2	16	2	1	1.1	.900
1963			5	12	.294	3.30	37	22	5	147.1	147	54	110	0	1	1	1	43	4	0	.093	7	30	3	4	1.1	.925
1964			10	7	.588	3.68	28	24	3	146.2	145	54	97	0	1	0	0	47	12	0	.255	5	34	6	2	1.6	.867
1965			4	9	.308	4.51	31	15	1	105.2	85	34	63	0	3	1	1	26	3	0	.115	3	23	1	0	0.9	.963
1966	SF	N	4	6	.400	3.67	37	10	1	81	86	16	48	0	1	3	1	15	3	0	.200	3	21	2	1	0.7	.923
1967			6	2	.750	3.07	28	10	3	82	65	33	63	1	1	0	1	24	1	0	.042	5	23	0	0	1.0	1.000
1968			1	2	.333	1.58	27	0	0	40	33	19	22	0	1	2	1	1	0	0	.000	2	7	0	0	0.3	1.000
1969	2 teams	SF N (16G 1–3)								PIT N (35G 5–1)																	
"	total		6	4	.600	2.40	51	0	0	71.1	53	30	44	0	6	4	11	8	0	0	.000	0	22	2	2	0.5	.917
1970	PIT	N	0	1	.000	4.83	41	0	0	41	44	24	26	0	0	1	5	3	0	0	.000	3	7	1	0	0.3	.909
1971	CIN	N	5	6	.455	2.95	50	0	0	64	54	32	34	0	5	6	11	1	0	0	.000	1	18	2	1	0.4	.905
1972	2 teams	CIN N (2G 0–0)								HOU N (9G 0–0)																	
"	total		0	0	–	11.74	11	0	0	7.2	16	6	5	0	0	0	0				–	2	3	0	0	0.5	1.000
13 yrs.			61	65	.484	3.52	419	127	20	1119.1	1053	414	743	4	23	19	32	263	38	0	.144	38	254	20	14	0.7	.936

LEAGUE CHAMPIONSHIP SERIES

Year	Team	Lg	W	L	PCT	ERA	G	GS	CG	IP	H	BB	SO	ShO	W	L	SV	AB	H	HR	BA	PO	A	E	DP	TC/G	FA
1970	PIT	N	0	0	–	0.00	2	0	0	.1	1	0	1	0	0	0	0	0	0	0	–	0	0	0	0	0.0	–

WORLD SERIES

Year	Team	Lg	W	L	PCT	ERA	G	GS	CG	IP	H	BB	SO	ShO	W	L	SV	AB	H	HR	BA	PO	A	E	DP	TC/G	FA
1960	PIT	N	0	0	–	9.00	2	0	0	3	4	1	2	0	0	0	0	0	0	0	–	1	0	0	0	0.5	1.000

Bob Gibson
GIBSON, ROBERT (Hoot)
B. Nov. 9, 1935, Omaha, Neb.
Hall of Fame 1981.
BR TR 6'1" 189 lbs.

Year	Team	Lg	W	L	PCT	ERA	G	GS	CG	IP	H	BB	SO	ShO	W	L	SV	AB	H	HR	BA	PO	A	E	DP	TC/G	FA
1959	STL	N	3	5	.375	3.33	13	9	2	75.2	77	39	48	1	1	0	0	26	3	0	.115	6	10	2	2	1.4	.889
1960			3	6	.333	5.61	27	12	2	86.2	97	48	69	0	1	0	0	28	5	0	.179	7	14	0	3	0.8	1.000
1961			13	12	.520	3.24	35	27	10	211.1	186	119	166	2	0	1	1	66	13	1	.197	14	35	2	4	1.5	.961
1962			15	13	.536	2.85	32	30	15	233.2	174	95	208	5	1	0	1	76	20	2	.263	18	35	3	6	1.8	.946
1963			18	9	.667	3.39	36	33	14	254.2	224	96	204	2	1	0	0	87	18	3	.207	27	28	5	0	1.7	.917
1964			19	12	.613	3.01	40	36	17	287.1	250	86	245	2	1	1	1	96	15	0	.156	24	36	6	4	1.7	.909
1965			20	12	.625	3.07	38	36	20	299	243	103	270	6	0	0	1	104	25	5	.240	27	33	3	1	1.7	.952
1966			21	12	.636	2.44	35	35	20	280.1	210	78	225	5	0	0	0	100	20	1	.200	26	28	2	4	1.6	.964
1967			13	7	.650	2.98	24	24	10	175.1	151	40	147	2	0	0	0	60	8	0	.133	19	23	0	0	1.8	1.000
1968			22	9	.710	1.12	34	34	28	304.2	198	62	268	13	0	0	0	94	16	0	.170	21	28	1	2	1.5	.980
1969			20	13	.606	2.18	35	35	28	314	251	95	269	4	0	0	0	118	29	1	.246	21	32	3	5	1.6	.946
1970			23	7	.767	3.12	34	34	23	294	262	88	274	3	0	0	0	109	33	2	.303	22	34	4	3	1.7	.931
1971			16	13	.552	3.04	31	31	20	246	215	76	185	5	0	0	0	87	15	2	.172	10	39	3	1	1.7	.942
1972			19	11	.633	2.46	34	34	23	278	226	88	208	4	0	0	0	103	20	5	.194	12	46	1	3	1.7	.983
1973			12	10	.545	2.77	25	25	13	195	159	57	142	1	0	0	0	65	12	2	.185	11	24	2	2	1.5	.946
1974			11	13	.458	3.83	33	33	9	240	236	104	129	1	0	0	0	81	17	0	.210	20	26	2	4	1.5	.958
1975			3	10	.231	5.04	22	14	1	109	120	62	60	0	1	2	2	28	5	0	.179	6	15	3	2	1.1	.875
17 yrs.			251	174	.591	2.91	528	482	255	3884.2	3279	1336	3117	56	6	4	6	1328	274	24	.206	291	484	42	46	1.5	.949
													10th														

WORLD SERIES

Year	Team	Lg	W	L	PCT	ERA	G	GS	CG	IP	H	BB	SO	ShO	W	L	SV	AB	H	HR	BA	PO	A	E	DP	TC/G	FA
1964	STL	N	2	1	.667	3.00	3	3	2	27	23	8	31	0	0	0	0	9	2	0	.222	1	2	0	0	1.0	1.000
1967			3	0	1.000	1.00	3	3	3	27	14	5	26	1	0	0	0	11	1	1	.091	2	3	0	0	1.7	1.000
1968			2	1	.667	1.67	3	3	3	27	18	4	35	0	0	0	0	8	1	1	.125	2	0	0	0	0.7	1.000
3 yrs.			7	2	.778	1.89	9	9	8	81	55	17	92	2	0	0	0	28	4	2	.143	5	5	0	0	1.1	1.000
			2nd				6th	3rd			6th		9th			2nd	4th										

Bob Gibson
GIBSON, ROBERT LOUIS
B. June 19, 1957, Philadelphia, Pa.
BR TR 6' 195 lbs.

Year	Team	Lg	W	L	PCT	ERA	G	GS	CG	IP	H	BB	SO	ShO	W	L	SV	AB	H	HR	BA	PO	A	E	DP	TC/G	FA
1983	MIL	A	3	4	.429	3.90	27	7	0	80.2	71	46	46	0	1	2	2	0	0	0	–	6	8	2	0	0.6	.875
1984			2	5	.286	4.96	18	9	1	69	61	47	54	1	0	0	0	0	0	0	–	11	7	0	0	1.0	1.000
1985			6	7	.462	3.90	41	1	0	92.1	86	49	53	0	6	6	11	0	0	0	–	8	10	0	2	0.4	1.000
1986			1	2	.333	4.73	11	1	0	26.2	23	23	11	0	1	1	0	0	0	0	–	4	1	0	0	0.5	1.000
1987	NY	N	0	0	–	0.00	1	0	0	1	0	1	2	0	0	0	0	0	0	0	–	1	0	0	0	1.0	1.000
5 yrs.			12	18	.400	4.24	98	18	1	269.2	241	166	166	1	8	9	13	0	0	0	–	30	26	2	2	0.6	.966

Bob Gibson
GIBSON, ROBERT MURRAY
B. Aug. 20, 1869, Duncansville, Pa. D. Dec. 19, 1949, Pittsburgh, Pa.
BR TR 6'3" 185 lbs.

Year	Team	W	L	PCT	ERA	G	GS	CG	IP	H	BB	SO	ShO	Relief Pitching W	L	SV	Batting AB	H	HR	BA	PO	A	E	DP	TC/G	FA

Bob Gibson *continued*

Year	Team	W	L	PCT	ERA	G	GS	CG	IP	H	BB	SO	ShO	W	L	SV	AB	H	HR	BA	PO	A	E	DP	TC/G	FA
1890	2 teams	CHI N (1G 1-0)				PIT N	(3G 0-3)																			
"	total	1	3	.250	9.86	4	4	3	21	30	25	4	0	0	0	0	17	3	0	.176	0	4	3	0	1.8	.571

Norwood Gibson

GIBSON, NORWOOD RINGOLD
B. Mar. 11, 1877, Peoria, Ill. D. July 7, 1959, Peoria, Ill.
BR TR 5'10" 165 lbs.

Year	Team	W	L	PCT	ERA	G	GS	CG	IP	H	BB	SO	ShO	W	L	SV	AB	H	HR	BA	PO	A	E	DP	TC/G	FA
1903	BOS A	13	9	.591	3.19	24	21	17	183.1	166	65	76	2	1	0	0	64	17	0	.266	10	55	4	2	2.9	.942
1904		17	14	.548	2.21	33	32	29	273	216	81	112	1	0	0	0	92	6	0	.065	5	83	6	2	2.8	.936
1905		4	7	.364	3.69	23	17	9	134	118	55	67	0	0	1	0	45	4	0	.089	11	28	3	2	1.8	.929
1906		0	2	.000	5.30	5	2	1	18.2	25	7	3	0	0	0	0	5	1	0	.200	0	5	0	0	1.0	1.000
4 yrs.		34	32	.515	2.93	85	72	56	609	525	208	258	3	1	1	0	206	28	0	.136	26	171	13	6	2.5	.938

Paul Gibson

GIBSON, PAUL MARSHALL
B. Jan. 4, 1960, Southampton, N. Y.
BR TL 6' 165 lbs.

Year	Team	W	L	PCT	ERA	G	GS	CG	IP	H	BB	SO	ShO	W	L	SV	AB	H	HR	BA	PO	A	E	DP	TC/G	FA
1988	DET A	4	2	.667	2.93	40	1	0	92	83	34	50	0	3	2	0	0	0	0	–	7	11	0	2	0.5	1.000
1989		4	8	.333	4.64	45	13	0	132	129	57	77	0	3	3	0	0	0	0	–	6	20	2	0	0.6	.929
2 yrs.		8	10	.444	3.94	85	14	0	224	212	91	127	0	6	5	0	0	0	0	–	13	31	2	2	0.5	.957

Sam Gibson

GIBSON, SAMUEL BRAXTON
B. Aug. 5, 1899, King, N. C. D. Jan. 31, 1983, High Point, N. C.
BL TR 6'2" 198 lbs.

Year	Team	W	L	PCT	ERA	G	GS	CG	IP	H	BB	SO	ShO	W	L	SV	AB	H	HR	BA	PO	A	E	DP	TC/G	FA
1926	DET A	12	9	.571	3.48	35	24	16	196.1	199	75	61	2	1	0	2	72	18	0	.250	4	50	1	3	1.6	.982
1927		11	12	.478	3.69	33	26	11	190.1	201	86	76	0	0	2	0	66	14	0	.212	7	38	3	0	1.5	.938
1928		5	8	.385	5.42	20	18	5	119.2	155	52	29	1	0	0	0	42	12	0	.286	7	24	1	2	1.6	.969
1930	NY A	0	1	.000	15.00	2	2	0	6	14	6	3	0	0	0	0	3	1	0	.333	1	1	0	0	1.0	1.000
1932	NY N	4	8	.333	4.85	41	5	1	81.2	107	30	39	1	2	5	3	19	5	0	.263	2	13	0	0	0.4	1.000
5 yrs.		32	38	.457	4.24	131	75	33	594	676	249	208	4	3	7	5	202	50	0	.248	21	126	5	5	1.2	.967

George Gick

GICK, GEORGE EDWARD
B. Oct. 18, 1915, Dunnington, Ind.
BB TR 6' 190 lbs.

Year	Team	W	L	PCT	ERA	G	GS	CG	IP	H	BB	SO	ShO	W	L	SV	AB	H	HR	BA	PO	A	E	DP	TC/G	FA
1937	CHI A	0	0	–	0.00	1	0	0	2	0	0	1	0	0	0	1	0	0	0	–	0	0	0	0	0.0	–
1938		0	0	–	0.00	1	0	0	1	0	0	1	0	0	0	0	0	0	0	–	0	0	0	0	0.0	–
2 yrs.		0	0	–	0.00	2	0	0	3	0	0	2	0	0	0	1	0	0	0	–	0	0	0	0	0.0	–

Brett Gideon

GIDEON, BYRON BRETT
B. Aug. 8, 1963, Ozona, Tex.
BR TR 6'2" 200 lbs.

Year	Team	W	L	PCT	ERA	G	GS	CG	IP	H	BB	SO	ShO	W	L	SV	AB	H	HR	BA	PO	A	E	DP	TC/G	FA
1987	PIT N	1	5	.167	4.66	29	0	0	36.2	34	10	31	0	1	5	3	1	1	0	1.000	1	5	0	0	0.2	1.000
1989	MON N	0	0	–	1.93	4	0	0	4.2	5	5	2	0	0	0	0	0	0	0	–	0	0	0	0	0.0	–
2 yrs.		1	5	.167	4.35	33	0	0	41.1	39	15	33	0	1	5	3	1	1	0	1.000	1	5	0	0	0.2	1.000

Jim Gideon

GIDEON, JAMES LESLIE
B. Sept. 26, 1953, Taylor, Tex.
BR TR 6'3" 190 lbs.

Year	Team	W	L	PCT	ERA	G	GS	CG	IP	H	BB	SO	ShO	W	L	SV	AB	H	HR	BA	PO	A	E	DP	TC/G	FA
1975	TEX A	0	0	–	7.94	1	1	0	5.2	7	5	2	0	0	0	0	0	0	0	–	0	0	0	0	0.0	–

Floyd Giebell

GIEBELL, FLOYD GEORGE
B. Dec. 10, 1909, Pennsboro, W. Va.
BL TR 6'2½" 172 lbs.

Year	Team	W	L	PCT	ERA	G	GS	CG	IP	H	BB	SO	ShO	W	L	SV	AB	H	HR	BA	PO	A	E	DP	TC/G	FA
1939	DET A	1	1	.500	2.93	9	0	0	15.1	19	12	9	0	1	1	0	2	0	0	.000	1	1	1	0	0.3	.667
1940		2	0	1.000	1.00	2	2	2	18	14	4	11	1	0	0	0	6	0	0	.000	2	2	0	0	2.0	1.000
1941		0	0	–	6.03	17	2	0	34.1	45	26	10	0	0	0	0	6	2	0	.333	1	7	1	0	0.5	.889
3 yrs.		3	1	.750	3.99	28	4	2	67.2	78	42	30	1	1	1	0	14	2	0	.143	4	10	2	0	0.6	.875

Paul Giel

GIEL, PAUL ROBERT
B. Sept. 29, 1932, Winona, Minn.
BR TR 5'11" 185 lbs.

Year	Team	W	L	PCT	ERA	G	GS	CG	IP	H	BB	SO	ShO	W	L	SV	AB	H	HR	BA	PO	A	E	DP	TC/G	FA
1954	NY N	0	0	–	8.31	6	0	0	4.1	8	2	4	0	0	0	0	0	0	0	–	0	0	0	0	0.0	–
1955		4	4	.500	3.39	34	2	0	82.1	70	50	47	0	4	3	0	19	1	0	.053	4	10	0	1	0.4	1.000
1958	SF N	4	5	.444	4.70	29	9	0	92	89	55	55	0	2	0	0	27	2	0	.074	8	18	0	2	0.9	1.000
1959	PIT N	0	0	–	14.09	4	0	0	7.2	17	6	3	0	0	0	0	0	0	0	–	0	2	0	0	0.5	1.000
1960		2	0	1.000	5.73	16	0	0	33	35	15	21	0	2	0	0	7	0	0	.000	2	3	1	0	0.4	.833
1961	2 teams	MIN A	(12G 1-0)				KC A	(1G 0-0)																		
"	total	1	0	1.000	12.00	13	0	0	21	30	20	15	0	1	0	0	2	1	0	.500	1	5	2	0	0.6	.750
6 yrs.		11	9	.550	5.39	102	11	0	240.1	249	148	145	0	9	3	0	55	4	0	.073	15	38	3	3	0.5	.946

Bob Giggie

GIGGIE, ROBERT THOMAS
B. Aug. 13, 1933, Dorchester, Mass.
BR TR 6'1" 200 lbs.

Year	Team	W	L	PCT	ERA	G	GS	CG	IP	H	BB	SO	ShO	W	L	SV	AB	H	HR	BA	PO	A	E	DP	TC/G	FA
1959	MIL N	1	0	1.000	4.05	13	0	0	20	24	10	15	0	1	0	1	1	0	0	.000	0	8	0	0	0.6	1.000
1960	2 teams	MIL N	(3G 0-0)				KC A	(10G 1-0)																		
"	total	1	0	1.000	5.48	13	0	0	23	29	19	13	0	1	0	0	2	0	0	.000	1	4	0	0	0.4	1.000
1962	KC A	1	1	.500	6.28	4	2	0	14.1	17	3	4	0	0	0	0	4	0	0	.000	1	0	0	0	0.3	1.000
3 yrs.		3	1	.750	5.18	30	2	0	57.1	70	32	32	0	2	0	1	7	0	0	.000	2	12	0	0	0.5	1.000

Bill Gilbert

GILBERT, WILMER M.
B. May 12, 1870, Havre de Grace, Md. Deceased.
6' 180 lbs.

Year	Team	W	L	PCT	ERA	G	GS	CG	IP	H	BB	SO	ShO	W	L	SV	AB	H	HR	BA	PO	A	E	DP	TC/G	FA
1892	BAL N	0	0	.000	5.79	2	1	1	14	14	17	5	0	0	0	0	6	2	0	.333	0	0	1	0	0.5	–

Joe Gilbert

GILBERT, JOE DENNIS
B. Apr. 20, 1952, Jasper, Tex.
BR TL 6'1" 167 lbs.

Year	Team	W	L	PCT	ERA	G	GS	CG	IP	H	BB	SO	ShO	W	L	SV	AB	H	HR	BA	PO	A	E	DP	TC/G	FA
1972	MON N	0	1	.000	8.45	22	0	0	33	41	18	25	0	0	1	0	3	0	0	.000	0	3	0	0	0.1	1.000
1973		1	2	.333	4.97	21	0	0	29	30	19	17	0	1	2	1	2	0	0	.000	1	5	0	0	0.3	1.000
2 yrs.		1	3	.250	6.82	43	0	0	62	71	37	42	0	1	3	1	5	0	0	.000	1	8	0	0	0.2	1.000

Year	Team		W	L	PCT	ERA	G	GS	CG	IP	H	BB	SO	ShO	Relief Pitching W	L	SV	Batting AB	H	HR	BA	PO	A	E	DP	TC/G	FA

Bill Gilbreth

GILBRETH, WILLIAM FREEMAN
B. Sept. 3, 1947, Abilene, Tex.   BL TL 6'   180 lbs.

1971	DET	A	2	1	.667	4.80	9	5	2	30	28	21	14	0	0	0	0	11	2	0	.182	1	7	0	0	0.9	1.000
1972			0	0	–	16.20	2	0	0	5	10	4	2	0	0	0	0	1	0	0	.000	0	1	0	0	0.5	1.000
1974	CAL	A	0	0	–	13.50	3	0	0	1.1	2	1	0	0	0	0	0	0	0	0	–	0	0	0	0	0.0	–
3 yrs.			2	1	.667	6.69	14	5	2	36.1	40	26	16	0	0	0	0	12	2	0	.167	1	8	0	0	0.6	1.000

Bob Gilks

GILKS, ROBERT JAMES
B. July 2, 1864, Cincinnati, Ohio. D. Aug. 21, 1944, Brunswick, Ga.   BR TR 5'8"   178 lbs.

1887	CLE	AA	7	5	.583	3.08	13	13	12	108	104	42	28	1	0	0	0	83	26	0	.313	8	29	5	2	3.2	.881
1888			0	2	.000	8.14	4	4	2	21	26	8	3	0	0	0	1	484	111	1	.229	2	3	0	0	1.3	1.000
1890	CLE	N	2	2	.500	4.26	4	3	3	31.2	34	9	5	0	1	0	0	544	116	0	.213	2	7	0	0	2.3	1.000
3 yrs.			9	9	.500	3.98	21	18	17	160.2	164	59	36	1	1	0	1	*				12	39	5	2	2.7	.911

Ed Gill

GILL, EDWARD JAMES
B. Aug. 7, 1896, Somerville, Mass.   BL TR 5'10"   165 lbs.

| 1919 | WAS | A | 1 | 1 | .500 | 4.82 | 16 | 2 | 0 | 37.1 | 38 | 21 | 7 | 0 | 0 | 1 | 0 | 7 | 0 | 0 | .000 | 1 | 8 | 1 | 0 | 0.6 | .900 |

George Gill

GILL, GEORGE LLOYD
B. Feb. 13, 1909, Catchings, Miss.   BR TR 6'1"   185 lbs.

1937	DET	A	11	4	.733	4.51	31	10	4	127.2	146	42	40	1	7	1	1	50	7	0	.140	3	32	2	3	1.2	.946
1938			12	9	.571	4.12	24	23	13	164	195	50	30	1	0	0	0	57	6	0	.105	3	32	1	10	1.5	.972
1939	2 teams	DET A (3G 0–1)				STL A (27G 1–12)																					
"	total		1	13	.071	7.21	30	12	5	103.2	153	37	25	0	0	4	0	28	4	0	.143	2	15	2	2	0.6	.895
3 yrs.			24	26	.480	5.05	85	45	22	395.1	494	129	95	2	7	5	1	135	17	0	.126	8	79	5	15	1.1	.946

Haddie Gill

GILL, HAROLD EDWARD
B. Jan. 23, 1899, Brockton, Mass. D. Aug. 1, 1932, Brockton, Mass.   BL TL 5'11"   165 lbs.

| 1923 | CIN | N | 0 | 0 | – | 0.00 | 1 | 0 | 0 | 1 | 1 | 1 | 1 | 0 | 0 | 0 | 0 | 0 | 0 | 0 | – | 0 | 0 | 0 | 0 | 0.0 | – |

Claral Gillenwater

GILLENWATER, CLARAL LEWIS
B. May 20, 1900, Sims, Ind. D. Feb. 26, 1978, Bradenton, Fla.   BR TR 6'   187 lbs.

| 1923 | CHI | A | 1 | 3 | .250 | 5.48 | 5 | 3 | 1 | 21.1 | 28 | 6 | 2 | 1 | 1 | 1 | 0 | 6 | 0 | 0 | .000 | 0 | 7 | 1 | 0 | 1.6 | .875 |

Bob Gillespie

GILLESPIE, ROBERT WILLIAM (Bunch)
B. Oct. 8, 1918, Columbus, Ohio.   BR TR 6'4"   187 lbs.

1944	DET	A	0	1	.000	6.55	7	0	0	11	7	12	4	0	0	0	0	2	0	0	.000	0	3	0	0	0.4	1.000
1947	CHI	A	5	8	.385	4.73	25	17	1	118	133	53	36	0	0	0	0	33	2	0	.061	4	35	1	0	1.6	.975
1948			0	4	.000	5.13	25	6	1	72	81	33	19	0	0	0	0	16	0	0	.000	3	13	0	0	0.6	1.000
1950	BOS	A	0	0	–	20.25	1	0	0	1.1	2	4	0	0	0	0	0	0	0	0	–	0	0	0	0	0.0	–
4 yrs.			5	13	.278	5.07	58	23	2	202.1	223	102	59	0	0	0	1	51	2	0	.039	7	51	1	0	1.0	.983

John Gillespie

GILLESPIE, JOHN PATRICK (Silent John)
B. Feb. 25, 1900, Oakland, Calif. D. Feb. 15, 1954, Vallejo, Calif.   BR TR 5'11½" 172 lbs.

| 1922 | CIN | N | 3 | 3 | .500 | 4.52 | 31 | 4 | 1 | 77.2 | 84 | 29 | 21 | 0 | 2 | 2 | 0 | 15 | 2 | 0 | .133 | 4 | 20 | 0 | 0 | 0.8 | 1.000 |

Paul Gilliford

GILLIFORD, PAUL GANT (Gorilla)
B. Jan. 12, 1945, Bryn Mawr, Pa.   BR TL 5'11"   210 lbs.

| 1967 | BAL | A | 0 | 0 | – | 12.00 | 2 | 0 | 0 | 3 | 6 | 1 | 2 | 0 | 0 | 0 | 0 | 0 | 0 | 0 | – | 0 | 2 | 0 | 0 | 1.0 | 1.000 |

Jack Gilligan

GILLIGAN, JOHN PATRICK
B. Oct. 18, 1885, Chicago, Ill.   D. Nov. 19, 1980, Modesto, Calif.   BB TR 6'   190 lbs.

1909	STL	A	1	2	.333	5.48	3	3	3	23	28	9	4	0	0	0	0	9	1	0	.111	0	5	0	0	1.7	1.000
1910			0	3	.000	3.66	9	5	2	39.1	37	28	10	0	0	0	1	15	3	0	.200	1	17	5	1	2.6	.783
2 yrs.			1	5	.167	4.33	12	8	5	62.1	65	37	14	0	0	0	1	24	4	0	.167	1	22	5	1	2.3	.821

George Gillpatrick

GILLPATRICK, GEORGE F.
B. Feb. 28, 1875, Holden, Mo.   D. Dec. 15, 1941, Kansas City, Mo.

| 1898 | STL | N | 0 | 2 | .000 | 6.94 | 7 | 3 | 1 | 35 | 42 | 19 | 12 | 0 | 0 | 0 | 0 | 16 | 2 | 0 | .125 | 2 | 6 | 4 | 0 | 1.7 | .667 |

Frank Gilmore

GILMORE, FRANK T.
B. Apr. 27, 1864, Webster, Mass.   D. July 21, 1929, Hartford, Conn.   BR

1886	WAS	N	4	4	.500	2.52	9	9	9	75	57	22	75	1	0	0	0	29	0	0	.000	2	8	0	0	1.1	1.000
1887			7	20	.259	3.87	28	27	27	234.2	247	92	114	1	0	0	0	93	6	0	.065	3	28	2	0	1.2	.939
1888			1	9	.100	6.59	12	11	10	95.2	131	29	23	0	0	0	0	41	1	0	.024	2	12	4	1	1.5	.778
3 yrs.			12	33	.267	4.26	49	47	46	405.1	435	143	212	2	0	0	0	163	7	0	.043	7	48	6	1	1.2	.902

Len Gilmore

GILMORE, LEONARD PRESTON (Meow)
B. Nov. 3, 1917, Clinton, Ind.   BR TR 6'3"   175 lbs.

| 1944 | PIT | N | 0 | 1 | .000 | 7.88 | 1 | 1 | 1 | 8 | 13 | 0 | 0 | 0 | 0 | 0 | 0 | 2 | 0 | 0 | .000 | 2 | 4 | 1 | 0 | 7.0 | .857 |

John Gilroy

GILROY, JOHN M.
B. Oct. 26, 1869, Washington, D. C.   D. Aug. 4, 1897, Norfolk, Va.

1895	WAS	N	1	4	.200	6.53	8	4	2	41.1	63	24	2	0	0	0	0	29	7	0	.241	6	10	1	0	2.1	.941
1896			0	0	–	0.00	1	0	0	2	0	1	0	0	0	0	0	1	0	0	.000	1	0	0	0	1.0	1.000
2 yrs.			1	4	.200	6.23	9	4	2	43.1	63	25	2	0	0	0	0	30	7	0	.233	7	10	1	0	2.0	.944

Year	Team	W	L	PCT	ERA	G	GS	CG	IP	H	BB	SO	ShO	Relief Pitching W	L	SV	Batting AB	H	HR	BA	PO	A	E	DP	TC/G	FA

Hal Gilson

GILSON, HAROLD (Lefty)
B. Feb. 9, 1942, Los Angeles, Calif.
BR TL 6'5" 195 lbs.

Year	Team	W	L	PCT	ERA	G	GS	CG	IP	H	BB	SO	ShO	W	L	SV	AB	H	HR	BA	PO	A	E	DP	TC/G	FA
1968	2 teams	STL N	(13G 0–2)		HOU N	(2G 0–0)																				
"	total	0	2	.000	4.97	15	0	0	25.1	34	12	20	0	0	2	2	4	0	0	.000	1	1	0	0	0.1	1.000

Billy Ging

GING, WILLIAM JOSEPH
B. Nov. 7, 1872, Elmira, N. Y.   D. Sept. 14, 1950, Elmira, N. Y.
BR TR 5'10" 170 lbs.

Year	Team	W	L	PCT	ERA	G	GS	CG	IP	H	BB	SO	ShO	W	L	SV	AB	H	HR	BA	PO	A	E	DP	TC/G	FA
1899	BOS N	1	0	1.000	1.13	1	1	1	8	5	5	2	0	0	0	0	2	0	0	.000	0	0	0	0	0.0	–

Joe Gingras

GINGRAS, JOSEPH JOHN
B. Jan. 10, 1893, New York, N. Y.   D. Sept. 6, 1947, Jersey City, N. J.
BR TR 6'2" 188 lbs.

Year	Team	W	L	PCT	ERA	G	GS	CG	IP	H	BB	SO	ShO	W	L	SV	AB	H	HR	BA	PO	A	E	DP	TC/G	FA
1915	KC F	0	0	–	6.75	2	0	0	4	6	1	2	0	0	0	0	1	0	0	.000	0	1	0	0	0.5	1.000

Charlie Girard

GIRARD, CHARLES AUGUST
B. Dec. 16, 1884, Brooklyn, N. Y.   D. Aug. 6, 1936, Brooklyn, N. Y.
BR TR 5'10" 175 lbs.

Year	Team	W	L	PCT	ERA	G	GS	CG	IP	H	BB	SO	ShO	W	L	SV	AB	H	HR	BA	PO	A	E	DP	TC/G	FA
1910	PHI N	0	2	.000	6.41	7	1	0	26.2	33	12	11	0	0	1	0	8	1	0	.125	2	2	2	0	0.9	.667

Dave Giusti

GIUSTI, DAVID JOHN
B. Nov. 27, 1939, Seneca Falls, N. Y.
BR TR 5'11" 190 lbs.

Year	Team	W	L	PCT	ERA	G	GS	CG	IP	H	BB	SO	ShO	W	L	SV	AB	H	HR	BA	PO	A	E	DP	TC/G	FA
1962	HOU N	2	3	.400	5.62	22	5	0	73.2	82	30	43	0	2	0	0	24	7	0	.292	8	13	1	2	1.0	.955
1964		0	0	–	3.16	8	0	0	25.2	24	8	16	0	0	0	0	7	2	0	.286	6	7	1	0	1.8	.929
1965		8	7	.533	4.32	38	13	4	131.1	132	46	92	1	4	3	3	35	6	1	.171	17	24	1	0	1.1	.976
1966		15	14	.517	4.20	34	33	9	210	215	54	131	4	0	0	0	74	17	0	.230	18	24	1	0	1.3	.977
1967		11	15	.423	4.18	37	33	8	221.2	231	58	157	1	0	1	1	84	13	3	.155	14	26	1	0	1.1	.976
1968		11	14	.440	3.19	37	34	12	251	226	67	186	2	0	0	1	82	15	0	.183	20	51	2	3	2.0	.973
1969	STL N	3	7	.300	3.60	22	12	0	100	96	37	62	0	1	0	0	25	5	0	.200	5	20	1	1	1.2	.962
1970	PIT N	9	3	.750	3.06	66	1	0	103	98	39	85	0	9	3	26	16	3	0	.188	5	14	0	1	0.3	1.000
1971		5	6	.455	2.93	58	0	0	86	79	31	55	0	5	6	30	17	1	0	.059	6	7	1	1	0.2	.929
1972		7	4	.636	1.93	54	0	0	74.2	59	20	54	0	7	4	22	10	0	0	.000	1	15	1	0	0.3	.941
1973		9	2	.818	2.37	67	0	0	98.2	89	37	64	0	9	2	20	13	4	0	.308	10	4	1	0	0.3	.933
1974		7	5	.583	3.31	64	2	0	106	101	40	53	0	6	5	12	9	1	0	.111	8	21	0	1	0.5	1.000
1975		5	4	.556	2.93	61	0	0	92	79	42	38	0	5	4	17	10	3	0	.300	4	17	3	0	0.4	.875
1976		5	4	.556	4.32	40	0	0	58.1	59	27	24	0	5	4	6	4	0	0	.000	4	11	1	0	0.4	.938
1977	2 teams	CHI N	(20G 0–2)		OAK A	(40G 3–3)																				
"	total	3	5	.375	3.92	60	0	0	85	84	34	43	0	3	5	7	2	0	0	.000	8	10	0	2	0.3	1.000
15 yrs.		100	93	.518	3.60	668	133	35	1717	1654	570	1103	9	55	37	145	412	77	4	.187	134	264	15	11	0.6	.964

LEAGUE CHAMPIONSHIP SERIES

Year	Team	W	L	PCT	ERA	G	GS	CG	IP	H	BB	SO	ShO	W	L	SV	AB	H	HR	BA	PO	A	E	DP	TC/G	FA
1970	PIT N	0	0	–	3.86	2	0	0	2.1	3	1	1	0	0	0	0	0	0	0	–	1	0	0	0	0.5	1.000
1971		0	0	–	0.00	4	0	0	5.1	1	2	3	0	0	0	3	1	0	0	.000	0	1	0	0	0.3	1.000
1972		0	1	.000	6.75	3	0	0	2.2	5	0	3	0	0	1	1	1	0	0	.000	1	0	0	0	0.3	1.000
1974		0	1	.000	21.60	3	0	0	3.1	13	5	1	0	0	1	0	0	0	0	–	1	2	0	0	1.0	1.000
1975		0	0	–	0.00	1	0	0	1.1	0	0	1	0	0	0	0	0	0	0	–	0	0	0	0	0.0	–
5 yrs.		0	2	.000	6.60	13	0	0	15	22	8	9	0	0	2	4	2	0	0	.000	3	3	0	0	0.5	1.000

WORLD SERIES

Year	Team	W	L	PCT	ERA	G	GS	CG	IP	H	BB	SO	ShO	W	L	SV	AB	H	HR	BA	PO	A	E	DP	TC/G	FA
1971	PIT N	0	0	–	0.00	3	0	0	5.1	3	2	4	0	0	0	1	0	0	0	–	0	0	0	0	0.0	–

Dan Gladden

GLADDEN, CLINTON DANIEL III
B. July 7, 1957, San Jose, Calif.
BR TR 5'11" 175 lbs.

Year	Team	W	L	PCT	ERA	G	GS	CG	IP	H	BB	SO	ShO	W	L	SV	AB	H	HR	BA	PO	A	E	DP	TC/G	FA
1988	MIN A	0	0	–	0.00	1	0	0	1	0	0	0	0	0	0	0	576	155	11	.269	0	0	0	0	0.0	–
1989		0	0	–	9.00	1	0	0	1	2	1	0	0	0	0	0	461	136	8	.295	0	0	0	0	0.0	–
2 yrs.		0	0	–	4.50	2	0	0	2	2	1	0	0	0	0	0	*				0	0	0	0	0.0	–

Fred Gladding

GLADDING, FRED EARL
B. June 28, 1936, Flat Rock, Mich.
BL TR 6'1" 220 lbs.

Year	Team	W	L	PCT	ERA	G	GS	CG	IP	H	BB	SO	ShO	W	L	SV	AB	H	HR	BA	PO	A	E	DP	TC/G	FA
1961	DET A	1	0	1.000	3.31	8	0	0	16.1	18	11	11	0	1	0	0	3	0	0	.000	1	1	0	0	0.4	.667
1962		0	0	–	0.00	6	0	0	5	3	2	4	0	0	0	0	0	0	0	–	0	2	0	0	0.3	1.000
1963		1	1	.500	1.98	22	0	0	27.1	19	14	24	0	1	1	1	1	0	0	.000	1	6	0	0	0.3	1.000
1964		7	4	.636	3.07	42	0	0	67.1	57	27	59	0	7	4	7	9	0	0	.000	3	9	0	0	0.3	1.000
1965		6	2	.750	2.83	46	0	0	70	63	29	43	0	6	2	5	7	0	0	.000	2	9	1	0	0.3	.917
1966		5	1	1.000	3.28	51	0	0	74	62	29	57	0	5	1	2	2	0	0	.000	1	11	2	0	0.3	.857
1967		6	4	.600	1.99	42	1	0	77	62	19	64	0	6	4	12	18	0	0	.000	5	9	1	1	0.4	.933
1968	HOU N	0	0	–	14.54	7	0	0	4.1	8	3	2	0	0	0	2	0	0	0	–	1	0	0	0	0.1	1.000
1969		4	8	.333	4.19	57	0	0	73	83	27	40	0	4	8	29	10	1	0	.100	5	12	0	0	0.3	1.000
1970		7	4	.636	4.06	63	0	0	71	84	24	48	0	7	4	18	6	0	0	.000	7	15	1	1	0.4	.957
1971		4	5	.444	2.12	48	0	0	51	51	25	17	0	4	5	12	2	0	0	.000	3	3	2	0	0.2	.750
1972		5	6	.455	2.77	42	0	0	48.2	38	12	18	0	5	6	14	5	0	0	.000	1	4	1	0	0.1	.833
1973		2	0	1.000	4.50	16	0	0	16	18	4	9	0	2	0	1	0	0	0	–	1	3	0	0	0.3	1.000
13 yrs.		48	34	.585	3.13	450	1	0	601	566	223	394	0	48	34	109	63	1	0	.016	33	87	9	2	0.3	.930

Fred Glade

GLADE, FREDERICK MONROE
B. Jan. 25, 1876, Dubuque, Iowa   D. Nov. 21, 1934, Grand Island, Neb.
BR TR 5'10" 175 lbs.

Year	Team	W	L	PCT	ERA	G	GS	CG	IP	H	BB	SO	ShO	W	L	SV	AB	H	HR	BA	PO	A	E	DP	TC/G	FA
1902	CHI N	0	1	.000	9.00	1	1	1	8	13	3	3	0	0	0	0	3	1	0	.333	1	2	0	0	3.0	1.000
1904	STL A	18	15	.545	2.27	35	34	30	289	248	58	156	6	0	0	1	102	19	0	.186	14	100	9	2	3.5	.927
1905		6	25	.194	2.81	32	32	28	275	257	58	127	2	0	0	0	98	9	0	.092	13	102	4	2	3.7	.966
1906		15	14	.517	2.36	35	32	28	266.2	215	59	96	4	0	0	0	95	13	0	.137	5	73	6	4	2.4	.929
1907		13	9	.591	2.67	24	22	18	202	187	45	71	2	0	1	0	73	15	0	.205	3	45	4	3	2.2	.923
1908	NY A	0	4	.000	4.22	5	5	2	32	30	14	11	0	0	0	0	10	0	0	.000	1	7	1	0	1.8	.889
6 yrs.		52	68	.433	2.62	132	126	107	1072.2	950	237	464	14	0	1	2	381	57	0	.150	37	329	24	11	3.0	.938

Year	Team		W	L	PCT	ERA	G	GS	CG	IP	H	BB	SO	ShO	W	L	SV	AB	H	HR	BA	PO	A	E	DP	TC/G	FA
															Relief Pitching			Batting									

John Glaiser

GLAISER, JOHN BURKE (Bert)
B. July 28, 1894, Yoakum, Tex.　D. Mar. 7, 1959, Houston, Tex.

BR TR 5'8"　165 lbs.

Year	Team		W	L	PCT	ERA	G	GS	CG	IP	H	BB	SO	ShO	W	L	SV	AB	H	HR	BA	PO	A	E	DP	TC/G	FA
1920	DET	A	0	0	–	6.35	9	1	0	17	23	8	3	0	0	0	1	3	0	0	.000	1	11	0	0	1.3	1.000

Tom Glass

GLASS, THOMAS JOSEPH
B. Apr. 29, 1898, Greensboro, N. C.　D. Dec. 15, 1981, Greensboro, N. C.

BR TR 6'3"　170 lbs.

| 1925 | PHI | A | 1 | 0 | 1.000 | 5.40 | 2 | 0 | 0 | 5 | 9 | 0 | 2 | 0 | 1 | 0 | 0 | 2 | 0 | 0 | .000 | 0 | 1 | 1 | 0 | 1.0 | .500 |

Jack Glasscock

GLASSCOCK, JOHN WESLEY (Old Battle Ax)
B. July 22, 1859, Wheeling, W. Va.　D. Feb. 24, 1947, Wheeling, W. Va.
Manager 1889, 1892.

BR TR 5'8"　160 lbs.

1884	CLE	N	0	0	–	5.40	2	0	0	5	8	2	1	0	0	0	0	453	142	3	.313	0	4	0	0	2.0	1.000
1887	IND	N	0	0	–	0.00	1	0	0	1	0	0	1	0	0	0	0	483	142	0	.294	0	0	0	0	0.0	–
1888			0	0	–	54.00	1	0	0	.1	1	2	1	0	0	0	0	442	119	1	.269	0	0	0	0	0.0	–
1889			0	0	–	0.00	1	0	0	.2	3	3	0	0	0	0	0	582	205	7	.352	0	0	0	0	0.0	–
4 yrs.			0	0	–	6.43	5	0	0	7	12	7	3	0	0	0	0	*				0	4	0	0	0.8	1.000

Luke Glavenich

GLAVENICH, LUKE FRANK
B. Jan. 17, 1893, Jackson, Calif.　D. May 22, 1935, Stockton, Calif.

BR TR 5'9½"　189 lbs.

| 1913 | CLE | A | 0 | 0 | – | 9.00 | 1 | 0 | 0 | 3 | 3 | 3 | 1 | 0 | 0 | 0 | 0 | – | 0 | 0 | – | 0 | 0 | 1 | 0 | 1.0 | .000 |

Tom Glavine

GLAVINE, THOMAS MICHAEL
B. Mar. 25, 1966, Concord, Mass.

BL TL 6'　175 lbs.

1987	ATL	N	2	4	.333	5.54	9	9	0	50.1	55	33	20	0	0	0	0	16	2	0	.125	1	13	1	0	1.7	.933
1988			7	17	.292	4.56	34	34	1	195.1	201	63	84	0	0	0	0	60	11	0	.183	12	41	4	3	1.7	.930
1989			14	8	.636	3.68	29	29	6	186	172	40	90	0	0	0	0	67	10	0	.149	7	37	4	4	1.7	.917
3 yrs.			23	29	.442	4.29	72	72	7	431.2	428	136	194	4	0	0	0	143	23	0	.161	20	91	9	7	1.7	.925

Ralph Glaze

GLAZE, DANIEL RALPH
B. Mar. 13, 1882, Denver, Colo.　D. Oct. 31, 1968, Atascadero, Calif.

BR TR 5'9"　165 lbs.

1906	BOS	A	4	6	.400	3.59	19	10	7	123	110	32	56	0	0	0	0	55	10	0	.182	12	33	2	2	2.5	.957
1907			8	13	.381	2.32	32	21	11	182.1	150	48	68	1	0	2	0	61	11	1	.180	8	40	2	1	1.6	.960
1908			2	2	.500	3.38	10	3	2	34.2	43	5	13	0	0	1	0	13	1	0	.077	1	7	0	0	0.8	1.000
3 yrs.			14	21	.400	2.89	61	34	20	340	303	85	137	1	0	3	0	129	22	1	.171	21	80	4	3	1.7	.962

Whitey Glazner

GLAZNER, CHARLES FRANKLIN
B. Sept. 17, 1893, Sycamore, Ala.　D. June 6, 1989, Orlando, Fla.

BR TR 5'9"　165 lbs.

1920	PIT	N	0	0	–	3.12	2	0	0	8.2	9	2	1	0	0	0	0	0	0	0	.000	0	1	0	0	0.5	1.000
1921			14	5	.737	2.77	36	25	15	234	214	58	88	0	0	1	1	76	10	0	.132	10	43	6	2	1.6	.898
1922			11	12	.478	4.38	34	26	10	193	238	52	77	1	1	0	1	65	16	1	.246	8	43	1	2	1.5	.981
1923	2 teams						PIT N (7G 2-1)				PHI N (28G 7-14)																	
"	total		9	15	.375	4.47	35	27	13	191.1	224	74	59	3	0	1	2	65	13	0	.200	6	43	3	6	1.5	.942
1924	PHI	N	7	16	.304	5.92	35	24	8	156.2	210	63	41	2	2	2	0	51	8	0	.157	5	43	2	5	1.4	.960
5 yrs.			41	48	.461	4.21	142	102	46	783.2	895	249	266	6	3	4	4	260	47	2	.181	29	173	12	15	1.5	.944

Bill Gleason

GLEASON, WILLIAM
B. 1868, Cleveland, Ohio　D. Dec. 2, 1893, Cleveland, Ohio

| 1890 | CLE | P | 0 | 1 | .000 | 27.00 | 1 | 1 | 0 | 4 | 14 | 6 | 0 | 0 | 0 | 0 | 0 | 2 | 0 | 0 | .000 | 0 | 0 | 0 | 0 | 0.0 | – |

Joe Gleason

GLEASON, JOSEPH PAUL
B. July 9, 1895, Phelps, N. Y.

BR TR 5'10½"　175 lbs.

1920	WAS	A	0	0	–	13.50	3	0	0	8	14	6	2	0	0	0	0	2	0	0	.000	0	3	0	0	1.0	1.000
1922			2	3	.400	4.65	8	5	3	40.2	53	18	12	0	0	1	0	14	2	0	.143	3	9	1	0	1.6	.923
2 yrs.			2	3	.400	6.10	11	5	3	48.2	67	24	14	0	0	1	0	16	2	0	.125	3	12	1	0	1.5	.938

Kid Gleason

GLEASON, WILLIAM J. (Youngster)
Brother of Harry Gleason.
B. Oct. 26, 1866, Camden, N. J.　D. Jan. 2, 1933, Philadelphia, Pa.
Manager 1919-23.

BB TR 5'7"　158 lbs.

1888	PHI	N	7	16	.304	2.84	24	23	23	199.2	199	53	89	1	0	0	0	83	17	0	.205	6	31	7	1	1.8	.841
1889			9	15	.375	5.58	29	21	15	205	242	97	64	0	2	2	1	99	25	0	.253	12	49	9	1	2.4	.871
1890			38	17	.691	2.63	60	55	54	506	479	167	222	6	1	0	2	224	47	0	.210	24	95	8	4	2.1	.937
1891			24	22	.522	3.51	53	44	40	418	431	165	100	1	1	2	1	214	53	0	.248	22	73	11	2	2.0	.896
1892	STL	N	16	24	.400	3.33	47	45	43	400	389	151	133	2	0	0	0	233	50	3	.215	0	0	0	0	0.0	–
1893			21	25	.457	4.61	48	45	37	380.1	436	187	86	1	1	1	1	199	51	0	.256	30	87	12	3	2.7	.907
1894	2 teams						STL N (8G 2-6)				BAL N (21G 15-5)																	
"	total		17	11	.607	4.85	29	28	25	230	299	65	44	0	0	0	0	114	37	0	.325	22	37	7	1	2.3	.894
1895	BAL	N	2	4	.333	6.97	9	5	3	50.1	77	21	6	0	1	2	1	421	130	0	.309	5	9	2	0	1.8	.875
8 yrs.			134	134	.500	3.79	299	266	240	2389.1	2552	906	744	11	6	7	6	*				121	381	56	12	1.9	.900

Jerry Don Gleaton

GLEATON, JERRY DON
B. Sept. 14, 1957, Brownwood, Tex.

BL TL 6'3"　205 lbs.

1979	TEX	A	0	1	.000	6.30	5	2	0	10	15	2	2	0	0	0	0	0	0	0	–	1	4	0	0	0.8	1.000
1980			0	0	–	2.57	5	0	0	7	5	4	2	0	0	0	0	0	0	0	–	1	2	0	0	0.6	1.000
1981	SEA	A	4	7	.364	4.76	20	13	1	85	88	38	31	0	0	0	0	0	0	0	–	5	12	1	0	0.9	.944
1982			0	0	–	13.50	3	0	0	4.2	7	2	1	0	0	0	0	0	0	0	–	1	0	0	0	0.3	1.000
1984	CHI	A	1	2	.333	3.44	11	1	0	18.1	20	6	4	0	0	0	1	0	0	0	–	1	1	0	0	0.3	.667
1985			1	0	1.000	5.76	31	0	0	29.2	37	13	22	0	1	0	1	0	0	0	–	0	4	0	0	0.1	1.000
1987	KC	A	4	4	.500	4.26	48	0	0	50.2	38	28	44	0	4	4	5	0	0	0	–	2	12	1	1	0.3	.933
1988			0	4	.000	3.55	42	0	0	38	33	17	29	0	0	4	3	0	0	0	–	3	3	0	0	0.1	1.000

Year	Team		W	L	PCT	ERA	G	GS	CG	IP	H	BB	SO	ShO	Relief Pitching W	L	SV	Batting AB	H	HR	BA	PO	A	E	DP	TC/G	FA

Jerry Don Gleaton *continued*

| 1989 | | | 0 | 0 | – | 5.65 | 15 | 0 | 0 | 14.1 | 20 | 6 | 9 | 0 | 0 | 0 | 0 | 0 | 0 | 0 | – | 0 | 2 | 0 | 0 | 0.1 | 1.000 |
| 9 yrs. | | | 10 | 18 | .357 | 4.72 | 180 | 16 | 1 | 257.2 | 263 | 116 | 144 | 0 | 6 | 9 | 11 | 0 | 0 | 0 | – | 13 | 40 | 3 | 1 | 0.3 | .946 |

Martin Glendon

GLENDON, MARTIN J.
B. Feb. 8, 1877, Milwaukee, Wis. D. Nov. 6, 1950, Chicago, Ill. 5'11" 180 lbs.

1902	CIN	N	0	1	.000	12.00	1	1	0	3	5	4	0	0	0	0	0	1	0	0	.000	0	2	1	0	3.0	.667
1903	CLE	A	1	2	.333	0.98	3	3	3	27.2	20	7	9	0	0	0	0	8	0	0	.000	3	11	0	0	4.7	1.000
2 yrs.			1	3	.250	2.05	4	4	3	30.2	25	11	9	0	0	0	0	9	0	0	.000	3	13	1	0	4.3	.941

Bob Glenn

GLENN, BURDETTE
B. June 16, 1894, West Sunbury, Pa. D. June 3, 1977, Richmond, Calif.

| 1920 | STL | N | 0 | 0 | – | 0.00 | 2 | 0 | 0 | 2 | 2 | 0 | 0 | 0 | 0 | 0 | 0 | 0 | 0 | 0 | – | 1 | 0 | 0 | 0 | 0.5 | 1.000 |

Sal Gliatto

GLIATTO, SALVADOR MICHAEL
B. May 7, 1902, Chicago, Ill. BB TR 5'8½" 150 lbs.

| 1930 | CLE | A | 0 | 0 | – | 6.60 | 8 | 0 | 0 | 15 | 21 | 9 | 7 | 0 | 0 | 0 | 2 | 2 | 0 | 0 | .000 | 0 | 2 | 2 | 0 | 0.5 | .500 |

Ed Glynn

GLYNN, EDWARD PAUL (The Flushing Flash)
B. June 3, 1953, New York, N. Y. BR TL 6'2" 180 lbs.

1975	DET	A	0	2	.000	4.30	3	1	0	14.2	11	8	8	0	0	1	0	0	0	0	–	1	3	1	1	1.7	.800
1976			1	3	.250	6.00	5	4	1	24	22	20	17	0	0	0	0	0	0	0	–	0	1	0	0	0.2	1.000
1977			2	1	.667	5.33	8	3	0	27	36	12	13	0	1	0	0	0	0	0	–	0	3	0	0	0.4	1.000
1978			0	0	–	3.07	10	0	0	14.2	11	4	9	0	0	0	0	0	0	0	–	0	6	0	0	0.6	1.000
1979	NY	N	1	4	.200	3.00	46	0	0	60	57	40	32	0	1	4	7	4	0	0	.000	5	3	0	0	0.2	1.000
1980			3	3	.500	4.15	38	0	0	52	49	23	32	0	3	3	1	6	0	0	.000	0	12	0	0	0.3	1.000
1981	CLE	A	0	0	–	1.13	4	0	0	8	5	4	4	0	0	0	0	0	0	0	–	0	0	0	0	0.0	
1982			5	2	.714	4.17	47	0	0	49.2	43	30	54	0	5	2	4	0	0	0	–	1	4	0	0	0.1	1.000
1983			0	2	.000	5.84	11	0	0	12.1	22	6	13	0	0	2	0	0	0	0	–	0	1	1	0	0.2	.500
1985	MON	N	0	0	–	19.29	3	0	0	2.1	5	4	2	0	0	0	0	0	0	0	–	0	0	0	0	0.0	
10 yrs.			12	17	.414	4.25	175	8	1	264.2	261	151	184	0	10	12	12	10	0	0	.000	7	33	2	1	0.2	.952

Jot Goar

GOAR, JOSHUA MERCER
B. Jan. 31, 1870, New Lisbon, Ind. D. Apr. 4, 1947, New Castle, Ind. BR TR 5'9" 160 lbs.

1896	PIT	N	0	1	.000	16.88	3	0	0	13.1	36	8	3	0	0	1	0	6	1	0	.167	0	2	2	0	1.3	.500
1898	CIN	N	0	0	–	9.00	1	0	0	2	4	1	0	0	0	0	0	0	0	0	–	0	1	0	0	1.0	1.000
2 yrs.			0	1	.000	15.85	4	0	0	15.1	40	9	3	0	0	1	0	6	1	0	.167	0	3	2	0	1.3	.600

George Goetz

GOETZ, GEORGE BURT
B. 1865, Greencastle, Ind. Deceased. 6'2" 180 lbs.

| 1889 | BAL | AA | 1 | 0 | 1.000 | 4.00 | 1 | 1 | 0 | 9 | 12 | 0 | 2 | 0 | 0 | 0 | 0 | 4 | 0 | 0 | .000 | 0 | 4 | 1 | 0 | 5.0 | .800 |

John Goetz

GOETZ, JOHN HARDY
B. Oct. 24, 1937, Goetzville, Mich. BR TR 6' 185 lbs.

| 1960 | CHI | N | 0 | 0 | – | 12.79 | 4 | 0 | 0 | 6.1 | 10 | 4 | 6 | 0 | 0 | 0 | 0 | 1 | 0 | 0 | .000 | 0 | 1 | 0 | 0 | 0.3 | 1.000 |

Bill Gogolewski

GOGOLEWSKI, WILLIAM JOSEPH
B. Oct. 26, 1947, Oshkosh, Wis. BL TR 6'4" 190 lbs.

1970	WAS	A	2	2	.500	4.76	8	5	0	34	33	25	19	0	0	0	0	7	0	0	.000	1	9	0	1	1.3	1.000
1971			6	5	.545	2.76	27	17	4	124	112	39	70	1	0	0	0	32	5	0	.156	10	18	1	1	1.1	.966
1972	TEX	A	4	11	.267	4.23	36	21	2	151	136	58	95	1	0	1	2	40	5	0	.125	7	21	0	2	0.8	1.000
1973			3	6	.333	4.21	49	1	0	124	139	48	77	0	3	6	6	0	0	0	–	9	28	2	2	0.8	.949
1974	CLE	A	0	0	–	4.50	5	0	0	14	15	2	3	0	0	0	0	0	0	0	–	1	8	0	1	1.8	1.000
1975	CHI	A	0	0	–	5.24	19	0	0	55	61	28	37	0	0	0	2	0	0	0	–	4	11	1	2	0.8	.938
6 yrs.			15	24	.385	4.02	144	44	6	502	496	200	301	2	3	7	10	79	10	0	.127	32	95	4	9	0.9	.969

Jim Golden

GOLDEN, JAMES EDWARD
B. Mar. 20, 1936, Eldon, Mo. BL TR 6' 175 lbs.

1960	LA	N	1	0	1.000	6.43	1	1	0	7	6	4	4	0	0	0	0	3	1	0	.333	0	1	0	0	1.0	1.000
1961			1	1	.500	5.79	28	1	0	42	52	20	18	0	1	1	0	3	0	0	.000	1	8	0	0	0.3	1.000
1962	HOU	N	7	11	.389	4.07	37	18	5	152.2	163	50	88	2	2	1	1	54	12	0	.222	10	29	2	1	1.1	.951
1963			0	1	.000	5.68	3	0	0	6.1	12	2	5	0	0	0	0	0	0	0	–	0	1	0	0	0.3	1.000
4 yrs.			9	13	.409	4.54	69	20	5	208	233	76	115	2	3	2	1	60	13	0	.217	11	39	2	1	0.8	.962

Mike Golden

GOLDEN, MICHAEL HENRY
B. Sept. 11, 1851, Shirley, Mass. D. Jan. 11, 1929, Rockford, Ill. BR TR 5'7" 166 lbs.

| 1878 | MIL | N | 3 | 13 | .188 | 4.14 | 22 | 18 | 15 | 161 | 217 | 33 | 52 | 0 | 0 | 0 | 0 | * | | | | 7 | 36 | 8 | 0 | 2.3 | .843 |

Roy Golden

GOLDEN, ROY KRAMER
B. July 12, 1888, Madisonville, Ohio D. Oct. 4, 1961, Norwood, Ohio BR TR 6'1" 195 lbs.

1910	STL	N	2	3	.400	4.43	7	6	3	42.2	44	33	31	0	0	0	0	15	4	0	.267	3	14	3	2	2.9	.850
1911			4	9	.308	5.02	30	25	6	148.2	127	129	81	0	0	0	0	44	5	0	.114	5	39	5	0	1.6	.898
2 yrs.			6	12	.333	4.89	37	31	9	191.1	171	162	112	0	0	0	0	59	9	0	.153	8	53	8	2	1.9	.884

Fred Goldsmith

GOLDSMITH, FRED ERNEST
B. May 15, 1852, New Haven, Conn. D. Mar. 28, 1939, Berkley, Mich. BR TR 6'1" 195 lbs.

1879	TRO	N	2	4	.333	1.57	8	7	7	63	61	1	31	0	0	0	0	38	9	0	.237	2	13	3	0	2.3	.833
1880	CHI	N	21	3	.875	1.75	26	24	22	210.1	189	18	90	4	0	0	1	142	37	0	.261	11	49	2	0	2.4	.968
1881			24	13	.649	2.59	39	39	37	330	328	44	76	5	0	0	0	158	38	0	.241	18	95	18	2	3.4	.863

Year	Team	W	L	PCT	ERA	G	GS	CG	IP	H	BB	SO	ShO	Relief Pitching W	L	SV	Batting AB	H	HR	BA	PO	A	E	DP	TC/G	FA

Fred Goldsmith *continued*

1882		28	16	.636	2.42	44	44	44	405	377	38	109	4	0	0	0	183	42	0	.230	7	0	1	0	0.2	.875
1883		25	19	.568	3.15	46	45	40	383.1	456	39	82	2	0	0	0	235	52	1	.221	23	86	17	3	2.7	.865
1884	2 teams	CHI N	(21G 9–11)		BAL AA	(4G 3–1)																				
"	total	12	12	.500	4.05	25	25	23	218	274	31	45	1	0	0	0	95	13	2	.137	16	41	14	0	2.8	.803
6 yrs.		112	67	.626	2.73	188	184	173	1609.2	1685	171	433	16	0	0	1	*				77	284	55	5	2.2	.868

Hal Goldsmith

GOLDSMITH, HAROLD EUGENE
B. Aug. 18, 1898, Peconic, N. Y.   BR TR 6'   174 lbs.

1926	BOS N	5	7	.417	4.37	19	15	5	101	135	28	16	0	1	1	1	38	8	0	.211	8	28	1	2	1.9	.973
1927		1	3	.250	3.52	22	5	1	71.2	83	26	13	0	0	1	1	21	5	0	.238	4	16	1	2	1.0	.952
1928		0	0	–	3.24	4	0	0	8.1	14	1	1	0	0	0	0	2	0	0	.000	1	4	1	0	1.5	.833
1929	STL N	0	0	–	6.75	2	0	0	4	3	1	0	0	0	0	0	1	0	0	.000	0	0	0	0	0.0	–
4 yrs.		6	10	.375	4.04	47	20	6	185	235	56	30	0	1	2	1	62	13	0	.210	13	48	3	4	1.4	.953

Izzy Goldstein

GOLDSTEIN, ISIDORE
B. June 6, 1908, New York, N. Y.   BB TR 6'   160 lbs.

| 1932 | DET A | 3 | 2 | .600 | 4.47 | 16 | 6 | 2 | 56.1 | 63 | 41 | 14 | 0 | 0 | 0 | 0 | 17 | 5 | 0 | .294 | 2 | 13 | 2 | 0 | 1.1 | .882 |

Dave Goltz

GOLTZ, DAVID ALLAN
B. June 23, 1949, Pelican Rapids, Minn.   BR TR 6'4"   200 lbs.

1972	MIN A	3	3	.500	2.67	15	11	2	91	75	26	38	0	0	0	1	29	3	0	.103	8	14	1	0	1.5	.957
1973		6	4	.600	5.25	32	10	1	106.1	138	32	66	0	3	0	1	0	0	0	–	7	17	1	4	0.8	.960
1974		10	10	.500	3.26	28	24	5	174	192	45	89	1	1	0	1	0	0	0	–	14	27	2	3	1.5	.953
1975		14	14	.500	3.67	32	32	15	243	235	72	128	1	0	0	0	0	0	0	–	20	38	3	4	1.9	.951
1976		14	14	.500	3.36	36	35	13	249.1	239	91	133	4	0	0	0	0	0	0	–	18	35	3	3	1.6	.946
1977		**20**	11	.645	3.36	39	**39**	19	303	**284**	91	186	2	0	0	0	0	0	0	–	20	41	5	4	1.7	.924
1978		15	10	.600	2.49	29	29	13	220.1	209	67	116	2	0	0	0	0	0	0	–	24	28	2	2	1.9	.963
1979		14	13	.519	4.16	36	35	12	251	282	69	132	1	0	0	0	0	0	0	–	16	34	2	3	1.4	.962
1980	LA N	7	11	.389	4.32	35	27	2	171	198	59	91	2	0	0	1	47	6	0	.128	11	24	1	1	1.0	.972
1981		2	7	.222	4.09	26	8	0	77	83	25	48	0	1	3	1	17	1	0	.059	6	14	0	1	0.8	1.000
1982	2 teams	LA N	(2G 0–1)		CAL A	(28G 8–5)																				
"	total	8	6	.571	4.12	30	8	1	89.2	88	32	52	0	4	4	3	1	0	0	.000	0	2	0	0	0.1	1.000
1983	CAL A	0	6	.000	6.22	15	6	0	63.2	81	37	27	0	0	2	0	0	0	0	–	4	8	1	1	0.9	.923
12 yrs.		113	109	.509	3.69	353	264	83	2039.1	2104	646	1106	13	9	9	8	94	10	0	.106	148	282	21	26	1.3	.953

LEAGUE CHAMPIONSHIP SERIES

| 1982 | CAL A | 0 | 0 | – | 7.36 | 1 | 0 | 0 | 3.2 | 4 | 2 | 2 | 0 | 0 | 0 | 0 | 0 | 0 | 0 | – | 0 | 0 | 0 | 0 | 0.0 | – |

WORLD SERIES

| 1981 | LA N | 0 | 0 | – | 5.40 | 2 | 0 | 0 | 3.1 | 4 | 1 | 2 | 0 | 0 | 0 | 0 | 0 | 0 | 0 | – | 0 | 0 | 0 | 0 | 0.0 | – |

Lefty Gomez

GOMEZ, VERNON LOUIS (Goofy, The Gay Castillion)
B. Nov. 26, 1908, Rodeo, Calif.   D. Feb. 17, 1989, Greenbrae, Calif.
Hall of Fame 1972.   BL TL 6'2"   173 lbs.

1930	NY A	2	5	.286	5.55	15	6	2	60	66	28	22	0	0	0	2	20	3	0	.150	1	18	0	0	1.3	1.000
1931		21	9	.700	2.63	40	26	17	243	206	85	150	1	3	2	3	83	11	0	.133	6	43	1	1	1.3	.980
1932		24	7	.774	4.21	37	31	21	265.1	266	105	176	1	1	2	1	104	18	0	.173	2	36	2	3	1.1	.950
1933		16	10	.615	3.18	35	30	14	234.2	218	106	163	4	0	2	2	80	9	0	.113	4	30	4	0	1.1	.895
1934		**26**	5	.839	2.33	38	33	**25**	281.2	223	96	**158**	6	1	2	1	99	13	0	.131	7	42	1	2	1.3	.980
1935		12	15	.444	3.18	34	30	15	246	223	86	138	2	0	1	1	83	10	0	.120	6	49	2	2	1.7	.965
1936		13	7	.650	4.39	31	30	10	188.2	184	122	105	0	0	0	0	69	10	0	.145	4	29	1	3	1.1	.971
1937		21	11	.656	2.33	34	34	25	278.1	233	93	**194**	6	0	0	0	105	21	0	.200	3	36	3	1	1.2	.929
1938		18	12	.600	3.35	32	32	20	239	239	99	129	4	0	0	0	86	13	0	.151	12	51	1	15	2.0	.984
1939		12	8	.600	3.41	26	26	14	198	173	84	102	2	0	0	0	73	11	0	.151	2	33	1	0	1.4	.972
1940		3	3	.500	6.59	9	5	2	27.1	37	18	14	0	1	0	0	9	0	0	.000	1	2	0	0	0.3	1.000
1941		15	5	.750	3.74	23	23	8	156.1	151	103	76	2	0	0	0	59	9	0	.153	6	11	2	2	0.8	.895
1942		6	4	.600	4.28	13	13	2	80	67	65	41	0	0	0	0	33	5	0	.152	2	9	1	0	0.9	.917
1943	WAS A	0	1	.000	5.79	1	1	0	4.2	5	5	0	0	0	0	0	0	0	0	.000	0	4	1	1	5.0	.800
14 yrs.		189	102	.649	3.34	368	320	173	2503	2290	1095	1468	28	5	12	9	904	133	0	.147	56	393	20	30	1.3	.957

WORLD SERIES

1932	NY A	1	0	1.000	1.00	1	1	1	9	9	1	8	0	0	0	0	3	0	0	.000	0	3	0	0	3.0	1.000
1936		2	0	1.000	4.70	2	2	1	15.1	14	11	9	0	0	0	0	8	2	0	.250	0	3	0	0	1.5	1.000
1937		2	0	1.000	1.50	2	2	2	18	16	2	8	0	0	0	0	6	1	0	.167	1	1	0	0	2.0	1.000
1938		1	0	1.000	3.86	1	1	0	7	9	1	5	0	0	0	0	2	0	0	.000	0	1	0	0	1.0	1.000
1939		0	0	–	9.00	1	1	0	1	3	1	0	0	0	0	0	0	0	0	–	0	0	0	0	0.0	–
5 yrs.		6	0	1.000	2.86	7	7	4	50.1	51	15	31	0	0	0	0	20	3	0	.150	1	10	0	0	1.6	1.000
		5th		1st																						

Luis Gomez

GOMEZ, LUIS
Born Luis Gomez y Sanchez.
B. Aug. 19, 1951, Guadalajara, Mexico   BR TR 5'9"   150 lbs.

| 1981 | ATL N | 0 | 0 | – | 27.00 | 1 | 0 | 0 | 1 | 3 | 2 | 0 | 0 | 0 | 0 | 0 | * | | | | 0 | 0 | 0 | 0 | 0.0 | – |

Ruben Gomez

GOMEZ, RUBEN
Born Ruben Gomez y Colon.
B. July 13, 1927, Arroyo, Puerto Rico   BR TR 6'   170 lbs.

1953	NY N	13	11	.542	3.40	29	26	13	204	166	101	113	3	0	0	0	72	15	0	.208	20	39	3	1	2.1	.952
1954		17	9	.654	2.88	37	32	10	221.2	202	109	106	4	0	2	0	81	14	2	.173	13	47	4	3	1.7	.938
1955		9	10	.474	4.56	33	31	9	185.1	207	63	79	3	0	1	1	60	18	0	.300	22	39	2	4	1.9	.968
1956		7	17	.292	4.58	40	31	4	196.1	191	77	76	2	1	0	0	60	11	0	.183	19	40	1	4	1.5	.983
1957		15	13	.536	3.78	38	36	16	238.1	233	71	92	1	0	0	0	87	16	1	.184	14	51	2	3	1.8	.970

Year	Team		W	L	PCT	ERA	G	GS	CG	IP	H	BB	SO	ShO	Relief Pitching W	L	SV	Batting AB	H	HR	BA	PO	A	E	DP	TC/G	FA

Ruben Gomez *continued*

Year	Team		W	L	PCT	ERA	G	GS	CG	IP	H	BB	SO	ShO	W	L	SV	AB	H	HR	BA	PO	A	E	DP	TC/G	FA
1958	SF	N	10	12	.455	4.38	42	30	8	207.2	204	77	112	1	0	2	1	70	14	0	.200	21	39	2	3	1.5	.968
1959	PHI	N	3	8	.273	6.10	20	12	2	72.1	90	24	37	1	1	1	1	17	3	0	.176	7	18	2	3	1.4	.926
1960			0	3	.000	5.33	22	1	0	52.1	68	9	24	0	0	3	1	12	1	0	.083	5	6	2	0	0.6	.846
1962	2 teams		CLE A	(15G 1-2)			MIN A	(6G 1-1)																			
"	total		2	3	.400	4.45	21	6	1	64.2	67	36	29	0	0	1	1	18	3	0	.167	5	13	1	2	0.9	.947
1967	PHI	N	0	0	–	3.97	7	0	0	11.1	8	7	9	0	0	0	0	0	0	0	–	1	5	0	1	0.9	1.000
10 yrs.			76	86	.469	4.09	289	205	63	1454	1436	574	677	15	2	10	5	477	95	3	.199	127	297	19	24	1.5	.957

WORLD SERIES

| 1954 | NY | N | 1 | 0 | 1.000 | 2.45 | 1 | 1 | 0 | 7.1 | 4 | 3 | 2 | 0 | 0 | 0 | 0 | 4 | 0 | 0 | .000 | 1 | 2 | 0 | 0 | 3.0 | 1.000 |

Joe Gonzales

GONZALES, JOE MADRID   BR TR 5'9"   175 lbs.
B. Mar. 19, 1915, San Francisco, Calif.

| 1937 | BOS | A | 1 | 2 | .333 | 4.35 | 8 | 2 | 2 | 31 | 37 | 11 | 11 | 0 | 1 | 0 | 0 | 10 | 0 | 0 | .000 | 0 | 6 | 0 | 1 | 0.8 | 1.000 |

Julio Gonzales

GONZALES, JULIO ENRIQUE   BR TR 5'11"   150 lbs.
B. Dec. 20, 1920, Havana, Cuba

| 1949 | WAS | A | 0 | 0 | – | 4.72 | 13 | 0 | 0 | 34.1 | 33 | 27 | 5 | 0 | 0 | 0 | 0 | 5 | 1 | 0 | .200 | 2 | 6 | 0 | 0 | 0.6 | 1.000 |

Vince Gonzales

GONZALES, WENCESLAO O'REILLY   BL TL 6'1"   165 lbs.
B. Sept. 28, 1925, Quivican, Cuba   D. Mar. 11, 1981, Ciudad del Carmen, Mex

| 1955 | WAS | A | 0 | 0 | – | 27.00 | 1 | 0 | 0 | 2 | 6 | 3 | 1 | 0 | 0 | 0 | 0 | 0 | 0 | 0 | – | 0 | 0 | 0 | 0 | 0.0 | – |

German Gonzalez

GONZALEZ, GERMAN JOSE   BR TR 6'   170 lbs.
Born German Jose Gonzalez y Caraballo.
B. Mar. 7, 1962, Rio Caribe, Venezuela

1988	MIN	A	0	0	–	3.38	16	0	0	21.1	20	8	19	0	0	0	1	0	0	0	–	3	2	0	0	0.3	1.000
1989			3	2	.600	4.66	22	0	0	29	32	11	25	0	3	2	0	0	0	0	–	4	2	0	0	0.3	1.000
2 yrs.			3	2	.600	4.11	38	0	0	50.1	52	19	44	0	3	2	1	0	0	0	–	7	4	0	0	0.3	1.000

Ralph Good

GOOD, RALPH NELSON   BR TR 6'   165 lbs.
B. Apr. 25, 1886, Monticello, Me.   D. Nov. 24, 1965, Waterville, Me.

| 1910 | BOS | N | 0 | 0 | – | 2.00 | 2 | 2 | 0 | 9 | 6 | 2 | 4 | 0 | 0 | 0 | 0 | 3 | 0 | 0 | .000 | 0 | 4 | 0 | 1 | 2.0 | 1.000 |

Wilbur Good

GOOD, WILBUR DAVID (Lefty)   BL TL 5'6"   165 lbs.
B. Sept. 28, 1885, Punxsutawney, Pa.   D. Dec. 30, 1963, Brooksville, Fla.

| 1905 | NY | A | 0 | 2 | .000 | 4.74 | 5 | 2 | 0 | 19 | 18 | 14 | 13 | 0 | 0 | 0 | 0 | * | | | | 1 | 7 | 1 | 0 | 1.8 | .889 |

Herb Goodall

GOODALL, HERBERT FRANK   BR TR 5'9"   180 lbs.
B. Mar. 10, 1870, Mansfield, Pa.   D. Jan. 20, 1938, Mansfield, Pa.

| 1890 | LOU | AA | 8 | 5 | .615 | 3.39 | 18 | 13 | 8 | 109 | 94 | 51 | 46 | 1 | 0 | 0 | 4 | 45 | 19 | 0 | .422 | 7 | 25 | 3 | 0 | 1.9 | .914 |

John Goodell

GOODELL, JOHN HENRY WILLIAM (Lefty)   BR TL 5'10"   165 lbs.
B. Apr. 5, 1907, Muskogee, Okla.

| 1928 | CHI | A | 0 | 0 | – | 18.00 | 2 | 0 | 0 | 3 | 6 | 2 | 0 | 0 | 0 | 0 | 0 | 0 | 0 | 0 | – | 0 | 1 | 0 | 0 | 0.5 | 1.000 |

Dwight Gooden

GOODEN, DWIGHT EUGENE (Doc, Dr. K)   BR TR 6'2"   190 lbs.
B. Nov. 16, 1964, Tampa, Fla.

1984	NY	N	17	9	.654	2.60	31	31	7	218	161	73	276	3	0	0	0	70	14	0	.200	21	22	2	0	1.5	.956
1985			24	4	.857	1.53	35	35	16	276.2	198	69	268	8	0	0	0	93	21	1	.226	25	38	2	6	1.9	.969
1986			17	6	.739	2.84	33	33	12	250	200	80	200	2	0	0	0	81	7	0	.086	36	36	2	5	2.2	.973
1987			15	7	.682	3.21	25	25	7	179.2	162	53	148	3	0	0	0	64	14	0	.219	15	22	3	3	1.6	.925
1988			18	9	.667	3.19	34	34	10	248.1	242	57	175	3	0	0	0	90	16	1	.178	27	56	5	3	2.6	.943
1989			9	4	.692	2.89	19	17	0	118.1	93	47	101	0	0	0	1	40	8	0	.200	8	16	3	0	1.4	.889
6 yrs.			100	39	.719	2.64	177	175	52	1291	1053	379	1168	19	0	0	1	438	80	2	.183	132	190	17	17	1.9	.950

LEAGUE CHAMPIONSHIP SERIES

1986	NY	N	0	1	.000	1.06	2	2	0	17	16	5	9	0	0	0	0	5	0	0	.000	3	2	0	0	2.5	1.000
1988			0	0	–	2.95	3	2	0	18.1	10	8	20	0	0	0	0	5	1	0	.200	1	3	0	0	1.3	1.000
2 yrs.			0	1	.000	2.04	5	4	0	35.1	26	13	29	0	0	0	0	10	1	0	.100	4	5	0	0	1.8	1.000

WORLD SERIES

| 1986 | NY | N | 0 | 2 | .000 | 8.00 | 2 | 2 | 0 | 9 | 17 | 4 | 9 | 0 | 0 | 0 | 0 | 2 | 1 | 0 | .500 | 1 | 2 | 0 | 0 | 1.5 | 1.000 |

Art Goodwin

GOODWIN, ARTHUR INGRAM
B. Feb. 27, 1876, Greene County, Pa.   D. June 19, 1943, Greene County, Pa.

| 1905 | NY | A | 0 | 0 | – | 81.00 | 1 | 0 | 0 | .1 | 2 | 2 | 0 | 0 | 0 | 0 | 0 | 0 | 0 | 0 | – | 0 | 0 | 0 | 0 | 0.0 | – |

Clyde Goodwin

GOODWIN, CLYDE SAMUEL   BR TR 5'11"   145 lbs.
B. Nov. 12, 1886, Shade, Ohio   D. Oct. 12, 1963, Dayton, Ohio

| 1906 | WAS | A | 0 | 2 | .000 | 4.43 | 4 | 3 | 1 | 22.1 | 20 | 13 | 9 | 0 | 0 | 0 | 0 | 5 | 1 | 0 | .200 | 0 | 4 | 0 | 0 | 1.0 | 1.000 |

Jim Goodwin

GOODWIN, JAMES PATRICK   BL TL 6'1"   170 lbs.
B. Aug. 15, 1926, St. Louis, Mo.

| 1948 | CHI | A | 0 | 0 | – | 8.71 | 8 | 0 | 0 | 10.1 | 9 | 12 | 3 | 0 | 0 | 0 | 1 | 2 | 1 | 0 | .500 | 1 | 2 | 0 | 0 | 0.4 | 1.000 |

Year	Team		W	L	PCT	ERA	G	GS	CG	IP	H	BB	SO	ShO	Relief Pitching W	L	SV	Batting AB	H	HR	BA	PO	A	E	DP	TC/G	FA

Marv Goodwin

GOODWIN, MARVIN MARDO
B. Jan. 16, 1891, Gordonsville, Va.   D. Oct. 22, 1925, Houston, Tex.
BR TR 5'11"   168 lbs.

Year	Team		W	L	PCT	ERA	G	GS	CG	IP	H	BB	SO	ShO	W	L	SV	AB	H	HR	BA	PO	A	E	DP	TC/G	FA
1916	WAS	A	0	0	–	3.18	3	0	0	5.2	5	3	1	0	0	0	0	1	0	0	.000	0	1	0	0	0.3	1.000
1917	STL	N	6	4	.600	2.21	14	12	6	85.1	70	19	38	3	0	1	0	23	4	0	.174	3	33	0	1	2.6	1.000
1919			11	9	.550	2.51	33	17	7	179	163	33	48	0	3	3	0	60	12	0	.200	3	52	4	1	1.8	.932
1920			3	8	.273	4.95	32	12	3	116.1	153	28	23	0	1	1	1	35	7	0	.200	3	25	6	0	1.1	.824
1921			1	2	.333	3.72	14	4	1	36.1	47	9	7	0	0	0	1	6	0	0	.000	2	11	1	1	1.0	.929
1922			0	0	–	2.25	2	0	0	4	3	3	0	0	0	0	0	0	0	0	–	1	2	1	0	2.0	.750
1925	CIN	N	0	2	.000	4.79	4	3	2	20.2	26	5	4	0	0	0	0	4	1	0	.250	2	9	0	1	2.8	.925
7 yrs.			21	25	.457	3.30	102	48	19	447.1	467	100	121	3	4	5	2	129	24	0	.186	14	133	12	5	1.6	.925

Ray Gordinier

GORDINIER, RAYMOND CORNELIUS
B. Apr. 11, 1892, Rochester, N. Y.
D. Nov. 15, 1960, Rochester, N. Y.
BR TR 5'8½"   170 lbs.
BB 1922

Year	Team		W	L	PCT	ERA	G	GS	CG	IP	H	BB	SO	ShO	W	L	SV	AB	H	HR	BA	PO	A	E	DP	TC/G	FA
1921	BKN	N	1	0	1.000	5.25	3	3	0	12	10	8	4	0	0	0	0	4	1	0	.250	0	4	1	1	1.7	.800
1922			0	0	–	8.74	5	0	0	11.1	13	8	5	0	0	0	0	2	0	0	.000	1	2	1	0	0.8	.750
2 yrs.			1	0	1.000	6.94	8	3	0	23.1	23	16	9	0	0	0	0	6	1	0	.167	1	6	2	1	1.1	.778

Don Gordon

GORDON, DONALD THOMAS
B. Oct. 10, 1959, New York, N. Y.
BR TR 6'1"   175 lbs.

Year	Team		W	L	PCT	ERA	G	GS	CG	IP	H	BB	SO	ShO	W	L	SV	AB	H	HR	BA	PO	A	E	DP	TC/G	FA
1986	TOR	A	0	1	.000	7.06	14	0	0	21.2	28	8	13	0	0	1	1	0	0	0	–	1	2	2	0	0.4	.600
1987	2 teams				TOR A	(5G 0–0)				CLE A	(21G 0–3)																
"	total		0	3	.000	4.09	26	0	0	50.2	57	15	23	0	0	3	1	0	0	0	–	3	11	2	1	0.6	.875
1988	CLE	A	3	4	.429	4.40	38	0	0	59.1	65	19	20	0	3	4	1	0	0	0	–	4	12	1	0	0.4	.941
3 yrs.			3	8	.273	4.72	78	0	0	131.2	150	42	56	0	3	8	3	0	0	0	–	8	25	5	1	0.5	.868

Tom Gordon

GORDON, THOMAS (Flash)
B. Nov. 18, 1967, Sebring, Fla.
BR TR 5'9"   160 lbs.

Year	Team		W	L	PCT	ERA	G	GS	CG	IP	H	BB	SO	ShO	W	L	SV	AB	H	HR	BA	PO	A	E	DP	TC/G	FA
1988	KC	A	0	2	.000	5.17	5	2	0	15.2	16	7	18	0	0	0	0	0	0	0	–	2	2	0	0	0.8	1.000
1989			17	9	.654	3.64	49	16	1	163	122	86	153	0	10	2	1	0	0	0	–	15	26	0	7	0.8	1.000
2 yrs.			17	11	.607	3.78	54	18	1	178.2	138	93	171	1	10	2	1	0	0	0	–	17	28	0	7	0.8	1.000

Charlie Gorin

GORIN, CHARLES PERRY
B. Feb. 6, 1928, Waco, Tex.
BL TL 5'10"   165 lbs.

Year	Team		W	L	PCT	ERA	G	GS	CG	IP	H	BB	SO	ShO	W	L	SV	AB	H	HR	BA	PO	A	E	DP	TC/G	FA
1954	MIL	N	0	1	.000	1.86	5	0	0	9.2	5	6	12	0	0	1	0	3	0	0	.000	1	0	0	0	0.2	1.000
1955			0	0	–	54.00	2	0	0	.1	1	3	0	0	0	0	0	0	0	0	–	0	0	0	0	0.0	–
2 yrs.			0	1	.000	3.60	7	0	0	10	6	9	12	0	0	1	0	3	0	0	.000	1	0	0	0	0.1	1.000

Jack Gorman

GORMAN, JOHN F. (Stooping Jack)
B. 1859, St. Louis, Mo.   D. Sept. 9, 1889, St. Louis, Mo.

Year	Team		W	L	PCT	ERA	G	GS	CG	IP	H	BB	SO	ShO	W	L	SV	AB	H	HR	BA	PO	A	E	DP	TC/G	FA
1884	PIT	AA	1	2	.333	4.68	3	3	3	25	22	5	10	0	0	0	0	*				0	6	2	0	2.7	.750

Tom Gorman

GORMAN, THOMAS ALOYSIUS
B. Jan. 4, 1925, New York, N. Y.
BR TR 6'1"   190 lbs.

Year	Team		W	L	PCT	ERA	G	GS	CG	IP	H	BB	SO	ShO	W	L	SV	AB	H	HR	BA	PO	A	E	DP	TC/G	FA
1952	NY	A	6	2	.750	4.60	12	6	1	60.2	63	22	31	1	3	0	1	23	2	0	.087	2	11	3	0	1.3	.813
1953			4	5	.444	3.39	40	1	0	77	65	32	38	0	4	4	6	15	2	0	.133	5	11	1	0	0.4	.941
1954			0	0	–	2.21	23	0	0	36.2	30	14	31	0	0	0	2	4	0	0	.000	2	6	0	1	0.3	1.000
1955	KC	A	7	6	.538	3.55	57	0	0	109	98	36	46	0	7	6	18	24	2	0	.083	8	13	3	1	0.8	.875
1956			9	10	.474	3.83	52	13	1	171.1	168	68	56	0	6	3	3	39	2	0	.051	11	29	3	1	0.8	.930
1957			5	9	.357	3.83	38	12	3	124.2	125	33	66	1	1	5	3	33	4	0	.121	10	19	2	0	0.8	.935
1958			4	4	.500	3.51	50	1	0	89.2	86	20	44	0	4	3	8	17	2	0	.118	2	11	0	0	0.3	1.000
1959			1	0	1.000	7.08	17	0	0	20.1	24	14	9	0	1	0	1	0	0	0	–	0	0	1	0	0.1	–
8 yrs.			36	36	.500	3.77	289	33	5	689.1	659	239	321	2	26	21	42	155	14	0	.090	40	100	13	3.	0.5	.915

WORLD SERIES

Year	Team		W	L	PCT	ERA	G	GS	CG	IP	H	BB	SO	ShO	W	L	SV	AB	H	HR	BA	PO	A	E	DP	TC/G	FA
1952	NY	A	0	0	–	0.00	1	0	0	.2	1	0	0	0	0	0	0	0	0	0	–	0	0	0	0	–	–
1953			0	0	–	3.00	1	0	0	3	4	0	1	0	0	0	0	1	0	0	.000	1	0	0	0	1.0	1.000
2 yrs.			0	0	–	2.45	2	0	0	3.2	5	0	1	0	0	0	0	1	0	0	.000	1	0	0	0	0.5	1.000

Tom Gorman

GORMAN, THOMAS DAVID (Big Tom)
B. Mar. 16, 1916, New York, N. Y.   D. Aug. 11, 1986, Closter, N. J.
BR TL 6'2"   200 lbs.

Year	Team		W	L	PCT	ERA	G	GS	CG	IP	H	BB	SO	ShO	W	L	SV	AB	H	HR	BA	PO	A	E	DP	TC/G	FA
1939	NY	N	0	0	–	7.20	4	0	0	5	7	1	2	0	0	0	0	1	0	0	.000	0	2	0	0	0.5	1.000

Tom Gorman

GORMAN, THOMAS PATRICK
B. Dec. 16, 1957, Portland, Ore.
BL TL 6'4"   194 lbs.

Year	Team		W	L	PCT	ERA	G	GS	CG	IP	H	BB	SO	ShO	W	L	SV	AB	H	HR	BA	PO	A	E	DP	TC/G	FA
1981	MON	N	0	0	–	4.20	9	0	0	15	12	6	13	0	0	0	0	0	0	0	–	0	6	0	1	0.7	1.000
1982	2 teams				MON N	(5G 1–0)				NY N	(3G 0–1)																
"	total		1	1	.500	2.76	8	1	0	16.1	16	4	13	0	1	0	0	1	0	0	.000	2	6	0	0	0.5	1.000
1983	NY	N	1	4	.200	4.93	25	4	0	49.1	45	15	30	0	1	0	0	4	1	0	.250	3	7	0	2	0.4	1.000
1984			6	0	1.000	2.97	36	0	0	57.2	51	18	40	0	6	0	0	3	0	0	.000	2	9	0	0	0.3	1.000
1985			4	4	.500	5.13	34	2	0	52.2	56	18	32	0	3	3	0	5	0	0	.000	3	14	0	1	0.5	1.000
1986	PHI	N	0	1	.000	7.71	8	0	0	11.2	21	5	4	0	0	1	0	0	0	0	.000	2	0	0	0	0.0	1.000
1987	SD	N	0	0	–	4.09	6	0	0	11	11	5	11	0	0	0	0	0	0	0	–	0	0	0	0	0.0	–
7 yrs.			12	10	.545	4.34	126	7	0	213.2	212	66	144	0	11	4	0	14	1	0	.071	12	40	0	3	0.4	1.000

Joe Gormley

GORMLEY, JOSEPH
B. Dec. 20, 1866, Summit Hill, Pa.   D. July 2, 1950, Summit Hill, Pa.
BL TL

Year	Team		W	L	PCT	ERA	G	GS	CG	IP	H	BB	SO	ShO	W	L	SV	AB	H	HR	BA	PO	A	E	DP	TC/G	FA
1891	PHI	N	0	1	.000	5.63	1	1	1	8	10	5	2	0	0	0	0	4	0	0	.000	0	3	0	0	3.0	1.000

Year	Team	W	L	PCT	ERA	G	GS	CG	IP	H	BB	SO	ShO	W	L	SV	AB	H	HR	BA	PO	A	E	DP	TC/G	FA
														Relief Pitching			**Batting**									

Hank Gornicki

GORNICKI, HENRY FRANK
B. Jan. 14, 1911, Niagara Falls, N. Y. BR TR 6' 145 lbs.

Year	Team	W	L	PCT	ERA	G	GS	CG	IP	H	BB	SO	ShO	W	L	SV	AB	H	HR	BA	PO	A	E	DP	TC/G	FA
1941	2 teams	STL N	(4G 1–0)			CHI N	(1G 0–0)																			
"	total	1	0	1.000	3.38	5	1	1	13.1	9	9	8	1	0	0	0	4	1	0	.250	0	3	0	1	0.6	1.000
1942	PIT N	5	6	.455	2.57	25	14	7	112	89	40	48	2	0	0	2	35	4	1	.114	6	18	2	0	1.0	.923
1943		9	13	.409	3.98	42	18	4	147	165	47	63	1	3	3	4	40	7	0	.175	7	25	2	1	0.8	.941
1946		0	0	–	3.55	7	0	0	12.2	12	11	4	0	0	0	0	3	0	0	.000	0	2	0	0	0.3	1.000
4 yrs.		15	19	.441	3.38	79	33	12	285	275	107	123	4	3	3	6	82	12	1	.146	13	48	4	2	0.8	.938

Johnny Gorsica

GORSICA, JOHN JOSEPH PERRY
Born John Joseph Perry Gorczyca.
B. Mar. 29, 1915, Bayonne, N. J. BR TR 6'2" 180 lbs.

Year	Team	W	L	PCT	ERA	G	GS	CG	IP	H	BB	SO	ShO	W	L	SV	AB	H	HR	BA	PO	A	E	DP	TC/G	FA
1940	DET A	7	7	.500	4.33	29	20	5	160	170	57	68	2	0	0	0	62	12	1	.194	15	53	4	2	2.5	.944
1941		9	11	.450	4.47	33	21	8	171	193	55	59	1	4	1	2	57	17	0	.298	10	52	2	3	1.9	.969
1942		3	2	.600	4.75	28	0	0	53	63	26	19	0	3	2	4	10	1	0	.100	1	29	1	0	1.3	.971
1943		4	5	.444	3.36	35	4	1	96.1	88	40	45	0	4	3	5	23	4	0	.174	10	30	0	3	1.1	1.000
1944		6	14	.300	4.11	34	19	8	162	192	32	47	1	1	2	1	52	7	0	.135	17	42	2	5	1.8	.967
1946		0	0	–	4.56	14	0	0	23.2	28	11	14	0	0	0	1	3	2	0	.667	2	1	1	0	0.4	.800
1947		2	0	1.000	3.75	31	0	0	57.2	44	26	20	0	2	0	1	10	2	0	.200	9	12	0	1	0.7	1.000
7 yrs.		31	39	.443	4.18	204	64	22	723.2	778	247	272	4	14	8	17	217	45	1	.207	68	220	10	14	1.5	.966

WORLD SERIES

Year	Team	W	L	PCT	ERA	G	GS	CG	IP	H	BB	SO	ShO	W	L	SV	AB	H	HR	BA	PO	A	E	DP	TC/G	FA
1940	DET A	0	0	–	0.79	2	0	0	11.1	6	4	4	0	0	0	0	4	0	0	.000	0	6	0	1	3.0	1.000

Goose Gossage

GOSSAGE, RICHARD MICHAEL
B. July 5, 1951, Colorado Springs, Colo. BR TR 6'3" 180 lbs.

Year	Team	W	L	PCT	ERA	G	GS	CG	IP	H	BB	SO	ShO	W	L	SV	AB	H	HR	BA	PO	A	E	DP	TC/G	FA
1972	CHI A	7	1	.875	4.28	36	1	0	80	72	44	57	0	7	0	2	16	0	0	.000	3	10	1	1	0.4	.929
1973		0	4	.000	7.43	20	4	1	49.2	57	37	33	0	0	0	0	0	0	0	–	5	5	1	0	0.6	.909
1974		4	6	.400	4.15	39	3	0	89	92	47	64	0	4	5	1	0	0	0	–	3	14	2	1	0.5	.895
1975		9	8	.529	1.84	62	0	0	141.2	99	70	130	0	9	8	**26**	0	0	0	–	3	25	3	0	0.5	.903
1976		9	17	.346	3.94	31	29	15	224	214	90	135	0	0	1	1	0	0	0	–	18	27	3	1	1.5	.938
1977	PIT N	11	9	.550	1.62	72	0	0	133	78	49	151	0	**11**	9	26	23	5	0	.217	4	10	1	0	0.2	.933
1978	NY A	10	11	.476	2.01	63	0	0	134.1	87	59	122	0	10	11	**27**	0	0	0	–	6	12	3	0	0.3	.857
1979		5	3	.625	2.64	36	0	0	58	48	19	41	0	5	3	18	0	0	0	–	1	4	0	0	0.1	1.000
1980		6	2	.750	2.27	64	0	0	99	74	37	103	0	6	2	**33**	0	0	0	–	1	10	2	0	0.2	.846
1981		3	2	.600	0.77	32	0	0	47	22	14	48	0	3	2	20	0	0	0	–	2	7	1	1	0.3	.900
1982		4	5	.444	2.23	56	0	0	93	63	28	102	0	4	5	30	0	0	0	–	2	6	0	1	0.1	1.000
1983		13	5	.722	2.27	57	0	0	87.1	82	25	90	0	13	5	22	0	0	0	–	2	3	1	0	0.1	.833
1984	SD N	10	6	.625	2.90	62	0	0	102.1	75	36	84	0	10	6	25	22	4	0	.182	5	8	0	0	0.2	1.000
1985		5	3	.625	1.82	50	0	0	79	64	17	52	0	5	3	26	11	0	0	.000	4	0	0	1	0.1	1.000
1986		5	7	.417	4.45	45	0	0	64.2	69	20	63	0	5	7	21	7	0	0	.000	2	5	0	0	0.2	1.000
1987		5	4	.556	3.12	40	0	0	52	47	19	44	0	5	4	11	4	0	0	.000	2	5	0	0	0.2	1.000
1988	CHI N	4	4	.500	4.33	46	0	0	43.2	50	15	30	0	4	4	13	1	0	0	.000	1	7	0	0	0.2	1.000
1989	2 teams	SF N	(31G 2–1)			NY A	(11G 1–0)																			
"	total	3	1	.750	2.95	42	0	0	58	46	30	30	0	3	1	5	1	0	0	.000	7	4	1	0	0.3	.917
18 yrs.		113	98	.536	2.92	853	37	16	1635.2	1339	656	1379	0	104	76	307	85	9	0	.106	67	169	19	10	0.3	.925
														4th		2nd										

DIVISIONAL PLAYOFF SERIES

Year	Team	W	L	PCT	ERA	G	GS	CG	IP	H	BB	SO	ShO	W	L	SV	AB	H	HR	BA	PO	A	E	DP	TC/G	FA
1981	NY A	0	0	–	0.00	3	0	0	6.2	3	2	8	0	0	0	3	0	0	0	–	0	0	0	0	0.0	–

LEAGUE CHAMPIONSHIP SERIES

Year	Team	W	L	PCT	ERA	G	GS	CG	IP	H	BB	SO	ShO	W	L	SV	AB	H	HR	BA	PO	A	E	DP	TC/G	FA
1978	NY A	1	0	1.000	4.50	2	0	0	4	3	0	3	0	1	0	1	0	0	0	–	0	1	0	0	0.5	1.000
1980		0	1	.000	54.00	1	0	0	.1	3	0	0	0	0	1	0	0	0	0	–	0	0	0	0	0.0	–
1981		0	0	–	0.00	2	0	0	2.1	1	2	2	0	0	0	0 .	0	0	0	–	0	0	0	0	0.0	–
1984	SD N	0	0	–	4.50	3	0	0	4	5	1	5	0	0	0	2	0	0	0	–	0	0	0	0	0.0	–
4 yrs.		1	1	.500	4.91	8	0	0	11	12	3	10	0	1	1	3	0	0	0	–	0	1	0	0	0.1	1.000

WORLD SERIES

Year	Team	W	L	PCT	ERA	G	GS	CG	IP	H	BB	SO	ShO	W	L	SV	AB	H	HR	BA	PO	A	E	DP	TC/G	FA
1978	NY A	1	0	1.000	0.00	3	0	0	6	1	4	1	0	1	0	0	0	0	0	–	0	0	0	0	0.0	–
1981		0	0	–	0.00	3	0	0	5	2	2	5	0	0	0	2	1	0	0	.000	0	0	0	0	0.0	–
1984	SD N	0	0	–	13.50	2	0	0	2.2	3	1	2	0	0	0	0	0	0	0	–	0	1	0	0	0.5	1.000
3 yrs.		1	0	1.000	2.63	8	0	0	13.2	6	4	11	0	1	0	2	1	0	0	.000	0	1	0	0	0.1	1.000

Jim Gott

GOTT, JAMES WILLIAM
B. Aug. 3, 1959, Hollywood, Calif. BR TR 6'4" 200 lbs.

Year	Team	W	L	PCT	ERA	G	GS	CG	IP	H	BB	SO	ShO	W	L	SV	AB	H	HR	BA	PO	A	E	DP	TC/G	FA
1982	TOR A	5	10	.333	4.43	30	23	1	136	134	66	82	1	0	0	0	0	0	0	–	6	18	1	2	0.8	.960
1983		9	14	.391	4.74	34	30	6	176.2	195	68	121	1	0	1	0	0	0	0	–	9	20	1	2	0.9	.967
1984		7	6	.538	4.02	35	12	1	109.2	93	49	73	1	2	1	2	0	0	0	–	6	9	1	0	0.5	.938
1985	SF N	7	10	.412	3.88	26	26	2	148.1	144	51	78	0	0	0	0	51	10	3	.196	9	28	0	0	1.4	1.000
1986		0	0	–	7.62	9	2	0	13	16	13	9	0	0	0	1	3	0	0	.000	0	2	0	0	0.2	1.000
1987	2 teams	SF N	(30G 1–0)			PIT N	(25G 0–2)																			
"	total	1	2	.333	3.41	55	3	0	87	81	40	90	0	1	2	13	11	1	1	.091	5	10	1	0	0.3	.938
1988	PIT N	6	6	.500	3.49	67	0	0	77.1	68	22	76	0	6	6	34	1	0	0	.000	4	8	0	0	0.2	1.000
1989		0	0	–	0.00	2	0	0	.2	1	1	1	0	0	0	0	0	0	0	–	0	0	0	0	0.0	–
8 yrs.		35	48	.422	4.17	257	96	10	748.2	732	310	530	3	9	10	50	66	11	4	.167	39	95	4	4	0.5	.971

Ted Goulait

GOULAIT, THEODORE LEE (Snooze)
B. Aug. 11, 1889, St. Clair, Mich. D. July 15, 1936, St. Clair, Mich. BR TR 5'9½" 172 lbs.

Year	Team	W	L	PCT	ERA	G	GS	CG	IP	H	BB	SO	ShO	W	L	SV	AB	H	HR	BA	PO	A	E	DP	TC/G	FA
1912	NY N	0	0	–	6.43	1	1	0	7	11	4	6	0	0	0	0	2	1	0	.500	1	1	0	0	2.0	1.000

Year	Team		W	L	PCT	ERA	G	GS	CG	IP	H	BB	SO	ShO	W	L	SV	AB	H	HR	BA	PO	A	E	DP	TC/G	FA

Al Gould

GOULD, ALBERT FRANK (Pudgy)
B. Jan. 20, 1893, Muscatine, Iowa   D. Aug. 8, 1982, San Jose, Calif.
BR TR 5'6½" 160 lbs.

Year	Team		W	L	PCT	ERA	G	GS	CG	IP	H	BB	SO	ShO	W	L	SV	AB	H	HR	BA	PO	A	E	DP	TC/G	FA
1916	CLE	A	5	7	.417	2.53	30	9	6	106.2	101	40	41	1	0	3	1	29	3	0	.103	3	29	2	0	1.1	.941
1917			4	4	.500	3.64	27	7	1	94	95	52	24	0	2	1	0	24	5	0	.208	3	37	1	0	1.5	.976
2 yrs.			9	11	.450	3.05	57	16	7	200.2	196	92	65	1	2	4	1	53	8	0	.151	6	66	3	0	1.3	.960

Charlie Gould

GOULD, CHARLES HARVEY
B. Aug. 21, 1847, Cincinnati, Ohio   D. Apr. 10, 1917, Flushing, N. Y.
Manager 1875-76.
BR TR 6' 172 lbs.

Year	Team		W	L	PCT	ERA	G	GS	CG	IP	H	BB	SO	ShO	W	L	SV	AB	H	HR	BA	PO	A	E	DP	TC/G	FA
1876	CIN	N	0	0	–	0.00	2	0	0	4.1	10	0	0	0	0	0	0	*				0	1	1	0	1.0	.500

Larry Gowell

GOWELL, LAWRENCE CLYDE
B. May 2, 1948, Lewiston, Me.
BR TR 6'2" 182 lbs.

Year	Team		W	L	PCT	ERA	G	GS	CG	IP	H	BB	SO	ShO	W	L	SV	AB	H	HR	BA	PO	A	E	DP	TC/G	FA
1972	NY	A	0	1	.000	1.29	2	1	0	7	3	2	7	0	0	0	0	1	1	0	1.000	0	1	0	0	0.5	1.000

Mauro Gozzo

GOZZO, MAURO PAUL (Goose)
B. Mar. 7, 1966, New Britain, Conn.
BR TR 6'2" 210 lbs.

Year	Team		W	L	PCT	ERA	G	GS	CG	IP	H	BB	SO	ShO	W	L	SV	AB	H	HR	BA	PO	A	E	DP	TC/G	FA
1989	TOR	A	4	1	.800	4.83	9	3	0	31.2	35	9	10	0	1	1	0	0	0	0	–	3	3	0	0	0.7	1.000

Al Grabowski

GRABOWSKI, ALFONS FRANCIS (Hook)
Brother of Reggie Grabowski.
B. Sept. 4, 1901, Syracuse, N. Y.   D. Oct. 29, 1966, Memphis, Tenn.
BL TL 5'11½" 175 lbs.

Year	Team		W	L	PCT	ERA	G	GS	CG	IP	H	BB	SO	ShO	W	L	SV	AB	H	HR	BA	PO	A	E	DP	TC/G	FA
1929	STL	N	3	2	.600	2.52	6	6	4	50	44	8	22	2	0	0	0	16	4	0	.250	6	8	0	0	2.3	1.000
1930			6	4	.600	4.84	33	8	1	106	121	50	45	0	2	3	1	33	12	0	.364	4	21	2	0	0.8	.926
2 yrs.			9	6	.600	4.10	39	14	5	156	165	58	67	2	2	3	1	49	16	0	.327	10	29	2	0	1.1	.951

Reggie Grabowski

GRABOWSKI, REGINALD JOHN
Brother of Al Grabowski.
B. July 16, 1907, Syracuse, N. Y.   D. Apr. 2, 1955, Syracuse, N. Y.
BR TR 6'½" 185 lbs.

Year	Team		W	L	PCT	ERA	G	GS	CG	IP	H	BB	SO	ShO	W	L	SV	AB	H	HR	BA	PO	A	E	DP	TC/G	FA
1932	PHI	N	2	2	.500	3.67	14	2	0	34.1	38	22	15	0	2	1	0	6	0	0	.000	1	5	1	0	0.5	.857
1933			1	3	.250	2.44	10	5	4	48	38	10	9	1	0	0	0	16	2	0	.125	4	5	0	0	0.9	1.000
1934			1	3	.250	9.23	27	5	0	65.1	114	23	13	0	1	0	0	18	1	0	.056	5	6	0	2	0.4	1.000
3 yrs.			4	8	.333	5.73	51	12	4	147.2	190	55	37	1	3	1	0	40	3	0	.075	10	16	1	2	0.5	.963

John Graff

GRAFF, JOHN F.
B. Philadelphia, Pa.   Deceased.

Year	Team		W	L	PCT	ERA	G	GS	CG	IP	H	BB	SO	ShO	W	L	SV	AB	H	HR	BA	PO	A	E	DP	TC/G	FA
1893	WAS	N	0	1	.000	11.25	2	1	1	12	21	13	4	0	0	0	0	5	1	0	.200	0	2	0	0	1.0	1.000

Bill Graham

GRAHAM, WILLIAM ALBERT
B. Jan. 21, 1937, Flemingsburg, Ky.
BR TR 6'3" 217 lbs.

Year	Team		W	L	PCT	ERA	G	GS	CG	IP	H	BB	SO	ShO	W	L	SV	AB	H	HR	BA	PO	A	E	DP	TC/G	FA
1966	DET	A	0	0	–	0.00	1	0	0	2	2	0	2	0	0	0	0	0	0	0	–	0	0	0	0	0.0	–
1967	NY	N	1	2	.333	2.63	5	3	1	27.1	20	11	14	0	0	0	0	8	1	0	.125	1	1	1	0	0.6	.667
2 yrs.			1	2	.333	2.45	6	3	1	29.1	22	11	16	0	0	0	0	8	1	0	.125	1	1	1	0	0.5	.667

Bill Graham

GRAHAM, WILLIAM JAMES
B. July 22, 1884, Owosso, Mich.   D. Feb. 15, 1936, Holt, Mich.
TL 6'

Year	Team		W	L	PCT	ERA	G	GS	CG	IP	H	BB	SO	ShO	W	L	SV	AB	H	HR	BA	PO	A	E	DP	TC/G	FA
1908	STL	A	6	7	.462	2.30	21	13	7	117.1	104	32	47	0	3	1	0	42	5	0	.119	9	35	2	2	2.0	.953
1909			8	14	.364	3.12	34	21	13	187.1	171	60	82	3	2	1	1	63	10	0	.159	9	58	4	5	2.1	.944
1910			0	8	.000	3.56	9	6	1	43	46	13	12	0	0	2	0	13	2	0	.154	1	8	4	0	1.4	.692
3 yrs.			14	29	.326	2.90	64	40	21	347.2	321	105	141	3	5	5	1	118	17	0	.144	16	101	10	7	2.0	.921

Kyle Graham

GRAHAM, KYLE (Skinny)
B. Aug. 14, 1899, Oak Grove, Ala.   D. Dec. 1, 1973, Oak Grove, Ala.
BR TR 6'2" 172 lbs.

Year	Team		W	L	PCT	ERA	G	GS	CG	IP	H	BB	SO	ShO	W	L	SV	AB	H	HR	BA	PO	A	E	DP	TC/G	FA
1924	BOS	N	0	4	.000	3.82	5	4	1	33	33	11	15	0	0	0	0	7	0	0	.000	1	6	0	1	1.4	1.000
1925			7	12	.368	4.41	34	23	5	157	177	62	32	0	1	1	1	44	6	0	.136	4	28	1	1	1.0	.970
1926			3	3	.500	7.93	15	4	1	36.1	54	19	7	0	2	2	0	12	2	0	.167	1	11	0	0	0.8	1.000
1929	DET	A	1	3	.250	5.57	13	6	2	51.2	70	33	7	0	0	1	1	19	2	1	.105	0	9	0	1	0.7	1.000
4 yrs.			11	22	.333	5.02	67	37	9	278	334	125	61	0	3	4	2	82	10	1	.122	6	54	1	3	0.9	.984

Oscar Graham

GRAHAM, OSCAR M.
B. July 20, 1878, Plattsmouth, Neb.   D. Oct. 15, 1931, Moline, Ill.
TL 6'½"

Year	Team		W	L	PCT	ERA	G	GS	CG	IP	H	BB	SO	ShO	W	L	SV	AB	H	HR	BA	PO	A	E	DP	TC/G	FA
1907	WAS	A	4	9	.308	3.98	20	14	6	104	116	29	44	0	0	1	0	48	11	1	.229	3	25	3	0	1.6	.903

Peaches Graham

GRAHAM, GEORGE FREDERICK
Father of Jack Graham.
B. Mar. 23, 1877, Aledo, Ill.   D. July 25, 1939, Long Beach, Calif.
BR TR 5'9" 180 lbs.

Year	Team		W	L	PCT	ERA	G	GS	CG	IP	H	BB	SO	ShO	W	L	SV	AB	H	HR	BA	PO	A	E	DP	TC/G	FA
1903	CHI	N	0	1	.000	5.40	1	1	0	5	9	3	4	0	0	0	0	*				0	3	0	0	3.0	1.000

Tommy Gramly

GRAMLY, BERT THOMAS
B. Apr. 19, 1945, Dallas, Tex.
BR TR 6'3" 175 lbs.

Year	Team		W	L	PCT	ERA	G	GS	CG	IP	H	BB	SO	ShO	W	L	SV	AB	H	HR	BA	PO	A	E	DP	TC/G	FA
1968	CLE	A	0	1	.000	2.70	3	0	0	3.1	3	2	1	0	0	1	0	0	0	0	–	0	0	0	0	0.0	–

Henry Grampp

GRAMPP, HENRY ERCHARDT
B. Sept. 28, 1903, New York, N. Y.   D. Mar. 24, 1986, New York, N. Y.
BR TR 6'1" 185 lbs.

Year	Team		W	L	PCT	ERA	G	GS	CG	IP	H	BB	SO	ShO	W	L	SV	AB	H	HR	BA	PO	A	E	DP	TC/G	FA
1927	CHI	N	0	0	–	9.00	2	0	0	3	4	1	3	0	0	0	0	0	0	0	–	0	1	0	0	0.5	1.000
1929			0	1	.000	27.00	1	1	0	2	4	3	0	0	0	0	0	0	0	0	–	0	0	0	0	0.0	–
2 yrs.			0	1	.000	16.20	3	1	0	5	8	4	3	0	0	0	0	0	0	0	–	0	1	0	0	0.3	1.000

Year	Team	W	L	PCT	ERA	G	GS	CG	IP	H	BB	SO	ShO	Relief Pitching W	L	SV	Batting AB	H	HR	BA	PO	A	E	DP	TC/G	FA

Jack Graney

GRANEY, JOHN GLADSTONE
B. June 10, 1886, St. Thomas, Ont., Canada D. Apr. 20, 1978, Louisiana, Mo.
BL TL 5'9" 180 lbs.

Year	Team	W	L	PCT	ERA	G	GS	CG	IP	H	BB	SO	ShO	W	L	SV	AB	H	HR	BA	PO	A	E	DP	TC/G	FA
1908	CLE A	0	0	–	5.40	2	0	0	3.1	6	1	0	0	0	0	0	*				0	0	0	0	0.0	–

Wayne Granger

GRANGER, WAYNE ALLAN
B. Mar. 15, 1944, Springfield, Mass.
BR TR 6'2" 165 lbs.

Year	Team	W	L	PCT	ERA	G	GS	CG	IP	H	BB	SO	ShO	W	L	SV	AB	H	HR	BA	PO	A	E	DP	TC/G	FA
1968	STL N	4	2	.667	2.25	34	0	0	44	40	12	27	0	4	2	4	5	1	0	.200	6	14	2	1	0.6	.909
1969	CIN N	9	6	.600	2.79	90	0	0	145	143	40	68	0	9	6	27	21	2	0	.095	14	29	2	3	0.5	.956
1970		6	5	.545	2.65	67	0	0	85	79	27	38	0	6	5	35	10	1	0	.100	8	22	4	4	0.5	.882
1971		7	6	.538	3.33	70	0	0	100	94	28	51	0	7	6	11	7	1	1	.143	9	29	0	1	0.5	1.000
1972	MIN A	4	6	.400	3.00	63	0	0	90	83	28	45	0	4	6	19	10	2	0	.200	5	14	2	0	0.3	.905
1973	2 teams		STL N	(33G 2–4)			NY A		(7G 0–1)																		
"	total	2	5	.286	3.63	40	0	0	62	69	24	24	0	2	5	5	3	0	0	.000	4	8	3	0	0.4	.800
1974	CHI A	0	0	–	7.88	5	0	0	8	16	3	4	0	0	0	0	0	0	0	–	1	2	0	1	0.6	1.000
1975	HOU N	2	5	.286	3.65	55	0	0	74	76	23	30	0	2	5	5	9	0	0	.000	2	18	3	1	0.4	.870
1976	MON N	1	0	1.000	3.66	27	0	0	32	32	16	16	0	1	0	2	3	0	0	.000	1	5	1	0	0.3	.857
9 yrs.		35	35	.500	3.14	451	0	0	640	632	201	303	0	35	35	108	68	7	1	.103	50	141	17	11	0.5	.918

LEAGUE CHAMPIONSHIP SERIES

Year	Team	W	L	PCT	ERA	G	GS	CG	IP	H	BB	SO	ShO	W	L	SV	AB	H	HR	BA	PO	A	E	DP	TC/G	FA
1970	CIN N	0	0	–	0.00	1	0	0	.2	1	0	0	0	0	0	0	0	0	0	–	0	0	0	0	0.0	–

WORLD SERIES

Year	Team	W	L	PCT	ERA	G	GS	CG	IP	H	BB	SO	ShO	W	L	SV	AB	H	HR	BA	PO	A	E	DP	TC/G	FA
1968	STL N	0	0	–	0.00	1	0	0	2	0	1	1	0	0	0	0	0	0	0	–	0	1	0	1	1.0	1.000
1970	CIN N	0	0	–	33.75	2	0	0	1.1	7	1	1	0	0	0	0	0	0	0	–	0	1	0	0	0.5	1.000
2 yrs.		0	0	–	13.50	3	0	0	3.1	7	2	2	0	0	0	0	0	0	0	–	0	2	0	1	0.7	1.000

George Grant

GRANT, GEORGE ADDISON
B. Jan. 6, 1903, East Tallassee, Ala. D. Mar. 25, 1986, Montgomery, Ala.
BR TR 5'11½" 175 lbs.

Year	Team	W	L	PCT	ERA	G	GS	CG	IP	H	BB	SO	ShO	W	L	SV	AB	H	HR	BA	PO	A	E	DP	TC/G	FA
1923	STL A	0	0	–	5.19	4	0	0	8.2	15	3	2	0	0	0	0	2	0	0	.000	0	4	0	0	1.0	1.000
1924		1	2	.333	6.26	21	2	0	50.1	67	25	11	0	1	0	0	13	0	0	.000	5	8	0	0	0.6	1.000
1925		0	2	.000	6.06	12	0	0	16.1	26	8	7	0	0	2	0	4	1	0	.250	1	5	1	1	0.6	.857
1927	CLE A	4	6	.400	4.46	25	3	2	74.2	85	40	19	0	3	4	1	21	2	0	.095	6	19	0	0	1.0	1.000
1928		10	8	.556	5.04	28	18	6	155.1	196	76	39	1	2	1	0	60	11	0	.183	9	46	0	2	2.0	1.000
1929		0	2	.000	10.50	12	0	0	24	41	23	5	0	0	2	0	2	0	0	.000	0	7	0	0	0.6	1.000
1931	PIT N	0	0	–	7.41	11	0	0	17	28	7	6	0	0	0	0	2	0	0	.000	2	4	1	1	0.6	.857
7 yrs.		15	20	.429	5.64	113	23	8	346.1	458	182	89	1	6	9	1	104	14	0	.135	23	93	3	4	1.0	.983

Jim Grant

GRANT, JAMES RONALD
B. Aug. 4, 1894, Coalville, Iowa D. Nov. 30, 1985, Des Moines, Iowa
BR TL 5'11" 180 lbs.

Year	Team	W	L	PCT	ERA	G	GS	CG	IP	H	BB	SO	ShO	W	L	SV	AB	H	HR	BA	PO	A	E	DP	TC/G	FA
1923	PHI N	0	0	–	13.50	2	0	0	4	10	4	0	0	0	0	0	1	0	0	.000	1	0	0	0	0.5	1.000

Mark Grant

GRANT, MARK ANDREW
B. Oct. 24, 1963, Aurora, Ill.
BR TR 6'2" 205 lbs.

Year	Team	W	L	PCT	ERA	G	GS	CG	IP	H	BB	SO	ShO	W	L	SV	AB	H	HR	BA	PO	A	E	DP	TC/G	FA
1984	SF N	1	4	.200	6.37	11	10	1	53.2	56	19	32	0	0	0	0	17	0	0	.000	6	6	1	0	1.2	.923
1986		1	1	.000	3.60	4	1	0	10	6	5	5	0	0	0	0	1	0	0	.000	0	1	0	1	0.3	1.000
1987	2 teams		SF N	(16G 1–2)			SD N		(17G 6–7)																		
"	total	7	9	.438	4.24	33	25	2	163.1	170	73	90	1	1	1	1	44	4	0	.091	10	21	4	0	1.1	.886
1988	SD N	2	8	.200	3.69	33	11	0	97.2	97	36	61	0	1	3	0	16	0	0	.000	4	16	0	1	0.6	1.000
1989		8	2	.800	3.33	50	0	0	116.1	105	32	69	0	8	2	2	20	1	0	.050	9	14	1	1	0.5	.958
5 yrs.		18	24	.429	4.12	131	47	2	441	434	165	257	1	10	6	4	98	5	0	.051	29	58	6	3	0.7	.935

Mudcat Grant

GRANT, JAMES TIMOTHY
B. Aug. 13, 1935, Lacoochee, Fla.
BR TR 6'1" 186 lbs.

Year	Team	W	L	PCT	ERA	G	GS	CG	IP	H	BB	SO	ShO	W	L	SV	AB	H	HR	BA	PO	A	E	DP	TC/G	FA
1958	CLE A	10	11	.476	3.84	44	28	11	204	173	104	111	1	2	2	4	66	5	0	.076	7	28	3	2	0.9	.921
1959		10	7	.588	4.14	38	19	6	165.1	140	81	85	1	1	1	3	55	11	1	.200	14	25	2	3	1.1	.951
1960		9	8	.529	4.40	33	19	5	159.2	147	78	75	0	1	3	0	57	16	0	.281	25	15	2	1	1.3	.952
1961		15	9	.625	3.86	35	35	11	244.2	207	109	146	3	0	0	0	88	15	1	.170	25	36	2	4	1.8	.968
1963		13	14	.481	3.69	38	32	10	229.1	213	87	157	2	1	0	1	69	13	1	.188	11	21	3	1	0.9	.914
1964	2 teams		CLE A	(13G 3–4)			MIN A		(26G 11–9)																		
"	total	14	13	.519	3.67	39	32	11	228	244	61	118	1	1	0	1	82	16	2	.195	19	35	0	6	1.4	1.000
1965	MIN A	21	7	.750	3.30	41	39	14	270.1	252	61	142	6	1	0	0	97	15	0	.155	16	50	2	6	1.7	.971
1966		13	13	.500	3.25	35	35	10	249	248	49	110	3	0	0	0	78	15	0	.192	9	53	3	6	1.9	.955
1967	LA N	5	6	.455	4.72	27	14	2	95.1	121	17	50	0	0	0	0	28	5	0	.179	3	7	1	3	0.4	.909
1968		6	4	.600	2.08	37	4	1	95	77	19	35	0	5	2	3	31	4	1	.129	4	21	0	0	0.7	1.000
1969	2 teams		MON N	(11G 1–6)			STL N		(30G 7–5)																		
"	total	8	11	.421	4.42	41	13	2	114	126	36	55	0	0	0	7	33	7	0	.212	9	16	1	0	0.6	.962
1970	2 teams		OAK A	(72G 6–2)			PIT N		(8G 2–1)																		
"	total	8	3	.727	1.87	80	0	0	135	112	32	58	0	8	3	24	11	2	0	.182	10	24	0	3	0.4	1.000
1971	2 teams		PIT N	(42G 5–3)			OAK A		(15G 1–0)																		
"	total	6	3	.667	3.18	57	0	0	102	104	34	35	0	6	3	10	11	3	0	.273	3	17	0	0	0.4	1.000
14 yrs.		145	119	.549	3.63	571	293	89	2441.1	2292	849	1267	18	25	15	53	759	135	6	.178	160	373	19	38	1.0	.966

LEAGUE CHAMPIONSHIP SERIES

Year	Team	W	L	PCT	ERA	G	GS	CG	IP	H	BB	SO	ShO	W	L	SV	AB	H	HR	BA	PO	A	E	DP	TC/G	FA
1971	OAK A	0	0	–	0.00	1	0	0	2	3	0	2	0	0	0	0	0	0	0	–	0	1	0	0	1.0	1.000

WORLD SERIES

Year	Team	W	L	PCT	ERA	G	GS	CG	IP	H	BB	SO	ShO	W	L	SV	AB	H	HR	BA	PO	A	E	DP	TC/G	FA
1965	MIN A	2	1	.667	2.74	3	3	2	23	22	2	12	0	0	0	0	8	2	1	.250	1	4	0	0	0.3	1.000

Dick Grapenthin

GRAPENTHIN, RICHARD RAY
B. Apr. 16, 1958, Linn Grove, Iowa
BR TR 6'2" 190 lbs.

Year	Team	W	L	PCT	ERA	G	GS	CG	IP	H	BB	SO	ShO	W	L	SV	AB	H	HR	BA	PO	A	E	DP	TC/G	FA
1983	MON N	0	1	.000	9.00	4	0	0	4	4	3	3	0	0	1	0	1	0	0	.000	0	4	0	0	1.0	1.000
1984		1	2	.333	3.52	13	1	0	23	19	7	9	0	1	1	2	5	1	0	.200	2	4	0	0	0.5	1.000

Year	Team	W	L	PCT	ERA	G	GS	CG	IP	H	BB	SO	ShO	Relief Pitching W	L	SV	Batting AB	H	HR	BA	PO	A	E	DP	TC/G	FA

Dick Grapenthin *continued*

Year		W	L	PCT	ERA	G	GS	CG	IP	H	BB	SO	ShO	W	L	SV	AB	H	HR	BA	PO	A	E	DP	TC/G	FA
1985		0	0	–	14.14	5	0	0	7	13	8	4	0	0	0	0	1	1	0	1.000	0	1	0	0	0.2	1.000
3 yrs.		1	3	.250	6.35	19	1	0	34	36	16	16	0	1	2	2	7	2	0	.286	2	6	0	0	0.4	1.000

Lou Grasmick

GRASMICK, LOUIS JUNIOR
B. Sept. 11, 1924, Baltimore, Md. BR TR 6' 195 lbs.

Year	Team	W	L	PCT	ERA	G	GS	CG	IP	H	BB	SO	ShO	W	L	SV	AB	H	HR	BA	PO	A	E	DP	TC/G	FA
1948	PHI N	0	0	–	7.20	2	0	0	5	3	8	2	0	0	0	0	1	1	0	1.000	1	1	0	0	1.0	1.000

Don Grate

GRATE, DONALD (Buckeye)
B. Aug. 27, 1923, Greenfield, Ohio BR TR 6'2½" 180 lbs.

Year	Team	W	L	PCT	ERA	G	GS	CG	IP	H	BB	SO	ShO	W	L	SV	AB	H	HR	BA	PO	A	E	DP	TC/G	FA
1945	PHI N	0	1	.000	17.28	4	2	0	8.1	18	12	6	0	0	0	0	3	0	0	.000	0	0	0	0	0.0	–
1946		1	0	1.000	1.13	3	0	0	8	4	2	2	0	1	0	0	1	0	0	.000	0	0	0	0	0.0	–
2 yrs.		1	1	.500	9.37	7	2	0	16.1	22	14	8	0	1	0	0	4	0	0	.000	0	0	0	0	0.0	–

Frank Graves

GRAVES, FRANK M.
B. Nov. 2, 1860, Cincinnati, Ohio Deceased. 6' 163 lbs.

Year	Team	W	L	PCT	ERA	G	GS	CG	IP	H	BB	SO	ShO	W	L	SV	AB	H	HR	BA	PO	A	E	DP	TC/G	FA
1886	STL N	0	0	–	9.00	1	0	0	7	10	1	2	0	0	0	0	*				0	1	0	0	1.0	1.000

Charlie Gray

GRAY, CHARLES
B. 1867, Indianapolis, Ind. Deceased.

Year	Team	W	L	PCT	ERA	G	GS	CG	IP	H	BB	SO	ShO	W	L	SV	AB	H	HR	BA	PO	A	E	DP	TC/G	FA
1890	PIT N	1	4	.200	7.55	5	4	3	31	48	24	10	0	1	0	0	15	3	0	.200	3	0	1	0	0.6	1.000

Chummy Gray

GRAY, GEORGE EDWARD
B. July 17, 1873, Rockland, Me. D. Aug. 14, 1913, Rockland, Me. TR 5'11½" 163 lbs.

Year	Team	W	L	PCT	ERA	G	GS	CG	IP	H	BB	SO	ShO	W	L	SV	AB	H	HR	BA	PO	A	E	DP	TC/G	FA
1899	PIT N	3	3	.500	3.44	9	7	6	70.2	85	24	9	0	0	0	0	26	1	0	.038	1	26	0	0	3.0	1.000

Dave Gray

GRAY, DAVID ALEXANDER
B. Jan. 7, 1943, Ogden, Utah BR TR 6'1" 190 lbs.

Year	Team	W	L	PCT	ERA	G	GS	CG	IP	H	BB	SO	ShO	W	L	SV	AB	H	HR	BA	PO	A	E	DP	TC/G	FA
1964	BOS A	0	0	–	9.00	9	1	0	13	18	20	17	0	0	0	0	1	1	0	1.000	0	3	0	0	0.3	1.000

Dolly Gray

GRAY, WILLIAM DENTON
B. Dec. 4, 1878, Ishpeming, Mich. D. Apr. 4, 1956, Yuba City, Calif. BL TL 6'2" 160 lbs.

Year	Team	W	L	PCT	ERA	G	GS	CG	IP	H	BB	SO	ShO	W	L	SV	AB	H	HR	BA	PO	A	E	DP	TC/G	FA
1909	WAS A	5	19	.208	3.59	36	26	19	218	210	77	87	0	0	0	0	89	13	0	.146	3	65	4	2	2.0	.944
1910		8	19	.296	2.63	34	29	21	229	216	64	84	3	0	0	2	85	21	0	.247	15	82	9	2	3.1	.915
1911		2	13	.133	5.06	28	15	6	121	160	40	42	0	0	0	3	44	10	0	.227	4	42	6	1	1.9	.885
3 yrs.		15	51	.227	3.52	98	70	46	568	586	181	213	3	0	0	5	218	44	0	.202	22	189	19	5	2.3	.917

Jeff Gray

GRAY, JEFFREY EDWARD
B. Apr. 10, 1963, Richmond, Va. BR TR 6'1" 175 lbs.

Year	Team	W	L	PCT	ERA	G	GS	CG	IP	H	BB	SO	ShO	W	L	SV	AB	H	HR	BA	PO	A	E	DP	TC/G	FA
1988	CIN N	0	0	–	3.86	5	0	0	9.1	12	4	5	0	0	0	0	1	0	0	.000	1	3	0	0	0.8	1.000

John Gray

GRAY, JOHN LEONARD
B. Dec. 11, 1927, West Palm Beach, Fla. BR TR 6'4" 226 lbs.

Year	Team	W	L	PCT	ERA	G	GS	CG	IP	H	BB	SO	ShO	W	L	SV	AB	H	HR	BA	PO	A	E	DP	TC/G	FA
1954	PHI A	3	12	.200	6.51	18	16	5	105	111	91	51	0	0	0	0	34	1	0	.029	11	14	1	2	1.4	.962
1955	KC A	0	3	.000	6.41	8	5	0	26.2	28	24	11	0	0	0	0	8	1	0	.125	2	1	0	0	0.4	1.000
1957	CLE A	1	3	.250	5.85	7	3	1	20	21	13	3	1	0	0	0	3	0	0	.000	3	3	1	0	1.0	.857
1958	PHI N	0	0	–	4.15	15	0	0	17.1	12	14	10	0	0	1	0	1	0	0	.000	0	3	0	0	0.2	1.000
4 yrs.		4	18	.182	6.18	48	24	6	169	172	142	75	1	0	1	0	47	2	0	.043	16	21	2	2	0.8	.949

Sam Gray

GRAY, SAMUEL DAVID (Sad Sam)
B. Oct. 15, 1897, Van Alstyne, Tex. D. Apr. 16, 1953, McKinney, Tex. BR TR 5'10" 175 lbs.

Year	Team	W	L	PCT	ERA	G	GS	CG	IP	H	BB	SO	ShO	W	L	SV	AB	H	HR	BA	PO	A	E	DP	TC/G	FA
1924	PHI A	8	7	.533	3.98	34	19	8	151.2	169	89	54	2	1	0	2	57	10	0	.175	5	31	1	2	1.1	.973
1925		16	8	.667	3.40	32	28	14	195.2	199	63	80	4	0	0	3	67	12	0	.179	8	37	3	1	1.5	.938
1926		11	12	.478	3.64	38	18	5	150.2	164	50	82	0	4	3	0	51	11	0	.216	5	29	7	2	1.1	.829
1927		9	6	.600	4.60	37	13	3	141	162	53	54	1	2	2	3	42	8	0	.190	8	32	3	2	1.2	.930
1928	STL A	20	12	.625	3.19	35	31	21	262.2	256	86	102	0	1	0	3	101	19	1	.188	20	67	2	6	2.5	.978
1929		18	15	.545	3.72	43	37	23	305	336	96	109	4	1	0	1	103	19	0	.184	9	61	3	4	1.7	.959
1930		4	15	.211	6.28	27	24	7	167.2	215	52	51	0	0	1	0	54	11	0	.204	3	33	5	2	1.5	.923
1931		11	24	.314	5.09	43	37	13	258	323	54	88	0	1	1	2	79	14	1	.177	11	49	8	0	1.6	.882
1932		8	12	.400	4.53	32	18	7	206.2	250	53	79	3	2	1	4	62	13	0	.210	9	39	4	1	1.0	.923
1933		7	4	.636	4.10	38	6	0	112	131	45	36	0	4	4	4	32	7	0	.219	3	21	2	2	0.7	.923
10 yrs.		112	115	.493	4.20	379	231	101	1951	2205	641	735	16	16	12	22	648	124	3	.191	81	399	38	22	1.4	.927

Ted Gray

GRAY, TED GLENN
B. Dec. 31, 1924, Detroit, Mich. BB TL 5'11" 175 lbs.

Year	Team	W	L	PCT	ERA	G	GS	CG	IP	H	BB	SO	ShO	W	L	SV	AB	H	HR	BA	PO	A	E	DP	TC/G	FA
1946	DET A	0	2	.000	8.49	3	2	0	11.2	17	5	5	0	0	0	1	3	0	0	.000	1	1	0	0	0.7	1.000
1948		6	2	.750	4.22	26	11	3	85.1	73	72	60	1	0	0	0	29	7	0	.241	3	11	0	1	0.5	1.000
1949		10	10	.500	3.51	34	27	8	195	163	103	96	3	0	0	0	63	8	0	.127	9	37	0	3	1.4	1.000
1950		10	7	.588	4.40	27	21	7	149.1	139	72	102	0	1	0	1	50	7	0	.140	5	16	1	0	0.8	.955
1951		7	14	.333	4.06	34	28	9	197.1	194	95	131	1	0	1	1	63	9	0	.143	10	25	3	2	1.1	.921
1952		12	17	.414	4.14	35	32	13	224	212	101	138	2	0	0	0	76	13	0	.171	14	40	2	3	1.6	.964
1953		10	15	.400	4.60	30	28	8	176	166	76	115	0	0	0	0	61	14	0	.230	9	22	2	0	1.1	.939
1954		3	5	.375	5.38	19	10	2	72	70	56	29	0	1	1	1	22	1	0	.045	0	9	1	1	0.5	.900
1955	4 teams	CHI A	(2G 0-0)		CLE A	(2G 0-0)		NY A	(1G 0-0)		BAL A	(9G 1-2)															
" total		1	2	.333	9.64	14	3	0	23.1	38	15	11	0	0	0	0	3	0	0	.000	1	7	0	1	0.6	1.000
9 yrs.		59	74	.444	4.37	222	162	50	1134	1072	595	687	7	2	2	4	370	59	0	.159	52	168	9	11	1.0	.961

Year	Team		W	L	PCT	ERA	G	GS	CG	IP	H	BB	SO	ShO	Relief Pitching W	L	SV	Batting AB	H	HR	BA	PO	A	E	DP	TC/G	FA

Eli Grba

GRBA, ELI
B. Aug. 9, 1934, Chicago, Ill.
BR TR 6'2" 205 lbs.

1959	NY	A	2	5	.286	6.44	19	6	0	50.1	52	39	23	0	1	1	0	14	3	0	.214	3	9	1	0	0.7	.923
1960			6	4	.600	3.68	24	9	1	80.2	65	46	32	0	5	0	1	21	5	1	.238	9	9	1	1	0.8	.947
1961	LA	A	11	13	.458	4.25	40	30	8	211.2	197	114	105	0	2	1	2	64	15	2	.234	11	31	2	2	1.1	.955
1962			8	9	.471	4.54	40	29	1	176.1	185	75	90	0	0	0	1	58	12	1	.207	9	37	7	3	1.3	.868
1963			1	2	.333	4.67	12	1	0	17.1	14	10	5	0	1	1	0	3	0	0	.000	2	3	0	1	0.4	1.000
5 yrs.			28	33	.459	4.48	135	75	10	536.1	513	284	255	0	9	3	4	160	35	4	.219	34	89	11	7	1.0	.918

Bill Greason

GREASON, WILLIAM HENRY (Booster)
B. Sept. 3, 1924, Atlanta, Ga.
BR TR 5'10" 170 lbs.

| 1954 | STL | N | 0 | 1 | .000 | 13.50 | 3 | 2 | 0 | 4 | 8 | 4 | 2 | 0 | 0 | 0 | 0 | 1 | 0 | 0 | .000 | 0 | 1 | 0 | 0 | 0.3 | 1.000 |

Chris Green

GREEN, CHRISTOPHER DeWAYNE
B. Sept. 5, 1960, Los Angeles, Calif.
BL TL 6'2" 180 lbs.

| 1984 | PIT | N | 0 | 0 | — | 6.00 | 4 | 0 | 0 | 3 | 5 | 1 | 3 | 0 | 0 | 0 | 0 | 0 | 0 | 0 | — | 0 | 1 | 0 | 0 | 0.3 | 1.000 |

Dallas Green

GREEN, GEORGE DALLAS
B. Aug. 4, 1934, Newport, Del.
Manager 1979-81, 1989.
BL TR 6'5" 210 lbs.

1960	PHI	N	3	6	.333	4.06	23	10	5	108.2	100	44	51	1	0	1	0	34	7	0	.206	11	15	0	1	1.1	1.000
1961			2	4	.333	4.85	42	10	1	128	160	47	51	0	1	1	1	33	5	0	.152	14	22	1	2	0.9	.973
1962			6	6	.500	3.83	37	10	2	129.1	145	43	58	0	3	1	1	32	2	0	.063	17	28	0	1	1.2	1.000
1963			7	5	.583	3.23	40	14	4	120	134	38	68	0	3	0	2	35	3	0	.086	11	26	1	1	1.0	.974
1964			2	1	.667	5.79	25	0	0	42	63	14	21	0	2	1	0	3	0	0	.000	0	8	3	0	0.4	.727
1965	WAS	A	0	0	—	3.14	6	2	0	14.1	14	3	6	0	0	0	0	4	0	0	.000	1	5	0	0	1.0	1.000
1966	NY	N	0	0	—	5.40	4	0	0	5	6	2	1	0	0	0	0	0	0	0	—	0	2	0	0	0.5	1.000
1967	PHI	N	0	0	—	9.00	8	0	0	15	25	6	12	0	0	0	0	1	0	0	.000	0	5	0	0	0.6	1.000
8 yrs.			20	22	.476	4.26	185	46	12	562.1	647	197	268	2	9	4	4	142	17	0	.120	56	109	5	4	0.9	.971

Ed Green

GREEN, EDWARD M.
B. 1850, Philadelphia, Pa. D. Mar. 22, 1917, Ogden, Utah

| 1890 | PHI | AA | 7 | 15 | .318 | 5.80 | 25 | 22 | 20 | 191 | 267 | 94 | 56 | 1 | 0 | 0 | 1 | 126 | 15 | 0 | .119 | 8 | 53 | 4 | 1 | 2.6 | .938 |

Freddie Green

GREEN, FRED ALLEN
Father of Gary Green.
B. Sept. 14, 1933, Titusville, N. J.
BR TL 6'4" 190 lbs.

1959	PIT	N	1	2	.333	3.13	17	1	0	37.1	37	15	20	0	1	1	1	6	0	0	.000	2	8	0	0	0.6	1.000
1960			8	4	.667	3.21	45	0	0	70	61	33	49	0	8	4	3	8	3	2	.375	4	9	1	0	0.3	.929
1961			0	0	—	4.79	13	0	0	20.2	27	9	4	0	0	0	0	3	0	0	.000	1	7	0	1	0.6	1.000
1962	WAS	A	0	1	.000	6.43	5	0	0	7	7	6	2	0	0	1	0	0	0	0	—	0	2	0	0	0.4	1.000
1964	PIT	N	0	0	—	1.23	8	0	0	7.1	10	0	2	0	0	0	0	0	0	0	—	0	0	1	0	0.1	—
5 yrs.			9	7	.563	3.48	88	1	0	142.1	142	63	77	0	9	6	4	17	3	2	.176	7	26	2	1	0.4	.943

WORLD SERIES

| 1960 | PIT | N | 0 | 0 | — | 22.50 | 3 | 0 | 0 | 4 | 11 | 1 | 3 | 0 | 0 | 0 | 0 | 1 | 0 | 0 | .000 | 0 | 0 | 0 | 0 | 0.0 | — |

Harvey Green

GREEN, HARVEY GEORGE (Buck)
B. Feb. 9, 1915, Kenosha, Wis. D. July 24, 1970, Franklin, La.
BB TR 6'2½" 185 lbs.

| 1935 | BKN | N | 0 | 0 | — | 9.00 | 2 | 0 | 1 | 4 | 1 | 2 | 3 | 0 | 0 | 0 | 0 | 0 | 0 | 0 | — | 0 | 0 | 0 | 0 | 0.0 | — |

June Greene

GREENE, JULIUS FOUST
B. June 25, 1899, Ramseur, N. C. D. Mar. 19, 1974, Glendora, Calif.
BL TR 6'2½" 185 lbs.

1928	PHI	N	0	0	—	9.00	1	0	0	2	5	0	0	0	0	0	0	6	3	0	.500	0	2	0	0	2.0	1.000
1929			0	0	—	19.76	5	0	0	13.2	33	9	4	0	0	0	0	19	4	0	.211	1	4	0	0	1.0	1.000
2 yrs.			0	0	—	18.38	6	0	0	15.2	38	9	4	0	0	0	0	*				1	6	0	0	1.2	1.000

Nelson Greene

GREENE, NELSON GEORGE (Lefty)
B. Sept. 20, 1900, Philadelphia, Pa. D. Apr. 6, 1983, Lebanon, Pa.
BL TL 6' 185 lbs.

1924	BKN	N	0	1	.000	4.00	4	1	0	9	14	2	3	0	0	0	0	1	0	0	.000	1	4	1	0	1.5	.833
1925			2	0	1.000	10.64	11	0	0	22	45	7	4	0	2	0	1	7	2	0	.286	0	6	0	1	0.5	1.000
2 yrs.			2	1	.667	8.71	15	1	0	31	59	9	7	0	2	0	1	8	2	0	.250	1	10	1	1	0.8	.917

Tommy Greene

GREENE, IRA THOMAS
B. Apr. 6, 1967, Lumberton, N. C.
BR TR 6'5" 225 lbs.

| 1989 | ATL | N | 1 | 2 | .333 | 4.10 | 4 | 4 | 1 | 26.1 | 22 | 6 | 17 | 0 | 0 | 0 | 0 | 10 | 1 | 0 | .100 | 2 | 0 | 0 | 0 | 1.0 | 1.000 |

Kent Greenfield

GREENFIELD, KENT
B. July 1, 1902, Guthrie, Ky. D. Mar. 14, 1978, Guthrie, Ky.
BR TR 6'1" 180 lbs.

1924	NY	N	0	1	.000	15.00	1	1	0	3	9	1	1	0	0	0	0	0	0	0	—	0	0	0	0	0.0	—
1925			12	8	.600	3.88	29	21	8	171.2	195	64	66	0	1	0	0	62	5	0	.081	4	43	2	2	1.7	.959
1926			13	12	.520	3.96	39	28	8	222.2	206	82	74	1	2	3	1	65	6	0	.092	6	46	3	1	1.4	.945
1927	2 teams		NY N	(12G 2-2)						BOS N	(27G 11-14)																
"	total		13	16	.448	4.37	39	27	11	210	242	72	63	1	2	2	0	66	11	0	.167	5	47	1	1	1.4	.981
1928	BOS	N	3	11	.214	5.32	32	23	5	143.2	173	60	30	0	0	0	0	38	2	0	.053	8	37	2	2	1.5	.957
1929	2 teams		BOS N	(6G 0-0)						BKN N	(6G 0-0)																
"	total		0	0	—	9.99	12	2	0	24.1	46	18	8	0	0	0	0	6	0	0	.000	1	10	0	0	0.9	1.000
6 yrs.			41	48	.461	4.54	152	102	36	775.1	871	297	242	2	5	5	1	237	24	0	.101	24	183	8	6	1.4	.963

Year	Team	W	L	PCT	ERA	G	GS	CG	IP	H	BB	SO	ShO	W	L	SV	AB	H	HR	BA	PO	A	E	DP	TC/G	FA
														Relief Pitching			**Batting**									

John Greening

GREENING, JOHN A.
Born John A. Greenig.
B. Philadelphia, Pa. Deceased.

| 1888 | WAS N | 0 | 1 | .000 | 11.00 | 1 | 1 | 1 | 9 | 17 | 4 | 2 | 0 | 0 | 0 | 0 | 3 | 0 | 0 | .000 | 0 | 1 | 0 | 0 | 1.0 | 1.000 |

Bob Greenwood

GREENWOOD, ROBERT CHANDLER (Greenie)
B. Mar. 13, 1928, Cananea, Mexico   BR TR 6'5"   200 lbs.

1954	PHI N	1	2	.333	3.19	11	4	0	36.2	28	18	9	0	0	0	0	9	0	0	.000	3	7	0	1	0.9	1.000
1955		0	0	–	15.43	1	0	0	2.1	7	0	0	0	0	0	0	1	0	0	.000	0	0	0	0	0.0	–
2 yrs.		1	2	.333	3.92	12	4	0	39	35	18	9	0	0	0	0	10	0	0	.000	3	7	0	1	0.8	1.000

Dave Gregg

GREGG, DAVID CHARLES (Highpockets)
Brother of Vean Gregg.
B. Mar. 14, 1891, Chehalis, Wash. D. Nov. 12, 1965, Clarkston, Wash.   BR TR 6'1"   185 lbs.

| 1913 | CLE A | 0 | 0 | – | 18.00 | 1 | 0 | 0 | 1 | 2 | 0 | 0 | 0 | 0 | 0 | 0 | 0 | 0 | 0 | – | 0 | 1 | 0 | 0 | 1.0 | 1.000 |

Hal Gregg

GREGG, HAROLD DANA
B. July 11, 1921, Anaheim, Calif.   BR TR 6'3½"   195 lbs.

1943	BKN N	0	3	.000	9.64	5	4	0	18.2	21	21	7	0	0	0	0	2	0	0	.000	1	3	0	0	0.8	1.000
1944		9	16	.360	5.46	39	31	6	197.2	201	**137**	92	0	1	0	2	68	14	0	.206	13	36	5	3	1.4	.907
1945		18	13	.581	3.47	42	34	13	254.1	221	**120**	139	2	1	2	2	91	20	1	.220	8	47	4	4	1.4	.932
1946		6	4	.600	2.99	26	16	4	117.1	103	44	54	2	1	1	2	32	4	0	.125	6	16	2	0	0.9	.917
1947		4	5	.444	5.87	37	16	2	104.1	115	55	59	1	1	0	1	34	9	0	.265	9	17	2	2	0.8	.929
1948	PIT N	2	4	.333	4.60	22	8	0	74.1	72	34	25	0	0	2	1	22	6	1	.273	7	10	0	1	0.8	1.000
1949		1	1	.500	3.38	8	1	0	18.2	20	8	9	0	1	0	0	5	0	0	.000	1	1	0	1	0.3	1.000
1950		0	1	.000	13.50	5	1	0	5.1	10	7	3	0	0	1	0	1	0	0	.000	0	2	1	0	0.2	1.000
1952	NY N	0	1	.000	4.71	16	4	0	36.1	42	17	13	0	0	0	1	8	1	0	.125	1	3	0	0	0.3	1.000
9 yrs.		40	48	.455	4.54	200	115	27	827	805	443	401	5	5	5	9	263	54	2	.205	46	134	13	12	1.0	.933

WORLD SERIES

| 1947 | BKN N | 0 | 1 | .000 | 3.55 | 3 | 1 | 0 | 12.2 | 9 | 8 | 10 | 0 | 0 | 0 | 0 | 3 | 0 | 0 | .000 | 1 | 3 | 0 | 1 | 1.3 | 1.000 |

Vean Gregg

GREGG, SYLVEANUS AUGUSTUS
Brother of Dave Gregg.
B. Apr. 13, 1885, Chehalis, Wash. D. July 29, 1964, Aberdeen, Wash.   BR TL 6'1"   185 lbs.

1911	CLE A	23	7	.767	**1.81**	34	26	22	244	172	86	125	5	5	0	0	85	14	0	.165	7	67	4	4	2.3	.949
1912		20	13	.606	2.59	37	34	26	271.1	242	90	184	1	0	1	2	97	17	0	.175	10	61	7	2	2.1	.910
1913		20	13	.606	2.24	44	34	23	285.2	258	**124**	166	3	2	0	2	99	13	0	.131	9	70	8	2	2.0	.908
1914	2 teams	CLE A	(17G 9–3)		BOS A	(12G 3–4)																				
"	total	12	7	.632	3.44	29	21	10	165	159	85	80	1	2	0	0	52	10	0	.192	5	40	3	5	1.7	.938
1915	BOS A	4	2	.667	3.36	18	9	3	75	71	32	43	1	0	0	3	20	7	0	.350	2	22	0	1	1.3	1.000
1916		2	5	.286	3.01	21	7	3	77.2	71	30	41	0	1	1	0	18	2	0	.111	5	19	0	0	1.1	1.000
1918	PHI A	8	14	.364	3.12	30	25	17	199.1	180	67	63	3	0	0	2	71	12	0	.169	9	48	1	2	1.9	.983
1925	WAS A	2	2	.500	4.12	26	5	1	74.1	87	38	18	0	1	1	2	14	3	0	.214	3	16	3	0	0.8	.864
8 yrs.		91	63	.591	2.70	239	161	105	1392.1	1240	552	720	14	11	3	12	456	78	0	.171	50	343	26	15	1.8	.938

Frank Gregory

GREGORY, FRANK ERNEST
B. July 25, 1888, Spring Valley, Wis. D. Nov. 5, 1955, Beloit, Wis.   BR TR 5'11"   185 lbs.

| 1912 | CIN N | 2 | 0 | 1.000 | 4.60 | 4 | 2 | 1 | 15.2 | 19 | 7 | 4 | 0 | 1 | 0 | 0 | 5 | 1 | 0 | .200 | 0 | 1 | 0 | 0 | 0.3 | 1.000 |

Howie Gregory

GREGORY, HOWARD WATTERSON
B. Nov. 18, 1886, Hannibal, Mo. D. May 30, 1970, Tulsa, Okla.   BL TR 6'   175 lbs.

| 1911 | STL A | 0 | 1 | .000 | 5.14 | 3 | 1 | 0 | 7 | 11 | 4 | 1 | 0 | 0 | 0 | 0 | 2 | 0 | 0 | .000 | 0 | 2 | 0 | 0 | 0.7 | 1.000 |

Lee Gregory

GREGORY, GROVER LeROY
B. June 2, 1938, Bakersfield, Calif.   BL TL 6'1"   180 lbs.

| 1964 | CHI N | 0 | 0 | – | 3.50 | 11 | 0 | 0 | 18 | 23 | 5 | 8 | 0 | 0 | 0 | 0 | 13 | 1 | 0 | .077 | 0 | 5 | 0 | 0 | 0.5 | 1.000 |

Paul Gregory

GREGORY, PAUL EDWIN (Pop)
B. July 9, 1908, Tomnolen, Miss.   BR TR 6'2"   180 lbs.

1932	CHI A	5	3	.625	4.51	33	9	3	117.2	125	51	39	0	2	0	0	38	3	0	.079	5	38	2	2	1.4	.956
1933		4	11	.267	4.95	23	17	5	103.2	124	47	18	0	0	0	0	35	5	0	.143	6	30	0	0	1.6	1.000
2 yrs.		9	14	.391	4.72	56	26	8	221.1	249	98	57	0	2	0	0	73	8	0	.110	11	68	2	2	1.4	.975

Bill Greif

GREIF, WILLIAM BRILEY
B. Apr. 25, 1950, Fort Stockton, Tex.   BB TR 6'4"   196 lbs.

1971	HOU N	1	1	.500	5.06	7	3	0	16	18	8	14	0	1	0	0	3	1	0	.333	0	3	0	0	0.4	1.000
1972	SD N	5	16	.238	5.60	34	22	2	125.1	143	47	91	1	1	0	2	33	1	0	.030	5	12	4	0	0.6	.810
1973		10	17	.370	3.21	36	31	9	199.1	181	62	120	3	0	0	1	61	6	0	.098	11	24	1	0	0.972	.972
1974		9	19	.321	4.66	43	35	7	226	244	95	137	1	0	0	1	56	4	0	.071	13	33	3	4	1.1	.939
1975		4	6	.400	3.88	59	1	0	72	74	38	43	0	4	6	9	1	0	0	.000	0	5	0	0	0.1	.833
1976	2 teams	SD N	(5G 1–3)		STL N	(47G 1–5)																				
"	total	2	8	.200	5.26	52	5	0	77	87	37	37	0	1	5	6	12	0	0	.000	6	9	0	0	0.3	1.000
6 yrs.		31	67	.316	4.41	231	97	18	715.2	747	287	442	5	7	11	19	166	12	0	.072	35	86	9	4	0.6	.931

Bill Grevell

GREVELL, WILLIAM J.
B. Mar. 5, 1898, Williamstown, N. J. D. June 21, 1923, Philadelphia, Pa.   BR TR 5'11"   170 lbs.

| 1919 | PHI A | 0 | 0 | – | 14.25 | 5 | 2 | 0 | 12 | 15 | 18 | 3 | 0 | 0 | 0 | 0 | 5 | 0 | 0 | .000 | 0 | 6 | 0 | 0 | 1.2 | 1.000 |

Year	Team		W	L	PCT	ERA	G	GS	CG	IP	H	BB	SO	ShO	Relief Pitching W	L	SV	Batting AB	H	HR	BA	PO	A	E	DP	TC/G	FA

Hank Griffin
GRIFFIN, JAMES LINTON (Pepper)
B. July 11, 1886, Whitehouse, Tex.   D. Feb. 11, 1950, Terrell, Tex.
BR TR 6'   170 lbs.

1911	2 teams	CHI N (1G 0–0)				BOS N	(15G 0–6)																				
"	total		0	6	.000	5.38	16	7	1	83.2	97	37	31	0	0	1	0	30	7	0	.233	3	24	2	0	1.8	.931
1912	BOS N		0	0	–	27.00	3	0	0	1.2	3	3	0	0	0	0	0	0	0	0	–	0	0	0	0	0.0	–
2 yrs.			0	6	.000	5.80	19	7	1	85.1	100	40	31	0	0	1	0	30	7	0	.233	3	24	2	0	1.5	.931

Marty Griffin
GRIFFIN, MARTIN JOHN
B. Sept. 2, 1901, San Francisco, Calif.   D. Nov. 19, 1951, Los Angeles, Calif.
BR TR 6'2"   200 lbs.

| 1928 | BOS A | | 0 | 3 | .000 | 5.02 | 11 | 3 | 0 | 37.2 | 42 | 17 | 9 | 0 | 0 | 0 | 0 | 13 | 4 | 0 | .308 | 1 | 8 | 0 | 0 | 0.8 | 1.000 |

Mike Griffin
GRIFFIN, MICHAEL LEROY
B. June 26, 1957, Colusa, Calif.
BR TR 6'4"   195 lbs.

1979	NY A		0	0	–	4.50	3	0	0	4	5	2	5	0	0	0	0	0	0	0	–	0	0	0	0	0.0	–
1980			2	4	.333	4.83	13	9	0	54	64	23	25	0	0	1	0	0	0	0	–	6	7	1	0	1.1	.929
1981	2 teams	NY A (2G 0–0)				CHI N	(16G 2–5)																				
"	total		2	5	.286	4.34	18	9	0	56	69	9	24	0	0	0	1	13	2	0	.154	1	13	0	0	0.8	1.000
1982	SD N		0	1	.000	3.48	7	0	0	10.1	9	3	4	0	0	1	0	1	0	0	.000	0	1	0	0	0.1	1.000
1987	BAL A		3	5	.375	4.36	23	6	1	74.1	78	33	42	0	0	2	1	0	0	0	–	6	8	2	0	0.7	.875
1989	CIN N		0	0	–	12.46	3	0	0	4.1	10	3	1	0	0	0	0	1	1	0	1.000	0	1	0	0	0.3	1.000
6 yrs.			7	15	.318	4.61	67	24	1	203	235	73	101	0	0	4	3	15	3	0	.200	13	30	3	0	0.7	.935

Pat Griffin
GRIFFIN, PATRICK RICHARD
B. May 6, 1893, Niles, Ohio   D. June 7, 1927, Youngstown, Ohio
BR TR 6'2"   180 lbs.

| 1914 | CIN N | | 0 | 0 | – | 9.00 | 1 | 0 | 0 | 1 | 3 | 2 | 0 | 0 | 0 | 0 | 0 | 0 | 0 | 0 | – | 0 | 2 | 0 | 0 | 2.0 | 1.000 |

Tom Griffin
GRIFFIN, THOMAS JAMES
B. Feb. 22, 1948, Los Angeles, Calif.
BR TR 6'3"   210 lbs.

1969	HOU N		11	10	.524	3.54	31	31	6	188	156	93	200	3	0	0	0	62	9	0	.145	8	16	2	1	0.8	.923
1970			3	13	.188	5.76	23	20	2	111	118	72	72	1	0	0	0	33	2	0	.061	8	10	1	0	0.8	.947
1971			0	6	.000	4.74	10	6	0	38	44	20	29	0	0	0	0	9	1	0	.111	0	10	0	0	1.0	1.000
1972			5	4	.556	3.24	39	5	1	94.1	92	38	83	1	4	3	0	25	7	1	.280	3	11	2	0	0.4	.875
1973			4	6	.400	4.15	25	12	4	99.2	83	46	69	0	1	0	0	28	3	1	.107	7	14	0	0	0.8	1.000
1974			14	10	.583	3.54	34	34	8	211	202	89	110	3	0	0	0	68	20	2	.294	19	35	8	2	1.8	.871
1975			3	8	.273	5.35	17	13	3	79	89	46	56	1	0	0	0	22	3	0	.136	5	14	1	2	1.2	.950
1976	2 teams	HOU N (20G 5–3)				SD N	(11G 4–3)																				
"	total		9	6	.600	4.10	31	13	2	112	100	79	69	0	5	1	0	31	2	0	.065	6	16	3	1	0.8	.880
1977	SD N		6	9	.400	4.47	38	20	0	151	144	88	79	0	2	1	0	45	6	2	.133	6	16	3	2	0.7	.880
1978	CAL A		3	4	.429	4.02	24	4	0	56	63	31	35	0	3	1	0	0	0	0	–	3	12	2	0	0.7	.882
1979	SF N		5	6	.455	3.93	59	3	0	94	83	46	82	0	5	3	2	14	1	0	.071	5	19	1	1	0.4	.960
1980			5	1	.833	2.75	42	4	0	108	80	49	79	0	3	1	0	18	2	1	.111	6	17	0	1	0.5	1.000
1981			8	8	.500	3.77	22	22	3	129	121	57	83	1	0	0	0	41	8	1	.195	9	29	3	0	1.9	.927
1982	PIT N		1	3	.250	8.87	6	4	0	22.1	32	15	8	0	0	0	0	9	2	0	.222	0	6	1	0	1.2	.857
14 yrs.			77	94	.450	4.07	401	191	29	1493.1	1407	769	1054	10	22	11	5	405	66	10	.163	85	225	27	10	0.8	.920

Clark Griffith
GRIFFITH, CLARK CALVIN (Griff, General)
B. Nov. 20, 1869, Clear Creek, Mo.   D. Oct. 27, 1955, Washington, D. C.
Manager 1901-20.
Hall of Fame 1946.
BR TR 5'6½"   156 lbs.

1891	2 teams	STL AA (27G 14–6)				BOS AA	(7G 3–1)																				
"	total		17	7	.708	3.74	34	21	15	226.1	242	73	88	0	7	0	0	100	16	2	.160	10	50	6	1	1.9	.909
1893	CHI N		1	2	.333	5.03	4	2	2	19.2	24	5	9	0	0	1	0	11	2	0	.182	2	6	0	0	2.0	1.000
1894			21	14	.600	4.92	36	30	28	261.1	328	85	71	0	3	3	0	142	33	0	.232	20	45	4	1	1.9	.942
1895			26	14	.650	3.93	42	41	39	353	434	91	79	0	1	0	0	144	46	1	.319	27	81	9	2	2.8	.923
1896			23	11	.676	3.54	36	35	35	317.2	370	70	81	0	0	0	0	135	36	1	.267	20	79	9	3	3.0	.917
1897			21	18	.538	3.72	41	38	38	343.2	410	86	102	1	1	0	1	162	38	0	.235	23	85	6	3	2.8	.947
1898			24	10	.706	1.88	38	38	36	325.2	305	64	97	4	0	0	0	122	20	0	.164	18	82	5	2	2.8	.952
1899			22	14	.611	2.79	38	38	35	319.2	329	65	73	0	0	0	0	120	31	0	.258	17	109	9	3	3.6	.933
1900			14	13	.519	3.05	30	30	27	248	245	51	61	4	0	0	0	95	24	1	.253	9	57	6	0	2.4	.917
1901	CHI A		24	7	.774	2.67	35	30	26	266.2	275	50	67	5	3	0	1	89	27	2	.303	9	78	5	3	2.6	.946
1902			15	9	.625	4.19	28	24	20	212.2	247	47	51	3	2	0	0	92	20	0	.217	10	55	0	1	2.3	1.000
1903	NY A		14	11	.560	2.70	25	24	22	213	201	33	69	3	1	0	0	69	11	0	.159	8	50	1	1	2.4	.983
1904			7	5	.583	2.87	16	11	8	100.1	91	16	36	1	1	0	0	42	6	0	.143	3	32	2	0	2.3	.946
1905			9	6	.600	1.67	25	7	4	102.2	82	15	46	2	6	3	1	32	7	0	.219	1	23	1	0	1.0	.960
1906			2	2	.500	3.02	17	2	1	59.2	58	15	16	0	1	2	2	18	2	0	.111	1	23	0	0	1.4	1.000
1907			0	0	–	8.64	4	0	0	8.1	15	6	5	0	0	0	0	2	0	0	.000	0	4	1	0	1.3	.800
1909	CIN N		0	1	.000	6.00	1	1	1	6	11	2	3	0	0	0	0	2	0	0	.000	0	5	0	0	5.0	1.000
1910			0	0	–	0.00	0	0	0	0	0	0	0	0	0	0	0	0	0	0	–	0	0	0	0	0.0	–
1912	WAS A		0	0	–	∞	1	0	0	0	1	0	0	0	0	0	0	1	0	0	.000	0	0	0	0	0.0	–
1913			0	0	–	0.00	1	0	0	1	0	0	1	0	0	0	0	0	0	0	–	0	0	0	0	0.0	–
1914			0	0	–	0.00	1	0	0	1	1	0	1	0	0	0	0	1	1	0	1.000	0	0	0	0	0.0	–
21 yrs.			240	144	.625	3.31	453	372	337	3386.1	3670	774	955	23	26	9	6	*				179	863	64	22	2.4	.942

Frank Griffith
GRIFFITH, FRANK WESLEY
B. Nov. 18, 1872, Gilman, Ill.   D. Dec. 13, 1908
BL TL   150 lbs.

1892	CHI N		0	1	.000	11.25	1	1	0	4	3	6	3	0	0	0	0	1	0	0	.000	0	0	0	0	0.0	–
1894	CLE N		1	2	.333	9.99	7	6	3	42.1	64	37	15	0	0	0	0	24	8	0	.333	0	8	1	0	1.3	.889
2 yrs.			1	3	.250	10.10	8	7	3	46.1	67	43	18	0	0	0	0	25	8	0	.320	0	8	1	0	1.1	.889

Year	Team	W	L	PCT	ERA	G	GS	CG	IP	H	BB	SO	ShO	W	L	SV	AB	H	HR	BA	PO	A	E	DP	TC/G	FA
														Relief Pitching			Batting									

Lee Griffith

GRIFFITH, LEON CLIFFORD
B. May 20, 1925, Carmel, N. Y.
BB TL 5'11½" 180 lbs.

Year	Team	W	L	PCT	ERA	G	GS	CG	IP	H	BB	SO	ShO	W	L	SV	AB	H	HR	BA	PO	A	E	DP	TC/G	FA
1946	PHI A	0	0	–	2.93	10	0	0	15.1	13	6	4	0	0	0	0	1	0	0	.000	2	1	0	0	0.3	1.000

Hal Griggs

GRIGGS, HAROLD LLOYD
B. Aug. 24, 1928, Shannon, Ga.
BR TR 6' 170 lbs.

Year	Team	W	L	PCT	ERA	G	GS	CG	IP	H	BB	SO	ShO	W	L	SV	AB	H	HR	BA	PO	A	E	DP	TC/G	FA
1956	WAS A	1	6	.143	6.02	34	12	1	98.2	120	76	48	0	0	0	1	16	0	0	.000	10	19	1	4	0.9	.967
1957		0	1	.000	3.29	2	2	0	13.2	11	7	12	0	0	0	0	4	1	0	.250	0	3	0	1	1.5	1.000
1958		3	11	.214	5.52	32	21	3	137	138	74	69	0	0	0	0	41	5	0	.122	6	22	2	3	0.9	.933
1959		2	8	.200	5.25	37	10	2	97.2	103	52	43	1	0	0	2	18	1	0	.056	1	18	1	1	0.5	.950
4 yrs.		6	26	.188	5.50	105	45	6	347	372	209	172	1	0	0	3	79	7	0	.089	17	62	4	9	0.8	.952

Guido Grilli

GRILLI, GUIDO JOHN
B. Jan. 9, 1939, Memphis, Tenn.
BL TL 6' 188 lbs.

Year	Team	W	L	PCT	ERA	G	GS	CG	IP	H	BB	SO	ShO	W	L	SV	AB	H	HR	BA	PO	A	E	DP	TC/G	FA
1966	2 teams	BOS A	(6G 0–1)		KC A	(16G 0–1)																				
"	total	0	2	.000	7.08	22	0	0	20.1	24	20	12	0	0	2	1	2	1	0	.500	1	2	2	0	0.2	.600

Steve Grilli

GRILLI, STEPHEN JOSEPH
B. May 2, 1949, Brooklyn, N. Y.
BR TR 6'2" 170 lbs.

Year	Team	W	L	PCT	ERA	G	GS	CG	IP	H	BB	SO	ShO	W	L	SV	AB	H	HR	BA	PO	A	E	DP	TC/G	FA
1975	DET A	0	0	–	1.35	3	0	0	6.2	3	6	5	0	0	0	0	0	0	0	–	1	0	0	0	0.3	1.000
1976		3	1	.750	4.64	36	0	0	66	63	41	36	0	3	1	3	0	0	0	–	5	18	1	1	0.7	.958
1977		1	2	.333	4.81	30	2	0	73	71	49	49	0	1	1	0	0	0	0	–	2	7	0	0	0.3	1.000
1979	TOR A	0	0	–	0.00	1	0	0	2	1	0	1	0	0	0	0	0	0	0	–	0	0	0	0	0.0	–
4 yrs.		4	3	.571	4.51	70	2	0	147.2	138	96	91	0	4	2	3	0	0	0	–	8	25	1	1	0.5	.971

Bob Grim

GRIM, ROBERT ANTON
B. Mar. 8, 1930, New York, N. Y.
BR TR 6'1" 175 lbs.

Year	Team	W	L	PCT	ERA	G	GS	CG	IP	H	BB	SO	ShO	W	L	SV	AB	H	HR	BA	PO	A	E	DP	TC/G	FA
1954	NY A	20	6	.769	3.26	37	37	8	199	175	85	108	1	8			70	10	1	.143	11	26	1	4	1.0	.974
1955		7	5	.583	4.19	26	11	1	92.1	81	42	63	1	3	3	4	25	3	0	.120	5	14	1	1	0.8	.950
1956		6	1	.857	2.77	26	6	1	74.2	64	31	48	0	3	0	5	16	1	0	.063	4	8	1	2	0.5	.923
1957		12	8	.600	2.63	46	0	0	72	60	36	52	0	12	8	19	9	1	0	.111	7	10	0	1	0.4	1.000
1958	2 teams	NY A	(11G 0–1)		KC A	(26G 7–6)																				
"	total	7	7	.500	3.81	37	14	5	130	130	51	65	1	0	3		33	6	0	.182	3	19	2	0	0.6	.917
1959	KC A	6	10	.375	4.09	40	9	1	125.1	124	57	65	1	2	6	4	32	3	1	.094	7	13	1	0	0.5	.952
1960	3 teams	CLE A	(3G 0–1)		CIN N	(26G 2–2)		STL N	(15G 1–0)																	
"	total	3	3	.500	4.22	44	0	0	53.1	60	20	39	0	3	3	2	2	0	0	.000	1	9	1	1	0.3	.909
1962	KC A	0	1	.000	6.23	12	0	0	13	14	8	3	0	0	1	3	2	0	0	.000	1	5	0	0	0.5	1.000
8 yrs.		61	41	.598	3.61	268	60	18	759.2	708	330	443	4	31	24	37	189	24	3	.127	39	104	7	10	0.6	.953

WORLD SERIES

Year	Team	W	L	PCT	ERA	G	GS	CG	IP	H	BB	SO	ShO	W	L	SV	AB	H	HR	BA	PO	A	E	DP	TC/G	FA
1955	NY A	0	1	.000	4.15	3	1	0	8.2	8	5	8	0	0	0	1	2	0	0	.000	1	1	0	0	0.7	1.000
1957		0	1	.000	7.71	2	0	0	2.1	3	0	2	0	0	1	0	0	0	0	–	0	0	0	0	0.0	–
2 yrs.		0	2	.000	4.91	5	1	0	11	11	5	10	0	0	1	1	2	0	0	.000	1	1	0	0	0.4	1.000

John Grim

GRIM, JOHN HELM
B. Aug. 9, 1867, Lebanon, Ky. D. July 28, 1961, Indianapolis, Ind.
BR TR 6'2" 175 lbs.

Year	Team	W	L	PCT	ERA	G	GS	CG	IP	H	BB	SO	ShO	W	L	SV	AB	H	HR	BA	PO	A	E	DP	TC/G	FA
1890	ROC AA	0	0	–	0.00	1	0	0	3.1	3	4	3	0	0	0	0	*				0	0	0	0	0.0	–

Burleigh Grimes

GRIMES, BURLEIGH ARLAND (Ol' Stubblebeard)
B. Aug. 9, 1893, Emerald, Wis. D. Dec. 6, 1985, Clear Lake, Wis.
Manager 1937-38.
Hall of Fame 1964.
BR TR 5'10" 175 lbs.

Year	Team	W	L	PCT	ERA	G	GS	CG	IP	H	BB	SO	ShO	W	L	SV	AB	H	HR	BA	PO	A	E	DP	TC/G	FA
1916	PIT N	2	3	.400	2.36	6	5	4	45.2	40	10	20	0	1	0	0	17	3	0	.176	1	16	3	1	3.3	.850
1917		3	16	.158	3.53	37	17	8	194	186	70	72	1	1	4	0	69	16	0	.232	9	62	6	3	2.1	.922
1918	BKN N	19	9	.679	2.14	41	28	19	269.2	210	76	113	7	1	1	1	90	18	0	.200	12	94	5	1	2.7	.955
1919		10	11	.476	3.47	25	21	13	181.1	179	60	82	1	1	1	1	69	17	0	.246	12	50	3	3	2.6	.954
1920		23	11	.676	2.22	40	33	25	303.2	271	67	131	5	2	1	2	111	34	0	.306	17	95	7	3	3.0	.941
1921		22	13	.629	2.83	37	35	30	302.1	313	76	136	2	0	1	0	114	27	1	.237	17	89	2	5	2.9	.981
1922		17	14	.548	4.76	36	34	18	259	324	84	99	1	1	0	1	93	22	0	.237	12	79	6	2	2.7	.938
1923		21	18	.538	3.58	39	38	33	327	356	100	119	2	0	0	0	126	30	0	.238	16	101	10	6	3.3	.921
1924		22	13	.629	3.82	38	36	30	310.2	351	91	135	1	0	0	1	124	37	0	.298	25	91	4	5	3.2	.967
1925		12	19	.387	5.04	33	31	19	246.2	305	102	73	1	0	1	0	96	24	1	.250	18	92	7	11	3.5	.940
1926		12	13	.480	3.71	30	29	18	225.1	238	88	64	1	0	0	0	81	18	0	.222	4	72	3	1	2.6	.962
1927	NY N	19	8	.704	3.54	39	34	15	259.2	274	87	102	2	1	0	2	96	18	0	.188	16	71	0	9	2.2	1.000
1928	PIT N	25	14	.641	2.99	48	37	28	330.2	311	77	97	4	4	1	3	131	42	0	.321	9	106	4	6	2.5	.966
1929		17	7	.708	3.13	33	29	18	232.2	245	70	62	2	0	1	2	91	26	0	.286	10	65	3	5	2.4	.962
1930	2 teams	BOS N	(11G 3–5)		STL N	(22G 13–6)																				
"	total	16	11	.593	4.07	33	28	11	201.1	246	65	73	1	2	0	0	73	18	0	.247	8	47	1	3	1.7	.982
1931	STL N	17	9	.654	3.65	29	28	17	212.1	240	59	67	3	1	0	0	76	14	0	.184	16	57	4	3	2.7	.948
1932	CHI N	6	11	.353	4.78	30	18	5	141.1	174	50	36	1	0	2	1	44	11	0	.250	12	33	2	4	1.6	.957
1933	2 teams	CHI N	(17G 3–6)		STL N	(4G 0–1)																				
"	total	3	7	.300	3.78	21	10	3	83.1	86	37	16	1	1	1	4	25	4	0	.160	6	16	1	2	1.1	.957
1934	3 teams	STL N	(4G 2–1)		PIT N	(8G 1–2)		NY A	(10G 1–2)																	
"	total	4	5	.444	6.11	22	4	1	53	63	26	15	0	4	3	1	9	1	0	.111	5	16	0	2	1.0	1.000
19 yrs.		270	212	.560	3.53	617	495	314	4179.2	4412	1295	1512	35	21	19	18	1535	380	2	.248	225	1252	71	74	2.5	.954

WORLD SERIES

Year	Team	W	L	PCT	ERA	G	GS	CG	IP	H	BB	SO	ShO	W	L	SV	AB	H	HR	BA	PO	A	E	DP	TC/G	FA
1920	BKN N	1	2	.333	4.19	3	3	1	19.1	23	9	4	0	0	0	0	6	2	0	.333	1	7	1	0	3.0	.889
1930	STL N	0	2	.000	3.71	2	2	2	17	10	6	13	0	0	0	0	5	2	0	.400	0	3	0	0	1.5	1.000
1931		2	0	1.000	2.04	2	2	1	17.2	9	9	11	0	0	0	0	7	2	0	.286	0	3	0	0	1.5	1.000
1932	CHI N	0	0	–	23.63	2	0	0	2.2	7	2	0	0	0	0	0	1	0	0	.000	0	0	0	0	0.0	–
4 yrs.		3	4	.429	4.29	9	7	4	56.2	49	26	28	0	0	0	0	19	6	0	.316	1	13	1	0	1.7	.933
				7th								8th														

Year	Team		W	L	PCT	ERA	G	GS	CG	IP	H	BB	SO	ShO	Relief Pitching W	L	SV	Batting AB	H	HR	BA	PO	A	E	DP	TC/G	FA

John Grimes

GRIMES, JOHN THOMAS
B. Apr. 17, 1869, Woodstock, Md.　D. Jan. 17, 1964, San Francisco, Calif.
BR　TR　5'11"　160 lbs.

Year	Team		W	L	PCT	ERA	G	GS	CG	IP	H	BB	SO	ShO	W	L	SV	AB	H	HR	BA	PO	A	E	DP	TC/G	FA
1897	STL	N	0	2	.000	5.95	3	1	1	19.2	24	8	4	0	0	1	0	7	2	0	.286	0	12	1	0	4.3	.923

Jason Grimsley

GRIMSLEY, JASON ALAN
B. Aug. 7, 1967, Cleveland, Tex.
BR　TR　6'3"　180 lbs.

Year	Team		W	L	PCT	ERA	G	GS	CG	IP	H	BB	SO	ShO	W	L	SV	AB	H	HR	BA	PO	A	E	DP	TC/G	FA
1989	PHI	N	1	3	.250	5.89	4	4	0	18.1	19	19	7	0	0	0	0	5	0	0	.000	1	4	1	1	1.5	.833

Ross Grimsley

GRIMSLEY, ROSS ALBERT II
Son of Ross Grimsley.
B. Jan. 7, 1950, Topeka, Kans.
BL　TL　6'3"　195 lbs.

Year	Team		W	L	PCT	ERA	G	GS	CG	IP	H	BB	SO	ShO	W	L	SV	AB	H	HR	BA	PO	A	E	DP	TC/G	FA
1971	CIN	N	10	7	.588	3.58	26	26	6	161	151	43	67	3	0	0	0	51	6	0	.118	5	25	0	0	1.2	1.000
1972			14	8	.636	3.05	30	28	4	197.2	194	50	79	1	0	0	1	66	8	0	.121	3	34	0	0	1.2	1.000
1973			13	10	.565	3.23	38	36	8	242.1	245	68	90	1	0	0	1	82	5	0	.061	11	33	0	3	1.2	1.000
1974	BAL	A	18	13	.581	3.07	40	39	17	296	267	76	158	4	0	0	1	0	0	0	—	3	51	2	1	1.4	.964
1975			10	13	.435	4.07	35	32	8	197	210	47	89	1	0	0	0	0	0	0	—	6	33	0	2	1.1	1.000
1976			8	7	.533	3.94	28	19	2	137	143	35	41	0	0	0	0	0	0	0	—	8	19	1	0	1.0	.964
1977			14	10	.583	3.96	34	34	11	218	230	74	53	2	0	0	0	0	0	0	—	8	52	3	4	1.9	.952
1978	MON	N	20	11	.645	3.05	36	36	19	263	237	67	84	3	0	0	0	90	13	0	.144	9	53	2	3	1.8	.969
1979			10	9	.526	5.36	32	27	2	151	199	41	42	0	0	1	0	55	11	0	.200	3	27	3	0	1.0	.909
1980	2 teams		MON N (11G 2–4)			CLE A	(14G 4–5)																				
"	total		6	9	.400	6.59	25	18	2	116	164	36	29	0	0	0	0	9	2	0	.222	2	19	1	0	0.9	.955
1982	BAL	A	1	2	.333	5.25	21	0	0	60	65	22	18	0	1	2	0	0	0	0	—	2	11	1	1	0.7	.929
11 yrs.			124	99	.556	3.81	345	295	79	2039	2105	559	750	15	1	3	3	353	45	0	.127	60	357	13	14	1.2	.970

LEAGUE CHAMPIONSHIP SERIES

Year	Team		W	L	PCT	ERA	G	GS	CG	IP	H	BB	SO	ShO	W	L	SV	AB	H	HR	BA	PO	A	E	DP	TC/G	FA
1972	CIN	N	1	0	1.000	1.00	1	1	1	9	2	0	5	0	0	0	0	4	2	0	.500	0	0	0	0	0.0	—
1973			0	1	.000	12.27	2	1	0	3.2	7	2	3	0	0	0	0	0	0	0	—	1	0	0	0	0.5	1.000
1974	BAL	A	0	0	—	1.69	2	0	0	5.1	1	2	2	0	0	0	0	0	0	0	—	0	1	0	0	0.5	1.000
3 yrs.			1	1	.500	3.50	5	2	1	18	10	4	10	0	0	0	0	4	2	0	.500	1	1	0	0	0.4	1.000

WORLD SERIES

Year	Team		W	L	PCT	ERA	G	GS	CG	IP	H	BB	SO	ShO	W	L	SV	AB	H	HR	BA	PO	A	E	DP	TC/G	FA
1972	CIN	N	2	1	.667	2.57	4	0	0	7	7	3	2	0	2	0	0	2	0	0	.000	0	2	0	0	0.5	1.000

2nd

Ross Grimsley

GRIMSLEY, ROSS ALBERT, SR. (Lefty)
Father of Ross Grimsley.
B. June 4, 1922, Americus, Kans.
BL　TL　6'　175 lbs.

Year	Team		W	L	PCT	ERA	G	GS	CG	IP	H	BB	SO	ShO	W	L	SV	AB	H	HR	BA	PO	A	E	DP	TC/G	FA
1951	CHI	A	0	0	—	3.86	7	0	0	14	12	10	8	0	0	0	0	2	0	0	.000	0	0	0	0	0.0	—

Dan Griner

GRINER, DONALD DEXTER (Rusty)
B. Mar. 7, 1888, Centerville, Tenn.　D. June 3, 1950, Bishopville, S. C.
BL　TR　6'1½"　200 lbs.

Year	Team		W	L	PCT	ERA	G	GS	CG	IP	H	BB	SO	ShO	W	L	SV	AB	H	HR	BA	PO	A	E	DP	TC/G	FA
1912	STL	N	3	4	.429	3.17	12	7	2	54	59	15	20	0	0	0	0	13	1	0	.077	1	8	0	0	0.8	1.000
1913			10	22	.313	5.08	34	34	18	225	279	66	79	1	0	0	0	81	21	0	.259	7	69	2	0	2.3	.974
1914			9	13	.409	2.51	37	16	11	179	163	57	74	2	1	1	2	55	14	0	.255	7	41	1	0	1.3	.980
1915			5	11	.313	2.81	37	18	9	150.1	137	46	46	3	0	3	3	52	14	0	.269	3	35	1	1	1.1	.974
1916			0	0	—	4.09	4	0	0	11	15	3	3	0	0	0	1	4	1	0	.250	0	3	0	0	0.8	1.000
1918	BKN	N	1	5	.167	2.15	11	6	3	54.1	47	15	22	1	0	0	0	14	1	0	.071	0	17	0	0	1.5	1.000
6 yrs.			28	55	.337	3.49	135	81	43	673.2	700	202	244	7	1	4	6	219	52	0	.237	18	173	4	1	1.4	.979

Lee Grissom

GRISSOM, LEE THEO (Lefty)
Brother of Marv Grissom.
B. Oct. 23, 1907, Sherman, Tex.
BB　TL　6'3"　200 lbs.
BR 1934,1937

Year	Team		W	L	PCT	ERA	G	GS	CG	IP	H	BB	SO	ShO	W	L	SV	AB	H	HR	BA	PO	A	E	DP	TC/G	FA
1934	CIN	N	0	1	.000	15.43	4	1	0	7	13	7	4	0	0	0	0	1	0	0	.000	0	1	0	0	0.3	1.000
1935			1	1	.500	3.86	3	3	1	21	31	4	13	0	0	0	0	7	0	0	.000	1	6	0	0	2.3	1.000
1936			1	1	.500	6.29	6	4	0	24.1	33	9	13	0	0	0	0	9	0	0	.000	2	4	0	0	1.0	1.000
1937			12	17	.414	3.26	50	30	14	223.2	193	93	149	5	1	1	6	64	7	0	.109	5	34	1	1	0.8	.975
1938			2	3	.400	5.29	14	7	0	51	60	22	16	0	0	0	0	16	3	0	.188	2	11	2	0	1.1	.867
1939			9	7	.563	4.10	33	21	3	153.2	145	56	53	0	1	1	0	47	4	0	.085	2	24	1	3	0.8	.963
1940	2 teams		NY A (5G 0–0)			BKN N	(14G 2–5)																				
"	total		2	5	.286	2.64	19	10	3	78.1	63	36	52	1	0	0	0	23	5	0	.217	3	11	2	1	0.8	.875
1941	2 teams		BKN N (4G 0–0)			PHI N	(29G 2–13)																				
"	total		2	13	.133	3.85	33	19	2	142.2	130	78	79	0	0	0	1	38	7	0	.184	1	26	2	0	0.9	.931
8 yrs.			29	48	.377	3.89	162	95	23	701.2	668	305	379	6	2	2	7	205	26	0	.127	16	117	8	5	0.9	.943

WORLD SERIES

Year	Team		W	L	PCT	ERA	G	GS	CG	IP	H	BB	SO	ShO	W	L	SV	AB	H	HR	BA	PO	A	E	DP	TC/G	FA
1939	CIN	N	0	0	—	0.00	1	0	0	1.1	0	1	0	0	0	0	0	0	0	0	—	0	0	0	0	0.0	—

Marv Grissom

GRISSOM, MARVIN EDWARD
Brother of Lee Grissom.
B. Mar. 31, 1918, Los Molinos, Calif.
BR　TR　6'3"　190 lbs.

Year	Team		W	L	PCT	ERA	G	GS	CG	IP	H	BB	SO	ShO	W	L	SV	AB	H	HR	BA	PO	A	E	DP	TC/G	FA
1946	NY	N	0	2	.000	4.34	4	3	0	18.2	17	13	9	0	0	0	0	5	1	0	.200	1	6	0	0	1.8	1.000
1949	DET	A	2	4	.333	6.41	27	2	0	39.1	56	34	17	0	2	3	0	9	2	0	.222	1	8	1	0	0.4	.900
1952	CHI	A	12	10	.545	3.74	28	24	7	166	156	79	97	1	0	1	0	53	8	0	.151	4	23	1	0	1.0	.964
1953	2 teams		BOS A (13G 2–6)			NY N	(21G 4–2)																				
"	total		6	8	.429	4.26	34	18	4	143.2	144	61	77	0	0	1	0	45	2	0	.044	9	23	1	3	1.0	.970
1954	NY	N	10	7	.588	2.35	56	3	1	122.1	100	50	64	0	9	7	19	32	5	0	.156	7	18	2	3	0.5	.926
1955			5	4	.556	2.92	55	0	0	89.1	76	41	49	0	5	4	8	13	2	0	.154	3	16	0	0	0.3	1.000
1956			1	1	.500	1.56	43	2	0	80.2	71	16	49	0	1	1	7	11	1	0	.091	1	12	0	0	0.3	1.000
1957			4	4	.500	2.61	55	0	0	82.2	74	23	51	0	4	4	14	12	2	0	.167	1	20	0	1	0.4	1.000
1958	SF	N	7	5	.583	3.99	51	0	0	65.1	71	26	46	0	7	5	10	9	0	0	.000	1	12	0	1	0.3	1.000

Year	Team		W	L	PCT	ERA	G	GS	CG	IP	H	BB	SO	ShO	Relief Pitching			Batting				PO	A	E	DP	TC/G	FA
															W	L	SV	AB	H	HR	BA						

Marv Grissom *continued*

| 1959 | STL | N | 0 | 0 | – | 22.50 | 3 | 0 | 0 | 2 | 6 | 0 | 0 | 0 | 0 | 0 | 0 | 0 | 0 | 0 | – | 0 | 1 | 0 | 0 | 0.3 | 1.000 |
| 10 yrs. | | | 47 | 45 | .511 | 3.41 | 356 | 52 | 12 | 810 | 771 | 343 | 459 | 3 | 28 | 26 | 58 | 189 | 23 | 0 | .122 | 28 | 139 | 5 | 8 | 0.5 | .971 |

WORLD SERIES

| 1954 | NY | N | 1 | 0 | 1.000 | 0.00 | 1 | 0 | 0 | 2.2 | 1 | 3 | 2 | 0 | 1 | 0 | 0 | 1 | 0 | 0 | .000 | 0 | 0 | 0 | 0 | 0.0 | – |

Connie Grob

GROB, CONRAD GEORGE
B. Nov. 9, 1932, Cross Plains, Wis.

BL TR 6'½" 180 lbs.

| 1956 | WAS | A | 4 | 5 | .444 | 7.83 | 37 | 1 | 0 | 79.1 | 121 | 26 | 27 | 0 | 4 | 5 | 1 | 18 | 6 | 0 | .333 | 6 | 18 | 2 | 1 | 0.7 | .923 |

Johnny Grodzicki

GRODZICKI, JOHN
B. Feb. 26, 1917, Nanticoke, Pa.

BR TR 6'2" 200 lbs.

1941	STL	N	2	1	.667	1.35	5	1	0	13.1	6	11	10	0	2	0	0	2	0	0	.000	0	2	0	0	0.4	1.000
1946			0	0	–	9.00	3	0	0	4	4	4	2	0	0	0	0	0	0	0	–	0	2	1	0	1.0	.667
1947			0	1	.000	5.40	16	0	0	23.1	21	19	8	0	0	1	0	1	0	0	.000	1	6	0	0	0.4	1.000
3 yrs.			2	2	.500	4.43	24	1	0	40.2	31	34	20	0	2	1	0	3	0	0	.000	1	10	1	0	0.5	.917

Steve Gromek

GROMEK, STEPHEN JOSEPH
B. Jan. 15, 1920, Hamtramck, Mich.

BB TR 6'2" 180 lbs.
BR 1941-49

1941	CLE	A	1	1	.500	4.24	9	2	1	23.1	25	11	19	0	0	0	2	6	1	0	.167	0	0	0	0	0.0	–
1942			2	0	1.000	3.65	14	0	0	44.1	46	23	14	0	2	0	0	15	5	0	.333	2	6	2	1	0.7	.800
1943			0	0	–	9.00	3	0	0	4	6	0	4	0	0	0	0	2	2	0	1.000	0	0	0	0	0.0	–
1944			10	9	.526	2.56	35	21	12	203.2	160	70	115	2	0	1	1	73	19	0	.260	10	22	3	3	1.0	.941
1945			19	9	.679	2.55	33	30	21	251	229	66	101	3	0	1	1	91	21	0	.231	15	31	2	1	1.5	.958
1946			5	15	.250	4.33	29	21	5	153.2	159	47	75	2	0	2	4	56	11	0	.196	10	21	1	2	1.1	.969
1947			3	5	.375	3.74	29	7	0	84.1	77	36	39	0	1	3	4	22	7	0	.318	2	13	1	0	0.6	.938
1948			9	3	.750	2.84	38	9	4	130	109	51	50	1	3	1	2	41	6	0	.146	8	17	2	3	0.7	.926
1949			4	6	.400	3.33	27	12	3	92	86	40	22	0	1	2	0	24	4	0	.167	8	18	1	1	1.0	.963
1950			10	7	.588	3.65	31	13	4	113.1	94	36	43	0	4	0	0	38	6	0	.158	11	31	4	3	0.8	1.000
1951			7	4	.636	2.77	27	8	1	107.1	98	29	40	1	3	2	1	27	8	0	.296	13	18	0	3	1.1	1.000
1952			7	7	.500	3.67	29	13	3	122.2	109	28	65	1	1	1	1	30	3	0	.100	7	9	0	0	0.6	1.000
1953	2 teams	CLE A	(5G 1–1)			DET A	(19G 6–8)																				
"	total		7	9	.438	4.41	24	18	6	136.2	149	39	67	0	1	0	1	43	3	0	.070	10	13	0	1	1.0	1.000
1954	DET	A	18	16	.529	2.74	36	32	17	252.2	236	57	102	4	2	0	1	79	15	0	.190	16	26	1	1	1.2	.977
1955			13	10	.565	3.98	28	25	8	181	183	37	73	2	2	0	0	54	9	0	.167	12	22	1	2	1.3	.971
1956			8	6	.571	4.28	40	13	4	141	142	47	64	0	3	0	4	27	4	0	.148	4	16	0	0	0.4	1.000
1957			0	1	.000	6.08	15	1	0	23.2	32	13	11	0	0	1	0	2	0	0	.000	1	2	0	0	0.2	1.000
17 yrs.			123	108	.532	3.41	447	225	92	2064.2	1940	630	904	17	23	14	23	630	124	0	.197	126	248	13	20	0.9	.966

WORLD SERIES

| 1948 | CLE | A | 1 | 0 | 1.000 | 1.00 | 1 | 1 | 1 | 9 | 7 | 1 | 2 | 0 | 0 | 0 | 0 | 3 | 0 | 0 | .000 | 1 | 1 | 0 | 1 | 2.0 | 1.000 |

Bob Groom

GROOM, ROBERT
B. Sept. 12, 1884, Belleville, Ill.   D. Feb. 19, 1948, Belleville, Ill.

BR TR 6'2" 175 lbs.

1909	WAS	A	7	26	.212	2.87	44	31	17	260.2	218	105	131	1	2	1	0	88	8	0	.091	8	98	11	3	2.7	.906
1910			12	17	.414	2.76	34	30	22	257.2	255	77	98	3	0	2	0	92	11	0	.120	10	77	6	0	2.7	.935
1911			13	17	.433	3.82	37	32	20	254.2	280	67	135	2	1	0	2	82	11	0	.134	8	73	5	0	2.3	.942
1912			24	13	.649	2.62	43	40	28	316	287	94	179	2	0	2	1	103	12	0	.117	13	77	9	2	2.3	.909
1913			16	16	.500	3.23	37	36	17	264.1	258	81	156	4	0	1	0	92	15	0	.163	14	75	5	3	2.5	.947
1914	STL	F	13	20	.394	3.24	42	34	23	280.2	281	75	167	3	0	3	1	94	15	0	.160	18	74	6	3	2.3	.939
1915			11	11	.500	3.27	37	26	11	209	200	73	111	4	0	0	0	66	10	0	.152	5	63	2	2	1.9	.971
1916	STL	A	13	9	.591	2.57	41	26	8	217.1	174	98	92	1	2	1	4	63	7	0	.111	10	72	6	2	2.1	.932
1917			8	19	.296	2.94	38	28	11	232.2	193	95	82	4	1	1	3	72	8	0	.111	9	59	1	3	1.8	.986
1918	CLE	A	2	2	.500	7.06	14	5	0	43.1	70	18	8	0	1	0	0	12	1	0	.083	0	14	0	0	1.0	1.000
10 yrs.			119	150	.442	3.10	367	288	157	2336.1	2216	783	1159	22	9	11	12	764	98	0	.128	95	682	51	18	2.3	.938

Don Gross

GROSS, DONALD JOHN
B. June 30, 1931, Weidman, Mich.

BL TL 5'11" 186 lbs.

1955	CIN	N	4	5	.444	4.14	17	11	2	67.1	79	16	33	1	0	0	0	19	3	0	.158	3	12	2	1	1.0	.882
1956			3	0	1.000	1.95	19	7	0	69.1	69	20	47	0	0	0	0	19	2	0	.105	6	13	0	3	1.0	1.000
1957			7	9	.438	4.31	43	16	5	148.1	152	33	73	0	1	4	1	46	5	0	.109	14	22	0	1	0.8	1.000
1958	PIT	N	5	7	.417	3.98	40	3	0	74.2	67	38	59	0	5	5	7	18	1	0	.056	5	14	0	1	0.5	1.000
1959			1	1	.500	3.55	21	0	0	33	28	10	15	0	1	1	2	2	0	0	.000	1	11	0	0	0.6	1.000
1960			0	0	–	3.38	5	0	0	5.1	5	0	3	0	0	0	0	0	0	0	–	0	0	0	0	0.0	–
6 yrs.			20	22	.476	3.73	145	37	9	398	400	117	230	1	7	12	10	104	11	0	.106	29	72	2	6	0.7	.981

Greg Gross

GROSS, GREGORY EUGENE
B. Aug. 1, 1952, York, Pa.

BL TL 5'10" 160 lbs.

1986	PHI	N	0	0	–	0.00	1	0	0	.2	1	1	2	0	0	0	0	101	25	0	.248	0	0	0	0	0.0	–
1989	HOU	N	0	0	–	18.00	1	0	0	1	3	1	1	0	0	0	0	75	15	0	.200	0	0	0	0	0.0	–
2 yrs.			0	0	–	10.80	2	0	0	1.2	4	2	3	0	0	0	0	*				0	0	0	0	0.0	–

Kevin Gross

GROSS, KEVIN FRANK
B. June 8, 1961, Downey, Calif.

BR TR 6'5" 200 lbs.

1983	PHI	N	4	6	.400	3.56	17	17	1	96	100	35	66	1	0	0	0	33	3	0	.091	11	13	0	0	1.4	1.000
1984			8	5	.615	4.12	44	14	1	129	140	44	84	0	4	0	1	30	2	0	.067	9	22	2	3	0.8	.939
1985			15	13	.536	3.41	38	31	6	205.2	194	81	151	2	1	0	0	65	9	1	.138	18	34	3	0	1.4	.945
1986			12	12	.500	4.02	37	36	7	241.2	240	94	154	2	0	0	0	80	15	1	.188	25	28	2	2	1.5	.964
1987			9	16	.360	4.35	34	33	3	200.2	205	87	110	1	1	0	0	63	12	1	.190	13	23	3	1	1.1	.923
1988			12	14	.462	3.69	33	33	5	231.2	209	89	162	1	0	0	0	75	13	0	.173	13	34	2	1	1.5	.959

Year	Team		W	L	PCT	ERA	G	GS	CG	IP	H	BB	SO	ShO	W	L	SV	AB	H	HR	BA	PO	A	E	DP	TC/G	FA
															Relief Pitching			Batting									

Kevin Gross *continued*

Year	Team		W	L	PCT	ERA	G	GS	CG	IP	H	BB	SO	ShO	W	L	SV	AB	H	HR	BA	PO	A	E	DP	TC/G	FA
1989	MON	N	11	12	.478	4.38	31	31	4	201.1	188	88	158	3	0	0	0	64	9	0	.141	15	25	2	1	1.4	.952
7 yrs.			71	78	.477	3.95	234	195	27	1306	1276	518	885	10	6	2	1	410	63	3	.154	104	179	14	9	1.3	.953

Wayne Gross

GROSS, WAYNE DALE
B. Jan. 14, 1952, Riverside, Calif.
BL TR 6'2" 210 lbs.

| 1983 | OAK | A | 0 | 0 | – | 0.00 | 1 | 0 | 0 | 2.1 | 2 | 1 | 0 | 0 | 0 | 0 | 0 | * | | | | 0 | 0 | 0 | 0 | 0.0 | – |

Harley Grossman

GROSSMAN, HARLEY JOSEPH
B. May 5, 1930, Evansville, Ind.
BR TR 6' 170 lbs.

| 1952 | WAS | A | 0 | 0 | – | 54.00 | 1 | 0 | 0 | .1 | 2 | 0 | 0 | 0 | 0 | 0 | 0 | 0 | 0 | 0 | – | 1 | 0 | 0 | 0 | 1.0 | 1.000 |

Ernie Groth

GROTH, ERNEST JOHN
B. Dec. 24, 1884, Cedarburg, Wis.   D. May 23, 1950, Milwaukee, Wis.
BR TR 5'11" 175 lbs.

| 1904 | CHI | N | 0 | 2 | .000 | 5.63 | 3 | 2 | 2 | 16 | 22 | 6 | 9 | 0 | 0 | 0 | 1 | 6 | 0 | 0 | .000 | 0 | 2 | 0 | 1 | 0.7 | 1.000 |

Ernie Groth

GROTH, ERNEST WILLIAM
B. May 3, 1922, Beaver Falls, Pa.
BR TR 5'9" 185 lbs.

1947	CLE	A	0	0	–	0.00	2	0	0	1.1	0	1	1	0	0	0	0	0	0	0	–	0	0	0	0	0.0	–
1948			0	0	–	9.00	1	0	0	1	1	2	0	0	0	0	0	0	0	0	–	0	0	0	0	0.0	–
1949	CHI	A	0	1	.000	5.40	3	0	0	5	2	3	1	0	0	1	0	0	0	0	–	1	0	1	0	0.7	.500
3 yrs.			0	1	.000	4.91	6	0	0	7.1	3	6	2	0	0	1	0	0	0	0	–	1	0	1	0	0.3	.500

Lefty Grove

GROVE, ROBERT MOSES (Mose)
B. Mar. 6, 1900, Lonaconing, Md.   D. May 22, 1975, Norwalk, Ohio
Hall of Fame 1947.
BL TL 6'3" 190 lbs.

1925	PHI	A	10	12	.455	4.75	45	18	5	197	207	131	116	0	5	3	1	65	8	0	.123	6	55	2	3	1.4	.968
1926			13	13	.500	2.51	45	33	20	258	227	101	194	1	1	1	6	81	8	0	.099	6	53	3	3	1.4	.952
1927			20	13	.606	3.19	51	28	14	262.1	251	79	174	1	3	5	9	80	10	2	.125	8	55	9	2	1.4	.875
1928			24	8	.750	2.58	39	31	24	261.2	228	64	183	4	1	0	4	88	15	1	.170	6	40	1	0	1.2	.979
1929			20	6	.769	2.81	42	37	21	275.1	278	81	170	2	0	0	4	102	22	1	.216	3	44	2	0	1.2	.959
1930			28	5	.848	2.54	50	32	22	291	273	60	209	2	5	2	9	110	22	2	.200	6	53	2	1	1.2	.967
1931			31	4	.886	2.06	41	30	27	288.2	249	62	175	4	4	1	5	115	23	0	.200	2	47	0	1	1.2	1.000
1932			25	10	.714	2.84	44	30	27	291.2	269	79	188	4	3	2	7	107	18	4	.168	3	46	1	1	1.2	.980
1933			24	8	.750	3.20	45	28	21	275.1	280	83	114	2	6	2	6	105	9	1	.086	9	58	2	5	1.5	.971
1934	BOS	A	8	8	.500	6.50	22	11	5	109.1	149	32	43	0	3	3	0	37	6	1	.162	3	18	2	1	1.0	.913
1935			20	12	.625	2.70	35	30	23	273	269	65	121	2	2	1	1	89	7	1	.079	1	63	2	6	1.9	.970
1936			17	12	.586	2.81	35	30	22	253.1	237	65	130	6	0	2	2	80	11	0	.138	3	49	2	0	1.5	.963
1937			17	9	.654	3.02	32	32	21	262	269	83	153	3	0	0	0	91	13	0	.143	6	43	1	0	1.6	.980
1938			14	4	.778	3.08	24	21	12	163.2	169	52	99	1	0	0	1	54	8	0	.148	0	29	0	1	1.2	1.000
1939			15	4	.789	2.54	23	23	17	191	180	58	81	2	0	0	0	67	9	1	.134	0	21	3	2	1.0	.875
1940			7	6	.538	3.99	22	21	9	153.1	159	50	62	1	0	0	0	53	8	1	.151	1	34	3	0	1.7	.921
1941			7	7	.500	4.37	21	21	10	134	155	42	54	0	0	0	0	45	5	0	.111	2	17	3	0	1.0	.864
17 yrs.			300	141	.680	3.06	616	456	300	3940.2	3849	1187	2266	35	33	22	55	1369	202	15	.148	65	725	38	26	1.3	.954
					4th																						

WORLD SERIES

1929	PHI	A	0	0	–	0.00	2	0	0	6.1	3	1	10	0	0	0	2	2	0	0	.000	0	0	0	0	0.5	1.000
1930			2	1	.667	1.42	3	2	2	19	15	3	10	0	1	0	0	6	0	0	.000	0	0	0	0	0.3	1.000
1931			2	1	.667	2.42	3	3	2	26	28	2	16	0	0	0	0	10	0	0	.000	0	2	0	0	0.0	–
3 yrs.			4	2	.667	1.75	8	5	4	51.1	46	6	36	0	1	0	2	18	0	0	.000	0	2	0	0	0.3	1.000

Orval Grove

GROVE, ORVAL LeROY
B. Aug. 29, 1919, Mineral, Kans.
BR TR 6'3" 196 lbs.

1940	CHI	A	0	0	–	3.00	3	0	0	6	4	4	1	0	0	0	0	1	0	0	.000	1	0	0	0	0.3	1.000
1941			0	0	–	10.29	2	0	0	7	9	5	5	0	0	0	0	2	0	0	.000	0	0	0	0	1.5	1.000
1942			4	6	.400	5.16	12	8	4	66.1	77	33	21	0	1	1	0	22	5	1	.227	8	16	1	1	2.1	.960
1943			15	9	.625	2.75	32	25	18	216.1	192	72	76	3	1	0	2	66	12	0	.182	21	43	1	0	2.0	.985
1944			14	15	.483	3.72	34	33	11	234.2	237	71	105	2	1	0	0	77	8	0	.104	6	64	3	3	2.1	.959
1945			14	12	.538	3.44	33	30	16	217	233	68	54	4	0	0	0	71	7	0	.099	12	55	5	3	2.2	.931
1946			8	13	.381	3.02	33	26	10	205.1	213	78	60	1	0	0	0	65	7	0	.108	8	49	4	1	1.8	.934
1947			6	8	.429	4.44	25	19	6	135.2	158	70	33	1	0	0	0	48	7	0	.146	11	19	1	1	1.2	.968
1948			2	10	.167	6.16	32	11	1	87.2	110	42	19	0	1	2	1	21	2	0	.095	5	26	3	1	1.1	.912
1949			0	0	–	54.00	1	0	0	.2	4	1	1	0	0	0	0	0	0	0	–	0	0	0	0	0.0	–
10 yrs.			63	73	.463	3.78	207	152	66	1176.2	1237	444	374	11	4	3	4	373	48	1	.129	72	275	18	14	1.8	.951

Charlie Grover

GROVER, CHARLES BYRD (Bugs)
B. June 20, 1890, Huntington Twp., Ohio   D. May 24, 1971, Emmett, Mich.
BL TR 6'1½" 185 lbs.

| 1913 | DET | A | 0 | 0 | – | 3.38 | 2 | 1 | 0 | 10.2 | 9 | 7 | 2 | 0 | 0 | 0 | 0 | 3 | 0 | 0 | .000 | 1 | 3 | 0 | 0 | 2.0 | 1.000 |

Tom Grubbs

GRUBBS, THOMAS DILLARD (Judge)
B. Feb. 22, 1894, Mt. Sterling, Ky.   D. Jan. 28, 1986, Mt. Sterling, Ky.
BR TR 6'2" 165 lbs.

| 1920 | NY | N | 0 | 1 | .000 | 7.20 | 1 | 1 | 0 | 5 | 9 | 0 | 0 | 0 | 0 | 0 | 0 | 1 | 0 | 0 | .000 | 0 | 0 | 0 | 0 | 0.0 | – |

Henry Gruber

GRUBER, HENRY JOHN (Hen)
B. Dec. 14, 1863, Hamden, Conn.   D. Sept. 26, 1932, New Haven, Conn.
BR TL

1887	DET	N	4	3	.571	2.74	7	7	7	62.1	63	21	12	0	0	0	0	24	4	0	.167	0	7	1	0	1.1	.875
1888			11	14	.440	2.29	27	25	25	240	196	41	71	3	1	1	0	92	13	0	.141	4	61	8	2	2.7	.890
1889	CLE	N	7	16	.304	3.64	25	23	23	205	198	94	74	0	1	0	0	69	7	0	.101	6	40	6	2	2.1	.885
1890	CLE	P	21	23	.477	4.27	48	44	39	383.1	464	204	110	1	0	0	1	163	36	0	.221	8	109	14	3	2.7	.893

Year	Team		W	L	PCT	ERA	G	GS	CG	IP	H	BB	SO	ShO	Relief Pitching W	L	SV	Batting AB	H	HR	BA	PO	A	E	DP	TC/G	FA

Henry Gruber *continued*

Year	Team		W	L	PCT	ERA	G	GS	CG	IP	H	BB	SO	ShO	W	L	SV	AB	H	HR	BA	PO	A	E	DP	TC/G	FA
1891	CLE	N	17	22	.436	4.13	44	40	35	348.2	407	119	79	1	2	1	0	141	23	1	.163	8	90	10	5	2.5	.907
5 yrs.			60	78	.435	3.67	151	139	129	1239.1	1328	479	346	5	4	2	2	489	83	1	.170	26	307	39	12	2.5	.895

Al Grunwald

GRUNWALD, ALFRED HENRY (Stretch)
B. Feb. 13, 1930, Los Angeles, Calif.

BL TL 6'4" 210 lbs.

Year	Team		W	L	PCT	ERA	G	GS	CG	IP	H	BB	SO	ShO	W	L	SV	AB	H	HR	BA	PO	A	E	DP	TC/G	FA
1955	PIT	N	0	0	–	4.70	3	0	0	7.2	7	7	2	0	0	0	0	4	2	0	.500	2	0	0	0	0.7	1.000
1959	KC	A	0	1	.000	7.94	6	1	0	11.1	18	11	9	0	0	0	1	4	0	0	.000	0	2	1	1	0.5	.667
2 yrs.			0	1	.000	6.63	9	1	0	19	25	18	11	0	0	0	1	8	2	0	.250	2	2	1	1	0.6	.800

Joe Grzenda

GRZENDA, JOSEPH CHARLES
B. June 8, 1937, Scranton, Pa.

BR TL 6'2" 180 lbs.

Year	Team		W	L	PCT	ERA	G	GS	CG	IP	H	BB	SO	ShO	W	L	SV	AB	H	HR	BA	PO	A	E	DP	TC/G	FA
1961	DET	A	1	0	1.000	7.94	4	0	0	5.2	9	2	0	0	1	0	0	1	1	0	1.000	1	2	0	0	0.8	1.000
1964	KC	A	0	2	.000	5.40	20	0	0	25	34	13	17	0	0	2	0	2	0	0	.000	0	10	0	0	0.5	1.000
1966			0	2	.000	3.27	21	0	0	22	28	12	14	0	0	2	0	1	0	0	.000	0	6	0	1	0.3	1.000
1967	NY	N	0	0	–	2.16	11	0	0	16.2	14	8	9	0	0	0	0	1	0	0	.000	0	1	0	0	0.1	1.000
1969	MIN	A	4	1	.800	3.88	38	0	0	48.2	52	17	24	0	4	1	3	5	0	0	.000	0	14	0	1	0.4	1.000
1970	WAS	A	3	6	.333	4.98	49	3	0	85	86	34	38	0	2	5	6	12	0	0	.000	3	16	0	1	0.4	1.000
1971			5	2	.714	1.93	46	0	0	70	54	17	56	0	5	2	5	7	1	0	.143	0	11	0	0	0.2	1.000
1972	STL	N	1	0	1.000	5.71	30	0	0	34.2	46	17	15	0	1	0	0	1	0	0	.000	2	6	0	0	0.3	1.000
8 yrs.			14	13	.519	4.01	219	3	0	307.2	323	120	173	0	13	12	14	30	2	0	.067	6	66	0	3	0.3	1.000

LEAGUE CHAMPIONSHIP SERIES

Year	Team		W	L	PCT	ERA	G	GS	CG	IP	H	BB	SO	ShO	W	L	SV	AB	H	HR	BA	PO	A	E	DP	TC/G	FA
1969	MIN	A	0	0	–	0.00	1	0	0	.2	0	0	0	0	0	0	0	0	0	0	–	0	0	0	0	0.0	

Cecilio Guante

GUANTE, CECILIO
Born Cecilio Guante y Magallane.
B. Feb. 1, 1960, Villa Mella, Dominican Republic

BR TR 6'3" 200 lbs.

Year	Team		W	L	PCT	ERA	G	GS	CG	IP	H	BB	SO	ShO	W	L	SV	AB	H	HR	BA	PO	A	E	DP	TC/G	FA
1982	PIT	N	0	0	–	3.33	10	0	0	27	28	5	26	0	0	0	0	5	0	0	.000	1	2	0	0	0.3	1.000
1983			2	6	.250	3.32	49	0	0	100.1	90	46	82	0	2	6	9	22	2	0	.091	5	9	2	0	0.3	.875
1984			2	3	.400	2.61	27	0	0	41.1	32	16	30	0	2	3	2	4	0	0	.000	2	3	0	0	0.2	1.000
1985			4	6	.400	2.72	63	0	0	109	84	40	92	0	4	6	5	17	1	0	.059	6	13	1	0	0.3	.950
1986			5	2	.714	3.35	52	0	0	78	65	29	63	0	5	2	4	1	0	0	.000	1	5	1	0	0.1	.857
1987	NY	A	3	2	.600	5.73	23	0	0	44	42	20	46	0	3	2	1	0	0	0	–	1	2	1	0	0.2	.750
1988	2 teams	NY A (56G 5–6)					TEX A	(7G 0–0)																			
"	total		5	6	.455	2.82	63	0	0	79.2	67	26	65	0	5	6	12	0	0	0	–	2	3	0	0	0.1	.833
1989	TEX	A	6	6	.500	3.91	50	0	0	69	66	36	69	0	6	6	2	0	0	0	–	4	5	0	0	0.2	1.000
8 yrs.			27	31	.466	3.35	337	0	0	548.1	474	218	473	0	27	31	35	49	3	0	.061	22	42	6	0	0.2	.914

Mark Gubicza

GUBICZA, MARK STEVEN
B. Aug. 14, 1962, Philadelphia, Pa.

BR TR 6'6" 215 lbs.

Year	Team		W	L	PCT	ERA	G	GS	CG	IP	H	BB	SO	ShO	W	L	SV	AB	H	HR	BA	PO	A	E	DP	TC/G	FA
1984	KC	A	10	14	.417	4.05	29	29	4	189	172	75	111	2	0	0	0	0	0	0	–	19	31	2	1	1.8	.962
1985			14	10	.583	4.06	29	28	0	177.1	160	77	99	0	1	0	0	0	0	0	–	23	26	0	4	1.7	1.000
1986			12	6	.667	3.64	35	24	3	180.2	155	84	118	2	1	1	0	0	0	0	–	17	32	0	3	1.4	1.000
1987			13	18	.419	3.98	35	35	10	241.2	231	120	166	2	0	0	0	0	0	0	–	32	40	2	7	2.1	.973
1988			20	8	.714	2.70	35	35	8	269.2	237	83	183	4	0	0	0	0	0	0	–	29	44	1	3	2.1	.986
1989			15	11	.577	3.04	36	**36**	8	255	252	63	173	2	0	0	0	0	0	0	–	18	49	5	0	2.0	.931
6 yrs.			84	67	.556	3.51	199	187	33	1313.1	1207	502	850	12	2	1	0	0	0	0	–	138	222	10	18	1.9	.973

LEAGUE CHAMPIONSHIP SERIES

Year	Team		W	L	PCT	ERA	G	GS	CG	IP	H	BB	SO	ShO	W	L	SV	AB	H	HR	BA	PO	A	E	DP	TC/G	FA
1985	KC	A	1	0	1.000	3.24	2	1	0	8.1	4	4	4	0	0	0	0	0	0	0	–	0	1	0	0	0.5	1.000

Marv Gudat

GUDAT, MARVIN JOHN
B. Aug. 27, 1905, Goliad, Tex. D. Mar. 1, 1954, Los Angeles, Calif.

BL TL 5'11" 162 lbs.

Year	Team		W	L	PCT	ERA	G	GS	CG	IP	H	BB	SO	ShO	W	L	SV	AB	H	HR	BA	PO	A	E	DP	TC/G	FA
1929	CIN	N	1	1	.500	3.38	7	2	2	26.2	29	4	0	0	0	0	0	10	2	0	.200	0	4	0	0	0.7	.800
1932	CHI	N	0	0	–	0.00	1	0	0	1	1	0	2	0	0	0	0	94	24	1	.255	0	0	0	0	0.0	–
2 yrs.			1	1	.500	3.25	8	2	2	27.2	30	4	2	0	0	0	0	*				0	4	1	0	0.6	.800

Whitey Guese

GUESE, THEODORE
B. Jan. 24, 1872, New Bremen, Ohio D. Apr. 8, 1951, Wapakoneta, Ohio

BR TR 6'½" 200 lbs.

Year	Team		W	L	PCT	ERA	G	GS	CG	IP	H	BB	SO	ShO	W	L	SV	AB	H	HR	BA	PO	A	E	DP	TC/G	FA
1901	CIN	N	1	4	.200	6.09	6	5	4	44.1	62	14	11	0	0	0	0	15	3	0	.200	1	6	3	0	1.7	.700

Lee Guetterman

GUETTERMAN, ARTHUR LEE
B. Nov. 22, 1958, Chattanooga, Tenn.

BL TL 6'8" 225 lbs.

Year	Team		W	L	PCT	ERA	G	GS	CG	IP	H	BB	SO	ShO	W	L	SV	AB	H	HR	BA	PO	A	E	DP	TC/G	FA
1984	SEA	A	0	0	–	4.15	3	0	0	4.1	9	2	2	0	0	0	0	0	0	0	–	0	1	0	1	0.3	1.000
1986			0	4	.000	7.34	41	4	0	76	108	30	38	0	0	4	0	0	0	0	–	5	12	2	1	0.5	.895
1987			11	4	.733	3.81	25	17	2	113.1	117	35	42	1	0	0	0	0	0	0	–	7	22	0	3	1.2	1.000
1988	NY	A	1	2	.333	4.65	20	2	0	40.2	49	14	15	0	1	0	0	0	0	0	–	2	5	0	0	0.4	1.000
1989			5	5	.500	2.45	70	0	0	103	98	26	51	0	5	5	13	0	0	0	–	6	24	3	4	0.5	.909
5 yrs.			17	15	.531	4.30	159	23	3	337.1	381	107	148	1	7	7	13	20	64	5	9						0.6	.944

Ron Guidry

GUIDRY, RONALD AMES (Louisiana Lightning, Gator)
B. Aug. 28, 1950, Lafayette, La.

BL TL 5'11" 161 lbs.

Year	Team		W	L	PCT	ERA	G	GS	CG	IP	H	BB	SO	ShO	W	L	SV	AB	H	HR	BA	PO	A	E	DP	TC/G	FA
1975	NY	A	0	1	.000	3.45	10	1	0	15.2	15	9	15	0	0	0	0	0	0	0	–	0	0	0	0	0.0	–
1976			0	0	–	5.63	7	0	0	16	20	4	12	0	0	0	0	0	0	0	–	0	4	0	0	0.6	1.000
1977			16	7	.696	2.82	31	25	9	211	174	65	176	5	1	0	1	0	0	0	–	7	27	1	2	1.1	.971
1978			25	3	.893	1.74	35	35	16	273.2	187	72	248	9	0	0	0	0	0	0	–	14	44	2	1	1.7	.967
1979			18	8	.692	2.78	33	30	15	236	203	71	201	2	1	0	2	0	0	0	–	11	29	1	1	1.2	.976
1980			17	10	.630	3.56	37	29	5	220	215	80	166	3	1	1	1	0	0	0	–	16	36	2	4	1.5	.963
1981			11	5	.688	2.76	23	21	0	127	100	26	104	0	1	0	0	0	0	0	–	13	17	0	1	1.3	1.000
1982			14	8	.636	3.81	34	33	6	222	216	69	162	0	0	0	0	0	0	0	–	7	19	0	1	0.8	1.000

Ron Guidry *continued*

Year	Team	Lg	W	L	PCT	ERA	G	GS	CG	IP	H	BB	SO	ShO	Relief Pitching W	L	SV	Batting AB	H	HR	BA	PO	A	E	DP	TC/G	FA
1983			21	9	.700	3.42	31	31	**21**	250.1	232	60	156	3	0	0	0	0	0	0	–	9	33	0	2	1.4	1.000
1984			10	11	.476	4.51	29	28	5	195.2	223	44	127	1	0	0	0	0	0	0	–	8	24	0	3	1.1	1.000
1985			**22**	6	**.786**	3.27	34	33	11	259	243	42	143	2	0	0	0	0	0	0	–	6	34	1	3	1.2	.976
1986			9	12	.429	3.98	30	30	5	192.1	202	38	140	0	0	0	0	0	0	0	–	9	21	1	0	1.0	.968
1987			5	8	.385	3.67	22	17	2	117.2	111	38	96	0	0	1	0	0	0	0	–	4	14	0	1	0.8	1.000
1988			2	3	.400	4.18	12	10	0	56	57	15	32	0	0	0	0	0	0	0	–	3	5	0	0	0.7	1.000
14 yrs.			170	91	.651	3.29	368	323	95	2392.1	2198	633	1778	26	3	2	4	0	0	0	–	107	307	8	19	1.1	.981

DIVISIONAL PLAYOFF SERIES

Year	Team	Lg	W	L	PCT	ERA	G	GS	CG	IP	H	BB	SO	ShO	W	L	SV	AB	H	HR	BA	PO	A	E	DP	TC/G	FA
1981	NY	A	0	0	–	5.40	2	2	0	8.1	11	3	8	0	0	0	0	0	0	0	–	0	0	0	0	0.0	–

LEAGUE CHAMPIONSHIP SERIES

Year	Team	Lg	W	L	PCT	ERA	G	GS	CG	IP	H	BB	SO	ShO	W	L	SV	AB	H	HR	BA	PO	A	E	DP	TC/G	FA
1977	NY	A	1	0	1.000	3.97	2	2	1	11.1	9	3	8	0	0	0	0	0	0	0	–	2	0	0	0	1.0	1.000
1978			1	0	1.000	1.13	1	1	0	8	7	1	7	0	0	0	0	0	0	0	–	0	0	0	0	0.0	–
1980			0	1	.000	12.00	1	1	0	3	5	4	2	0	0	0	0	0	0	0	–	0	1	0	0	1.0	1.000
3 yrs.			2	1	.667	4.03	4	4	1	22.1	21	8	17	0	0	0	0	0	0	0	–	2	1	0	0	0.8	1.000

WORLD SERIES

Year	Team	Lg	W	L	PCT	ERA	G	GS	CG	IP	H	BB	SO	ShO	W	L	SV	AB	H	HR	BA	PO	A	E	DP	TC/G	FA
1977	NY	A	1	0	1.000	2.00	1	1	1	9	4	3	7	0	0	0	0	2	0	0	.000	0	0	0	0	0.0	–
1978			1	0	1.000	1.00	1	1	1	9	8	7	4	0	0	0	0	0	0	0	–	1	1	0	0	2.0	1.000
1981			1	1	.500	1.93	2	2	0	14	8	4	15	0	0	0	0	5	0	0	.000	0	0	0	0	0.0	–
3 yrs.			3	1	.750	1.69	4	4	2	32	20	14	26	0	0	0	0	7	0	0	.000	1	1	0	0	0.5	1.000

Skip Guinn

GUINN, DRANNON EUGENE
B. Oct. 25, 1944, St. Charles, Mo.

BR TL 5'10" 180 lbs.

Year	Team	Lg	W	L	PCT	ERA	G	GS	CG	IP	H	BB	SO	ShO	W	L	SV	AB	H	HR	BA	PO	A	E	DP	TC/G	FA
1968	ATL	N	0	0	–	3.60	3	0	0	5	3	3	4	0	0	0	0	0	0	0	–	0	0	0	0	0.0	–
1969	HOU	N	1	2	.333	6.67	28	0	0	27	34	21	33	0	1	2	0	3	0	0	.000	1	3	0	0	0.1	1.000
1971			0	0	–	0.00	4	0	0	5	1	3	3	0	0	0	1	0	0	0	–	1	0	0	0	0.3	1.000
3 yrs.			1	2	.333	5.35	35	0	0	37	38	27	40	0	1	2	1	3	0	0	.000	2	3	0	0	0.1	1.000

Witt Guise

GUISE, WITT ORISON (Lefty)
B. Sept. 18, 1909, Driggs, Ark. D. Aug. 13, 1968, Little Rock, Ark.

BL TL 6'2" 172 lbs.

Year	Team	Lg	W	L	PCT	ERA	G	GS	CG	IP	H	BB	SO	ShO	W	L	SV	AB	H	HR	BA	PO	A	E	DP	TC/G	FA
1940	CIN	N	0	0	–	1.17	2	0	0	7.2	8	5	1	0	0	0	0	3	1	0	.333	0	3	0	0	1.5	1.000

Don Gullett

GULLETT, DONALD EDWARD
B. Jan. 6, 1951, Lynn, Ky.

BR TL 6' 210 lbs.

Year	Team	Lg	W	L	PCT	ERA	G	GS	CG	IP	H	BB	SO	ShO	W	L	SV	AB	H	HR	BA	PO	A	E	DP	TC/G	FA
1970	CIN	N	5	2	.714	2.42	44	2	0	78	54	44	76	0	4	1	6	19	4	0	.211	2	5	0	1	0.2	1.000
1971			16	6	**.727**	2.64	35	31	4	218	196	64	107	3	0	0	0	75	9	0	.120	6	25	1	2	0.9	.969
1972			9	10	.474	3.94	31	16	2	134.2	127	43	96	0	3	2	2	38	8	0	.211	4	11	1	0	0.5	.938
1973			18	8	.692	3.51	45	30	7	228.1	198	69	153	4	5	1	2	64	12	0	.188	12	31	0	2	1.0	1.000
1974			17	11	.607	3.04	36	35	10	243	201	88	183	3	0	1	0	80	19	0	.238	8	36	1	0	1.3	.978
1975			15	4	.789	2.42	22	22	8	160	127	56	98	3	0	0	0	62	14	0	.226	2	22	0	0	1.1	1.000
1976			11	3	.786	3.00	23	20	4	126	119	48	64	0	1	0	1	44	8	0	.182	4	20	0	1	1.0	1.000
1977	NY	A	14	4	.778	3.59	22	22	7	158	137	69	116	1	0	0	0	0	0	0	–	9	15	1	1	1.1	.960
1978			4	2	.667	3.63	8	8	2	44.2	46	20	28	0	0	0	0	0	0	0	–	2	8	2	0	1.5	.833
9 yrs.			109	50	.686	3.11	266	186	44	1390.2	1205	501	921	14	13	5	11	382	74	0	.194	49	173	6	7	0.9	.974

LEAGUE CHAMPIONSHIP SERIES

Year	Team	Lg	W	L	PCT	ERA	G	GS	CG	IP	H	BB	SO	ShO	W	L	SV	AB	H	HR	BA	PO	A	E	DP	TC/G	FA
1970	CIN	N	0	0	–	0.00	2	0	0	3.2	1	2	3	0	0	0	2	1	0	0	.000	0	0	0	0	0.0	–
1972			0	1	.000	8.00	2	2	0	9	12	0	5	0	0	0	0	2	1	0	.500	0	0	0	0	0.0	–
1973			0	1	.000	2.00	3	1	0	9	4	3	6	0	0	0	0	1	0	0	.000	1	0	0	0	0.3	1.000
1975			1	0	1.000	3.00	1	1	1	9	8	2	5	0	0	0	0	4	2	1	.500	4	1	0	0	5.0	1.000
1976			1	0	1.000	1.13	1	1	0	8	2	3	4	0	0	0	0	4	2	0	.500	0	0	0	0	0.0	–
1977	NY	A	0	1	.000	18.00	1	1	0	2	4	2	0	0	0	0	0	0	0	0	–	0	0	0	0	0.0	–
6 yrs.			2	3	.400	3.98	10	6	1	40.2	31	12	23	0	0	0	2	12	5	1	.417	5	1	0	0	0.6	1.000

WORLD SERIES

Year	Team	Lg	W	L	PCT	ERA	G	GS	CG	IP	H	BB	SO	ShO	W	L	SV	AB	H	HR	BA	PO	A	E	DP	TC/G	FA
1970	CIN	N	0	0	–	1.35	3	0	0	6.2	5	4	4	0	0	0	0	1	0	0	.000	0	0	0	0	0.0	–
1972			0	0	–	1.29	1	1	0	7	5	2	4	0	0	0	0	2	0	0	.000	0	1	0	0	1.0	1.000
1975			1	1	.500	4.34	3	3	0	18.2	19	10	15	0	0	0	0	7	2	0	.286	0	0	0	0	0.0	–
1976			1	0	1.000	1.23	1	1	0	7.1	5	3	4	0	0	0	0	0	0	0	–	0	1	0	0	1.0	1.000
1977	NY	A	0	1	.000	6.39	2	2	0	12.2	13	7	10	0	0	0	0	2	0	0	.000	1	2	0	0	1.5	1.000
5 yrs.			2	2	.500	3.61	10	7	0	52.1	47	26 8th	37	0	0	0	0	12	2	0	.167	1	4	0	0	0.5	1.000

Bill Gullickson

GULLICKSON, WILLIAM LEE
B. Feb. 20, 1959, Marshall, Minn.

BR TR 6'3" 200 lbs.

Year	Team	Lg	W	L	PCT	ERA	G	GS	CG	IP	H	BB	SO	ShO	W	L	SV	AB	H	HR	BA	PO	A	E	DP	TC/G	FA
1979	MON	N	0	0	–	0.00	1	0	0	1	2	0	0	0	0	0	0	0	0	0	–	0	0	0	0	0.0	–
1980			10	5	.667	3.00	24	19	5	141	127	50	120	2	0	1	0	40	7	0	.175	4	21	1	2	1.1	.962
1981			7	9	.438	2.81	22	22	3	157	142	34	115	2	0	0	0	46	7	0	.152	12	16	1	2	1.3	.966
1982			12	14	.462	3.57	34	34	6	236.2	231	61	155	0	0	0	0	82	10	0	.122	16	18	3	1	1.1	.919
1983			17	12	.586	3.75	34	34	10	242.1	230	59	120	1	0	0	0	82	11	1	.134	27	25	1	3	1.6	.981
1984			12	9	.571	3.61	32	32	3	226.2	230	37	100	0	0	0	0	73	8	0	.110	14	19	4	2	1.2	.892
1985			14	12	.538	3.52	29	29	4	181.1	187	47	68	1	0	0	0	64	12	0	.188	10	26	1	0	1.3	.973
1986	CIN	N	15	12	.556	3.38	37	37	6	244.2	245	60	121	2	0	0	0	79	6	0	.076	14	32	3	3	1.3	.939
1987	2 teams		CIN N (27G 10–11)			NY A (8G 4–2)																					
"	total		14	13	.519	4.86	35	35	4	213	218	50	117	1	0	0	0	53	11	1	.208	16	21	0	0	1.1	1.000
9 yrs.			101	86	.540	3.61	248	242	41	1643.2	1612	398	916	9	0	1	0	519	72	2	.139	113	178	14	13	1.2	.954

DIVISIONAL PLAYOFF SERIES

Year	Team	Lg	W	L	PCT	ERA	G	GS	CG	IP	H	BB	SO	ShO	W	L	SV	AB	H	HR	BA	PO	A	E	DP	TC/G	FA
1981	MON	N	1	0	1.000	1.17	1	1	0	7.2	6	1	3	0	0	0	0	3	0	0	.000	0	0	0	0	0.0	–

LEAGUE CHAMPIONSHIP SERIES

Year	Team	Lg	W	L	PCT	ERA	G	GS	CG	IP	H	BB	SO	ShO	W	L	SV	AB	H	HR	BA	PO	A	E	DP	TC/G	FA
1981	MON	N	0	2	.000	2.51	2	2	0	14.1	12	6	12	0	0	0	0	3	0	0	.000	0	0	0	0	0.0	–

Year	Team		W	L	PCT	ERA	G	GS	CG	IP	H	BB	SO	ShO	Relief Pitching W	L	SV	Batting AB	H	HR	BA	PO	A	E	DP	TC/G	FA

Ad Gumbert

GUMBERT, ADDISON COURTNEY
Brother of Billy Gumbert.
B. Oct. 10, 1868, Pittsburgh, Pa.   D. Apr. 23, 1925, Pittsburgh, Pa.

BR TR 5'10" 200 lbs.

Year	Team		W	L	PCT	ERA	G	GS	CG	IP	H	BB	SO	ShO	W	L	SV	AB	H	HR	BA	PO	A	E	DP	TC/G	FA
1888	CHI	N	3	3	.500	3.14	6	6	5	48.2	44	10	16	0	0	0	0	24	8	0	.333	1	8	1	0	1.7	.900
1889			16	13	.552	3.62	31	28	25	246.1	258	76	91	2	2	0	0	153	44	7	.288	17	44	6	1	2.2	.910
1890	BOS	P	22	12	.647	3.96	39	33	27	277.1	338	86	81	1	3	1	0	145	35	3	.241	15	83	13	0	2.8	.883
1891	CHI	N	17	11	.607	3.58	32	31	24	256.1	282	90	73	1	0	0	0	105	32	0	.305	18	55	8	3	2.5	.901
1892			22	19	.537	3.41	46	45	39	382.2	399	107	118	0	0	0	0	178	42	1	.236	10	97	9	1	2.5	.922
1893	PIT	N	12	7	.632	5.15	22	20	16	162.2	207	78	40	2	1	0	0	95	21	0	.221	12	23	0	3	1.6	1.000
1894			15	14	.517	6.02	37	31	26	269	372	84	65	0	0	0	0	113	33	1	.292	18	49	4	3	1.9	.944
1895	BKN	N	11	16	.407	5.08	33	26	20	234	288	69	45	0	1	1	0	97	35	2	.361	15	48	5	0	2.1	.926
1896	2 teams		BKN N (5G 0-4)			PHI N (11G 5-3)																						
"	total		5	7	.417	4.32	16	14	9	108.1	133	34	17	1	0	0	0	45	11	0	.244	5	28	2	1	2.2	.943
9 yrs.			123	102	.547	4.27	262	234	191	1985.1	2321	634	546	7	8	2	1	*				111	435	48	12	2.3	.919

Billy Gumbert

GUMBERT, WILLIAM SKEEN
Brother of Ad Gumbert.
B. Aug. 8, 1865, Pittsburgh, Pa.   D. Apr. 13, 1946, Pittsburgh, Pa.

BR TR 6'1½" 200 lbs.

Year	Team		W	L	PCT	ERA	G	GS	CG	IP	H	BB	SO	ShO	W	L	SV	AB	H	HR	BA	PO	A	E	DP	TC/G	FA
1890	PIT	N	4	6	.400	5.22	10	10	8	79.1	96	31	18	0	0	0	0	37	9	1	.243	6	18	3	1	2.7	.889
1892			3	2	.600	1.36	6	3	2	39.2	30	23	3	0	1	0	0	18	2	0	.111	1	7	5	0	2.2	.615
1893	LOU	N	0	0	-	27.00	1	1	0	.2	2	5	0	0	0	0	0	1	1	0	1.000	0	0	0	0	0.0	-
3 yrs.			7	8	.467	4.06	17	14	10	119.2	128	59	21	0	1	0	0	56	12	1	.214	7	25	8	1	2.4	.800

Harry Gumbert

GUMBERT, HARRY EDWARD (Gunboat)
B. Nov. 5, 1909, Elizabeth, Pa.

BR TR 6'2" 185 lbs.

Year	Team		W	L	PCT	ERA	G	GS	CG	IP	H	BB	SO	ShO	W	L	SV	AB	H	HR	BA	PO	A	E	DP	TC/G	FA
1935	NY	N	1	2	.333	6.08	6	3	1	23.2	35	10	11	0	0	0	0	8	0	0	.000	1	4	1	0	1.0	.833
1936			11	3	.786	3.90	39	15	1	140.2	157	54	52	0	4	0	0	44	11	0	.250	12	44	1	1	1.5	.982
1937			10	11	.476	3.68	34	24	10	200.1	194	62	65	1	0	0	0	72	13	1	.181	16	80	2	2	2.9	.980
1938			15	13	.536	4.01	38	33	14	235.2	238	84	81	1	0	0	0	84	13	0	.155	18	85	1	7	2.5	.989
1939			18	11	.621	4.32	36	34	14	243.2	257	81	81	2	0	1	0	90	18	0	.200	18	76	3	4	2.7	.969
1940			12	14	.462	3.76	35	30	14	237	230	81	77	2	2	0	2	87	17	1	.195	11	65	0	4	2.2	1.000
1941	2 teams		NY N (5G 1-1)			STL N (33G 11-5)																						
"	total		12	6	.667	3.06	38	22	9	176.2	173	48	62	3	4	0	1	65	19	2	.292	13	57	3	3	1.9	.959
1942	STL	N	9	5	.643	3.26	38	19	5	163	156	59	52	0	4	0	5	54	6	0	.111	6	60	0	2	1.7	1.000
1943			10	5	.667	2.84	21	19	7	133	115	32	40	2	0	0	0	45	7	0	.156	10	35	1	0	2.2	.978
1944	2 teams		STL N (10G 4-2)			CIN N (24G 10-8)																						
"	total		14	10	.583	3.07	34	26	14	216.2	217	59	56	2	1	2	3	73	9	0	.123	20	52	3	9	2.2	.960
1946	CIN	N	6	8	.429	3.24	36	10	5	119.1	112	42	44	0	4	4	4	32	8	0	.250	5	29	0	2	0.9	1.000
1947			10	10	.500	3.89	46	0	0	90.1	88	47	43	0	10	10	10	22	6	0	.273	2	17	1	3	0.4	.950
1948			10	8	.556	3.47	61	0	0	106.1	123	34	25	0	10	8	17	25	1	1	.040	4	40	1	3	0.7	.978
1949	2 teams		CIN N (29G 4-3)			PIT N (16G 1-4)																						
"	total		5	7	.417	5.64	45	0	0	68.2	88	26	17	0	5	7	5	6	1	0	.167	3	24	0	1	0.6	1.000
1950	PIT	N	0	0	-	5.40	1	0	0	1.2	3	2	0	0	0	0	0	1	1	0	1.000	0	2	0	0	2.0	1.000
15 yrs.			143	113	.559	3.68	508	235	94	2156.2	2186	721	709	13	44	28	48	708	130	5	.184	129	670	17	42	1.6	.979

WORLD SERIES

Year	Team		W	L	PCT	ERA	G	GS	CG	IP	H	BB	SO	ShO	W	L	SV	AB	H	HR	BA	PO	A	E	DP	TC/G	FA
1936	NY	N	0	0	-	36.00	2	0	0	2	7	4	2	0	0	0	0	0	0	0	-	0	0	0	0	0.0	-
1937			0	0	-	27.00	2	0	0	1.1	4	1	1	0	0	0	0	0	0	0	-	0	0	0	0	0.0	-
1942	STL	N	0	0	-	0.00	2	0	0	.2	1	0	0	0	0	0	0	0	0	0	-	0	1	0	0	0.5	1.000
3 yrs.			0	0	-	27.00	6	0	0	4	12	5	3	0	0	0	0	0	0	0	-	0	1	0	0	0.0	1.000

Dave Gumpert

GUMPERT, DAVID LAWRENCE
B. May 5, 1958, South Haven, Mich.

BR TR 6'1" 190 lbs.

Year	Team		W	L	PCT	ERA	G	GS	CG	IP	H	BB	SO	ShO	W	L	SV	AB	H	HR	BA	PO	A	E	DP	TC/G	FA
1982	DET	A	0	0	-	27.00	5	1	0	2	7	2	0	0	0	0	1	0	0	0	-	0	0	0	0	0.0	-
1983			0	2	.000	2.64	26	0	0	44.1	43	7	14	0	0	2	2	0	0	0	-	2	3	0	0	0.2	1.000
1985	CHI	N	1	0	1.000	3.48	9	0	0	10.1	12	7	4	0	1	0	0	1	0	0	.000	0	0	0	0	0.2	-
1986			2	0	1.000	4.37	38	0	0	59.2	60	28	45	0	0	0	2	5	0	0	.000	3	4	0	0	0.2	1.000
1987	KC	A	0	0	-	6.05	8	0	0	19.1	27	6	13	0	0	0	1	0	0	0	-	1	4	0	0	0.6	1.000
5 yrs.			3	2	.600	4.31	86	1	0	135.2	149	50	76	0	1	2	5	6	0	0	.000	6	11	0	0	0.2	1.000

Randy Gumpert

GUMPERT, RANDALL PENNINGTON
B. Jan. 23, 1918, Monocacy, Pa.

BR TR 6'3" 185 lbs.

Year	Team		W	L	PCT	ERA	G	GS	CG	IP	H	BB	SO	ShO	W	L	SV	AB	H	HR	BA	PO	A	E	DP	TC/G	FA
1936	PHI	A	1	2	.333	4.76	22	3	2	62.1	74	32	9	0	0	0	2	22	6	0	.273	1	9	0	0	0.4	1.000
1937			0	0	-	12.00	10	1	0	12	16	15	5	0	0	0	0	3	1	0	.333	1	3	0	0	0.4	1.000
1938			0	2	.000	10.95	4	2	0	12.1	24	10	1	0	0	0	0	4	1	0	.250	1	5	0	0	1.5	1.000
1946	NY	A	11	3	.786	2.31	33	12	4	132.2	113	32	63	0	3	0	1	47	6	0	.128	4	21	3	4	0.8	.893
1947			4	1	.800	5.43	24	6	2	56.1	71	28	50	0	0	0	0	14	1	0	.071	2	9	0	1	0.5	1.000
1948	2 teams		NY A (15G 1-0)			CHI A (16G 2-6)																						
"	total		3	6	.333	3.60	31	11	6	122.1	130	19	43	1	3	0	1	29	4	0	.138	3	18	1	1	0.7	.955
1949	CHI	A	13	16	.448	3.81	34	32	18	234	223	83	78	3	0	0	1	84	16	0	.190	15	43	1	6	1.7	.983
1950			5	12	.294	4.75	40	17	6	155.1	165	58	48	1	2	2	0	42	3	0	.071	10	24	1	3	0.9	.971
1951			8	5	.529	4.32	33	16	7	141.2	156	34	45	1	2	3	2	45	15	0	.333	2	16	3	1	0.6	.857
1952	2 teams		BOS A (10G 1-0)			WAS A (20G 4-9)																						
"	total		5	9	.357	4.22	30	13	2	123.2	127	35	35	0	2	1	2	39	7	0	.179	6	21	2	1	1.0	.931
10 yrs.			51	59	.464	4.17	261	113	47	1052.2	1099	346	352	6	11	10	7	329	60	0	.182	44	169	11	17	0.9	.951

Red Gunkel

GUNKEL, WOODWARD WILLIAM
B. Apr. 15, 1894, Sheffield, Ill.   D. Apr. 19, 1954, Chicago, Ill.

BB TR 5'8" 158 lbs.

Year	Team		W	L	PCT	ERA	G	GS	CG	IP	H	BB	SO	ShO	W	L	SV	AB	H	HR	BA	PO	A	E	DP	TC/G	FA
1916	CLE	A	0	0	-	0.00	1	0	0	1	0	1	1	0	0	0	0	0	0	0	-	0	0	0	0	0.0	-

Larry Gura

GURA, LAWRENCE CYRIL
B. Nov. 26, 1947, Joliet, Ill.

BB TL 6' 170 lbs.

Year	Team		W	L	PCT	ERA	G	GS	CG	IP	H	BB	SO	ShO	W	L	SV	AB	H	HR	BA	PO	A	E	DP	TC/G	FA
1970	CHI	N	1	3	.250	3.79	20	3	1	38	35	23	21	0	0	0	1	10	0	0	.000	1	6	0	1	0.4	1.000
1971			0	0	-	6.00	6	0	0	3	6	1	2	0	0	0	1	0	0	0	.000	0	0	0	0	0.0	-

Year	Team		W	L	PCT	ERA	G	GS	CG	IP	H	BB	SO	ShO	W	L	SV	AB	H	HR	BA	PO	A	E	DP	TC/G	FA

Larry Gura *continued*

Year	Team		W	L	PCT	ERA	G	GS	CG	IP	H	BB	SO	ShO	W	L	SV	AB	H	HR	BA	PO	A	E	DP	TC/G	FA
1972			0	0	–	3.75	7	0	0	12	11	3	13	0	0	0	0	1	0	0	.000	0	3	0	0	0.4	1.000
1973			2	4	.333	4.85	21	7	0	65	79	11	43	0	0	1	0	15	3	0	.200	7	13	0	0	1.0	1.000
1974	NY	A	5	1	.833	2.41	8	8	4	56	54	12	17	0	0	0	0	0	0	0	–	4	8	0	0	1.5	1.000
1975			7	8	.467	3.51	26	20	5	151.1	173	41	65	0	0	0	0	0	0	0	–	8	21	0	2	1.1	1.000
1976	KC	A	4	0	1.000	2.29	20	2	1	63	47	20	22	1	3	0	1	0	0	0	–	4	12	0	2	0.8	1.000
1977			8	5	.615	3.14	52	6	1	106	108	28	46	1	5	3	10	0	0	0	–	6	18	2	1	0.5	.923
1978			16	4	.800	2.72	35	26	8	221.2	183	60	81	2	2	0	0	0	0	0	–	13	44	1	2	1.7	.983
1979			13	12	.520	4.46	39	33	7	234	226	73	85	1	1	0	0	0	0	0	–	15	38	2	5	1.4	.964
1980			18	10	.643	2.96	36	36	16	283	272	76	113	4	0	0	0	0	0	0	–	9	50	0	3	1.6	1.000
1981			11	8	.579	2.72	23	23	12	172	139	35	61	2	0	0	0	0	0	0	–	9	30	0	4	1.7	1.000
1982			18	12	.600	4.03	37	37	8	248	251	64	98	3	0	0	0	0	0	0	–	7	50	2	6	1.6	.966
1983			11	18	.379	4.90	34	31	5	200.1	220	76	57	0	1	0	0	0	0	0	–	12	42	0	5	1.6	1.000
1984			12	9	.571	5.18	31	25	3	168.2	175	67	68	0	1	0	0	0	0	0	–	6	30	0	1	1.2	1.000
1985	2 teams		KC A	(3G 0–0)		CHI N	(5G 0–3)																					
"	total		0	3	.000	9.12	8	4	0	24.2	41	10	9	0	0	0	1	6	0	0	.000	6	4	0	0	1.3	1.000
16 yrs.			126	97	.565	3.76	403	261	71	2046.2	2020	600	801	14	13	5	14	33	3	0	.091	107	369	7	32	1.2	.986

DIVISIONAL PLAYOFF SERIES

Year	Team		W	L	PCT	ERA	G	GS	CG	IP	H	BB	SO	ShO	W	L	SV	AB	H	HR	BA	PO	A	E	DP	TC/G	FA
1981	KC	A	0	1	.000	7.36	1	1	0	3.2	7	3	3	0	0	0	0	0	0	0	–	0	0	0	0	0.0	–

LEAGUE CHAMPIONSHIP SERIES

Year	Team		W	L	PCT	ERA	G	GS	CG	IP	H	BB	SO	ShO	W	L	SV	AB	H	HR	BA	PO	A	E	DP	TC/G	FA
1976	KC	A	0	1	.000	4.22	2	2	0	10.2	18	1	4	0	0	0	0	0	0	0	–	0	0	0	0	0.0	–
1977			0	1	.000	18.00	2	1	0	2	7	1	2	0	0	0	0	0	0	0	–	0	0	0	0	0.0	–
1978			1	0	1.000	2.84	1	1	0	6.1	8	2	2	0	0	0	0	0	0	0	–	1	4	0	0	5.0	1.000
1980			1	0	1.000	2.00	1	1	1	9	10	1	4	0	0	0	0	0	0	0	–	0	1	0	0	1.0	1.000
4 yrs.			2	2	.500	4.18	6	5	1	28	43	5	12	0	0	0	0	0	0	0	–	1	5	0	0	1.0	1.000

WORLD SERIES

Year	Team		W	L	PCT	ERA	G	GS	CG	IP	H	BB	SO	ShO	W	L	SV	AB	H	HR	BA	PO	A	E	DP	TC/G	FA
1980	KC	A	0	0	–	2.19	2	2	0	12.1	8	3	4	0	0	0	0	0	0	0	–	2	4	0	2	3.0	1.000

Charlie Guth

GUTH, CHARLES J.
B. 1856, Chicago, Ill. D. July 5, 1883, Boston, Mass.

Year	Team		W	L	PCT	ERA	G	GS	CG	IP	H	BB	SO	ShO	W	L	SV	AB	H	HR	BA	PO	A	E	DP	TC/G	FA
1880	CHI	N	1	0	1.000	5.00	1	1	1	9	12	1	7	0	0	0	0	4	1	0	.250	0	0	0	0	0.0	–

Mark Guthrie

GUTHRIE, MARK ANTHONY
B. Sept. 22, 1965, Buffalo, N. Y.   BR TR 5'11" 192 lbs.

Year	Team		W	L	PCT	ERA	G	GS	CG	IP	H	BB	SO	ShO	W	L	SV	AB	H	HR	BA	PO	A	E	DP	TC/G	FA
1989	MIN	A	2	4	.333	4.55	13	8	0	57.1	66	21	38	0	0	0	0	0	0	0	–	2	8	0	0	0.8	1.000

Jose Guzman

GUZMAN, JOSE ALBERTO
Born Jose Alberto Guzman y Mirabel.
B. Apr. 9, 1963, Santa Isabel, Puerto Rico   BR TR 6'2" 172 lbs.

Year	Team		W	L	PCT	ERA	G	GS	CG	IP	H	BB	SO	ShO	W	L	SV	AB	H	HR	BA	PO	A	E	DP	TC/G	FA
1985	TEX	A	3	2	.600	2.76	5	5	0	32.2	27	14	24	0	0	0	0	0	5	0	–	0	5	0	0	1.0	1.000
1986			9	15	.375	4.54	29	29	2	172.1	199	60	87	0	0	0	0	0	0	0	–	13	24	0	0	1.3	1.000
1987			14	14	.500	4.67	37	30	6	208.1	196	82	143	0	3	0	0	0	0	0	–	14	34	2	3	1.4	.960
1988			11	13	.458	3.70	30	30	6	206.2	180	82	157	2	0	0	0	0	0	0	–	15	24	3	1	1.4	.929
4 yrs.			37	44	.457	4.21	101	94	14	620	602	238	411	2	3	0	0	0	0	0	–	42	87	5	4	1.3	.963

Santiago Guzman

GUZMAN, SANTIAGO
Born Santiago Donovan y Guzman.
B. July 25, 1949, San Pedro de Macoris, Dominican Republic   BR TR 6'2" 180 lbs.

Year	Team		W	L	PCT	ERA	G	GS	CG	IP	H	BB	SO	ShO	W	L	SV	AB	H	HR	BA	PO	A	E	DP	TC/G	FA
1969	STL	N	0	1	.000	5.14	1	1	0	7	9	3	7	0	0	0	0	3	1	0	.333	1	0	0	0	1.0	1.000
1970			1	1	.500	7.07	8	3	1	14	14	13	9	0	0	1	0	5	1	0	.200	0	2	0	1	0.3	1.000
1971			0	0	–	0.00	2	1	0	10	6	2	13	0	0	0	0	1	0	0	.000	0	0	0	0	0.0	–
1972			0	0	–	9.00	1	0	0	1	1	0	0	0	0	0	0	0	0	0	–	0	0	0	0	0.0	–
4 yrs.			1	2	.333	4.50	12	5	1	32	30	18	29	0	0	1	0	9	2	0	.222	1	2	0	1	0.3	1.000

Bruno Haas

HAAS, BRUNO PHILIP (Boon)
B. May 5, 1891, Worcester, Mass. D. June 5, 1952, Sarasota, Fla.   BB TL 5'10" 180 lbs.

Year	Team		W	L	PCT	ERA	G	GS	CG	IP	H	BB	SO	ShO	W	L	SV	AB	H	HR	BA	PO	A	E	DP	TC/G	FA
1915	PHI	A	0	1	.000	11.93	6	2	1	14.1	23	28	7	0	0	0	0	18	1	0	.056	1	6	1	0	1.3	.875

Moose Haas

HAAS, BRYAN EDMUND
B. Apr. 22, 1956, Baltimore, Md.   BR TR 6' 180 lbs.

Year	Team		W	L	PCT	ERA	G	GS	CG	IP	H	BB	SO	ShO	W	L	SV	AB	H	HR	BA	PO	A	E	DP	TC/G	FA
1976	MIL	A	0	1	.000	3.94	5	2	0	16	12	12	9	0	0	0	0	0	0	0	–	2	5	1	1	1.6	.875
1977			10	12	.455	4.32	32	32	6	198	195	84	113	0	0	0	0	0	0	0	–	20	13	2	3	1.1	.943
1978			2	3	.400	6.16	7	6	2	30.2	33	8	32	0	0	0	1	0	0	0	–	4	2	1	0	1.0	.857
1979			11	11	.500	4.77	29	28	8	185	198	59	95	1	0	0	0	0	0	0	–	14	21	1	3	1.2	.972
1980			16	15	.516	3.11	33	33	14	252	246	56	146	3	0	0	0	0	0	0	–	19	31	3	6	1.6	.943
1981			11	7	.611	4.47	24	22	5	137	146	40	64	0	1	0	0	0	0	0	–	16	5	1	1	1.3	.969
1982			11	8	.579	4.47	32	27	3	193.1	232	39	104	0	1	0	0	0	0	0	–	14	18	0	1	1.0	1.000
1983			13	3	.813	3.27	25	25	7	179	170	42	75	3	0	0	0	0	0	0	–	12	22	0	1	1.4	1.000
1984			9	11	.450	3.99	31	30	4	189.1	205	43	84	0	0	0	0	0	0	0	–	19	36	0	2	1.8	1.000
1985			8	8	.500	3.84	27	26	6	161.2	165	25	78	1	0	0	0	0	0	0	–	17	15	4	1	1.3	.889
1986	OAK	A	7	2	.778	2.74	12	12	1	72.1	58	19	40	0	0	0	0	0	0	0	–	4	8	0	0	1.0	1.000
1987			2	2	.500	5.75	9	9	0	40.2	57	9	13	0	0	0	0	0	0	0	–	2	5	0	0	0.8	1.000
12 yrs.			100	83	.546	4.01	266	252	56	1655	1717	436	853	8	2	0	2	0	0	0	–	143	191	13	21	1.3	.963

DIVISIONAL PLAYOFF SERIES

Year	Team		W	L	PCT	ERA	G	GS	CG	IP	H	BB	SO	ShO	W	L	SV	AB	H	HR	BA	PO	A	E	DP	TC/G	FA
1981	MIL	A	0	2	.000	9.45	2	2	0	6.2	13	1	1	0	0	0	0	0	0	0	–	0	0	0	0	0.0	–

LEAGUE CHAMPIONSHIP SERIES

Year	Team		W	L	PCT	ERA	G	GS	CG	IP	H	BB	SO	ShO	W	L	SV	AB	H	HR	BA	PO	A	E	DP	TC/G	FA
1982	MIL	A	1	0	1.000	4.91	1	1	0	7.1	5	5	7	0	0	0	0	0	0	0	–	0	0	0	0	0.0	–

Year	Team	W	L	PCT	ERA	G	GS	CG	IP	H	BB	SO	ShO	W	L	SV	AB	H	HR	BA	PO	A	E	DP	TC/G	FA

Column group headers: **Relief Pitching** (W L SV) · **Batting** (AB H HR BA)

Moose Haas *continued*

WORLD SERIES

Year	Team	W	L	PCT	ERA	G	GS	CG	IP	H	BB	SO	ShO	W	L	SV	AB	H	HR	BA	PO	A	E	DP	TC/G	FA
1982	MIL A	0	0	–	7.36	2	1	0	7.1	8	3	4	0	0	0	0	0	0	0	–	1	2	0	0	1.5	1.000

Bob Habenicht

HABENICHT, ROBERT JULIUS (Hobby)
B. Feb. 13, 1926, St. Louis, Mo. D. Dec. 24, 1980, Richmond, Va.   BR TR 6'2" 185 lbs.

Year	Team	W	L	PCT	ERA	G	GS	CG	IP	H	BB	SO	ShO	W	L	SV	AB	H	HR	BA	PO	A	E	DP	TC/G	FA
1951	STL N	0	0	–	7.20	3	0	0	5	5	9	1	0	0	0	0	1	0	0	.000	1	1	0	1	0.7	1.000
1953	STL A	0	0	–	5.40	1	0	0	1.2	1	1	1	0	0	0	0	0	0	0	–	0	0	0	0	0.0	–
2 yrs.		0	0	–	6.75	4	0	0	6.2	6	10	2	0	0	0	0	1	0	0	.000	1	1	0	1	0.5	1.000

John Habyan

HABYAN, JOHN GABRIEL
B. Jan. 29, 1963, Bay Shore, N. Y.   BR TR 6'1" 195 lbs.

Year	Team	W	L	PCT	ERA	G	GS	CG	IP	H	BB	SO	ShO	W	L	SV	AB	H	HR	BA	PO	A	E	DP	TC/G	FA
1985	BAL A	1	0	1.000	0.00	2	0	0	2.2	3	0	2	0	1	0	0	0	0	0	–	1	0	0	0	0.5	1.000
1986		1	3	.250	4.44	6	5	0	26.1	24	18	14	0	0	0	0	0	0	0	–	1	3	0	0	0.7	1.000
1987		6	7	.462	4.80	27	13	0	116.1	110	40	64	0	4	0	1	0	0	0	–	15	17	0	2	1.2	1.000
1988		1	0	1.000	4.30	7	0	0	14.2	22	4	4	0	1	0	0	0	0	0	–	5	1	0	0	0.9	1.000
4 yrs.		9	10	.474	4.61	42	18	0	160	159	62	84	0	6	0	1	0	0	0	–	22	21	0	2	1.0	1.000

Warren Hacker

HACKER, WARREN LOUIS
B. Nov. 21, 1924, Marissa, Ill.   BR TR 6'1" 185 lbs.

Year	Team	W	L	PCT	ERA	G	GS	CG	IP	H	BB	SO	ShO	W	L	SV	AB	H	HR	BA	PO	A	E	DP	TC/G	FA
1948	CHI N	0	1	.000	21.00	3	1	0	3	7	3	0	0	0	0	0	0	0	0	–	0	1	0	0	0.3	1.000
1949		5	8	.385	4.23	30	12	3	125.2	141	53	40	0	3	1	0	38	7	0	.184	10	25	3	0	1.3	.921
1950		0	1	.000	5.28	5	3	1	15.1	20	8	5	0	0	0	1	5	0	0	.000	0	7	0	0	1.4	1.000
1951		0	0	–	13.50	2	0	0	1.1	3	0	2	0	0	0	0	0	0	0	–	0	0	0	0	0.0	–
1952		15	9	.625	2.58	33	20	12	185	144	31	84	5	2	2	1	58	7	0	.121	7	19	0	0	0.8	1.000
1953		12	19	.387	4.38	39	32	9	221.2	225	54	106	0	1	2	2	78	17	0	.218	10	24	0	2	1.0	.949
1954		6	13	.316	4.25	39	18	4	158.2	157	37	80	1	1	2	2	55	13	0	.236	4	20	0	2	0.8	1.000
1955		11	15	.423	4.27	35	30	13	213	202	43	80	0	1	0	3	72	18	0	.250	14	20	3	0	1.1	.919
1956		3	13	.188	4.66	34	24	4	168	190	44	65	0	0	0	0	54	8	0	.148	5	18	0	2	0.7	1.000
1957	2 teams	CIN N	(15G 3–2)		PHI N	(20G 4–4)																				
"	total	7	6	.538	4.76	35	16	1	117.1	122	31	51	0	1	0	0	31	7	0	.226	7	13	0	1	0.6	1.000
1958	PHI N	0	1	.000	7.41	9	1	0	17	24	8	4	0	0	0	0	1	0	0	.000	0	2	0	0	0.2	1.000
1961	CHI A	3	3	.500	3.77	42	0	0	57.1	62	8	40	0	3	3	8	9	1	0	.111	1	4	0	0	0.1	1.000
12 yrs.		62	89	.411	4.21	306	157	47	1283.1	1297	320	557	6	12	14	17	401	78	0	.195	64	156	8	5	0.7	.965

Jim Hackett

HACKETT, JAMES JOSEPH (Sunny Jim)
B. Oct. 1, 1877, Jacksonville, Ill. D. Mar. 28, 1961, Douglas, Mich.   BR TR 6'2" 185 lbs.

Year	Team	W	L	PCT	ERA	G	GS	CG	IP	H	BB	SO	ShO	W	L	SV	AB	H	HR	BA	PO	A	E	DP	TC/G	FA
1902	STL N	0	3	.000	6.23	4	3	3	30.1	46	16	7	0	0	0	0	21	6	0	.286	3	7	2	0	3.0	.833
1903		1	4	.200	3.72	7	6	5	48.1	47	18	21	0	0	0	1	351	80	0	.228	2	13	1	0	2.3	.938
2 yrs.		1	7	.125	4.69	11	9	8	78.2	93	34	28	0	0	0	1	*				5	20	3	0	2.5	.893

Harvey Haddix

HADDIX, HARVEY (The Kitten)
B. Sept. 18, 1925, Medway, Ohio   BL TL 5'9½" 170 lbs.

Year	Team	W	L	PCT	ERA	G	GS	CG	IP	H	BB	SO	ShO	W	L	SV	AB	H	HR	BA	PO	A	E	DP	TC/G	FA
1952	STL N	2	2	.500	2.79	7	6	3	42	31	10	31	0	0	0	0	14	3	0	.214	0	5	1	0	0.9	.833
1953		20	9	.690	3.06	36	33	19	253	220	69	163	6	0	0	1	97	28	1	.289	15	43	2	5	1.7	.967
1954		18	13	.581	3.57	43	35	13	259.2	247	77	184	3	1	1	4	93	18	0	.194	14	39	3	3	1.3	.946
1955		12	16	.429	4.46	37	30	9	208	216	62	150	2	1	1	1	73	12	1	.164	14	38	4	2	1.5	.929
1956	2 teams	STL N	(4G 1–0)		PHI N	(31G 12–8)																				
"	total	13	8	.619	3.67	35	30	12	230.1	224	65	170	3	0	0	2	102	24	0	.235	10	31	1	1	1.2	.976
1957	PHI N	10	13	.435	4.06	27	25	8	170.2	176	39	136	1	1	0	0	68	21	0	.309	10	15	2	0	1.0	.926
1958	CIN N	8	7	.533	3.52	29	26	8	184	191	43	110	1	0	0	1	61	11	1	.180	10	26	1	1	1.3	.973
1959	PIT N	12	12	.500	3.13	31	29	14	224.1	189	49	149	2	0	0	0	83	12	0	.145	8	35	0	3	1.4	1.000
1960		11	10	.524	3.97	29	28	4	172.1	189	38	101	0	0	0	1	67	17	0	.254	9	46	1	2	1.9	.982
1961		10	6	.625	4.10	29	22	5	156	159	41	99	2	3	0	0	56	8	0	.143	5	29	2	4	1.2	.944
1962		9	6	.600	4.20	28	20	4	141.1	146	42	101	1	2	1	0	52	13	1	.250	10	19	2	2	1.1	.935
1963		3	4	.429	3.34	49	1	0	70	67	20	70	0	3	4	1	11	2	0	.182	5	10	1	0	0.3	.938
1964	BAL A	5	5	.500	2.31	49	0	0	89.2	68	23	90	0	5	5	10	19	0	0	.000	4	16	0	1	0.4	1.000
1965		3	2	.600	3.48	24	0	0	33.2	31	23	21	0	3	2	1	2	0	0	.000	1	6	1	0	0.3	.875
14 yrs.		136	113	.546	3.63	453	285	99	2235	2154	601	1575	20	19	14	21	*				115	358	21	24	1.1	.957

WORLD SERIES

Year	Team	W	L	PCT	ERA	G	GS	CG	IP	H	BB	SO	ShO	W	L	SV	AB	H	HR	BA	PO	A	E	DP	TC/G	FA
1960	PIT N	2	0	1.000	2.45	2	1	0	7.1	6	2	6	0	1	0	0	3	1	0	.333	1	1	0	0	1.0	1.000

George Haddock

HADDOCK, GEORGE SILAS (Gentleman George)
B. Dec. 25, 1866, Portsmouth, N. H. D. Apr. 18, 1926, Boston, Mass.   BR TR 5'11" 155 lbs.

Year	Team	W	L	PCT	ERA	G	GS	CG	IP	H	BB	SO	ShO	W	L	SV	AB	H	HR	BA	PO	A	E	DP	TC/G	FA
1888	WAS N	0	2	.000	2.25	2	2	2	16	9	2	3	0	0	0	0	5	1	0	.200	2	8	1	0	5.5	.909
1889		11	19	.367	4.20	33	31	30	276.1	299	123	106	0	0	0	0	112	25	2	.223	12	54	9	3	2.3	.880
1890	BUF P	9	26	.257	5.76	35	34	31	290.2	366	149	123	0	1	0	0	146	36	0	.247	20	86	8	2	3.3	.930
1891	BOS AA	34	11	.756	2.49	51	47	37	379.2	330	137	169	5	2	0	1	185	45	3	.243	21	116	12	2	2.9	.919
1892	BKN N	29	13	.690	3.14	46	44	39	381.1	340	163	153	3	0	1	0	158	28	0	.177	21	80	11	5	2.4	.902
1893		8	9	.471	5.60	23	20	12	151	193	89	37	0	1	0	0	85	24	1	.282	10	19	7	0	1.6	.806
1894	2 teams	PHI N	(10G 4–3)		WAS N	(4G 0–4)																				
"	total	4	7	.364	6.78	14	11	9	85	113	51	8	0	0	0	0	45	8	0	.178	4	20	1	0	1.8	.960
7 yrs.		95	87	.522	4.07	204	189	160	1580	1650	714	599	8	4	0	2	*				90	383	49	12	2.6	.906

Bump Hadley

HADLEY, IRVING DARIUS
B. July 5, 1904, Lynn, Mass. D. Feb. 15, 1963, Lynn, Mass.   BR TR 5'11" 190 lbs.

Year	Team	W	L	PCT	ERA	G	GS	CG	IP	H	BB	SO	ShO	W	L	SV	AB	H	HR	BA	PO	A	E	DP	TC/G	FA
1926	WAS A	0	0	–	12.00	1	0	0	3	6	2	0	0	0	0	0	0	0	0	–	0	0	0	0	0.0	–
1927		14	6	.700	2.85	30	27	13	198.2	177	86	60	0	0	0	0	70	19	0	.271	9	50	2	0	2.0	.967
1928		12	13	.480	3.54	33	31	16	231.2	236	100	80	3	0	0	0	81	17	0	.210	8	52	2	2	1.9	.968
1929		6	16	.273	5.65	37	27	6	194.1	196	85	98	1	0	0	0	62	6	0	.097	9	41	2	3	1.4	.962
1930		15	11	.577	3.73	42	34	15	260.1	242	105	162	1	1	1	2	93	21	0	.226	9	43	2	1	1.3	.963

Year	Team	W	L	PCT	ERA	G	GS	CG	IP	H	BB	SO	ShO	W	L	SV	AB	H	HR	BA	PO	A	E	DP	TC/G	FA
														Relief Pitching			Batting									

Bump Hadley *continued*

Year	Team		W	L	PCT	ERA	G	GS	CG	IP	H	BB	SO	ShO	W	L	SV	AB	H	HR	BA	PO	A	E	DP	TC/G	FA
1931			11	10	.524	3.06	**55**	11	2	179.2	145	92	124	1	**8**	5	8	54	9	0	.167	6	39	1	5	0.8	.978
1932	2 teams	CHI A (3G 1–1)					STL A	(40G 13–20)																			
"	total		14	21	.400	5.40	43	35	13	248.1	261	**171**	145	1	0	3	2	84	23	0	.274	15	29	2	0	1.1	.957
1933	STL A		15	20	.429	3.92	45	36	19	316.2	309	141	149	2	2	1	3	109	17	0	.156	12	51	2	0	1.4	.969
1934			10	16	.385	4.35	39	32	7	213	212	127	79	0	0	2	1	64	13	0	.203	9	40	2	1	1.3	.961
1935	WAS A		10	15	.400	4.92	35	32	13	230.1	268	102	77	0	0	0	1	77	15	0	.195	13	47	3	3	1.8	.952
1936	NY A		14	4	.778	4.35	31	17	8	173.2	194	89	74	1	3	1	1	68	16	0	.235	13	32	0	4	1.5	1.000
1937			11	8	.579	5.30	29	25	6	178.1	199	83	70	0	0	1	0	65	11	0	.169	7	37	4	3	1.7	.917
1938			9	8	.529	3.60	29	17	8	167.1	165	66	61	1	1	1	1	54	5	0	.093	17	40	0	3	2.0	1.000
1939			12	6	.667	2.98	26	18	7	154	132	85	65	1	2	0	2	62	11	0	.177	8	35	4	4	1.8	.915
1940			3	5	.375	5.74	25	2	0	80	88	52	39	0	3	3	2	27	3	0	.111	2	16	0	0	0.7	1.000
1941	2 teams	NY N (3G 1–0)					PHI A	(25G 4–6)																			
"	total		5	6	.455	5.15	28	11	1	115.1	150	56	35	0	1	1	3	34	4	0	.118	3	21	2	0	0.9	.923
16 yrs.			161	165	.494	4.25	528	355	134	2944.2	2980	1442	1318	14	21	23	25	1004	190	0	.189	140	573	28	30	1.4	.962
												10th															

WORLD SERIES

Year	Team	W	L	PCT	ERA	G	GS	CG	IP	H	BB	SO	ShO	W	L	SV	AB	H	HR	BA	PO	A	E	DP	TC/G	FA
1936	NY A	1	0	1.000	1.13	1	1	0	8	10	1	2	0	0	0	0	2	0	0	.000	0	3	0	0	3.0	1.000
1937		0	1	.000	33.75	1	1	0	1.1	6	0	0	0	0	0	0	0	0	0	–	0	0	0	0	0.0	–
1939		1	0	1.000	2.25	1	0	0	8	7	3	2	0	1	0	0	3	0	0	.000	1	1	1	0	3.0	.667
3 yrs.		2	1	.667	4.15	3	2	0	17.1	23	4	4	0	1	0	0	5	0	0	.000	1	4	1	0	2.0	.833

Mickey Haefner

HAEFNER, MILTON ARNOLD
B. Oct. 9, 1912, Lenzburg, Ill.   BL TL 5'8"   160 lbs.

Year	Team		W	L	PCT	ERA	G	GS	CG	IP	H	BB	SO	ShO	W	L	SV	AB	H	HR	BA	PO	A	E	DP	TC/G	FA
1943	WAS A		11	5	.688	2.29	36	13	8	165.1	126	60	65	1	3	1	6	45	6	0	.133	7	31	0	3	1.1	1.000
1944			12	15	.444	3.04	31	28	18	228	221	71	86	3	0	1	1	70	11	0	.157	8	45	1	5	1.7	.981
1945			16	14	.533	3.47	37	28	19	238.1	226	69	83	1	2	0	3	82	20	0	.244	10	53	3	1	1.8	.955
1946			14	11	.560	2.85	33	27	17	227.2	220	80	85	2	0	1	1	74	15	0	.203	13	36	3	2	1.6	.942
1947			10	14	.417	3.64	31	28	14	193	195	85	77	4	0	0	1	59	8	0	.136	7	27	0	3	1.1	1.000
1948			5	13	.278	4.02	28	20	4	147.2	151	61	45	0	1	1	0	43	7	0	.163	4	38	1	2	1.5	.977
1949	2 teams	WAS A (19G 5–5)					CHI A	(14G 4–6)																			
"	total		9	11	.450	4.40	33	24	8	172	169	94	40	2	0	1	1	48	11	0	.229	2	43	3	3	1.5	.938
1950	2 teams	CHI A (24G 1–6)					BOS N	(8G 0–2)																			
"	total		1	8	.111	5.70	32	11	3	94.2	106	57	27	0	0	0	0	27	6	0	.222	2	14	0	3	0.5	1.000
8 yrs.			78	91	.462	3.50	261	179	91	1466.2	1414	577	508	13	6	5	13	448	84	0	.188	53	287	11	22	1.3	.969

Bud Hafey

HAFEY, DANIEL ALBERT
Brother of Tom Hafey.   BR TR 6'   185 lbs.
B. Aug. 6, 1912, Berkeley, Calif.   D. July 27, 1986, Sacramento, Calif.

Year	Team		W	L	PCT	ERA	G	GS	CG	IP	H	BB	SO	ShO	W	L	SV	AB	H	HR	BA	PO	A	E	DP	TC/G	FA
1939	2 teams	CIN N (0G 0–0)					PHI N	(2G 0–0)																			
"	total		0	0	–	33.75	2	0	0	1.1	7	1	1	0	0	0	0	*				0	1	0	0	0.5	1.000

Leo Hafford

HAFFORD, LEO EDGAR
B. Sept. 17, 1883, Somerville, Mass.   D. Oct. 2, 1911, Willimantic, Conn.   TR 6'   170 lbs.

Year	Team	W	L	PCT	ERA	G	GS	CG	IP	H	BB	SO	ShO	W	L	SV	AB	H	HR	BA	PO	A	E	DP	TC/G	FA
1906	CIN N	1	1	.500	0.95	3	1	1	19	13	11	5	0	0	1	0	9	2	0	.222	1	2	0	0	1.0	1.000

Frank Hafner

HAFNER, FRANK R.
B. Aug., 1867, Mo.   D. Mar. 2, 1957, Hannibal, Mo.

Year	Team	W	L	PCT	ERA	G	GS	CG	IP	H	BB	SO	ShO	W	L	SV	AB	H	HR	BA	PO	A	E	DP	TC/G	FA
1888	KC AA	0	2	.000	7.00	2	2	2	18	24	16	5	0	0	0	0	6	0	0	.000	2	2	0	0	2.0	1.000

Art Hagan

HAGAN, ARTHUR CHARLES
B. Mar. 17, 1863, Providence, R. I.   D. Mar. 25, 1936, Providence, R. I.   TR

Year	Team		W	L	PCT	ERA	G	GS	CG	IP	H	BB	SO	ShO	W	L	SV	AB	H	HR	BA	PO	A	E	DP	TC/G	FA
1883	2 teams	PHI N (17G 1–14)					BUF N	(2G 0–2)																			
"	total		1	16	.059	5.27	19	18	16	152	224	39	46	0	0	0	0	66	6	0	.091	12	25	9	2	2.4	.804
1884	BUF N		1	2	.333	5.88	3	3	3	26	53	4	4	0	0	0	0	13	4	0	.308	0	3	2	0	1.7	.600
2 yrs.			2	18	.100	5.36	22	21	19	178	277	43	50	0	0	0	0	79	10	0	.127	12	28	11	2	2.3	.784

Casey Hageman

HAGEMAN, KURT MORITZ
B. May 12, 1887, Mt. Oliver, Pa.   D. Apr. 1, 1964, New Bedford, Pa.   BR TR 5'10½" 186 lbs.

Year	Team		W	L	PCT	ERA	G	GS	CG	IP	H	BB	SO	ShO	W	L	SV	AB	H	HR	BA	PO	A	E	DP	TC/G	FA
1911	BOS A		0	2	.000	2.12	2	2	2	17	16	5	8	0	0	0	0	4	0	0	.000	0	0	1	0	0.5	–
1912			0	0	–	27.00	2	1	0	1.1	5	3	1	0	0	0	0	0	0	0	–	0	0	0	0	0.0	–
1914	2 teams	STL N (12G 1–4)					CHI N	(16G 2–1)																			
"	total		3	5	.375	2.91	28	8	1	102	87	32	38	0	2	1	1	31	9	0	.290	2	27	2	1	1.1	.935
3 yrs.			3	7	.300	3.07	32	11	3	120.1	108	40	47	0	2	1	1	35	9	0	.257	2	27	3	1	1.0	.906

Kevin Hagen

HAGEN, KEVIN EUGENE
B. Mar. 8, 1960, Renton, Wash.   BR TR 6'2"   180 lbs.

Year	Team	W	L	PCT	ERA	G	GS	CG	IP	H	BB	SO	ShO	W	L	SV	AB	H	HR	BA	PO	A	E	DP	TC/G	FA
1983	STL N	2	2	.500	4.84	9	4	0	22.1	34	7	7	0	0	1	0	5	0	0	.000	2	4	0	0	0.7	1.000
1984		1	0	1.000	2.45	4	0	0	7.1	9	1	2	0	1	0	0	0	0	0	–	0	1	1	0	0.5	.500
2 yrs.		3	2	.600	4.25	13	4	0	29.2	43	8	9	0	1	1	0	5	0	0	.000	2	5	1	0	0.6	.875

Rip Hagerman

HAGERMAN, ZERIAH ZEQUIEL
B. June 20, 1888, Linden, Kans.   D. Jan. 30, 1930, Albuquerque, N. M.   BR TR 6'2"   200 lbs.

Year	Team	W	L	PCT	ERA	G	GS	CG	IP	H	BB	SO	ShO	W	L	SV	AB	H	HR	BA	PO	A	E	DP	TC/G	FA
1909	CHI N	4	4	.500	1.82	13	7	4	79	64	28	32	1	1	0	0	23	3	0	.130	4	19	0	1	1.8	1.000
1914	CLE A	9	15	.375	3.09	37	26	12	198	189	118	112	3	1	2	0	61	1	0	.016	3	42	6	3	1.4	.882
1915		6	14	.300	3.52	29	22	7	151	156	77	69	0	1	1	0	38	4	0	.105	3	31	3	0	1.3	.919
1916		0	0	–	12.27	2	0	0	3.2	5	2	1	0	0	0	0	1	0	0	.000	0	1	0	0	0.5	1.000
4 yrs.		19	33	.365	3.09	81	55	23	431.2	414	225	214	4	3	3	0	123	8	0	.065	10	93	9	4	1.4	.920

Year	Team	W	L	PCT	ERA	G	GS	CG	IP	H	BB	SO	ShO	Relief Pitching W	L	SV	Batting AB	H	HR	BA	PO	A	E	DP	TC/G	FA

Fred Hahn

HAHN, FREDERICK ALOYS
B. Feb. 16, 1929, Nyack, N. Y.   D. Aug. 16, 1984, Valhalla, N. Y.
BR TL 6'3"   174 lbs.

| 1952 | STL | N | 0 | 0 | — | 0.00 | 1 | 0 | 0 | 2 | 2 | 1 | 0 | 0 | 0 | 0 | 0 | 0 | 0 | 0 | — | 0 | 1 | 0 | 0 | 1.0 | 1.000 |

Noodles Hahn

HAHN, FRANK GEORGE
B. Apr. 29, 1879, Nashville, Tenn.   D. Feb. 6, 1960, Candler, N. C.
BL TL 5'9"   160 lbs.

1899	CIN	N	23	8	.742	2.68	38	34	32	309	280	68	145	4	1	0	0	109	16	0	.147	12	51	13	3	2.0	.829
1900			16	19	.457	3.29	38	36	28	303.1	296	88	127	4	0	1	0	111	23	2	.207	9	74	6	1	2.3	.933
1901			22	19	.537	2.71	42	42	41	375.1	370	69	239	2	0	0	0	141	24	0	.170	14	85	6	4	2.5	.943
1902			22	12	.647	1.76	36	35	34	312	274	57	138	6	0	0	0	119	22	0	.185	14	69	9	1	2.6	.902
1903			22	12	.647	2.52	34	34	34	296	297	47	127	5	0	0	0	112	18	0	.161	26	67	7	3	2.9	.930
1904			16	18	.471	2.06	35	34	33	297.2	258	35	98	2	1	0	0	99	17	0	.172	21	80	9	4	3.1	.918
1905			5	3	.625	2.81	13	8	5	77	85	9	17	1	1	0	0	24	4	0	.167	2	12	2	0	1.2	.875
1906	NY	A	3	2	.600	3.86	6	6	3	42	38	6	17	1	0	0	0	12	4	0	.333	3	9	1	0	2.2	.923
8 yrs.			129	93	.581	2.55	242	229	210	2012.1	1898	379	908	25	3	1	0	727	128	2	.176	101	447	53	16	2.5	.912

Hal Haid

HAID, HAROLD AUGUSTINE
B. Dec. 21, 1897, Barberton, Ohio   D. Aug. 13, 1952, Los Angeles, Calif.
BR TR 5'10½"   150 lbs.

1919	STL	A	0	0	—	18.00	1	0	0	2	5	3	1	0	0	0	0	0	0	0	—	0	1	1	0	2.0	.500
1928	STL	N	2	2	.500	2.30	27	0	0	47	39	11	21	0	2	2	5	8	3	0	.375	2	11	0	0	0.5	1.000
1929			9	9	.500	4.07	38	12	8	154.2	171	66	41	0	4	3	4	49	4	0	.082	3	32	4	5	1.0	.897
1930			3	2	.600	4.09	20	0	0	33	38	14	13	0	3	2	2	3	0	0	.000	3	9	1	2	0.7	.923
1931	BOS	N	0	2	.000	4.50	27	0	0	56	59	16	20	0	0	2	1	8	1	0	.125	5	21	1	0	1.0	.963
1933	CHI	A	0	0	—	7.98	6	0	0	14.2	18	13	7	0	0	0	0	4	1	0	.250	1	4	0	0	0.8	1.000
6 yrs.			14	15	.483	4.16	119	12	8	307.1	330	123	103	0	9	9	12	72	9	0	.125	14	78	7	7	0.8	.929

Jesse Haines

HAINES, JESSE JOSEPH (Pop)
B. July 22, 1893, Clayton, Ohio   D. Aug. 5, 1978, Dayton, Ohio
Hall of Fame 1970.
BR TR 6'   190 lbs.

1918	CIN	N	0	0	—	1.80	1	0	0	5	5	1	2	0	0	0	0	1	1	0	1.000	1	1	0	0	2.0	1.000
1920	STL	N	13	20	.394	2.98	47	37	19	301.2	303	80	120	4	2	2	0	108	19	1	.176	13	57	4	1	1.6	.946
1921			18	12	.600	3.50	37	29	14	244.1	261	56	84	3	3	0	0	94	17	0	.181	7	72	4	5	2.2	.952
1922			11	9	.550	3.84	29	26	11	183	207	45	62	2	0	1	0	72	12	0	.167	11	42	2	1	1.9	.964
1923			20	13	.606	3.11	37	36	23	266	283	75	73	1	1	0	0	99	20	0	.202	13	64	3	1	2.2	.963
1924			8	19	.296	4.41	35	31	16	222.2	275	66	69	1	0	1	0	74	14	0	.189	3	52	3	3	1.7	.948
1925			13	14	.481	4.57	29	25	15	207	234	52	63	1	0	1	0	74	13	0	.176	9	43	2	1	1.9	.963
1926			13	4	.765	3.25	33	21	14	183	186	48	46	3	0	0	1	61	13	0	.213	4	32	2	1	1.2	.947
1927			24	10	.706	2.72	38	36	25	300.2	273	77	89	6	1	0	1	114	23	0	.202	5	72	1	3	2.1	.987
1928			20	8	.714	3.18	33	28	20	240.1	238	72	77	1	1	1	0	87	16	0	.184	3	43	0	2	1.4	1.000
1929			13	10	.565	5.71	28	25	12	179.2	230	73	59	0	0	0	0	69	11	1	.159	4	20	0	3	0.9	1.000
1930			13	8	.619	4.30	29	24	14	182	215	54	68	0	0	0	0	65	16	0	.246	6	22	1	3	1.0	.966
1931			12	3	.800	3.02	19	17	8	122.1	134	28	27	2	1	0	0	45	6	0	.133	5	21	1	0	1.4	.963
1932			3	5	.375	4.75	20	10	4	85.1	116	16	27	1	0	1	0	27	5	1	.185	2	14	0	2	0.8	1.000
1933			9	6	.600	2.50	32	10	5	115.1	113	37	37	0	5	2	1	30	2	0	.067	3	19	1	0	0.7	.957
1934			4	4	.500	3.50	37	6	0	90	86	19	17	0	4	2	1	19	3	0	.158	7	27	0	0	0.9	1.000
1935			6	5	.545	3.59	30	12	3	115.1	110	28	24	1	1	2	2	33	9	0	.273	4	16	1	2	0.8	.957
1936			7	5	.583	3.90	25	9	4	99.1	110	21	19	0	4	1	1	30	5	0	.167	3	24	2	0	1.2	.931
1937			3	3	.500	4.52	16	6	2	65.2	81	23	18	0	1	0	0	22	4	0	.182	2	10	0	0	0.8	1.000
19 yrs.			210	158	.571	3.64	555	388	209	3208.2	3460	871	981	24	25	14	10	1124	209	3	.186	107	651	27	32	1.4	.966

WORLD SERIES

1926	STL	N	2	0	1.000	1.08	3	2	1	16.2	13	9	5	1	0	0	0	5	3	1	.600	0	6	0	0	2.0	1.000
1928			0	1	.000	4.50	1	1	0	6	6	3	3	0	0	0	0	2	0	0	.000	0	1	0	0	1.0	1.000
1930			1	0	1.000	1.00	1	1	1	9	4	4	2	0	0	0	0	2	1	0	.500	0	1	0	0	1.0	1.000
1934			0	0	—	0.00	1	0	0	.2	1	0	2	0	0	0	0	0	0	0	—	0	0	0	0	0.0	—
4 yrs.			3	1	.750	1.67	6	4	2	32.1	24	16	12	1	0	0	0	9	4	1	.444	0	8	0	0	1.3	1.000

Jim Haislip

HAISLIP, JAMES CLIFTON
B. Aug. 4, 1891, Farmersville, Tex.   D. Jan. 22, 1970, Dallas, Tex.
BR TR 6'3"   186 lbs.

| 1913 | PHI | N | 0 | 0 | — | 6.00 | 1 | 0 | 0 | 3 | 4 | 3 | 0 | 0 | 0 | 0 | 0 | 1 | 0 | 0 | .000 | 0 | 0 | 0 | 0 | 0.0 | — |

Ed Halbriter

HALBRITER, EDWARD L.
B. Feb. 2, 1860, Auburn, N. Y.   D. Aug. 9, 1936, Los Angeles, Calif.

| 1882 | PHI | AA | 0 | 1 | .000 | 7.88 | 1 | 1 | 1 | 8 | 17 | 4 | 4 | 0 | 0 | 0 | 0 | 4 | 0 | 0 | .000 | 1 | 2 | 0 | 4.0 | .500 |

Dad Hale

HALE, RAY LUTHER
B. Feb. 18, 1879, Allegan, Mich.   D. Feb. 1, 1946, Allegan, Mich.
BR TR 5'10"   180 lbs.

| 1902 | 2 teams | BOS N | (8G 1–4) | | | BAL A | (3G 0–1) | | | | | | | | | | | | | | | | | | | | |
| " | total | | 1 | 5 | .167 | 5.90 | 11 | 8 | 4 | 61 | 90 | 24 | 18 | 0 | 0 | 0 | 0 | 20 | 0 | 0 | .000 | 1 | 15 | 5 | 0 | 1.9 | .762 |

Ed Halicki

HALICKI, EDWARD LOUIS
B. Oct. 4, 1950, Kearny, N. J.
BR TR 6'7"   220 lbs.

1974	SF	N	1	8	.111	4.26	16	11	2	74	84	31	40	0	0	0	0	25	6	1	.240	7	8	4	0	1.2	.789
1975			9	13	.409	3.49	24	23	7	160	143	59	153	2	0	1	0	53	6	0	.113	7	20	5	0	1.3	.844
1976			12	14	.462	3.62	32	31	8	186.1	171	61	130	4	0	1	0	53	9	0	.170	16	22	5	3	1.3	.884
1977			16	12	.571	3.31	37	37	7	258	241	70	168	2	0	0	0	85	15	2	.176	15	24	3	1	1.1	.929
1978			9	10	.474	2.85	29	28	9	199	166	45	105	4	0	0	1	66	9	0	.136	13	22	5	0	1.0	.875
1979			5	8	.385	4.57	33	19	3	126	134	47	81	1	0	0	0	34	7	0	.206	9	19	4	1	1.0	.875
1980	2 teams	SF N	(11G 0–0)			CAL A	(10G 3–1)																				
"	total		3	1	.750	5.10	21	8	0	60	68	21	30	0	1	1	0	6	1	0	.167	4	5	0	1	0.4	1.000
7 yrs.			55	66	.455	3.62	192	157	36	1063.1	1007	334	707	13	1	1	2	322	53	3	.165	71	120	26	7	1.1	.880

1880

Year	Team	W	L	PCT	ERA	G	GS	CG	IP	H	BB	SO	ShO	W	L	SV	AB	H	HR	BA	PO	A	E	DP	TC/G	FA

Bert Hall — HALL, HERBERT ERNEST
B. Oct. 15, 1888, Portland, Ore. D. July 18, 1948, Seattle, Wash.   BR TR 5'10" 178 lbs.

| 1911 | PHI N | 0 | 1 | .000 | 4.00 | 7 | 1 | 0 | 18 | 19 | 13 | 8 | 0 | 0 | 1 | 0 | 3 | 1 | 0 | .333 | 0 | 2 | 0 | 0 | 0.3 | 1.000 |

Bill Hall — HALL, WILLIAM BERNARD (Beanie)
B. Feb. 22, 1894, Charleston, W. Va. D. Aug. 15, 1947, Newport, Ky.   BR TR 6'2" 250 lbs.

| 1913 | BKN N | 0 | 0 | – | 5.79 | 3 | 0 | 0 | 4.2 | 4 | 5 | 3 | 0 | 0 | 0 | 0 | 1 | 0 | 0 | .000 | 0 | 1 | 0 | 0 | 0.3 | 1.000 |

Bob Hall — HALL, ROBERT LEWIS
B. Dec. 22, 1923, Swissvale, Pa. D. Mar. 12, 1983, St. Petersburg, Fla.   BR TR 6'2" 195 lbs.

1949	BOS N	6	4	.600	4.36	31	6	2	74.1	77	41	43	0	5	0	0	22	8	0	.364	3	3	2	0	0.3	.750
1950		0	2	.000	6.97	21	4	0	50.1	58	33	22	0	0	1	0	12	1	0	.083	4	7	1	0	0.6	.917
1953	PIT N	3	12	.200	5.39	37	17	6	152	172	72	68	1	0	1	1	38	6	1	.158	10	23	4	2	1.0	.892
3 yrs.		9	18	.333	5.40	89	27	8	276.2	307	146	133	1	5	2	1	72	15	1	.208	17	33	7	2	0.6	.877

Charley Hall — HALL, CHARLES LOUIS (Sea Lion)
Born Carlos Clolo.
B. July 27, 1885, Ventura, Calif. D. Dec. 6, 1943, Ventura, Calif.   BL TR 6'1" 187 lbs.

1906	CIN N	4	6	.400	3.32	14	9	9	95	86	50	49	1	0	1	1	47	6	0	.128	2	27	1	2	2.1	.967
1907		4	2	.667	2.51	11	8	5	68	51	43	25	0	1	0	0	26	7	0	.269	3	14	1	0	1.6	.944
1909	BOS A	6	4	.600	2.56	11	7	3	59.2	59	17	27	0	3	0	0	19	3	0	.158	5	16	1	2	2.0	.955
1910		12	9	.571	1.91	35	16	13	188.2	142	73	95	0	6	1	2	82	17	0	.207	8	61	3	0	2.1	.958
1911		8	7	.533	3.73	32	10	6	147.1	149	72	83	0	4	3	4	64	9	1	.141	4	30	2	0	1.1	.944
1912		15	8	.652	3.02	34	21	9	191	178	70	83	2	6	0	2	75	20	1	.267	9	59	3	0	2.1	.958
1913		4	4	.500	3.43	35	4	2	105	97	46	48	0	4	0	3	42	9	0	.214	6	25	2	1	0.9	.939
1916	STL N	0	4	.000	5.48	10	5	2	42.2	45	14	15	0	0	0	0	14	2	0	.143	1	13	2	2	1.6	.875
1918	DET A	0	1	.000	6.75	6	1	0	13.1	14	6	2	0	0	0	0	2	0	0	.000	1	1	1	1	0.5	.667
9 yrs.		53	45	.541	3.08	188	81	49	910.2	821	391	427	3	24	5	13	*				39	246	16	8	1.6	.947

WORLD SERIES

| 1912 | BOS A | 0 | 0 | – | 3.38 | 2 | 0 | 0 | 10.2 | 11 | 9 | 1 | 0 | 0 | 0 | 0 | 4 | 3 | 0 | .750 | 0 | 5 | 1 | 0 | 3.0 | .833 |

Dick Hall — HALL, RICHARD WALLACE
B. Sept. 27, 1930, St. Louis, Mo.   BR TR 6'6" 200 lbs.

1952	PIT N	0	0	–	0.00	0	0	0	0	0	0	0	0	0	0	0	80	11	0	.138	0	0	0	0	0.0	–
1953		0	0	–	0.00	0	0	0	0	0	0	0	0	0	0	0	24	4	0	.167	0	0	0	0	0.0	–
1954		0	0	–	0.00	0	0	0	0	0	0	0	0	0	0	0	310	74	2	.239	0	0	0	0	0.0	–
1955		6	6	.500	3.91	15	13	4	94.1	92	28	46	0	0	0	0	40	7	1	.175	6	6	0	0	0.8	1.000
1956		0	7	.000	4.76	19	9	1	62.1	64	21	27	0	0	1	1	29	10	0	.345	2	6	0	0	0.4	1.000
1957		0	0	–	10.80	8	0	0	10	17	5	7	0	0	0	0	1	0	0	.000	0	0	0	0	0.0	–
1959		0	0	–	3.12	2	1	0	8.2	12	1	3	0	0	0	0	2	0	0	.000	0	1	0	0	0.5	1.000
1960	KC A	8	13	.381	4.05	29	28	9	182.1	183	38	79	1	0	1	0	56	6	0	.107	9	28	3	1	1.4	.925
1961	BAL A	7	5	.583	3.09	29	13	4	122.1	102	30	92	2	2	1	4	36	5	0	.139	9	23	1	1	1.1	.970
1962		6	6	.500	2.28	43	6	1	118.1	102	19	71	0	4	3	6	24	4	0	.167	9	17	0	1	0.6	1.000
1963		5	5	.500	2.98	47	3	0	111.2	91	16	74	0	5	2	12	28	13	1	.464	7	21	0	1	0.6	1.000
1964		9	1	.900	1.85	45	0	0	87.2	58	16	52	0	9	1	7	16	2	0	.125	7	12	0	1	0.4	1.000
1965		11	8	.579	3.07	48	0	0	93.2	84	11	79	0	11	8	12	15	5	0	.333	4	8	1	2	0.3	.923
1966		6	2	.750	3.95	32	0	0	66	59	8	44	0	6	2	7	12	2	0	.167	4	4	0	0	0.3	1.000
1967	PHI N	10	8	.556	2.20	48	1	1	86	83	12	49	0	9	8	8	14	1	0	.071	2	21	0	1	0.5	1.000
1968		4	1	.800	4.89	32	0	0	46	53	5	31	0	4	1	0	3	1	0	.333	2	6	0	0	0.3	1.000
1969	BAL A	5	2	.714	1.92	39	0	0	65.2	49	9	31	0	5	2	6	7	2	0	.286	4	6	2	0	0.3	1.000
1970		10	5	.667	3.10	32	0	0	61	51	6	30	0	10	5	3	12	1	0	.083	3	3	0	0	0.2	1.000
1971		6	6	.500	5.02	27	0	0	43	52	11	26	0	6	6	1	5	2	0	.400	1	3	1	0	0.2	.800
19 yrs.		93	75	.554	3.32	495	74	20	1259	1152	236	741	3	71	41	68	*				69	171	6	10	0.5	.976

LEAGUE CHAMPIONSHIP SERIES

1969	BAL A	1	0	1.000	0.00	1	0	0	.2	0	0	1	0	1	0	0	0	0	0	–	0	0	0	0	0.0	–
1970		1	0	1.000	0.00	1	0	0	4.2	1	0	3	0	1	0	0	2	1	0	.500	0	0	0	0	0.0	–
2 yrs.		2	0	1.000	0.00	2	0	0	5.1	1	0	4	0	2	0	0	2	1	0	.500	0	0	0	0	0.0	–

WORLD SERIES

1969	BAL A	0	1	.000	0.00	1	0	0	1	1	1	0	0	0	1	0	0	0	0	–	0	0	0	0	0.0	–
1970		0	0	–	0.00	1	0	0	2.1	0	0	0	0	0	0	1	1	0	0	.000	0	0	0	0	0.0	–
1971		0	0	–	0.00	1	0	0	1	1	0	0	0	0	0	0	0	0	0	–	1	0	0	0	1.0	1.000
3 yrs.		0	1	.000	0.00	3	0	0	3.1	2	1	0	0	0	1	2	1	0	0	.000	1	0	0	0	0.3	1.000

Drew Hall — HALL, ANDREW CLARK
B. Mar. 27, 1963, Louisville, Ky.   BL TL 6'4" 220 lbs.

1986	CHI N	1	2	.333	4.56	5	4	0	23.2	24	10	21	0	0	0	0	7	1	0	.143	0	2	0	0	0.4	1.000
1987		1	1	.500	6.89	21	0	0	32.2	40	14	20	0	1	1	0	4	0	0	.000	3	3	0	0	0.3	1.000
1988		1	1	.500	7.66	19	0	0	22.1	26	9	22	0	1	1	0	1	0	0	.000	0	0	0	0	0.0	–
1989	TEX A	2	1	.667	3.70	38	0	0	58.1	42	33	45	0	2	1	0	0	0	0	–	2	8	0	1	0.3	1.000
4 yrs.		5	5	.500	5.26	83	4	1	137	132	66	108	0	4	3	2	12	1	0	.083	5	17	0	1	0.3	1.000

Herb Hall — HALL, HERBERT SILAS (Iron Duke)
B. June 5, 1893, Steelville, Ill. D. July 1, 1970, Fresno, Calif.   BB TR 6'4" 220 lbs.

| 1918 | DET A | 0 | 0 | – | 15.00 | 3 | 0 | 0 | 6 | 12 | 7 | 1 | 0 | 0 | 0 | 0 | 1 | 0 | 0 | .000 | 0 | 2 | 0 | 0 | 0.7 | 1.000 |

Johnny Hall — HALL, JOHN SYLVESTER
B. Jan. 9, 1924, Muskogee, Okla.   BR TR 6'2½" 170 lbs.

| 1948 | BKN N | 0 | 0 | – | 6.23 | 3 | 0 | 0 | 4.1 | 4 | 2 | 2 | 0 | 0 | 0 | 0 | 0 | 0 | 0 | – | 0 | 0 | 0 | 0 | 0.3 | 1.000 |

Year	Team		W	L	PCT	ERA	G	GS	CG	IP	H	BB	SO	ShO	Relief Pitching W	L	SV	Batting AB	H	HR	BA	PO	A	E	DP	TC/G	FA

Marc Hall

HALL, MARCUS
B. Aug. 12, 1887, Joplin, Mo. D. Feb. 24, 1915, Joplin, Mo.
BR TR 6'1½'' 190 lbs.

Year	Team		W	L	PCT	ERA	G	GS	CG	IP	H	BB	SO	ShO	W	L	SV	AB	H	HR	BA	PO	A	E	DP	TC/G	FA
1910	STL	A	1	7	.125	4.27	8	7	5	46.1	50	31	25	0	1	0	0	15	1	0	.067	3	18	3	1	3.0	.875
1913	DET	A	10	12	.455	3.27	30	21	8	165	154	79	69	1	2	3	0	45	4	0	.089	7	48	1	2	1.9	.982
1914			4	6	.400	2.69	25	8	1	90.1	88	27	18	0	0	3	0	23	1	0	.043	4	29	0	0	1.3	1.000
3 yrs.			15	25	.375	3.25	63	36	14	301.2	292	137	112	1	3	6	0	83	6	0	.072	14	95	4	3	1.8	.965

Tom Hall

HALL, TOM EDWARD (The Blade)
B. Nov. 23, 1947, Thomasville, N. C.
BL TL 6' 150 lbs.

Year	Team		W	L	PCT	ERA	G	GS	CG	IP	H	BB	SO	ShO	W	L	SV	AB	H	HR	BA	PO	A	E	DP	TC/G	FA
1968	MIN	A	2	1	.667	2.43	8	4	0	29.2	27	12	18	0	1	0	0	9	0	0	.000	1	4	1	0	0.8	.833
1969			8	7	.533	3.33	31	18	5	140.2	129	50	92	2	0	2	0	43	8	0	.186	1	13	0	0	0.5	1.000
1970			11	6	.647	2.55	52	11	0	155	94	66	184	0	4	2	4	44	8	0	.182	2	9	2	1	0.3	.846
1971			4	7	.364	3.32	48	11	0	130	104	58	137	0	3	3	9	34	9	0	.265	8	11	1	0	0.6	.964
1972	CIN	N	10	1	.909	2.61	47	7	1	124.1	77	56	134	1	7	1	8	30	3	0	.100	1	10	2	0	0.3	.833
1973			8	5	.615	3.47	54	7	0	103.2	74	48	96	0	7	4	8	22	1	0	.045	3	6	0	0	0.2	1.000
1974			3	1	.750	4.08	40	1	0	64	54	30	48	0	2	1	1	5	0	0	.000	1	9	0	0	0.3	1.000
1975	2 teams		CIN N	(2G 0-0)		NY N	(34G 4-3)																					
"	total		4	3	.571	4.57	36	4	0	63	60	33	51	0	2	2	1	5	2	0	.400	2	7	0	0	0.3	1.000
1976	2 teams		NY N	(5G 1-1)		KC A	(31G 1-1)																					
"	total		2	2	.500	4.63	36	0	0	35	33	23	27	0	2	2	1	0	0	0	—	0	2	0	0	0.1	1.000
1977	KC	A	0	0	—	3.38	6	0	0	8	4	6	10	0	0	0	0	0	0	0	—	0	2	0	0	0.3	1.000
10 yrs.			52	33	.612	3.27	358	63	7	853.1	656	382	797	3	28	17	32	192	31	0	.161	18	81	6	1	0.3	.943

LEAGUE CHAMPIONSHIP SERIES

Year	Team		W	L	PCT	ERA	G	GS	CG	IP	H	BB	SO	ShO	W	L	SV	AB	H	HR	BA	PO	A	E	DP	TC/G	FA
1969	MIN	A	0	0	—	0.00	1	0	0	.2	0	0	0	0	0	0	0	0	0	0	—	0	0	0	0	0.0	—
1970			0	1	.000	6.75	2	0	0	5.1	6	4	6	0	0	0	0	1	0	0	.000	0	0	0	0	0.0	—
1972	CIN	N	1	0	1.000	1.23	2	0	0	7.1	3	3	8	0	1	0	0	1	0	0	.000	0	1	0	0	0.5	1.000
1973			0	0	—	67.50	3	0	0	.2	3	4	1	0	0	0	0	0	0	0	—	1	0	0	0	0.3	1.000
1976	KC	A	0	0	—	0.00	1	0	0	.1	1	0	0	0	0	0	0	0	0	0	—	0	0	0	0	0.0	—
5 yrs.			1	1	.500	6.28	9	0	0	14.1	13	11	15	0	1	0	0	2	0	0	.000	2	0	0	0	0.2	1.000

WORLD SERIES

Year	Team		W	L	PCT	ERA	G	GS	CG	IP	H	BB	SO	ShO	W	L	SV	AB	H	HR	BA	PO	A	E	DP	TC/G	FA
1972	CIN	N	0	0	—	0.00	4	0	0	8.1	6	2	7	0	0	0	1	2	0	0	.000	0	2	0	0	0.5	1.000

John Halla

HALLA, JOHN ARTHUR
B. May 13, 1884, St. Louis, Mo. D. Sept. 30, 1947, Redondo Beach, Calif.
BL TL 5'11'' 175 lbs.

Year	Team		W	L	PCT	ERA	G	GS	CG	IP	H	BB	SO	ShO	W	L	SV	AB	H	HR	BA	PO	A	E	DP	TC/G	FA
1905	CLE	A	0	0	—	2.84	3	0	0	12.2	12	0	4	0	0	0	0	4	1	0	.250	0	4	0	0	1.3	1.000

Bill Hallahan

HALLAHAN, WILLIAM ANTHONY (Wild Bill)
B. Aug. 4, 1902, Binghamton, N. Y. D. July 8, 1981, Binghamton, N. Y.
BR TL 5'10½'' 170 lbs.

Year	Team		W	L	PCT	ERA	G	GS	CG	IP	H	BB	SO	ShO	W	L	SV	AB	H	HR	BA	PO	A	E	DP	TC/G	FA
1925	STL	N	1	0	1.000	3.52	6	0	0	15.1	14	11	8	0	1	0	0	3	1	0	.333	1	5	1	0	1.2	.857
1926			1	4	.200	3.65	19	3	0	56.2	45	32	28	0	1	2	0	16	4	0	.250	1	12	4	1	0.9	.765
1929			4	4	.500	4.42	20	12	5	93.2	94	60	52	0	0	0	0	26	4	0	.154	2	25	1	0	1.4	.964
1930			15	9	.625	4.66	35	32	13	237.1	233	**126**	**177**	2	0	0	2	81	10	0	.123	8	41	3	2	1.5	.942
1931			**19**	9	.679	3.29	37	30	16	248.2	242	112	159	3	0	0	1	81	8	0	.099	10	34	1	3	1.2	.978
1932			12	7	.632	3.11	25	22	13	176.1	169	69	108	1	0	0	0	56	12	0	.214	7	27	2	10	1.4	.944
1933			16	13	.552	3.50	36	32	16	244.1	245	**98**	93	2	1	1	0	80	12	0	.150	11	39	6	2	1.6	.893
1934			8	12	.400	4.26	32	26	10	162.2	195	66	70	0	0	0	0	55	10	0	.182	5	34	4	2	1.3	.907
1935			15	8	.652	3.42	40	23	8	181.1	196	57	73	1	3	2	1	56	8	0	.143	9	34	4	4	1.2	.915
1936	2 teams		STL N	(9G 2-2)		CIN N	(23G 5-9)																					
"	total		7	11	.389	4.76	32	25	6	172	178	77	48	2	0	0	0	56	14	0	.250	10	42	2	2	1.7	.963
1937	CIN	N	3	9	.250	6.14	21	9	2	63	90	29	18	0	1	3	0	21	2	0	.095	2	18	3	1	1.0	.864
1938	PHI	N	1	8	.111	5.46	21	10	1	89	107	45	22	0	0	0	0	26	5	0	.192	2	19	1	1	1.0	.955
12 yrs.			102	94	.520	4.03	324	224	90	1740.1	1808	782	856	14	9	14	8	557	90	2	.162	67	330	32	28	1.3	.925

WORLD SERIES

Year	Team		W	L	PCT	ERA	G	GS	CG	IP	H	BB	SO	ShO	W	L	SV	AB	H	HR	BA	PO	A	E	DP	TC/G	FA
1926	STL	N	0	0	—	4.50	1	0	0	2	2	3	1	0	0	0	0	0	0	0	—	1	0	0	0	1.0	1.000
1930			1	1	.500	1.64	2	2	1	11	9	8	8	1	0	0	0	2	0	0	.000	0	1	0	0	0.5	1.000
1931			2	0	1.000	0.49	3	2	2	18.1	12	8	12	1	0	0	1	6	0	0	.000	0	0	0	0	0.0	—
1934			0	0	—	2.16	1	1	0	8.1	6	4	6	0	0	0	0	3	0	0	.000	1	3	1	0	5.0	.800
4 yrs.			3	1	.750	1.36	7	5	3	39.2	29	23	27	2	0	0	1	11	0	0	.000	2	4	1	0	1.0	.857

4th

Jack Hallett

HALLETT, JACK PRICE
B. Nov. 13, 1914, Toledo, Ohio D. June 11, 1982, Toledo, Ohio
BR TR 6'4'' 215 lbs.

Year	Team		W	L	PCT	ERA	G	GS	CG	IP	H	BB	SO	ShO	W	L	SV	AB	H	HR	BA	PO	A	E	DP	TC/G	FA
1940	CHI	A	1	1	.500	6.43	2	2	1	14	15	6	9	0	0	0	0	5	2	0	.400	1	2	0	0	1.5	1.000
1941			5	5	.500	6.03	22	6	3	74.2	96	38	25	0	3	1	0	26	4	0	.154	2	14	0	1	0.7	1.000
1942	PIT	N	0	1	.000	4.84	3	3	2	22.1	23	8	16	0	0	0	0	8	3	1	.375	0	5	0	0	1.7	1.000
1943			1	2	.333	1.70	9	4	2	47.2	36	11	11	1	0	1	0	14	4	0	.286	3	5	0	1	0.9	1.000
1946			5	7	.417	3.29	35	9	3	115	107	39	64	1	3	2	0	26	6	0	.231	8	20	0	0	0.8	1.000
1948	NY	N	0	0	—	4.50	2	0	0	4	3	4	3	0	0	0	0	1	0	0	.000	0	0	0	0	0.0	—
6 yrs.			12	16	.429	4.05	73	24	11	277.2	280	106	128	2	6	4	0	80	19	1	.238	14	46	0	4	0.8	1.000

Bill Hallman

HALLMAN, WILLIAM WILSON
B. Mar. 31, 1867, Pittsburgh, Pa. D. Sept. 11, 1920, Philadelphia, Pa.
Manager 1897.
BR TR 5'8''

Year	Team		W	L	PCT	ERA	G	GS	CG	IP	H	BB	SO	ShO	W	L	SV	AB	H	HR	BA	PO	A	E	DP	TC/G	FA
1896	PHI	N	0	0	—	18.00	1	0	0	2	4	2	0	0	0	0	0	*					0	0	0	0	0.0	—

Charlie Hallstrom

HALLSTROM, CHARLES E. (Swedish Wonder)
B. Jan. 22, 1864, Jonkoping, Sweden D. May 6, 1949, Chicago, Ill.

Year	Team		W	L	PCT	ERA	G	GS	CG	IP	H	BB	SO	ShO	W	L	SV	AB	H	HR	BA	PO	A	E	DP	TC/G	FA
1885	PRO	N	0	1	.000	11.00	1	1	1	9	18	6	0	0	0	0	0	4	0	0	.000	0	1	1	0	2.0	.500

Year	Team	W	L	PCT	ERA	G	GS	CG	IP	H	BB	SO	ShO	W	L	SV	AB	H	HR	BA	PO	A	E	DP	TC/G	FA

Doc Hamann

HAMANN, ELMER JOSEPH
B. Dec. 21, 1900, New Ulm, Minn. D. Jan. 11, 1973, Milwaukee, Wis. BR TR 6'1" 180 lbs.

Year	Team	W	L	PCT	ERA	G	GS	CG	IP	H	BB	SO	ShO	W	L	SV	AB	H	HR	BA	PO	A	E	DP	TC/G	FA
1922	CLE A	0	0	–	∞	1	0	0		3	3	0	0	0	0	0	0	0	0	–	0	0	0	0	0.0	–

Roger Hambright

HAMBRIGHT, ROGER DEE
B. Mar. 26, 1949, Sunnywise, Wash. BR TR 5'10" 180 lbs.

Year	Team	W	L	PCT	ERA	G	GS	CG	IP	H	BB	SO	ShO	W	L	SV	AB	H	HR	BA	PO	A	E	DP	TC/G	FA
1971	NY A	3	1	.750	4.33	18	0	0	27	22	10	14	0	3	1	2	2	1	0	.500	1	5	0	0	0.3	1.000

John Hamill

HAMILL, JOHN ALEXANDER CHARLES
B. Dec. 18, 1860, New York, N. Y. D. Dec. 6, 1911, Bristol, R. I. BR TR 5'8" 158 lbs.

Year	Team	W	L	PCT	ERA	G	GS	CG	IP	H	BB	SO	ShO	W	L	SV	AB	H	HR	BA	PO	A	E	DP	TC/G	FA
1884	WAS AA	2	17	.105	4.48	19	19	18	156.2	197	43	50	1	0	0	0	71	7	0	.099	14	31	17	0	3.3	.726

Dave Hamilton

HAMILTON, DAVID EDWARD
B. Dec. 13, 1947, Seattle, Wash. BL TL 6' 180 lbs.

Year	Team	W	L	PCT	ERA	G	GS	CG	IP	H	BB	SO	ShO	W	L	SV	AB	H	HR	BA	PO	A	E	DP	TC/G	FA
1972	OAK A	6	6	.500	2.93	25	14	1	101.1	94	31	55	0	0	1	0	26	4	0	.154	4	17	1	0	0.9	.955
1973		6	4	.600	4.39	16	11	1	69.2	74	24	34	0	1	0	0	0	0	0	–	2	7	0	0	0.6	1.000
1974		7	4	.636	3.15	29	18	1	117	104	48	69	1	1	0	0	0	0	0	–	3	17	2	1	0.8	.909
1975	2 teams	OAK A	(11G 1–2)		CHI A	(30G 6–5)																				
"	total	7	7	.500	3.25	41	5	0	105.1	105	47	71	0	7	4	0	0	0	0	–	3	15	0	3	0.4	1.000
1976	CHI A	6	6	.500	3.60	45	1	0	90	81	45	62	0	6	5	10	0	0	0	–	4	9	1	1	0.3	.929
1977		4	5	.444	3.63	55	0	0	67	71	33	45	0	4	5	9	0	0	0	–	4	10	1	1	0.3	.933
1978	2 teams	STL N	(13G 0–0)		PIT N	(16G 0–2)																				
"	total	0	2	.000	4.46	29	0	0	40.1	39	18	23	0	0	2	1	7	0	0	.000	3	5	0	0	0.3	1.000
1979	OAK A	3	4	.429	3.69	40	7	1	83	80	43	52	0	2	0	5	0	0	0	–	3	15	0	0	0.5	1.000
1980		0	3	.000	11.40	21	1	0	30	44	28	23	0	0	3	0	0	0	0	–	2	3	0	0	0.2	1.000
9 yrs.		39	41	.488	3.85	301	57	4	703.2	692	317	434	1	21	20	31	33	4	0	.121	28	98	5	6	0.4	.962

LEAGUE CHAMPIONSHIP SERIES

Year	Team	W	L	PCT	ERA	G	GS	CG	IP	H	BB	SO	ShO	W	L	SV	AB	H	HR	BA	PO	A	E	DP	TC/G	FA
1972	OAK A	0	0	–	0.00	1	0	0	1	1	0	0	0	0	0	0	0	0	0	–	0	0	0	0	0.0	–

WORLD SERIES

Year	Team	W	L	PCT	ERA	G	GS	CG	IP	H	BB	SO	ShO	W	L	SV	AB	H	HR	BA	PO	A	E	DP	TC/G	FA
1972	OAK A	0	0	–	27.00	2	0	0	1.1	3	1	1	0	0	0	0	0	0	0	–	0	0	0	0	0.0	–

Earl Hamilton

HAMILTON, EARL ANDREW
B. July 19, 1891, Gibson City, Ill. D. Nov. 17, 1968, Anaheim, Calif. BL TL 5'8" 160 lbs.

Year	Team	W	L	PCT	ERA	G	GS	CG	IP	H	BB	SO	ShO	W	L	SV	AB	H	HR	BA	PO	A	E	DP	TC/G	FA
1911	STL A	5	12	.294	3.97	32	17	10	177	191	69	55	1	1	1	0	56	6	0	.107	13	51	2	2	2.1	.970
1912		11	14	.440	3.24	41	26	17	249.2	228	86	139	1	1	1	2	73	13	0	.178	9	57	5	2	1.7	.930
1913		13	12	.520	2.57	31	24	19	217.1	197	83	101	3	0	2	1	74	10	0	.135	15	53	4	2	2.3	.944
1914		17	18	.486	2.50	44	35	20	302.1	265	100	111	5	1	2	2	85	15	0	.176	16	64	3	3	1.9	.964
1915		9	17	.346	2.87	35	27	13	204	203	69	63	1	0	1	0	62	7	0	.113	7	50	2	3	1.7	.966
1916	3 teams	STL A	(1G 0–0)		DET A	(5G 1–2)			STL A	(22G 5–7)																
"	total	6	9	.400	3.12	28	17	6	132.2	135	52	32	0	2	2	0	37	1	0	.027	3	40	2	1	1.6	.956
1917	STL A	0	9	.000	3.14	27	8	2	83	86	41	19	0	1	0	0	19	7	0	.368	8	18	0	1	1.0	1.000
1918	PIT N	6	0	1.000	0.83	6	6	6	54	47	13	20	1	0	0	0	21	6	0	.286	4	13	1	2	3.0	.944
1919		8	11	.421	3.31	28	19	10	160.1	167	49	39	1	1	0	1	52	7	0	.135	11	51	3	6	2.3	.954
1920		10	13	.435	3.24	39	23	12	230.2	223	69	74	0	3	2	3	67	10	0	.149	10	62	1	0	1.9	.986
1921		13	15	.464	3.36	35	30	12	225	237	58	59	2	0	3	0	75	12	0	.160	15	74	3	1	2.6	.967
1922		11	7	.611	3.99	33	14	9	160	183	40	34	1	3	3	2	58	9	0	.155	4	35	0	1	1.2	1.000
1923		7	9	.438	3.77	28	15	5	141	148	42	42	0	2	3	1	52	9	0	.173	9	42	1	7	1.9	.981
1924	PHI N	0	1	.000	10.50	3	0	0	6	9	2	2	0	0	1	0	2	0	0	.000	0	2	0	0	0.7	1.000
14 yrs.		116	147	.441	3.16	410	261	141	2343	2319	773	790	16	14	24	13	733	112	0	.153	124	612	27	29	1.9	.965

Jack Hamilton

HAMILTON, JACK EDWIN (Hairbreadth Harry)
B. Dec. 25, 1938, Burlington, Iowa BR TR 6' 200 lbs.

Year	Team	W	L	PCT	ERA	G	GS	CG	IP	H	BB	SO	ShO	W	L	SV	AB	H	HR	BA	PO	A	E	DP	TC/G	FA
1962	PHI N	9	12	.429	5.09	41	26	4	182	185	107	101	1	2	0	2	54	3	0	.056	16	39	3	6	1.4	.948
1963		2	1	.667	5.40	19	1	0	30	22	17	23	0	2	0	1	3	0	0	.000	1	8	0	0	0.5	1.000
1964	DET A	0	1	.000	8.40	5	1	0	15	24	8	5	0	0	0	0	3	0	0	.000	1	5	0	0	1.2	1.000
1965		1	1	.500	14.54	4	1	0	4.1	6	4	3	0	1	0	0	0	0	0	–	1	2	0	0	0.8	1.000
1966	NY N	6	13	.316	3.93	57	13	3	148.2	138	88	93	1	2	6	13	38	5	0	.132	16	25	2	2	0.8	.953
1967	2 teams	NY N	(17G 2–0)		CAL A	(26G 9–6)																				
"	total	11	6	.647	3.35	43	21	0	150.2	128	79	96	0	3	0	1	43	7	1	.163	5	24	2	2	0.7	.935
1968	CAL A	3	1	.750	3.32	21	2	1	38	34	15	18	0	2	0	2	7	1	0	.143	4	4	0	1	0.4	1.000
1969	2 teams	CLE A	(20G 0–2)		CHI A	(8G 0–3)																				
"	total	0	5	.000	6.49	28	0	0	43	60	30	18	0	0	5	1	2	0	0	.000	1	6	0	0	0.3	1.000
8 yrs.		32	40	.444	4.53	218	65	8	611.2	597	348	357	2	12	11	20	150	16	1	.107	45	113	7	10	0.8	.958

Jeff Hamilton

HAMILTON, JEFFREY ROBERT
B. Mar. 19, 1964, Flint, Mich. BR TR 6'3" 190 lbs.

Year	Team	W	L	PCT	ERA	G	GS	CG	IP	H	BB	SO	ShO	W	L	SV	AB	H	HR	BA	PO	A	E	DP	TC/G	FA
1989	LA N	0	1	.000	5.40	1	0	0	1.2	2	1	2	0	0	1	0	*				0	1	0	0	1.0	1.000

Steve Hamilton

HAMILTON, STEVE ABSHER
B. Nov. 30, 1935, Columbia, Ky. BL TL 6'6" 190 lbs.

Year	Team	W	L	PCT	ERA	G	GS	CG	IP	H	BB	SO	ShO	W	L	SV	AB	H	HR	BA	PO	A	E	DP	TC/G	FA
1961	CLE A	0	0	–	2.70	2	0	0	3.1	2	3	4	0	0	0	0	1	1	0	1.000	1	1	0	0	1.0	1.000
1962	WAS A	3	8	.273	3.77	41	10	1	107.1	103	39	83	0	2	4	2	26	2	0	.077	8	22	2	0	0.8	.938
1963	2 teams	WAS A	(3G 0–1)		NY A	(34G 5–1)																				
"	total	5	2	.714	2.94	37	0	0	64.1	54	26	64	0	5	2	4	14	4	0	.286	0	1	0	0	0.0	1.000
1964	NY A	7	2	.778	3.28	30	3	1	60.1	55	15	49	0	5	2	4	20	4	0	.200	3	9	0	1	0.4	1.000
1965		3	1	.750	1.39	46	1	0	58.1	47	16	51	0	3	1	5	6	1	0	.167	0	3	1	0	0.1	.750
1966		8	3	.727	3.00	44	3	1	90	69	22	57	0	7	2	3	19	1	0	.053	2	12	2	0	0.4	.875
1967		2	4	.333	3.48	44	0	0	62	57	23	55	0	2	4	4	9	1	0	.111	0	12	0	0	0.3	1.000
1968		2	2	.500	2.13	40	0	0	50.2	37	13	42	0	2	2	11	3	0	0	.000	2	9	0	1	0.3	1.000
1969		3	4	.429	3.32	38	0	0	57	39	21	39	0	3	4	2	3	0	0	.000	0	3	0	0	0.1	1.000

Year	Team		W	L	PCT	ERA	G	GS	CG	IP	H	BB	SO	ShO	Relief Pitching W	L	SV	Batting AB	H	HR	BA	PO	A	E	DP	TC/G	FA

Steve Hamilton *continued*

1970	2 teams	NY A (35G 4–3)				CHI A	(3G 0–0)																				
"	total		4	3	.571	2.98	38	0	0	48.1	40	17	36	0	4	3	3	6	0	0	.000	0	11	1	0	0.3	.917
1971	SF	N	2	2	.500	3.00	39	0	0	45	29	11	38	0	2	2	4	2	0	0	.000	3	4	0	0	0.2	1.000
1972	CHI	N	1	0	1.000	4.76	22	0	0	17	24	8	13	0	1	0	0	1	0	0	.000	0	2	0	0	0.1	1.000
	12 yrs.		40	31	.563	3.05	421	17	3	663.2	556	214	531	1	36	26	42	112	14	0	.125	19	90	6	2	0.3	.948

LEAGUE CHAMPIONSHIP SERIES

| 1971 | SF | N | 0 | 0 | – | 9.00 | 1 | 0 | 0 | 1 | 1 | 0 | 3 | 0 | 0 | 0 | 0 | 0 | 0 | 0 | – | 0 | 0 | 0 | 0 | 0.0 | – |

WORLD SERIES

1963	NY	A	0	0	–	0.00	1	0	0	1	0	0	1	0	0	0	0	0	0	0	–	0	0	0	0	0.0	–
1964			0	0	–	4.50	2	0	0	2	3	0	2	0	0	0	1	0	0	0	–	0	0	0	0	0.0	–
	2 yrs.		0	0	–	3.00	3	0	0	3	3	0	3	0	0	0	1	0	0	0	–	0	0	0	0	0.0	–

Luke Hamlin

HAMLIN, LUKE DANIEL (Hot Potato)
B. July 3, 1904, Ferris Center, Mich.   D. Feb. 18, 1978, Clare, Mich.

BL TR 6'2"   168 lbs.

1933	DET	A	1	0	1.000	4.86	3	3	0	16.2	20	10	10	0	0	0	0	5	2	0	.400	1	0	2	0	1.0	.333
1934			2	3	.400	5.38	20	5	1	75.1	87	44	30	0	0	3	1	26	6	0	.231	4	12	0	1	0.8	1.000
1937	BKN	N	11	13	.458	3.59	39	25	11	185.2	183	48	93	1	2	2	1	59	11	0	.186	7	26	6	1	1.0	.846
1938			12	15	.444	3.68	44	30	10	237.1	243	65	97	3	1	1	6	78	11	0	.141	8	29	2	1	0.9	.949
1939			20	13	.606	3.64	40	36	19	269.2	255	54	88	2	2	0	0	103	13	1	.126	13	33	1	1	1.2	.979
1940			9	8	.529	3.06	33	25	9	182.1	183	34	91	2	0	0	0	58	5	0	.086	5	19	2	3	0.8	.923
1941			8	8	.500	4.24	30	20	5	136	139	41	58	1	1	0	1	41	6	0	.146	9	18	0	2	0.9	1.000
1942	PIT	N	4	4	.500	3.94	23	14	6	112	128	19	38	1	0	1	0	37	9	0	.243	4	15	2	0	0.9	.905
1944	PHI	A	6	12	.333	3.74	29	23	9	190	204	38	58	2	0	1	0	56	13	0	.232	1	19	4	0	0.8	.833
	9 yrs.		73	76	.490	3.77	261	181	70	1405	1442	353	563	12	6	7	9	463	76	1	.164	52	171	19	8	0.9	.921

Pete Hamm

HAMM, PETER WHITFIELD
B. Sept. 20, 1947, Buffalo, N. Y.

BR TR 6'5"   210 lbs.

1970	MIN	A	0	2	.000	5.63	10	0	0	16	17	7	3	0	0	2	0	1	0	0	.000	1	0	0	0	0.1	1.000
1971			2	4	.333	6.75	13	8	1	44	55	18	16	0	0	1	0	11	3	0	.273	6	7	0	0	1.0	1.000
	2 yrs.		2	6	.250	6.45	23	8	1	60	72	25	19	0	0	3	0	12	3	0	.250	7	7	0	0	0.6	1.000

Atlee Hammaker

HAMMAKER, CHARLTON ATLEE
B. Jan. 24, 1958, Carmel, Calif.

BB TL 6'3"   200 lbs.

1981	KC	A	1	3	.250	5.54	10	6	0	39	44	12	11	0	0	0	0	0	0	0	–	1	4	0	1	0.5	1.000
1982	SF	N	12	8	.600	4.11	29	27	4	175	189	28	102	1	0	0	0	59	4	0	.068	5	35	1	0	1.4	.976
1983			10	9	.526	2.25	23	23	8	172.1	147	32	127	3	0	0	0	59	6	0	.102	3	31	3	2	1.6	.919
1984			2	0	1.000	2.18	6	6	0	33	32	9	24	0	0	0	0	11	2	0	.182	0	6	0	0	1.0	1.000
1985			5	12	.294	3.74	29	29	1	170.2	161	47	100	1	0	0	0	47	4	0	.085	6	32	1	1	1.3	.974
1987			10	10	.500	3.58	31	27	0	168.1	159	57	107	0	1	0	0	57	7	0	.123	7	23	0	0	1.0	1.000
1988			9	9	.500	3.73	43	17	3	144.2	136	41	65	1	4	2	5	33	4	0	.121	7	33	3	3	0.9	1.000
1989			6	6	.500	3.76	28	9	0	76.2	78	23	30	0	3	3	0	19	7	0	.368	3	9	1	0	0.5	.923
	8 yrs.		55	57	.491	3.54	199	144	18	979.2	946	249	566	6	8	5	5	285	34	0	.119	32	173	6	8	1.1	.972

LEAGUE CHAMPIONSHIP SERIES

1987	SF	N	0	1	.000	7.88	2	2	0	8	12	0	7	0	0	0	0	3	0	0	.000	0	1	0	0	0.5	1.000
1989			0	0	–	0.00	1	0	0	1	1	0	0	0	0	0	0	0	0	0	–	0	0	0	0	0.0	–
	2 yrs.		0	1	.000	7.00	3	2	0	9	13	0	7	0	0	0	0	3	0	0	.000	0	1	0	0	0.3	1.000

WORLD SERIES

| 1989 | SF | N | 0 | 0 | – | 15.43 | 2 | 0 | 0 | 2.1 | 8 | 0 | 2 | 0 | 0 | 0 | 0 | 0 | 0 | 0 | – | 1 | 0 | 0 | 0 | 0.5 | 1.000 |

Granny Hamner

HAMNER, GRANVILLE WILBUR
Brother of Garvin Hamner.
B. Apr. 26, 1927, Richmond, Va.

BR TR 5'10"   163 lbs.

1956	PHI	N	0	1	.000	4.32	3	1	0	8.1	10	2	4	0	0	0	0	401	90	4	.224	0	1	0	0	0.3	1.000
1957			0	0	–	0.00	1	0	0	1	1	0	1	0	0	0	0	502	114	10	.227	0	0	0	0	0.3	1.000
1962	KC	A	0	1	.000	9.00	3	0	0	4	10	6	0	0	0	1	0	0	0	0	–	0	1	0	0	0.3	1.000
	3 yrs.		0	2	.000	5.40	7	1	0	13.1	21	8	5	0	0	1	0	*				0	2	0	0	0.3	1.000

Ralph Hamner

HAMNER, RALPH CONANT (Bruz)
B. Sept. 12, 1916, Gibsland, La.

BR TR 6'3"   165 lbs.

1946	CHI	A	2	7	.222	4.42	25	7	1	71.1	80	39	29	0	0	0	1	18	3	0	.167	3	10	1	0	0.6	.929
1947	CHI	N	1	2	.333	2.52	3	3	2	25	24	16	14	0	0	0	0	8	1	0	.125	2	1	0	1	1.7	.800
1948			5	9	.357	4.69	27	17	5	111.1	110	69	53	0	0	0	1	33	6	1	.182	7	26	1	3	1.3	.971
1949			0	2	.000	8.76	6	1	0	12.1	22	8	3	0	0	0	0	2	0	0	.000	3	6	0	0	1.5	1.000
	4 yrs.		8	20	.286	4.58	61	28	8	220	236	132	99	0	0	0	2	61	10	1	.164	15	44	3	3	1.0	.952

Garry Hancock

HANCOCK, RONALD GARRY
B. Jan. 23, 1954, Tampa, Fla.

BL TL 6'   175 lbs.

| 1984 | OAK | A | 0 | 0 | – | 0.00 | 1 | 0 | 0 | 1.1 | 0 | 0 | 0 | 0 | 0 | 0 | 0 | * | | | | 0 | 0 | 0 | 0 | 0.0 | – |

Rich Hand

HAND, RICHARD ALLEN
B. July 10, 1948, Bellevue, Wash.

BR TR 6'1"   185 lbs.

1970	CLE	A	6	13	.316	3.83	35	25	3	160	132	69	110	1	0	0	3	41	6	0	.146	11	22	2	2	1.0	.943
1971			2	6	.250	5.75	15	12	0	61	74	38	26	0	0	1	0	16	2	0	.125	4	5	0	0	0.6	1.000
1972	TEX	A	10	14	.417	3.32	30	28	3	170.2	139	103	109	1	0	0	0	52	8	0	.154	10	25	3	2	1.3	.921
1973	2 teams	TEX A (8G 2–3)				CAL A	(16G 4–3)																				
"	total		6	6	.500	4.39	24	13	1	96.1	107	40	33	0	2	2	0	–				8	16	2	0	1.1	.923
	4 yrs.		24	39	.381	4.00	104	78	6	488	452	250	278	2	2	3	3	109	16	0	.147	33	68	7	4	1.0	.935

Year	Team		W	L	PCT	ERA	G	GS	CG	IP	H	BB	SO	ShO	Relief Pitching W	L	SV	Batting AB	H	HR	BA	PO	A	E	DP	TC/G	FA

Jim Handiboe

HANDIBOE, JAMES EDWARD (Nick)
B. July 17, 1866, Columbus, Ohio D. Nov. 8, 1942, Columbus, Ohio
BR TR 5'11" 160 lbs.

| 1886 | PIT | AA | 7 | 7 | .500 | 3.32 | 14 | 14 | 12 | 114 | 82 | 33 | 83 | 1 | 0 | 0 | 0 | 44 | 5 | 0 | .114 | 5 | 17 | 6 | 0 | 2.0 | .786 |

Vern Handrahan

HANDRAHAN, JAMES VERNON
B. Nov. 27, 1938, Charlottetown, P. E. I., Canada
BL TR 6'2" 185 lbs.

1964	KC	A	0	1	.000	6.06	18	1	0	35.2	33	25	18	0	0	0	0	9	2	0	.222	1	6	0	1	0.4	1.000
1966			0	1	.000	4.26	16	1	0	25.1	20	15	18	0	0	0	1	3	0	0	.000	2	4	0	1	0.4	1.000
2 yrs.			0	2	.000	5.31	34	2	0	61	53	40	36	0	0	0	1	12	2	0	.167	3	10	0	2	0.4	1.000

Bill Hands

HANDS, WILLIAM ALFRED
B. May 6, 1940, Hackensack, N. J.
BR TR 6'2" 185 lbs.

1965	SF	N	0	2	.000	16.50	4	2	0	6	13	6	5	0	0	0	0	1	0	0	.000	0	2	0	0	0.5	1.000
1966	CHI	N	8	13	.381	4.58	41	26	0	159	168	59	93	0	4	0	2	49	2	0	.041	12	33	4	1	1.2	.918
1967			7	8	.467	2.46	49	11	3	150	134	48	84	1	3	6	6	38	4	0	.105	11	24	1	1	0.7	.972
1968			16	10	.615	2.89	38	34	11	258.2	221	36	148	4	0	1	0	82	5	0	.061	21	39	1	0	1.6	.984
1969			20	14	.588	2.49	41	41	18	300	268	73	181	3	0	0	0	98	9	0	.092	16	56	3	2	1.8	.960
1970			18	15	.545	3.70	39	38	12	265	278	76	170	2	0	0	0	75	10	0	.133	22	42	3	2	1.7	.955
1971			12	18	.400	3.42	36	35	14	242	248	50	128	1	0	0	0	72	6	0	.083	21	32	2	2	1.5	.964
1972			11	8	.579	2.99	32	28	6	189.1	168	47	96	3	0	1	0	57	1	0	.018	12	21	5	1	1.2	.868
1973	MIN	A	7	10	.412	3.49	39	15	3	142	138	41	78	1	2	3	2	4	20	2	2	0.7	.923			
1974	2 teams	MIN A	(35G 4–5)				TEX A	(2G 2–0)																			
"	total		9	5	.545	4.19	37	12	1	129	141	28	78	1	2	0	3	0	0	0	–	10	12	0	0	0.6	1.000
1975	TEX	A	6	7	.462	4.02	18	18	4	109.2	118	28	67	1	0	0	0	0	0	0	–	11	16	3	1	1.7	.900
11 yrs.			111	110	.502	3.35	374	260	72	1950.2	1895	492	1128	17	11	11	14	472	37	0	.078	140	297	24	12	1.2	.948

Don Hankins

HANKINS, DONALD WAYNE
B. Feb. 9, 1902, Pendleton, Ind. D. May 16, 1963, Winston-Salem, N. C.
BR TR 6'3" 183 lbs.

| 1927 | DET | A | 2 | 1 | .667 | 6.48 | 20 | 1 | 0 | 41.2 | 67 | 13 | 10 | 0 | 2 | 0 | 2 | 7 | 1 | 0 | .143 | 4 | 10 | 0 | 0 | 0.7 | 1.000 |

Frank Hankinson

HANKINSON, FRANK EDWARD
B. Apr. 29, 1856, New York, N. Y. D. Apr. 5, 1911, Palisades Park, N. J.
BR TR 5'11" 168 lbs.

1878	CHI	N	0	1	.000	6.00	1	1	1	9	11	0	4	0	0	0	0	240	64	1	.267	1	0	0	0	1.0	1.000
1879			15	10	.600	2.50	26	25	25	230.2	248	27	69	2	1	0	0	171	31	0	.181	16	67	6	1	3.4	.933
1880	CLE	N	1	1	.500	1.08	4	2	2	25	20	3	8	0	0	0	1	263	55	0	.209	2	10	0	0	3.0	1.000
1885	NY	AA	0	0	–	4.50	1	0	0	2	2	1	0	0	0	0	0	362	81	2	.224	0	0	0	0	0.0	–
4 yrs.			16	12	.571	2.50	32	28	28	266.2	281	31	81	2	1	0	1	*				19	77	6	1	3.2	.941

Jim Hanley

HANLEY, JAMES PATRICK
B. Oct. 13, 1885, Providence, R. I. D. May 1, 1961, Elmhurst, N. Y.
BR TL 5'11" 165 lbs.

| 1913 | NY | A | 0 | 0 | – | 6.75 | 1 | 0 | 0 | 4 | 5 | 4 | 2 | 0 | 0 | 0 | 0 | 1 | 0 | 0 | .000 | 2 | 0 | 0 | 0 | 2.0 | 1.000 |

Preston Hanna

HANNA, PRESTON LEE
B. Sept. 10, 1954, Pensacola, Fla.
BR TR 6'1" 195 lbs.

1975	ATL	N	0	0	–	1.50	4	0	0	6	7	5	2	0	0	0	0	0	0	0	–	0	0	0	0	0.0	–
1976			0	0	–	4.50	5	0	0	8	11	4	3	0	0	0	0	1	0	0	.000	1	0	0	0	0.2	1.000
1977			2	6	.250	4.95	17	9	1	60	69	34	37	0	0	0	1	14	1	0	.071	2	18	3	0	1.4	.870
1978			7	13	.350	5.14	29	28	0	140	132	93	90	0	0	0	0	49	9	1	.184	10	18	0	1	1.0	1.000
1979			1	1	.500	3.00	6	4	0	24	27	15	15	0	0	0	0	6	0	0	.000	0	8	0	1	1.3	1.000
1980			2	0	1.000	3.19	32	2	0	79	63	44	35	0	2	0	0	14	2	0	.143	6	8	0	0	0.4	1.000
1981			2	1	.667	6.43	20	1	0	35	45	23	22	0	2	0	0	4	1	0	.250	3	12	0	2	0.8	1.000
1982	2 teams	ATL N	(20G 3–0)				OAK A	(23G 0–4)																			
"	total		3	4	.429	4.80	43	3	1	84.1	90	61	49	0	3	2	0	5	2	0	.400	2	8	1	1	0.3	.909
8 yrs.			17	25	.405	4.62	156	47	2	436.1	444	279	253	0	6	2	1	93	15	1	.161	24	72	4	5	0.6	.960

Gerald Hannahs

HANNAHS, GERALD ELLIS
B. Mar. 6, 1953, Binghamton, N. Y.
BL TL 6'3" 210 lbs.

1976	MON	N	2	0	1.000	6.75	3	3	0	16	20	12	10	0	0	0	0	8	3	0	.375	0	2	0	0	0.7	1.000
1977			1	5	.167	4.86	8	7	0	37	43	17	21	0	0	0	0	7	0	0	.000	1	6	2	0	1.1	.778
1978	LA	N	0	0	–	9.00	1	0	0	2	3	0	5	0	0	0	0	0	0	0	–	0	0	0	0	0.0	–
1979			0	2	.000	3.38	4	2	0	16	10	13	6	0	0	0	0	4	1	0	.250	0	3	0	0	0.8	1.000
4 yrs.			3	7	.300	5.07	16	12	0	71	76	42	42	0	0	0	1	19	4	0	.211	1	11	2	0	0.9	.857

Jim Hannan

HANNAN, JAMES JOHN
B. Jan. 7, 1940, Jersey City, N. J.
BR TR 6'3" 205 lbs.

1962	WAS	A	2	4	.333	3.31	42	3	0	68	56	49	39	0	1	2	4	11	1	0	.091	5	12	1	0	0.4	.944
1963			2	2	.500	4.88	13	2	0	27.2	23	17	14	0	1	1	0	6	0	0	.000	1	7	1	0	0.7	.889
1964			4	7	.364	4.16	49	7	0	106	108	45	67	0	4	3	3	20	3	0	.150	4	15	0	0	0.4	1.000
1965			1	1	.500	4.91	4	1	1	14.2	18	6	5	1	0	1	0	3	0	0	.000	1	0	0	0	0.3	1.000
1966			3	9	.250	4.26	30	18	2	114	125	59	68	0	0	1	0	30	2	0	.067	7	18	1	0	0.9	.962
1967			1	1	.500	5.40	8	2	0	21.2	28	7	14	0	0	0	0	4	0	0	.000	2	4	1	0	0.9	.857
1968			10	6	.625	3.01	25	22	4	140.1	147	50	75	1	0	0	0	47	3	0	.064	8	20	1	2	1.2	.966
1969			7	6	.538	3.64	35	28	1	158.1	138	91	72	1	0	0	0	52	6	0	.115	11	21	0	2	0.9	1.000
1970			9	11	.450	4.01	17	17	1	128	119	54	61	1	0	4	3	31	4	0	.129	7	25	1	0	0.8	.970
1971	2 teams	DET A	(7G 1–0)				MIL A	(21G 1–1)																			
"	total		2	1	.667	4.57	28	1	0	43.1	45	28	23	0	2	0	0	5	0	0	.000	4	8	1	1	0.5	.923
10 yrs.			41	48	.461	3.88	276	101	9	822	807	406	438	4	13	10	7	209	19	0	.091	50	130	7	5	0.7	.963

Loy Hanning

HANNING, LOY VERNON
B. Oct. 18, 1917, Bunker, Mo. D. June 24, 1986, Anaconda, Mo.
BR TR 6'2" 175 lbs.

| 1939 | STL | A | 0 | 1 | .000 | 3.60 | 4 | 1 | 0 | 10 | 6 | 4 | 8 | 0 | 0 | 0 | 0 | 1 | 0 | 0 | .000 | 1 | 1 | 0 | 0 | 0.5 | 1.000 |

Year	Team		W	L	PCT	ERA	G	GS	CG	IP	H	BB	SO	ShO	W	L	SV	AB	H	HR	BA	PO	A	E	DP	TC/G	FA
															Relief Pitching			**Batting**									

Andy Hansen

HANSEN, ANDREW VIGGO (Swede)
B. Nov. 12, 1924, Lake Worth, Fla.

BR TR 6'3" 185 lbs.

Year	Team		W	L	PCT	ERA	G	GS	CG	IP	H	BB	SO	ShO	W	L	SV	AB	H	HR	BA	PO	A	E	DP	TC/G	FA
1944	NY	N	3	3	.500	6.49	23	4	0	52.2	63	32	15	0	3	0	1	12	2	0	.167	4	14	0	2	0.8	1.000
1945			4	3	.571	4.66	23	13	4	92.2	98	28	37	0	0	0	3	25	0	0	.000	2	26	0	1	1.2	1.000
1947			1	5	.167	4.37	27	9	1	82.1	78	38	18	0	0	1	0	21	4	0	.190	7	18	0	1	0.9	1.000
1948			5	3	.625	2.97	36	9	3	100	96	36	27	0	2	0	1	20	1	0	.050	7	13	0	0	0.6	1.000
1949			2	6	.250	4.61	33	2	0	66.1	58	28	26	0	2	5	1	12	0	0	.000	6	11	0	2	0.5	1.000
1950			0	1	.000	5.53	31	1	0	57	64	26	19	0	0	0	3	7	0	0	.000	6	8	0	1	0.5	1.000
1951	PHI	N	3	1	.750	2.54	24	0	0	39	34	7	11	0	3	1	0	3	1	0	.333	5	10	0	1	0.6	1.000
1952			5	6	.455	3.26	43	0	0	77.1	76	27	18	0	5	6	4	11	2	0	.182	6	19	1	2	0.6	.962
1953			0	2	.000	4.03	30	1	0	51.1	60	24	17	0	0	1	3	7	2	0	.286	4	11	1	2	0.5	.938
9 yrs.			23	30	.434	4.22	270	39	8	618.2	627	246	188	0	15	14	16	118	12	0	.102	47	130	2	12	0.7	.989

Roy Hansen

HANSEN, ROY INGLOF (Ing)
B. Mar. 6, 1898, Beloit, Wis. D. Feb. 9, 1977, Beloit, Wis.

BR TR 6' 165 lbs.

Year	Team		W	L	PCT	ERA	G	GS	CG	IP	H	BB	SO	ShO	W	L	SV	AB	H	HR	BA	PO	A	E	DP	TC/G	FA
1918	WAS	A	1	0	1.000	3.00	5	0	0	9	10	3	2	0	1	0	0	0	0	0	—	0	4	0	0	0.8	1.000

Snipe Hansen

HANSEN, ROY EMIL FREDERICK
B. Feb. 21, 1907, Chicago, Ill.
D. Sept. 11, 1978, Chicago, Ill.

BB TL 6'3" 195 lbs.
BL 1930,
BR 1932

Year	Team		W	L	PCT	ERA	G	GS	CG	IP	H	BB	SO	ShO	W	L	SV	AB	H	HR	BA	PO	A	E	DP	TC/G	FA
1930	PHI	N	0	7	.000	6.72	22	9	1	84.1	123	38	25	0	0	0	0	27	3	0	.111	2	16	0	0	0.9	.900
1932			10	10	.500	3.72	39	23	5	191	215	51	56	0	0	0	2	63	8	0	.127	9	32	1	0	1.1	.976
1933			6	14	.300	4.44	32	22	8	168.1	199	30	47	0	0	1	1	58	9	0	.155	5	34	4	1	1.3	.907
1934			6	12	.333	5.42	50	16	5	151	194	61	40	2	2	4	3	43	10	0	.233	2	39	0	3	0.8	1.000
1935	2 teams		PHI N	(2G 0–1)		STL A	(10G 0–1)																					
"	total		0	2	.000	9.29	12	1	0	31	52	14	8	0	0	0	0	9	1	0	.111	0	5	1	0	0.5	.833
5 yrs.			22	45	.328	5.01	155	71	19	625.2	783	194	176	2	2	7	6	200	31	0	.155	18	126	8	4	1.0	.947

F. C. Hansford

HANSFORD, F. C.
Deceased.

TL 6' 180 lbs.

Year	Team		W	L	PCT	ERA	G	GS	CG	IP	H	BB	SO	ShO	W	L	SV	AB	H	HR	BA	PO	A	E	DP	TC/G	FA
1898	BKN	N	0	0	—	3.86	1	0	0	7	10	5	0	0	0	0	0	3	0	0	.000	0	0	0	0	0.0	—

Don Hanski

HANSKI, DONALD THOMAS
Born Donald Thomas Hanyzewski.
B. Feb. 27, 1916, LaPorte, Ind. D. Sept. 2, 1957, Worth, Ill.

BL TL 5'11" 180 lbs.

Year	Team		W	L	PCT	ERA	G	GS	CG	IP	H	BB	SO	ShO	W	L	SV	AB	H	HR	BA	PO	A	E	DP	TC/G	FA
1943	CHI	A	0	0	—	0.00	1	0	0	1	1	1	0	0	0	0	0	21	5	0	.238	37	3	2	5	42.0	.952
1944			0	0	—	12.00	2	0	0	3	5	2	0	0	0	0	0	1	0	0	.000	0	0	0	0	0.0	—
2 yrs.			0	0	—	9.00	3	0	0	4	6	3	0	0	0	0	0	*				*					

Erik Hanson

HANSON, ERIK BRIAN
B. May 18, 1965, Kinnelon, N. J.

BR TR 6'6" 210 lbs.

Year	Team		W	L	PCT	ERA	G	GS	CG	IP	H	BB	SO	ShO	W	L	SV	AB	H	HR	BA	PO	A	E	DP	TC/G	FA
1988	SEA	A	2	3	.400	3.24	6	6	0	41.2	35	12	36	0	0	0	0	0	0	0	—	0	4	0	1	0.7	1.000
1989			9	5	.643	3.18	17	17	1	113.1	103	32	75	0	0	0	0	0	0	0	—	8	16	0	0	1.4	1.000
2 yrs.			11	8	.579	3.19	23	23	1	155	138	44	111	0	0	0	0	0	0	0	—	8	20	0	1	1.2	1.000

Ollie Hanson

HANSON, EARL SYLVESTER
B. Jan. 19, 1896, Holbrook, Mass. D. Aug. 19, 1951, Clifton, N. J.

BR TR 5'11" 178 lbs.

Year	Team		W	L	PCT	ERA	G	GS	CG	IP	H	BB	SO	ShO	W	L	SV	AB	H	HR	BA	PO	A	E	DP	TC/G	FA
1921	CHI	N	0	2	.000	7.00	2	2	1	9	9	6	2	0	0	0	0	3	0	0	.000	0	4	0	0	2.0	1.000

Ed Hanyzewski

HANYZEWSKI, EDWARD MICHAEL
B. Sept. 18, 1920, Union Mills, Ind.

BR TR 6'1" 200 lbs.

Year	Team		W	L	PCT	ERA	G	GS	CG	IP	H	BB	SO	ShO	W	L	SV	AB	H	HR	BA	PO	A	E	DP	TC/G	FA
1942	CHI	N	1	1	.500	3.79	6	1	0	19	17	8	6	0	1	0	0	5	1	0	.200	1	5	0	0	1.0	1.000
1943			8	7	.533	2.56	33	16	3	130	120	45	55	0	4	0	0	41	2	0	.049	10	33	1	1	1.3	.977
1944			2	5	.286	4.47	14	7	3	58.1	61	20	19	0	0	1	0	17	1	0	.059	2	26	0	1	2.0	1.000
1945			0	0	—	5.79	2	1	0	4.2	7	1	0	0	0	0	0	1	0	0	.000	0	2	1	0	1.5	.667
1946			1	0	1.000	4.50	3	0	0	6	8	5	1	0	1	0	0	1	0	0	.000	2	1	0	0	1.0	1.000
5 yrs.			12	13	.480	3.30	58	25	6	218	213	79	81	0	6	1	0	65	4	0	.062	15	67	2	2	1.4	.976

Mel Harder

HARDER, MELVIN LeROY (Chief, Wimpy)
B. Oct. 15, 1909, Beemer, Neb.
Manager 1961.

BR TR 6'1" 195 lbs.

Year	Team		W	L	PCT	ERA	G	GS	CG	IP	H	BB	SO	ShO	W	L	SV	AB	H	HR	BA	PO	A	E	DP	TC/G	FA
1928	CLE	A	0	2	.000	6.61	23	1	0	49	64	32	15	0	0	1	1	8	0	0	.000	0	8	2	0	0.4	.800
1929			1	0	1.000	5.60	11	0	0	17.2	24	5	4	0	1	0	0	1	0	0	.000	0	3	1	0	0.4	.750
1930			11	10	.524	4.21	36	19	7	175.1	205	68	44	0	3	3	2	63	9	0	.143	9	32	7	3	1.3	.854
1931			13	14	.481	4.36	40	24	9	194	229	72	63	0	3	0	1	75	19	0	.253	14	38	4	4	1.4	.929
1932			15	13	.536	3.75	39	32	17	254.2	277	68	90	1	0	2	0	94	17	0	.181	18	65	2	0	2.2	.976
1933			15	17	.469	2.95	43	31	14	253	254	67	81	2	3	1	4	84	16	1	.190	22	87	3	4	2.6	.973
1934			20	12	.625	2.61	44	29	17	255.1	246	81	91	6	4	2	4	87	14	0	.161	10	61	7	2	1.8	.910
1935			22	11	.667	3.29	42	35	17	287.1	313	53	95	4	2	0	2	102	21	2	.206	18	81	4	0	2.5	.961
1936			15	15	.500	5.17	36	30	13	224.2	294	71	84	0	3	0	1	80	11	0	.138	13	38	3	3	1.5	.944
1937			15	12	.556	4.28	38	30	13	233.2	269	86	95	0	2	2	2	86	15	0	.174	12	48	1	3	1.6	.984
1938			17	10	.630	3.83	38	29	15	240	257	62	102	2	1	0	4	88	10	0	.114	21	49	1	2	1.9	.986
1939			15	9	.625	3.50	29	26	9	208	213	64	67	1	0	1	1	72	10	0	.139	14	26	1	1	1.4	.976
1940			12	11	.522	4.06	35	25	5	186.1	200	59	76	0	1	0	1	62	11	0	.177	9	38	2	4	1.6	.959
1941			5	4	.556	5.24	15	10	1	68.2	76	37	21	0	0	0	1	25	2	0	.080	7	16	1	0	1.6	.958
1942			13	14	.481	3.44	29	29	13	198.2	179	82	74	4	0	0	0	67	8	0	.119	14	44	3	5	2.1	.951
1943			8	7	.533	3.06	19	18	6	135.1	126	61	40	1	0	0	0	47	10	0	.213	6	27	0	2	1.7	1.000
1944			12	10	.545	3.71	30	27	12	196.1	211	69	64	2	0	0	0	74	16	0	.216	11	34	2	3	1.6	.957
1945			3	7	.300	3.67	11	11	2	76	93	23	16	0	0	0	0	25	2	0	.080	6	19	0	1	2.3	1.000
1946			5	4	.556	3.41	13	12	4	92.1	85	31	21	0	0	0	0	35	3	0	.086	5	9	0	1	1.1	1.000

Year	Team	W	L	PCT	ERA	G	GS	CG	IP	H	BB	SO	ShO	W	L	SV	AB	H	HR	BA	PO	A	E	DP	TC/G	FA

Mel Harder *continued*

Year	Team	W	L	PCT	ERA	G	GS	CG	IP	H	BB	SO	ShO	W	L	SV	AB	H	HR	BA	PO	A	E	DP	TC/G	FA
1943		8	7	.533	3.06	19	18	6	135.1	126	61	40	1	0	0	0	47	10	0	.213	6	27	0	2	1.7	1.000
1944		12	10	.545	3.71	30	27	12	196.1	211	69	64	2	0	0	0	74	16	0	.216	11	34	2	3	1.6	.957
1945		3	7	.300	3.67	11	11	2	76	93	23	16	0	0	0	0	25	2	0	.080	6	19	0	1	2.3	1.000
1946		5	4	.556	3.41	13	12	4	92.1	85	31	21	1	0	1	0	35	3	0	.086	5	9	0	1	1.1	1.000
1947		6	4	.600	4.50	15	15	4	80	91	27	17	1	0	0	0	28	5	0	.179	0	11	1	0	0.8	.917
20 yrs.		223	186	.545	3.80	582	433	181	3426.1	3706	1118	1160	25	23	16	23	1203	199	4	.165	209	734	45	38	1.7	.954

Jim Hardin

HARDIN, JAMES WARREN
B. Aug. 6, 1943, Morris Chapel, Tenn.   BR TR 6'   175 lbs.

Year	Team	W	L	PCT	ERA	G	GS	CG	IP	H	BB	SO	ShO	W	L	SV	AB	H	HR	BA	PO	A	E	DP	TC/G	FA
1967	BAL A	8	3	.727	2.27	19	14	5	111	85	27	64	2	0	0	0	37	5	0	.135	13	9	0	1	1.2	1.000
1968		18	13	.581	2.51	35	35	16	244	188	70	160	2	0	0	0	82	7	0	.085	19	32	1	2	1.5	.981
1969		6	7	.462	3.60	30	20	3	137.2	128	43	64	1	1	1	1	45	7	2	.156	12	16	2	1	1.0	.933
1970		6	5	.545	3.54	36	19	3	145	150	26	78	2	3	0	1	45	3	0	.067	9	14	0	0	0.6	1.000
1971	2 teams	BAL A	(6G 0–0)		NY A	(12G 0–2)																				
"	total	0	2	.000	5.03	18	3	0	34	47	12	17	0	0	1	0	4	0	0	.000	4	4	0	0	0.4	1.000
1972	ATL N	5	2	.714	4.39	26	9	1	80	93	24	25	0	2	0	2	21	2	1	.095	3	10	0	1	0.5	1.000
6 yrs.		43	32	.573	3.18	164	100	28	751.2	691	202	408	7	6	2	4	234	24	3	.103	60	85	3	5	0.9	.980

Charlie Harding

HARDING, CHARLES HAROLD (Slim)
B. Jan. 3, 1891, Nashville, Tenn.   D. Oct. 30, 1971, Bold Springs, Tenn.   BR TR 6'2½"   172 lbs.

Year	Team	W	L	PCT	ERA	G	GS	CG	IP	H	BB	SO	ShO	W	L	SV	AB	H	HR	BA	PO	A	E	DP	TC/G	FA
1913	DET A	0	0	–	4.50	1	0	0	2	3	1	0	0	0	0	0	0	0	0	–	0	1	0	0	1.0	1.000

Alex Hardy

HARDY, DAVID ALEXANDER
B. Sept. 29, 1877, Toronto, Ont., Canada   D. Apr. 22, 1940, Toronto, Ont., Canada   TL

Year	Team	W	L	PCT	ERA	G	GS	CG	IP	H	BB	SO	ShO	W	L	SV	AB	H	HR	BA	PO	A	E	DP	TC/G	FA
1902	CHI N	2	2	.500	3.60	4	4	4	35	29	12	12	1	0	0	0	14	3	0	.214	1	6	1	0	2.0	.875
1903		2	1	.667	6.39	3	3	1	12.2	21	7	4	0	0	0	0	6	1	0	.167	0	6	0	0	2.0	1.000
2 yrs.		4	3	.571	4.34	7	7	5	47.2	50	19	16	1	0	0	0	20	4	0	.200	1	12	1	0	2.0	.929

Harry Hardy

HARDY, HARRY
B. Nov. 5, 1875, Steubenville, Ohio   D. Sept. 4, 1943, Steubenville, Ohio   BL TL 5'6"   155 lbs.

Year	Team	W	L	PCT	ERA	G	GS	CG	IP	H	BB	SO	ShO	W	L	SV	AB	H	HR	BA	PO	A	E	DP	TC/G	FA
1905	WAS A	1	1	.500	1.88	3	2	2	24	20	6	10	0	0	0	0	9	1	0	.111	0	1	0	0	0.3	1.000
1906		0	3	.000	9.00	5	3	2	20	35	12	4	0	0	0	0	6	0	0	.000	2	11	0	0	2.6	1.000
2 yrs.		1	4	.200	5.11	8	5	4	44	55	18	14	0	0	0	0	15	1	0	.067	2	12	0	0	1.8	1.000

Jack Hardy

HARDY, JOHN GRAYDON
B. Dec. 8, 1959, St. Petersburg, Fla.   BR TR 6'2"   175 lbs.

Year	Team	W	L	PCT	ERA	G	GS	CG	IP	H	BB	SO	ShO	W	L	SV	AB	H	HR	BA	PO	A	E	DP	TC/G	FA
1989	CHI A	0	0	–	6.57	5	0	0	12.1	14	5	4	0	0	0	0	0	0	0	–	3	4	0	1	1.4	1.000

Larry Hardy

HARDY, HOWARD LAWRENCE
B. Jan. 10, 1948, Goose Creek, Tex.   BR TR 5'10"   180 lbs.

Year	Team	W	L	PCT	ERA	G	GS	CG	IP	H	BB	SO	ShO	W	L	SV	AB	H	HR	BA	PO	A	E	DP	TC/G	FA
1974	SD N	9	4	.692	4.68	76	1	0	102	129	44	57	0	9	3	2	10	0	0	.000	6	22	2	2	0.4	.933
1975		0	0	–	12.00	3	0	0	3	8	2	3	0	0	0	0	0	0	0		0	0	1	0	0.3	–
1976	HOU N	0	0	–	6.95	15	0	0	22	34	10	10	0	0	0	3	2	0	0	.000	0	4	0	1	0.3	1.000
3 yrs.		9	4	.692	5.24	94	1	0	127	171	56	70	0	9	3	5	12	0	0	.000	6	26	3	3	0.4	.914

Red Hardy

HARDY, FRANCIS JOSEPH
B. Jan. 6, 1923, Marmarth, N. D.   BR TR 5'11"   175 lbs.

Year	Team	W	L	PCT	ERA	G	GS	CG	IP	H	BB	SO	ShO	W	L	SV	AB	H	HR	BA	PO	A	E	DP	TC/G	FA
1951	NY N	0	0	–	6.75	2	0	0	1.1	4	1	0	0	0	0	0	0	0	0	–	0	1	0	0	0.5	1.000

Steve Hargan

HARGAN, STEVEN LOWELL
B. Sept. 8, 1942, Fort Wayne, Ind.   BR TR 6'3"   170 lbs.

Year	Team	W	L	PCT	ERA	G	GS	CG	IP	H	BB	SO	ShO	W	L	SV	AB	H	HR	BA	PO	A	E	DP	TC/G	FA
1965	CLE A	4	3	.571	3.43	17	8	1	60.1	55	28	37	0	2	0	2	19	1	0	.053	5	12	2	0	1.1	.895
1966		13	10	.565	2.48	38	21	7	192	173	45	132	3	2	2	0	58	7	0	.121	9	35	3	0	1.2	.936
1967		14	13	.519	2.62	30	29	15	223	180	72	141	6	0	1	0	67	11	1	.164	21	37	3	6	2.0	.951
1968		8	15	.348	4.15	32	27	4	158.1	139	81	78	2	1	1	0	51	9	0	.176	14	16	3	1	1.0	.909
1969		5	14	.263	5.70	32	23	1	143.2	145	81	76	1	0	1	0	44	7	0	.159	13	26	1	4	1.3	.975
1970		11	3	.786	2.90	23	19	8	143	101	53	72	1	0	0	0	45	5	0	.111	13	24	0	3	1.6	1.000
1971		1	13	.071	6.21	37	16	1	113	138	56	52	0	0	1	1	32	2	0	.063	7	12	1	0	0.5	.950
1972		0	3	.000	5.85	12	1	0	20	23	15	10	0	0	2	0	3	0	0	.000	3	5	0	2	0.7	1.000
1974	TEX A	12	9	.571	3.95	37	27	8	187	202	48	98	2	1	0	0	0	0	0	–	16	33	5	3	1.5	.907
1975		9	10	.474	3.80	33	26	8	189.1	203	62	93	1	1	0	0	0	0	0	–	19	36	5	4	1.8	.917
1976		8	8	.500	3.63	35	24	8	124	127	38	63	1	4	4	1	0	0	0	–	6	18	2	1	0.7	.923
1977	3 teams	TOR A	(6G 1–3)		TEX A	(6G 1–0)		ATL N	(16G 0–3)																	
"	total	2	6	.250	6.52	28	10	1	78.2	107	35	39	0	2	2	0	6	0	0	.000	4	18	2	1	0.9	.917
12 yrs.		87	107	.448	3.92	354	215	56	1632.1	1593	614	891	17	13	14	4	325	42	1	.129	130	272	27	25	1.2	.937

Alan Hargesheimer

HARGESHEIMER, ALAN ROBERT
B. Nov. 21, 1956, Chicago, Ill.   BR TR 6'3"   195 lbs.

Year	Team	W	L	PCT	ERA	G	GS	CG	IP	H	BB	SO	ShO	W	L	SV	AB	H	HR	BA	PO	A	E	DP	TC/G	FA
1980	SF N	4	6	.400	4.32	15	13	0	75	82	32	40	0	0	0	0	22	4	0	.182	2	10	0	0	0.8	1.000
1981		1	2	.333	4.26	6	3	0	19	20	9	6	0	0	0	0	5	1	0	.200	2	5	0	0	1.2	1.000
1983	CHI N	0	0	–	9.00	5	0	0	4	6	2	5	0	0	0	0	0	0	0	–	0	0	0	0	0.0	–
1986	KC A	0	1	.000	6.23	5	1	0	13	18	7	4	0	0	1	0	0	0	0	–	0	1	0	0	0.2	1.000
4 yrs.		5	9	.357	4.70	31	17	0	111	126	50	55	0	0	1	0	27	5	0	.185	4	16	0	0	0.6	1.000

Mike Harkey

HARKEY, MICHAEL ANTHONY
B. Oct. 25, 1966, San Diego, Calif.   BR TR 6'5"   220 lbs.

Year	Team	W	L	PCT	ERA	G	GS	CG	IP	H	BB	SO	ShO	W	L	SV	AB	H	HR	BA	PO	A	E	DP	TC/G	FA
1988	CHI N	0	3	.000	2.60	5	5	0	34.2	33	15	18	0	0	0	0	11	1	0	.091	2	3	2	0	1.4	.714

Year	Team		W	L	PCT	ERA	G	GS	CG	IP	H	BB	SO	ShO	Relief Pitching W	L	SV	Batting AB	H	HR	BA	PO	A	E	DP	TC/G	FA

John Harkins

HARKINS, JOHN JOSEPH (Pa)
B. Apr. 12, 1859, New Brunswick, N. J. D. Nov. 18, 1940, New Brunswick, N. J.
BR TR 6'1" 205 lbs.

Year	Team		W	L	PCT	ERA	G	GS	CG	IP	H	BB	SO	ShO	W	L	SV	AB	H	HR	BA	PO	A	E	DP	TC/G	FA
1884	CLE	N	12	32	.273	3.68	46	45	42	391	399	108	192	3	0	0	0	229	47	0	.205	15	81	17	3	2.5	.850
1885	BKN	AA	14	20	.412	3.75	34	34	33	293	303	56	141	1	0	0	0	159	42	1	.264	36	63	16	0	3.4	.861
1886			15	16	.484	3.60	34	33	33	292.1	286	114	118	0	0	0	0	142	32	1	.225	24	61	8	2	2.7	.914
1887			10	14	.417	6.02	24	24	22	199	262	77	36	0	0	0	0	98	23	0	.235	10	37	5	1	2.2	.904
1888	BAL	AA	0	1	.000	6.75	1	1	1	8	12	3	2	0	0	0	0	3	0	0	.000	0	4	0	0	4.0	1.000
5 yrs.			51	83	.381	4.09	139	137	131	1183.1	1262	358	489	4	0	0	0	*				85	246	46	6	2.7	.878

Specs Harkness

HARKNESS, FREDERICK HARVEY
B. Dec. 13, 1887, Los Angeles, Calif. D. May 18, 1952, Compton, Calif.
BR TR 5'11" 180 lbs.

Year	Team		W	L	PCT	ERA	G	GS	CG	IP	H	BB	SO	ShO	W	L	SV	AB	H	HR	BA	PO	A	E	DP	TC/G	FA
1910	CLE	A	10	7	.588	3.04	26	16	6	136.1	132	55	60	1	5	0	1	50	7	0	.140	5	39	2	1	1.8	.957
1911			2	2	.500	4.30	12	6	3	52.1	62	21	25	0	0	0	0	19	6	0	.316	0	6	0	0	0.5	1.000
2 yrs.			12	9	.571	3.39	38	22	9	188.2	194	76	85	1	5	0	1	69	13	0	.188	5	45	2	1	1.4	.962

Dick Harley

HARLEY, HENRY RISK
B. Aug. 18, 1874, Springfield, Ohio D. May 16, 1961, Springfield, Ohio
BR TR

Year	Team		W	L	PCT	ERA	G	GS	CG	IP	H	BB	SO	ShO	W	L	SV	AB	H	HR	BA	PO	A	E	DP	TC/G	FA
1905	BOS	N	2	5	.286	4.64	9	4	4	66	72	19	19	1	0	2	0	22	1	0	.045	8	24	1	1	3.7	.970

Larry Harlow

HARLOW, LARRY DUANE
B. Nov. 13, 1951, Colorado Springs, Colo.
BL TL 6'2" 185 lbs.

Year	Team		W	L	PCT	ERA	G	GS	CG	IP	H	BB	SO	ShO	W	L	SV	AB	H	HR	BA	PO	A	E	DP	TC/G	FA
1978	BAL	A	0	0	–	67.50	1	0	0	.2	2	4	1	0	0	0	0	*				0	0	0	0	0.0	–

Bill Harman

HARMAN, WILLIAM BELL
B. Jan. 2, 1919, Bridgewater, Va.
BR TR 6'4" 200 lbs.

Year	Team		W	L	PCT	ERA	G	GS	CG	IP	H	BB	SO	ShO	W	L	SV	AB	H	HR	BA	PO	A	E	DP	TC/G	FA
1941	PHI	N	0	0	–	4.85	5	0	0	13	15	8	3	0	0	0	0	*				0	2	0	0	0.4	1.000

Bob Harmon

HARMON, ROBERT GREEN (Hickory Bob)
B. Oct. 15, 1887, Liberal, Mo. D. Nov. 27, 1961, Monroe, La.
BB TR 6' 187 lbs.

Year	Team		W	L	PCT	ERA	G	GS	CG	IP	H	BB	SO	ShO	W	L	SV	AB	H	HR	BA	PO	A	E	DP	TC/G	FA
1909	STL	N	6	11	.353	3.68	21	17	10	159	155	65	48	0	1	1	0	51	13	0	.255	6	45	3	1	2.6	.944
1910			13	15	.464	4.46	43	33	15	236	227	133	87	0	3	1	2	76	14	0	.184	11	74	7	4	2.1	.924
1911			23	16	.590	3.13	51	41	28	348	290	181	144	2	1	1	4	111	17	0	.153	11	98	3	4	2.2	.973
1912			18	18	.500	3.93	43	34	15	268	284	116	73	3	3	2	0	99	23	0	.232	11	87	3	3	2.3	.970
1913			8	21	.276	3.92	42	27	16	273.1	291	99	66	1	3	6	1	92	24	0	.261	22	75	3	3	2.4	.970
1914	PIT	N	13	17	.433	2.53	37	30	19	245	226	55	61	2	1	0	3	86	12	1	.140	11	59	1	1	1.9	.986
1915			16	17	.485	2.50	37	32	25	269.2	242	62	86	5	0	1	1	95	14	0	.147	9	92	4	2	2.8	.962
1916			8	11	.421	2.81	31	17	10	172.2	175	39	62	2	1	3	0	55	6	0	.109	4	64	2	2	2.3	.971
1918			2	7	.222	2.62	16	9	5	82.1	76	12	7	0	0	1	0	27	4	0	.148	3	26	0	2	1.8	1.000
9 yrs.			107	133	.446	3.33	321	240	143	2054	1966	762	634	15	13	16	11	692	127	1	.184	88	620	26	22	2.3	.965

Pete Harnisch

HARNISCH, PETER THOMAS
B. Sept. 23, 1966, Commack, N. Y.
BB TR 6'1" 195 lbs.

Year	Team		W	L	PCT	ERA	G	GS	CG	IP	H	BB	SO	ShO	W	L	SV	AB	H	HR	BA	PO	A	E	DP	TC/G	FA
1988	BAL	A	0	2	.000	5.54	2	2	0	13	13	9	10	0	0	0	0	0	0	0	–	2	2	0	0	2.0	1.000
1989			5	9	.357	4.62	18	17	2	103.1	97	64	70	0	0	0	0	0	0	0	–	7	9	0	2	0.9	1.000
2 yrs.			5	11	.313	4.72	20	19	2	116.1	110	73	80	0	0	0	0	0	0	0	–	9	11	0	2	1.0	1.000

Bill Harper

HARPER, WILLIAM HOMER (Blue Sleeve)
B. June 14, 1889, Bertrand, Mo. D. June 17, 1951, Somerville, Tenn.
BB TR 6'1" 180 lbs.

Year	Team		W	L	PCT	ERA	G	GS	CG	IP	H	BB	SO	ShO	W	L	SV	AB	H	HR	BA	PO	A	E	DP	TC/G	FA
1911	STL	A	0	0	–	6.75	2	0	0	9	8	4	6	0	0	0	0	3	0	0	.000	0	2	0	0	1.0	1.000

George Harper

HARPER, GEORGE B.
B. Aug. 17, 1866, Milwaukee, Wis. D. Dec. 11, 1931, Stockton, Calif.

Year	Team		W	L	PCT	ERA	G	GS	CG	IP	H	BB	SO	ShO	W	L	SV	AB	H	HR	BA	PO	A	E	DP	TC/G	FA
1894	PHI	N	6	6	.500	5.32	12	9	7	86.1	128	49	24	0	1	2	0	40	6	0	.150	4	12	1	1	1.4	.941
1896	BKN	N	4	8	.333	5.55	16	11	7	86	106	39	22	0	1	1	0	37	6	0	.162	5	24	1	0	1.9	.967
2 yrs.			10	14	.417	5.43	28	20	14	172.1	234	88	46	0	2	3	0	77	12	0	.156	9	36	2	1	1.7	.957

Harry Harper

HARPER, HARRY CLAYTON
B. Apr. 24, 1895, Hackensack, N. J. D. Apr. 23, 1963, Layton, N. J.
BL TL 6'2" 165 lbs.

Year	Team		W	L	PCT	ERA	G	GS	CG	IP	H	BB	SO	ShO	W	L	SV	AB	H	HR	BA	PO	A	E	DP	TC/G	FA
1913	WAS	A	0	0	–	3.55	4	0	0	12.2	10	5	9	0	0	0	0	4	1	0	.250	1	4	2	1	1.8	.714
1914			2	1	.667	3.47	23	3	1	57	45	35	50	0	1	0	2	12	3	0	.250	0	11	3	0	0.6	.786
1915			4	4	.500	1.77	19	10	5	86.1	66	40	54	0	1	0	2	25	0	0	.000	0	15	2	0	0.9	.882
1916			14	10	.583	2.45	36	34	12	249.2	209	101	149	2	0	0	0	87	18	0	.207	8	46	4	4	1.6	.931
1917			11	12	.478	3.01	31	31	10	179.1	145	106	99	4	0	0	0	60	7	0	.117	6	37	9	5	1.7	.827
1918			11	10	.524	2.18	35	32	14	244	182	104	78	3	0	0	0	82	11	0	.134	9	45	2	2	1.6	.947
1919			6	21	.222	3.72	35	30	8	208	220	97	87	0	0	0	0	65	11	0	.169	10	47	3	2	1.7	.950
1920	BOS	A	5	14	.263	3.04	27	22	11	162.2	163	66	71	1	0	0	0	50	6	0	.120	1	31	3	1	1.3	.914
1921	NY	A	4	3	.571	3.76	8	7	4	52.2	52	25	22	0	0	0	0	16	2	0	.125	5	4	0	0	1.1	1.000
1923	BKN	N	0	1	.000	14.73	1	1	0	3.2	8	3	4	0	0	0	0	1	0	0	.000	0	0	0	0	0.0	–
10 yrs.			57	76	.429	2.87	219	170	65	1256	1100	582	623	12	1	0	5	402	59	0	.147	40	240	29	14	1.4	.906

WORLD SERIES

Year	Team		W	L	PCT	ERA	G	GS	CG	IP	H	BB	SO	ShO	W	L	SV	AB	H	HR	BA	PO	A	E	DP	TC/G	FA
1921	NY	A	0	0	–	20.25	1	1	0	1.1	3	2	1	0	0	0	0	0	0	0	–	0	0	0	0	0.0	–

Jack Harper

HARPER, CHARLES WILLIAM
B. Apr. 2, 1878, Galloway, Pa. D. Sept. 30, 1950, Jamestown, N. Y.
BR TR 6' 178 lbs.

Year	Team		W	L	PCT	ERA	G	GS	CG	IP	H	BB	SO	ShO	W	L	SV	AB	H	HR	BA	PO	A	E	DP	TC/G	FA
1899	CLE	N	1	4	.200	3.89	5	5	5	37	44	12	14	0	0	0	0	11	2	0	.182	1	7	0	0	1.6	1.000
1900	STL	N	0	1	.000	12.00	1	1	0	3	4	2	0	0	0	0	0	1	0	0	.000	0	1	0	0	1.0	1.000
1901			23	13	.639	3.62	39	37	28	308.2	294	99	128	1	1	0	0	116	20	1	.172	13	82	4	3	2.5	.960
1902	STL	A	15	11	.577	4.13	29	26	20	222.1	224	81	74	2	1	1	0	83	17	0	.205	8	70	6	3	2.9	.929
1903	CIN	N	6	8	.429	4.33	17	15	13	135	143	70	45	0	2	0	0	56	14	0	.250	7	43	4	2	3.2	.926

Jack Harper *continued*

Year	Team	W	L	PCT	ERA	G	GS	CG	IP	H	BB	SO	ShO	Relief Pitching W	L	SV	Batting AB	H	HR	BA	PO	A	E	DP	TC/G	FA
1904		23	9	.719	2.37	35	35	31	284.2	262	85	125	6	0	0	0	113	18	0	.159	12	58	5	1	2.1	.933
1905		10	13	.435	3.87	26	23	15	179	189	69	70	1	1	0	0	60	10	0	.167	6	49	4	1	2.3	.932
1906	2 teams	CIN N	(5G 1-4)			CHI N	(1G 0-0)																			
"	total	1	4	.200	4.06	6	6	3	37.2	38	20	10	0	0	0	0	11	3	0	.273	2	7	1	0	1.7	.900
8 yrs.		79	63	.556	3.58	158	148	115	1207.1	1198	438	466	10	3	3	0	451	84	1	.186	49	317	24	10	2.5	.938

Jack Harper

HARPER, JOHN WESLEY
B. Aug. 5, 1893, Hendricks, W. Va. D. June 18, 1927, Halstead, Kans. BR TR 5'11" 180 lbs.

Year	Team	W	L	PCT	ERA	G	GS	CG	IP	H	BB	SO	ShO	W	L	SV	AB	H	HR	BA	PO	A	E	DP	TC/G	FA
1915	PHI A	0	0	-	3.12	3	0	0	8.2	5	1	3	0	0	0	0	2	0	0	.000	0	4	0	0	1.3	1.000

Ray Harrell

HARRELL, RAYMOND JAMES (Cowboy)
B. Feb. 16, 1912, Petrolia, Tex. D. Jan. 28, 1984, Alexandria, La. BR TR 6'1" 185 lbs.

Year	Team	W	L	PCT	ERA	G	GS	CG	IP	H	BB	SO	ShO	W	L	SV	AB	H	HR	BA	PO	A	E	DP	TC/G	FA
1935	STL N	1	1	.500	6.67	11	1	0	29.2	39	11	13	0	1	1	0	4	0	0	.000	2	5	0	0	0.6	1.000
1937		3	7	.300	5.87	35	15	1	96.2	99	59	41	1	1	0	1	22	1	0	.045	3	17	3	1	0.7	.870
1938		2	3	.400	4.86	32	3	1	63	78	29	32	0	1	3	2	10	0	0	.000	0	14	0	2	0.4	1.000
1939	2 teams	CHI N	(4G 0-2)			PHI N	(22G 3-7)																			
"	total	3	9	.250	5.87	26	12	4	112	127	62	40	0	1	0	0	31	3	0	.097	4	11	3	0	0.7	.833
1940	PIT N	0	0	-	8.10	3	0	0	3.1	5	2	3	0	0	0	0	0	0	0	-	0	0	0	0	0.0	-
1945	NY N	0	0	-	4.97	12	0	0	25.1	34	14	7	0	0	0	0	5	1	0	.200	2	6	0	1	0.7	1.000
6 yrs.		9	20	.310	5.70	119	31	6	330	382	177	136	1	4	4	3	72	5	0	.069	11	53	6	4	0.6	.914

Slim Harrell

HARRELL, OSCAR MARTIN
B. July 31, 1890, Grandview, Tex. D. Apr. 30, 1971, Hillsboro, Tex. BR TR 6'3" 180 lbs.

Year	Team	W	L	PCT	ERA	G	GS	CG	IP	H	BB	SO	ShO	W	L	SV	AB	H	HR	BA	PO	A	E	DP	TC/G	FA
1912	PHI A	0	0	-	0.00	1	0	0	3	4	0	1	0	0	0	0	1	0	0	.000	0	0	0	0	0.0	-

Bill Harrelson

HARRELSON, WILLIAM CHARLES
B. Nov. 17, 1945, Tahlequah, Okla. BB TR 6'5" 215 lbs:

Year	Team	W	L	PCT	ERA	G	GS	CG	IP	H	BB	SO	ShO	W	L	SV	AB	H	HR	BA	PO	A	E	DP	TC/G	FA
1968	CAL A	1	6	.143	5.08	10	5	1	33.2	28	26	22	0	0	2	0	10	1	0	.100	1	3	0	1	0.4	1.000

Andy Harrington

HARRINGTON, ANDREW FRANCIS
B. Nov. 13, 1888, Wakefield, Mass. D. Nov. 12, 1938, Malden, Mass. BR TR 6' 193 lbs.

Year	Team	W	L	PCT	ERA	G	GS	CG	IP	H	BB	SO	ShO	W	L	SV	AB	H	HR	BA	PO	A	E	DP	TC/G	FA
1913	CIN N	0	0	-	9.00	1	0	0	4	6	1	0	0	0	0	0	2	1	0	.500	1	0	0	0	1.0	1.000

Bill Harrington

HARRINGTON, WILLIAM WOMBLE
B. Oct. 3, 1927, Sanford, N. C. BR TR 5'11" 160 lbs.

Year	Team	W	L	PCT	ERA	G	GS	CG	IP	H	BB	SO	ShO	W	L	SV	AB	H	HR	BA	PO	A	E	DP	TC/G	FA
1953	PHI A	0	0	-	13.50	1	0	0	2	5	0	0	0	0	0	0	0	0	0	-	0	0	0	0	0.0	-
1955	KC A	3	3	.500	4.11	34	1	0	76.2	69	41	26	0	3	2	2	17	2	0	.118	4	11	0	0	0.4	1.000
1956		2	2	.500	6.45	23	1	0	37.2	40	26	14	0	2	2	1	7	0	0	.000	3	5	0	1	0.3	1.000
3 yrs.		5	5	.500	5.03	58	2	0	116.1	114	67	40	0	5	4	3	24	2	0	.083	7	16	0	1	0.4	1.000

Ben Harris

HARRIS, BEN FRANKLIN
B. Dec. 17, 1889, Donelson, Tenn. D. Apr. 1, 1927, St. Louis, Mo. BR TR 6' 220 lbs.

Year	Team	W	L	PCT	ERA	G	GS	CG	IP	H	BB	SO	ShO	W	L	SV	AB	H	HR	BA	PO	A	E	DP	TC/G	FA
1914	KC F	7	8	.467	4.09	31	14	5	154	179	41	40	0	2	1	1	45	9	0	.200	12	51	1	0	2.1	.984
1915		0	0	-	0.00	1	0	0	2	1	0	0	0	0	0	0	0	0	0	-	0	2	0	0	2.0	1.000
2 yrs.		7	8	.467	4.04	32	14	5	156	180	41	40	0	2	1	1	45	9	0	.200	12	53	1	0	2.1	.985

Bill Harris

HARRIS, WILLIAM MILTON
B. June 23, 1900, Wylie, Tex. D. Aug. 21, 1965, Indian Trail, N. C. BR TR 6'1½" 180 lbs.

Year	Team	W	L	PCT	ERA	G	GS	CG	IP	H	BB	SO	ShO	W	L	SV	AB	H	HR	BA	PO	A	E	DP	TC/G	FA
1923	CIN N	3	2	.600	5.17	22	3	1	69.2	79	18	18	0	2	0	0	17	6	0	.353	4	17	2	0	1.0	.913
1924		0	0	-	9.00	3	0	0	7	10	2	5	0	0	0	0	1	1	0	1.000	0	3	1	0	1.3	.750
1931	PIT N	2	2	.500	0.87	4	4	3	31	21	9	10	1	0	0	0	11	1	0	.091	2	7	0	0	2.3	1.000
1932		10	9	.526	3.64	37	17	4	168	178	38	63	0	7	1	2	55	10	0	.182	2	30	1	0	0.9	.970
1933		4	4	.500	3.22	31	0	0	58.2	68	14	19	0	4	4	5	9	0	0	.000	3	9	0	1	0.4	1.000
1934		0	0	-	6.63	11	2	0	19	28	7	9	0	0	0	0	2	1	0	.500	1	5	0	0	0.5	1.000
1938	BOS A	5	5	.500	4.03	13	11	5	80.1	83	21	26	1	0	0	1	28	6	0	.214	2	14	0	2	1.2	1.000
7 yrs.		24	22	.522	3.92	121	37	13	433.2	467	109	149	2	13	5	8	123	25	0	.203	14	85	4	3	0.9	.961

Bill Harris

HARRIS, WILLIAM THOMAS (Billy)
B. Dec. 3, 1931, Duguayville, N. B., Canada BL TR 5'8" 187 lbs.

Year	Team	W	L	PCT	ERA	G	GS	CG	IP	H	BB	SO	ShO	W	L	SV	AB	H	HR	BA	PO	A	E	DP	TC/G	FA
1957	BKN N	0	1	.000	3.86	1	1	0	7	9	1	3	0	0	0	0	2	1	0	.500	0	2	0	0	2.0	1.000
1959	LA N	0	0	-	0.00	1	0	0	1.2	0	3	0	0	0	0	0	0	0	0	-	0	1	0	0	1.0	1.000
2 yrs.		0	1	.000	3.12	2	1	0	8.2	9	4	3	0	0	0	0	2	1	0	.500	0	3	0	0	1.5	1.000

Bob Harris

HARRIS, ROBERT ARTHUR
B. May 1, 1916, Gillette, Wyo. BR TR 6' 185 lbs.

Year	Team	W	L	PCT	ERA	G	GS	CG	IP	H	BB	SO	ShO	W	L	SV	AB	H	HR	BA	PO	A	E	DP	TC/G	FA
1938	DET A	1	0	1.000	7.20	3	1	1	10	14	4	7	0	0	0	0	3	1	0	.333	2	3	0	0	1.7	1.000
1939	2 teams	DET A	(5G 1-2)			STL A	(28G 3-12)																			
"	total	4	13	.235	5.50	33	17	6	144	180	79	57	0	2	0	0	42	9	0	.214	8	35	2	5	1.4	.956
1940	STL A	11	15	.423	4.93	35	28	8	193.2	225	85	49	1	2	1	1	60	15	0	.250	10	36	1	1	1.3	.979
1941		12	14	.462	5.21	34	29	9	186.2	237	85	57	2	1	1	1	61	7	0	.115	10	27	1	2	1.1	.974
1942	2 teams	STL A	(6G 1-5)			PHI A	(16G 1-5)																			
"	total	2	10	.167	3.71	22	14	2	111.2	114	41	35	1	0	2	0	36	7	0	.194	5	31	0	0	1.6	1.000
5 yrs.		30	52	.366	4.96	127	89	26	646	770	294	205	4	5	5	2	202	39	0	.193	35	132	4	8	1.3	.977

Buddy Harris

HARRIS, WALTER FRANCIS, JR.
B. Dec. 5, 1948, Philadelphia, Pa. BR TR 6'7" 245 lbs.

Year	Team	W	L	PCT	ERA	G	GS	CG	IP	H	BB	SO	ShO	W	L	SV	AB	H	HR	BA	PO	A	E	DP	TC/G	FA
1970	HOU N	0	0	-	6.00	2	0	0	6	6	0	2	0	0	0	0	1	0	0	.000	1	0	0	0	0.5	1.000

Year	Team		W	L	PCT	ERA	G	GS	CG	IP	H	BB	SO	ShO	Relief Pitching W	L	SV	Batting AB	H	HR	BA	PO	A	E	DP	TC/G	FA

Chuck Hartenstein

HARTENSTEIN, CHARLES OSCAR (Twiggy)
B. May 26, 1942, Seguin, Tex.   BR TR 5'11" 165 lbs.

Year	Team		W	L	PCT	ERA	G	GS	CG	IP	H	BB	SO	ShO	W	L	SV	AB	H	HR	BA	PO	A	E	DP	TC/G	FA
1965	CHI	N	0	0	–	0.00	0	0	0		0	0	0	0	0	0	0	0	0	0	–	0	0	0	0	0.0	
1966			0	0	–	1.93	5	0	0	9.1	8	3	4	0	0	0	0	0	0	0	–	2	2	0	0	0.8	1.000
1967			9	5	.643	3.08	45	0	0	73	74	17	20	0	9	5	10	16	1	0	.063	5	14	1	0	0.4	.950
1968			2	4	.333	4.54	28	0	0	35.2	41	11	17	0	2	4	1	2	0	0	.000	4	5	2	1	0.4	.818
1969	PIT	N	5	4	.556	3.94	56	0	0	96	84	27	44	0	5	4	10	14	1	0	.071	8	22	0	1	0.5	1.000
1970	3 teams		PIT N (17G 1–1)			STL N (6G 0–0)				BOS A (17G 0–3)																	
"	total		1	4	.200	6.75	40	0	0	56	70	25	35	0	1	4	2	5	0	0	.000	2	11	1	1	0.4	.929
1977	TOR	A	0	2	.000	6.67	13	0	0	27	40	6	15	0	0	2	0	0	0	0	–	1	4	0	0	0.4	1.000
7 yrs.			17	19	.472	4.52	187	0	0	297	317	89	135	0	17	19	23	37	2	0	.054	22	58	4	3	0.4	.952

Frank Harter

HARTER, FRANKLIN PIERCE (Chief)
B. Sept. 19, 1886, Keyesport, Ill.   D. Apr. 14, 1959, Breese, Ill.   BR TR 5'11" 165 lbs.

Year	Team		W	L	PCT	ERA	G	GS	CG	IP	H	BB	SO	ShO	W	L	SV	AB	H	HR	BA	PO	A	E	DP	TC/G	FA
1912	CIN	N	1	2	.333	3.07	6	3	1	29.1	25	11	12	0	0	0	0	11	1	0	.091	0	3	0	0	0.5	1.000
1913			1	1	.500	3.86	17	2	0	46.2	47	19	10	0	1	0	0	14	2	0	.143	0	10	1	0	0.6	.909
1914	IND	F	1	2	.333	4.01	6	1	1	24.2	33	7	8	0	0	2	0	8	0	0	.000	1	6	0	0	1.2	1.000
3 yrs.			3	5	.375	3.67	29	6	2	100.2	105	37	30	0	1	2	0	33	3	0	.091	1	19	1	0	0.7	.952

Mike Hartley

HARTLEY, MICHAEL EDWARD
B. Aug. 31, 1961, Hawthorne, Calif.   BR TR 6'1" 192 lbs.

Year	Team		W	L	PCT	ERA	G	GS	CG	IP	H	BB	SO	ShO	W	L	SV	AB	H	HR	BA	PO	A	E	DP	TC/G	FA
1989	LA	N	0	1	.000	1.50	5	0	0	6	2	0	4	0	0	1	0	1	0	0	.000	2	0	0	0	0.4	1.000

Bob Hartman

HARTMAN, ROBERT LOUIS
B. Aug. 28, 1937, Kenosha, Wis.   BR TL 5'11" 185 lbs.

Year	Team		W	L	PCT	ERA	G	GS	CG	IP	H	BB	SO	ShO	W	L	SV	AB	H	HR	BA	PO	A	E	DP	TC/G	FA
1959	MIL	N	0	0	–	27.00	3	0	0	1.2	6	2	1	0	0	0	0	0	0	0	–	0	0	0	0	0.0	–
1962	CLE	A	0	1	.000	3.12	8	2	0	17.1	14	8	11	0	0	0	0	7	0	0	.000	1	1	0	0	0.3	1.000
2 yrs.			0	1	.000	5.21	11	2	0	19	20	10	12	0	0	0	0	7	0	0	.000	1	1	0	0	0.2	1.000

Charlie Hartman

HARTMAN, CHARLES OTTO
B. Aug. 10, 1888, Los Angeles, Calif.   D. Oct. 22, 1960, Los Angeles, Calif.

Year	Team		W	L	PCT	ERA	G	GS	CG	IP	H	BB	SO	ShO	W	L	SV	AB	H	HR	BA	PO	A	E	DP	TC/G	FA
1908	BOS	A	0	0	–	4.50	1	0	0	2	1	2	1	0	0	0	0	0	0	0	–	1	2	0	0	3.0	1.000

Ray Hartranft

HARTRANFT, RAYMOND JOSEPH
B. Sept. 19, 1890, Quakertown, Pa.   D. Feb. 10, 1955, Spring City, Pa.   BL TL 6'1" 195 lbs.

Year	Team		W	L	PCT	ERA	G	GS	CG	IP	H	BB	SO	ShO	W	L	SV	AB	H	HR	BA	PO	A	E	DP	TC/G	FA
1913	PHI	N	0	0	–	9.00	1	0	0	1	3	1	1	0	0	0	0	0	0	0	–	0	0	0	0	0.0	–

Clint Hartung

HARTUNG, CLINTON CLARENCE (Floppy, The Hondo Hurricane)
B. Aug. 10, 1922, Hondo, Tex.   BR TR 6'5" 210 lbs.

Year	Team		W	L	PCT	ERA	G	GS	CG	IP	H	BB	SO	ShO	W	L	SV	AB	H	HR	BA	PO	A	E	DP	TC/G	FA
1947	NY	N	9	7	.563	4.57	23	20	8	138	140	69	54	1	0	0	0	94	29	4	.309	5	22	0	0	1.2	1.000
1948			8	8	.500	4.75	36	19	6	153.1	146	72	42	2	2	2	1	56	10	0	.179	6	29	0	1	1.0	1.000
1949			9	11	.450	5.00	33	25	8	154.2	156	86	48	0	1	0	0	63	12	4	.190	9	36	2	1	1.4	.957
1950			3	3	.500	6.61	20	8	1	65.1	87	44	23	0	2	0	0	43	13	3	.302	8	23	2	0	1.7	.939
1951			0	0	–	0.00	0	0	0	0	0	0	0	0	0	0	0	44	9	0	.205	0	0	0	0	0.0	–
1952			0	0	–	0.00	0	0	0	0	0	0	0	0	0	0	0	78	17	3	.218	0	0	0	0	0.0	–
6 yrs.			29	29	.500	5.02	112	72	23	511.1	529	271	167	3	5	2	1	*				28	110	4	2	1.3	.972

Paul Hartzell

HARTZELL, PAUL FRANKLIN
B. Nov. 2, 1953, Bloomsburg, Pa.   BR TR 6'5" 200 lbs.

Year	Team		W	L	PCT	ERA	G	GS	CG	IP	H	BB	SO	ShO	W	L	SV	AB	H	HR	BA	PO	A	E	DP	TC/G	FA
1976	CAL	A	7	4	.636	2.77	37	15	7	166	166	43	51	2	0	2	2	0	0	0	–	13	32	3	1	1.3	.938
1977			8	12	.400	3.57	41	23	6	189.1	200	38	79	0	2	3	4	0	0	0	–	23	30	5	1	1.4	.914
1978			6	10	.375	3.44	54	12	5	157	168	41	55	0	1	5	6	0	0	0	–	15	27	0	2	0.8	1.000
1979	MIN	A	6	10	.375	5.36	28	26	4	163	193	44	44	0	0	0	0	0	0	0	–	14	30	3	1	1.7	.936
1980	BAL	A	0	2	.000	6.50	6	0	0	18	22	9	5	0	0	2	0	0	0	0	–	0	1	0	0	0.2	1.000
1984	MIL	A	0	1	.000	7.84	4	1	0	10.1	17	6	3	0	0	0	0	0	0	0	–	0	2	0	0	0.5	1.000
6 yrs.			27	39	.409	3.90	170	77	22	703.2	766	181	237	2	3	12	12	0	0	0	–	65	122	11	5	1.2	.944

Bryan Harvey

HARVEY, BRYAN STANLEY
B. June 2, 1963, Chattanooga, Tenn.   BR TR 6'3" 235 lbs.

Year	Team		W	L	PCT	ERA	G	GS	CG	IP	H	BB	SO	ShO	W	L	SV	AB	H	HR	BA	PO	A	E	DP	TC/G	FA
1987	CAL	A	0	0	–	0.00	3	0	0	5	6	2	3	0	0	0	0	0	0	0	–	0	0	0	0	0.0	.857
1988			7	5	.583	2.13	50	0	0	76	59	20	67	0	7	5	17	0	0	0	–	4	2	1	0	0.1	.857
1989			3	3	.500	3.44	51	0	0	55	36	41	78	0	3	3	25	0	0	0	–	1	7	1	0	0.2	.889
3 yrs.			10	8	.556	2.58	104	0	0	136	101	63	148	0	10	8	42	0	0	0	–	5	9	2	0	0.2	.875

Ervin Harvey

HARVEY, ERVIN KING (Zaza)
B. Jan. 5, 1879, Saratoga, Calif.   D. June 3, 1954, Santa Monica, Calif.   BL TL

Year	Team		W	L	PCT	ERA	G	GS	CG	IP	H	BB	SO	ShO	W	L	SV	AB	H	HR	BA	PO	A	E	DP	TC/G	FA
1900	CHI	N	0	0	–	0.00	1	0	0	4	3	1	0	0	0	0	0	3	0	0	.000	1	0	0	0	1.0	1.000
1901	CHI	A	3	6	.333	3.62	16	9	5	92	91	34	27	0	2	0	1	210	70	1	.333	5	35	3	2	2.7	.930
2 yrs.			3	6	.333	3.47	17	9	5	96	94	35	27	0	2	0	1	*				6	35	3	2	2.6	.932

Herb Hash

HASH, HERBERT HOWARD
B. Feb. 13, 1911, Woolwine, Va.   BR TR 6'1" 180 lbs.

Year	Team		W	L	PCT	ERA	G	GS	CG	IP	H	BB	SO	ShO	W	L	SV	AB	H	HR	BA	PO	A	E	DP	TC/G	FA
1940	BOS	A	7	7	.500	4.95	34	12	3	120	123	84	36	1	4	3	3	40	7	0	.175	12	26	2	0	1.2	.950
1941			1	0	1.000	5.40	4	0	0	8.1	7	7	3	0	1	0	1	2	0	0	.000	1	2	0	0	0.8	1.000
2 yrs.			8	7	.533	4.98	38	12	3	128.1	130	91	39	1	5	3	4	42	7	0	.167	13	28	2	0	1.1	.953

Andy Hassler

HASSLER, ANDREW EARL
B. Oct. 18, 1951, Texas City, Tex.   BL TL 6'5" 220 lbs.

Year	Team		W	L	PCT	ERA	G	GS	CG	IP	H	BB	SO	ShO	W	L	SV	AB	H	HR	BA	PO	A	E	DP	TC/G	FA
1971	CAL	A	0	3	.000	3.79	6	4	0	19	25	15	13	0	0	0	0	5	0	0	.000	1	3	0	2	0.7	1.000
1973			0	4	.000	3.69	7	4	1	31.2	33	19	19	0	0	0	0	0	0	0	–	1	4	0	0	0.7	1.000

Year	Team	W	L	PCT	ERA	G	GS	CG	IP	H	BB	SO	ShO	Relief Pitching W	L	SV	Batting AB	H	HR	BA	PO	A	E	DP	TC/G	FA

Andy Hassler *continued*

Year	Team		W	L	PCT	ERA	G	GS	CG	IP	H	BB	SO	ShO	W	L	SV	AB	H	HR	BA	PO	A	E	DP	TC/G	FA
1974			7	11	.389	2.61	23	22	10	162	132	79	76	2	0	0	1	0	0	0	–	1	29	1	2	1.3	.968
1975			3	12	.200	5.94	30	18	6	133.1	158	53	82	1	0	0	0	0	0	0	–	6	23	1	1	1.0	.967
1976	2 teams	CAL A (14G 0–6)						KC A	(19G 5–6)																		
"	total		5	12	.294	3.61	33	18	4	147	139	56	61	1	0	3	0	0	0	0	–	4	27	1	3	1.0	.969
1977	KC A		9	6	.600	4.21	29	27	3	156	166	75	83	1	0	0	0	0	0	0	–	6	28	3	2	1.3	.919
1978	2 teams	KC A (11G 1–4)						BOS A	(13G 2–1)																		
"	total		3	5	.375	3.89	24	11	1	88	114	37	49	0	2	1	1	0	0	0	–	3	11	2	1	0.7	.875
1979	2 teams	BOS A (8G 1–2)						NY N	(29G 4–5)																		
"	total		5	7	.417	4.55	37	8	1	95	97	49	60	0	2	3	4	22	2	0	.000	3	16	1	0	0.5	.950
1980	2 teams	PIT N (6G 0–0)						CAL A	(41G 5–1)																		
"	total		5	1	.833	2.65	47	0	0	95	76	41	79	0	5	1	10	2	0	0	.000	5	12	0	0	0.4	1.000
1981	CAL A		4	3	.571	3.20	42	0	0	76	72	33	44	0	4	3	5	0	0	0	–	4	14	0	1	0.4	1.000
1982			2	1	.667	2.78	54	0	0	71.1	58	40	38	0	2	1	4	0	0	0	–	2	19	1	2	0.4	.955
1983			0	5	.000	5.45	42	0	0	36.1	42	17	20	0	0	5	4	0	0	0	–	3	8	1	2	0.3	.917
1984	STL N		1	0	1.000	11.57	3	0	0	2.1	4	2	1	0	1	0	0	0	0	0	–	0	1	0	0	0.3	1.000
1985			0	1	.000	1.80	10	0	0	10	9	4	5	0	0	1	0	0	0	0	–	2	0	1	0	0.3	.667
14 yrs.			44	71	.383	3.83	387	112	26	1123	1125	520	630	5	16	18	29	29	0	0	.000	41	195	12	16	0.6	.952

LEAGUE CHAMPIONSHIP SERIES

Year	Team		W	L	PCT	ERA	G	GS	CG	IP	H	BB	SO	ShO	W	L	SV	AB	H	HR	BA	PO	A	E	DP	TC/G	FA
1976	KC A		0	1	.000	6.14	2	1	0	7.1	8	6	4	0	1	1	1	0	0	0	–	0	0	0	0	0.0	–
1977			0	1	.000	4.76	1	1	0	5.2	5	0	3	0	0	0	0	0	0	0	–	1	0	0	0	1.0	1.000
1982	CAL A		0	0	–	0.00	2	0	0	2.2	0	0	2	0	0	0	0	0	0	0	–	0	0	0	0	0.0	–
3 yrs.			0	2	.000	4.60	5	2	0	15.2	13	6	9	0	0	0	0	0	0	0	–	1	0	0	0	0.2	1.000

Charlie Hastings

HASTINGS, CHARLES MORTON
B. Nov. 11, 1870, Ironton, Ohio   D. Aug. 3, 1934, Parkersburg, W. Va.   5'11"   179 lbs.

Year	Team	W	L	PCT	ERA	G	GS	CG	IP	H	BB	SO	ShO	W	L	SV	AB	H	HR	BA	PO	A	E	DP	TC/G	FA
1893	CLE N	4	5	.444	4.70	15	9	6	92	128	33	14	0	1	1	1	39	7	0	.179	4	14	2	0	1.3	.900
1896	PIT N	5	10	.333	5.88	17	13	9	104	126	44	19	0	1	1	1	37	8	0	.216	8	29	5	3	2.5	.881
1897		5	4	.556	4.58	16	10	9	118	138	47	42	0	0	1	0	43	10	1	.233	10	17	0	1	1.7	1.000
1898		4	10	.286	3.41	19	13	12	137.1	142	52	40	0	0	2	0	43	10	0	.233	6	37	3	2	2.4	.935
4 yrs.		18	29	.383	4.55	67	45	36	451.1	534	176	115	0	2	5	2	162	35	1	.216	28	97	10	6	2.0	.926

Bob Hasty

HASTY, ROBERT KELLER
B. May 3, 1896, Canton, Ga.   D. May 28, 1972, Dallas, Ga.   BR TR 6'3"   210 lbs.

Year	Team	W	L	PCT	ERA	G	GS	CG	IP	H	BB	SO	ShO	W	L	SV	AB	H	HR	BA	PO	A	E	DP	TC/G	FA
1919	PHI A	0	2	.000	5.25	2	2	1	12	15	4	5	0	0	0	0	3	1	0	.333	1	0	1	0	1.0	.500
1920		1	3	.250	5.02	19	4	1	71.2	91	28	12	0	0	0	0	24	6	0	.250	3	27	1	0	1.6	.968
1921		5	16	.238	4.87	35	22	9	179.1	238	40	46	0	1	0	0	68	20	0	.294	3	53	5	2	1.7	.918
1922		9	14	.391	4.25	28	26	14	192.2	225	41	33	1	0	0	0	75	15	1	.200	8	41	7	1	2.0	.875
1923		13	15	.464	4.44	44	36	10	243.1	274	72	56	1	2	1	1	88	17	0	.193	9	61	6	4	1.7	.921
1924		1	3	.250	5.64	18	4	0	52.2	57	30	15	0	1	0	0	13	1	0	.077	5	19	2	3	1.4	.923
6 yrs.		29	53	.354	4.65	146	94	35	751.2	900	215	167	2	4	1	1	271	60	1	.221	29	201	22	10	1.7	.913

Mickey Hatcher

HATCHER, MICHAEL VAUGHN, JR.
B. Mar. 15, 1955, Cleveland, Ohio   BR TR 6'2"   200 lbs.

Year	Team	W	L	PCT	ERA	G	GS	CG	IP	H	BB	SO	ShO	W	L	SV	AB	H	HR	BA	PO	A	E	DP	TC/G	FA
1989	LA N	0	0	–	9.00	1	0	0	1	0	3	0	0	0	0	0	*				0	0	0	0	0.0	–

Gil Hatfield

HATFIELD, GILBERT
Brother of John Hatfield.
B. Jan. 27, 1855, Hoboken, N. J.   D. May 27, 1921, Hoboken, N. J.   TR 5'9"   168 lbs.

Year	Team	W	L	PCT	ERA	G	GS	CG	IP	H	BB	SO	ShO	W	L	SV	AB	H	HR	BA	PO	A	E	DP	TC/G	FA
1889	NY N	2	4	.333	3.98	6	5	5	52	53	25	28	0	1	0	0	125	23	1	.184	3	11	1	0	2.5	.933
1890	NY P	1	1	.500	3.52	3	0	0	7.2	8	4	3	0	1	1	1	287	80	1	.279	0	0	0	0	0.0	–
1891	WAS AA	0	0	–	11.00	4	0	0	18	29	14	3	0	0	0	0	500	128	1	.256	1	4	1	0	1.5	.833
3 yrs.		3	5	.375	5.56	13	5	5	77.2	90	43	34	0	2	1	1	*				4	15	2	0	1.6	.905

Ray Hathaway

HATHAWAY, RAY WILSON
B. Oct. 13, 1916, Greenville, Ohio   BR TR 6'   165 lbs.

Year	Team	W	L	PCT	ERA	G	GS	CG	IP	H	BB	SO	ShO	W	L	SV	AB	H	HR	BA	PO	A	E	DP	TC/G	FA
1945	BKN N	0	1	.000	4.00	4	1	0	9	11	6	3	0	0	0	0	2	0	0	.000	3	3	1	0	1.8	.857

Joe Hatten

HATTEN, JOSEPH HILARIAN
B. Nov. 7, 1916, Bancroft, Iowa   D. Dec. 16, 1988, Redding, Calif.   BR TL 6'   176 lbs.

Year	Team		W	L	PCT	ERA	G	GS	CG	IP	H	BB	SO	ShO	W	L	SV	AB	H	HR	BA	PO	A	E	DP	TC/G	FA
1946	BKN N		14	11	.560	2.84	42	30	13	222	207	110	85	1	1	1	2	79	6	0	.076	13	36	6	4	1.3	.891
1947			17	8	.680	3.63	42	32	11	225.1	211	105	76	3	2	0	0	83	17	0	.205	15	52	0	4	1.6	1.000
1948			13	10	.565	3.58	42	30	11	208.2	228	94	73	1	0	1	0	63	13	0	.206	11	57	3	5	1.7	.958
1949			12	8	.600	4.18	37	29	11	187.1	194	69	58	2	2	0	2	67	12	0	.179	12	32	2	5	1.2	.957
1950			2	2	.500	4.59	23	8	2	68.2	82	31	29	1	0	0	0	18	2	0	.111	5	10	1	0	0.7	.938
1951	2 teams	BKN N (11G 1–0)							CHI N	(23G 2–6)																		
"	total		3	6	.333	4.91	34	12	1	124.2	137	58	45	0	2	1	0	32	6	0	.188	11	23	1	4	1.0	.971
1952	CHI N		4	4	.500	6.08	13	8	2	50.1	65	25	15	0	2	0	0	15	1	0	.067	3	14	0	3	1.3	1.000
7 yrs.			65	49	.570	3.87	233	149	51	1087	1124	492	381	8	9	3	4	357	57	0	.160	70	224	13	25	1.3	.958

WORLD SERIES

Year	Team		W	L	PCT	ERA	G	GS	CG	IP	H	BB	SO	ShO	W	L	SV	AB	H	HR	BA	PO	A	E	DP	TC/G	FA
1947	BKN N		0	0	–	7.00	4	1	0	9	12	7	5	0	0	0	0	3	1	0	.333	0	0	0	0	0.0	–
1949			0	0	–	16.20	2	0	0	1.2	4	2	0	0	0	0	0	0	0	0	–	0	0	0	0	0.0	–
2 yrs.			0	0	–	8.44	6	1	0	10.2	16	9	5	0	0	0	0	3	1	0	.333	0	0	0	0	0.0	–

Clyde Hatter

HATTER, CLYDE MELNO (Mad)
B. Aug. 7, 1908, Poplar Hill, Ky.   D. Oct. 16, 1937, Yosemite, Ky.   BR TL 5'11"   170 lbs.

Year	Team	W	L	PCT	ERA	G	GS	CG	IP	H	BB	SO	ShO	W	L	SV	AB	H	HR	BA	PO	A	E	DP	TC/G	FA
1935	DET A	0	0	–	7.56	8	2	0	33.1	44	30	15	0	0	0	0	10	3	0	.300	1	2	1	0	0.5	.750
1937		1	0	1.000	11.57	3	0	0	9.1	17	11	4	0	1	0	0	3	0	0	.000	0	1	0	0	0.3	1.000
2 yrs.		1	0	1.000	8.44	11	2	0	42.2	61	41	19	0	1	0	0	13	3	0	.231	1	3	1	0	0.5	.800

Year	Team		W	L	PCT	ERA	G	GS	CG	IP	H	BB	SO	ShO	Relief Pitching W	L	SV	Batting AB	H	HR	BA	PO	A	E	DP	TC/G	FA

Chris Haughey

HAUGHEY, CHRISTOPHER FRANCIS (Bud)
B. Oct. 3, 1925, Astoria, N. Y. BR TR 6'1" 180 lbs.

Year	Team		W	L	PCT	ERA	G	GS	CG	IP	H	BB	SO	ShO	W	L	SV	AB	H	HR	BA	PO	A	E	DP	TC/G	FA
1943	BKN	N	0	1	.000	3.86	1	0	0	7	5	10	0	0	0	1	0	3	0	0	.000	0	2	1	0	3.0	.667

Phil Haugstad

HAUGSTAD, PHILIP DONALD
B. Feb. 23, 1924, Black River Falls, Wis. BR TR 6'2" 165 lbs.

Year	Team		W	L	PCT	ERA	G	GS	CG	IP	H	BB	SO	ShO	W	L	SV	AB	H	HR	BA	PO	A	E	DP	TC/G	FA
1947	BKN	N	1	0	1.000	2.84	6	1	0	12.2	14	4	4	0	1	0	0	2	0	0	.000	0	2	0	0	0.3	1.000
1948			0	0	–	0.00	1	0	0	1	1	0	0	0	0	0	0	0	0	0	–	0	2	0	0	2.0	1.000
1951			0	1	.000	6.46	21	1	0	30.2	28	24	22	0	0	1	0	1	0	0	.000	1	7	0	0	0.4	1.000
1952	CIN	N	0	0	–	6.75	9	0	0	12	8	13	2	0	0	0	0	1	0	0	.000	0	4	1	0	0.6	.800
4 yrs.			1	1	.500	5.59	37	2	0	56.1	51	41	28	0	1	1	0	4	0	0	.000	1	15	1	0	0.5	.941

Tom Hausman

HAUSMAN, THOMAS MATTHEW
B. Mar. 31, 1953, Mobridge, S. D. BR TR 6'4" 190 lbs.

Year	Team		W	L	PCT	ERA	G	GS	CG	IP	H	BB	SO	ShO	W	L	SV	AB	H	HR	BA	PO	A	E	DP	TC/G	FA
1975	MIL	A	3	6	.333	4.10	29	9	1	112	110	47	46	0	3	1	0	0	0	0	–	8	19	1	1	0.9	1.000
1976			0	0	–	5.40	3	0	0	3.1	3	3	1	0	0	0	0	0	0	0	–	1	2	0	0	1.0	1.000
1978	NY	N	3	3	.500	4.67	10	10	0	52	58	9	16	0	0	0	0	17	3	0	.176	6	8	1	0	1.5	.933
1979			2	6	.250	2.73	19	10	1	79	65	19	33	0	0	2	2	26	3	0	.115	10	11	0	0	1.1	1.000
1980			6	5	.545	3.98	55	4	0	122	125	26	53	0	4	4	1	16	1	0	.063	11	23	3	4	0.7	.919
1981			0	1	.000	2.18	20	0	0	33	28	7	13	0	0	1	0	2	0	0	.000	2	6	0	0	0.4	1.000
1982	2 teams	NY N (21G 1–2)		ATL N	(3G 0–0)																						
"	total		1	2	.333	4.46	24	0	0	40.1	50	10	18	0	1	2	0	4	0	0	.000	4	5	1	1	0.4	.900
7 yrs.			15	23	.395	3.79	160	33	2	441.2	439	121	180	0	8	10	3	63	7	0	.111	42	74	5	6	0.8	.959

Clem Hausmann

HAUSMANN, CLEMENS RAYMOND
B. Aug. 17, 1919, Houston, Tex. D. Aug. 29, 1972, Baytown, Tex. BR TR 5'9" 165 lbs.

Year	Team		W	L	PCT	ERA	G	GS	CG	IP	H	BB	SO	ShO	W	L	SV	AB	H	HR	BA	PO	A	E	DP	TC/G	FA
1944	BOS	A	4	7	.364	3.42	32	12	3	137	139	69	43	0	1	2	2	38	3	0	.079	8	25	0	0	1.0	1.000
1945			5	7	.417	5.04	31	13	4	125	131	60	30	2	1	2	2	39	4	0	.103	13	30	1	2	1.4	.977
1949	PHI	A	0	0	–	9.00	1	0	0	1	0	2	0	0	0	0	0	0	0	0	–	0	1	0	1	1.0	1.000
3 yrs.			9	14	.391	4.21	64	25	7	263	270	131	73	2	2	4	4	77	7	0	.091	21	56	1	3	1.2	.987

Brad Havens

HAVENS, BRADLEY DAVID
B. Nov. 17, 1959, Highland Park, Mich. BL TL 6'1" 180 lbs.

Year	Team		W	L	PCT	ERA	G	GS	CG	IP	H	BB	SO	ShO	W	L	SV	AB	H	HR	BA	PO	A	E	DP	TC/G	FA
1981	MIN	A	3	6	.333	3.58	14	12	1	78	76	24	44	1	0	0	0	–	1	11	0	1	0.9	1.000			
1982			10	14	.417	4.31	33	32	4	208.2	201	80	129	1	0	1	0	–	4	18	0	0	0.7	1.000			
1983			5	8	.385	8.18	16	14	0	80.1	110	38	40	0	0	0	0	–	0	2	0	0	0.1	1.000			
1985	BAL	A	0	1	.000	8.79	8	1	0	14.1	20	10	19	0	0	0	0	–	0	1	0	0	0.1	1.000			
1986			3	3	.500	4.56	46	0	0	71	64	29	57	0	3	3	1	–	4	13	1	0	0.4	.944			
1987	LA	N	0	0	–	4.33	31	1	0	35.1	30	23	23	0	0	0	1	2	0	0	.000	1	3	0	0	0.1	1.000
1988	2 teams	LA N (9G 0–0)		CLE A	(28G 2–3)																						
"	total		2	3	.400	3.36	37	0	0	67	77	21	38	0	2	3	1	0	0	0	.000	7	10	0	0	0.5	1.000
1989	2 teams	CLE A (7G 0–0)		DET A	(13G 1–2)																						
"	total		1	2	.333	5.00	20	1	0	36	46	21	21	0	1	1	0	–	4	7	0	3	0.6	1.000
8 yrs.			24	37	.393	4.81	205	61	6	590.2	624	246	370	2	6	9	3	3	0	0	.000	21	65	1	4	0.4	.989

Ed Hawk

HAWK, EDWARD
B. May 11, 1890, Neosho, Mo. D. Mar. 26, 1936, Neosho, Mo. BL TR 5'11" 175 lbs.

Year	Team		W	L	PCT	ERA	G	GS	CG	IP	H	BB	SO	ShO	W	L	SV	AB	H	HR	BA	PO	A	E	DP	TC/G	FA
1911	STL	A	0	4	.000	3.35	5	4	4	37.2	38	8	14	0	0	0	0	13	2	0	.154	0	12	1	1	2.6	.923

Bill Hawke

HAWKE, WILLIAM VICTOR (Dick)
B. Apr. 28, 1870, Elsmere, Del. D. Dec. 11, 1902, Wilmington, Del. BR TR 5'8½" 169 lbs.

Year	Team		W	L	PCT	ERA	G	GS	CG	IP	H	BB	SO	ShO	W	L	SV	AB	H	HR	BA	PO	A	E	DP	TC/G	FA
1892	STL	N	4	5	.444	3.70	14	11	10	97.1	108	45	55	1	0	1	0	45	4	0	.089	8	17	0	0	1.8	1.000
1893	2 teams	STL N (1G 0–1)		BAL N	(29G 11–16)																						
"	total		11	17	.393	4.77	30	30	22	230.1	257	111	70	1	0	0	0	96	17	1	.177	18	48	10	0	2.5	.868
1894	BAL	N	16	9	.640	5.84	32	25	17	205	264	78	68	0	2	0	3	92	28	1	.304	9	41	5	3	1.7	.909
3 yrs.			31	31	.500	4.98	76	66	49	532.2	629	234	193	2	2	1	3	233	49	2	.210	35	106	15	3	2.1	.904

Andy Hawkins

HAWKINS, MELTON ANDREW
B. Jan. 21, 1960, Waco, Tex. BR TR 6'4" 200 lbs.

Year	Team		W	L	PCT	ERA	G	GS	CG	IP	H	BB	SO	ShO	W	L	SV	AB	H	HR	BA	PO	A	E	DP	TC/G	FA
1982	SD	N	2	5	.286	4.10	15	10	1	63.2	66	27	25	0	0	0	0	15	0	0	.000	6	6	1	0	0.9	.923
1983			5	7	.417	2.93	21	19	4	119.2	106	48	59	1	0	0	0	31	2	0	.065	13	18	1	2	1.5	.969
1984			8	9	.471	4.68	36	22	2	146	143	72	77	1	2	1	0	41	8	0	.195	10	16	2	1	0.8	.929
1985			18	8	.692	3.15	33	33	5	228.2	229	65	69	2	0	0	0	77	6	0	.078	21	30	1	3	1.6	.981
1986			10	8	.556	4.30	37	35	3	209.1	218	75	117	1	1	0	0	67	10	0	.149	7	28	0	0	0.9	1.000
1987			3	10	.231	5.05	24	20	0	117.2	131	49	51	0	0	0	0	32	5	0	.156	8	18	0	1	1.1	1.000
1988			14	11	.560	3.35	33	33	4	217.2	196	76	91	2	0	0	0	62	7	0	.113	14	23	2	4	1.2	.949
1989	NY	A	15	15	.500	4.80	34	34	5	208.1	238	76	98	2	0	0	0	0	0	0	–	8	20	1	0	0.9	.933
8 yrs.			75	73	.507	4.00	233	206	24	1311	1327	488	587	9	3	1	0	325	38	0	.117	87	159	9	14	1.1	.965

LEAGUE CHAMPIONSHIP SERIES

Year	Team		W	L	PCT	ERA	G	GS	CG	IP	H	BB	SO	ShO	W	L	SV	AB	H	HR	BA	PO	A	E	DP	TC/G	FA
1984	SD	N	0	0	–	0.00	3	0	0	3.2	0	2	1	0	0	0	0	0	0	0	–	0	1	0	0	0.3	1.000

WORLD SERIES

Year	Team		W	L	PCT	ERA	G	GS	CG	IP	H	BB	SO	ShO	W	L	SV	AB	H	HR	BA	PO	A	E	DP	TC/G	FA
1984	SD	N	1	1	.500	0.75	2	0	0	12	4	6	4	0	1	1	0	0	0	0	–	0	1	0	0	0.3	1.000

Wynn Hawkins

HAWKINS, WYNN FIRTH (Hawk)
B. Feb. 20, 1936, E. Palestine, Ohio BR TR 6'3" 195 lbs.

Year	Team		W	L	PCT	ERA	G	GS	CG	IP	H	BB	SO	ShO	W	L	SV	AB	H	HR	BA	PO	A	E	DP	TC/G	FA
1960	CLE	A	4	4	.500	4.23	15	9	1	66	68	39	39	0	0	0	0	20	2	0	.100	9	11	0	1	1.3	1.000
1961			7	9	.438	4.06	30	21	3	133	139	59	51	1	3	0	1	37	4	0	.108	11	18	3	1	1.1	.906
1962			1	0	1.000	7.36	3	0	0	3.2	9	1	0	0	1	0	0	0	0	0	–	0	0	0	0	0.0	–
3 yrs.			12	13	.480	4.17	48	30	4	202.2	216	99	90	1	4	0	1	57	6	0	.105	20	29	3	2	1.1	.942

Year	Team		W	L	PCT	ERA	G	GS	CG	IP	H	BB	SO	ShO	W	L	SV	AB	H	HR	BA	PO	A	E	DP	TC/G	FA
															Relief Pitching			**Batting**									

Pink Hawley

HAWLEY, EMERSON P.
B. Dec. 5, 1872, Beaver Dam, Wis.   D. Sept. 19, 1938, Beaver Dam, Wis.
BL TR 5'10"   185 lbs.

Year	Team		W	L	PCT	ERA	G	GS	CG	IP	H	BB	SO	ShO	W	L	SV	AB	H	HR	BA	PO	A	E	DP	TC/G	FA
1892	STL	N	6	14	.300	3.19	20	20	18	166.1	160	63	63	0	0	0	0	71	12	1	.169	9	26	4	1	2.0	.897
1893			5	17	.227	4.60	31	24	21	227	249	103	73	0	0	0	1	91	26	0	.286	8	40	10	1	1.9	.828
1894			19	**26**	.422	4.90	53	41	36	392.2	481	149	120	0	2	5	0	163	43	2	.264	29	77	12	2	2.2	.898
1895	PIT	N	31	22	.585	3.18	56	50	44	444.1	449	149	120	4	3	2	1	185	57	5	.308	16	110	13	2	2.5	.906
1896			22	21	.512	3.57	49	43	37	378	382	157	**137**	2	3	1	0	163	39	1	.239	12	108	10	2	2.7	.923
1897			18	18	.500	4.80	40	39	33	311.1	362	94	88	0	0	0	0	130	30	0	.231	11	69	4	3	2.1	.952
1898	CIN	N	27	11	.711	3.37	43	37	32	331	357	91	69	3	4	0	0	130	24	1	.185	11	58	4	0	1.7	.945
1899			14	17	.452	4.24	34	29	25	250.1	289	65	46	0	1	3	1	101	22	0	.218	13	50	5	2	2.0	.926
1900	NY	N	18	18	.500	3.53	41	38	**34**	329.1	377	89	80	1	0	1	0	123	25	1	.203	14	95	4	5	2.8	.965
1901	MIL	A	7	14	.333	4.59	26	23	17	182.1	228	41	50	0	0	0	0	73	19	0	.260	6	55	4	1	2.5	.938
10 yrs.			167	178	.484	3.96	393	344	297	3012.2	3334	974	868	10	13	12	3	1230	297	11	.241	129	688	70	19	2.3	.921

Scott Hawley

HAWLEY, SCOTT
Deceased.

Year	Team		W	L	PCT	ERA	G	GS	CG	IP	H	BB	SO	ShO	W	L	SV	AB	H	HR	BA	PO	A	E	DP	TC/G	FA
1894	BOS	N	0	1	.000	7.71	1	1	1	7	10	7	1	0	0	0	0	3	0	0	.000	1	2	0	1	3.0	1.000

Hal Haydel

HAYDEL, JOHN HAROLD
B. July 9, 1944, Houma, La.
BR TR 6'   190 lbs.

Year	Team		W	L	PCT	ERA	G	GS	CG	IP	H	BB	SO	ShO	W	L	SV	AB	H	HR	BA	PO	A	E	DP	TC/G	FA
1970	MIN	A	2	0	1.000	3.00	4	0	0	9	7	4	4	0	2	0	0	3	2	1	.667	0	1	0	0	0.3	1.000
1971			4	2	.667	4.28	31	0	0	40	33	20	29	0	4	2	1	3	1	0	.333	1	7	1	0	0.3	.889
2 yrs.			6	2	.750	4.04	35	0	0	49	40	24	33	0	6	2	1	6	3	1	.500	1	8	1	0	0.3	.900

Gene Hayden

HAYDEN, EUGENE FRANKLIN (Lefty)
B. Apr. 14, 1935, San Francisco, Calif.
BL TL 6'2"   175 lbs.

Year	Team		W	L	PCT	ERA	G	GS	CG	IP	H	BB	SO	ShO	W	L	SV	AB	H	HR	BA	PO	A	E	DP	TC/G	FA
1958	CIN	N	0	0	—	4.91	3	0	0	3.2	5	1	3	0	0	0	0	0	0	0	—	0	0	0	0	0.0	—

Ben Hayes

HAYES, BEN JOSEPH
B. Aug. 4, 1957, Niagara Falls, N. Y.
BR TR 6'1"   180 lbs.

Year	Team		W	L	PCT	ERA	G	GS	CG	IP	H	BB	SO	ShO	W	L	SV	AB	H	HR	BA	PO	A	E	DP	TC/G	FA
1982	CIN	N	2	0	1.000	1.97	26	0	0	45.2	37	22	38	0	2	0	2	4	0	0	.000	1	4	0	0	0.2	1.000
1983			4	6	.400	6.49	60	0	0	69.1	82	37	44	0	4	6	7	5	0	0	.000	3	11	0	0	0.2	1.000
2 yrs.			6	6	.500	4.70	86	0	0	115	119	59	82	0	6	6	9	9	0	0	.000	4	15	0	0	0.2	1.000

Jim Hayes

HAYES, JAMES MILLARD (Whitey)
B. Feb. 11, 1913, Montevallo, Ala.
BL TR 6'1"   168 lbs.

Year	Team		W	L	PCT	ERA	G	GS	CG	IP	H	BB	SO	ShO	W	L	SV	AB	H	HR	BA	PO	A	E	DP	TC/G	FA
1935	WAS	A	2	4	.333	8.36	7	4	1	28	38	23	9	0	1	1	0	8	2	0	.250	1	2	1	0	0.6	.750

Joe Haynes

HAYNES, JOSEPH WALTON
B. Sept. 21, 1917, Lincolnton, Ga.   D. Jan. 6, 1967, Hopkins, Minn.
BR TR 6'2½"   190 lbs.

Year	Team		W	L	PCT	ERA	G	GS	CG	IP	H	BB	SO	ShO	W	L	SV	AB	H	HR	BA	PO	A	E	DP	TC/G	FA
1939	WAS	A	8	12	.400	5.36	27	20	10	173	186	78	64	1	2	0	0	67	14	0	.209	10	23	1	1	1.3	.971
1940			3	6	.333	6.54	22	7	1	63.1	85	34	23	0	2	3	0	19	2	0	.105	2	9	2	1	0.6	.846
1941	CHI	A	0	0	—	3.86	8	0	0	28	30	11	18	0	0	0	0	11	3	0	.273	1	3	0	0	0.5	1.000
1942			8	5	.615	2.62	**40**	1	1	103	88	47	35	0	8	4	6	28	5	0	.179	6	22	0	0	0.7	1.000
1943			7	2	.778	2.96	35	2	1	109.1	114	32	37	0	5	2	3	34	9	0	.265	4	21	1	0	0.7	.962
1944			5	6	.455	2.57	33	12	8	154.1	148	43	44	0	2	0	2	50	10	0	.200	10	31	3	1	1.3	.932
1945			5	5	.500	3.55	14	13	8	104	92	29	34	1	0	0	1	40	7	0	.175	2	22	0	1	2.2	1.000
1946			7	9	.438	3.76	32	23	9	177.1	203	60	60	0	0	0	2	57	14	0	.246	4	39	0	1	1.3	1.000
1947			14	6	.700	2.42	29	22	7	182	174	61	50	2	3	0	0	65	17	0	.262	12	29	2	5	1.5	.953
1948			9	10	.474	3.97	27	22	6	149.2	167	52	40	1	0	0	0	50	8	0	.160	6	19	2	1	1.0	.926
1949	WAS	A	2	9	.182	6.26	37	10	0	96.1	106	55	19	0	0	5	2	25	6	0	.240	6	23	1	0	0.8	.967
1950			7	5	.583	5.84	27	10	1	101.2	124	46	15	1	3	0	0	35	7	0	.200	9	20	1	1	1.1	.967
1951			1	4	.200	4.56	26	3	1	73	85	37	18	0	1	3	2	21	7	1	.333	2	11	0	0	0.5	1.000
1952			0	3	.000	4.50	22	2	0	66	70	35	18	0	0	1	3	19	2	0	.105	3	10	0	0	0.6	1.000
14 yrs.			76	82	.481	4.01	379	147	53	1581	1672	620	475	5	27	19	21	521	111	1	.213	83	283	13	12	1.0	.966

Ray Hayward

HAYWARD, RAYMOND ALTON
B. Apr. 27, 1961, Enid, Okla.
BL TL 6'1"   190 lbs.

Year	Team		W	L	PCT	ERA	G	GS	CG	IP	H	BB	SO	ShO	W	L	SV	AB	H	HR	BA	PO	A	E	DP	TC/G	FA
1986	SD	N	0	2	.000	9.00	3	3	0	10	16	4	6	0	0	0	0	4	0	0	.000	0	1	1	0	0.7	.500
1987			0	0	—	16.50	4	0	0	6	12	3	2	0	0	0	0	1	0	0	.000	1	3	0	1	1.0	1.000
1988	TEX	A	4	6	.400	5.46	12	12	1	62.2	63	35	37	1	0	0	0	0	0	0	—	5	12	2	3	1.6	.895
3 yrs.			4	8	.333	6.75	19	15	1	78.2	91	42	45	1	0	0	0	5	0	0	.000	6	16	3	4	1.3	.880

Bill Haywood

HAYWOOD, WILLIAM KIERNAN
B. Apr. 21, 1937, Colon, Panama
BR TR 6'3"   205 lbs.

Year	Team		W	L	PCT	ERA	G	GS	CG	IP	H	BB	SO	ShO	W	L	SV	AB	H	HR	BA	PO	A	E	DP	TC/G	FA
1968	WAS	A	0	0	—	4.63	14	0	0	23.1	27	12	10	0	0	0	0	0	0	0	—	0	4	0	0	0.3	1.000

Ed Head

HEAD, EDWARD MARVIN
B. Jan. 25, 1918, Selma, La.   D. Jan. 31, 1980, Bastrop, La.
BR TR 6'1"   175 lbs.

Year	Team		W	L	PCT	ERA	G	GS	CG	IP	H	BB	SO	ShO	W	L	SV	AB	H	HR	BA	PO	A	E	DP	TC/G	FA
1940	BKN	N	1	2	.333	4.12	13	5	2	39.1	40	18	13	0	0	0	0	11	2	0	.182	0	3	0	0	0.2	1.000
1942			10	6	.625	3.56	36	15	5	136.2	118	47	78	1	3	1	4	39	13	0	.333	9	29	3	1	1.1	.927
1943			9	10	.474	3.66	47	18	7	169.2	166	66	83	3	2	3	6	46	7	0	.152	6	40	3	2	1.0	.939
1944			4	3	.571	2.70	9	8	5	63.1	54	19	17	0	0	0	0	19	5	0	.263	4	6	1	0	1.1	1.000
1946			3	2	.600	3.21	13	7	3	56	56	24	17	1	0	0	1	16	5	0	.313	2	9	1	1	0.9	.917
5 yrs.			27	23	.540	3.48	118	53	22	465	434	174	208	5	5	4	11	131	32	0	.244	21	87	7	4	1.0	.939

Ralph Head

HEAD, RALPH
B. Aug. 30, 1893, Tallapoosa, Ga.   D. Oct. 8, 1962, Muscadine, Ala.
BR TR 5'10"   175 lbs.

Year	Team		W	L	PCT	ERA	G	GS	CG	IP	H	BB	SO	ShO	W	L	SV	AB	H	HR	BA	PO	A	E	DP	TC/G	FA
1923	PHI	N	2	9	.182	6.66	35	13	5	132.1	185	57	24	0	1	0	0	42	3	0	.071	2	30	0	1	0.9	1.000

Year	Team		W	L	PCT	ERA	G	GS	CG	IP	H	BB	SO	ShO	Relief Pitching W	L	SV	Batting AB	H	HR	BA	PO	A	E	DP	TC/G	FA

Tom Healey

HEALEY, THOMAS F.
B. 1853, Cranston, R. I. D. Feb. 6, 1891, Lewiston, Me.   TR

| 1878 | 2 teams | PRO N | (3G 0–3) | | IND N | (11G 6–4) | | | | | | | | | | | | | | | | | | | | | | |
| " | total | | 6 | 7 | .462 | 2.39 | 14 | 13 | 12 | 113 | 125 | 20 | 20 | 0 | 0 | 0 | 1 | 54 | 10 | 0 | .185 | 6 | 24 | 4 | 0 | 2.4 | .882 |

Egyptian Healy

HEALY, JOHN J. (Long John)
B. Oct. 27, 1866, Cairo, Ill. D. Mar. 16, 1899, St. Louis, Mo.   BR TR 6'2" 158 lbs.

1885	STL	N	1	7	.125	3.00	8	8	8	66	54	20	32	0	0	0	0	24	1	0	.042	6	16	4	1	3.3	.846
1886			17	23	.425	2.88	42	41	39	353.2	315	118	213	3	1	0	0	145	14	0	.097	6	62	4	2	1.7	.944
1887	IND	N	12	29	.293	5.17	41	41	40	341	415	108	75	3	0	0	0	138	24	3	.174	7	51	12	0	1.7	.829
1888			12	24	.333	3.89	37	37	36	321.1	347	87	124	1	0	0	0	131	30	0	.229	5	79	15	3	2.7	.848
1889	2 teams	WAS N	(13G 1–11)		CHI N	(5G 1–4)																						
"	total		2	15	.118	5.69	18	17	15	147	187	56	71	0	0	0	0	65	12	1	.185	6	36	6	0	2.7	.875
1890	TOL	AA	22	21	.512	2.89	46	46	44	389	326	127	225	2	0	0	0	156	34	1	.218	24	62	14	2	2.2	.860
1891	BAL	AA	9	10	.474	3.75	23	22	19	170.1	179	57	54	0	0	0	0	64	9	0	.141	17	2	1	0	0.8	.895
1892	2 teams	BAL N	(9G 3–6)		LOU N	(2G 1–1)																						
"	total		4	7	.364	4.15	11	10	7	86.2	97	26	28	0	1	0	0	34	8	0	.235	3	17	4	1	2.2	.833
	8 yrs.		79	136	.367	3.84	226	222	208	1875	1920	599	822	9	2	0	0	757	132	5	.174	57	340	61	10	2.0	.867

Charlie Heard

HEARD, CHARLES
B. Jan. 30, 1872, Philadelphia, Pa. D. Feb. 20, 1945, Philadelphia, Pa.   BR TR 6'2" 190 lbs.

| 1890 | PIT | N | 0 | 6 | .000 | 8.39 | 6 | 6 | 5 | 44 | 75 | 32 | 13 | 0 | 0 | 0 | 0 | 43 | 8 | 0 | .186 | 1 | 6 | 2 | 1 | 1.5 | .778 |

Jay Heard

HEARD, JEHOSIE
B. Jan. 17, 1920, Atlanta, Ga.   BL TL 5'7" 155 lbs.

| 1954 | BAL | A | 0 | 0 | – | 13.50 | 2 | 0 | 0 | 3.1 | 6 | 3 | 2 | 0 | 0 | 0 | 0 | 0 | 0 | 0 | – | 0 | 1 | 0 | 0 | 0.5 | 1.000 |

Bunny Hearn

HEARN, BUNN
B. May 21, 1891, Chapel Hill, N. C. D. Oct. 10, 1959, Wilson, N. C.   BL TL 5'11½" 190 lbs.

1910	STL	N	1	3	.250	5.08	5	5	4	39	49	16	14	0	0	0	0	15	2	1	.133	2	7	0	1	1.8	1.000
1911			0	0	–	13.50	2	0	0	2.2	7	1	0	0	0	0	0	1	0	0	.000	0	0	0	0	0.0	–
1913	NY	N	1	1	.500	2.77	2	2	1	13	13	7	8	0	0	0	0	5	2	0	.400	1	2	0	0	1.5	1.000
1915	PIT	F	6	11	.353	3.38	29	17	8	175.2	187	37	49	1	1	1	0	53	10	0	.189	7	50	0	1	2.0	1.000
1918	BOS	N	5	6	.455	2.49	17	12	9	126.1	119	29	30	1	0	0	0	45	8	0	.178	3	43	0	0	2.7	1.000
1920			0	3	.000	5.65	11	4	2	43	54	11	9	0	0	0	0	14	2	0	.143	2	15	3	0	1.8	.850
	6 yrs.		13	24	.351	3.56	66	40	24	399.2	429	100	111	2	1	1	0	133	24	1	.180	15	117	3	2	2.0	.978

Bunny Hearn

HEARN, ELMER LAFAYETTE
B. Jan. 13, 1904, Brooklyn, N. Y. D. Mar. 31, 1974, Venice, Fla.   BL TL 5'8" 160 lbs.

1926	BOS	N	4	9	.308	4.22	34	12	3	117.1	121	56	40	0	2	3	2	30	3	0	.100	2	38	0	1	1.2	1.000
1927			0	2	.000	4.26	8	0	0	12.2	16	9	5	0	0	2	0	5	2	0	.400	0	4	1	1	0.6	.800
1928			1	0	1.000	6.30	7	0	0	10	6	8	8	0	1	0	0	1	0	0	.000	0	1	0	0	0.1	1.000
1929			2	0	1.000	4.42	10	1	0	18.1	18	9	12	0	2	0	0	2	0	0	.000	1	5	0	2	0.6	1.000
	4 yrs.		7	11	.389	4.38	59	13	3	158.1	161	82	65	0	5	5	2	38	5	0	.132	3	48	1	4	0.9	.981

Jim Hearn

HEARN, JAMES TOLBERT
B. Apr. 11, 1921, Atlanta, Ga.   BR TR 6'3" 205 lbs.

1947	STL	N	12	7	.632	3.22	37	21	4	162	151	63	57	1	3	2	1	55	8	0	.145	6	25	1	2	0.9	.969
1948			8	6	.571	4.22	34	13	3	89.2	92	35	27	0	5	2	1	25	5	0	.200	1	8	0	0	0.3	1.000
1949			1	3	.250	5.14	17	4	0	42	48	23	18	0	1	1	0	10	1	0	.100	4	8	1	0	0.8	.923
1950	2 teams	STL N	(6G 0–1)		NY N	(16G 11–3)																						
"	total		11	4	.733	2.49	22	16	11	134	84	44	58	5	0	1	0	45	7	0	.156	9	23	1	2	1.5	.970
1951	NY	N	17	9	.654	3.62	34	34	11	211.1	204	82	66	0	0	0	0	74	12	1	.162	16	61	2	7	2.3	.975
1952			14	7	.667	3.78	37	34	11	223.2	208	97	89	1	0	0	1	77	14	3	.182	14	57	0	6	1.9	1.000
1953			9	12	.429	4.53	36	32	6	196.2	206	84	77	0	0	1	0	66	9	0	.136	9	44	3	2	1.6	.946
1954			8	8	.500	4.15	29	18	3	130	137	66	45	2	1	1	1	45	5	1	.111	8	29	2	3	1.3	.949
1955			14	16	.467	3.73	39	33	11	226.2	225	66	86	1	2	1	0	77	12	4	.156	19	48	5	6	1.8	.931
1956			5	11	.313	3.97	30	19	2	129.1	124	44	66	0	0	1	1	41	4	0	.098	7	22	3	2	1.1	.906
1957	PHI	N	5	1	.833	3.65	36	1	0	74	79	18	46	0	4	0	3	17	0	0	.000	9	16	3	1	0.8	.893
1958			5	3	.625	4.17	39	1	0	73.1	88	27	33	0	4	3	0	14	0	0	.000	3	10	1	2	0.4	.929
1959			0	2	.000	5.73	6	0	0	11	15	6	1	0	0	2	0	2	0	0	.000	1	4	0	0	0.8	1.000
	13 yrs.		109	89	.551	3.81	396	229	63	1703.2	1661	655	669	10	20	15	8	548	77	9	.141	106	355	22	33	1.2	.954

WORLD SERIES

| 1951 | NY | N | 1 | 0 | 1.000 | 1.04 | 2 | 1 | 0 | 8.2 | 5 | 8 | 1 | 0 | 0 | 0 | 0 | 0 | 0 | 0 | .000 | 0 | 2 | 0 | 1 | 1.0 | 1.000 |

Spencer Heath

HEATH, SPENCER PAUL
B. Nov. 5, 1894, Chicago, Ill. D. Jan. 25, 1930, Chicago, Ill.   BB TR 6' 170 lbs.

| 1920 | CHI | A | 0 | 0 | – | 15.43 | 4 | 0 | 0 | 7 | 19 | 2 | 0 | 0 | 0 | 0 | 0 | 3 | 0 | 0 | .000 | 0 | 3 | 3 | 0 | 1.5 | .500 |

Jeff Heathcock

HEATHCOCK, RONALD JEFFREY
B. Nov. 18, 1959, Covina, Calif.   BR TR 6'4" 195 lbs.

1983	HOU	N	2	1	.667	3.21	6	3	0	28	19	4	12	0	0	0	0	6	0	0	.000	3	4	0	1	1.2	1.000
1985			3	1	.750	3.36	14	7	1	56.1	50	13	25	0	1	1	1	16	1	0	.063	4	9	1	0	0.9	1.000
1987			4	2	.667	3.16	19	2	0	42.2	44	9	15	0	3	1	1	10	0	0	.000	3	7	1	0	0.6	.909
1988			0	5	.000	5.81	17	1	0	31	33	16	12	0	0	4	1	3	0	0	.000	3	7	1	0	0.6	.909
	4 yrs.		9	9	.500	3.76	56	13	1	158	146	42	64	0	4	6	3	35	1	0	.029	13	27	2	1	0.8	.952

Neal Heaton

HEATON, NEAL
B. Mar. 3, 1960, Jamaica, N. Y.   BL TL 6'2" 197 lbs.

| 1982 | CLE | A | 0 | 2 | .000 | 5.23 | 8 | 4 | 0 | 31 | 32 | 16 | 14 | 0 | 0 | 0 | 0 | 0 | 0 | 0 | – | 2 | 3 | 0 | 0 | 0.6 | 1.000 |
| 1983 | | | 11 | 7 | .611 | 4.16 | 39 | 16 | 4 | 149.1 | 157 | 44 | 75 | 3 | 4 | 2 | 7 | 0 | 0 | 0 | – | 7 | 14 | 0 | 0 | 0.5 | 1.000 |

Year	Team	W	L	PCT	ERA	G	GS	CG	IP	H	BB	SO	ShO	W	L	SV	AB	H	HR	BA	PO	A	E	DP	TC/G	FA

Neal Heaton *continued*

Year	Team	W	L	PCT	ERA	G	GS	CG	IP	H	BB	SO	ShO	W	L	SV	AB	H	HR	BA	PO	A	E	DP	TC/G	FA
1984		12	15	.444	5.21	38	34	4	198.2	231	75	75	1	0	0	0	0	0	0	–	9	19	2	0	0.8	.933
1985		9	17	.346	4.90	36	33	5	207.2	244	80	82	1	0	1	0	0	0	0	–	8	21	1	0	0.8	.967
1986	2 teams	CLE A	(12G 3–6)		MIN A	(21G 4–9)																				
"	total	7	15	.318	4.08	33	29	5	198.2	201	81	90	0	0	0	1	0	0	0	–	13	24	1	1	1.2	.974
1987	MON N	13	10	.565	4.52	32	32	3	193.1	207	37	105	1	0	0	0	67	14	0	.209	5	28	3	1	1.1	.917
1988		3	10	.231	4.99	32	11	0	97.1	98	43	43	0	1	4	2	21	3	0	.143	6	14	1	2	0.7	.952
1989	PIT N	6	7	.462	3.05	42	18	1	147.1	127	55	67	0	2	0	0	42	9	0	.214	6	28	1	1	0.8	.971
8 yrs.		61	83	.424	4.46	260	177	22	1223.1	1297	431	551	6	7	8	10	130	26	0	.200	56	151	9	6	0.8	.958

Dave Heaverlo

HEAVERLO, DAVID WALLACE
B. Aug. 25, 1950, Ellensburg, Wash.

BR TR 6'2" 220 lbs.

Year	Team	W	L	PCT	ERA	G	GS	CG	IP	H	BB	SO	ShO	W	L	SV	AB	H	HR	BA	PO	A	E	DP	TC/G	FA
1975	SF N	3	1	.750	2.39	42	0	0	64	62	31	35	0	3	1	1	4	2	0	.500	7	10	1	1	0.4	.944
1976		4	4	.500	4.44	61	0	0	75	85	15	40	0	4	4	1	3	1	0	.333	7	15	2	1	0.4	.917
1977		5	1	.833	2.55	56	0	0	99	92	21	58	0	5	1	1	5	0	0	.000	10	20	1	2	0.6	.968
1978	OAK A	3	6	.333	3.25	69	0	0	130	141	41	71	0	3	6	10	0	0	0	–	9	30	0	3	0.6	1.000
1979		4	11	.267	4.19	62	0	0	86	97	42	40	0	4	11	9	1	0	0	.000	9	13	2	1	0.4	.917
1980	SEA A	6	3	.667	3.87	60	0	0	79	75	35	42	0	6	3	4	0	0	0	–	7	5	4	0	0.3	.750
1981	OAK A	1	0	1.000	1.50	6	0	0	6	7	3	2	0	1	0	0	0	0	0	–	0	0	0	0	0.0	–
7 yrs.		26	26	.500	3.41	356	0	0	539	559	188	288	0	26	26	26	13	3	0	.231	49	93	10	8	0.4	.934

Wally Hebert

HEBERT, WALLACE ANDREW (Preacher)
B. Aug. 21, 1907, Lake Charles, La.

BL TL 6'1" 195 lbs.

Year	Team	W	L	PCT	ERA	G	GS	CG	IP	H	BB	SO	ShO	W	L	SV	AB	H	HR	BA	PO	A	E	DP	TC/G	FA
1931	STL A	6	7	.462	5.07	23	13	5	103	128	43	26	0	0	1	0	43	9	0	.209	7	11	0	0	0.8	1.000
1932		1	12	.077	6.48	35	15	2	108.1	145	45	29	0	0	1	1	34	12	0	.353	9	22	1	0	0.9	.969
1933		4	6	.400	5.30	33	10	3	88.1	114	35	19	0	2	1	0	23	9	0	.391	7	13	0	1	0.6	1.000
1943	PIT N	10	11	.476	2.98	34	23	12	184	197	45	41	1	1	1	0	59	13	0	.220	13	43	4	5	1.8	.933
4 yrs.		21	36	.368	4.63	125	61	22	483.2	584	168	115	1	3	4	1	159	43	0	.270	36	89	5	6	1.0	.962

Guy Hecker

HECKER, GUY JACKSON (Blond Guy)
B. Apr. 3, 1856, Youngville, Pa.   D. Dec. 3, 1938, Wooster, Ohio
Manager 1890.

BR TR 6' 190 lbs.

Year	Team	W	L	PCT	ERA	G	GS	CG	IP	H	BB	SO	ShO	W	L	SV	AB	H	HR	BA	PO	A	E	DP	TC/G	FA
1882	LOU AA	6	6	.500	1.30	13	11	10	104	75	5	33	0	1	0	0	340	94	3	.276	9	46	0	0	4.2	1.000
1883		28	25	.528	3.33	55	54	53	451	509	72	153	3	0	0	0	322	88	1	.273	39	93	19	4	2.7	.874
1884		52	20	.722	1.80	76	73	72	670.2	526	56	385	6	1	0	1	316	94	4	.297	50	145	10	3	2.7	.951
1885		30	23	.566	2.18	54	53	51	480	454	54	209	2	0	0	0	297	81	2	.273	30	105	10	1	2.7	.931
1886		26	23	.531	2.87	52	48	45	420.2	390	118	133	2	1	0	0	343	117	4	.341	15	2	3	1	0.4	.850
1887		18	12	.600	4.16	33	32	32	285.1	325	50	58	2	0	0	1	370	118	4	.319	19	1	6	0	0.8	.769
1888		8	17	.320	3.39	28	25	25	223.1	251	43	63	0	0	0	0	211	48	0	.227	0	0	0	0	0.0	–
1889		5	11	.313	5.59	17	16	15	151.1	215	47	33	0	0	1	0	327	93	1	.284	609	23	20	43	38.4	.969
1890	PIT N	2	9	.182	5.11	14	12	11	119.2	160	44	32	0	0	0	0	340	77	0	.226	9	19	3	0	2.2	.903
9 yrs.		175	146	.545	2.92	342	324	314	2906	2905	489	1099	15	4	2	1	*				780	434	71	52	3.8	.945

Harry Hedgepath

HEDGEPATH, HARRY MALCOLM
B. Sept. 4, 1888, Fayetteville, N. C.   D. July 30, 1966, Richmond, Va.

BL TL 6'1½" 194 lbs.

Year	Team	W	L	PCT	ERA	G	GS	CG	IP	H	BB	SO	ShO	W	L	SV	AB	H	HR	BA	PO	A	E	DP	TC/G	FA
1913	WAS A	0	0	–	0.00	1	0	0	1	1	0	0	0	0	0	1	0	0	0	–	0	2	0	0	2.0	1.000

Mike Hedlund

HEDLUND, MICHAEL DAVID (Red)
B. Aug. 11, 1946, Dallas, Tex.

BB TR 6'1" 182 lbs.

Year	Team	W	L	PCT	ERA	G	GS	CG	IP	H	BB	SO	ShO	W	L	SV	AB	H	HR	BA	PO	A	E	DP	TC/G	FA
1965	CLE A	0	0	–	5.06	6	0	0	5.1	6	5	4	0	0	0	0	1	0	0	.000	0	0	0	0	0.0	–
1968		0	0	–	10.80	3	0	0	1.2	6	2	0	0	0	0	0	0	0	0	–	0	1	0	0	0.3	1.000
1969	KC A	3	6	.333	3.24	34	16	1	125	123	40	74	0	0	0	0	33	5	0	.152	9	24	1	3	1.0	.971
1970		2	3	.400	7.20	9	0	0	15	18	7	5	0	2	3	0	4	0	0	.000	0	1	0	0	0.1	1.000
1971		15	8	.652	2.71	32	30	7	206	168	72	76	1	0	0	0	68	6	0	.088	16	47	2	5	2.0	.969
1972		5	7	.417	4.78	29	16	1	113	119	41	52	0	1	0	0	32	6	0	.188	12	19	0	3	1.1	1.000
6 yrs.		25	24	.510	3.55	113	62	9	466	440	167	211	1	3	3	2	138	17	0	.123	37	92	3	11	1.2	.977

Danny Heep

HEEP, DANIEL WILLIAM
B. July 3, 1957, San Antonio, Tex.

BL TL 5'11" 185 lbs.

Year	Team	W	L	PCT	ERA	G	GS	CG	IP	H	BB	SO	ShO	W	L	SV	AB	H	HR	BA	PO	A	E	DP	TC/G	FA
1988	LA N	0	0	–	9.00	1	0	0	2	2	0	0	0	0	0	0	*				0	0	0	0	0.0	–

Bob Heffner

HEFFNER, ROBERT FREDERIC (Butch)
B. Sept. 13, 1938, Allentown, Pa.

BR TR 6'4" 200 lbs.

Year	Team	W	L	PCT	ERA	G	GS	CG	IP	H	BB	SO	ShO	W	L	SV	AB	H	HR	BA	PO	A	E	DP	TC/G	FA
1963	BOS A	4	9	.308	4.26	20	19	3	124.2	131	36	77	1	0	0	0	43	5	0	.116	15	16	1	0	1.6	.969
1964		7	9	.438	4.08	55	10	1	158.2	152	44	112	1	6	4	6	44	7	1	.159	15	17	2	1	0.6	.941
1965		0	2	.000	7.16	27	1	0	49	59	18	42	0	0	2	0	6	0	0	.000	3	4	0	0	0.3	1.000
1966	CLE A	0	1	.000	3.46	5	1	0	13	12	3	7	0	0	0	0	1	0	0	.000	0	0	0	0	0.0	–
1968	CAL A	0	0	–	2.25	7	0	0	8	6	6	3	0	0	0	0	0	0	0	–	0	1	0	0	0.1	1.000
5 yrs.		11	21	.344	4.51	114	31	4	353.1	360	107	241	2	6	6	6	94	12	1	.128	33	38	3	1	0.6	.959

Randy Heflin

HEFLIN, RANDOLPH RUTHERFORD
B. Sept. 11, 1918, Fredericksburg, Va.

BL TR 6' 185 lbs.

Year	Team	W	L	PCT	ERA	G	GS	CG	IP	H	BB	SO	ShO	W	L	SV	AB	H	HR	BA	PO	A	E	DP	TC/G	FA
1945	BOS A	4	10	.286	4.06	20	14	6	102	102	61	39	2	0	0	0	35	3	0	.086	8	26	3	2	1.9	.919
1946		0	1	.000	2.45	5	1	0	14.2	16	12	6	0	0	1	0	3	2	0	.667	0	7	0	0	1.4	1.000
2 yrs.		4	11	.267	3.86	25	15	6	116.2	118	73	45	2	0	2	0	38	5	0	.132	8	33	3	2	1.8	.932

Jake Hehl

HEHL, HERMAN JACOB
B. Dec. 8, 1899, Brooklyn, N. Y.   D. July 4, 1961, Brooklyn, N. Y.

BR TR 5'11" 180 lbs.

Year	Team	W	L	PCT	ERA	G	GS	CG	IP	H	BB	SO	ShO	W	L	SV	AB	H	HR	BA	PO	A	E	DP	TC/G	FA
1918	BKN N	0	0	–	0.00	1	0	0	1	0	0	0	0	0	0	0	0	0	0	–	0	1	0	0	1.0	1.000

Year	Team		W	L	PCT	ERA	G	GS	CG	IP	H	BB	SO	ShO	Relief Pitching W	L	SV	Batting AB	H	HR	BA	PO	A	E	DP	TC/G	FA

Emmett Heidrick

HEIDRICK, JOHN EMMETT (Snags)
B. July 29, 1876, Queenstown, Pa. D. Jan. 20, 1916, Clarion, Pa.
BL TR 6' 185 lbs.

Year	Team	W	L	PCT	ERA	G	GS	CG	IP	H	BB	SO	ShO	W	L	SV	AB	H	HR	BA	PO	A	E	DP	TC/G	FA
1902	STL A	0	0	–	0.00	1	0	0	1	0	0	0	0	0	0	0	*				0	0	0	0	0.0	–

Fred Heimach

HEIMACH, FREDERICK AMOS (Lefty)
B. Jan. 27, 1901, Camden, N. J. D. June 1, 1973, Fort Myers, Fla.
BL TL 6' 175 lbs.

Year	Team	W	L	PCT	ERA	G	GS	CG	IP	H	BB	SO	ShO	W	L	SV	AB	H	HR	BA	PO	A	E	DP	TC/G	FA
1920	PHI A	0	1	.000	14.40	1	1	0	5	13	1	0	0	0	0	0	1	0	0	.000	1	5	0	0	6.0	1.000
1921		1	0	1.000	0.00	1	1	1	9	7	1	1	1	0	0	0	4	1	0	.250	1	5	0	0	6.0	1.000
1922		7	11	.389	5.03	37	19	7	171.2	220	63	47	0	3	2	1	60	15	0	.250	7	46	3	4	1.5	.946
1923		6	12	.333	4.32	40	19	10	208.1	238	69	63	0	1	1	0	118	30	1	.254	14	54	4	2	1.8	.944
1924		14	12	.538	4.73	40	26	10	198	243	60	60	0	3	0	0	90	29	0	.322	11	57	2	1	1.8	.971
1925		0	1	.000	3.98	10	0	0	20.1	24	9	6	0	0	1	0	6	1	0	.167	1	6	0	1	0.7	1.000
1926	2 teams				PHI A (13G 1–0)				BOS A	(20G 2–9)																
"	total	3	9	.250	4.98	33	14	6	133.2	147	47	25	0	1	1	0	54	14	0	.259	8	58	4	3	2.1	.943
1928	NY A	2	3	.400	3.31	13	9	5	68	66	16	25	0	0	0	0	30	5	0	.167	0	16	0	2	1.2	1.000
1929		11	6	.647	4.01	35	10	3	134.2	141	29	26	3	7	2	4	49	9	1	.184	6	37	0	1	1.2	1.000
1930	BKN N	0	2	.000	4.91	9	0	0	7.1	14	3	1	0	0	1	0	4	1	0	.250	0	3	0	1	0.3	1.000
1931		9	7	.563	3.46	31	10	7	135.1	145	23	43	1	4	2	1	61	12	0	.197	8	44	0	3	1.7	1.000
1932		9	4	.692	3.97	36	15	7	167.2	203	28	30	0	3	0	0	55	9	1	.164	10	41	0	1	1.4	1.000
1933		0	1	.000	10.01	10	3	0	29.2	49	11	7	0	0	0	0	10	2	0	.200	1	6	0	0	0.6	1.000
13 yrs.		62	69	.473	4.46	296	127	56	1288.2	1510	360	334	5	22	14	7	*				67	378	13	20	1.5	.972

Gorman Heimueller

HEIMUELLER, GORMAN JOHN
B. Sept. 24, 1955, Los Angeles, Calif.
BL TL 6'4" 195 lbs.

Year	Team	W	L	PCT	ERA	G	GS	CG	IP	H	BB	SO	ShO	W	L	SV	AB	H	HR	BA	PO	A	E	DP	TC/G	FA
1983	OAK A	3	5	.375	4.41	16	14	2	83.2	93	29	31	1	0	0	0	0	0	0	–	7	23	0	1	1.9	1.000
1984		0	1	.000	6.14	6	0	0	14.2	21	7	3	0	0	1	0	0	0	0	–	1	3	0	1	0.7	1.000
2 yrs.		3	6	.333	4.67	22	14	2	98.1	114	36	34	1	0	1	0	0	0	0	–	8	26	0	2	1.5	1.000

Don Heinkel

HEINKEL, DONALD ELLIOTT
B. Oct. 20, 1959, Racine, Wis.
BL TR 6' 185 lbs.

Year	Team	W	L	PCT	ERA	G	GS	CG	IP	H	BB	SO	ShO	W	L	SV	AB	H	HR	BA	PO	A	E	DP	TC/G	FA
1988	DET A	0	0	–	3.96	21	0	0	36.1	30	12	30	0	0	0	1	0	0	0	–	3	3	0	1	0.3	1.000
1989	STL N	1	1	.500	5.81	7	5	0	26.1	40	7	16	0	0	0	0	6	0	0	.000	3	3	0	1	0.9	1.000
2 yrs.		1	1	.500	4.74	28	5	0	62.2	70	19	46	0	0	0	1	6	0	0	.000	6	6	0	2	0.4	1.000

Ken Heintzelman

HEINTZELMAN, KENNETH ALPHONSE
Father of Tom Heintzelman.
B. Oct. 14, 1915, Peruque, Mo.
BR TL 5'11½" 185 lbs.

Year	Team	W	L	PCT	ERA	G	GS	CG	IP	H	BB	SO	ShO	W	L	SV	AB	H	HR	BA	PO	A	E	DP	TC/G	FA
1937	PIT N	1	0	1.000	2.00	1	1	1	9	6	3	4	0	0	0	0	4	0	0	.000	0	0	1	0	1.0	–
1938		0	0	–	9.00	1	0	0	3	1	3	1	0	0	0	0	0	0	0	–	0	1	0	0	1.0	1.000
1939		1	1	.500	5.05	17	2	1	35.2	35	18	18	1	0	0	0	9	2	0	.222	2	5	0	0	0.4	1.000
1940		8	8	.500	4.47	39	16	5	165	193	65	71	2	3	2	3	54	9	0	.167	4	45	1	4	1.3	.980
1941		11	11	.500	3.44	35	24	13	196	206	83	81	2	1	3	0	63	8	0	.127	8	44	2	4	1.5	.963
1942		8	11	.421	4.57	27	18	5	130	143	63	39	3	3	1	0	35	3	0	.086	1	23	0	1	0.9	1.000
1946		8	12	.400	3.77	32	24	6	157.2	165	86	57	2	1	1	0	44	6	0	.136	7	39	0	3	1.4	1.000
1947	2 teams				PIT N (2G 0–0)				PHI N	(24G 7–10)																
"	total	7	10	.412	4.50	26	20	8	140	153	52	57	0	1	0	1	43	5	0	.116	2	14	2	1	0.7	.889
1948	PHI N	6	11	.353	4.29	27	16	5	130	117	45	57	2	1	0	0	37	5	0	.135	2	21	0	1	0.9	1.000
1949		17	10	.630	3.02	33	32	15	250	239	93	65	5	0	1	0	83	13	0	.157	4	38	1	4	1.3	.977
1950		3	9	.250	4.09	23	17	4	125.1	122	54	39	1	0	0	0	38	2	0	.053	1	16	0	1	0.7	1.000
1951		6	12	.333	4.18	35	12	3	118.1	119	53	55	1	3	4	2	28	3	0	.107	4	17	0	3	0.6	1.000
1952		1	3	.250	3.16	23	1	0	42.2	41	12	20	0	1	2	1	2	0	0	.000	2	3	0	1	0.2	1.000
13 yrs.		77	98	.440	3.93	319	183	66	1501.2	1540	630	564	19	15	13	10	440	56	0	.127	37	267	7	23	1.0	.977

WORLD SERIES

Year	Team	W	L	PCT	ERA	G	GS	CG	IP	H	BB	SO	ShO	W	L	SV	AB	H	HR	BA	PO	A	E	DP	TC/G	FA
1950	PHI N	0	0	–	1.17	1	1	0	7.2	4	6	3	0	0	0	0	2	0	0	.000	0	2	0	0	2.0	1.000

Clarence Heise

HEISE, CLARENCE EDWARD (Lefty)
B. Aug. 7, 1907, Topeka, Kans.
BL TL 5'10" 172 lbs.

Year	Team	W	L	PCT	ERA	G	GS	CG	IP	H	BB	SO	ShO	W	L	SV	AB	H	HR	BA	PO	A	E	DP	TC/G	FA
1934	STL N	0	0	–	4.50	1	0	0	2	3	0	1	0	0	0	0	0	0	0	–	0	0	0	0	0.0	–

Jim Heise

HEISE, JAMES EDWARD
B. Oct. 2, 1932, Scottsdale, Pa.
BR TR 6'1" 185 lbs.

Year	Team	W	L	PCT	ERA	G	GS	CG	IP	H	BB	SO	ShO	W	L	SV	AB	H	HR	BA	PO	A	E	DP	TC/G	FA
1957	WAS A	0	3	.000	8.05	8	2	0	19	25	16	8	0	0	1	0	4	0	0	.000	1	3	1	1	0.6	.800

Roy Heiser

HEISER, LEROY BARTON
B. June 22, 1942, Baltimore, Md.
BR TR 6'4" 190 lbs.

Year	Team	W	L	PCT	ERA	G	GS	CG	IP	H	BB	SO	ShO	W	L	SV	AB	H	HR	BA	PO	A	E	DP	TC/G	FA
1961	WAS A	0	0	–	6.35	3	0	0	5.2	6	9	1	0	0	0	0	2	0	0	.000	0	1	0	0	0.3	–

Crese Heisman

HEISMAN, CHRISTIAN ERNEST
B. Apr. 16, 1880, Cincinnati, Ohio D. Nov. 19, 1951, Cincinnati, Ohio
BR TL 6'2" 175 lbs.

Year	Team	W	L	PCT	ERA	G	GS	CG	IP	H	BB	SO	ShO	W	L	SV	AB	H	HR	BA	PO	A	E	DP	TC/G	FA
1901	CIN N	0	2	.000	5.93	3	2	1	13.2	18	6	6	0	0	0	0	5	2	0	.400	1	1	0	0	0.7	1.000
1902	2 teams				CIN N (5G 2–1)				BAL A	(3G 0–3)																
"	total	2	4	.333	4.41	8	6	4	49	53	22	17	0	0	0	0	21	4	0	.190	3	11	0	0	1.8	1.000
2 yrs.		2	6	.250	4.74	11	8	5	62.2	71	28	23	0	0	0	0	26	6	0	.231	4	12	0	0	1.5	1.000

Henry Heitmann

HEITMANN, HARRY ANTON
B. Oct. 6, 1896, Albany, N. Y. D. Dec. 15, 1958, Brooklyn, N. Y.
BR TR 6' 175 lbs.

Year	Team	W	L	PCT	ERA	G	GS	CG	IP	H	BB	SO	ShO	W	L	SV	AB	H	HR	BA	PO	A	E	DP	TC/G	FA
1918	BKN N	0	1	.000	108.00	1	1	0	.1	4	0	0	0	0	0	0	0	0	0	–	0	0	0	0	0.0	–

Year	Team	W	L	PCT	ERA	G	GS	CG	IP	H	BB	SO	ShO	W	L	SV	AB	H	HR	BA	PO	A	E	DP	TC/G	FA

Mel Held

HELD, MELVIN NICHOLAS (Country)
B. Apr. 12, 1929, Edon, Ohio. BR TR 6'1" 178 lbs.

| 1956 | BAL A | 0 | 0 | – | 5.14 | 4 | 0 | 0 | 7 | 7 | 3 | 4 | 0 | 0 | 0 | 0 | 0 | 0 | 0 | – | 0 | 3 | 0 | 1 | 0.8 | 1.000 |

Horace Helmbold

HELMBOLD, HORACE WILLING
B. Aug. 27, 1867, Philadelphia, Pa. Deceased.

| 1890 | PHI AA | 0 | 1 | .000 | 14.14 | 1 | 1 | 1 | 7 | 17 | 6 | 3 | 0 | 0 | 0 | 0 | 3 | 0 | 0 | .000 | 1 | 2 | 1 | 0 | 4.0 | .750 |

Russ Heman

HEMAN, RUSSELL FREDERICK
B. Feb. 10, 1933, Olive, Calif. BR TR 6'4" 200 lbs.

| 1961 | 2 teams | | | CLE A | (6G 0–0) | | | | LA A | (6G 0–0) | | | | | | | | | | | | | | | | |
| " | total | 0 | 0 | – | 2.70 | 12 | 0 | 0 | 20 | 12 | 10 | 6 | 0 | 0 | 0 | 1 | 2 | 0 | 0 | .000 | 1 | 4 | 0 | 0 | 0.4 | 1.000 |

George Hemming

HEMMING, GEORGE EARL (Old Wax Figger)
B. Dec. 15, 1868, Carrollton, Ohio D. June 3, 1930, Springfield, Mass. BR TR 5'11" 170 lbs.

1890	2 teams			CLE P	(3G 0–1)				BKN P	(19G 8–4)																
"	total	8	5	.615	4.25	22	12	12	144	142	78	35	0	1	0	3	68	11	0	.162	4	42	3	1	2.2	.939
1891	BKN N	8	15	.348	4.96	27	22	19	199.2	231	84	83	1	0	1	1	82	13	0	.159	9	44	6	1	2.2	.898
1892	2 teams			CIN N	(1G 0–1)				LOU N	(4G 2–2)																
"	total	2	3	.400	5.05	5	4	4	41	46	19	12	0	1	0	0	16	2	0	.125	3	10	1	1	2.8	.929
1893	LOU N	18	17	.514	5.18	41	33	33	332	373	176	79	1	2	0	1	158	32	0	.203	19	80	7	2	2.6	.934
1894	2 teams			LOU N	(35G 13–19)				BAL N	(6G 4–0)																
"	total	17	19	.472	4.27	41	38	36	339.2	406	159	70	1	0	1	1	152	39	2	.257	19	55	5	1	1.9	.937
1895	BAL N	20	13	.606	4.05	34	31	26	262.1	288	96	43	1	0	2	0	117	33	1	.282	7	46	4	2	1.7	.930
1896	" "	15	6	.714	4.19	25	21	20	202	233	54	33	3	1	0	0	97	25	0	.258	11	37	3	2	2.0	.941
1897	LOU N	3	4	.429	5.10	9	8	7	67	80	25	7	0	0	0	0	28	5	0	.179	9	16	2	0	3.0	.926
8 yrs.		91	82	.526	4.55	204	169	157	1587.2	1799	691	362	7	4	4	6	718	160	3	.223	81	330	31	10	2.2	.930

Bernie Henderson

HENDERSON, BERNARD (Barnyard)
B. Apr. 12, 1899, Douglasville, Tex. D. June 4, 1966, Linden, Tex. BL TR 5'9" 175 lbs.

| 1921 | CLE A | 0 | 1 | .000 | 9.00 | 2 | 1 | 0 | 3 | 5 | 0 | 1 | 0 | 0 | 0 | 0 | 1 | 0 | 0 | .000 | 0 | 0 | 0 | 0 | 0.0 | – |

Bill Henderson

HENDERSON, WILLIAM MAXWELL
B. Nov. 4, 1901, Pensacola, Fla. D. Oct. 6, 1966, Pensacola, Fla. BR TR 6' 190 lbs.

| 1930 | NY A | 0 | 0 | – | 4.50 | 3 | 0 | 0 | 8 | 7 | 4 | 2 | 0 | 0 | 0 | 0 | 2 | 1 | 0 | .500 | 0 | 2 | 0 | 0 | 0.7 | 1.000 |

Ed Henderson

HENDERSON, EDWARD J.
Born Eugene J. Ball.
B. Dec. 25, 1884, Newark, N. J. D. Jan. 15, 1964, New York, N. Y. BL TL 5'9" 168 lbs.

| 1914 | 2 teams | | | PIT F | (6G 0–1) | | | | IND F | (2G 1–0) | | | | | | | | | | | | | | | | |
| " | total | 1 | 1 | .500 | 4.15 | 8 | 2 | 2 | 26 | 22 | 12 | 5 | 0 | 0 | 0 | 0 | 7 | 0 | 0 | .000 | 2 | 4 | 0 | 0 | 0.8 | 1.000 |

Hardie Henderson

HENDERSON, JAMES HARDING
B. Oct. 31, 1862, Philadelphia, Pa. D. Feb. 6, 1903, Philadelphia, Pa. BR TR

1883	2 teams			PHI N	(1G 0–1)				BAL AA	(45G 10–32)																
"	total	10	33	.233		46	43	39	367.1	409	89	147	0	0	0	1	199	33	1	.166	24	60	22	3	2.3	.792
1884	BAL AA	27	23	.540	2.62	52	52	50	439.1	382	116	346	4	0	0	0	203	46	0	.227	27	78	22	3	2.4	.827
1885	" "	25	35	.417	3.19	61	61	59	539.1	539	117	263	0	0	0	0	229	51	1	.223	28	81	14	4	2.0	.886
1886	2 teams			BAL AA	(19G 3–15)				BKN AA	(14G 10–4)																
"	total	13	19	.406	3.90	33	33	33	295.1	300	117	137	0	0	0	0	118	25	0	.212	22	55	5	3	2.5	.939
1887	BKN AA	5	8	.385	3.95	13	12	12	111.2	127	63	28	0	1	0	0	41	5	0	.122	5	32	1	0	2.9	.974
1888	PIT N	1	3	.250	5.35	5	5	4	35.1	43	20	9	0	0	0	0	18	5	0	.278	1	8	1	1	2.0	.900
6 yrs.		81	121	.401	3.50	210	206	197	1788.1	1800	522	930	4	1	1	0	808	165	2	.204	107	314	65	14	2.3	.866

Joe Henderson

HENDERSON, JOSEPH LEE
B. July 4, 1946, Lake Cormorant, Miss. BL TR 6'2" 195 lbs.

1974	CHI A	1	0	1.000	8.40	5	3	0	15	21	11	12	0	1	0	0	1	0	0	.000	0	3	1	0	0.8	.750
1976	CIN N	2	0	1.000	0.00	4	0	0	11	9	8	7	0	2	0	0	0	0	0	–	1	2	0	0	0.8	1.000
1977	" "	0	2	.000	12.00	7	0	0	9	17	6	8	0	0	2	0	1	0	0	.000	0	0	0	0	0.0	–
3 yrs.		3	2	.600	6.69	16	3	0	35	47	25	27	0	3	2	0	2	0	0	.000	1	5	1	0	0.4	.857

Bob Hendley

HENDLEY, CHARLES ROBERT
B. Apr. 30, 1939, Macon, Ga. BR TL 6'2" 190 lbs.

1961	MIL N	5	7	.417	3.90	19	13	3	97	96	39	44	0	1	0	0	31	1	0	.032	6	24	1	0	1.6	.968
1962	" "	11	13	.458	3.60	35	29	7	200	188	59	112	2	0	1	1	59	7	1	.119	7	41	5	1	1.5	.906
1963	" "	9	9	.500	3.93	41	24	7	169.1	153	64	105	3	0	2	3	47	5	0	.106	3	39	0	1	1.0	1.000
1964	SF N	10	11	.476	3.64	30	29	4	163.1	161	59	104	1	0	0	0	47	5	0	.106	6	21	2	3	1.0	.931
1965	2 teams			SF N	(8G 0–0)				CHI N	(18G 4–4)																
"	total	4	4	.500	5.96	26	12	2	77	86	38	46	0	0	0	0	17	0	0	.000	4	19	2	0	1.0	.920
1966	CHI N	4	5	.444	3.91	43	6	0	89.2	98	39	65	0	4	3	7	18	3	0	.167	3	18	1	1	0.5	.955
1967	2 teams			CHI N	(7G 2–0)				NY N	(15G 3–3)																
"	total	5	3	.625	3.90	22	13	2	83	82	31	46	0	2	0	0	24	2	0	.083	1	5	0	0	0.3	1.000
7 yrs.		48	52	.480	3.97	216	126	25	879.1	864	329	522	6	8	7	12	243	23	1	.095	30	167	11	5	1.0	.947

Ed Hendricks

HENDRICKS, EDWARD (Big Ed)
B. June 20, 1886, Zeeland, Mich. D. Nov. 28, 1930, Jackson, Mich. BL TL 6'3" 200 lbs.

| 1910 | NY N | 0 | 1 | .000 | 3.75 | 4 | 1 | 1 | 12 | 12 | 4 | 2 | 0 | 0 | 0 | 0 | 4 | 0 | 0 | .000 | 1 | 1 | 0 | 0 | 0.5 | 1.000 |

Year	Team		W	L	PCT	ERA	G	GS	CG	IP	H	BB	SO	ShO	Relief Pitching W	L	SV	Batting AB	H	HR	BA	PO	A	E	DP	TC/G	FA

Ellie Hendricks

HENDRICKS, ELROD JEROME
B. Dec. 22, 1940, Charlotte Amalie, Virgin Islands — BL TR 6'1" 175 lbs.

Year	Team		W	L	PCT	ERA	G	GS	CG	IP	H	BB	SO	ShO	W	L	SV	AB	H	HR	BA	PO	A	E	DP	TC/G	FA
1978	BAL	A	0	0	—	0.00	1	0	0	2.1	1	1	0	0	0	0	0	*				0	0	0	0	0.0	—

Don Hendrickson

HENDRICKSON, DONALD WILLIAM
B. July 14, 1915, Kewanna, Ind. D. Jan. 19, 1977, Norfolk, Va. — BR TR 6'2" 204 lbs.

1945	BOS	N	4	8	.333	4.91	37	2	1	73.1	74	39	14	0	3	8	5	18	3	0	.167	1	14	2	1	0.5	.882
1946			0	1	.000	4.50	2	0	0	2	4	2	2	0	0	1	0	1	0	0	.000	0	0	0	0	0.0	—
2 yrs.			4	9	.308	4.90	39	2	1	75.1	78	41	16	0	3	9	5	19	3	0	.158	1	14	2	1	0.4	.882

Claude Hendrix

HENDRIX, CLAUDE RAYMOND
B. Apr. 13, 1889, Olathe, Kans. D. Mar. 22, 1944, Allentown, Pa. — BR TR 6' 195 lbs.

1911	PIT	N	4	6	.400	2.73	22	12	6	118.2	85	53	57	1	0	1	1	41	4	0	.098	12	45	1	2	2.6	.983
1912			24	9	.727	2.59	39	32	25	288.2	256	105	176	4	3	1	1	121	39	1	.322	7	91	3	2	2.6	.970
1913			14	15	.483	2.84	42	25	17	241	216	89	138	2	4	2	3	99	27	1	.273	6	67	4	6	1.8	.948
1914	CHI	F	29	11	.725	1.69	49	37	34	362	262	77	189	6	3	5	5	130	30	2	.231	10	137	5	5	3.1	.967
1915			16	15	.516	3.00	40	31	26	285	256	84	107	5	2	0	4	113	30	4	.265	11	69	3	2	2.1	.964
1916	CHI	N	8	16	.333	2.68	36	24	15	218	193	67	117	3	1	1	2	80	16	1	.200	10	65	4	2	2.2	.949
1917			10	12	.455	2.60	40	21	13	215	202	72	81	1	3	2	1	86	22	0	.256	6	52	4	1	1.6	.935
1918			19	7	.731	2.78	32	27	21	233	229	54	86	3	1	0	0	91	24	3	.264	6	75	2	1	2.6	.976
1919			10	14	.417	2.62	33	25	15	206.1	208	42	69	2	1	0	1	78	15	1	.192	5	67	1	0	2.2	.986
1920			9	12	.429	3.58	27	23	12	203.2	216	54	72	0	1	0	0	83	15	0	.181	4	56	5	1	2.4	.923
10 yrs.			143	117	.550	2.65	360	257	184	2371.1	2123	697	1092	27	19	10	17	*				77	724	32	22	2.3	.962

WORLD SERIES

| 1918 | CHI | N | 0 | 0 | — | 0.00 | 1 | 0 | 0 | 1 | 0 | 0 | 0 | 0 | 0 | 0 | 0 | 1 | 1 | 0 | 1.000 | 0 | 0 | 0 | 0 | 0.0 | — |

Lafayette Henion

HENION, LAFAYETTE MARION
B. June 7, 1899, Eureka, Calif. D. July 22, 1955, San Luis Obispo, Calif. — BR TR 5'11" 154 lbs.

| 1919 | BKN | N | 0 | 0 | — | 6.00 | 1 | 0 | 0 | 3 | 2 | 2 | 2 | 0 | 0 | 0 | 0 | 1 | 0 | 0 | .000 | 1 | 0 | 0 | 0 | 1.0 | 1.000 |

Tom Henke

HENKE, THOMAS ANTHONY (The Terminator)
B. Dec. 21, 1957, Kansas City, Mo. — BR TR 6'5" 215 lbs.

1982	TEX	A	1	0	1.000	1.15	8	0	0	15.2	14	8	9	0	1	0	0	0	0	0	—	2	2	0	0	0.5	1.000
1983			1	0	1.000	3.38	8	0	0	16	16	4	17	0	1	0	1	0	0	0	—	0	3	1	0	0.5	.750
1984			1	1	.500	6.35	25	0	0	28.1	36	20	25	0	1	1	2	0	0	0	—	1	2	0	0	0.1	1.000
1985	TOR	A	3	3	.500	2.03	28	0	0	40	29	8	42	0	3	3	13	0	0	0	—	3	3	0	0	0.2	1.000
1986			9	5	.643	3.35	63	0	0	91.1	63	32	118	0	9	5	27	0	0	0	—	2	2	0	1	0.1	1.000
1987			0	6	.000	2.49	72	0	0	94	62	25	128	0	0	6	34	0	0	0	—	9	12	0	0	0.3	1.000
1988			4	4	.500	2.91	52	0	0	68	60	24	66	0	4	4	25	0	0	0	—	1	9	0	1	0.2	1.000
1989			8	3	.727	1.92	64	0	0	89	66	25	116	0	8	3	20	0	0	0	—	3	10	1	0	0.2	.929
8 yrs.			27	22	.551	2.81	320	0	0	442.1	346	146	521	0	27	22	122	0	0	0	—	21	43	2	3	0.2	.970

LEAGUE CHAMPIONSHIP SERIES

1985	TOR	A	2	0	1.000	4.26	3	0	0	6.1	5	4	4	0	2	0	0	0	0	0	—	1	0	0	0	0.3	1.000
1989			0	0	—	0.00	3	0	0	2.2	0	0	3	0	0	0	0	0	0	0	—	0	1	0	0	0.3	1.000
2 yrs.			2	0	1.000	3.00	6	0	0	9	5	4	7	0	2	0	0	0	0	0	—	1	1	0	0	0.3	1.000

Weldon Henley

HENLEY, WELDON
B. Oct. 20, 1880, Jasper, Ga. D. Nov. 17, 1960, Palatka, Fla. — BR TR 6' 175 lbs.

1903	PHI	A	12	9	.571	3.91	29	21	13	186.1	186	67	86	1	2	0	0	68	9	0	.132	8	52	3	2	2.2	.952
1904			15	17	.469	2.53	36	34	31	295.2	245	76	130	5	0	0	0	108	24	0	.222	16	115	7	3	3.8	.949
1905			4	12	.250	2.60	25	19	12	183.2	155	67	82	2	0	0	0	65	11	0	.169	10	77	6	1	3.7	.935
1907	BKN	N	1	5	.167	3.05	7	7	5	56	54	21	11	0	0	0	0	20	4	0	.200	5	24	2	0	4.4	.935
4 yrs.			32	43	.427	2.94	97	81	61	721.2	640	231	309	8	2	0	0	261	48	0	.184	39	268	18	6	3.4	.945

Mike Henneman

HENNEMAN, MICHAEL ALAN
B. Dec. 11, 1961, St. Charles, Mo. — BR TR 6'4" 205 lbs.

1987	DET	A	11	3	.786	2.98	55	0	0	96.2	86	30	75	0	11	3	7	1	0	0	.000	8	11	0	2	0.3	1.000
1988			9	6	.600	1.87	65	0	0	91.1	72	24	58	0	9	6	22	0	0	0	—	4	8	1	0	0.2	.923
1989			11	4	.733	3.70	60	0	0	90	84	51	69	0	11	4	8	0	0	0	.000	5	12	0	2	0.3	1.000
3 yrs.			31	13	.705	2.85	180	0	0	278	242	105	202	0	31	13	37	1	0	0	.000	17	31	1	4	0.3	.980

LEAGUE CHAMPIONSHIP SERIES

| 1987 | DET | A | 1 | 0 | 1.000 | 10.80 | 3 | 0 | 0 | 5 | 6 | 6 | 3 | 0 | 1 | 0 | 0 | 0 | 0 | 0 | — | 0 | 2 | 0 | 0 | 0.7 | 1.000 |

George Hennessey

HENNESSEY, GEORGE (Three Star)
B. Oct. 28, 1907, Slatington, Pa. D. Jan. 15, 1988, Princeton, N. J. — BR TR 5'10" 168 lbs.

1937	STL	A	0	1	.000	10.29	5	1	0	7	15	6	4	0	0	1	0	0	0	0	—	0	2	0	0	0.4	1.000
1942	PHI	N	1	1	.500	2.65	5	1	0	17	11	10	2	0	1	0	0	5	0	0	.000	1	2	0	0	0.6	1.000
1945	CHI	N	0	0	—	7.36	2	0	0	3.2	7	1	2	0	0	0	0	0	0	0	—	1	1	0	0	1.0	1.000
3 yrs.			1	2	.333	5.20	12	1	0	27.2	33	17	8	0	1	1	0	5	0	0	.000	2	5	0	0	0.6	1.000

Phil Hennigan

HENNIGAN, PHILLIP WINSTON
B. Apr. 10, 1946, Jasper, Tex. — BR TR 5'11½" 185 lbs.

1969	CLE	A	2	1	.667	3.31	9	0	0	16.1	14	4	10	0	2	1	0	2	0	0	.000	0	0	0	0	0.0	—
1970			6	3	.667	4.00	42	1	0	72	69	44	43	0	6	2	3	7	1	0	.143	12	11	0	1	0.5	1.000
1971			4	3	.571	4.94	57	0	0	82	80	51	69	0	4	3	14	6	0	0	.000	5	8	0	1	0.2	1.000
1972			5	3	.625	2.69	38	1	0	67	54	18	44	0	5	2	6	12	1	0	.083	3	5	0	0	0.2	1.000

Year	Team		W	L	PCT	ERA	G	GS	CG	IP	H	BB	SO	ShO	W	L	SV	AB	H	HR	BA	PO	A	E	DP	TC/G	FA
															Relief Pitching			Batting									

Phil Hennigan *continued*

Year	Team		W	L	PCT	ERA	G	GS	CG	IP	H	BB	SO	ShO	W	L	SV	AB	H	HR	BA	PO	A	E	DP	TC/G	FA
1973	NY	N	0	4	.000	6.23	30	0	0	43.1	50	16	22	0	0	4	3	3	1	0	.333	4	4	1	0	0.3	.889
5 yrs.			17	14	.548	4.26	176	2	0	280.2	267	133	188	0	17	12	26	30	3	0	.100	22	28	1	2	0.3	.980

Pete Henning

HENNING, ERNEST HERMAN
B. Dec. 28, 1887, Crown Point, Ind.   D. Nov. 4, 1939, Dyer, Ind.

BR TR 5'11" 185 lbs.

Year	Team		W	L	PCT	ERA	G	GS	CG	IP	H	BB	SO	ShO	W	L	SV	AB	H	HR	BA	PO	A	E	DP	TC/G	FA
1914	KC	F	6	12	.333	4.83	28	14	7	138	153	58	45	0	1	5	1	44	8	0	.182	6	44	5	1	2.0	.909
1915			8	16	.333	3.17	40	20	15	207	181	76	73	1	2	3	2	68	14	0	.206	10	80	1	3	2.3	.989
2 yrs.			14	28	.333	3.83	68	34	22	345	334	134	118	1	3	8	3	112	22	0	.196	16	124	6	4	2.1	.959

Rick Henninger

HENNINGER, RICHARD LEE
B. Jan. 11, 1948, Hastings, Neb.

BR TR 6'6" 225 lbs.

Year	Team		W	L	PCT	ERA	G	GS	CG	IP	H	BB	SO	ShO	W	L	SV	AB	H	HR	BA	PO	A	E	DP	TC/G	FA
1973	TEX	A	1	0	1.000	2.74	6	2	0	23	23	11	6	0	1	0	0	0	0	0	—	1	1	0	0	0.3	1.000

Bill Henry

HENRY, WILLIAM FRANCIS
B. Feb. 15, 1942, Long Beach, Calif.

BL TL 6'3" 195 lbs.

Year	Team		W	L	PCT	ERA	G	GS	CG	IP	H	BB	SO	ShO	W	L	SV	AB	H	HR	BA	PO	A	E	DP	TC/G	FA
1966	NY	A	0	0	—	0.00	2	0	0	3	0	2	3	0	0	0	0	0	0	0	—	0	2	0	0	1.0	1.000

Bill Henry

HENRY, WILLIAM RODMAN
B. Oct. 15, 1927, Alice, Tex.

BL TL 6'2" 180 lbs.

Year	Team		W	L	PCT	ERA	G	GS	CG	IP	H	BB	SO	ShO	W	L	SV	AB	H	HR	BA	PO	A	E	DP	TC/G	FA
1952	BOS	A	5	4	.556	3.87	13	10	5	76.2	75	36	23	0	0	0	0	31	8	0	.258	5	7	0	1	0.9	1.000
1953			5	5	.500	3.26	21	12	4	85.2	86	33	56	1	1	0	1	32	6	0	.188	4	11	1	0	0.8	.938
1954			3	7	.300	4.52	24	13	3	95.2	104	49	38	1	0	1	0	34	4	0	.118	4	13	0	0	0.7	1.000
1955			2	4	.333	3.32	17	7	0	59.2	56	21	23	0	1	1	0	19	2	0	.105	4	11	0	1	0.9	1.000
1958	CHI	N	5	4	.556	2.88	44	0	0	81.1	63	17	58	0	5	4	6	17	4	0	.235	2	8	0	1	0.2	1.000
1959			9	8	.529	2.68	65	0	0	134.1	111	26	115	0	9	8	12	31	6	0	.194	2	18	1	2	0.3	.952
1960	CIN	N	1	5	.167	3.19	51	0	0	67.2	62	20	58	0	1	5	17	8	0	0	.000	5	13	1	2	0.4	.947
1961			2	1	.667	2.19	47	0	0	53.1	50	15	53	0	2	1	16	5	0	0	.000	4	7	0	0	0.2	1.000
1962			4	2	.667	4.58	40	0	0	37.1	40	20	35	0	4	2	11	3	1	0	.333	2	2	0	0	0.1	1.000
1963			1	3	.250	4.15	47	0	0	52	55	11	45	0	1	3	14	6	1	0	.167	2	9	2	1	0.3	.846
1964			2	2	.500	0.87	37	0	0	52	31	12	28	0	2	2	6	6	3	0	.500	6	7	0	0	0.4	1.000
1965	2 teams	CIN N (3G 2–0)				SF N (35G 2–2)																					
"	total		4	2	.667	3.26	38	0	0	47	43	9	40	0	4	2	4	5	1	0	.200	4	8	0	0	0.2	1.000
1966	SF	N	1	1	.500	2.49	35	0	0	21.2	15	10	15	0	1	1	1	2	0	0	.000	1	3	0	0	0.1	1.000
1967			2	0	1.000	2.05	28	1	0	22	16	9	23	0	2	0	2	1	0	0	.000	1	1	0	0	0.1	1.000
1968	2 teams	SF N (7G 0–2)				PIT N (10G 0–0)																					
"	total		0	2	.000	7.48	17	1	0	21.2	33	6	9	0	0	2	0	3	0	0	.000	2	1	0	0	0.2	1.000
1969	HOU	N	0	0	—	0.00	3	0	0	5	2	2	2	0	0	0	0	0	0	0	—	0	0	0	0	0.0	—
16 yrs.			46	50	.479	3.26	527	44	12	913	842	296	621	2	33	31	90	203	36	0	.177	48	115	5	9	0.3	.970

WORLD SERIES

Year	Team		W	L	PCT	ERA	G	GS	CG	IP	H	BB	SO	ShO	W	L	SV	AB	H	HR	BA	PO	A	E	DP	TC/G	FA
1961	CIN	N	0	0	—	19.29	2	0	0	2.1	4	2	3	0	0	0	0	0	0	0	—	0	1	0	0	0.5	1.000

Dutch Henry

HENRY, FRANK JOHN
B. May 12, 1902, Cleveland, Ohio   D. Aug. 23, 1968, Cleveland, Ohio

BL TL 6'1" 173 lbs.

Year	Team		W	L	PCT	ERA	G	GS	CG	IP	H	BB	SO	ShO	W	L	SV	AB	H	HR	BA	PO	A	E	DP	TC/G	FA
1921	STL	A	0	0	—	4.50	1	0	0	2	2	0	1	0	0	0	0	1	1	0	1.000	1	0	0	0	1.0	1.000
1922			0	0	—	5.40	4	0	0	5	7	5	3	0	0	0	0	0	0	0	—	0	1	0	0	0.3	1.000
1923	BKN	N	4	6	.400	3.91	17	9	5	94.1	105	28	28	2	1	1	0	35	8	0	.229	2	21	1	2	1.4	.958
1924			1	2	.333	5.67	16	4	0	46	69	15	11	0	1	1	0	20	5	0	.250	3	12	0	0	0.9	1.000
1927	NY	N	11	6	.647	4.23	45	15	7	163.2	184	31	40	1	6	2	4	55	13	0	.236	5	30	0	0	0.8	1.000
1928			3	6	.333	3.80	17	8	4	64	82	25	23	0	0	1	0	19	3	0	.158	4	17	1	5	1.3	.955
1929	2 teams	NY N (27G 5–6)				CHI A (2G 1–0)																					
"	total		6	6	.500	4.10	29	10	5	116.1	149	38	29	0	3	3	1	35	8	0	.229	8	17	1	2	0.9	.962
1930	CHI	A	2	17	.105	4.88	35	16	4	155	211	48	35	0	2	2	0	51	12	0	.235	11	42	1	3	1.5	.981
8 yrs.			27	43	.386	4.39	164	62	25	646.1	809	190	170	3	11	10	6	216	50	0	.231	34	140	4	12	1.1	.978

Dwayne Henry

HENRY, DWAYNE ALLEN
B. Feb. 16, 1962, Elkton, Md.

BR TR 6'3" 210 lbs.

Year	Team		W	L	PCT	ERA	G	GS	CG	IP	H	BB	SO	ShO	W	L	SV	AB	H	HR	BA	PO	A	E	DP	TC/G	FA
1984	TEX	A	0	1	.000	8.31	3	0	0	4.1	5	7	2	0	0	0	0	0	0	0	—	0	0	0	0	0.0	—
1985			2	2	.500	2.57	16	0	0	21	16	7	20	0	2	2	3	0	0	0	—	1	2	1	1	0.3	.750
1986			1	0	1.000	4.66	19	0	0	19.1	14	22	17	0	1	0	0	0	0	0	—	0	4	0	0	0.2	1.000
1987			0	0	—	9.00	5	0	0	10	12	9	7	0	0	0	0	0	0	0	—	2	1	0	0	0.6	1.000
1988			0	1	.000	8.71	11	0	0	10.1	15	9	10	0	0	1	1	0	0	0	—	1	0	0	0	0.1	1.000
1989	ATL	N	0	2	.000	4.26	12	0	0	12.2	12	5	16	0	0	2	1	0	0	0	—	1	0	1	0	0.2	.500
6 yrs.			3	6	.333	5.33	66	0	0	77.2	74	59	72	0	3	5	5	0	0	0	—	5	7	2	1	0.2	.857

Earl Henry

HENRY, EARL CLIFFORD (Hook)
B. June 10, 1917, Roseville, Ohio

BL TL 5'11" 172 lbs.

Year	Team		W	L	PCT	ERA	G	GS	CG	IP	H	BB	SO	ShO	W	L	SV	AB	H	HR	BA	PO	A	E	DP	TC/G	FA
1944	CLE	A	1	1	.500	4.58	2	2	1	17.2	18	3	5	0	0	0	0	5	0	0	.000	1	4	0	0	2.5	1.000
1945			0	3	.000	5.40	15	1	0	21.2	20	20	10	0	0	2	0	4	2	0	.500	3	6	0	0	0.6	1.000
2 yrs.			1	4	.200	5.03	17	3	1	39.1	38	23	15	0	0	2	0	9	2	0	.222	4	10	0	0	0.8	1.000

Jim Henry

HENRY, JAMES FRANCIS
B. June 26, 1910, Danville, Va.   D. Aug. 15, 1976, Memphis, Tenn.

BR TR 6'2" 175 lbs.

Year	Team		W	L	PCT	ERA	G	GS	CG	IP	H	BB	SO	ShO	W	L	SV	AB	H	HR	BA	PO	A	E	DP	TC/G	FA
1936	BOS	A	5	1	.833	4.60	21	8	2	76.1	75	40	36	0	2	0	0	26	3	0	.115	3	13	0	0	0.8	1.000
1937			1	0	1.000	5.17	3	2	1	15.2	15	11	8	0	0	0	0	5	0	0	.000	0	2	0	1	0.7	1.000
1939	PHI	N	0	1	.000	5.09	9	1	0	23	24	8	7	0	0	1	1	5	0	0	.000	0	3	1	0	0.4	.750
3 yrs.			6	2	.750	4.77	33	11	3	115	114	59	51	0	2	1	1	36	3	0	.083	3	18	1	1	0.7	.955

Year	Team		W	L	PCT	ERA	G	GS	CG	IP	H	BB	SO	ShO	Relief Pitching W	L	SV	Batting AB	H	HR	BA	PO	A	E	DP	TC/G	FA

John Henry

HENRY, JOHN MICHAEL   B. Sept. 2, 1863, Springfield, Mass.   D. June 11, 1939, Hartford, Conn.   TL

Year	Team		W	L	PCT	ERA	G	GS	CG	IP	H	BB	SO	ShO	W	L	SV	AB	H	HR	BA	PO	A	E	DP	TC/G	FA
1884	CLE	N	1	4	.200	3.64	5	5	5	42	46	26	23	1	0	0	0	26	4	0	.154	4	11	0	0	3.0	1.000
1885	BAL	AA	2	7	.222	4.31	9	9	9	71	71	13	31	0	0	0	0	34	9	0	.265	9	18	2	1	3.2	.931
1886	WAS	N	1	3	.250	4.23	4	4	4	27.2	35	15	19	0	0	0	0	14	5	0	.357	2	3	1	0	1.5	.833
3 yrs.			4	14	.222	4.09	18	18	18	140.2	152	54	73	1	0	0	0	*				15	32	3	1	2.8	.940

Roy Henshaw

HENSHAW, ROY KNIKLEBINE   B. July 29, 1911, Chicago, Ill.   BR TL 5'8" 155 lbs.

Year	Team		W	L	PCT	ERA	G	GS	CG	IP	H	BB	SO	ShO	W	L	SV	AB	H	HR	BA	PO	A	E	DP	TC/G	FA
1933	CHI	N	2	1	.667	4.19	21	0	0	38.2	32	20	16	0	2	1	0	10	2	0	.200	1	5	1	0	0.3	.857
1935			13	5	.722	3.28	31	18	7	142.2	135	68	53	3	4	0	1	51	13	0	.255	6	15	4	2	0.8	.840
1936			6	5	.545	3.97	39	14	6	129.1	152	56	69	2	1	3	1	44	6	0	.136	4	16	3	1	0.6	.870
1937	BKN	N	5	12	.294	5.07	42	16	5	156.1	176	69	98	0	1	3	2	48	8	0	.167	4	32	3	2	0.9	.923
1938	STL	N	5	11	.313	4.02	27	15	4	130	132	48	34	0	2	1	0	41	9	0	.220	3	23	1	0	1.0	.963
1942	DET	A	2	4	.333	4.09	23	2	0	61.2	63	27	24	0	2	3	1	12	1	0	.083	4	10	2	0	0.7	.875
1943			0	2	.000	3.79	26	3	0	71.1	75	33	33	0	0	1	2	18	2	0	.111	9	13	1	0	0.9	.957
1944			0	0	–	8.76	7	1	0	12.1	17	6	10	0	0	0	0	5	0	0	.000	3	2	0	0	0.7	1.000
8 yrs.			33	40	.452	4.16	216	69	22	742.1	782	327	337	5	12	12	7	229	41	0	.179	34	116	15	5	0.8	.909

WORLD SERIES

Year	Team		W	L	PCT	ERA	G	GS	CG	IP	H	BB	SO	ShO	W	L	SV	AB	H	HR	BA	PO	A	E	DP	TC/G	FA
1935	CHI	N	0	0	–	7.36	1	0	0	3.2	2	5	2	0	0	0	0	1	0	0	.000	0	1	0	0	1.0	1.000

Phil Hensiek

HENSIEK, PHILIP FRANK (Sid)   B. Oct. 13, 1901, St. Louis, Mo.   D. Feb. 21, 1972, St. Louis, Mo.   BR TR 6' 160 lbs.

Year	Team		W	L	PCT	ERA	G	GS	CG	IP	H	BB	SO	ShO	W	L	SV	AB	H	HR	BA	PO	A	E	DP	TC/G	FA
1935	WAS	A	0	3	.000	9.69	6	1	0	13	21	9	6	0	0	2	1	3	2	0	.667	0	3	2	0	0.8	.600

Chuck Hensley

HENSLEY, CHARLES FLOYD   B. Mar. 11, 1959, Tulare, Calif.   BL TL 6'3" 190 lbs.

Year	Team		W	L	PCT	ERA	G	GS	CG	IP	H	BB	SO	ShO	W	L	SV	AB	H	HR	BA	PO	A	E	DP	TC/G	FA
1986	SF	N	0	0	–	2.45	11	0	0	7.1	5	2	6	0	0	0	1	0	0	0	–	0	1	0	0	0.1	1.000

Bill Hepler

HEPLER, WILLIAM LEWIS   B. Sept. 25, 1945, Covington, Va.   BL TL 6' 160 lbs.

Year	Team		W	L	PCT	ERA	G	GS	CG	IP	H	BB	SO	ShO	W	L	SV	AB	H	HR	BA	PO	A	E	DP	TC/G	FA
1966	NY	N	3	3	.500	3.52	37	3	0	69	71	51	25	0	3	1	0	14	3	0	.214	3	11	2	0	0.4	.875

Ron Herbel

HERBEL, RONALD SAMUEL   B. Jan. 16, 1938, Denver, Colo.   BR TR 6'1" 195 lbs.

Year	Team		W	L	PCT	ERA	G	GS	CG	IP	H	BB	SO	ShO	W	L	SV	AB	H	HR	BA	PO	A	E	DP	TC/G	FA
1963	SF	N	0	0	–	6.75	2	0	0	1.1	1	1	1	0	0	0	0	0	0	0	–	0	0	0	0	0.0	–
1964			9	9	.500	3.07	40	22	7	161	162	61	98	2	0	1	1	47	0	0	.000	12	39	2	1	1.3	.962
1965			12	9	.571	3.85	47	21	1	170.2	172	47	106	0	4	2	1	49	1	0	.020	14	39	3	1	1.2	.946
1966			4	5	.444	4.16	32	18	0	129.2	149	39	55	0	0	1	1	38	1	0	.026	4	22	3	2	0.9	.897
1967			4	5	.444	3.08	42	11	1	125.2	125	35	52	1	2	1	1	28	3	0	.107	11	37	0	7	1.1	1.000
1968			0	0	–	3.35	28	2	0	43	55	15	18	0	0	0	0	3	0	0	.000	3	11	0	0	0.5	1.000
1969			4	1	.800	4.03	39	4	2	87	92	23	34	0	2	1	1	17	0	0	.000	8	16	1	1	0.6	.960
1970	2 teams	SD N	(64G 7–5)				NY N	(12G 2–2)																			
"	total		9	7	.563	4.57	76	0	0	124	128	41	61	0	9	6	10	13	0	0	.000	8	17	2	0	0.4	.926
1971	ATL	N	0	1	.000	5.19	25	0	0	52	61	23	22	0	0	1	1	11	1	0	.091	3	7	0	3	0.4	1.000
9 yrs.			42	37	.532	3.82	331	79	11	894.1	945	285	447	3	17	13	16	206	6	0	.029	63	188	11	15	0.8	.958

Ernie Herbert

HERBERT, ERNIE ALBERT (Tex)   B. Jan. 30, 1887, Hale, Mo.   D. Jan. 13, 1968, Dallas, Tex.   BR TR 5'10" 165 lbs.

Year	Team		W	L	PCT	ERA	G	GS	CG	IP	H	BB	SO	ShO	W	L	SV	AB	H	HR	BA	PO	A	E	DP	TC/G	FA
1913	CIN	N	0	0	–	2.08	6	0	0	17.1	12	5	5	0	0	0	0	4	1	0	.250	0	1	0	0	0.2	1.000
1914	STL	F	1	1	.500	3.75	18	2	0	50.1	56	27	24	0	0	0	1	13	7	0	.538	1	3	0	1	0.2	1.000
1915			1	0	1.000	3.38	11	1	1	48	48	18	23	0	0	0	0	18	5	0	.278	0	12	0	0	1.1	1.000
3 yrs.			2	1	.667	3.35	35	3	1	115.2	116	50	52	0	0	0	1	35	13	0	.371	1	16	0	1	0.5	1.000

Fred Herbert

HERBERT, FREDERICK   Born Herbert Frederick Kemman.   B. Mar. 4, 1887, LaGrange, Ill.   D. May 29, 1963, Tice, Fla.   BR TR 6' 185 lbs.

Year	Team		W	L	PCT	ERA	G	GS	CG	IP	H	BB	SO	ShO	W	L	SV	AB	H	HR	BA	PO	A	E	DP	TC/G	FA
1915	NY	N	1	1	.500	1.06	2	2	1	17	12	4	6	0	0	0	0	6	1	0	.167	0	5	0	0	2.5	1.000

Ray Herbert

HERBERT, RAYMOND ERNEST   B. Dec. 15, 1929, Detroit, Mich.   BR TR 5'11" 185 lbs.

Year	Team		W	L	PCT	ERA	G	GS	CG	IP	H	BB	SO	ShO	W	L	SV	AB	H	HR	BA	PO	A	E	DP	TC/G	FA
1950	DET	A	1	2	.333	3.63	8	3	1	22.1	20	12	5	0	1	0	1	7	2	0	.286	1	8	0	1	1.1	1.000
1951			4	0	1.000	1.42	5	0	0	12.2	8	9	9	0	4	0	0	4	0	0	.000	0	1	1	0	0.4	.500
1953			4	6	.400	5.24	43	3	0	87.2	109	46	37	0	4	4	6	19	3	0	.158	9	28	2	2	0.9	.949
1954			3	6	.333	5.87	42	4	0	84.1	114	50	44	0	3	3	0	17	3	1	.176	7	24	1	2	0.8	.969
1955	KC	A	1	8	.111	6.26	23	11	2	87.2	99	40	30	0	0	0	0	21	4	0	.190	8	24	0	0	1.4	1.000
1958			8	8	.500	3.50	42	16	5	175	161	55	108	0	1	3	3	52	10	0	.192	13	23	1	4	1.2	.939
1959			11	11	.500	4.85	37	26	10	183.2	196	62	99	2	0	1	1	57	12	1	.211	8	55	2	6	1.8	.969
1960			14	15	.483	3.28	37	33	14	252.2	256	72	122	0	0	1	0	76	13	0	.171	8	55	2	6	1.8	.969
1961	2 teams	KC A	(13G 3–6)				CHI A	(21G 9–6)																			
"	total		12	12	.500	4.55	34	32	5	221.1	245	66	84	0	1	0	0	81	15	2	.185	20	39	2	4	1.8	.967
1962	CHI	A	20	9	.690	3.27	35	35	12	236.2	228	74	115	2	0	0	0	82	16	2	.195	21	50	0	8	2.0	1.000
1963			13	10	.565	3.24	33	33	14	224.2	230	35	105	7	0	0	0	63	14	1	.222	18	48	1	1	2.0	.985
1964			6	7	.462	3.47	20	19	1	111.2	117	17	40	1	0	0	0	36	5	0	.139	3	18	0	1	1.1	1.000
1965	PHI	N	5	8	.385	3.86	25	19	2	130.2	162	19	51	1	0	0	0	41	11	0	.268	2	24	0	1	1.3	1.000
1966			2	5	.286	4.29	23	2	0	50.1	55	14	15	0	4	0	2	13	1	0	.077	1	1	0	0	0.4	1.000
14 yrs.			104	107	.493	4.01	407	236	68	1881.1	2000	571	864	13	16	17	15	569	109	7	.192	126	389	13	42	1.3	.975

Year	Team		W	L	PCT	ERA	G	GS	CG	IP	H	BB	SO	ShO	Relief Pitching W	L	SV	Batting AB	H	HR	BA	PO	A	E	DP	TC/G	FA

Ubaldo Heredia

HEREDIA, UBALDO JOSE
Born Ubaldo Jose Heredia y Martinez.
B. May 4, 1956, Ciudad Bolivar, Venezuela

BR TR 6'2" 180 lbs.

Year	Team	W	L	PCT	ERA	G	GS	CG	IP	H	BB	SO	ShO	W	L	SV	AB	H	HR	BA	PO	A	E	DP	TC/G	FA
1987	MON N	0	1	.000	5.40	2	2	0	10	10	3	6	0	0	0	0	2	0	0	.000	0	2	0	1	1.0	1.000

Art Herman

HERMAN, ARTHUR
B. May 11, 1871, Louisville, Ky. D. Sept. 20, 1955, Los Angeles, Calif.

Year	Team	W	L	PCT	ERA	G	GS	CG	IP	H	BB	SO	ShO	W	L	SV	AB	H	HR	BA	PO	A	E	DP	TC/G	FA
1896	LOU N	4	6	.400	5.63	14	12	9	94.1	122	36	13	0	0	0	0	36	5	0	.139	1	20	4	1	1.8	.840
1897		0	1	.000	4.00	3	2	1	18	23	5	4	0	0	0	0	6	2	0	.333	0	6	0	0	2.0	1.000
2 yrs.		4	7	.364	5.37	17	14	10	112.1	145	41	17	0	0	0	0	42	7	0	.167	1	26	4	1	1.8	.871

Jesus Hernaiz

HERNAIZ, JESUS RAFAEL
Born Jesus Rafael Hernaiz y Rodriguez.
B. Jan. 8, 1948, Santurce, Puerto Rico

BR TR 6'2" 175 lbs.

Year	Team	W	L	PCT	ERA	G	GS	CG	IP	H	BB	SO	ShO	W	L	SV	AB	H	HR	BA	PO	A	E	DP	TC/G	FA
1974	PHI N	2	3	.400	5.93	27	0	0	41	53	25	16	0	2	3	1	2	0	0	.000	4	6	3	0	0.5	.769

Evelio Hernandez

HERNANDEZ, GREGORIO EVELIO
Born Gregorio Evelio Hernandez y Lopez.
B. Dec. 24, 1930, Guanabacoa, Cuba

BR TR 6'1" 180 lbs.

Year	Team	W	L	PCT	ERA	G	GS	CG	IP	H	BB	SO	ShO	W	L	SV	AB	H	HR	BA	PO	A	E	DP	TC/G	FA
1956	WAS A	1	1	.500	4.76	4	4	1	22.2	24	8	9	0	0	0	0	11	2	0	.182	1	3	0	0	1.0	1.000
1957		0	0		4.25	14	2	0	36	38	20	15	0	0	0	0	6	0	0	.000	2	3	1	0	0.4	.833
2 yrs.		1	1	.500	4.45	18	6	1	58.2	62	28	24	0	0	0	0	17	2	0	.118	3	6	1	0	0.6	.900

Guillermo Hernandez

HERNANDEZ, GUILLERMO (Willie)
Born Guillermo Hernandez y Villanueva.
B. Nov. 14, 1954, Aguada, Puerto Rico

BL TL 6'3" 180 lbs.

Year	Team	W	L	PCT	ERA	G	GS	CG	IP	H	BB	SO	ShO	W	L	SV	AB	H	HR	BA	PO	A	E	DP	TC/G	FA
1977	CHI N	8	7	.533	3.03	67	1	0	110	94	28	78	0	8	6	4	16	1	0	.063	8	27	0	2	0.5	1.000
1978		8	2	.800	3.75	54	0	0	60	57	35	38	0	8	2	3	1	0	0	.000	2	12	0	0	0.3	1.000
1979		4	4	.500	5.01	51	2	0	79	85	39	53	0	4	3	0	8	2	0	.250	4	11	1	0	0.3	.938
1980		1	9	.100	4.42	53	7	0	108	115	45	75	0	1	3	0	19	4	0	.211	12	20	2	0	0.6	1.000
1981		0	0	—	3.86	12	0	0	14	14	8	13	0	0	0	2	0	0	0		0	3	0	0	0.3	1.000
1982		4	6	.400	3.00	75	0	0	75	74	24	54	0	4	6	10	3	0	0	.000	5	22	1	1	0.4	.964
1983	2 teams	CHI N	(11G 1-0)		PHI N	(63G 8-4)																				
"	total	9	4	.692	3.28	74	1	0	115.1	109	32	93	0	9	4	8	15	6	0	.400	2	17	0	3	0.3	1.000
1984	DET A	9	3	.750	1.92	80	0	0	140.1	96	36	112	0	9	3	32	0	0	0	—	5	14	0	1	0.2	1.000
1985		8	10	.444	2.70	74	0	0	106.2	82	14	76	0	8	10	31	1	0	0	.000	7	7	1	0	0.2	.933
1986		8	7	.533	3.55	64	0	0	88.2	87	21	77	0	8	7	24	0	0	0	—	6	13	0	0	0.3	1.000
1987		3	4	.429	3.67	45	0	0	49	53	20	30	0	3	4	8	0	0	0	—	2	4	1	1	0.2	.857
1988		6	5	.545	3.06	63	0	0	67.2	50	31	59	0	6	5	10	0	0	0	—	3	15	0	1	0.3	1.000
1989		2	2	.500	5.74	32	0	0	31.1	36	16	30	0	2	2	15	0	0	0	—	2	4	0	1	0.2	1.000
13 yrs.		70	63	.526	3.38	744	11	0	1045	952	349	788	0	70	55	147	63	13	0	.206	58	169	4	12	0.3	.983

LEAGUE CHAMPIONSHIP SERIES

Year	Team	W	L	PCT	ERA	G	GS	CG	IP	H	BB	SO	ShO	W	L	SV	AB	H	HR	BA	PO	A	E	DP	TC/G	FA
1984	DET A	0	0	—	2.25	3	0	0	4	3	1	3	0	0	0	1	0	0	0	—	0	0	0	0	0.0	—
1987		0	0	—	0.00	1	0	0	.1	2	0	0	0	0	0	0	0	0	0	—	0	0	0	0	0.0	—
2 yrs.		0	0	—	2.08	4	0	0	4.1	5	1	3	0	0	0	1	0	0	0	—	0	0	0	0	0.0	—

WORLD SERIES

Year	Team	W	L	PCT	ERA	G	GS	CG	IP	H	BB	SO	ShO	W	L	SV	AB	H	HR	BA	PO	A	E	DP	TC/G	FA
1983	PHI N	0	0	—	0.00	3	0	0	4	0	1	4	0	0	0	0	0	0	0	—	1	0	0	0	0.3	1.000
1984	DET A	0	0	—	1.69	3	0	0	5.1	4	0	0	0	0	0	2	0	0	0	—	0	1	0	0	0.3	1.000
2 yrs.		0	0	—	0.96	6	0	0	9.1	4	1	4	0	0	0	2	0	0	0	—	1	1	0	0	0.3	1.000

Manny Hernandez

HERNANDEZ, MANUEL ANTONIO
Born Manuel Antonio Hernandez y Montas.
B. May 7, 1961, La Romana, Dominican Republic

BR TR 6' 150 lbs.

Year	Team	W	L	PCT	ERA	G	GS	CG	IP	H	BB	SO	ShO	W	L	SV	AB	H	HR	BA	PO	A	E	DP	TC/G	FA
1986	HOU N	2	3	.400	3.90	9	4	0	27.2	33	12	9	0	1	0	0	6	0	0	.000	1	5	0	0	0.7	1.000
1987		0	4	.000	5.40	6	3	0	21.2	25	5	12	0	0	2	0	5	0	0	.000	2	4	1	0	1.2	.857
1989	NY N	0	0	—	5.40	1	0	0	1	0	0	1	0	0	0	0	0	0	0	—	0	0	0	0	0.0	—
3 yrs.		2	7	.222	4.47	16	7	0	50.1	58	17	22	0	1	2	0	11	0	0	.000	3	9	1	0	0.8	.923

Ramon Hernandez

HERNANDEZ, RAMON
Born Ramon Hernandez y Gonzalez.
B. Aug. 31, 1940, Carolina, Puerto Rico

BB TL 5'11" 165 lbs.

Year	Team	W	L	PCT	ERA	G	GS	CG	IP	H	BB	SO	ShO	W	L	SV	AB	H	HR	BA	PO	A	E	DP	TC/G	FA
1967	ATL N	0	2	.000	4.18	46	0	0	51.2	60	14	28	0	0	2	5	4	0	0	.000	2	12	0	1	0.3	1.000
1968	CHI N	0	0	—	9.00	8	0	0	9	14	0	3	0	0	0	0	0	0	0	—	0	3	1	0	0.5	.750
1971	PIT N	0	1	.000	0.75	10	0	0	12	5	2	7	0	0	1	4	2	1	0	.500	2	2	0	0	0.4	1.000
1972		5	0	1.000	1.67	53	0	0	70	50	22	47	0	5	0	14	12	2	0	.167	3	11	0	0	0.3	1.000
1973		4	5	.444	2.41	59	0	0	89.2	71	25	64	0	4	5	11	8	1	0	.125	3	16	1	2	0.3	.950
1974		5	2	.714	2.74	58	0	0	69	68	18	33	0	5	2	2	4	1	0	.250	2	9	1	1	0.2	.917
1975		7	2	.778	2.95	46	0	0	64	62	28	43	0	7	2	5	6	0	0	.000	1	13	0	0	0.3	1.000
1976	2 teams	PIT N	(37G 2-2)		CHI N	(2G 0-0)																				
"	total	2	2	.500	3.43	39	0	0	44.2	44	16	18	0	2	2	3	2	0	0	.000	0	7	2	1	0.2	.778
1977	2 teams	CHI N	(6G 0-0)		BOS A	(12G 0-1)																				
"	total	0	1	.000	6.53	18	0	0	20.2	25	10	12	0	0	1	2	1	0	0	.000	0	5	0	0	0.3	1.000
9 yrs.		23	15	.605	3.03	337	0	0	430.2	399	135	255	0	23	15	46	40	5	0	.125	13	78	5	5	0.3	.948

LEAGUE CHAMPIONSHIP SERIES

Year	Team	W	L	PCT	ERA	G	GS	CG	IP	H	BB	SO	ShO	W	L	SV	AB	H	HR	BA	PO	A	E	DP	TC/G	FA
1972	PIT N	0	0	—	2.70	3	0	0	3.1	1	0	3	0	0	0	0	0	0	0	—	0	2	0	0	0.7	1.000
1974		0	0	—	0.00	2	0	0	4.1	3	1	2	0	0	0	1	1	0	0	.000	0	1	0	0	0.5	1.000
1975		0	1	.000	27.00	1	0	0	.2	3	0	0	0	0	1	0	0	0	0	—	0	0	0	0	0.0	—
3 yrs.		0	1	.000	3.24	6	0	0	8.1	7	1	5	0	0	1	1	1	0	0	.000	0	3	0	0	0.5	1.000

Year	Team	W	L	PCT	ERA	G	GS	CG	IP	H	BB	SO	ShO	Relief Pitching W	L	SV	Batting AB	H	HR	BA	PO	A	E	DP	TC/G	FA

Rudy Hernandez

HERNANDEZ, RUDOLPH ALBERT
Born Rudolph Albert Hernandez y Fuentes.
B. Dec. 10, 1931, Santiago, Dominican Republic

BR TR 6'3" 185 lbs.

Year	Team	W	L	PCT	ERA	G	GS	CG	IP	H	BB	SO	ShO	W	L	SV	AB	H	HR	BA	PO	A	E	DP	TC/G	FA
1960	WAS A	4	1	.800	4.41	21	0	0	34.2	34	21	22	0	4	1	0	6	1	0	.167	1	4	1	1	0.3	.833
1961		0	1	.000	3.00	7	0	0	9	8	3	4	0	0	1	0	0	0	0	–	1	3	0	0	0.6	1.000
2 yrs.		4	2	.667	4.12	28	0	0	43.2	42	24	26	0	4	2	0	6	1	0	.167	2	7	1	1	0.4	.900

Xavier Hernandez

HERNANDEZ, FRANCIS XAVIER
B. Aug. 16, 1965, Port Arthur, Tex.

BL TR 6'2" 185 lbs.

Year	Team	W	L	PCT	ERA	G	GS	CG	IP	H	BB	SO	ShO	W	L	SV	AB	H	HR	BA	PO	A	E	DP	TC/G	FA
1989	TOR A	1	0	1.000	4.76	7	0	0	22.2	25	8	7	0	1	0	0	0	0	0	–	1	2	1	0	0.6	.750

Walt Herrell

HERRELL, WALTER WILLIAM
B. Feb. 19, 1889, Rockville, Md. D. Jan. 23, 1949, Front Royal, Va.

Year	Team	W	L	PCT	ERA	G	GS	CG	IP	H	BB	SO	ShO	W	L	SV	AB	H	HR	BA	PO	A	E	DP	TC/G	FA
1911	WAS A	0	0	–	18.00	1	0	0	2	5	2	0	0	0	0	0	1	0	0	.000	1	0	0	0	1.0	1.000

Tito Herrera

HERRERA, PROCOPIO (Bobby)
Born Procopio Herrera y Rodriguez.
·B. July 26, 1926, Nuevo Laredo, Mexico

BR TR 6' 184 lbs.

Year	Team	W	L	PCT	ERA	G	GS	CG	IP	H	BB	SO	ShO	W	L	SV	AB	H	HR	BA	PO	A	E	DP	TC/G	FA
1951	STL A	0	0	–	27.00	3	0	0	2.1	6	4	1	0	0	0	0	0	0	0	–	0	0	0	0	0.0	–

Troy Herriage

HERRIAGE, WILLIAM TROY (Dutch)
B. Dec. 20, 1930, Tipton, Okla.

BR TR 6'1" 170 lbs.

Year	Team	W	L	PCT	ERA	G	GS	CG	IP	H	BB	SO	ShO	W	L	SV	AB	H	HR	BA	PO	A	E	DP	TC/G	FA
1956	KC A	1	13	.071	6.64	31	16	1	103	135	64	59	0	0	1	0	25	3	0	.120	0	11	3	0	0.5	.786

Tom Herrin

HERRIN, THOMAS EDWARD
B. Sept. 12, 1929, Shreveport, La.

BR TR 6'3" 190 lbs.

Year	Team	W	L	PCT	ERA	G	GS	CG	IP	H	BB	SO	ShO	W	L	SV	AB	H	HR	BA	PO	A	E	DP	TC/G	FA
1954	BOS A	1	2	.333	7.31	14	1	0	28.1	34	22	8	0	1	1	0	8	1	0	.125	4	9	0	2	0.9	1.000

Art Herring

HERRING, ARTHUR L (Sandy)
B. Mar. 10, 1907, Altus, Okla.

BR TR 5'7" 168 lbs.

Year	Team	W	L	PCT	ERA	G	GS	CG	IP	H	BB	SO	ShO	W	L	SV	AB	H	HR	BA	PO	A	E	DP	TC/G	FA
1929	DET A	2	1	.667	4.78	4	4	2	32	38	19	15	0	0	0	0	14	3	0	.214	2	7	0	0	2.3	1.000
1930		3	3	.500	5.33	23	6	1	77.2	97	36	16	0	1	0	0	23	3	0	.130	4	14	0	1	0.8	1.000
1931		7	13	.350	4.31	35	16	9	165	186	67	64	0	1	4	1	55	11	0	.200	9	39	2	6	1.4	.960
1932		1	2	.333	5.24	12	0	0	22.1	25	15	12	0	1	2	2	4	0	0	.000	0	6	0	1	0.5	1.000
1933		1	2	.333	3.84	24	0	0	61	61	20	20	0	0	2	0	13	1	0	.077	0	11	0	2	0.5	1.000
1934	BKN N	2	4	.333	6.20	14	4	2	49.1	63	29	15	0	1	3	0	14	2	0	.143	3	9	1	0	0.9	.923
1939	CHI A	0	0	–	5.65	7	0	0	14.1	13	5	8	0	0	0	0	4	0	0	.000	0	3	0	0	0.4	1.000
1944	BKN N	3	4	.429	3.42	12	6	3	55.1	59	17	19	1	1	0	1	15	3	0	.200	3	11	0	1	1.2	1.000
1945		7	4	.636	3.48	22	15	7	124	103	43	34	2	1	0	2	42	4	0	.095	5	25	2	2	1.5	.938
1946		7	2	.778	3.35	35	2	0	86	91	29	34	0	5	2	5	22	4	0	.182	5	25	2	2	0.9	.938
1947	PIT N	1	3	.250	8.44	11	0	0	10.2	18	4	6	0	1	3	2	2	0	0	.000	0	1	0	0	0.1	1.000
11 yrs.		34	38	.472	4.32	199	56	25	697.2	754	284	243	3	12	16	13	208	31	0	.149	33	153	5	17	1.0	.974

Bill Herring

HERRING, WILLIAM FRANCIS (Smoke)
B. Oct. 31, 1893, New York, N. Y. D. Sept. 10, 1962, Honesdale, Pa.

BR TR 6'3" 185 lbs.

Year	Team	W	L	PCT	ERA	G	GS	CG	IP	H	BB	SO	ShO	W	L	SV	AB	H	HR	BA	PO	A	E	DP	TC/G	FA
1915	BKN F	0	0	–	15.00	3	0	0	3	5	2	3	0	0	0	0	0	0	0	–	0	0	0	0	0.0	–

Herb Herring

HERRING, HERBERT LEE
B. July 22, 1891, Danville, Ark. D. Apr. 22, 1964, Tucson, Ariz.

BR TR 5'11" 178 lbs.

Year	Team	W	L	PCT	ERA	G	GS	CG	IP	H	BB	SO	ShO	W	L	SV	AB	H	HR	BA	PO	A	E	DP	TC/G	FA
1912	WAS A	0	0	–	0.00	1	0	0	1	1	1	0	0	0	0	0	0	0	0	–	0	0	0	0	0.0	–

Lefty Herring

HERRING, SILAS CLARKE
B. Mar. 4, 1880, Philadelphia, Pa. D. Feb. 11, 1965, Massapequa, N. Y.

BL TL 5'11" 160 lbs.

Year	Team	W	L	PCT	ERA	G	GS	CG	IP	H	BB	SO	ShO	W	L	SV	AB	H	HR	BA	PO	A	E	DP	TC/G	FA
1899	WAS N	0	0	–	0.00	2	0	0	2	0	2	0	0	0	0	0	*				0	1	0	0	0.5	1.000

LeRoy Herrmann

HERRMANN, LeROY GEORGE
B. Feb. 27, 1906, Steward, Ill. D. July 3, 1972, Livermore, Calif.

BR TR 5'10" 185 lbs.

Year	Team	W	L	PCT	ERA	G	GS	CG	IP	H	BB	SO	ShO	W	L	SV	AB	H	HR	BA	PO	A	E	DP	TC/G	FA
1932	CHI N	2	1	.667	6.39	7	0	0	12.2	18	9	5	0	2	1	0	2	1	0	.500	2	1	0	1	0.4	1.000
1933		0	1	.000	5.57	9	1	0	21	26	8	4	0	0	0	0	6	1	0	.167	1	1	0	0	0.3	.667
1935	CIN N	3	5	.375	3.58	29	8	2	108	124	31	30	0	1	0	0	30	8	0	.267	4	23	1	1	1.0	.964
3 yrs.		5	7	.417	4.13	45	9	2	141.2	168	48	39	0	3	1	1	38	10	0	.263	7	25	2	2	0.8	.941

Marty Herrmann

HERRMANN, MARTIN JOHN (Lefty)
B. Jan. 10, 1893, Oldenburg, Ind. D. Sept. 11, 1956, Cincinnati, Ohio

BL TL 5'10" 150 lbs.

Year	Team	W	L	PCT	ERA	G	GS	CG	IP	H	BB	SO	ShO	W	L	SV	AB	H	HR	BA	PO	A	E	DP	TC/G	FA
1918	BKN N	0	0	–	0.00	1	0	0	1	0	1	0	0	0	0	0	0	0	0	–	0	0	0	0	0.0	–

Frank Hershey

HERSHEY, FRANK
B. Dec. 13, 1877, Gorham, N. Y. D. Dec. 15, 1949, Canandaigua, N. Y.

TR 175 lbs.

Year	Team	W	L	PCT	ERA	G	GS	CG	IP	H	BB	SO	ShO	W	L	SV	AB	H	HR	BA	PO	A	E	DP	TC/G	FA
1905	BOS N	0	1	.000	6.75	1	1	0	4	5	2	1	0	0	0	0	0	0	0	.000	0	0	0	0	0.0	–

Orel Hershiser

HERSHISER, OREL LEONARD QUINTON IV (Bulldog)
B. Sept. 16, 1958, Buffalo, N. Y.

BR TR 6'3" 190 lbs.

Year	Team	W	L	PCT	ERA	G	GS	CG	IP	H	BB	SO	ShO	W	L	SV	AB	H	HR	BA	PO	A	E	DP	TC/G	FA
1983	LA N	0	0	–	3.38	8	0	0	8	7	6	5	0	0	0	1	0	0	0	–	0	2	0	1	0.3	1.000
1984		11	8	.579	2.66	45	20	8	189.2	160	50	150	4	3	0	2	50	10	0	.200	17	28	5	2	1.1	.900
1985		19	3	**.864**	2.03	36	34	9	239.2	179	68	157	5	1	0	0	76	15	0	.197	20	45	7	4	2.0	.903
1986		14	14	.500	3.85	35	35	8	231.1	213	86	153	1	0	0	0	71	17	0	.239	22	36	3	6	1.7	.951
1987		16	16	.500	3.06	37	35	10	264.2	247	74	190	1	1	0	1	90	19	0	.211	37	34	5	6	2.1	.934
1988		**23**	8	.742	2.26	35	34	**15**	267	208	73	178	8	0	0	1	85	11	0	.129	32	60	6	6	2.8	.939

Year	Team		W	L	PCT	ERA	G	GS	CG	IP	H	BB	SO	ShO	W	L	SV	AB	H	HR	BA	PO	A	E	DP	TC/G	FA

Orel Hershiser *continued*

Year	Team		W	L	PCT	ERA	G	GS	CG	IP	H	BB	SO	ShO	W	L	SV	AB	H	HR	BA	PO	A	E	DP	TC/G	FA
1989			15	**15**	.500	2.31	35	33	8	**256.2**	226	77	178	4	0	0	0	77	14	0	.182	24	51	4	2	2.3	.949
7 yrs.			98	64	.605	2.69	231	191	58	1457	1240	434	1011	23	4	1	5	449	86	0	.192	152	256	30	27	1.9	.932

LEAGUE CHAMPIONSHIP SERIES

Year	Team		W	L	PCT	ERA	G	GS	CG	IP	H	BB	SO	ShO	W	L	SV	AB	H	HR	BA	PO	A	E	DP	TC/G	FA
1985	LA	N	1	0	1.000	3.52	2	2	1	15.1	17	6	5	0	0	0	0	7	2	0	.286	2	2	0	1	2.0	1.000
1988			1	0	1.000	1.09	4	3	1	24.2	18	7	15	1	0	0	1	9	0	0	.000	3	3	0	0	1.5	1.000
2 yrs.			2	0	1.000	2.03	6	5	2	40	35	13	20	1	0	0	1	16	2	0	.125	5	5	0	1	1.7	1.000

WORLD SERIES

Year	Team		W	L	PCT	ERA	G	GS	CG	IP	H	BB	SO	ShO	W	L	SV	AB	H	HR	BA	PO	A	E	DP	TC/G	FA
1988	LA	N	2	0	1.000	1.00	2	2	2	18	7	6	17	1	0	0	0	3	3	0	1.000	1	1	0	0	1.0	1.000

Joe Hesketh

HESKETH, JOSEPH THOMAS
B. Feb. 15, 1959, Lackawanna, N. Y.

BL TL 6'2" 165 lbs.

Year	Team		W	L	PCT	ERA	G	GS	CG	IP	H	BB	SO	ShO	W	L	SV	AB	H	HR	BA	PO	A	E	DP	TC/G	FA
1984	MON	N	2	2	.500	1.80	11	5	1	45	38	15	32	1	0	0	0	10	1	0	.100	2	6	1	1	0.8	.889
1985			10	5	.667	2.49	25	25	2	155.1	125	45	113	1	0	0	0	44	4	0	.091	3	22	0	0	1.0	1.000
1986			6	5	.545	5.01	15	15	0	82.2	92	31	67	0	0	0	0	23	0	0	.000	2	8	1	0	0.7	.909
1987			0	0	—	3.14	18	0	0	28.2	23	15	31	0	0	0	1	4	0	0	.000	1	1	1	0	0.2	.667
1988			4	3	.571	2.85	60	0	0	72.2	63	35	64	0	4	3	9	2	0	0	.000	6	14	0	2	0.3	1.000
1989			6	4	.600	5.77	43	0	0	48.1	54	26	44	0	6	4	3	2	1	0	.500	3	9	1	3	0.3	.923
6 yrs.			28	19	.596	3.37	172	45	3	432.2	395	167	351	2	10	8	14	85	6	0	.071	17	60	4	6	0.5	.951

Otto Hess

HESS, OTTO C.
B. Nov. 13, 1878, Berne, Switzerland   D. Feb. 24, 1926, Tucson, Ariz.

BL TL 6'1" 170 lbs.

Year	Team		W	L	PCT	ERA	G	GS	CG	IP	H	BB	SO	ShO	W	L	SV	AB	H	HR	BA	PO	A	E	DP	TC/G	FA
1902	CLE	A	2	4	.333	5.98	7	4	4	43.2	67	23	13	0	0	**2**	0	14	1	0	.071	4	16	3	0	3.3	.870
1904			8	7	.533	1.67	21	16	15	151.1	134	31	64	4	1	0	0	100	12	0	.120	13	45	3	0	2.9	.951
1905			10	15	.400	3.16	26	25	22	213.2	179	72	109	4	0	1	0	175	44	2	.251	22	62	6	0	3.5	.933
1906			20	17	.541	1.83	43	36	33	334	274	85	167	7	0	0	**3**	154	31	0	.201	25	86	6	4	2.7	.949
1907			6	6	.500	2.89	17	14	7	93.1	84	37	36	0	0	0	1	30	4	0	.133	6	26	2	0	2.0	.941
1908			0	0	—	5.14	4	0	0	7	11	1	2	0	0	0	0	14	0	0	.000	1	3	0	0	1.0	1.000
1912	BOS	N	12	17	.414	3.76	33	31	21	254	270	90	80	0	0	2	0	94	23	0	.245	11	47	3	3	1.8	.951
1913			7	17	.292	3.83	29	27	19	218.1	231	70	80	2	0	0	0	83	26	2	.313	11	58	4	2	2.5	.945
1914			5	6	.455	3.03	14	11	7	89	89	33	24	1	1	0	1	47	11	1	.234	3	33	2	2	2.7	.947
1915			0	1	.000	3.86	4	1	1	14	16	6	5	0	0	0	0	5	2	0	.400	1	4	1	0	1.3	.800
10 yrs.			70	90	.438	2.98	198	165	129	1418.1	1355	448	580	18	3	5	5	*				96	380	30	11	2.6	.941

George Hesselbacher

HESSELBACHER, GEORGE EDWARD
B. Jan. 18, 1895, Philadelphia, Pa.   D. Feb. 18, 1980, Rydal, Pa.

BR TR 6'2" 175 lbs.

Year	Team		W	L	PCT	ERA	G	GS	CG	IP	H	BB	SO	ShO	W	L	SV	AB	H	HR	BA	PO	A	E	DP	TC/G	FA
1916	PHI	A	0	4	.000	7.27	6	4	2	26	37	22	6	0	0	0	0	8	1	0	.125	0	14	0	0	2.3	1.000

Larry Hesterfer

HESTERFER, LAWRENCE
B. June 9, 1878, Newark, N. J.   D. Sept. 22, 1943, Cedar Grove, N. Y.

BR TL 5'8" 145 lbs.

Year	Team		W	L	PCT	ERA	G	GS	CG	IP	H	BB	SO	ShO	W	L	SV	AB	H	HR	BA	PO	A	E	DP	TC/G	FA
1901	NY	N	0	1	.000	7.50	1	1	1	6	15	3	2	0	0	0	0	2	0	0	.000	0	1	0	0	1.0	1.000

Johnny Hetki

HETKI, JOHN EDWARD
B. May 12, 1922, Leavenworth, Kans.

BR TR 6'1" 202 lbs.

Year	Team		W	L	PCT	ERA	G	GS	CG	IP	H	BB	SO	ShO	W	L	SV	AB	H	HR	BA	PO	A	E	DP	TC/G	FA
1945	CIN	N	1	2	.333	3.58	5	2	2	32.2	28	11	9	0	1	0	0	11	1	0	.091	2	9	0	0	2.2	1.000
1946			6	6	.500	2.99	32	11	4	126.1	121	31	41	0	2	1	1	33	11	0	.333	6	24	1	0	1.0	.968
1947			3	4	.429	5.81	37	5	2	96	110	48	33	0	2	0	0	27	6	0	.222	3	19	0	0	0.6	1.000
1948			0	1	.000	9.45	3	0	0	6.2	8	3	3	0	0	1	0	1	0	0	.000	0	0	0	0	0.0	—
1950			1	2	.333	5.09	22	1	0	53	53	27	21	0	1	1	0	9	2	0	.222	1	8	0	1	0.4	1.000
1952	STL	A	0	1	.000	3.86	3	1	0	9.1	15	2	4	0	0	0	0	1	0	0	.000	1	0	0	0	1.0	1.000
1953	PIT	N	3	6	.333	3.95	54	2	0	118.1	120	33	37	0	3	5	3	24	5	0	.208	9	20	0	1	0.5	1.000
1954			4	4	.500	4.99	58	1	0	83	102	30	27	0	4	3	9	9	2	0	.222	3	11	0	0	0.2	1.000
8 yrs.			18	26	.409	4.39	214	23	8	525.1	557	185	175	0	12	12	13	115	27	0	.235	25	93	1	2	0.6	.992

Eric Hetzel

HETZEL, ERIC PAUL
B. Sept. 25, 1963, Crowley, La.

BR TR 6'3" 175 lbs.

Year	Team		W	L	PCT	ERA	G	GS	CG	IP	H	BB	SO	ShO	W	L	SV	AB	H	HR	BA	PO	A	E	DP	TC/G	FA
1989	BOS	A	2	3	.400	6.26	12	11	0	50.1	61	28	33	0	0	1	0	0	0	0	—	3	1	0	1	0.3	1.000

Ed Heusser

HEUSSER, EDWARD BURLTON (The Wild Elk of the Wasatch)
B. May 7, 1909, Mill Creek, Utah
D. Mar. 1, 1956, Aurora, Colo.

BB TR 6'½" 187 lbs.
BR 1935-38

Year	Team		W	L	PCT	ERA	G	GS	CG	IP	H	BB	SO	ShO	W	L	SV	AB	H	HR	BA	PO	A	E	DP	TC/G	FA
1935	STL	N	5	5	.500	2.92	33	11	2	123.1	125	27	39	0	2	1	2	34	4	0	.118	7	20	1	3	0.8	.964
1936			7	3	.700	5.43	42	3	0	104.1	130	38	26	0	6	2	3	26	7	1	.269	2	24	4	2	0.7	.867
1938	PHI	N	0	0	—	27.00	1	0	0	1	2	1	0	0	0	0	0	0	0	0	—	0	0	0	0	0.0	—
1940	PHI	A	6	13	.316	4.99	41	6	2	110	144	42	39	0	4	9	5	30	5	1	.167	9	21	1	1	0.8	.968
1943	CIN	N	4	3	.571	3.46	26	10	2	91	97	23	28	0	2	0	0	27	5	0	.185	6	14	0	1	0.8	1.000
1944			13	11	.542	**2.38**	30	23	17	192.2	165	42	42	4	2	1	2	69	15	0	.217	11	33	1	1	1.5	.978
1945			11	16	.407	3.71	31	30	18	223	248	60	56	4	0	1	1	77	19	0	.247	9	45	1	2	1.8	.982
1946			7	14	.333	3.22	29	21	9	167.2	167	39	47	0	1	1	0	53	11	0	.208	7	26	3	3	1.2	.917
1948	PHI	N	3	2	.600	4.99	33	0	0	74	89	28	22	0	3	2	3	19	3	0	.158	5	15	1	0	0.6	.952
9 yrs.			56	67	.455	3.69	266	104	50	1087	1167	300	299	10	19	16	18	335	69	3	.206	56	198	12	13	1.0	.955

Joe Heving

HEVING, JOSEPH WILLIAM
Brother of Johnnie Heving.
B. Sept. 2, 1900, Covington, Ky.   D. Apr. 11, 1970, Covington, Ky.

BR TR 6'1" 185 lbs.

Year	Team		W	L	PCT	ERA	G	GS	CG	IP	H	BB	SO	ShO	W	L	SV	AB	H	HR	BA	PO	A	E	DP	TC/G	FA
1930	NY	N	7	5	.583	5.22	41	2	0	89.2	109	27	37	0	**7**	**5**	6	22	5	0	.227	11	33	2	2	1.1	.957
1931			1	6	.143	4.89	22	0	0	42.1	48	11	26	0	1	**6**	3	8	1	0	.125	2	12	0	0	0.6	1.000
1933	CHI	A	7	5	.583	2.67	40	6	3	118	113	27	47	1	5	1	6	38	8	0	.211	3	28	1	1	0.8	.969

Year	Team	W	L	PCT	ERA	G	GS	CG	IP	H	BB	SO	ShO	W	L	SV	AB	H	HR	BA	PO	A	E	DP	TC/G	FA
														Relief Pitching			Batting									

Joe Heving *continued*

Year	Team		W	L	PCT	ERA	G	GS	CG	IP	H	BB	SO	ShO	W	L	SV	AB	H	HR	BA	PO	A	E	DP	TC/G	FA
1934			1	7	.125	7.26	33	2	0	88	133	48	40	0	1	5	4	27	5	0	.185	10	18	2	2	0.9	.933
1937	CLE	A	8	4	.667	4.83	40	0	0	72.2	92	30	35	0	8	4	5	19	5	0	.263	3	18	0	1	0.5	1.000
1938	2 teams	CLE A (3G 1–1)					BOS A (16G 8–1)																				
"	total		9	2	.818	4.09	19	11	7	88	104	27	34	1	1	1	2	31	4	0	.129	8	22	1	4	1.6	.968
1939	BOS	A	11	3	.786	3.70	46	5	1	107	124	34	43	0	11	2	7	32	6	0	.188	8	17	3	2	0.6	.893
1940			12	7	.632	4.01	39	7	4	119	129	42	55	0	8	4	3	40	8	0	.200	8	22	4	3	0.9	.882
1941	CLE	A	5	2	.714	2.29	27	3	2	70.2	63	31	18	1	3	2	5	15	0	0	.000	8	22	0	0	1.1	1.000
1942			5	3	.625	4.86	27	2	0	46.1	52	25	13	0	5	2	3	7	0	0	.000	3	10	2	1	0.6	.867
1943			1	1	.500	2.75	30	1	0	72	58	34	34	0	1	1	9	14	1	0	.071	8	20	0	0	0.9	1.000
1944			8	3	.727	1.96	63	1	0	119.1	106	41	46	0	8	2	10	22	4	0	.182	5	29	4	0	0.6	.895
1945	BOS	N	1	0	1.000	3.38	3	0	0	5.1	5	3	1	0	1	0	0	1	0	0	.000	0	4	0	0	1.3	1.000
13 yrs.			76	48	.613	3.90	430	40	17	1038.1	1136	380	429	3	60	35	63	276	47	0	.170	77	255	19	16	0.8	.946

Jake Hewitt

HEWITT, CHARLES JACOB
B. June 6, 1870, Madisonville, W. Va.   D. May 18, 1959, Morgantown, W. Va.

BL TL 5'7"   150 lbs.

Year	Team		W	L	PCT	ERA	G	GS	CG	IP	H	BB	SO	ShO	W	L	SV	AB	H	HR	BA	PO	A	E	DP	TC/G	FA
1895	PIT	N	1	0	1.000	4.15	4	2	1	13	13	2	4	0	0	0	2	6	1	0	.167	0	2	1	0	0.8	.667

Greg Heydeman

HEYDEMAN, GREGORY GEORGE
B. Jan. 2, 1952, Carmel, Calif.

BR TR 6'   180 lbs.

Year	Team		W	L	PCT	ERA	G	GS	CG	IP	H	BB	SO	ShO	W	L	SV	AB	H	HR	BA	PO	A	E	DP	TC/G	FA
1973	LA	N	0	0	–	4.50	1	0	0	2	2	1	1	0	0	0	0	0	0	0	–	0	0	0	0	0.0	–

John Heyner

HEYNER, JOHN
B. Hyde Park, Ill.   Deceased.

Year	Team		W	L	PCT	ERA	G	GS	CG	IP	H	BB	SO	ShO	W	L	SV	AB	H	HR	BA	PO	A	E	DP	TC/G	FA
1890	PIT	N	0	0	–	13.50	1	0	0	4	7	5	1	0	0	0	0	2	0	0	.000	0	1	0	0	1.0	1.000

Greg Hibbard

HIBBARD, JAMES GREGORY
B. Sept. 13, 1964, New Orleans, La.

BL TL 6'   180 lbs.

Year	Team		W	L	PCT	ERA	G	GS	CG	IP	H	BB	SO	ShO	W	L	SV	AB	H	HR	BA	PO	A	E	DP	TC/G	FA
1989	CHI	A	6	7	.462	3.21	23	23	2	137.1	142	41	55	0	0	0	0	0	0	0	–	5	27	0	4	1.4	1.000

John Hibbard

HIBBARD, JOHN DENISON
B. Dec. 2, 1864, Chicago, Ill.   D. Nov. 17, 1937, Hollywood, Calif.

TL

Year	Team		W	L	PCT	ERA	G	GS	CG	IP	H	BB	SO	ShO	W	L	SV	AB	H	HR	BA	PO	A	E	DP	TC/G	FA
1884	CHI	N	1	1	.500	2.65	2	2	2	17	18	9	4	1	0	0	0	7	0	0	.000	1	3	0	0	2.0	1.000

Jim Hickey

HICKEY, JAMES ROBERT (Sid)
B. Oct. 22, 1920, North Abington, Mass.

BR TR 6'1"   204 lbs.

Year	Team		W	L	PCT	ERA	G	GS	CG	IP	H	BB	SO	ShO	W	L	SV	AB	H	HR	BA	PO	A	E	DP	TC/G	FA
1942	BOS	N	0	1	.000	20.25	1	1	0	1.1	4	2	0	0	0	0	0	1	0	0	.000	0	0	0	0	0.0	–
1944			0	0	–	4.82	8	0	0	9.1	15	5	3	0	0	0	0	1	0	0	.000	0	3	0	0	0.4	1.000
2 yrs.			0	1	.000	6.75	9	1	0	10.2	19	7	3	0	0	0	0	2	0	0	.000	0	3	0	0	0.3	1.000

John Hickey

HICKEY, JOHN WILLIAM
B. Nov. 3, 1881, Minneapolis, Minn.   D. Dec. 28, 1941, Seattle, Wash.

BR TL

Year	Team		W	L	PCT	ERA	G	GS	CG	IP	H	BB	SO	ShO	W	L	SV	AB	H	HR	BA	PO	A	E	DP	TC/G	FA
1904	CLE	A	0	1	.000	7.30	2	1	0	12.1	14	11	5	0	0	0	0	5	0	0	.000	0	5	0	0	2.5	1.000

Kevin Hickey

HICKEY, KEVIN JOHN
B. Feb. 25, 1956, Chicago, Ill.

BL TL 6'1"   170 lbs.

Year	Team		W	L	PCT	ERA	G	GS	CG	IP	H	BB	SO	ShO	W	L	SV	AB	H	HR	BA	PO	A	E	DP	TC/G	FA
1981	CHI	A	0	2	.000	3.68	41	0	0	44	38	18	17	0	0	2	3	0	0	0	–	3	11	0	0	0.3	1.000
1982			4	4	.500	3.00	60	0	0	78	73	30	38	0	4	4	6	0	0	0	–	5	20	1	4	0.4	.962
1983			1	2	.333	5.23	23	0	0	20.2	23	11	8	0	1	2	5	0	0	0	–	1	3	0	0	0.2	1.000
1989	BAL	A	2	3	.400	2.92	51	0	0	49.1	38	23	28	0	2	3	2	0	0	0	–	2	6	0	0	0.2	1.000
4 yrs.			7	11	.389	3.38	175	0	0	192	172	82	91	0	7	11	16	0	0	0	–	11	40	1	4	0.3	.981

Ernie Hickman

HICKMAN, ERNEST P.
B. 1856, East St. Louis, Ill.   D. Nov. 19, 1891, East St. Louis, Ill.

Year	Team		W	L	PCT	ERA	G	GS	CG	IP	H	BB	SO	ShO	W	L	SV	AB	H	HR	BA	PO	A	E	DP	TC/G	FA
1884	KC	U	4	13	.235	4.52	17	17	15	137.1	172	36	68	0	0	0	0	72	12	0	.167	7	31	12	0	2.9	.760

Jess Hickman

HICKMAN, JESSE OWENS
B. Feb. 18, 1939, Lecompte, La.

BR TR 6'2"   186 lbs.

Year	Team		W	L	PCT	ERA	G	GS	CG	IP	H	BB	SO	ShO	W	L	SV	AB	H	HR	BA	PO	A	E	DP	TC/G	FA
1965	KC	A	0	1	.000	5.87	12	0	0	15.1	9	8	16	0	0	1	0	0	0	0	–	2	1	0	0	0.3	1.000
1966			0	0	–	0.00	1	0	0	1	0	1	0	0	0	0	0	0	0	0	–	0	0	0	0	0.0	–
2 yrs.			0	1	.000	5.51	13	0	0	16.1	9	9	16	0	0	1	0	0	0	0	–	2	1	0	0	0.2	1.000

Jim Hickman

HICKMAN, JAMES LUCIUS
B. May 10, 1937, Henning, Tenn.

BR TR 6'3"   192 lbs.

Year	Team		W	L	PCT	ERA	G	GS	CG	IP	H	BB	SO	ShO	W	L	SV	AB	H	HR	BA	PO	A	E	DP	TC/G	FA
1967	LA	N	0	0	–	4.50	1	0	0	2	2	0	0	0	0	0	0	*				0	0	0	0	0.0	–

Piano Legs Hickman

HICKMAN, CHARLES TAYLOR
B. Mar. 4, 1876, Taylortown, Pa.   D. Apr. 19, 1934, Morgantown, W. Va.

BR TR 5'11½"   215 lbs.

Year	Team		W	L	PCT	ERA	G	GS	CG	IP	H	BB	SO	ShO	W	L	SV	AB	H	HR	BA	PO	A	E	DP	TC/G	FA
1897	BOS	N	0	0	–	5.87	2	0	0	7.2	10	5	0	0	0	0	0	3	2	1	.667	1	1	0	1	1.0	1.000
1898			1	2	.333	2.18	6	3	3	33	22	13	9	1	0	0	2	58	15	0	.259	3	2	0	0	0.8	1.000
1899			6	0	1.000	4.48	11	9	5	66.1	52	40	14	2	0	0	1	63	25	0	.397	4	12	1	1	1.5	.941
1901	NY	N	3	5	.375	4.57	9	9	6	65	76	26	11	0	0	0	0	401	113	4	.282	6	19	2	2	3.0	.926
1902	2 teams	BOS A (0G 0–0)					CLE A (1G 0–1)																				
"	total		0	1	.000	7.88	1	1	1	8	11	5	1	0	0	0	0	534	194	11	.363	0	1	0	0	1.0	1.000
1907	2 teams	WAS A (1G 0–0)					CHI A (0G 0–0)																				
"	total		0	0	–	3.60	1	0	0	5	4	5	2	0	0	0	0	216	61	1	.282	0	4	0	0	4.0	1.000
6 yrs.			10	8	.556	4.28	30	22	15	185	175	94	37	3	0	0	4	*				14	39	3	4	1.9	.946

Year	Team		W	L	PCT	ERA	G	GS	CG	IP	H	BB	SO	ShO	Relief Pitching			Batting			BA	PO	A	E	DP	TC/G	FA
															W	L	SV	AB	H	HR							

Kirby Higbe

HIGBE, WALTER KIRBY
B. Apr. 8, 1915, Columbia, S. C. D. May 6, 1985, Columbia, S. C. BR TR 5'11" 190 lbs.

Year	Team		W	L	PCT	ERA	G	GS	CG	IP	H	BB	SO	ShO	W	L	SV	AB	H	HR	BA	PO	A	E	DP	TC/G	FA
1937	CHI	N	1	0	1.000	5.40	1	1	0	5	4	1	2	0	1	0	0	3	0	0	.000	0	0	0	0	0.0	–
1938			0	0	–	5.40	2	2	0	10	10	6	4	0	0	0	0	3	0	0	.000	1	4	0	1	2.5	1.000
1939	2 teams		CHI N	(9G 2–1)		PHI N	(34G 10–14)																				
"	total		12	15	.444	4.67	43	28	14	210	220	**123**	95	1	1	1	2	73	13	0	.178	9	19	0	0	0.7	1.000
1940	PHI	N	14	19	.424	3.72	41	36	20	283	242	121	**137**	1	1	0	1	103	17	0	.165	15	47	3	4	1.6	.954
1941	BKN	N	**22**	9	.710	3.14	**48**	**39**	19	298	244	**132**	121	2	1	2	3	112	21	0	.188	13	39	1	2	1.1	.981
1942			16	11	.593	3.25	38	32	13	221.2	180	106	115	2	1	2	0	77	8	0	.104	12	36	2	5	1.3	.960
1943			13	10	.565	3.70	35	27	8	185	189	95	108	1	1	2	0	65	9	1	.138	9	27	0	2	1.0	1.000
1946			17	8	.680	3.03	42	29	11	210.2	178	107	134	3	2	2	1	77	10	0	.130	13	40	3	2	1.3	.946
1947	2 teams		BKN N	(4G 2–0)		PIT N	(46G 11–17)																				
"	total		13	17	.433	3.81	50	33	10	240.2	222	**122**	109	1	2	1	5	77	11	1	.143	10	26	1	0	0.7	.973
1948	PIT	N	8	7	.533	3.36	56	8	3	158	140	83	86	0	6	4	10	48	10	1	.208	5	22	1	0	0.5	.964
1949	2 teams		PIT N	(7G 0–2)		NY N	(37G 2–0)																				
"	total		2	2	.500	5.08	44	3	0	95.2	97	53	43	0	2	1	2	18	1	0	.056	2	14	0	1	0.4	1.000
1950	NY	N	0	3	.000	4.93	18	1	0	34.2	37	30	17	0	0	2	0	4	1	0	.250	3	11	0	0	0.8	1.000
12 yrs.			118	101	.539	3.69	418	238	98	1952.1	1763	979	971	11	18	17	24	660	101	3	.153	92	285	11	17	0.9	.972

WORLD SERIES

| 1941 | BKN | N | 0 | 0 | – | 7.36 | 1 | 0 | 0 | 3.2 | 6 | 2 | 1 | 0 | 0 | 0 | 0 | 1 | 1 | 0 | 1.000 | 0 | 1 | 0 | 0 | 1.0 | 1.000 |

Irv Higginbotham

HIGGINBOTHAM, IRVING CLINTON
B. Apr. 26, 1882, Homer, Neb. D. June 12, 1959, Seattle, Wash. BR TR 6'1" 196 lbs.

Year	Team		W	L	PCT	ERA	G	GS	CG	IP	H	BB	SO	ShO	W	L	SV	AB	H	HR	BA	PO	A	E	DP	TC/G	FA
1906	STL	N	1	4	.200	3.23	7	6	4	47.1	50	11	14	0	0	0	0	18	4	0	.222	1	18	2	0	3.0	.905
1908			3	8	.273	3.20	19	11	7	107	113	33	38	1	0	1	0	38	5	0	.132	2	27	1	0	1.6	.967
1909	2 teams		STL N	(3G 1–0)		CHI N	(19G 5–2)																				
"	total		6	2	.750	2.12	22	7	5	89.1	69	22	34	0	3	1	0	29	6	0	.207	4	17	3	0	1.1	.875
3 yrs.			10	14	.417	2.81	48	24	16	243.2	232	66	86	1	3	2	0	85	15	0	.176	7	62	6	0	1.6	.920

Dennis Higgins

HIGGINS, DENNIS DEAN
B. Aug. 4, 1939, Jefferson City, Mo. BR TR 6'3" 180 lbs.

Year	Team		W	L	PCT	ERA	G	GS	CG	IP	H	BB	SO	ShO	W	L	SV	AB	H	HR	BA	PO	A	E	DP	TC/G	FA
1966	CHI	A	1	0	1.000	2.52	42	1	0	93	66	33	86	0	0	0	5	17	3	0	.176	4	15	0	2	0.5	1.000
1967			1	2	.333	5.84	9	0	0	12.1	13	10	8	0	1	2	0	1	0	0	.000	2	2	0	0	0.4	1.000
1968	WAS	A	4	4	.500	3.25	59	0	0	99.2	81	46	66	0	4	4	13	15	2	0	.133	2	11	0	0	0.2	1.000
1969			10	9	.526	3.48	55	0	0	85.1	79	56	71	0	10	9	16	11	1	0	.091	4	7	0	0	0.2	1.000
1970	CLE	A	4	6	.400	4.00	58	0	0	90	82	54	82	0	4	6	11	12	3	0	.250	7	14	1	0	0.4	.955
1971	STL	N	1	0	1.000	3.86	3	0	0	7	6	2	6	0	1	0	0	1	0	0	.000	1	1	0	0	0.7	1.000
1972			1	2	.333	3.97	15	0	0	22.2	19	22	20	0	1	1	1	1	0	0	.000	2	1	0	0	0.2	1.000
7 yrs.			22	23	.489	3.42	241	2	0	410	346	223	339	0	21	22	46	58	9	0	.155	22	51	1	2	0.3	.986

Thomas Higgins

HIGGINS, THOMAS EDWARD (Eddie, Irish)
B. Mar. 18, 1888, Nevada, Ill. D. Feb. 14, 1959, Elgin, Ill. BR TR 6'1½" 174 lbs.

Year	Team		W	L	PCT	ERA	G	GS	CG	IP	H	BB	SO	ShO	W	L	SV	AB	H	HR	BA	PO	A	E	DP	TC/G	FA
1909	STL	N	3	3	.500	4.50	16	5	5	66	68	17	15	0	1	0	0	21	4	0	.190	4	20	0	0	1.5	1.000
1910			0	1	.000	4.35	2	0	0	10.1	15	7	1	0	0	1	0	5	2	0	.400	1	6	0	0	3.5	1.000
2 yrs.			3	4	.429	4.48	18	5	5	76.1	83	24	16	0	1	1	0	26	6	0	.231	5	26	0	0	1.7	1.000

Ed High

HIGH, EDWARD THOMAS (Lefty)
B. Dec. 26, 1876, Baltimore, Md. D. Feb. 20, 1926, Baltimore, Md. TL

Year	Team		W	L	PCT	ERA	G	GS	CG	IP	H	BB	SO	ShO	W	L	SV	AB	H	HR	BA	PO	A	E	DP	TC/G	FA
1901	DET	A	1	0	1.000	3.50	4	1	1	18	21	6	4	0	0	0	0	7	0	0	.000	2	3	0	1	1.3	1.000

Ted Higuera

HIGUERA, TEODORO VALENZUELA
Born Teodoro Valenzuela Higuera y Valenzuela.
B. Nov. 9, 1958, Los Mochis, Mexico BB TL 5'10" 180 lbs.

Year	Team		W	L	PCT	ERA	G	GS	CG	IP	H	BB	SO	ShO	W	L	SV	AB	H	HR	BA	PO	A	E	DP	TC/G	FA
1985	MIL	A	15	8	.652	3.90	32	30	7	212.1	186	63	127	2	0	0	0	0	0	0	–	8	18	1	2	0.8	.963
1986			20	11	.645	2.79	34	34	15	248.1	226	74	207	4	0	0	0	0	0	0	–	9	26	0	1	1.0	1.000
1987			18	10	.643	3.85	35	35	14	261.2	236	87	240	3	0	0	0	0	0	0	–	9	23	2	3	1.0	.941
1988			16	9	.640	2.45	31	31	8	227.1	168	59	192	1	0	0	0	0	0	0	–	12	33	0	1	1.5	1.000
1989			9	6	.600	3.46	22	22	2	135.1	125	48	91	1	0	0	0	0	0	0	–	5	10	1	0	0.7	.938
5 yrs.			78	44	.639	3.28	154	152	46	1085	941	331	857	11	0	0	0	0	0	0	–	43	110	4	7	1.0	.975

Whitey Hilcher

HILCHER, WALTER FRANK
B. Feb. 28, 1909, Chicago, Ill. D. Nov. 21, 1962, Minneapolis, Minn. BR TR 6' 174 lbs.

Year	Team		W	L	PCT	ERA	G	GS	CG	IP	H	BB	SO	ShO	W	L	SV	AB	H	HR	BA	PO	A	E	DP	TC/G	FA
1931	CIN	N	0	1	.000	3.00	2	1	0	12	16	4	5	0	0	0	0	4	0	0	.000	0	1	0	0	0.5	1.000
1932			0	3	.000	7.71	11	2	0	18.2	24	10	4	0	0	1	0	3	1	0	.333	3	3	0	0	0.5	1.000
1935			2	0	1.000	2.79	4	2	1	19.1	19	5	9	0	1	0	0	6	1	0	.167	1	8	0	0	2.3	1.000
1936			1	2	.333	6.17	14	1	0	35	44	14	10	0	1	2	0	8	0	0	.000	1	5	1	1	0.5	.857
4 yrs.			3	6	.333	5.29	31	6	1	85	103	33	28	0	2	3	0	21	2	0	.095	5	17	1	1	0.7	.957

Oral Hildebrand

HILDEBRAND, ORAL CLYDE
B. Apr. 7, 1907, Indianapolis, Ind. D. Sept. 8, 1977, Southport, Ind. BR TR 6'3" 175 lbs.

Year	Team		W	L	PCT	ERA	G	GS	CG	IP	H	BB	SO	ShO	W	L	SV	AB	H	HR	BA	PO	A	E	DP	TC/G	FA
1931	CLE	A	2	1	.667	4.39	5	2	2	26.2	25	13	6	0	1	0	0	11	2	0	.182	1	4	0	0	1.0	1.000
1932			8	6	.571	3.69	27	15	7	129.1	124	62	49	0	2	0	0	48	7	0	.146	9	13	1	2	0.9	.957
1933			16	11	.593	3.76	36	31	15	220.1	205	88	90	**6**	1	1	0	84	16	0	.190	11	43	2	4	1.6	.964
1934			11	9	.550	4.50	33	28	10	198	225	99	72	1	0	1	0	76	13	0	.171	5	44	0	1	1.5	1.000
1935			9	8	.529	3.94	34	20	8	171.1	171	63	49	0	3	0	5	55	9	0	.164	6	35	2	1	1.3	.953
1936			10	11	.476	4.90	36	21	9	174.2	197	83	65	0	4	4	1	63	12	0	.190	4	26	0	0	0.8	1.000
1937	STL	A	8	17	.320	5.14	30	27	12	201.1	228	87	75	1	1	1	0	70	14	0	.200	5	36	2	1	1.4	.953
1938			8	10	.444	5.69	23	23	10	163	194	73	66	0	0	0	0	59	15	0	.254	5	14	1	0	0.9	.950
1939	NY	A	10	4	.714	3.06	21	15	7	126.2	102	41	50	1	0	0	2	44	8	0	.182	5	18	1	1	1.1	.958

Year	Team		W	L	PCT	ERA	G	GS	CG	IP	H	BB	SO	ShO	Relief Pitching W	L	SV	Batting AB	H	HR	BA	PO	A	E	DP	TC/G	FA

Oral Hildebrand *continued*

Year	Team		W	L	PCT	ERA	G	GS	CG	IP	H	BB	SO	ShO	W	L	SV	AB	H	HR	BA	PO	A	E	DP	TC/G	FA
1940			1	1	.500	1.86	13	0	0	19.1	19	14	5	0	1	1	0	3	0	0	.000	1	3	1	0	0.4	.800
10 yrs.			83	78	.516	4.35	258	182	80	1430.2	1490	623	527	9	13	4	13	513	96	0	.187	52	236	10	11	1.2	.966

WORLD SERIES

| 1939 | NY | A | 0 | 0 | — | 0.00 | 1 | 1 | 0 | 4 | 2 | 0 | 3 | 0 | 0 | 0 | 0 | 1 | 0 | 0 | .000 | 0 | 0 | 0 | 0 | 0.0 | — |

Tom Hilgendorf

HILGENDORF, THOMAS EUGENE
B. Mar. 10, 1942, Clinton, Iowa

BB TL 6'1½" 187 lbs.

1969	STL	N	0	0	—	1.50	6	0	0	6	3	2	2	0	0	0	2	1	1	0	1.000	0	1	0	0	0.2	1.000
1970			0	4	.000	3.86	23	0	0	21	22	13	13	0	0	4	3	1	0	0	.000	0	5	0	0	0.2	1.000
1972	CLE	A	3	1	.750	2.68	19	5	1	47	51	21	25	0	1	0	0	13	1	0	.077	2	10	1	0	0.7	.923
1973			5	3	.625	3.14	48	1	1	94.2	87	36	58	0	5	2	6	0	0	0	—	4	20	1	1	0.5	.960
1974			4	3	.571	4.88	35	0	0	48	58	17	23	0	4	3	3	0	0	0	—	3	8	0	0	0.3	1.000
1975	PHI	N	7	3	.700	2.13	53	0	0	97	82	38	52	0	7	3	0	12	3	0	.250	5	18	0	1	0.4	1.000
6 yrs.			19	14	.576	3.04	184	6	2	313.2	303	127	173	0	17	12	14	27	5	0	.185	14	62	2	2	0.4	.974

Carmen Hill

HILL, CARMEN PROCTOR (Specs, Bunker)
B. Oct. 1, 1895, Royalton, Minn.

BR TR 6'1" 180 lbs.

1915	PIT	N	2	1	.667	1.15	8	3	2	47	42	13	24	1	0	0	0	13	2	0	.154	3	14	0	1	2.1	1.000
1916			0	0	—	8.53	2	0	0	6.1	11	5	5	0	0	0	0	0	0	0	—	0	0	0	0	0.0	—
1918			2	3	.400	1.24	6	4	3	43.2	24	17	15	0	1	0	0	12	2	0	.167	1	13	0	1	2.3	1.000
1919			0	0	—	9.00	4	0	0	5	12	1	1	0	0	0	0	0	0	0	—	0	2	0	1	0.5	1.000
1922	NY	N	2	1	.667	4.76	8	4	0	28.1	33	5	6	0	1	0	0	11	2	0	.182	1	11	0	0	1.5	1.000
1926	PIT	N	3	3	.500	3.40	6	6	4	39.2	42	9	8	1	0	0	0	17	3	0	.176	2	16	0	1	3.0	1.000
1927			22	11	.667	3.24	43	31	22	277.2	260	80	95	2	4	0	0	104	22	0	.212	11	64	4	0	1.8	.949
1928			16	10	.615	3.53	36	31	16	237	229	81	73	1	1	1	2	86	20	0	.233	7	44	5	2	1.6	.911
1929	2 teams		PIT N	(27G 2–3)		STL N	(3G 0–0)																					
"	total		2	3	.400	4.41	30	4	0	87.2	104	43	29	0	2	1	3	31	1	0	.032	3	22	3	1	0.9	.893
1930	STL	N	0	1	.000	7.36	4	2	0	14.2	12	13	8	0	0	0	0	3	1	0	.333	1	2	0	0	0.8	1.000
10 yrs.			49	33	.598	3.44	147	85	47	787	769	267	264	5	9	2	8	277	53	0	.191	29	188	12	6	1.6	.948

WORLD SERIES

| 1927 | PIT | N | 0 | 0 | — | 4.50 | 1 | 0 | 0 | 6 | 9 | 1 | 6 | 0 | 0 | 0 | 0 | 0 | 0 | 0 | .000 | 0 | 0 | 0 | 0 | 0.0 | — |

Dave Hill

HILL, DAVID BURNHAM
B. Nov. 11, 1937, New Orleans, La.

BR TL 6'2" 170 lbs.

| 1957 | KC | A | 0 | 0 | — | 27.00 | 2 | 0 | 0 | 2.1 | 6 | 3 | 1 | 0 | 0 | 0 | 0 | 0 | 0 | 0 | — | 0 | 0 | 0 | 0 | 0.0 | — |

Garry Hill

HILL, GARRY ALTON
B. Nov. 3, 1946, Rutherfordton, N. C.

BR TR 6'2" 195 lbs.

| 1969 | ATL | N | 0 | 1 | .000 | 18.00 | 1 | 1 | 0 | 2 | 6 | 1 | 2 | 0 | 0 | 0 | 0 | 0 | 0 | 0 | — | 0 | 1 | 0 | 0 | 1.0 | 1.000 |

Herbert Hill

HILL, HERBERT LEE
B. Aug. 19, 1892, Hutchins, Tex.   D. Sept. 2, 1970, Farmer's Branch, Tex.

BR TR 5'11" 175 lbs.

| 1915 | CLE | A | 0 | 0 | — | 0.00 | 1 | 0 | 0 | 2 | 1 | 2 | 0 | 0 | 0 | 0 | 0 | 0 | 0 | 0 | — | 0 | 0 | 0 | 0 | 0.0 | — |

Ken Hill

HILL, KENNETH WADE (Thrill)
B. Dec. 14, 1965, Lynn, Mass.

BR TR 6'4" 200 lbs.

1988	STL	N	0	1	.000	5.14	4	1	0	14	16	6	6	0	0	0	0	3	0	0	.000	0	3	0	0	0.8	1.000
1989			7	15	.318	3.80	33	33	2	196.2	186	99	112	1	0	0	0	59	9	0	.153	12	31	1	1	1.3	.977
2 yrs.			7	16	.304	3.89	37	34	2	210.2	202	105	118	1	0	0	0	62	9	0	.145	12	34	1	1	1.3	.979

Red Hill

HILL, CLIFFORD JOSEPH
B. Jan. 20, 1893, Marshall, Tex.   D. Aug. 11, 1938, El Paso, Tex.

BB TL

| 1917 | PHI | A | 0 | 0 | — | 6.75 | 1 | 0 | 0 | 2.2 | 5 | 1 | 0 | 0 | 0 | 0 | 0 | 0 | 0 | 0 | — | 0 | 2 | 0 | 0 | 2.0 | 1.000 |

Still Bill Hill

HILL, WILLIAM CICERO
Brother of Hugh Hill.
B. Aug. 2, 1874, Chattanooga, Tenn.   D. Jan. 28, 1938, Cincinnati, Ohio

BL TL 6'1" 201 lbs.

1896	LOU	N	9	28	.243	4.31	43	39	32	319.2	353	155	104	0	0	0	2	116	24	0	.207	13	95	13	5	2.8	.893
1897			7	17	.292	3.62	27	26	20	199	209	69	55	1	0	0	0	74	7	0	.095	14	53	12	1	2.9	.848
1898	CIN	N	13	14	.481	3.98	33	32	26	262	261	119	75	2	0	0	0	98	13	0	.133	6	67	1	7	2.2	.986
1899	3 teams		CLE N	(11G 3–6)		BAL N	(8G 3–4)		BKN	N	(2G 1–0)																	
"	total		7	10	.412	4.93	21	18	14	144.1	171	63	46	0	0	0	1	60	14	0	.233	4	40	8	2	2.5	.846
4 yrs.			36	69	.343	4.16	124	115	92	925	994	406	280	3	0	0	3	348	58	0	.167	37	255	34	15	2.6	.896

Homer Hillebrand

HILLEBRAND, HOMER HILLER HENRY
B. Oct. 10, 1879, Freeport, Ill.   D. Jan. 20, 1974, Elsinore, Calif.

BR TL 5'8" 165 lbs.

1905	PIT	N	4	2	.667	2.82	10	6	4	60.2	43	19	37	0	1	0	0	110	26	0	.236	4	11	0	0	1.5	1.000
1906			3	2	.600	2.21	7	5	4	53	42	21	32	1	1	0	0	21	5	0	.238	4	19	0	2	3.3	1.000
1908			0	0	—	0.00	1	0	0	1	1	0	1	0	0	0	0	0	0	0	—	0	0	0	0	0.0	—
3 yrs.			7	4	.636	2.51	18	11	8	114.2	86	40	70	1	2	0	0	*				8	30	0	2	2.1	1.000

Shawn Hillegas

HILLEGAS, SHAWN PATRICK
B. Aug. 21, 1964, Dos Palos, Calif.

BR TR 6'3" 205 lbs.

1987	LA	N	4	3	.571	3.57	12	10	0	58	52	31	51	0	0	0	0	14	0	0	.000	4	2	1	0	0.6	.857
1988	2 teams		LA N	(11G 3–4)		CHI A	(6G 3–2)																					
"	total		6	6	.500	3.72	17	16	0	96.2	84	35	56	0	0	0	0	15	2	0	.133	10	8	1	0	1.1	.947

Year	Team		W	L	PCT	ERA	G	GS	CG	IP	H	BB	SO	ShO	Relief Pitching W	L	SV	Batting AB	H	HR	BA	PO	A	E	DP	TC/G	FA

Shawn Hillegas *continued*

Year	Team		W	L	PCT	ERA	G	GS	CG	IP	H	BB	SO	ShO	W	L	SV	AB	H	HR	BA	PO	A	E	DP	TC/G	FA
1989	CHI	A	7	11	.389	4.74	50	13	0	119.2	132	51	76	0	5	4	3	0	0	0	–	5	13	3	1	0.4	.857
3 yrs.			17	20	.459	4.13	79	39	0	274.1	268	117	183	0	5	4	3	29	2	0	.069	19	23	5	1	0.6	.894

Frank Hiller

HILLER, FRANK WALTER (Dutch)
B. July 13, 1920, Newark, N. J.   D. Jan. 8, 1987, West Chester, Pa.

BR TR 6'   200 lbs.

Year	Team		W	L	PCT	ERA	G	GS	CG	IP	H	BB	SO	ShO	W	L	SV	AB	H	HR	BA	PO	A	E	DP	TC/G	FA
1946	NY	A	0	2	.000	4.76	3	1	0	11.1	13	6	4	0	0	0	0	4	1	0	.250	0	2	0	0	0.7	1.000
1948			5	2	.714	4.04	22	5	1	62.1	59	30	25	0	3	1	0	16	6	0	.375	3	11	0	0	0.6	1.000
1949			0	2	.000	5.87	4	0	0	7.2	9	7	3	0	0	2	1	2	1	0	.500	0	1	0	0	0.3	1.000
1950	CHI	N	12	5	.706	3.53	38	17	9	153	153	32	55	2	2	1	1	44	5	0	.114	14	29	1	0	1.2	.977
1951			6	12	.333	4.84	24	21	6	141.1	147	31	50	2	0	0	1	48	6	0	.125	13	30	1	2	1.8	.977
1952	CIN	N	5	8	.385	4.63	28	15	6	124.1	129	37	50	1	0	3	1	30	5	0	.167	9	25	1	0	1.3	.971
1953	NY	N	2	1	.667	6.15	19	1	0	33.2	43	15	10	0	2	0	0	4	2	0	.500	5	10	2	0	0.9	.882
7 yrs.			30	32	.484	4.42	138	60	22	533.2	553	158	197	5	7	7	4	148	26	0	.176	44	108	5	2	1.1	.968

John Hiller

HILLER, JOHN FREDERICK
B. Apr. 8, 1943, Toronto, Ont., Canada

BR TL 6'1"   185 lbs.

Year	Team		W	L	PCT	ERA	G	GS	CG	IP	H	BB	SO	ShO	W	L	SV	AB	H	HR	BA	PO	A	E	DP	TC/G	FA
1965	DET	A	0	0	–	0.00	5	0	0	6	5	1	4	0	0	0	1	0	0	0	–	0	0	0	0	0.0	–
1966			0	0	–	9.00	1	0	0	2	2	2	1	0	0	0	0	0	0	0	–	0	0	0	0	0.0	–
1967			4	3	.571	2.63	23	6	2	65	57	9	49	2	1	1	3	15	2	0	.133	4	9	1	0	0.6	.929
1968			9	6	.600	2.39	39	12	4	128	92	51	78	1	4	3	2	37	3	0	.081	12	15	0	1	0.7	1.000
1969			4	4	.500	3.99	40	8	1	99.1	97	44	74	1	3	1	4	21	6	0	.286	2	11	1	0	0.4	.929
1970			6	6	.500	3.03	47	5	1	104	82	46	89	1	5	3	3	23	0	0	.000	3	10	0	0	0.3	1.000
1972			1	2	.333	2.05	24	3	1	44	39	13	26	0	0	0	0	4	0	0	.000	1	9	0	2	0.4	1.000
1973			10	5	.667	1.44	65	0	0	125	89	39	124	0	10	5	38	0	0	0	–	8	16	1	1	0.4	.960
1974			17	14	.548	2.64	59	0	0	150	127	62	134	0	17	14	13	0	0	0	–	2	11	1	0	0.2	.929
1975			2	3	.400	2.17	36	0	0	70.2	52	36	87	0	2	3	14	0	0	0	–	1	8	0	0	0.3	1.000
1976			12	8	.600	2.38	56	1	1	121	93	67	117	1	11	8	13	1	0	0	.000	2	13	1	0	0.3	.938
1977			8	14	.364	3.56	45	8	3	124	120	61	115	0	5	9	7	0	0	0	–	4	11	2	1	0.4	.882
1978			9	4	.692	2.34	51	0	0	92.1	64	35	74	0	9	4	15	0	0	0	–	1	9	0	0	0.2	1.000
1979			4	7	.364	5.24	43	0	0	79	83	55	46	0	4	7	9	0	0	0	–	4	10	0	0	0.3	1.000
1980			1	0	1.000	4.35	11	0	0	31	38	14	18	0	1	0	0	0	0	0	–	1	4	1	0	0.5	.833
15 yrs.			87	76	.534	2.83	545	43	13	1241.1	1040	535	1036	6	72	58	125	101	11	0	.109	45	136	8	5	0.3	.958

LEAGUE CHAMPIONSHIP SERIES

Year	Team		W	L	PCT	ERA	G	GS	CG	IP	H	BB	SO	ShO	W	L	SV	AB	H	HR	BA	PO	A	E	DP	TC/G	FA
1972	DET	A	1	0	1.000	0.00	3	0	0	3.1	1	1	1	0	1	0	0	0	0	0	–	0	0	0	0	0.0	–

WORLD SERIES

Year	Team		W	L	PCT	ERA	G	GS	CG	IP	H	BB	SO	ShO	W	L	SV	AB	H	HR	BA	PO	A	E	DP	TC/G	FA
1968	DET	A	0	0	–	13.50	2	0	0	2	6	3	1	0	0	0	0	0	0	0	–	1	0	0	0	0.5	1.000

Dave Hillman

HILLMAN, DARIUS DUTTON
B. Sept. 14, 1927, Dungannon, Va.

BR TR 5'11"   168 lbs.

Year	Team		W	L	PCT	ERA	G	GS	CG	IP	H	BB	SO	ShO	W	L	SV	AB	H	HR	BA	PO	A	E	DP	TC/G	FA
1955	CHI	N	0	0	–	5.31	25	3	0	57.2	63	25	23	0	0	0	0	10	1	0	.100	4	10	1	1	0.6	.933
1956			0	2	.000	2.19	2	2	0	12.1	11	5	6	0	0	0	0	4	0	0	.000	0	4	0	0	2.0	1.000
1957			6	11	.353	4.35	32	14	1	103.1	115	37	53	0	3	3	1	24	0	0	.000	11	12	1	3	0.8	.958
1958			4	8	.333	3.15	31	16	3	125.2	132	31	65	0	0	1	1	41	6	0	.146	7	20	1	0	0.9	.964
1959			8	11	.421	3.53	39	24	4	191	178	43	88	1	3	1	0	60	9	0	.150	28	31	2	0	1.6	.967
1960	BOS	A	0	3	.000	5.65	16	3	0	36.2	41	12	14	0	0	1	0	6	0	0	.000	3	0	0	0	0.6	1.000
1961			2	1	.600	2.77	28	1	0	78	70	23	39	0	2	0	0	17	0	0	.000	1	15	0	0	0.6	1.000
1962	2 teams		CIN N (2G 0–0)				NY N (13G 0–0)																					
"	total		0	0	–	6.98	15	1	0	19.1	29	9	8	0	0	0	1	1	0	0	.000	2	3	0	0	0.3	1.000
8 yrs.			21	37	.362	3.87	188	64	8	624	639	185	296	1	9	8	3	163	16	0	.098	54	104	5	4	0.9	.969

Charlie Hilsey

HILSEY, CHARLES T.
B. Mar. 23, 1864, Philadelphia, Pa.   D. Oct. 31, 1918, Philadelphia, Pa.

5'7"   180 lbs.

Year	Team		W	L	PCT	ERA	G	GS	CG	IP	H	BB	SO	ShO	W	L	SV	AB	H	HR	BA	PO	A	E	DP	TC/G	FA
1883	PHI	N	0	3	.000	5.54	3	3	3	26	36	4	8	0	0	0	0	10	1	0	.100	1	4	2	0	2.3	.714
1884	PHI	AA	2	1	.667	4.67	3	3	3	27	29	5	10	0	0	0	0	24	5	0	.208	1	8	1	0	3.3	.900
2 yrs.			2	4	.333	5.09	6	6	6	53	65	9	18	0	0	0	0	34	6	0	.176	2	12	3	0	2.8	.824

Sam Hinds

HINDS, SAMUEL RUSSELL
B. July 11, 1953, Frederick, Md.

BR TR 6'6"   215 lbs.

Year	Team		W	L	PCT	ERA	G	GS	CG	IP	H	BB	SO	ShO	W	L	SV	AB	H	HR	BA	PO	A	E	DP	TC/G	FA
1977	MIL	A	0	3	.000	4.75	29	1	0	72	72	40	46	0	0	2	2	0	0	0	–	5	8	0	0	0.4	1.000

Paul Hines

HINES, PAUL A.
B. Mar. 1, 1852, Washington, D. C.   D. July 10, 1935, Hyattsville, Md.

BR TR 5'9½"   173 lbs.

Year	Team		W	L	PCT	ERA	G	GS	CG	IP	H	BB	SO	ShO	W	L	SV	AB	H	HR	BA	PO	A	E	DP	TC/G	FA
1884	PRO	N	0	0	–	0.00	1	0	0	1	3	0	0	0	0	0	0	0	0	0	*	0	0	0	0	0.0	

Dutch Hinrichs

HINRICHS, WILLIAM LOUIS
B. Apr. 27, 1889, Orange, Calif.   D. Aug. 18, 1972, Kingsburg, Calif.

BR TR 6'3"   195 lbs.

Year	Team		W	L	PCT	ERA	G	GS	CG	IP	H	BB	SO	ShO	W	L	SV	AB	H	HR	BA	PO	A	E	DP	TC/G	FA
1910	WAS	A	0	1	.000	2.57	3	0	0	7	10	3	5	0	0	1	1	4	0	0	.000	0	0	0	0	0.0	–

Paul Hinrichs

HINRICHS, PAUL EDWIN (Herky)
B. Aug. 31, 1925, Marengo, Iowa

BR TR 6'   180 lbs.

Year	Team		W	L	PCT	ERA	G	GS	CG	IP	H	BB	SO	ShO	W	L	SV	AB	H	HR	BA	PO	A	E	DP	TC/G	FA
1951	BOS	A	0	0	–	21.60	4	0	0	3.1	7	4	1	0	0	0	0	0	0	0	–	0	1	0	0	0.3	1.000

Jerry Hinsley

HINSLEY, JERRY DEAN
B. Apr. 9, 1944, Hugo, Okla.

BR TR 5'11"   165 lbs.

Year	Team		W	L	PCT	ERA	G	GS	CG	IP	H	BB	SO	ShO	W	L	SV	AB	H	HR	BA	PO	A	E	DP	TC/G	FA
1964	NY	N	0	2	.000	8.22	9	2	0	15.1	21	7	11	0	0	0	1	1	0	0	.000	0	1	0	0	0.2	.500

Year	Team	W	L	PCT	ERA	G	GS	CG	IP	H	BB	SO	ShO	W	L	SV	AB	H	HR	BA	PO	A	E	DP	TC/G	FA

Jerry Hinsley *continued*

Year	Team	W	L	PCT	ERA	G	GS	CG	IP	H	BB	SO	ShO	W	L	SV	AB	H	HR	BA	PO	A	E	DP	TC/G	FA
1967		0	0	–	3.60	2	0	0	5	6	4	3	0	0	0	0	0	0	0	–	1	0	0	1	0.5	1.000
2 yrs.		0	2	.000	7.08	11	2	0	20.1	27	11	14	0	0	1	0	1	0	0	.000	1	1	1	1	0.3	.667

Rich Hinton

HINTON, RICHARD MICHAEL
B. May 22, 1947, Tucson, Ariz.   BL TL 6'2"   185 lbs.

Year	Team	W	L	PCT	ERA	G	GS	CG	IP	H	BB	SO	ShO	W	L	SV	AB	H	HR	BA	PO	A	E	DP	TC/G	FA
1971	CHI A	2	4	.333	4.50	18	2	0	24	27	6	15	0	2	2	0	1	0	0	.000	0	7	0	1	0.4	1.000
1972	2 teams	NY A	(7G 1–0)		TEX A	(5G 0–1)																				
"	total	1	1	.500	3.86	12	3	0	28	27	18	17	0	0	1	0	5	1	0	.200	2	3	0	0	0.4	1.000
1975	CHI A	1	0	1.000	4.82	15	0	0	37.1	41	15	30	0	1	0	0	0	0	0	–	1	9	0	1	0.7	1.000
1976	CIN N	1	2	.333	7.50	12	1	0	18	30	11	8	0	1	2	0	1	0	0	.000	0	2	1	0	0.3	.667
1978	CHI A	2	6	.250	4.02	29	4	2	80.2	78	28	48	0	1	2	1	0	0	0	–	3	8	1	0	0.4	.917
1979	2 teams	CHI A	(16G 1–2)		SEA A	(14G 0–2)																				
"	total	1	4	.200	5.81	30	3	0	62	80	13	34	0	1	1	2	0	0	0	–	6	10	1	1	0.6	.941
6 yrs.		8	17	.320	4.86	116	13	2	250	283	91	152	0	6	8	3	7	1	0	.143	12	39	3	3	0.5	.944

Herb Hippauf

HIPPAUF, HERBERT AUGUST
B. May 9, 1940, New York, N. Y.   BR TL 6'   180 lbs.

Year	Team	W	L	PCT	ERA	G	GS	CG	IP	H	BB	SO	ShO	W	L	SV	AB	H	HR	BA	PO	A	E	DP	TC/G	FA
1966	ATL N	0	1	.000	13.50	3	0	0	2.2	6	1	1	0	0	1	0	0	0	0	–	0	0	1	0	0.3	–

Harley Hisner

HISNER, HARLEY PARNELL
B. Nov. 6, 1926, Naples, Ind.   BR TR 6'1"   185 lbs.

Year	Team	W	L	PCT	ERA	G	GS	CG	IP	H	BB	SO	ShO	W	L	SV	AB	H	HR	BA	PO	A	E	DP	TC/G	FA
1951	BOS A	0	1	.000	4.50	1	1	0	6	7	4	3	0	0	0	0	2	1	0	.500	0	1	0	1	1.0	1.000

Bruce Hitt

HITT, BRUCE SMITH
B. Mar. 14, 1897, Comanche, Tex.   D. Nov. 10, 1973, Portland, Ore.   BR TR 6'1"   190 lbs.

Year	Team	W	L	PCT	ERA	G	GS	CG	IP	H	BB	SO	ShO	W	L	SV	AB	H	HR	BA	PO	A	E	DP	TC/G	FA
1917	STL N	0	0	–	9.00	2	0	0	4	7	1	1	0	0	0	0	1	0	0	.000	0	2	0	0	1.0	1.000

Roy Hitt

HITT, ROY WESLEY (Rhino)
B. June 22, 1887, Carleton, Neb.   D. Feb. 8, 1956, Pomona, Calif.   BL TL 5'10"   200 lbs.

Year	Team	W	L	PCT	ERA	G	GS	CG	IP	H	BB	SO	ShO	W	L	SV	AB	H	HR	BA	PO	A	E	DP	TC/G	FA
1907	CIN N	6	10	.375	3.40	21	18	14	153.1	143	56	63	2	0	0	0	56	10	0	.179	3	37	1	0	2.0	.976

Lloyd Hittle

HITTLE, LLOYD ELDON (Red)
B. Feb. 21, 1924, Lodi, Calif.   BR TL 5'10½" 164 lbs.

Year	Team	W	L	PCT	ERA	G	GS	CG	IP	H	BB	SO	ShO	W	L	SV	AB	H	HR	BA	PO	A	E	DP	TC/G	FA
1949	WAS A	5	7	.417	4.21	36	9	3	109	123	57	32	2	3	2	0	28	4	0	.143	5	17	1	0	0.6	.957
1950		2	4	.333	4.98	11	4	1	43.1	60	17	9	0	1	3	0	13	1	0	.077	3	14	1	1	1.6	.944
2 yrs.		7	11	.389	4.43	47	13	4	152.1	183	74	41	2	4	5	0	41	5	0	.122	8	31	2	1	0.9	.951

Myril Hoag

HOAG, MYRIL OLIVER
B. Mar. 9, 1908, Davis, Calif.   D. July 28, 1971, High Springs, Fla.   BR TR 5'11"   180 lbs.

Year	Team	W	L	PCT	ERA	G	GS	CG	IP	H	BB	SO	ShO	W	L	SV	AB	H	HR	BA	PO	A	E	DP	TC/G	FA
1939	STL A	0	0	–	0.00	1	0	0	1	0	0	0	0	0	0	0	482	142	10	.295	0	0	0	0	0.0	–
1945	CLE A	0	0	–	0.00	2	0	0	3	3	1	0	0	0	0	0	128	27	0	.211	0	1	0	0	0.5	1.000
2 yrs.		0	0	–	0.00	3	0	0	4	3	1	0	0	0	0	0	*				0	1	0	0	0.3	1.000

Ed Hobaugh

HOBAUGH, EDWARD RUSSELL
B. June 27, 1934, Kittanning, Pa.   BR TR 6'   176 lbs.

Year	Team	W	L	PCT	ERA	G	GS	CG	IP	H	BB	SO	ShO	W	L	SV	AB	H	HR	BA	PO	A	E	DP	TC/G	FA
1961	WAS A	7	9	.438	4.42	26	18	3	126.1	142	64	67	0	0	2	0	41	4	0	.098	7	22	2	3	1.2	.935
1962		2	1	.667	3.76	26	2	0	69.1	66	25	37	0	2	0	1	12	2	0	.167	1	8	0	1	0.3	1.000
1963		0	0	–	6.19	9	1	0	16	20	6	11	0	0	0	0	2	1	1	.500	1	3	0	0	0.4	1.000
3 yrs.		9	10	.474	4.34	61	21	3	211.2	228	95	115	0	2	2	1	55	7	1	.127	9	33	2	5	0.7	.955

Glen Hobbie

HOBBIE, GLEN FREDERICK
B. Apr. 24, 1936, Witt, Ill.   BR TR 6'2"   195 lbs.

Year	Team	W	L	PCT	ERA	G	GS	CG	IP	H	BB	SO	ShO	W	L	SV	AB	H	HR	BA	PO	A	E	DP	TC/G	FA
1957	CHI N	0	0	–	10.38	2	0	0	4.1	6	5	3	0	0	0	0	2	0	0	.000	1	0	0	0	0.5	1.000
1958		10	6	.625	3.74	55	16	2	168.1	163	93	91	1	6	1	2	48	7	0	.146	12	44	5	5	1.1	.918
1959		16	13	.552	3.69	46	33	10	234	204	106	138	3	0	1	0	79	9	0	.114	18	40	4	2	1.3	.935
1960		16	20	.444	3.97	46	36	16	258.2	253	101	134	4	2	3	1	86	13	1	.151	19	67	5	4	2.0	.945
1961		7	13	.350	4.26	36	29	7	198.2	207	54	103	2	1	0	2	66	11	2	.167	16	53	4	1	2.0	.945
1962		5	14	.263	5.22	42	23	5	162	198	62	87	0	0	2	0	49	6	0	.122	8	31	0	0	0.9	1.000
1963		7	10	.412	3.92	36	24	4	165.1	172	49	94	1	1	0	0	50	4	0	.080	6	29	4	1	1.1	.897
1964	2 teams	CHI N	(8G 0–3)		STL N	(13G 1–2)																				
"	total	1	5	.167	5.65	21	9	1	71.2	80	25	32	0	0	0	1	18	2	1	.111	6	18	0	0	1.1	1.000
8 yrs.		62	81	.434	4.20	284	170	45	1263	1283	495	682	11	10	7	6	398	52	4	.131	86	282	22	14	1.4	.944

Jack Hobbs

HOBBS, JOHN DOUGLAS
B. Nov. 11, 1955, Philadelphia, Pa.   BR TL 6'3"   190 lbs.

Year	Team	W	L	PCT	ERA	G	GS	CG	IP	H	BB	SO	ShO	W	L	SV	AB	H	HR	BA	PO	A	E	DP	TC/G	FA
1981	MIN A	0	0	–	3.00	4	0	0	6	5	6	1	0	0	0	0	0	0	0	–	1	0	0	0	0.3	1.000

Harry Hoch

HOCH, HARRY KELLER
B. Jan. 9, 1887, Woodside, Del.   D. Oct. 26, 1981, Lewes, Del.   BR TR 5'10½" 165 lbs.

Year	Team	W	L	PCT	ERA	G	GS	CG	IP	H	BB	SO	ShO	W	L	SV	AB	H	HR	BA	PO	A	E	DP	TC/G	FA
1908	PHI N	2	1	.667	2.77	3	3	2	26	20	13	4	0	0	0	0	5	1	0	.200	2	9	0	1	3.7	1.000
1914	STL A	0	2	.000	3.00	15	2	1	54	55	27	13	0	0	0	0	18	1	0	.056	4	23	0	1	1.8	1.000
1915		0	4	.000	7.20	12	3	1	40	52	26	9	0	0	1	0	10	2	0	.200	2	11	2	1	1.3	.867
3 yrs.		2	7	.222	4.35	30	8	4	120	127	66	26	0	0	1	0	33	4	0	.121	8	43	2	3	1.8	.962

Chuck Hockenbery

HOCKENBERY, CHARLES MARION
B. Dec. 15, 1950, La Crosse, Wis.   BB TR 6'1"   195 lbs.

Year	Team	W	L	PCT	ERA	G	GS	CG	IP	H	BB	SO	ShO	W	L	SV	AB	H	HR	BA	PO	A	E	DP	TC/G	FA
1975	CAL A	0	5	.000	5.27	16	4	0	41	48	19	15	0	0	1	1	0	0	0	–	1	6	0	1	0.4	1.000

Year	Team	W	L	PCT	ERA	G	GS	CG	IP	H	BB	SO	ShO	W	L	SV	AB	H	HR	BA	PO	A	E	DP	TC/G	FA

George Hockette

HOCKETTE, GEORGE EDWARD (Lefty)
B. Apr. 7, 1908, Perth, Miss. D. Jan. 20, 1974, Plantation, Fla. BL TL 6' 174 lbs.

Year	Team	W	L	PCT	ERA	G	GS	CG	IP	H	BB	SO	ShO	W	L	SV	AB	H	HR	BA	PO	A	E	DP	TC/G	FA
1934	BOS A	2	1	.667	1.65	3	3	3	27.1	22	6	14	2	0	0	0	11	3	0	.273	2	3	1	0	2.0	.833
1935		2	3	.400	5.16	23	4	0	61	83	12	11	0	2	1	0	14	2	0	.143	5	27	2	1	1.5	.941
2 yrs.		4	4	.500	4.08	26	7	3	88.1	105	18	25	2	2	1	0	25	5	0	.200	7	30	3	1	1.5	.925

Ed Hodge

HODGE, ED OLIVER
B. Apr. 19, 1958, Bellflower, Calif. BL TL 6'2" 185 lbs.

Year	Team	W	L	PCT	ERA	G	GS	CG	IP	H	BB	SO	ShO	W	L	SV	AB	H	HR	BA	PO	A	E	DP	TC/G	FA
1984	MIN A	4	3	.571	4.77	25	15	0	100	116	29	59	0	0	0	0	0	0	0	–	2	6	0	0	0.3	1.000

Shovel Hodge

HODGE, CLARENCE CLEMENT
B. July 6, 1893, Mount Andrew, Ala. D. Dec. 31, 1967, Ft. Walton Beach, Fla. BL TR 6'4" 190 lbs.

Year	Team	W	L	PCT	ERA	G	GS	CG	IP	H	BB	SO	ShO	W	L	SV	AB	H	HR	BA	PO	A	E	DP	TC/G	FA
1920	CHI A	1	1	.500	2.29	4	3	1	19.2	15	12	5	0	0	0	0	6	0	0	.000	0	3	0	0	0.8	1.000
1921		6	8	.429	6.56	36	11	6	142.2	191	54	25	0	4	1	2	52	17	0	.327	10	52	2	1	1.8	.969
1922		7	6	.538	4.14	35	8	2	139	154	65	37	0	5	2	1	58	12	0	.207	0	46	3	3	1.4	.939
3 yrs.		14	15	.483	5.17	75	21	9	301.1	360	131	67	0	9	3	3	116	29	0	.250	10	101	5	4	1.5	.957

Eli Hodkey

HODKEY, ALOYSIUS JOSEPH
B. Nov. 3, 1917, Lorain, Ohio BL TL 6'4" 185 lbs.

Year	Team	W	L	PCT	ERA	G	GS	CG	IP	H	BB	SO	ShO	W	L	SV	AB	H	HR	BA	PO	A	E	DP	TC/G	FA
1946	PHI N	0	1	.000	12.46	2	1	0	4.1	9	5	0	0	0	1	0	2	0	0	.000	0	0	0	0	0.0	–

Charlie Hodnett

HODNETT, CHARLES
B. 1861, St. Louis, Mo. Deceased.

Year	Team	W	L	PCT	ERA	G	GS	CG	IP	H	BB	SO	ShO	W	L	SV	AB	H	HR	BA	PO	A	E	DP	TC/G	FA
1883	STL AA	2	2	.500	1.41	4	4	3	32	28	7	6	0	0	0	0	11	2	0	.182	0	6	0	0	1.5	1.000
1884	STL U	12	2	.857	2.01	14	14	12	121	121	16	41	1	0	0	0	58	12	0	.207	3	22	6	1	2.2	.806
2 yrs.		14	4	.778	1.88	18	18	15	153	149	23	47	1	0	0	0	69	14	0	.203	3	28	6	1	2.1	.838

George Hodson

HODSON, GEORGE S.
B. 1876, Hartford, Conn. Deceased.

Year	Team	W	L	PCT	ERA	G	GS	CG	IP	H	BB	SO	ShO	W	L	SV	AB	H	HR	BA	PO	A	E	DP	TC/G	FA
1894	BOS N	4	4	.500	5.84	12	11	8	74	103	35	12	0	0	0	0	30	3	0	.100	1	10	4	1	1.3	.733
1895	PHI N	1	2	.333	9.53	4	2	1	17	27	9	6	0	1	0	0	5	0	0	.000	1	1	0	0	0.5	1.000
2 yrs.		5	6	.455	6.53	16	13	9	91	130	44	18	0	1	0	0	35	3	0	.086	2	11	4	1	1.1	.765

Billy Hoeft

HOEFT, WILLIAM FREDERICK
B. May 17, 1932, Oshkosh, Wis. BL TL 6'3" 180 lbs.

Year	Team	W	L	PCT	ERA	G	GS	CG	IP	H	BB	SO	ShO	W	L	SV	AB	H	HR	BA	PO	A	E	DP	TC/G	FA
1952	DET A	2	7	.222	4.32	34	10	1	125	123	63	67	0	0	2	4	40	6	0	.150	5	25	2	4	0.9	.938
1953		9	14	.391	4.83	29	27	9	197.2	223	58	90	0	0	2	2	64	11	0	.172	14	24	2	0	1.4	.950
1954		7	15	.318	4.58	34	25	10	175	180	59	114	4	1	1	1	52	10	0	.192	6	18	1	2	0.7	.960
1955		16	7	.696	2.99	32	29	17	220	187	75	133	7	0	1	0	82	17	0	.207	7	21	0	2	0.9	1.000
1956		20	14	.588	4.06	38	34	18	248	276	104	172	4	2	0	0	80	20	0	.250	5	28	1	1	0.9	.971
1957		9	11	.450	3.48	34	28	10	207	188	69	111	1	0	0	1	67	10	3	.149	8	28	2	2	1.1	.947
1958		10	9	.526	4.15	36	21	6	143	148	49	94	0	1	2	3	44	12	0	.273	6	15	3	2	0.7	.875
1959	3 teams	DET A	(2G 1–1)		BOS A	(5G 0–3)		BAL A	(16G 1–1)																		
"	total	2	5	.286	5.59	23	8	1	67.2	78	31	40	0	1	4	0	18	4	0	.222	4	12	1	0	0.7	.941
1960	BAL A	2	1	.667	4.34	19	0	0	18.2	18	14	14	0	2	1	0	1	0	0	.000	3	3	0	1	0.3	1.000
1961		7	4	.636	2.02	35	12	3	138	106	55	100	1	2	1	3	39	7	0	.179	9	25	0	2	1.0	1.000
1962		4	8	.333	4.59	57	4	0	113.2	103	43	73	0	4	6	7	19	3	0	.158	10	17	2	2	0.5	.931
1963	SF N	2	0	1.000	4.44	23	0	0	24.1	26	10	8	0	2	0	4	1	1	0	1.000	1	4	2	0	0.3	.714
1964	MIL N	4	0	1.000	3.80	42	0	0	73.1	76	18	47	0	4	0	4	9	2	0	.222	4	14	0	0	0.4	1.000
1965	CHI N	2	2	.500	2.81	29	2	1	51.1	41	20	44	0	1	1	1	11	3	0	.273	0	7	1	0	0.3	.875
1966	2 teams	CHI N	(36G 1–2)		SF N	(4G 0–2)																				
"	total	1	4	.200	4.84	40	0	0	44.2	47	17	33	0	1	4	3	4	1	0	.250	5	8	0	0	0.3	1.000
15 yrs.		97	101	.490	3.94	505	200	75	1847.1	1820	685	1140	17	20	19	33	531	107	3	.202	87	249	17	19	0.7	.952

Art Hoelskoetter

HOELSKOETTER, ARTHUR H.
B. Sept. 30, 1882, St. Louis, Mo. D. Aug. 3, 1954, St. Louis, Mo. BR TR 6'2"

Year	Team	W	L	PCT	ERA	G	GS	CG	IP	H	BB	SO	ShO	W	L	SV	AB	H	HR	BA	PO	A	E	DP	TC/G	FA
1905	STL N	0	1	.000	1.50	1	1	1	6	4	5	4	0	0	0	0	83	20	0	.241	0	3	0	0	3.0	1.000
1906		2	4	.333	4.63	12	3	2	58.1	53	34	20	0	0	0	0	317	71	0	.224	5	13	1	0	1.6	.947
1907		0	0	–	5.73	2	0	0	11	9	10	8	0	0	0	0	396	98	2	.247	0	0	0	0	–	–
3 yrs.		2	5	.286	4.54	15	4	3	75.1	68	49	32	0	1	0	0	*				5	16	1	0	1.5	.955

Joe Hoerner

HOERNER, JOSEPH WALTER
B. Nov. 12, 1936, Dubuque, Iowa BR TL 6'1" 200 lbs.

Year	Team	W	L	PCT	ERA	G	GS	CG	IP	H	BB	SO	ShO	W	L	SV	AB	H	HR	BA	PO	A	E	DP	TC/G	FA
1963	HOU N	0	0	–	0.00	1	0	0	3	2	0	2	0	0	0	0	1	0	0	.000	0	1	0	0	1.0	1.000
1964		0	0	–	4.91	7	0	0	11	13	6	4	0	0	0	0	1	0	0	.000	1	3	1	0	0.7	.800
1966	STL N	5	1	.833	1.54	57	0	0	76	57	21	63	0	5	1	13	8	1	1	.125	5	9	2	0	0.3	.875
1967		4	4	.500	2.59	57	0	0	66	52	20	50	0	4	4	15	11	2	0	.182	3	10	0	0	0.2	1.000
1968		8	2	.800	1.47	47	0	0	49	34	12	42	0	8	2	17	6	0	0	.000	2	6	1	0	0.2	.889
1969		2	3	.400	2.89	45	0	0	53	44	9	35	0	2	3	15	5	0	0	.000	3	9	0	1	0.3	1.000
1970	PHI N	9	5	.643	2.64	44	0	0	58	53	20	39	0	9	5	9	10	2	0	.200	2	1	1	0	0.1	.750
1971		4	5	.444	1.97	49	0	0	73	57	21	57	0	4	5	9	10	1	0	.100	2	10	2	0	0.3	.857
1972	2 teams	PHI N	(15G 0–2)		ATL N	(25G 1–3)																				
"	total	1	5	.167	4.40	40	0	0	45	55	13	31	0	1	5	5	5	0	0	.000	1	3	1	0	0.1	.800
1973	2 teams	ATL N	(20G 2–2)		KC A	(22G 2–0)																				
"	total	4	2	.667	5.63	42	0	0	32	45	17	25	0	4	2	6	–				2	3	1	0	0.1	.800
1974	KC A	2	3	.400	3.86	30	0	0	35	32	12	24	0	2	3	2	–				1	0	0	0	0.0	1.000
1975	PHI N	0	0	–	2.57	25	0	0	21	25	8	20	0	0	0	0	2	0	0	.000	0	0	0	0	0.0	–
1976	TEX A	0	4	.000	5.14	41	0	0	35	41	19	15	0	0	4	8	–				3	0	0	0	0.1	1.000
1977	CIN N	0	0	–	12.00	8	0	0	6	9	3	5	0	0	0	0	–				0	0	0	0	0.0	–
14 yrs.		39	34	.534	2.99	493	0	0	563	519	181	412	0	39	34	99	59	6	1	.102	19	57	8	1	0.2	.905

Year	Team		W	L	PCT	ERA	G	GS	CG	IP	H	BB	SO	ShO	Relief Pitching W	L	SV	Batting AB	H	HR	BA	PO	A	E	DP	TC/G	FA

Joe Hoerner *continued*

WORLD SERIES

1967	STL	N	0	0	–	40.50	2	0	0	.2	4	1	0	0	0	0	0	0	0	0	–	0	0	0	0	0.0	–
1968			0	1	.000	3.86	3	0	0	4.2	5	5	3	0	0	1	1	2	1	0	.500	0	0	0	0	0.0	–
2 yrs.			0	1	.000	8.44	5	0	0	5.1	9	6	3	0	0	1	1	2	1	0	.500	0	0	0	0	0.0	–

Frank Hoerst

HOERST, FRANCIS JOSEPH (Lefty)
B. Aug. 11, 1917, Philadelphia, Pa.
BL TL 6'3" 192 lbs.

1940	PHI	N	1	0	1.000	5.25	6	0	0	12	12	8	3	0	1	0	0	2	0	0	.000	1	6	0	1	1.2	1.000
1941			3	10	.231	5.20	37	11	1	105.2	111	50	33	0	1	1	0	22	4	0	.182	3	31	4	2	1.0	.895
1942			4	16	.200	5.20	33	22	5	150.2	162	78	52	0	0	0	1	46	7	0	.152	11	40	2	2	1.6	.962
1946			1	6	.143	4.61	18	7	2	68.1	77	36	17	0	1	0	0	17	1	0	.059	5	9	0	0	0.8	1.000
1947			1	1	.500	7.94	4	1	0	11.1	19	3	0	0	0	1	0	4	2	0	.500	2	2	0	0	1.0	1.000
5 yrs.			10	33	.233	5.17	98	41	8	348	381	175	105	0	3	2	1	91	14	0	.154	22	88	6	5	1.2	.948

Red Hoff

HOFF, CHESTER CORNELIUS
B. May 8, 1891, Ossining, N. Y.
BL TL 5'9" 162 lbs.

1911	NY	A	0	1	.000	2.18	5	1	0	20.2	21	7	10	0	0	0	0	11	3	0	.273	2	11	1	0	2.8	.929
1912			0	1	.000	6.89	5	1	0	15.2	20	6	14	0	0	0	0	5	1	0	.200	0	4	1	0	1.0	.800
1913			0	0	–	0.00	2	0	0	3	0	1	2	0	0	0	0	1	0	0	.000	0	0	0	0	0.0	–
1915	STL	A	2	2	.500	1.24	11	3	2	43.2	26	24	23	0	1	0	0	17	3	0	.176	2	17	3	0	2.0	.864
4 yrs.			2	4	.333	2.49	23	5	2	83	67	38	49	0	1	0	0	34	7	0	.206	4	32	5	0	1.8	.878

Bill Hoffer

HOFFER, WILLIAM LEOPOLD (Wizard)
B. Nov. 8, 1870, Cedar Rapids, Iowa   D. July 21, 1959, Cedar Rapids, Iowa
BR TR 5'9" 155 lbs.

1895	BAL	N	31	6	.838	3.21	41	38	32	314	296	124	80	4	2	1	0	126	27	0	.214	15	55	2	2	1.8	.972
1896			25	7	.781	3.38	35	35	32	309	317	95	93	3	0	0	0	125	38	0	.304	15	83	9	6	3.1	.916
1897			22	11	.667	4.30	38	33	29	303.1	350	104	62	1	1	2	0	139	33	1	.237	22	64	4	4	2.4	.956
1898	2 teams		3	4	.429	BAL N (4G 0–4)					PIT N (4G 3–0)																	
"	total		3	4	.429	4.68	8	7	7	65.1	88	31	16	0	0	0	0	35	6	0	.171	3	13	0	0	2.0	1.000
1899	PIT	N	8	10	.444	3.63	23	19	15	163.2	169	64	44	2	1	1	0	91	18	0	.198	13	37	5	2	2.4	.909
1901	CLE	A	3	8	.273	4.55	16	10	10	99	113	35	19	0	0	1	3	44	6	0	.136	5	29	1	1	2.2	.971
6 yrs.			92	46	.667	3.75	161	142	125	1254.1	1333	453	314	10	4	5	3	560	128	1	.229	73	281	21	15	2.3	.944

Bill Hoffman

HOFFMAN, WILLIAM JOSEPH
B. Mar. 3, 1918, Philadelphia, Pa.
BL TL 5'9" 170 lbs.

| 1939 | PHI | N | 0 | 0 | – | 13.50 | 3 | 0 | 0 | 6 | 8 | 7 | 1 | 0 | 0 | 0 | 0 | 1 | 0 | 0 | .000 | 0 | 0 | 0 | 0 | 0.0 | – |

Danny Hoffman

HOFFMAN, DANIEL JOHN
B. Mar. 12, 1880, Canaan, Conn.   D. Mar. 14, 1922, Manchester, Conn.
BL TL 5'9" 175 lbs.

| 1903 | PHI | A | 0 | 0 | – | 2.70 | 1 | 0 | 0 | 3.1 | 2 | 2 | 0 | 0 | 0 | 0 | 0 | * | | | | 0 | 0 | 0 | 0 | 0.0 | – |

Frank Hoffman

HOFFMAN, FRANK J. (The Texas Wonder)
B. Houston, Tex.   Deceased.

| 1888 | KC | AA | 3 | 9 | .250 | 2.77 | 12 | 12 | 12 | 104 | 102 | 42 | 38 | 0 | 0 | 0 | 0 | 39 | 6 | 0 | .154 | 7 | 24 | 6 | 1 | 3.1 | .838 |

Guy Hoffman

HOFFMAN, GUY ALAN
B. July 9, 1956, Ottawa, Ill.
BL TL 5'9" 175 lbs.

1979	CHI	A	0	5	.000	5.40	24	0	0	30	30	23	18	0	0	5	2	0	0	–	1	5	0	1	0.3	1.000
1980			1	0	1.000	2.61	23	1	0	38	38	17	24	0	1	0	1	0	0	–	1	1	0	0	0.1	1.000
1983			1	0	1.000	7.50	11	0	0	6	14	2	2	0	1	0	0	0	0	–	1	0	0	0	0.1	1.000
1986	CHI	N	6	2	.750	3.86	32	8	1	84	92	29	47	0	4	0	0	15	1	0	.067	1	9	1	0	0.3	.909
1987	CIN	N	9	10	.474	4.37	36	22	0	158.2	160	49	87	0	3	0	0	45	5	0	.111	3	21	0	0	0.7	1.000
1988	TEX		0	0	–	5.24	11	0	0	22.1	22	8	9	0	0	0	0					1	4	0	0	0.5	1.000
6 yrs.			17	17	.500	4.25	137	31	1	339	356	128	187	0	9	5	3	60	6	0	.100	8	40	1	1	0.4	.980

John Hofford

HOFFORD, JOHN WILLIAM
B. May 25, 1863, Philadelphia, Pa.   D. Dec. 16, 1915, Philadelphia, Pa.

1885	PIT	AA	0	3	.000	3.60	3	3	3	25	28	9	21	0	0	0	0	8	1	0	.125	1	5	0	0	2.0	1.000
1886			3	6	.333	4.33	9	9	9	81	88	40	25	0	0	0	0	34	10	0	.294	5	17	2	0	2.7	.917
2 yrs.			3	9	.250	4.16	12	12	12	106	116	49	46	0	0	0	0	42	11	0	.262	6	22	2	0	2.5	.933

Eddie Hogan

HOGAN, ROBERT EDWARD
B. Apr., 1860, St. Louis, Mo.   Deceased.
BR 5'7" 153 lbs.

| 1882 | STL | AA | 0 | 1 | .000 | 1.13 | 1 | 1 | 1 | 8 | 10 | 0 | 4 | 0 | 0 | 0 | 0 | * | | | | 0 | 1 | 2 | 0 | 3.0 | .333 |

George Hogan

HOGAN, GEORGE A.
Brother of Happy Hogan.
B. Sept. 25, 1885, Marion, Ohio   D. Feb. 22, 1922, Bartlesville, Okla.
BR TR 6' 160 lbs.

| 1914 | KC | F | 0 | 1 | .000 | 4.15 | 4 | 1 | 0 | 13 | 12 | 7 | 7 | 0 | 0 | 0 | 0 | 4 | 0 | 0 | .000 | 0 | 5 | 1 | 1 | 1.5 | .833 |

Bill Hogg

HOGG, WILLIAM (Buffalo Bill)
B. 1880, Port Huron, Mich.   D. Dec. 8, 1909, New Orleans, La.
BR TR 6'

1905	NY	A	9	13	.409	3.20	39	22	9	205	178	101	125	3	4	3	1	67	4	0	.060	5	35	2	3	1.1	.952
1906			14	13	.519	2.93	28	25	15	206	171	72	107	3	3	0	0	72	9	0	.125	5	35	1	4	1.5	.976
1907			10	8	.556	3.08	25	21	13	166.2	173	83	64	0	0	0	0	64	11	1	.172	7	47	2	0	2.2	.964
1908			4	16	.200	3.01	24	21	6	152.1	155	63	72	0	0	0	0	43	4	0	.093	5	37	1	0	1.8	.977
4 yrs.			37	50	.425	3.06	116	89	43	730	677	319	368	6	7	3	1	246	28	1	.114	22	154	6	7	1.6	.967

Year	Team	W	L	PCT	ERA	G	GS	CG	IP	H	BB	SO	ShO	Relief Pitching W	L	SV	Batting AB	H	HR	BA	PO	A	E	DP	TC/G	FA

Brad Hogg

HOGG, CARTER BRADLEY
B. Mar. 26, 1888, Buena Vista, Ga.   D. Apr. 2, 1935, Buena Vista, Ga.   BR TR 6'   185 lbs.

Year	Team	W	L	PCT	ERA	G	GS	CG	IP	H	BB	SO	ShO	W	L	SV	AB	H	HR	BA	PO	A	E	DP	TC/G	FA
1911	BOS N	0	3	.000	6.66	8	3	2	25.2	33	14	8	0	0	1	0	9	4	0	.444	2	8	1	0	1.4	.909
1912		1	1	.500	6.97	10	1	0	31	37	16	12	0	1	1	0	11	1	0	.091	0	6	0	0	0.6	1.000
1915	CHI N	1	0	1.000	2.08	2	2	1	13	12	6	0	1	0	0	0	3	0	0	.000	0	6	0	0	3.0	1.000
1918	PHI N	13	13	.500	2.53	29	25	17	228	201	61	81	3	1	0	1	79	18	0	.228	8	73	1	7	2.8	.988
1919		5	12	.294	4.43	22	19	13	150.1	163	55	48	0	1	0	1	60	17	0	.283	3	34	0	0	1.7	1.000
5 yrs.		20	29	.408	3.70	71	50	33	448	446	152	149	4	2	3	1	162	40	0	.247	13	127	2	7	2.0	.986

Chief Hogsett

HOGSETT, ELON CHESTER
B. Nov. 2, 1903, Brownell, Kans.   BL TL 6'   190 lbs.

Year	Team	W	L	PCT	ERA	G	GS	CG	IP	H	BB	SO	ShO	W	L	SV	AB	H	HR	BA	PO	A	E	DP	TC/G	FA
1929	DET A	1	2	.333	2.83	4	4	2	28.2	34	9	9	1	0	0	0	10	2	0	.200	1	8	0	1	2.3	1.000
1930		9	8	.529	5.42	33	17	4	146	174	63	54	0	2	1	1	58	17	1	.293	10	37	5	1	1.6	.904
1931		3	9	.250	5.93	22	12	5	112.1	150	33	47	0	2	2	2	47	11	0	.234	8	23	1	0	1.5	.969
1932		11	9	.550	3.54	47	15	7	178	201	66	56	0	6	3	7	57	14	2	.246	8	46	3	4	1.2	.947
1933		6	10	.375	4.50	45	2	0	116	137	56	39	0	6	9	9	38	8	0	.211	4	31	1	2	0.8	.972
1934		3	2	.600	4.29	26	0	0	50.1	61	19	23	0	3	2	3	13	3	0	.231	4	11	0	0	0.6	1.000
1935		6	6	.500	3.54	40	0	0	96.2	109	49	39	0	6	6	5	23	6	2	.261	5	31	2	2	1.0	.947
1936	2 teams	DET A	(3G 0–1)			STL A	(39G 13–15)																			
"	total	13	16	.448	5.58	42	29	10	219.1	286	91	68	0	1	0	1	70	10	0	.143	2	51	6	2	1.4	.898
1937	STL A	6	19	.240	6.29	37	26	8	177.1	245	75	68	1	1	0	2	62	13	1	.210	8	28	3	2	1.1	.923
1938	WAS A	5	6	.455	6.03	31	9	1	91	107	36	33	0	3	2	3	23	7	0	.304	7	18	2	2	0.9	.926
1944	DET A	0	0	–	0.00	3	0	0	6.1	7	4	5	0	0	0	0	2	0	0	.000	0	1	0	0	0.7	.500
11 yrs.		63	87	.420	5.02	330	114	37	1222	1511	501	441	2	28	27	33	403	91	6	.226	57	285	24	16	1.1	.934

WORLD SERIES

Year	Team	W	L	PCT	ERA	G	GS	CG	IP	H	BB	SO	ShO	W	L	SV	AB	H	HR	BA	PO	A	E	DP	TC/G	FA
1934	DET A	0	0	–	1.23	3	0	0	7.1	6	3	3	0	0	0	0	3	0	0	.000	0	2	0	0	0.7	1.000
1935		0	0	–	0.00	1	0	0	1	0	1	0	0	0	0	0	0	0	0	–	1	0	0	0	1.0	1.000
2 yrs.		0	0	–	1.08	4	0	0	8.1	6	4	3	0	0	0	0	3	0	0	.000	1	2	0	0	0.8	1.000

Bobby Hogue

HOGUE, ROBERT CLINTON
B. Apr. 5, 1921, Miami, Fla.   D. Dec. 22, 1987, Miami, Fla.   BR TR 5'10"   195 lbs.

Year	Team	W	L	PCT	ERA	G	GS	CG	IP	H	BB	SO	ShO	W	L	SV	AB	H	HR	BA	PO	A	E	DP	TC/G	FA
1948	BOS N	8	2	.800	3.23	40	1	0	86.1	88	19	43	0	8	2	4	21	2	0	.095	4	11	0	1	0.4	1.000
1949		2	2	.500	3.13	33	1	0	72	78	25	23	0	2	2	3	21	6	0	.286	3	21	0	1	0.7	1.000
1950		3	5	.375	5.03	36	1	0	62.2	69	31	15	0	3	5	7	13	3	0	.231	1	14	0	4	0.4	1.000
1951	3 teams	BOS N	(3G 0–0)			STL A	(18G 1–1)		NY A	(7G 1–0)																
"	total	2	1	.667	4.29	28	0	0	42	39	29	13	0	2	1	1	5	3	0	.600	2	9	0	2	0.4	1.000
1952	2 teams	NY A	(27G 3–5)			STL A	(8G 0–1)																			
"	total	3	6	.333	4.66	35	0	0	63.2	62	38	14	0	3	5	4	13	3	0	.231	0	10	3	0	0.4	.769
5 yrs.		18	16	.529	3.97	172	3	0	326.2	336	142	108	0	18	15	17	73	17	0	.233	10	65	3	8	0.5	.962

WORLD SERIES

Year	Team	W	L	PCT	ERA	G	GS	CG	IP	H	BB	SO	ShO	W	L	SV	AB	H	HR	BA	PO	A	E	DP	TC/G	FA
1951	NY A	0	0	–	0.00	2	0	0	2.2	1	0	0	0	0	0	0	0	0	0	–	0	1	0	0	0.5	1.000

Cal Hogue

HOGUE, CALVIN GREY
B. Oct. 24, 1927, Dayton, Ohio   BR TR 6'   185 lbs.

Year	Team	W	L	PCT	ERA	G	GS	CG	IP	H	BB	SO	ShO	W	L	SV	AB	H	HR	BA	PO	A	E	DP	TC/G	FA
1952	PIT N	1	8	.111	4.84	19	12	3	83.2	79	68	34	0	0	0	0	24	6	0	.250	4	9	2	1	0.8	.867
1953		1	1	.500	5.21	3	2	2	19	19	16	10	0	0	0	0	5	0	0	.000	1	3	0	1	1.3	1.000
1954		0	1	.000	4.91	3	2	0	11	11	12	7	0	0	0	0	3	0	0	.000	0	2	0	0	0.7	1.000
3 yrs.		2	10	.167	4.91	25	16	5	113.2	109	96	51	0	0	0	0	32	6	0	.188	5	14	2	2	0.8	.905

Wally Holborow

HOLBOROW, WALTER ALBERT
B. Nov. 30, 1913, New York, N. Y.   D. July 14, 1986, Ft. Lauderdale, Fla.   BR TR 5'11"   187 lbs.

Year	Team	W	L	PCT	ERA	G	GS	CG	IP	H	BB	SO	ShO	W	L	SV	AB	H	HR	BA	PO	A	E	DP	TC/G	FA
1944	WAS A	0	0	–	0.00	1	0	0	3	0	2	1	0	0	0	0	–	1	0	0	0	1.0	1.000			
1945		1	1	.500	2.30	15	1	0	31.1	20	16	14	1	0	1	0	2	0	0	.000	1	3	1	0	0.3	.800
1948	PHI A	1	2	.333	5.71	5	1	1	17.1	32	7	3	0	1	0	0	4	2	0	.500	2	6	1	1	1.8	.889
3 yrs.		2	3	.400	3.31	21	2	1	51.2	52	25	18	1	1	1	0	6	2	0	.333	4	9	2	1	0.7	.867

Ken Holcombe

HOLCOMBE, KENNETH EDWARD
B. Aug. 23, 1918, Burnsville, N. C.   BR TR 5'11½"   169 lbs.

Year	Team	W	L	PCT	ERA	G	GS	CG	IP	H	BB	SO	ShO	W	L	SV	AB	H	HR	BA	PO	A	E	DP	TC/G	FA
1945	NY A	3	3	.500	1.79	23	2	0	55.1	43	27	20	0	3	2	0	15	2	0	.133	2	10	1	1	0.6	.923
1948	CIN N	0	0	–	7.71	2	0	0	2.1	3	2	2	0	0	0	0	0	0	0	–	0	0	0	0	0.0	–
1950	CHI A	3	10	.231	4.59	24	15	5	96	122	45	37	0	0	1	1	32	5	0	.156	4	16	2	1	1.0	.917
1951		11	12	.478	3.78	28	23	12	159.1	142	68	39	2	1	0	0	44	11	0	.250	8	43	3	5	1.9	.943
1952	2 teams	CHI A	(7G 0–5)			STL A	(12G 0–2)																			
"	total	0	7	.000	5.30	19	8	1	56	58	27	19	0	0	0	0	13	1	0	.077	4	15	2	0	1.0	.895
1953	BOS A	1	0	1.000	6.00	3	0	0	6	9	3	1	0	1	0	1	2	0	0	.000	1	0	0	0	0.7	1.000
6 yrs.		18	32	.360	3.98	99	48	18	375	377	170	118	2	5	4	2	106	19	0	.179	19	84	8	7	1.1	.928

Fred Holdsworth

HOLDSWORTH, FREDERICK WILLIAM
B. May 29, 1952, Detroit, Mich.   BR TR 6'1"   190 lbs.

Year	Team	W	L	PCT	ERA	G	GS	CG	IP	H	BB	SO	ShO	W	L	SV	AB	H	HR	BA	PO	A	E	DP	TC/G	FA
1972	DET A	0	1	.000	12.86	2	2	0	7	13	2	5	0	0	0	0	3	1	0	.333	1	0	0	0	0.5	1.000
1973		0	1	.000	6.60	5	2	0	15	13	6	9	0	0	0	0	0	0	0	–	2	0	1	0	0.6	.667
1974		0	3	.000	4.25	8	5	0	36	40	14	16	0	0	0	0	0	0	0	–	0	2	0	0	0.5	.500
1976	BAL A	4	1	.800	2.03	16	0	0	40	24	13	24	0	4	1	2	0	0	0	–	4	3	0	0	0.4	1.000
1977	2 teams	BAL A	(12G 0–1)			MON N	(14G 3–3)																			
"	total	3	4	.429	4.02	26	6	0	56	52	34	25	0	1	0	0	10	0	0	.000	5	6	0	2	0.4	1.000
1978	MON N	0	0	–	7.00	6	0	0	9	16	8	3	0	0	0	0	0	0	0	–	0	1	2	0	0.5	.667
1980	MIL A	0	0	–	4.50	9	0	0	20	24	9	12	0	0	0	0	0	0	0	–	0	5	0	0	0.6	1.000
7 yrs.		7	10	.412	4.38	72	15	0	183	182	86	94	0	4	2	2	13	1	0	.077	12	18	4	2	0.5	.882

Walter Holke

HOLKE, WALTER HENRY (Union Man)
B. Dec. 25, 1892, St. Louis, Mo.   D. Oct. 12, 1954, St. Louis, Mo.   BB TL 6'1½"   185 lbs.

Year	Team	W	L	PCT	ERA	G	GS	CG	IP	H	BB	SO	ShO	W	L	SV	AB	H	HR	BA	PO	A	E	DP	TC/G	FA
1923	PHI N	0	0	–	0.00	1	0	0	1	1	0	0	0	0	0	0	*				0	0	0	0	0.0	–

Year	Team		W	L	PCT	ERA	G	GS	CG	IP	H	BB	SO	ShO	Relief Pitching W	L	SV	Batting AB	H	HR	BA	PO	A	E	DP	TC/G	FA

Al Holland

HOLLAND, ALFRED WILLIS
B. Aug. 16, 1952, Roanoke, Va.   BR TL 5'11" 207 lbs.

Year	Team		W	L	PCT	ERA	G	GS	CG	IP	H	BB	SO	ShO	W	L	SV	AB	H	HR	BA	PO	A	E	DP	TC/G	FA
1977	PIT	N	0	0	–	9.00	2	0	0	2	4	0	1	0	0	0	0	0	0	0	–	1	0	0	0	0.5	1.000
1979	SF	N	0	0	–	0.00	3	0	0	7	3	5	7	0	0	0	0	0	0	0	–	0	0	0	0	0.0	–
1980			5	3	.625	1.76	54	0	0	82	71	34	65	0	5	3	7	5	1	0	.200	3	15	3	1	0.4	.857
1981			7	5	.583	2.41	47	3	0	101	87	44	78	0	6	5	7	16	1	0	.063	7	11	4	0	0.5	.818
1982			7	3	.700	3.33	58	7	0	129.2	115	40	97	0	5	0	5	34	2	0	.059	2	22	2	1	0.4	.923
1983	PHI	N	8	4	.667	2.26	68	0	0	91.2	63	30	100	0	8	4	25	7	0	0	.000	0	5	0	0	0.1	1.000
1984			5	10	.333	3.39	68	0	0	98.1	82	30	61	0	5	10	29	5	0	0	.000	1	8	0	0	0.1	1.000
1985	3 teams		PHI N	(3G 0–1)		PIT N	(38G 1–3)		CAL A	(15G 0–1)																	
"	total		1	5	.167	2.90	56	0	0	87	70	31	62	0	1	5	5	5	2	0	.400	4	9	0	1	0.2	1.000
1986	NY	A	1	0	1.000	5.09	25	1	0	40.2	44	9	37	0	1	0	0	0	0	0	–	0	2	2	0	0.2	.500
1987			0	0	–	14.21	3	0	0	6.1	9	9	5	0	0	0	0	0	0	0	–	0	1	0	0	0.3	1.000
10 yrs.			34	30	.531	2.98	384	11	0	645.2	548	232	513	0	31	27	78	72	6	0	.083	18	73	11	3	0.3	.892

LEAGUE CHAMPIONSHIP SERIES

Year	Team		W	L	PCT	ERA	G	GS	CG	IP	H	BB	SO	ShO	W	L	SV	AB	H	HR	BA	PO	A	E	DP	TC/G	FA
1983	PHI	N	0	0	–	0.00	2	0	0	1	0	3	0	0	0	0	0	0	0	–	0	0	0	0	0.0	–

WORLD SERIES

Year	Team		W	L	PCT	ERA	G	GS	CG	IP	H	BB	SO	ShO	W	L	SV	AB	H	HR	BA	PO	A	E	DP	TC/G	FA
1983	PHI	N	0	0	–	0.00	2	0	0	3.2	1	0	5	0	0	0	1	0	0	0	–	0	0	0	0	0.0	–

Bill Holland

HOLLAND, WILLIAM DAVID
B. June 4, 1915, Varina, N. C.   BL TL 6'1" 190 lbs.

Year	Team		W	L	PCT	ERA	G	GS	CG	IP	H	BB	SO	ShO	W	L	SV	AB	H	HR	BA	PO	A	E	DP	TC/G	FA
1939	WAS	A	0	1	.000	11.25	3	0	0	4	6	5	2	0	0	1	0	0	0	0	–	1	0	1	0	0.3	1.000

Mul Holland

HOLLAND, HOWARD ARTHUR
B. Jan. 6, 1903, Franklin, Va.   D. Feb. 16, 1969, Winchester, Va.   BR TR 6'4" 185 lbs.

Year	Team		W	L	PCT	ERA	G	GS	CG	IP	H	BB	SO	ShO	W	L	SV	AB	H	HR	BA	PO	A	E	DP	TC/G	FA
1926	CIN	N	0	0	–	1.35	3	0	0	6.2	3	5	0	0	0	0	0	2	1	0	.500	1	5	0	0	2.0	1.000
1927	NY	N	1	0	1.000	0.00	2	0	0	2	0	3	0	0	1	0	0	0	0	0	–	0	0	0	0	0.0	–
1929	STL	N	0	1	.000	9.42	8	0	0	14.1	13	7	5	0	0	1	0	4	1	0	.250	0	2	0	1	0.3	1.000
3 yrs.			1	1	.500	6.26	13	0	0	23	16	15	5	0	1	1	0	6	2	0	.333	1	7	0	1	0.6	1.000

Ed Holley

HOLLEY, EDWARD EDGAR
B. July 23, 1899, Benton, Ky.   D. Oct. 26, 1986, Paducah, Ky.   BR TR 6'1½" 195 lbs.

Year	Team		W	L	PCT	ERA	G	GS	CG	IP	H	BB	SO	ShO	W	L	SV	AB	H	HR	BA	PO	A	E	DP	TC/G	FA
1928	CHI	N	0	0	–	3.77	13	1	0	31	31	16	10	0	0	0	0	5	0	0	.000	0	5	0	0	0.4	1.000
1932	PHI	N	11	14	.440	3.95	34	30	16	228	247	55	87	2	0	0	0	91	12	0	.132	11	39	5	3	1.6	.909
1933			13	15	.464	3.53	30	28	12	206.2	219	62	56	3	0	1	0	74	12	0	.162	8	32	0	2	1.3	1.000
1934	2 teams		PHI N	(15G 1–8)		PIT N	(5G 0–3)																				
"	total		1	11	.083	8.12	20	17	2	82	105	37	16	0	0	0	0	26	7	0	.269	0	13	2	2	0.8	.867
4 yrs.			25	40	.385	4.40	97	76	30	547.2	602	170	169	5	0	1	0	196	31	0	.158	19	89	7	7	1.2	.939

Bug Holliday

HOLLIDAY, JAMES WEAR
B. Feb. 8, 1867, St. Louis, Mo.   D. Feb. 15, 1910, Cincinnati, Ohio   BR TR 5'11" 151 lbs.

Year	Team		W	L	PCT	ERA	G	GS	CG	IP	H	BB	SO	ShO	W	L	SV	AB	H	HR	BA	PO	A	E	DP	TC/G	FA
1892	CIN	N	0	0	–	11.25	1	0	0	4	13	1	0	0	0	0	0	602	176	13	.292	0	1	0	0	1.0	1.000
1896			0	0	–	0.00	1	0	0	1	4	2	0	0	0	0	0	84	27	0	.321	0	0	0	0	0.0	–
2 yrs.			0	0	–	9.00	2	0	0	5	17	3	0	0	0	0	0	*				0	1	0	0	0.5	1.000

Carl Holling

HOLLING, CARL
B. July 9, 1896, Dana, Calif.   D. July 18, 1962, Sonoma, Calif.   BR TR 6'1" 172 lbs.

Year	Team		W	L	PCT	ERA	G	GS	CG	IP	H	BB	SO	ShO	W	L	SV	AB	H	HR	BA	PO	A	E	DP	TC/G	FA
1921	DET	A	3	7	.300	4.30	35	11	4	136	162	58	38	0	1	3	4	48	13	0	.271	13	39	1	3	1.5	.981
1922			1	1	.500	15.43	5	1	0	9.1	21	5	2	0	1	0	0	2	0	0	.000	0	3	0	0	0.6	1.000
2 yrs.			4	8	.333	5.02	40	12	4	145.1	183	63	40	0	2	3	4	50	13	0	.260	13	42	1	3	1.4	.982

Al Hollingsworth

HOLLINGSWORTH, ALBERT WAYNE (Boots)
B. Feb. 25, 1908, St. Louis, Mo.   BL TL 6' 174 lbs.

Year	Team		W	L	PCT	ERA	G	GS	CG	IP	H	BB	SO	ShO	W	L	SV	AB	H	HR	BA	PO	A	E	DP	TC/G	FA
1935	CIN	N	6	13	.316	3.89	38	22	8	173.1	165	76	89	0	1	1	0	54	8	0	.148	9	39	4	0	1.4	.923
1936			9	10	.474	4.16	29	25	9	184	204	66	76	0	1	1	1	73	23	0	.315	10	28	2	2	1.4	.950
1937			9	15	.375	3.91	43	24	11	202.1	229	73	74	1	2	3	5	76	19	0	.250	4	51	4	2	1.4	.932
1938	2 teams		CIN N	(9G 2–2)		PHI N	(24G 5–16)																				
"	total		7	18	.280	4.36	33	25	12	208.1	220	89	93	1	2	1	0	79	18	0	.228	10	28	0	3	1.2	1.000
1939	2 teams		PHI N	(15G 1–9)		BKN N	(8G 1–2)																				
"	total		2	11	.154	5.67	23	15	4	87.1	111	38	35	0	1	1	0	28	3	0	.107	3	20	0	1	1.0	1.000
1940	WAS	A	1	0	1.000	5.50	3	2	0	18	18	11	7	0	0	0	0	6	1	0	.167	1	7	0	1	2.7	1.000
1942	STL	A	10	6	.625	2.96	33	18	7	161	173	52	60	1	1	2	4	56	10	0	.179	6	36	1	2	1.3	.977
1943			6	13	.316	4.21	35	20	9	154	169	51	63	1	1	2	3	50	7	0	.140	7	27	2	3	1.0	.944
1944			5	7	.417	4.47	26	10	3	92.2	108	37	22	0	1	1	1	28	2	0	.071	3	14	0	0	0.7	1.000
1945			12	9	.571	2.70	26	22	15	173.1	164	64	64	1	1	1	1	61	12	0	.197	14	38	0	2	2.0	1.000
1946	2 teams		STL A	(5G 0–0)		CHI A	(21G 3–2)																				
"	total		3	2	.600	4.91	26	2	0	66	86	26	25	0	3	1	1	14	0	0	.000	0	3	0	0	0.3	1.000
11 yrs.			70	104	.402	3.99	315	185	78	1520.1	1647	587	608	7	15	14	15	525	103	2	.196	67	297	13	16	1.2	.966

WORLD SERIES

Year	Team		W	L	PCT	ERA	G	GS	CG	IP	H	BB	SO	ShO	W	L	SV	AB	H	HR	BA	PO	A	E	DP	TC/G	FA
1944	STL	A	0	0	–	2.25	1	0	0	4	5	2	1	0	0	0	0	1	0	0	.000	0	1	0	0	1.0	1.000

Bonnie Hollingsworth

HOLLINGSWORTH, JOHN BURNETTE
B. Dec. 26, 1895, Jacksboro, Tenn.   BR TR 5'10½" 170 lbs.

Year	Team		W	L	PCT	ERA	G	GS	CG	IP	H	BB	SO	ShO	W	L	SV	AB	H	HR	BA	PO	A	E	DP	TC/G	FA
1922	PIT	N	0	0	–	7.90	9	0	0	13.2	17	8	7	0	0	0	0	0	0	0	–	1	1	0	0	0.2	1.000
1923	WAS	A	3	7	.300	4.09	17	8	1	72.2	72	50	26	0	0	0	0	22	2	0	.091	3	14	1	0	1.1	.944
1924	BKN	N	1	0	1.000	6.75	3	1	1	8	7	9	6	0	0	0	0	3	0	0	.000	0	3	0	0	1.0	1.000
1928	BOS	N	0	2	.000	5.24	7	2	0	22.1	30	13	10	0	0	2	0	6	1	0	.167	0	7	0	0	1.0	1.000
4 yrs.			4	9	.308	4.94	36	11	2	116.2	126	80	49	0	0	2	0	31	3	0	.097	4	25	1	0	0.8	.967

Year	Team	W	L	PCT	ERA	G	GS	CG	IP	H	BB	SO	ShO	W	L	SV	AB	H	HR	BA	PO	A	E	DP	TC/G	FA

John Hollison

HOLLISON, JOHN HENRY (Swede)
B. May 3, 1870, Chicago, Ill. D. Aug. 19, 1969, Chicago, Ill.
BR TL 5'8" 162 lbs.

Year	Team	W	L	PCT	ERA	G	GS	CG	IP	H	BB	SO	ShO	W	L	SV	AB	H	HR	BA	PO	A	E	DP	TC/G	FA
1892	CHI N	0	0	–	2.25	1	0	0	4	1	0	2	0	0	0	0	3	0	0	.000	0	1	0	0	1.0	1.000

Bobo Holloman

HOLLOMAN, ALVA LEE
B. Mar. 7, 1925, Thomaston, Ga. D. May 1, 1987, Athens, Ga.
BR TR 6'2" 207 lbs.

Year	Team	W	L	PCT	ERA	G	GS	CG	IP	H	BB	SO	ShO	W	L	SV	AB	H	HR	BA	PO	A	E	DP	TC/G	FA
1953	STL A	3	7	.300	5.23	22	10	1	65.1	69	50	25	1	0	2	0	19	2	0	.105	8	9	3	1	0.9	.850

Jim Holloway

HOLLOWAY, JAMES MADISON
B. Sept. 22, 1908, Plaquemine, La.
BR TR 6'1" 165 lbs.

Year	Team	W	L	PCT	ERA	G	GS	CG	IP	H	BB	SO	ShO	W	L	SV	AB	H	HR	BA	PO	A	E	DP	TC/G	FA
1929	PHI N	0	0	–	13.50	3	0	0	4.2	10	5	1	0	0	0	0	1	1	0	1.000	1	0	0	0	0.3	1.000

Ken Holloway

HOLLOWAY, KENNETH EUGENE
Born Kenneth Eugene Hallaway.
B. Aug. 8, 1897, Thomas County, Ga. D. Sept. 25, 1968, Thomasville, Ga.
BR TR 6' 185 lbs.

Year	Team	W	L	PCT	ERA	G	GS	CG	IP	H	BB	SO	ShO	W	L	SV	AB	H	HR	BA	PO	A	E	DP	TC/G	FA
1922	DET A	0	0	–	0.00	1	0	0	1	1	0	1	0	0	0	0	0	0	0	–	0	0	0	0	0.0	–
1923		11	10	.524	4.45	42	24	7	194	232	75	55	1	3	1	1	65	8	0	.123	15	54	2	2	1.7	.972
1924		14	6	.700	4.07	49	14	5	181.1	209	61	46	0	9	2	3	58	11	0	.190	13	53	4	2	1.4	.943
1925		13	4	.765	4.62	38	14	6	157.2	170	67	29	0	4	0	2	48	11	0	.229	7	32	1	1	1.1	.975
1926		4	6	.400	5.12	36	12	3	139	192	42	43	0	0	2	2	46	11	0	.239	3	37	0	1	1.1	1.000
1927		11	12	.478	4.07	36	23	11	183.1	210	61	36	1	1	2	6	62	8	0	.129	9	55	3	1	1.9	.955
1928		4	8	.333	4.34	30	11	5	120.1	137	32	32	0	1	1	2	33	4	0	.121	7	34	3	2	1.5	.932
1929	CLE A	6	5	.545	3.03	25	11	6	119	118	37	32	2	1	0	0	41	7	0	.171	4	18	2	3	1.0	.917
1930	2 teams	CLE A	(12G 1–1)		NY A	(16G 0–0)																				
"	total	1	1	.500	6.72	28	2	0	64.1	101	22	19	0	0	0	0	25	3	0	.120	3	18	2	0	0.8	.913
9 yrs.		64	52	.552	4.40	285	111	43	1160	1370	397	293	4	19	8	18	378	63	0	.167	61	301	17	12	1.3	.955

Jeff Holly

HOLLY, JEFFREY OWEN
B. Mar. 1, 1953, San Pedro, Calif.
BL TL 6'5" 210 lbs.

Year	Team	W	L	PCT	ERA	G	GS	CG	IP	H	BB	SO	ShO	W	L	SV	AB	H	HR	BA	PO	A	E	DP	TC/G	FA
1977	MIN A	2	3	.400	6.94	18	5	0	48	57	12	32	0	1	0	0	0	0	0	–	4	4	1	0	0.5	.889
1978		1	1	.500	3.57	15	1	0	35.1	28	18	12	0	1	0	0	0	0	0	–	0	8	0	0	0.5	1.000
1979		0	0	–	7.50	6	0	0	6	10	3	5	0	0	0	0	0	0	0	–	0	1	0	0	0.2	1.000
3 yrs.		3	4	.429	5.64	39	6	0	89.1	95	33	49	0	2	0	0	0	0	0	–	4	13	1	0	0.5	.944

Brian Holman

HOLMAN, BRIAN SCOTT
B. Jan. 25, 1965, Denver, Colo.
BR TR 6'4" 185 lbs.

Year	Team	W	L	PCT	ERA	G	GS	CG	IP	H	BB	SO	ShO	W	L	SV	AB	H	HR	BA	PO	A	E	DP	TC/G	FA
1988	MON N	4	8	.333	3.23	18	16	1	100.1	101	34	58	1	0	0	0	28	3	0	.107	4	11	1	0	0.9	.938
1989	2 teams	MON N	(10G 1–2)		SEA A	(23G 8–10)																				
"	total	9	12	.429	3.67	33	25	6	191.1	194	77	105	2	0	0	0	8	1	0	.125	11	31	2	3	1.3	.955
2 yrs.		13	20	.394	3.52	51	41	7	291.2	295	111	163	3	0	0	0	36	4	0	.111	15	42	3	3	1.2	.950

Scott Holman

HOLMAN, RANDY SCOTT
B. Sept. 18, 1958, Santa Paula, Calif.
BR TR 6'1" 190 lbs.

Year	Team	W	L	PCT	ERA	G	GS	CG	IP	H	BB	SO	ShO	W	L	SV	AB	H	HR	BA	PO	A	E	DP	TC/G	FA
1980	NY N	0	0	–	1.29	4	0	0	7	6	1	3	0	0	0	0	0	0	0	–	0	0	1	0	0.3	–
1982		2	1	.667	2.36	4	4	1	26.2	23	7	11	0	0	0	0	9	2	0	.222	1	6	0	0	2.3	1.000
1983		1	7	.125	3.74	35	10	0	101	90	52	44	0	0	1	0	23	5	0	.217	16	22	2	1	1.1	.950
3 yrs.		3	8	.273	3.34	43	14	1	134.2	119	60	58	0	0	1	0	32	7	0	.219	17	30	3	1	1.2	.940

Shawn Holman

HOLMAN, SHAWN LEROY
B. Nov. 10, 1964, Sewickley, Pa.
BR TR 6'2" 185 lbs.

Year	Team	W	L	PCT	ERA	G	GS	CG	IP	H	BB	SO	ShO	W	L	SV	AB	H	HR	BA	PO	A	E	DP	TC/G	FA
1989	DET A	0	0	–	1.80	5	0	0	10	8	11	9	0	0	0	0	0	0	0	–	0	1	0	0	0.2	1.000

Ducky Holmes

HOLMES, JAMES WILLIAM
B. Jan. 28, 1869, Des Moines, Iowa D. Aug. 6, 1932, Truro, Iowa
BL TR 5'6" 170 lbs.

Year	Team	W	L	PCT	ERA	G	GS	CG	IP	H	BB	SO	ShO	W	L	SV	AB	H	HR	BA	PO	A	E	DP	TC/G	FA
1895	LOU N	1	0	1.000	5.79	2	1	1	14	16	4	0	0	0	0	0	161	60	3	.373	1	4	0	0	2.5	1.000
1896		0	1	.000	7.50	2	1	0	12	26	8	3	0	0	0	0	141	38	0	.270	0	3	0	0	1.5	1.000
2 yrs.		1	1	.500	6.58	4	2	1	26	42	12	3	0	0	0	0	*				1	7	0	0	2.0	1.000

Ed Holmes

HOLMES, ELWOOD MARTER (Chick)
B. Mar. 22, 1896, Beverly, N. J. D. Apr. 15, 1954, Camden, N. J.
TR

Year	Team	W	L	PCT	ERA	G	GS	CG	IP	H	BB	SO	ShO	W	L	SV	AB	H	HR	BA	PO	A	E	DP	TC/G	FA
1918	PHI A	0	0	–	13.50	2	0	0	2	4	1	0	0	0	0	0	0	0	0	–	0	0	0	0	0.0	–

Jim Holmes

HOLMES, JAMES SCOTT
B. Aug. 2, 1882, Lawrenceburg, Ky. D. Mar. 10, 1960, Jacksonville, Fla.

Year	Team	W	L	PCT	ERA	G	GS	CG	IP	H	BB	SO	ShO	W	L	SV	AB	H	HR	BA	PO	A	E	DP	TC/G	FA
1906	PHI A	0	1	.000	4.00	3	1	0	9	10	8	1	0	0	0	0	5	3	0	.600	1	3	0	0	1.3	1.000
1908	BKN N	1	4	.200	3.38	13	1	1	40	37	20	10	0	1	3	0	13	1	0	.077	0	4	2	0	0.5	.667
2 yrs.		1	5	.167	3.49	16	2	1	49	47	28	11	0	1	3	0	18	4	0	.222	1	7	2	0	0.6	.800

Herm Holshouser

HOLSHOUSER, HERMAN ALEXANDER
B. Jan. 20, 1907, Rockwell, N. C.
BR TR 6' 170 lbs.

Year	Team	W	L	PCT	ERA	G	GS	CG	IP	H	BB	SO	ShO	W	L	SV	AB	H	HR	BA	PO	A	E	DP	TC/G	FA
1930	STL A	0	1	.000	7.80	25	1	0	62.1	103	28	37	0	0	1	1	16	2	0	.125	1	11	1	0	0.5	.923

Vern Holtgrave

HOLTGRAVE, LAVERN GEORGE (Woody)
B. Oct. 18, 1942, Aviston, Ill.
BR TR 6'1" 183 lbs.

Year	Team	W	L	PCT	ERA	G	GS	CG	IP	H	BB	SO	ShO	W	L	SV	AB	H	HR	BA	PO	A	E	DP	TC/G	FA
1965	DET A	0	0	–	6.00	1	0	0	3	4	2	2	0	0	0	0	0	0	0	–	0	0	0	0	0.0	–

Year	Team		W	L	PCT	ERA	G	GS	CG	IP	H	BB	SO	ShO	W	L	SV	AB	H	HR	BA	PO	A	E	DP	TC/G	FA
															Relief Pitching			Batting									

Brian Holton

HOLTON, BRIAN JOHN
B. Nov. 29, 1959, McKeesport, Pa. BR TR 6'3'' 190 lbs.

Year	Team		W	L	PCT	ERA	G	GS	CG	IP	H	BB	SO	ShO	W	L	SV	AB	H	HR	BA	PO	A	E	DP	TC/G	FA
1985	LA	N	1	1	.500	9.00	3	0	0	4	9	1	1	0	1	1	0	0	0	0	–	0	1	0	0	0.3	1.000
1986			2	3	.400	4.44	12	3	0	24.1	28	6	24	0	2	1	0	5	0	0	.000	3	3	0	0	0.5	1.000
1987			3	2	.600	3.89	53	1	0	83.1	87	32	58	0	3	2	2	5	1	0	.200	8	14	0	2	0.4	1.000
1988			7	3	.700	1.70	45	0	0	84.2	69	26	49	0	7	3	1	10	0	0	.000	8	11	0	0	0.4	1.000
1989	BAL	A	5	7	.417	4.02	39	12	0	116.1	140	39	51	0	2	4	0	0	0	0	–	22	9	1	0	0.8	.969
5 yrs.			18	16	.529	3.45	152	16	0	312.2	333	104	183	0	15	11	3	20	1	0	.050	41	38	1	3	0.5	.988

LEAGUE CHAMPIONSHIP SERIES

| 1988 | LA | N | 0 | 0 | – | 2.25 | 3 | 0 | 0 | 4 | 2 | 1 | 2 | 0 | 0 | 0 | 1 | 1 | 1 | 0 | 1.000 | 0 | 1 | 0 | 0 | 0.3 | 1.000 |

WORLD SERIES

| 1988 | LA | N | 0 | 0 | – | 0.00 | 1 | 0 | 0 | 2 | 0 | 1 | 0 | 0 | 0 | 0 | 0 | 0 | 0 | 0 | – | 0 | 1 | 0 | 0 | 1.0 | 1.000 |

Ken Holtzman

HOLTZMAN, KENNETH DALE
B. Nov. 3, 1945, St. Louis, Mo. BR TL 6'2'' 175 lbs.

1965	CHI	N	0	0		2.25	3	0	0	4	2	3	3	0	0	0	0	0	0	0		0	1	0	0	0.3	1.000
1966			11	16	.407	3.79	34	33	9	220.2	194	68	171	0	0	0	0	73	9	0	.123	12	24	4	2	1.2	.900
1967			9	0	1.000	2.53	12	12	3	92.2	76	44	62	0	0	0	0	35	7	0	.200	4	17	0	0	1.8	1.000
1968			11	14	.440	3.35	34	32	6	215	201	76	151	3	0	0	1	80	10	0	.125	4	42	1	3	1.3	.978
1969			17	13	.567	3.59	39	39	12	261	248	93	176	6	0	0	0	100	15	1	.150	6	40	3	2	1.3	.939
1970			17	11	.607	3.38	39	38	15	288	271	94	202	3	0	0	0	105	21	0	.200	11	44	2	1	1.5	.965
1971			9	15	.375	4.48	30	29	9	195	213	64	143	3	0	0	0	69	9	1	.130	6	28	3	2	1.2	.919
1972	OAK	A	19	11	.633	2.51	39	37	16	265	232	52	134	4	1	0	0	90	16	0	.178	7	47	1	4	1.4	.982
1973			21	13	.618	2.97	40	40	16	297.1	275	66	157	4	0	0	0	0	0	0	–	15	42	5	2	1.6	.919
1974			19	17	.528	3.07	39	38	9	255	273	51	117	3	0	1	0	0	0	0	–	5	43	1	2	1.3	.980
1975			18	14	.563	3.14	39	38	13	266.1	217	108	122	2	1	0	0	2	0	0	.000	11	58	1	3	1.8	.986
1976	2 teams		BAL A	(13G 5–4)		NY A	(21G 9–7)																					
"	total		14	11	.560	3.65	34	34	16	246.2	265	70	66	3	0	0	0	0	0	0	–	19	42	3	2	1.9	.953
1977	NY	A	2	3	.400	5.75	18	11	0	72	105	24	14	0	0	0	0	0	0	0	–	8	21	1	1	1.7	.967
1978	2 teams		NY A	(5G 1–0)		CHI N	(23G 0–3)																					
"	total		1	3	.250	5.60	28	9	0	70.2	82	44	39	0	0	0	0	10	2	0	.200	3	11	0	1	0.5	1.000
1979	CHI	N	6	9	.400	4.58	23	20	3	118	133	53	44	2	0	0	0	43	10	0	.233	8	11	1	0	0.9	.950
15 yrs.			174	150	.537	3.49	451	410	127	2867.1	2787	910	1601	31	2	1	3	607	99	2	.163	117	471	26	25	1.4	.958

LEAGUE CHAMPIONSHIP SERIES

1972	OAK	A	0	1	.000	4.50	1	1	0	4	4	2	2	0	0	0	0	1	0	0	.000	0	1	0	0	1.0	1.000
1973			1	0	1.000	0.82	1	1	1	11	3	1	7	0	0	0	0	0	0	0	–	1	2	0	1	3.0	1.000
1974			1	0	1.000	0.00	1	1	1	9	5	2	3	1	0	0	0	0	0	0	–	0	1	0	0	1.0	1.000
1975			0	2	.000	4.09	2	2	0	11	12	1	7	0	0	0	0	0	0	0	–	1	1	0	0	1.0	1.000
4 yrs.			2	3	.400	2.06	5	5	2	35	24	6	19	1	0	0	0	1	0	0	.000	2	5	0	1	1.4	1.000

WORLD SERIES

1972	OAK	A	1	0	1.000	2.13	3	2	0	12.2	11	3	4	0	0	0	0	5	0	0	.000	0	3	1	1	1.3	.750
1973			2	1	.667	4.22	3	3	0	10.2	13	5	6	0	0	0	0	3	2	0	.667	1	3	0	1	1.3	1.000
1974			1	0	1.000	1.50	2	2	0	12	13	4	10	0	0	0	0	4	2	1	.500	0	3	0	0	1.5	1.000
3 yrs.			4	1	.800	2.55	8	7	0	35.1	37	12	20	0	0	0	0	12	4	1	.333	1	9	1	2	1.4	.909

Rick Honeycutt

HONEYCUTT, FREDERICK WAYNE
B. June 29, 1952, Chattanooga, Tenn. BL TL 6'1'' 185 lbs.

1977	SEA	A	0	1	.000	4.34	10	3	0	29	26	11	17	0	0	0	0	0	0	0	–	0	2	0	0	0.2	1.000
1978			5	11	.313	4.89	26	24	4	134.1	150	49	50	1	0	0	0	0	0	0	–	9	28	2	1	1.5	.949
1979			11	12	.478	4.04	33	28	8	194	201	67	83	1	1	3	0	0	0	0	–	6	28	5	2	1.2	.872
1980			10	17	.370	3.95	30	30	9	203	221	60	79	1	0	0	0	0	0	0	–	9	32	2	1	1.4	.953
1981	TEX	A	11	6	.647	3.30	20	20	8	128	120	17	40	2	0	0	0	0	0	0	–	3	30	3	1	1.8	.917
1982			5	17	.227	5.27	30	26	4	164	201	54	64	1	0	0	0	0	0	0	–	3	35	2	0	1.3	.950
1983	2 teams		TEX A	(25G 14–8)		LA N	(9G 2–3)																					
"	total		16	11	.593	3.03	34	32	6	213.2	214	50	74	2	0	0	0	12	1	0	.083	13	55	1	5	2.0	.986
1984	LA	N	10	9	.526	2.84	29	28	6	183.2	180	51	75	2	0	0	0	56	8	0	.143	10	42	3	2	1.9	.945
1985			8	12	.400	3.42	31	25	1	142	141	49	67	0	0	1	1	38	5	0	.132	9	37	2	1	1.5	.958
1986			11	9	.550	3.32	32	28	0	171	164	45	100	0	1	0	0	43	3	0	.070	9	35	1	2	1.4	.978
1987	2 teams		LA N	(27G 2–12)		OAK A	(7G 1–4)																					
"	total		3	16	.158	4.72	34	24	1	139.1	158	54	102	1	0	0	0	30	7	0	.233	5	20	2	0	0.8	.926
1988	OAK	A	3	2	.600	3.50	55	0	0	79.2	74	25	47	0	3	2	7	0	0	0	–	3	18	2	3	0.4	.913
1989			2	2	.500	2.35	64	0	0	76.2	56	26	52	0	2	2	12	0	0	0	–	4	16	1	1	0.3	.952
13 yrs.			95	125	.432	3.76	428	268	47	1858.1	1906	558	850	11	7	9	20	179	24	0	.134	83	378	26	19	1.1	.947

LEAGUE CHAMPIONSHIP SERIES

1983	LA	N	0	0	–	21.60	2	0	0	1.2	4	0	2	0	0	0	0	0	0	0	–	1	0	0	0	0.5	1.000
1985			0	0	–	13.50	2	0	0	1.1	2	1	1	0	0	0	0	0	0	0	–	0	1	0	0	0.5	1.000
1988	OAK	A	1	0	1.000	0.00	3	0	0	2	0	2	0	0	1	0	0	0	0	0	–	0	0	0	0	0.0	–
1989			0	0	–	32.40	3	0	0	1.2	6	5	1	0	0	0	1	0	0	0	–	0	0	0	0	0.0	–
4 yrs.			1	0	1.000	16.20	10	0	0	6.2	14	9	4	0	1	0	0	0	0	0	–	1	1	0	0	0.2	1.000

WORLD SERIES

1988	OAK	A	1	0	1.000	0.00	3	0	0	3.1	0	0	5	0	1	0	0	0	0	0	–	0	0	0	0	0.0	–
1989			0	0	–	6.75	3	0	0	2.2	4	0	2	0	0	0	0	0	0	0	–	0	0	0	0	0.0	–
2 yrs.			1	0	1.000	3.00	6	0	0	6	4	0	7	0	1	0	0	0	0	0	–	0	0	0	0	0.0	–

Don Hood

HOOD, DONALD HARRIS
B. Oct. 16, 1949, Florence, S. C. BL TL 6'2'' 180 lbs.

1973	BAL	A	3	2	.600	3.94	8	4	0	32	31	6	18	1	2	0	1	0	0	0	–	1	3	2	1	0.8	.667
1974			1	1	.500	3.47	20	2	0	57	47	20	26	0	1	1	0	0	0	0	–	1	9	1	0	0.6	.909
1975	CLE	A	6	10	.375	4.39	29	19	2	135.1	136	57	51	0	1	1	0	0	0	0	–	7	15	3	0	0.9	.880
1976			3	5	.375	4.85	33	6	0	78	89	41	32	0	2	1	1	0	0	0	–	10	12	2	0	0.7	.917

Don Hood *continued*

Year	Team		W	L	PCT	ERA	G	GS	CG	IP	H	BB	SO	ShO	W	L	SV	AB	H	HR	BA	PO	A	E	DP	TC/G	FA
1977			2	1	.667	3.00	41	5	1	105	87	49	62	0	1	0	0	0	0	0	—	4	10	2	1	0.4	.875
1978			5	6	.455	4.47	36	19	1	155	166	77	73	0	0	1	0	0	0	0	—	6	26	1	2	0.9	.970
1979	2 teams	CLE A (13G 1-0)								NY A	(27G 3-1)																
"	total		4	1	.800	3.24	40	6	0	89	75	44	29	0	2	1	2	0	0	0	—	5	18	0	2	0.6	1.000
1980	STL	N	4	6	.400	3.40	33	8	1	82	90	34	35	0	1	4	0	20	4	0	.200	7	15	1	1	0.7	.957
1982	KC	A	4	0	1.000	3.51	30	3	0	66.2	71	22	31	0	1	0	1	0	0	0	—	6	11	1	0	0.6	.944
1983			2	3	.400	2.27	27	0	0	47.2	48	14	17	0	2	3	0	0	0	0	—	3	14	3	3	0.7	.850
10 yrs.			34	35	.493	3.79	297	72	6	847.2	840	364	374	1	13	11	6	20	4	0	.200	50	133	16	10	0.7	.920

Wally Hood

HOOD, WALLACE JAMES, JR.
Son of Wally Hood.
B. Sept. 24, 1925, Los Angeles, Calif.

BR TR 6'1" 190 lbs.

Year	Team		W	L	PCT	ERA	G	GS	CG	IP	H	BB	SO	ShO	W	L	SV	AB	H	HR	BA	PO	A	E	DP	TC/G	FA
1949	NY	A	0	0	—	0.00	2	0	0	2.1	0	1	2	0	0	0	0	0	0	0	—	0	0	0	0	0.0	—

Jay Hook

HOOK, JAMES WESLEY
B. Nov. 18, 1936, Waukegan, Ill.

BL TR 6'2" 182 lbs.

Year	Team		W	L	PCT	ERA	G	GS	CG	IP	H	BB	SO	ShO	W	L	SV	AB	H	HR	BA	PO	A	E	DP	TC/G	FA
1957	CIN	N	0	1	.000	4.50	3	2	0	10	6	8	6	0	0	0	0	3	0	0	.000	2	1	0	0	1.0	1.000
1958			0	1	.000	12.00	1	1	0	3	3	2	5	0	0	0	0	1	0	0	.000	0	0	0	0	0.0	—
1959			5	5	.500	5.13	17	15	4	79	79	39	37	0	0	0	0	24	3	0	.125	7	8	1	2	0.9	.938
1960			11	18	.379	4.50	36	33	10	222	222	73	103	2	0	0	0	72	6	0	.083	19	30	1	5	1.4	.980
1961			1	3	.250	7.76	22	5	0	62.2	83	22	36	0	1	0	0	15	2	0	.133	10	4	0	0	0.6	1.000
1962	NY	N	8	19	.296	4.84	37	34	13	213.2	230	71	113	0	1	0	0	69	14	0	.203	22	31	3	2	1.5	.946
1963			4	14	.222	5.48	41	20	3	152.2	168	53	89	0	1	0	1	38	9	0	.237	11	20	3	1	0.8	.912
1964			0	1	.000	9.31	3	2	0	9.2	17	7	5	0	0	0	0	3	0	0	.000	1	3	0	0	1.3	1.000
8 yrs.			29	62	.319	5.23	160	112	30	752.2	808	275	394	2	3	0	1	225	34	0	.151	72	97	8	10	1.1	.955

Cy Hooker

HOOKER, WILLIAM EDWARD
Also known as William Edward Hoch.
B. Aug. 28, 1880, Richmond, Va. D. July 2, 1929, Richmond, Va.

TR 5'6"

Year	Team		W	L	PCT	ERA	G	GS	CG	IP	H	BB	SO	ShO	W	L	SV	AB	H	HR	BA	PO	A	E	DP	TC/G	FA
1902	CIN	N	0	1	.000	4.50	1	1	0	8	11	0	0	0	0	0	0	3	0	0	.000	0	1	1	0	2.0	.500
1903			0	0	—	0.00	1	0	0	2.1	2	2	0	0	0	0	0	1	0	0	.000	0	0	0	0	0.0	—
2 yrs.			0	1	.000	3.48	2	1	0	10.1	13	2	0	0	0	0	0	4	0	0	.000	0	1	1	0	1.0	.500

Bob Hooper

HOOPER, ROBERT NELSON
B. May 30, 1922, Leamington, Ontario, Canada D. Mar. 17, 1980, New Brunswick, N. J.

BR TR 5'11" 195 lbs.

Year	Team		W	L	PCT	ERA	G	GS	CG	IP	H	BB	SO	ShO	W	L	SV	AB	H	HR	BA	PO	A	E	DP	TC/G	FA
1950	PHI	A	15	10	.600	5.02	45	20	3	170.1	181	91	58	0	3	6	5	56	7	1	.125	19	37	2	10	1.3	.966
1951			12	10	.545	4.38	38	23	9	189	192	61	64	0	1	5	3	72	15	1	.208	18	37	3	3	1.5	.948
1952			8	15	.348	5.18	43	14	4	144.1	158	68	40	0	6	4	6	41	8	2	.195	22	32	1	5	1.3	.982
1953	CLE	A	5	4	.556	4.02	43	0	0	69.1	50	38	16	0	5	4	7	12	1	0	.083	3	16	0	2	0.4	1.000
1954			0	0	—	4.93	17	0	0	34.2	39	16	12	0	0	0	2	5	0	0	.000	2	6	0	0	0.5	1.000
1955	CIN	N	0	2	.000	7.62	8	0	0	13	20	6	6	0	0	2	0	1	0	0	.000	0	4	0	0	0.5	1.000
6 yrs.			40	41	.494	4.80	194	57	16	620.2	640	280	196	0	15	17	25	187	31	4	.166	64	132	6	20	1.0	.970

Harry Hooper

HOOPER, HARRY BARTHOLOMEW
B. Aug. 24, 1887, Bell Station, Calif. D. Dec. 18, 1974, Santa Cruz, Calif.
Hall of Fame 1971.

BL TR 5'10" 168 lbs.

Year	Team		W	L	PCT	ERA	G	GS	CG	IP	H	BB	SO	ShO	W	L	SV	AB	H	HR	BA	PO	A	E	DP	TC/G	FA
1913	BOS	A	0	0	—	0.00	1	0	0	1	0	1	0	0	0	0	0				*			0	0	0	0	0.0	—

Leon Hooten

HOOTEN, MICHAEL LEON
B. Apr. 4, 1948, Downey, Calif.

BR TR 5'11" 180 lbs.

Year	Team		W	L	PCT	ERA	G	GS	CG	IP	H	BB	SO	ShO	W	L	SV	AB	H	HR	BA	PO	A	E	DP	TC/G	FA
1974	OAK	A	0	0	—	3.12	6	0	0	8.2	6	4	1	0	0	0	0	0	0	0	—	0	2	0	0	0.3	1.000

Burt Hooton

HOOTON, BURT CARLTON (Happy)
B. Feb. 17, 1950, Greenville, Tex.

BR TR 6'1" 210 lbs.

Year	Team		W	L	PCT	ERA	G	GS	CG	IP	H	BB	SO	ShO	W	L	SV	AB	H	HR	BA	PO	A	E	DP	TC/G	FA
1971	CHI	N	2	0	1.000	2.14	3	3	2	21	8	10	22	1	0	0	0	7	0	0	.000	3	0	1	0	1.3	.750
1972			11	14	.440	2.80	33	31	9	218.1	201	81	132	3	1	0	0	72	9	1	.125	13	35	1	2	1.5	.980
1973			14	17	.452	3.68	42	34	9	240	248	73	134	2	1	2	0	70	9	0	.129	21	32	4	0	1.4	.930
1974			7	11	.389	4.81	48	21	3	176	214	51	94	1	2	2	1	50	3	0	.060	15	39	1	1	1.1	.982
1975	2 teams	CHI N (3G 0-2)								LA N	(31G 18-7)																
"	total		18	9	.667	3.07	34	33	12	234.2	190	68	153	4	0	1	0	73	9	1	.123	13	29	1	3	1.3	.977
1976	LA	N	11	15	.423	3.26	33	33	8	226.2	203	60	116	4	0	0	0	62	6	0	.097	6	31	0	0	1.1	1.000
1977			12	7	.632	2.62	32	31	6	223	184	60	153	2	0	0	0	67	11	0	.164	11	31	0	4	1.3	1.000
1978			19	10	.655	2.71	32	32	10	236	196	61	104	3	0	0	0	67	10	0	.149	12	33	1	4	1.4	.978
1979			11	10	.524	2.97	29	29	12	212	191	63	129	1	0	0	0	75	11	0	.147	12	26	0	3	1.3	1.000
1980			14	8	.636	3.65	34	33	4	207	194	64	118	0	0	0	0	64	4	1	.063	23	26	4	2	1.6	.925
1981			11	6	.647	2.28	23	23	5	142	124	33	74	4	0	0	0	42	8	0	.190	4	18	0	2	1.0	1.000
1982			4	7	.364	4.03	21	21	0	120.2	130	33	51	2	0	0	0	35	3	1	.086	9	21	0	1	1.4	1.000
1983			9	8	.529	4.22	33	27	2	160	156	59	87	0	0	0	0	50	8	0	.160	8	24	2	1	1.0	.941
1984			3	6	.333	3.44	54	6	0	110	109	43	62	0	3	4	4	14	1	0	.071	6	15	0	1	0.4	1.000
1985	TEX	A	5	8	.385	5.23	29	20	2	124	149	40	62	0	0	0	0	0	0	0	—	9	13	1	0	0.8	.957
15 yrs.			151	136	.526	3.38	480	377	86	2651.1	2497	799	1491	29	7	9	7	748	92	4	.123	165	373	16	21	1.2	.971

DIVISIONAL PLAYOFF SERIES

Year	Team		W	L	PCT	ERA	G	GS	CG	IP	H	BB	SO	ShO	W	L	SV	AB	H	HR	BA	PO	A	E	DP	TC/G	FA
1981	LA	N	1	0	1.000	1.29	1	1	0	7	3	3	2	0	0	0	0	3	0	0	.000	0	0	0	0	0.0	—

LEAGUE CHAMPIONSHIP SERIES

Year	Team		W	L	PCT	ERA	G	GS	CG	IP	H	BB	SO	ShO	W	L	SV	AB	H	HR	BA	PO	A	E	DP	TC/G	FA
1977	LA	N	0	0	—	16.20	1	1	0	1.2	2	4	1	0	0	0	0	1	1	0	1.000	0	1	0	0	1.0	1.000
1978			0	0	—	7.71	1	1	0	4.2	10	0	5	0	0	0	0	2	0	0	.000	1	0	0	0	1.0	1.000
1981			2	0	1.000	0.00	2	2	0	14.2	11	6	7	0	0	0	0	5	0	0	.000	0	0	0	0	0.0	—
3 yrs.			2	0	1.000	3.00	4	4	0	21	23	10	13	0	0	0	0	8	1	0	.125	1	1	0	0	0.5	1.000

Year	Team		W	L	PCT	ERA	G	GS	CG	IP	H	BB	SO	ShO	Relief Pitching W	L	SV	Batting AB	H	HR	BA	PO	A	E	DP	TC/G	FA

Burt Hooton *continued*

WORLD SERIES

Year	Team		W	L	PCT	ERA	G	GS	CG	IP	H	BB	SO	ShO	W	L	SV	AB	H	HR	BA	PO	A	E	DP	TC/G	FA
1977	LA	N	1	1	.500	3.75	2	2	1	12	8	2	9	0	0	0	0	5	0	0	.000	0	0	0	0	0.0	–
1978			1	1	.500	6.48	2	2	0	8.1	13	3	6	0	0	0	0	0	0	0	–	0	1	0	0	0.5	1.000
1981			1	1	.500	1.59	2	2	0	11.1	8	9	3	0	0	0	0	4	0	0	.000	1	0	0	0	0.5	1.000
3 yrs.			3	3	.500	3.69	6	6	1	31.2	29	14	18	0	0	0	0	9	0	0	.000	2	0	0	0	0.3	1.000

Dick Hoover

HOOVER, RICHARD LLOYD
B. Dec. 11, 1925, Columbus, Ohio D. Apr. 12, 1981, Lake Placid, Fla. BL TL 6' 170 lbs.

Year	Team		W	L	PCT	ERA	G	GS	CG	IP	H	BB	SO	ShO	W	L	SV	AB	H	HR	BA	PO	A	E	DP	TC/G	FA
1952	BOS	N	0	0	–	7.71	2	0	0	4.2	8	3	0	0	0	0	0	0	0	0	–	1	0	0	0	0.5	1.000

Sam Hope

HOPE, SAMUEL
B. Dec. 4, 1878, Brooklyn, N. Y. D. June 30, 1946, Greenport, N. Y. BR TR 5'10"

Year	Team		W	L	PCT	ERA	G	GS	CG	IP	H	BB	SO	ShO	W	L	SV	AB	H	HR	BA	PO	A	E	DP	TC/G	FA
1907	PHI	A	0	0	–	0.00	1	0	0	.1	3	0	0	0	0	0	0	0	0	0	–	0	1	0	0	1.0	1.000

Paul Hopkins

HOPKINS, PAUL HENRY
B. Sept. 25, 1904, Chester, Pa. BR TR 6' 175 lbs.

Year	Team		W	L	PCT	ERA	G	GS	CG	IP	H	BB	SO	ShO	W	L	SV	AB	H	HR	BA	PO	A	E	DP	TC/G	FA
1927	WAS	A	1	0	1.000	5.00	2	1	0	9	13	4	5	0	0	0	0	3	2	0	.667	0	4	0	0	2.0	1.000
1929	2 teams		WAS A	(7G 0–1)			STL A	(2G 0–0)																				
"	total		0	1	.000	1.96	9	0	0	18.1	15	11	6	0	0	1	0	3	0	0	.000	1	2	0	0	0.3	1.000
2 yrs.			1	1	.500	2.96	11	1	0	27.1	28	15	11	0	0	1	0	6	2	0	.333	1	6	0	0	0.6	1.000

Bill Hopper

HOPPER, WILLIAM BOOTH (Bird Dog)
B. Aug. 26, 1890, Jackson, Tenn. D. Jan. 14, 1965, Allen Park, Mich. BR TR 6' 175 lbs.

Year	Team		W	L	PCT	ERA	G	GS	CG	IP	H	BB	SO	ShO	W	L	SV	AB	H	HR	BA	PO	A	E	DP	TC/G	FA
1913	STL	N	0	3	.000	3.75	3	3	2	24	20	8	3	0	0	0	0	8	3	0	.375	1	6	1	0	2.7	.875
1914			0	0	–	3.60	3	0	0	5	6	5	1	0	0	0	0	0	0	0	–	0	2	0	0	0.7	1.000
1915	WAS	A	0	1	.000	4.60	13	0	0	31.1	39	16	8	0	0	1	1	5	1	0	.200	3	13	2	1	1.4	.889
3 yrs.			0	4	.000	4.18	19	3	2	60.1	65	29	12	0	0	1	1	13	4	0	.308	4	21	3	1	1.5	.893

Jim Hopper

HOPPER, JAMES McDANIEL
B. Sept. 1, 1919, Charlotte, N. C. D. Jan. 23, 1982, Charlotte, N. C. BR TR 6'1" 175 lbs.

Year	Team		W	L	PCT	ERA	G	GS	CG	IP	H	BB	SO	ShO	W	L	SV	AB	H	HR	BA	PO	A	E	DP	TC/G	FA
1946	PIT	N	0	1	.000	10.38	2	1	0	4.1	6	3	1	0	0	0	0	0	0	0	–	1	0	0	0	0.5	1.000

Lefty Hopper

HOPPER, CLARENCE F.
B. Ridgewood, N. J. Deceased. TL

Year	Team		W	L	PCT	ERA	G	GS	CG	IP	H	BB	SO	ShO	W	L	SV	AB	H	HR	BA	PO	A	E	DP	TC/G	FA
1898	BKN	N	0	2	.000	4.91	2	2	2	11	14	5	5	0	0	0	0	4	0	0	.000	4	1	0	0	2.5	.800

John Horan

HORAN, JOHN J.
B. 1863, Ireland D. Dec. 21, 1905, Chicago, Ill.

Year	Team		W	L	PCT	ERA	G	GS	CG	IP	H	BB	SO	ShO	W	L	SV	AB	H	HR	BA	PO	A	E	DP	TC/G	FA
1884	CHI	U	3	6	.333	3.40	13	10	9	98	94	24	55	0	0	0	0	68	6	0	.088	6	19	8	1	2.5	.758

Joe Horlen

HORLEN, JOEL EDWARD
B. Aug. 14, 1937, San Antonio, Tex. BR TR 6' 170 lbs.

Year	Team		W	L	PCT	ERA	G	GS	CG	IP	H	BB	SO	ShO	W	L	SV	AB	H	HR	BA	PO	A	E	DP	TC/G	FA
1961	CHI	A	1	3	.250	6.62	5	4	0	17.2	25	13	11	0	1	0	0	7	0	0	.000	3	3	0	1	1.2	1.000
1962			7	6	.538	4.89	20	19	5	108.2	108	43	63	1	0	0	0	38	2	0	.053	10	28	1	0	2.0	.974
1963			11	7	.611	3.27	33	21	3	124	122	55	61	0	2	0	2	40	9	0	.225	4	30	0	1	1.0	1.000
1964			13	9	.591	1.88	32	28	9	210.2	142	55	138	2	1	0	0	69	11	0	.159	14	46	3	3	1.9	.944
1965			13	13	.500	2.88	34	34	7	219	203	39	125	4	0	0	0	68	9	0	.132	10	41	3	0	1.6	.944
1966			10	13	.435	2.43	37	29	4	211	185	53	124	2	1	0	1	60	4	0	.067	25	57	3	5	2.3	.965
1967			19	7	**.731**	**2.06**	35	35	13	258	188	58	103	6	0	0	0	83	14	0	.169	29	53	0	4	2.3	1.000
1968			12	14	.462	2.37	35	35	4	223.2	197	70	102	1	0	0	0	67	7	0	.104	14	47	3	3	1.8	.953
1969			13	16	.448	3.78	36	35	7	235.2	237	77	121	2	0	0	0	77	14	0	.182	13	32	3	0	1.3	.938
1970			6	16	.273	4.87	28	26	4	172	198	41	77	0	0	0	0	52	6	0	.115	22	42	1	1	2.3	.985
1971			8	9	.471	4.27	34	18	3	137	150	30	82	0	1	2	2	40	4	0	.100	10	27	2	0	1.1	.949
1972	OAK	A	3	4	.429	3.00	32	6	0	84	74	20	58	0	2	0	1	17	3	0	.176	5	15	0	0	0.6	1.000
12 yrs.			116	117	.498	3.11	361	290	59	2001.1	1829	554	1065	18	6	4	4	618	83	0	.134	159	421	16	17	1.7	.973

LEAGUE CHAMPIONSHIP SERIES

Year	Team		W	L	PCT	ERA	G	GS	CG	IP	H	BB	SO	ShO	W	L	SV	AB	H	HR	BA	PO	A	E	DP	TC/G	FA
1972	OAK	A	0	1	.000	∞	1	0	0	0	1	0	0	0	0	1	0	0	0	0	–	0	0	0	0	0.0	–

WORLD SERIES

Year	Team		W	L	PCT	ERA	G	GS	CG	IP	H	BB	SO	ShO	W	L	SV	AB	H	HR	BA	PO	A	E	DP	TC/G	FA
1972	OAK	A	0	0	–	6.75	1	0	0	1.1	2	2	1	0	0	0	0	0	0	0	–	1	0	0	0	1.0	1.000

Trader Horne

HORNE, BERLYN DALE (Sonny)
B. Apr. 12, 1899, Bachman, Ohio D. Feb. 3, 1983, Franklin, Ohio BB TR 5'9" 155 lbs.

Year	Team		W	L	PCT	ERA	G	GS	CG	IP	H	BB	SO	ShO	W	L	SV	AB	H	HR	BA	PO	A	E	DP	TC/G	FA
1929	CHI	N	1	1	.500	5.09	11	1	0	23	24	21	6	0	1	1	0	5	2	0	.400	2	6	0	0	0.7	1.000

Jack Horner

HORNER, WILLIAM FRANK
B. Sept. 21, 1863, Baltimore, Md. D. July 14, 1910, New Orleans, La.

Year	Team		W	L	PCT	ERA	G	GS	CG	IP	H	BB	SO	ShO	W	L	SV	AB	H	HR	BA	PO	A	E	DP	TC/G	FA
1894	BAL	N	0	1	.000	9.00	2	1	1	11	15	7	2	0	0	0	0	6	1	0	.167	0	3	1	0	2.0	.750

Joe Hornung

HORNUNG, MICHAEL JOSEPH (Ubbo Ubbo)
B. June 12, 1857, Carthage, N. Y. D. Oct. 30, 1931, New York, N. Y. BR TR 5'8½" 164 lbs.

Year	Team		W	L	PCT	ERA	G	GS	CG	IP	H	BB	SO	ShO	W	L	SV	AB	H	HR	BA	PO	A	E	DP	TC/G	FA
1880	BUF	N	0	0	–	6.00	1	0	0	3	2	1	0	0	0	0	0	*				0	1	0	0	1.0	1.000

Hanson Horsey

HORSEY, HANSON
B. Nov. 26, 1889, Galena, Md. D. Dec. 1, 1949, Millington, Md. BR TR 5'11" 165 lbs.

Year	Team		W	L	PCT	ERA	G	GS	CG	IP	H	BB	SO	ShO	W	L	SV	AB	H	HR	BA	PO	A	E	DP	TC/G	FA
1912	CIN	N	0	0	–	22.50	1	0	0	4	14	3	0	0	0	0	0	2	0	0	.000	0	0	0	0	0.0	–

Year	Team	W	L	PCT	ERA	G	GS	CG	IP	H	BB	SO	ShO	W	L	SV	AB	H	HR	BA	PO	A	E	DP	TC/G	FA

Oscar Horstmann

HORSTMANN, OSCAR THEODORE
B. June 2, 1891, Alma, Mo. D. May 11, 1977, Salina, Kans. — BR TR 5'11" 165 lbs.

Year	Team	W	L	PCT	ERA	G	GS	CG	IP	H	BB	SO	ShO	W	L	SV	AB	H	HR	BA	PO	A	E	DP	TC/G	FA
1917	STL N	9	4	.692	3.45	35	11	4	138.1	111	54	50	1	4	0	1	46	9	0	.196	3	40	2	2	1.3	.956
1918		0	2	.000	5.48	9	2	0	23	29	14	6	0	0	1	0	4	0	0	.000	1	12	0	0	1.4	1.000
1919		0	1	.000	3.00	6	2	0	15	14	12	5	0	0	0	0	2	1	0	.500	1	5	0	0	1.0	1.000
3 yrs.		9	7	.563	3.67	50	15	4	176.1	154	80	61	1	4	1	1	52	10	0	.192	5	57	2	2	1.3	.969

Elmer Horton

HORTON, ELMER E. (Herky Jerky)
B. Sept. 4, 1869, Hamilton, Ohio D. Aug. 12, 1920, Vienna, Ohio

Year	Team	W	L	PCT	ERA	G	GS	CG	IP	H	BB	SO	ShO	W	L	SV	AB	H	HR	BA	PO	A	E	DP	TC/G	FA
1896	PIT N	0	2	.000	9.60	2	2	1	15	22	9	3	0	0	0	0	7	0	0	.000	4	0	2	0	3.0	.667
1898	BKN N	0	1	.000	10.00	1	1	1	9	16	6	0	0	0	0	0	4	1	0	.250	0	2	0	0	2.0	1.000
2 yrs.		0	3	.000	9.75	3	3	3	24	38	15	3	0	0	0	0	11	1	0	.091	4	2	2	0	2.7	.750

Ricky Horton

HORTON, RICKY NEAL
B. July 30, 1959, Poughkeepsie, N. Y. — BL TL 6'2" 197 lbs.

Year	Team	W	L	PCT	ERA	G	GS	CG	IP	H	BB	SO	ShO	W	L	SV	AB	H	HR	BA	PO	A	E	DP	TC/G	FA
1984	STL N	9	4	.692	3.44	37	18	1	125.2	140	39	76	1	1	0	1	31	2	0	.065	5	35	3	3	1.2	.930
1985		3	2	.600	2.91	49	3	0	89.2	84	34	59	0	2	2	1	16	1	0	.063	9	21	2	0	0.7	.938
1986		4	3	.571	2.24	42	9	1	100.1	77	26	49	0	1	0	3	18	1	0	.056	4	24	0	3	0.7	1.000
1987		8	3	.727	3.82	67	6	0	125	127	42	55	0	6	2	7	29	5	0	.172	12	31	2	2	0.7	.956
1988	2 teams	CHI A (52G 6–10)		LA N (12G 1–1)																						
"	total	7	11	.389	4.87	64	9	1	118.1	131	38	36	0	4	5	2	29	0	0	—	5	27	4	4	0.5	.941
1989	2 teams	LA N (23G 0–0)		STL N (11G 0–3)																						
"	total	0	3	.000	4.85	34	8	0	72.1	85	21	26	0	0	0	0	12	3	0	.250	2	13	0	2	0.4	1.000
6 yrs.		31	26	.544	3.68	293	53	3	631.1	644	200	301	1	14	9	14	106	12	0	.113	37	151	9	14	0.7	.954

LEAGUE CHAMPIONSHIP SERIES

Year	Team	W	L	PCT	ERA	G	GS	CG	IP	H	BB	SO	ShO	W	L	SV	AB	H	HR	BA	PO	A	E	DP	TC/G	FA
1985	STL N	0	0	—	9.00	3	0	0	3	4	2	1	0	0	0	0	0	0	0	—	1	2	0	0	1.0	1.000
1987		0	0	—	0.00	1	0	0	3	2	0	2	0	0	0	0	0	0	0	—	0	0	0	0	—	—
1988	LA N	0	0	—	0.00	4	0	0	4.1	4	2	3	0	0	0	0	0	0	0	—	0	1	1	0	0.3	1.000
3 yrs.		0	0	—	2.61	8	0	0	10.1	10	4	6	0	0	0	0	0	0	0	—	1	3	1	0	0.5	1.000

WORLD SERIES

Year	Team	W	L	PCT	ERA	G	GS	CG	IP	H	BB	SO	ShO	W	L	SV	AB	H	HR	BA	PO	A	E	DP	TC/G	FA
1985	STL N	0	0	—	6.75	3	0	0	4	4	5	5	0	0	0	0	1	0	0	.000	2	0	0	0	0.7	1.000
1987		0	0	—	6.00	2	0	0	3	5	0	1	0	0	0	0	0	0	0	—	0	1	0	0	0.5	1.000
2 yrs.		0	0	—	6.43	5	0	0	7	9	5	6	0	0	0	0	1	0	0	.000	2	1	0	0	0.6	1.000

Dave Hoskins

HOSKINS, DAVID TAYLOR
B. Aug. 3, 1925, Greenwood, Miss. D. Apr. 2, 1970, Flint, Mich. — BL TR 6'1" 180 lbs.

Year	Team	W	L	PCT	ERA	G	GS	CG	IP	H	BB	SO	ShO	W	L	SV	AB	H	HR	BA	PO	A	E	DP	TC/G	FA
1953	CLE A	9	3	.750	3.99	26	7	3	112.2	102	38	55	0	6	1	0	58	15	1	.259	7	18	0	1	1.0	1.000
1954		0	1	.000	3.04	14	1	0	26.2	29	10	9	0	0	1	0	8	0	0	.000	2	4	0	0	0.4	1.000
2 yrs.		9	4	.692	3.81	40	8	3	139.1	131	48	64	0	6	2	1	66	15	1	.227	9	22	0	1	0.8	1.000

Gene Host

HOST, EUGENE EARL (Twinkles, Slick)
B. Jan. 1, 1933, Leeper, Pa. — BB TL 5'11" 190 lbs.

Year	Team	W	L	PCT	ERA	G	GS	CG	IP	H	BB	SO	ShO	W	L	SV	AB	H	HR	BA	PO	A	E	DP	TC/G	FA
1956	DET A	0	0	—	7.71	1	1	0	4.2	9	2	5	0	0	0	0	2	0	0	.000	0	0	0	0	0.0	—
1957	KC A	0	2	.000	7.23	11	2	0	23.2	29	14	9	0	0	1	0	5	0	0	.000	0	6	0	0	0.5	1.000
2 yrs.		0	2	.000	7.31	12	3	0	28.1	38	16	14	0	0	1	0	7	0	0	.000	0	6	0	0	0.5	1.000

Byron Houck

HOUCK, BYRON SIMON (Duke)
B. Aug. 28, 1891, Prosper, Minn. D. June 17, 1969, Santa Cruz, Calif. — BR TR 6' 175 lbs.

Year	Team	W	L	PCT	ERA	G	GS	CG	IP	H	BB	SO	ShO	W	L	SV	AB	H	HR	BA	PO	A	E	DP	TC/G	FA
1912	PHI A	8	8	.500	2.94	30	17	12	180.2	148	74	75	0	0	0	0	62	4	0	.065	7	50	4	2	2.0	.934
1913		14	6	.700	4.14	41	19	4	176	147	122	71	1	8	2	0	60	5	0	.083	12	42	1	1	1.3	.982
1914	2 teams	PHI A (3G 0–0)		BKN F (17G 2–6)																						
"	total	2	6	.250	3.15	20	12	3	103	109	49	49	0	0	0	0	33	8	1	.242	1	18	4	0	1.2	.826
1918	STL A	2	4	.333	2.39	27	2	0	71.2	58	29	29	0	1	3	2	20	3	0	.150	5	18	4	1	1.0	.852
4 yrs.		26	24	.520	3.30	118	50	19	531.1	462	274	224	1	9	7	2	175	20	1	.114	25	128	13	4	1.4	.922

Charlie Hough

HOUGH, CHARLES OLIVER
B. Jan. 5, 1948, Honolulu, Hawaii — BR TR 6'2" 190 lbs.

Year	Team	W	L	PCT	ERA	G	GS	CG	IP	H	BB	SO	ShO	W	L	SV	AB	H	HR	BA	PO	A	E	DP	TC/G	FA
1970	LA N	0	0	—	5.29	8	0	0	17	18	11	8	0	0	0	2	3	1	0	.333	1	3	0	0	0.5	1.000
1971		0	0	—	4.50	4	0	0	4	3	3	4	0	0	0	0	3	0	0	—	0	1	0	0	0.3	1.000
1972		0	0	—	3.38	2	0	0	2.2	2	2	4	0	0	0	0	0	0	0	—	0	1	0	0	0.5	1.000
1973		4	2	.667	2.76	37	0	0	71.2	52	45	70	0	4	2	5	14	3	0	.214	4	11	1	1	0.4	.938
1974		9	4	.692	3.75	49	0	0	96	65	40	63	0	9	4	1	12	0	0	.000	3	14	1	1	0.4	.944
1975		3	7	.300	2.95	38	0	0	61	43	34	34	0	3	7	4	6	2	0	.333	4	7	2	0	0.3	.846
1976		12	8	.600	2.21	77	0	0	142.2	102	77	81	0	12	8	18	21	6	0	.286	3	22	1	0	0.3	.962
1977		6	12	.333	3.33	70	1	0	127	98	70	105	0	5	12	22	22	4	0	.182	6	15	1	1	0.3	.955
1978		5	5	.500	3.29	55	0	0	93	69	48	66	0	5	5	7	12	4	0	.333	5	11	0	2	0.3	1.000
1979		7	5	.583	4.77	42	14	0	151	152	66	76	0	1	2	0	38	6	0	.158	5	26	1	0	0.8	.969
1980	2 teams	LA N (19G 1–3)		TEX A (16G 2–2)																						
"	total	3	5	.375	4.55	35	3	2	93	91	58	72	1	2	3	1	2	1	0	.500	2	10	1	0	0.4	.923
1981	TEX A	4	1	.800	2.96	21	5	2	82	61	31	69	0	0	0	0	0	0	0	—	2	8	0	1	0.5	1.000
1982		16	13	.552	3.95	34	34	12	228	217	72	128	0	0	0	0	0	0	0	—	14	35	1	4	1.5	.980
1983		15	13	.536	3.18	34	33	11	252	219	95	152	3	0	0	0	0	0	0	—	25	46	2	0	2.1	.973
1984		16	14	.533	3.76	36	36	17	266	260	94	165	1	0	0	0	0	0	0	—	12	51	1	2	1.8	.984
1985		14	16	.467	3.31	34	34	14	250.1	198	83	141	1	0	0	0	0	0	0	—	18	35	2	5	1.6	.964
1986		17	10	.630	3.79	33	33	7	230.1	188	89	146	2	0	0	0	0	0	0	—	20	32	1	0	1.6	.981
1987		18	13	.581	3.79	40	40	13	285.1	238	124	223	0	0	0	0	0	0	0	—	30	46	1	3	1.9	.987
1988		15	16	.484	3.32	34	34	10	252	202	126	174	0	0	0	0	0	0	0	—	27	43	1	4	2.1	.986
1989		10	13	.435	4.35	30	30	5	182	168	95	94	1	0	0	0	0	0	0	—	13	18	1	3	1.1	.969
20 yrs.		174	157	.526	3.60	713	297	93	2887	2446	1263	1875	11	42	43	61	130	27	1	.208	194	435	18	33	0.9	.972

LEAGUE CHAMPIONSHIP SERIES

Year	Team	W	L	PCT	ERA	G	GS	CG	IP	H	BB	SO	ShO	W	L	SV	AB	H	HR	BA	PO	A	E	DP	TC/G	FA
1974	LA N	0	0	—	7.71	1	0	0	2.1	4	0	2	0	0	0	0	0	0	0	—	0	1	0	0	1.0	—

Year	Team	W	L	PCT	ERA	G	GS	CG	IP	H	BB	SO	ShO	W	L	SV	AB	H	HR	BA	PO	A	E	DP	TC/G	FA

Charlie Hough *continued*

Year	Team	W	L	PCT	ERA	G	GS	CG	IP	H	BB	SO	ShO	W	L	SV	AB	H	HR	BA	PO	A	E	DP	TC/G	FA
1977		0	0	–	4.50	1	0	0	2	2	0	3	0	0	0	0	0	0	0	–	0	1	0	0	1.0	1.000
1978		0	0	–	4.50	1	0	0	2	1	0	1	0	0	0	0	0	0	0	–	1	0	0	0	2.0	1.000
3 yrs.		0	0	–	5.68	3	0	0	6.1	7	0	6	0	0	0	0	0	0	0	–	1	2	1	0	1.3	.750

WORLD SERIES

Year	Team	W	L	PCT	ERA	G	GS	CG	IP	H	BB	SO	ShO	W	L	SV	AB	H	HR	BA	PO	A	E	DP	TC/G	FA
1974	LA N	0	0	–	0.00	1	0	0	2	0	1	4	0	0	0	0	0	0	0	–	0	0	0	0	0.0	–
1977		0	0	–	1.80	2	0	0	5	3	0	5	0	0	0	0	0	0	0	–	0	0	0	0	0.5	1.000
1978		0	0	–	8.44	2	0	0	5.1	10	2	5	0	0	0	0	0	0	0	–	1	0	0	0	0.2	1.000
3 yrs.		0	0	–	4.38	5	0	0	12.1	13	3	14	0	0	0	0	0	0	0	–	1	0	0	0	0.2	1.000

Fred House

HOUSE, WILLARD EDWIN
B. Oct. 3, 1890, Cabool, Mo.   D. Nov. 16, 1923, Kansas City, Mo.

BR TR 6'3"   190 lbs.

Year	Team	W	L	PCT	ERA	G	GS	CG	IP	H	BB	SO	ShO	W	L	SV	AB	H	HR	BA	PO	A	E	DP	TC/G	FA
1913	DET A	1	2	.333	5.20	19	2	0	53.2	64	17	16	0	1	1	0	10	0	0	.000	0	27	2	0	1.5	.931

Pat House

HOUSE, PATRICK LORY
B. Sept. 1, 1940, Boise, Ida.

BL TL 6'3"   185 lbs.

Year	Team	W	L	PCT	ERA	G	GS	CG	IP	H	BB	SO	ShO	W	L	SV	AB	H	HR	BA	PO	A	E	DP	TC/G	FA
1967	HOU N	1	0	1.000	4.50	6	0	0	4	3	0	2	0	1	0	1	0	0	0	–	1	2	0	0	0.5	1.000
1968		1	1	.500	7.71	18	0	0	16.1	21	6	6	0	1	1	0	0	0	0	–	1	2	0	0	0.2	1.000
2 yrs.		2	1	.667	7.08	24	0	0	20.1	24	6	8	0	2	1	1	0	0	0	–	2	4	0	0	0.3	1.000

Tom House

HOUSE, THOMAS ROSS
B. Apr. 29, 1947, Seattle, Wash.

BL TL 5'11"   190 lbs.

Year	Team	W	L	PCT	ERA	G	GS	CG	IP	H	BB	SO	ShO	W	L	SV	AB	H	HR	BA	PO	A	E	DP	TC/G	FA
1971	ATL N	1	0	1.000	3.00	11	1	0	21	20	3	11	0	0	0	0	5	2	0	.400	0	4	0	0	0.4	1.000
1972		0	0	–	3.00	8	0	0	9	7	6	7	0	0	0	2	1	0	0	.000	0	2	0	0	0.3	1.000
1973		4	2	.667	4.70	52	0	0	67	58	31	42	0	4	2	4	10	2	0	.200	1	10	0	0	0.2	1.000
1974		6	2	.750	1.92	56	0	0	103	74	27	64	0	6	2	11	10	4	0	.400	6	23	3	0	0.6	.906
1975		7	7	.500	3.19	58	0	0	79	79	36	36	0	7	7	11	9	1	0	.111	7	16	4	0	0.5	.852
1976	BOS A	1	3	.250	4.30	36	0	0	44	39	19	27	0	1	3	4	0	0	0	–	3	11	1	0	0.4	.933
1977	2 teams	BOS A		(8G 1–0)				SEA A	(26G 4–5)																		
"	total	5	5	.500	4.64	34	11	1	97	109	25	45	0	1	1	1	0	0	0	–	1	11	1	1	0.4	.923
1978	SEA A	5	4	.556	4.66	34	9	3	116	130	35	29	0	2	0	0	0	0	0	.257	3	19	0	0	0.6	1.000
8 yrs.		29	23	.558	3.79	289	21	4	536	516	182	261	0	21	15	33	35	9	0	.257	21	96	9	1	0.4	.929

Charlie Householder

HOUSEHOLDER, CHARLES F.
B. 1856, Harrisburg, Pa.   Deceased.

BR TR 5'7"   150 lbs.

Year	Team	W	L	PCT	ERA	G	GS	CG	IP	H	BB	SO	ShO	W	L	SV	AB	H	HR	BA	PO	A	E	DP	TC/G	FA
1884	CHI U	0	0	–	3.00	2	0	0	3	4	0	3	0	0	0	0	*				0	0	0	0	0.0	–

Frank Houseman

HOUSEMAN, FRANK
B. Baltimore, Md.   Deceased.

Year	Team	W	L	PCT	ERA	G	GS	CG	IP	H	BB	SO	ShO	W	L	SV	AB	H	HR	BA	PO	A	E	DP	TC/G	FA
1886	BAL AA	0	1	.000	3.38	1	1	1	8	6	1	5	0	0	0	0	4	1	0	.250	2	1	0	0	3.0	1.000

Joe Houser

HOUSER, JOSEPH WILLIAM
B. July 3, 1891, Steubenville, Ohio   D. Jan. 3, 1953, Orlando, Fla.

BL TL 5'9½"   160 lbs.

Year	Team	W	L	PCT	ERA	G	GS	CG	IP	H	BB	SO	ShO	W	L	SV	AB	H	HR	BA	PO	A	E	DP	TC/G	FA
1914	BUF F	0	1	.000	5.48	7	2	0	23	21	20	6	0	0	0	0	7	1	0	.143	1	11	0	0	1.7	1.000

Art Houtteman

HOUTTEMAN, ARTHUR JOSEPH
B. Aug. 7, 1927, Detroit, Mich.

BR TR 6'2"   188 lbs.

Year	Team	W	L	PCT	ERA	G	GS	CG	IP	H	BB	SO	ShO	W	L	SV	AB	H	HR	BA	PO	A	E	DP	TC/G	FA
1945	DET A	0	2	.000	5.33	13	0	0	25.1	27	11	9	0	0	2	0	5	0	0	.000	2	8	0	1	0.8	1.000
1946		0	1	.000	9.00	1	1	0	8	15	0	2	0	0	0	0	2	1	0	.500	0	1	0	0	1.0	1.000
1947		7	2	.778	3.42	23	9	7	110.2	106	36	58	2	1	0	0	40	12	0	.300	4	17	2	2	1.0	.913
1948		2	16	.111	4.66	43	20	4	164.1	186	52	74	0	1	2	10	56	11	0	.196	9	47	4	5	1.4	.933
1949		15	10	.600	3.71	34	25	13	203.2	227	59	85	2	3	2	0	78	19	0	.244	14	59	2	7	2.2	.973
1950		19	12	.613	3.54	41	34	21	274.2	257	99	88	4	2	0	4	93	14	0	.151	15	63	4	2	2.0	.951
1952		8	20	.286	4.36	35	28	10	221	218	65	109	2	1	2	1	69	7	0	.101	16	40	1	3	1.6	.982
1953	2 teams	DET A		(16G 2–6)				CLE A	(22G 7–7)																		
"	total	9	13	.409	4.61	38	22	9	177.2	200	54	68	2	2	2	4	53	8	1	.151	11	28	1	1	1.1	.975
1954	CLE A	15	7	.682	3.35	32	25	11	188	198	59	68	1	1	2	0	65	18	1	.277	17	38	2	3	1.8	.965
1955		10	6	.625	3.98	35	12	3	124.1	126	44	53	1	6	1	0	38	6	0	.158	14	27	1	4	1.2	.976
1956		2	2	.500	6.56	22	4	0	46.2	60	31	19	0	1	0	1	12	2	0	.167	3	9	0	0	0.5	1.000
1957	2 teams	CLE A		(3G 0–0)				BAL A	(5G 0–0)																		
"	total	0	0	–	13.50	8	1	0	10.2	26	6	6	0	0	0	0	2	1	0	.500	0	2	0	0	0.3	1.000
12 yrs.		87	91	.489	4.14	325	181	78	1555	1646	516	639	14	18	13	20	513	99	2	.193	105	339	17	28	1.4	.963

WORLD SERIES

Year	Team	W	L	PCT	ERA	G	GS	CG	IP	H	BB	SO	ShO	W	L	SV	AB	H	HR	BA	PO	A	E	DP	TC/G	FA
1954	CLE A	0	0	–	4.50	1	0	0	2	2	1	1	0	0	0	0	0	0	0	–	0	0	0	0	0.0	–

Hick Hovlik

HOVLIK, EDWARD CHARLES
Brother of Joe Hovlik.
B. Aug. 20, 1891, Cleveland, Ohio   D. Mar. 19, 1955, Painesville, Ohio

BR TR 6'   180 lbs.

Year	Team	W	L	PCT	ERA	G	GS	CG	IP	H	BB	SO	ShO	W	L	SV	AB	H	HR	BA	PO	A	E	DP	TC/G	FA
1918	WAS A	2	1	.667	1.29	8	2	1	28	25	10	10	0	1	1	0	8	1	0	.125	2	5	0	0	0.9	1.000
1919		0	0	–	12.71	3	0	0	5.2	12	9	3	0	0	0	1	2	0	0	.000	0	3	0	0	1.0	1.000
2 yrs.		2	1	.667	3.21	11	2	1	33.2	37	19	13	0	1	1	1	10	1	0	.100	2	8	0	0	0.9	1.000

Joe Hovlik

HOVLIK, JOSEPH
Brother of Hick Hovlik.
B. Aug. 16, 1884, Austria-Hungary   D. Nov. 3, 1951, Oxford Junction, Iowa

BR TR 5'10½"   194 lbs.

Year	Team	W	L	PCT	ERA	G	GS	CG	IP	H	BB	SO	ShO	W	L	SV	AB	H	HR	BA	PO	A	E	DP	TC/G	FA
1909	WAS A	0	0	–	4.50	3	0	0	6	13	3	1	0	0	0	0	2	0	0	.000	0	3	0	0	1.0	1.000
1910		0	0	–	16.20	1	0	0	1.2	6	0	0	0	0	0	0	0	0	0	–	0	1	1	0	2.0	.500

Year	Team		W	L	PCT	ERA	G	GS	CG	IP	H	BB	SO	ShO	W	L	SV	AB	H	HR	BA	PO	A	E	DP	TC/G	FA
															Relief Pitching			Batting									

Joe Hovlik *continued*

Year	Team		W	L	PCT	ERA	G	GS	CG	IP	H	BB	SO	ShO	W	L	SV	AB	H	HR	BA	PO	A	E	DP	TC/G	FA
1911	CHI	A	2	0	1.000	3.06	12	3	1	47	47	20	24	1	1	0	0	13	1	0	.077	2	18	0	0	1.7	1.000
3 yrs.			2	0	1.000	3.62	16	3	1	54.2	66	23	25	1	1	0	0	15	1	0	.067	2	22	1	0	1.6	.960

Bruce Howard

HOWARD, BRUCE ERNEST
B. Mar. 23, 1943, Salisbury, Md. — BB TR 6'2" 180 lbs.

Year	Team		W	L	PCT	ERA	G	GS	CG	IP	H	BB	SO	ShO	W	L	SV	AB	H	HR	BA	PO	A	E	DP	TC/G	FA
1963	CHI	A	2	1	.667	2.65	7	0	0	17	12	14	9	0	2	1	1	4	1	0	.250	1	1	0	0	0.3	1.000
1964			2	1	.667	0.81	3	3	1	22.1	10	8	17	1	0	0	0	8	0	0	.000	1	3	0	0	1.3	1.000
1965			9	8	.529	3.47	30	22	1	148	123	72	120	1	2	1	0	41	6	0	.146	5	22	1	0	0.9	.964
1966			9	5	.643	2.30	27	21	4	149	110	44	85	2	1	0	0	43	3	0	.070	10	27	3	1	1.5	.925
1967			3	10	.231	3.43	30	17	1	112.2	102	52	76	0	1	1	0	28	5	0	.179	7	23	0	3	1.0	1.000
1968	2 teams		BAL A	(10G 0–2)		WAS A	(13G 1–4)																				
"	total		1	6	.143	4.74	23	12	0	79.2	92	49	42	0	0	0	0	23	2	1	.087	2	18	0	2	0.9	1.000
6 yrs.			26	31	.456	3.18	120	75	7	528.2	449	239	349	4	6	3	1	147	17	1	.116	26	94	4	6	1.0	.968

Del Howard

HOWARD, GEORGE ELMER
Brother of Ivon Howard.
B. Dec. 24, 1877, Kenney, Ill. D. Dec. 24, 1956, Seattle, Wash. — BL TR 6' 180 lbs.

Year	Team		W	L	PCT	ERA	G	GS	CG	IP	H	BB	SO	ShO	W	L	SV	AB	H	HR	BA	PO	A	E	DP	TC/G	FA
1905	PIT	N	0	0	–	0.00	1	0	0	6	4	1	0	0	0	0	0	*				0	2	0	1	2.0	1.000

Earl Howard

HOWARD, EARL NYCUM
B. June 25, 1896, Everett, Pa. D. Apr. 4, 1937, Everett, Pa. — BR TR 6'1" 160 lbs.

Year	Team		W	L	PCT	ERA	G	GS	CG	IP	H	BB	SO	ShO	W	L	SV	AB	H	HR	BA	PO	A	E	DP	TC/G	FA
1918	STL	N	0	0	–	0.00	1	0	0	2	0	2	0	0	0	0	0	0	0	0	–	1	2	0	1	3.0	1.000

Fred Howard

HOWARD, FRED IRVING III
B. Sept. 2, 1956, Portland, Me. — BR TR 6'3" 190 lbs.

Year	Team		W	L	PCT	ERA	G	GS	CG	IP	H	BB	SO	ShO	W	L	SV	AB	H	HR	BA	PO	A	E	DP	TC/G	FA
1979	CHI	A	1	5	.167	3.57	28	6	0	68	73	32	36	0	0	1	0	0	0	0	–	7	4	0	0	0.4	1.000

Lee Howard

HOWARD, LEE VINCENT
B. Nov. 11, 1923, Staten Island, N. Y. — BL TL 6'2" 175 lbs.

Year	Team		W	L	PCT	ERA	G	GS	CG	IP	H	BB	SO	ShO	W	L	SV	AB	H	HR	BA	PO	A	E	DP	TC/G	FA
1946	PIT	N	0	1	.000	2.03	3	2	1	13.1	14	9	6	0	0	0	0	5	0	0	.000	0	2	1	1	1.0	.667
1947			0	0	–	3.38	2	0	0	2.2	4	0	2	0	0	0	0	0	0	0	–	0	0	0	0	0.0	–
2 yrs.			0	1	.000	2.25	5	2	1	16	18	9	8	0	0	0	0	5	0	0	.000	0	2	1	1	0.6	.667

Cal Howe

HOWE, CALVIN EARL
B. Nov. 27, 1924, Rock Falls, Ill. — BL TL 6'3" 205 lbs.

Year	Team		W	L	PCT	ERA	G	GS	CG	IP	H	BB	SO	ShO	W	L	SV	AB	H	HR	BA	PO	A	E	DP	TC/G	FA
1952	CHI	N	0	0	–	0.00	1	0	0	2	0	1	2	0	0	0	0	0	0	0	–	0	0	0	0	0.0	–

Les Howe

HOWE, LESTER CURTIS (Lucky)
B. Aug. 24, 1895, Brooklyn, N. Y. D. July 16, 1976, Woodmere, N. Y. — BR TR 5'11½" 170 lbs.

Year	Team		W	L	PCT	ERA	G	GS	CG	IP	H	BB	SO	ShO	W	L	SV	AB	H	HR	BA	PO	A	E	DP	TC/G	FA
1923	BOS	A	1	0	1.000	2.40	12	2	0	30	23	7	7	0	1	0	0	6	0	0	.000	2	10	2	0	1.2	.857
1924			1	0	1.000	7.36	4	0	0	7.1	11	2	3	0	1	0	0	2	1	0	.500	0	2	0	0	0.5	1.000
2 yrs.			2	0	1.000	3.38	16	2	0	37.1	34	9	10	0	2	0	0	8	1	0	.125	2	12	2	0	1.0	.875

Steve Howe

HOWE, STEVEN ROY
B. Mar. 10, 1958, Pontiac, Mich. — BL TL 6'1" 180 lbs.

Year	Team		W	L	PCT	ERA	G	GS	CG	IP	H	BB	SO	ShO	W	L	SV	AB	H	HR	BA	PO	A	E	DP	TC/G	FA
1980	LA	N	7	9	.438	2.65	59	0	0	85	83	22	39	0	7	9	17	11	1	0	.091	3	20	1	0	0.4	.958
1981			5	3	.625	2.50	41	0	0	54	51	18	32	0	5	3	8	1	0	0	.000	1	5	0	0	0.1	1.000
1982			7	5	.583	2.08	66	0	0	99.1	87	17	49	0	7	5	13	7	0	0	.000	2	17	1	0	0.3	.950
1983			4	7	.364	1.44	46	0	0	68.2	55	12	52	0	4	7	18	8	1	0	.125	4	15	0	0	0.4	1.000
1985	2 teams		LA N	(19G 1–1)		MIN A	(13G 2–3)																				
"	total		3	4	.429	5.49	32	0	0	41	58	12	21	0	3	4	2	0	0	0	–	3	7	1	0	0.3	.909
1987	TEX	A	3	3	.500	4.31	24	0	0	31.1	33	8	19	0	3	3	1	0	0	0	–	4	4	0	0	0.3	1.000
6 yrs.			29	31	.483	2.70	268	0	0	379.1	367	89	212	0	29	31	60	27	2	0	.074	17	68	3	0	0.3	.966

DIVISIONAL PLAYOFF SERIES

Year	Team		W	L	PCT	ERA	G	GS	CG	IP	H	BB	SO	ShO	W	L	SV	AB	H	HR	BA	PO	A	E	DP	TC/G	FA
1981	LA	N	0	0	–	0.00	2	0	0	2	1	0	2	0	0	0	0	0	0	0	–	0	0	0	0	0.0	–

LEAGUE CHAMPIONSHIP SERIES

Year	Team		W	L	PCT	ERA	G	GS	CG	IP	H	BB	SO	ShO	W	L	SV	AB	H	HR	BA	PO	A	E	DP	TC/G	FA
1981	LA	N	0	0	–	0.00	2	0	0	2	1	0	2	0	0	0	0	0	0	0	–	0	0	0	0	0.0	–

WORLD SERIES

Year	Team		W	L	PCT	ERA	G	GS	CG	IP	H	BB	SO	ShO	W	L	SV	AB	H	HR	BA	PO	A	E	DP	TC/G	FA
1981	LA	N	1	0	1.000	3.86	3	0	0	7	7	1	4	0	1	0	1	2	0	0	.000	0	1	1	0	0.7	.500

Dixie Howell

HOWELL, MILLARD
B. Jan. 7, 1920, Bowman, Ky. D. Mar. 18, 1960, Hollywood, Fla. — BL TR 6'2" 210 lbs.

Year	Team		W	L	PCT	ERA	G	GS	CG	IP	H	BB	SO	ShO	W	L	SV	AB	H	HR	BA	PO	A	E	DP	TC/G	FA
1940	CLE	A	0	0	–	1.80	3	0	0	5	2	4	2	0	0	0	0	0	0	0	–	0	1	0	0	0.3	1.000
1949	CIN	N	0	1	.000	8.10	5	1	0	13.1	21	8	7	0	0	0	0	9	1	0	.111	0	3	0	0	0.6	1.000
1955	CHI	A	8	3	.727	2.93	35	0	0	73.2	70	25	25	0	8	3	9	21	8	0	.381	4	21	3	0	0.8	.893
1956			5	6	.455	4.62	34	1	0	64.1	79	36	28	0	4	6	4	17	4	2	.235	2	12	2	2	0.5	.875
1957			6	5	.545	3.29	37	0	0	68.1	64	30	37	0	6	5	6	27	5	3	.185	4	14	0	1	0.5	1.000
1958			0	0	–	0.00	1	0	0	1.2	0	0	0	0	0	0	0	0	0	0	–	0	1	0	0	1.0	1.000
6 yrs.			19	15	.559	3.78	115	2	0	226.1	236	103	99	0	18	14	19	74	18	5	.243	10	52	5	3	0.6	.925

Harry Howell

HOWELL, HENRY HARRY (Handsome Harry)
B. Nov. 14, 1876, New Jersey D. May 22, 1956, Spokane, Wash. — BR TR 5'9"

Year	Team		W	L	PCT	ERA	G	GS	CG	IP	H	BB	SO	ShO	W	L	SV	AB	H	HR	BA	PO	A	E	DP	TC/G	FA
1898	BKN	N	2	0	1.000	5.00	2	2	2	18	15	11	2	0				8	2	0	.250	1	5	0	1	3.0	1.000
1899	BAL	N	13	8	.619	3.91	28	25	21	209.1	248	69	58	0	1	0	1	82	12	0	.146	10	53	4	1	2.4	.940
1900	BKN	N	6	5	.545	3.75	21	10	7	110.1	131	36	26	2	1	0	1	42	12	0	.286	6	31	2	1	1.9	.949
1901	BAL	A	14	21	.400	3.67	37	34	32	294.2	333	79	93	1	1	1	0	188	41	2	.218	13	73	9	5	2.6	.905
1902			9	15	.375	4.12	26	23	19	199	243	48	33	1				347	93	2	.268	24	74	5	0	4.0	.951

Year	Team	W	L	PCT	ERA	G	GS	CG	IP	H	BB	SO	ShO	Relief Pitching W	L	SV	Batting AB	H	HR	BA	PO	A	E	DP	TC/G	FA

Carl Hubbell *continued*

| 1937 | | 1 | 1 | .500 | 3.77 | 2 | 2 | 1 | 14.1 | 12 | 4 | 7 | 0 | 0 | 0 | 0 | 6 | 0 | 0 | .000 | 0 | 3 | 0 | 1 | 1.5 | 1.000 |
| 3 yrs. | | 4 | 2 | .667 | 1.79 | 6 | 6 | 4 | 50.1 | 40 | 12 | 32 | 0 | 0 | 0 | 0 | 19 | 4 | 0 | .211 | 3 | 9 | 2 | 1 | 2.3 | .857 |

Earl Huckleberry

HUCKLEBERRY, EARL EUGENE
B. May 23, 1910, Konawa, Okla.

BR TR 5'11" 165 lbs.

| 1935 | PHI A | 1 | 0 | 1.000 | 9.45 | 1 | 1 | 0 | 6.2 | 8 | 4 | 2 | 0 | 0 | 0 | 0 | 3 | 0 | 0 | .000 | 1 | 1 | 1 | 0 | 3.0 | .667 |

Willis Hudlin

HUDLIN, GEORGE WILLIS (Ace)
B. May 23, 1906, Wagoner, Okla.

BR TR 6' 190 lbs.

1926	CLE A	1	3	.250	2.78	8	2	1	32.1	25	13	6	0	1	1	0	8	1	0	.125	6	15	0	0	2.6	1.000
1927		18	12	.600	4.01	43	30	18	264.2	**291**	83	65	1	4	0	0	96	24	1	.250	12	80	1	4	2.2	.989
1928		14	14	.500	4.04	42	26	10	220.1	231	90	62	0	6	0	7	72	14	0	.194	16	60	7	3	2.0	.916
1929		17	15	.531	3.34	40	33	22	280.1	299	73	60	2	3	1	1	97	19	0	.196	24	88	5	8	2.9	.957
1930		13	16	.448	4.57	37	33	13	216.2	255	76	60	1	1	2	1	73	16	0	.219	8	67	5	6	2.2	.938
1931		15	14	.517	4.60	44	34	15	254.1	313	88	83	1	1	1	4	100	20	0	.200	14	65	4	10	1.9	.952
1932		12	8	.600	4.71	33	21	12	181.2	204	59	65	0	1	1	2	64	13	0	.203	3	47	2	1	1.6	.962
1933		5	13	.278	3.97	34	17	6	147.1	161	61	44	0	0	2	1	41	6	1	.146	8	48	1	2	1.7	.982
1934		15	10	.600	4.75	36	26	15	195	210	65	58	1	1	3	4	68	14	1	.206	10	62	1	8	2.0	.986
1935		15	11	.577	3.69	36	29	14	231.2	252	61	45	3	0	1	5	86	24	1	.279	11	48	1	2	1.7	.983
1936		1	5	.167	9.00	27	7	1	64	112	31	20	0	1	0	0	18	2	0	.111	2	15	1	1	0.7	.944
1937		12	11	.522	4.10	35	23	10	175.2	213	40	31	2	4	0	2	59	10	0	.169	4	51	4	4	1.7	.932
1938		8	8	.500	4.89	29	15	8	127	182	45	27	0	2	4	1	43	5	0	.116	7	29	3	3	1.3	.923
1939		9	10	.474	4.91	27	20	7	143	175	42	28	0	1	2	3	48	9	1	.188	21	42	1	2	2.4	.984
1940	4 teams	CLE A	(4G 2–1)		WAS A	(8G 1–2)		STL A		(6G 0–1)		NY	N	(1G 0–1)												
"	total	3	5	.375	6.98	19	12	3	77.1	109	16	22	0	0	0	0	21	3	0	.143	4	17	2	0	1.2	.913
1944	STL A	0	1	.000	4.50	1	0	0	2	3	0	1	0	0	0	0	0	0	0	–	0	0	0	0	0.0	–
16 yrs.		158	156	.503	4.41	491	328	155	2613.1	3011	843	677	11	26	19	31	894	180	5	.201	150	734	38	54	1.9	.959

Charles Hudson

HUDSON, CHARLES
B. Aug. 18, 1949, Ada, Okla.

BL TL 6'3" 185 lbs.

1972	STL N	1	0	1.000	5.11	12	0	0	12.1	10	7	4	0	1	0	0	0	0	0	–	1	3	0	0	0.3	1.000
1973	TEX A	4	2	.667	4.65	25	4	1	62	59	31	34	0	2	1	1	0	0	0	–	3	10	1	0	0.6	.929
1975	CAL A	0	1	.000	9.53	3	1	0	5.2	7	4	0	0	0	0	0	0	0	0	–	0	2	1	0	1.0	.667
3 yrs.		5	3	.625	5.06	40	5	1	80	76	42	38	0	3	1	1	0	0	0	–	4	15	2	0	0.5	.905

Charles Hudson

HUDSON, CHARLES LYNN
B. Mar. 16, 1959, Ennis, Tex.

BB TR 6'3" 185 lbs.

1983	PHI N	8	8	.500	3.35	26	26	3	169.1	158	53	101	0	0	0	0	54	5	0	.093	14	19	1	3	1.3	.971
1984		9	11	.450	4.04	30	30	1	173.2	181	52	94	1	0	0	0	56	5	0	.089	4	20	2	1	0.9	.923
1985		8	13	.381	3.78	38	26	3	193	188	74	122	0	0	2	0	57	8	0	.140	14	18	0	1	0.8	1.000
1986		7	10	.412	4.94	33	23	0	144	165	58	82	0	1	0	0	43	2	0	.047	12	20	1	0	1.0	.970
1987	NY A	11	7	.611	3.61	35	16	6	154.2	137	57	100	2	5	2	0	0	0	0	–	9	14	0	1	0.7	1.000
1988		6	6	.500	4.49	28	12	1	106.1	93	36	58	0	2	2	2	0	0	0	–	9	10	0	3	0.7	1.000
1989	DET A	1	5	.167	6.35	18	7	0	66.2	75	31	23	0	0	0	0	0	0	0	–	7	5	1	1	0.7	.923
7 yrs.		50	60	.455	4.14	208	140	14	1007.2	997	361	580	3	8	8	2	210	20	0	.095	69	106	5	10	0.9	.972

LEAGUE CHAMPIONSHIP SERIES

| 1983 | PHI N | 1 | 0 | 1.000 | 2.00 | 1 | 1 | 1 | 9 | 4 | 2 | 9 | 0 | 0 | 0 | 0 | 4 | 0 | 0 | .000 | 0 | 0 | 0 | 0 | 0.0 | |

WORLD SERIES

| 1983 | PHI N | 0 | 2 | .000 | 8.64 | 2 | 2 | 0 | 8.1 | 9 | 1 | 6 | 0 | 0 | 0 | 0 | 2 | 0 | 0 | .000 | 0 | 0 | 0 | 0 | 0.0 | |

Hal Hudson

HUDSON, HAL CAMPBELL (Lefty)
B. May 4, 1927, Grosse Pointe, Mich.

BL TL 5'10" 175 lbs.

1952	2 teams	STL A	(3G 0–0)		CHI A	(2G 0–0)																				
"	total	0	0	–	8.38	5	0	0	9.2	16	7	4	0	0	0	0	1	0	0	.000	0	0	0	0	0.0	–
1953	CHI A	0	0	–	0.00	1	0	0	.2	0	0	0	0	0	0	0	0	0	0	–	0	0	0	0	0.0	–
2 yrs.		0	0	–	7.84	6	0	0	10.1	16	7	4	0	0	0	0	1	0	0	–	0	0	0	0	0.0	–

Jesse Hudson

HUDSON, JESSE JAMES
B. July 22, 1948, Mansfield, La.

BL TL 6'2" 165 lbs.

| 1969 | NY N | 0 | 0 | – | 4.50 | 1 | 0 | 0 | 2 | 2 | 2 | 3 | 0 | 0 | 0 | 0 | 0 | 0 | 0 | – | 0 | 1 | 0 | 0 | 1.0 | 1.000 |

Nat Hudson

HUDSON, NATHANIEL P.
B. Jan. 12, 1869, Chicago, Ill. D. Mar. 14, 1928, Chicago, Ill.

TR

1886	STL AA	16	10	.615	3.03	29	27	25	234.1	224	62	100	0	1	0	1	150	35	0	.233	18	33	4	0	1.9	.927
1887		4	4	.500	4.97	9	9	7	67	91	20	15	0	0	0	0	48	12	0	.250	5	6	2	0	1.4	.846
1888		25	10	**.714**	2.54	39	37	36	333	283	59	130	5	1	0	0	196	50	2	.255	42	53	6	3	2.6	.941
1889		3	2	.600	4.20	9	5	4	60	71	15	13	0	1	0	0	52	13	1	.250	2	11	2	0	1.7	.867
4 yrs.		48	26	.649	3.08	86	78	72	694.1	669	156	258	5	3	0	1	*				67	103	14	3	2.1	.924

Rex Hudson

HUDSON, REX HAUGHTON
B. Aug. 11, 1953, Tulsa, Okla.

BB TR 5'11" 165 lbs.

| 1974 | LA N | 0 | 0 | – | 22.50 | 1 | 0 | 0 | 2 | 6 | 0 | 0 | 0 | 0 | 0 | 0 | 0 | 0 | 0 | – | 0 | 0 | 0 | 0 | 0.0 | – |

Sid Hudson

HUDSON, SIDNEY CHARLES
B. Jan. 3, 1917, Coalfield, Tenn.

BR TR 6'4" 180 lbs.

1940	WAS A	17	16	.515	4.57	38	31	19	252	272	81	96	3	0	2	1	93	22	0	.237	14	50	4	1	1.8	.941
1941		13	14	.481	3.46	33	33	17	249.2	242	97	108	3	0	0	0	86	16	0	.186	11	57	7	4	2.3	.907
1942		10	17	.370	4.36	35	31	19	239.1	266	70	72	1	1	1	2	89	19	0	.213	14	67	6	3	2.5	.931

Year	Team	W	L	PCT	ERA	G	GS	CG	IP	H	BB	SO	ShO	Relief Pitching W	L	SV	Batting AB	H	HR	BA	PO	A	E	DP	TC/G	FA

Sid Hudson *continued*

Year	Team	W	L	PCT	ERA	G	GS	CG	IP	H	BB	SO	ShO	W	L	SV	AB	H	HR	BA	PO	A	E	DP	TC/G	FA
1946		8	11	.421	3.60	31	15	6	142.1	160	37	35	1	5	1	1	43	12	0	.279	9	36	0	1	1.5	1.000
1947		6	9	.400	5.60	20	17	5	106	113	58	37	1	1	0	0	39	12	0	.308	7	20	0	1	1.4	1.000
1948		4	16	.200	5.88	39	29	4	182	217	107	53	0	0	0	1	59	14	0	.237	15	44	3	5	1.6	.952
1949		8	17	.320	4.22	40	27	11	209	234	91	54	2	1	1	1	67	16	0	.239	18	53	1	5	1.8	.986
1950		14	14	.500	4.09	30	30	17	237.2	261	98	75	0	0	0	0	93	20	0	.215	11	55	3	7	2.3	.957
1951		5	12	.294	5.13	23	19	8	138.2	168	52	43	0	0	0	0	44	12	0	.273	10	35	1	4	2.0	.978
1952	2 teams	WAS A	(7G 3–4)		BOS A	(21G 7–9)																				
"	total	10	13	.435	3.34	28	25	13	197	204	65	74	0	0	0	0	70	12	0	.171	23	57	3	7	3.0	.964
1953	BOS A	6	9	.400	3.52	30	17	4	156	164	49	60	0	2	1	2	50	7	0	.140	13	26	1	2	1.3	.975
1954		3	4	.429	4.42	33	5	0	71.1	83	30	27	0	3	1	5	13	2	0	.154	6	14	2	1	0.7	.909
12 yrs.		104	152	.406	4.28	380	279	123	2181	2384	835	734	11	13	7	13	746	164	0	.220	151	514	31	41	1.8	.955

Al Huenke

HUENKE, ALBERT A.
B. June 26, 1891, New Bremen, Ohio   D. Sept. 20, 1974, St. Mary's, Ohio

BR TR 6'   175 lbs.

Year	Team	W	L	PCT	ERA	G	GS	CG	IP	H	BB	SO	ShO	W	L	SV	AB	H	HR	BA	PO	A	E	DP	TC/G	FA
1914	NY N	0	0	–	4.50	1	0	0	2	2	0	2	0	0	0	0	1	0	0	.000	0	0	0	0	0.0	–

Phil Huffman

HUFFMAN, PHILLIP LEE
B. June 20, 1958, Freeport, Tex.

BR TR 6'2"   180 lbs.

Year	Team	W	L	PCT	ERA	G	GS	CG	IP	H	BB	SO	ShO	W	L	SV	AB	H	HR	BA	PO	A	E	DP	TC/G	FA
1979	TOR A	6	18	.250	5.77	31	31	2	173	220	68	56	1	0	0	0	0	0	0	–	7	30	0	0	1.2	1.000
1985	BAL A	0	0	–	15.43	2	1	0	4.2	7	5	2	0	0	0	0	0	0	0	–	2	0	0	0	1.0	1.000
2 yrs.		6	18	.250	6.03	33	32	2	177.2	227	73	58	1	0	0	0	0	0	0	–	9	30	0	0	1.2	1.000

Bill Hughes

HUGHES, WILLIAM NESBERT
B. Nov. 18, 1896, Philadelphia, Pa.   D. Feb. 25, 1963, Birmingham, Ala.

BR TR 5'10½" 155 lbs.

Year	Team	W	L	PCT	ERA	G	GS	CG	IP	H	BB	SO	ShO	W	L	SV	AB	H	HR	BA	PO	A	E	DP	TC/G	FA
1921	PIT N	0	0	–	4.50	1	0	0	2	3	1	2	0	0	0	0	0	0	0	–	0	1	0	0	1.0	1.000

Bill Hughes

HUGHES, WILLIAM R.
B. Nov. 25, 1866, Bladensville, Ill.   D. Aug. 25, 1943, Santa Ana, Calif.

BL TL

Year	Team	W	L	PCT	ERA	G	GS	CG	IP	H	BB	SO	ShO	W	L	SV	AB	H	HR	BA	PO	A	E	DP	TC/G	FA
1885	PHI AA	0	2	.000	4.86	2	2	2	16.2	18	10	4	0	0	0	0	*				1	2	0	0	1.5	1.000

Dick Hughes

HUGHES, RICHARD HENRY
B. Feb. 13, 1938, Stephens, Ark.

BR TR 6'3"   195 lbs.

Year	Team	W	L	PCT	ERA	G	GS	CG	IP	H	BB	SO	ShO	W	L	SV	AB	H	HR	BA	PO	A	E	DP	TC/G	FA
1966	STL N	2	1	.667	1.71	6	2	1	21	12	7	20	1	1	0	0	5	2	0	.400	1	4	0	0	0.8	1.000
1967		16	6	.727	2.67	37	27	12	222.1	164	48	161	3	1	0	3	78	10	0	.128	10	28	1	1	1.1	.974
1968		2	2	.500	3.53	25	5	0	63.2	45	21	49	0	1	1	4	15	0	0	.000	7	10	0	3	0.7	1.000
3 yrs.		20	9	.690	2.79	68	34	13	307	221	76	230	4	3	2	8	98	12	0	.122	18	42	1	4	0.9	.984

WORLD SERIES

Year	Team	W	L	PCT	ERA	G	GS	CG	IP	H	BB	SO	ShO	W	L	SV	AB	H	HR	BA	PO	A	E	DP	TC/G	FA
1967	STL N	0	1	.000	5.00	2	2	0	9	9	3	7	0	0	0	0	3	0	0	.000	1	0	0	0	0.5	1.000
1968		0	0	–	0.00	1	0	0	.1	2	0	0	0	0	0	0	0	0	0	–	0	0	0	0	0.0	–
2 yrs.		0	1	.000	4.82	3	2	0	9.1	11	3	7	0	0	0	0	3	0	0	.000	1	0	0	0	0.3	1.000

Ed Hughes

HUGHES, EDWARD J.
Brother of Long Tom Hughes.
B. Oct. 5, 1880, Chicago, Ill.   D. Oct. 11, 1927, McHenry, Ill.

BR TR 6'1"   180 lbs.

Year	Team	W	L	PCT	ERA	G	GS	CG	IP	H	BB	SO	ShO	W	L	SV	AB	H	HR	BA	PO	A	E	DP	TC/G	FA
1902	CHI A	0	0	–	0.00	0	0	0					0	0	0	0	4	1	0	.250	0	0	0	0	0.0	–
1905	BOS A	3	2	.600	4.59	6	4	2	33.1	38	9	8	0	0	1	0	14	3	0	.214	0	5	5	0	1.7	.500
1906		0	0	–	5.40	2	0	0	10	15	3	3	0	0	0	0	3	0	0	.000	0	3	1	0	2.0	.750
3 yrs.		3	2	.600	4.78	8	4	2	43.1	53	12	11	0	0	1	0	21	4	0	.190	0	8	6	0	1.8	.571

Jim Hughes

HUGHES, JAMES JAY
Brother of Mickey Hughes.
B. Jan. 22, 1874, Sacramento, Calif.   D. June 2, 1924, Sacramento, Calif.

BR TR

Year	Team	W	L	PCT	ERA	G	GS	CG	IP	H	BB	SO	ShO	W	L	SV	AB	H	HR	BA	PO	A	E	DP	TC/G	FA
1898	BAL N	23	12	.657	3.20	38	35	31	300.2	268	100	81	3				164	37	2	.226	29	78	11	1	3.1	.907
1899	BKN N	28	6	.824	2.68	35	35	30	291.2	250	119	99	3	0	0	0	107	27	0	.252	19	74	7	4	2.9	.930
1901		17	12	.586	3.27	31	29	24	250.2	265	102	96	1	0	0	0	91	16	0	.176	18	66	6	5	2.9	.933
1902		15	11	.577	2.87	31	30	27	254	228	55	94	1	0	0	0	94	20	1	.213	20	70	4	5	3.0	.957
4 yrs.		83	41	.669	3.00	135	129	112	1097	1011	376	370	8	3	1	0	456	100	3	.219	86	288	28	15	3.0	.930

Jim Hughes

HUGHES, JAMES MICHAEL
B. Aug. 11, 1951, Los Angeles, Calif.

BR TR 6'3"   190 lbs.

Year	Team	W	L	PCT	ERA	G	GS	CG	IP	H	BB	SO	ShO	W	L	SV	AB	H	HR	BA	PO	A	E	DP	TC/G	FA
1974	MIN A	0	2	.000	5.40	2	2	1	10	8	4	8	0	0	0	0	0	0	0	–	1	1	0	0	1.0	1.000
1975		16	14	.533	3.82	37	34	12	249.2	241	127	130	2	1	0	0	0	0	0	–	18	41	6	1	1.8	.908
1976		9	14	.391	4.98	37	26	3	177	190	73	87	0	2	1	0	0	0	0	–	13	21	5	2	1.1	.872
1977		0	0	–	2.25	2	0	0	4	4	1	1	0	0	0	0	0	0	0	–	0	0	0	0	0.0	–
4 yrs.		25	30	.455	4.31	78	62	16	440.2	443	205	226	2	3	1	0	0	0	0	–	32	63	11	3	1.4	.896

Jim Hughes

HUGHES, JAMES ROBERT
B. Mar. 21, 1923, Chicago, Ill.

BR TR 6'1½" 200 lbs.

Year	Team	W	L	PCT	ERA	G	GS	CG	IP	H	BB	SO	ShO	W	L	SV	AB	H	HR	BA	PO	A	E	DP	TC/G	FA
1952	BKN N	2	1	.667	1.45	6	0	0	18.2	16	11	8	0	2	1	0	4	0	0	.000	0	1	0	0	0.2	1.000
1953		4	3	.571	3.47	48	0	0	85.2	80	41	49	0	4	3	9	14	4	0	.286	8	9	0	0	0.4	1.000
1954		8	4	.667	3.22	60	0	0	86.2	76	44	58	0	8	4	24	16	3	0	.188	4	10	2	1	0.3	.875
1955		0	2	.000	4.22	24	0	0	42.2	41	19	20	0	0	2	6	0	0	0	.000	4	8	1	1	0.5	.909
1956	2 teams	BKN N	(5G 0–0)		CHI N	(25G 1–3)																				
"	total	1	3	.250	5.18	30	0	0	57.1	53	34	28	0	1	2	0	9	2	0	.222	2	5	0	2	0.2	1.000
1957	CHI A	0	0	–	10.80	4	0	0	5	12	3	2	0	0	0	0	0	0	0	–	0	1	0	0	0.3	1.000
6 yrs.		15	13	.536	3.83	172	1	0	296	278	152	165	0	15	12	39	53	9	0	.170	16	34	3	4	0.3	.943

WORLD SERIES

Year	Team	W	L	PCT	ERA	G	GS	CG	IP	H	BB	SO	ShO	W	L	SV	AB	H	HR	BA	PO	A	E	DP	TC/G	FA
1953	BKN N	0	0	–	2.25	1	0	0	4	3	1	3	0	0	0	0	1	0	0	.000	0	0	1	0	1.0	–

Year	Team		W	L	PCT	ERA	G	GS	CG	IP	H	BB	SO	ShO	Relief Pitching W	L	SV	Batting AB	H	HR	BA	PO	A	E	DP	TC/G	FA

Long Tom Hughes

HUGHES, THOMAS JAMES
Brother of Ed Hughes.
B. Nov. 29, 1878, Chicago, Ill.   D. Feb. 8, 1956, Chicago, Ill.

BR TR 6'1"

Year	Team		W	L	PCT	ERA	G	GS	CG	IP	H	BB	SO	ShO	W	L	SV	AB	H	HR	BA	PO	A	E	DP	TC/G	FA
1900	CHI	N	1	1	.500	5.14	3	3	3	21	31	7	12	0	0	0	0	6	0	0	.000	0	6	0	0	2.0	1.000
1901			11	21	.344	3.24	37	35	32	308.1	309	115	225	1	1	0	0	118	14	0	.119	12	58	6	4	2.1	.921
1902	2 teams	BAL A	(13G 7–6)				BOS A	(9G 3–3)																			
"	total		10	9	.526	3.71	22	21	16	157.2	171	56	60	1	0	0	0	73	17	0	.233	11	45	3	1	2.7	.949
1903	BOS	A	20	7	.741	2.57	33	31	25	244.2	232	60	112	5	0	1	0	93	26	1	.280	7	52	3	3	1.9	.952
1904	2 teams	NY A	(19G 7–11)				WAS A	(16G 2–13)																			
"	total		9	24	.273	3.59	35	32	26	260.2	274	82	123	2	0	2	1	111	26	1	.234	11	69	6	1	2.5	.930
1905	WAS	A	16	20	.444	2.35	39	35	26	291.1	239	79	149	5	2	1	0	104	22	1	.212	9	69	5	0	2.1	.940
1906			7	17	.292	3.62	30	24	18	204	230	81	90	1	1	1	0	66	14	1	.212	6	43	5	1	1.8	.907
1907			7	14	.333	3.11	34	23	18	211	206	47	102	2	0	0	4	87	17	0	.195	8	87	11	4	2.5	.896
1908			18	15	.545	2.21	43	31	24	276.1	224	77	165	3	3	1	4	87	17	0	.195	8	87	11	4	2.5	.896
1909			4	7	.364	2.69	22	13	7	120.1	113	33	77	0	2	1	0	36	3	0	.083	2	36	6	0	2.0	.864
1911			11	17	.393	3.47	34	27	17	223	251	77	86	2	2	1	0	81	15	0	.185	8	51	5	3	1.9	.922
1912			13	10	.565	2.94	31	26	11	196	201	78	108	1	3	1	0	67	13	0	.194	6	57	7	1	2.3	.900
1913			4	12	.250	4.30	36	13	4	129.2	129	61	59	0	2	3	6	36	4	0	.111	9	41	5	1	1.5	.909
	13 yrs.		131	174	.430	3.09	399	314	227	2644	2610	853	1368	25	14	12	17	958	190	6	.198	95	675	63	19	2.1	.924

WORLD SERIES

| 1903 | BOS | A | 0 | 1 | .000 | 9.00 | 1 | 1 | 0 | 2 | 4 | 2 | 0 | 0 | 0 | 0 | 0 | 0 | 0 | 0 | – | 0 | 0 | 0 | 0 | 0.0 | – |

Mickey Hughes

HUGHES, MICHAEL F.
Brother of Jim Hughes.
B. Oct. 25, 1866, New York, N. Y.   D. Apr. 10, 1931, Jersey City, N. J.

TR 5'6"   165 lbs.

1888	BKN	AA	25	13	.658	2.13	40	40	40	363	281	98	159	2	0	0	0	139	19	0	.137	13	83	15	3	2.8	.865
1889			9	8	.529	4.35	20	17	13	153	172	86	54	0	0	0	0	68	12	0	.176	3	33	0	1	1.8	1.000
1890	2 teams	BKN N	(9G 4–4)				PHI AA	(6G 1–3)																			
"	total		5	7	.417	5.27	15	13	10	107.2	141	51	37	0	0	0	0	42	3	0	.071	2	20	7	2	1.9	.759
	3 yrs.		39	28	.582	3.22	75	70	63	623.2	594	235	250	2	0	0	0	249	34	0	.137	18	136	22	6	2.3	.875

Tom Hughes

HUGHES, THOMAS EDWARD
B. Sept. 13, 1934, Ancon, Canal Zone

BL TR 6'2"   180 lbs.

1959	STL	N	0	2	.000	15.75	2	2	0	4	9	2	2	0	0	0	0	1	0	0	.000	0	0	0	0	0.0	–

Tom Hughes

HUGHES, THOMAS L.
B. Jan. 28, 1884, Coal Creek, Colo.   D. Nov. 1, 1961, Los Angeles, Calif.

BR TR 6'2"   175 lbs.

1906	NY	A	1	0	1.000	4.20	3	1	1	15	11	11	5	0	0	0	0	5	1	0	.200	0	1	0	0	0.3	1.000
1907			2	0	1.000	2.67	4	3	2	27	16	11	10	0	0	0	0	7	1	0	.143	1	4	0	0	1.3	1.000
1909			7	8	.467	2.65	24	16	9	118.2	109	37	69	2	1	0	1	39	5	1	.128	8	29	1	0	1.6	.974
1910			7	9	.438	3.50	23	15	11	151.2	153	37	64	0	1	1	1	55	9	0	.164	4	57	4	1	2.8	.938
1914	BOS	N	1	0	1.000	2.65	2	2	1	17	14	4	11	0	0	0	0	7	0	0	.000	2	6	0	0	4.0	1.000
1915			16	14	.533	2.12	50	25	17	280.1	208	58	171	4	6	0	5	90	9	1	.100	6	59	3	2	1.4	.956
1916			16	3	.842	2.35	40	14	7	161	121	51	97	1	9	2	5	52	10	0	.192	8	31	0	0	1.0	1.000
1917			5	3	.625	1.95	11	8	6	74	54	30	40	2	0	0	0	24	0	0	.000	4	17	1	1	2.0	.955
1918			0	2	.000	3.44	3	3	1	18.1	17	6	9	0	0	0	0	6	2	1	.333	0	7	0	0	2.3	1.000
	9 yrs.		55	39	.585	2.56	160	87	55	863	703	235	476	9	17	3	12	285	37	3	.130	33	211	9	4	1.6	.964

Tommy Hughes

HUGHES, THOMAS OWEN
B. Oct. 7, 1919, Wilkes-Barre, Pa.

BR TR 6'1"   190 lbs.

1941	PHI	N	9	14	.391	4.45	34	24	5	170	187	82	59	0	2	2	0	55	11	0	.200	11	36	2	1	1.4	.959
1942			12	18	.400	3.06	40	31	19	253	224	99	77	0	1	0	1	80	8	0	.100	9	69	3	2	2.0	.975
1946			6	9	.400	4.38	29	13	3	111	123	44	34	2	2	0	1	31	3	0	.097	5	17	1	2	0.8	.957
1947			4	11	.267	3.47	29	15	4	127	121	59	44	1	1	1	1	40	2	0	.050	4	25	0	1	1.0	1.000
1948	CIN	N	0	4	.000	9.00	12	4	0	27	43	24	7	0	1	0	0	7	1	0	.143	2	4	0	0	0.5	1.000
	5 yrs.		31	56	.356	3.92	144	87	31	688	698	308	221	5	7	3	3	213	25	0	.117	31	151	5	8	1.3	.973

Vern Hughes

HUGHES, VERNON ALEXANDER (Lefty)
B. Apr. 15, 1893, Etna, Pa.   D. Sept. 26, 1961, Sewickley, Pa.

BL TL 5'10"   155 lbs.

1914	BAL	F	0	0	–	3.18	3	0	0	5.2	5	3	0	0	0	0	0	1	0	0	.000	0	2	1	0	1.0	.667

Jim Hughey

HUGHEY, JAMES ULYSSES (Cold Water Jim)
B. Mar. 8, 1869, Wakashma, Mich.   D. Mar. 29, 1945, Coldwater, Mich.

TR 6'

1891	MIL	AA	1	0	1.000	3.00	2	1	1	15	18	3	9	0	0	0	0	7	1	0	.143	0	5	0	0	2.5	1.000
1893	CHI	N	0	1	.000	11.00	2	2	1	9	14	3	4	0	0	0	0	4	0	0	.000	0	3	1	0	2.0	.750
1896	PIT	N	6	8	.429	4.99	25	14	11	155	171	67	48	0	0	2	0	65	14	0	.215	5	23	3	1	1.2	.909
1897			6	10	.375	5.06	25	17	13	149.1	193	45	38	0	1	1	1	63	8	0	.127	4	26	3	0	1.3	.909
1898	STL	N	7	24	.226	3.93	35	33	31	283.2	325	71	74	0	0	0	0	97	11	1	.113	8	67	11	2	2.5	.872
1899	CLE	N	4	30	.118	5.41	36	34	32	283	403	88	54	0	0	0	0	111	18	0	.162	9	48	12	3	1.9	.826
1900	STL	N	5	7	.417	5.19	20	12	11	112.2	147	40	23	0	0	0	0	41	7	0	.171	1	24	5	0	1.5	.833
	7 yrs.		29	80	.266	4.87	145	113	100	1007.2	1271	317	250	0	3	3	1	386	59	1	.153	27	196	35	6	1.8	.864

Tex Hughson

HUGHSON, CECIL CARLTON
B. Feb. 9, 1916, Kyle, Tex.

BR TR 6'3"   198 lbs.

1941	BOS	A	5	3	.625	4.13	12	8	4	61	70	13	22	0	1	0	0	17	1	0	.059	3	11	0	1	1.2	1.000
1942			22	6	.786	2.59	38	30	22	281	258	75	113	4	0	0	2	102	18	0	.176	16	59	1	7	2.0	.987
1943			12	15	.444	2.64	35	32	20	266	242	73	114	4	0	1	0	86	9	0	.105	10	61	2	3	2.1	.973
1944			18	5	.783	2.26	28	23	19	203.1	172	41	112	2	0	0	5	66	10	0	.152	9	35	2	0	1.6	.957
1946			20	11	.645	2.75	39	35	21	278	252	51	172	6	0	0	3	91	12	0	.132	18	34	1	0	1.4	.972
1947			12	11	.522	3.33	29	26	13	189.1	173	71	119	0	3	1	0	61	2	0	.033	10	25	1	3	1.2	.972
1948			3	1	.750	5.12	15	0	0	19.1	21	7	6	0	3	1	0	2	0	0	.000	1	1	0	0	0.2	.667

Year	Team		W	L	PCT	ERA	G	GS	CG	IP	H	BB	SO	ShO	W	L	SV	AB	H	HR	BA	PO	A	E	DP	TC/G	FA

Tex Hughson *continued*

| 1949 | | | 4 | 2 | .667 | 5.33 | 29 | 2 | 0 | 77.2 | 82 | 41 | 35 | 0 | 4 | 1 | 3 | 22 | 1 | 0 | .045 | 3 | 5 | 0 | 2 | 0.3 | 1.000 |
| 8 yrs. | | | 96 | 54 | .640 | 2.94 | 225 | 156 | 99 | 1375.2 | 1270 | 372 | 693 | 19 | 9 | 3 | 17 | 447 | 53 | 0 | .119 | 70 | 231 | 8 | 16 | 1.4 | .974 |

WORLD SERIES

| 1946 | BOS | A | 0 | 1 | .000 | 3.14 | 3 | 2 | 0 | 14.1 | 14 | 3 | 8 | 0 | 0 | 0 | 0 | 3 | 1 | 0 | .333 | 0 | 1 | 1 | 0 | 0.7 | .500 |

Mark Huismann

HUISMANN, MARK LAWRENCE
B. May 11, 1958, Lincoln, Neb.   BR TR 6'3" 195 lbs.

1983	KC	A	2	1	.667	5.58	13	0	0	30.2	29	17	20	0	2	1	0	0	0	0	–	1	2	0	0	0.2	1.000
1984			3	3	.500	4.08	38	0	0	75	83	21	54	0	3	3	3	0	0	0	–	7	10	3	0	0.5	.850
1985			1	0	1.000	1.93	9	0	0	18.2	14	3	9	0	1	0	0	0	0	0	–	1	3	0	0	0.4	1.000
1986	2 teams					KC A (10G 0-1)				SEA A (36G 3-3)																	
"	total		3	4	.429	3.79	46	1	0	97.1	98	25	72	0	3	3	5	0	0	0	–	12	12	3	1	0.6	.889
1987	2 teams					SEA A (6G 0-0)				CLE A (20G 2-3)																	
"	total		2	3	.400	5.04	26	0	0	50	48	12	38	0	2	3	2	0	0	0	–	4	8	3	0	0.6	.800
1988	DET	A	1	0	1.000	5.06	5	0	0	5.1	6	2	6	0	1	0	0	0	0	0	–	2	0	1	0	0.4	1.000
1989	BAL	A	0	0	–	6.35	8	0	0	11.1	13	0	13	0	0	0	1	0	0	0	–	3	0	0	0	0.8	1.000
7 yrs.			12	11	.522	4.28	145	1	0	288.1	291	80	212	0	12	10	11	0	0	0	–	28	40	9	2	0.5	.883

LEAGUE CHAMPIONSHIP SERIES

| 1984 | KC | A | 0 | 0 | – | 10.13 | 1 | 0 | 0 | 2.2 | 6 | 1 | 2 | 0 | 0 | 0 | 0 | 0 | 0 | 0 | – | 0 | 0 | 0 | 0 | 0.0 | – |

Harry Hulihan

HULIHAN, HARRY JOSEPH
B. Apr. 18, 1899, Rutland, Vt. D. Sept. 11, 1980, Rutland, Vt.   BR TL 5'11" 170 lbs.

| 1922 | BOS | N | 2 | 3 | .400 | 3.15 | 7 | 6 | 2 | 40 | 40 | 26 | 16 | 0 | 0 | 0 | 0 | 13 | 2 | 0 | .154 | 0 | 6 | 1 | 0 | 1.0 | .857 |

Jim Hulvey

HULVEY, JAMES HENSEL
B. July 18, 1897, Mount Sidney, Va. D. Apr. 9, 1982, Mount Sidney, Va.   BB TR 6' 180 lbs.

| 1923 | PHI | A | 0 | 1 | .000 | 7.71 | 1 | 1 | 0 | 7 | 10 | 2 | 2 | 0 | 0 | 0 | 0 | 2 | 1 | 0 | .500 | 0 | 2 | 0 | 0 | 2.0 | 1.000 |

Tom Hume

HUME, THOMAS HUBERT
B. Mar. 29, 1953, Cincinnati, Ohio   BR TR 6'1" 185 lbs.

1977	CIN	N	3	3	.500	7.12	14	5	0	43	54	17	22	0	1	0	0	10	2	0	.200	1	6	0	0	0.5	1.000
1978			8	11	.421	4.14	42	23	3	174	198	50	90	0	2	0	1	45	3	0	.067	8	30	1	1	0.9	.974
1979			10	9	.526	2.76	57	12	2	163	162	33	80	0	5	5	17	46	8	0	.174	6	27	2	1	0.6	.943
1980			9	10	.474	2.56	78	0	0	137	121	38	68	0	9	10	25	16	3	0	.188	9	32	0	3	0.5	1.000
1981			9	4	.692	3.44	51	0	0	68	63	31	27	0	9	4	13	4	0	0	.000	2	12	0	0	0.3	1.000
1982			2	6	.250	3.11	46	0	0	63.2	57	21	22	0	2	6	17	5	0	0	.000	3	9	1	0	0.3	.923
1983			3	5	.375	4.77	48	0	0	66	66	41	34	0	3	5	5	5	0	0	.000	3	14	1	3	0.4	.944
1984			4	13	.235	5.64	54	8	0	113.1	142	41	59	0	3	8	3	22	3	0	.136	14	17	0	1	0.6	1.000
1985			3	5	.375	3.26	56	0	0	80	65	35	50	0	3	5	3	5	0	0	.000	4	12	1	1	0.3	.941
1986	PHI	N	4	1	.800	2.77	48	1	0	94.1	89	34	51	0	3	1	4	11	0	0	.000	8	19	1	1	0.6	.964
1987	2 teams					PHI N (38G 1-4)				CIN N (11G 1-0)																	
"	total		2	4	.333	5.36	49	6	0	84	89	43	33	0	1	1	0	15	3	0	.200	2	17	0	0	0.4	1.000
11 yrs.			57	71	.445	3.85	543	55	5	1086.1	1106	384	536	0	41	46	92	184	22	1	.120	60	195	7	11	0.5	.973

LEAGUE CHAMPIONSHIP SERIES

| 1979 | CIN | N | 0 | 1 | .000 | 6.75 | 3 | 0 | 0 | 4 | 6 | 0 | 2 | 0 | 0 | 1 | 0 | 1 | 0 | 0 | .000 | 0 | 2 | 0 | 0 | 0.7 | 1.000 |

Bill Humphrey

HUMPHREY, BYRON WILLIAM
B. June 17, 1911, Vienna, Mo.   BR TR 6' 180 lbs.

| 1938 | BOS | A | 0 | 0 | – | 9.00 | 2 | 0 | 0 | 2 | 5 | 1 | 0 | 0 | 0 | 0 | 0 | 0 | 0 | 0 | – | 0 | 0 | 0 | 0 | 0.0 | – |

Bob Humphreys

HUMPHREYS, ROBERT WILLIAM
B. Aug. 18, 1935, Covington, Va.   BR TR 5'11" 165 lbs.

1962	DET	A	0	1	.000	7.20	4	0	0	5	8	2	3	0	0	1	1	0	0	0	–	1	1	0	0	0.5	1.000
1963	STL	N	0	1	.000	5.06	9	0	0	10.2	11	7	8	0	0	1	0	0	0	0	–	0	2	0	0	0.2	1.000
1964			2	0	1.000	2.53	28	0	0	42.2	32	15	36	0	2	0	2	4	1	0	.250	3	5	0	1	0.3	1.000
1965	CHI	N	2	0	1.000	3.15	41	0	0	65.2	59	27	38	0	2	0	0	3	0	0	.000	2	8	0	0	0.2	1.000
1966	WAS	A	7	3	.700	2.82	58	1	0	111.2	91	28	88	0	6	3	3	12	2	0	.167	8	13	0	2	0.4	1.000
1967			6	2	.750	4.17	48	2	0	105.2	93	41	54	0	5	1	4	15	2	0	.133	7	11	2	2	0.4	.900
1968			5	7	.417	3.69	56	0	0	92.2	78	30	56	0	5	7	2	5	2	0	.400	8	16	0	2	0.4	1.000
1969			3	3	.500	3.05	24	0	0	79.2	69	38	43	0	3	3	5	13	1	0	.077	1	16	1	0	0.4	.944
1970	2 teams					WAS A (5G 0-0)				MIL A (23G 2-4)																	
"	total		2	4	.333	2.92	28	1	0	52.1	41	31	38	0	2	4	3	9	0	0	.000	5	6	0	1	0.4	1.000
9 yrs.			27	21	.563	3.36	319	4	0	566	482	219	364	0	25	20	20	61	8	0	.131	35	78	3	8	0.4	.974

WORLD SERIES

| 1964 | STL | N | 0 | 0 | – | 0.00 | 1 | 0 | 0 | 1 | 0 | 0 | 1 | 0 | 0 | 0 | 0 | 0 | 0 | 0 | – | 0 | 0 | 0 | 0 | 0.0 | – |

Bert Humphries

HUMPHRIES, ALBERT
B. Sept. 26, 1880, California, Pa. D. Sept. 21, 1945, Orlando, Fla.   BR TR 5'11½" 182 lbs.

1910	PHI	N				4.66	5	0	0	9.2	13	3	3	0	0	0	1	2	0	0	.000	0	4	0	1	0.8	1.000
1911	2 teams					PHI N (11G 3-1)				CIN N (14G 4-3)																	
"	total		7	4	.636	3.06	25	12	5	106	118	28	29	0	0	1	1	31	6	0	.194	4	29	1	1	1.4	.971
1912	CIN	N	9	11	.450	3.23	30	15	9	158.2	162	36	58	1	4	3	2	51	7	0	.137	6	33	3	1	1.4	.929
1913	CHI	N	16	4	.800	2.69	28	20	13	181	169	24	61	2	2	1	0	62	12	0	.194	8	37	4	1	1.8	.918
1914			10	11	.476	2.68	34	22	8	171	162	37	62	4	2	2	0	55	13	0	.236	10	55	2	1	2.0	.970
1915			8	13	.381	2.31	31	22	10	171.2	183	23	45	4	1	1	2	46	8	0	.174	4	38	4	4	1.5	.913
6 yrs.			50	43	.538	2.79	153	91	45	798	807	151	258	9	9	8	6	247	46	0	.186	32	196	14	9	1.6	.942

Year	Team		W	L	PCT	ERA	G	GS	CG	IP	H	BB	SO	ShO	Relief Pitching W	L	SV	Batting AB	H	HR	BA	PO	A	E	DP	TC/G	FA

John Humphries

HUMPHRIES, JOHN WILLIAM
B. June 23, 1915, Clifton Forge, Va. D. June 24, 1965, New Orleans, La.
BR TR 6'1" 185 lbs.

Year	Team		W	L	PCT	ERA	G	GS	CG	IP	H	BB	SO	ShO	W	L	SV	AB	H	HR	BA	PO	A	E	DP	TC/G	FA
1938	CLE	A	9	8	.529	5.23	45	6	1	103.1	105	63	56	0	8	3	6	29	3	0	.103	3	15	2	1	0.4	.900
1939			2	4	.333	8.26	15	1	0	28.1	30	32	12	0	2	3	2	7	0	0	.000	1	4	1	0	0.4	.833
1940			0	2	.000	8.29	19	1	1	33.2	35	29	17	0	0	1	1	6	0	0	.000	0	4	1	0	0.3	.800
1941	CHI	A	4	2	.667	1.84	14	6	4	73.1	63	22	25	4	0	0	1	23	2	0	.087	4	7	0	1	0.8	1.000
1942			12	12	.500	2.68	28	28	17	228.1	227	59	71	2	0	0	0	80	18	0	.225	11	41	2	1	1.9	.963
1943			11	11	.500	3.30	28	27	8	188.1	198	54	51	2	0	0	0	69	20	0	.290	6	36	3	1	1.6	.933
1944			8	10	.444	3.67	30	20	8	169	170	57	42	0	2	1	1	53	10	0	.189	3	22	2	0	0.9	.926
1945			6	14	.300	4.24	22	21	10	153	172	48	33	1	0	0	1	54	8	0	.148	3	19	6	0	1.3	.786
1946	PHI	N	0	0	–	4.01	10	1	0	24.2	24	9	10	0	0	0	0	8	2	0	.250	0	0	0	0	0.0	–
9 yrs.			52	63	.452	3.78	211	111	49	1002	1024	373	317	9	12	8	12	329	63	0	.191	31	148	17	4	0.9	.913

Ben Hunt

HUNT, BENJAMIN FRANKLIN (Highpockets)
B. 1888, Eufaula, Okla.
BL TL 6'5" 190 lbs.

Year	Team		W	L	PCT	ERA	G	GS	CG	IP	H	BB	SO	ShO	W	L	SV	AB	H	HR	BA	PO	A	E	DP	TC/G	FA
1910	BOS	A	2	3	.400	4.05	7	7	3	46.2	45	20	19	0	0	0	0	18	1	0	.056	1	14	2	0	2.4	.882
1913	STL	N	0	1	.000	3.38	2	1	0	8	6	9	6	0	0	0	0	2	0	0	.000	1	4	0	0	2.5	1.000
2 yrs.			2	4	.333	3.95	9	8	3	54.2	51	29	25	0	0	0	0	20	1	0	.050	2	18	2	0	2.4	.909

Ken Hunt

HUNT, KENNETH RAYMOND
B. Dec. 14, 1938, Ogden, Utah
BR TR 6'4" 200 lbs.

Year	Team		W	L	PCT	ERA	G	GS	CG	IP	H	BB	SO	ShO	W	L	SV	AB	H	HR	BA	PO	A	E	DP	TC/G	FA
1961	CIN	N	9	10	.474	3.96	29	22	4	136.1	130	66	75	0	0	0	0	39	7	0	.179	10	19	5	2	1.2	.853

WORLD SERIES

Year	Team		W	L	PCT	ERA	G	GS	CG	IP	H	BB	SO	ShO	W	L	SV	AB	H	HR	BA	PO	A	E	DP	TC/G	FA
1961	CIN	N	0	0	–	0.00	1	0	0	1	0	1	1	0	0	0	0	0	0	0	–	0	1	0	0	1.0	1.000

Catfish Hunter

HUNTER, JAMES AUGUSTUS
B. Apr. 8, 1946, Hertford, N. C.
Hall of Fame 1987.
BR TR 6' 190 lbs.

Year	Team		W	L	PCT	ERA	G	GS	CG	IP	H	BB	SO	ShO	W	L	SV	AB	H	HR	BA	PO	A	E	DP	TC/G	FA
1965	KC	A	8	8	.500	4.26	32	20	3	133	124	46	82	2	1	0	0	40	6	0	.150	4	16	2	1	0.7	.909
1966			9	11	.450	4.02	30	25	4	176.2	158	64	103	0	0	0	0	59	9	0	.153	10	14	3	1	0.9	.889
1967			13	17	.433	2.81	35	35	13	259.2	209	84	196	5	0	0	0	92	18	2	.196	15	16	1	1	0.9	.969
1968	OAK	A	13	13	.500	3.35	36	34	11	234	210	69	172	2	0	0	1	82	19	1	.232	16	20	4	0	1.1	.900
1969			12	15	.444	3.35	38	35	10	247	210	85	150	3	0	0	0	85	19	1	.224	17	32	1	4	1.3	1.000
1970			18	14	.563	3.81	40	40	9	262	253	74	178	1	0	0	0	90	18	1	.200	17	24	1	3	1.1	.976
1971			21	11	.656	2.96	37	37	16	274	225	80	181	4	0	0	0	103	36	1	.350	15	26	0	1	1.1	1.000
1972			21	7	.750	2.04	38	37	16	295	200	70	191	5	1	0	0	105	23	0	.219	23	30	2	1	1.4	.964
1973			21	5	.808	3.34	36	36	11	256.1	222	69	124	3	0	0	0	1	1	0	1.000	11	24	1	0	1.0	.972
1974			25	12	.676	2.49	41	41	23	318	268	46	143	6	0	0	0	0	0	0	–	25	37	3	1	1.3	.945
1975	NY	A	23	14	.622	2.58	39	39	30	328	248	83	177	7	0	0	0	0	0	0	–	23	26	3	0	1.3	.942
1976			17	15	.531	3.53	36	36	21	298.2	268	68	173	2	0	0	0	1	0	0	.000	24	30	2	2	1.6	.964
1977			9	9	.500	4.72	22	22	8	143	137	47	52	1	0	0	0	0	0	0	–	4	11	0	1	0.7	1.000
1978			12	6	.667	3.58	21	20	5	118	98	35	56	1	0	0	0	0	0	0	–	11	13	0	1	1.1	1.000
1979			2	9	.182	5.31	21	19	1	105	128	34	34	0	0	0	0	0	0	0	–	10	10	1	0	1.1	.952
15 yrs.			224	166	.574	3.26	500	476	181	3448.1	2958	954	2012	42	2	0	1	658	149	6	.226	225	319	23	16	1.1	.959

LEAGUE CHAMPIONSHIP SERIES

Year	Team		W	L	PCT	ERA	G	GS	CG	IP	H	BB	SO	ShO	W	L	SV	AB	H	HR	BA	PO	A	E	DP	TC/G	FA
1971	OAK	A	0	1	.000	5.63	1	1	0	8	7	2	6	0	0	0	0	3	0	0	.000	0	0	0	0	0.0	–
1972			0	0	–	1.17	2	2	0	15.1	10	5	9	0	0	0	0	6	1	0	.167	0	1	0	0	0.5	1.000
1973			2	0	1.000	1.65	2	2	1	16.1	12	5	6	0	0	0	0	0	0	0	–	3	2	0	0	2.5	1.000
1974			1	1	.500	4.63	2	2	0	11.2	11	2	6	0	0	0	0	0	0	0	–	0	3	0	0	1.5	1.000
1976	NY	A	1	1	.500	4.50	2	2	1	12	10	3	5	0	0	0	0	0	0	0	–	0	1	0	0	1.0	1.000
1978			0	0	–	4.50	1	1	0	6	7	3	5	0	0	0	0	0	0	0	–	1	0	0	0	1.0	1.000
6 yrs.			4	3	.571	3.25	10	10	3	69.1	57	18	37	0	0	0	0	9	1	0	.111	4	6	0	0	1.0	1.000

WORLD SERIES

Year	Team		W	L	PCT	ERA	G	GS	CG	IP	H	BB	SO	ShO	W	L	SV	AB	H	HR	BA	PO	A	E	DP	TC/G	FA
1972	OAK	A	2	0	1.000	2.81	3	2	0	16	12	6	11	0	0	0	0	5	1	0	.200	0	3	1	0	1.3	.750
1973			1	0	1.000	2.03	2	2	0	13.1	11	4	6	0	0	0	0	5	0	0	.000	1	2	1	0	2.0	.750
1974			1	0	1.000	1.17	2	1	1	7.2	5	2	5	0	0	0	1	2	0	0	.000	0	1	0	0	1.0	1.000
1976	NY	A	0	1	.000	3.12	1	1	1	8.2	10	4	5	0	0	0	0	0	0	0	–	0	1	0	0	0.5	1.000
1977			0	1	.000	10.38	2	1	0	4.1	6	1	1	0	0	0	0	0	0	0	–	2	0	0	0	1.0	1.000
1978			1	1	.500	4.15	2	2	0	13	13	1	5	0	0	0	0	2	0	0	.000	1	0	0	0	0.5	1.000
6 yrs.			5	3	.625	3.29	12	9	1	63	57	17	33	0	0	0	1	12	1	0	.083	5	7	2	0	1.2	.857
	8th						7th	6th		10th	7th																

George Hunter

HUNTER, GEORGE HENRY
Brother of Bill Hunter.
B. July 8, 1887, Buffalo, N. Y. D. Jan. 11, 1968, Harrisburg, Pa.
BB TL 5'8½" 165 lbs.

Year	Team		W	L	PCT	ERA	G	GS	CG	IP	H	BB	SO	ShO	W	L	SV	AB	H	HR	BA	PO	A	E	DP	TC/G	FA
1909	BKN	N	4	10	.286	2.46	16	13	10	113.1	104	38	43	0	1	0	2	0			*		5	31	3	2	2.4	.923

Lem Hunter

HUNTER, ROBERT LEMUEL
B. Jan. 16, 1863, Warren, Ohio D. Nov. 9, 1956, West Lafayette, Ohio
BR TL 6'2" 180 lbs.

Year	Team		W	L	PCT	ERA	G	GS	CG	IP	H	BB	SO	ShO	W	L	SV	AB	H	HR	BA	PO	A	E	DP	TC/G	FA
1883	CLE	N	0	0	–	1.42	1	0	0	6.1	10	2	4	0	0	0	0	4	1	0	.250	0	1	0	0	1.0	1.000

Willard Hunter

HUNTER, WILLARD MITCHELL
B. Mar. 8, 1934, Newark, N. J.
BR TL 6'2" 180 lbs.

Year	Team		W	L	PCT	ERA	G	GS	CG	IP	H	BB	SO	ShO	W	L	SV	AB	H	HR	BA	PO	A	E	DP	TC/G	FA
1962	2 teams	LA N (1G 0–0)				NY N (27G 1–6)																					
"	total		1	6	.143	6.65	28	6	1	65	73	38	41	0	1	0	0	13	3	0	.231	5	7	1	0	0.5	.923
1964	NY	N	3	3	.500	4.41	41	0	0	49	54	9	22	0	3	3	5	1	1	0	1.000	2	8	0	1	0.2	1.000
2 yrs.			4	9	.308	5.68	69	6	1	114	127	47	63	0	4	3	5	14	4	0	.286	7	15	1	1	0.3	.957

Year	Team	W	L	PCT	ERA	G	GS	CG	IP	H	BB	SO	ShO	W	L	SV	AB	H	HR	BA	PO	A	E	DP	TC/G	FA

Walter Huntzinger

HUNTZINGER, WALTER HENRY (Shakes)
B. Feb. 6, 1899, Pottsville, Pa. D. Aug. 11, 1981, Upper Darby, Pa.   BR TR 6'   150 lbs.

Year	Team	W	L	PCT	ERA	G	GS	CG	IP	H	BB	SO	ShO	W	L	SV	AB	H	HR	BA	PO	A	E	DP	TC/G	FA
1923	NY N	0	1	.000	7.88	2	1	0	8	9	1	2	0	0	1	0	2	0	0	.000	0	1	0	0	0.5	1.000
1924		1	1	.500	4.45	12	2	0	32.1	41	9	6	0	0	0	1	8	4	0	.500	0	7	1	0	0.7	.875
1925		5	1	.833	3.50	26	1	0	64.1	68	17	19	0	5	1	0	11	1	0	.091	1	11	0	1	0.5	1.000
1926	2 teams	STL N		(9G 0–4)		CHI N		(11G 1–1)																		
"	total	1	5	.167	2.73	20	4	2	62.2	61	22	13	0	1	2	2	15	1	0	.067	2	20	1	1	1.2	.957
4 yrs.		7	8	.467	3.60	60	8	2	167.1	179	49	40	0	6	4	3	36	6	0	.167	3	39	2	2	0.7	.955

Tom Hurd

HURD, THOMAS CARR (Whitey)
B. May 27, 1924, Danville, Va. D. Sept. 5, 1982, Waterloo, Iowa   BR TR 5'9"   155 lbs.

Year	Team	W	L	PCT	ERA	G	GS	CG	IP	H	BB	SO	ShO	W	L	SV	AB	H	HR	BA	PO	A	E	DP	TC/G	FA
1954	BOS A	2	0	1.000	3.03	16	0	0	29.2	21	12	14	0	2	0	0	3	1	0	.333	3	6	0	0	0.6	1.000
1955		8	6	.571	3.01	43	0	0	80.2	72	38	48	0	8	6	5	14	1	0	.071	4	12	0	1	0.4	1.000
1956		3	4	.429	5.33	40	0	0	76	84	47	34	0	3	4	5	12	6	0	.500	3	9	0	0	0.3	1.000
3 yrs.		13	10	.565	3.96	99	0	0	186.1	177	97	96	0	13	10	11	29	8	0	.276	10	27	0	1	0.4	1.000

Bruce Hurst

HURST, BRUCE VEE
B. Mar. 24, 1958, St. George, Utah   BL TL 6'4"   200 lbs.

Year	Team	W	L	PCT	ERA	G	GS	CG	IP	H	BB	SO	ShO	W	L	SV	AB	H	HR	BA	PO	A	E	DP	TC/G	FA
1980	BOS A	2	2	.500	9.00	12	7	0	31	39	16	16	0	0	0	0	0	0	0	–	1	4	0	0	0.4	1.000
1981		2	0	1.000	4.30	5	5	0	23	23	12	11	0	0	0	0	0	0	0	–	0	2	0	0	0.4	1.000
1982		3	7	.300	5.77	28	19	0	117	161	40	53	0	0	1	0	0	0	0	–	6	22	1	1	1.0	.966
1983		12	12	.500	4.09	33	32	6	211.1	241	62	115	2	0	0	0	0	0	0	–	12	34	2	2	1.5	.958
1984		12	12	.500	3.92	33	33	9	218	232	88	136	2	0	0	0	0	0	0	–	10	30	0	1	1.2	1.000
1985		11	13	.458	4.51	35	31	6	229.1	243	70	189	1	0	2	0	0	0	0	–	11	32	3	0	1.3	.935
1986		13	8	.619	2.99	25	25	11	174.1	169	50	167	4	0	0	0	0	0	0	–	7	18	2	2	1.1	.926
1987		15	13	.536	4.41	33	33	15	238.2	239	76	190	3	0	0	0	0	0	0	–	12	34	3	2	1.5	.939
1988		18	6	.750	3.66	33	32	7	216.2	222	65	166	1	0	0	0	0	0	0	–	7	31	0	2	1.2	1.000
1989	SD N	15	11	.577	2.69	33	33	10	244.2	214	66	179	2	0	0	0	70	5	0	.071	8	42	0	2	1.5	1.000
10 yrs.		103	84	.551	4.01	270	250	64	1704	1783	545	1222	15	0	3	0	70	5	0	.071	74	249	11	10	1.2	.967

LEAGUE CHAMPIONSHIP SERIES

Year	Team	W	L	PCT	ERA	G	GS	CG	IP	H	BB	SO	ShO	W	L	SV	AB	H	HR	BA	PO	A	E	DP	TC/G	FA
1986	BOS A	1	0	1.000	2.40	2	2	1	15	18	1	8	0	0	0	0	0	0	0	–	1	2	0	0	1.5	1.000
1988		0	2	.000	2.77	2	2	1	13	10	5	12	0	0	0	0	0	0	0	–	0	4	0	0	2.0	1.000
2 yrs.		1	2	.333	2.57	4	4	2	28	28	6	20	0	0	0	0	0	0	0	–	1	6	0	0	1.8	1.000

WORLD SERIES

Year	Team	W	L	PCT	ERA	G	GS	CG	IP	H	BB	SO	ShO	W	L	SV	AB	H	HR	BA	PO	A	E	DP	TC/G	FA
1986	BOS A	2	0	1.000	1.96	3	3	1	23	18	6	17	0	0	0	0	3	0	0	.000	1	3	0	0	1.3	1.000

Bill Husted

HUSTED, WILLIAM J.
B. Oct. 11, 1866, Gloucester, N. J. D. May 17, 1941, Gloucester, N. J.

Year	Team	W	L	PCT	ERA	G	GS	CG	IP	H	BB	SO	ShO	W	L	SV	AB	H	HR	BA	PO	A	E	DP	TC/G	FA
1890	PHI P	5	12	.294	4.88	18	17	12	129	148	67	33	0	0	0	0	56	6	0	.107	3	24	5	1	1.8	.844

Bert Husting

HUSTING, BERTHOLD JUNEAU (Pete)
B. Mar. 6, 1878, Fond du Lac, Wis. D. Sept. 3, 1948, Milwaukee, Wis.   BR TR

Year	Team	W	L	PCT	ERA	G	GS	CG	IP	H	BB	SO	ShO	W	L	SV	AB	H	HR	BA	PO	A	E	DP	TC/G	FA
1900	PIT N	0	0	–	5.63	2	2	0	8	10	5	7	0	0	0	0	3	0	0	.000	1	4	0	0	2.5	1.000
1901	MIL A	10	15	.400	4.27	34	26	19	217.1	234	95	67	0	1	1	1	94	19	1	.202	16	82	8	4	3.1	.925
1902	2 teams	BOS A		(1G 0–1)		PHI A		(32G 14–5)																		
"	total	14	6	.700	3.99	33	28	18	212	255	99	48	1	1	0	0	86	14	0	.163	20	74	12	3	3.2	.887
3 yrs.		24	21	.533	4.16	69	54	37	437.1	499	199	122	1	2	1	1	183	33	1	.180	37	160	20	7	3.1	.908

Johnny Hutchings

HUTCHINGS, JOHN RICHARD JOSEPH
B. Apr. 14, 1916, Chicago, Ill.
D. Apr. 27, 1963, Indianapolis, Ind.   BB TR 6'2"   250 lbs.
BR 1944,1946

Year	Team	W	L	PCT	ERA	G	GS	CG	IP	H	BB	SO	ShO	W	L	SV	AB	H	HR	BA	PO	A	E	DP	TC/G	FA
1940	CIN N	2	1	.667	3.50	19	4	0	54	53	18	18	0	2	0	0	13	2	0	.154	1	6	0	0	0.4	1.000
1941	2 teams	CIN N		(8G 0–0)		BOS N		(36G 1–6)																		
"	total	1	6	.143	4.13	44	7	1	106.2	122	26	41	0	0	2	0	27	4	0	.148	2	23	1	5	0.6	.962
1942	BOS N	1	0	1.000	4.39	20	3	0	65.2	66	34	27	0	0	0	0	20	1	0	.050	3	10	1	1	0.7	.929
1944		1	4	.200	3.97	14	7	1	56.2	55	26	26	0	1	1	0	15	1	0	.067	1	8	0	1	0.6	1.000
1945		7	6	.538	3.75	57	12	3	185	173	75	99	2	3	3	3	54	13	0	.241	7	36	3	0	0.8	.935
1946		0	1	.000	9.00	1	1	0	3	5	1	1	0	0	0	0	1	0	0	.000	0	0	0	0	0.0	–
6 yrs.		12	18	.400	3.96	155	34	5	471	474	180	212	2	5	6	3	130	21	0	.162	14	83	5	8	0.7	.951

WORLD SERIES

Year	Team	W	L	PCT	ERA	G	GS	CG	IP	H	BB	SO	ShO	W	L	SV	AB	H	HR	BA	PO	A	E	DP	TC/G	FA
1940	CIN N	0	0	–	9.00	1	0	0	1	2	1	0	0	0	0	0	0	0	0	–	0	1	0	0	1.0	1.000

Bill Hutchinson

HUTCHINSON, WILLIAM FORREST (Wild Bill)
B. Dec. 17, 1859, New Haven, Conn. D. Mar. 19, 1926, Kansas City, Mo.   BR TR 5'9"   175 lbs.

Year	Team	W	L	PCT	ERA	G	GS	CG	IP	H	BB	SO	ShO	W	L	SV	AB	H	HR	BA	PO	A	E	DP	TC/G	FA
1884	KC U	1	1	.500	2.65	2	2	2	17	14	1	5	0	0	0	0	8	2	0	.250	1	12	0	0	6.5	1.000
1889	CHI N	16	17	.485	3.54	37	36	33	318	306	117	136	3	0	0	0	133	21	1	.158	18	86	13	3	3.2	.889
1890		42	25	.627	2.70	71	66	65	603	505	199	289	5	1	1	2	261	53	2	.203	44	128	14	5	2.6	.925
1891		44	19	.698	2.81	66	56	56	561	508	178	261	4	7	0	1	243	45	2	.185	22	103	13	0	2.1	.906
1892		37	36	.507	2.74	75	71	67	627	572	187	316	5	1	2	0	263	57	1	.217	21	156	13	4	2.5	.932
1893		16	24	.400	4.75	44	40	38	348.1	420	156	80	2	0	1	0	162	41	0	.253	13	62	7	3	1.9	.915
1894		14	16	.467	6.06	36	34	28	277.2	373	140	59	0	0	0	0	136	42	6	.309	10	45	5	1	1.7	.917
1895		13	21	.382	4.73	38	35	30	291	371	129	85	0	1	0	0	126	25	0	.198	9	65	8	1	2.2	.902
1897	STL N	1	4	.200	6.08	6	5	2	40	55	22	5	0	0	0	0	18	5	0	.278	0	7	1	0	1.3	.875
9 yrs.		184	163	.530	3.58	375	347	321	3083	3124	1129	1236	21	10	4	3	1350	291	12	.216	138	664	74	17	2.3	.916

Fred Hutchinson

HUTCHINSON, FREDERICK CHARLES
B. Aug. 12, 1919, Seattle, Wash. D. Nov. 12, 1964, Bradenton, Fla.   BL TR 6'2"   190 lbs.
Manager 1952-54, 1956-64.

Year	Team	W	L	PCT	ERA	G	GS	CG	IP	H	BB	SO	ShO	W	L	SV	AB	H	HR	BA	PO	A	E	DP	TC/G	FA
1939	DET A	3	6	.333	5.21	13	12	3	84.2	95	51	22	0	0	0	0	34	13	0	.382	6	13	0	1	1.5	1.000
1940		3	7	.300	5.68	17	10	1	76	85	26	32	0	1	2	0	30	8	0	.267	2	16	2	1	1.2	.900

Year	Team	W	L	PCT	ERA	G	GS	CG	IP	H	BB	SO	ShO	Relief Pitching W	L	SV	Batting AB	H	HR	BA	PO	A	E	DP	TC/G	FA

Fred Hutchinson *continued*

Year	Team	W	L	PCT	ERA	G	GS	CG	IP	H	BB	SO	ShO	W	L	SV	AB	H	HR	BA	PO	A	E	DP	TC/G	FA
1941		0	0		0.00	0	0	0	0	0	0	0	0	0	0	0	2	0	0	.000	0	0	0	0	0.0	
1946		14	11	.560	3.09	28	26	16	207	184	66	138	3	0	0	2	89	28	0	.315	11	47	1	3	2.1	.983
1947		18	10	.643	3.03	33	25	18	219.2	211	61	113	3	2	1	2	106	32	2	.302	15	40	1	1	1.7	.982
1948		13	11	.542	4.32	33	28	15	221	223	48	92	0	0	0	0	112	23	1	.205	19	45	0	5	1.9	1.000
1949		15	7	.682	2.96	33	21	9	188.2	167	52	54	4	3	2	1	73	18	0	.247	18	39	1	5	1.8	.983
1950		17	8	.680	3.96	39	26	10	231.2	269	48	71	1	4	1	0	95	31	0	.326	17	50	4	6	1.8	.944
1951		10	10	.500	3.68	31	20	9	188.1	204	27	53	2	4	1	2	85	16	0	.188	17	45	4	1	2.1	.939
1952		2	1	.667	3.38	12	1	0	37.1	48	9	12	0	2	0	0	18	1	0	.056	1	15	0	1	1.3	1.000
1953		0	0	—	2.79	3	0	0	9.2	9	0	4	0	0	0	0	6	1	1	.167	2	0	0	0	0.7	1.000
11 yrs.		95	71	.572	3.73	242	169	81	1464	1487	388	591	13	16	7	7	*				108	310	13	24	1.8	.970

WORLD SERIES

Year	Team		W	L	PCT	ERA	G	GS	CG	IP	H	BB	SO	ShO	W	L	SV	AB	H	HR	BA	PO	A	E	DP	TC/G	FA
1940	DET	A	0	0	—	9.00	1	0	0	1	1	1	1	0	0	0	0	0	0	0	—	0	0	0	0	0.0	—

Ira Hutchinson

HUTCHINSON, IRA KENDALL BR TR 5'10½" 180 lbs.
B. Aug. 31, 1910, Chicago, Ill. D. Aug. 21, 1973, Chicago, Ill.

Year	Team		W	L	PCT	ERA	G	GS	CG	IP	H	BB	SO	ShO	W	L	SV	AB	H	HR	BA	PO	A	E	DP	TC/G	FA
1933	CHI	A	0	0		13.50	1	1	0	4	7	3	2	0	0	0	0	2	1	0	.500	0	0	0	0	0.0	
1937	BOS	N	4	6	.400	3.73	31	8	1	91.2	99	35	29	0	4	0	0	26	3	0	.115	5	24	1	1	1.0	.967
1938			9	8	.529	2.74	36	12	4	151	150	61	38	1	5	3	4	52	9	0	.173	14	33	1	4	1.3	.979
1939	BKN	N	5	2	.714	4.34	41	1	0	105.2	103	51	46	0	5	2	1	27	1	0	.037	3	28	0	2	0.8	1.000
1940	STL	N	4	2	.667	3.13	20	2	1	63.1	68	19	19	0	2	2	1	18	4	0	.222	2	14	1	1	0.9	.941
1941			1	5	.167	3.86	29	0	0	46.2	32	19	19	0	1	5	5	8	2	0	.250	2	10	2	3	0.5	.857
1944	BOS	N	9	7	.563	4.21	40	8	1	119.2	136	53	22	1	6	4	1	29	4	0	.138	3	29	0	4	0.8	1.000
1945			2	3	.400	5.02	11	0	0	28.2	33	8	4	0	2	3	1	9	0	0	.000	0	9	0	1	0.8	1.000
8 yrs.			34	33	.507	3.76	209	32	7	610.2	628	249	179	2	25	19	13	171	24	0	.140	29	147	5	16	0.9	.972

Herb Hutson

HUTSON, GEORGE HERBERT BR TR 6'2" 205 lbs.
B. July 17, 1949, Savannah, Ga.

Year	Team		W	L	PCT	ERA	G	GS	CG	IP	H	BB	SO	ShO	W	L	SV	AB	H	HR	BA	PO	A	E	DP	TC/G	FA
1974	CHI	N	0	2	.000	3.41	20	2	0	29	24	15	22	0	0	0	0	0	0	0	.000	1	2	0	0	0.2	1.000

Tom Hutton

HUTTON, THOMAS GEORGE BL TL 5'11" 180 lbs.
B. Apr. 20, 1946, Los Angeles, Calif.

Year	Team		W	L	PCT	ERA	G	GS	CG	IP	H	BB	SO	ShO	W	L	SV	AB	H	HR	BA	PO	A	E	DP	TC/G	FA
1980	MON	N	0	0	—	27.00	1	0	0	1	3	1	1	0	0	0	0	*				0	0	0	0	0.0	—

Dick Hyde

HYDE, RICHARD ELDE BR TR 5'11" 170 lbs.
B. Aug. 3, 1928, Hindsboro, Ill.

Year	Team		W	L	PCT	ERA	G	GS	CG	IP	H	BB	SO	ShO	W	L	SV	AB	H	HR	BA	PO	A	E	DP	TC/G	FA
1955	WAS	A	0	0	—	4.50	3	0	0	2	2	1	1	0	0	0	0	0	0	0	—	0	0	0	0	0.0	
1957			4	3	.571	4.12	52	2	0	109.1	104	56	46	0	4	3	1	18	3	0	.167	5	23	0	3	0.5	1.000
1958			10	3	.769	1.75	53	0	0	103	82	35	49	0	10	3	18	18	0	0	.000	7	25	1	1	0.6	.970
1959			2	5	.286	4.97	37	0	0	54.1	56	27	29	0	2	5	4	6	0	0	.000	3	20	3	0	0.7	.885
1960			0	1	.000	4.15	9	0	0	8.2	11	5	4	0	0	1	0	0	0	0	—	0	1	0	0	0.1	1.000
1961	BAL	A	1	2	.333	5.57	15	0	0	21	18	13	15	0	1	2	0	1	1	0	1.000	1	10	1	1	0.8	.917
6 yrs.			17	14	.548	3.56	169	2	0	298.1	273	137	144	0	17	14	23	43	4	0	.093	16	79	5	5	0.6	.950

Jim Hyndman

HYNDMAN, JAMES WILLIAM
B. 1864, Kingston, Pa. Deceased.

Year	Team		W	L	PCT	ERA	G	GS	CG	IP	H	BB	SO	ShO	W	L	SV	AB	H	HR	BA	PO	A	E	DP	TC/G	FA
1886	PHI	AA	0	1	.000	27.00	1	1	0	2	5	5	1	0	0	0	0	4	0	0	.000	3	1	1	0	5.0	.800

Pat Hynes

HYNES, PATRICK J. TL
B. Mar. 12, 1884, St. Louis, Mo. D. Mar. 12, 1907, St. Louis, Mo.

Year	Team		W	L	PCT	ERA	G	GS	CG	IP	H	BB	SO	ShO	W	L	SV	AB	H	HR	BA	PO	A	E	DP	TC/G	FA
1903	STL	N	0	1	.000	4.00	1	1	1	9	10	6	1	0	0	0	0	3	0	0	.000	1	0	1	0	2.0	.500
1904	STL	A	1	0	1.000	6.23	5	2	1	26	35	7	6	0	0	0	0	254	60	0	.236	1	4	0	0	1.0	1.000
2 yrs.			1	1	.500	5.66	6	3	2	35	45	13	7	0	0	0	0	*				2	4	1	0	1.2	.857

Ham Iburg

IBURG, HERMAN EDWARD BR TR 5'11½" 165 lbs.
B. Oct. 29, 1877, San Francisco, Calif. D. Feb. 11, 1945, San Francisco, Calif.

Year	Team		W	L	PCT	ERA	G	GS	CG	IP	H	BB	SO	ShO	W	L	SV	AB	H	HR	BA	PO	A	E	DP	TC/G	FA
1902	PHI	N	11	18	.379	3.89	30	30	20	236	286	62	106	1	0	0	0	87	12	0	.138	8	59	4	1	2.4	.944

Gary Ignasiak

IGNASIAK, GARY RAYMOND BR TL 5'11" 185 lbs.
B. Sept. 1, 1949, Mt. Clemens, Mich.

Year	Team		W	L	PCT	ERA	G	GS	CG	IP	H	BB	SO	ShO	W	L	SV	AB	H	HR	BA	PO	A	E	DP	TC/G	FA
1973	DET	A	0	0	—	3.60	3	0	0	5	5	3	4	0	0	0	0	0	0	0	—	0	1	0	0	0.3	1.000

Doc Imlay

IMLAY, HARRY MILLER BR TR 5'11" 168 lbs.
B. Jan. 12, 1889, Allentown, N. J. D. Oct. 7, 1948, Bordentown, N. J.

Year	Team		W	L	PCT	ERA	G	GS	CG	IP	H	BB	SO	ShO	W	L	SV	AB	H	HR	BA	PO	A	E	DP	TC/G	FA
1913	PHI	N	0	0	—	7.24	9	0	0	13.2	19	7	7	0	0	0	0	3	0	0	.000	1	5	0	0	0.7	1.000

Bob Ingersoll

INGERSOLL, ROBERT RANDOLPH BR TR 5'11½" 175 lbs.
B. Jan. 8, 1883, Rapid City, S. D. D. Jan. 13, 1927, Minneapolis, Minn.

Year	Team		W	L	PCT	ERA	G	GS	CG	IP	H	BB	SO	ShO	W	L	SV	AB	H	HR	BA	PO	A	E	DP	TC/G	FA
1914	CIN	N	0	0	—	3.00	4	0	0	6	5	5	2	0	0	0	0	1	0	0	1.000	0	1	0	0	0.3	1.000

Bert Inks

INKS, ALBERT PRESTON BL TL 6'3" 175 lbs.
Born Albert Preston Inkstein.
B. Jan. 27, 1871, Ligonier, Ind. D. Oct. 3, 1941, Ligonier, Ind.

Year	Team		W	L	PCT	ERA	G	GS	CG	IP	H	BB	SO	ShO	W	L	SV	AB	H	HR	BA	PO	A	E	DP	TC/G	FA
1891	BKN	N	3	10	.231	4.02	13	13	11	96.1	99	43	47	1	0	0	0	35	10	0	.286	2	18	2	0	1.7	.909
1892	2 teams					BKN N (9G 4–2)				WAS N (3G 1–2)																	
"	total		5	4	.556	4.22	12	11	7	79	77	43	36	1	0	0	0	35	13	0	.371	3	18	4	0	2.1	.840

Year	Team		W	L	PCT	ERA	G	GS	CG	IP	H	BB	SO	ShO	Relief Pitching			Batting			BA	PO	A	E	DP	TC/G	FA
															W	L	SV	AB	H	HR							

Bert Inks *continued*

Year	Team		W	L	PCT	ERA	G	GS	CG	IP	H	BB	SO	ShO	W	L	SV	AB	H	HR	BA	PO	A	E	DP	TC/G	FA
1894	2 teams	BAL N (22G 9–4)				LOU N (8G 2–6)																					
"	total		11	10	.524	5.84	30	22	18	192.2	268	88	38	0	1	0	1	84	30	0	.357	11	33	8	0	1.7	.846
1895	LOU	N	7	20	.259	6.40	28	27	21	205.1	294	78	42	0	0	0	0	84	21	0	.250	5	53	6	0	2.3	.906
1896	2 teams	PHI N (3G 0–1)				CIN N (3G 1–1)																					
"	total		1	2	.333	5.64	6	4	2	30.1	42	14	4	0	0	0	0	12	1	0	.083	2	2	1	0	0.8	.800
5 yrs.			27	46	.370	5.52	89	77	59	603.2	780	266	167	2	1	0	1	250	75	0	.300	23	124	21	0	1.9	.875

Jeff Innis

INNIS, JEFFREY DAVID
B. July 5, 1962, Decatur, Ill.

BR TR 6'1" 170 lbs.

Year	Team		W	L	PCT	ERA	G	GS	CG	IP	H	BB	SO	ShO	W	L	SV	AB	H	HR	BA	PO	A	E	DP	TC/G	FA
1987	NY	N	0	1	.000	3.16	17	1	0	25.2	29	4	28	0	0	1	0	3	0	0	.000	3	2	0	0	0.3	1.000
1988			1	1	.500	1.89	12	0	0	19	19	2	14	0	1	1	0	0	0	0	–	0	0	0	0	0.0	–
1989			0	1	.000	3.18	29	0	0	39.2	38	8	16	0	0	1	0	2	0	0	.000	7	8	1	0	0.6	.938
3 yrs.			1	3	.250	2.88	58	1	0	84.1	86	14	58	0	1	3	0	5	0	0	.000	10	10	1	0	0.4	.952

Dane Iorg

IORG, DANE CHARLES
Brother of Garth Iorg.
B. May 11, 1950, Eureka, Calif.

BL TR 6' 180 lbs.

Year	Team		W	L	PCT	ERA	G	GS	CG	IP	H	BB	SO	ShO	W	L	SV	AB	H	HR	BA	PO	A	E	DP	TC/G	FA
1986	SD	N	0	0	–	6.00	2	0	0	3	5	1	2	0	0	0	0	*				0	0	0	0	0.0	–

Hooks Iott

IOTT, CLARENCE EUGENE
B. Dec. 3, 1919, Mountain Grove, Mo. D. Aug. 17, 1980, St. Petersburg, Fla.

BB TL 6'2" 200 lbs.

Year	Team		W	L	PCT	ERA	G	GS	CG	IP	H	BB	SO	ShO	W	L	SV	AB	H	HR	BA	PO	A	E	DP	TC/G	FA
1941	STL	A	0	0	–	9.00	2	0	0	2	2	1	1	0	0	0	0	0	0	0	–	0	1	0	0	0.5	1.000
1947	2 teams	STL A (4G 0–1)				NY N (20G 3–8)																					
"	total		3	9	.250	7.00	24	9	2	79.2	82	66	52	1	1	5	0	23	3	0	.130	2	13	0	1	0.6	1.000
2 yrs.			3	9	.250	7.05	26	9	2	81.2	84	67	53	1	1	5	0	23	3	0	.130	2	14	0	1	0.6	1.000

Arthur Irwin

IRWIN, ARTHUR ALBERT
Brother of John Irwin.
B. Feb. 14, 1858, Toronto, Ont., Canada D. July 16, 1921, Atlantic Ocean
Manager 1889, 1891-92, 1894-96, 1898-99.

BL TR 5'8½" 158 lbs.

Year	Team		W	L	PCT	ERA	G	GS	CG	IP	H	BB	SO	ShO	W	L	SV	AB	H	HR	BA	PO	A	E	DP	TC/G	FA
1884	PRO	N	0	0	–	3.00	1	0	0	3	5	1	0	0	0	0	0	404	97	2	.240	0	1	0	0	1.0	1.000
1889	PHI	N	0	0	–	0.00	1	0	0	1	1	0	0	0	0	0	0	386	89	0	.231	0	0	0	0	0.0	–
2 yrs.			0	0	–	2.25	2	0	0	4	6	1	0	0	0	0	0	*				0	1	0	0	0.5	1.000

Bill Irwin

IRWIN, WILLIAM FRANKLIN (Phil)
B. Sept. 16, 1859, Neville, Ohio D. Aug. 7, 1933, Ft. Thomas, Ky.

BR TR 6' 195 lbs.

Year	Team		W	L	PCT	ERA	G	GS	CG	IP	H	BB	SO	ShO	W	L	SV	AB	H	HR	BA	PO	A	E	DP	TC/G	FA
1886	CIN	AA	0	2	.000	5.82	2	2	2	17	18	8	6	0	0	0	0	6	0	0	.000	1	5	0	0	3.0	1.000

Frank Isbell

ISBELL, WILLIAM FRANK (Bald Eagle)
B. Aug. 21, 1875, Delevan, N. Y. D. July 15, 1941, Wichita, Kans.

BL TR 5'11" 190 lbs.

Year	Team		W	L	PCT	ERA	G	GS	CG	IP	H	BB	SO	ShO	W	L	SV	AB	H	HR	BA	PO	A	E	DP	TC/G	FA
1898	CHI	N	4	7	.364	3.56	13	9	7	81	86	42	16	0	1	1	0	159	37	0	.233	7	19	6	2	2.5	.813
1901	CHI	A	0	0	–	9.00	1	1	0	1	2	0	0	0	0	0	0	556	143	3	.257	0	1	0	0	1.0	1.000
1902			0	0	–	9.00	1	1	0	1	3	1	1	0	0	0	0	515	130	4	.252	0	3	0	0	3.0	1.000
1906			0	0	–	0.00	1	0	0	2	0	0	2	0	0	0	0	549	153	0	.279	0	0	0	0	0.0	–
1907			0	0	–	0.00	1	0	0	.1	1	0	0	0	0	0	1	486	118	0	.243	0	1	0	1	1.0	1.000
5 yrs.			4	7	.364	3.59	17	10	7	85.1	92	43	19	0	1	1	1	*				7	24	6	3	2.2	.838

Pete Jablonowski

Playing record listed under Pete Appleton

Al Jackson

JACKSON, ALVIN NEIL
B. Dec. 25, 1935, Waco, Tex.

BL TL 5'10" 169 lbs.

Year	Team		W	L	PCT	ERA	G	GS	CG	IP	H	BB	SO	ShO	W	L	SV	AB	H	HR	BA	PO	A	E	DP	TC/G	FA
1959	PIT	N	0	0	–	6.50	8	3	0	18	30	8	13	0	0	0	0	5	1	0	.200	2	2	0	0	0.5	1.000
1961			1	0	1.000	3.42	3	2	1	23.2	20	4	15	0	0	0	0	8	0	0	.000	2	7	0	0	3.0	1.000
1962	NY	N	8	20	.286	4.40	36	33	12	231.1	244	78	118	4	0	0	0	73	5	0	.068	21	59	2	1	2.3	.976
1963			13	17	.433	3.96	37	34	11	227	237	84	142	0	0	0	1	79	16	0	.203	15	46	3	5	1.7	.953
1964			11	16	.407	4.26	40	31	11	213.1	229	60	112	3	2	0	1	72	11	1	.153	23	36	4	2	1.6	.937
1965			8	20	.286	4.34	37	31	7	205.1	217	61	120	3	0	0	1	60	7	0	.117	10	48	3	2	1.6	.951
1966	STL	N	13	15	.464	2.51	36	30	11	232.2	222	45	90	3	0	0	0	74	13	0	.176	16	63	5	4	2.3	.940
1967			9	4	.692	3.95	38	11	1	107	117	29	43	1	4	1	0	31	8	0	.258	10	29	1	2	1.1	.975
1968	NY	N	3	7	.300	3.69	25	9	0	92.2	88	17	59	0	1	1	3	28	7	0	.250	7	17	0	1	1.0	1.000
1969	2 teams	NY N (9G 0–0)				CIN N (33G 1–0)																					
"	total		0	1	1.000	6.81	42	0	0	38.1	45	21	26	0	0	0	3	5	1	0	.200	7	4	2	0	0.3	.846
10 yrs.			67	99	.404	3.98	302	184	54	1389.1	1449	407	738	14	9	3	10	435	69	1	.159	113	311	20	18	1.5	.955

Charlie Jackson

JACKSON, CHARLES BERNARD
B. Aug. 4, 1876, Versailles, Ohio D. Nov. 23, 1957, Scottsbluff, Neb.

TR

Year	Team		W	L	PCT	ERA	G	GS	CG	IP	H	BB	SO	ShO	W	L	SV	AB	H	HR	BA	PO	A	E	DP	TC/G	FA
1905	DET	A	0	2	.000	5.73	2	2	1	11	14	7	3	0	0	0	0	4	1	0	.250	1	2	1	0	2.0	.750

Danny Jackson

JACKSON, DANNY LYNN
B. Jan. 5, 1962, San Antonio, Tex.

BR TL 6' 205 lbs.

Year	Team		W	L	PCT	ERA	G	GS	CG	IP	H	BB	SO	ShO	W	L	SV	AB	H	HR	BA	PO	A	E	DP	TC/G	FA
1983	KC	A	1	1	.500	5.21	4	3	0	19	26	6	9	0	0	0	0	0	0	0	–	2	3	0	0	1.3	1.000
1984			2	6	.250	4.26	15	11	1	76	84	35	40	0	1	0	0	0	0	0	–	6	7	1	2	0.9	.929
1985			14	12	.538	3.42	32	32	4	208	209	76	114	3	0	0	0	0	0	0	–	8	27	3	2	1.2	.921
1986			11	12	.478	3.20	32	27	4	185.2	177	79	115	1	0	0	1	0	0	0	–	14	21	2	1	1.2	.946
1987			9	18	.333	4.02	36	34	11	224	219	109	152	2	0	0	0	0	0	0	–	13	23	2	1	1.1	.947
1988	CIN	N	23	8	.742	2.73	35	35	15	260.2	206	71	161	6	0	0	0	90	13	0	.144	10	52	3	2	1.9	.954

Year	Team	W	L	PCT	ERA	G	GS	CG	IP	H	BB	SO	ShO	Relief Pitching W	L	SV	Batting AB	H	HR	BA	PO	A	E	DP	TC/G	FA

Paul Jaeckel
JAECKEL, PAUL HENRY (Jake)
B. Apr. 1, 1942, East Los Angeles, Calif.   BR TR 5'10" 170 lbs.

| 1964 | CHI N | 1 | 0 | 1.000 | 0.00 | 4 | 0 | 0 | 8 | 4 | 3 | 2 | 0 | 1 | 0 | 1 | 1 | 0 | 0 | .000 | 1 | 1 | 0 | 0 | 0.5 | 1.000 |

Charlie Jaeger
JAEGER, CHARLES THOMAS
B. Apr. 17, 1875, Ottawa, Ill.   D. Sept. 27, 1942, Ottawa, Ill.   BR TR 6'1" 195 lbs.

| 1904 | DET A | 3 | 3 | .500 | 2.57 | 8 | 6 | 5 | 49 | 49 | 15 | 13 | 0 | 0 | 0 | 0 | 17 | 1 | 0 | .059 | 2 | 15 | 2 | 0 | 2.4 | .895 |

Joe Jaeger
JAEGER, JOSEPH PETER (Zip)
B. Mar. 3, 1895, St. Cloud, Minn.   D. Dec. 13, 1963, Hampton, Iowa   BR TR 6'3" 180 lbs.

| 1920 | CHI N | 0 | 0 | — | 12.00 | 2 | 0 | 0 | 3 | 6 | 4 | 0 | 0 | 0 | 0 | 0 | 1 | 0 | 0 | .000 | 0 | 1 | 0 | 0 | 0.5 | 1.000 |

Sig Jakucki
JAKUCKI, SIGMUND (Jack)
B. Aug. 20, 1909, Camden, N. J.   D. May 29, 1979, Galveston, Tex.   BR TR 6'2½" 198 lbs.

1936	STL A	0	3	.000	8.71	7	2	0	20.2	32	12	9	0	0	1	0	6	0	0	.000	1	4	1	1	0.9	.833
1944		13	9	.591	3.55	35	24	12	198	211	54	67	4	1	2	3	73	11	1	.151	7	44	0	2	1.5	.980
1945		12	10	.545	3.51	30	24	15	192.1	188	65	55	1	2	0	2	70	13	2	.186	7	42	1	0	1.7	.980
3 yrs.		25	22	.532	3.79	72	50	27	411	431	131	131	5	3	3	5	149	24	3	.161	15	90	2	3	1.5	.981

WORLD SERIES

| 1944 | STL A | 0 | 1 | .000 | 9.00 | 1 | 1 | 0 | 3 | 5 | 0 | 4 | 0 | 0 | 0 | 0 | 0 | 0 | 0 | — | 0 | 1 | 0 | 0 | 1.0 | 1.000 |

Charlie Jamerson
JAMERSON, CHARLES DEWEY (Lefty)
B. Jan. 26, 1900, Enfield, Ill.   D. Aug. 4, 1980, Mockville, N. C.   BL TL 6'1" 195 lbs.

| 1924 | BOS A | 0 | 0 | — | 18.00 | 1 | 0 | 0 | 1 | 1 | 3 | 0 | 0 | 0 | 0 | 0 | 0 | 0 | 0 | — | 0 | 0 | 0 | 0 | 0.0 | — |

Bill James
JAMES, WILLIAM HENRY (Big Bill)
B. Jan. 20, 1887, Detroit, Mich.   D. May 24, 1942, Venice, Calif.   BB TR 6'4" 195 lbs.

1911	CLE A	2	4	.333	4.88	8	6	4	51.2	58	32	21	0	0	0	0	17	1	0	.059	4	11	1	0	2.0	.938
1912		0	0	—	4.61	3	0	0	13.2	15	9	5	0	0	0	0	3	0	0	.000	1	2	3	0	2.0	.500
1914	STL A	15	14	.517	2.85	44	35	20	284	269	109	109	3	0	0	1	89	10	0	.112	11	106	3	5	2.7	.975
1915	2 teams	STL A	(34G 7–10)		DET A	(11G 7–3)																				
"	total	14	13	.519	3.26	45	32	11	237.1	212	125	82	1	2	0	1	63	14	0	.222	14	84	8	3	2.4	.925
1916	DET A	8	12	.400	3.68	30	20	8	151.2	141	79	61	0	2	0	1	44	3	0	.068	4	46	6	1	1.9	.893
1917		13	10	.565	2.09	34	23	10	198	163	96	62	2	2	1	1	57	12	0	.211	4	61	5	1	2.1	.929
1918		6	11	.353	3.76	19	18	8	122	127	68	42	1	1	0	0	46	5	0	.109	5	43	1	3	2.6	.980
1919	3 teams	DET A	(2G 1–0)		BOS A	(13G 3–5)		CHI A	(5G 3–2)																	
"	total	7	7	.500	3.71	20	13	7	121.1	129	58	26	2	0	2	0	39	6	0	.154	1	2	0	0	0.2	1.000
8 yrs.		65	71	.478	3.20	203	147	68	1179.2	1114	576	408	9	7	4	5	358	51	0	.142	44	355	27	13	2.1	.937

WORLD SERIES

| 1919 | CHI A | 0 | 0 | — | 5.79 | 1 | 0 | 0 | 4.2 | 8 | 3 | 2 | 0 | 0 | 0 | 0 | 2 | 0 | 0 | .000 | 0 | 0 | 0 | 0 | 0.0 | — |

Bill James
JAMES, WILLIAM LAWRENCE (Seattle Bill)
B. Mar. 12, 1892, Iowa Hill, Calif.   D. Mar. 10, 1971, Oroville, Calif.   BR TR 6'3" 196 lbs.

1913	BOS N	6	10	.375	2.79	24	14	10	135.2	134	57	73	1	1	1	0	47	12	0	.255	7	35	7	2	2.0	.857
1914		26	7	.788	1.90	46	37	30	332.1	261	118	156	4	1	1	2	129	33	0	.256	4	85	10	7	2.2	.899
1915		5	4	.556	3.03	13	10	4	68.1	68	22	23	0	0	0	0	21	1	0	.048	0	25	0	0	2.1	1.000
1919		0	0	—	3.38	1	0	0	5.1	6	2	1	0	0	0	0	2	0	0	.000	0	3	0	0	3.0	1.000
4 yrs.		37	21	.638	2.28	84	61	44	541.2	469	199	253	5	2	3	2	199	46	0	.231	13	148	17	9	2.1	.904

WORLD SERIES

| 1914 | BOS N | 2 | 0 | 1.000 | 0.00 | 2 | 1 | 1 | 11 | 2 | 6 | 9 | 1 | 1 | 0 | 0 | 4 | 0 | 0 | .000 | 0 | 5 | 0 | 0 | 2.5 | 1.000 |

Bob James
JAMES, ROBERT HARVEY
B. Aug. 15, 1958, Glendale, Calif.   BR TR 6'4" 215 lbs.

1978	MON N	0	1	.000	9.00	4	1	0	4	4	4	3	0	0	0	0	0	0	0	—	0	1	0	0	0.3	1.000
1979		0	0	—	13.50	2	0	0	2	2	3	1	0	0	0	0	0	0	0	—	0	0	0	0	0.0	—
1982	2 teams	MON N	(7G 0–0)		DET A	(12G 0–2)																				
"	total	0	2	.000	5.34	19	1	0	28.2	32	16	31	0	0	2	0	0	0	0	—	1	4	3	0	0.4	.625
1983	2 teams	DET A	(4G 0–0)		MON N	(27G 1–0)																				
"	total	1	0	1.000	3.50	31	0	0	54	42	26	60	0	1	0	7	7	2	0	.286	4	12	2	1	0.6	.889
1984	MON N	6	6	.500	3.66	62	0	0	96	92	45	91	0	6	6	10	14	2	0	.143	5	7	4	0	0.3	.750
1985	CHI A	8	7	.533	2.13	69	0	0	110	90	23	88	0	8	7	32	0	0	0	—	12	8	1	0	0.3	.952
1986		5	4	.556	5.25	49	0	0	58.1	63	23	32	0	5	4	14	0	0	0	—	3	6	0	0	0.2	1.000
1987		4	6	.400	4.67	43	0	0	54	54	17	34	0	4	6	10	0	0	0	—	3	9	3	1	0.3	.800
8 yrs.		24	26	.480	3.80	279	2	0	407	377	157	340	0	24	25	73	21	4	0	.190	28	47	13	2	0.3	.852

Jeff James
JAMES, JEFFREY LYNN (Jesse)
B. Sept. 29, 1941, Indianapolis, Ind.   BR TR 6'3" 195 lbs.

1968	PHI N	4	4	.500	4.28	29	13	1	115.2	112	46	83	1	0	0	0	33	4	0	.121	10	18	3	2	1.1	.903
1969		2	2	.500	5.34	6	5	1	32	36	14	21	0	0	0	0	11	2	0	.182	2	3	0	0	0.8	1.000
2 yrs.		6	6	.500	4.51	35	18	2	147.2	148	60	104	1	0	0	0	44	6	0	.136	12	21	3	2	1.0	.917

Johnny James
JAMES, JOHN PHILLIP
B. July 23, 1933, Bonner's Ferry, Ida.   BL TR 5'10" 160 lbs.

1958	NY A	0	0	—	0.00	1	0	0	3	2	4	1	0	0	0	0	1	0	0	.000	1	0	0	0	1.0	1.000
1960		5	1	.833	4.36	28	0	0	43.1	38	26	29	0	5	1	2	3	0	0	.000	2	9	0	0	0.4	1.000
1961	2 teams	NY A	(1G 0–0)		LA A	(36G 0–2)																				
"	total	0	2	.000	5.20	37	3	0	72.2	67	54	43	0	0	2	2	13	0	0	.000	1	12	0	1	0.4	1.000
3 yrs.		5	3	.625	4.76	66	3	0	119	107	84	73	0	5	3	4	17	0	0	.000	4	21	0	1	0.4	1.000

Year	Team		W	L	PCT	ERA	G	GS	CG	IP	H	BB	SO	ShO	Relief Pitching W	L	SV	Batting AB	H	HR	BA	PO	A	E	DP	TC/G	FA

Lefty James

JAMES, L   B. July 1, 1889, Glenroy, Ohio   D. May 3, 1933, Portsmouth, Ohio   BR TL 5'11½" 175 lbs.

Year	Team		W	L	PCT	ERA	G	GS	CG	IP	H	BB	SO	ShO	W	L	SV	AB	H	HR	BA	PO	A	E	DP	TC/G	FA
1912	CLE	A	0	1	.000	7.50	3	1	0	6	8	4	2	0	0	0	1	3	0	0	.000	0	2	1	0	1.0	.667
1913			2	2	.500	3.00	11	4	4	39	42	9	18	0	0	0	0	13	3	0	.231	0	8	3	0	1.0	.727
1914			0	3	.000	3.20	17	6	1	50.2	44	32	16	0	0	0	1	12	0	0	.000	3	21	0	0	1.4	1.000
3 yrs.			2	6	.250	3.39	31	11	5	95.2	94	45	36	0	0	0	2	28	3	0	.107	3	31	4	0	1.2	.895

Rick James

JAMES, RICHARD LEE   B. Oct. 11, 1947, Sheffield, Ala.   BR TR 6'2½" 205 lbs.

Year	Team		W	L	PCT	ERA	G	GS	CG	IP	H	BB	SO	ShO	W	L	SV	AB	H	HR	BA	PO	A	E	DP	TC/G	FA
1967	CHI	N	0	1	.000	13.50	3	1	0	4.2	9	2	2	0	0	0	0	1	0	0	.000	0	0	0	0	0.0	–

Charlie Jamieson

JAMIESON, CHARLES DEVINE   B. Feb. 7, 1893, Paterson, N. J.   D. Oct. 27, 1969, Paterson, N. J.   BL TL 5'8½" 165 lbs.

Year	Team		W	L	PCT	ERA	G	GS	CG	IP	H	BB	SO	ShO	W	L	SV	AB	H	HR	BA	PO	A	E	DP	TC/G	FA
1916	WAS	A	0	0	–	4.50	1	0	0	4	2	3	1	0	0	0	0	145	36	0	.248	2	1	0	0	3.0	1.000
1917	2 teams		WAS A	(1G 0-0)			PHI A	(0G 0-0)																			
"	total		0	0	–	38.57	1	0	0	2.1	10	2	1	0	0	0	0	382	98	0	.257	0	0	0	0	0.0	–
1918	PHI	A	2	1	.667	4.30	5	2	1	23	24	13	2	0	1	0	0	416	84	0	.202	2	6	4	0	2.4	.667
1919	CLE	A	0	0	–	5.54	4	1	0	13	12	8	0	0	0	0	0	17	6	0	.353	1	2	1	0	1.0	.750
1922			0	0	–	3.18	2	0	0	5.2	7	4	2	0	0	0	0	567	183	3	.323	0	0	0	0	0.0	–
5 yrs.			2	1	.667	6.19	13	3	1	48	55	30	7	0	1	0	0	*				5	9	5	0	1.5	.737

Gerry Janeski

JANESKI, GERALD JOSEPH   B. Apr. 18, 1946, Pasadena, Calif.   BR TR 6'4" 205 lbs.

Year	Team		W	L	PCT	ERA	G	GS	CG	IP	H	BB	SO	ShO	W	L	SV	AB	H	HR	BA	PO	A	E	DP	TC/G	FA
1970	CHI	A	10	17	.370	4.76	35	35	4	206	247	63	79	1	0	0	0	66	5	0	.076	15	37	5	6	1.6	.912
1971	WAS	A	1	5	.167	4.94	23	10	0	62	72	34	19	0	1	0	1	14	3	0	.214	7	12	0	2	0.8	1.000
1972	TEX	A	0	1	.000	2.77	4	1	0	13	11	7	7	0	0	0	0	2	0	0	.000	1	3	0	0	1.0	1.000
3 yrs.			11	23	.324	4.71	62	46	4	281	330	104	105	1	1	0	1	82	8	0	.098	23	52	5	8	1.3	.938

Larry Jansen

JANSEN, LAWRENCE JOSEPH   B. July 16, 1920, Verboort, Ore.   BR TR 6'2" 190 lbs.

Year	Team		W	L	PCT	ERA	G	GS	CG	IP	H	BB	SO	ShO	W	L	SV	AB	H	HR	BA	PO	A	E	DP	TC/G	FA
1947	NY	N	21	5	.808	3.16	42	30	20	248	241	57	104	1	1	1	1	86	16	0	.186	19	42	4	3	1.5	.938
1948			18	12	.600	3.61	42	36	15	277	283	54	126	4	1	0	2	95	13	0	.137	20	56	1	7	1.8	.987
1949			15	16	.484	3.85	37	35	17	259.2	271	62	113	3	0	0	0	97	16	0	.165	14	57	1	1	1.9	.986
1950			19	13	.594	3.01	40	35	21	275	238	55	161	5	0	0	3	96	16	1	.167	30	45	1	7	1.9	.987
1951			23	11	.676	3.04	39	34	18	278.1	254	56	145	3	4	1	0	96	9	0	.094	29	54	1	3	2.2	.988
1952			11	11	.500	4.09	34	27	8	167.1	183	47	74	1	1	0	2	45	8	0	.178	9	38	3	5	1.5	.940
1953			11	16	.407	4.14	36	26	6	184.2	185	55	88	0	2	1	1	60	8	0	.133	11	27	0	2	1.1	1.000
1954			2	2	.500	5.98	13	7	0	40.2	57	15	15	0	1	1	0	14	4	0	.286	3	12	0	3	1.2	1.000
1956	CIN	N	2	3	.400	5.19	8	7	2	34.2	39	9	16	0	0	0	1	11	0	0	.000	3	4	0	0	0.9	1.000
9 yrs.			122	89	.578	3.58	291	237	107	1765.1	1751	410	842	17	10	5	10	600	90	1	.150	138	335	11	31	1.7	.977

WORLD SERIES

Year	Team		W	L	PCT	ERA	G	GS	CG	IP	H	BB	SO	ShO	W	L	SV	AB	H	HR	BA	PO	A	E	DP	TC/G	FA
1951	NY	N	0	2	.000	6.30	3	2	0	10	8	4	6	0	0	0	0	2	0	0	.000	1	2	0	0	1.0	1.000

Pat Jarvis

JARVIS, ROBERT PATRICK   B. Mar. 18, 1941, Carlyle, Ill.   BR TR 5'10½" 180 lbs.

Year	Team		W	L	PCT	ERA	G	GS	CG	IP	H	BB	SO	ShO	W	L	SV	AB	H	HR	BA	PO	A	E	DP	TC/G	FA
1966	ATL	N	6	2	.750	2.31	10	9	3	62.1	46	12	41	1	0	0	0	22	0	0	.000	1	7	0	0	0.8	1.000
1967			15	10	.600	3.66	32	30	7	194	195	62	118	1	2	0	0	71	6	0	.085	11	24	4	1	1.2	.897
1968			16	12	.571	2.60	34	34	14	256	202	50	157	1	0	0	0	85	12	0	.141	18	29	2	2	1.4	.959
1969			13	11	.542	4.44	37	33	4	217	204	73	123	1	0	0	0	71	8	0	.113	19	31	0	1	1.4	1.000
1970			16	16	.500	3.61	36	34	11	254	240	72	173	1	0	0	1	82	15	0	.183	29	38	1	0	1.9	.985
1971			6	14	.300	4.11	35	23	3	162	162	51	68	3	2	1	1	47	5	0	.106	16	27	1	1	1.3	.977
1972			11	7	.611	4.09	37	6	0	99	94	44	56	0	8	5	2	24	3	0	.125	5	19	1	1	0.7	.960
1973	MON	N	2	1	.667	3.20	28	0	0	39.1	37	16	19	0	2	1	0	3	0	0	.000	4	5	2	0	0.4	.818
8 yrs.			85	73	.538	3.58	249	169	42	1283.2	1180	380	755	8	14	8	3	405	49	0	.121	103	180	11	6	1.2	.963

LEAGUE CHAMPIONSHIP SERIES

Year	Team		W	L	PCT	ERA	G	GS	CG	IP	H	BB	SO	ShO	W	L	SV	AB	H	HR	BA	PO	A	E	DP	TC/G	FA
1969	ATL	N	0	1	.000	12.46	1	1	0	4.1	10	0	6	0	0	0	0	2	0	0	.000	1	2	0	1	3.0	1.000

Ray Jarvis

JARVIS, RAYMOND ARNOLD   B. May 10, 1946, Providence, R. I.   BR TR 6'2" 198 lbs.

Year	Team		W	L	PCT	ERA	G	GS	CG	IP	H	BB	SO	ShO	W	L	SV	AB	H	HR	BA	PO	A	E	DP	TC/G	FA
1969	BOS	A	5	6	.455	4.75	29	12	2	100.1	105	43	36	0	2	0	1	29	2	0	.069	9	19	3	1	1.1	.903
1970			0	1	.000	3.94	15	0	0	16	17	14	8	0	0	1	0	0	0	0	–	1	3	1	0	0.3	.800
2 yrs.			5	7	.417	4.64	44	12	2	116.1	122	57	44	0	2	1	1	29	2	0	.069	10	22	4	1	0.8	.889

Hi Jasper

JASPER, HENRY W.   B. Nov. 15, 1880, St. Louis, Mo.   D. May 22, 1937, St. Louis, Mo.   BR TR 5'11" 180 lbs.

Year	Team		W	L	PCT	ERA	G	GS	CG	IP	H	BB	SO	ShO	W	L	SV	AB	H	HR	BA	PO	A	E	DP	TC/G	FA
1914	CHI	A	1	0	1.000	3.34	16	0	0	32.1	22	20	19	0	1	0	0	5	0	0	.000	2	13	0	1	0.9	1.000
1915			0	1	.000	4.60	3	2	0	15.2	8	9	15	0	0	0	0	7	2	0	.286	0	11	1	0	4.0	.917
1916	STL	N	5	6	.455	3.28	21	11	2	107	97	42	37	0	3	1	1	33	7	1	.212	3	35	0	2	1.8	1.000
1919	CLE	A	4	5	.444	3.59	12	10	5	82.2	83	28	25	0	1	0	0	29	3	0	.103	2	30	4	0	3.0	.889
4 yrs.			10	12	.455	3.48	52	23	8	237.2	210	99	96	0	5	1	1	74	12	0	.162	7	89	5	3	1.9	.950

Larry Jaster

JASTER, LARRY EDWARD   B. Jan. 13, 1944, Midland, Mich.   BL TL 6'3" 190 lbs.

Year	Team		W	L	PCT	ERA	G	GS	CG	IP	H	BB	SO	ShO	W	L	SV	AB	H	HR	BA	PO	A	E	DP	TC/G	FA
1965	STL	N	3	0	1.000	1.61	4	3	3	28	21	7	10	0	0	0	0	10	2	0	.200	1	3	0	0	0.8	1.000
1966			11	5	.688	3.26	26	21	6	151.2	124	45	92	5	1	0	0	45	8	1	.178	6	20	0	3	1.0	1.000
1967			9	7	.563	3.01	34	23	2	152.1	141	44	87	1	1	0	3	50	5	0	.100	1	18	2	3	0.6	.905
1968			9	13	.409	3.51	31	21	3	153.2	153	38	70	1	2	1	0	43	6	1	.140	5	20	0	1	0.8	1.000
1969	MON	N	1	6	.143	5.49	24	11	0	77	95	28	39	0	0	0	0	19	8	0	.421	7	6	6	0	0.8	.684
1970	ATL	N	1	1	.500	6.95	14	0	0	22	33	8	9	0	1	1	0	3	0	0	.000	0	8	0	0	0.6	1.000

Year	Team		W	L	PCT	ERA	G	GS	CG	IP	H	BB	SO	ShO	W	L	SV	AB	H	HR	BA	PO	A	E	DP	TC/G	FA
															Relief Pitching			**Batting**									

Tommy John *continued*

Year	Team		W	L	PCT	ERA	G	GS	CG	IP	H	BB	SO	ShO	W	L	SV	AB	H	HR	BA	PO	A	E	DP	TC/G	FA
1976			10	10	.500	3.09	31	31	6	207	207	61	91	2	0	0	0	64	7	0	.109	3	33	1	2	1.2	.973
1977			20	7	.741	2.78	31	31	11	220	225	50	123	3	0	0	0	79	14	1	.177	6	47	1	5	1.7	.981
1978			17	10	.630	3.30	33	30	7	213	230	53	124	0	1	0	1	66	8	0	.121	8	45	3	1	1.7	.946
1979	NY	A	21	9	.700	2.97	37	36	17	276	268	65	111	3	1	0	0	0	0	0	–	15	51	3	5	1.9	.957
1980			22	9	.710	3.43	36	36	16	265	270	56	78	6	0	0	0	0	0	0	–	16	46	1	4	1.8	.984
1981			9	8	.529	2.64	20	20	7	140	135	39	50	0	0	0	0	0	0	0	–	11	27	0	2	1.9	1.000
1982	2 teams	NY A (30G 10–10)													CAL A (7G 4–2)												
"	total		14	12	.538	3.69	37	33	10	221.2	239	39	68	2	0	0	0	0	0	0	–	8	40	2	1	1.4	.960
1983	CAL	A	11	13	.458	4.33	34	34	9	234.2	287	49	65	0	0	0	0	0	0	0	–	16	39	0	4	1.6	1.000
1984			7	13	.350	4.52	32	29	4	181.1	223	56	47	1	0	0	0	0	0	0	–	15	27	0	2	1.3	1.000
1985	2 teams	CAL A (12G 2–4)													OAK A (11G 2–6)												
"	total		4	10	.286	5.53	23	17	0	86.1	117	28	25	0	1	1	0	0	0	0	–	8	22	0	2	1.3	1.000
1986	NY	A	5	3	.625	2.93	13	10	1	70.2	73	15	28	0	0	0	0	0	0	0	–	4	15	3	2	1.7	.864
1987			13	6	.684	4.03	33	33	3	187.2	212	47	63	0	0	0	0	0	0	0	–	4	31	5	1	1.2	.875
1988			9	8	.529	4.49	35	32	0	176.1	221	46	81	0	0	0	0	0	0	0	–	4	40	4	2	1.4	.917
1989			2	7	.222	5.80	10	10	0	63.2	87	22	18	0	0	0	0	0	0	0	–	3	21	0	0	2.4	1.000
26 yrs.			288	231	.555	3.34	760	700	162	4708.1	4783	1259	2245	46	4	3	4	900	141	5	.157	235	1020	49	69	1.7	.962
								3rd																			

DIVISIONAL PLAYOFF SERIES

Year	Team		W	L	PCT	ERA	G	GS	CG	IP	H	BB	SO	ShO	W	L	SV	AB	H	HR	BA	PO	A	E	DP	TC/G	FA
1981	NY	A	0	1	.000	6.43	1	1	0	7	8	2	0	0	0	0	0	0	0	0	–	0	0	0	0	0.0	–

LEAGUE CHAMPIONSHIP SERIES

Year	Team		W	L	PCT	ERA	G	GS	CG	IP	H	BB	SO	ShO	W	L	SV	AB	H	HR	BA	PO	A	E	DP	TC/G	FA
1977	LA	N	1	0	1.000	0.66	2	2	1	13.2	11	5	11	0	0	0	0	5	1	0	.200	0	1	0	0	0.5	1.000
1978			1	0	1.000	0.00	1	1	1	9	4	2	4	1	0	0	0	3	0	0	.000	0	0	0	0	0.0	–
1980	NY	A	0	0	–	2.70	1	1	0	6.2	8	1	3	0	0	0	0	0	0	0	–	0	1	0	0	1.0	1.000
1981			1	0	1.000	1.50	1	1	0	6	6	1	3	0	0	0	0	0	0	0	–	0	0	0	0	0.0	–
1982	CAL	A	1	1	.500	5.11	2	2	1	12.1	11	6	6	0	0	0	0	0	0	0	–	2	0	0	0	0.3	1.000
5 yrs.			4	1	.800	2.08	7	7	3	47.2	40	15	27	1	0	0	0	8	1	0	.125	2	2	0	0	0.5	1.000

WORLD SERIES

Year	Team		W	L	PCT	ERA	G	GS	CG	IP	H	BB	SO	ShO	W	L	SV	AB	H	HR	BA	PO	A	E	DP	TC/G	FA
1977	LA	N	0	1	.000	6.00	1	1	0	6	9	3	7	0	0	0	0	2	0	0	.000	0	0	0	0	0.0	–
1978			1	0	1.000	3.07	2	2	0	14.2	14	4	6	0	0	0	0	0	0	0	–	0	4	0	0	2.0	1.000
1981	NY	A	1	0	1.000	0.69	3	2	0	13	11	0	8	0	0	0	0	2	0	0	.000	0	3	0	0	1.0	1.000
3 yrs.			2	1	.667	2.67	6	5	0	33.2	34	7	21	0	0	0	0	4	0	0	.000	0	7	0	0	1.2	1.000

Augie Johns

JOHNS, AUGUSTUS FRANCIS (Lefty)
B. Sept. 10, 1899, St. Louis, Mo. D. Sept. 12, 1975, San Antonio, Tex.

BL TL 5'8½" 170 lbs.

Year	Team		W	L	PCT	ERA	G	GS	CG	IP	H	BB	SO	ShO	W	L	SV	AB	H	HR	BA	PO	A	E	DP	TC/G	FA
1926	DET	A	6	4	.600	5.35	35	14	3	112.2	117	69	40	1	2	0	1	28	4	0	.143	4	16	0	0	0.6	1.000
1927			0	0	–	9.00	1	0	0	1	1	1	1	0	0	0	0	0	0	0	–	0	1	0	0	1.0	1.000
2 yrs.			6	4	.600	5.38	36	14	3	113.2	118	70	41	1	2	0	1	28	4	0	.143	4	17	0	0	0.6	1.000

Ollie Johns

JOHNS, OLIVER TRACY
B. Aug. 21, 1879, Trenton, Ohio D. June 17, 1961, Hamilton, Ohio

BL TL

Year	Team		W	L	PCT	ERA	G	GS	CG	IP	H	BB	SO	ShO	W	L	SV	AB	H	HR	BA	PO	A	E	DP	TC/G	FA
1905	CIN	N	1	0	1.000	3.50	4	1	1	18	31	4	8	0	0	0	1	5	1	0	.200	2	4	1	0	1.8	.857

Abe Johnson

JOHNSON, ABRAHAM
B. London, Ont., Canada Deceased.

Year	Team		W	L	PCT	ERA	G	GS	CG	IP	H	BB	SO	ShO	W	L	SV	AB	H	HR	BA	PO	A	E	DP	TC/G	FA
1893	CHI	N	0	0	–	36.00	1	0	0	1	2	2	0	0	0	0	0	0	0	0	–	0	0	0	0	0.0	–

Adam Johnson

JOHNSON, ADAM RANKIN, SR. (Tex)
Father of Adam Johnson.
B. Feb. 4, 1888, Burnet, Tex. D. July 2, 1972, Williamsport, Pa.

BR TR 6'1½" 185 lbs.

Year	Team		W	L	PCT	ERA	G	GS	CG	IP	H	BB	SO	ShO	W	L	SV	AB	H	HR	BA	PO	A	E	DP	TC/G	FA
1914	2 teams	BOS A (16G 4–9)													CHI F (16G 9–5)												
"	total		13	14	.481	2.26	32	27	16	219.1	180	63	84	4	1	1	0	67	8	0	.119	6	51	2	4	1.8	.966
1915	2 teams	CHI F (11G 2–4)													BAL F (23G 7–11)												
"	total		9	15	.375	3.64	34	25	15	207.2	201	81	81	2	1	2	2	73	9	0	.123	2	40	0	2	1.2	1.000
1918	STL	N	1	1	.500	2.74	6	1	0	23	20	7	4	0	1	0	0	4	1	0	.250	0	13	2	0	2.5	.867
3 yrs.			23	30	.434	2.92	72	53	31	450	401	151	169	6	3	3	2	144	18	0	.125	8	104	4	6	1.6	.966

Adam Johnson

JOHNSON, ADAM RANKIN, JR.
Son of Adam Johnson.
B. Mar. 1, 1917, Hayden, Ariz.

BR TR 6'3" 177 lbs.

Year	Team		W	L	PCT	ERA	G	GS	CG	IP	H	BB	SO	ShO	W	L	SV	AB	H	HR	BA	PO	A	E	DP	TC/G	FA
1941	PHI	A	1	0	1.000	3.60	7	0	0	10	14	3	0	0	1	0	0	1	0	0	.000	1	3	0	0	0.6	1.000

Art Johnson

JOHNSON, ARTHUR GILBERT
B. Feb. 15, 1897, Warren, Pa. D. June 7, 1982, Sarasota, Fla.

BB TL 6'1" 167 lbs.

Year	Team		W	L	PCT	ERA	G	GS	CG	IP	H	BB	SO	ShO	W	L	SV	AB	H	HR	BA	PO	A	E	DP	TC/G	FA
1927	NY	N	0	0	–	0.00	1	0	0	3	1	1	0	0	0	0	0	0	0	0	–	0	1	1	0	2.0	.500

Art Johnson

JOHNSON, ARTHUR HENRY (Lefty)
B. July 16, 1916, Winchester, Mass.

BL TL 6'2" 185 lbs.

Year	Team		W	L	PCT	ERA	G	GS	CG	IP	H	BB	SO	ShO	W	L	SV	AB	H	HR	BA	PO	A	E	DP	TC/G	FA
1940	BOS	N	0	1	.000	10.50	2	1	0	6	10	3	1	0	0	0	0	1	0	0	.000	0	3	0	0	1.5	1.000
1941			7	15	.318	3.53	43	18	6	183.1	189	71	70	0	1	4	1	55	8	0	.145	7	40	4	4	1.2	.922
1942			0	0	–	1.42	4	0	0	6.1	4	5	0	0	0	0	0	1	0	0	.000	0	1	0	0	0.3	1.000
3 yrs.			7	16	.304	3.68	49	19	6	195.2	203	79	71	0	1	4	1	57	8	0	.140	7	44	4	4	1.1	.927

Bart Johnson

JOHNSON, CLAIR BARTH
B. Jan. 3, 1950, Torrance, Calif.

BR TR 6'5" 190 lbs.

Year	Team		W	L	PCT	ERA	G	GS	CG	IP	H	BB	SO	ShO	W	L	SV	AB	H	HR	BA	PO	A	E	DP	TC/G	FA
1969	CHI	A	1	3	.250	3.22	4	3	0	22.1	22	6	18	0	0	1	0	6	1	0	.167	2	2	1	0	1.3	.800
1970			4	7	.364	4.80	18	15	2	90	92	46	71	1	0	0	0	29	8	0	.276	4	11	0	2	0.8	1.000
1971			12	10	.545	2.93	53	16	4	178	148	111	153	0	4	4	14	57	11	0	.193	12	19	3	0	0.6	.912

Year	Team	W	L	PCT	ERA	G	GS	CG	IP	H	BB	SO	ShO	Relief Pitching W	L	SV	Batting AB	H	HR	BA	PO	A	E	DP	TC/G	FA

Bart Johnson *continued*

Year	Team	W	L	PCT	ERA	G	GS	CG	IP	H	BB	SO	ShO	W	L	SV	AB	H	HR	BA	PO	A	E	DP	TC/G	FA
1972		0	3	.000	9.22	9	0	0	13.2	18	13	9	0	0	3	1	1	0	0	.000	0	3	0	0	0.3	1.000
1973		3	3	.500	4.13	22	9	0	80.2	76	40	56	0	1	0	0	0	0	0	–	4	10	0	0	0.6	1.000
1974		10	4	.714	2.73	18	18	8	122	105	32	76	2	0	0	0	0	0	0	–	6	7	0	0	0.7	1.000
1976		9	16	.360	4.73	32	32	8	211	231	62	91	3	0	0	0	0	0	0	–	22	30	1	0	1.7	.981
1977		4	5	.444	4.01	29	4	0	92	114	38	46	0	3	2	2	0	0	0	–	8	12	1	1	0.7	.952
8 yrs.		43	51	.457	3.93	185	97	22	809.2	806	348	520	6	8	10	17	93	20	0	.215	58	94	6	3	0.9	.962

Ben Johnson

JOHNSON, BENJAMIN FRANKLIN
B. May 15, 1931, Greenwood, S. C.

BR TR 6'2" 190 lbs.

Year	Team	W	L	PCT	ERA	G	GS	CG	IP	H	BB	SO	ShO	W	L	SV	AB	H	HR	BA	PO	A	E	DP	TC/G	FA
1959	CHI N	0	0	–	2.16	4	0	0	16.2	17	4	6	0	0	0	0	4	0	0	.000	2	1	0	0	0.8	1.000
1960		2	1	.667	4.91	17	0	0	29.1	39	11	9	0	2	1	1	2	0	0	.000	2	8	0	1	0.6	1.000
2 yrs.		2	1	.667	3.91	21	2	0	46	56	15	15	0	2	1	1	6	0	0	.000	4	9	0	1	0.6	1.000

Bill Johnson

JOHNSON, WILLIAM CHARLES
B. Oct. 6, 1960, Wilmington, Del.

BR TR 6'5" 205 lbs.

Year	Team	W	L	PCT	ERA	G	GS	CG	IP	H	BB	SO	ShO	W	L	SV	AB	H	HR	BA	PO	A	E	DP	TC/G	FA
1983	CHI N	1	0	1.000	4.38	10	0	0	12.1	17	3	4	0	1	0	0	0	0	0	–	1	4	0	0	0.5	1.000
1984		0	0	–	1.69	4	0	0	5.1	4	1	3	0	0	0	0	0	0	0	–	0	3	0	0	0.8	1.000
2 yrs.		1	0	1.000	3.57	14	0	0	17.2	21	4	7	0	1	0	0	0	0	0	–	1	7	0	0	0.6	1.000

Bob Johnson

JOHNSON, ROBERT DALE
B. Apr. 25, 1943, Aurora, Ind.

BL TR 6'4" 220 lbs.

Year	Team	W	L	PCT	ERA	G	GS	CG	IP	H	BB	SO	ShO	W	L	SV	AB	H	HR	BA	PO	A	E	DP	TC/G	FA
1969	NY N	0	0	–	0.00	2	0	0	1.2	1	1	1	0	0	0	1	0	0	0		0	0	0	0	0.0	–
1970	KC A	8	13	.381	3.07	40	26	10	214	178	82	206	1	0	1	4	57	6	0	.105	13	20	0	0	0.8	1.000
1971	PIT N	9	10	.474	3.45	31	27	7	175	170	55	101	1	0	0	0	48	3	0	.063	14	20	3	2	1.2	.919
1972		4	4	.500	2.96	31	11	1	115.2	98	46	79	0	2	3	3	35	5	0	.143	6	7	1	1	0.5	.929
1973		4	2	.667	3.62	50	2	0	92	98	34	68	0	4	1	4	14	0	0	.000	2	4	1	1	0.1	.857
1974	CLE A	3	4	.429	4.38	14	10	0	72	75	37	36	0	0	0	0	0	0	0	–	2	11	0	0	0.9	1.000
1977	ATL N	0	1	.000	7.36	15	0	0	22	24	14	16	0	0	1	0	3	1	0	.333	0	1	0	0	0.1	1.000
7 yrs.		28	34	.452	3.48	183	76	18	692.1	644	269	507	2	6	5	12	157	15	0	.096	37	63	5	4	0.6	.952

LEAGUE CHAMPIONSHIP SERIES

Year	Team	W	L	PCT	ERA	G	GS	CG	IP	H	BB	SO	ShO	W	L	SV	AB	H	HR	BA	PO	A	E	DP	TC/G	FA
1971	PIT N	1	0	1.000	0.00	1	1	0	8	5	3	7	0	0	0	0	2	0	0	.000	0	0	0	0	0.0	–
1972		0	0	–	3.00	2	0	0	6	4	2	7	0	0	0	0	1	0	0	.000	0	0	0	0	0.0	–
2 yrs.		1	0	1.000	1.29	3	1	0	14	9	5	14	0	0	0	0	3	0	0	.000	0	0	0	0	0.0	–

WORLD SERIES

Year	Team	W	L	PCT	ERA	G	GS	CG	IP	H	BB	SO	ShO	W	L	SV	AB	H	HR	BA	PO	A	E	DP	TC/G	FA
1971	PIT N	0	1	.000	9.00	2	1	0	5	5	3	3	0	0	0	0	3	0	0	.000	2	0	0	0	1.0	1.000

Chet Johnson

JOHNSON, CHESTER LILLIS
Brother of Earl Johnson.
B. Aug. 1, 1917, Redmond, Wash.   D. Apr. 10, 1983, Seattle, Wash.

BL TL 6' 175 lbs.

Year	Team	W	L	PCT	ERA	G	GS	CG	IP	H	BB	SO	ShO	W	L	SV	AB	H	HR	BA	PO	A	E	DP	TC/G	FA
1946	STL A	0	0	–	5.00	5	3	0	18	20	13	8	0	0	0	0	6	0	0	.000	0	0	0	0	0.0	–

Chief Johnson

JOHNSON, GEORGE HOWARD
B. Mar. 30, 1886, Winnebago, Neb.   D. June 11, 1922, Des Moines, Iowa

BR TR 5'11½" 190 lbs.

Year	Team	W	L	PCT	ERA	G	GS	CG	IP	H	BB	SO	ShO	W	L	SV	AB	H	HR	BA	PO	A	E	DP	TC/G	FA
1913	CIN N	14	16	.467	3.01	44	31	13	269	251	86	107	3	2	2	0	88	10	1	.114	1	75	6	2	1.9	.927
1914	2 teams				CIN N	(1G 0-0)				KC F	(20G 9-10)																
"	total	9	10	.474	3.26	21	20	12	138	163	35	79	1	0	0	0	49	6	0	.122	1	27	4	1	1.5	.875
1915	KC F	18	17	.514	2.75	46	34	19	281.1	253	71	118	4	4	0	1	87	11	1	.126	13	94	12	4	2.6	.899
3 yrs.		41	43	.488	2.95	111	85	44	688.1	667	192	304	9	6	2	1	224	27	3	.121	15	196	22	7	2.1	.906

Connie Johnson

JOHNSON, CLIFFORD
B. Dec. 27, 1922, Stone Mountain, Ga.

BR TR 6'4" 200 lbs.

Year	Team	W	L	PCT	ERA	G	GS	CG	IP	H	BB	SO	ShO	W	L	SV	AB	H	HR	BA	PO	A	E	DP	TC/G	FA
1953	CHI A	4	4	.500	3.56	14	10	2	60.2	55	38	44	1	0	0	0	20	1	0	.050	1	6	0	0	0.5	1.000
1955		7	4	.636	3.45	17	16	5	99	95	52	72	2	0	0	0	33	5	0	.152	3	9	0	0	0.7	1.000
1956	2 teams				CHI A	(5G 0-1)				BAL A	(26G 9-10)																
"	total	9	11	.450	3.44	31	27	9	196	176	69	136	2	0	0	0	61	15	0	.246	9	16	1	0	0.8	.962
1957	BAL A	14	11	.560	3.20	35	30	14	242	212	66	177	3	0	1	0	89	12	0	.135	10	22	1	0	0.9	.970
1958		6	9	.400	3.88	26	17	4	118.1	116	32	68	0	1	1	1	34	7	0	.206	3	13	0	0	0.6	1.000
5 yrs.		40	39	.506	3.44	123	100	34	716	654	257	497	8	1	2	1	237	40	0	.169	26	66	2	0	0.8	.979

Dave Johnson

JOHNSON, DAVID CHARLES
B. Oct. 4, 1948, Abilene, Tex.

BR TR 6'1" 183 lbs.

Year	Team	W	L	PCT	ERA	G	GS	CG	IP	H	BB	SO	ShO	W	L	SV	AB	H	HR	BA	PO	A	E	DP	TC/G	FA
1974	BAL A	2	2	.500	3.00	11	0	0	15	17	5	6	0	2	2	2	0	0	0	–	1	1	0	0	0.2	1.000
1975		0	1	.000	4.15	6	0	0	8.2	8	7	4	0	0	1	0	0	0	0	–	1	1	0	0	0.3	1.000
1977	MIN A	2	5	.286	4.56	30	6	0	73	86	23	33	0	1	3	0	0	0	0	–	5	11	0	2	0.5	1.000
1978		0	2	.000	7.50	6	1	0	12	15	9	7	0	0	1	0	0	0	0	–	2	1	0	0	0.5	1.000
4 yrs.		4	10	.286	4.64	53	7	0	108.2	126	44	50	0	3	7	2	0	0	0	–	9	14	0	2	0.4	1.000

Dave Johnson

JOHNSON, DAVID WAYNE
B. Oct. 24, 1959, Baltimore, Md.

BR TR 5'10" 180 lbs.

Year	Team	W	L	PCT	ERA	G	GS	CG	IP	H	BB	SO	ShO	W	L	SV	AB	H	HR	BA	PO	A	E	DP	TC/G	FA
1987	PIT N	0	0	–	9.95	5	0	0	6.1	13	2	4	0	0	0	0	0	0	0	–	1	0	0	1	0.4	1.000
1989	BAL A	4	7	.364	4.23	14	14	4	89.1	90	28	26	0	0	0	0	0	0	0	–	6	6	0	0	0.8	1.000
2 yrs.		4	7	.364	4.61	19	14	4	95.2	103	30	30	0	0	0	0	0	0	0	–	7	6	0	1	0.7	1.000

Don Johnson

JOHNSON, DONALD ROY
B. Nov. 12, 1926, Portland, Ore.

BR TR 6'3" 200 lbs.

Year	Team	W	L	PCT	ERA	G	GS	CG	IP	H	BB	SO	ShO	W	L	SV	AB	H	HR	BA	PO	A	E	DP	TC/G	FA
1947	NY A	4	3	.571	3.64	15	8	2	54.1	57	23	16	0	1	1	0	13	0	0	.000	2	7	2	2	0.7	.818

Year	Team	W	L	PCT	ERA	G	GS	CG	IP	H	BB	SO	ShO	Relief Pitching W	L	SV	Batting AB	H	HR	BA	PO	A	E	DP	TC/G	FA

Don Johnson *continued*

Year	Team	W	L	PCT	ERA	G	GS	CG	IP	H	BB	SO	ShO	W	L	SV	AB	H	HR	BA	PO	A	E	DP	TC/G	FA
1950	2 teams	NY A (8G 1–0)			STL A	(25G 5–6)																				
"	total	6	6	.500	6.71	33	12	4	114	161	67	40	0	2	0	1	32	2	0	.063	2	19	3	0	0.7	.875
1951	2 teams	STL A (6G 0–1)			WAS A	(21G 7–11)																				
"	total	7	12	.368	4.76	27	23	8	158.2	165	76	60	1	0	0	0	50	5	0	.100	3	27	0	5	1.1	1.000
1952	WAS A	0	5	.000	4.43	29	6	0	69	80	33	37	0	0	2	2	13	1	0	.077	6	9	0	0	0.5	1.000
1954	CHI A	8	7	.533	3.13	46	16	3	144	129	43	68	3	2	3	7	35	1	0	.029	8	24	1	1	0.7	.970
1955	BAL A	2	4	.333	5.82	31	5	0	68	89	35	27	0	2	1	1	10	0	0	.000	0	14	1	2	0.5	.933
1958	SF N	0	1	.000	6.26	17	0	0	23	31	8	14	0	0	1	1	2	0	0	.000	1	3	0	0	0.2	1.000
7 yrs.		27	38	.415	4.78	198	70	17	631	712	285	262	4	7	8	12	155	9	0	.058	22	103	7	10	0.7	.947

Earl Johnson

JOHNSON, EARL DOUGLAS (Lefty)
Brother of Chet Johnson.
B. Apr. 2, 1919, Redmond, Wash.

BL TL 6'3" 190 lbs.

Year	Team	W	L	PCT	ERA	G	GS	CG	IP	H	BB	SO	ShO	W	L	SV	AB	H	HR	BA	PO	A	E	DP	TC/G	FA
1940	BOS A	6	2	.750	4.09	17	10	2	70.1	69	39	26	0	2	1	0	27	2	0	.074	2	19	0	1	1.2	1.000
1941		4	5	.444	4.52	17	12	4	93.2	90	51	46	0	1	0	0	34	10	0	.294	3	27	0	3	1.8	1.000
1946		5	4	.556	3.71	29	5	1	80	78	39	40	1	5	3	3	22	5	0	.227	5	12	1	1	0.6	.944
1947		12	11	.522	2.97	45	17	6	142.1	129	62	65	3	4	3	8	44	12	0	.273	4	31	2	5	0.8	.946
1948		10	4	.714	4.53	35	3	1	91.1	98	42	45	0	9	2	5	31	3	0	.097	6	25	0	2	0.9	1.000
1949		3	6	.333	7.48	19	3	0	49.1	65	29	20	0	3	4	0	11	0	0	.000	3	5	1	0	0.5	.889
1950		0	0	–	7.24	11	0	0	13.2	18	8	6	0	0	0	1	2	0	0	.000	0	6	0	0	0.5	1.000
1951	DET A	0	0	–	6.35	6	0	0	5.2	9	2	2	0	0	0	1	0	0	0	–	1	1	0	1	0.3	1.000
8 yrs.		40	32	.556	4.30	179	50	14	546.1	556	272	250	4	24	13	17	171	32	0	.187	24	126	4	13	0.9	.974

WORLD SERIES

Year	Team	W	L	PCT	ERA	G	GS	CG	IP	H	BB	SO	ShO	W	L	SV	AB	H	HR	BA	PO	A	E	DP	TC/G	FA
1946	BOS A	1	0	1.000	2.70	3	0	0	3.1	1	2	1	0	1	0	1	0	0	0	.000	0	2	0	0	0.7	1.000

Ellis Johnson

JOHNSON, ELLIS WALTER
B. Dec. 8, 1892, Minneapolis, Minn. D. Jan. 14, 1965, Minneapolis, Minn.

BR TR 6'½" 180 lbs.

Year	Team	W	L	PCT	ERA	G	GS	CG	IP	H	BB	SO	ShO	W	L	SV	AB	H	HR	BA	PO	A	E	DP	TC/G	FA
1912	CHI A	0	0	–	3.29	4	0	0	13.2	11	10	8	0	0	0	0	3	0	0	.000	1	2	0	0	0.8	1.000
1915		0	0	–	9.00	1	0	0	2	3	0	3	0	0	0	0	0	0	0	–	0	0	0	0	0.0	–
1917	PHI A	0	2	.000	7.24	4	2	0	13.2	15	5	8	0	0	0	0	1	0	0	.000	0	5	0	0	1.3	1.000
3 yrs.		0	2	.000	5.52	9	2	0	29.1	29	15	19	0	0	0	0	4	0	0	.000	1	7	0	0	0.9	1.000

Ernie Johnson

JOHNSON, ERNEST THORWALD
B. June 16, 1924, Brattleboro, Vt.

BR TR 6'3½" 190 lbs.

Year	Team	W	L	PCT	ERA	G	GS	CG	IP	H	BB	SO	ShO	W	L	SV	AB	H	HR	BA	PO	A	E	DP	TC/G	FA
1950	BOS N	2	0	1.000	6.97	16	1	0	20.2	37	13	15	0	2	0	0	2	1	0	.500	1	10	0	0	0.7	1.000
1952		6	3	.667	4.11	29	10	2	92	100	31	45	1	2	0	1	22	2	0	.091	9	21	1	3	1.1	.968
1953	MIL N	4	3	.571	2.67	36	1	0	81	79	22	36	0	4	2	0	14	1	0	.071	4	15	2	1	0.6	.905
1954		5	2	.714	2.81	40	4	1	99.1	77	34	68	0	4	1	2	13	3	0	.231	4	22	0	2	0.7	1.000
1955		5	7	.417	3.42	40	2	0	92	81	55	43	0	5	5	4	20	2	0	.100	7	14	3	0	0.6	.875
1956		4	3	.571	3.71	36	0	0	51	54	21	26	0	4	3	6	4	1	0	.250	4	10	1	0	0.4	.933
1957		7	3	.700	3.88	30	0	0	65	67	26	44	0	7	3	4	17	6	1	.353	6	13	0	0	0.6	1.000
1958		3	1	.750	8.10	15	0	0	23.1	35	10	13	0	3	1	1	2	0	0	.000	2	4	1	0	0.5	.857
1959	BAL A	4	1	.800	4.11	31	1	0	50.1	57	19	29	0	4	1	1	6	2	0	.333	1	10	1	0	0.4	.917
9 yrs.		40	23	.635	3.77	273	19	3	574.2	587	231	319	1	35	16	19	100	18	1	.180	38	119	9	6	0.6	.946

WORLD SERIES

Year	Team	W	L	PCT	ERA	G	GS	CG	IP	H	BB	SO	ShO	W	L	SV	AB	H	HR	BA	PO	A	E	DP	TC/G	FA
1957	MIL N	0	1	.000	1.29	3	0	0	7	2	1	8	0	0	1	0	1	0	0	.000	1	4	0	0	1.7	1.000

Fred Johnson

JOHNSON, FREDERICK EDWARD (Cactus)
B. Mar. 10, 1894, Tolar, Tex. D. June 14, 1973, Kerrville, Tex.

BR TR 6' 185 lbs.

Year	Team	W	L	PCT	ERA	G	GS	CG	IP	H	BB	SO	ShO	W	L	SV	AB	H	HR	BA	PO	A	E	DP	TC/G	FA
1922	NY N	0	2	.000	4.00	2	2	1	18	20	1	7	0	0	0	0	4	0	0	.000	1	3	0	0	2.0	1.000
1923		2	0	1.000	4.24	3	2	1	17	11	7	5	0	1	0	0	6	0	0	.000	0	9	0	1	3.0	1.000
1938	STL A	3	7	.300	5.61	17	6	3	69	91	27	24	0	5	5	3	25	6	0	.240	0	7	3	1	0.6	.700
1939		0	1	.000	6.43	5	2	1	14	23	9	2	0	0	0	0	4	0	0	.000	0	7	0	0	1.4	1.000
4 yrs.		5	10	.333	5.26	27	12	6	118	145	44	39	0	1	5	3	39	6	0	.154	1	26	3	2	1.1	.900

Hank Johnson

JOHNSON, HENRY WARD
B. May 21, 1906, Bradenton, Fla.
D. Aug. 20, 1982, Bradenton, Fla.

BR TR 5'11½" 175 lbs.
BB 1933

Year	Team	W	L	PCT	ERA	G	GS	CG	IP	H	BB	SO	ShO	W	L	SV	AB	H	HR	BA	PO	A	E	DP	TC/G	FA
1925	NY A	1	3	.250	6.85	24	4	2	67	88	37	25	1	0	1	0	17	1	0	.059	0	21	1	1	0.9	.955
1926		0	0	–	18.00	1	0	0	1	2	2	0	0	0	0	0	0	0	0	–	0	1	0	0	1.0	1.000
1928		14	9	.609	4.30	31	22	10	199	188	104	110	1	2	0	0	79	19	1	.241	9	42	2	1	1.7	.962
1929		3	3	.500	5.06	12	8	2	42.2	37	39	24	0	0	0	0	14	1	0	.071	1	5	1	0	0.6	.857
1930		14	11	.560	4.67	44	15	7	175.1	177	104	115	1	9	5	2	64	17	1	.266	5	40	2	3	1.1	.957
1931		13	8	.619	4.72	40	23	8	196.1	176	102	106	0	3	1	4	77	15	0	.195	4	24	0	0	0.7	1.000
1932		2	2	.500	4.88	5	4	2	31.1	34	15	27	0	0	0	0	13	3	0	.231	1	5	0	0	1.2	1.000
1933	BOS A	8	6	.571	4.06	25	21	7	155.1	156	74	65	0	1	0	0	52	12	0	.231	3	25	0	0	1.1	1.000
1934		6	8	.429	5.36	31	14	7	124.1	162	53	66	1	0	2	1	43	10	0	.233	3	18	0	1	0.7	1.000
1935		2	1	.667	5.52	13	2	0	31	41	14	14	0	2	0	1	8	0	0	.000	2	1	0	0	0.2	1.000
1936	PHI A	0	2	.000	7.71	3	3	0	11.2	16	10	6	0	0	0	0	4	1	0	.250	1	1	0	0	1.0	.667
1939	CIN N	0	3	.000	2.01	20	0	0	31.1	30	13	10	0	0	3	1	5	2	0	.400	2	0	0	0	0.1	1.000
12 yrs.		63	56	.529	4.75	249	116	45	1066.1	1107	567	568	4	16	12	11	376	81	2	.215	29	185	7	9	0.9	.968

Jerry Johnson

JOHNSON, JERRY MICHAEL
B. Dec. 3, 1943, Miami, Fla.

BR TR 6'3" 200 lbs.

Year	Team	W	L	PCT	ERA	G	GS	CG	IP	H	BB	SO	ShO	W	L	SV	AB	H	HR	BA	PO	A	E	DP	TC/G	FA
1968	PHI N	4	4	.500	3.24	16	11	2	80.2	82	29	40	0	0	0	0	25	2	0	.080	4	17	0	3	1.3	1.000
1969		6	13	.316	4.29	33	21	4	147	151	57	82	2	0	0	1	43	9	0	.209	6	22	1	1	0.9	.966
1970	2 teams	STL N (7G 2–0)			SF N	(33G 3–4)																				
"	total	5	4	.556	4.11	40	1	0	76.2	73	41	49	0	5	3	4	16	1	0	.063	3	9	1	0	0.3	.923
1971	SF N	12	9	.571	2.97	67	0	0	109	93	48	85	0	12	9	18	13	2	0	.154	6	15	1	0	0.3	.955
1972		8	6	.571	4.44	48	0	0	73	73	40	57	0	8	6	8	9	0	0	.000	5	12	2	0	0.4	.895

Year	Team		W	L	PCT	ERA	G	GS	CG	IP	H	BB	SO	ShO	Relief Pitching W	L	SV	Batting AB	H	HR	BA	PO	A	E	DP	TC/G	FA

Jerry Johnson *continued*

1973	CLE	A	5	6	.455	6.18	39	1	0	59.2	70	39	45	0	5	6	5	0	0	0	–	3	11	1	0	0.4	.933
1974	HOU	N	2	1	.667	4.80	34	0	0	45	47	24	32	0	2	1	0	1	0	0	.000	3	6	2	2	0.3	.818
1975	SD	N	3	1	.750	5.17	21	4	0	54	60	31	60	0	2	0	0	12	1	0	.083	6	5	1	0	0.6	.917
1976			1	3	.250	5.31	24	1	0	39	39	26	27	0	1	2	0	3	0	0	.000	4	3	1	0	0.3	.875
1977	TOR	A	2	4	.333	4.60	43	0	0	86	91	54	54	0	2	4	5	0	0	0	–	4	11	1	2	0.4	.938
10 yrs.			48	51	.485	4.31	365	39	6	770	779	389	489	2	37	31	41	122	15	0	.123	44	111	11	8	0.5	.934

LEAGUE CHAMPIONSHIP SERIES

| 1971 | SF | N | 0 | 0 | – | 13.50 | 1 | 0 | 0 | 1.1 | 1 | 1 | 2 | 0 | 0 | 0 | 0 | 0 | 0 | 0 | – | 0 | 0 | 0 | 0 | 0.0 | – |

Jim Johnson

JOHNSON, JAMES BRIAN
B. Nov. 3, 1945, Muskegon, Mich.

BL TL 5'11" 175 lbs.

| 1970 | SF | N | 1 | 0 | 1.000 | 7.71 | 3 | 0 | 0 | 7 | 8 | 5 | 2 | 0 | 1 | 0 | 0 | 2 | 0 | 0 | .000 | 0 | 2 | 0 | 0 | 0.7 | 1.000 |

Jing Johnson

JOHNSON, RUSSELL CONWELL
B. Oct. 9, 1894, Parker Ford, Pa. D. Dec. 6, 1950, Pottstown, Pa.

BR TR 5'9" 172 lbs.

1916	PHI	A	2	8	.200	3.74	12	12	8	84.1	90	39	25	0	0	0	0	27	2	1	.074	6	34	1	3	3.4	.976
1917			9	12	.429	2.78	34	23	13	191	184	56	55	0	0	0	0	59	12	0	.203	14	64	3	0	2.4	.963
1919			9	15	.375	3.61	34	25	12	202	222	62	67	0	2	1	0	72	14	1	.194	12	76	4	2	2.7	.957
1927			4	2	.667	3.48	17	3	2	51.2	42	16	16	0	2	1	0	12	2	0	.167	1	18	1	2	1.2	.950
1928			0	0	–	5.06	3	0	0	10.2	13	5	3	0	0	0	0	4	2	0	.500	1	3	0	1	1.3	1.000
5 yrs.			24	37	.393	3.35	100	63	35	539.2	551	178	166	0	4	2	0	174	32	2	.184	34	195	9	8	2.4	.962

Joe Johnson

JOHNSON, JOSEPH RICHARD
B. Oct. 30, 1961, Brookline, Mass.

BR TR 6'2" 195 lbs.

1985	ATL	N	4	4	.500	4.10	15	14	1	85.2	95	24	34	0	0	0	0	23	1	0	.043	4	7	1	0	0.8	.917
1986	2 teams	ATL N (17G 6–7)								TOR A (16G 7–2)																	
"	total		13	9	.591	4.42	33	30	2	175	195	57	88	0	0	0	0	26	3	0	.115	11	29	2	1	1.3	.952
1987	TOR	A	3	5	.375	5.13	14	14	0	66.2	77	18	27	0	0	0	0	0	0	0	–	7	8	0	0	1.1	1.000
3 yrs.			20	18	.526	4.48	62	58	3	327.1	367	99	149	0	0	0	0	49	4	0	.082	22	44	3	2	1.1	.957

John Johnson

JOHNSON, JOHN LOUIS
Born John Louis Mercer.
B. Nov. 18, 1869, Pekin, Ill. D. Jan. 28, 1941, Kansas City, Mo.

TL 165 lbs.

| 1894 | PHI | N | 1 | 1 | .500 | 6.06 | 4 | 3 | 2 | 32.2 | 44 | 15 | 10 | 0 | 0 | 0 | 0 | 16 | 3 | 0 | .188 | 0 | 8 | 2 | 0 | 2.5 | .800 |

John Henry Johnson

JOHNSON, JOHN HENRY
B. Aug. 21, 1956, Houston, Tex.

BL TL 6'2" 190 lbs.

1978	OAK	A	11	10	.524	3.39	33	30	7	186	164	82	91	0	0	0	0	0	0	0	–	8	16	4	0	0.8	.857
1979	2 teams	OAK A (14G 2–8)								TEX A (17G 2–6)																	
"	total		4	14	.222	4.63	31	25	2	167	168	72	96	0	1	0	0	0	0	0	–	5	18	0	3	0.7	1.000
1980	TEX	A	2	2	.500	2.31	33	0	0	39	27	15	44	0	2	2	4	0	0	0	–	0	5	0	0	0.2	1.000
1981			3	1	.750	2.63	24	0	0	24	19	6	8	0	3	1	2	0	0	0	–	1	7	0	1	0.3	1.000
1983	BOS	A	3	2	.600	3.71	34	1	0	53.1	58	20	51	0	3	1	1	0	0	0	–	2	5	1	0	0.2	.875
1984			1	2	.333	3.53	30	3	0	63.2	64	27	57	0	1	1	1	0	0	0	–	0	8	0	0	0.3	1.000
1986	MIL	A	2	1	.667	2.66	19	0	0	44	43	10	42	0	2	1	1	0	0	0	–	2	3	1	0	0.3	.833
1987			0	1	.000	9.57	10	2	0	26.1	42	18	18	0	0	0	0	0	0	0	–	0	5	0	1	0.5	1.000
8 yrs.			26	33	.441	3.89	214	61	9	603.1	585	250	407	2	12	6	9	0	0	0	–	18	67	6	5	0.4	.934

Johnny Johnson

JOHNSON, JOHN CLIFFORD (Swede)
B. Sept. 29, 1914, Belmore, Ohio

BL TL 6' 182 lbs.

1944	NY	A	0	2	.000	4.05	22	1	0	26.2	25	24	11	0	0	1	3	6	3	0	.500	2	1	1	0	0.2	.750
1945	CHI	A	3	0	1.000	4.26	29	0	0	69.2	85	35	38	0	3	0	4	14	4	0	.286	1	10	1	1	0.4	.917
2 yrs.			3	2	.600	4.20	51	1	0	96.1	110	59	49	0	3	1	7	20	7	0	.350	3	11	2	1	0.3	.875

Ken Johnson

JOHNSON, KENNETH TRAVIS
B. June 16, 1933, West Palm Beach, Fla.

BR TR 6'4" 210 lbs.

1958	KC	A	0	0	–	27.00	2	0	0	2.1	6	3	1	0	0	0	0	0	0	0	–	1	1	0	0	1.0	1.000
1959			1	1	.500	4.09	2	2	0	11	11	5	8	0	0	0	0	3	0	0	.000	0	3	0	0	1.5	1.000
1960			5	10	.333	4.26	42	4	2	120.1	120	45	83	0	3	6	3	30	5	0	.167	6	27	0	0	0.8	1.000
1961	2 teams	KC A (6G 0–4)								CIN N (15G 6–2)																	
"	total		6	6	.500	4.00	21	12	3	92.1	82	29	46	1	0	3	1	26	6	0	.231	10	23	0	1	1.6	1.000
1962	HOU	N	7	16	.304	3.84	33	31	5	197	195	46	178	1	0	0	0	52	4	0	.077	9	37	4	1	1.5	.920
1963			11	17	.393	2.65	37	32	6	224	204	50	148	1	1	1	1	74	5	0	.068	8	51	1	4	1.6	.983
1964			11	16	.407	3.63	35	35	7	218	209	44	117	0	0	0	0	76	6	0	.079	9	50	6	4	1.9	.908
1965	2 teams	HOU N (8G 3–2)								MIL N (29G 13–8)																	
"	total		16	10	.615	3.42	37	34	9	231.1	217	48	151	1	0	0	0	79	9	0	.114	16	30	2	1	1.3	.958
1966	ATL	N	14	8	.636	3.30	32	31	11	215.2	213	46	105	2	0	0	0	70	10	1	.143	14	35	1	4	1.6	.980
1967			13	9	.591	2.74	29	29	6	210.1	191	38	85	0	0	0	0	71	9	0	.127	9	33	1	0	1.5	.977
1968			5	8	.385	3.47	31	16	1	135	145	25	57	0	1	2	0	40	7	0	.175	7	18	1	3	0.8	.962
1969	3 teams	ATL N (9G 0–1)								NY A (12G 1–2)				CHI N (9G 1–2)												
"	total		2	5	.286	3.89	30	3	0	74	68	33	59	0	1	2	2	13	0	0	.000	3	13	0	1	0.5	1.000
1970	MON	N	0	0	–	7.50	3	0	0	6	9	1	4	0	0	0	0	0	0	0	–	1	1	0	0	0.7	1.000
13 yrs.			91	106	.462	3.46	334	231	50	1737.1	1670	413	1042	7	6	14	9	534	61	2	.114	93	322	16	19	1.3	.963

WORLD SERIES

| 1961 | CIN | N | 0 | 0 | – | 0.00 | 1 | 0 | 0 | 0 | 0 | 0 | 0 | 0 | 0 | 0 | 0 | 0 | 0 | 0 | – | 0 | 0 | 0 | 0 | 0.0 | – |

Ken Johnson

JOHNSON, KENNETH WANDERSEE (Hooks)
B. Jan. 14, 1923, Topeka, Kans.

BL TL 6'1" 185 lbs.

| 1947 | STL | N | 1 | 0 | 1.000 | 0.00 | 2 | 1 | 0 | 10 | 2 | 5 | 8 | 0 | 0 | 0 | 0 | 4 | 2 | 0 | .500 | 0 | 2 | 0 | 0 | 1.0 | 1.000 |

Year	Team	W	L	PCT	ERA	G	GS	CG	IP	H	BB	SO	ShO	Relief Pitching W	L	SV	Batting AB	H	HR	BA	PO	A	E	DP	TC/G	FA

Ken Johnson *continued*

Year	Team	W	L	PCT	ERA	G	GS	CG	IP	H	BB	SO	ShO	W	L	SV	AB	H	HR	BA	PO	A	E	DP	TC/G	FA
1948		2	4	.333	4.76	13	4	0	45.1	43	30	20	0	2	1	0	20	6	0	.300	0	8	1	0	0.7	.889
1949		0	1	.000	6.42	14	2	0	33.2	29	35	18	0	0	0	0	8	2	0	.250	1	13	2	1	1.1	.875
1950	2 teams	STL N	(2G 0–0)		PHI N	(14G 4–1)																				
"	total	4	1	.800	3.88	16	9	3	62.2	62	46	33	1	1	0	0	19	3	0	.158	0	1	0	0	0.1	1.000
1951	PHI N	5	8	.385	4.57	20	18	4	106.1	103	68	58	3	0	0	0	35	5	0	.143	4	15	0	4	1.0	1.000
1952	DET A	0	0	–	6.35	9	1	0	11.1	12	11	10	0	0	0	0	3	1	0	.333	1	2	0	0	0.3	1.000
6 yrs.		12	14	.462	4.58	74	35	8	269.1	251	195	147	4	3	1	0	89	19	0	.213	6	41	3	5	0.7	.940

Lloyd Johnson

JOHNSON, LLOYD WILLIAM (Eppa)
B. Dec. 24, 1910, Santa Rosa, Calif.   D. Oct. 8, 1980, Stockton, Calif.   BL TL 6'4''   204 lbs.

Year	Team	W	L	PCT	ERA	G	GS	CG	IP	H	BB	SO	ShO	W	L	SV	AB	H	HR	BA	PO	A	E	DP	TC/G	FA
1934	PIT N	0	0	–	0.00	1	0	0	1	1	0	0	0	0	0	0	0	0	0	–	0	0	0	0	0.0	–

Mike Johnson

JOHNSON, MICHAEL NORTON
B. Mar. 2, 1951, Slayton, Minn.   BR TR 6'1''   185 lbs.

Year	Team	W	L	PCT	ERA	G	GS	CG	IP	H	BB	SO	ShO	W	L	SV	AB	H	HR	BA	PO	A	E	DP	TC/G	FA
1974	SD N	0	2	.000	4.71	18	0	0	21	29	15	15	0	0	2	0	0	0	0	–	0	2	0	1	0.1	1.000

Randy Johnson

JOHNSON, RANDALL DAVID
B. Sept. 10, 1963, Walnut Creek, Calif.   BL TR 6'10''   225 lbs.

Year	Team	W	L	PCT	ERA	G	GS	CG	IP	H	BB	SO	ShO	W	L	SV	AB	H	HR	BA	PO	A	E	DP	TC/G	FA
1988	MON N	3	0	1.000	2.42	4	4	1	26	23	7	25	0	0	0	0	9	1	0	.111	0	0	1	0	0.3	–
1989	2 teams	MON N	(7G 0–4)		SEA A	(22G 7–9)																				
"	total	7	13	.350	4.82	29	28	2	160.2	147	96	130	0	0	0	0	7	1	0	.143	8	26	7	1	1.4	.829
2 yrs.		10	13	.435	4.48	33	32	3	186.2	170	103	155	0	0	0	0	16	2	0	.125	8	26	8	1	1.3	.810

Roy Johnson

JOHNSON, ROY J. (Hardrock)
B. Oct. 1, 1895, Madill, Okla.   D. Jan. 10, 1986, Scottsdale, Ariz.   BR TR 6'   185 lbs.

Year	Team	W	L	PCT	ERA	G	GS	CG	IP	H	BB	SO	ShO	W	L	SV	AB	H	HR	BA	PO	A	E	DP	TC/G	FA
1918	PHI A	1	5	.167	3.42	10	8	3	50	47	27	14	0	0	0	0	15	1	0	.067	2	13	1	1	1.6	.938

Si Johnson

JOHNSON, SILAS KENNETH
B. Oct. 5, 1906, Marseilles, Ill.   BR TR 5'11½''   185 lbs.

Year	Team	W	L	PCT	ERA	G	GS	CG	IP	H	BB	SO	ShO	W	L	SV	AB	H	HR	BA	PO	A	E	DP	TC/G	FA
1928	CIN N	0	0	–	4.35	3	1	0	10.1	9	5	1	0	0	0	0	4	1	0	.250	0	4	0	0	1.3	1.000
1929		0	0	–	4.50	1	0	0	2	2	1	0	0	0	0	0	0	0	0	–	0	0	0	0	0.0	–
1930		3	1	.750	4.94	35	3	0	78.1	86	31	47	0	2	1	0	17	4	0	.235	4	12	1	1	0.5	.941
1931		11	19	.367	3.77	42	33	14	262.1	273	74	95	0	0	2	0	87	13	0	.149	2	34	0	0	0.9	1.000
1932		13	15	.464	3.27	42	27	14	245	246	57	94	2	1	0	2	80	10	0	.125	7	55	7	1	1.6	.899
1933		7	18	.280	3.49	34	28	14	211.1	212	54	51	4	0	0	1	72	3	0	.042	3	44	3	3	1.5	.940
1934		7	22	.241	5.22	46	31	9	215.2	264	84	89	0	0	2	3	72	10	0	.139	6	32	0	1	0.8	1.000
1935		5	11	.313	6.23	30	20	4	130	155	59	40	1	0	0	0	41	1	0	.024	3	24	0	2	0.9	1.000
1936	2 teams	CIN N	(2G 0–0)		STL N	(12G 5–3)																				
"	total	5	3	.625	4.93	14	9	3	65.2	89	11	23	1	1	1	0	21	4	0	.190	1	8	0	1	0.6	1.000
1937	STL N	12	12	.500	3.32	38	21	12	192.1	222	43	64	1	3	3	1	65	9	0	.138	5	36	1	2	1.1	.976
1938		0	3	.000	7.47	6	3	0	15.2	27	6	4	0	0	0	0	1	0	0	.000	0	2	0	0	0.7	1.000
1940	PHI N	5	14	.263	4.88	37	14	5	138.1	145	42	58	0	1	6	1	43	6	0	.140	5	16	0	1	0.6	1.000
1941		5	12	.294	4.52	39	21	6	163.1	207	54	80	1	0	3	2	47	7	0	.149	4	27	0	1	0.8	1.000
1942		8	19	.296	3.69	29	26	10	195.1	198	72	78	1	1	1	0	58	6	0	.103	3	30	0	2	0.8	1.000
1943		8	3	.727	3.27	21	14	9	113	110	25	46	1	0	0	2	33	6	0	.182	4	21	1	1	1.2	.962
1946	2 teams	PHI N	(1G 0–0)		BOS N	(28G 6–5)																				
"	total	6	5	.545	2.77	29	12	5	130	141	35	43	1	0	1	1	38	6	0	.158	6	21	1	0	1.0	.964
1947	BOS N	6	8	.429	4.23	36	10	3	112.2	124	34	27	0	2	2	2	30	1	0	.033	3	36	0	3	1.1	1.000
17 yrs.		101	165	.380	4.09	492	272	108	2281.1	2510	687	840	13	11	21	15	709	87	0	.123	56	404	14	19	1.0	.970

Syl Johnson

JOHNSON, SYLVESTER
B. Dec. 31, 1900, Portland, Ore.   D. Feb. 20, 1985, Portland, Ore.   BR TR 5'11½''   180 lbs.

Year	Team	W	L	PCT	ERA	G	GS	CG	IP	H	BB	SO	ShO	W	L	SV	AB	H	HR	BA	PO	A	E	DP	TC/G	FA
1922	DET A	7	3	.700	3.71	29	8	3	97	99	30	29	0	3	1	0	36	8	0	.222	3	17	2	0	0.8	.909
1923		12	7	.632	3.98	37	18	7	176.1	181	47	93	1	5	2	0	62	10	1	.161	5	17	1	0	0.6	.957
1924		5	4	.556	4.93	29	9	2	104	117	42	55	0	2	3	3	34	7	0	.206	2	17	0	0	0.7	1.000
1925		0	2	.000	3.46	6	0	0	13	11	10	5	0	0	2	0	3	0	0	.000	2	4	0	0	0.5	1.000
1926	STL N	0	3	.000	4.22	19	6	1	49	54	15	10	0	0	0	1	12	0	0	.000	0	10	0	1	0.5	1.000
1927		0	0	–	6.00	2	0	0	3	3	0	2	0	0	0	0	1	0	0	.000	0	1	0	0	0.5	1.000
1928		8	4	.667	3.90	34	6	2	120	117	33	66	0	4	3	3	38	6	0	.158	3	20	1	2	0.7	.958
1929		13	7	.650	3.60	42	19	12	182.1	186	56	80	3	3	3	2	60	7	1	.117	5	19	1	0	0.6	.960
1930		12	10	.545	4.65	32	24	9	187.2	215	38	92	2	2	1	2	70	15	0	.214	4	21	1	3	0.8	.962
1931		11	9	.550	3.00	32	24	12	186	186	29	82	2	1	0	2	60	14	0	.233	3	24	3	2	0.9	.900
1932		5	14	.263	4.92	32	22	7	164.2	199	35	70	1	1	1	1	51	10	0	.196	3	30	0	1	1.0	1.000
1933		3	3	.500	4.29	35	1	0	84	89	16	28	0	2	3	3	21	5	0	.238	1	12	0	1	0.4	1.000
1934	2 teams	CIN N	(2G 0–0)		PHI N	(42G 5–9)																				
"	total	5	9	.357	3.46	44	10	4	140.1	131	24	54	3	2	5	3	43	9	0	.209	5	10	1	1	0.4	.938
1935	PHI N	10	8	.556	3.56	37	18	8	174.2	182	31	89	1	3	1	6	58	14	0	.241	6	20	2	1	0.8	.929
1936		5	7	.417	4.30	39	8	1	111	129	29	48	0	1	4	7	36	9	0	.250	4	13	0	0	0.4	1.000
1937		4	10	.286	5.02	32	15	4	138	155	22	46	0	1	3	2	48	7	0	.146	2	25	1	2	1.1	.971
1938		2	7	.222	4.23	22	6	2	83	87	11	21	0	1	3	0	29	1	0	.034	2	9	0	0	0.5	1.000
1939		8	8	.500	3.81	22	13	6	111	112	15	37	0	2	0	2	33	5	0	.152	3	17	0	1	0.9	1.000
1940		2	2	.500	4.20	17	2	2	40.2	37	5	13	0	1	2	2	8	0	0	.000	3	6	0	1	0.5	1.000
19 yrs.		112	117	.489	4.06	542	209	82	2165.2	2290	488	920	13	33	33	43	702	127	4	.181	63	291	13	13	0.7	.965

WORLD SERIES

Year	Team	W	L	PCT	ERA	G	GS	CG	IP	H	BB	SO	ShO	W	L	SV	AB	H	HR	BA	PO	A	E	DP	TC/G	FA
1928	STL N	0	0	–	4.50	2	0	0	2	4	1	1	0	0	0	0	0	0	0	–	0	0	0	0	0.0	–
1930		0	0	–	7.20	2	0	0	5	4	3	4	0	0	0	0	0	0	0	–	0	0	0	0	0.0	–
1931		0	1	.000	3.00	3	1	0	9	10	1	6	0	0	0	0	2	0	0	.000	0	1	0	0	0.3	1.000
3 yrs.		0	1	.000	4.50	7	1	0	16	18	5	11	0	0	0	0	2	0	0	.000	0	1	0	0	0.1	1.000

Year	Team		W	L	PCT	ERA	G	GS	CG	IP	H	BB	SO	ShO	Relief Pitching W	L	SV	Batting AB	H	HR	BA	PO	A	E	DP	TC/G	FA

Tom Johnson

JOHNSON, THOMAS RAYMOND
B. Apr. 2, 1951, St. Paul, Minn.
BR TR 6'1" 185 lbs.

Year	Team		W	L	PCT	ERA	G	GS	CG	IP	H	BB	SO	ShO	W	L	SV	AB	H	HR	BA	PO	A	E	DP	TC/G	FA
1974	MIN	A	2	0	1.000	0.00	4	0	0	7	4	0	4	0	2	0	1	0	0	0	–	0	1	1	0	0.5	.500
1975			1	2	.333	4.19	18	0	0	38.2	40	21	17	0	1	2	3	0	0	0	–	5	5	1	0	0.6	.909
1976			3	1	.750	2.61	18	1	0	48.1	44	8	37	0	3	0	0	0	0	0	–	1	7	0	0	0.4	1.000
1977			16	7	.696	3.12	71	0	0	147	152	47	87	0	16	7	15	0	0	0	–	9	26	1	0	0.5	.972
1978			1	4	.200	5.51	18	0	0	32.2	42	17	21	0	1	4	3	0	0	0	–	0	6	0	0	0.3	1.000
5 yrs.			23	14	.622	3.39	129	1	0	273.2	282	93	166	0	23	13	22	0	0	0	–	15	45	3	0	0.5	.952

Vic Johnson

JOHNSON, VICTOR OSCAR
B. Aug. 3, 1920, Eau Claire, Wis.
BR TL 6' 160 lbs.

Year	Team		W	L	PCT	ERA	G	GS	CG	IP	H	BB	SO	ShO	W	L	SV	AB	H	HR	BA	PO	A	E	DP	TC/G	FA
1944	BOS	A	0	3	.000	6.26	7	5	0	27.1	42	15	7	0	0	0	0	10	0	0	.000	1	9	1	1	1.6	.909
1945			6	4	.600	4.01	26	9	4	85.1	90	46	21	1	3	0	2	30	5	0	.167	4	23	2	2	1.1	.931
1946	CLE	A	0	1	.000	9.22	9	1	0	13.2	20	8	3	0	0	0	0	2	0	0	.000	1	5	1	1	0.8	.857
3 yrs.			6	8	.429	5.06	42	15	4	126.1	152	69	31	1	3	0	2	42	5	0	.119	6	37	4	4	1.1	.915

Walter Johnson

JOHNSON, WALTER PERRY (The Big Train, Barney)
B. Nov. 6, 1887, Humboldt, Kans. D. Dec. 10, 1946, Washington, D. C.
Manager 1929-35.
Hall of Fame 1936.
BR TR 6'1" 200 lbs.

Year	Team		W	L	PCT	ERA	G	GS	CG	IP	H	BB	SO	ShO	W	L	SV	AB	H	HR	BA	PO	A	E	DP	TC/G	FA
1907	WAS	A	5	9	.357	1.87	14	12	11	110.2	98	17	70	2	0	2	0	36	4	0	.111	5	20	3	1	2.0	.893
1908			14	14	.500	1.64	36	29	23	257.1	194	53	160	6	0	1	1	79	13	0	.165	4	56	4	3	1.8	.938
1909			13	25	.342	2.21	40	36	27	297	247	84	164	4	1	2	1	101	13	1	.129	15	73	7	2	2.4	.926
1910			25	17	.595	1.35	45	42	38	373	269	76	313	8	1	1	1	137	24	2	.175	23	90	6	3	2.6	.950
1911			25	13	.658	1.89	40	37	36	323.1	292	70	207	6	1	1	1	128	30	1	.234	14	95	4	8	2.8	.964
1912			32	12	.727	1.39	50	37	34	368	259	76	303	7	5	2	2	144	38	2	.264	15	93	4	4	2.2	.964
1913			36	7	.837	1.09	47	36	29	346	230	38	243	11	7	0	2	134	35	2	.261	21	82	0	7	2.2	1.000
1914			28	18	.609	1.72	51	40	33	371.2	287	74	225	9	4	3	1	136	30	3	.221	30	102	5	6	2.7	.964
1915			27	13	.675	1.55	47	39	35	336.2	258	56	203	7	2	0	4	147	34	2	.231	22	95	6	7	2.6	.951
1916			25	20	.556	1.89	48	38	36	371	290	82	228	3	4	3	1	142	33	1	.232	17	72	6	2	2.0	.937
1917			23	16	.590	2.30	47	34	30	328	259	67	188	8	5	1	3	130	33	0	.254	16	82	0	2	2.1	1.000
1918			23	13	.639	1.27	39	29	29	325	241	70	162	8	3	4	3	150	40	1	.267	17	70	2	4	2.3	.978
1919			20	14	.588	1.49	39	29	27	290.1	235	51	147	7	2	4	2	125	24	1	.192	16	69	1	5	2.2	.988
1920			8	10	.444	3.13	21	15	12	143.2	135	27	78	4	1	2	3	69	18	1	.261	5	28	1	0	1.6	.971
1921			17	14	.548	3.51	35	32	25	264	265	92	143	1	1	1	1	111	30	0	.270	4	51	1	1	1.6	.982
1922			15	16	.484	2.99	41	31	23	280	283	99	105	4	1	1	4	108	22	1	.204	11	66	0	2	1.9	1.000
1923			17	12	.586	3.48	42	35	18	261.1	263	69	130	3	1	2	4	93	18	0	.194	13	51	2	7	1.6	.970
1924			23	7	.767	2.72	38	38	20	277.2	233	77	158	6	0	0	0	113	32	1	.283	9	53	0	2	1.6	1.000
1925			20	7	.741	3.07	30	29	16	229	211	78	108	3	0	0	0	97	42	2	.433	5	37	0	1	1.4	1.000
1926			15	16	.484	3.61	33	33	22	261.2	259	73	125	2	0	0	0	103	20	1	.194	11	38	1	1	1.5	.980
1927			5	6	.455	5.10	18	15	7	107.2	113	26	48	1	0	0	0	46	16	2	.348	5	25	0	3	1.7	1.000
21 yrs.			416	279	.599	2.17	801	666	531	5923	4921	1355	3508	110	40	30	34	*				278	1348	53	72	2.1	.968
			2nd	3rd		7th			5th		3rd		7th	1st													

WORLD SERIES

Year	Team		W	L	PCT	ERA	G	GS	CG	IP	H	BB	SO	ShO	W	L	SV	AB	H	HR	BA	PO	A	E	DP	TC/G	FA
1924	WAS	A	1	2	.333	2.63	3	2	2	24	30	11	20	0	1	0	0	9	1	0	.111	1	4	1	2	2.0	.833
1925			2	1	.667	2.08	3	3	3	26	26	4	15	1	0	0	0	11	1	0	.091	0	4	0	0	1.3	1.000
2 yrs.			3	3	.500	2.34	6	5	5	50	56	15	35	1	1	0	0	20	2	0	.100	1	8	1	2	1.7	.900
									10th		8th																

Youngy Johnson

JOHNSON, JOHN GODFRED
B. July 22, 1877, San Francisco, Calif. D. Aug. 28, 1936, Berkeley, Calif.
TR

Year	Team		W	L	PCT	ERA	G	GS	CG	IP	H	BB	SO	ShO	W	L	SV	AB	H	HR	BA	PO	A	E	DP	TC/G	FA
1897	PHI	N	1	2	.333	4.66	5	2	1	29	39	12	7	0	0	0	0	13	1	0	.077	2	4	0	1	1.2	1.000
1899	NY	N	0	0	–	0.00	1	0	0	2	0	2	1	0	0	0	0	1	0	0	.000	0	1	1	0	2.0	.500
2 yrs.			1	2	.333	4.35	6	2	1	31	39	14	8	0	0	0	0	14	1	0	.071	2	5	1	1	1.3	.875

Roy Joiner

JOINER, ROY MERRILL (Pop)
B. Oct. 30, 1906, Red Bluff, Calif.
BL TL 6' 170 lbs.

Year	Team		W	L	PCT	ERA	G	GS	CG	IP	H	BB	SO	ShO	W	L	SV	AB	H	HR	BA	PO	A	E	DP	TC/G	FA
1934	CHI	N	0	1	.000	8.21	20	2	0	34	61	8	9	0	0	0	0	10	2	0	.200	1	7	1	0	0.5	.889
1935			0	0	–	5.40	2	0	0	3.1	6	2	0	0	0	0	0	1	0	0	.000	0	3	0	0	1.5	1.000
1940	NY	N	3	2	.600	3.40	30	2	0	53	66	17	25	0	2	1	1	11	3	0	.273	4	11	2	0	0.6	.882
3 yrs.			3	3	.500	5.28	52	4	0	90.1	133	27	34	0	2	1	1	22	5	0	.227	5	21	3	0	0.6	.897

Dave Jolly

JOLLY, DAVID (Gabby)
B. Oct. 14, 1924, Stony Point, N. C. D. May 27, 1963, Durham, N. C.
BR TR 6' 170 lbs.

Year	Team		W	L	PCT	ERA	G	GS	CG	IP	H	BB	SO	ShO	W	L	SV	AB	H	HR	BA	PO	A	E	DP	TC/G	FA
1953	MIL	N	0	1	.000	3.52	24	0	0	38.1	34	27	23	0	0	1	0	2	1	0	.500	2	6	0	0	0.3	1.000
1954			11	6	.647	2.43	47	1	0	111.1	87	64	62	0	11	6	10	31	9	1	.290	4	21	1	3	0.6	.962
1955			2	3	.400	5.71	36	0	0	58.1	58	51	23	0	2	3	1	6	1	0	.167	2	15	2	2	0.5	.895
1956			2	3	.400	3.74	29	0	0	45.2	39	35	20	0	2	3	7	4	0	0	.000	0	5	1	1	0.2	.833
1957			1	1	.500	5.02	23	0	0	37.2	37	21	27	0	1	1	1	5	3	0	.600	1	7	0	0	0.3	1.000
5 yrs.			16	14	.533	3.77	159	1	0	291.1	255	198	155	0	16	14	19	48	14	1	.292	9	54	4	6	0.4	.940

Al Jones

JONES, ALFORNIA
B. Feb. 10, 1959, Charleston, Miss.
BR TR 6'4" 210 lbs.

Year	Team		W	L	PCT	ERA	G	GS	CG	IP	H	BB	SO	ShO	W	L	SV	AB	H	HR	BA	PO	A	E	DP	TC/G	FA
1983	CHI	A	0	0	–	3.86	2	0	0	2.1	3	2	2	0	0	0	0	0	0	0	–	0	0	0	0	0.0	–
1984			1	1	.500	4.43	20	0	0	20.1	23	11	15	0	1	1	5	0	0	0	–	0	3	0	0	0.2	1.000
1985			1	0	1.000	1.50	5	0	0	6	3	3	2	0	1	0	0	0	0	0	–	1	1	0	0	0.4	1.000
3 yrs.			2	1	.667	3.77	27	0	0	28.2	29	16	19	0	2	1	5	0	0	0	–	1	4	0	0	0.2	1.000

Alex Jones

JONES, ALEXANDER H.
B. Dec. 25, 1869, Bradford, Pa. D. Apr. 4, 1941, Woodville, Pa.
BL TL 5'6" 135 lbs.

Year	Team		W	L	PCT	ERA	G	GS	CG	IP	H	BB	SO	ShO	W	L	SV	AB	H	HR	BA	PO	A	E	DP	TC/G	FA
1889	PIT	N	1	0	1.000	3.00	1	1	1	9	7	1	10	0	0	0	0	5	1	0	.200	0	3	0	1	3.0	1.000

Year	Team		W	L	PCT	ERA	G	GS	CG	IP	H	BB	SO	ShO	Relief Pitching W	L	SV	Batting AB	H	HR	BA	PO	A	E	DP	TC/G	FA

Mike Jones *continued*

Year	Team		W	L	PCT	ERA	G	GS	CG	IP	H	BB	SO	ShO	W	L	SV	AB	H	HR	BA	PO	A	E	DP	TC/G	FA
1981			6	3	.667	3.20	12	11	0	76	74	28	29	0	0	0	0	0	0	0	–	3	14	0	0	1.4	1.000
1984			2	3	.400	4.89	23	12	0	81	86	36	43	0	0	0	0	0	0	0	–	2	7	0	0	0.4	1.000
1985			3	3	.500	4.78	33	1	0	64	62	39	32	0	3	2	0	0	0	0	–	6	8	0	0	0.4	1.000
4 yrs.			11	10	.524	4.42	71	25	0	226	228	108	106	0	3	2	0	0	0	0	–	11	29	0	0	0.6	1.000

DIVISIONAL PLAYOFF SERIES

| 1981 | KC | A | 0 | 1 | .000 | 2.25 | 1 | 1 | 0 | 8 | 9 | 0 | 2 | 0 | 0 | 0 | 0 | 0 | 0 | 0 | – | 0 | 0 | 0 | 0 | 0.0 | – |

LEAGUE CHAMPIONSHIP SERIES

| 1984 | KC | A | 0 | 0 | – | 6.75 | 1 | 0 | 0 | 1.1 | 1 | 0 | 0 | 0 | 0 | 0 | 0 | 0 | 0 | 0 | – | 0 | 0 | 0 | 0 | 0.0 | – |

Odell Jones

JONES, ODELL
B. Jan. 13, 1953, Tulare, Calif.   BR TR 6'3" 175 lbs.

Year	Team		W	L	PCT	ERA	G	GS	CG	IP	H	BB	SO	ShO	W	L	SV	AB	H	HR	BA	PO	A	E	DP	TC/G	FA
1975	PIT	N	0	0	–	0.00	2	0	0	3	1	0	2	0	0	0	0	0	0	0	–	0	1	0	0	0.5	1.000
1977			3	7	.300	5.08	34	15	1	108	118	31	66	0	1	1	0	28	4	0	.143	2	8	0	0	0.3	1.000
1978			2	0	1.000	2.00	3	1	0	9	7	4	10	0	1	0	0	1	0	0	.000	0	1	0	0	0.3	1.000
1979	SEA	A	3	11	.214	6.05	25	19	3	119	151	58	72	0	0	2	0	0	0	0	–	8	9	4	0	0.8	.810
1981	PIT	N	4	5	.444	3.33	13	8	0	54	51	23	30	0	1	1	0	10	2	0	.200	3	10	0	0	1.0	1.000
1983	TEX	A	3	6	.333	3.09	42	0	0	67	56	22	50	0	3	6	10	0	0	0	–	3	5	0	0	0.2	1.000
1984			2	4	.333	3.64	33	0	0	59.1	62	23	28	0	2	4	2	0	0	0	–	5	10	0	1	0.5	1.000
1986	BAL	A	2	2	.500	3.83	21	0	0	49.1	58	23	32	0	2	2	0	0	0	0	–	2	5	0	0	0.3	1.000
1988	MIL	A	5	0	1.000	4.35	28	2	0	80.2	75	29	48	0	4	0	1	0	0	0	–	3	8	1	0	0.4	.917
9 yrs.			24	35	.407	4.42	201	45	4	549.1	579	213	338	0	14	16	13	39	6	0	.154	26	57	5	1	0.4	.943

Oscar Jones

JONES, OSCAR WINFIELD (Flip Flap)
B. Jan. 21, 1879, London Grove, Pa.   D. Oct. 8, 1946, Perkasie, Pa.   BR TR 5'7" 163 lbs.

Year	Team		W	L	PCT	ERA	G	GS	CG	IP	H	BB	SO	ShO	W	L	SV	AB	H	HR	BA	PO	A	E	DP	TC/G	FA
1903	BKN	N	20	16	.556	2.94	38	36	31	324.1	320	77	95	4	0	1	0	125	32	0	.256	13	75	9	2	2.6	.907
1904			17	25	.405	2.75	46	41	38	377	387	92	96	0	1	0	0	137	24	0	.175	16	78	10	2	2.3	.904
1905			8	15	.348	4.66	29	20	14	174	197	56	66	0	2	1	0	65	13	0	.200	3	32	4	0	1.3	.897
3 yrs.			45	56	.446	3.20	113	97	83	875.1	904	225	257	4	3	2	1	327	69	0	.211	32	185	23	4	2.1	.904

Percy Jones

JONES, PERCY LEE
B. Oct. 28, 1899, Harwood, Tex.   D. Mar. 18, 1979, Dallas, Tex.   BR TL 5'11½" 175 lbs.

Year	Team		W	L	PCT	ERA	G	GS	CG	IP	H	BB	SO	ShO	W	L	SV	AB	H	HR	BA	PO	A	E	DP	TC/G	FA
1920	CHI	N	0	0	–	11.57	4	0	0	7	15	3	0	0	0	0	0	2	0	0	.000	0	2	0	0	0.5	1.000
1921			3	5	.375	4.56	32	5	1	98.2	116	39	46	0	2	3	0	27	6	0	.222	6	14	0	0	0.6	1.000
1922			8	9	.471	4.72	44	26	7	164	197	69	46	2	2	0	1	47	4	0	.085	3	42	4	1	1.1	.918
1925			6	6	.500	4.65	28	13	6	124	123	71	60	1	2	1	0	39	6	0	.154	4	38	3	1	1.6	.933
1926			12	7	.632	3.09	30	20	10	160.1	151	90	80	2	4	0	2	50	13	0	.260	2	34	5	0	1.4	.878
1927			7	8	.467	4.07	30	11	5	112.2	123	72	37	1	3	1	0	40	14	0	.350	3	33	2	2	1.3	.947
1928			10	6	.625	4.03	39	18	9	154	164	56	41	1	3	0	3	56	11	0	.196	3	36	2	2	1.1	.951
1929	BOS	N	7	15	.318	4.64	35	22	11	188.1	219	84	69	1	2	1	0	61	9	0	.148	14	42	1	2	1.6	.982
1930	PIT	N	0	1	.000	6.63	9	2	0	19	26	11	3	0	0	0	0	2	0	0	.000	0	2	0	0	0.2	1.000
9 yrs.			53	57	.482	4.33	251	117	49	1028	1134	495	382	8	18	6	6	324	63	0	.194	35	243	17	8	1.2	.942

Randy Jones

JONES, RANDALL LEO
B. Jan. 12, 1950, Fullerton, Calif.   BR TL 6' 178 lbs.

Year	Team		W	L	PCT	ERA	G	GS	CG	IP	H	BB	SO	ShO	W	L	SV	AB	H	HR	BA	PO	A	E	DP	TC/G	FA
1973	SD	N	7	6	.538	3.16	20	19	6	139.2	129	37	77	1	0	0	0	48	8	0	.167	3	24	1	0	1.4	.964
1974			8	22	.267	4.46	40	34	4	208	217	78	124	1	0	1	2	65	10	0	.154	7	44	2	3	1.3	.962
1975			20	12	.625	2.24	37	36	18	285	242	56	103	6	1	0	0	83	11	0	.133	14	70	4	5	2.4	.955
1976			22	14	.611	2.74	40	40	25	315.1	274	50	93	5	0	0	0	103	6	0	.058	31	81	0	12	2.8	1.000
1977			6	12	.333	4.59	27	25	1	147	173	36	44	0	0	0	0	43	5	0	.116	8	47	2	0	2.1	.965
1978			13	14	.481	2.88	37	36	7	253	263	64	71	2	1	0	0	82	15	0	.183	15	51	4	5	1.9	.943
1979			11	12	.478	3.63	39	39	6	263	257	64	112	0	0	0	0	86	15	0	.174	15	60	3	2	2.0	.962
1980			5	13	.278	3.92	24	24	4	154	165	29	53	3	0	0	0	45	3	0	.067	12	38	1	0	2.1	1.000
1981	NY	N	1	8	.111	4.88	13	12	0	59	65	38	14	0	0	0	0	17	2	0	.118	2	19	0	1	1.6	1.000
1982			7	10	.412	4.60	28	20	2	107.2	130	51	44	1	0	0	0	27	4	0	.148	7	31	1	3	1.4	.974
10 yrs.			100	123	.448	3.42	305	285	73	1931.2	1915	503	735	19	2	2	2	599	79	0	.132	114	465	18	30	2.0	.970

Rick Jones

JONES, THOMAS FREDERICK
B. Apr. 16, 1955, Jacksonville, Fla.   BL TL 6'5" 190 lbs.

Year	Team		W	L	PCT	ERA	G	GS	CG	IP	H	BB	SO	ShO	W	L	SV	AB	H	HR	BA	PO	A	E	DP	TC/G	FA
1976	BOS	A	5	3	.625	3.38	24	14	1	104	133	26	45	0	1	0	0	0	0	0	–	8	13	0	2	0.9	1.000
1977	SEA	A	1	4	.200	5.14	10	10	0	42	47	37	16	0	0	0	0	0	0	0	–	1	7	0	1	0.8	1.000
1978			0	2	.000	5.84	3	2	0	12.1	17	7	11	0	0	0	0	0	0	0	–	0	0	0	0	0.0	–
3 yrs.			6	9	.400	4.04	37	26	1	158.1	197	70	72	0	1	0	0	0	0	0	–	9	20	0	3	0.8	1.000

Sad Sam Jones

JONES, SAMUEL POND
B. July 26, 1892, Woodsfield, Ohio   D. July 6, 1966, Barnesville, Ohio   BR TR 6' 170 lbs.

Year	Team		W	L	PCT	ERA	G	GS	CG	IP	H	BB	SO	ShO	W	L	SV	AB	H	HR	BA	PO	A	E	DP	TC/G	FA
1914	CLE	A	0	0	–	2.70	1	0	0	3.1	2	2	0	0	0	0	0	2	1	0	.500	0	1	0	0	1.0	1.000
1915			4	9	.308	3.65	48	9	2	145.2	131	63	42	0	2	3	4	32	5	0	.156	6	46	4	2	1.2	.929
1916	BOS	A	0	1	.000	3.67	12	0	0	27	25	10	7	0	0	1	1	6	2	0	.333	3	8	0	0	0.9	1.000
1917			0	1	.000	4.41	9	1	0	16.1	15	6	5	0	0	0	0	4	0	0	.000	3	5	0	2	0.9	1.000
1918			16	5	.762	2.25	24	21	16	184	151	70	44	0	5	0	0	57	10	0	.175	11	41	2	5	2.3	.963
1919			12	20	.375	3.75	35	31	21	245	258	95	67	5	0	3	1	81	11	0	.136	12	81	5	2	2.8	.949
1920			13	16	.448	3.94	37	33	20	274	302	79	86	3	0	2	0	92	20	0	.217	8	68	5	2	2.2	.938
1921			23	16	.590	3.22	40	38	25	298.2	318	78	98	5	0	1	0	100	24	2	.240	14	59	4	2	1.9	.948
1922	NY	A	13	13	.500	3.67	45	28	21	260	270	76	81	0	1	0	8	87	23	0	.264	11	60	3	5	1.6	.959
1923			21	8	.724	3.63	39	27	18	243	239	69	68	3	2	2	4	85	19	0	.224	7	68	1	1	1.9	.987
1924			9	6	.600	3.63	36	21	8	178.2	187	76	53	3	2	1	3	51	9	1	.176	6	40	4	1	1.4	.920
1925			15	21	.417	4.63	43	31	14	246.2	267	104	92	1	2	2	1	80	13	0	.163	17	56	3	4	1.8	.961
1926			9	8	.529	4.98	39	23	6	161	186	80	69	1	2	1	5	49	10	0	.204	4	33	2	1	1.0	.949
1927	STL	A	8	14	.364	4.32	30	26	11	189.2	211	102	72	0	0	0	0	55	6	0	.109	12	35	2	0	1.6	.959

Year	Team		W	L	PCT	ERA	G	GS	CG	IP	H	BB	SO	ShO	Relief Pitching W	L	SV	Batting AB	H	HR	BA	PO	A	E	DP	TC/G	FA

Sad Sam Jones *continued*

Year	Team		W	L	PCT	ERA	G	GS	CG	IP	H	BB	SO	ShO	W	L	SV	AB	H	HR	BA	PO	A	E	DP	TC/G	FA
1928	WAS	A	17	7	.708	2.84	30	27	19	224.2	209	78	63	4	0	0	0	79	20	2	.253	16	49	0	5	2.2	1.000
1929			9	9	.500	3.92	24	24	8	153.2	156	49	36	1	0	0	0	51	8	0	.157	10	26	3	1	1.6	.923
1930			15	7	.682	4.07	25	25	14	183.1	195	61	60	1	0	0	0	61	9	0	.148	11	32	4	2	1.9	.915
1931			9	10	.474	4.32	25	24	8	148	185	47	58	1	0	0	0	48	15	0	.313	6	28	2	2	1.4	.944
1932	CHI	A	10	15	.400	4.22	30	28	10	200.1	217	75	64	0	2	0	0	57	11	0	.193	17	50	3	2	2.3	.957
1933			10	12	.455	3.36	27	25	11	176.2	181	65	60	2	0	1	0	58	9	0	.155	6	34	3	3	1.6	.930
1934			8	12	.400	5.11	27	26	11	183.1	217	60	60	1	0	0	0	60	12	0	.200	11	27	2	1	1.5	.950
1935			8	7	.533	4.05	21	19	7	140	162	51	38	0	0	0	0	48	8	0	.167	5	29	0	1	1.6	1.000
22 yrs.			229	217	.513	3.84	647	487	250	3883	4084	1396	1223	36	16	17	31	1243	245	6	.197	196	876	52	48	1.7	.954

WORLD SERIES

Year	Team		W	L	PCT	ERA	G	GS	CG	IP	H	BB	SO	ShO	W	L	SV	AB	H	HR	BA	PO	A	E	DP	TC/G	FA
1918	BOS	A	0	1	.000	3.00	1	1	1	9	7	5	5	1	0	0	0	1	0	0	.000	0	4	0	0	4.0	1.000
1922	NY	A	0	0	–	0.00	2	0	0	2	1	1	0	0	0	0	0	0	0	0	–	0	1	0	0	0.5	1.000
1923			0	1	.000	0.90	2	1	0	10	5	2	3	0	0	0	1	2	0	0	.000	0	3	0	1	1.5	1.000
1926			0	0	–	9.00	1	0	0	1	2	2	1	0	0	0	0	0	0	0	–	0	0	0	0	0.0	–
4 yrs.			0	2	.000	2.05	6	2	1	22	15	10	9	1	0	0	1	3	0	0	.000	0	8	0	1	1.3	1.000

Sam Jones

JONES, SAMUEL (Toothpick Sam, Sad Sam)   BR TR 6'4"   192 lbs.
B. Dec. 14, 1925, Stewartsville, Ohio   D. Nov. 5, 1971, Morgantown, W. Va.

Year	Team		W	L	PCT	ERA	G	GS	CG	IP	H	BB	SO	ShO	W	L	SV	AB	H	HR	BA	PO	A	E	DP	TC/G	FA
1951	CLE	A	0	1	.000	2.08	2	1	0	8.2	4	5	4	0	0	0	0	2	0	0	.000	1	1	0	0	1.0	1.000
1952			2	3	.400	7.25	14	4	0	36	38	37	28	0	1	0	1	10	1	0	.100	0	4	0	0	0.3	1.000
1955	CHI	N	14	**20**	.412	4.10	36	34	12	241.2	175	**185**	198	4	1	1	0	77	14	0	.182	14	36	5	1	1.5	.909
1956			9	14	.391	3.91	33	28	8	188.2	155	**115**	176	2	1	0	0	57	10	0	.175	7	21	4	3	1.0	.875
1957	STL	N	12	9	.571	3.60	28	27	10	182.2	164	71	154	2	1	0	0	63	10	0	.159	13	27	1	1	1.5	.976
1958			14	13	.519	2.88	35	35	14	250	204	**107**	**225**	4	0	0	0	90	9	0	.100	14	31	1	3	1.3	.978
1959	SF	N	**21**	15	.583	**2.83**	50	35	16	270.2	232	109	209	**4**	4	1	4	85	11	0	.129	10	34	3	2	0.9	.936
1960			18	14	.563	3.19	39	35	13	234	200	91	190	3	2	1	0	80	16	0	.200	6	34	5	1	1.2	.889
1961			8	8	.500	4.49	37	17	2	128.1	134	57	105	0	2	1	1	36	5	0	.139	7	11	1	1	0.5	.947
1962	DET	A	2	4	.333	3.65	30	6	1	81.1	77	35	73	0	1	1	1	21	2	1	.095	11	8	1	0	0.7	.950
1963	STL	N	2	0	1.000	9.00	11	0	0	11	15	5	8	0	2	0	2	1	0	0	.000	1	1	0	0	0.2	1.000
1964	BAL	A	0	0	–	2.61	7	0	0	10.1	5	5	6	0	0	0	0	0	0	0	–	0	1	0	1	0.1	1.000
12 yrs.			102	101	.502	3.59	322	222	76	1643.1	1403	822	1376	17	15	5	9	522	78	1	.149	84	209	21	13	1.0	.933

Sheldon Jones

JONES, SHELDON LESLIE (Available)   BR TR 6'   180 lbs.
B. Feb. 2, 1922, Tecumseh, Neb.

Year	Team		W	L	PCT	ERA	G	GS	CG	IP	H	BB	SO	ShO	W	L	SV	AB	H	HR	BA	PO	A	E	DP	TC/G	FA
1946	NY	N	1	2	.333	3.21	6	4	1	28	21	17	24	0	0	0	0	8	2	0	.250	1	4	0	0	0.8	1.000
1947			2	2	.500	3.88	15	6	0	55.2	51	29	24	0	2	0	0	16	2	0	.125	4	5	1	0	0.7	.900
1948			16	8	.667	3.35	55	21	8	201.1	204	90	82	2	5	4	5	64	13	0	.203	10	38	2	1	0.9	.960
1949			15	12	.556	3.34	42	27	11	207.1	198	88	79	1	5	0	0	66	8	0	.121	11	35	1	2	1.1	.979
1950			13	16	.448	4.61	40	28	11	199	188	90	97	2	3	2	2	57	6	0	.105	8	25	0	0	0.8	1.000
1951			6	11	.353	4.26	41	12	2	120.1	119	52	58	0	4	4	4	31	3	0	.097	5	23	2	2	0.7	.933
1952	BOS	N	1	4	.200	4.76	39	1	0	70	81	31	40	0	1	3	1	8	1	0	.125	4	13	1	1	0.5	.944
1953	CHI	N	0	2	.000	5.40	22	2	0	38.1	47	16	9	0	0	1	0	7	0	0	.000	4	6	1	2	0.5	.909
8 yrs.			54	57	.486	3.96	260	101	33	920	909	413	413	5	19	15	12	257	35	0	.136	47	149	8	8	0.8	.961

WORLD SERIES

Year	Team		W	L	PCT	ERA	G	GS	CG	IP	H	BB	SO	ShO	W	L	SV	AB	H	HR	BA	PO	A	E	DP	TC/G	FA
1951	NY	N	0	0	–	2.08	2	0	0	4.1	5	1	2	0	0	0	0	0	0	0	–	0	1	0	0	0.5	1.000

Sherman Jones

JONES, SHERMAN JARVIS (Roadblock)   BL TR 6'4"   205 lbs.
B. Feb. 10, 1935, Winton, N. C.

Year	Team		W	L	PCT	ERA	G	GS	CG	IP	H	BB	SO	ShO	W	L	SV	AB	H	HR	BA	PO	A	E	DP	TC/G	FA
1960	SF	N	1	1	.500	3.09	16	0	0	32	37	11	10	0	1	1	1	7	2	0	.286	0	4	1	0	0.3	.800
1961	CIN	N	1	1	.500	4.42	24	2	0	55	51	27	32	0	0	1	2	11	2	0	.182	5	8	0	0	0.5	1.000
1962	NY	N	0	4	.000	7.71	8	3	0	23.1	31	8	11	0	0	1	0	7	3	0	.429	3	5	0	0	1.0	1.000
3 yrs.			2	6	.250	4.73	48	5	0	110.1	119	46	53	0	1	3	3	25	7	0	.280	8	17	1	0	0.5	.962

WORLD SERIES

Year	Team		W	L	PCT	ERA	G	GS	CG	IP	H	BB	SO	ShO	W	L	SV	AB	H	HR	BA	PO	A	E	DP	TC/G	FA
1961	CIN	N	0	0	–	0.00	1	0	0	.2	0	0	0	0	0	0	0	0	0	0	–	0	0	0	0	0.0	–

Steve Jones

JONES, STEVEN HOWELL   BL TL 5'10"   175 lbs.
Brother of Gary Jones.
B. Apr. 22, 1941, Huntington Park, Calif.

Year	Team		W	L	PCT	ERA	G	GS	CG	IP	H	BB	SO	ShO	W	L	SV	AB	H	HR	BA	PO	A	E	DP	TC/G	FA
1967	CHI	A	2	2	.500	4.21	11	3	0	25.2	21	12	17	0	1	0	0	4	1	0	.250	0	4	1	0	0.5	.800
1968	WAS	A	1	2	.333	5.91	7	0	0	10.2	8	7	11	0	1	2	0	1	0	0	.000	0	0	1	0	0.1	–
1969	KC	A	2	3	.400	4.23	20	4	0	44.2	45	24	31	0	0	1	0	8	1	0	.125	7	6	1	0	0.7	.929
3 yrs.			5	7	.417	4.44	38	7	0	81	74	43	59	0	2	3	0	13	2	0	.154	7	10	3	0	0.5	.850

Tim Jones

JONES, TIMOTHY BRYON   BB TR 6'5"   220 lbs.
B. Jan. 24, 1954, Sacramento, Calif.

Year	Team		W	L	PCT	ERA	G	GS	CG	IP	H	BB	SO	ShO	W	L	SV	AB	H	HR	BA	PO	A	E	DP	TC/G	FA
1977	PIT	N	1	0	1.000	0.00	3	1	0	10	4	3	5	0	0	0	0	2	0	0	.000	1	0	0	0	0.3	1.000

Claude Jonnard

JONNARD, CLAUDE ALFRED   BR TR 6'1"   165 lbs.
Brother of Bubber Jonnard.
B. Nov. 23, 1897, Nashville, Tenn.   D. Aug. 27, 1959, Nashville, Tenn.

Year	Team		W	L	PCT	ERA	G	GS	CG	IP	H	BB	SO	ShO	W	L	SV	AB	H	HR	BA	PO	A	E	DP	TC/G	FA
1921	NY	N	0	0	–	0.00	1	0	0	4	4	0	7	0	0	0	0	0	0	0	.000	0	0	0	0	0.0	–
1922			6	1	.857	3.84	33	0	0	96	96	28	44	0	6	1	**5**	24	1	0	.042	0	15	1	1	0.5	.938
1923			4	3	.571	3.28	**45**	1	1	96	105	35	45	0	3	3	**5**	26	1	0	.038	3	17	1	0	0.5	.952
1924			4	5	.444	2.41	34	3	1	89.2	86	24	40	0	4	3	5	22	1	0	.045	2	20	0	0	0.6	1.000
1926	STL	A	0	2	.000	6.00	12	2	0	36	46	24	13	0	0	0	0	7	0	0	.000	0	17	2	0	1.6	.895
1929	CHI	N	0	1	.000	7.48	12	0	0	27.2	41	11	11	0	0	0	0	10	2	0	.200	0	8	2	0	0.8	.800
6 yrs.			14	12	.538	3.79	137	9	2	349.1	372	122	160	0	13	7	17	90	5	0	.056	5	77	6	1	0.6	.932

Year	Team	W	L	PCT	ERA	G	GS	CG	IP	H	BB	SO	ShO	Relief Pitching W	L	SV	Batting AB	H	HR	BA	PO	A	E	DP	TC/G	FA

Claude Jonnard *continued*

WORLD SERIES

Year	Team	W	L	PCT	ERA	G	GS	CG	IP	H	BB	SO	ShO	W	L	SV	AB	H	HR	BA	PO	A	E	DP	TC/G	FA
1923	NY N	0	0	–	0.00	2	0	0	2	1	1	1	0	0	0	0	0	0	0	–	0	1	0	0	0.5	1.000
1924		0	0	–	0.00	1	0	0		0	1	0	0	0	0	0	0	0	0	–	0	0	0	0	0.0	–
2 yrs.		0	0	–	0.00	3	0	0	2	1	2	1	0	0	0	0	0	0	0	–	0	1	0	0	0.3	1.000

Charlie Jordan

JORDAN, CHARLES T.
B. Oct. 4, 1871, Baltimore, Md.   D. June 1, 1928, Hazleton, Pa.

Year	Team	W	L	PCT	ERA	G	GS	CG	IP	H	BB	SO	ShO	W	L	SV	AB	H	HR	BA	PO	A	E	DP	TC/G	FA
1896	PHI N	0	0	–	7.71	2	0	0	4.2	9	2	3	0	0	0	0	2	1	0	.500	0	1	0	0	0.5	1.000

Harry Jordan

JORDAN, HARRY J.
B. Feb. 14, 1873, Titusville, Pa.   D. Mar. 1, 1920, Pittsburgh, Pa.

Year	Team	W	L	PCT	ERA	G	GS	CG	IP	H	BB	SO	ShO	W	L	SV	AB	H	HR	BA	PO	A	E	DP	TC/G	FA
1894	PIT N	1	0	1.000	4.00	1	1	1	9	10	1	0	0	0	0	0	3	0	0	.000	2	0	0	0	2.0	1.000
1895		0	2	.000	4.24	2	2	2	17	24	6	4	0	0	0	0	7	2	0	.286	1	2	1	0	2.0	.750
2 yrs.		1	2	.333	4.15	3	3	3	26	34	8	5	0	0	0	0	10	2	0	.200	3	2	1	0	2.0	.833

Milt Jordan

JORDAN, MILTON MIGNOT
B. May 24, 1927, Mineral Springs, Pa.   BR TR 6'2½" 207 lbs.

Year	Team	W	L	PCT	ERA	G	GS	CG	IP	H	BB	SO	ShO	W	L	SV	AB	H	HR	BA	PO	A	E	DP	TC/G	FA
1953	DET A	0	1	.000	5.82	8	1	0	17	26	5	4	0	0	0	0	2	1	0	.500	0	6	2	0	1.0	.750

Niles Jordan

JORDAN, NILES CHAPMAN
B. Dec. 1, 1925, Lyman, Wash.   BL TL 5'11" 180 lbs.

Year	Team	W	L	PCT	ERA	G	GS	CG	IP	H	BB	SO	ShO	W	L	SV	AB	H	HR	BA	PO	A	E	DP	TC/G	FA
1951	PHI N	2	3	.400	3.19	5	5	2	36.2	35	8	11	1	0	0	0	13	1	0	.077	3	4	0	0	1.4	1.000
1952	CIN N	0	1	.000	9.95	3	1	0	6.1	14	3	2	0	0	0	0	1	0	0	.000	0	1	0	1	0.3	1.000
2 yrs.		2	4	.333	4.19	8	6	2	43	49	11	13	1	0	0	0	14	1	0	.071	3	5	0	1	1.0	1.000

Rip Jordan

JORDAN, RAYMOND WILLIS (Lanky)
B. Sept. 28, 1889, Portland, Me.   D. June 5, 1960, Meriden, Conn.   BL TR 6' 172 lbs.

Year	Team	W	L	PCT	ERA	G	GS	CG	IP	H	BB	SO	ShO	W	L	SV	AB	H	HR	BA	PO	A	E	DP	TC/G	FA
1912	CHI A	0	0	–	6.10	3	0	0	10.1	13	0	0	0	0	0	0	4	0	0	.000	0	2	0	0	0.7	1.000
1919	WAS A	0	0	–	11.25	1	1	0	4	6	2	2	0	0	0	0	1	0	0	.000	0	0	0	1	0.0	–
2 yrs.		0	0	–	7.53	4	1	0	14.1	19	2	2	0	0	0	0	5	0	0	.000	0	2	0	1	0.5	1.000

Orville Jorgens

JORGENS, ORVILLE EDWARD
Brother of Arndt Jorgens.
B. June 4, 1908, Rockford, Ill.   BR TR 6'1" 180 lbs.

Year	Team	W	L	PCT	ERA	G	GS	CG	IP	H	BB	SO	ShO	W	L	SV	AB	H	HR	BA	PO	A	E	DP	TC/G	FA
1935	PHI N	10	15	.400	4.83	**53**	24	6	188.1	216	96	57	0	4	3	2	62	6	0	.097	9	55	2	0	1.2	.970
1936		8	8	.500	4.79	39	21	4	167.1	196	69	58	0	0	1	0	60	12	0	.200	5	39	3	1	1.1	1.000
1937		3	4	.429	4.41	52	11	1	140.2	159	68	34	0	2	0	3	35	5	0	.143	8	40	3	2	1.0	.941
3 yrs.		21	27	.438	4.70	144	56	11	496.1	571	233	149	0	6	4	5	157	23	0	.146	22	134	5	5	1.1	.969

Addie Joss

JOSS, ADRIAN
B. Apr. 12, 1880, Woodland, Wis.   D. Apr. 14, 1911, Toledo, Ohio   BR TR 6'3" 185 lbs.
Hall of Fame 1978.

Year	Team	W	L	PCT	ERA	G	GS	CG	IP	H	BB	SO	ShO	W	L	SV	AB	H	HR	BA	PO	A	E	DP	TC/G	FA
1902	CLE A	17	13	.567	2.77	32	29	28	269.1	225	75	106	**5**	1	0	0	103	12	0	.117	9	106	6	2	3.8	.950
1903		18	13	.581	2.15	32	31	31	292.2	239	43	126	3	0	0	0	117	22	0	.188	13	112	7	3	4.1	.947
1904		14	10	.583	**1.59**	25	24	20	192.1	160	30	83	6	0	0	1	76	10	0	.132	11	61	3	2	3.0	.960
1905		20	12	.625	2.01	33	32	31	286	246	46	132	3	0	1	0	94	13	0	.138	22	106	4	1	4.0	.970
1906		21	9	.700	1.72	34	31	28	282	220	43	106	9	0	1	1	100	21	0	.210	26	93	4	2	3.6	.967
1907		**27**	11	.711	1.83	42	38	34	338.2	279	54	127	6	2	0	2	114	13	0	.114	21	143	3	6	4.0	.982
1908		24	11	.686	**1.16**	42	35	29	325	232	30	130	9	2	0	2	97	15	0	.155	23	109	5	3	3.3	.964
1909		14	13	.519	1.71	33	28	24	242.2	198	31	67	4	0	1	0	80	8	1	.100	12	78	2	0	2.8	.978
1910		5	5	.500	2.26	13	12	9	107.1	96	18	49	1	0	0	0	36	4	0	.111	7	42	2	1	3.9	.961
9 yrs.		160	97	.623	1.88 2nd	286	260	234	2336	1895	370	926	46	5	4	5	817	118	1	.144	144	850	36	20	3.6	.965

Bob Joyce

JOYCE, ROBERT EMMETT
B. Jan. 14, 1915, Stockton, Calif.   D. Dec. 10, 1981, San Francisco, Calif.   BR TR 6'1" 180 lbs.

Year	Team	W	L	PCT	ERA	G	GS	CG	IP	H	BB	SO	ShO	W	L	SV	AB	H	HR	BA	PO	A	E	DP	TC/G	FA
1939	PHI A	3	5	.375	6.69	30	6	1	107.2	156	37	25	0	3	1	0	35	3	0	.086	3	24	0	1	0.9	1.000
1946	NY N	3	4	.429	5.34	14	7	2	60.2	79	20	24	0	0	0	0	19	3	1	.158	4	14	0	0	1.3	1.000
2 yrs.		6	9	.400	6.20	44	13	3	168.1	235	57	49	0	3	1	0	54	6	1	.111	7	38	0	1	1.0	1.000

Dick Joyce

JOYCE, RICHARD EDWARD
B. Nov. 18, 1943, Portland, Me.   BL TL 6'5" 225 lbs.

Year	Team	W	L	PCT	ERA	G	GS	CG	IP	H	BB	SO	ShO	W	L	SV	AB	H	HR	BA	PO	A	E	DP	TC/G	FA
1965	KC A	0	1	.000	2.77	5	3	0	13	12	4	7	0	0	0	0	4	0	0	.000	0	2	0	0	0.4	1.000

Mike Joyce

JOYCE, MICHAEL LEWIS
B. Feb. 12, 1941, Detroit, Mich.   BR TR 6'2" 193 lbs.

Year	Team	W	L	PCT	ERA	G	GS	CG	IP	H	BB	SO	ShO	W	L	SV	AB	H	HR	BA	PO	A	E	DP	TC/G	FA
1962	CHI A	2	1	.667	3.32	25	1	0	43.1	40	14	9	0	2	1	2	7	3	0	.429	2	9	0	1	0.4	1.000
1963		0	0	–	8.44	6	0	0	10.2	13	8	7	0	0	0	0	0	0	0	–	0	1	0	0	0.2	1.000
2 yrs.		2	1	.667	4.33	31	1	0	54	53	22	16	0	2	1	2	7	3	0	.429	2	10	0	1	0.4	1.000

Oscar Judd

JUDD, THOMAS WILLIAM OSCAR (Ossie)
B. Feb. 14, 1908, London, Ontario, Canada   BL TL 6'½" 180 lbs.

Year	Team	W	L	PCT	ERA	G	GS	CG	IP	H	BB	SO	ShO	W	L	SV	AB	H	HR	BA	PO	A	E	DP	TC/G	FA
1941	BOS A	0	0	–	8.76	7	0	0	12.1	15	10	5	0	0	0	1	4	2	0	.500	0	4	1	0	0.7	.800
1942		8	10	.444	3.89	31	19	11	150.1	135	90	70	0	0	2	2	67	18	2	.269	6	29	1	1	1.2	.972
1943		11	6	.647	2.90	23	20	8	155.1	131	69	53	1	0	1	0	54	14	0	.259	9	41	3	4	2.3	.943
1944		1	1	.500	3.60	9	6	1	30	30	15	9	0	0	0	0	11	2	0	.182	1	4	0	0	0.6	1.000

Year	Team	W	L	PCT	ERA	G	GS	CG	IP	H	BB	SO	ShO	Relief Pitching W	L	SV	Batting AB	H	HR	BA	PO	A	E	DP	TC/G	FA

Oscar Judd *continued*

Year	Team	W	L	PCT	ERA	G	GS	CG	IP	H	BB	SO	ShO	W	L	SV	AB	H	HR	BA	PO	A	E	DP	TC/G	FA
1945	2 teams	BOS A	(2G 0–1)		PHI N	(23G 5–4)																				
"	total	5	5	.500	4.13	25	10	3	89.1	90	43	41	1	0	0	2	32	9	0	.281	4	23	0	0	1.1	1.000
1946	PHI N	11	12	.478	3.53	30	24	12	173.1	169	90	65	1	0	1	2	79	25	1	.316	10	50	0	0	1.0	1.000
1947		4	15	.211	4.60	32	19	8	146.2	155	69	54	1	0	2	0	64	12	0	.188	7	33	1	3	1.3	.976
1948		0	2	.000	6.91	4	1	0	14.1	19	11	7	0	0	2	0	6	1	0	.167	1	2	1	0	1.0	.750
8 yrs.		40	51	.440	3.90	161	99	43	771.2	744	397	304	4	0	8	7	*				38	186	7	8	1.4	.970

Ralph Judd

JUDD, RALPH WESLEY
B. Dec. 7, 1901, Perrysburg, Ohio   D. May 6, 1957, Lapeer, Mich.

BL TR 5'10"   170 lbs.

Year	Team	W	L	PCT	ERA	G	GS	CG	IP	H	BB	SO	ShO	W	L	SV	AB	H	HR	BA	PO	A	E	DP	TC/G	FA
1927	WAS A	0	0	–	6.75	1	0	0	4	8	2	2	0	0	0	1	1	0	0	.000	0	0	0	0	0.0	–
1929	NY N	3	0	1.000	2.66	18	0	0	50.2	49	11	21	0	3	0	0	14	0	0	.000	2	12	0	1	0.8	1.000
1930		0	0	–	5.87	2	0	0	7.2	13	3	0	0	0	0	0	3	0	0	.000	0	2	1	0	1.5	.667
3 yrs.		3	0	1.000	3.32	21	0	0	62.1	70	16	23	0	3	0	1	18	0	0	.000	2	14	1	1	0.8	.941

Howie Judson

JUDSON, HOWARD KOLLS
B. Feb. 16, 1926, Hebron, Ill.

BR TR 6'1"   195 lbs.

Year	Team	W	L	PCT	ERA	G	GS	CG	IP	H	BB	SO	ShO	W	L	SV	AB	H	HR	BA	PO	A	E	DP	TC/G	FA
1948	CHI A	4	5	.444	4.78	40	5	1	107.1	102	56	38	0	4	2	8	29	3	0	.103	2	22	1	2	0.6	.960
1949		1	14	.067	4.58	26	13	3	108	114	70	36	0	0	4	1	31	2	0	.065	3	24	2	0	1.1	.929
1950		2	3	.400	3.94	46	3	1	112	105	63	34	0	2	0	0	20	2	0	.100	6	14	1	1	0.5	.833
1951		5	6	.455	3.77	27	14	3	121.2	124	55	43	0	0	1	1	33	4	0	.121	2	25	1	2	1.0	.964
1952		0	1	.000	4.24	21	0	0	34	30	22	15	0	0	1	1	4	0	0	.000	1	6	1	0	0.4	.875
1953	CIN N	0	1	.000	5.59	10	6	0	38.2	58	11	11	0	0	0	0	9	1	0	.111	1	8	0	1	1.0	1.000
1954		5	7	.417	3.95	37	8	0	93.1	86	42	27	0	1	3	3	24	2	0	.083	4	10	1	1	0.4	.933
7 yrs.		17	37	.315	4.29	207	48	8	615	619	319	204	0	7	13	14	150	14	0	.093	17	109	10	7	0.7	.926

Ken Jungels

JUNGELS, KENNETH PETER (Curly)
B. June 23, 1916, Aurora, Ill.   D. Sept. 9, 1975, West Bend, Wis.

BR TR 6'1"   180 lbs.

Year	Team	W	L	PCT	ERA	G	GS	CG	IP	H	BB	SO	ShO	W	L	SV	AB	H	HR	BA	PO	A	E	DP	TC/G	FA
1937	CLE A	0	0	–	0.00	2	0	0	3	3	1	0	0	0	0	0	0	0	0	–	1	0	0	0	0.5	1.000
1938		1	0	1.000	8.80	9	0	0	15.1	21	18	7	0	1	0	0	5	0	0	.000	1	2	0	0	0.3	1.000
1940		0	0	–	2.70	2	0	0	3.1	3	1	1	0	0	0	0	1	0	0	.000	0	1	0	0	0.5	1.000
1941		0	0	–	7.24	6	0	0	13.2	17	8	6	0	0	0	0	2	0	0	.000	0	1	0	0	0.2	1.000
1942	PIT N	0	0	–	6.59	6	0	0	13.2	12	4	7	0	0	1	0	2	1	0	.500	1	3	0	0	0.7	1.000
5 yrs.		1	0	1.000	6.80	25	0	0	49	56	32	21	0	1	0	0	10	1	0	.100	3	7	0	0	0.4	1.000

Mike Jurewicz

JUREWICZ, MICHAEL ALLEN
B. Sept. 20, 1945, Buffalo, N. Y.

BB TL 6'3"   205 lbs.

Year	Team	W	L	PCT	ERA	G	GS	CG	IP	H	BB	SO	ShO	W	L	SV	AB	H	HR	BA	PO	A	E	DP	TC/G	FA
1965	NY A	0	0	–	7.71	2	0	0	2.1	5	1	2	0	0	0	0	0	0	0	–	0	0	0	0	0.0	–

Al Jurisich

JURISICH, ALVIN JOSEPH
B. Aug. 25, 1921, New Orleans, La.   D. Nov. 3, 1981, New Orleans, La.

BR TR 6'2"   193 lbs.

Year	Team	W	L	PCT	ERA	G	GS	CG	IP	H	BB	SO	ShO	W	L	SV	AB	H	HR	BA	PO	A	E	DP	TC/G	FA
1944	STL N	7	9	.438	3.39	30	14	5	130	102	65	53	2	2	0	1	45	8	0	.178	5	18	1	2	0.8	.958
1945		3	3	.500	5.15	27	6	1	71.2	61	41	42	0	1	1	0	23	2	0	.087	3	8	0	0	0.4	1.000
1946	PHI N	4	3	.571	3.69	13	10	2	68.1	71	31	34	1	0	0	1	23	3	0	.130	5	5	1	1	0.8	.909
1947		1	7	.125	4.94	34	12	5	118.1	110	52	48	0	1	2	3	31	1	0	.032	1	16	0	1	0.5	1.000
4 yrs.		15	22	.405	4.24	104	42	13	388.1	344	189	177	3	4	3	5	122	14	0	.115	14	47	2	4	0.6	.968

WORLD SERIES

Year	Team	W	L	PCT	ERA	G	GS	CG	IP	H	BB	SO	ShO	W	L	SV	AB	H	HR	BA	PO	A	E	DP	TC/G	FA
1944	STL N	0	0	–	27.00	1	0	0	.2	2	1	0	0	0	0	0	0	0	0	–	0	0	0	0	0.0	–

Walt Justis

JUSTIS, WALTER NEWTON (Smoke)
B. Aug. 17, 1883, Moore's Hill, Ind.   D. Oct. 4, 1941, Lawrenceburg, Ind.

BR TR 5'11½" 195 lbs.

Year	Team	W	L	PCT	ERA	G	GS	CG	IP	H	BB	SO	ShO	W	L	SV	AB	H	HR	BA	PO	A	E	DP	TC/G	FA
1905	DET A	0	0	–	8.10	2	0	0	3.1	4	6	0	0	0	0	0				–	0	0	0	0	0.0	–

Earl Juul

JUUL, EARL HEROLD
B. May 21, 1893, Chicago, Ill.   D. Jan. 4, 1942, Chicago, Ill.

BR TR 5'9½" 150 lbs.

Year	Team	W	L	PCT	ERA	G	GS	CG	IP	H	BB	SO	ShO	W	L	SV	AB	H	HR	BA	PO	A	E	DP	TC/G	FA
1914	BKN F	0	3	.000	6.21	9	3	0	29	26	31	16	0	0	0	0	9	2	0	.222	0	7	1	0	0.9	.875

Herb Juul

JUUL, HERBERT VICTOR
B. Feb. 2, 1886, Chicago, Ill.   D. Nov. 14, 1928, Chicago, Ill.

BL TL 5'11" 150 lbs.

Year	Team	W	L	PCT	ERA	G	GS	CG	IP	H	BB	SO	ShO	W	L	SV	AB	H	HR	BA	PO	A	E	DP	TC/G	FA
1911	CIN N	0	0	–	4.50	1	0	0	4	3	4	2	0	0	0	0	2	0	0	.000	0	0	0	0	0.0	–

Jim Kaat

KAAT, JAMES LEE
B. Nov. 7, 1938, Zeeland, Mich.

BL TL 6'4½" 205 lbs.

Year	Team	W	L	PCT	ERA	G	GS	CG	IP	H	BB	SO	ShO	W	L	SV	AB	H	HR	BA	PO	A	E	DP	TC/G	FA
1959	WAS A	0	2	.000	12.60	3	2	0	5	7	4	2	0	0	0	0	1	0	0	.000	0	1	0	0	0.3	1.000
1960		1	5	.167	5.58	13	9	0	50	48	31	25	0	0	0	0	14	2	0	.143	0	11	0	1	0.8	1.000
1961	MIN A	9	17	.346	3.90	36	29	8	200.2	188	82	122	1	0	0	1	63	15	0	.238	19	41	2	8	1.7	.968
1962		18	14	.563	3.14	39	35	16	269	243	75	173	5	1	0	1	100	18	1	.180	16	72	3	6	2.3	.967
1963		10	10	.500	4.19	31	27	7	178.1	195	38	105	1	0	1	1	61	8	1	.131	19	43	1	5	2.0	.984
1964		17	11	.607	3.22	36	34	13	243	231	60	171	0	0	1	1	83	14	3	.169	16	48	5	6	1.9	.928
1965		18	11	.621	2.83	45	42	7	264.1	267	63	154	2	0	0	2	93	23	1	.247	15	64	6	3	1.9	.929
1966		25	13	.658	2.75	41	41	19	304.2	271	55	205	3	0	0	0	118	23	2	.195	19	46	3	5	1.7	.956
1967		16	13	.552	3.04	42	38	13	263.1	269	42	211	2	0	0	0	99	17	1	.172	13	46	3	0	1.5	.952
1968		14	12	.538	2.94	30	29	9	208	192	40	130	2	0	0	0	77	12	0	.156	10	31	1	0	1.4	.976
1969		14	13	.519	3.49	40	32	10	242.1	252	75	139	0	3	1	1	87	18	2	.207	9	29	8	4	1.2	.826
1970		14	10	.583	3.56	45	34	4	230	244	58	120	1	1	0	1	76	15	1	.197	15	43	4	1	1.4	.935
1971		13	14	.481	3.32	39	38	15	260	275	47	137	0	0	0	0	93	15	1	.161	13	41	1	4	1.4	.982
1972		10	2	.833	2.07	15	15	5	113	94	20	64	0	0	0	0	45	13	2	.289	5	19	2	0	1.7	.923

Year	Team	W	L	PCT	ERA	G	GS	CG	IP	H	BB	SO	ShO	W	L	SV	AB	H	HR	BA	PO	A	E	DP	TC/G	FA

Jim Kaat *continued*

Year	Team		W	L	PCT	ERA	G	GS	CG	IP	H	BB	SO	ShO	W	L	SV	AB	H	HR	BA	PO	A	E	DP	TC/G	FA
1973	2 teams	MIN A (29G 11–12)								CHI A (7G 4–1)																	
"	total		15	13	.536	4.37	36	35	10	224.1	250	43	109	3	1	0	0	0	0	0	–	10	26	1	2	1.0	.973
1974	CHI	A	21	13	.618	2.92	42	39	15	277	263	63	142	3	1	0	0	1	0	0	.000	14	33	2	3	1.2	.959
1975			20	14	.588	3.11	43	41	12	303.2	321	77	142	1	0	0	0	0	0	0	–	15	39	1	2	1.3	.982
1976	PHI	N	12	14	.462	3.48	38	35	7	227.2	241	32	83	1	0	1	0	79	14	1	.177	18	19	2	3	1.0	.949
1977			6	11	.353	5.40	35	27	2	160	211	40	55	0	0	1	0	53	10	0	.189	7	19	3	1	0.8	.897
1978			8	5	.615	4.11	26	24	2	140	150	32	48	1	0	0	0	48	7	0	.146	5	15	0	4	0.8	1.000
1979	2 teams	PHI N (3G 1–0)								NY A (40G 2–3)																	
"	total		3	3	.500	3.95	43	1	0	66	73	19	25	0	3	3	2	1	0	0	.000	5	6	1	0	0.3	.917
1980	2 teams	NY A (4G 0–1)								STL N (49G 8–7)																	
"	total		8	8	.500	3.93	53	14	6	135	148	37	37	1	3	3	4	35	5	1	.143	5	19	2	2	0.5	.923
1981	STL	N	6	6	.500	3.40	41	1	0	53	60	17	8	0	6	5	4	8	3	0	.375	4	13	2	1	0.5	.895
1982			5	3	.625	4.08	62	2	0	75	79	23	35	0	5	3	2	12	0	0	.000	8	14	2	0	0.4	.917
1983			0	0	–	3.89	24	0	0	34.2	48	10	19	0	0	0	0	4	0	0	.000	2	6	1	0	0.4	.889
25 yrs.			283	237	.544	3.45	898	625	180	4528	4620	1083	2461	31	24	20	18	1251	232	16	.185	262	744	56	65	1.2	.947
								8th																			

LEAGUE CHAMPIONSHIP SERIES

Year	Team		W	L	PCT	ERA	G	GS	CG	IP	H	BB	SO	ShO	W	L	SV	AB	H	HR	BA	PO	A	E	DP	TC/G	FA
1970	MIN	A	0	1	.000	9.00	1	1	0	2	6	2	1	0	0	0	0	1	0	0	.000	0	0	0	0	0.0	–
1976	PHI	N	0	0	–	3.00	1	1	0	6	2	2	1	0	0	0	0	2	1	0	.500	0	1	0	0	1.0	1.000
2 yrs.			0	1	.000	4.50	2	2	0	8	8	4	2	0	0	0	0	3	1	0	.333	0	1	0	0	0.5	1.000

WORLD SERIES

Year	Team		W	L	PCT	ERA	G	GS	CG	IP	H	BB	SO	ShO	W	L	SV	AB	H	HR	BA	PO	A	E	DP	TC/G	FA
1965	MIN	A	1	2	.333	3.77	3	3	1	14.1	18	2	6	0	0	0	0	6	1	0	.167	5	2	0	0	2.3	1.000
1982	STL	N	0	0	–	3.86	4	0	0	2.1	4	2	2	0	0	0	0	0	0	0	–	0	0	0	0	0.0	–
2 yrs.			1	2	.333	3.78	7	3	1	16.2	22	4	8	0	0	0	0	6	1	0	.167	5	2	0	0	1.0	1.000

George Kahler

KAHLER, GEORGE RANNELS (Krum)
B. Sept. 6, 1889, Athens, Ohio   D. Feb. 14, 1924, Battle Creek, Mich.
BR TR 6'   183 lbs.

Year	Team		W	L	PCT	ERA	G	GS	CG	IP	H	BB	SO	ShO	W	L	SV	AB	H	HR	BA	PO	A	E	DP	TC/G	FA
1910	CLE	A	6	4	.600	1.60	12	12	8	95.1	80	46	38	2	0	0	0	35	5	0	.143	4	29	3	1	3.0	.917
1911			9	8	.529	3.27	30	17	10	154.1	153	66	97	0	1	0	1	54	9	0	.167	9	35	2	0	1.5	.957
1912			12	19	.387	3.69	41	32	17	246.1	263	121	104	3	0	0	1	80	9	0	.113	12	54	2	4	1.7	.971
1913			5	9	.357	3.14	24	15	5	117.2	118	32	43	0	0	2	0	33	2	0	.061	5	21	2	0	1.2	.929
1914			0	1	.000	3.86	2	1	1	14	17	7	3	0	0	0	0	5	0	0	.000	0	3	0	0	1.5	1.000
5 yrs.			32	41	.438	3.17	109	77	41	627.2	631	272	285	5	1	2	2	207	25	0	.121	30	142	9	5	1.7	.950

Don Kainer

KAINER, DONALD WAYNE
B. Sept. 3, 1955, Houston, Tex.
BR TR 6'3"   205 lbs.

Year	Team		W	L	PCT	ERA	G	GS	CG	IP	H	BB	SO	ShO	W	L	SV	AB	H	HR	BA	PO	A	E	DP	TC/G	FA
1980	TEX	A	0	0	–	1.80	4	3	0	20	22	9	10	0	0	0	0	0	0	0	–	1	9	0	1	2.5	1.000

Bob Kaiser

KAISER, ROBERT THOMAS
B. Apr. 29, 1950, Cincinnati, Ohio
BR TL 5'10"   175 lbs.

Year	Team		W	L	PCT	ERA	G	GS	CG	IP	H	BB	SO	ShO	W	L	SV	AB	H	HR	BA	PO	A	E	DP	TC/G	FA
1971	CLE	A	0	0	–	4.50	5	0	0	8	6	3	4	0	0	0	0	0	0	0	–	0	1	0	0	0.2	1.000

Don Kaiser

KAISER, CLYDE DONALD (Tiger)
B. Feb. 3, 1935, Byng, Okla.
BR TR 6'5"   195 lbs.

Year	Team		W	L	PCT	ERA	G	GS	CG	IP	H	BB	SO	ShO	W	L	SV	AB	H	HR	BA	PO	A	E	DP	TC/G	FA
1955	CHI	N	0	0	–	5.40	11	0	0	18.1	20	5	11	0	0	0	0	2	0	0	.000	0	2	1	0	0.3	.667
1956			4	9	.308	3.59	27	22	5	150.1	144	52	74	1	0	0	0	47	2	0	.043	7	26	3	1	1.3	.917
1957			2	6	.250	5.00	20	13	1	72	91	28	23	0	0	0	0	19	2	0	.105	5	20	1	4	1.3	.962
3 yrs.			6	15	.286	4.15	58	35	6	240.2	255	85	108	1	0	0	0	68	4	0	.059	12	48	5	5	1.1	.923

Jeff Kaiser

KAISER, JEFFREY PATRICK
B. July 24, 1960, Wyandotte, Mich.
BR TL 6'3"   195 lbs.

Year	Team		W	L	PCT	ERA	G	GS	CG	IP	H	BB	SO	ShO	W	L	SV	AB	H	HR	BA	PO	A	E	DP	TC/G	FA
1985	OAK	A	0	0	–	14.58	15	0	0	16.2	25	20	10	0	0	0	0	0	0	0	–	4	3	0	1	0.5	1.000
1987	CLE	A	0	0	–	16.20	2	0	0	3.1	4	3	2	0	0	0	0	0	0	0	–	1	0	0	0	0.5	1.000
1988			0	0	–	0.00	3	0	0	2.2	2	1	0	0	0	0	0	0	0	0	–	0	2	0	0	0.7	1.000
1989			0	1	.000	7.36	6	0	0	3.2	5	5	4	0	0	0	1	0	0	0	–	0	0	0	0	0.0	–
4 yrs.			0	1	.000	12.30	26	0	0	26.1	36	29	16	0	0	0	1	0	0	0	–	5	5	0	1	0.4	1.000

George Kaiserling

KAISERLING, GEORGE
B. May 12, 1893, Steubenville, Ohio   D. Mar. 2, 1918, Steubenville, Ohio
BR TR 6'   175 lbs.

Year	Team		W	L	PCT	ERA	G	GS	CG	IP	H	BB	SO	ShO	W	L	SV	AB	H	HR	BA	PO	A	E	DP	TC/G	FA
1914	IND	F	17	10	.630	3.11	37	33	20	275.1	288	72	75	1	1	1	0	98	11	0	.112	10	70	2	3	2.2	.976
1915	NWK	F	13	14	.481	2.24	41	29	16	261.1	246	73	75	5	1	0	2	79	12	0	.152	6	81	5	2	2.2	.946
2 yrs.			30	24	.556	2.68	78	62	36	536.2	534	145	150	6	2	1	2	177	23	0	.130	16	151	7	5	2.2	.960

Bill Kalfass

KALFASS, WILLIAM PHILIP (Lefty)
B. Mar. 3, 1916, New York, N. Y.   D. Sept. 8, 1968, Brooklyn, N. Y.
BR TL 6'3½"   190 lbs.

Year	Team		W	L	PCT	ERA	G	GS	CG	IP	H	BB	SO	ShO	W	L	SV	AB	H	HR	BA	PO	A	E	DP	TC/G	FA
1937	PHI	A	1	0	1.000	3.00	3	1	0	12	10	10	9	0	0	0	0	4	0	0	.000	0	1	0	0	0.3	1.000

Rudy Kallio

KALLIO, RUDOLPH
B. Dec. 14, 1892, Portland, Ore.   D. Apr. 6, 1979, Newport, Ore.
BR TR 5'10"   160 lbs.

Year	Team		W	L	PCT	ERA	G	GS	CG	IP	H	BB	SO	ShO	W	L	SV	AB	H	HR	BA	PO	A	E	DP	TC/G	FA
1918	DET	A	8	14	.364	3.62	30	22	10	181.1	178	76	70	2	1	2	0	56	9	0	.161	10	47	5	0	2.1	.919
1919			0	0	–	5.64	12	1	0	22.1	28	8	3	0	0	0	1	4	0	0	.000	1	4	0	1	0.4	1.000
1925	BOS	A	1	4	.200	7.71	7	4	0	18.2	28	9	2	0	0	1	0	6	2	0	.333	1	4	0	0	0.7	1.000
3 yrs.			9	18	.333	4.17	49	27	10	222.1	234	93	75	2	1	3	1	66	11	0	.167	12	55	5	1	1.5	.931

Bob Kammeyer

KAMMEYER, ROBERT LYNN
B. Dec. 2, 1950, Kansas City, Mo.
BR TR 6'4"   210 lbs.

Year	Team		W	L	PCT	ERA	G	GS	CG	IP	H	BB	SO	ShO	W	L	SV	AB	H	HR	BA	PO	A	E	DP	TC/G	FA
1978	NY	A	0	0	–	5.82	7	0	0	21.2	24	6	11	0	0	0	0	0	0	0	–	0	7	0	0	1.0	1.000

Year	Team	W	L	PCT	ERA	G	GS	CG	IP	H	BB	SO	ShO	W	L	SV	AB	H	HR	BA	PO	A	E	DP	TC/G	FA

Bob Kammeyer *continued*

Year	Team	W	L	PCT	ERA	G	GS	CG	IP	H	BB	SO	ShO	W	L	SV	AB	H	HR	BA	PO	A	E	DP	TC/G	FA
1979		0	0	–	∞	1	0	0	7	0	0	0	0	0	0	0	0	0	0	–	0	0	0	0	0.0	–
2 yrs.		0	0	–	9.14	8	0	0	21.2	31	6	11	0	0	0	0	0	0	0	–	0	7	0	0	0.9	1.000

Ike Kamp

KAMP, ALPHONSE FRANCIS
B. Sept. 5, 1900, Roxbury, Mass. D. Feb. 25, 1955, Boston, Mass.

BB TL 6'   170 lbs.

Year	Team	W	L	PCT	ERA	G	GS	CG	IP	H	BB	SO	ShO	W	L	SV	AB	H	HR	BA	PO	A	E	DP	TC/G	FA
1924	BOS N	0	1	.000	5.14	1	1	0	7	9	5	4	0	0	0	0	1	0	0	.000	0	3	0	0	3.0	1.000
1925		2	4	.333	5.09	24	4	1	58.1	68	35	20	0	1	2	0	12	2	0	.167	4	14	1	1	0.8	.947
2 yrs.		2	5	.286	5.10	25	5	1	65.1	77	40	24	0	1	2	0	13	2	0	.154	4	17	1	1	0.9	.955

Harry Kane

KANE, HARRY (Klondike)
Born Harry Cohen.
B. July 27, 1883, Hamburg, Ark. D. Sept. 15, 1932, Portland, Ore.

BL TL

Year	Team	W	L	PCT	ERA	G	GS	CG	IP	H	BB	SO	ShO	W	L	SV	AB	H	HR	BA	PO	A	E	DP	TC/G	FA
1902	STL A	0	1	.000	5.48	4	1	1	23	34	16	7	0	0	0	0	9	1	0	.111	1	6	0	0	1.8	1.000
1903	DET A	0	2	.000	8.50	3	3	2	18	26	8	10	0	0	0	0	7	1	0	.143	0	3	1	0	1.3	.750
1905	PHI N	1	1	.500	1.59	2	2	2	17	12	8	12	1	0	0	0	6	1	0	.167	1	2	0	0	1.5	1.000
1906		1	3	.250	3.86	6	3	2	28	28	18	14	0	1	1	0	8	0	0	.000	2	9	0	0	1.8	1.000
4 yrs.		2	7	.222	4.81	15	9	7	86	100	50	43	1	1	1	0	30	3	0	.100	4	20	1	0	1.7	.960

Erv Kantlehner

KANTLEHNER, ERVING LESLIE
B. July 31, 1892, San Jose, Calif.

BL TL 6'   190 lbs.

Year	Team	W	L	PCT	ERA	G	GS	CG	IP	H	BB	SO	ShO	W	L	SV	AB	H	HR	BA	PO	A	E	DP	TC/G	FA
1914	PIT N	3	2	.600	3.09	21	5	3	67	51	39	26	2	0	0	0	15	1	0	.067	3	17	2	1	1.0	.909
1915		5	12	.294	2.26	29	18	10	163	135	58	64	1	1	2	2	52	15	0	.288	3	49	1	1	1.8	.981
1916	2 teams			PIT N	(34G 5–15)		PHI N	(3G 0–0)																		
"	total	5	15	.250	3.30	37	21	7	169	158	60	51	2	2	3	2	46	8	0	.174	8	53	3	2	1.7	.953
3 yrs.		13	29	.310	2.84	87	44	20	399	344	157	141	5	3	6	4	113	24	0	.212	14	119	6	4	1.6	.957

Paul Kardow

KARDOW, PAUL OTTO (Tex)
B. Sept. 19, 1915, Humble, Tex. D. Apr. 27, 1968, San Antonio, Tex.

BR TR 6'6"   210 lbs.

Year	Team	W	L	PCT	ERA	G	GS	CG	IP	H	BB	SO	ShO	W	L	SV	AB	H	HR	BA	PO	A	E	DP	TC/G	FA
1936	CLE A	0	0	–	4.50	2	0	0	2	1	2	0	0	0	0	0	0	0	0	–	0	0	0	0	0.0	–

Ed Karger

KARGER, EDWIN (Loose)
B. May 6, 1883, San Angelo, Tex. D. Sept. 9, 1957, Delta, Colo.

BR TL 5'11"   185 lbs.

Year	Team	W	L	PCT	ERA	G	GS	CG	IP	H	BB	SO	ShO	W	L	SV	AB	H	HR	BA	PO	A	E	DP	TC/G	FA
1906	2 teams			PIT N	(6G 2–3)		STL N	(25G 5–16)																		
"	total	7	19	.269	2.62	31	22	17	219.2	214	52	81	0	1	4	1	84	18	1	.214	21	81	5	2	3.5	.953
1907	STL N	15	19	.441	2.03	38	31	28	310	251	64	132	6	1	2	1	111	19	2	.171	29	96	6	4	3.4	.954
1908		4	9	.308	3.06	22	15	9	141.1	148	50	34	1	0	0	0	54	13	0	.241	10	33	2	5	2.0	.956
1909	2 teams			CIN N	(9G 1–3)		BOS A	(12G 5–2)																		
"	total	6	5	.545	3.61	21	11	4	102.1	97	52	25	0	2	0	0	35	6	0	.171	5	33	6	0	2.1	.864
1910	BOS A	11	7	.611	3.19	27	25	16	183.1	162	53	81	1	0	0	1	68	20	2	.294	7	47	2	2	2.1	.964
1911		5	8	.385	3.37	25	18	6	131	134	42	57	1	0	0	0	47	11	1	.234	6	35	3	2	1.8	.932
6 yrs.		48	67	.417	2.79	164	122	80	1087.2	1006	313	410	9	4	8	3	399	87	6	.218	78	325	24	15	2.6	.944

Andy Karl

KARL, ANTON ANDREW
B. Apr. 8, 1914, Mount Vernon, N. Y. D. Apr. 8, 1989, San Diego, Calif.

BR TR 6'1½"   175 lbs.

Year	Team	W	L	PCT	ERA	G	GS	CG	IP	H	BB	SO	ShO	W	L	SV	AB	H	HR	BA	PO	A	E	DP	TC/G	FA
1943	2 teams			BOS A	(11G 1–1)		PHI N	(9G 1–2)																		
"	total	2	3	.400	5.30	20	2	0	52.2	75	24	10	0	1	1	0	15	4	0	.267	6	19	1	0	1.3	.962
1944	PHI N	3	2	.600	2.33	38	0	0	89	76	21	26	0	3	2	2	15	3	0	.200	4	22	0	0	0.7	1.000
1945		9	8	.529	2.99	67	2	1	180.2	175	50	51	0	9	6	15	49	7	0	.143	10	38	2	3	0.7	.960
1946		3	7	.300	4.96	39	0	0	65.1	84	22	5	0	3	7	5	10	1	0	.100	3	17	0	0	0.5	1.000
1947	BOS N	2	3	.400	3.86	27	0	0	35	41	13	5	0	2	3	2	6	1	0	.167	5	13	0	2	0.7	1.000
5 yrs.		19	23	.452	3.51	191	4	1	422.2	451	130	107	0	18	19	26	95	16	0	.168	28	109	3	5	0.7	.979

Bill Karns

KARNS, WILLIAM ARTHUR
B. Chicago, Ill. Deceased.

TL

Year	Team	W	L	PCT	ERA	G	GS	CG	IP	H	BB	SO	ShO	W	L	SV	AB	H	HR	BA	PO	A	E	DP	TC/G	FA
1901	BAL A	1	0	1.000	6.35	3	1	1	17	30	9	5	0	0	0	0	7	1	0	.143	1	3	0	0	1.3	1.000

Herb Karpel

KARPEL, HERBERT (Lefty)
B. Dec. 27, 1917, Brooklyn, N. Y.

BL TL 5'9½"   180 lbs.

Year	Team	W	L	PCT	ERA	G	GS	CG	IP	H	BB	SO	ShO	W	L	SV	AB	H	HR	BA	PO	A	E	DP	TC/G	FA
1946	NY A	0	0	–	10.80	2	0	0	1.2	4	0	0	0	0	0	0	0	0	0	–	0	0	0	0	0.0	–

Benn Karr

KARR, BENJAMIN JOYCE (Baldy)
B. Nov. 28, 1893, Mt. Pleasant, Miss. D. Dec. 8, 1968, Memphis, Tenn.

BL TR 6'   175 lbs.

Year	Team	W	L	PCT	ERA	G	GS	CG	IP	H	BB	SO	ShO	W	L	SV	AB	H	HR	BA	PO	A	E	DP	TC/G	FA
1920	BOS A	3	8	.273	4.81	26	2	0	91.2	109	24	21	0	3	6	1				.280	5	18	2	0	1.0	.920
1921		8	7	.533	3.67	26	7	5	117.2	123	38	37	0	5	3	0	62	16	0	.258	2	30	2	0	1.3	.941
1922		5	12	.294	4.47	41	13	7	183.1	212	45	41	0	0	5	1	98	21	0	.214	9	44	5	3	1.4	.914
1925	CLE A	11	12	.478	4.78	32	24	12	197.2	248	80	41	1	5	1	0	92	24	1	.261	14	54	4	5	2.3	.947
1926		5	6	.455	5.00	30	7	4	113.1	137	41	23	0	2	4	1	45	10	0	.222	6	35	2	0	1.4	.953
1927		3	3	.500	5.05	22	5	1	76.2	92	32	17	0	1	0	2	20	4	0	.200	4	29	2	0	1.6	.943
6 yrs.		35	48	.422	4.60	177	58	29	780.1	921	260	180	1	16	19	5	*				40	213	17	8	1.5	.937

John Katoll

KATOLL, JOHN (Katy)
B. June 24, 1872, Germany D. June 18, 1955, Hartland, Ill.

BR TR 5'11"   195 lbs.

Year	Team	W	L	PCT	ERA	G	GS	CG	IP	H	BB	SO	ShO	W	L	SV	AB	H	HR	BA	PO	A	E	DP	TC/G	FA
1898	CHI N	0	1	.000	0.82	2	1	1	11	8	1	3	0	0	0	0	4	0	0	.000	0	2	0	0	1.0	1.000
1899		1	1	.500	6.00	2	2	2	18	17	4	1	0	0	0	0	7	0	0	.000	0	6	2	0	4.0	.750
1901	CHI A	11	10	.524	2.81	27	25	19	208	231	53	59	0	0	0	0	80	10	1	.125	11	71	8	1	3.3	.911
1902	2 teams			CHI A	(1G 0–0)		BAL A	(15G 5–10)																		
"	total	5	10	.333	3.99	16	13	13	124	176	32	27	0	0	0	0	58	10	0	.172	9	55	5	0	4.3	.928
4 yrs.		17	22	.436	3.32	47	41	35	361	432	90	90	0	0	0	0	149	20	1	.134	20	134	15	1	3.6	.911

Year	Team		W	L	PCT	ERA	G	GS	CG	IP	H	BB	SO	ShO	Relief Pitching W	L	SV	Batting AB	H	HR	BA	PO	A	E	DP	TC/G	FA

Bob Katz

KATZ, ROBERT CLYDE
B. Jan. 30, 1911, Lancaster, Pa. D. Dec. 14, 1962, St. Joseph, Mich.
BR TR 5'11½" 190 lbs.

Year	Team		W	L	PCT	ERA	G	GS	CG	IP	H	BB	SO	ShO	W	L	SV	AB	H	HR	BA	PO	A	E	DP	TC/G	FA
1944	CIN	N	0	1	.000	3.93	6	2	0	18.1	17	7	4	0	0	0	0	4	0	0	.000	1	6	0	1	1.2	1.000

Curt Kaufman

KAUFMAN, CURT GERRARD
B. July 19, 1957, Omaha, Neb.
BR TR 6'2" 175 lbs.

Year	Team		W	L	PCT	ERA	G	GS	CG	IP	H	BB	SO	ShO	W	L	SV	AB	H	HR	BA	PO	A	E	DP	TC/G	FA
1982	NY	A	1	0	1.000	5.19	7	0	0	8.2	9	6	1	0	1	0	0	0	0	0	—	1	0	0	0	0.1	1.000
1983			0	0	—	3.12	4	0	0	8.2	10	4	8	0	0	0	0	0	0	0	—	0	1	0	0	0.3	1.000
1984	CAL	A	2	3	.400	4.57	29	1	0	69	68	20	41	0	2	3	1	0	0	0	—	1	12	0	2	0.4	1.000
3 yrs.			3	3	.500	4.48	40	1	0	86.1	87	30	50	0	3	3	1	0	0	0	—	2	13	0	2	0.4	1.000

Tony Kaufmann

KAUFMANN, ANTHONY CHARLES
B. Dec. 16, 1900, Chicago, Ill. D. June 4, 1982, Elgin, Ill.
BR TR 5'11" 165 lbs.

Year	Team		W	L	PCT	ERA	G	GS	CG	IP	H	BB	SO	ShO	W	L	SV	AB	H	HR	BA	PO	A	E	DP	TC/G	FA
1921	CHI	N	1	0	1.000	4.15	2	1	1	13	12	3	6	0	0	0	0	5	2	0	.400	0	1	0	0	0.5	1.000
1922			7	13	.350	4.06	37	9	4	153	161	57	45	1	1	6	3	45	9	1	.200	14	28	3	0	1.2	.933
1923			14	10	.583	3.10	33	24	18	206.1	209	67	72	2	1	0	3	74	16	2	.216	9	41	2	3	1.6	.962
1924			16	11	.593	4.02	34	26	16	208.1	218	66	79	3	1	2	0	76	24	1	.316	14	38	1	3	1.6	.981
1925			13	13	.500	4.50	31	23	14	196	221	77	49	2	2	3	2	78	15	2	.192	9	43	1	6	1.7	.981
1926			9	7	.563	3.02	26	21	14	169.2	169	44	52	1	0	0	2	60	15	1	.250	4	34	0	1	1.5	1.000
1927	3 teams		CHI N	(9G 3–3)		PHI N	(5G 0–3)		STL N	(1G 0–0)																		
"	total		3	6	.333	7.84	15	11	4	72.1	116	28	25	0	0	0	0	23	6	2	.261	3	21	0	1	1.6	1.000
1928	STL	N	0	0	—	9.64	4	1	0	4.2	8	4	2	0	0	0	0	0	0	0	—	0	1	0	0	0.3	1.000
1929	NY	N	0	0	—	0.00	0	0	0	0	0	0	0	0	0	0	0	32	1	0	.031	0	0	0	0	0.0	—
1930	STL	N	0	1	.000	7.84	2	1	0	10.1	15	4	2	0	0	0	0	3	1	0	.333	0	1	0	0	0.5	1.000
1931			1	1	.500	6.06	15	1	0	49	65	17	13	0	1	1	1	18	2	0	.111	2	11	1	0	0.9	.929
1935			0	0	—	2.45	3	0	0	3.2	4	1	0	0	0	0	0	0	0	0	—	0	1	0	0	0.3	1.000
12 yrs.			64	62	.508	4.18	202	118	71	1086.1	1198	368	345	9	6	12	12	414	91	9	.220	55	220	8	15	1.4	.972

Steve Kealey

KEALEY, STEVEN WILLIAM
B. May 13, 1947, Torrance, Calif.
BR TR 6' 185 lbs.

Year	Team		W	L	PCT	ERA	G	GS	CG	IP	H	BB	SO	ShO	W	L	SV	AB	H	HR	BA	PO	A	E	DP	TC/G	FA
1968	CAL	A	0	1	.000	2.70	6	0	0	10	10	5	4	0	0	0	0	0	0	0	—	0	0	1	0	0.2	—
1969			2	0	1.000	3.93	15	3	1	36.2	48	13	17	1	1	0	0	9	0	0	.000	1	2	0	0	0.2	1.000
1970			1	0	1.000	4.09	17	0	0	22	19	6	14	0	1	0	1	4	1	0	.250	1	0	1	0	0.1	.500
1971	CHI	A	2	2	.500	3.86	54	1	0	77	69	26	50	0	2	2	6	10	2	1	.200	5	11	2	0	0.3	.889
1972			3	2	.600	3.30	40	0	0	57.1	50	12	37	0	3	2	4	3	0	0	.000	3	6	2	0	0.3	.818
1973			0	0	—	15.09	7	0	0	11.1	23	7	4	0	0	0	0	0	0	0	—	0	1	0	0	0.1	1.000
6 yrs.			8	5	.615	4.28	139	4	1	214.1	219	69	126	1	7	5	11	26	3	1	.115	10	20	6	0	0.3	.833

Ed Keas

KEAS, EDWARD JAMES
B. Feb. 2, 1863, Dubuque, Iowa D. Jan. 12, 1940, Dubuque, Iowa

Year	Team		W	L	PCT	ERA	G	GS	CG	IP	H	BB	SO	ShO	W	L	SV	AB	H	HR	BA	PO	A	E	DP	TC/G	FA
1888	CLE	AA	3	3	.500	2.29	6	6	6	51	53	12	18	0	0	0	0	23	2	0	.087	5	13	1	1	3.2	.947

Ed Keating

KEATING, ROBERT EDWARD
B. Sept. 22, 1862, Springfield, Mass. D. Jan. 19, 1922, Springfield, Mass.
BL TL 6'4"

Year	Team		W	L	PCT	ERA	G	GS	CG	IP	H	BB	SO	ShO	W	L	SV	AB	H	HR	BA	PO	A	E	DP	TC/G	FA
1887	BAL	AA	0	1	.000	11.00	1	1	1	9	16	6	0	0	0	0	0	4	1	0	.250	0	4	0	0	4.0	1.000

Ray Keating

KEATING, RAYMOND HERBERT
B. July 21, 1891, Bridgeport, Conn. D. Nov. 28, 1963, Sacramento, Calif.
BR TR 5'11" 185 lbs.

Year	Team		W	L	PCT	ERA	G	GS	CG	IP	H	BB	SO	ShO	W	L	SV	AB	H	HR	BA	PO	A	E	DP	TC/G	FA
1912	NY	A	0	3	.000	5.80	6	5	3	35.2	36	18	21	0	0	0	0	16	6	0	.375	0	11	1	0	2.0	.917
1913			6	12	.333	3.21	28	21	9	151.1	146	51	83	2	0	0	0	43	3	0	.070	3	39	9	0	1.8	.824
1914			7	11	.389	2.96	34	25	14	210	198	67	109	0	1	0	1	71	12	0	.169	9	68	3	2	2.4	.963
1915			3	6	.333	3.63	11	10	8	79.1	66	45	37	1	1	0	0	26	4	0	.154	0	28	2	0	2.7	.933
1916			5	6	.455	3.07	14	12	6	91	91	37	35	0	0	0	0	29	7	0	.241	7	35	5	3	3.4	.894
1918			2	2	.500	3.91	15	6	1	48.1	39	30	16	0	0	1	0	16	3	0	.188	3	13	0	1	1.1	1.000
1919	BOS	N	7	11	.389	2.98	22	13	9	136	129	45	48	1	1	1	0	46	7	1	.152	7	44	1	4	2.4	.981
7 yrs.			30	51	.370	3.29	130	92	50	751.2	705	293	349	4	4	2	1	247	42	1	.170	29	238	21	10	2.2	.927

Cactus Keck

KECK, FRANK JOSEPH
B. Jan. 13, 1899, St. Louis, Mo. D. Feb. 6, 1981, St. Louis, Mo.
BR TR 5'11" 170 lbs.

Year	Team		W	L	PCT	ERA	G	GS	CG	IP	H	BB	SO	ShO	W	L	SV	AB	H	HR	BA	PO	A	E	DP	TC/G	FA
1922	CIN	N	7	6	.538	3.37	27	15	5	131	138	29	27	1	2	2	1	44	7	0	.159	2	17	4	2	0.9	.826
1923			3	6	.333	3.72	35	6	1	87	84	32	16	0	3	1	2	17	1	0	.059	5	25	3	1	0.9	.909
2 yrs.			10	12	.455	3.51	62	21	6	218	222	61	43	1	5	3	3	61	8	0	.131	7	42	7	3	0.9	.875

Bob Keefe

KEEFE, ROBERT FRANCIS
B. June 16, 1882, Folsom, Calif. D. Dec. 7, 1964, Sacramento, Calif.
BR TR 5'11" 155 lbs.

Year	Team		W	L	PCT	ERA	G	GS	CG	IP	H	BB	SO	ShO	W	L	SV	AB	H	HR	BA	PO	A	E	DP	TC/G	FA
1907	NY	A	3	5	.375	2.50	19	3	0	57.2	60	20	20	0	3	5	3	19	1	0	.053	1	20	2	0	1.2	.913
1911	CIN	N	12	13	.480	2.69	39	26	15	234.1	196	76	105	0	1	1	3	70	6	0	.086	13	36	8	1	1.5	.860
1912			1	3	.250	5.24	17	6	0	68.2	78	33	29	0	0	1	2	18	3	0	.167	3	18	4	1	1.5	.840
3 yrs.			16	21	.432	3.14	75	35	15	360.2	334	129	154	0	4	4	8	107	10	0	.093	17	74	14	2	1.4	.867

Dave Keefe

KEEFE, DAVID EDWIN
B. Jan. 9, 1897, Williston, Vt. D. Feb. 4, 1978, Kansas City, Mo.
BL TR 5'9" 165 lbs.

Year	Team		W	L	PCT	ERA	G	GS	CG	IP	H	BB	SO	ShO	W	L	SV	AB	H	HR	BA	PO	A	E	DP	TC/G	FA
1917	PHI	A	1	0	1.000	1.80	3	0	0	5	5	4	1	0	1	0	0	0	0	0	.000	0	2	0	0	0.7	1.000
1919			0	1	.000	4.00	1	1	1	9	8	3	5	0	0	0	0	3	0	0	.000	0	3	0	0	3.0	1.000
1920			6	7	.462	2.97	31	13	7	130.1	129	30	41	1	3	0	0	40	10	0	.250	4	39	3	2	1.5	.935
1921			2	9	.182	4.68	44	12	4	173	214	64	68	0	1	2	1	57	10	0	.175	5	37	7	2	1.1	.857
1922	CLE	A	0	0	—	6.19	18	1	0	36.1	47	12	11	0	0	0	0	6	2	0	.333	2	8	1	1	0.6	.909
5 yrs.			9	17	.346	4.15	97	27	12	353.2	403	113	126	1	5	2	1	107	22	0	.206	11	89	11	5	1.1	.901

Year	Team		W	L	PCT	ERA	G	GS	CG	IP	H	BB	SO	ShO	W	L	SV	AB	H	HR	BA	PO	A	E	DP	TC/G	FA
															Relief Pitching			**Batting**									

George Keefe

KEEFE, GEORGE WASHINGTON
B. Jan. 7, 1867, Washington, D. C. D. Aug. 24, 1935, Washington, D. C.

BL TL 5'9" 168 lbs.

Year	Team		W	L	PCT	ERA	G	GS	CG	IP	H	BB	SO	ShO	W	L	SV	AB	H	HR	BA	PO	A	E	DP	TC/G	FA
1886	WAS	N	0	3	.000	5.17	4	4	4	31.1	28	15	5	0	0	0	0	14	0	0	.000	2	2	0	0	1.0	1.000
1887			0	1	.000	9.00	1	1	1	8	16	4	0	0	0	0	0	3	0	0	.000	0	0	1	0	1.0	–
1888			6	7	.462	2.84	13	13	13	114	87	43	52	1	0	0	0	42	9	0	.214	2	28	2	0	2.5	.938
1889			8	18	.308	5.13	30	27	24	230	266	143	90	0	1	0	0	98	16	0	.163	6	33	3	0	1.4	.929
1890	BUF	P	6	16	.273	6.52	25	22	22	196	280	138	55	0	0	0	0	79	16	0	.203	2	49	10	1	2.4	.836
1891	WAS	AA	0	3	.000	2.68	5	4	4	37	44	17	11	0	0	0	1	14	2	0	.143	1	12	2	0	3.0	.867
6 yrs.			20	48	.294	5.05	78	71	68	616.1	721	360	213	1	1	0	1	250	43	0	.172	13	124	18	1	2.0	.884

John Keefe

KEEFE, JOHN THOMAS
B. May 5, 1867, Fitchburg, Mass. D. Aug. 9, 1937, Fitchburg, Mass.

TL

Year	Team		W	L	PCT	ERA	G	GS	CG	IP	H	BB	SO	ShO	W	L	SV	AB	H	HR	BA	PO	A	E	DP	TC/G	FA
1890	SYR	AA	17	24	.415	4.32	43	41	36	352.1	355	148	120	2	1	0	0	157	30	0	.191	14	71	4	2	2.1	.955

Tim Keefe

KEEFE, TIMOTHY JOHN (Sir Timothy)
B. Jan. 1, 1857, Cambridge, Mass. D. Apr. 23, 1933, Cambridge, Mass.
Hall of Fame 1964.

BR TR 5'10½" 185 lbs.

Year	Team		W	L	PCT	ERA	G	GS	CG	IP	H	BB	SO	ShO	W	L	SV	AB	H	HR	BA	PO	A	E	DP	TC/G	FA
1880	TRO	N	6	6	.500	0.86	12	12	12	105	71	17	43	0	0	0	0	43	10	0	.233	7	22	0	0	2.4	1.000
1881			18	27	.400	3.25	45	45	45	402	442	81	103	4	0	0	0	152	35	0	.230	23	79	17	5	2.6	.857
1882			17	26	.395	2.50	43	42	41	375	368	81	116	1	1	0	0	189	43	1	.228	32	89	11	4	3.1	.917
1883	NY	AA	41	27	.603	2.41	68	68	68	619	486	98	361	5	0	0	0	259	57	0	.220	31	148	59	3	3.5	.752
1884			37	17	.685	2.29	58	58	57	491.2	388	75	323	4	0	0	0	213	50	3	.235	18	95	30	2	2.5	.790
1885	NY	N	32	13	.711	1.58	46	46	45	398	297	103	230	7	0	0	0	166	27	0	.163	30	80	13	0	2.7	.894
1886			42	20	.677	2.53	64	64	62	540	478	100	291	2	0	0	0	205	35	1	.171	29	107	15	3	2.4	.901
1887			35	19	.648	3.10	56	56	54	478.2	447	108	186	2	0	0	0	191	42	2	.220	17	102	15	1	2.4	.888
1888			35	12	.745	1.74	51	51	51	434.1	316	91	333	8	0	0	0	181	23	2	.127	29	79	10	1	2.3	.915
1889			28	13	.683	3.31	47	45	38	364	310	151	209	3	0	0	1	149	23	0	.154	10	78	8	3	2.0	.917
1890	NY	P	17	11	.607	3.38	30	30	23	229	228	85	88	1	0	0	0	92	10	2	.109	15	61	4	2	2.7	.950
1891	2 teams		NY N (8G 2–5)				PHI N (11G 3–6)																				
"	total		5	11	.313	4.46	19	17	13	133.1	155	55	64	0	0	0	1	50	7	0	.140	6	28	2	1	1.9	.944
1892	PHI	N	19	16	.543	2.36	39	38	31	313.1	264	100	127	3	1	0	0	117	10	1	.085	8	68	13	2	2.3	.854
1893			10	7	.588	4.40	22	22	17	178	202	79	53	0	0	0	0	79	18	0	.228	5	32	6	1	2.0	.860
14 yrs.			342	225	.603	2.62	600	594	557	5061.1	4452	1224	2527	40	2	0	2	2086	390	12	.187	260	1068	203	28	2.6	.867
			8th							3rd																		

Bob Keegan

KEEGAN, ROBERT CHARLES (Smiley)
B. Aug. 4, 1920, Rochester, N. Y.

BR TR 6'2½" 207 lbs.

Year	Team		W	L	PCT	ERA	G	GS	CG	IP	H	BB	SO	ShO	W	L	SV	AB	H	HR	BA	PO	A	E	DP	TC/G	FA
1953	CHI	A	7	5	.583	2.74	22	11	4	98.2	80	33	32	2	2	0	1	28	9	0	.321	7	20	0	2	1.2	1.000
1954			16	9	.640	3.09	31	27	14	209.2	211	82	61	2	0	0	2	75	9	0	.120	5	36	1	3	1.4	.976
1955			2	5	.286	5.83	18	11	1	58.2	83	28	29	0	0	1	0	18	6	0	.333	2	11	1	0	0.8	.929
1956			5	7	.417	3.93	20	16	4	105.1	119	35	32	0	1	0	0	32	4	0	.125	6	18	1	0	1.3	.960
1957			10	8	.556	3.53	30	20	6	142.2	131	37	36	2	2	2	2	39	4	0	.103	5	23	0	1	0.9	1.000
1958			0	2	.000	6.07	14	2	0	29.2	44	18	8	0	0	2	0	4	0	0	.000	0	9	0	0	0.6	1.000
6 yrs.			40	36	.526	3.66	135	87	29	644.2	668	233	198	6	5	5	5	196	32	0	.163	25	117	3	6	1.1	.979

Ed Keegan

KEEGAN, EDWARD CHARLES
B. July 8, 1939, Camden, N. J.

BR TR 6'3" 165 lbs.

Year	Team		W	L	PCT	ERA	G	GS	CG	IP	H	BB	SO	ShO	W	L	SV	AB	H	HR	BA	PO	A	E	DP	TC/G	FA
1959	PHI	N	0	3	.000	18.00	3	3	0	9	19	13	3	0	0	0	0	3	0	0	.000	0	1	0	0	0.3	1.000
1961	KC	A	0	0	–	4.50	6	0	0	6	6	5	3	0	0	0	1	0	0	0	–	1	0	0	0	0.2	1.000
1962	PHI	N	0	0	–	2.25	4	0	0	8	6	5	5	0	0	0	0	0	0	0	–	0	0	0	0	–	–
3 yrs.			0	3	.000	9.00	13	3	0	23	31	23	11	0	0	0	1	3	0	0	.000	1	1	0	0	0.2	1.000

Burt Keeley

KEELEY, BURTON ELWOOD (Speed)
B. Nov. 2, 1879, Wilmington, Ill. D. May 3, 1952, Ely, Minn.

BR TR 5'9" 170 lbs.

Year	Team		W	L	PCT	ERA	G	GS	CG	IP	H	BB	SO	ShO	W	L	SV	AB	H	HR	BA	PO	A	E	DP	TC/G	FA
1908	WAS	A	6	11	.353	2.97	28	17	12	169.2	173	48	68	1	0	3	1	49	5	0	.102	6	64	10	2	2.9	.875
1909			0	0	–	11.57	2	0	0	7	12	1	0	0	0	0	0	2	1	0	.500	0	7	0	0	3.5	1.000
2 yrs.			6	11	.353	3.31	30	17	12	176.2	185	49	68	1	0	3	1	51	6	0	.118	6	71	10	2	2.9	.885

Vic Keen

KEEN, HOWARD VICTOR
B. Mar. 16, 1899, Bel Air, Md. D. Dec. 10, 1976, Salisbury, Md.

BR TR 5'9" 165 lbs.

Year	Team		W	L	PCT	ERA	G	GS	CG	IP	H	BB	SO	ShO	W	L	SV	AB	H	HR	BA	PO	A	E	DP	TC/G	FA
1918	PHI	A	0	1	.000	3.38	1	1	0	8	9	1	1	0	0	0	0	1	0	0	.000	0	0	0	0	0.0	–
1921	CHI	N	0	3	.000	4.68	5	4	1	25	29	9	9	0	0	0	0	5	0	0	.000	0	7	1	1	1.6	.875
1922			1	2	.333	3.89	7	3	2	34.2	36	10	11	0	0	1	0	12	4	0	.333	0	8	1	0	1.3	.889
1923			12	8	.600	3.00	35	17	10	177	169	57	46	0	3	2	1	53	8	0	.151	5	35	3	2	1.2	.930
1924			15	14	.517	3.80	40	28	15	234.2	242	80	75	0	1	1	3	77	12	0	.156	6	42	1	1	1.2	.980
1925			2	6	.250	6.26	30	8	1	83.1	125	41	19	0	2	1	1	25	6	0	.240	1	26	1	2	0.9	.964
1926	STL	N	10	9	.526	4.56	26	21	12	152	179	42	29	1	0	1	0	53	3	0	.057	7	29	0	4	1.4	1.000
1927			2	1	.667	4.81	21	0	0	33.2	39	8	12	0	2	1	0	4	1	0	.250	1	8	0	0	0.4	1.000
8 yrs.			42	44	.488	4.11	165	82	41	748.1	828	248	202	1	9	7	6	230	34	0	.148	20	155	7	10	1.1	.962

WORLD SERIES

Year	Team		W	L	PCT	ERA	G	GS	CG	IP	H	BB	SO	ShO	W	L	SV	AB	H	HR	BA	PO	A	E	DP	TC/G	FA
1926	STL	N	0	0	–	0.00	1	0	0	1	0	0	0	0	0	0	0	0	0	0	–	0	1	0	0	1.0	1.000

Jim Keenan

KEENAN, JAMES WILLIAM
B. Feb. 10, 1858, New Haven, Conn. D. Sept. 21, 1926, Cincinnati, Ohio

BR TR 5'10" 186 lbs.

Year	Team		W	L	PCT	ERA	G	GS	CG	IP	H	BB	SO	ShO	W	L	SV	AB	H	HR	BA	PO	A	E	DP	TC/G	FA
1884	IND	AA	0	0	–	3.00	1	0	0	3	2	0	0	0	0	0	0	249	73	3	.293	0	0	0	0	0.0	–
1885	CIN	AA	0	0	–	1.13	1	0	0	8	7	1	0	0	0	0	0	132	35	1	.265	1	1	0	0	2.0	1.000
1886			0	1	.000	3.38	2	0	0	8	8	3	2	0	0	1	0	148	40	3	.270	0	1	0	0	0.5	1.000
3 yrs.			0	1	.000	2.37	4	0	0	19	17	4	2	0	0	1	0	*				1	2	0	0	0.8	1.000

Year	Team	W	L	PCT	ERA	G	GS	CG	IP	H	BB	SO	ShO	W	L	SV	AB	H	HR	BA	PO	A	E	DP	TC/G	FA

Bob Kelly *continued*

Year	Team	W	L	PCT	ERA	G	GS	CG	IP	H	BB	SO	ShO	W	L	SV	AB	H	HR	BA	PO	A	E	DP	TC/G	FA
1958	2 teams	CIN N	(2G 0–0)		CLE A	(13G 0–2)																				
"	total	0	2	.000	5.16	15	4	0	29.2	32	16	13	0	0	1	0	4	1	0	.250	0	6	0	1	0.4	1.000
4 yrs.		12	18	.400	4.50	123	35	7	362	374	152	146	2	2	6	2	90	16	0	.178	24	71	5	5	0.8	.950

Bryan Kelly

KELLY, BRYAN KEITH BR TR 6'2" 195 lbs.
B. Feb. 24, 1959, Silver Spring, Md.

Year	Team	W	L	PCT	ERA	G	GS	CG	IP	H	BB	SO	ShO	W	L	SV	AB	H	HR	BA	PO	A	E	DP	TC/G	FA
1986	DET A	1	2	.333	4.50	6	4	0	20	21	10	18	0	0	1	0	0	0	0	–	2	4	1	0	1.2	.857
1987		0	1	.000	5.06	5	0	0	10.2	12	7	10	0	0	1	0	0	0	0	–	0	0	0	0	0.0	–
2 yrs.		1	3	.250	4.70	11	4	0	30.2	33	17	28	0	0	2	0	0	0	0	–	2	4	1	0	0.6	.857

Ed Kelly

KELLY, EDWARD LEO BR TR 5'11½" 173 lbs.
B. Dec. 10, 1888, Pawtucket, R. I. D. Nov. 4, 1928, Red Lodge, Mont.

Year	Team	W	L	PCT	ERA	G	GS	CG	IP	H	BB	SO	ShO	W	L	SV	AB	H	HR	BA	PO	A	E	DP	TC/G	FA
1914	BOS A	0	0	–	0.00	3	0	0	2.1	1	1	4	0	0	0	0	1	0	0	.000	0	1	0	0	0.3	1.000

George Kelly

KELLY, GEORGE LANGE (Highpockets) BR TR 6'4" 190 lbs.
Brother of Ren Kelly.
B. Sept. 10, 1895, San Francisco, Calif. D. Oct. 13, 1984, Burlingame, Calif.
Hall of Fame 1973.

Year	Team	W	L	PCT	ERA	G	GS	CG	IP	H	BB	SO	ShO	W	L	SV	AB	H	HR	BA	PO	A	E	DP	TC/G	FA
1917	NY N	1	0	1.000	0.00	1	0	0	5	4	1	2	0	1	0	0	*				0	0	0	0	0.0	–

Herb Kelly

KELLY, HERBERT BARRETT BL TL 5'9" 160 lbs.
B. June 4, 1892, Mobile, Ala. D. May 18, 1973, Torrance, Calif.

Year	Team	W	L	PCT	ERA	G	GS	CG	IP	H	BB	SO	ShO	W	L	SV	AB	H	HR	BA	PO	A	E	DP	TC/G	FA
1914	PIT N	0	2	.000	2.45	5	2	2	25.2	24	7	6	0	0	0	0	9	2	0	.222	2	6	0	0	1.6	1.000
1915		1	1	.500	4.09	5	1	0	11	10	4	6	0	1	0	0	2	1	0	.500	1	8	1	1	2.0	.900
2 yrs.		1	3	.250	2.95	10	3	2	36.2	34	11	12	0	1	0	0	11	3	0	.273	3	14	1	1	1.8	.944

King Kelly

KELLY, MICHAEL JOSEPH BR TR 5'10" 170 lbs.
B. Dec. 31, 1857, Troy, N. Y. D. Nov. 8, 1894, Boston, Mass.
Manager 1887, 1890-91.
Hall of Fame 1945.

Year	Team	W	L	PCT	ERA	G	GS	CG	IP	H	BB	SO	ShO	W	L	SV	AB	H	HR	BA	PO	A	E	DP	TC/G	FA
1880	CHI N	0	0	–	0.00	1	0	0	3	3	1	1	0	0	0	0	344	100	1	.291	0	0	0	0	0.0	–
1883		0	0	–	0.00	1	0	0	1	1	0	0	0	0	0	0	428	109	3	.255	0	1	0	0	1.0	1.000
1884		0	1	.000	8.44	2	0	0	5.1	12	2	1	0	0	1	0	452	160	13	.354	0	0	0	0	0.0	–
1887	BOS N	1	0	1.000	3.46	3	0	0	13	17	14	0	0	1	0	0	484	156	8	.322	0	4	2	0	2.0	.667
1890	BOS P	1	0	1.000	4.50	1	0	0	2	1	2	2	0	1	0	0	340	111	4	.326	0	0	0	0	0.0	–
1891	3 teams	CIN AA	(3G 0–1)		BOS AA	(0G 0–0)		BOS N	(0G 0–0)																	
"	total	0	1	.000	5.28	3	0	0	15.1	21	7	0	0	0	1	0	350	100	2	.286	0	5	0	0	1.7	1.000
1892	BOS N	0	0	–	1.50	1	0	0	6	8	4	0	0	0	0	0	281	53	2	.189	0	0	0	0	0.0	–
7 yrs.		2	2	.500	4.14	12	0	0	45.2	63	30	4	0	2	2	0	*				0	10	2	0	1.0	.833

Mike Kelly

KELLY, MICHAEL J. BR TR 6'1" 178 lbs.
B. Nov. 9, 1902, St. Louis, Mo.

Year	Team	W	L	PCT	ERA	G	GS	CG	IP	H	BB	SO	ShO	W	L	SV	AB	H	HR	BA	PO	A	E	DP	TC/G	FA
1926	PHI N	0	0	–	9.45	4	0	0	6.2	9	4	2	0	0	0	0	3	0	0	.000	0	0	0	0	0.0	–

Ren Kelly

KELLY, REYNOLDS JOSEPH BR TR 6' 183 lbs.
Brother of George Kelly.
B. Nov. 18, 1899, San Francisco, Calif. D. Aug. 24, 1963, Millbrae, Calif.

Year	Team	W	L	PCT	ERA	G	GS	CG	IP	H	BB	SO	ShO	W	L	SV	AB	H	HR	BA	PO	A	E	DP	TC/G	FA
1923	PHI A	0	0	–	2.57	1	0	0	7	7	4	1	0	0	0	0	3	0	0	.000	0	0	0	0	0.0	–

Bill Kelso

KELSO, WILLIAM EUGENE BR TR 6'4" 215 lbs.
B. Feb. 19, 1940, Kansas City, Mo.

Year	Team	W	L	PCT	ERA	G	GS	CG	IP	H	BB	SO	ShO	W	L	SV	AB	H	HR	BA	PO	A	E	DP	TC/G	FA
1964	LA A	2	0	1.000	2.28	10	1	1	23.2	19	9	21	1	1	0	0	6	0	0	.000	0	5	0	0	0.5	1.000
1966	CAL A	1	1	.500	2.38	5	0	0	11.1	11	6	11	0	1	1	0	1	0	0	.000	0	1	0	0	0.4	1.000
1967		5	3	.625	2.97	69	1	0	112	85	63	91	0	5	2	11	19	2	0	.105	5	20	2	1	0.4	.926
1968	CIN N	4	1	.800	3.98	35	0	0	54.1	56	15	39	0	4	1	1	8	0	0	.000	1	6	0	0	0.2	1.000
4 yrs.		12	5	.706	3.13	119	2	1	201.1	171	93	162	1	11	4	12	34	2	0	.059	7	32	2	1	0.3	.951

Russ Kemmerer

KEMMERER, RUSSELL PAUL (Rusty, Dutch) BR TR 6'2" 198 lbs.
B. Nov. 1, 1931, Pittsburgh, Pa.

Year	Team	W	L	PCT	ERA	G	GS	CG	IP	H	BB	SO	ShO	W	L	SV	AB	H	HR	BA	PO	A	E	DP	TC/G	FA
1954	BOS A	5	3	.625	3.82	19	9	2	75.1	71	41	37	1	2	0	0	21	3	0	.143	4	14	2	2	1.1	.900
1955		1	1	.500	7.27	7	2	0	17.1	18	15	13	0	1	0	0	3	0	0	.000	0	2	0	0	0.3	1.000
1957	2 teams	BOS A	(1G 0–0)		WAS A	(39G 7–11)																				
"	total	7	11	.389	4.95	40	26	6	176.1	219	73	82	0	1	0	0	46	3	2	.065	4	20	3	2	0.7	.889
1958	WAS A	6	15	.286	4.61	40	30	6	224.1	234	74	111	0	0	0	0	69	11	0	.159	13	37	2	1	1.3	.962
1959		8	17	.320	4.50	37	28	8	206	221	71	89	0	0	0	0	60	8	0	.133	18	36	3	1	1.5	.947
1960	2 teams	WAS A	(3G 0–2)		CHI A	(36G 6–3)																				
"	total	6	5	.545	3.59	39	10	2	138	129	55	86	1	4	2	2	33	0	0	.000	12	22	1	1	0.9	.971
1961	CHI A	3	3	.500	4.38	47	2	0	96.2	102	26	35	0	3	3	2	15	3	0	.200	8	21	2	2	0.7	.935
1962	2 teams	CHI A	(20G 2–1)		HOU N	(36G 5–3)																				
"	total	7	4	.636	4.03	56	2	0	96	102	26	40	0	7	3	2	11	4	0	.364	8	21	2	1	0.6	.935
1963	HOU N	0	0	–	5.65	17	0	0	36.2	48	8	12	0	0	1	0	7	2	0	.286	5	8	0	1	0.8	1.000
9 yrs.		43	59	.422	4.46	302	109	24	1066.2	1144	389	505	2	18	7	8	265	34	2	.128	72	181	15	12	0.9	.944

Dutch Kemner

KEMNER, HERMAN JOHN BR TR 5'10½" 175 lbs.
B. Mar. 4, 1899, Quincy, Ill. D. Jan. 16, 1988, Quincy, Ill.

Year	Team	W	L	PCT	ERA	G	GS	CG	IP	H	BB	SO	ShO	W	L	SV	AB	H	HR	BA	PO	A	E	DP	TC/G	FA
1929	CIN N	0	0	–	7.63	9	0	0	15.1	19	8	10	0	0	0	1	4	1	0	.250	0	4	1	0	0.6	.800

Year	Team	W	L	PCT	ERA	G	GS	CG	IP	H	BB	SO	ShO	W	L	SV	AB	H	HR	BA	PO	A	E	DP	TC/G	FA
														Relief Pitching			Batting									

Ed Kenna

KENNA, EDWARD BENNINGHAUS (The Pitching Poet)
B. Oct. 17, 1877, Charleston, W. Va. D. Mar. 22, 1912, Grant, Fla. TR 6' 180 lbs.

Year	Team	W	L	PCT	ERA	G	GS	CG	IP	H	BB	SO	ShO	W	L	SV	AB	H	HR	BA	PO	A	E	DP	TC/G	FA
1902	PHI A	1	1	.500	5.29	2	1	1	17	19	11	5	0	1	0	0	8	1	0	.125	1	7	1	0	4.5	.889

Bill Kennedy

KENNEDY, WILLIAM AULTON (Lefty)
B. Mar. 14, 1921, Carnesville, Ga. D. Apr. 9, 1983, Seattle, Wash. BL TL 6'2" 195 lbs.

Year	Team	W	L	PCT	ERA	G	GS	CG	IP	H	BB	SO	ShO	W	L	SV	AB	H	HR	BA	PO	A	E	DP	TC/G	FA
1948	2 teams	CLE A	(6G 1–0)		STL A	(26G 7–8)																				
"	total	8	8	.500	5.21	32	23	3	143.1	148	117	89	0	0	0	0	47	13	0	.277	3	21	0	0	0.8	1.000
1949	STL A	4	11	.267	4.69	48	16	2	153.2	172	73	69	0	2	1	1	40	6	0	.150	4	23	3	0	0.6	.900
1950		0	0	–	0.00	1	0	0	2	1	2	1	0	0	0	0	0	0	0	–	0	0	1	0	1.0	–
1951		1	5	.167	5.63	19	5	1	56	76	37	29	0	0	2	0	16	2	0	.125	3	14	1	2	0.9	.944
1952	CHI A	2	2	.500	2.80	47	1	0	70.2	54	38	46	0	2	1	5	13	3	0	.231	5	8	1	1	0.3	.929
1953	BOS A	0	0	–	3.70	16	0	0	24.1	24	17	14	0	0	0	2	2	1	0	.500	2	3	0	0	0.4	.714
1956	CIN N	0	0	–	18.00	1	0	0	2	6	0	0	0	0	0	0	0	0	0	–	0	0	0	0	0.0	–
1957		0	2	.000	6.39	8	0	0	12.2	16	5	8	0	0	2	3	2	0	0	.000	0	3	0	1	0.4	1.000
	8 yrs.	15	28	.349	4.71	172	45	6	464.2	497	289	256	0	4	6	11	120	25	0	.208	17	72	8	4	0.6	.918

Bill Kennedy

KENNEDY, WILLIAM GORMAN
B. Dec. 22, 1918, Alexandria, Va. BL TL 6'1" 175 lbs.

Year	Team	W	L	PCT	ERA	G	GS	CG	IP	H	BB	SO	ShO	W	L	SV	AB	H	HR	BA	PO	A	E	DP	TC/G	FA
1942	WAS A	0	1	.000	8.00	8	2	1	18	21	10	4	0	0	0	2	4	0	0	.000	1	6	0	1	0.9	1.000
1946		1	2	.333	6.00	21	2	0	39	40	29	18	0	1	1	3	8	1	0	.125	2	7	2	0	0.5	.818
1947		0	0	–	8.10	2	0	0	6.2	10	5	1	0	0	0	0	2	0	0	.000	0	2	0	0	1.0	1.000
	3 yrs.	1	3	.250	6.79	31	4	1	63.2	71	44	23	0	1	1	5	14	1	0	.071	3	15	2	1	0.6	.900

Brickyard Kennedy

KENNEDY, WILLIAM P.
B. Oct. 7, 1867, Bellaire, Ohio D. Sept. 23, 1915, Bellaire, Ohio BR TR 5'11" 160 lbs.

Year	Team	W	L	PCT	ERA	G	GS	CG	IP	H	BB	SO	ShO	W	L	SV	AB	H	HR	BA	PO	A	E	DP	TC/G	FA
1892	BKN N	13	8	.619	3.86	26	21	18	191	189	95	108	0	1	0	1	85	14	0	.165	17	32	2	1	2.0	.961
1893		25	20	.556	3.72	46	44	40	382.2	376	168	107	0	2	0	1	157	39	0	.248	12	109	10	6	2.8	.924
1894		24	20	.545	4.92	48	41	34	360.2	445	149	107	0	4	0	2	161	49	0	.304	7	82	8	4	2.0	.918
1895		19	12	.613	5.12	39	33	26	279.2	335	93	39	2	3	0	1	127	39	0	.307	5	66	5	1	1.9	.934
1896		17	20	.459	4.42	42	38	28	305.2	334	130	76	1	0	0	1	122	23	0	.189	10	87	5	2	2.4	.951
1897		18	20	.474	3.91	44	40	36	343.1	370	149	81	2	1	1	1	147	40	1	.272	14	87	4	4	2.4	.962
1898		16	22	.421	3.37	40	39	38	339.1	360	123	73	0	0	0	0	135	34	0	.252	15	108	6	5	3.2	.953
1899		22	9	.710	2.79	40	33	27	277.1	297	86	55	2	1	0	2	109	27	0	.248	14	67	8	2	2.2	.910
1900		20	13	.606	3.91	42	35	26	292	316	111	75	2	2	0	0	123	37	0	.301	20	73	5	3	2.3	.949
1901		3	5	.375	3.06	14	8	6	85.1	80	24	28	0	0	0	0	36	6	0	.167	3	20	1	1	1.7	.958
1902	NY N	1	4	.200	3.96	6	6	4	38.2	44	16	9	1	0	0	0	15	4	0	.267	4	7	2	0	2.2	.846
1903	PIT N	9	6	.600	3.45	18	15	10	125.1	130	57	39	1	0	0	1	58	21	0	.362	3	29	1	0	1.8	.969
	12 yrs.	187	159	.540	3.96	405	353	293	3021	3276	1201	797	13	12	3	9	1275	333	1	.261	123	767	57	29	2.3	.940

WORLD SERIES

Year	Team	W	L	PCT	ERA	G	GS	CG	IP	H	BB	SO	ShO	W	L	SV	AB	H	HR	BA	PO	A	E	DP	TC/G	FA
1903	PIT N	0	1	.000	5.14	1	1	0	7	11	3	3	0	0	0	0	2	1	0	.500	0	1	0	0	1.0	1.000

Monte Kennedy

KENNEDY, MONTIA CALVIN (Lefty)
B. May 11, 1922, Amelia, Va. BR TL 6'2" 185 lbs.

Year	Team	W	L	PCT	ERA	G	GS	CG	IP	H	BB	SO	ShO	W	L	SV	AB	H	HR	BA	PO	A	E	DP	TC/G	FA
1946	NY N	9	10	.474	3.42	38	27	10	186.2	153	116	71	1	0	0	1	64	15	0	.234	10	35	2	2	1.2	.957
1947		9	12	.429	4.85	34	24	9	148.1	158	88	60	0	1	1	0	48	8	0	.167	7	26	1	1	1.0	.971
1948		3	9	.250	4.01	25	16	7	114.1	118	57	63	1	0	1	0	31	4	0	.129	3	17	1	0	0.8	.952
1949		12	14	.462	3.43	38	32	14	223.1	208	100	95	4	0	0	1	83	12	1	.145	2	30	2	4	0.9	.941
1950		5	4	.556	4.72	36	17	5	114.1	120	53	41	0	2	0	2	36	2	0	.056	5	20	1	2	0.7	.962
1951		1	2	.333	2.25	29	5	1	68	68	31	22	0	1	0	1	15	3	0	.200	4	13	2	0	0.7	.895
1952		3	4	.429	3.02	31	6	2	83.1	73	31	48	1	2	1	0	22	2	0	.091	6	15	1	4	0.7	.955
1953		0	0	–	7.15	18	0	0	22.2	30	19	11	0	0	0	0	2	0	0	.000	2	4	0	2	0.3	1.000
	8 yrs.	42	55	.433	3.84	249	127	48	961	928	495	411	7	5	3	4	301	46	1	.153	39	160	10	15	0.8	.952

WORLD SERIES

Year	Team	W	L	PCT	ERA	G	GS	CG	IP	H	BB	SO	ShO	W	L	SV	AB	H	HR	BA	PO	A	E	DP	TC/G	FA
1951	NY N	0	0	–	6.00	2	0	0	3	3	1	4	0	0	0	0	0	0	0	–	0	1	0	0	0.5	1.000

Ted Kennedy

KENNEDY, THEODORE A.
B. Feb., 1865, Henry, Ill. D. Oct. 31, 1907, St. Louis, Mo. BL

Year	Team	W	L	PCT	ERA	G	GS	CG	IP	H	BB	SO	ShO	W	L	SV	AB	H	HR	BA	PO	A	E	DP	TC/G	FA
1885	CHI N	7	2	.778	3.43	9	9	8	78.2	91	28	36	0	0	0	0	36	3	0	.083	3	17	2	0	2.4	.909
1886	2 teams	PHI AA	(20G 5–15)		LOU AA	(4G 0–4)																				
"	total	5	19	.208	4.66	24	23	23	204.2	249	81	82	0	0	1	0	81	4	0	.049	8	37	6	1	2.1	.882
	2 yrs.	12	21	.364	4.32	33	32	31	283.1	340	109	118	0	0	1	0	117	7	0	.060	11	54	8	1	2.2	.890

Vern Kennedy

KENNEDY, LLOYD VERNON
B. Mar. 20, 1907, Kansas City, Mo. BL TR 6' 175 lbs.

Year	Team	W	L	PCT	ERA	G	GS	CG	IP	H	BB	SO	ShO	W	L	SV	AB	H	HR	BA	PO	A	E	DP	TC/G	FA
1934	CHI A	0	2	.000	3.72	3	3	1	19.1	21	9	7	0	0	0	0	7	2	0	.286	1	6	0	0	2.3	1.000
1935		11	11	.500	3.91	31	25	16	211.2	211	95	65	2	0	1	1	73	18	0	.247	8	54	2	3	2.1	.969
1936		21	9	.700	4.63	35	34	20	274.1	282	147	99	1	1	0	0	113	32	0	.283	13	50	2	5	1.9	.969
1937		14	13	.519	5.09	32	30	15	221	238	124	114	1	0	0	0	87	20	3	.230	9	40	3	1	1.6	.942
1938	DET A	12	9	.571	5.06	33	26	11	190.1	215	113	53	0	1	0	2	79	23	0	.291	6	46	4	4	1.7	.945
1939	2 teams	DET A	(4G 0–3)		STL A	(33G 9–17)																				
"	total	9	20	.310	5.80	37	31	13	212.2	254	124	64	1	0	1	0	74	12	0	.162	8	37	1	2	1.2	.978
1940	STL A	5	9	.357	4.59	34	32	18	222.1	263	122	70	0	1	0	0	84	25	2	.298	13	50	0	0	1.9	1.000
1941	2 teams	STL A	(6G 2–4)		WAS A	(17G 1–7)																				
"	total	3	11	.214	5.17	23	13	4	111.1	121	66	28	0	1	0	0	36	9	0	.250	5	24	2	1	1.3	.935
1942	CLE A	4	8	.333	4.08	28	13	4	108	99	50	37	0	3	0	0	30	6	0	.200	4	24	3	1	1.1	.903
1943		10	7	.588	2.45	28	17	8	146.2	130	59	63	1	3	0	1	52	12	0	.231	8	36	2	1	1.6	.978
1944	2 teams	CLE A	(12G 2–5)		PHI N	(12G 1–5)																				
"	total	3	10	.231	4.64	24	17	5	114.1	126	57	40	0	0	0	0	44	8	0	.182	8	25	3	1	1.5	.917

Year	Team	W	L	PCT	ERA	G	GS	CG	IP	H	BB	SO	ShO	W	L	SV	AB	H	HR	BA	PO	A	E	DP	TC/G	FA
														Relief Pitching			**Batting**									

Vern Kennedy *continued*

Year	Team	W	L	PCT	ERA	G	GS	CG	IP	H	BB	SO	ShO	W	L	SV	AB	H	HR	BA	PO	A	E	DP	TC/G	FA
1945	2 teams	PHI N (12G 0–3)			CIN N (24G 5–12)																					
"	total	5	15	.250	4.28	36	23	11	193.2	213	83	51	1	0	2	1	64	14	0	.219	16	47	2	2	1.8	.969
12 yrs.		104	132	.441	4.67	344	263	126	2025.2	2173	1049	691	7	8	9	5	743	181	4	.244	99	439	22	28	1.6	.961

Art Kenney

KENNEY, ARTHUR JOSEPH
B. Apr. 29, 1916, Milford, Mass.
BL TL 6' 175 lbs.

Year	Team	W	L	PCT	ERA	G	GS	CG	IP	H	BB	SO	ShO	W	L	SV	AB	H	HR	BA	PO	A	E	DP	TC/G	FA
1938	BOS N	0	0	–	15.43	2	0	0	2.1	3	8	2	0	0	0	0	0	0	0	–	0	1	0	0	0.5	1.000

Ed Kent

KENT, EDWARD C.
B. 1859, New York, N. Y. Deceased.
TL 5'6½" 152 lbs.

Year	Team	W	L	PCT	ERA	G	GS	CG	IP	H	BB	SO	ShO	W	L	SV	AB	H	HR	BA	PO	A	E	DP	TC/G	FA
1884	TOL AA	0	1	.000	6.00	1	1	1	9	14	3	4	0	0	0	0	4	0	0	.000	1	4	1	0	6.0	.833

Maury Kent

KENT, MAURICE ALLEN
B. Sept. 17, 1885, Marshalltown, Iowa D. Apr. 19, 1966, Iowa City, Iowa
BB TR 6' 168 lbs.

Year	Team	W	L	PCT	ERA	G	GS	CG	IP	H	BB	SO	ShO	W	L	SV	AB	H	HR	BA	PO	A	E	DP	TC/G	FA
1912	BKN N	5	5	.500	4.84	20	9	2	93	107	46	24	1	1	1	0	35	8	0	.229	2	29	2	1	1.7	.939
1913		0	0	–	2.45	3	0	0	7.1	5	3	1	0	0	0	0	3	0	0	.000	0	1	0	0	0.3	1.000
2 yrs.		5	5	.500	4.66	23	9	2	100.1	112	49	25	1	1	1	0	38	8	0	.211	2	30	2	1	1.5	.941

Matt Keough

KEOUGH, MATTHEW LON
Son of Marty Keough.
B. July 3, 1955, Pomona, Calif.
BR TR 6'3" 190 lbs.

Year	Team	W	L	PCT	ERA	G	GS	CG	IP	H	BB	SO	ShO	W	L	SV	AB	H	HR	BA	PO	A	E	DP	TC/G	FA
1977	OAK A	1	3	.250	4.81	7	6	0	43	39	22	23	0	0	0	0	–	3	4	1	0	1.1	.875		
1978		8	15	.348	3.24	32	32	6	197.1	178	85	108	0	0	0	0	0	0	0	–	21	31	2	2	1.7	.963
1979		2	17	.105	5.03	30	28	7	177	220	78	95	1	0	0	0	0	0	0	–	23	28	3	5	1.8	.944
1980		16	13	.552	2.92	34	32	20	250	218	94	121	2	0	0	0	0	0	0	–	23	28	3	2	1.6	.944
1981		10	6	.625	3.41	19	19	10	140	125	45	60	2	0	0	0	0	0	0	–	10	13	2	2	1.3	.920
1982		11	18	.379	5.72	34	34	10	209.1	233	101	75	2	0	0	0	0	0	0	–	9	20	3	2	0.9	.906
1983	2 teams	OAK A (14G 2–3)			NY A (12G 3–4)																					
"	total	5	7	.417	5.33	26	16	0	99.2	109	51	54	0	2	0	0	0	0	0	–	6	9	1	0	0.6	.938
1985	STL N	0	1	.000	4.50	4	1	0	10	10	4	10	0	0	0	0	2	0	0	.000	0	2	0	0	0.5	1.000
1986	2 teams	CHI N (19G 2–2)			HOU N (10G 3–2)																					
"	total	5	4	.556	3.94	29	7	0	64	58	30	44	0	3	0	0	16	6	0	.375	3	6	1	2	0.3	.900
9 yrs.		58	84	.408	4.17	215	175	53	1190.1	1190	510	590	7	5	0	0	18	6	0	.333	98	141	16	15	1.2	.937

LEAGUE CHAMPIONSHIP SERIES

Year	Team	W	L	PCT	ERA	G	GS	CG	IP	H	BB	SO	ShO	W	L	SV	AB	H	HR	BA	PO	A	E	DP	TC/G	FA
1981	OAK A	0	1	.000	1.08	1	1	0	8.1	7	6	2	0	0	0	0	–	0	0	0	0	0.0	–		

Kurt Kepshire

KEPSHIRE, KURT DAVID
B. July 3, 1959, Bridgeport, Conn.
BL TR 6'1" 180 lbs.

Year	Team	W	L	PCT	ERA	G	GS	CG	IP	H	BB	SO	ShO	W	L	SV	AB	H	HR	BA	PO	A	E	DP	TC/G	FA
1984	STL N	6	5	.545	3.30	17	16	2	109	100	44	71	2	0	0	0	36	2	0	.056	4	10	3	0	1.0	.824
1985		10	9	.526	4.75	32	29	0	153.1	155	71	67	0	0	0	0	51	6	0	.118	5	19	1	1	0.8	.960
1986		0	1	.000	4.50	2	1	0	8	8	4	6	0	0	0	0	1	0	0	.000	1	2	0	0	1.5	1.000
3 yrs.		16	15	.516	4.16	51	46	2	270.1	263	119	144	2	0	0	0	88	8	0	.091	10	31	4	1	0.9	.911

Charlie Kerfeld

KERFELD, CHARLES PATRICK
B. Sept. 28, 1963, Knob Noster, Mo.
BR TR 6'6" 225 lbs.

Year	Team	W	L	PCT	ERA	G	GS	CG	IP	H	BB	SO	ShO	W	L	SV	AB	H	HR	BA	PO	A	E	DP	TC/G	FA
1985	HOU N	4	2	.667	4.06	11	6	0	44.1	44	25	30	0	2	0	0	14	0	0	.000	5	2	1	1	0.7	.875
1986		11	2	.846	2.59	61	0	0	93.2	71	42	77	0	11	2	7	9	1	0	.111	7	9	0	1	0.3	1.000
1987		0	2	.000	6.67	21	0	0	29.2	34	21	17	0	0	2	0	3	0	0	.000	5	3	1	0	0.4	.889
3 yrs.		15	6	.714	3.70	93	6	0	167.2	149	88	124	0	13	4	7	26	1	0	.038	17	14	2	2	0.4	.939

LEAGUE CHAMPIONSHIP SERIES

Year	Team	W	L	PCT	ERA	G	GS	CG	IP	H	BB	SO	ShO	W	L	SV	AB	H	HR	BA	PO	A	E	DP	TC/G	FA
1986	HOU N	0	1	.000	2.25	3	0	0	4	2	1	4	0	0	0	0	–	0	0	1	0	0.3	–		

Gus Keriazakos

KERIAZAKOS, CONSTANTINE NICHOLAS
B. July 28, 1931, West Orange, N. J.
BR TR 6'3" 187 lbs.

Year	Team	W	L	PCT	ERA	G	GS	CG	IP	H	BB	SO	ShO	W	L	SV	AB	H	HR	BA	PO	A	E	DP	TC/G	FA
1950	CHI A	0	1	.000	19.29	1	1	0	2.1	7	5	1	0	0	0	0	1	1	0	1.000	0	0	0	0	0.0	–
1954	WAS A	2	3	.400	3.77	22	3	2	59.2	59	30	33	0	1	1	0	15	1	0	.067	7	7	0	1	0.6	1.000
1955	KC A	0	1	.000	12.34	5	1	0	11.2	15	7	8	0	0	1	0	3	0	0	.000	0	1	0	0	0.2	1.000
3 yrs.		2	5	.286	5.62	28	5	2	73.2	81	42	42	0	1	2	0	19	2	0	.105	7	8	0	1	0.5	1.000

Bill Kerksieck

KERKSIECK, WAYMAN WILLIAM
B. Dec. 6, 1913, Ulm, Ark. D. Mar. 11, 1970, Stuttgart, Ark.
BR TR 6'1" 183 lbs.

Year	Team	W	L	PCT	ERA	G	GS	CG	IP	H	BB	SO	ShO	W	L	SV	AB	H	HR	BA	PO	A	E	DP	TC/G	FA
1939	PHI N	0	2	.000	7.18	23	2	1	62.2	81	32	13	0	0	0	0	12	1	0	.083	1	11	0	1	0.5	1.000

Jim Kern

KERN, JAMES LESTER
B. Mar. 15, 1949, Gladwin, Mich.
BR TR 6'5" 185 lbs.

Year	Team	W	L	PCT	ERA	G	GS	CG	IP	H	BB	SO	ShO	W	L	SV	AB	H	HR	BA	PO	A	E	DP	TC/G	FA
1974	CLE A	0	1	.000	4.70	4	3	1	15.1	16	14	11	0	0	0	0	0	0	0	–	0	1	0	0	0.3	1.000
1975		1	2	.333	3.77	13	7	0	71.2	60	45	55	0	0	0	0	0	0	0	–	4	11	2	0	1.3	.882
1976		10	7	.588	2.36	50	2	0	118	91	50	111	0	9	6	15	0	0	0	–	7	14	3	2	0.5	.875
1977		8	10	.444	3.42	60	0	0	92	85	47	91	0	8	10	18	0	0	0	–	5	13	3	2	0.4	.857
1978		10	10	.500	3.08	58	0	0	99.1	77	58	95	0	10	10	13	0	0	0	.000	4	16	0	0	0.3	1.000
1979	TEX A	13	5	.722	1.57	71	0	0	143	99	62	136	0	13	5	29	0	0	0	–	9	16	7	1	0.5	.781
1980		3	11	.214	4.86	38	1	0	63	65	45	40	0	3	11	2	0	0	0	–	0	12	0	1	0.3	1.000
1981		1	2	.333	2.70	30	0	0	30	21	22	20	0	1	2	6	0	0	0	–	3	3	1	0	0.3	.857
1982	2 teams	CIN N (50G 3–5)			CHI A (13G 2–1)																					
"	total	5	6	.455	3.46	63	1	0	104	81	60	66	0	4	6	5	7	0	0	.000	6	18	0	0	0.4	1.000
1983	CHI A	0	0	–	0.00	1	0	0	.2	1	0	0	0	0	0	0	0	0	0	–	0	0	0	0	0.0	–

Year	Team		W	L	PCT	ERA	G	GS	CG	IP	H	BB	SO	ShO	Relief Pitching W	L	SV	Batting AB	H	HR	BA	PO	A	E	DP	TC/G	FA

Jim Kern *continued*

1984	2 teams	PHI N (8G 0–1)				MIL A (6G 1–0)																					
"	total		1	1	.500	7.50	14	0	0	18	26	13	12	0	1	1	0	1	0	0	.000	1	2	0	0	0.2	1.000
1985	MIL	A	0	1	.000	6.55	5	0	0	11	14	5	3	0	0	1	0	0	0	0	–	2	3	0	1	1.0	1.000
1986	CLE	A	1	1	.500	7.90	16	0	0	27.1	34	23	11	0	1	1	0	0	0	0	–	2	6	0	0	0.5	1.000
13 yrs.			53	57	.482	3.32	416	14	1	793.1	670	444	651	0	50	53	88	9	0	0	.000	43	115	16	7	0.4	.908

Dickie Kerr

KERR, RICHARD HENRY
B. July 3, 1893, St. Louis, Mo.   D. May 4, 1963, Houston, Tex.
BL TL 5'7"   155 lbs.

1919	CHI	A	13	7	.650	2.88	39	17	10	212.1	208	64	79	1	7	1	0	68	17	0	.250	7	66	4	0	2.0	.948
1920			21	9	.700	3.37	45	28	20	253.2	266	72	72	3	3	1	5	90	14	0	.156	8	81	1	2	2.2	.989
1921			19	17	.528	4.72	44	37	25	308.2	357	96	80	3	3	0	1	105	25	0	.238	10	81	7	4	2.2	.929
1925			0	1	.000	5.15	12	2	0	36.2	45	18	4	0	0	0	0	12	4	0	.333	1	11	1	3	1.1	.923
4 yrs.			53	34	.609	3.84	140	84	55	811.1	876	250	235	7	13	2	6	275	60	0	.218	26	239	13	9	2.0	.953

WORLD SERIES

| 1919 | CHI | A | 2 | 0 | 1.000 | 1.42 | 2 | 2 | 2 | 19 | 14 | 3 | 6 | 1 | 0 | 0 | 0 | 6 | 1 | 0 | .167 | 1 | 4 | 0 | 0 | 2.5 | 1.000 |

Joe Kerrigan

KERRIGAN, JOSEPH THOMAS
B. Nov. 30, 1954, Philadelphia, Pa.
BR TR 6'5"   205 lbs.

1976	MON	N	2	6	.250	3.81	38	0	0	56.2	63	23	22	0	2	6	1	2	0	0	.000	7	9	1	2	0.4	.941
1977			3	5	.375	3.24	66	0	0	89	80	33	43	0	3	5	11	8	0	0	.000	6	16	2	3	0.4	.917
1978	BAL	A	3	1	.750	4.77	26	2	0	71.2	75	36	41	0	2	1	3	0	0	0	–	1	19	1	0	0.8	.952
1980			0	0	–	4.50	1	0	0	2	3	0	1	0	0	0	0	0	0	0	–	0	2	0	0	2.0	1.000
4 yrs.			8	12	.400	3.90	131	2	0	219.1	221	92	107	0	7	12	15	10	0	0	.000	14	46	4	5	0.5	.938

Rick Kester

KESTER, RICHARD LEE
B. July 7, 1946, Iola, Kans.
BR TR 6'   190 lbs.

1968	ATL	N	0	0	–	5.68	5	0	0	6.1	8	3	9	0	0	0	0	0	0	0	–	0	0	0	0	0.0	–
1969			0	0	–	13.50	1	0	0	2	5	0	2	0	0	0	0	0	0	0	–	0	0	0	0	0.0	–
1970			0	0	–	5.63	15	0	0	32	36	19	20	0	0	0	0	9	0	0	.000	0	3	2	0	0.3	.600
3 yrs.			0	0	–	6.02	21	0	0	40.1	49	22	31	0	0	0	0	9	0	0	.000	0	3	2	0	0.2	.600

Gus Ketchum

KETCHUM, AUGUSTUS FRANKLIN
B. Mar. 21, 1897, Royce City, Tex.   D. Sept. 6, 1980, Oklahoma City, Okla.
BR TR 5'9½"   170 lbs.

| 1922 | PHI | A | 0 | 1 | .000 | 5.63 | 6 | 0 | 0 | 16 | 19 | 8 | 4 | 0 | 0 | 1 | 0 | 4 | 0 | 0 | .000 | 0 | 1 | 0 | 0 | 0.2 | 1.000 |

Hank Keupper

KEUPPER, HENRY J.
B. June 24, 1887, Staunton, Ill.   D. Aug. 14, 1960, Marion, Ill.
BL TL 6'1"   185 lbs.

| 1914 | STL | F | 8 | 20 | .286 | 4.27 | 42 | 25 | 12 | 213 | 256 | 49 | 70 | 1 | 3 | 0 | 0 | 68 | 17 | 0 | .250 | 10 | 74 | 4 | 1 | 2.1 | .955 |

Jimmy Key

KEY, JAMES EDWARD
B. Apr. 22, 1961, Huntsville, Ala.
BR TL 6'1"   180 lbs.

1984	TOR	A	4	5	.444	4.65	63	0	0	62	70	32	44	0	4	5	10	0	0	0	–	9	11	1	0	0.3	.952
1985			14	6	.700	3.00	35	32	3	212.2	188	50	85	0	1	0	0	0	0	0	–	15	52	3	3	2.0	.957
1986			14	11	.560	3.57	36	35	4	232	222	74	141	0	0	0	0	0	0	0	–	18	42	0	4	1.7	1.000
1987			17	8	.680	2.76	36	36	8	261	210	66	161	1	0	0	0	0	0	0	–	17	44	3	5	1.8	.953
1988			12	5	.706	3.29	21	21	2	131.1	127	30	65	2	0	0	0	0	0	0	–	5	19	0	1	1.1	1.000
1989			13	14	.481	3.88	33	33	5	216	226	27	118	0	0	0	0	0	0	0	–	11	44	2	2	1.7	.965
6 yrs.			74	49	.602	3.36	224	157	22	1115	1043	279	614	6	5	5	10	0	0	0	–	75	212	9	15	1.3	.970

LEAGUE CHAMPIONSHIP SERIES

1985	TOR	A	0	1	.000	5.19	2	2	0	8.2	15	2	5	0	0	0	0	0	0	0	–	0	3	0	0	1.5	1.000
1989			1	0	1.000	4.50	1	1	0	6	7	2	2	0	0	0	0	0	0	0	–	0	0	0	0	0.0	–
2 yrs.			1	1	.500	4.91	3	3	0	14.2	22	4	7	0	0	0	0	0	0	0	–	0	3	0	0	1.0	1.000

Joe Kiefer

KIEFER, JOSEPH WILLIAM (Smoke, Harlem Joe)
B. July 19, 1899, West Leyden, N. Y.   D. July 5, 1975, Utica, N. Y.
BR TR 5'11"   190 lbs.

1920	CHI	A	0	1	.000	15.43	2	1	0	4.2	7	5	1	0	0	0	0	2	0	0	.000	0	0	0	0	0.0	–
1925	BOS	A	0	2	.000	6.00	2	2	0	15	20	9	4	0	0	0	0	4	0	0	.000	1	7	1	0	4.5	.889
1926			0	2	.000	4.80	11	1	0	30	29	16	4	0	0	1	0	7	1	0	.143	0	10	1	1	1.0	.909
3 yrs.			0	5	.000	6.16	15	4	0	49.2	56	30	9	0	0	1	0	13	1	0	.077	1	17	2	1	1.3	.900

Leo Kiely

KIELY, LEO PATRICK
B. Nov. 30, 1929, Hoboken, N. J.   D. Jan. 18, 1984, Montclair, N. J.
BL TL 6'2"   180 lbs.

1951	BOS	A	7	7	.500	3.34	17	16	4	113.1	106	39	46	0	0	1	0	35	5	0	.143	4	29	2	0	2.1	.943
1954			5	8	.385	3.50	28	19	4	131	153	58	59	1	0	1	1	50	9	1	.180	7	20	5	1	1.1	.844
1955			3	3	.500	2.80	33	4	0	90	91	37	36	0	3	2	6	26	5	0	.192	6	19	0	4	0.8	1.000
1956			2	2	.500	5.17	23	0	0	31.1	47	14	9	0	2	2	3	6	1	0	.167	2	1	0	0	0.3	1.000
1958			5	2	.714	3.00	47	0	0	81	77	18	26	0	5	2	12	13	0	0	.000	4	19	1	0	0.5	.958
1959			3	3	.500	4.20	41	0	0	55.2	67	18	30	0	3	3	7	8	0	0	.000	7	12	0	0	0.5	1.000
1960	KC	A	1	2	.333	1.74	20	0	0	20.2	21	5	6	0	1	2	1	1	0	0	.000	2	9	0	0	0.6	1.000
7 yrs.			26	27	.491	3.37	209	39	8	523	562	189	212	1	14	12	29	139	20	1	.144	33	113	8	8	0.7	.948

John Kiley

KILEY, JOHN FREDERICK
B. July 1, 1859, South Dedham, Mass.   D. Dec. 18, 1940, Norwood, Mass.
BL TL

| 1891 | BOS | N | 0 | 1 | .000 | 6.75 | 1 | 1 | 1 | 8 | 13 | 5 | 1 | 0 | 0 | 0 | 0 | * | | | | 0 | 2 | 0 | 0 | 2.0 | 1.000 |

Paul Kilgus

KILGUS, PAUL NELSON
B. Feb. 2, 1962, Bowling Green, Ky.
BL TL 6'1"   175 lbs.

| 1987 | TEX | A | 2 | 7 | .222 | 4.13 | 25 | 12 | 0 | 89.1 | 95 | 31 | 42 | 0 | 0 | 2 | 0 | 0 | 0 | 0 | – | 7 | 9 | 4 | 2 | 0.8 | .800 |

Year	Team		W	L	PCT	ERA	G	GS	CG	IP	H	BB	SO	ShO	Relief Pitching W	L	SV	Batting AB	H	HR	BA	PO	A	E	DP	TC/G	FA

Paul Kilgus *continued*

Year	Team		W	L	PCT	ERA	G	GS	CG	IP	H	BB	SO	ShO	W	L	SV	AB	H	HR	BA	PO	A	E	DP	TC/G	FA
1988			12	15	.444	4.16	32	32	5	203.1	190	71	88	3	0	0	0	0	0	0	–	11	34	2	4	1.5	.957
1989	CHI	N	6	10	.375	4.39	35	23	0	145.2	164	49	61	0	0	0	2	41	3	0	.073	10	25	2	0	1.1	.946
3 yrs.			20	32	.385	4.23	92	67	5	438.1	449	151	191	3	0	2	2	41	3	0	.073	28	68	8	6	1.1	.923

LEAGUE CHAMPIONSHIP SERIES

| 1989 | CHI | N | 0 | 0 | – | 0.00 | 1 | 0 | 0 | 3 | 4 | 1 | 1 | 0 | 0 | 0 | 0 | 0 | 0 | 0 | – | 0 | 0 | 0 | 0 | 0.0 | – |

Mike Kilkenny

KILKENNY, MICHAEL DAVID BR TL 6'3½" 175 lbs.
B. Apr. 11, 1945, Bradford Ont., Canada

1969	DET	A	8	6	.571	3.37	39	15	6	128.1	99	63	97	4	1	1	2	37	2	0	.054	5	19	1	0	0.6	.960
1970			7	6	.538	5.16	36	21	3	129	141	70	105	0	0	1	0	39	3	0	.077	6	20	1	1	0.8	.963
1971			4	5	.444	5.02	30	11	2	86	83	44	47	0	0	0	1	24	2	0	.083	4	14	2	0	0.7	.900
1972	4 teams		DET A (1G 0–0)		OAK A (1G 0–0)			CLE A (22G 4–1)			SD N (5G 0–0)																
"	total		4	1	.800	3.78	29	7	1	64.1	59	42	49	0	2	0	1	14	1	0	.071	4	11	0	2	0.5	1.000
1973	CLE	A	0	0	–	22.50	5	0	0	2	5	5	3	0	0	0	0	0	0	0	–	0	1	0	0	0.2	1.000
5 yrs.			23	18	.561	4.44	139	54	12	409.2	387	224	301	4	4	1	4	114	8	0	.070	19	65	4	3	0.6	.955

Evans Killeen

KILLEEN, EVANS HENRY BR TR 6' 190 lbs.
B. Feb. 27, 1936, Brooklyn, N. Y.

| 1959 | KC | A | 0 | 0 | – | 4.76 | 4 | 0 | 0 | 5.2 | 4 | 4 | 1 | 0 | 0 | 0 | 0 | 0 | 0 | 0 | – | 0 | 0 | 0 | 0 | 0.0 | – |

Henry Killeen

KILLEEN, HENRY
B. 1871, Troy, N. Y. Deceased.

| 1891 | CLE | N | 0 | 1 | .000 | 6.23 | 1 | 1 | 1 | 8.2 | 11 | 8 | 3 | 0 | 0 | 0 | 0 | 3 | 0 | 0 | .000 | 0 | 3 | 0 | 0 | 3.0 | 1.000 |

Frank Killen

KILLEN, FRANK BISSELL (Lefty) BL TL 6'1" 200 lbs.
B. Nov. 30, 1870, Pittsburgh, Pa. D. Dec. 3, 1939, Pittsburgh, Pa.

1891	MIL	AA	7	4	.636	1.68	11	11	11	96.1	73	51	38	2	0	0	0	35	8	0	.229	3	22	3	1	2.5	.893
1892	WAS	N	29	26	.527	3.31	60	52	46	459.2	448	182	147	2	1	3	0	186	37	4	.199	20	121	22	2	2.7	.865
1893	PIT	N	34	14	.708	3.64	55	48	38	415	401	140	99	2	5	1	0	171	47	4	.275	16	103	14	2	2.4	.895
1894			14	11	.560	4.50	28	28	20	204	261	86	62	1	0	0	0	80	21	0	.263	6	44	5	2	2.0	.909
1895			5	5	.500	5.49	13	11	6	95	113	57	25	0	1	1	0	38	13	0	.342	1	26	0	1	2.1	1.000
1896			30	18	.625	3.41	52	50	44	432.1	476	119	134	5	0	0	0	173	40	2	.231	15	115	10	1	2.7	.929
1897			17	23	.425	4.46	42	41	38	337.1	417	76	99	1	0	1	0	129	32	1	.248	17	73	13	2	2.5	.874
1898	2 teams		PIT N (23G 10–11)			WAS N (17G 6–9)																					
"	total		16	20	.444	3.68	40	39	32	306	350	70	91	0	0	0	0	120	32	0	.267	12	69	8	3	2.2	.910
1899	2 teams		WAS N (2G 0–2)			BOS N (12G 7–5)																					
"	total		7	7	.500	4.45	14	14	12	111.1	126	30	26	0	0	0	0	46	8	0	.174	6	24	5	0	2.5	.857
1900	CHI	N	3	3	.500	4.67	6	6	6	54	65	11	4	0	0	0	0	20	3	0	.150	0	15	2	0	2.8	.882
10 yrs.			162	131	.553	3.78	321	300	253	2511	2730	822	725	13	8	6	0	998	241	11	.241	96	612	82	14	2.5	.896

Ed Killian

KILLIAN, EDWIN HENRY (Twilight Ed) BL TL 5'11" 170 lbs.
B. Nov. 12, 1876, Racine, Wis. D. July 18, 1928, Detroit, Mich.

1903	CLE	A	3	4	.429	2.48	9	8	7	61.2	61	13	18	3	0	0	0	28	5	0	.179	2	20	2	0	2.7	.917
1904	DET	A	14	20	.412	2.44	40	34	32	331.2	293	93	124	4	0	2	1	126	18	0	.143	20	85	8	3	2.8	.929
1905			23	14	.622	2.27	39	37	33	313.1	263	102	110	8	2	0	0	118	32	0	.271	14	79	7	3	2.6	.930
1906			10	6	.625	3.43	21	16	14	149.2	165	54	47	0	1	0	2	53	9	0	.170	2	38	2	2	2.0	.952
1907			25	13	.658	1.78	41	34	29	314	286	91	96	3	1	0	1	122	39	0	.320	11	94	4	1	2.7	.963
1908			12	9	.571	2.99	27	23	15	180.2	170	53	47	0	0	0	0	73	10	0	.137	15	71	3	0	3.3	.966
1909			11	9	.550	1.71	25	19	14	173.1	150	49	54	3	1	0	1	62	10	0	.161	11	49	1	1	2.4	.984
1910			4	3	.571	3.04	11	9	5	74	75	27	20	1	0	1	0	27	4	0	.148	7	19	0	0	2.4	1.000
8 yrs.			102	78	.567	2.38	213	180	149	1598.1	1463	482	516	22	5	3	6	609	127	0	.209	82	455	27	10	2.6	.952

WORLD SERIES

1907	DET	A	0	0	–	2.25	1	0	0	4	3	1	1	0	0	0	0	2	1	0	.500	0	0	0	0	0.0	–
1908			0	0	–	7.71	1	1	0	2.1	5	3	1	0	0	0	0	0	0	0	–	0	1	0	0	1.0	1.000
2 yrs.			0	0	–	4.26	2	1	0	6.1	8	4	2	0	0	0	0	2	1	0	.500	0	1	0	0	0.5	1.000

Jack Killilay

KILLILAY, JOHN WILLIAM BR TR 5'11" 165 lbs.
B. May 24, 1887, Leavenworth, Kans. D. Oct. 21, 1968, Tulsa, Okla.

| 1911 | BOS | A | 4 | 2 | .667 | 3.54 | 14 | 7 | 1 | 61 | 65 | 36 | 28 | 0 | 2 | 0 | 0 | 24 | 1 | 0 | .042 | 1 | 17 | 0 | 0 | 1.3 | 1.000 |

Matt Kilroy

KILROY, MATTHEW ALOYSIUS (Matches) BL TL 5'9" 175 lbs.
Brother of Mike Kilroy.
B. June 21, 1866, Philadelphia, Pa. D. Mar. 2, 1940, Philadelphia, Pa.

1886	BAL	AA	29	34	.460	3.37	68	68	66	583	476	182	513	5	0	0	0	218	38	0	.174	32	116	28	1	2.6	.841
1887			46	19	.708	3.07	69	69	66	589.1	585	157	217	6	0	0	0	239	59	0	.247	37	167	20	2	3.2	.911
1888			17	21	.447	4.04	40	40	35	321	347	79	135	2	0	0	0	145	26	0	.179	17	60	6	2	2.1	.928
1889			29	25	.537	2.85	59	56	55	480.2	476	142	217	5	0	0	0	208	57	1	.274	25	139	17	4	3.1	.906
1890	BOS	P	10	15	.400	4.26	30	27	18	217.2	268	87	48	0	2	1	0	93	20	0	.215	25	55	8	2	2.9	.909
1891	CIN	AA	1	4	.200	2.98	7	6	4	45.1	51	19	6	0	0	0	0	20	3	0	.150	3	14	2	0	2.7	.895
1892	WAS	N	1	1	.500	2.39	4	3	2	26.1	20	15	1	0	0	0	0	10	2	0	.200	3	14	2	0	4.8	.895
1893	LOU	N	3	2	.600	9.00	5	5	5	35	57	23	2	0	0	0	0	16	7	0	.438	1	12	1	0	2.8	.929
1894			0	5	.000	3.89	8	7	3	37	46	20	11	0	0	0	0	17	2	0	.118	6	13	4	0	2.9	.826
1898	CHI	N	6	7	.462	4.31	13	11	10	100.1	119	30	18	0	0	1	0	96	22	0	.229	7	29	3	1	3.0	.923
10 yrs.			142	133	.516	3.47	303	292	264	2435.2	2445	754	1170	19	3	2	0	*				156	619	91	12	2.9	.895

Mike Kilroy

KILROY, MICHAEL JOSEPH BR TR
Brother of Matt Kilroy.
B. Nov. 4, 1872, Philadelphia, Pa. D. Oct. 2, 1960, Philadelphia, Pa.

Year	Team		W	L	PCT	ERA	G	GS	CG	IP	H	BB	SO	ShO	Relief Pitching W	L	SV	Batting AB	H	HR	BA	PO	A	E	DP	TC/G	FA

Mike Kilroy *continued*

1888	BAL	AA	0	1	.000	8.00	1	1	1	9	12	5	1	0	0	0	0	4	0	0	.000	1	1	0	0	2.0	1.000
1891	PHI	N	0	2	.000	9.90	3	1	0	10	15	4	3	0	0	1	0	5	2	0	.400	1	1	0	0	0.7	1.000
2 yrs.			0	3	.000	9.00	4	2	1	19	27	9	4	0	0	1	0	9	2	0	.222	2	2	0	0	1.0	1.000

Newt Kimball

KIMBALL, NEWELL W.
B. Mar. 27, 1915, Logan, Utah   BR TR 6'2½" 190 lbs.

1937	CHI	N	0	0	–	10.80	2	0	0	5	12	1	0	0	0	0	0	1	0	0	.000	0	2	0	0	1.0	1.000
1938			0	0	–	9.00	1	0	0	1	3	0	1	0	0	0	0	0	0	0	–	0	0	0	0	0.0	–
1940	2 teams	BKN N	(21G 3-1)			STL N	(2G 1-0)																					
"	total		4	1	.800	3.02	23	1	1	47.2	40	21	27	0	3	1	1	11	2	0	.182	4	5	0	0	0.4	1.000
1941	BKN	N	3	1	.750	3.63	15	5	1	52	43	29	17	0	1	0	1	14	3	0	.214	4	10	0	0	0.9	1.000
1942			2	0	1.000	3.68	14	1	0	29.1	27	19	8	0	1	0	0	5	1	0	.200	0	0	0	0	0.0	–
1943	2 teams	BKN N	(5G 1-1)			PHI N	(34G 1-6)																					
"	total		2	7	.222	3.84	39	6	2	100.2	94	47	35	0	1	4	3	19	3	0	.158	5	10	4	2	0.5	.789
6 yrs.			11	9	.550	3.78	94	13	4	235.2	219	117	88	0	6	5	5	50	9	0	.180	13	27	4	2	0.5	.909

Sam Kimber

KIMBER, SAMUEL JACKSON
B. Oct. 29, 1852, Philadelphia, Pa.   D. Nov. 7, 1925, Philadelphia, Pa.   BR TR 5'10½" 168 lbs.

1884	BKN	AA	17	20	.459	3.91	40	40	40	352.1	363	69	119	3	0	0	0	138	20	0	.145	32	67	30	0	3.2	.767
1885	PRO	N	0	1	.000	11.25	1	1	1	8	15	5	4	0	0	0	0	3	0	0	.000	0	4	1	0	5.0	.800
2 yrs.			17	21	.447	4.07	41	41	41	360.1	378	74	123	3	0	0	0	141	20	0	.142	32	71	31	0	3.3	.769

Harry Kimberlin

KIMBERLIN, HARRY LYDLE (Murphy)
B. Mar. 13, 1909, Sullivan, Mo.   BR TR 6'3" 175 lbs.   BB 1938

1936	STL	A	0	0	–	5.40	13	0	0	20	24	16	4	0	0	0	0	1	0	0	.000	0	2	0	0	0.2	1.000
1937			0	2	.000	2.35	3	2	1	15.1	16	9	5	0	0	0	0	5	1	0	.200	0	3	1	0	1.3	.750
1938			0	0	–	3.38	1	1	1	8	8	3	1	0	0	0	0	1	0	0	.000	0	0	0	0	0.0	–
1939			1	2	.333	5.49	17	3	0	41	59	19	11	0	1	0	0	9	3	0	.333	2	8	1	0	0.6	.909
4 yrs.			1	4	.200	4.70	34	6	2	84.1	107	47	21	0	1	0	0	16	4	0	.250	2	13	2	0	0.5	.882

Hal Kime

KIME, HAROLD LEE (Lefty)
B. Mar. 15, 1899, West Salem, Ohio   D. May 16, 1939, Columbus, Ohio   BL TL 5'9" 160 lbs.

| 1920 | STL | N | 0 | 0 | – | 2.57 | 4 | 0 | 0 | 7 | 9 | 2 | 1 | 0 | 0 | 0 | 0 | 1 | 0 | 0 | .000 | 0 | 3 | 0 | 0 | 0.8 | 1.000 |

Chad Kimsey

KIMSEY, CLYDE ELIAS
B. Aug. 6, 1906, Copperhill, Tenn.   D. Dec. 3, 1942, Pryor, Okla.   BL TR 6'3½" 200 lbs.

1929	STL	A	3	6	.333	5.04	24	3	1	64.1	88	19	13	0	1	5	1	30	8	2	.267	7	25	1	2	1.4	.970
1930			6	10	.375	6.35	42	4	1	113.1	139	45	32	0	6	7	1	70	24	2	.343	2	32	2	0	0.9	.944
1931			4	6	.400	4.39	42	1	0	94.1	121	27	27	0	4	5	7	37	10	2	.270	6	31	3	1	1.0	.925
1932	2 teams	STL A	(33G 4-2)			CHI A	(7G 1-1)																					
"	total		5	3	.625	3.83	40	0	0	89.1	93	38	19	0	5	3	5	20	6	0	.300	4	30	2	2	0.9	.944
1933	CHI	A	4	1	.800	5.53	28	2	0	96	124	36	19	0	4	0	0	33	5	0	.152	2	28	0	2	1.1	1.000
1936	DET	A	2	3	.400	4.85	22	0	0	52	58	29	11	0	2	3	3	16	5	0	.313	3	18	1	0	1.0	.955
6 yrs.			24	29	.453	5.07	198	10	2	509.1	623	194	121	0	22	23	17	*				24	164	9	7	1.0	.954

Ellis Kinder

KINDER, ELLIS RAYMOND (Old Folks)
B. July 26, 1914, Atkins, Ark.   D. Oct. 16, 1968, Jackson, Tenn.   BR TR 6' 215 lbs.

1946	STL	A	3	3	.500	3.32	33	7	1	86.2	78	36	59	0	0	0	0	19	1	0	.053	2	10	0	2	0.4	1.000
1947			8	15	.348	4.49	34	26	10	194.1	201	82	110	2	0	0	1	62	8	0	.129	5	18	2	2	0.7	.920
1948	BOS	A	10	7	.588	3.74	28	22	10	178	183	63	53	1	1	2	0	62	6	0	.097	5	20	1	2	0.9	.962
1949			23	6	**.793**	3.36	43	30	19	252	251	99	138	6	2	1	4	92	12	0	.130	7	28	1	1	0.8	.972
1950			14	12	.538	4.26	48	23	11	207	212	78	95	1	3	4	9	71	13	1	.183	7	30	3	0	0.8	.925
1951			11	2	.846	2.55	**63**	2	1	127	108	46	84	0	10	1	14	34	4	0	.118	5	13	0	1	0.3	1.000
1952			5	6	.455	2.58	23	10	4	97.2	85	28	50	0	1	2	4	32	0	0	.000	4	16	0	2	0.9	1.000
1953			10	6	.625	1.85	**69**	0	0	107	84	38	39	0	10	6	27	29	11	0	.379	10	18	0	0	0.4	1.000
1954			8	8	.500	3.62	48	2	0	107	106	36	67	0	7	8	15	27	5	0	.185	2	11	2	0	0.3	.867
1955			5	5	.500	2.84	43	0	0	66.2	57	15	31	0	5	5	18	12	3	0	.250	2	7	0	1	0.2	1.000
1956	2 teams	STL N	(22G 2-0)			CHI A	(29G 3-1)																					
"	total		5	1	.833	3.09	51	0	0	55.1	56	17	23	0	5	1	9	4	0	0	.000	3	6	0	0	0.1	1.000
1957	CHI	A	0	0	–	0.00	1	0	0	1	0	0	1	0	0	0	0	0	0	0	–	0	0	0	0	0.0	–
12 yrs.			102	71	.590	3.43	484	122	56	1479.2	1421	539	749	10	44	30	102	444	63	1	.142	52	174	9	11	0.5	.962

Clyde King

KING, CLYDE EDWARD
B. May 23, 1925, Goldsboro, N.C.
Manager 1969-70, 1974-75, 1982.   BB TR 6'1" 175 lbs.

1944	BKN	N	2	1	.667	3.09	14	3	1	43.2	42	12	14	0	0	0	0	10	2	0	.200	0	3	0	0	0.2	1.000
1945			5	5	.500	4.09	42	2	0	112.1	131	48	29	0	0	1	3	32	4	0	.125	5	27	2	2	0.8	.941
1947			6	5	.545	2.77	29	9	2	87.2	85	29	31	0	2	2	0	26	3	0	.115	5	11	1	1	0.6	.941
1948			0	1	.000	8.03	9	0	0	12.1	14	6	5	0	0	1	0	2	0	0	.000	0	4	0	0	0.4	1.000
1951			14	7	.667	4.15	48	3	1	121.1	118	50	33	0	13	6	6	29	4	0	.138	12	21	0	4	0.7	1.000
1952			2	0	1.000	5.06	23	0	0	42.2	52	12	17	0	2	0	0	5	0	0	.000	6	11	1	1	0.8	.944
1953	CIN	N	3	6	.333	5.21	35	4	0	76	78	32	21	0	2	4	2	10	0	0	.000	6	11	0	3	0.5	1.000
7 yrs.			32	25	.561	4.14	200	21	4	496	524	189	150	0	19	14	11	114	13	0	.114	34	88	4	11	0.6	.968

Eric King

KING, ERIC STEVEN
B. Apr. 10, 1964, Oxnard, Calif.   BR TR 6'2" 180 lbs.

1986	DET	A	11	4	.733	3.51	33	16	3	138.1	108	63	79	1	3	0	3	0	0	0	–	19	15	1	0	1.1	.971
1987			6	9	.400	4.89	55	4	0	116	111	60	89	0	6	7	9	0	0	0	–	15	22	1	3	0.7	.974
1988			4	1	.800	3.41	23	5	0	68.2	60	34	45	0	1	0	3	0	0	0	–	3	8	2	0	0.6	.846

Year	Team		W	L	PCT	ERA	G	GS	CG	IP	H	BB	SO	ShO	W	L	SV	AB	H	HR	BA	PO	A	E	DP	TC/G	FA
															Relief Pitching			**Batting**									

Eric King *continued*

Year	Team		W	L	PCT	ERA	G	GS	CG	IP	H	BB	SO	ShO	W	L	SV	AB	H	HR	BA	PO	A	E	DP	TC/G	FA
1989	CHI	A	9	10	.474	3.39	25	25	1	159.1	144	64	72	1	0	0	0	0	0	0	–	15	20	3	2	1.5	.921
4 yrs.			30	24	.556	3.79	136	50	4	482.1	423	221	285	2	10	7	15	0	0	0	–	52	65	7	5	0.9	.944

LEAGUE CHAMPIONSHIP SERIES

Year	Team		W	L	PCT	ERA	G	GS	CG	IP	H	BB	SO	ShO	W	L	SV	AB	H	HR	BA	PO	A	E	DP	TC/G	FA
1987	DET	A	0	0	–	1.69	2	0	0	5.1	3	2	4	0	0	0	0	0	0	0	–	1	1	0	0	1.0	1.000

Nellie King

KING, NELSON JOSEPH
B. Mar. 15, 1928, Shenandoah, Pa.   BR TR 6'6"   185 lbs.

Year	Team		W	L	PCT	ERA	G	GS	CG	IP	H	BB	SO	ShO	W	L	SV	AB	H	HR	BA	PO	A	E	DP	TC/G	FA
1954	PIT	N	0	0	–	5.14	4	0	0	7	10	1	3	0	0	0	0	0	0	0	–	3	0	1	0	0.8	1.000
1955			1	3	.250	2.98	17	4	0	54.1	60	14	21	0	0	1	0	12	0	0	.000	7	6	0	1	0.8	1.000
1956			4	1	.800	3.15	38	0	0	60	54	19	25	0	4	1	5	6	0	0	.000	6	5	0	0	0.3	1.000
1957			2	1	.667	4.50	36	0	0	52	69	16	23	0	2	1	1	5	0	0	.000	6	6	0	0	0.3	1.000
4 yrs.			7	5	.583	3.58	95	4	0	173.1	193	50	72	0	6	3	6	23	0	0	.000	19	20	0	2	0.4	1.000

Silver King

KING, CHARLES FREDERICK
Born Charles Frederick Koenig.
B. Jan. 11, 1868, St. Louis, Mo.   D. May 21, 1938, St. Louis, Mo.   BR TR 6'   170 lbs.

Year	Team		W	L	PCT	ERA	G	GS	CG	IP	H	BB	SO	ShO	W	L	SV	AB	H	HR	BA	PO	A	E	DP	TC/G	FA
1886	KC	N	1	3	.250	4.85	5	5	5	39	43	9	23	0				22	1	0	.045	0	13	1	0	2.8	.929
1887	STL	AA	34	11	.756	3.78	46	44	43	390	401	109	128	2	1	0	1	222	46	0	.207	16	69	6	0	2.0	.934
1888			45	21	.682	1.64	66	65	64	585.2	437	76	258	6	1	0	0	207	43	1	.208	32	119	12	4	2.5	.926
1889			33	17	.660	3.14	56	53	47	458	462	125	188	3	0	1	1	189	43	0	.228	19	91	5	2	2.1	.957
1890	CHI	P	32	22	.593	2.69	56	56	48	461	420	163	185	4	0	1	0	185	31	1	.168	22	139	6	5	3.0	.964
1891	PIT	N	14	29	.326	3.11	48	44	40	384.1	382	144	160	3	0	0	1	148	25	0	.169	19	67	10	5	2.0	.896
1892	NY	N	23	24	.489	3.24	52	47	46	419.1	397	174	177	1	0	1	0	167	35	2	.210	22	81	11	4	2.2	.904
1893	2 teams		NY N	(7G 3–4)			CIN N	(17G 5–6)																			
"	total		8	10	.444	6.08	24	22	12	154	188	82	43	1	0	0	1	54	9	0	.167	8	32	3	1	1.8	.930
1896	WAS	N	10	7	.588	4.09	22	16	12	145.1	179	43	35	0	3	1	1	58	16	0	.276	6	19	1	0	1.2	.962
1897			7	8	.467	4.79	23	19	12	154	196	45	32	0	0	1	1	57	11	0	.193	2	40	2	1	1.9	.955
10 yrs.			207	152	.577	3.18	398	371	329	3190.2	3105	970	1229	20	6	3	6	*				146	670	57	22	2.2	.935

Brian Kingman

KINGMAN, BRIAN PAUL
B. July 27, 1954, Los Angeles, Calif.   BR TR 6'2"   200 lbs.

Year	Team		W	L	PCT	ERA	G	GS	CG	IP	H	BB	SO	ShO	W	L	SV	AB	H	HR	BA	PO	A	E	DP	TC/G	FA
1979	OAK	A	8	7	.533	4.30	18	17	5	113	113	33	58	1	1	0	0	0	0	0	–	8	8	2	0	1.0	.889
1980			8	20	.286	3.84	32	30	10	211	209	82	116	1	0	1	0	0	0	0	–	7	22	3	2	1.0	.906
1981			3	6	.333	3.96	18	15	3	100	112	32	52	1	0	0	0	0	0	0	–	4	9	2	0	0.8	.867
1982			4	12	.250	4.48	23	20	3	122.2	131	57	46	0	1	0	1	0	0	0	–	3	9	1	0	0.6	.923
1983	SF	N	0	0	–	7.71	3	0	0	4.2	10	1	1	0	0	0	0	0	0	0	–	0	0	0	0	0.0	–
5 yrs.			23	45	.338	4.13	94	82	21	551.1	575	205	273	3	2	1	1	0	0	0	–	22	48	8	2	0.8	.897

LEAGUE CHAMPIONSHIP SERIES

Year	Team		W	L	PCT	ERA	G	GS	CG	IP	H	BB	SO	ShO	W	L	SV	AB	H	HR	BA	PO	A	E	DP	TC/G	FA
1981	OAK	A	0	0	–	81.00	1	0	0	.1	3	0	0	0	0	0	0	0	0	0	–	0	0	0	0	0.0	–

Dave Kingman

KINGMAN, DAVID ARTHUR (Kong)
B. Dec. 21, 1948, Pendleton, Ore.   BR TR 6'6"   210 lbs.

Year	Team		W	L	PCT	ERA	G	GS	CG	IP	H	BB	SO	ShO	W	L	SV	AB	H	HR	BA	PO	A	E	DP	TC/G	FA
1973	SF	N	0	0	–	9.00	2	0	0	4	3	6	4	0	0	0	0	*				0	0	0	0	0.0	–

Dennis Kinney

KINNEY, DENNIS PAUL
B. Feb. 26, 1952, Toledo, Ohio   BL TL 6'1"   175 lbs.

Year	Team		W	L	PCT	ERA	G	GS	CG	IP	H	BB	SO	ShO	W	L	SV	AB	H	HR	BA	PO	A	E	DP	TC/G	FA
1978	2 teams		CLE A	(18G 0–2)			SD N	(7G 0–1)																			
"	total		0	3	.000	4.73	25	0	0	45.2	43	18	21	0	0	3	0	4	0	0	.000	4	4	1	1	0.4	.889
1979	SD	N	0	0	–	3.50	13	0	0	18	17	8	11	0	0	0	0	1	0	0	.000	0	2	1	0	0.2	.667
1980			4	6	.400	4.23	50	0	0	83	79	37	40	0	4	6	1	12	1	0	.083	2	13	0	0	0.3	1.000
1981	DET	A	0	0	–	9.00	6	0	0	4	5	4	3	0	0	0	0	0	0	0	–	1	0	0	0	0.2	1.000
1982	OAK	A	0	0	–	8.31	3	0	0	4.1	9	4	0	0	0	0	0	0	0	0	–	0	1	0	0	0.3	1.000
5 yrs.			4	9	.308	4.53	97	0	0	155	153	71	75	0	4	9	6	14	1	0	.071	7	20	2	1	0.3	.931

Walt Kinney

KINNEY, WALTER WILLIAM
B. Sept. 9, 1893, Denison, Tex.   D. July 1, 1971, Escondido, Calif.   BL TL 6'2"   186 lbs.

Year	Team		W	L	PCT	ERA	G	GS	CG	IP	H	BB	SO	ShO	W	L	SV	AB	H	HR	BA	PO	A	E	DP	TC/G	FA
1918	BOS	A	0	0	–	1.80	5	0	0	15	5	8	4	0	0	0	0	5	0	0	.000	2	3	0	0	1.0	1.000
1919	PHI	A	9	15	.375	3.64	43	21	13	202.2	199	91	97	0	3	2	2	88	25	1	.284	14	63	5	3	1.9	.939
1920			2	4	.333	3.10	10	8	5	61	59	28	19	1	0	0	0	26	9	0	.346	4	15	1	0	2.0	.950
1923			0	1	.000	7.50	5	1	0	12	11	9	9	0	0	1	0	6	1	0	.167	1	1	0	0	0.4	1.000
4 yrs.			11	20	.355	3.59	63	30	18	290.2	274	136	129	1	3	3	2	125	35	2	.280	21	82	6	3	1.7	.945

Mike Kinnunen

KINNUNEN, MICHAEL JOHN
B. Apr. 1, 1958, Seattle, Wash.   BL TL 6'1"   185 lbs.

Year	Team		W	L	PCT	ERA	G	GS	CG	IP	H	BB	SO	ShO	W	L	SV	AB	H	HR	BA	PO	A	E	DP	TC/G	FA
1980	MIN	A	0	0	–	5.04	21	0	0	25	29	9	8	0	0	0	0	0	0	0	–	6	3	0	0	0.4	1.000
1986	BAL	A	0	0	–	6.43	9	0	0	7	8	5	1	0	0	0	0	0	0	0	–	1	2	0	0	0.3	1.000
1987			0	0	–	4.95	18	0	0	20	27	16	14	0	0	0	0	0	0	0	–	0	2	0	0	0.1	1.000
3 yrs.			0	0	–	5.19	48	0	0	52	64	30	23	0	0	0	0	0	0	0	–	7	7	0	0	0.3	1.000

Ed Kinsella

KINSELLA, EDWARD WILLIAM (Rube)
B. Jan. 15, 1882, Lexington, Ill.   D. Jan. 17, 1976, Bloomington, Ill.   BR TR 6'1½"   175 lbs.

Year	Team		W	L	PCT	ERA	G	GS	CG	IP	H	BB	SO	ShO	W	L	SV	AB	H	HR	BA	PO	A	E	DP	TC/G	FA
1905	PIT	N	0	1	.000	2.65	3	2	2	17	19	3	11	0	0	0	0	3	0	0	.000	0	1	1	0	0.7	.500
1910	STL	A	1	3	.250	3.78	10	5	2	50	62	16	10	0	0	0	0	12	3	0	.250	0	22	2	2	2.4	.917
2 yrs.			1	4	.200	3.49	13	7	4	67	81	19	21	0	0	0	0	15	3	0	.200	0	23	3	2	2.0	.885

Matt Kinzer

KINZER, MATTHEW ROY
B. June 17, 1963, Indianapolis, Ind.   BR TR 6'2"   210 lbs.

Year	Team		W	L	PCT	ERA	G	GS	CG	IP	H	BB	SO	ShO	W	L	SV	AB	H	HR	BA	PO	A	E	DP	TC/G	FA
1989	STL	N	0	2	.000	12.83	8	1	0	13.1	25	4	8	0	0	1	0	1	0	0	.000	0	0	0	0	0.0	–

Year	Team	W	L	PCT	ERA	G	GS	CG	IP	H	BB	SO	ShO	W	L	SV	AB	H	HR	BA	PO	A	E	DP	TC/G	FA

Harry Kinzy

KINZY, HENRY HERSHEL (Slim)
B. July 19, 1910, Hallsville, Tex.   BR TR 6'4" 185 lbs.

Year	Team	W	L	PCT	ERA	G	GS	CG	IP	H	BB	SO	ShO	W	L	SV	AB	H	HR	BA	PO	A	E	DP	TC/G	FA
1934	CHI A	0	1	.000	4.98	13	2	1	34.1	38	31	12	0	0	0	0	10	3	0	.300	1	6	1	0	0.6	.875

Fred Kipp

KIPP, FRED LEO
B. Oct. 1, 1931, Piqua, Kans.   BL TL 6'4" 200 lbs.

Year	Team	W	L	PCT	ERA	G	GS	CG	IP	H	BB	SO	ShO	W	L	SV	AB	H	HR	BA	PO	A	E	DP	TC/G	FA
1957	BKN N	0	0	–	9.00	1	0	0	4	6	0	3	0	0	0	0	1	0	0	.000	0	1	0	0	1.0	1.000
1958	LA N	6	6	.500	5.01	40	9	0	102.1	107	45	58	0	2	3	0	36	9	0	.250	7	18	0	0	0.6	1.000
1959		0	0	–	0.00	2	0	0	2.2	2	3	1	0	0	0	0	0	0	0	–	0	2	0	0	1.0	1.000
1960	NY A	0	1	.000	6.23	4	0	0	4.1	4	0	2	0	0	1	0	0	0	0	–	0	1	0	0	0.3	1.000
4 yrs.		6	7	.462	5.08	47	9	0	113.1	119	48	64	0	2	4	0	37	9	0	.243	7	22	0	0	0.6	1.000

Bob Kipper

KIPPER, ROBERT WAYNE
B. July 8, 1964, Aurora, Ill.   BR TL 6'2" 190 lbs.

Year	Team	W	L	PCT	ERA	G	GS	CG	IP	H	BB	SO	ShO	W	L	SV	AB	H	HR	BA	PO	A	E	DP	TC/G	FA
1985	2 teams	CAL A	(2G 0–1)		PIT N	(5G 1–2)																				
"	total	1	3	.250	7.07	7	5	0	28	28	10	13	0	0	0	0	8	2	0	.250	1	5	1	0	1.0	.857
1986	PIT N	6	8	.429	4.03	20	19	0	114	123	34	81	0	0	0	0	33	1	0	.030	1	15	1	2	0.9	.941
1987		5	9	.357	5.94	24	20	1	110.2	117	52	83	1	0	0	0	33	8	0	.242	3	16	0	1	0.8	1.000
1988		2	6	.250	3.74	50	0	0	65	54	26	39	0	2	6	0	4	0	0	.000	4	16	0	1	0.4	1.000
1989		3	4	.429	2.93	52	0	0	83	55	33	58	0	3	4	4	9	1	0	.111	3	10	2	1	0.3	.867
5 yrs.		17	30	.362	4.49	153	44	1	400.2	377	155	274	1	5	10	4	87	12	0	.138	12	62	4	5	0.5	.949

Thornton Kipper

KIPPER, THORNTON JOHN
B. Sept. 27, 1928, Bagley, Wis.   BR TR 6'3" 190 lbs.

Year	Team	W	L	PCT	ERA	G	GS	CG	IP	H	BB	SO	ShO	W	L	SV	AB	H	HR	BA	PO	A	E	DP	TC/G	FA
1953	PHI N	3	3	.500	4.73	20	3	0	45.2	59	12	15	0	3	0	0	11	1	0	.091	6	5	0	1	0.6	1.000
1954		0	0	–	7.90	11	0	0	13.2	22	12	5	0	0	0	1	2	0	0	.000	0	4	0	0	0.4	1.000
1955		0	1	.000	4.99	24	0	0	39.2	47	22	15	0	0	1	0	3	1	0	.333	1	5	0	0	0.3	1.000
3 yrs.		3	4	.429	5.27	55	3	0	99	128	46	35	0	3	1	1	16	2	0	.125	7	14	0	1	0.4	1.000

Clay Kirby

KIRBY, CLAYTON LAWS
B. June 25, 1948, Washington, D. C.   BR TR 6'3" 175 lbs.

Year	Team	W	L	PCT	ERA	G	GS	CG	IP	H	BB	SO	ShO	W	L	SV	AB	H	HR	BA	PO	A	E	DP	TC/G	FA
1969	SD N	7	20	.259	3.79	35	35	2	216	204	100	113	0	0	0	0	66	4	0	.061	17	23	4	4	1.3	.909
1970		10	16	.385	4.52	36	34	6	215	198	120	154	1	0	0	0	74	11	0	.149	6	23	2	1	0.9	.935
1971		15	13	.536	2.83	38	36	13	267	213	103	231	2	0	0	0	86	8	0	.093	17	33	2	1	1.4	.962
1972		12	14	.462	3.13	34	34	9	238.2	197	116	175	2	0	0	0	74	5	0	.068	11	29	5	3	1.3	.889
1973		8	18	.308	4.79	34	31	4	191.2	214	66	129	2	0	0	0	54	5	0	.093	9	19	3	1	0.9	.903
1974	CIN N	12	9	.571	3.27	36	35	7	231	210	91	160	1	0	0	0	74	7	0	.095	11	27	10	1	1.3	.792
1975		10	6	.625	4.70	26	19	1	111	113	54	48	1	0	3	1	32	6	0	.188	7	9	3	0	0.7	.842
1976	MON N	1	8	.111	5.72	22	15	0	78.2	81	63	51	0	0	0	0	18	1	0	.056	1	9	0	1	0.5	1.000
8 yrs.		75	104	.419	3.83	261	239	42	1549	1430	713	1061	8	3	1	0	478	47	0	.098	79	172	29	12	1.1	.896

John Kirby

KIRBY, JOHN F. (Chickenhearted)
B. Jan. 13, 1865, St. Louis, Mo.   D. Oct. 6, 1931, St. Louis, Mo.   TR 5'8" 172 lbs.

Year	Team	W	L	PCT	ERA	G	GS	CG	IP	H	BB	SO	ShO	W	L	SV	AB	H	HR	BA	PO	A	E	DP	TC/G	FA
1884	KC U	0	1	.000	4.09	2	2	1	11	13	2	5	0	0	0	0	7	1	0	.143	1	6	1	0	4.0	.875
1885	STL N	5	8	.385	3.55	14	14	14	129.1	118	44	46	0	0	0	0	50	3	0	.060	5	22	7	1	2.4	.794
1886		11	25	.306	3.30	41	41	38	325	329	134	129	1	0	0	0	136	15	0	.110	14	61	9	2	2.0	.893
1887	2 teams	IND N	(8G 1–6)		CLE AA	(5G 0–5)																				
"	total	1	11	.083	7.25	13	13	10	103	132	71	13	0	0	0	0	47	7	0	.149	2	18	2	0	1.7	.909
1888	KC AA	1	4	.200	4.19	5	5	5	43	48	7	11	0	0	0	0	16	1	0	.063	1	11	3	0	3.0	.800
5 yrs.		18	49	.269	4.09	75	75	68	611.1	640	258	200	1	0	0	0	256	27	0	.105	23	118	22	3	2.2	.865

LaRue Kirby

KIRBY, LaRUE
B. Dec. 30, 1889, Eureka, Mich.   D. June 10, 1961, Lansing, Mich.   BB TR 6' 185 lbs.

Year	Team	W	L	PCT	ERA	G	GS	CG	IP	H	BB	SO	ShO	W	L	SV	AB	H	HR	BA	PO	A	E	DP	TC/G	FA
1912	NY N	1	0	1.000	5.73	3	1	1	11	13	6	2	0	0	0	0	5	1	0	.200	2	3	0	0	1.7	1.000
1915	STL F	0	0	–	5.14	1	0	0	7	7	2	7	0	0	0	0	178	38	0	.213	1	0	1	0	2.0	.500
2 yrs.		1	0	1.000	5.50	4	1	1	18	20	8	9	0	0	0	0	*				3	3	1	0	1.8	.857

Mike Kircher

KIRCHER, MICHAEL ANDREW
Born Wolfgang Andrew Kerscher.
B. Sept. 30, 1897, Rochester, N. Y.   D. June 26, 1972, Rochester, N. Y.   BB TR 6' 180 lbs.

Year	Team	W	L	PCT	ERA	G	GS	CG	IP	H	BB	SO	ShO	W	L	SV	AB	H	HR	BA	PO	A	E	DP	TC/G	FA
1919	PHI A	0	0	–	7.88	2	0	0	8	15	3	2	0	0	0	0	3	0	0	.000	0	0	0	0	0.0	–
1920	STL N	2	1	.667	5.40	9	3	1	36.2	50	5	5	0	1	0	0	11	3	0	.273	3	4	1	0	0.9	.875
1921		0	1	.000	8.10	3	0	0	3.1	4	1	2	0	0	1	0	0	0	0	–	0	0	0	0	0.0	–
3 yrs.		2	2	.500	6.00	14	3	1	48	69	9	9	0	1	1	0	14	3	0	.214	3	4	1	0	0.6	.875

Bill Kirk

KIRK, WILLIAM PARTLEMORE
B. July 19, 1935, Coatesville, Pa.   BL TL 6' 165 lbs.

Year	Team	W	L	PCT	ERA	G	GS	CG	IP	H	BB	SO	ShO	W	L	SV	AB	H	HR	BA	PO	A	E	DP	TC/G	FA
1961	KC A	0	0	–	12.00	1	1	0	3	6	1	3	0	0	0	0	0	0	0	–	0	0	0	0	0.0	–

Don Kirkwood

KIRKWOOD, DONALD PAUL
B. Sept. 24, 1949, Pontiac, Mich.   BR TR 6'3" 175 lbs.

Year	Team	W	L	PCT	ERA	G	GS	CG	IP	H	BB	SO	ShO	W	L	SV	AB	H	HR	BA	PO	A	E	DP	TC/G	FA
1974	CAL A	0	0	–	9.00	3	0	0	7	12	6	4	0	0	0	0	0	0	0	–	0	0	0	0	0.0	–
1975		6	5	.545	3.11	44	2	0	84	85	28	49	0	6	4	7	0	0	0	–	3	12	3	1	0.4	.833
1976		4	12	.333	4.61	28	26	4	158	167	57	78	0	0	0	0	0	0	0	–	18	26	5	3	1.8	.898
1977	2 teams	CAL A	(13G 1–0)		CHI A	(16G 1–1)																				
"	total	2	1	.667	5.15	29	0	0	57.2	69	19	34	0	2	1	1	0	0	0	–	5	14	1	1	0.7	.950
1978	TOR A	4	5	.444	4.24	16	9	3	68	76	25	29	0	1	1	0	0	0	0	–	4	12	0	1	1.0	1.000
5 yrs.		18	23	.439	4.37	120	37	7	374.2	409	135	194	0	9	7	8	0	0	0	–	30	64	9	5	0.9	.913

Year	Team		W	L	PCT	ERA	G	GS	CG	IP	H	BB	SO	ShO	Relief Pitching W	L	SV	Batting AB	H	HR	BA	PO	A	E	DP	TC/G	FA

Ron Kline

KLINE, RONALD LEE — BR TR 6'3" 205 lbs.
B. Mar. 9, 1932, Callery, Pa.

Year	Team		W	L	PCT	ERA	G	GS	CG	IP	H	BB	SO	ShO	W	L	SV	AB	H	HR	BA	PO	A	E	DP	TC/G	FA
1952	PIT	N	0	7	.000	5.49	27	11	0	78.2	74	66	27	0	0	1	0	19	0	0	.000	3	8	0	2	0.4	1.000
1955			6	13	.316	4.15	36	19	2	136.2	161	53	48	1	2	0	2	38	5	0	.132	20	30	2	2	1.4	.962
1956			14	18	.438	3.38	44	39	9	264	263	81	125	2	0	0	2	79	10	0	.127	17	42	4	3	1.4	.937
1957			9	16	.360	4.04	40	31	11	205	214	61	88	2	0	1	0	66	4	0	.061	18	27	1	2	1.2	.978
1958			13	16	.448	3.53	32	32	11	237.1	220	92	109	2	0	0	0	74	2	0	.027	20	40	3	4	2.0	.952
1959			11	13	.458	4.26	33	29	7	186	186	70	91	0	1	0	0	59	8	0	.136	15	27	2	1	1.3	.955
1960	STL	N	4	9	.308	6.04	34	17	1	117.2	133	43	54	0	1	2	1	35	5	0	.143	8	23	0	1	0.9	1.000
1961	2 teams		LA A	(26G 3–6)		DET A	(10G 5–3)																				
"	total		8	9	.471	4.14	36	20	3	161	172	61	97	1	1	3	1	49	6	0	.122	10	28	3	2	1.1	.927
1962	DET	A	3	6	.333	4.31	36	4	0	77.1	88	28	47	0	3	3	2	16	2	0	.125	13	11	2	2	0.7	.923
1963	WAS	A	3	8	.273	2.79	62	1	0	93.2	85	30	49	0	3	8	17	11	1	0	.091	3	14	1	2	0.3	.944
1964			10	7	.588	2.32	61	0	0	81.1	81	21	40	0	10	7	14	6	1	0	.167	2	13	1	1	0.3	.938
1965			7	6	.538	2.63	74	0	0	99.1	106	32	52	0	7	6	29	7	0	0	.000	3	13	0	1	0.2	1.000
1966			6	4	.600	2.39	63	0	0	90.1	79	17	46	0	6	4	23	6	1	0	.167	6	7	1	0	0.2	.929
1967	MIN	A	7	1	.875	3.77	54	0	0	71.2	71	15	36	0	7	1	5	5	0	0	.000	2	11	0	0	0.2	1.000
1968	PIT	N	12	5	.706	1.68	56	0	0	112.2	94	31	48	0	12	5	7	16	0	0	.000	4	15	0	0	0.3	1.000
1969	3 teams		PIT N	(20G 1–3)		SF N	(7G 0–2)		BOS A	(16G 0–1)																	
"	total		1	6	.143	5.19	43	0	0	59	77	28	29	0	1	6	4	5	0	0	.000	3	10	0	1	0.3	1.000
1970	ATL	N	0	0	–	7.50	5	0	0	6	9	2	3	0	0	0	1	0	0	0	–	0	0	0	0	0.0	–
17 yrs.			114	144	.442	3.75	736	203	44	2077.2	2113	731	989	8	54	47	108	491	45	0	.092	147	319	20	24	0.7	.959

Steve Kline

KLINE, STEVEN JACK — BR TR 6'3" 205 lbs.
B. Oct. 6, 1947, Wenatchee, Wash.

Year	Team		W	L	PCT	ERA	G	GS	CG	IP	H	BB	SO	ShO	W	L	SV	AB	H	HR	BA	PO	A	E	DP	TC/G	FA
1970	NY	A	6	6	.500	3.42	16	15	5	100	99	24	49	0	0	0	0	28	5	0	.179	14	14	0	2	1.8	1.000
1971			12	13	.480	2.96	31	30	15	222	206	37	81	1	0	0	0	66	9	0	.136	24	49	1	1	2.4	.986
1972			16	9	.640	2.40	32	32	11	236	210	44	58	4	0	0	0	76	7	0	.092	20	50	7	3	2.4	.909
1973			4	7	.364	4.01	14	13	2	74	76	31	19	1	0	0	0	0	0	0	–	1	12	0	0	0.9	1.000
1974	2 teams		NY A	(4G 2–2)		CLE A	(16G 3–8)																				
"	total		5	10	.333	4.64	20	15	1	97	96	36	23	0	0	0	0	0	0	0	–	5	17	0	4	1.1	1.000
1977	ATL	N	0	0	–	6.75	16	0	0	20	21	12	10	0	0	0	1	0	0	0	–	0	2	1	0	0.2	.667
6 yrs.			43	45	.489	3.27	129	105	34	749	708	184	240	6	0	0	1	170	21	0	.124	64	144	9	10	1.7	.959

Bill Kling

KLING, WILLIAM — BL TR 6' 190 lbs.
Brother of Johnny Kling.
B. Jan. 14, 1867, Kansas City, Mo.   D. Aug. 26, 1934, Kansas City, Mo.

Year	Team		W	L	PCT	ERA	G	GS	CG	IP	H	BB	SO	ShO	W	L	SV	AB	H	HR	BA	PO	A	E	DP	TC/G	FA
1891	PHI	N	4	2	.667	4.32	12	7	4	75	90	32	26	0	0	0	0	31	6	0	.194	1	12	1	0	1.2	.929
1892	BAL	N	0	2	.000	11.45	2	2	0	11	17	7	7	0	0	0	0	4	1	0	.250	0	2	0	0	1.0	1.000
1895	LOU	N	0	0	–	0.00	1	0	0	1	0	1	0	0	0	0	0	1	0	0	.000	0	0	0	0	0.0	–
3 yrs.			4	4	.500	5.17	15	9	4	87	107	40	33	0	0	0	0	36	7	0	.194	1	14	1	0	1.1	.938

Bob Klinger

KLINGER, ROBERT HAROLD — BR TR 6' 180 lbs.
B. June 4, 1908, Allenton, Mo.   D. Aug. 19, 1977, Villa Ridge, Mo.

Year	Team		W	L	PCT	ERA	G	GS	CG	IP	H	BB	SO	ShO	W	L	SV	AB	H	HR	BA	PO	A	E	DP	TC/G	FA
1938	PIT	N	12	5	.706	2.99	28	21	10	159.1	152	42	58	1	1	0	0	60	10	0	.167	4	34	0	2	1.4	1.000
1939			14	17	.452	4.36	37	33	10	225	251	81	64	2	1	1	0	84	17	0	.202	7	62	3	5	1.9	.958
1940			8	13	.381	5.39	39	22	3	142	196	53	48	0	2	0	3	42	6	0	.143	6	33	0	1	1.0	1.000
1941			9	4	.692	3.93	35	9	3	116.2	127	30	36	0	7	0	4	32	8	0	.250	6	25	1	3	0.9	.967
1942			8	11	.421	3.24	37	19	8	152.2	151	45	58	1	1	2	1	40	8	0	.200	14	35	1	0	1.4	.980
1943			11	8	.579	2.72	33	25	14	195	185	58	65	3	0	2	0	65	16	0	.246	14	37	0	4	1.5	1.000
1946	BOS	A	3	2	.600	2.37	28	1	0	57	49	25	16	0	3	2	9	16	5	0	.313	1	11	1	0	0.5	.923
1947			1	1	.500	3.86	28	0	0	42	42	24	12	0	1	1	5	9	1	0	.111	4	4	0	0	0.3	1.000
8 yrs.			66	61	.520	3.68	265	130	48	1089.2	1153	358	357	7	17	8	23	348	71	0	.204	54	241	6	13	1.1	.980

WORLD SERIES

Year	Team		W	L	PCT	ERA	G	GS	CG	IP	H	BB	SO	ShO	W	L	SV	AB	H	HR	BA	PO	A	E	DP	TC/G	FA
1946	BOS	A	0	1	.000	13.50	1	0	0	.2	2	1	0	0	0	1	0	0	0	0	–	1	0	0	0	1.0	1.000

Joe Klink

KLINK, JOSEPH CHARLES — BL TL 5'11" 170 lbs.
B. Feb. 3, 1962, Johnstown, Pa.

Year	Team		W	L	PCT	ERA	G	GS	CG	IP	H	BB	SO	ShO	W	L	SV	AB	H	HR	BA	PO	A	E	DP	TC/G	FA
1987	MIN	A	0	1	.000	6.65	12	0	0	23	37	11	17	0	0	1	0	0	0	0	–	0	2	0	1	0.2	1.000

Johnny Klippstein

KLIPPSTEIN, JOHN CALVIN — BR TR 6'1" 173 lbs.
B. Oct. 17, 1927, Washington, D. C.

Year	Team		W	L	PCT	ERA	G	GS	CG	IP	H	BB	SO	ShO	W	L	SV	AB	H	HR	BA	PO	A	E	DP	TC/G	FA
1950	CHI	N	2	9	.182	5.25	33	11	3	104.2	112	64	51	0	1	1	1	33	11	1	.333	7	15	3	3	0.8	.880
1951			6	6	.500	4.29	35	11	3	123.2	125	53	56	1	4	0	2	37	4	1	.108	4	23	0	3	0.8	1.000
1952			9	14	.391	4.44	41	25	7	202.2	208	89	110	2	4	0	3	63	11	1	.175	6	43	0	4	1.2	1.000
1953			10	11	.476	4.83	48	20	5	167.2	169	107	113	0	4	2	6	58	9	1	.155	5	21	2	1	0.6	.929
1954			4	11	.267	5.29	36	21	4	148	155	96	69	0	0	2	1	45	6	0	.133	15	27	0	3	1.2	1.000
1955	CIN	N	9	10	.474	3.39	39	14	3	138	120	60	68	2	4	2	0	31	2	0	.065	9	23	3	0	0.9	.914
1956			12	11	.522	4.09	37	29	11	211	219	82	86	0	2	0	1	71	7	0	.099	10	42	1	3	1.4	.981
1957			8	11	.421	5.05	46	18	0	146	146	68	99	1	3	2	3	41	3	0	.073	10	17	0	0	0.6	1.000
1958	2 teams		CIN N	(12G 3–2)		LA N	(45G 3–5)																				
"	total		6	7	.462	4.10	57	4	0	123	118	58	95	0	5	6	10	28	2	0	.071	8	11	0	3	0.3	1.000
1959	LA	N	4	0	1.000	5.91	28	0	0	45.2	48	33	30	0	4	0	2	7	1	0	.143	2	7	2	0	0.4	.818
1960	CLE	A	5	5	.500	2.91	49	0	0	74.1	53	35	46	0	5	5	14	14	2	0	.143	13	9	1	0	0.5	.957
1961	WAS	A	2	2	.500	6.78	42	1	0	71.2	83	43	41	0	2	1	0	7	1	0	.143	3	14	0	2	0.4	1.000
1962	CIN	N	7	6	.538	4.47	40	7	0	108.2	113	64	67	0	6	3	4	24	3	1	.125	3	22	0	1	0.6	1.000
1963	PHI	N	5	6	.455	1.93	49	0	0	112	80	46	86	0	5	5	8	26	1	0	.038	5	15	0	0	0.4	1.000
1964	2 teams		PHI N	(11G 2–1)		MIN A	(33G 0–4)																				
"	total		2	5	.286	2.65	44	0	0	68	66	28	52	0	2	5	5	6	0	0	.000	2	19	1	2	0.5	.955
1965	MIN	A	9	3	.750	2.24	56	0	0	76.1	59	31	59	0	9	3	5	8	0	0	.000	0	11	2	0	0.2	.846
1966			1	1	.500	3.40	26	0	0	39.2	35	20	26	0	1	1	3	3	1	0	.000	2	10	0	1	0.3	1.000

Year	Team		W	L	PCT	ERA	G	GS	CG	IP	H	BB	SO	ShO	Relief Pitching W	L	SV	Batting AB	H	HR	BA	PO	A	E	DP	TC/G	FA

Johnny Klippstein *continued*

| 1967 | DET | A | 0 | 0 | – | 5.40 | 5 | 0 | 0 | 6.2 | 6 | 1 | 4 | 0 | 0 | 0 | 0 | 0 | 0 | 0 | – | 0 | 1 | 0 | 0 | 0.2 | 1.000 |
| 18 yrs. | | | 101 | 118 | .461 | 4.24 | 711 | 162 | 37 | 1967.2 | 1915 | 978 | 1158 | 6 | 59 | 40 | 66 | 502 | 63 | 5 | .125 | 106 | 324 | 15 | 23 | 0.6 | .966 |

WORLD SERIES

1959	LA	N	0	0	–	0.00	1	0	0	2	1	0	2	0	0	0	0	0	0	0	–	0	1	0	0	1.0	1.000
1965	MIN	A	0	0	–	0.00	2	0	0	2.2	2	2	3	0	0	0	0	0	0	0	–	0	0	0	0	0.0	–
2 yrs.			0	0	–	0.00	3	0	0	4.2	3	2	5	0	0	0	0	0	0	0	–	0	1	0	0	0.3	1.000

Fred Klobedanz

KLOBEDANZ, FREDERICK AUGUSTUS (Kloby)
B. June 13, 1871, Waterbury, Conn. D. Apr. 12, 1940, Waterbury, Conn. BL TL 5'11" 190 lbs.

1896	BOS	N	6	4	.600	3.01	10	9	9	80.2	69	31	26	0	1	0	0	41	13	2	.317	3	15	2	1	2.0	.900
1897			26	7	.788	4.60	38	37	30	309.1	344	125	92	2	0	0	0	148	48	1	.324	8	47	2	4	1.5	.965
1898			19	10	.655	3.89	35	33	25	270.2	281	99	51	0	0	0	0	127	27	3	.213	8	66	5	2	2.3	.937
1899			1	4	.200	4.86	5	5	4	33.1	39	9	8	0	0	0	0	11	2	1	.182	0	11	0	0	2.2	1.000
1902			1	0	1.000	1.13	1	1	1	8	9	2	4	0	0	0	0	2	1	0	.500	1	0	0	0	1.0	1.000
5 yrs.			53	25	.679	4.12	89	85	69	702	742	266	181	2	1	0	0	329	91	7	.277	20	139	9	7	1.9	.946

Stan Klopp

KLOPP, STANLEY HAROLD (Betz)
B. Dec. 22, 1910, Womelsdorf, Pa. D. Mar. 11, 1980, Robesonia, Pa. BR TR 6'1½" 180 lbs.

| 1944 | BOS | N | 1 | 2 | .333 | 4.27 | 24 | 0 | 0 | 46.1 | 47 | 33 | 17 | 0 | 1 | 2 | 0 | 7 | 2 | 0 | .286 | 1 | 6 | 1 | 0 | 0.3 | .875 |

Chris Knapp

KNAPP, ROBERT CHRISTIAN
B. Sept. 16, 1953, Cherry Point, N. C. BR TR 6'5" 195 lbs.

1975	CHI	A	0	0	–	4.50	2	0	0	2	2	4	3	0	0	0	0	0	0	0	–	0	0	0	0	0.0	–
1976			3	1	.750	4.85	11	6	1	52	54	32	41	0	1	0	0	0	0	0	–	2	5	1	1	0.7	.875
1977			12	7	.632	4.81	27	26	4	146	166	61	103	0	0	0	0	0	0	0	–	8	19	2	1	1.1	.931
1978	CAL	A	14	8	.636	4.21	30	29	6	188.1	178	67	126	0	0	0	0	0	0	0	–	4	20	4	1	0.9	.857
1979			5	5	.500	5.51	20	18	3	98	109	35	36	0	0	0	0	0	0	0	–	8	14	1	1	1.2	.957
1980			2	11	.154	6.15	32	20	1	117	133	51	46	0	1	1	1	0	0	0	–	2	14	1	0	0.5	.941
6 yrs.			36	32	.529	5.00	122	99	15	603.1	642	250	355	0	2	1	1	0	0	0	–	24	72	9	4	0.9	.914

LEAGUE CHAMPIONSHIP SERIES

| 1979 | CAL | A | 0 | 1 | .000 | 7.71 | 1 | 1 | 0 | 2.1 | 5 | 1 | 0 | 0 | 0 | 0 | 0 | 0 | 0 | 0 | – | 0 | 0 | 0 | 0 | 0.0 | – |

Frank Knauss

KNAUSS, FRANK H.
B. 1868, Cleveland, Ohio Deceased. BL TL 170 lbs.

1890	COL	AA	17	12	.586	*2.81*	37	34	28	275.2	206	106	148	3	0	0	2	106	24	1	.226	9	48	5	1	1.7	.919
1891	CLE	N	0	3	.000	7.20	3	3	1	15	23	8	6	0	0	0	0	6	1	0	.167	1	3	0	0	1.3	1.000
1892	CIN	N	0	0	–	3.38	1	0	0	8	13	5	2	0	0	0	0	3	1	0	.333	1	2	1	1	4.0	.750
1894	CLE	N	0	1	.000	5.73	2	2	1	11	7	14	2	0	0	0	0	4	0	0	.000	0	5	0	0	2.5	1.000
1895	NY	N	0	0	–	17.18	1	1	0	3.2	9	2	1	0	0	0	0	1	0	0	.000	0	1	2	0	3.0	.333
5 yrs.			17	16	.515	3.30	44	40	30	313.1	258	135	159	3	0	0	2	120	26	1	.217	11	59	8	2	1.8	.897

Rudy Kneisch

KNEISCH, RUDOLPH FRANK
B. Apr. 10, 1899, Baltimore, Md. D. Apr. 6, 1965, Baltimore, Md. BR TL 5'10½" 175 lbs.

| 1926 | DET | A | 0 | 1 | .000 | 2.65 | 2 | 2 | 1 | 17 | 18 | 6 | 4 | 0 | 0 | 0 | 0 | 5 | 0 | 0 | .000 | 2 | 5 | 0 | 1 | 3.5 | 1.000 |

Phil Knell

KNELL, PHILIP H.
B. Mar. 2, 1865, Mill Valley, Calif. D. June 5, 1944, Santa Monica, Calif. BR TL 5'7½" 154 lbs.

1888	PIT	N	1	2	.333	3.76	3	3	3	26.1	20	18	15	0	0	0	0	11	1	0	.091	2	5	2	0	3.0	.778
1890	PHI	P	22	11	.667	3.83	35	31	30	286.2	287	166	99	2	2	1	0	132	29	0	.220	24	67	10	4	2.9	.901
1891	COL	AA	22	11	.667	2.92	58	52	47	462	363	226	228	5	1	2	0	215	34	0	.158	40	119	10	1	2.9	.941
1892	2 teams		WAS N	(22G 9–13)		PHI N	(11G 5–5)																					
"	total		14	18	.438	3.78	33	30	24	250	243	111	117	1	2	0	0	102	11	0	.108	21	40	9	1	2.1	.871
1894	2 teams		PIT N	(1G 0–0)		LOU N	(32G 7–21)																					
"	total		7	21	.250	5.49	33	28	25	254	341	110	67	0	0	0	0	116	31	1	.267	16	38	13	2	2.0	.806
1895	2 teams		LOU N	(10G 0–6)		CLE N	(20G 7–5)																					
"	total		7	11	.389	5.76	30	19	12	173.1	224	74	49	0	2	1	0	81	17	0	.210	15	41	7	2	2.1	.889
6 yrs.			79	90	.467	4.05	192	163	141	1452.1	1478	705	575	8	7	4	0	657	123	1	.187	118	310	51	10	2.5	.894

Bob Knepper

KNEPPER, ROBERT WESLEY
B. May 25, 1954, Akron, Ohio BL TL 6'3" 195 lbs.

1976	SF	N	1	2	.333	3.24	4	4	0	25	26	7	11	0	0	0	0	9	1	0	.111	1	4	0	1	1.3	1.000
1977			11	9	.550	3.36	27	27	6	166	151	72	100	2	0	0	0	55	10	0	.182	10	21	1	1	1.2	.969
1978			17	11	.607	2.63	36	35	16	260	218	85	147	6	0	0	0	79	5	0	.063	4	33	0	3	1.0	1.000
1979			9	12	.429	4.65	34	34	6	207	241	77	123	0	0	0	0	66	12	1	.182	8	26	5	1	1.1	.872
1980			9	16	.360	4.10	35	33	8	215	242	61	103	1	0	0	0	66	10	0	.152	7	45	3	3	1.6	.945
1981	HOU	N	9	5	.643	2.18	22	22	6	157	128	38	75	5	0	0	0	47	7	1	.149	6	26	3	1	1.6	.914
1982			5	15	.250	4.45	33	29	4	180	193	60	108	0	0	0	0	52	3	0	.058	8	32	1	3	1.2	.976
1983			6	13	.316	3.19	35	29	8	203	202	71	125	3	1	1	0	66	12	1	.182	2	40	3	4	1.3	.933
1984			15	10	.600	3.20	35	34	11	233.2	223	55	140	3	0	0	0	76	13	1	.171	7	32	2	0	1.2	.951
1985			15	13	.536	3.55	37	37	4	241	253	54	131	0	0	0	0	78	11	1	.141	5	30	3	1	1.0	.921
1986			17	12	.586	3.14	40	38	8	258	232	62	143	5	0	0	0	91	9	0	.099	23	47	3	6	1.8	.959
1987			8	17	.320	5.27	33	31	1	177.2	226	54	76	0	0	0	0	51	5	0	.098	7	39	2	1	1.5	.958
1988			14	5	.737	3.14	27	27	3	175	156	67	103	2	0	0	0	48	6	0	.125	6	39	2	3	1.7	.957
1989	2 teams		HOU N	(22G 4–10)		SF N	(13G 3–2)																					
"	total		7	12	.368	5.13	35	26	3	165	190	75	64	1	1	0	0	43	8	0	.186	8	29	2	1	1.1	.949
14 yrs.			143	152	.485	3.64	433	406	78	2663.1	2681	838	1449	30	3	1	0	827	112	6	.135	102	443	30	32	1.3	.948

DIVISIONAL PLAYOFF SERIES

| 1981 | HOU | N | 0 | 1 | .000 | 5.40 | 1 | 1 | 0 | 5 | 6 | 2 | 4 | 0 | 0 | 0 | 0 | 1 | 0 | 0 | .000 | 0 | 0 | 0 | 0 | 0.0 | – |

Year	Team		W	L	PCT	ERA	G	GS	CG	IP	H	BB	SO	ShO	Relief Pitching W	L	SV	Batting AB	H	HR	BA	PO	A	E	DP	TC/G	FA

Elmer Koestner

KOESTNER, ELMER JOSEPH (Bob)
B. Nov. 30, 1885, Piper City, Ill. D. Oct. 27, 1959, Fairbury, Ill. BR TR 6'1½" 175 lbs.

Year	Team		W	L	PCT	ERA	G	GS	CG	IP	H	BB	SO	ShO	W	L	SV	AB	H	HR	BA	PO	A	E	DP	TC/G	FA
1910	CLE	A	5	10	.333	3.04	27	13	8	145	145	63	44	1	2	4	2	48	15	0	.313	9	41	4	3	2.0	.926
1914	2 teams		CHI N		(4G 0-0)		CIN N		(5G 0-0)																		
"	total		0	0	—	4.01	9	1	0	24.2	24	13	12	0	0	0	0	6	2	0	.333	1	6	1	1	0.9	.875
2 yrs.			5	10	.333	3.18	36	14	8	169.2	169	76	56	1	2	4	2	54	17	0	.315	10	47	5	4	1.7	.919

Joe Kohlman

KOHLMAN, JOSEPH JAMES (Blackie)
B. Jan. 28, 1913, Philadelphia, Pa. D. Mar. 16, 1974, Philadelphia, Pa. BR TR 6' 160 lbs.

Year	Team		W	L	PCT	ERA	G	GS	CG	IP	H	BB	SO	ShO	W	L	SV	AB	H	HR	BA	PO	A	E	DP	TC/G	FA
1937	WAS	A	1	0	1.000	4.15	2	2	1	13	15	3	3	0	0	0	0	5	1	0	.200	0	1	0	0	0.5	1.000
1938			0	0	—	6.28	7	0	0	14.1	12	11	5	0	0	0	0	3	0	0	.000	2	3	0	1	0.7	1.000
2 yrs.			1	0	1.000	5.27	9	2	1	27.1	27	14	8	0	0	0	0	8	1	0	.125	2	4	0	1	0.7	1.000

Eddie Kolb

KOLB, EDWARD WILLIAM
B. July 20, 1880, Cincinnati, Ohio Deceased. BR TR

Year	Team		W	L	PCT	ERA	G	GS	CG	IP	H	BB	SO	ShO	W	L	SV	AB	H	HR	BA	PO	A	E	DP	TC/G	FA
1899	CLE	N	0	1	.000	10.13	1	1	1	8	18	5	1	0	0	0	0	4	1	0	.250	0	0	1	0	1.0	—

Ray Kolp

KOLP, RAYMOND CARL (Jockey)
B. Oct. 1, 1894, New Berlin, Ohio D. July 29, 1967, New Orleans, La. BR TR 5'10½" 187 lbs.

Year	Team		W	L	PCT	ERA	G	GS	CG	IP	H	BB	SO	ShO	W	L	SV	AB	H	HR	BA	PO	A	E	DP	TC/G	FA
1921	STL	A	8	7	.533	4.97	37	18	5	166.2	208	51	43	1	2	1	0	55	7	0	.127	12	43	0	3	1.5	1.000
1922			14	4	.778	3.93	32	18	9	169.2	199	36	54	1	2	1	0	57	17	0	.298	13	18	1	0	1.0	.969
1923			5	12	.294	3.89	34	17	11	171.1	178	54	44	1	0	2	1	54	6	0	.111	10	37	5	2	1.5	.904
1924			5	7	.417	5.68	25	12	5	96.2	131	25	29	1	2	0	0	30	6	0	.200	7	18	0	1	1.0	1.000
1927	CIN	N	3	3	.500	3.06	24	5	2	82.1	86	29	28	1	1	2	3	30	6	0	.200	4	17	0	3	0.9	1.000
1928			13	10	.565	3.19	44	24	12	209	219	55	61	1	3	1	3	70	15	1	.214	11	50	1	4	1.4	.984
1929			8	10	.444	4.03	30	16	4	145.1	151	39	27	1	2	1	0	49	8	0	.163	7	38	2	1	1.6	.957
1930			7	12	.368	4.22	37	19	5	168.1	180	34	40	2	1	2	3	49	12	1	.245	8	30	1	0	1.1	.974
1931			4	9	.308	4.96	30	10	2	107	144	39	24	0	2	1	1	32	4	0	.125	3	17	0	2	0.7	1.000
1932			6	10	.375	3.89	32	19	7	159.2	176	27	42	2	0	0	1	49	9	0	.184	6	23	0	3	0.9	1.000
1933			6	9	.400	3.53	30	14	4	150.1	168	23	28	0	3	3	3	45	7	0	.156	5	39	2	0	1.5	.957
1934			0	2	.000	4.52	28	2	0	61.2	78	12	19	0	0	0	3	12	1	0	.083	0	21	0	3	0.8	1.000
12 yrs.			79	95	.454	4.08	383	174	66	1688	1918	424	439	11	17	14	18	532	98	2	.184	86	351	12	22	1.2	.973

Hal Kolstad

KOLSTAD, HAROLD EVERETTE
B. June 1, 1935, Rice Lake, Wis. BR TR 5'9" 190 lbs.

Year	Team		W	L	PCT	ERA	G	GS	CG	IP	H	BB	SO	ShO	W	L	SV	AB	H	HR	BA	PO	A	E	DP	TC/G	FA
1962	BOS	A	0	2	.000	5.43	27	2	0	61.1	65	35	36	0	0	2	2	18	1	0	.056	6	10	1	1	0.6	.941
1963			0	2	.000	13.09	7	0	0	11	16	6	6	0	0	2	0	1	0	0	.000	1	1	0	0	0.3	1.000
2 yrs.			0	4	.000	6.59	34	2	0	72.1	81	41	42	0	0	4	2	19	1	0	.053	7	11	1	1	0.6	.947

Ed Konetchy

KONETCHY, EDWARD JOSEPH (Big Ed)
B. Sept. 3, 1885, LaCrosse, Wis. D. May 27, 1947, Fort Worth, Tex. BR TR 6'2½" 195 lbs.

Year	Team		W	L	PCT	ERA	G	GS	CG	IP	H	BB	SO	ShO	W	L	SV	AB	H	HR	BA	PO	A	E	DP	TC/G	FA
1910	STL	N	0	0	—	4.50	1	0	0	4	4	1	0	0	0	0	0	520	157	3	.302	0	0	0	0	0.0	—
1913			1	0	1.000	0.00	1	0	0	4.2	1	4	3	0	1	0	0	502	137	7	.273	0	0	0	0	0.0	—
1918	BOS	N	0	1	.000	6.75	1	1	1	8	14	2	3	0	0	0	0	437	103	2	.236	0	1	0	0	1.0	1.000
3 yrs.			1	1	.500	4.32	3	1	1	16.2	19	7	6	0	1	0	0	*				0	1	0	0	0.3	1.000

Doug Konieczny

KONIECZNY, DOUGLAS JAMES
B. Sept. 27, 1951, Detroit, Mich. BR TR 6'4" 220 lbs.

Year	Team		W	L	PCT	ERA	G	GS	CG	IP	H	BB	SO	ShO	W	L	SV	AB	H	HR	BA	PO	A	E	DP	TC/G	FA
1973	HOU	N	0	1	.000	5.54	2	2	0	13	12	4	6	0	0	0	0	4	0	0	.000	1	1	0	0	1.0	1.000
1974			0	3	.000	7.88	6	3	0	16	18	12	8	0	0	0	0	4	0	0	.000	1	2	0	0	0.5	1.000
1975			6	13	.316	4.47	32	29	4	171	184	87	89	1	0	0	0	50	8	0	.160	7	21	4	1	1.0	.875
1977			1	1	.500	6.00	4	4	0	21	26	8	7	0	0	0	0	7	1	0	.143	5	3	0	0	2.0	1.000
4 yrs.			7	18	.280	4.93	44	38	4	221	240	111	110	1	0	0	0	65	9	0	.138	14	27	4	1	1.0	.911

Alex Konikowski

KONIKOWSKI, ALEXANDER JAMES (Whitey)
B. June 8, 1928, Throop, Pa. BR TR 6'1" 187 lbs.

Year	Team		W	L	PCT	ERA	G	GS	CG	IP	H	BB	SO	ShO	W	L	SV	AB	H	HR	BA	PO	A	E	DP	TC/G	FA
1948	NY	N	2	3	.400	7.56	22	1	0	33.1	46	17	9	0	2	2	1	2	0	0	.000	3	8	0	1	0.5	1.000
1951			0	0	—	0.00	3	0	0	4	2	0	5	0	0	0	0	0	0	0	—	1	0	0	0	0.3	1.000
1954			0	0	—	7.50	10	0	0	12	10	12	6	0	0	0	0	1	0	0	.000	0	1	0	0	0.1	1.000
3 yrs.			2	3	.400	6.93	35	1	0	49.1	58	29	20	0	2	2	1	3	0	0	.000	4	9	0	1	0.4	1.000

WORLD SERIES

Year	Team		W	L	PCT	ERA	G	GS	CG	IP	H	BB	SO	ShO	W	L	SV	AB	H	HR	BA	PO	A	E	DP	TC/G	FA
1951	NY	N	0	0	—	0.00	1	0	0	1	1	0	0	0	0	0	0	0	0	0	—	0	0	0	0	0.0	

Jim Konstanty

KONSTANTY, CASIMIR JAMES
B. Mar. 2, 1917, Strykersville, N. Y. D. June 11, 1976, Oneonta, N. Y. BR TR 6'1½" 202 lbs.

Year	Team		W	L	PCT	ERA	G	GS	CG	IP	H	BB	SO	ShO	W	L	SV	AB	H	HR	BA	PO	A	E	DP	TC/G	FA
1944	CIN	N	6	4	.600	2.80	20	12	5	112.2	113	33	19	1	2	1	0	34	10	0	.294	10	25	0	1	1.8	1.000
1946	BOS	N	0	1	.000	5.28	10	1	0	15.1	17	7	9	0	0	0	0	2	0	0	.000	2	5	0	1	0.7	1.000
1948	PHI	N	1	0	1.000	0.93	6	0	0	9.2	7	2	7	0	1	0	2	3	0	0	.000	0	1	0	0	0.2	1.000
1949			9	5	.643	3.25	53	0	0	97	98	29	43	0	9	5	7	17	3	0	.176	3	25	2	0	0.6	.933
1950			16	7	.696	2.66	74	0	0	152	108	50	56	0	16	7	22	37	4	0	.108	12	22	3	2	0.5	.944
1951			4	11	.267	4.05	58	1	0	115.2	127	31	27	0	4	10	9	19	3	0	.158	8	29	1	1	0.7	.974
1952			5	3	.625	3.94	42	2	2	80	87	21	16	1	4	2	6	14	1	0	.071	6	16	3	1	0.6	.880
1953			14	10	.583	4.43	48	19	7	170.2	198	42	45	0	4	3	5	50	11	0	.220	6	33	0	5	0.8	1.000
1954	2 teams		PHI N		(33G 2-3)		NY A		(9G 1-1)																		
"	total		3	4	.429	3.01	42	1	0	68.2	73	18	14	0	3	4	5	16	0	0	.000	5	9	1	0	0.4	1.000
1955	NY	A	7	2	.778	2.32	45	0	0	73.2	68	24	19	0	7	2	11	8	1	0	.125	6	11	2	1	0.5	.905
1956	2 teams		NY A		(8G 0-0)		STL N		(27G 1-1)																		
"	total		1	1	.500	4.65	35	0	0	50.1	61	12	13	0	1	1	7	2	0	0	.000	5	5	0	0	0.2	1.000
11 yrs.			66	48	.579	3.46	433	36	14	945.2	957	269	268	2	51	35	74	202	33	0	.163	61	185	10	14	0.6	.961

Year	Team		W	L	PCT	ERA	G	GS	CG	IP	H	BB	SO	ShO	Relief Pitching W	L	SV	Batting AB	H	HR	BA	PO	A	E	DP	TC/G	FA

Jim Konstanty *continued*

WORLD SERIES

Year	Team		W	L	PCT	ERA	G	GS	CG	IP	H	BB	SO	ShO	W	L	SV	AB	H	HR	BA	PO	A	E	DP	TC/G	FA
1950	PHI	N	0	1	.000	2.40	3	1	0	15	9	4	3	0	0	0	0	4	1	0	.250	1	1	0	0	0.7	1.000

Ernie Koob

KOOB, ERNEST GERALD
B. Sept. 11, 1893, Keeler, Mich.   D. Nov. 12, 1941, Lemay, Mo.

BL TL 5'10"   160 lbs.

Year	Team		W	L	PCT	ERA	G	GS	CG	IP	H	BB	SO	ShO	W	L	SV	AB	H	HR	BA	PO	A	E	DP	TC/G	FA
1915	STL	A	4	5	.444	2.36	28	13	6	133.2	119	50	37	0	0	0	1	37	5	0	.135	3	32	0	3	1.3	1.000
1916			11	8	.579	2.54	33	20	10	166.2	153	56	26	2	2	1	2	41	0	0	.000	4	36	0	1	1.2	1.000
1917			6	14	.300	3.91	39	18	3	133.2	139	57	47	1	1	2	1	35	4	0	.114	4	44	7	3	1.4	.873
1919			2	3	.400	4.64	25	4	0	66	77	23	11	0	2	1	0	15	0	0	.000	2	21	1	2	1.0	.958
4 yrs.			23	30	.434	3.13	125	55	19	500	488	186	121	3	5	4	4	128	9	0	.070	13	133	8	9	1.2	.948

Cal Koonce

KOONCE, CALVIN LEE
B. Nov. 18, 1940, Fayetteville, N. C.

BR TR 6'1"   185 lbs.

Year	Team		W	L	PCT	ERA	G	GS	CG	IP	H	BB	SO	ShO	W	L	SV	AB	H	HR	BA	PO	A	E	DP	TC/G	FA
1962	CHI	N	10	10	.500	3.97	35	30	3	190.2	200	86	84	1	0	0	0	64	6	0	.094	17	29	3	1	1.4	.939
1963			2	6	.250	4.58	21	13	0	72.2	75	32	44	0	0	0	0	19	2	0	.105	2	18	0	1	1.0	1.000
1964			3	0	1.000	2.03	6	2	0	31	30	7	17	0	1	0	0	10	0	0	.000	0	14	0	2	2.3	1.000
1965			7	9	.438	3.69	38	23	3	173	181	52	88	0	1	0	0	49	5	0	.102	8	31	0	3	1.0	1.000
1966			5	5	.500	3.81	45	5	0	108.2	113	35	65	0	4	4	2	23	3	0	.130	6	25	1	1	0.7	.969
1967	2 teams		CHI N	(34G 2–2)				NY N		(11G 3–3)																	
"	total		5	5	.500	3.75	45	6	2	96	97	28	52	1	2	2	2	20	2	0	.100	13	21	0	3	0.8	1.000
1968	NY	N	6	4	.600	2.42	55	2	0	96.2	80	32	50	0	5	4	11	14	0	0	.000	13	11	0	0	0.4	1.000
1969			6	3	.667	4.99	40	0	0	83	85	42	48	0	6	3	7	17	4	0	.235	7	18	0	2	0.6	1.000
1970	2 teams		NY N	(13G 0–2)				BOS A		(23G 3–4)																	
"	total		3	6	.333	3.49	36	8	1	98	89	43	47	0	0	2	2	22	2	0	.091	10	24	1	2	1.0	.971
1971	BOS	A	0	1	.000	5.57	13	1	0	21	22	11	9	0	0	0	0	1	0	0	.000	5	4	0	1	0.7	1.000
10 yrs.			47	49	.490	3.78	334	90	9	970.2	972	368	504	3	18	15	24	239	24	0	.100	81	195	5	16	0.8	.982

Jerry Koosman

KOOSMAN, JEROME MARTIN (Kooz)
B. Dec. 23, 1942, Appleton, Minn.

BR TL 6'2"   205 lbs.

Year	Team		W	L	PCT	ERA	G	GS	CG	IP	H	BB	SO	ShO	W	L	SV	AB	H	HR	BA	PO	A	E	DP	TC/G	FA
1967	NY	N	0	2	.000	6.04	9	3	0	22.1	22	19	11	0	0	0	0	2	0	0	.000	0	5	0	1	0.6	1.000
1968			19	12	.613	2.08	35	34	17	263.2	221	69	178	7	0	0	0	91	7	1	.077	5	42	0	2	1.3	1.000
1969			17	9	.654	2.28	32	32	16	241	187	68	180	6	0	0	0	84	4	0	.048	4	37	1	3	1.3	.976
1970			12	7	.632	3.14	30	29	5	212	189	71	118	1	1	0	0	70	6	0	.086	7	20	0	1	0.9	1.000
1971			6	11	.353	3.04	26	24	4	166	160	51	96	0	0	0	0	50	8	0	.160	6	23	1	2	1.2	.967
1972			11	12	.478	4.14	34	24	4	163	155	52	147	1	2	0	1	47	4	0	.085	4	23	1	1	0.8	.964
1973			14	15	.483	2.84	35	35	12	263	234	76	156	3	0	0	0	78	8	0	.103	5	41	2	1	1.4	.958
1974			15	11	.577	3.36	35	35	13	265	258	85	188	0	0	0	0	86	16	0	.186	8	41	4	2	1.5	.925
1975			14	13	.519	3.41	36	34	11	240	234	98	173	4	0	0	2	78	14	0	.179	10	32	3	3	1.3	.933
1976			21	10	.677	2.70	34	32	17	247	205	66	200	3	0	0	0	79	17	0	.215	5	39	3	3	1.4	.936
1977			8	20	.286	3.49	32	32	6	227	195	81	192	1	0	0	0	72	8	1	.111	4	25	4	0	1.0	.879
1978			3	15	.167	3.75	38	32	5	235	221	84	160	0	0	0	2	70	6	0	.086	4	48	6	1	1.5	.897
1979	MIN	A	20	13	.606	3.38	37	36	10	264	268	83	157	2	0	0	0	0	0	0	–	10	50	5	6	1.8	.923
1980			16	13	.552	4.04	38	34	8	243	252	69	149	0	1	1	2	0	0	0	–	7	41	3	2	1.3	.941
1981	2 teams		MIN A	(19G 3–9)				CHI A		(8G 1–4)																	
"	total		4	13	.235	4.02	27	16	3	121	125	41	76	1	0	2	5	0	0	0	–	7	17	1	0	0.9	.960
1982	CHI	A	11	7	.611	3.84	42	19	3	173.1	194	38	88	1	2	3	3	0	0	0	–	12	24	1	3	0.9	.973
1983			11	7	.611	4.77	37	24	2	169.2	176	53	90	1	1	0	2	0	0	0	–	5	26	2	2	0.9	.939
1984	PHI	N	14	15	.483	3.25	36	34	3	224	232	60	137	1	0	0	0	74	8	0	.108	9	34	4	1	1.3	.915
1985			6	4	.600	4.62	19	18	3	99.1	107	34	60	0	0	0	0	34	3	0	.088	4	14	1	1	1.0	.947
19 yrs.			222	209	.515	3.36	612	527	140	3839.1	3635	1198	2556	33	7	6	17	915	109	2	.119	116	582	42	36	1.2	.943

LEAGUE CHAMPIONSHIP SERIES

Year	Team		W	L	PCT	ERA	G	GS	CG	IP	H	BB	SO	ShO	W	L	SV	AB	H	HR	BA	PO	A	E	DP	TC/G	FA
1969	NY	N	0	0	–	11.57	1	1	0	4.2	7	4	5	0	0	0	0	2	0	0	.000	0	1	0	0	1.0	1.000
1973			1	0	1.000	2.00	1	1	1	9	8	0	9	0	0	0	0	4	2	0	.500	0	0	0	0	0.0	–
1983	CHI	A	0	0	–	54.00	1	0	0	.1	1	2	0	0	0	0	0	0	0	0	–	0	0	0	0	0.0	–
3 yrs.			1	0	1.000	6.43	3	2	1	14	16	6	14	0	0	0	0	6	2	0	.333	0	1	0	0	0.3	1.000

WORLD SERIES

Year	Team		W	L	PCT	ERA	G	GS	CG	IP	H	BB	SO	ShO	W	L	SV	AB	H	HR	BA	PO	A	E	DP	TC/G	FA
1969	NY	N	2	0	1.000	2.04	2	2	0	17.2	7	4	9	0	0	0	0	7	1	0	.143	0	2	0	0	1.0	1.000
1973			1	0	1.000	3.12	2	2	0	8.2	9	7	8	0	0	0	0	4	0	0	.000	0	1	0	0	1.0	.500
2 yrs.			3	0	1.000	2.39	4	4	1	26.1	16	11	17	0	0	0	0	11	1	0	.091	0	3	0	0	1.0	.750
					1st																					

Howie Koplitz

KOPLITZ, HOWARD DEAN
B. May 4, 1938, Oshkosh, Wis.

BR TR 5'10½"   190 lbs.

Year	Team		W	L	PCT	ERA	G	GS	CG	IP	H	BB	SO	ShO	W	L	SV	AB	H	HR	BA	PO	A	E	DP	TC/G	FA
1961	DET	A	2	0	1.000	2.25	4	1	1	12	16	8	9	0	1	0	0	4	0	0	.000	0	1	0	0	0.3	1.000
1962			3	0	1.000	5.26	10	6	1	37.2	54	10	10	0	0	0	0	13	3	0	.231	3	7	0	1	1.0	1.000
1964	WAS	A	0	0	–	4.76	6	1	0	17	20	13	9	0	0	0	0	4	0	0	.000	1	3	0	0	0.7	1.000
1965			4	7	.364	4.05	33	11	0	106.2	97	48	59	0	2	2	1	30	3	0	.100	8	23	0	2	0.9	1.000
1966			0	0	–	0.00	1	0	0	2	0	1	0	0	0	0	0	0	0	0	–	0	1	0	0	1.0	1.000
5 yrs.			9	7	.563	4.21	54	19	2	175.1	187	80	87	0	3	2	1	51	6	0	.118	12	35	0	3	0.9	1.000

George Korince

KORINCE, GEORGE EUGENE (Moose)
B. Jan. 10, 1946, Ottawa, Ont., Canada

BR TR 6'3"   210 lbs.

Year	Team		W	L	PCT	ERA	G	GS	CG	IP	H	BB	SO	ShO	W	L	SV	AB	H	HR	BA	PO	A	E	DP	TC/G	FA
1966	DET	A	0	0	–	0.00	2	0	0	3	1	3	2	0	0	0	0	0	0	0	–	0	0	0	0	0.0	–
1967			1	0	1.000	5.14	9	0	0	14	10	11	11	0	1	0	0	1	0	0	.000	1	2	0	0	0.3	1.000
2 yrs.			1	0	1.000	4.24	11	0	0	17	11	14	13	0	1	0	0	1	0	0	.000	1	2	0	0	0.3	1.000

Jim Korwan

KORWAN, JAMES
B. Mar. 4, 1874, Brooklyn, N. Y.   D. Aug., 1899, Brooklyn, N. Y.

BR TR 6'1"   181 lbs.

Year	Team		W	L	PCT	ERA	G	GS	CG	IP	H	BB	SO	ShO	W	L	SV	AB	H	HR	BA	PO	A	E	DP	TC/G	FA
1894	BKN	N	0	0	–	14.40	1	0	0	5	9	5	2	0	0	0	0	2	0	0	.000	0	1	0	0	1.0	1.000

Year	Team		W	L	PCT	ERA	G	GS	CG	IP	H	BB	SO	ShO	Relief Pitching W	L	SV	Batting AB	H	HR	BA	PO	A	E	DP	TC/G	FA

Harry Krause

KRAUSE, HARRY WILLIAM (Hal)
B. July 12, 1887, San Francisco, Calif. D. Oct. 23, 1940, San Francisco, Calif.
BB TL 5'10" 165 lbs.

Year	Team	W	L	PCT	ERA	G	GS	CG	IP	H	BB	SO	ShO	W	L	SV	AB	H	HR	BA	PO	A	E	DP	TC/G	FA
1908	PHI A	1	1	.500	2.57	4	2	2	21	20	4	10	0	0	0	0	7	0	0	.000	3	1	2	0	1.5	.667
1909		18	8	.692	**1.39**	32	21	16	213	151	49	139	7	4	2	0	77	12	0	.156	7	48	4	3	1.8	.932
1910		6	6	.500	2.88	16	11	9	112.1	99	42	60	2	0	1	0	38	8	0	.211	7	24	4	1	2.2	.886
1911		11	8	.579	3.04	27	19	12	169	155	47	85	1	2	1	2	59	15	0	.254	5	31	2	0	1.4	.947
1912	2 teams	PHI A	(4G 0–2)		CLE A	(2G 0–1)																				
"	total	0	3	.000	12.60	6	4	0	10	21	4	4	0	0	0	0	4	1	0	.250	0	2	0	0	0.3	1.000
	5 yrs.	36	26	.581	2.50	85	57	39	525.1	446	146	298	10	6	4	2	185	36	0	.195	22	106	12	4	1.6	.914

Lew Krausse

KRAUSSE, LEWIS BERNARD, SR.
Father of Lew Krausse.
B. June 8, 1912, Media, Pa. D. Sept. 6, 1988, Sarasota, Fla.
BR TR 6'½" 167 lbs.

Year	Team	W	L	PCT	ERA	G	GS	CG	IP	H	BB	SO	ShO	W	L	SV	AB	H	HR	BA	PO	A	E	DP	TC/G	FA
1931	PHI A	1	0	1.000	3.97	3	1	1	11.1	6	6	1	0	0	0	0	2	0	0	.000	1	3	0	1	1.3	1.000
1932		4	1	.800	4.58	20	3	2	57	64	24	16	1	2	1	0	15	2	0	.133	3	17	1	1	1.1	.952
	2 yrs.	5	1	.833	4.48	23	4	3	68.1	70	30	17	1	2	1	0	17	2	0	.118	4	20	1	2	1.1	.960

Lew Krausse

KRAUSSE, LEWIS BERNARD, JR.
Son of Lew Krausse.
B. Apr. 25, 1943, Media, Pa.
BR TR 6' 175 lbs.

Year	Team	W	L	PCT	ERA	G	GS	CG	IP	H	BB	SO	ShO	W	L	SV	AB	H	HR	BA	PO	A	E	DP	TC/G	FA
1961	KC A	2	5	.286	4.85	12	8	2	55.2	49	46	32	1	0	0	0	17	2	0	.118	1	4	1	0	0.5	.833
1964		0	2	.000	7.36	5	4	0	14.2	22	9	9	0	0	0	0	2	0	0	.000	1	2	1	0	0.8	.750
1965		2	4	.333	5.04	7	5	0	25	29	8	22	0	0	1	0	7	0	0	.000	2	0	0	0	0.3	1.000
1966		14	9	.609	2.99	36	22	4	177.2	144	63	87	1	1	3	3	52	8	0	.154	11	15	1	1	0.8	.963
1967		7	17	.292	4.28	48	19	0	160	140	67	96	0	3	3	6	41	6	1	.146	5	26	2	2	0.7	.939
1968	OAK A	10	11	.476	3.11	36	25	2	185	147	62	105	0	2	1	4	56	9	0	.161	11	20	0	2	0.9	1.000
1969		7	7	.500	4.44	43	16	4	140	134	48	85	0	2	1	3	48	8	4	.167	5	17	1	4	0.5	.957
1970	MIL A	13	18	.419	4.75	37	35	8	216	235	67	130	1	0	0	0	65	9	0	.138	21	27	1	0	1.3	.980
1971		8	12	.400	2.95	43	22	1	180	164	62	92	0	1	2	0	44	1	0	.023	17	22	2	0	1.0	.951
1972	BOS A	1	3	.250	6.34	24	7	0	61	74	28	35	0	0	0	1	16	2	0	.125	5	11	0	0	0.7	1.000
1973	STL N	0	0	–	0.00	1	0	0	2	2	1	1	0	0	0	0	0	0	0	–	0	1	0	0	1.0	1.000
1974	ATL N	4	3	.571	4.16	29	4	0	67	65	32	27	0	3	2	0	6	2	1	.333	5	8	0	0	0.4	1.000
	12 yrs.	68	91	.428	4.00	321	167	21	1284	1205	493	721	5	11	15	21	354	47	6	.133	84	153	9	9	0.8	.963

Ken Kravec

KRAVEC, KENNETH PETER
B. July 29, 1951, Cleveland, Ohio
BL TL 6'2" 185 lbs.

Year	Team	W	L	PCT	ERA	G	GS	CG	IP	H	BB	SO	ShO	W	L	SV	AB	H	HR	BA	PO	A	E	DP	TC/G	FA
1975	CHI A	0	1	.000	6.23	2	1	0	4.1	1	8	1	0	0	0	0	0	0	0	–	0	4	0	0	2.0	1.000
1976		1	5	.167	4.86	9	8	1	50	49	32	38	0	0	0	0	0	0	0	–	0	7	1	0	0.9	.875
1977		11	8	.579	4.10	26	25	6	167	161	57	125	1	0	0	0	0	0	0	–	6	26	1	2	1.3	.970
1978		11	16	.407	4.08	30	30	7	203	188	95	154	2	0	0	0	0	0	0	–	7	25	3	1	1.2	.914
1979		15	13	.536	3.74	36	35	10	250	208	111	132	3	0	0	1	0	0	0	–	8	35	1	1	1.2	.977
1980		3	6	.333	6.91	20	15	0	82	100	44	37	0	0	0	0	0	0	0	–	7	13	0	0	1.0	1.000
1981	CHI N	1	6	.143	5.08	24	12	0	78	80	39	50	0	0	1	0	15	0	0	.000	3	16	1	0	0.8	.950
1982		1	1	.500	6.12	13	2	0	25	27	18	20	0	1	1	0	3	0	0	.000	1	3	0	0	0.3	1.000
	8 yrs.	43	56	.434	4.46	160	128	24	859.1	814	404	557	6	1	2	1	18	0	0	.000	32	129	7	4	1.1	.958

Ray Krawczyk

KRAWCZYK, RAYMOND ALLEN
B. Oct. 9, 1959, Sewickley, Pa.
BR TR 6'2" 190 lbs.

Year	Team	W	L	PCT	ERA	G	GS	CG	IP	H	BB	SO	ShO	W	L	SV	AB	H	HR	BA	PO	A	E	DP	TC/G	FA
1984	PIT N	0	0	–	3.38	4	0	0	5.1	7	4	3	0	0	0	0	0	0	0	–	0	0	0	0	0.0	–
1985		0	2	.000	14.04	8	0	0	8.1	20	6	9	0	0	2	0	0	0	0	–	0	2	1	1	0.4	.667
1986		0	1	.000	7.30	12	0	0	12.1	17	10	7	0	0	1	0	0	0	0	–	2	0	1	0	0.3	.667
1988	CAL A	0	1	.000	4.81	14	1	0	24.1	29	8	17	0	0	0	1	0	0	0	–	2	6	0	0	0.6	1.000
1989	MIL A	0	0	–	13.50	1	0	0	2	4	1	6	0	0	0	0	0	0	0	–	0	0	0	0	0.0	–
	5 yrs.	0	4	.000	7.05	39	1	0	52.1	77	29	42	0	0	3	1	0	0	0	–	4	8	2	1	0.4	.857

Ray Kremer

KREMER, REMY PETER (Wiz)
B. Mar. 23, 1893, Oakland, Calif. D. Feb. 8, 1965, Pinole, Calif.
BR TR 6'1" 190 lbs.

Year	Team	W	L	PCT	ERA	G	GS	CG	IP	H	BB	SO	ShO	W	L	SV	AB	H	HR	BA	PO	A	E	DP	TC/G	FA
1924	PIT N	18	10	.643	3.19	41	30	17	259.1	262	51	64	4	3	1	1	86	13	0	.151	3	59	2	2	1.6	.969
1925		17	8	.680	3.69	40	27	14	214.2	232	47	62	0	3	2	2	71	14	0	.197	1	39	0	1	1.0	1.000
1926		**20**	6	.769	**2.61**	37	26	18	231.1	221	51	74	3	2	0	5	83	21	1	.253	4	46	1	0	1.4	.980
1927		19	8	.704	2.47	35	28	18	226	205	53	63	3	2	2	2	83	14	2	.169	7	37	1	0	1.3	.978
1928		15	13	.536	4.64	34	31	17	219	253	68	61	1	0	0	0	78	14	0	.179	7	33	2	0	1.2	.952
1929		18	10	.643	4.26	34	27	14	221.2	226	60	66	0	3	0	0	86	11	1	.128	4	39	0	0	1.3	1.000
1930		**20**	12	.625	5.02	39	**38**	18	276	366	63	58	1	0	1	0	102	16	1	.157	7	38	2	7	1.2	.957
1931		11	15	.423	3.33	30	30	15	230	246	65	58	1	0	0	0	75	17	0	.227	1	27	1	1	1.0	.966
1932		4	3	.571	4.29	11	10	3	56.2	61	16	6	1	0	0	0	19	2	0	.105	1	7	1	0	0.8	.889
1933		1	0	1.000	10.35	7	0	0	20	36	9	4	0	1	0	0	4	0	0	.000	2	6	0	2	1.1	1.000
	10 yrs.	143	85	.627	3.76	308	247	134	1954.2	2108	483	516	14	14	6	10	687	122	5	.178	37	331	10	13	1.2	.974

WORLD SERIES

Year	Team	W	L	PCT	ERA	G	GS	CG	IP	H	BB	SO	ShO	W	L	SV	AB	H	HR	BA	PO	A	E	DP	TC/G	FA
1925	PIT N	2	1	.667	3.00	3	2	2	21	17	4	9	0	1	0	0	7	1	0	.143	2	5	1	0	2.7	.875
1927		0	1	.000	3.60	1	1	0	5	5	3	1	0	0	0	0	2	1	0	.500	0	0	0	0	0.0	–
	2 yrs.	2	2	.500	3.12	4	3	2	26	22	7	10	0	1	0	0	9	2	0	.222	2	5	1	0	2.0	.875

Jim Kremmel

KREMMEL, JAMES LOUIS
B. Feb. 28, 1948, Belleville, Ill.
BL TL 6' 175 lbs.

Year	Team	W	L	PCT	ERA	G	GS	CG	IP	H	BB	SO	ShO	W	L	SV	AB	H	HR	BA	PO	A	E	DP	TC/G	FA
1973	TEX A	0	2	.000	9.00	4	2	0	9	15	6	6	0	0	0	0	0	0	0	–	1	0	0	0	0.3	1.000
1974	CHI N	0	2	.000	5.23	23	2	0	31	37	18	22	0	0	1	0	3	0	0	.000	0	4	1	1	0.3	.833
	2 yrs.	0	4	.000	6.08	27	4	0	40	52	24	28	0	0	1	0	3	0	0	.000	1	5	1	1	0.3	.857

Year	Team		W	L	PCT	ERA	G	GS	CG	IP	H	BB	SO	ShO	Relief Pitching W	L	SV	Batting AB	H	HR	BA	PO	A	E	DP	TC/G	FA

Red Kress

KRESS, RALPH
B. Jan. 2, 1907, Columbia, Calif.   D. Nov. 29, 1962, Los Angeles, Calif.
BR TR 5'11½" 165 lbs.

1935	WAS	A	0	0	–	12.71	3	0	0	5.2	8	5	5	0	0	0	0	252	75	2	.298	0	3	0	0	1.0	1.000
1946	NY	N	0	0	–	12.27	1	0	0	3.2	5	1	1	0	0	0	0	1	0	0	.000	2	3	0	0	5.0	1.000
2 yrs.			0	0	–	12.54	4	0	0	9.1	13	6	6	0	0	0	0	*				2	6	0	0	2.0	1.000

Lou Kretlow

KRETLOW, LOUIS HENRY
B. June 27, 1923, Apache, Okla.
BR TR 6'2" 185 lbs.

1946	DET	A	1	0	1.000	3.00	2	1	1	9	7	2	4	0	0	0	0	4	2	0	.500	0	1	0	0	1.0	1.000
1948			2	1	.667	4.63	5	2	1	23.1	21	11	9	0	1	0	0	8	4	0	.500	0	5	0	0	1.0	1.000
1949			3	2	.600	6.16	25	10	1	76	85	69	40	0	2	1	0	26	0	0	.000	2	23	2	1	1.1	.926
1950	2 teams		STL A	(9G 0–2)		CHI A	(11G 0–0)																				
"	total		0	2	.000	7.07	20	3	0	35.2	42	45	24	0	0	1	0	7	0	0	.000	0	3	0	0	0.2	1.000
1951	CHI	A	6	9	.400	4.20	26	18	7	137	129	74	89	1	0	1	0	48	4	0	.083	5	22	3	2	1.2	.900
1952			4	4	.500	2.96	19	11	4	79	52	56	63	2	0	0	1	20	1	0	.050	1	9	0	2	0.5	1.000
1953	2 teams		CHI A	(9G 0–0)		STL A	(22G 1–5)																				
"	total		1	5	.167	4.78	31	14	0	101.2	105	82	52	0	0	0	0	29	5	0	.172	6	13	4	1	0.7	.826
1954	BAL	A	6	11	.353	4.37	32	20	5	166.2	169	82	82	0	0	1	0	51	8	0	.157	4	30	0	2	1.1	1.000
1955			0	4	.000	8.22	15	5	0	38.1	50	27	26	0	0	0	0	11	1	0	.091	1	11	0	0	0.8	1.000
1956	KC	A	4	9	.308	5.31	25	20	3	118.2	121	74	61	0	0	0	0	33	2	0	.061	5	16	2	1	0.9	.913
10 yrs.			27	47	.365	4.87	199	104	22	785.1	781	522	450	3	3	4	1	237	27	0	.114	24	133	11	9	0.8	.935

Rick Kreuger

KREUGER, RICHARD ALLEN
B. Nov. 3, 1948, Grand Rapids, Mich.
BR TL 6'2" 185 lbs.

1975	BOS	A	0	0	–	4.50	2	0	0	4	3	1	1	0	0	0	0	0	0	0	–	1	2	0	1	1.5	1.000
1976			2	1	.667	4.06	8	4	1	31	31	16	12	0	0	0	0	0	0	0	–	1	8	0	1	1.1	1.000
1977			0	1	.000	∞	1	0	0	0	2	0	0	0	0	1	0	0	0	0	–	0	0	0	0	0.0	–
1978	CLE	A	0	0	–	3.86	6	0	0	9.1	6	3	7	0	0	0	0	0	0	0	–	1	1	0	0	0.3	1.000
4 yrs.			2	2	.500	4.47	17	4	1	44.1	42	20	20	0	0	1	0	0	0	0	–	3	11	0	1	0.8	1.000

Frank Kreutzer

KREUTZER, FRANKLIN JAMES
B. Feb. 7, 1939, Buffalo, N. Y.
BR TL 6'1" 175 lbs.

1962	CHI	A	0	0	–	0.00	1	0	0	1.1	0	1	1	0	0	0	0	0	0	0	–	0	0	0	0	0.0	–
1963			1	0	1.000	1.80	1	1	0	5	3	1	0	0	0	0	0	2	0	0	.000	0	1	0	0	1.0	1.000
1964	2 teams		CHI A	(17G 3–1)		WAS A	(13G 2–6)																				
"	total		5	7	.417	4.10	30	11	0	85.2	85	41	59	0	2	3	1	19	1	0	.053	8	16	1	0	0.8	.960
1965	WAS	A	2	6	.250	4.32	33	14	2	85.1	73	54	65	1	0	1	0	22	1	1	.045	4	6	3	0	0.4	.769
1966			0	5	.000	6.03	9	6	0	31.1	30	10	24	0	0	0	0	8	2	0	.250	4	4	0	0	0.9	1.000
1969			0	0	–	4.50	4	0	0	2	3	2	2	0	0	0	0	0	0	0	–	0	1	0	0	0.3	1.000
6 yrs.			8	18	.308	4.40	78	32	2	210.2	194	109	151	1	2	3	1	51	4	1	.078	16	28	4	0	0.6	.917

Krieger

KRIEGER,
Deceased.

| 1884 | KC | U | 0 | 1 | .000 | 0.00 | 1 | 1 | 0 | 7 | 9 | 5 | 3 | 0 | 0 | 0 | 0 | 3 | 0 | 0 | .000 | 1 | 1 | 0 | 0 | 2.0 | 1.000 |

Kurt Krieger

KRIEGER, KURT FERDINAND (Dutch)
B. Sept. 16, 1926, Traisen, Austria   D. Aug. 16, 1970, St. Louis, Mo.
BR TR 6'3" 212 lbs.

1949	STL	N	0	0	–	0.00	1	0	0	1	0	1	0	0	0	0	0	0	0	0	–	0	0	0	0	0.0	–
1951			0	0	–	15.75	2	0	0	4	6	5	3	0	0	0	0	0	0	0	–	0	1	0	0	0.5	1.000
2 yrs.			0	0	–	12.60	3	0	0	5	6	6	3	0	0	0	0	0	0	0	–	0	1	0	0	0.3	1.000

Howie Krist

KRIST, HOWARD WILBUR (Spud)
B. Feb. 28, 1916, West Henrietta, N. Y.   D. Apr. 23, 1989, Buffalo, N. Y.
BL TR 6'1" 175 lbs.

1937	STL	N	3	1	.750	4.23	6	4	1	27.2	34	10	6	0	1	0	0	9	0	0	.000	2	3	0	0	0.8	1.000
1938			0	0	–	0.00	2	0	0	1.1	1	0	1	0	0	0	0	0	0	0	–	0	0	0	0	0.0	–
1941			10	0	1.000	4.03	37	8	2	114	107	35	36	0	6	0	2	38	9	0	.237	4	19	0	0	0.6	1.000
1942			13	3	.813	2.51	34	8	3	118.1	103	43	47	0	8	2	1	42	6	0	.143	2	16	1	1	0.6	.947
1943			11	5	.688	2.90	34	17	9	164.1	141	62	57	3	2	1	3	60	10	0	.167	1	13	3	1	0.5	.824
1946			0	2	.000	6.75	15	0	0	18.2	22	8	3	0	0	2	0	0	0	0	–	0	4	0	1	0.3	1.000
6 yrs.			37	11	.771	3.32	128	37	15	444.1	408	158	150	3	17	5	6	149	25	0	.168	9	55	4	3	0.5	.941

WORLD SERIES

| 1943 | STL | N | 0 | 0 | – | 0.00 | 1 | 0 | 0 | | 1 | 0 | 0 | 0 | 0 | 0 | 0 | 0 | 0 | 0 | – | 0 | 0 | 0 | 0 | 0.0 | – |

Gus Krock

KROCK, AUGUST H.
B. May 9, 1866, Milwaukee, Wis.   D. Mar. 22, 1905, Pasadena, Calif.
TL 6' 196 lbs.

1888	CHI	N	25	14	.641	2.44	39	39	39	339.2	295	45	161	4	0	0	0	134	22	1	.164	4	61	12	1	2.0	.844
1889	3 teams		CHI N	(7G 3–3)		IND N	(4G 2–2)		WAS N	(6G 2–4)																	
"	total		7	9	.438	5.57	17	17	14	140.2	199	50	43	0	0	0	0	61	11	0	.180	4	25	6	0	2.1	.829
1890	BUF	P	0	3	.000	6.12	4	3	3	25	43	15	5	0	0	0	0	12	1	0	.083	0	9	0	0	2.3	1.000
3 yrs.			32	26	.552	3.49	60	59	56	505.1	537	110	209	4	0	0	0	207	34	1	.164	8	95	18	1	2.0	.851

Rube Kroh

KROH, FLOYD MYRON
B. Aug. 25, 1886, Friendship, N. Y.   D. Mar. 17, 1944, New Orleans, La.
BL TL 6'2" 186 lbs.

1906	BOS	A	1	0	1.000	0.00	1	1	1	9	2	4	5	1	0	0	0	3	0	0	.000	0	4	0	0	4.0	1.000
1907			1	4	.200	2.62	7	5	1	34.1	33	8	8	0	0	0	0	11	3	0	.273	1	12	2	0	2.1	.867
1908	CHI	N	0	0	–	1.50	2	1	0	12	9	4	11	0	0	0	0	4	0	0	.000	0	4	0	0	2.0	1.000
1909			9	4	.692	1.65	17	13	10	120.1	97	30	51	2	0	0	0	40	6	0	.150	6	37	1	2	2.6	.977
1910			3	1	.750	4.46	6	4	1	34.1	33	15	16	0	2	0	0	12	3	0	.250	0	12	0	0	2.0	1.000
1912	BOS	N	0	0	–	5.68	3	1	0	6.1	8	6	1	0	0	0	0	2	1	0	.500	0	4	0	0	1.3	1.000
6 yrs.			14	9	.609	2.29	36	25	13	216.1	182	67	92	3	2	0	0	72	13	0	.181	7	73	3	2	2.3	.964

Year	Team	W	L	PCT	ERA	G	GS	CG	IP	H	BB	SO	ShO	Relief Pitching W	L	SV	Batting AB	H	HR	BA	PO	A	E	DP	TC/G	FA

Gary Kroll
KROLL, GARY MELVIN
B. July 8, 1941, Culver City, Calif.   BR TR 6'6" 220 lbs.

Year	Team	W	L	PCT	ERA	G	GS	CG	IP	H	BB	SO	ShO	W	L	SV	AB	H	HR	BA	PO	A	E	DP	TC/G	FA
1964	2 teams	PHI N		(2G 0–0)		NY N		(8G 0–1)																		
"	total	0	1	.000	4.01	10	2	0	24.2	22	17	26	0	0	0	0	3	1	0	.333	1	8	1	0	1.0	.900
1965	NY N	6	6	.500	4.45	32	11	1	87	83	41	62	0	4	1	1	26	3	0	.115	4	14	2	3	0.6	.900
1966	HOU N	0	0	–	3.80	10	0	0	23.2	26	11	22	0	0	0	0	3	0	0	.000	1	4	0	0	0.5	1.000
1969	CLE A	0	0	–	4.13	19	0	0	24	16	22	28	0	0	0	0	0	0	0	–	0	3	0	0	0.2	1.000
4 yrs.		6	7	.462	4.24	71	13	1	159.1	147	91	138	0	4	1	1	32	4	0	.125	6	29	3	3	0.5	.921

Bill Krueger
KRUEGER, WILLIAM CULP
B. Apr. 24, 1958, Waukegan, Ill.   BL TL 6'5" 205 lbs.

Year	Team	W	L	PCT	ERA	G	GS	CG	IP	H	BB	SO	ShO	W	L	SV	AB	H	HR	BA	PO	A	E	DP	TC/G	FA
1983	OAK A	7	6	.538	3.61	17	16	2	109.2	104	53	58	0	0	0	0	0	0	0	–	3	7	1	0	0.6	.909
1984		10	10	.500	4.75	26	24	1	142	156	85	61	0	0	0	0	0	0	0	–	6	12	0	1	0.7	1.000
1985		9	10	.474	4.52	32	23	2	151.1	165	69	56	0	1	0	0	0	0	0	–	3	23	2	0	0.9	.929
1986		1	2	.333	6.03	11	3	0	34.1	40	13	10	0	0	1	1	0	0	0	–	2	8	1	1	1.0	.909
1987	2 teams	OAK A		(9G 0–3)		LA N		(2G 0–0)																		
"	total	0	3	.000	6.75	11	0	0	8	12	9	4	0	0	3	0	0	0	0	–	0	0	0	0	0.0	–
1988	LA N	0	0	–	11.57	1	1	0	2.1	4	2	1	0	0	0	0	0	0	0	–	0	2	0	0	2.0	1.000
1989	MIL A	3	2	.600	3.84	34	5	0	93.2	96	33	72	0	1	0	3	0	0	0	–	5	11	0	0	0.5	1.000
7 yrs.		30	33	.476	4.44	132	72	5	541.1	577	264	262	0	3	4	4	0	0	0	–	19	63	4	2	0.7	.953

Abe Kruger
KRUGER, ABRAHAM
B. Feb. 14, 1885, Morris Run, Pa. D. July 4, 1962, Elmira, N. Y.   BR TR 6'2" 190 lbs.

Year	Team	W	L	PCT	ERA	G	GS	CG	IP	H	BB	SO	ShO	W	L	SV	AB	H	HR	BA	PO	A	E	DP	TC/G	FA
1908	BKN N	0	1	.000	4.26	2	1	0	6.1	5	3	2	0	0	0	0	2	0	0	.000	0	6	0	0	3.0	1.000

Mike Krukow
KRUKOW, MICHAEL EDWARD
B. Jan. 21, 1952, Long Beach, Calif.   BR TR 6'5" 205 lbs.

Year	Team	W	L	PCT	ERA	G	GS	CG	IP	H	BB	SO	ShO	W	L	SV	AB	H	HR	BA	PO	A	E	DP	TC/G	FA
1976	CHI N	0	0	–	9.00	2	0	0	4	6	2	1	0	0	0	0	1	0	0	.000	0	0	0	0	0.0	–
1977		8	14	.364	4.40	34	33	1	172	195	61	106	1	0	0	0	55	11	0	.200	15	26	3	3	1.3	.932
1978		9	3	.750	3.91	27	20	3	138	125	53	81	1	0	0	0	45	11	0	.244	9	19	0	1	1.0	1.000
1979		9	9	.500	4.20	28	28	0	165	172	81	119	0	0	0	0	51	16	1	.314	11	12	0	3	0.8	1.000
1980		10	15	.400	4.39	34	34	3	205	200	80	130	0	0	0	0	65	16	1	.246	10	19	5	3	1.0	.853
1981		9	9	.500	3.69	25	25	2	144	146	55	101	1	0	0	0	50	9	0	.180	13	21	2	2	1.4	.944
1982	PHI N	13	11	.542	3.12	33	33	7	208	211	82	138	2	0	0	0	72	13	0	.181	19	35	1	1	1.7	.982
1983	SF N	11	11	.500	3.95	31	31	2	184.1	189	76	136	1	0	0	0	63	16	1	.254	13	18	5	1	1.2	.861
1984		11	12	.478	4.56	35	33	3	199.1	234	78	141	1	0	0	0	72	10	0	.139	12	20	1	3	0.9	.970
1985		8	11	.421	3.38	28	28	6	194.2	176	49	150	1	0	0	0	55	12	1	.218	6	27	1	3	1.2	.971
1986		20	9	.690	3.05	34	34	10	245	204	55	178	2	0	0	0	82	12	0	.146	17	33	4	1	1.6	.926
1987		5	6	.455	4.80	30	28	3	163	182	46	104	0	0	0	0	54	9	0	.167	9	30	1	5	1.3	.975
1988		7	4	.636	3.54	20	20	1	124.2	111	31	75	0	0	0	0	41	3	0	.073	8	18	0	0	1.3	1.000
1989		4	3	.571	3.98	8	8	0	43	37	18	18	0	0	0	0	16	1	0	.063	4	6	0	1	1.3	1.000
14 yrs.		124	117	.515	3.90	369	355	41	2190	2188	767	1478	10	0	0	1	722	139	5	.193	146	284	23	27	1.2	.949

LEAGUE CHAMPIONSHIP SERIES

Year	Team	W	L	PCT	ERA	G	GS	CG	IP	H	BB	SO	ShO	W	L	SV	AB	H	HR	BA	PO	A	E	DP	TC/G	FA
1987	SF N	1	0	1.000	2.00	1	1	1	9	9	1	3	0	0	0	0	2	0	0	.000	2	2	0	1	4.0	1.000

Al Krumm
KRUMM, ALBERT
B. Columbus, Ohio   Deceased.   TR

Year	Team	W	L	PCT	ERA	G	GS	CG	IP	H	BB	SO	ShO	W	L	SV	AB	H	HR	BA	PO	A	E	DP	TC/G	FA
1889	PIT N	0	1	.000	10.00	1	1	1	9	8	10	4	0	0	0	0	0	0	0	.000	0	0	0	0	0.0	–

Johnny Kucab
KUCAB, JOHN ALBERT
B. Dec. 17, 1919, Olyphant, Pa. D. May 26, 1977, Youngstown, Ohio   BR TR 6'2" 185 lbs.

Year	Team	W	L	PCT	ERA	G	GS	CG	IP	H	BB	SO	ShO	W	L	SV	AB	H	HR	BA	PO	A	E	DP	TC/G	FA
1950	PHI A	1	1	.500	3.46	4	2	2	26	29	8	8	0	0	0	0	9	1	0	.111	0	3	0	0	0.8	1.000
1951		4	3	.571	4.22	30	1	0	74.2	76	23	23	0	4	2	4	16	0	0	.000	3	6	1	1	0.3	.900
1952		0	1	.000	5.26	25	0	0	51.1	64	20	17	0	0	1	2	10	2	0	.200	3	9	2	1	0.6	.857
3 yrs.		5	5	.500	4.44	59	3	2	152	169	51	48	0	4	3	6	35	3	0	.086	6	18	3	2	0.5	.889

Jack Kucek
KUCEK, JOHN ANDREW CHARLES
B. June 8, 1953, Warren, Ohio   BR TR 6'2" 200 lbs.

Year	Team	W	L	PCT	ERA	G	GS	CG	IP	H	BB	SO	ShO	W	L	SV	AB	H	HR	BA	PO	A	E	DP	TC/G	FA
1974	CHI A	1	4	.200	5.21	9	7	0	38	48	21	25	0	0	0	0	0	0	0	–	4	8	0	0	1.3	1.000
1975		0	0	–	4.91	2	0	0	3.2	9	4	2	0	0	0	0	0	0	0	–	0	0	0	0	0.0	–
1976		0	0	–	9.00	2	0	0	5	9	4	2	0	0	0	0	0	0	0	–	0	0	0	0	0.0	–
1977		0	1	.000	3.60	8	3	0	35	35	10	25	0	0	0	0	0	0	0	–	7	8	1	0	2.0	.938
1978		2	3	.400	3.29	10	5	3	52	42	27	30	0	0	0	1	0	0	0	–	4	5	0	0	0.9	1.000
1979	2 teams	CHI A		(1G 0–0)		PHI N		(4G 1–0)																		
"	total	1	0	1.000	7.20	5	0	0	5	6	4	2	0	0	0	0	0	0	0	–	0	0	0	0	0.0	–
1980	TOR A	3	8	.273	6.75	23	12	0	68	83	41	35	0	1	2	1	0	0	0	–	1	10	4	1	0.7	.733
7 yrs.		7	16	.304	5.10	59	27	3	206.2	232	111	121	0	2	2	2	0	0	0	–	16	31	5	1	0.9	.904

Johnny Kucks
KUCKS, JOHN CHARLES
B. July 27, 1933, Hoboken, N. J.   BR TR 6'3" 170 lbs.

Year	Team	W	L	PCT	ERA	G	GS	CG	IP	H	BB	SO	ShO	W	L	SV	AB	H	HR	BA	PO	A	E	DP	TC/G	FA
1955	NY A	8	7	.533	3.41	29	13	3	126.2	122	44	49	1	2	3	0	40	2	0	.050	3	24	3	0	1.0	.900
1956		18	9	.667	3.85	34	31	12	224.1	223	72	67	3	2	0	0	77	11	0	.143	13	40	5	5	1.7	.914
1957		8	10	.444	3.56	37	23	4	179.1	169	59	78	1	1	1	2	55	6	0	.109	9	47	1	5	1.5	.982
1958		8	8	.500	3.93	34	16	4	126	132	39	46	1	2	5	4	40	5	0	.125	6	25	1	2	0.9	.969
1959	2 teams	NY A		(9G 0–1)		KC A		(33G 8–11)																		
"	total	8	12	.400	4.34	42	24	6	168	184	51	60	0	0	1	1	49	4	0	.082	11	36	1	4	1.1	.979
1960	KC A	4	10	.286	6.00	31	17	1	114	140	43	38	0	2	0	0	30	4	0	.133	3	22	3	1	0.9	.893
6 yrs.		54	56	.491	4.10	207	123	30	938.1	970	308	338	7	9	10	7	291	32	0	.110	45	194	14	17	1.2	.945

WORLD SERIES

Year	Team	W	L	PCT	ERA	G	GS	CG	IP	H	BB	SO	ShO	W	L	SV	AB	H	HR	BA	PO	A	E	DP	TC/G	FA
1955	NY A	0	0	–	6.00	1	0	0	3	3	1	0	0	0	0	0	1	0	0	–	0	1	0	0	0.5	1.000
1956		1	0	1.000	0.82	3	1	1	11	6	3	2	1	0	0	0	3	0	0	.000	1	2	0	1	1.0	1.000

Year	Team		W	L	PCT	ERA	G	GS	CG	IP	H	BB	SO	ShO	Relief Pitching W	L	SV	Batting AB	H	HR	BA	PO	A	E	DP	TC/G	FA

Johnny Kucks *continued*

1957			0	0	–	0.00	1	0	0	.2	1	1	1	0	0	0	0	0	0	0	–	0	0	0	0	0.0	–
1958			0	0	–	2.08	2	0	0	4.1	4	1	0	0	0	0	0	1	1	0	1.000	0	0	0	0	0.0	–
4 yrs.			1	0	1.000	1.89	8	1	1	19	15	6	4	1	0	0	0	4	1	0	.250	1	3	0	1	0.5	1.000

Bert Kuczynski

KUCZYNSKI, BERNARD CARL
B. Jan. 8, 1920, Philadelphia, Pa.
BR TR 6' 195 lbs.

| 1943 | PHI | A | 0 | 1 | .000 | 4.01 | 6 | 1 | 0 | 24.2 | 36 | 9 | 8 | 0 | 0 | 0 | 0 | 6 | 0 | 0 | .000 | 0 | 5 | 0 | 0 | 0.8 | 1.000 |

Fred Kuhaulua

KUHAULUA, FRED MAHELE
B. Feb. 23, 1953, Honolulu, Hawaii
BL TL 5'11" 175 lbs.

1977	CAL	A	0	0	–	15.63	3	1	0	6.1	15	7	3	0	0	0	0	0	0	0	.000	0	0	0	0	0.3	1.000
1981	SD	N	1	0	1.000	2.48	5	4	0	29	28	9	16	0	0	0	0	9	1	0	.111	0	2	0	0	0.2	1.000
2 yrs.			1	0	1.000	4.84	8	5	0	35.1	43	16	19	0	0	0	0	9	1	0	.111	0	2	0	0	0.3	1.000

Bub Kuhn

KUHN, BERNARD DANIEL
B. Oct. 12, 1899, Vicksburg, Mich.   D. Nov. 20, 1956, Detroit, Mich.
BL TR 6'4" 182 lbs.

| 1924 | CLE | A | 0 | 1 | .000 | 27.00 | 1 | 0 | 0 | 1 | 4 | 0 | 0 | 0 | 0 | 0 | 0 | 0 | 0 | 0 | – | 0 | 0 | 0 | 0 | 1.0 | 1.000 |

John Kull

KULL, JOHN A.
B. June 24, 1882, Shenandoah, Pa.   D. Mar. 30, 1936, Schuylkill, Pa.
BL TL 6'2" 190 lbs.

| 1909 | PHI | A | 1 | 0 | 1.000 | 3.00 | 1 | 0 | 0 | 3 | 3 | 5 | 4 | 0 | 1 | 0 | 0 | 1 | 1 | 0 | 1.000 | 0 | 1 | 0 | 0 | 1.0 | 1.000 |

John Kume

KUME, JOHN MICHAEL
B. May 19, 1926, Premier, W. Va.
BR TR 6'1" 200 lbs.

| 1955 | KC | A | 0 | 2 | .000 | 7.99 | 6 | 4 | 0 | 23.2 | 35 | 15 | 7 | 0 | 0 | 0 | 0 | 8 | 1 | 0 | .125 | 1 | 4 | 0 | 0 | 0.8 | 1.000 |

Bill Kunkel

KUNKEL, WILLIAM GUSTAVE JAMES
Father of Jeff Kunkel.
B. July 7, 1936, Hoboken, N. J.   D. May 4, 1985, Red Bank, N. J.
BR TR 6'1" 187 lbs.

1961	KC	A	3	4	.429	5.18	58	2	0	88.2	103	32	46	0	3	2	4	8	1	0	.125	10	13	3	2	0.4	.885
1962			0	0	–	3.52	9	0	0	7.2	8	4	6	0	0	0	0	0	0	0	–	0	1	0	0	0.1	1.000
1963	NY	A	3	2	.600	2.72	22	0	0	46.1	42	13	31	0	3	2	0	6	2	0	.333	2	4	0	0	0.3	1.000
3 yrs.			6	6	.500	4.29	89	2	0	142.2	153	49	83	0	6	4	4	14	3	0	.214	12	18	3	2	0.4	.909

Jeff Kunkel

KUNKEL, JEFFREY WILLIAM
Son of Bill Kunkel.
B. Mar. 25, 1962, West Palm Beach, Fla.
BR TR 6'2" 175 lbs.

1988	TEX	A	0	0	–	0.00	1	0	0	1	0	0	0	0	0	0	0	154	35	2	.227	0	0	0	0	0.0	–
1989			0	0	–	21.60	1	0	0	1.2	4	3	0	0	0	0	0	293	79	8	.270	1	0	0	0	1.0	1.000
2 yrs.			0	0	–	13.50	2	0	0	2.2	4	3	1	0	0	0	0	*				1	0	0	0	0.5	1.000

Earl Kunz

KUNZ, EARL DEWEY (Pinch)
B. Dec. 25, 1899, Sacramento, Calif.   D. Apr. 14, 1963, Sacramento, Calif.
BR TR 5'10" 170 lbs.

| 1923 | PIT | N | 1 | 2 | .333 | 5.52 | 21 | 2 | 1 | 45.2 | 48 | 24 | 12 | 0 | 1 | 1 | 1 | 12 | 1 | 0 | .083 | 1 | 8 | 4 | 0 | 0.6 | .692 |

Ryan Kurosaki

KUROSAKI, RYAN YOSHITOMO
B. July 3, 1952, Honolulu, Hawaii
BR TR 5'10" 160 lbs.

| 1975 | STL | N | 0 | 0 | – | 7.62 | 7 | 0 | 0 | 13 | 15 | 7 | 6 | 0 | 0 | 0 | 0 | 1 | 0 | 0 | .000 | 0 | 1 | 0 | 0 | 0.1 | 1.000 |

Hal Kurtz

KURTZ, HAROLD JAMES (Bud)
B. Aug. 20, 1943, Washington, D. C.
BR TR 6'3" 205 lbs.

| 1968 | CLE | A | 1 | 0 | 1.000 | 5.21 | 28 | 0 | 0 | 38 | 37 | 15 | 16 | 0 | 1 | 0 | 1 | 4 | 0 | 0 | .000 | 0 | 5 | 1 | 1 | 0.2 | .833 |

Ed Kusel

KUSEL, EDWARD D.
B. Feb. 15, 1886, Cleveland, Ohio   D. Oct. 20, 1948, Cleveland, Ohio
TR 6' 165 lbs.

| 1909 | STL | A | 0 | 3 | .000 | 7.13 | 3 | 3 | 3 | 24 | 43 | 1 | 2 | 0 | 0 | 0 | 0 | 10 | 3 | 0 | .300 | 2 | 5 | 0 | 0 | 2.3 | 1.000 |

Emil Kush

KUSH, EMIL BENEDICT (Moe)
B. Nov. 4, 1916, Chicago, Ill.   D. Nov. 26, 1969, River Grove, Ill.
BR TR 5'11" 185 lbs.

1941	CHI	N	0	0	–	2.25	2	0	0	4	2	0	2	0	0	0	0	1	0	0	.000	0	0	0	0	0.0	–
1942			0	0	–	0.00	1	0	0	2	1	1	1	0	0	0	0	1	0	0	.000	0	2	0	0	2.0	1.000
1946			9	2	.818	3.05	40	6	1	129.2	120	43	50	1	8	0	2	38	8	0	.211	9	37	2	2	1.2	.958
1947			8	3	.727	3.36	47	1	1	91	80	53	44	0	7	2	5	20	5	0	.250	5	21	1	1	0.6	.963
1948			1	4	.200	4.38	34	1	0	72	70	37	31	0	1	3	3	13	2	0	.154	6	15	1	0	0.6	.955
1949			3	3	.500	3.78	26	0	0	47.2	51	24	22	0	3	3	2	9	3	0	.333	6	10	0	2	0.6	1.000
6 yrs.			21	12	.636	3.48	150	8	2	346.1	324	158	150	1	19	8	12	82	18	0	.220	26	85	4	5	0.8	.965

Craig Kusick

KUSICK, CRAIG ROBERT
B. Sept. 30, 1948, Milwaukee, Wis.
BR TR 6'3" 210 lbs.

| 1979 | MIN | A | 0 | 0 | – | 4.50 | 1 | 0 | 0 | 4 | 3 | 0 | 0 | 0 | 0 | 0 | 0 | * | | | | 0 | 0 | 0 | 0 | 0.0 | – |

Marty Kutyna

KUTYNA, MARION JOHN
B. Nov. 14, 1932, Philadelphia, Pa.
BR TR 6' 190 lbs.

1959	KC	A	0	0	–	0.00	4	0	0	7.1	7	1	1	0	0	0	0	0	0	0	–	1	3	0	0	1.0	1.000
1960			3	2	.600	3.94	51	0	0	61.2	64	32	20	0	3	2	4	5	1	0	.200	3	12	1	1	0.3	.938
1961	WAS	A	6	8	.429	3.97	50	6	0	143	147	48	64	0	5	4	3	34	7	0	.206	13	36	1	4	1.0	.980

Year	Team		W	L	PCT	ERA	G	GS	CG	IP	H	BB	SO	ShO	Relief Pitching W	L	SV	Batting AB	H	HR	BA	PO	A	E	DP	TC/G	FA

Marty Kutyna *continued*

| 1962 | | | 5 | 6 | .455 | 4.04 | 54 | 0 | 0 | 78 | 83 | 27 | 25 | 0 | 5 | 6 | 0 | 8 | 1 | 0 | .125 | 6 | 18 | 1 | 0 | 0.5 | .960 |
| 4 yrs. | | | 14 | 16 | .467 | 3.88 | 159 | 6 | 0 | 290 | 301 | 108 | 110 | 0 | 13 | 12 | 8 | 47 | 9 | 0 | .191 | 23 | 69 | 3 | 5 | 0.6 | .968 |

Bob Kuzava

KUZAVA, ROBERT LeROY (Sarge)
B. May 28, 1923, Wyandotte, Mich.

BB TL 6'2" 202 lbs.
BR 1946

1946	CLE	A	1	0	1.000	3.00	2	2	0	12	9	11	4	0	0	0	0	5	1	0	.200	0	4	0	0	2.5	.800
1947			1	1	.500	4.15	4	4	1	21.2	22	9	9	1	0	0	0	9	1	0	.111	0	8	0	0	2.0	1.000
1949	CHI	A	10	6	.625	4.02	29	18	9	156.2	139	91	83	0	2	0	0	56	2	0	.036	8	17	3	1	1.0	.893
1950	2 teams		CHI A	(10G 1–3)		WAS A	(22G 8–7)																				
"	total		9	10	.474	4.33	32	29	9	199.1	199	102	105	1	0	0	0	62	6	1	.097	8	30	3	5	1.3	.927
1951	2 teams		WAS A	(8G 3–3)		NY A	(23G 8–4)																				
"	total		11	7	.611	3.61	31	16	7	134.2	133	55	72	1	5	1	5	39	6	0	.154	3	9	0	0	0.4	1.000
1952	NY	A	8	8	.500	3.45	28	12	6	133	115	63	67	1	3	2	3	43	4	0	.093	4	16	0	2	0.7	1.000
1953			6	5	.545	3.31	33	6	2	92.1	92	34	48	2	4	1	1	21	1	0	.048	1	8	0	0	0.3	1.000
1954	2 teams		NY A	(20G 1–3)		BAL A	(4G 1–3)																				
"	total		2	6	.250	4.97	24	7	0	63.1	76	29	37	0	4	4	1	13	0	0	.000	0	5	0	1	0.2	1.000
1955	2 teams		BAL A	(6G 0–1)		PHI N	(17G 1–0)																				
"	total		1	1	.500	6.25	23	5	0	44.2	57	16	18	0	1	1	0	8	1	0	.125	3	6	0	0	0.4	1.000
1957	2 teams		PIT N	(4G 0–0)		STL N	(3G 0–0)																				
"	total		0	0	–	6.23	7	0	0	4.1	7	5	3	0	0	0	0	0	0	0	–	0	1	0	0	0.1	1.000
10 yrs.			49	44	.527	4.05	213	99	34	862	849	415	446	7	15	5	13	256	22	1	.086	27	104	7	9	0.6	.949

WORLD SERIES

1951	NY	A	0	0	–	0.00	1	0	0	1	0	0	0	0	0	0	0	0	0	0	–	0	0	0	0	0.0	–
1952			0	0	–	0.00	1	0	0	2.2	0	0	2	0	0	0	1	1	0	0	.000	0	0	0	0	0.0	–
1953			0	0	–	13.50	1	0	0	.2	2	0	1	0	0	0	1	1	0	0	.000	0	0	0	0	0.0	–
3 yrs.			0	0	–	2.08	3	0	0	4.1	2	0	3	0	0	0	2	2	0	0	.000	0	0	0	0	0.0	–

Clem Labine

LABINE, CLEMENT WALTER
B. Aug. 6, 1926, Lincoln, R. I.

BR TR 6' 180 lbs.

1950	BKN	N	0	0	–	4.50	2	1	0	2	2	1	0	0	0	0	0	0	0	0	–	0	0	0	0	0.0	–
1951			5	1	.833	2.20	14	6	5	65.1	52	20	39	2	0	0	0	21	3	0	.143	6	1	1	1	0.9	.923
1952			8	4	.667	5.14	25	9	0	77	76	47	43	0	6	1	0	22	1	0	.045	8	17	1	1	0.9	.962
1953			11	6	.647	2.77	37	7	0	110.1	92	30	44	0	10	4	7	28	2	0	.071	8	19	0	2	0.7	1.000
1954			7	6	.538	4.15	47	2	0	108.1	101	56	43	0	6	5	5	30	1	0	.033	7	24	3	1	0.7	.912
1955			13	5	.722	3.24	60	8	1	144.1	121	55	67	0	10	2	11	31	3	3	.097	21	30	1	0	0.9	.981
1956			10	6	.625	3.35	62	3	1	115.2	111	39	75	0	9	6	19	23	2	0	.087	13	18	2	1	0.5	.939
1957			5	7	.417	3.44	58	0	0	104.2	104	27	67	0	5	7	17	20	2	0	.100	6	28	1	2	0.6	.971
1958	LA	N	6	6	.500	4.15	52	2	0	104	112	33	43	0	5	5	14	18	1	0	.056	3	21	2	2	0.5	.923
1959			5	10	.333	3.93	56	0	0	84.2	91	25	37	0	5	10	9	16	0	0	.000	9	18	0	2	0.5	1.000
1960	3 teams		LA N	(13G 0–1)		DET A	(14G 0–3)		PIT N	(15G 3–0)																	
"	total		3	4	.429	3.65	42	0	0	66.2	74	31	42	0	3	4	0	8	1	0	.125	4	12	1	0	0.4	.889
1961	PIT	N	4	1	.800	3.69	56	1	0	92.1	102	31	49	0	4	1	8	10	1	0	.100	12	12	1	0	0.4	.960
1962	NY	N	0	0	–	11.25	3	0	0	4	5	1	1	0	0	0	0	0	0	0	–	0	2	0	0	0.7	1.000
13 yrs.			77	56	.579	3.63	513	38	7	1079.2	1043	396	551	2	63	45	96	227	17	3	.075	97	207	14	15	0.6	.956

WORLD SERIES

1953	BKN	N	0	2	.000	3.60	3	0	0	5	10	1	3	0	0	0	0	2	0	0	.000	0	2	0	1	0.7	1.000
1955			1	0	1.000	2.89	4	0	0	9.1	6	2	2	0	1	0	1	4	0	0	.000	0	3	0	0	0.8	1.000
1956			1	0	1.000	0.00	2	1	0	7	12	8	3	1	0	0	0	4	1	0	.250	0	3	0	0	1.5	1.000
1959	LA	N	0	0	–	0.00	1	0	0	1	0	0	1	0	0	0	0	0	0	0	–	0	0	0	0	0.0	–
1960	PIT	N	0	0	–	13.50	3	0	0	4	13	1	0	0	0	0	1	0	0	0	–	0	2	0	0	0.7	1.000
5 yrs.			2	2	.500	3.16	13	1	0	31.1	37	7	15	1	1	2	1	10	1	0	.100	0	10	0	1	0.8	1.000
							6th						**2nd**														

Bob Lacey

LACEY, ROBERT JOSEPH
B. Aug. 25, 1953, Fredericksburg, Va.

BR TL 6'5" 210 lbs.

1977	OAK	A	6	8	.429	3.02	64	0	0	122	100	43	69	0	6	8	7	0	0	0	–	3	38	3	1	0.7	.932
1978			8	9	.471	3.01	74	0	0	119.2	126	35	60	0	8	9	5	0	0	0	–	8	27	3	1	0.5	.921
1979			1	5	.167	5.81	42	0	0	48	66	24	33	0	1	5	4	0	0	0	–	3	7	0	0	0.2	1.000
1980			3	2	.600	2.93	47	1	1	80	68	21	45	1	2	2	6	0	0	0	–	3	12	0	0	0.3	1.000
1981	2 teams		CLE A	(14G 0–0)		TEX A	(1G 0–0)																				
"	total		0	0	–	7.77	15	0	0	22	37	3	11	0	0	0	0	0	0	0	–	1	3	0	0	0.3	1.000
1983	CAL	A	1	2	.333	5.19	8	0	0	8.2	12	0	7	0	1	2	0	0	0	0	–	0	1	0	0	0.1	1.000
1984	SF	N	1	3	.250	3.88	34	1	0	51	55	13	26	0	1	3	0	6	2	0	.333	1	10	0	0	0.3	1.000
7 yrs.			20	29	.408	3.67	284	2	1	451.1	464	139	251	1	19	28	22	6	2	0	.333	19	98	6	2	0.4	.951

Marcel Lachemann

LACHEMANN, MARCEL ERNEST
Brother of Rene Lachemann.
B. June 13, 1941, Los Angeles, Calif.

BR TR 6'1" 185 lbs.

1969	OAK	A	4	1	.800	3.95	28	0	0	43.1	43	19	16	0	4	1	2	2	0	0	.000	2	10	1	0	0.5	.923
1970			3	3	.500	2.79	41	0	0	58	58	18	39	0	3	3	3	8	0	0	.000	1	15	1	1	0.4	.941
1971			0	0	–	54.00	1	0	0	.1	2	1	0	0	0	0	0	0	0	0	–	0	1	0	0	1.0	1.000
3 yrs.			7	4	.636	3.45	70	0	0	101.2	103	38	55	0	7	4	5	10	0	0	.000	3	26	2	2	0.4	.935

Al Lachowicz

LACHOWICZ, ALLEN ROBERT
B. Sept. 6, 1960, Pittsburgh, Pa.

BR TR 6'3" 185 lbs.

| 1983 | TEX | A | 0 | 1 | .000 | 2.25 | 2 | 1 | 0 | 8 | 9 | 2 | 8 | 0 | 0 | 0 | 0 | 0 | 0 | 0 | – | 1 | 0 | 1 | 0 | 1.0 | 1.000 |

George LaClaire

LaCLAIRE, GEORGE LEWIS
B. Oct. 18, 1886, Milton, Vt. D. Oct. 10, 1918, Farnham, Que., Canada

BR TR 5'9" 170 lbs.

| 1914 | PIT | F | 5 | 2 | .714 | 4.01 | 22 | 7 | 5 | 103.1 | 99 | 25 | 49 | 1 | 2 | 0 | 0 | 34 | 5 | 0 | .147 | 6 | 28 | 0 | 2 | 1.5 | 1.000 |

Year	Team	W	L	PCT	ERA	G	GS	CG	IP	H	BB	SO	ShO	Relief Pitching W	L	SV	Batting AB	H	HR	BA	PO	A	E	DP	TC/G	FA

George LaClaire *continued*

Year	Team	W	L	PCT	ERA	G	GS	CG	IP	H	BB	SO	ShO	W	L	SV	AB	H	HR	BA	PO	A	E	DP	TC/G	FA
1915	3 teams	PIT F	(14G 1-0)		BUF F	(1G 0-0)		BAL F	(18G 2-8)																		
"	total	3	8	.273	2.85	33	12	7	132.2	123	36	42	1	1	2	1	37	4	0	.108	0	46	0	2	1.4	1.000
2 yrs.		8	10	.444	3.36	55	19	12	236	222	61	91	2	3	2	1	71	9	0	.127	6	74	0	4	1.5	1.000

Frank LaCorte
LaCORTE, FRANK JOSEPH
B. Oct. 13, 1951, San Jose, Calif. BR TR 6'1" 180 lbs.

Year	Team	W	L	PCT	ERA	G	GS	CG	IP	H	BB	SO	ShO	W	L	SV	AB	H	HR	BA	PO	A	E	DP	TC/G	FA
1975	ATL N	0	3	.000	5.14	3	2	0	14	13	6	10	0	0	1	0	5	0	0	.000	0	2	0	1	0.7	1.000
1976		3	12	.200	4.71	19	17	1	105	97	53	79	0	0	1	0	33	3	0	.091	5	14	3	0	1.2	.864
1977		1	8	.111	11.68	14	7	0	37	67	29	28	0	0	2	0	10	2	0	.200	2	6	0	0	0.6	1.000
1978		0	1	.000	3.60	2	2	0	15	9	4	7	0	0	0	0	4	0	0	.000	0	1	0	0	0.5	1.000
1979	2 teams	ATL N	(6G 0-0)		HOU N	(12G 1-2)																				
"	total	1	2	.333	5.60	18	3	0	35.1	30	15	30	0	0	0	0	4	0	0	.000	0	1	1	0	0.1	.500
1980	HOU N	8	5	.615	2.82	55	0	0	83	61	43	66	0	8	5	11	6	1	0	.167	1	3	1	0	0.1	.800
1981		4	2	.667	3.64	37	0	0	42	41	21	40	0	4	2	5	3	1	0	.333	2	4	0	0	0.2	1.000
1982		1	5	.167	4.48	55	0	0	76.1	71	46	51	0	1	5	7	7	0	0	.000	2	4	2	0	0.1	.750
1983		4	4	.500	5.06	37	0	0	53.1	35	28	48	0	4	4	3	5	1	0	.200	1	6	0	0	0.2	1.000
1984	CAL A	1	2	.333	7.06	13	0	0	29.1	33	13	13	0	0	2	0	0	0	0	–	0	4	1	0	0.4	.800
10 yrs.		23	44	.343	5.01	253	32	1	490.1	457	258	372	0	17	22	26	77	8	0	.104	13	45	8	1	0.3	.879

DIVISIONAL PLAYOFF SERIES

Year	Team	W	L	PCT	ERA	G	GS	CG	IP	H	BB	SO	ShO	W	L	SV	AB	H	HR	BA	PO	A	E	DP	TC/G	FA
1981	HOU N	0	0	–	0.00	2	0	0	3.2	2	1	5	0	0	0	0	0	0	0	–	0	0	0	0	0.0	–

LEAGUE CHAMPIONSHIP SERIES

Year	Team	W	L	PCT	ERA	G	GS	CG	IP	H	BB	SO	ShO	W	L	SV	AB	H	HR	BA	PO	A	E	DP	TC/G	FA
1980	HOU N	1	1	.500	3.00	2	0	0	3	7	2	2	0	1	1	0	1	0	0	.000	0	0	0	0	0.0	–

Mike LaCoss
LaCOSS, MICHAEL JAMES
B. May 30, 1956, Glendale, Calif. BR TR 6'5" 185 lbs.

Year	Team	W	L	PCT	ERA	G	GS	CG	IP	H	BB	SO	ShO	W	L	SV	AB	H	HR	BA	PO	A	E	DP	TC/G	FA
1978	CIN N	4	8	.333	4.50	16	15	2	96	104	46	31	1	0	0	0	30	2	0	.067	8	13	0	4	1.3	1.000
1979		14	8	.636	3.50	35	32	6	206	202	79	73	1	0	0	0	70	9	0	.129	15	34	2	4	1.5	.961
1980		10	12	.455	4.63	34	29	4	169	207	68	59	2	2	0	0	55	5	0	.091	9	34	3	4	1.4	.935
1981		4	7	.364	6.12	20	13	1	78	102	30	22	1	2	0	1	19	0	0	.000	6	14	1	0	1.1	.952
1982	HOU N	6	6	.500	2.90	41	8	0	115	107	54	51	0	3	3	0	24	6	0	.250	7	16	3	3	0.6	.885
1983		5	7	.417	4.43	38	17	2	138	142	56	53	0	0	1	0	35	3	0	.086	6	27	0	1	0.9	1.000
1984		7	5	.583	4.02	39	18	2	132	132	55	86	0	1	0	3	31	4	0	.129	9	20	2	2	0.8	.935
1985	KC A	1	1	.500	5.09	21	0	0	40.2	49	29	26	0	1	1	1	0	0	0	–	1	8	0	1	0.4	1.000
1986	SF N	10	13	.435	3.57	37	31	6	204.1	179	70	86	1	0	0	0	61	14	2	.230	19	34	1	2	1.5	.981
1987		13	10	.565	3.68	39	26	2	171	184	63	79	1	1	0	0	50	3	0	.060	15	43	2	4	1.5	.967
1988		7	7	.500	3.62	19	19	1	114.1	99	47	70	1	0	0	0	33	8	0	.242	10	32	0	1	2.2	1.000
1989		10	10	.500	3.17	45	18	1	150.1	143	65	78	0	3	5	6	41	3	0	.073	12	20	4	1	0.8	.889
12 yrs.		91	94	.492	3.93	384	226	25	1614.2	1650	662	714	9	13	10	12	449	57	2	.127	117	295	18	23	1.1	.958

LEAGUE CHAMPIONSHIP SERIES

Year	Team	W	L	PCT	ERA	G	GS	CG	IP	H	BB	SO	ShO	W	L	SV	AB	H	HR	BA	PO	A	E	DP	TC/G	FA
1979	CIN N	0	1	.000	10.80	1	1	0	1.2	4	4	0	0	0	0	0	0	0	0	–	0	1	0	0	1.0	1.000
1987	SF N	0	0	–	0.00	2	0	0	3.1	1	3	2	0	0	0	0	0	0	0	–	0	2	0	0	1.0	1.000
1989		0	0	–	9.00	1	1	0	3	7	0	2	0	0	0	0	1	0	0	.000	0	0	0	0	1.0	–
3 yrs.		0	1	.000	5.63	4	2	0	8	9	7	4	0	0	0	0	1	0	0	.000	0	3	0	0	1.0	.750

WORLD SERIES

Year	Team	W	L	PCT	ERA	G	GS	CG	IP	H	BB	SO	ShO	W	L	SV	AB	H	HR	BA	PO	A	E	DP	TC/G	FA
1989	SF N	0	0	–	6.23	2	0	0	4.1	4	3	2	0	0	0	0	1	0	0	.000	0	0	0	0	0.5	1.000

Pete Ladd
LADD, PETER LINWOOD (Bigfoot)
B. July 17, 1956, Portland, Me. BR TR 6'3" 228 lbs.

Year	Team	W	L	PCT	ERA	G	GS	CG	IP	H	BB	SO	ShO	W	L	SV	AB	H	HR	BA	PO	A	E	DP	TC/G	FA
1979	HOU N	1	1	.500	3.00	10	0	0	12	8	8	6	0	1	1	0	1	0	0	.000	3	2	0	0	0.5	1.000
1982	MIL A	1	3	.250	4.00	16	0	0	18	16	6	12	0	1	3	3	0	0	0	–	1	0	0	0	0.1	1.000
1983		3	4	.429	2.55	44	0	0	49.1	30	16	41	0	3	4	25	0	0	0	–	1	5	0	0	0.1	1.000
1984		4	9	.308	5.24	54	1	0	91	94	38	75	0	4	8	3	0	0	0	–	5	4	1	0	0.2	.900
1985		0	0	–	4.53	29	0	0	45.2	58	10	22	0	0	0	2	0	0	0	–	3	5	1	0	0.3	.889
1986	SEA A	8	6	.571	3.82	52	0	0	70.2	69	18	53	0	8	6	6	0	0	0	–	2	5	1	0	0.2	.875
6 yrs.		17	23	.425	4.14	205	1	0	286.2	275	96	209	0	17	22	39	1	0	0	.000	15	21	3	0	0.2	.923

LEAGUE CHAMPIONSHIP SERIES

Year	Team	W	L	PCT	ERA	G	GS	CG	IP	H	BB	SO	ShO	W	L	SV	AB	H	HR	BA	PO	A	E	DP	TC/G	FA
1982	MIL A	0	0	–	0.00	3	0	0	3.1	0	0	5	0	0	0	2	0	0	0	–	0	0	0	0	0.0	–

WORLD SERIES

Year	Team	W	L	PCT	ERA	G	GS	CG	IP	H	BB	SO	ShO	W	L	SV	AB	H	HR	BA	PO	A	E	DP	TC/G	FA
1982	MIL A	0	0	–	0.00	1	0	0	.2	1	2	0	0	0	0	0	0	0	0	–	0	0	0	0	0.0	–

Doyle Lade
LADE, DOYLE MARION (Porky)
B. Feb. 17, 1921, Fairbury, Neb. BR TR 5'10" 183 lbs.
BB 1946-47

Year	Team	W	L	PCT	ERA	G	GS	CG	IP	H	BB	SO	ShO	W	L	SV	AB	H	HR	BA	PO	A	E	DP	TC/G	FA
1946	CHI N	0	2	.000	4.11	3	2	0	15.1	15	3	8	0	0	0	0	5	1	0	.200	0	4	0	0	1.3	1.000
1947		11	10	.524	3.94	34	25	7	187.1	202	79	62	1	0	0	0	60	13	0	.217	10	46	1	2	1.7	.982
1948		5	6	.455	4.02	19	12	6	87.1	99	31	29	0	0	0	0	32	5	0	.156	11	19	0	1	1.6	1.000
1949		4	5	.444	5.00	36	13	5	129.2	141	58	43	0	0	0	1	32	7	0	.219	10	23	1	0	0.9	.971
1950		5	6	.455	4.74	34	12	2	117.2	126	50	36	1	2	1	2	35	10	0	.286	10	36	0	2	1.4	1.000
5 yrs.		25	29	.463	4.39	126	64	20	537.1	583	221	178	2	2	1	3	164	36	0	.220	41	128	2	5	1.4	.988

Steve Ladew
LADEW, STEPHEN
B. St. Louis, Mo. Deceased.

Year	Team	W	L	PCT	ERA	G	GS	CG	IP	H	BB	SO	ShO	W	L	SV	AB	H	HR	BA	PO	A	E	DP	TC/G	FA
1889	KC AA	0	0	–	4.50	1	0	0	2	1	3	0	0	0	0	0	4	0	0	.000	0	1	0	0	1.0	1.000

Flip Lafferty
LAFFERTY, FRANK BERNARD
B. May 4, 1854, Scranton, Pa. D. Feb. 8, 1910, Wilmington, Del. TR

Year	Team	W	L	PCT	ERA	G	GS	CG	IP	H	BB	SO	ShO	W	L	SV	AB	H	HR	BA	PO	A	E	DP	TC/G	FA
1876	PHI N	0	1	.000	0.00	1	1	1	9	5	0	0	0	0	0	0	*				1	2	1	1	4.0	.750

Year	Team		W	L	PCT	ERA	G	GS	CG	IP	H	BB	SO	ShO	Relief Pitching W	L	SV	Batting AB	H	HR	BA	PO	A	E	DP	TC/G	FA

Ed Lafitte
LAFITTE, EDWARD FRANCIS (Doc)
B. Apr. 7, 1886, New Orleans, La.   D. Apr. 12, 1971, Jenkintown, Pa.   BR TR 6'2" 188 lbs.

Year	Team		W	L	PCT	ERA	G	GS	CG	IP	H	BB	SO	ShO	W	L	SV	AB	H	HR	BA	PO	A	E	DP	TC/G	FA
1909	DET	A	0	1	.000	3.86	3	1	1	14	22	2	11	0	0	0	1	4	1	0	.250	1	4	0	0	1.7	1.000
1911			11	8	.579	3.92	29	20	15	172.1	205	52	63	0	0	1	1	70	11	1	.157	9	41	4	0	1.9	.926
1912			0	0	–	16.20	1	0	0	1.2	2	2	0	0	0	0	0	0	0	0		1	1	0	0	2.0	1.000
1914	BKN	F	16	16	.500	2.63	42	33	23	290.2	260	**127**	137	0	1	2	2	101	26	1	.257	11	101	4	3	2.8	.966
1915	2 teams		BKN	F	(17G 6–9)	BUF	F	(14G 2–2)																			
"	total		8	11	.421	3.80	31	21	8	168	179	79	51	0	0	1	1	70	16	0	.229	4	44	2	0	1.6	.960
5 yrs.			35	36	.493	3.34	106	75	47	646.2	668	262	262	0	1	4	5	245	54	2	.220	26	191	10	3	2.1	.956

Ed Lagger
LAGGER, EDWIN JOSEPH
B. July 14, 1912, Joliet, Ill.   D. Nov. 10, 1981, Joliet, Ill.   BR TR 6'3" 200 lbs.

Year	Team		W	L	PCT	ERA	G	GS	CG	IP	H	BB	SO	ShO	W	L	SV	AB	H	HR	BA	PO	A	E	DP	TC/G	FA
1934	PHI	A	0	0	–	11.00	8	0	0	18	27	14	2	0	0	0	0	6	0	0	.000	2	9	1	1	1.5	.917

Lerrin LaGrow
LaGROW, LERRIN HARRIS
B. July 8, 1948, Phoenix, Ariz.   BR TR 6'5" 220 lbs.

Year	Team		W	L	PCT	ERA	G	GS	CG	IP	H	BB	SO	ShO	W	L	SV	AB	H	HR	BA	PO	A	E	DP	TC/G	FA
1970	DET	A	0	1	.000	7.50	10	0	0	12	16	6	7	0	0	1	0	1	0	0	.000	1	1	0	0	0.2	1.000
1972			0	1	.000	1.33	16	0	0	27	22	6	9	0	0	1	0	2	0	0	–	2	4	0	0	0.4	1.000
1973			1	5	.167	4.33	21	3	0	54	54	23	33	0	0	3	3	0	0	0	–	5	11	2	0	0.9	.889
1974			8	19	.296	4.67	37	34	11	216	245	80	85	0	0	0	0	0	0	0	–	12	48	4	1	1.7	.938
1975			7	14	.333	4.38	32	26	7	164.1	183	66	75	2	0	0	0	0	0	0	–	6	17	4	3	0.8	.852
1976	STL	N	0	1	.000	1.48	8	2	1	24.1	7	7	10	0	0	0	0	5	0	0	.000	1	4	0	0	0.6	1.000
1977	CHI	A	7	3	.700	2.45	66	0	0	99	81	35	63	0	7	3	25	0	0	0	–	5	17	1	2	0.3	.957
1978			6	5	.545	4.40	52	0	0	88	85	38	41	0	6	5	16	0	0	0	–	4	20	1	3	0.5	.960
1979	2 teams		CHI	A	(11G 0–3)	LA	N	(31G 5–1)																			
"	total		5	4	.556	5.24	42	2	0	55	65	34	31	0	5	2	3	3	1	0	.333	0	8	1	0	0.2	.889
1980	PHI	N	0	2	.000	4.15	25	0	0	39	42	17	21	0	0	2	1	4	1	0	.250	1	6	0	0	0.3	1.000
10 yrs.			34	55	.382	4.11	309	67	19	778.2	814	312	375	2	18	17	54	13	2	0	.154	37	136	13	9	0.6	.930

LEAGUE CHAMPIONSHIP SERIES

Year	Team		W	L	PCT	ERA	G	GS	CG	IP	H	BB	SO	ShO	W	L	SV	AB	H	HR	BA	PO	A	E	DP	TC/G	FA
1972	DET	A	0	0	–	0.00	1	0	0	1	0	0	1	0	0	0	0	0	0	0	–	0	0	0	0	0.0	–

Jeff Lahti
LAHTI, JEFFREY ALLEN
B. Oct. 8, 1956, Oregon City, Ore.   BR TR 6' 180 lbs.

Year	Team		W	L	PCT	ERA	G	GS	CG	IP	H	BB	SO	ShO	W	L	SV	AB	H	HR	BA	PO	A	E	DP	TC/G	FA
1982	STL	N	5	4	.556	3.81	33	1	0	56.2	53	21	22	0	5	3	0	13	1	0	.077	9	15	1	1	0.8	.960
1983			3	3	.500	3.16	53	0	0	74	64	29	26	0	3	3	0	10	0	0	.000	6	14	0	3	0.4	1.000
1984			4	2	.667	3.72	63	0	0	84.2	69	34	45	0	4	2	1	6	1	0	.167	4	15	1	0	0.3	.950
1985			5	2	.714	1.84	52	0	0	68.1	63	26	41	0	5	2	19	9	0	0	.000	5	9	1	1	0.3	.933
1986			0	0	–	0.00	4	0	0	2.1	3	1	3	0	0	0	0	0	0	0	–	0	0	0	0	0.0	–
5 yrs.			17	11	.607	3.12	205	1	0	286	252	111	137	0	17	10	20	38	2	0	.053	24	53	3	6	0.4	.963

LEAGUE CHAMPIONSHIP SERIES

Year	Team		W	L	PCT	ERA	G	GS	CG	IP	H	BB	SO	ShO	W	L	SV	AB	H	HR	BA	PO	A	E	DP	TC/G	FA
1985	STL	N	1	0	1.000	0.00	2	0	0	2	0	1	0	0	1	0	0	0	0	0	–	0	0	0	0	0.0	–

WORLD SERIES

Year	Team		W	L	PCT	ERA	G	GS	CG	IP	H	BB	SO	ShO	W	L	SV	AB	H	HR	BA	PO	A	E	DP	TC/G	FA
1982	STL	N	0	0	–	10.80	2	0	0	1.2	4	1	0	0	0	0	0	0	0	0	–	0	1	0	0	0.5	1.000
1985			0	0	–	12.27	3	0	0	3.2	10	0	2	0	0	0	0	0	0	0	–	0	0	0	0	0.0	–
2 yrs.			0	0	–	11.81	5	0	0	5.1	14	1	3	0	0	0	0	0	0	0	–	0	1	0	0	0.2	1.000

Eddie Lake
LAKE, EDWARD ERVING
B. Mar. 18, 1916, Antioch, Calif.   BR TR 5'7" 159 lbs.

Year	Team		W	L	PCT	ERA	G	GS	CG	IP	H	BB	SO	ShO	W	L	SV	AB	H	HR	BA	PO	A	E	DP	TC/G	FA
1944	BOS	A	0	0	–	4.19	6	0	0	19.1	20	11	7	0	0	0	0	*				0	6	1	0	1.2	.857

Joe Lake
LAKE, JOSEPH HENRY
B. Dec. 6, 1881, Brooklyn, N. Y.   D. June 30, 1950, Brooklyn, N. Y.   BR TR 6' 185 lbs.

Year	Team		W	L	PCT	ERA	G	GS	CG	IP	H	BB	SO	ShO	W	L	SV	AB	H	HR	BA	PO	A	E	DP	TC/G	FA
1908	NY	A	9	**22**	.290	3.17	38	27	19	269.1	252	77	118	2	2	2	0	112	21	1	.188	9	64	10	1	2.2	.880
1909			14	11	.560	1.88	31	26	17	215.1	180	59	117	3	2	0	1	81	14	0	.173	3	94	10	2	3.5	.907
1910	STL	A	11	17	.393	2.20	35	29	24	261.1	243	77	141	1	1	1	2	81	21	0	.259	5	88	9	2	2.9	.912
1911			10	15	.400	3.30	30	25	14	215.1	245	40	69	2	1	1	0	80	21	1	.263	15	88	7	0	3.7	.936
1912	2 teams		STL	A	(11G 1–7)	DET	A	(26G 9–11)																			
"	total		10	18	.357	3.44	37	20	15	219.2	260	55	114	0	5	4	1	81	12	1	.148	4	73	5	1	2.2	.939
1913	DET	A	8	7	.533	3.28	28	12	6	137	149	24	35	0	4	1	1	45	12	1	.267	6	59	4	1	2.5	.942
6 yrs.			62	90	.408	2.85	199	139	95	1318	1329	332	594	8	15	9	5	480	101	3	.210	42	466	45	7	2.8	.919

Al Lakeman
LAKEMAN, ALBERT WESLEY (Moose)
B. Dec. 31, 1918, Cincinnati, Ohio   D. May 25, 1976, Spartanburg, S. C.   BR TR 6'2" 195 lbs.

Year	Team		W	L	PCT	ERA	G	GS	CG	IP	H	BB	SO	ShO	W	L	SV	AB	H	HR	BA	PO	A	E	DP	TC/G	FA
1948	PHI	N	0	0	–	13.50	1	0	0	.2	1	0	0	0	0	0	0	*				0	0	0	0	0.0	–

Jack Lamabe
LAMABE, JOHN ALEXANDER
B. Oct. 3, 1936, Farmingdale, N. Y.   BR TR 6'1" 198 lbs.

Year	Team		W	L	PCT	ERA	G	GS	CG	IP	H	BB	SO	ShO	W	L	SV	AB	H	HR	BA	PO	A	E	DP	TC/G	FA
1962	PIT	N	3	1	.750	2.88	46	0	0	78	70	40	56	0	3	1	2	9	0	0	.000	3	17	0	1	0.4	1.000
1963	BOS	A	7	4	.636	3.15	65	2	0	151.1	139	46	93	0	7	3	6	32	3	1	.094	11	26	1	0	0.6	.974
1964			9	13	.409	5.89	39	25	3	177.1	209	57	109	0	1	2	1	52	6	0	.115	12	26	3	1	1.1	.927
1965	2 teams		BOS	A	(14G 0–3)	HOU	N	(3G 0–2)																			
"	total		0	5	.000	6.87	17	2	0	38	51	17	23	0	0	3	0	8	1	0	.125	2	7	0	1	0.5	1.000
1966	CHI	A	7	9	.438	3.93	34	17	3	121.1	116	35	67	0	2	0	0	35	2	0	.057	13	16	0	0	0.9	1.000
1967	3 teams		CHI	A	(3G 1–0)	NY	N	(16G 0–3)	STL	N	(23G 3–4)																
"	total		4	7	.364	3.20	42	3	1	84.1	79	19	56	0	3	5	5	15	2	0	.133	5	13	1	0	0.5	.947
1968	CHI	N	3	2	.600	4.30	42	0	0	60.2	68	24	30	0	3	2	1	5	1	0	.200	3	8	0	1	0.3	1.000
7 yrs.			33	41	.446	4.24	285	49	7	711	753	238	434	3	19	16	15	156	15	1	.096	49	113	5	4	0.6	.970

WORLD SERIES

Year	Team		W	L	PCT	ERA	G	GS	CG	IP	H	BB	SO	ShO	W	L	SV	AB	H	HR	BA	PO	A	E	DP	TC/G	FA
1967	STL	N	0	1	.000	6.75	3	0	0	2.2	5	0	4	0	0	1	0	0	0	0	–	1	0	1	0	0.3	1.000

Year	Team	W	L	PCT	ERA	G	GS	CG	IP	H	BB	SO	ShO	Relief Pitching W	L	SV	Batting AB	H	HR	BA	PO	A	E	DP	TC/G	FA

Al LaMacchia

LaMACCHIA, ALFRED ANTHONY
B. July 22, 1921, St. Louis, Mo.

BR TR 5'10½" 190 lbs.

Year	Team	W	L	PCT	ERA	G	GS	CG	IP	H	BB	SO	ShO	W	L	SV	AB	H	HR	BA	PO	A	E	DP	TC/G	FA
1943	STL A	0	1	.000	11.25	1	1	0	4	9	2	2	0	0	0	0	2	0	0	.000	0	1	0	0	0.0	—
1945		2	0	1.000	2.00	5	0	0	9	6	3	2	0	2	0	0	1	0	0	.000	0	2	0	0	0.4	1.000
1946	2 teams			STL A	(8G 0-0)			WAS A	(2G 0-1)																		
"	total	0	1	—	7.64	10	0	0	17.2	23	9	3	0	0	1	0	3	0	0	.000	1	1	0	0	0.2	1.000
	3 yrs.	2	2	.500	6.46	16	1	0	30.2	38	14	7	0	2	1	0	6	0	0	.000	1	3	0	0	0.3	1.000

Frank LaManna

LaMANNA, FRANK (Hank)
B. Aug. 22, 1919, Watertown, Pa. D. Sept. 1, 1980, Syracuse, N. Y.

BR TR 6'2½" 195 lbs.

Year	Team	W	L	PCT	ERA	G	GS	CG	IP	H	BB	SO	ShO	W	L	SV	AB	H	HR	BA	PO	A	E	DP	TC/G	FA
1940	BOS N	1	0	1.000	4.73	5	1	0	13.1	13	8	3	0	0	0	0	5	1	0	.200	2	2	1	1	1.0	.800
1941		5	4	.556	5.33	35	4	0	72.2	77	56	23	0	4	2	1	32	9	0	.281	2	20	1	1	0.7	.957
1942		0	1	.000	5.40	5	0	0	6.2	5	3	2	0	0	1	0	2	0	0	.000	0	1	0	0	0.2	1.000
	3 yrs.	6	5	.545	5.24	45	5	1	92.2	95	67	28	0	4	3	1	39	10	0	.256	4	23	2	2	0.6	.931

Frank Lamanske

LAMANSKE, FRANK JAMES (Lefty)
B. Sept. 30, 1906, Oglesby, Ill. D. Aug. 4, 1971, Olney, Ill.

BL TL 5'11" 170 lbs.

Year	Team	W	L	PCT	ERA	G	GS	CG	IP	H	BB	SO	ShO	W	L	SV	AB	H	HR	BA	PO	A	E	DP	TC/G	FA
1935	BKN N	0	0	—	7.36	2	0	0	3.2	5	1	1	0	0	0	0	0	0	0	.000	1	0	0	0	1.0	1.000

Wayne LaMaster

LaMASTER, WAYNE LEE
B. Feb. 13, 1907, Speed, Ind.

BL TL 5'8" 170 lbs.

Year	Team	W	L	PCT	ERA	G	GS	CG	IP	H	BB	SO	ShO	W	L	SV	AB	H	HR	BA	PO	A	E	DP	TC/G	FA
1937	PHI N	15	19	.441	5.31	50	30	10	220.1	255	82	135	1	3	4	4	79	15	0	.190	10	23	4	1	0.7	.892
1938	2 teams			PHI N	(18G 4-7)			BKN N	(3G 0-1)																		
"	total	4	8	.333	7.32	21	12	1	75	97	34	38	1	0	2	0	28	10	0	.357	7	15	0	1	1.0	1.000
	2 yrs.	19	27	.413	5.82	71	42	11	295.1	352	116	173	2	3	6	4	107	25	0	.234	17	38	4	2	0.8	.932

John Lamb

LAMB, JOHN ANDREW
B. July 20, 1946, Sharon, Conn.

BR TR 6'3" 180 lbs.

Year	Team	W	L	PCT	ERA	G	GS	CG	IP	H	BB	SO	ShO	W	L	SV	AB	H	HR	BA	PO	A	E	DP	TC/G	FA
1970	PIT N	0	1	.000	2.81	23	0	0	32	23	13	24	0	0	1	3	3	0	0	.000	0	2	0	0	0.1	1.000
1971		0	0	—	0.00	2	0	0	4	3	1	1	0	0	0	0	1	0	0	.000	0	1	0	0	0.5	1.000
1973		0	1	.000	6.07	22	0	0	29.2	37	10	11	0	0	1	2	3	0	0	.000	3	5	0	0	0.4	1.000
	3 yrs.	0	2	.000	4.11	47	0	0	65.2	63	24	36	0	0	2	5	7	0	0	.000	3	8	0	0	0.2	1.000

Ray Lamb

LAMB, RAYMOND RICHARD
B. Dec. 28, 1944, Glendale, Calif.

BR TR 6'1" 170 lbs.

Year	Team	W	L	PCT	ERA	G	GS	CG	IP	H	BB	SO	ShO	W	L	SV	AB	H	HR	BA	PO	A	E	DP	TC/G	FA
1969	LA N	0	0	.000	1.80	10	0	0	15	12	7	11	0	0	0	1	1	0	0	.000	2	3	0	0	0.5	1.000
1970		6	1	.857	3.79	35	0	0	57	59	27	32	0	6	1	0	4	0	0	.000	3	3	0	1	0.2	1.000
1971	CLE A	6	12	.333	3.36	43	21	3	158	147	69	91	1	0	2	1	43	4	0	.093	6	19	2	0	0.6	.926
1972		5	6	.455	3.08	34	9	0	108	101	29	64	0	4	1	0	21	0	0	.000	2	13	1	0	0.5	.938
1973		3	3	.500	4.60	32	1	0	86	98	42	60	0	3	2	2	0	0	0	—	5	10	1	1	0.5	.938
	5 yrs.	20	23	.465	3.54	154	31	3	424	417	174	258	1	13	7	4	69	4	0	.058	18	48	4	2	0.5	.943

Clay Lambert

LAMBERT, CLAYTON PATRICK
B. Mar. 26, 1917, Summit, Ill. D. Apr. 3, 1981, Ogden, Utah

BR TR 6'2" 185 lbs.

Year	Team	W	L	PCT	ERA	G	GS	CG	IP	H	BB	SO	ShO	W	L	SV	AB	H	HR	BA	PO	A	E	DP	TC/G	FA
1946	CIN N	2	2	.500	4.27	23	4	2	52.2	48	20	20	0	1	1	1	13	2	0	.154	1	6	0	0	0.3	1.000
1947		0	0	—	15.88	3	0	0	5.2	12	6	1	0	0	0	0	1	0	0	.000	0	2	0	0	0.7	1.000
	2 yrs.	2	2	.500	5.40	26	4	2	58.1	60	26	21	0	1	1	1	14	2	0	.143	1	8	0	0	0.3	1.000

Gene Lambert

LAMBERT, EUGENE MARION
B. Apr. 26, 1921, Crenshaw, Miss.

BR TR 5'11" 175 lbs.

Year	Team	W	L	PCT	ERA	G	GS	CG	IP	H	BB	SO	ShO	W	L	SV	AB	H	HR	BA	PO	A	E	DP	TC/G	FA
1941	PHI N	0	1	.000	2.00	2	1	0	9	11	2	3	0	0	0	0	2	0	0	.000	0	1	0	0	0.5	1.000
1942		0	0	—	9.00	1	0	0	1	3	0	1	0	0	0	0	0	0	0	—	0	1	0	0	1.0	1.000
	2 yrs.	0	1	.000	2.70	3	1	0	10	14	2	4	0	0	0	0	2	0	0	.000	0	2	0	0	0.7	1.000

Otis Lambeth

LAMBETH, OTIS SAMUEL
B. May 13, 1890, Berlin, Kans. D. June 5, 1976, Moran, Kans.

BR TR 6' 175 lbs.

Year	Team	W	L	PCT	ERA	G	GS	CG	IP	H	BB	SO	ShO	W	L	SV	AB	H	HR	BA	PO	A	E	DP	TC/G	FA
1916	CLE A	4	3	.571	2.92	15	9	3	74	69	38	28	0	1	0	1	27	3	0	.111	2	14	3	1	1.3	.842
1917		7	6	.538	3.14	26	10	2	97.1	97	30	27	0	3	3	2	32	6	0	.188	6	23	3	1	1.2	.906
1918		0	0	—	6.43	2	0	0	7	10	6	3	0	0	0	0	1	1	0	1.000	0	2	0	0	1.0	1.000
	3 yrs.	11	9	.550	3.18	43	19	5	178.1	176	74	58	0	4	3	3	60	10	0	.167	8	39	6	2	1.2	.887

Fred Lamline

LAMLINE, FREDERICK ARTHUR (Dutch)
Born Frederick Arthur Lamlein.
B. Aug. 14, 1887, Port Huron, Mich. D. Sept. 20, 1970, Port Huron, Mich.

BR TR 5'11" 171 lbs.

Year	Team	W	L	PCT	ERA	G	GS	CG	IP	H	BB	SO	ShO	W	L	SV	AB	H	HR	BA	PO	A	E	DP	TC/G	FA
1912	CHI A	0	0	—	31.50	1	0	0	2	7	2	1	0	0	0	0	0	0	0	—	0	1	0	0	1.0	1.000
1915	STL N	0	0	—	2.84	4	0	0	19	21	3	11	0	0	0	0	8	1	0	.125	0	5	0	0	1.3	1.000
	2 yrs.	0	0	—	5.57	5	0	0	21	28	5	12	0	0	0	0	8	1	0	.125	0	6	0	0	1.2	1.000

Dennis Lamp

LAMP, DENNIS PATRICK
B. Sept. 23, 1952, Los Angeles, Calif.

BR TR 6'4" 200 lbs.

Year	Team	W	L	PCT	ERA	G	GS	CG	IP	H	BB	SO	ShO	W	L	SV	AB	H	HR	BA	PO	A	E	DP	TC/G	FA
1977	CHI N	0	2	.000	6.30	11	3	0	30	43	8	12	0	0	1	0	8	3	0	.375	1	8	1	0	0.9	.900
1978		7	15	.318	3.29	37	36	6	224	221	56	73	3	0	0	0	73	15	0	.205	18	51	1	1	1.9	.986
1979		11	10	.524	3.51	38	32	6	200	223	46	86	1	0	0	0	58	9	0	.155	17	45	3	3	1.7	.954
1980		10	14	.417	5.19	41	37	2	203	259	82	83	1	1	2	0	61	6	0	.098	8	47	2	3	1.4	.965
1981	CHI A	7	6	.538	2.41	27	10	3	127	103	43	71	0	3	1	0	0	0	0	—	5	23	1	4	1.1	.966
1982		11	8	.579	3.99	44	27	3	189.2	206	59	78	2	1	1	5	0	0	0	—	9	39	5	1	1.2	.906
1983		7	7	.500	3.71	49	5	1	116.1	123	29	44	0	4	5	15	0	0	0	—	9	16	0	2	0.5	1.000
1984	TOR A	8	8	.500	4.55	56	4	0	85	97	38	45	0	5	7	9	0	0	0	—	9	15	2	3	0.5	.923
1985		11	0	1.000	3.32	53	1	0	105.2	96	27	68	0	11	0	2	0	0	0	—	11	21	0	3	0.6	1.000
1986		2	6	.250	5.05	40	2	0	73	93	23	30	0	2	4	2	0	0	0	—	5	11	1	2	0.4	.941
1987	OAK A	1	3	.250	5.08	36	5	0	56.2	76	22	36	0	0	0	0	0	0	0	—	1	9	0	0	0.3	1.000

Year	Team		W	L	PCT	ERA	G	GS	CG	IP	H	BB	SO	ShO	Relief Pitching W	L	SV	Batting AB	H	HR	BA	PO	A	E	DP	TC/G	FA

Dennis Lamp *continued*

1988	BOS	A	7	6	.538	3.48	46	0	0	82.2	92	19	49	0	7	6	0	0	0	0	–	5	18	1	0	0.5	.958
1989			4	2	.667	2.32	42	0	0	112.1	96	27	61	0	4	2	2	0	0	0	–	12	20	0	3	0.8	1.000
13 yrs.			86	87	.497	3.81	520	162	21	1605.1	1728	479	736	7	38	29	35	200	33	0	.165	110	323	17	25	0.9	.962

LEAGUE CHAMPIONSHIP SERIES

1983	CHI	A	0	0	–	0.00	3	0	0	2	0	2	1	0	0	0	0	0	0	0	–	0	0	0	0	0.0	
1985	TOR	A	0	0	–	0.00	3	0	0	9.1	2	1	10	0	0	0	0	0	0	0	–	0	0	0	0	0.0	–
2 yrs.			0	0	–	0.00	6	0	0	11.1	2	3	11	0	0	0	0	0	0	0	–	0	0	0	0	0.0	–

Henry Lampe

LAMPE, HENRY JOSEPH
B. Sept. 19, 1872, Boston, Mass. D. Sept. 16, 1936, Dorchester, Mass.
BR TL 5'11½" 175 lbs.

1894	BOS	N	0	1	.000	11.81	2	1	0	5.1	17	7	1	0	0	0	0	2	0	0	.000	1	2	1	0	2.0	.750
1895	PHI	N	0	2	.000	7.57	7	3	2	44	68	33	18	0	0	0	0	16	2	0	.125	1	11	4	0	2.3	.750
2 yrs.			0	3	.000	8.03	9	4	2	49.1	85	40	19	0	0	0	0	18	2	0	.111	2	13	5	0	2.2	.750

Dick Lanahan

LANAHAN, RICHARD ANTHONY
B. Sept. 27, 1911, Washington, D. C. D. Mar. 12, 1975, Rochester, Minn.
BL TL 6' 186 lbs.

1935	WAS	A	0	3	.000	5.66	3	3	0	20.2	27	17	10	0	0	0	0	6	1	0	.167	0	4	0	0	1.3	1.000
1937			0	1	.000	12.71	6	1	0	11.1	16	13	2	0	0	0	0	1	0	0	.000	1	4	0	0	0.8	1.000
1940	PIT	N	6	8	.429	4.25	40	8	4	108	121	42	45	0	2	6	2	34	4	0	.118	3	22	1	3	0.7	.962
1941			0	1	.000	5.25	7	0	0	12	13	3	5	0	0	1	0	1	0	0	.000	0	2	0	0	0.3	1.000
4 yrs.			6	13	.316	5.15	56	13	4	152	177	75	62	0	2	7	2	42	5	0	.119	4	32	1	3	0.7	.973

Les Lancaster

LANCASTER, LESTER WAYNE
B. Apr. 21, 1962, Dallas, Tex.
BR TR 6'2" 200 lbs.

1987	CHI	N	8	3	.727	4.90	27	18	0	132.1	138	51	78	0	1	0	0	49	4	0	.082	12	14	0	0	1.0	1.000
1988			4	6	.400	3.78	44	3	1	85.2	89	34	36	0	3	6	5	20	1	0	.050	6	17	0	0	0.5	1.000
1989			4	2	.667	1.36	42	0	0	72.2	60	15	56	0	4	2	8	11	2	0	.182	8	5	0	1	0.3	1.000
3 yrs.			16	11	.593	3.68	113	21	1	290.2	287	100	170	0	8	8	13	80	7	0	.088	26	36	0	1	0.5	1.000

LEAGUE CHAMPIONSHIP SERIES

| 1989 | CHI | N | 1 | 1 | .500 | 6.00 | 3 | 0 | 0 | 6 | 6 | 1 | 3 | 0 | 1 | 1 | 0 | 1 | 0 | 0 | .000 | 0 | 1 | 0 | 0 | 0.3 | 1.000 |

Gary Lance

LANCE, GARY DEAN
B. Sept. 21, 1948, Greenville, S. C.
BB TR 6'3" 195 lbs.

| 1977 | KC | A | 0 | 1 | .000 | 4.50 | 1 | 0 | 0 | 2 | 2 | 2 | 2 | 0 | 0 | 1 | 0 | 0 | 0 | 0 | – | 0 | 0 | 0 | 0 | 0.0 | – |

Bill Landis

LANDIS, WILLIAM HENRY
B. Oct. 8, 1942, Hanford, Calif.
BL TL 6'2" 178 lbs.

1963	KC	A	0	0	–	0.00	1	0	0	1.2	0	1	3	0	0	0	0	0	0	0	–	0	0	0	0	0.0	–
1967	BOS	A	1	0	1.000	5.26	18	1	0	25.2	24	11	23	0	1	0	0	2	0	0	.000	0	1	0	0	0.1	1.000
1968			3	3	.500	3.15	38	1	0	60	48	30	59	0	3	3	3	6	0	0	.000	2	3	0	0	0.1	1.000
1969			5	5	.500	5.25	45	5	0	82.1	82	49	50	0	4	3	1	11	0	0	.000	2	16	2	0	0.4	.900
4 yrs.			9	8	.529	4.46	102	7	0	169.2	154	91	135	0	8	5	4	19	0	0	.000	4	20	2	0	0.3	.923

Doc Landis

LANDIS, SAMUEL H.
B. Aug. 16, 1854, Philadelphia, Pa. Deceased.
5'11" 172 lbs.

| 1882 | 2 teams | PHI AA (2G 1–1) | | | | | | BAL AA (42G 11–27) | | | | | | | | | | | | | | | | | | |
| " | total | | 12 | 28 | .300 | 3.32 | 44 | 41 | 37 | 358 | 425 | 47 | 75 | 0 | 0 | 0 | 0 | 187 | 31 | 0 | .166 | 19 | 105 | 14 | 3 | 3.1 | .899 |

Larry Landreth

LANDRETH, LARRY ROBERT
B. Mar. 11, 1955, Stratford, Ontario, Canada
BR TR 6'1" 175 lbs.

1976	MON	N	1	2	.333	4.09	3	3	0	11	13	10	7	0	0	0	0	3	0	0	.000	0	1	0	0	0.3	1.000
1977			0	2	.000	10.00	4	1	0	9	16	8	5	0	0	1	0	2	0	0	.000	0	0	0	0	0.0	–
2 yrs.			1	4	.200	6.75	7	4	0	20	29	18	12	0	0	1	0	5	0	0	.000	0	1	0	0	0.1	1.000

Bill Landrum

LANDRUM, THOMAS WILLIAM
Son of Joe Landrum.
B. Aug. 17, 1957, Columbia, S. C.
BR TR 6'2" 185 lbs.

1986	CIN	N	0	0	–	6.75	10	0	0	13.1	23	4	14	0	0	0	0	2	0	0	.000	0	1	0	0	0.1	1.000
1987			3	2	.600	4.71	44	2	0	65	68	34	42	0	3	1	2	5	1	0	.200	3	12	0	4	0.3	1.000
1988	CHI	N	1	0	1.000	5.84	7	0	0	12.1	19	3	6	0	1	0	0	2	0	0	.000	2	0	0	0	0.3	1.000
1989	PIT	N	2	3	.400	1.67	56	0	0	81	60	28	51	0	2	3	26	3	0	0	.000	8	10	0	0	0.3	1.000
4 yrs.			6	5	.545	3.51	117	2	0	171.2	170	69	113	0	6	4	28	12	1	0	.083	13	23	0	4	0.3	1.000

Joe Landrum

LANDRUM, JOSEPH BUTLER
Father of Bill Landrum.
B. Dec. 13, 1928, Columbia, S. C.
BR TR 5'11" 180 lbs.

1950	BKN	N	0	0	–	8.10	7	0	0	6.2	12	1	5	0	0	0	1	0	0	0	–	1	3	0	0	0.6	1.000
1952			1	3	.250	5.21	9	5	2	38	46	10	17	0	0	0	0	8	1	0	.125	4	5	1	0	1.1	.900
2 yrs.			1	3	.250	5.64	16	5	2	44.2	58	11	22	0	0	0	1	8	1	0	.125	5	8	1	0	0.9	.929

Jerry Lane

LANE, JERALD HAL
B. Feb. 7, 1926, Ashland, N. Y. D. July 24, 1988, Chattanooga, Tenn.
BR TR 6'½" 205 lbs.

1953	WAS	A	1	4	.200	4.92	20	2	0	56.2	64	16	26	0	1	2	0	9	1	0	.111	1	8	0	0	0.5	1.000
1954	CIN	N	1	0	1.000	1.69	3	0	0	10.2	9	3	2	0	1	0	1	4	0	0	.000	0	0	0	0	0.0	–
1955			0	2	.000	4.91	8	0	0	11	11	6	5	0	0	2	1	0	0	0	–	1	3	0	0	0.5	1.000
3 yrs.			2	6	.250	4.48	31	2	0	78.1	84	25	33	0	2	4	1	13	1	0	.077	2	11	0	0	0.4	1.000

Year	Team	W	L	PCT	ERA	G	GS	CG	IP	H	BB	SO	ShO	Relief Pitching W	L	SV	Batting AB	H	HR	BA	PO	A	E	DP	TC/G	FA

Sam Lanford

LANFORD, LEWIS GROVER
B. Jan. 8, 1886, Woodruff, S. C.   D. Sept. 14, 1970, Woodruff, S. C.
BL TR 5'9"   155 lbs.

Year	Team	W	L	PCT	ERA	G	GS	CG	IP	H	BB	SO	ShO	W	L	SV	AB	H	HR	BA	PO	A	E	DP	TC/G	FA
1907	WAS A	0	1	.000	5.14	2	1	0	7	10	5	2	0	0	0	0	3	1	0	.333	0	2	1	0	1.5	.667

Walt Lanfranconi

LANFRANCONI, WALTER OSWALD
B. Nov. 9, 1916, Barre, Vt.   D. Aug. 18, 1986, Barre, Vt.
BR TR 5'7½"   155 lbs.

Year	Team	W	L	PCT	ERA	G	GS	CG	IP	H	BB	SO	ShO	W	L	SV	AB	H	HR	BA	PO	A	E	DP	TC/G	FA
1941	CHI N	0	1	.000	3.00	2	1	0	6	7	2	1	0	0	0	0	1	0	0	.000	0	1	0	0	0.5	1.000
1947	BOS N	4	4	.500	2.95	36	4	1	64	65	27	18	0	3	0	1	10	0	0	.000	1	20	0	0	0.6	1.000
2 yrs.		4	5	.444	2.96	38	5	1	70	72	29	19	0	3	0	1	11	0	0	.000	1	21	0	0	0.6	1.000

Chip Lang

LANG, ROBERT DAVID
B. Aug. 21, 1952, Pittsburgh, Pa.
BR TR 6'4"   210 lbs.

Year	Team	W	L	PCT	ERA	G	GS	CG	IP	H	BB	SO	ShO	W	L	SV	AB	H	HR	BA	PO	A	E	DP	TC/G	FA
1975	MON N	0	0	–	9.00	1	0	0	2	3	3	2	0	0	0	0	0	0	0	–	0	0	0	0	0.0	–
1976		1	3	.250	4.19	29	2	0	62.1	56	34	30	0	1	1	0	6	1	0	.167	6	10	1	1	0.6	.941
2 yrs.		1	3	.250	4.34	30	3	0	64.1	58	37	32	0	1	1	0	6	1	0	.167	6	10	1	1	0.6	.941

Marty Lang

LANG, MARTIN JOHN (Lefty)
B. Sept. 27, 1905, Hooper, Neb.   D. Jan. 13, 1968, Lakewood, Colo.
BR TL 5'11"   160 lbs.

Year	Team	W	L	PCT	ERA	G	GS	CG	IP	H	BB	SO	ShO	W	L	SV	AB	H	HR	BA	PO	A	E	DP	TC/G	FA
1930	PIT N	0	0	–	54.00	2	0	0	1.2	9	3	2	0	0	0	0	0	0	0	–	0	0	0	0	0.0	–

Dick Lange

LANGE, RICHARD OTTO
B. Sept. 1, 1948, Harbor Beach, Mich.
BR TR 5'10"   185 lbs.

Year	Team	W	L	PCT	ERA	G	GS	CG	IP	H	BB	SO	ShO	W	L	SV	AB	H	HR	BA	PO	A	E	DP	TC/G	FA
1972	CAL A	0	0	–	4.50	2	1	0	8	7	2	8	0	0	0	0	3	0	0	.000	0	2	0	0	1.0	1.000
1973		2	1	.667	4.44	17	4	1	52.2	61	21	27	0	1	0	0	0	0	0	–	3	7	0	2	0.6	1.000
1974		3	8	.273	3.79	21	18	1	114	111	47	57	0	0	0	0	0	0	0	–	5	11	1	1	0.8	.941
1975		4	6	.400	5.21	30	8	1	102	119	53	45	0	2	2	1	0	0	0	–	6	13	0	2	0.6	1.000
4 yrs.		9	15	.375	4.46	70	31	3	276.2	298	123	137	0	3	2	1	3	0	0	.000	14	33	1	5	0.7	.979

Erv Lange

LANGE, ERWIN HENRY
B. Aug. 12, 1887, Forest Park Ill.   D. Apr. 24, 1971, Maywood, Ill.
BR TR 5'10"   170 lbs.

Year	Team	W	L	PCT	ERA	G	GS	CG	IP	H	BB	SO	ShO	W	L	SV	AB	H	HR	BA	PO	A	E	DP	TC/G	FA
1914	CHI F	12	10	.545	2.23	36	22	10	190	162	55	87	2	3	1	2	51	9	0	.176	4	43	5	3	1.4	.904

Frank Lange

LANGE, FRANK HERMAN (Seagan)
B. Oct. 28, 1883, Columbus, Wis.   D. Dec. 26, 1945, Madison, Wis.
BR TR 5'11"   180 lbs.

Year	Team	W	L	PCT	ERA	G	GS	CG	IP	H	BB	SO	ShO	W	L	SV	AB	H	HR	BA	PO	A	E	DP	TC/G	FA
1910	CHI A	9	4	.692	1.65	23	15	6	130.2	93	54	98	1	1	0	0	51	13	0	.255	5	29	5	1	1.7	.872
1911		8	8	.500	3.23	29	22	8	161.2	151	77	104	1	0	1	0	76	22	0	.289	7	41	9	2	2.0	.842
1912		10	10	.500	3.27	31	21	11	165.1	165	68	96	2	3	1	3	65	14	0	.215	6	42	5	1	1.7	.906
1913		1	3	.250	4.87	12	3	0	40.2	46	20	20	0	0	1	0	18	3	0	.167	1	17	0	3	1.5	1.000
4 yrs.		28	25	.528	2.96	95	61	25	498.1	455	219	318	4	4	3	3	*				19	129	19	7	1.8	.886

Rick Langford

LANGFORD, JAMES RICK
B. Mar. 20, 1952, Farmville, Va.
BR TR 6'   180 lbs.

Year	Team	W	L	PCT	ERA	G	GS	CG	IP	H	BB	SO	ShO	W	L	SV	AB	H	HR	BA	PO	A	E	DP	TC/G	FA
1976	PIT N	0	1	.000	6.26	12	1	0	23	27	14	17	0	0	1	0	5	1	0	.200	2	4	0	1	0.5	1.000
1977	OAK A	8	19	.296	4.02	37	31	6	208	223	73	141	1	1	0	0	0	0	0	–	23	29	0	3	1.4	1.000
1978		7	13	.350	3.43	37	24	4	175.2	169	56	92	2	1	1	0	0	0	0	–	27	23	0	1	1.4	1.000
1979		12	16	.429	4.27	34	29	14	219	233	57	101	1	1	0	0	0	0	0	–	26	36	0	3	1.8	1.000
1980		19	12	.613	3.26	35	33	**28**	**290**	276	64	102	2	1	0	0	0	0	0	–	28	45	1	1	2.1	.986
1981		12	10	.545	3.00	24	24	**18**	195	190	58	84	2	0	0	0	0	0	0	–	16	23	3	3	1.8	.929
1982		11	16	.407	4.21	32	31	15	237.1	265	49	79	2	0	0	0	1	0	0	.000	15	39	2	3	1.8	.964
1983		0	4	.000	12.15	7	7	0	20	43	10	2	0	0	0	0	0	0	0	–	1	2	0	0	0.4	1.000
1984		0	0	–	8.31	3	1	0	8.2	15	2	2	0	0	0	0	0	0	0	–	0	0	0	0	0.0	–
1985		3	5	.375	3.51	23	3	0	59	60	15	21	0	3	3	0	0	0	0	–	2	5	0	0	0.5	1.000
1986		1	10	.091	7.36	16	11	0	55	69	18	30	0	0	2	0	0	0	0	–	5	1	0	0	0.4	1.000
11 yrs.		73	106	.408	4.01	260	195	85	1490.2	1570	416	671	10	7	7	0	6	1	0	.167	145	211	6	17	1.4	.983

DIVISIONAL PLAYOFF SERIES

Year	Team	W	L	PCT	ERA	G	GS	CG	IP	H	BB	SO	ShO	W	L	SV	AB	H	HR	BA	PO	A	E	DP	TC/G	FA
1981	OAK A	1	0	1.000	1.23	1	1	0	7.1	10	0	3	0	0	0	0	0	0	0	–	0	0	0	0	0.0	–

Mark Langston

LANGSTON, MARK EDWARD
B. Aug. 20, 1960, San Diego, Calif.
BB TL 6'2"   175 lbs.

Year	Team	W	L	PCT	ERA	G	GS	CG	IP	H	BB	SO	ShO	W	L	SV	AB	H	HR	BA	PO	A	E	DP	TC/G	FA
1984	SEA A	17	10	.630	3.40	35	33	5	225	188	**118**	**204**	2	1	0	0	0	0	0	–	15	30	2	2	1.3	.957
1985		7	14	.333	5.47	24	24	2	126.2	122	91	72	0	0	0	0	0	0	0	–	9	26	2	4	1.5	.946
1986		12	14	.462	4.85	37	36	9	239.1	234	123	**245**	0	0	0	0	0	0	0	–	7	27	6	3	1.1	.850
1987		19	13	.594	3.84	35	35	14	272	242	114	**262**	3	0	0	0	0	0	0	–	8	41	2	3	1.5	.961
1988		15	11	.577	3.34	35	35	9	261.1	222	110	235	3	0	0	0	0	0	0	–	11	45	4	6	1.7	.933
1989	2 teams	SEA A	(10G 4–5)		MON N	(24G 12–9)																				
"	total	16	14	.533	2.74	34	34	8	250	198	112	235	5	0	0	0	64	11	0	.172	15	28	2	2	1.3	.956
6 yrs.		86	76	.531	3.80	200	197	47	1374.1	1206	668	1253	13	1	0	0	64	11	0	.172	65	197	18	20	1.4	.936

Max Lanier

LANIER, HUBERT MAX
Father of Hal Lanier.
B. Aug. 18, 1915, Denton, N. C.
BR TL 5'11"   180 lbs.

Year	Team	W	L	PCT	ERA	G	GS	CG	IP	H	BB	SO	ShO	W	L	SV	AB	H	HR	BA	PO	A	E	DP	TC/G	FA
1938	STL N	0	3	.000	4.20	18	3	1	45	57	28	14	0	0	2	0	10	1	0	.100	3	9	2	1	0.8	.857
1939		2	1	.667	2.39	7	6	2	37.2	29	13	14	0	0	0	0	14	4	0	.286	1	6	0	0	1.0	1.000
1940		9	6	.600	3.34	35	11	4	105	113	38	49	2	5	3	3	30	6	0	.200	5	26	3	1	1.0	.912
1941		10	8	.556	2.82	35	18	8	153	126	59	93	2	5	3	2	52	10	0	.192	10	37	0	2	1.3	1.000
1942		13	8	.619	2.98	34	20	8	160	137	60	93	2	5	2	2	47	12	0	.255	5	38	2	1	1.3	.956
1943		15	7	.682	1.90	32	25	14	213.1	195	75	123	2	2	0	3	73	12	0	.164	8	43	1	2	1.6	.981
1944		17	12	.586	2.65	33	30	16	224.1	192	71	141	5	3	0	1	77	14	0	.182	8	39	3	3	1.5	.940
1945		2	2	.500	1.73	4	3	3	26	22	8	16	0	1	0	0	11	2	0	.182	2	4	0	0	1.0	1.000
1946		6	0	1.000	1.93	6	6	4	56	45	19	36	2	0	0	0	25	5	0	.200	1	10	0	1	1.8	1.000

Year	Team	W	L	PCT	ERA	G	GS	CG	IP	H	BB	SO	ShO	Relief Pitching W	L	SV	Batting AB	H	HR	BA	PO	A	E	DP	TC/G	FA

Max Lanier *continued*

Year	Team	W	L	PCT	ERA	G	GS	CG	IP	H	BB	SO	ShO	W	L	SV	AB	H	HR	BA	PO	A	E	DP	TC/G	FA
1949		5	4	.556	3.82	15	15	4	92	92	35	37	1	0	0	0	27	2	0	.074	2	12	0	2	0.9	1.000
1950		11	9	.550	3.13	27	27	10	181.1	173	68	89	2	0	0	0	68	11	0	.162	12	31	1	2	1.6	.977
1951		11	9	.550	3.26	31	23	9	160	149	50	59	2	1	0	1	53	8	0	.151	9	28	2	5	1.3	.949
1952	NY N	7	12	.368	3.94	37	16	6	137	124	65	47	1	2	3	5	41	11	0	.268	13	37	3	4	1.4	.943
1953	2 teams	NY N	(3G 0–0)		STL A	(10G 0–1)																				
"	total	0	1	.000	7.16	13	1	0	27.2	36	22	10	0	0	0	0	7	1	0	.143	1	4	0	1	0.4	1.000
14 yrs.		108	82	.568	3.01	327	204	91	1618.1	1490	611	821	21	20	12	17	535	99	0	.185	78	324	17	25	1.3	.959

WORLD SERIES

Year	Team	W	L	PCT	ERA	G	GS	CG	IP	H	BB	SO	ShO	W	L	SV	AB	H	HR	BA	PO	A	E	DP	TC/G	FA
1942	STL N	1	0	1.000	0.00	2	0	0	4	3	1	1	0	1	0	0	1	1	0	1.000	0	1	2	0	1.5	.333
1943		0	1	.000	1.76	3	2	0	15.1	13	3	13	0	0	0	0	4	1	0	.250	1	3	1	0	1.3	.750
1944		1	0	1.000	2.19	2	2	0	12.1	8	8	11	0	0	0	0	4	2	0	.500	1	1	0	1	1.0	1.000
3 yrs.		2	1	.667	1.71	7	4	0	31.2	24	12	25	0	1	0	0	9	4	0	.444	1	5	3	1	1.3	.667

Johnny Lanning

LANNING, JOHN YOUNG (Tobacco Chewin' Johnny)
Brother of Tom Lanning.
B. Sept. 6, 1910, Asheville, N. C.
BR TR 6'1" 185 lbs.

Year	Team	W	L	PCT	ERA	G	GS	CG	IP	H	BB	SO	ShO	W	L	SV	AB	H	HR	BA	PO	A	E	DP	TC/G	FA
1936	BOS N	7	11	.389	3.65	28	20	3	153	154	55	33	1	1	1	0	52	7	1	.135	8	28	3	1	1.4	.923
1937		5	7	.417	3.93	32	11	4	116.2	107	40	37	1	2	0	2	33	4	0	.121	7	23	0	3	0.9	1.000
1938		8	7	.533	3.72	32	18	4	138	146	52	39	1	3	1	0	48	9	0	.188	7	24	3	3	1.1	.912
1939		5	6	.455	3.42	37	6	3	129	120	53	45	0	3	4	4	42	6	0	.143	12	25	3	0	1.1	.925
1940	PIT N	8	4	.667	4.05	38	7	2	115.2	119	39	42	0	5	2	2	35	7	0	.200	8	22	3	2	0.9	.909
1941		11	11	.500	3.13	34	23	9	175.2	175	47	41	0	3	2	1	56	6	0	.107	12	41	0	2	1.6	1.000
1942		6	8	.429	3.32	34	8	2	119.1	125	26	31	0	4	2	1	29	4	0	.138	13	20	1	4	1.0	.971
1943		4	1	.800	2.33	12	2	0	27	23	9	11	0	4	0	2	6	1	0	.167	1	3	2	0	0.5	.667
1945		0	0	–	36.00	1	0	0	2	8	0	0	0	0	0	0				–	0	1	0	0	1.0	1.000
1946		4	5	.444	3.07	27	9	3	91	97	31	16	0	2	2	1	21	3	0	.143	5	22	0	1	1.0	1.000
1947	BOS N	0	0	–	9.82	3	0	0	3.2	4	6	0	0	0	0	0	0	0	0	–	0	3	0	0	1.0	1.000
11 yrs.		58	60	.492	3.58	278	104	30	1071	1078	358	295	4	26	10	13	322	47	1	.146	73	212	15	16	1.1	.950

Les Lanning

LANNING, LESTER ALFRED (Red)
B. May 13, 1895, Harvard, Ill. D. June 13, 1962, Bristol, Conn.
BL TL 5'9" 165 lbs.

Year	Team	W	L	PCT	ERA	G	GS	CG	IP	H	BB	SO	ShO	W	L	SV	AB	H	HR	BA	PO	A	E	DP	TC/G	FA
1916	PHI A	0	3	.000	8.14	6	3	1	24.1	38	17	9	0	0	0	0	*				0	8	0	0	1.3	1.000

Tom Lanning

LANNING, THOMAS NEWTON
Brother of Johnny Lanning.
B. Apr. 22, 1907, Biltmore, N. C. D. Nov. 4, 1967, Marietta, Ga.
BL TL 6'1" 165 lbs.

Year	Team	W	L	PCT	ERA	G	GS	CG	IP	H	BB	SO	ShO	W	L	SV	AB	H	HR	BA	PO	A	E	DP	TC/G	FA
1938	PHI N	0	1	.000	6.43	3	1	0	7	9	2	2	0	0	0	0	1	1	0	1.000	1	0	0	0	0.3	1.000

Gene Lansing

LANSING, EUGENE HEWITT (Jigger)
B. Jan. 11, 1898, Albany, N. Y. D. Jan. 18, 1945, Rensselaer, N. Y.
BR TR 6'1" 185 lbs.

Year	Team	W	L	PCT	ERA	G	GS	CG	IP	H	BB	SO	ShO	W	L	SV	AB	H	HR	BA	PO	A	E	DP	TC/G	FA
1922	BOS N	0	1	.000	5.98	15	1	0	40.2	46	22	14	0	0	1	0	11	0	0	.000	1	8	1	0	0.7	.900

Paul LaPalme

LaPALME, PAUL EDMORE (Lefty)
B. Dec. 14, 1923, Springfield, Mass.
BL TL 5'10" 175 lbs.

Year	Team	W	L	PCT	ERA	G	GS	CG	IP	H	BB	SO	ShO	W	L	SV	AB	H	HR	BA	PO	A	E	DP	TC/G	FA
1951	PIT N	1	5	.167	6.29	22	8	1	54.1	79	31	24	1	0	2	0	10	1	0	.100	4	6	0	0	0.5	1.000
1952		1	2	.333	3.92	31	2	0	59.2	56	37	25	0	1	2	0	10	1	0	.100	1	15	1	1	0.5	.941
1953		8	16	.333	4.59	35	24	7	176.1	191	64	86	1	1	1	2	59	5	0	.085	5	23	4	1	0.9	.875
1954		4	10	.286	5.52	33	15	2	120.2	147	54	57	0	1	1	0	35	5	0	.143	7	19	0	1	0.8	1.000
1955	STL N	4	3	.571	2.75	56	0	0	91.2	76	34	39	0	4	3	3	19	4	0	.211	7	19	1	1	0.5	.963
1956	3 teams	STL N	(1G 0–0)		CIN N	(11G 2–4)			CHI A	(29G 3–1)																	
"	total	5	5	.500	3.93	41	2	0	73.1	61	33	27	0	4	4	0	10	2	0	.200	1	16	0	2	0.4	1.000
1957	CHI A	1	4	.200	3.35	35	0	0	40.1	35	19	19	0	1	4	7	4	2	0	.500	4	10	1	2	0.4	.933
7 yrs.		24	45	.348	4.42	253	51	10	616.1	645	272	277	2	12	17	14	147	20	0	.136	29	108	7	8	0.6	.951

Andy Lapihuska

LAPIHUSKA, ANDREW (Apples)
B. Nov. 1, 1922, Delmont, N. J.
BL TR 5'10½" 175 lbs.

Year	Team	W	L	PCT	ERA	G	GS	CG	IP	H	BB	SO	ShO	W	L	SV	AB	H	HR	BA	PO	A	E	DP	TC/G	FA
1942	PHI N	0	2	.000	5.23	3	2	0	20.2	17	13	8	0	0	0	0	7	2	0	.286	1	5	0	0	2.0	1.000
1943		0	0	–	23.14	1	0	0	2.1	5	3	0	0	0	0	0	2	0	0	.000	0	0	0	0	0.0	–
2 yrs.		0	2	.000	7.04	4	2	0	23	22	16	8	0	0	0	0	9	2	0	.222	1	5	0	0	1.5	1.000

Dave LaPoint

LaPOINT, DAVID JEFFREY
B. July 29, 1959, Glens Falls, N. Y.
BL TL 6'3" 205 lbs.

Year	Team	W	L	PCT	ERA	G	GS	CG	IP	H	BB	SO	ShO	W	L	SV	AB	H	HR	BA	PO	A	E	DP	TC/G	FA
1980	MIL A	1	0	1.000	6.00	5	3	0	15	17	13	5	0	1	0	1	0	0	0	–	0	0	0	0	0.0	–
1981	STL N	1	0	1.000	4.09	3	2	0	11	12	2	4	0	0	0	0	5	0	0	.000	1	2	0	0	1.0	1.000
1982		9	3	.750	3.42	42	21	0	152.2	170	52	81	0	1	0	0	38	2	0	.053	2	13	1	0	0.4	.938
1983		12	9	.571	3.95	37	29	1	191.1	191	84	113	0	2	1	0	59	9	0	.153	11	24	0	1	0.9	1.000
1984		12	10	.545	3.96	33	33	2	193	205	77	130	1	0	0	0	59	4	0	.068	4	23	1	4	0.8	.962
1985	SF N	7	17	.292	3.57	31	31	2	206.2	215	74	122	1	0	0	0	60	10	0	.167	8	23	1	1	1.0	.969
1986	2 teams	DET A	(16G 3–6)		SD N	(24G 1–4)																				
"	total	4	10	.286	5.02	40	12	0	129	152	56	77	0	3	0	0	0	0	0	.000	5	16	1	2	0.6	.955
1987	2 teams	STL N	(6G 1–1)		CHI A	(14G 6–3)																				
"	total	7	4	.636	3.56	20	14	2	98.2	95	36	51	0	0	0	0	4	0	0	.000	2	26	0	1	1.5	.966
1988	2 teams	CHI A	(25G 10–11)		PIT N	(8G 4–2)																				
"	total	14	13	.519	3.25	33	33	2	213.1	205	57	98	1	0	0	0	16	1	0	.063	7	24	1	1	1.0	.969
1989	NY A	6	9	.400	5.62	20	20	0	113.2	146	45	51	0	0	0	0	0	0	0	–	2	10	0	1	0.6	1.000
10 yrs.		73	75	.493	3.96	264	198	9	1324.1	1408	496	732	4	5	5	1	249	26	0	.104	40	161	6	10	0.8	.971

WORLD SERIES

Year	Team	W	L	PCT	ERA	G	GS	CG	IP	H	BB	SO	ShO	W	L	SV	AB	H	HR	BA	PO	A	E	DP	TC/G	FA
1982	STL N	0	0	–	3.24	2	1	0	8.1	10	2	3	0	0	0	0	0	0	0	–	0	2	1	0	1.5	.667

Year	Team		W	L	PCT	ERA	G	GS	CG	IP	H	BB	SO	ShO	Relief Pitching W	L	SV	Batting AB	H	HR	BA	PO	A	E	DP	TC/G	FA

Pat Larkin

LARKIN, PATRICK CLIBORN
B. June 14, 1960, Arcadia, Calif.   BL TL 6'   180 lbs.

| 1983 | SF | N | 0 | 0 | – | 4.35 | 5 | 0 | 0 | 10.1 | 13 | 3 | 6 | 0 | 0 | 0 | 0 | 1 | 0 | 0 | .000 | 0 | 2 | 1 | 0 | 0.6 | .667 |

Steve Larkin

LARKIN, STEPHEN PATRICK
B. Dec. 9, 1910, Cincinnati, Ohio   D. May 2, 1969, Norristown, Pa.   BR TR 6'1"   195 lbs.

| 1934 | DET | A | 0 | 0 | – | 1.50 | 2 | 1 | 0 | 6 | 8 | 5 | 8 | 0 | 0 | 0 | 0 | 3 | 1 | 0 | .333 | 1 | 2 | 1 | 0 | 2.0 | .750 |

Terry Larkin

LARKIN, FRANK S.
B. 1856, Brooklyn, N. Y.   D. Sept. 16, 1894, Brooklyn N. Y.,   BR TR

1876	NY	N	0	1	.000	3.00	1	1	1	9	9	0	0	0	0	0	0	4	0	0	.000	26	2	2	0	4.0	.500
1877	HAR	N	29	25	.537	2.14	56	56	55	501	510	4	53	96	0	0	0	0	228	52	1	.228	26	89	15	0	2.3	.885
1878	CHI	N	29	26	.527	2.24	56	56	56	506	511	31	163	1	0	0	0	226	65	0	.288	19	90	18	0	2.3	.858
1879			31	23	.574	2.44	58	58	57	513.1	514	30	142	3	0	0	0	228	50	0	.219	10	79	8	1	1.7	.918
1880	TRO	N	0	5	.000	8.76	5	5	3	38	83	10	5	0	0	0	0	20	3	0	.150	4	8	0	1	2.4	1.000
1884	RIC	AA	0	0	–	0.00	0	0	0	0	0	0	0	0	0	0	0	209	45	0	.215	0	0	0	0	–	
6 yrs.			89	80	.527	2.43	176	176	172	1567.1	1627	124	406	8	0	0	0	*				59	268	43	2	2.1	.884

Dave LaRoche

LaROCHE, DAVID EUGENE
B. May 14, 1948, Colorado Springs, Colo.   BL TL 6'2"   200 lbs.

1970	CAL	A	4	1	.800	3.42	38	0	0	50	41	21	44	0	4	1	4	8	2	0	.250	5	7	0	1	0.3	1.000
1971			5	1	.833	2.50	56	0	0	72	55	27	63	0	5	1	9	11	1	0	.091	0	8	1	0	0.2	.889
1972	MIN	A	5	7	.417	2.84	62	0	0	95	72	39	79	0	5	7	10	11	1	0	.091	2	15	0	1	0.3	1.000
1973	CHI	N	4	1	.800	5.83	45	0	0	54	55	29	34	0	4	1	4	4	2	0	.500	5	13	3	1	0.5	.857
1974			5	6	.455	4.79	49	4	0	92	103	47	49	0	4	5	5	27	9	0	.333	3	14	0	0	0.3	1.000
1975	CLE	A	5	3	.625	2.19	61	0	0	82.1	61	57	94	0	5	3	17	0	0	0	–	3	13	0	0	0.3	1.000
1976			1	4	.200	2.25	61	0	0	96	57	49	104	0	1	4	21	0	0	0	–	3	9	3	0	0.2	.800
1977	2 teams		CLE A	(13G 2–2)			CAL A	(46G 6–5)																				
"	total		8	7	.533	3.51	59	0	0	100	79	44	79	0	8	7	17	0	0	0	–	6	10	0	0	0.3	1.000
1978	CAL	A	10	9	.526	2.81	59	0	0	96	73	48	70	0	10	9	25	0	0	0	–	2	14	0	0	0.3	1.000
1979			7	11	.389	5.55	53	1	0	86	107	32	59	0	6	11	10	0	0	0	–	4	17	0	0	0.4	1.000
1980			3	5	.375	4.08	52	9	1	128	122	39	89	0	2	0	4	0	0	0	–	5	16	1	0	0.4	.955
1981	NY	A	4	1	.800	2.49	26	1	0	47	38	16	24	0	4	1	0	0	0	0	–	5	4	0	0	0.3	1.000
1982			4	2	.667	3.42	25	0	0	50	54	11	31	0	4	2	0	0	0	0	–	1	3	0	0	0.2	1.000
1983			0	0	–	18.00	1	0	0	1	2	1	0	0	0	0	0	0	0	0	–	1	0	0	0	1.0	1.000
14 yrs.			65	58	.528	3.53	647	15	1	1049.1	919	459	819	0	62	52	126	61	15	0	.246	48	144	8	5	0.3	.960

LEAGUE CHAMPIONSHIP SERIES

| 1979 | CAL | A | 0 | 0 | – | 6.75 | 1 | 0 | 0 | 1.1 | 2 | 1 | 1 | 0 | 0 | 0 | 0 | 0 | 0 | 0 | – | 0 | 0 | 0 | 0 | 0.0 | – |

WORLD SERIES

| 1981 | NY | A | 0 | 0 | – | 0.00 | 1 | 0 | 0 | 1 | 0 | 0 | 2 | 0 | 0 | 0 | 0 | 0 | 0 | 0 | – | 0 | 0 | 0 | 0 | 0.0 | – |

John LaRose

LaROSE, HENRY JOHN
B. Oct. 25, 1951, Pawtucket, R. I.   BL TL 6'1"   185 lbs.

| 1978 | BOS | A | 0 | 0 | – | 22.50 | 1 | 0 | 0 | 2 | 3 | 3 | 0 | 0 | 0 | 0 | 0 | 0 | 0 | 0 | – | 0 | 1 | 0 | 0 | 1.0 | 1.000 |

Don Larsen

LARSEN, DON JAMES
B. Aug. 7, 1929, Michigan City, Ind.   BR TR 6'4"   215 lbs.

1953	STL	A	7	12	.368	4.16	38	22	7	192.2	201	64	96	2	1	2	2	81	23	3	.284	8	29	2	1	1.0	.949
1954	BAL	A	3	21	.125	4.37	29	28	12	201.2	213	89	80	1	0	1	0	88	22	1	.250	14	34	1	3	1.7	.980
1955	NY	A	9	2	.818	3.06	19	13	5	97	81	51	44	1	2	1	2	41	6	2	.146	5	13	1	3	1.0	.947
1956			11	5	.688	3.26	38	20	6	179.2	133	96	107	1	2	1	1	79	19	2	.241	13	23	3	3	1.0	.923
1957			10	4	.714	3.74	27	20	4	139.2	113	87	81	1	2	0	1	56	14	0	.250	10	20	2	2	1.2	.938
1958			9	6	.600	3.07	19	19	5	114.1	100	55	55	3	0	0	4	49	15	4	.306	5	14	2	2	1.1	.905
1959			6	7	.462	4.33	25	18	3	124.2	122	76	69	0	0	0	0	47	12	0	.255	5	22	2	1	1.2	.931
1960	KC	A	1	10	.091	5.38	22	15	0	83.2	97	42	43	0	0	1	0	29	6	0	.207	4	8	1	1	0.6	.923
1961	2 teams		KC A	(8G 1–0)			CHI A	(25G 7–2)																				
"	total		8	2	.800	4.13	33	4	0	89.1	85	40	66	0	1	0	1	45	14	2	.311	5	17	0	0	0.7	1.000
1962	SF	N	5	4	.556	4.38	49	0	0	86.1	83	47	58	0	5	4	11	25	5	0	.200	4	15	0	3	0.4	1.000
1963			7	7	.500	3.05	46	0	0	62	46	30	44	0	7	7	3	11	2	0	.182	4	12	1	0	0.4	.941
1964	2 teams		SF N	(6G 0–1)			HOU N	(30G 4–8)																				
"	total		4	9	.308	2.45	36	10	2	113.2	102	26	64	1	4	1	2	32	3	0	.094	9	19	1	1	0.8	.966
1965	2 teams		HOU N	(1G 0–0)			BAL A	(27G 1–2)																				
"	total		1	2	.333	2.88	28	2	0	59.1	61	23	41	0	1	1	0	13	3	0	.231	6	16	1	1	0.8	.957
1967	CHI	N	0	0	–	9.00	3	0	0	4	5	2	1	0	0	0	0	0	0	0	–	0	2	0	1	0.7	1.000
14 yrs.			81	91	.471	3.78	412	171	44	1548	1442	725	849	11	26	23	23	*				92	244	17	22	0.9	.952

WORLD SERIES

1955	NY	A	0	1	.000	11.25	1	1	0	4	5	2	2	0	0	0	0	2	0	0	.000	0	1	0	0	1.0	1.000
1956			1	0	1.000	0.00	2	2	1	10.2	1	4	7	1	0	0	0	3	1	0	.333	0	1	0	0	0.5	1.000
1957			1	1	.500	3.72	2	1	0	9.2	8	5	6	0	1	0	0	2	0	0	.000	0	1	0	0	0.5	1.000
1958			1	0	1.000	0.96	2	2	0	9.1	9	6	9	0	0	0	0	1	0	0	.000	1	0	0	0	0.5	1.000
1962	SF	N	1	0	1.000	3.86	3	0	0	2.1	1	2	0	0	1	0	0	0	0	0	–	1	0	0	0	0.3	1.000
5 yrs.			4	2	.667	2.75	10	6	1	36	24	19	24	1	2	0	0	9	1	0	.111	2	3	0	0	0.5	1.000

2nd

Dan Larson

LARSON, DANIEL JAMES
B. July 4, 1954, Los Angeles, Calif.   BR TR 6'   175 lbs.

1976	HOU	N	5	8	.385	3.03	13	13	5	92	81	28	42	0	0	0	0	31	9	0	.290	7	13	0	2	1.5	1.000
1977			1	7	.125	5.79	32	10	1	98	108	45	44	0	1	3	1	28	6	0	.214	11	14	2	0	0.8	.926
1978	PHI	N	0	0	–	9.00	1	0	0	1	1	1	2	0	0	0	0	0	0	0	–	0	0	0	0	0.0	–
1979			1	1	.500	4.26	3	3	0	19	17	9	9	0	0	0	0	5	0	0	.000	1	4	0	1	1.7	1.000
1980			0	5	.000	3.13	12	7	0	46	46	24	17	0	0	0	0	13	2	0	.154	4	4	0	0	0.7	1.000

Year	Team		W	L	PCT	ERA	G	GS	CG	IP	H	BB	SO	ShO	Relief Pitching W	L	SV	Batting AB	H	HR	BA	PO	A	E	DP	TC/G	FA

Dan Larson *continued*

1981			3	0	1.000	4.18	5	4	1	28	27	15	15	0	0	0	0	9	1	0	.111	6	2	0	0	1.6	1.000
1982	CHI	N	0	4	.000	5.67	12	6	0	39.2	51	18	22	0	0	0	0	11	3	0	.273	10	7	0	2	1.4	1.000
7 yrs.			10	25	.286	4.39	78	43	7	323.2	331	140	151	0	1	3	1	97	21	0	.216	39	44	2	5	1.1	.976

Al Lary

LARY, ALFRED ALLEN
Brother of Frank Lary.
B. Sept. 26, 1929, Northport, Ala.

BR TR 6'3" 185 lbs.

1954	CHI	N	0	0	–	3.00	1	1	0	6	3	7	4	0	0	0	0	2	1	0	.500	1	1	0	0	2.0	1.000
1955			0	0	–	0.00	0	0	0	0	0	0	0	0	0	0	0	0	0	0	–	0	0	0	0	0.0	–
1962			0	1	.000	7.15	15	3	0	34	42	15	18	0	0	0	0	6	1	0	.167	1	5	1	0	0.5	.857
3 yrs.			0	1	.000	6.53	16	4	0	40	45	22	22	0	0	0	0	8	2	0	.250	2	6	1	0	0.6	.889

Frank Lary

LARY, FRANK STRONG (Mule, The Yankee Killer)
Brother of Al Lary.
B. Apr. 10, 1930, Northport, Ala.

BR TR 5'11" 175 lbs.

1954	DET	A	0	0	–	2.45	3	0	0	3.2	4	3	5	0	0	0	0	0	0	0	–	0	0	0	0	0.0	–
1955			14	15	.483	3.10	36	31	16	235	232	89	98	2	1	1	1	82	16	0	.195	14	46	3	4	1.8	.952
1956			21	13	.618	3.15	41	38	20	294	289	116	165	3	0	0	1	103	19	1	.184	15	45	3	3	1.5	.952
1957			11	16	.407	3.98	40	35	12	237.2	250	72	107	2	0	1	3	73	9	0	.123	14	43	1	4	1.5	.983
1958			16	15	.516	2.90	39	34	19	260.1	249	68	131	3	0	2	1	88	15	1	.170	20	39	1	1	1.5	.983
1959			17	10	.630	3.55	32	32	11	223	225	46	137	3	0	0	0	80	10	1	.125	15	34	3	1	1.6	.942
1960			15	15	.500	3.51	38	36	15	274.1	262	62	149	2	0	0	0	93	17	2	.183	14	37	4	2	1.4	.927
1961			23	9	.719	3.24	36	36	22	275.1	252	66	146	4	0	0	1	108	25	1	.231	32	55	1	5	2.4	.989
1962			2	6	.250	5.74	17	14	2	80	98	21	41	1	0	1	0	24	4	0	.167	7	8	3	0	1.1	.833
1963			4	9	.308	3.27	16	14	6	107.1	90	26	46	0	0	0	0	35	8	0	.229	26	14	0	1	2.5	1.000
1964	3 teams	DET A (6G 0–2)				NY N (13G 2–3)				MIL N (5G 1–0)																	
"	total		3	5	.375	5.03	24	4	0	87.2	101	24	37	1	0	0	1	27	2	0	.074	11	13	1	1	1.0	.960
1965	2 teams	NY N (14G 1–3)				CHI A (14G 1–0)																					
"	total		2	3	.400	3.32	28	8	0	84	71	23	37	0	0	0	0	21	5	0	.238	6	17	1	1	0.9	.958
12 yrs.			128	116	.525	3.49	350	292	126	2162.1	2123	616	1099	21	1	5	11	734	130	6	.177	174	351	21	23	1.6	.962

Fred Lasher

LASHER, FREDERICK WALTER
B. Aug. 19, 1941, Poughkeepsie, N. Y.

BR TR 6'3" 190 lbs.

1963	MIN	A	0	0	–	4.76	11	0	0	11.1	12	11	10	0	0	0	0	1	0	0	.000	1	4	1	0	0.5	.833
1967	DET	A	2	1	.667	3.90	17	0	0	30	25	11	28	0	2	1	9	9	1	0	.111	1	4	0	0	0.3	1.000
1968			5	1	.833	3.33	34	0	0	48.2	37	22	32	0	5	1	5	9	1	0	.111	3	10	1	1	0.4	.929
1969			2	1	.667	3.07	32	0	0	44	34	22	16	0	2	1	0	4	0	0	.000	2	8	0	0	0.3	1.000
1970	2 teams	DET A (12G 1–3)				CLE A (43G 1–7)																					
"	total		2	10	.167	4.19	55	1	0	66.2	67	42	52	0	2	9	8	9	0	0	.000	1	8	4	0	0.2	.692
1971	CAL	A	0	0	–	36.00	2	0	0	1	4	2	0	0	0	0	0	0	0	0	–	0	0	0	0	0.0	–
6 yrs.			11	13	.458	3.88	151	1	0	201.2	179	110	148	0	11	12	22	32	2	0	.063	8	34	6	1	0.3	.875

WORLD SERIES

| 1968 | DET | A | 0 | 0 | – | 0.00 | 1 | 0 | 0 | 1 | 0 | 0 | 1 | 0 | 0 | 0 | 0 | 0 | 0 | 0 | – | 0 | 1 | 0 | 0 | 1.0 | 1.000 |

Bill Laskey

LASKEY, WILLIAM ALAN
B. Dec. 20, 1957, Toledo, Ohio

BR TR 6'5" 190 lbs.

1982	SF	N	13	12	.520	3.14	32	31	7	189.1	186	43	88	1	0	0	0	62	8	0	.129	17	30	2	2	1.5	.959
1983			13	10	.565	4.19	25	25	1	148.1	151	45	81	0	0	0	0	47	5	0	.106	11	16	1	0	1.1	.964
1984			9	14	.391	4.33	35	34	2	207.2	222	50	71	0	1	0	0	63	4	0	.063	12	23	0	0	1.0	1.000
1985	2 teams	SF N (19G 5–11)				MON N (11G 0–5)																					
"	total		5	16	.238	4.91	30	26	0	148.1	165	53	60	0	0	0	0	37	5	0	.135	12	26	2	1	1.3	.950
1986	SF	N	1	1	.500	4.28	20	0	0	27.1	28	13	8	0	1	1	1	1	0	0	.000	3	6	1	0	0.5	.900
1988	CLE	A	1	0	1.000	5.18	17	0	0	24.1	32	6	17	0	1	0	1	0	0	0	–	0	4	0	0	0.2	1.000
6 yrs.			42	53	.442	4.14	159	116	10	745.1	784	210	325	1	3	1	2	210	22	0	.105	55	105	6	4	1.0	.964

Bill Lasley

LASLEY, WILLARD ALMOND
B. July 13, 1902, Marietta, Ohio

BR TR 6' 175 lbs.

| 1924 | STL | A | 0 | 0 | – | 6.75 | 2 | 0 | 0 | 4 | 7 | 2 | 0 | 0 | 0 | 0 | 0 | 1 | 0 | 0 | .000 | 0 | 0 | 0 | 0 | 0.0 | – |

Tom Lasorda

LASORDA, THOMAS CHARLES
B. Sept. 22, 1927, Norristown, Pa.
Manager 1976-89.

BL TL 5'10" 175 lbs.

1954	BKN	N	0	0	–	5.00	4	0	0	9	8	5	5	0	0	0	0	1	0	0	.000	0	0	0	0	0.3	1.000
1955			0	0	–	13.50	4	1	0	4	5	6	4	0	0	0	0	0	0	0	–	0	0	0	0	0.0	–
1956	KC	A	0	4	.000	6.15	18	5	0	45.1	40	45	28	0	0	0	1	13	1	0	.077	3	9	1	0	0.7	.923
3 yrs.			0	4	.000	6.48	26	6	0	58.1	53	56	37	0	0	0	1	14	1	0	.071	3	10	1	0	0.5	.929

Bill Latham

LATHAM, WILLIAM CAROL, JR.
B. Aug. 29, 1960, Birmingham, Ala.

BL TL 6'2" 190 lbs.

1985	NY	N	1	3	.250	3.97	7	3	0	22.2	21	7	10	0	0	1	0	3	1	0	.333	0	7	0	0	1.0	1.000
1986	MIN	A	0	1	.000	7.31	7	2	0	16	24	6	8	0	0	0	0	0	0	0	–	0	1	0	0	0.3	.500
2 yrs.			1	4	.200	5.35	14	5	0	38.2	45	13	18	0	0	1	0	3	1	0	.333	0	8	0	0	0.6	.889

Bill Lathrop

LATHROP, WILLIAM GEORGE
B. Aug. 12, 1891, Hanover, Wis. D. Nov. 20, 1958, Janesville, Wis.

BR TR 6'2½" 184 lbs.

1913	CHI	A	0	1	.000	4.24	6	0	0	17	16	12	9	0	0	0	0	4	0	0	.000	0	6	0	0	1.0	1.000
1914			1	2	.333	2.64	19	1	0	47.2	41	19	7	0	1	0	0	12	0	0	.000	0	19	0	0	1.0	1.000
2 yrs.			1	3	.250	3.06	25	1	0	64.2	57	31	16	0	1	2	0	16	0	0	.000	0	25	0	0	1.0	1.000

Year	Team		W	L	PCT	ERA	G	GS	CG	IP	H	BB	SO	ShO	Relief W	L	SV	AB	H	HR	BA	PO	A	E	DP	TC/G	FA

Barry Latman

LATMAN, ARNOLD BARRY   B. May 21, 1936, Los Angeles, Calif.   BR TR 6'3" 210 lbs.

Year	Team	Lg	W	L	PCT	ERA	G	GS	CG	IP	H	BB	SO	ShO	W	L	SV	AB	H	HR	BA	PO	A	E	DP	TC/G	FA
1957	CHI	A	1	2	.333	8.03	7	2	0	12.1	12	13	9	0	1	1	0	1	0	0	.000	1	2	0	0	0.4	1.000
1958			3	0	1.000	0.76	13	3	1	47.2	27	17	28	1	1	0	0	12	1	0	.083	2	5	1	0	0.6	.875
1959			8	5	.615	3.75	37	21	5	156	138	72	97	2	0	0	0	47	6	0	.128	5	13	1	1	0.5	.947
1960	CLE	A	7	7	.500	4.03	31	20	4	147.1	146	72	94	0	1	0	0	41	9	0	.220	10	18	1	0	0.9	.966
1961			13	5	.722	4.02	45	18	4	176.2	163	54	108	2	6	0	5	55	4	0	.073	10	13	2	2	0.6	.920
1962			8	13	.381	4.17	45	21	7	179.1	179	72	117	1	2	2	5	53	10	1	.189	17	22	7	3	1.0	.848
1963			7	12	.368	4.94	38	21	7	149.1	146	52	133	2	1	1	2	44	8	1	.182	18	31	3	1	1.4	.942
1964	LA	A	6	10	.375	3.85	40	18	2	138	128	52	81	1	3	2	2	40	5	0	.125	9	17	3	2	0.7	.897
1965	CAL	A	1	1	.500	2.84	18	0	0	31.2	30	16	18	0	1	0	0	2	0	0	.000	0	2	1	0	0.2	.667
1966	HOU	N	2	7	.222	2.71	31	9	1	103	88	35	74	1	1	2	1	26	4	0	.154	5	16	1	0	0.7	.955
1967			3	6	.333	4.52	39	1	0	77.2	73	34	70	0	3	6	0	11	1	0	.091	2	13	0	0	0.4	1.000
11 yrs.			59	68	.465	3.91	344	134	28	1219	1130	489	829	10	20	16	16	332	48	2	.145	79	152	20	10	0.7	.920

Bill Lattimore

LATTIMORE, WILLIAM HERSHEL (Slothful Bill)   B. May 5, 1884, Roxton, Tex.   D. Oct. 30, 1919, Colorado Springs, Colo.   BL TL 5'9" 165 lbs.

Year	Team	Lg	W	L	PCT	ERA	G	GS	CG	IP	H	BB	SO	ShO	W	L	SV	AB	H	HR	BA	PO	A	E	DP	TC/G	FA
1908	CLE	A	1	2	.333	4.50	4	4	1	24	24	7	5	1	0	0	0	9	4	0	.444	0	5	0	0	1.3	1.000

Chuck Lauer

LAUER, JOHN CHARLES   B. 1865, Pittsburgh, Pa.   Deceased.   TR

Year	Team	Lg	W	L	PCT	ERA	G	GS	CG	IP	H	BB	SO	ShO	W	L	SV	AB	H	HR	BA	PO	A	E	DP	TC/G	FA
1884	PIT	AA	0	2	.000	7.58	3	3	2	19	23	9	8	0	0	0	0	*				1	1	1	0	1.0	.667

George Lauzerique

LAUZERIQUE, GEORGE ALBERT   B. July 22, 1947, Havana, Cuba   BR TR 6'1" 180 lbs.

Year	Team	Lg	W	L	PCT	ERA	G	GS	CG	IP	H	BB	SO	ShO	W	L	SV	AB	H	HR	BA	PO	A	E	DP	TC/G	FA
1967	KC	A	0	2	.000	2.25	3	2	0	16	11	6	10	0	0	0	0	3	0	0	.000	0	1	0	0	1.0	1.000
1968	OAK	A	0	0	-	0.00	1	0	0	1	0	1	0	0	0	0	0	0	0	0	-	0	1	0	0	1.0	1.000
1969			3	4	.429	4.70	19	8	1	61.1	58	27	39	0	0	2	0	20	2	0	.100	2	14	0	1	0.8	1.000
1970	MIL	A	1	2	.333	6.94	11	4	1	35	41	14	24	0	0	0	0	10	2	1	.200	3	3	0	0	0.5	1.000
4 yrs.			4	8	.333	5.00	34	14	2	113.1	110	48	73	0	0	2	0	33	4	1	.121	5	21	0	1	0.8	1.000

Gary Lavelle

LAVELLE, GARY ROBERT   B. Jan. 3, 1949, Scranton, Pa.   BB TL 6'2" 190 lbs.

Year	Team	Lg	W	L	PCT	ERA	G	GS	CG	IP	H	BB	SO	ShO	W	L	SV	AB	H	HR	BA	PO	A	E	DP	TC/G	FA
1974	SF	N	0	3	.000	2.12	10	0	0	17	14	10	12	0	0	0	0	2	0	0	.000	0	2	1	0	0.3	.667
1975			6	3	.667	2.96	65	0	0	82	80	48	51	0	6	3	8	9	1	0	.111	6	11	1	2	0.3	.944
1976			10	6	.625	2.69	65	0	0	110.1	102	52	71	0	10	6	12	13	1	0	.077	5	11	4	0	0.3	.800
1977			7	7	.500	2.06	73	0	0	118	106	37	93	0	7	7	20	14	0	0	.000	5	20	1	2	0.4	.962
1978			13	10	.565	3.31	67	0	0	98	96	44	63	0	13	10	14	15	1	0	.067	2	19	2	1	0.3	.913
1979			7	9	.438	2.51	70	0	0	97	86	42	80	0	7	9	20	4	1	0	.250	4	13	1	0	0.3	.944
1980			6	8	.429	3.42	62	0	0	100	106	36	66	0	6	8	9	11	0	0	.000	3	16	0	0	0.3	1.000
1981			2	6	.250	3.82	34	3	0	66	58	23	45	0	2	4	4	11	3	0	.273	3	16	1	3	0.6	.950
1982			10	7	.588	2.67	68	0	0	104.2	97	29	76	0	10	7	8	13	2	0	.154	8	26	2	0	0.5	.944
1983			7	4	.636	2.59	56	0	0	87	73	19	68	0	7	4	20	14	0	0	.000	5	20	1	2	0.5	.962
1984			5	4	.556	2.76	77	0	0	101	92	42	71	0	5	4	12	5	0	0	.000	1	13	0	0	0.2	1.000
1985	TOR	A	5	7	.417	3.10	69	0	0	72.2	54	36	50	0	5	7	8	-	0	0	-	2	9	0	1	0.2	1.000
1987	2 teams		TOR A (23G 2–3)							OAK A (6G 0–0)																		
"	total		2	3	.400	5.91	29	0	0	32	40	22	23	0	2	3	1	0	0	0	-	4	5	0	0	0.3	1.000
13 yrs.			80	77	.510	2.93	745	3	0	1085.2	1004	440	769	0	80	75	136	111	9	0	.081	48	181	14	11	0.3	.942

LEAGUE CHAMPIONSHIP SERIES

Year	Team	Lg	W	L	PCT	ERA	G	GS	CG	IP	H	BB	SO	ShO	W	L	SV	AB	H	HR	BA	PO	A	E	DP	TC/G	FA
1985	TOR	A	0	0	-	0.00	1	0	0	0	1	0	0	0	0	0	0	0	0	0	-	0	0	0	0	0.0	-

Jimmy Lavender

LAVENDER, JAMES SANFORD   B. Mar. 25, 1884, Barnesville, Ga.   D. Jan. 12, 1960, Cartersville, Ga.   BR TR 5'11" 165 lbs.

Year	Team	Lg	W	L	PCT	ERA	G	GS	CG	IP	H	BB	SO	ShO	W	L	SV	AB	H	HR	BA	PO	A	E	DP	TC/G	FA
1912	CHI	N	16	13	.552	3.04	42	31	15	251.2	240	89	109	3	1	1	3	87	13	0	.149	8	64	4	5	1.8	.947
1913			10	14	.417	3.66	40	20	10	204	206	98	91	0	3	2	2	68	8	0	.118	2	46	2	0	1.3	.960
1914			11	11	.500	3.07	37	28	11	214.1	191	87	87	2	1	2	0	63	11	0	.175	5	71	2	0	2.1	.974
1915			10	16	.385	2.58	41	24	13	220	178	67	117	1	2	4	3	67	9	0	.134	14	67	1	3	2.0	.988
1916			10	14	.417	2.82	36	25	9	188	163	62	91	4	1	1	2	53	8	0	.151	3	47	2	0	1.4	.962
1917	PHI	N	5	8	.385	3.55	28	14	7	129.1	119	44	52	0	1	0	1	36	5	0	.139	3	30	3	0	1.3	.917
6 yrs.			62	76	.449	3.09	224	142	65	1207.1	1097	447	547	10	9	10	11	374	54	0	.144	35	325	14	8	1.7	.963

Ron Law

LAW, RONALD DAVID   B. Mar. 14, 1946, Hamilton, Ont., Canada   BR TR 6'2" 165 lbs.

Year	Team	Lg	W	L	PCT	ERA	G	GS	CG	IP	H	BB	SO	ShO	W	L	SV	AB	H	HR	BA	PO	A	E	DP	TC/G	FA
1969	CLE	A	3	4	.429	4.99	35	1	0	52.1	68	34	29	0	3	4	1	7	1	0	.143	4	9	1	1	0.4	.929

Vance Law

LAW, VANCE AARON   Son of Vern Law.   B. Oct. 1, 1956, Boise, Ida.   BR TR 6'2" 185 lbs.

Year	Team	Lg	W	L	PCT	ERA	G	GS	CG	IP	H	BB	SO	ShO	W	L	SV	AB	H	HR	BA	PO	A	E	DP	TC/G	FA
1986	MON	N	0	0	-	2.25	3	0	0	4	3	2	0	0	0	0	0	360	81	5	.225	0	0	0	0	0.3	1.000
1987			0	0	-	5.40	3	0	0	3.1	5	0	2	0	0	0	0	436	119	12	.273	1	0	0	0	0.3	1.000
2 yrs.			0	0	-	3.68	6	0	0	7.1	8	2	2	0	0	0	0	*				0	2	0	0	0.3	1.000

Vern Law

LAW, VERNON SANDERS (Deacon)   Father of Vance Law.   B. Mar. 12, 1930, Meridian, Ida.   BR TR 6'2" 195 lbs.

Year	Team	Lg	W	L	PCT	ERA	G	GS	CG	IP	H	BB	SO	ShO	W	L	SV	AB	H	HR	BA	PO	A	E	DP	TC/G	FA
1950	PIT	N	7	9	.438	4.92	27	17	5	128	137	49	57	1	1	0	0	41	3	0	.073	5	15	2	1	0.8	.909
1951			6	9	.400	4.50	28	14	2	114	109	51	41	0	3	3	2	32	11	1	.344	10	15	2	2	1.0	.926
1954			9	13	.409	5.51	39	18	7	161.2	201	56	57	0	4	0	3	52	12	1	.231	11	23	1	2	0.9	.971
1955			10	10	.500	3.81	43	24	8	200.2	221	61	82	1	1	1	0	63	16	1	.254	14	35	4	3	1.2	.925
1956			8	16	.333	4.32	39	32	6	195.2	218	49	60	0	1	3	2	57	10	1	.175	12	31	0	3	1.1	1.000

Year	Team	W	L	PCT	ERA	G	GS	CG	IP	H	BB	SO	ShO	Relief Pitching W	L	SV	Batting AB	H	HR	BA	PO	A	E	DP	TC/G	FA

Vern Law *continued*

Year	Team	W	L	PCT	ERA	G	GS	CG	IP	H	BB	SO	ShO	W	L	SV	AB	H	HR	BA	PO	A	E	DP	TC/G	FA
1957		10	8	.556	2.87	31	25	9	172.2	172	32	55	3	2	0	1	63	12	0	.190	13	23	2	2	1.2	.947
1958		14	12	.538	3.96	35	29	6	202.1	235	39	56	1	2	0	3	62	12	2	.194	16	31	0	3	1.3	1.000
1959		18	9	.667	2.98	34	33	20	266	245	53	110	2	0	0	1	96	16	1	.167	20	47	1	5	2.0	.985
1960		20	9	.690	3.08	35	35	**18**	271.2	266	40	120	3	0	0	0	94	17	1	.181	28	50	2	6	2.3	.975
1961		3	4	.429	4.70	11	10	1	59.1	72	18	20	0	0	0	0	19	5	0	.263	7	13	0	1	1.8	1.000
1962		10	7	.588	3.94	23	20	7	139.1	156	27	78	2	0	0	0	45	14	0	.311	7	27	2	3	1.6	.944
1963		4	5	.444	4.93	18	12	1	76.2	91	13	31	1	0	1	0	23	5	0	.217	5	20	0	1	1.4	1.000
1964		12	13	.480	3.61	35	29	7	192	203	32	93	5	0	1	0	61	19	1	.311	16	36	1	3	1.5	.981
1965		17	9	.654	2.15	29	28	13	217.1	182	35	101	4	1	0	0	82	20	1	.244	29	36	1	2	2.3	.985
1966		12	8	.600	4.05	31	28	8	177.2	203	24	88	4	2	0	0	66	16	1	.242	11	36	0	4	1.5	1.000
1967		2	6	.250	4.18	25	10	1	97	122	18	43	0	0	2	0	27	3	0	.111	8	15	1	0	1.0	.958
16 yrs.		162	147	.524	3.77	483	364	119	2672	2833	597	1092	28	17	11	13	883	191	11	.216	212	453	19	41	1.4	.972

WORLD SERIES

Year	Team	W	L	PCT	ERA	G	GS	CG	IP	H	BB	SO	ShO	W	L	SV	AB	H	HR	BA	PO	A	E	DP	TC/G	FA
1960	PIT N	2	0	1.000	3.44	3	3	0	18.1	22	3	8	0	0	0	0	6	2	0	.333	0	6	0	0	2.0	1.000

Bob Lawrence

LAWRENCE, ROBERT ANDREW (Larry)
B. Dec. 14, 1899, Brooklyn, N. Y. D. Nov. 6, 1983, Jamaica, N. Y. BR TR 5'11" 180 lbs.

Year	Team	W	L	PCT	ERA	G	GS	CG	IP	H	BB	SO	ShO	W	L	SV	AB	H	HR	BA	PO	A	E	DP	TC/G	FA
1924	CHI A	0	0	—	9.00	1	0	0	1	1	1	1	0	0	0	0	0	0	0	—	0	0	0	0	0.0	—

Brooks Lawrence

LAWRENCE, BROOKS ULYSSES (Bull)
B. Jan. 30, 1925, Springfield, Ohio BR TR 6' 205 lbs.

Year	Team	W	L	PCT	ERA	G	GS	CG	IP	H	BB	SO	ShO	W	L	SV	AB	H	HR	BA	PO	A	E	DP	TC/G	FA
1954	STL N	15	6	.714	3.74	35	18	8	158.2	141	72	72	0	6	4	1	53	10	0	.189	13	26	1	4	1.1	.975
1955		3	8	.273	6.56	46	10	2	96	102	58	52	1	1	3	1	21	2	0	.095	11	16	1	2	0.6	.964
1956	CIN N	19	10	.655	3.99	49	30	11	218.2	210	71	96	1	6	1	0	70	11	0	.157	13	53	2	5	1.4	.971
1957		16	13	.552	3.52	49	32	12	250.1	234	76	121	1	1	2	4	82	14	0	.171	34	32	4	3	1.4	.943
1958		8	13	.381	4.13	46	23	6	181	194	55	74	2	5	5	5	53	6	0	.113	6	33	2	2	0.9	.951
1959		7	12	.368	4.77	43	14	3	128.1	144	45	64	0	4	5	10	40	6	0	.150	7	22	3	1	0.7	.906
1960		1	0	1.000	10.57	7	0	0	7.2	9	8	2	0	1	0	1	0	0	0	—	0	3	0	0	0.4	1.000
7 yrs.		69	62	.527	4.25	275	127	42	1040.2	1034	385	481	5	21	20	22	319	49	0	.154	84	185	13	17	1.0	.954

Al Lawson

LAWSON, ALFRED WILLIAM
B. Mar. 24, 1869, London, England D. Nov. 29, 1954, San Antonio, Tex. BR TR 5'11" 165 lbs.

Year	Team	W	L	PCT	ERA	G	GS	CG	IP	H	BB	SO	ShO	W	L	SV	AB	H	HR	BA	PO	A	E	DP	TC/G	FA
1890	2 teams	BOS N	(1G 0–1)		PIT N	(2G 0–2)																				
"	total	0	3	.000	6.63	3	3	2	19	27	14	3	0	0	0	0	6	0	0	.000	0	5	3	0	2.7	.625

Bob Lawson

LAWSON, ROBERT BAKER
B. Aug. 23, 1876, Brookneal, Va. D. Oct. 28, 1952, Chapel Hill, N. C. BR TR 5'10" 170 lbs.

Year	Team	W	L	PCT	ERA	G	GS	CG	IP	H	BB	SO	ShO	W	L	SV	AB	H	HR	BA	PO	A	E	DP	TC/G	FA
1901	BOS N	2	2	.500	3.33	6	4	4	46	45	28	12	0	0	0	0	27	4	1	.148	1	17	2	0	3.3	.900
1902	BAL A	0	2	.000	4.85	3	2	1	13	21	3	5	0	0	0	0	6	1	0	.167	0	7	0	0	2.3	1.000
2 yrs.		2	4	.333	3.66	9	6	5	59	66	31	17	0	0	0	0	33	5	1	.152	1	24	2	0	3.0	.926

Roxie Lawson

LAWSON, ALFRED VOYLE
B. Apr. 13, 1906, Donnellson, Iowa D. Apr. 9, 1977, Stockport, Iowa BR TR 6' 170 lbs.

Year	Team	W	L	PCT	ERA	G	GS	CG	IP	H	BB	SO	ShO	W	L	SV	AB	H	HR	BA	PO	A	E	DP	TC/G	FA
1930	CLE A	1	2	.333	6.15	7	4	2	33.2	46	23	10	0	0	0	0	11	1	0	.091	2	6	0	0	1.1	1.000
1931		0	0	.000	7.60	17	3	0	55.2	72	36	20	0	0	0	0	14	2	0	.143	5	7	1	1	0.8	.923
1933	DET A	0	1	.000	7.31	4	2	0	16	17	17	6	0	0	0	0	5	0	0	.000	0	5	0	0	1.3	1.000
1935		3	1	.750	1.58	7	4	4	40	34	24	16	2	0	0	0	13	4	0	.308	2	1	0	0	0.7	.800
1936		8	6	.571	5.48	41	8	3	128	139	71	34	0	5	5	3	45	10	0	.222	7	28	1	1	0.9	.972
1937		18	7	.720	5.26	37	29	15	217.1	236	115	68	0	3	1	1	81	21	0	.259	16	33	2	2	1.4	.961
1938		8	9	.471	5.46	27	16	5	127	154	82	39	0	3	0	0	45	2	0	.044	9	26	2	0	1.4	.946
1939	2 teams	DET A	(2G 1–1)		STL A	(36G 3–7)																				
"	total	4	8	.333	5.28	38	15	5	162	188	90	47	0	2	0	0	47	8	0	.170	8	26	1	1	0.9	.971
1940	STL A	5	3	.625	5.13	30	2	0	72	77	54	18	0	5	1	4	22	1	0	.045	3	12	0	2	0.5	1.000
9 yrs.		47	39	.547	5.37	208	83	34	851.2	963	512	258	2	18	7	11	283	49	0	.173	52	145	8	7	1.0	.961

Steve Lawson

LAWSON, STEVEN GEORGE
B. Dec. 28, 1950, Oakland, Calif. BR TL 6'1" 175 lbs.

Year	Team	W	L	PCT	ERA	G	GS	CG	IP	H	BB	SO	ShO	W	L	SV	AB	H	HR	BA	PO	A	E	DP	TC/G	FA
1972	TEX A	0	0	—	2.81	13	0	0	16	13	10	13	0	0	0	1	1	1	0	1.000	0	2	0	0	0.2	1.000

Bill Laxton

LAXTON, WILLIAM HENRY
B. Jan. 5, 1948, Camden, N. J. BL TL 6'1" 190 lbs.

Year	Team	W	L	PCT	ERA	G	GS	CG	IP	H	BB	SO	ShO	W	L	SV	AB	H	HR	BA	PO	A	E	DP	TC/G	FA
1970	PHI N	0	0	—	13.50	2	0	0	2	2	2	2	0	0	0	0	0	0	0	—	0	0	0	0	0.0	—
1971	SD N	0	2	.000	6.75	18	0	0	28	32	26	23	0	0	2	0	0	0	0	—	1	4	0	0	0.3	1.000
1974		0	1	.000	4.00	30	1	0	45	37	38	40	0	0	1	0	5	1	0	.200	2	4	0	0	0.2	1.000
1976	DET A	0	5	.000	4.09	26	3	0	94.2	77	51	74	0	0	2	0	4	5	2	0	.818	0	4	5	2	0.4	.818
1977	2 teams	SEA A	(43G 3–2)		CLE A	(2G 0–0)																				
"	total	3	2	.600	4.96	45	0	0	74.1	64	41	50	0	3	2	3	0	0	0	—	3	6	0	0	0.2	1.000
5 yrs.		3	10	.231	4.72	121	4	0	244	212	158	189	0	3	7	5	5	1	0	.200	10	19	2	0	0.3	.935

Danny Lazar

LAZAR, JOHN DANIEL
B. Nov. 14, 1943, East Chicago, Ind. BL TL 6'1" 190 lbs.

Year	Team	W	L	PCT	ERA	G	GS	CG	IP	H	BB	SO	ShO	W	L	SV	AB	H	HR	BA	PO	A	E	DP	TC/G	FA
1968	CHI A	0	1	.000	4.05	8	1	0	13.1	14	4	11	0	0	0	0	2	0	0	.000	1	2	0	0	0.4	1.000
1969		0	0	—	6.53	9	3	0	20.2	21	11	9	0	0	0	0	4	0	0	.000	2	2	0	0	0.4	1.000
2 yrs.		0	1	.000	5.56	17	4	0	34	35	15	20	0	0	0	0	6	0	0	.000	3	4	0	0	0.4	1.000

Jack Lazorko

LAZORKO, JACK THOMAS
B. Mar. 30, 1956, Hoboken, N. J. BR TR 5'11" 198 lbs.

Year	Team	W	L	PCT	ERA	G	GS	CG	IP	H	BB	SO	ShO	W	L	SV	AB	H	HR	BA	PO	A	E	DP	TC/G	FA
1984	MIL A	0	1	.000	4.31	15	1	0	39.2	37	22	24	0	0	0	1	0	0	0	—	3	5	0	0	0.5	1.000
1985	SEA A	0	0	—	3.54	15	0	0	20.1	23	8	7	0	0	0	0	0	0	0	—	4	4	0	1	0.5	1.000

Year	Team		W	L	PCT	ERA	G	GS	CG	IP	H	BB	SO	ShO	Relief Pitching			Batting			BA	PO	A	E	DP	TC/G	FA
															W	L	SV	AB	H	HR							
Jack Lazorko	*continued*																										
1986	DET	A	0	0	–	4.05	3	0	0	6.2	8	4	3	0	0	0	0	0	0	0	–	1	1	0	0	0.7	1.000
1987	CAL	A	5	6	.455	4.59	26	11	2	117.2	108	44	55	0	2	1	0	0	0	0	–	8	25	0	1	1.3	1.000
1988			0	1	.000	3.35	10	3	0	37.2	37	16	19	0	0	0	0	0	0	0	–	2	7	0	0	0.9	1.000
5 yrs.			5	8	.385	4.22	69	15	2	222	213	94	108	0	2	2	2	0	0	0	–	18	42	0	2	0.9	1.000

Charlie Lea

LEA, CHARLES WILLIAM
B. Dec. 25, 1956, Orleans, France

BR TR 6'4" 194 lbs.

Year	Team		W	L	PCT	ERA	G	GS	CG	IP	H	BB	SO	ShO	W	L	SV	AB	H	HR	BA	PO	A	E	DP	TC/G	FA
1980	MON	N	7	5	.583	3.72	21	9	0	104	103	55	56	0	0	0	0	37	3	0	.081	4	10	0	0	0.7	1.000
1981			5	4	.556	4.64	16	11	2	64	63	26	31	2	0	0	0	15	2	0	.133	5	8	0	2	0.8	1.000
1982			12	10	.545	3.24	27	27	4	177.2	145	56	115	2	0	0	0	65	8	0	.123	6	22	1	1	1.1	.966
1983			16	11	.593	3.12	33	33	8	222	195	84	137	4	0	0	0	70	8	0	.114	19	27	2	0	1.5	.958
1984			15	10	.600	2.89	30	30	8	224.1	198	68	123	0	0	0	0	72	8	0	.111	19	33	1	1	1.8	.981
1987			0	1	.000	36.00	1	1	0	1	4	2	1	0	0	0	0	0	0	0	–	0	0	0	0	0.0	–
1988	MIN	A	7	7	.500	4.85	24	23	0	130	156	50	72	0	0	0	0	0	0	0	–	12	12	0	1	1.0	1.000
7 yrs.			62	48	.564	3.54	152	144	22	923	864	341	535	8	0	0	0	259	29	0	.112	65	112	4	5	1.2	.978

Rick Leach

LEACH, RICHARD MAX
B. May 4, 1957, Ann Arbor, Mich.

BL TL 6'1" 180 lbs.

Year	Team		W	L	PCT	ERA	G	GS	CG	IP	H	BB	SO	ShO	W	L	SV	AB	H	HR	BA	PO	A	E	DP	TC/G	FA
1984	TOR	A	0	0	–	27.00	1	0	0	1	2	2	0	0	0	0	0	*				0	0	0	0	0.0	–

Terry Leach

LEACH, TERRY HESTER
B. Mar. 13, 1954, Selma, Ala.

BR TR 6' 215 lbs.

Year	Team		W	L	PCT	ERA	G	GS	CG	IP	H	BB	SO	ShO	W	L	SV	AB	H	HR	BA	PO	A	E	DP	TC/G	FA
1981	NY	N	1	1	.500	2.57	21	1	0	35	26	12	16	0	1	0	0	1	0	0	.000	4	7	0	0	0.5	1.000
1982			2	1	.667	4.17	21	1	1	45.1	46	18	30	1	1	1	3	8	1	0	.125	0	8	1	0	0.4	.889
1985			3	4	.429	2.91	22	4	1	55.2	48	14	30	1	0	3	1	12	2	0	.167	5	14	0	0	0.9	1.000
1986			0	0	–	2.70	6	0	0	6.2	6	3	4	0	0	0	0	0	0	0	–	0	2	0	0	0.3	1.000
1987			11	1	.917	3.22	44	12	1	131.1	132	29	61	1	4	0	0	33	2	0	.061	18	21	2	3	0.9	.951
1988			7	2	.778	2.54	52	0	0	92	95	24	51	0	7	2	3	14	2	0	.143	10	22	0	0	0.6	1.000
1989	2 teams		NY N	(10G 0–0)		KC A	(30G 5–6)																				
"	total		5	6	.455	4.17	40	3	0	95	97	40	36	0	4	4	0	4	0	0	.000	7	25	4	0	0.9	.889
7 yrs.			29	15	.659	3.28	206	21	3	461	450	140	228	3	17	10	7	72	7	0	.097	44	99	7	3	0.7	.953

LEAGUE CHAMPIONSHIP SERIES

Year	Team		W	L	PCT	ERA	G	GS	CG	IP	H	BB	SO	ShO	W	L	SV	AB	H	HR	BA	PO	A	E	DP	TC/G	FA
1988	NY	N	0	0	–	0.00	3	0	0	5	4	1	4	0	0	0	0	0	0	0	–	1	0	0	0	0.3	1.000

Luis Leal

LEAL, LUIS ENRIQUE
Born Luis Enrique Albardo y Leal.
B. Mar. 21, 1957, Barquisimento, Venezuela

BR TR 6'3" 205 lbs.

Year	Team		W	L	PCT	ERA	G	GS	CG	IP	H	BB	SO	ShO	W	L	SV	AB	H	HR	BA	PO	A	E	DP	TC/G	FA
1980	TOR	A	3	4	.429	4.50	13	10	1	60	72	31	26	0	0	0	0	0	0	0	–	3	7	1	0	0.8	.909
1981			7	13	.350	3.67	29	19	3	130	127	44	71	0	1	3	0	0	0	0	–	4	19	0	0	0.8	1.000
1982			12	15	.444	3.93	38	38	10	249.2	250	79	111	0	0	0	0	0	0	0	–	17	31	0	2	1.3	1.000
1983			13	12	.520	4.31	35	35	7	217.1	216	65	116	1	0	0	0	0	0	0	–	20	23	1	2	1.3	.977
1984			13	8	.619	3.89	35	35	6	222.1	221	77	134	2	0	0	0	0	0	0	–	12	30	0	3	1.2	1.000
1985			3	6	.333	5.75	15	14	0	67.1	82	24	33	0	0	1	0	0	0	0	–	5	10	1	1	1.1	.938
6 yrs.			51	58	.468	4.14	165	151	27	946.2	968	320	491	3	1	4	1	0	0	0	–	61	120	3	8	1.1	.984

King Lear

LEAR, CHARLES BERNARD
B. Jan. 23, 1891, Greencastle, Pa. D. Oct. 31, 1976, Greencastle, Pa.

BR TR 6' 175 lbs.

Year	Team		W	L	PCT	ERA	G	GS	CG	IP	H	BB	SO	ShO	W	L	SV	AB	H	HR	BA	PO	A	E	DP	TC/G	FA
1914	CIN	N	1	2	.333	3.07	17	4	3	55.2	55	19	20	1	0	0	0	16	3	0	.188	1	14	1	0	0.9	.938
1915			6	10	.375	3.01	40	15	9	167.2	169	45	46	0	1	3	0	47	8	0	.170	4	29	3	2	0.9	.917
2 yrs.			7	12	.368	3.02	57	19	12	223.1	224	64	66	1	1	3	0	63	11	0	.175	5	43	4	2	0.9	.923

Frank Leary

LEARY, FRANCIS PATRICK
B. Feb. 26, 1881, Wayland, Mass. D. Oct. 4, 1907, Natick, Mass.

Year	Team		W	L	PCT	ERA	G	GS	CG	IP	H	BB	SO	ShO	W	L	SV	AB	H	HR	BA	PO	A	E	DP	TC/G	FA
1907	CIN	N	0	1	.000	1.13	2	1	0	8	7	6	4	0	0	1	0	2	0	0	.000	0	4	0	0	2.0	1.000

Jack Leary

LEARY, JOHN J.
B. 1858, New Haven, Conn. Deceased.

TL 5'11" 186 lbs.

Year	Team		W	L	PCT	ERA	G	GS	CG	IP	H	BB	SO	ShO	W	L	SV	AB	H	HR	BA	PO	A	E	DP	TC/G	FA
1880	BOS	N	0	1	.000	15.00	1	1	0	3	8	0	1	0	0	0	0	3	0	0	.000	0	0	0	0	1.0	1.000
1881	DET	N	0	2	.000	4.15	2	2	1	13	13	2	2	0	0	0	0	11	3	0	.273	1	1	1	0	1.5	.667
1882	2 teams		PIT AA	(3G 1–0)		BAL AA	(3G 2–1)																				
"	total		3	1	.750	3.43	6	5	4	44.2	57	11	21	0	0	0	0	275	79	2	.287	1	17	3	1	3.5	.857
1884	2 teams		ALT U	(3G 0–3)		CHI U	(2G 0–2)																				
"	total		0	5	.000	5.29	5	4	3	34	45	7	13	0	0	1	0	73	10	0	.137	2	9	4	0	3.0	.733
4 yrs.			3	9	.250	4.56	14	12	8	94.2	123	20	23	0	0	1	0	*				4	28	8	1	2.9	.800

Tim Leary

LEARY, TIMOTHY JAMES
B. Mar. 21, 1958, Santa Monica, Calif.

BR TR 6'3" 205 lbs.

Year	Team		W	L	PCT	ERA	G	GS	CG	IP	H	BB	SO	ShO	W	L	SV	AB	H	HR	BA	PO	A	E	DP	TC/G	FA
1981	NY	N	0	0	–	0.00	1	1	0	2	0	1	3	0	0	0	0	1	0	0	.000	0	0	0	0	0.0	–
1983			1	1	.500	3.38	2	2	1	10.2	15	4	9	0	0	0	0	3	1	0	.333	1	3	0	0	2.0	1.000
1984			3	3	.500	4.02	20	7	0	53.2	61	18	29	0	0	3	0	10	3	1	.300	3	4	1	0	0.4	.875
1985	MIL	A	1	4	.200	4.05	5	5	0	33.1	40	8	29	0	0	0	0	0	0	0	–	1	0	0	0	1.6	1.000
1986			12	12	.500	4.21	33	30	3	188.1	216	53	110	2	0	0	0	0	0	0	–	22	26	1	1	1.5	.980
1987	LA	N	3	11	.214	4.76	39	12	0	107.2	121	36	61	0	1	4	0	23	7	0	.304	9	18	0	2	0.7	1.000
1988			17	11	.607	2.91	34	33	9	228.2	201	56	180	6	0	0	0	67	18	0	.269	24	34	1	4	1.7	.983
1989	2 teams		LA N	(19G 6–7)		CIN N	(14G 2–7)																				
"	total		8	14	.364	3.52	33	31	2	207	205	68	123	0	1	1	0	59	7	0	.119	20	31	2	2	1.6	.962
8 yrs.			45	56	.446	3.71	168	122	15	831.1	859	244	544	8	5	5	1	163	36	1	.221	80	123	5	9	1.2	.976

Year	Team		W	L	PCT	ERA	G	GS	CG	IP	H	BB	SO	ShO	Relief Pitching W	L	SV	Batting AB	H	HR	BA	PO	A	E	DP	TC/G	FA

Tim Leary *continued*

LEAGUE CHAMPIONSHIP SERIES

Year	Team		W	L	PCT	ERA	G	GS	CG	IP	H	BB	SO	ShO	W	L	SV	AB	H	HR	BA	PO	A	E	DP	TC/G	FA
1988	LA	N	0	1	.000	6.23	2	1	0	4.1	8	3	3	0	0	0	0	1	0	0	.000	0	1	0	0	0.5	1.000

WORLD SERIES

| 1988 | LA | N | 0 | 0 | – | 1.35 | 2 | 0 | 0 | 6.2 | 6 | 2 | 4 | 0 | 0 | 0 | 0 | 0 | 0 | 0 | – | 1 | 3 | 0 | 1 | 2.0 | 1.000 |

Razor Ledbetter

LEDBETTER, RALPH OVERTON BR TR 6'3" 190 lbs.
B. Dec. 8, 1894, Rutherford College, N. C. D. Feb. 1, 1969, West Palm Beach, Fla.

| 1915 | DET | A | 0 | 0 | – | 0.00 | 1 | 0 | 0 | 1 | 1 | 0 | 0 | 0 | 0 | 0 | 0 | 0 | 0 | 0 | – | 0 | 1 | 0 | 0 | 1.0 | 1.000 |

Bill Lee

LEE, WILLIAM CRUTCHER (Big Bill) BR TR 6'3" 195 lbs.
B. Oct. 21, 1909, Plaquemine, La. D. June 15, 1977, Plaquemine, La.

Year	Team		W	L	PCT	ERA	G	GS	CG	IP	H	BB	SO	ShO	W	L	SV	AB	H	HR	BA	PO	A	E	DP	TC/G	FA
1934	CHI	N	13	14	.481	3.40	35	29	16	214.1	218	74	104	4	0	0	1	76	10	0	.132	15	48	4	2	1.9	.940
1935			20	6	**.769**	2.96	39	32	18	252	241	84	100	3	2	0	1	102	24	0	.235	12	52	7	4	1.8	.901
1936			18	11	.621	3.31	43	33	20	258.2	238	93	102	4	1	2	1	87	12	1	.138	12	61	7	5	1.9	.913
1937			14	15	.483	3.54	42	33	17	272.1	289	73	108	2	0	1	3	87	15	1	.172	20	70	5	5	2.3	.947
1938			**22**	9	**.710**	**2.66**	44	**37**	19	291	281	74	121	**9**	1	1	2	101	20	0	.198	18	61	5	3	1.9	.940
1939			19	15	.559	3.44	37	**36**	20	282.1	295	85	105	1	0	1	0	103	13	1	.126	15	80	5	3	2.7	.950
1940			9	17	.346	5.03	37	30	9	211.1	246	70	70	1	1	0	0	76	10	0	.132	10	42	6	3	1.6	.897
1941			8	14	.364	3.76	28	22	12	167.1	179	43	62	0	0	1	1	59	11	2	.186	10	39	6	3	2.0	.891
1942			13	13	.500	3.85	32	30	18	219.2	221	67	75	1	0	0	0	69	11	0	.159	10	55	2	2	2.1	.970
1943	2 teams	CHI N (13G 3–7)		PHI N	(13G 1–5)																						
"	total		4	12	.250	4.01	26	19	6	139	153	48	35	0	0	0	0	43	8	0	.186	9	21	3	1	1.3	.909
1944	PHI	N	10	11	.476	3.15	31	28	11	208.1	199	57	50	3	0	0	1	72	14	0	.194	17	47	4	2	2.2	.941
1945	2 teams	PHI N (13G 3–6)		BOS N	(16G 6–3)																						
"	total		9	9	.500	3.58	29	26	8	183.2	219	66	25	1	0	0	0	55	8	0	.145	5	46	1	1	1.8	.981
1946	BOS	N	10	9	.526	4.18	25	21	8	140	148	45	32	0	1	0	0	47	8	0	.170	6	35	1	0	1.7	.976
1947	CHI	N	0	2	.000	4.50	14	2	0	24	26	14	9	0	0	0	0	3	1	0	.333	4	5	2	0	0.8	.818
	14 yrs.		169	157	.518	3.54	462	378	182	2864	2953	893	998	29	6	7	13	980	165	5	.168	163	662	58	34	1.9	.934

WORLD SERIES

1935	CHI	N	0	0	–	3.48	2	1	0	10.1	11	5	5	0	0	0	0	1	0	0	.000	1	0	0	0	1.0	1.000
1938			0	2	.000	2.45	2	2	0	11	15	1	8	0	0	0	1	3	0	0	.000	1	0	0	0	0.5	1.000
	2 yrs.		0	2	.000	2.95	4	3	0	21.1	26	6	13	0	0	0	1	4	0	0	.000	2	1	0	0	0.8	1.000

Bill Lee

LEE, WILLIAM FRANCIS (Spaceman) BL TL 6'3" 205 lbs.
B. Dec. 28, 1946, Burbank, Calif.

Year	Team		W	L	PCT	ERA	G	GS	CG	IP	H	BB	SO	ShO	W	L	SV	AB	H	HR	BA	PO	A	E	DP	TC/G	FA
1969	BOS	A	1	3	.250	4.50	20	1	0	52	56	28	45	0	1	2	0	10	0	0	.000	2	6	1	0	0.5	.889
1970			2	2	.500	4.62	11	5	0	37	48	14	19	0	0	0	1	11	0	0	.000	1	10	0	1	1.0	1.000
1971			9	2	.818	2.74	47	3	0	102	102	46	74	0	8	2	5	23	5	0	.217	2	19	1	0	0.5	.955
1972			7	4	.636	3.20	47	0	0	84.1	75	32	43	0	7	4	5	16	3	1	.188	6	24	0	2	0.6	1.000
1973			17	11	.607	2.74	38	33	18	285.1	275	76	120	1	1	0	1	0	0	0	–	10	57	6	2	1.9	.918
1974			17	15	.531	3.51	38	37	16	282	**320**	67	95	1	0	0	0	0	0	0	–	9	69	8	3	2.3	.907
1975			17	9	.654	3.95	41	34	17	260	274	69	78	4	0	0	0	0	0	0	–	9	54	5	4	1.7	.926
1976			5	7	.417	5.63	24	14	1	96	124	28	29	0	1	0	3	0	0	0	–	2	22	2	1	1.1	.923
1977			9	5	.643	4.42	27	16	4	128.1	155	29	31	0	1	0	1	0	0	0	–	3	32	1	4	1.3	.972
1978			10	10	.500	3.46	28	24	8	177	198	59	44	1	0	0	0	0	0	0	–	9	32	3	2	1.6	.932
1979	MON	N	16	10	.615	3.04	33	33	6	222	230	46	59	3	0	0	0	74	16	0	.216	11	41	1	2	1.6	.981
1980			4	6	.400	4.96	24	18	2	118	156	22	34	0	1	0	0	41	9	0	.220	7	19	0	2	1.1	1.000
1981			5	6	.455	2.93	31	7	0	89	90	14	34	0	3	3	6	22	8	1	.364	12	27	0	1	1.3	1.000
1982			0	0	–	4.38	7	0	0	12.1	19	1	8	0	0	0	0	0	0	0	–	0	3	0	0	0.4	1.000
	14 yrs.		119	90	.569	3.62	416	225	72	1945.1	2122	531	713	10	22	13	19	197	41	2	.208	83	415	28	24	1.3	.947

DIVISIONAL PLAYOFF SERIES

| 1981 | MON | N | 0 | 0 | – | 0.00 | 1 | 0 | 0 | .2 | 2 | 0 | 1 | 0 | 0 | 0 | 0 | – | – | – | – | 0 | 0 | 0 | 0 | 0.0 | – |

LEAGUE CHAMPIONSHIP SERIES

| 1981 | MON | N | 0 | 0 | – | 0.00 | 1 | 0 | 0 | .1 | 1 | 0 | 0 | 0 | 0 | 0 | 0 | – | – | – | – | 0 | 0 | 0 | 0 | 0.0 | – |

WORLD SERIES

| 1975 | BOS | A | 0 | 0 | – | 3.14 | 2 | 2 | 0 | 14.1 | 12 | 3 | 7 | 0 | 0 | 0 | 0 | 6 | 1 | 0 | .167 | 1 | 0 | 0 | 0 | 0.5 | 1.000 |

Bob Lee

LEE, ROBERT DEAN (Moose, Horse) BR TR 6'3" 225 lbs.
B. Nov. 26, 1937, Ottumwa, Iowa

Year	Team		W	L	PCT	ERA	G	GS	CG	IP	H	BB	SO	ShO	W	L	SV	AB	H	HR	BA	PO	A	E	DP	TC/G	FA
1964	LA	A	6	5	.545	1.51	64	5	0	137	87	58	111	0	5	4	19	22	0	0	.000	9	10	2	1	0.3	.905
1965	CAL	A	9	7	.563	1.92	69	0	0	131.1	95	42	89	0	9	7	23	21	3	1	.143	3	18	0	0	0.3	1.000
1966			5	4	.556	2.74	61	0	0	101.2	90	31	46	0	5	4	16	11	0	0	.000	4	16	1	0	0.3	.952
1967	2 teams	LA N (4G 0–0)		CIN N	(27G 3–3)																						
"	total		3	3	.500	4.55	31	1	0	57.1	57	28	35	0	2	3	4	8	3	0	.375	3	6	1	1	0.3	.900
1968	CIN	N	2	4	.333	5.15	44	1	0	64.2	73	37	34	0	2	4	3	5	1	0	.200	4	5	0	0	0.2	1.000
	5 yrs.		25	23	.521	2.71	269	7	0	492	402	196	315	0	23	22	63	67	7	1	.104	23	55	4	3	0.3	.951

Don Lee

LEE, DONALD EDWARD BR TR 6'4" 205 lbs.
Son of Thornton Lee.
B. Feb. 26, 1934, Globe, Ariz.

Year	Team		W	L	PCT	ERA	G	GS	CG	IP	H	BB	SO	ShO	W	L	SV	AB	H	HR	BA	PO	A	E	DP	TC/G	FA
1957	DET	A	1	3	.250	4.66	11	6	0	38.2	48	18	19	0	0	1	0	12	2	0	.167	1	6	0	0	0.6	1.000
1958			0	0	–	9.00	1	0	0	2	1	1	0	0	0	0	0	0	0	0	–	0	0	0	0	0.0	–
1960	WAS	A	8	7	.533	3.44	44	20	1	165	160	64	88	0	3	2	3	43	5	1	.116	4	31	0	3	0.8	1.000
1961	MIN	A	3	6	.333	3.52	37	10	4	115	93	35	65	0	1	2	1	30	2	0	.067	8	29	2	1	1.1	.949
1962	2 teams	MIN A (9G 3–3)		LA A	(27G 8–8)																						
"	total		11	11	.500	3.46	36	31	5	205.1	204	63	102	2	0	0	0	68	13	0	.191	13	28	1	1	1.2	.976
1963	LA	A	8	11	.421	3.68	40	23	3	154	148	51	89	2	0	1	0	45	7	0	.156	8	21	1	4	0.8	.967
1964			5	4	.556	2.72	33	8	0	89.1	99	25	73	0	3	1	2	23	6	0	.261	1	12	0	0	0.4	1.000

Year	Team	W	L	PCT	ERA	G	GS	CG	IP	H	BB	SO	ShO	Relief Pitching W	L	SV	Batting AB	H	HR	BA	PO	A	E	DP	TC/G	FA

Don Lee *continued*

Year	Team	W	L	PCT	ERA	G	GS	CG	IP	H	BB	SO	ShO	W	L	SV	AB	H	HR	BA	PO	A	E	DP	TC/G	FA
1965	2 teams	CAL A	(10G 0–1)		HOU N	(7G 0–0)																				
"	total	0	1	.000	5.32	17	0	0	22	29	8	15	0	0	1	0	4	1	0	.250	3	4	1	0	0.5	.875
1966	2 teams	HOU N	(9G 2–0)		CHI N	(16G 2–1)																				
"	total	4	1	.800	4.86	25	0	0	37	45	16	16	0	4	1	0	1	1	0	1.000	3	9	1	2	0.5	.923
9 yrs.		40	44	.476	3.61	244	97	13	828.1	827	281	467	4	13	7	11	226	37	1	.164	43	140	6	11	0.8	.968

Mark Lee

LEE, MARK LINDEN B. June 14, 1953, Inglewood, Calif. BR TR 6'4" 225 lbs.

Year	Team	W	L	PCT	ERA	G	GS	CG	IP	H	BB	SO	ShO	W	L	SV	AB	H	HR	BA	PO	A	E	DP	TC/G	FA
1978	SD N	5	1	.833	3.28	56	0	0	85	74	36	31	0	5	1	2	5	0	0	.000	5	22	1	0	0.5	.964
1979		2	4	.333	4.29	46	1	0	65	88	25	25	0	2	3	5	6	2	0	.333	3	14	1	1	0.4	.944
1980	PIT N	0	1	.000	4.50	4	0	0	6	5	3	2	0	0	1	0	0	0	0	–	2	2	0	0	1.0	1.000
1981		0	2	.000	2.70	12	0	0	20	17	5	5	0	0	2	2	2	1	0	.500	6	7	1	0	1.2	.929
4 yrs.		7	8	.467	3.63	118	1	0	176	184	69	63	0	7	7	9	13	3	0	.231	16	45	3	1	0.5	.953

Mark Lee

LEE, MARK OWEN B. July 20, 1964, Williston, N. D. BL TL 6'3" 198 lbs.

Year	Team	W	L	PCT	ERA	G	GS	CG	IP	H	BB	SO	ShO	W	L	SV	AB	H	HR	BA	PO	A	E	DP	TC/G	FA
1988	KC A	0	0	–	3.60	4	0	0	5	6	1	0	0	0	0	0	0	0	0	–	0	1	0	1	0.3	1.000

Mike Lee

LEE, MICHAEL RANDALL B. May 19, 1941, Bell, Calif. BL TL 6'5" 220 lbs.

Year	Team	W	L	PCT	ERA	G	GS	CG	IP	H	BB	SO	ShO	W	L	SV	AB	H	HR	BA	PO	A	E	DP	TC/G	FA
1960	CLE A	0	0	–	2.00	7	0	0	9	6	11	6	0	0	0	0	0	0	0	–	0	0	0	0	0.0	–
1963	LA A	1	1	.500	3.81	6	4	0	26	30	14	11	0	0	0	0	7	0	0	.000	1	10	0	0	1.8	1.000
2 yrs.		1	1	.500	3.34	13	4	0	35	36	25	17	0	0	0	0	7	0	0	.000	1	10	0	0	0.8	1.000

Roy Lee

LEE, ROY EDWIN B. Sept. 28, 1917, Elmira, N. Y. D. Nov. 11, 1985, St. Louis, Mo. BL TL 5'11½" 175 lbs.

Year	Team	W	L	PCT	ERA	G	GS	CG	IP	H	BB	SO	ShO	W	L	SV	AB	H	HR	BA	PO	A	E	DP	TC/G	FA
1945	NY N	0	2	.000	11.57	3	1	0	7	8	3	0	0	0	1	0	1	0	0	.000	0	0	0	0	0.0	–

Thornton Lee

LEE, THORNTON STARR (Lefty) Father of Don Lee. B. Sept. 13, 1906, Sonoma, Calif. BL TL 6'3" 205 lbs.

Year	Team	W	L	PCT	ERA	G	GS	CG	IP	H	BB	SO	ShO	W	L	SV	AB	H	HR	BA	PO	A	E	DP	TC/G	FA
1933	CLE A	1	1	.500	4.15	3	2	2	17.1	13	11	7	0	0	0	0	8	3	0	.375	0	3	0	0	1.0	1.000
1934		1	1	.500	5.04	24	6	2	85.2	105	44	41	0	0	0	0	21	2	0	.095	4	18	2	1	1.0	.917
1935		7	10	.412	4.04	32	20	8	180.2	179	91	81	1	2	1	1	61	12	0	.197	11	41	3	3	1.7	.945
1936		3	5	.375	4.89	43	8	2	127	138	67	49	0	1	2	3	41	5	0	.122	3	35	2	0	0.9	.950
1937	CHI A	12	10	.545	3.52	30	25	13	204.2	209	60	80	2	0	0	0	71	15	0	.211	9	34	3	0	1.5	.935
1938		13	12	.520	3.49	33	30	18	245.1	252	94	77	1	0	1	1	97	25	4	.258	1	46	5	2	1.6	.904
1939		15	11	.577	4.21	33	29	15	235	260	70	81	2	0	1	3	91	15	0	.165	6	45	2	0	1.6	.962
1940		12	13	.480	3.47	28	27	24	228	223	56	87	1	0	0	0	84	23	0	.274	5	31	4	2	1.4	.900
1941		22	11	.667	2.37	35	34	30	300.1	258	92	130	3	0	0	1	114	29	0	.254	10	52	5	2	1.9	.925
1942		2	6	.250	3.32	11	8	6	76	82	31	25	1	0	0	0	30	6	0	.200	1	7	1	2	0.8	.889
1943		5	9	.357	4.18	19	19	7	127	129	50	35	1	0	0	0	42	3	0	.071	3	17	3	1	1.2	.870
1944		3	9	.250	3.02	15	14	6	113.1	105	25	39	0	0	0	0	42	4	0	.095	3	32	2	2	2.5	.946
1945		15	12	.556	2.44	29	28	19	228.1	208	76	108	1	1	0	0	78	14	0	.179	6	38	2	4	1.6	.957
1946		2	4	.333	3.53	7	7	2	43.1	39	23	23	0	0	0	0	15	4	0	.267	0	7	2	1	1.3	.778
1947		3	7	.300	4.47	21	11	2	86.2	86	56	57	0	0	3	1	29	6	0	.207	4	2	1	1	1.0	.905
1948	NY N	1	3	.250	4.41	11	4	1	32.1	41	12	17	0	0	1	0	11	1	0	.091	1	7	0	0	0.7	1.000
16 yrs.		117	124	.485	3.56	374	272	155	2331.1	2327	838	937	14	4	9	10	835	167	4	.200	67	428	38	21	1.4	.929

Tom Lee

LEE, THOMAS FRANK B. June 8, 1862, Milwaukee, Wis. D. Mar. 4, 1886, Milwaukee, Wis.

Year	Team	W	L	PCT	ERA	G	GS	CG	IP	H	BB	SO	ShO	W	L	SV	AB	H	HR	BA	PO	A	E	DP	TC/G	FA
1884	2 teams	CHI N	(5G 1–4)		BAL U	(15G 5–8)																				
"	total	6	12	.333	3.50	20	19	17	167.1	176	44	95	0	0	0	0	106	26	0	.245	15	34	6	1	2.8	.891

Watty Lee

LEE, WYATT ARNOLD (Indian) B. Aug. 12, 1879, Lynch's Station, Va. D. Mar. 6, 1936, Washington, D. C. BL TL 5'10½" 171 lbs.

Year	Team	W	L	PCT	ERA	G	GS	CG	IP	H	BB	SO	ShO	W	L	SV	AB	H	HR	BA	PO	A	E	DP	TC/G	FA
1901	WAS A	16	16	.500	4.40	36	33	25	262	328	45	63	2	0	0	0	129	33	0	.256	11	81	5	3	2.7	.948
1902		5	7	.417	5.05	13	10	10	98	118	20	24	0	1	1	0	391	100	4	.256	5	32	2	0	3.0	.949
1903		8	12	.400	3.08	22	20	15	166.2	169	40	70	2	1	0	0	231	48	0	.208	13	58	1	3	3.3	.986
1904	PIT N	1	2	.333	8.74	5	3	1	22.2	34	9	5	0	1	0	0	12	4	0	.333	1	7	1	0	1.8	.889
4 yrs.		30	37	.448	4.29	76	66	51	549.1	649	114	162	4	3	3	0	*				30	178	9	6	2.9	.959

Sam Leever

LEEVER, SAMUEL (The Goshen Schoolmaster) B. Dec. 23, 1871, Goshen, Ohio D. May 19, 1953, Goshen, Ohio BR TR 5'10½" 175 lbs.

Year	Team	W	L	PCT	ERA	G	GS	CG	IP	H	BB	SO	ShO	W	L	SV	AB	H	HR	BA	PO	A	E	DP	TC/G	FA
1898	PIT N	1	0	1.000	2.45	5	5	3	33	26	5	15	0	0	0	0	12	3	0	.250	3	5	0	0	1.6	1.000
1899		21	23	.477	3.18	51	39	35	379	353	122	121	4	2	5	3	146	33	0	.226	10	100	6	2	2.3	.948
1900		15	13	.536	2.71	30	29	25	232.2	236	48	84	3	0	0	0	88	18	1	.205	8	52	4	0	2.1	.938
1901		14	5	.737	2.86	21	20	18	176	182	39	82	2	1	0	0	71	13	0	.183	3	54	2	0	2.8	.966
1902		16	7	.696	2.39	28	26	23	222	203	31	86	4	0	0	2	90	16	0	.178	3	42	2	0	1.7	.957
1903		25	7	.781	2.06	36	34	30	284.1	255	60	90	7	0	0	1	115	19	0	.165	12	76	4	1	2.6	.957
1904		18	11	.621	2.17	34	32	26	253.1	224	54	63	1	1	0	0	99	26	1	.263	11	67	1	2	2.3	.987
1905		19	6	.760	2.70	33	29	20	230	199	54	81	3	1	0	0	88	9	0	.102	7	70	8	1	2.6	.906
1906		22	7	.759	2.32	36	31	25	260.1	229	48	76	6	1	1	0	95	20	0	.211	11	52	3	1	1.8	.955
1907		14	9	.609	1.66	31	24	17	216.2	182	46	65	5	2	1	0	73	11	0	.151	4	39	2	1	1.5	.956
1908		15	7	.682	2.10	38	20	14	192.2	179	41	28	4	2	2	2	61	9	0	.148	8	44	2	0	1.4	.963
1909		8	1	.889	2.83	19	4	2	70	74	14	23	0	6	1	2	24	4	0	.167	0	23	0	0	1.2	1.000
1910		6	5	.545	2.76	26	8	4	111	104	25	33	0	3	2	2	31	2	0	.065	3	35	0	1	1.5	1.000
13 yrs.		194	101	.658	2.47	388	299	241	2661	2449	587	847	39	19	12	12	993	183	2	.184	83	659	34	11	2.0	.956
					8th																					

Year	Team		W	L	PCT	ERA	G	GS	CG	IP	H	BB	SO	ShO	Relief Pitching W	L	SV	Batting AB	H	HR	BA	PO	A	E	DP	TC/G	FA

Sam Leever *continued*

WORLD SERIES

Year	Team		W	L	PCT	ERA	G	GS	CG	IP	H	BB	SO	ShO	W	L	SV	AB	H	HR	BA	PO	A	E	DP	TC/G	FA
1903	PIT	N	0	2	.000	6.30	2	2	1	10	13	3	2	0	0	0	0	4	0	0	.000	0	2	0	0	1.0	1.000

Bill LeFebvre

LeFEBVRE, WILFRID HENRY (Lefty)
B. Nov. 11, 1915, Natick, R. I. — BL TL 5'11½" 180 lbs.

Year	Team		W	L	PCT	ERA	G	GS	CG	IP	H	BB	SO	ShO	W	L	SV	AB	H	HR	BA	PO	A	E	DP	TC/G	FA
1938	BOS	A	0	0	–	13.50	1	0	0	4	8	0	0	0	0	0	0	1	1	1	1.000	0	0	0	0	0.0	–
1939			1	1	.500	5.81	5	3	0	26.1	35	14	8	0	0	0	0	10	3	0	.300	1	2	0	0	0.6	1.000
1943	WAS	A	2	0	1.000	4.45	6	3	1	32.1	33	16	10	0	1	0	0	14	4	0	.286	1	6	0	1	1.2	1.000
1944			2	4	.333	4.52	24	4	2	69.2	86	21	18	0	1	1	3	62	16	0	.258	1	13	1	2	0.6	.933
4 yrs.			5	5	.500	5.03	36	10	3	132.1	162	51	36	0	2	1	3	*				3	21	1	3	0.7	.960

Craig Lefferts

LEFFERTS, CRAIG LINDSAY
B. Sept. 29, 1957, Munich, West Germany — BL TL 6'1" 180 lbs.

Year	Team		W	L	PCT	ERA	G	GS	CG	IP	H	BB	SO	ShO	W	L	SV	AB	H	HR	BA	PO	A	E	DP	TC/G	FA
1983	CHI	N	3	4	.429	3.13	56	5	0	89	80	29	60	0	2	3	1	18	2	0	.111	8	13	1	0	0.4	.955
1984	SD	N	3	4	.429	2.13	62	0	0	105.2	88	24	56	0	3	4	10	17	5	0	.294	5	10	1	2	0.3	.938
1985			7	6	.538	3.35	60	0	0	83.1	75	30	48	0	7	6	2	4	1	0	.250	4	11	0	1	0.3	1.000
1986			9	8	.529	3.09	**83**	0	0	107.2	98	44	72	0	9	8	4	8	1	0	.125	3	24	0	3	0.3	1.000
1987	2 teams					SD N (33G 2–2)				SF N (44G 3–3)																	
"	total		5	5	.500	3.83	77	0	0	98.2	92	33	57	0	5	5	6	7	2	0	.286	5	11	2	1	0.2	.889
1988	SF	N	3	8	.273	2.92	64	0	0	92.1	74	23	58	0	3	8	11	9	0	0	.000	2	11	0	0	0.2	1.000
1989			2	4	.333	2.69	70	0	0	107	93	22	71	0	2	4	20	7	0	0	.000	5	9	0	2	0.2	1.000
7 yrs.			32	39	.451	3.00	472	5	0	683.2	600	205	422	0	31	38	54	70	11	1	.157	32	89	4	9	0.3	.968

LEAGUE CHAMPIONSHIP SERIES

Year	Team		W	L	PCT	ERA	G	GS	CG	IP	H	BB	SO	ShO	W	L	SV	AB	H	HR	BA	PO	A	E	DP	TC/G	FA
1984	SD	N	2	0	1.000	0.00	3	0	0	4	1	1	1	0	2	0	0	0	0	0	–	0	0	0	0	0.0	–
1987	SF	N	0	0	–	0.00	3	0	0	2	3	1	1	0	0	0	0	0	0	0	–	0	2	0	1	0.7	1.000
1989			0	0	–	9.00	2	0	0	1	1	2	1	0	0	0	0	0	0	0	–	0	0	0	0	0.0	–
3 yrs.			2	0	1.000	1.29	8	0	0	7	5	4	2	0	2	0	0	0	0	0	–	0	2	0	1	0.3	1.000

WORLD SERIES

Year	Team		W	L	PCT	ERA	G	GS	CG	IP	H	BB	SO	ShO	W	L	SV	AB	H	HR	BA	PO	A	E	DP	TC/G	FA
1984	SD	N	0	0	–	0.00	3	0	0	6	2	1	7	0	0	0	0	0	0	0	–	0	0	0	0	0.0	–
1989	SF	N	0	0	–	3.38	3	0	0	2.2	2	2	1	0	0	0	1	0	0	0	–	0	1	1	0	0.7	.500
2 yrs.			0	0	–	1.04	6	0	0	8.2	4	3	8	0	0	0	1	0	0	0	–	0	1	1	0	0.3	.500

Regis Leheny

LEHENY, REGIS FRANCIS
B. Jan. 5, 1908, Pittsburgh, Pa. D. Nov. 2, 1976, Pittsburgh, Pa. — BL TL 6'½" 180 lbs.

Year	Team		W	L	PCT	ERA	G	GS	CG	IP	H	BB	SO	ShO	W	L	SV	AB	H	HR	BA	PO	A	E	DP	TC/G	FA
1932	BOS	A	0	0	–	16.88	2	0	0	2.2	5	3	1	0	0	0	0	1	0	0	.000	0	2	0	0	1.0	1.000

Jim Lehew

LEHEW, JAMES ANTHONY
B. Aug. 19, 1937, Baltimore, Md. — BR TR 6' 185 lbs.

Year	Team		W	L	PCT	ERA	G	GS	CG	IP	H	BB	SO	ShO	W	L	SV	AB	H	HR	BA	PO	A	E	DP	TC/G	FA
1961	BAL	A	0	0	–	0.00	2	0	0	2	1	0	0	0	0	0	0	0	0	0	–	0	1	0	0	0.5	1.000
1962			0	0	–	1.86	6	0	0	9.2	10	3	2	0	0	0	0	1	0	0	.000	0	4	0	0	0.7	1.000
2 yrs.			0	0	–	1.54	8	0	0	11.2	11	3	2	0	0	0	0	1	0	0	.000	0	5	0	0	0.6	1.000

Ken Lehman

LEHMAN, KENNETH KARL
B. June 10, 1928, Seattle, Wash. — BL TL 6' 170 lbs.

Year	Team		W	L	PCT	ERA	G	GS	CG	IP	H	BB	SO	ShO	W	L	SV	AB	H	HR	BA	PO	A	E	DP	TC/G	FA
1952	BKN	N	1	2	.333	5.28	4	3	0	15.1	19	6	7	0	1	0	0	4	0	0	.000	0	4	0	0	1.0	1.000
1956			2	3	.400	5.66	25	4	0	49.1	65	23	29	0	2	1	0	10	3	0	.300	4	11	1	0	0.6	.938
1957	2 teams		BKN N (3G 0–0)			BAL A (30G 8–3)																					
"	total		8	3	.727	2.52	33	3	1	75	64	23	35	0	7	1	6	22	5	0	.227	8	9	3	3	0.6	.850
1958	BAL	A	2	1	.667	3.48	31	1	1	62	64	18	36	0	2	1	0	14	1	0	.071	3	11	0	0	0.5	1.000
1961	PHI	N	1	1	.500	4.26	41	2	0	63.1	61	25	27	0	1	0	1	6	0	0	.000	6	16	0	1	0.5	1.000
5 yrs.			14	10	.583	3.91	134	13	2	265	273	95	134	0	13	3	7	56	9	0	.161	21	51	4	4	0.6	.947

WORLD SERIES

Year	Team		W	L	PCT	ERA	G	GS	CG	IP	H	BB	SO	ShO	W	L	SV	AB	H	HR	BA	PO	A	E	DP	TC/G	FA
1952	BKN	N	0	0	–	0.00	1	0	0	2	2	1	0	0	0	0	0	0	0	0	–	0	1	0	0	1.0	1.000

Norm Lehr

LEHR, NORMAN CARL MICHAEL (King)
B. May 28, 1901, Rochester, N. Y. D. July 17, 1968, Livonia, N. Y. — BR TR 6' 168 lbs.

Year	Team		W	L	PCT	ERA	G	GS	CG	IP	H	BB	SO	ShO	W	L	SV	AB	H	HR	BA	PO	A	E	DP	TC/G	FA
1926	CLE	A	0	0	–	3.07	4	0	0	14.2	11	4	4	0	0	0	0	4	0	0	.000	1	7	1	0	2.3	.889

Hank Leiber

LEIBER, HENRY EDWARD
B. Jan. 17, 1911, Phoenix, Ariz. — BR TR 6'1½" 205 lbs.

Year	Team		W	L	PCT	ERA	G	GS	CG	IP	H	BB	SO	ShO	W	L	SV	AB	H	HR	BA	PO	A	E	DP	TC/G	FA
1942	NY	N	0	1	.000	6.00	1	1	1	9	9	5	5	0	0	0	0	*				0	4	1	0	5.0	.800

Charlie Leibrandt

LEIBRANDT, CHARLES LOUIS, JR.
B. Oct. 4, 1956, Chicago, Ill. — BR TL 6'3" 195 lbs.

Year	Team		W	L	PCT	ERA	G	GS	CG	IP	H	BB	SO	ShO	W	L	SV	AB	H	HR	BA	PO	A	E	DP	TC/G	FA
1979	CIN	N	0	0	–	0.00	3	0	0	4	2	2	1	0	0	0	0	0	0	0	–	1	0	0	1	0.3	1.000
1980			10	9	.526	4.24	36	27	5	174	200	54	62	2	0	0	0	56	11	0	.196	10	35	3	3	1.3	.938
1981			1	1	.500	3.60	7	4	1	30	28	15	9	1	0	0	0	8	0	0	.000	0	7	0	0	1.0	1.000
1982			5	7	.417	5.10	36	11	0	107.2	130	48	34	0	2	1	2	25	2	0	.080	5	18	1	0	0.7	.958
1984	KC	A	11	7	.611	3.63	23	23	3	143.2	158	38	53	0	0	0	0	0	0	0	–	9	15	3	1	1.2	.889
1985			17	9	.654	2.69	33	33	8	237.2	223	68	108	3	0	0	0	0	0	0	–	19	53	1	2	2.2	.986
1986			14	11	.560	4.09	35	34	8	231.1	238	63	108	1	0	0	0	0	0	0	–	14	43	1	3	1.7	.983
1987			16	11	.593	3.41	35	35	8	240.1	235	74	151	3	0	0	0	0	0	0	–	15	55	4	4	2.1	.946
1988			13	12	.520	3.19	35	35	7	243	244	62	125	2	0	0	0	0	0	0	–	19	43	3	2	1.9	.954
1989			5	11	.313	5.14	33	27	3	161	196	54	73	0	0	0	0	0	0	0	–	6	26	2	0	1.0	.941
10 yrs.			92	78	.541	3.77	276	229	40	1572.2	1654	478	724	13	2	1	2	89	13	0	.146	98	295	18	16	1.5	.956

Year	Team		W	L	PCT	ERA	G	GS	CG	IP	H	BB	SO	ShO	Relief Pitching W	L	SV	Batting AB	H	HR	BA	PO	A	E	DP	TC/G	FA

Charlie Leibrandt *continued*

LEAGUE CHAMPIONSHIP SERIES

Year	Team		W	L	PCT	ERA	G	GS	CG	IP	H	BB	SO	ShO	W	L	SV	AB	H	HR	BA	PO	A	E	DP	TC/G	FA
1979	CIN	N	0	0	–	0.00	1	0	0	.1	0	0	0	0	0	0	0	0	0	0	–	0	0	0	0	0.0	
1984	KC	A	0	1	.000	1.13	1	1	1	8	3	4	6	0	0	0	0	0	0	0	–	1	2	0	0	3.0	1.000
1985			1	2	.333	5.28	3	2	0	15.1	17	4	6	0	1	0	0	0	0	0	–	3	7	0	0	3.3	1.000
3 yrs.			1	3	.250	3.80	5	3	1	23.2	20	8	12	0	1	0	0	0	0	0	–	4	9	0	0	2.6	1.000

WORLD SERIES

Year	Team		W	L	PCT	ERA	G	GS	CG	IP	H	BB	SO	ShO	W	L	SV	AB	H	HR	BA	PO	A	E	DP	TC/G	FA
1985	KC	A	0	1	.000	2.76	2	2	0	16.1	10	4	10	0	0	0	0	4	0	0	.000	1	2	0	0	1.5	1.000

Lefty Leifield

LEIFIELD, ALBERT PETER BL TL 6'1" 165 lbs.
B. Sept. 5, 1883, Trenton, Ill. D. Oct. 10, 1970, Alexandria, Va.

Year	Team		W	L	PCT	ERA	G	GS	CG	IP	H	BB	SO	ShO	W	L	SV	AB	H	HR	BA	PO	A	E	DP	TC/G	FA
1905	PIT	N	5	2	.714	2.89	8	7	6	56	52	14	10	1	0	0	0	20	7	0	.350	5	19	0	0	3.0	1.000
1906			18	13	.581	1.87	37	31	24	255.2	214	68	111	8	3	0	1	88	11	0	.125	12	78	3	3	2.5	.968
1907			20	16	.556	2.33	40	33	24	286	270	100	112	6	3	2	0	102	15	0	.147	18	94	6	3	3.0	.949
1908			15	14	.517	2.10	34	26	18	218.2	168	86	87	5	2	1	2	75	17	0	.227	6	62	5	4	2.1	.932
1909			19	8	.704	2.37	32	27	13	201.2	172	54	43	3	3	1	0	73	14	0	.192	6	53	3	1	1.9	.952
1910			15	12	.556	2.64	40	30	13	218.1	197	67	64	3	5	0	0	60	11	0	.183	13	75	2	2	2.3	.978
1911			16	16	.500	2.63	42	37	26	318	301	82	111	3	0	0	1	102	24	0	.235	12	82	7	6	2.4	.931
1912	2 teams		PIT N	(6G 1–2)		CHI N	(13G 7–2)																				
"	total		8	4	.667	2.86	19	10	5	94.1	97	31	31	1	3	1	0	33	4	0	.121	10	31	1	2	2.2	.976
1913	CHI	N	0	1	.000	5.48	6	1	0	21.1	28	5	4	0	0	0	0	7	0	0	.000	0	10	0	0	1.7	1.000
1918	STL	A	2	6	.250	2.55	15	6	3	67	61	19	22	1	1	0	0	19	1	0	.053	2	23	0	1	1.7	1.000
1919			6	4	.600	2.93	19	9	6	92	96	25	18	2	1	1	0	30	3	0	.100	1	30	0	1	1.6	1.000
1920			0	0	–	7.00	4	0	0	9	17	3	3	0	0	0	0	2	0	0	.000	0	1	0	0	0.3	1.000
12 yrs.			124	96	.564	2.47	296	217	138	1838	1673	554	616	32	21	8	5	611	107	0	.175	85	558	27	23	2.3	.960

WORLD SERIES

Year	Team		W	L	PCT	ERA	G	GS	CG	IP	H	BB	SO	ShO	W	L	SV	AB	H	HR	BA	PO	A	E	DP	TC/G	FA
1909	PIT	N	0	1	.000	11.25	1	1	0	4	7	1	0	0	0	0	0	1	0	0	.000	0	5	0	0	5.0	1.000

Dave Leiper

LEIPER, DAVID PAUL BL TL 6'1" 160 lbs.
B. June 18, 1962, Whittier, Calif.

Year	Team		W	L	PCT	ERA	G	GS	CG	IP	H	BB	SO	ShO	W	L	SV	AB	H	HR	BA	PO	A	E	DP	TC/G	FA
1984	OAK	A	1	0	1.000	9.00	8	0	0	7	12	5	3	0	1	0	0	0	0	0	–	1	2	0	0	0.4	1.000
1986			2	2	.500	4.83	33	0	0	31.2	28	18	15	0	2	2	1	0	0	0	–	0	6	0	0	0.2	1.000
1987	2 teams		OAK A	(45G 2–1)		SD N	(12G 1–0)																				
"	total		3	1	.750	3.95	57	0	0	68.1	65	23	43	0	3	1	0	0	0	0	–	5	14	2	1	0.4	.905
1988	SD	N	3	0	1.000	2.17	35	0	0	54	45	14	33	0	3	0	1	2	1	0	.500	3	9	0	1	0.3	1.000
1989			0	1	.000	5.02	22	0	0	28.2	40	20	7	0	0	1	0	1	0	0	.000	4	7	1	0	0.5	.917
5 yrs.			9	4	.692	3.94	155	0	0	189.2	190	80	101	0	9	4	3	3	1	0	.333	13	38	3	2	0.3	.944

Jack Leiper

LEIPER, JOHN HENRY THOMAS BL TL 5'11"
B. Dec. 23, 1867, Chester, Pa. D. Aug. 23, 1960, West Goshen, Pa.

Year	Team		W	L	PCT	ERA	G	GS	CG	IP	H	BB	SO	ShO	W	L	SV	AB	H	HR	BA	PO	A	E	DP	TC/G	FA
1891	COL	AA	2	2	.500	5.40	6	5	4	45	41	39	19	0	0	0	0	21	3	0	.143	3	8	3	1	2.3	.786

John Leister

LEISTER, JOHN WILLIAM BR TR 6'2" 200 lbs.
B. Jan. 3, 1961, San Antonio, Tex.

Year	Team		W	L	PCT	ERA	G	GS	CG	IP	H	BB	SO	ShO	W	L	SV	AB	H	HR	BA	PO	A	E	DP	TC/G	FA
1987	BOS	A	0	2	.000	9.20	8	6	0	30.1	49	12	16	0	0	0	0	0	0	0	–	2	2	0	0	0.5	1.000

Al Leiter

LEITER, ALOIS TERRY BL TL 6'2" 200 lbs.
B. Oct. 23, 1965, Toms River, N. J.

Year	Team		W	L	PCT	ERA	G	GS	CG	IP	H	BB	SO	ShO	W	L	SV	AB	H	HR	BA	PO	A	E	DP	TC/G	FA
1987	NY	A	2	2	.500	6.35	4	4	0	22.2	24	15	28	0	0	0	0	0	0	0	–	0	2	0	0	0.5	1.000
1988			4	4	.500	3.92	14	14	0	57.1	49	33	60	0	0	0	0	0	0	0	–	0	11	1	0	0.9	.917
1989	2 teams		NY A	(4G 1–2)		TOR A	(1G 0–0)																				
"	total		1	2	.333	5.67	5	5	0	33.1	32	23	26	0	0	0	0	0	0	0	–	1	2	0	0	0.6	1.000
3 yrs.			7	8	.467	4.92	23	23	0	113.1	105	71	114	0	0	0	0	0	0	0	–	1	15	1	0	0.7	.941

Bill Leith

LEITH, WILLIAM (Shady Bill) TL
B. May 31, 1873, Mattequam, N. Y. D. July 16, 1940, Beacon, N. Y.

Year	Team		W	L	PCT	ERA	G	GS	CG	IP	H	BB	SO	ShO	W	L	SV	AB	H	HR	BA	PO	A	E	DP	TC/G	FA
1899	WAS	N	0	0	–	18.00	1	0	0	2	4	2	1	0	0	0	0	1	0	0	.000	0	1	0	0	1.0	–

Doc Leitner

LEITNER, GEORGE ALOYSIUS BR TR 5'11½" 185 lbs.
B. Sept. 14, 1865, Piermont, N. Y. D. May 18, 1937, New York, N. Y.

Year	Team		W	L	PCT	ERA	G	GS	CG	IP	H	BB	SO	ShO	W	L	SV	AB	H	HR	BA	PO	A	E	DP	TC/G	FA
1887	IND	N	2	6	.250	5.68	8	8	8	65	69	41	27	0	0	0	0	27	4	0	.148	0	5	3	0	1.0	.625

Dummy Leitner

LEITNER, GEORGE MICHAEL BL TR 5'7" 120 lbs.
B. June 19, 1871, Parkton, Md. D. Feb. 20, 1960, Baltimore, Md.

Year	Team		W	L	PCT	ERA	G	GS	CG	IP	H	BB	SO	ShO	W	L	SV	AB	H	HR	BA	PO	A	E	DP	TC/G	FA
1901	2 teams		PHI A	(1G 0–0)		NY N	(2G 0–2)																				
"	total		0	2	.000	4.05	3	2	2	20	28	5	4	0	0	0	0	8	1	0	.125	0	3	0	0	1.0	1.000
1902	2 teams		CLE A	(1G 0–0)		CHI A	(1G 0–0)																				
"	total		0	0	–	7.50	2	1	0	12	20	3	0	0	0	0	0	7	1	0	.143	1	5	0	2	3.0	1.000
2 yrs.			0	2	.000	5.34	5	3	2	32	48	8	4	0	0	0	0	15	2	0	.133	1	8	0	2	1.8	1.000

Bill Lelivelt

LELIVELT, WILLIAM JOHN BR TR 6' 195 lbs.
Brother of Jack Lelivelt.
B. Oct. 21, 1884, Chicago, Ill. D. Feb. 14, 1968, Chicago, Ill.

Year	Team		W	L	PCT	ERA	G	GS	CG	IP	H	BB	SO	ShO	W	L	SV	AB	H	HR	BA	PO	A	E	DP	TC/G	FA
1909	DET	A	0	1	.000	4.50	4	2	1	20	27	2	4	0	0	0	1	6	2	0	.333	1	7	0	0	2.0	1.000
1910			0	1	.000	1.00	1	1	1	9	6	3	2	0	0	0	0	2	1	0	.500	0	3	0	1	3.0	1.000
2 yrs.			0	2	.000	3.41	5	3	2	29	33	5	6	0	0	0	1	8	3	0	.375	1	10	0	1	2.2	1.000

Year	Team	W	L	PCT	ERA	G	GS	CG	IP	H	BB	SO	ShO	W	L	SV	AB	H	HR	BA	PO	A	E	DP	TC/G	FA
														Relief Pitching			**Batting**									

Dave Lemanczyk

LEMANCZYK, DAVID LAWRENCE
B. Aug. 17, 1950, Syracuse, N. Y.

BR TR 6'4" 235 lbs.

Year	Team	W	L	PCT	ERA	G	GS	CG	IP	H	BB	SO	ShO	W	L	SV	AB	H	HR	BA	PO	A	E	DP	TC/G	FA
1973	DET A	0	0	–	13.50	1	0	0	2	4	0	0	0	0	0	0	0	0	0	–	0	0	0	0	0.0	–
1974		2	1	.667	3.99	22	3	0	79	79	44	52	0	1	0	0	0	0	0	–	6	12	0	1	0.8	1.000
1975		2	7	.222	4.46	26	6	4	109	120	46	67	0	2	1	0	0	0	0	–	9	14	1	1	0.9	.958
1976		4	6	.400	5.11	20	10	1	81	86	34	51	0	2	0	0	0	0	0	–	8	14	2	0	1.2	.917
1977	TOR A	13	16	.448	4.25	34	34	11	252	278	87	105	0	0	0	0	0	0	0	–	25	37	4	4	1.9	.939
1978		4	14	.222	6.26	29	20	3	136.2	170	65	62	0	0	0	0	0	0	0	–	2	22	2	1	0.9	.923
1979		8	10	.444	3.71	22	20	11	143	137	45	63	3	0	0	0	0	0	0	–	12	20	2	2	1.5	.941
1980	2 teams	TOR A (10G 2-5)			CAL A	(21G 2-4)																				
"	total	4	9	.308	4.75	31	10	0	110	138	42	29	0	1	3	0	0	0	0	–	5	15	0	1	0.6	1.000
8 yrs.		37	63	.370	4.62	185	103	30	912.2	1012	363	429	3	6	4	0	0	0	0	–	67	134	11	10	1.1	.948

Denny Lemaster

LEMASTER, DENVER CLAYTON
B. Feb. 25, 1939, Corona, Calif.

BR TL 6'1" 182 lbs.

Year	Team	W	L	PCT	ERA	G	GS	CG	IP	H	BB	SO	ShO	W	L	SV	AB	H	HR	BA	PO	A	E	DP	TC/G	FA
1962	MIL N	3	4	.429	3.01	17	12	4	86.2	75	32	69	1	0	0	0	33	4	0	.121	3	7	3	0	0.8	.769
1963		11	14	.440	3.04	46	31	10	237	199	85	190	1	1	0	1	74	14	2	.189	12	26	2	1	0.9	.950
1964		17	11	.607	4.15	39	35	9	221	216	75	185	3	1	0	1	67	9	0	.134	11	35	3	1	1.2	1.000
1965		7	13	.350	4.43	32	23	4	146.1	140	58	111	1	0	1	0	45	4	0	.089	10	23	3	1	1.1	.917
1966	ATL N	11	8	.579	3.74	27	27	10	171	170	41	139	3	0	0	0	59	7	0	.119	7	18	0	0	0.9	1.000
1967		9	9	.500	3.34	31	31	8	215.1	184	72	148	2	0	0	0	67	7	0	.104	7	35	0	0	1.4	1.000
1968	HOU N	10	15	.400	2.81	33	32	7	224	231	72	146	2	0	0	0	65	2	0	.031	7	27	4	1	1.2	.895
1969		13	17	.433	3.16	38	37	11	245	232	72	173	1	0	0	1	88	15	1	.170	12	33	0	1	1.2	1.000
1970		7	12	.368	4.56	39	21	3	162	169	65	103	0	1	1	3	45	8	1	.178	8	11	0	1	0.7	.962
1971		0	2	.000	3.45	42	0	0	60	59	22	28	0	0	2	2	6	1	0	.167	1	10	0	1	0.3	1.000
1972	MON N	2	0	1.000	7.78	13	0	0	19.2	28	6	13	0	2	0	0	3	1	0	.333	0	1	0	0	0.1	1.000
11 yrs.		90	105	.462	3.58	357	249	66	1788	1703	600	1305	14	5	4	8	552	72	4	.130	78	232	13	9	0.9	.960

Dick LeMay

LeMAY, RICHARD PAUL
B. Aug. 28, 1938, Cincinnati, Ohio

BL TL 6'3" 190 lbs.

Year	Team	W	L	PCT	ERA	G	GS	CG	IP	H	BB	SO	ShO	W	L	SV	AB	H	HR	BA	PO	A	E	DP	TC/G	FA
1961	SF N	3	6	.333	3.56	27	5	1	83.1	65	36	54	0	2	6	3	26	2	0	.077	3	15	2	1	0.7	.900
1962		0	1	.000	7.71	9	0	0	9.1	9	9	5	0	0	1	1	0	0	0	–	0	2	0	0	0.2	1.000
1963	CHI N	0	1	.000	5.28	9	1	0	15.1	26	4	10	0	0	1	0	2	0	0	.000	0	3	1	0	0.4	.750
3 yrs.		3	8	.273	4.17	45	6	1	108	100	49	69	0	2	8	4	28	2	0	.071	3	20	3	1	0.6	.885

Bob Lemon

LEMON, ROBERT GRANVILLE
B. Sept. 22, 1920, San Bernardino, Calif.
Manager 1970-72, 1977-79, 1981-82.
Hall of Fame 1976.

BL TR 6' 180 lbs.

Year	Team	W	L	PCT	ERA	G	GS	CG	IP	H	BB	SO	ShO	W	L	SV	AB	H	HR	BA	PO	A	E	DP	TC/G	FA
1941	CLE A	0	0	–	0.00	0	0	0	0	0	0	0	0	0	0	0	4	1	0	.250	0	0	0	0	0.0	–
1942		0	0	–	0.00	0	0	0	0	0	0	0	0	0	0	0	5	0	0	.000	0	0	0	0	0.0	–
1946		4	5	.444	2.49	32	5	1	94	77	68	39	0	3	2	1	89	16	1	.180	13	28	1	5	1.3	.976
1947		11	5	.688	3.44	37	15	6	167.1	150	97	65	1	1	2	3	56	18	2	.321	12	46	1	4	1.6	.983
1948		20	14	.588	2.82	43	37	20	293.2	231	129	147	10	1	1	2	119	34	5	.286	23	86	4	8	2.6	.965
1949		22	10	.688	2.99	37	33	22	279.2	211	137	138	2	1	1	1	108	29	7	.269	34	71	4	5	2.9	.963
1950		23	11	.676	3.84	44	37	22	288	281	146	170	3	1	0	3	136	37	6	.272	22	66	4	6	2.1	.957
1951		17	14	.548	3.52	42	34	17	263.1	244	124	132	1	0	0	2	102	21	3	.206	21	60	2	5	2.0	.976
1952		22	11	.667	2.50	42	36	28	309.2	236	105	131	5	0	1	4	124	28	2	.226	32	79	2	7	2.7	.982
1953		21	15	.583	3.36	41	36	23	286.2	283	110	98	5	1	1	1	112	26	2	.232	31	74	3	15	2.6	.972
1954		23	7	.767	2.72	36	33	21	258.1	228	92	110	2	1	0	0	98	21	2	.214	22	57	3	8	2.3	.963
1955		18	10	.643	3.88	35	31	5	211.1	218	74	100	0	1	0	2	78	19	1	.244	16	43	1	3	1.7	.983
1956		20	14	.588	3.03	39	35	21	255.1	230	89	94	2	0	0	3	93	18	5	.194	24	61	6	6	2.3	.934
1957		6	11	.353	4.60	21	17	2	117.1	129	64	45	0	1	2	0	46	3	1	.065	12	31	0	5	2.0	1.000
1958		0	1	.000	5.33	11	1	0	25.1	41	16	8	0	0	0	0	13	3	0	.231	1	7	0	1	0.7	1.000
15 yrs.		207	128	.618	3.23	460	350	188	2850	2559	1251	1277	31	12	10	22	*				263	709	31	78	2.2	.969

WORLD SERIES

Year	Team	W	L	PCT	ERA	G	GS	CG	IP	H	BB	SO	ShO	W	L	SV	AB	H	HR	BA	PO	A	E	DP	TC/G	FA
1948	CLE A	2	0	1.000	1.65	2	2	1	16.1	16	7	6	0	0	0	0	7	0	0	.000	3	9	0	1	6.0	1.000
1954		0	2	.000	6.75	2	2	1	13.1	16	8	11	0	0	0	0	6	0	0	.000	2	2	0	0	2.0	1.000
2 yrs.		2	2	.500	3.94	4	4	2	29.2	32	15	17	0	0	0	0	13	0	0	.000	5	11	0	1	4.0	1.000

Dave Lemonds

LEMONDS, DAVID LEE
B. July 5, 1948, Charlotte, N. C.

BL TL 6'1½" 180 lbs.

Year	Team	W	L	PCT	ERA	G	GS	CG	IP	H	BB	SO	ShO	W	L	SV	AB	H	HR	BA	PO	A	E	DP	TC/G	FA
1969	CHI N	0	1	.000	3.60	2	1	0	5	5	5	0	0	0	0	0	1	0	0	.000	0	0	0	0	0.5	1.000
1972	CHI A	4	7	.364	2.95	31	18	0	94.2	87	38	69	0	1	1	0	25	3	0	.120	7	11	0	2	0.6	1.000
2 yrs.		4	8	.333	2.98	33	19	0	99.2	92	43	69	0	1	1	0	26	3	0	.115	7	12	0	2	0.6	1.000

Mark Lemongello

LEMONGELLO, MARK
B. July 21, 1955, Jersey City, N. J.

BR TR 6'1" 180 lbs.

Year	Team	W	L	PCT	ERA	G	GS	CG	IP	H	BB	SO	ShO	W	L	SV	AB	H	HR	BA	PO	A	E	DP	TC/G	FA
1976	HOU N	3	1	.750	2.79	4	4	0	29	26	7	9	0	0	0	0	8	0	0	.000	1	9	0	0	2.5	1.000
1977		9	14	.391	3.47	34	30	5	215	237	52	83	0	0	0	1	69	6	0	.087	23	30	5	1	1.7	.914
1978		9	14	.391	3.94	33	30	9	210	204	66	77	1	0	0	0	64	11	0	.172	15	34	2	1	1.5	.961
1979	TOR A	1	9	.100	6.29	18	10	2	83	97	34	40	0	1	2	0	0	0	0	–	8	15	2	0	1.4	.920
4 yrs.		22	38	.367	4.06	89	74	17	537	564	159	209	1	1	3	1	141	17	0	.121	47	88	9	2	1.6	.938

Ed Lennon

LENNON, EDWARD FRANCIS
B. Aug. 17, 1897, Philadelphia, Pa.   D. Sept. 13, 1947, Philadelphia, Pa.

BR TR 5'11" 170 lbs.

Year	Team	W	L	PCT	ERA	G	GS	CG	IP	H	BB	SO	ShO	W	L	SV	AB	H	HR	BA	PO	A	E	DP	TC/G	FA
1928	PHI N	0	0	–	8.76	5	0	0	12.1	19	10	6	0	0	0	0	4	0	0	.000	0	1	1	0	0.4	.500

Max Leon

LEON, MAXIMINO
Born Maximino Leon y Molino.
B. Feb. 4, 1950, Pozo Hondo, Mexico

BR TR 5'10" 145 lbs.

Year	Team	W	L	PCT	ERA	G	GS	CG	IP	H	BB	SO	ShO	Relief Pitching W	L	SV	Batting AB	H	HR	BA	PO	A	E	DP	TC/G	FA

Max Leon *continued*

Year	Team	W	L	PCT	ERA	G	GS	CG	IP	H	BB	SO	ShO	W	L	SV	AB	H	HR	BA	PO	A	E	DP	TC/G	FA
1973	ATL N	2	2	.500	5.33	12	1	1	27	30	9	18	0	1	2	0	7	2	0	.286	1	2	0	0	0.3	1.000
1974		4	7	.364	2.64	34	2	1	75	68	14	38	1	3	6	3	15	2	0	.133	4	15	1	2	0.6	.950
1975		2	1	.667	4.13	50	1	0	85	90	33	53	0	1	1	6	9	3	0	.333	3	19	3	0	0.5	.880
1976		2	4	.333	2.75	30	0	0	36	32	15	16	0	2	4	3	2	0	0	.000	1	3	0	0	0.1	1.000
1977		4	4	.500	3.95	31	9	0	82	89	25	44	0	2	2	1	19	6	0	.316	9	12	1	0	0.7	.955
1978		0	0	–	6.00	5	0	0	6	6	4	1	0	0	0	0	0	0	0	–	0	1	0	0	0.2	1.000
6 yrs.		14	18	.438	3.70	162	13	2	311	315	100	170	1	9	15	13	52	13	0	.250	18	52	5	2	0.5	.933

Sid Leon

LEON, ISIDORO (Izzy)
Born Isidoro Leon y Becerra.
B. Jan. 4, 1911, Cruces, Cuba

BR TR 5'10" 160 lbs.

Year	Team	W	L	PCT	ERA	G	GS	CG	IP	H	BB	SO	ShO	W	L	SV	AB	H	HR	BA	PO	A	E	DP	TC/G	FA
1945	PHI N	0	4	.000	5.35	14	4	0	38.2	49	19	11	0	0	0	0	9	1	0	.111	2	8	1	0	0.8	.909

Dennis Leonard

LEONARD, DENNIS PATRICK
B. May 8, 1951, Brooklyn, N. Y.

BR TR 6'1" 190 lbs.

Year	Team	W	L	PCT	ERA	G	GS	CG	IP	H	BB	SO	ShO	W	L	SV	AB	H	HR	BA	PO	A	E	DP	TC/G	FA
1974	KC A	0	4	.000	5.32	5	4	0	22	28	12	8	0	0	0	0	0	0	0	–	3	7	0	1	2.0	1.000
1975		15	7	.682	3.77	32	30	8	212.1	212	90	146	0	1	0	0	0	0	0	–	14	28	2	4	1.4	.955
1976		17	10	.630	3.51	35	34	16	259	247	70	150	2	0	0	0	0	0	0	–	11	23	6	2	1.1	.850
1977		**20**	12	.625	3.04	38	37	21	293	246	79	244	5	0	0	1	0	0	0	–	21	29	4	2	1.4	.926
1978		21	17	.553	3.33	40	**40**	20	294.2	**283**	78	183	4	0	0	0	0	0	0	–	16	43	1	2	1.5	.983
1979		14	12	.538	4.08	32	32	12	236	226	56	126	5	0	0	0	0	0	0	–	19	32	1	2	1.6	.981
1980		20	11	.645	3.79	38	**38**	9	280	271	80	155	3	0	0	0	0	0	0	–	9	41	1	4	1.3	.980
1981		13	11	.542	2.99	26	**26**	9	**202**	**202**	41	107	2	0	0	0	0	0	0	–	13	31	0	3	1.7	1.000
1982		10	6	.625	5.10	21	21	2	130.2	145	46	58	0	0	0	0	0	0	0	–	16	18	3	2	1.8	.919
1983		6	3	.667	3.71	10	10	1	63	69	19	31	0	0	0	0	0	0	0	–	2	11	2	2	1.5	.867
1985		0	0	–	0.00	2	0	0	2	1	0	1	0	0	0	0	0	0	0	–	0	0	0	0	0.0	–
1986		8	13	.381	4.44	33	30	5	192.2	207	51	114	2	0	0	0	0	0	0	–	11	29	4	4	1.3	.909
12 yrs.		144	106	.576	3.69	312	302	103	2187.1	2137	622	1323	23	1	0	1	0	0	0	–	135	292	24	28	1.4	.947

DIVISIONAL PLAYOFF SERIES

Year	Team	W	L	PCT	ERA	G	GS	CG	IP	H	BB	SO	ShO	W	L	SV	AB	H	HR	BA	PO	A	E	DP	TC/G	FA
1981	KC A	0	1	.000	1.13	1	1	0	8	7	1	3	0	0	0	0	0	0	0	–	0	0	0	0	0.0	–

LEAGUE CHAMPIONSHIP SERIES

Year	Team	W	L	PCT	ERA	G	GS	CG	IP	H	BB	SO	ShO	W	L	SV	AB	H	HR	BA	PO	A	E	DP	TC/G	FA
1976	KC A	0	0	–	19.29	2	2	0	2.1	9	2	4	0	0	0	0	0	0	0	–	0	0	0	0	0.0	–
1977		1	1	.500	3.00	2	1	1	9	5	2	4	0	0	0	0	0	0	0	–	0	0	0	0	0.0	–
1978		0	2	.000	3.75	2	2	1	12	13	2	11	0	0	0	0	0	0	0	–	1	0	0	0	0.5	1.000
1980		1	0	1.000	2.25	1	1	0	8	7	1	8	0	0	0	0	0	0	0	–	0	0	0	0	0.0	–
4 yrs.		2	3	.400	4.31	7	6	2	31.1	34	7	23	0	0	0	0	0	0	0	–	1	0	0	0	0.1	1.000

WORLD SERIES

Year	Team	W	L	PCT	ERA	G	GS	CG	IP	H	BB	SO	ShO	W	L	SV	AB	H	HR	BA	PO	A	E	DP	TC/G	FA
1980	KC A	1	1	.500	6.75	2	2	0	10.2	15	2	5	0	0	0	0	0	0	0	–	0	0	1	0	0.5	–

Dutch Leonard

LEONARD, EMIL JOHN
B. Mar. 25, 1909, Auburn, Ill. D. Apr. 17, 1983, Springfield, Ill.

BR TR 6' 175 lbs.

Year	Team	W	L	PCT	ERA	G	GS	CG	IP	H	BB	SO	ShO	W	L	SV	AB	H	HR	BA	PO	A	E	DP	TC/G	FA
1933	BKN N	2	3	.400	2.93	10	3	2	40	42	10	6	0	1	1	0	11	0	0	.000	4	10	2	0	1.6	.875
1934		14	11	.560	3.28	44	20	11	183.2	210	34	58	2	5	3	5	67	12	0	.179	11	42	0	4	1.2	1.000
1935		2	9	.182	3.92	43	11	4	137.2	152	29	41	0	0	4	**8**	39	1	0	.026	2	26	1	0	0.7	.966
1936		0	0	–	3.66	16	0	0	32	34	5	8	0	0	0	1	5	2	0	.400	1	12	0	0	0.8	1.000
1938	WAS A	12	15	.444	3.43	33	31	15	223.1	221	53	68	3	1	0	0	82	19	0	.232	9	46	4	3	1.8	.932
1939		20	8	.714	3.54	34	34	21	269.1	**273**	59	88	2	0	0	0	95	21	0	.221	10	56	2	3	2.0	.971
1940		14	**19**	.424	3.49	35	35	23	289	**328**	78	124	2	0	0	0	101	16	0	.158	15	72	4	7	2.6	.956
1941		18	13	.581	3.45	34	33	19	256	271	54	91	4	0	0	0	88	9	0	.102	20	37	3	7	1.8	.950
1942		2	2	.500	4.11	6	6	1	35	28	5	15	1	0	0	0	10	1	0	.100	1	7	0	1	1.3	1.000
1943		11	13	.458	3.28	31	30	15	219.2	218	46	51	2	0	0	1	67	7	0	.104	10	55	2	5	2.2	.970
1944		14	14	.500	3.06	32	31	17	229.1	222	37	62	3	0	1	0	79	18	0	.228	7	53	3	2	2.0	.952
1945		17	7	.708	2.13	31	29	12	216	208	35	96	4	1	0	1	78	18	0	.231	8	44	2	0	1.7	.963
1946		10	10	.500	3.56	26	23	7	161.2	182	36	62	2	0	0	0	53	9	0	.170	4	47	3	2	2.1	.944
1947	PHI N	17	12	.586	2.68	32	29	19	235	224	57	103	3	1	1	0	80	14	0	.175	18	51	0	2	2.2	1.000
1948		11	**18**	.379	2.51	34	30	16	225.2	226	54	92	1	1	1	0	83	12	0	.145	15	57	2	2	2.2	.973
1949	CHI N	7	16	.304	4.15	33	28	10	180	198	43	83	1	0	0	0	59	12	0	.203	13	36	3	1	1.6	.942
1950		5	1	.833	3.77	35	1	0	74	70	27	28	0	4	1	6	16	1	0	.063	6	0	0	0	0.6	1.000
1951		10	6	.625	2.64	41	1	0	81.2	69	28	30	0	10	5	3	21	0	0	.000	6	21	0	2	0.7	1.000
1952		2	2	.500	2.16	45	0	0	66.2	56	24	37	0	2	2	11	10	2	0	.200	6	22	1	0	0.6	.966
1953		2	3	.400	4.60	45	0	0	62.2	72	24	27	0	2	3	8	10	3	0	.300	9	10	0	0	0.4	1.000
20 yrs.		190	182	.511	3.25	640	374	192	3218.1	3304	738	1170	30	28	22	44	1054	177	0	.168	174	719	32	41	1.4	.965

Dutch Leonard

LEONARD, HUBERT BENJAMIN
B. Apr. 16, 1892, Birmingham, Ohio D. July 11, 1952, Fresno, Calif.

BL TL 5'10½" 185 lbs.

Year	Team	W	L	PCT	ERA	G	GS	CG	IP	H	BB	SO	ShO	W	L	SV	AB	H	HR	BA	PO	A	E	DP	TC/G	FA
1913	BOS A	14	16	.467	2.39	42	27	14	259.1	245	94	144	2	3	**3**	1	83	15	0	.181	6	62	8	0	1.8	.895
1914		19	5	.792	**1.01**	36	25	17	222.2	141	60	174	7	4	0	3	69	10	0	.145	6	41	2	1	1.4	.959
1915		15	7	.682	2.36	32	21	10	183.1	130	67	116	2	4	0	0	53	14	0	.264	3	30	2	0	1.1	.943
1916		18	12	.600	2.36	48	34	17	274	244	66	144	6	2	0	6	85	17	0	.200	7	49	3	1	1.2	.949
1917		16	17	.485	2.17	37	36	26	294.1	257	72	144	4	0	0	1	104	9	0	.087	5	60	1	2	1.8	.985
1918		8	6	.571	2.72	16	16	12	125.2	119	53	47	3	0	0	0	43	8	0	.186	4	25	2	2	1.9	.935
1919	DET A	14	13	.519	2.77	29	28	19	217.1	212	65	102	4	0	1	0	71	11	0	.155	7	40	3	1	1.7	.940
1920		10	17	.370	4.33	28	27	10	191.1	192	63	76	3	0	1	0	57	12	0	.211	7	42	2	0	1.8	.960
1921		11	13	.458	3.75	36	32	16	245	273	63	120	1	0	2	1	82	14	0	.171	4	50	3	1	1.6	.947
1924		3	2	.600	4.56	9	7	3	51.1	69	17	26	0	0	0	0	19	4	0	.211	0	11	1	0	1.3	.917
1925		11	4	.733	4.51	18	18	8	125.2	143	43	65	0	0	2	0	50	10	0	.200	5	17	1	0	1.3	.957
11 yrs.		139	112	.554	2.77	331	271	152	2190	2025	663	1158	32	13	9	13	716	124	0	.173	54	426	28	8	1.5	.945

Year	Team	W	L	PCT	ERA	G	GS	CG	IP	H	BB	SO	ShO	W	L	SV	AB	H	HR	BA	PO	A	E	DP	TC/G	FA
														Relief Pitching			**Batting**									

Dutch Leonard *continued*

WORLD SERIES

Year	Team	W	L	PCT	ERA	G	GS	CG	IP	H	BB	SO	ShO	W	L	SV	AB	H	HR	BA	PO	A	E	DP	TC/G	FA
1915	BOS A	1	0	1.000	1.00	1	1	1	9	3	0	6	0	0	0	0	3	0	0	.000	0	2	0	0	2.0	1.000
1916		1	0	1.000	1.00	1	1	1	9	5	4	3	0	0	0	0	3	0	0	.000	0	1	0	0	1.0	1.000
2 yrs.		2	0	1.000	1.00	2	2	2	18	8	4	9	0	0	0	0	6	0	0	.000	0	3	0	0	1.5	1.000

Elmer Leonard

LEONARD, ELMER ELLSWORTH (Tiny)
B. Nov. 12, 1888, Napa, Calif. D. May 27, 1981, Napa, Calif. BR TR 6'3½" 210 lbs.

Year	Team	W	L	PCT	ERA	G	GS	CG	IP	H	BB	SO	ShO	W	L	SV	AB	H	HR	BA	PO	A	E	DP	TC/G	FA
1911	PHI A	2	2	.500	2.84	5	1	1	19	26	10	10	0	1	2	0	7	2	0	.286	0	3	0	0	0.6	1.000

Dave Leonhard

LEONHARD, DAVID PAUL
B. Jan. 22, 1942, Arlington, Va. BR TR 5'11" 165 lbs.

Year	Team	W	L	PCT	ERA	G	GS	CG	IP	H	BB	SO	ShO	W	L	SV	AB	H	HR	BA	PO	A	E	DP	TC/G	FA
1967	BAL A	0	0	–	3.14	3	2	0	14.1	11	6	9	0	0	0	1	5	0	0	.000	3	3	0	0	2.0	1.000
1968		7	7	.500	3.13	28	18	5	126.1	95	57	61	2	1	0	1	31	4	0	.129	10	26	2	1	1.4	.947
1969		7	4	.636	2.49	37	3	1	94	78	38	37	1	6	2	1	21	2	0	.095	9	11	0	1	0.5	1.000
1970		0	0	–	5.14	23	0	0	28	32	18	14	0	0	0	1	1	0	0	.000	0	9	0	1	0.4	1.000
1971		2	3	.400	2.83	12	6	1	54	51	19	18	1	1	0	1	18	5	0	.278	3	13	0	0	1.3	1.000
1972		0	0	–	4.50	14	0	0	20	20	12	7	0	0	0	0	1	1	0	1.000	2	3	0	0	0.4	1.000
6 yrs.		16	14	.533	3.15	117	29	7	336.2	287	150	146	4	8	2	5	77	12	0	.156	27	65	2	3	0.8	.979

WORLD SERIES

Year	Team	W	L	PCT	ERA	G	GS	CG	IP	H	BB	SO	ShO	W	L	SV	AB	H	HR	BA	PO	A	E	DP	TC/G	FA
1969	BAL A	0	0	–	4.50	1	0	0	2	1	1	1	0	0	0	0	0	0	0	–	0	1	0	0	1.0	1.000
1971		0	0	–	0.00	1	0	0	1	0	1	0	0	0	0	0	0	0	0	–	0	0	0	0	0.0	–
2 yrs.		0	0	–	3.00	2	0	0	3	1	2	1	0	0	0	0	0	0	0	–	0	1	0	0	0.5	1.000

Rudy Leopold

LEOPOLD, RUDOLPH MATAS
B. July 27, 1905, Grand Cane, La. D. Sept. 3, 1965, Baton Rouge, La. BL TL 6' 160 lbs.

Year	Team	W	L	PCT	ERA	G	GS	CG	IP	H	BB	SO	ShO	W	L	SV	AB	H	HR	BA	PO	A	E	DP	TC/G	FA
1928	CHI A	0	0	–	3.86	2	0	0	2.1	3	0	0	0	0	0	0	1	0	0	.000	0	0	1	0	0.5	–

Randy Lerch

LERCH, RANDY LOUIS
B. Oct. 9, 1954, Sacramento, Calif. BL TL 6'5" 195 lbs.

Year	Team	W	L	PCT	ERA	G	GS	CG	IP	H	BB	SO	ShO	W	L	SV	AB	H	HR	BA	PO	A	E	DP	TC/G	FA
1975	PHI N	0	0	–	6.43	3	0	0	7	6	1	8	0	0	0	0	0	0	0	–	0	0	0	0	0.0	–
1976		0	0	–	3.00	1	0	0	3	3	0	0	0	0	0	1	1	1	0	1.000	0	0	0	0	0.0	–
1977		10	6	.625	5.06	32	28	3	169	207	75	81	0	0	0	0	54	9	0	.167	16	33	2	4	1.6	.961
1978		11	8	.579	3.96	33	28	5	184	183	70	96	0	0	0	0	60	15	3	.250	9	32	2	3	1.3	.953
1979		10	13	.435	3.74	37	35	6	214	228	60	92	1	0	0	0	72	11	1	.153	13	38	1	5	1.4	.981
1980		4	14	.222	5.16	30	22	2	150	178	55	57	0	1	0	0	45	12	0	.267	8	29	1	1	1.3	.974
1981	MIL A	7	9	.438	4.30	23	18	1	111	134	43	53	0	2	1	0					4	21	1	1	1.1	.962
1982	2 teams	MIL A	(21G 8–7)		MON N	(6G 2–0)																				
"	total	10	7	.588	4.69	27	24	1	132.1	149	59	37	1	0	0	0	8	2	0	.250	5	17	2	0	0.9	.917
1983	2 teams	MON N	(19G 1–3)		SF N	(7G 1–0)																				
"	total	2	3	.400	6.02	26	5	0	49.1	54	26	30	0	1	1	0	9	2	0	.222	3	6	0	0	0.3	1.000
1984	SF N	5	3	.625	4.23	37	4	0	72.1	80	36	48	0	5	2	2	15	2	0	.133	5	12	0	1	0.5	1.000
1986	PHI N	1	1	.500	7.88	4	0	0	8	10	7	5	0	1	1	0	3	1	0	.333	1	0	0	0	0.3	1.000
11 yrs.		60	64	.484	4.52	253	164	18	1100	1232	432	507	2	11	5	3	267	55	4	.206	63	189	9	16	1.0	.966

DIVISIONAL PLAYOFF SERIES

Year	Team	W	L	PCT	ERA	G	GS	CG	IP	H	BB	SO	ShO	W	L	SV	AB	H	HR	BA	PO	A	E	DP	TC/G	FA
1981	MIL A	0	0	–	1.50	1	1	0	6	3	4	3	0	0	0	0					0	0	0	0	0.0	–

LEAGUE CHAMPIONSHIP SERIES

Year	Team	W	L	PCT	ERA	G	GS	CG	IP	H	BB	SO	ShO	W	L	SV	AB	H	HR	BA	PO	A	E	DP	TC/G	FA
1978	PHI N	0	0	–	5.06	1	1	0	5.1	7	0	0	0	0	0	0	2	0	0	.000	1	0	0	0	1.0	1.000

Louis LeRoy

LeROY, LOUIS PAUL
B. Feb. 18, 1879, Ormo Village, Wis. D. Oct. 10, 1944, Shawano, Wis. BR TR 5'10" 180 lbs.

Year	Team	W	L	PCT	ERA	G	GS	CG	IP	H	BB	SO	ShO	W	L	SV	AB	H	HR	BA	PO	A	E	DP	TC/G	FA
1905	NY A	1	1	.500	3.75	3	3	2	24	26	1	8	0	0	0	0	8	1	0	.125	2	5	0	0	2.3	1.000
1906		2	0	1.000	2.22	11	2	1	44.2	33	12	28	0	1	0	1	14	2	0	.143	2	17	0	0	1.7	1.000
1910	BOS A	0	0	–	11.25	1	0	0	4	7	2	3	0	0	0	0	1	0	0	.000	0	1	0	0	1.0	1.000
3 yrs.		3	1	.750	3.22	15	5	3	72.2	66	15	39	0	1	0	1	23	3	0	.130	4	23	0	0	1.8	1.000

Barry Lersch

LERSCH, BARRY LEE
B. Sept. 7, 1944, Denver, Colo. BB TR 6' 175 lbs.

Year	Team	W	L	PCT	ERA	G	GS	CG	IP	H	BB	SO	ShO	W	L	SV	AB	H	HR	BA	PO	A	E	DP	TC/G	FA
1969	PHI N	0	3	.000	7.00	10	0	0	18	20	10	13	0	0	3	2	3	0	0	.000	2	6	0	0	0.8	1.000
1970		6	3	.667	3.26	42	11	3	138	119	47	92	0	2	0	3	31	2	0	.065	6	18	2	3	0.6	.923
1971		5	14	.263	3.79	38	30	3	214	203	50	113	0	0	0	0	59	10	0	.169	14	30	2	1	1.2	.957
1972		4	6	.400	3.04	36	8	3	100.2	86	33	48	1	0	2	0	23	0	0	.000	7	15	2	0	0.7	.917
1973		3	6	.333	4.39	42	4	0	98.1	105	27	51	0	3	4	1	17	3	0	.176	5	13	1	2	0.5	.947
1974	STL N	0	0	–	54.00	1	0	0	1	3	5	0	0	0	0	0	0	0	0	–	0	0	0	0	0.0	–
6 yrs.		18	32	.360	3.82	169	53	9	570	536	172	317	1	5	9	6	133	15	0	.113	34	82	7	7	0.7	.943

Don Leshnock

LESHNOCK, DONALD LEE
B. Nov. 25, 1946, Youngstown, Ohio BR TL 6'3" 195 lbs.

Year	Team	W	L	PCT	ERA	G	GS	CG	IP	H	BB	SO	ShO	W	L	SV	AB	H	HR	BA	PO	A	E	DP	TC/G	FA
1972	DET A	0	0	–	0.00	1	0	0	2	0	2	0	0	0	0	0	0	0	0	–	0	0	0	0	0.0	–

Brad Lesley

LESLEY, BRADLEY JAY (The Animal)
B. Sept. 11, 1958, Turlock, Calif. BR TR 6'6" 220 lbs.

Year	Team	W	L	PCT	ERA	G	GS	CG	IP	H	BB	SO	ShO	W	L	SV	AB	H	HR	BA	PO	A	E	DP	TC/G	FA
1982	CIN N	0	2	.000	2.58	28	0	0	38.1	27	13	29	0	0	2	4	1	0	0	.000	2	5	0	0	0.3	1.000
1983		0	0	–	2.16	5	0	0	8.1	9	0	5	0	0	0	0	0	0	0	–	0	1	0	0	0.2	1.000
1984		0	1	.000	5.12	16	0	0	19.1	17	14	7	0	0	1	2	2	1	0	.500	1	4	1	0	0.4	.833
1985	MIL A	1	0	1.000	9.95	5	0	0	6.1	8	2	5	0	1	0	0	0	0	0	–	0	1	0	0	0.2	1.000
4 yrs.		1	3	.250	3.86	54	0	0	72.1	61	29	46	0	1	3	6	3	1	0	.333	3	11	1	0	0.3	.933

Year	Team		W	L	PCT	ERA	G	GS	CG	IP	H	BB	SO	ShO	Relief Pitching W	L	SV	Batting AB	H	HR	BA	PO	A	E	DP	TC/G	FA

Walt Leverenz

LEVERENZ, WALTER FRED (Tiny)
B. July 21, 1887, Chicago, Ill. D. Mar. 19, 1973, Atascadero, Calif.   BL TL 5'10"   175 lbs.

Year	Team		W	L	PCT	ERA	G	GS	CG	IP	H	BB	SO	ShO	W	L	SV	AB	H	HR	BA	PO	A	E	DP	TC/G	FA
1913	STL	A	6	17	.261	2.58	30	27	13	202.2	159	89	87	2	0	0	1	68	12	0	.176	11	52	5	2	2.3	.926
1914			1	12	.077	3.80	27	16	5	111.1	107	63	41	0	0	2	0	33	6	0	.182	6	28	6	0	1.5	.850
1915			0	2	.000	8.00	5	1	0	9	11	8	3	0	0	1	1	1	0	0	.000	0	3	0	0	0.6	1.000
3 yrs.			7	31	.184	3.15	62	44	18	323	277	160	131	2	0	3	2	102	18	0	.176	17	83	11	2	1.8	.901

Dixie Leverett

LEVERETT, GORHAM VANCE
B. Mar. 29, 1894, Georgetown, Tex. D. Feb. 20, 1957, Beaverton, Ore.   BR TR 5'11"   190 lbs.

Year	Team		W	L	PCT	ERA	G	GS	CG	IP	H	BB	SO	ShO	W	L	SV	AB	H	HR	BA	PO	A	E	DP	TC/G	FA
1922	CHI	A	13	10	.565	3.32	33	27	16	224.2	224	79	60	4	0	0	2	83	21	0	.253	12	51	2	2	2.0	.969
1923			10	13	.435	4.06	38	24	9	192.2	212	64	64	0	1	3	3	60	16	0	.267	6	49	3	2	1.5	.948
1924			2	3	.400	5.82	21	11	4	99	123	41	29	0	0	0	0	32	6	0	.188	4	25	2	1	1.5	.935
1926			1	1	.500	6.00	6	3	1	24	31	7	12	0	0	0	0	7	1	0	.143	1	7	1	1	1.5	.889
1929	BOS	N	3	7	.300	6.36	24	12	3	97.2	135	30	28	0	0	1	1	32	6	0	.188	5	20	1	0	1.1	.962
5 yrs.			29	34	.460	4.50	122	77	33	638	725	221	193	4	1	4	6	214	50	0	.234	28	152	9	6	1.5	.952

Hod Leverette

LEVERETTE, HORACE WILBUR
B. Feb. 4, 1889, Shreveport, La. D. Apr. 10, 1958, St. Petersburg, Fla.   BR TR 6'   180 lbs.

Year	Team		W	L	PCT	ERA	G	GS	CG	IP	H	BB	SO	ShO	W	L	SV	AB	H	HR	BA	PO	A	E	DP	TC/G	FA
1920	STL	A	0	2	.000	5.23	3	2	0	10.1	9	12	0	0	0	0	0	3	0	0	.000	0	7	0	0	2.3	1.000

Dutch Levsen

LEVSEN, EMIL HENRY
B. Apr. 29, 1898, Wyoming, Iowa D. Mar. 12, 1972, St. Louis Park, Minn.   BR TR 6'   180 lbs.

Year	Team		W	L	PCT	ERA	G	GS	CG	IP	H	BB	SO	ShO	W	L	SV	AB	H	HR	BA	PO	A	E	DP	TC/G	FA
1923	CLE	A	0	0	–	0.00	3	0	0	4.1	4	0	1	0	0	0	0	1	0	0	.000	0	6	0	0	2.0	1.000
1924			1	1	.500	4.41	4	1	1	16.1	22	4	3	0	0	1	0	5	0	0	.000	2	4	0	0	1.5	1.000
1925			1	2	.333	5.55	4	3	2	24.1	30	16	9	0	0	0	0	8	2	0	.250	1	2	1	0	1.0	.750
1926			16	13	.552	3.41	33	31	18	237.1	235	85	53	2	0	2	0	83	17	0	.205	12	55	2	7	2.1	.971
1927			3	7	.300	5.49	25	13	2	80.1	96	37	15	1	0	1	0	25	5	0	.200	2	27	2	3	1.2	.935
1928			0	3	.000	5.44	11	3	0	41.1	39	31	7	0	0	1	0	13	0	0	.000	0	12	3	0	1.4	.800
6 yrs.			21	26	.447	4.17	80	51	23	404	426	173	88	3	0	5	0	135	24	0	.178	17	106	8	10	1.6	.939

Dennis Lewallyn

LEWALLYN, DENNIS DALE
B. Aug. 11, 1953, Pensacola, Fla.   BR TR 6'4"   195 lbs.

Year	Team		W	L	PCT	ERA	G	GS	CG	IP	H	BB	SO	ShO	W	L	SV	AB	H	HR	BA	PO	A	E	DP	TC/G	FA
1975	LA	N	0	0	–	0.00	3	0	0	3	0	0	0	0	0	0	0	0	0	0	–	1	0	0	0	0.5	1.000
1976			1	1	.500	2.16	4	2	0	16.2	12	6	4	0	0	0	0	5	0	0	.000	0	5	0	0	1.3	1.000
1977			3	1	.750	4.24	5	1	0	17	22	4	8	0	2	1	1	6	0	0	.000	2	1	0	0	0.6	1.000
1978			0	0	–	0.00	1	0	0	2	2	0	0	0	0	0	0	0	0	0	–	0	0	0	0	0.0	–
1979			0	1	.000	5.25	7	0	0	12	19	5	1	0	0	1	0	2	1	0	.500	1	4	0	0	0.7	1.000
1980	TEX	A	0	0	–	7.50	4	0	0	6	7	4	1	0	0	0	0	0	0	0	–	0	2	0	0	0.5	1.000
1981	CLE	A	0	0	–	5.54	7	0	0	13	16	2	11	0	0	0	0	0	0	0	–	0	1	0	0	0.1	1.000
1982			0	1	.000	6.97	4	0	0	10.1	13	1	3	0	0	1	0	0	0	0	–	2	0	0	0	0.5	1.000
8 yrs.			4	4	.500	4.50	34	3	0	80	92	22	28	0	2	3	1	13	1	0	.077	6	13	0	0	0.6	1.000

Dan Lewandowski

LEWANDOWSKI, DANIEL WILLIAM
B. Jan. 6, 1928, Buffalo, N. Y.   BR TR 6'   180 lbs.

Year	Team		W	L	PCT	ERA	G	GS	CG	IP	H	BB	SO	ShO	W	L	SV	AB	H	HR	BA	PO	A	E	DP	TC/G	FA
1951	STL	N	0	1	.000	9.00	2	0	0	1	3	1	1	0	0	0	0	0	0	0	–	0	0	0	0	0.0	–

Lewis

LEWIS,
B. Brooklyn, N. Y. Deceased.

Year	Team		W	L	PCT	ERA	G	GS	CG	IP	H	BB	SO	ShO	W	L	SV	AB	H	HR	BA	PO	A	E	DP	TC/G	FA
1890	BUF	P	0	1	.000	60.00	1	1	0	3	13	7	1	0	0	0	0	5	1	0	.200	2	3	0	0	5.0	1.000

Burt Lewis

LEWIS, WILLIAM BURTON
B. Oct. 3, 1895, Tonawanda, N. Y. D. Mar. 24, 1950, Tonawanda, N. Y.   BR TR 6'2"   176 lbs.

Year	Team		W	L	PCT	ERA	G	GS	CG	IP	H	BB	SO	ShO	W	L	SV	AB	H	HR	BA	PO	A	E	DP	TC/G	FA
1924	PHI	N	0	0	–	6.00	12	0	0	18	23	7	3	0	0	0	0	5	0	0	.000	2	4	0	1	0.5	1.000

Duffy Lewis

LEWIS, GEORGE EDWARD
B. Apr. 18, 1888, San Francisco, Calif. D. June 17, 1979, Salem, N. H.   BR TR 5'10½" 165 lbs.

Year	Team		W	L	PCT	ERA	G	GS	CG	IP	H	BB	SO	ShO	W	L	SV	AB	H	HR	BA	PO	A	E	DP	TC/G	FA
1913	BOS	A	0	0	–	0.00	1	0	0	1	0	1	0	0	0	0	0	*				0	0	0	0	0.0	–

Jim Lewis

LEWIS, JAMES MARTIN
B. Oct. 12, 1955, Miami, Fla.   BR TR 6'3"   190 lbs.

Year	Team		W	L	PCT	ERA	G	GS	CG	IP	H	BB	SO	ShO	W	L	SV	AB	H	HR	BA	PO	A	E	DP	TC/G	FA
1979	SEA	A	0	0	–	18.00	2	0	0	2	10	1	0	0	0	0	0	0	0	0	–	0	0	1	0	0.5	–
1982	NY	A	0	0	–	54.00	1	0	0	.2	3	3	0	0	0	0	0	0	0	0	–	0	0	0	0	0.0	–
1983	MIN	A	0	0	–	6.50	6	0	0	18	24	7	8	0	0	0	0	0	0	0	–	1	3	0	0	0.7	1.000
1985	SEA	A	0	1	.000	7.71	2	1	0	4.2	8	1	1	0	0	0	0	0	0	0	–	0	0	0	0	0.0	–
4 yrs.			0	1	.000	8.88	11	1	0	25.1	45	12	9	0	0	0	0	0	0	0	–	1	3	1	0	0.5	.800

Ted Lewis

LEWIS, EDWARD MORGAN (Parson)
B. Dec. 25, 1872, Machynlleth, Wales D. May 24, 1936, Durham, N. H.   BR TR 5'10½" 158 lbs.

Year	Team		W	L	PCT	ERA	G	GS	CG	IP	H	BB	SO	ShO	W	L	SV	AB	H	HR	BA	PO	A	E	DP	TC/G	FA
1896	BOS	N	1	4	.200	3.24	6	5	4	41.2	37	27	12	0	0	0	0	18	2	0	.111	6	10	1	1	2.7	1.000
1897			21	12	.636	3.85	38	34	30	290	316	125	65	2	1	1	1	113	28	0	.248	6	46	3	1	1.4	.945
1898			26	8	.765	2.90	41	33	29	313.1	267	109	72	1	0	2	2	131	37	0	.282	13	71	4	4	2.1	.955
1899			17	11	.607	3.49	29	25	23	234.2	245	73	60	2	3	1	0	96	25	0	.260	17	35	6	0	2.0	.897
1900	BOS	A	13	12	.520	4.13	30	22	19	209	215	86	66	1	4	0	0	73	10	0	.137	8	36	5	1	1.6	.898
1901			16	17	.485	3.53	39	34	31	316.1	299	91	103	1	0	2	1	121	21	0	.174	7	84	7	1	2.5	.929
6 yrs.			94	64	.595	3.53	183	153	136	1405	1379	511	378	7	11	4	4	552	123	0	.223	57	282	25	8	2.0	.931

Terry Ley

LEY, TERRENCE RICHARD
B. Feb. 21, 1947, Portland, Ore.   BL TL 6'   190 lbs.

Year	Team		W	L	PCT	ERA	G	GS	CG	IP	H	BB	SO	ShO	W	L	SV	AB	H	HR	BA	PO	A	E	DP	TC/G	FA
1971	NY	A	0	0	–	5.00	6	0	0	9	9	9	7	0	0	0	0	0	0	0	–	1	3	1	0	0.8	.800

Year	Team		W	L	PCT	ERA	G	GS	CG	IP	H	BB	SO	ShO	Relief Pitching W	L	SV	Batting AB	H	HR	BA	PO	A	E	DP	TC/G	FA

Al Libke

LIBKE, ALBERT WALTER (Big Al)
B. Sept. 12, 1918, Tacoma, Wash.

BL TR 6'4" 215 lbs.

Year	Team		W	L	PCT	ERA	G	GS	CG	IP	H	BB	SO	ShO	W	L	SV	AB	H	HR	BA	PO	A	E	DP	TC/G	FA
1945	CIN	N	0	0	–	0.00	4	0	0	4.1	3	3	2	0	0	0	0	449	127	4	.283	0	2	0	0	0.5	1.000
1946			0	0	–	3.60	1	1	0	5	4	3	2	0	0	0	0	431	109	5	.253	0	0	0	0	0.0	–
2 yrs.			0	0	–	1.93	5	1	0	9.1	7	6	4	0	0	0	0	*				0	2	0	0	0.4	1.000

Don Liddle

LIDDLE, DONALD EUGENE
B. May 25, 1925, Mt. Carmel, Ill.

BL TL 5'10" 165 lbs.

Year	Team		W	L	PCT	ERA	G	GS	CG	IP	H	BB	SO	ShO	W	L	SV	AB	H	HR	BA	PO	A	E	DP	TC/G	FA
1953	MIL	N	7	6	.538	3.08	31	15	4	128.2	119	55	63	0	3	1	2	34	3	0	.088	5	20	2	2	0.9	.926
1954	NY	N	9	4	.692	3.06	28	19	4	126.2	100	55	44	3	1	0	1	37	7	0	.189	6	19	1	1	0.9	.962
1955			10	4	.714	4.23	33	13	4	106.1	97	61	56	0	4	1	1	27	5	0	.185	5	15	1	0	0.6	.952
1956	2 teams		NY N (11G 1–2)			STL N (14G 1–2)																					
"	total		2	4	.333	5.59	25	7	1	66	81	32	35	0	1	1	0	14	2	0	.143	7	10	1	1	0.7	.944
4 yrs.			28	18	.609	3.75	117	54	13	427.2	397	203	198	3	9	3	4	112	17	0	.152	23	64	5	4	0.8	.946

WORLD SERIES

Year	Team		W	L	PCT	ERA	G	GS	CG	IP	H	BB	SO	ShO	W	L	SV	AB	H	HR	BA	PO	A	E	DP	TC/G	FA
1954	NY	N	1	0	1.000	1.29	2	1	0	7	5	1	2	0	0	0	0				.000	0	1	1	0	1.0	.500

Dutch Lieber

LIEBER, CHARLES EDWIN
B. Feb. 1, 1910, Alameda, Calif.   D. Dec. 31, 1961, Sawtelle, Calif.

BR TR 6'½" 180 lbs.

Year	Team		W	L	PCT	ERA	G	GS	CG	IP	H	BB	SO	ShO	W	L	SV	AB	H	HR	BA	PO	A	E	DP	TC/G	FA
1935	PHI	A	1	1	.500	3.09	18	1	0	46.2	45	19	14	0	1	1	2	14	2	0	.143	3	10	1	1	0.8	.929
1936			0	1	.000	7.71	3	0	0	11.2	17	6	1	0	0	0	0	3	0	0	.000	0	5	0	0	1.7	1.000
2 yrs.			1	2	.333	4.01	21	1	0	58.1	62	25	15	0	1	1	2	17	2	0	.118	3	15	1	1	0.9	.947

Glenn Liebhardt

LIEBHARDT, GLENN IGNATIUS (Sandy)
Son of Glenn Liebhardt.
B. July 31, 1910, Cleveland, Ohio

BR TR 5'10½" 170 lbs.

Year	Team		W	L	PCT	ERA	G	GS	CG	IP	H	BB	SO	ShO	W	L	SV	AB	H	HR	BA	PO	A	E	DP	TC/G	FA
1930	PHI	A	0	1	.000	11.00	5	0	0	9	14	8	2	0	0	1	0	2	0	0	.000	0	1	1	0	0.4	.500
1936	STL	A	0	0	–	8.78	24	0	0	55.1	98	27	20	0	0	0	0	11	0	0	.000	0	4	1	0	0.2	.800
1938			0	0	–	6.00	2	0	0	3	4	0	1	0	0	0	0	0	0	0	–	0	1	0	0	0.5	1.000
3 yrs.			0	1	.000	8.96	31	0	0	67.1	116	35	23	0	0	1	0	13	0	0	.000	0	6	2	0	0.3	.750

Glenn Liebhardt

LIEBHARDT, GLENN JOHN
Father of Glenn Liebhardt.
B. Mar. 10, 1883, Milton, Ind.   D. July 13, 1956, Cleveland, Ohio

BR TR 5'10" 175 lbs.

Year	Team		W	L	PCT	ERA	G	GS	CG	IP	H	BB	SO	ShO	W	L	SV	AB	H	HR	BA	PO	A	E	DP	TC/G	FA
1906	CLE	A	2	0	1.000	1.50	2	2	2	18	13	1	9	0	0	0	0	8	0	0	.000	0	7	0	0	3.5	1.000
1907			18	14	.563	2.05	38	34	27	280.1	254	85	110	4	0	0	1	87	14	0	.161	9	92	4	3	2.8	.962
1908			15	16	.484	2.20	39	26	19	262	222	81	146	3	3	2	0	80	14	0	.175	14	78	4	4	2.5	.958
1909			1	5	.167	2.92	12	4	1	52.1	54	16	15	0	1	1	1	15	0	0	.000	5	7	1	0	1.1	.923
4 yrs.			36	35	.507	2.17	91	66	49	612.2	543	183	280	7	4	3	2	190	28	0	.147	28	184	9	7	2.4	.959

Gene Lillard

LILLARD, ROBERT EUGENE
Brother of Bill Lillard.
B. Nov. 12, 1913, Santa Barbara, Calif.

BR TR 5'10½" 178 lbs.

Year	Team		W	L	PCT	ERA	G	GS	CG	IP	H	BB	SO	ShO	W	L	SV	AB	H	HR	BA	PO	A	E	DP	TC/G	FA
1939	CHI	N	3	5	.375	6.55	20	7	2	55	68	36	31	0	1	0	1	10	1	0	.100	2	11	0	0	0.7	1.000
1940	STL	N	0	1	.000	13.50	2	1	0	4.2	8	4	2	0	0	0	0	0	0	0	–	0	1	0	0	0.5	1.000
2 yrs.			3	6	.333	7.09	22	8	2	59.2	76	40	33	0	1	2	0	44	8	0	.182	2	12	0	0	0.6	1.000

Jim Lillie

LILLIE, JAMES J. (Grasshopper)
B. 1862, New Haven, Conn.   D. Nov. 9, 1890, Kansas City, Mo.

Year	Team		W	L	PCT	ERA	G	GS	CG	IP	H	BB	SO	ShO	W	L	SV	AB	H	HR	BA	PO	A	E	DP	TC/G	FA
1883	BUF	N	0	1	.000	3.00	3	0	0	12	16	2	4	0	0	0	0	201	47	1	.234	0	2	0	1	0.7	1.000
1884			0	1	.000	6.23	2	0	0	13	22	5	4	0	0	0	0	471	105	3	.223	0	5	0	0	2.5	1.000
1886	KC	N	0	0	–	4.50	1	0	0	6	8	1	0	0	0	0	0	416	73	0	.175	0	2	0	0	2.0	1.000
3 yrs.			0	2	.000	4.65	6	1	0	31	46	8	8	0	0	0	0	*				0	9	0	1	1.5	1.000

Derek Lilliquist

LILLIQUIST, DEREK JANSEN
B. Feb. 20, 1966, Winter Park, Fla.

BL TL 6' 200 lbs.

Year	Team		W	L	PCT	ERA	G	GS	CG	IP	H	BB	SO	ShO	W	L	SV	AB	H	HR	BA	PO	A	E	DP	TC/G	FA
1989	ATL	N	8	10	.444	3.97	32	30	0	165.2	202	34	79	0	0	0	0	63	12	0	.190	9	20	2	1	1.0	.935

Ezra Lincoln

LINCOLN, EZRA PERRY
B. Nov. 17, 1868, Raynham, Mass.   D. May 7, 1951, Taunton, Mass.

BL TL 5'11" 160 lbs.

Year	Team		W	L	PCT	ERA	G	GS	CG	IP	H	BB	SO	ShO	W	L	SV	AB	H	HR	BA	PO	A	E	DP	TC/G	FA
1890	2 teams		CLE N (15G 3–11)			SYR AA (3G 0–3)																					
"	total		3	14	.176	5.28	18	18	15	138	190	57	28	0	0	0	0	59	8	0	.136	6	29	2	0	2.1	.946

Vive Lindaman

LINDAMAN, VIVIAN ALEXANDER
B. Oct. 28, 1877, Charles City, Iowa   D. Feb. 13, 1927, Charles City, Iowa

BR TR 6'1" 200 lbs.

Year	Team		W	L	PCT	ERA	G	GS	CG	IP	H	BB	SO	ShO	W	L	SV	AB	H	HR	BA	PO	A	E	DP	TC/G	FA
1906	BOS	N	12	23	.343	2.43	39	37	32	307.1	303	90	115	2	0	0	0	106	14	0	.132	13	85	14	2	2.9	.875
1907			11	15	.423	3.63	34	28	24	260	252	108	90	2	0	1	0	90	11	0	.122	12	62	4	1	2.3	.949
1908			12	16	.429	2.36	43	30	21	270.2	246	70	68	2	0	1	2	85	15	0	.176	9	68	2	0	1.8	.975
1909			1	6	.143	4.64	15	6	6	66	75	28	13	1	0	1	0	22	6	0	.273	2	16	2	0	1.3	.900
4 yrs.			36	60	.375	2.92	131	101	83	904	876	296	286	7	0	3	2	303	46	0	.152	36	231	22	3	2.2	.924

Paul Lindblad

LINDBLAD, PAUL AARON
B. Aug. 9, 1941, Chanute, Kans.

BL TL 6'1" 185 lbs.

Year	Team		W	L	PCT	ERA	G	GS	CG	IP	H	BB	SO	ShO	W	L	SV	AB	H	HR	BA	PO	A	E	DP	TC/G	FA
1965	KC	A	0	1	.000	11.05	4	0	0	7.1	12	0	12	0	0	0	0	1	0	0	.000	1	3	1	0	1.3	.800
1966			5	10	.333	4.17	38	14	0	121	138	37	69	0	3	3	2	34	5	0	.147	6	22	1	1	0.8	.966
1967			5	8	.385	3.58	46	10	0	115.2	106	35	83	1	3	3	6	34	7	1	.206	4	17	0	1	0.5	1.000
1968	OAK	A	4	3	.571	2.40	47	1	0	56.1	51	14	42	0	4	2	2	8	3	0	.375	4	9	0	1	0.3	1.000
1969			9	6	.600	4.14	60	0	0	78.1	72	33	64	0	9	6	9	12	4	0	.333	2	11	0	0	0.2	1.000
1970			8	2	.800	2.71	62	0	0	63	52	28	42	0	8	2	3	6	0	0	.000	1	10	0	0	0.2	1.000

Year	Team	W	L	PCT	ERA	G	GS	CG	IP	H	BB	SO	ShO	Relief Pitching W	L	SV	Batting AB	H	HR	BA	PO	A	E	DP	TC/G	FA

Paul Lindblad *continued*

Year	Team	W	L	PCT	ERA	G	GS	CG	IP	H	BB	SO	ShO	W	L	SV	AB	H	HR	BA	PO	A	E	DP	TC/G	FA
1971	2 teams	OAK A	(8G 1–0)		WAS A	(43G 6–4)																				
"	total	7	4	.636	2.80	51	0	0	99.2	76	31	54	0	7	4	8	22	4	0	.182	4	21	0	1	0.5	1.000
1972	TEX A	5	8	.385	2.61	66	0	0	100	95	29	51	0	5	8	9	15	3	0	.200	0	15	0	1	0.2	1.000
1973	OAK A	1	5	.167	3.69	36	3	0	78	89	28	33	0	1	2	2	0	0	0	–	5	9	0	0	0.4	1.000
1974		4	4	.500	2.05	45	2	0	101	90	30	46	0	3	3	6	0	0	0	–	1	19	1	1	0.5	.952
1975		9	1	.900	2.72	68	0	0	122.1	105	43	58	0	9	1	7	1	0	0	.000	10	23	2	3	0.5	.943
1976		6	5	.545	3.05	65	0	0	115	111	24	37	0	6	5	5	0	0	0	–	9	21	1	1	0.5	.968
1977	TEX A	4	5	.444	4.18	42	1	0	99	103	29	46	0	4	4	4	0	0	0	–	7	16	0	1	0.5	1.000
1978	2 teams	TEX A	(18G 1–1)		NY A	(7G 0–0)																				
"	total	1	1	.500	3.88	25	1	0	58	62	23	34	0	1	1	2	0	0	0	–	0	5	0	1	0.2	1.000
14 yrs.		68	63	.519	3.28	655	32	1	1214.2	1157	384	671	0	62	45	64	133	26	1	.195	54	201	6	11	0.4	.977

LEAGUE CHAMPIONSHIP SERIES

Year	Team	W	L	PCT	ERA	G	GS	CG	IP	H	BB	SO	ShO	W	L	SV	AB	H	HR	BA	PO	A	E	DP	TC/G	FA
1975	OAK A	0	0	–	0.00	2	0	0	4.2	5	1	0	0	0	0	0	0	0	0	–	1	4	0	0	2.5	1.000

WORLD SERIES

Year	Team	W	L	PCT	ERA	G	GS	CG	IP	H	BB	SO	ShO	W	L	SV	AB	H	HR	BA	PO	A	E	DP	TC/G	FA
1973	OAK A	1	0	1.000	0.00	3	0	0	3.1	4	1	0	0	1	0	0	1	0	0	.000	0	0	0	0	0.0	–
1978	NY A	0	0	–	11.57	1	0	0	2.1	4	0	1	0	0	0	0	0	0	0	–	0	0	0	0	0.0	–
2 yrs.		1	0	1.000	4.76	4	0	0	5.2	8	1	2	0	1	0	0	1	0	0	.000	0	0	0	0	0.0	–

Lymie Linde   LINDE, LYMAN GILBERT   BR TR 5'11" 185 lbs.
B. Sept. 20, 1920, Beaver Dam, Wis.

Year	Team	W	L	PCT	ERA	G	GS	CG	IP	H	BB	SO	ShO	W	L	SV	AB	H	HR	BA	PO	A	E	DP	TC/G	FA
1947	CLE A	0	0	–	27.00	1	0	0	.2	3	1	0	0	0	0	0	0	0	0	–	0	0	0	0	0.0	–
1948		0	0	–	5.40	3	0	0	10	9	4	0	0	0	0	0	2	0	0	.000	0	1	1	0	0.7	.500
2 yrs.		0	0	–	6.75	4	0	0	10.2	12	5	0	0	0	0	0	2	0	0	.000	0	1	1	0	0.5	.500

Johnny Lindell   LINDELL, JOHN HARLAN   BR TR 6'4½" 217 lbs.
B. Aug. 30, 1916, Greeley, Colo.   D. Aug. 27, 1985, Newport Beach, Calif.

Year	Team	W	L	PCT	ERA	G	GS	CG	IP	H	BB	SO	ShO	W	L	SV	AB	H	HR	BA	PO	A	E	DP	TC/G	FA
1942	NY A	2	1	.667	3.76	23	4	0	52.2	52	22	28	0	2	0	1	24	6	0	.250	5	7	1	2	0.6	.923
1953	2 teams	PIT N	(27G 5–16)		PHI N	(5G 1–1)																				
"	total	6	17	.261	4.66	32	26	15	199	195	139	118	1	1	0	0	109	33	4	.303	8	45	2	1	1.7	.964
2 yrs.		8	18	.308	4.47	55	28	15	251.2	247	161	146	1	3	0	1	*				13	52	3	4	1.2	.956

Ernie Lindemann   LINDEMANN, ERNEST   BR TR
B. June 10, 1883, New York, N. Y.   D. Dec. 27, 1951, Brooklyn, N. Y.

Year	Team	W	L	PCT	ERA	G	GS	CG	IP	H	BB	SO	ShO	W	L	SV	AB	H	HR	BA	PO	A	E	DP	TC/G	FA
1907	BOS N	0	0	–	5.68	1	1	0	6.1	6	4	3	0	0	0	0	2	1	0	.500	0	3	0	0	3.0	1.000

Carl Lindquist   LINDQUIST, CARL EMIL (Lindy)   BR TR 6'2" 185 lbs.
B. May 9, 1919, Morris Run, Pa.

Year	Team	W	L	PCT	ERA	G	GS	CG	IP	H	BB	SO	ShO	W	L	SV	AB	H	HR	BA	PO	A	E	DP	TC/G	FA
1943	BOS N	0	2	.000	6.23	2	2	0	13	17	4	1	0	0	0	0	4	0	0	.000	1	4	0	0	2.5	1.000
1944		0	0	–	3.12	5	0	0	8.2	8	2	4	0	0	0	0	1	0	0	.000	1	0	0	0	0.2	1.000
2 yrs.		0	2	.000	4.98	7	2	0	21.2	25	6	5	0	0	0	0	5	0	0	.000	2	4	0	0	0.9	1.000

Jim Lindsey   LINDSEY, JAMES KENDRICK   BR TR 6'1" 175 lbs.
B. Jan. 24, 1898, Greensburg, La.   D. Oct. 25, 1963, Jackson, La.

Year	Team	W	L	PCT	ERA	G	GS	CG	IP	H	BB	SO	ShO	W	L	SV	AB	H	HR	BA	PO	A	E	DP	TC/G	FA
1922	CLE A	4	5	.444	6.02	29	5	0	83.2	105	24	29	0	4	2	1	24	4	0	.167	1	17	1	0	0.7	.947
1924		0	0	–	21.00	3	0	0	3	8	3	0	0	0	0	0	0	0	0	–	0	3	0	0	0.3	1.000
1929	STL N	1	1	.500	5.51	2	2	1	16.1	20	2	8	0	0	0	0	5	1	0	.200	0	3	0	0	1.5	1.000
1930		7	5	.583	4.43	39	6	3	105.2	131	46	50	0	4	2	5	28	8	0	.286	1	9	1	0	0.3	.909
1931		6	4	.600	2.77	35	2	1	74.2	77	45	32	1	5	4	7	9	1	0	.111	0	15	1	1	0.5	.938
1932		3	3	.500	4.94	33	5	0	89.1	96	38	31	0	3	3	3	21	3	0	.143	1	16	1	1	0.5	.941
1933		0	0	–	4.50	1	0	0	2	2	1	1	0	0	0	0	0	0	0	–	0	0	0	0	0.0	–
1934	2 teams	CIN N	(4G 0–0)		STL N	(11G 0–1)																				
"	total	0	1	.000	6.00	15	0	0	18	25	5	9	0	0	1	0	5	0	0	.000	0	3	0	0	0.2	1.000
1937	BKN N	0	1	.000	3.52	20	0	0	38.1	43	12	15	0	0	1	2	6	1	0	.167	0	7	1	0	0.4	.875
9 yrs.		21	20	.512	4.70	177	20	5	431	507	176	175	1	16	12	19	94	18	0	.191	2	71	5	3	0.4	.936

WORLD SERIES

Year	Team	W	L	PCT	ERA	G	GS	CG	IP	H	BB	SO	ShO	W	L	SV	AB	H	HR	BA	PO	A	E	DP	TC/G	FA
1930	STL N	0	0	–	1.93	2	0	0	4.2	1	1	2	0	0	0	0	1	1	0	1.000	0	1	0	0	0.5	1.000
1931		0	0	–	5.40	2	0	0	3.1	4	3	2	0	0	0	0	0	0	0	–	0	0	0	0	0.0	–
2 yrs.		0	0	–	3.38	4	0	0	8	5	4	4	0	0	0	0	1	1	0	1.000	0	1	0	0	0.3	1.000

Axel Lindstrom   LINDSTROM, AXEL OLAF   BR TR 5'10" 180 lbs.
B. Aug. 26, 1895, Gustavberg, Sweden   D. June 24, 1940, Asheville, N. C.

Year	Team	W	L	PCT	ERA	G	GS	CG	IP	H	BB	SO	ShO	W	L	SV	AB	H	HR	BA	PO	A	E	DP	TC/G	FA
1916	PHI A	0	0	–	4.50	1	0	0	4	2	0	1	0	0	0	1	2	1	0	.500	0	1	0	0	1.0	1.000

Dick Lines   LINES, RICHARD GEORGE   BR TL 6'1" 175 lbs.
B. Aug. 17, 1938, Montreal, Que., Canada

Year	Team	W	L	PCT	ERA	G	GS	CG	IP	H	BB	SO	ShO	W	L	SV	AB	H	HR	BA	PO	A	E	DP	TC/G	FA
1966	WAS A	5	2	.714	2.28	53	0	0	83	63	24	49	0	5	2	2	10	0	0	.000	4	23	1	3	0.5	.964
1967		2	5	.286	3.36	54	0	0	85.2	83	24	54	0	2	5	4	9	1	0	.111	5	16	3	2	0.4	.875
2 yrs.		7	7	.500	2.83	107	0	0	168.2	146	48	103	0	7	7	6	19	1	0	.053	9	39	4	5	0.5	.923

Fred Link   LINK, FREDERICK THEODORE (Laddie)   BL TL 6' 170 lbs.
B. Mar. 11, 1886, Columbus, Ohio   D. May 22, 1939, Houston, Tex.

Year	Team	W	L	PCT	ERA	G	GS	CG	IP	H	BB	SO	ShO	W	L	SV	AB	H	HR	BA	PO	A	E	DP	TC/G	FA
1910	2 teams	CLE A	(22G 5–6)		STL A	(3G 0–1)																				
"	total	5	7	.417	3.42	25	16	6	139.2	139	62	57	1	1	0	1	49	8	0	.163	4	42	4	0	2.0	.920

Ed Linke   LINKE, EDWARD KARL   BR TR 5'11" 180 lbs.
B. Nov. 9, 1911, Chicago, Ill.   D. June 21, 1988, Chicago, Ill.

Year	Team	W	L	PCT	ERA	G	GS	CG	IP	H	BB	SO	ShO	W	L	SV	AB	H	HR	BA	PO	A	E	DP	TC/G	FA
1933	WAS A	1	0	1.000	5.06	3	2	0	16	15	11	6	0	0	0	0	6	1	0	.167	2	3	1	0	2.0	.833

Year	Team		W	L	PCT	ERA	G	GS	CG	IP	H	BB	SO	ShO	Relief Pitching W	L	SV	Batting AB	H	HR	BA	PO	A	E	DP	TC/G	FA

Ed Linke *continued*

Year	Team		W	L	PCT	ERA	G	GS	CG	IP	H	BB	SO	ShO	W	L	SV	AB	H	HR	BA	PO	A	E	DP	TC/G	FA
1934			2	2	.500	4.15	7	4	2	34.2	38	9	9	0	0	0	0	11	2	0	.182	3	7	0	0	1.4	1.000
1935			11	7	.611	5.01	40	22	10	178	211	80	51	1	2	3	3	68	20	1	.294	4	30	2	3	0.9	.944
1936			1	5	.167	7.10	13	6	1	52	73	14	11	0	1	1	0	15	6	1	.400	1	17	1	1	1.5	.947
1937			6	1	.857	5.60	36	7	0	128.2	158	59	61	0	3	1	3	46	10	0	.217	1	23	1	1	0.7	.960
1938	STL	A	1	7	.125	7.94	21	2	0	39.2	60	33	18	0	1	5	0	10	2	0	.200	1	11	1	1	0.6	.923
6 yrs.			22	22	.500	5.61	120	43	13	449	555	206	156	1	7	8	6	156	41	2	.263	12	91	6	6	0.9	.945

Royce Lint

LINT, ROYCE JAMES
B. Jan. 1, 1921, Birmingham, Ala.
BL TL 6'1" 165 lbs.

Year	Team		W	L	PCT	ERA	G	GS	CG	IP	H	BB	SO	ShO	W	L	SV	AB	H	HR	BA	PO	A	E	DP	TC/G	FA
1954	STL	N	2	3	.400	4.86	30	4	1	70.1	75	30	36	1	1	3	0	10	1	0	.100	8	14	3	0	0.8	.880

Frank Linzy

LINZY, FRANK ALFRED
B. Sept. 15, 1940, Fort Gibson, Okla.
BR TR 6'1" 190 lbs.

Year	Team		W	L	PCT	ERA	G	GS	CG	IP	H	BB	SO	ShO	W	L	SV	AB	H	HR	BA	PO	A	E	DP	TC/G	FA
1963	SF	N	0	0	–	4.86	8	1	0	16.2	22	10	14	0	0	0	0	3	0	0	.000	2	4	0	0	0.8	1.000
1965			9	3	.750	1.43	57	0	0	81.2	76	23	35	0	9	3	21	18	4	1	.222	8	39	0	2	0.8	1.000
1966			7	11	.389	2.96	51	0	0	100.1	107	34	57	0	7	11	16	20	3	0	.150	6	21	3	1	0.6	.900
1967			7	7	.500	1.51	57	0	0	95.2	67	34	38	0	7	7	17	15	0	0	.000	8	32	0	2	0.7	1.000
1968			9	8	.529	2.08	57	0	0	95.1	76	27	36	0	9	8	12	11	0	0	.000	7	33	0	4	0.7	1.000
1969			14	9	.609	3.65	58	0	0	116	129	38	62	0	14	9	11	30	8	0	.267	6	37	3	2	0.8	.935
1970	2 teams		SF N	(20G 2–1)		STL N	(47G 3–5)																				
"	total		5	6	.455	4.66	67	0	0	87	99	34	35	0	5	6	3	11	0	0	.000	3	20	0	1	0.3	1.000
1971	STL	N	4	3	.571	2.14	50	0	0	59	49	27	24	0	4	3	6	4	2	0	.500	6	13	0	0	0.4	1.000
1972	MIL	A	2	2	.500	3.04	47	0	0	77	70	27	24	0	2	2	12	9	1	0	.111	2	18	1	3	0.4	.952
1973			2	6	.250	3.57	42	1	0	63	68	21	21	0	2	6	13	0	0	0	–	3	12	2	1	0.4	.882
1974	PHI	N	3	2	.600	3.24	22	0	0	25	27	7	12	0	3	2	0	0	0	0	–	0	7	0	1	0.3	1.000
11 yrs.			62	57	.521	2.85	516	2	0	816.2	790	282	358	0	62	57	111	121	18	1	.149	51	236	9	17	0.6	.970

Angelo LiPetri

LiPETRI, MICHAEL ANGELO
B. July 6, 1930, Brooklyn, N. Y.
BR TR 6'1½" 180 lbs.

Year	Team		W	L	PCT	ERA	G	GS	CG	IP	H	BB	SO	ShO	W	L	SV	AB	H	HR	BA	PO	A	E	DP	TC/G	FA
1956	PHI	N	0	0	–	3.27	6	0	0	11	7	3	8	0	0	0	0	1	0	0	.000	1	2	0	0	0.5	1.000
1958			0	0	–	11.25	4	0	0	4	6	0	1	0	0	0	0	0	0	0	–	1	1	0	0	0.5	1.000
2 yrs.			0	0	–	5.40	10	0	0	15	13	3	9	0	0	0	0	1	0	0	.000	2	3	0	0	0.5	1.000

Tom Lipp

LIPP, THOMAS C.
B. June 4, 1870, Baltimore, Md. D. May 30, 1932, Baltimore, Md.
5'11½" 170 lbs.

Year	Team		W	L	PCT	ERA	G	GS	CG	IP	H	BB	SO	ShO	W	L	SV	AB	H	HR	BA	PO	A	E	DP	TC/G	FA
1897	PHI	N	0	1	.000	15.00	1	1	0	3	8	2	1	0	0	0	0	1	1	0	1.000	0	0	0	0	0.0	–

Nig Lipscomb

LIPSCOMB, GERARD
B. Feb. 24, 1911, Rutherfordton, N. C. D. Feb. 27, 1978, Huntersville, N. C.
BR TR 6' 175 lbs.

Year	Team		W	L	PCT	ERA	G	GS	CG	IP	H	BB	SO	ShO	W	L	SV	AB	H	HR	BA	PO	A	E	DP	TC/G	FA
1937	STL	A	0	0	–	6.52	3	0	0	9.2	13	5	1	0	0	0	0	*				0	0	0	0	0.0	–

Hod Lisenbee

LISENBEE, HORACE MILTON
B. Sept. 23, 1898, Clarksville, Tenn. D. Nov. 14, 1987, Clarksville, Tenn.
BR TR 5'11" 170 lbs.

Year	Team		W	L	PCT	ERA	G	GS	CG	IP	H	BB	SO	ShO	W	L	SV	AB	H	HR	BA	PO	A	E	DP	TC/G	FA
1927	WAS	A	18	9	.667	3.57	39	34	17	242	221	78	105	4	2	1	0	83	11	0	.133	11	45	4	2	1.5	.933
1928			2	6	.250	6.08	16	9	3	77	102	32	13	0	1	0	0	23	4	0	.174	2	15	1	0	1.1	.944
1929	BOS	A	0	0	–	5.19	5	0	0	8.2	10	4	2	0	0	0	0	2	0	0	.000	0	3	0	0	0.6	1.000
1930			10	17	.370	4.40	37	31	15	237.1	254	86	47	0	1	0	0	75	20	0	.267	3	37	4	1	1.2	.909
1931			5	12	.294	5.19	41	17	6	164.2	190	49	42	0	2	1	0	53	12	0	.226	7	30	5	0	1.0	.881
1932			0	4	.000	5.65	19	6	3	73.1	87	25	13	0	0	0	0	21	1	0	.048	2	12	1	0	0.8	.933
1936	PHI	A	1	7	.125	6.20	19	7	4	85.2	115	24	17	0	0	1	0	25	3	0	.120	2	15	2	0	1.0	.895
1945	CIN	N	1	3	.250	5.49	31	3	0	80.1	97	16	14	0	1	2	1	19	0	0	.000	2	11	0	0	0.4	1.000
8 yrs.			37	58	.389	4.81	207	107	48	969	1076	314	253	4	7	5	1	301	51	0	.169	29	168	17	3	1.0	.921

Ad Liska

LISKA, ADOLPH JAMES
B. July 10, 1906, Dwight, Neb.
BR TR 5'11½" 160 lbs.

Year	Team		W	L	PCT	ERA	G	GS	CG	IP	H	BB	SO	ShO	W	L	SV	AB	H	HR	BA	PO	A	E	DP	TC/G	FA
1929	WAS	A	3	9	.250	4.77	24	10	4	94.1	87	42	33	0	0	3	0	29	5	0	.172	7	34	0	0	1.7	1.000
1930			9	7	.563	3.29	32	16	7	150.2	140	71	40	1	0	1	1	52	5	0	.096	14	56	0	4	2.2	1.000
1931			0	1	.000	6.75	2	1	0	4	9	1	2	0	0	0	0	1	0	0	.000	0	2	0	0	1.0	1.000
1932	PHI	N	2	0	1.000	1.69	8	0	0	26.2	22	10	6	0	2	0	0	7	0	0	.000	2	12	1	0	1.9	.933
1933			3	1	.750	4.52	45	1	0	75.2	96	26	23	0	3	1	1	14	1	0	.071	4	33	1	3	0.8	.974
5 yrs.			17	18	.486	3.87	111	28	11	351.1	354	150	104	1	5	5	3	103	11	0	.107	27	137	2	7	1.5	.988

Mark Littell

LITTELL, MARK ALAN
B. Jan. 17, 1953, Cape Girardeau, Mo.
BL TR 6'3" 210 lbs.

Year	Team		W	L	PCT	ERA	G	GS	CG	IP	H	BB	SO	ShO	W	L	SV	AB	H	HR	BA	PO	A	E	DP	TC/G	FA
1973	KC	A	1	3	.250	5.68	8	7	1	38	44	23	16	0	0	0	0	0	0	0	–	2	5	0	0	0.9	1.000
1975			1	2	.333	3.70	7	3	1	24.1	19	15	19	0	1	0	0	0	0	0	–	4	6	1	0	1.6	.909
1976			8	4	.667	2.08	60	1	0	104	68	60	92	0	8	3	16	1	0	0	.000	3	9	0	0	0.2	1.000
1977			8	4	.667	3.60	48	5	0	105	73	55	106	0	6	4	12	1	0	0	.000	7	7	1	1	0.3	.933
1978	STL	N	4	8	.333	2.80	72	2	0	106	80	59	130	0	4	8	11	7	0	0	.000	4	10	1	0	0.2	.933
1979			9	4	.692	2.20	63	0	0	82	60	39	67	0	9	4	13	14	0	0	.000	6	7	1	1	0.2	.929
1980			0	2	.000	9.00	14	0	0	11	14	7	7	0	0	2	2	0	0	0	–	0	1	0	0	0.1	1.000
1981			1	3	.250	4.39	28	1	0	41	36	31	22	0	1	2	2	8	2	0	.250	5	4	2	0	0.4	.818
1982			0	1	.000	5.23	16	0	0	20.2	22	15	7	0	0	1	0	2	0	0	.000	0	2	1	0	0.2	.667
9 yrs.			32	31	.508	3.32	316	19	2	532	416	304	466	0	29	24	56	34	2	0	.059	31	51	7	3	0.3	.921

LEAGUE CHAMPIONSHIP SERIES

Year	Team		W	L	PCT	ERA	G	GS	CG	IP	H	BB	SO	ShO	W	L	SV	AB	H	HR	BA	PO	A	E	DP	TC/G	FA
1976	KC	A	0	1	.000	1.93	3	0	0	4.2	4	1	3	0	0	1	0	0	0	0	–	0	1	0	0	0.3	1.000
1977			0	0	–	3.00	2	0	0	3	5	3	1	0	0	0	0	0	0	0	–	0	0	0	0	0.0	–
2 yrs.			0	1	.000	2.35	5	0	0	7.2	9	4	4	0	0	1	0	0	0	0	–	0	1	0	0	0.2	1.000

Year	Team		W	L	PCT	ERA	G	GS	CG	IP	H	BB	SO	ShO	Relief Pitching W	L	SV	Batting AB	H	HR	BA	PO	A	E	DP	TC/G	FA

Jeff Little

LITTLE, DONALD JEFFREY
B. Dec. 25, 1954, Fremont, Ohio — BR TL 6'6" 220 lbs.

Year	Team		W	L	PCT	ERA	G	GS	CG	IP	H	BB	SO	ShO	W	L	SV	AB	H	HR	BA	PO	A	E	DP	TC/G	FA
1980	STL	N	1	1	.500	3.79	7	2	0	19	18	9	17	0	0	0	0	6	1	0	.167	0	1	0	0	0.1	1.000
1982	MIN	A	2	0	1.000	4.21	33	0	0	36.1	33	27	26	0	2	0	0	0	0	0	–	0	3	0	0	0.1	1.000
2 yrs.			3	1	.750	4.07	40	2	0	55.1	51	36	43	0	2	0	0	6	1	0	.167	0	4	0	0	0.1	1.000

Dick Littlefield

LITTLEFIELD, RICHARD BERNARD
B. Mar. 18, 1926, Detroit, Mich. — BL TL 6' 180 lbs.

Year	Team		W	L	PCT	ERA	G	GS	CG	IP	H	BB	SO	ShO	W	L	SV	AB	H	HR	BA	PO	A	E	DP	TC/G	FA
1950	BOS	A	2	2	.500	9.26	15	2	0	23.1	27	24	13	0	2	0	1	4	0	0	.000	1	6	0	1	0.5	1.000
1951	CHI	A	1	1	.500	8.38	4	2	0	9.2	9	17	7	0	1	0	0	1	0	0	.000	1	1	0	1	0.5	1.000
1952	2 teams	DET A (28G 0–3)				STL A	(7G 2–3)																				
"	total		2	6	.250	3.54	35	6	3	94	81	42	66	0	2	0	1	23	2	0	.087	4	4	0	1	0.2	1.000
1953	STL	A	7	12	.368	5.08	36	22	2	152.1	153	84	104	0	2	1	0	42	8	0	.190	9	19	0	0	0.8	1.000
1954	2 teams	BAL A (3G 0–0)				PIT N	(23G 10–11)																				
"	total		10	11	.476	3.86	26	21	0	161	148	91	97	0	1	1	0	50	8	0	.160	5	14	3	0	0.8	.864
1955	PIT	N	5	12	.294	5.12	35	17	4	130	148	68	70	0	1	3	0	34	6	0	.176	7	12	3	1	0.6	.864
1956	3 teams	PIT N (6G 0–0)				STL N	(3G 0–2)	NY	N	(31G 4–4)																	
"	total		4	6	.400	4.37	40	11	0	119.1	101	49	80	0	1	2	2	28	2	0	.071	10	14	1	1	0.6	.960
1957	CHI	N	2	3	.400	5.35	48	2	0	65.2	76	37	51	0	1	3	4	11	2	0	.182	2	7	4	0	0.3	.692
1958	MIL	N	0	1	.000	4.26	4	0	0	6.1	7	1	7	0	0	1	0	0	0	0	–	0	0	0	0	0.0	–
9 yrs.			33	54	.379	4.71	243	83	16	761.2	750	413	495	2	11	11	9	193	28	0	.145	39	77	11	5	0.5	.913

John Littlefield

LITTLEFIELD, JOHN ANDREW
B. Jan. 5, 1954, Covina, Calif. — BR TR 6'2" 200 lbs.

Year	Team		W	L	PCT	ERA	G	GS	CG	IP	H	BB	SO	ShO	W	L	SV	AB	H	HR	BA	PO	A	E	DP	TC/G	FA
1980	STL	N	5	5	.500	3.14	52	0	0	66	71	20	22	0	5	5	9	11	0	0	.000	2	12	1	3	0.3	.933
1981	SD	N	2	3	.400	3.66	42	0	0	64	53	28	21	0	2	3	2	1	0	0	.000	6	9	1	1	0.4	.938
2 yrs.			7	8	.467	3.39	94	0	0	130	124	48	43	0	7	8	11	12	0	0	.000	8	21	2	4	0.3	.935

Carlisle Littlejohn

LITTLEJOHN, CHARLES CARLISLE
B. Oct. 6, 1901, Irene, Tex. D. Oct. 27, 1977, Kansas City, Mo. — BR TR 5'10" 175 lbs.

Year	Team		W	L	PCT	ERA	G	GS	CG	IP	H	BB	SO	ShO	W	L	SV	AB	H	HR	BA	PO	A	E	DP	TC/G	FA
1927	STL	N	3	1	.750	4.50	14	2	1	42	47	14	16	0	2	0	0	12	5	0	.417	1	5	1	0	0.5	.857
1928			2	1	.667	3.66	12	2	1	32	36	14	6	0	1	0	0	11	0	0	.000	0	8	1	0	0.8	.889
2 yrs.			5	2	.714	4.14	26	4	2	74	83	28	22	0	3	0	0	23	5	0	.217	1	13	2	0	0.6	.875

Bud Lively

LIVELY, EVERETT ADRIAN (Red)
Son of Jack Lively.
B. Feb. 14, 1925, Birmingham, Ala. — BR TR 6'½" 200 lbs.

Year	Team		W	L	PCT	ERA	G	GS	CG	IP	H	BB	SO	ShO	W	L	SV	AB	H	HR	BA	PO	A	E	DP	TC/G	FA
1947	CIN	N	4	7	.364	4.68	38	17	3	123	126	63	52	1	0	1	0	32	6	0	.188	8	21	2	0	0.8	.935
1948			0	0	–	2.38	10	0	0	22.2	13	11	12	0	0	0	0	2	0	0	.000	1	1	0	1	0.2	1.000
1949			4	6	.400	3.92	31	10	3	103.1	91	53	30	1	0	1	1	26	4	0	.154	4	15	1	1	0.6	.950
3 yrs.			8	13	.381	4.16	79	27	6	249	230	127	94	2	0	2	1	60	10	0	.167	13	37	3	2	0.7	.943

Jack Lively

LIVELY, HENRY EVERETT
Father of Bud Lively.
B. May 29, 1885, Joppa, Ala. D. Dec. 5, 1967, Arab, Ala. — BR TR 5'9" 185 lbs.

Year	Team		W	L	PCT	ERA	G	GS	CG	IP	H	BB	SO	ShO	W	L	SV	AB	H	HR	BA	PO	A	E	DP	TC/G	FA
1911	DET	A	7	5	.583	4.59	18	14	10	113.2	143	34	45	0	1	0	0	43	11	0	.256	2	31	2	0	1.9	.943

Wes Livengood

LIVENGOOD, WESLEY AMOS
B. July 18, 1910, Salisbury, N. C. — BR TR 6'2" 172 lbs.

Year	Team		W	L	PCT	ERA	G	GS	CG	IP	H	BB	SO	ShO	W	L	SV	AB	H	HR	BA	PO	A	E	DP	TC/G	FA
1939	CIN	N	0	0	–	9.53	5	0	0	5.2	9	3	4	0	0	0	0	0	0	0	–	0	1	0	0	0.2	1.000

Jake Livingstone

LIVINGSTONE, JACOB M.
B. Jan. 1, 1886, Petrograd, Russia D. Mar. 22, 1949, Wassaic, N. Y.

Year	Team		W	L	PCT	ERA	G	GS	CG	IP	H	BB	SO	ShO	W	L	SV	AB	H	HR	BA	PO	A	E	DP	TC/G	FA
1901	NY	N	0	0	–	9.00	2	0	0	12	26	7	6	0	0	0	0	6	1	0	.167	0	1	0	0	0.5	1.000

Clem Llewellyn

LLEWELLYN, CLEMENT MANLEY (Lew)
B. Aug. 1, 1895, Dobson, N. C. D. Nov. 26, 1969, Concord, N. C. — BL TR 6'2" 195 lbs.

Year	Team		W	L	PCT	ERA	G	GS	CG	IP	H	BB	SO	ShO	W	L	SV	AB	H	HR	BA	PO	A	E	DP	TC/G	FA
1922	NY	A	0	0	–	0.00	1	0	0	1	1	0	0	0	0	0	0	0	0	0	–	0	0	0	0	0.0	–

Harry Lochhead

LOCHHEAD, ROBERT HENRY
B. Mar. 29, 1876, Stockton, Calif. D. Aug. 22, 1909, Stockton, Calif. — TR

Year	Team		W	L	PCT	ERA	G	GS	CG	IP	H	BB	SO	ShO	W	L	SV	AB	H	HR	BA	PO	A	E	DP	TC/G	FA
1899	CLE	N	0	0	–	0.00	1	0	0	3.2	4	2	0	0	0	0	0				*		0	0	0	0	0.0	–

Charlie Locke

LOCKE, CHARLES EDWARD (Chuck)
B. May 5, 1932, Malden, Mo. — BR TR 5'11" 185 lbs.

Year	Team		W	L	PCT	ERA	G	GS	CG	IP	H	BB	SO	ShO	W	L	SV	AB	H	HR	BA	PO	A	E	DP	TC/G	FA
1955	BAL	A	0	0	–	0.00	2	0	0	2	0	1	1	0	0	0	0	0	0	0	–	0	1	0	0	0.5	1.000

Larry Locke

LOCKE, LAWRENCE DONALD (Bobby)
B. Mar. 3, 1934, Rowe's Run, Pa. — BR TR 5'11" 185 lbs.

Year	Team		W	L	PCT	ERA	G	GS	CG	IP	H	BB	SO	ShO	W	L	SV	AB	H	HR	BA	PO	A	E	DP	TC/G	FA
1959	CLE	A	3	2	.600	3.13	24	7	0	77.2	66	41	40	0	1	0	2	24	8	1	.333	9	11	1	1	0.9	.952
1960			3	5	.375	3.37	32	11	2	123	121	37	53	2	0	3	2	38	9	0	.237	10	30	2	2	1.3	.952
1961			4	4	.500	4.53	37	4	0	95.1	112	40	37	0	3	4	2	19	4	0	.211	9	20	0	0	0.8	1.000
1962	2 teams	STL N (1G 0–0)				PHI N	(5G 1–0)																				
"	total		1	0	1.000	5.09	6	0	0	17.2	17	12	10	0	1	0	0	7	2	0	.286	1	6	0	1	1.2	1.000
1963	PHI	N	0	0	–	5.91	9	0	0	10.2	10	5	7	0	0	0	0	2	0	0	.000	2	0	0	0	0.2	1.000
1964			0	0	–	2.79	8	0	0	19.1	21	6	11	0	0	0	0	3	0	0	.000	3	3	0	0	0.8	1.000
1965	CIN	N	0	1	.000	5.71	11	0	0	17.1	20	8	8	0	0	1	0	3	0	0	.000	2	5	0	0	0.6	1.000
1967	CAL	A	3	0	1.000	2.33	9	1	0	19.1	14	3	7	0	2	0	0	3	2	0	.667	1	5	0	0	0.7	1.000

Year	Team	W	L	PCT	ERA	G	GS	CG	IP	H	BB	SO	ShO	W	L	SV	AB	H	HR	BA	PO	A	E	DP	TC/G	FA

Larry Locke *continued*

Year	Team	W	L	PCT	ERA	G	GS	CG	IP	H	BB	SO	ShO	W	L	SV	AB	H	HR	BA	PO	A	E	DP	TC/G	FA
1968		2	3	.400	6.44	29	0	0	36.1	51	13	21	0	2	3	2	3	0	0	.000	2	3	1	1	0.2	.833
9 yrs.		16	15	.516	4.02	165	23	2	416.2	432	165	194	2	9	11	10	98	25	1	.255	39	83	4	6	0.8	.968

Ron Locke

LOCKE, RONALD THOMAS
B. Apr. 4, 1942, Wakefield, R. I.   BR TL 5'11" 168 lbs.

Year	Team	W	L	PCT	ERA	G	GS	CG	IP	H	BB	SO	ShO	W	L	SV	AB	H	HR	BA	PO	A	E	DP	TC/G	FA
1964	NY N	1	2	.333	3.48	25	3	0	41.1	46	22	17	0	0	0	0	5	0	0	.000	2	8	1	0	0.4	.909

Bob Locker

LOCKER, ROBERT AWTRY
B. Mar. 15, 1938, George, Iowa   BR TR 6'3" 200 lbs.
BB 1968

Year	Team	W	L	PCT	ERA	G	GS	CG	IP	H	BB	SO	ShO	W	L	SV	AB	H	HR	BA	PO	A	E	DP	TC/G	FA
1965	CHI A	5	2	.714	3.15	51	0	0	91.1	71	30	69	0	5	2	2	14	0	0	.000	10	28	0	3	0.7	1.000
1966		9	8	.529	2.46	56	0	0	95	73	23	70	0	9	8	12	16	4	0	.250	11	25	1	1	0.7	.973
1967		7	5	.583	2.09	77	0	0	124.2	102	23	80	0	7	5	20	10	0	0	.000	13	43	3	3	0.8	.948
1968		5	4	.556	2.29	70	0	0	90.1	78	27	62	0	5	4	10	8	0	0	.000	6	25	1	1	0.5	.969
1969	2 teams					CHI A	(17G 2–3)		SEA A	(51G 3–3)																
"	total	5	6	.455	3.14	68	0	0	100.1	95	32	61	0	5	6	10	13	1	0	.077	11	23	1	0	0.5	.971
1970	2 teams					MIL A	(28G 0–1)		OAK A	(38G 3–3)																
"	total	3	4	.429	3.07	66	0	0	88	86	29	52	0	3	4	7	7	1	0	.143	3	17	3	0	0.3	.870
1971	OAK A	7	2	.778	2.88	47	0	0	72	68	19	46	0	7	2	6	6	0	0	.000	3	20	2	0	0.5	.920
1972		6	1	.857	2.65	56	0	0	78	69	16	47	0	6	1	10	6	0	0	.000	5	9	1	0	0.3	.933
1973	CHI N	10	6	.625	2.55	63	0	0	106	96	42	76	0	10	6	18	15	1	0	.067	10	21	4	3	0.6	.886
1975		0	1	.000	4.91	22	0	0	33	38	16	14	0	0	1	0	0	0	0	–	5	6	0	0	0.5	1.000
10 yrs.		57	39	.594	2.76	576	0	0	878.2	776	257	577	0	57	39	95	95	7	0	.074	77	216	16	11	0.5	.948

LEAGUE CHAMPIONSHIP SERIES

Year	Team	W	L	PCT	ERA	G	GS	CG	IP	H	BB	SO	ShO	W	L	SV	AB	H	HR	BA	PO	A	E	DP	TC/G	FA
1971	OAK A	0	0	–	0.00	1	0	0	.2	0	2	0	0	0	0	0	0	0	0	–	0	0	0	0	0.0	–
1972		0	0	–	13.50	2	0	0	2	4	0	1	0	0	0	0	0	0	0	–	0	0	0	0	0.0	–
2 yrs.		0	0	–	10.13	3	0	0	2.2	4	2	1	0	0	0	0	0	0	0	–	0	0	0	0	0.0	–

WORLD SERIES

Year	Team	W	L	PCT	ERA	G	GS	CG	IP	H	BB	SO	ShO	W	L	SV	AB	H	HR	BA	PO	A	E	DP	TC/G	FA
1972	OAK A	0	0	–	0.00	1	0	0	.1	1	0	0	0	0	0	0	0	0	0	–	0	0	0	0	0.0	–

Milo Lockwood

LOCKWOOD, MILO HATHAWAY
B. Apr. 7, 1858, Solon, Ohio D. Oct. 9, 1897, Economy, Pa.   5'10" 160 lbs.

Year	Team	W	L	PCT	ERA	G	GS	CG	IP	H	BB	SO	ShO	W	L	SV	AB	H	HR	BA	PO	A	E	DP	TC/G	FA
1884	WAS U	1	9	.100	7.32	11	10	6	67.2	99	15	48	0	0	0	0	67	14	0	.209	5	19	3	0	2.5	.889

Skip Lockwood

LOCKWOOD, CLAUDE EDWARD
B. Aug. 17, 1946, Roslindale, Mass.   BR TR 6'1" 175 lbs.

Year	Team	W	L	PCT	ERA	G	GS	CG	IP	H	BB	SO	ShO	W	L	SV	AB	H	HR	BA	PO	A	E	DP	TC/G	FA
1965	KC A	0	0	–	0.00	0	0	0	0	0	0	0	0	0	0	0	33	4	0	.121	0	0	0	0	0.0	–
1969	SEA A	0	1	.000	3.52	6	3	0	23	24	6	10	0	0	0	0	7	0	0	.000	2	5	0	1	1.2	1.000
1970	MIL A	5	12	.294	4.29	27	26	3	174	173	79	93	1	0	0	0	53	12	1	.226	14	18	1	1	1.2	.970
1971		10	15	.400	3.33	33	32	5	208	191	91	115	0	0	0	0	62	5	1	.081	9	18	0	2	0.8	1.000
1972		8	15	.348	3.60	29	27	5	170	148	71	106	3	0	0	0	53	7	0	.132	10	13	1	1	0.8	.958
1973		5	12	.294	3.90	37	15	3	154.2	164	59	87	0	3	3	0	0	0	0	–	11	23	2	1	1.0	.944
1974	CAL A	2	5	.286	4.32	37	2	0	81.1	81	32	39	0	4	0	1	0	0	0	–	3	11	0	1	0.4	1.000
1975	NY N	1	3	.250	1.50	24	0	0	48	28	25	61	0	1	3	2	6	1	0	.167	1	3	1	0	0.2	.800
1976		10	7	.588	2.67	56	0	0	94.1	62	34	108	0	10	7	19	18	6	0	.333	2	11	2	1	0.3	.867
1977		4	8	.333	3.38	63	0	0	104	87	31	84	0	4	8	20	15	3	0	.200	1	6	1	0	0.1	.875
1978		7	13	.350	3.56	57	0	0	91	78	31	73	0	7	13	15	11	2	1	.182	4	5	1	1	0.2	.900
1979		2	5	.286	1.50	27	0	0	42	33	14	42	0	2	5	9	2	0	0	.000	3	1	1	0	0.2	.800
1980	BOS A	3	1	.750	5.28	24	1	0	46	62	17	11	0	3	1	2	0	0	0	–	3	1	0	0	0.3	1.000
13 yrs.		57	97	.370	3.55	420	106	16	1236.1	1130	490	829	5	30	44	68	*				61	119	10	10	0.5	.947

Billy Loes

LOES, WILLIAM
B. Dec. 13, 1929, Long Island City, N. Y.   BR TR 6'1" 165 lbs.

Year	Team	W	L	PCT	ERA	G	GS	CG	IP	H	BB	SO	ShO	W	L	SV	AB	H	HR	BA	PO	A	E	DP	TC/G	FA
1950	BKN N	0	0	–	7.82	10	0	0	12.1	6	5	2	0	0	0	0	1	0	0	.000	0	2	1	0	0.3	.667
1952		13	8	.619	2.69	39	21	8	187.1	154	71	115	4	5	2	1	54	5	0	.093	14	27	1	5	1.1	.976
1953		14	8	.636	4.54	32	25	9	162.2	165	53	75	2	3	1	0	56	7	0	.125	14	37	1	5	1.6	.981
1954		13	5	.722	4.14	28	21	6	147.2	154	60	97	0	2	0	2	51	6	0	.118	9	21	1	1	1.1	.968
1955		10	4	.714	3.59	22	19	6	128	116	46	85	0	0	2	0	44	4	0	.091	6	20	1	1	1.2	.963
1956	2 teams					BKN N	(1G 0–1)		BAL A	(21G 2–7)																
"	total	2	8	.200	5.59	22	7	1	58	70	24	24	0	1	6	3	17	3	0	.176	7	12	0	0	0.9	1.000
1957	BAL A	12	7	.632	3.24	31	18	8	155.1	142	37	86	3	2	1	4	50	4	0	.080	7	33	1	4	1.3	.976
1958		3	9	.250	3.63	32	10	1	114	106	44	44	0	3	3	5	30	2	0	.067	9	21	4	1	1.1	.882
1959		4	7	.364	4.06	37	0	0	64.1	58	25	34	0	4	7	14	8	1	0	.125	3	15	0	3	0.5	1.000
1960	SF N	3	2	.600	4.93	37	0	0	45.2	40	17	28	0	3	2	5	4	1	0	.250	2	12	1	1	0.4	.933
1961		6	5	.545	4.24	26	18	3	114.2	114	39	55	1	1	0	0	32	5	0	.156	9	23	2	1	1.3	.941
11 yrs.		80	63	.559	3.89	316	139	42	1190.1	1135	421	645	9	25	26	32	347	38	0	.110	80	223	13	22	1.0	.959

WORLD SERIES

Year	Team	W	L	PCT	ERA	G	GS	CG	IP	H	BB	SO	ShO	W	L	SV	AB	H	HR	BA	PO	A	E	DP	TC/G	FA
1952	BKN N	0	1	.000	4.35	2	1	0	10.1	11	5	5	0	0	1	0	3	1	0	.333	0	2	0	0	1.0	1.000
1953		1	0	1.000	3.38	1	1	0	8	8	2	8	0	0	0	0	3	2	0	.667	0	0	0	0	0.0	–
1955		0	1	.000	9.82	1	1	0	3.2	7	1	5	0	0	0	0	1	0	0	.000	0	0	0	0	0.0	–
3 yrs.		1	2	.333	4.91	4	3	0	22	26	8	18	0	0	1	0	7	3	0	.429	0	2	0	0	0.5	1.000

Frank Loftus

LOFTUS, FRANCIS PATRICK
B. Mar. 10, 1898, Scranton, Pa. D. Oct. 27, 1980, Belchertown, Mass.   BR TR 5'9" 190 lbs.

Year	Team	W	L	PCT	ERA	G	GS	CG	IP	H	BB	SO	ShO	W	L	SV	AB	H	HR	BA	PO	A	E	DP	TC/G	FA
1926	WAS A	0	0	–	9.00	1	0	0	3	3	2	0	0	0	0	0	0	0	0	–	0	0	0	0	0.0	–

Bob Logan

LOGAN, ROBERT DEAN (Lefty)
B. Feb. 10, 1910, Thompson, Neb. D. May 20, 1978, Indianapolis, Ind.   BR TL 5'10" 170 lbs.

Year	Team	W	L	PCT	ERA	G	GS	CG	IP	H	BB	SO	ShO	W	L	SV	AB	H	HR	BA	PO	A	E	DP	TC/G	FA
1935	BKN N	0	1	.000	3.38	2	0	0	2.2	2	1	1	0	0	1	0	0	0	0	–	0	2	0	0	1.0	1.000

Year	Team	W	L	PCT	ERA	G	GS	CG	IP	H	BB	SO	ShO	Relief Pitching W	L	SV	Batting AB	H	HR	BA	PO	A	E	DP	TC/G	FA

Bob Logan *continued*

Year	Team	W	L	PCT	ERA	G	GS	CG	IP	H	BB	SO	ShO	W	L	SV	AB	H	HR	BA	PO	A	E	DP	TC/G	FA
1937	2 teams	DET A	(1G 0–0)		CHI N	(4G 0–0)																				
"	total	0	0	–	1.29	5	0	0	7	7	5	3	0	0	0	1	1	0	0	.000	1	0	0	0	0.2	1.000
1938	CHI N	0	2	.000	2.78	14	0	0	22.2	18	17	10	0	0	2	2	3	0	0	.000	3	2	1	0	0.4	.833
1941	CIN N	0	1	.000	8.10	2	0	0	3.1	5	5	0	0	0	1	0	0	0	0	–	0	2	0	0	1.0	1.000
1945	BOS N	7	11	.389	3.18	34	25	5	187	213	53	53	1	0	2	1	61	13	0	.213	7	38	2	7	1.4	.957
5 yrs.		7	15	.318	3.15	57	25	5	222.2	245	81	67	1	0	6	4	65	13	0	.200	11	44	3	7	1.0	.948

Bill Lohrman

LOHRMAN, WILLIAM LeROY
B. May 22, 1913, Brooklyn, N. Y.   BR TR 6'1"   185 lbs.

Year	Team	W	L	PCT	ERA	G	GS	CG	IP	H	BB	SO	ShO	W	L	SV	AB	H	HR	BA	PO	A	E	DP	TC/G	FA
1934	PHI N	0	1	.000	4.50	4	0	0	6	5	1	2	0	0	1	1	2	1	0	.500	0	2	0	0	0.5	1.000
1937	NY N	1	0	1.000	0.90	2	1	1	10	5	2	3	0	0	0	1	2	0	0	.000	1	3	0	1	2.0	1.000
1938		9	6	.600	3.32	31	14	3	152	152	33	52	0	4	0	0	49	4	0	.082	4	40	1	3	1.5	.978
1939		12	13	.480	4.07	38	24	9	185.2	200	45	70	1	2	2	1	60	14	2	.233	3	38	3	5	1.2	.932
1940		10	15	.400	3.78	31	27	11	195	200	43	73	5	1	0	1	65	8	0	.123	4	52	1	4	1.8	.982
1941		9	10	.474	4.02	33	20	6	159	184	40	61	2	1	3	3	48	11	0	.229	10	33	3	4	1.4	.935
1942	2 teams	STL N	(5G 1–1)		NY N	(26G 13–4)																				
"	total	14	5	.737	2.48	31	19	12	170.2	154	35	47	2	0	1	0	61	9	0	.148	7	34	2	3	1.4	.953
1943	2 teams	NY N	(17G 5–6)		BKN N	(6G 0–2)																				
"	total	5	8	.385	4.75	23	14	5	108	139	35	21	0	1	1	1	34	2	0	.059	3	18	0	1	0.9	1.000
1944	2 teams	BKN N	(3G 0–0)		CIN N	(2G 0–1)																				
"	total	0	1	.000	10.38	5	1	0	4.1	9	6	1	0	0	0	0	0	0	0	–	0	0	0	0	0.0	–
9 yrs.		60	59	.504	3.69	198	120	47	990.2	1048	240	330	10	11	8	8	321	49	2	.153	32	220	10	22	1.3	.962

Mickey Lolich

LOLICH, MICHAEL STEPHEN
B. Sept. 12, 1940, Portland, Ore.   BB TL 6'1"   170 lbs.

Year	Team	W	L	PCT	ERA	G	GS	CG	IP	H	BB	SO	ShO	W	L	SV	AB	H	HR	BA	PO	A	E	DP	TC/G	FA
1963	DET A	5	9	.357	3.55	33	18	4	144.1	145	56	103	0	0	2	0	36	2	0	.056	4	22	3	1	0.9	.897
1964		18	9	.667	3.26	44	33	8	232	196	64	192	6	2	1	2	64	7	0	.109	7	28	3	0	0.9	.921
1965		15	9	.625	3.44	43	37	7	243.2	216	72	226	3	1	0	3	86	5	0	.058	11	27	5	2	1.0	.884
1966		14	14	.500	4.77	40	33	5	203.2	204	83	173	1	0	1	3	64	9	0	.141	4	21	3	1	0.7	.893
1967		14	13	.519	3.04	31	30	11	204	165	56	174	6	0	0	0	61	12	0	.197	10	33	1	1	1.1	.914
1968		17	9	.654	3.19	39	32	8	220	178	65	197	4	4	0	0	70	8	0	.114	5	26	3	0	0.9	.912
1969		19	11	.633	3.14	37	36	15	280.2	214	122	271	1	0	0	0	91	8	0	.088	5	41	4	1	1.4	.920
1970		14	19	.424	3.79	40	39	13	273	272	109	230	3	0	0	0	82	11	0	.134	9	46	2	1	1.4	.965
1971		25	14	.641	2.92	45	45	29	376	336	92	308	4	0	0	0	115	15	0	.130	9	40	1	2	1.1	.980
1972		22	14	.611	2.50	41	41	23	327	282	74	250	4	0	0	0	89	6	0	.067	4	32	2	2	0.9	.947
1973		16	15	.516	3.82	42	42	17	309	315	79	214	3	0	0	0	0	0	0	–	11	40	1	3	1.2	.981
1974		16	21	.432	4.15	41	41	27	308	310	78	202	3	0	0	0	0	0	0	–	9	29	2	1	1.0	.950
1975		12	18	.400	3.78	32	32	19	240.2	260	64	139	1	0	0	0	0	0	0	–	2	32	0	1	1.1	1.000
1976	NY N	8	13	.381	3.22	31	30	5	193	184	52	120	2	0	0	0	54	7	0	.130	9	27	6	1	1.4	.857
1978	SD N	2	1	.667	1.54	20	2	0	35	30	11	13	0	1	0	1	3	0	0	.000	1	6	0	0	0.4	1.000
1979		0	2	.000	4.78	27	5	0	49	59	22	20	0	0	0	0	6	0	0	.000	0	9	0	0	0.3	1.000
16 yrs.		217	191	.532	3.44	586	496	195	3639	3366	1099	2832	41	8	4	11	821	90	0	.110	100	448	38	16	1.0	.935

LEAGUE CHAMPIONSHIP SERIES

Year	Team	W	L	PCT	ERA	G	GS	CG	IP	H	BB	SO	ShO	W	L	SV	AB	H	HR	BA	PO	A	E	DP	TC/G	FA
1972	DET A	0	1	.000	1.42	2	2	0	19	14	5	10	0	0	0	0	7	0	0	.000	1	3	0	0	2.0	1.000

WORLD SERIES

Year	Team	W	L	PCT	ERA	G	GS	CG	IP	H	BB	SO	ShO	W	L	SV	AB	H	HR	BA	PO	A	E	DP	TC/G	FA
1968	DET A	3	0	1.000	1.67	3	3	3	27	20	6	21	0	0	0	0	12	3	1	.250	1	4	0	0	1.7	1.000
	1st																									

Tim Lollar

LOLLAR, WILLIAM TIMOTHY
B. Mar. 17, 1956, Poplar Bluff, Mo.   BL TL 6'3"   200 lbs.

Year	Team	W	L	PCT	ERA	G	GS	CG	IP	H	BB	SO	ShO	W	L	SV	AB	H	HR	BA	PO	A	E	DP	TC/G	FA
1980	NY A	1	0	1.000	3.38	14	1	0	32	33	20	13	0	0	0	2	0	0	0	–	1	7	1	1	0.6	.889
1981	SD N	2	8	.200	6.08	24	11	0	77	87	51	38	0	1	2	1	18	3	1	.167	4	22	1	1	1.1	.963
1982		16	9	.640	3.13	34	34	4	232.2	192	87	150	2	0	0	0	85	21	3	.247	7	38	0	4	1.3	1.000
1983		7	12	.368	4.61	30	30	1	175.2	170	85	135	0	0	0	0	58	14	1	.241	4	19	0	1	0.8	1.000
1984		11	13	.458	3.91	31	31	3	195.2	168	105	131	0	0	0	0	68	15	3	.221	1	22	0	1	0.7	1.000
1985	2 teams	CHI A	(18G 3–5)		BOS A	(16G 5–5)																				
"	total	8	10	.444	4.62	34	23	1	150	140	98	105	1	0	1	0	1	0	0	.000	8	13	0	0	0.6	1.000
1986	BOS A	2	0	1.000	6.91	32	1	0	43	51	34	28	0	1	0	0	1	1	0	1.000	4	7	0	1	0.3	1.000
7 yrs.		47	52	.475	4.27	199	131	9	906	841	480	600	4	3	2	4	231	54	8	.234	29	128	2	9	0.8	.987

LEAGUE CHAMPIONSHIP SERIES

Year	Team	W	L	PCT	ERA	G	GS	CG	IP	H	BB	SO	ShO	W	L	SV	AB	H	HR	BA	PO	A	E	DP	TC/G	FA
1984	SD N	0	0	–	6.23	1	1	0	4.1	3	4	3	0	0	0	0	1	0	0	.000	0	0	0	0	0.0	–

WORLD SERIES

Year	Team	W	L	PCT	ERA	G	GS	CG	IP	H	BB	SO	ShO	W	L	SV	AB	H	HR	BA	PO	A	E	DP	TC/G	FA
1984	SD N	0	1	.000	21.60	1	1	0	1.2	4	4	0	0	0	0	0	0	0	0	–	0	0	0	0	0.0	–

Vic Lombardi

LOMBARDI, VICTOR ALVIN
B. Sept. 20, 1922, Reedley, Calif.   BL TL 5'7"   158 lbs.

Year	Team	W	L	PCT	ERA	G	GS	CG	IP	H	BB	SO	ShO	W	L	SV	AB	H	HR	BA	PO	A	E	DP	TC/G	FA
1945	BKN N	10	11	.476	3.31	38	24	9	203.2	195	86	64	0	3	1	4	71	13	0	.183	8	38	3	5	1.3	.939
1946		13	10	.565	2.89	41	25	13	193	170	84	60	2	1	2	3	61	14	0	.230	4	44	3	1	1.2	.941
1947		12	11	.522	2.99	33	20	7	174.2	156	65	72	3	3	1	3	66	16	0	.242	8	35	0	2	1.3	1.000
1948	PIT N	10	9	.526	3.70	38	17	9	163	156	67	54	0	3	1	4	48	10	0	.208	3	37	0	1	1.1	1.000
1949		5	5	.500	4.57	34	12	4	134	149	68	64	0	1	2	1	49	17	0	.347	9	28	0	1	1.1	1.000
1950		0	5	.000	6.60	39	2	0	76.1	93	48	26	0	0	3	1	16	4	0	.250	4	15	0	2	0.5	1.000
6 yrs.		50	51	.495	3.68	223	100	42	944.2	919	418	340	5	11	10	16	311	74	0	.238	36	197	6	12	1.1	.975

WORLD SERIES

Year	Team	W	L	PCT	ERA	G	GS	CG	IP	H	BB	SO	ShO	W	L	SV	AB	H	HR	BA	PO	A	E	DP	TC/G	FA
1947	BKN N	0	1	.000	12.15	2	2	0	6.2	14	1	5	0	0	0	0	3	0	0	.000	0	0	0	0	0.0	–

Lou Lombardo

LOMBARDO, LOUIS
B. Nov. 18, 1928, Carlstadt, N. J.   BL TL 6'2"   210 lbs.

Year	Team	W	L	PCT	ERA	G	GS	CG	IP	H	BB	SO	ShO	W	L	SV	AB	H	HR	BA	PO	A	E	DP	TC/G	FA
1948	NY N	0	0	–	6.75	2	0	0	5.1	5	5	0	0	0	0	0	2	0	0	.000	0	2	0	0	1.0	1.000

Year	Team	W	L	PCT	ERA	G	GS	CG	IP	H	BB	SO	ShO	Relief Pitching W	L	SV	Batting AB	H	HR	BA	PO	A	E	DP	TC/G	FA

Jim Lonborg

LONBORG, JAMES REYNOLD
B. Apr. 16, 1942, Santa Maria, Calif.
BR TR 6'5" 200 lbs.

Year	Team	W	L	PCT	ERA	G	GS	CG	IP	H	BB	SO	ShO	W	L	SV	AB	H	HR	BA	PO	A	E	DP	TC/G	FA
1965	BOS A	9	17	.346	4.47	32	31	7	185.1	193	65	113	1	0	0	0	59	8	0	.136	12	24	5	0	1.3	.878
1966		10	10	.500	3.86	45	23	3	181.2	173	55	131	1	1	1	2	54	5	0	.093	18	21	2	2	0.9	.951
1967		22	9	.710	3.16	39	39	15	273.1	228	83	246	2	0	0	0	99	14	0	.141	19	24	1	2	1.1	.977
1968		6	10	.375	4.29	23	17	4	113.1	89	59	73	1	0	2	0	39	11	1	.282	8	6	0	0	0.6	1.000
1969		7	11	.389	4.51	29	23	4	143.2	148	65	100	0	1	0	0	41	4	0	.098	13	18	2	1	1.1	.939
1970		4	1	.800	3.18	9	4	0	34	33	9	21	0	2	0	0	9	4	1	.444	2	5	0	1	0.8	1.000
1971		10	7	.588	4.13	27	26	5	168	167	67	100	1	1	0	0	53	9	0	.170	15	28	1	3	1.6	.977
1972	MIL A	14	12	.538	2.83	33	30	11	223	197	76	143	2	0	0	1	69	10	0	.145	9	25	3	2	1.1	.919
1973	PHI N	13	16	.448	4.88	38	30	6	199.1	218	80	106	1	0	2	0	59	8	0	.136	10	26	5	2	1.1	.878
1974		17	13	.567	3.21	39	39	16	283	280	70	121	3	0	0	0	94	9	1	.096	16	26	2	1	1.1	.955
1975		8	6	.571	4.13	27	26	6	159	161	45	72	2	0	0	0	44	1	0	.023	24	18	1	0	1.6	.977
1976		18	10	.643	3.08	33	32	8	222	210	50	118	1	0	0	0	67	11	0	.164	21	16	0	1	1.1	1.000
1977		11	4	.733	4.10	25	25	4	158	157	50	76	1	0	0	0	48	5	0	.104	10	17	0	3	1.1	1.000
1978		8	10	.444	5.21	22	22	1	114	132	45	48	0	0	0	0	34	6	0	.176	11	14	0	1	1.1	1.000
1979		0	1	.000	11.57	4	1	0	7	14	4	7	0	0	0	0	3	0	0	.000	1	0	0	0	0.3	1.000
15 yrs.		157	137	.534	3.86	425	368	90	2464.2	2400	823	1475	15	7	4	4	770	105	3	.136	189	268	22	18	1.1	.954

LEAGUE CHAMPIONSHIP SERIES

Year	Team	W	L	PCT	ERA	G	GS	CG	IP	H	BB	SO	ShO	W	L	SV	AB	H	HR	BA	PO	A	E	DP	TC/G	FA
1976	PHI N	0	1	.000	1.69	1	1	0	5.1	2	2	2	0	0	0	0	1	0	0	.000	0	2	0	0	2.0	1.000
1977		0	1	.000	11.25	1	1	0	4	5	1	1	0	0	0	0	1	0	0	.000	0	2	0	0	2.0	1.000
2 yrs.		0	2	.000	5.79	2	2	0	9.1	7	3	3	0	0	0	0	2	0	0	.000	0	4	0	0	2.0	1.000

WORLD SERIES

Year	Team	W	L	PCT	ERA	G	GS	CG	IP	H	BB	SO	ShO	W	L	SV	AB	H	HR	BA	PO	A	E	DP	TC/G	FA
1967	BOS A	2	1	.667	2.63	3	3	0	24	14	2	11	0	0	0	0	9	0	0	.000	1	2	0	0	1.0	1.000

Bill Long

LONG, WILLIAM DOUGLAS
B. Feb. 29, 1960, Cincinnati, Ohio
BR TR 6' 185 lbs.

Year	Team	W	L	PCT	ERA	G	GS	CG	IP	H	BB	SO	ShO	W	L	SV	AB	H	HR	BA	PO	A	E	DP	TC/G	FA
1985	CHI A	0	1	.000	10.29	4	3	0	14	25	5	13	0	0	0	0	0	0	0	—	2	3	0	0	1.3	1.000
1987		8	8	.500	4.37	29	23	5	169	179	28	72	2	1	1	1	0	0	0	—	14	25	3	2	1.4	.929
1988		8	11	.421	4.03	47	18	3	174	187	43	77	0	2	2	1	0	0	0	—	7	25	0	0	0.7	1.000
1989		5	5	.500	3.92	30	8	0	98.2	101	37	51	0	2	0	1	0	0	0	—	9	15	0	0	0.8	1.000
4 yrs.		21	25	.457	4.33	110	52	8	455.2	492	113	213	2	5	3	4	0	0	0	—	32	68	3	2	0.9	.971

Bob Long

LONG, ROBERT EARL
B. Nov. 11, 1954, Jasper, Tenn.
BR TR 6'3" 178 lbs.

Year	Team	W	L	PCT	ERA	G	GS	CG	IP	H	BB	SO	ShO	W	L	SV	AB	H	HR	BA	PO	A	E	DP	TC/G	FA
1981	PIT N	1	2	.333	5.85	5	3	0	20	23	10	8	0	0	0	0	4	0	0	.000	1	1	0	0	0.4	1.000
1985	SEA A	0	0	—	3.76	28	0	0	38.1	30	17	29	0	0	0	0	0	0	0	—	3	3	0	0	0.2	1.000
2 yrs.		1	2	.333	4.47	33	3	0	58.1	53	27	37	0	0	0	0	4	0	0	.000	4	4	0	0	0.2	1.000

Lep Long

LONG, LESTER
B. July 12, 1888, Summit, N. J. D. Oct. 21, 1958, Birmingham, Ala.
BR TR 5'10" 153 lbs.

Year	Team	W	L	PCT	ERA	G	GS	CG	IP	H	BB	SO	ShO	W	L	SV	AB	H	HR	BA	PO	A	E	DP	TC/G	FA
1911	PHI A	0	0	—	4.50	4	0	0	8	15	5	4	0	0	0	0	3	0	0	.000	1	2	0	0	0.8	1.000

Red Long

LONG, NELSON
B. Sept. 28, 1876, Burlington, Ont., Canada D. Aug. 11, 1929, Hamilton, Ont., Canada
BR TR 6'1" 190 lbs.

Year	Team	W	L	PCT	ERA	G	GS	CG	IP	H	BB	SO	ShO	W	L	SV	AB	H	HR	BA	PO	A	E	DP	TC/G	FA
1902	BOS N	0	0	—	1.13	1	1	1	8	4	3	5	0	0	0	0	*				1	0	0	0	1.0	1.000

Tom Long

LONG, THOMAS FRANCIS
B. Apr. 22, 1898, Memphis, Tenn. D. Sept. 16, 1973, Louisville, Ky.
BL TL 5'9" 154 lbs.

Year	Team	W	L	PCT	ERA	G	GS	CG	IP	H	BB	SO	ShO	W	L	SV	AB	H	HR	BA	PO	A	E	DP	TC/G	FA
1924	BKN N	0	0	—	9.00	1	0	0	2	2	2	0	0	0	0	0	0	0	0	—	0	0	0	0	0.0	—

Pete Loos

LOOS, IVAN
B. Mar. 23, 1878, Philadelphia, Pa. D. Feb. 23, 1956, Darby, Pa.
TR

Year	Team	W	L	PCT	ERA	G	GS	CG	IP	H	BB	SO	ShO	W	L	SV	AB	H	HR	BA	PO	A	E	DP	TC/G	FA
1901	PHI A	0	1	.000	27.00	1	1	0	2	4	0	0	0	0	0	0	0	0	0	—	0	1	0	0	1.0	1.000

Ed Lopat

LOPAT, EDMUND WALTER (Steady Eddie)
Born Edmund Walter Lopatynski.
B. June 21, 1918, New York, N. Y.
Manager 1963-64.
BL TL 5'10" 185 lbs.

Year	Team	W	L	PCT	ERA	G	GS	CG	IP	H	BB	SO	ShO	W	L	SV	AB	H	HR	BA	PO	A	E	DP	TC/G	FA
1944	CHI A	11	10	.524	3.26	27	25	13	210	217	59	75	1	0	0	0	81	25	0	.309	9	44	0	4	2.0	1.000
1945		10	13	.435	4.11	26	24	17	199.1	226	56	74	1	0	0	1	82	24	1	.293	15	32	2	0	1.9	.959
1946		13	13	.500	2.73	29	29	20	231	216	48	89	2	0	0	0	87	22	0	.253	8	48	0	4	1.9	1.000
1947		16	13	.552	2.81	31	31	22	252.2	241	73	109	3	0	0	0	96	19	0	.198	12	36	2	0	1.6	.960
1948	NY A	17	11	.607	3.65	33	31	13	226.2	246	66	83	3	1	0	0	81	14	0	.173	6	50	3	3	1.8	.949
1949		15	10	.600	3.26	31	30	14	215.1	222	69	70	4	0	0	1	76	20	1	.263	7	42	2	5	1.6	.961
1950		18	8	.692	3.47	35	32	15	236.1	244	65	72	3	1	0	0	82	19	0	.232	10	47	2	0	1.7	.966
1951		21	9	.700	2.91	31	31	20	234.2	209	71	93	5	0	0	0	84	15	3	.179	9	50	3	4	2.0	.952
1952		10	5	.667	2.53	20	19	10	149.1	127	53	56	2	0	0	0	52	9	0	.173	6	30	1	2	1.9	.973
1953		16	4	.800	2.42	25	24	9	178.1	169	32	50	3	0	0	0	63	12	0	.190	8	38	2	1	1.9	.958
1954		12	4	.750	3.55	26	23	7	170	189	33	54	0	0	0	0	57	1	0	.018	3	28	1	1	1.2	.969
1955	2 teams	NY A	(16G 4-8)		BAL A	(10G 3-4)																				
"	total	7	12	.368	3.91	26	19	4	135.2	158	25	34	1	0	0	0	46	7	0	.152	7	23	1	2	1.2	.968
12 yrs.		166	112	.597	3.21	340	318	164	2439.1	2464	650	859	28	2	3	3	887	187	5	.211	100	468	19	30	1.7	.968

WORLD SERIES

Year	Team	W	L	PCT	ERA	G	GS	CG	IP	H	BB	SO	ShO	W	L	SV	AB	H	HR	BA	PO	A	E	DP	TC/G	FA
1949	NY A	1	0	1.000	6.35	1	1	0	5.2	9	1	4	0	0	0	0	3	1	0	.333	0	1	0	0	1.0	1.000
1950		0	0	—	2.25	1	1	0	8	9	0	5	0	0	0	0	2	1	0	.500	1	4	0	0	5.0	1.000
1951		2	0	1.000	0.50	2	2	2	18	10	3	4	1	0	0	0	8	1	0	.125	1	8	0	1	3.0	1.000
1952		0	1	.000	4.76	2	2	0	11.1	14	4	3	0	0	0	0	3	1	0	.333	0	1	0	0	0.5	1.000

Year	Team.	W	L	PCT	ERA	G	GS	CG	IP	H	BB	SO	ShO	Relief Pitching W	L	SV	Batting AB	H	HR	BA	PO	A	E	DP	TC/G	FA

Ed Lopat *continued*

Year	Team.	W	L	PCT	ERA	G	GS	CG	IP	H	BB	SO	ShO	W	L	SV	AB	H	HR	BA	PO	A	E	DP	TC/G	FA
1953		1	0	1.000	2.00	1	1	1	9	9	4	3	0	0	0	0	3	0	0	.000	0	2	0	0	2.0	1.000
5 yrs.		4	1	.800	2.60	7	7	3	52	51	12	19	0	0	0	0	19	4	0	.211	3	12	0	1	2.1	1.000

Art Lopatka

LOPATKA, ARTHUR JOSEPH
B. May 28, 1919, Chicago, Ill.

BB TL 5'10" 170 lbs.
BB 1946

Year	Team.	W	L	PCT	ERA	G	GS	CG	IP	H	BB	SO	ShO	W	L	SV	AB	H	HR	BA	PO	A	E	DP	TC/G	FA
1945	STL N	1	0	1.000	1.54	4	1	1	11.2	7	3	5	0	0	0	0	4	1	0	.250	1	0	0	0	0.3	1.000
1946	PHI N	0	1	.000	16.88	4	1	0	5.1	13	4	4	0	0	0	0	0	0	0	–	0	1	0	0	0.3	1.000
2 yrs.		1	1	.500	6.35	8	2	1	17	20	7	9	0	0	0	0	4	1	0	.250	1	1	0	0	0.3	1.000

Aurelio Lopez

LOPEZ, AURELIO ALEJANDRO
Born Aurelio Alejandro Lopez y Rios.
B. Sept. 21, 1948, Tecamachalco, Mexico

BR TR 6' 185 lbs.

Year	Team.	W	L	PCT	ERA	G	GS	CG	IP	H	BB	SO	ShO	W	L	SV	AB	H	HR	BA	PO	A	E	DP	TC/G	FA
1974	KC A	0	0	–	5.63	8	0	0	16	21	10	5	0	0	0	0	0	0	0	–	0	4	2	0	0.8	.667
1978	STL N	4	2	.667	4.29	25	4	0	65	52	32	46	0	2	1	0	14	3	0	.214	0	5	1	0	0.2	.833
1979	DET A	10	5	.667	2.41	61	0	0	127	95	51	106	0	10	5	21	0	0	0	–	9	15	1	1	0.4	.960
1980		13	6	.684	3.77	67	1	0	124	125	45	97	0	13	5	21	0	0	0	–	5	11	1	0	0.3	.941
1981		5	2	.714	3.62	29	3	0	82	70	31	53	0	3	2	3	0	0	0	–	5	10	0	1	0.5	1.000
1982		3	1	.750	5.27	19	0	0	41	41	19	26	0	3	1	3	0	0	0	–	3	5	0	0	0.4	1.000
1983		9	8	.529	2.81	57	0	0	115.1	87	49	90	0	9	8	18	0	0	0	–	2	13	1	0	0.3	.938
1984		10	1	.909	2.94	71	0	0	137.2	109	52	94	0	10	1	14	0	0	0	–	6	11	2	2	0.3	.895
1985		3	7	.300	4.80	51	0	0	86.1	82	41	53	0	3	7	5	0	0	0	–	5	10	1	1	0.3	.938
1986	HOU N	3	3	.500	3.46	45	0	0	78	64	25	44	0	3	3	7	9	0	0	.000	2	6	2	0	0.2	.800
1987		2	1	.667	4.50	26	0	0	38	39	12	21	0	2	1	1	1	0	0	.000	0	7	1	0	0.3	.875
11 yrs.		62	36	.633	3.56	459	9	0	910.1	785	367	635	0	58	34	93	24	3	0	.125	37	97	12	6	0.3	.918

LEAGUE CHAMPIONSHIP SERIES

Year	Team.	W	L	PCT	ERA	G	GS	CG	IP	H	BB	SO	ShO	W	L	SV	AB	H	HR	BA	PO	A	E	DP	TC/G	FA
1984	DET A	1	0	1.000	0.00	1	0	0	3	4	1	2	0	1	0	0	0	0	0	–	0	0	0	0	0.0	–
1986	HOU N	0	1	.000	8.10	2	0	0	3.1	7	4	3	0	0	1	0	0	0	0	–	0	0	0	0	0.0	–
2 yrs.		1	1	.500	4.26	3	0	0	6.1	11	5	5	0	1	1	0	0	0	0	–	0	0	0	0	0.0	–

WORLD SERIES

Year	Team.	W	L	PCT	ERA	G	GS	CG	IP	H	BB	SO	ShO	W	L	SV	AB	H	HR	BA	PO	A	E	DP	TC/G	FA
1984	DET A	1	0	1.000	0.00	2	0	0	3	1	1	4	0	1	0	0	0	0	0	–	0	0	0	0	0.0	–

Marcelino Lopez

LOPEZ, MARCELINO PONS
B. Sept. 23, 1943, Havana, Cuba

BR TL 6'3" 195 lbs.

Year	Team.	W	L	PCT	ERA	G	GS	CG	IP	H	BB	SO	ShO	W	L	SV	AB	H	HR	BA	PO	A	E	DP	TC/G	FA
1963	PHI N	1	0	1.000	6.00	4	2	0	6	8	7	2	0	0	0	0	2	0	0	.000	1	2	0	0	0.8	1.000
1965	CAL A	14	13	.519	2.93	35	32	8	215.1	185	82	122	1	0	0	1	69	14	1	.203	12	57	2	4	2.0	.972
1966		7	14	.333	3.93	37	32	6	199	188	68	132	2	0	0	1	58	11	0	.190	17	40	2	1	1.6	.966
1967	2 teams	CAL A	(4G 0–2)			BAL A	(4G 1–0)																			
"	total	1	2	.333	4.73	8	7	0	26.2	26	19	21	0	0	0	0	7	1	0	.143	0	1	2	0	0.4	.333
1969	BAL A	5	3	.625	4.41	27	4	0	69.1	65	34	57	0	4	2	0	14	3	0	.214	2	4	1	1	0.3	.857
1970		1	1	.500	2.07	25	3	0	61	47	37	49	0	0	1	0	13	1	0	.077	2	6	4	1	0.5	.667
1971	MIL A	2	7	.222	4.63	31	11	0	68	64	60	42	0	1	3	0	17	1	0	.059	5	13	1	2	0.6	.947
1972	CLE A	0	0	–	5.63	4	2	0	8	8	10	1	0	0	0	0	1	0	0	.000	0	0	0	0	0.3	1.000
8 yrs.		31	40	.437	3.62	171	93	14	653.1	591	317	426	3	5	6	2	181	31	1	.171	39	124	12	9	1.0	.931

LEAGUE CHAMPIONSHIP SERIES

Year	Team.	W	L	PCT	ERA	G	GS	CG	IP	H	BB	SO	ShO	W	L	SV	AB	H	HR	BA	PO	A	E	DP	TC/G	FA
1969	BAL A	0	0	–	0.00	1	0	0	.1	1	2	0	0	0	0	0	0	0	0	–	0	0	0	0	0.0	–

WORLD SERIES

Year	Team.	W	L	PCT	ERA	G	GS	CG	IP	H	BB	SO	ShO	W	L	SV	AB	H	HR	BA	PO	A	E	DP	TC/G	FA
1970	BAL A	0	0	–	0.00	1	0	0	.1	0	0	0	0	0	0	0	0	0	0	–	0	0	0	0	0.0	–

Ramon Lopez

LOPEZ, JOSE RAMON
Born Jose Roman Lopez y Hevia.
B. May 26, 1933, Las Villas, Cuba   D. Sept. 4, 1982, Miami, Fla.

BR TR 6' 175 lbs.

Year	Team.	W	L	PCT	ERA	G	GS	CG	IP	H	BB	SO	ShO	W	L	SV	AB	H	HR	BA	PO	A	E	DP	TC/G	FA
1966	CAL A	0	1	.000	5.14	4	1	0	7	4	4	2	0	0	0	0	0	0	0	–	2	0	1	0	0.8	.667

Bris Lord

LORD, BRISCOE ROBOTHAM (The Human Eyeball)
B. Sept. 21, 1883, Upland, Pa.   D. Nov. 13, 1964, Annapolis, Md.

BR TR 5'9" 185 lbs.

Year	Team.	W	L	PCT	ERA	G	GS	CG	IP	H	BB	SO	ShO	W	L	SV	AB	H	HR	BA	PO	A	E	DP	TC/G	FA
1907	PHI A	0	0	–	9.00	1	0	0	3	3	0	0	0	0	0	0	*				0	0	0	0	0.0	–

Lefty Lorenzen

LORENZEN, ADOLPH ANDREAS
B. Jan. 12, 1893, Davenport, Iowa   D. Mar. 5, 1963, Davenport, Iowa

BL TL 5'10" 164 lbs.

Year	Team.	W	L	PCT	ERA	G	GS	CG	IP	H	BB	SO	ShO	W	L	SV	AB	H	HR	BA	PO	A	E	DP	TC/G	FA
1913	DET A	0	0	–	18.00	1	0	0	2	4	3	0	0	0	0	0	2	1	0	.500	0	3	0	1	3.0	1.000

Joe Lotz

LOTZ, JOSEPH PETER (Smokey)
B. Jan. 2, 1891, Remsen, Iowa   D. Jan. 1, 1971, Castro Valley, Calif.

BR TR 5'8½" 175 lbs.

Year	Team.	W	L	PCT	ERA	G	GS	CG	IP	H	BB	SO	ShO	W	L	SV	AB	H	HR	BA	PO	A	E	DP	TC/G	FA
1916	STL N	0	3	.000	4.28	12	3	1	40	31	17	18	0	0	0	0	12	4	0	.333	1	8	0	0	0.8	1.000

Art Loudell

LOUDELL, ARTHUR
Born Arthur Laudel.
B. May 10, 1882, Latham, Mo.   D. Feb. 19, 1961, Kansas City, Mo.

BR TR 5'11" 173 lbs.

Year	Team.	W	L	PCT	ERA	G	GS	CG	IP	H	BB	SO	ShO	W	L	SV	AB	H	HR	BA	PO	A	E	DP	TC/G	FA
1910	DET A	1	1	.500	3.38	5	2	1	21.1	23	14	12	0	0	0	0	7	1	0	.143	0	3	0	0	0.6	1.000

Larry Loughlin

LOUGHLIN, LARRY JOHN
B. Aug. 16, 1941, Tacoma, Wash.

BL TL 6'1" 190 lbs.

Year	Team.	W	L	PCT	ERA	G	GS	CG	IP	H	BB	SO	ShO	W	L	SV	AB	H	HR	BA	PO	A	E	DP	TC/G	FA
1967	PHI N	0	0	–	15.19	3	0	0	5.1	9	4	5	0	0	0	0	1	1	0	1.000	0	0	1	0	0.3	–

Year	Team	W	L	PCT	ERA	G	GS	CG	IP	H	BB	SO	ShO	Relief Pitching W	L	SV	Batting AB	H	HR	BA	PO	A	E	DP	TC/G	FA

Don Loun
LOUN, DONALD NELSON B. Nov. 9, 1940, Frederick, Md. — BR TL 6'2" 185 lbs.

Year	Team	W	L	PCT	ERA	G	GS	CG	IP	H	BB	SO	ShO	W	L	SV	AB	H	HR	BA	PO	A	E	DP	TC/G	FA
1964	WAS A	1	1	.500	2.08	2	2	1	13	13	3	3	1	0	0	0	4	0	0	.000	2	4	0	0	3.0	1.000

Slim Love
LOVE, EDWARD HAUGHTON B. Aug. 1, 1890, Love, Miss. D. Nov. 30, 1942, Memphis, Tenn. — BL TL 6'7" 195 lbs.

Year	Team	W	L	PCT	ERA	G	GS	CG	IP	H	BB	SO	ShO	W	L	SV	AB	H	HR	BA	PO	A	E	DP	TC/G	FA
1913	WAS A	1	0	1.000	1.62	5	1	0	16.2	14	6	5	0	0	0	0	5	1	0	.200	0	1	2	0	0.6	.333
1916	NY A	2	0	1.000	4.91	20	1	0	47.2	46	23	21	0	1	0	0	14	0	0	.000	0	14	1	0	0.8	.933
1917		6	5	.545	2.35	33	9	2	130.1	115	57	82	0	4	0	1	36	6	0	.167	3	27	3	1	1.0	.909
1918		13	12	.520	3.07	38	29	13	228.2	207	116	95	1	1	1	1	74	17	0	.230	7	39	4	5	1.3	.920
1919	DET A	6	4	.600	3.01	22	8	4	89.2	92	40	46	0	3	1	1	27	6	0	.222	1	15	2	3	0.8	.889
1920		0	0	—	8.31	1	0	0	4.1	6	4	2	0	0	0	0	0	0	0	—	0	1	0	0	1.0	1.000
6 yrs.		28	21	.571	3.04	119	48	19	517.1	480	246	251	1	9	2	4	156	30	0	.192	11	97	12	9	1.0	.900

Vance Lovelace
LOVELACE, VANCE ODELL B. Aug. 9, 1963, Tampa, Fla. — BL TL 6'5" 205 lbs.

Year	Team	W	L	PCT	ERA	G	GS	CG	IP	H	BB	SO	ShO	W	L	SV	AB	H	HR	BA	PO	A	E	DP	TC/G	FA
1988	CAL A	0	0	—	13.50	3	0	0	1.1	2	3	0	0	0	0	0	0	0	0	—	0	0	0	0	0.0	—
1989		0	0	—	0.00	1	0	0	1	0	1	1	0	0	0	0	0	0	0	—	0	0	0	0	0.0	—
2 yrs.		0	0	—	7.71	4	0	0	2.1	2	4	1	0	0	0	0	0	0	0	—	0	0	0	0	0.0	—

Lynn Lovenguth
LOVENGUTH, LYNN RICHARD B. Nov. 29, 1922, Camden, N. J. — BL TR 5'10½" 170 lbs.

Year	Team	W	L	PCT	ERA	G	GS	CG	IP	H	BB	SO	ShO	W	L	SV	AB	H	HR	BA	PO	A	E	DP	TC/G	FA
1955	PHI N	0	1	.000	4.50	14	0	0	18	17	10	14	0	0	1	0	2	0	0	.000	0	1	0	1	0.1	1.000
1957	STL N	0	1	.000	2.00	2	1	0	9	6	6	6	0	0	0	0	2	0	0	.000	0	0	0	0	0.0	—
2 yrs.		0	2	.000	3.67	16	1	0	27	23	16	20	0	0	1	0	4	0	0	.000	0	1	0	1	0.1	1.000

John Lovett
LOVETT, JOHN B. May 6, 1878, Monday, Ohio D. Dec. 5, 1937, Murray City, Ohio

Year	Team	W	L	PCT	ERA	G	GS	CG	IP	H	BB	SO	ShO	W	L	SV	AB	H	HR	BA	PO	A	E	DP	TC/G	FA
1903	STL N	0	1	.000	5.40	3	1	0	5	6	5	3	0	0	0	0	3	1	0	.333	0	1	0	0	0.3	1.000

Tom Lovett
LOVETT, THOMAS JOSEPH B. Dec. 7, 1863, Providence, R. I. D. Mar. 20, 1928, Providence, R. I. — BR 5'8" 165 lbs.

Year	Team	W	L	PCT	ERA	G	GS	CG	IP	H	BB	SO	ShO	W	L	SV	AB	H	HR	BA	PO	A	E	DP	TC/G	FA
1885	PHI AA	7	8	.467	3.70	16	15	15	138.2	130	38	56	0	0	0	0	58	13	0	.224	8	20	12	0	2.5	.700
1889	BKN AA	17	10	.630	4.32	29	28	23	229	234	65	92	1	0	0	0	100	19	2	.190	8	49	3	2	2.1	.950
1890	BKN N	30	11	.732	2.78	44	41	39	372	327	141	124	4	1	0	0	164	33	1	.201	10	79	10	3	2.2	.899
1891		23	19	.548	3.69	44	43	39	365.2	361	129	129	3	0	0	0	153	25	0	.163	23	59	6	2	2.0	.932
1893		3	5	.375	6.56	14	8	6	96	134	35	15	0	1	0	1	50	9	0	.180	8	16	3	2	1.9	.889
1894	BOS N	8	6	.571	5.97	15	13	10	104	155	36	23	0	1	1	0	49	7	1	.143	6	14	1	1	1.4	.952
6 yrs.		88	59	.599	3.94	162	149	132	1305.1	1341	444	439	9	3	1	1	574	106	4	.185	63	237	35	10	2.1	.896

Pete Lovrich
LOVRICH, PETER B. Oct. 16, 1942, Blue Island, Ill. — BR TR 6'4" 200 lbs.

Year	Team	W	L	PCT	ERA	G	GS	CG	IP	H	BB	SO	ShO	W	L	SV	AB	H	HR	BA	PO	A	E	DP	TC/G	FA
1963	KC A	1	1	.500	7.84	20	1	0	20.2	25	10	16	0	1	0	0	0	0	0	—	0	1	0	0	0.1	1.000

Grover Lowdermilk
LOWDERMILK, GROVER CLEVELAND (Slim) Brother of Lou Lowdermilk. B. Jan. 15, 1885, Sandborn, Ind. D. Mar. 31, 1968, Odin, Ill. — BR TR 6'4" 190 lbs.

Year	Team	W	L	PCT	ERA	G	GS	CG	IP	H	BB	SO	ShO	W	L	SV	AB	H	HR	BA	PO	A	E	DP	TC/G	FA
1909	STL N	0	2	.000	6.21	7	3	1	29	28	30	14	0	0	0	0	10	1	0	.100	0	8	1	0	1.3	.889
1911		0	1	.000	7.29	11	2	1	33.1	37	33	15	0	0	0	0	9	1	0	.111	0	11	0	0	1.0	1.000
1912	CHI N	0	1	.000	9.69	2	1	1	13	17	14	8	0	0	0	0	4	0	0	.000	0	4	3	0	3.5	.571
1915	2 teams STL A (38G 9–17) DET A (7G 4–1)																									
"	total	13	18	.419	3.24	45	34	14	250.1	200	157	148	1	3	0	0	80	10	0	.125	6	73	9	3	2.0	.898
1916	2 teams DET A (1G 0–0) CLE A (10G 1–5)																									
"	total	1	5	.167	3.14	11	9	2	51.2	52	48	28	0	0	0	0	18	3	0	.167	2	15	2	1	1.7	.895
1917	STL A	2	1	.667	1.42	3	2	2	19	16	4	9	1	0	1	0	7	0	0	.000	1	5	0	0	2.0	1.000
1918		2	6	.250	3.15	13	11	4	80	74	38	25	0	0	0	0	28	7	0	.250	5	33	1	1	3.0	.974
1919	2 teams STL A (7G 0–0) CHI A (20G 5–5)																									
"	total	5	5	.500	2.57	27	11	5	108.2	101	47	49	0	0	2	0	35	3	0	.086	0	4	0	0	0.1	1.000
1920	CHI A	0	0	—	6.75	3	0	0	5.1	9	5	0	0	0	0	0	0	0	0	—	1	4	1	0	2.0	.833
9 yrs.		23	39	.371	3.58	122	73	30	590.1	534	376	296	2	3	5	0	191	25	0	.131	15	157	17	5	1.5	.910

WORLD SERIES

Year	Team	W	L	PCT	ERA	G	GS	CG	IP	H	BB	SO	ShO	W	L	SV	AB	H	HR	BA	PO	A	E	DP	TC/G	FA
1919	CHI A	0	0	—	9.00	1	0	0	1	2	1	0	0	0	0	0	0	0	0	—	0	1	0	0	1.0	1.000

Lou Lowdermilk
LOWDERMILK, LOUIS BAILEY Brother of Grover Lowdermilk. B. Feb. 23, 1887, Sandborn, Ind. D. Dec. 27, 1975, Centralia, Ill. — BR TL 6'1" 180 lbs.

Year	Team	W	L	PCT	ERA	G	GS	CG	IP	H	BB	SO	ShO	W	L	SV	AB	H	HR	BA	PO	A	E	DP	TC/G	FA
1911	STL N	3	4	.429	3.46	16	3	3	65	72	29	20	1	2	2	0	18	2	0	.111	0	11	1	0	0.8	.917
1912		1	1	.500	3.00	4	1	1	15	14	9	2	0	0	1	1	4	1	0	.250	0	5	0	0	1.3	1.000
2 yrs.		4	5	.444	3.38	20	4	4	80	86	38	22	1	2	3	1	22	3	0	.136	0	16	1	0	0.9	.941

Bobby Lowe
LOWE, ROBERT LINCOLN (Link) B. July 10, 1868, Pittsburg, Pa. D. Dec. 8, 1951, Detroit, Mich. Manager 1904. — BR TR 5'10" 150 lbs.

Year	Team	W	L	PCT	ERA	G	GS	CG	IP	H	BB	SO	ShO	W	L	SV	AB	H	HR	BA	PO	A	E	DP	TC/G	FA
1891	BOS N	0	0	—	9.00	1	0	0	1	3	1	0	0	0	0	0	0	*				0	0	0	0	0.0	—

George Lowe
LOWE, GEORGE WESLEY B. Apr. 25, 1895, Ridgefield Park, N. J. D. Sept. 3, 1981, Somers Point, N. J. — BR TR 6'2" 180 lbs.

Year	Team	W	L	PCT	ERA	G	GS	CG	IP	H	BB	SO	ShO	W	L	SV	AB	H	HR	BA	PO	A	E	DP	TC/G	FA
1920	CIN N	0	0	—	0.00	1	0	0	2	1	1	0	0	0	0	0	0	0	0	—	0	0	0	0	0.0	—

Year	Team		W	L	PCT	ERA	G	GS	CG	IP	H	BB	SO	ShO	W	L	SV	AB	H	HR	BA	PO	A	E	DP	TC/G	FA
															Relief Pitching			Batting									

Turk Lown

LOWN, OMAR JOSEPH
B. May 30, 1924, Brooklyn, N. Y.   BR TR 6' 180 lbs.

Year	Team		W	L	PCT	ERA	G	GS	CG	IP	H	BB	SO	ShO	W	L	SV	AB	H	HR	BA	PO	A	E	DP	TC/G	FA
1951	CHI	N	4	9	.308	5.46	31	18	3	127	125	90	39	1	1	2	0	39	8	0	.205	9	23	0	1	1.0	1.000
1952			4	11	.267	4.37	33	19	5	156.2	154	93	73	0	1	2	0	50	7	0	.140	12	33	1	2	1.4	.978
1953			8	7	.533	5.16	49	12	2	148.1	166	84	76	0	7	3	3	48	6	0	.125	12	33	0	4	0.9	1.000
1954			0	2	.000	6.14	15	0	0	22	23	15	16	0	0	2	0	0	0	0	–	2	6	1	0	0.6	.889
1956			9	8	.529	3.58	61	0	0	110.2	95	78	74	0	9	8	13	23	5	1	.217	9	13	1	1	0.4	.957
1957			5	7	.417	3.77	67	0	0	93	74	51	51	0	5	7	12	10	2	0	.200	5	22	1	4	0.4	.964
1958	3 teams	CHI N	(4G 0–0)			CIN N	(11G 0–2)			CHI A	(27G 3–3)																
"	total		3	5	.375	4.31	42	0	0	56.1	63	43	53	0	3	5	8	10	3	0	.300	6	5	1	1	0.3	.917
1959	CHI	A	9	2	.818	2.89	60	0	0	93.1	73	42	63	0	9	2	15	12	3	0	.250	2	21	1	0	0.4	.958
1960			2	3	.400	3.88	45	0	0	67.1	60	34	39	0	2	3	5	5	1	0	.200	4	13	2	1	0.4	.895
1961			7	5	.583	2.76	59	0	0	101	87	35	50	0	7	5	11	14	0	0	.000	6	15	2	1	0.4	.913
1962			4	2	.667	3.04	42	0	0	56.1	58	25	40	0	4	2	6	3	0	0	.000	7	14	1	1	0.5	.955
11 yrs.			55	61	.474	4.12	504	49	10	1032	978	590	574	1	48	41	73	214	35	1	.164	74	198	11	16	0.6	.961

WORLD SERIES

Year	Team		W	L	PCT	ERA	G	GS	CG	IP	H	BB	SO	ShO	W	L	SV	AB	H	HR	BA	PO	A	E	DP	TC/G	FA
1959	CHI	A	0	0	–	0.00	3	0	0	3.1	2	1	3	0	0	0	0	0	0	0	–	0	0	0	0	0.0	

Sam Lowry

LOWRY, SAMUEL JOSEPH (Mose)
B. Mar. 25, 1920, Philadelphia, Pa.   BR TR 5'11" 160 lbs.

Year	Team		W	L	PCT	ERA	G	GS	CG	IP	H	BB	SO	ShO	W	L	SV	AB	H	HR	BA	PO	A	E	DP	TC/G	FA
1942	PHI	A	0	0	–	6.00	1	0	0	3	3	1	0	0	0	0	0	1	0	0	.000	0	0	0	0	0.0	–
1943			0	0	–	5.00	5	0	0	18	18	9	3	0	0	0	0	6	1	0	.167	1	5	0	0	1.2	1.000
2 yrs.			0	0	–	5.14	6	0	0	21	21	10	3	0	0	0	0	7	1	0	.143	1	5	0	0	1.0	1.000

Mike Loynd

LOYND, MICHAEL WALLACE
B. Mar. 26, 1964, St. Louis, Mo.   BR TR 6'4" 210 lbs.

Year	Team		W	L	PCT	ERA	G	GS	CG	IP	H	BB	SO	ShO	W	L	SV	AB	H	HR	BA	PO	A	E	DP	TC/G	FA
1986	TEX	A	2	2	.500	5.36	9	8	0	42	49	19	33	0	0	0	0	0	0	0	–	5	5	1	0	1.2	.909
1987			1	5	.167	6.10	26	8	0	69.1	82	38	48	0	1	0	1	0	0	0	–	5	6	3	0	0.5	.786
2 yrs.			3	7	.300	5.82	35	16	0	111.1	131	57	81	0	1	0	2	0	0	0	–	10	11	4	0	0.7	.840

Pat Luby

LUBY, JOHN PERKINS
B. 1868, Charleston, S. C.   D. Apr. 24, 1899, Charleston, S. C.   TR 6' 185 lbs.

Year	Team		W	L	PCT	ERA	G	GS	CG	IP	H	BB	SO	ShO	W	L	SV	AB	H	HR	BA	PO	A	E	DP	TC/G	FA
1890	CHI	N	20	9	.690	3.19	34	31	26	267.2	226	95	85	0	0	0	1	116	31	3	.267	12	42	2	0	1.6	.964
1891			8	11	.421	4.76	30	24	18	206	221	94	52	0	1	0	1	98	24	2	.245	8	42	2	2	1.7	.962
1892			10	16	.385	3.13	31	26	24	247.1	247	106	64	1	2	0	1	163	31	2	.190	11	61	7	3	2.5	.911
1895	LOU	N	1	5	.167	6.81	11	6	5	71.1	115	19	12	0	0	0	0	53	15	0	.283	2	21	5	1	2.5	.821
4 yrs.			39	41	.488	3.91	106	87	73	792.1	809	314	213	1	3	0	3	*				33	166	16	6	2.0	.926

Gary Lucas

LUCAS, GARY PAUL
B. Nov. 8, 1954, Riverside, Calif.   BL TL 6'5" 200 lbs.

Year	Team		W	L	PCT	ERA	G	GS	CG	IP	H	BB	SO	ShO	W	L	SV	AB	H	HR	BA	PO	A	E	DP	TC/G	FA
1980	SD	N	5	8	.385	3.24	46	18	0	150	138	43	85	0	1	1	3	35	6	0	.171	9	23	0	4	0.7	1.000
1981			7	7	.500	2.00	57	0	0	90	78	36	53	0	7	7	13	10	1	0	.100	5	15	0	0	0.4	1.000
1982			1	10	.091	3.24	65	0	0	97.1	89	29	64	0	1	10	16	14	0	0	.000	6	19	0	0	0.4	1.000
1983			5	8	.385	2.87	62	0	0	91	85	34	60	0	5	8	17	12	0	0	.000	5	10	3	1	0.3	.833
1984	MON	N	0	3	.000	2.72	55	0	0	53	54	20	42	0	0	3	8	4	0	0	.000	2	15	0	1	0.3	1.000
1985			6	2	.750	3.19	49	0	0	67.2	63	24	31	0	6	2	2	5	0	0	.000	2	11	0	1	0.3	1.000
1986	CAL	A	4	1	.800	3.15	27	0	0	45.2	45	6	31	0	4	1	2	0	0	0	–	6	9	0	0	0.6	1.000
1987			1	5	.167	3.63	48	0	0	74.1	66	35	44	0	1	5	3	0	0	0	–	3	17	2	1	0.5	.909
8 yrs.			29	44	.397	3.01	409	18	0	669	618	227	410	0	25	37	64	80	7	0	.088	38	119	5	8	0.4	.969

LEAGUE CHAMPIONSHIP SERIES

Year	Team		W	L	PCT	ERA	G	GS	CG	IP	H	BB	SO	ShO	W	L	SV	AB	H	HR	BA	PO	A	E	DP	TC/G	FA
1986	CAL	A	0	0	–	11.57	4	0	0	2.1	3	1	2	0	0	0	0	0	0	0	–	0	0	0	0	0.0	–

Ray Lucas

LUCAS, RAY WESLEY (Luke)
B. Oct. 2, 1908, Springfield, Ohio   D. Oct. 9, 1969, Harrison, Mich.   BR TR 6'2" 175 lbs.

Year	Team		W	L	PCT	ERA	G	GS	CG	IP	H	BB	SO	ShO	W	L	SV	AB	H	HR	BA	PO	A	E	DP	TC/G	FA
1929	NY	N	0	0	–	0.00	3	0	0	8	3	3	1	0	0	0	0	2	1	0	.500	0	3	0	1	1.0	1.000
1930			0	0	–	6.97	6	0	0	10.1	9	10	1	0	0	0	1	1	0	0	.000	0	6	0	0	1.0	1.000
1931			0	0	–	4.50	1	0	0	2	1	1	0	0	0	0	0	0	0	0	–	0	0	0	0	0.0	–
1933	BKN	N	0	0	–	7.20	2	0	0	5	6	4	0	0	0	0	0	0	0	0	–	1	0	0	1	1.0	1.000
1934			1	1	.500	6.75	10	2	0	30.2	39	14	3	0	1	0	0	6	2	0	.333	2	12	1	1	1.5	.933
5 yrs.			1	1	.500	5.79	22	2	0	56	58	32	5	0	1	0	1	9	3	0	.333	3	22	1	2	1.2	.962

Red Lucas

LUCAS, CHARLES FREDERICK (The Nashville Narcissus)
B. Apr. 28, 1902, Columbia, Tenn.   D. July 9, 1986, Nashville, Tenn.   BL TR 5'9½" 170 lbs.

Year	Team		W	L	PCT	ERA	G	GS	CG	IP	H	BB	SO	ShO	W	L	SV	AB	H	HR	BA	PO	A	E	DP	TC/G	FA
1923	NY	N	0	0	–	0.00	3	0	0	5.1	9	4	3	0	0	0	0	2	0	0	.000	1	3	0	0	1.3	1.000
1924	BOS	N	1	4	.200	5.16	27	4	1	83.2	112	18	30	0	1	1	0	33	11	0	.333	5	22	0	1	1.0	1.000
1926	CIN	N	8	5	.615	3.68	39	11	7	154	161	30	34	1	3	1	2	76	23	0	.303	6	36	0	1	1.1	1.000
1927			18	11	.621	3.38	37	23	19	239.2	231	39	51	4	4	3	2	150	47	0	.313	7	51	1	2	1.6	.983
1928			13	9	.591	3.39	27	19	13	167.1	164	42	35	4	3	2	1	73	23	0	.315	8	37	0	0	1.7	1.000
1929			19	12	.613	3.60	32	32	28	270	267	58	72	2	0	0	0	140	41	0	.293	12	63	4	3	2.5	.949
1930			14	16	.467	5.38	33	28	18	210.2	270	44	53	1	0	0	1	113	38	2	.336	8	30	0	0	1.2	1.000
1931			14	13	.519	3.59	29	29	24	238	261	39	56	0	0	0	0	153	43	0	.281	8	54	1	3	2.2	.984
1932			13	17	.433	2.94	31	31	28	269.1	261	35	63	0	0	0	0	150	43	0	.287	17	55	2	4	2.4	.973
1933			10	16	.385	3.40	29	29	21	219.2	248	18	40	3	0	0	0	122	35	1	.287	3	52	0	5	1.9	1.000
1934	PIT	N	10	9	.526	4.38	29	21	12	172.2	198	40	44	0	0	0	0	105	23	0	.219	7	24	2	1	1.1	.939
1935			8	6	.571	3.44	20	19	8	125.2	136	23	29	2	0	0	0	66	21	1	.318	7	23	1	1	1.6	.968
1936			15	4	.789	3.18	27	22	12	175.2	178	26	53	0	3	0	0	108	26	0	.241	8	33	1	4	1.6	.976
1937			8	10	.444	4.27	20	20	9	126.1	150	23	20	1	0	0	0	82	22	0	.268	9	19	0	1	1.4	1.000
1938			6	3	.667	3.54	13	13	4	84	90	16	19	0	0	0	0	46	5	0	.109	3	14	0	1	1.3	1.000
15 yrs.			157	135	.538	3.72	396	301	204	2542	2736	455	602	19	14	10	7	*				109	516	12	31	1.6	.981

Year	Team		W	L	PCT	ERA	G	GS	CG	IP	H	BB	SO	ShO	Relief Pitching W	L	SV	Batting AB	H	HR	BA	PO	A	E	DP	TC/G	FA

Joe Lucey

LUCEY, JOSEPH EARL (Scootch)
B. Mar. 27, 1897, Holyoke, Mass. D. July 30, 1980, Holyoke, Mass.   BR TR 6'   168 lbs.

1920	NY	A	0	0	–	0.00	0	0	0	0	0	0	0	0	0	0	0	3	0	0	.000	0	0	0	0	0.0	–
1925	BOS	A	0	1	.000	9.00	7	2	0	11	18	14	2	0	0	0	0	15	2	0	.133	7	5	4	2	2.3	.750
2 yrs.			0	1	.000	9.00	7	2	0	11	18	14	2	0	0	0	0	18	2	0	.111	7	5	4	2	2.3	.750

Con Lucid

LUCID, CORNELIUS CECIL
B. Feb. 24, 1874, Dublin, Ireland D. June 25, 1931, Houston, Tex.

1893	LOU	N	0	1	.000	15.00	2	1	0	6	10	10	0	0	0	0	0	3	1	0	.333	0	1	1	0	1.0	.500
1894	BKN	N	5	3	.625	6.56	10	9	7	71.1	87	44	15	0	0	0	0	33	7	0	.212	3	3	2	0	0.8	.750
1895	2 teams		BKN N	(21G 10–7)		PHI N	(10G 6–3)																				
"	total		16	10	.615	5.66	31	29	19	206.2	244	107	43	3	1	0	0	82	23	0	.280	8	36	4	1	1.5	.917
1896	PHI	N	1	4	.200	8.36	5	5	5	42	75	17	3	0	0	0	0	16	2	0	.125	3	4	1	1	1.6	.875
1897	STL	N	1	5	.167	3.67	6	6	5	49	66	26	4	0	0	0	0	17	3	0	.176	2	16	4	1	3.7	.818
5 yrs.			23	23	.500	6.02	54	50	36	375	482	204	65	3	1	0	0	151	36	0	.238	16	60	12	3	1.6	.864

Lou Lucier

LUCIER, LOUIS JOSEPH
B. Mar. 23, 1918, Northbridge, Mass.   BR TR 5'8"   160 lbs.

1943	BOS	A	3	4	.429	3.89	16	9	3	74	94	33	23	0	0	0	0	20	4	0	.200	7	29	1	4	2.3	.973
1944	2 teams		BOS A	(3G 0–0)		PHI N	(1G 0–0)																				
"	total		0	0	–	7.36	4	0	0	7.1	10	9	3	0	0	0	0	1	0	0	.000	0	0	0	0	0.0	–
1945	PHI	N	0	1	.000	2.21	13	0	0	20.1	14	5	5	0	0	1	1	4	1	0	.250	1	8	0	1	0.7	1.000
3 yrs.			3	5	.375	3.81	33	9	3	101.2	118	47	31	0	0	1	1	25	5	0	.200	8	37	1	5	1.4	.978

Howard Luckey

LUCKEY, HOWARD J.
B. Philadelphia, Pa. Deceased.

| 1890 | PHI | AA | 0 | 0 | – | 9.00 | 1 | 0 | 0 | 2 | 1 | 0 | 3 | 1 | 0 | 0 | 0 | 1 | 0 | 0 | .000 | 0 | 0 | 0 | 0 | 0.0 | – |

Willie Ludolph

LUDOLPH, WILLIAM FRANCIS (Wee Willie)
B. Jan. 21, 1900, San Francisco, Calif. D. Apr. 8, 1952, Oakland, Calif.   BR TR 6'1½" 170 lbs.

| 1924 | DET | A | 0 | 0 | – | 4.76 | 3 | 0 | 0 | 5.2 | 5 | 2 | 1 | 0 | 0 | 0 | 0 | 0 | 0 | 0 | .000 | 1 | 2 | 0 | 0 | 1.0 | 1.000 |

Steve Luebber

LUEBBER, STEPHEN LEE
B. July 9, 1949, Clinton, Mo.   BR TR 6'3"   185 lbs.

1971	MIN	A	2	5	.286	5.03	18	12	0	68	73	37	35	0	1	0	1	19	1	0	.053	2	12	0	1	0.8	1.000
1972			0	0	–	0.00	2	0	0	2	3	2	1	0	0	0	0	0	0	0	–	0	1	0	0	0.5	1.000
1976			4	5	.444	4.00	38	12	2	119.1	109	62	45	1	0	1	2	0	0	0	–	5	17	6	1	0.7	.786
1979	TOR	A	0	0	–	∞	1	0	0	0	2	1	0	0	0	0	0	0	0	0	–	0	0	0	0	0.0	–
1981	BAL	A	0	0	–	7.41	7	0	0	17	26	4	12	0	0	0	0	0	0	0	–	3	3	0	0	0.9	1.000
5 yrs.			6	10	.375	4.62	66	24	2	206.1	213	106	93	1	1	1	3	19	1	0	.053	10	33	6	2	0.7	.878

Dick Luebke

LUEBKE, RICHARD RAYMOND
B. Apr. 8, 1935, Chicago, Ill. D. Dec. 4, 1974, San Diego, Calif.   BR TL 6'4"   200 lbs.

| 1962 | BAL | A | 0 | 1 | .000 | 2.70 | 10 | 0 | 0 | 13.1 | 12 | 6 | 7 | 0 | 0 | 0 | 1 | 0 | 0 | 0 | – | 1 | 0 | 0 | 0 | 0.1 | 1.000 |

Rick Luecken

LUECKEN, RICHARD FRED
B. Nov. 15, 1960, McAllen, Tex.   BR TR 6'6"   210 lbs.

| 1989 | KC | A | 2 | 1 | .667 | 3.42 | 19 | 0 | 0 | 23.2 | 23 | 13 | 16 | 0 | 2 | 1 | 1 | 0 | 0 | 0 | – | 2 | 2 | 0 | 0 | 0.2 | 1.000 |

Urbano Lugo

LUGO, URBANO RAFAEL
Born Urbano Rafael Lugo y Colina.
B. Aug. 12, 1962, Punto Fijo, Venezuela   BR TR 6'   185 lbs.

1985	CAL	A	3	4	.429	3.69	20	10	1	83	86	29	42	0	0	0	0	0	0	0	–	4	13	2	2	1.0	.895
1986			1	1	.500	3.80	6	3	0	21.1	21	6	9	0	0	0	0	0	0	0	–	2	2	0	0	0.7	1.000
1987			0	2	.000	9.32	7	5	0	28	42	18	24	0	0	0	0	0	0	0	–	2	2	0	0	0.6	1.000
1988			0	0	–	9.00	1	0	0	2	2	1	1	0	0	0	0	0	0	0	–	0	0	0	0	0.0	–
1989	MON	N	0	0	–	6.75	3	0	0	4	4	0	3	0	0	0	0	0	0	0	–	1	0	0	0	0.3	1.000
5 yrs.			4	7	.364	5.01	37	18	1	138.1	155	54	79	0	0	0	0	0	0	0	–	9	17	2	2	0.8	.929

Bill Luhrsen

LUHRSEN, WILLIAM FERDINAND (Wild Bill)
B. Apr. 14, 1884, Buckley, Ill. D. Aug. 15, 1973, Little Rock, Ark.   BR TR 5'9"   165 lbs.

| 1913 | PIT | N | 3 | 1 | .750 | 2.48 | 5 | 3 | 2 | 29 | 25 | 16 | 11 | 0 | 1 | 0 | 0 | 10 | 0 | 0 | .000 | 1 | 12 | 0 | 1 | 2.6 | 1.000 |

Al Lukens

LUKENS, ALBERT P.
B. 1872, Vineland, N. J. Deceased.

| 1894 | PHI | N | 0 | 1 | .000 | 10.20 | 3 | 2 | 1 | 15 | 26 | 10 | 0 | 0 | 0 | 0 | 0 | 8 | 0 | 0 | .000 | 0 | 1 | 0 | 0 | 0.3 | 1.000 |

Ralph Lumenti

LUMENTI, RAPHAEL ANTHONY (Commuter)
B. Dec. 21, 1936, Milford, Mass.   BL TL 6'3"   185 lbs.

1957	WAS	A	0	1	.000	6.75	3	2	0	9.1	9	5	8	0	0	0	0	2	0	0	.000	0	1	0	1	0.3	1.000
1958			1	2	.333	8.57	8	4	0	21	21	36	20	0	0	0	0	8	2	0	.250	0	4	0	0	0.5	1.000
1959			0	0	–	0.00	2	0	0	3	2	1	2	0	0	0	0	0	0	0	–	0	0	0	0	0.0	–
3 yrs.			1	3	.250	7.29	13	6	0	33.1	32	42	30	0	0	0	0	10	2	0	.200	0	5	0	1	0.4	1.000

Memo Luna

LUNA, GUILLERMO ROMERO
B. June 25, 1930, Tacubaya, Mexico   BL TL 6'   168 lbs.

| 1954 | STL | N | 0 | 1 | .000 | 27.00 | 1 | 1 | 0 | .2 | 2 | 2 | 0 | 0 | 0 | 0 | 0 | 0 | 0 | 0 | – | 0 | 0 | 0 | 0 | 0.0 | – |

Year	Team		W	L	PCT	ERA	G	GS	CG	IP	H	BB	SO	ShO	Relief Pitching W	L	SV	Batting AB	H	HR	BA	PO	A	E	DP	TC/G	FA

Jack Lundbom
LUNDBOM, JOHN FREDERICK   BR TR 6'2"   187 lbs.
B. Mar. 10, 1877, Manistee, Mich.   D. Oct. 31, 1949, Manistee, Mich.

Year	Team		W	L	PCT	ERA	G	GS	CG	IP	H	BB	SO	ShO	W	L	SV	AB	H	HR	BA	PO	A	E	DP	TC/G	FA
1902	CLE	A	1	1	.500	6.62	8	3	1	34	48	16	7	0	1	0	0	15	4	0	.267	0	8	0	1	1.0	1.000

Carl Lundgren
LUNDGREN, CARL LEONARD   BR TR 5'11"   175 lbs.
B. Feb. 16, 1880, Marengo, Ill.   D. Aug. 21, 1934, Marengo, Ill.

Year	Team		W	L	PCT	ERA	G	GS	CG	IP	H	BB	SO	ShO	W	L	SV	AB	H	HR	BA	PO	A	E	DP	TC/G	FA
1902	CHI	N	9	9	.500	1.97	18	18	17	160	158	45	68	1	0	0	0	66	7	0	.106	8	27	5	2	2.2	.875
1903			10	9	.526	2.94	27	20	16	193	191	60	67	0	1	0	3	61	7	0	.115	8	40	1	0	1.8	.980
1904			17	10	.630	2.60	31	27	25	242	203	77	106	2	1	0	1	90	20	0	.222	21	56	4	2	2.6	.951
1905			13	4	.765	2.24	23	19	16	169	132	53	69	3	0	0	0	61	11	0	.180	11	51	3	1	2.4	.954
1906			17	6	.739	2.21	27	24	21	207.2	160	89	103	5	0	0	2	67	12	0	.179	10	53	1	2	2.4	.984
1907			18	7	.720	1.17	28	25	21	207	130	92	84	7	3	0	0	66	7	0	.106	6	56	1	1	2.3	.984
1908			6	9	.400	4.22	23	15	9	138.2	149	56	38	1	1	0	0	47	7	0	.149	6	24	1	0	1.3	.968
1909			0	1	.000	4.15	2	1	0	4.1	6	4	0	0	0	0	0	2	1	0	.500	0	0	0	0	0.0	—
8 yrs.			90	55	.621	2.42	179	149	125	1321.2	1129	476	535	19	6	0	6	460	72	0	.157	70	307	16	9	2.2	.959

Del Lundgren
LUNDGREN, EBIN DELMAR   BR TR 5'8"   160 lbs.
B. Sept. 21, 1899, Lindsborg, Kans.   D. Oct. 19, 1984, Lindsborg, Kans.

Year	Team		W	L	PCT	ERA	G	GS	CG	IP	H	BB	SO	ShO	W	L	SV	AB	H	HR	BA	PO	A	E	DP	TC/G	FA
1924	PIT	N	0	1	.000	6.48	8	1	0	16.2	25	3	4	0	0	0	0	3	0	0	.000	0	6	0	0	0.8	1.000
1926	BOS	A	0	2	.000	8.07	17	1	0	29	35	24	10	0	0	1	0	4	0	0	.000	1	9	1	0	0.6	.909
1927			5	12	.294	6.27	30	17	5	136.1	160	87	39	2	0	2	0	44	7	0	.159	6	22	0	1	0.9	1.000
3 yrs.			5	15	.250	6.58	55	19	5	182	220	114	53	2	0	3	0	51	7	0	.137	7	37	1	1	0.8	.978

Dolf Luque
LUQUE, ADOLFO (The Pride Of Havana)   BR TR 5'7"   160 lbs.
B. Aug. 4, 1890, Havana, Cuba   D. July 3, 1957, Havana, Cuba

Year	Team		W	L	PCT	ERA	G	GS	CG	IP	H	BB	SO	ShO	W	L	SV	AB	H	HR	BA	PO	A	E	DP	TC/G	FA
1914	BOS	N	0	1	.000	4.15	2	1	1	8.2	5	4	1	0	0	0	0	2	0	0	.000	1	0	0	0	0.5	1.000
1915			0	0	—	3.60	2	1	0	5	6	4	3	0	0	0	0	2	0	0	.000	2	0	0	0	1.0	1.000
1918	CIN	N	6	3	.667	3.80	12	10	9	83	84	32	26	1	0	0	0	28	9	0	.321	2	23	1	1	2.2	.962
1919			9	3	.750	2.63	30	9	6	106	89	36	40	2	3	0	3	32	4	0	.125	6	34	0	1	1.3	1.000
1920			13	9	.591	2.51	37	23	10	207.2	168	60	72	1	1	1	1	64	17	0	.266	11	47	4	2	1.7	.935
1921			17	19	.472	3.38	41	36	25	304	318	64	102	3	0	1	3	111	30	0	.270	21	76	5	3	2.5	.951
1922			13	23	.361	3.31	39	32	18	261	266	72	79	0	3	2	0	86	18	0	.209	13	61	3	0	2.0	.961
1923			27	8	.771	1.93	41	37	28	322	279	88	151	6	1	0	2	104	21	1	.202	17	71	2	4	2.2	.978
1924			10	15	.400	3.16	31	28	13	219.1	229	53	86	2	0	0	0	73	13	1	.178	11	57	6	1	2.4	.919
1925			16	18	.471	2.63	36	36	22	291	263	78	140	4	0	0	0	102	26	2	.255	15	84	7	3	2.9	.934
1926			13	16	.448	3.43	34	30	16	233.2	231	77	83	1	1	0	0	78	27	0	.346	12	65	3	2	2.4	.963
1927			13	12	.520	3.20	29	27	17	230.2	225	56	76	2	1	0	0	83	18	0	.217	18	64	5	4	3.0	.943
1928			11	10	.524	3.57	33	29	11	234.1	254	84	72	1	0	0	1	67	8	0	.119	15	43	3	3	1.8	.950
1929			5	16	.238	4.50	32	22	8	176	213	56	43	1	0	1	0	54	15	1	.278	9	40	0	2	1.5	1.000
1930	BKN	N	14	8	.636	4.30	31	24	16	199	221	58	62	2	1	0	2	75	18	0	.240	8	45	1	0	1.7	.981
1931			7	6	.538	4.56	19	15	5	102.2	122	27	25	0	2	0	0	30	4	0	.133	3	19	0	1	1.2	1.000
1932	NY	N	6	7	.462	4.01	38	5	1	110	128	32	32	0	6	3	5	25	1	0	.040	19	23	1	2	1.1	.977
1933			8	2	.800	2.69	35	0	0	80.1	75	19	23	0	8	2	4	19	5	0	.263	3	19	0	0	0.6	1.000
1934			4	3	.571	3.83	26	0	0	42.1	54	17	12	0	4	3	7	7	2	0	.286	4	14	2	1	0.8	.900
1935			1	0	1.000	0.00	2	0	0	3.2	1	1	2	0	1	0	0	1	1	0	1.000	0	0	0	0	0.0	—
20 yrs.			193	179	.519	3.24	550	365	206	3220.1	3231	918	1130	26	32	16	28	1043	237	5	.227	188	786	43	29	1.8	.958

WORLD SERIES

Year	Team		W	L	PCT	ERA	G	GS	CG	IP	H	BB	SO	ShO	W	L	SV	AB	H	HR	BA	PO	A	E	DP	TC/G	FA
1919	CIN	N	0	0	—	0.00	2	0	0	5	1	0	6	0	0	0	0	1	0	0	.000	1	0	0	0	0.5	1.000
1933	NY	N	1	0	1.000	0.00	1	0	0	4.1	2	2	5	0	1	0	0	1	1	0	1.000	1	0	0	0	1.0	1.000
2 yrs.			1	0	1.000	0.00	3	0	0	9.1	3	2	11	0	1	0	0	2	1	0	.500	2	0	0	0	0.7	1.000

Johnny Lush
LUSH, JOHN CHARLES   BL TL 5'9½"   165 lbs.
B. Oct. 8, 1885, Williamsport, Pa.   D. Nov. 18, 1946, Beverly Hills, Calif.

Year	Team		W	L	PCT	ERA	G	GS	CG	IP	H	BB	SO	ShO	W	L	SV	AB	H	HR	BA	PO	A	E	DP	TC/G	FA
1904	PHI	N	0	6	.000	3.59	7	6	3	42.2	52	27	27	0	0	0	0	369	102	2	.276	3	13	1	1	2.4	.941
1905			2	0	1.000	1.59	2	2	1	17	12	8	8	0	0	0	0	16	5	0	.313	0	6	1	0	3.5	.857
1906			18	15	.545	2.37	37	35	24	281	254	119	151	5	0	0	0	212	56	0	.264	18	89	11	2	3.2	.907
1907	2 teams	PHI N (8G 3-5)						STL N	(20G 7-10)																		
"	total		10	15	.400	2.64	28	27	20	201.1	180	63	91	6	0	0	1	122	31	0	.254	11	53	4	4	2.4	.941
1908	STL	N	11	18	.379	2.12	38	32	23	250.2	221	57	93	3	1	0	1	89	15	0	.169	15	73	7	0	2.5	.926
1909			11	18	.379	3.13	34	28	21	221.1	215	69	66	2	0	1	0	92	22	0	.239	5	64	4	0	2.1	.945
1910			14	13	.519	3.20	36	24	13	225.1	235	70	54	1	0	0	0	93	21	0	.226	2	56	5	2	1.9	.928
7 yrs.			66	85	.437	2.68	182	154	105	1239.1	1169	413	490	17	5	4	2	*				60	354	33	9	2.5	.926

Jim Lyle
LYLE, JAMES CHARLES   BR TR 6'1"   180 lbs.
B. July 24, 1900, Lake, Miss.   D. Oct. 10, 1977, Williamsport, Pa.

Year	Team		W	L	PCT	ERA	G	GS	CG	IP	H	BB	SO	ShO	W	L	SV	AB	H	HR	BA	PO	A	E	DP	TC/G	FA
1925	WAS	A	0	0	—	6.00	1	0	0	3	5	1	3	0	0	0	0	1	0	0	.000	0	0	0	0	0.0	—

Sparky Lyle
LYLE, ALBERT WALTER   BL TL 6'1"   182 lbs.
B. July 22, 1944, DuBois, Pa.

Year	Team		W	L	PCT	ERA	G	GS	CG	IP	H	BB	SO	ShO	W	L	SV	AB	H	HR	BA	PO	A	E	DP	TC/G	FA
1967	BOS	A	1	2	.333	2.28	27	0	0	43.1	33	14	42	0	1	2	5	8	2	0	.250	2	5	0	0	0.3	1.000
1968			6	1	.857	2.74	49	0	0	65.2	67	14	52	0	6	1	11	8	1	0	.125	5	6	3	0	0.3	.786
1969			8	3	.727	2.54	71	0	0	102.2	91	48	93	0	8	3	17	17	2	0	.118	3	19	3	3	0.4	.880
1970			1	7	.125	3.90	63	0	0	67	62	34	51	0	1	7	20	13	0	0	.000	1	7	0	0	0.1	1.000
1971			6	4	.600	2.77	50	0	0	52	41	23	37	0	6	4	16	3	3	0	1.000	2	10	0	1	0.2	1.000
1972	NY	A	9	5	.643	1.91	59	0	0	108.1	84	29	75	0	9	5	35	21	4	0	.190	4	11	0	0	0.3	1.000
1973			5	9	.357	2.51	51	0	0	82.1	66	18	63	0	5	9	27	0	0	0	—	2	13	2	2	0.3	.882
1974			9	3	.750	1.66	66	0	0	114	93	43	89	0	9	3	15	0	0	0	—	2	11	1	2	0.2	.933
1975			5	7	.417	3.12	49	0	0	89.1	94	36	65	0	5	7	6	0	0	0	—	2	16	4	1	0.4	.818
1976			7	8	.467	2.26	64	0	0	103.2	82	42	61	0	7	8	23	0	0	0	—	3	11	2	1	0.3	.875
1977			13	5	.722	2.17	72	0	0	137	131	33	68	0	13	5	26	0	0	0	—	2	22	2	0	0.4	.923
1978			9	3	.750	3.47	59	0	0	111.2	116	33	33	0	9	3	9	0	0	0	—	9	18	1	3	0.5	.964

Year	Team		W	L	PCT	ERA	G	GS	CG	IP	H	BB	SO	ShO	Relief Pitching W	L	SV	Batting AB	H	HR	BA	PO	A	E	DP	TC/G	FA

Sparky Lyle *continued*

Year	Team		W	L	PCT	ERA	G	GS	CG	IP	H	BB	SO	ShO	W	L	SV	AB	H	HR	BA	PO	A	E	DP	TC/G	FA
1979	TEX	A	5	8	.385	3.13	67	0	0	95	78	28	48	0	5	8	13	0	0	0	–	2	11	2	0	0.2	.867
1980	2 teams	TEX A	(49G 3–2)			PHI N	(10G 0–0)																				
"	total		3	2	.600	4.26	59	0	0	95	108	34	49	0	3	2	10	0	0	0	–	4	10	0	0	0.2	1.000
1981	PHI	N	9	6	.600	4.44	48	0	0	75	85	33	29	0	9	6	2	5	2	0	.400	6	17	0	0	0.5	1.000
1982	2 teams	PHI N	(34G 3–3)			CHI A	(11G 0–0)																				
"	total		3	3	.500	4.62	45	0	0	48.2	61	19	18	0	3	3	3	2	1	0	.500	4	11	1	1	0.4	.938
16 yrs.			99	76	.566	2.88	899	0	0	1390.2	1292	481	873	0	99	76	238	78	15	0	.192	54	198	21	14	0.3	.923
						7th									5th		6th										

DIVISIONAL PLAYOFF SERIES

Year	Team		W	L	PCT	ERA	G	GS	CG	IP	H	BB	SO	ShO	W	L	SV	AB	H	HR	BA	PO	A	E	DP	TC/G	FA
1981	PHI	N	0	0	–	0.00	3	0	0	2.1	4	2	1	0	0	0	0	0	0	0	–	0	0	0	0	0.0	–

LEAGUE CHAMPIONSHIP SERIES

Year	Team		W	L	PCT	ERA	G	GS	CG	IP	H	BB	SO	ShO	W	L	SV	AB	H	HR	BA	PO	A	E	DP	TC/G	FA
1976	NY	A	0	0	–	0.00	1	0	0	1	0	1	0	0	0	0	1	0	0	0	–	0	0	0	0	0.0	–
1977			2	0	1.000	0.96	4	0	0	9.1	7	0	3	0	2	0	0	0	0	0	–	0	0	0	0	0.0	–
1978			0	0	–	13.50	1	0	0	1.1	3	0	0	0	0	0	0	0	0	0	–	1	1	0	0	2.0	1.000
3 yrs.			2	0	1.000	2.31	6	0	0	11.2	10	1	3	0	2	0	1	0	0	0	–	1	1	0	0	0.3	1.000

WORLD SERIES

Year	Team		W	L	PCT	ERA	G	GS	CG	IP	H	BB	SO	ShO	W	L	SV	AB	H	HR	BA	PO	A	E	DP	TC/G	FA
1976	NY	A	0	0	–	0.00	2	0	0	2.2	1	0	2	0	0	0	0	0	0	0	.000	0	0	0	0	0.0	–
1977			1	0	1.000	1.93	2	0	0	4.2	2	0	3	0	1	0	0	2	0	0	.000	0	0	0	0	0.0	–
2 yrs.			1	0	1.000	1.23	4	0	0	7.1	3	0	5	0	1	0	0	2	0	0	.000	0	0	0	0	0.0	–

Adrian Lynch

LYNCH, ADRIAN RYAN
B. Feb. 9, 1897, Laurens, Iowa D. Mar. 16, 1934, Davenport, Iowa
BB TR 6'1½" 185 lbs.

Year	Team		W	L	PCT	ERA	G	GS	CG	IP	H	BB	SO	ShO	W	L	SV	AB	H	HR	BA	PO	A	E	DP	TC/G	FA
1920	STL	A	2	0	1.000	5.24	5	3	1	22.1	23	17	8	0	0	0	0	9	2	0	.222	0	4	1	0	1.0	.800

Ed Lynch

LYNCH, EDWARD FRANCIS
B. Feb. 25, 1956, Brooklyn, N. Y.
BR TR 6'5" 210 lbs.

Year	Team		W	L	PCT	ERA	G	GS	CG	IP	H	BB	SO	ShO	W	L	SV	AB	H	HR	BA	PO	A	E	DP	TC/G	FA
1980	NY	N	1	1	.500	5.21	5	4	0	19	24	5	9	0	0	0	0	6	2	0	.333	1	3	0	1	0.8	1.000
1981			4	5	.444	2.93	17	13	0	80	79	21	27	0	0	1	0	21	3	0	.143	7	9	1	0	1.0	.941
1982			4	8	.333	3.55	43	12	0	139.1	145	40	51	0	1	3	2	33	0	0	.000	6	18	0	0	0.6	1.000
1983			10	10	.500	4.28	30	27	1	174.2	208	41	44	0	1	0	0	52	8	0	.154	10	24	0	0	1.1	1.000
1984			9	8	.529	4.50	40	13	0	124	169	24	62	0	5	0	2	27	6	0	.222	9	13	1	0	0.6	.957
1985			10	8	.556	3.44	31	29	6	191	188	27	65	0	1	0	0	52	4	0	.077	15	14	2	2	1.0	.935
1986	2 teams	NY N	(1G 0–0)			CHI N	(23G 7–5)																				
"	total		7	5	.583	3.73	24	13	1	101.1	107	23	58	1	3	1	0	30	1	0	.033	7	12	0	2	0.8	1.000
1987	CHI	N	2	9	.182	5.38	58	8	0	110.1	130	48	80	0	0	5	4	16	3	0	.188	9	17	0	2	0.4	1.000
8 yrs.			47	54	.465	4.00	248	119	8	939.2	1050	229	396	2	10	10	8	237	27	0	.114	64	110	4	7	0.7	.978

Jack Lynch

LYNCH, JOHN H.
B. Feb. 5, 1857, New York, N. Y. D. Apr. 19, 1923, Bronx, N. Y.
BR TR 5'8" 185 lbs.

Year	Team		W	L	PCT	ERA	G	GS	CG	IP	H	BB	SO	ShO	W	L	SV	AB	H	HR	BA	PO	A	E	DP	TC/G	FA
1881	BUF	N	10	9	.526	3.59	20	19	17	165.2	203	29	32	1	0	0	0	78	13	0	.167	9	39	4	0	2.6	.923
1883	NY	AA	13	15	.464	4.09	29	29	29	255	263	25	119	1	0	0	0	107	20	0	.187	18	46	20	0	2.9	.738
1884			37	15	.712	2.64	54	53	53	487	410	42	286	5	1	0	1	195	30	0	.154	24	80	37	3	2.6	.738
1885			23	21	.523	3.61	44	43	43	379	410	42	177	1	1	0	0	153	30	0	.196	11	34	4	0	1.1	.918
1886			20	30	.400	3.95	51	50	50	432.2	485	116	193	1	0	0	0	169	27	0	.160	9	65	11	0	1.7	.871
1887			7	14	.333	5.10	21	21	21	187	245	36	45	0	0	0	0	83	14	0	.169	7	59	6	1	3.4	.917
1890	BKN	AA	0	1	.000	12.00	1	1	1	9	22	5	1	0	0	0	0	4	3	0	.750	2	5	0	0	7.0	1.000
7 yrs.			110	105	.512	3.69	220	216	214	1915.1	2038	295	853	8	1	1	0	789	137	0	.174	80	328	82	4	2.2	.833

Mike Lynch

LYNCH, MICHAEL JOSEPH
B. June 28, 1880, Holyoke, Mass. D. Apr. 2, 1927, Garrison, N. Y.
BR TR 5'10" 155 lbs.

Year	Team		W	L	PCT	ERA	G	GS	CG	IP	H	BB	SO	ShO	W	L	SV	AB	H	HR	BA	PO	A	E	DP	TC/G	FA
1904	PIT	N	15	11	.577	2.71	27	24	24	222.2	200	91	95	1	1	1	0	87	20	0	.230	11	49	6	1	2.4	.909
1905			17	8	.680	3.80	33	22	13	206	191	107	106	1	5	1	2	81	11	0	.136	16	53	3	2	2.2	.958
1906			6	5	.545	2.42	18	12	7	119	101	31	48	1	2	0	0	39	8	0	.205	4	31	1	1	2.0	.972
1907	2 teams	PIT N	(7G 2–2)			NY N	(12G 3–6)																				
"	total		5	8	.385	3.00	19	14	9	108	105	52	43	0	0	0	0	39	11	0	.282	7	35	0	3	2.2	1.000
4 yrs.			43	32	.573	3.05	97	72	53	655.2	597	281	292	1	8	2	2	246	50	0	.203	38	168	10	7	2.2	.954

Thomas Lynch

LYNCH, THOMAS S.
B. 1863, Peru, Ill. D. May 13, 1923, Peru, Ill.
BL 5'11" 175 lbs.

Year	Team		W	L	PCT	ERA	G	GS	CG	IP	H	BB	SO	ShO	W	L	SV	AB	H	HR	BA	PO	A	E	DP	TC/G	FA
1884	CHI	N	0	0	–	2.57	1	1	0	7	7	3	2	0	0	0	0	4	0	0	.000	3	1	0	0	4.0	1.000

Red Lynn

LYNN, JAPHET MONROE
B. Dec. 27, 1913, Kenney, Tex. D. Oct. 27, 1977, Bellville, Tex.
BR TR 6' 162 lbs.

Year	Team		W	L	PCT	ERA	G	GS	CG	IP	H	BB	SO	ShO	W	L	SV	AB	H	HR	BA	PO	A	E	DP	TC/G	FA
1939	2 teams	DET A	(4G 0–1)			NY N	(26G 1–0)																				
"	total		1	1	.500	3.88	30	0	0	58	55	24	25	0	1	1	1	8	0	0	.000	2	6	2	0	0.3	.800
1940	NY	N	4	3	.571	3.83	33	0	0	42.1	40	24	25	0	4	3	3	4	0	0	.000	1	3	0	0	0.1	1.000
1944	CHI	N	5	4	.556	4.06	22	7	4	84.1	80	37	35	1	0	2	1	29	6	0	.207	7	20	0	2	1.2	1.000
3 yrs.			10	8	.556	3.95	85	7	4	184.2	175	85	85	1	5	6	5	41	6	0	.146	10	29	2	2	0.5	.951

Al Lyons

LYONS, ALBERT HAROLD
B. July 18, 1918, St. Joseph, Mo. D. Dec. 20, 1965, Inglewood, Calif.
BR TR 6'2" 195 lbs.

Year	Team		W	L	PCT	ERA	G	GS	CG	IP	H	BB	SO	ShO	W	L	SV	AB	H	HR	BA	PO	A	E	DP	TC/G	FA
1944	NY	A	0	0	–	4.54	11	0	0	39.2	43	24	14	0	0	0	0	26	9	0	.346	1	4	0	0	0.5	1.000
1946			0	1	.000	5.40	7	0	0	8.1	11	6	4	0	0	1	0	4	0	0	.000	1	2	0	0	1.5	1.000
1947	2 teams	NY A	(6G 1–0)			PIT N	(13G 1–2)																				
"	total		2	2	.500	7.78	19	0	0	39.1	54	21	23	0	2	2	0	16	6	1	.375	4	11	1	2	0.8	.938
1948	BOS	N	1	0	1.000	7.82	2	0	0	12.2	17	8	5	0	1	0	0	12	2	0	.167	3	8	0	0	1.6	1.000
4 yrs.			3	3	.500	6.30	39	0	0	100	125	59	46	0	3	2	0	58	17	1	.293	9	25	1	2	0.9	.971

George Lyons

LYONS, GEORGE TONY (Smooth)
B. Jan. 25, 1891, Bible Grove, Ill.   D. Aug. 12, 1981, Nevada, Mo.
BR TR   5'11''   180 lbs.

Year	Team	W	L	PCT	ERA	G	GS	CG	IP	H	BB	SO	ShO	Relief W	Relief L	Relief SV	AB	H	HR	BA	PO	A	E	DP	TC/G	FA
1920	STL N	2	1	.667	3.09	7	2	1	23.1	21	9	5	0	1	0	0	7	1	0	.143	1	9	0	1	1.4	1.000
1924	STL A	3	2	.600	4.93	25	6	2	76.2	95	44	25	0	1	0	0	20	5	0	.250	5	24	0	0	1.2	1.000
2 yrs.		5	3	.625	4.50	32	8	3	100	116	53	30	0	2	0	0	27	6	0	.222	6	33	0	1	1.2	1.000

Harry Lyons

LYONS, HARRY P.
B. Mar. 25, 1866, Chester, Pa.   D. June 30, 1912, Mauricetown, N. J.
BR TR   5'10½''   157 lbs.

Year	Team	W	L	PCT	ERA	G	GS	CG	IP	H	BB	SO	ShO	Relief W	Relief L	Relief SV	AB	H	HR	BA	PO	A	E	DP	TC/G	FA
1890	ROC AA	0	0	-	12.27	1	0	0	3.2	8	1	2	0	0	0	0	*				0	2	0	0	2.0	1.000

Hersh Lyons

LYONS, HERSCHEL ENGLEBERT
B. July 23, 1915, Fresno, Calif.
BR TR   5'11''   195 lbs.

Year	Team	W	L	PCT	ERA	G	GS	CG	IP	H	BB	SO	ShO	Relief W	Relief L	Relief SV	AB	H	HR	BA	PO	A	E	DP	TC/G	FA
1941	STL N	0	0	-	0.00	1	0	0	1.1	3	1	3	0	0	0	0	0	0	0	-	0	0	0	0	0.0	-

Ted Lyons

LYONS, THEODORE AMAR
B. Dec. 28, 1900, Lake Charles, La.
D. July 25, 1986, Sulphur, La.
Manager 1946-48.
Hall of Fame 1955.
BB TR   5'11''   200 lbs.
BR 1925-27

Year	Team	W	L	PCT	ERA	G	GS	CG	IP	H	BB	SO	ShO	Relief W	Relief L	Relief SV	AB	H	HR	BA	PO	A	E	DP	TC/G	FA
1923	CHI A	2	1	.667	6.35	9	1	0	22.2	30	15	6	0	2	0	0	5	1	0	.200	3	7	0	1	1.1	1.000
1924		12	11	.522	4.87	41	22	12	216.1	279	72	52	0	1	1	3	77	17	0	.221	3	45	5	2	1.3	.906
1925		21	11	.656	3.26	43	32	19	262.2	274	83	45	5	2	2	3	97	18	0	.186	8	80	4	3	2.1	.957
1926		18	16	.529	3.01	39	31	24	283.2	268	106	51	3	1	3	2	104	22	0	.212	16	91	5	3	2.9	.955
1927		22	14	.611	2.84	39	34	30	307.2	291	67	71	2	0	2	2	110	28	1	.255	13	79	2	3	2.4	.979
1928		15	14	.517	3.98	39	27	21	240	276	68	60	0	3	1	6	91	23	0	.253	20	60	7	6	2.2	.920
1929		14	20	.412	4.10	37	31	21	259.1	276	76	57	1	1	3	2	91	20	0	.220	21	66	5	4	2.5	.946
1930		22	15	.595	3.78	42	36	29	297.2	331	57	69	1	0	1	1	122	38	1	.311	14	77	6	5	2.3	.938
1931		4	6	.400	4.01	22	12	7	101	117	33	16	0	1	1	0	33	5	0	.152	4	18	1	3	1.0	.957
1932		10	15	.400	3.28	33	26	19	230.2	243	71	58	1	0	1	2	73	19	1	.260	11	42	2	1	1.7	.964
1933		10	21	.323	4.38	36	27	14	228	260	74	74	2	4	3	1	91	26	1	.286	10	49	1	3	1.7	.983
1934		11	13	.458	4.87	30	24	21	205.1	249	66	53	0	1	1	1	97	20	1	.206	12	50	4	4	2.2	.939
1935		15	8	.652	3.02	23	22	19	190.2	194	56	54	3	0	0	1	82	18	0	.220	9	31	0	1	1.7	1.000
1936		10	13	.435	5.14	26	24	15	182	227	45	48	1	0	0	0	70	11	0	.157	12	38	0	1	1.9	1.000
1937		12	7	.632	4.15	22	22	11	169.1	182	45	45	0	0	0	0	57	12	0	.211	6	33	0	3	1.8	1.000
1938		9	11	.450	3.70	23	23	17	194.2	238	52	54	1	0	0	0	72	14	0	.194	9	46	1	1	2.4	.982
1939		14	6	.700	2.76	21	21	16	172.2	162	26	65	0	0	0	0	61	18	0	.295	9	22	3	3	1.6	.912
1940		12	8	.600	3.24	22	22	17	186.1	188	37	72	4	0	0	0	75	18	0	.240	12	24	3	1	1.8	.923
1941		12	10	.545	3.70	22	22	19	187.1	199	37	63	2	0	0	0	74	20	0	.270	17	36	1	3	2.5	.981
1942		14	6	.700	2.10	20	20	20	180.1	167	26	50	1	0	0	0	67	16	0	.239	8	41	1	4	2.5	.980
1946		1	4	.200	2.32	5	5	5	42.2	38	9	10	0	0	0	0	14	0	0	.000					2.4	1.000
21 yrs.		260	230	.531	3.67	594	484	356	4161	4489	1121	1073	27	17	21	23	*				219	945	51	57	2.0	.958

Toby Lyons

LYONS, THOMAS A.
B. Mar. 27, 1869, Cambridge, Mass.   D. Aug. 27, 1920, Boston, Mass.

Year	Team	W	L	PCT	ERA	G	GS	CG	IP	H	BB	SO	ShO	Relief W	Relief L	Relief SV	AB	H	HR	BA	PO	A	E	DP	TC/G	FA
1890	SYR AA	0	2	.000	10.48	3	3	2	22.1	40	21	6	0	0	0	0	12	4	0	.333	1	6	0	0	2.3	1.000

Rick Lysander

LYSANDER, RICHARD EUGENE
B. Feb. 21, 1953, Huntington Park, Calif.
BR TR   6'2''   195 lbs.

Year	Team	W	L	PCT	ERA	G	GS	CG	IP	H	BB	SO	ShO	Relief W	Relief L	Relief SV	AB	H	HR	BA	PO	A	E	DP	TC/G	FA
1980	OAK A	0	0	-	7.71	5	0	0	14	24	4	5	0	0	0	0	0	0	0	-	2	3	0	0	1.0	1.000
1983	MIN A	5	12	.294	3.38	61	4	1	125	132	43	58	1	4	9	3	0	0	0	-	19	14	1	2	0.6	.971
1984		4	3	.571	3.65	36	0	0	56.2	62	27	22	0	4	3	5	0	0	0	-	8	6	1	1	0.4	.933
1985		0	2	.000	6.05	35	1	0	61	72	22	26	0	0	1	3	0	0	0	-	7	5	0	0	0.3	1.000
4 yrs.		9	17	.346	4.31	137	5	1	256.2	290	96	111	1	8	13	11	0	0	0	-	36	28	2	3	0.5	.970

Bill Lyston

LYSTON, WILLIAM EDWARD
B. 1863, Baltimore, Md.   D. Aug. 4, 1944, Baltimore, Md.
TR

Year	Team	W	L	PCT	ERA	G	GS	CG	IP	H	BB	SO	ShO	Relief W	Relief L	Relief SV	AB	H	HR	BA	PO	A	E	DP	TC/G	FA
1891	COL AA	0	1	.000	10.50	1	1	1	6	10	6	1	0	0	0	0	2	0	0	.000	1	0	0	0	1.0	1.000
1894	CLE N	0	1	.000	9.82	1	1	0	3.2	5	4	0	0	0	0	0	2	0	0	.000	0	0	0	0	0.0	-
2 yrs.		0	2	.000	10.24	2	2	1	9.2	15	10	1	0	0	0	0	4	0	0	.000	1	0	0	0	0.5	1.000

Duke Maas

MAAS, DUANE FREDERICK
B. Jan. 31, 1929, Utica, Mich.   D. Dec. 7, 1976, Mt. Clemens, Mich.
BR TR   5'10''   170 lbs.

Year	Team	W	L	PCT	ERA	G	GS	CG	IP	H	BB	SO	ShO	Relief W	Relief L	Relief SV	AB	H	HR	BA	PO	A	E	DP	TC/G	FA
1955	DET A	5	6	.455	4.88	18	16	5	86.2	91	50	42	2	0	0	0	30	5	0	.167	2	17	0	0	1.1	1.000
1956		0	7	.000	6.54	26	7	0	63.1	81	32	34	0	0	0	1	16	3	0	.188	5	8	2	0	0.6	.867
1957		10	14	.417	3.28	45	26	8	219.1	210	65	116	2	1	2	6	71	6	1	.085	8	41	1	2	1.1	.980
1958	2 teams		KC A	(10G 4-5)	NY A	(22G 7-3)																				
"	total	11	8	.579	3.85	32	20	5	156.2	142	49	69	2	5	0	4	51	6	0	.118	12	19	1	0	1.0	.969
1959	NY A	14	8	.636	4.43	38	21	3	138	149	53	67	1	5	0	4	40	5	0	.125	5	28	1	2	0.9	.971
1960		5	1	.833	4.09	35	1	0	70.1	70	35	28	0	5	0	0	6	0	0	.000	8	13	2	3	0.7	.913
1961		0	0	-	54.00	1	0	0	.1	3	1	0	0	0	0	0	0	0	0	-	0	0	0	0	0.0	-
7 yrs.		45	44	.506	4.19	195	91	21	734.2	745	284	356	7	13	5	15	214	25	1	.117	40	126	7	7	0.9	.960

WORLD SERIES

Year	Team	W	L	PCT	ERA	G	GS	CG	IP	H	BB	SO	ShO	Relief W	Relief L	Relief SV	AB	H	HR	BA	PO	A	E	DP	TC/G	FA
1958	NY A	0	0	-	81.00	1	0	0	.1	1	0	0	0	0	0	0	-				0	0	0	0	0.0	-
1960		0	0	-	4.50	1	0	0	2	3	1	1	0	0	0	0	-				0	0	0	0	0.0	-
2 yrs.		0	0	-	15.43	2	0	0	2.1	4	1	1	0	0	0	0	-				0	0	0	0	0.0	-

Bob Mabe

MABE, ROBERT LEE
B. Oct. 8, 1929, Danville, Va.
BR TR   5'11''   165 lbs.

Year	Team	W	L	PCT	ERA	G	GS	CG	IP	H	BB	SO	ShO	Relief W	Relief L	Relief SV	AB	H	HR	BA	PO	A	E	DP	TC/G	FA
1958	STL N	3	9	.250	4.51	31	13	4	111.2	113	41	74	1	1	0	1	24	1	0	.042	11	17	1	1	0.9	.966
1959	CIN N	4	2	.667	5.46	18	1	0	29.2	29	19	8	0	4	2	3	7	0	0	.000	1	3	0	2	0.2	1.000

Year	Team		W	L	PCT	ERA	G	GS	CG	IP	H	BB	SO	ShO	Relief Pitching W	L	SV	Batting AB	H	HR	BA	PO	A	E	DP	TC/G	FA

Bob Mabe *continued*

Year	Team		W	L	PCT	ERA	G	GS	CG	IP	H	BB	SO	ShO	W	L	SV	AB	H	HR	BA	PO	A	E	DP	TC/G	FA
1960	BAL	A	0	0	–	27.00	2	0	0	.2	4	1	0	0	0	0	0	0	0	0	–	0	0	0	0	0.0	–
3 yrs.			7	11	.389	4.82	51	14	4	142	146	61	82	0	5	3	3	31	1	0	.032	12	20	1	3	0.6	.970

Mac MacArthur

MacARTHUR, MALCOLM M. TR
B. Jan. 19, 1862, Glasgow, Scotland D. Oct. 18, 1932, Detroit, Mich.

Year	Team		W	L	PCT	ERA	G	GS	CG	IP	H	BB	SO	ShO	W	L	SV	AB	H	HR	BA	PO	A	E	DP	TC/G	FA
1884	IND	AA	1	5	.167	5.02	6	6	6	52	57	21	19	0	0	0	0	21	2	0	.095	1	12	5	1	3.0	.722

Frank MacCormick

MacCORMICK, FRANK LOUIS BR TR 6'4" 210 lbs.
B. Sept. 21, 1954, Jersey City, N. J.

Year	Team		W	L	PCT	ERA	G	GS	CG	IP	H	BB	SO	ShO	W	L	SV	AB	H	HR	BA	PO	A	E	DP	TC/G	FA
1976	DET	A	0	5	.000	5.73	9	8	0	33	35	34	14	0	0	0	0	3	0	0	.000	4	3	0	0	0.8	1.000
1977	SEA	A	0	0	–	3.86	3	3	0	7	4	12	4	0	0	0	0	0	0	0	–	0	1	0	0	0.3	1.000
2 yrs.			0	5	.000	5.40	12	11	0	40	39	46	18	0	0	0	0	3	0	0	.000	4	4	0	0	0.7	1.000

Bill MacDonald

MacDONALD, WILLIAM PAUL BR TR 5'10" 170 lbs.
B. Mar. 28, 1929, Alameda, Calif.

Year	Team		W	L	PCT	ERA	G	GS	CG	IP	H	BB	SO	ShO	W	L	SV	AB	H	HR	BA	PO	A	E	DP	TC/G	FA
1950	PIT	N	8	10	.444	4.29	32	20	6	153	138	88	60	2	1	1	1	49	6	0	.122	5	15	1	1	0.7	.952
1953			0	1	.000	12.27	4	1	0	7.1	12	8	4	0	0	0	0	0	0	0	–	0	1	0	0	0.3	1.000
2 yrs.			8	11	.421	4.66	36	21	6	160.1	150	96	64	2	1	1	1	49	6	0	.122	5	16	1	1	0.6	.955

Harry Mace

MACE, HARRY F. 5'11" 185 lbs.
B. 1870, Washington, D. C. Deceased.

Year	Team		W	L	PCT	ERA	G	GS	CG	IP	H	BB	SO	ShO	W	L	SV	AB	H	HR	BA	PO	A	E	DP	TC/G	FA
1891	WAS	AA	0	1	.000	7.31	3	1	1	16	18	8	3	0	0	0	0	6	0	0	.000	0	4	1	0	1.7	.800

Danny MacFayden

MacFAYDEN, DANIEL KNOWLES (Deacon Danny) BR TR 5'11" 170 lbs.
B. June 10, 1905, North Truro, Mass. D. Aug. 26, 1972, Brunswick, Me.

Year	Team		W	L	PCT	ERA	G	GS	CG	IP	H	BB	SO	ShO	W	L	SV	AB	H	HR	BA	PO	A	E	DP	TC/G	FA
1926	BOS	A	0	1	.000	4.85	3	1	1	13	10	7	1	0	0	0	0	3	1	0	.333	1	6	0	2	2.3	1.000
1927			5	8	.385	4.27	34	16	6	160.1	176	59	42	1	2	1	2	46	13	1	.283	3	35	3	0	1.2	.927
1928			9	15	.375	4.75	33	28	9	195	215	78	61	0	1	0	0	63	9	0	.143	8	42	0	1	1.5	1.000
1929			10	18	.357	3.62	32	26	14	221	225	81	61	4	0	0	0	74	13	0	.176	6	60	3	2	2.2	.957
1930			11	14	.440	4.21	36	33	18	269.1	293	93	76	1	0	2	0	92	13	0	.141	17	60	3	4	2.2	.963
1931			16	12	.571	4.02	35	32	17	230.2	263	79	74	2	1	0	0	81	10	0	.123	12	56	1	5	2.0	.986
1932	2 teams		BOS A	(12G 1–10)		NY A	(17G 7–5)																					
"	total		8	15	.348	4.39	29	26	14	199	228	70	62	0	0	0	1	74	8	0	.108	11	35	7	4	1.8	.868
1933	NY	A	3	2	.600	5.88	25	6	2	90.1	120	37	28	0	0	0	1	34	1	0	.029	4	19	2	2	1.0	.920
1934			4	3	.571	4.50	22	11	4	96	110	31	41	0	0	0	0	39	4	0	.103	3	15	1	1	0.9	.947
1935	2 teams		CIN N	(7G 1–2)		BOS N	(28G 5–13)																					
"	total		6	15	.286	5.04	35	24	8	187.2	239	47	59	1	0	2	0	62	9	0	.145	8	55	4	2	1.9	.940
1936	BOS	N	17	13	.567	2.87	37	31	21	266.2	268	66	86	2	2	1	0	83	8	0	.096	9	75	4	5	2.4	.955
1937			14	14	.500	2.93	32	32	16	246	250	60	70	2	0	0	0	83	13	0	.157	13	62	4	3	2.5	.949
1938			14	9	.609	2.95	29	29	19	219.2	211	64	58	5	0	0	0	77	9	0	.117	11	41	1	2	1.8	.981
1939			8	14	.364	3.90	33	28	8	191.2	221	59	46	0	0	0	2	67	12	0	.179	9	47	3	0	1.8	.949
1940	PIT	N	5	4	.556	3.55	35	8	0	91.1	112	27	24	0	4	2	2	28	5	0	.179	2	22	1	2	0.7	.960
1941	WAS	A	0	1	.000	10.29	5	0	0	7	12	5	3	0	0	1	0	0	0	0	–	0	3	0	1	0.6	1.000
1943	BOS	N	2	1	.667	5.91	10	1	0	21.1	31	9	5	0	2	1	0	4	1	0	.250	1	4	0	0	0.5	1.000
17 yrs.			132	159	.454	3.96	465	332	157	2706	2984	872	797	18	12	11	9	910	129	1	.142	118	637	37	36	1.7	.953

Julio Machado

MACHADO, JULIO SEGUNDO (Iguana Man) BR TR 6' 175 lbs.
B. Dec. 1, 1965, Zulia, Venezuela

Year	Team		W	L	PCT	ERA	G	GS	CG	IP	H	BB	SO	ShO	W	L	SV	AB	H	HR	BA	PO	A	E	DP	TC/G	FA
1989	NY	N	0	1	.000	3.27	10	0	0	11	9	3	14	0	0	1	0	0	0	0	–	2	0	0	0	0.2	1.000

Chuck Machemehl

MACHEMEHL, CHARLES WALTER BR TR 6'4" 200 lbs.
B. Apr. 20, 1947, Brenham, Tex.

Year	Team		W	L	PCT	ERA	G	GS	CG	IP	H	BB	SO	ShO	W	L	SV	AB	H	HR	BA	PO	A	E	DP	TC/G	FA
1971	CLE	A	0	2	.000	6.50	14	0	0	18	16	15	9	0	0	2	3	2	1	0	.500	1	3	0	0	0.3	1.000

Bill Mack

MACK, WILLIAM FRANCIS BL TL 6'1" 155 lbs.
B. Feb. 12, 1885, Elmira, N. Y. D. Sept. 30, 1971, Elmira, N. Y.

Year	Team		W	L	PCT	ERA	G	GS	CG	IP	H	BB	SO	ShO	W	L	SV	AB	H	HR	BA	PO	A	E	DP	TC/G	FA
1908	CHI	N	0	0	–	2.84	2	0	0	6.1	5	1	2	0	0	0	0	3	2	0	.667	0	2	1	0	1.5	.667

Frank Mack

MACK, FRANK GEORGE (Stubby) BR TR 6'1½" 180 lbs.
B. Feb. 2, 1900, Oklahoma City, Okla. D. July 2, 1971, Clearwater, Fla.

Year	Team		W	L	PCT	ERA	G	GS	CG	IP	H	BB	SO	ShO	W	L	SV	AB	H	HR	BA	PO	A	E	DP	TC/G	FA
1922	CHI	A	2	2	.500	3.67	8	2	2	34.1	36	16	11	1	0	0	0	12	3	0	.250	2	5	0	0	0.9	1.000
1923			0	1	.000	4.24	11	0	0	23.1	23	11	6	0	0	0	1	6	0	0	.000	0	7	0	1	0.6	1.000
1925			0	0	–	9.45	8	0	0	13.1	24	13	6	0	0	0	0	3	1	0	.333	0	2	0	0	0.3	1.000
3 yrs.			2	3	.400	4.94	27	2	2	71	83	40	23	1	0	0	1	21	4	0	.190	2	14	0	1	0.6	1.000

Tony Mack

MACK, TONY LYNN BR TR 5'10" 175 lbs.
B. Apr. 30, 1961, Lexington, Ky.

Year	Team		W	L	PCT	ERA	G	GS	CG	IP	H	BB	SO	ShO	W	L	SV	AB	H	HR	BA	PO	A	E	DP	TC/G	FA
1985	CAL	A	0	1	.000	15.43	1	1	0	2.1	8	1	0	0	0	0	0	0	0	0	–	0	0	0	0	0.0	–

Ken MacKenzie

MacKENZIE, KENNETH PURVIS BR TL 6' 185 lbs.
B. Mar. 10, 1934, Gore Bay, Ont., Canada

Year	Team		W	L	PCT	ERA	G	GS	CG	IP	H	BB	SO	ShO	W	L	SV	AB	H	HR	BA	PO	A	E	DP	TC/G	FA
1960	MIL	N	0	1	.000	6.48	9	0	0	8.1	9	3	9	0	0	1	0	1	0	0	.000	1	0	0	0	0.1	1.000
1961			0	0	–	5.14	5	0	0	7	8	2	7	0	0	0	0	2	0	0	.000	0	3	0	0	0.6	1.000
1962	NY	N	5	4	.556	4.95	42	1	0	80	87	34	51	0	5	3	1	12	1	0	.083	3	16	2	3	0.5	.905
1963	2 teams		NY N	(34G 3–1)		STL N	(8G 0–0)																					
"	total		3	1	.750	4.88	42	0	0	66.1	72	15	48	0	3	1	1	9	0	0	.000	3	6	2	0	0.3	.818
1964	SF	N	0	0	–	5.00	10	0	0	9	9	3	3	0	0	0	0	1	0	0	–	1	3	0	0	0.4	1.000

Year	Team		W	L	PCT	ERA	G	GS	CG	IP	H	BB	SO	ShO	Relief Pitching W	L	SV	Batting AB	H	HR	BA	PO	A	E	DP	TC/G	FA

Ken MacKenzie *continued*

Year	Team		W	L	PCT	ERA	G	GS	CG	IP	H	BB	SO	ShO	W	L	SV	AB	H	HR	BA	PO	A	E	DP	TC/G	FA
1965	HOU	N	0	3	.000	3.86	21	0	0	37.1	46	6	26	0	0	3	0	11	3	0	.273	0	6	0	1	0.3	1.000
6 yrs.			8	10	.444	4.80	129	1	0	208	231	63	142	0	8	9	5	36	4	0	.111	8	34	4	4	0.4	.913

Johnny Mackinson

MACKINSON, JOHN JOSEPH
B. Oct. 29, 1923, Orange, N. J. D. Oct. 17, 1989, Reseda, Calif.

BR TR 5'10½" 160 lbs.

Year	Team		W	L	PCT	ERA	G	GS	CG	IP	H	BB	SO	ShO	W	L	SV	AB	H	HR	BA	PO	A	E	DP	TC/G	FA
1953	PHI	A	0	0	—	0.00	1	0	0	1.1	1	2	0	0	0	0	0	0	0	0	—	0	0	0	0	0.0	—
1955	STL	N	0	1	.000	7.84	8	1	0	20.2	24	10	8	0	0	1	0	4	0	0	.000	0	4	0	0	0.5	1.000
2 yrs.			0	1	.000	7.36	9	1	0	22	25	12	8	0	0	1	0	4	0	0	.000	0	4	0	0	0.4	1.000

Bill MacLeod

MacLEOD, WILLIAM DANIEL
B. May 13, 1942, Gloucester, Mass.

BL TL 6'2" 190 lbs.

Year	Team		W	L	PCT	ERA	G	GS	CG	IP	H	BB	SO	ShO	W	L	SV	AB	H	HR	BA	PO	A	E	DP	TC/G	FA
1962	BOS	A	0	1	.000	5.40	2	0	0	1.2	4	1	2	0	0	1	0	0	0	0	—	0	0	0	0	—	—

Max Macon

MACON, MAX CULLEN
B. Oct. 14, 1915, Pensacola, Fla. D. Aug. 5, 1989, Jupiter, Fla.

BL TL 6'3" 175 lbs.

Year	Team		W	L	PCT	ERA	G	GS	CG	IP	H	BB	SO	ShO	W	L	SV	AB	H	HR	BA	PO	A	E	DP	TC/G	FA
1938	STL	N	4	11	.267	4.11	38	12	5	129.1	133	61	39	1	2	2	2	36	11	0	.306	3	32	2	2	1.0	.946
1940	BKN	N	1	0	1.000	22.50	2	0	0	2	2	1	0	0	1	0	0	1	1	0	1.000	0	0	0	0	0.0	—
1942			5	3	.625	1.93	14	8	4	84	67	33	27	1	2	0	1	43	12	0	.279	9	15	1	0	1.8	.960
1943			7	5	.583	5.96	25	9	0	77	89	32	21	0	3	2	0	55	9	0	.164	3	19	0	2	0.9	1.000
1944	BOS	N	0	0	—	21.00	1	0	0	3	10	1	1	0	0	0	0	366	100	3	.273	0	1	0	0	1.0	1.000
1947			0	0	—	0.00	1	0	0	2	1	1	0	0	0	0	0	1	0	0	.000	0	1	0	0	1.0	1.000
6 yrs.			17	19	.472	4.24	81	29	9	297.1	305	128	90	2	8	4	3	*				15	68	3	4	1.1	.965

Harry MacPherson

MacPHERSON, HARRY WILLIAM
B. July 10, 1926, North Andover, Mass.

BR TR 5'10" 150 lbs.

Year	Team		W	L	PCT	ERA	G	GS	CG	IP	H	BB	SO	ShO	W	L	SV	AB	H	HR	BA	PO	A	E	DP	TC/G	FA
1944	BOS	N	0	0	—	0.00	1	0	0	1	0	1	1	0	0	0	0	0	0	0	—	0	0	0	0	0.0	—

Jimmy Macullar

MACULLAR, JAMES F. (Little Mac)
B. Jan. 16, 1855, Boston, Mass. D. Apr. 8, 1924, Baltimore, Md.
Manager 1879.

BR TL

Year	Team		W	L	PCT	ERA	G	GS	CG	IP	H	BB	SO	ShO	W	L	SV	AB	H	HR	BA	PO	A	E	DP	TC/G	FA
1886	BAL	AA	0	0	—	9.00	1	0	0	2	4	0	1	0	0	0	0	*				0	0	0	0	0.0	—

Keith MacWhorter

MacWHORTER, KEITH
B. Dec. 30, 1955, Worcester, Mass.

BR TR 6'4" 190 lbs.

Year	Team		W	L	PCT	ERA	G	GS	CG	IP	H	BB	SO	ShO	W	L	SV	AB	H	HR	BA	PO	A	E	DP	TC/G	FA
1980	BOS	A	0	3	.000	5.57	14	2	0	42	46	18	21	0	0	1	0	0	0	0	—	5	7	1	1	0.9	.923

Kid Madden

MADDEN, MICHAEL JOSEPH
B. Oct. 22, 1867, Portland, Me. D. Mar. 16, 1896, Portland, Me.

TL 5'7½" 130 lbs.

Year	Team		W	L	PCT	ERA	G	GS	CG	IP	H	BB	SO	ShO	W	L	SV	AB	H	HR	BA	PO	A	E	DP	TC/G	FA
1887	BOS	N	21	14	.600	3.79	37	37	36	321	317	122	81	3	0	0	0	132	32	1	.242	4	59	13	1	2.1	.829
1888			7	11	.389	2.95	20	18	17	165	142	24	53	1	0	0	0	67	11	0	.164	4	41	4	0	2.5	.918
1889			10	10	.500	4.40	22	19	18	178	194	71	64	1	1	0	1	86	25	0	.291	6	35	4	2	2.0	.911
1890	BOS	P	3	2	.600	4.79	10	7	5	62	85	25	24	1	0	0	1	38	7	0	.184	5	16	2	2	2.3	.913
1891	2 teams		BOS AA	(1G 0–1)			BAL AA	(32G 13–12)																			
"	total		13	13	.500	4.19	33	28	21	232	249	94	62	1	1	0	1	110	31	1	.282	11	77	10	5	3.0	.898
5 yrs.			54	50	.519	3.92	122	109	97	958	987	336	284	7	2	0	3	433	106	2	.245	30	228	33	10	2.4	.887

Len Madden

MADDEN, LEONARD JOSEPH (Lefty)
B. July 2, 1890, Toledo, Ohio D. Sept. 9, 1949, Toledo, Ohio

BL TL 6'2" 165 lbs.

Year	Team		W	L	PCT	ERA	G	GS	CG	IP	H	BB	SO	ShO	W	L	SV	AB	H	HR	BA	PO	A	E	DP	TC/G	FA
1912	CHI	N	0	1	.000	2.92	6	2	0	12.1	16	9	5	0	0	0	0	4	1	0	.250	0	3	2	0	0.8	.600

Mike Madden

MADDEN, MICHAEL ANTHONY
B. Jan. 13, 1957, Denver, Colo.

BL TL 6'1" 185 lbs.

Year	Team		W	L	PCT	ERA	G	GS	CG	IP	H	BB	SO	ShO	W	L	SV	AB	H	HR	BA	PO	A	E	DP	TC/G	FA
1983	HOU	N	9	5	.643	3.14	28	13	0	94.2	76	45	44	0·	3	0	0	22	1	0	.045	7	15	1	4	0.8	.957
1984			2	3	.400	5.53	17	7	0	40.2	46	35	29	0	1	0	0	6	2	0	.333	0	2	0	0	0.1	1.000
1985			0	0	—	4.26	13	0	0	19	29	11	16	0	0	0	0	0	0	0	—	2	1	0	0	0.2	1.000
1986			1	2	.333	4.08	13	6	0	39.2	47	22	30	0	1	0	0	9	0	0	.000	1	5	0	0	0.5	1.000
4 yrs.			12	10	.545	3.94	71	26	0	194	198	113	119	0	5	0	0	37	3	0	.081	10	23	1	4	0.5	.971

Morris Madden

MADDEN, MORRIS DeWAYNE
B. Aug. 31, 1960, Laurens, S. C.

BL TL 6' 155 lbs.

Year	Team		W	L	PCT	ERA	G	GS	CG	IP	H	BB	SO	ShO	W	L	SV	AB	H	HR	BA	PO	A	E	DP	TC/G	FA
1987	DET	A	0	0	—	16.20	2	0	0	1.2	4	3	0	0	0	0	0	0	0	0	—	0	0	0	0	0.0	—
1988	PIT	N	0	0	—	0.00	5	0	0	5.2	5	7	3	0	0	0	0	0	0	0	—	0	2	0	0	0.4	1.000
1989			2	2	.500	7.07	9	3	0	14	17	13	6	0	1	0	0	1	0	0	.000	1	0	2	0	0.3	.333
3 yrs.			2	2	.500	5.91	16	3	0	21.1	26	23	9	0	1	0	0	1	0	0	.000	1	2	2	0	0.3	.600

Nick Maddox

MADDOX, NICHOLAS
B. Nov. 9, 1886, Gavanstown, Md. D. Nov. 27, 1954, Pittsburgh, Pa.

BL TR 6' 175 lbs.

Year	Team		W	L	PCT	ERA	G	GS	CG	IP	H	BB	SO	ShO	W	L	SV	AB	H	HR	BA	PO	A	E	DP	TC/G	FA
1907	PIT	N	5	1	.833	0.83	6	6	6	54	32	13	38	1	0	0	0	20	5	0	.250	2	12	1	0	2.5	.933
1908			23	8	.742	2.28	36	32	22	260.2	209	90	70	4	2	0	1	94	25	0	.266	8	77	3	3	2.4	.966
1909			13	8	.619	2.21	31	27	17	203.1	173	39	56	4	1	0	0	67	15	0	.224	6	54	2	3	2.0	.968
1910			2	3	.400	3.40	20	7	2	87.1	73	28	29	0	1	1	0	28	6	0	.214	1	24	1	2	1.3	.962
4 yrs.			43	20	.683	2.29	93	72	47	605.1	487	170	193	9	4	1	1	209	51	0	.244	17	167	7	8	2.1	.963

WORLD SERIES

Year	Team		W	L	PCT	ERA	G	GS	CG	IP	H	BB	SO	ShO	W	L	SV	AB	H	HR	BA	PO	A	E	DP	TC/G	FA
1909	PIT	N	1	0	1.000	1.00	1	1	1	9	10	2	4	0	0	0	0	4	0	0	.000	0	1	0	0	1.0	1.000

Year	Team	W	L	PCT	ERA	G	GS	CG	IP	H	BB	SO	ShO	Relief Pitching W	L	SV	Batting AB	H	HR	BA	PO	A	E	DP	TC/G	FA

Greg Maddux

MADDUX, GREGORY ALAN
Brother of Mike Maddux.
B. Apr. 14, 1966, San Angelo, Tex.

BR TR 6' 170 lbs.

Year	Team	W	L	PCT	ERA	G	GS	CG	IP	H	BB	SO	ShO	W	L	SV	AB	H	HR	BA	PO	A	E	DP	TC/G	FA
1986	CHI N	2	4	.333	5.52	6	5	1	31	44	11	20	0	0	1	0	12	4	0	.333	1	6	1	0	1.3	.875
1987		6	14	.300	5.61	30	27	1	155.2	181	74	101	1	0	0	0	42	5	0	.119	16	50	4	7	2.3	.943
1988		18	8	.692	3.18	34	34	9	249	230	81	140	3	0	0	0	96	19	0	.198	28	45	3	3	2.2	.961
1989		19	12	.613	2.95	35	35	7	238.1	222	82	135	1	0	0	0	81	17	0	.210	35	41	3	4	2.3	.962
4 yrs.		45	38	.542	3.77	105	101	18	674	677	248	396	5	0	1	0	231	45	0	.195	80	142	11	14	2.2	.953

LEAGUE CHAMPIONSHIP SERIES

| 1989 | CHI N | 0 | 1 | .000 | 13.50 | 2 | 2 | 0 | 7.1 | 13 | 4 | 5 | 0 | 0 | 0 | 0 | 3 | 0 | 0 | .000 | 0 | 0 | 1 | 0 | 0.5 | — |

Mike Maddux

MADDUX, MICHAEL AUSLEY
Brother of Greg Maddux.
B. Aug. 27, 1961, Dayton, Ohio

BL TR 6'2" 180 lbs.

Year	Team	W	L	PCT	ERA	G	GS	CG	IP	H	BB	SO	ShO	W	L	SV	AB	H	HR	BA	PO	A	E	DP	TC/G	FA
1986	PHI N	3	7	.300	5.42	16	16	0	78	88	34	44	0	0	0	0	22	1	0	.045	5	10	2	0	1.1	.882
1987		2	0	1.000	2.65	7	2	0	17	17	5	15	0	1	0	0	3	0	0	.000	1	1	0	0	0.4	.667
1988		4	3	.571	3.76	25	11	0	88.2	91	34	59	0	2	0	0	23	3	0	.130	8	18	4	1	1.2	.867
1989		1	3	.250	5.15	16	4	0	43.2	52	14	26	1	0	1	1	10	0	0	.000	7	12	1	1	1.2	1.000
4 yrs.		10	13	.435	4.51	64	33	2	227.1	248	87	144	1	3	1	1	58	4	0	.069	21	41	7	2	1.1	.899

Tony Madigan

MADIGAN, WILLIAM J.
B. 1868, Washington, D. C. D. Dec. 4, 1954, Washington, D. C.

TR 5'5½" 126 lbs.

Year	Team	W	L	PCT	ERA	G	GS	CG	IP	H	BB	SO	ShO	W	L	SV	AB	H	HR	BA	PO	A	E	DP	TC/G	FA
1886	WAS N	1	13	.071	5.06	14	14	13	115.2	159	44	29	0	0	0	0	48	4	0	.083	3	28	3	1	2.4	.912

Dave Madison

MADISON, DAVID PLEDGER
B. Feb. 1, 1921, Brooksville, Miss. D. Dec. 8, 1985, Macon, Miss.

BR TR 6'3" 190 lbs.

Year	Team	W	L	PCT	ERA	G	GS	CG	IP	H	BB	SO	ShO	W	L	SV	AB	H	HR	BA	PO	A	E	DP	TC/G	FA
1950	NY A	0	0	—	6.00	1	0	0	3	3	1	1	0	0	0	0	0	0	0	—	0	0	0	0	0.0	—
1952	2 teams	STL A		(31G 4–2)		DET A		(10G 1–1)																		
"	total	5	3	.625	4.94	41	5	0	93	94	58	42	0	3	0	0	19	2	0	.105	2	17	1	0	0.5	.950
1953	DET A	3	4	.429	6.82	32	1	0	62	76	44	27	0	3	3	0	11	1	0	.091	2	13	2	0	0.5	.882
3 yrs.		8	7	.533	5.70	74	6	0	158	173	103	70	0	6	5	0	30	3	0	.100	4	30	3	0	0.5	.919

Alex Madrid

MADRID, ALEXANDER
B. Apr. 18, 1963, Springerville, Ariz.

BR TR 6'3" 200 lbs.

Year	Team	W	L	PCT	ERA	G	GS	CG	IP	H	BB	SO	ShO	W	L	SV	AB	H	HR	BA	PO	A	E	DP	TC/G	FA
1987	MIL A	0	0	—	15.19	3	0	0	5.1	11	1	1	0	0	0	0	0	0	0	—	0	0	0	0	0.0	—
1988	PHI N	1	1	.500	2.76	5	2	1	16.1	15	6	2	0	0	0	0	3	0	0	.000	0	2	0	0	0.4	1.000
1989		1	2	.333	5.47	6	3	0	24.2	32	14	13	0	0	0	0	6	0	0	.000	0	2	0	0	0.3	1.000
3 yrs.		2	3	.400	5.63	14	5	1	46.1	58	21	16	0	0	0	0	9	0	0	.000	0	4	0	0	0.3	1.000

Hector Maestri

MAESTRI, HECTOR ANIBAL
Born Hector Anibal Maestri y Garcia.
B. Apr. 19, 1935, Havana, Cuba

BR TR 5'10" 170 lbs.

Year	Team	W	L	PCT	ERA	G	GS	CG	IP	H	BB	SO	ShO	W	L	SV	AB	H	HR	BA	PO	A	E	DP	TC/G	FA
1960	WAS A	0	0	—	0.00	1	0	0	2	1	1	1	0	0	0	0	0	0	0	—	0	0	0	0	0.0	—
1961		0	1	.000	1.50	1	1	0	6	6	2	2	0	0	0	0	1	0	0	.000	0	1	0	0	1.0	1.000
2 yrs.		0	1	.000	1.13	2	1	0	8	7	3	3	0	0	0	0	1	0	0	.000	0	1	0	0	0.5	1.000

Bill Magee

MAGEE, WILLIAM J.
B. 1875, Cambridge, Mass. Deceased.

BR TR 5'10" 154 lbs.

Year	Team	W	L	PCT	ERA	G	GS	CG	IP	H	BB	SO	ShO	W	L	SV	AB	H	HR	BA	PO	A	E	DP	TC/G	FA
1897	LOU N	4	12	.250	5.39	22	16	13	155.1	186	99	44	1	0	1	0	62	13	0	.210	4	42	7	1	2.4	.868
1898		16	15	.516	4.05	38	33	29	295.1	294	129	55	3	0	1	0	111	14	0	.126	11	65	6	3	2.2	.927
1899	3 teams	LOU N		(12G 3–7)		PHI N		(9G 3–5)		WAS N		(8G 1–4)														
"	total	7	16	.304	6.15	29	26	17	183	227	88	28	1	0	0	0	73	13	0	.178	8	51	7	0	2.3	.894
1901	2 teams	STL N		(1G 0–0)		NY N		(6G 0–4)																		
"	total	0	4	.000	5.72	7	4	1	50.1	64	15	17	0	0	0	0	18	4	0	.222	4	10	0	0	2.0	1.000
1902	2 teams	NY N		(2G 0–0)		PHI N		(8G 2–4)																		
"	total	2	4	.333	3.68	10	7	6	58.2	66	19	17	0	0	0	0	20	4	0	.200	4	16	4	1	2.0	.800
5 yrs.		29	51	.363	4.93	106	88	69	742.2	837	350	161	5	0	3	0	284	48	0	.169	27	184	24	5	2.2	.898

Sal Maglie

MAGLIE, SALVATORE ANTHONY (The Barber)
B. Apr. 26, 1917, Niagara Falls, N. Y.

BR TR 6'2" 180 lbs.

Year	Team	W	L	PCT	ERA	G	GS	CG	IP	H	BB	SO	ShO	W	L	SV	AB	H	HR	BA	PO	A	E	DP	TC/G	FA
1945	NY N	5	4	.556	2.35	13	10	7	84.1	72	22	32	3	0	1	0	30	5	0	.167	1	17	0	1	1.4	1.000
1950		18	4	.818	2.71	47	16	12	206	169	86	96	5	5	2	1	66	8	0	.121	12	51	1	3	1.4	.984
1951		23	6	.793	2.93	42	37	22	298	254	86	146	3	1	0	4	112	17	1	.152	23	53	0	7	1.8	1.000
1952		18	8	.692	2.92	35	31	12	216	199	75	112	5	1	1	0	69	5	0	.072	18	41	3	3	1.8	.958
1953		8	9	.471	4.15	27	24	9	145.1	158	47	80	3	0	1	0	48	13	0	.271	8	15	1	0	0.9	.958
1954		14	6	.700	3.26	34	32	9	218.1	222	70	117	1	0	0	2	63	8	0	.127	4	41	2	3	1.4	.957
1955	2 teams	NY N		(23G 9–5)		CLE A		(10G 0–2)																		
"	total	9	7	.563	3.77	33	23	6	155.1	168	55	82	0	1	0	1	45	5	0	.111	6	14	1	2	0.6	.952
1956	2 teams	CLE A		(2G 0–0)		BKN N		(28G 13–5)																		
"	total	13	5	.722	2.89	30	26	9	196	160	54	110	3	0	0	0	70	9	0	.129	9	20	0	5	1.0	1.000
1957	2 teams	BKN N		(19G 6–6)		NY A		(6G 2–0)																		
"	total	8	6	.571	2.69	25	20	5	127.1	116	33	59	2	0	0	4	37	3	0	.081	10	17	1	1	1.1	.964
1958	2 teams	NY A		(7G 1–1)		STL N		(10G 2–6)																		
"	total	3	7	.300	4.72	17	13	2	76.1	73	34	28	0	0	0	0	23	3	0	.130	5	11	0	0	1.0	.941
10 yrs.		119	62	.657	3.15	303	232	93	1723	1591	562	862	25	8	4	14	563	76	2	.135	96	280	10	26	1.3	.974
					9th																					

WORLD SERIES

| 1951 | NY N | 0 | 1 | .000 | 7.20 | 1 | 1 | 0 | 5 | 7 | 5 | 3 | 0 | 0 | 0 | 0 | 1 | 0 | 0 | .000 | 1 | 0 | 0 | 0 | 1.0 | — |
| 1954 | | 0 | 0 | — | 2.57 | 1 | 1 | 0 | 7 | 7 | 2 | 2 | 0 | 0 | 0 | 0 | 3 | 0 | 0 | .000 | 0 | 2 | 0 | 0 | 2.0 | 1.000 |

Year	Team		W	L	PCT	ERA	G	GS	CG	IP	H	BB	SO	ShO	Relief Pitching W	L	SV	Batting AB	H	HR	BA	PO	A	E	DP	TC/G	FA

Sal Maglie *continued*

| 1956 | BKN | N | 1 | 1 | .500 | 2.65 | 2 | 2 | 2 | 17 | 14 | 6 | 15 | 0 | 0 | 0 | 0 | 5 | 0 | 0 | .000 | 0 | 1 | 0 | 0 | 0.5 | 1.000 |
| | 3 yrs. | | 1 | 2 | .333 | 3.41 | 4 | 4 | 2 | 29 | 29 | 10 | 20 | 0 | 0 | 0 | 0 | 9 | 0 | 0 | .000 | 0 | 3 | 0 | 0 | 0.8 | 1.000 |

Jim Magnuson

MAGNUSON, JAMES ROBERT
B. Aug. 18, 1946, Marinette, Wis. BR TL 6'2" 190 lbs.

1970	CHI	A	1	5	.167	4.80	13	6	0	45	45	16	20	0	0	0	0	11	0	0	.000	3	6	0	0	0.7	1.000
1971			2	1	.667	4.50	15	4	0	30	30	16	11	0	0	0	0	4	0	0	.000	2	4	0	1	0.4	1.000
1973	NY	A	0	1	.000	4.28	8	0	0	27.1	38	9	9	0	0	1	0	0	0	0	–	3	5	1	2	1.1	.889
	3 yrs.		3	7	.300	4.57	36	10	0	102.1	113	41	40	0	0	1	0	15	0	0	.000	8	15	1	3	0.7	.958

Joe Magrane

MAGRANE, JOSEPH DAVID
B. July 2, 1964, Des Moines, Iowa BR TL 6'6" 225 lbs.

1987	STL	N	9	7	.563	3.54	27	26	4	170.1	157	60	101	2	0	0	0	52	7	1	.135	10	26	3	3	1.4	.923
1988			5	9	.357	2.18	24	24	4	165.1	133	51	100	3	0	0	0	48	8	1	.167	16	37	5	0	2.4	.914
1989			18	9	.667	2.91	34	33	9	234.2	219	72	127	3	0	0	0	80	11	1	.138	11	31	2	1	1.3	.955
	3 yrs.		32	25	.561	2.89	85	83	17	570.1	509	183	328	8	0	0	0	180	26	3	.144	37	94	10	4	1.7	.929

LEAGUE CHAMPIONSHIP SERIES

| 1987 | STL | N | 0 | 0 | – | 9.00 | 1 | 1 | 0 | 4 | 4 | 2 | 3 | 0 | 0 | 0 | 0 | 0 | 0 | 0 | .000 | 0 | 1 | 0 | 0 | 1.0 | 1.000 |

WORLD SERIES

| 1987 | STL | N | 0 | 1 | .000 | 8.59 | 2 | 2 | 0 | 7.1 | 9 | 5 | 5 | 0 | 0 | 0 | 0 | 0 | 0 | 0 | – | 1 | 1 | 0 | 0 | 1.0 | 1.000 |

Pete Magrini

MAGRINI, PETER ALEXANDER
B. June 8, 1942, San Francisco, Calif. BR TR 6' 195 lbs.

| 1966 | BOS | A | 0 | 1 | .000 | 9.82 | 3 | 1 | 0 | 7.1 | 8 | 8 | 3 | 0 | 0 | 0 | 0 | 3 | 0 | 0 | .000 | 0 | 1 | 1 | 0 | 0.7 | .500 |

Art Mahaffey

MAHAFFEY, ARTHUR
B. June 4, 1938, Cincinnati, Ohio BR TR 6'1" 185 lbs.

1960	PHI	N	7	3	.700	2.31	14	12	5	93.1	78	34	56	1	0	0	0	30	3	0	.100	6	13	0	0	1.4	1.000
1961			11	19	.367	4.10	36	32	12	219.1	205	70	158	3	0	1	0	63	8	0	.127	14	28	3	2	1.3	.933
1962			19	14	.576	3.94	41	39	20	274	253	81	177	2	0	1	0	92	13	2	.141	14	24	0	1	0.9	1.000
1963			7	10	.412	3.99	26	22	6	149	143	48	97	1	1	0	0	50	10	0	.200	11	22	1	0	1.3	.971
1964			12	9	.571	4.52	34	29	2	157.1	161	82	80	2	1	0	0	50	6	1	.120	6	19	0	2	0.7	1.000
1965			2	5	.286	6.21	22	9	1	71	82	32	52	0	0	0	0	21	2	0	.095	4	6	1	0	0.5	.909
1966	STL	N	1	4	.200	6.43	12	5	0	35	37	21	19	0	0	0	0	7	0	0	.000	1	4	0	0	0.4	1.000
	7 yrs.		59	64	.480	4.17	185	148	46	999	959	368	639	9	2	2	1	313	42	3	.134	56	116	5	5	1.0	.972

Lou Mahaffey

MAHAFFEY, LOUIS WOOD
B. Jan. 3, 1874, Madison, Wis. D. Oct. 26, 1949, Torrance, Calif. 5'9" 170 lbs.

| 1898 | LOU | N | 0 | 1 | .000 | 3.00 | 1 | 1 | 1 | 9 | 10 | 5 | 1 | 0 | 0 | 0 | 0 | 4 | 0 | 0 | .000 | 0 | 1 | 0 | 0 | 1.0 | 1.000 |

Roy Mahaffey

MAHAFFEY, LEE ROY (Popeye)
B. Feb. 9, 1903, Belton, S. C. D. July 23, 1969, Anderson, S. C. BR TR 6' 180 lbs.

1926	PIT	N	0	0	–	0.00	4	0	0	4.2	5	1	3	0	0	0	0	2	0	0	.000	0	1	0	0	0.3	–
1927			1	0	1.000	7.71	2	1	0	9.1	9	4	4	0	0	0	0	5	2	0	.400	0	1	0	0	0.5	1.000
1930	PHI	A	9	5	.643	5.01	33	16	6	152.2	186	53	38	0	0	0	0	59	7	1	.119	5	25	2	4	1.0	.938
1931			15	4	.789	4.21	30	20	8	162.1	161	82	59	0	3	0	2	63	12	2	.190	4	19	1	0	0.8	.958
1932			13	13	.500	5.09	37	28	13	222.2	245	96	106	0	2	3	0	87	15	1	.172	11	35	3	3	1.3	.939
1933			13	10	.565	5.17	33	23	9	179.1	198	74	66	0	0	1	0	65	14	0	.215	7	29	1	1	1.1	.973
1934			6	7	.462	5.37	37	14	3	129	142	55	37	0	0	0	0	48	13	0	.271	5	19	2	0	0.7	.923
1935			8	4	.667	3.90	27	17	5	136	153	42	39	0	2	0	2	51	9	0	.176	2	21	1	3	0.9	.958
1936	STL	A	2	6	.250	8.10	21	9	1	60	82	40	13	0	1	0	1	16	1	0	.063	0	3	1	0	0.2	.750
	9 yrs.		67	49	.578	5.01	224	128	45	1056	1181	452	365	0	12	5	5	396	73	4	.184	34	152	12	11	0.9	.939

WORLD SERIES

| 1931 | PHI | A | 0 | 0 | – | 9.00 | 1 | 0 | 0 | 1 | 1 | 1 | 0 | 0 | 0 | 0 | 0 | 0 | 0 | 0 | – | 0 | 1 | 0 | 0 | 1.0 | 1.000 |

Art Mahan

MAHAN, ARTHUR LEO
B. June 8, 1913, Somerville, Mass. BL TL 5'11" 178 lbs.

| 1940 | PHI | N | 0 | 0 | – | 0.00 | 1 | 0 | 0 | 1 | 1 | 0 | 0 | 0 | 0 | 0 | 0 | * | | | | 0 | 0 | 0 | 0 | 0.0 | – |

Mickey Mahler

MAHLER, MICHAEL JAMES
Brother of Rick Mahler.
B. July 30, 1952, Montgomery, Ala. BB TL 6'3" 189 lbs.

1977	ATL	N	1	2	.333	6.26	5	5	0	23	31	9	14	0	0	0	0	6	3	0	.500	0	3	1	1	0.8	.750
1978			4	11	.267	4.67	34	21	1	135	130	66	92	0	0	0	0	41	4	0	.098	4	15	0	1	0.6	1.000
1979			5	11	.313	5.85	26	18	1	100	123	47	71	0	2	0	0	27	3	0	.111	4	13	1	1	0.7	.944
1980	PIT	N	0	0	–	63.00	2	0	0	1	4	3	1	0	0	0	0	0	0	0	–	0	0	0	0	0.0	–
1981	CAL	A	0	0	–	0.00	6	0	0	6	1	2	5	0	0	0	0	0	0	0	–	0	0	0	0	0.0	–
1982			2	0	1.000	1.13	6	0	0	8	9	6	5	0	2	0	0	0	0	0	–	0	1	0	0	0.2	1.000
1985	2 teams	MON N (9G 1–4)								DET A	(3G 1–2)																
"	total		2	6	.250	3.00	12	9	1	69	59	28	46	1	1	0	1	16	3	0	.188	2	6	2	2	0.8	.800
1986	2 teams	TEX A (29G 0–2)								TOR A	(2G 0–0)																
"	total		0	2	.000	4.08	31	5	0	64	72	29	28	0	0	0	3	0	0	0	–	1	9	0	2	0.4	1.000
	8 yrs.		14	32	.304	4.68	122	58	3	406	429	190	262	1	5	0	4	90	13	0	.144	13	48	4	7	0.5	.938

Rick Mahler

MAHLER, RICHARD KEITH
Brother of Mickey Mahler.
B. Aug. 5, 1953, Austin, Tex. BR TR 6'1" 195 lbs.

Year	Team		W	L	PCT	ERA	G	GS	CG	IP	H	BB	SO	ShO	Relief Pitching W	L	SV	Batting AB	H	HR	BA	PO	A	E	DP	TC/G	FA

Rick Mahler *continued*

Year	Team		W	L	PCT	ERA	G	GS	CG	IP	H	BB	SO	ShO	W	L	SV	AB	H	HR	BA	PO	A	E	DP	TC/G	FA
1979	ATL	N	0	0	–	6.14	15	0	0	22	28	11	12	0	0	0	0	2	1	0	.500	1	3	1	0	0.3	.800
1980			0	0	–	2.25	2	0	0	4	2	0	1	0	0	0	0	0	0	0	–	0	1	0	0	0.5	1.000
1981			8	6	.571	2.81	34	14	1	112	109	43	54	0	2	0	2	27	4	0	.148	14	19	2	0	1.0	.943
1982			9	10	.474	4.21	39	33	5	205.1	213	62	105	2	0	0	0	58	11	1	.190	19	36	1	5	1.4	.982
1983			0	0	–	5.02	10	0	0	14.1	16	9	7	0	0	0	0	2	0	0	.000	1	1	1	1	0.3	.667
1984			13	10	.565	3.12	38	29	9	222	209	62	106	1	0	0	0	71	21	0	.296	20	42	2	5	1.7	.969
1985			17	15	.531	3.48	39	**39**	6	266.2	272	79	107	1	0	0	0	90	14	0	.156	21	45	4	9	1.8	.943
1986			14	**18**	.438	4.88	39	**39**	7	237.2	283	95	137	1	0	0	0	83	16	0	.193	23	41	3	2	1.7	.955
1987			8	13	.381	4.98	39	28	3	197	212	85	95	1	2	1	0	65	11	0	.169	13	42	1	2	1.4	.982
1988			9	16	.360	3.69	39	34	5	249	**279**	42	131	0	2	0	0	72	9	0	.125	22	43	3	4	1.7	.956
1989	CIN	N	9	13	.409	3.83	40	31	5	220.2	242	51	102	0	0	0	0	62	11	0	.177	8	35	1	2	1.1	.977
	11 yrs.		87	101	.463	3.95	334	247	41	1750.2	1865	539	857	8	6	1	2	532	98	1	.184	142	308	19	30	1.4	.959

LEAGUE CHAMPIONSHIP SERIES

Year	Team		W	L	PCT	ERA	G	GS	CG	IP	H	BB	SO	ShO	W	L	SV	AB	H	HR	BA	PO	A	E	DP	TC/G	FA
1982	ATL	N	0	0	–	0.00	1	0	0	1.2	3	2	0	0	0	0	0	0	0	0	–	0	0	0	0	0.0	

Al Mahon

MAHON, ALFRED GWINN (Lefty)
B. Sept. 23, 1909, Albion, Neb.   D. Dec. 26, 1977, New Haven, Conn.   BL TL 5'11" 160 lbs.

Year	Team		W	L	PCT	ERA	G	GS	CG	IP	H	BB	SO	ShO	W	L	SV	AB	H	HR	BA	PO	A	E	DP	TC/G	FA
1930	PHI	A	0	0	–	22.85	3	0	0	4.1	11	7	0	0	0	0	0	1	0	0	.000	0	2	0	0	0.7	1.000

Bob Mahoney

MAHONEY, ROBERT PAUL
B. June 20, 1928, LeRoy, Minn.   BR TR 6'1" 185 lbs.

Year	Team		W	L	PCT	ERA	G	GS	CG	IP	H	BB	SO	ShO	W	L	SV	AB	H	HR	BA	PO	A	E	DP	TC/G	FA
1951	2 teams	CHI A (3G 0–0)				STL A	(30G 2–5)																					
"	total		2	5	.286	4.52	33	4	0	87.2	91	46	33	0	2	2	0	18	4	0	.222	4	12	1	2	0.5	.941
1952	STL	A	0	0	–	18.00	3	0	0	3	8	4	1	0	0	0	0	0	0	0	–	0	0	0	0	0.0	–
	2 yrs.		2	5	.286	4.96	36	4	0	90.2	99	50	34	0	2	2	0	18	4	0	.222	4	12	1	2	0.5	.941

Chris Mahoney

MAHONEY, CHRISTOPHER JOHN
B. June 11, 1885, Milton, Mass.   D. July 15, 1954, Visalia, Calif.   BR TR 5'9" 160 lbs.

Year	Team		W	L	PCT	ERA	G	GS	CG	IP	H	BB	SO	ShO	W	L	SV	AB	H	HR	BA	PO	A	E	DP	TC/G	FA
1910	BOS	A	0	1	.000	3.27	2	1	0	11	16	5	6	0	0	0	1	7	1	0	.143	1	6	0	1	3.5	1.000

Mike Mahoney

MAHONEY, GEORGE W.
B. Dec. 5, 1873, Boston, Mass.   D. Jan. 3, 1940, Boston, Mass.   6'4" 220 lbs.

Year	Team		W	L	PCT	ERA	G	GS	CG	IP	H	BB	SO	ShO	W	L	SV	AB	H	HR	BA	PO	A	E	DP	TC/G	FA
1897	BOS	N	0	0	–	18.00	1	0	0	3	1	1	0	0	0	0	0	*					0	1	0	0	1.0	1.000

Duster Mails

MAILS, JOHN WALTER (The Great)
B. Oct. 1, 1895, San Quentin, Calif.   D. July 5, 1974, San Francisco, Calif.   BL TL 6' 195 lbs.

Year	Team		W	L	PCT	ERA	G	GS	CG	IP	H	BB	SO	ShO	W	L	SV	AB	H	HR	BA	PO	A	E	DP	TC/G	FA
1915	BKN	N	0	1	.000	3.60	2	0	0	5	6	5	3	0	0	0	0	0	0	0	.000	0	2	0	0	1.0	1.000
1916			0	1	.000	3.63	11	2	0	17.1	15	9	13	0	0	0	0	4	1	0	.250	0	2	0	0	0.2	1.000
1920	CLE	A	7	0	1.000	1.85	9	8	6	63.1	54	18	25	2	0	0	0	20	4	0	.200	3	10	0	0	1.4	1.000
1921			14	8	.636	3.94	34	24	10	194.1	210	89	87	2	2	1	2	64	6	0	.094	7	33	2	0	1.2	.952
1922			4	7	.364	5.28	26	13	4	104	122	40	54	1	1	1	0	31	5	0	.161	6	24	0	1	1.2	1.000
1925	STL	N	7	7	.500	4.60	21	14	9	131	145	58	49	0	0	0	0	45	6	0	.133	4	24	3	1	1.5	.903
1926			0	1	.000	0.00	1	0	0	1	2	1	1	0	0	0	0	1	0	0	–	0	1	1	0	2.0	.500
	7 yrs.		32	25	.561	4.10	104	59	29	516	554	220	232	5	3	6	2	165	22	0	.133	20	96	6	2	1.2	.951

WORLD SERIES

Year	Team		W	L	PCT	ERA	G	GS	CG	IP	H	BB	SO	ShO	W	L	SV	AB	H	HR	BA	PO	A	E	DP	TC/G	FA
1920	CLE	A	1	0	1.000	0.00	2	1	1	15.2	6	6	6	1	0	0	0	5	0	0	.000	1	4	0	1	2.5	1.000

Alex Main

MAIN, MILES GRANT
B. May 13, 1884, Montrose, Mich.   D. Dec. 29, 1965, Royal Oak, Mich.   BL TR 6'5" 195 lbs.

Year	Team		W	L	PCT	ERA	G	GS	CG	IP	H	BB	SO	ShO	W	L	SV	AB	H	HR	BA	PO	A	E	DP	TC/G	FA
1914	DET	A	6	6	.500	2.67	32	12	6	138.1	131	59	55	1	1	1	3	40	4	0	.100	6	60	4	5	2.2	.943
1915	KC	F	13	14	.481	2.54	35	28	18	230	181	75	91	2	1	0	3	76	15	0	.197	8	86	5	3	2.8	.949
1918	PHI	N	2	2	.500	4.63	8	4	0	35	30	16	14	1	0	0	0	11	1	0	.091	1	10	0	1	1.4	1.000
	3 yrs.		21	22	.488	2.77	75	44	24	403.1	342	150	160	4	2	1	6	127	20	0	.157	15	156	9	9	2.4	.950

Woody Main

MAIN, FORREST HARRY
B. Feb. 12, 1922, Delano, Calif.   BR TR 6'3½" 195 lbs.

Year	Team		W	L	PCT	ERA	G	GS	CG	IP	H	BB	SO	ShO	W	L	SV	AB	H	HR	BA	PO	A	E	DP	TC/G	FA
1948	PIT	N	1	1	.500	8.33	17	0	0	27	35	19	12	0	1	1	0	2	0	0	.000	2	6	0	0	0.5	1.000
1950			1	0	1.000	4.87	12	0	0	20.1	21	11	12	0	1	0	1	5	2	0	.400	1	4	0	0	0.4	1.000
1952			2	12	.143	4.46	48	11	2	153.1	149	52	79	0	0	7	2	37	2	0	.054	8	15	4	0	0.6	.852
1953			0	0	–	11.25	2	0	0	4	5	2	4	0	0	0	0	0	0	0	–	0	0	0	0	0.0	–
	4 yrs.		4	13	.235	5.14	79	11	2	204.2	210	84	107	0	2	8	3	44	4	0	.091	11	25	4	0	0.5	.900

Jim Mains

MAINS, JAMES ROYAL
B. June 12, 1922, Bridgton, Me.   D. Mar. 17, 1969, Bridgton, Me.   BR TR 6'2" 190 lbs.

Year	Team		W	L	PCT	ERA	G	GS	CG	IP	H	BB	SO	ShO	W	L	SV	AB	H	HR	BA	PO	A	E	DP	TC/G	FA
1943	PHI	A	0	1	.000	5.63	1	1	1	8	9	3	4	0	0	0	0	2	0	0	.000	0	1	0	0	1.0	1.000

Willard Mains

MAINS, WILLARD EBEN (Grasshopper)
B. July 7, 1868, North Windham, Me.   D. May 23, 1923, Bridgton, Me.   TR 6'2" 190 lbs.

Year	Team		W	L	PCT	ERA	G	GS	CG	IP	H	BB	SO	ShO	W	L	SV	AB	H	HR	BA	PO	A	E	DP	TC/G	FA
1888	CHI	N	1	1	.500	4.91	2	2	1	11	8	6	5	0	0	0	0	7	1	0	.143	0	2	0	0	1.0	1.000
1891	2 teams	CIN AA (30G 12–12)				MIL AA	(2G 0–2)																					
"	total		12	14	.462	3.07	32	28	20	214	210	117	78	0	1	2	0	95	25	0	.263	4	70	7	1	2.5	.914
1896	BOS	N	3	2	.600	5.48	8	5	3	42.2	43	31	13	0	0	0	1	22	6	1	.273	2	9	0	0	1.4	1.000
	3 yrs.		16	17	.485	3.53	42	32	24	267.2	261	154	96	0	1	2	1	124	32	1	.258	6	81	7	1	2.2	.926

Frank Makosky

MAKOSKY, FRANK (Dins)
B. Jan. 20, 1910, Boonton, N.J.   D. Jan. 10, 1987, Stroudsburg, Pa.   BR TR 6'1" 185 lbs.

Year	Team		W	L	PCT	ERA	G	GS	CG	IP	H	BB	SO	ShO	W	L	SV	AB	H	HR	BA	PO	A	E	DP	TC/G	FA
1937	NY	A	5	2	.714	4.97	26	1	1	58	64	24	27	0	5	1	3	16	5	0	.313	3	21	0	0	0.9	1.000

Year	Team		W	L	PCT	ERA	G	GS	CG	IP	H	BB	SO	ShO	W	L	SV	AB	H	HR	BA	PO	A	E	DP	TC/G	FA
															Relief Pitching			Batting									

Tom Makowski

MAKOWSKI, THOMAS ANTHONY
B. Dec. 22, 1950, Buffalo, N. Y.
BR TL 5'11" 185 lbs.

Year	Team		W	L	PCT	ERA	G	GS	CG	IP	H	BB	SO	ShO	W	L	SV	AB	H	HR	BA	PO	A	E	DP	TC/G	FA
1975	DET	A	0	0	—	4.82	3	0	0	9.1	10	9	3	0	0	0	0	0	0	0	—	0	4	1	0	1.7	.800

Bill Malarkey

MALARKEY, WILLIAM JOHN
B. Nov. 26, 1878, Port Byron, Ill. D. Dec. 12, 1956, Phoenix, Ariz.
BR TR 5'10" 185 lbs.

Year	Team		W	L	PCT	ERA	G	GS	CG	IP	H	BB	SO	ShO	W	L	SV	AB	H	HR	BA	PO	A	E	DP	TC/G	FA
1908	NY	N	0	2	.000	2.57	15	0	0	35	31	10	12	0	0	2	1	6	0	0	.000	1	9	1	0	0.7	.909

John Malarkey

MALARKEY, JOHN S.
B. May 4, 1872, Springfield, Ohio D. Oct. 29, 1949, Cincinnati, Ohio
TR 5'11" 155 lbs.

Year	Team		W	L	PCT	ERA	G	GS	CG	IP	H	BB	SO	ShO	W	L	SV	AB	H	HR	BA	PO	A	E	DP	TC/G	FA
1894	WAS	N	2	1	.667	4.15	3	3	3	26	42	5	3	0	0	0	0	14	1	0	.071	1	1	0	0	0.7	1.000
1895			0	8	.000	5.99	22	8	5	100.2	135	60	32	0	0	1	2	37	5	0	.135	3	15	1	0	0.9	.947
1896			0	1	.000	1.29	1	1	0	7	9	3	0	0	0	0	0	2	1	0	.500	2	1	0	0	3.0	1.000
1899	CHI	N	0	1	.000	13.00	1	1	1	9	19	5	7	0	0	0	0	5	1	0	.200	0	4	0	0	4.0	1.000
1902	BOS	N	8	10	.444	2.59	21	19	17	170.1	158	58	39	1	1	0	1	62	13	1	.210	8	59	8	1	3.6	.893
1903			11	16	.407	3.09	32	27	25	253	266	96	98	2	0	2	0	87	14	0	.161	16	75	11	5	3.2	.892
6 yrs.			21	37	.362	3.64	80	59	51	566	629	227	179	3	1	3	3	207	35	1	.169	30	155	20	6	2.6	.902

Cy Malis

MALIS, CYRUS SOL
B. Feb. 26, 1907, Philadelphia, Pa. D. Jan. 12, 1971, North Hollywood, Calif.
BR TR 5'11" 175 lbs.

Year	Team		W	L	PCT	ERA	G	GS	CG	IP	H	BB	SO	ShO	W	L	SV	AB	H	HR	BA	PO	A	E	DP	TC/G	FA
1934	PHI	N	0	0	—	4.91	1	0	0	3.2	4	2	1	0	0	0	0	0	0	0	—	1	0	0	0	1.0	1.000

Mal Mallette

MALLETTE, MALCOLM FRANCIS
B. Jan. 30, 1922, Syracuse, N. Y.
BL TL 6'2" 200 lbs.

Year	Team		W	L	PCT	ERA	G	GS	CG	IP	H	BB	SO	ShO	W	L	SV	AB	H	HR	BA	PO	A	E	DP	TC/G	FA
1950	BKN	N	0	0	—	0.00	2	0	0	1.1	2	1	2	0	0	0	0	0	0	0	—	0	0	0	0	0.0	—

Rob Mallicoat

MALLICOAT, ROBBIN DALE
B. Nov. 16, 1964, St. Helens, Ore.
BL TL 6'3" 180 lbs.

Year	Team		W	L	PCT	ERA	G	GS	CG	IP	H	BB	SO	ShO	W	L	SV	AB	H	HR	BA	PO	A	E	DP	TC/G	FA
1987	HOU	N	0	0	—	6.75	4	1	0	6.2	8	6	4	0	0	0	0	0	0	0	—	1	1	0	0	0.5	1.000

Alex Malloy

MALLOY, ARCHIBALD ALEXANDER (Lick)
B. Oct. 31, 1886, Laurinburg, N. C. D. Mar. 1, 1961, Ferris, Tex.
BR TR 6'2" 180 lbs.

Year	Team		W	L	PCT	ERA	G	GS	CG	IP	H	BB	SO	ShO	W	L	SV	AB	H	HR	BA	PO	A	E	DP	TC/G	FA
1910	STL	A	0	6	.000	2.56	7	6	4	52.2	47	17	27	0	0	0	0	16	1	0	.063	2	17	2	1	3.0	.905

Bob Malloy

MALLOY, ROBERT PAUL
B. May 28, 1918, Canonsburg, Pa. D. Mar. 18, 1976, Sandusky, Ohio
BR TR 5'11" 185 lbs.

Year	Team		W	L	PCT	ERA	G	GS	CG	IP	H	BB	SO	ShO	W	L	SV	AB	H	HR	BA	PO	A	E	DP	TC/G	FA
1943	CIN	N	0	0	—	6.30	6	0	0	10	14	8	4	0	0	0	0	3	2	0	.667	0	1	0	0	0.2	1.000
1944			1	1	.500	3.09	9	0	0	23.1	22	11	4	0	1	1	0	7	0	0	.000	1	6	0	1	0.8	1.000
1946			2	5	.286	2.75	27	3	1	72	71	26	24	0	1	4	2	18	5	0	.278	0	13	4	11	0.6	.765
1947			0	0	—	18.00	1	0	0	1	3	0	1	0	0	0	0	0	0	0	—	0	0	0	0	0.0	—
1949	STL	A	1	1	.500	2.79	5	0	0	9.2	6	7	2	0	1	1	0	3	0	0	.000	2	1	0	0	0.6	1.000
5 yrs.			4	7	.364	3.26	48	3	1	116	116	52	35	0	3	6	2	31	7	0	.226	3	21	4	12	0.6	.857

Bob Malloy

MALLOY, ROBERT WILLIAM
B. Nov. 24, 1964, Garland, Tex.
BR TR 6'5" 200 lbs.

Year	Team		W	L	PCT	ERA	G	GS	CG	IP	H	BB	SO	ShO	W	L	SV	AB	H	HR	BA	PO	A	E	DP	TC/G	FA
1987	TEX	A	0	0	—	6.55	2	2	0	11	13	3	8	0	0	0	0	0	0	0	—	0	1	0	0	0.5	1.000

Herm Malloy

MALLOY, HERMAN
B. June 1, 1885, Massillon, Ohio D. May 9, 1942, Nimishillen, Ohio
BR TR 6'

Year	Team		W	L	PCT	ERA	G	GS	CG	IP	H	BB	SO	ShO	W	L	SV	AB	H	HR	BA	PO	A	E	DP	TC/G	FA
1907	DET	A	0	1	.000	5.63	1	1	1	8	13	5	6	0	0	0	0	4	0	0	.000	0	2	0	0	2.0	1.000
1908			0	2	.000	3.71	3	2	2	17	20	4	8	0	0	0	0	9	3	0	.333	2	10	1	0	4.3	.923
2 yrs.			0	3	.000	4.32	4	3	3	25	33	9	14	0	0	0	0	13	3	0	.231	2	12	1	0	3.8	.933

Pat Malone

MALONE, PERCE LEIGH
B. Sept. 25, 1902, Altoona, Pa.
D. May 13, 1943, Altoona, Pa.
BL TR 6' 200 lbs.
BB 1935-37

Year	Team		W	L	PCT	ERA	G	GS	CG	IP	H	BB	SO	ShO	W	L	SV	AB	H	HR	BA	PO	A	E	DP	TC/G	FA
1928	CHI	N	18	13	.581	2.84	42	25	16	250.2	218	99	155	2	2	4	2	95	18	1	.189	5	54	3	2	1.5	.952
1929			22	10	.688	3.57	40	30	19	267	283	102	166	5	4	1	2	105	22	2	.210	10	35	1	5	1.2	.978
1930			20	9	.690	3.94	45	35	22	271.2	290	96	142	2	1	1	4	105	26	4	.248	16	40	1	1	1.3	.982
1931			16	9	.640	3.90	36	30	12	228.1	229	88	112	2	3	0	0	79	17	1	.215	6	46	2	2	1.5	.963
1932			15	17	.469	3.38	37	33	17	237	222	78	120	2	1	1	0	78	14	1	.179	8	33	2	1	1.2	.953
1933			10	14	.417	3.91	31	26	13	186.1	186	59	72	2	2	0	0	63	10	0	.159	11	35	2	1	1.5	.958
1934			14	7	.667	3.53	34	21	8	191	200	55	111	1	2	0	0	64	11	0	.172	4	32	0	1	1.1	1.000
1935	NY	A	3	5	.375	5.43	29	2	0	56.1	53	33	25	0	3	4	3	15	0	0	.000	1	10	2	0	0.4	.846
1936			12	4	.750	3.81	35	9	5	134.2	144	60	72	0	8	2	9	51	10	0	.196	1	17	1	0	0.5	.947
1937			4	4	.500	5.48	28	9	3	92	109	35	49	0	1	3	6	33	1	0	.030	1	9	0	0	0.4	1.000
10 yrs.			134	92	.593	3.74	357	220	115	1915	1934	705	1024	16	27	16	26	688	129	9	.188	63	311	14	14	1.1	.964

WORLD SERIES

Year	Team		W	L	PCT	ERA	G	GS	CG	IP	H	BB	SO	ShO	W	L	SV	AB	H	HR	BA	PO	A	E	DP	TC/G	FA
1929	CHI	N	0	2	.000	4.15	3	2	1	13	12	7	11	0	0	0	0	4	1	0	.250	0	1	0	0	0.3	1.000
1932			0	0	—	0.00	1	0	0	2.2	1	4	4	0	0	0	0	0	0	0	—	0	0	0	0	0.0	—
1936	NY	A	0	1	.000	1.80	2	0	0	5	2	1	2	0	0	0	0	1	1	0	1.000	0	2	0	0	1.0	1.000
3 yrs.			0	3	.000	3.05	6	2	1	20.2	15	12	17	0	0	0	0	5	2	0	.400	0	3	0	0	0.5	1.000

Charlie Maloney

MALONEY, CHARLES MICHAEL
B. May 22, 1886, Cambridge, Mass. D. Jan. 17, 1967, Arlington, Mass.
BR TR 5'8" 155 lbs.

Year	Team		W	L	PCT	ERA	G	GS	CG	IP	H	BB	SO	ShO	W	L	SV	AB	H	HR	BA	PO	A	E	DP	TC/G	FA
1908	BOS	N	0	0	—	4.50	1	0	0	2	3	1	0	0	0	0	0	0	0	0	—	0	1	0	0	1.0	1.000

Year	Team		W	L	PCT	ERA	G	GS	CG	IP	H	BB	SO	ShO	Relief Pitching W	L	SV	Batting AB	H	HR	BA	PO	A	E	DP	TC/G	FA

Jim Maloney

MALONEY, JAMES WILLIAM
B. June 2, 1940, Fresno, Calif.

BL TR 6'2" 190 lbs.

Year	Team		W	L	PCT	ERA	G	GS	CG	IP	H	BB	SO	ShO	W	L	SV	AB	H	HR	BA	PO	A	E	DP	TC/G	FA
1960	CIN	N	2	6	.250	4.66	11	10	2	63.2	61	37	48	1	0	0	0	18	2	0	.111	3	9	0	1	1.1	1.000
1961			6	7	.462	4.37	27	11	1	94.2	86	59	57	0	1	3	2	29	11	1	.379	5	13	1	0	0.7	.947
1962			9	7	.563	3.51	22	17	3	115.1	90	66	105	2	2	0	1	43	8	0	.186	7	10	2	1	0.9	.895
1963			23	7	.767	2.77	33	33	13	250.1	183	88	265	6	0	0	0	89	15	0	.169	8	30	3	1	1.2	.927
1964			15	10	.600	2.71	31	31	11	216	175	83	214	2	0	0	0	73	11	1	.151	10	23	2	1	1.1	.943
1965			20	9	.690	2.54	33	33	14	255.1	189	110	244	5	0	0	0	89	20	0	.225	18	33	1	0	1.6	.981
1966			16	8	.667	2.80	32	32	10	224.2	174	90	216	5	0	0	0	81	18	0	.222	12	29	2	3	1.3	.953
1967			15	11	.577	3.25	30	29	6	196.1	181	72	153	3	0	1	0	69	11	0	.159	7	29	1	0	1.2	.973
1968			16	10	.615	3.61	33	32	8	207	183	80	181	5	1	0	0	74	18	2	.243	16	21	2	1	1.2	.949
1969			12	5	.706	2.77	30	27	6	179	135	86	102	3	0	0	0	55	11	3	.200	13	25	1	2	1.3	.974
1970			0	1	.000	11.12	7	3	0	17	26	15	7	0	0	0	1	3	0	0	.000	0	5	0	0	0.7	1.000
1971	CAL	A	0	3	.000	5.10	13	4	0	30	35	24	13	0	0	0	0	5	1	0	.200	1	5	0	0	0.5	1.000
12 yrs.			134	84	.615	3.19	302	262	74	1849.1	1518	810	1605	30	4	4	4	628	126	7	.201	100	232	15	10	1.1	.957

WORLD SERIES

| 1961 | CIN | N | 0 | 0 | — | 27.00 | 1 | 0 | 0 | .2 | 4 | 1 | 1 | 0 | 0 | 0 | 0 | 0 | 0 | 0 | — | 0 | 0 | 0 | 0 | 0.0 | — |

Paul Maloy

MALOY, PAUL AUGUSTUS (Biff)
B. June 4, 1892, Bascom, Ohio. D. Mar. 18, 1976, Sandusky, Ohio

BR TR 5'11" 185 lbs.

| 1913 | BOS | A | 0 | 0 | — | 9.00 | 2 | 0 | 0 | 2 | 2 | 1 | 0 | 0 | 0 | 0 | 0 | 0 | 0 | 0 | — | 0 | 0 | 1 | 0 | 0.5 | — |

Gordon Maltzberger

MALTZBERGER, GORDON RALPH (Maltzy)
B. Sept. 4, 1912, Utopia, Tex. D. Dec. 11, 1974, Rialto, Calif.

BR TR 6' 170 lbs.

1943	CHI	A	7	4	.636	2.46	37	0	0	98.2	86	24	48	0	7	4	14	25	3	0	.120	5	20	0	2	0.7	1.000
1944			10	5	.667	2.96	46	0	0	91.1	81	19	49	0	10	5	12	22	3	0	.136	1	16	2	0	0.4	.895
1946			2	0	1.000	1.59	19	0	0	39.2	30	6	17	0	2	0	2	6	0	0	.000	1	4	0	1	0.3	1.000
1947			1	4	.200	3.39	33	0	0	63.2	61	25	22	0	1	4	5	7	1	0	.143	4	14	0	1	0.5	1.000
4 yrs.			20	13	.606	2.70	135	0	0	293.1	258	74	136	0	20	13	33	60	7	0	.117	11	54	2	4	0.5	.970

Al Mamaux

MAMAUX, ALBERT LEON
B. May 30, 1894, Pittsburgh, Pa. D. Jan. 2, 1963, Santa Monica, Calif.

BR TR 6'½" 168 lbs.

1913	PIT	N	0	0	—	3.00	1	0	0	3	2	2	2	0	0	0	0	1	0	0	.000	0	1	0	0	1.0	1.000
1914			5	2	.714	1.71	13	6	4	63	41	24	30	2	1	1	0	20	5	0	.250	4	23	2	0	2.2	.931
1915			21	8	.724	2.04	38	31	17	251.2	182	96	152	8	3	0	0	92	15	0	.163	5	48	2	2	1.4	.964
1916			21	15	.583	2.53	45	38	26	310	264	136	163	1	1	0	2	110	21	0	.191	7	82	1	1	2.0	.989
1917			2	11	.154	5.25	16	13	5	85.2	92	50	22	0	0	1	0	31	7	0	.226	3	20	1	0	1.5	.958
1918	BKN	N	0	1	.000	6.75	2	1	0	8	14	2	2	0	0	0	0	2	0	0	.000	0	6	0	0	3.0	1.000
1919			10	12	.455	2.66	30	22	16	199.1	174	66	80	2	1	0	0	63	11	0	.175	4	56	3	0	2.1	.952
1920			12	8	.600	2.69	41	18	9	190.2	172	63	101	2	5	1	4	60	10	0	.167	6	46	3	1	1.3	.945
1921			3	3	.500	3.14	12	1	0	43	36	13	21	0	3	2	1	11	2	0	.182	1	14	1	0	1.3	.938
1922			1	4	.200	3.70	37	7	1	87.2	97	33	35	0	0	2	3	17	4	1	.235	2	22	0	0	0.6	1.000
1923			0	2	.000	8.31	5	0	0	13	20	6	5	0	0	2	0	2	1	0	.500	0	3	0	1	0.6	1.000
1924	NY	A	1	1	.500	5.68	14	2	0	38	44	20	12	0	1	0	0	13	1	0	.077	1	6	2	0	0.6	.778
12 yrs.			76	67	.531	2.90	254	140	78	1293	1138	511	625	15	14	9	10	422	77	1	.182	33	327	15	5	1.5	.960

WORLD SERIES

| 1920 | BKN | N | 0 | 0 | — | 4.50 | 3 | 0 | 0 | 4 | 2 | 0 | 5 | 0 | 0 | 0 | 0 | 1 | 0 | 0 | .000 | 0 | 1 | 0 | 0 | 0.3 | 1.000 |

Hal Manders

MANDERS, HAROLD CARL
B. June 14, 1917, Waukee, Iowa

BR TR 6' 187 lbs.

1941	DET	A	1	0	1.000	2.35	8	0	0	15.1	13	8	7	0	1	0	0	4	0	0	.000	1	2	0	0	0.3	1.000
1942			2	0	1.000	4.09	18	0	0	33	39	15	14	0	2	0	0	4	1	0	.250	1	7	0	0	0.4	1.000
1946	2 teams		DET A	(2G 0–0)		CHI N	(2G 0–1)																				
"	total		0	1	.000	9.75	4	1	0	12	19	5	7	0	0	0	0	4	1	0	.250	0	0	0	0	0.0	—
3 yrs.			3	1	.750	4.77	30	1	0	60.1	71	28	28	0	3	0	0	12	2	0	.167	1	9	0	0	0.3	1.000

Leo Mangum

MANGUM, LEO ALLAN (Blackie)
B. May 24, 1896, Durham, N. C. D. July 9, 1974, Lima, Ohio

BR TR 6'1" 187 lbs.

1924	CHI	A	1	4	.200	7.09	13	7	1	47	69	25	12	0	1	0	0	14	1	0	.071	3	11	2	1	1.2	.875
1925			1	0	1.000	7.80	7	0	0	15	25	6	6	0	1	0	0	4	2	0	.500	1	2	0	1	0.3	1.000
1928	NY	N	0	0	—	15.00	1	1	0	3	6	5	1	0	0	0	0	1	1	0	1.000	0	3	0	1	3.0	1.000
1932	BOS	N	0	0	—	5.23	7	0	0	10.1	17	0	3	0	0	0	0	2	0	0	.000	2	6	0	1	1.1	1.000
1933			4	3	.571	3.32	25	5	2	84	93	11	28	1	2	1	0	22	2	0	.091	2	27	0	1	1.2	1.000
1934			5	3	.625	5.72	29	3	1	94.1	127	23	28	0	4	2	1	32	9	0	.281	2	27	1	2	1.0	.967
1935			0	0	—	3.86	3	0	0	4.2	6	2	0	0	0	0	0	0	0	0	—	0	1	0	0	0.3	1.000
7 yrs.			11	10	.524	5.37	85	16	4	258.1	343	72	78	1	8	3	1	75	15	0	.200	9	77	3	6	1.0	.966

Ernie Manning

MANNING, ERNEST DEVON (Ed)
B. Oct. 9, 1890, Florala, Ala. D. Apr. 28, 1973, Pensacola, Fla.

BL TR 6' 175 lbs.

| 1914 | STL | A | 0 | 0 | — | 3.60 | 4 | 0 | 0 | 10 | 11 | 3 | 3 | 0 | 0 | 0 | 0 | 4 | 0 | 0 | .000 | 1 | 3 | 0 | 0 | 1.0 | 1.000 |

Jack Manning

MANNING, JOHN E.
B. Dec. 20, 1853, Braintree, Mass. D. Aug. 15, 1929, Boston, Mass.

BR TR 5'8½" 158 lbs.

1876	BOS	N	18	5	.783	2.14	34	20	13	197.1	213	32	24	0	4	0	5	288	76	2	.264	10	30	0	3	1.2	1.000
1877	CIN	N	0	4	.000	6.95	10	4	2	44	83	7	6	0	0	0	0	252	80	0	.317	1	11	3	1	1.5	.800
1878	BOS	N	1	0	1.000	14.29	3	1	1	11.1	24	5	2	0	0	0	1	248	63	0	.254	0	3	0	0	1.0	1.000
3 yrs.			19	9	.679	3.53	47	25	16	252.2	320	44	32	0	4	0	6	*				11	44	3	4	1.2	.948

Year	Team		W	L	PCT	ERA	G	GS	CG	IP	H	BB	SO	ShO	Relief Pitching W	L	SV	Batting AB	H	HR	BA	PO	A	E	DP	TC/G	FA

Jim Manning

MANNING, JAMES BENJAMIN
B. July 21, 1943, L'Anse, Mich.
BR TR 6'1" 185 lbs.

| 1962 | MIN | A | 0 | 0 | – | 5.14 | 5 | 1 | 0 | 7 | 14 | 1 | 3 | 0 | 0 | 0 | 0 | 1 | 0 | 0 | .000 | 3 | 1 | 0 | 0 | 0.8 | 1.000 |

Rube Manning

MANNING, WALTER S.
B. Apr. 29, 1883, Chambersburg, Pa.   D. Apr. 23, 1930, Williamsport, Pa.
BR TR 6' 180 lbs.

1907	NY	A	0	1	.000	3.00	1	1	1	9	8	3	3	0	0	0	0	3	0	0	.000	0	2	0	0	2.0	1.000
1908			13	16	.448	2.94	41	26	19	245	228	86	113	2	4	1	1	91	17	0	.187	3	70	2	0	1.8	.973
1909			7	11	.389	3.17	26	21	11	173	167	48	71	2	1	1	1	60	11	0	.183	5	51	1	0	2.2	.982
1910			2	4	.333	3.70	16	9	4	75.1	80	25	25	0	0	0	0	26	5	0	.192	1	22	0	2	1.4	1.000
4 yrs.			22	32	.407	3.14	84	57	35	502.1	483	162	212	4	5	2	2	180	33	0	.183	9	145	3	2	1.9	.981

Tom Mansell

MANSELL, THOMAS E.
Brother of Mike Mansell.   Brother of John Mansell.
B. Jan. 1, 1855, Auburn, N. Y.   D. Oct. 6, 1934, Auburn, N. Y.
BL TL 5'8" 160 lbs.

| 1883 | DET | N | 0 | 0 | – | 16.20 | 1 | 0 | 0 | 6.2 | 21 | 5 | 3 | 0 | 0 | 0 | 0 | * | | | | 1 | 0 | 1 | 0 | 2.0 | .500 |

Lou Manske

MANSKE, LOUIS HUGO
B. July 4, 1884, Milwaukee, Wis.   D. Apr. 27, 1963, Milwaukee, Wis.
BL TL 6'

| 1906 | PIT | N | 1 | 0 | 1.000 | 5.63 | 2 | 1 | 0 | 8 | 12 | 5 | 6 | 0 | 0 | 0 | 0 | 4 | 0 | 0 | .000 | 0 | 0 | 0 | 0 | 0.0 | – |

Moxie Manuel

MANUEL, MARK GARFIELD
B. Oct. 16, 1881, Metropolis, Ill.   D. Apr. 26, 1924, Memphis, Tenn.
BR TB 5'11" 170 lbs.

1905	WAS	A	0	1	.000	5.40	3	1	1	10	9	3	3	0	0	1	0	4	1	0	.250	1	5	2	0	2.7	.750
1908	CHI	A	3	4	.429	3.28	18	6	3	60.1	52	25	25	0	2	1	1	16	1	0	.063	3	22	3	1	1.6	.893
2 yrs.			3	5	.375	3.58	21	7	4	70.1	61	28	28	0	2	2	1	20	2	0	.100	4	27	5	1	1.7	.861

Dick Manville

MANVILLE, RICHARD WESLEY
B. Dec. 25, 1926, Des Moines, Iowa
BR TR 6'4" 192 lbs.

1950	BOS	N	0	0	–	0.00	1	0	0	2	0	3	2	0	0	0	0	–	0	0	–	0	0	0	0	0.0	–
1952	CHI	N	0	0	–	7.94	11	0	0	17	25	12	6	0	0	0	0	2	1	0	.500	2	4	0	0	0.5	1.000
2 yrs.			0	0	–	7.11	12	0	0	19	25	15	8	0	0	0	0	2	1	0	.500	2	4	0	0	0.5	1.000

Ravelo Manzanillo

MANZANILLO, RAVELO
Born Ravelo Manzanillo y Adams.
B. Oct. 17, 1963, San Pedro de Macoris, Dominican Republic
BL TL 6' 210 lbs.

| 1988 | CHI | A | 0 | 1 | .000 | 5.79 | 2 | 2 | 0 | 9.1 | 7 | 12 | 10 | 0 | 0 | 0 | 0 | 0 | 0 | 0 | – | 0 | 1 | 0 | 0 | 0.5 | 1.000 |

Rolla Mapel

MAPEL, ROLLA HAMILTON (Lefty)
B. Mar. 9, 1890, Lee's Summit, Mo.   D. Apr. 6, 1966, San Diego, Calif.
BL TL 5'11½" 165 lbs.

| 1919 | STL | A | 0 | 3 | .000 | 4.50 | 4 | 3 | 2 | 20 | 17 | 17 | 2 | 0 | 0 | 0 | 0 | 6 | 1 | 0 | .167 | 0 | 11 | 0 | 0 | 2.8 | 1.000 |

Georges Maranda

MARANDA, GEORGES HENRI
B. Jan. 15, 1932, Levis, Que., Canada
BR TR 6'2" 195 lbs.

1960	SF	N	1	4	.200	4.62	17	4	0	50.2	50	30	28	0	0	1	0	12	2	0	.167	5	17	1	1	1.4	.957
1962	MIN	A	1	3	.250	4.46	32	4	0	72.2	69	35	36	0	0	2	0	16	4	0	.250	3	16	1	2	0.6	.950
2 yrs.			2	7	.222	4.52	49	8	0	123.1	119	65	64	0	0	3	0	28	6	0	.214	8	33	2	3	0.9	.953

Firpo Marberry

MARBERRY, FREDERICK
B. Nov. 30, 1898, Streetman, Tex.   D. June 30, 1976, Mexia, Tex.
BR TR 6'1" 190 lbs.

1923	WAS	A	4	0	1.000	2.82	11	4	2	44.2	42	17	18	0	1	0	0	14	2	0	.143	1	10	1	0	1.1	.917
1924			11	12	.478	3.09	50	15	6	195.1	190	70	68	0	6	5	15	59	8	0	.136	8	39	2	3	1.0	.959
1925			8	6	.571	3.47	55	0	0	93.1	84	45	53	0	8	6	15	19	5	0	.263	6	26	0	1	0.6	1.000
1926			12	7	.632	3.00	64	5	3	138	120	66	43	0	9	5	22	34	6	0	.176	5	31	2	2	0.6	.947
1927			10	7	.588	4.64	56	10	2	155.1	177	68	74	0	8	2	9	41	5	0	.122	9	25	0	4	0.6	1.000
1928			13	13	.500	3.85	48	11	7	161.1	160	42	76	1	7	9	3	46	5	0	.109	8	27	1	2	0.8	.972
1929			19	12	.613	3.06	49	26	16	250.1	233	69	121	0	3	4	11	82	19	0	.232	15	35	0	1	1.0	1.000
1930			15	5	.750	4.09	33	22	9	185	190	53	56	0	3	1	1	73	24	0	.329	7	33	1	2	1.2	.976
1931			16	4	.800	3.45	45	25	11	219	211	63	88	2	3	1	7	82	19	1	.232	3	36	1	4	0.9	.975
1932			8	4	.667	4.01	54	15	8	197.2	202	72	66	1	1	1	13	66	11	0	.167	9	45	1	5	1.0	.982
1933	DET	A	16	11	.593	3.29	37	32	15	238.1	232	61	84	1	2	0	2	90	11	0	.122	11	37	4	3	1.4	.923
1934			15	5	.750	4.57	38	19	6	155.2	174	48	64	1	0	0	0	55	12	0	.218	10	20	2	2	0.8	.938
1935			0	1	.000	4.26	5	2	1	19	22	9	7	0	0	1	0	5	1	0	.200	0	3	0	0	0.6	1.000
1936	2 teams		NY N (1G 0-0)			WAS A (5G 0-2)																					
"	total		0	2	.000	3.77	6	1	0	14.1	12	9	4	0	0	0	0	3	0	0	.000	0	3	2	0	0.8	.600
14 yrs.			147	89	.623	3.63	551	187	86	2067.1	2049	686	822	8	53	37	101	669	128	1	.191	92	370	17	29	0.9	.965

WORLD SERIES

1924	WAS	A	0	1	.000	1.13	4	1	0	8	9	4	10	0	0	0	0	2	0	0	.000	1	1	0	0	0.5	1.000
1925			0	0	–	0.00	2	0	0	2.1	3	0	2	0	0	0	1	0	0	0	–	0	0	0	0	0.0	–
1934	DET	A	0	0	–	21.60	2	0	0	1.2	5	1	0	0	0	0	0	0	0	0	–	0	0	0	0	0.0	1.000
3 yrs.			0	1	.000	3.75	8	1	0	12	17	5	12	0	0	0	3	2	0	0	.000	1	1	0	0	0.4	1.000

4th

Walt Marbet

MARBET, WALTER WILLIAM
B. Sept. 13, 1890, Plymouth County, Iowa   D. Sept. 24, 1956, Hohenwald, Tenn.
BR TR 6'1" 175 lbs.

| 1913 | STL | N | 0 | 1 | .000 | 16.20 | 3 | 1 | 0 | 3.1 | 9 | 4 | 1 | 0 | 0 | 0 | 0 | – | 0 | 0 | – | 0 | 0 | 0 | 0 | 0.0 | – |

Year	Team		W	L	PCT	ERA	G	GS	CG	IP	H	BB	SO	ShO	W	L	SV	AB	H	HR	BA	PO	A	E	DP	TC/G	FA
															Relief Pitching			**Batting**									

Phil Marchildon

MARCHILDON, PHILIP JOSEPH
B. Oct. 25, 1913, Penetanguishene, Ont., Canada

BR TR 5'10½" 170 lbs.

Year	Team		W	L	PCT	ERA	G	GS	CG	IP	H	BB	SO	ShO	W	L	SV	AB	H	HR	BA	PO	A	E	DP	TC/G	FA
1940	PHI	A	0	2	.000	7.20	2	2	1	10	12	8	4	0	0	0	0	2	0	0	.000	0	3	0	0	1.5	1.000
1941			10	15	.400	3.57	30	27	14	204.1	188	118	74	1	1	1	0	66	11	0	.167	11	22	1	1	1.1	.971
1942			17	14	.548	4.20	38	31	18	244	215	140	110	1	2	1	1	84	20	0	.238	13	35	2	3	1.3	.960
1945			0	1	.000	4.00	3	2	0	9	5	11	2	0	0	0	0	2	1	0	.500	1	2	0	0	1.0	1.000
1946			13	**16**	.448	3.49	36	29	16	226.2	197	114	95	1	2	0	1	75	5	0	.067	9	33	4	0	1.3	.913
1947			19	9	.679	3.22	35	35	21	276.2	228	**141**	128	2	0	0	0	98	15	1	.153	7	34	3	2	1.3	.932
1948			9	15	.375	4.53	33	30	12	226.1	214	131	66	1	0	0	1	72	5	0	.069	10	36	4	5	1.5	.920
1949			0	3	.000	11.81	7	6	0	16	24	19	2	0	0	0	0	6	1	0	.167	1	3	1	0	0.7	.800
1950	BOS	A	0	0	–	6.75	1	0	0	1.1	1	2	0	0	0	0	0	0	0	0	–	0	0	0	0	0.0	–
9 yrs.			68	75	.476	3.93	185	162	82	1214.1	1084	684	481	6	5	3	2	405	58	1	.143	52	168	15	11	1.3	.936

Johnny Marcum

MARCUM, JOHN ALFRED (Footsie)
B. Sept. 9, 1909, Campbellsburg, Ky. D. Sept. 10, 1984, Louisville, Ky.

BL TR 5'11" 197 lbs.

Year	Team		W	L	PCT	ERA	G	GS	CG	IP	H	BB	SO	ShO	W	L	SV	AB	H	HR	BA	PO	A	E	DP	TC/G	FA
1933	PHI	A	3	2	.600	1.95	5	4	4	37	28	20	14	2	0	0	0	12	2	0	.167	5	6	0	0	2.2	1.000
1934			14	11	.560	4.50	37	31	17	232	257	88	92	2	1	2	0	112	30	1	.268	14	42	3	2	1.6	.949
1935			17	12	.586	4.08	39	27	19	242.2	256	83	99	2	2	0	3	119	37	2	.311	11	32	5	1	1.2	.896
1936	BOS	A	8	13	.381	4.81	31	23	9	174	194	52	57	1	1	2	1	88	18	2	.205	7	31	2	3	1.3	.950
1937			13	11	.542	4.85	37	23	9	183.2	230	47	59	1	5	1	3	86	23	0	.267	13	38	1	1	1.4	.981
1938			5	6	.455	4.09	15	11	7	92.1	113	25	25	0	1	0	0	37	5	0	.135	3	15	0	0	1.2	1.000
1939	2 teams		STL A		(12G 2–5)					CHI A		(19G 3–3)															
"	total		5	8	.385	6.60	31	12	4	137.2	191	29	46	0	0	3	0	79	26	0	.329	8	17	1	2	0.8	.962
7 yrs.			65	63	.508	4.66	195	132	69	1099.1	1269	344	392	8	10	8	7	*				61	181	12	9	1.3	.953

Leo Marentette

MARENTETTE, LEO JOHN
B. Feb. 18, 1941, Detroit, Mich.

BR TR 6'2" 200 lbs.

Year	Team		W	L	PCT	ERA	G	GS	CG	IP	H	BB	SO	ShO	W	L	SV	AB	H	HR	BA	PO	A	E	DP	TC/G	FA
1965	DET	A	0	0	–	0.00	2	0	0	3	1	1	3	0	0	0	0	0	0	0	–	0	1	0	0	0.5	1.000
1969	MON	N	0	0	–	6.75	3	0	0	5.1	9	1	4	0	0	0	0	1	0	0	.000	2	0	0	0	0.7	1.000
2 yrs.			0	0	–	4.32	5	0	0	8.1	10	2	7	0	0	0	0	1	0	0	.000	2	1	0	0	0.6	1.000

Joe Margoneri

MARGONERI, JOSEPH EMANUEL
B. Jan. 13, 1930, Somerset, Pa.

BL TL 6' 185 lbs.

Year	Team		W	L	PCT	ERA	G	GS	CG	IP	H	BB	SO	ShO	W	L	SV	AB	H	HR	BA	PO	A	E	DP	TC/G	FA
1956	NY	N	6	6	.500	3.93	23	13	2	91.2	88	49	49	0	1	1	0	29	3	1	.103	3	15	1	0	0.8	.947
1957			1	1	.500	5.24	13	2	1	34.1	44	21	18	0	0	1	0	8	0	0	.000	1	5	0	1	0.5	1.000
2 yrs.			7	7	.500	4.29	36	15	3	126	132	70	67	0	1	2	0	37	3	1	.081	4	20	1	1	0.7	.960

Juan Marichal

MARICHAL, JUAN ANTONIO (Manito, The Dominican Dandy)
Born Juan Antonio Marichal y Sanchez.
B. Oct. 20, 1937, Laguna Verde, Dominican Republic
Hall of Fame 1983.

BR TR 6' 185 lbs.

Year	Team		W	L	PCT	ERA	G	GS	CG	IP	H	BB	SO	ShO	W	L	SV	AB	H	HR	BA	PO	A	E	DP	TC/G	FA
1960	SF	N	6	2	.750	2.66	11	11	6	81.1	59	28	58	1	0	0	0	31	4	0	.129	5	13	0	1	1.6	1.000
1961			13	10	.565	3.89	29	27	9	185	183	48	124	3	1	1	0	59	7	0	.119	10	27	3	1	1.4	.925
1962			18	11	.621	3.36	37	36	18	262.2	233	90	153	3	0	0	1	89	21	0	.236	15	43	4	0	1.7	.935
1963			**25**	8	.758	2.41	41	40	18	**321.1**	259	61	248	5	1	0	0	112	20	1	.179	18	39	2	1	1.4	.966
1964			21	8	.724	2.48	33	33	**22**	269	241	52	206	4	0	0	0	97	14	0	.144	29	42	3	2	2.2	.959
1965			22	13	.629	2.13	39	37	24	295.1	224	46	240	**10**	1	0	1	98	17	0	.173	23	43	3	3	1.8	.957
1966			25	**6**	.806	2.23	37	36	25	307.1	228	36	222	4	1	0	0	112	28	1	.250	23	47	4	2	2.0	.946
1967			14	10	.583	2.76	26	26	18	202.1	195	42	166	2	0	0	0	79	14	0	.177	15	22	2	1	1.5	.949
1968			**26**	9	.743	2.43	38	38	**30**	325.2	295	46	218	5	0	0	0	123	20	0	.163	33	64	6	3	2.7	.942
1969			21	11	.656	**2.10**	37	36	27	300	244	54	205	**8**	0	0	0	109	15	0	.138	21	64	2	3	2.4	.977
1970			12	10	.545	4.11	34	33	14	243	269	48	123	1	0	0	0	85	5	0	.059	25	43	1	1	2.0	.986
1971			18	11	.621	2.94	37	37	18	279	244	56	159	4	0	0	0	105	14	2	.133	28	52	7	3	2.4	.920
1972			6	16	.273	3.71	25	24	6	165	176	46	72	0	0	1	0	51	10	0	.196	17	24	6	1	1.9	.872
1973			11	15	.423	3.79	34	32	9	209	231	37	87	2	0	0	0	69	13	0	.188	25	44	4	5	2.1	.945
1974	BOS	A	5	1	.833	4.87	11	9	0	57.1	61	14	21	0	0	0	0	–				4	8	0	0	1.1	1.000
1975	LA	N	0	1	.000	13.50	2	2	0	6	11	5	1	0	0	0	0	0	0	0	.000	0	2	0	0	1.0	1.000
16 yrs.			243	142	.631	2.89	471	457	244	3509.1	3153	709	2303	52	5	2	2	1221	202	4	.165	291	577	47	27	1.9	.949

LEAGUE CHAMPIONSHIP SERIES

Year	Team		W	L	PCT	ERA	G	GS	CG	IP	H	BB	SO	ShO	W	L	SV	AB	H	HR	BA	PO	A	E	DP	TC/G	FA
1971	SF	N	0	1	.000	2.25	1	1	1	8	4	0	6	0	0	0	0	3	0	0	.000	2	4	0	0	6.0	1.000

WORLD SERIES

Year	Team		W	L	PCT	ERA	G	GS	CG	IP	H	BB	SO	ShO	W	L	SV	AB	H	HR	BA	PO	A	E	DP	TC/G	FA
1962	SF	N	0	0	–	0.00	1	1	0	4	2	2	4	0	0	0	0	2	0	0	.000	1	0	1	0	1.0	1.000

Dan Marion

MARION, DONALD G.
B. July 31, 1890, Cleveland, Ohio D. Jan. 18, 1933, Milwaukee, Wis.

BR TR 6'1" 187 lbs.

Year	Team		W	L	PCT	ERA	G	GS	CG	IP	H	BB	SO	ShO	W	L	SV	AB	H	HR	BA	PO	A	E	DP	TC/G	FA
1914	BKN	F	3	2	.600	3.93	17	9	4	89.1	97	38	41	0	0	0	0	36	7	0	.194	3	21	2	0	1.5	.923
1915			10	9	.526	3.20	35	25	15	208.1	193	64	46	2	0	1	0	74	13	0	.176	8	66	6	2	2.3	.925
2 yrs.			13	11	.542	3.42	52	34	19	297.2	290	102	87	2	0	1	0	110	20	0	.182	11	87	8	2	2.0	.925

Duke Markell

MARKELL, HARRY DUQUESNE
Born Harry Duquesne Makowsky.
B. Aug. 17, 1923, Paris, France D. June 14, 1984, Fort Lauderdale, Fla.

BR TR 6'1½" 209 lbs.

Year	Team		W	L	PCT	ERA	G	GS	CG	IP	H	BB	SO	ShO	W	L	SV	AB	H	HR	BA	PO	A	E	DP	TC/G	FA
1951	STL	A	1	1	.500	6.33	5	2	1	21.1	25	20	10	0	0	0	0	6	1	0	.167	1	1	0	0	0.4	1.000

Cliff Markle

MARKLE, CLIFFORD MONROE
B. May 3, 1894, Dravosburg, Pa. D. May 24, 1974, Temple City, Calif.

BR TR 5'8½" 160 lbs.

Year	Team		W	L	PCT	ERA	G	GS	CG	IP	H	BB	SO	ShO	W	L	SV	AB	H	HR	BA	PO	A	E	DP	TC/G	FA
1915	NY	A	2	0	1.000	0.39	3	2	2	23	15	6	12	0	0	0	0				.000	1	4	1	0	2.0	.833
1916			4	3	.571	4.53	11	7	3	45.2	41	31	14	1	0	1	0	13	0	0	.000	1	12	0	0	1.2	1.000
1921	CIN	N	2	6	.250	3.76	10	6	5	67	75	20	23	0	1	0	0	24	3	0	.125	6	11	2	1	1.9	.895
1922			4	5	.444	3.81	25	3	2	75.2	75	33	34	1	3	3	0	20	3	0	.150	4	15	0	0	0.8	1.000

Year	Team	W	L	PCT	ERA	G	GS	CG	IP	H	BB	SO	ShO	Relief Pitching W	L	SV	Batting AB	H	HR	BA	PO	A	E	DP	TC/G	FA

Cliff Markle *continued*

Year	Team	W	L	PCT	ERA	G	GS	CG	IP	H	BB	SO	ShO	W	L	SV	AB	H	HR	BA	PO	A	E	DP	TC/G	FA
1924	NY A	0	3	.000	8.87	7	3	0	23.1	29	20	7	0	0	0	0	8	0	0	.000	1	3	1	0	0.7	.800
5 yrs.		12	17	.414	4.10	56	21	12	234.2	235	110	90	2	4	5	0	69	6	0	.087	13	45	4	1	1.1	.935

Dick Marlowe

MARLOWE, RICHARD BURTON
B. June 27, 1929, Hickory, N. C.   D. Dec. 30, 1968, Toledo, Ohio

BR TR 6'2"   165 lbs.

Year	Team	W	L	PCT	ERA	G	GS	CG	IP	H	BB	SO	ShO	W	L	SV	AB	H	HR	BA	PO	A	E	DP	TC/G	FA
1951	DET A	0	1	.000	32.40	2	1	0	1.2	5	2	1	0	0	0	0	0	0	0	–	0	0	0	0	0.0	–
1952		0	2	.000	7.36	4	1	0	11	11	3	3	0	0	1	0	2	0	0	.000	1	2	0	0	0.3	1.000
1953		6	7	.462	5.26	42	11	2	119.2	152	42	52	0	3	1	0	32	7	0	.219	7	17	1	0	0.6	.960
1954		5	4	.556	4.18	38	2	0	84	76	40	39	0	5	2	2	18	3	0	.167	5	11	1	0	0.4	.941
1955		1	0	1.000	1.80	4	1	1	15	12	4	9	0	0	0	0	4	0	0	.000	0	0	0	0	0.3	1.000
1956	2 teams	DET A	(7G 1–1)			CHI A	(1G 0–0)																			
"	total	1	1	.500	6.00	8	1	0	12	14	10	4	0	1	0	0	1	0	0	.000	2	0	0	0	0.4	1.000
6 yrs.		13	15	.464	4.99	98	17	3	243.1	280	101	108	0	9	4	3	57	10	0	.175	15	30	2	0	0.5	.957

Lou Marone

MARONE, LOUIS STEPHEN
B. Dec. 3, 1945, San Diego, Calif.

BB TL 5'11"   185 lbs.

Year	Team	W	L	PCT	ERA	G	GS	CG	IP	H	BB	SO	ShO	W	L	SV	AB	H	HR	BA	PO	A	E	DP	TC/G	FA
1969	PIT N	1	1	.500	2.57	29	0	0	35	24	13	25	0	1	1	0	0	0	0	–	1	4	1	0	0.2	.833
1970		0	0	–	4.50	1	0	0	2	2	0	0	0	0	0	0	0	0	0	–	0	0	0	0	0.0	–
2 yrs.		1	1	.500	2.68	30	0	0	37	26	13	25	0	1	1	0	0	0	0	–	1	4	1	0	0.2	.833

Rube Marquard

MARQUARD, RICHARD WILLIAM
B. Oct. 9, 1889, Cleveland, Ohio
D. June 1, 1980, Baltimore, Md.
Hall of Fame 1971.

BB TL 6'3"   180 lbs.
BL 1925

Year	Team	W	L	PCT	ERA	G	GS	CG	IP	H	BB	SO	ShO	W	L	SV	AB	H	HR	BA	PO	A	E	DP	TC/G	FA
1908	NY N	0	1	.000	3.60	1	1	0	5	6	2	2	0	0	0	0	1	0	0	.000	0	1	0	0	1.0	1.000
1909		5	13	.278	2.60	29	21	8	173	155	73	109	0	2	0	0	54	8	0	.148	3	45	4	1	1.8	.923
1910		4	4	.500	4.46	13	8	2	70.2	65	40	52	0	0	1	0	27	3	0	.111	0	17	2	1	1.5	.895
1911		24	7	**.774**	2.50	45	33	22	277.2	221	106	**237**	5	2	1	2	104	17	1	.163	6	46	4	1	1.2	.929
1912		26	11	.703	2.57	43	38	22	294.2	286	80	175	1	2	0	0	96	21	0	.219	2	58	1	0	1.4	.984
1913		23	10	.697	2.50	42	33	20	288	248	49	151	4	5	0	2	105	23	0	.219	4	46	2	2	1.2	.962
1914		12	22	.353	3.06	39	33	15	268	261	47	92	4	1	0	2	84	15	0	.179	5	77	3	0	2.2	.965
1915	2 teams	NY N	(27G 9–8)			BKN N	(6G 2–2)																			
"	total	11	10	.524	4.04	33	23	10	193.2	207	38	92	2	1	2	0	63	7	0	.111	6	51	6	2	1.9	.905
1916	BKN N	13	6	.684	1.58	36	20	15	205	169	38	107	2	3	0	5	63	9	0	.143	4	35	2	1	1.1	.951
1917		19	12	.613	2.55	37	29	14	232.2	200	60	117	2	5	1	0	75	15	0	.200	5	47	3	1	1.5	.945
1918		9	18	.333	2.64	34	29	19	239	231	59	89	4	0	0	0	76	13	0	.171	5	58	3	1	1.9	.955
1919		3	3	.500	2.29	8	7	3	59	54	10	29	0	0	0	0	23	6	0	.261	1	11	0	0	1.5	1.000
1920		10	7	.588	3.23	28	26	10	189.2	181	35	89	1	0	0	0	59	10	0	.169	7	30	1	2	1.4	.974
1921	CIN N	17	14	.548	3.39	39	35	18	265.2	291	50	88	2	0	1	0	95	19	0	.200	7	51	1	6	1.5	.983
1922	BOS N	11	15	.423	5.09	39	24	7	198	255	66	57	0	3	1	1	63	14	0	.222	4	51	4	4	1.5	.932
1923		11	14	.440	3.73	38	29	11	239	265	65	78	3	0	2	0	86	12	0	.140	0	58	2	5	1.6	.967
1924		1	2	.333	3.00	6	6	1	36	33	13	10	0	0	0	0	11	3	0	.273	0	9	0	0	1.5	1.000
1925		2	8	.200	5.75	26	8	0	72	105	27	19	0	0	4	0	22	3	0	.136	4	6	1	0	0.4	.909
18 yrs.		201	177	.532	3.08	536	403	197	3306.2	3233	858	1593	30	27	12	14	1107	198	1	.179	63	697	39	27	1.5	.951

WORLD SERIES

Year	Team	W	L	PCT	ERA	G	GS	CG	IP	H	BB	SO	ShO	W	L	SV	AB	H	HR	BA	PO	A	E	DP	TC/G	FA
1911	NY N	0	1	.000	1.54	3	2	1	11.2	9	1	8	0	0	0	0	2	0	0	.000	0	2	0	0	0.7	1.000
1912		2	0	1.000	0.50	3	2	2	18	14	2	9	0	0	0	0	4	0	0	.000	0	4	1	0	2.5	.800
1913		0	1	.000	7.00	2	1	0	9	10	3	3	0	0	0	0	1	0	0	.000	0	8	0	0	4.0	1.000
1916	BKN N	0	2	.000	4.91	2	2	0	11	12	6	9	0	0	0	0	3	0	0	.000	0	2	0	0	1.0	1.000
1920		0	1	.000	2.00	2	1	0	9	7	3	6	0	0	0	0	1	0	0	.000	0	1	0	0	0.5	1.000
5 yrs.		2	5	.286	2.76	11	8	4	58.2	52	15	35	0	0	0	0	11	0	0	.000	0	17	1	0	1.6	.944
				2nd			10th	10th																		

Jim Marquis

MARQUIS, JAMES MILBURN
B. Nov. 18, 1900, Yoakum, Tex.

BR TR 5'11"   174 lbs.

Year	Team	W	L	PCT	ERA	G	GS	CG	IP	H	BB	SO	ShO	W	L	SV	AB	H	HR	BA	PO	A	E	DP	TC/G	FA
1925	NY A	0	0	–	9.82	2	2	0	7.1	12	6	0	0	0	0	0	2	0	0	.000	0	4	1	0	2.5	.800

Connie Marrero

MARRERO, CONRADO EUGENIO
Born Conrado Eugenio Marrero y Ramos.
B. Apr. 25, 1911, Las Villas, Cuba

BR TR 5'7"   158 lbs.

Year	Team	W	L	PCT	ERA	G	GS	CG	IP	H	BB	SO	ShO	W	L	SV	AB	H	HR	BA	PO	A	E	DP	TC/G	FA
1950	WAS A	6	10	.375	4.50	27	19	8	152	159	55	63	1	1	0	1	49	6	0	.122	4	14	0	0	0.7	1.000
1951		11	9	.550	3.90	25	25	16	187	198	71	66	2	0	0	0	61	10	0	.164	5	29	3	1	1.5	.919
1952		11	8	.579	2.88	22	22	16	184.1	175	53	77	2	0	0	0	63	5	0	.079	7	18	1	2	1.2	.962
1953		8	7	.533	3.03	22	20	10	145.2	130	48	65	2	0	0	0	48	6	0	.125	5	19	2	1	1.2	.923
1954		3	6	.333	4.75	22	8	1	66.1	74	22	26	0	2	2	2	15	0	0	.000	1	9	0	1	0.5	1.000
5 yrs.		39	40	.494	3.67	118	94	51	735.1	736	249	297	7	3	2	3	236	27	0	.114	22	89	6	5	1.0	.949

Buck Marrow

MARROW, CHARLES KENNON
B. Aug. 29, 1909, Tarboro, N. C.   D. Nov. 21, 1982, Newport News, Va.

BR TR 6'4"   200 lbs.

Year	Team	W	L	PCT	ERA	G	GS	CG	IP	H	BB	SO	ShO	W	L	SV	AB	H	HR	BA	PO	A	E	DP	TC/G	FA
1932	DET A	2	5	.286	4.81	18	7	2	63.2	70	29	31	0	1	0	1	19	3	0	.158	6	14	1	0	1.2	.952
1937	BKN N	1	2	.333	6.61	6	3	1	16.1	19	9	2	0	0	1	0	5	0	0	.000	1	4	0	1	0.8	1.000
1938		0	1	.000	4.58	15	0	0	19.2	23	11	6	0	0	0	0	1	0	0	.000	2	4	0	1	0.4	1.000
3 yrs.		3	8	.273	5.06	39	10	3	99.2	112	49	39	0	1	1	1	25	3	0	.120	9	22	1	1	0.8	.969

Ed Mars

MARS, EDWARD M.
B. Dec. 4, 1866, Chicago, Ill.   D. Dec. 9, 1941, Chicago, Ill.

5'9"   166 lbs.

Year	Team	W	L	PCT	ERA	G	GS	CG	IP	H	BB	SO	ShO	W	L	SV	AB	H	HR	BA	PO	A	E	DP	TC/G	FA
1890	SYR AA	9	5	.643	4.67	16	14	14	121.1	132	49	59	0	0	0	0	51	14	0	.275	3	28	2	1	2.1	.939

Year	Team		W	L	PCT	ERA	G	GS	CG	IP	H	BB	SO	ShO	Relief Pitching W	L	SV	Batting AB	H	HR	BA	PO	A	E	DP	TC/G	FA

Cuddles Marshall

MARSHALL, CLARENCE WESTLY
B. Apr. 28, 1925, Bellingham, Wash.　　　　　　BR TR 6'3" 200 lbs.

Year	Team		W	L	PCT	ERA	G	GS	CG	IP	H	BB	SO	ShO	W	L	SV	AB	H	HR	BA	PO	A	E	DP	TC/G	FA
1946	NY	A	3	4	.429	5.33	23	11	1	81	96	56	32	0	2	0	0	28	4	0	.143	2	18	0	2	0.9	1.000
1948			0	0	–	0.00	1	0	0	1	0	3	0	0	0	0	0	0	0	0	–	0	0	0	0	0.0	–
1949			3	0	1.000	5.11	21	2	0	49.1	48	48	13	0	3	0	3	9	1	0	.111	0	14	1	1	0.7	.933
1950	STL	A	1	3	.250	7.88	28	2	0	53.2	72	51	24	0	1	2	1	12	4	0	.333	0	5	2	0	0.3	.714
4 yrs.			7	7	.500	5.98	73	15	1	185	216	158	69	0	6	2	4	49	9	0	.184	2	37	3	3	0.6	.929

Mike Marshall

MARSHALL, MICHAEL GRANT
B. Jan. 15, 1943, Adrian, Mich.　　　　　　BR TR 5'10" 180 lbs.

Year	Team		W	L	PCT	ERA	G	GS	CG	IP	H	BB	SO	ShO	W	L	SV	AB	H	HR	BA	PO	A	E	DP	TC/G	FA
1967	DET	A	1	3	.250	1.98	37	0	0	59	51	20	41	0	1	3	10	9	2	0	.222	11	8	0	0	0.5	1.000
1969	SEA	A	3	10	.231	5.13	20	14	3	87.2	99	35	47	1	0	1	0	27	7	1	.259	14	22	2	2	1.9	.947
1970	2 teams		HOU N (4G 0–1)			MON N (24G 3–7)																					
"	total		3	8	.273	3.86	28	5	0	70	64	33	43	0	3	4	3	11	1	0	.091	4	20	0	2	0.9	1.000
1971	MON	N	5	8	.385	4.30	66	0	0	111	100	50	85	0	5	8	23	16	3	0	.188	6	30	2	2	0.6	.947
1972			14	8	.636	1.78	65	0	0	116	82	47	95	0	14	8	18	22	3	0	.136	5	17	1	0	0.4	.957
1973			14	11	.560	2.66	92	0	0	179	163	75	124	0	14	11	31	33	8	0	.242	14	37	1	2	0.6	.981
1974	LA	N	15	12	.556	2.42	106¹	0	0	208	191	56	143	0	15	12	21	34	8	0	.235	9	33	2	4	0.4	.955
1975			9	14	.391	3.30	57	0	0	109	98	39	64	0	9	14	13	15	1	0	.067	6	23	3	6	0.6	.906
1976	2 teams		LA N (30G 4–3)			ATL N (24G 2–1)																					
"	total		6	4	.600	3.99	54	0	0	99.1	99	39	56	0	6	4	14	11	1	0	.091	7	24	0	1	0.6	1.000
1977	2 teams		ATL N (4G 1–0)			TEX A (12G 2–2)																					
"	total		3	2	.600	4.71	16	4	0	42	54	15	24	0	1	2	1	1	1	0	1.000	2	7	1	1	0.6	.900
1978	MIN	A	10	12	.455	2.36	54	0	0	99	80	37	56	0	10	12	21	0	0	0	–	9	19	1	1	0.5	.966
1979			10	15	.400	2.64	90	1	0	143	132	48	81	0	10	14	32	0	0	0	–	11	31	1	4	0.5	.977
1980			1	3	.250	6.19	18	0	0	32	42	12	13	0	1	3	1	0	0	0	–	4	7	0	0	0.6	1.000
1981	NY	N	3	2	.600	2.61	20	0	0	31	26	8	17	0	3	2	0	0	0	0	–	3	5	1	0	0.5	.889
14 yrs.			97	112	.464	3.14	723	24	3	1386	1281	514	880	1	92	98	188	179	35	1	.196	105	283	15	25	0.6	.963
															9th												

LEAGUE CHAMPIONSHIP SERIES

Year	Team		W	L	PCT	ERA	G	GS	CG	IP	H	BB	SO	ShO	W	L	SV	AB	H	HR	BA	PO	A	E	DP	TC/G	FA
1974	LA	N	0	0	–	0.00	2	0	0	3	0	0	1	0	0	0	0	0	0	0	–	0	0	0	0	0.0	–

WORLD SERIES

Year	Team		W	L	PCT	ERA	G	GS	CG	IP	H	BB	SO	ShO	W	L	SV	AB	H	HR	BA	PO	A	E	DP	TC/G	FA
1974	LA	N	0	1	.000	1.00	5	0	0	9	6	1	10	0	0	1	1	0	0	0	–	0	4	0	0	0.8	1.000

Rube Marshall

MARSHALL, ROY DeVERNE (Cy)
B. July 19, 1890, Salineville, Ohio　 D. June 11, 1980, Dover, Ohio　　　BR TR 5'11" 170 lbs.

Year	Team		W	L	PCT	ERA	G	GS	CG	IP	H	BB	SO	ShO	W	L	SV	AB	H	HR	BA	PO	A	E	DP	TC/G	FA
1912	PHI	N	0	1	.000	21.00	2	1	0	3	12	1	2	0	0	0	0				–	0	1	0	0	0.5	1.000
1913			0	1	.000	4.57	14	3	0	45.1	54	22	18	0	0	0	1	11	1	0	.091	0	13	0	0	0.9	1.000
1914			6	7	.462	3.75	27	19	7	134.1	144	50	49	0	1	0	1	43	6	0	.140	7	38	3	1	1.8	.938
1915	BUF	F	3	1	.750	3.94	21	4	2	59.1	62	33	21	0	0	0	0	17	5	0	.294	0	15	1	0	0.8	.938
4 yrs.			9	10	.474	4.17	64	27	9	242	272	106	90	0	1	0	2	71	12	0	.169	7	67	4	1	1.2	.949

Barney Martin

MARTIN, BARNES ROBERTSON
Father of Jerry Martin.
B. Mar. 3, 1923, Columbia, S. C.　　　　　　BR TR 5'11" 170 lbs.

Year	Team		W	L	PCT	ERA	G	GS	CG	IP	H	BB	SO	ShO	W	L	SV	AB	H	HR	BA	PO	A	E	DP	TC/G	FA
1953	CIN	N	0	0	–	9.00	1	0	0	2	3	1	1	0	0	0	0	0	0	0	–	0	0	0	0	0.0	–

Doc Martin

MARTIN, HAROLD WINTHROP
B. Sept. 23, 1887, Roxbury, Mass.　 D. Apr. 14, 1935, Milton, Mass.　　BR TR 5'11" 165 lbs.

Year	Team		W	L	PCT	ERA	G	GS	CG	IP	H	BB	SO	ShO	W	L	SV	AB	H	HR	BA	PO	A	E	DP	TC/G	FA
1908	PHI	A	0	1	.000	13.50	1	1	0	2	2	3	2	0	0	0	0	1	0	0	.000	0	0	0	0	0.0	–
1911			1	1	.500	4.50	11	3	1	38	40	17	21	0	0	0	0	14	3	0	.214	1	12	2	0	1.4	.867
1912			0	0	–	10.38	2	0	0	4.1	5	5	4	0	0	0	0	3	0	0	.000	0	3	0	0	1.5	1.000
3 yrs.			1	2	.333	5.48	14	4	1	44.1	47	25	27	0	0	0	0	18	3	0	.167	1	15	2	0	1.3	.889

Freddie Martin

MARTIN, FRED TURNER
B. June 27, 1915, Williams, Okla.　 D. June 11, 1979, Chicago, Ill.　　BR TR 6'1" 185 lbs.

Year	Team		W	L	PCT	ERA	G	GS	CG	IP	H	BB	SO	ShO	W	L	SV	AB	H	HR	BA	PO	A	E	DP	TC/G	FA
1946	STL	N	2	1	.667	4.08	6	3	2	28.2	29	8	19	0	0	0	1	11	3	0	.273	2	7	1	1	1.7	.900
1949			6	0	1.000	2.44	21	5	3	70	65	20	30	0	2	0	0	20	6	0	.300	4	13	1	0	0.9	.944
1950			4	2	.667	5.12	30	2	0	63.1	87	30	19	0	4	0	0	15	4	0	.267	8	13	1	0	0.7	.955
3 yrs.			12	3	.800	3.78	57	10	5	162	181	58	68	0	6	0	1	46	13	0	.283	14	33	3	1	0.9	.940

John Martin

MARTIN, JOHN ROBERT
B. Apr. 11, 1956, Wyandotte, Mich.　　　　　　BB TL 6' 190 lbs.

Year	Team		W	L	PCT	ERA	G	GS	CG	IP	H	BB	SO	ShO	W	L	SV	AB	H	HR	BA	PO	A	E	DP	TC/G	FA
1980	STL	N	2	3	.400	4.29	9	5	1	42	39	9	23	0	0	0	0	11	3	0	.273	0	5	0	0	0.6	1.000
1981			8	5	.615	3.41	17	15	4	103	85	26	36	0	0	0	0	33	7	0	.212	3	20	0	1	1.4	1.000
1982			4	5	.444	4.23	24	7	0	66	56	30	21	0	1	2	0	11	1	0	.091	2	8	1	0	0.5	.909
1983	2 teams		STL N (26G 3–1)			DET A (15G 0–0)																					
"	total		3	1	.750	4.18	41	0	0	79.2	75	30	40	0	2	0	1	18	4	0	.222	3	16	1	0	0.5	.950
4 yrs.			17	14	.548	3.93	91	32	5	290.2	255	95	120	0	3	3	1	73	15	0	.205	8	49	2	0	0.6	.966

Morrie Martin

MARTIN, MORRIS WEBSTER
B. Sept. 3, 1922, Dixon, Mo.　　　　　　BL TL 6' 173 lbs.

Year	Team		W	L	PCT	ERA	G	GS	CG	IP	H	BB	SO	ShO	W	L	SV	AB	H	HR	BA	PO	A	E	DP	TC/G	FA
1949	BKN	N	1	3	.250	7.04	10	4	0	30.2	39	15	15	0	1	0	0	10	2	0	.200	0	7	1	0	0.8	.875
1951	PHI	A	11	4	.733	3.78	35	13	3	138	139	63	35	1	5	0	0	50	11	0	.220	6	33	2	5	1.2	.951
1952			0	2	.000	6.39	5	5	0	25.1	32	15	13	0	0	0	0	9	1	0	.111	0	3	0	0	0.6	1.000
1953			10	12	.455	4.43	58	11	2	156.1	158	59	64	0	8	5	7	42	4	0	.095	2	26	0	4	0.5	1.000
1954	2 teams		PHI A (13G 2–4)			CHI A (35G 5–4)																					
"	total		7	8	.467	3.52	48	8	3	122.2	109	43	55	0	4	5	5	32	6	0	.188	4	19	1	1	0.5	.958
1955	CHI	A	2	3	.400	3.63	37	0	0	52	50	22	22	0	2	3	2	10	3	0	.300	2	15	0	0	0.5	1.000

Year	Team	W	L	PCT	ERA	G	GS	CG	IP	H	BB	SO	ShO	Relief Pitching W	L	SV	Batting AB	H	HR	BA	PO	A	E	DP	TC/G	FA

Morrie Martin *continued*

Year	Team	W	L	PCT	ERA	G	GS	CG	IP	H	BB	SO	ShO	W	L	SV	AB	H	HR	BA	PO	A	E	DP	TC/G	FA
1956	2 teams	CHI A	(10G 1–0)		BAL A	(9G 1–1)																				
"	total	2	1	.667	6.17	19	0	0	23.1	31	9	12	0	2	1	0	5	1	0	.200	1	4	1	1	0.3	.833
1957	STL N	0	0	–	2.53	4	1	0	10.2	5	4	7	0	0	0	0	2	0	0	.000	1	3	0	0	1.0	1.000
1958	2 teams	STL N	(17G 3–1)		CLE A	(14G 2–0)																				
"	total	5	1	.833	3.74	31	0	0	43.1	39	20	21	0	5	1	1	5	0	0	.000	2	5	0	2	0.2	1.000
1959	CHI N	0	0	–	19.29	3	0	0	2.1	5	1	1	0	0	0	0	0	0	0	–	0	1	0	0	0.3	1.000
	10 yrs.	38	34	.528	4.29	250	42	8	604.2	607	251	245	1	27	15	15	165	28	0	.170	18	116	5	13	0.6	.964

Pat Martin

MARTIN, PATRICK FRANCIS
B. Apr. 13, 1894, Brooklyn, N. Y.   D. Feb. 4, 1949, Brooklyn, N. Y.

BL TL 5'11½" 170 lbs.

Year	Team	W	L	PCT	ERA	G	GS	CG	IP	H	BB	SO	ShO	W	L	SV	AB	H	HR	BA	PO	A	E	DP	TC/G	FA
1919	PHI A	0	2	.000	4.09	2	2	1	11	11	8	6	0	0	0	0	3	0	0	.000	0	2	1	0	1.5	.667
1920		1	4	.200	6.12	8	5	2	32.1	48	25	14	0	0	0	0	10	4	0	.400	0	6	3	0	1.1	.667
	2 yrs.	1	6	.143	5.61	10	7	3	43.1	59	33	20	0	0	0	0	13	4	0	.308	0	8	4	0	1.2	.667

Paul Martin

MARTIN, PAUL CHARLES
B. Mar. 10, 1932, Brownstone, Pa.

BR TR 6'6" 235 lbs.

Year	Team	W	L	PCT	ERA	G	GS	CG	IP	H	BB	SO	ShO	W	L	SV	AB	H	HR	BA	PO	A	E	DP	TC/G	FA
1955	PIT N	0	1	.000	13.50	7	1	0	7.1	13	17	3	0	0	0	0	0	0	0	–	0	1	0	0	0.1	1.000

Pepper Martin

MARTIN, JOHN LEONARD ROOSEVELT (The Wild Hoss Of The Osage)
B. Feb. 29, 1904, Temple, Okla.   D. Mar. 5, 1965, McAlester, Okla.

BR TR 5'8" 170 lbs.

Year	Team	W	L	PCT	ERA	G	GS	CG	IP	H	BB	SO	ShO	W	L	SV	AB	H	HR	BA	PO	A	E	DP	TC/G	FA
1934	STL N	0	0	–	4.50	1	0	0	2	1	0	0	0	0	0	0	454	131	5	.289	0	1	0	0	1.0	1.000
1936		0	0	–	0.00	1	0	0	2	1	2	0	0	0	0	0	572	177	11	.309	0	0	0	0	0.0	–
	2 yrs.	0	0	–	2.25	2	0	0	4	2	2	0	0	0	0	0	*				0	1	0	0	0.5	1.000

Ray Martin

MARTIN, RAYMOND JOSEPH
B. Mar. 13, 1925, Norwood, Mass.

BR TR 6'2" 177 lbs.

Year	Team	W	L	PCT	ERA	G	GS	CG	IP	H	BB	SO	ShO	W	L	SV	AB	H	HR	BA	PO	A	E	DP	TC/G	FA
1943	BOS N	0	0	–	8.10	2	0	0	3.1	3	1	1	0	0	0	0	1	0	0	.000	0	2	0	0	1.0	1.000
1947		1	0	1.000	1.00	1	1	1	9	7	4	2	0	0	0	0	3	0	0	.000	3	2	0	0	5.0	1.000
1948		0	0	–	0.00	2	0	0	2.1	0	1	0	0	0	0	0	0	0	0	–	0	0	0	0	0.0	–
	3 yrs.	1	0	1.000	2.45	5	1	1	14.2	10	6	3	0	0	0	0	4	0	0	.000	3	4	0	0	1.4	1.000

Renie Martin

MARTIN, DONALD RENIE
B. Aug. 30, 1955, Dover, Del.

BR TR 6'4" 190 lbs.

Year	Team	W	L	PCT	ERA	G	GS	CG	IP	H	BB	SO	ShO	W	L	SV	AB	H	HR	BA	PO	A	E	DP	TC/G	FA
1979	KC A	0	3	.000	5.14	25	0	0	35	32	14	25	0	0	3	0		5	8	1	0	0.6	.929			
1980		10	10	.500	4.40	32	20	2	137	133	70	68	0	2	0	2	0	0	0	–	10	18	4	5	1.0	.875
1981		4	5	.444	2.76	29	0	0	62	55	29	25	0	4	5	4	0	0	0	–	3	15	2	2	0.7	.900
1982	SF N	7	10	.412	4.66	29	25	1	141	148	64	63	0	0	0	0	49	13	0	.265	8	28	5	2	1.4	.878
1983		2	4	.333	4.20	37	6	0	94.1	95	51	43	0	2	1	1	26	9	0	.346	15	16	0	0	0.8	1.000
1984	2 teams	SF N	(12G 1–1)		PHI N	(9G 0–2)																				
"	total	1	3	.250	4.15	21	0	0	39	46	28	13	0	1	3	5	8	3	0	.375	3	14	0	1	0.8	1.000
	6 yrs.	24	35	.407	4.27	173	51	3	508.1	509	256	237	0	9	12	12	83	25	0	.301	44	99	12	10	0.9	.923

DIVISIONAL PLAYOFF SERIES

Year	Team	W	L	PCT	ERA	G	GS	CG	IP	H	BB	SO	ShO	W	L	SV	AB	H	HR	BA	PO	A	E	DP	TC/G	FA
1981	KC A	0	0	–	0.00	2	0	0	5.1	1	2	2	0	0	0	0	0	0	0	–	0	0	0	0	0.0	–

WORLD SERIES

Year	Team	W	L	PCT	ERA	G	GS	CG	IP	H	BB	SO	ShO	W	L	SV	AB	H	HR	BA	PO	A	E	DP	TC/G	FA
1980	KC A	0	0	–	2.79	3	0	0	9.2	11	3	2	0	0	0	0	0	0	0	–	0	0	0	0	0.0	–

Speed Martin

MARTIN, ELWOOD GOOD
B. Sept. 15, 1893, Wawawai, Wash.   D. June 14, 1983, Lemon Grove, Calif.

BR TR 6' 165 lbs.

Year	Team	W	L	PCT	ERA	G	GS	CG	IP	H	BB	SO	ShO	W	L	SV	AB	H	HR	BA	PO	A	E	DP	TC/G	FA
1917	STL A	0	2	.000	5.74	9	2	0	15.2	20	5	5	0	0	0	0	2	0	0	.000	3	11	1	0	1.7	.933
1918	CHI N	6	2	.750	1.84	9	5	4	53.2	47	14	16	1	3	0	0	16	3	0	.188	4	18	1	1	2.6	.957
1919		8	8	.500	2.47	35	14	7	163.2	158	52	54	2	3	1	2	44	8	0	.182	9	53	3	3	1.9	.954
1920		4	15	.211	4.83	35	13	6	136	160	50	44	0	1	5	2	44	7	1	.159	6	44	4	1	1.5	.926
1921		11	15	.423	4.35	37	28	13	217.1	245	68	86	1	2	1	1	73	17	0	.233	9	65	1	1	2.0	.987
1922		1	0	1.000	7.50	1	1	0	6	10	2	2	0	0	0	0	1	0	0	.000	0	0	0	0	0.0	–
	6 yrs.	30	42	.417	3.78	126	63	30	592.1	645	191	207	4	8	7	5	180	35	1	.194	31	191	10	6	1.8	.957

Joe Martina

MARTINA, JOHN JOSEPH (Oyster Joe)
B. July 8, 1889, New Orleans, La.   D. Mar. 22, 1962, New Orleans, La.

BR TR 6' 183 lbs.

Year	Team	W	L	PCT	ERA	G	GS	CG	IP	H	BB	SO	ShO	W	L	SV	AB	H	HR	BA	PO	A	E	DP	TC/G	FA
1924	WAS A	6	8	.429	4.67	24	13	8	125.1	129	56	57	0	2	2	0	43	14	0	.326	0	19	0	1	0.8	1.000

WORLD SERIES

Year	Team	W	L	PCT	ERA	G	GS	CG	IP	H	BB	SO	ShO	W	L	SV	AB	H	HR	BA	PO	A	E	DP	TC/G	FA
1924	WAS A	0	0	–	0.00	1	0	0	1	0	1	1	0	0	0	0	0	0	0	–	0	0	0	0	0.0	–

Buck Martinez

MARTINEZ, JOHN ALBERT
B. Nov. 7, 1948, Redding, Calif.

BR TR 5'10" 190 lbs.

Year	Team	W	L	PCT	ERA	G	GS	CG	IP	H	BB	SO	ShO	W	L	SV	AB	H	HR	BA	PO	A	E	DP	TC/G	FA
1979	MIL A	0	0	–	9.00	1	0	0	1	1	1	0	0	0	0	0	*				0	0	0	0	0.0	–

Dennis Martinez

MARTINEZ, JOSE DENNIS
Born Jose Dennis Martinez y Emilia.
B. May 14, 1955, Granada, Nicaragua

BR TR 6'1" 175 lbs.

Year	Team	W	L	PCT	ERA	G	GS	CG	IP	H	BB	SO	ShO	W	L	SV	AB	H	HR	BA	PO	A	E	DP	TC/G	FA
1976	BAL A	1	2	.333	2.57	4	2	1	28	23	8	18	0	1	0	0		3	4	0	0	1.8	1.000			
1977		14	7	.667	4.10	42	13	5	167	157	64	107	0	8	4	4	0	0	0	–	9	26	1	2	0.9	.972
1978		16	11	.593	3.52	40	38	15	276.1	257	93	142	2	0	0	0	0	0	0	–	27	51	1	6	2.0	.987
1979		15	16	.484	3.67	40	39	18	292	279	78	132	3	0	0	0	0	0	0	–	26	59	5	3	2.3	.944
1980		6	4	.600	3.96	25	12	2	100	103	44	42	0	0	1	0	0	0	0	–	5	16	0	1	0.8	1.000
1981		14	5	.737	3.32	25	24	9	179	173	62	88	2	0	0	0	0	0	0	–	20	44	2	4	2.6	.970
1982		16	12	.571	4.21	40	39	10	252	262	87	111	0	0	0	0	0	0	0	–	13	38	1	2	1.3	.981
1983		7	16	.304	5.53	32	25	4	153	209	45	71	0	1	0	0	0	0	0	–	16	42	1	0	1.8	.983
1984		6	9	.400	5.02	34	20	2	141.2	145	37	77	0	1	2	0	0	0	0	–	17	19	2	4	1.1	.947

Year	Team	W	L	PCT	ERA	G	GS	CG	IP	H	BB	SO	ShO	W	L	SV	AB	H	HR	BA	PO	A	E	DP	TC/G	FA
														Relief Pitching			**Batting**									

Dennis Martinez *continued*

Year	Team	W	L	PCT	ERA	G	GS	CG	IP	H	BB	SO	ShO	W	L	SV	AB	H	HR	BA	PO	A	E	DP	TC/G	FA
1985		13	11	.542	5.15	33	31	3	180	203	63	68	1	1	0	0	0	0	0	–	17	26	1	0	1.3	.977
1986	2 teams	BAL A	(4G 0-0)			MON N	(19G 3-6)																			
"	total	3	6	.333	4.73	23	15	0	104.2	114	30	65	1	0	0	0	30	3	0	.100	4	25	1	0	1.3	.967
1987	MON N	11	4	.733	3.30	22	22	2	144.2	133	40	84	1	0	0	0	46	3	0	.065	10	23	1	3	1.5	.971
1988		15	13	.536	2.72	34	34	9	235.1	215	55	120	2	0	0	0	78	15	0	.192	19	39	6	3	1.9	.906
1989		16	7	.696	3.18	34	33	5	232	227	49	142	2	0	1	0	72	9	0	.125	11	50	2	6	1.9	.968
14 yrs.		153	123	.554	3.90	428	347	86	2485.2	2500	755	1267	16	12	8	5	226	30	0	.133	197	462	24	34	1.6	.965

LEAGUE CHAMPIONSHIP SERIES

Year	Team	W	L	PCT	ERA	G	GS	CG	IP	H	BB	SO	ShO	W	L	SV	AB	H	HR	BA	PO	A	E	DP	TC/G	FA
1979	BAL A	0	0	–	3.24	1	1	0	8.1	8	0	4	0	0	0	0	0	0	0	–	2	0	0	0	2.0	1.000

WORLD SERIES

Year	Team	W	L	PCT	ERA	G	GS	CG	IP	H	BB	SO	ShO	W	L	SV	AB	H	HR	BA	PO	A	E	DP	TC/G	FA
1979	BAL A	0	0	–	18.00	2	1	0	2	6	0	0	0	0	0	0	0	0	0	–	0	1	0	1	0.5	1.000

Fred Martinez

MARTINEZ, ALFREDO
B. Mar. 15, 1957, Los Angeles, Calif.

BR TR 6'3" 185 lbs.

Year	Team	W	L	PCT	ERA	G	GS	CG	IP	H	BB	SO	ShO	W	L	SV	AB	H	HR	BA	PO	A	E	DP	TC/G	FA
1980	CAL A	7	9	.438	4.53	30	23	4	149	150	59	57	1	0	0	0	0	0	0	–	3	17	2	0	0.7	.909
1981					3.00	2	0	0	6	5	3	4	0	0	0	0	0	0	0	–	0	2	0	0	1.0	1.000
2 yrs.		7	9	.438	4.47	32	23	4	155	155	62	61	1	0	0	0	0	0	0	–	3	19	2	0	0.8	.917

Marty Martinez

MARTINEZ, ORLANDO
Born Orlando Martinez y Oliva.
B. Aug. 23, 1941, Havana, Cuba
Manager 1986.

BB TR 6' 170 lbs.
BR 1962

Year	Team	W	L	PCT	ERA	G	GS	CG	IP	H	BB	SO	ShO	W	L	SV	AB	H	HR	BA	PO	A	E	DP	TC/G	FA
1969	HOU N	0	0	–	9.00	1	0	0	1	1	0	0	0	0	0	0	*				0	0	0	0	0.0	–

Ramon Martinez

MARTINEZ, RAMON JAIME
Born Ramon Jaime y Martinez.
B. Mar. 22, 1968, Santo Domingo, Dominican Republic

BR TR 6'4" 165 lbs.

Year	Team	W	L	PCT	ERA	G	GS	CG	IP	H	BB	SO	ShO	W	L	SV	AB	H	HR	BA	PO	A	E	DP	TC/G	FA
1988	LA N	1	3	.250	3.79	9	6	0	35.2	27	22	23	0	0	0	0	7	0	0	.000	1	5	0	0	0.7	1.000
1989		6	4	.600	3.19	15	15	2	98.2	79	41	89	2	0	0	0	37	6	0	.162	11	14	0	1	1.7	1.000
2 yrs.		7	7	.500	3.35	24	21	2	134.1	106	63	112	2	0	0	0	44	6	0	.136	12	19	0	1	1.3	1.000

Rogelio Martinez

MARTINEZ, ROGELIO ULLOA (Limonar)
Born Rogelio Martinez y Ulloa.
B. Nov. 5, 1918, Cidra, Cuba

BR TR 6' 180 lbs.

Year	Team	W	L	PCT	ERA	G	GS	CG	IP	H	BB	SO	ShO	W	L	SV	AB	H	HR	BA	PO	A	E	DP	TC/G	FA
1950	WAS A	0	1	.000	27.00	2	1	0	1.1	4	2	0	0	0	0	0	0	0	0	–	0	0	0	0	0.0	–

Silvio Martinez

MARTINEZ, SILVIO RAMON
Born Silvio Ramon Martinez y Cabrera.
B. Aug. 19, 1955, Santiago, Dominican Republic

BR TR 5'10" 170 lbs.

Year	Team	W	L	PCT	ERA	G	GS	CG	IP	H	BB	SO	ShO	W	L	SV	AB	H	HR	BA	PO	A	E	DP	TC/G	FA
1977	CHI A	0	1	.000	5.57	10	0	0	21	28	12	10	0	0	1	1	0	0	0	–	2	4	1	1	0.7	.857
1978	STL N	9	8	.529	3.65	22	22	5	138	114	71	45	2	0	0	0	47	8	0	.170	9	18	3	0	1.4	.900
1979		15	8	.652	3.26	32	29	7	207	204	67	102	2	0	0	0	62	8	0	.129	17	15	4	3	1.1	.889
1980		5	10	.333	4.80	25	20	2	120	127	48	39	0	1	0	0	35	3	0	.086	4	12	2	2	0.7	.889
1981		2	5	.286	3.99	18	16	0	97	95	39	34	0	0	0	0	35	7	0	.200	6	13	1	0	1.1	.950
5 yrs.		31	32	.492	3.87	107	87	14	583	568	237	230	4	1	1	1	179	26	0	.145	38	62	11	6	1.0	.901

Tippy Martinez

MARTINEZ, FELIX ANTHONY
B. May 31, 1950, LaJunta, Colo.

BL TL 5'10" 180 lbs.

Year	Team	W	L	PCT	ERA	G	GS	CG	IP	H	BB	SO	ShO	W	L	SV	AB	H	HR	BA	PO	A	E	DP	TC/G	FA
1974	NY A	0	0	–	4.15	10	0	0	13	14	9	10	0	0	0	0	0	0	0	–	1	1	0	0	0.2	1.000
1975		1	2	.333	2.68	23	2	0	37	27	32	20	0	1	0	8	0	0	0	–	2	2	1	0	0.2	.800
1976	2 teams	NY A	(11G 2-0)			BAL A	(28G 3-1)																			
"	total	5	1	.833	2.33	39	0	0	69.2	50	42	45	0	5	1	10	0	0	0	–	11	15	0	1	0.7	1.000
1977	BAL A	5	1	.833	2.70	41	0	0	50	47	27	29	0	5	1	9	0	0	0	–	2	12	0	3	0.3	1.000
1978		3	3	.500	4.83	42	0	0	69	77	40	57	0	3	3	5	0	0	0	–	8	13	0	1	0.5	1.000
1979		10	3	.769	2.88	39	0	0	78	59	31	61	0	10	3	3	0	0	0	–	4	13	1	2	0.5	.944
1980		4	4	.500	3.00	53	0	0	81	69	34	68	0	4	4	10	0	0	0	–	5	16	0	3	0.4	1.000
1981		3	3	.500	2.90	37	0	0	59	48	32	50	0	3	3	11	0	0	0	–	3	13	3	0	0.5	.842
1982		8	8	.500	3.41	76	0	0	95	81	37	78	0	8	8	16	0	0	0	–	6	10	1	1	0.2	1.000
1983		9	3	.750	2.35	65	0	0	103.1	76	37	81	0	9	3	21	0	0	0	–	5	23	0	1	0.4	1.000
1984		4	9	.308	3.91	55	0	0	89.2	88	51	71	0	4	9	17	0	0	0	–	2	14	2	0	0.3	.889
1985		3	3	.500	5.40	49	0	0	70	70	37	47	0	3	3	4	0	0	0	–	9	10	1	1	0.4	.950
1986		0	2	.000	5.63	14	0	0	16	18	12	11	0	0	2	1	0	0	0	–	0	3	1	0	0.3	.750
1988	MIN A	0	0	–	18.00	3	0	0	4	8	4	3	0	0	0	0	0	0	0	–	0	0	0	0	0.0	–
14 yrs.		55	42	.567	3.45	546	2	0	834.2	732	425	631	0	55	40	115	0	0	0	–	58	145	9	13	0.4	.958

LEAGUE CHAMPIONSHIP SERIES

Year	Team	W	L	PCT	ERA	G	GS	CG	IP	H	BB	SO	ShO	W	L	SV	AB	H	HR	BA	PO	A	E	DP	TC/G	FA
1983	BAL A	1	0	1.000	0.00	2	0	0	6	5	3	5	0	1	0	0	0	0	0	–	0	2	0	0	1.0	1.000

WORLD SERIES

Year	Team	W	L	PCT	ERA	G	GS	CG	IP	H	BB	SO	ShO	W	L	SV	AB	H	HR	BA	PO	A	E	DP	TC/G	FA
1979	BAL A	0	0	–	6.75	3	0	0	1.1	3	0	1	0	0	0	1	0	0	0	–	0	0	0	0	0.0	–
1983		0	0	–	3.00	3	0	0	3	3	0	0	0	0	0	2	0	0	0	–	0	0	0	0	0.0	–
2 yrs.		0	0	–	4.15	6	0	0	4.1	6	0	1	0	0	0	0	0	0	0	–	0	0	0	0	0.0	–

Wedo Martini

MARTINI, GUIDO JOE (Southern)
B. July 1, 1913, Birmingham, Ala.   D. Oct. 28, 1970, Philadelphia, Pa.

BR TR 5'10" 165 lbs.

Year	Team	W	L	PCT	ERA	G	GS	CG	IP	H	BB	SO	ShO	W	L	SV	AB	H	HR	BA	PO	A	E	DP	TC/G	FA
1935	PHI A	0	2	.000	17.05	3	2	0	6.1	8	11	1	0	0	0	0	2	0	0	.000	0	4	0	0	1.3	1.000

Year	Team	W	L	PCT	ERA	G	GS	CG	IP	H	BB	SO	ShO	Relief Pitching W	L	SV	Batting AB	H	HR	BA	PO	A	E	DP	TC/G	FA

Joe Marty

MARTY, JOSEPH ANTON
B. Sept. 1, 1913, Sacramento, Calif.   D. Oct. 4, 1984, Sacramento, Calif.
BR TR 6'   182 lbs.

| 1939 | CHI N | 0 | 0 | — | 4.50 | 1 | 0 | 0 | 4 | 2 | 3 | 1 | 0 | 0 | 0 | 0 | * | | | | 0 | 0 | 0 | 0 | 0.0 | — |

Randy Martz

MARTZ, RANDY CARL
B. May 28, 1956, Harrisburg, Pa.
BL TR 6'4"   210 lbs.

1980	CHI N	1	2	.333	2.10	6	6	0	30	28	11	5	0	0	0	0	9	1	0	.111	7	6	0	0	2.2	1.000
1981		5	7	.417	3.67	33	14	1	108	103	49	32	0	2	0	6	28	6	0	.214	7	18	0	2	0.8	1.000
1982		11	10	.524	4.21	28	24	1	147.2	157	36	40	0	1	1	1	42	6	0	.143	15	27	1	1	1.5	.977
1983	CHI A	0	0	—	3.60	1	1	0	5	4	4	1	0	0	0	0	0	0	0	—	1	0	0	0	1.0	1.000
4 yrs.		17	19	.472	3.78	68	45	2	290.2	292	100	78	0	3	1	7	79	13	0	.165	30	51	1	3	1.2	.988

Del Mason

MASON, ADELBERT WILLIAM
B. Oct. 29, 1883, Newfane, N. Y.   D. Dec. 31, 1962, Winter Park, Fla.
BR TR 6'   160 lbs.

1904	WAS A	0	3	.000	6.00	5	3	2	33	45	13	16	0	0	1	0	15	0	0	.000	3	6	0	0	1.8	1.000
1906	CIN N	0	1	.000	4.50	2	1	1	12	10	6	4	0	0	0	0	5	0	0	.000	1	2	0	0	1.5	1.000
1907		5	12	.294	3.14	25	17	13	146	144	55	45	1	2	1	0	44	8	0	.182	6	44	1	4	2.0	.980
3 yrs.		5	16	.238	3.72	32	21	16	191	199	74	65	1	2	2	0	64	8	0	.125	10	52	1	4	2.0	.984

Ernie Mason

MASON, ERNEST
B. New Orleans, La.   D. July 30, 1904, Covington, La.

| 1894 | STL N | 0 | 2 | .000 | 7.15 | 4 | 2 | 2 | 22.2 | 34 | 10 | 3 | 0 | 0 | 0 | 1 | 12 | 3 | 0 | .250 | 2 | 2 | 1 | 0 | 1.3 | .800 |

Hank Mason

MASON, HENRY
B. June 19, 1931, Marshall, Mo.
BR TR 6'   185 lbs.

1958	PHI N	0	0	—	10.80	1	0	0	5	7	2	3	0	0	0	0	2	0	0	.000	0	0	0	0	0.0	—
1960		0	0	—	9.53	3	0	0	5.2	9	5	3	0	0	0	0	1	0	0	.000	0	1	0	0	0.3	1.000
2 yrs.		0	0	—	10.13	4	0	0	10.2	16	7	6	0	0	0	0	3	0	0	.000	0	1	0	0	0.3	1.000

Mike Mason

MASON, MICHAEL PAUL
B. Nov. 21, 1958, Fairbault, Minn.
BL TL 6'2"   205 lbs.

1982	TEX A	1	2	.333	5.09	4	4	0	23	21	9	8	0	0	0	0	0	0	0	—	1	5	0	0	1.5	1.000
1983		0	2	.000	5.91	5	0	0	10.2	10	6	9	0	0	2	0	0	0	0	—	1	2	0	0	0.6	1.000
1984		9	13	.409	3.61	36	24	4	184.1	159	51	113	0	3	0	0	0	0	0	—	4	22	0	0	0.7	1.000
1985		8	15	.348	4.83	38	30	1	179	212	73	92	1	0	0	0	0	0	0	—	4	30	4	0	1.0	.895
1986		7	3	.700	4.33	27	22	2	135	135	56	85	0	0	0	0	0	0	0	—	9	19	0	1	1.0	1.000
1987	2 teams	TEX A	(8G 0–2)			CHI N	(17G 4–1)																			
"	total	4	3	.571	5.64	25	10	0	67	80	45	49	0	2	0	0	9	2	0	.222	2	10	1	2	0.5	.923
1988	MIN A	0	1	.000	10.80	5	0	0	6.2	8	9	7	0	0	1	0	0	0	0	—	0	0	0	0	0.0	—
7 yrs.		29	39	.426	4.53	140	90	7	605.2	625	249	363	2	5	3	0	9	2	0	.222	21	88	5	3	0.8	.956

Roger Mason

MASON, ROGER LeROY
B. Sept. 18, 1958, Bellaire, Mich.
BR TR 6'6"   215 lbs.

1984	DET A	1	1	.500	3.86	4	2	0	21	20	10	14	0	0	0	0	0	0	0	—	5	1	0	0	1.5	1.000
1985	SF N	1	3	.250	2.12	5	5	1	29.2	28	11	26	1	0	0	0	11	1	0	.091	4	2	0	0	1.2	1.000
1986		3	4	.429	4.80	11	11	1	60	56	30	43	0	0	0	0	21	1	0	.048	6	4	1	0	1.0	.909
1987		1	1	.500	4.50	5	5	0	26	30	10	18	0	0	0	0	8	1	0	.125	3	3	0	2	1.2	1.000
1989	HOU N	0	0	—	20.25	2	0	0	1.1	2	2	3	0	0	0	0	0	0	0	—	1	0	0	0	0.5	1.000
5 yrs.		6	9	.400	4.17	27	23	2	138	136	63	104	1	0	0	1	40	3	0	.075	19	10	1	2	1.1	.967

Walt Masters

MASTERS, WALTER THOMAS
B. Mar. 28, 1907, Pen Argyl, Pa.
BR TR 5'10½" 180 lbs.

1931	WAS A	0	0	—	2.00	3	0	0	9	7	4	1	0	0	0	0	2	0	0	.000	0	4	0	1	1.3	1.000
1937	PHI N	0	0	—	36.00	1	0	0	1	5	1	0	0	0	0	0	0	0	0	—	0	0	0	0	0.0	—
1939	PHI A	0	0	—	6.55	4	0	0	11	15	8	2	0	0	0	0	2	0	0	.000	0	3	1	0	1.0	.750
3 yrs.		0	0	—	6.00	8	0	0	21	27	13	3	0	0	0	1	4	0	0	.000	0	7	1	1	1.0	.875

Paul Masterson

MASTERSON, PAUL NICKALIS (Lefty)
B. Oct. 16, 1915, Chicago, Ill.
BL TL 5'11"   165 lbs.

1940	PHI N	0	0	—	7.20	2	0	0	5	5	2	3	0	0	0	0	1	0	0	.000	0	1	0	0	0.5	1.000
1941		1	0	1.000	4.76	2	1	1	11.1	11	6	8	0	0	0	0	4	0	0	.000	0	2	0	0	1.0	1.000
1942		0	0	—	6.48	4	0	0	8.1	10	5	3	0	0	0	0	0	0	0	—	0	2	0	0	0.5	1.000
3 yrs.		1	0	1.000	5.84	8	1	1	24.2	26	13	14	0	0	0	0	5	0	0	.000	0	5	0	0	0.6	1.000

Walt Masterson

MASTERSON, WALTER EDWARD
B. June 22, 1920, Philadelphia, Pa.
BR TR 6'2"   189 lbs.

1939	WAS A	2	2	.500	5.55	24	5	1	58.1	66	48	12	0	1	0	0	13	2	0	.154	2	9	2	0	0.5	.846
1940		3	13	.188	4.90	31	19	3	130.1	128	88	68	0	1	1	2	38	7	0	.184	5	16	1	0	0.7	.955
1941		4	3	.571	5.97	34	6	1	78.1	101	53	40	0	2	0	3	19	2	0	.105	4	17	1	2	0.6	.955
1942		5	9	.357	3.34	25	15	8	142.2	138	54	63	4	0	2	2	45	7	0	.156	8	22	7	0	1.5	.811
1945		1	2	.333	1.08	4	2	1	25	21	10	14	1	0	2	0	9	1	0	.111	2	4	0	1	1.5	1.000
1946		5	6	.455	6.01	29	9	2	91.1	105	67	61	0	4	2	1	25	2	0	.080	5	15	1	0	0.7	.952
1947		12	16	.429	3.13	35	31	14	253	215	97	135	4	2	2	0	83	11	0	.133	14	51	6	4	2.0	.915
1948		8	15	.348	3.83	33	27	9	188	171	122	72	2	0	2	2	57	11	0	.193	10	24	3	1	1.1	.919
1949	2 teams	WAS A	(10G 3–2)			BOS A	(18G 3–4)																			
"	total	6	6	.500	3.75	28	14	7	108	100	56	36	0	2	1	0	35	3	0	.086	4	21	1	1	0.9	.962
1950	BOS A	8	6	.571	5.64	33	15	6	129.1	145	82	60	0	1	2	1	44	6	0	.136	8	26	2	6	1.1	.944
1951		3	0	1.000	3.34	30	1	0	59.1	53	32	39	0	3	0	2	11	2	0	.182	1	12	1	0	0.5	.929
1952	2 teams	BOS A	(5G 1–1)			WAS A	(24G 9–8)																			
"	total	10	9	.526	4.13	29	22	11	170	171	83	92	1	1	0	0	52	6	0	.115	16	31	1	3	1.7	.979
1953	WAS A	10	12	.455	3.63	29	20	10	166.1	145	62	95	4	1	0	1	51	7	0	.137	10	27	4	1	1.4	.902

Year	Team		W	L	PCT	ERA	G	GS	CG	IP	H	BB	SO	ShO	Relief Pitching			Batting			BA	PO	A	E	DP	TC/G	FA
															W	L	SV	AB	H	HR							

Walt Masterson *continued*

| 1956 | DET | A | 1 | 1 | .500 | 4.17 | 35 | 0 | 0 | 49.2 | 54 | 32 | 28 | 0 | 1 | 1 | 0 | 4 | 1 | 0 | .250 | 3 | 6 | 2 | 1 | 0.3 | .818 |
| 14 yrs. | | | 78 | 100 | .438 | 4.15 | 399 | 184 | 70 | 1649.2 | 1613 | 886 | 815 | 15 | 17 | 14 | 20 | 486 | 68 | 0 | .140 | 92 | 281 | 32 | 19 | 1.0 | .921 |

Len Matarazzo

MATARAZZO, LEONARD   BR TR 6'4"   195 lbs.
B. Sept. 12, 1928, New Castle, Pa.

| 1952 | PHI | A | 0 | 0 | – | 0.00 | 1 | 0 | 0 | 1 | 1 | 1 | 0 | 0 | 0 | 0 | 0 | 0 | 0 | 0 | – | 0 | 0 | 0 | 0 | 0.0 | – |

Bobby Mathews

MATHEWS, ROBERT T.   BR TR 5'5½"   140 lbs.
B. Nov. 21, 1851, Baltimore, Md.   D. Apr. 17, 1898, Baltimore, Md.

1876	NY	N	21	34	.382	2.86	56	56	55	516	**693**	24	37	2	0	0	0	218	40	0	.183	41	78	28	0	2.6	.810
1877	CIN	N	3	12	.200	4.04	15	15	13	129.1	208	17	9	0	0	0	0	59	10	0	.169	7	18	4	0	1.9	.862
1879	PRO	N	12	8	.600	2.29	27	25	15	189	194	26	90	0	0	0	1	173	35	1	.202	4	40	2	0	1.7	.957
1881	2 teams			PRO N	(14G 4–8)		BOS N	(5G 1–0)																			
"	total		5	8	.385	3.02	19	15	11	125.1	143	32	33	1	0	0	2	128	23	0	.180	3	18	4	2	1.3	.840
1882	BOS	N	19	15	.559	2.87	34	32	31	285	278	22	153	0	1	1	0	169	38	0	.225	5	34	6	1	1.3	.867
1883	PHI	AA	30	13	.698	2.46	44	44	41	381	396	31	203	1	0	0	0	167	31	0	.186	15	68	12	2	2.2	.874
1884			30	18	.625	3.32	49	49	48	430.2	401	49	286	3	0	0	0	184	34	0	.185	8	78	25	1	2.3	.775
1885			30	17	.638	2.43	48	48	46	422.1	394	57	286	2	0	0	0	179	30	0	.168	7	67	10	1	1.8	.881
1886			13	9	.591	3.96	24	24	22	197.2	226	53	93	0	0	0	0	88	21	0	.239	5	46	8	3	2.5	.864
1887			3	4	.429	6.67	7	7	7	58	75	25	9	0	0	0	0	25	5	0	.200	2	14	2	1	2.6	.889
10 yrs.			166	138	.546	3.00	323	315	289	2734.1	3008	336	1199	9	1	1	3	*					97	461	101	11	2.0	.847

Greg Mathews

MATHEWS, GREGORY INMAN   BB TL 6'2"   180 lbs.
B. May 17, 1962, Harbor City, Calif.

1986	STL	N	11	8	.579	3.65	23	22	1	145.1	139	44	67	0	0	0	0	43	2	0	.047	3	17	0	1	0.9	1.000
1987			11	11	.500	3.73	32	32	2	197.2	184	71	108	1	0	0	0	68	13	0	.191	3	31	4	2	1.2	.895
1988			4	6	.400	4.24	13	13	1	68	61	33	31	0	0	0	0	23	4	0	.174	3	13	2	0	1.4	.889
3 yrs.			26	25	.510	3.79	68	67	4	411	384	148	206	1	0	0	0	134	19	0	.142	9	61	6	3	1.1	.921

LEAGUE CHAMPIONSHIP SERIES

| 1987 | STL | N | 1 | 0 | 1.000 | 3.48 | 2 | 2 | 0 | 10.1 | 9 | 3 | 10 | 0 | 0 | 0 | 0 | 2 | 2 | 0 | 1.000 | 0 | 0 | 0 | 0 | 0.0 | – |

WORLD SERIES

| 1987 | STL | N | 0 | 0 | – | 2.45 | 1 | 1 | 0 | 3.2 | 2 | 2 | 3 | 0 | 0 | 0 | 0 | 1 | 0 | 0 | .000 | 0 | 1 | 0 | 0 | 1.0 | 1.000 |

Christy Mathewson

MATHEWSON, CHRISTOPHER (Big Six, Matty)   BR TR 6'1½"   195 lbs.
Brother of Henry Mathewson.
B. Aug. 12, 1880, Factoryville, Pa.   D. Oct. 7, 1925, Saranac Lake, N. Y.
Manager 1916-18.
Hall of Fame 1936.

1900	NY	N	0	3	.000	4.76	5	1	1	34	35	14	15	0	0	2	0	11	2	0	.182	1	9	0	0	2.0	1.000
1901			20	17	.541	2.41	40	38	36	336	288	97	221	5	0	1	0	130	28	0	.215	21	108	1	1	3.3	.992
1902			14	17	.452	2.11	34	32	29	276.2	241	73	159	8	1	0	0	127	26	2	.205	17	79	6	5	3.0	.941
1903			30	13	.698	2.26	45	42	37	366.1	321	100	**267**	3	1	0	0	124	28	1	.226	18	93	3	0	2.5	.974
1904			33	12	.733	2.03	48	**46**	33	367.2	306	78	**212**	4	**2**	0	0	133	30	0	.226	32	116	6	0	3.2	.961
1905			**31**	8	**.795**	**1.27**	43	37	33	339	252	64	**206**	8	3	1	2	127	30	2	.236	15	116	4	4	3.1	.970
1906			22	12	.647	2.97	38	35	22	266.2	262	77	128	6	1	0	1	91	24	0	.264	15	90	1	1	2.8	.991
1907			24	13	.649	1.99	41	36	31	316	250	53	178	8	1	0	2	107	20	0	.187	16	87	6	0	2.7	.945
1908			**37**	11	**.771**	**1.43**	56	44	34	390.2	285	42	**259**	12	3	1	5	129	20	0	.155	27	141	2	1	3.0	.988
1909			25	6	**.806**	**1.14**	37	33	26	275.1	192	36	149	8	2	0	2	95	25	1	.263	19	96	4	3	3.2	.966
1910			**27**	9	.750	1.90	38	35	**27**	318	292	60	184	2	2	1	0	107	25	1	.234	12	114	4	6	3.4	.969
1911			26	13	.667	**1.99**	45	37	29	307	**303**	38	141	5	2	0	3	112	22	0	.196	31	107	2	2	3.1	.986
1912			23	12	.657	2.12	43	34	27	310	311	34	134	0	0	1	2	110	29	0	.264	15	74	4	4	2.2	.957
1913			25	11	.694	**2.06**	40	35	25	306	**291**	21	93	4	3	0	2	103	19	0	.184	13	100	3	3	2.9	.974
1914			24	13	.649	3.00	41	35	29	312	314	23	80	5	3	0	2	105	23	0	.219	15	91	5	7	2.7	.955
1915			8	14	.364	3.58	27	24	11	186	199	20	57	1	0	0	0	51	8	0	.157	8	54	1	3	2.3	.984
1916	2 teams			NY N	(12G 3–4)		CIN N	(1G 1–0)																			
"	total		4	4	.500	3.01	13	7	5	74.2	74	8	19	1	1	2	2	22	3	0	.136	6	28	0	1	2.6	1.000
17 yrs.			373	188	.665	2.13	634	551	435	4782	4216	838	2502	80	26	10	27	1684	362	7	.215	281	1503	52	41	2.9	.972
			3rd		6th	5th								3rd													

WORLD SERIES

1905	NY	N	3	0	1.000	0.00	3	3	3	27	14	1	18	3	0	0	0	8	2	0	.250	2	8	1	0	3.7	.909
1911			1	2	.333	2.00	3	3	2	27	25	2	13	0	0	0	0	7	2	0	.286	2	9	1	0	4.0	1.000
1912			0	2	.000	1.57	3	3	3	28.2	23	5	10	0	0	0	0	12	2	0	.167	1	12	0	0	4.3	1.000
1913			1	1	.500	0.95	2	2	2	19	14	2	7	1	0	0	0	5	3	0	.600	1	5	0	0	3.0	1.000
4 yrs.			5	5	.500	1.15	11	11	10	101.2	76	10	48	4	0	0	0	32	9	0	.281	6	34	2	0	3.8	.952
			8th	2nd		8th	10th	2nd	1st		2nd	3rd		9th	1st												

Henry Mathewson

MATHEWSON, HENRY   BR TR 6'3"   175 lbs.
Brother of Christy Mathewson.
B. Dec. 24, 1886, Factoryville, Pa.   D. July 1, 1917, Factoryville, Pa.

1906	NY	N	0	1	.000	5.40	2	1	1	10	7	14	1	0	0	0	1	2	0	0	.000	0	4	0	2	2.0	1.000
1907			0	0	–	0.00	1	0	0	1	1	0	0	0	0	0	1	0	0	0	–	0	0	0	0	0.0	–
2 yrs.			0	1	.000	4.91	3	1	1	11	8	14	2	0	0	0	2	2	0	0	.000	0	4	0	2	1.3	1.000

Carl Mathias

MATHIAS, CARL LYNWOOD (Stubby)   BR TL 5'11"   195 lbs.
B. June 13, 1936, Bechtelsville, Pa.   BB 1960

| 1960 | CLE | A | 0 | 1 | .000 | 3.52 | 7 | 0 | 0 | 15.1 | 14 | 8 | 13 | 0 | 0 | 0 | 1 | 0 | 1 | 0 | 0 | .000 | 1 | 3 | 0 | 0 | 0.6 | 1.000 |

Year	Team	W	L	PCT	ERA	G	GS	CG	IP	H	BB	SO	ShO	W	L	SV	AB	H	HR	BA	PO	A	E	DP	TC/G	FA

Carl Mathias *continued*

Year	Team	W	L	PCT	ERA	G	GS	CG	IP	H	BB	SO	ShO	W	L	SV	AB	H	HR	BA	PO	A	E	DP	TC/G	FA
1961	WAS A	0	1	.000	11.20	4	3	0	13.2	22	4	7	0	0	0	0	5	1	0	.200	1	2	0	0	0.8	1.000
2 yrs.		0	2	.000	7.14	11	3	0	29	36	12	20	0	0	0	0	6	1	0	.167	2	5	0	0	0.6	1.000

Ron Mathis

MATHIS, RONALD VANCE
B. Sept. 25, 1958, Kansas City, Mo.   BR TR 6'   180 lbs.

Year	Team	W	L	PCT	ERA	G	GS	CG	IP	H	BB	SO	ShO	W	L	SV	AB	H	HR	BA	PO	A	E	DP	TC/G	FA
1985	HOU N	3	5	.375	6.04	23	8	0	70	83	27	34	0	0	2	1	14	1	0	.071	5	10	1	0	0.7	.938
1987		0	1	.000	5.25	8	0	0	12	10	11	8	0	0	1	0	2	0	0	.000	2	2	1	0	0.6	.800
2 yrs.		3	6	.333	5.93	31	8	0	82	93	38	42	0	0	3	1	16	1	0	.063	7	12	2	0	0.7	.905

Jon Matlack

MATLACK, JONATHAN TRUMPBOUR
B. Jan. 19, 1950, West Chester, Pa.   BL TL 6'3"   205 lbs.

Year	Team	W	L	PCT	ERA	G	GS	CG	IP	H	BB	SO	ShO	W	L	SV	AB	H	HR	BA	PO	A	E	DP	TC/G	FA
1971	NY N	0	3	.000	4.14	7	6	0	37	31	15	24	0	0	0	0	11	3	0	.273	1	2	0	0	0.4	1.000
1972		15	10	.600	2.32	34	32	8	244	215	71	169	4	1	0	0	78	10	0	.128	8	33	1	1	1.2	.976
1973		14	16	.467	3.20	34	34	14	242	210	99	205	3	0	0	0	65	9	0	.138	4	40	1	3	1.3	.978
1974		13	15	.464	2.41	34	34	14	265	221	76	195	7	0	0	0	79	8	0	.101	5	40	1	1	1.3	1.000
1975		16	12	.571	3.38	33	32	8	229	224	58	154	3	0	0	0	70	7	0	.100	3	28	3	1	1.0	.912
1976		17	10	.630	2.95	35	35	16	262	236	57	153	6	0	0	0	88	17	0	.193	10	35	1	0	1.3	.978
1977		7	15	.318	4.21	26	26	5	169	175	43	123	3	0	0	0	50	3	0	.060	4	27	1	1	1.2	.969
1978	TEX A	15	13	.536	2.27	35	33	18	270	252	51	157	2	0	0	1	0	0	0	—	17	42	5	2	1.8	.922
1979		5	4	.556	4.13	13	13	2	85	98	15	35	0	0	0	0	0	0	0	—	3	16	2	1	1.6	.905
1980		10	10	.500	3.68	35	34	8	235	265	48	142	1	0	0	1	0	0	0	—	5	25	4	0	1.0	.882
1981		4	7	.364	4.15	17	16	1	104	101	41	43	1	0	0	0	0	0	0	—	2	20	2	0	1.4	.917
1982		7	7	.500	3.53	33	14	1	147.2	158	37	78	0	2	2	1	0	0	0	—	1	24	0	1	0.8	1.000
1983		4	4	.333	4.66	25	9	2	73.1	90	27	38	0	0	1	0	0	0	0	—	2	14	1	3	0.7	.941
13 yrs.		125	126	.498	3.18	361	318	97	2363	2276	638	1516	30	3	3	3	441	57	0	.129	68	346	21	14	1.2	.952

LEAGUE CHAMPIONSHIP SERIES

Year	Team	W	L	PCT	ERA	G	GS	CG	IP	H	BB	SO	ShO	W	L	SV	AB	H	HR	BA	PO	A	E	DP	TC/G	FA
1973	NY N	1	0	1.000	0.00	1	1	1	9	2	3	9	1	0	0	0	2	0	0	.000	0	0	0	0	1.0	1.000

WORLD SERIES

Year	Team	W	L	PCT	ERA	G	GS	CG	IP	H	BB	SO	ShO	W	L	SV	AB	H	HR	BA	PO	A	E	DP	TC/G	FA
1973	NY N	1	2	.333	2.16	3	3	0	16.2	10	5	11	0	0	0	0	4	1	0	.250	0	1	0	0	0.3	1.000

Al Mattern

MATTERN, ALONZO ALBERT
B. June 16, 1883, West Rush, N. Y.   D. Nov. 6, 1958, West Rush, N. Y.   BL TR 5'10"   165 lbs.

Year	Team	W	L	PCT	ERA	G	GS	CG	IP	H	BB	SO	ShO	W	L	SV	AB	H	HR	BA	PO	A	E	DP	TC/G	FA
1908	BOS N	1	3	.250	2.08	5	3	1	30.1	30	6	15	0	1	0	0	8	1	0	.125	1	8	0	0	1.8	1.000
1909		16	20	.444	2.85	47	32	24	316.1	322	108	98	2	3	4	3	101	17	0	.168	21	100	10	2	2.8	.924
1910		16	19	.457	2.98	51	37	17	305	288	121	94	6	4	2	1	98	16	0	.163	12	90	3	1	2.1	.971
1911		4	15	.211	4.97	33	21	11	186.1	228	63	51	1	0	3	0	63	11	0	.175	6	61	2	0	2.1	.971
1912		0	1	.000	7.11	2	1	0	6.1	10	1	3	0	0	0	0	2	0	0	.000	0	2	0	0	1.0	1.000
5 yrs.		37	58	.389	3.37	138	94	53	844.1	878	299	254	9	7	9	4	272	45	0	.165	40	261	15	3	2.3	.953

C. V. Matterson

MATTERSON, C. V.
B. Ohio   Deceased.

Year	Team	W	L	PCT	ERA	G	GS	CG	IP	H	BB	SO	ShO	W	L	SV	AB	H	HR	BA	PO	A	E	DP	TC/G	FA
1884	STL U	1	0	1.000	9.00	1	1	0	6	9	3	3	0	0	0	0	4	0	0	.000	0	0	0	0	0.0	—

Henry Matteson

MATTESON, HENRY EDSON
B. Sept. 7, 1884, Guy's Mills, Pa.   D. Sept. 1, 1943, Westfield, N. Y.   BR TR 5'10½" 160 lbs.

Year	Team	W	L	PCT	ERA	G	GS	CG	IP	H	BB	SO	ShO	W	L	SV	AB	H	HR	BA	PO	A	E	DP	TC/G	FA
1914	PHI N	3	2	.600	3.10	15	3	2	58	58	23	28	1	2	0	1	22	4	0	.182	1	7	0	0	0.5	1.000
1918	WAS A	5	3	.625	1.73	14	6	2	67.2	57	15	17	0	3	1	0	19	2	0	.105	2	15	1	1	1.3	.944
2 yrs.		8	5	.615	2.36	29	9	4	125.2	115	38	45	1	5	2	0	41	6	0	.146	3	22	1	1	0.9	.962

Bill Matthews

MATTHEWS, WILLIAM CALVIN
B. Jan. 12, 1878, Mahanoy City, Pa.   D. Jan. 23, 1946, Mahanoy City, Pa.   TR

Year	Team	W	L	PCT	ERA	G	GS	CG	IP	H	BB	SO	ShO	W	L	SV	AB	H	HR	BA	PO	A	E	DP	TC/G	FA
1909	BOS A	0	0	—	3.24	5	1	0	16.2	16	10	6	0	0	0	0	8	0	0	.000	1	3	0	0	0.8	1.000

Joe Matthews

MATTHEWS, JOHN JOSEPH (Lefty)
B. Sept. 29, 1898, Baltimore, Md.   D. Feb. 8, 1968, Hagerstown, Md.   BB TL 6'   170 lbs.

Year	Team	W	L	PCT	ERA	G	GS	CG	IP	H	BB	SO	ShO	W	L	SV	AB	H	HR	BA	PO	A	E	DP	TC/G	FA
1922	BOS N	0	1	.000	3.60	3	1	0	10	5	6	0	0	0	0	0	2	0	0	.000	0	1	0	0	0.3	1.000

Steve Matthias

MATTHIAS, DALE WESLEY
B. May 15, 1923, Catasauqua, Pa.   D. Feb. 20, 1984, Blairsville, Ga.   BR TR 5'11½" 145 lbs.

Year	Team	W	L	PCT	ERA	G	GS	CG	IP	H	BB	SO	ShO	W	L	SV	AB	H	HR	BA	PO	A	E	DP	TC/G	FA
1943	PHI N	0	3	.000	4.85	11	1	0	26	26	8	8	0	0	2	0	0	0	0	.000	1	4	0	1	0.5	1.000
1944		0	0	—	3.94	17	0	0	32	27	16	8	0	0	0	0	3	1	0	.333	3	5	1	0	0.5	.889
2 yrs.		0	3	.000	4.34	28	1	0	58	53	24	16	0	0	2	0	*				4	9	1	1	0.5	.929

Mike Mattimore

MATTIMORE, MICHAEL JOSEPH
B. 1859, Renovo, Pa.   D. Apr. 28, 1931, Butte, Mont.   BL TL 5'8½" 160 lbs.

Year	Team	W	L	PCT	ERA	G	GS	CG	IP	H	BB	SO	ShO	W	L	SV	AB	H	HR	BA	PO	A	E	DP	TC/G	FA
1887	NY N	3	3	.500	2.35	7	7	6	57.1	47	28	12	0	0	0	0	32	8	0	.250	3	5	1	0	1.3	.889
1888	PHI AA	15	10	.600	3.38	26	24	24	221	221	65	80	4	0	1	0	142	38	0	.268	8	67	7	4	3.2	.915
1889	2 teams	PHI AA (5G 2-1)			KC AA (1G 0-0)																					
"	total	2	1	.667	5.56	6	1	1	34	46	15	7	0	2	0	1	148	29	1	.196	1	6	2	0	1.5	.778
1890	BKN AA	6	13	.316	4.44	19	19	19	178.1	201	76	33	1	0	0	0	129	17	0	.132	9	38	6	0	2.8	.887
4 yrs.		26	27	.491	3.80	58	51	50	490.2	515	184	132	5	2	1	1	*				21	116	16	4	2.6	.895

Earl Mattingly

MATTINGLY, LAURENCE EARL
B. Nov. 4, 1904, Newport, Md.   BR TR 5'10½" 164 lbs.

Year	Team	W	L	PCT	ERA	G	GS	CG	IP	H	BB	SO	ShO	W	L	SV	AB	H	HR	BA	PO	A	E	DP	TC/G	FA
1931	BKN N	0	1	.000	2.51	8	0	0	14.1	15	10	6	0	0	1	0	3	0	0	.000	0	5	0	1	0.6	1.000

Year	Team		W	L	PCT	ERA	G	GS	CG	IP	H	BB	SO	ShO	Relief Pitching W	L	SV	Batting AB	H	HR	BA	PO	A	E	DP	TC/G	FA

Rick Matula

MATULA, RICHARD CARLTON
B. Nov. 22, 1953, Wharton, Tex. BR TR 6' 190 lbs.

1979	ATL N	8	10	.444	4.16	28	28	1	171	193	64	67	0	0	0	0	53	5	0	.094	15	23	0	6	1.4	1.000
1980		11	13	.458	4.58	33	30	3	177	195	60	62	1	0	0	0	57	6	0	.105	20	28	1	5	1.5	.980
1981		0	0	—	6.43	5	0	0	7	8	2	0	0	0	0	0	1	0	0	.000	1	1	0	0	0.4	1.000
3 yrs.		19	23	.452	4.41	66	58	4	355	396	126	129	1	0	0	0	111	11	0	.099	36	52	1	11	1.3	.989

Harry Matuzak

MATUZAK, HENRY GEORGE (Matty)
B. Jan. 27, 1910, Omer, Mich. D. Nov. 16, 1978, Fairhope, Ala. BR TR 5'11½" 185 lbs.

1934	PHI A	0	3	.000	4.88	11	0	0	24	28	10	9	0	0	3	0	6	1	0	.167	0	7	1	0	0.7	.875
1936		0	1	.000	7.20	6	1	0	15	21	4	8	0	0	1	0	3	0	0	.000	0	3	1	0	0.7	.750
2 yrs.		0	4	.000	5.77	17	1	0	39	49	14	17	0	0	4	0	9	1	0	.111	0	10	2	0	0.7	.833

Hal Mauck

MAUCK, ALFRED MARIS
B. Mar. 6, 1869, Princeton, Ind. D. Apr. 27, 1921, Princeton, Ind. BR TR 5'11" 185 lbs.

| 1893 | CHI N | 8 | 10 | .444 | 4.41 | 23 | 18 | 12 | 143 | 168 | 60 | 23 | 1 | 2 | 1 | 0 | 61 | 9 | 0 | .148 | 2 | 32 | 4 | 0 | 1.7 | .895 |

Al Maul

MAUL, ALBERT JOSEPH (Smiling Al)
B. Oct. 9, 1865, Philadelphia, Pa. D. May 3, 1958, Philadelphia, Pa. BR TR 6' 175 lbs.

1884	PHI U	0	1	.000	4.50	1	1	1	8	10	1	7	0	0	0	0	4	0	0	.000	0	1	0	0	1.0	1.000
1887	PHI N	4	2	.667	5.54	7	5	4	50.1	72	15	18	0	2	0	0	56	17	1	.304	1	10	1	0	1.7	.917
1888	PIT N	0	2	.000	6.35	3	1	1	17	26	5	12	0	0	0	0	259	54	0	.208	1	4	2	0	2.3	.714
1889		1	4	.200	9.86	6	4	4	42	64	28	11	0	0	1	0	257	71	4	.276	2	15	2	1	3.2	.895
1890	PIT P	16	12	.571	3.79	30	28	26	246.2	258	104	81	2	0	1	0	162	42	0	.259	25	79	11	4	3.8	.904
1891	PIT N	1	2	.333	2.31	8	3	3	39	44	16	13	0	0	0	1	149	28	0	.188	3	6	0	1	1.1	1.000
1893	WAS N	12	21	.364	5.30	37	33	29	297	355	144	72	1	1	0	0	134	34	0	.254	11	69	10	1	2.4	.889
1894		11	15	.423	5.98	28	26	21	201.2	272	73	34	0	0	0	0	124	30	2	.242	8	49	8	0	2.3	.877
1895		10	5	.667	2.45	16	16	14	135.2	136	37	34	0	0	0	0	72	18	0	.250	10	32	3	3	2.8	.933
1896		5	2	.714	3.63	8	8	7	62	75	20	18	0	0	0	0	28	8	0	.286	2	10	1	1	1.6	.923
1897	2 teams							WAS N (1G 0–1)				BAL N	(2G 0–0)													
"	total	0	1	.000	7.45	3	3	3	9.2	13	9	2	0	0	0	0	4	1	0	.250	0	2	0	0	0.7	1.000
1898	BAL N	20	7	.741	2.10	28	28	26	239.2	207	49	31	1	0	0	0	93	19	0	.204	7	38	1	0	1.6	.978
1899	BKN N	2	0	1.000	4.50	4	4	2	26	35	6	2	0	0	0	0	11	3	0	.273	0	9	1	0	2.5	.900
1900	PHI N	2	3	.400	6.16	5	4	3	38	53	6	3	0	1	0	0	15	3	0	.200	0	11	1	0	2.4	.917
1901	NY N	0	2	.000	11.37	3	3	2	19	39	8	5	0	0	0	0	8	3	0	.375	1	7	0	0	2.7	1.000
15 yrs.		84	79	.515	4.43	187	167	143	1431.2	1659	518	346	4	4	3	1	*				71	342	41	11	2.4	.910

Ernie Maun

MAUN, ERNEST GERALD
B. Feb. 3, 1901, Clearwater, Kans. D. Jan. 1, 1987, Corpus Christi, Tex. BR TR 6' 165 lbs.

1924	NY N	1	1	.500	5.91	22	5	0	35	46	10	5	0	1	1	1	3	2	0	.667	1	6	0	0	0.3	1.000
1926	PHI N	1	4	.200	6.45	14	5	0	37.2	57	18	9	0	1	1	0	12	3	0	.250	1	9	0	0	0.7	1.000
2 yrs.		2	5	.286	6.19	36	5	0	72.2	103	28	14	0	2	2	1	15	5	0	.333	2	15	0	0	0.5	1.000

Dick Mauney

MAUNEY, RICHARD
B. Jan. 26, 1920, Concord, N. C. D. Feb. 6, 1970, Albemarle, N. C. BR TR 5'11½" 164 lbs.

1945	PHI N	6	10	.375	3.08	20	16	6	122.2	127	27	35	0	1	2	2	41	6	0	.146	8	29	2	0	2.0	.949
1946		6	4	.600	2.70	24	7	3	90	98	18	31	1	3	2	2	24	4	0	.167	8	17	0	0	1.0	1.000
1947		0	0	—	3.86	9	1	0	16.1	15	7	6	0	0	0	1	2	0	0	.000	1	7	1	0	1.0	.889
3 yrs.		12	14	.462	2.99	53	24	9	229	240	52	72	1	3	4	4	67	10	0	.149	17	53	3	0	1.4	.959

Harry Maupin

MAUPIN, HENRY CARR
B. July 11, 1872, Wellesville, Mo. TR

1898	STL N	0	2	.000	5.50	2	2	1	18	22	3	3	0	0	0	0	7	3	0	.429	0	1	0	0	0.5	1.000
1899	CLE N	0	3	.000	12.60	5	3	2	25	55	7	3	0	0	0	0	10	0	0	.000	0	2	1	0	0.6	.667
2 yrs.		0	5	.000	9.63	7	5	4	43	77	10	6	0	0	0	0	17	3	0	.176	0	3	1	0	0.6	.750

Ralph Mauriello

MAURIELLO, RALPH (Tami)
B. Aug. 25, 1934, Brooklyn, N. Y. BR TR 6'3" 195 lbs.

| 1958 | LA N | 1 | 1 | .500 | 4.63 | 3 | 2 | 0 | 11.2 | 10 | 8 | 11 | 0 | 0 | 0 | 0 | 4 | 0 | 0 | .000 | 1 | 0 | 0 | 0 | 0.3 | 1.000 |

Larry Maxie

MAXIE, LARRY HANS
B. Oct. 10, 1940, Upland, Calif. BR TR 6'4" 220 lbs.

| 1969 | ATL N | 0 | 0 | — | 3.00 | 2 | 0 | 0 | 3 | 1 | 1 | 1 | 0 | 0 | 0 | 0 | 0 | 0 | 0 | — | 0 | 2 | 0 | 0 | 1.0 | 1.000 |

Bert Maxwell

MAXWELL, JAMES ALBERT
B. Oct. 17, 1886, Texarkana, Ark. D. Dec. 10, 1961, Brady, Tex. BB TR 6' 180 lbs.

1906	PIT N	0	1	.000	5.63	1	1	0	8	2	1	0	0	0	0	0	3	0	0	.000	0	3	0	1	3.0	1.000
1908	PHI A	0	0	—	11.08	4	0	0	13	23	9	7	0	0	0	0	5	0	0	.000	1	3	0	0	1.0	1.000
1911	NY N	1	2	.333	2.90	4	3	3	31	37	7	8	0	0	0	0	9	1	0	.111	3	11	1	1	3.8	.933
1914	BKN F	3	4	.429	3.28	12	8	6	71.1	76	24	19	1	0	0	0	23	2	0	.087	5	23	1	2	2.4	.966
4 yrs.		4	7	.364	4.16	21	12	9	123.1	144	42	35	1	0	0	0	40	3	0	.075	9	40	2	4	2.4	.961

Buckshot May

MAY, WILLIAM HERBERT
B. Dec. 13, 1899, Bakersfield, Calif. D. Mar. 15, 1984, Bakersfield, Calif. BR TR 6'2" 169 lbs.

| 1924 | PIT N | 0 | 0 | — | 0.00 | 1 | 0 | 0 | 2 | 2 | 0 | 1 | 0 | 0 | 0 | 0 | 0 | 0 | 0 | — | 0 | 0 | 0 | 0 | 0.0 | — |

Jakie May

MAY, FRANK SPRUIELL
B. Nov. 25, 1895, Youngville, N. C. D. June 3, 1970, Wendell, N. C. BR TL 5'8" 178 lbs.

| 1917 | STL N | 0 | 0 | — | 3.38 | 15 | 1 | 0 | 29.1 | 29 | 11 | 18 | 0 | 0 | 0 | 0 | 4 | 0 | 0 | .000 | 3 | 14 | 0 | 1 | 1.1 | 1.000 |
| 1918 | | 5 | 6 | .455 | 3.83 | 29 | 16 | 6 | 152.2 | 149 | 69 | 61 | 0 | 2 | 0 | 0 | 45 | 3 | 1 | .067 | 6 | 33 | 2 | 0 | 1.4 | .951 |

Jakie May *continued*

Year	Team	W	L	PCT	ERA	G	GS	CG	IP	H	BB	SO	ShO	Relief Pitching W	L	SV	Batting AB	H	HR	BA	PO	A	E	DP	TC/G	FA
1919		3	12	.200	3.22	28	19	8	125.2	99	87	58	1	0	1	0	37	6	0	.162	1	30	1	0	1.1	.969
1920		1	4	.200	3.06	16	5	3	70.2	65	37	33	0	0	1	0	22	5	0	.227	0	10	0	0	0.6	1.000
1921		1	3	.250	4.71	5	5	1	21	29	12	5	0	0	0	0	6	2	0	.333	0	3	1	0	0.8	.750
1924	CIN N	3	3	.500	3.00	38	4	2	99	104	29	59	0	2	2	6	27	3	1	.111	2	21	0	0	0.6	1.000
1925		8	9	.471	3.87	36	12	7	137.1	146	45	74	1	2	4	2	43	8	0	.186	5	30	0	2	1.0	1.000
1926		13	9	.591	3.22	45	15	9	167.2	175	44	103	1	5	4	3	48	7	0	.146	6	30	1	5	0.8	.973
1927		15	12	.556	3.51	44	28	17	235.2	242	70	121	2	2	0	1	76	14	0	.184	6	51	0	2	1.3	1.000
1928		3	5	.375	4.42	21	11	1	79.1	99	35	39	1	2	2	1	27	8	0	.296	4	12	0	1	0.8	1.000
1929		10	14	.417	4.61	41	24	10	199	219	75	92	0	4	1	3	64	13	0	.203	6	40	1	2	1.1	.979
1930		3	11	.214	5.77	26	18	5	112.1	147	41	44	1	0	1	0	39	5	0	.128	6	23	1	1	1.2	.967
1931	CHI N	5	5	.500	3.87	31	4	1	79	81	43	38	0	3	4	2	22	5	0	.227	4	14	0	3	0.6	1.000
1932		2	2	.500	4.36	35	0	0	53.2	61	19	20	0	2	2	1	8	1	0	.125	4	10	2	0	0.5	.875
14 yrs.		72	95	.431	3.88	410	162	70	1562.1	1645	617	765	7	24	22	19	468	80	2	.171	53	321	9	17	0.9	.977

WORLD SERIES

Year	Team	W	L	PCT	ERA	G	GS	CG	IP	H	BB	SO	ShO	W	L	SV	AB	H	HR	BA	PO	A	E	DP	TC/G	FA
1932	CHI N	0	1	.000	11.57	2	0	0	4.2	9	3	4	0	0	1	0	2	0	0	.000	1	0	0	0	0.5	1.000

Rudy May

MAY, RUDOLPH
B. July 18, 1944, Coffeyville, Kans.

BL TL 6'2" 205 lbs.

Year	Team	W	L	PCT	ERA	G	GS	CG	IP	H	BB	SO	ShO	W	L	SV	AB	H	HR	BA	PO	A	E	DP	TC/G	FA
1965	CAL A	4	9	.308	3.92	30	19	2	124	111	78	76	1				30	6	0	.200	4	15	0	0	0.6	1.000
1969		10	13	.435	3.44	43	25	4	180.1	142	66	133	0	3	2	2	49	4	0	.082	6	26	6	3	0.9	.842
1970		7	13	.350	4.00	38	34	2	209	190	81	164	2	1	1	0	69	6	0	.087	5	33	3	1	1.1	.927
1971		11	12	.478	3.03	32	31	7	208	160	87	156	2	0	1	0	68	10	0	.147	7	31	4	3	1.3	.905
1972		12	11	.522	2.94	35	30	10	205	162	82	169	3	1	0	1	62	7	0	.113	2	24	5	2	0.9	.839
1973		7	17	.292	4.38	34	28	10	185	177	80	134	4	0	2	0	0	0	0	—	2	39	1	0	1.2	.976
1974	2 teams	CAL A	(18G 0–1)		NY A	(17G 8–4)																				
"	total	8	5	.615	3.19	35	18	8	141	104	58	102	2	1	0	2	0	0	0	—	4	19	0	0	0.7	1.000
1975	NY A	14	12	.538	3.06	32	31	13	212	179	99	145	1	0	0	0	0	0	0	—	9	25	2	0	1.1	.944
1976	2 teams	NY A	(11G 4–3)		BAL A	(24G 11–7)																				
"	total	15	10	.600	3.72	35	32	7	220.1	205	70	109	2	0	0	0	0	0	0	—	13	31	5	3	1.4	.898
1977	BAL A	18	14	.563	3.61	37	37	11	252	243	78	105	4	0	0	0	0	0	0	—	6	33	4	1	1.2	.907
1978	MON N	8	10	.444	3.88	27	23	4	144	141	42	87	1	0	1	0	42	6	0	.143	5	13	3	2	0.9	.870
1979		10	3	.769	2.30	33	7	2	94	88	31	67	1	6	1	0	21	3	0	.143	6	15	0	0	0.6	1.000
1980	NY A	15	5	.750	2.47	41	17	3	175	144	39	133	1	4	2	3	0	0	0	—	5	26	2	2	0.8	.939
1981		6	11	.353	4.14	27	22	4	148	137	41	79	0	0	1	1	0	0	0	—	11	28	1	0	1.5	.975
1982		6	6	.500	2.89	41	6	0	106	109	14	85	0	4	3	3	0	0	0	—	2	19	1	1	0.5	.955
1983		1	5	.167	6.87	15	0	0	18.1	22	12	16	0	1	5	0	0	0	0	—	0	3	0	0	0.2	1.000
16 yrs.		152	156	.494	3.46	535	360	87	2622	2314	958	1760	24	21	19	12	341	42	0	.123	87	382	37	18	0.9	.927

DIVISIONAL PLAYOFF SERIES

Year	Team	W	L	PCT	ERA	G	GS	CG	IP	H	BB	SO	ShO	W	L	SV	AB	H	HR	BA	PO	A	E	DP	TC/G	FA
1981	NY A	0	0	—	0.00	1	0	0	2	1	0	1	0	0	0	0	0	0	0	—	0	1	0	0	1.0	—

LEAGUE CHAMPIONSHIP SERIES

Year	Team	W	L	PCT	ERA	G	GS	CG	IP	H	BB	SO	ShO	W	L	SV	AB	H	HR	BA	PO	A	E	DP	TC/G	FA
1980	NY A	0	1	.000	3.38	1	1	1	8	6	3	4	0	0	0	0	0	0	0	—	2	0	0	0	4.0	1.000
1981		0	0	—	8.10	1	1	0	3.1	6	0	5	0	0	0	0	0	0	0	—	0	0	0	0	0.0	—
2 yrs.		0	1	.000	4.76	2	2	1	11.1	12	3	9	0	0	0	0	0	0	0	—	2	0	0	0	2.0	1.000

WORLD SERIES

Year	Team	W	L	PCT	ERA	G	GS	CG	IP	H	BB	SO	ShO	W	L	SV	AB	H	HR	BA	PO	A	E	DP	TC/G	FA
1981	NY A	0	0	—	2.84	3	0	0	6.1	5	1	0	0	0	0	0	1	0	0	.000	1	0	0	0	0.3	1.000

Scott May

MAY, SCOTT FRANCIS
B. Nov. 11, 1961, West Bend, Wis.

BR TR 6'1" 185 lbs.

Year	Team	W	L	PCT	ERA	G	GS	CG	IP	H	BB	SO	ShO	W	L	SV	AB	H	HR	BA	PO	A	E	DP	TC/G	FA
1988	TEX A	0	0	—	8.59	3	1	0	7.1	8	4	4	0	0	0	0	0	0	0	—	1	0	0	1	0.3	1.000

Ed Mayer

MAYER, EDWIN DAVID
B. Nov. 30, 1931, San Francisco, Calif.

BL TL 6'2" 185 lbs.

Year	Team	W	L	PCT	ERA	G	GS	CG	IP	H	BB	SO	ShO	W	L	SV	AB	H	HR	BA	PO	A	E	DP	TC/G	FA
1957	CHI N	0	0	—	5.87	3	1	0	7.2	8	2	3	0	0	0	0	2	1	0	.500	1	3	0	0	1.3	1.000
1958		2	2	.500	3.80	19	0	0	23.2	15	16	14	0	2	2	1	5	1	0	.200	1	3	1	0	0.3	.800
2 yrs.		2	2	.500	4.31	22	1	0	31.1	23	18	17	0	2	2	1	7	2	0	.286	2	6	1	0	0.4	.889

Erskine Mayer

MAYER, ERSKINE JOHN
Born James Erskine. Brother of Sam Mayer.
B. Jan. 16, 1889, Atlanta, Ga. D. Mar. 10, 1957, Los Angeles, Calif.

BR TR 6' 168 lbs.

Year	Team	W	L	PCT	ERA	G	GS	CG	IP	H	BB	SO	ShO	W	L	SV	AB	H	HR	BA	PO	A	E	DP	TC/G	FA
1912	PHI N	0	1	.000	6.33	7	1	0	21.1	27	7	5	0	0	0	0	3	0	0	.000	1	6	1	2	1.1	.875
1913		9	9	.500	3.11	39	20	7	170.2	172	46	51	2	3	1	1	50	6	0	.120	3	48	1	2	1.3	.981
1914		21	19	.525	2.58	48	39	24	321	308	91	116	4	3	1	2	108	21	1	.194	14	105	5	1	2.6	.960
1915		21	15	.583	2.36	43	33	20	274.2	240	59	114	2	4	1	2	88	21	1	.239	14	74	2	3	2.1	.978
1916		7	7	.500	3.15	28	16	7	140	148	33	62	2	1	0	0	38	5	0	.132	9	50	3	3	2.2	.952
1917		11	6	.647	2.76	28	18	11	160	160	33	64	1	1	1	0	51	10	0	.196	5	43	3	4	1.8	.941
1918	2 teams	PHI N	(13G 7–4)		PIT N	(15G 9–3)																				
"	total	16	7	.696	2.65	28	27	18	227.1	230	53	41	1	0	0	0	79	15	0	.190	10	58	0	2	2.4	1.000
1919	2 teams	PIT N	(18G 5–3)		CHI A	(6G 1–3)																				
"	total	6	6	.500	5.30	24	12	6	112	130	23	29	0	2	1	0	36	6	0	.167	2	21	1	0	1.0	.958
8 yrs.		91	70	.565	2.96	245	166	93	1427	1415	345	482	12	14	5	6	453	84	2	.185	58	405	16	17	2.0	.967

WORLD SERIES

Year	Team	W	L	PCT	ERA	G	GS	CG	IP	H	BB	SO	ShO	W	L	SV	AB	H	HR	BA	PO	A	E	DP	TC/G	FA
1915	PHI N	0	1	.000	2.38	2	2	1	11.1	16	2	7	0	0	0	0	4	0	0	.000	2	3	0	1	2.5	1.000
1919	CHI A	0	0	—	0.00	1	0	0	1	0	1	0	0	0	0	0	0	0	0	—	0	0	0	0	0.0	—
2 yrs.		0	1	.000	2.19	3	2	1	12.1	16	3	7	0	0	0	0	4	0	0	.000	2	3	0	1	1.7	1.000

Sam Mayer

MAYER, SAMUEL FRANKEL
Born Samuel Frankel Erskine. Brother of Erskine Mayer.
B. Feb. 28, 1893, Atlanta, Ga. D. July 1, 1962, Atlanta, Ga.

BR TL 5'10" 164 lbs.

Year	Team		W	L	PCT	ERA	G	GS	CG	IP	H	BB	SO	ShO	W	L	SV	AB	H	HR	BA	PO	A	E	DP	TC/G	FA
															Relief Pitching			Batting									

Sam Mayer *continued*

Year	Team		W	L	PCT	ERA	G	GS	CG	IP	H	BB	SO	ShO	W	L	SV	AB	H	HR	BA	PO	A	E	DP	TC/G	FA
1915	WAS	A	0	0	–	0.00	1	0	0	0	2	0	0	0	0	0	0	*				0	0	0	0	0.0	–

Al Mays

MAYS, ALBERT C.　　　　　　　　　　　　　　　　　　　BR
B. May 17, 1865, Canal Dover, Ohio　D. May 17, 1905, Parkersburg, W. Va.

Year	Team		W	L	PCT	ERA	G	GS	CG	IP	H	BB	SO	ShO	W	L	SV	AB	H	HR	BA	PO	A	E	DP	TC/G	FA
1885	LOU	AA	6	11	.353	2.76	17	17	17	150	129	43	61	0	0	0	0	61	13	0	.213	5	23	0	0	1.6	1.000
1886	NY	AA	11	28	.282	3.39	41	41	39	350	330	140	163	1	0	0	0	135	16	1	.119	9	71	11	3	2.2	.879
1887			17	34	.333	4.73	52	52	50	441.1	551	136	124	0	0	0	0	221	45	2	.204	21	144	24	4	3.6	.873
1888	BKN	AA	9	9	.500	2.80	18	18	17	160.2	150	32	67	1	0	0	0	63	5	0	.079	7	45	6	2	3.2	.897
1889	COL	AA	10	7	.588	4.82	21	19	13	140	167	56	52	1	0	0	0	54	7	0	.130	5	36	4	1	2.1	.911
1890			0	1	.000	8.00	1	1	1	9	14	8	2	0	0	0	0	3	0	0	.000	0	0	1	0	1.0	–
6 yrs.			53	90	.371	3.91	150	148	137	1251	1341	415	469	3	0	0	0	537	86	3	.160	47	319	46	10	2.7	.888

Carl Mays

MAYS, CARL WILLIAM (Sub)　　　　　　　　　　　BL　TR　5'11½"　195 lbs.
B. Nov. 12, 1891, Liberty, Ky.　D. Apr. 4, 1971, El Cajon, Calif.

Year	Team		W	L	PCT	ERA	G	GS	CG	IP	H	BB	SO	ShO	W	L	SV	AB	H	HR	BA	PO	A	E	DP	TC/G	FA
1915	BOS	A	6	5	.545	2.60	38	6	2	131.2	119	21	65	0	5	3	7	38	9	0	.237	9	44	2	0	1.4	.964
1916			18	13	.581	2.39	44	24	14	245	208	74	76	2	6	3	3	77	18	0	.234	13	117	6	5	3.1	.956
1917			22	9	.710	1.74	35	33	27	289	230	74	91	2	1	0	0	107	27	0	.252	22	118	1	5	4.0	.993
1918			21	13	.618	2.21	35	33	30	293.1	230	81	114	8	0	1	0	104	30	0	.288	16	122	8	3	4.2	.945
1919	2 teams		BOS	A	(21G 5–11)		NY	A	(13G 9–3)																		
"	total		14	14	.500	2.11	34	29	26	265	227	77	107	3	0	0	0	98	22	0	.224	19	86	5	6	3.2	.955
1920	NY	A	26	11	.703	3.06	45	37	26	312	310	84	92	6	4	0	0	109	26	0	.239	19	106	1	5	2.8	.992
1921			27	9	.750	3.05	49	38	30	336.2	332	76	70	1	1	0	7	143	49	2	.343	8	104	2	4	2.3	.982
1922			13	14	.481	3.60	34	29	21	240	257	50	41	1	0	1	2	92	23	0	.250	8	94	5	4	3.1	.953
1923			5	2	.714	6.20	23	7	2	81.1	119	32	16	0	2	0	0	27	4	1	.148	8	32	1	2	1.8	.976
1924	CIN	N	20	9	.690	3.15	37	27	15	226	238	36	63	2	4	1	0	83	24	1	.289	13	94	5	5	3.0	.955
1925			3	5	.375	3.31	12	5	3	51.2	60	13	10	0	1	2	2	16	4	0	.250	3	15	2	3	1.7	.900
1926			19	12	.613	3.14	39	33	24	281	286	53	58	3	0	1	1	98	22	0	.224	16	117	4	10	3.5	.971
1927			3	7	.300	3.51	14	9	6	82	89	10	17	0	1	0	0	32	13	1	.406	3	38	0	1	3.1	1.000
1928			4	1	.800	3.88	14	7	4	62.2	67	22	10	1	0	0	1	27	8	0	.296	3	17	1	0	1.5	.952
1929	NY	N	7	2	.778	4.32	37	8	1	123	140	31	32	0	6	1	4	34	12	0	.353	12	34	1	3	1.3	.979
15 yrs.			208	126	.623	2.92	490	325	231	3020.1	2912	734	862	29	31	13	31	1085	291	5	.268	174	1138	44	56	2.8	.968

WORLD SERIES

Year	Team		W	L	PCT	ERA	G	GS	CG	IP	H	BB	SO	ShO	W	L	SV	AB	H	HR	BA	PO	A	E	DP	TC/G	FA
1916	BOS	A	0	1	.000	5.06	2	1	0	5.1	8	3	2	0	0	0	0	1	0	0	.000	0	4	0	0	2.0	1.000
1918			2	0	1.000	1.00	2	2	2	18	10	3	5	0	0	0	0	5	1	0	.200	0	8	0	0	4.0	1.000
1921	NY	A	1	2	.333	1.73	3	3	3	26	20	0	9	1	0	0	0	9	1	0	.111	0	8	0	0	2.7	1.000
1922			0	1	.000	4.50	1	1	0	8	9	2	1	0	0	0	0	2	0	0	.000	0	4	0	0	4.0	1.000
4 yrs.			3	4	.429	2.20	8	7	5	57.1	47	8	17	1	0	0	0	17	2	0	.118	0	24	0	0	3.0	1.000
					7th				10th																		

Jack McAdams

McADAMS, GEORGE D.　　　　　　　　　　　　　　　BR　TR　6'1½"　170 lbs.
B. Dec. 17, 1886, Benton, Ark.　D. May 21, 1937, San Francisco, Calif.

Year	Team		W	L	PCT	ERA	G	GS	CG	IP	H	BB	SO	ShO	W	L	SV	AB	H	HR	BA	PO	A	E	DP	TC/G	FA
1911	STL	N	0	0	–	3.72	6	0	0	9.2	7	5	4	0	0	0	0	1	0	0	.000	2	2	0	0	0.7	1.000

Bill McAfee

McAFEE, WILLIAM FORT　　　　　　　　　　　　　　BR　TR　6'2"　186 lbs.
B. Sept. 7, 1907, Smithville, Ga.　D. July 8, 1958, Culpeper, Va.

Year	Team		W	L	PCT	ERA	G	GS	CG	IP	H	BB	SO	ShO	W	L	SV	AB	H	HR	BA	PO	A	E	DP	TC/G	FA
1930	CHI	N	0	0	–	0.00	2	0	0	3	3	2	0	0	0	0	0	0	0	0	–	0	0	0	0	0.0	–
1931	BOS	N	0	1	.000	6.37	18	1	0	29.2	39	10	9	0	0	0	0	3	0	0	.000	0	8	2	0	0.4	1.000
1932	WAS	A	6	1	.857	3.92	8	5	2	41.1	47	22	10	0	3	0	0	18	2	0	.111	2	14	0	0	2.0	1.000
1933			3	2	.600	6.62	27	1	0	53	64	21	14	0	3	2	5	15	4	1	.267	1	12	1	2	0.5	.929
1934	STL	A	1	0	1.000	5.84	28	0	0	61.2	84	26	11	0	1	0	0	16	3	0	.188	3	10	2	0	0.5	.867
5 yrs.			10	4	.714	5.69	83	7	2	186.2	237	81	44	0	7	2	5	52	9	1	.173	6	44	3	4	0.6	.943

Jimmy McAleer

McALEER, JAMES ROBERT　　　　　　　　　　　　　BR　TR　6'　175 lbs.
B. July 10, 1864, Youngstown, Ohio　D. Apr. 29, 1931, Youngstown, Ohio
Manager 1901–11.

Year	Team		W	L	PCT	ERA	G	GS	CG	IP	H	BB	SO	ShO	W	L	SV	AB	H	HR	BA	PO	A	E	DP	TC/G	FA
1901	CLE	A	0	0	–	0.00	1	0	0	.1	2	3	0	0	0	0	0	*				0	0	0	0	0.0	–

John McAleese

McALEESE, JOHN JAMES　　　　　　　　　　　　　　BR　TR　5'8"
B. Aug. 22, 1878, Sharon, Pa.　D. Nov. 14, 1950, New York, N. Y.

Year	Team		W	L	PCT	ERA	G	GS	CG	IP	H	BB	SO	ShO	W	L	SV	AB	H	HR	BA	PO	A	E	DP	TC/G	FA
1901	CHI	A	0	0	–	9.00	1	0	0	3	7	1	1	0	0	0	0	*				1	0	0	0	1.0	1.000

Jack McAllister

Playing record listed under Andy Coakley

Sport McAllister

McALLISTER, LEWIS WILLIAM　　　　　　　　　　BB　TR　5'11"　180 lbs.
B. July 23, 1874, Austin, Miss.　D. July 17, 1962, Wyandotte, Mich.

Year	Team		W	L	PCT	ERA	G	GS	CG	IP	H	BB	SO	ShO	W	L	SV	AB	H	HR	BA	PO	A	E	DP	TC/G	FA
1896	CLE	N	0	0	–	6.75	1	0	0	4	9	2	0	0	0	0	0	27	6	0	.222	0	2	0	0	2.0	1.000
1897			1	2	.333	4.50	4	3	3	28	29	9	10	0	0	0	0	137	30	0	.219	3	8	0	0	2.8	1.000
1898			3	4	.429	4.55	9	7	6	65.1	73	23	9	0	0	0	0	57	13	0	.228	2	14	1	0	1.9	.941
1899			0	1	.000	9.56	3	1	1	16	29	10	2	0	0	0	0	418	99	1	.237	0	3	0	0	1.0	1.000
4 yrs.			4	7	.364	5.32	17	11	10	113.1	140	44	21	0	0	0	0	*				5	27	1	0	1.9	.970

Ernie McAnally

McANALLY, ERNEST LEE　　　　　　　　　　　　　　BR　TR　6'1"　190 lbs.
B. Aug. 15, 1946, Pittsburg, Tex.

Year	Team		W	L	PCT	ERA	G	GS	CG	IP	H	BB	SO	ShO	W	L	SV	AB	H	HR	BA	PO	A	E	DP	TC/G	FA
1971	MON	N	11	12	.478	3.89	31	25	8	178	150	87	98	2	0	0	0	60	7	1	.117	12	28	6	2	1.5	.870
1972			6	15	.286	3.81	29	27	4	170	165	71	102	2	0	0	0	53	6	0	.113	9	40	4	1	1.8	.925
1973			7	9	.438	4.04	27	24	4	147	158	54	72	0	0	0	0	49	9	0	.184	4	25	7	4	1.3	.806

Year	Team		W	L	PCT	ERA	G	GS	CG	IP	H	BB	SO	ShO	Relief Pitching W	L	SV	Batting AB	H	HR	BA	PO	A	E	DP	TC/G	FA

Ernie McAnally *continued*

Year	Team		W	L	PCT	ERA	G	GS	CG	IP	H	BB	SO	ShO	W	L	SV	AB	H	HR	BA	PO	A	E	DP	TC/G	FA
1974			6	13	.316	4.47	25	21	5	129	126	56	79	2	0	1	0	42	5	0	.119	5	24	1	1	1.2	.967
4 yrs.			30	49	.380	4.02	112	97	21	624	599	268	351	6	0	1	0	204	27	1	.132	30	117	18	8	1.5	.891

Jim McAndrew
McANDREW, JAMES CLEMENT
B. Jan. 11, 1944, Lost Nation, Iowa   BR TR 6'2"   185 lbs.

Year	Team		W	L	PCT	ERA	G	GS	CG	IP	H	BB	SO	ShO	W	L	SV	AB	H	HR	BA	PO	A	E	DP	TC/G	FA
1968	NY	N	4	7	.364	2.28	12	12	2	79	66	17	46	1	0	0	0	22	1	0	.045	8	8	0	2	1.3	1.000
1969			6	7	.462	3.47	27	21	4	135	112	44	90	2	0	0	0	37	5	0	.135	10	14	0	1	0.9	1.000
1970			10	14	.417	3.57	32	27	9	184	166	38	111	3	0	1	2	54	8	0	.148	13	17	0	1	0.9	1.000
1971			2	5	.286	4.40	24	10	0	90	78	32	42	0	1	0	1	23	1	0	.043	10	17	4	1	1.3	.871
1972			11	8	.579	2.80	28	23	4	160.2	133	38	81	0	1	0	1	43	2	0	.047	16	16	1	0	1.2	.970
1973			3	8	.273	5.38	23	12	0	80.1	109	31	38	0	0	1	0	15	2	0	.133	3	9	2	0	0.6	.857
1974	SD	N	1	4	.200	5.57	15	5	1	42	48	13	16	0	0	1	0	7	1	0	.143	5	5	0	0	0.3	1.000
7 yrs.			37	53	.411	3.65	161	110	20	771	712	213	424	6	1	4	4	201	20	0	.100	60	86	7	5	1.0	.954

Dixie McArthur
McARTHUR, OLAND ALEXANDER
B. Feb. 1, 1892, Vernon, Ala.   D. May 31, 1986, West Point, Miss.   BR TR 6'1"   185 lbs.

Year	Team		W	L	PCT	ERA	G	GS	CG	IP	H	BB	SO	ShO	W	L	SV	AB	H	HR	BA	PO	A	E	DP	TC/G	FA
1914	PIT	N	0	0	–	0.00	1	0	0	1	1	1	0	1	0	0	0	0	0	0	–	0	0	0	0	0.0	–

Tom McAvoy
McAVOY, THOMAS JOHN
B. Aug. 12, 1936, Brooklyn, N. Y.   BL TL 6'3"   200 lbs.

Year	Team		W	L	PCT	ERA	G	GS	CG	IP	H	BB	SO	ShO	W	L	SV	AB	H	HR	BA	PO	A	E	DP	TC/G	FA
1959	WAS	A	0	0	–	0.00	1	0	0	2.2	1	2	0	0	0	0	0	1	0	0	.000	0	1	0	0	1.0	1.000

Wickey McAvoy
McAVOY, JAMES EUGENE
B. Oct. 20, 1894, Rochester, N. Y.   D. July 5, 1973, Rochester, N. Y.   BR TR 5'11"   172 lbs.

Year	Team		W	L	PCT	ERA	G	GS	CG	IP	H	BB	SO	ShO	W	L	SV	AB	H	HR	BA	PO	A	E	DP	TC/G	FA
1918	PHI	A	0	0	–	0.00	1	0	0	.2	0	0	0	0	0	0	0	*				0	0	0	0		

Al McBean
McBEAN, ALVIN O'NEAL
B. May 15, 1938, Charlotte Amalie, Virgin Islands   BR TR 5'11½" 165 lbs.

Year	Team		W	L	PCT	ERA	G	GS	CG	IP	H	BB	SO	ShO	W	L	SV	AB	H	HR	BA	PO	A	E	DP	TC/G	FA
1961	PIT	N	3	2	.600	3.75	27	2	0	74.1	72	42	49	0	0	3	1	15	4	1	.267	4	23	1	1	1.0	.964
1962			15	10	.600	3.70	33	29	6	189.2	212	65	119	2	0	0	0	67	14	0	.209	17	31	5	4	1.6	.906
1963			13	3	.813	2.57	55	7	2	122.1	100	39	74	1	11	2	11	31	6	1	.194	11	29	6	2	0.8	.870
1964			8	3	.727	1.91	58	0	0	89.2	76	17	41	0	8	3	22	12	1	0	.083	3	38	4	5	0.8	.911
1965			6	6	.500	2.29	62	1	0	114	111	42	54	0	5	6	18	27	6	0	.222	6	27	1	1	0.5	.971
1966			4	3	.571	3.22	47	0	0	86.2	95	24	54	0	4	3	3	10	1	0	.100	7	17	1	0	0.5	.960
1967			7	4	.636	2.54	51	8	5	131	118	43	54	0	3	2	4	29	6	0	.207	9	26	2	1	0.7	.946
1968			9	12	.429	3.58	36	28	9	198.1	204	63	100	2	0	1	0	67	13	1	.194	16	54	3	3	2.0	.959
1969	2 teams	SD N (1G 0–1)														LA N	(31G 2–6)										
"	total		2	7	.222	4.07	32	2	0	55.1	56	23	27	0	2	6	4	5	1	0	.200	0	5	1	0	0.2	.833
1970	2 teams	LA N (1G 0–0)														PIT N	(7G 0–0)										
"	total		0	0	–	7.36	8	0	0	11	14	7	3	0	0	0	1	1	0	0	.000	0	2	0	1	0.3	1.000
10 yrs.			67	50	.573	3.13	409	76	22	1072.1	1058	365	575	5	36	24	63	264	52	3	.197	73	252	24	18	0.9	.931

Pryor McBee
McBEE, PRYOR EDWARD (Lefty)
B. June 20, 1901, Blanco, Okla.   D. Apr. 19, 1963, Roseville, Calif.   BR TL 6'1"   190 lbs.

Year	Team		W	L	PCT	ERA	G	GS	CG	IP	H	BB	SO	ShO	W	L	SV	AB	H	HR	BA	PO	A	E	DP	TC/G	FA
1926	CHI	A	0	0	–	6.75	1	0	0	1.1	1	3	1	0	0	0	0	0	0	0	–	0	0	0	0	0.0	–

Dick McBride
McBRIDE, JAMES DICKSON
B. 1845, Philadelphia, Pa.   D. Oct. 10, 1916, Philadelphia, Pa.
Manager 1871-75.   TR 5'9"   150 lbs.

Year	Team		W	L	PCT	ERA	G	GS	CG	IP	H	BB	SO	ShO	W	L	SV	AB	H	HR	BA	PO	A	E	DP	TC/G	FA
1876	BOS	N	0	4	.000	2.73	4	4	3	33	53	5	2	0	0	0	0	16	3	0	.188	0	5	1	0	1.5	.833

Ken McBride
McBRIDE, KENNETH FAYE
B. Aug. 12, 1935, Huntsville, Ala.   BR TR 6'1"   190 lbs.

Year	Team		W	L	PCT	ERA	G	GS	CG	IP	H	BB	SO	ShO	W	L	SV	AB	H	HR	BA	PO	A	E	DP	TC/G	FA
1959	CHI	A	0	1	.000	3.18	11	2	0	22.2	20	17	12	0	0	0	1	6	1	0	.167	0	9	1	0	0.9	.900
1960			0	1	.000	3.86	5	0	0	4.2	6	3	4	0	0	1	0	0	0	0	–	1	0	0	0	0.2	1.000
1961	LA	A	12	15	.444	3.65	38	36	11	241.2	229	102	180	1	0	1	1	83	7	0	.084	19	53	2	5	1.9	.973
1962			11	5	.688	3.50	24	23	6	149.1	136	70	83	4	0	0	0	55	9	1	.164	20	41	2	7	2.6	.968
1963			13	12	.520	3.26	36	36	11	251	198	82	147	5	0	0	0	87	15	0	.172	22	52	3	3	2.1	.961
1964			4	13	.235	5.26	29	21	0	116.1	104	75	66	0	0	1	0	28	6	0	.214	13	29	1	4	1.5	.977
1965	CAL	A	0	3	.000	6.14	8	4	0	22	24	14	11	0	0	0	0	5	0	0	.000	3	1	0	0	0.5	1.000
7 yrs.			40	50	.444	3.79	151	122	28	807.2	717	363	503	7	1	2	3	264	38	1	.144	78	185	9	19	1.8	.967

Pete McBride
McBRIDE, PETER WILLIAM
B. July 9, 1875, Adams, Mass.   D. July 3, 1944, North Adams, Mass.   BR TR 5'10"   170 lbs.

Year	Team		W	L	PCT	ERA	G	GS	CG	IP	H	BB	SO	ShO	W	L	SV	AB	H	HR	BA	PO	A	E	DP	TC/G	FA
1898	CLE	N	0	1	.000	6.43	1	1	1	7	9	4	6	0	0	0	0	2	2	0	1.000	0	1	0	0	1.0	1.000
1899	STL	N	2	4	.333	4.08	11	6	4	64	65	40	26	0	0	0	0	27	5	1	.185	3	13	6	0	2.0	.727
2 yrs.			2	5	.286	4.31	12	7	5	71	74	44	32	0	0	0	0	29	7	1	.241	3	14	6	0	1.9	.739

Dick McCabe
McCABE, RICHARD JAMES
B. Feb. 21, 1896, Mamaroneck, N. Y.   D. Apr. 11, 1950, Buffalo, N. Y.   BR TR 5'10½" 159 lbs.

Year	Team		W	L	PCT	ERA	G	GS	CG	IP	H	BB	SO	ShO	W	L	SV	AB	H	HR	BA	PO	A	E	DP	TC/G	FA
1918	BOS	A	0	1	.000	2.79	3	1	0	9.2	13	2	3	0	0	0	0	2	0	0	.000	1	3	0	0	1.3	1.000
1922	CHI	A	1	0	1.000	5.40	3	0	0	3.1	4	0	1	0	1	0	0	0	0	0	–	0	0	0	0	0.0	–
2 yrs.			1	1	.500	3.46	6	1	0	13	17	2	4	0	1	0	0	2	0	0	.000	1	3	0	0	0.7	1.000

Ralph McCabe
McCABE, RALPH HERBERT
B. Oct. 21, 1918, Napanee, Ont., Canada   D. May 3, 1974, Windsor, Ont., Canada   BR TR 6'4"   195 lbs.

Year	Team		W	L	PCT	ERA	G	GS	CG	IP	H	BB	SO	ShO	W	L	SV	AB	H	HR	BA	PO	A	E	DP	TC/G	FA
1946	CLE	A	0	1	.000	11.25	1	1	0	4	5	2	3	0	0	0	0	1	0	0	.000	1	0	0	0	1.0	1.000

Year	Team		W	L	PCT	ERA	G	GS	CG	IP	H	BB	SO	ShO	Relief Pitching W	L	SV	Batting AB	H	HR	BA	PO	A	E	DP	TC/G	FA

Tim McCabe
McCABE, TIMOTHY J.
B. Oct. 19, 1894, Ironton, Mo. D. Apr. 12, 1977, Ironton, Mo.
BR TR 6' 190 lbs.

Year	Team		W	L	PCT	ERA	G	GS	CG	IP	H	BB	SO	ShO	W	L	SV	AB	H	HR	BA	PO	A	E	DP	TC/G	FA
1915	STL	A	3	1	.750	2.38	7	4	4	41.2	25	9	17	1	0	0	0	15	1	0	.067	0	10	1	0	1.6	.909
1916			2	0	1.000	3.16	13	0	0	25.2	29	7	7	0	2	0	0	4	0	0	.000	1	14	0	0	1.2	1.000
1917			0	0	–	23.14	1	0	0	2.1	4	4	2	0	0	0	0	0	0	0	–	0	1	0	0	1.0	1.000
1918			0	0	–	13.50	1	0	0	1.1	2	1	0	0	0	0	0	0	0	0	–	0	0	0	0	0.0	–
4 yrs.			5	1	.833	3.55	22	4	4	71	60	21	26	1	2	0	0	19	1	0	.053	1	25	1	0	1.2	.963

Harry McCaffrey
McCAFFREY, HARRY CHARLES
B. Nov. 25, 1858, St. Louis, Mo. D. Apr. 19, 1928, St. Louis, Mo.
BR TR 5'10½" 185 lbs.

Year	Team		W	L	PCT	ERA	G	GS	CG	IP	H	BB	SO	ShO	W	L	SV	AB	H	HR	BA	PO	A	E	DP	TC/G	FA
1885	CIN	AA	1	0	1.000	6.00	1	1	1	9	13	2	2	0	0	0	0	*				0	1	0	1	1.0	–

Bill McCahan
McCAHAN, WILLIAM GLENN
B. June 7, 1921, Philadelphia, Pa. D. July 3, 1986, Fort Worth, Tex.
BR TR 5'11" 200 lbs.

Year	Team		W	L	PCT	ERA	G	GS	CG	IP	H	BB	SO	ShO	W	L	SV	AB	H	HR	BA	PO	A	E	DP	TC/G	FA
1946	PHI	A	1	1	.500	1.00	4	2	2	18	16	9	6	1	0	0	0	5	2	0	.400	1	3	0	0	1.0	1.000
1947			10	5	.667	3.32	29	19	10	165.1	160	62	47	1	1	0	0	55	9	0	.164	7	33	1	4	1.4	.976
1948			4	7	.364	5.71	17	15	5	86.2	98	65	20	0	0	0	0	31	8	0	.258	6	10	1	0	1.0	.941
1949			1	1	.500	2.61	7	4	0	20.2	23	9	3	0	0	0	0	5	1	0	.200	0	3	0	0	0.4	1.000
4 yrs.			16	14	.533	3.84	57	40	17	290.2	297	145	76	2	1	0	0	96	20	0	.208	14	49	2	4	1.1	.969

Dutch McCall
McCALL, ROBERT LEONARD
B. Dec. 27, 1920, Columbia, Tenn.
BL TL 6'1½" 185 lbs.

Year	Team		W	L	PCT	ERA	G	GS	CG	IP	H	BB	SO	ShO	W	L	SV	AB	H	HR	BA	PO	A	E	DP	TC/G	FA
1948	CHI	N	4	13	.235	4.82	30	20	5	151.1	158	85	89	0	0	3	0	53	9	0	.170	5	31	3	5	1.3	.923

Larry McCall
McCALL, LARRY STEPHEN
B. Sept. 8, 1952, Asheville, N. C.
BL TR 6'2" 195 lbs.

Year	Team		W	L	PCT	ERA	G	GS	CG	IP	H	BB	SO	ShO	W	L	SV	AB	H	HR	BA	PO	A	E	DP	TC/G	FA
1977	NY	A	0	1	.000	7.50	2	0	0	6	12	1	0	0	0	1	0	0	0	0	–	1	1	0	1	1.0	.500
1978			1	1	.500	5.63	5	1	0	16	20	6	7	0	0	1	0	0	0	0	–	0	4	0	1	0.8	1.000
1979	TEX	A	1	0	1.000	2.25	2	1	0	8	7	3	3	0	1	0	0	0	0	0	–	0	1	0	1	0.5	1.000
3 yrs.			2	2	.500	5.10	9	2	0	30	39	10	10	0	1	2	0	0	0	0	–	1	5	1	2	0.8	.857

Windy McCall
McCALL, JOHN WILLIAM
B. July 18, 1925, San Francisco, Calif.
BL TL 6' 180 lbs.

Year	Team		W	L	PCT	ERA	G	GS	CG	IP	H	BB	SO	ShO	W	L	SV	AB	H	HR	BA	PO	A	E	DP	TC/G	FA
1948	BOS	A	0	1	.000	20.25	1	1	0	1.1	6	1	1	0	0	0	0	0	0	0	–	0	1	0	0	1.0	1.000
1949			0	0	–	11.57	5	0	0	9.1	13	10	8	0	0	0	0	3	2	0	.667	0	0	0	0	0.0	–
1950	PIT	N	0	0	–	9.45	2	0	0	6.2	12	4	5	0	0	0	0	2	0	0	.000	1	1	0	0	1.0	1.000
1954	NY	N	2	5	.286	3.25	33	4	0	61	50	29	38	0	2	3	2	11	0	0	.000	3	5	3	0	0.3	.727
1955			6	5	.545	3.69	42	6	4	95	86	37	50	0	3	3	3	17	2	0	.118	6	16	1	4	0.5	1.000
1956			3	4	.429	3.61	46	4	0	77.1	74	20	41	0	1	1	7	15	3	0	.200	4	6	1	0	0.2	.909
1957			0	0	–	15.00	5	0	0	3	8	2	1	0	0	0	0	0	0	0	–	0	0	0	0	0.0	–
7 yrs.			11	15	.423	4.22	134	15	4	253.2	249	103	144	0	8	7	12	48	7	0	.146	14	29	4	4	0.4	.915

Randy McCament
McCAMENT, LARRY RANDALL
B. July 29, 1962, Albuquerque, N. M.
BR TR 6'3" 195 lbs.

Year	Team		W	L	PCT	ERA	G	GS	CG	IP	H	BB	SO	ShO	W	L	SV	AB	H	HR	BA	PO	A	E	DP	TC/G	FA
1989	SF	N	1	1	.500	3.93	25	0	0	36.2	32	23	12	0	1	1	0	3	1	0	.333	3	8	1	1	0.5	.917

Gene McCann
McCANN, HENRY EUGENE
B. June 13, 1876, Baltimore, Md. D. Apr. 26, 1943, New York, N. Y.
TR 5'10"

Year	Team		W	L	PCT	ERA	G	GS	CG	IP	H	BB	SO	ShO	W	L	SV	AB	H	HR	BA	PO	A	E	DP	TC/G	FA
1901	BKN	N	2	3	.400	3.44	6	5	3	34	34	16	9	0	0	0	0	10	0	0	.000	2	11	2	0	2.5	.867
1902			1	2	.333	2.40	3	3	3	30	32	12	9	0	0	0	0	12	1	0	.083	4	10	1	0	5.0	.933
2 yrs.			3	5	.375	2.95	9	8	6	64	66	28	18	0	0	0	0	22	1	0	.045	6	21	3	0	3.3	.900

Arch McCarthy
McCARTHY, ARCHIBALD JOSEPH
B. Jan. 21, 1881, Ypsilanti, Mich. Deceased.

Year	Team		W	L	PCT	ERA	G	GS	CG	IP	H	BB	SO	ShO	W	L	SV	AB	H	HR	BA	PO	A	E	DP	TC/G	FA
1902	DET	A	2	7	.222	6.13	10	8	8	72	90	31	10	0	1	0	0	28	2	0	.071	2	13	3	1	1.8	.833

Bill McCarthy
McCARTHY, WILLIAM THOMAS
B. Apr. 11, 1882, Ashland, Mass. D. May 29, 1939, Boston, Mass.
BR TR 5'11" 180 lbs.

Year	Team		W	L	PCT	ERA	G	GS	CG	IP	H	BB	SO	ShO	W	L	SV	AB	H	HR	BA	PO	A	E	DP	TC/G	FA
1906	BOS	N	0	0	–	9.00	1	0	0	2	2	3	0	0	0	0	0	1	0	0	.000	0	0	0	0	0.0	–

Johnny McCarthy
McCARTHY, JOHN JOSEPH
B. Jan. 7, 1910, Chicago, Ill. D. Sept. 13, 1973, Mundelein, Ill.
BL TL 6'1½" 185 lbs.

Year	Team		W	L	PCT	ERA	G	GS	CG	IP	H	BB	SO	ShO	W	L	SV	AB	H	HR	BA	PO	A	E	DP	TC/G	FA
1939	NY	N	0	0	–	7.20	1	0	0	5	8	2	0	0	0	0	0	*				0	2	0	0	2.0	1.000

Tom McCarthy
McCARTHY, THOMAS MICHAEL
B. June 18, 1961, Lundsthal, West Germany
BR TR 6' 180 lbs.

Year	Team		W	L	PCT	ERA	G	GS	CG	IP	H	BB	SO	ShO	W	L	SV	AB	H	HR	BA	PO	A	E	DP	TC/G	FA
1985	BOS	A	0	0	–	10.80	3	0	0	5	7	4	2	0	0	0	0	0	0	0	–	1	0	0	0	0.3	1.000
1988	CHI	A	2	0	1.000	1.38	6	0	0	13	9	2	5	0	2	0	1	0	0	0	–	1	3	0	0	0.7	1.000
1989			1	2	.333	3.51	31	0	0	66.2	72	20	27	0	1	2	0	0	0	0	–	4	13	0	2	0.5	1.000
3 yrs.			3	2	.600	3.61	40	0	0	84.2	88	26	34	0	3	2	1	0	0	0	–	6	16	0	2	0.6	1.000

Tom McCarthy
McCARTHY, THOMAS PATRICK
B. May 22, 1884, Fort Wayne, Ind. D. Mar. 28, 1933, Mishawaka, Ind.
TR 5'7" 170 lbs.

Year	Team		W	L	PCT	ERA	G	GS	CG	IP	H	BB	SO	ShO	W	L	SV	AB	H	HR	BA	PO	A	E	DP	TC/G	FA
1908	3 teams		CIN N (1G 0–1)			PIT N (2G 0–0)			BOS N (14G 6–3)																		
"	total		6	4	.600	1.82	17	13	7	103.2	86	37	31	2	0	0	0	41	6	0	.146	4	36	1	0	2.4	.976
1909	BOS	N	0	5	.000	3.50	8	7	3	46.1	47	28	11	0	0	0	0	16	2	0	.125	3	14	1	0	2.3	.944
2 yrs.			6	9	.400	2.34	25	20	10	150	133	65	42	2	0	0	0	57	8	0	.140	7	50	2	0	2.4	.966

Year	Team		W	L	PCT	ERA	G	GS	CG	IP	H	BB	SO	ShO	Relief Pitching W	L	SV	Batting AB	H	HR	BA	PO	A	E	DP	TC/G	FA

Tommy McCarthy

McCARTHY, THOMAS FRANCIS MICHAEL
B. July 24, 1863, Boston, Mass.   D. Aug. 5, 1922, Boston, Mass.
Manager 1890.
Hall of Fame 1946.

BR TR 5'7"   170 lbs.

Year	Team		W	L	PCT	ERA	G	GS	CG	IP	H	BB	SO	ShO	W	L	SV	AB	H	HR	BA	PO	A	E	DP	TC/G	FA
1884	BOS	U	0	7	.000	4.82	7	6	5	56	73	14	18	0	0	1	0	209	45	0	.215	6	19	5	1	4.3	.833
1886	PHI	N	0	0	—	0.00	1	0	0	1	0	1	1	0	0	0	0	27	5	0	.185	0	0	0	0	0.0	—
1888	STL	AA	0	0	—	4.15	2	0	0	4.1	3	2	1	0	0	0	0	511	140	1	.274	0	0	0	0	0.0	—
1889			0	0	—	7.20	1	0	0	5	4	6	1	0	0	0	0	604	176	2	.291	0	0	0	0	0.0	—
1891			0	0	—	9.00	1	0	0	1	2	0	0	0	0	0	0	578	179	8	.310	0	0	0	0	0.0	—
1894	BOS	N	0	0	—	4.50	1	0	0	2	1	3	0	0	0	0	0	539	188	13	.349	0	0	0	0	0.0	—
6 yrs.			0	7	.000	4.93	13	6	5	69.1	83	26	21	0	0	1	0	*				6	19	5	1	2.3	.833

John McCarty

McCARTY, JOHN A.
B. St. Louis, Mo.   Deceased.

TR

Year	Team		W	L	PCT	ERA	G	GS	CG	IP	H	BB	SO	ShO	W	L	SV	AB	H	HR	BA	PO	A	E	DP	TC/G	FA
1889	KC	AA	8	6	.571	3.91	15	14	13	119.2	147	61	36	0	0	0	0	79	18	0	.228	3	30	10	0	2.9	.767

Kirk McCaskill

McCASKILL, KIRK EDWARD
B. Apr. 9, 1961, Kapuskasing, Ont., Canada

BR TR 6'1"   185 lbs.

Year	Team		W	L	PCT	ERA	G	GS	CG	IP	H	BB	SO	ShO	W	L	SV	AB	H	HR	BA	PO	A	E	DP	TC/G	FA
1985	CAL	A	12	12	.500	4.70	30	29	6	189.2	189	64	102	1	0	0	0	0	0	0	—	11	27	3	1	1.4	.927
1986			17	10	.630	3.36	34	33	10	246.1	207	92	202	2	0	0	0	0	0	0	—	24	26	1	0	1.5	.980
1987			4	6	.400	5.67	14	13	1	74.2	84	34	56	1	0	0	0	0	0	0	—	8	12	1	1	1.5	.952
1988			8	6	.571	4.31	23	23	4	146.1	155	61	98	2	0	0	0	0	0	0	—	12	18	3	2	1.4	.909
1989			15	10	.600	2.93	32	32	6	212	202	59	107	4	0	0	0	0	0	0	—	16	42	3	5	1.9	.951
5 yrs.			56	44	.560	3.90	133	130	27	869	837	310	565	10	0	0	0	0	0	0	—	71	125	11	9	1.6	.947

LEAGUE CHAMPIONSHIP SERIES

| 1986 | CAL | A | 0 | 2 | .000 | 7.71 | 2 | 2 | 0 | 9.1 | 16 | 5 | 7 | 0 | 0 | 0 | 0 | 0 | 0 | 0 | — | 0 | 0 | 0 | 0 | 0.0 | — |

Steve McCatty

McCATTY, STEVEN EARL
B. Mar. 20, 1954, Detroit, Mich.

BR TR 6'3"   195 lbs.

Year	Team		W	L	PCT	ERA	G	GS	CG	IP	H	BB	SO	ShO	W	L	SV	AB	H	HR	BA	PO	A	E	DP	TC/G	FA
1977	OAK	A	0	0	—	5.14	4	2	0	14	16	7	9	0	0	0	0	0	0	0	—	0	0	0	0	0.0	—
1978			0	0	—	4.50	9	0	0	20	26	9	10	0	0	0	0	0	0	0	—	2	1	0	0	0.4	.750
1979			11	12	.478	4.21	31	23	8	186	207	80	87	0	0	0	0	0	0	0	—	12	20	3	1	1.1	.914
1980			14	14	.500	3.85	33	31	11	222	202	99	114	0	1	0	0	0	0	0	—	13	26	1	2	1.2	.975
1981			14	7	.667	2.32	22	22	16	186	140	61	91	4	0	0	0	0	0	0	—	11	26	1	2	1.7	.974
1982			6	3	.667	3.99	21	20	2	128.2	124	70	66	0	0	0	0	0	0	0	—	12	13	0	1	1.2	1.000
1983			6	9	.400	3.99	38	24	3	167	156	82	65	2	0	0	0	0	0	0	—	7	16	1	1	0.6	.958
1984			8	14	.364	4.76	33	30	4	179.2	206	71	63	0	1	0	5	0	0	0	—	15	16	2	1	1.0	.939
1985			4	4	.500	5.57	30	9	1	85.2	95	41	36	0	1	0	0	0	0	0	—	4	13	1	4	0.6	.944
9 yrs.			63	63	.500	3.99	221	161	45	1189	1172	520	541	7	4	4	5	0	0	0	—	76	131	10	13	1.0	.954

DIVISIONAL PLAYOFF SERIES

| 1981 | OAK | A | 1 | 0 | 1.000 | 1.00 | 1 | 1 | 1 | 9 | 6 | 4 | 3 | 0 | 0 | 0 | 0 | 0 | 0 | 0 | — | 0 | 0 | 0 | 0 | 0.0 | — |

LEAGUE CHAMPIONSHIP SERIES

| 1981 | OAK | A | 0 | 1 | .000 | 13.50 | 1 | 1 | 0 | 3.1 | 6 | 2 | 2 | 0 | 0 | 0 | 0 | 0 | 0 | 0 | — | 0 | 0 | 0 | 0 | 0.0 | — |

Al McCauley

McCAULEY, ALLEN A.
B. Mar. 4, 1863, Indianapolis, Ind.   D. Aug. 24, 1917, Indianapolis, Ind.

BL TL 6'   180 lbs.

Year	Team		W	L	PCT	ERA	G	GS	CG	IP	H	BB	SO	ShO	W	L	SV	AB	H	HR	BA	PO	A	E	DP	TC/G	FA
1884	IND	AA	2	7	.222	5.09	10	9	9	76	87	25	34	0	0	0	0	*				5	22	0	1	2.7	1.000

Joe McClain

McCLAIN, JOSEPH FRED
B. May 5, 1933, Johnson City, Tenn.

BR TR 6'   183 lbs.

Year	Team		W	L	PCT	ERA	G	GS	CG	IP	H	BB	SO	ShO	W	L	SV	AB	H	HR	BA	PO	A	E	DP	TC/G	FA
1961	WAS	A	8	18	.308	3.86	33	29	7	212	221	48	76	2	0	0	0	68	14	0	.206	15	24	1	0	1.2	.975
1962			0	4	.000	9.38	10	4	0	24	33	11	6	0	0	0	0	7	1	0	.143	1	5	0	1	0.6	1.000
2 yrs.			8	22	.267	4.42	43	33	7	236	254	59	82	2	0	0	0	75	15	0	.200	16	29	1	1	1.1	.978

Jim McCloskey

McCLOSKEY, JAMES ELLWOOD
B. May 26, 1910, Danville, Pa.   D. Aug. 18, 1971, Jersey City, N. J.

BL TL 5'9½"   180 lbs.

Year	Team		W	L	PCT	ERA	G	GS	CG	IP	H	BB	SO	ShO	W	L	SV	AB	H	HR	BA	PO	A	E	DP	TC/G	FA
1936	BOS	N	0	0	—	11.25	4	1	0	8	14	3	2	0	0	0	1	1	0	0	.000	0	3	0	0	0.8	1.000

John McCloskey

McCLOSKEY, JAMES JOHN
B. Aug. 20, 1882, Wyoming, Pa.   D. Mar. 1, 1919, Lewisburg, Pa.

Year	Team		W	L	PCT	ERA	G	GS	CG	IP	H	BB	SO	ShO	W	L	SV	AB	H	HR	BA	PO	A	E	DP	TC/G	FA
1906	PHI	N	3	2	.600	2.85	9	4	3	41	46	9	6	0	1	0	0	15	3	0	.200	0	10	0	0	1.1	1.000
1907			0	0	—	7.00	3	0	0	9	15	6	3	0	0	0	0	4	0	0	.000	0	3	1	0	1.3	.750
2 yrs.			3	2	.600	3.60	12	4	3	50	61	15	9	0	1	0	0	19	3	0	.158	0	13	1	0	1.2	.929

Bob McClure

McCLURE, ROBERT CRAIG
B. Apr. 29, 1952, Oakland, Calif.

BB TL 5'11"   170 lbs.

Year	Team		W	L	PCT	ERA	G	GS	CG	IP	H	BB	SO	ShO	W	L	SV	AB	H	HR	BA	PO	A	E	DP	TC/G	FA
1975	KC	A	1	0	1.000	0.00	12	0	0	15.1	4	14	15	0	1	0	1	0	0	0	—	0	0	0	0	0.0	—
1976			0	0	—	9.00	8	0	0	4	8	3	3	0	0	1	0	0	0	0	—	0	0	0	0	0.0	—
1977	MIL	A	2	1	.667	2.54	68	0	0	71	64	34	57	0	2	1	6	0	0	0	—	2	19	2	2	0.3	.913
1978			2	6	.250	3.74	44	0	0	65	53	30	47	0	2	6	9	0	0	0	—	1	8	1	0	0.2	.900
1979			5	2	.714	3.88	36	0	0	51	53	24	37	0	5	2	5	0	0	0	—	1	7	3	1	0.3	.727
1980			5	8	.385	3.07	52	5	2	91	83	37	47	0	1	7	10	0	0	0	—	3	9	0	0	0.2	1.000
1981			0	0	—	3.38	4	0	0	8	7	4	6	0	0	0	0	0	0	0	—	1	0	0	0	0.3	1.000
1982			12	7	.632	4.22	34	26	5	172.2	160	74	99	0	2	0	0	0	0	0	—	4	23	3	3	0.9	.900
1983			9	9	.500	4.50	24	23	4	142	152	68	68	0	0	0	0	0	0	0	—	4	19	1	1	1.0	.958
1984			4	8	.333	4.38	39	18	1	139.2	154	52	68	0	1	0	0	0	0	0	—	4	21	2	2	0.7	.926
1985			4	1	.800	4.31	38	1	0	85.2	91	30	57	0	4	3	3	0	0	0	—	3	11	0	2	0.4	1.000

Year	Team	W	L	PCT	ERA	G	GS	CG	IP	H	BB	SO	ShO	W	L	SV	AB	H	HR	BA	PO	A	E	DP	TC/G	FA

Bob McClure *continued*

Year	Team	W	L	PCT	ERA	G	GS	CG	IP	H	BB	SO	ShO	W	L	SV	AB	H	HR	BA	PO	A	E	DP	TC/G	FA
1986	2 teams	MIL A	(13G 2–1)		MON N	(52G 2–5)																				
"	total	4	6	.400	3.19	65	0	0	79	71	33	53	0	4	6	6	4	1	0	.250	2	12	1	1	0.2	.933
1987	MON N	6	1	.857	3.44	52	0	0	52.1	47	20	33	0	6	1	5	2	0	0	.000	3	8	0	0	0.2	1.000
1988	2 teams	MON N	(19G 1–3)		NY N	(14G 1–0)																				
"	total	2	3	.400	5.40	33	0	0	30	35	8	19	0	2	3	3	0	0	0	.000	0	5	0	0	0.2	1.000
1989	CAL A	6	1	.857	1.55	48	0	0	52.1	39	15	36	0	6	1	3	0	0	0	–	2	4	0	0	0.1	1.000
15 yrs.		62	53	.539	3.76	557	73	12	1059	1016	451	645	1	35	30	52	8	1	0	.125	30	146	13	12	0.3	.931

DIVISIONAL PLAYOFF SERIES

| 1981 | MIL A | 0 | 0 | – | 0.00 | 3 | 0 | 0 | 3.1 | 4 | 0 | 2 | 0 | 0 | 0 | 0 | 0 | 0 | 0 | – | 0 | 0 | 0 | 0 | 0.0 | – |

LEAGUE CHAMPIONSHIP SERIES

| 1982 | MIL A | 1 | 0 | 1.000 | 0.00 | 1 | 0 | 0 | 1.2 | 2 | 0 | 0 | 0 | 1 | 0 | 0 | 0 | 0 | 0 | – | 0 | 0 | 0 | 0 | 0.0 | – |

WORLD SERIES

| 1982 | MIL A | 0 | 2 | .000 | 4.15 | 5 | 0 | 0 | 4.1 | 5 | 3 | 5 | 0 | 0 | 2 | 2 | 0 | 0 | 0 | – | 0 | 0 | 0 | 0 | 0.0 | – |

2nd

Harry McCluskey

McCLUSKEY, HARRY ROBERT (Lefty)
B. May 29, 1892, Clay Center, Ohio   D. June 7, 1962, Toledo, Ohio

BL TL 5'11½" 173 lbs.

| 1915 | CIN N | 0 | 0 | – | 5.40 | 3 | 0 | 0 | 5 | 4 | 0 | 2 | 0 | 0 | 0 | 0 | 2 | 0 | 0 | .000 | 0 | 0 | 0 | 0 | 0.0 | – |

Alex McColl

McCOLL, ALEXANDER BOYD (Red)
B. Mar. 29, 1894, Eagleville, Ohio

BB TR 6'1" 178 lbs.

1933	WAS A	1	0	1.000	2.65	4	1	1	17	13	7	5	0	0	0	0	6	2	0	.333	0	4	1	0	1.3	.800
1934		3	4	.429	3.86	42	2	1	112	129	36	29	0	2	3	1	31	3	0	.097	6	32	2	3	1.0	.950
2 yrs.		4	4	.500	3.70	46	3	2	129	142	43	34	0				37	5	0	.135	6	36	3	3	1.0	.933

WORLD SERIES

| 1933 | WAS A | 0 | 0 | – | 0.00 | 1 | 0 | 0 | 2 | 0 | 0 | 0 | 0 | 0 | 0 | 0 | 0 | 0 | 0 | – | 0 | 1 | 0 | 0 | 1.0 | 1.000 |

Ralph McConnaughey

McCONNAUGHEY, RALPH JAMES
B. Aug. 5, 1889, Pa.   D. June 4, 1966, Detroit, Mich.

BR TR 5'8½" 166 lbs.

| 1914 | IND F | 0 | 2 | .000 | 4.85 | 7 | 2 | 1 | 26 | 23 | 16 | 7 | 0 | 0 | 0 | 0 | 8 | 1 | 0 | .125 | 0 | 7 | 0 | 1 | 1.0 | 1.000 |

George McConnell

McCONNELL, GEORGE NEELY
B. Sept. 16, 1877, Shelbyville, Tenn.   D. May 10, 1964, Chattanooga, Tenn.

BR TR 6'3" 190 lbs.

1909	NY A	0	1	.000	2.25	2	1	0	4	3	3	4	0	0	1	0	43	9	0	.209	1	3	0	0	2.0	1.000
1912		8	12	.400	2.75	23	20	19	176.2	172	52	91	0	0	0	0	91	27	0	.297	9	75	8	3	4.0	.913
1913		4	15	.211	3.20	35	20	8	180	162	60	72	0	0	0	3	67	12	0	.179	9	74	3	2	2.5	.965
1914	CHI N	0	1	.000	1.29	1	1	0	7	3	3	3	0	0	0	0	2	0	0	.000	0	3	0	0	3.0	1.000
1915	CHI F	25	10	.714	2.20	44	35	23	303	262	89	151	4	3	1	1	125	31	1	.248	8	105	3	4	2.6	.974
1916	CHI N	4	12	.250	2.57	28	20	8	171.1	137	35	82	1	0	2	0	57	9	0	.158	9	50	3	3	2.2	.952
6 yrs.		41	51	.446	2.60	133	97	58	842	739	242	403	5	3	5	4	*				36	310	17	12	2.7	.953

Billy McCool

McCOOL, WILLIAM JOHN
B. July 14, 1944, Batesville, Ind.

BR TL 6'2" 195 lbs.

1964	CIN N	6	5	.545	2.42	40	3	0	89.1	66	29	87	0	5	2	7	17	0	0	.000	1	8	0	0	0.2	1.000
1965		9	10	.474	4.27	62	2	0	105.1	93	47	120	0	9	8	21	27	1	0	.037	2	15	0	0	0.3	1.000
1966		8	8	.500	2.48	57	0	0	105.1	76	41	104	0	8	8	18	18	3	0	.167	3	25	0	3	0.5	.882
1967		3	7	.300	3.42	31	11	0	97.1	92	56	83	0	0	3	2	26	2	0	.077	1	14	2	0	0.5	.818
1968		3	4	.429	4.97	30	4	0	50.2	59	41	30	0	3	4	7	8	1	0	.125	3	6	2	0	0.4	.818
1969	SD N	3	5	.375	4.27	54	0	0	59	59	42	35	0	3	5	7	1	0	0	.000	0	10	1	0	0.2	.909
1970	STL N	0	3	.000	6.14	18	0	0	22	20	16	12	0	0	3	1	4	0	0	.000	0	5	0	0	0.3	1.000
7 yrs.		32	42	.432	3.59	292	20	0	529	465	272	471	0	27	32	58	101	7	0	.069	10	83	5	3	0.3	.949

Harry McCormick

McCORMICK, PATRICK HENRY
B. Oct. 25, 1855, Syracuse, N. Y.   D. Aug. 8, 1889, Syracuse, N. Y.

BR TR 5'9" 155 lbs.

1879	SYR N	18	33	.353	2.99	54	54	49	457.1	517	31	96	5	0	0	0	230	51	1	.222	13	68	8	0	1.6	.910
1881	WOR N	1	8	.111	3.56	9	9	9	78.1	89	15	7	1	0	0	0	45	6	0	.133	6	10	1	0	1.9	.941
1882	CIN AA	14	11	.560	1.52	25	25	24	219.2	177	42	33	1	0	0	0	93	12	0	.129	12	76	5	0	3.7	.946
1883		8	6	.571	2.87	15	15	14	128.2	139	27	21	1	0	0	0	55	17	0	.309	6	32	4	0	2.8	.905
4 yrs.		41	58	.414	2.66	103	103	96	884	922	115	157	10	0	0	0	423	86	1	.203	37	186	18	0	2.3	.925

Jerry McCormick

McCORMICK, JOHN
B. Philadelphia, Pa.   D. Sept. 19, 1905, Philadelphia, Pa.

| 1884 | PHI U | 0 | 0 | – | 9.00 | 1 | 0 | 0 | 2 | 5 | 0 | 3 | 0 | 0 | 0 | 0 | * | | | | 0 | 0 | 0 | 0 | 0.0 | – |

Jim McCormick

McCORMICK, JAMES
B. 1856, Glasgow, Scotland   D. Mar. 10, 1918, Paterson, N. J.
Manager 1879-82.

BR TR 5'10½" 215 lbs.

1878	IND N	5	8	.385	1.69	14	14	12	117	128	15	36	1	0	0	0	56	8	0	.143	6	32	2	2	2.9	.950
1879	CLE N	20	40	.333	2.42	62	60	59	546.1	582	74	197	3	1	0	0	282	62	0	.220	39	119	9	4	2.7	.886
1880		45	28	.616	1.85	74	74	72	657.2	585	75	260	7	0	0	0	289	71	0	.246	34	135	22	3	2.6	.898
1881		26	30	.464	2.45	59	58	57	526	484	84	178	2	0	0	0	309	79	0	.256	34	81	13	4	2.2	.917
1882		36	29	.554	2.37	68	67	65	595.2	550	103	200	4	1	0	0	262	57	2	.218	43	100	13	1	2.3	.917
1883		28	12	.700	1.84	43	41	36	342	316	65	145	1	1	0	1	157	37	0	.236	28	101	16	4	3.4	.890
1884	2 teams	CLE N	(42G 19–22)		CIN U	(26G 21–3)																				
"	total	40	25	.615	2.37	68	68	63	569	508	89	343	10	0	0	0	300	77	0	.257	31	117	7	5	2.3	.955

Year	Team		W	L	PCT	ERA	G	GS	CG	IP	H	BB	SO	ShO	W	L	SV	AB	H	HR	BA	PO	A	E	DP	TC/G	FA
															Relief Pitching			Batting									

Jim McCormick *continued*

Year	Team		W	L	PCT	ERA	G	GS	CG	IP	H	BB	SO	ShO	W	L	SV	AB	H	HR	BA	PO	A	E	DP	TC/G	FA
1885	2 teams	PRO N (4G 1–3)													CHI N		(24G 20–4)										
"	total		21	7	.750	2.43	28	28	28	252	221	60	96	3	0	0	0	117	26	0	.222	22	75	5	3	3.6	.951
1886	CHI	N	31	11	.738	2.82	42	42	38	347.2	341	100	172	2	0	0	0	174	41	2	.236	21	74	6	3	2.4	.941
1887	PIT	N	13	23	.361	4.30	36	36	36	322.1	377	84	77	0	0	0	0	136	33	0	.243	13	88	8	1	3.0	.927
10 yrs.			265	213	.554	2.43	494	488	466	4275.2	4092	749	1704	33	3	0	1	*				273	922	101	30	2.6	.922
													10th														

Mike McCormick

McCORMICK, MICHAEL FRANCIS
B. Sept. 29, 1938, Pasadena, Calif.　　　BL TL 6'2"　195 lbs.

Year	Team		W	L	PCT	ERA	G	GS	CG	IP	H	BB	SO	ShO	W	L	SV	AB	H	HR	BA	PO	A	E	DP	TC/G	FA
1956	NY	N	0	1	.000	9.45	3	2	0	6.2	7	10	4	0	0	0	0	1	0	0	.000	0	1	0	0	0.3	1.000
1957			3	1	.750	4.10	24	5	1	74.2	79	32	50	0	2	0	0	22	6	0	.273	3	9	1	2	0.5	.923
1958	SF	N	11	8	.579	4.59	42	28	8	178.1	192	60	82	2	2	0	1	54	12	0	.222	11	37	2	5	1.2	.960
1959			12	16	.429	3.99	47	31	7	225.2	213	86	151	3	2	0	4	66	7	0	.106	12	43	1	1	1.2	.947
1960			15	12	.556	2.70	40	34	15	253	228	65	154	4	0	2	3	88	16	0	.182	12	55	2	7	1.7	.971
1961			13	16	.448	3.20	40	35	13	250	235	75	163	3	0	2	0	80	15	0	.188	12	37	0	1	1.2	1.000
1962			5	5	.500	5.38	28	15	1	98.2	112	45	42	0	0	0	0	28	3	1	.107	1	18	1	1	0.7	.950
1963	BAL	A	6	8	.429	4.30	25	21	2	136	132	66	75	0	0	0	0	46	8	1	.174	9	21	2	0	1.3	.938
1964			0	2	.000	5.19	4	2	0	17.1	21	8	13	0	0	0	0	6	1	0	.167	1	2	0	0	0.8	1.000
1965	WAS	A	8	8	.500	3.36	44	21	3	158	158	38	88	1	1	2	1	41	3	0	.073	8	22	0	1	0.7	1.000
1966			11	14	.440	3.46	41	32	8	216	193	51	101	3	1	0	0	66	14	2	.212	5	34	0	1	1.0	1.000
1967	SF	N	22	10	.688	2.85	40	35	14	262.1	220	81	150	5	2	1	0	84	10	1	.119	10	36	0	0	1.2	1.000
1968			12	14	.462	3.58	38	28	9	198.1	196	49	121	2	3	1	1	58	6	1	.103	9	23	1	0	0.9	.970
1969			11	9	.550	3.34	32	28	9	197	175	77	76	0	0	0	0	66	9	1	.136	3	33	0	3	1.1	1.000
1970	2 teams	SF N (23G 3–4)													NY A		(9G 2–0)										
"	total		5	4	.556	6.18	32	15	1	99	106	49	49	0	1	0	2	30	5	0	.167	5	16	0	2	0.7	1.000
1971	KC	A	0	0	–	9.00	4	1	0	10	14	5	2	0	0	0	0	2	0	0	.000	1	8	0	0	2.3	1.000
16 yrs.			134	128	.511	3.73	484	333	91	2381	2281	795	1321	23	14	10	12	738	115	7	.156	102	394	12	24	1.0	.976

Bill McCorry

McCORRY, WILLIAM CHARLES
B. July 9, 1887, Saranac Lake, N. Y.　D. Mar. 22, 1973, Augusta, Ga.　　BL TR 5'9"　157 lbs.

Year	Team		W	L	PCT	ERA	G	GS	CG	IP	H	BB	SO	ShO	W	L	SV	AB	H	HR	BA	PO	A	E	DP	TC/G	FA
1909	STL	A	0	2	.000	9.00	2	2	2	15	29	6	10	0	0	0	0	5	0	0	.000	0	1	0	0	0.5	1.000

Les McCrabb

McCRABB, LESTER WILLIAM (Buster)
B. Nov. 4, 1914, Wakefield, Pa.　　　BR TR 5'11"　175 lbs.

Year	Team		W	L	PCT	ERA	G	GS	CG	IP	H	BB	SO	ShO	W	L	SV	AB	H	HR	BA	PO	A	E	DP	TC/G	FA
1939	PHI	A	1	2	.333	4.04	5	4	2	35.2	42	10	11	0	0	0	0	13	0	0	.000	1	6	0	0	1.4	1.000
1940			0	0	–	6.94	4	0	0	11.2	19	2	4	0	0	0	0	4	1	0	.250	0	4	0	0	1.0	1.000
1941			9	13	.409	5.49	26	23	11	157.1	188	49	40	1	1	0	2	56	8	0	.143	9	24	4	1	1.4	.892
1942			0	0	–	31.50	1	0	0	4	14	2	0	0	0	0	0	1	0	0	.000	0	2	0	0	2.0	1.000
1950			0	0	–	27.00	2	0	0	1.1	7	0	2	0	0	0	0	0	0	0	–	0	0	0	0	0.0	–
5 yrs.			10	15	.400	5.96	38	27	13	210	270	63	57	1	1	0	2	74	9	0	.122	10	36	4	1	1.3	.920

Ed McCreery

McCREERY, ESLEY PORTERFIELD
B. Dec. 24, 1889, Cripple Creek, Colo.　D. Oct. 19, 1960, Sacramento, Calif.　　BR TR 6'1"　195 lbs.

Year	Team		W	L	PCT	ERA	G	GS	CG	IP	H	BB	SO	ShO	W	L	SV	AB	H	HR	BA	PO	A	E	DP	TC/G	FA
1914	DET	A	1	0	1.000	11.25	3	1	0	4	6	3	4	0	0	0	0	1	0	0	.000	0	1	0	0	0.3	1.000

Tom McCreery

McCREERY, THOMAS LIVINGSTON
B. Oct. 19, 1874, Beaver, Pa.　D. July 3, 1941, Beaver, Pa.　　BB TR 5'11"　180 lbs.

Year	Team		W	L	PCT	ERA	G	GS	CG	IP	H	BB	SO	ShO	W	L	SV	AB	H	HR	BA	PO	A	E	DP	TC/G	FA
1895	LOU	N	3	1	.750	5.36	8	4	3	48.2	51	38	14	1	0	0	0	108	35	0	.324	4	14	0	3	2.3	1.000
1896			0	1	.000	36.00	1	1	0	1	4	5	0	0	0	0	0	441	155	7	.351	0	1	0	0	1.0	1.000
1900	PIT	N	0	0	–	12.00	1	0	0	3	3	1	0	0	0	0	0	132	29	1	.220	0	1	0	0	1.0	1.000
3 yrs.			3	2	.600	6.32	10	5	3	52.2	58	44	14	1	0	0	1	*				4	16	0	3	2.0	1.000

Lance McCullers

McCULLERS, LANCE GRAYE
B. Mar. 8, 1964, Tampa, Fla.　　　BB TR 6'1"　185 lbs.

Year	Team		W	L	PCT	ERA	G	GS	CG	IP	H	BB	SO	ShO	W	L	SV	AB	H	HR	BA	PO	A	E	DP	TC/G	FA
1985	SD	N	0	0	.000	2.31	21	0	0	35	23	16	27	0	0	0	5	4	0	0	.000	2	6	2	0	0.5	.800
1986			10	10	.500	2.78	70	7	0	136	103	58	92	0	9	6	5	22	2	0	.091	6	16	2	1	0.3	.917
1987			8	10	.444	3.72	78	0	0	123.1	115	59	126	0	8	10	16	14	1	0	.071	9	17	2	1	0.4	.929
1988			3	6	.333	2.49	60	0	0	97.2	70	55	81	0	3	6	10	8	2	0	.250	6	14	2	1	0.4	.909
1989	NY	A	4	3	.571	4.57	52	1	0	84.2	83	37	82	0	4	3	3	–				5	10	2	0	0.3	.882
5 yrs.			25	31	.446	3.25	281	8	0	476.2	394	225	408	0	24	26	39	48	5	0	.104	28	63	10	3	0.4	.901

Charlie McCullough

McCULLOUGH, CHARLES F.
B. 1867, Dublin, Ireland　Deceased.

Year	Team		W	L	PCT	ERA	G	GS	CG	IP	H	BB	SO	ShO	W	L	SV	AB	H	HR	BA	PO	A	E	DP	TC/G	FA
1890	2 teams	BKN AA (26G 4–21)													SYR AA		(3G 1–2)										
"	total		5	23	.179	4.88	29	28	27	241.2	276	116	69	0	0	0	0	95	3	0	.032	4	42	6	0	1.8	.885

Paul McCullough

McCULLOUGH, PAUL WILLARD
B. July 28, 1898, New Castle, Pa.　D. Nov. 7, 1970, New Castle, Pa.　　BR TR 5'9½"　190 lbs.

Year	Team		W	L	PCT	ERA	G	GS	CG	IP	H	BB	SO	ShO	W	L	SV	AB	H	HR	BA	PO	A	E	DP	TC/G	FA
1929	WAS	A	0	0	–	8.59	3	0	0	7.1	7	2	3	0	0	0	0	1	0	0	.000	0	0	0	0	0.0	–

Phil McCullough

McCULLOUGH, PINSON LAMAR
B. July 22, 1917, Stockbridge, Ga.　　　BR TR 6'4"　204 lbs.

Year	Team		W	L	PCT	ERA	G	GS	CG	IP	H	BB	SO	ShO	W	L	SV	AB	H	HR	BA	PO	A	E	DP	TC/G	FA
1942	WAS	A	0	0	–	6.00	1	0	0	3	5	2	2	0	0	0	0	1	0	0	.000	0	0	0	0	1.0	1.000

Lindy McDaniel

McDANIEL, LYNDALL DALE
Brother of Von McDaniel.
B. Dec. 13, 1935, Hollis, Okla.　　　BR TR 6'3"　195 lbs.

Year	Team		W	L	PCT	ERA	G	GS	CG	IP	H	BB	SO	ShO	W	L	SV	AB	H	HR	BA	PO	A	E	DP	TC/G	FA
1955	STL	N	0	0	–	4.74	4	2	0	19	22	7	7	0	0	0	0	5	1	0	.200	3	3	0	0	1.5	1.000
1956			7	6	.538	3.40	39	7	1	116.1	121	42	59	0	5	2	0	32	7	0	.219	9	24	3	0	0.9	.917

Year	Team	W	L	PCT	ERA	G	GS	CG	IP	H	BB	SO	ShO	Relief Pitching W	L	SV	Batting AB	H	HR	BA	PO	A	E	DP	TC/G	FA

Lindy McDaniel *continued*

Year	Team	W	L	PCT	ERA	G	GS	CG	IP	H	BB	SO	ShO	W	L	SV	AB	H	HR	BA	PO	A	E	DP	TC/G	FA
1957		15	9	.625	3.49	30	26	10	191	196	53	75	1	3	0	0	74	19	1	.257	12	33	1	3	1.5	.978
1958		5	7	.417	5.80	26	17	2	108.2	139	31	47	1	0	2	0	30	2	0	.067	4	26	1	3	1.2	.968
1959		14	12	.538	3.82	62	7	1	132	144	41	86	0	13	8	15	29	1	0	.034	7	31	3	3	0.7	.927
1960		12	4	.750	2.09	65	2	1	116.1	85	24	105	0	12	2	26	26	6	0	.231	5	21	0	2	0.4	1.000
1961		10	6	.625	4.87	55	0	0	94.1	117	31	65	0	10	6	9	17	4	0	.235	5	22	0	1	0.5	1.000
1962		3	10	.231	4.12	55	2	0	107	96	29	79	0	2	9	14	21	2	0	.095	10	25	1	2	0.7	.972
1963	CHI N	13	7	.650	2.86	57	0	0	88	82	27	75	0	13	7	22	22	2	1	.091	3	16	1	0	0.3	.950
1964		1	7	.125	3.88	63	0	0	95	104	23	71	0	1	7	15	16	2	0	.125	3	18	1	1	0.3	.955
1965		5	6	.455	2.59	71	0	0	128.2	115	47	92	0	5	6	2	8	0	0	.000	5	30	0	1	0.5	1.000
1966	SF N	10	5	.667	2.66	64	0	0	121.2	103	35	93	0	10	5	6	22	2	0	.091	8	24	0	0	0.5	1.000
1967		2	6	.250	3.72	41	3	0	72.2	69	24	48	0	2	4	3	11	1	0	.091	5	19	0	1	0.6	1.000
1968	2 teams	SF N	(12G 0–0)			NY A	(24G 4–1)																			
"	total	4	1	.800	3.31	36	0	0	70.2	60	17	52	0	4	1	10	15	0	0	.000	10	20	1	0	0.9	.968
1969	NY A	5	6	.455	3.55	51	0	0	83.2	84	23	60	0	5	6	5	8	0	0	.000	3	21	2	0	0.5	.923
1970		9	5	.643	2.01	62	0	0	112	88	23	81	0	9	5	29	24	4	0	.167	7	19	3	2	0.5	.897
1971		5	10	.333	5.01	44	0	0	70	82	24	39	0	5	10	4	9	1	0	.111	4	14	0	0	0.4	1.000
1972		3	1	.750	2.25	37	0	0	68	54	25	47	0	3	1	1	7	2	1	.286	5	14	1	2	0.5	.950
1973		12	6	.667	2.86	47	3	1	160.1	148	49	93	0	12	4	10	2	0	0	.000	9	35	1	7	1.0	.978
1974	KC A	1	4	.200	3.45	38	5	2	107	109	24	47	0	0	2	1	0	0	0	–	8	21	1	0	0.8	.967
1975		5	1	.833	4.15	40	0	0	78	81	24	40	0	5	1	1	0	0	0	–	4	11	2	0	0.4	.882
21 yrs.		141	119	.542	3.45	987	74	18	2140.1	2099	623	1361	2	119	88	172	378	56	3	.148	127	447	22	28	0.6	.963
					3rd									2nd												

Von McDaniel

McDANIEL, MAX VON
Brother of Lindy McDaniel.
B. Apr. 18, 1939, Hollis, Okla.

BR TR 6'2½" 180 lbs.

Year	Team	W	L	PCT	ERA	G	GS	CG	IP	H	BB	SO	ShO	W	L	SV	AB	H	HR	BA	PO	A	E	DP	TC/G	FA
1957	STL N	7	5	.583	3.22	17	13	4	86.2	71	31	45	2	1	0	0	26	0	0	.000	3	9	0	3	0.7	1.000
1958		0	0	–	13.50	2	1	0	2	5	5	0	0	0	0	0	0	0	0	–	0	0	0	0	0.0	–
2 yrs.		7	5	.583	3.45	19	14	4	88.2	76	36	45	2	1	0	0	26	0	0	.000	3	9	0	3	0.6	1.000

Mickey McDermott

McDERMOTT, MAURICE JOSEPH
B. Aug. 29, 1928, Poughkeepsie, N. Y.

BL TL 6'2" 170 lbs.

Year	Team	W	L	PCT	ERA	G	GS	CG	IP	H	BB	SO	ShO	W	L	SV	AB	H	HR	BA	PO	A	E	DP	TC/G	FA
1948	BOS A	0	0	–	6.17	7	0	0	23.1	16	35	17	0	0	0	0	8	3	0	.375	1	8	0	0	1.3	1.000
1949		5	4	.556	4.05	12	12	6	80	63	52	50	2	0	0	0	33	7	0	.212	2	14	1	0	1.4	.941
1950		7	3	.700	5.19	38	15	4	130	119	124	96	0	3	0	5	44	16	0	.364	4	25	2	1	0.8	.938
1951		8	8	.500	3.35	34	19	5	172	141	92	127	1	0	0	3	66	18	1	.273	4	34	2	5	1.2	.950
1952		10	9	.526	3.72	30	21	7	162	139	92	117	2	2	3	0	62	14	1	.226	10	24	2	1	1.2	.944
1953		18	10	.643	3.01	32	30	8	206.1	169	109	92	4	0	0	0	93	28	1	.301	5	40	2	3	1.5	.957
1954	WAS A	7	15	.318	3.44	30	26	11	196.1	172	110	95	1	0	0	0	95	19	0	.200	3	39	2	1	1.5	.955
1955		10	10	.500	3.75	31	20	8	156	140	102	78	1	2	1	1	95	25	1	.263	3	30	2	1	1.1	.943
1956	NY A	2	6	.250	4.24	23	9	1	87	85	47	38	0	0	0	0	52	11	1	.212	7	17	1	0	0.7	1.000
1957	KC A	1	4	.200	5.48	29	4	0	69	68	50	29	0	0	0	4	49	12	4	.245	7	17	1	0	0.9	.960
1958	DET A	0	0	–	9.00	2	0	0	2	6	2	0	0	0	0	0	3	1	0	.333	0	0	0	0	0.0	–
1961	2 teams	STL N	(19G 1–0)			KC A	(4G 0–0)																			
"	total	1	0	1.000	5.51	23	0	0	32.2	43	25	18	0	1	0	4	19	2	0	.105	2	3	1	0	0.3	.833
12 yrs.		69	69	.500	3.91	291	156	54	1316.2	1161	840	757	11	9	7	14	*				44	247	15	15	1.1	.951

WORLD SERIES

Year	Team	W	L	PCT	ERA	G	GS	CG	IP	H	BB	SO	ShO	W	L	SV	AB	H	HR	BA	PO	A	E	DP	TC/G	FA
1956	NY A	0	0	–	3.00	1	0	0	3	2	3	3	0	0	0	0	1	1	0	1.000	0	0	0	0	0.0	–

Mike McDermott

McDERMOTT, MICHAEL JOSEPH
B. Sept. 7, 1862, St. Louis, Mo. D. June 30, 1943, St. Louis, Mo.

TR 5'8" 145 lbs.

Year	Team	W	L	PCT	ERA	G	GS	CG	IP	H	BB	SO	ShO	W	L	SV	AB	H	HR	BA	PO	A	E	DP	TC/G	FA
1889	LOU AA	1	8	.111	4.16	9	9	9	84.1	108	34	22	0	0	0	0	33	6	0	.182	1	17	1	1	2.1	.947
1895	LOU N	4	19	.174	5.99	33	26	18	207.1	258	103	42	0	0	0	0	82	13	0	.159	6	57	14	2	2.3	.818
1896		2	7	.222	7.34	12	10	4	65	87	44	12	1	0	0	0	27	8	0	.296	5	20	4	0	2.4	.862
1897	2 teams	CLE N	(9G 4–5)			STL N	(4G 1–2)																			
"	total	5	7	.417	5.72	13	11	5	83.1	98	44	15	0	2	0	0	34	10	0	.294	4	28	1	1	2.5	.970
4 yrs.		12	41	.226	5.79	67	56	36	440	551	225	91	1	2	0	0	176	37	0	.210	16	122	20	4	2.4	.873

Danny McDevitt

McDEVITT, DANIEL EUGENE
B. Nov. 18, 1932, New York, N. Y.

BL TL 5'10" 175 lbs.

Year	Team	W	L	PCT	ERA	G	GS	CG	IP	H	BB	SO	ShO	W	L	SV	AB	H	HR	BA	PO	A	E	DP	TC/G	FA
1957	BKN N	7	4	.636	3.25	22	17	5	119	105	72	90	0	0	0	0	39	6	0	.154	11	26	4	1	1.9	.902
1958	LA N	2	6	.250	7.45	13	10	2	48.1	71	31	26	0	0	0	0	15	2	0	.133	0	8	3	0	0.8	.727
1959		10	8	.556	3.97	39	22	6	145	149	51	106	2	1	0	4	46	5	0	.109	11	22	4	2	0.9	.892
1960		0	4	.000	4.25	24	7	0	53	51	42	30	0	0	2	0	10	2	0	.200	2	9	0	0	0.5	1.000
1961	2 teams	NY A	(8G 1–2)			MIN A	(16G 1–0)																			
"	total	2	2	.500	4.08	24	0	0	39.2	38	27	23	0	2	0	1	4	0	0	.000	1	10	1	0	0.5	.917
1962	KC A	0	3	.000	5.82	33	1	0	51	47	41	28	0	0	2	2	9	2	0	.222	4	12	1	1	0.5	.941
6 yrs.		21	27	.438	4.40	155	60	13	456	461	264	303	4	3	4	7	123	17	0	.138	29	87	13	4	0.8	.899

Ben McDonald

McDONALD, LARRY BENARD
B. Nov. 14, 1967, Baton Rouge, La.

BR TR 6'7" 212 lbs.

Year	Team	W	L	PCT	ERA	G	GS	CG	IP	H	BB	SO	ShO	W	L	SV	AB	H	HR	BA	PO	A	E	DP	TC/G	FA
1989	BAL A	1	0	1.000	8.59	6	0	0	7.1	8	4	3	0	1	0	0	0	0	0	–	0	2	0	0	0.3	1.000

Hank McDonald

McDONALD, HENRY MONROE
B. Jan. 16, 1911, Santa Monica, Calif. D. Oct. 17, 1982, Hemet, Calif.

BR TR 6'3½" 200 lbs.

Year	Team	W	L	PCT	ERA	G	GS	CG	IP	H	BB	SO	ShO	W	L	SV	AB	H	HR	BA	PO	A	E	DP	TC/G	FA
1931	PHI A	2	4	.333	3.71	19	10	1	70.1	62	41	23	1	1	1	0	21	2	0	.095	5	9	1	0	0.8	.933
1933	2 teams	PHI A	(4G 1–1)			STL A	(25G 0–4)																			
"	total	1	5	.167	8.02	29	6	0	70.2	97	38	23	0	1	1	2	18	2	0	.111	6	14	1	1	0.7	.952
2 yrs.		3	9	.250	5.87	48	16	1	141	159	79	46	1	2	2	2	39	4	0	.103	11	23	2	1	0.8	.944

Year	Team	W	L	PCT	ERA	G	GS	CG	IP	H	BB	SO	ShO	W	L	SV	AB	H	HR	BA	PO	A	E	DP	TC/G	FA

Jim McDonald

McDONALD, JIMMIE LeROY (Hot Rod)
B. May 17, 1927, Grant's Pass, Ore.

BR TR 5'10½" 185 lbs.
BB 1950-51

Year	Team	W	L	PCT	ERA	G	GS	CG	IP	H	BB	SO	ShO	W	L	SV	AB	H	HR	BA	PO	A	E	DP	TC/G	FA
1950	BOS A	1	0	1.000	3.79	9	0	0	19	23	10	5	0	1	0	0	3	1	0	.333	3	7	0	0	1.1	1.000
1951	STL A	4	7	.364	4.07	16	11	5	84	84	46	28	0	0	0	1	29	6	0	.207	9	16	2	1	1.7	.926
1952	NY A	3	4	.429	3.50	26	5	1	69.1	71	40	20	0	2	3	0	19	6	0	.316	7	24	0	1	1.2	1.000
1953		9	7	.563	3.82	27	18	6	129.2	128	39	43	2	1	1	0	41	4	0	.098	7	30	1	6	1.4	.974
1954		4	1	.800	3.17	16	10	3	71	54	45	20	1	0	0	0	19	4	0	.211	7	14	0	2	1.3	1.000
1955	BAL A	3	5	.375	7.14	21	8	0	51.2	76	30	20	0	1	0	0	11	2	0	.182	2	15	1	2	0.9	.944
1956	CHI A	0	2	.000	8.68	8	3	0	18.2	29	7	10	0	0	0	0	5	0	0	.000	1	3	0	0	0.6	.800
1957		0	1	.000	2.01	10	0	0	22.1	18	10	12	0	0	0	0	1	0	0	.000	3	3	1	0	0.7	.857
1958		0	0	–	19.29	3	0	0	2.1	6	4	0	0	0	0	0	0	0	0	–	0	1	0	1	0.7	
9 yrs.		24	27	.471	4.27	136	55	15	468	489	231	158	3	5	5	1	128	23	0	.180	39	113	6	13	1.2	.962

WORLD SERIES

Year	Team	W	L	PCT	ERA	G	GS	CG	IP	H	BB	SO	ShO	W	L	SV	AB	H	HR	BA	PO	A	E	DP	TC/G	FA
1953	NY A	1	0	1.000	5.87	1	1	0	7.2	9	0	3	0	0	0	0	2	1	0	.500	3	0	0	0	3.0	1.000

John McDonald

McDONALD, JOHN JOSEPH
Born John Joseph McDonnell.
B. Jan. 27, 1883, Throop, Pa. D. Apr. 9, 1950, Roselle, N. J.

TR 6'1" 170 lbs.

Year	Team	W	L	PCT	ERA	G	GS	CG	IP	H	BB	SO	ShO	W	L	SV	AB	H	HR	BA	PO	A	E	DP	TC/G	FA
1907	WAS A	0	0	–	9.00	1	0	0	6	12	2	3	0	0	0	0	3	1	0	.333	0	2	1	0	3.0	.667

John McDougal

McDOUGAL, JOHN H.
B. Sept. 19, 1871, Aledo, Ill. D. Apr. 28, 1936, Galesburg, Ill.

170 lbs.

Year	Team	W	L	PCT	ERA	G	GS	CG	IP	H	BB	SO	ShO	W	L	SV	AB	H	HR	BA	PO	A	E	DP	TC/G	FA
1895	STL N	4	10	.286	8.32	18	14	10	114.2	187	46	23	0	0	0	1	41	6	0	.146	6	21	4	0	1.7	.871
1896		0	1	.000	8.10	3	1	0	10	13	4	0	0	0	0	0	3	0	0	.000	1	6	1	0	2.7	.875
2 yrs.		4	11	.267	8.30	21	15	10	124.2	200	50	23	0	0	0	1	44	6	0	.136	7	27	5	0	1.9	.872

Sandy McDougal

McDOUGAL, JOHN AUCHANBOLT
B. May 21, 1874, Buffalo, N. Y. D. Oct. 2, 1910, Buffalo, N. Y.

BR TR 5'10" 155 lbs.

Year	Team	W	L	PCT	ERA	G	GS	CG	IP	H	BB	SO	ShO	W	L	SV	AB	H	HR	BA	PO	A	E	DP	TC/G	FA
1895	BKN N	0	0	–	12.00	1	0	0	3	3	5	2	0	0	0	0	1	0	0	.000	0	0	0	0	0.0	–
1905	STL N	1	4	.200	3.43	5	5	5	44.2	50	12	10	0	0	0	0	15	2	0	.133	0	27	0	0	5.4	1.000
2 yrs.		1	4	.200	3.97	6	5	5	47.2	53	17	12	0	0	0	0	16	2	0	.125	0	27	0	0	4.5	1.000

Jack McDowell

McDOWELL, JACK BURNS
B. Jan. 16, 1966, Van Nuys, Calif.

BR TR 6'5" 180 lbs.

Year	Team	W	L	PCT	ERA	G	GS	CG	IP	H	BB	SO	ShO	W	L	SV	AB	H	HR	BA	PO	A	E	DP	TC/G	FA
1987	CHI A	3	0	1.000	1.93	4	4	0	28	16	6	15	0	0	0	0	0	0	0	–	1	6	0	0	1.8	1.000
1988		5	10	.333	3.97	26	26	1	158.2	147	68	84	0	0	0	0	0	0	0	–	12	16	5	1	1.3	.848
2 yrs.		8	10	.444	3.66	30	30	1	186.2	163	74	99	0	0	0	0	0	0	0	–	13	22	5	1	1.3	.875

Roger McDowell

McDOWELL, ROGER ALAN
B. Dec. 21, 1960, Cincinnati, Ohio

BR TR 6'1" 175 lbs.

Year	Team	W	L	PCT	ERA	G	GS	CG	IP	H	BB	SO	ShO	W	L	SV	AB	H	HR	BA	PO	A	E	DP	TC/G	FA
1985	NY N	6	5	.545	2.83	62	2	0	127.1	108	37	70	0	6	4	17	19	3	0	.158	17	27	4	2	0.8	.917
1986		14	9	.609	3.02	75	0	0	128	107	42	65	0	14	9	22	18	5	0	.278	17	30	0	0	0.6	1.000
1987		7	5	.583	4.16	56	0	0	88.2	95	28	32	0	7	5	25	13	3	0	.231	10	17	0	1	0.5	1.000
1988		5	5	.500	2.63	62	0	0	89	80	31	46	0	5	5	16	9	3	0	.333	11	19	1	2	0.5	.968
1989	2 teams					NY N	(25G 1–5)		PHI N	(44G 3–3)																
"	total	4	8	.333	1.96	69	0	0	92	79	38	47	0	4	8	23	3	1	0	.333	17	25	3	0	0.7	.933
5 yrs.		36	32	.529	2.91	324	2	0	525	469	176	260	0	36	31	103	62	15	0	.242	72	118	8	8	0.6	.960

LEAGUE CHAMPIONSHIP SERIES

Year	Team	W	L	PCT	ERA	G	GS	CG	IP	H	BB	SO	ShO	W	L	SV	AB	H	HR	BA	PO	A	E	DP	TC/G	FA
1986	NY N	0	0	–	0.00	2	0	0	7	1	0	3	0	0	0	0	1	0	0	.000	3	1	0	0	2.0	1.000
1988		0	1	.000	4.50	4	0	0	6	6	2	5	0	0	1	0	0	0	0	–	0	3	1	0	1.0	.750
2 yrs.		0	1	.000	2.08	6	0	0	13	7	2	8	0	0	1	0	1	0	0	.000	3	4	1	0	1.3	.875

WORLD SERIES

Year	Team	W	L	PCT	ERA	G	GS	CG	IP	H	BB	SO	ShO	W	L	SV	AB	H	HR	BA	PO	A	E	DP	TC/G	FA
1986	NY N	1	0	1.000	4.91	5	0	0	7.1	10	6	2	0	1	0	0	0	0	0	–	1	4	0	0	1.0	1.000

Sam McDowell

McDOWELL, SAMUEL EDWARD (Sudden Sam)
B. Sept. 21, 1942, Pittsburgh, Pa.

BL TL 6'5" 190 lbs.

Year	Team	W	L	PCT	ERA	G	GS	CG	IP	H	BB	SO	ShO	W	L	SV	AB	H	HR	BA	PO	A	E	DP	TC/G	FA
1961	CLE A	0	0	–	0.00	1	1	0	6.1	3	5	5	0	0	0	0	2	0	0	.000	0	2	0	1	2.0	1.000
1962		3	7	.300	6.06	25	13	0	87.2	81	70	70	0	2	0	1	26	4	0	.154	4	14	2	0	0.8	.900
1963		3	5	.375	4.85	14	13	3	65	63	44	63	1	0	0	0	19	4	0	.211	4	7	0	0	0.8	1.000
1964		11	6	.647	2.70	31	24	6	173.1	148	100	177	2	2	0	1	56	8	0	.143	7	20	2	1	0.9	.931
1965		17	11	.607	2.18	42	35	14	273	178	132	325	3	1	0	4	95	12	0	.126	6	46	4	0	1.3	.929
1966		9	8	.529	2.87	35	28	8	194.1	130	102	225	5	0	0	3	60	12	0	.200	11	30	2	2	1.2	.953
1967		13	15	.464	3.85	37	37	10	236.1	201	123	236	1	0	0	0	82	15	1	.183	9	31	5	2	1.2	.889
1968		15	14	.517	1.81	38	37	11	269	181	110	283	3	0	0	0	85	13	0	.153	10	30	4	7	1.2	.909
1969		18	14	.563	2.94	39	38	18	285	222	102	279	4	0	0	1	92	16	0	.174	5	39	4	5	1.2	.917
1970		20	12	.625	2.92	39	39	19	305	236	131	304	1	0	0	0	105	13	0	.124	3	35	4	1	1.1	.905
1971		13	17	.433	3.39	35	31	8	215	160	153	192	2	0	0	0	73	13	0	.178	3	26	4	2	0.9	.879
1972	SF N	10	8	.556	4.34	28	25	4	164	155	86	122	0	0	0	0	59	7	0	.119	8	21	1	0	1.1	.967
1973	2 teams					SF N	(18G 1–2)		NY A	(16G 5–8)																
"	total	6	10	.375	4.11	34	18	2	135.2	118	93	110	1	2	3	0	12	2	0	.167	7	20	1	0	0.8	.964
1974	NY A	1	6	.143	4.69	13	7	0	48	42	41	33	0	0	1	0	0	0	0	–	1	2	1	0	0.3	.750
1975	PIT N	2	1	.667	2.83	14	1	0	35	30	20	29	0	1	0	0	8	0	0	.000	1	5	0	2	0.4	1.000
15 yrs.		141	134	.513	3.17	425	346	103	2492.2	1948	1312	2453	23	8	3	14	774	119	2	.154	79	328	33	23	1.0	.925

Chuck McElroy

McELROY, CHARLES DWAYNE
B. Oct. 1, 1967, Galveston, Tex.

BL TL 6' 160 lbs.

Year	Team	W	L	PCT	ERA	G	GS	CG	IP	H	BB	SO	ShO	W	L	SV	AB	H	HR	BA	PO	A	E	DP	TC/G	FA
1989	PHI N	0	0	–	1.74	11	0	0	10.1	12	4	8	0	0	0	0	0	0	0	–	1	0	0	0	0.1	1.000

Year	Team	W	L	PCT	ERA	G	GS	CG	IP	H	BB	SO	ShO	Relief Pitching W	L	SV	Batting AB	H	HR	BA	PO	A	E	DP	TC/G	FA

Jim McElroy

McELROY, JAMES D.
B. 1863, San Francisco, Calif. D. Feb. 24, 1889, Albuquerque, N. M.

| 1884 | 2 teams | PHI N (13G 1–12) | | | | WIL U (1G 0–1) | | | | | | | | | | | | | | | | | | | | | |
| " | total | 1 | 13 | .071 | 5.12 | 14 | 14 | 13 | 116 | 125 | 54 | 48 | 0 | 0 | 0 | 0 | 50 | 7 | 0 | .140 | 7 | 25 | 7 | 1 | 2.8 | .821 |

Will McEnaney

McENANEY, WILLIAM HENRY
B. Feb. 14, 1952, Springfield, Ohio

BL TL 6' 180 lbs.

1974	CIN	N	2	1	.667	4.33	24	0	0	27	24	9	13	0	2	1	2	0	0	0	–	0	1	0	0	0.0	1.000
1975			5	2	.714	2.47	70	0	0	91	92	23	48	0	5	2	15	14	0	0	.000	6	8	0	0	0.2	1.000
1976			2	6	.250	4.88	55	0	0	72	97	23	28	0	2	6	7	6	1	0	.167	4	13	3	1	0.4	.850
1977	MON	N	3	5	.375	3.93	69	0	0	87	92	22	38	0	3	5	3	8	0	0	.000	5	12	0	1	0.2	1.000
1978	PIT	N	0	0	–	10.00	6	0	0	9	15	2	6	0	0	0	0	0	0	0	–	1	1	0	0	0.3	1.000
1979	STL	N	0	3	.000	2.95	45	0	0	64	60	16	15	0	0	3	2	3	0	0	.000	2	19	0	2	0.5	1.000
6 yrs.			12	17	.414	3.75	269	0	0	350	380	95	148	0	12	17	29	31	1	0	.032	18	54	3	4	0.3	.960

LEAGUE CHAMPIONSHIP SERIES

| 1975 | CIN | N | 0 | 0 | – | 6.75 | 1 | 0 | 0 | 1.1 | 1 | 1 | 0 | 0 | 1 | 0 | 0 | 0 | 0 | 0 | – | 0 | 0 | 0 | 0 | 0.0 | – |

WORLD SERIES

1975	CIN	N	0	0	–	2.70	5	0	0	6.2	3	2	5	0	0	0	1	1	1	0	1.000	0	0	0	0	0.0	–
1976			0	0	–	0.00	2	0	0	4.2	2	1	2	0	0	0	2	0	0	0	–	1	0	0	0	0.5	1.000
2 yrs.			0	0	–	1.59	7	0	0	11.1	5	3	7	0	0	0	3	1	1	0	1.000	1	0	0	0	0.1	1.000

4th

Lou McEvoy

McEVOY, LOUIS ANTHONY
B. May 30, 1902, Williamsburg, Kans. D. Dec. 17, 1953, Webster Groves, Mo.

BR TR 6'2½" 203 lbs.

1930	NY	A	1	3	.250	6.71	28	1	0	52.1	64	29	14	0	1	2	3	16	2	0	.125	2	8	3	0	0.5	.769
1931			0	0	–	12.41	6	0	0	12.1	19	12	3	0	0	0	1	4	0	0	.000	1	4	0	0	0.8	1.000
2 yrs.			1	3	.250	7.79	34	1	0	64.2	83	41	17	0	1	2	4	20	2	0	.100	3	12	3	0	0.5	.833

Barney McFadden

McFADDEN, BERNARD JOSEPH
B. Feb. 22, 1874, Eckley, Pa. D. Apr. 28, 1924, Mauch Chunk, Pa.

BR TR 6'1" 195 lbs.

1901	CIN	N	3	3	.500	6.07	8	5	4	46	54	40	11	0	0	0	0	20	3	0	.150	4	15	3	3	2.8	.864
1902	PHI	N	0	1	.000	8.00	1	1	1	9	14	7	3	0	0	0	0	3	0	0	.000	0	2	0	1	2.0	1.000
2 yrs.			3	4	.429	6.38	9	6	5	55	68	47	14	0	0	0	0	23	3	0	.130	4	17	3	4	2.7	.875

Dan McFarlan

McFARLAN, ANDERSON DANIEL
Brother of Alex McFarlan.
B. Nov. 26, 1874, Gainesville, Tex. D. Sept. 24, 1924, Louisville, Ky.

1895	LOU	N	0	7	.000	6.65	7	7	6	46	80	15	10	0	0	0	0	21	5	0	.238	3	13	0	0	2.3	1.000
1899	2 teams	BKN N (1G 0–0)					WAS N (32G 8–18)																				
"	total	8	18	.308	4.67	33	28	22	217.2	274	67	41	1	0	0	0	88	16	0	.182	9	51	8	4	2.1	.882
2 yrs.			8	25	.242	5.02	40	35	28	263.2	354	82	51	1	0	0	0	109	21	0	.193	12	64	8	4	2.1	.905

Chappie McFarland

McFARLAND, CHARLES A.
Brother of Monte McFarland.
B. Mar. 13, 1875, White Hill, Ill. D. Dec. 14, 1924, Houston, Tex.

TR 6'1"

1902	STL	N	0	1	.000	5.73	2	1	1	11	11	3	3	0	0	0	0	4	0	0	.000	0	5	0	0	2.5	1.000
1903			9	18	.333	3.07	28	26	25	229	253	48	76	1	0	2	0	74	8	0	.108	5	75	6	5	3.1	.930
1904			14	17	.452	3.21	32	31	28	269.1	266	56	111	1	0	0	0	99	13	0	.131	13	106	6	3	3.9	.952
1905			8	18	.308	3.82	31	28	22	250	281	65	85	3	0	0	1	85	14	0	.165	12	75	4	1	2.9	.956
1906	3 teams	STL N (6G 2–1)					PIT N (6G 1–3)			BKN N (1G 0–1)																	
"	total	3	5	.375	2.87	13	10	5	81.2	82	20	32	1	0	0	1	31	7	0	.226	5	25	1	1	2.4	.968
5 yrs.			34	59	.366	3.35	106	96	81	841	893	192	307	6	0	2	2	293	42	0	.143	35	286	17	10	3.2	.950

Chris McFarland

McFARLAND, CHRISTOPHER
B. Aug. 17, 1861, Fall River, Mass. D. May 24, 1918, New Bedford, Mass.

5'9" 170 lbs.

| 1884 | BAL | U | 0 | 1 | .000 | 15.00 | 1 | 1 | 0 | 3 | 9 | 1 | 3 | 0 | 0 | 0 | 0 | * | | | | 0 | 0 | 0 | 0 | 0.0 | – |

Monte McFarland

McFARLAND, LAMONT A.
Brother of Chappie McFarland.
B. 1871, Illinois D. Nov. 15, 1913, Peoria, Ill.

1895	CHI	N	2	0	1.000	5.14	2	2	2	14	21	5	5	0	0	0	0	7	1	0	.143	0	4	0	0	2.0	1.000
1896			0	4	.000	7.20	4	3	2	25	32	21	3	0	0	1	0	12	0	0	.000	2	8	0	0	2.5	1.000
2 yrs.			2	4	.333	6.46	6	5	4	39	53	26	8	0	0	1	0	19	1	0	.053	2	12	0	0	2.3	1.000

Jack McFetridge

McFETRIDGE, JOHN REED
B. Aug. 25, 1869, Philadelphia, Pa. D. Jan. 10, 1917, Philadelphia, Pa.

6' 175 lbs.

1890	PHI	N	1	0	1.000	1.00	1	1	1	9	5	2	4	0	0	0	0	4	3	0	.750	0	1	0	0	1.0	1.000
1903			1	11	.083	4.91	14	13	11	102.2	120	49	31	0	0	0	0	34	6	0	.176	2	24	3	0	2.1	.897
2 yrs.			2	11	.154	4.59	15	14	12	111.2	125	51	35	0	0	0	0	38	9	0	.237	2	25	3	0	2.0	.900

Andy McGaffigan

McGAFFIGAN, ANDREW JOSEPH
B. Oct. 25, 1956, West Palm Beach, Fla.

BR TR 6'3" 185 lbs.

1981	NY	A	0	0	–	2.57	2	0	0	7	5	3	2	0	0	0	0	0	0	0	–	0	0	0	0	0.0	–
1982	SF	N	1	0	1.000	0.00	4	0	0	8	5	1	4	0	1	0	0	1	0	0	.000	0	0	0	0	0.0	–
1983			3	9	.250	4.29	43	16	0	134.1	131	39	93	0	1	0	2	30	2	0	.067	8	4	2	0	0.3	.857
1984	2 teams	MON N (21G 3–4)					CIN N (9G 0–2)																				
"	total	3	6	.333	3.52	30	0	0	69	60	23	57	0	0	0	0	10	0	0	.000	3	6	1	1	0.3	.900
1985	CIN	N	3	3	.500	3.72	15	15	2	94.1	88	30	83	0	0	0	0	29	1	0	.034	8	12	1	1	1.4	.952
1986	MON	N	10	5	.667	2.65	48	14	1	142.2	114	55	104	0	5	2	2	33	2	0	.061	6	17	5	1	0.6	.821
1987			5	2	.714	2.39	69	0	0	120.1	105	42	100	0	5	2	12	17	0	0	.000	5	17	4	2	0.4	.846

Year	Team	W	L	PCT	ERA	G	GS	CG	IP	H	BB	SO	ShO	W	L	SV	AB	H	HR	BA	PO	A	E	DP	TC/G	FA
														Relief Pitching			Batting									

Andy McGaffigan *continued*

Year	Team	W	L	PCT	ERA	G	GS	CG	IP	H	BB	SO	ShO	W	L	SV	AB	H	HR	BA	PO	A	E	DP	TC/G	FA
1988		6	0	1.000	2.76	63	0	0	91.1	81	37	71	0	6	0	4	5	0	0	.000	7	8	1	0	0.3	.938
1989		3	5	.375	4.68	57	0	0	75	85	30	40	0	3	5	2	1	1	0	1.000	3	8	2	0	0.2	.846
9 yrs.		34	30	.531	3.31	331	51	3	742	674	260	554	1	22	11	23	126	6	0	.048	40	72	16	6	0.4	.875

Jack McGeachy

McGEACHY, JOHN CHARLES
B. May 13, 1864, Clinton, Mass. D. Apr. 5, 1930, Cambridge, Mass.　　　　BR TR 5'8"　165 lbs.

Year	Team	W	L	PCT	ERA	G	GS	CG	IP	H	BB	SO	ShO	W	L	SV	AB	H	HR	BA	PO	A	E	DP	TC/G	FA
1887	IND N	0	1	.000	11.37	1	0	0	6.1	13	4	3	0	0	1	0	405	109	1	.269	0	1	0	0	1.0	1.000
1888		0	0	—	7.20	1	0	0	5	5	3	0	0	0	0	0	452	99	0	.219	0	1	0	0	1.0	1.000
1889		0	0	—	11.57	3	0	0	4.2	7	6	3	0	0	0	0	532	142	2	.267	0	0	0	0	0.0	—
3 yrs.		0	1	.000	10.13	5	0	0	16	25	13	6	0	0	1	0	*				0	2	0	0	0.4	1.000

Bill McGee

McGEE, WILLIAM HENRY (Fiddler Bill)
B. Nov. 16, 1909, Batchtown, Ill. D. Feb. 11, 1987, St. Louis, Mo.　　　BR TR 6'1"　215 lbs.

Year	Team	W	L	PCT	ERA	G	GS	CG	IP	H	BB	SO	ShO	W	L	SV	AB	H	HR	BA	PO	A	E	DP	TC/G	FA
1935	STL N	1	0	1.000	1.00	1	1	1	9	3	1	2	0	0	0	0	3	1	0	.333	0	0	0	0	0.0	—
1936		1	1	.500	8.04	7	2	0	15.2	23	4	8	0	0	0	0	4	1	0	.250	0	5	0	0	0.7	1.000
1937		1	0	1.000	2.63	4	1	1	13.2	13	4	9	0	0	0	0	5	1	0	.200	0	4	0	0	1.0	1.000
1938		7	12	.368	3.21	47	25	10	216	216	78	104	1	1	2	5	67	14	0	.209	11	39	3	2	1.1	.943
1939		12	5	.706	3.81	43	17	5	156	155	59	56	4	4	3	0	55	8	0	.145	3	33	0	0	0.8	1.000
1940		16	10	.615	3.80	38	31	11	217.2	222	96	78	3	0	1	0	73	13	0	.178	8	33	2	1	1.1	.953
1941	2 teams	STL N	(4G 0–1)			NY N	(22G 2–9)																			
"	total	2	10	.167	4.92	26	17	1	120.2	134	67	43	0	0	1	0	35	5	0	.143	3	17	0	0	0.8	1.000
1942	NY N	6	3	.667	2.93	31	8	2	104.1	95	46	40	1	4	0	1	29	3	0	.103	6	16	1	1	0.7	.957
8 yrs.		46	41	.529	3.74	197	102	31	853	861	355	340	9	10	8	6	271	46	0	.170	31	147	6	7	0.9	.967

Connie McGeehan

McGEEHAN, CORNELIUS BERNARD
Brother of Dan McGeehan.
B. Aug. 25, 1882, Drifton, Pa. D. July 4, 1907, Hazleton, Pa.

Year	Team	W	L	PCT	ERA	G	GS	CG	IP	H	BB	SO	ShO	W	L	SV	AB	H	HR	BA	PO	A	E	DP	TC/G	FA
1903	PHI A	1	0	1.000	4.50	3	0	0	10	9	1	4	0	1	0	0	6	0	0	.000	0	4	0	0	1.3	1.000

Pat McGehee

McGEHEE, PATRICK HENRY
B. July 2, 1888, Meadville, Miss. D. Dec. 30, 1946, Paducah, Ky.　　　BL TR 6'2½"　180 lbs.

Year	Team	W	L	PCT	ERA	G	GS	CG	IP	H	BB	SO	ShO	W	L	SV	AB	H	HR	BA	PO	A	E	DP	TC/G	FA
1912	DET A	0	0	—	0.00	1	1	0	1	1	1	0	0	0	0	0	0	0	0	—	0	0	0	0	0.0	—

Randy McGilberry

McGILBERRY, RANDALL KENT
B. Oct. 29, 1953, Mobile, Ala.　　　BB TR 6'1"　195 lbs.

Year	Team	W	L	PCT	ERA	G	GS	CG	IP	H	BB	SO	ShO	W	L	SV	AB	H	HR	BA	PO	A	E	DP	TC/G	FA
1977	KC A	0	1	.000	5.14	3	0	0	7	7	1	1	0	0	1	0	0	0	0	—	1	2	0	0	1.0	1.000
1978		0	1	.000	4.56	18	0	0	25.2	27	18	12	0	0	1	0	0	0	0	—	2	6	3	0	0.6	.727
2 yrs.		0	2	.000	4.68	21	0	0	32.2	34	19	13	0	0	2	0	0	0	0	—	3	8	3	0	0.7	.786

Bill McGill

McGILL, WILLIAM JOHN (Parson)
B. June 29, 1880, Galva, Kans. D. Aug. 7, 1959, Alva, Okla.　　　BR TR 6'2"

Year	Team	W	L	PCT	ERA	G	GS	CG	IP	H	BB	SO	ShO	W	L	SV	AB	H	HR	BA	PO	A	E	DP	TC/G	FA
1907	STL A	1	0	1.000	3.44	2	2	1	18.1	22	2	8	0	0	0	0	9	0	0	.000	2	5	1	0	4.0	.875

Willie McGill

McGILL, WILLIAM VANESS (Kid)
B. Nov. 10, 1873, Atlanta, Ga. D. Aug. 29, 1944, Indianapolis, Ind.　　　TL 5'6½"　170 lbs.

Year	Team	W	L	PCT	ERA	G	GS	CG	IP	H	BB	SO	ShO	W	L	SV	AB	H	HR	BA	PO	A	E	DP	TC/G	FA
1890	CLE P	11	9	.550	4.12	24	20	19	183.2	222	96	82	0	1	0	0	68	10	0	.147	5	52	4	1	2.5	.934
1891	2 teams	CIN AA	(8G 2–5)			STL AA	(35G 18–10)																			
"	total	20	15	.571	3.36	43	39	28	313.2	294	168	173	1	1	1	1	107	16	0	.150	8	48	9	0	1.5	.862
1892	CIN N	1	1	.500	5.29	3	3	1	17	18	5	7	0	0	0	0	7	2	0	.286	0	4	0	0	1.3	1.000
1893	CHI N	17	18	.486	4.61	39	34	26	302.2	311	181	91	1	1	2	0	124	29	0	.234	7	42	6	3	1.4	.891
1894		7	19	.269	5.84	27	23	22	208	272	117	58	0	0	0	0	82	20	0	.244	4	30	4	1	1.4	.895
1895	PHI N	10	8	.556	5.55	20	20	13	146	177	81	70	0	0	0	0	63	14	0	.222	3	32	4	1	2.0	.897
1896		5	4	.556	5.31	12	11	7	79.2	87	53	29	0	0	0	0	29	6	0	.207	0	22	4	0	2.2	.846
7 yrs.		71	74	.490	4.59	168	150	116	1250.2	1381	701	510	2	5	4	1	480	97	0	.202	27	230	31	5	1.7	.892

John McGillen

McGILLEN, JOHN JOSEPH
B. Aug. 6, 1917, Eddystone, Pa.　　　BL TL 6'1"　175 lbs.

Year	Team	W	L	PCT	ERA	G	GS	CG	IP	H	BB	SO	ShO	W	L	SV	AB	H	HR	BA	PO	A	E	DP	TC/G	FA
1944	PHI A	0	0	—	18.00	2	0	0	1	1	2	0	0	0	0	0	0	0	0	—	0	0	0	0	0.0	—

Jim McGinley

McGINLEY, JAMES WILLIAM
B. Oct. 2, 1878, Groveland, Mass. D. Sept. 20, 1961, Haverhill, Mass.　　　BR TR 5'9½"　165 lbs.

Year	Team	W	L	PCT	ERA	G	GS	CG	IP	H	BB	SO	ShO	W	L	SV	AB	H	HR	BA	PO	A	E	DP	TC/G	FA
1904	STL N	2	1	.667	2.00	3	3	3	27	28	6	6	0	0	0	0	11	1	0	.091	0	1	0	0	0.3	1.000
1905		0	1	.000	15.00	1	1	0	3	5	2	0	0	0	0	0	1	1	0	1.000	0	0	0	0	0.0	—
2 yrs.		2	2	.500	3.30	4	4	3	30	33	8	6	0	0	0	0	12	2	0	.167	0	1	0	0	0.3	1.000

Dan McGinn

McGINN, DANIEL MICHAEL
B. Nov. 29, 1943, Omaha, Neb.　　　BL TL 6'　185 lbs.

Year	Team	W	L	PCT	ERA	G	GS	CG	IP	H	BB	SO	ShO	W	L	SV	AB	H	HR	BA	PO	A	E	DP	TC/G	FA
1968	CIN N	0	1	.000	5.25	14	0	0	12	13	11	16	0	0	1	0	2	0	0	.000	0	3	1	0	0.3	.750
1969	MON N	7	10	.412	3.94	74	1	0	132.1	123	65	112	0	7	10	6	29	5	1	.172	3	30	6	0	0.5	.846
1970		7	10	.412	5.43	52	19	3	131	154	78	83	2	1	2	3	35	4	0	.114	6	29	3	1	0.7	.921
1971		1	4	.200	5.96	28	6	1	71	74	42	40	0	0	2	1	17	4	0	.235	4	15	1	3	0.7	.950
1972	CHI N	0	5	.000	5.86	42	2	0	63	78	29	42	0	1	1	0	8	2	0	.250	2	6	1	0	0.2	.889
5 yrs.		15	30	.333	5.10	210	28	4	409.1	442	225	293	2	9	16	10	91	15	1	.165	15	83	12	4	0.5	.891

Gus Mcginnis

MCGINNIS, GUS
B. 1871, Painesville, Ohio　Deceased.　　　TL 5'11"　168 lbs.

Year	Team	W	L	PCT	ERA	G	GS	CG	IP	H	BB	SO	ShO	Relief Pitching W	L	SV	Batting AB	H	HR	BA	PO	A	E	DP	TC/G	FA

Gus Mcginnis *continued*

Year	Team	W	L	PCT	ERA	G	GS	CG	IP	H	BB	SO	ShO	W	L	SV	AB	H	HR	BA	PO	A	E	DP	TC/G	FA
1893	2 teams	CHI N	(13G 2–5)		PHI N	(5G 1–3)																				
"	total	3	8	.273	4.99	18	9	7	104.2	124	48	25	1	1	1	0	40	9	0	.225	3	27	1	1	1.7	.968

Jumbo McGinnis

McGINNIS, GEORGE WASHINGTON   5'10" 197 lbs.
B. Feb. 22, 1864, Alton, Ill.   D. May 18, 1934, St. Louis, Mo.

Year	Team	W	L	PCT	ERA	G	GS	CG	IP	H	BB	SO	ShO	W	L	SV	AB	H	HR	BA	PO	A	E	DP	TC/G	FA
1882	STL AA	25	17	.595	2.47	44	44	42	379.1	376	52	134	3	0	0	0	203	44	0	.217	13	97	11	2	2.8	.909
1883		28	16	.636	2.33	45	45	41	382.2	325	69	128	6	0	0	0	180	36	0	.200	14	80	21	3	2.6	.817
1884		24	16	.600	2.84	40	40	39	354.1	331	35	141	5	0	0	0	146	34	0	.233	8	71	12	1	2.3	.868
1885		6	6	.500	3.38	13	13	12	112	98	19	41	3	0	0	0	50	11	0	.220	1	15	6	1	1.7	.727
1886	2 teams	STL AA	(10G 5–5)		BAL AA	(26G 11–13)																				
"	total	16	18	.471	3.58	36	35	34	297	342	75	100	1	0	0	0	122	23	1	.189	12	54	11	1	2.1	.857
1887	CIN AA	3	5	.375	5.45	8	8	8	69.1	85	43	18	0	0	0	0	31	6	0	.194	1	14	1	0	2.0	.938
6 yrs.		102	78	.567	2.92	186	185	176	1594.2	1557	293	562	18	0	0	0	732	154	1	.210	49	331	62	8	2.4	.860

Joe McGinnity

McGINNITY, JOSEPH JEROME (Iron Man)   BR TR 5'11" 206 lbs.
B. Mar. 19, 1871, Rock Island, Ill.   D. Nov. 14, 1929, Brooklyn, N. Y.
Hall of Fame 1946.

Year	Team	W	L	PCT	ERA	G	GS	CG	IP	H	BB	SO	ShO	W	L	SV	AB	H	HR	BA	PO	A	E	DP	TC/G	FA
1899	BAL N	28	17	.622	2.58	48	41	38	380	358	93	74	4	3	2	2	145	28	0	.193	19	96	10	0	2.6	.920
1900	BKN N	29	9	.763	2.90	44	37	32	347	350	113	93	1	3	0	0	145	28	0	.193	15	75	12	4	2.3	.882
1901	BAL A	26	20	.565	3.56	48	43	39	382	412	96	75	1	2	1	1	148	31	0	.209	15	104	9	2	2.7	.930
1902	2 teams	BAL A	(25G 13–10)		NY N	(19G 8–8)																				
"	total	21	18	.538	2.84	44	39	35	351.2	341	78	106	1	0	0	0	153	33	0	.216	21	90	11	4	2.8	.910
1903	NY N	31	20	.608	2.43	55	48	44	434	391	109	171	3	2	2	2	165	34	0	.206	31	94	16	3	2.6	.887
1904		35	8	.814	1.61	51	44	38	408	307	86	144	9	2	0	5	142	25	0	.176	28	127	13	1	3.3	.923
1905		21	15	.583	2.87	46	38	26	320	289	71	125	2	0	1	3	120	28	0	.233	23	94	7	3	2.7	.944
1906		27	12	.692	2.25	45	37	32	339.2	316	71	105	3	2	1	4	115	15	0	.130	22	105	13	4	3.1	.907
1907		18	18	.500	3.16	47	34	23	310.1	320	58	120	3	3	4	4	103	18	0	.175	18	94	4	0	2.5	.966
1908		11	7	.611	2.27	37	20	7	186	192	37	55	5	4	1	4	61	11	0	.180	10	50	5	4	1.8	.923
10 yrs.		247	144	.632	2.64	465	381	314	3458.2	3276	812	1068	32	21	13	23	1297	251	0	.194	202	929	100	25	2.6	.919

WORLD SERIES

Year	Team	W	L	PCT	ERA	G	GS	CG	IP	H	BB	SO	ShO	W	L	SV	AB	H	HR	BA	PO	A	E	DP	TC/G	FA
1905	NY N	1	1	.500	0.00	2	2	1	17	10	3	6	1	0	0	0	5	0	0	.000	0	6	0	0	3.0	1.000

Lynn McGlothen

McGLOTHEN, LYNN EVERETT   BL TR 6'2" 185 lbs.
B. Mar. 27, 1950, Monroe, La.   D. Aug. 14, 1984, Dubach, La.

Year	Team	W	L	PCT	ERA	G	GS	CG	IP	H	BB	SO	ShO	W	L	SV	AB	H	HR	BA	PO	A	E	DP	TC/G	FA
1972	BOS A	8	7	.533	3.41	22	22	4	145.1	135	59	112	1	0	0	0	53	10	0	.189	17	31	0	2	2.2	1.000
1973		1	2	.333	8.22	6	3	0	23	39	8	16	0	0	0	0	3	2	0	–	3	0	0	0	0.8	1.000
1974	STL N	16	12	.571	2.70	31	31	8	237	212	89	142	3	0	0	0	83	15	0	.181	19	37	1	3	1.8	.982
1975		15	13	.536	3.92	35	34	9	239	231	97	146	2	0	0	0	80	7	0	.088	10	25	2	3	1.1	.946
1976		13	15	.464	3.91	33	32	9	205	209	68	106	4	0	0	0	71	15	0	.211	20	18	0	3	1.2	1.000
1977	SF N	2	9	.182	5.63	29	13	0	80	94	52	42	0	1	0	0	19	2	0	.105	3	4	1	0	0.4	.875
1978	2 teams	SF N	(5G 0–0)		CHI N	(49G 5–3)																				
"	total	5	3	.625	3.30	54	2	0	92.2	92	43	69	0	5	2	0	16	3	0	.188	1	7	1	1	0.2	.889
1979	CHI N	13	14	.481	4.12	42	29	6	212	236	55	147	1	3	1	2	71	16	0	.225	15	15	0	0	0.7	1.000
1980		12	14	.462	4.80	39	27	2	182	211	64	119	2	0	1	0	51	10	0	.196	3	21	2	0	0.7	.923
1981	2 teams	CHI N	(20G 1–4)		CHI A	(11G 0–0)																				
"	total	1	4	.200	4.56	31	6	0	77	85	35	38	0	1	1	0	12	1	0	.083	6	13	0	0	0.6	1.000
1982	NY A	0	0	–	10.80	4	0	0	5	9	2	2	0	0	0	0	0	0	0	–	1	1	0	0	0.5	1.000
11 yrs.		86	93	.480	3.98	318	201	41	1498	1553	572	939	13	9	7	2	456	79	0	.173	98	174	7	12	0.9	.975

Pat McGlothin

McGLOTHIN, EZRA MAC   BL TR 6'3½" 180 lbs.
B. Oct. 20, 1920, Coalfield, Tenn.

Year	Team	W	L	PCT	ERA	G	GS	CG	IP	H	BB	SO	ShO	W	L	SV	AB	H	HR	BA	PO	A	E	DP	TC/G	FA
1949	BKN N	1	1	.500	4.60	7	0	0	15.2	13	5	11	0	1	1	0	3	0	0	.000	3	5	1	0	1.3	.889
1950		0	0	–	13.50	1	0	0	2	5	1	2	0	0	0	0	0	0	0	–	0	0	0	0	0.0	
2 yrs.		1	1	.500	5.60	8	0	0	17.2	18	6	13	0	1	1	0	3	0	0	.000	3	5	1	0	1.1	.889

Jim McGlothlin

McGLOTHLIN, JAMES MILTON (Red)   BR TR 6'1" 185 lbs.
B. Oct. 6, 1943, Los Angeles, Calif.   D. Dec. 23, 1975, Union, Ky.

Year	Team	W	L	PCT	ERA	G	GS	CG	IP	H	BB	SO	ShO	W	L	SV	AB	H	HR	BA	PO	A	E	DP	TC/G	FA
1965	CAL A	0	3	.000	3.50	3	3	1	18	18	7	9	0	0	0	0	6	0	0	.000	1	1	0	1	0.7	1.000
1966		3	1	.750	4.52	19	11	0	67.2	79	19	41	0	0	0	0	17	1	0	.059	10	7	1	0	0.9	.944
1967		12	8	.600	2.96	32	29	9	197.1	163	56	137	6	1	0	0	57	8	0	.140	15	33	4	4	1.6	.923
1968		10	15	.400	3.54	40	32	8	208.1	187	60	135	0	0	0	3	63	7	0	.111	19	35	1	4	1.4	.982
1969		8	16	.333	3.18	37	35	4	201	188	58	96	1	0	0	0	58	7	0	.121	14	38	2	0	1.5	.963
1970	CIN N	14	10	.583	3.58	35	34	9	211	192	54	97	3	0	0	0	66	8	1	.121	16	55	0	6	2.0	1.000
1971		8	12	.400	3.21	30	26	6	171	151	47	93	0	0	0	0	51	7	1	.137	11	33	4	1	1.6	.917
1972		9	8	.529	3.91	31	21	3	145	165	49	69	1	1	1	0	46	8	1	.174	10	22	4	2	1.2	.889
1973	2 teams	CIN N	(24G 3–3)		CHI A	(5G 0–1)																				
"	total	3	4	.429	6.06	29	10	0	81.2	104	36	32	0	1	1	0	16	2	0	.125	3	19	0	1	0.8	1.000
9 yrs.		67	77	.465	3.61	256	201	36	1301	1247	418	709	11	2	3	3	380	48	3	.126	99	243	16	21	1.4	.955

LEAGUE CHAMPIONSHIP SERIES

Year	Team	W	L	PCT	ERA	G	GS	CG	IP	H	BB	SO	ShO	W	L	SV	AB	H	HR	BA	PO	A	E	DP	TC/G	FA
1972	CIN N	0	0	–	0.00	1	0	0	1	0	0	0	0	0	0	0	0	0	0	–	0	0	0	0	0.0	–

WORLD SERIES

Year	Team	W	L	PCT	ERA	G	GS	CG	IP	H	BB	SO	ShO	W	L	SV	AB	H	HR	BA	PO	A	E	DP	TC/G	FA
1970	CIN N	0	0	–	8.31	1	1	0	4.1	6	2	2	0	0	0	0	2	0	0	.000	0	1	0	0	1.0	1.000
1972		0	0	–	12.00	1	1	0	3	2	2	3	0	0	0	0	1	0	0	.000	1	0	0	0	0.5	1.000
2 yrs.		0	0	–	9.82	2	2	0	7.1	8	4	5	0	0	0	0	3	0	0	.000	1	1	0	0	0.5	1.000

Stoney McGlynn

McGLYNN, ULYSSES SIMPSON GRANT   BR TR 5'11" 185 lbs.
B. May 26, 1872, Lancaster, Pa.   D. Aug. 26, 1941, Manitowoc, Wis.

Year	Team	W	L	PCT	ERA	G	GS	CG	IP	H	BB	SO	ShO	W	L	SV	AB	H	HR	BA	PO	A	E	DP	TC/G	FA
1906	STL N	2	2	.500	2.44	6	6	6	48	43	15	25	1	0	0	0	17	1	0	.059	1	23	1	1	4.2	.960
1907		14	25	.359	2.91	45	39	33	352.1	329	112	109	3	1	1	1	125	25	0	.200	22	94	12	4	2.8	.906

Year	Team		W	L	PCT	ERA	G	GS	CG	IP	H	BB	SO	ShO	Relief Pitching W	L	SV	Batting AB	H	HR	BA	PO	A	E	DP	TC/G	FA

Stoney McGlynn *continued*

Year	Team		W	L	PCT	ERA	G	GS	CG	IP	H	BB	SO	ShO	W	L	SV	AB	H	HR	BA	PO	A	E	DP	TC/G	FA
1908			1	6	.143	3.45	16	6	4	75.2	76	17	23	0	1	0	1	26	2	0	.077	1	29	4	1	2.1	.882
3 yrs.			17	33	.340	2.95	67	51	43	476	448	144	157	3	2	1	2	168	28	0	.167	24	146	17	6	2.8	.909

Mickey McGowan
McGOWAN, TULLIS EARL
B. Nov. 26, 1921, Dothan, Ala.   BL TL 6'2"   200 lbs.

| 1948 | NY | N | 0 | 0 | – | 7.36 | 3 | 0 | 0 | 3.2 | 3 | 4 | 2 | 0 | 0 | 0 | 0 | 1 | 0 | 0 | .000 | 0 | 1 | 0 | 0 | 0.3 | 1.000 |

Howard McGraner
McGRANER, HOWARD (Muck)
B. Sept. 11, 1889, Hamley Run, Ohio   D. Oct. 22, 1952, Zaleski, Ohio   BL TL 5'7"   155 lbs.

| 1912 | CIN | N | 1 | 0 | 1.000 | 7.11 | 4 | 0 | 0 | 19 | 22 | 7 | 5 | 0 | 1 | 0 | 0 | 8 | 2 | 0 | .250 | 0 | 8 | 0 | 0 | 2.0 | 1.000 |

Bob McGraw
McGRAW, ROBERT EMMETT
B. Apr. 10, 1895, La Veta, Colo.   D. June 2, 1978, Seal Beach, Calif.   BR TR 6'2"   160 lbs.

1917	NY	A	0	1	.000	0.82	2	2	1	11	9	3	3	0	0	0	0	3	0	0	.000	0	2	0	0	1.0	1.000
1918			0	1	.000	∞	1	1	0	0	0	4	0	0	0	0	0	0	0	0	–	0	0	0	0	0.0	–
1919	2 teams									NY A (6G 1-0)				BOS A (10G 0-2)													
"	total		1	2	.333	5.44	16	1	0	43	44	27	9	0	1	1	0	13	1	0	.077	0	9	0	0	0.6	1.000
1920	NY	A	0	0	–	4.67	15	0	0	27	24	20	11	0	0	0	0	7	0	0	.000	2	3	0	0	0.3	1.000
1925	BKN	N	0	2	.000	3.20	2	2	2	19.2	14	13	3	0	0	0	0	6	1	0	.167	0	2	0	0	1.0	1.000
1926			9	13	.409	4.59	33	21	10	174.1	197	67	49	0	1	2	1	55	8	0	.145	7	37	2	0	1.4	.957
1927	2 teams									BKN N (1G 0-1)				STL N (18G 4-5)													
"	total		4	6	.400	5.23	19	13	4	98	126	32	39	1	0	1	0	34	6	1	.176	5	25	1	0	1.6	.968
1928	PHI	N	7	8	.467	4.64	39	3	0	132	150	56	28	0	5	8	1	36	4	0	.111	2	29	2	1	0.8	.939
1929			5	5	.500	5.73	41	4	0	86.1	113	43	22	0	4	4	4	20	4	0	.200	5	24	2	4	0.8	.935
9 yrs.			26	38	.406	4.89	168	47	17	591.1	677	265	164	1	11	16	6	174	24	1	.138	21	131	7	5	0.9	.956

Jim McGraw
McGRAW, JOHN
B. 1890   BR TR   190 lbs.

| 1914 | BKN | F | 0 | 0 | – | 0.00 | 1 | 0 | 0 | 2 | 0 | 0 | 2 | 0 | 0 | 0 | 0 | 0 | 0 | 0 | – | 0 | 0 | 0 | 0 | 0.0 | – |

Tug McGraw
McGRAW, FRANK EDWIN
B. Aug. 30, 1944, Martinez, Calif.   BR TL 6'   170 lbs.

1965	NY	N	2	7	.222	3.32	37	9	2	97.2	88	48	57	0	0	1	1	23	3	0	.130	5	14	3	2	0.6	.864
1966			2	9	.182	5.34	15	12	1	62.1	72	25	34	0	0	0	0	17	4	0	.235	3	9	0	0	0.8	1.000
1967			0	3	.000	7.79	4	4	0	17.1	13	13	18	0	0	0	0	4	1	0	.250	1	4	0	0	1.3	1.000
1969			9	3	.750	2.24	42	4	1	100.1	89	47	92	0	8	2	12	24	4	0	.167	6	19	4	2	0.7	.862
1970			4	6	.400	3.26	57	0	0	91	77	49	81	0	4	6	10	13	4	0	.308	9	17	3	0	0.5	.897
1971			11	4	.733	1.70	51	1	0	111	73	41	109	0	11	4	8	18	4	1	.222	2	12	1	2	0.3	.933
1972			8	6	.571	1.70	54	0	0	106	71	40	92	0	8	6	27	20	2	0	.100	6	13	0	0	0.4	1.000
1973			5	6	.455	3.87	60	2	0	118.2	106	55	81	0	5	6	25	24	4	0	.167	8	19	1	1	0.5	.964
1974			6	11	.353	4.15	41	4	1	89	96	32	54	1	4	9	3	14	1	0	.071	2	13	3	0	0.4	.833
1975	PHI	N	9	6	.600	2.97	56	0	0	103	84	36	55	0	9	6	14	13	2	0	.154	4	15	1	2	0.4	.950
1976			7	6	.538	2.50	58	0	0	97.1	81	42	76	0	7	6	11	7	1	0	.143	4	12	4	0	0.3	.800
1977			7	3	.700	2.62	45	0	0	79	62	24	58	0	7	3	9	10	4	0	.400	2	13	0	2	0.3	1.000
1978			8	7	.533	3.20	55	1	0	90	82	23	63	0	8	6	9	4	0	0	.000	4	13	1	2	0.3	.944
1979			4	3	.571	5.14	65	1	0	84	83	29	57	0	4	3	16	6	1	0	.167	6	4	0	0	0.2	1.000
1980			5	4	.556	1.47	57	0	0	92	62	23	75	0	5	4	20	8	2	0	.250	3	5	0	1	0.3	1.000
1981			2	4	.333	2.66	34	0	0	44	35	14	26	0	2	4	10	1	0	0	.000	3	4	0	0	0.2	1.000
1982			3	3	.500	4.31	34	0	0	39.2	50	12	25	0	3	3	5	2	0	0	.000	4	7	0	1	0.3	1.000
1983			2	1	.667	3.56	34	0	0	55.2	58	19	30	0	2	0	0	3	1	0	.333	1	10	1	1	0.4	.917
1984			2	0	1.000	3.79	25	0	0	38	36	10	26	0	2	0	0	3	1	0	.333	2	6	1	0	0.4	.889
19 yrs.			96	92	.511	3.13	824	39	5	1516	1318	582	1109	1	89	69	180	214	39	1	.182	75	219	23	16	0.4	.927

DIVISIONAL PLAYOFF SERIES

| 1981 | PHI | N | 1 | 0 | 1.000 | 0.00 | 2 | 0 | 0 | 4 | 2 | 0 | 2 | 0 | 1 | 0 | 0 | 0 | 0 | 0 | – | 0 | 0 | 0 | 0 | 0.0 | – |

LEAGUE CHAMPIONSHIP SERIES

1969	NY	N	0	0	–	0.00	1	0	0	3	1	1	1	0	0	0	1	0	0	0	–	0	0	0	0	0.0	–
1973			0	0	–	0.00	2	0	0	5	4	3	3	0	0	0	1	1	0	0	.000	2	0	1	0	1.5	.667
1976	PHI	N	0	0	–	11.57	2	0	0	2.1	4	1	5	0	0	0	0	0	0	0	–	0	1	0	0	0.5	1.000
1977			0	0	–	0.00	2	0	0	4	1	2	3	0	0	0	1	0	0	0	–	0	0	0	0	0.0	–
1978			0	1	.000	1.59	3	0	0	5.2	3	5	5	0	0	1	0	0	0	0	–	0	0	0	0	0.0	–
1980			0	1	.000	4.50	5	0	0	8	8	4	5	0	0	1	2	1	0	0	.000	0	0	0	0	0.0	–
6 yrs.			0	2	.000	2.67	15	0	0	27	21	16	22	0	0	2	5	2	0	0	.000	2	1	1	0	0.3	.750

WORLD SERIES

1973	NY	N	1	0	1.000	2.63	5	0	0	13.2	8	9	14	0	1	0	1	3	1	0	.333	0	3	0	0	0.6	1.000
1980	PHI	N	1	1	.500	1.17	4	0	0	7.2	7	8	10	0	1	1	2	0	0	0	–	0	1	0	0	0.3	1.000
2 yrs.			2	1	.667	2.11	9	0	0	21.1	15	17	24	0	2	1	3	3	1	0	.333	0	4	0	0	0.4	1.000
															2nd	4th											

Scott McGregor
McGREGOR, SCOTT HOUSTON
B. Jan. 18, 1954, Inglewood, Calif.   BB TL 6'1"   190 lbs.

1976	BAL	A	0	1	.000	3.60	3	2	0	15	17	5	6	0	0	0	0	0	0	0	–	2	3	0	0	1.7	1.000
1977			3	5	.375	4.42	29	5	1	114	119	30	55	0	1	4	4	0	0	0	–	3	15	1	0	0.7	.947
1978			15	13	.536	3.32	35	32	13	233	217	47	94	4	1	0	1	0	0	0	–	11	38	2	5	1.5	.961
1979			13	6	.684	3.34	27	23	7	175	165	23	81	2	0	0	0	0	0	0	–	10	21	0	0	1.1	1.000
1980			20	8	.714	3.32	36	36	12	252	254	58	119	4	0	0	0	0	0	0	–	8	28	0	0	1.0	1.000
1981			13	5	.722	3.26	24	22	8	160	167	40	82	3	0	0	0	0	0	0	–	8	29	0	2	1.5	1.000
1982			14	12	.538	4.61	37	37	7	226.1	238	52	84	1	0	0	0	0	0	0	–	11	30	0	1	1.1	1.000
1983			18	7	.720	3.18	36	36	12	260	271	45	86	2	0	0	0	0	0	0	–	19	35	2	2	1.6	.964

Year	Team		W	L	PCT	ERA	G	GS	CG	IP	H	BB	SO	ShO	Relief Pitching W	L	SV	Batting AB	H	HR	BA	PO	A	E	DP	TC/G	FA
Scott McGregor	*continued*																										
1984			15	12	.556	3.94	30	30	10	196.1	216	54	67	3	0	0	0	0	0	0	–	14	35	1	2	1.7	.980
1985			14	14	.500	4.81	35	34	8	204	226	65	86	1	0	0	0	0	0	0	–	13	26	1	2	1.1	.975
1986			11	15	.423	4.52	34	33	4	203	216	57	95	2	0	0	0	0	0	0	–	12	27	1	2	1.2	.975
1987			2	7	.222	6.64	26	15	1	85.1	112	35	39	1	0	0	0	0	0	0	–	7	25	1	1	1.3	.970
1988			0	3	.000	8.83	4	4	0	17.1	27	7	10	0	0	0	0	0	0	0	–	1	5	0	0	1.5	1.000
13 yrs.			138	108	.561	3.99	356	309	83	2141.1	2245	518	904	23	2	4	5	0	0	0	–	119	317	9	18	1.3	.980
LEAGUE CHAMPIONSHIP SERIES																											
1979	BAL	A	1	0	1.000	0.00	1	1	1	9	6	1	4	1	0	0	0	0	0	0	–	0	0	0	0	0.0	–
1983			0	1	.000	1.35	1	1	0	6.2	6	3	2	0	0	0	0	0	0	0	–	1	1	0	0	2.0	1.000
2 yrs.			1	1	.500	0.57	2	2	1	15.2	12	4	6	1	0	0	0	0	0	0	–	1	1	0	0	1.0	1.000
WORLD SERIES																											
1979	BAL	A	1	1	.500	3.18	2	2	1	17	16	2	8	0	0	0	0	4	0	0	.000	1	2	0	0	1.5	1.000
1983			1	1	.500	1.06	2	2	1	17	9	2	12	1	0	0	0	5	0	0	.000	0	0	0	0	0.0	–
2 yrs.			2	2	.500	2.12	4	4	2	34	25	4	20	1	0	0	0	9	0	0	.000	1	2	0	0	0.8	1.000

Slim McGrew

McGREW, WALTER HOWARD
B. Aug. 5, 1899, Yoakum, Tex. D. Aug. 21, 1967, Houston, Tex.
BR TR 6'7½" 235 lbs.

Year	Team		W	L	PCT	ERA	G	GS	CG	IP	H	BB	SO	ShO	W	L	SV	AB	H	HR	BA	PO	A	E	DP	TC/G	FA
1922	WAS	A	0	0	–	10.80	1	0	0	1.2	4	2	1	0	0	0	0	1	0	0	.000	0	2	0	0	2.0	1.000
1923			0	0	–	12.60	3	0	0	5	11	3	1	0	0	0	0	1	0	0	.000	0	3	1	0	1.3	.750
1924			0	1	.000	5.01	6	2	0	23.1	25	12	8	0	0	0	0	8	0	0	.000	0	3	0	0	0.5	1.000
3 yrs.			0	1	.000	6.60	10	2	0	30	40	17	10	0	0	0	0	10	0	0	.000	0	8	1	0	0.9	.889

Deacon McGuire

McGUIRE, JAMES THOMAS
B. Nov. 18, 1863, Youngstown, Ohio D. Oct. 31, 1936, Albion, Mich.
Manager 1898, 1907-11.
BR TL 6'1" 185 lbs.

Year	Team		W	L	PCT	ERA	G	GS	CG	IP	H	BB	SO	ShO	W	L	SV	AB	H	HR	BA	PO	A	E	DP	TC/G	FA
1890	ROC	AA	0	0	–	6.75	1	0	0	4	10	1	1	0	0	0	0	*				1	1	0	0	2.0	1.000

Murray McGuire

McGUIRE,
TL

Year	Team		W	L	PCT	ERA	G	GS	CG	IP	H	BB	SO	ShO	W	L	SV	AB	H	HR	BA	PO	A	E	DP	TC/G	FA
1894	CIN	N	0	0	–	10.50	1	0	0	6	15	5	1	0	0	0	0	4	1	0	.250	0	2	0	0	2.0	1.000

Tom McGuire

McGUIRE, THOMAS PATRICK (Elmer)
B. Feb. 1, 1892, Chicago, Ill. D. Dec. 7, 1959, Phoenix, Ariz.
BR TR 6' 175 lbs.

Year	Team		W	L	PCT	ERA	G	GS	CG	IP	H	BB	SO	ShO	W	L	SV	AB	H	HR	BA	PO	A	E	DP	TC/G	FA
1914	CHI	F	5	7	.417	3.70	24	12	7	131.1	143	57	37	0	0	0	3	70	19	1	.271	1	45	3	2	2.0	.939
1919	CHI	A	0	0	–	9.00	1	0	0	3	5	3	0	0	0	0	0	1	0	0	.000	0	3	0	0	3.0	1.000
2 yrs.			5	7	.417	3.82	25	12	7	134.1	148	60	37	0	0	0	3	71	19	1	.268	1	48	3	2	2.1	.942

Bill McGunnigle

McGUNNIGLE, WILLIAM HENRY (Gunner)
B. Jan. 1, 1855, Boston, Mass. D. Mar. 9, 1899, Brockton, Mass.
Manager 1880, 1888-91, 1896.
BR TR 5'9" 155 lbs.

Year	Team		W	L	PCT	ERA	G	GS	CG	IP	H	BB	SO	ShO	W	L	SV	AB	H	HR	BA	PO	A	E	DP	TC/G	FA
1879	BUF	N	9	5	.643	2.63	14	13	13	120	113	16	62	2	0	1	0	171	30	0	.175	3	29	3	2	2.5	.914
1880			2	3	.400	3.41	5	5	4	37	43	8	3	1	0	0	0	26	4	0	.154	1	4	0	0	1.0	1.000
2 yrs.			11	8	.579	2.81	19	18	17	157	156	24	65	3	0	1	0	*				4	33	3	2	2.1	.925

Marty McHale

McHALE, MARTIN JOSEPH
B. Oct. 30, 1888, Stoneham, Mass. D. May 7, 1979, Hempstead, N. Y.
BR TR 5'11½" 174 lbs.

Year	Team		W	L	PCT	ERA	G	GS	CG	IP	H	BB	SO	ShO	W	L	SV	AB	H	HR	BA	PO	A	E	DP	TC/G	FA
1910	BOS	A	0	2	.000	4.61	2	2	1	13.2	15	6	14	0	0	0	0	6	0	0	.000	0	3	0	0	1.5	1.000
1911			0	0	–	9.64	4	1	0	9.1	19	3	3	0	0	0	0	3	0	0	.000	0	4	0	0	1.0	1.000
1913	NY	A	2	4	.333	2.96	7	6	4	48.2	49	10	11	1	0	0	0	15	0	0	.000	3	11	1	2	1.7	.917
1914			7	16	.304	2.97	31	23	12	191	195	33	75	0	1	0	1	60	12	0	.200	3	45	9	2	1.8	.842
1915			3	7	.300	4.25	11	11	6	78.1	86	19	25	0	0	0	0	21	3	0	.143	7	22	1	0	2.3	.967
1916	2 teams	BOS A	(2G 0–1)			CLE A		(5G 0–0)																			
"	total		0	1	.000	4.67	7	1	0	17.1	17	10	3	0	0	0	0	2	0	0	.000	1	5	0	0	0.9	1.000
6 yrs.			12	30	.286	3.57	64	44	23	358.1	381	81	131	1	1	0	1	107	15	0	.140	11	90	11	4	1.8	.902

Vance McIlree

McILREE, VANCE ELMER
B. Oct. 14, 1897, Riverside, Iowa D. May 6, 1959, Kansas City, Mo.
BR TR 6' 160 lbs.

Year	Team		W	L	PCT	ERA	G	GS	CG	IP	H	BB	SO	ShO	W	L	SV	AB	H	HR	BA	PO	A	E	DP	TC/G	FA
1921	WAS	A	0	0	–	9.00	1	0	0	1	1	1	0	0	0	0	0	0	0	0	–	0	0	0	0	0.0	–

Irish McIlveen

McILVEEN, HENRY COOKE
B. July 27, 1880, Belfast, Ireland D. Oct. 18, 1960, Lorain, Ohio
BL TL 5'11½" 180 lbs.

Year	Team		W	L	PCT	ERA	G	GS	CG	IP	H	BB	SO	ShO	W	L	SV	AB	H	HR	BA	PO	A	E	DP	TC/G	FA
1906	PIT	N	0	1	.000	7.71	2	1	0	7	10	2	3	0	0	0	0	*				1	2	0	0	1.5	1.000

Stover McIlwain

McILWAIN, STOVER WILLIAM (Smokey)
B. Sept. 22, 1939, Savannah, Ga. D. Jan. 15, 1966, Buffalo, N. Y.
BR TR 6'2" 195 lbs.

Year	Team		W	L	PCT	ERA	G	GS	CG	IP	H	BB	SO	ShO	W	L	SV	AB	H	HR	BA	PO	A	E	DP	TC/G	FA
1957	CHI	A	0	0	–	0.00	1	0	0	1	2	1	0	0	0	0	0	0	0	0	–	0	0	0	0	0.0	–
1958			0	0	–	2.25	1	1	0	4	4	0	4	0	0	0	0	1	0	0	.000	1	0	0	0	1.0	1.000
2 yrs.			0	0	–	1.80	2	1	0	5	6	1	4	0	0	0	0	1	0	0	.000	1	0	0	0	0.5	1.000

Harry McIntire

McINTIRE, JOHN REID (Rocks)
B. Jan. 11, 1879, Dayton, Ohio D. Jan. 9, 1949, Daytona Beach, Fla.
BR TR 5'11" 180 lbs.

Year	Team		W	L	PCT	ERA	G	GS	CG	IP	H	BB	SO	ShO	W	L	SV	AB	H	HR	BA	PO	A	E	DP	TC/G	FA
1905	BKN	N	8	25	.242	3.70	40	35	29	309	**340**	101	135	4	0	0	0	138	34	1	.246	10	73	10	2	2.3	.892
1906			13	21	.382	2.97	39	31	25	276	254	89	121	4	2	3	3	103	18	0	.175	3	78	3	4	2.2	.964
1907			7	15	.318	2.39	28	22	19	199.2	178	79	49	3	1	0	0	69	15	0	.217	7	56	6	2	2.5	.913
1908			11	20	.355	2.69	40	35	26	288	259	90	108	4	0	1	2	100	20	0	.200	6	76	4	5	2.2	.953
1909			7	17	.292	3.63	32	26	20	228	200	91	84	2	0	1	0	76	13	0	.171	6	62	4	3	2.3	.944
1910	CHI	N	13	9	.591	3.07	28	19	10	176	152	50	65	2	4	0	3	66	17	1	.258	4	48	3	0	2.0	.945
1911			11	7	.611	4.11	25	17	9	149	147	33	56	1	2	0	0	53	14	0	.264	1	42	0	0	1.7	1.000

Year	Team		W	L	PCT	ERA	G	GS	CG	IP	H	BB	SO	ShO	Relief Pitching W	L	SV	Batting AB	H	HR	BA	PO	A	E	DP	TC/G	FA

Harry McIntire *continued*

1912			1	2	.333	3.80	4	3	2	23.2	22	6	8	0	0	1	0	10	3	0	.300	1	6	1	0	2.0	.875
1913	CIN	N	0	1	.000	27.00	1	0	0	1	3	0	0	0	0	1	0	0	0	0	–	0	0	0	0	0.0	–
9 yrs.			71	117	.378	3.22	237	188	140	1650.1	1555	539	626	17	9	8	6	615	134	2	.218	38	441	31	16	2.2	.939

WORLD SERIES

| 1910 | CHI | N | 0 | 1 | .000 | 6.75 | 2 | 0 | 0 | 5.1 | 4 | 3 | 3 | 0 | 0 | 1 | 0 | 1 | 0 | 0 | .000 | 0 | 2 | 1 | 0 | 1.5 | .667 |

Joe McIntosh

McINTOSH, JOSEPH ANTHONY
B. Aug. 4, 1951, Billings, Mont.   BB TR 6'2" 185 lbs.

1974	SD	N	0	4	.000	3.65	10	5	0	37	36	17	22	0	0	0	0	10	0	0	.000	1	4	0	1	0.5	1.000
1975			8	15	.348	3.69	37	28	4	183	195	60	71	1	1	3	0	48	9	0	.188	12	26	0	1	1.0	1.000
2 yrs.			8	19	.296	3.68	47	33	4	220	231	77	93	1	1	3	0	58	9	0	.155	13	30	0	2	0.9	1.000

Frank McIntyre

McINTYRE, FRANK W.
B. Detroit, Mich.   D. July 8, 1887, Detroit, Mich.

| 1883 | 2 teams | | | DET | N | (1G 1-0) | | COL | AA | (2G 1-1) | | | | | | | | | | | | | | | | | |
| " | total | | 2 | 1 | .667 | 3.60 | 3 | 3 | 3 | 30 | 31 | 8 | 6 | 0 | 0 | 0 | 0 | 11 | 0 | 0 | .000 | 0 | 4 | 0 | 0 | 1.3 | 1.000 |

Doc McJames

McJAMES, JAMES McCUTCHEN
Born James McCutchen James.   TR
B. Aug. 27, 1873, Williamsburg, S. C.   D. Sept. 23, 1901, Charleston, S. C.

1895	WAS	N	1	1	.500	1.59	2	2	2	17	17	16	9	0	0	0	0	7	1	0	.143	0	4	0	0	2.0	1.000
1896			12	20	.375	4.27	37	33	29	280.1	310	135	103	0	0	0	1	111	18	0	.162	9	66	9	2	2.3	.893
1897			15	23	.395	3.61	44	39	33	323.2	361	137	156	3	2	1	2	124	21	0	.169	7	72	7	1	2.0	.919
1898	BAL	N	27	15	.643	2.36	45	42	40	374	327	113	178	2	1	1	0	149	27	0	.181	12	70	7	1	2.0	.921
1899	BKN	N	19	15	.559	3.50	37	34	27	275.1	295	122	105	1	1	0	1	112	19	0	.170	6	78	7	3	2.5	.923
1901			5	6	.455	4.75	13	12	6	91	104	40	42	0	0	0	0	34	1	0	.029	2	17	5	0	1.8	.792
6 yrs.			79	80	.497	3.43	178	162	137	1361.1	1414	563	593	6	4	3	4	537	87	0	.162	36	307	35	7	2.1	.907

Archie McKain

McKAIN, ARCHIE RICHARD (Happy)
B. May 12, 1911, Delphos, Kans.   BB TL 5'10" 175 lbs.
D. May 21, 1985, Salina, Kans.   BL 1941,1943

1937	BOS	A	8	8	.500	4.66	36	18	3	137	152	64	66	0	2	0	2	49	13	0	.265	4	27	3	0	0.9	.912
1938			5	4	.556	4.52	37	5	1	99.2	119	44	27	0	3	3	6	31	2	0	.065	10	26	2	1	1.0	.947
1939	DET	A	5	6	.455	3.68	32	11	4	129.2	120	54	49	0	4	2	4	41	9	2	.220	1	15	2	0	0.6	.889
1940			5	0	1.000	2.82	27	0	0	51	48	25	24	0	5	0	3	7	1	0	.143	2	16	0	0	0.7	1.000
1941	2 teams			DET	A	(15G 2-1)		STL	A	(8G 0-1)																	
"	total		2	2	.500	5.60	23	0	0	53	74	15	16	0	2	1	1	13	0	0	.000	2	24	0	2	1.1	1.000
1943	STL	A	1	1	.500	3.94	10	0	0	16	16	6	6	0	1	1	0	1	0	0	.000	1	4	1	0	0.6	.833
6 yrs.			26	21	.553	4.26	165	34	8	486.1	529	208	188	1	17	8	16	142	25	2	.176	20	112	8	3	0.8	.943

WORLD SERIES

| 1940 | DET | A | 0 | 0 | – | 3.00 | 1 | 0 | 0 | 3 | 4 | 0 | 0 | 0 | 0 | 0 | 0 | 0 | 0 | 0 | – | 0 | 1 | 0 | 0 | 1.0 | 1.000 |

Hal McKain

McKAIN, HAROLD LEROY
B. July 10, 1906, Logan, Iowa   D. Jan. 24, 1970, Sacramento, Calif.   BL TR 5'11" 185 lbs.

1927	CLE	A	0	1	.000	4.09	2	1	0	11	18	4	5	0	0	0	0	0	0	0	.000	0	5	0	0	2.5	1.000
1929	CHI	A	6	9	.400	3.65	34	10	4	158	158	85	33	1	3	4	1	44	10	0	.227	4	54	3	4	1.8	.951
1930			6	4	.600	5.56	32	5	0	89	108	42	52	0	0	3	5	31	13	0	.419	2	23	2	0	0.8	.926
1931			6	9	.400	5.71	27	8	3	112	134	57	39	0	0	6	0	42	5	0	.119	5	31	2	0	1.4	.947
1932			0	0	–	11.12	8	0	0	11.1	17	5	7	0	0	0	0	1	0	0	.000	1	4	1	0	0.8	.833
5 yrs.			18	23	.439	4.93	103	24	7	381.1	435	193	136	1	3	13	6	122	28	0	.230	12	117	8	4	1.3	.942

Reeve McKay

McKAY, REEVE STEWART
B. Nov. 16, 1881, Morgan, Tex.   D. Jan. 18, 1946, Dallas, Tex.   TR 6'1½" 168 lbs.

| 1915 | STL | A | 0 | 0 | – | 9.00 | 1 | 0 | 0 | 1 | 1 | 0 | 0 | 0 | 0 | 0 | 0 | 0 | 0 | 0 | – | 0 | 1 | 0 | 0 | 1.0 | 1.000 |

Jim McKee

McKEE, JAMES MARION
B. Feb. 1, 1947, Columbus, Ohio   BR TR 6'7" 215 lbs.

1972	PIT	N	1	0	1.000	0.00	2	0	0	5	2	1	4	0	1	0	0	0	0	0	–	0	0	0	0	0.0	–
1973			0	1	.000	5.67	15	1	0	27	31	17	13	0	0	1	0	4	0	0	.000	0	4	2	0	0.4	.667
2 yrs.			1	1	.500	4.78	17	1	0	32	33	18	17	0	1	1	0	4	0	0	.000	0	4	2	0	0.4	.667

Rogers McKee

McKEE, ROGERS HORNSBY
B. Sept. 16, 1926, Shelby, N. C.   BL TL 6'1" 160 lbs.

1943	PHI	N	1	0	1.000	6.08	4	1	1	13.1	12	10	1	0	0	0	0	5	1	0	.200	0	4	0	0	1.0	1.000
1944			0	0	–	4.50	1	0	0	2	2	1	0	0	0	0	0	0	0	0	–	1	0	0	0	1.0	1.000
2 yrs.			1	0	1.000	5.87	5	1	1	15.1	14	11	1	0	0	0	0	5	1	0	.200	1	4	0	0	1.0	1.000

Tim McKeithan

McKEITHAN, EMMETT JAMES
B. Nov. 2, 1906, Lawndale, N. C.   D. Aug. 20, 1969, Forest City, N. C.   BR TR 6'2" 182 lbs.

1932	PHI	A	0	1	.000	7.11	4	2	0	12.2	18	5	0	0	0	0	0	3	0	0	.000	0	4	0	0	1.0	1.000
1933			1	0	1.000	4.00	3	1	0	9	10	4	3	0	1	0	0	3	1	0	.333	1	2	0	0	1.0	1.000
1934			0	0	–	15.75	3	0	0	4	7	5	0	0	0	0	0	1	0	0	.000	0	0	0	0	0.0	–
3 yrs.			1	1	.500	7.36	10	3	0	25.2	35	14	3	0	1	0	0	7	1	0	.143	1	6	0	0	0.7	1.000

Russ McKelvey

McKELVEY, RUSSELL ERRETT
B. Sept. 8, 1856, Meadville, Pa.   D. Oct. 19, 1915, Omaha, Neb.   BR TR

| 1878 | IND | N | 0 | 2 | .000 | 2.16 | 4 | 1 | 1 | 25 | 38 | 3 | 3 | 0 | 0 | 1 | 0 | * | | | | 2 | 9 | 3 | 0 | 3.5 | .786 |

Year	Team		W	L	PCT	ERA	G	GS	CG	IP	H	BB	SO	ShO	Relief Pitching W	L	SV	Batting AB	H	HR	BA	PO	A	E	DP	TC/G	FA

Kit McKenna

McKENNA, JAMES WILLIAM
B. Feb. 10, 1873, Lynchburg, Va.   D. Mar. 31, 1941, Lynchburg, Va.

Year	Team		W	L	PCT	ERA	G	GS	CG	IP	H	BB	SO	ShO	W	L	SV	AB	H	HR	BA	PO	A	E	DP	TC/G	FA
1898	BKN	N	2	6	.250	5.63	14	9	7	100.2	118	57	27	0	1	0	0	40	9	0	.225	1	34	1	0	2.6	.972
1899	BAL	N	2	3	.400	4.60	8	4	4	45	66	19	7	0	1	0	1	17	1	0	.059	1	10	0	0	1.4	1.000
2 yrs.			4	9	.308	5.31	22	13	11	145.2	184	76	34	0	2	0	1	57	10	0	.175	2	44	1	0	2.1	.979

Limb McKenry

McKENRY, FRANK GORDON (Big Pete)
B. Aug. 13, 1888, Piney Flats, Tenn.   D. Nov. 1, 1956, Fresno, Calif.

BR TR 6'   205 lbs.

Year	Team		W	L	PCT	ERA	G	GS	CG	IP	H	BB	SO	ShO	W	L	SV	AB	H	HR	BA	PO	A	E	DP	TC/G	FA
1915	CIN	N	5	5	.500	2.94	21	11	5	110.1	94	39	37	1	1	0	0	33	5	0	.152	3	36	2	3	2.0	.951
1916			1	1	.500	4.30	6	1	0	14.2	14	8	2	0	0	0	0	5	2	0	.400	0	4	0	0	0.7	1.000
2 yrs.			6	6	.500	3.10	27	12	5	125	108	47	39	0	1	0	0	38	7	0	.184	3	40	2	3	1.7	.956

Joel McKeon

McKEON, JOEL JACOB
B. Feb. 25, 1963, Covington, Ky.

BL TL 6'   185 lbs.

Year	Team		W	L	PCT	ERA	G	GS	CG	IP	H	BB	SO	ShO	W	L	SV	AB	H	HR	BA	PO	A	E	DP	TC/G	FA
1986	CHI	A	3	1	.750	2.45	30	0	0	33	18	17	18	0	3	1	1	0	0	0	–	2	2	0	0	0.1	1.000
1987			1	2	.333	9.43	13	0	0	21	27	15	14	0	1	2	0	0	0	0	–	4	0	0	0	0.3	1.000
2 yrs.			4	3	.571	5.17	43	0	0	54	45	32	32	0	4	3	1	0	0	0	–	6	2	0	0	0.2	1.000

Larry McKeon

McKEON, LAWRENCE G.
B. Mar. 25, 1866, New York, N. Y.   D. July 18, 1915, Indianapolis, Ind.

5'10"   168 lbs.

Year	Team		W	L	PCT	ERA	G	GS	CG	IP	H	BB	SO	ShO	W	L	SV	AB	H	HR	BA	PO	A	E	DP	TC/G	FA
1884	IND	AA	18	41	.305	3.50	61	60	59	512	488	94	308	2	0	0	0	247	53	0	.215	35	124	20	1	2.9	.888
1885	CIN	AA	20	13	.606	2.86	33	33	32	290	273	50	117	2	0	0	0	121	20	0	.165	18	41	1	0	1.8	.983
1886	2 teams	CIN AA (19G 8–8)					KC N	(3G 0–2)																			
"	total		8	10	.444	5.75	22	22	19	177	218	62	49	0	0	0	0	84	19	0	.226	9	37	2	1	2.2	.958
3 yrs.			46	64	.418	3.71	116	115	110	979	979	206	474	4	0	0	0	452	92	0	.204	62	202	23	2	2.5	.920

Denny McLain

McLAIN, DENNIS DALE
B. Mar. 29, 1944, Chicago, Ill.

BR TR 6'1"   185 lbs.

Year	Team		W	L	PCT	ERA	G	GS	CG	IP	H	BB	SO	ShO	W	L	SV	AB	H	HR	BA	PO	A	E	DP	TC/G	FA
1963	DET	A	2	1	.667	4.29	3	3	2	21	20	16	22	0	0	0	0	5	1	1	.200	0	6	2	2	2.7	.750
1964			4	5	.444	4.05	19	16	3	100	84	37	70	0	0	1	0	37	5	0	.135	4	6	1	0	0.6	.909
1965			16	6	.727	2.61	33	29	13	220.1	174	62	192	4	1	0	1	74	4	0	.054	17	30	1	1	1.5	.979
1966			20	14	.588	3.92	38	38	14	264.1	205	104	192	4	0	0	0	93	17	0	.183	14	34	0	2	1.3	1.000
1967			17	16	.515	3.79	37	37	10	235	209	73	161	3	0	0	0	85	10	0	.118	21	22	5	4	1.3	.896
1968			**31**	6	**.838**	1.96	41	**41**	**28**	**336**	241	63	280	6	0	0	0	111	18	0	.162	36	40	1	3	1.9	.987
1969			24	9	.727	2.80	42	**41**	23	**325**	**288**	67	181	9	0	0	0	106	17	0	.160	26	24	2	1	1.2	.962
1970			3	5	.375	4.65	14	14	1	91	100	28	52	0	0	0	0	31	2	0	.065	7	14	0	1	1.5	1.000
1971	WAS	A	10	22	.313	4.27	33	32	9	217	233	72	103	3	1	0	0	58	6	0	.103	27	26	0	1	1.6	1.000
1972	2 teams	OAK A (5G 1–2)					ATL N	(15G 3–5)																			
"	total		4	7	.364	6.39	20	13	2	76	92	26	29	0	1	1	1	16	2	0	.125	2	10	1	0	0.7	.923
10 yrs.			131	91	.590	3.39	280	264	105	1885.2	1646	548	1282	29	3	2	2	616	82	1	.133	154	212	13	15	1.4	.966

WORLD SERIES

Year	Team		W	L	PCT	ERA	G	GS	CG	IP	H	BB	SO	ShO	W	L	SV	AB	H	HR	BA	PO	A	E	DP	TC/G	FA
1968	DET	A	1	2	.333	3.24	3	3	1	16.2	18	4	13	0	0	0	0	6	0	0	.000	0	3	1	0	1.3	.750

Barney McLaughlin

McLAUGHLIN, BERNARD
Brother of Frank McLaughlin.
B. 1857, Ireland   D. Feb. 13, 1921, Lowell, Mass.

BR TR 5'8"   163 lbs.

Year	Team		W	L	PCT	ERA	G	GS	CG	IP	H	BB	SO	ShO	W	L	SV	AB	H	HR	BA	PO	A	E	DP	TC/G	FA
1884	KC	U	1	3	.250	5.36	7	4	4	48.2	62	15	14	0	1	0	0	*				4	12	3	1	2.7	.842

Bo McLaughlin

McLAUGHLIN, MICHAEL DUANE
B. Oct. 23, 1953, Oakland, Calif.

BR TR 6'5"   210 lbs.

Year	Team		W	L	PCT	ERA	G	GS	CG	IP	H	BB	SO	ShO	W	L	SV	AB	H	HR	BA	PO	A	E	DP	TC/G	FA
1976	HOU	N	4	5	.444	2.85	17	11	4	79	71	17	32	2	0	0	1	19	0	0	.000	10	10	0	2	1.2	1.000
1977			4	7	.364	4.24	46	6	0	85	81	34	59	0	3	4	5	9	0	0	.000	7	15	2	1	0.5	.917
1978			0	1	.000	5.09	12	1	0	23	30	16	10	0	0	0	2	3	0	0	.000	1	3	0	0	0.3	1.000
1979	2 teams	HOU N (12G 1–2)					ATL N	(37G 1–1)																			
"	total		2	3	.400	5.05	49	1	0	66	85	20	57	0	1	3	0	6	0	0	.000	3	4	1	0	0.2	.875
1981	OAK	A	0	0	–	11.25	11	0	0	12	17	9	3	0	0	0	1	0	0	0	–	2	1	0	0	0.3	1.000
1982			0	4	.000	0.00	21	2	1	48.1	51	27	27	0	0	2	0	0	0	0		0	0	0	0	0.0	–
6 yrs.			10	20	.333	3.73	156	21	5	313.1	335	123	188	2	4	9	9	37	0	0	.000	23	33	3	3	0.4	.949

Byron McLaughlin

McLAUGHLIN, BYRON SCOTT
B. Sept. 29, 1955, Van Nuys, Calif.

BR TR 6'1"   175 lbs.

Year	Team		W	L	PCT	ERA	G	GS	CG	IP	H	BB	SO	ShO	W	L	SV	AB	H	HR	BA	PO	A	E	DP	TC/G	FA
1977	SEA	A	0	0	–	36.00	1	0	0	1	5	0	1	0	0	0	0	0	0	0	–	0	0	0	0	0.0	–
1978			4	8	.333	4.37	20	17	4	107	97	39	87	0	0	0	0	0	0	0	–	3	8	2	0	0.7	.846
1979			7	7	.500	4.21	47	7	1	124	114	60	74	0	6	2	14	0	0	0	–	6	11	1	0	0.4	.944
1980			3	6	.333	6.82	45	4	0	91	124	50	41	0	2	4	2	0	0	0	–	1	8	1	1	0.2	.900
1982	OAK	A	0	0	–	0.00	0	0	0	0	0	0	0	0	0	0	0	0	0	0	–	0	0	0	0	0.0	–
1983	CAL	A	2	4	.333	5.17	16	7	0	55.2	63	22	45	0	0	1	0	0	0	0	–	0	8	0	0	0.5	1.000
6 yrs.			16	25	.390	5.11	129	35	5	378.2	403	171	248	0	8	7	16	0	0	0	–	10	35	4	1	0.4	.918

Frank McLaughlin

McLAUGHLIN, FRANCIS EDWARD
Brother of Barney McLaughlin.
B. June 19, 1856, Lowell, Mass.   D. Apr. 5, 1917, Lowell, Mass.

BR TR 5'9"   160 lbs.

Year	Team		W	L	PCT	ERA	G	GS	CG	IP	H	BB	SO	ShO	W	L	SV	AB	H	HR	BA	PO	A	E	DP	TC/G	FA
1883	PIT	AA	0	0	–	13.00	2	0	0	9	14	3	1	0	0	0	0	114	25	1	.219	0	0	0	0	0.0	
1884	2 teams	CIN U (0G 0–0)					U	(0G 0–0)																			
"	total		0	0	–	5.40	2	1	0	10	15	2	3	0	0	0	0	257	60	3	.233	0	0	0	0	0.0	–
2 yrs.			0	0	–	9.00	4	1	0	19	29	5	4	0	0	0	0	*				0	0	0	0	0.0	

Jim McLaughlin

McLAUGHLIN, JAMES C.
B. 1860, Cleveland, Ohio   D. Nov. 16, 1895, Cleveland, Ohio

TL

Year	Team		W	L	PCT	ERA	G	GS	CG	IP	H	BB	SO	ShO	W	L	SV	AB	H	HR	BA	PO	A	E	DP	TC/G	FA
1884	BAL	AA	1	2	.333	3.68	3	2	2	22	27	11	8	0	0	1	0	*				1	4	0	0	1.7	1.000

Year	Team	W	L	PCT	ERA	G	GS	CG	IP	H	BB	SO	ShO	Relief Pitching W	L	SV	Batting AB	H	HR	BA	PO	A	E	DP	TC/G	FA

Joey McLaughlin

McLAUGHLIN, JOEY RICHARD
B. July 11, 1956, Tulsa, Okla.   BR TR 6'2"   205 lbs.

Year	Team	W	L	PCT	ERA	G	GS	CG	IP	H	BB	SO	ShO	W	L	SV	AB	H	HR	BA	PO	A	E	DP	TC/G	FA
1977	ATL N	0	0	–	15.00	3	0	0	6	10	3	0	0	0	0	0	1	0	0	.000	0	3	0	0	1.0	1.000
1979		5	3	.625	2.48	37	0	0	69	54	34	40	0	5	3	5	11	2	0	.182	4	8	2	0	0.4	.857
1980	TOR A	6	9	.400	4.50	55	10	0	136	159	53	70	0	4	5	4	0	0	0	–	12	15	0	2	0.5	1.000
1981		1	5	.167	2.85	40	0	0	60	55	21	38	0	1	5	10	0	0	0	–	7	6	0	0	0.3	1.000
1982		8	6	.571	3.21	44	0	0	70	54	30	49	0	8	6	8	0	0	0	–	6	10	0	3	0.4	1.000
1983		7	4	.636	4.45	50	0	0	64.2	63	37	47	0	7	4	9	0	0	0	–	6	6	0	1	0.2	1.000
1984	2 teams					TOR A	(6G 0–0)		TEX A	(15G 2–1)																
"	total	2	1	.667	3.95	21	0	0	43.1	45	20	24	0	2	1	0	0	0	0	–	3	5	1	2	0.4	.889
7 yrs.		29	28	.509	3.85	250	12	0	449	440	198	268	0	27	24	36	12	2	0	.167	38	53	3	8	0.4	.968

Jud McLaughlin

McLAUGHLIN, JUSTIN THEODORE
B. Mar. 24, 1912, Brighton, Mass.   D. Sept. 27, 1964, Cambridge, Mass.   BL TL 5'11"   155 lbs.

Year	Team	W	L	PCT	ERA	G	GS	CG	IP	H	BB	SO	ShO	W	L	SV	AB	H	HR	BA	PO	A	E	DP	TC/G	FA
1931	BOS A	0	0	–	12.00	9	0	0	12	23	8	3	0	0	0	0	0	0	0	–	1	4	1	1	0.7	.833
1932		0	0	–	15.00	1	0	0	3	5	4	0	0	0	0	0	1	0	0	.000	0	1	0	0	1.0	1.000
1933		0	0	–	6.23	6	0	0	8.2	14	5	1	0	0	0	0	0	0	0	–	0	1	0	0	0.2	1.000
3 yrs.		0	0	–	10.27	16	0	0	23.2	42	17	4	0	0	0	0	1	0	0	.000	1	6	1	1	0.5	.875

Pat McLaughlin

McLAUGHLIN, PATRICK ELMER
B. Aug. 17, 1910, Taylor, Tex.   BR TR 6'2"   175 lbs.

Year	Team	W	L	PCT	ERA	G	GS	CG	IP	H	BB	SO	ShO	W	L	SV	AB	H	HR	BA	PO	A	E	DP	TC/G	FA
1937	DET A	0	2	.000	6.34	10	3	0	32.2	39	16	8	0	0	0	0	10	1	0	.100	1	3	0	0	0.4	1.000
1940	PHI A	0	0	–	16.20	1	0	0	1.2	4	1	0	0	0	0	0	0	0	0	–	0	1	0	0	1.0	1.000
1945	DET A	0	0	–	9.00	1	0	0	1	2	0	0	0	0	0	0	0	0	0	–	0	0	1	0	1.0	
3 yrs.		0	2	.000	6.88	12	3	0	35.1	45	17	8	0	0	0	0	10	1	0	.100	1	4	1	0	0.5	.833

Warren McLaughlin

McLAUGHLIN, WARREN A.
B. Jan. 22, 1876, N. Plainfield, N. J.   D. Oct. 22, 1923, Plainfield, N. J.   TL

Year	Team	W	L	PCT	ERA	G	GS	CG	IP	H	BB	SO	ShO	W	L	SV	AB	H	HR	BA	PO	A	E	DP	TC/G	FA
1900	PHI N	0	0	–	4.50	1	0	0	6	4	6	1	0	0	0	0	2	1	0	.500	0	2	1	0	3.0	.667
1902	PIT N	3	0	1.000	2.77	3	3	3	26	27	9	13	0	0	0	0	11	4	0	.364	1	1	0	0	0.7	1.000
1903	PHI N	0	2	.000	7.04	3	2	2	23	38	11	3	0	0	1	0	10	2	0	.200	0	4	0	0	1.3	1.000
3 yrs.		3	2	.600	4.75	7	5	5	55	69	26	17	0	0	1	0	23	7	0	.304	1	7	1	0	1.3	.889

Mac McLean

McLEAN, ALBERT ELDON
B. Sept. 20, 1912, Chicago, Ill.   BR TR 6'   175 lbs.

Year	Team	W	L	PCT	ERA	G	GS	CG	IP	H	BB	SO	ShO	W	L	SV	AB	H	HR	BA	PO	A	E	DP	TC/G	FA
1935	WAS A	0	0	–	7.27	4	0	0	8.2	12	5	3	0	0	0	0	2	0	0	.000	0	0	0	0	0.0	–

Wayne McLeland

McLELAND, WAYNE GAFFNEY (Nubbin)
B. Aug. 29, 1924, Milton, Iowa   BR TR 6'   180 lbs.

Year	Team	W	L	PCT	ERA	G	GS	CG	IP	H	BB	SO	ShO	W	L	SV	AB	H	HR	BA	PO	A	E	DP	TC/G	FA
1951	DET A	0	1	.000	8.18	6	1	0	11	20	4	0	0	0	0	0	1	0	0	.000	2	3	1	0	1.0	.833
1952		0	0	–	10.13	4	0	0	2.2	4	6	0	0	0	0	0	0	0	0	–	0	0	0	0	0.0	
2 yrs.		0	1	.000	8.56	10	1	0	13.2	24	10	0	0	0	0	0	1	0	0	.000	2	3	1	0	0.6	.833

Cal McLish

McLISH, CALVIN COOLIDGE JULIUS CAESAR TUSKAHOMA (Buster)
B. Dec. 1, 1925, Anadarko, Okla.   BB TR 6'   179 lbs.

Year	Team	W	L	PCT	ERA	G	GS	CG	IP	H	BB	SO	ShO	W	L	SV	AB	H	HR	BA	PO	A	E	DP	TC/G	FA
1944	BKN N	3	10	.231	7.82	23	13	3	84	110	48	24	0	0	2	0	32	7	0	.219	3	9	0	0	0.5	1.000
1946		0	0	–	∞	1	0	0	1	1	0	0	0	0	0	0	0	0	0	–	0	0	0	0	0.0	–
1947	PIT N	0	0	–	18.00	1	0	0	1	2	0	0	0	0	0	0	0	0	0	–	1	1	0	0	2.0	1.000
1948		0	0	–	9.00	2	1	0	5	8	2	1	0	0	0	0	1	0	0	.000	0	2	0	0	1.0	1.000
1949	CHI N	1	1	.500	5.87	8	2	0	23	31	12	6	0	0	0	0	9	3	1	.333	3	6	1	1	1.3	.900
1951		4	10	.286	4.45	30	17	5	145.2	159	52	46	1	0	1	0	42	5	0	.119	14	22	1	6	1.2	.973
1956	CLE A	2	4	.333	4.96	37	2	0	61.2	67	32	27	0	1	3	1	9	1	0	.111	5	14	0	0	0.5	1.000
1957		9	7	.563	2.74	42	7	2	144.1	117	67	88	0	7	5	1	43	8	2	.186	6	27	1	2	0.8	.971
1958		16	8	.667	2.99	39	30	13	225.2	214	70	97	0	0	0	0	64	6	0	.094	15	38	1	4	1.4	.981
1959		19	8	.704	3.63	35	32	13	235.1	**253**	72	113	0	0	0	0	74	14	0	.189	25	49	2	4	2.2	.974
1960	CIN N	4	14	.222	4.16	37	21	2	151.1	170	48	56	1	0	3	0	41	2	0	.049	13	33	1	0	1.3	.979
1961	CHI A	10	13	.435	4.38	31	27	4	162.1	178	47	80	0	1	0	0	54	9	0	.167	16	32	0	1	1.5	1.000
1962	PHI N	11	5	.688	4.25	32	24	5	154.2	184	45	71	1	1	0	1	51	4	0	.078	17	20	0	2	1.2	1.000
1963		13	11	.542	3.26	32	32	10	209.2	184	56	98	2	0	0	0	69	14	0	.203	13	47	4	7	2.0	.938
1964		0	1	.000	3.38	2	1	0	5.1	6	1	6	0	0	0	0	1	0	0	–	0	2	0	0	1.0	1.000
15 yrs.		92	92	.500	4.01	352	209	57	1609	1684	552	713	5	9	14	6	490	73	3	.149	131	302	11	27	1.3	.975

Sam McMackin

McMACKIN, SAMUEL
B. 1872, Cleveland, Ohio   D. Feb. 11, 1903, Columbus, Ohio   TL

Year	Team	W	L	PCT	ERA	G	GS	CG	IP	H	BB	SO	ShO	W	L	SV	AB	H	HR	BA	PO	A	E	DP	TC/G	FA
1902	2 teams					CHI A	(1G 0–0)		DET A	(1G 0–1)																
"	total	0	1	.000	2.38	2	1	1	11.1	10	4	4	0	0	0	0	5	2	0	.400	1	6	0	0	3.5	1.000

Jack McMahan

McMAHAN, JACK WALLY
B. July 22, 1932, Hot Springs, Ark.   BR TL 6'   175 lbs.

Year	Team	W	L	PCT	ERA	G	GS	CG	IP	H	BB	SO	ShO	W	L	SV	AB	H	HR	BA	PO	A	E	DP	TC/G	FA
1956	2 teams					PIT N	(11G 0–0)		KC A	(23G 0–5)																
"	total	0	5	.000	5.04	34	9	0	75	87	40	22	0	0	0	0	15	0	0	.000	3	14	0	1	0.5	1.000

Doc McMahon

McMAHON, HENRY JOHN
B. Dec. 19, 1886, Woburn, Mass.   D. Dec. 11, 1929, Woburn, Mass.

Year	Team	W	L	PCT	ERA	G	GS	CG	IP	H	BB	SO	ShO	W	L	SV	AB	H	HR	BA	PO	A	E	DP	TC/G	FA
1908	BOS A	1	0	1.000	3.00	1	1	1	9	14	0	3	0	0	0	0	5	2	0	.400	1	2	1	0	4.0	.750

Don McMahon

McMAHON, DONALD JOHN
B. Jan. 4, 1930, Brooklyn, N. Y.   D. July 22, 1987, Los Angeles, Calif.   BR TR 6'2"   215 lbs.

Year	Team	W	L	PCT	ERA	G	GS	CG	IP	H	BB	SO	ShO	W	L	SV	AB	H	HR	BA	PO	A	E	DP	TC/G	FA
1957	MIL N	2	3	.400	1.54	32	0	0	46.2	33	29	46	0	2	3	9	8	2	0	.250	1	5	1	1	0.2	.857
1958		7	2	.778	3.68	38	0	0	58.2	50	29	37	0	7	2	8	9	1	0	.111	5	7	1	0	0.3	.923

Year	Team		W	L	PCT	ERA	G	GS	CG	IP	H	BB	SO	ShO	Relief Pitching W	L	SV	Batting AB	H	HR	BA	PO	A	E	DP	TC/G	FA

Don McMahon *continued*

Year	Team		W	L	PCT	ERA	G	GS	CG	IP	H	BB	SO	ShO	W	L	SV	AB	H	HR	BA	PO	A	E	DP	TC/G	FA
1959			5	3	.625	2.57	60	0	0	80.2	81	37	55	0	5	3	**15**	9	2	0	.222	4	10	2	0	0.3	.875
1960			3	6	.333	5.94	48	0	0	63.2	66	32	50	0	3	6	10	11	0	0	.000	1	13	1	0	0.3	.933
1961			6	4	.600	2.84	53	0	0	92	84	51	55	0	6	4	8	16	3	0	.188	7	23	3	1	0.6	.909
1962	2 teams	MIL N (2G 0–1)					HOU N (51G 5–5)																				
"	total		5	6	.455	1.69	53	0	0	79.2	56	33	72	0	5	6	8	12	1	0	.083	4	11	0	0	0.3	1.000
1963	HOU	N	1	5	.167	4.05	49	2	0	80	83	26	51	0	1	3	5	12	1	0	.083	5	12	1	2	0.4	.944
1964	CLE	A	6	4	.600	2.41	70	0	0	101	67	52	92	0	6	4	16	14	2	0	.143	5	10	0	0	0.2	1.000
1965			3	3	.500	3.28	58	0	0	85	79	37	60	0	3	3	11	9	2	0	.222	10	15	0	3	0.4	1.000
1966	2 teams	CLE A (12G 1–1)					BOS A (49G 8–7)																				
"	total		9	8	.529	2.69	61	0	0	90.1	73	44	62	0	9	8	10	13	1	0	.077	7	10	0	1	0.3	1.000
1967	2 teams	BOS A (11G 1–2)					CHI A (52G 5–0)																				
"	total		6	2	.750	1.98	63	0	0	109.1	68	40	84	0	6	2	5	13	2	0	.154	7	16	1	1	0.4	.958
1968	2 teams	CHI A (25G 2–1)					DET A (20G 3–1)																				
"	total		5	2	.714	1.98	45	0	0	81.2	53	30	65	0	5	2	1	7	1	0	.143	3	8	0	0	0.2	1.000
1969	2 teams	DET A (34G 3–5)					SF N (13G 3–1)																				
"	total		6	6	.500	3.54	47	0	0	61	38	27	59	0	6	6	13	9	1	0	.111	8	11	0	1	0.2	1.000
1970	SF	N	9	5	.643	2.97	61	0	0	94	70	45	74	0	9	5	19	14	2	0	.143	8	9	0	0	0.3	1.000
1971			10	6	.625	4.06	61	0	0	82	73	37	71	0	10	6	4	7	0	0	.000	8	14	0	1	0.4	1.000
1972			3	3	.500	3.71	44	0	0	63	46	21	45	0	3	3	3	4	1	0	.250	3	5	0	0	0.3	1.000
1973			4	0	1.000	1.50	22	0	0	30	21	7	20	0	4	0	6	1	1	0	1.000	2	5	0	0	0.3	1.000
1974			0	0	—	3.00	9	0	0	12	13	2	5	0	0	0	0	0	0	0	—	1	1	0	0	0.2	1.000
18 yrs.			90	68	.570	2.96	874 9th	2	0	1310.2	1054	579	1003 10th	0	90	66	153	168	23	0	.137	83	187	10	12	0.3	.964

LEAGUE CHAMPIONSHIP SERIES

| 1971 | SF | N | 0 | 0 | — | 0.00 | 2 | 0 | 0 | 3 | 0 | 0 | 3 | 0 | 0 | 0 | 0 | 0 | 0 | 0 | — | 1 | 1 | 0 | 0 | 1.0 | 1.000 |

WORLD SERIES

1957	MIL	N	0	0	—	0.00	3	0	0	5	3	3	5	0	0	0	0	0	0	0	—	0	2	0	0	0.7	1.000
1958			0	0	—	5.40	3	0	0	3.1	3	3	5	0	0	0	0	0	0	0	—	1	0	0	0	0.3	1.000
1968	DET	A	0	0	—	13.50	2	0	0	2	4	0	1	0	0	0	0	0	0	0	—	1	0	0	0	0.5	1.000
3 yrs.			0	0	—	4.35	8	0	0	10.1	10	6	11	0	0	0	0	0	0	0	—	2	2	0	0	0.5	1.000

Sadie McMahon

McMAHON, JOHN JOSEPH
B. Sept. 19, 1867, Wilmington, Del. D. Feb. 20, 1954, Delaware City, Del.　　　BR TR 5'9"　165 lbs.

1889	PHI	AA	16	12	.571	3.35	30	29	29	255	265	104	117	2	0	1	0	104	16	0	.154	7	62	5	6	2.5	.932
1890	2 teams	PHI AA (48G 29–18)					BAL AA (12G 7–3)																				
"	total		36	21	.632	3.29	60	57	55	509	498	166	291	1	0	1	1	214	44	2	.206	31	139	11	7	3.0	.939
1891	BAL	AA	34	25	.576	2.81	61	58	53	503	493	149	219	5	2	0	1	210	43	1	.205	14	141	11	4	2.7	.934
1892	BAL	N	20	25	.444	3.24	48	46	44	397	430	145	118	2	1	0	0	177	25	0	.141	7	94	12	2	2.4	.894
1893			23	18	.561	4.37	43	40	33	346.1	378	156	79	0	0	1	1	148	36	0	.243	16	75	18	2	2.5	.835
1894			25	8	.758	4.21	35	33	26	275.2	317	111	60	0	0	1	0	126	36	0	.286	17	62	5	2	2.4	.940
1895			10	4	.714	2.94	15	15	15	122.1	110	32	37	4	0	0	0	51	16	0	.314	3	23	2	0	1.9	.929
1896			11	9	.550	3.48	22	22	19	175.2	195	55	33	0	0	0	0	73	9	0	.123	5	48	5	1	2.5	.911
1897	BKN	N	0	5	.000	5.86	9	7	5	63	75	29	13	0	0	1	0	25	5	0	.200	3	16	1	0	2.2	.950
9 yrs.			175	127	.579	3.49	323	307	281	2647	2761	947	967	14	3	5	3	1128	230	3	.204	101	660	70	24	2.6	.916

John McMakin

McMAKIN, JOHN WEAVER (Spartanburg John)
B. Mar. 6, 1878, Spartanburg, S. C. D. Sept. 25, 1956, Lyman, S. C.　　　BR TL 5'11"　165 lbs.

| 1902 | BKN | N | 2 | 2 | .500 | 3.09 | 4 | 4 | 4 | 32 | 34 | 11 | 6 | 0 | 0 | 0 | 0 | 11 | 2 | 0 | .182 | 0 | 9 | 0 | 0 | 2.3 | 1.000 |

Joe McManus

McMANUS, JOAB LOGAN
B. Sept. 7, 1887, Palmyra, Ill. D. Dec. 23, 1955, Beckley, W. Va.　　　BR TR 6'1"　185 lbs.

| 1913 | CIN | N | 0 | 0 | — | 18.00 | 1 | 0 | 0 | 3 | 3 | 4 | 1 | 0 | 0 | 0 | 0 | 0 | 0 | 0 | — | 0 | 1 | 0 | 0 | 1.0 | 1.000 |

Pat McManus

McMANUS, PATRICK
B. Ireland D. Oct. 6, 1917, Brooklyn, N. Y.

| 1879 | TRO | | 0 | 2 | .000 | 3.00 | 2 | 2 | 2 | 21 | 24 | 1 | 6 | 0 | 0 | 0 | 0 | 8 | 1 | 0 | .125 | 2 | 5 | 0 | 0 | 3.5 | 1.000 |

George McMullen

McMULLEN, GEORGE
B. Calif. Deceased.

| 1887 | NY | AA | 2 | 1 | .667 | 7.71 | 3 | 3 | 2 | 21 | 25 | 19 | 2 | 0 | 0 | 0 | 0 | 12 | 1 | 0 | .083 | 1 | 6 | 3 | 0 | 3.3 | .700 |

Craig McMurtry

McMURTRY, JOE CRAIG
B. Nov. 5, 1959, Temple, Tex.　　　BR TR 6'5"　195 lbs.

1983	ATL	N	15	9	.625	3.08	36	35	6	224.2	204	88	105	3	0	0	0	70	6	0	.086	15	51	3	3	1.9	.957
1984			9	17	.346	4.32	37	30	0	183.1	184	102	99	0	0	2	0	52	6	0	.115	10	48	1	2	1.6	.983
1985			0	3	.000	6.60	17	6	0	45	56	27	28	0	0	0	1	14	1	0	.071	2	12	0	0	0.9	.875
1986			1	6	.143	4.74	37	5	0	79.2	82	43	50	0	1	3	0	16	2	0	.125	6	11	0	1	0.5	1.000
1988	TEX	A	3	3	.500	2.25	32	0	0	60	37	24	35	0	3	3	3	0	0	0	—	8	10	2	3	0.6	.900
1989			0	0	—	7.43	19	0	0	23	29	13	14	0	0	0	0	0	0	0	—	1	5	1	0	0.4	.857
6 yrs.			28	38	.424	4.01	178	76	6	615.2	592	297	331	3	4	8	4	152	15	0	.099	42	137	9	9	1.1	.952

Edgar McNabb

McNABB, EDGAR J.
B. Oct. 24, 1865, Mt. Vernon, Ohio D. Feb. 28, 1894, Pittsburgh, Pa.　　　TL 5'11½"　170 lbs.

| 1893 | BAL | N | 8 | 7 | .533 | 4.12 | 21 | 14 | 12 | 142 | 167 | 53 | 18 | 0 | 1 | 1 | 0 | 67 | 13 | 0 | .194 | 11 | 31 | 5 | 1 | 2.2 | .894 |

Dave McNally

McNALLY, DAVID ARTHUR
B. Oct. 31, 1942, Billings, Mont.　　　BR TL 5'11"　185 lbs.

| 1962 | BAL | A | 1 | 0 | 1.000 | 0.00 | 1 | 1 | 1 | 9 | 2 | 3 | 4 | 1 | 0 | 0 | 0 | 3 | 0 | 0 | .000 | 0 | 2 | 0 | 0 | 2.0 | 1.000 |
| 1963 | | | 7 | 8 | .467 | 4.58 | 29 | 20 | 2 | 125.2 | 133 | 55 | 78 | 0 | 0 | 0 | 1 | 38 | 2 | 0 | .053 | 6 | 16 | 0 | 0 | 0.8 | 1.000 |

Year	Team		W	L	PCT	ERA	G	GS	CG	IP	H	BB	SO	ShO	Relief Pitching W	L	SV	Batting AB	H	HR	BA	PO	A	E	DP	TC/G	FA

Dave McNally *continued*

Year	Team		W	L	PCT	ERA	G	GS	CG	IP	H	BB	SO	ShO	W	L	SV	AB	H	HR	BA	PO	A	E	DP	TC/G	FA
1964			9	11	.450	3.67	30	23	5	159.1	157	51	88	3	1	0	0	51	7	0	.137	5	26	1	6	1.1	.969
1965			11	6	.647	2.85	35	29	6	198.2	163	73	116	2	0	0	0	65	6	0	.092	6	38	2	3	1.3	.957
1966			13	6	.684	3.17	34	33	5	213	212	64	158	1	0	0	0	77	15	0	.195	7	36	0	2	1.3	1.000
1967			7	7	.500	4.54	24	22	3	119	134	39	70	1	0	0	0	38	6	0	.158	3	11	1	2	0.6	.933
1968			22	10	.688	1.95	35	35	18	273	175	55	202	5	0	0	0	86	11	3	.128	6	28	1	1	1.0	.971
1969			20	7	.741	3.22	41	40	11	268.2	232	84	166	4	0	0	0	94	8	1	.085	6	28	1	2	0.9	.971
1970			24	9	.727	3.22	40	40	16	296	277	78	185	1	0	0	0	105	14	1	.133	10	37	1	4	1.2	.979
1971			21	5	.808	2.89	30	30	11	224	188	58	91	1	0	0	0	74	12	2	.162	10	39	1	1	1.7	.980
1972			13	17	.433	2.95	36	36	12	241	220	68	120	6	0	0	0	79	12	2	.152	9	43	3	5	1.5	.945
1973			17	17	.500	3.21	38	38	17	266	247	81	87	4	0	0	0	0	0	0	–	13	51	2	4	1.7	.970
1974			16	10	.615	3.58	39	37	13	259	260	81	111	4	0	0	1	0	0	0	–	13	50	5	7	1.7	.926
1975	MON	N	3	6	.333	5.26	12	12	0	77	88	36	36	0	0	0	0	21	4	0	.190	3	12	3	0	1.5	.833
14 yrs.			184	119	.607	3.24	424	396	120	2729.1	2488	826	1512	33	1	0	2	731	97	9	.133	97	417	21	37	1.3	.961

LEAGUE CHAMPIONSHIP SERIES

Year	Team		W	L	PCT	ERA	G	GS	CG	IP	H	BB	SO	ShO	W	L	SV	AB	H	HR	BA	PO	A	E	DP	TC/G	FA
1969	BAL	A	1	0	1.000	0.00	1	1	1	11	3	5	11	1	0	0	0	4	0	0	.000	0	0	0	0	0.0	–
1970			1	0	1.000	3.00	1	1	1	9	6	5	5	0	0	0	0	5	2	0	.400	0	0	0	0	0.0	–
1971			1	0	1.000	3.86	1	1	0	7	7	1	5	0	0	0	0	2	0	0	.000	0	2	0	0	2.0	1.000
1973			0	1	.000	5.87	1	1	0	7.2	7	2	7	0	0	0	0	0	0	0	–	0	0	0	0	0.0	–
1974			0	1	.000	1.59	1	1	0	5.2	6	2	2	0	0	0	0	0	0	0	–	0	0	0	0	0.0	–
5 yrs.			3	2	.600	2.68	5	5	2	40.1	29	15	30	1	0	0	0	11	2	0	.182	0	2	0	0	0.4	1.000

WORLD SERIES

Year	Team		W	L	PCT	ERA	G	GS	CG	IP	H	BB	SO	ShO	W	L	SV	AB	H	HR	BA	PO	A	E	DP	TC/G	FA
1966	BAL	A	1	0	1.000	1.59	2	2	1	11.1	6	7	5	1	0	0	0	3	0	0	.000	0	0	0	0	0.0	–
1969			0	1	.000	2.81	2	2	1	16	11	5	13	0	0	0	0	5	1	1	.200	1	0	0	0	1.0	1.000
1970			1	0	1.000	3.00	1	1	1	9	9	2	5	0	0	0	0	4	1	1	.250	0	0	0	0	1.0	1.000
1971			2	1	.667	1.98	4	2	1	13.2	10	5	12	0	0	0	0	4	0	0	.000	0	4	0	0	0.5	1.000
4 yrs.			4	2	.667	2.34	9	7	4	50	36	19	35	1	0	0	0	16	2	2	.125	1	4	0	0	0.6	1.000

Tim McNamara

McNAMARA, TIMOTHY AUGUSTINE
B. Nov. 20, 1898, Millville, Mass.　　　BR TR 5'11"　170 lbs.

Year	Team		W	L	PCT	ERA	G	GS	CG	IP	H	BB	SO	ShO	W	L	SV	AB	H	HR	BA	PO	A	E	DP	TC/G	FA
1922	BOS	N	3	4	.429	2.42	24	5	4	70.2	55	26	16	2	0	3	0	17	2	0	.118	3	14	0	0	0.7	1.000
1923			3	13	.188	4.91	32	16	6	139.1	185	29	32	1	1	1	0	39	7	0	.179	7	23	2	2	1.0	.938
1924			8	12	.400	5.18	35	21	6	179	242	31	35	1	2	0	0	43	6	0	.140	12	45	0	2	1.6	1.000
1925			0	0	–	81.00	1	0	0	.2	6	2	1	0	0	0	0	0	0	0	–	0	0	0	0	0.0	–
1926	NY	N	0	0	–	9.00	6	0	0	6	7	4	4	0	0	0	0	0	0	0	–	0	2	0	0	0.3	1.000
5 yrs.			14	29	.326	4.78	98	42	13	395.2	495	92	88	4	3	4	0	99	15	0	.152	22	84	2	4	1.1	.981

Gordon McNaughton

McNAUGHTON, GORDON JOSEPH (Big Train)
B. July 31, 1910, Chicago, Ill. D. Aug. 6, 1942, Chicago, Ill.　　　BR TR 6'1"　190 lbs.

Year	Team		W	L	PCT	ERA	G	GS	CG	IP	H	BB	SO	ShO	W	L	SV	AB	H	HR	BA	PO	A	E	DP	TC/G	FA
1932	BOS	A	0	1	.000	6.43	6	2	0	21	21	22	6	0	0	0	0	8	2	0	.250	2	6	0	1	1.3	1.000

Harry McNeal

McNEAL, JOHN HARLEY (The Cleveland Kid)
B. Aug. 11, 1877, Iberia, Ohio D. Jan. 11, 1945, Cleveland, Ohio　　　BR TR 6'3"　175 lbs.

Year	Team		W	L	PCT	ERA	G	GS	CG	IP	H	BB	SO	ShO	W	L	SV	AB	H	HR	BA	PO	A	E	DP	TC/G	FA
1901	CLE	A	5	5	.500	4.43	12	10	9	85.1	120	30	15	0	0	0	0	37	6	0	.162	2	15	2	0	1.6	.895

Ed McNichol

McNICHOL, EDWIN BRIGGS
B. Jan. 10, 1879, Martin's Ferry, Ohio D. Nov. 1, 1952, Salineville, Ohio　　　BR TR 5'5"　170 lbs.

Year	Team		W	L	PCT	ERA	G	GS	CG	IP	H	BB	SO	ShO	W	L	SV	AB	H	HR	BA	PO	A	E	DP	TC/G	FA
1904	BOS	N	2	12	.143	4.28	17	15	12	122	120	74	39	1	0	0	0	43	4	0	.093	1	28	1	1	1.8	.967

Frank McPartlin

McPARTLIN, FRANK
B. Feb. 16, 1872, Hoosick Falls, N. Y. D. Nov. 13, 1943, New York, N. Y.　　　TR 6'　180 lbs.

Year	Team		W	L	PCT	ERA	G	GS	CG	IP	H	BB	SO	ShO	W	L	SV	AB	H	HR	BA	PO	A	E	DP	TC/G	FA
1899	NY	N	0	0	–	4.50	1	0	0	4	4	3	2	0	0	0	0	1	0	0	.000	0	2	1	0	3.0	.667

John McPherson

McPHERSON, JOHN JACOB
B. Mar. 9, 1869, Easton, Pa. D. Sept. 30, 1941, Easton, Pa.

Year	Team		W	L	PCT	ERA	G	GS	CG	IP	H	BB	SO	ShO	W	L	SV	AB	H	HR	BA	PO	A	E	DP	TC/G	FA
1901	PHI	A	0	1	.000	11.25	1	1	0	4	7	4	0	0	0	0	0	1	0	0	.000	0	3	1	1	4.0	.750
1904	PHI	N	1	10	.091	3.66	15	12	11	128	130	46	32	1	0	0	0	47	3	0	.064	7	38	2	0	3.1	.957
2 yrs.			1	11	.083	3.89	16	13	11	132	137	50	32	1	0	0	0	48	3	0	.063	7	41	3	1	3.2	.941

Herb McQuaid

McQUAID, HERBERT GEORGE
B. Mar. 29, 1899, San Francisco, Calif. D. Apr. 4, 1966, Richmond, Calif.　　　BR TR 6'2"　185 lbs.

Year	Team		W	L	PCT	ERA	G	GS	CG	IP	H	BB	SO	ShO	W	L	SV	AB	H	HR	BA	PO	A	E	DP	TC/G	FA
1923	CIN	N	1	0	1.000	2.36	12	1	0	34.1	31	10	9	0	0	0	0	7	0	0	.000	1	12	0	1	1.1	1.000
1926	NY	A	1	0	1.000	6.10	17	1	0	38.1	48	13	6	0	1	0	0	7	0	0	.000	2	12	0	0	0.8	1.000
2 yrs.			2	0	1.000	4.33	29	2	0	72.2	79	23	15	0	1	0	0	14	0	0	.000	3	24	0	1	0.9	1.000

Mike McQueen

McQUEEN, MICHAEL ROBERT
B. Aug. 30, 1950, Oklahoma City, Okla.　　　BL TL 6'　188 lbs.

Year	Team		W	L	PCT	ERA	G	GS	CG	IP	H	BB	SO	ShO	W	L	SV	AB	H	HR	BA	PO	A	E	DP	TC/G	FA
1969	ATL	N	0	0	–	3.00	1	1	0	3	2	3	3	0	0	0	0	0	0	0	–	0	0	0	0	0.0	–
1970			1	5	.167	5.59	22	8	1	66	67	31	54	0	0	0	1	20	6	0	.300	0	7	1	0	0.4	.875
1971			4	1	.800	3.54	17	3	0	56	47	23	38	0	2	0	0	19	4	0	.211	1	4	0	1	0.3	1.000
1972			0	5	.000	4.62	23	7	1	78	79	44	40	0	0	0	1	23	2	0	.087	0	8	1	1	0.4	.889
1974	CIN	N	0	0	–	5.40	10	0	0	15	17	11	5	0	0	0	1	1	1	0	1.000	1	0	0	0	0.1	1.000
5 yrs.			5	11	.313	4.67	73	19	2	218	212	112	140	0	2	0	3	63	13	0	.206	2	19	2	2	0.3	.913

George McQuillan

McQUILLAN, GEORGE WATT
B. May 1, 1885, Brooklyn, N. Y. D. Mar. 30, 1940, Columbus, Ohio　　　BR TR 5'11½"　175 lbs.

Year	Team		W	L	PCT	ERA	G	GS	CG	IP	H	BB	SO	ShO	W	L	SV	AB	H	HR	BA	PO	A	E	DP	TC/G	FA
1907	PHI	N	4	0	1.000	0.66	6	5	5	41	21	11	28	3	0	0	0	11	4	0	.364	1	2	0	0	0.5	1.000
1908			23	17	.575	1.53	48	42	32	359.2	263	91	114	7	0	0	2	119	18	0	.151	14	95	6	1	2.4	.948

Year	Team		W	L	PCT	ERA	G	GS	CG	IP	H	BB	SO	ShO	W	L	SV	AB	H	HR	BA	PO	A	E	DP	TC/G	FA

George McQuillan *continued*

Year	Team		W	L	PCT	ERA	G	GS	CG	IP	H	BB	SO	ShO	W	L	SV	AB	H	HR	BA	PO	A	E	DP	TC/G	FA
1909			13	16	.448	2.14	41	28	16	247.2	202	54	96	4	2	2	2	76	9	0	.118	8	56	0	2	1.6	1.000
1910			9	6	.600	1.60	24	17	13	152.1	109	50	71	3	0	1	1	47	7	0	.149	3	39	1	3	1.8	.977
1911	CIN	N	2	6	.250	4.68	19	5	2	77	92	31	28	0	1	2	0	22	2	0	.091	3	16	2	1	1.1	.905
1913	PIT	N	8	6	.571	3.43	25	16	7	141.2	144	35	59	0	2	0	1	39	4	0	.103	6	32	0	0	1.5	1.000
1914			13	17	.433	2.98	45	28	15	259.1	248	60	96	0	1	2	4	73	5	0	.068	11	68	2	3	1.8	.975
1915	2 teams		PIT N	(30G 8–10)		PHI N	(9G 4–3)																				
"	total		12	13	.480	2.62	39	28	14	212.2	220	50	69	0	1	0	1	67	5	0	.075	5	58	4	0	1.7	.940
1916	PHI	N	1	7	.125	2.76	21	3	1	62	58	15	22	0	1	4	2	11	1	0	.091	0	17	2	0	0.9	1.000
1918	CLE	A	0	1	.000	2.35	5	1	0	23	25	4	7	0	0	0	1	4	0	0	.000	2	7	0	0	1.8	1.000
10 yrs.			85	89	.489	2.38	273	173	105	1576.1	1382	401	590	17	8	11	14	469	55	0	.117	53	390	17	10	1.7	.963

Hugh McQuillan

McQUILLAN, HUGH A. (Handsome Hugh)
B. Sept. 15, 1897, New York, N. Y.   D. Aug. 26, 1947, New York, N. Y.   BR TR 6'   170 lbs.

Year	Team		W	L	PCT	ERA	G	GS	CG	IP	H	BB	SO	ShO	W	L	SV	AB	H	HR	BA	PO	A	E	DP	TC/G	FA
1918	BOS	N	1	0	1.000	3.00	1	1	1	9	7	3	1	0	0	0	0	4	1	0	.250	0	3	0	1	3.0	1.000
1919			2	3	.400	3.45	16	7	2	60	66	14	13	0	0	0	1	18	4	0	.222	6	14	4	1	1.5	.833
1920			11	15	.423	3.55	38	27	17	225.2	230	70	53	0	1	1	5	74	19	1	.257	5	76	5	4	2.3	.942
1921			13	17	.433	4.00	45	31	13	250	284	90	94	2	2	1	5	88	18	1	.205	10	68	9	2	1.9	.897
1922	2 teams		BOS N	(28G 5–10)		NY N	(15G 6–5)																				
"	total		11	15	.423	4.06	43	30	8	230.1	265	90	57	0	3	2	1	79	14	0	.177	5	55	9	4	1.6	.870
1923	NY	N	15	14	.517	3.41	38	32	15	229.2	224	66	75	5	2	0	0	82	14	0	.171	8	48	2	3	1.5	.966
1924			14	8	.636	2.69	27	23	14	184	179	43	49	1	0	0	3	67	14	0	.209	2	39	4	1	1.7	.911
1925			2	3	.400	6.04	14	11	2	70	95	23	23	0	0	0	0	21	3	0	.143	2	20	0	2	1.6	1.000
1926			11	10	.524	3.72	33	22	12	167	171	42	47	1	0	2	0	53	7	0	.132	10	46	2	5	1.8	.966
1927	2 teams		NY N	(11G 5–4)		BOS N	(13G 3–5)																				
"	total		8	9	.471	5.11	24	20	7	135.2	182	46	34	0	1	2	0	41	9	0	.220	4	35	4	1	1.8	.907
10 yrs.			88	94	.484	3.83	279	204	91	1561.1	1703	489	446	10	9	8	16	527	103	2	.195	52	404	39	24	1.8	.921

WORLD SERIES

Year	Team		W	L	PCT	ERA	G	GS	CG	IP	H	BB	SO	ShO	W	L	SV	AB	H	HR	BA	PO	A	E	DP	TC/G	FA
1922	NY	N	1	0	1.000	3.00	1	1	1	9	8	2	4	0	0	0	0	4	1	0	.250	0	0	0	0	0.0	—
1923			0	1	.000	5.00	2	1	0	9	11	4	3	0	0	0	0	3	0	0	.000	0	1	0	0	0.5	1.000
1924			0	0	—	2.57	3	1	0	7	2	6	2	0	0	0	1	1	1	0	1.000	0	2	0	1	0.7	1.000
3 yrs.			1	1	.500	3.60	6	3	1	25	21	12	9	0	0	0	1	8	2	0	.250	0	3	0	1	0.5	1.000

Norm McRae

McRAE, NORMAN
B. Sept. 26, 1947, Elizabeth, N. J.   BR TR 6'1"   195 lbs.

Year	Team		W	L	PCT	ERA	G	GS	CG	IP	H	BB	SO	ShO	W	L	SV	AB	H	HR	BA	PO	A	E	DP	TC/G	FA
1969	DET	A	0	0	—	6.00	3	0	0	3	2	1	3	0	0	0	0	0	0	0	—	0	0	0	0	0.0	—
1970			0	0	—	2.90	19	0	0	31	26	25	16	0	0	0	0	1	0	0	.000	3	7	2	1	0.6	.833
2 yrs.			0	0	—	3.18	22	0	0	34	28	26	19	0	0	0	0	1	0	0	.000	3	7	2	1	0.5	.833

Trick McSorley

McSORLEY, JOHN BERNARD
B. Dec. 16, 1858, St. Louis, Mo.   D. Feb. 9, 1936, St. Louis, Mo.   TR 5'4"   142 lbs.

Year	Team		W	L	PCT	ERA	G	GS	CG	IP	H	BB	SO	ShO	W	L	SV	AB	H	HR	BA	PO	A	E	DP	TC/G	FA
1884	TOL	AA	0	0	—	4.50	1	0	0	2	5	1	0	0	0	0	0	*				0	0	0	0	0.0	—

Bill McTigue

McTIGUE, WILLIAM PATRICK
B. Jan. 3, 1891, Nashville, Tenn.   D. May 8, 1920, Nashville, Tenn.   BL TL 6'1½"   175 lbs.

Year	Team		W	L	PCT	ERA	G	GS	CG	IP	H	BB	SO	ShO	W	L	SV	AB	H	HR	BA	PO	A	E	DP	TC/G	FA
1911	BOS	N	0	5	.000	7.05	14	8	0	37	37	49	23	0	0	0	0	12	1	0	.083	1	6	1	0	0.6	.875
1912			2	0	1.000	5.45	10	1	1	34.2	39	18	17	0	1	0	0	13	1	0	.077	1	10	0	2	1.1	1.000
1916	DET	A	0	0	—	5.06	3	0	0	5.1	5	5	1	0	0	0	0	1	0	0	.000	1	3	0	0	1.3	1.000
3 yrs.			2	5	.286	6.19	27	9	1	77	81	72	41	0	1	0	0	26	2	0	.077	3	19	1	2	0.9	.957

Cal McVey

McVEY, CALVIN ALEXANDER
B. Aug. 30, 1850, Montrose, Iowa   D. Aug. 20, 1926, San Francisco, Calif.
Manager 1873, 1878–79.   BR TR 5'9"   170 lbs.

Year	Team		W	L	PCT	ERA	G	GS	CG	IP	H	BB	SO	ShO	W	L	SV	AB	H	HR	BA	PO	A	E	DP	TC/G	FA
1876	CHI	N	5	1	.833	1.52	11	6	5	59.1	57	2	9	0	0	0	2	308	107	1	.347	1	13	4	0	1.6	.778
1877			4	8	.333	4.50	17	10	6	92	129	11	20	0	1	1	2	266	98	0	.368	6	14	5	0	1.5	.800
1879	CIN	N	0	2	.000	8.36	3	1	1	14	34	2	7	0	0	1	0	354	105	0	.297	0	3	0	0	1.0	1.000
3 yrs.			9	11	.450	3.76	31	17	12	165.1	220	15	36	0	1	2	4	*				7	30	9	0	1.5	.804

Doug McWeeny

McWEENY, DOUGLAS LAWRENCE (Buzz)
B. Aug. 17, 1896, Chicago, Ill.   D. Jan. 1, 1953, Melrose Park, Ill.   BR TR 6'2"   190 lbs.

Year	Team		W	L	PCT	ERA	G	GS	CG	IP	H	BB	SO	ShO	W	L	SV	AB	H	HR	BA	PO	A	E	DP	TC/G	FA
1921	CHI	A	3	6	.333	6.08	27	9	4	97.2	127	45	46	0	0	0	2	31	1	0	.032	3	21	1	0	0.9	.960
1922			0	1	.000	5.91	4	1	0	10.2	13	7	5	0	0	0	0	1	0	0	.000	0	1	0	0	0.3	1.000
1924			1	3	.250	4.57	13	5	2	43.1	47	17	18	0	1	0	0	9	0	0	.000	1	22	0	0	1.9	1.000
1926	BKN	N	11	13	.458	3.04	42	25	10	216.1	213	84	96	1	2	0	1	64	7	0	.109	12	44	5	1	1.5	.918
1927			4	8	.333	3.56	34	22	6	164.1	167	70	73	0	0	1	1	47	2	0	.043	10	38	5	0	1.6	.906
1928			14	14	.500	3.17	42	32	12	244	218	114	79	4	0	2	1	81	14	0	.173	7	72	3	2	2.0	.963
1929			4	10	.286	6.10	36	24	4	146	167	93	59	0	0	2	1	48	5	0	.104	7	23	2	1	0.9	1.000
1930	CIN	N	0	2	.000	7.36	8	2	0	25.2	28	20	10	0	1	0	0	7	1	0	.143	1	5	0	0	0.8	1.000
8 yrs.			37	57	.394	4.17	206	120	38	948	980	450	386	5	4	6	5	288	30	0	.104	43	226	16	5	1.4	.944

Larry McWilliams

McWILLIAMS, LARRY DEAN
B. Feb. 10, 1954, Wichita, Kans.   BL TL 6'5"   180 lbs.

Year	Team		W	L	PCT	ERA	G	GS	CG	IP	H	BB	SO	ShO	W	L	SV	AB	H	HR	BA	PO	A	E	DP	TC/G	FA
1978	ATL	N	9	3	.750	2.82	15	15	3	99	84	35	42	1	0	0	0	32	2	0	.063	10	19	0	1	1.9	1.000
1979			3	2	.600	5.59	13	13	1	66	69	22	32	0	0	0	0	24	5	0	.208	2	17	1	2	1.5	.950
1980			9	14	.391	4.94	30	30	4	164	188	39	77	1	0	0	0	51	8	0	.157	11	24	3	1	1.3	.921
1981			2	1	.667	3.08	6	5	2	38	31	8	23	1	0	0	0	10	1	0	.100	4	9	0	2	2.2	1.000
1982	2 teams		ATL N	(27G 2–3)		PIT N	(19G 6–5)																				
"	total		8	8	.500	3.84	46	20	2	159.1	158	44	118	2	2	2	2	38	7	0	.184	9	40	0	2	1.1	1.000
1983	PIT	N	15	8	.652	3.25	35	35	8	238	205	87	199	4	0	0	0	79	9	0	.114	10	40	5	5	1.6	.909
1984			12	11	.522	2.93	34	32	7	227.1	226	78	149	2	0	0	0	74	9	0	.122	15	32	0	4	1.4	1.000
1985			7	9	.438	4.70	30	19	2	126.1	139	62	52	0	1	1	0	40	5	0	.125	4	21	0	0	0.8	1.000
1986			3	11	.214	5.15	49	15	0	122.1	129	49	80	0	2	3	0	29	4	0	.138	7	17	0	2	0.5	1.000

Year	Team		W	L	PCT	ERA	G	GS	CG	IP	H	BB	SO	ShO	W	L	SV	AB	H	HR	BA	PO	A	E	DP	TC/G	FA
															Relief Pitching			**Batting**									

Larry McWilliams *continued*

Year	Team		W	L	PCT	ERA	G	GS	CG	IP	H	BB	SO	ShO	W	L	SV	AB	H	HR	BA	PO	A	E	DP	TC/G	FA
1987	ATL	N	0	1	.000	5.75	9	2	0	20.1	25	7	13	0	0	0	0	5	1	0	.200	1	3	0	1	0.4	1.000
1988	STL	N	6	9	.400	3.90	42	17	2	136	130	45	70	1	1	3	1	37	6	0	.162	5	24	2	0	0.7	.935
1989	2 teams	PHI N (40G 2–11)				KC A	(8G 2–2)																				
"	total		4	13	.235	4.11	48	21	3	153.1	154	57	78	1	0	1	0	27	3	0	.111	7	26	2	2	0.7	.943
12 yrs.			78	90	.464	3.95	357	224	34	1550	1538	533	933	13	6	10	3	446	60	0	.135	85	272	13	22	1.0	.965

Johnny Meador

MEADOR, JOHN DAVIS   BR TR 5'10½" 165 lbs.
B. Dec. 4, 1892, Madison, N. C.   D. Apr. 11, 1970, Winston-Salem, N. C.

Year	Team		W	L	PCT	ERA	G	GS	CG	IP	H	BB	SO	ShO	W	L	SV	AB	H	HR	BA	PO	A	E	DP	TC/G	FA
1920	PIT	N	0	2	.000	4.21	12	2	0	36.1	48	7	5	0	0	0	0	6	1	0	.167	2	13	0	0	1.3	1.000

Lee Meadows

MEADOWS, HENRY LEE (Specs)   BL TR 5'9" 190 lbs.   BR 1920-21, BB 1926,1929
B. July 12, 1894, Oxford, N. C.
D. Jan. 29, 1963, Daytona Beach, Fla.

Year	Team		W	L	PCT	ERA	G	GS	CG	IP	H	BB	SO	ShO	W	L	SV	AB	H	HR	BA	PO	A	E	DP	TC/G	FA
1915	STL	N	13	11	.542	2.99	39	26	14	244	232	88	104	1	3	0	0	83	8	0	.096	3	53	3	2	1.5	.949
1916			12	23	.343	2.58	51	36	11	289	261	119	120	1	5	3	2	95	15	0	.158	4	83	6	2	1.9	.937
1917			15	9	.625	3.09	43	37	18	265.1	253	90	100	4	3	0	2	89	9	0	.101	4	66	4	0	1.7	.946
1918			8	14	.364	3.59	30	21	12	165.1	176	56	49	0	1	1	0	55	7	0	.127	6	41	4	4	1.7	.922
1919	2 teams	STL N (22G 4–10)				PHI N	(18G 8–10)																				
"	total		12	20	.375	2.69	40	29	18	241.1	228	79	116	4	3	0	0	80	9	0	.113	7	81	8	0	2.4	.917
1920	PHI	N	16	14	.533	2.84	35	33	19	247	249	90	95	3	1	0	0	82	14	0	.171	4	70	7	1	2.5	.920
1921			11	16	.407	4.31	28	27	15	194.1	226	62	52	2	1	0	0	62	13	3	.210	9	69	6	6	3.0	.929
1922			12	18	.400	4.03	33	33	19	237	264	71	62	2	0	0	0	86	27	0	.314	8	71	1	2	2.4	.988
1923	2 teams	PHI N (8G 1–3)				PIT N	(31G 16–10)																				
"	total		17	13	.567	3.83	39	30	17	246.2	290	59	76	1	1	1	1	98	26	1	.265	8	64	1	7	1.9	.986
1924	PIT	N	13	12	.520	3.26	36	30	15	229.1	240	51	61	3	1	1	0	82	16	0	.195	3	55	4	0	1.7	.935
1925			19	10	.655	3.67	35	31	20	255.1	272	67	87	1	1	2	1	97	17	1	.175	6	62	0	4	1.9	1.000
1926			**20**	9	.690	3.97	36	31	15	226.2	254	52	54	1	3	0	0	88	20	0	.227	9	69	3	6	2.3	.963
1927			19	10	.655	3.40	40	**38**	**25**	299.1	315	66	84	2	0	0	0	115	18	0	.157	5	64	5	5	1.9	.932
1928			1	1	.500	8.10	4	1	0	10	18	5	3	0	0	0	0	4	2	0	.500	0	0	0	0	0.5	1.000
1929			0	0	–	13.50	1	0	0	.2	2	1	0	0	0	0	0	1	0	0	.000	0	0	0	0	0.0	–
15 yrs.			188	180	.511	3.38	490	404	219	3151.1	3280	956	1063	25	22	11	7	1117	201	5	.180	84	850	52	39	2.0	.947

WORLD SERIES

Year	Team		W	L	PCT	ERA	G	GS	CG	IP	H	BB	SO	ShO	W	L	SV	AB	H	HR	BA	PO	A	E	DP	TC/G	FA
1925	PIT	N	0	1	.000	3.38	1	1	0	8	6	0	4	0	0	0	0	1	0	0	.000	0	2	0	0	2.0	1.000
1927			0	1	.000	9.95	1	1	0	6.1	7	1	6	0	0	0	0	2	0	0	.000	0	1	0	0	1.0	1.000
2 yrs.			0	2	.000	6.28	2	2	0	14.1	13	1	10	0	0	0	0	3	0	0	.000	0	3	0	0	1.5	1.000

Rufe Meadows

MEADOWS, RUFUS RIVERS   BL TL 5'11" 175 lbs.
B. Aug. 25, 1907, Chase City, Va.   D. May 10, 1970, Wichita, Kans.

Year	Team		W	L	PCT	ERA	G	GS	CG	IP	H	BB	SO	ShO	W	L	SV	AB	H	HR	BA	PO	A	E	DP	TC/G	FA
1926	CIN	N	0	0	–	0.00	1	0	0	.1	0	0	0	0	0	0	0	1	0	0	.000	0	0	0	0	0.0	–

Dave Meads

MEADS, DAVID DONALD   BL TL 6'½" 175 lbs.
B. Jan. 7, 1964, Montclair, N. J.

Year	Team		W	L	PCT	ERA	G	GS	CG	IP	H	BB	SO	ShO	W	L	SV	AB	H	HR	BA	PO	A	E	DP	TC/G	FA
1987	HOU	N	5	3	.625	5.55	45	0	0	48.2	60	16	32	0	5	3	0	3	1	0	.333	1	4	0	1	0.1	1.000
1988			3	1	.750	3.18	22	2	0	39.2	37	14	27	0	2	0	0	4	1	0	.250	3	6	1	0	0.5	.900
2 yrs.			8	4	.667	4.48	67	2	0	88.1	97	30	59	0	7	3	0	7	2	0	.286	4	10	1	1	0.2	.933

George Meakim

MEAKIM, GEORGE CLINTON   BR TR 5'7½" 154 lbs.
B. July 11, 1865, Brooklyn, N. Y.   D. Feb. 17, 1923, Queens, N. Y.

Year	Team		W	L	PCT	ERA	G	GS	CG	IP	H	BB	SO	ShO	W	L	SV	AB	H	HR	BA	PO	A	E	DP	TC/G	FA
1890	LOU	AA	12	7	.632	2.91	28	21	16	192	173	63	123	3	1	0	1	72	11	0	.153	15	28	8	2	1.8	.843
1891	PHI	AA	1	4	.200	6.94	6	6	4	35	51	22	13	0	0	0	0	15	3	0	.200	6	18	4	1	4.7	.857
1892	2 teams	CHI N (1G 0–1)				CIN N	(3G 1–1)																				
"	total		1	2	.333	9.53	4	4	2	22.2	37	11	4	0	0	0	0	10	2	0	.200	3	3	1	0	1.8	.857
1895	LOU	N	1	0	1.000	2.57	1	1	1	7	7	4	2	0	0	0	0	3	1	0	.333	1	1	0	0	2.0	1.000
4 yrs.			15	13	.536	4.03	39	32	23	256.2	268	100	142	3	1	0	1	100	17	0	.170	25	50	13	3	2.3	.852

Doc Medich

MEDICH, GEORGE FRANCIS   BR TR 6'5" 225 lbs.
B. Dec. 9, 1948, Aliquippa, Pa.

Year	Team		W	L	PCT	ERA	G	GS	CG	IP	H	BB	SO	ShO	W	L	SV	AB	H	HR	BA	PO	A	E	DP	TC/G	FA
1972	NY	A	0	0	–	∞	1	1	0		2	2	0	0	0	0	0	0	0	0	–	0	0	0	0	0.0	–
1973			14	9	.609	2.95	34	32	11	235	217	74	145	3	0	0	0	0	0	0	–	14	25	5	0	1.3	.886
1974			19	15	.559	3.60	38	38	17	280	275	91	154	4	0	0	0	0	0	0	–	18	35	3	3	1.5	.946
1975	PIT	N	16	16	.500	3.50	38	37	15	272.1	271	72	132	2	0	0	0	0	0	0	–	18	27	2	1	1.2	.957
1976			8	11	.421	3.51	29	29	3	179.1	193	48	86	0	0	0	0	52	5	0	.096	6	36	2	2	1.5	.955
1977	3 teams	OAK A (26G 10–6)				SEA A (3G 2–0)	NY N (1G 0–1)																				
"	total		12	7	.632	4.53	30	30	9	177	187	54	80	1	0	0	0	0	0	0	.000	12	18	2	0	1.1	.938
1978	TEX	A	9	8	.529	3.74	28	22	6	171	166	52	71	1	0	0	0	0	0	0	–	11	31	1	2	1.5	.977
1979			10	7	.588	4.17	29	19	4	149	156	49	58	1	0	2	0	0	0	0	–	6	33	2	0	1.4	.951
1980			14	11	.560	3.93	34	32	6	204	230	56	91	0	0	0	0	0	0	0	–	9	27	3	3	1.1	.923
1981			10	6	.625	3.08	24	19	3	143	136	33	65	4	0	0	0	0	0	0	–	15	26	1	3	2.1	.976
1982	2 teams	TEX A (21G 7–11)				MIL A	(10G 5–4)																				
"	total		12	15	.444	5.04	31	30	3	185.2	203	93	73	0	0	0	0	0	0	0	–	5	21	0	0	0.8	1.000
11 yrs.			124	105	.541	3.78	312	287	71	1996.1	2036	624	955	16	1	2	2	54	5	0	.093	114	279	21	12	1.3	.949

WORLD SERIES

Year	Team		W	L	PCT	ERA	G	GS	CG	IP	H	BB	SO	ShO	W	L	SV	AB	H	HR	BA	PO	A	E	DP	TC/G	FA
1982	MIL	A	0	0	–	18.00	1	0	0	2	5	1	0	0	0	0	0	0	0	0	–	0	0	0	0	0.0	–

Irv Medlinger

MEDLINGER, IRVING JOHN   BL TL 5'11" 185 lbs.
B. June 18, 1927, Chicago, Ill.   D. Sept. 3, 1975, Wheeling, Ill.

Year	Team		W	L	PCT	ERA	G	GS	CG	IP	H	BB	SO	ShO	W	L	SV	AB	H	HR	BA	PO	A	E	DP	TC/G	FA
1949	STL	A	0	0	–	27.00	3	0	0	4	11	3	4	0	0	0	0	0	0	0	–	0	0	0	0	0.0	–
1951			0	0	–	8.38	6	0	0	9.2	10	12	5	0	0	0	0	0	0	0	–	0	1	0	0	0.2	1.000
2 yrs.			0	0	–	13.83	9	0	0	13.2	21	15	9	0	0	0	0	0	0	0	–	0	1	0	0	0.1	1.000

Year	Team		W	L	PCT	ERA	G	GS	CG	IP	H	BB	SO	ShO	Relief Pitching W	L	SV	Batting AB	H	HR	BA	PO	A	E	DP	TC/G	FA

Scott Medvin
MEDVIN, SCOTT HOWARD
B. Sept. 16, 1961, North Olmsted, Ohio
BR TR 6'1" 195 lbs.

Year	Team		W	L	PCT	ERA	G	GS	CG	IP	H	BB	SO	ShO	W	L	SV	AB	H	HR	BA	PO	A	E	DP	TC/G	FA
1988	PIT	N	3	0	1.000	4.88	17	0	0	27.2	23	9	16	0	3	0	0	3	0	0	.000	0	6	0	0	0.4	1.000
1989			0	1	.000	5.68	6	0	0	6.1	6	5	4	0	0	1	0	0	0	0	–	1	2	0	0	0.5	1.000
2 yrs.			3	1	.750	5.03	23	0	0	34	29	14	20	0	3	1	0	3	0	0	.000	1	8	0	0	0.4	1.000

Pete Meegan
MEEGAN, PETER J. (Steady Pete)
B. Nov. 13, 1863, San Francisco, Calif.   D. Mar. 15, 1905, San Francisco, Calif.

Year	Team		W	L	PCT	ERA	G	GS	CG	IP	H	BB	SO	ShO	W	L	SV	AB	H	HR	BA	PO	A	E	DP	TC/G	FA
1884	RIC	AA	5	9	.357	4.37	17	17	17	140	140	27	71	1	0	0	0	59	8	0	.136	6	34	9	0	2.9	.816
1885	PIT	AA	7	8	.467	3.39	18	16	14	146	146	38	58	1	1	0	0	67	13	0	.194	8	27	8	0	2.4	.814
2 yrs.			12	17	.414	3.87	35	33	31	286	286	65	129	2	1	0	0	126	21	0	.167	14	61	17	0	2.6	.815

Bill Meehan
MEEHAN, WILLIAM THOMAS
B. Sept. 4, 1889, Osceola Mills, Pa.   D. Oct. 8, 1982, Douglas, Wyo.
BR TR 5'9" 155 lbs.

Year	Team		W	L	PCT	ERA	G	GS	CG	IP	H	BB	SO	ShO	W	L	SV	AB	H	HR	BA	PO	A	E	DP	TC/G	FA
1915	PHI	A	0	1	.000	11.25	1	1	0	4	7	3	4	0	0	0	0	1	1	0	1.000	1	2	0	0	3.0	1.000

Roy Meeker
MEEKER, CHARLES ROY (Lefty)
B. Sept. 15, 1900, Lead Mines, Mo.   D. Mar. 25, 1929, Orlando, Fla.
BL TL 5'9" 175 lbs.

Year	Team		W	L	PCT	ERA	G	GS	CG	IP	H	BB	SO	ShO	W	L	SV	AB	H	HR	BA	PO	A	E	DP	TC/G	FA
1923	PHI	A	3	0	1.000	3.60	5	2	2	25	24	13	12	0	1	0	0	9	1	0	.111	0	5	0	0	1.0	1.000
1924			5	12	.294	4.68	30	14	5	146	166	81	37	1	1	2	0	48	11	0	.229	7	28	1	2	1.2	.972
1926	CIN	N	0	2	.000	6.43	7	1	1	21	24	9	5	0	0	1	0	6	0	0	.000	0	6	0	0	0.9	1.000
3 yrs.			8	14	.364	4.73	42	17	8	192	214	103	54	1	2	3	0	63	12	0	.190	7	39	1	2	1.1	.979

Jouett Meekin
MEEKIN, JOUETT
B. Feb. 21, 1867, New Albany, Ind.   D. Dec. 14, 1944, New Albany, Ind.
BR TR 6'1" 180 lbs.

Year	Team		W	L	PCT	ERA	G	GS	CG	IP	H	BB	SO	ShO	W	L	SV	AB	H	HR	BA	PO	A	E	DP	TC/G	FA
1891	LOU	AA	10	16	.385	4.30	29	26	25	228	227	113	144	2	0	0	0	97	21	1	.216	10	38	3	3	1.7	.960
1892	2 teams		LOU N	(19G 7–10)		WAS N	(14G 3–10)																					
"	total		10	20	.333	3.79	33	32	30	268.1	280	126	125	1	0	0	0	109	11	2	.101	14	56	7	1	2.3	.909
1893	WAS	N	10	15	.400	4.96	31	28	24	245	289	140	91	1	0	0	0	113	29	3	.257	12	53	7	3	2.3	.903
1894	NY	N	33	9	.786	3.70	52	48	40	409	404	171	133	1	1	1	2	170	48	5	.282	15	60	4	3	1.5	.949
1895			16	11	.593	5.30	29	29	24	225.2	296	73	76	1	0	0	0	96	28	1	.292	10	44	5	1	2.0	.915
1896			26	14	.650	3.82	42	41	34	334.1	378	127	110	0	0	0	0	144	43	2	.299	17	62	8	3	1.9	.908
1897			20	11	.645	3.76	37	34	30	303.2	328	99	83	2	0	0	0	137	41	0	.299	14	56	11	2	2.2	.864
1898			16	18	.471	3.77	38	37	34	320	329	108	82	1	0	0	0	129	27	0	.209	18	51	9	0	2.1	.885
1899	2 teams		NY N	(18G 5–11)		BOS N	(13G 7–6)																					
"	total		12	17	.414	3.72	31	31	28	256.1	280	93	53	0	0	0	1	99	19	1	.192	7	37	5	1	1.6	.898
1900	PIT	N	0	2	.000	6.92	2	2	1	13	20	8	3	0	0	0	0	4	0	0	.000	0	0	2	0	1.0	–
10 yrs.			153	133	.535	4.07	324	308	270	2603.1	2831	1058	900	9	1	3	2	1098	267	15	.243	117	457	60	17	2.0	.905

Phil Meeler
MEELER, CHARLES PHILIP JR.
B. July 23, 1948, South Boston, Va.
BR TR 6'5" 215 lbs.

Year	Team		W	L	PCT	ERA	G	GS	CG	IP	H	BB	SO	ShO	W	L	SV	AB	H	HR	BA	PO	A	E	DP	TC/G	FA
1972	DET	A	0	1	.000	4.50	7	0	0	8	10	7	5	0	0	1	0	2	0	0	.000	1	1	0	0	0.3	1.000

Russ Meers
MEERS, RUSSELL HARLAN (Babe)
B. Nov. 28, 1918, Tilton, Ill.
BL TL 5'10" 170 lbs.

Year	Team		W	L	PCT	ERA	G	GS	CG	IP	H	BB	SO	ShO	W	L	SV	AB	H	HR	BA	PO	A	E	DP	TC/G	FA
1941	CHI	N	0	1	.000	1.13	1	1	0	8	5	0	5	0	0	0	0	2	0	0	.000	1	0	0	0	1.0	1.000
1946			1	2	.333	3.18	7	2	0	11.1	10	10	2	0	1	0	0	1	1	0	1.000	0	3	0	0	0.4	1.000
1947			2	0	1.000	4.48	35	1	0	64.1	61	38	28	0	2	0	0	14	2	0	.143	3	12	2	0	0.5	.882
3 yrs.			3	3	.500	3.98	43	4	0	83.2	76	48	35	0	3	0	0	17	3	0	.176	4	15	2	0	0.5	.905

Heinie Meine
MEINE, HENRY WILLIAM (The Count of Luxemburg)
B. May 1, 1896, St. Louis, Mo.   D. Mar. 18, 1968, St. Louis, Mo.
BR TR 5'11" 180 lbs.

Year	Team		W	L	PCT	ERA	G	GS	CG	IP	H	BB	SO	ShO	W	L	SV	AB	H	HR	BA	PO	A	E	DP	TC/G	FA
1922	STL	A	0	0	–	4.50	1	0	0	4	5	2	0	0	0	0	0	1	0	0	.000	1	2	0	0	3.0	1.000
1929	PIT	N	7	6	.538	4.50	22	13	7	108	120	34	19	1	1	1	1	39	4	0	.103	2	19	1	1	1.0	.955
1930			6	8	.429	6.14	20	16	8	117.1	168	44	18	0	0	0	1	41	5	0	.122	6	35	0	5	2.1	1.000
1931			19	13	.594	2.98	36	35	22	284	278	87	58	3	1	0	1	96	14	0	.146	15	59	4	7	2.2	.949
1932			12	9	.571	3.86	28	25	13	172.1	193	45	32	1	0	1	0	61	10	0	.164	7	35	4	3	1.6	.913
1933			15	8	.652	3.65	32	29	8	207.1	227	50	50	2	2	0	0	75	13	0	.173	11	31	1	1	1.3	.977
1934			7	6	.538	4.32	26	14	2	106.1	134	25	22	0	3	0	0	28	3	0	.107	3	19	1	0	0.9	.957
7 yrs.			66	50	.569	3.95	165	132	60	999.1	1125	287	199	7	6	2	3	341	49	0	.144	45	200	11	17	1.6	.957

Frank Meinke
MEINKE, FRANK LOUIS
Father of Bob Meinke.
B. Oct. 18, 1863, Chicago, Ill.   D. Nov. 8, 1931, Chicago, Ill.
5'10½" 172 lbs.

Year	Team		W	L	PCT	ERA	G	GS	CG	IP	H	BB	SO	ShO	W	L	SV	AB	H	HR	BA	PO	A	E	DP	TC/G	FA
1884	DET	N	8	22	.267	3.18	35	31	31	289	341	63	124	1	0	1	0	341	56	6	.164	11	47	0	3	1.7	1.000
1885			0	1	.000	3.60	1	1	0	5	13	4	0	0	0	0	0	3	0	0	.000	0	2	0	0	2.0	1.000
2 yrs.			8	23	.258	3.18	36	32	31	294	354	67	124	1	0	1	0	*				11	49	0	3	1.7	1.000

Sam Mejias
MEJIAS, SAMUEL ELIAS
B. May 9, 1952, Santiago, Dominican Republic
BR TR 6' 170 lbs.

Year	Team		W	L	PCT	ERA	G	GS	CG	IP	H	BB	SO	ShO	W	L	SV	AB	H	HR	BA	PO	A	E	DP	TC/G	FA
1978	MON	N	0	0	–	0.00	1	0	0	1	0	1	0	0	0	0	0	*				0	0	0	0	0.0	–

Steve Melter
MELTER, STEPHEN BLAZIUS
B. Jan. 2, 1886, Cherokee, Iowa   D. Jan. 28, 1962, Mishawaka, Ind.
BR TR 6'2" 180 lbs.

Year	Team		W	L	PCT	ERA	G	GS	CG	IP	H	BB	SO	ShO	W	L	SV	AB	H	HR	BA	PO	A	E	DP	TC/G	FA
1909	STL	N	0	1	.000	3.50	23	1	0	64.1	79	20	24	0	0	1	1	15	2	0	.133	5	21	0	2	1.1	1.000

Cliff Melton
MELTON, CLIFFORD GEORGE (Mountain Music)
B. Jan. 3, 1912, Brevard, N.C.   D. July 28, 1986, Baltimore, Md.
BL TL 6'5½" 203 lbs.

Year	Team		W	L	PCT	ERA	G	GS	CG	IP	H	BB	SO	ShO	W	L	SV	AB	H	HR	BA	PO	A	E	DP	TC/G	FA
1937	NY	N	20	9	.690	2.61	46	27	14	248	216	55	142	2	4	1	7	82	10	0	.122	10	68	1	3	1.7	.987

Year	Team	W	L	PCT	ERA	G	GS	CG	IP	H	BB	SO	ShO	Relief Pitching W	L	SV	Batting AB	H	HR	BA	PO	A	E	DP	TC/G	FA

Cliff Melton *continued*

Year	Team	W	L	PCT	ERA	G	GS	CG	IP	H	BB	SO	ShO	W	L	SV	AB	H	HR	BA	PO	A	E	DP	TC/G	FA
1938		14	14	.500	3.89	36	31	10	243	266	61	101	1	1	0	0	80	14	0	.175	5	64	4	1	2.0	.945
1939		12	15	.444	3.56	41	23	9	207.1	214	65	95	2	3	2	5	66	12	0	.182	6	49	4	0	1.4	.932
1940		10	11	.476	4.91	37	21	4	166.2	185	68	91	1	3	2	2	54	12	0	.222	6	38	0	4	1.2	1.000
1941		8	11	.421	3.01	42	22	9	194.1	181	61	100	3	1	1	1	61	7	0	.115	4	58	2	1	1.5	.969
1942		11	5	.688	2.63	23	17	12	143.2	122	33	61	2	0	0	1	47	11	0	.234	7	44	1	1	2.3	.981
1943		9	13	.409	3.19	34	28	6	186.1	184	69	55	2	0	1	0	54	8	0	.148	6	57	3	4	1.9	.955
1944		2	2	.500	4.06	13	10	1	64.1	78	19	15	0	0	0	0	25	3	0	.120	1	19	1	1	1.6	.952
8 yrs.		86	80	.518	3.42	272	179	65	1453.2	1446	431	660	13	12	7	16	469	77	0	.164	45	397	16	15	1.7	.965

WORLD SERIES

Year	Team	W	L	PCT	ERA	G	GS	CG	IP	H	BB	SO	ShO	W	L	SV	AB	H	HR	BA	PO	A	E	DP	TC/G	FA
1937	NY N	0	2	.000	4.91	3	2	0	11	12	6	7	0	0	0	0	2	0	0	.000	0	0	1	0	0.3	—

Rube Melton

MELTON, REUBEN FRANKLIN
B. Feb. 27, 1917, Cramerton, N. C.   D. Sept. 11, 1971, Greer, S. C.   BR TR 6'5"   205 lbs.

Year	Team	W	L	PCT	ERA	G	GS	CG	IP	H	BB	SO	ShO	W	L	SV	AB	H	HR	BA	PO	A	E	DP	TC/G	FA
1941	PHI N	1	5	.167	4.73	25	5	2	83.2	81	47	57	0	1	1	2	19	2	0	.105	0	11	2	0	0.5	.846
1942		9	20	.310	3.70	42	29	10	209.1	180	114	107	1	1	1	4	65	8	1	.123	8	33	1	2	1.0	.976
1943	BKN N	5	8	.385	3.92	30	17	4	119.1	102	79	63	2	1	1	0	38	4	0	.105	1	20	3	1	0.8	.875
1944		9	13	.409	3.46	37	23	6	187.1	178	96	91	1	2	0	0	57	7	0	.123	8	34	2	2	1.2	.955
1946		6	3	.667	1.99	24	12	3	99.2	72	52	44	2	1	1	1	28	3	0	.107	1	20	1	0	0.9	.955
1947		0	1	.000	13.50	4	1	0	4.2	7	7	1	0	0	0	0	1	1	0	1.000	0	0	0	0	0.0	—
6 yrs.		30	50	.375	3.62	162	87	25	704	620	395	363	6	6	5	5	208	25	1	.120	18	118	9	5	0.9	.938

Mario Mendoza

MENDOZA, MARIO
Born Mario Mendoza y Aizpuru.
B. Dec. 26, 1950, Chihuahua, Mexico   BR TR 5'11"   170 lbs.

Year	Team	W	L	PCT	ERA	G	GS	CG	IP	H	BB	SO	ShO	W	L	SV	AB	H	HR	BA	PO	A	E	DP	TC/G	FA
1977	PIT N	0	0	—	13.50	1	0	0	2	3	2	0	0	0	0	0	*				0	1	0	0	1.0	1.000

Mike Mendoza

MENDOZA, MICHAEL JOSEPH
B. Nov. 26, 1955, Inglewood, Calif.   BR TR 6'5"   215 lbs.

Year	Team	W	L	PCT	ERA	G	GS	CG	IP	H	BB	SO	ShO	W	L	SV	AB	H	HR	BA	PO	A	E	DP	TC/G	FA
1979	HOU N	0	0	—	0.00	1	0	0	1	0	0	0	0	0	0	0	0	0	0	—	0	0	0	0	0.0	—

Jock Menefee

MENEFEE, JOHN
B. Jan. 15, 1868, West Virginia   D. Mar. 11, 1953, Belle Vernon, Pa.   BR TR 6'

Year	Team	W	L	PCT	ERA	G	GS	CG	IP	H	BB	SO	ShO	W	L	SV	AB	H	HR	BA	PO	A	E	DP	TC/G	FA
1892	PIT N	0	0	—	11.25	1	1	0	4	10	2	0	0	0	0	0	3	0	0	.000	0	2	0	0	2.0	1.000
1893	LOU N	8	7	.533	4.24	15	15	14	129.1	150	40	30	1	0	0	0	73	20	0	.274	6	36	4	1	3.1	.913
1894	2 teams						LOU N	(28G 8–17)			PIT N	(13G 5–8)														
"	total	13	25	.342	4.68	41	37	33	323.1	417	89	76	1	0	0	0	126	25	0	.198	28	75	8	0	2.7	.928
1895	PIT N	0	1	.000	16.20	2	1	0	1.2	2	7	0	0	0	0	0	0	0	0	—	1	1	1	0	1.5	.667
1898	NY N	0	1	.000	4.82	1	1	1	9.1	11	2	3	0	0	0	0	5	0	0	.000	0	3	1	0	4.0	.750
1900	CHI N	9	4	.692	3.85	16	13	11	117	140	35	30	0	0	0	0	46	5	0	.109	3	21	3	1	1.7	.889
1901		8	13	.381	3.80	21	20	17	182.1	201	34	55	0	0	0	1	152	39	0	.257	13	44	4	0	2.9	.934
1902		12	10	.545	2.42	22	21	20	197.1	202	26	60	5	1	0	0	216	50	0	.231	13	45	3	2	2.8	.951
1903		8	8	.500	3.00	20	17	13	147	157	38	39	1	1	1	0	64	13	0	.203	13	56	8	0	3.9	.896
9 yrs.		58	69	.457	3.81	139	125	111	1111.1	1290	273	293	8	3	3	0	*				77	283	32	4	2.8	.918

Mike Meola

MEOLA, EMILE MICHAEL
B. Oct. 19, 1905, New York, N. Y.   D. Sept. 1, 1976, Fair Lawn, N. J.   BR TR 5'11"   175 lbs.

Year	Team	W	L	PCT	ERA	G	GS	CG	IP	H	BB	SO	ShO	W	L	SV	AB	H	HR	BA	PO	A	E	DP	TC/G	FA
1933	BOS A	0	0	—	23.14	3	0	0	2.1	5	2	1	0	0	0	0	0	0	0	—	0	0	0	0	0.0	—
1936	2 teams		STL A	(9G 0–1)			BOS A	(6G 0–2)																		
"	total	0	3	.000	7.30	15	3	1	40.2	58	23	14	0	0	1	1	9	2	0	.222	1	11	0	0	0.8	1.000
2 yrs.		0	3	.000	8.16	18	3	1	43	63	25	15	0	0	1	1	9	2	0	.222	1	11	0	0	0.7	1.000

Jack Mercer

MERCER, HARRY VERNON
B. Mar. 10, 1889, Zanesville, Ohio   D. June 25, 1945, Dayton, Ohio

Year	Team	W	L	PCT	ERA	G	GS	CG	IP	H	BB	SO	ShO	W	L	SV	AB	H	HR	BA	PO	A	E	DP	TC/G	FA
1910	PIT N	0	0	—	0.00	1	0	0	1	0	2	1	0	0	0	0	0	0	0	—	0	0	0	0	0.0	—

Mark Mercer

MERCER, MARK KENNETH
B. May 22, 1954, Fort Bragg, N. C.   BL TL 6'5"   220 lbs.

Year	Team	W	L	PCT	ERA	G	GS	CG	IP	H	BB	SO	ShO	W	L	SV	AB	H	HR	BA	PO	A	E	DP	TC/G	FA
1981	TEX A	0	1	.000	4.50	7	0	0	8	7	7	8	0	0	1	2	0	0	0	—	0	2	0	0	0.3	1.000

Win Mercer

MERCER, GEORGE BARCLAY
B. June 20, 1874, Chester, W. Va.   D. Jan. 12, 1903, San Francisco, Calif.   BR TR 5'7"   140 lbs.

Year	Team	W	L	PCT	ERA	G	GS	CG	IP	H	BB	SO	ShO	W	L	SV	AB	H	HR	BA	PO	A	E	DP	TC/G	FA
1894	WAS N	17	23	.425	3.76	49	38	30	333	431	125	69	0	2	1	3	162	46	2	.284	14	68	5	1	1.8	.943
1895		13	23	.361	4.46	43	38	32	311	430	96	84	0	1	1	2	196	50	1	.255	25	58	12	2	2.2	.874
1896		25	18	.581	4.13	46	45	38	366.1	456	117	94	2	1	0	0	156	38	1	.244	36	89	21	3	3.2	.856
1897		20	20	.500	3.25	45	42	34	332	395	102	88	3	0	1	2	135	43	0	.319	0	0	0	0	0.0	—
1898		12	18	.400	4.81	33	30	24	233.2	309	71	52	0	0	0	0	249	80	2	.321	14	49	10	2	2.2	.863
1899		7	14	.333	4.60	23	21	21	186	234	53	28	0	0	0	0	375	112	1	.299	9	59	3	1	3.1	.958
1900	NY N	13	17	.433	3.86	32	29	26	242.1	303	58	39	1	0	0	0	248	73	0	.294	14	67	6	3	2.7	.931
1901	WAS A	9	13	.409	4.56	24	22	19	179.2	217	50	31	1	1	0	0	140	42	0	.300	17	50	4	1	3.0	.944
1902	DET A	15	18	.455	3.04	35	33	28	281.2	282	80	40	4	0	0	1	100	18	0	.180	13	103	8	2	3.5	.935
9 yrs.		131	164	.444	3.98	330	298	252	2465.2	3057	752	525	11	3	5	9	*				142	543	69	15	2.3	.908

Kent Mercker

MERCKER, KENT FRANKLIN
B. Feb. 1, 1968, Dublin, Ohio   BL TL 6'1"   175 lbs.

Year	Team	W	L	PCT	ERA	G	GS	CG	IP	H	BB	SO	ShO	W	L	SV	AB	H	HR	BA	PO	A	E	DP	TC/G	FA
1989	ATL N	0	0	—	12.46	2	1	0	4.1	8	6	4	0	0	0	0	1	0	0	.000	0	0	0	0	0.0	—

Year	Team		W	L	PCT	ERA	G	GS	CG	IP	H	BB	SO	ShO	Relief Pitching W	L	SV	Batting AB	H	HR	BA	PO	A	E	DP	TC/G	FA

Spike Merena

MERENA, JOHN JOSEPH
B. Nov. 18, 1909, Paterson, N. J. D. Mar. 9, 1977, Bridgeport, Conn.
BL TL 6' 185 lbs.

Year	Team	W	L	PCT	ERA	G	GS	CG	IP	H	BB	SO	ShO	W	L	SV	AB	H	HR	BA	PO	A	E	DP	TC/G	FA
1934	BOS A	1	2	.333	2.92	4	3	2	24.2	20	16	7	0	0	0	0	7	1	0	.143	0	2	0	0	0.5	1.000

Ron Meridith

MERIDITH, RONALD KNOX
B. Nov. 26, 1956, San Pedro, Calif.
BL TL 6' 175 lbs.

Year	Team	W	L	PCT	ERA	G	GS	CG	IP	H	BB	SO	ShO	W	L	SV	AB	H	HR	BA	PO	A	E	DP	TC/G	FA
1984	CHI N	0	0	—	3.38	3	0	0	5.1	6	2	4	0	0	0	0	0	0	0	—	1	0	0	0	0.3	1.000
1985		3	2	.600	4.47	32	0	0	46.1	53	24	23	0	3	2	1	4	1	0	.250	0	9	0	1	0.3	1.000
1986	TEX A	1	0	1.000	3.00	5	0	0	3	2	1	2	0	1	0	0	0	0	0	—	0	2	0	0	0.4	1.000
1987		1	0	1.000	6.10	11	0	0	20.2	25	12	17	0	1	0	0	0	0	0	—	0	5	0	1	0.5	1.000
4 yrs.		5	2	.714	4.78	51	0	0	75.1	86	39	46	0	5	2	1	4	1	0	.250	1	16	0	2	0.3	1.000

George Merritt

MERRITT, GEORGE WASHINGTON
B. Apr. 14, 1880, Paterson, N. J. D. Feb. 21, 1938, Memphis, Tenn.
TR 6' 160 lbs.

Year	Team	W	L	PCT	ERA	G	GS	CG	IP	H	BB	SO	ShO	W	L	SV	AB	H	HR	BA	PO	A	E	DP	TC/G	FA
1901	PIT N	3	0	1.000	4.88	3	3	3	24	28	5	5	0	0	0	0	11	3	0	.273	1	5	0	0	2.0	1.000
1903		0	0	—	2.25	1	0	0	4	4	1	2	0	0	0	0	27	4	0	.148	1	0	0	0	1.0	1.000
2 yrs.		3	0	1.000	4.50	4	3	3	28	32	6	7	0	0	0	0	*				2	5	0	0	1.8	1.000

Jim Merritt

MERRITT, JAMES JOSEPH
B. Dec. 9, 1943, Altadena, Calif.
BL TL 6'3" 175 lbs.

Year	Team	W	L	PCT	ERA	G	GS	CG	IP	H	BB	SO	ShO	W	L	SV	AB	H	HR	BA	PO	A	E	DP	TC/G	FA
1965	MIN A	5	4	.556	3.17	16	9	3	76.2	68	20	61	0	1	1	2	22	3	0	.136	2	13	1	1	1.0	.938
1966		7	14	.333	3.38	31	18	5	144	112	33	124	1	0	3	3	39	4	0	.103	7	20	0	0	0.9	1.000
1967		13	7	.650	2.53	37	28	11	227.2	196	30	161	4	1	0	0	74	10	0	.135	4	32	3	1	1.1	.923
1968		12	16	.429	3.25	38	34	11	238.1	207	52	181	1	1	0	1	71	10	0	.141	7	38	0	2	1.2	1.000
1969	CIN N	17	9	.654	4.37	42	36	9	251	269	61	144	1	0	0	0	77	11	1	.143	7	33	1	1	1.0	.976
1970		20	12	.625	4.08	35	35	12	234	248	53	136	1	0	0	0	83	14	3	.169	5	30	2	1	1.1	.946
1971		1	11	.083	4.37	28	11	0	107	115	31	38	0	0	1	2	29	4	0	.138	1	10	1	1	0.6	.938
1972		1	0	1.000	4.50	4	1	0	8	13	2	4	0	0	1	0	2	0	0	.000	0	1	0	0	0.3	1.000
1973	TEX A	5	13	.278	4.05	35	19	8	160	191	34	65	1	0	2	1	0	0	0	—	1	22	2	1	0.9	.935
1974		0	0	—	4.09	26	1	0	33	46	6	18	0	0	0	0	0	0	0	—	1	4	3	0	0.3	.625
1975		0	0	—	0.00	5	0	0	3.2	3	0	0	0	0	0	0	0	0	0	—	0	0	0	0	0.0	—
11 yrs.		81	86	.485	3.65	297	192	56	1483.1	1468	322	932	9	5	8	7	397	56	4	.141	45	203	13	8	0.9	.950

LEAGUE CHAMPIONSHIP SERIES

Year	Team	W	L	PCT	ERA	G	GS	CG	IP	H	BB	SO	ShO	W	L	SV	AB	H	HR	BA	PO	A	E	DP	TC/G	FA
1970	CIN N	1	0	1.000	1.69	1	1	0	5.1	3	0	2	0	0	0	0	2	0	0	.000	0	2	0	0	2.0	1.000

WORLD SERIES

Year	Team	W	L	PCT	ERA	G	GS	CG	IP	H	BB	SO	ShO	W	L	SV	AB	H	HR	BA	PO	A	E	DP	TC/G	FA
1965	MIN A	0	0	—	2.70	2	0	0	3.1	2	1	1	0	0	0	0	0	0	0	—	0	2	0	0	1.0	1.000
1970	CIN N	0	1	.000	21.60	1	1	0	1.2	3	0	0	0	0	0	0	1	0	0	.000	0	0	0	0	0.0	—
2 yrs.		0	1	.000	9.00	3	1	0	5	5	1	1	0	0	0	0	1	0	0	.000	0	2	0	0	0.7	1.000

Lloyd Merritt

MERRITT, LLOYD WESLEY
B. Apr. 8, 1933, St. Louis, Mo.
BR TR 6' 189 lbs.

Year	Team	W	L	PCT	ERA	G	GS	CG	IP	H	BB	SO	ShO	W	L	SV	AB	H	HR	BA	PO	A	E	DP	TC/G	FA
1957	STL N	1	2	.333	3.31	44	0	0	65.1	60	28	35	0	1	2	7	7	0	0	.000	3	13	2	0	0.4	.889

Sam Mertes

MERTES, SAMUEL BLAIR (Sandow)
B. Aug. 6, 1872, San Francisco, Calif. D. Mar. 11, 1945, San Francisco, Calif.
BR TR 5'10" 185 lbs.

Year	Team	W	L	PCT	ERA	G	GS	CG	IP	H	BB	SO	ShO	W	L	SV	AB	H	HR	BA	PO	A	E	DP	TC/G	FA
1902	CHI A	1	0	1.000	1.17	1	0	0	7.2	6	0	0	0	1	0	0	*				0	0	0	0	0.0	—

Jim Mertz

MERTZ, JAMES VERLIN
B. Aug. 10, 1916, Lima, Ohio
BR TR 5'10½" 170 lbs.

Year	Team	W	L	PCT	ERA	G	GS	CG	IP	H	BB	SO	ShO	W	L	SV	AB	H	HR	BA	PO	A	E	DP	TC/G	FA
1943	WAS A	5	7	.417	4.63	33	10	2	116.2	109	58	53	0	2	1	3	38	7	0	.184	3	26	3	2	1.0	.906

Jose Mesa

MESA, JOSE RAMON
B. May 22, 1966, Pueblo Viejo, Dominican Republic
BR TR 6'3" 170 lbs.

Year	Team	W	L	PCT	ERA	G	GS	CG	IP	H	BB	SO	ShO	W	L	SV	AB	H	HR	BA	PO	A	E	DP	TC/G	FA
1987	BAL A	1	3	.250	6.03	6	5	0	31.1	38	15	17	0	0	0	0	0	0	0	—	1	1	0	0	0.3	1.000

Bud Messenger

MESSENGER, ANDREW WARREN
B. Feb. 1, 1898, Grand Blanc, Mich. D. Nov. 4, 1971, Lansing, Mich.
BR TR 6' 175 lbs.

Year	Team	W	L	PCT	ERA	G	GS	CG	IP	H	BB	SO	ShO	W	L	SV	AB	H	HR	BA	PO	A	E	DP	TC/G	FA
1924	CLE A	2	0	1.000	4.32	5	2	1	25	28	14	4	0	1	0	0	8	1	0	.125	0	6	0	0	1.2	1.000

Andy Messersmith

MESSERSMITH, JOHN ALEXANDER
B. Aug. 6, 1945, Toms River, N. J.
BR TR 6'1" 200 lbs.

Year	Team	W	L	PCT	ERA	G	GS	CG	IP	H	BB	SO	ShO	W	L	SV	AB	H	HR	BA	PO	A	E	DP	TC/G	FA
1968	CAL A	4	2	.667	2.21	28	5	2	81.1	44	35	74	1	2	0	4	20	2	0	.100	6	12	1	0	0.7	.947
1969		16	11	.593	2.52	40	33	10	250	169	100	211	2	0	0	2	77	12	0	.156	17	29	5	2	1.3	.902
1970		11	10	.524	3.00	37	26	6	195	144	78	162	1	3	0	5	70	11	1	.157	12	23	4	3	1.1	.897
1971		20	13	.606	2.99	38	38	14	277	224	121	179	4	0	0	0	93	16	2	.172	18	49	5	2	1.9	.931
1972		8	11	.421	2.81	25	21	10	170	125	68	142	3	0	0	2	53	10	0	.189	9	24	0	0	1.3	1.000
1973	LA N	14	10	.583	2.70	33	33	10	249.2	196	77	177	3	0	0	0	89	15	0	.169	19	35	5	0	1.8	.915
1974		20	6	.769	2.59	39	39	13	292	227	94	221	3	0	0	0	96	23	1	.240	18	44	9	3	1.8	.873
1975		19	14	.576	2.29	42	40	19	322	244	96	213	7	0	0	1	108	17	0	.157	11	43	5	1	1.4	.915
1976	ATL N	11	11	.500	3.04	29	28	12	207	166	74	135	3	0	0	0	67	12	0	.179	14	33	5	2	1.8	.904
1977		5	4	.556	4.41	16	16	1	102	101	39	69	0	0	0	0	34	4	1	.118	5	15	2	1	1.4	.909
1978	NY A	0	3	.000	5.64	6	5	0	22.1	24	15	16	0	0	0	0	0	0	0	—	2	2	0	4	0.7	1.000
1979	LA N	2	4	.333	4.94	11	11	1	62	55	34	26	0	0	0	0	22	2	0	.091	5	9	0	1	1.3	1.000
12 yrs.		130	99	.568	2.86	344	295	98	2230.1	1719	831	1625	27	5	0	15	729	124	5	.170	136	318	41	19	1.4	.917

LEAGUE CHAMPIONSHIP SERIES

Year	Team	W	L	PCT	ERA	G	GS	CG	IP	H	BB	SO	ShO	W	L	SV	AB	H	HR	BA	PO	A	E	DP	TC/G	FA
1974	LA N	1	0	1.000	2.57	1	1	1	7	8	3	0	0	0	0	0	3	0	0	.000	1	2	0	0	3.0	1.000

Year	Team	W	L	PCT	ERA	G	GS	CG	IP	H	BB	SO	ShO	Relief Pitching W	L	SV	Batting AB	H	HR	BA	PO	A	E	DP	TC/G	FA

Andy Messersmith *continued*
WORLD SERIES

| 1974 | LA | N | 0 | 2 | .000 | 4.50 | 2 | 2 | 0 | 14 | 11 | 7 | 12 | 0 | 0 | 0 | 0 | 4 | 2 | 0 | .500 | 1 | 4 | 1 | 0 | 3.0 | .833 |

Tom Metcalf
METCALF, THOMAS JOHN
B. July 16, 1940, Amherst, Wis.
BR TR 6'2½" 174 lbs.

| 1963 | NY | A | 1 | 0 | 1.000 | 2.77 | 8 | 0 | 0 | 13 | 12 | 3 | 3 | 0 | 1 | 0 | 0 | 0 | 0 | 0 | — | 0 | 2 | 0 | 0 | 0.3 | 1.000 |

Dewey Metivier
METIVIER, GEORGE DEWEY
B. May 6, 1898, Cambridge, Mass.
D. Mar. 2, 1947, Cambridge, Mass.
BB TR 5'11" 175 lbs.
BL 1922

1922	CLE	A	2	0	1.000	4.50	2	2	0	18	18	3	1	0	0	0	0	6	1	0	.167	1	2	0	0	1.5	1.000
1923			4	2	.667	6.50	26	5	1	73.1	111	38	9	0	3	1	1	20	3	0	.150	2	22	1	2	1.0	.960
1924			1	5	.167	5.31	26	6	1	76.1	110	34	14	0	1	1	3	24	3	0	.125	5	14	0	1	0.7	1.000
3 yrs.			7	7	.500	5.74	54	13	4	167.2	239	75	24	0	4	2	4	50	7	0	.140	8	38	1	3	0.9	.979

Butch Metzger
METZGER, CLARENCE EDWARD
B. May 23, 1952, Lafayette, Ind.
BR TR 6'1" 185 lbs.

1974	SF	N	1	0	1.000	3.46	10	0	0	13	11	12	5	0	1	0	0		1	1	0	—	1	1	0	0	0.2	1.000
1975	SD	N	1	0	1.000	7.20	4	0	0	5	6	4	6	0	1	0	0	0	0	0	—	0	1	0	0	0.3	1.000
1976			11	4	.733	2.92	77	0	0	123.1	119	52	89	0	11	4	16	8	0	0	.000	5	17	1	0	0.3	.957
1977	2 teams	SD N	(17G 0–0)			STL N	(58G 4–2)																					
"	total		4	2	.667	3.59	75	0	0	115.1	105	50	54	0	4	2	7	7	0	0	.000	5	12	0	1	0.2	1.000
1978	NY	N	1	3	.250	6.57	25	0	0	37	48	22	21	0	1	3	0	0	0	0	—	1	4	0	0	0.2	1.000
5 yrs.			18	9	.667	3.74	191	0	0	293.2	289	140	175	0	18	9	23	15	0	0	.000	12	35	1	1	0.3	.979

Bob Meyer
MEYER, ROBERT BERNARD
B. Aug. 4, 1939, Toledo, Ohio
BR TL 6'2" 185 lbs.

1964	3 teams	NY A	(7G 0–3)			LA A	(6G 1–1)			KC A	(9G 1–4)																	
"	total		2	8	.200	4.37	22	13	2	78.1	78	58	55	0	0	0	0	21	0	0	.000	4	10	1	1	0.7	.933
1969	SEA	A	0	3	.000	3.31	6	5	1	32.2	30	10	17	0	0	0	0	11	1	0	.091	0	3	3	0	1.0	.500
1970	MIL	A	0	1	.000	6.50	10	0	0	18	24	12	20	0	0	0	0	3	1	0	.333	0	3	0	0	0.3	1.000
3 yrs.			2	12	.143	4.40	38	18	3	129	132	80	92	0	0	2	0	35	2	0	.057	4	16	4	1	0.6	.833

Brian Meyer
MEYER, BRIAN SCOTT
B. Jan. 29, 1963, Camden, N. J.
BR TR 6'1" 190 lbs.

1988	HOU	N	0	0	—	1.46	8	0	0	12.1	9	4	10	0	0	0	0	0	0	0	—	0	5	0	0	0.6	1.000
1989			0	1	.000	4.50	12	0	0	18	16	13	13	0	0	1	1	0	0	0	—	2	2	0	0	0.3	1.000
2 yrs.			0	1	.000	3.26	20	0	0	30.1	25	17	23	0	0	1	1	0	0	0	—	2	7	0	0	0.5	1.000

Jack Meyer
MEYER, JOHN ROBERT
B. Mar. 23, 1932, Philadelphia, Pa. D. Mar. 9, 1967, Philadelphia, Pa.
BR TR 6'1" 175 lbs.

1955	PHI	N	6	11	.353	3.43	50	5	0	110.1	75	66	97	0	5	7	16	20	2	0	.100	6	13	1	0	0.4	.950
1956			7	11	.389	4.41	41	7	2	96	86	51	66	0	6	6	2	20	4	1	.200	4	17	1	2	0.5	.955
1957			0	2	.000	5.73	19	2	0	37.2	44	28	34	0	0	2	0	6	1	0	.167	5	6	0	0	0.6	1.000
1958			3	6	.333	3.59	37	5	1	90.1	77	33	87	0	3	2	2	18	5	0	.278	4	7	1	1	0.3	.917
1959			5	3	.625	3.36	47	1	1	93.2	76	53	71	0	5	2	1	14	1	0	.071	4	14	1	2	0.4	.947
1960			3	1	.750	4.32	7	4	0	25	25	11	18	0	1	0	0	8	1	0	.125	1	4	0	0	0.7	1.000
1961			0	0	—	9.00	1	0	0	2	2	2	2	0	0	0	0	0	0	0	—	0	0	0	0	0.0	—
7 yrs.			24	34	.414	3.92	202	24	4	455	385	244	375	0	20	19	21	86	14	1	.163	24	61	4	5	0.4	.955

Russ Meyer
MEYER, RUSSELL CHARLES (The Mad Monk)
B. Oct. 25, 1923, Peru, Ill.
BB TR 6'1" 175 lbs.

1946	CHI	N	0	0	—	3.18	4	1	0	17	21	10	10	0	0	0	0	5	1	0	.200	0	4	0	0	1.0	1.000
1947			3	2	.600	3.40	23	2	1	45	43	14	22	0	3	1	0	12	3	0	.250	1	6	0	0	0.3	1.000
1948			10	10	.500	3.66	29	26	8	164.2	157	77	89	3	0	2	0	56	6	0	.107	12	26	1	0	1.3	.974
1949	PHI	N	17	8	.680	3.08	37	28	14	213	199	70	78	2	2	1	1	70	10	0	.143	14	28	1	3	1.2	.977
1950			9	11	.450	5.30	32	25	3	159.2	193	67	74	0	0	1	0	50	7	0	.140	8	31	0	4	1.2	1.000
1951			8	9	.471	3.48	28	24	7	168	172	55	65	2	0	1	0	48	5	0	.104	5	21	1	1	1.0	.963
1952			13	14	.481	3.14	37	32	14	232.1	235	65	92	1	0	1	0	79	7	1	.089	8	37	4	6	1.3	.918
1953	BKN	N	15	5	.750	4.56	34	32	10	191.1	201	63	106	2	1	0	0	75	11	0	.147	8	33	3	1	1.3	.932
1954			11	6	.647	3.99	36	28	6	180.1	193	49	70	0	0	0	0	47	2	0	.043	5	27	3	0	1.0	.914
1955			6	2	.750	5.42	18	11	2	73	86	31	26	1	1	1	0	27	1	0	.037	1	21	0	1	1.2	1.000
1956	2 teams	CHI N	(20G 1–6)			CIN N	(1G 0–0)																					
"	total		1	6	.143	6.21	21	9	0	58	72	26	29	0	0	0	0	12	1	0	.083	4	18	0	2	1.0	1.000
1957	BOS	A	0	0	—	5.40	2	1	0	5	10	3	1	0	0	0	0	1	1	0	1.000	0	4	0	0	2.0	1.000
1959	KC	A	1	0	1.000	4.50	18	0	0	24	24	11	10	0	1	0	1	2	0	0	.000	2	2	0	0	0.2	1.000
13 yrs.			94	73	.563	3.99	319	219	65	1531.1	1606	541	672	13	7	10	5	484	55	1	.114	68	258	13	18	1.1	.962

WORLD SERIES

1950	PHI	N	0	1	.000	5.40	2	0	0	1.2	4	0	1	0	0	0	0	0	0	0	—	0	1	0	0	0.5	1.000
1953	BKN	N	0	0	—	6.23	1	0	0	4.1	8	4	5	0	0	0	0	1	0	0	.000	0	1	0	0	1.0	1.000
1955			0	0	—	0.00	1	0	0	5.2	4	2	4	0	0	0	0	2	0	0	.000	0	1	0	0	1.0	1.000
3 yrs.			0	1	.000	3.09	4	0	0	11.2	16	6	10	0	0	0	0	3	0	0	.000	0	3	0	0	0.8	1.000

Levi Meyerle
MEYERLE, LEVI SAMUEL (Long Levi)
B. July, 1845, Philadelphia, Pa. D. Nov. 4, 1921, Philadelphia, Pa.
BR TR 6'1" 177 lbs.

| 1876 | PHI | N | 0 | 2 | .000 | 5.00 | 2 | 2 | 2 | 18 | 28 | 1 | 0 | 0 | 0 | 0 | 0 | * | | | | 3 | 1 | 0 | 0 | 2.0 | 1.000 |

Year	Team	W	L	PCT	ERA	G	GS	CG	IP	H	BB	SO	ShO	W	L	SV	AB	H	HR	BA	PO	A	E	DP	TC/G	FA

Gene Michael
MICHAEL, EUGENE RICHARD (Stick)
B. June 2, 1938, Kent, Ohio
Manager 1981-82, 1986-87.
BB TR 6'2" 183 lbs.

Year	Team	W	L	PCT	ERA	G	GS	CG	IP	H	BB	SO	ShO	W	L	SV	AB	H	HR	BA	PO	A	E	DP	TC/G	FA
1968	NY A	0	0	–	0.00	1	0	0	3	5	0	3	0	0	0	0	*				1	0	0	0	1.0	1.000

John Michaels
MICHAELS, JOHN JOSEPH
B. July 10, 1907, Bridgeport, Conn.
BL TL 5'10½" 154 lbs.

Year	Team	W	L	PCT	ERA	G	GS	CG	IP	H	BB	SO	ShO	W	L	SV	AB	H	HR	BA	PO	A	E	DP	TC/G	FA
1932	BOS A	1	6	.143	5.13	28	8	2	80.2	101	27	16	0				21	3	0	.143	5	24	3	1	1.1	.906

John Michaelson
MICHAELSON, JOHN AUGUST (Mike)
B. Aug. 12, 1893, Tivalkoski, Finland D. Apr. 16, 1968, Woodruff, Wis.
BR TR 5'9" 165 lbs.

Year	Team	W	L	PCT	ERA	G	GS	CG	IP	H	BB	SO	ShO	W	L	SV	AB	H	HR	BA	PO	A	E	DP	TC/G	FA
1921	CHI A	0	0	–	10.13	2	0	0	2.2	4	1	1	0	0	0	0	0	0	0	–	0	0	0	0	0.0	–

Glenn Mickens
MICKENS, GLENN ROGER
B. July 26, 1930, Wilmar, Calif.
BR TR 6' 175 lbs.

Year	Team	W	L	PCT	ERA	G	GS	CG	IP	H	BB	SO	ShO	W	L	SV	AB	H	HR	BA	PO	A	E	DP	TC/G	FA
1953	BKN N	0	1	.000	11.37	4	2	0	6.1	11	4	5	0	0	0	0	2	0	0	.000	0	2	1	0	0.8	.667

Jim Middleton
MIDDLETON, JAMES BLAINE (Rifle Jim)
B. May 28, 1889, Argos, Ind. D. Jan. 12, 1974, Argos, Ind.
BR TR 5'11½" 165 lbs.

Year	Team	W	L	PCT	ERA	G	GS	CG	IP	H	BB	SO	ShO	W	L	SV	AB	H	HR	BA	PO	A	E	DP	TC/G	FA
1917	NY N	1	1	.500	2.75	13	0	0	36	35	8	9	0	1	1	1	8	0	0	.000	2	13	0	0	1.2	1.000
1921	DET A	6	11	.353	5.03	38	10	2	121.2	149	44	31	0	4	8	7	34	5	0	.147	9	38	2	0	1.3	.959
2 yrs.		7	12	.368	4.51	51	10	2	157.2	184	52	40	0	5	9	8	42	5	0	.119	11	51	2	0	1.3	.969

John Middleton
MIDDLETON, JOHN WAYNE (Lefty)
B. Apr. 11, 1900, Mt. Calm, Tex. D. Nov. 3, 1986, Amarillo, Tex.
BL TL 6'1" 185 lbs.

Year	Team	W	L	PCT	ERA	G	GS	CG	IP	H	BB	SO	ShO	W	L	SV	AB	H	HR	BA	PO	A	E	DP	TC/G	FA
1922	CLE A	0	1	.000	7.36	2	1	0	7.1	8	6	2	0	0	0	0	3	1	0	.333	0	2	0	0	1.0	1.000

Dick Midkiff
MIDKIFF, RICHARD JAMES
B. Sept. 28, 1914, Gonzales, Tex. D. Oct. 30, 1956, Temple, Tex.
BR TR 6'2" 195 lbs.

Year	Team	W	L	PCT	ERA	G	GS	CG	IP	H	BB	SO	ShO	W	L	SV	AB	H	HR	BA	PO	A	E	DP	TC/G	FA
1938	BOS A	1	1	.500	5.09	13	2	0	35.1	43	21	10	0	0	0	0	10	2	0	.200	2	7	0	0	0.7	1.000

Gary Mielke
MIELKE, GARY ROGER
B. Jan. 28, 1963, St. James, Minn.
BR TR 6'3" 185 lbs.

Year	Team	W	L	PCT	ERA	G	GS	CG	IP	H	BB	SO	ShO	W	L	SV	AB	H	HR	BA	PO	A	E	DP	TC/G	FA
1987	TEX A	0	0	–	6.00	3	0	0	3	3	1	3	0	0	0	0	0	0	0	–	0	0	0	0	0.0	–
1989		1	0	1.000	3.26	43	0	0	49.2	52	25	26	0	1	0	1	0	0	0	–	3	6	1	0	0.2	.900
2 yrs.		1	0	1.000	3.42	46	0	0	52.2	55	26	29	0	1	0	1	0	0	0	–	3	6	1	0	0.2	.900

Pete Mikkelsen
MIKKELSEN, PETER JAMES
B. Oct. 25, 1939, Staten Island, N. Y.
BR TR 6'2" 210 lbs.

Year	Team	W	L	PCT	ERA	G	GS	CG	IP	H	BB	SO	ShO	W	L	SV	AB	H	HR	BA	PO	A	E	DP	TC/G	FA
1964	NY A	7	4	.636	3.56	50	0	0	86	79	41	63	0	7	4	12	16	1	0	.063	9	17	0	1	0.5	1.000
1965		4	9	.308	3.28	41	3	0	82.1	78	36	69	0	4	6	1	10	1	0	.100	5	20	4	1	0.7	.862
1966	PIT N	9	8	.529	3.07	71	0	0	126	106	51	76	0	9	8	14	20	3	0	.150	7	20	1	0	0.4	.964
1967	2 teams	PIT N	(32G 1–2)		CHI N	(7G 0–0)																				
"	total	1	2	.333	4.55	39	0	0	63.1	59	24	30	0	1	2	2	4	0	0	.000	3	6	2	0	0.3	.818
1968	2 teams	CHI N	(3G 0–0)		STL N	(5G 0–0)																				
"	total	0	0	–	2.61	8	0	0	20.2	17	8	13	0	0	0	0	4	1	0	.250	0	3	2	0	0.6	.600
1969	LA N	7	5	.583	2.78	48	0	0	81	57	30	51	0	7	5	4	6	1	0	.167	7	17	2	0	0.5	1.000
1970		4	2	.667	2.76	33	0	0	62	48	20	47	0	4	2	6	6	2	0	.333	5	10	0	0	0.5	1.000
1971		8	5	.615	3.65	41	0	0	74	67	17	46	0	8	5	5	10	2	0	.200	1	9	1	0	0.6	.917
1972		5	5	.500	4.06	33	0	0	57.2	65	23	41	0	5	5	5	7	0	0	.000	1	9	1	0	0.3	.909
9 yrs.		45	40	.529	3.38	364	3	0	653	576	250	436	0	45	37	49	83	11	0	.133	46	115	14	2	0.5	.920

WORLD SERIES

Year	Team	W	L	PCT	ERA	G	GS	CG	IP	H	BB	SO	ShO	W	L	SV	AB	H	HR	BA	PO	A	E	DP	TC/G	FA
1964	NY A	0	1	.000	5.79	4	0	0	4.2	4	2	4	0	0	1	0	2	0	0	–	0	2	0	0	0.5	1.000

John Miklos
MIKLOS, JOHN JOSEPH (Hank)
B. Nov. 27, 1910, Chicago, Ill.
BL TL 5'11" 185 lbs.

Year	Team	W	L	PCT	ERA	G	GS	CG	IP	H	BB	SO	ShO	W	L	SV	AB	H	HR	BA	PO	A	E	DP	TC/G	FA
1944	CHI N	0	0	–	7.71	2	0	0	7	9	3	0	0	0	0	0	2	0	0	.000	0	4	0	0	2.0	1.000

Bob Milacki
MILACKI, ROBERT
B. July 28, 1964, Trenton, N. J.
BR TR 6'4" 220 lbs.

Year	Team	W	L	PCT	ERA	G	GS	CG	IP	H	BB	SO	ShO	W	L	SV	AB	H	HR	BA	PO	A	E	DP	TC/G	FA
1988	BAL A	2	0	1.000	0.72	3	3	1	25	9	9	18	1	0	0	0	0	0	0	–	4	3	0	1	2.3	1.000
1989		14	12	.538	3.74	37	36	3	243	233	88	113	2	0	0	0	0	0	0	–	27	28	2	5	1.5	.965
2 yrs.		16	12	.571	3.46	40	39	4	268	242	97	131	3	0	0	0	0	0	0	–	31	31	2	6	1.6	.969

Carl Miles
MILES, CARL THOMAS
B. Mar. 22, 1918, Trenton, Mo.
BB TL 5'11" 178 lbs.

Year	Team	W	L	PCT	ERA	G	GS	CG	IP	H	BB	SO	ShO	W	L	SV	AB	H	HR	BA	PO	A	E	DP	TC/G	FA
1940	PHI A	0	0	–	13.50	2	0	0	8	9	8	6	0	0	0	0	4	3	0	.750	0	1	0	0	0.5	1.000

Jim Miles
MILES, JAMES CHARLIE
B. Aug. 8, 1943, Grenada, Miss.
BR TR 6'2" 210 lbs.

Year	Team	W	L	PCT	ERA	G	GS	CG	IP	H	BB	SO	ShO	W	L	SV	AB	H	HR	BA	PO	A	E	DP	TC/G	FA
1968	WAS A	0	0	–	12.46	3	0	0	4.1	8	2	5	0	0	0	0	0	0	0	–	0	0	0	0	0.0	1.000
1969		0	1	.000	6.20	10	1	0	20.1	19	15	15	0	0	0	0	3	1	0	.333	2	5	1	0	0.7	1.000
2 yrs.		0	1	.000	7.30	13	1	0	24.2	27	17	20	0	0	0	0	3	1	0	.333	2	5	1	0	0.5	1.000

Johnny Miljus
MILJUS, JOHN KENNETH (Big Serb)
B. June 30, 1895, Pittsburgh, Pa. D. Feb. 11, 1976, Polson, Mont.
BR TR 6'1" 178 lbs.

Year	Team	W	L	PCT	ERA	G	GS	CG	IP	H	BB	SO	ShO	W	L	SV	AB	H	HR	BA	PO	A	E	DP	TC/G	FA
1915	PIT F	0	0	–	0.00	1	0	0	1	0	1	0	0	0	0	0	0	0	0	–	0	1	0	0	1.0	1.000
1917	BKN N	0	1	.000	0.60	4	1	1	15	14	8	9	0	0	0	0	5	0	0	.000	0	4	2	0	1.5	.667

Year	Team	W	L	PCT	ERA	G	GS	CG	IP	H	BB	SO	ShO	Relief Pitching W	L	SV	Batting AB	H	HR	BA	PO	A	E	DP	TC/G	FA

Johnny Miljus *continued*

Year	Team	W	L	PCT	ERA	G	GS	CG	IP	H	BB	SO	ShO	W	L	SV	AB	H	HR	BA	PO	A	E	DP	TC/G	FA
1920		1	0	1.000	3.09	9	0	0	23.1	24	4	9	0	1	0	0	6	2	0	.333	0	9	0	1	1.0	1.000
1921		6	3	.667	4.23	28	9	3	93.2	115	27	37	0	2	0	1	30	5	0	.167	4	33	1	1	1.4	.974
1927	PIT N	8	3	.727	1.90	19	6	3	75.2	62	17	24	2	4	1	0	28	5	0	.179	4	23	0	2	1.4	1.000
1928	2 teams	PIT N	(21G 5–7)		CLE A	(11G 1–4)																				
"	total	6	11	.353	4.19	32	14	4	120.1	136	53	45	0	3	2	0	41	11	0	.268	5	25	1	1	1.0	.968
1929	CLE A	8	8	.500	5.19	34	15	4	128.1	174	64	42	0	4	1	2	43	11	0	.256	9	28	3	1	1.2	.925
7 yrs.		29	26	.527	3.92	127	45	15	457.1	526	173	166	2	14	4	5	153	34	0	.222	22	123	7	6	1.2	.954

WORLD SERIES

Year	Team	W	L	PCT	ERA	G	GS	CG	IP	H	BB	SO	ShO	W	L	SV	AB	H	HR	BA	PO	A	E	DP	TC/G	FA
1927	PIT N	0	1	.000	1.35	2	0	0	6.2	4	4	6	0	0	1	0	2	0	0	.000	1	2	0	0	1.5	1.000

Bill Miller

MILLER, WILLIAM FRANCIS (Wild Bill)
B. Apr. 12, 1910, Hannibal, Mo.   D. Feb. 26, 1982, Hannibal, Mo.   BR TR 6'   180 lbs.

Year	Team	W	L	PCT	ERA	G	GS	CG	IP	H	BB	SO	ShO	W	L	SV	AB	H	HR	BA	PO	A	E	DP	TC/G	FA
1937	STL A	0	1	.000	13.50	1	1	0	4	7	4	1	0	0	0	0	1	0	0	.000	0	1	0	0	1.0	1.000

Bill Miller

MILLER, WILLIAM PAUL (Hooks)
B. July 26, 1927, Minersville, Pa.   BL TL 6'   175 lbs.

Year	Team	W	L	PCT	ERA	G	GS	CG	IP	H	BB	SO	ShO	W	L	SV	AB	H	HR	BA	PO	A	E	DP	TC/G	FA
1952	NY A	4	6	.400	3.48	21	13	5	88	78	49	45	2	0	1	0	28	6	0	.214	2	15	1	0	0.9	.944
1953		2	1	.667	4.76	13	3	0	34	46	19	17	0	1	0	1	10	2	0	.200	1	10	0	0	0.8	1.000
1954		0	1	.000	6.35	2	1	0	5.2	9	1	6	0	0	0	0	1	0	0	.000	0	0	0	0	0.0	—
1955	BAL A	0	1	.000	13.50	5	1	0	4	3	10	4	0	0	0	0	1	1	0	1.000	0	1	0	0	0.2	1.000
4 yrs.		6	9	.400	4.24	41	18	5	131.2	136	79	72	2	1	1	1	40	9	0	.225	3	26	1	0	0.7	.967

Bob Miller

MILLER, ROBERT GERALD
B. July 15, 1935, Berwyn, Ill.   BR TL 6'1"   185 lbs.

Year	Team	W	L	PCT	ERA	G	GS	CG	IP	H	BB	SO	ShO	W	L	SV	AB	H	HR	BA	PO	A	E	DP	TC/G	FA
1953	DET A	1	2	.333	5.94	13	1	0	36.1	43	21	9	0	0	0	0	8	1	0	.125	5	7	0	0	0.9	1.000
1954		1	1	.500	2.45	32	1	0	69.2	62	26	27	0	1	1	1	15	2	0	.133	4	9	1	0	0.4	.929
1955		2	1	.667	2.49	7	3	1	25.1	26	12	11	0	0	0	0	9	2	0	.222	1	3	0	0	0.6	1.000
1956		0	2	.000	5.68	11	3	0	31.2	37	22	16	0	0	0	0	7	1	0	.143	2	3	2	1	0.6	.714
1962	2 teams	CIN N	(6G 0–0)		NY N	(17G 2–2)																				
"	total	2	2	.500	10.17	23	0	0	25.2	38	11	12	0	2	2	0	2	0	0	.000	2	4	0	1	0.3	1.000
5 yrs.		6	8	.429	4.72	86	8	1	188.2	206	92	75	0	4	4	1	41	6	0	.146	14	26	3	2	0.5	.930

Bob Miller

MILLER, ROBERT JOHN
B. June 16, 1926, Detroit, Mich.   BR TR 6'3"   190 lbs.

Year	Team	W	L	PCT	ERA	G	GS	CG	IP	H	BB	SO	ShO	W	L	SV	AB	H	HR	BA	PO	A	E	DP	TC/G	FA
1949	PHI N	0	0	–	0.00	3	0	0	2.2	2	2	0	0	0	0	0	0	0	0	–	0	1	0	0	0.3	1.000
1950		11	6	.647	3.57	35	21	7	174	190	57	44	2	0	0	1	61	11	0	.180	15	40	0	2	1.6	1.000
1951		2	1	.667	6.82	17	3	0	34.1	47	18	10	0	1	1	0	7	3	0	.429	1	3	0	0	0.2	1.000
1952		0	1	.000	6.00	3	1	0	9	13	1	2	0	0	0	0	1	0	0	.000	1	3	0	0	1.3	1.000
1953		8	9	.471	4.00	35	20	8	157.1	169	42	63	3	2	1	2	55	10	0	.182	8	24	0	3	0.9	1.000
1954		7	9	.438	4.56	30	16	5	150	176	39	42	0	4	1	0	50	8	1	.160	13	31	2	4	1.5	.957
1955		8	4	.667	2.41	40	0	0	89.2	80	28	28	0	8	4	1	18	5	0	.278	3	17	0	1	0.5	1.000
1956		3	6	.333	3.24	49	6	3	122.1	115	34	53	1	1	4	5	22	2	0	.091	9	19	0	1	0.6	1.000
1957		2	5	.286	2.69	32	1	0	60.1	61	17	12	0	2	5	6	8	2	1	.250	4	7	0	2	0.3	1.000
1958		1	1	.500	11.69	17	0	0	22.1	36	9	9	0	1	1	0	1	0	0	.000	1	3	0	0	0.2	1.000
10 yrs.		42	42	.500	3.96	261	68	23	822	889	247	263	6	19	17	15	223	41	2	.184	55	148	2	13	0.8	.990

WORLD SERIES

Year	Team	W	L	PCT	ERA	G	GS	CG	IP	H	BB	SO	ShO	W	L	SV	AB	H	HR	BA	PO	A	E	DP	TC/G	FA
1950	PHI N	0	1	.000	27.00	1	1	0	.1	2	0	0	0	0	0	0	0	0	0	–	0	0	0	0	0.0	–

Bob Miller

MILLER, ROBERT LANE
B. Feb. 18, 1939, St. Louis, Mo.   BR TR 6'1"   180 lbs.

Year	Team	W	L	PCT	ERA	G	GS	CG	IP	H	BB	SO	ShO	W	L	SV	AB	H	HR	BA	PO	A	E	DP	TC/G	FA
1957	STL N	0	0	–	7.00	5	0	0	9	13	5	7	0	0	0	0	0	0	0	–	1	2	0	0	0.6	1.000
1959		4	3	.571	3.31	11	10	3	70.2	66	21	43	0	0	0	0	24	5	0	.208	6	16	0	1	2.0	1.000
1960		4	3	.571	3.42	15	7	0	52.2	53	17	33	0	1	0	0	14	2	0	.143	3	11	0	0	0.9	1.000
1961		1	3	.250	4.24	34	5	0	74.1	82	46	39	0	1	1	3	14	5	0	.357	2	18	3	3	0.7	.870
1962	NY N	1	12	.077	4.89	33	21	1	143.2	146	62	91	0	0	1	0	41	5	0	.122	14	32	2	3	1.5	.958
1963	LA N	10	8	.556	2.89	42	23	2	187	171	65	125	0	4	2	0	57	4	0	.070	15	54	2	5	1.7	.972
1964		7	7	.500	2.62	74	2	0	137.2	115	63	94	0	6	7	9	19	3	0	.158	8	36	1	2	0.6	.978
1965		6	7	.462	2.97	61	6	0	103	82	26	77	0	6	6	9	16	0	0	.000	2	29	4	0	0.6	.886
1966		4	2	.667	2.77	46	0	0	84.1	70	29	58	0	4	2	5	13	1	0	.077	3	10	5	1	0.4	.722
1967		2	9	.182	4.31	52	4	0	85.2	88	27	32	0	2	6	0	8	1	0	.125	6	21	3	1	0.6	.900
1968	MIN A	0	3	.000	2.74	45	0	0	72.1	65	24	41	0	0	3	6	7	1	0	.143	3	15	0	2	0.4	1.000
1969		5	5	.500	3.02	48	11	1	119.1	118	32	57	0	0	4	3	31	0	0	.000	7	25	0	0	0.7	1.000
1970	3 teams	CLE A	(15G 2–2)		CHI N	(7G 0–0)		CHI A	(15G 4–6)																	
"	total	6	8	.429	4.79	37	15	0	107	129	54	55	0	2	0	3	28	5	0	.179	7	22	0	2	0.8	1.000
1971	3 teams	CHI N	(2G 0–0)		SD N	(38G 7–3)		PIT N	(16G 1–2)																	
"	total	8	5	.615	1.64	56	0	0	98.2	83	40	51	0	8	5	10	12	0	0	.000	10	11	0	2	0.4	1.000
1972	PIT N	5	2	.714	2.65	36	0	0	54.1	58	24	18	0	5	2	4	4	0	0	.000	2	8	1	1	0.3	.909
1973	3 teams	DET A	(22G 4–2)		SD N	(18G 0–0)		NY N	(1G 0–0)																	
"	total	4	2	.667	3.67	41	0	0	73.2	63	34	39	0	4	2	1	9	1	0	.000	4	7	0	1	0.3	1.000
1974	NY N	2	2	.500	3.58	58	0	0	78	89	39	35	0	2	2	2	9	1	0	.111	2	7	0	0	0.2	1.000
17 yrs.		69	81	.460	3.37	694	99	7	1551.1	1487	608	895	0	45	43	52	299	33	0	.110	100	329	21	26	0.6	.953

LEAGUE CHAMPIONSHIP SERIES

Year	Team	W	L	PCT	ERA	G	GS	CG	IP	H	BB	SO	ShO	W	L	SV	AB	H	HR	BA	PO	A	E	DP	TC/G	FA
1969	MIN A	0	1	.000	5.40	1	1	0	1.2	5	0	0	0	0	0	0	0	0	0	–	0	0	0	0	0.0	–
1971	PIT N	0	0	–	6.00	3	0	0	3	3	3	3	0	0	0	0	1	0	0	.000	1	0	0	0	1.0	1.000
1972		0	0	–	0.00	1	0	0	1	0	0	1	0	0	0	0	0	0	0	–	0	0	0	0	0.0	–
3 yrs.		0	1	.000	4.76	3	1	0	5.2	8	3	4	0	0	0	0	1	0	0	.000	1	0	0	0	0.3	1.000

WORLD SERIES

Year	Team	W	L	PCT	ERA	G	GS	CG	IP	H	BB	SO	ShO	W	L	SV	AB	H	HR	BA	PO	A	E	DP	TC/G	FA
1965	LA N	0	0	–	0.00	2	0	0	1.1	1	0	1	0	0	0	0	0	0	0	–	0	0	0	0	0.0	–
1966		0	0	–	0.00	1	0	0	3	2	2	1	0	0	0	0	0	0	0	–	0	1	0	0	1.0	1.000

Year	Team	W	L	PCT	ERA	G	GS	CG	IP	H	BB	SO	ShO	Relief Pitching W	L	SV	Batting AB	H	HR	BA	PO	A	E	DP	TC/G	FA

Bob Miller *continued*

Year	Team	W	L	PCT	ERA	G	GS	CG	IP	H	BB	SO	ShO	W	L	SV	AB	H	HR	BA	PO	A	E	DP	TC/G	FA
1971	PIT N	0	1	.000	3.86	3	0	0	4.2	7	1	2	0	0	0	0	0	0	0	–	1	1	0	0	0.7	1.000
3 yrs.		0	1	.000	2.00	6	0	0	9	9	3	3	0	0	0	0	0	0	0	–	1	2	0	0	0.5	1.000

Bob Miller

MILLER, ROBERT W.
B. 1862 Deceased.

Year	Team	W	L	PCT	ERA	G	GS	CG	IP	H	BB	SO	ShO	W	L	SV	AB	H	HR	BA	PO	A	E	DP	TC/G	FA
1890	ROC AA	3	7	.300	4.29	13	12	11	92.1	89	26	20	0	0	0	1	40	6	0	.150	0	22	2	0	1.8	.917
1891	WAS AA	2	5	.286	4.29	7	7	3	42	53	24	13	0	0	0	0	18	2	0	.111	3	13	2	0	2.6	.889
2 yrs.		5	12	.294	4.29	20	19	14	134.1	142	50	33	0	0	0	1	58	8	0	.138	3	35	4	0	2.1	.905

Burt Miller

MILLER, BURT
B. Kalamazoo, Mich. Deceased.

Year	Team	W	L	PCT	ERA	G	GS	CG	IP	H	BB	SO	ShO	W	L	SV	AB	H	HR	BA	PO	A	E	DP	TC/G	FA
1897	LOU N	0	1	.000	7.94	4	1	1	17	32	3	3	0	0	0	0	6	1	0	.167	1	4	0	0	1.3	1.000

Cyclone Miller

MILLER, JOSEPH H.   TL 5'9½" 165 lbs.
B. Sept. 24, 1859, Springfield, Mass. D. Oct. 13, 1916, New London, Conn.

Year	Team	W	L	PCT	ERA	G	GS	CG	IP	H	BB	SO	ShO	W	L	SV	AB	H	HR	BA	PO	A	E	DP	TC/G	FA
1884	3 teams	CHI U (1G 1–0)			PRO N	(6G 2–2)			PHI N	(1G 0–1)																
"	total	3	3	.500	3.25	8	7	4	52.2	57	17	26	0	0	0	1	31	2	0	.065	0	13	0	0	1.6	1.000
1886	PHI AA	10	8	.556	2.97	19	19	19	169.2	158	59	99	1	0	0	0	66	9	0	.136	4	38	0	1	2.2	1.000
2 yrs.		13	11	.542	3.04	27	26	23	222.1	215	76	125	1	0	0	1	97	11	0	.113	4	51	0	1	2.0	1.000

Dyar Miller

MILLER, DYAR K   BR TR 6'1" 195 lbs.
B. May 29, 1946, Batesville, Ind.

Year	Team	W	L	PCT	ERA	G	GS	CG	IP	H	BB	SO	ShO	W	L	SV	AB	H	HR	BA	PO	A	E	DP	TC/G	FA
1975	BAL A	6	3	.667	2.72	30	0	0	46.1	32	16	33	0	6	3	8	0	0	0	–	1	8	1	0	0.3	.900
1976		2	4	.333	2.93	49	0	0	89	79	36	37	0	2	4	7	0	0	0	–	1	10	2	1	0.3	.846
1977	2 teams	BAL A	(12G 2–2)		CAL A	(41G 4–4)																				
"	total	6	6	.500	3.53	53	0	0	114.2	106	40	58	0	6	6	5	0	0	0	–	9	11	0	1	0.4	1.000
1978	CAL A	6	2	.750	2.66	41	0	0	84.2	85	41	34	0	6	2	1	0	0	0	–	6	4	1	0	0.3	.909
1979	2 teams	CAL A	(14G 1–0)		TOR A	(10G 0–0)																				
"	total	1	0	1.000	5.58	24	1	0	50	71	18	23	0	1	0	0	0	0	0	–	4	3	0	0	0.3	1.000
1980	NY N	1	2	.333	1.93	31	0	0	42	37	11	28	0	1	2	1	1	0	0	.000	0	4	2	1	0.2	.667
1981		1	0	1.000	3.32	23	0	0	38	49	15	22	0	1	0	0	3	1	0	.333	2	2	1	0	0.2	.800
7 yrs.		23	17	.575	3.23	251	1	0	464.2	459	177	235	0	23	17	22	4	1	0	.250	23	42	7	4	0.3	.903

Elmer Miller

MILLER, ELMER JOSEPH   BL TL 5'11" 189 lbs.
B. Apr. 17, 1904, Detroit, Mich. D. Jan. 8, 1987, Corona, Calif.

Year	Team	W	L	PCT	ERA	G	GS	CG	IP	H	BB	SO	ShO	W	L	SV	AB	H	HR	BA	PO	A	E	DP	TC/G	FA
1929	PHI N	0	1	.000	11.12	8	2	0	11.1	12	21	5	0	0	0	0	*				1	2	1	0	0.5	.750

Frank Miller

MILLER, FRANK LEE (Bullet)   BR TR 6' 188 lbs.
B. Mar. 13, 1886, Allegan, Mich. D. Feb. 19, 1974, Allegan, Mich.

Year	Team	W	L	PCT	ERA	G	GS	CG	IP	H	BB	SO	ShO	W	L	SV	AB	H	HR	BA	PO	A	E	DP	TC/G	FA
1913	CHI A	0	1	.000	27.00	1	1	0	1.2	4	3	2	0	0	0	0	0	0	0	–	0	1	0	0	1.0	1.000
1916	PIT N	7	10	.412	2.29	30	20	10	173	135	49	88	2	2	0	1	51	7	0	.137	3	44	3	0	1.7	.940
1917		10	19	.345	3.13	38	28	14	224	216	60	92	5	1	2	1	76	9	0	.118	4	69	1	0	1.9	.986
1918		11	8	.579	2.38	23	23	14	170.1	152	37	47	2	0	0	0	57	6	0	.105	2	53	3	1	2.5	.948
1919		13	12	.520	3.03	32	26	16	201.2	170	34	59	3	0	0	0	66	7	0	.106	10	63	2	0	2.3	.973
1922	BOS N	11	13	.458	3.51	31	23	14	200	213	60	65	2	2	1	1	68	8	0	.118	4	51	3	0	1.9	.948
1923		0	3	.000	4.58	8	6	0	39.1	54	11	6	0	0	1	0	7	1	0	.143	1	5	0	0	0.8	1.000
7 yrs.		52	66	.441	3.01	163	127	68	1010	944	254	359	14	3	5	4	325	38	0	.117	24	286	12	3	2.0	.963

Fred Miller

MILLER, FREDERICK HOLMAN (Speedy)   BL TL 6'2" 190 lbs.
B. June 28, 1886, Fairfield, Ind. D. May 2, 1953, Brookville, Ind.

Year	Team	W	L	PCT	ERA	G	GS	CG	IP	H	BB	SO	ShO	W	L	SV	AB	H	HR	BA	PO	A	E	DP	TC/G	FA
1910	BKN N	1	1	.500	4.71	6	2	0	21	25	13	2	0	0	0	0	8	2	0	.250	0	9	0	0	1.5	1.000

Jake Miller

MILLER, JACOB WALTER   BL TL 6'2" 170 lbs.
Brother of Russ Miller.
B. Feb. 28, 1898, Wagram, Ohio D. Aug. 20, 1975, Venice, Fla.

Year	Team	W	L	PCT	ERA	G	GS	CG	IP	H	BB	SO	ShO	W	L	SV	AB	H	HR	BA	PO	A	E	DP	TC/G	FA
1924	CLE A	0	1	.000	3.00	2	2	1	12	13	5	4	0	0	0	0	5	0	0	.000	1	3	1	1	2.5	.800
1925		10	13	.435	3.31	32	22	13	190.1	207	62	51	0	2	2	2	71	13	0	.183	22	43	3	1	2.1	.956
1926		7	4	.636	3.27	18	11	5	82.2	99	18	24	3	2	0	1	24	2	0	.083	8	16	0	0	1.3	1.000
1927		10	8	.556	3.21	34	23	11	185.1	189	48	53	0	0	1	0	58	8	0	.138	9	48	3	2	1.8	.950
1928		8	9	.471	4.44	25	23	8	158	203	43	37	0	0	0	0	52	7	0	.135	11	39	1	2	2.0	.980
1929		14	12	.538	3.58	29	29	14	206	227	60	58	2	0	0	0	75	15	0	.200	15	47	5	3	2.3	.925
1930		4	5	.444	7.13	24	9	1	88.1	147	38	31	0	2	0	0	33	10	0	.303	10	26	5	1	1.7	.878
1931		2	1	.667	4.35	10	5	1	41.1	45	19	17	1	1	0	0	13	1	0	.077	5	11	1	0	1.7	.941
1933	CHI A	5	6	.455	5.62	26	14	4	105.2	130	47	30	2	0	0	0	37	7	0	.189	2	31	3	1	1.4	.917
9 yrs.		60	59	.504	4.09	200	138	58	1069.2	1260	340	305	8	7	4	3	368	63	0	.171	83	264	22	11	1.8	.940

John Miller

MILLER, JOHN ERNEST   BR TR 6'2" 210 lbs.
B. May 30, 1941, Baltimore, Md.

Year	Team	W	L	PCT	ERA	G	GS	CG	IP	H	BB	SO	ShO	W	L	SV	AB	H	HR	BA	PO	A	E	DP	TC/G	FA
1962	BAL A	1	1	.500	0.90	2	1	0	10	2	5	4	0	1	0	0	3	0	0	.000	0	3	0	0	1.5	1.000
1963		1	1	.500	3.18	3	2	0	17	12	14	16	0	0	0	0	6	0	0	.000	1	0	0	0	1.0	1.000
1965		6	4	.600	3.18	16	16	1	93.1	75	58	71	0	0	0	0	30	3	0	.100	4	17	2	1	1.4	.913
1966		4	8	.333	4.74	23	16	0	100.2	92	58	81	0	2	1	0	34	4	0	.118	8	16	0	2	1.0	1.000
1967		0	0	–	7.50	2	0	0	6	7	3	6	0	0	0	0	0	0	0	–	1	0	0	0	0.5	1.000
5 yrs.		12	14	.462	3.89	46	35	1	227	188	138	178	0	3	1	0	73	7	0	.096	14	38	2	3	1.2	.963

Ken Miller

MILLER, KENNETH ALBERT (Whitey)   BR TR 6'1" 195 lbs.
B. May 2, 1915, St. Louis, Mo.

Year	Team	W	L	PCT	ERA	G	GS	CG	IP	H	BB	SO	ShO	W	L	SV	AB	H	HR	BA	PO	A	E	DP	TC/G	FA
1944	NY N	0	1	.000	0.00	4	0	0	5	1	4	2	0	0	1	0	1	0	0	.000	1	1	0	0	0.8	.667

Year	Team		W	L	PCT	ERA	G	GS	CG	IP	H	BB	SO	ShO	Relief Pitching W	L	SV	Batting AB	H	HR	BA	PO	A	E	DP	TC/G	FA

Larry Miller

MILLER, LARRY DON
B. June 19, 1937, Topeka, Kans.   BL TL 6'   195 lbs.

Year	Team		W	L	PCT	ERA	G	GS	CG	IP	H	BB	SO	ShO	W	L	SV	AB	H	HR	BA	PO	A	E	DP	TC/G	FA
1964	LA	N	4	8	.333	4.18	16	14	1	79.2	87	28	50	0	1	0	0	26	7	0	.269	3	12	0	0	0.9	1.000
1965	NY	N	1	4	.200	5.02	28	5	0	57.1	66	25	36	0	1	0	0	11	2	0	.182	4	9	3	0	0.6	.813
1966			0	2	.000	7.56	4	1	0	8.1	9	4	7	0	0	1	0	2	1	0	.500	0	0	0	0	0.0	–
3 yrs.			5	14	.263	4.71	48	20	1	145.1	162	57	93	0	2	1	0	39	10	0	.256	7	21	3	0	0.6	.903

Ox Miller

MILLER, JOHN ANTHONY
B. May 4, 1915, Gause, Tex.   BR TR 6'1"   190 lbs.

Year	Team		W	L	PCT	ERA	G	GS	CG	IP	H	BB	SO	ShO	W	L	SV	AB	H	HR	BA	PO	A	E	DP	TC/G	FA
1943	2 teams	WAS A (3G 0–0)					STL A	(2G 0–0)																			
"	total		0	0	–	11.25	5	0	0	12	17	8	4	0	0	0	0	2	0	0	.000	2	7	0	0	1.8	1.000
1945	STL	A	2	1	.667	1.59	4	3	3	28.1	23	5	4	0	0	0	0	11	2	0	.182	0	2	1	0	0.8	.667
1946			1	3	.250	6.88	11	3	0	35.1	52	15	12	0	0	0	1	7	2	0	.286	7	7	0	1	1.3	1.000
1947	CHI	N	1	2	.333	10.13	4	4	1	16	31	5	7	0	0	0	0	7	3	1	.429	1	1	0	0	0.5	1.000
4 yrs.			4	6	.400	6.38	24	10	4	91.2	123	33	27	0	0	0	1	27	7	1	.259	10	17	1	1	1.2	.964

Ralph Miller

MILLER, RALPH DARWIN
B. Mar. 15, 1873, Cincinnati, Ohio   D. Cincinnati, Ohio   BR TR 5'11"   170 lbs.

Year	Team		W	L	PCT	ERA	G	GS	CG	IP	H	BB	SO	ShO	W	L	SV	AB	H	HR	BA	PO	A	E	DP	TC/G	FA
1898	BKN	N	4	14	.222	5.34	23	21	16	151.2	161	86	43	0	1	0	0	62	12	0	.194	9	49	5	0	2.7	.921
1899	BAL	N	1	3	.250	4.76	5	4	3	34	42	13	3	0	1	0	0	11	2	0	.182	0	7	2	0	1.8	.778
2 yrs.			5	17	.227	5.24	28	25	19	185.2	203	99	46	0	2	0	0	73	14	0	.192	9	56	7	0	2.6	.903

Ralph Miller

MILLER, RALPH HENRY (Lefty)
Brother of Bing Miller.
B. Jan. 14, 1899, Vinton, Iowa   D. Feb. 18, 1967, White Bear Lake, Minn.   BR TL 6'1½"   190 lbs.

Year	Team		W	L	PCT	ERA	G	GS	CG	IP	H	BB	SO	ShO	W	L	SV	AB	H	HR	BA	PO	A	E	DP	TC/G	FA
1921	WAS	A	0	0	–	0.00	1	0	0	1	0	0	0	0	0	0	0	0	0	0	–	0	0	0	0	0.0	–

Randy Miller

MILLER, RANDALL SCOTT
B. Mar. 18, 1953, Oxnard, Calif.   BR TR 6'1"   180 lbs.

Year	Team		W	L	PCT	ERA	G	GS	CG	IP	H	BB	SO	ShO	W	L	SV	AB	H	HR	BA	PO	A	E	DP	TC/G	FA
1977	BAL	A	0	0	–	27.00	1	0	0	1	4	0	0	0	0	0	0	0	0	0	–	0	0	0	0	0.0	–
1978	MON	N	0	1	.000	10.29	5	0	0	7	11	3	6	0	0	1	0	1	0	0	.000	0	2	1	0	0.6	.667
2 yrs.			0	1	.000	12.38	6	0	0	8	15	3	6	0	0	1	0	1	0	0	.000	0	2	1	0	0.5	.667

Red Miller

MILLER, LEO ALPHONSO
B. Feb. 11, 1897, Philadelphia, Pa.   D. Oct. 20, 1973, Orlando, Fla.   BR TR 5'11"   195 lbs.

Year	Team		W	L	PCT	ERA	G	GS	CG	IP	H	BB	SO	ShO	W	L	SV	AB	H	HR	BA	PO	A	E	DP	TC/G	FA
1923	PHI	N	0	0	–	32.40	1	0	0	1.2	6	1	0	0	0	0	0	1	0	0	.000	0	0	0	0	0.0	–

Roger Miller

MILLER, ROGER WESLEY
B. Aug. 1, 1954, Connellsville, Pa.   BR TR 6'3"   200 lbs.

Year	Team		W	L	PCT	ERA	G	GS	CG	IP	H	BB	SO	ShO	W	L	SV	AB	H	HR	BA	PO	A	E	DP	TC/G	FA
1974	MIL	A	0	0	–	13.50	2	0	0	2	3	1	0	2	0	0	0	0	0	0	–	0	0	0	0	0.0	–

Ronnie Miller

MILLER, RONALD ARTHUR
B. Aug. 28, 1918, Mason City, Iowa   BB TR 5'11"   167 lbs.

Year	Team		W	L	PCT	ERA	G	GS	CG	IP	H	BB	SO	ShO	W	L	SV	AB	H	HR	BA	PO	A	E	DP	TC/G	FA
1941	WAS	A	0	0	–	4.50	1	0	0	2	2	1	0	0	0	0	0	0	0	0	–	0	0	0	0	0.0	–

Roscoe Miller

MILLER, ROSCOE CLYDE (Roxy, Rubberlegs)
B. Dec. 2, 1876, Greenville, Ind.   D. Apr. 18, 1913, Corydon, Ind.   BR TR 6'2"   190 lbs.

Year	Team		W	L	PCT	ERA	G	GS	CG	IP	H	BB	SO	ShO	W	L	SV	AB	H	HR	BA	PO	A	E	DP	TC/G	FA
1901	DET	A	23	13	.639	2.95	38	36	35	332	339	98	79	3	1	0	1	130	27	0	.208	19	112	5	4	3.6	.963
1902	2 teams	DET A (20G 6–12)					NY N	(10G 1–8)																			
"	total		7	20	.259	3.98	30	27	22	221.1	235	68	54	1	0	0	1	81	12	0	.148	21	53	4	4	2.6	.949
1903	NY	N	2	5	.286	4.13	15	8	6	85	101	24	30	0	0	0	3	31	5	0	.161	8	17	2	1	1.8	.926
1904	PIT	N	7	8	.467	3.35	19	17	11	134.1	133	39	35	2	0	0	0	46	2	0	.043	2	34	2	0	2.0	.947
4 yrs.			39	46	.459	3.45	102	88	74	772.2	808	229	198	6	1	0	5	288	46	0	.160	50	216	13	9	2.7	.953

Russ Miller

MILLER, RUSSELL LEWIS
Brother of Jake Miller.
B. Mar. 25, 1900, Etna, Ohio   D. Apr. 30, 1962, Bucyrus, Ohio   BR TR 5'11"   165 lbs.

Year	Team		W	L	PCT	ERA	G	GS	CG	IP	H	BB	SO	ShO	W	L	SV	AB	H	HR	BA	PO	A	E	DP	TC/G	FA
1927	PHI	N	1	1	.500	5.28	2	2	1	15.1	21	3	4	0	0	0	0	3	1	0	.333	0	3	0	0	1.5	1.000
1928			0	12	.000	5.42	33	12	1	108	137	34	19	0	0	3	1	27	4	0	.148	6	27	1	0	1.0	.971
2 yrs.			1	13	.071	5.40	35	14	2	123.1	158	37	23	0	0	3	1	30	5	0	.167	6	30	1	0	1.1	.973

Stu Miller

MILLER, STUART LEONARD
B. Dec. 26, 1927, Northampton, Mass.   BR TR 5'11½"   165 lbs.

Year	Team		W	L	PCT	ERA	G	GS	CG	IP	H	BB	SO	ShO	W	L	SV	AB	H	HR	BA	PO	A	E	DP	TC/G	FA
1952	STL	N	6	3	.667	2.05	12	11	6	88	63	26	64	2	1	0	0	25	3	0	.120	12	24	1	2	3.1	.973
1953			7	8	.467	5.56	40	18	8	137.2	161	47	79	2	0	1	4	43	8	0	.186	22	38	3	4	1.6	.952
1954			2	3	.400	5.79	19	4	0	46.2	55	29	22	0	1	2	2	13	4	0	.308	8	16	1	3	1.3	.960
1956	2 teams	STL N (3G 0–1)					PHI N	(24G 5–8)																			
"	total		5	9	.357	4.50	27	15	2	114	121	56	60	0	2	1	1	26	4	0	.154	9	19	0	1	1.0	1.000
1957	NY	N	7	9	.438	3.63	38	13	0	124	110	45	60	0	6	3	1	35	2	0	.057	12	34	1	6	1.0	.973
1958	SF	N	6	9	.400	2.47	41	20	4	182	160	49	119	1	0	3	0	50	6	0	.120	9	34	1	4	1.1	.977
1959			8	7	.533	2.84	59	9	2	167.2	164	57	95	0	7	4	8	45	2	0	.044	15	40	2	1	1.0	.965
1960			7	6	.538	3.90	47	3	2	101.2	100	31	65	0	5	5	2	25	5	0	.200	5	22	2	2	0.7	.938
1961			14	5	.737	2.66	63	0	0	122	95	37	89	0	14	5	17	20	4	0	.200	10	29	0	1	0.6	1.000
1962			5	8	.385	4.12	59	0	0	107	107	42	78	0	5	8	19	16	2	0	.125	6	17	0	1	0.4	1.000
1963	BAL	A	5	8	.385	2.24	71	0	0	112.1	93	53	114	0	5	8	27	16	5	0	.313	7	22	1	1	0.4	.967
1964			7	7	.500	3.06	66	0	0	97	77	34	87	0	7	7	23	9	1	0	.111	2	16	2	2	0.4	.920
1965			14	7	.667	1.89	67	0	0	119.1	87	32	104	0	14	7	24	16	1	0	.063	18	16	0	2	0.5	1.000
1966			9	4	.692	2.25	51	0	0	92	65	22	67	0	9	4	18	19	2	0	.105	5	11	0	1	0.3	1.000
1967			3	10	.231	2.55	42	0	0	81.1	63	36	60	0	3	10	8	11	0	0	.000	6	10	0	0	0.4	1.000

Year	Team	W	L	PCT	ERA	G	GS	CG	IP	H	BB	SO	ShO	W	L	SV	AB	H	HR	BA	PO	A	E	DP	TC/G	FA

Stu Miller *continued*

Year	Team	W	L	PCT	ERA	G	GS	CG	IP	H	BB	SO	ShO	W	L	SV	AB	H	HR	BA	PO	A	E	DP	TC/G	FA
1968	ATL N	0	0	–	54.00	2	0	0	.2	1	4	1	0	0	0	0	0	0	0	–	0	1	0	0	0.5	1.000
16 yrs.		105	103	.505	3.24	704	93	24	1693.1	1522	600	1164	5	79	67	154	369	49	0	.133	152	341	14	35	0.7	.972

WORLD SERIES

Year	Team	W	L	PCT	ERA	G	GS	CG	IP	H	BB	SO	ShO	W	L	SV	AB	H	HR	BA	PO	A	E	DP	TC/G	FA
1962	SF N	0	0	–	0.00	2	0	0	1.1	1	2	0	0	0	0	0	0	0	0	–	0	1	0	0	0.5	1.000

Walt Miller

MILLER, WALTER W.
B. Oct. 19, 1884, Gas City, Ind.   D. Mar. 1, 1956, Marion, Ind.

BR TR 5'11½" 180 lbs.

Year	Team	W	L	PCT	ERA	G	GS	CG	IP	H	BB	SO	ShO	W	L	SV	AB	H	HR	BA	PO	A	E	DP	TC/G	FA
1911	BKN N	0	1	.000	6.55	3	2	0	11	16	6	0	0	0	0	0	4	0	0	.000	0	2	0	1	0.7	1.000

Billy Milligan

MILLIGAN, WILLIAM JOSEPH
B. Aug. 19, 1878, Buffalo, N. Y.   D. Oct. 14, 1928, Buffalo, N. Y.

BR TL 5'7"

Year	Team	W	L	PCT	ERA	G	GS	CG	IP	H	BB	SO	ShO	W	L	SV	AB	H	HR	BA	PO	A	E	DP	TC/G	FA
1901	PHI A	0	3	.000	4.36	6	3	2	33	43	14	5	0	0	1	0	15	5	1	.333	1	8	0	0	1.5	1.000
1904	NY N	0	1	.000	5.40	5	1	1	25	36	4	6	0	0	0	2	9	1	0	.111	1	7	1	0	1.8	.889
2 yrs.		0	4	.000	4.81	11	4	3	58	79	18	11	0	0	1	2	24	6	1	.250	2	15	1	0	1.6	.944

Jocko Milligan

MILLIGAN, JOHN
B. Aug. 8, 1861, Philadelphia, Pa.   D. Aug. 29, 1923, Philadelphia, Pa.

BR TR 6'   195 lbs.

Year	Team	W	L	PCT	ERA	G	GS	CG	IP	H	BB	SO	ShO	W	L	SV	AB	H	HR	BA	PO	A	E	DP	TC/G	FA
1890	PHI P	0	0	–	0.00	1	0	0	0	0	0	0	0	0	0	0	*				0	0	0	0	0.0	–

John Milligan

MILLIGAN, JOHN ALEXANDER
B. Jan. 22, 1904, Schuylerville, N. Y.   D. May 15, 1972, Fort Pierce, Fla.

BR TL 5'10"   172 lbs.

Year	Team	W	L	PCT	ERA	G	GS	CG	IP	H	BB	SO	ShO	W	L	SV	AB	H	HR	BA	PO	A	E	DP	TC/G	FA
1928	PHI N	2	5	.286	4.37	13	7	3	68	69	32	22	0	0	1	0	20	1	0	.050	4	20	2	0	2.0	.923
1929		0	1	.000	16.76	8	3	0	9.2	29	10	2	0	0	1	0	3	1	0	.333	0	4	0	0	0.5	1.000
1930		1	2	.333	3.18	9	2	1	28.1	26	21	7	0	0	1	0	9	1	0	.111	3	11	0	1	1.6	1.000
1931		0	0	–	3.38	3	0	0	8	11	4	6	0	0	0	0	2	0	0	.000	0	0	0	0	0.0	–
1934	WAS A	0	0	–	10.13	2	0	0	2.2	6	0	1	0	0	0	0	0	0	0	–	0	1	0	0	0.5	1.000
5 yrs.		3	8	.273	5.17	35	12	4	116.2	141	67	38	0	0	3	0	34	3	0	.088	7	36	2	1	1.3	.956

Bob Milliken

MILLIKEN, ROBERT FOGLE (Bobo)
B. Aug. 25, 1926, Majorsville, W. Va.

BR TR 6'   195 lbs.

Year	Team	W	L	PCT	ERA	G	GS	CG	IP	H	BB	SO	ShO	W	L	SV	AB	H	HR	BA	PO	A	E	DP	TC/G	FA
1953	BKN N	8	4	.667	3.37	37	10	3	117.2	94	42	65	0	5	2	2	34	4	0	.118	3	11	0	1	0.4	1.000
1954		5	2	.714	4.02	24	3	0	62.2	58	18	25	0	5	0	2	17	3	0	.176	3	5	0	1	0.3	1.000
2 yrs.		13	6	.684	3.59	61	13	3	180.1	152	60	90	0	10	2	4	51	7	0	.137	6	16	0	2	0.4	1.000

WORLD SERIES

Year	Team	W	L	PCT	ERA	G	GS	CG	IP	H	BB	SO	ShO	W	L	SV	AB	H	HR	BA	PO	A	E	DP	TC/G	FA
1953	BKN N	0	0	–	0.00	1	0	0	2	2	1	0	0	0	0	0	0	0	0	–	0	0	0	0	0.0	–

Art Mills

MILLS, ARTHUR GRANT
Son of Willie Mills.
B. Mar. 2, 1903, Utica, N. Y.   D. July 23, 1975, Utica, N. Y.

BR TR 5'10"   155 lbs.

Year	Team	W	L	PCT	ERA	G	GS	CG	IP	H	BB	SO	ShO	W	L	SV	AB	H	HR	BA	PO	A	E	DP	TC/G	FA
1927	BOS N	0	1	.000	3.82	15	1	0	37.2	41	18	7	0	0	1	0	7	0	0	.000	6	12	0	0	1.2	1.000
1928		0	0	–	12.91	4	0	0	7.2	17	8	0	0	0	0	0	1	0	0	.000	1	1	0	0	0.5	1.000
2 yrs.		0	1	.000	5.36	19	1	0	45.1	58	26	7	0	0	1	0	8	0	0	.000	7	13	0	0	1.1	1.000

Dick Mills

MILLS, RICHARD ALAN
B. Jan. 29, 1945, Boston, Mass.

BR TR 6'3"   195 lbs.

Year	Team	W	L	PCT	ERA	G	GS	CG	IP	H	BB	SO	ShO	W	L	SV	AB	H	HR	BA	PO	A	E	DP	TC/G	FA
1970	BOS A	0	0	–	2.25	2	0	0	4	6	3	3	0	0	0	0	0	0	0	–	0	1	1	0	1.0	.500

Lefty Mills

MILLS, HOWARD ROBINSON
B. May 12, 1910, Dedham, Mass.   D. Sept. 23, 1982, Riverside, Calif.

BL TL 6'1"   187 lbs.

Year	Team	W	L	PCT	ERA	G	GS	CG	IP	H	BB	SO	ShO	W	L	SV	AB	H	HR	BA	PO	A	E	DP	TC/G	FA
1934	STL A	0	0	–	4.15	4	0	0	8.2	10	11	2	0	0	0	0	3	1	0	.333	0	1	0	0	0.3	1.000
1937		1	1	.500	6.39	2	2	1	12.2	16	10	10	0	0	0	0	5	0	0	.000	0	3	1	0	2.0	.750
1938		10	12	.455	5.31	30	27	15	210.1	216	116	134	1	0	0	0	66	6	0	.091	4	28	5	1	1.2	.865
1939		4	11	.267	6.55	34	14	4	144.1	147	113	103	0	2	2	2	47	11	1	.234	2	20	3	0	0.7	.880
1940		0	6	.000	7.78	26	5	1	59	64	52	18	0	0	1	0	13	2	0	.154	3	13	1	1	0.7	.941
5 yrs.		15	30	.333	6.06	96	48	21	435	453	302	267	1	2	3	2	134	20	1	.149	9	65	10	2	0.9	.881

Willie Mills

MILLS, WILLIAM GRANT (Wee Willie)
Father of Art Mills.
B. Aug. 15, 1877, Schenevus, N. Y.   D. July 5, 1914, Norwood, N. Y.

BR TR 5'7"   150 lbs.

Year	Team	W	L	PCT	ERA	G	GS	CG	IP	H	BB	SO	ShO	W	L	SV	AB	H	HR	BA	PO	A	E	DP	TC/G	FA
1901	NY N	0	2	.000	8.44	2	2	2	16	21	4	3	0	0	0	0	6	1	0	.167	1	2	0	0	1.5	1.000

Al Milnar

MILNAR, ALBERT JOSEPH (Happy)
B. Dec. 26, 1913, Cleveland, Ohio

BL TL 6'2"   195 lbs.

Year	Team	W	L	PCT	ERA	G	GS	CG	IP	H	BB	SO	ShO	W	L	SV	AB	H	HR	BA	PO	A	E	DP	TC/G	FA
1936	CLE A	1	2	.333	7.36	4	3	1	22	26	18	9	0	0	0	0	10	3	0	.300	0	5	1	1	1.5	.833
1938		3	1	.750	5.00	23	5	2	68.1	90	26	29	0	2	0	1	26	4	1	.154	2	12	0	2	0.6	1.000
1939		14	12	.538	3.79	37	26	12	209	212	99	76	2	2	1	3	79	20	0	.253	6	37	0	1	1.2	1.000
1940		18	10	.643	3.27	37	33	15	242.1	242	99	99	4	0	0	3	94	17	0	.181	2	26	4	2	0.9	.875
1941		12	19	.387	4.36	35	30	9	229.1	236	116	82	1	0	3	0	82	14	2	.171	10	29	1	3	1.1	.975
1942		6	8	.429	4.13	28	19	8	157	146	85	35	2	1	0	0	70	12	1	.171	5	38	1	3	1.6	.977
1943	2 teams	CLE A	(16G 1-3)		STL A	(3G 1-2)																				
"	total	2	5	.286	7.38	19	8	1	53.2	74	44	19	0	1	1	0	25	6	0	.240	4	13	0	0	0.9	1.000
1946	2 teams	STL A	(4G 1-1)		PHI N	(1G 0-0)																				
"	total	1	1	.500	4.91	5	3	1	14.2	17	8	1	0	0	0	0	4	3	0	.750	0	3	0	0	0.6	1.000
8 yrs.		57	58	.496	4.22	188	127	49	996.1	1043	495	350	10	6	5	7	390	79	4	.203	29	163	7	12	1.1	.965

Year	Team	W	L	PCT	ERA	G	GS	CG	IP	H	BB	SO	ShO	W	L	SV	AB	H	HR	BA	PO	A	E	DP	TC/G	FA
														Relief Pitching			**Batting**									

George Milstead

MILSTEAD, GEORGE EARL (Cowboy)
B. Sept. 26, 1903, Cleburne, Tex.   D. Aug. 9, 1977, Cleburne, Tex.   BL TL 5'10"   144 lbs.

Year	Team	W	L	PCT	ERA	G	GS	CG	IP	H	BB	SO	ShO	W	L	SV	AB	H	HR	BA	PO	A	E	DP	TC/G	FA
1924	CHI N	1	1	.500	6.07	13	2	1	29.2	41	13	6	0	0	0	0	6	1	0	.167	1	9	0	0	0.8	1.000
1925		1	1	.500	3.00	5	3	1	21	26	8	7	0	0	0	0	7	0	0	.000	0	5	0	2	1.0	1.000
1926		1	5	.167	3.58	18	4	0	55.1	63	24	14	0	1	2	2	19	1	0	.053	5	24	1	2	1.7	.967
3 yrs.		3	7	.300	4.16	36	9	2	106	130	45	27	0	1	2	2	32	2	0	.063	6	38	1	4	1.3	.978

Larry Milton

MILTON, SAMUEL LAWRENCE
B. May 4, 1879, Owensboro, Ky.   D. May 16, 1942, Tulsa, Okla.   TR

Year	Team	W	L	PCT	ERA	G	GS	CG	IP	H	BB	SO	ShO	W	L	SV	AB	H	HR	BA	PO	A	E	DP	TC/G	FA
1903	STL N	0	0	—	2.25	1	0	0	4	3	1	0	0	0	0	0	2	1	0	.500	0	3	0	0	3.0	1.000

Cotton Minahan

MINAHAN, EDMUND JOSEPH
B. Dec. 10, 1882, Springfield, Ohio   D. May 20, 1958, East Orange, N. J.   BR TR 6'   190 lbs.

Year	Team	W	L	PCT	ERA	G	GS	CG	IP	H	BB	SO	ShO	W	L	SV	AB	H	HR	BA	PO	A	E	DP	TC/G	FA
1907	CIN N	0	2	.000	1.29	2	2	1	14	12	13	4	0	0	0	0	5	0	0	.000	0	2	1	0	1.5	.667

Rudy Minarcin

MINARCIN, RUDY ANTHONY (Buster)
B. Mar. 25, 1930, North Vandergrift, Pa.   BR TR 6'   195 lbs.

Year	Team	W	L	PCT	ERA	G	GS	CG	IP	H	BB	SO	ShO	W	L	SV	AB	H	HR	BA	PO	A	E	DP	TC/G	FA
1955	CIN N	5	9	.357	4.90	41	12	3	115.2	116	51	45	1	2	1	1	28	5	0	.179	8	28	1	2	0.9	.973
1956	BOS A	1	0	1.000	2.79	3	1	0	9.2	9	8	5	0	1	0	0	2	1	0	.500	0	3	0	0	1.0	1.000
1957		0	0		4.43	26	0	0	44.2	44	30	20	0	0	0	2	2	0	0	.000	2	7	0	1	0.3	1.000
3 yrs.		6	9	.400	4.66	70	13	3	170	169	89	70	1	3	1	3	32	6	0	.188	10	38	1	3	0.7	.980

Ray Miner

MINER, RAYMOND THEODORE (Lefty)
B. Apr. 4, 1897, Glen Falls, N. Y.   D. Sept. 15, 1963, Glen Ridge, N. Y.   BR TL 5'11"   160 lbs.

Year	Team	W	L	PCT	ERA	G	GS	CG	IP	H	BB	SO	ShO	W	L	SV	AB	H	HR	BA	PO	A	E	DP	TC/G	FA
1921	PHI A	0	0	—	36.00	1	0	0	1	2	3	0	0	0	0	0	0	0	0	—	0	0	0	0	0.0	—

Craig Minetto

MINETTO, CRAIG STEPHEN
B. Apr. 25, 1954, Stockton, Calif.   BL TL 6'   185 lbs.

Year	Team	W	L	PCT	ERA	G	GS	CG	IP	H	BB	SO	ShO	W	L	SV	AB	H	HR	BA	PO	A	E	DP	TC/G	FA
1978	OAK A	0	0	—	3.75	4	1	0	12	13	7	3	0	0	0	0	0	0	0	—	2	1	0	0	0.8	1.000
1979		1	5	.167	5.57	36	13	0	118	131	58	64	0	0	0	0	0	0	0	—	4	10	0	0	0.4	1.000
1980		0	2	.000	7.88	7	1	0	8	11	3	5	0	0	1	1	0	0	0	—	0	0	0	0	0.0	—
1981		0	0	—	2.57	8	0	0	7	7	4	4	0	0	0	0	0	0	0	—	0	0	0	0	0.0	—
4 yrs.		1	7	.125	5.40	55	15	0	145	162	72	76	0	0	1	1	0	0	0	—	6	11	0	0	0.3	1.000

Steve Mingori

MINGORI, STEPHEN BERNARD
B. Feb. 29, 1944, Kansas City, Mo.   BL TL 5'10"   165 lbs.

Year	Team	W	L	PCT	ERA	G	GS	CG	IP	H	BB	SO	ShO	W	L	SV	AB	H	HR	BA	PO	A	E	DP	TC/G	FA
1970	CLE A	1	0	1.000	2.70	21	0	0	20	17	12	16	0	1	0	1	1	0	0	.000	3	3	1	0	0.3	.857
1971		1	2	.333	1.42	54	0	0	57	31	24	45	0	1	2	4	2	1	0	.500	2	12	0	1	0.3	1.000
1972		0	6	.000	3.95	41	0	0	57	67	36	47	0	0	6	10	8	1	0	.125	4	11	1	0	0.4	.938
1973	2 teams	CLE A	(5G 0–0)		KC A	(19G 3–3)																				
"	total	3	3	.500	3.57	24	1	0	68	69	33	50	0	3	2	1	0	0	0	—	5	10	0	0	0.6	1.000
1974	KC A	2	3	.400	2.82	36	0	0	67	53	23	43	0	2	3	2	0	0	0	—	6	16	0	3	0.6	1.000
1975		0	3	.000	2.52	36	0	0	50	42	20	25	0	0	3	2	1	0	0	.000	3	9	2	2	0.4	.857
1976		5	5	.500	2.33	55	0	0	85	73	25	38	0	5	5	10	0	0	0	—	9	24	0	1	0.6	1.000
1977		2	4	.333	3.09	43	0	0	64	59	19	19	0	2	4	4	0	0	0	—	3	14	1	1	0.4	.944
1978		1	4	.200	2.74	45	0	0	69	64	16	28	0	1	4	7	0	0	0	—	3	13	1	0	0.4	.941
1979		3	3	.500	5.74	30	1	0	47	69	17	18	0	3	2	1	0	0	0	—	6	4	2	0	0.4	.833
10 yrs.		18	33	.353	3.04	385	2	0	584	544	225	329	0	18	31	42	12	2	0	.167	44	116	8	11	0.4	.952

LEAGUE CHAMPIONSHIP SERIES

Year	Team	W	L	PCT	ERA	G	GS	CG	IP	H	BB	SO	ShO	W	L	SV	AB	H	HR	BA	PO	A	E	DP	TC/G	FA
1976	KC A	0	0	—	2.70	3	0	0	3.1	4	0	1	0	0	0	0	0	0	0	—	0	0	0	0	0.0	—
1977		0	0	—	0.00	3	0	0	1.1	0	0	1	0	0	0	0	0	0	0	—	0	0	0	0	0.0	—
1978		0	0	—	7.36	1	0	0	3.2	5	3	0	0	0	0	1	0	0	0	—	0	0	0	0	0.0	—
3 yrs.		0	0	—	4.32	7	0	0	8.1	9	3	2	0	0	0	1	0	0	0	—	0	0	0	0	0.0	—

Paul Minner

MINNER, PAUL EDISON (Lefty)
B. July 30, 1923, New Wilmington, Pa.   BL TL 6'5"   200 lbs.

Year	Team	W	L	PCT	ERA	G	GS	CG	IP	H	BB	SO	ShO	W	L	SV	AB	H	HR	BA	PO	A	E	DP	TC/G	FA
1946	BKN N	0	1	.000	6.75	3	0	0	4	6	3	3	0	0	1	0	0	0	0	—	0	1	0	0	0.3	—
1948		4	3	.571	2.44	28	2	0	62.2	61	26	23	0	3	3	1	21	4	0	.190	2	14	1	2	0.6	.941
1949		3	1	.750	3.80	27	1	0	47.1	49	18	17	0	3	1	2	14	3	0	.214	2	11	1	0	0.5	.929
1950	CHI N	8	13	.381	4.11	39	24	9	190.1	217	72	99	1	0	0	4	65	14	1	.215	12	45	2	4	1.5	.966
1951		6	17	.261	3.79	33	28	11	201.2	219	64	68	3	0	0	1	71	18	1	.254	10	53	1	6	1.9	.984
1952		14	9	.609	3.74	28	27	12	180.2	180	54	61	2	0	0	0	64	15	1	.234	15	40	1	3	2.0	.982
1953		12	15	.444	4.21	31	27	9	201	227	40	64	2	2	0	1	68	15	1	.221	11	56	3	2	2.3	.957
1954		11	11	.500	3.96	32	29	12	218	236	50	79	0	0	1	1	76	13	2	.171	15	42	1	6	1.8	.983
1955		9	9	.500	3.48	22	22	7	157.2	173	47	53	1	0	0	0	56	13	0	.232	4	39	1	3	2.0	.977
1956		2	5	.286	6.89	10	9	1	47	60	19	14	0	0	0	0	12	3	0	.250	4	10	1	0	1.5	.933
10 yrs.		69	84	.451	3.94	253	169	64	1310.1	1428	393	481	9	8	6	10	447	98	6	.219	75	310	13	26	1.6	.967

WORLD SERIES

Year	Team	W	L	PCT	ERA	G	GS	CG	IP	H	BB	SO	ShO	W	L	SV	AB	H	HR	BA	PO	A	E	DP	TC/G	FA
1949	BKN N	0	0	—	0.00	1	0	0	2	0	0	0	0	0	0	0	0	0	0	—	0	1	0	0	1.0	1.000

Don Minnick

MINNICK, DONALD ATHEY
B. Apr. 14, 1931, Lynchburg, Va.   BR TR 6'3"   195 lbs.

Year	Team	W	L	PCT	ERA	G	GS	CG	IP	H	BB	SO	ShO	W	L	SV	AB	H	HR	BA	PO	A	E	DP	TC/G	FA
1957	WAS A	0	1	.000	4.82	2	1	0	9.1	14	2	7	0	0	0	0	2	0	0	.000	1	0	0	0	0.5	1.000

Jim Minshall

MINSHALL, JAMES EDWARD
B. July 4, 1947, Covington, Ky.   BB TR 6'6"   215 lbs.

Year	Team	W	L	PCT	ERA	G	GS	CG	IP	H	BB	SO	ShO	W	L	SV	AB	H	HR	BA	PO	A	E	DP	TC/G	FA
1974	PIT N	0	1	.000	0.00	5	0	0	4	1	2	3	0	0	1	0	0	0	0	—	0	0	0	0	0.0	—

Year	Team		W	L	PCT	ERA	G	GS	CG	IP	H	BB	SO	ShO	W	L	SV	AB	H	HR	BA	PO	A	E	DP	TC/G	FA
															Relief Pitching			**Batting**									

Jim Minshall *continued*

Year	Team		W	L	PCT	ERA	G	GS	CG	IP	H	BB	SO	ShO	W	L	SV	AB	H	HR	BA	PO	A	E	DP	TC/G	FA
1975			0	0	–	0.00	1	0	0	1	0	2	2	0	0	0	0	0	0	0	–	0	0	0	0	0.0	–
2 yrs.			0	1	.000	0.00	6	0	0	5	1	4	5	0	0	1	0	0	0	0	–	0	0	0	0	0.0	–

Greg Minton

MINTON, GREGORY BRIAN (Moon Man)
B. July 29, 1951, Lubbock, Tex.
BB TR 6'2" 180 lbs.

Year	Team		W	L	PCT	ERA	G	GS	CG	IP	H	BB	SO	ShO	W	L	SV	AB	H	HR	BA	PO	A	E	DP	TC/G	FA
1975	SF	N	1	1	.500	6.88	7	2	0	17	19	11	6	0	0	0	0	6	0	0	.000	2	4	0	1	1.5	1.000
1976			0	3	.000	4.91	10	2	0	25.2	32	12	7	0	0	2	0	5	1	0	.200	3	4	2	0	0.9	.778
1977			1	1	.500	4.50	2	2	0	14	14	4	5	0	0	0	0	3	1	0	.333	2	4	0	0	3.0	1.000
1978			0	1	.000	7.88	11	0	0	16	22	8	6	0	0	1	0	1	0	0	.000	2	2	0	1	0.4	1.000
1979			4	3	.571	1.80	46	0	0	80	59	27	33	0	4	3	4	4	0	0	.000	3	23	1	2	0.6	.963
1980			4	6	.400	2.47	68	0	0	91	81	34	42	0	4	6	19	8	1	0	.125	8	21	1	2	0.4	.967
1981			4	5	.444	2.89	55	0	0	84	84	36	29	0	4	5	21	12	0	0	.000	11	25	0	1	0.7	1.000
1982			10	4	.714	1.83	78	0	0	123	108	42	58	0	10	4	30	17	3	0	.176	11	22	3	2	0.5	.917
1983			7	11	.389	3.54	73	0	0	106.2	117	47	38	0	7	11	22	11	6	1	.545	5	18	1	0	0.3	.958
1984			4	9	.308	3.76	74	1	0	124.1	130	57	48	0	3	9	19	21	1	0	.048	8	31	2	1	0.6	.951
1985			5	4	.556	3.54	68	0	0	96.2	98	54	37	0	5	4	9	8	0	0	.000	7	27	1	1	0.5	.971
1986			4	4	.500	3.93	48	0	0	68.2	63	34	34	0	4	4	5	5	2	0	.400	7	19	2	1	0.6	.929
1987	2 teams	SF N (15G 1–0)				CAL A	(41G 5–4)																				
"	total		6	4	.600	3.17	56	0	0	99.1	101	39	44	0	6	4	11	2	0	0	.000	7	23	0	2	0.5	1.000
1988	CAL	A	4	5	.444	2.85	44	0	0	79	67	34	46	0	4	5	7	0	0	0	–	11	15	0	3	0.6	1.000
1989			4	3	.571	2.20	62	0	0	90	76	37	42	0	4	3	8	0	0	0	–	8	20	0	0	0.5	1.000
15 yrs.			58	64	.475	3.11	699	7	0	1115.1	1071	476	475	0	55	61	150	103	15	1	.146	95	258	13	17	0.5	.964

Paul Mirabella

MIRABELLA, PAUL THOMAS
B. Mar. 20, 1954, Belleville, N. J.
BL TL 6'1" 190 lbs.

Year	Team		W	L	PCT	ERA	G	GS	CG	IP	H	BB	SO	ShO	W	L	SV	AB	H	HR	BA	PO	A	E	DP	TC/G	FA
1978	TEX	A	3	2	.600	5.79	10	4	0	28	30	17	23	0	1	1	1	0	0	0	–	0	3	0	0	0.3	1.000
1979	NY	A	0	4	.000	9.00	10	1	0	14	16	10	4	0	0	3	0	0	0	0	–	0	2	0	0	0.2	1.000
1980	TOR	A	5	12	.294	4.33	33	22	3	131	151	66	53	1	0	0	0	0	0	0	–	9	20	1	1	0.9	.967
1981			0	0	–	7.20	8	1	0	15	20	7	9	0	0	0	0	0	0	0	–	1	0	0	0	0.1	1.000
1982	TEX	A	1	1	.500	4.80	40	0	0	50.2	46	22	29	0	1	1	3	0	0	0	–	2	6	1	2	0.2	.889
1983	BAL	A	0	0	–	5.59	3	2	0	9.2	9	7	4	0	0	0	0	0	0	0	–	0	1	1	0	0.7	.500
1984	SEA	A	2	5	.286	4.37	52	1	0	68	74	32	41	0	2	4	3	0	0	0	–	4	11	0	1	0.3	1.000
1985			0	0	–	1.32	10	0	0	13.2	9	4	8	0	0	0	0	0	0	0	–	0	1	0	0	0.1	1.000
1986			0	0	–	8.53	8	0	0	6.1	13	3	6	0	0	0	0	0	0	0	–	0	1	0	0	0.1	1.000
1987	MIL	A	2	1	.667	4.91	29	0	0	29.1	30	16	14	0	2	1	0	0	0	0	–	7	5	1	1	0.4	.923
1988			2	2	.500	1.65	38	0	0	60	44	21	33	0	2	2	4	0	0	0	–	6	10	0	1	0.4	1.000
1989			0	0	–	7.63	13	0	0	15.1	18	7	6	0	0	0	0	0	0	0	–	0	6	2	0	0.6	.750
12 yrs.			15	27	.357	4.51	254	31	3	441	460	212	230	1	8	12	13	0	0	0	–	29	66	6	6	0.4	.941

Bobby Mitchell

MITCHELL, ROBERT McKASHA
B. Feb. 6, 1856, Cincinnati, Ohio D. May 1, 1933, Springfield, Ohio
BL TL 5'5" 135 lbs.

Year	Team		W	L	PCT	ERA	G	GS	CG	IP	H	BB	SO	ShO	W	L	SV	AB	H	HR	BA	PO	A	E	DP	TC/G	FA
1877	CIN	N	6	5	.545	3.51	12	12	11	100	123	11	41	1	0	0	0	49	10	0	.204	9	14	2	0	2.1	.920
1878			7	2	.778	2.14	9	9	9	80	69	18	51	1	0	0	0	49	12	0	.245	3	14	1	1	2.0	.944
1879	CLE	N	7	15	.318	3.28	23	22	20	194.2	236	42	90	0	0	1	0	109	16	0	.147	11	24	14	0	2.1	.714
1882	STL	AA	0	1	.000	7.71	1	1	0	7	12	2	2	0	0	0	0	4	0	0	.000	0	2	1	0	3.0	.667
4 yrs.			20	23	.465	3.18	45	44	40	381.2	440	73	184	2	0	1	0	211	38	0	.180	23	54	18	1	2.1	.811

Charlie Mitchell

MITCHELL, CHARLES ROSS
Brother of John Mitchell.
B. June 24, 1962, Dickson, Tenn.
BR TR 6'3" 170 lbs.

Year	Team		W	L	PCT	ERA	G	GS	CG	IP	H	BB	SO	ShO	W	L	SV	AB	H	HR	BA	PO	A	E	DP	TC/G	FA
1984	BOS	A	0	0	–	2.76	10	0	0	16.1	14	6	7	0	0	0	0	0	0	0	–	1	3	1	0	0.5	.800
1985			0	0	–	16.20	2	0	0	1.2	5	0	2	0	0	0	0	0	0	0	–	1	1	0	0	1.0	1.000
2 yrs.			0	0	–	4.00	12	0	0	18	19	6	9	0	0	0	0	0	0	0	–	2	4	1	0	0.6	.857

Clarence Mitchell

MITCHELL, CLARENCE ELMER
B. Feb. 22, 1891, Franklin, Neb. D. Nov. 6, 1963, Grand Island, Neb.
BL TL 5'11½" 190 lbs.

Year	Team		W	L	PCT	ERA	G	GS	CG	IP	H	BB	SO	ShO	W	L	SV	AB	H	HR	BA	PO	A	E	DP	TC/G	FA
1911	DET	A	1	0	1.000	8.16	5	1	0	14.1	20	7	4	0	1	0	0	4	2	0	.500	0	2	0	0	0.4	1.000
1916	CIN	N	11	10	.524	3.14	29	24	17	194.2	211	45	52	1	0	1	0	117	28	0	.239	10	55	1	5	2.3	.985
1917			9	15	.375	3.22	32	20	10	159.1	166	34	37	2	2	3	1	90	25	0	.278	10	45	1	2	1.8	.982
1918	BKN	N	0	1	.000	108.00	1	1	0	.1	4	0	0	0	0	0	0	24	6	0	.250	0	0	0	0	0.0	–
1919			7	5	.583	3.06	23	11	9	108.2	123	23	43	0	1	0	1	49	18	1	.367	4	36	1	1	1.8	.976
1920			5	2	.714	3.09	19	7	3	78.2	85	23	18	1	0	1	0	107	25	0	.234	2	30	0	0	1.7	1.000
1921			11	9	.550	2.89	37	18	13	190	206	46	39	3	2	2	2	91	24	0	.264	6	63	4	6	2.0	.945
1922			0	3	.000	14.21	5	3	0	12.2	28	7	1	0	0	0	0	155	45	3	.290	1	7	0	0	1.6	1.000
1923	PHI	N	9	10	.474	4.72	29	19	8	139.1	170	46	42	1	1	1	0	78	21	1	.269	4	18	3	2	0.9	.880
1924			6	13	.316	5.62	30	26	9	165	223	58	36	0	0	1	0	102	26	0	.255	10	51	0	0	2.0	1.000
1925			10	17	.370	5.28	32	26	12	199.1	245	51	46	1	0	0	0	92	18	0	.196	13	62	0	3	2.3	1.000
1926			9	14	.391	4.58	28	25	12	178.2	232	55	52	1	0	1	1	78	19	0	.244	11	62	1	3	2.6	.986
1927			6	3	.667	4.09	13	12	8	94.2	99	28	17	1	0	0	0	42	10	1	.238	1	25	1	1	2.1	.963
1928	2 teams	PHI N (3G 0–0)				STL N	(19G 8–9)																				
"	total		8	9	.471	3.53	22	18	9	155.2	162	40	31	1	1	0	0	60	8	0	.133	6	51	1	3	2.6	.983
1929	STL	N	8	11	.421	4.27	25	22	16	173	221	60	39	0	0	0	0	66	18	0	.273	1	37	1	1	1.6	.974
1930	2 teams	STL N (1G 1–0)				NY N	(24G 10–3)																				
"	total		11	3	.786	4.02	25	17	5	132	156	38	41	0	1	0	2	49	13	0	.265	10	35	0	1	1.8	1.000
1931	NY	N	13	11	.542	4.07	27	25	13	190.1	221	52	39	0	0	0	0	73	16	1	.219	13	33	6	2	1.9	.885
1932			1	3	.250	4.15	8	3	1	30.1	41	11	7	0	0	1	2	10	2	0	.200	2	3	1	0	0.8	.833
18 yrs.			125	139	.473	4.12	390	278	145	2217	2613	624	544	12	10	13	9	*				104	615	21	39	1.9	.972

WORLD SERIES

Year	Team		W	L	PCT	ERA	G	GS	CG	IP	H	BB	SO	ShO	W	L	SV	AB	H	HR	BA	PO	A	E	DP	TC/G	FA
1920	BKN	N	0	0	–	0.00	1	0	0	4.2	3	3	1	0	0	0	0	3	1	0	.333	1	0	0	0	1.0	1.000

Year	Team		W	L	PCT	ERA	G	GS	CG	IP	H	BB	SO	ShO	Relief Pitching W	L	SV	Batting AB	H	HR	BA	PO	A	E	DP	TC/G	FA

Clarence Mitchell *continued*

Year	Team		W	L	PCT	ERA	G	GS	CG	IP	H	BB	SO	ShO	W	L	SV	AB	H	HR	BA	PO	A	E	DP	TC/G	FA
1928	STL	N	0	0	–	1.59	1	0	0	5.2	2	2	2	0	0	0	0	2	0	0	.000	0	1	1	0	2.0	.500
2 yrs.			0	0	–	0.87	2	0	0	10.1	5	5	3	0	0	0	0	5	1	0	.200	1	1	1	0	1.5	.667

Craig Mitchell

MITCHELL, CRAIG SETON
B. Apr. 14, 1954, Santa Rosa, Calif.
BR TR 6'3" 180 lbs.

Year	Team		W	L	PCT	ERA	G	GS	CG	IP	H	BB	SO	ShO	W	L	SV	AB	H	HR	BA	PO	A	E	DP	TC/G	FA
1975	OAK	A	0	1	.000	12.27	1	1	0	3.2	6	4	2	0	0	0	0	0	0	0	–	1	1	0	1	2.0	1.000
1976			0	0	–	3.00	1	0	0	3	3	0	0	0	0	0	0	0	0	0	–	0	1	1	0	2.0	.500
1977			0	1	.000	7.50	3	1	0	6	9	2	1	0	0	0	0	0	0	0	–	1	1	1	0	1.0	.667
3 yrs.			0	2	.000	7.82	5	2	0	12.2	18	4	3	0	0	0	0	0	0	0	–	2	3	2	1	1.4	.714

Fred Mitchell

MITCHELL, FREDERICK FRANCIS
Born Frederick Francis Yapp.
B. June 5, 1878, Cambridge, Mass. D. Oct. 13, 1970, Newton, Mass.
Manager 1917-23.
BR TR 5'9½" 185 lbs.

Year	Team		W	L	PCT	ERA	G	GS	CG	IP	H	BB	SO	ShO	W	L	SV	AB	H	HR	BA	PO	A	E	DP	TC/G	FA
1901	BOS	A	6	6	.500	3.81	17	13	10	108.2	115	51	34	0	1	0	0	44	7	0	.159	2	33	5	2	2.4	.875
1902	2 teams	BOS A (1G 0–1)							PHI A (18G 5–7)																		
"	total		5	8	.385	3.87	19	14	9	111.2	128	64	24	0	1	1	1	49	9	0	.184	6	45	4	4	2.9	.927
1903	PHI	N	11	15	.423	4.48	28	28	24	227	250	102	69	0	0	0	0	95	19	0	.200	10	50	10	3	2.5	.857
1904	2 teams	PHI N (13G 4–7)							BKN N (8G 2–5)																		
"	total		6	12	.333	3.56	21	21	19	174.2	206	48	45	1	0	0	0	106	24	0	.226	11	69	4	2	4.0	.952
1905	BKN	N	3	7	.300	4.78	12	10	9	96	107	38	44	0	0	0	0	79	15	0	.190	4	33	5	1	3.5	.881
5 yrs.			31	48	.392	4.10	97	86	71	718	806	303	216	2	2	1	1	*				33	230	28	12	3.0	.904

John Mitchell

MITCHELL, JOHN KYLE
Brother of Charlie Mitchell.
B. Aug. 11, 1965, Dickson, Tenn.
BR TR 6'2" 165 lbs.

Year	Team		W	L	PCT	ERA	G	GS	CG	IP	H	BB	SO	ShO	W	L	SV	AB	H	HR	BA	PO	A	E	DP	TC/G	FA
1986	NY	N	0	1	.000	3.60	4	1	0	10	10	4	2	0	0	0	0	2	0	0	.000	3	1	0	0	1.0	1.000
1987			3	6	.333	4.11	20	19	1	111.2	124	36	57	0	0	0	0	35	4	0	.114	16	21	6	3	2.2	.860
1988			0	0	–	0.00	1	0	0	1	2	1	1	0	0	0	0	1	0	0	.000	0	0	0	0	0.0	–
1989			0	1	.000	6.00	2	0	0	3	3	4	4	0	0	0	1	0	0	0	–	0	0	0	0	0.0	–
4 yrs.			3	8	.273	4.08	27	20	1	125.2	139	45	64	0	0	0	1	38	4	0	.105	19	22	6	3	1.7	.872

Monroe Mitchell

MITCHELL, MONROE BARR
B. Sept. 11, 1901, Starkville, Miss. D. Sept. 4, 1976, Valdosta, Ga.
BR TR 6'1½" 170 lbs.

Year	Team		W	L	PCT	ERA	G	GS	CG	IP	H	BB	SO	ShO	W	L	SV	AB	H	HR	BA	PO	A	E	DP	TC/G	FA
1923	WAS	A	2	4	.333	6.48	10	6	3	41.2	57	22	8	1	0	0	2	12	3	0	.250	3	8	1	0	1.2	.917

Paul Mitchell

MITCHELL, PAUL MICHAEL
B. Aug. 19, 1949, Worcester, Mass.
BR TR 6'1" 195 lbs.

Year	Team		W	L	PCT	ERA	G	GS	CG	IP	H	BB	SO	ShO	W	L	SV	AB	H	HR	BA	PO	A	E	DP	TC/G	FA
1975	BAL	A	3	0	1.000	3.63	11	4	1	57	41	19	31	2	0	0	0	0	0	0	–	2	5	0	0	0.6	1.000
1976	OAK	A	9	7	.563	4.25	26	26	4	142	169	30	67	1	0	0	0	0	0	0	–	7	17	0	0	0.9	1.000
1977	2 teams	OAK A (5G 0–3)							SEA A (9G 3–3)																		
"	total		3	6	.333	6.41	14	12	0	53.1	71	23	25	0	0	0	0	0	0	0	–	5	11	0	0	1.1	1.000
1978	SEA	A	8	14	.364	4.18	29	29	4	168	173	79	75	2	0	0	0	0	0	0	–	7	20	0	2	0.9	1.000
1979	2 teams	SEA A (10G 1–4)							MIL A (18G 3–3)																		
"	total		4	7	.364	5.30	28	14	1	112	127	25	50	0	0	0	0	0	0	0	–	5	13	0	1	0.6	1.000
1980	MIL	A	5	5	.500	3.54	17	11	1	89	92	15	29	1	0	0	1	0	0	0	–	6	16	0	0	1.3	1.000
6 yrs.			32	39	.451	4.45	125	96	11	621.1	673	191	277	4	2	0	1	0	0	0	–	32	82	0	3	0.9	1.000

Roy Mitchell

MITCHELL, ALBERT ROY
B. Apr. 19, 1885, Belton, Tex. D. Sept. 8, 1959, Temple, Tex.
BR TR 5'9½" 170 lbs.

Year	Team		W	L	PCT	ERA	G	GS	CG	IP	H	BB	SO	ShO	W	L	SV	AB	H	HR	BA	PO	A	E	DP	TC/G	FA
1910	STL	A	4	2	.667	2.60	6	6	6	52	43	12	23	0	0	0	0	19	4	0	.211	0	20	0	1	3.3	1.000
1911			4	8	.333	3.84	28	12	8	133.2	134	45	40	1	1	1	0	49	11	0	.224	5	39	5	0	1.8	.898
1912			3	4	.429	4.65	13	8	5	62	81	17	22	0	1	0	0	19	6	0	.316	3	11	0	1	1.1	1.000
1913			13	16	.448	3.01	33	27	21	245.1	265	47	59	2	1	1	1	88	13	0	.148	17	69	6	2	2.8	.935
1914			4	5	.444	4.35	28	9	4	103.1	134	38	38	0	2	1	4	34	7	0	.206	5	32	3	0	1.4	.925
1918	2 teams	CHI A (2G 0–1)							CIN N (5G 4–0)																		
"	total		4	1	.800	2.42	7	5	3	48.1	45	9	12	1	0	0	0	16	3	0	.188	2	14	2	0	2.6	.889
1919	CIN	N	0	1	.000	2.32	7	1	0	31	32	9	10	0	0	0	0	10	0	0	.000	1	15	1	0	2.4	.941
7 yrs.			32	37	.464	3.42	122	68	47	675.2	734	177	204	7	7	2	5	235	44	0	.187	33	200	17	4	2.0	.932

Willie Mitchell

MITCHELL, WILLIAM
B. Dec. 1, 1889, Pleasant Grove, Miss. D. Nov. 23, 1973, Sardis, Miss.
BR TL 6' 176 lbs.

Year	Team		W	L	PCT	ERA	G	GS	CG	IP	H	BB	SO	ShO	W	L	SV	AB	H	HR	BA	PO	A	E	DP	TC/G	FA
1909	CLE	A	1	2	.333	1.57	3	3	3	23	18	10	8	0	0	0	0	7	2	0	.286	2	7	1	1	3.3	.900
1910			12	8	.600	2.60	35	18	11	183.2	155	55	102	1	2	2	0	63	10	0	.159	9	46	4	1	1.7	.932
1911			7	14	.333	3.76	30	22	9	177.1	190	60	78	0	1	2	0	64	7	0	.109	9	47	6	0	2.1	.903
1912			5	8	.385	2.80	29	15	8	163.2	149	56	94	0	1	1	0	53	6	0	.113	8	30	6	1	1.5	.864
1913			14	8	.636	1.74	34	22	14	217	153	88	141	4	4	1	0	70	10	0	.143	10	44	4	3	1.7	.931
1914			12	17	.414	3.19	39	32	16	257	228	124	179	3	0	1	1	81	7	0	.086	4	46	6	1	1.4	.893
1915			11	14	.440	2.82	36	30	12	236	210	84	149	1	1	1	1	79	10	0	.127	3	48	8	1	1.6	.864
1916	2 teams	CLE A (12G 2–5)							DET A (23G 7–5)																		
"	total		9	10	.474	3.78	35	23	8	171.1	174	67	84	2	1	1	2	47	9	0	.191	5	30	4	1	1.1	.897
1917	DET	A	12	8	.600	2.19	30	22	12	185.1	172	46	80	5	0	0	0	59	7	0	.119	11	40	4	2	1.8	.927
1918			0	1	.000	9.00	1	1	0	4	3	5	2	0	0	0	0	2	0	0	.000	1	2	0	0	3.0	1.000
1919			1	2	.333	5.27	3	2	0	13.2	12	10	4	0	0	0	0	5	1	0	.200	1	4	0	0	1.7	1.000
11 yrs.			84	92	.477	2.86	275	190	93	1632	1464	605	921	16	10	9	4	530	69	0	.130	63	344	43	10	1.6	.904

Vinegar Bend Mizell

MIZELL, WILMER DAVID
B. Aug. 13, 1930, Leakesville, Miss.
BR TL 6'3½" 205 lbs.

Year	Team		W	L	PCT	ERA	G	GS	CG	IP	H	BB	SO	ShO	W	L	SV	AB	H	HR	BA	PO	A	E	DP	TC/G	FA
1952	STL	N	10	8	.556	3.65	30	30	7	190	171	103	146	2	0	0	0	68	3	0	.044	7	25	4	1	1.2	.889
1953			13	11	.542	3.49	33	33	10	224.1	193	114	173	1	0	0	0	83	7	1	.084	13	35	7	2	1.7	.873
1956			14	14	.500	3.62	33	33	11	208.2	172	92	153	3	0	0	0	75	8	0	.107	19	30	2	1	1.5	.961

Year	Team	W	L	PCT	ERA	G	GS	CG	IP	H	BB	SO	ShO	W	L	SV	AB	H	HR	BA	PO	A	E	DP	TC/G	FA

Vinegar Bend Mizell *continued*

Year	Team	W	L	PCT	ERA	G	GS	CG	IP	H	BB	SO	ShO	W	L	SV	AB	H	HR	BA	PO	A	E	DP	TC/G	FA
1957		8	10	.444	3.74	33	21	7	149.1	136	51	87	2	1	1	0	45	4	0	.089	8	29	0	3	1.1	1.000
1958		10	14	.417	3.42	30	29	8	189.2	178	91	80	2	0	0	0	61	7	0	.115	6	31	3	3	1.3	.925
1959		13	10	.565	4.20	31	30	8	201.1	196	89	108	1	1	0	0	75	14	0	.187	9	23	3	1	1.1	.914
1960	2 teams	STL N	(9G 1–3)		PIT N	(23G 13–5)																				
"	total	14	8	.636	3.50	32	32	8	211	205	74	113	3	1	0	0	69	9	0	.130	2	11	0	0	0.4	1.000
1961	PIT N	7	10	.412	5.04	25	17	2	100	120	31	37	1	1	0	0	23	3	0	.130	6	7	2	1	0.6	.867
1962	2 teams	PIT N	(4G 1–1)		NY N	(17G 0–2)																				
"	total	1	3	.250	6.63	21	5	0	54.1	63	35	21	0	0	0	0	14	2	0	.143	2	9	0	0	0.5	1.000
9 yrs.		90	88	.506	3.85	268	230	61	1528.2	1434	680	918	15	3	3	0	513	57	1	.111	72	200	21	13	1.1	.928

WORLD SERIES

Year	Team	W	L	PCT	ERA	G	GS	CG	IP	H	BB	SO	ShO	W	L	SV	AB	H	HR	BA	PO	A	E	DP	TC/G	FA
1960	PIT N	0	1	.000	15.43	2	1	0	2.1	4	2	1	0	0	0	0	0	0	0	–	0	0	0	0	0.0	–

Kevin Mmahat

MMAHAT, KEVIN PAUL
B. Nov. 9, 1964, Memphis, Tenn.

BL TL 6'5" 220 lbs.

Year	Team	W	L	PCT	ERA	G	GS	CG	IP	H	BB	SO	ShO	W	L	SV	AB	H	HR	BA	PO	A	E	DP	TC/G	FA
1989	NY A	0	2	.000	12.91	4	2	0	7.2	13	8	3	0	0	0	0	0	0	0	–	0	1	1	0	0.5	.500

Mike Modak

MODAK, MICHAEL JOSEPH ALOYSIUS
B. May 18, 1922, Campbell, Ohio

BR TR 5'10½" 195 lbs.

Year	Team	W	L	PCT	ERA	G	GS	CG	IP	H	BB	SO	ShO	W	L	SV	AB	H	HR	BA	PO	A	E	DP	TC/G	FA
1945	CIN N	1	2	.333	5.74	20	3	1	42.1	52	23	7	1	0	1	1	10	1	0	.100	0	5	1	0	0.3	.833

Joe Moeller

MOELLER, JOSEPH DOUGLAS
B. Feb. 15, 1943, Blue Island, Ill.

BR TR 6'5" 192 lbs.

Year	Team	W	L	PCT	ERA	G	GS	CG	IP	H	BB	SO	ShO	W	L	SV	AB	H	HR	BA	PO	A	E	DP	TC/G	FA
1962	LA N	6	5	.545	5.25	19	15	1	85.2	87	58	46	0	0	1	1	33	7	0	.212	6	18	0	2	1.3	1.000
1964		7	13	.350	4.21	27	24	1	145.1	153	31	97	0	0	0	0	45	3	0	.067	9	24	1	1	1.3	.971
1966		2	4	.333	2.52	29	8	0	78.2	73	14	31	0	1	1	0	12	2	0	.167	5	21	1	1	0.9	.963
1967		0	0	–	9.00	6	0	0	5	9	3	2	0	0	0	0	0	0	0	–	0	1	0	0	0.2	1.000
1968		1	1	.500	5.06	3	3	0	16	17	2	11	0	0	0	0	7	0	0	.000	0	3	0	0	1.0	1.000
1969		1	0	1.000	3.35	23	4	0	51	54	13	25	0	0	0	0	10	2	0	.200	6	13	0	1	0.8	1.000
1970		7	9	.438	3.93	31	19	2	135	131	43	63	1	1	0	4	39	6	0	.154	6	15	2	1	0.7	.913
1971		2	4	.333	3.82	28	1	0	66	72	12	32	0	2	3	1	9	0	0	.000	3	14	1	1	0.6	.944
8 yrs.		26	36	.419	4.02	166	74	4	582.2	596	176	307	1	4	5	7	155	20	0	.129	35	109	5	7	0.9	.966

WORLD SERIES

Year	Team	W	L	PCT	ERA	G	GS	CG	IP	H	BB	SO	ShO	W	L	SV	AB	H	HR	BA	PO	A	E	DP	TC/G	FA
1966	LA N	0	0	–	4.50	1	0	0	2	1	1	0	0	0	0	0	0	0	0	–	0	0	0	0	0.0	–

Ron Moeller

MOELLER, RONALD RALPH (The Kid)
B. Oct. 13, 1938, Cincinnati, Ohio

BL TL 6' 180 lbs.

Year	Team	W	L	PCT	ERA	G	GS	CG	IP	H	BB	SO	ShO	W	L	SV	AB	H	HR	BA	PO	A	E	DP	TC/G	FA
1956	BAL A	0	1	.000	4.15	4	1	0	8.2	10	3	2	0	0	0	0	0	0	0	.000	0	1	0	0	0.3	1.000
1958		0	0	–	4.15	4	0	0	4.1	6	3	3	0	0	0	0	0	0	0	–	0	2	0	0	0.5	1.000
1961	LA A	4	8	.333	5.83	33	18	1	112.2	122	83	87	1	0	1	0	29	6	0	.207	5	21	3	2	0.9	.897
1963	2 teams	LA A	(3G 0–0)		WAS A	(8G 2–0)																				
"	total	2	0	1.000	6.33	11	3	0	27	36	11	12	0	0	0	0	9	2	0	.222	0	3	0	0	0.3	1.000
4 yrs.		6	9	.400	5.78	52	22	1	152.2	174	100	104	1	0	1	0	39	8	0	.205	5	27	3	2	0.7	.914

Sam Moffett

MOFFETT, SAMUEL R.
Brother of Joe Moffett.
B. Mar. 14, 1857, Wheeling, W. Va. D. May 5, 1907, Butte, Mont.

TR

Year	Team	W	L	PCT	ERA	G	GS	CG	IP	H	BB	SO	ShO	W	L	SV	AB	H	HR	BA	PO	A	E	DP	TC/G	FA
1884	CLE N	3	19	.136	3.87	24	22	21	197.2	236	58	84	0	0	0	0	256	47	0	.184	13	49	6	2	2.8	.912
1887	IND N	1	5	.167	3.78	6	6	6	50	47	23	3	0	0	0	0	41	5	0	.122	5	7	2	0	2.3	.857
1888		2	5	.286	4.66	7	7	6	56	62	17	7	1	0	0	0	35	4	0	.114	1	5	2	1	1.1	.750
3 yrs.		6	29	.171	4.00	37	35	33	303.2	345	98	94	1	0	0	0	*				19	61	10	3	2.4	.889

Randy Moffitt

MOFFITT, RANDALL JAMES
B. Oct. 13, 1948, Long Beach, Calif.

BR TR 6'3" 190 lbs.

Year	Team	W	L	PCT	ERA	G	GS	CG	IP	H	BB	SO	ShO	W	L	SV	AB	H	HR	BA	PO	A	E	DP	TC/G	FA
1972	SF N	1	5	.167	3.68	40	0	0	71	72	30	37	0	1	5	4	8	0	0	.000	4	12	1	0	0.4	.941
1973		4	4	.500	2.43	60	0	0	100	86	31	65	0	4	4	14	17	1	0	.059	6	10	3	2	0.3	.842
1974		5	7	.417	4.50	61	1	0	102	99	29	49	0	5	7	15	16	5	0	.313	12	16	0	1	0.5	1.000
1975		4	5	.444	3.89	55	0	0	74	73	32	39	0	4	5	11	14	3	0	.214	4	10	3	1	0.3	.824
1976		6	6	.500	2.27	58	0	0	103	92	35	50	0	6	6	14	14	2	0	.143	11	13	3	0	0.5	.889
1977		4	9	.308	3.58	64	0	0	88	91	39	68	0	4	9	11	3	0	0	.000	8	15	1	1	0.4	.958
1978		8	4	.667	3.29	70	0	0	82	79	33	52	0	8	4	12	7	1	0	.143	3	7	1	0	0.2	.909
1979		2	5	.286	7.71	28	0	0	35	53	14	16	0	2	5	2	4	0	0	.000	1	5	0	0	0.2	1.000
1980		1	1	.500	4.76	13	0	0	17	18	4	10	0	1	1	0	0	0	0	.000	0	1	0	0	0.1	1.000
1981		0	0	–	8.18	10	0	0	11	15	2	11	0	0	0	0	0	0	0	–	0	0	1	0	0.1	–
1982	HOU N	2	4	.333	3.02	30	0	0	41.2	36	13	20	0	2	4	3	2	0	0	.000	3	2	0	0	0.2	1.000
1983	TOR A	6	2	.750	3.77	45	0	0	57.1	52	24	38	0	6	2	10	0	0	0	–	1	8	1	0	0.2	1.000
12 yrs.		43	52	.453	3.65	534	1	0	782	766	286	455	0	43	52	96	86	12	0	.140	53	101	13	7	0.3	.922

Herb Moford

MOFORD, HERBERT
B. Aug. 6, 1928, Brooksville, Ky.

BR TR 6'1" 175 lbs.

Year	Team	W	L	PCT	ERA	G	GS	CG	IP	H	BB	SO	ShO	W	L	SV	AB	H	HR	BA	PO	A	E	DP	TC/G	FA
1955	STL N	1	1	.500	7.88	14	1	0	24	29	15	8	0	1	0	2	2	0	0	.000	1	9	0	0	0.7	1.000
1958	DET A	4	9	.308	3.61	25	11	6	109.2	83	42	58	0	0	2	1	37	1	0	.027	5	24	0	2	1.2	1.000
1959	BOS A	0	2	.000	11.42	4	2	0	8.2	10	6	7	0	0	0	0	1	0	0	.000	2	0	0	0	0.5	1.000
1962	NY N	0	1	.000	7.20	7	0	0	15	21	1	5	0	0	1	0	4	1	0	.250	0	3	0	0	0.4	1.000
4 yrs.		5	13	.278	5.03	50	14	6	157.1	143	64	78	0	1	3	3	44	2	0	.045	8	36	0	2	0.9	1.000

George Mogridge

MOGRIDGE, GEORGE ANTHONY
B. Feb. 18, 1889, Rochester, N. Y. D. Mar. 4, 1962, Rochester, N. Y.

BL TL 6'2" 165 lbs.

Year	Team	W	L	PCT	ERA	G	GS	CG	IP	H	BB	SO	ShO	W	L	SV	AB	H	HR	BA	PO	A	E	DP	TC/G	FA
1911	CHI A	0	2	.000	4.97	4	1	0	12.2	12	1	5	0	0	1	0	5	2	0	.400	3	2	0	0	1.3	1.000

Year	Team	W	L	PCT	ERA	G	GS	CG	IP	H	BB	SO	ShO	Relief Pitching W	L	SV	Batting AB	H	HR	BA	PO	A	E	DP	TC/G	FA

George Mogridge *continued*

Year	Team	W	L	PCT	ERA	G	GS	CG	IP	H	BB	SO	ShO	W	L	SV	AB	H	HR	BA	PO	A	E	DP	TC/G	FA
1912		3	4	.429	4.04	17	7	2	64.2	69	15	31	0	1	1	3	16	2	0	.125	4	16	2	0	1.3	.909
1915	NY A	2	3	.400	1.76	6	6	3	41	33	11	11	1	0	0	0	12	1	0	.083	1	11	1	0	2.2	.923
1916		6	12	.333	2.31	30	21	10	194.2	174	45	66	2	1	0	0	66	14	0	.212	15	61	4	2	2.7	.950
1917		9	11	.450	2.98	29	25	15	196.1	185	39	46	1	1	0	0	69	11	0	.159	16	61	0	1	2.7	1.000
1918		16	13	.552	2.27	45	19	13	230.1	232	43	62	1	4	7	7	79	15	0	.190	13	76	1	5	2.0	.989
1919		10	7	.588	2.50	35	18	13	187	159	46	58	3	1	1	0	48	6	0	.125	10	51	2	2	1.8	.968
1920		5	9	.357	4.31	26	15	8	125.1	146	36	35	0	1	1	1	42	7	0	.167	3	37	1	1	1.6	.976
1921	WAS A	18	14	.563	3.00	38	36	21	288	301	66	101	4	1	0	0	98	15	0	.153	18	78	2	3	2.6	.980
1922		18	13	.581	3.58	34	32	18	251.2	300	72	61	3	0	2	0	86	21	1	.244	12	59	6	5	2.3	.922
1923		13	13	.500	3.11	33	28	17	211	228	56	62	3	0	1	1	75	17	0	.227	11	60	5	6	2.3	.934
1924		16	11	.593	3.76	30	30	13	213	217	61	48	2	0	0	0	74	13	0	.176	7	53	2	4	2.1	.968
1925	2 teams	WAS A	(10G 4–3)		STL A	(2G 1–1)																				
"	total	5	4	.556	3.95	12	10	4	68.1	73	23	21	0	0	1	0	23	2	0	.087	3	18	3	1	2.0	.875
1926	BOS N	6	10	.375	4.50	39	10	2	142	173	36	46	0	5	3	3	46	8	0	.174	10	43	3	5	1.4	.946
1927		6	4	.600	3.70	20	1	0	48.2	48	15	26	0	6	3	5	15	3	0	.200	1	13	0	0	0.7	1.000
15 yrs.		133	130	.506	3.20	398	259	138	2274.2	2350	565	679	20	20	21	20	754	137	1	.182	127	639	32	35	2.0	.960

WORLD SERIES

Year	Team	W	L	PCT	ERA	G	GS	CG	IP	H	BB	SO	ShO	W	L	SV	AB	H	HR	BA	PO	A	E	DP	TC/G	FA
1924	WAS A	1	0	1.000	2.25	2	1	0	12	7	6	5	0	0	0	0	5	0	0	.000	0	0	0	0	0.0	–

George Mohart

MOHART, GEORGE BENJAMIN
B. Mar. 6, 1892, Buffalo, N. Y.   D. Oct. 2, 1970, Silver Creek, N. Y.   BR TR 5'9"   165 lbs.

Year	Team	W	L	PCT	ERA	G	GS	CG	IP	H	BB	SO	ShO	W	L	SV	AB	H	HR	BA	PO	A	E	DP	TC/G	FA
1920	BKN N	0	1	.000	1.77	13	1	0	35.2	33	7	13	0	0	1	0	8	1	0	.125	3	13	0	0	1.2	1.000
1921		0	0	–	3.86	2	0	0	7	8	1	1	0	0	0	0	2	1	0	.500	0	1	0	0	0.5	1.000
2 yrs.		0	1	.000	2.11	15	1	0	42.2	41	8	14	0	0	1	0	10	2	0	.200	3	14	0	0	1.1	1.000

Dale Mohorcic

MOHORCIC, DALE ROBERT
B. Jan. 25, 1956, Cleveland, Ohio   BR TR 6'3"   220 lbs.

Year	Team	W	L	PCT	ERA	G	GS	CG	IP	H	BB	SO	ShO	W	L	SV	AB	H	HR	BA	PO	A	E	DP	TC/G	FA
1986	TEX A	2	4	.333	2.51	58	0	0	79	86	15	29	0	2	4	7	0	0	0	–	5	12	0	3	0.3	1.000
1987		7	6	.538	2.99	74	0	0	99.1	88	19	48	0	7	6	16	0	0	0	–	9	23	2	3	0.5	.941
1988	2 teams	TEX A	(43G 2–6)		NY A	(13G 2–2)																				
"	total	4	8	.333	4.22	56	0	0	74.2	83	29	44	0	4	8	6	0	0	0	–	7	9	1	0	0.3	.941
1989	NY A	2	1	.667	4.99	32	0	0	57.2	65	18	24	0	2	1	2	0	0	0	–	5	10	0	2	0.5	1.000
4 yrs.		15	19	.441	3.53	220	0	0	310.2	322	81	145	0	15	19	31	0	0	0	–	26	54	3	8	0.4	.964

Bill Moisan

MOISAN, WILLIAM JOSEPH
B. July 30, 1925, Bradford, Mass.   BL TR 6'1"   170 lbs.

Year	Team	W	L	PCT	ERA	G	GS	CG	IP	H	BB	SO	ShO	W	L	SV	AB	H	HR	BA	PO	A	E	DP	TC/G	FA
1953	CHI N	0	0	–	5.40	3	0	0	5	5	2	1	0	0	0	0	0	0	0	–	0	1	0	0	0.3	1.000

Carlton Molesworth

MOLESWORTH, CARLTON
B. Feb. 15, 1876, Frederick, Md.   D. July 25, 1961, Frederick, Md.   BL TL 5'6"   200 lbs.

Year	Team	W	L	PCT	ERA	G	GS	CG	IP	H	BB	SO	ShO	W	L	SV	AB	H	HR	BA	PO	A	E	DP	TC/G	FA
1895	WAS N	0	2	.000	14.63	4	3	1	16	33	15	7	0	0	0	0	7	1	0	.143	0	2	0	0	0.5	1.000

Rich Moloney

MOLONEY, RICHARD HENRY
B. June 7, 1950, Brookline, Mass.   BR TR 6'3"   185 lbs.

Year	Team	W	L	PCT	ERA	G	GS	CG	IP	H	BB	SO	ShO	W	L	SV	AB	H	HR	BA	PO	A	E	DP	TC/G	FA
1970	CHI A	0	0	–	0.00	1	0	0	1	2	0	1	0	0	0	0	0	0	0	–	0	0	0	0	0.0	–

Vince Molyneaux

MOLYNEAUX, VINCENT LEO
B. Aug. 17, 1888, Lewiston, N. Y.   D. May 4, 1950, Stamford, Conn.   BR TR 6'   180 lbs.

Year	Team	W	L	PCT	ERA	G	GS	CG	IP	H	BB	SO	ShO	W	L	SV	AB	H	HR	BA	PO	A	E	DP	TC/G	FA
1917	STL A	0	0	–	4.91	7	0	0	22	18	20	4	0	0	0	0	4	0	0	.000	0	9	0	0	1.3	1.000
1918	BOS A	1	0	1.000	3.38	6	0	0	10.2	3	8	1	0	1	0	0	2	0	0	.000	1	3	0	1	0.7	1.000
2 yrs.		1	0	1.000	4.41	13	0	0	32.2	21	28	5	0	1	0	0	6	0	0	.000	1	12	0	1	1.0	1.000

Rinty Monahan

MONAHAN, EDWARD FRANCIS
B. Apr. 28, 1928, Brooklyn, N. Y.   BR TR 6'1"   195 lbs.

Year	Team	W	L	PCT	ERA	G	GS	CG	IP	H	BB	SO	ShO	W	L	SV	AB	H	HR	BA	PO	A	E	DP	TC/G	FA
1953	PHI A	0	0	–	4.22	4	0	0	10.2	11	7	2	0	0	0	0	2	0	0	.000	0	1	0	0	0.3	1.000

Bill Monbouquette

MONBOUQUETTE, WILLIAM CHARLES
B. Aug. 11, 1936, Medford, Mass.   BR TR 5'11"   190 lbs.

Year	Team	W	L	PCT	ERA	G	GS	CG	IP	H	BB	SO	ShO	W	L	SV	AB	H	HR	BA	PO	A	E	DP	TC/G	FA
1958	BOS A	3	4	.429	3.31	10	8	3	54.1	52	20	30	0	0	0	0	17	3	0	.176	1	7	1	1	0.9	.889
1959		7	7	.500	4.15	34	17	4	151.2	165	33	87	0	2	1	0	46	3	0	.065	11	22	0	3	1.0	1.000
1960		14	11	.560	3.64	35	30	12	215	217	68	134	3	2	0	0	65	6	0	.092	18	28	0	3	1.3	1.000
1961		14	14	.500	3.39	32	32	12	236.1	233	100	161	1	0	0	0	69	9	0	.130	16	28	1	2	1.4	.978
1962		15	13	.536	3.33	35	35	11	235.1	227	65	153	4	0	0	0	73	7	0	.096	7	21	1	0	0.8	.966
1963		20	10	.667	3.81	37	36	13	266.2	258	42	174	1	0	1	0	88	10	0	.114	31	37	0	0	1.8	1.000
1964		13	14	.481	4.04	36	35	7	234	258	40	120	5	0	1	0	72	6	0	.083	15	38	0	2	1.5	1.000
1965		10	18	.357	3.70	35	35	10	228.2	239	40	110	2	0	0	0	68	4	0	.059	21	38	2	2	1.7	.967
1966	DET A	7	8	.467	4.73	30	14	2	102.2	120	22	61	3	0	0	0	26	4	0	.154	11	16	1	1	0.7	.955
1967	2 teams	DET A	(2G 0–0)		NY A	(33G 6–5)																				
"	total	6	5	.545	2.33	35	10	2	135.1	123	17	55	1	2	1	1	32	5	0	.156	11	19	1	1	0.9	.968
1968	2 teams	NY A	(17G 5–7)		SF N	(7G 0–1)																				
"	total	5	8	.385	4.35	24	11	2	101.1	103	15	37	0	1	4	1	26	3	0	.115	13	18	1	1	1.3	1.000
11 yrs.		114	112	.504	3.68	343	263	78	1961.1	1995	462	1122	18	10	7	3	582	60	0	.103	155	266	7	19	1.2	.984

Sid Monge

MONGE, ISIDRO PEDROZA
B. Apr. 11, 1951, Agua Prieta, Mexico   BB TL 6'2"   185 lbs.

Year	Team	W	L	PCT	ERA	G	GS	CG	IP	H	BB	SO	ShO	W	L	SV	AB	H	HR	BA	PO	A	E	DP	TC/G	FA
1975	CAL A	0	2	.000	4.18	4	2	0	23.2	22	10	17	0	0	0	0	0	0	0	–	1	2	0	0	0.8	1.000
1976		6	7	.462	3.36	32	13	2	118	108	49	53	0	2	2	0	0	0	0	–	6	15	2	1	0.7	.913

Year	Team	W	L	PCT	ERA	G	GS	CG	IP	H	BB	SO	ShO	Relief Pitching W	L	SV	Batting AB	H	HR	BA	PO	A	E	DP	TC/G	FA

Sid Monge *continued*

Year	Team	W	L	PCT	ERA	G	GS	CG	IP	H	BB	SO	ShO	W	L	SV	AB	H	HR	BA	PO	A	E	DP	TC/G	FA
1977	2 teams	CAL A	(4G 0–1)		CLE A	(33G 1–2)																					
"	total	1	3	.250	5.44	37	0	0	51.1	61	33	29	0	1	3	4	0	0	0	–	1	7	2	1	0.3	.800
1978	CLE A	4	3	.571	2.76	48	2	0	84.2	71	51	54	0	4	2	6	0	0	0	–	4	11	2	1	0.4	.882
1979		12	10	.545	2.40	76	0	0	131	96	64	108	0	12	10	19	0	0	0	–	6	17	3	2	0.3	.885
1980		3	5	.375	3.54	67	0	0	94	80	40	61	0	3	5	14	0	0	0	–	4	6	0	0	0.1	1.000
1981		3	5	.375	4.34	31	0	0	58	58	21	41	0	3	5	4	0	0	0	–	5	4	0	0	0.3	1.000
1982	PHI N	7	1	.875	3.75	47	0	0	72	70	22	43	0	7	1	2	9	1	0	.111	5	14	1	0	0.4	.950
1983	2 teams	PHI N	(14G 3–0)		SD N	(47G 7–3)																					
"	total	10	3	.769	3.70	61	0	0	80.1	85	37	39	0	10	3	7	11	1	0	.091	4	10	0	0	0.2	1.000
1984	2 teams	SD N	(13G 2–1)		DET A	(19G 1–0)																					
"	total	3	1	.750	4.41	32	0	0	51	57	29	26	0	3	1	0	1	0	0	.000	1	3	1	0	0.2	.800
10 yrs.		49	40	.551	3.53	435	17	4	764	708	356	471	0	45	32	56	21	2	0	.095	37	89	11	5	0.3	.920

Ed Monroe

MONROE, EDWARD OLIVER (Peck)
B. Feb. 22, 1895, Louisville, Ky. D. Apr. 29, 1969, Louisville, Ky.
BR TR 6'5" 187 lbs.

Year	Team	W	L	PCT	ERA	G	GS	CG	IP	H	BB	SO	ShO	W	L	SV	AB	H	HR	BA	PO	A	E	DP	TC/G	FA
1917	NY A	1	0	1.000	3.45	9	1	1	28.2	35	6	12	0	0	0	1	12	2	0	.167	0	9	2	1	1.2	.818
1918		0	0	–	4.50	1	0	0	2	1	2	1	0	0	0	0	0	0	0	–	0	1	1	1	2.0	.500
2 yrs.		1	0	1.000	3.52	10	1	1	30.2	36	8	13	0	0	0	1	12	2	0	.167	0	10	3	2	1.3	.769

Larry Monroe

MONROE, LAWRENCE JAMES
B. June 20, 1956, Detroit, Mich.
BR TR 6'4" 200 lbs.

Year	Team	W	L	PCT	ERA	G	GS	CG	IP	H	BB	SO	ShO	W	L	SV	AB	H	HR	BA	PO	A	E	DP	TC/G	FA
1976	CHI A	0	1	.000	4.09	8	2	0	22	23	13	9	0	0	0	0	0	0	0	–	5	1	0	0	0.8	1.000

Zack Monroe

MONROE, ZACHARY CHARLES
B. July 8, 1931, Peoria, Ill.
BR TR 6' 198 lbs.

Year	Team	W	L	PCT	ERA	G	GS	CG	IP	H	BB	SO	ShO	W	L	SV	AB	H	HR	BA	PO	A	E	DP	TC/G	FA
1958	NY A	4	2	.667	3.26	21	6	1	58	57	27	18	0	1	1	1	17	2	0	.118	7	10	1	2	0.9	.944
1959		0	0	–	5.40	3	0	0	3.1	3	2	1	0	0	0	0	0	0	0	–	0	1	0	0	0.3	1.000
2 yrs.		4	2	.667	3.38	24	6	1	61.1	60	29	19	0	1	1	1	17	2	0	.118	7	11	1	2	0.8	.947

WORLD SERIES

Year	Team	W	L	PCT	ERA	G	GS	CG	IP	H	BB	SO	ShO	W	L	SV	AB	H	HR	BA	PO	A	E	DP	TC/G	FA
1958	NY A	0	0	–	27.00	1	0	0	1	3	1	1	0	0	0	0	0	0	0	–	0	0	0	0	0.0	–

John Montague

MONTAGUE, JOHN EVANS
B. Sept. 12, 1947, Newport News, Va.
BR TR 6'2" 213 lbs.

Year	Team	W	L	PCT	ERA	G	GS	CG	IP	H	BB	SO	ShO	W	L	SV	AB	H	HR	BA	PO	A	E	DP	TC/G	FA
1973	MON N	0	0	–	3.52	4	0	0	7.2	8	2	7	0	0	0	0	1	0	0	.000	0	0	0	0	0.0	–
1974		3	4	.429	3.14	46	1	0	83	73	38	43	0	3	3	3	10	1	0	.100	6	5	3	1	0.3	.786
1975	2 teams	MON N	(12G 0–1)		PHI N	(3G 0–0)																					
"	total	0	1	.000	6.35	15	0	0	22.2	31	10	10	0	0	1	2	1	0	0	.000	0	5	1	1	0.4	.833
1977	SEA A	8	12	.400	4.30	47	15	2	182	193	75	98	0	4	4	4	0	0	0	–	11	33	0	1	0.9	1.000
1978		1	3	.250	6.18	19	0	0	43.2	52	24	14	0	1	3	2	0	0	0	–	2	5	1	0	0.4	.875
1979	2 teams	SEA A	(41G 6–4)		CAL A	(14G 2–0)																					
"	total	8	4	.667	5.51	55	0	0	134	141	56	66	0	8	3	7	0	0	0	–	6	23	0	0	0.5	.967
1980	CAL A	4	2	.667	5.11	37	0	0	74	97	21	22	0	4	2	3	0	0	0	–	4	13	0	1	0.5	1.000
7 yrs.		24	26	.480	4.76	223	17	2	547	595	226	260	0	20	16	21	12	1	0	.083	29	84	4	4	0.5	.950

LEAGUE CHAMPIONSHIP SERIES

Year	Team	W	L	PCT	ERA	G	GS	CG	IP	H	BB	SO	ShO	W	L	SV	AB	H	HR	BA	PO	A	E	DP	TC/G	FA
1979	CAL A	0	1	.000	9.00	2	0	0	4	4	2	2	0	0	1	0	0	0	0	–	1	2	0	0	1.5	1.000

Rafael Montalvo

MONTALVO, RAFAEL EDGARDO
Born Rafael Edgardo Montalvo y Torres.
B. Mar. 31, 1964, Rio Piedras, Puerto Rico
BR TR 6' 185 lbs.

Year	Team	W	L	PCT	ERA	G	GS	CG	IP	H	BB	SO	ShO	W	L	SV	AB	H	HR	BA	PO	A	E	DP	TC/G	FA
1986	HOU N	0	0	–	9.00	1	0	0	2	1	2	0	0	0	0	0	0	0	0	–	1	1	0	0	2.0	1.000

Aurelio Monteagudo

MONTEAGUDO, AURELIO FAUSTINO
Born Aurelio Faustino Monteagudo y Cintra. Son of Rene Monteagudo.
B. Nov. 19, 1943, Caibarien, Cuba
BR TR 5'11" 180 lbs.

Year	Team	W	L	PCT	ERA	G	GS	CG	IP	H	BB	SO	ShO	W	L	SV	AB	H	HR	BA	PO	A	E	DP	TC/G	FA
1963	KC A	0	0	–	2.57	4	0	0	7	3	3	3	0	0	0	0	0	0	0	–	0	3	0	0	0.8	1.000
1964		0	4	.000	8.90	11	6	0	31.1	40	10	14	0	0	0	0	7	2	0	.286	3	3	1	1	0.6	.857
1965		0	0	–	3.86	4	0	0	7	5	4	5	0	0	0	0	0	0	0	–	0	0	0	0	0.0	–
1966	2 teams	KC A	(6G 0–0)		HOU N	(10G 0–0)																					
"	total	0	0	–	3.86	16	0	0	28	26	18	10	0	0	0	1	1	0	0	.000	0	4	0	2	0.3	1.000
1967	CHI A	0	1	.000	20.25	1	1	0	1.1	4	2	0	0	0	0	0	0	0	0	–	0	0	0	0	0.0	–
1970	KC A	1	1	.500	3.00	21	0	0	27	20	9	18	0	1	1	0	2	0	0	.000	1	2	1	0	0.2	.750
1973	CAL A	2	1	.667	4.20	15	0	0	30	23	16	8	0	2	1	3	0	0	0	–	6	3	1	0	0.6	1.000
7 yrs.		3	7	.300	5.06	72	7	0	131.2	122	62	58	0	3	2	4	10	2	0	.200	10	15	4	4	0.4	.926

Rene Monteagudo

MONTEAGUDO, RENE
Born Rene Monteagudo y Miranda. Father of Aurelio Monteagudo.
B. Mar. 12, 1916, Havana, Cuba D. Sept. 14, 1973, Hialeah, Fla.
BL TL 5'7" 165 lbs.

Year	Team	W	L	PCT	ERA	G	GS	CG	IP	H	BB	SO	ShO	W	L	SV	AB	H	HR	BA	PO	A	E	DP	TC/G	FA
1938	WAS A	1	1	.500	5.73	5	3	2	22	26	15	13	0	0	0	0	6	3	0	.500	0	1	0	0	0.2	1.000
1940		2	6	.250	6.08	27	8	3	100.2	128	52	64	0	0	0	1	33	6	0	.182	5	11	1	1	0.6	.941
1945	PHI N	0	0	–	7.49	14	0	0	45.2	67	28	16	0	0	0	0	193	58	0	.301	1	6	2	1	0.6	.778
3 yrs.		3	7	.300	6.42	46	11	5	168.1	221	95	93	0	0	0	2	*				6	18	3	2	0.6	.889

John Montefusco

MONTEFUSCO, JOHN JOSEPH (The Count)
B. May 25, 1950, Long Branch, N. J.
BR TR 6'1" 180 lbs.

Year	Team	W	L	PCT	ERA	G	GS	CG	IP	H	BB	SO	ShO	W	L	SV	AB	H	HR	BA	PO	A	E	DP	TC/G	FA
1974	SF N	3	2	.600	4.85	7	5	1	39	41	19	34	1	1	0	0	14	4	2	.286	0	4	0	0	0.6	1.000
1975		15	9	.625	2.88	35	34	10	244	210	86	215	4	0	0	0	80	7	1	.088	11	25	1	0	1.1	.973
1976		16	14	.533	2.84	37	36	11	253.1	224	74	172	6	0	0	0	78	8	0	.103	12	21	3	0	1.0	.917
1977		7	12	.368	3.50	26	25	4	157	170	46	110	0	0	0	0	49	6	1	.122	10	12	1	0	0.9	.957
1978		11	9	.550	3.80	36	36	3	239	233	68	177	0	0	0	0	70	4	0	.057	8	28	2	1	1.1	.947

Year	Team		W	L	PCT	ERA	G	GS	CG	IP	H	BB	SO	ShO	Relief Pitching W	L	SV	Batting AB	H	HR	BA	PO	A	E	DP	TC/G	FA

John Montefusco *continued*

Year	Team		W	L	PCT	ERA	G	GS	CG	IP	H	BB	SO	ShO	W	L	SV	AB	H	HR	BA	PO	A	E	DP	TC/G	FA
1979			3	8	.273	3.94	22	22	0	137	145	51	76	0	0	0	0	42	7	0	.167	9	20	1	2	1.4	.967
1980			4	8	.333	4.38	22	17	1	113	120	39	85	0	1	0	0	30	1	0	.033	6	9	0	1	0.7	1.000
1981	ATL	N	2	3	.400	3.51	26	9	0	77	75	27	34	0	0	0	1	15	1	0	.067	6	12	1	1	0.7	.947
1982	SD	N	10	11	.476	4.00	32	32	1	184.1	177	41	83	0	0	0	0	58	5	0	.086	11	29	3	0	1.3	.930
1983	2 teams		SD	N	(31G 9–4)		NY	A	(6G 5–0)																		
"	total		14	4	.778	3.31	37	16	1	133.1	133	42	67	0	6	1	4	19	1	0	.053	5	16	3	0	0.6	.875
1984	NY	A	5	3	.625	3.58	11	11	0	55.1	55	13	23	0	0	0	0				–	1	7	1	1	0.8	.889
1985			0	0	–	10.29	3	1	0	7	12	2	2	0	0	0	0	0	0	0	–	1	0	0	0	0.7	1.000
1986			0	0	–	2.19	4	0	0	12.1	9	5	3	0	0	0	0	0	0	0	–	2	3	0	1	1.3	1.000
13 yrs.			90	83	.520	3.54	298	244	32	1651.2	1604	513	1081	11	8	1	5	455	44	4	.097	82	187	16	8	1.0	.944

Manny Montejo

MONTEJO, MANUEL (Pete)
Born Manuel Montejo y Bofill.
B. Oct. 16, 1935, Caibarien, Cuba

BR TR 5'11" 150 lbs.

Year	Team		W	L	PCT	ERA	G	GS	CG	IP	H	BB	SO	ShO	W	L	SV	AB	H	HR	BA	PO	A	E	DP	TC/G	FA
1961	DET	A	0	0	–	3.86	12	0	0	16.1	13	6	15	0	0	0	0	0	0	0	–	0	0	0	0	0.0	–

Rich Monteleone

MONTELEONE, RICHARD
B. Mar. 22, 1963, Tampa, Fla.

BR TR 6'2" 205 lbs.

Year	Team		W	L	PCT	ERA	G	GS	CG	IP	H	BB	SO	ShO	W	L	SV	AB	H	HR	BA	PO	A	E	DP	TC/G	FA
1987	SEA	A	0	0	–	6.43	3	0	0	7	10	4	2	0	0	0	0	0	0	0	–	0	3	0	0	1.0	1.000
1988	CAL	A	0	0	–	0.00	3	0	0	4.1	4	1	3	0	0	0	0	0	0	0	–	0	1	0	0	0.3	1.000
1989			2	2	.500	3.18	24	0	0	39.2	39	13	27	0	2	2	0	0	0	0	–	1	9	1	1	0.5	.909
3 yrs.			2	2	.500	3.35	30	0	0	51	53	18	32	0	2	2	0	0	0	0	–	1	13	1	1	0.5	.933

Jeff Montgomery

MONTGOMERY, JEFFREY THOMAS
B. Jan. 7, 1962, Wellston, Ohio

BR TR 5'11" 170 lbs.

Year	Team		W	L	PCT	ERA	G	GS	CG	IP	H	BB	SO	ShO	W	L	SV	AB	H	HR	BA	PO	A	E	DP	TC/G	FA
1987	CIN	N	2	2	.500	6.52	14	1	0	19.1	25	9	13	0	2	1	0	2	0	0	.000	1	3	0	0	0.3	1.000
1988	KC	A	7	2	.778	3.45	45	0	0	62.2	54	30	47	0	7	2	1	0	0	0	–	3	10	1	0	0.3	.929
1989			7	3	.700	1.37	63	0	0	92	66	25	94	0	7	3	18	0	0	0	–	11	6	2	1	0.3	.895
3 yrs.			16	7	.696	2.69	122	1	0	174	145	64	154	0	16	6	19	2	0	0	.000	15	19	3	1	0.3	.919

Monty Montgomery

MONTGOMERY, MONTY BRYSON
B. Sept. 1, 1946, Albemarle, N. C.

BR TR 6'3" 200 lbs.

Year	Team		W	L	PCT	ERA	G	GS	CG	IP	H	BB	SO	ShO	W	L	SV	AB	H	HR	BA	PO	A	E	DP	TC/G	FA
1971	KC	A	3	0	1.000	2.14	3	2	0	21	16	3	12	0	1	0	0	7	0	0	.000	2	5	0	0	1.7	1.000
1972			3	3	.500	3.05	9	8	1	56	55	17	24	1	0	0	0	17	3	0	.176	3	7	0	2	1.1	1.000
2 yrs.			6	3	.667	2.81	12	10	1	77	71	20	36	1	1	0	0	24	3	0	.125	5	10	0	2	1.3	1.000

Ray Monzant

MONZANT, RAMON SEGUNDO
Born Ramon Segundo Monzant y Espina.
B. Jan. 4, 1933, Maracaibo, Venezuela

BR TR 6' 160 lbs.

Year	Team		W	L	PCT	ERA	G	GS	CG	IP	H	BB	SO	ShO	W	L	SV	AB	H	HR	BA	PO	A	E	DP	TC/G	FA
1954	NY	N	0	0	–	4.70	6	1	0	7.2	8	11	5	0	0	0	0	2	0	0	.000	0	0	1	0	0.2	–
1955			4	8	.333	3.99	28	12	3	94.2	98	43	54	0	2	1	0	24	3	0	.125	7	10	2	0	0.7	.895
1956			1	0	1.000	4.15	4	1	1	13	8	7	11	0	0	0	0	4	0	0	.000	0	2	0	0	0.5	1.000
1957			3	2	.600	3.99	24	2	0	49.2	55	16	37	0	3	0	0	10	3	0	.300	1	2	0	0	0.1	1.000
1958	SF	N	8	11	.421	4.72	43	16	4	150.2	160	57	93	1	3	5	1	49	8	0	.163	16	26	2	4	1.0	.955
1960			0	0	–	9.00	1	0	0	1	1	0	1	0	0	0	0	0	0	0	–	0	1	0	0	1.0	1.000
6 yrs.			16	21	.432	4.38	106	32	8	316.2	330	134	201	1	8	6	1	89	14	0	.157	24	41	5	4	0.7	.929

Leo Moon

MOON, LEO (Lefty)
B. June 22, 1899, Belmont, N. C.   D. Aug. 25, 1970, New Orleans, La.

BR TL 5'11" 165 lbs.

Year	Team		W	L	PCT	ERA	G	GS	CG	IP	H	BB	SO	ShO	W	L	SV	AB	H	HR	BA	PO	A	E	DP	TC/G	FA
1932	CLE	A	0	0	–	11.12	1	0	0	5.2	11	7	1	0	0	0	0	2	1	0	.500	0	2	0	0	2.0	1.000

Jim Mooney

MOONEY, JIM IRVING
B. Sept. 4, 1906, Mooresburg, Tenn.   D. Apr. 27, 1979, Johnson City, Tenn.

BR TL 5'11" 168 lbs.

Year	Team		W	L	PCT	ERA	G	GS	CG	IP	H	BB	SO	ShO	W	L	SV	AB	H	HR	BA	PO	A	E	DP	TC/G	FA
1931	NY	N	7	1	.875	2.01	10	8	4	71.2	71	16	38	2	1	0	0	25	4	0	.160	1	10	0	1	1.1	1.000
1932			6	10	.375	5.05	29	18	4	124.2	154	42	37	1	0	1	0	41	5	0	.122	2	21	2	2	0.9	.920
1933	STL	N	2	5	.286	3.72	21	8	2	77.1	87	26	14	0	0	1	1	20	1	0	.050	2	22	1	0	1.2	.960
1934			2	4	.333	5.47	32	7	1	82.1	114	49	27	0	2	0	1	19	1	0	.053	3	12	2	0	0.5	.882
4 yrs.			17	20	.459	4.25	92	41	13	356	426	133	116	3	3	2	2	105	11	0	.105	8	65	5	3	0.9	.936

WORLD SERIES

Year	Team		W	L	PCT	ERA	G	GS	CG	IP	H	BB	SO	ShO	W	L	SV	AB	H	HR	BA	PO	A	E	DP	TC/G	FA
1934	STL	N	0	0	–	0.00	1	0	0	1	1	0	0	0	0	0	0	0	0	0	–	0	1	0	0	1.0	1.000

Bill Mooneyham

MOONEYHAM, WILLIAM CRAIG
B. Aug. 16, 1960, Livermore, Calif.

BR TR 6' 175 lbs.

Year	Team		W	L	PCT	ERA	G	GS	CG	IP	H	BB	SO	ShO	W	L	SV	AB	H	HR	BA	PO	A	E	DP	TC/G	FA
1986	OAK	A	4	5	.444	4.52	45	6	0	99.2	103	67	75	0	4	3	2	0	0	0	–	5	17	2	1	0.5	.917

Balor Moore

MOORE, BALOR LILBON
B. Jan. 25, 1951, Smithville, Tex.

BL TL 6'2" 178 lbs.

Year	Team		W	L	PCT	ERA	G	GS	CG	IP	H	BB	SO	ShO	W	L	SV	AB	H	HR	BA	PO	A	E	DP	TC/G	FA
1970	MON	N	0	2	.000	7.20	6	2	0	10	14	8	6	0	0	0	0	3	1	0	.333	1	2	1	1	0.7	.750
1972			9	9	.500	3.47	22	22	6	147.2	122	59	161	3	0	0	0	55	8	0	.145	4	21	3	0	1.3	.893
1973			7	16	.304	4.49	35	32	3	176.1	151	109	151	1	0	0	0	53	3	0	.057	11	19	4	2	1.0	.882
1974			0	2	.000	3.86	8	2	0	14	13	15	16	0	0	0	0	2	0	0	.000	0	1	0	0	0.3	.500
1977	CAL	A	0	2	.000	3.97	7	3	0	22.2	28	10	14	0	0	0	0	0	0	0	–	0	2	0	0	0.4	.667
1978	TOR	A	6	9	.400	4.86	37	18	2	144.1	165	54	75	0	0	0	0				–	4	29	3	2	1.0	.917
1979			5	7	.417	4.86	34	16	5	139	135	79	51	0	0	0	0				–	4	22	4	1	0.9	.867
1980			1	1	.500	5.26	31	3	0	65	76	31	22	0	3	0	1				–	2	10	2	1	0.5	.857
8 yrs.			28	48	.368	4.51	180	98	16	719	704	365	496	4	3	0	1	113	12	0	.106	26	106	19	7	0.8	.874

Year	Team	W	L	PCT	ERA	G	GS	CG	IP	H	BB	SO	ShO	W	L	SV	AB	H	HR	BA	PO	A	E	DP	TC/G	FA

Barry Moore

MOORE, ROBERT BARRY   BL TL 6'1"   190 lbs.
B. Apr. 3, 1943, Statesville, N. C.

Year	Team	W	L	PCT	ERA	G	GS	CG	IP	H	BB	SO	ShO	W	L	SV	AB	H	HR	BA	PO	A	E	DP	TC/G	FA
1965	WAS A	0	0	–	0.00	1	0	0	1	1	1	0	0	0	0	0	0	0	0	–	0	0	0	0	0.0	
1966		3	3	.500	3.75	12	11	1	62.1	55	39	28	0	0	0	0	19	2	0	.105	2	13	0	1	1.3	1.000
1967		7	11	.389	3.76	27	26	3	143.2	127	71	74	1	0	0	0	46	6	0	.130	6	31	2	2	1.4	.949
1968		4	6	.400	3.37	32	18	0	117.2	116	42	56	0	0	0	3	31	3	0	.097	9	24	1	1	1.1	.971
1969		9	8	.529	4.30	31	25	4	134	123	67	51	0	0	0	2	43	9	0	.209	3	14	1	2	0.6	.944
1970	2 teams	CLE A	(13G 3–5)			CHI A	(24G 0–4)																			
"	total	3	9	.250	5.30	37	19	0	141	155	80	69	0	0	0	0	40	7	0	.175	11	28	2	1	1.1	.951
6 yrs.		26	37	.413	4.16	140	99	8	599.2	577	300	278	1	0	2	3	179	27	0	.151	31	110	6	6	1.1	.959

Bill Moore

MOORE, WILLIAM CHRISTOPHER   BR TR 6'3"   195 lbs.
B. Sept. 3, 1902, Corning, N. Y.   D. Jan. 24, 1984, Corning, N. Y.

Year	Team	W	L	PCT	ERA	G	GS	CG	IP	H	BB	SO	ShO	W	L	SV	AB	H	HR	BA	PO	A	E	DP	TC/G	FA
1925	DET A	0	0	–	∞	1	0	0	0	3	0	0	0	0	0	0	0	0	0	–	0	0	0	0	0.0	–

Bob Moore

MOORE, ROBERT DEVELL   BR TR 6'5"   215 lbs.
B. Nov. 8, 1958, Sweetwater, La.

Year	Team	W	L	PCT	ERA	G	GS	CG	IP	H	BB	SO	ShO	W	L	SV	AB	H	HR	BA	PO	A	E	DP	TC/G	FA
1985	SF N	0	0	–	3.24	11	0	0	16.2	18	10	10	0	0	0	0	2	0	0	.000	0	1	1	0	0.2	.500

Brad Moore

MOORE, BRADLEY ALAN   BR TR 6'1"   185 lbs.
B. June 21, 1964, Loveland, Colo.

Year	Team	W	L	PCT	ERA	G	GS	CG	IP	H	BB	SO	ShO	W	L	SV	AB	H	HR	BA	PO	A	E	DP	TC/G	FA
1988	PHI N	0	0	–	0.00	5	0	0	5.2	4	4	2	0	0	0	0	0	0	0	–	2	1	0	0	0.6	1.000

Carlos Moore

MOORE, CARLOS WHITMAN   BR TR 6'1½"   180 lbs.
B. Aug. 13, 1906, Clinton, Tenn.   D. July 2, 1958, New Orleans, La.

Year	Team	W	L	PCT	ERA	G	GS	CG	IP	H	BB	SO	ShO	W	L	SV	AB	H	HR	BA	PO	A	E	DP	TC/G	FA
1930	WAS A	0	0	–	2.31	4	0	0	11.2	9	4	0	0	0	0	0	4	0	0	.000	2	1	0	0	0.8	1.000

Cy Moore

MOORE, WILLIAM AUSTIN   BR TR 6'1"   190 lbs.
B. Feb. 7, 1905, Elberton, Ga.   D. Mar. 28, 1972, Augusta, Ga.

Year	Team	W	L	PCT	ERA	G	GS	CG	IP	H	BB	SO	ShO	W	L	SV	AB	H	HR	BA	PO	A	E	DP	TC/G	FA
1929	BKN N	3	3	.500	5.56	32	4	0	68	87	31	17	0	2	1	2	16	3	0	.188	2	11	0	1	0.4	1.000
1930		0	0	–	0.00	1	0	0	2	2	0	0	0	0	0	0	0	0	0	–	0	0	0	0	0.0	–
1931		1	2	.333	3.79	23	1	1	61.2	62	13	35	0	1	1	0	13	2	0	.154	2	12	0	0	0.6	1.000
1932		0	3	.000	4.81	20	2	0	48.2	56	17	23	0	0	2	0	14	3	0	.214	5	11	1	0	0.9	.941
1933	PHI N	8	9	.471	3.74	36	18	9	161.1	177	42	53	3	2	0	1	48	3	0	.063	6	35	1	1	1.2	.976
1934		4	9	.308	6.47	35	15	3	126.2	163	65	55	0	2	0	0	42	6	0	.143	2	21	2	2	0.7	.920
6 yrs.		16	26	.381	4.86	147	40	13	466.1	547	168	183	3	7	4	3	133	17	0	.128	17	90	4	4	0.8	.964

Dee Moore

MOORE, D C   BR TR 6'   200 lbs.
B. Apr. 6, 1914, Hedley, Tex.

Year	Team	W	L	PCT	ERA	G	GS	CG	IP	H	BB	SO	ShO	W	L	SV	AB	H	HR	BA	PO	A	E	DP	TC/G	FA
1936	CIN N	0	0	–	0.00	2	1	0	7	3	2	3	0	0	0	0	*				0	3	0	0	1.5	1.000

Donnie Moore

MOORE, DONNIE RAY   BL TR 6'   175 lbs.
B. Feb. 13, 1954, Lubbock, Tex.   D. July 18, 1989, Anaheim, Calif.

Year	Team	W	L	PCT	ERA	G	GS	CG	IP	H	BB	SO	ShO	W	L	SV	AB	H	HR	BA	PO	A	E	DP	TC/G	FA
1975	CHI N	0	0	–	4.00	4	0	0	9	12	4	4	0	0	0	0	3	0	0	.000	2	0	0	0	0.5	1.000
1977		4	2	.667	4.04	27	1	0	49	51	18	34	0	4	2	0	10	3	0	.300	4	11	2	1	0.6	.882
1978		9	7	.563	4.11	71	1	0	103	117	31	50	0	9	7	4	15	4	0	.267	10	16	2	0	0.4	.929
1979		1	4	.200	5.18	39	1	0	73	95	25	43	0	1	3	1	13	2	0	.154	6	15	2	0	0.6	.913
1980	STL N	1	1	.500	6.14	11	0	0	22	25	5	10	0	1	1	0	4	3	0	.750	1	1	1	0	0.3	.667
1981	MIL A	0	0	–	6.75	3	0	0	4	4	4	2	0	0	0	0					1	0	0	0	0.7	1.000
1982	ATL N	3	1	.750	4.23	16	0	0	27.2	32	7	17	0	3	1	1	1	0	0	.000	7	3	0	1	0.6	1.000
1983		2	3	.400	3.67	43	0	0	68.2	72	10	41	0	2	3	6	8	4	0	.500	2	8	0	0	0.3	1.000
1984		4	5	.444	2.94	47	0	0	64.1	63	18	47	0	4	5	16	3	0	0	.000	3	10	1	1	0.3	.929
1985	CAL A	8	8	.500	1.92	65	0	0	103	91	21	72	0	8	8	31	0	0	0	–	4	12	2	1	0.3	.889
1986		4	5	.444	2.97	49	0	0	72.2	60	22	53	0	4	5	21	0	0	0	–	2	7	1	0	0.2	.900
1987		2	2	.500	2.70	14	0	0	26.2	28	13	17	0	2	2	5	0	0	0	–	1	4	0	0	0.3	1.000
1988		5	2	.714	4.91	27	0	0	33	48	8	22	0	5	2	4	0	0	0	–	3	4	0	0	0.3	1.000
13 yrs.		43	40	.518	3.66	416	4	0	656	698	186	416	0	43	39	89	57	16	0	.281	45	90	11	4	0.4	.925

LEAGUE CHAMPIONSHIP SERIES

Year	Team	W	L	PCT	ERA	G	GS	CG	IP	H	BB	SO	ShO	W	L	SV	AB	H	HR	BA	PO	A	E	DP	TC/G	FA
1982	ATL A	0	0	–	0.00	2	0	0	2.2	2	0	1	0	0	0	0	0	0	0	–	0	0	0	0	0.0	–
1986	CAL A	0	1	.000	7.20	3	0	0	5	8	2	0	0	0	1	1	0	0	0	–	1	0	0	0	0.3	1.000
2 yrs.		0	1	.000	4.70	5	0	0	7.2	10	2	1	0	0	1	1	0	0	0	–	1	0	0	0	0.2	1.000

Earl Moore

MOORE, EARL ALONZO (Steam Engine In Boots)   BR TR 6'   195 lbs.
B. July 29, 1879, Pickerington, Ohio   D. Nov. 28, 1961, Columbus, Ohio

Year	Team	W	L	PCT	ERA	G	GS	CG	IP	H	BB	SO	ShO	W	L	SV	AB	H	HR	BA	PO	A	E	DP	TC/G	FA
1901	CLE A	16	14	.533	2.90	31	30	28	251.1	234	107	99	4	0	0	0	99	16	0	.162	9	45	7	2	2.0	.885
1902		17	17	.500	2.95	36	34	29	293	304	101	84	4	1	0	1	113	24	0	.212	7	79	3	4	2.5	.966
1903		19	9	.679	1.77	29	27	27	238.2	189	56	142	3	0	1	1	84	8	0	.095	5	56	5	0	2.3	.924
1904		12	11	.522	2.25	26	24	22	227.2	186	61	139	1	0	1	0	86	12	0	.140	6	40	8	1	2.1	.852
1905		15	15	.500	2.64	31	30	28	269	232	92	131	3	0	0	0	94	10	0	.106	14	72	7	0	3.0	.925
1906		1	1	.500	3.94	5	4	2	29.2	27	18	8	0	0	0	0	10	0	0	.000	0	6	1	1	1.4	.857
1907	2 teams	CLE A	(3G 1–1)			NY A	(12G 2–6)																			
"	total	3	7	.300	4.10	15	11	4	83.1	90	38	35	0	0	0	1	29	6	0	.207	1	27	2	0	2.0	.933
1908	PHI N	2	1	.667	0.00	3	3	3	26	20	8	16	1	0	0	0	9	2	0	.222	0	4	0	0	1.3	1.000
1909		18	12	.600	2.10	38	34	24	299.2	238	108	173	4	2	1	0	96	9	0	.094	10	54	6	1	1.8	.914
1910		22	15	.595	2.58	46	35	19	283	228	121	185	6	3	3	0	87	20	0	.230	3	57	4	2	1.4	.938
1911		15	19	.441	2.63	42	36	21	308.1	265	164	174	1	0	0	0	101	11	0	.109	3	63	5	2	1.7	.930
1912		9	14	.391	3.31	31	24	10	182.1	186	77	79	1	2	0	0	56	6	0	.107	4	34	3	2	1.3	.927

Year	Team	W	L	PCT	ERA	G	GS	CG	IP	H	BB	SO	ShO	W	L	SV	AB	H	HR	BA	PO	A	E	DP	TC/G	FA
														Relief Pitching			**Batting**									

Earl Moore continued

Year	Team	W	L	PCT	ERA	G	GS	CG	IP	H	BB	SO	ShO	W	L	SV	AB	H	HR	BA	PO	A	E	DP	TC/G	FA
1913	**2 teams**						PHI N (12G 1–3)		CHI N (7G 1–1)																	
"	total	2	4	.333	4.82	19	6	0	80.1	84	52	36	0	0	0	1	24	1	0	.042	2	29	2	1	1.7	.939
1914	BUF F	10	14	.417	4.30	36	27	14	194.2	184	99	96	2	0	1	2	56	9	0	.161	2	51	7	1	1.7	.883
14 yrs.		161	153	.513	2.78	388	325	231	2767	2467	1102	1397	34	8	9	7	944	134	0	.142	66	617	60	17	1.9	.919

Euel Moore

MOORE, EUEL WALTON (Chief)   BR TR 6'2"   185 lbs.
B. May 27, 1908, Reagan, Okla. D. Feb. 12, 1989, Tishomingo, Okla.

Year	Team	W	L	PCT	ERA	G	GS	CG	IP	H	BB	SO	ShO	W	L	SV	AB	H	HR	BA	PO	A	E	DP	TC/G	FA
1934	PHI N	5	7	.417	4.05	20	16	3	122.1	145	41	38	0	0	1	1	46	5	0	.109	0	22	2	0	1.2	.917
1935	**2 teams**						PHI N (15G 1–6)		NY N (6G 1–0)																	
"	total	2	6	.250	7.45	21	8	1	48.1	72	24	18	0	1	0	1	17	6	0	.353	0	12	2	2	0.7	.857
1936	PHI N	2	3	.400	6.96	20	5	1	54.1	76	12	19	0	0	2	1	18	4	0	.222	1	7	4	1	0.6	.667
3 yrs.		9	16	.360	5.48	61	29	5	225	293	77	75	0	1	3	3	81	15	0	.185	1	41	8	3	0.8	.840

Gene Moore

MOORE, EUGENE SR. (Blue Goose)   BL TL 6'2"   185 lbs.
Father of Gene Moore.
B. Nov. 9, 1885, Lancaster, Tex. D. Aug. 31, 1938, Dallas, Tex.

Year	Team	W	L	PCT	ERA	G	GS	CG	IP	H	BB	SO	ShO	W	L	SV	AB	H	HR	BA	PO	A	E	DP	TC/G	FA
1909	PIT N	0	0	–	18.00	1	0	0	2	4	3	2	0	0	0	0	1	0	0	.000	0	0	0	0	0.0	–
1910		2	1	.667	3.12	4	1	0	17.1	19	7	9	0	2	1	0	6	0	0	.000	1	5	0	1	1.5	1.000
1912	CIN N	0	1	.000	4.91	5	2	0	14.2	17	11	6	0	0	0	1	4	0	0	.000	0	3	0	0	0.6	1.000
3 yrs.		2	2	.500	4.76	10	3	0	34	40	21	17	0	2	1	1	11	0	0	.000	1	8	0	1	0.9	1.000

George Moore

MOORE, GEORGE RAYMOND   BB TR 5'10"   165 lbs.
B. Nov. 25, 1872, Cambridge, Mass. D. Nov. 17, 1948, Barnstable, Mass.

Year	Team	W	L	PCT	ERA	G	GS	CG	IP	H	BB	SO	ShO	W	L	SV	AB	H	HR	BA	PO	A	E	DP	TC/G	FA
1905	PIT N	0	0	–	0.00	1	0	0	3	2	0	1	0	0	0	0	1	0	0	.000	0	0	0	0	0.0	–

Jim Moore

MOORE, JAMES STANFORD   BR TR 6'   165 lbs.
B. Dec. 14, 1903, Prescott, Ark. D. May 19, 1973, Seattle, Wash.

Year	Team	W	L	PCT	ERA	G	GS	CG	IP	H	BB	SO	ShO	W	L	SV	AB	H	HR	BA	PO	A	E	DP	TC/G	FA
1928	CLE A	0	1	.000	2.00	1	1	1	9	5	5	1	0	0	0	0	3	0	0	.000	0	1	0	0	1.0	1.000
1929		0	0	–	9.53	2	0	0	5.2	6	4	0	0	0	0	0	2	0	0	.000	0	3	0	0	1.5	1.000
1930	CHI A	2	1	.667	3.60	9	5	2	40	42	12	11	0	0	0	1	13	3	0	.231	1	8	0	0	1.0	1.000
1931		0	2	.000	4.95	33	4	0	83.2	93	27	15	0	0	0	0	16	1	0	.063	2	25	3	1	0.9	.900
1932		0	0	–	0.00	1	0	0	1	1	1	2	0	0	0	0	1	0	0	.000	0	0	0	0	0.0	–
5 yrs.		2	4	.333	4.52	46	10	3	139.1	147	49	29	0	0	0	1	35	4	0	.114	3	37	3	1	0.9	.930

Mike Moore

MOORE, MICHAEL WAYNE   BR TR 6'4"   205 lbs.
B. Nov. 26, 1959, Carnegie, Okla.

Year	Team	W	L	PCT	ERA	G	GS	CG	IP	H	BB	SO	ShO	W	L	SV	AB	H	HR	BA	PO	A	E	DP	TC/G	FA
1982	SEA A	7	14	.333	5.36	28	27	1	144.1	159	79	73	1	0	0	0	0	0	0	–	13	27	5	2	1.6	.889
1983		6	8	.429	4.71	22	21	3	128	130	60	108	2	0	0	0	0	0	0	–	7	24	1	0	1.5	.969
1984		7	17	.292	4.97	34	33	6	212	236	85	158	0	0	0	0	0	0	0	–	18	41	7	0	1.9	.894
1985		17	10	.630	3.46	35	34	14	247	230	70	155	2	0	0	0	0	0	0	–	21	43	2	1	1.9	.970
1986		11	13	.458	4.30	38	**37**	11	266	**279**	94	146	1	0	0	0	0	0	0	–	23	33	4	1	1.6	.933
1987		9	**19**	.321	4.71	33	33	12	231	**268**	84	115	0	0	0	0	1	0	0	.000	22	34	2	4	1.8	.966
1988		9	15	.375	3.78	37	32	9	228.2	196	63	182	3	1	0	1	0	0	0	–	19	29	1	3	1.3	.980
1989	OAK A	19	11	.633	2.61	35	35	6	241.2	193	83	172	3	0	0	0	0	0	0	–	25	37	2	5	1.8	.969
8 yrs.		85	107	.443	4.13	262	252	62	1698.2	1691	618	1109	12	1	0	2	1	0	0	.000	148	268	24	16	1.7	.945

LEAGUE CHAMPIONSHIP SERIES

Year	Team	W	L	PCT	ERA	G	GS	CG	IP	H	BB	SO	ShO	W	L	SV	AB	H	HR	BA	PO	A	E	DP	TC/G	FA
1989	OAK A	1	0	1.000	0.00	1	1	0	7	3	2	3	0	0	0	0	0	0	0	–	0	1	0	0	1.0	1.000

WORLD SERIES

Year	Team	W	L	PCT	ERA	G	GS	CG	IP	H	BB	SO	ShO	W	L	SV	AB	H	HR	BA	PO	A	E	DP	TC/G	FA
1989	OAK A	2	0	1.000	2.08	2	2	0	13	9	3	10	0	0	0	0	3	1	0	.333	0	3	0	0	1.5	1.000

Ray Moore

MOORE, RAYMOND LEROY (Farmer)   BR TR 6'   195 lbs.
B. June 1, 1926, Meadows, Md.

Year	Team	W	L	PCT	ERA	G	GS	CG	IP	H	BB	SO	ShO	W	L	SV	AB	H	HR	BA	PO	A	E	DP	TC/G	FA
1952	BKN N	1	2	.333	4.76	14	2	0	28.1	29	26	11	0	1	0	0	3	0	0	.000	0	5	0	1	0.4	1.000
1953		0	1	.000	3.38	1	1	1	8	6	4	4	0	0	0	0	3	0	0	.000	1	0	1	0	2.0	.500
1955	BAL A	10	10	.500	3.92	46	14	3	151.2	128	80	80	1	3	**7**	6	44	6	0	.136	3	20	3	2	0.6	.885
1956		12	7	.632	4.18	32	27	9	185	161	99	105	1	1	1	1	70	19	2	.271	6	22	4	4	1.0	.875
1957		11	13	.458	3.72	34	32	7	227.1	197	**112**	117	1	0	1	0	84	18	3	.214	3	30	0	5	1.0	1.000
1958	CHI A	9	7	.563	3.82	32	20	4	136.2	107	70	73	2	2	3	2	44	9	1	.205	6	20	0	0	0.8	1.000
1959		3	6	.333	4.12	29	8	0	89.2	86	46	49	0	2	1	0	23	2	0	.087	3	14	1	0	0.6	.944
1960	**2 teams**						CHI A (14G 1–1)		WAS A (37G 3–2)																	
"	total	4	3	.571	3.54	51	0	0	86.1	68	38	32	0	4	3	13	16	1	0	.063	5	7	0	0	0.3	1.000
1961	MIN A	4	4	.500	3.67	46	0	0	56.1	49	38	45	0	4	4	14	4	0	0	.000	6	6	0	0	0.3	1.000
1962		8	3	.727	4.73	49	0	0	64.2	55	30	58	0	8	3	9	5	0	0	.000	3	6	0	2	0.2	1.000
1963		1	3	.250	6.98	31	1	0	38.2	50	17	38	0	1	2	2	3	1	0	.333	2	6	1	0	0.3	.889
11 yrs.		63	59	.516	4.06	365	105	24	1072.2	935	560	612	5	26	25	46	299	56	6	.187	41	133	10	14	0.5	.946

WORLD SERIES

Year	Team	W	L	PCT	ERA	G	GS	CG	IP	H	BB	SO	ShO	W	L	SV	AB	H	HR	BA	PO	A	E	DP	TC/G	FA
1959	CHI A	0	0	–	9.00	1	0	0	1	1	0	1	0	0	0	0	0	0	0	–	0	0	0	0	0.0	–

Roy Moore

MOORE, ROY DANIEL   BB TL 6'   185 lbs.
B. Dec. 26, 1898, Austin, Tex.   BL 1921,1923
D. Apr. 5, 1951, Seattle, Wash.

Year	Team	W	L	PCT	ERA	G	GS	CG	IP	H	BB	SO	ShO	W	L	SV	AB	H	HR	BA	PO	A	E	DP	TC/G	FA
1920	PHI A	1	13	.071	4.68	24	16	7	132.2	161	64	45	0	0	0	0	50	10	1	.200	5	40	3	4	2.0	.938
1921		10	10	.500	4.51	29	26	12	191.2	206	122	64	0	0	0	0	74	19	3	.257	9	60	4	5	2.5	.945
1922	**2 teams**						PHI A (15G 0–3)		DET A (9G 0–0)																	
"	total	0	3	.000	7.17	24	6	0	70.1	94	42	38	0	0	1	2	26	8	0	.308	4	14	2	1	0.8	.900
1923	DET A	0	0	–	3.00	3	0	0	12	15	11	7	0	0	0	0	5	0	0	.000	0	6	0	0	2.0	1.000
4 yrs.		11	26	.297	4.98	80	48	19	406.2	476	239	154	0	0	1	3	155	37	4	.239	18	120	9	10	1.8	.939

Year	Team	W	L	PCT	ERA	G	GS	CG	IP	H	BB	SO	ShO	Relief Pitching W	L	SV	Batting AB	H	HR	BA	PO	A	E	DP	TC/G	FA

Terry Moore

MOORE, TERRY BLUFORD
B. May 27, 1912, Vernon, Ala.
Manager 1954.

BR TR 5'11" 195 lbs.

| 1939 | STL N | 0 | 0 | — | 0.00 | 1 | 0 | 0 | 1 | 0 | 0 | 1 | 0 | 0 | 0 | 0 | * | | | | 0 | 1 | 0 | 0 | 1.0 | 1.000 |

Tommy Moore

MOORE, TOMMY JOE
B. July 7, 1948, Lynwood, Calif.

BR TR 5'11" 175 lbs.

1972	NY N	0	0	—	2.92	3	1	0	12.1	12	1	5	0	0	0	0	3	1	0	.333	1	2	0	0	1.0	1.000
1973		0	1	.000	10.80	3	1	0	3.1	6	3	1	0	0	0	0	0	0	0	—	1	0	1	0	0.7	.500
1975	2 teams	STL N	(10G 0–0)		TEX A	(12G 0–2)																				
"	total	0	2	.000	6.08	22	0	0	40	46	24	21	0	0	2	0	2	1	0	.500	5	8	2	1	0.7	.867
1977	SEA A	2	1	.667	4.91	14	1	0	33	36	21	13	0	2	0	0	0	0	0	—	2	2	0	0	0.3	1.000
4 yrs.		2	4	.333	5.38	42	3	0	88.2	100	49	40	0	2	2	0	5	2	0	.400	9	12	3	1	0.6	.875

Whitey Moore

MOORE, LLOYD ALBERT
B. June 10, 1912, Tuscarawas, Ohio   D. Dec. 10, 1987, Uhrichsville, Ohio

BR TR 6'1" 195 lbs.

1936	CIN N	1	0	1.000	5.40	1	0	0	5	3	3	4	0	1	0	0	2	0	0	.000	0	0	0	0	0.0	
1937		0	3	.000	4.89	13	6	0	38.2	32	39	27	0	0	0	0	8	0	0	.000	1	7	0	0	0.6	1.000
1938		6	4	.600	3.49	19	11	3	90.1	66	42	38	1	2	0	0	26	2	0	.077	2	15	1	1	0.9	.944
1939		13	12	.520	3.45	42	24	9	187.2	177	95	81	2	4	3	3	61	6	0	.098	9	32	1	0	1.0	.976
1940		8	8	.500	3.63	25	15	5	116.2	100	56	60	1	2	2	1	39	5	0	.128	3	9	1	0	0.5	.923
1941		2	1	.667	4.38	23	4	1	61.2	62	45	17	0	1	0	0	18	3	0	.167	2	10	2	2	0.6	.857
1942	2 teams	CIN N	(1G 0–0)		STL N	(9G 0–1)																				
"	total	0	1	.000	4.05	10	0	0	13.1	10	12	1	0	0	1	0	2	0	0	.000	1	0	0	0	0.1	1.000
7 yrs.		30	29	.508	3.75	133	60	18	513.1	450	292	228	4	10	3	4	156	16	0	.103	18	73	5	3	0.7	.948

WORLD SERIES

1939	CIN N	0	0	—	0.00	1	0	0	3	0	0	2	0	0	0	0	1	0	0	.000	0	0	0	0	2.0	1.000
1940		0	0	—	3.24	3	0	0	8.1	8	6	7	0	0	0	0	2	0	0	.000	0	1	0	0	0.3	1.000
2 yrs.		0	0	—	2.38	4	0	0	11.1	8	6	9	0	0	0	0	3	0	0	.000	0	3	0	0	0.8	1.000

Wilcy Moore

MOORE, WILLIAM WILCY (Cy)
B. May 20, 1897, Bonita, Tex.   D. Mar. 29, 1963, Hollis, Okla.

BR TR 6' 195 lbs.

1927	NY A	19	7	.731	2.28	50	12	6	213	185	59	75	1	13	3	13	75	6	1	.080	18	89	1	1	2.2	.991
1928		4	4	.500	4.18	35	2	0	60.1	71	31	18	0	3	3	2	14	2	0	.143	4	21	3	1	0.8	.893
1929		6	4	.600	4.06	41	0	0	62	64	19	21	0	6	4	8	15	1	0	.067	1	25	2	0	0.7	.929
1931	BOS A	11	13	.458	3.88	53	15	8	185.1	195	55	37	1	7	8	10	56	9	0	.161	2	70	1	2	1.4	.986
1932	2 teams	BOS A	(37G 4–10)		NY A	(10G 2–0)																				
"	total	6	10	.375	4.61	47	3	0	109.1	125	48	36	0	5	8	8	30	1	0	.033	6	34	1	3	0.9	.976
1933	NY A	5	6	.455	5.52	35	0	0	62	92	20	17	0	5	6	8	15	2	0	.133	3	15	3	1	0.6	.857
6 yrs.		51	44	.537	3.69	261	32	14	692	732	232	204	2	39	26	49	205	21	1	.102	34	254	11	8	1.1	.963

WORLD SERIES

1927	NY A	1	0	1.000	0.84	2	1	1	10.2	11	2	2	0	0	0	0	5	1	0	.200	0	5	1	0	3.0	.833
1932		1	0	1.000	0.00	1	0	0	5.1	2	0	1	0	1	0	0	3	1	0	.333	0	1	0	0	1.0	1.000
2 yrs.		2	0	1.000	0.56	3	1	1	16	13	2	3	0	1	0	1	8	2	0	.250	0	6	1	0	2.3	.857

Bob Moorhead

MOORHEAD, CHARLES ROBERT
B. Jan. 23, 1938, Chambersburg, Pa.   D. Dec. 3, 1986, Lemoyne, Pa.

BR TR 6'1" 208 lbs.

1962	NY N	0	2	.000	4.53	38	7	0	105.1	118	42	63	0	0	1	0	22	1	0	.045	7	28	4	4	1.0	.897
1965		0	1	.000	4.40	9	0	0	14.1	16	5	5	0	0	1	0	0	0	0	—	0	5	0	0	0.6	1.000
2 yrs.		0	3	.000	4.51	47	7	0	119.2	134	47	68	0	0	2	0	22	1	0	.045	7	33	4	4	0.9	.909

Bob Moose

MOOSE, ROBERT RALPH
B. Oct. 9, 1947, Export, Pa.   D. Oct. 9, 1976, Martin's Ferry, Ohio

BR TR 6' 200 lbs.

1967	PIT N	1	0	1.000	3.68	2	2	1	14.2	14	4	7	0	0	0	0	6	2	0	.333	3	1	0	0	2.0	1.000
1968		8	12	.400	2.74	38	22	3	170.2	136	41	126	3	0	4	3	54	5	0	.093	13	36	3	4	1.4	.942
1969		14	3	.824	2.91	44	19	6	170	149	62	165	1	0	0	4	53	4	0	.075	7	31	4	0	1.0	.905
1970		11	10	.524	3.98	28	27	9	190	186	64	119	2	0	0	0	66	12	0	.182	10	23	3	2	1.3	.914
1971		11	7	.611	4.11	30	18	3	140	169	35	68	1	4	1	1	39	4	0	.103	11	24	4	2	1.3	.897
1972		13	10	.565	2.91	31	30	6	226	213	47	144	3	0	0	1	71	12	0	.169	20	33	2	1	1.8	.964
1973		12	13	.480	3.53	38	29	6	201.1	219	70	111	3	1	1	0	67	9	0	.134	13	39	2	7	1.6	.963
1974		1	5	.167	7.50	7	6	0	36	59	7	15	0	0	0	0	11	2	0	.182	1	15	0	1	2.3	1.000
1975		2	2	.500	3.71	23	5	1	68	63	25	34	0	1	2	4	18	3	0	.167	6	16	1	2	1.0	.957
1976		3	9	.250	3.70	53	2	0	87.2	100	32	38	0	3	7	10	12	3	1	.250	3	14	2	0	0.4	.895
10 yrs.		76	71	.517	3.50	289	160	35	1304.1	1308	387	827	13	9	13	19	397	56	1	.141	87	231	21	19	1.2	.938

LEAGUE CHAMPIONSHIP SERIES

1970	PIT N	0	1	.000	3.52	1	1	0	7.2	4	2	4	0	0	0	0	4	0	0	.000	1	2	0	0	3.0	1.000
1971		0	0	—	0.00	1	0	0	2	0	0	0	0	0	0	0	0	0	0	—	0	0	0	0	0.0	—
1972		0	1	.000	54.00	2	1	0	.2	5	0	0	0	0	0	0	0	0	0	—	0	0	0	0	0.0	—
3 yrs.		0	2	.000	6.10	4	2	0	10.1	9	2	4	0	0	0	0	4	0	0	.000	1	2	0	0	0.8	1.000

WORLD SERIES

| 1971 | PIT N | 0 | 0 | — | 6.52 | 3 | 0 | 0 | 9.2 | 12 | 2 | 7 | 0 | 0 | 0 | 0 | 2 | 0 | 0 | .000 | 0 | 3 | 0 | 0 | 1.0 | 1.000 |

Jake Mooty

MOOTY, J T
B. Apr. 13, 1913, Bennett, Tex.   D. Apr. 20, 1970, Fort Worth, Tex.

BR TR 5'10½" 170 lbs.

1936	CIN N	0	0	—	3.95	8	0	0	13.2	10	4	11	0	0	0	1	1	0	0	.000	0	1	0	0	0.1	1.000
1937		0	3	.000	8.31	14	2	0	39	54	22	11	0	0	1	0	8	0	0	.000	4	8	2	0	1.0	.857
1940	CHI N	6	6	.500	2.92	20	12	6	114	101	49	42	0	2	0	1	38	10	0	.263	5	16	1	0	1.1	.955
1941		8	9	.471	3.35	33	14	7	153.1	143	56	45	1	3	0	4	50	10	0	.200	3	36	0	6	1.2	1.000
1942		2	5	.286	4.70	19	10	1	84.1	89	44	28	0	0	1	1	28	6	0	.214	3	22	2	0	1.4	.926
1943		0	0	—	0.00	2	0	0	1	2	1	0	0	0	0	0	0	0	0	—	0	0	0	0	0.0	—

Year	Team		W	L	PCT	ERA	G	GS	CG	IP	H	BB	SO	ShO	W	L	SV	AB	H	HR	BA	PO	A	E	DP	TC/G	FA
															Relief Pitching			**Batting**									

Jake Mooty *continued*

Year	Team		W	L	PCT	ERA	G	GS	CG	IP	H	BB	SO	ShO	W	L	SV	AB	H	HR	BA	PO	A	E	DP	TC/G	FA
1944	DET	A	0	0	–	4.45	15	0	0	28.1	35	18	7	0	0	0	0	7	1	0	.143	3	4	1	0	0.5	.875
7 yrs.			16	23	.410	4.03	111	38	14	433.2	434	194	145	1	5	2	8	132	27	0	.205	18	87	6	6	1.0	.946

Carl Moran

MORAN, CARL WILLIAM (Bugs)
B. Sept. 26, 1950, Portsmouth, Va.   BR TR 6'4"   210 lbs.

Year	Team		W	L	PCT	ERA	G	GS	CG	IP	H	BB	SO	ShO	W	L	SV	AB	H	HR	BA	PO	A	E	DP	TC/G	FA
1974	CHI	A	1	3	.250	4.70	15	5	0	46	57	23	17	0	0	1	0	0	0	0	–	2	3	0	1	0.3	1.000

Charley Moran

MORAN, CHARLES BARTHELL (Uncle Charlie)
B. Feb. 22, 1878, Nashville, Tenn.   D. June 14, 1949, Horse Cave, Ky.   BR TR 5'8"   180 lbs.

Year	Team		W	L	PCT	ERA	G	GS	CG	IP	H	BB	SO	ShO	W	L	SV	AB	H	HR	BA	PO	A	E	DP	TC/G	FA
1903	STL	N	0	1	.000	5.25	3	2	2	24	30	19	7	0	0	0	0	*				1	3	0	0	1.3	1.000

Harry Moran

MORAN, HARRY EDWIN
B. Apr. 2, 1889, Slater, W. Va.   D. Nov. 28, 1962, Beckley, W. Va.   BL TL 6'1"   165 lbs.

Year	Team		W	L	PCT	ERA	G	GS	CG	IP	H	BB	SO	ShO	W	L	SV	AB	H	HR	BA	PO	A	E	DP	TC/G	FA
1912	DET	A	0	1	.000	4.91	5	2	1	14.2	19	12	3	0	0	0	0	5	1	0	.200	1	4	0	0	1.0	1.000
1914	BUF	F	11	8	.579	4.27	34	16	7	154	159	53	73	2	3	1	1	51	10	0	.196	5	37	2	4	1.3	.955
1915	NWK	F	13	10	.565	2.54	34	23	13	205.2	193	66	87	2	2	0	0	61	11	0	.180	9	72	7	1	2.6	.920
3 yrs.			24	19	.558	3.34	73	41	21	374.1	371	131	163	4	5	1	1	117	22	0	.188	15	113	9	5	1.9	.934

Hiker Moran

MORAN, ALBERT THOMAS
B. Jan. 1, 1912, Rochester, N. Y.   BR TR 6'4½"   185 lbs.

Year	Team		W	L	PCT	ERA	G	GS	CG	IP	H	BB	SO	ShO	W	L	SV	AB	H	HR	BA	PO	A	E	DP	TC/G	FA
1938	BOS	N	0	0	–	0.00	1	0	0	3	1	1	0	0	0	0	0	0	0	0	–	0	0	0	0	0.0	–
1939			1	1	.500	4.50	6	2	1	20	21	11	4	0	0	0	0	5	1	0	.200	1	3	1	0	0.8	.800
2 yrs.			1	1	.500	3.91	7	2	1	23	22	12	4	0	0	0	0	5	1	0	.200	1	3	1	0	0.7	.800

Sam Moran

MORAN, SAMUEL
B. Sept. 16, 1870, Rochester, N. Y.   D. Aug. 29, 1897, Rochester, N. Y.   TL   160 lbs.

Year	Team		W	L	PCT	ERA	G	GS	CG	IP	H	BB	SO	ShO	W	L	SV	AB	H	HR	BA	PO	A	E	DP	TC/G	FA
1895	PIT	N	2	4	.333	7.47	10	6	6	62.2	78	51	19	0	0	0	0	26	4	1	.154	1	15	1	1	1.7	.941

Forrest More

MORE, FORREST T.
B. Sept. 30, 1883, Hayden, Ind.   D. Aug. 17, 1968, Columbus, Ind.   BR TR 6'   180 lbs.

Year	Team		W	L	PCT	ERA	G	GS	CG	IP	H	BB	SO	ShO	W	L	SV	AB	H	HR	BA	PO	A	E	DP	TC/G	FA
1909	2 teams	STL N (15G 1–5)									BOS N (10G 0–4)																	
"	total		1	9	.100	4.74	25	7	4	98.2	95	40	27	0	0	5	0	28	3	0	.107	2	34	2	1	1.5	.947

Dave Morehead

MOREHEAD, DAVID MICHAEL (Moe)
B. Sept. 5, 1942, San Diego, Calif.   BR TR 6'1"   185 lbs.

Year	Team		W	L	PCT	ERA	G	GS	CG	IP	H	BB	SO	ShO	W	L	SV	AB	H	HR	BA	PO	A	E	DP	TC/G	FA
1963	BOS	A	10	13	.435	3.81	29	29	6	174.2	137	99	136	1	0	0	0	57	6	0	.105	17	26	2	4	1.6	.956
1964			8	15	.348	4.97	32	30	3	166.2	156	112	139	1	0	0	0	54	5	0	.093	9	18	1	1	0.9	.964
1965			10	18	.357	4.06	34	33	5	192.2	157	113	163	2	0	0	0	61	8	0	.131	16	17	1	1	1.0	.971
1966			1	2	.333	5.46	12	5	0	28	31	7	20	0	0	0	0	6	3	0	.500	2	2	0	0	0.3	1.000
1967			5	4	.556	4.34	10	7	1	47.2	48	22	40	1	1	0	0	12	1	0	.083	2	4	0	1	0.6	1.000
1968			1	4	.200	2.45	11	9	3	55	52	20	28	1	0	0	0	16	2	0	.125	2	3	0	0	0.5	1.000
1969	KC	A	2	3	.400	5.73	21	2	0	33	28	28	32	0	2	1	0	2	0	0	.000	1	3	0	0	0.2	1.000
1970			3	5	.375	3.61	28	17	1	122	121	62	69	0	0	1	0	36	6	0	.167	7	10	2	0	0.7	.895
8 yrs.			40	64	.385	4.15	177	134	19	819.2	730	463	627	6	3	2	1	244	31	0	.127	56	83	7	8	0.8	.952

WORLD SERIES

Year	Team		W	L	PCT	ERA	G	GS	CG	IP	H	BB	SO	ShO	W	L	SV	AB	H	HR	BA	PO	A	E	DP	TC/G	FA
1967	BOS	A	0	0	–	0.00	2	0	0	3.1	0	4	3	0	0	0	0	0	0	0	–	0	0	0	0	0.0	–

Seth Morehead

MOREHEAD, SETH MARVIN (Moe)
B. Aug. 15, 1934, Houston, Tex.   BL TL 6'½"   195 lbs.

Year	Team		W	L	PCT	ERA	G	GS	CG	IP	H	BB	SO	ShO	W	L	SV	AB	H	HR	BA	PO	A	E	DP	TC/G	FA
1957	PHI	N	1	1	.500	3.68	34	1	1	58.2	57	20	36	0	0	1	0	6	0	0	.000	3	7	1	0	0.3	.909
1958			1	6	.143	5.85	27	11	0	92.1	91	26	54	0	1	0	0	22	4	0	.182	3	10	5	1	0.7	.722
1959	2 teams	PHI N (3G 0–2)									CHI N (11G 0–1)																	
"	total		0	3	.000	6.59	14	5	0	28.2	40	11	17	0	0	0	0	5	1	0	.200	1	0	0	0	0.1	1.000
1960	CHI	N	2	9	.182	3.94	45	7	2	123.1	123	46	64	0	2	4	4	29	4	0	.138	8	19	0	1	0.6	1.000
1961	MIL	N	1	0	1.000	6.46	12	0	0	15.1	16	7	13	0	1	0	0	0	0	0	–	0	2	0	0	0.2	1.000
5 yrs.			5	19	.208	4.81	132	24	3	318.1	357	110	184	0	3	5	5	62	9	0	.145	15	39	6	2	0.5	.900

Lew Moren

MOREN, LEWIS HOWARD (Hicks)
B. Aug. 4, 1883, Pittsburgh, Pa.   D. Nov. 2, 1966, Pittsburgh, Pa.   BR TR 5'11"   150 lbs.

Year	Team		W	L	PCT	ERA	G	GS	CG	IP	H	BB	SO	ShO	W	L	SV	AB	H	HR	BA	PO	A	E	DP	TC/G	FA
1903	PIT	N	0	1	.000	9.00	1	1	1	6	9	2	2	0	0	0	0	2	0	0	.000	1	1	0	0	2.0	1.000
1904			0	0	–	9.00	1	0	0	4	7	4	0	0	0	0	0	2	0	0	.000	0	3	0	0	3.0	1.000
1907	PHI	N	11	18	.379	2.54	37	31	21	255	202	101	98	3	0	1	1	74	6	0	.081	3	72	2	3	2.1	.974
1908			8	9	.471	2.92	28	16	9	154	146	49	72	1	1	0	0	49	12	0	.245	6	43	2	1	1.8	.961
1909			16	15	.516	2.66	39	31	19	253.2	223	91	108	2	3	3	1	90	10	0	.111	8	46	5	3	1.5	.915
1910			13	14	.481	3.55	34	26	12	205.1	207	82	74	1	3	2	1	74	11	0	.149	11	56	5	2	2.1	.931
6 yrs.			48	57	.457	2.95	140	105	62	878	794	329	354	10	7	7	3	291	39	0	.134	29	221	14	9	1.9	.947

Angel Moreno

MORENO, ANGEL
Born Angel Moreno y Veneroso.
B. June 6, 1955, La Mendosa, Mexico   BL TL 5'9"   165 lbs.

Year	Team		W	L	PCT	ERA	G	GS	CG	IP	H	BB	SO	ShO	W	L	SV	AB	H	HR	BA	PO	A	E	DP	TC/G	FA
1981	CAL	A	1	3	.250	2.90	8	4	1	31	27	14	12	0	0	0	0	0	0	0	–	0	5	1	0	0.8	.833
1982			3	7	.300	4.74	13	8	2	49.1	55	23	22	0	0	1	1	0	0	0	–	2	8	2	0	0.9	.833
2 yrs.			4	10	.286	4.03	21	12	3	80.1	82	37	34	0	0	1	1	0	0	0	–	2	13	3	0	0.9	.833

Julio Moreno

MORENO, JULIO
Born Julio Moreno y Gonzalez.
B. Jan. 28, 1921, Guines, Cuba   D. Jan. 2, 1987, Miami, Fla.   BR TR 5'8"   165 lbs.

Year	Team		W	L	PCT	ERA	G	GS	CG	IP	H	BB	SO	ShO	Relief Pitching W	L	SV	Batting AB	H	HR	BA	PO	A	E	DP	TC/G	FA

Julio Moreno *continued*

Year	Team		W	L	PCT	ERA	G	GS	CG	IP	H	BB	SO	ShO	W	L	SV	AB	H	HR	BA	PO	A	E	DP	TC/G	FA
1950	WAS	A	1	1	.500	4.64	4	3	1	21.1	22	12	7	0	0	0	0	8	1	0	.125	3	3	0	0	1.5	1.000
1951			5	11	.313	4.88	31	18	5	132.2	132	80	37	0	1	2	2	40	7	0	.175	10	24	0	1	1.1	1.000
1952			9	9	.500	3.97	26	22	7	147.1	154	52	62	0	0	1	0	49	6	0	.122	8	21	1	0	1.2	.967
1953			3	1	.750	2.80	12	2	1	35.1	41	13	13	0	2	1	0	9	0	0	.000	1	5	0	0	0.5	1.000
4 yrs.			18	22	.450	4.25	73	45	14	336.2	349	157	119	0	3	4	2	106	14	0	.132	22	53	1	1	1.0	.987

Roger Moret

MORET, ROGELIO
Born Rogelio Moret y Torres.
B. Sept. 16, 1949, Guayama, Puerto Rico

BB TL 6'4" 170 lbs.

Year	Team		W	L	PCT	ERA	G	GS	CG	IP	H	BB	SO	ShO	W	L	SV	AB	H	HR	BA	PO	A	E	DP	TC/G	FA
1970	BOS	A	1	0	1.000	3.38	3	1	0	8	7	4	2	0	1	0	0	3	0	0	.000	0	1	0	0	0.3	1.000
1971			4	3	.571	2.92	13	7	4	71	50	40	47	1	0	1	0	23	2	0	.087	1	11	0	1	0.9	1.000
1972			0	0	—	3.60	3	0	0	5	5	6	4	0	0	0	0	1	0	0	.000	0	0	0	0	0.0	—
1973			13	2	.867	3.17	30	15	5	156	138	67	90	2	1	0	3	0	0	0	—	5	22	1	3	0.9	.964
1974			9	10	.474	3.75	31	21	10	173	158	79	111	1	1	1	2	0	0	0	—	4	16	1	1	0.7	.952
1975			14	3	.824	3.60	36	16	4	145	132	76	80	1	4	0	1	0	0	0	—	2	18	0	1	0.6	1.000
1976	ATL	N	3	5	.375	5.03	27	12	1	77	84	27	30	0	0	0	1	23	3	0	.130	0	13	0	1	0.5	1.000
1977	TEX	A	3	3	.500	3.75	18	8	0	72	59	38	39	0	1	0	4	0	0	0	—	0	1	0	0	0.3	1.000
1978			0	1	.000	4.91	7	2	0	14.2	23	2	5	0	0	0	1	0	0	0	—	0	7	0	0	0.6	.981
9 yrs.			47	27	.635	3.67	168	82	24	721.2	656	339	408	5	8	2	12	50	5	0	.100	14	89	2	7	0.6	.981

LEAGUE CHAMPIONSHIP SERIES

Year	Team		W	L	PCT	ERA	G	GS	CG	IP	H	BB	SO	ShO	W	L	SV	AB	H	HR	BA	PO	A	E	DP	TC/G	FA
1975	BOS	A	1	0	1.000	0.00	1	0	0	1	1	1	0	0	0	0	0	0	0	0	—	0	0	0	0	0.0	—

WORLD SERIES

Year	Team		W	L	PCT	ERA	G	GS	CG	IP	H	BB	SO	ShO	W	L	SV	AB	H	HR	BA	PO	A	E	DP	TC/G	FA
1975	BOS	A	0	0	—	0.00	3	0	0	1.2	2	3	1	0	0	0	0	0	0	0	—	0	1	0	0	0.3	1.000

Dave Morey

MOREY, DAVID BEALE
B. Feb. 25, 1889, Malden, Mass.   D. Jan. 4, 1986, Oak Bluff, Mass.

BL TR 6'   185 lbs.

Year	Team		W	L	PCT	ERA	G	GS	CG	IP	H	BB	SO	ShO	W	L	SV	AB	H	HR	BA	PO	A	E	DP	TC/G	FA
1913	PHI	A	0	0	—	4.50	2	0	0	4	2	2	1	0	0	0	0	1	0	0	.000	0	2	0	0	1.0	1.000

Bill Morgan

MORGAN, HENRY WILLIAM
B. Brooklyn, N. Y.   Deceased.

Year	Team		W	L	PCT	ERA	G	GS	CG	IP	H	BB	SO	ShO	W	L	SV	AB	H	HR	BA	PO	A	E	DP	TC/G	FA
1884	RIC	AA	2	3	.400	4.15	5	5	5	39	37	2	35	0	0	0	0	*				2	9	3	0	2.8	.786

Cy Morgan

MORGAN, CYRIL ARLON
B. Dec. 11, 1896, Lakeville, Mass.   D. Sept. 11, 1946, Lakeville, Mass.

BR TR 6'   170 lbs.

Year	Team		W	L	PCT	ERA	G	GS	CG	IP	H	BB	SO	ShO	W	L	SV	AB	H	HR	BA	PO	A	E	DP	TC/G	FA
1921	BOS	N	1	1	.500	6.53	17	0	0	30.1	37	17	8	0	1	1	1	5	0	0	.000	0	13	0	0	0.8	1.000
1922			0	0	—	27.00	2	0	0	1.1	8	2	0	0	0	0	0	0	0	0	—	0	0	0	0	0.0	—
2 yrs.			1	1	.500	7.39	19	0	0	31.2	45	19	8	0	1	1	1	5	0	0	.000	0	13	0	0	0.7	1.000

Cy Morgan

MORGAN, HARRY RICHARD
B. Nov. 10, 1878, Pomeroy, Ohio   D. June 28, 1962, Wheeling, W. Va.

BR TR 6'   175 lbs.

Year	Team		W	L	PCT	ERA	G	GS	CG	IP	H	BB	SO	ShO	W	L	SV	AB	H	HR	BA	PO	A	E	DP	TC/G	FA
1903	STL	A	0	2	.000	4.15	2	1	1	13	12	6	6	0	0	1	0	4	1	0	.250	1	2	0	0	1.5	1.000
1904			0	2	.000	3.71	8	3	2	51	51	10	24	0	0	0	0	18	1	0	.056	3	22	1	0	3.3	.962
1905			2	5	.286	3.61	13	8	5	77.1	82	37	44	1	0	0	0	31	8	0	.258	5	34	8	1	3.6	.830
1907	2 teams					STL A	(10G 2–5)			BOS A	(16G 6–6)																
"	total		8	11	.421	3.30	26	19	13	169.1	154	51	64	2	1	0	0	55	4	0	.073	6	57	4	3	2.6	.940
1908	BOS	A	14	13	.519	2.46	30	26	17	205	166	90	99	2	1	1	1	63	8	0	.127	11	65	2	1	2.6	.974
1909	2 teams					BOS A	(12G 2–6)			PHI A	(28G 16–11)																
"	total		18	17	.514	1.81	40	36	26	293.1	204	102	111	5	1	1	1	94	9	0	.096	6	100	4	1	2.8	.964
1910	PHI	A	18	12	.600	1.55	36	34	23	290.2	214	117	134	3	0	1	1	99	14	0	.141	5	104	4	1	3.1	.965
1911			15	7	.682	2.70	38	30	15	249.2	217	113	136	2	1	0	1	94	15	0	.160	14	81	5	2	2.6	.950
1912			3	8	.273	3.75	16	14	5	93.2	75	51	47	0	1	0	0	30	1	0	.033	2	41	5	0	3.0	.896
1913	CIN	N	0	1	.000	15.43	1	1	0	2.1	5	1	2	0	0	0	0	1	0	0	.000	0	2	0	0	2.0	1.000
10 yrs.			78	78	.500	2.51	210	172	107	1445.1	1180	578	667	15	5	5	3	489	61	0	.125	53	508	33	9	2.8	.944

Mike Morgan

MORGAN, MICHAEL THOMAS
B. Oct. 8, 1959, Tulare, Calif.

BR TR 6'3"   195 lbs.

Year	Team		W	L	PCT	ERA	G	GS	CG	IP	H	BB	SO	ShO	W	L	SV	AB	H	HR	BA	PO	A	E	DP	TC/G	FA
1978	OAK	A	0	3	.000	7.30	3	3	1	12.1	19	8	0	0	0	0	0				—	1	4	0	1	1.7	1.000
1979			2	10	.167	5.96	13	13	2	77	102	50	17	0	0	0	0				—	9	15	1	0	1.9	.960
1982	NY	A	7	11	.389	4.37	30	23	9	150.1	167	67	71	0	2	1	0				—	4	26	0	3	1.0	1.000
1983	TOR	A	0	3	.000	5.16	16	4	0	45.1	48	21	22	0	0	1	0				—	2	10	1	0	0.8	.923
1985	SEA	A	1	1	.500	12.00	2	2	0	6	11	5	2	0	0	0	0				—	0	1	0	0	0.5	1.000
1986			11	17	.393	4.53	37	33	9	216.1	243	86	116	1	0	0	1	0	0	0	—	14	27	2	5	1.2	.953
1987			12	17	.414	4.65	34	31	8	207	245	53	85	2	0	0	0				—	18	35	2	5	1.6	.964
1988	BAL	A	1	6	.143	5.43	22	10	2	71.1	70	23	29	0	0	1	0				—	9	9	1	0	0.8	1.000
1989	LA	N	8	11	.421	2.53	40	19	0	152.2	130	33	72	0	2	0	0	36	3	0	.083	20	41	2	1	1.6	.968
9 yrs.			42	79	.347	4.51	197	138	24	938.1	1035	346	414	3	5	2	2	36	3	0	.083	77	168	8	17	1.3	.968

Tom Morgan

MORGAN, TOM STEPHEN (Plowboy)
B. May 20, 1930, El Monte, Calif.   D. Jan. 13, 1987, Anaheim, Calif.

BR TR 6'1"   180 lbs.

Year	Team		W	L	PCT	ERA	G	GS	CG	IP	H	BB	SO	ShO	W	L	SV	AB	H	HR	BA	PO	A	E	DP	TC/G	FA
1951	NY	A	9	3	.750	3.68	27	16	4	124.2	119	36	57	1	2	0	2	44	12	1	.273	12	27	4	2	1.6	.907
1952			5	4	.556	3.07	16	12	2	93.2	86	33	35	1	1	0	2	33	6	1	.182	6	29	0	3	2.2	1.000
1954			11	5	.688	3.34	32	17	7	143	149	40	34	1	3	1	1	49	7	1	.143	11	38	0	2	1.5	1.000
1955			7	3	.700	3.25	40	0	0	72	72	24	17	0	7	3	10	18	4	0	.222	6	24	1	2	0.8	.968
1956			6	7	.462	4.16	41	0	0	71.1	74	27	20	0	6	7	11	13	2	0	.154	2	18	2	5	0.5	.909
1957	KC	A	9	7	.563	4.64	46	13	5	143.2	160	61	32	0	6	5	2	33	3	0	.091	20	37	1	6	1.3	.983
1958	DET	A	2	5	.286	3.16	39	6	0	62.2	70	4	32	0	2	4	0	10	2	0	.200	4	15	2	0	0.3	.917
1959			1	4	.200	3.98	46	0	0	92.2	94	18	39	0	1	4	9	23	9	2	.391	4	15	0	2	0.4	1.000

Year	Team		W	L	PCT	ERA	G	GS	CG	IP	H	BB	SO	ShO	Relief Pitching W	L	SV	Batting AB	H	HR	BA	PO	A	E	DP	TC/G	FA

Tom Morgan *continued*

Year	Team		W	L	PCT	ERA	G	GS	CG	IP	H	BB	SO	ShO	W	L	SV	AB	H	HR	BA	PO	A	E	DP	TC/G	FA
1960	2 teams	DET A (22G 3–2)				WAS A (14G 1–3)																					
"	total		4	5	.444	4.25	36	0	0	53	69	15	23	0	4	5	1	5	0	0	.000	4	10	0	1	0.4	1.000
1961	LA	A	8	2	.800	2.36	59	0	0	91.2	74	17	39	0	8	2	10	12	1	0	.083	8	18	2	2	0.5	.929
1962			5	2	.714	2.91	48	0	0	58.2	53	19	29	0	5	2	9	6	0	0	.000	1	6	0	1	0.1	1.000
1963			0	0	–	5.51	13	0	0	16.1	20	6	7	0	0	0	1	1	0	0	.000	0	2	0	0	0.2	1.000
12 yrs.			67	47	.588	3.61	443	61	18	1023.1	1040	300	364	7	40	25	64	247	46	5	.186	76	233	11	27	0.7	.966

WORLD SERIES

Year	Team		W	L	PCT	ERA	G	GS	CG	IP	H	BB	SO	ShO	W	L	SV	AB	H	HR	BA	PO	A	E	DP	TC/G	FA
1951	NY	A	0	0	–	0.00	1	0	0	2	2	1	3	0	0	0	0	0	0	0	–	0	1	0	0	1.0	1.000
1955			0	0	–	4.91	2	0	0	3.2	3	3	1	0	0	0	0	0	0	0	–	0	0	0	0	0.0	–
1956			0	1	.000	9.00	2	0	0	4	6	4	3	0	0	1	0	1	1	0	1.000	0	0	0	0	0.0	–
3 yrs.			0	1	.000	5.59	5	0	0	9.2	11	8	7	0	0	1	0	1	1	0	1.000	0	1	0	0	0.2	1.000

Gene Moriarity

MORIARITY, EUGENE JOHN
B. Holyoke, Mass. Deceased.
BL TL 5'8" 190 lbs.

Year	Team		W	L	PCT	ERA	G	GS	CG	IP	H	BB	SO	ShO	W	L	SV	AB	H	HR	BA	PO	A	E	DP	TC/G	FA
1884	BOS	N	0	2	.000	5.27	2	2	2	13.2	16	7	4	0	0	0	0	53	9	0	.170	2	4	0	0	3.0	1.000
1885	DET	N	0	0	–	9.00	1	0	0	2	3	1	1	0	0	0	0	39	1	0	.026	0	0	1	0	1.0	–
2 yrs.			0	2	.000	5.74	3	2	2	15.2	19	8	5	0	0	0	0	*				2	4	1	0	2.3	.857

John Morlan

MORLAN, JOHN GLEN
B. Nov. 22, 1947, Columbus, Ohio
BR TR 6' 178 lbs.

Year	Team		W	L	PCT	ERA	G	GS	CG	IP	H	BB	SO	ShO	W	L	SV	AB	H	HR	BA	PO	A	E	DP	TC/G	FA
1973	PIT	N	2	2	.500	3.95	10	7	1	41	42	23	23	0	0	0	0	11	2	0	.182	3	3	0	0	0.6	1.000
1974			0	3	.000	4.29	39	0	0	65	54	48	38	0	0	3	0	7	0	0	.000	4	6	1	0	0.3	.909
2 yrs.			2	5	.286	4.16	49	7	1	106	96	71	61	0	0	3	0	18	2	0	.111	7	9	1	0	0.3	.941

Dan Morogiello

MOROGIELLO, DANIEL JOSEPH
B. Mar. 26, 1955, Brooklyn, N. Y.
BL TL 6'1" 200 lbs.

Year	Team		W	L	PCT	ERA	G	GS	CG	IP	H	BB	SO	ShO	W	L	SV	AB	H	HR	BA	PO	A	E	DP	TC/G	FA
1983	BAL	A	0	1	.000	2.39	22	0	0	37.2	39	10	15	0	0	1	1	0	0	0	–	0	3	1	0	0.2	.750

Jim Moroney

MORONEY, JAMES FRANCIS
B. Dec. 4, 1885, Boston, Mass. D. Feb. 26, 1929, Philadelphia, Pa.
BL TL 6'1" 175 lbs.

Year	Team		W	L	PCT	ERA	G	GS	CG	IP	H	BB	SO	ShO	W	L	SV	AB	H	HR	BA	PO	A	E	DP	TC/G	FA
1906	BOS	N	0	3	.000	5.33	3	3	3	27	28	12	11	0	0	0	0	10	1	0	.100	0	9	0	0	3.3	.900
1910	PHI	N	1	2	.333	2.14	12	2	1	42	43	11	13	0	1	0	1	10	0	0	.000	1	11	2	0	1.2	.857
1912	CHI	N	1	1	.500	4.56	10	3	1	23.2	25	17	5	0	0	1	0	6	3	0	.500	0	7	2	0	0.9	.778
3 yrs.			2	6	.250	3.69	25	8	5	92.2	96	40	29	0	1	1	2	26	4	0	.154	1	27	5	0	1.3	.848

Bill Morrell

MORRELL, WILLARD BLACKMER
B. Apr. 9, 1900, Boston, Mass.
D. Aug. 5, 1975, Birmingham, Ala.
BL TR 6' 172 lbs.
BR 1926

Year	Team		W	L	PCT	ERA	G	GS	CG	IP	H	BB	SO	ShO	W	L	SV	AB	H	HR	BA	PO	A	E	DP	TC/G	FA
1926	WAS	A	3	3	.500	5.30	26	2	1	69.2	83	29	16	0	2	2	1	17	4	0	.235	3	15	1	0	0.7	.947
1930	NY	N	0	0	–	1.13	2	0	0	8	6	1	3	0	0	0	0	2	0	0	.000	2	1	0	0	1.5	1.000
1931			5	3	.625	4.36	20	7	2	66	83	27	16	0	1	1	1	18	2	0	.111	6	10	1	2	0.9	.941
3 yrs.			8	6	.571	4.64	48	9	3	143.2	172	57	35	0	3	3	2	37	6	0	.162	11	26	2	2	0.8	.949

John Morrill

MORRILL, JOHN FRANCIS (Honest John)
B. Feb. 19, 1855, Boston, Mass. D. Apr. 2, 1932, Boston, Mass.
Manager 1882–89.
BR TR 5'10½" 155 lbs.

Year	Team		W	L	PCT	ERA	G	GS	CG	IP	H	BB	SO	ShO	W	L	SV	AB	H	HR	BA	PO	A	E	DP	TC/G	FA
1880	BOS	N	0	0	–	0.84	3	0	0	10.2	9	1	0	0	0	0	0	342	81	2	.237	1	3	0	0	1.3	1.000
1881			0	1	.000	6.35	3	0	0	5.2	9	1	0	0	0	1	1	311	90	1	.289	0	0	0	0	0.0	–
1882			0	0	–	0.00	1	0	0	2	3	0	2	0	0	0	0	349	101	2	.289	0	1	0	0	1.0	1.000
1883			1	0	1.000	2.77	2	1	1	13	15	4	5	0	0	0	0	404	129	6	.319	0	2	1	0	1.5	.667
1884			0	1	.000	7.43	7	1	1	23	34	6	13	0	0	0	2	438	114	3	.260	1	5	0	0	0.9	1.000
1886			0	0	–	0.00	1	0	0	4	5	0	2	0	0	0	0	430	106	7	.247	0	2	0	0	2.0	1.000
1889	WAS	N	0	0	–	0.00	1	0	0	.1	1	0	0	0	0	0	0	146	27	2	.185	0	0	0	0	0.0	–
7 yrs.			1	2	.333	4.30	18	2	2	58.2	75	12	22	0	0	1	3	*				2	13	1	0	0.9	.938

Bugs Morris

Playing record listed under Bugs Bennett

Danny Morris

MORRIS, DANNY WALKER
B. June 11, 1946, Greenville, Ky.
BR TR 6'1" 200 lbs.

Year	Team		W	L	PCT	ERA	G	GS	CG	IP	H	BB	SO	ShO	W	L	SV	AB	H	HR	BA	PO	A	E	DP	TC/G	FA
1968	MIN	A	0	1	.000	1.69	3	2	0	10.2	11	4	6	0	0	0	0	3	0	0	.000	0	2	0	1	0.7	1.000
1969			0	1	.000	5.06	3	1	0	5.1	5	4	1	0	0	0	0	0	0	0	–	0	1	0	0	0.3	1.000
2 yrs.			0	2	.000	2.81	6	3	0	16	16	8	7	0	0	0	0	3	0	0	.000	0	3	0	1	0.5	1.000

E. Morris

MORRIS, E.
B. Trenton, N. J. Deceased.

Year	Team		W	L	PCT	ERA	G	GS	CG	IP	H	BB	SO	ShO	W	L	SV	AB	H	HR	BA	PO	A	E	DP	TC/G	FA
1884	BAL	U	0	0	–	9.00	1	1	0	1	2	2	0	0	0	0	0	3	0	0	.000	0	0	2	0	2.0	–

Ed Morris

MORRIS, EDWARD (Cannonball)
B. Sept. 29, 1862, Brooklyn, N. Y. D. Apr. 12, 1937, Pittsburgh, Pa.
BR TL 165 lbs.

Year	Team		W	L	PCT	ERA	G	GS	CG	IP	H	BB	SO	ShO	W	L	SV	AB	H	HR	BA	PO	A	E	DP	TC/G	FA
1884	COL	AA	34	13	.723	2.18	52	52	47	429.2	335	51	302	3	0	0	0	199	37	0	.186	19	88	23	3	2.5	.823
1885	PIT	AA	39	24	.619	2.35	63	63	63	581	459	101	298	6	0	0	0	237	44	0	.186	24	93	20	4	2.2	.854
1886			41	20	.672	2.45	64	63	63	555.1	455	118	326	12	0	0	1	227	38	1	.167	21	90	10	2	1.9	.917
1887	PIT	N	14	22	.389	4.31	38	38	37	317.2	375	71	91	1	0	0	0	126	25	0	.198	5	52	5	1	1.6	.919
1888			29	24	.547	2.31	55	55	54	480	470	74	135	5	0	0	0	189	19	0	.101	20	106	8	3	2.4	.940
1889			6	13	.316	4.13	21	21	18	170	196	48	40	0	0	0	0	72	7	0	.097	5	27	1	0	1.6	.970

Year	Team	W	L	PCT	ERA	G	GS	CG	IP	H	BB	SO	ShO	W	L	SV	AB	H	HR	BA	PO	A	E	DP	TC/G	FA

Ed Morris *continued*

Year	Team	W	L	PCT	ERA	G	GS	CG	IP	H	BB	SO	ShO	W	L	SV	AB	H	HR	BA	PO	A	E	DP	TC/G	FA
1890	PIT P	8	7	.533	4.86	18	15	15	144.1	178	35	25	1	0	0	0	63	9	0	.143	3	28	4	1	1.9	.886
7 yrs.		171	123	.582	2.82	311	307	297	2678	2468	498	1217	28	0	0	1	1113	179	1	.161	97	484	71	14	2.1	.891

Ed Morris

MORRIS, WALTER EDWARD BR TR 6'2" 185 lbs.
B. Dec. 7, 1899, Foshee, Ala. D. Mar. 3, 1932, Century, Fla.

Year	Team	W	L	PCT	ERA	G	GS	CG	IP	H	BB	SO	ShO	W	L	SV	AB	H	HR	BA	PO	A	E	DP	TC/G	FA
1922	CHI N	0	0	–	8.25	5	0	0	12	22	6	5	0	0	0	0	4	1	0	.250	0	3	2	0	1.0	.600
1928	BOS A	19	15	.559	3.53	47	29	20	257.2	255	80	104	0	3	2	5	91	14	0	.154	4	48	0	4	1.1	1.000
1929		14	14	.500	4.45	33	26	17	208.1	227	95	73	2	2	1	1	69	16	1	.232	6	38	3	1	1.4	.936
1930		4	9	.308	4.13	18	9	3	65.1	67	38	28	0	2	2	0	19	6	0	.316	4	11	2	0	0.9	.882
1931		5	7	.417	4.75	37	14	3	130.2	131	74	46	0	1	1	0	38	6	0	.158	11	27	5	1	1.2	.884
5 yrs.		42	45	.483	4.19	140	78	43	674	702	293	256	2	8	6	6	221	43	1	.195	25	127	12	6	1.2	.927

Jack Morris

MORRIS, JOHN SCOTT BR TR 6'3" 195 lbs.
B. May 16, 1955, St. Paul, Minn.

Year	Team	W	L	PCT	ERA	G	GS	CG	IP	H	BB	SO	ShO	W	L	SV	AB	H	HR	BA	PO	A	E	DP	TC/G	FA
1977	DET A	1	1	.500	3.72	7	6	1	46	38	23	28	0	0	0	0	0	0	0	–	2	8	0	0	1.4	1.000
1978		3	5	.375	4.33	28	7	0	106	107	49	48	0	3	3	0	0	0	0	–	5	15	2	3	0.8	.909
1979		17	7	.708	3.27	27	27	9	198	179	59	113	1	0	0	0	0	0	0	–	14	23	2	1	1.4	.949
1980		16	15	.516	4.18	36	36	11	250	252	87	112	2	0	0	0	0	0	0	–	31	43	2	2	2.1	.974
1981		14	7	.667	3.05	25	25	15	198	153	78	97	1	0	0	0	0	0	0	–	16	28	0	2	1.8	1.000
1982		17	16	.515	4.06	37	37	17	266.1	247	96	135	3	0	0	0	0	0	0	–	26	31	1	2	1.6	.983
1983		20	13	.606	3.34	37	37	20	293.2	257	83	232	1	0	0	0	0	0	0	–	29	26	2	1	1.5	.965
1984		19	11	.633	3.60	35	35	9	241.1	224	87	149	1	0	0	0	0	0	0	–	29	32	3	4	1.8	.953
1985		16	11	.593	3.33	35	35	13	257	212	110	191	4	0	0	0	0	0	0	–	25	25	4	2	1.5	.926
1986		21	8	.724	3.27	35	35	15	267	229	82	223	6	0	0	0	0	0	0	–	27	27	2	4	1.6	.964
1987		18	11	.621	3.38	34	34	13	266	227	93	208	0	0	0	0	1	0	0	.000	31	18	0	1	1.4	1.000
1988		15	13	.536	3.94	34	34	10	235	225	83	168	2	0	0	0	0	0	0	–	31	21	1	1	1.6	.981
1989		6	14	.300	4.86	24	24	10	170.1	189	59	115	0	0	0	0	0	0	0	–	17	22	1	3	1.7	.975
13 yrs.		183	132	.581	3.67	394	372	143	2794.2	2539	989	1819	21	3	3	0	1	0	0	.000	283	319	20	29	1.6	.968

LEAGUE CHAMPIONSHIP SERIES

Year	Team	W	L	PCT	ERA	G	GS	CG	IP	H	BB	SO	ShO	W	L	SV	AB	H	HR	BA	PO	A	E	DP	TC/G	FA
1984	DET A	1	0	1.000	1.29	1	1	0	7	5	1	4	0	0	0	0	0	0	0	–	1	1	0	0	2.0	1.000
1987		0	1	.000	6.75	1	1	1	8	6	3	7	0	0	0	0	0	0	0	–	0	0	0	0	0.0	–
2 yrs.		1	1	.500	4.20	2	2	1	15	11	4	11	0	0	0	0	0	0	0	–	1	1	0	0	1.0	1.000

WORLD SERIES

Year	Team	W	L	PCT	ERA	G	GS	CG	IP	H	BB	SO	ShO	W	L	SV	AB	H	HR	BA	PO	A	E	DP	TC/G	FA
1984	DET A	2	0	1.000	2.00	2	2	2	18	13	3	13	0	0	0	0	0	0	0	–	5	1	0	0	3.0	1.000

John Morris

MORRIS, JOHN WALLACE BR TL 6'2" 195 lbs.
B. Aug. 23, 1941, Lewes, Del.

Year	Team	W	L	PCT	ERA	G	GS	CG	IP	H	BB	SO	ShO	W	L	SV	AB	H	HR	BA	PO	A	E	DP	TC/G	FA
1966	PHI N	1	1	.500	5.27	13	0	0	13.2	15	3	8	0	1	1	0	0	0	0	–	1	3	0	0	0.3	1.000
1968	BAL A	2	0	1.000	2.56	19	0	0	31.2	19	17	22	0	2	0	0	6	0	0	.000	1	5	0	0	0.3	1.000
1969	SEA A	0	0	–	6.39	6	0	0	12.2	16	8	8	0	0	0	0	1	1	0	1.000	2	6	0	1	1.3	1.000
1970	MIL A	4	3	.571	3.95	20	9	2	73	70	22	40	0	1	0	0	17	3	0	.176	2	15	0	3	0.9	1.000
1971		2	2	.500	3.71	43	1	0	68	69	27	42	0	2	2	1	5	1	0	.200	0	3	1	1	0.5	.950
1972	SF N	0	0	–	4.50	7	0	0	6	9	2	5	0	0	0	0	1	0	0	–	0	1	0	0	0.1	1.000
1973		1	0	1.000	9.00	7	0	0	6	12	3	3	0	1	0	0	1	0	0	.000	0	1	0	0	0.1	1.000
1974		1	1	.500	3.00	17	0	0	21	17	4	9	0	1	1	0	1	0	0	1.000	0	14	0	0	0.1	1.000
8 yrs.		11	7	.611	3.96	132	10	2	232	227	86	137	0	8	4	2	31	6	0	.194	9	48	1	5	0.4	.983

Bill Morrisette

MORRISETTE, WILLIAM LEE BR TR 6' 176 lbs.
B. Jan. 17, 1893, Baltimore, Md. D. Mar. 25, 1966, Virginia Beach, Va.

Year	Team	W	L	PCT	ERA	G	GS	CG	IP	H	BB	SO	ShO	W	L	SV	AB	H	HR	BA	PO	A	E	DP	TC/G	FA
1915	PHI A	2	0	1.000	1.35	4	1	1	20	15	5	11	0	1	0	0	7	2	0	.286	1	6	1	0	2.0	.875
1916		0	0	–	6.75	1	0	0	4	6	5	2	0	0	0	0	1	0	0	.000	0	4	0	0	4.0	1.000
1920	DET A	1	1	.500	4.33	8	3	1	27	25	19	15	0	0	0	0	8	0	0	.000	0	5	0	0	0.6	1.000
3 yrs.		3	1	.750	3.35	13	4	2	51	46	29	28	0	1	0	0	16	2	0	.125	1	15	1	0	1.3	.941

Guy Morrison

MORRISON, WALTER GUY BR TR 5'11" 185 lbs.
B. Aug. 29, 1895, Hinton, W. Va. D. Aug. 14, 1934, Grand Rapids, Mich.

Year	Team	W	L	PCT	ERA	G	GS	CG	IP	H	BB	SO	ShO	W	L	SV	AB	H	HR	BA	PO	A	E	DP	TC/G	FA
1927	BOS N	1	2	.333	4.46	11	3	1	34.1	40	15	6	0	0	0	0	8	1	1	.125	2	14	3	0	1.7	.842
1928		0	0	–	12.00	1	0	0	3	4	3	0	0	0	0	0	0	0	0	–	0	2	0	0	2.0	1.000
2 yrs.		1	2	.333	5.06	12	3	1	37.1	44	18	6	0	0	0	0	8	1	1	.125	2	16	3	0	1.8	.857

Hank Morrison

MORRISON, STEPHEN HENRY BR TR 5'10" 180 lbs.
B. May 22, 1866, Olneyville, R. I. D. Sept. 30, 1927, Attleboro, Mass.

Year	Team	W	L	PCT	ERA	G	GS	CG	IP	H	BB	SO	ShO	W	L	SV	AB	H	HR	BA	PO	A	E	DP	TC/G	FA
1887	IND N	3	4	.429	7.58	7	7	5	57	79	27	13	0	0	0	0	26	3	0	.115	1	4	1	0	0.9	.833

Jim Morrison

MORRISON, JAMES FORREST BR TR 5'11" 175 lbs.
B. Sept. 23, 1952, Pensacola, Fla.

Year	Team	W	L	PCT	ERA	G	GS	CG	IP	H	BB	SO	ShO	W	L	SV	AB	H	HR	BA	PO	A	E	DP	TC/G	FA
1988	ATL N	0	0	–	0.00	3	0	0	3.2	3	2	1	0	0	0	0	*				0	0	0	0	0.0	–

Johnny Morrison

MORRISON, JOHN DEWEY (Jughandle Johnny) BR TR 5'11" 188 lbs.
Brother of Phil Morrison.
B. Oct. 22, 1895, Pelleville, Ky. D. Mar. 20, 1966, Louisville, Ky.

Year	Team	W	L	PCT	ERA	G	GS	CG	IP	H	BB	SO	ShO	W	L	SV	AB	H	HR	BA	PO	A	E	DP	TC/G	FA
1920	PIT N	1	0	1.000	0.00	2	1	1	7	4	1	3	1	0	0	0	3	0	0	.000	0	2	0	0	1.0	1.000
1921		9	7	.563	2.88	21	17	11	144	131	33	52	3	0	0	0	42	5	0	.119	3	37	0	2	1.9	1.000
1922		17	11	.607	3.43	45	33	20	286.1	315	87	104	5	1	1	1	101	20	0	.198	3	69	2	0	1.6	.973
1923		25	13	.658	3.49	42	37	27	301.2	287	110	114	2	1	0	2	115	21	0	.183	5	70	2	1	1.8	.974
1924		11	16	.407	3.75	41	25	10	237.2	213	73	85	0	1	1	0	77	13	0	.169	3	50	3	2	1.4	.946
1925		17	14	.548	3.88	44	26	10	211	245	60	60	0	6	3	4	73	13	0	.178	1	43	2	1	1.0	.957
1926		6	8	.429	3.38	26	14	6	122.1	119	44	39	1	2	1	3	39	3	0	.077	2	20	0	3	0.8	1.000

Year	Team		W	L	PCT	ERA	G	GS	CG	IP	H	BB	SO	ShO	Relief Pitching W	L	SV	AB	H	HR	BA	PO	A	E	DP	TC/G	FA

Johnny Morrison *continued*

1927			3	2	.600	4.19	21	2	1	53.2	63	21	21	0	2	0	3	13	2	0	.154	0	6	1	1	0.3	.857
1929	BKN	N	13	7	.650	4.48	39	10	4	136.2	150	61	57	0	**10**	2	**8**	43	7	0	.163	1	15	1	0	0.5	.889
1930			1	2	.333	5.45	16	0	0	34.2	47	16	11	0	1	2	1	5	0	0	.000	1	6	1	0	0.5	.875
10 yrs.			103	80	.563	3.65	297	165	90	1535	1574	506	546	13	28	12	23	511	84	0	.164	19	318	13	12	1.2	.963
WORLD SERIES																											
1925	PIT	N	0	0	—	2.89	3	0	0	9.1	11	1	7	0	0	0	0	2	1	0	.500	0	3	0	0	1.0	1.000

Mike Morrison

MORRISON, MICHAEL
B. Feb. 6, 1867, Erie, Pa.   D. June 16, 1955, Erie, Pa.   BR TR 5'8½" 156 lbs.

1887	CLE	AA	12	25	.324	4.92	40	40	35	316.2	385	**205**	158	0	0	0	0	141	27	0	.191	14	109	11	4	3.4	.918
1888			1	3	.250	5.40	4	4	4	35	40	19	14	0	0	0	0	17	4	0	.235	5	7	3	0	3.8	.800
1890	2 teams	SYR AA (17G 6–9)				BAL	AA	(4G 1–2)																			
"	total		7	11	.389	5.53	21	18	16	153	146	101	82	1	1	0	0	129	30	1	.233	20	38	4	3	3.0	.935
3 yrs.			20	39	.339	5.14	65	62	55	504.2	571	325	254	1	1	0	0	287	61	1	.213	39	154	18	7	3.2	.915

Phil Morrison

MORRISON, PHILIP MELVIN
Brother of Johnny Morrison.
B. Oct. 18, 1894, Rockport, Ind.   D. Jan. 18, 1955, Lexington, Ky.   BB TR 6'2" 190 lbs.

| 1921 | PIT | N | 0 | 0 | — | 0.00 | 1 | 0 | 0 | .2 | 0 | 1 | 0 | 0 | 0 | 0 | 0 | 0 | 0 | 0 | — | 0 | 0 | 0 | 0 | 0.0 | — |

Deacon Morrissey

MORRISSEY, MICHAEL JOSEPH
B. May 3, 1876, Baltimore, Md.   D. Feb. 22, 1939, Baltimore, Md.   TR 5'4" 140 lbs.

1901	BOS	A	0	0	—	2.08	1	0	0	4.1	5	2	1	0	0	0	0	3	0	0	.000	0	2	0	0	2.0	1.000
1902	CHI	N	1	3	.250	2.25	5	5	5	40	40	8	13	0	0	0	0	22	2	0	.091	2	12	0	0	2.8	1.000
2 yrs.			1	3	.250	2.23	6	5	5	44.1	45	10	14	0	0	0	0	25	2	0	.080	2	14	0	0	2.7	1.000

Carl Morton

MORTON, CARL WENDLE
B. Jan. 18, 1944, Kansas City, Mo.   D. Apr. 12, 1983, Tulsa, Okla.   BR TR 6' 200 lbs.

1969	MON	N	0	3	.000	4.66	8	5	0	29	29	18	16	0	0	0	1	7	0	0	.000	3	7	0	0	1.3	1.000
1970			18	11	.621	3.60	43	37	10	285	281	**125**	154	4	0	0	0	93	15	0	.161	29	42	2	2	1.7	.973
1971			10	18	.357	4.79	36	35	9	214	252	83	84	0	0	0	1	77	14	2	.182	28	37	2	4	1.9	.970
1972			7	13	.350	3.92	27	27	3	172	170	53	51	1	0	0	0	52	7	0	.135	24	25	1	0	1.9	.980
1973	ATL	N	15	10	.600	3.41	38	37	10	256.1	254	70	112	4	0	0	0	94	17	3	.181	26	36	2	2	1.7	.969
1974			16	12	.571	3.14	38	38	7	275	**293**	89	113	1	0	0	0	89	10	0	.112	25	36	1	3	1.6	.984
1975			17	16	.515	3.50	39	39	11	278	**302**	82	78	2	0	0	0	94	15	0	.160	29	40	2	3	1.8	.972
1976			4	9	.308	4.18	26	24	1	140	172	45	42	1	0	0	0	45	8	0	.178	18	26	1	1	1.7	.978
8 yrs.			87	92	.486	3.73	255	242	51	1649.1	1753	565	650	13	0	0	2	551	86	7	.156	182	249	11	15	1.7	.975

Charlie Morton

MORTON, CHARLES HAZEN
B. Oct. 12, 1854, Kingsville, Ohio   D. Dec. 9, 1921, Massillon, Ohio
Manager 1884-85, 1890.   TR

| 1884 | TOL | AA | 0 | 1 | .000 | 3.09 | 3 | 1 | 1 | 23.1 | 18 | 5 | 7 | 0 | 0 | 0 | 0 | * | | | | 0 | 1 | 0 | 0 | 0.3 | 1.000 |

Guy Morton

MORTON, GUY, SR. (Alabama Blossom)
Father of Guy Morton.
B. June 1, 1893, Vernon, Ala.   D. Oct. 18, 1934, Sheffield, Ala.   BR TR 6'1" 175 lbs.

1914	CLE	A	1	13	.071	3.02	25	13	5	128	116	55	80	0	0	2	1	35	1	0	.029	2	30	5	1	1.5	.865
1915			16	15	.516	2.14	34	27	15	240	189	60	134	6	2	2	1	82	12	0	.146	3	69	4	2	2.2	.947
1916			12	8	.600	2.89	27	18	9	149.2	139	42	88	0	1	3	0	57	12	0	.211	7	38	6	0	1.9	.882
1917			10	10	.500	2.74	35	18	6	161	158	59	62	1	3	3	2	47	4	0	.085	5	42	6	0	1.5	.887
1918			14	8	.636	2.64	30	28	13	214.2	189	77	123	1	1	0	1	77	12	0	.156	6	52	7	2	2.2	.892
1919			9	9	.500	2.81	26	20	9	147.1	128	47	64	1	1	0	0	56	9	0	.161	1	40	6	0	1.8	.872
1920			8	6	.571	4.47	29	17	5	137	140	57	72	1	2	0	1	46	10	0	.217	2	25	6	0	1.1	.818
1921			8	3	.727	2.76	30	6	2	107.2	98	32	45	2	**5**	1	0	35	6	0	.171	1	20	2	1	0.8	.913
1922			14	9	.609	4.00	38	23	13	202.2	218	85	102	3	2	2	0	68	13	0	.191	6	64	3	3	1.9	.959
1923			6	6	.500	4.24	33	14	3	129.1	133	56	54	2	1	1	1	44	7	0	.159	2	32	3	0	1.1	.919
1924			0	1	.000	6.57	10	0	0	12.1	12	13	6	0	0	1	0	1	0	0	.000	0	3	2	0	0.5	.600
11 yrs.			98	88	.527	3.13	317	184	80	1629.2	1520	583	830	19	18	16	6	548	86	0	.157	35	415	50	10	1.6	.900

Sparrow Morton

MORTON, WILLIAM P
Deceased.   TL

| 1884 | PHI | N | 0 | 2 | .000 | 5.29 | 2 | 2 | 2 | 17 | 16 | 11 | 5 | 0 | 0 | 0 | 0 | 8 | 3 | 0 | .375 | 2 | 3 | 2 | 0 | 3.5 | .714 |

Earl Moseley

MOSELEY, EARL VICTOR
B. Sept. 7, 1884, Middleburg, Ohio   D. July 1, 1963, Alliance, Ohio   BR TR 5'9½" 168 lbs.

1913	BOS	A	9	5	.643	3.13	24	15	7	120.2	105	49	62	3	1	1	1	37	3	0	.081	8	37	2	1	2.0	.957
1914	IND	F	19	18	.514	3.47	43	38	29	316.2	303	123	205	4	1	2	1	109	12	0	.110	13	86	7	3	2.5	.934
1915	NWK	F	16	16	.500	1.91	38	32	22	268	222	99	142	5	1	2	0	88	13	0	.148	7	63	4	1	1.9	.946
1916	CIN	N	7	10	.412	3.89	31	15	7	150.1	145	69	60	0	2	2	0	46	4	0	.087	2	33	1	2	1.2	.972
4 yrs.			51	49	.510	3.01	136	100	65	855.2	775	340	469	12	5	7	2	280	32	0	.114	30	219	14	7	1.9	.947

Walter Moser

MOSER, WALTER FREDERICK
B. Feb. 27, 1881, Concord, N. C.   D. Dec. 10, 1946, Philadelphia, Pa.   BR TR 5'9" 170 lbs.

1906	PHI	N	0	4	.000	3.59	6	4	4	42.2	49	15	17	0	0	0	0	14	0	0	.000	3	14	2	1	2.2	.846
1911	2 teams	BOS A (6G 0–1)				STL	A	(2G 0–2)																			
"	total		0	3	.000	6.11	8	5	1	28	48	15	13	0	0	0	0	8	1	0	.125	1	3	2	0	1.5	.833
2 yrs.			0	7	.000	4.58	14	9	5	70.2	97	30	30	0	0	0	0	22	1	0	.045	4	17	4	1	1.8	.840

Year	Team		W	L	PCT	ERA	G	GS	CG	IP	H	BB	SO	ShO	Relief Pitching W	L	SV	Batting AB	H	HR	BA	PO	A	E	DP	TC/G	FA

John Moses

MOSES, JOHN WILLIAM
B. Aug. 9, 1957, Los Angeles, Calif.　　BB TL 5'10" 165 lbs.

Year	Team		W	L	PCT	ERA	G	GS	CG	IP	H	BB	SO	ShO	W	L	SV	AB	H	HR	BA	PO	A	E	DP	TC/G	FA
1989	MIN	A	0	0	–	0.00	1	0	0	1	0	1	0	0	0	0	0	*				0	0	0	0	0.0	–

Paul Moskau

MOSKAU, PAUL RICHARD
B. Dec. 20, 1953, St. Joseph, Mo.　　BR TR 6'2" 200 lbs.

Year	Team		W	L	PCT	ERA	G	GS	CG	IP	H	BB	SO	ShO	W	L	SV	AB	H	HR	BA	PO	A	E	DP	TC/G	FA
1977	CIN	N	6	6	.500	4.00	20	19	2	108	116	40	71	2	0	0	0	38	7	1	.184	6	19	0	1	1.3	1.000
1978			6	4	.600	3.97	26	25	2	145	139	57	88	1	0	0	1	49	10	1	.204	5	13	0	1	0.7	1.000
1979			5	4	.556	3.91	21	15	1	106	107	51	58	0	1	0	0	37	3	0	.081	3	19	2	3	1.1	.917
1980			9	7	.563	4.00	33	19	2	153	147	41	94	1	5	0	2	44	7	0	.159	11	22	3	4	1.1	.917
1981			2	1	.667	4.91	27	1	0	55	54	32	32	0	2	1	2	6	0	0	.000	4	12	1	0	0.6	.941
1982	PIT	N	1	3	.250	4.37	13	5	0	35	43	8	15	0	0	1	0	11	1	0	.091	3	4	0	0	0.5	1.000
1983	CHI	N	3	2	.600	6.75	8	8	0	32	44	14	16	0	0	0	0	11	2	0	.182	3	5	2	0	1.3	.800
7 yrs.			32	27	.542	4.22	148	92	7	634	650	243	374	4	8	2	5	196	30	2	.153	35	94	8	9	0.9	.942

Jim Mosolf

MOSOLF, JAMES FREDERICK
B. Aug. 21, 1905, Puyallup, Wash.　D. Dec. 28, 1979, Dallas, Ore.　　BL TR 5'10" 186 lbs.

Year	Team		W	L	PCT	ERA	G	GS	CG	IP	H	BB	SO	ShO	W	L	SV	AB	H	HR	BA	PO	A	E	DP	TC/G	FA
1930	PIT	N	0	0	–	27.00	1	0	0	.1	1	0	1	0	0	0	0	*				0	0	0	0	0.0	–

Mal Moss

MOSS, CHARLES MALCOLM
B. Apr. 18, 1905, Sullivan, Ind.　D. Feb. 6, 1983, Savannah, Ga.　　BR TL 6' 175 lbs.

Year	Team		W	L	PCT	ERA	G	GS	CG	IP	H	BB	SO	ShO	W	L	SV	AB	H	HR	BA	PO	A	E	DP	TC/G	FA
1930	CHI	N	0	0	–	6.27	12	1	0	18.2	18	14	4	0	0	0	1	11	3	0	.273	3	4	0	0	0.6	1.000

Ray Moss

MOSS, RAYMOND EARL
B. Dec. 5, 1901, Chattanooga, Tenn.　　BR TR 6'1" 185 lbs.

Year	Team		W	L	PCT	ERA	G	GS	CG	IP	H	BB	SO	ShO	W	L	SV	AB	H	HR	BA	PO	A	E	DP	TC/G	FA
1926	BKN	N	0	0	–	9.00	1	0	0	1	3	0	0	0	0	0	0	1	0	0	.000	0	0	0	0	0.0	–
1927			1	0	1.000	3.24	1	1	0	8.1	11	1	1	0	0	0	0	3	1	0	.333	0	1	0	0	1.0	1.000
1928			0	3	.000	4.92	22	5	1	60.1	62	35	5	1	0	1	1	25	8	0	.320	3	15	2	1	0.9	.900
1929			11	6	.647	5.04	39	20	7	182	214	81	59	2	2	1	0	66	5	0	.076	5	32	1	0	1.0	.974
1930			9	6	.600	5.10	36	11	5	118.1	127	55	30	0	3	3	1	39	6	0	.154	4	16	1	2	0.6	.952
1931	2 teams		BKN N (1G 0–0)			BOS N (12G 1–3)																					
"	total		1	3	.250	4.50	13	5	0	46	57	17	14	0	1	0	0	15	2	0	.133	1	10	0	0	0.8	1.000
6 yrs.			22	18	.550	4.95	112	42	13	416	474	189	109	3	6	5	2	149	22	0	.148	13	74	4	3	0.8	.956

Don Mossi

MOSSI, DONALD LOUIS (The Sphinx)
B. Jan. 11, 1929, St. Helena, Calif.　　BL TL 6'1" 195 lbs.

Year	Team		W	L	PCT	ERA	G	GS	CG	IP	H	BB	SO	ShO	W	L	SV	AB	H	HR	BA	PO	A	E	DP	TC/G	FA
1954	CLE	A	6	1	.857	1.94	40	1	0	93	56	39	55	0	4	0	7	19	3	0	.158	4	11	0	1	0.4	1.000
1955			4	3	.571	2.42	57	1	0	81.2	81	18	69	0	4	3	9	9	1	0	.111	7	19	0	2	0.5	1.000
1956			6	5	.545	3.59	48	3	0	87.2	79	33	59	0	0	4	11	20	3	0	.150	3	15	1	1	0.4	.947
1957			11	10	.524	4.13	36	22	6	159	166	57	97	1	1	1	2	55	12	0	.218	7	21	0	2	0.8	1.000
1958			7	8	.467	3.90	43	5	0	101.2	106	30	55	0	7	4	3	26	3	0	.115	8	17	0	1	0.6	1.000
1959	DET	A	17	9	.654	3.36	34	30	15	228	210	49	125	3	0	0	0	77	13	1	.169	12	38	1	5	1.5	.980
1960			9	8	.529	3.47	23	22	9	158.1	158	32	69	2	1	0	0	43	5	0	.116	2	27	0	2	1.3	1.000
1961			15	7	.682	2.96	35	34	12	240.1	237	47	137	1	0	0	1	79	13	1	.165	7	40	1	8	1.4	.979
1962			11	13	.458	4.19	35	27	8	180.1	195	36	121	1	0	2	1	55	9	0	.164	9	19	0	3	0.8	1.000
1963			7	7	.500	3.74	24	16	3	122.2	110	17	68	0	2	0	2	39	8	0	.205	6	20	0	1	1.1	1.000
1964	CHI	A	3	1	.750	2.93	34	0	0	40	37	7	36	0	3	1	7	6	1	0	.167	2	5	0	0	0.2	1.000
1965	KC	A	5	8	.385	3.74	51	0	0	55.1	59	20	41	0	5	8	7	8	0	0	.000	2	7	0	2	0.2	1.000
12 yrs.			101	80	.558	3.43	460	165	55	1548	1494	385	932	8	27	24	50	436	71	2	.163	69	239	3	28	0.7	.990

WORLD SERIES

Year	Team		W	L	PCT	ERA	G	GS	CG	IP	H	BB	SO	ShO	W	L	SV	AB	H	HR	BA	PO	A	E	DP	TC/G	FA
1954	CLE	A	0	0	–	0.00	3	0	0	4	3	0	1	0	0	0	0	0	0	0	–	0	2	0	1	0.7	1.000

Earl Mossor

MOSSOR, EARL DALTON
B. July 21, 1925, Forbes, Tenn.　　BL TR 6'1" 175 lbs.

Year	Team		W	L	PCT	ERA	G	GS	CG	IP	H	BB	SO	ShO	W	L	SV	AB	H	HR	BA	PO	A	E	DP	TC/G	FA
1951	BKN	N	0	0	–	32.40	3	0	0	1.2	2	7	1	0	0	0	0	1	1	0	1.000	0	0	0	0	0.0	–

Glen Moulder

MOULDER, GLEN HUBERT
B. Sept. 28, 1917, Cleveland, Okla.　　BR TR 6' 180 lbs.

Year	Team		W	L	PCT	ERA	G	GS	CG	IP	H	BB	SO	ShO	W	L	SV	AB	H	HR	BA	PO	A	E	DP	TC/G	FA
1946	BKN	N	0	0	–	4.50	1	0	0	2	2	1	1	0	0	0	0	0	0	0	–	0	0	0	0	0.0	–
1947	STL	A	4	2	.667	3.82	32	2	0	73	78	43	23	0	3	1	2	17	4	0	.235	4	16	1	1	0.7	.952
1948	CHI	A	3	6	.333	6.41	33	9	0	85.2	108	54	26	0	1	2	2	20	6	0	.300	3	17	3	0	0.7	.870
3 yrs.			7	8	.467	5.21	66	11	0	160.2	188	98	50	0	4	3	4	37	10	0	.270	7	33	4	1	0.7	.909

Frank Mountain

MOUNTAIN, FRANK HENRY
B. May 17, 1860, Ft. Edward, N. Y.　D. Nov. 19, 1939, Schenectady, N. Y.　　BR TR 5'11" 185 lbs.

Year	Team		W	L	PCT	ERA	G	GS	CG	IP	H	BB	SO	ShO	W	L	SV	AB	H	HR	BA	PO	A	E	DP	TC/G	FA
1880	TRO	N	1	1	.500	5.29	2	2	2	17	23	6	2	0	0	0	0	9	2	0	.222	0	4	0	0	2.0	1.000
1881	DET	N	3	4	.429	5.25	7	7	7	60	80	18	13	0	0	0	0	25	4	0	.160	6	6	1	0	1.9	.923
1882	3 teams		WOR N (5G 0–5)			PHI AA (8G 2–5)				WOR N (13G 2–11)																	
"	total		4	21	.160	3.76	26	26	24	213	257	46	44	0	0	0	0	122	32	2	.262	8	53	7	1	2.6	.897
1883	COL	AA	26	33	.441	3.60	59	59	57	503	546	123	159	4	0	0	0	276	60	3	.217	31	105	24	3	2.7	.850
1884			23	17	.575	2.45	42	41	40	360.2	289	78	156	5	0	0	1	210	50	4	.238	14	88	9	0	2.6	.919
1885	PIT	AA	1	4	.200	4.30	5	5	5	46	56	24	7	0	0	0	0	20	2	0	.100	1	10	2	0	2.6	.846
1886			0	2	.000	7.88	2	2	2	16	22	14	2	0	0	0	0	55	8	0	.145	1	4	2	0	3.5	.714
7 yrs.			58	82	.414	3.47	143	142	137	1215.2	1273	309	383	9	0	0	1	*				61	270	45	4	2.6	.880

Billy Mountjoy

MOUNTJOY, WILLIAM R. (Medicine Bill)
B. 1857, Port Huron, Mich.　D. May 19, 1934, London, Ont., Canada　　TR

Year	Team		W	L	PCT	ERA	G	GS	CG	IP	H	BB	SO	ShO	W	L	SV	AB	H	HR	BA	PO	A	E	DP	TC/G	FA
1883	CIN	AA	0	1	.000	2.25	1	1	1	8	9	2	3	0	0	0	0	3	0	0	.000	0	1	0	1	1.0	1.000
1884			19	12	.613	2.93	33	33	32	289	274	43	96	3	0	0	0	119	18	0	.151	13	64	6	2	2.5	.928

Year	Team		W	L	PCT	ERA	G	GS	CG	IP	H	BB	SO	ShO	Relief Pitching W	L	SV	Batting AB	H	HR	BA	PO	A	E	DP	TC/G	FA

Billy Mountjoy *continued*

Year	Team		W	L	PCT	ERA	G	GS	CG	IP	H	BB	SO	ShO	W	L	SV	AB	H	HR	BA	PO	A	E	DP	TC/G	FA
1885	2 teams	CIN AA (17G 10–7)	BAL AA (6G 2–4)																								
"	total		12	11	.522	3.75	23	23	23	206.2	221	65	65	2	0	0	0	78	11	0	.141	3	37	5	1	2.0	.889
	3 yrs.		31	24	.564	3.25	57	57	56	503.2	504	110	164	5	0	0	0	200	29	0	.145	16	102	11	3	2.3	.915

Charlie Moyer

MOYER, CHARLES EDWARD
B. Aug. 15, 1885, Andover, Ohio   D. Nov. 18, 1962, Jacksonville, Fla.

Year	Team		W	L	PCT	ERA	G	GS	CG	IP	H	BB	SO	ShO	W	L	SV	AB	H	HR	BA	PO	A	E	DP	TC/G	FA
1910	WAS	A	0	3	.000	3.24	6	3	2	25	22	13	3	0	0	0	0	8	1	0	.125	0	16	0	0	2.7	1.000

Jamie Moyer

MOYER, JAMIE
B. Nov. 11, 1962, Sellersville, Pa.   BL TL 6'   170 lbs.

Year	Team		W	L	PCT	ERA	G	GS	CG	IP	H	BB	SO	ShO	W	L	SV	AB	H	HR	BA	PO	A	E	DP	TC/G	FA
1986	CHI	N	7	4	.636	5.05	16	16	1	87.1	107	42	45	1	0	0	0	22	2	0	.091	2	22	0	0	1.5	1.000
1987			12	15	.444	5.10	35	33	1	201	210	97	147	0	1	0	0	61	14	0	.230	15	37	4	3	1.6	.929
1988			9	15	.375	3.48	34	30	3	202	212	55	121	1	1	0	0	60	5	0	.083	11	45	1	3	1.7	.982
1989	TEX	A	4	9	.308	4.86	15	15	1	76	84	33	44	0	0	0	0	0	0	0	–	5	14	0	2	1.3	1.000
	4 yrs.		32	43	.427	4.48	100	94	6	566.1	613	227	357	2	2	0	0	143	21	0	.147	33	118	5	8	1.6	.968

Ron Mrozinski

MROZINSKI, RONALD FRANK
B. Sept. 16, 1930, White Haven, Pa.   BR TL 5'11"   160 lbs.

Year	Team		W	L	PCT	ERA	G	GS	CG	IP	H	BB	SO	ShO	W	L	SV	AB	H	HR	BA	PO	A	E	DP	TC/G	FA
1954	PHI	N	1	1	.500	4.50	15	4	1	48	49	25	26	0	0	0	0	12	1	0	.083	3	3	0	1	0.4	1.000
1955			0	2	.000	6.55	22	1	0	34.1	38	19	18	0	0	0	1	4	0	0	.000	0	5	1	2	0.3	.833
	2 yrs.		1	3	.250	5.36	37	5	1	82.1	87	44	44	0	0	0	1	16	1	0	.063	3	8	1	3	0.3	.917

Phil Mudrock

MUDROCK, PHILIP RAY
B. June 12, 1937, Louisville, Colo.   BR TR 6'1"   190 lbs.

Year	Team		W	L	PCT	ERA	G	GS	CG	IP	H	BB	SO	ShO	W	L	SV	AB	H	HR	BA	PO	A	E	DP	TC/G	FA
1963	CHI	N	0	0	–	9.00	1	0	0	1	2	0	0	0	0	0	0	0	0	0	–	0	0	0	0	0.0	–

Gordy Mueller

MUELLER, JOSEPH GORDON
B. Dec. 10, 1922, Baltimore, Md.   BR TR 6'4"   200 lbs.

Year	Team		W	L	PCT	ERA	G	GS	CG	IP	H	BB	SO	ShO	W	L	SV	AB	H	HR	BA	PO	A	E	DP	TC/G	FA
1950	BOS	A	0	0	–	10.29	8	0	0	7	11	13	1	0	0	0	0	1	0	0	.000	2	1	0	0	0.4	1.000

Les Mueller

MUELLER, LESLIE CLYDE
B. Mar. 4, 1919, Belleville, Ill.   BR TR 6'3"   190 lbs.

Year	Team		W	L	PCT	ERA	G	GS	CG	IP	H	BB	SO	ShO	W	L	SV	AB	H	HR	BA	PO	A	E	DP	TC/G	FA
1941	DET	A	0	0	–	4.85	4	0	0	13	9	10	8	0	0	0	0	3	0	0	.000	0	3	0	0	0.8	1.000
1945			6	8	.429	3.68	26	18	6	134.2	117	58	42	2	0	0	1	44	8	1	.182	6	20	3	0	1.1	.897
	2 yrs.		6	8	.429	3.78	30	18	6	147.2	126	68	50	2	0	0	1	47	8	1	.170	6	23	3	0	1.1	.906

WORLD SERIES

Year	Team		W	L	PCT	ERA	G	GS	CG	IP	H	BB	SO	ShO	W	L	SV	AB	H	HR	BA	PO	A	E	DP	TC/G	FA
1945	DET	A	0	0	–	0.00	1	0	0	2	0	1	1	0	0	0	0	0	0	0	–	0	0	0	0	0.0	–

Willie Mueller

MUELLER, WILLARD LAWRENCE
B. Aug. 30, 1956, West Bend, Wis.   BR TR 6'4"   220 lbs.

Year	Team		W	L	PCT	ERA	G	GS	CG	IP	H	BB	SO	ShO	W	L	SV	AB	H	HR	BA	PO	A	E	DP	TC/G	FA
1978	MIL	A	1	0	1.000	6.39	5	0	0	12.2	16	6	6	0	1	0	0	0	0	0	–	1	2	0	0	0.6	1.000
1981			0	0	–	4.50	1	0	0	2	4	0	1	0	0	0	0	0	0	0	–	1	0	0	0	1.0	1.000
	2 yrs.		1	0	1.000	6.14	6	0	0	14.2	20	6	7	0	1	0	0	0	0	0	–	2	2	0	0	0.7	1.000

Billy Muffett

MUFFETT, BILLY ARNOLD (Muff)
B. Sept. 21, 1930, Hammond, Ind.   BR TR 6'1"   198 lbs.

Year	Team		W	L	PCT	ERA	G	GS	CG	IP	H	BB	SO	ShO	W	L	SV	AB	H	HR	BA	PO	A	E	DP	TC/G	FA
1957	STL	N	3	2	.600	2.25	23	0	0	44	35	13	21	0	3	2	8	7	0	0	.000	2	4	1	1	0.3	.857
1958			4	6	.400	4.93	35	6	1	84	107	42	41	0	3	3	5	20	4	0	.200	3	12	1	1	0.5	.938
1959	SF	N	0	0	–	5.40	5	0	0	6.2	11	3	3	0	0	0	0	0	0	0	–	0	1	0	0	0.2	1.000
1960	BOS	A	6	4	.600	3.24	23	14	4	125	116	36	75	1	1	1	0	41	11	0	.268	11	17	1	1	1.3	.966
1961			3	11	.214	5.67	38	11	2	112.2	130	36	47	0	2	3	2	23	5	1	.217	6	18	0	1	0.6	1.000
1962			0	0	–	4.33	1	1	0	4	8	2	1	0	0	0	0	1	0	0	.000	0	0	0	0	0.0	–
	6 yrs.		16	23	.410	4.33	125	32	7	376.1	407	132	188	1	9	9	15	92	20	1	.217	22	52	3	4	0.6	.961

Joe Muich

MUICH, IGNATIUS ANDREW
B. Nov. 23, 1903, St. Louis, Mo.   BR TR 6'2"   175 lbs.

Year	Team		W	L	PCT	ERA	G	GS	CG	IP	H	BB	SO	ShO	W	L	SV	AB	H	HR	BA	PO	A	E	DP	TC/G	FA
1924	BOS	N	0	0	–	11.00	3	0	0	9	19	5	1	0	0	0	0	3	0	0	.000	0	2	0	0	0.7	1.000

Joe Muir

MUIR, JOSEPH ALLEN
B. Nov. 26, 1922, Oriole, Md.   D. June 25, 1980, Baltimore, Md.   BL TL 6'1"   172 lbs.

Year	Team		W	L	PCT	ERA	G	GS	CG	IP	H	BB	SO	ShO	W	L	SV	AB	H	HR	BA	PO	A	E	DP	TC/G	FA
1951	PIT	N	0	2	.000	2.76	9	1	0	16.1	11	7	5	0	0	2	0	1	0	0	.000	1	7	0	0	0.9	1.000
1952			2	3	.400	6.31	12	5	1	35.2	42	18	17	0	0	1	0	9	1	0	.111	4	5	1	1	0.8	.900
	2 yrs.		2	5	.286	5.19	21	6	1	52	53	25	22	0	0	3	0	10	1	0	.100	5	12	1	1	0.9	.944

Hugh Mulcahy

MULCAHY, HUGH NOYES (Losing Pitcher)
B. Sept. 9, 1913, Brighton, Mass.   BR TR 6'2"   190 lbs.

Year	Team		W	L	PCT	ERA	G	GS	CG	IP	H	BB	SO	ShO	W	L	SV	AB	H	HR	BA	PO	A	E	DP	TC/G	FA
1935	PHI	N	1	5	.167	4.78	18	5	0	52.2	62	25	11	0	1	1	1	17	0	0	.000	4	17	3	0	1.3	.875
1936			1	1	.500	3.22	3	2	2	22.1	20	12	2	0	0	0	0	8	2	0	.250	2	6	1	0	3.0	.889
1937			8	18	.308	5.13	56	25	9	215.2	256	97	54	1	1	5	3	73	11	0	.151	13	64	3	1	1.4	.963
1938			10	20	.333	4.61	46	34	15	267.1	294	120	90	0	0	0	0	94	16	0	.170	13	54	0	4	1.5	1.000
1939			9	16	.360	4.99	38	32	14	225.2	246	93	59	1	0	2	4	76	12	0	.158	12	48	6	1	1.7	.909
1940			13	22	.371	3.60	36	36	21	280	283	91	82	3	0	0	0	94	19	0	.202	22	65	1	9	2.4	.989
1945			1	3	.250	3.81	5	4	1	28.1	33	14	7	0	0	0	0	7	0	0	.000	3	10	1	0	2.8	.929
1946			2	4	.333	4.45	16	5	1	62.2	69	33	12	0	0	2	0	16	3	0	.188	5	18	0	0	1.4	1.000
1947	PIT	N	0	0	–	4.05	2	1	0	6.2	8	2	7	0	0	0	0	3	1	0	.333	1	3	0	1	2.0	1.000
	9 yrs.		45	89	.336	4.49	220	144	63	1161.1	1271	487	314	5	3	11	9	388	64	0	.165	75	285	15	18	1.7	.960

Year	Team	W	L	PCT	ERA	G	GS	CG	IP	H	BB	SO	ShO	Relief Pitching W	L	SV	Batting AB	H	HR	BA	PO	A	E	DP	TC/G	FA

Terry Mulholland

MULHOLLAND, TERENCE JOHN
B. Mar. 9, 1963, Uniontown, Pa.

BR TL 6'3" 200 lbs.

Year	Team		W	L	PCT	ERA	G	GS	CG	IP	H	BB	SO	ShO	W	L	SV	AB	H	HR	BA	PO	A	E	DP	TC/G	FA
1986	SF	N	1	7	.125	4.94	15	10	0	54.2	51	35	27	0	0	0	0	19	1	0	.053	1	9	3	0	0.9	.769
1988			2	1	.667	3.72	9	6	2	46	50	7	18	1	0	0	0	14	0	0	.000	7	7	0	0	1.6	1.000
1989	2 teams	SF N (5G 0–0)				PHI N (20G 4–7)																					
"	total		4	7	.364	4.92	25	18	2	115.1	137	36	66	1	0	0	0	36	2	0	.056	2	25	4	1	1.2	.871
3 yrs.			7	15	.318	4.67	49	34	4	216	238	78	111	2	0	0	0	69	3	0	.043	10	41	7	1	1.2	.879

Tony Mullane

MULLANE, ANTHONY JOHN (Count, The Apollo of the Box)
B. Jan. 30, 1859, Cork, Ireland
D. Apr. 25, 1944, Chicago, Ill.

BB TB 5'10½" 165 lbs.
BL 1882

Year	Team		W	L	PCT	ERA	G	GS	CG	IP	H	BB	SO	ShO	W	L	SV	AB	H	HR	BA	PO	A	E	DP	TC/G	FA
1881	DET	N	1	4	.200	4.91	5	5	5	44	55	17	7	0	0	0	0	19	5	0	.263	8	7	2	0	3.4	.882
1882	LOU	AA	30	24	.556	1.88	55	55	51	460.1	418	78	170	5	0	0	0	303	78	0	.257	54	177	10	6	4.4	.959
1883	STL	AA	35	15	.700	2.19	53	49	49	460.2	372	74	191	3	1	0	1	307	69	0	.225	24	96	21	4	2.7	.851
1884	TOL	AA	37	26	.587	2.48	68	66	65	576	485	90	334	8	0	1	0	352	97	3	.276	42	132	14	7	2.9	.879
1886	CIN	AA	33	27	.550	3.70	63	56	55	529.2	501	166	250	1	4	0	0	324	73	0	.225	40	104	14	7	2.5	.911
1887			31	17	.646	3.24	48	48	47	416.1	414	121	97	6	0	0	0	199	44	3	.221	29	72	6	5	2.2	.944
1888			26	16	.619	2.84	44	42	41	380.1	341	75	186	4	1	0	0	175	44	1	.251	22	81	13	1	2.6	.888
1889			11	9	.550	2.99	33	24	17	220	218	89	112	0	1	0	5	196	58	0	.296	10	42	4	0	1.7	.929
1890	CIN	N	12	10	.545	2.24	25	21	21	209	175	96	91	0	1	0	1	286	79	0	.276	16	36	3	0	2.2	.945
1891			23	26	.469	3.23	51	47	42	426.1	390	187	124	1	2	2	0	209	31	0	.148	22	93	5	2	2.4	.958
1892			21	13	.618	2.59	37	34	30	295	222	127	109	3	2	0	0	118	20	0	.169	26	87	9	4	3.3	.926
1893	2 teams	CIN N (15G 6–6)				BAL N (34G 12–16)																					
"	total		18	22	.450	4.44	49	39	34	367	407	189	95	0	3	1	2	166	41	1	.247	24	89	7	3	2.4	.942
1894	2 teams	BAL N (21G 6–9)				CLE N (4G 1–2)																					
"	total		7	11	.389	6.59	25	19	12	155.2	201	100	46	0	0	1	4	66	22	0	.333	10	31	4	2	1.8	.911
13 yrs.			285	220	.564	3.05	556	505	469	4540.1	4199	1409	1812	31	15	5	15	*				327	1047	122	41	2.7	.918
									9th																		

Dick Mulligan

MULLIGAN, RICHARD CHARLES
B. Mar. 18, 1918, Wilkes-Barre, Pa.

BL TL 6' 167 lbs.

Year	Team		W	L	PCT	ERA	G	GS	CG	IP	H	BB	SO	ShO	W	L	SV	AB	H	HR	BA	PO	A	E	DP	TC/G	FA
1941	WAS	A	0	1	.000	5.00	1	1	1	9	11	2	2	0	0	0	0	3	0	0	.000	0	2	0	0	2.0	1.000
1946	2 teams	PHI N (19G 2–2)				BOS N (4G 1–0)																					
"	total		3	2	.600	4.24	23	5	1	70	67	36	20	0	1	0	0	15	0	0	.000	4	13	0	0	0.7	1.000
1947	BOS	N	0	0	–	9.00	1	0	0	2	4	1	1	0	0	0	0	0	0	0	–	0	0	0	0	0.0	–
3 yrs.			3	3	.500	4.44	25	6	2	81	82	39	23	0	1	0	0	18	0	0	.000	4	15	0	0	0.8	1.000

Joe Mulligan

MULLIGAN, JOSEPH IGNATIUS (Big Joe)
B. July 31, 1913, East Weymouth, Mass.   D. June 5, 1986, West Roxbury, Mass.

BR TR 6'4" 210 lbs.

Year	Team		W	L	PCT	ERA	G	GS	CG	IP	H	BB	SO	ShO	W	L	SV	AB	H	HR	BA	PO	A	E	DP	TC/G	FA
1934	BOS	A	1	0	1.000	3.63	14	2	1	44.2	46	27	13	0	0	0	0	12	0	0	.000	2	10	0	1	0.9	1.000

George Mullin

MULLIN, GEORGE JOSEPH (Wabash George)
B. July 4, 1880, Toledo, Ohio   D. Jan. 7, 1944, Wabash, Ind.

BR TR 5'11" 188 lbs.

Year	Team		W	L	PCT	ERA	G	GS	CG	IP	H	BB	SO	ShO	W	L	SV	AB	H	HR	BA	PO	A	E	DP	TC/G	FA
1902	DET	A	13	16	.448	3.67	35	30	25	260	282	95	78	0	1	1	0	120	39	0	.325	26	79	9	3	3.3	.921
1903			19	15	.559	2.25	41	36	31	320.2	284	106	170	6	1	1	2	126	35	1	.278	38	108	10	1	3.8	.936
1904			17	23	.425	2.40	45	44	42	382.1	345	131	161	7	1	0	0	151	45	0	.298	28	163	13	5	4.5	.936
1905			21	21	.500	2.51	44	41	35	347.2	303	138	168	1	1	1	0	135	35	0	.259	20	134	6	7	3.6	.963
1906			21	18	.538	2.78	40	40	35	330	315	108	123	2	0	0	0	142	32	0	.225	21	113	6	2	3.5	.957
1907			20	20	.500	2.59	46	42	35	357.1	346	106	146	5	1	1	0	157	34	0	.217	15	133	6	1	3.3	.961
1908			17	13	.567	3.10	39	30	26	290.2	301	71	121	1	1	0	1	125	32	1	.256	11	102	5	2	3.3	.961
1909			29	8	.784	2.22	40	35	29	303.2	258	78	124	3	4	0	1	126	27	0	.214	11	99	3	2	2.8	.973
1910			21	12	.636	2.87	38	32	27	289	260	102	98	5	2	0	0	129	33	1	.256	20	97	7	1	3.3	.944
1911			18	10	.643	3.07	30	29	25	234.1	245	61	87	2	0	1	0	98	28	0	.286	9	55	4	2	2.3	.941
1912			12	17	.414	3.54	30	29	22	226	214	92	88	2	0	1	0	90	25	0	.278	8	70	6	1	2.8	.929
1913	2 teams	DET A (7G 1–6)				WAS A (12G 3–5)																					
"	total		4	11	.267	3.94	19	16	7	109.2	122	43	30	0	1	0	0	41	11	0	.268	2	41	2	1	2.4	.956
1914	IND	F	14	10	.583	2.70	36	20	11	203	202	91	74	1	8	0	2	77	24	0	.312	9	45	5	1	1.6	.915
1915	NWK	F	2	2	.500	5.85	5	4	3	32.1	41	16	14	0	0	0	0	10	1	0	.100	1	5	0	0	1.2	1.000
14 yrs.			228	196	.538	2.82	488	428	353	3686.2	3518	1238	1482	35	23	5	8	*				229	1244	82	30	3.2	.947

WORLD SERIES

Year	Team		W	L	PCT	ERA	G	GS	CG	IP	H	BB	SO	ShO	W	L	SV	AB	H	HR	BA	PO	A	E	DP	TC/G	FA
1907	DET	A	0	2	.000	2.12	2	2	1	17	16	6	7	0	0	0	0	6	0	0	.000	1	4	0	0	2.5	1.000
1908			1	0	1.000	1.00	1	1	1	9	7	1	8	0	0	0	0	3	1	0	.333	0	2	0	0	2.0	1.000
1909			2	1	.667	2.25	4	3	3	32	22	8	20	1	0	0	0	16	3	0	.188	0	12	0	0	3.0	1.000
3 yrs.			3	3	.500	2.02	7	6	6	58	45	15	35	1	0	0	0	25	4	0	.160	1	18	0	0	2.7	1.000
									6th																		

Dominic Mulrenan

MULRENAN, DOMINIC JOSEPH
B. Dec. 18, 1893, Woburn, Mass.   D. July 27, 1964, Melrose, Mass.

BR TR 5'11" 170 lbs.

Year	Team		W	L	PCT	ERA	G	GS	CG	IP	H	BB	SO	ShO	W	L	SV	AB	H	HR	BA	PO	A	E	DP	TC/G	FA
1921	CHI	A	2	8	.200	7.23	12	10	3	56	84	36	10	0	0	1	0	20	3	0	.150	4	17	2	0	1.9	.913

Frank Mulroney

MULRONEY, FRANCIS JOSEPH
B. Apr. 8, 1903, Mallard, Iowa   D. Nov. 11, 1985, Aberdeen, Wash.

BR TR 6' 170 lbs.

Year	Team		W	L	PCT	ERA	G	GS	CG	IP	H	BB	SO	ShO	W	L	SV	AB	H	HR	BA	PO	A	E	DP	TC/G	FA
1930	BOS	A	0	1	.000	3.00	2	0	0	3	3	1	0	2	0	0	1	0	0	0	–	0	1	0	0	0.5	1.000

Bob Muncrief

MUNCRIEF, ROBERT CLEVELAND
B. Jan. 28, 1916, Madill, Okla.

BR TR 6'2" 190 lbs.

Year	Team		W	L	PCT	ERA	G	GS	CG	IP	H	BB	SO	ShO	W	L	SV	AB	H	HR	BA	PO	A	E	DP	TC/G	FA
1937	STL	A	0	0	–	4.50	1	1	0	2	3	2	0	0	0	0	0	0	0	0	–	0	0	0	0	0.0	–
1939			0	0	–	15.00	2	0	0	3	7	3	1	0	0	0	0	0	0	0	–	0	0	0	0	0.0	–
1941			13	9	.591	3.65	36	24	12	214.1	221	53	67	2	1	0	1	76	18	0	.237	13	36	2	2	1.4	.961
1942			6	8	.429	3.89	24	18	7	134.1	149	31	39	1	0	0	1	45	5	0	.111	9	25	0	2	1.4	1.000
1943			13	12	.520	2.81	35	27	12	205	211	48	80	3	1	1	1	66	10	0	.152	10	28	1	2	1.1	.974

Year	Team	W	L	PCT	ERA	G	GS	CG	IP	H	BB	SO	ShO	Relief Pitching W	L	SV	Batting AB	H	HR	BA	PO	A	E	DP	TC/G	FA

Bob Muncrief *continued*

1944		13	8	.619	3.08	33	27	12	219.1	216	50	88	3	0	1	1	78	18	0	.231	16	35	1	1	1.6	.981
1945		13	4	.765	2.72	27	15	10	145.2	132	44	54	0	3	2	1	45	3	0	.067	9	22	2	1	1.2	.939
1946		3	12	.200	4.99	29	14	4	115.1	149	31	49	1	0	1	0	32	1	0	.031	7	13	2	1	0.8	.909
1947		8	14	.364	4.90	31	23	7	176.1	210	51	74	0	2	1	0	57	6	0	.105	6	29	0	2	1.1	1.000
1948	CLE A	5	4	.556	3.98	21	9	1	72.1	76	31	24	1	2	0	0	18	2	0	.111	4	10	0	2	0.7	1.000
1949	2 teams	PIT N	(13G 1–5)			CHI N	(34G 5–6)																			
"	total	6	11	.353	5.12	47	7	2	110.2	124	44	47	0	4	5	5	21	5	0	.238	5	22	0	1	0.6	1.000
1951	NY A	0	0	–	9.00	2	0	0	3	5	4	2	0	0	0	0	0	0	0	–	1	2	1	0	2.0	.750
12 yrs.		80	82	.494	3.80	288	165	67	1401.1	1503	392	525	11	13	13	9	438	68	0	.155	80	222	9	14	1.1	.971

WORLD SERIES

1944	STL A	0	1	.000	1.35	2	0	0	6.2	5	4	4	0	0	1	0	1	0	0	.000	0	1	0	0	0.5	1.000
1948	CLE A	0	0	–	0.00	1	0	0	2	1	0	0	0	0	0	0	0	0	0	–	1	0	0	0	1.0	1.000
2 yrs.		0	1	.000	1.04	3	0	0	8.2	6	4	4	0	0	1	0	1	0	0	.000	1	1	0	0	0.7	1.000

George Munger

MUNGER, GEORGE DAVID (Red)
B. Oct. 4, 1918, Houston, Tex.

BR TR 6'2" 210 lbs.

1943	STL N	9	5	.643	3.95	32	9	2	93.1	101	42	45	0	4	2	2	28	6	0	.214	3	24	1	3	0.9	.964
1944		11	3	.786	1.34	21	12	7	121	92	41	55	2	2	1	2	44	5	0	.114	8	33	2	5	2.0	.953
1946		2	2	.500	3.33	10	7	2	48.2	47	12	28	0	0	0	1	16	4	0	.250	1	16	0	3	1.7	1.000
1947		16	5	.762	3.37	40	31	13	224.1	218	76	123	6	0	0	3	81	15	0	.185	5	55	1	1	1.6	.968
1948		10	11	.476	4.50	39	25	7	166	179	74	72	2	0	2	0	50	8	0	.160	8	37	0	5	1.2	1.000
1949		15	8	.652	3.87	35	28	12	188.1	179	87	82	2	2	0	2	66	17	1	.258	4	38	1	2	1.2	.977
1950		7	8	.467	3.90	32	20	8	154.2	158	70	61	1	1	1	0	51	7	0	.137	3	32	0	2	1.1	1.000
1951		4	6	.400	5.32	23	11	3	94.2	106	46	44	0	2	2	0	29	5	0	.172	7	25	1	2	1.4	.970
1952	2 teams	STL N	(1G 0–1)			PIT N	(5G 0–3)																			
"	total	0	4	–	7.92	6	5	0	30.2	37	11	9	0	0	0	0	9	0	0	.000	1	12	0	3	2.2	1.000
1956	PIT N	3	4	.429	4.04	35	13	0	107	126	41	45	0	1	1	2	28	3	0	.107	4	16	2	1	0.6	.909
10 yrs.		77	56	.579	3.83	273	161	54	1228.2	1243	500	564	13	10	11	12	402	70	1	.174	44	288	9	27	1.2	.974

WORLD SERIES

| 1946 | STL N | 1 | 0 | 1.000 | 1.00 | 1 | 1 | 1 | 9 | 9 | 3 | 2 | 0 | 0 | 0 | 0 | 4 | 1 | 0 | .250 | 1 | 0 | 0 | 0 | 1.0 | 1.000 |

Van Lingle Mungo

MUNGO, VAN LINGLE
B. June 8, 1911, Pageland, S. C.   D. Feb. 12, 1985, Pageland, S. C.

BR TR 6'2" 185 lbs.

1931	BKN N	3	1	.750	2.32	5	4	2	31	27	13	12	1	0	0	0	12	3	0	.250	1	4	0	0	1.0	1.000
1932		13	11	.542	4.43	39	33	11	223.1	224	115	107	1	0	1	2	79	16	0	.203	15	48	2	4	1.7	.969
1933		16	15	.516	2.72	41	28	18	248	223	84	110	3	2	2	0	84	15	0	.179	15	55	3	1	1.8	.959
1934		18	16	.529	3.37	45	38	22	315.1	300	104	184	3	1	1	3	121	30	0	.248	14	67	3	3	1.9	.964
1935		16	10	.615	3.65	37	26	18	214.1	205	90	143	4	1	2	2	90	26	0	.289	10	45	2	1	1.5	.965
1936		18	19	.486	3.35	45	37	22	311.2	275	118	238	2	1	2	3	123	22	0	.179	11	67	8	7	1.9	.907
1937		9	11	.450	2.91	25	21	14	161	136	56	122	0	0	0	3	64	16	0	.250	12	41	0	0	2.1	1.000
1938		4	11	.267	3.92	24	18	6	133.1	133	72	72	2	1	1	0	47	9	0	.191	4	31	0	2	1.5	1.000
1939		4	5	.444	3.26	14	10	1	77.1	70	33	34	0	1	0	0	29	10	0	.345	4	10	0	0	1.0	1.000
1940		1	0	1.000	2.45	7	0	0	22	24	10	9	0	1	0	0	7	0	0	.000	0	3	0	0	0.4	1.000
1941		0	0	–	4.50	2	0	0	2	1	2	1	0	0	0	0	0	0	0	–	0	1	0	0	0.5	1.000
1942	NY N	1	2	.333	5.94	9	5	0	36.1	38	21	27	0	0	0	0	14	3	0	.214	2	6	0	2	0.9	1.000
1943		3	7	.300	3.91	45	13	2	154.1	140	79	83	2	3	7	2	44	7	0	.159	5	36	0	1	0.9	1.000
1945		14	7	.667	3.20	26	26	7	183	161	71	101	2	0	0	0	73	17	0	.233	6	34	5	1	1.7	.889
14 yrs.		120	115	.511	3.47	364	259	123	2113	1957	868	1242	20	11	16	16	787	174	0	.221	99	448	23	22	1.6	.960

Manny Muniz

MUNIZ, MANUEL
Born Manuel Muniz y Rodriguez.
B. Dec. 31, 1947, Caguas, Puerto Rico

BR TR 5'11" 190 lbs.

| 1971 | PHI N | 0 | 1 | .000 | 7.20 | 5 | 0 | 0 | 10 | 9 | 8 | 6 | 0 | 0 | 1 | 0 | 1 | 0 | 0 | .000 | 0 | 1 | 0 | 0 | 0.2 | 1.000 |

Scott Munninghoff

MUNNINGHOFF, SCOTT ANDREW
B. Dec. 5, 1958, Cincinnati, Ohio

BR TR 6' 175 lbs.

| 1980 | PHI N | 0 | 0 | – | 4.50 | 4 | 0 | 0 | 6 | 8 | 5 | 2 | 0 | 0 | 0 | 0 | 1 | 1 | 0 | 1.000 | 2 | 1 | 0 | 0 | 0.8 | 1.000 |

Les Munns

MUNNS, LESLIE ERNEST (Nemo, Big Ed)
B. Dec. 1, 1908, Fort Bragg, Calif.

BR TR 6'5" 212 lbs.

1934	BKN N	3	7	.300	4.71	33	9	4	99.1	106	60	41	0	1	1	0	29	7	0	.241	7	29	1	0	1.1	.973
1935		1	3	.250	5.55	21	5	0	58.1	74	33	13	0	1	0	1	16	3	0	.188	7	4	3	0	0.7	.786
1936	STL N	0	3	.000	3.00	7	1	0	24	23	12	4	0	0	3	1	9	1	0	.111	2	10	0	0	1.7	1.000
3 yrs.		4	13	.235	4.76	61	15	4	181.2	203	105	58	0	2	4	2	54	11	0	.204	16	43	4	0	1.0	.937

Mike Munoz

MUNOZ, MICHAEL ANTHONY
B. July 12, 1965, Baldwin Park, Calif.

BL TL 6'2" 190 lbs.

| 1989 | LA N | 0 | 0 | – | 16.88 | 3 | 0 | 0 | 2 | 5 | 2 | 3 | 0 | 0 | 0 | 0 | 0 | 0 | 0 | – | 1 | 1 | 0 | 0 | 0.7 | 1.000 |

Steve Mura

MURA, STEPHEN ANDREW
B. Feb. 12, 1955, New Orleans, La.

BR TR 6'2" 188 lbs.

1978	SD N	0	2	.000	11.25	5	2	0	8	15	5	5	0	0	0	0	1	0	0	.000	0	2	1	0	0.6	.333
1979		4	4	.500	3.08	38	5	0	73	57	37	59	0	3	2	1	10	0	0	.000	5	8	1	0	0.4	.929
1980		8	7	.533	3.67	37	23	3	169	149	86	109	1	0	0	0	51	7	0	.137	9	26	1	3	1.0	.972
1981		5	14	.263	4.27	23	22	2	139	156	50	70	0	0	1	0	44	6	0	.136	14	26	1	0	1.8	.976
1982	STL N	12	11	.522	4.05	35	30	7	184.1	196	80	84	1	0	0	0	53	3	0	.057	14	22	2	3	1.1	.947
1983	CHI A	0	0	–	4.38	6	0	0	12.1	13	6	4	0	0	0	0	0	0	0	–	0	1	1	0	0.3	.500

Year	Team		W	L	PCT	ERA	G	GS	CG	IP	H	BB	SO	ShO	Relief Pitching W	L	SV	Batting AB	H	HR	BA	PO	A	E	DP	TC/G	FA

Steve Mura *continued*

Year	Team		W	L	PCT	ERA	G	GS	CG	IP	H	BB	SO	ShO	W	L	SV	AB	H	HR	BA	PO	A	E	DP	TC/G	FA
1985	OAK	A	1	1	.500	4.13	23	1	0	48	41	25	29	0	1	1	1	0	0	0	–	2	6	1	0	0.4	.889
7 yrs.			30	39	.435	3.99	167	83	12	633.2	627	289	360	2	4	4	5	159	16	0	.101	44	90	9	6	0.9	.937

Masanori Murakami

MURAKAMI, MASANORI
B. May 6, 1944, Otsuki, Japan

BL TL 6'   180 lbs.

Year	Team		W	L	PCT	ERA	G	GS	CG	IP	H	BB	SO	ShO	W	L	SV	AB	H	HR	BA	PO	A	E	DP	TC/G	FA
1964	SF	N	1	0	1.000	1.80	9	0	0	15	8	1	15	0	1	0	1	3	0	0	.000	0	0	0	0	0.0	–
1965			4	1	.800	3.75	45	1	0	74.1	57	22	85	0	4	1	8	13	2	0	.154	0	4	0	0	0.1	1.000
2 yrs.			5	1	.833	3.43	54	1	0	89.1	65	23	100	0	5	1	9	16	2	0	.125	0	4	0	0	0.1	1.000

Tim Murchison

MURCHISON, THOMAS MALCOLM
B. Oct. 8, 1896, Liberty, N. C.   D. Oct. 20, 1962, Liberty, N. C.

BR TL 6'   185 lbs.

Year	Team		W	L	PCT	ERA	G	GS	CG	IP	H	BB	SO	ShO	W	L	SV	AB	H	HR	BA	PO	A	E	DP	TC/G	FA
1917	STL	N	0	0	–	0.00	1	0	0	1	0	2	2	0	0	0	0	0	0	0	–	0	0	0	0	0.0	–
1920	CLE	A	0	0	–	0.00	2	0	0	5	3	4	0	0	0	0	0	1	0	0	.000	0	4	0	0	2.0	1.000
2 yrs.			0	0	–	0.00	3	0	0	6	3	6	2	0	0	0	0	1	0	0	.000	0	4	0	0	1.3	1.000

Red Murff

MURFF, JOHN ROBERT
B. Apr. 1, 1921, Burlington, Tex.

BR TR 6'3"   195 lbs.

Year	Team		W	L	PCT	ERA	G	GS	CG	IP	H	BB	SO	ShO	W	L	SV	AB	H	HR	BA	PO	A	E	DP	TC/G	FA
1956	MIL	N	0	0	–	4.44	14	1	0	24.1	25	7	18	0	0	0	1	5	1	0	.200	4	4	1	0	0.6	.889
1957			2	2	.500	4.85	12	1	0	26	31	11	13	0	2	2	2	6	0	0	.000	1	7	0	0	0.7	1.000
2 yrs.			2	2	.500	4.65	26	2	0	50.1	56	18	31	0	2	2	3	11	1	0	.091	5	11	1	0	0.7	.941

Bob Murphy

MURPHY, ROBERT J.
B. Dec. 26, 1866, Dutchess County, N. Y.   Deceased.

Year	Team		W	L	PCT	ERA	G	GS	CG	IP	H	BB	SO	ShO	W	L	SV	AB	H	HR	BA	PO	A	E	DP	TC/G	FA
1890	NY	N	1	0	1.000	5.50	3	2	1	18	23	10	8	0	0	0	0	9	1	0	.111	0	2	0	0	0.7	1.000

Con Murphy

MURPHY, CORNELIUS B. (Razzle Dazzle)
B. Oct. 15, 1863, Worcester, Mass.   D. Aug. 1, 1914, Worcester, Mass.

TR 5'9"   130 lbs.

Year	Team		W	L	PCT	ERA	G	GS	CG	IP	H	BB	SO	ShO	W	L	SV	AB	H	HR	BA	PO	A	E	DP	TC/G	FA
1884	PHI	N	0	3	.000	6.58	3	3	3	26	37	6	10	0	0	0	0	10	0	0	.000	0	8	0	0	2.7	1.000
1890	2 teams	BKN P	(20G 4–10)			BKN AA	(12G 3–9)																				
"	total		7	19	.269	5.19	32	26	21	234	289	128	55	0	0	2	2	119	24	1	.202	8	66	5	3	2.5	.937
2 yrs.			7	22	.241	5.33	35	29	24	260	326	134	65	0	0	2	2	129	24	1	.186	8	74	5	3	2.5	.943

Dan Murphy

MURPHY, DANIEL LEE
B. Sept. 18, 1964, Artesia, Calif.

BR TR 6'2"   195 lbs.

Year	Team		W	L	PCT	ERA	G	GS	CG	IP	H	BB	SO	ShO	W	L	SV	AB	H	HR	BA	PO	A	E	DP	TC/G	FA
1989	SD	N	0	0	–	5.68	7	0	0	6.1	6	4	1	0	0	0	0	0	0	0	–	0	1	0	0	0.1	1.000

Danny Murphy

MURPHY, DANIEL FRANCIS
B. Aug. 23, 1942, Beverly, Mass.

BL TR 5'11"   185 lbs.

Year	Team		W	L	PCT	ERA	G	GS	CG	IP	H	BB	SO	ShO	W	L	SV	AB	H	HR	BA	PO	A	E	DP	TC/G	FA
1960	CHI	N	0	0	–	0.00	0	0	0	0	0	0	0	0	0	0	0	75	9	1	.120	0	0	0	0	0.0	–
1961			0	0	–	0.00	0	0	0	0	0	0	0	0	0	0	0	13	5	2	.385	0	0	0	0	0.0	–
1962			0	0	–	0.00	0	0	0	0	0	0	0	0	0	0	0	35	7	0	.200	0	0	0	0	0.0	–
1969	CHI	A	2	1	.667	2.01	17	0	0	31.1	28	10	16	0	2	1	4	1	0	0	.000	0	4	0	0	0.2	1.000
1970			2	3	.400	5.67	51	0	0	81	82	49	42	0	2	3	5	6	2	1	.333	4	10	1	1	0.3	.933
5 yrs.			4	4	.500	4.65	68	0	0	112.1	110	59	58	0	4	4	9	*				4	14	1	1	0.3	.947

Ed Murphy

MURPHY, EDWARD J.
B. Jan. 22, 1877, Auburn, N. Y.   D. Jan. 29, 1935, Weedsport, N. Y.

TR 6'1"   186 lbs.

Year	Team		W	L	PCT	ERA	G	GS	CG	IP	H	BB	SO	ShO	W	L	SV	AB	H	HR	BA	PO	A	E	DP	TC/G	FA
1898	PHI	N	1	2	.333	5.10	7	3	2	30	41	10	8	0	0	0	0	14	5	0	.357	3	12	2	2	2.4	.882
1901	STL	N	10	9	.526	4.20	23	21	16	165	201	32	42	0	0	0	0	64	16	1	.250	7	52	1	1	2.6	.983
1902			9	7	.563	3.02	23	17	12	164	187	31	37	1	1	0	1	61	16	0	.262	8	52	3	1	2.7	.952
1903			4	8	.333	3.31	15	12	9	106	108	38	16	0	1	1	0	64	13	0	.203	3	31	0	1	2.3	1.000
4 yrs.			24	26	.480	3.64	68	53	39	465	537	111	103	1	2	1	1	203	50	1	.246	21	147	6	5	2.6	.966

Joe Murphy

MURPHY, JOSEPH AKIN
B. Sept. 7, 1866, St. Louis, Mo.   D. Mar. 28, 1951, Coral Gables, Fla.

5'11"   160 lbs.

Year	Team		W	L	PCT	ERA	G	GS	CG	IP	H	BB	SO	ShO	W	L	SV	AB	H	HR	BA	PO	A	E	DP	TC/G	FA
1886	3 teams	CIN AA	(5G 2–3)			STL N	(4G 0–4)			STL AA	(1G 1–0)																
"	total		3	7	.300	6.07	10	10	9	86	100	40	25	0	0	0	0	35	3	0	.086	2	8	1	0	1.1	.909
1887	STL	AA	1	0	1.000	5.00	1	1	1	9	13	4	5	0	0	0	0	6	1	0	.167	1	3	0	1	4.0	1.000
2 yrs.			4	7	.364	5.97	11	11	10	95	113	44	30	0	0	0	0	41	4	0	.098	3	11	1	1	1.4	.933

John Murphy

MURPHY, JOHN H.
B. Mar. 8, 1867, Philadelphia, Pa.   Deceased.

Year	Team		W	L	PCT	ERA	G	GS	CG	IP	H	BB	SO	ShO	W	L	SV	AB	H	HR	BA	PO	A	E	DP	TC/G	FA
1884	2 teams	ALT U	(14G 5–6)			WIL U	(7G 0–6)																				
"	total		5	12	.294	3.61	21	16	15	159.2	193	11	73	0	1	0	0	125	16	0	.128	9	40	10	2	2.8	.831

Johnny Murphy

MURPHY, JOHN JOSEPH (Fireman, Grandma, Fordham Johnny)
B. July 14, 1908, New York, N. Y.   D. Jan. 14, 1970, New York, N. Y.

BR TR 6'2"   190 lbs.

Year	Team		W	L	PCT	ERA	G	GS	CG	IP	H	BB	SO	ShO	W	L	SV	AB	H	HR	BA	PO	A	E	DP	TC/G	FA
1932	NY	A	0	0	–	16.20	2	0	0	3.1	7	3	2	0	0	0	0	1	1	0	1.000	0	1	0	0	0.5	1.000
1934			14	10	.583	3.12	40	20	10	207.2	193	76	70	0	3	2	4	71	7	0	.099	19	41	3	6	1.6	.952
1935			10	5	.667	4.08	40	8	4	117	110	55	28	0	6	4	5	32	5	0	.156	6	21	2	0	0.7	.931
1936			9	3	.750	3.38	27	5	2	88	90	36	34	0	5	2	5	36	13	0	.361	9	19	3	4	1.1	.903
1937			13	4	.765	4.17	39	4	0	110	121	50	36	0	12	4	10	35	8	0	.229	9	39	3	1	1.3	.941
1938			8	2	.800	4.24	32	2	1	91.1	90	41	43	0	8	2	11	32	2	0	.063	7	21	1	0	0.9	.966
1939			3	6	.333	4.40	38	0	0	61.1	57	28	30	0	3	6	19	11	2	0	.182	3	12	1	1	0.4	.938
1940			8	4	.667	3.69	35	1	0	63.1	58	15	23	0	8	4	9	13	1	0	.077	2	15	0	0	0.5	1.000
1941			8	3	.727	1.98	35	0	0	77.1	68	40	29	0	8	3	15	18	1	0	.056	3	11	1	1	0.4	.933
1942			4	10	.286	3.41	31	0	0	58	66	23	24	0	4	10	11	13	2	0	.154	4	13	3	1	0.6	.850
1943			12	4	.750	2.51	37	0	0	68	44	30	31	0	12	4	8	19	1	0	.053	4	12	2	1	0.5	.889

Year	Team	W	L	PCT	ERA	G	GS	CG	IP	H	BB	SO	ShO	Relief Pitching W	L	SV	Batting AB	H	HR	BA	PO	A	E	DP	TC/G	FA

Johnny Murphy *continued*

Year	Team	W	L	PCT	ERA	G	GS	CG	IP	H	BB	SO	ShO	W	L	SV	AB	H	HR	BA	PO	A	E	DP	TC/G	FA
1946		4	2	.667	3.40	27	0	0	45	40	19	19	0	4	2	7	6	0	0	.000	6	11	2	2	0.7	.895
1947	BOS A	0	0		2.80	32	0	0	54.2	41	28	9	0	0	0	3	11	3	0	.273	5	10	1	0	0.5	.938
13 yrs.		93	53	.637	3.50	415	40	17	1045	985	444	378	0	73	42	107	298	46	0	.154	77	226	22	17	0.8	.932

WORLD SERIES

Year	Team	W	L	PCT	ERA	G	GS	CG	IP	H	BB	SO	ShO	W	L	SV	AB	H	HR	BA	PO	A	E	DP	TC/G	FA
1936	NY A	0	0	—	3.38	1	0	0	2.2	1	1	1	0	0	0	1	2	1	0	.500	0	0	0	0	0.0	—
1937		0	0	—	0.00	1	0	0	.1	0	0	0	0	0	0	0	0	0	0	—	0	0	0	0	0.0	—
1938		0	0	—	0.00	1	0	0	2	2	1	1	0	0	0	1	0	0	0	—	0	0	0	0	0.0	—
1939		1	0	1.000	2.70	1	0	0	3.1	5	0	2	0	1	0	0	2	0	0	.000	3	0	0	0	3.0	1.000
1941		1	0	1.000	0.00	2	0	0	6	2	1	3	0	1	0	0	2	0	0	.000	1	0	0	0	0.5	1.000
1943		0	0		0.00	2	0	0	2	1	1	1	0	0	0	1	0	0	0	—	0	1	0	0	0.5	1.000
6 yrs.		2	0	1.000	1.10	8	0	0	16.1	11	4	8	0	2 2nd	0	4 2nd	6	1	0	.167	1	4	0	0	0.6	1.000

Rob Murphy

MURPHY, ROBERT ALBERT, JR.
B. May 26, 1960, Miami, Fla.

BL TL 6'2" 200 lbs.

Year	Team	W	L	PCT	ERA	G	GS	CG	IP	H	BB	SO	ShO	W	L	SV	AB	H	HR	BA	PO	A	E	DP	TC/G	FA
1985	CIN N	0	0	—	6.00	2	0	0	3	2	2	1	0	0	0	0	0	0	0	—	0	0	0	0	0.0	—
1986		6	0	1.000	0.72	34	0	0	50.1	26	21	36	0	6	0	1	3	0	0	.000	1	9	0	0	0.3	1.000
1987		8	5	.615	3.04	87	0	0	100.2	91	32	99	0	8	5	3	5	1	0	.200	7	14	0	0	0.2	1.000
1988		0	6	.000	3.08	76	0	0	84.2	69	38	74	0	0	6	3	0	0	0	—	4	14	0	2	0.2	1.000
1989	BOS A	5	7	.417	2.74	74	0	0	105	97	41	107	0	5	7	9	0	0	0	—	7	15	0	1	0.3	1.000
5 yrs.		19	18	.514	2.65	273	0	0	343.2	285	134	317	0	19	18	16	8	1	0	.125	19	52	0	3	0.3	1.000

Tom Murphy

MURPHY, THOMAS ANDREW
B. Dec. 30, 1945, Cleveland, Ohio

BR TR 6'3" 185 lbs.

Year	Team	W	L	PCT	ERA	G	GS	CG	IP	H	BB	SO	ShO	W	L	SV	AB	H	HR	BA	PO	A	E	DP	TC/G	FA
1968	CAL A	5	6	.455	2.17	15	15	3	99.1	67	28	56	0	0	0	0	28	0	0	.000	5	11	3	0	1.3	.842
1969		10	16	.385	4.21	36	35	4	215.2	213	69	100	0	0	0	0	71	10	0	.141	14	38	5	6	1.6	.912
1970		16	13	.552	4.24	39	38	5	227	223	81	99	2	0	0	0	76	14	1	.184	22	29	5	3	1.4	.911
1971		6	17	.261	3.78	37	36	7	243	228	82	89	1	0	0	0	75	13	0	.173	19	49	4	2	1.9	.944
1972	2 teams			CAL A (6G 0–0)				KC A (18G 4–4)																		
"	total	4	4	.500	3.36	24	9	1	80.1	90	24	36	1	1	0	1	14	0	0	.000	3	20	1	1	1.0	.958
1973	STL N	3	7	.300	3.76	19	13	2	88.2	89	22	42	0	1	0	0	23	4	0	.174	8	16	1	0	1.3	.960
1974	MIL A	10	10	.500	1.90	70	0	0	123	97	51	47	0	10	10	20	2	1	0	.500	4	30	0	2	0.5	.895
1975		1	9	.100	4.60	52	0	0	72.1	85	27	32	0	1	9	20	0	0	0	—	6	11	2	1	0.4	.895
1976	2 teams			MIL A (15G 0–1)				BOS A (37G 4–5)																		
"	total	4	6	.400	4.17	52	0	0	99.1	116	34	39	0	4	6	9	0	0	0	—	7	16	2	1	0.5	.920
1977	2 teams			BOS A (16G 0–1)				TOR A (19G 2–1)																		
"	total	2	2	.500	4.79	35	1	0	82.2	107	30	39	0	1	2	2	0	0	0	—	5	14	0	1	0.5	1.000
1978	TOR A	6	9	.400	3.93	50	1	0	94	87	37	36	0	6	9	7	0	0	0	—	4	24	0	1	0.6	1.000
1979		1	2	.333	5.50	10	0	0	18	23	8	6	0	1	2	0	0	0	0	—	3	5	0	1	0.8	1.000
12 yrs.		68	101	.402	3.78	439	147	22	1443.1	1425	493	621	3	25	38	59	289	42	1	.145	100	263	23	18	0.9	.940

Walter Murphy

MURPHY, WALTER JOSEPH
B. Sept. 27, 1907, New York, N. Y.

BR TR 6'1½" 180 lbs.

Year	Team	W	L	PCT	ERA	G	GS	CG	IP	H	BB	SO	ShO	W	L	SV	AB	H	HR	BA	PO	A	E	DP	TC/G	FA
1931	BOS A	0	0	—	9.00	2	0	0	2	4	1	0	0	0	0	0	0	0	0	—	0	0	0	0	0.0	—

Amby Murray

MURRAY, JOSEPH AMBROSE
B. June 14, 1913, Fall River, Mass.

BL TL 5'7" 150 lbs.

Year	Team	W	L	PCT	ERA	G	GS	CG	IP	H	BB	SO	ShO	W	L	SV	AB	H	HR	BA	PO	A	E	DP	TC/G	FA
1936	BOS N	0	0	—	4.09	4	1	0	11	15	3	2	0	0	0	0	4	1	0	.250	0	3	0	0	0.8	1.000

Dale Murray

MURRAY, DALE ALBERT
B. Feb. 2, 1950, Cuero, Tex.

BR TR 6'4" 205 lbs.

Year	Team	W	L	PCT	ERA	G	GS	CG	IP	H	BB	SO	ShO	W	L	SV	AB	H	HR	BA	PO	A	E	DP	TC/G	FA
1974	MON N	1	1	.500	1.03	32	0	0	70	46	23	31	0	1	1	10	10	0	0	.000	3	13	2	0	0.6	.889
1975		15	8	.652	3.97	63	0	0	111	134	39	43	0	15	8	9	14	3	0	.214	9	30	3	1	0.7	.929
1976		4	9	.308	3.26	81	0	0	113.1	117	37	35	0	4	9	13	8	0	0	.000	8	38	1	3	0.6	.979
1977	CIN N	7	2	.778	4.94	61	1	0	102	125	46	42	0	7	2	4	12	2	0	.167	8	17	5	3	0.5	.833
1978	2 teams			CIN N (15G 1–1)				NY N (53G 8–5)																		
"	total	9	6	.600	3.78	68	0	0	119	119	53	62	0	9	6	7	10	0	0	.000	9	30	4	1	0.6	.907
1979	2 teams			NY N (58G 4–8)				MON N (9G 1–2)																		
"	total	5	10	.333	4.57	67	0	0	110.1	119	55	41	0	5	10	5	8	0	0	.000	5	19	1	0	0.4	.960
1980	MON N	0	1	.000	6.21	16	0	0	29	39	12	16	0	0	1	0	3	0	0	.000	4	1	1	0	0.4	.833
1981	TOR A	1	0	1.000	1.20	11	0	0	15	12	5	12	0	1	0	0	0	0	0	—	2	6	1	0	0.8	.889
1982		8	7	.533	3.16	56	0	0	111	115	32	60	0	8	7	11	0	0	0	—	5	32	2	2	0.7	.949
1983	NY A	2	4	.333	4.48	40	0	0	94.1	113	22	45	0	2	4	1	0	0	0	—	5	15	2	1	0.6	.909
1984		1	2	.333	4.94	19	0	0	23.2	30	5	13	0	1	2	0	0	0	0	—	4	1	0	0	0.3	.800
1985	2 teams			NY A (3G 0–0)				TEX A (1G 0–0)																		
"	total	0	0	—	15.00	4	0	0	3	7	0	0	0	0	0	0	0	0	0	—	0	1	0	0	0.3	1.000
12 yrs.		53	50	.515	3.85	518	1	0	901.2	976	329	400	0	53	50	60	65	5	0	.077	58	206	23	14	0.6	.920

George Murray

MURRAY, GEORGE KING (Smiler)
B. Sept. 23, 1898, Charlotte, N. C. D. Oct. 18, 1955, Memphis, Tenn.

BR TR 6'2" 200 lbs.

Year	Team	W	L	PCT	ERA	G	GS	CG	IP	H	BB	SO	ShO	W	L	SV	AB	H	HR	BA	PO	A	E	DP	TC/G	FA
1922	NY A	4	2	.667	3.97	22	3	0	56.2	53	26	14	0	4	1	0	18	5	1	.278	0	15	1	2	0.7	.938
1923	BOS A	7	11	.389	4.91	39	18	5	177.2	190	87	40	0	3	1	0	55	9	0	.164	5	41	3	1	1.3	.939
1924		2	9	.182	6.72	28	7	0	80.1	97	32	27	0	1	3	0	22	4	0	.182	2	20	2	0	0.9	.917
1926	WAS A	6	3	.667	5.64	12	12	5	81.1	89	37	28	0	0	0	0	36	5	0	.139	3	17	0	1	1.7	1.000
1927		1	1	.500	7.00	7	3	0	18	18	15	5	0	0	0	0	6	1	0	.167	0	0	0	0	0.0	—
1933	CHI A	0	0		7.71	2	0	0	2.1	3	2	0	0	0	0	0	0	0	0	—	0	1	0	0	0.5	1.000
6 yrs.		20	26	.435	5.38	110	43	10	416.1	450	199	114	0	8	6	0	137	24	1	.175	10	94	6	4	1.0	.945

Jim Murray

MURRAY, JAMES FRANCIS (Big Jim)
B. Dec. 31, 1900, Scranton, Pa. D. July 15, 1973, New York, N. Y.

BB TL 6'2" 200 lbs.

Year	Team	W	L	PCT	ERA	G	GS	CG	IP	H	BB	SO	ShO	W	L	SV	AB	H	HR	BA	PO	A	E	DP	TC/G	FA
1922	BKN N	0	0	—	4.50	4	0	0	6	8	3	3	0	0	0	1	2	1	0	.500	1	0	0	0	0.3	1.000

Year	Team		W	L	PCT	ERA	G	GS	CG	IP	H	BB	SO	ShO	Relief Pitching W	L	SV	Batting AB	H	HR	BA	PO	A	E	DP	TC/G	FA

Joe Murray

MURRAY, JOSEPH AMBROSE
B. Nov. 11, 1920, Wilkes-Barre, Pa.

BL TL 6' 165 lbs.

| 1950 | PHI | A | 0 | 3 | .000 | 5.70 | 8 | 2 | 0 | 30 | 34 | 21 | 8 | 0 | 0 | 1 | 0 | 11 | 0 | 0 | .000 | 3 | 7 | 0 | 0 | 1.3 | 1.000 |

Pat Murray

MURRAY, PATRICK JOSEPH
B. July 18, 1897, Scottsville, N. Y. D. Nov. 5, 1983, Rochester, N. Y.

BR TL 6' 175 lbs.

| 1919 | PHI | N | 0 | 2 | .000 | 6.29 | 8 | 2 | 1 | 34.1 | 50 | 12 | 11 | 0 | 0 | 0 | 0 | 12 | 0 | 0 | .000 | 1 | 9 | 1 | 0 | 1.4 | .909 |

Dennis Musgraves

MUSGRAVES, DENNIS EUGENE
B. Dec. 25, 1943, Indianapolis, Ind.

BR TR 6'4" 188 lbs.

| 1965 | NY | N | 0 | 0 | – | 0.56 | 5 | 1 | 0 | 16 | 11 | 7 | 11 | 0 | 0 | 0 | 0 | 2 | 0 | 0 | .000 | 1 | 2 | 0 | 0 | 0.6 | 1.000 |

Stan Musial

MUSIAL, STANLEY FRANK (Stan the Man)
B. Nov. 21, 1920, Donora, Pa.
Hall of Fame 1969.

BL TL 6' 175 lbs.

| 1952 | STL | N | 0 | 0 | – | 0.00 | 1 | 0 | 0 | 0 | 0 | 0 | 0 | 0 | 0 | 0 | 0 | * | | | | 0 | 0 | 0 | 0 | 0.0 | |

Jeff Musselman

MUSSELMAN, JEFFREY JOSEPH
B. June 21, 1963, Doylestown, Pa.

BL TL 6' 180 lbs.

1986	TOR	A	0	0	–	10.13	6	0	0	5.1	8	5	4	0	0	0	0	0	0	0	–	1	1	0	0	0.3	1.000
1987			12	5	.706	4.15	68	1	0	89	75	54	54	0	12	5	3	0	0	0	–	9	15	0	2	0.4	1.000
1988			8	5	.615	3.18	15	15	0	85	80	30	39	0	0	0	0	0	0	0	–	3	8	1	1	0.8	.917
1989	2 teams	TOR A	(5G 0–1)			NY N	(20G 3–2)																				
"	total		3	3	.500	5.30	25	3	0	37.1	46	23	14	0	3	2	0	0	0	0	–	6	12	2	0	0.8	.900
4 yrs.			23	13	.639	4.11	114	19	0	216.2	209	112	111	0	15	7	3	0	0	0	–	19	36	3	3	0.5	.948

Ron Musselman

MUSSELMAN, RALPH RONALD
B. Nov. 11, 1954, Wilmington, N. C.

BR TR 6'2" 185 lbs.

1982	SEA	A	1	0	1.000	3.45	12	0	0	15.2	18	6	9	0	1	0	0	0	0	0	–	1	4	1	0	0.5	.833
1984	TOR	A	0	2	.000	2.11	11	0	0	21.1	18	10	9	0	0	2	1	0	0	0	–	0	3	0	0	0.3	1.000
1985			3	0	1.000	4.47	25	4	0	52.1	59	24	29	0	3	0	0	0	0	0	–	2	4	1	0	0.3	.857
3 yrs.			4	2	.667	3.73	48	4	0	89.1	95	40	47	0	4	2	1	0	0	0	–	3	11	2	0	0.3	.875

Paul Musser

MUSSER, PAUL
B. June 24, 1889, Millheim, Pa. D. July 7, 1973, State College, Pa.

BR TR 6' 175 lbs.

1912	WAS	A	1	0	1.000	2.61	7	2	0	20.2	16	16	10	0	0	0	1	7	0	0	.000	3	6	0	0	1.3	1.000
1919	BOS	A	0	2	.000	4.12	5	4	1	19.2	26	8	14	0	0	0	0	8	0	0	.000	2	3	0	0	1.0	1.000
2 yrs.			1	2	.333	3.35	12	6	1	40.1	42	24	24	0	0	0	1	15	0	0	.000	5	9	0	0	1.2	1.000

Barney Mussill

MUSSILL, BERNARD JAMES
B. Oct. 1, 1919, Woodville, Pa.

BR TL 6'1" 200 lbs.

| 1944 | PHI | N | 0 | 1 | .000 | 6.05 | 16 | 0 | 0 | 19.1 | 20 | 13 | 5 | 0 | 0 | 1 | 0 | 1 | 0 | 0 | .000 | 0 | 4 | 0 | 0 | 0.3 | 1.000 |

Alex Mustaikis

MUSTAIKIS, ALEXANDER DOMINICK
B. Mar. 26, 1909, Chelsea, Mass. D. Jan. 17, 1970, Scranton, Pa.

BR TR 6'3" 180 lbs.

| 1940 | BOS | A | 0 | 1 | .000 | 9.00 | 6 | 1 | 0 | 15 | 15 | 15 | 6 | 0 | 0 | 0 | 0 | 6 | 2 | 0 | .333 | 2 | 7 | 1 | 1 | 1.7 | .900 |

Elmer Myers

MYERS, ELMER GLENN
B. Mar. 2, 1894, York Springs, Pa. D. July 29, 1976, Collingwood, N. J.

BR TR 6'2" 185 lbs.

1915	PHI	A	1	0	1.000	0.00	1	1	1	9	2	5	12	0	0	0	0	3	0	0	.000	1	0	1	0	2.0	.500
1916			14	23	.378	3.66	44	35	31	315	280	168	182	2	1	1	1	126	27	0	.214	16	106	5	4	2.9	.961
1917			9	16	.360	4.42	38	23	13	201.2	221	79	88	2	1	2	3	73	18	0	.247	15	60	4	0	2.1	.949
1918			4	8	.333	4.63	18	15	5	95.1	101	42	17	1	0	0	1	35	5	0	.143	4	35	2	3	2.3	.951
1919	CLE	A	8	7	.533	3.74	23	15	6	134.2	134	43	38	1	2	0	1	46	11	0	.239	12	38	1	1	2.2	.980
1920	2 teams	CLE A	(16G 2–4)			BOS A	(12G 9–1)																				
"	total		11	5	.688	3.27	28	17	11	167.2	183	47	50	1	0	1	1	63	18	0	.286	10	39	4	0	1.9	.925
1921	BOS	A	8	12	.400	4.87	30	20	11	172	217	53	40	0	3	3	0	65	14	0	.215	7	45	1	4	1.8	.981
1922			0	1	.000	17.47	3	1	0	5.2	10	3	1	0	0	0	0	1	0	0	.000	0	2	0	0	0.7	1.000
8 yrs.			55	72	.433	4.06	185	127	78	1101	1148	440	428	8	7	7	7	412	93	0	.226	65	325	18	12	2.2	.956

Henry Myers

MYERS, HENRY C.
B. May, 1858, Philadelphia, Pa. D. Apr. 18, 1895, Philadelphia, Pa.
Manager 1882.

BR TR 5'9" 159 lbs.

| 1882 | BAL | AA | 0 | 2 | .000 | 6.58 | 6 | 2 | 1 | 26 | 30 | 4 | 7 | 0 | 0 | 0 | 0 | * | | | | 0 | 7 | 0 | 0 | 1.2 | 1.000 |

Joe Myers

MYERS, JOSEPH WILLIAM
B. Mar. 18, 1882, Wilmington, Del. D. Feb. 11, 1956, Delaware City, Del.

BR TR 5'10½" 205 lbs.

| 1905 | PHI | A | 0 | 0 | – | 3.60 | 1 | 1 | 1 | 5 | 3 | 3 | 5 | 0 | 0 | 0 | 0 | 2 | 0 | 0 | .000 | 0 | 1 | 0 | 0 | 1.0 | 1.000 |

Randy Myers

MYERS, RANDALL KIRK
B. Sept. 19, 1962, Vancouver, Wash.

BL TL 6'1" 190 lbs.

1985	NY	N	0	0	–	0.00	1	0	0	2	1	1	2	0	0	0	0	0	0	0	–	0	1	0	0	1.0	1.000
1986			0	0	–	4.22	10	0	0	10.2	11	9	13	0	0	0	0	0	0	0	–	0	2	0	0	0.2	1.000
1987			3	6	.333	3.96	54	0	0	75	61	30	92	0	3	6	6	7	2	0	.286	5	9	1	0	0.3	.933
1988			7	3	.700	1.72	55	0	0	68	45	17	69	0	7	3	26	4	1	0	.250	3	3	0	1	0.1	1.000
1989			7	4	.636	2.35	65	0	0	84.1	62	40	88	0	7	4	24	5	0	0	.000	4	11	0	0	0.2	1.000
5 yrs.			17	13	.567	2.74	185	0	0	240	179	97	264	0	17	13	56	16	3	0	.188	12	26	1	1	0.2	.974

Year	Team	W	L	PCT	ERA	G	GS	CG	IP	H	BB	SO	ShO	Relief Pitching W	L	SV	Batting AB	H	HR	BA	PO	A	E	DP	TC/G	FA

Randy Myers *continued*
LEAGUE CHAMPIONSHIP SERIES

| 1988 | NY | N | 2 | 0 | 1.000 | 0.00 | 3 | 0 | 0 | 4.2 | 1 | 2 | 0 | 0 | 2 | 0 | 0 | 0 | 0 | 0 | – | 0 | 1 | 0 | 0 | 0.3 | 1.000 |

Bob Myrick
MYRICK, ROBERT HOWARD
B. Oct. 1, 1952, Hattiesburg, Miss.   BR TL 6'1" 195 lbs.

1976	NY	N	1	1	.500	3.21	21	1	0	28	34	13	11	0	1	0	0	3	0	0	.000	0	7	0	1	0.3	1.000
1977			2	2	.500	3.62	44	4	0	87	86	33	49	0	2	1	2	11	2	0	.182	3	15	0	0	0.4	1.000
1978			0	3	.000	3.24	17	0	0	25	18	13	13	0	0	3	0	2	0	0	.000	1	5	0	1	0.4	1.000
3 yrs.			3	6	.333	3.47	82	5	0	140	138	59	73	0	3	4	2	16	2	0	.125	4	27	0	2	0.4	1.000

Jack Nabors
NABORS, HERMAN JOHN
B. Nov. 19, 1887, Montevallo, Ala.   D. Nov. 20, 1923, Wilton, Ala.   BR TR 6'3" 185 lbs.

1915	PHI	A	0	5	.000	5.50	10	7	2	54	58	35	18	0	0	0	0	16	2	0	.125	2	18	5	0	2.5	.800
1916			1	20	.048	3.47	40	30	11	212.2	206	95	74	0	0	0	1	69	7	0	.101	4	58	13	0	1.9	.827
1917			0	0	–	3.00	2	0	0	3	2	1	2	0	0	0	0	0	0	0	–	0	2	0	0	1.0	1.000
3 yrs.			1	25	.038	3.87	52	37	13	269.2	266	131	94	0	0	0	1	85	9	0	.106	6	78	18	0	2.0	.824

Bill Nagel
NAGEL, WILLIAM TAYLOR
B. Aug. 19, 1915, Memphis, Tenn.   D. Oct. 8, 1981, Freehold, N. J.   BR TR 6'1" 190 lbs.

| 1939 | PHI | A | 0 | 0 | – | 12.00 | 1 | 0 | 0 | 3 | 7 | 1 | 0 | 0 | 0 | 0 | 0 | * | | | | 0 | 0 | 0 | 0 | 0.0 | – |

Judge Nagle
NAGLE, WALTER HAROLD (Lucky)
B. Mar. 10, 1880, Santa Rosa, Calif.   D. May 27, 1971, Santa Rosa, Calif.   BR TR 6' 176 lbs.

| 1911 | 2 teams | PIT N | (8G 4-2) | | | BOS A | (5G 1-1) | | | | | | | | | | | | | | | | | | | | |
| " | total | | 5 | 3 | .625 | 3.48 | 13 | 4 | 1 | 54.1 | 60 | 12 | 23 | 0 | 3 | 0 | 1 | 17 | 2 | 0 | .118 | 3 | 11 | 0 | 1 | 1.1 | 1.000 |

Mike Nagy
NAGY, MICHAEL TIMOTHY
B. Mar. 25, 1948, New York, N. Y.   BR TR 6'3" 195 lbs.

1969	BOS	A	12	2	.857	3.11	33	28	7	196.2	183	106	84	1	0	0	0	65	5	0	.077	17	29	3	6	1.5	.939
1970			6	5	.545	4.47	23	20	4	129	138	64	56	0	0	0	0	44	11	0	.250	12	15	1	1	1.2	.964
1971			1	3	.250	6.63	12	7	0	38	46	20	9	0	0	1	0	12	1	0	.083	3	5	0	1	0.7	1.000
1972			0	0	–	9.00	1	0	0	2	3	0	2	0	0	0	0	0	0	0	–	0	0	0	0	0.0	–
1973	STL	N	0	2	.000	4.20	7	7	0	40.2	44	15	14	0	0	0	0	11	1	0	.091	1	5	0	1	0.7	1.000
1974	HOU	N	1	1	.500	8.53	9	0	0	12.2	17	5	5	0	1	1	0	1	0	0	.000	0	2	0	0	0.2	1.000
6 yrs.			20	13	.606	4.15	87	62	11	419	431	210	170	1	1	2	0	133	18	0	.135	33	56	4	9	1.1	.957

Steve Nagy
NAGY, STEPHEN
B. May 28, 1919, Franklin, N. J.   BL TL 5'9" 174 lbs.

1947	PIT	N	1	3	.250	5.79	6	1	0	14	18	9	4	0	1	2	0	4	1	0	.250	2	2	0	0	0.7	1.000
1950	WAS	A	2	5	.286	6.58	9	9	2	53.1	69	29	17	0	0	0	0	22	5	1	.227	3	8	0	0	1.2	1.000
2 yrs.			3	8	.273	6.42	15	10	2	67.1	87	38	21	0	1	2	0	26	6	1	.231	5	10	0	0	1.0	1.000

Sam Nahem
NAHEM, SAMUEL RALPH (Subway)
B. Oct. 19, 1915, New York, N. Y.   BR TR 6'1½" 190 lbs.

1938	BKN	N	1	0	1.000	3.00	1	1	1	9	6	4	2	0	0	0	0	5	2	0	.400	0	1	0	0	1.0	1.000
1941	STL	N	5	2	.714	2.98	26	8	2	81.2	76	38	31	0	1	1	1	23	4	0	.174	6	21	2	1	1.1	.931
1942	PHI	N	1	3	.250	4.94	35	2	0	74.2	72	40	38	0	1	2	0	20	2	0	.100	6	19	1	2	0.7	.962
1948			3	3	.500	7.02	28	1	0	59	68	45	30	0	3	2	0	13	2	0	.154	1	9	4	0	0.5	.714
4 yrs.			10	8	.556	4.69	90	12	3	224.1	222	127	101	0	5	5	1	61	10	0	.164	13	50	7	2	0.8	.900

Pete Naktenis
NAKTENIS, PETER ERNEST
B. June 12, 1914, Aberdeen, Wash.   BL TL 6'1" 185 lbs.

1936	PHI	A	0	1	.000	12.54	7	1	0	18.2	24	27	18	0	0	0	0	5	1	0	.200	1	0	0	0	0.1	1.000
1939	CIN	N	0	0	–	2.25	3	0	0	4	2	0	1	0	0	0	0	0	0	0	–	0	2	0	0	0.7	1.000
2 yrs.			0	1	.000	10.72	10	1	0	22.2	26	27	19	0	0	0	0	5	1	0	.200	1	2	0	0	0.3	1.000

Buddy Napier
NAPIER, SKELTON LeROY
B. Dec. 18, 1889, Byronville, Ga.   D. Mar. 29, 1968, Hutchins, Tex.   BR TR 5'11" 165 lbs.

1912	STL	A	1	2	.333	4.97	7	2	0	25.1	33	5	10	0	1	0	0	7	0	0	.000	0	7	0	0	1.0	1.000
1918	CHI	N	0	0	–	5.40	1	0	0	6.2	10	4	2	0	0	0	0	3	1	0	.333	1	1	0	0	2.0	1.000
1920	CIN	N	4	2	.667	1.29	9	5	5	49	47	7	17	1	1	0	0	14	3	0	.214	4	12	0	1	1.8	1.000
1921			0	2	.000	5.56	22	6	1	56.2	72	13	14	0	0	0	1	14	2	0	.143	4	20	1	0	1.1	.960
4 yrs.			5	6	.455	3.92	39	13	6	137.2	162	29	43	1	2	0	1	38	6	0	.158	9	40	1	1	1.3	.980

Cholly Naranjo
NARANJO, LAZARO RAMON GONZALO
B. Nov. 25, 1934, Havana, Cuba   BL TR 5'11½" 165 lbs.

| 1956 | PIT | N | 1 | 2 | .333 | 4.46 | 17 | 3 | 0 | 34.1 | 37 | 17 | 26 | 0 | 1 | 0 | 0 | 7 | 1 | 0 | .143 | 8 | 9 | 0 | 0 | 1.0 | 1.000 |

Ray Narleski
NARLESKI, RAYMOND EDMOND
Son of Bill Narleski.
B. Nov. 25, 1928, Camden, N. J.   BR TR 6'1" 175 lbs.

1954	CLE	A	3	3	.500	2.22	42	1	1	89	59	44	52	0	3	2	13	16	0	0	.000	5	10	2	2	0.4	.882
1955			9	1	.900	3.71	60	1	1	111.2	91	52	94	0	8	1	19	24	7	0	.292	1	11	2	0	0.2	.857
1956			3	2	.600	1.52	32	0	0	59.1	36	19	42	0	3	2	4	8	2	0	.250	2	5	0	1	0.2	1.000
1957			11	5	.688	3.09	46	15	7	154.1	136	70	93	1	5	0	16	43	4	1	.093	4	10	2	0	0.3	.875
1958			13	10	.565	4.07	44	24	7	183.1	179	91	102	0	2	1	1	54	11	0	.204	6	16	1	0	0.5	.957
1959	DET	A	4	12	.250	5.78	42	10	1	104.1	105	59	71	0	2	7	5	21	2	0	.095	4	8	2	0	0.3	.857
6 yrs.			43	33	.566	3.60	266	52	17	702	606	335	454	1	23	13	58	166	26	1	.157	22	60	9	3	0.3	.901

Year	Team		W	L	PCT	ERA	G	GS	CG	IP	H	BB	SO	ShO	W	L	SV	AB	H	HR	BA	PO	A	E	DP	TC/G	FA
															Relief Pitching			**Batting**									

Ray Narleski *continued*

WORLD SERIES

Year	Team		W	L	PCT	ERA	G	GS	CG	IP	H	BB	SO	ShO	W	L	SV	AB	H	HR	BA	PO	A	E	DP	TC/G	FA
1954	CLE	A	0	0	–	2.25	2	0	0	4	1	1	2	0	0	0	0	0	0	0	–	0	1	0	0	0.5	1.000

Buster Narum

NARUM, LESLIE FERDINAND
B. Nov. 16, 1940, Philadelphia, Pa.
BR TR 6'1" 194 lbs.

Year	Team		W	L	PCT	ERA	G	GS	CG	IP	H	BB	SO	ShO	W	L	SV	AB	H	HR	BA	PO	A	E	DP	TC/G	FA
1963	BAL	A	0	0	–	3.00	7	0	0	9	8	5	5	0	0	0	0	1	1	1	1.000	1	2	0	0	0.4	1.000
1964	WAS	A	9	15	.375	4.30	38	32	7	199	195	73	121	2	0	0	0	66	4	1	.061	9	16	1	2	0.7	.962
1965			4	12	.250	4.46	46	24	2	173.2	176	91	86	0	1	1	0	46	2	1	.043	17	39	3	2	1.3	.949
1966			0	0	–	21.60	3	0	0	3.1	11	4	0	0	0	0	0	0	0	0	–	0	0	0	0	0.0	–
1967			1	0	1.000	3.09	2	2	0	11.2	8	4	8	0	0	0	0	5	0	0	.000	1	1	0	0	1.0	1.000
5 yrs.			14	27	.341	4.45	96	58	9	396.2	398	177	220	2	1	1	0	118	7	3	.059	28	58	4	4	0.9	.956

Billy Nash

NASH, WILLIAM MITCHELL
B. June 24, 1865, Richmond, Va. D. Nov. 15, 1929, East Orange, N. J.
Manager 1896.
BR TR 5'8½" 167 lbs.

Year	Team		W	L	PCT	ERA	G	GS	CG	IP	H	BB	SO	ShO	W	L	SV	AB	H	HR	BA	PO	A	E	DP	TC/G	FA
1889	BOS	N	0	0	–	0.00	1	0	0	1	0	1	0	0	0	0	0	481	132	3	.274	0	0	0	0	0.0	–
1890	BOS	P	0	0	–	0.00	1	0	0	.1	1	0	0	0	0	0	0	488	130	5	.266	0	0	0	0	0.0	–
2 yrs.			0	0	–	0.00	2	0	0	1.1	1	1	0	0	0	0	0	*				0	0	0	0	0.0	–

Jim Nash

NASH, JAMES EDWIN
B. Feb. 9, 1945, Hawthorne, Nev.
BR TR 6'5" 215 lbs.

Year	Team		W	L	PCT	ERA	G	GS	CG	IP	H	BB	SO	ShO	W	L	SV	AB	H	HR	BA	PO	A	E	DP	TC/G	FA
1966	KC	A	12	1	.923	2.06	18	17	5	127	95	47	98	0	0	0	1	49	5	0	.102	6	5	0	0	0.6	1.000
1967			12	17	.414	3.76	37	34	8	222.1	200	87	186	2	0	0	0	70	7	0	.100	9	23	1	1	0.9	.970
1968	OAK	A	13	13	.500	2.28	34	33	12	228.2	185	55	169	6	0	0	0	74	5	2	.068	9	20	1	2	0.9	.967
1969			8	8	.500	3.67	26	19	3	115.1	112	30	75	1	2	0	0	36	4	0	.111	9	14	3	0	1.0	.885
1970	ATL	N	13	9	.591	4.08	34	33	6	212	211	90	153	2	0	1	0	80	7	2	.088	18	27	2	1	1.4	.957
1971			9	7	.563	4.94	32	19	2	133	166	50	65	0	0	1	2	47	7	0	.149	7	16	2	1	0.8	.920
1972	2 teams		ATL N	(11G 1–1)		PHI N	(9G 0–8)																					
"	total		1	9	.100	5.90	20	12	0	68.2	81	42	25	0	1	0	0	19	3	0	.158	2	10	1	2	0.7	.923
7 yrs.			68	64	.515	3.59	201	167	36	1107	1050	401	771	11	3	2	4	375	38	4	.101	60	115	10	7	0.9	.946

Phil Nastu

NASTU, PHILIP
B. Mar. 8, 1955, Bridgeport, Conn.
BL TL 6'2" 180 lbs.

Year	Team		W	L	PCT	ERA	G	GS	CG	IP	H	BB	SO	ShO	W	L	SV	AB	H	HR	BA	PO	A	E	DP	TC/G	FA
1978	SF	N	0	1	.000	5.63	3	1	0	8	8	2	5	0	0	0	0	1	0	0	.000	1	0	0	0	0.3	1.000
1979			3	4	.429	4.32	25	14	1	100	105	41	47	0	0	0	0	24	1	0	.042	6	14	1	4	0.8	.952
1980			0	0	–	6.00	6	0	0	6	10	5	1	0	0	0	0	0	0	0	–	1	2	0	0	0.5	1.000
3 yrs.			3	5	.375	4.50	34	15	1	114	123	48	53	0	0	0	0	25	1	0	.040	8	16	1	4	0.7	.960

Jaime Navarro

NAVARRO, JAIME
Born Jaime Navarro y Cintron. Son of Julio Navarro.
B. Mar. 27, 1967, Bayamon, Puerto Rico
BR TR 6'4" 210 lbs.

Year	Team		W	L	PCT	ERA	G	GS	CG	IP	H	BB	SO	ShO	W	L	SV	AB	H	HR	BA	PO	A	E	DP	TC/G	FA
1989	MIL	A	7	8	.467	3.12	19	17	1	109.2	119	32	56	0	1	0	0	0	0	0	–	6	16	2	0	1.3	.917

Julio Navarro

NAVARRO, JULIO (Whiplash)
Born Julio Navarro y Ventura. Father of Jaime Navarro.
B. Jan. 9, 1936, Vieques, Puerto Rico
BR TR 6' 175 lbs.

Year	Team		W	L	PCT	ERA	G	GS	CG	IP	H	BB	SO	ShO	W	L	SV	AB	H	HR	BA	PO	A	E	DP	TC/G	FA
1962	LA	A	1	1	.500	4.70	9	0	0	15.1	20	4	11	0	1	1	0	2	1	0	.500	2	0	0	0	0.2	1.000
1963			4	5	.444	2.89	57	0	0	90.1	75	32	53	0	4	5	12	15	3	0	.200	5	20	1	3	0.5	.962
1964	2 teams		LA A	(5G 0–0)		DET A	(26G 2–1)																					
"	total		2	1	.667	3.58	31	0	0	50.1	45	21	44	0	2	1	3	7	0	0	.000	2	7	0	1	0.3	1.000
1965	DET	A	0	2	.000	4.20	15	1	0	30	25	12	22	0	0	2	1	4	0	0	.000	2	6	0	0	0.5	1.000
1966			0	0	–	∞	1	0	0		2	0	0	0	0	0	0	0	0	0	–	0	0	0	0	0.0	–
1970	ATL	N	0	0	–	4.15	17	0	0	26	24	1	21	0	0	0	1	6	1	0	.167	2	3	0	0	0.3	1.000
6 yrs.			7	9	.438	3.65	130	1	0	212	191	70	151	0	7	9	17	34	5	0	.147	11	38	1	4	0.4	.980

Earl Naylor

NAYLOR, EARL EUGENE
B. May 19, 1919, Kansas City, Mo.
BR TR 6' 190 lbs.

Year	Team		W	L	PCT	ERA	G	GS	CG	IP	H	BB	SO	ShO	W	L	SV	AB	H	HR	BA	PO	A	E	DP	TC/G	FA
1942	PHI	N	0	5	.000	6.12	20	4	1	60.1	68	29	19	0	0	2	0	*				7	10	0	0	0.9	1.000

Rollie Naylor

NAYLOR, ROLEINE CECIL
B. Feb. 4, 1892, Crum, Tex. D. June 18, 1966, Fort Worth, Tex.
BR TR 6'1½" 180 lbs.

Year	Team		W	L	PCT	ERA	G	GS	CG	IP	H	BB	SO	ShO	W	L	SV	AB	H	HR	BA	PO	A	E	DP	TC/G	FA
1917	PHI	A	2	2	.500	1.64	5	5	3	33	30	11	11	0	0	0	0	11	1	0	.091	7	11	0	0	3.6	1.000
1919			5	18	.217	3.34	31	23	17	204.2	210	64	68	0	1	0	0	71	12	0	.169	14	50	5	5	2.2	.928
1920			10	23	.303	3.47	42	36	20	251.1	306	86	90	0	2	0	0	86	14	0	.163	13	70	2	4	2.0	.976
1921			3	13	.188	4.84	32	19	6	169.1	214	55	39	0	0	1	0	52	6	0	.115	6	38	2	1	1.4	.957
1922			10	15	.400	4.73	35	26	11	171.1	212	51	37	0	0	2	0	55	11	1	.200	10	46	0	3	1.6	1.000
1923			12	7	.632	3.46	26	20	9	143	149	59	27	0	1	0	0	45	11	0	.244	9	29	4	4	1.6	.905
1924			0	5	.000	6.34	10	7	1	38.1	53	20	10	0	0	0	0	8	3	0	.375	0	12	0	0	1.2	1.000
7 yrs.			42	83	.336	3.93	181	136	67	1011	1174	346	282	0	4	4	0	328	58	1	.177	59	256	13	17	1.8	.960

Mike Naymick

NAYMICK, MICHAEL JOHN
B. Sept. 6, 1917, Berlin, Pa.
BR TR 6'8" 225 lbs.

Year	Team		W	L	PCT	ERA	G	GS	CG	IP	H	BB	SO	ShO	W	L	SV	AB	H	HR	BA	PO	A	E	DP	TC/G	FA
1939	CLE	A	0	1	.000	1.93	2	1	1	4.2	3	5	3	0	0	0	0	3	0	0	.000	0	0	0	0	0.0	–
1940			1	2	.333	5.10	13	4	0	30	36	17	15	0	0	0	0	6	1	0	.167	2	9	0	0	0.8	1.000
1943			4	4	.500	2.30	29	4	0	62.2	32	47	41	0	4	1	2	16	3	0	.188	2	17	4	0	0.8	.826
1944	2 teams		CLE A	(7G 0–0)		STL N	(1G 0–0)																					
"	total		0	0	–	9.00	8	0	0	15	18	11	5	0	0	0	0	1	0	0	.000	2	3	1	1	0.8	.833
4 yrs.			5	7	.417	3.93	52	9	1	112.1	89	80	64	0	4	1	2	26	4	0	.154	6	29	5	1	0.8	.875

Year	Team		W	L	PCT	ERA	G	GS	CG	IP	H	BB	SO	ShO	Relief Pitching W	L	SV	Batting AB	H	HR	BA	PO	A	E	DP	TC/G	FA

Jack Neagle

NEAGLE, JOHN HENRY
B. Jan. 2, 1858, Syracuse, N. Y. D. Sept. 20, 1904, Syracuse, N. Y.

BR TR 5'6" 155 lbs.

Year	Team		W	L	PCT	ERA	G	GS	CG	IP	H	BB	SO	ShO	W	L	SV	AB	H	HR	BA	PO	A	E	DP	TC/G	FA
1879	CIN	N	0	1	.000	3.46	2	2	1	13	13	5	4	0	0	0	0	12	2	0	.167	1	2	2	0	2.5	.600
1883	3 teams	PHI N (8G 1–7)				BAL AA	(6G 1–4)		PIT AA	(16G 3–12)																	
"	total		5	23	.179	5.94	30	28	22	221.1	292	66	63	0	0	0	1	209	41	0	.196	8	37	8	0	1.8	.849
1884	PIT	AA	11	26	.297	3.73	38	38	37	326	354	70	85	2	0	0	0	148	22	0	.149	19	57	24	1	2.6	.760
3 yrs.			16	50	.242	4.59	70	68	60	560.1	659	141	152	2	0	1	0	*				28	96	34	1	2.3	.785

Joe Neale

NEALE, JOSEPH HUNT
B. May 7, 1866, Wadsworth, Ohio D. Dec. 30, 1913, Akron, Ohio

BR TR 5'8" 153 lbs.

Year	Team		W	L	PCT	ERA	G	GS	CG	IP	H	BB	SO	ShO	W	L	SV	AB	H	HR	BA	PO	A	E	DP	TC/G	FA
1886	LOU	AA	0	1	.000	7.71	1	1	0	7	11	7	0	0	0	0	0	5	0	0	.000	0	5	0	0	5.0	1.000
1887			1	4	.200	6.97	5	4	4	41.1	60	15	11	0	1	0	0	19	1	0	.053	1	11	2	1	2.8	.857
1890	STL	AA	5	3	.625	3.39	10	9	8	69	53	15	23	0	0	0	0	30	2	0	.067	3	6	0	0	0.9	1.000
1891			8	4	.667	4.24	15	11	9	110.1	109	36	24	1	2	0	1	51	6	1	.118	6	36	3	0	3.0	.933
4 yrs.			14	12	.538	4.59	31	25	21	227.2	233	73	58	1	3	0	1	105	9	1	.086	10	58	5	1	2.4	.932

Ron Necciai

NECCIAI, RONALD ANDREW
B. June 18, 1932, Manown, Pa.

BR TR 6'5" 185 lbs.

Year	Team		W	L	PCT	ERA	G	GS	CG	IP	H	BB	SO	ShO	W	L	SV	AB	H	HR	BA	PO	A	E	DP	TC/G	FA
1952	PIT	N	1	6	.143	7.08	12	9	0	54.2	63	32	31	0	0	0	0	17	1	0	.059	4	7	2	2	1.1	.846

Ron Negray

NEGRAY, RONALD ALVIN
B. Feb. 26, 1930, Akron, Ohio

BR TR 6'1" 185 lbs.

Year	Team		W	L	PCT	ERA	G	GS	CG	IP	H	BB	SO	ShO	W	L	SV	AB	H	HR	BA	PO	A	E	DP	TC/G	FA
1952	BKN	N	0	0	–	3.46	4	1	0	13	15	5	5	0	0	0	0	2	0	0	.000	0	2	0	0	0.5	1.000
1955	PHI	N	4	3	.571	3.52	19	10	2	71.2	71	21	30	0	1	0	0	24	0	0	.000	5	9	0	2	0.7	1.000
1956			2	3	.400	4.19	39	4	0	66.2	72	24	44	0	2	2	3	7	3	0	.429	4	11	1	1	0.4	.938
1958	LA	N	0	0	–	7.15	4	0	0	11.1	12	7	2	0	0	0	0	2	0	0	.000	0	2	0	0	0.5	1.000
4 yrs.			6	6	.500	4.04	66	15	2	162.2	170	57	81	0	3	2	3	35	3	0	.086	9	24	1	3	0.5	.971

Jim Neher

NEHER, JAMES GILMORE
B. Feb. 5, 1889, Rochester, N. Y. D. Nov. 11, 1951, Buffalo, N. Y.

BR TR 5'11" 185 lbs.

Year	Team		W	L	PCT	ERA	G	GS	CG	IP	H	BB	SO	ShO	W	L	SV	AB	H	HR	BA	PO	A	E	DP	TC/G	FA
1912	CLE	A	0	0	–	0.00	1	0	0	1	0	0	0	0	0	0	0	0	0	0	–	0	0	0	0	0.0	–

Art Nehf

NEHF, ARTHUR NEUKOM
B. July 31, 1892, Terre Haute, Ind. D. Dec. 18, 1960, Phoenix, Ariz.

BL TL 5'9½" 176 lbs.

Year	Team		W	L	PCT	ERA	G	GS	CG	IP	H	BB	SO	ShO	W	L	SV	AB	H	HR	BA	PO	A	E	DP	TC/G	FA
1915	BOS	N	5	4	.556	2.53	12	10	6	78.1	60	21	39	4	0	0	0	28	4	0	.143	7	17	2	3	2.2	.923
1916			7	5	.583	2.01	22	12	6	121	110	20	36	1	1	1	0	40	5	0	.125	7	29	2	2	1.7	.947
1917			17	8	.680	2.16	38	23	17	233.1	197	39	101	5	4	2	0	70	12	0	.171	9	63	1	3	1.9	.986
1918			15	15	.500	2.69	32	31	28	284.1	274	76	96	2	0	0	0	95	16	0	.168	13	97	3	2	3.5	.973
1919	2 teams	BOS N (22G 8–9)				NY N	(13G 9–2)																				
"	total		17	11	.607	2.49	35	31	22	270.2	221	59	77	3	0	0	0	98	21	1	.214	14	77	2	2	2.7	.978
1920	NY	N	21	12	.636	3.08	40	33	22	280.2	273	45	79	5	2	0	0	97	26	0	.268	18	83	2	11	2.6	.981
1921			20	10	.667	3.63	41	34	18	260.2	266	55	67	2	1	1	1	89	18	0	.202	17	77	2	3	2.3	.979
1922			19	13	.594	3.29	37	35	20	268.1	286	64	60	3	1	1	1	98	25	1	.255	14	64	3	3	2.2	.963
1923			13	10	.565	4.50	34	27	7	196	219	49	50	1	1	1	2	63	12	0	.190	14	47	1	5	1.8	.984
1924			14	4	.778	3.62	30	20	11	171.2	167	42	72	0	1	0	2	57	13	5	.228	6	50	1	2	1.9	.982
1925			11	9	.550	3.77	29	20	8	155	193	50	63	1	4	1	1	51	11	0	.216	8	42	0	5	1.7	1.000
1926	2 teams	NY N (2G 0–0)				CIN N	(7G 0–1)																				
"	total		0	1	.000	4.34	9	0	0	18.2	27	6	4	0	0	0	1	6	1	0	.167	0	9	1	0	1.1	.900
1927	2 teams	CIN N (21G 3–5)				CHI N	(8G 1–1)																				
"	total		4	6	.400	4.02	29	7	3	71.2	84	23	33	1	3	1	5	20	4	0	.200	3	19	0	0	0.8	1.000
1928	CHI	N	13	7	.650	2.65	31	21	10	176.2	190	52	40	2	2	0	1	58	11	1	.190	3	48	2	3	1.7	.962
1929			8	5	.615	5.59	32	15	4	120.2	148	39	27	0	1	2	1	45	13	0	.289	9	27	0	3	1.1	1.000
15 yrs.			184	120	.605	3.20	451	319	182	2707.2	2715	640	844	30	18	14	13	915	192	8	.210	142	749	22	47	2.0	.976

WORLD SERIES

Year	Team		W	L	PCT	ERA	G	GS	CG	IP	H	BB	SO	ShO	W	L	SV	AB	H	HR	BA	PO	A	E	DP	TC/G	FA
1921	NY	N	1	2	.333	1.38	3	3	3	26	13	13	8	1	0	0	0	9	0	0	.000	1	4	1	0	2.0	.833
1922			1	0	1.000	2.25	2	2	1	16	11	3	6	0	0	0	0	3	0	0	.000	0	3	1	0	2.0	.750
1923			1	1	.500	2.76	2	2	1	16.1	10	6	7	1	0	0	0	6	1	0	.167	0	6	0	1	3.0	1.000
1924			1	1	.500	1.83	3	2	1	19.2	15	9	7	0	0	0	0	7	3	0	.429	0	6	0	0	2.0	1.000
1929	CHI	N	0	0	–	18.00	2	0	0	1	1	1	0	0	0	0	0	0	0	0	–	0	0	0	0	0.0	–
5 yrs.			4	4	.500	2.16	12	9	6	79	50	32	28	2	0	0	0	25	4	0	.160	1	19	2	1	1.8	.909
					7th																						
						7th	6th	6th	7th			2nd		4th													

Gary Neibauer

NEIBAUER, GARY WAYNE
B. Oct. 29, 1944, Billings, Mont.

BR TR 6'3" 200 lbs.

Year	Team		W	L	PCT	ERA	G	GS	CG	IP	H	BB	SO	ShO	W	L	SV	AB	H	HR	BA	PO	A	E	DP	TC/G	FA
1969	ATL	N	1	2	.333	3.88	29	0	0	58	42	31	42	0	1	2	0	10	0	0	.000	4	7	0	1	0.4	1.000
1970			0	3	.000	4.85	7	0	0	13	11	9	9	0	0	2	0	2	0	0	.000	1	0	0	0	0.1	1.000
1971			1	0	1.000	2.14	6	1	0	21	14	9	6	0	1	0	1	5	0	0	.000	2	3	0	1	0.8	1.000
1972	2 teams	ATL N (8G 0–0)				PHI N	(9G 0–2)																				
"	total		0	2	.000	6.25	17	2	0	36	44	20	15	0	0	0	0	8	1	0	.125	0	4	0	0	0.2	1.000
1973	ATL	N	2	1	.667	7.29	16	1	0	21	24	19	9	0	2	1	0	4	1	1	.250	2	0	0	0	0.1	1.000
5 yrs.			4	8	.333	4.77	75	4	0	149	135	87	81	0	4	5	1	29	2	1	.069	8	15	0	2	0.3	1.000

LEAGUE CHAMPIONSHIP SERIES

Year	Team		W	L	PCT	ERA	G	GS	CG	IP	H	BB	SO	ShO	W	L	SV	AB	H	HR	BA	PO	A	E	DP	TC/G	FA
1969	ATL	N	0	0	–	0.00	1	0	0	1	0	0	1	0	0	0	0	0	0	0	–	0	0	0	0	0.0	–

Al Neiger

NEIGER, ALVIN EDWARD
B. Mar. 26, 1939, Wilmington, Del.

BL TL 6' 195 lbs.

Year	Team		W	L	PCT	ERA	G	GS	CG	IP	H	BB	SO	ShO	W	L	SV	AB	H	HR	BA	PO	A	E	DP	TC/G	FA
1960	PHI	N	0	0	–	5.68	6	0	0	12.2	16	4	3	0	0	0	0	2	1	0	.500	1	2	0	0	0.5	1.000

Ernie Neitzke

NEITZKE, ERNEST FREDERICK
B. Nov. 13, 1894, Toledo, Ohio D. Apr. 27, 1977, Sylvania, Ohio

BR TR 5'10" 180 lbs.

Year	Team		W	L	PCT	ERA	G	GS	CG	IP	H	BB	SO	ShO	W	L	SV	AB	H	HR	BA	PO	A	E	DP	TC/G	FA
1921	BOS	A	0	0	–	6.14	2	0	0	7.1	8	4	1	0	0	0	0	*				0	3	0	0	1.5	1.000

Year	Team		W	L	PCT	ERA	G	GS	CG	IP	H	BB	SO	ShO	Relief Pitching W	L	SV	Batting AB	H	HR	BA	PO	A	E	DP	TC/G	FA

Bots Nekola

NEKOLA, FRANCIS JOSEPH
B. Dec. 10, 1906, New York, N. Y.   D. Mar. 11, 1987, Rockville Centre, N. Y.   BL TL 5'11½" 175 lbs.

Year	Team		W	L	PCT	ERA	G	GS	CG	IP	H	BB	SO	ShO	W	L	SV	AB	H	HR	BA	PO	A	E	DP	TC/G	FA
1929	NY	A	0	0	–	4.34	9	1	0	18.2	21	15	2	0	0	0	0	4	2	0	.500	1	8	0	1	1.0	1.000
1933	DET	A	0	0	–	27.00	2	0	0	1.1	4	1	0	0	0	0	0	0	0	0	–	0	0	0	0	0.0	–
2 yrs.			0	0	–	5.85	11	1	0	20	25	16	2	0	0	0	0	4	2	0	.500	1	8	0	1	0.8	1.000

Andy Nelson

NELSON, ANDREW
B. St. Paul Minn.,   TL

Year	Team		W	L	PCT	ERA	G	GS	CG	IP	H	BB	SO	ShO	W	L	SV	AB	H	HR	BA	PO	A	E	DP	TC/G	FA
1908	CHI	A	0	0	–	2.00	2	1	0	9	11	4	1	0	0	0	0	2	0	0	.000	1	0	0	0	0.5	1.000

Bill Nelson

NELSON, WILLIAM F.
B. Sept. 28, 1863, Terre Haute, Ind.   D. June 23, 1941, Terre Haute, Ind.   TR

Year	Team		W	L	PCT	ERA	G	GS	CG	IP	H	BB	SO	ShO	W	L	SV	AB	H	HR	BA	PO	A	E	DP	TC/G	FA
1884	PIT	AA	1	2	.333	4.50	3	3	3	26	26	8	6	0	0	0	0	12	2	0	.167	4	5	5	0	4.7	.643

Emmett Nelson

NELSON, GEORGE EMMETT (Ramrod)
B. Feb. 26, 1905, Viborg, S. D.   D. Aug. 25, 1967, Sioux Falls, S. D.   BR TR 6'3" 180 lbs.

Year	Team		W	L	PCT	ERA	G	GS	CG	IP	H	BB	SO	ShO	W	L	SV	AB	H	HR	BA	PO	A	E	DP	TC/G	FA
1935	CIN	N	4	4	.500	4.33	19	7	3	60.1	70	23	14	1	1	1	1	15	2	0	.133	2	16	0	1	0.9	1.000
1936			1	0	1.000	3.18	6	1	0	17	24	4	3	0	1	0	0	6	1	0	.167	1	3	0	1	0.7	1.000
2 yrs.			5	4	.556	4.07	25	8	3	77.1	94	27	17	1	2	1	1	21	3	0	.143	3	19	0	2	0.9	1.000

Gene Nelson

NELSON, WAYLAND EUGENE
B. Dec. 3, 1960, Tampa, Fla.   BR TR 6' 172 lbs.

Year	Team		W	L	PCT	ERA	G	GS	CG	IP	H	BB	SO	ShO	W	L	SV	AB	H	HR	BA	PO	A	E	DP	TC/G	FA
1981	NY	A	3	1	.750	4.85	8	7	0	39	40	23	16	0	0	0	0	0	0	0	–	3	6	1	0	1.3	.900
1982	SEA	A	6	9	.400	4.62	22	19	2	122.2	133	60	71	1	0	1	0	0	0	0	–	10	20	1	2	1.4	.968
1983			0	3	.000	7.88	10	5	1	32	38	21	11	0	0	0	0	0	0	0	–	5	6	1	0	1.2	.917
1984	CHI	A	3	5	.375	4.46	20	9	2	74.2	72	17	36	0	2	0	1	0	0	0	–	11	8	0	1	1.0	1.000
1985			10	10	.500	4.26	46	18	1	145.2	144	67	101	0	4	3	2	1	0	0	.000	10	19	1	0	0.7	.967
1986			6	6	.500	3.85	54	1	0	114.2	118	41	70	0	6	5	6	0	0	0	–	8	17	0	3	0.5	1.000
1987	OAK	A	6	5	.545	3.93	54	6	0	123.2	120	35	94	0	5	2	3	0	0	0	–	8	13	2	0	0.4	.913
1988			9	6	.600	3.06	54	1	0	111.2	93	38	67	0	9	5	3	0	0	0	–	4	11	0	1	0.3	1.000
1989			3	5	.375	3.26	50	0	0	80	60	30	70	0	3	5	3	0	0	0	–	6	3	0	0	0.2	1.000
9 yrs.			46	50	.479	4.14	318	66	6	844	818	332	536	1	29	21	18	1	0	0	.000	65	103	6	7	0.5	.966

LEAGUE CHAMPIONSHIP SERIES

Year	Team		W	L	PCT	ERA	G	GS	CG	IP	H	BB	SO	ShO	W	L	SV	AB	H	HR	BA	PO	A	E	DP	TC/G	FA
1988	OAK	A	2	0	1.000	0.00	2	0	0	4.2	5	1	0	0	2	0	0	0	0	0	–	0	0	0	0	0.0	–
1989			0	0	–	0.00	1	0	0	1.1	1	0	2	0	0	0	0	0	0	0	–	0	0	0	0	0.0	–
2 yrs.			2	0	1.000	0.00	3	0	0	6	6	1	2	0	2	0	0	0	0	0	–	0	0	0	0	0.0	–

WORLD SERIES

Year	Team		W	L	PCT	ERA	G	GS	CG	IP	H	BB	SO	ShO	W	L	SV	AB	H	HR	BA	PO	A	E	DP	TC/G	FA
1988	OAK	A	0	0	–	1.42	3	0	0	6.1	4	3	3	0	0	0	0	0	0	0	–	1	2	0	0	1.0	1.000
1989			0	0	–	54.00	2	0	0	1	4	2	1	0	0	0	0	0	0	0	–	0	0	0	0	0.0	–
2 yrs.			0	0	–	8.59	5	0	0	7.1	8	5	4	0	0	0	0	0	0	0	–	1	2	0	0	0.6	1.000

Jim Nelson

NELSON, JAMES LORIN
B. July 4, 1947, Birmingham, Ala.   BR TR 6' 180 lbs.

Year	Team		W	L	PCT	ERA	G	GS	CG	IP	H	BB	SO	ShO	W	L	SV	AB	H	HR	BA	PO	A	E	DP	TC/G	FA
1970	PIT	N	4	2	.667	3.44	15	10	1	68	64	38	42	1	0	0	0	20	4	0	.200	7	4	2	1	0.9	.846
1971			2	2	.500	2.31	17	2	0	35	27	26	11	0	2	1	0	6	3	0	.500	4	3	0	0	0.4	1.000
2 yrs.			6	4	.600	3.06	32	12	1	103	91	64	53	1	2	1	0	26	7	0	.269	11	7	2	1	0.6	.900

Luke Nelson

NELSON, LUTHER MARTIN
B. Dec. 4, 1893, Cable, Ill.   D. Nov. 14, 1985, Moline, Ill.   BR TR 6' 180 lbs.

Year	Team		W	L	PCT	ERA	G	GS	CG	IP	H	BB	SO	ShO	W	L	SV	AB	H	HR	BA	PO	A	E	DP	TC/G	FA
1919	NY	A	3	0	1.000	2.96	9	1	0	24.1	22	11	11	0	2	0	0	7	1	0	.143	1	5	0	0	0.7	1.000

Lynn Nelson

NELSON, LYNN BERNARD (Line Drive)
B. Feb. 24, 1905, Sheldon, N. D.   D. Feb. 15, 1955, Kansas City, Mo.   BL TR 5'10½" 170 lbs.

Year	Team		W	L	PCT	ERA	G	GS	CG	IP	H	BB	SO	ShO	W	L	SV	AB	H	HR	BA	PO	A	E	DP	TC/G	FA
1930	CHI	N	3	2	.600	5.09	37	3	0	81.1	97	28	29	0	2	0	0	18	4	0	.222	6	22	1	1	0.8	.966
1933			5	5	.500	3.21	24	3	3	75.2	65	30	20	0	4	3	1	21	5	0	.238	1	20	0	1	0.9	1.000
1934			0	1	.000	36.00	2	1	0	1	4	1	0	0	0	0	0	0	0	0	–	0	0	0	0	0.0	–
1937	PHI	A	4	9	.308	5.90	30	4	1	116	140	51	49	0	4	7	2	113	40	4	.354	3	14	0	0	0.6	1.000
1938			10	11	.476	5.65	32	23	13	191	215	79	75	0	2	2	2	112	31	0	.277	4	36	2	0	1.3	.952
1939			10	13	.435	4.78	35	24	12	197.2	233	64	75	2	0	2	1	80	15	0	.188	11	27	2	6	1.1	.950
1940	DET	A	1	1	.500	10.93	6	2	0	14	23	9	7	0	1	0	0	23	8	1	.348	0	3	0	0	0.5	1.000
7 yrs.			33	42	.440	5.25	166	60	29	676.2	777	262	255	2	13	14	6	*				25	122	5	8	0.9	.967

Mel Nelson

NELSON, MELVIN FREDERICK
B. May 30, 1936, San Diego, Calif.   BR TL 6' 185 lbs.

Year	Team		W	L	PCT	ERA	G	GS	CG	IP	H	BB	SO	ShO	W	L	SV	AB	H	HR	BA	PO	A	E	DP	TC/G	FA
1960	STL	N	0	1	.000	3.38	2	2	0	8	7	2	7	0	0	0	0	2	1	0	.500	0	1	0	0	0.5	1.000
1963	LA	A	2	3	.400	5.30	36	3	0	52.2	55	32	41	0	2	0	1	11	1	0	.091	1	15	0	0	0.4	1.000
1965	MIN	A	0	4	.000	4.12	28	3	0	54.2	57	23	31	0	0	3	3	9	1	0	.111	2	8	0	0	0.4	1.000
1967			0	0	–	54.00	1	0	0	.1	3	0	0	0	0	0	0	0	0	0	–	0	0	0	0	0.0	–
1968	STL	N	2	1	.667	2.91	18	4	1	52.2	49	9	16	0	0	1	1	12	2	0	.167	3	9	0	0	0.7	1.000
1969			0	1	.000	12.60	8	0	0	5	13	3	3	0	0	1	0	0	0	0	–	1	0	0	0	0.1	1.000
6 yrs.			4	10	.286	4.41	93	11	1	173.1	184	69	98	0	2	5	5	34	5	0	.147	7	33	0	0	0.4	1.000

WORLD SERIES

Year	Team		W	L	PCT	ERA	G	GS	CG	IP	H	BB	SO	ShO	W	L	SV	AB	H	HR	BA	PO	A	E	DP	TC/G	FA
1968	STL	N	0	0	–	0.00	1	0	0	1	0	1	0	0	0	0	0	0	0	0	–	0	0	0	0	0.0	–

Red Nelson

NELSON, ALBERT FRANCIS
Born Albert W. Horazdovsky.
B. May 19, 1886, Cleveland, Ohio   D. Oct. 26, 1956, St. Petersburg, Fla.   BR TR 5'11" 190 lbs.

Year	Team		W	L	PCT	ERA	G	GS	CG	IP	H	BB	SO	ShO	W	L	SV	AB	H	HR	BA	PO	A	E	DP	TC/G	FA

Red Nelson *continued*

Year	Team		W	L	PCT	ERA	G	GS	CG	IP	H	BB	SO	ShO	W	L	SV	AB	H	HR	BA	PO	A	E	DP	TC/G	FA
1910	STL	A	5	1	.833	2.55	7	6	6	60	57	14	30	1	0	0	0	23	6	1	.261	4	36	1	1	5.9	.976
1911			3	9	.250	5.22	16	13	6	81	103	44	24	0	1	0	0	27	3	0	.111	0	22	2	0	1.5	.917
1912	2 teams	STL A (8G 0-2)					PHI N (4G 2-0)																				
"	total		2	2	.500	5.30	12	5	1	37.1	46	19	11	0	0	0	1	13	2	0	.154	0	8	1	0	0.8	.889
1913	2 teams	PHI N (2G 0-0)					CIN N (2G 0-0)																				
"	total		0	0	—	8.10	4	0	0	10	15	8	3	0	0	0	0	3	1	0	.333	0	4	0	0	1.0	1.000
4 yrs.			10	12	.455	4.54	39	24	13	188.1	221	85	68	1	1	0	1	66	12	1	.182	4	70	4	1	2.0	.949

Roger Nelson

NELSON, ROGER EUGENE (Spider)
B. June 7, 1944, Altadena, Calif. BR TR 6'3" 200 lbs.

Year	Team		W	L	PCT	ERA	G	GS	CG	IP	H	BB	SO	ShO	W	L	SV	AB	H	HR	BA	PO	A	E	DP	TC/G	FA
1967	CHI	A	0	1	.000	1.29	5	0	0	7	4	0	4	0	0	0	0	0	0	0	—	1	2	0	1	0.6	1.000
1968	BAL	A	4	3	.571	2.41	19	6	0	71	49	26	70	0	2	1	1	16	1	0	.063	3	8	0	0	0.6	1.000
1969	KC	A	7	13	.350	3.31	29	29	8	193.1	170	65	82	1	0	0	0	58	8	0	.138	19	25	5	3	1.7	.898
1970			0	2	.000	10.00	4	2	0	9	18	0	3	0	0	0	0	0	0	0	—	0	3	0	0	0.8	1.000
1971			0	1	.000	5.29	13	1	0	34	35	5	29	0	0	1	0	6	2	0	.333	2	9	0	0	0.8	1.000
1972			11	6	.647	2.08	34	19	10	173.1	120	31	120	6	1	1	2	54	5	0	.093	8	33	1	1	1.2	.976
1973	CIN	N	3	2	.600	3.46	14	8	1	54.2	49	24	17	0	0	0	0	18	2	0	.111	3	12	0	2	1.1	1.000
1974			4	4	.500	3.39	14	12	1	85	67	35	42	0	0	1	0	28	5	0	.179	6	10	2	1	1.3	.889
1976	KC	A	0	0	—	2.00	3	0	0	9	4	4	4	0	0	0	0	0	0	0	—	1	1	0	0	0.7	1.000
9 yrs.			29	32	.475	3.06	135	77	20	636.1	516	190	371	7	3	4	4	180	23	0	.128	43	103	8	8	1.1	.948

LEAGUE CHAMPIONSHIP SERIES

Year	Team		W	L	PCT	ERA	G	GS	CG	IP	H	BB	SO	ShO	W	L	SV	AB	H	HR	BA	PO	A	E	DP	TC/G	FA
1973	CIN	N	0	0	—	0.00	1	0	0	2.1	0	1	0	0	0	0	0	1	0	0	.000	0	0	0	0	0.0	—

Hal Neubauer

NEUBAUER, HAROLD CHARLES
B. May 13, 1902, Hoboken, N. J. D. Sept. 9, 1949, Barrington, R. I. BR TR 6'½" 185 lbs.

Year	Team		W	L	PCT	ERA	G	GS	CG	IP	H	BB	SO	ShO	W	L	SV	AB	H	HR	BA	PO	A	E	DP	TC/G	FA
1925	BOS	A	1	0	1.000	12.19	7	0	0	10.1	17	11	4	0	1	0	0	0	0	0	—	0	3	0	0	0.4	1.000

Tex Neuer

NEUER, JOHN S.
B. June 8, 1877, Fremont, Ohio D. Jan. 14, 1966, Northumberland, Pa. TL

Year	Team		W	L	PCT	ERA	G	GS	CG	IP	H	BB	SO	ShO	W	L	SV	AB	H	HR	BA	PO	A	E	DP	TC/G	FA
1907	NY	A	4	2	.667	2.17	7	6	6	54	40	19	22	3	0	0	0	21	2	0	.095	4	11	1	0	2.3	.938

Dan Neumeier

NEUMEIER, DANIEL GEORGE
B. Mar. 9, 1948, Shawano, Wis. BR TR 6'5" 205 lbs.

Year	Team		W	L	PCT	ERA	G	GS	CG	IP	H	BB	SO	ShO	W	L	SV	AB	H	HR	BA	PO	A	E	DP	TC/G	FA
1972	CHI	A	0	0	—	7.36	3	0	0	3.2	2	3	0	0	0	0	0	1	0	0	.000	0	0	0	0	0.0	—

Ernie Nevel

NEVEL, ERNIE WYRE
B. Aug. 17, 1919, Charleston, Mo. D. July 10, 1988, Springfield, Mo. BR TR 5'11" 190 lbs.

Year	Team		W	L	PCT	ERA	G	GS	CG	IP	H	BB	SO	ShO	W	L	SV	AB	H	HR	BA	PO	A	E	DP	TC/G	FA
1950	NY	A	0	1	.000	9.95	3	1	0	6.1	10	6	3	0	0	0	0	1	0	0	.000	0	2	0	0	0.7	1.000
1951			0	0	—	0.00	1	0	0	4	1	1	1	0	0	0	1	1	0	0	.000	0	0	0	0	0.0	—
1953	CIN	N	0	0	—	6.10	10	0	0	10.1	16	1	5	0	0	0	0	0	0	0	—	0	2	0	0	0.2	1.000
3 yrs.			0	1	.000	6.10	14	1	0	20.2	27	8	9	0	0	0	1	2	0	0	.000	0	4	0	0	0.3	1.000

Ernie Nevers

NEVERS, ERNEST ALONZO
B. June 11, 1903, Willow River, Minn. D. May 3, 1976, San Rafael, Calif. BR TR 6' 205 lbs.

Year	Team		W	L	PCT	ERA	G	GS	CG	IP	H	BB	SO	ShO	W	L	SV	AB	H	HR	BA	PO	A	E	DP	TC/G	FA
1926	STL	A	2	4	.333	4.46	11	7	4	74.2	82	24	16	0	0	0	0	27	5	0	.185	8	27	0	1	3.2	1.000
1927			3	8	.273	4.94	27	5	2	94.2	105	35	22	0	3	4	2	32	7	0	.219	5	31	4	0	1.5	.900
1928			1	0	1.000	3.00	6	0	0	9	9	2	1	0	1	0	0	1	0	0	.000	1	2	0	0	0.5	1.000
3 yrs.			6	12	.333	4.64	44	12	6	178.1	196	61	39	0	4	4	2	60	12	0	.200	14	60	4	1	1.8	.949

Don Newcombe

NEWCOMBE, DONALD (Newk)
B. June 14, 1926, Madison, N. J. BL TR 6'4" 220 lbs.

Year	Team		W	L	PCT	ERA	G	GS	CG	IP	H	BB	SO	ShO	W	L	SV	AB	H	HR	BA	PO	A	E	DP	TC/G	FA
1949	BKN	N	17	8	.680	3.17	38	31	19	244.1	223	73	149	5	0	0	1	96	22	0	.229	17	40	0	2	1.5	1.000
1950			19	11	.633	3.70	40	35	20	267.1	258	75	130	4	0	0	3	97	24	1	.247	19	43	2	3	1.6	.969
1951			20	9	.690	3.28	40	36	18	272	235	91	164	3	1	1	0	103	23	0	.223	24	45	3	3	1.8	.958
1954			9	8	.529	4.55	29	25	6	144.1	158	49	82	0	0	0	0	47	15	0	.319	11	16	2	2	1.0	.931
1955			20	5	.800	3.20	34	31	17	233.2	222	38	143	1	1	0	0	117	42	7	.359	15	24	4	5	1.3	.907
1956			27	7	.794	3.06	38	36	18	268	219	46	139	5	2	0	0	111	26	2	.234	25	39	1	0	1.7	.985
1957			11	12	.478	3.49	28	28	12	198.2	199	33	90	0	0	0	0	74	17	1	.230	13	41	2	1	2.0	.964
1958	2 teams	LA N (11G 0-6)					CIN N (20G 7-7)																				
"	total		7	13	.350	4.67	31	26	8	167.2	212	36	69	0	0	1	0	72	26	1	.361	11	19	2	1	1.0	1.000
1959	CIN	N	13	8	.619	3.16	30	29	17	222	216	27	100	0	0	1	0	105	32	3	.305	14	31	1	4	1.5	.978
1960	2 teams	CIN N (16G 4-6)					CLE A (20G 2-3)																				
"	total		6	9	.400	4.48	36	17	1	136.2	160	22	63	0	2	1	1	56	11	0	.196	10	15	3	0	0.8	.893
10 yrs.			149	90	.623	3.56	344	294	136	2154.2	2102	490	1129	24	6	3	7	*				159	313	18	27	1.4	.963

WORLD SERIES

Year	Team		W	L	PCT	ERA	G	GS	CG	IP	H	BB	SO	ShO	W	L	SV	AB	H	HR	BA	PO	A	E	DP	TC/G	FA
1949	BKN	N	0	2	.000	3.09	2	2	1	11.2	10	3	11	0	0	0	0	4	0	0	.000	1	1	0	0	1.0	1.000
1955			0	1	.000	9.53	1	1	0	5.2	8	2	4	0	0	0	0	3	0	0	.000	0	1	0	0	1.0	1.000
1956			0	1	.000	21.21	2	2	0	4.2	11	3	4	0	0	0	0	1	0	0	.000	0	2	0	0	1.0	1.000
3 yrs.			0	4	.000	8.59	5	5	1	22	29	8	19	0	0	0	0	8	0	0	.000	1	4	0	0	1.0	1.000
	7th																										

Tom Newell

NEWELL, THOMAS DEAN
B. May 17, 1963, Monrovia, Calif. BR TR 6'1" 185 lbs.

Year	Team		W	L	PCT	ERA	G	GS	CG	IP	H	BB	SO	ShO	W	L	SV	AB	H	HR	BA	PO	A	E	DP	TC/G	FA
1987	PHI	N	0	0	—	108.00	2	0	0	.1	4	3	1	0	0	0	0	0	0	0	—	0	0	0	0	0.0	—

Don Newhauser

NEWHAUSER, DONALD LOUIS
B. Nov. 7, 1947, Miami, Fla. BR TR 6'4" 200 lbs.

Year	Team		W	L	PCT	ERA	G	GS	CG	IP	H	BB	SO	ShO	W	L	SV	AB	H	HR	BA	PO	A	E	DP	TC/G	FA
1972	BOS	A	4	2	.667	2.43	31	0	0	37	30	25	27	0	4	2	4	2	0	0	.000	0	6	0	0	0.2	1.000

Year	Team	W	L	PCT	ERA	G	GS	CG	IP	H	BB	SO	ShO	Relief Pitching W	L	SV	Batting AB	H	HR	BA	PO	A	E	DP	TC/G	FA

Don Newhauser *continued*

1973		0	0		0.00	9	0	0	12	9	13	8	0	0	0	1	0	0	0	–	0	0	0	0	0.0	
1974		0	1	.000	9.00	2	0	0	4	5	4	2	0	0	1	0	0	0	0	–	1	1	0	0	1.0	1.000
3 yrs.		4	3	.571	2.38	42	0	0	53	44	42	37	0	4	3	5	2	0	0	.000	1	7	0	0	0.2	1.000

Hal Newhouser

NEWHOUSER, HAROLD (Prince Hal)
B. May 20, 1921, Detroit, Mich.

BL TL 6'2" 180 lbs.

1939	DET A	0	1	.000	5.40	1	1	1	5	3	4	4	0	0	0	0	1	0	0	.000	0	1	0	0	1.0	1.000
1940		9	9	.500	4.86	28	20	7	133.1	149	76	89	0	1	0	0	40	8	0	.200	5	31	1	0	1.3	.973
1941		9	11	.450	4.79	33	27	5	173	166	137	106	1	0	1	0	60	9	0	.150	4	37	0	4	1.2	.973
1942		8	14	.364	2.45	38	23	11	183.2	137	114	103	1	0	2	5	52	8	0	.154	10	45	1	3	1.5	.982
1943		8	17	.320	3.04	37	25	10	195.2	163	111	144	1	1	1	1	65	12	0	.185	8	49	1	1	1.6	.983
1944		**29**	9	.763	2.22	47	34	25	312.1	264	102	**187**	6	4	2	2	120	29	0	.242	9	61	1	5	1.5	.986
1945		**25**	9	**.735**	**1.81**	40	**36**	**29**	313.1	239	110	**212**	8	1	1	2	109	28	0	.257	16	66	0	5	2.1	1.000
1946		**26**	9	.743	**1.94**	37	34	29	292.1	215	98	275	6	0	1	1	103	13	2	.126	15	47	3	4	1.8	.954
1947		17	**17**	.500	2.87	40	36	**24**	285	268	110	176	3	0	1	2	96	19	0	.198	23	52	4	3	2.0	.949
1948		**21**	12	.636	3.01	39	35	19	272.1	249	99	143	2	1	1	1	92	19	0	.207	11	52	1	5	1.6	.984
1949		18	11	.621	3.36	38	35	22	292	**277**	111	144	3	1	0	1	91	18	0	.198	7	69	3	3	2.1	.962
1950		15	13	.536	4.34	35	30	15	213.2	232	81	87	1	1	0	3	74	13	0	.176	10	37	2	1	1.4	.959
1951		6	6	.500	3.92	15	14	7	96.1	98	19	37	1	0	0	0	29	9	0	.310	3	22	2	4	1.8	.926
1952		9	9	.500	3.74	25	19	8	154	148	47	57	0	3	0	0	46	10	0	.217	10	31	3	2	1.8	.932
1953		0	1	.000	7.06	7	4	0	21.2	31	6	6	0	0	1	0	8	4	0	.500	1	4	0	0	0.7	1.000
1954	CLE A	7	2	.778	2.51	26	1	0	46.2	34	18	25	0	7	1	7	13	2	0	.154	3	7	0	0	0.4	1.000
1955		0	0	–	0.00	2	0	0	2.1	1	4	1	0	0	0	0	0	0	0	–	0	0	0	0	0.0	–
17 yrs.		207	150	.580	3.06	488	374	212	2992.2	2674	1249	1796	33	20	10	26	999	201	2	.201	135	611	22	40	1.6	.971

WORLD SERIES

1945	DET A	2	1	.667	6.10	3	3	2	20.2	25	4	22	0	0	0	0	8	0	0	.000	2	6	1	0	3.0	.889
1954	CLE A	0	0	–	∞	1	0	0		1	1	0	0	0	0	0	0	0	0	–	0	0	0	0	0.0	–
2 yrs.		2	1	.667	6.53	4	3	2	20.2	26	5	22	0	0	0	0	8	0	0	.000	2	6	1	0	2.3	.889

Floyd Newkirk

NEWKIRK, FLOYD ELMO (Three-Finger)
Brother of Joel Newkirk.
B. July 16, 1908, Norris City, Ill. D. Apr. 15, 1976, Clayton, Mo.

BR TR 5'11" 178 lbs.

| 1934 | NY A | 0 | 0 | – | 0.00 | 1 | 0 | 0 | 1 | 1 | 1 | 0 | 0 | 0 | 0 | 0 | 0 | 0 | 0 | – | 0 | 2 | 0 | 0 | 2.0 | 1.000 |

Joel Newkirk

NEWKIRK, JOEL IVAN (Sailor)
Brother of Floyd Newkirk.
B. June 1, 1896, Kyana, Ind. D. Jan. 22, 1966, El Dorado, Ill.

BR TR 6' 180 lbs.

1919	CHI N	0	0	–	13.50	1	0	0	2	2	3	1	0	0	0	0	1	0	0	.000	0	1	0	0	1.0	1.000
1920		0	1	.000	5.40	2	1	0	6.2	8	6	2	0	0	0	0	3	0	0	.000	0	0	1	0	0.5	–
2 yrs.		0	1	.000	7.27	3	1	0	8.2	10	9	3	0	0	0	0	4	0	0	.000	0	1	1	0	0.7	.500

Maury Newlin

NEWLIN, MAURICE MILTON (Newt, Newley)
B. June 22, 1914, Bloomingdale, Ind. D. Aug. 14, 1978, Houston, Tex.

BR TR 6' 176 lbs.

1940	STL A	1	0	1.000	6.00	1	1	0	6	4	2	3	0	0	0	0	2	1	0	.500	0	0	0	0	0.0	–
1941		0	2	.000	6.51	14	0	0	27.2	43	12	10	0	0	2	1	6	0	0	.000	0	9	1	0	0.7	.900
2 yrs.		1	2	.333	6.42	15	1	0	33.2	47	14	13	0	0	2	1	8	1	0	.125	0	9	1	0	0.7	.900

Fred Newman

NEWMAN, FREDERICK WILLIAM
B. Feb. 21, 1942, Boston, Mass. D. June 24, 1987, Framingham, Mass.

BR TR 6'3" 180 lbs.

1962	LA A	0	1	.000	9.95	4	1	0	6.1	11	3	4	0	0	0	0	1	0	0	.000	0	0	0	0	0.0	–
1963		1	5	.167	5.32	12	8	0	44	56	15	16	0	0	0	0	16	4	0	.250	3	6	1	0	0.8	.900
1964		13	10	.565	2.75	32	28	7	190	177	39	83	2	0	0	0	61	11	1	.180	16	49	3	6	2.1	.956
1965	CAL A	14	16	.467	2.93	36	36	10	260.2	225	64	109	2	0	0	0	74	7	1	.095	25	83	3	4	3.1	.973
1966		4	7	.364	4.73	21	19	1	102.2	112	31	42	0	0	0	0	30	6	0	.200	8	21	1	1	1.4	.967
1967		1	0	1.000	1.42	3	1	0	6.1	8	2	0	0	1	0	0	1	0	0	.000	0	0	0	0	0.0	–
6 yrs.		33	39	.458	3.41	108	93	18	610	589	154	254	4	1	0	0	183	28	2	.153	52	159	8	11	2.0	.963

Jeff Newman

NEWMAN, JEFFREY LYNN
B. Sept. 11, 1948, Ft. Worth, Tex.
Manager 1986.

BR TR 6'2" 215 lbs.

| 1977 | OAK A | 0 | 0 | – | 0.00 | 1 | 0 | 0 | 1 | 1 | 0 | 0 | 0 | 0 | 0 | 0 | * | | | | 0 | 0 | 0 | 0 | 0.0 | – |

Ray Newman

NEWMAN, RAYMOND FRANCIS
B. June 20, 1945, Evansville, Ind.

BL TL 6'5" 205 lbs.

1971	CHI N	1	2	.333	3.55	30	0	0	38	30	17	35	0	1	2	2	6	0	0	.000	1	6	0	0	0.2	1.000
1972	MIL A	0	0	–	0.00	4	0	0	7	4	2	1	0	0	0	0	1	1	0	1.000	0	2	0	0	0.5	1.000
1973		2	1	.667	2.95	11	0	0	18.1	19	5	10	0	2	1	2	0	0	0	–	0	6	0	0	0.5	1.000
3 yrs.		3	3	.500	2.98	45	0	0	63.1	53	24	46	0	3	3	4	7	1	0	.143	1	14	0	0	0.3	1.000

Bobo Newsom

NEWSOM, LOUIS NORMAN (Buck)
B. Aug. 11, 1907, Hartsville, S. C. D. Dec. 7, 1962, Orlando, Fla.

BR TR 6'3" 200 lbs.

1929	BKN N	0	3	.000	10.61	3	2	0	9.1	15	5	6	0	0	0	0	2	0	0	.000	0	2	0	1	0.7	1.000
1930		0	0	–	0.00	2	0	0	3	2	2	1	0	0	0	0	0	0	0	–	0	0	0	0	0.0	–
1932	CHI N	0	0	–	0.00	1	0	0	1	0	1	0	0	0	0	0	0	0	0	–	0	0	0	0	0.0	–
1934	STL A	16	**20**	.444	4.01	47	32	15	262.1	259	**149**	135	2	3	4	5	93	17	0	.183	13	49	2	1	1.4	.969
1935	2 teams	STL A	(7G 0–6)			WAS A	(28G 11–12)																				
"	total	11	18	.379	4.52	35	29	18	241	276	97	87	2	0	0	0	84	23	0	.274	6	37	2	4	1.3	.956
1936	WAS A	17	15	.531	4.32	43	**38**	24	285.2	294	146	156	4	0	0	2	108	23	0	.213	11	50	1	5	1.4	.984

Year	Team	W	L	PCT	ERA	G	GS	CG	IP	H	BB	SO	ShO	Relief Pitching W	L	SV	Batting AB	H	HR	BA	PO	A	E	DP	TC/G	FA

Bobo Newsom *continued*

Year	Team	W	L	PCT	ERA	G	GS	CG	IP	H	BB	SO	ShO	W	L	SV	AB	H	HR	BA	PO	A	E	DP	TC/G	FA
1937	2 teams						**37**				**167**															
	WAS A (11G 3–4) BOS A (30G 13–10)																									
"	total	16	14	.533	4.74	41	37	17	275.1	271	167	166	1	1	1	0	100	22	1	.220	11	41	3	1	1.3	.945
1938	STL A	20	16	.556	5.08	44	**40**	31	329.2	334	192	226	0	0	0	1	124	31	0	.250	11	38	2	1	1.2	.961
1939	2 teams						37																			
	STL A (6G 3–1) DET A (35G 17–10)																									
"	total	20	11	.645	3.58	41	37	24	291.2	280	126	192	3	0	0	2	115	22	0	.191	12	39	3	1	1.3	.944
1940	DET A	21	5	.808	2.83	36	34	20	264	235	100	164	3	1	1	0	107	23	0	.215	3	32	3	3	1.1	.921
1941		12	**20**	.375	4.60	43	36	12	250.1	265	118	175	2	1	1	2	88	9	0	.102	5	36	2	2	1.0	.953
1942	2 teams						34					**134**														
	WAS A (30G 11–17) BKN N (6G 2–2)																									
"	total	13	19	.406	4.73	36	34	17	245.2	264	106	134	3	1	0	0	86	12	0	.140	6	34	5	3	1.3	.889
1943	3 teams						34																			
	BKN N (22G 9–4) STL A (10G 1–6) WAS A (6G 3–3)																									
"	total	13	13	.500	4.22	38	34	17	217.1	220	113	123	1	4	1	1	74	18	0	.243	5	34	0	0	1.0	1.000
1944	PHI A	13	15	.464	2.82	37	33	18	265	243	82	142	2	0	0	1	88	10	0	.114	3	45	0	0	1.3	1.000
1945		8	**20**	.286	3.29	36	34	16	257.1	255	103	127	3	0	1	0	86	14	0	.163	12	28	2	1	1.2	.952
1946	2 teams						31																			
	PHI A (10G 3–5) WAS A (24G 11–8)																									
"	total	14	13	.519	2.93	34	31	17	236.2	224	90	114	0	0	0	1	81	12	0	.148	4	25	0	1	0.9	1.000
1947	2 teams						28																			
	WAS A (14G 4–6) NY A (17G 7–5)																									
"	total	11	11	.500	3.34	31	28	7	199.1	208	67	82	2	0	0	0	71	11	0	.155	2	7	2	0	0.4	.818
1948	NY N	0	4	.000	4.21	11	4	0	25.2	35	13	9	0	0	1	0	7	3	0	.429	1	4	1	0	0.5	.833
1952	2 teams						5																			
	WAS A (10G 1–1) PHI A (14G 3–3)																									
"	total	4	4	.500	3.88	24	5	1	60.1	54	32	27	0	3	2	3	17	2	0	.118	3	14	0	1	0.7	1.000
1953	PHI A	2	1	.667	4.89	17	2	1	38.2	44	24	16	0	1	0	0	6	1	0	.167	1	7	0	1	0.5	1.000
20 yrs.		211	222	.487	3.98	600	483	246	3759.1	3771	1732	2082	31	15	15	21	1337	253	1	.189	109	523	28	30	1.1	.958
												6th														

WORLD SERIES

Year	Team	W	L	PCT	ERA	G	GS	CG	IP	H	BB	SO	ShO	W	L	SV	AB	H	HR	BA	PO	A	E	DP	TC/G	FA
1940	DET A	2	1	.667	1.38	3	3	3	26	18	4	17	1	0	0	0	10	1	0	.100	2	0	0	0	0.7	1.000
1947	NY A	0	1	.000	19.29	2	1	0	2.1	6	2	0	0	0	0	0	0	0	0	–	0	1	0	0	0.5	1.000
2 yrs.		2	2	.500	2.86	5	4	3	28.1	24	6	17	1	0	0	0	10	1	0	.100	2	1	0	0	0.6	1.000

Dick Newsome

NEWSOME, HEBER HAMPTON
B. Dec. 13, 1909, Ahoskie, N. C.   D. Dec. 15, 1965, Ahoskie, N. C.

BR TR 6'   185 lbs.

Year	Team	W	L	PCT	ERA	G	GS	CG	IP	H	BB	SO	ShO	W	L	SV	AB	H	HR	BA	PO	A	E	DP	TC/G	FA
1941	BOS A	19	10	.655	4.13	36	29	17	213.2	235	79	58	2	2	0	0	78	19	0	.244	19	53	2	5	2.1	.973
1942		8	10	.444	5.01	24	23	11	158	174	67	40	0	0	0	0	55	13	0	.236	11	36	4	4	2.1	.922
1943		8	13	.381	4.49	25	22	8	154.1	166	68	40	2	0	1	0	48	7	0	.146	8	25	1	2	1.4	.971
3 yrs.		35	33	.515	4.50	85	74	36	526	575	214	138	4	2	1	0	181	39	0	.215	38	114	7	11	1.9	.956

Doc Newton

NEWTON, EUSTACE JAMES
B. Oct. 26, 1877, Indianapolis, Ind.   D. May 14, 1931, Memphis, Tenn.

BL TL 6'   185 lbs.

Year	Team	W	L	PCT	ERA	G	GS	CG	IP	H	BB	SO	ShO	W	L	SV	AB	H	HR	BA	PO	A	E	DP	TC/G	FA
1900	CIN N	9	15	.375	4.14	35	27	22	234.2	255	100	88	1	2	1	0	86	17	0	.198	6	50	10	0	1.9	.848
1901	2 teams						30																			
	CIN N (20G 4–14) BKN N (13G 6–5)																									
"	total	10	19	.345	3.62	33	30	26	273.1	300	89	110	0	0	1	0	110	18	0	.164	14	78	18	3	3.3	.836
1902	BKN N	15	14	.517	2.42	31	28	26	264.1	208	87	107	5	2	0	0	109	19	0	.174	9	58	3	1	2.3	.957
1905	NY A	2	2	.500	2.11	11	7	5	59.2	61	24	15	0	0	0	0	22	3	0	.136	1	16	5	0	2.0	.773
1906		6	5	.545	3.17	21	15	6	125	118	33	52	2	1	0	0	41	9	0	.220	2	50	6	1	2.8	.897
1907		7	10	.412	3.18	19	15	10	133	132	31	70	0	2	0	0	37	4	0	.108	6	43	4	2	2.8	.925
1908		4	5	.444	2.95	23	13	6	88.1	78	41	49	1	0	1	1	25	4	0	.160	2	27	3	0	1.4	.906
1909		0	3	.000	2.82	4	4	1	22.1	27	11	11	0	0	0	0	6	1	0	.167	1	11	4	0	4.0	.750
8 yrs.		53	73	.421	3.22	177	139	99	1200.2	1179	416	502	9	7	3	1	436	75	0	.172	41	333	53	7	2.4	.876

Chet Nichols

NICHOLS, CHESTER RAYMOND, SR.
Father of Chet Nichols.
B. July 3, 1897, Woonsocket, R. I.   D. July 11, 1982, Pawtucket, R. I.

BR TR 5'10"   160 lbs.

Year	Team	W	L	PCT	ERA	G	GS	CG	IP	H	BB	SO	ShO	W	L	SV	AB	H	HR	BA	PO	A	E	DP	TC/G	FA
1926	PIT N	0	0	–	8.22	3	0	0	7.2	13	5	2	0	0	0	0	3	1	0	.333	0	3	0	0	1.0	1.000
1927		0	3	.000	5.86	8	0	0	27.2	34	17	9	0	0	3	0	9	1	0	.111	0	6	0	0	0.8	1.000
1928	NY N	0	0	–	23.63	3	0	0	2.2	11	3	1	0	0	0	0	0	0	0	–	0	0	0	0	0.3	1.000
1930	PHI N	1	2	.333	6.79	16	5	1	59.2	76	16	15	0	0	0	0	20	6	0	.300	1	17	0	0	1.1	1.000
1931		0	1	.000	9.53	3	0	0	5.2	10	1	1	0	0	1	0	2	0	0	.000	1	1	0	0	0.7	1.000
1932		0	2	.000	6.98	11	0	0	19.1	23	14	5	0	0	2	1	4	0	0	.000	2	5	0	1	0.6	1.000
6 yrs.		1	8	.111	7.19	44	5	1	122.2	167	56	33	0	0	6	1	38	8	0	.211	4	33	0	1	0.8	1.000

Chet Nichols

NICHOLS, CHESTER RAYMOND, JR.
Son of Chet Nichols.
B. Feb. 22, 1931, Providence, R. I.

BB TL 6'1½"   165 lbs.
BR 1951,
BL 1954,1961

Year	Team	W	L	PCT	ERA	G	GS	CG	IP	H	BB	SO	ShO	W	L	SV	AB	H	HR	BA	PO	A	E	DP	TC/G	FA
1951	BOS N	11	8	.579	**2.88**	33	19	12	156	142	69	71	3	2	1	2	51	7	0	.137	6	36	0	2	1.3	1.000
1954	MIL N	9	11	.450	4.41	35	20	5	122.1	132	65	55	1	2	3	1	35	3	0	.086	3	27	0	3	0.9	1.000
1955		9	8	.529	4.00	34	21	6	144	139	67	44	0	1	1	1	52	8	0	.154	6	35	2	3	1.3	.953
1956		0	1	.000	6.75	2	0	0	4	9	3	2	0	0	1	0	1	0	0	.000	0	2	0	0	1.0	1.000
1960	BOS A	0	2	.000	4.26	6	1	0	12.2	12	4	11	0	0	1	0	3	0	0	.000	0	4	0	0	0.7	1.000
1961		3	2	.600	2.09	26	2	0	51.2	40	26	20	0	3	1	3	9	1	0	.111	3	23	0	1	1.0	1.000
1962		1	1	.500	3.00	29	1	0	57	57	22	33	0	1	1	0	9	0	0	.000	2	10	0	2	0.7	1.000
1963		1	3	.250	4.78	21	7	0	52.2	61	24	27	0	0	0	0	13	3	0	.231	2	8	1	1	0.5	.909
1964	CIN N	0	0	–	6.00	3	0	0	3	4	0	3	0	0	0	0	0	0	0	–	0	0	0	0	0.0	–
9 yrs.		34	36	.486	3.64	189	71	23	603.1	600	280	266	4	8	9	10	173	22	0	.127	24	150	3	12	0.9	.983

Dolan Nichols

NICHOLS, DOLAN LEVON (Nick)
B. Feb. 28, 1930, Tishomingo, Miss.

BR TR 6'   195 lbs.

Year	Team	W	L	PCT	ERA	G	GS	CG	IP	H	BB	SO	ShO	W	L	SV	AB	H	HR	BA	PO	A	E	DP	TC/G	FA
1958	CHI N	0	4	.000	5.01	24	0	0	41.1	46	16	9	0	0	4	1	5	0	0	.000	1	13	0	0	0.5	1.000

Kid Nichols

NICHOLS, CHARLES AUGUSTUS (Nick)
B. Sept. 14, 1869, Madison, Wis.   D. Apr. 11, 1953, Kansas City, Mo.
Manager 1904-05.
Hall of Fame 1949.

BB TR 5'10½"   175 lbs.

Year	Team	W	L	PCT	ERA	G	GS	CG	IP	H	BB	SO	ShO	W	L	SV	AB	H	HR	BA	PO	A	E	DP	TC/G	FA

Kid Nichols *continued*

Year	Team	W	L	PCT	ERA	G	GS	CG	IP	H	BB	SO	ShO	W	L	SV	AB	H	HR	BA	PO	A	E	DP	TC/G	FA
1890	BOS N	27	19	.587	2.21	48	47	47	427	374	112	222	7	0	0	0	174	43	0	.247	14	85	13	1	2.3	.884
1891		30	17	.638	2.39	52	48	45	425.2	413	103	240	5	0	1	3	183	36	1	.197	30	100	7	5	2.6	.949
1892		35	16	.686	2.83	53	51	50	454	404	121	187	5	1	0	0	197	39	2	.198	25	88	4	4	2.2	.966
1893		34	14	.708	3.52	52	44	43	425	426	118	94	1	4	1	1	177	39	2	.220	21	81	5	5	2.1	.953
1894		32	13	.711	4.75	50	46	40	407	488	121	113	3	1	1	0	170	50	4	.294	34	67	7	3	2.2	.935
1895		26	16	.619	3.29	47	42	42	394	417	86	140	1	0	0	3	157	37	0	.236	29	73	4	2	2.3	.962
1896		30	14	.682	2.81	49	43	37	375	387	101	102	3	2	1	1	147	28	1	.190	19	92	0	3	2.3	1.000
1897		31	11	.738	2.64	46	40	37	368	362	72	136	2	2	0	3	147	39	3	.265	29	62	3	1	2.0	.968
1898		31	12	.721	2.13	50	42	40	388	316	85	138	5	2	0	4	158	38	2	.241	21	78	4	1	2.1	.961
1899		21	19	.525	2.94	42	37	37	349	326	82	108	4	1	2	1	136	26	1	.191	25	71	5	5	2.4	.950
1900		13	16	.448	3.07	29	27	25	231.1	215	72	53	4	0	2	0	90	18	1	.200	19	48	1	1	2.3	.985
1901		19	16	.543	3.22	38	34	33	321	306	90	143	4	2	1	0	163	46	4	.282	27	69	4	1	2.6	.960
1904	STL N	21	13	.618	2.02	36	35	35	317	268	50	134	3	0	0	1	109	17	0	.156	13	84	5	1	2.8	.951
1905	2 teams		STL N	(7G 1–5)		PHI N	(17G 10–6)																			
"	total	11	11	.500	3.11	24	23	20	191	193	46	66	1	0	0	0	75	15	0	.200	5	32	5	1	1.8	.881
1906	PHI N	0	1	.000	9.82	4	2	1	11	17	13	1	0	0	0	0	3	0	0	.000	0	1	0	0	0.3	1.000
15 yrs.		361	208	.634	2.94	620	561	532	5084	4912	1272	1877	48	15	9	17	*				311	1031	67	34	2.3	.952
				6th					4th	10th																

Rod Nichols

NICHOLS, RODNEY LEA
B. Dec. 29, 1964, Burlington, Iowa   BR TR 6'2"   190 lbs.

Year	Team	W	L	PCT	ERA	G	GS	CG	IP	H	BB	SO	ShO	W	L	SV	AB	H	HR	BA	PO	A	E	DP	TC/G	FA
1988	CLE A	1	7	.125	5.06	11	10	3	69.1	73	23	31	0	0	1	0	0	0	0	–	5	9	1	0	1.4	.933
1989		4	6	.400	4.40	15	11	0	71.2	81	24	42	0	0	2	0	0	0	0	–	4	8	0	2	0.8	1.000
2 yrs.		5	13	.278	4.72	26	21	3	141	154	47	73	0	0	3	0	0	0	0	–	9	17	1	2	1.0	.963

Tricky Nichols

NICHOLS, FREDERICK C.
B. July 26, 1850, Bridgeport, Conn.   D. Aug. 22, 1897, Bridgeport Conn.,   BR TR 5'7½"   150 lbs.

Year	Team	W	L	PCT	ERA	G	GS	CG	IP	H	BB	SO	ShO	W	L	SV	AB	H	HR	BA	PO	A	E	DP	TC/G	FA
1876	BOS N	1	0	1.000	1.00	1	1	1	9	7	0	0	0	0	0	0	4	0	0	.000	0	2	0	0	2.0	1.000
1877	STL N	18	23	.439	2.60	42	39	35	350	376	53	80	1	2	0	0	186	31	0	.167	14	62	4	1	1.9	.950
1878	PRO N	4	7	.364	4.22	11	10	10	98	157	8	21	0	0	1	0	49	9	0	.184	6	27	1	2	3.1	.971
1880	WOR N	0	2	.000	4.08	2	2	2	17.2	29	4	4	0	0	0	0	7	0	0	.000	0	3	3	0	3.0	.500
1882	BAL AA	1	12	.077	5.02	16	13	12	118.1	155	17	21	0	0	0	0	95	15	0	.158	5	34	8	0	2.9	.830
5 yrs.		24	44	.353	3.37	72	65	60	593	724	82	126	1	2	1	0	*				25	128	16	3	2.3	.905

Frank Nicholson

NICHOLSON, FRANK COLLINS
B. Aug. 29, 1889, Berlin, Pa.   D. Nov. 10, 1972, Jersey Shore, Pa.   BR TR 6'2"   175 lbs.

Year	Team	W	L	PCT	ERA	G	GS	CG	IP	H	BB	SO	ShO	W	L	SV	AB	H	HR	BA	PO	A	E	DP	TC/G	FA
1912	PHI N	0	0	–	6.75	2	0	0	4	8	2	1	0	0	0	0	0	0	0	–	0	1	0	0	0.5	1.000

George Nicol

NICOL, GEORGE EDWARD
B. Oct. 17, 1870, Barry, Ill.   D. Aug. 10, 1924, Milwaukee, Wis.   TL 5'7"   155 lbs.

Year	Team	W	L	PCT	ERA	G	GS	CG	IP	H	BB	SO	ShO	W	L	SV	AB	H	HR	BA	PO	A	E	DP	TC/G	FA
1890	STL AA	2	1	.667	4.76	3	3	2	17	11	19	16	0	0	0	0	7	2	0	.286	2	0	0	0	0.7	1.000
1891	CHI N	0	1	.000	4.91	3	2	0	11	14	10	12	0	0	1	0	6	2	0	.333	0	0	3	0	1.0	–
1894	2 teams		PIT N	(8G 3–4)		LOU N	(1G 0–1)																			
"	total	3	5	.375	7.93	9	6	4	53.1	76	38	14	0	2	0	0	128	47	0	.367	0	7	1	0	0.9	.875
3 yrs.		5	7	.417	6.86	15	11	6	81.1	101	67	42	0	2	1	0	*				2	7	4	0	0.9	.692

Tom Niedenfuer

NIEDENFUER, THOMAS EDWARD
B. Aug. 13, 1959, St. Louis Park, Minn.   BR TR 6'5"   225 lbs.

Year	Team	W	L	PCT	ERA	G	GS	CG	IP	H	BB	SO	ShO	W	L	SV	AB	H	HR	BA	PO	A	E	DP	TC/G	FA
1981	LA N	3	1	.750	3.81	17	0	0	26	25	6	12	0	3	1	2	0	0	0	–	4	2	0	0	0.4	1.000
1982		3	4	.429	2.71	55	0	0	69.2	71	25	60	0	3	4	9	3	0	0	.000	1	7	0	0	0.1	1.000
1983		8	3	.727	1.90	66	0	0	94.2	55	29	66	0	8	3	11	4	0	0	.000	8	8	1	0	0.3	.941
1984		2	5	.286	2.47	33	0	0	47.1	39	23	45	0	2	5	11	3	0	0	.000	1	5	1	0	0.2	.857
1985		7	9	.438	2.71	64	0	0	106.1	86	24	102	0	7	9	19	9	1	0	.111	8	7	0	0	0.2	1.000
1986		6	6	.500	3.71	60	0	0	80	86	29	55	0	6	6	11	4	2	0	.500	9	10	1	1	0.3	.950
1987	2 teams		LA N	(15G 1–0)		BAL A	(45G 3–5)																			
"	total	4	5	.444	4.46	60	0	0	68.2	68	31	47	0	4	5	14	0	0	0	–	7	6	1	2	0.2	.929
1988	BAL A	3	4	.429	3.51	52	0	0	59	59	19	40	0	3	4	18	0	0	0	–	3	5	1	1	0.2	.889
1989	SEA A	0	3	.000	6.69	25	0	0	36.1	46	15	15	0	0	3	0	0	0	0	–	6	5	2	0	0.5	.846
9 yrs.		36	40	.474	3.28	432	0	0	588	535	201	442	0	36	40	95	23	3	0	.130	47	55	7	4	0.3	.936

DIVISIONAL PLAYOFF SERIES

Year	Team	W	L	PCT	ERA	G	GS	CG	IP	H	BB	SO	ShO	W	L	SV	AB	H	HR	BA	PO	A	E	DP	TC/G	FA
1981	LA N	0	0	–	0.00	1	0	0	.1	1	1	1	0	0	0	0	0	0	0	–	0	0	0	0	0.0	–

LEAGUE CHAMPIONSHIP SERIES

Year	Team	W	L	PCT	ERA	G	GS	CG	IP	H	BB	SO	ShO	W	L	SV	AB	H	HR	BA	PO	A	E	DP	TC/G	FA
1981	LA N	0	0	–	0.00	1	0	0	.1	2	0	0	0	0	0	0	0	0	0	–	0	0	0	0	0.0	–
1983		0	0	–	0.00	2	0	0	2	0	1	3	0	0	0	0	0	0	0	–	0	1	0	0	0.5	1.000
1985		0	2	.000	6.35	3	0	0	5.2	5	2	5	0	0	2	1	1	0	0	.000	2	0	0	0	0.7	1.000
3 yrs.		0	2	.000	4.50	6	0	0	8	7	3	8	0	0	2	1	1	0	0	.000	2	1	0	0	0.5	1.000

WORLD SERIES

Year	Team	W	L	PCT	ERA	G	GS	CG	IP	H	BB	SO	ShO	W	L	SV	AB	H	HR	BA	PO	A	E	DP	TC/G	FA
1981	LA N	0	0	–	0.00	2	0	0	3	1	3	1	0	0	0	0	0	0	0	–	0	0	0	0	0.0	–

Dick Niehaus

NIEHAUS, RICHARD J.
B. Oct. 24, 1892, Covington, Ky.   D. Mar. 12, 1957, Atlanta, Ga.   BL TL 5'11"   165 lbs.

Year	Team	W	L	PCT	ERA	G	GS	CG	IP	H	BB	SO	ShO	W	L	SV	AB	H	HR	BA	PO	A	E	DP	TC/G	FA
1913	STL N	0	2	.000	4.13	3	3	2	24	20	13	4	0	0	0	0	7	2	0	.286	0	9	1	0	3.3	.900
1914		1	0	1.000	3.12	8	1	1	17.1	18	8	6	0	0	0	0	4	1	0	.250	1	3	2	0	0.8	.667
1915		2	1	.667	3.97	15	2	0	45.1	48	22	21	0	1	0	0	14	1	0	.071	1	14	2	0	1.1	.882
1920	CLE A	1	2	.333	3.60	19	3	0	40	42	16	12	0	1	0	2	9	4	0	.444	0	5	0	0	0.3	1.000
4 yrs.		4	5	.444	3.77	45	9	3	126.2	128	59	43	0	2	0	2	34	8	0	.235	2	31	5	0	0.8	.868

Year	Team		W	L	PCT	ERA	G	GS	CG	IP	H	BB	SO	ShO	Relief Pitching W	L	SV	Batting AB	H	HR	BA	PO	A	E	DP	TC/G	FA

Joe Niekro

NIEKRO, JOSEPH FRANKLIN
Brother of Phil Niekro.
B. Nov. 7, 1944, Martin's Ferry, Ohio

BR TR 6'1" 185 lbs.

Year	Team		W	L	PCT	ERA	G	GS	CG	IP	H	BB	SO	ShO	W	L	SV	AB	H	HR	BA	PO	A	E	DP	TC/G	FA
1967	CHI	N	10	7	.588	3.34	36	22	7	169.2	171	32	77	2	1	1	0	46	9	0	.196	10	26	0	1	1.0	1.000
1968			14	10	.583	4.31	34	29	2	177.1	204	59	65	1	1	0	2	60	6	0	.100	9	33	0	2	1.2	1.000
1969	2 teams		CHI N	(4G 0–1)		SD N	(37G 8–17)																				
"	total		8	18	.308	3.70	41	34	8	221.1	237	51	62	3	0	0	0	56	7	0	.125	21	34	5	2	1.5	.917
1970	DET	A	12	13	.480	4.06	38	34	6	213	221	72	101	2	1	0	0	66	13	0	.197	17	35	1	1	1.4	.981
1971			6	7	.462	4.50	31	15	0	122	136	49	43	0	2	0	1	30	4	0	.133	9	25	1	1	1.1	.971
1972			3	2	.600	3.83	18	7	1	47	62	8	24	0	0	1	1	12	3	0	.250	5	4	0	1	0.5	1.000
1973	ATL	N	2	4	.333	4.13	20	0	0	24	23	11	12	0	2	4	3	3	1	0	.333	2	5	0	2	0.4	1.000
1974			3	2	.600	3.56	27	2	0	43	36	18	31	0	3	2	0	5	0	0	.000	4	8	0	1	0.4	1.000
1975	HOU	N	6	4	.600	3.07	40	4	1	88	79	39	54	1	3	4	4	14	3	0	.214	7	13	0	0	0.5	1.000
1976			4	8	.333	3.36	36	13	0	118	107	56	77	0	0	2	0	27	5	1	.185	9	34	3	1	0.7	.880
1977			13	8	.619	3.03	44	14	9	181	155	64	101	2	4	5	5	50	7	0	.140	11	31	0	7	1.0	1.000
1978			14	14	.500	3.86	35	29	10	203	190	73	97	1	1	0	0	65	9	0	.138	18	21	0	3	1.1	1.000
1979			**21**	11	.656	3.00	38	38	11	264	221	107	119	**5**	0	0	0	83	10	0	.120	14	39	0	4	1.4	1.000
1980			20	12	.625	3.55	37	36	11	256	268	79	127	2	1	0	0	80	22	0	.275	17	37	2	2	1.5	.964
1981			9	9	.500	2.82	24	24	5	166	150	47	77	2	0	0	0	51	9	0	.176	11	23	0	1	1.4	1.000
1982			17	12	.586	2.47	35	35	16	270	224	64	130	5	0	0	0	89	8	0	.090	22	42	3	2	1.9	.955
1983			15	14	.517	3.48	38	**38**	9	263.2	238	101	152	1	0	0	0	85	8	0	.094	9	36	4	0	1.3	.918
1984			16	12	.571	3.04	38	**38**	6	248.1	223	89	127	1	0	0	0	83	11	0	.133	19	39	2	5	1.6	.967
1985	2 teams		HOU N	(32G 9–12)		NY A	(3G 2–1)																				
"	total		11	13	.458	3.83	35	35	4	225.1	211	107	121	1	0	0	0	68	17	0	.250	17	36	1	1	1.5	.981
1986	NY	A	9	10	.474	4.87	25	25	0	125.2	139	63	59	0	0	0	0	0	0	0	—	9	13	1	2	0.9	.957
1987	2 teams		NY A	(8G 3–4)		MIN A	(19G 4–9)																				
"	total		7	13	.350	5.33	27	26	1	147	155	64	84	0	0	0	0	0	0	0	—	5	6	1	0	0.4	.917
1988	MIN	A	1	1	.500	10.03	5	2	0	11.2	16	9	7	0	1	0	0	0	0	0	—	2	3	0	1	1.0	1.000
22 yrs.			221	204	.520	3.59	702	500	107	3585	3466	1262	1747	29	20	18	16	973	152	1	.156	247	522	24	40	1.1	.970

DIVISIONAL PLAYOFF SERIES

| 1981 | HOU | N | 0 | 0 | — | 0.00 | 1 | 1 | 0 | 8 | 7 | 3 | 4 | 0 | 0 | 0 | 0 | 2 | 0 | 0 | .000 | 0 | 0 | 0 | 0 | 0.0 | — |

LEAGUE CHAMPIONSHIP SERIES

| 1980 | HOU | N | 0 | 0 | — | 0.00 | 1 | 1 | 0 | 10 | 6 | 1 | 2 | 0 | 0 | 0 | 0 | 3 | 0 | 0 | .000 | 1 | 0 | 0 | 0 | 1.0 | 1.000 |

WORLD SERIES

| 1987 | MIN | A | 0 | 0 | — | 0.00 | 1 | 1 | 0 | 2 | 1 | 1 | 1 | 0 | 0 | 0 | 0 | 0 | 0 | 0 | — | 0 | 1 | 0 | 0 | 1.0 | 1.000 |

Phil Niekro

NIEKRO, PHILIP HENRY (Knucksie)
Brother of Joe Niekro.
B. Apr. 1, 1939, Blaine, Ohio

BR TR 6'1" 180 lbs.

Year	Team		W	L	PCT	ERA	G	GS	CG	IP	H	BB	SO	ShO	W	L	SV	AB	H	HR	BA	PO	A	E	DP	TC/G	FA
1964	MIL	N	0	0	—	4.80	10	0	0	15	15	7	8	0	0	0	0	0	0	0	—	0	2	0	1	0.2	1.000
1965			2	3	.400	2.89	41	1	0	74.2	73	26	49	0	1	3	6	10	1	0	.100	6	17	1	2	0.6	.958
1966	ATL	N	4	3	.571	4.11	28	0	0	50.1	48	23	17	0	4	3	2	8	0	0	.000	2	18	0	1	0.7	1.000
1967			11	9	.550	**1.87**	46	20	10	207	164	55	129	1	1	2	9	57	7	0	.123	10	40	4	4	1.2	.926
1968			14	12	.538	2.59	37	34	15	256.2	228	45	140	5	0	1	2	77	8	2	.104	18	59	4	4	2.2	.951
1969			23	13	.639	2.57	40	35	21	284	235	57	193	4	0	0	1	95	20	0	.211	24	51	3	4	2.0	.962
1970			12	18	.400	4.27	34	32	10	230	222	68	168	3	1	0	0	79	12	1	.152	14	38	1	4	1.6	.981
1971			15	14	.517	2.98	42	36	18	269	248	70	173	4	1	0	0	92	14	0	.152	19	44	2	6	1.5	.969
1972			16	12	.571	3.06	38	36	17	282	254	53	164	1	0	1	0	93	18	1	.194	26	40	4	4	1.8	.943
1973			13	10	.565	3.31	42	30	9	245	214	89	131	1	2	1	4	82	10	1	.122	30	41	4	4	1.8	.947
1974			**20**	13	.606	2.38	41	39	18	**302**	249	88	195	6	0	0	1	104	20	0	.192	22	42	0	3	1.6	1.000
1975			15	15	.500	3.20	39	37	13	276	285	72	144	1	0	1	1	99	17	0	.172	21	41	0	3	1.6	1.000
1976			17	11	.607	3.29	38	37	10	271	249	101	173	2	0	0	0	94	18	1	.191	19	41	2	2	1.6	.968
1977			16	**20**	.444	4.04	44	**43**	20	**330**	315	164	262	2	1	0	0	109	19	0	.174	20	51	0	5	1.6	1.000
1978			19	18	.514	2.88	44	**42**	**22**	**334**	295	102	248	4	0	1	0	120	27	0	.225	17	65	2	4	1.9	.976
1979			**21**	20	.512	3.39	44	**44**	**23**	**342**	311	113	208	1	0	0	0	123	24	0	.195	31	56	1	3	2.0	.989
1980			15	18	.455	3.63	40	**38**	11	275	256	85	176	3	1	0	1	90	12	0	.133	18	40	1	6	1.5	.983
1981			7	7	.500	3.11	22	22	3	139	120	56	62	1	0	0	0	52	4	0	.077	10	22	0	2	1.5	1.000
1982			17	4	**.810**	3.61	35	35	4	234.1	225	73	144	2	0	0	0	87	17	1	.195	18	38	1	4	1.6	.982
1983			11	10	.524	3.97	34	33	2	201.2	212	105	128	1	0	0	0	65	12	0	.185	15	27	2	6	1.3	.955
1984	NY	A	16	8	.667	3.09	32	31	5	215.2	219	76	136	1	0	0	0	0	0	0	—	13	36	1	4	1.6	.980
1985			16	12	.571	4.09	33	33	7	220	203	**120**	149	1	0	0	0	0	0	0	—	11	20	0	5	0.9	1.000
1986	CLE	A	11	11	.500	4.32	34	32	5	210.1	214	95	81	0	0	0	0	0	0	0	—	9	32	4	2	1.3	.911
1987	3 teams		CLE A	(22G 7–11)		TOR A	(3G 0–2)		ATL N	(1G 0–0)																	
"	total		7	13	.350	6.30	26	26	2	138.2	163	66	64	0	0	0	0	1	0	0	.000	13	17	0	1	1.2	1.000
24 yrs.			318	274	.537	3.35	864	716	245	5403.1	5044	1809	3342	45	14	12	30	1537	260	7	.169	386	878	37	83	1.5	.972
					4th				10th			4th	3rd	8th														

LEAGUE CHAMPIONSHIP SERIES

1969	ATL	N	0	1	.000	4.50	1	1	0	8	9	4	4	0	0	0	0	3	0	0	.000	0	3	0	0	3.0	1.000
1982			0	0	—	3.00	1	1	0	6	6	4	5	0	0	0	0	0	0	0	—	0	0	0	0	0.0	—
2 yrs.			0	1	.000	3.86	2	2	0	14	15	8	9	0	0	0	0	3	0	0	.000	0	3	0	0	1.5	1.000

Scott Nielsen

NIELSEN, JEFFREY SCOTT
B. Dec. 18, 1958, Salt Lake City, Utah

BR TR 6'1" 190 lbs.

Year	Team		W	L	PCT	ERA	G	GS	CG	IP	H	BB	SO	ShO	W	L	SV	AB	H	HR	BA	PO	A	E	DP	TC/G	FA
1986	NY	A	4	4	.500	4.02	10	9	2	56	66	12	20	1	0	0	0	0	0	0	—	0	5	0	2	0.5	1.000
1987	CHI	A	3	5	.375	6.24	19	7	1	66.1	83	25	23	1	1	0	2	0	0	0	—	4	9	2	0	0.8	.867
1988	NY	A	1	2	.333	6.86	7	2	0	19.2	27	13	4	0	1	0	0	0	0	0	—	0	5	0	2	0.7	1.000
1989			1	0	1.000	13.50	2	0	0	.2	2	1	0	0	1	0	0	0	0	0	—	0	0	0	0	0.0	—
4 yrs.			9	11	.450	5.49	38	18	3	142.2	178	51	47	3	3	0	2	0	0	0	—	4	19	2	4	0.7	.920

Randy Niemann

NIEMANN, RANDAL HAROLD
B. Nov. 15, 1955, Scotia, Calif. BL TL 6'4" 200 lbs.

Year	Team		W	L	PCT	ERA	G	GS	CG	IP	H	BB	SO	ShO	W	L	SV	AB	H	HR	BA	PO	A	E	DP	TC/G	FA
1979	HOU	N	3	2	.600	3.76	26	7	3	67	68	22	24	2	0	1	1	15	2	0	.133	1	7	0	0	0.3	1.000
1980			0	1	.000	5.45	22	1	0	33	40	12	18	0	0	1	1	6	2	0	.333	4	8	0	0	0.5	1.000
1982	PIT	N	1	1	.500	5.09	20	0	0	35.1	34	17	26	0	1	1	1	2	1	0	1.000	2	7	0	0	0.6	1.000
1983			0	1	.000	9.22	8	1	0	13.2	20	7	8	0	0	0	0	1	0	0	.000	2	2	0	1	0.5	1.000
1984	CHI	A	0	0	–	1.69	5	0	0	5.1	5	5	5	0	0	0	0	0	0	0	–	2	1	0	0	0.6	1.000
1985	NY	N	0	0	–	0.00	4	0	0	4.2	5	0	4	0	0	0	0	0	0	0	–	0	2	0	0	0.5	1.000
1986			2	3	.400	3.79	31	1	0	35.2	44	12	18	0	1	3	0	6	2	0	.333	3	9	0	1	0.4	1.000
1987	MIN	A	1	0	1.000	8.44	6	0	0	5.1	3	7	1	0	1	0	0	0	0	0	–	0	1	0	0	0.2	1.000
8 yrs.			7	8	.467	4.64	122	10	3	200	219	82	102	2	3	6	3	30	8	0	.267	16	37	0	2	0.4	1.000

Jack Niemes

NIEMES, JACOB LELAND
B. Oct. 19, 1919, Cincinnati, Ohio D. Mar. 4, 1966, Hamilton, Ohio BR TL 6'1" 180 lbs.

Year	Team		W	L	PCT	ERA	G	GS	CG	IP	H	BB	SO	ShO	W	L	SV	AB	H	HR	BA	PO	A	E	DP	TC/G	FA
1943	CIN	N	0	0	–	6.00	3	0	0	3	5	2	1	0	0	0	0	0	0	0	–	0	0	0	0	0.0	–

Chuck Nieson

NIESON, CHARLES BASSETT
B. Sept. 24, 1942, Hanford, Calif. BR TR 6'2" 185 lbs.

Year	Team		W	L	PCT	ERA	G	GS	CG	IP	H	BB	SO	ShO	W	L	SV	AB	H	HR	BA	PO	A	E	DP	TC/G	FA
1964	MIN	A	0	0	–	4.50	2	0	0	2	1	1	5	0	0	0	0	0	0	0	–	0	0	0	0	0.0	–

Juan Nieves

NIEVES, JUAN MANUEL
Born Juan Manuel Nieves y Cruz.
B. Jan. 5, 1965, Santurce, Puerto Rico BL TL 6'3" 175 lbs.

Year	Team		W	L	PCT	ERA	G	GS	CG	IP	H	BB	SO	ShO	W	L	SV	AB	H	HR	BA	PO	A	E	DP	TC/G	FA
1986	MIL	A	11	12	.478	4.92	35	33	4	184.2	224	77	116	3	1	0	0	0	0	0	–	4	18	2	2	0.7	.917
1987			14	8	.636	4.88	34	33	3	195.2	199	100	163	1	0	0	0	0	0	0	–	6	23	5	2	1.0	.853
1988			7	5	.583	4.08	25	15	1	110.1	84	50	73	1	1	0	1	0	0	0	–	4	14	1	0	0.8	.947
3 yrs.			32	25	.561	4.71	94	81	8	490.2	507	227	352	5	2	0	1	0	0	0	–	14	55	8	4	0.8	.896

Johnny Niggeling

NIGGELING, JOHN ARNOLD
B. July 10, 1903, Remsen, Iowa D. Sept. 16, 1963, Le Mars, Iowa BR TR 6' 170 lbs.

Year	Team		W	L	PCT	ERA	G	GS	CG	IP	H	BB	SO	ShO	W	L	SV	AB	H	HR	BA	PO	A	E	DP	TC/G	FA
1938	BOS	N	1	0	1.000	9.00	2	0	0	2	4	1	1	0	1	0	0	0	0	0	–	0	0	0	0	0.0	–
1939	CIN	N	2	1	.667	5.80	10	5	2	40.1	37	13	20	1	0	0	0	13	2	0	.154	1	6	2	2	0.9	.778
1940	STL	A	7	11	.389	4.45	28	20	10	153.2	148	69	82	1	0	0	0	51	9	0	.176	9	22	2	5	1.2	.939
1941			7	9	.438	3.80	24	20	13	168.1	168	63	68	1	0	0	1	60	10	0	.167	9	28	0	0	1.5	1.000
1942			15	11	.577	2.66	28	27	16	206.1	173	93	107	3	0	0	0	72	10	0	.139	3	36	0	0	1.4	1.000
1943	2 teams		STL A (20G 6–8)			WAS A (6G 4–2)																						
"	total		10	10	.500	2.59	26	26	12	201.1	149	74	97	3	0	0	0	67	8	0	.119	10	38	0	4	1.5	1.000
1944	WAS	A	10	8	.556	2.32	24	24	14	206	164	88	121	3	0	0	0	69	9	0	.130	7	29	0	2	1.5	1.000
1945			7	12	.368	3.16	26	25	8	176.2	161	73	90	2	0	0	0	59	7	0	.119	6	25	2	2	1.3	.939
1946	2 teams		WAS A (8G 3–2)			BOS N (8G 2–5)																						
"	total		5	7	.417	3.56	16	14	6	96	93	42	34	0	0	1	0	29	4	0	.138	5	19	1	1	1.6	.960
9 yrs.			64	69	.481	3.22	184	161	81	1250.2	1111	516	620	13	1	2	0	420	59	0	.140	50	203	7	16	1.4	.973

Al Nipper

NIPPER, ALBERT SAMUEL
B. Apr. 2, 1959, San Diego, Calif. BR TR 6' 188 lbs.

Year	Team		W	L	PCT	ERA	G	GS	CG	IP	H	BB	SO	ShO	W	L	SV	AB	H	HR	BA	PO	A	E	DP	TC/G	FA
1983	BOS	A	1	1	.500	2.25	3	2	1	16	17	7	5	0	0	0	0	0	0	0	–	1	2	0	0	1.0	1.000
1984			11	6	.647	3.89	29	24	6	182.2	183	52	84	0	0	0	0	0	0	0	–	28	31	1	0	2.1	.983
1985			9	12	.429	4.06	25	25	5	162	157	82	85	0	0	0	0	0	0	0	–	24	28	5	4	2.3	.912
1986			10	12	.455	5.38	26	26	3	159	186	47	79	0	0	0	0	0	0	0	–	28	28	1	4	2.2	.982
1987			11	12	.478	5.43	30	30	6	174	196	62	89	0	0	0	0	0	0	0	–	20	27	2	2	1.6	.959
1988	CHI	N	2	4	.333	3.04	22	12	0	80	72	34	27	0	0	1	1	23	2	0	.087	4	7	1	1	0.5	.917
6 yrs.			44	47	.484	4.46	135	119	21	773.2	811	284	369	0	0	1	1	23	2	0	.087	105	123	10	11	1.8	.958

WORLD SERIES

Year	Team		W	L	PCT	ERA	G	GS	CG	IP	H	BB	SO	ShO	W	L	SV	AB	H	HR	BA	PO	A	E	DP	TC/G	FA
1986	BOS	A	0	1	.000	7.11	2	1	0	6.1	10	2	2	0	0	0	0	0	0	0	–	0	2	0	0	1.5	1.000

Merlin Nippert

NIPPERT, MERLIN LEE
B. Sept. 1, 1938, Mangum, Okla. BR TR 6'1" 175 lbs.

Year	Team		W	L	PCT	ERA	G	GS	CG	IP	H	BB	SO	ShO	W	L	SV	AB	H	HR	BA	PO	A	E	DP	TC/G	FA
1962	BOS	A	0	0	–	4.50	4	0	0	6	4	4	3	0	0	0	0	0	0	0	–	0	1	1	0	0.5	.500

Ron Nischwitz

NISCHWITZ, RONALD LEE
B. July 1, 1937, Dayton, Ohio BB TL 6'3" 205 lbs.

Year	Team		W	L	PCT	ERA	G	GS	CG	IP	H	BB	SO	ShO	W	L	SV	AB	H	HR	BA	PO	A	E	DP	TC/G	FA
1961	DET	A	0	1	.000	5.56	6	0	0	11.1	13	8	8	0	0	0	0	2	0	0	.000	1	1	1	0	0.5	.667
1962			4	5	.444	3.90	48	0	0	64.2	73	26	28	0	4	5	4	12	5	0	.417	2	13	1	2	0.3	.938
1963	CLE	A	0	2	.000	6.48	14	0	0	16.2	17	8	10	0	0	0	0	1	0	0	.000	2	3	1	1	0.4	.833
1965	DET	A	1	0	1.000	2.78	20	0	0	22.2	21	6	12	0	1	0	1	3	0	0	.000	2	3	0	0	0.3	1.000
4 yrs.			5	8	.385	4.21	88	1	0	115.1	124	48	58	0	5	7	6	18	5	0	.278	7	20	3	3	0.3	.900

Otho Nitcholas

NITCHOLAS, OTHO JAMES (Nick)
B. Sept. 13, 1908, McKinney, Tex. BR TR 6' 195 lbs.

Year	Team		W	L	PCT	ERA	G	GS	CG	IP	H	BB	SO	ShO	W	L	SV	AB	H	HR	BA	PO	A	E	DP	TC/G	FA
1945	BKN	N	1	0	1.000	5.30	7	0	0	18.2	19	1	4	0	1	0	0	4	1	0	.250	1	3	0	0	0.6	1.000

Willard Nixon

NIXON, WILLARD LEE
B. June 17, 1928, Taylorsville, Ga. BL TR 6'2" 195 lbs.

Year	Team		W	L	PCT	ERA	G	GS	CG	IP	H	BB	SO	ShO	W	L	SV	AB	H	HR	BA	PO	A	E	DP	TC/G	FA
1950	BOS	A	8	6	.571	6.04	22	15	2	101.1	126	58	57	0	2	0	2	36	5	0	.139	7	14	1	3	1.0	.955
1951			7	4	.636	4.90	33	14	2	125	136	56	70	1	2	0	1	45	13	1	.289	2	23	1	1	0.8	.962
1952			5	4	.556	4.86	23	13	5	103.2	115	61	50	0	0	0	0	53	11	0	.208	7	18	0	4	1.1	1.000
1953			4	8	.333	3.93	23	15	5	116.2	114	59	57	1	0	0	1	42	8	0	.190	7	18	2	1	1.2	.926
1954			11	12	.478	4.06	31	30	9	199.2	182	87	102	2	0	0	0	68	18	1	.265	17	34	1	6	1.7	.981
1955			12	10	.545	4.07	31	31	7	208	207	85	95	3	0	0	0	69	18	0	.261	18	43	1	3	2.0	.984
1956			9	8	.529	4.21	23	22	9	145.1	142	57	74	1	0	0	0	54	11	0	.204	7	31	1	4	1.7	.974

Year	Team		W	L	PCT	ERA	G	GS	CG	IP	H	BB	SO	ShO	W	L	SV	AB	H	HR	BA	PO	A	E	DP	TC/G	FA

Relief Pitching: W L SV — **Batting:** AB H HR BA

Willard Nixon *continued*

Year	Team	W	L	PCT	ERA	G	GS	CG	IP	H	BB	SO	ShO	W	L	SV	AB	H	HR	BA	PO	A	E	DP	TC/G	FA
1957		12	13	.480	3.68	29	29	11	191	207	56	96	1	0	0	0	75	22	0	.293	8	28	0	4	1.2	1.000
1958		1	7	.125	6.02	10	8	2	43.1	48	11	15	0	1	0	0	17	5	0	.294	1	8	0	1	0.9	1.000
9 yrs.		69	72	.489	4.39	225	177	51	1234	1277	530	616	9	5	1	3	459	111	2	.242	74	217	7	27	1.3	.977

Gary Nolan

NOLAN, GARY LYNN
B. May 27, 1948, Herlong, Calif.   BR TR 6'2½" 197 lbs.

Year	Team	W	L	PCT	ERA	G	GS	CG	IP	H	BB	SO	ShO	W	L	SV	AB	H	HR	BA	PO	A	E	DP	TC/G	FA
1967	CIN N	14	8	.636	2.58	33	32	8	226.2	193	62	206	5	1	0	0	67	7	0	.104	12	28	1	1	1.2	.976
1968		9	4	.692	2.40	23	22	4	150	105	49	111	2	0	0	0	46	6	1	.130	5	16	0	1	0.9	1.000
1969		8	8	.500	3.55	16	15	2	109	102	40	83	1	0	0	0	35	8	0	.229	4	10	0	1	0.9	1.000
1970		18	7	.720	3.26	37	37	4	251	226	96	181	2	0	0	0	82	13	0	.159	17	28	1	1	1.2	.978
1971		12	15	.444	3.16	35	35	9	245	208	59	146	0	0	0	0	75	11	0	.147	15	38	0	4	1.5	1.000
1972		15	5	**.750**	1.99	25	25	6	176	147	30	90	2	0	0	0	60	7	0	.117	14	19	0	1	1.3	1.000
1973		0	1	.000	3.48	2	2	0	10.1	6	7	3	0	0	0	0	2	0	0	.000	0	1	0	0	0.5	1.000
1975		15	9	.625	3.16	32	32	5	211	202	29	74	1	0	0	0	68	12	0	.176	12	22	0	1	1.1	1.000
1976		15	9	.625	3.46	34	34	7	239	232	27	113	1	0	0	0	79	8	0	.101	9	22	0	0	0.9	1.000
1977	2 teams	CIN N	(8G 4–1)			CAL A	(5G 0–3)																			
"	total	4	4	.500	6.16	13	13	0	57	84	14	32	0	0	0	0	15	1	0	.067	7	5	1	0	1.0	.923
10 yrs.		110	70	.611	3.08	250	247	45	1675	1505	413	1039	14	1	0	0	529	73	1	.138	95	189	3	11	1.1	.990

LEAGUE CHAMPIONSHIP SERIES

Year	Team	W	L	PCT	ERA	G	GS	CG	IP	H	BB	SO	ShO	W	L	SV	AB	H	HR	BA	PO	A	E	DP	TC/G	FA
1970	CIN N	1	0	1.000	0.00	1	1	1	9	8	4	6	0	0	0	0	3	1	0	.333	0	2	0	0	2.0	1.000
1972		0	0	–	1.50	1	1	0	6	4	1	4	0	0	0	0	2	0	0	.000	0	0	0	0	0.0	
1975		0	0	–	3.00	1	1	0	6	5	0	5	0	0	0	0	2	0	0	.000	0	0	0	0	0.0	
1976		0	0	–	1.59	1	1	0	5.2	6	2	1	0	0	0	0	0	0	0	–	1	0	0	0	1.0	1.000
4 yrs.		1	0	1.000	1.35	4	4	1	26.2	23	7	16	0	0	0	0	7	1	0	.143	1	2	0	0	0.8	1.000

WORLD SERIES

Year	Team	W	L	PCT	ERA	G	GS	CG	IP	H	BB	SO	ShO	W	L	SV	AB	H	HR	BA	PO	A	E	DP	TC/G	FA
1970	CIN N	0	1	.000	7.71	2	2	0	9.1	9	3	9	0	0	0	0	3	0	0	.000	0	1	0	0	0.5	1.000
1972		0	1	.000	3.38	2	2	0	10.2	7	2	3	0	0	0	0	3	0	0	.000	0	2	0	0	1.0	1.000
1975		0	0	–	6.00	2	2	0	6	6	1	2	0	0	0	0	1	0	0	.000	1	0	0	0	0.5	1.000
1976		1	0	1.000	2.70	1	1	0	6.2	8	1	1	0	0	0	0	0	0	0	–	0	1	0	0	1.0	1.000
4 yrs.		1	2	.333	4.96	7	7	0	32.2	30	7	15	0	0	0	0	7	0	0	.000	1	4	0	0	0.7	1.000

The Only Nolan

NOLAN, EDWARD SYLVESTER
B. Nov. 7, 1857, Paterson, N. J.   D. May 18, 1913, Paterson, N. J.   BL TR 5'8" 171 lbs.

Year	Team	W	L	PCT	ERA	G	GS	CG	IP	H	BB	SO	ShO	W	L	SV	AB	H	HR	BA	PO	A	E	DP	TC/G	FA
1878	IND N	13	22	.371	2.57	38	38	37	347	357	56	125	1	0	0	0	152	37	0	.243	19	80	11	5	2.9	.900
1881	CLE N	8	14	.364	3.05	22	21	20	180	183	38	54	0	0	0	1	0	168	41	0	.244	9	28	4	0	1.9	.902
1883	PIT AA	0	7	.000	4.25	7	7	6	55	81	10	23	0	0	0	0	26	8	0	.308	2	11	5	0	2.6	.722
1884	WIL U	1	4	.200	2.93	5	5	5	40	44	7	52	0	0	0	0	33	9	0	.273	1	11	1	0	2.6	.923
1885	PHI N	1	5	.167	4.17	7	7	6	54	55	24	20	0	0	0	0	26	2	0	.077	0	10	2	0	1.7	.833
5 yrs.		23	52	.307	2.98	79	78	74	676	720	135	274	1	0	1	0	*				31	140	23	5	2.5	.881

Dick Nold

NOLD, RICHARD LOUIS
B. May 4, 1943, San Francisco, Calif.   BR TR 6'2" 190 lbs.

Year	Team	W	L	PCT	ERA	G	GS	CG	IP	H	BB	SO	ShO	W	L	SV	AB	H	HR	BA	PO	A	E	DP	TC/G	FA
1967	WAS A	0	2	.000	4.87	7	3	0	20.1	19	13	10	0	0	0	0	3	0	0	.000	1	2	0	0	0.4	1.000

Dickie Noles

NOLES, DICKIE RAY
B. Nov. 19, 1956, Charlotte, N. C.   BR TR 6'2" 160 lbs.

Year	Team		W	L	PCT	ERA	G	GS	CG	IP	H	BB	SO	ShO	W	L	SV	AB	H	HR	BA	PO	A	E	DP	TC/G	FA
1979	PHI N		3	4	.429	3.80	14	14	0	90	80	38	42	0	0	0	0	30	3	0	.100	4	17	1	1	1.6	.955
1980			1	4	.200	3.89	48	3	0	81	80	42	57	0	0	4	6	13	4	0	.308	8	10	2	0	0.4	.900
1981			2	2	.500	4.19	13	8	0	58	57	23	34	0	0	0	0	19	2	0	.105	1	5	2	0	0.6	.750
1982	CHI N		10	13	.435	4.42	31	30	2	171	180	61	85	2	0	0	0	56	6	0	.107	14	26	2	0	1.4	.952
1983			5	10	.333	4.72	24	18	0	116.1	133	37	59	1	0	1	0	38	9	0	.237	11	14	1	0	1.1	.962
1984	2 teams	CHI N	(21G 2–2)				TEX A	(18G 2–3)																			
"	total		4	5	.444	5.15	39	7	0	108.1	120	46	53	0	4	3	0	10	0	0	.000	2	6	1	1	0.2	.889
1985	TEX A		4	8	.333	5.06	28	13	0	110.1	129	33	59	0	1	1	1	33	4	0	–	13	16	3	2	1.1	.906
1986	CLE A		3	2	.600	5.10	32	0	0	54.2	56	30	32	0	3	2	0	0	0	0	–	5	8	0	0	0.4	1.000
1987	2 teams	CHI N	(41G 4–2)				DET A	(4G 0–0)																			
"	total		4	2	.667	3.53	45	1	0	66.1	61	28	33	0	1	1	4	11	0	0	.000	6	15	0	1	0.5	1.000
1988	BAL A		0	2	.000	24.30	2	2	0	3.1	11	0	1	0	0	0	0	0	0	0	–	0	0	0	0	0.0	–
10 yrs.			36	52	.409	4.56	276	96	3	859.1	907	338	455	3	12	12	11	177	24	0	.136	64	117	12	4	0.7	.938

DIVISIONAL PLAYOFF SERIES

Year	Team	W	L	PCT	ERA	G	GS	CG	IP	H	BB	SO	ShO	W	L	SV	AB	H	HR	BA	PO	A	E	DP	TC/G	FA
1981	PHI N	0	0	–	4.50	1	1	0	4	4	2	5	0	0	0	0	0	0	0	–	0	0	0	0	0.0	–

LEAGUE CHAMPIONSHIP SERIES

Year	Team	W	L	PCT	ERA	G	GS	CG	IP	H	BB	SO	ShO	W	L	SV	AB	H	HR	BA	PO	A	E	DP	TC/G	FA
1980	PHI N	0	0	–	0.00	2	0	0	2.2	1	3	0	0	0	0	0	0	0	0	–	1	2	0	1	1.5	1.000

WORLD SERIES

Year	Team	W	L	PCT	ERA	G	GS	CG	IP	H	BB	SO	ShO	W	L	SV	AB	H	HR	BA	PO	A	E	DP	TC/G	FA
1980	PHI N	0	0	–	1.93	1	0	0	4.2	5	2	6	0	0	0	0	0	0	0	–	1	0	0	0	1.0	1.000

Eric Nolte

NOLTE, ERIC CARL
B. Apr. 28, 1964, Canoga Park, Calif.   BL TL 6'3" 205 lbs.

Year	Team	W	L	PCT	ERA	G	GS	CG	IP	H	BB	SO	ShO	W	L	SV	AB	H	HR	BA	PO	A	E	DP	TC/G	FA
1987	SD N	2	6	.250	3.21	12	12	1	67.1	57	36	44	0	0	0	0	21	2	0	.095	5	7	0	1	1.0	1.000
1988		0	0	–	6.00	2	0	0	3	3	2	1	0	0	0	0	0	0	0	–	0	0	0	0	0.0	–
1989		0	0	–	11.00	3	1	0	9	15	7	8	0	0	0	0	2	0	0	.000	0	3	0	0	1.0	1.000
3 yrs.		2	6	.250	4.20	17	13	1	79.1	75	45	53	0	0	0	0	23	2	0	.087	5	10	0	1	0.9	1.000

Jerry Nops

NOPS, JEREMIAH H.
B. June 23, 1875, Toledo, Ohio   D. Mar. 26, 1937, Camden, N. J.   TL

Year	Team		W	L	PCT	ERA	G	GS	CG	IP	H	BB	SO	ShO	W	L	SV	AB	H	HR	BA	PO	A	E	DP	TC/G	FA
1896	2 teams	PHI N	(1G 1–0)				BAL N	(3G 2–1)																			
"	total		3	1	.750	5.90	4	4	4	29	40	3	9	0	0	0	0	13	1	0	.077	1	6	2	0	2.3	.778
1897	BAL N		20	6	.769	2.81	30	25	23	220.2	235	52	69	1	1	1	0	92	18	0	.196	10	38	4	0	1.7	.923
1898			16	9	.640	3.56	33	29	23	235	241	78	91	2	0	0	0	91	20	0	.220	6	36	8	0	1.5	.840

Year	Team		W	L	PCT	ERA	G	GS	CG	IP	H	BB	SO	ShO	Relief Pitching W	L	SV	Batting AB	H	HR	BA	PO	A	E	DP	TC/G	FA

Jerry Nops *continued*

Year	Team		W	L	PCT	ERA	G	GS	CG	IP	H	BB	SO	ShO	W	L	SV	AB	H	HR	BA	PO	A	E	DP	TC/G	FA
1899			17	11	.607	4.03	33	33	26	259	296	71	60	2	0	0	0	105	29	0	.276	7	53	7	1	2.0	.896
1900	BKN	N	4	4	.500	3.84	9	8	6	68	79	18	22	1	0	0	0	25	4	0	.160	5	12	5	2	2.4	.773
1901	BAL	A	11	10	.524	4.08	27	23	17	176.2	192	59	43	1	0	0	1	59	13	0	.220	2	34	10	0	1.7	.783
6 yrs.			71	41	.634	3.70	136	122	99	988.1	1083	281	294	7	2	1	1	385	85	0	.221	31	179	36	3	1.8	.854

Wayne Nordhagen

NORDHAGEN, WAYNE OREN
B. July 4, 1948, Thief River Falls, Minn.

BR TR 6'2" 205 lbs.

Year	Team		W	L	PCT	ERA	G	GS	CG	IP	H	BB	SO	ShO	W	L	SV	AB	H	HR	BA	PO	A	E	DP	TC/G	FA
1979	CHI	A	0	0	—	9.00	2	0	0	2	2	1	2	0	0	0	0	*				0	0	0	0	0.0	—

John Noriega

NORIEGA, JOHN ALAN
B. Dec. 20, 1943, Ogden, Utah

BR TR 6'4" 185 lbs.

Year	Team		W	L	PCT	ERA	G	GS	CG	IP	H	BB	SO	ShO	W	L	SV	AB	H	HR	BA	PO	A	E	DP	TC/G	FA
1969	CIN	N	0	0	—	5.63	5	0	0	8	12	3	4	0	0	0	0	0	0	0	—	0	1	1	0	0.4	.500
1970			0	0	—	8.00	8	0	0	18	25	10	6	0	0	0	0	4	1	0	.250	1	7	0	0	1.0	1.000
2 yrs.			0	0	—	7.27	13	0	0	26	37	13	10	0	0	0	0	4	1	0	.250	1	8	1	0	0.8	.900

Fred Norman

NORMAN, FREDIE HUBERT
B. Aug. 20, 1942, San Antonio, Tex.

BL TL 5'8" 155 lbs.

Year	Team		W	L	PCT	ERA	G	GS	CG	IP	H	BB	SO	ShO	W	L	SV	AB	H	HR	BA	PO	A	E	DP	TC/G	FA
1962	KC	A	0	0	—	2.25	2	0	0	4	4	1	2	0	0	0	0	0	0	0	—	0	0	0	0	0.0	—
1963			0	1	.000	11.37	2	2	0	6.1	9	7	6	0	0	0	0	1	0	0	.000	1	1	0	0	1.0	1.000
1964	CHI	N	0	4	.000	6.54	8	5	0	31.2	34	21	20	0	0	0	0	11	1	0	.091	2	4	0	1	0.8	1.000
1966			0	0	—	4.50	2	0	0	4	5	2	6	0	0	0	0	0	0	0	—	0	0	0	0	0.0	—
1967			0	0	—	0.00	1	0	0	1	0	0	3	0	0	0	0	0	0	0	—	0	0	0	0	0.0	—
1970 2 teams	LA N	(30G 2-0)				STL N		(1G 0-0)																			
" total			2	0	1.000	5.14	31	0	0	63	66	33	47	0	2	0	1	7	1	0	.143	2	8	3	0	0.4	.769
1971 2 teams	STL N	(4G 0-0)				SD N		(20G 3-12)																			
" total			3	12	.200	3.57	24	18	5	131	121	63	81	0	0	0	0	38	9	0	.237	3	18	3	0	1.0	.875
1972	SD	N	9	11	.450	3.44	42	28	10	211.2	195	88	167	6	1	0	2	64	8	0	.125	9	24	2	4	0.8	.943
1973 2 teams	SD N	(12G 1-7)				CIN N		(24G 12-6)																			
" total			13	13	.500	3.60	36	35	8	240.1	208	101	161	3	0	0	0	80	6	0	.075	5	14	0	0	0.5	1.000
1974	CIN	N	13	12	.520	3.15	35	26	8	186	170	68	141	2	0	3	0	61	8	0	.131	5	14	2	1	0.6	.905
1975			12	4	.750	3.73	34	26	2	188	163	84	119	0	1	0	0	60	7	0	.117	4	19	2	2	0.9	.933
1976			12	7	.632	3.10	33	24	8	180	153	70	126	3	1	0	0	50	7	0	.140	4	14	0	0	0.5	1.000
1977			14	13	.519	3.38	35	34	8	221	200	98	160	1	0	0	0	73	8	0	.110	9	31	4	2	1.3	.909
1978			11	9	.550	3.71	36	31	0	177	173	82	111	0	1	0	0	50	7	0	.140	6	25	2	0	0.9	.939
1979			11	13	.458	3.65	34	31	5	195	193	57	95	0	0	1	0	59	9	0	.153	4	26	3	1	1.0	.909
1980	MON	N	4	4	.500	4.05	48	8	2	98.6	96	40	58	0	0	1	4	20	1	0	.050	1	11	1	0	0.3	.923
16 yrs.			104	103	.502	3.64	403	268	56	1938.6	1790	815	1303	15	6	5	8	574	72	0	.125	60	209	22	11	0.7	.924

LEAGUE CHAMPIONSHIP SERIES

Year	Team		W	L	PCT	ERA	G	GS	CG	IP	H	BB	SO	ShO	W	L	SV	AB	H	HR	BA	PO	A	E	DP	TC/G	FA
1973	CIN	N	0	0	—	1.80	1	1	0	5	1	3	3	0	0	0	0	1	0	0	.000	1	0	0	0	1.0	1.000
1975			1	0	1.000	1.50	1	1	0	6	4	5	4	0	0	0	0	1	0	0	.000	0	1	0	0	1.0	1.000
1979			0	0	—	18.00	1	0	0	2	4	1	1	0	0	0	0	1	0	0	.000	0	0	0	0	0.0	—
3 yrs.			1	0	1.000	4.15	3	2	0	13	9	9	8	0	0	0	0	3	0	0	.000	1	1	0	0	0.7	1.000

WORLD SERIES

Year	Team		W	L	PCT	ERA	G	GS	CG	IP	H	BB	SO	ShO	W	L	SV	AB	H	HR	BA	PO	A	E	DP	TC/G	FA
1975	CIN	N	0	1	.000	9.00	2	1	0	4	8	3	2	0	0	0	0	1	0	0	.000	0	0	0	0	0.0	—
1976			0	0	—	4.26	1	1	0	6.1	9	2	2	0	0	0	0	0	0	0	—	0	1	0	0	1.0	1.000
2 yrs.			0	1	.000	6.10	3	2	0	10.1	17	5	4	0	0	0	0	1	0	0	.000	0	1	0	0	0.3	1.000

Mike Norris

NORRIS, MICHAEL KELVIN
B. Mar. 19, 1955, San Francisco, Calif.

BR TR 6'2" 175 lbs.

Year	Team		W	L	PCT	ERA	G	GS	CG	IP	H	BB	SO	ShO	W	L	SV	AB	H	HR	BA	PO	A	E	DP	TC/G	FA
1975	OAK	A	1	0	1.000	0.00	4	3	1	16.2	6	8	5	1	0	0	0	0	0	0	—	1	4	1	0	1.5	.833
1976			4	5	.444	4.78	24	19	1	96	91	56	44	1	0	0	0	0	0	0	—	11	29	2	1	1.8	.952
1977			2	7	.222	4.79	16	12	1	77	77	31	35	1	0	0	0	1	0	0	.000	8	17	2	1	1.7	.926
1978			0	5	.000	5.51	14	5	1	49	46	35	36	0	0	0	0	0	0	0	—	5	5	2	0	0.9	.833
1979			5	8	.385	4.81	29	18	3	146	146	94	96	0	0	0	0	0	0	0	—	6	17	1	0	0.8	.958
1980			22	9	.710	2.54	33	33	24	284	215	83	180	1	0	0	0	0	0	0	—	25	52	3	3	2.4	.963
1981			12	9	.571	3.75	23	23	12	173	145	63	78	2	0	0	0	0	0	0	—	16	25	1	0	1.8	.976
1982			7	11	.389	4.76	28	28	7	166.1	154	84	83	1	0	0	0	0	0	0	—	22	21	2	1	1.6	.956
1983			4	5	.444	3.76	16	16	2	88.2	68	36	63	0	0	0	0	0	0	0	—	3	4	1	0	0.5	.875
9 yrs.			57	59	.491	3.91	187	157	52	1096.2	948	490	620	7	0	0	0	1	0	0	.000	97	174	15	7	1.5	.948

DIVISIONAL PLAYOFF SERIES

Year	Team		W	L	PCT	ERA	G	GS	CG	IP	H	BB	SO	ShO	W	L	SV	AB	H	HR	BA	PO	A	E	DP	TC/G	FA
1981	OAK	A	1	0	1.000	0.00	1	1	1	9	4	3	2	1	0	0	0	0	0	0	—	0	1	0	0	1.0	—

LEAGUE CHAMPIONSHIP SERIES

Year	Team		W	L	PCT	ERA	G	GS	CG	IP	H	BB	SO	ShO	W	L	SV	AB	H	HR	BA	PO	A	E	DP	TC/G	FA
1981	OAK	A	0	1	.000	3.68	1	1	0	7.1	7	2	4	0	0	0	0	0	0	0	—	0	0	0	0	0.0	—

Lou North

NORTH, LOUIS ALEXANDER
B. June 15, 1891, Elgin, Ill. D. May 16, 1974, Shelton, Conn.

BR TR 5'11" 175 lbs.

Year	Team		W	L	PCT	ERA	G	GS	CG	IP	H	BB	SO	ShO	W	L	SV	AB	H	HR	BA	PO	A	E	DP	TC/G	FA
1913	DET	A	0	1	.000	15.00	1	1	0	6	10	9	3	0	0	0	0	2	0	0	.000	0	1	1	0	2.0	.500
1917	STL	N	0	0	—	3.97	5	0	0	11.1	14	4	4	0	0	0	0	3	0	0	.000	0	5	0	0	1.0	1.000
1920			3	2	.600	3.27	24	6	3	88	90	32	37	0	1	1	1	31	7	0	.226	2	18	1	0	0.9	.952
1921			4	4	.500	3.54	40	0	0	86.1	81	32	28	0	4	4	7	19	3	0	.158	4	11	2	1	0.4	.882
1922			10	3	.769	4.45	53	11	4	149.2	164	64	84	0	5	1	4	47	11	1	.234	9	49	1	3	1.1	.983
1923			3	4	.429	5.15	34	4	0	71.2	90	31	24	0	2	4	1	22	4	0	.182	3	18	0	2	0.6	1.000
1924 2 teams	STL N	(6G 0-0)				BOS N		(9G 1-2)																			
" total			1	2	.333	5.76	15	4	1	50	60	28	19	0	0	0	0	13	2	0	.154	2	8	2	0	0.8	.833
7 yrs.			21	16	.568	4.43	172	25	8	463	509	200	199	0	12	10	13	137	27	1	.197	20	110	7	6	0.8	.949

Jake Northrop

NORTHROP, GEORGE HOWARD
B. Mar. 5, 1888, Monroeton, Pa. D. Nov. 16, 1945, Monroeton, Pa.

BL TR 5'11" 170 lbs.

Year	Team		W	L	PCT	ERA	G	GS	CG	IP	H	BB	SO	ShO	W	L	SV	AB	H	HR	BA	PO	A	E	DP	TC/G	FA
1918	BOS	N	5	1	.833	1.35	7	4	4	40	26	3	4	1	2	0	0	13	2	0	.154	0	14	0	0	2.0	1.000

Year	Team	W	L	PCT	ERA	G	GS	CG	IP	H	BB	SO	ShO	W	L	SV	AB	H	HR	BA	PO	A	E	DP	TC/G	FA

Jake Northrop *continued*

Year	Team	W	L	PCT	ERA	G	GS	CG	IP	H	BB	SO	ShO	W	L	SV	AB	H	HR	BA	PO	A	E	DP	TC/G	FA
1919		1	5	.167	4.58	11	3	2	37.1	43	10	9	0	0	3	0	8	4	0	.500	7	14	0	1	1.9	1.000
2 yrs.		6	6	.500	2.91	18	7	6	77.1	69	13	13	1	2	3	0	21	6	0	.286	7	28	0	1	1.9	1.000

Elisha Norton

NORTON, ELISHA STRONG
B. Aug. 17, 1873, Conneaut, Ohio D. Mar. 5, 1950, Aspinwall, Pa. BR TR

Year	Team	W	L	PCT	ERA	G	GS	CG	IP	H	BB	SO	ShO	W	L	SV	AB	H	HR	BA	PO	A	E	DP	TC/G	FA
1896	WAS N	3	1	.750	3.07	8	5	2	44	49	14	13	0	1	0	0	19	4	0	.211	0	10	1	0	1.4	.909
1897		2	1	.667	6.88	4	2	1	17	31	11	3	0	1	0	0	18	5	0	.278	2	2	2	0	1.5	.667
2 yrs.		5	2	.714	4.13	12	7	3	61	80	25	16	0	2	0	0	37	9	0	.243	2	12	3	0	1.4	.824

Tom Norton

NORTON, THOMAS JOHN
B. Apr. 26, 1950, Elyria, Ohio BR TR 6'1" 200 lbs.

Year	Team	W	L	PCT	ERA	G	GS	CG	IP	H	BB	SO	ShO	W	L	SV	AB	H	HR	BA	PO	A	E	DP	TC/G	FA
1972	MIN A	0	1	.000	2.81	21	0	0	32	31	14	22	0	0	0	0	0	0	0	—	4	9	0	0	0.6	1.000

Randy Nosek

NOSEK, RANDALL WILLIAM
B. Jan. 8, 1967, Omaha, Neb. BR TR 6'4" 215 lbs.

Year	Team	W	L	PCT	ERA	G	GS	CG	IP	H	BB	SO	ShO	W	L	SV	AB	H	HR	BA	PO	A	E	DP	TC/G	FA
1989	DET A	0	2	.000	13.50	2	2	0	5.1	7	10	4	0	0	0	0	0	0	0	—	0	0	0	0	0.0	—

Don Nottebart

NOTTEBART, DONALD EDWARD
B. Jan. 23, 1936, West Newton, Mass. BR TR 6'1" 190 lbs.

Year	Team	W	L	PCT	ERA	G	GS	CG	IP	H	BB	SO	ShO	W	L	SV	AB	H	HR	BA	PO	A	E	DP	TC/G	FA
1960	MIL N	1	0	1.000	4.11	5	1	0	15.1	14	15	8	0	1	0	1	5	0	0	.000	2	6	0	0	1.6	1.000
1961		6	7	.462	4.06	38	11	2	126.1	117	48	66	0	3	2	3	38	7	0	.184	9	31	1	1	1.1	.976
1962		2	2	.500	3.23	39	0	0	64	64	20	36	0	2	2	2	6	2	0	.333	4	17	0	3	0.5	1.000
1963	HOU N	11	8	.579	3.17	31	27	9	193	170	39	118	2	0	0	0	66	11	0	.167	14	30	1	2	1.5	.978
1964		6	11	.353	3.90	28	24	2	157	165	37	90	0	1	0	0	47	3	0	.064	14	44	3	3	2.2	.951
1965		4	15	.211	4.67	29	25	3	158	166	55	77	0	0	1	0	48	5	0	.104	8	40	1	1	1.7	.980
1966	CIN N	5	4	.556	3.07	59	1	0	111.1	97	43	69	0	5	4	11	24	4	0	.167	9	20	0	1	0.5	1.000
1967		0	3	.000	1.93	47	0	0	79.1	75	19	48	0	0	3	4	3	0	0	.000	4	17	2	2	0.5	.913
1969	2 teams																									
"	NY A (4G 0–0)					CHI N (16G 1–1)																				
"	total	1	1	.500	6.38	20	0	0	24	34	7	13	0	1	0	0	1	0	0	.000	2	4	0	0	0.3	1.000
9 yrs.		36	51	.414	3.65	296	89	16	928.1	902	283	525	2	13	13	21	238	32	0	.134	66	209	8	13	1.0	.972

Chet Nourse

NOURSE, CHESTER LINWOOD
B. Aug. 7, 1887, Ipswich, Mass. D. Apr. 20, 1958, Clearwater, Fla. BR TR 6'3" 185 lbs.

Year	Team	W	L	PCT	ERA	G	GS	CG	IP	H	BB	SO	ShO	W	L	SV	AB	H	HR	BA	PO	A	E	DP	TC/G	FA
1909	BOS A	0	0	—	7.20	3	0	0	5	5	5	3	0	0	0	0	2	0	0	.000	1	2	2	0	1.7	.600

Wynn Noyes

NOYES, WINFIELD CHARLES
B. June 16, 1889, Pleasanton, Neb. D. Apr. 8, 1969, Cashmere, Wash. BR TR 6' 180 lbs.

Year	Team	W	L	PCT	ERA	G	GS	CG	IP	H	BB	SO	ShO	W	L	SV	AB	H	HR	BA	PO	A	E	DP	TC/G	FA
1913	BOS N	0	0	—	4.79	11	0	0	20.2	22	6	5	0	0	0	0	4	1	0	.250	2	5	0	0	0.6	1.000
1917	PHI A	10	10	.500	2.95	27	22	11	171	156	77	64	1	1	1	1	52	6	0	.115	7	43	4	4	2.0	.926
1919	2 teams	PHI A (10G 1–5)				CHI A (1G 0–0)																				
"	total	1	5	.167	5.89	11	7	3	55	76	15	24	0	0	0	0	18	3	0	.167	2	16	1	0	1.7	.947
3 yrs.		11	15	.423	3.76	49	29	14	246.2	254	98	93	1	1	1	1	74	10	0	.135	11	64	5	4	1.6	.938

Edwin Nunez

NUNEZ, EDWIN
Born Edwin Nunez y Martinez.
B. May 27, 1963, Humacao, Puerto Rico BR TR 6'5" 207 lbs.

Year	Team	W	L	PCT	ERA	G	GS	CG	IP	H	BB	SO	ShO	W	L	SV	AB	H	HR	BA	PO	A	E	DP	TC/G	FA
1982	SEA A	1	2	.333	4.58	8	5	0	35.1	36	16	27	0	0	0	0	0	0	0	—	2	5	0	0	1.0	.875
1983		0	4	.000	4.38	14	5	0	37	40	22	35	0	0	0	0	0	0	0	—	0	6	0	1	0.4	1.000
1984		2	2	.500	3.18	37	0	0	68	56	21	57	0	2	2	7	0	0	0	—	4	6	1	0	0.3	.909
1985		7	3	.700	3.09	70	0	0	90.1	79	34	58	0	7	3	16	0	0	0	—	5	12	0	1	0.2	1.000
1986		1	2	.333	5.82	14	1	0	21.2	25	5	17	0	0	2	0	0	0	0	—	1	1	0	0	0.1	1.000
1987		3	4	.429	3.80	48	0	0	47.1	45	18	34	0	3	4	12	0	0	0	—	2	5	0	0	0.1	1.000
1988	2 teams	SEA A (14G 1–4)				NY N (10G 1–0)																				
"	total	2	4	.333	6.85	24	3	0	43.1	66	17	27	0	2	1	0	0	0	0	—	6	8	2	1	0.7	.875
1989	DET A	3	4	.429	4.17	27	0	0	54	49	36	41	0	3	4	1	0	0	0	—	3	9	0	2	0.4	1.000
8 yrs.		19	25	.432	4.15	242	14	0	397	395	169	296	0	17	16	36	0	0	0	—	23	52	4	5	0.3	.949

Jose Nunez

NUNEZ, JOSE
Born Jose Nunez y Jiminez.
B. Jan. 13, 1964, Jarabacoa, Dominican Republic BR TR 6'3" 175 lbs.

Year	Team	W	L	PCT	ERA	G	GS	CG	IP	H	BB	SO	ShO	W	L	SV	AB	H	HR	BA	PO	A	E	DP	TC/G	FA
1987	TOR A	5	2	.714	5.01	37	9	0	97	91	58	99	0	3	1	0	0	0	0	—	5	7	0	0	0.3	1.000
1988		0	1	.000	3.07	13	2	0	29.1	28	17	18	0	0	1	0	0	0	0	—	1	4	0	0	0.4	1.000
1989		0	0	—	2.53	6	1	0	10.2	8	2	14	0	0	0	0	0	0	0	—	1	0	1	0	0.3	.500
3 yrs.		5	3	.625	4.40	56	12	0	137	127	77	131	0	3	2	0	0	0	0	—	7	11	1	1	0.3	.947

Howie Nunn

NUNN, HOWARD RALPH
B. Oct. 18, 1935, Westfield, N. C. BR TR 6' 173 lbs.

Year	Team	W	L	PCT	ERA	G	GS	CG	IP	H	BB	SO	ShO	W	L	SV	AB	H	HR	BA	PO	A	E	DP	TC/G	FA
1959	STL N	2	2	.500	7.59	16	0	0	21.1	23	15	20	0	2	2	0	1	0	0	.000	0	6	0	0	0.4	1.000
1961	CIN N	2	1	.667	3.58	24	0	0	37.2	35	24	26	0	2	1	0	8	2	0	.250	1	6	0	1	0.3	1.000
1962		0	0	—	5.59	6	0	0	9.2	15	3	4	0	0	0	0	1	0	0	.000	2	2	0	1	0.7	1.000
3 yrs.		4	3	.571	5.11	46	0	0	68.2	73	42	50	0	4	3	0	10	2	0	.200	3	14	0	2	0.4	1.000

Joe Nuxhall

NUXHALL, JOSEPH HENRY
B. July 30, 1928, Hamilton, Ohio BL TL 6'3" 195 lbs.

Year	Team	W	L	PCT	ERA	G	GS	CG	IP	H	BB	SO	ShO	W	L	SV	AB	H	HR	BA	PO	A	E	DP	TC/G	FA
1944	CIN N	0	0	—	67.50	1	0	0	.2	2	5	0	0	0	0	0	0	0	0	—	0	0	0	0	0.0	—
1952		1	4	.200	3.22	37	5	2	92.1	83	42	52	0	1	2	1	23	2	0	.087	3	24	1	4	0.8	.964
1953		9	11	.450	4.32	30	17	5	141.2	136	69	52	1	2	2	2	49	16	3	.327	6	18	3	0	0.9	.889
1954		12	5	.706	3.89	35	14	5	166.2	188	59	85	1	5	0	3	52	9	3	.173	4	29	1	5	1.0	.971
1955		17	12	**.586**	3.47	50	33	14	257	240	78	98	5	5	0	3	86	17	3	.198	12	35	3	4	1.0	.940

Year	Team		W	L	PCT	ERA	G	GS	CG	IP	H	BB	SO	ShO	Relief Pitching W	L	SV	Batting AB	H	HR	BA	PO	A	E	DP	TC/G	FA

Joe Nuxhall *continued*

Year	Team		W	L	PCT	ERA	G	GS	CG	IP	H	BB	SO	ShO	W	L	SV	AB	H	HR	BA	PO	A	E	DP	TC/G	FA
1956			13	11	.542	3.72	44	32	10	200.2	196	87	120	2	2	0	3	59	11	2	.186	6	31	2	3	0.9	.949
1957			10	10	.500	4.75	39	28	6	174.1	192	53	99	2	1	0	1	59	14	0	.237	11	20	4	1	0.9	.886
1958			12	11	.522	3.79	36	26	5	175.2	169	63	111	0	4	0	0	62	13	0	.210	6	29	3	3	1.1	.921
1959			9	9	.500	4.24	28	21	6	131.2	155	35	75	1	2	0	1	44	11	0	.250	6	19	1	1	0.9	.962
1960			1	8	.111	4.42	38	6	0	112	130	27	72	0	0	3	0	26	2	0	.077	8	26	1	4	0.9	.971
1961	KC	A	5	8	.385	5.34	37	13	1	128	135	65	81	0	1	2	1	65	19	2	.292	10	13	3	1	0.7	.885
1962	2 teams				LA A (5G 0–0)				CIN N (12G 5–0)																	
"	total		5	0	1.000	3.03	17	9	1	71.1	66	30	59	0	1	0	1	26	7	1	.269	2	11	0	1	0.8	1.000
1963	CIN	N	15	8	.652	2.61	35	29	14	217.1	194	39	169	2	0	0	2	76	12	0	.158	5	33	5	2	0.8	.884
1964			9	8	.529	4.07	32	22	7	154.2	146	51	111	4	1	1	2	54	7	1	.130	5	20	2	1	0.8	.926
1965			11	4	.733	3.45	32	16	5	148.2	142	31	117	1	1	1	2	45	8	0	.178	5	13	0	0	0.6	1.000
1966			6	8	.429	4.50	35	16	2	130	136	42	71	1	2	1	0	40	4	0	.100	6	20	3	1	0.8	.897
16 yrs.			135	117	.536	3.90	526	287	83	2302.2	2310	776	1372	20	25	13	19	766	152	15	.198	95	341	32	31	0.9	.932

Rich Nye

NYE, RICHARD RAYMOND
B. Aug. 4, 1944, Oakland, Calif.
BL TL 6'4" 185 lbs.

Year	Team		W	L	PCT	ERA	G	GS	CG	IP	H	BB	SO	ShO	W	L	SV	AB	H	HR	BA	PO	A	E	DP	TC/G	FA
1966	CHI	N	0	2	.000	2.12	3	3	0	17	16	7	9	0	0	0	0	4	1	0	.250	0	1	0	0	0.3	1.000
1967			13	10	.565	3.20	35	30	7	205	179	52	119	0	0	0	0	75	16	0	.213	10	35	1	2	1.3	.978
1968			7	12	.368	3.80	27	20	6	132.2	145	34	74	1	1	0	1	44	8	0	.182	6	22	2	1	1.1	.933
1969			3	5	.375	5.09	34	5	1	69	72	21	39	0	0	0	3	16	1	0	.063	1	10	0	0	0.3	1.000
1970	2 teams				MON N (8G 3–2)				STL N (6G 0–0)																	
"	total		3	2	.600	4.14	14	4	2	54.1	60	26	26	0	0	0	0	19	4	0	.211	5	7	0	1	0.9	1.000
5 yrs.			26	31	.456	3.71	113	63	16	478	472	140	267	1	1	1	4	158	30	0	.190	22	75	3	5	0.9	.970

Jerry Nyman

NYMAN, GERALD SMITH
B. Nov. 23, 1942, Logan, Utah
BL TL 5'10" 165 lbs.

Year	Team		W	L	PCT	ERA	G	GS	CG	IP	H	BB	SO	ShO	W	L	SV	AB	H	HR	BA	PO	A	E	DP	TC/G	FA
1968	CHI	A	2	1	.667	2.01	8	7	1	40.1	38	16	27	1	0	0	0	13	2	0	.154	2	6	2	1	1.3	.800
1969			4	4	.500	5.29	20	10	2	64.2	58	39	40	1	0	0	0	20	1	0	.050	0	9	0	0	0.5	1.000
1970	SD	N	0	2	.000	16.20	2	2	0	5	8	2	2	0	0	0	0	0	0	0	—	0	0	0	0	0.0	—
3 yrs.			6	7	.462	4.58	30	19	3	110	104	57	69	2	0	0	0	33	3	0	.091	2	15	2	1	0.6	.895

Prince Oana

OANA, HENRY KAUHANE
B. Jan. 22, 1908, Waipahu, Hawaii D. June 19, 1976, Austin, Tex.
BR TR 6'2" 193 lbs.

Year	Team		W	L	PCT	ERA	G	GS	CG	IP	H	BB	SO	ShO	W	L	SV	AB	H	HR	BA	PO	A	E	DP	TC/G	FA
1943	DET	A	3	2	.600	4.50	10	1	0	34	34	19	15	0	3	2	1	26	10	1	.385	0	6	2	0	0.8	.750
1945			0	0	—	1.59	3	1	0	11.1	3	7	3	0	0	0	1	5	1	0	.200	0	1	0	0	0.3	1.000
2 yrs.			3	2	.600	3.77	13	1	0	45.1	37	26	18	0	3	2	1	*				0	7	2	0	0.7	.778

Henry Oberbeck

OBERBECK, HENRY A.
B. May 17, 1858, St. Louis, Mo. D. Aug. 26, 1921, St. Louis, Mo.

Year	Team		W	L	PCT	ERA	G	GS	CG	IP	H	BB	SO	ShO	W	L	SV	AB	H	HR	BA	PO	A	E	DP	TC/G	FA
1884	2 teams				BAL U (2G 0–0)				KC U (6G 0–5)																	
"	total		0	5	.000	5.30	8	5	3	35.2	56	5	7	0	1	0	1	*				1	6	2	0	1.1	.778

Doc Oberlander

OBERLANDER, HARTMAN LOUIS
B. May 12, 1864, Waukegan, Ill. D. Nov. 14, 1922, Pryor, Okla.
TL

Year	Team		W	L	PCT	ERA	G	GS	CG	IP	H	BB	SO	ShO	W	L	SV	AB	H	HR	BA	PO	A	E	DP	TC/G	FA
1888	CLE	AA	1	2	.333	5.26	3	3	3	25.2	27	18	23	0	0	0	0	14	3	0	.214	0	4	1	0	1.7	.800

Frank Oberlin

OBERLIN, FRANK RUFUS (Flossie)
B. Mar. 29, 1876, Elsie, Mich. D. Jan. 6, 1952, Ashley, Ind.
BR TR 6'1" 165 lbs.

Year	Team		W	L	PCT	ERA	G	GS	CG	IP	H	BB	SO	ShO	W	L	SV	AB	H	HR	BA	PO	A	E	DP	TC/G	FA
1906	BOS	A	1	3	.250	3.18	4	4	4	34	38	13	13	0	0	0	0	13	2	0	.154	1	16	2	0	4.8	.895
1907	2 teams				BOS A (12G 1–5)				WAS A (11G 2–6)																	
"	total		3	11	.214	4.47	23	12	5	94.2	105	36	36	0	1	2	0	31	3	0	.097	0	26	5	0	1.3	.839
1909	WAS	A	1	4	.200	3.73	9	4	1	41	41	16	13	0	1	0	0	14	2	0	.143	1	8	0	0	1.0	1.000
1910			0	6	.000	2.98	8	6	6	57.1	52	23	18	0	0	0	0	19	1	0	.053	3	17	5	0	3.1	.800
4 yrs.			5	24	.172	3.77	44	26	16	227	236	88	80	0	2	2	0	77	8	0	.104	5	67	12	0	1.9	.857

Billy O'Brien

O'BRIEN, WILLIAM SMITH
B. Mar. 14, 1860, Albany, N. Y. D. May 26, 1911, Kansas City, Mo.
BR 6' 185 lbs.

Year	Team		W	L	PCT	ERA	G	GS	CG	IP	H	BB	SO	ShO	W	L	SV	AB	H	HR	BA	PO	A	E	DP	TC/G	FA
1884	KC	U	1	0	1.000	1.80	2	0	0	10	8	3	7	0	1	0	0	*				0	4	3	1	3.5	.571

Bob O'Brien

O'BRIEN, ROBERT ALLEN
B. Apr. 23, 1949, Pittsburgh, Pa.
BL TL 5'10" 170 lbs.

Year	Team		W	L	PCT	ERA	G	GS	CG	IP	H	BB	SO	ShO	W	L	SV	AB	H	HR	BA	PO	A	E	DP	TC/G	FA
1971	LA	N	2	2	.500	3.00	14	4	1	42	42	13	15	1	1	1	0	9	1	0	.111	1	3	0	0	0.3	1.000

Buck O'Brien

O'BRIEN, THOMAS JOSEPH
B. May 9, 1882, Brockton, Mass. D. July 25, 1959, Dorchester, Mass.
BR TR 5'10" 188 lbs.

Year	Team		W	L	PCT	ERA	G	GS	CG	IP	H	BB	SO	ShO	W	L	SV	AB	H	HR	BA	PO	A	E	DP	TC/G	FA
1911	BOS	A	5	1	.833	0.38	6	5	5	47.2	30	21	31	2	0	0	0	16	2	0	.125	3	14	0	1	2.8	1.000
1912			20	13	.606	2.58	37	34	25	275.2	237	90	115	2	1	0	0	94	13	0	.138	10	83	5	1	2.6	.949
1913	2 teams				BOS A (15G 4–9)				CHI A (6G 0–2)																	
"	total		4	11	.267	3.73	21	15	6	108.2	124	48	58	0	2	2	0	33	5	0	.152	2	33	0	0	1.7	1.000
3 yrs.			29	25	.537	2.63	64	54	36	432	391	159	204	4	3	2	0	143	20	0	.140	15	130	5	2	2.3	.967

WORLD SERIES

Year	Team		W	L	PCT	ERA	G	GS	CG	IP	H	BB	SO	ShO	W	L	SV	AB	H	HR	BA	PO	A	E	DP	TC/G	FA
1912	BOS	A	0	2	.000	7.00	2	2	0	9	12	3	4	0	0	0	0	2	0	0	.000	1	6	0	0	3.5	1.000

Dan O'Brien

O'BRIEN, DANIEL JOQUES
B. Apr. 22, 1954, St. Petersburg, Fla.
BR TR 6'4" 215 lbs.

Year	Team		W	L	PCT	ERA	G	GS	CG	IP	H	BB	SO	ShO	W	L	SV	AB	H	HR	BA	PO	A	E	DP	TC/G	FA
1978	STL	N	0	2	.000	4.50	7	2	0	18	22	8	12	0	0	1	0	3	0	0	.000	0	2	0	0	0.3	1.000
1979			1	1	.500	8.18	6	0	0	11	21	3	5	0	1	1	0	2	0	0	.000	0	0	0	0	0.0	—
2 yrs.			1	3	.250	5.90	13	2	0	29	43	11	17	0	1	2	0	5	0	0	.000	0	2	0	0	0.2	1.000

Year	Team		W	L	PCT	ERA	G	GS	CG	IP	H	BB	SO	ShO	Relief Pitching W	L	SV	Batting AB	H	HR	BA	PO	A	E	DP	TC/G	FA

Darby O'Brien

O'BRIEN, JOHN F.
B. Apr. 15, 1867, Troy, N. Y. D. Mar. 11, 1892, West Troy, N. Y.
BR TR 5'10" 165 lbs.

Year	Team		W	L	PCT	ERA	G	GS	CG	IP	H	BB	SO	ShO	W	L	SV	AB	H	HR	BA	PO	A	E	DP	TC/G	FA
1888	CLE	AA	11	19	.367	3.30	30	30	30	259	245	99	135	1	0	0	0	109	20	0	.183	16	62	9	2	2.9	.897
1889	CLE	N	22	17	.564	4.15	41	41	39	346.2	345	167	122	1	0	0	0	140	35	0	.250	25	70	7	3	2.5	.931
1890	CLE	P	8	16	.333	3.40	25	25	22	206.1	229	93	54	0	0	0	0	96	15	0	.156	9	45	2	2	2.2	.964
1891	BOS	AA	18	13	.581	3.65	40	30	22	268.2	300	127	87	0	3	1	2	128	30	0	.234	11	50	4	4	1.6	.938
4 yrs.			59	65	.476	3.68	136	126	113	1080.2	1119	486	398	2	3	1	2	473	100	0	.211	61	227	22	11	2.3	.929

Darby O'Brien

O'BRIEN, WILLIAM D.
B. Sept. 1, 1863, Peoria, Ill. D. June 15, 1893, Peoria, Ill.
BR TR 6'1" 186 lbs.

Year	Team		W	L	PCT	ERA	G	GS	CG	IP	H	BB	SO	ShO	W	L	SV	AB	H	HR	BA	PO	A	E	DP	TC/G	FA
1887	NY	AA	0	0	–	7.36	1	0	0	3.2	4	5	0	0	0	0	0	*				0	0	0	0	0.0	–

Eddie O'Brien

O'BRIEN, EDWARD JOSEPH
Brother of Johnny O'Brien.
B. Dec. 11, 1930, South Amboy, N. J.
BR TR 5'9" 165 lbs.

Year	Team		W	L	PCT	ERA	G	GS	CG	IP	H	BB	SO	ShO	W	L	SV	AB	H	HR	BA	PO	A	E	DP	TC/G	FA
1956	PIT	N	0	0	–	0.00	1	0	0	2	1	0	0	0	0	0	0	53	14	0	.264	0	0	0	0	0.0	–
1957			1	0	1.000	2.19	3	1	1	12.1	11	3	10	0	0	0	0	4	0	0	.000	0	2	0	1	0.7	1.000
1958			0	0	–	13.50	1	0	0	2	4	1	1	0	0	0	0	0	0	0	–	0	0	0	0	0.0	–
3 yrs.			1	0	1.000	3.31	5	1	1	16.1	16	4	11	0	0	0	0	*				0	2	0	1	0.4	1.000

Johnny O'Brien

O'BRIEN, JOHN THOMAS
Brother of Eddie O'Brien.
B. Dec. 11, 1930, South Amboy, N. J.
BR TR 5'9" 170 lbs.

Year	Team		W	L	PCT	ERA	G	GS	CG	IP	H	BB	SO	ShO	W	L	SV	AB	H	HR	BA	PO	A	E	DP	TC/G	FA
1956	PIT	N	1	0	1.000	2.84	8	0	0	19	8	9	9	0	1	0	0	104	18	0	.173	0	0	2	0	0.3	–
1957			0	3	.000	6.08	16	1	0	40	46	24	19	0	0	2	0	35	11	0	.314	2	4	1	0	0.4	.857
1958	2 teams	PIT N	(0G 0–0)			22.50	STL N	(1G 0–0)																			
"	total		0	0	–	22.50	2	0	0	2	7	2	2	0	0	0	0	3	0	0	.000	0	0	0	0	0.0	–
3 yrs.			1	3	.250	5.61	25	1	0	61	61	35	30	0	1	2	0	*				2	4	3	0	0.4	.667

Tom O'Brien

O'BRIEN, THOMAS H.
B. June 22, 1860, Salem, Mass. D. Apr. 21, 1921, Worcester, Mass.
BR TR

Year	Team		W	L	PCT	ERA	G	GS	CG	IP	H	BB	SO	ShO	W	L	SV	AB	H	HR	BA	PO	A	E	DP	TC/G	FA
1887	NY	AA	0	0	–	0.00	1	0	0	1	1	1	0	0	0	0	0	*				0	0	0	0	0.0	–

Walter Ockey

OCKEY, WALTER ANDREW (Footie)
Born Walter Andrew Okypch.
B. Jan. 4, 1920, New York, N. Y. D. Dec. 4, 1971, Staten Island, N. Y.
BR TR 6' 175 lbs.

Year	Team		W	L	PCT	ERA	G	GS	CG	IP	H	BB	SO	ShO	W	L	SV	AB	H	HR	BA	PO	A	E	DP	TC/G	FA
1944	NY	N	0	0	–	3.38	2	0	0	2.2	2	2	1	0	0	0	0	0	0	0	–	0	2	0	0	1.0	1.000

Pat O'Connell

O'CONNELL, PATRICK H.
B. June 10, 1861, Bangor, Me. D. Jan. 24, 1943, Lewiston, Me.
BL TR 5'10" 175 lbs.

Year	Team		W	L	PCT	ERA	G	GS	CG	IP	H	BB	SO	ShO	W	L	SV	AB	H	HR	BA	PO	A	E	DP	TC/G	FA
1886	BAL	AA	0	0	–	6.00	1	0	0	3	4	2	1	0	0	0	0	*				0	0	0	0	0.0	–

Andy O'Connor

O'CONNOR, ANDREW JAMES
B. Sept. 14, 1884, Roxbury, Mass. D. Sept. 26, 1980, Norwood, Mass.
BR TR 6' 160 lbs.

Year	Team		W	L	PCT	ERA	G	GS	CG	IP	H	BB	SO	ShO	W	L	SV	AB	H	HR	BA	PO	A	E	DP	TC/G	FA
1908	NY	A	0	1	.000	10.13	1	1	0	8	15	7	5	0	0	0	0	3	0	0	.000	0	2	1	0	3.0	.667

Frank O'Connor

O'CONNOR, FRANK HENRY
B. Sept. 15, 1870, Keeseville, N. Y. D. Dec. 26, 1913, Brattleboro, Vt.
BL TL 6' 185 lbs.

Year	Team		W	L	PCT	ERA	G	GS	CG	IP	H	BB	SO	ShO	W	L	SV	AB	H	HR	BA	PO	A	E	DP	TC/G	FA
1893	PHI	N	0	0	–	11.25	3	1	0	4	2	9	0	0	0	0	1	2	2	1	1.000	0	1	0	0	0.3	1.000

Jack O'Connor

O'CONNOR, JACK WILLIAM
B. June 2, 1958, Twenty-Nine Palms, Calif.
BL TL 6'3" 215 lbs.

Year	Team		W	L	PCT	ERA	G	GS	CG	IP	H	BB	SO	ShO	W	L	SV	AB	H	HR	BA	PO	A	E	DP	TC/G	FA
1981	MIN	A	3	2	.600	5.91	28	0	0	35	46	30	16	0	3	2	0	0	0	0	–	2	8	2	3	0.4	.833
1982			8	9	.471	4.29	23	19	6	126	122	57	56	1	0	0	0	0	0	0	–	3	6	0	0	0.4	1.000
1983			2	3	.400	5.86	27	8	0	83	107	36	56	0	1	0	0	0	0	0	–	2	6	0	0	0.3	1.000
1984			0	0	–	1.93	2	0	0	4.2	1	4	0	0	0	0	0	0	0	0	–	0	0	0	0	0.0	–
1985	MON	N	0	2	.000	4.94	20	1	0	23.2	21	13	16	0	0	1	0	0	0	0	–	0	1	0	1	0.1	1.000
1987	BAL	A	1	1	.500	4.30	29	0	0	46	46	23	33	0	1	1	2	0	0	0	–	3	2	1	1	0.2	.833
6 yrs.			14	17	.452	4.89	129	28	6	318.1	343	163	177	1	5	4	2	0	0	0	–	10	23	3	5	0.3	.917

Hank O'Day

O'DAY, HENRY FRANCIS (Peep)
B. July 8, 1862, Chicago, Ill. D. July 2, 1935, Chicago, Ill.
Manager 1912, 1914.
TR

Year	Team		W	L	PCT	ERA	G	GS	CG	IP	H	BB	SO	ShO	W	L	SV	AB	H	HR	BA	PO	A	E	DP	TC/G	FA
1884	TOL	AA	7	28	.200	3.97	39	38	33	308.2	326	65	154	0	0	0	1	242	51	0	.211	15	82	15	2	2.9	.866
1885	PIT	AA	5	7	.417	3.67	12	12	10	103	110	16	36	0	0	0	0	49	12	0	.245	6	19	4	2	2.4	.862
1886	WAS	N	1	2	.333	1.65	6	6	6	49	41	17	47	0	0	0	0	19	1	0	.053	4	14	2	1	3.3	.900
1887			8	20	.286	4.17	30	30	29	254.2	255	109	86	0	0	0	0	116	23	0	.198	11	47	3	3	2.0	.951
1888			16	29	.356	3.10	46	46	46	403	359	117	186	3	0	0	0	166	23	0	.139	19	64	7	1	2.0	.922
1889	2 teams	WAS N	(13G 2–10)				NY N	(10G 9–1)																			
"	total		11	11	.500	4.31	23	23	19	186	200	92	51	0	0	0	0	75	11	0	.147	12	34	3	1	2.1	.939
1890	NY	P	22	13	.629	4.21	43	35	32	329	356	163	94	1	1	0	3	150	34	1	.227	11	71	7	0	2.1	.921
7 yrs.			70	110	.389	3.79	199	190	175	1633.1	1647	579	654	4	1	0	4	*				78	331	41	10	2.3	.909

Paul O'Dea

O'DEA, PAUL (Lefty)
B. July 3, 1920, Cleveland, Ohio D. Dec. 11, 1978, Cleveland, Ohio
BL TL 6' 200 lbs.

Year	Team		W	L	PCT	ERA	G	GS	CG	IP	H	BB	SO	ShO	W	L	SV	AB	H	HR	BA	PO	A	E	DP	TC/G	FA
1944	CLE	A	0	0	–	2.08	3	0	0	4.1	5	6	0	0	0	0	0	173	55	0	.318	0	0	1	0	0.3	–
1945			0	0	–	13.50	1	0	0	2	4	2	0	0	0	0	0	221	52	1	.235	0	1	0	0	1.0	1.000
2 yrs.			0	0	–	5.68	4	0	0	6.1	9	8	0	0	0	0	0	*				0	1	1	0	0.5	.500

Year	Team		W	L	PCT	ERA	G	GS	CG	IP	H	BB	SO	ShO	Relief Pitching			Batting				PO	A	E	DP	TC/G	FA
															W	L	SV	AB	H	HR	BA						

Billy O'Dell

O'DELL, WILLIAM OLIVER (Digger)   BB TL 5'11"   170 lbs.
B. Feb. 10, 1933, Whitmere, S. C.

Year	Team		W	L	PCT	ERA	G	GS	CG	IP	H	BB	SO	ShO	W	L	SV	AB	H	HR	BA	PO	A	E	DP	TC/G	FA
1954	BAL	A	1	1	.500	2.76	7	2	1	16.1	15	5	6	0	0	0	0	3	0	0	.000	0	5	0	0	0.7	1.000
1956			0	0	—	1.13	4	1	0	8	6	6	6	0	0	0	0	1	0	0	.000	0	0	0	0	0.0	—
1957			4	10	.286	2.69	35	15	2	140.1	107	39	97	1	0	1	4	34	5	0	.147	5	14	2	1	0.6	.905
1958			14	11	.560	2.97	41	25	12	221.1	201	51	137	3	2	1	8	72	8	1	.111	12	32	0	2	1.1	1.000
1959			10	12	.455	2.93	38	24	6	199.1	163	67	88	2	2	4	1	60	5	1	.083	7	44	3	3	1.4	.944
1960	SF	N	8	13	.381	3.20	43	24	6	202.2	198	72	145	1	1	3	2	56	6	0	.107	9	29	1	0	0.9	.974
1961			7	5	.583	3.59	46	14	4	130.1	132	33	110	1	3	2	2	39	4	0	.103	8	17	0	1	0.5	1.000
1962			19	14	.576	3.53	43	43	20	280.2	**282**	66	195	2	1	0	0	90	12	0	.133	15	39	5	0	1.4	.915
1963			14	10	.583	3.16	36	33	10	222.1	218	70	116	3	0	1	1	78	16	0	.205	5	27	1	0	0.9	.970
1964			8	7	.533	5.40	36	8	1	85	82	35	54	0	**8**	3	2	22	0	0	.000	5	10	1	0	0.4	.938
1965	MIL	N	10	6	.625	2.18	62	1	0	111.1	87	30	78	0	**10**	5	18	23	4	0	.174	12	13	0	1	0.4	1.000
1966	2 teams		ATL N	(24G 2–3)		PIT N	(37G 3–2)																					
"	total		5	5	.500	2.64	61	2	0	112.2	118	41	67	0	4	5	10	24	3	0	.125	7	10	0	2	0.3	1.000
1967	PIT	N	5	6	.455	5.82	27	1	1	86.2	88	41	34	0	1	1	0	26	3	0	.115	3	12	1	0	0.6	1.000
13 yrs.			105	100	.512	3.29	479	199	63	1817	1697	556	1133	13	32	26	48	528	66	2	.125	88	252	13	11	0.7	.963

WORLD SERIES

Year	Team		W	L	PCT	ERA	G	GS	CG	IP	H	BB	SO	ShO	W	L	SV	AB	H	HR	BA	PO	A	E	DP	TC/G	FA
1962	SF	N	0	1	.000	4.38	3	1	0	12.1	12	3	9	0	0	0	1	3	1	0	.333	0	0	0	0	0.0	—

Ted Odenwald

ODENWALD, THEODORE JOSEPH (Lefty)   BR TL 5'10"   147 lbs.
B. Jan. 4, 1902, Hudson, Wis.   D. Oct. 23, 1965, Shakopee, Minn.

Year	Team		W	L	PCT	ERA	G	GS	CG	IP	H	BB	SO	ShO	W	L	SV	AB	H	HR	BA	PO	A	E	DP	TC/G	FA
1921	CLE	A	1	0	1.000	1.56	10	0	0	17.1	16	6	4	0	1	0	0	3	0	0	.000	0	5	0	0	0.5	1.000
1922			0	0	—	40.50	1	0	0	1.1	6	2	2	0	0	0	0	0	0	0	—	1	0	0	0	1.0	1.000
2 yrs.			1	0	1.000	4.34	11	0	0	18.2	22	8	6	0	1	0	0	3	0	0	.000	1	5	0	0	0.5	1.000

Blue Moon Odom

ODOM, JOHNNY LEE   BR TR 6'   178 lbs.
B. May 29, 1945, Macon, Ga.

Year	Team		W	L	PCT	ERA	G	GS	CG	IP	H	BB	SO	ShO	W	L	SV	AB	H	HR	BA	PO	A	E	DP	TC/G	FA
1964	KC	A	1	2	.333	10.06	5	5	1	17	29	11	10	1	0	0	0	5	0	0	.000	2	1	1	0	1.0	.800
1965			0	0	—	9.00	1	0	0	1	2	2	0	0	0	0	0	0	0	0	—	0	1	0	0	1.0	1.000
1966			5	5	.500	2.49	14	14	4	90.1	70	53	47	2	0	0	0	31	3	0	.097	12	20	1	2	2.4	.970
1967			3	8	.273	5.04	29	17	0	103.2	94	68	67	0	0	0	0	28	8	0	.286	9	17	3	2	1.0	.897
1968	OAK	A	16	10	.615	2.45	32	31	9	231.1	179	98	143	4	0	0	0	78	17	1	.218	10	43	2	1	1.7	.964
1969			15	6	.714	2.92	32	32	10	231.1	179	112	150	3	0	0	0	79	21	5	.266	27	32	4	4	2.0	.937
1970			9	8	.529	3.81	29	29	4	156	128	100	88	1	0	0	0	54	13	3	.241	22	30	4	2	1.9	.929
1971			10	12	.455	4.28	25	25	3	141	147	71	69	1	0	0	0	50	8	1	.160	15	19	6	3	1.6	.850
1972			15	6	.714	2.50	31	30	7	194.1	164	87	86	2	0	0	0	66	8	2	.121	15	33	7	2	1.8	.873
1973			5	12	.294	4.49	30	24	3	150.1	153	67	83	0	1	0	0	1	0	0	.000	8	20	4	3	1.1	.875
1974			1	5	.167	3.83	34	1	0	87	85	52	52	0	1	0	0	0	0	0	—	7	16	5	1	0.8	.821
1975	3 teams		OAK A	(7G 0–2)		CLE A	(3G 1–0)		ATL N	(15G 1–7)																		
"	total		2	9	.182	7.22	25	13	1	77.1	101	47	44	1	0	0	0	13	1	0	.077	13	8	2	0	0.9	.913
1976	CHI	A	2	2	.500	5.79	8	4	0	28	31	20	18	0	0	0	0	0	0	0	—	1	2	2	0	0.6	.600
13 yrs.			84	85	.497	3.70	295	229	40	1508.2	1362	788	857	15	2	1	1	405	79	12	.195	141	243	41	21	1.4	.904

LEAGUE CHAMPIONSHIP SERIES

Year	Team		W	L	PCT	ERA	G	GS	CG	IP	H	BB	SO	ShO	W	L	SV	AB	H	HR	BA	PO	A	E	DP	TC/G	FA
1972	OAK	A	2	0	1.000	0.00	2	2	1	14	5	2	5	1	0	0	0	4	1	0	.250	2	1	0	0	1.5	1.000
1973			0	0	—	1.80	1	0	0	5	6	2	4	0	0	0	0	0	0	0	—	0	1	0	0	1.0	1.000
1974			0	0	—	0.00	1	0	0	3.1	1	0	1	0	0	0	0	0	0	0	—	0	0	0	0	0.0	—
3 yrs.			2	0	1.000	0.40	4	2	1	22.1	12	4	10	1	0	0	0	4	1	0	.250	2	2	0	0	1.0	1.000

WORLD SERIES

Year	Team		W	L	PCT	ERA	G	GS	CG	IP	H	BB	SO	ShO	W	L	SV	AB	H	HR	BA	PO	A	E	DP	TC/G	FA
1972	OAK	A	0	1	.000	1.59	2	2	0	11.1	5	6	13	0	0	0	0	4	0	0	.000	1	3	0	0	2.0	1.000
1973			0	0	—	3.86	2	0	0	4.2	5	2	2	0	0	0	0	1	0	0	.000	0	1	0	0	0.5	1.000
1974			1	0	1.000	0.00	2	0	0	1.1	0	1	2	0	1	0	0	0	0	0	—	0	0	0	0	0.0	—
3 yrs.			1	1	.500	2.08	6	2	0	17.1	10	9	17	0	1	0	0	5	0	0	.000	1	4	0	0	0.8	1.000

Dave Odom

ODOM, DAVID EVERETT (Porky)   BR TR 6'1"   220 lbs.
B. June 5, 1918, Dinuba, Calif.

Year	Team		W	L	PCT	ERA	G	GS	CG	IP	H	BB	SO	ShO	W	L	SV	AB	H	HR	BA	PO	A	E	DP	TC/G	FA
1943	BOS	N	0	3	.000	5.27	22	3	1	54.2	54	30	17	0	0	0	2	12	0	0	.000	3	5	0	1	0.4	.889

George O'Donnell

O'DONNELL, GEORGE DANA   BR TR 6'3"   175 lbs.
B. May 27, 1929, Winchester, Ill.

Year	Team		W	L	PCT	ERA	G	GS	CG	IP	H	BB	SO	ShO	W	L	SV	AB	H	HR	BA	PO	A	E	DP	TC/G	FA
1954	PIT	N	3	9	.250	4.53	21	10	3	87.1	105	21	8	0	1	1	1	23	2	1	.087	7	19	0	1	1.2	1.000

John O'Donoghue

O'DONOGHUE, JOHN EUGENE   BR TL 6'4"   203 lbs.
B. Oct. 7, 1939, Kansas City, Mo.

Year	Team		W	L	PCT	ERA	G	GS	CG	IP	H	BB	SO	ShO	W	L	SV	AB	H	HR	BA	PO	A	E	DP	TC/G	FA
1963	KC	A	0	1	.000	1.50	1	1	0	6	6	2	1	0	0	0	0	2	0	0	.000	0	0	0	0	0.0	—
1964			10	14	.417	4.92	39	32	2	173.2	202	65	79	1	1	0	0	55	13	1	.236	8	27	3	4	1.0	.921
1965			9	**18**	.333	3.95	34	30	4	177.2	183	66	82	1	0	2	0	55	12	1	.218	8	36	4	2	1.4	.917
1966	CLE	A	6	8	.429	3.83	32	13	2	108	109	23	49	0	2	2	0	33	5	0	.152	5	24	0	0	0.9	1.000
1967			8	9	.471	3.24	33	17	5	130.2	120	33	81	0	1	2	2	40	4	1	.100	7	35	0	3	1.3	1.000
1968	BAL	A	0	0	—	6.14	16	0	0	22	34	7	11	0	0	0	0	0	0	0	.000	0	8	0	0	0.3	1.000
1969	SEA	A	2	2	.500	2.96	55	0	0	70	58	37	48	0	2	2	6	13	1	0	.077	3	9	1	2	0.2	.923
1970	2 teams		MIL A	(25G 2–0)		MON N	(9G 2–3)																					
"	total		4	3	.571	5.20	34	3	0	45	49	20	19	0	4	1	1	6	0	0	.000	2	11	1	2	0.4	.929
1971	MON	N	0	0	—	4.76	13	0	0	17	19	7	7	0	0	0	0	0	0	0	—	2	2	0	0	0.3	1.000
9 yrs.			39	55	.415	4.08	257	96	13	750	780	260	377	4	10	7	10	206	35	3	.170	35	149	9	13	0.8	.953

Lefty O'Doul

O'DOUL, FRANCIS JOSEPH   BL TL 6'   180 lbs.
B. Mar. 4, 1897, San Francisco, Calif.   D. Dec. 7, 1969, San Francisco, Calif.

Year	Team		W	L	PCT	ERA	G	GS	CG	IP	H	BB	SO	ShO	W	L	SV	AB	H	HR	BA	PO	A	E	DP	TC/G	FA
1919	NY	A	0	0	—	3.60	3	0	0	5	7	4	2	0	0	0	0	16	4	0	.250	1	1	0	0	0.7	1.000
1920			0	0	—	4.91	2	0	0	3.2	4	2	2	0	0	0	0	12	2	0	.167	0	0	0	0	0.0	—

Year	Team	W	L	PCT	ERA	G	GS	CG	IP	H	BB	SO	ShO	Relief Pitching W	L	SV	Batting AB	H	HR	BA	PO	A	E	DP	TC/G	FA

Lefty O'Doul *continued*

Year	Team	W	L	PCT	ERA	G	GS	CG	IP	H	BB	SO	ShO	W	L	SV	AB	H	HR	BA	PO	A	E	DP	TC/G	FA
1922		0	0	–	3.38	6	0	0	16	24	12	5	0	0	0	0	9	3	0	.333	1	4	0	1	0.8	1.000
1923	BOS A	1	1	.500	5.43	23	0	0	53	69	31	10	0	1	1	0	35	5	0	.143	2	21	1	0	1.0	.958
4 yrs.		1	1	.500	4.87	34	0	0	77.2	104	49	19	0	1	1	0	*				4	26	1	1	0.9	.968

Bryan Oelkers

OELKERS, BRYAN ALOIS
B. Mar. 11, 1961, Zaragoza, Spain

BL TL 6'2" 190 lbs.

Year	Team	W	L	PCT	ERA	G	GS	CG	IP	H	BB	SO	ShO	W	L	SV	AB	H	HR	BA	PO	A	E	DP	TC/G	FA
1983	MIN A	0	5	.000	8.65	10	8	0	34.1	56	17	13	0	0	0	0	0	0	0	–	1	1	0	0	0.2	1.000
1986	CLE A	3	3	.500	4.70	35	4	0	69	70	40	33	0	3	2	1	0	0	0	–	5	4	0	0	0.3	1.000
2 yrs.		3	8	.273	6.01	45	12	0	103.1	126	57	46	0	3	2	1	0	0	0	–	6	5	0	0	0.2	1.000

Joe Oeschger

OESCHGER, JOSEPH CARL
B. May 24, 1891, Chicago, Ill.   D. July 29, 1986, Rohnert Park, Calif.

BR TR 6' 190 lbs.

Year	Team	W	L	PCT	ERA	G	GS	CG	IP	H	BB	SO	ShO	W	L	SV	AB	H	HR	BA	PO	A	E	DP	TC/G	FA
1914	PHI N	4	8	.333	3.77	32	10	5	124	129	54	47	0	3	0	1	40	3	0	.075	4	29	3	0	1.1	.917
1915		1	0	1.000	3.42	6	1	1	23.2	21	9	8	0	0	0	0	7	0	0	.000	1	6	0	0	1.2	1.000
1916		1	0	1.000	2.37	14	0	0	30.1	18	14	17	0	1	0	0	5	0	0	.000	1	10	0	0	0.8	1.000
1917		16	14	.533	2.75	42	30	18	262	241	72	123	0	3	0	0	88	10	0	.114	5	57	2	2	1.5	.969
1918		6	18	.250	3.03	30	23	13	184	159	83	60	5	2	0	3	60	5	0	.083	8	45	3	2	1.9	.946
1919	3 teams	PHI N	(5G 0–1)		NY N	(5G 0–1)		BOS N	(7G 4–2)																		
"	total	4	4	.500	3.94	17	12	6	102.2	127	39	24	1	0	1	0	38	2	0	.053	6	22	1	0	1.7	.966
1920	BOS N	15	13	.536	3.46	38	30	20	299	294	99	80	5	0	1	0	101	18	0	.178	10	70	5	3	2.2	.941
1921		20	14	.588	3.52	46	36	19	299	303	97	68	3	2	1	0	110	28	0	.255	11	93	5	2	2.4	.954
1922		6	21	.222	5.06	46	23	10	195.2	234	81	51	1	2	3	1	63	12	0	.190	6	51	1	3	1.3	.983
1923		5	15	.250	5.68	44	19	6	166.1	227	54	33	1	2	2	2	52	12	0	.231	7	38	0	3	1.0	1.000
1924	2 teams	NY N	(10G 2–0)		PHI N	(19G 2–7)																				
"	total	4	7	.364	4.01	29	10	0	94.1	123	30	18	0	2	0	0	27	8	0	.296	3	18	1	2	0.8	.955
1925	BKN N	1	2	.333	6.08	21	3	1	37	60	19	6	0	0	1	0	8	1	0	.125	2	8	1	0	0.5	.909
12 yrs.		83	116	.417	3.81	365	197	99	1818	1936	651	535	18	15	14	7	599	99	0	.165	64	447	22	19	1.5	.959

Curly Ogden

OGDEN, WARREN HARVEY
Brother of Jack Ogden.
B. Jan. 24, 1901, Ogden, Pa.   D. Aug. 6, 1964, Chester, Pa.

BR TR 6'1½" 180 lbs.

Year	Team	W	L	PCT	ERA	G	GS	CG	IP	H	BB	SO	ShO	W	L	SV	AB	H	HR	BA	PO	A	E	DP	TC/G	FA
1922	PHI A	1	4	.200	3.11	15	6	4	72.1	59	33	20	0	0	0	0	29	7	0	.241	5	16	2	0	1.5	.913
1923		1	2	.333	5.63	18	2	0	46.1	63	32	14	0	1	0	0	17	5	0	.294	3	13	1	0	0.9	.941
1924	2 teams	PHI A	(5G 0–3)		WAS A	(16G 9–5)																				
"	total	9	8	.529	2.83	21	17	9	120.2	97	58	27	3	0	2	0	50	13	0	.260	7	24	0	1	1.5	1.000
1925	WAS A	3	1	.750	4.50	17	4	2	42	45	18	6	1	1	0	0	12	3	0	.250	1	10	1	0	0.7	.917
1926		4	4	.500	4.30	22	9	4	96.1	114	45	21	0	1	1	0	27	5	0	.185	7	18	1	0	1.2	.962
5 yrs.		18	19	.486	3.79	93	38	19	377.2	378	186	88	4	3	3	0	135	33	0	.244	23	81	5	0	1.2	.954

WORLD SERIES

Year	Team	W	L	PCT	ERA	G	GS	CG	IP	H	BB	SO	ShO	W	L	SV	AB	H	HR	BA	PO	A	E	DP	TC/G	FA
1924	WAS A	0	0	–	0.00	1	1	0	.1	0	1	1	0	0	0	0	0	0	0	–	0	0	0	0	0.0	–

Jack Ogden

OGDEN, JOHN MAHLON
Brother of Curly Ogden.
B. Nov. 5, 1897, Ogden, Pa.   D. Nov. 9, 1977, Philadelphia, Pa.

BR TR 6' 190 lbs.

Year	Team	W	L	PCT	ERA	G	GS	CG	IP	H	BB	SO	ShO	W	L	SV	AB	H	HR	BA	PO	A	E	DP	TC/G	FA
1918	NY N	0	0	–	3.12	5	0	0	8.2	8	3	1	0	0	0	0	1	0	0	.000	0	1	0	0	0.2	1.000
1928	STL A	15	16	.484	4.15	38	31	18	242.2	257	80	67	1	2	1	2	85	17	0	.200	15	35	1	3	1.3	.980
1929		4	8	.333	4.93	34	14	7	131.1	154	44	32	0	0	2	0	45	11	0	.244	6	28	2	4	1.1	.944
1931	CIN N	4	8	.333	2.93	22	9	3	89	79	32	24	1	1	3	1	27	4	0	.148	8	15	4	0	1.2	.852
1932		2	2	.500	5.21	24	3	1	57	72	22	20	0	1	1	0	12	2	0	.167	4	14	1	0	0.8	.947
5 yrs.		25	34	.424	4.24	123	57	29	528.2	570	181	144	3	4	7	3	170	34	0	.200	33	93	8	7	1.1	.940

Joe Ogrodowski

OGRODOWSKI, JOSEPH ANTHONY
B. Nov. 20, 1906, Hoytville, Pa.   D. June 24, 1959, Elmira, N. Y.

BR TR 5'11" 165 lbs.

Year	Team	W	L	PCT	ERA	G	GS	CG	IP	H	BB	SO	ShO	W	L	SV	AB	H	HR	BA	PO	A	E	DP	TC/G	FA
1925	BOS N	0	0	–	54.00	1	0	0	1	6	3	0	0	0	0	0	0	0	0	–	0	0	0	0	0.0	–

Bill O'Hara

O'HARA, WILLIAM ALEXANDER
B. Aug. 14, 1883, Toronto, Ont., Canada   D. June 15, 1931, Jersey City, N. J.

BL TR 5'10"

Year	Team	W	L	PCT	ERA	G	GS	CG	IP	H	BB	SO	ShO	W	L	SV	AB	H	HR	BA	PO	A	E	DP	TC/G	FA
1910	STL N	0	0	–	0.00	1	0	0	1	0	1	0	0	0	0	0	0	0	0	*	0	0	0	0	0.0	–

Joe Ohl

OHL, JOSEPH EARL
B. Jan. 10, 1888, Jobstown N. J.   D. Dec. 18, 1951, Camden, N. J.

BL TL

Year	Team	W	L	PCT	ERA	G	GS	CG	IP	H	BB	SO	ShO	W	L	SV	AB	H	HR	BA	PO	A	E	DP	TC/G	FA
1909	WAS A	0	0	–	2.08	4	0	0	8.2	7	1	2	0	0	0	0	2	0	0	.000	5	0	0	0	1.3	1.000

Bob Ojeda

OJEDA, ROBERT MICHAEL (Bobby O.)
B. Dec. 17, 1957, Los Angeles, Calif.

BL TL 6'1" 185 lbs.

Year	Team	W	L	PCT	ERA	G	GS	CG	IP	H	BB	SO	ShO	W	L	SV	AB	H	HR	BA	PO	A	E	DP	TC/G	FA
1980	BOS A	1	1	.500	6.92	7	7	0	26	39	14	12	0	0	0	0	0	0	0	–	1	3	0	0	0.6	1.000
1981		6	2	.750	3.14	10	10	2	66	50	25	28	0	0	0	0	0	0	0	–	3	10	1	1	1.4	.929
1982		4	6	.400	5.63	22	14	0	78.1	95	29	52	0	1	0	0	0	0	0	–	2	7	1	0	0.5	.900
1983		12	7	.632	4.04	29	28	5	173.2	173	73	94	0	0	0	0	0	0	0	–	11	23	1	2	1.2	.971
1984		12	12	.500	3.99	33	32	8	216.2	211	96	137	5	0	0	0	0	0	0	–	10	32	3	3	1.3	.955
1985		9	11	.450	4.00	39	22	5	157.2	166	48	102	0	2	1	1	0	0	0	–	13	23	3	0	1.0	.923
1986	NY N	18	5	.783	2.57	32	30	7	217.1	185	52	148	2	1	0	0	71	8	0	.113	9	37	1	3	1.5	.979
1987		3	5	.375	3.88	10	7	0	46.1	45	10	21	0	0	0	0	14	1	0	.071	5	6	0	2	1.1	1.000
1988		10	13	.435	2.88	29	29	5	190.1	158	33	133	5	0	0	0	61	10	0	.164	13	36	2	5	1.8	.961
1989		13	11	.542	3.47	31	31	5	192	179	78	95	2	0	0	0	66	7	0	.106	16	36	1	3	1.7	.981
10 yrs.		88	73	.547	3.65	242	210	37	1364.1	1301	458	822	14	4	2	1	212	26	0	.123	83	213	12	19	1.3	.961

LEAGUE CHAMPIONSHIP SERIES

Year	Team	W	L	PCT	ERA	G	GS	CG	IP	H	BB	SO	ShO	W	L	SV	AB	H	HR	BA	PO	A	E	DP	TC/G	FA
1986	NY N	1	0	1.000	2.57	2	2	1	14	15	4	6	0	0	0	0	5	0	0	.000	2	4	0	0	3.0	1.000

Year	Team		W	L	PCT	ERA	G	GS	CG	IP	H	BB	SO	ShO	W	L	SV	AB	H	HR	BA	PO	A	E	DP	TC/G	FA
															Relief Pitching			Batting									

Bob Ojeda *continued*

WORLD SERIES

Year	Team		W	L	PCT	ERA	G	GS	CG	IP	H	BB	SO	ShO	W	L	SV	AB	H	HR	BA	PO	A	E	DP	TC/G	FA
1986	NY	N	1	0	1.000	2.08	2	2	0	13	13	5	9	0	0	0	0	2	0	0	.000	0	2	0	0	1.0	1.000

Frank Okrie

OKRIE, FRANK ANTHONY (Lefty)
Father of Len Okrie.
B. Oct. 28, 1896, Detroit, Mich. D. Oct. 16, 1959, Detroit, Mich.

BL TL 5'11½" 175 lbs.

| 1920 | DET | A | 1 | 2 | .333 | 5.27 | 21 | 1 | 1 | 41 | 44 | 18 | 9 | 0 | 1 | 1 | 0 | 5 | 1 | 0 | .200 | 0 | 41 | 1 | 0 | 2.0 | .976 |

Red Oldham

OLDHAM, JOHN CYRUS
B. July 15, 1893, Zion, Md. D. Jan. 28, 1961, Costa Mesa, Calif.

BB TL 6' 176 lbs.

1914	DET	A	2	4	.333	3.38	9	7	3	45.1	42	8	23	0	0	0	0	15	4	0	.267	1	10	4	0	1.7	.733
1915			3	0	1.000	2.81	17	2	1	57.2	52	17	17	0	2	0	4	14	2	0	.143	0	18	3	0	1.2	.857
1920			8	13	.381	3.85	39	23	11	215.1	248	91	62	1	1	1	2	69	12	0	.174	6	78	4	1	2.3	.955
1921			11	14	.440	4.24	40	28	12	229.1	258	81	67	1	0	5	1	85	19	2	.224	6	66	4	2	1.9	.947
1922			10	13	.435	4.67	43	27	9	212	256	59	72	0	1	3	3	73	19	0	.260	7	57	3	1	1.6	.955
1925	PIT	N	3	2	.600	3.91	11	3	3	53	66	18	10	0	1	1	1	18	6	0	.333	1	15	1	1	1.5	.941
1926			2	2	.500	5.62	17	2	0	41.2	56	18	16	0	2	1	2	9	2	0	.222	3	9	1	1	0.8	.923
7 yrs.			39	48	.448	4.15	176	93	39	854.1	978	292	267	2	7	10	12	283	64	2	.226	24	253	20	6	1.7	.933

WORLD SERIES

| 1925 | PIT | N | 0 | 0 | — | 0.00 | 1 | 0 | 0 | 1 | 0 | 0 | 2 | 0 | 0 | 0 | 1 | 0 | 0 | 0 | — | 0 | 0 | 0 | 0 | 0.0 | — |

Steve Olin

OLIN, STEVEN ROBERT
B. Oct. 4, 1965, Portland, Ore.

BR TR 6'3" 185 lbs.

| 1989 | CLE | A | 1 | 4 | .200 | 3.75 | 25 | 0 | 0 | 36 | 35 | 14 | 24 | 0 | 1 | 4 | 1 | 0 | 0 | 0 | — | 2 | 5 | 0 | 0 | 0.3 | 1.000 |

Dick Oliver

Playing record listed under Dick Barrett

Francisco Oliveras

OLIVERAS, FRANCISCO JAVIER
Born Francisco Javier Oliveras y Noa.
B. Jan. 31, 1963, Santurce, Puerto Rico

BR TR 5'10" 170 lbs.

| 1989 | MIN | A | 3 | 4 | .429 | 4.53 | 12 | 8 | 1 | 55.2 | 64 | 15 | 24 | 0 | 0 | 1 | 0 | 0 | 0 | 0 | — | 0 | 6 | 1 | 2 | 0.6 | .857 |

Chi Chi Olivo

OLIVO, FEDERICO EMILIO
Born Federico Emilio Olivo y Maldonado. Brother of Diomedes Olivo.
B. Mar. 18, 1928, Guayubin, Dominican Republic
D. Feb. 3, 1977, Guayubin, Dominican Republic

BR TR 6'2" 215 lbs.

1961	MIL	N	0	0	—	18.00	3	0	0	2	3	5	1	0	0	0	0	0	0	0	—	0	0	0	0	0.0	—
1964			2	1	.667	3.75	38	0	0	60	55	21	45	0	2	1	5	4	1	0	.250	3	13	0	0	0.4	1.000
1965			0	1	.000	1.38	8	0	0	13	12	5	11	0	0	1	0	0	0	0	—	0	1	0	0	0.1	1.000
1966	ATL	N	5	4	.556	4.23	47	0	0	66	59	19	41	0	5	4	7	9	1	0	.111	0	9	0	0	0.2	1.000
4 yrs.			7	6	.538	3.96	96	0	0	141	129	50	98	0	7	6	12	13	2	0	.154	3	23	0	0	0.3	1.000

Diomedes Olivo

OLIVO, DIOMEDES ANTONIO
Born Diomedes Antonio Olivo y Maldonado. Brother of Chi Chi Olivo.
B. Jan. 22, 1919, Guayubin, Dominican Republic D. Feb. 15, 1977, Santo Domingo, Dominican Republic

BL TL 6'1" 195 lbs.

1960	PIT	N	0	0	—	2.79	4	0	0	9.2	8	5	10	0	0	0	0	1	0	0	.000	0	1	0	0	0.3	1.000
1962			5	1	.833	2.77	62	1	0	84.1	88	25	66	0	5	1	7	16	3	0	.188	6	10	1	0	0.3	.941
1963	STL	N	0	5	.000	5.40	19	0	0	13.1	16	9	9	0	0	5	0	0	0	0	—	1	4	0	0	0.3	1.000
3 yrs.			5	6	.455	3.10	85	1	0	107.1	112	39	85	0	5	6	7	17	3	0	.176	7	15	1	0	0.3	.957

Jim Ollom

OLLOM, JAMES DONALD
B. July 8, 1945, Snohomish, Wash.

BL TR 6'4" 210 lbs.
BR 1967

1966	MIN	A	0	0	—	3.60	3	1	0	10	6	1	11	0	0	0	0	2	0	0	.000	0	1	0	0	0.3	1.000
1967			0	1	.000	5.40	21	2	0	35	33	11	17	0	0	0	0	5	1	0	.200	1	6	1	0	0.4	.875
2 yrs.			0	1	.000	5.00	24	3	0	45	39	12	28	0	0	0	0	7	1	0	.143	1	7	1	0	0.4	.889

Fred Olmstead

OLMSTEAD, FREDERIC WILLIAM
B. July 3, 1881, Grand Rapids, Mich. D. Oct. 22, 1936, Muskogee, Okla.

BR TR 5'11" 170 lbs.

1908	CHI	A	0	0	—	13.50	1	0	0	2	6	1	1	0	0	0	0	0	0	0	.000	0	0	0	0	0.0	—
1909			3	2	.600	1.81	8	6	5	54.2	52	12	21	0	0	0	0	21	2	0	.095	1	17	0	0	2.3	1.000
1910			10	12	.455	1.95	32	20	14	184.1	174	50	68	4	2	1	0	65	10	0	.154	8	66	6	2	2.5	.925
1911			6	6	.500	4.21	25	11	7	117.2	146	30	45	1	3	0	2	37	7	0	.189	7	29	2	0	1.5	.947
4 yrs.			19	20	.487	2.74	66	37	26	358.2	378	93	135	5	5	1	2	124	19	0	.153	16	112	8	2	2.1	.941

Al Olmsted

OLMSTED, ALAN RAY
B. Mar. 18, 1957, St. Louis, Mo.

BR TL 6'2" 195 lbs.

| 1980 | STL | N | 1 | 1 | .500 | 2.83 | 5 | 5 | 0 | 35 | 32 | 14 | 14 | 0 | 0 | 0 | 0 | 11 | 2 | 0 | .182 | 2 | 9 | 0 | 0 | 2.2 | 1.000 |

Hank Olmsted

OLMSTED, HENRY THEODORE
B. Jan. 12, 1879, Saginaw Bay, Mich. D. Jan. 6, 1969, Brandenton, Fla.

BR TR 5'8½" 147 lbs.

| 1905 | BOS | A | 1 | 2 | .333 | 3.24 | 3 | 3 | 3 | 25 | 18 | 2 | 6 | 0 | 0 | 0 | 0 | 8 | 1 | 0 | .125 | 3 | 5 | 1 | 0 | 3.0 | .889 |

Ole Olsen

OLSEN, ARTHUR
B. Sept. 12, 1894, South Norwalk, Conn. D. Sept. 12, 1980, Norwalk, Conn.

BR TR 5'10" 163 lbs.

| 1922 | DET | A | 7 | 6 | .538 | 4.53 | 37 | 15 | 5 | 137 | 147 | 40 | 52 | 0 | 1 | 3 | 3 | 39 | 7 | 0 | .179 | 8 | 36 | 1 | 2 | 1.2 | .978 |

Year	Team	W	L	PCT	ERA	G	GS	CG	IP	H	BB	SO	ShO	Relief Pitching			Batting				PO	A	E	DP	TC/G	FA
														W	L	SV	AB	H	HR	BA						

Ole Olsen *continued*

| 1923 | | 1 | 1 | .500 | 6.31 | 17 | 2 | 1 | 41.1 | 42 | 17 | 12 | 0 | 0 | 0 | 0 | 8 | 1 | 0 | .125 | 1 | 6 | 2 | 0 | 0.5 | .778 |
| 2 yrs. | | 8 | 7 | .533 | 4.95 | 54 | 17 | 6 | 178.1 | 189 | 57 | 64 | 0 | 1 | 3 | 3 | 47 | 8 | 0 | .170 | 9 | 42 | 3 | 2 | 1.0 | .944 |

Vern Olsen

OLSEN, VERN JARL
B. Mar. 16, 1918, Hillsboro, Ore. D. July 13, 1989, Maywood, Ill. BR TL 6'½" 175 lbs.

1939	CHI N	1	0	1.000	0.00	4	0	0	7.2	2	7	3	0	1	0	0	1	0	0	.000	0	1	0	0	0.3	1.000
1940		13	9	.591	2.97	34	20	9	172.2	172	62	71	4	2	1	0	57	15	0	.263	9	53	0	1	1.8	1.000
1941		10	8	.556	3.15	37	23	10	185.2	202	59	73	2	0	0	1	63	15	1	.238	9	48	2	2	1.6	.966
1942		6	9	.400	4.49	32	17	4	140.1	161	55	46	1	0	2	1	48	9	0	.188	8	37	0	1	1.4	1.000
1946		0	0		2.79	5	0	0	9.2	10	9	8	0	0	0	0	0	0	0	–	0	2	0	0	0.4	1.000
5 yrs.		30	26	.536	3.40	112	60	23	516	547	192	201	7	3	3	2	169	39	1	.231	26	141	2	4	1.5	.988

Gregg Olson

OLSON, GREGGORY WILLIAM
B. Oct. 11, 1966, Scribner, Neb. BR TR 6'4" 210 lbs.

1988	BAL A	1	1	.500	3.27	10	0	0	11	10	10	9	0	1	0	0	0	0	0	–	1	2	0	0	0.3	1.000
1989		5	2	.714	1.69	64	0	0	85	57	46	90	0	5	2	27	0	0	0	–	5	12	1	0	0.3	.944
2 yrs.		6	3	.667	1.88	74	0	0	96	67	56	99	0	6	3	27	0	0	0	–	6	14	1	0	0.3	.952

Ted Olson

OLSON, THEODORE OTTO
B. Aug. 27, 1912, Quincy, Mass. D. Dec. 9, 1980, Weymouth, Mass. BR TR 6'2½" 185 lbs.

1936	BOS A	1	1	.500	7.36	5	3	1	18.1	24	8	5	0	0	0	0	7	1	0	.143	1	4	0	0	1.0	1.000
1937		0	0		7.24	11	0	0	32.1	42	15	11	0	0	0	0	10	3	0	.300	3	11	2	0	1.5	.875
1938		0	0		6.43	2	0	0	7	9	2	2	0	0	0	0	1	0	0	.000	0	1	0	0	0.5	1.000
3 yrs.		1	1	.500	7.18	18	3	1	57.2	75	25	18	0	0	0	0	18	4	0	.222	4	16	2	0	1.2	.909

Ed Olwine

OLWINE, EDWARD R.
B. May 28, 1958, Greenville, Ohio BR TL 6'2" 165 lbs.

1986	ATL N	0	0		3.40	37	0	0	47.2	35	17	37	0	0	0	1	3	1	0	.333	3	5	0	0	0.2	1.000
1987		0	1	.000	5.01	27	0	0	23.1	25	8	12	0	0	1	1	0	0	0	–	0	3	1	0	0.1	.750
1988		0	0		6.75	16	0	0	18.2	22	4	5	0	0	0	1	0	0	0	–	1	1	0	0	0.1	1.000
3 yrs.		0	1	.000	4.52	80	0	0	89.2	82	29	54	0	0	1	3	3	1	0	.333	4	9	1	0	0.2	.929

Randy O'Neal

O'NEAL, RANDALL JEFFREY
B. Aug. 30, 1960, Ashland, Ky. BR TR 6'2" 195 lbs.

1984	DET A	2	1	.667	3.38	4	3	0	18.2	16	6	12	0	0	0	0	0	0	0	–	2	1	0	0	1.0	.750
1985		5	5	.500	3.24	28	12	1	94.1	82	36	52	0	0	0	1	0	0	0	–	9	17	2	1	1.0	.929
1986		3	7	.300	4.33	37	11	1	122.2	121	44	68	0	0	3	2	0	0	0	–	15	19	2	0	1.0	.944
1987	2 teams				ATL N	(16G 4–2)			STL N	(1G 0–0)																
"	total	4	2	.667	5.32	17	11	0	66	81	26	37	0	0	0	0	20	3	0	.150	4	17	0	1	1.2	1.000
1988	STL N	2	3	.400	4.58	10	8	0	53	57	10	20	0	0	1	0	19	0	0	.000	3	14	0	1	1.7	1.000
1989	PHI N	0	1	.000	6.23	20	1	0	39	46	9	29	0	0	1	0	5	0	0	.000	2	9	1	0	0.6	.917
6 yrs.		16	19	.457	4.41	116	46	2	393.2	403	131	218	0	0	5	3	44	3	0	.068	35	77	6	3	1.0	.949

Skinny O'Neal

O'NEAL, ORAN HERBERT
B. May 2, 1899, Gatewood, Mo. D. June 2, 1981, Springfield, Mo. BR TR 5'11" 160 lbs.

1925	PHI N	0	0		9.30	11	1	0	20.1	35	12	6	0	0	0	0	6	1	0	.167	0	3	0	0	0.4	1.000
1927		0	0		9.00	2	0	0	5	9	2	2	0	0	0	0	1	0	0	.000	1	4	0	0	2.0	1.000
2 yrs.		0	0		9.24	13	1	0	25.1	44	14	8	0	0	0	0	7	1	0	.143	1	7	0	0	0.6	1.000

Ed O'Neill

O'NEILL, EDWARD J.
B. Mar. 11, 1859, Fall River, Mass. D. Sept. 30, 1892, Fall River, Mass. TR 5'11" 180 lbs.

| 1890 | 2 teams | | | | TOL AA | (2G 0–1) | | | PHI AA | (6G 0–6) | | | | | | | | | | | | | | | | |
| " | total | 0 | 7 | .000 | 9.26 | 8 | 8 | 8 | 68 | 111 | 45 | 19 | 0 | 0 | 0 | 0 | 40 | 5 | 0 | .125 | 3 | 18 | 2 | 0 | 2.9 | .913 |

Emmett O'Neill

O'NEILL, ROBERT EMMETT (Pinky)
B. Jan. 13, 1918, San Mateo, Calif. BR TR 6'3" 185 lbs.

1943	BOS A	1	4	.200	4.53	11	5	1	57.2	56	46	20	0	1	0	0	16	3	0	.188	3	13	0	0	1.5	1.000
1944		6	11	.353	4.63	28	22	8	151.2	154	89	68	1	0	0	0	55	10	0	.182	3	19	1	0	0.8	.957
1945		8	11	.421	5.15	24	22	10	141.2	134	117	55	1	0	0	0	50	9	1	.180	5	31	3	3	1.6	.923
1946	2 teams				CHI N	(1G 0–0)			CHI A	(2G 0–0)																
"	total	0	0		0.00	3	0	0	4.2	4	8	1	0	0	0	0	1	0	0	.000	0	1	1	1	0.7	.500
4 yrs.		15	26	.366	4.76	66	49	19	355.2	348	260	144	2	1	0	0	122	22	1	.180	11	64	5	4	1.2	.938

Harry O'Neill

O'NEILL, JOSEPH HENRY
B. Feb. 20, 1897, Ridgetown, Ont., Canada D. Sept. 5, 1969, Ridgetown, Ont., Canada BR TR 6' 180 lbs.

1922	PHI A	0	0		3.00	1	0	0	3	2	1	0	0	0	0	0	0	0	0	.000	0	2	0	0	2.0	1.000
1923		0	0			3	0	0	2	1	3	2	0	0	0	0	0	0	0	–	0	0	0	0	0.0	–
2 yrs.		0	0		1.80	4	0	0	5	3	4	2	0	0	0	0	1	0	0	.000	0	2	0	0	0.5	1.000

Mike O'Neill

O'NEILL, MICHAEL JOYCE
Played as Mike Joyce in 1901. Brother of Jim O'Neill.
Brother of Jack O'Neill. Brother of Steve O'Neill.
B. Sept. 7, 1877, Galway, Ireland D. Aug. 12, 1959, Scranton, Pa. BR TR 5'11" 185 lbs.

1901	STL N	2	2	.500	1.32	5	4	4	41	29	10	16	1	0	0	0	15	6	0	.400	1	6	1	0	1.6	.875
1902		18	14	.563	2.93	36	32	29	288.1	297	66	105	2	2	0	0	135	43	2	.319	19	73	8	0	2.8	.920
1903		4	13	.235	4.77	19	17	12	115	184	43	39	0	0	0	0	110	25	0	.227	6	39	6	3	2.7	.882
1904		10	14	.417	2.09	25	24	23	220	229	50	68	0	0	0	0	91	21	0	.231	13	68	8	3	3.6	.910
1907	CIN N	0	0		0.00	0	0	0	0	0	0	0	0	0	0	0	29	2	0	.069	0	0	0	0	0.0	–
5 yrs.		34	43	.442	2.87	85	77	68	664.1	739	169	228	4	2	0	0	*				39	186	23	6	2.9	.907

Year	Team		W	L	PCT	ERA	G	GS	CG	IP	H	BB	SO	ShO	Relief Pitching W	L	SV	Batting AB	H	HR	BA	PO	A	E	DP	TC/G	FA

Paul O'Neill

O'NEILL, PAUL ANDREW
B. Feb. 25, 1963, Columbus, Ohio

BL TL 6'4" 200 lbs.

| 1987 | CIN | N | 0 | 0 | – | 13.50 | 1 | 0 | 0 | 2 | 2 | 4 | 2 | 0 | 0 | 0 | 0 | * | | | | 0 | 0 | 0 | 0 | 0.0 | – |

Tip O'Neill

O'NEILL, JAMES EDWARD
B. May 25, 1858, Woodstock, Ont., Canada D. Dec. 31, 1915, Montreal Que., Canada

BR TR 6'1½" 167 lbs.

1883	NY	N	5	12	.294	4.07	19	19	15	148	182	64	55	0	0	0	0	76	15	0	.197	10	23	3	0	1.9	.917
1884	STL	AA	11	4	.733	2.68	17	14	14	141	125	51	36	0	1	0	0	297	82	3	.276	6	31	5	0	2.5	.881
2 yrs.			16	16	.500	3.39	36	33	29	289	307	115	91	0	1	0	0	*				16	54	8	0	2.2	.897

Steve Ontiveros

ONTIVEROS, STEVEN
B. Mar. 5, 1961, Tularosa, N. M.

BR TR 6' 180 lbs.

1985	OAK	A	1	3	.250	1.93	39	0	0	74.2	45	19	36	0	1	3	8	0	0	0	–	7	14	1	1	0.6	.955
1986			2	2	.500	4.71	46	0	0	72.2	72	25	54	0	2	2	10	0	0	0	–	2	10	0	1	0.3	1.000
1987			10	8	.556	4.00	35	22	2	150.2	141	50	97	1	1	2	1	0	0	0	–	14	29	1	0	1.3	.977
1988			3	4	.429	4.61	10	10	0	54.2	57	21	30	0	0	0	0	0	0	0	–	6	12	0	0	1.8	1.000
1989	PHI	N	2	1	.667	3.82	6	5	0	30.2	34	15	12	0	0	0	0	12	1	0	.083	4	9	0	2	2.2	1.000
5 yrs.			18	18	.500	3.80	136	37	2	383.1	349	130	229	1	4	7	19	12	1	0	.083	33	74	2	4	0.8	.982

Jose Oquendo

OQUENDO, JOSE MANUEL
Born Jose Manuel Oquendo y Contreras.
B. July 4, 1963, Rio Peidras, Puerto Rico

BB TR 5'10" 160 lbs.
BR 1984

1987	STL	N	0	0	–	27.00	1	0	0	1	4	1	0	0	0	0	0	248	71	1	.286	0	0	0	0	0.0	–
1988			0	1	.000	4.50	1	0	0	4	4	6	1	0	0	0	1	451	125	7	.277	0	0	0	0	0.0	–
2 yrs.			0	1	.000	9.00	2	0	0	5	8	7	1	0	0	0	1	*				0	0	0	0	0.0	–

Don O'Riley

O'RILEY, DONALD LEE
B. Mar. 12, 1945, Topeka, Kans.

BR TR 6'3" 205 lbs.

1969	KC	A	1	1	.500	6.94	18	0	0	23.1	32	15	10	0	1	1	1	3	0	0	.000	3	1	0	0	0.2	1.000
1970			0	0	–	5.48	9	2	0	23	26	9	13	0	0	0	0	3	0	0	.000	2	1	0	0	0.3	1.000
2 yrs.			1	1	.500	6.22	27	2	0	46.1	58	24	23	0	1	1	1	6	0	0	.000	5	2	0	0	0.2	1.000

Jesse Orosco

OROSCO, JESSE RUSSELL
B. Apr. 21, 1957, Santa Barbara, Calif.

BR TL 6'2" 174 lbs.

1979	NY	N	1	2	.333	4.89	18	2	0	35	33	22	22	0	1	2	0	6	0	0	.000	2	9	0	1	0.6	1.000
1981			0	1	.000	1.59	8	0	0	17	13	6	18	0	0	1	1	2	0	0	.000	1	2	0	0	0.4	1.000
1982			4	10	.286	2.72	54	2	0	109.1	92	40	89	0	4	8	4	14	2	0	.143	4	16	0	1	0.4	1.000
1983			13	7	.650	1.47	62	0	0	110	76	38	84	0	13	7	17	12	4	0	.333	5	19	0	0	0.4	1.000
1984			10	6	.625	2.59	60	0	0	87	58	34	85	0	10	6	31	4	1	0	.250	2	11	1	1	0.2	.929
1985			8	6	.571	2.73	54	0	0	79	66	34	68	0	8	6	17	7	3	0	.429	3	8	1	2	0.2	.917
1986			8	6	.571	2.33	58	0	0	81	64	35	62	0	8	6	21	3	0	0	.000	4	8	0	0	0.2	1.000
1987			3	9	.250	4.44	58	0	0	77	78	31	78	0	3	9	16	8	0	0	.000	4	9	0	1	0.2	1.000
1988	LA	N	3	2	.600	2.72	55	0	0	53	41	30	43	0	3	2	9	2	0	0	.000	1	10	0	1	0.2	1.000
1989	CLE	A	3	4	.429	2.08	69	0	0	78	54	26	79	0	3	4	3	0	0	0	–	6	13	0	1	0.3	1.000
10 yrs.			53	53	.500	2.66	496	4	0	726.1	575	296	628	0	53	51	119	58	10	0	.172	32	105	2	8	0.3	.986

LEAGUE CHAMPIONSHIP SERIES

1986	NY	N	3	0	1.000	3.38	4	0	0	8	5	2	10	0	3	0	0	0	0	0	–	1	1	0	0	0.5	1.000
1988	LA	N	0	0	–	7.71	4	0	0	2.1	4	3	0	0	0	0	0	0	0	0	–	1	0	0	0	0.3	1.000
2 yrs.			3	0	1.000	4.35	8	0	0	10.1	9	5	10	0	3	0	0	0	0	0	–	2	1	0	0	0.4	1.000

WORLD SERIES

| 1986 | NY | N | 0 | 0 | – | 0.00 | 4 | 0 | 0 | 5.2 | 2 | 0 | 6 | 0 | 0 | 0 | 2 | 1 | 1 | 0 | 1.000 | 0 | 0 | 0 | 0 | 0.0 | – |

Jim O'Rourke

O'ROURKE, JAMES HENRY (Orator Jim)
Brother of John O'Rourke.
B. Sept. 1, 1850, Bridgeport, Conn.   D. Jan. 8, 1919, Bridgeport, Conn.
Manager 1881-84, 1893.
Hall of Fame 1945.

BR TR 5'8" 185 lbs.

1883	BUF	N	0	0	–	6.43	2	0	0	7	10	1	1	0	0	0	1	436	143	1	.328	0	0	0	0	0.0	–
1884			0	1	.000	2.84	4	0	0	12.2	7	1	3	0	0	1	1	467	162	5	.347	0	2	0	0	0.5	1.000
2 yrs.			0	1	.000	4.12	6	0	0	19.2	17	2	4	0	0	1	2	*				0	2	0	0	0.3	1.000

Mike O'Rourke

O'ROURKE, MICHAEL J
Deceased.

| 1890 | BAL | AA | 1 | 2 | .333 | 3.95 | 5 | 5 | 5 | 41 | 45 | 10 | 8 | 0 | 0 | 0 | 0 | 26 | 3 | 0 | .115 | 0 | 12 | 0 | 0 | 2.4 | 1.000 |

Dave Orr

ORR, DAVID L.
B. Sept. 29, 1859, New York, N. Y.   D. June 3, 1915, Brooklyn, N. Y.
Manager 1887.

BL TR 5'11" 250 lbs.

| 1885 | NY | AA | 0 | 0 | – | 7.20 | 3 | 0 | 0 | 10 | 11 | 5 | 1 | 0 | 0 | 0 | 0 | * | | | | 0 | 0 | 0 | 0 | 0.0 | – |

Joe Orrell

ORRELL, FORREST GORDON
B. Oct. 6, 1917, National City, Calif.

BR TR 6'4" 210 lbs.

1943	DET	A	0	0	–	3.72	10	0	0	19.1	18	11	2	0	0	0	0	4	1	0	.250	2	3	0	0	0.5	1.000
1944			2	1	.667	2.42	10	2	0	22.1	26	11	10	0	1	0	0	4	1	0	.250	1	8	0	0	0.9	1.000
1945			2	3	.400	3.00	12	5	1	48	46	24	14	0	1	0	1	15	2	0	.133	4	8	1	0	1.1	.923
3 yrs.			4	4	.500	3.01	32	7	1	89.2	90	46	26	0	1	1	1	23	4	0	.174	7	19	1	0	0.8	.963

Year	Team		W	L	PCT	ERA	G	GS	CG	IP	H	BB	SO	ShO	W	L	SV	AB	H	HR	BA	PO	A	E	DP	TC/G	FA
															Relief Pitching			Batting									

Phil Ortega

ORTEGA, FILOMENO CORONADO (Kemo)
B. Oct. 7, 1939, Gilbert, Ariz.
BR TR 6'2" 170 lbs.

Year	Team		W	L	PCT	ERA	G	GS	CG	IP	H	BB	SO	ShO	W	L	SV	AB	H	HR	BA	PO	A	E	DP	TC/G	FA
1960	LA	N	0	0	–	17.05	3	1	0	6.1	12	5	4	0	0	0	0	1	0	0	.000	0	1	0	0	0.3	1.000
1961			0	2	.000	5.54	4	2	1	13	10	2	15	0	0	0	0	4	1	0	.250	0	1	0	0	0.3	1.000
1962			0	2	.000	6.88	24	3	0	53.2	60	39	30	0	0	0	1	7	0	0	.000	2	7	1	0	0.4	.900
1963			0	0	–	18.00	1	0	0	1	2	0	1	0	0	0	0	0	0	0	–	0	0	0	0	0.0	–
1964			7	9	.438	4.00	34	25	4	157.1	149	56	107	3	1	0	1	44	6	0	.136	6	18	2	1	0.8	.923
1965	WAS	A	12	15	.444	5.11	35	29	4	179.2	176	97	88	2	2	0	0	53	11	0	.208	11	26	1	1	1.1	.974
1966			12	12	.500	3.92	33	31	5	197.1	158	53	121	1	1	0	0	54	3	0	.056	11	28	3	1	1.3	.929
1967			10	10	.500	3.03	34	34	5	219.2	189	57	122	2	0	0	0	66	4	0	.061	13	33	1	2	1.4	.979
1968			5	12	.294	4.98	31	16	1	115.2	115	62	57	1	1	3	0	24	4	0	.167	4	20	4	3	0.9	.857
1969	CAL	A	0	0	–	10.13	5	0	0	8	13	7	4	0	0	0	0	0	0	0	–	1	1	0	0	0.4	1.000
10 yrs.			46	62	.426	4.43	204	141	20	951.2	884	378	549	9	5	3	2	253	29	0	.115	48	135	12	9	1.0	.938

Al Orth

ORTH, ALBERT LEWIS (The Curveless Wonder)
B. Sept. 5, 1872, Tipton, Ind. D. Oct. 8, 1948, Lynchburg, Va.
BL TR 6' 200 lbs.

Year	Team		W	L	PCT	ERA	G	GS	CG	IP	H	BB	SO	ShO	W	L	SV	AB	H	HR	BA	PO	A	E	DP	TC/G	FA
1895	PHI	N	8	1	.889	3.89	11	10	9	88	103	22	25	0	0	0	1	45	16	1	.356	2	14	3	0	1.7	.842
1896			15	10	.600	4.41	25	23	19	196	244	46	23	0	2	0	0	82	21	1	.256	10	54	7	2	2.8	.901
1897			14	19	.424	4.62	36	34	29	282.1	349	82	64	2	0	1	0	152	50	1	.329	9	69	6	1	2.3	.929
1898			15	13	.536	3.02	32	28	25	250	290	53	52	1	0	1	0	123	36	1	.293	8	62	3	1	2.3	.959
1899			14	3	.824	2.49	21	15	13	144.2	149	19	35	3	3	0	1	62	13	1	.210	4	19	6	0	1.4	.793
1900			12	13	.480	3.78	33	30	24	262	302	60	68	1	1	1	1	129	40	1	.310	15	68	5	3	2.7	.943
1901			20	12	.625	2.27	35	33	30	281.2	250	32	92	6	1	1	0	128	36	1	.281	21	83	6	2	3.1	.945
1902	WAS	A	19	18	.514	3.97	38	37	36	324	332	40	76	1	0	0	0	175	38	2	.217	25	95	10	3	3.4	.923
1903			10	22	.313	4.34	36	32	30	279.2	326	62	88	2	0	0	2	162	49	0	.302	17	86	9	0	3.1	.920
1904	2 teams		WAS A (10G 3–4)						NY A	(20G 11–6)																		
"	total		14	10	.583	3.41	30	25	18	211.1	210	34	70	1	0	0	0	166	41	0	.247	20	73	3	1	3.2	.969
1905	NY	A	18	16	.529	2.86	40	37	26	305.1	273	61	121	6	1	1	0	131	24	1	.183	13	96	7	1	2.9	.940
1906			27	17	.614	2.34	45	39	36	338.2	317	66	133	3	5	0	0	135	37	1	.274	13	101	8	1	2.7	.934
1907			14	21	.400	2.61	36	33	21	248.2	244	53	78	2	1	2	0	105	34	1	.324	7	95	8	1	3.1	.927
1908			2	13	.133	3.42	21	17	8	139.1	134	30	22	1	0	1	0	69	20	0	.290	6	42	1	2	2.3	.980
1909			0	0	–	12.00	1	1	0	3	6	1	1	0	0	0	0	34	9	0	.265	0	0	0	0	0.0	–
15 yrs.			202	188	.518	3.37	440	394	324	3354.2	3564	661	948	31	14	9	5	*				170	957	82	18	2.7	.932

Baby Ortiz

ORTIZ, OLIVERIO
Born Oliverio Ortiz y Nunez. Brother of Roberto Ortiz.
B. Dec. 5, 1919, Camaguey, Cuba D. Mar. 27, 1984, Central Senado, Cuba
BR TR 6' 190 lbs.

Year	Team		W	L	PCT	ERA	G	GS	CG	IP	H	BB	SO	ShO	W	L	SV	AB	H	HR	BA	PO	A	E	DP	TC/G	FA
1944	WAS	A	0	2	.000	6.23	2	2	1	13	13	6	4	0	0	0	0	6	1	0	.167	0	0	0	0	0.0	–

Ossie Orwoll

ORWOLL, OSWALD CHRISTIAN
B. Nov. 17, 1900, Portland, Ore. D. May 8, 1967, Decorah, Iowa
BL TL 6' 174 lbs.

Year	Team		W	L	PCT	ERA	G	GS	CG	IP	H	BB	SO	ShO	W	L	SV	AB	H	HR	BA	PO	A	E	DP	TC/G	FA
1928	PHI	A	6	5	.545	4.58	27	8	3	106	110	50	53	0	3	0	2	170	52	0	.306	6	20	1	0	1.0	.963
1929			0	2	.000	4.80	12	0	0	30	32	6	12	0	0	2	1	51	13	0	.255	0	6	0	1	0.5	1.000
2 yrs.			6	7	.462	4.63	39	8	3	136	142	56	65	0	3	2	3	*				6	26	1	1	0.8	.970

Bob Osborn

OSBORN, JOHN BODE
B. Apr. 17, 1903, San Diego, Tex. D. Apr. 19, 1960, Paris, Tex.
BR TR 6'1" 175 lbs.

Year	Team		W	L	PCT	ERA	G	GS	CG	IP	H	BB	SO	ShO	W	L	SV	AB	H	HR	BA	PO	A	E	DP	TC/G	FA
1925	CHI	N	0	0	–	0.00	1	0	0	2	6	0	0	0	0	0	0	0	0	0	–	0	1	0	0	1.0	1.000
1926			6	5	.545	3.63	31	15	6	136.1	157	58	43	0	2	0	1	41	6	0	.146	9	39	1	4	1.6	.980
1927			5	5	.500	4.18	24	12	2	107.2	125	48	45	0	1	1	0	39	8	0	.205	8	19	3	1	1.3	.900
1929			0	0	–	3.00	3	1	0	9	8	2	1	0	0	0	0	4	1	0	.250	0	1	0	0	0.3	1.000
1930			10	6	.625	4.97	35	13	3	126.2	147	53	42	0	5	3	1	42	4	0	.095	10	34	1	2	1.3	.978
1931	PIT	N	6	1	.857	5.01	27	2	0	64.2	85	20	9	0	6	1	0	18	3	0	.167	2	12	1	0	0.6	.933
6 yrs.			27	17	.614	4.32	121	43	11	446.1	528	181	140	0	14	5	2	144	22	0	.153	29	106	6	7	1.0	.957

Danny Osborn

OSBORN, DANNY LEON
B. June 19, 1946, Springfield, Mo.
BR TR 6'2" 195 lbs.

Year	Team		W	L	PCT	ERA	G	GS	CG	IP	H	BB	SO	ShO	W	L	SV	AB	H	HR	BA	PO	A	E	DP	TC/G	FA
1975	CHI	A	3	0	1.000	4.50	24	0	0	58	57	37	38	0	3	0	0	0	0	0	–	3	5	1	0	0.4	.889

Fred Osborne

OSBORNE, FREDERICK W.
B. May, 1865, Canada Deceased.
TL

Year	Team		W	L	PCT	ERA	G	GS	CG	IP	H	BB	SO	ShO	W	L	SV	AB	H	HR	BA	PO	A	E	DP	TC/G	FA
1890	PIT	N	0	5	.000	8.38	8	5	5	58	82	45	14	0	0	0	0	*				3	11	3	0	2.1	.824

Tiny Osborne

OSBORNE, EARNEST PRESTON
Father of Bobo Osborne.
B. Apr. 9, 1893, Porterdale, Ga. D. Jan. 5, 1969, Atlanta, Ga.
BL TR 6'4½" 215 lbs.

Year	Team		W	L	PCT	ERA	G	GS	CG	IP	H	BB	SO	ShO	W	L	SV	AB	H	HR	BA	PO	A	E	DP	TC/G	FA
1922	CHI	N	9	5	.643	4.50	41	14	7	184	183	95	81	1	2	1	3	67	9	0	.134	3	26	0	0	0.7	1.000
1923			8	15	.348	4.56	37	25	8	179.2	174	89	69	1	1	3	1	60	12	0	.200	3	39	2	0	1.2	.955
1924	2 teams		CHI N	(2G 0–0)					BKN N	(21G 6–5)																		
"	total		6	5	.545	5.03	23	13	6	107.1	126	56	54	0	2	1	1	36	9	0	.250	2	21	3	0	1.1	.885
1925	BKN	N	8	15	.348	4.94	41	22	10	175	210	75	59	0	2	4	1	57	14	0	.246	3	34	1	1	0.9	.974
4 yrs.			31	40	.437	4.72	142	74	31	646	693	315	263	2	6	8	6	220	44	0	.200	11	120	6	2	1.0	.956

Wayne Osborne

OSBORNE, WAYNE HAROLD (Ossie)
B. Oct. 11, 1912, Watsonville, Calif. D. Mar. 13, 1987, Vancouver, Wash.
BL TR 6'2½" 172 lbs.

Year	Team		W	L	PCT	ERA	G	GS	CG	IP	H	BB	SO	ShO	W	L	SV	AB	H	HR	BA	PO	A	E	DP	TC/G	FA
1935	PIT	N	0	0	–	6.75	2	0	0	1.1	1	1	0	0	0	0	0	0	0	0	–	0	1	0	0	0.5	1.000
1936	BOS	N	1	1	.500	5.85	5	3	0	20	31	9	8	0	0	0	0	8	2	0	.250	1	4	0	1	1.0	1.000
2 yrs.			1	1	.500	5.91	7	3	0	21.1	32	9	9	0	0	0	0	8	2	0	.250	1	5	0	1	0.9	1.000

Year	Team	W	L	PCT	ERA	G	GS	CG	IP	H	BB	SO	ShO	Relief Pitching W	L	SV	Batting AB	H	HR	BA	PO	A	E	DP	TC/G	FA

Pat Osburn

OSBURN, LARRY PATRICK
B. May 4, 1949, Murray, Ky.

BL TL 6'4" 195 lbs.

Year	Team	W	L	PCT	ERA	G	GS	CG	IP	H	BB	SO	ShO	W	L	SV	AB	H	HR	BA	PO	A	E	DP	TC/G	FA
1974	CIN N	0	0	–	8.00	6	0	0	9	11	4	4	0	0	0	0	2	0	0	.000	1	3	0	0	0.7	1.000
1975	MIL A	0	1	.000	6.17	6	1	0	11.2	19	9	1	0	0	0	0	0	0	0	–	2	3	0	0	0.8	1.000
2 yrs.		0	1	.000	6.97	12	1	0	20.2	30	13	5	0	0	0	0	2	0	0	.000	3	6	0	0	0.8	1.000

Charlie Osgood

OSGOOD, CHARLES BENJAMIN
B. Nov. 23, 1926, Somerville, Mass.

BR TR 5'10" 180 lbs.

Year	Team	W	L	PCT	ERA	G	GS	CG	IP	H	BB	SO	ShO	W	L	SV	AB	H	HR	BA	PO	A	E	DP	TC/G	FA
1944	BKN N	0	0	–	3.00	1	0	0	3	2	3	0	0	0	0	0	0	0	0	–	0	0	0	0	0.0	–

Dan Osinski

OSINSKI, DANIEL
B. Nov. 17, 1933, Chicago, Ill.

BR TR 6'1½" 190 lbs.

Year	Team	W	L	PCT	ERA	G	GS	CG	IP	H	BB	SO	ShO	W	L	SV	AB	H	HR	BA	PO	A	E	DP	TC/G	FA
1962	2 teams					KC A	(4G 0–0)			LA A	(33G 6–4)															
"	total	6	4	.600	3.97	37	0	0	59	53	38	48	0	6	4	0	11	0	0	.000	3	10	1	0	0.4	.929
1963	LA A	8	8	.500	3.28	47	16	4	159.1	145	80	100	1	4	2	0	45	5	0	.111	8	21	3	2	0.7	.906
1964		3	3	.500	3.48	47	4	1	93	87	39	88	0	2	2	2	18	1	0	.056	6	19	1	0	0.6	.962
1965	MIL N	0	3	.000	2.82	61	0	0	83	81	40	54	0	0	3	6	6	1	0	.167	5	12	0	0	0.3	1.000
1966	BOS A	4	3	.571	3.61	44	1	0	67.1	68	28	44	0	4	3	2	6	2	0	.333	4	8	0	0	0.3	1.000
1967		3	1	.750	2.54	34	0	0	63.2	61	14	38	0	3	1	2	9	3	0	.333	3	9	0	1	0.4	1.000
1969	CHI A	5	5	.500	3.56	51	0	0	60.2	56	23	27	0	5	5	2	3	0	0	.000	1	21	0	1	0.4	1.000
1970	HOU N	0	1	.000	9.00	3	0	0	4	5	2	1	0	0	0	0	0	0	0	–	0	0	0	0	0.0	–
8 yrs.		29	28	.509	3.34	324	21	5	590	556	264	400	2	23	21	18	98	12	0	.122	30	100	5	3	0.4	.963

WORLD SERIES

Year	Team	W	L	PCT	ERA	G	GS	CG	IP	H	BB	SO	ShO	W	L	SV	AB	H	HR	BA	PO	A	E	DP	TC/G	FA
1967	BOS A	0	0	–	6.75	2	0	0	1.1	2	0	0	0	0	0	0	0	0	0	–	0	0	0	0	0.0	–

Claude Osteen

OSTEEN, CLAUDE WILSON
B. Aug. 9, 1939, Caney Springs, Tenn.

BL TL 5'11" 160 lbs.

Year	Team	W	L	PCT	ERA	G	GS	CG	IP	H	BB	SO	ShO	W	L	SV	AB	H	HR	BA	PO	A	E	DP	TC/G	FA
1957	CIN N	0	0	–	2.25	3	0	0	4	4	3	3	0	0	0	0	1	0	0	.000	0	0	0	0	0.0	–
1959		0	0	–	7.04	2	0	0	7.2	11	9	3	0	0	0	0	2	0	0	.000	0	1	0	0	0.5	1.000
1960		0	1	.000	5.03	20	3	0	48.1	53	30	51	0	0	0	0	12	1	0	.083	0	13	1	0	0.7	.929
1961	2 teams					CIN N	(1G 0–0)			WAS A	(3G 1–1)															
"	total	1	1	.500	4.82	4	3	0	18.2	14	9	14	0	0	0	0	7	1	0	.143	0	3	0	1	0.8	1.000
1962	WAS A	8	13	.381	3.65	28	22	7	150.1	140	47	59	2	0	0	1	48	10	0	.208	4	30	0	2	1.2	1.000
1963		9	14	.391	3.35	40	29	8	212.1	222	60	109	2	1	1	0	70	12	0	.171	11	30	3	2	1.1	.932
1964		15	13	.536	3.33	37	36	13	257	256	64	133	0	0	0	0	90	14	1	.156	9	51	0	5	1.6	1.000
1965	LA N	15	15	.500	2.79	40	40	9	287	253	78	162	1	0	0	0	99	12	0	.121	11	82	3	6	2.4	.969
1966		17	14	.548	2.85	39	38	8	240.1	238	65	137	3	0	0	0	76	16	1	.211	10	49	4	0	1.6	.937
1967		17	17	.500	3.22	39	39	14	288.1	298	52	152	5	0	0	0	101	18	2	.178	11	53	2	1	1.7	.970
1968		12	18	.400	3.08	39	36	5	254	267	54	119	3	0	0	0	84	15	0	.179	11	50	1	2	1.6	.984
1969		20	15	.571	2.66	41	41	16	321	293	74	183	7	0	0	0	111	24	1	.216	19	69	3	0	2.2	.967
1970		16	14	.533	3.82	37	37	11	259	280	52	114	4	0	0	0	93	19	1	.204	10	40	1	5	1.4	.980
1971		14	11	.560	3.51	38	38	11	259	262	63	109	4	0	0	0	86	16	0	.186	22	66	1	4	2.3	.989
1972		20	11	.645	2.64	33	33	14	252	232	69	100	4	0	0	0	88	24	1	.273	9	40	1	2	1.5	.980
1973		16	11	.593	3.31	33	33	12	236.2	227	61	86	3	0	0	0	78	12	0	.154	9	53	2	3	1.9	.969
1974	2 teams					HOU N	(23G 9–9)			STL N	(8G 0–2)															
"	total	9	11	.450	3.80	31	23	7	161	184	58	51	2	0	1	0	53	13	0	.245	11	28	2	1	1.3	.951
1975	CHI A	7	16	.304	4.36	37	37	5	204.1	237	92	63	0	0	0	0	0	0	0	–	12	41	2	1	1.5	.964
18 yrs.		196	195	.501	3.30	541	488	140	3461	3471	940	1612	40	1	2	1	1099	207	8	.188	159	699	26	37	1.6	.971

WORLD SERIES

Year	Team	W	L	PCT	ERA	G	GS	CG	IP	H	BB	SO	ShO	W	L	SV	AB	H	HR	BA	PO	A	E	DP	TC/G	FA
1965	LA N	1	1	.500	0.64	2	2	1	14	9	5	4	1	0	0	0	3	1	0	.333	2	3	0	1	2.5	1.000
1966		0	1	.000	1.29	1	1	0	7	3	1	3	0	0	0	0	2	0	0	.000	1	0	0	0	1.0	1.000
2 yrs.		1	2	.333	0.86	3	3	1	21	12	6	7	1	0	0	0	5	1	0	.200	3	3	0	1	2.0	1.000

Darrell Osteen

OSTEEN, MILTON DARRELL
B. Feb. 14, 1943, Oklahoma City, Okla.

BR TR 6'1" 170 lbs.

Year	Team	W	L	PCT	ERA	G	GS	CG	IP	H	BB	SO	ShO	W	L	SV	AB	H	HR	BA	PO	A	E	DP	TC/G	FA
1965	CIN N	0	0	–	0.00	3	0	0	3	2	4	1	0	0	0	0	0	0	0	–	0	1	0	0	0.3	1.000
1966		0	2	.000	12.00	13	0	0	15	26	9	17	0	0	2	1	2	1	0	.500	0	1	0	0	0.1	1.000
1967		0	2	.000	6.28	10	0	0	14.1	10	13	13	0	0	2	2	1	0	0	.000	1	3	0	0	0.4	1.000
1970	OAK A	1	0	1.000	6.00	3	1	0	6	9	3	3	0	0	0	0	2	0	0	.000	0	0	0	0	0.0	–
4 yrs.		1	4	.200	7.98	29	1	0	38.1	47	29	34	0	0	4	3	5	1	0	.200	1	5	0	0	0.2	1.000

Fred Ostendorf

OSTENDORF, FREDERICK K.
B. Aug. 5, 1890, Baltimore, Md. D. Mar. 2, 1965, Kecoughtan, Va.

BL TL 6'½" 169 lbs.

Year	Team	W	L	PCT	ERA	G	GS	CG	IP	H	BB	SO	ShO	W	L	SV	AB	H	HR	BA	PO	A	E	DP	TC/G	FA
1914	IND F	0	0	–	22.50	1	0	0	2	5	2	0	0	0	0	0	0	0	0	.000	0	1	0	0	1.0	1.000

Bill Oster

OSTER, WILLIAM CHARLES
B. Jan. 2, 1933, New York, N. Y.

BL TL 6'3" 198 lbs.

Year	Team	W	L	PCT	ERA	G	GS	CG	IP	H	BB	SO	ShO	W	L	SV	AB	H	HR	BA	PO	A	E	DP	TC/G	FA
1954	PHI A	0	1	.000	6.32	8	1	0	15.2	19	12	5	0	0	0	0	3	1	0	.333	0	3	0	0	0.4	1.000

Fritz Ostermueller

OSTERMUELLER, FREDERICK RAYMOND
B. Sept. 15, 1907, Quincy, Ill. D. Dec. 17, 1957, Quincy, Ill.

BL TL 5'11" 175 lbs.

Year	Team	W	L	PCT	ERA	G	GS	CG	IP	H	BB	SO	ShO	W	L	SV	AB	H	HR	BA	PO	A	E	DP	TC/G	FA
1934	BOS A	10	13	.435	3.49	33	24	10	198.2	200	99	75	0	4	0	3	78	13	0	.167	8	52	2	2	1.9	.968
1935		7	8	.467	3.92	22	19	10	137.2	135	78	41	0	0	0	1	49	14	0	.286	9	27	5	1	1.9	.878
1936		10	16	.385	4.87	43	23	7	181	210	84	90	1	2	4	2	64	15	0	.234	10	42	1	1	1.2	.981
1937		3	7	.300	4.98	25	7	2	86.2	101	44	29	0	1	4	1	33	11	0	.333	9	17	3	0	1.2	.897
1938		13	5	.722	4.58	31	18	10	176.2	199	58	46	1	3	1	2	74	16	0	.216	15	30	4	3	1.6	.918
1939		11	7	.611	4.24	34	20	8	159.1	173	58	61	0	3	0	4	56	9	0	.161	12	22	2	1	1.1	.944
1940		5	9	.357	4.95	31	16	5	143.2	166	70	80	0	2	1	0	54	17	0	.315	2	21	1	0	0.8	.958
1941	STL A	0	3	.000	4.50	15	2	0	46	45	23	20	0	0	3	1	14	3	0	.214	2	10	1	0	0.9	.929
1942		3	1	.750	3.71	10	4	2	43.2	46	17	21	0	0	1	0	16	3	0	.188	2	6	0	0	0.8	1.000

Year	Team		W	L	PCT	ERA	G	GS	CG	IP	H	BB	SO	ShO	W	L	SV	AB	H	HR	BA	PO	A	E	DP	TC/G	FA
															Relief Pitching			**Batting**									

Fritz Ostermueller *continued*

Year	Team		W	L	PCT	ERA	G	GS	CG	IP	H	BB	SO	ShO	W	L	SV	AB	H	HR	BA	PO	A	E	DP	TC/G	FA
1943	2 teams	STL A (11G 0-2)	BKN N	(7G 1-1)																							
"	total		1	3	.250	4.18	18	4	0	56	57	25	19	0	0	1	2	18	2	0	.111	0	12	0	0	0.7	1.000
1944	2 teams	BKN N (10G 2-1)	PIT N	(28G 11-7)																							
"	total		13	8	.619	2.81	38	28	17	246.1	247	77	97	1	0	0	2	93	22	0	.237	9	41	2	2	1.4	.962
1945	PIT	N	5	4	.556	4.57	14	11	4	80.2	74	37	29	1	0	0	0	28	9	0	.321	8	14	1	0	1.6	.957
1946			13	10	.565	2.84	27	25	16	193.1	193	56	57	2	0	0	0	64	21	0	.328	9	33	1	0	1.6	.977
1947			12	10	.545	3.84	26	24	12	183	181	68	66	3	0	0	0	64	12	0	.188	9	25	0	4	1.3	1.000
1948			8	11	.421	4.42	23	22	10	134.1	143	41	43	2	0	0	0	44	8	0	.182	3	21	0	0	1.0	1.000
15 yrs.			114	115	.498	3.99	390	247	113	2067	2170	835	774	11	15	17	15	749	175	0	.234	108	373	23	15	1.3	.954

Joe Ostrowski

OSTROWSKI, JOSEPH PAUL (Professor)
B. Nov. 15, 1916, West Wyoming, Pa.   BL TL 6'   180 lbs.

Year	Team		W	L	PCT	ERA	G	GS	CG	IP	H	BB	SO	ShO	W	L	SV	AB	H	HR	BA	PO	A	E	DP	TC/G	FA
1948	STL	A	4	6	.400	5.97	26	9	3	78.1	108	17	20	0	0	0	3	18	4	0	.222	5	23	0	0	1.1	1.000
1949			8	8	.500	4.79	40	13	4	141	185	27	34	0	2	2	2	37	7	0	.189	8	22	1	0	0.8	.968
1950	2 teams	STL A (9G 2-4)	NY A	(21G 1-1)																							
"	total		3	5	.375	3.65	30	11	3	101	107	22	30	0	1	0	3	27	5	0	.185	4	16	1	0	0.7	.952
1951	NY	A	6	4	.600	3.49	34	3	2	95.1	103	18	30	0	4	4	5	28	3	0	.107	5	14	0	1	0.6	1.000
1952			2	2	.500	5.63	20	1	0	40	56	14	17	0	2	2	2	8	0	0	.000	2	3	0	1	0.3	1.000
5 yrs.			23	25	.479	4.54	150	37	12	455.2	559	98	131	0	10	8	15	118	19	0	.161	24	78	2	4	0.7	.981

WORLD SERIES

Year	Team		W	L	PCT	ERA	G	GS	CG	IP	H	BB	SO	ShO	W	L	SV	AB	H	HR	BA	PO	A	E	DP	TC/G	FA
1951	NY	A	0	0	–	0.00	1	0	0	2	1	0	1	0	0	0	0	0	0	0	–	0	0	0	0	0.0	–

Bill Otey

OTEY, WILLIAM TILFORD (Steamboat Bill)
B. Dec. 16, 1886, Dayton, Ohio D. Apr. 23, 1931, Dayton, Ohio   BL TL 6'2½"   181 lbs.

Year	Team		W	L	PCT	ERA	G	GS	CG	IP	H	BB	SO	ShO	W	L	SV	AB	H	HR	BA	PO	A	E	DP	TC/G	FA
1907	PIT	N	0	1	.000	4.41	3	2	1	16.1	23	4	5	0	0	0	0	4	1	0	.250	0	3	1	0	1.3	.750
1910	WAS	A	0	1	.000	3.38	9	1	1	34.2	40	6	12	0	0	0	0	13	5	0	.385	3	5	1	0	1.0	.889
1911			1	3	.250	6.34	12	2	0	49.2	68	15	16	0	1	2	0	17	1	0	.059	3	19	4	0	2.2	.846
3 yrs.			1	5	.167	5.01	24	5	2	100.2	131	25	33	0	1	2	0	34	7	0	.206	6	27	6	0	1.6	.846

Harry Otis

OTIS, HARRY GEORGE (Cannonball)
B. Oct. 5, 1886, W. New York, N. J. D. Jan. 29, 1976, Trenton, N. J.   BR TL 6'   180 lbs.

Year	Team		W	L	PCT	ERA	G	GS	CG	IP	H	BB	SO	ShO	W	L	SV	AB	H	HR	BA	PO	A	E	DP	TC/G	FA
1909	CLE	A	2	2	.500	1.37	5	3	0	26.1	26	18	6	0	1	0	0	9	1	0	.111	0	9	1	0	2.0	.900

Denny O'Toole

O'TOOLE, DENNIS JOSEPH
Brother of Jim O'Toole.
B. Mar. 13, 1949, Chicago, Ill.   BR TR 6'3"   195 lbs.

Year	Team		W	L	PCT	ERA	G	GS	CG	IP	H	BB	SO	ShO	W	L	SV	AB	H	HR	BA	PO	A	E	DP	TC/G	FA
1969	CHI	A	0	0	–	6.75	2	0	0	4	5	2	4	0	0	0	0	0	0	0	–	0	0	0	0	0.0	–
1970			0	0	–	3.00	3	0	0	3	5	2	3	0	0	0	0	0	0	0	–	0	0	0	0	0.0	–
1971			0	0	–	0.00	1	0	0	2	0	1	2	0	0	0	0	0	0	0	–	0	0	0	0	0.0	–
1972			0	0	–	5.40	3	0	0	5	10	2	5	0	0	0	0	0	0	0	–	0	1	0	0	0.3	1.000
1973			0	0	–	5.63	6	0	0	16	23	3	8	0	0	0	0	0	0	0	–	0	3	0	0	0.5	1.000
5 yrs.			0	0	–	5.10	15	0	0	30	43	10	22	0	0	0	0	0	0	0	–	0	4	0	0	0.3	1.000

Jim O'Toole

O'TOOLE, JAMES JEROME
Brother of Denny O'Toole.
B. Jan. 10, 1937, Chicago, Ill.   BB TL 6'   190 lbs.

Year	Team		W	L	PCT	ERA	G	GS	CG	IP	H	BB	SO	ShO	W	L	SV	AB	H	HR	BA	PO	A	E	DP	TC/G	FA
1958	CIN	N	0	1	.000	1.29	1	1	1	7	4	5	4	0	0	0	0	2	0	0	.000	0	0	0	0	0.0	–
1959			5	8	.385	5.15	28	19	3	129.1	144	73	68	1	0	0	0	37	5	0	.135	5	24	0	2	1.0	1.000
1960			12	12	.500	3.80	34	31	7	196.1	198	66	124	2	0	0	0	66	7	0	.106	8	23	5	1	1.1	.861
1961			19	9	.679	3.10	39	35	11	252.2	229	93	178	3	1	0	0	93	16	0	.172	16	42	2	1	1.5	.967
1962			16	13	.552	3.50	36	34	11	251.2	222	87	170	3	2	0	0	91	10	0	.110	10	33	1	1	1.2	.977
1963			17	14	.548	2.88	33	32	12	234.1	208	57	146	5	0	0	0	74	11	0	.149	14	29	5	1	1.5	.896
1964			17	7	.708	2.66	30	30	9	220	194	51	145	3	0	0	0	70	7	0	.100	12	29	2	1	1.4	.953
1965			3	10	.231	5.92	29	22	2	127.2	154	47	71	0	0	0	1	45	4	0	.089	5	17	2	1	0.8	.917
1966			5	7	.417	3.55	25	24	2	142	139	49	96	1	0	0	0	47	6	0	.128	5	20	1	0	1.0	.962
1967	CHI	A	4	3	.571	2.82	15	10	1	54.1	53	18	37	1	0	0	0	13	1	0	.077	5	6	2	1	0.9	.846
10 yrs.			98	84	.538	3.57	270	238	58	1615.1	1545	546	1039	18	3	0	4	538	67	0	.125	80	223	20	10	1.2	.938

WORLD SERIES

Year	Team		W	L	PCT	ERA	G	GS	CG	IP	H	BB	SO	ShO	W	L	SV	AB	H	HR	BA	PO	A	E	DP	TC/G	FA
1961	CIN	N	0	2	.000	3.00	2	2	0	12	11	7	4	0	0	0	0	3	0	0	.000	1	0	0	0	0.5	1.000

Marty O'Toole

O'TOOLE, MARTIN JAMES
B. Nov. 27, 1888, William Penn, Pa. D. Feb. 18, 1949, Aberdeen, Wash.   BR TR 5'11"   175 lbs.

Year	Team		W	L	PCT	ERA	G	GS	CG	IP	H	BB	SO	ShO	W	L	SV	AB	H	HR	BA	PO	A	E	DP	TC/G	FA
1908	CIN	N	1	0	1.000	2.40	3	2	1	15	15	7	5	0	0	0	0	5	1	0	.200	2	3	0	0	1.7	1.000
1911	PIT	N	3	2	.600	2.37	5	5	3	38	28	20	34	0	0	0	0	14	5	0	.357	4	9	1	0	2.8	.929
1912			15	17	.469	2.71	37	36	17	275.1	237	159	150	6	0	1	0	99	22	0	.222	3	75	3	1	2.2	.963
1913			6	8	.429	3.30	26	15	7	144.2	148	55	58	0	0	2	1	53	7	0	.132	5	36	2	2	1.7	.953
1914	2 teams	PIT N (19G 1-8)	NY N	(10G 1-1)																							
"	total		2	9	.182	4.56	29	14	3	126.1	126	59	49	0	0	2	0	40	8	0	.200	1	28	0	0	1.0	1.000
5 yrs.			27	36	.429	3.21	100	72	31	599.1	554	300	296	6	0	5	1	211	43	0	.204	15	151	6	3	1.7	.965

Jim Otten

OTTEN, JAMES EDWARD
B. July 1, 1951, Lewiston, Mont.   BR TR 6'2"   195 lbs.

Year	Team		W	L	PCT	ERA	G	GS	CG	IP	H	BB	SO	ShO	W	L	SV	AB	H	HR	BA	PO	A	E	DP	TC/G	FA
1974	CHI	A	0	1	.000	5.63	5	1	0	16	22	12	11	0	0	0	0	0	0	0	–	0	2	0	0	0.4	1.000
1975			0	0	–	6.75	2	0	0	5.1	4	7	3	0	0	0	0	0	0	0	–	0	1	0	0	0.5	1.000
1976			0	0	–	4.50	2	0	0	6	9	2	3	0	0	0	0	0	0	0	–	0	0	0	0	0.0	–
1980	STL	N	0	5	.000	5.56	31	4	0	55	71	26	38	0	0	1	0	5	1	0	.200	0	11	1	0	0.4	1.000
1981			1	0	1.000	5.25	24	0	0	36	44	20	20	0	1	0	2	2	0	0	.000	0	3	1	2	0.2	.750
5 yrs.			1	6	.143	5.48	64	5	0	118.1	150	67	75	0	1	1	2	7	1	0	.143	0	17	1	2	0.3	.944

Year	Team		W	L	PCT	ERA	G	GS	CG	IP	H	BB	SO	ShO	Relief Pitching W	L	SV	Batting AB	H	HR	BA	PO	A	E	DP	TC/G	FA

Dave Otto

OTTO, DAVID ALAN
B. Nov. 12, 1964, Chicago, Ill.   BL TL 6'7"   210 lbs.

Year	Team		W	L	PCT	ERA	G	GS	CG	IP	H	BB	SO	ShO	W	L	SV	AB	H	HR	BA	PO	A	E	DP	TC/G	FA
1987	OAK	A	0	0	–	9.00	3	0	0	6	7	1	3	0	0	0	0	0	0	0	–	1	0	0	0	0.3	1.000
1988			0	0	–	1.80	3	2	0	10	9	6	7	0	0	0	0	0	0	0	–	1	1	0	0	0.7	1.000
1989			0	0	–	2.70	1	1	0	6.2	6	2	4	0	0	0	0	0	0	0	–	0	1	0	0	1.0	1.000
3 yrs.			0	0	–	3.97	7	3	0	22.2	22	9	14	0	0	0	0	0	0	0	–	2	2	0	0	0.6	1.000

Orval Overall

OVERALL, ORVAL
B. Feb. 2, 1881, Farmersville, Calif.   D. July 14, 1947, Fresno, Calif.   BB TR 6'2"   214 lbs.

Year	Team		W	L	PCT	ERA	G	GS	CG	IP	H	BB	SO	ShO	W	L	SV	AB	H	HR	BA	PO	A	E	DP	TC/G	FA
1905	CIN	N	17	22	.436	2.86	42	39	32	318	290	147	173	2	1	1	0	117	17	0	.145	10	82	13	2	2.5	.876
1906	2 teams		CIN N	(13G 3–5)			CHI N	(18G 12–3)																			
"	total		15	8	.652	2.74	31	24	19	226.1	193	97	127	2	2	0	1	84	15	0	.179	2	20	3	1	0.8	.880
1907	CHI	N	23	8	.742	1.70	35	29	26	265.1	199	69	139	8	1	2	3	94	20	0	.213	14	76	3	2	2.7	.968
1908			15	11	.577	1.92	37	27	16	225	165	78	167	4	3	0	2	70	9	0	.129	13	51	5	1	1.9	.928
1909			20	11	.645	1.42	38	32	23	285	204	80	205	9	1	0	2	96	22	0	.229	12	69	3	3	2.2	.964
1910			12	6	.667	2.68	23	21	11	144.2	106	54	92	4	0	1	1	41	5	0	.122	5	43	0	0	2.1	1.000
1913			4	5	.444	3.31	11	9	6	68	73	26	30	1	0	0	0	24	6	0	.250	2	24	0	0	2.4	1.000
7 yrs.			106	71	.599	2.24	217	181	133	1532.1	1230	551	933	30	8	4	9	526	94	2	.179	58	365	27	9	2.1	.940
						8th																					

WORLD SERIES

Year	Team		W	L	PCT	ERA	G	GS	CG	IP	H	BB	SO	ShO	W	L	SV	AB	H	HR	BA	PO	A	E	DP	TC/G	FA
1906	CHI	N	0	0	–	1.50	2	0	0	12	10	3	8	0	0	0	0	4	1	0	.250	0	2	0	0	1.0	1.000
1907			1	0	1.000	1.00	2	2	1	18	14	4	11	0	0	0	0	5	1	0	.200	0	6	0	0	3.0	1.000
1908			2	0	1.000	0.98	3	2	2	18.1	7	7	15	1	0	0	0	6	2	0	.333	0	3	0	0	1.0	1.000
1910			0	1	.000	9.00	1	1	0	3	6	1	1	0	0	0	0	1	0	0	.000	0	0	0	0	0.0	–
4 yrs.			3	1	.750	1.58	8	5	3	51.1	37	15	35	1	0	0	0	16	4	0	.250	0	11	0	0	1.4	1.000

Stubby Overmire

OVERMIRE, FRANK
B. May 16, 1919, Moline, Mich.   D. Mar. 3, 1977, Lakeland, Fla.   BR TL 5'7"   170 lbs.

Year	Team		W	L	PCT	ERA	G	GS	CG	IP	H	BB	SO	ShO	W	L	SV	AB	H	HR	BA	PO	A	E	DP	TC/G	FA
1943	DET	A	7	6	.538	3.18	29	18	8	147	135	38	48	3	0	0	1	42	7	0	.167	10	23	0	2	1.1	1.000
1944			11	11	.500	3.07	32	28	11	199.2	214	41	57	3	0	0	1	63	11	0	.175	12	46	1	3	1.8	.983
1945			9	9	.500	3.88	31	22	9	162.1	189	42	36	0	0	0	4	53	10	0	.189	11	33	2	1	1.5	.957
1946			5	7	.417	4.62	24	13	3	97.1	106	29	34	0	1	3	1	33	5	0	.152	5	25	2	0	1.3	.938
1947			11	5	.688	3.77	28	17	7	140.2	142	44	33	3	3	0	0	47	7	0	.149	10	21	1	2	1.1	.969
1948			3	4	.429	5.97	37	4	0	66.1	89	31	14	0	3	3	3	14	1	0	.071	6	16	0	1	0.6	1.000
1949			1	3	.250	9.87	14	1	0	17.1	29	9	3	0	1	2	0	3	1	0	.333	1	5	0	0	0.4	1.000
1950	STL	A	9	12	.429	4.19	31	19	8	161	200	45	39	2	1	2	0	48	8	0	.167	4	24	1	0	0.9	.966
1951	2 teams		STL A	(8G 1–6)		NY A	(15G 1–1)																				
"	total		2	7	.222	4.04	23	11	4	98	111	39	27	0	0	0	0	21	2	0	.095	9	14	3	1	1.1	.885
1952	STL	A	0	3	.000	3.73	17	4	0	41	44	7	10	0	0	0	0	11	2	0	.182	2	10	0	1	0.7	1.000
10 yrs.			58	67	.464	3.96	266	137	50	1130.2	1259	325	301	11	9	12	10	335	54	0	.161	70	217	10	11	1.1	.966

WORLD SERIES

Year	Team		W	L	PCT	ERA	G	GS	CG	IP	H	BB	SO	ShO	W	L	SV	AB	H	HR	BA	PO	A	E	DP	TC/G	FA
1945	DET	A	0	1	.000	3.00	1	1	0	6	4	2	2	0	0	0	0	1	0	0	.000	0	1	0	1	1.0	1.000

Mike Overy

OVERY, HARRY MICHAEL
B. Jan. 27, 1951, Clinton, Ill.   BR TR 6'2"   190 lbs.

Year	Team		W	L	PCT	ERA	G	GS	CG	IP	H	BB	SO	ShO	W	L	SV	AB	H	HR	BA	PO	A	E	DP	TC/G	FA
1976	CAL	A	0	2	.000	6.43	5	0	0	7	6	3	8	0	0	0	2	0	0	0	–	0	2	1	0	0.6	.667

Ernie Ovitz

OVITZ, ERNEST GAYHEART
B. Oct. 7, 1885, Mineral Point, Wis.   D. Sept. 11, 1980, Green Bay, Wis.   BR TR 5'8½"   156 lbs.

Year	Team		W	L	PCT	ERA	G	GS	CG	IP	H	BB	SO	ShO	W	L	SV	AB	H	HR	BA	PO	A	E	DP	TC/G	FA
1911	CHI	N	0	0	–	4.50	1	0	0	2	3	3	0	0	0	0	0	0	0	0	–	0	0	0	0	0.0	–

Bob Owchinko

OWCHINKO, ROBERT DENNIS
B. Jan. 1, 1955, Detroit, Mich.   BL TL 6'2"   190 lbs.

Year	Team		W	L	PCT	ERA	G	GS	CG	IP	H	BB	SO	ShO	W	L	SV	AB	H	HR	BA	PO	A	E	DP	TC/G	FA
1976	SD	N	0	2	.000	16.62	2	2	0	4.1	11	3	4	0	0	0	0	1	0	0	.000	0	1	0	0	0.5	1.000
1977			9	12	.429	4.45	30	28	3	170	191	67	101	2	1	0	0	49	4	0	.082	2	21	0	1	0.8	1.000
1978			10	13	.435	3.56	36	33	4	202	198	78	94	1	0	0	0	63	11	0	.175	6	30	0	3	1.0	1.000
1979			6	12	.333	3.74	42	20	2	149	144	55	66	0	2	5	0	33	4	0	.121	3	24	2	2	0.7	.929
1980	CLE	A	2	9	.182	5.29	29	14	1	114	138	47	66	1	1	0	0	0	0	0	–	3	18	1	0	0.7	.955
1981	OAK	A	4	3	.571	3.23	29	0	0	39	34	19	26	0	4	3	2	0	0	0	–	0	6	1	1	0.2	.857
1982			2	4	.333	5.21	54	0	0	102	111	52	67	0	2	4	3	0	0	0	–	7	7	0	1	0.3	1.000
1983	PIT	N	0	0	∞		1	0	0		2	0	0	0	0	0	0	0	0	0	–	0	0	0	0	0.0	–
1984	CIN	N	3	5	.375	4.12	49	4	0	94	91	39	60	0	2	3	2	12	2	0	.167	4	11	0	0	0.3	1.000
1986	MON	N	1	0	1.000	3.60	3	3	0	15	17	3	6	0	0	0	0	5	1	0	.200	2	0	0	0	0.7	1.000
10 yrs.			37	60	.381	4.29	275	104	10	889.1	937	363	490	4	12	15	7	163	22	0	.135	24	120	4	8	0.5	.973

LEAGUE CHAMPIONSHIP SERIES

Year	Team		W	L	PCT	ERA	G	GS	CG	IP	H	BB	SO	ShO	W	L	SV	AB	H	HR	BA	PO	A	E	DP	TC/G	FA
1981	OAK	A	0	0	–	5.40	1	0	0	1.2	3	0	0	0	0	0	0	0	0	0	–	0	0	0	0	0.0	–

Frank Owen

OWEN, FRANK MALCOLM (Yip)
B. Dec. 23, 1879, Ypsilanti, Mich.   D. Nov. 24, 1942, Dearborn, Mich.   BL TR

Year	Team		W	L	PCT	ERA	G	GS	CG	IP	H	BB	SO	ShO	W	L	SV	AB	H	HR	BA	PO	A	E	DP	TC/G	FA
1901	DET	A	1	3	.250	4.34	8	5	3	56	70	30	17	0	0	0	0	20	1	0	.050	7	24	1	2	4.0	.969
1903	CHI	A	8	12	.400	3.50	26	20	15	167.1	167	44	66	1	1	2	1	57	7	0	.123	11	68	3	4	3.2	.963
1904			21	15	.583	1.94	37	36	34	315	243	61	103	4	0	0	1	107	23	2	.215	21	130	0	8	4.1	1.000
1905			21	13	.618	2.10	42	38	32	334	276	56	125	3	0	0	0	124	18	0	.145	20	120	3	1	3.4	.979
1906			22	13	.629	2.33	42	36	27	293	289	54	66	7	3	1	2	103	14	0	.136	22	110	3	1	3.2	.978
1907			2	3	.400	2.49	11	4	2	47	43	13	15	0	0	0	0	16	4	0	.250	5	16	0	0	1.9	1.000
1908			6	7	.462	3.41	25	14	5	140	142	37	48	1	2	0	1	50	9	0	.180	6	54	4	2	2.6	.938
1909			1	1	.500	4.50	3	2	1	16	19	3	3	0	0	0	0	6	1	0	.167	1	5	0	0	1.7	1.000
8 yrs.			82	67	.550	2.55	194	155	119	1368.1	1249	298	443	16	6	5	4	483	77	2	.159	92	527	14	18	3.3	.978

WORLD SERIES

Year	Team		W	L	PCT	ERA	G	GS	CG	IP	H	BB	SO	ShO	W	L	SV	AB	H	HR	BA	PO	A	E	DP	TC/G	FA
1906	CHI	A	0	0	–	3.00	1	0	0	6	6	3	2	0	0	0	0	2	0	0	.000	1	4	0	0	5.0	1.000

Year	Team		W	L	PCT	ERA	G	GS	CG	IP	H	BB	SO	ShO	Relief Pitching W	L	SV	Batting AB	H	HR	BA	PO	A	E	DP	TC/G	FA

Jim Owens

OWENS, JAMES PHILIP (Bear)
B. Jan. 16, 1934, Gifford, Pa. BR TR 5'11" 180 lbs.

Year	Team		W	L	PCT	ERA	G	GS	CG	IP	H	BB	SO	ShO	W	L	SV	AB	H	HR	BA	PO	A	E	DP	TC/G	FA
1955	PHI	N	0	2	.000	8.31	3	2	0	8.2	13	7	6	0	0	0	0	1	0	0	.000	0	1	0	0	0.3	1.000
1956			0	4	.000	7.28	10	5	0	29.2	35	22	22	0	0	1	0	6	1	0	.167	2	5	0	2	0.7	1.000
1958			1	0	1.000	2.57	1	1	0	7	4	5	3	0	0	0	0	2	0	0	.000	0	1	0	0	1.0	1.000
1959			12	12	.500	3.21	31	30	11	221.1	203	73	135	1	0	0	1	75	9	0	.120	8	33	1	4	1.4	.976
1960			4	14	.222	5.04	31	22	6	150	182	64	83	0	0	1	0	44	3	0	.068	6	22	2	0	1.0	.933
1961			5	10	.333	4.47	20	17	3	106.2	119	32	38	0	0	1	0	27	2	0	.074	4	13	2	3	1.0	.895
1962			2	4	.333	6.33	23	12	1	69.2	90	33	21	0	0	0	0	14	2	0	.143	5	8	0	0	0.6	1.000
1963	CIN	N	0	2	.000	5.31	19	3	0	42.1	42	24	29	0	0	1	0	8	1	0	.125	4	9	1	0	0.7	.929
1964	HOU	N	8	7	.533	3.28	48	11	0	118	115	32	88	0	6	2	6	29	3	0	.103	2	17	2	0	0.4	.905
1965			6	5	.545	3.28	50	0	0	71.1	64	29	53	0	6	5	8	8	1	0	.125	2	11	0	0	0.3	1.000
1966			4	7	.364	4.68	40	0	0	50	53	17	32	0	4	7	2	4	0	0	.000	0	12	0	1	0.3	1.000
1967			0	1	.000	4.22	10	0	0	10.2	12	2	6	0	0	1	0	0	0	0	–	0	0	0	0	0.0	–
12 yrs.			42	68	.382	4.31	286	103	21	885.1	932	340	516	1	16	19	21	218	22	0	.101	33	132	8	10	0.6	.954

Rick Ownbey

OWNBEY, RICHARD WAYNE
B. Oct. 20, 1957, Corona, Calif. BR TR 6'3" 185 lbs.

Year	Team		W	L	PCT	ERA	G	GS	CG	IP	H	BB	SO	ShO	W	L	SV	AB	H	HR	BA	PO	A	E	DP	TC/G	FA
1982	NY	N	1	2	.333	3.75	8	8	1	50.1	44	43	28	0	0	0	0	15	3	0	.200	1	7	2	0	1.3	.800
1983			1	3	.250	4.67	10	4	0	34.2	31	21	19	0	1	0	0	9	1	0	.111	1	6	1	1	0.8	.875
1984	STL	N	0	3	.000	4.74	4	4	0	19	23	8	11	0	0	2	0	4	0	0	.000	1	1	0	0	0.5	1.000
1986			1	3	.250	3.80	17	3	0	42.2	47	19	25	0	0	2	0	7	0	0	.000	4	4	2	0	0.6	.800
4 yrs.			3	11	.214	4.11	39	19	2	146.2	145	91	83	0	1	2	0	35	4	0	.114	7	18	5	1	0.8	.833

Doc Ozmer

OZMER, HORACE ROBERT
B. May 25, 1901, Atlanta, Ga. D. Dec. 28, 1970, Atlanta, Ga. BR TR 5'10½" 185 lbs.

Year	Team		W	L	PCT	ERA	G	GS	CG	IP	H	BB	SO	ShO	W	L	SV	AB	H	HR	BA	PO	A	E	DP	TC/G	FA
1923	PHI	A	0	0	–	4.50	1	0	0	2	1	1	1	0	0	0	0	0	0	0	–	1	1	0	0	2.0	1.000

John Pacella

PACELLA, JOHN LEWIS
B. Sept. 15, 1956, Brooklyn, N. Y. BR TR 6'3" 195 lbs.

Year	Team		W	L	PCT	ERA	G	GS	CG	IP	H	BB	SO	ShO	W	L	SV	AB	H	HR	BA	PO	A	E	DP	TC/G	FA
1977	NY	N	0	0	–	0.00	3	0	0	4	2	2	1	0	0	0	0	0	0	0	–	0	0	1	0	0.3	–
1979			0	2	.000	4.50	4	0	0	16	16	4	12	0	0	0	0	4	0	0	.000	2	1	0	0	0.8	1.000
1980			3	4	.429	5.14	32	15	0	84	89	59	68	0	0	0	0	20	2	0	.100	6	9	1	0	0.5	.938
1982	2 teams	NY A (3G 0–1)	MIN A (21G 1–2)																								
"	total		1	3	.250	7.30	24	2	0	61.2	74	46	22	0	1	1	0	0	0	0	–	3	2	0	0	0.2	1.000
1984	BAL	A	0	1	.000	6.75	6	1	0	14.2	15	9	8	0	0	1	0	0	0	0	–	0	1	1	0	0.3	.500
1986	DET	A	0	0	–	4.09	5	0	0	11	10	13	5	0	0	0	1	0	0	0	–	3	4	0	0	1.4	1.000
6 yrs.			4	10	.286	5.74	74	21	0	191.1	206	133	116	0	1	2	3	24	2	0	.083	14	17	3	0	0.5	.912

Pat Pacillo

PACILLO, PATRICK MICHAEL
B. July 23, 1963, Jersey City, N. J. BR TR 6'2" 205 lbs.

Year	Team		W	L	PCT	ERA	G	GS	CG	IP	H	BB	SO	ShO	W	L	SV	AB	H	HR	BA	PO	A	E	DP	TC/G	FA
1987	CIN	N	3	3	.500	6.13	12	7	0	39.2	41	19	23	0	1	1	0	11	1	0	.091	2	5	0	0	0.6	1.000
1988			1	0	1.000	5.06	6	0	0	10.2	14	4	11	0	1	0	0	1	0	0	.000	0	1	0	0	0.3	.500
2 yrs.			4	3	.571	5.90	18	7	0	50.1	55	23	34	0	2	1	0	12	1	0	.083	2	6	1	0	0.5	.889

Gene Packard

PACKARD, EUGENE MILO
B. July 13, 1887, Colorado Springs, Colo. D. May 19, 1959, Riverside, Calif. BL TL 5'10" 155 lbs.

Year	Team		W	L	PCT	ERA	G	GS	CG	IP	H	BB	SO	ShO	W	L	SV	AB	H	HR	BA	PO	A	E	DP	TC/G	FA
1912	CIN	N	1	0	1.000	3.00	1	1	1	9	7	4	2	0	0	0	0	4	1	0	.250	1	2	0	0	3.0	1.000
1913			7	11	.389	2.97	39	21	9	190.2	208	64	73	2	1	2	0	61	11	0	.180	7	46	5	1	1.5	.914
1914	KC	F	21	13	.618	2.89	42	34	24	302	282	88	154	4	3	0	4	116	28	1	.241	25	121	6	7	3.6	.961
1915			20	11	.645	2.68	42	31	21	281.2	250	74	108	5	2	2	2	95	22	1	.232	23	114	7	3	3.4	.951
1916	CHI	N	10	6	.625	2.78	37	15	5	155.1	154	38	36	2	0	0	0	54	7	0	.130	14	64	2	2	2.2	.975
1917	2 teams	CHI N (2G 0–0)	STL N (34G 9–6)																								
"	total		9	6	.600	2.55	36	11	6	155	141	25	45	0	6	0	0	52	15	0	.288	5	43	0	2	1.3	1.000
1918	STL	N	12	12	.500	3.50	30	23	10	182.1	184	33	46	1	3	1	2	69	12	0	.174	1	50	2	5	1.8	.962
1919	PHI	N	6	8	.429	4.15	21	16	10	134.1	167	30	24	1	0	1	1	51	7	0	.137	9	36	0	3	2.1	1.000
8 yrs.			86	67	.562	3.01	248	152	86	1410.1	1393	356	488	15	19	7	16	502	103	2	.205	85	476	22	23	2.4	.962

Joe Pactwa

PACTWA, JOSEPH MARTIN
B. June 2, 1948, Hammond, Ind. BL TL 5'11" 185 lbs.

Year	Team		W	L	PCT	ERA	G	GS	CG	IP	H	BB	SO	ShO	W	L	SV	AB	H	HR	BA	PO	A	E	DP	TC/G	FA
1975	CAL	A	1	0	1.000	3.86	4	3	0	16.1	23	10	3	0	0	0	0	0	0	0	–	0	2	0	0	0.5	1.000

Dave Pagan

PAGAN, DAVID PERCY
B. Sept. 15, 1949, Nipawin, Sask., Canada BR TR 6'2" 175 lbs.

Year	Team		W	L	PCT	ERA	G	GS	CG	IP	H	BB	SO	ShO	W	L	SV	AB	H	HR	BA	PO	A	E	DP	TC/G	FA
1973	NY	A	0	0	–	2.84	4	1	0	12.2	16	1	9	0	0	0	0	0	0	0	–	2	1	0	0	0.8	1.000
1974			1	3	.250	5.14	16	6	1	49	49	28	39	0	0	0	0	0	0	0	–	3	5	0	0	0.5	1.000
1975			0	0	–	4.06	13	0	0	31	30	13	18	0	0	0	1	0	0	0	–	5	1	1	0	0.5	.857
1976	2 teams	NY A (7G 1–1)	BAL A (20G 1–4)																								
"	total		2	5	.286	4.73	27	7	1	70.1	72	27	47	0	0	3	0	0	0	0	–	6	2	1	0	0.3	.889
1977	2 teams	SEA A (24G 1–1)	PIT N (1G 0–0)																								
"	total		1	1	.500	5.87	25	4	1	69	87	26	34	1	0	1	2	0	0	0	–	3	11	0	0	0.6	1.000
5 yrs.			4	9	.308	4.97	85	18	3	232	254	95	147	1	0	5	4	0	0	0	–	19	20	2	0	0.5	.951

Joe Page

PAGE, JOSEPH FRANCIS (Fireman, The Gay Reliever)
B. Oct. 28, 1917, Cherry Valley, Pa. D. Apr. 21, 1980, Latrobe, Pa. BL TL 6'3" 200 lbs.

Year	Team		W	L	PCT	ERA	G	GS	CG	IP	H	BB	SO	ShO	W	L	SV	AB	H	HR	BA	PO	A	E	DP	TC/G	FA
1944	NY	A	5	7	.417	4.56	19	16	4	102.2	100	52	63	0	0	0	0	32	5	0	.156	3	14	1	0	0.9	.944
1945			6	3	.667	2.82	20	7	4	102	95	46	50	0	2	0	0	36	9	0	.250	2	12	1	1	0.8	.933
1946			9	8	.529	3.57	31	17	6	136	126	72	77	1	2	4	3	43	7	1	.163	2	23	5	1	1.0	.833
1947			14	8	.636	2.48	56	2	0	141.1	105	72	116	0	14	7	17	46	10	1	.217	2	18	0	0	0.4	1.000
1948			7	8	.467	4.26	55	1	0	107.2	116	66	77	0	7	8	16	24	7	0	.292	3	14	0	0	0.3	1.000
1949			13	8	.619	2.59	60	0	0	135.1	103	75	99	0	13	8	27	40	7	0	.175	4	15	1	1	0.3	.950
1950			3	7	.300	5.04	37	0	0	55.1	66	31	33	0	3	7	13	8	2	0	.250	1	6	0	0	0.2	1.000

Year	Team	W	L	PCT	ERA	G	GS	CG	IP	H	BB	SO	ShO	Relief Pitching W	L	SV	Batting AB	H	HR	BA	PO	A	E	DP	TC/G	FA

Joe Page *continued*

Year	Team	W	L	PCT	ERA	G	GS	CG	IP	H	BB	SO	ShO	W	L	SV	AB	H	HR	BA	PO	A	E	DP	TC/G	FA
1954	PIT N	0	0	–	11.17	7	0	0	9.2	16	7	4	0	0	0	0	0	0	0	–	0	2	0	0	0.3	1.000
8 yrs.		57	49	.538	3.53	285	45	14	790	727	421	519	1	41	34	76	229	47	2	.205	17	104	8	4	0.5	.938
WORLD SERIES																										
1947	NY A	1	1	.500	4.15	4	0	0	13	12	2	7	0	1	1	1	4	0	0	.000	1	2	0	0	0.8	1.000
1949		1	0	1.000	2.00	3	0	0	9	6	3	8	0	1	0	1	4	0	0	.000	0	2	0	1	0.7	1.000
2 yrs.		2	1	.667	3.27	7	0	0	22	18	5	15	0	2 (2nd)	1	2	8	0	0	.000	1	4	0	1	0.7	1.000

Phil Page

PAGE, PHILIPPE RAUSAC
B. Aug. 23, 1905, Springfield, Mass.   D. July 27, 1958, Springfield, Mass.

BR TL 6'2"   175 lbs.

Year	Team	W	L	PCT	ERA	G	GS	CG	IP	H	BB	SO	ShO	W	L	SV	AB	H	HR	BA	PO	A	E	DP	TC/G	FA
1928	DET A	2	0	1.000	2.45	3	2	2	22	21	10	3	0	0	0	0	9	2	0	.222	4	5	0	3	3.0	1.000
1929		0	2	.000	8.17	10	4	1	25.1	29	19	6	0	0	1	0	8	1	0	.125	2	2	1	0	0.5	.800
1930		0	1	.000	9.75	12	0	0	12	23	9	2	0	0	1	0	0	0	0	–	1	4	0	0	0.4	1.000
1934	BKN N	1	0	1.000	5.40	6	0	0	10	13	6	4	0	1	0	0	1	0	0	.000	2	5	1	0	1.3	.875
4 yrs.		3	3	.500	6.23	31	6	3	69.1	86	44	15	0	1	2	0	18	3	0	.167	9	16	2	3	0.9	.926

Sam Page

PAGE, SAMUEL WALTER
B. Feb. 11, 1916, Woodruff, S. C.

BL TR 6'   172 lbs.

Year	Team	W	L	PCT	ERA	G	GS	CG	IP	H	BB	SO	ShO	W	L	SV	AB	H	HR	BA	PO	A	E	DP	TC/G	FA
1939	PHI A	0	3	.000	6.95	4	3	1	22	34	15	11	0	0	1	0	7	3	0	.429	0	6	0	1	1.5	1.000

Vance Page

PAGE, VANCE LINWOOD
B. Sept. 15, 1905, Elm City, N. C.   D. July 14, 1951, Wilson, N. C.

BR TR 6'   180 lbs.

Year	Team	W	L	PCT	ERA	G	GS	CG	IP	H	BB	SO	ShO	W	L	SV	AB	H	HR	BA	PO	A	E	DP	TC/G	FA
1938	CHI N	5	4	.556	3.84	13	9	3	68	90	13	18	0	0	0	1	26	4	0	.154	9	25	0	1	2.6	1.000
1939		7	7	.500	3.88	27	17	8	139.1	169	37	43	1	1	0	1	47	12	0	.255	4	33	0	1	1.4	1.000
1940		1	3	.250	4.42	30	1	0	59	65	26	22	0	1	3	2	13	4	0	.308	1	15	1	0	0.6	.941
1941		2	2	.500	4.28	25	3	1	48.1	48	30	17	0	2	1	1	7	2	0	.286	2	12	0	0	0.6	1.000
4 yrs.		15	16	.484	4.03	95	30	12	314.2	372	106	100	1	4	5	5	93	22	0	.237	16	85	1	2	1.1	.990
WORLD SERIES																										
1938	CHI N	0	0	–	13.50	1	0	0	1.1	2	0	0	0	0	0	0	0	0	0	–	0	1	0	0	1.0	1.000

Pat Paige

PAIGE, GEORGE LYNN
B. May 5, 1883, Paw Paw, Mich.   D. June 8, 1939, Berlin, Wis.

BL TR 5'10"   175 lbs.

Year	Team	W	L	PCT	ERA	G	GS	CG	IP	H	BB	SO	ShO	W	L	SV	AB	H	HR	BA	PO	A	E	DP	TC/G	FA
1911	CLE A	1	0	1.000	4.50	2	1	1	16	21	7	6	0	0	0	0	7	1	0	.143	2	7	0	0	4.5	1.000

Satchel Paige

PAIGE, LEROY ROBERT
B. July 7, 1906, Mobile, Ala.   D. June 8, 1982, Kansas City, Mo.
Hall of Fame 1971.

BR TR 6'3½"   180 lbs.

Year	Team	W	L	PCT	ERA	G	GS	CG	IP	H	BB	SO	ShO	W	L	SV	AB	H	HR	BA	PO	A	E	DP	TC/G	FA
1948	CLE A	6	1	.857	2.48	21	7	3	72.2	61	25	45	2	2	1	1	23	2	0	.087	2	12	0	0	0.7	1.000
1949		4	7	.364	3.04	31	5	1	83	70	33	54	0	3	4	5	16	1	0	.063	5	10	0	0	0.5	1.000
1951	STL A	3	4	.429	4.79	23	3	0	62	67	29	48	0	3	2	5	16	2	0	.125	2	5	0	0	0.3	1.000
1952		12	10	.545	3.07	46	6	3	138	116	57	91	2	8	8	10	39	5	0	.128	5	23	0	2	0.6	1.000
1953		3	9	.250	3.53	57	4	0	117.1	114	39	51	0	2	8	11	29	2	0	.069	3	12	0	1	0.3	1.000
1965	KC A	0	0	–	0.00	1	1	0	3	1	0	1	0	0	0	0	1	0	0	.000	0	0	0	0	0.0	–
6 yrs.		28	31	.475	3.29	179	26	7	476	429	183	290	4	18	23	32	124	12	0	.097	17	62	0	3	0.4	1.000
WORLD SERIES																										
1948	CLE A	0	0	–	0.00	1	0	0	.2	0	0	0	0	0	0	0	0	0	0	–	0	0	0	0	0.0	–

Phil Paine

PAINE, PHILLIPS STEERE (Flip)
B. June 8, 1930, Chepachet, R. I.   D. Feb. 19, 1978, Lebanon, Pa.

BR TR 6'2"   180 lbs.

Year	Team	W	L	PCT	ERA	G	GS	CG	IP	H	BB	SO	ShO	W	L	SV	AB	H	HR	BA	PO	A	E	DP	TC/G	FA
1951	BOS N	2	0	1.000	3.06	21	0	0	35.1	36	20	17	0	2	0	0	4	0	0	.000	2	5	0	0	0.3	1.000
1954	MIL N	1	0	1.000	3.86	11	0	0	14	14	12	11	0	1	0	0	0	0	0	–	0	1	1	0	0.2	.500
1955		2	0	1.000	2.49	15	0	0	25.1	20	14	26	0	2	0	0	3	1	0	.333	1	6	2	0	0.6	.778
1956		0	0	–	∞	1	0	0	0	3	0	0	0	0	0	0	0	0	0	–	0	1	0	0	1.0	1.000
1957		0	0	–	0.00	1	0	0	2	1	3	2	0	0	0	0	0	0	0	–	0	1	0	0	1.0	1.000
1958	STL N	5	1	.833	3.56	46	0	0	73.1	70	31	45	0	5	1	1	7	2	0	.286	6	12	1	0	0.4	.947
6 yrs.		10	1	.909	3.36	95	0	0	150	144	80	101	0	10	1	1	14	3	0	.214	9	25	4	0	0.4	.895

Vicente Palacios

PALACIOS, VICENTE
Born Vicente Palacios y Hernandez.
B. July 19, 1963, Veracruz, Mexico

BR TR 6'3"   165 lbs.

Year	Team	W	L	PCT	ERA	G	GS	CG	IP	H	BB	SO	ShO	W	L	SV	AB	H	HR	BA	PO	A	E	DP	TC/G	FA
1987	PIT N	2	1	.667	4.30	6	4	0	29.1	27	9	13	0	0	0	0	9	1	0	.111	2	1	0	0	0.5	1.000
1988		1	2	.333	6.66	7	3	0	24.1	28	15	15	0	0	0	0	8	0	0	.000	3	5	0	0	1.1	1.000
2 yrs.		3	3	.500	5.37	13	7	0	53.2	55	24	28	0	0	0	0	17	1	0	.059	5	6	0	0	0.8	1.000

Mike Palagyi

PALAGYI, MICHAEL RAYMOND
B. July 4, 1917, Conneaut, Ohio

BR TR 6'2"   185 lbs.

Year	Team	W	L	PCT	ERA	G	GS	CG	IP	H	BB	SO	ShO	W	L	SV	AB	H	HR	BA	PO	A	E	DP	TC/G	FA
1939	WAS A	0	0	–	∞	1	0	0	0	0	3	0	0	0	0	0	0	0	0	–	0	0	0	0	0.0	–

Erv Palica

PALICA, ERVIN MARTIN
Born Ervin Martin Pavliecivich.
B. Feb. 9, 1928, Lomita, Calif.   D. May 29, 1982, Huntington Beach, Calif.

BR TR 6'1½"   180 lbs.

Year	Team	W	L	PCT	ERA	G	GS	CG	IP	H	BB	SO	ShO	W	L	SV	AB	H	HR	BA	PO	A	E	DP	TC/G	FA
1945	BKN N	0	0	–	0.00	0	0	0	0	0	0	0	0	0	0	0	0	0	0	–	0	0	0	0	0.0	–
1947		0	1	.000	3.00	3	0	0	3	2	2	1	0	0	1	0	0	0	0	–	0	0	0	0	0.0	–
1948		6	6	.500	4.45	41	10	3	125.1	111	58	74	0	3	3	3	39	5	0	.128	5	16	0	1	0.5	1.000
1949		8	9	.471	3.62	49	1	0	97	93	49	44	0	8	8	6	19	3	0	.158	3	18	3	2	0.5	.875
1950		13	8	.619	3.58	43	19	10	201.1	176	98	131	2	2	2	1	68	15	1	.221	8	16	3	1	0.6	.889
1951		2	6	.250	4.75	19	8	0	53	55	20	15	0	2	1	0	13	2	0	.154	5	12	0	0	0.9	1.000

Year	Team	W	L	PCT	ERA	G	GS	CG	IP	H	BB	SO	ShO	W	L	SV	AB	H	HR	BA	PO	A	E	DP	TC/G	FA
														Relief Pitching			**Batting**									

Erv Palica *continued*

Year	Team	W	L	PCT	ERA	G	GS	CG	IP	H	BB	SO	ShO	W	L	SV	AB	H	HR	BA	PO	A	E	DP	TC/G	FA
1953		0	0	–	12.00	4	0	0	6	10	8	3	0	0	0	0	1	1	0	1.000	0	2	0	0	0.5	1.000
1954		3	3	.500	5.32	25	3	0	67.2	77	31	25	0	3	2	0	16	4	0	.250	1	6	1	0	0.3	.875
1955	BAL A	5	11	.313	4.14	33	25	5	169.2	165	83	68	1	0	0	2	55	13	0	.236	15	23	4	2	1.3	.905
1956		4	11	.267	4.49	29	14	2	116.1	117	50	62	0	2	3	0	32	5	0	.156	2	20	2	2	0.8	.917
10 yrs.		41	55	.427	4.22	246	80	20	839.1	806	399	423	3	20	20	12	243	48	1	.198	39	113	13	8	0.7	.921

WORLD SERIES

Year	Team	W	L	PCT	ERA	G	GS	CG	IP	H	BB	SO	ShO	W	L	SV	AB	H	HR	BA	PO	A	E	DP	TC/G	FA
1949	BKN N	0	0	–	0.00	1	0	0	2	1	1	1	0	0	0	0	0	0	0	–	0	1	0	0	1.0	1.000

Donn Pall

PALL, DONN STEVEN
B. Jan. 11, 1962, Chicago, Ill.
BR TR 6'2" 185 lbs.

Year	Team	W	L	PCT	ERA	G	GS	CG	IP	H	BB	SO	ShO	W	L	SV	AB	H	HR	BA	PO	A	E	DP	TC/G	FA
1988	CHI A	0	2	.000	3.45	17	0	0	28.2	39	8	16	0	0	2	0	0	0	0	–	4	6	0	1	0.6	1.000
1989		4	5	.444	3.31	53	0	0	87	90	19	58	0	4	5	6	0	0	0	–	5	7	2	0	0.3	.857
2 yrs.		4	7	.364	3.35	70	0	0	115.2	129	27	74	0	4	7	6	0	0	0	–	9	13	2	1	0.3	.917

Mike Palm

PALM, RICHARD PAUL
B. Feb. 13, 1925, Boston, Mass.
BR TR 6'3½" 190 lbs.

Year	Team	W	L	PCT	ERA	G	GS	CG	IP	H	BB	SO	ShO	W	L	SV	AB	H	HR	BA	PO	A	E	DP	TC/G	FA
1948	BOS A	0	0	–	6.00	3	0	0	3	6	5	1	0	0	0	0	3	0	0	.000	0	0	0	0	0.0	–

Palmer

PALMER,
B. St. Louis, Mo. Deceased.

Year	Team	W	L	PCT	ERA	G	GS	CG	IP	H	BB	SO	ShO	W	L	SV	AB	H	HR	BA	PO	A	E	DP	TC/G	FA
1885	STL N	0	4	.000	*3.44*	4	4	4	34	46	20	9	0	0	0	0	11	1	0	.091	1	2	1	0	1.0	.750

David Palmer

PALMER, DAVID WILLIAM
B. Aug. 19, 1957, Glens Falls, N. Y.
BR TR 6'1" 195 lbs.

Year	Team	W	L	PCT	ERA	G	GS	CG	IP	H	BB	SO	ShO	W	L	SV	AB	H	HR	BA	PO	A	E	DP	TC/G	FA
1978	MON N	0	1	.000	2.70	5	1	0	10	9	2	7	0	0	0	0	1	0	0	.000	0	5	1	0	1.2	.833
1979		10	2	.833	2.63	36	11	2	123	110	30	72	1	1	0	2	31	1	0	.032	7	17	1	0	0.7	.960
1980		8	6	.571	2.98	24	19	3	130	124	30	73	1	0	0	0	45	9	0	.200	9	26	2	0	1.5	.946
1982		6	4	.600	3.18	13	13	1	73.2	60	36	46	0	0	0	0	24	1	0	.042	7	10	1	1	1.4	.944
1984		7	3	.700	3.84	20	19	1	105.1	101	44	66	1	0	1	0	33	5	1	.152	20	13	1	1	1.7	.971
1985		7	10	.412	3.71	24	23	0	135.2	128	67	106	0	0	0	0	36	4	0	.111	17	21	1	5	1.6	.974
1986	ATL N	11	10	.524	3.65	35	35	2	209.2	181	102	170	0	0	0	0	66	12	1	.182	18	33	0	3	1.5	1.000
1987		8	11	.421	4.90	28	28	0	152.1	169	64	111	0	0	0	0	48	6	1	.125	9	25	1	2	1.3	.971
1988	PHI N	7	9	.438	4.47	22	22	1	129	129	48	85	1	0	0	2	39	10	2	.256	14	12	1	2	1.2	.963
1989	DET A	0	3	.000	7.79	11	5	0	17.1	25	11	12	0	0	0	0	0	0	0	–	2	1	1	0	0.8	.750
10 yrs.		64	59	.520	3.78	212	176	10	1086	1036	434	748	4	1	1	2	323	48	5	.149	103	163	10	14	1.3	.964

Jim Palmer

PALMER, JAMES ALVIN
B. Oct. 15, 1945, New York, N. Y.
BR TR 6'3" 190 lbs.

Year	Team	W	L	PCT	ERA	G	GS	CG	IP	H	BB	SO	ShO	W	L	SV	AB	H	HR	BA	PO	A	E	DP	TC/G	FA
1965	BAL A	5	4	.556	3.72	27	6	0	92	75	56	75	0	4	2	1	26	5	1	.192	6	17	3	1	1.0	.885
1966		15	10	.600	3.46	30	30	6	208.1	176	91	147	0	0	0	0	73	7	1	.096	14	26	1	2	1.4	.976
1967		3	1	.750	2.94	9	9	2	49	34	20	23	1	0	0	0	13	1	0	.077	2	9	0	1	1.2	1.000
1969		16	4	**.800**	2.34	26	23	11	181	131	64	123	6	2	0	0	64	13	0	.203	7	11	1	0	0.7	.947
1970		20	10	.667	2.71	39	39	17	305	263	100	199	5	0	0	0	113	17	1	.150	21	42	2	4	1.7	.969
1971		20	9	.690	2.68	37	37	20	282	231	106	184	3	0	0	0	102	20	0	.196	27	41	5	3	2.0	.932
1972		21	10	.677	2.07	36	36	18	274.1	219	70	184	3	0	0	0	98	22	0	.224	14	37	3	4	1.5	.944
1973		22	9	.710	**2.40**	38	37	19	296	225	113	158	6	0	0	1	0	0	0	–	24	35	2	3	1.6	.967
1974		7	12	.368	3.27	26	26	5	179	176	69	84	2	0	0	0	0	0	0	–	15	33	1	2	1.9	.980
1975		**23**	11	.676	**2.09**	39	38	25	323	253	80	193	**10**	0	0	1	0	0	0	–	30	52	6	7	2.3	.932
1976		**22**	13	.629	2.51	40	**40**	23	315	255	84	159	6	0	0	0	0	0	0	–	27	49	1	2	1.9	.987
1977		20	11	.645	2.91	39	**39**	22	319	263	99	193	3	0	0	0	0	0	0	–	20	48	2	5	1.8	.971
1978		21	12	.636	2.46	38	38	19	**296**	246	97	138	6	0	0	0	0	0	0	–	27	43	2	5	1.9	.972
1979		10	6	.625	3.29	23	22	7	156	144	43	67	0	0	0	0	0	0	0	–	10	23	0	1	1.4	1.000
1980		16	10	.615	3.98	34	33	4	224	238	74	109	0	0	0	0	0	0	0	–	14	37	2	6	1.6	.962
1981		7	8	.467	3.76	22	22	5	127	117	46	35	0	0	0	0	0	0	0	–	12	26	0	2	1.7	1.000
1982		15	5	**.750**	3.13	36	32	8	227	195	63	103	2	0	1	1	0	0	0	–	16	37	2	3	1.5	.964
1983		5	4	.556	4.23	14	11	0	76.2	86	19	34	0	0	0	0	0	0	0	–	5	8	1	0	1.0	.929
1984		0	3	.000	9.17	5	3	0	17.2	22	17	4	0	0	1	0	0	0	0	–	1	3	0	1	0.8	1.000
19 yrs.		268	152	.638	2.86	558	521	211	3948	3349	1311	2212	53	6	4	4	489	85	3	.174	292	577	34	53	1.6	.962

LEAGUE CHAMPIONSHIP SERIES

Year	Team	W	L	PCT	ERA	G	GS	CG	IP	H	BB	SO	ShO	W	L	SV	AB	H	HR	BA	PO	A	E	DP	TC/G	FA
1969	BAL A	1	0	1.000	2.00	1	1	1	9	10	2	4	0	0	0	0	5	0	0	.000	0	1	0	0	1.0	1.000
1970		1	0	1.000	1.00	1	1	1	9	7	3	12	0	0	0	0	4	1	0	.250	1	1	0	0	2.0	1.000
1971		1	0	1.000	3.00	1	1	1	9	7	8	8	0	0	0	0	5	1	0	.200	1	0	0	0	1.0	1.000
1973		1	0	1.000	1.84	3	2	1	14.2	11	8	15	1	0	0	0	1	0	0	–	1	0	0	1	0.7	1.000
1974		0	1	.000	1.00	1	1	1	9	4	1	4	0	0	0	0	0	0	0	–	0	2	0	0	2.0	1.000
1979		0	0	–	3.00	1	1	0	9	7	2	3	0	0	0	0	0	0	0	–	1	1	0	0	2.0	1.000
6 yrs.		4	1	.800	1.96	8	7	5	59.2	46	19	46	1	0	0	0	14	2	0	.143	4	6	0	1	1.3	1.000

WORLD SERIES

Year	Team	W	L	PCT	ERA	G	GS	CG	IP	H	BB	SO	ShO	W	L	SV	AB	H	HR	BA	PO	A	E	DP	TC/G	FA
1966	BAL A	1	0	1.000	0.00	1	1	1	9	4	3	6	1	0	0	0	4	0	0	.000	0	2	0	0	2.0	1.000
1969		0	1	.000	6.00	1	1	0	6	5	4	5	0	0	0	0	2	0	0	.000	1	0	1	0	2.0	.500
1970		1	0	1.000	4.60	2	2	0	15.2	11	9	9	0	0	0	0	7	1	0	.143	0	0	0	0	0.0	–
1971		1	0	1.000	2.65	2	2	0	17	15	9	15	0	0	0	0	4	0	0	.000	2	1	0	0	1.5	1.000
1979		0	1	.000	3.60	2	2	0	15	18	5	8	0	0	0	0	4	0	0	.000	2	1	0	0	1.5	1.000
1983		1	0	1.000	0.00	1	0	0	2	2	1	1	0	1	0	0	0	0	0	–	0	0	0	0	0.0	–
6 yrs.		4	2	.667	3.20	9	8	1	64.2	55	31	44	1	1	0	0	21	1	0	.048	5	4	1	1	1.1	.900

10th 9th 9th 4th

Year	Team		W	L	PCT	ERA	G	GS	CG	IP	H	BB	SO	ShO	Relief Pitching W	L	SV	Batting AB	H	HR	BA	PO	A	E	DP	TC/G	FA

Lowell Palmer

PALMER, LOWELL RAYMOND
B. Aug. 18, 1947, Sacramento, Calif.   BR TR 6'1" 190 lbs.

Year	Team		W	L	PCT	ERA	G	GS	CG	IP	H	BB	SO	ShO	RP W	L	SV	AB	H	HR	BA	PO	A	E	DP	TC/G	FA
1969	PHI	N	2	8	.200	5.20	26	9	1	90	91	47	68	1	0	0	0	22	3	1	.136	4	13	0	1	0.7	1.000
1970			1	2	.333	5.47	38	5	0	102	98	55	85	0	1	1	0	27	4	0	.148	7	10	0	1	0.4	1.000
1971			0	0	–	6.00	3	1	0	15	13	13	6	0	0	0	0	5	1	0	.200	2	1	0	0	1.0	1.000
1972	2 teams					CLE A	(1G 0–0)			STL N	(16G 0–3)																
"	total		0	3	.000	3.89	17	2	0	37	32	28	28	0	0	1	0	5	0	0	.000	3	4	0	0	0.4	1.000
1974	SD	N	2	5	.286	5.67	22	8	1	73	68	59	52	0	1	2	0	23	2	0	.087	1	9	1	1	0.5	.909
5 yrs.			5	18	.217	5.28	106	25	2	317	302	202	239	1	2	4	0	82	10	1	.122	17	37	1	3	0.5	.982

Emilio Palmero

PALMERO, EMILIO ANTONIO
B. June 13, 1895, Guanabocoa, Cuba
D. July 15, 1970, Toledo, Ohio   BB TL 5'11" 157 lbs.   BL 1928

Year	Team		W	L	PCT	ERA	G	GS	CG	IP	H	BB	SO	ShO	RP W	L	SV	AB	H	HR	BA	PO	A	E	DP	TC/G	FA
1915	NY	N	0	2	.000	3.09	3	2	1	11.2	10	9	8	0	0	0	0	4	1	0	.250	0	5	0	0	1.7	1.000
1916			0	3	.000	8.04	4	1	0	15.2	17	8	8	0	0	2	0	3	0	0	.000	0	7	0	0	1.8	1.000
1921	STL	A	4	7	.364	5.00	24	9	4	90	109	49	26	0	2	1	0	37	8	0	.216	2	31	2	2	1.5	.943
1926	WAS	A	2	2	.500	4.76	7	3	0	17	22	15	6	0	1	0	0	3	1	0	.333	0	4	1	0	0.7	.800
1928	BOS	N	0	1	.000	5.40	3	1	0	6.2	14	2	0	0	0	0	0	1	0	0	.000	0	1	0	0	0.3	1.000
5 yrs.			6	15	.286	5.17	41	16	5	141	172	83	48	0	3	3	0	48	10	0	.208	2	48	3	2	1.3	.943

Ed Palmquist

PALMQUIST, EDWIN LEE
B. June 10, 1933, Los Angeles, Calif.   BR TR 6'3" 195 lbs.

Year	Team		W	L	PCT	ERA	G	GS	CG	IP	H	BB	SO	ShO	RP W	L	SV	AB	H	HR	BA	PO	A	E	DP	TC/G	FA
1960	LA	N	0	1	.000	2.54	22	0	0	39	34	16	23	0	0	1	0	7	0	0	.000	1	7	0	1	0.4	1.000
1961	2 teams					LA N	(5G 0–1)			MIN A	(9G 1–1)																
"	total		1	2	.333	8.49	14	2	0	29.2	43	20	18	0	1	1	1	3	0	0	.000	2	6	1	1	0.6	.889
2 yrs.			1	3	.250	5.11	36	2	0	68.2	77	36	41	0	1	2	1	10	0	0	.000	3	13	1	2	0.5	.941

Jim Panther

PANTHER, JAMES EDWARD
B. Mar. 1, 1945, Burlington, Iowa   BR TR 6'1" 190 lbs.

Year	Team		W	L	PCT	ERA	G	GS	CG	IP	H	BB	SO	ShO	RP W	L	SV	AB	H	HR	BA	PO	A	E	DP	TC/G	FA
1971	OAK	A	0	1	.000	10.50	4	0	0	6	10	5	4	0	0	1	0	1	0	0	.000	1	1	0	0	0.5	1.000
1972	TEX	A	5	9	.357	4.12	58	4	0	94	101	46	44	0	5	5	0	8	1	0	.125	5	17	1	0	0.4	.957
1973	ATL	N	2	3	.400	7.55	23	0	0	31	45	9	8	0	2	3	0	0	0	0	–	2	1	1	0	0.2	.750
3 yrs.			7	13	.350	5.22	85	4	0	131	156	60	56	0	7	9	0	9	1	0	.111	8	19	2	0	0.3	.931

John Papa

PAPA, JOHN PAUL
B. Dec. 5, 1940, Bridgeport, Conn.   BR TR 5'11" 190 lbs.

Year	Team		W	L	PCT	ERA	G	GS	CG	IP	H	BB	SO	ShO	RP W	L	SV	AB	H	HR	BA	PO	A	E	DP	TC/G	FA
1961	BAL	A	0	0	–	18.00	2	0	0	1	3	3	3	0	0	0	0	0	0	0	–	0	0	0	0	0.0	
1962			0	0	–	27.00	1	0	0	1	3	1	0	0	0	0	0	0	0	0	–	0	0	0	0	0.0	
2 yrs.			0	0	–	22.50	3	0	0	2	5	4	3	0	0	0	0	0	0	0	–	0	0	0	0	0.0	

Al Papai

PAPAI, ALFRED THOMAS
B. May 7, 1919, Divernon, Ill.   BR TR 6'3" 185 lbs.

Year	Team		W	L	PCT	ERA	G	GS	CG	IP	H	BB	SO	ShO	RP W	L	SV	AB	H	HR	BA	PO	A	E	DP	TC/G	FA
1948	STL	N	0	1	.000	5.06	10	0	0	16	14	7	8	0	0	1	0	2	0	0	.000	1	4	0	0	0.5	1.000
1949	STL	A	4	11	.267	5.06	42	15	6	142.1	175	81	31	0	2	3	2	38	3	0	.079	13	39	2	4	1.3	.963
1950	2 teams					BOS A	(16G 4–2)			STL N	(13G 1–0)																
"	total		5	2	.714	6.33	29	3	2	69.2	82	42	26	0	4	0	0	20	3	0	.150	2	11	0	2	0.4	1.000
1955	CHI	A	0	0	–	3.86	7	0	0	11.2	10	8	5	0	0	0	0	2	0	0	.000	2	7	1	0	1.4	.900
4 yrs.			9	14	.391	5.37	88	18	8	239.2	281	138	70	0	6	4	4	62	6	0	.097	18	61	3	6	0.9	.963

Larry Pape

PAPE, LAURENCE ALBERT
B. July 21, 1883, Norwood, Ohio   D. July 21, 1918, Swissvale, Pa.   BR TR 5'11" 175 lbs.

Year	Team		W	L	PCT	ERA	G	GS	CG	IP	H	BB	SO	ShO	RP W	L	SV	AB	H	HR	BA	PO	A	E	DP	TC/G	FA
1909	BOS	A	2	0	1.000	2.01	11	3	2	58.1	46	12	18	1	0	0	2	21	3	0	.143	3	6	1	0	0.9	.900
1911			10	8	.556	2.45	27	19	10	176.1	167	63	49	1	0	0	0	64	13	0	.203	8	76	7	0	3.4	.923
1912			1	1	.500	4.99	13	2	1	48.2	74	16	17	0	1	0	1	17	4	0	.235	1	17	1	0	1.5	.947
3 yrs.			13	9	.591	2.80	51	24	13	283.1	287	91	84	2	2	0	3	102	20	0	.196	12	99	9	0	2.4	.925

Frank Papish

PAPISH, FRANK RICHARD (Pap)
B. Oct. 21, 1917, Pueblo, Colo.   D. Aug. 30, 1965, Pueblo, Colo.   BR TL 6'2" 192 lbs.

Year	Team		W	L	PCT	ERA	G	GS	CG	IP	H	BB	SO	ShO	RP W	L	SV	AB	H	HR	BA	PO	A	E	DP	TC/G	FA
1945	CHI	A	4	4	.500	3.74	19	5	3	84.1	75	40	45	0	4	4	1	26	6	0	.231	2	24	1	0	1.4	.963
1946			7	5	.583	2.74	31	15	6	138	122	63	66	2	0	1	0	43	8	0	.186	11	23	3	2	1.2	.919
1947			12	12	.500	3.26	38	26	6	199	185	98	79	1	2	0	3	58	5	0	.086	11	27	2	2	1.1	.950
1948			2	8	.200	5.00	32	14	2	95.1	97	75	41	0	0	1	4	27	5	0	.185	2	14	1	2	0.5	.941
1949	CLE	A	1	0	1.000	3.19	25	3	1	62	54	39	23	0	1	0	1	8	1	0	.125	1	14	0	2	0.6	1.000
1950	PIT	N	0	0	–	27.00	4	1	0	2.1	8	4	1	0	0	0	0	0	0	0	–	1	0	0	0	0.3	1.000
6 yrs.			26	29	.473	3.58	149	64	18	581	541	319	255	3	7	6	9	162	25	0	.154	28	102	7	8	0.9	.949

John Pappalau

PAPPALAU, JOHN JOSEPH
B. Apr. 3, 1875, Albany, N. Y.   D. May 12, 1944, Albany, N. Y.   BR TR 6' 175 lbs.

Year	Team		W	L	PCT	ERA	G	GS	CG	IP	H	BB	SO	ShO	RP W	L	SV	AB	H	HR	BA	PO	A	E	DP	TC/G	FA
1897	CLE	N	0	1	.000	10.50	2	1	1	12	22	6	3	0	0	0	0	5	0	0	.000	1	3	0	0	2.0	1.000

Milt Pappas

PAPPAS, MILTON STEPHEN (Gimpy)
Born Miltiades Stergios Papastegios.
B. May 11, 1939, Detroit, Mich.   BR TR 6'3" 190 lbs.

Year	Team		W	L	PCT	ERA	G	GS	CG	IP	H	BB	SO	ShO	RP W	L	SV	AB	H	HR	BA	PO	A	E	DP	TC/G	FA
1957	BAL	A	0	0	–	1.00	4	0	0	9	6	3	3	0	0	0	0	1	0	0	.000	0	2	0	0	0.5	1.000
1958			10	10	.500	4.06	31	21	3	135.1	135	48	72	0	1	1	0	42	6	1	.143	9	28	2	3	1.3	.949
1959			15	9	.625	3.27	33	27	15	209.1	175	75	120	4	1	0	3	79	11	0	.139	6	36	3	2	1.4	.933
1960			15	11	.577	3.37	30	27	11	205.2	184	83	126	3	2	1	0	70	3	1	.043	8	36	1	3	1.5	.978
1961			13	9	.591	3.04	26	23	11	177.2	134	78	89	4	1	0	1	66	9	3	.136	24	34	1	2	2.3	.983
1962			12	10	.545	4.03	35	32	9	205.1	200	75	130	1	0	0	0	69	6	4	.087	20	38	3	3	1.7	.951
1963			16	9	.640	3.03	34	32	11	216.2	186	69	120	4	0	0	0	71	9	2	.127	26	41	2	4	2.0	.971
1964			16	7	.696	2.97	37	36	13	251.2	225	48	157	7	0	0	0	93	12	0	.129	25	30	0	2	1.5	1.000

Year	Team		W	L	PCT	ERA	G	GS	CG	IP	H	BB	SO	ShO	Relief Pitching W	L	SV	Batting AB	H	HR	BA	PO	A	E	DP	TC/G	FA

Milt Pappas *continued*

Year	Team		W	L	PCT	ERA	G	GS	CG	IP	H	BB	SO	ShO	W	L	SV	AB	H	HR	BA	PO	A	E	DP	TC/G	FA
1965			13	9	.591	2.60	34	34	9	221.1	192	52	127	3	0	0	0	70	5	0	.071	15	21	3	4	1.1	.923
1966	CIN	N	12	11	.522	4.29	33	32	6	209.2	224	39	133	2	0	1	0	75	8	1	.107	16	32	1	2	1.5	.980
1967			16	13	.552	3.35	34	32	5	217.2	218	38	129	3	2	0	0	72	7	1	.097	13	36	0	3	1.4	1.000
1968	2 teams	CIN N	(15G 2–5)			ATL N	(22G 10–8)																				
"	total		12	13	.480	3.47	37	30	3	184	181	32	118	1	0	1	0	53	7	1	.132	4	29	1	0	0.9	.971
1969	ATL	N	6	10	.375	3.63	26	24	1	144	149	44	72	0	0	0	0	45	7	2	.156	17	20	2	1	1.5	.949
1970	2 teams	ATL N	(11G 2–2)			CHI N	(21G 10–8)																				
"	total		12	10	.545	3.34	32	23	7	180.1	179	43	105	2	1	0	0	60	12	0	.200	12	21	1	4	1.1	.971
1971	CHI	N	17	14	.548	3.52	35	35	14	261	279	62	99	5	0	0	0	91	14	0	.154	19	30	0	1	1.4	1.000
1972			17	7	.708	2.77	29	28	10	195	187	29	80	3	0	0	0	68	13	1	.191	20	27	0	2	1.6	1.000
1973			7	12	.368	4.28	30	29	1	162	192	40	48	1	0	0	0	48	3	1	.063	11	25	3	2	1.3	.923
17 yrs.			209	164	.560	3.40	520	465	129	3185.2	3046	858	1728	43	8	4	4	1073	132	20	.123	245	486	23	38	1.5	.969

LEAGUE CHAMPIONSHIP SERIES

Year	Team		W	L	PCT	ERA	G	GS	CG	IP	H	BB	SO	ShO	W	L	SV	AB	H	HR	BA	PO	A	E	DP	TC/G	FA
1969	ATL	N	0	0	–	11.57	1	0	0	2.1	4	0	4	0	0	0	0	1	0	0	.000	0	0	0	0	0.0	–

Jim Park

PARK, JAMES
B. Nov. 10, 1892, Richmond, Ky.   D. Dec. 17, 1970, Lexington, Ky.

BR TR 6'2"   175 lbs.

Year	Team		W	L	PCT	ERA	G	GS	CG	IP	H	BB	SO	ShO	W	L	SV	AB	H	HR	BA	PO	A	E	DP	TC/G	FA
1915	STL	A	2	0	1.000	1.19	3	3	1	22.2	18	9	5	0	0	0	0	10	4	0	.400	1	4	0	0	1.7	1.000
1916			1	4	.200	2.62	26	6	1	79	69	25	26	0	1	0	0	20	2	0	.100	3	17	3	1	0.9	.870
1917			1	1	.500	6.64	13	0	0	20.1	27	12	9	0	1	1	0	2	0	0	.000	0	7	1	0	0.6	.875
3 yrs.			4	5	.444	3.02	42	9	2	122	114	46	40	0	2	1	0	32	6	0	.188	4	28	4	1	0.9	.889

Clay Parker

PARKER, JAMES CLAYTON
B. Dec. 19, 1962, Columbia, La.

BR TR 6'1"   185 lbs.

Year	Team		W	L	PCT	ERA	G	GS	CG	IP	H	BB	SO	ShO	W	L	SV	AB	H	HR	BA	PO	A	E	DP	TC/G	FA
1987	SEA	A	0	0	–	10.57	3	1	0	7.2	15	4	8	0	0	0	0	0	0	0	–	0	1	0	0	0.3	1.000
1989	NY	A	4	5	.444	3.68	22	17	2	120	123	31	53	0	0	0	0	0	0	0	–	7	20	0	1	1.2	1.000
2 yrs.			4	5	.444	4.09	25	18	2	127.2	138	35	61	0	0	0	0	0	0	0	–	7	21	0	1	1.1	1.000

Doc Parker

PARKER, HARLEY PARK
Brother of Jay Parker.
B. June 14, 1872, Theresa, N. Y.   D. Mar. 3, 1941, Chicago, Ill.

BR TR 6'2"   200 lbs.

Year	Team		W	L	PCT	ERA	G	GS	CG	IP	H	BB	SO	ShO	W	L	SV	AB	H	HR	BA	PO	A	E	DP	TC/G	FA
1893	CHI	N	0	0	–	13.50	1	0	0	2	5	1	0	0	0	0	1	0	0	0	.000	0	0	0	0	0.0	–
1895			4	2	.667	3.68	7	6	5	51.1	65	9	9	1	0	0	0	22	7	0	.318	3	12	1	1	2.3	.938
1896			1	5	.167	6.16	9	7	7	73	100	27	15	0	0	0	0	36	10	0	.278	4	22	3	1	3.2	.897
1901	CIN	N	0	1	.000	15.75	1	1	1	8	26	2	0	0	0	0	0	3	0	0	.000	1	1	0	1	2.0	1.000
4 yrs.			5	8	.385	5.90	18	14	13	134.1	196	39	24	1	0	0	1	62	17	0	.274	8	35	4	3	2.6	.915

Harry Parker

PARKER, HARRY WILLIAM
B. Sept. 14, 1947, Highland, Ill.

BR TR 6'3"   190 lbs.

Year	Team		W	L	PCT	ERA	G	GS	CG	IP	H	BB	SO	ShO	W	L	SV	AB	H	HR	BA	PO	A	E	DP	TC/G	FA
1970	STL	N	1	1	.500	3.27	7	4	0	22	24	15	9	0	1	1	0	8	2	0	.250	4	4	0	0	1.1	1.000
1971			0	0	–	7.20	4	0	0	5	6	2	2	0	0	0	0	0	0	0	–	0	0	0	0	0.0	–
1973	NY	N	8	4	.667	3.35	38	9	0	96.2	79	36	63	0	4	2	5	23	4	0	.174	4	14	0	0	0.5	1.000
1974			4	12	.250	3.92	40	16	1	131	145	46	58	0	0	2	4	36	0	0	.000	5	15	1	1	0.5	.952
1975	2 teams	NY N	(18G 2–3)			STL N	(14G 0–1)																				
"	total		2	4	.333	5.06	32	1	0	53.1	58	29	35	0	2	3	3	3	0	0	.000	0	11	0	0	0.3	1.000
1976	CLE	A	0	0	–	0.00	3	0	0	7	3	0	5	0	0	0	0	0	0	0	–	1	1	0	0	0.7	1.000
6 yrs.			15	21	.417	3.86	124	30	1	315	315	128	172	0	7	8	12	70	6	0	.086	14	45	1	1	0.5	.983

LEAGUE CHAMPIONSHIP SERIES

Year	Team		W	L	PCT	ERA	G	GS	CG	IP	H	BB	SO	ShO	W	L	SV	AB	H	HR	BA	PO	A	E	DP	TC/G	FA
1973	NY	N	0	1	.000	9.00	1	0	0	1	1	0	0	0	0	1	0	0	0	0	–	0	0	0	0	0.0	–

WORLD SERIES

Year	Team		W	L	PCT	ERA	G	GS	CG	IP	H	BB	SO	ShO	W	L	SV	AB	H	HR	BA	PO	A	E	DP	TC/G	FA
1973	NY	N	0	1	.000	0.00	3	0	0	3.1	2	2	2	0	0	1	0	0	0	0	–	0	0	0	0	0.0	–

Jay Parker

PARKER, JAY
Brother of Doc Parker.
B. July 8, 1874, Theresa, N. Y.   D. June 8, 1935, Hartford, Mich.

BR TR 5'11"   185 lbs.

Year	Team		W	L	PCT	ERA	G	GS	CG	IP	H	BB	SO	ShO	W	L	SV	AB	H	HR	BA	PO	A	E	DP	TC/G	FA
1899	PIT	N	0	0	–	∞	1	1	0	0	2	0	0	0	0	0	0	0	0	0	–	0	0	0	0	0.0	–

Roy Parker

PARKER, ROY W.
B. 1897

BR TR 6'2"   185 lbs.

Year	Team		W	L	PCT	ERA	G	GS	CG	IP	H	BB	SO	ShO	W	L	SV	AB	H	HR	BA	PO	A	E	DP	TC/G	FA
1919	STL	N	0	0	–	31.50	2	0	0	2	6	1	0	0	0	0	0	0	0	0	–	0	1	0	0	0.5	1.000

Slicker Parks

PARKS, VERNON HENRY
B. Nov. 10, 1895, Dallas, Mich.   D. Feb. 21, 1978, Royal Oak, Mich.

BR TR 5'10"   158 lbs.

Year	Team		W	L	PCT	ERA	G	GS	CG	IP	H	BB	SO	ShO	W	L	SV	AB	H	HR	BA	PO	A	E	DP	TC/G	FA
1921	DET	A	3	2	.600	5.68	10	1	0	25.1	33	16	10	0	3	2	0	9	1	0	.111	0	3	0	0	0.3	1.000

Roy Parmelee

PARMELEE, LeROY EARL (Bud)
B. Apr. 25, 1907, Lambertville, Mich.   D. Aug. 31, 1981, Monroe, Mich.

BR TR 6'1"   190 lbs.

Year	Team		W	L	PCT	ERA	G	GS	CG	IP	H	BB	SO	ShO	W	L	SV	AB	H	HR	BA	PO	A	E	DP	TC/G	FA
1929	NY	N	1	0	1.000	9.00	2	1	0	7	13	3	1	0	0	0	0	2	1	0	.500	0	2	0	0	1.0	1.000
1930			0	1	.000	9.43	11	1	0	21	18	26	19	0	0	0	0	4	1	0	.250	1	4	1	0	0.5	.833
1931			2	2	.500	3.68	13	5	4	58.2	47	33	30	0	0	0	0	20	4	0	.200	5	11	0	1	1.2	1.000
1932			0	3	.000	3.91	8	3	0	25.1	25	14	23	0	0	0	0	5	2	0	.400	1	6	1	0	1.0	.875
1933			13	8	.619	3.17	32	32	14	218.1	191	77	132	3	0	0	0	81	19	1	.235	8	44	4	4	1.8	.929
1934			10	6	.625	3.42	22	20	7	152.2	134	60	83	3	0	0	0	55	11	2	.200	9	39	1	1	2.2	.980
1935			14	10	.583	4.22	34	31	13	226	214	97	79	0	0	1	0	86	18	0	.209	16	55	5	2	2.2	.934
1936	STL	N	11	11	.500	4.56	37	28	9	221	226	107	79	0	0	1	2	76	15	0	.197	16	42	2	1	1.6	.967
1937	CHI	N	7	8	.467	5.13	33	18	8	145.2	165	79	55	0	2	1	2	52	9	2	.173	13	33	2	2	1.5	.958

Year	Team		W	L	PCT	ERA	G	GS	CG	IP	H	BB	SO	ShO	Relief W	Relief L	SV	AB	H	HR	BA	PO	A	E	DP	TC/G	FA

Roy Parmelee *continued*

Year	Team		W	L	PCT	ERA	G	GS	CG	IP	H	BB	SO	ShO	W	L	SV	AB	H	HR	BA	PO	A	E	DP	TC/G	FA
1939	PHI	A	1	6	.143	6.45	14	5	0	44.2	42	35	13	0	1	2	1	15	2	0	.133	2	10	1	0	0.9	.923
	10 yrs.		59	55	.518	4.27	206	144	55	1120.1	1075	531	514	6	2	4	3	396	82	5	.207	71	246	17	11	1.6	.949

Mel Parnell

PARNELL, MELVIN LLOYD (Dusty) BL TL 6' 180 lbs.
B. June 13, 1922, New Orleans, La.

Year	Team		W	L	PCT	ERA	G	GS	CG	IP	H	BB	SO	ShO	W	L	SV	AB	H	HR	BA	PO	A	E	DP	TC/G	FA
1947	BOS	A	2	3	.400	6.39	15	5	1	50.2	60	27	23	0	1	1	0	18	1	0	.056	0	7	1	0	0.5	.875
1948			15	8	.652	3.14	35	27	16	212	205	90	77	1	0	2	0	80	13	0	.163	9	48	1	3	1.7	.983
1949			25	7	.781	2.77	39	33	27	295.1	258	134	122	4	1	1	2	114	29	0	.254	8	53	0	5	1.6	1.000
1950			18	10	.643	3.61	40	31	21	249	244	106	93	2	0	1	3	98	19	0	.194	7	67	1	6	1.9	.987
1951			18	11	.621	3.26	36	29	11	221	229	77	77	3	2	0	2	81	25	0	.309	8	42	3	2	1.5	.943
1952			12	12	.500	3.62	33	29	15	214	207	89	107	3	0	0	2	84	8	1	.095	15	38	0	4	1.6	1.000
1953			21	8	.724	3.06	38	34	12	241	217	116	136	5	1	0	0	94	21	0	.223	10	27	2	4	1.0	.949
1954			3	7	.300	3.70	19	15	4	92.1	104	35	38	1	0	0	0	34	3	0	.088	3	17	1	1	1.1	.952
1955			2	3	.400	7.83	13	9	0	46	62	25	18	0	0	1	0	19	6	0	.316	2	9	1	0	0.9	.917
1956			7	6	.538	3.77	21	20	6	131.1	129	59	41	1	0	1	0	46	7	0	.152	7	19	2	2	1.3	.929
	10 yrs.		123	75	.621	3.50	289	232	113	1752.2	1715	758	732	20	5	6	10	668	132	1	.198	69	327	12	27	1.4	.971

Rube Parnham

PARNHAM, JAMES ARTHUR BR TR 6'3" 185 lbs.
B. Feb. 1, 1894, Heidelberg, Pa.   D. Nov. 25, 1963, McKeesport, Pa.

Year	Team		W	L	PCT	ERA	G	GS	CG	IP	H	BB	SO	ShO	W	L	SV	AB	H	HR	BA	PO	A	E	DP	TC/G	FA
1916	PHI	A	2	1	.667	0.36	4	3	2	24.2	27	13	8	0	0	0	0	11	3	0	.273	1	12	0	0	3.3	1.000
1917			0	1	.000	4.09	2	2	0	11	12	9	4	0	0	0	0	3	0	0	.000	1	3	0	0	2.0	1.000
	2 yrs.		2	2	.500	1.51	6	5	2	35.2	39	22	12	0	0	0	0	14	3	0	.214	2	15	0	0	2.8	1.000

Jeff Parrett

PARRETT, JEFFREY DALE BR TR 6'4" 185 lbs.
B. Aug. 26, 1961, Indianapolis, Ind.

Year	Team		W	L	PCT	ERA	G	GS	CG	IP	H	BB	SO	ShO	W	L	SV	AB	H	HR	BA	PO	A	E	DP	TC/G	FA
1986	MON	N	0	1	.000	4.87	12	0	0	20.1	19	13	21	0	0	1	0	2	1	0	.500	1	2	0	1	0.3	1.000
1987			7	6	.538	4.21	45	0	0	62	53	30	56	0	7	6	6	5	0	0	.000	3	9	2	1	0.3	.857
1988			12	4	.750	2.65	61	0	0	91.2	66	45	62	0	12	4	6	0	0	0	—	7	9	1	0	0.2	.941
1989	PHI	N	12	6	.667	2.98	72	0	0	105.2	90	44	98	0	12	6	6	5	0	0	.000	2	9	0	0	0.2	1.000
	4 yrs.		31	17	.646	3.28	190	0	0	279.2	228	132	237	0	31	17	18	12	1	0	.083	13	29	3	2	0.2	.933

Mike Parrott

PARROTT, MICHAEL EVERETT BR TR 6'4" 210 lbs.
B. Dec. 6, 1954, Oxnard, Calif.

Year	Team		W	L	PCT	ERA	G	GS	CG	IP	H	BB	SO	ShO	W	L	SV	AB	H	HR	BA	PO	A	E	DP	TC/G	FA
1977	BAL	A	0	0	—	2.25	3	0	0	4	4	2	2	0	0	0	0		1	0	0	—	1	3	0	0	0.3	1.000
1978	SEA	A	1	5	.167	5.14	27	10	0	82.1	108	32	41	0	0	1	1	0	0	0	—	7	11	1	1	0.7	.947
1979			14	12	.538	3.77	38	30	13	229	231	86	127	2	1	0	0	0	0	0	—	27	39	0	1	1.7	1.000
1980			1	16	.059	7.28	27	16	1	94	136	42	53	0	0	2	3	0	0	0	—	11	28	2	2	1.5	.951
1981			3	6	.333	5.08	24	12	0	85	102	28	43	0	0	0	1	0	0	0	—	6	15	0	0	0.9	1.000
	5 yrs.		19	39	.328	4.88	119	68	14	494.1	581	190	266	2	1	3	5	0	0	0	—	52	93	3	4	1.2	.980

Tom Parrott

PARROTT, THOMAS WILLIAM (Tacky Tom) BR TR 5'10½" 170 lbs.
Brother of Jiggs Parrott.
B. Apr. 10, 1868, Portland, Ore.   D. Jan. 1, 1932, Dundee, Ore.

Year	Team		W	L	PCT	ERA	G	GS	CG	IP	H	BB	SO	ShO	W	L	SV	AB	H	HR	BA	PO	A	E	DP	TC/G	FA
1893	2 teams	CHI N (4G 0–3)									CIN N (22G 10–7)																	
"	total		10	10	.500	4.48	26	20	13	181	209	87	40	1	3	0	0	95	20	1	.211	17	41	6	1	2.5	.906
1894	CIN	N	17	19	.472	5.60	41	36	31	308.2	402	126	61	1	0	1	1	229	74	4	.323	25	66	7	2	2.4	.929
1895			11	18	.379	5.47	41	31	23	263.1	382	76	57	0	3	1	3	201	69	3	.343	30	64	8	2	2.5	.922
1896	STL	N	1	1	.500	6.21	7	2	2	42	62	18	8	0	0	0	0	474	138	7	.291	7	6	1	0	2.0	.929
	4 yrs.		39	48	.448	5.33	115	89	69	795	1055	307	166	2	6	2	4	*				79	177	22	5	2.4	.921

Jiggs Parson

PARSON, WILLIAM EDWIN BR TR 6'2" 180 lbs.
B. Dec. 28, 1885, Parker, S. D.   D. May 19, 1967, Los Angeles, Calif.

Year	Team		W	L	PCT	ERA	G	GS	CG	IP	H	BB	SO	ShO	W	L	SV	AB	H	HR	BA	PO	A	E	DP	TC/G	FA
1910	BOS	N	0	2	.000	3.82	10	4	0	35.1	35	26	7	0	0	1	0	12	1	0	.083	0	11	1	0	1.2	.917
1911			0	1	.000	6.48	7	0	0	25	36	15	7	0	0	1	0	10	2	0	.200	0	5	1	0	0.9	.833
	2 yrs.		0	3	.000	4.92	17	4	0	60.1	71	41	14	0	0	2	0	22	3	0	.136	0	16	2	0	1.1	.889

Bill Parsons

PARSONS, WILLIAM RAYMOND BR TR 6'6" 195 lbs.
B. Aug. 17, 1948, Riverside, Calif.

Year	Team		W	L	PCT	ERA	G	GS	CG	IP	H	BB	SO	ShO	W	L	SV	AB	H	HR	BA	PO	A	E	DP	TC/G	FA
1971	MIL	A	13	17	.433	3.20	36	35	12	245	219	93	139	4	0	0	0	72	12	0	.167	22	35	0	4	1.6	1.000
1972			13	13	.500	3.91	33	30	10	214	194	68	111	2	0	0	0	67	11	0	.164	8	22	0	1	0.9	1.000
1973			3	6	.333	6.79	20	17	0	59.2	59	67	30	0	0	0	0	0	0	0	—	2	9	1	0	0.6	.917
1974	OAK	A	0	0	—	0.00	4	0	0	2	1	3	2	0	0	0	0	0	0	0	—	0	0	0	0	0.0	—
	4 yrs.		29	36	.446	3.89	93	82	22	520.2	473	231	282	6	0	0	0	139	23	1	.165	32	66	1	5	1.1	.990

Charlie Parsons

PARSONS, CHARLES JAMES BL TL 5'10" 160 lbs.
B. July 18, 1863, Cherry Flats, Pa.   D. Mar. 24, 1936, Mansfield, Pa.

Year	Team		W	L	PCT	ERA	G	GS	CG	IP	H	BB	SO	ShO	W	L	SV	AB	H	HR	BA	PO	A	E	DP	TC/G	FA
1886	BOS	N	0	2	.000	3.94	2	2	2	16	20	4	5	0	0	0	0	8	3	0	.375	0	1	0	0	0.5	1.000
1887	NY	AA	1	1	.500	4.50	4	4	4	34	51	6	5	0	0	0	0	15	3	0	.200	1	8	2	0	2.8	.818
1890	CLE	N	0	1	.000	6.00	2	1	0	9	12	6	2	0	0	0	0	4	3	0	.750	0	2	3	0	2.5	.400
	3 yrs.		1	4	.200	4.58	8	7	6	59	83	16	12	0	0	0	0	27	9	0	.333	1	11	5	0	2.1	.706

Tom Parsons

PARSONS, THOMAS ANTHONY (Long Tom) BR TR 6'7" 210 lbs.
B. Sept. 13, 1939, Lakeville, Conn.

Year	Team		W	L	PCT	ERA	G	GS	CG	IP	H	BB	SO	ShO	W	L	SV	AB	H	HR	BA	PO	A	E	DP	TC/G	FA
1963	PIT	N	0	1	.000	8.31	1	1	0	4.1	7	2	2	0	0	0	0	2	0	0	.000	0	1	0	0	1.0	1.000
1964	NY	N	1	2	.333	4.19	4	2	1	19.1	20	6	10	0	1	0	0	7	0	0	.000	0	2	0	0	0.5	1.000
1965			1	10	.091	4.67	35	11	1	90.2	108	17	58	0	0	3	1	18	1	0	.056	4	22	0	1	0.7	1.000
	3 yrs.		2	13	.133	4.72	40	14	2	114.1	135	25	70	0	1	3	1	27	1	0	.037	4	25	0	1	0.7	1.000

Year	Team	W	L	PCT	ERA	G	GS	CG	IP	H	BB	SO	ShO	W	L	SV	AB	H	HR	BA	PO	A	E	DP	TC/G	FA
														Relief Pitching			Batting									

Stan Partenheimer

PARTENHEIMER, STANWOOD WENDELL (Party)
Son of Steve Partenheimer.
B. Oct. 21, 1922, Chicopee Falls, Mass. D. Jan. 28, 1989, Wilson, N. C.

BR TL 5'11" 175 lbs.
BL 1944

Year	Team	W	L	PCT	ERA	G	GS	CG	IP	H	BB	SO	ShO	W	L	SV	AB	H	HR	BA	PO	A	E	DP	TC/G	FA
1944	BOS A	0	0	–	18.00	1	1	0	1	3	2	0	0	0	0	0	1	0	0	.000	0	0	0	0	0.0	–
1945	STL N	0	0	–	6.08	8	2	0	13.1	12	16	6	0	0	0	0	3	0	0	.000	0	4	0	0	0.5	1.000
2 yrs.		0	0	–	6.91	9	3	0	14.1	15	18	6	0	0	0	0	4	0	0	.000	0	4	0	0	0.4	1.000

Bill Paschall

PASCHALL, WILLIAM HERBERT
B. Apr. 22, 1954, Norfolk, Va.

BR TR 6' 175 lbs.

Year	Team	W	L	PCT	ERA	G	GS	CG	IP	H	BB	SO	ShO	W	L	SV	AB	H	HR	BA	PO	A	E	DP	TC/G	FA
1978	KC A	0	1	.000	3.38	2	0	0	8	6	0	5	0	0	1	1	0	0	0	–	0	0	0	0	0.0	–
1979		0	1	.000	6.43	7	0	0	14	18	5	3	0	0	1	0	0	0	0	–	0	2	0	0	0.3	1.000
1981		0	0	–	4.50	2	0	0	2	2	0	1	0	0	0	0	0	0	0	–	0	0	0	0	0.0	–
3 yrs.		0	2	.000	5.25	11	0	0	24	26	5	9	0	0	2	1	0	0	0	–	0	2	0	0	0.2	1.000

Camilo Pascual

PASCUAL, CAMILO ALBERTO (Little Patato)
Born Camilo Alberto Pascual y Lus. Brother of Carlos Pascual.
B. Jan. 20, 1934, Havana, Cuba

BR TR 5'11" 175 lbs.

Year	Team	W	L	PCT	ERA	G	GS	CG	IP	H	BB	SO	ShO	W	L	SV	AB	H	HR	BA	PO	A	E	DP	TC/G	FA
1954	WAS A	4	7	.364	4.22	48	4	1	119.1	126	61	60	0	4	4	3	30	4	0	.133	6	34	0	2	0.8	1.000
1955		2	12	.143	6.14	43	16	1	129	158	70	82	0	0	4	3	32	7	0	.219	8	31	2	1	1.0	.951
1956		6	18	.250	5.87	39	27	6	188.2	194	89	162	0	1	1	2	58	8	0	.138	8	31	2	1	1.1	.951
1957		8	17	.320	4.10	29	26	8	175.2	168	76	113	2	0	3	0	50	7	0	.140	7	37	1	1	1.6	.978
1958		8	12	.400	3.15	31	27	6	177.1	166	60	146	2	0	0	0	57	9	0	.158	12	27	3	2	1.4	.929
1959		17	10	.630	2.64	32	30	17	238.2	202	69	185	6	0	0	0	86	26	0	.302	18	55	0	4	2.3	1.000
1960		12	8	.600	3.03	26	22	8	151.2	139	53	143	3	0	1	2	51	9	1	.176	6	21	0	1	1.0	1.000
1961	MIN A	15	16	.484	3.46	35	33	15	252.1	205	100	221	8	0	1	0	85	14	0	.165	14	40	1	0	1.6	.982
1962		20	11	.645	3.32	34	33	18	257.2	236	59	206	5	0	0	0	97	26	2	.268	28	32	1	4	1.8	.984
1963		21	9	.700	2.46	31	31	18	248.1	205	81	202	3	0	0	0	92	23	0	.250	20	29	2	2	1.6	.961
1964		15	12	.556	3.30	36	36	14	267.1	245	98	213	1	0	0	0	94	17	0	.181	19	38	4	2	1.7	.934
1965		9	3	.750	3.35	27	27	5	156	126	63	96	1	0	0	0	60	12	2	.200	14	32	1	1	1.7	.979
1966		8	6	.571	4.89	21	19	2	103	113	30	56	0	0	0	0	37	8	0	.216	11	25	0	1	1.7	1.000
1967	WAS A	12	10	.545	3.28	28	27	5	164.2	147	43	106	1	0	0	0	51	9	0	.176	11	25	1	1	1.3	.972
1968		13	12	.520	2.69	31	31	8	201	181	59	111	4	0	0	0	65	12	0	.185	19	35	0	0	1.7	1.000
1969	2 teams		WAS A	(14G 2–5)		CIN N	(5G 0–0)																				
"	total	2	5	.286	7.07	19	14	0	62.1	63	42	37	0	0	0	0	17	4	0	.235	5	7	0	0	0.6	1.000
1970	LA N	0	0	–	2.57	10	0	0	14	12	5	8	0	0	0	0	0	0	0	–	1	3	0	1	0.4	1.000
1971	CLE A	2	2	.500	3.13	9	1	0	23	17	11	20	0	2	1	0	5	3	0	.600	4	5	2	1	1.2	.818
18 yrs.		174	170	.506	3.63	529	404	132	2930	2703	1069	2167	36	7	15	10	967	198	5	.205	210	507	20	26	1.4	.973

WORLD SERIES

Year	Team	W	L	PCT	ERA	G	GS	CG	IP	H	BB	SO	ShO	W	L	SV	AB	H	HR	BA	PO	A	E	DP	TC/G	FA
1965	MIN A	0	1	.000	5.40	1	1	0	5	8	1	0	0	0	0	0	1	0	0	.000	0	1	0	0	1.0	1.000

Carlos Pascual

PASCUAL, CARLOS ALBERTO (Patato)
Born Carlos Alberto Pascual y Lus. Brother of Camilo Pascual.
B. Mar. 13, 1931, Havana, Cuba

BR TR 5'6" 165 lbs.

Year	Team	W	L	PCT	ERA	G	GS	CG	IP	H	BB	SO	ShO	W	L	SV	AB	H	HR	BA	PO	A	E	DP	TC/G	FA
1950	WAS A	1	1	.500	2.12	2	2	2	17	12	8	3	0	0	0	0	4	1	0	.250	0	1	1	0	1.0	.500

Larry Pashnick

PASHNICK, LARRY JOHN
B. Apr. 25, 1956, Lincoln Park, Mich.

BR TR 6'3" 205 lbs.

Year	Team	W	L	PCT	ERA	G	GS	CG	IP	H	BB	SO	ShO	W	L	SV	AB	H	HR	BA	PO	A	E	DP	TC/G	FA
1982	DET A	4	4	.500	4.01	28	13	1	94.1	110	25	19	0	1	0	0	0	0	0	–	6	12	0	1	0.6	1.000
1983		1	3	.250	5.26	12	6	0	37.2	48	18	17	0	1	0	0	0	0	0	–	6	6	0	0	1.0	1.000
1984	MIN A	2	1	.667	3.52	13	1	0	38.1	38	11	10	0	2	0	0	0	0	0	–	3	6	0	0	0.7	1.000
3 yrs.		7	8	.467	4.17	53	20	1	170.1	196	54	46	0	4	0	0	0	0	0	–	15	24	0	1	0.7	1.000

Claude Passeau

PASSEAU, CLAUDE WILLIAM
B. Apr. 9, 1909, Waynesboro, Miss.

BR TR 6'3" 198 lbs.

Year	Team	W	L	PCT	ERA	G	GS	CG	IP	H	BB	SO	ShO	W	L	SV	AB	H	HR	BA	PO	A	E	DP	TC/G	FA
1935	PIT N	0	1	.000	12.00	1	1	0	3	7	2	1	0	0	0	0	1	0	0	.000	0	2	0	1	2.0	1.000
1936	PHI N	11	15	.423	3.48	49	21	8	217.1	247	55	85	2	3	7	3	78	22	2	.282	7	49	2	4	1.2	.966
1937		14	18	.438	4.34	50	34	18	292.1	348	79	135	1	2	1	2	107	21	1	.196	14	60	1	3	1.5	.987
1938		11	18	.379	4.52	44	33	15	239	281	93	100	0	0	0	1	80	13	0	.163	14	60	4	4	1.8	.949
1939	2 teams		PHI N	(8G 2–4)		CHI N	(34G 13–9)																				
"	total	15	13	.536	3.28	42	35	17	274.1	269	73	137	2	1	2	3	97	16	1	.165	11	58	0	2	1.6	1.000
1940	CHI N	20	13	.606	2.50	46	31	20	280.2	259	59	124	4	4	1	5	98	20	1	.204	17	62	7	0	1.9	.919
1941		14	14	.500	3.35	34	30	20	231	262	52	80	3	1	1	0	86	19	3	.221	6	45	1	4	1.5	.981
1942		19	14	.576	2.68	35	34	24	278.1	284	74	89	3	0	0	0	105	19	2	.181	12	61	0	9	2.1	1.000
1943		15	12	.556	2.91	35	31	18	257	245	66	93	2	0	1	1	96	19	0	.198	13	55	0	3	1.9	1.000
1944		15	9	.625	2.89	34	27	18	227	234	50	89	2	0	0	3	80	13	0	.163	12	42	0	5	1.6	1.000
1945		17	9	.654	2.46	34	27	19	227	205	59	98	5	1	0	1	91	17	2	.187	17	52	0	3	2.0	1.000
1946		9	8	.529	3.13	21	21	10	129.1	118	42	47	2	0	0	0	49	10	3	.204	6	30	1	3	1.8	.973
1947		2	6	.250	6.25	19	6	1	63.1	97	24	26	1	1	0	2	14	0	0	.000	7	7	1	1	0.5	.889
13 yrs.		162	150	.519	3.32	444	331	188	2719.2	2856	728	1104	27	13	13	21	982	189	15	.192	130	583	17	44	1.6	.977

WORLD SERIES

Year	Team	W	L	PCT	ERA	G	GS	CG	IP	H	BB	SO	ShO	W	L	SV	AB	H	HR	BA	PO	A	E	DP	TC/G	FA
1945	CHI N	1	0	1.000	2.70	3	2	1	16.2	7	8	3	1	0	0	0	7	0	0	.000	1	3	0	2	1.3	1.000

Frank Pastore

PASTORE, FRANK ENRICO
B. Aug. 21, 1957, Alhambra, Calif.

BR TR 6'2" 188 lbs.

Year	Team	W	L	PCT	ERA	G	GS	CG	IP	H	BB	SO	ShO	W	L	SV	AB	H	HR	BA	PO	A	E	DP	TC/G	FA
1979	CIN N	6	7	.462	4.26	30	9	2	95	102	23	63	1	2	3	4	25	4	0	.160	5	13	0	2	0.6	1.000
1980		13	7	.650	3.26	27	27	9	185	161	42	110	2	0	0	0	64	10	0	.156	10	25	3	1	1.4	.921
1981		4	9	.308	4.02	22	22	2	132	125	35	81	1	0	0	0	44	5	0	.114	5	13	0	0	0.8	1.000
1982		8	13	.381	3.97	31	29	3	188.1	210	57	94	2	0	0	0	58	10	1	.172	6	24	1	2	1.0	.968
1983		9	12	.429	4.88	36	29	4	184.1	207	64	93	1	0	0	0	59	11	1	.186	15	19	0	3	0.9	1.000
1984		3	8	.273	6.50	24	16	1	98.1	110	40	53	0	1	0	0	28	2	0	.071	6	16	1	1	1.0	.957
1985		2	1	.667	3.83	17	6	1	54	60	16	29	0	1	0	0	14	2	0	.143	3	9	1	1	0.8	.923

Year	Team		W	L	PCT	ERA	G	GS	CG	IP	H	BB	SO	ShO	Relief Pitching W	L	SV	Batting AB	H	HR	BA	PO	A	E	DP	TC/G	FA

Frank Pastore *continued*

| 1986 | MIN | A | 3 | 1 | .750 | 4.01 | 33 | 1 | 0 | 49.1 | 54 | 24 | 18 | 0 | 3 | 1 | 2 | 0 | 0 | 0 | – | 1 | 5 | 0 | 0 | 0.2 | 1.000 |
| 8 yrs. | | | 48 | 58 | .453 | 4.29 | 220 | 139 | 22 | 986.1 | 1029 | 301 | 541 | 7 | 7 | 4 | 6 | 292 | 44 | 2 | .151 | 51 | 124 | 6 | 11 | 0.8 | .967 |

LEAGUE CHAMPIONSHIP SERIES

| 1979 | CIN | N | 0 | 0 | – | 2.57 | 1 | 1 | 0 | 7 | 7 | 3 | 1 | 0 | 0 | 0 | 0 | 0 | 0 | 0 | – | 0 | 0 | 0 | 0 | 0.0 | |

Jim Pastorius

PASTORIUS, JAMES W.
B. July 12, 1881, Pittsburgh, Pa.   D. May 10, 1941, Pittsburgh, Pa.

BL TL 5'9"   165 lbs.

1906	BKN	N	10	14	.417	3.61	29	24	16	211.2	225	69	58	3	1	2	0	71	10	0	.141	11	56	3	4	2.4	.957
1907			16	12	.571	2.35	28	26	20	222	218	77	70	4	2	0	0	73	15	0	.205	7	60	2	4	2.5	.971
1908			4	20	.167	2.44	28	25	16	213.2	171	74	54	2	0	1	0	62	8	0	.129	6	66	2	1	2.6	.973
1909			1	9	.100	5.76	12	9	5	79.2	91	58	23	1	0	1	0	25	2	0	.080	4	26	3	1	2.8	.909
4 yrs.			31	55	.360	3.12	97	84	57	727	705	278	205	10	3	4	0	231	35	0	.152	28	208	10	10	2.5	.959

Joe Pate

PATE, JOSEPH WILLIAM
B. June 6, 1892, Alice, Tex.   D. Dec. 26, 1948, Fort Worth, Tex.

BL TL 5'10"   184 lbs.

1926	PHI	A	9	0	1.000	2.71	47	2	0	113	109	51	24	0	9	0	6	27	4	0	.148	4	46	0	2	1.1	1.000
1927			0	3	.000	5.20	32	0	0	53.2	67	21	14	0	0	3	6	10	3	0	.300	1	16	2	0	0.6	.895
2 yrs.			9	3	.750	3.51	79	2	0	166.2	176	72	38	0	9	3	12	37	7	0	.189	5	62	2	2	0.9	.971

Casey Patten

PATTEN, CASE LYMAN (Pat)
B. May 7, 1876, Westport, N.Y.   D. May 31, 1935, Rochester, N.Y.

BB TL 6'   175 lbs.

1901	WAS	A	18	10	.643	3.93	32	30	26	254.1	285	74	109	4	0	1	0	96	13	1	.135	21	60	4	2	2.7	.953
1902			17	16	.515	4.05	36	34	33	299.2	331	89	92	1	0	0	1	125	12	0	.096	19	82	10	1	3.1	.910
1903			11	22	.333	3.60	36	34	32	300	313	80	133	0	0	0	1	106	14	0	.132	16	91	7	1	3.2	.939
1904			14	23	.378	3.07	45	39	37	357.2	**367**	79	150	2	0	2	3	126	16	0	.127	32	111	7	5	3.3	.953
1905			14	21	.400	3.14	42	37	29	309.2	300	86	113	2	1	2	0	106	16	0	.151	28	81	9	3	2.8	.924
1906			19	16	.543	2.17	38	32	28	282.2	253	79	96	6	1	2	0	94	11	0	.117	18	80	4	2	2.7	.961
1907			12	16	.429	3.56	39	29	20	237.1	272	63	58	1	0	1	0	87	11	0	.126	12	58	12	1	2.3	.854
1908	2 teams		WAS A		(4G 0–2)			BOS A		(1G 0–1)																	
"	total		0	3	.000	5.14	5	4	1	21	33	7	6	0	0	0	0	6	1	0	.167	0	5	1	1	1.2	.833
8 yrs.			105	127	.453	3.36	270	239	206	2062.1	2154	557	757	16	2	8	5	746	94	2	.126	146	568	54	16	2.8	.930

Bob Patterson

PATTERSON, ROBERT CHANDLER
B. May 16, 1959, Jacksonville, Fla.

BR TR 6'2"   185 lbs.

1985	SD	N	0	0	–	24.75	3	0	0	4	13	3	1	0	0	0	0	0	0	0	–	0	0	0	0	0.0	
1986	PIT	N	2	3	.400	4.95	11	5	0	36.1	49	5	20	0	1	2	0	8	1	0	.125	1	9	0	1	0.9	1.000
1987			1	4	.200	6.70	15	7	0	43	49	22	27	0	0	0	0	12	1	0	.083	0	7	0	0	0.5	1.000
1989			4	3	.571	4.05	12	3	0	26.2	23	8	20	0	3	1	1	3	0	0	.000	1	2	0	0	0.3	1.000
4 yrs.			7	10	.412	6.14	41	15	0	110	134	38	68	0	4	3	1	23	2	0	.087	2	18	0	1	0.5	1.000

Daryl Patterson

PATTERSON, DARYL ALAN
B. Nov. 21, 1943, Coalinga, Calif.

BL TR 6'4"   192 lbs.

1968	DET	A	2	3	.400	2.12	38	1	0	68	53	27	49	0	0	0	7	13	0	0	.000	4	9	1	0	0.4	.929
1969			0	2	.000	2.82	18	0	0	22.1	15	19	12	0	0	2	0	1	0	0	.000	1	0	0	0	0.1	1.000
1970			7	1	.875	4.85	43	0	0	78	81	39	55	0	7	1	2	11	0	0	.000	5	8	1	0	0.3	.929
1971	3 teams		DET A		(12G 0–1)			OAK A		(4G 0–0)			STL N		(13G 0–1)												
"	total		0	2	.000	4.93	29	2	0	42	39	25	18	0	0	2	1	6	0	0	.000	3	3	1	0	0.2	.857
1974	PIT	N	2	1	.667	7.29	14	0	0	21	35	9	8	0	2	1	1	4	0	0	.000	0	4	0	0	0.3	1.000
5 yrs.			11	9	.550	4.09	142	3	0	231.1	223	119	142	0	9	6	11	35	0	0	.000	13	24	3	0	0.3	.925

WORLD SERIES

| 1968 | DET | A | 0 | 0 | – | 0.00 | 2 | 0 | 0 | 3 | 1 | 1 | 0 | 0 | 0 | 0 | 0 | 0 | 0 | 0 | – | 0 | 1 | 0 | 0 | 0.5 | 1.000 |

Dave Patterson

PATTERSON, DAVID GLENN
B. July 25, 1956, Springfield, Mo.

BR TR 6'   170 lbs.

| 1979 | LA | N | 4 | 1 | .800 | 5.26 | 36 | 0 | 0 | 53 | 62 | 22 | 34 | 0 | 4 | 1 | 6 | 7 | 1 | 0 | .143 | 6 | 5 | 0 | 1 | 0.3 | 1.000 |

Gil Patterson

PATTERSON, GILBERT THOMAS
B. Sept. 5, 1955, Philadelphia, Pa.

BR TR 6'1"   185 lbs.

| 1977 | NY | A | 1 | 2 | .333 | 5.45 | 10 | 6 | 0 | 33 | 38 | 20 | 29 | 0 | 0 | 0 | 0 | 0 | 0 | 0 | – | 5 | 6 | 1 | 0 | 1.2 | .917 |

Ken Patterson

PATTERSON, KENNETH BRIAN
B. July 8, 1964, Costa Mesa, Calif.

BL TL 6'4"   210 lbs.

1988	CHI	A	0	2	.000	4.79	9	2	0	20.2	25	7	8	0	0	1	1	0	0	0	–	1	2	0	0	0.3	1.000
1989			6	1	.857	4.52	50	1	0	65.2	64	28	43	0	6	1	0	0	0	0	–	3	4	0	1	0.1	1.000
2 yrs.			6	3	.667	4.59	59	3	0	86.1	89	35	51	0	6	2	1	0	0	0	–	4	6	0	1	0.2	1.000

Reggie Patterson

PATTERSON, REGINALD ALLEN
B. Nov. 7, 1958, Birmingham, Ala.

BR TR 6'4"   180 lbs.

1981	CHI	A	0	1	.000	14.14	6	1	0	7	14	6	2	0	0	0	0	0	0	0	–	0	3	0	0	0.5	1.000
1983	CHI	N	1	2	.333	4.82	5	2	0	18.2	17	6	10	0	0	1	0	6	0	0	.000	3	1	0	1	0.8	1.000
1984			0	1	.000	10.50	3	1	0	6	10	2	5	0	0	0	0	2	0	0	.000	1	1	0	0	0.7	1.000
1985			3	0	1.000	3.00	8	5	1	39	36	10	17	0	0	0	0	10	1	0	.100	4	4	0	0	1.0	1.000
4 yrs.			4	4	.500	5.22	22	9	1	70.2	77	24	34	0	0	1	0	18	1	0	.056	8	9	0	1	0.8	1.000

Roy Patterson

PATTERSON, ROY LEWIS (Pat)
B. Dec. 17, 1876, Stoddard, Wis.   D. Apr. 14, 1953, St. Croix Falls, Wis.

BR TR 6'   185 lbs.

| 1901 | CHI | A | 20 | 16 | .556 | 3.37 | 41 | 35 | 30 | 312.1 | 345 | 62 | 127 | 4 | 2 | 2 | 0 | 117 | 26 | 1 | .222 | 9 | 88 | 6 | 2 | 2.5 | .942 |
| 1902 | | | 19 | 14 | .576 | 3.06 | 34 | 30 | 26 | 268 | 262 | 67 | 61 | 2 | 2 | 2 | 0 | 105 | 20 | 0 | .190 | 17 | 83 | 6 | 4 | 3.1 | .943 |

Year	Team		W	L	PCT	ERA	G	GS	CG	IP	H	BB	SO	ShO	Relief Pitching W	L	SV	Batting AB	H	HR	BA	PO	A	E	DP	TC/G	FA

Roy Patterson *continued*

Year	Team	W	L	PCT	ERA	G	GS	CG	IP	H	BB	SO	ShO	W	L	SV	AB	H	HR	BA	PO	A	E	DP	TC/G	FA
1903		15	15	.500	2.70	34	30	26	293	275	69	89	2	1	0	1	105	11	0	.105	23	98	6	2	3.7	.953
1904		9	9	.500	2.29	22	17	14	165	148	24	64	4	1	0	0	58	6	0	.103	7	49	2	2	2.6	.966
1905		4	5	.444	1.83	13	9	7	88.2	73	16	29	1	0	1	0	30	8	0	.267	5	32	1	2	2.9	.974
1906		10	7	.588	2.09	21	18	12	142	119	17	45	3	0	0	1	49	3	0	.061	9	46	2	0	2.7	.965
1907		4	6	.400	2.63	19	13	4	96	105	18	27	1	0	0	0	31	3	0	.097	5	36	0	0	2.2	1.000
7 yrs.		81	72	.529	2.75	184	152	119	1365	1327	273	442	17	6	5	2	495	77	1	.156	75	432	23	12	2.9	.957

Marty Pattin

PATTIN, MARTIN WILLIAM
B. Apr. 6, 1943, Charleston, Ill.   BR TR 5'11"   180 lbs.

Year	Team		W	L	PCT	ERA	G	GS	CG	IP	H	BB	SO	ShO	W	L	SV	AB	H	HR	BA	PO	A	E	DP	TC/G	FA
1968	CAL	A	4	4	.500	2.79	52	4	0	84	67	37	66	0	3	3	3	12	1	0	.083	6	5	0	0	0.2	1.000
1969	SEA	A	7	12	.368	5.62	34	27	2	158.2	166	71	126	1	0	0	0	58	9	0	.155	5	18	2	2	0.7	.920
1970	MIL	A	14	12	.538	3.40	37	29	11	233	204	71	161	0	1	1	0	70	9	0	.129	18	40	1	3	1.6	.983
1971			14	14	.500	3.12	36	36	9	265	225	73	169	5	0	0	0	83	7	0	.084	18	36	1	0	1.5	.982
1972	BOS	A	17	13	.567	3.23	38	35	13	253.1	232	65	168	4	0	1	0	86	12	2	.140	19	38	1	2	1.5	.983
1973			15	15	.500	4.31	34	30	11	219.1	238	69	119	2	1	0	1	0	0	0	–	13	36	2	3	1.5	.961
1974	KC	A	3	7	.300	4.00	25	11	2	117	121	28	50	0	2	3	0	0	0	0	–	5	14	1	1	0.8	.950
1975			10	10	.500	3.25	44	15	5	177	173	45	89	1	4	4	5	0	0	0	–	13	22	3	1	0.9	.921
1976			8	14	.364	2.49	44	15	4	141	114	38	65	1	1	8	5	0	0	0	–	9	20	1	1	0.7	.967
1977			10	3	.769	3.59	31	10	4	128	115	37	55	0	5	1	0	0	0	0	–	6	19	0	0	0.8	1.000
1978			3	3	.500	3.32	32	5	2	78.2	72	25	30	0	1	1	4	0	0	0	–	3	4	0	2	0.2	1.000
1979			5	2	.714	4.60	31	7	1	94	109	21	41	0	2	1	3	0	0	0	–	4	13	1	0	0.6	.944
1980			4	0	1.000	3.64	37	0	0	89	97	23	40	0	4	0	4	0	0	0	–	4	9	1	1	0.4	.929
13 yrs.			114	109	.511	3.62	475	224	64	2038	1933	603	1179	14	24	23	25	309	38	2	.123	123	274	14	16	0.9	.966

LEAGUE CHAMPIONSHIP SERIES

Year	Team		W	L	PCT	ERA	G	GS	CG	IP	H	BB	SO	ShO	W	L	SV	AB	H	HR	BA	PO	A	E	DP	TC/G	FA
1976	KC	A	0	0	–	27.00	2	0	0	.1	1	0	1	0	0	0	0	0	0	0	–	0	0	0	0	0.0	–
1977			0	0	–	1.50	1	0	0	6	6	0	0	0	0	0	0	0	0	0	–	1	2	0	1	3.0	1.000
1978			0	0	–	27.00	1	0	0	.2	2	0	0	0	0	0	0	0	0	0	–	0	0	0	0	0.0	–
3 yrs.			0	0	–	5.14	4	0	0	7	8	1	1	0	0	0	0	0	0	0	–	1	2	0	1	0.8	1.000

WORLD SERIES

Year	Team		W	L	PCT	ERA	G	GS	CG	IP	H	BB	SO	ShO	W	L	SV	AB	H	HR	BA	PO	A	E	DP	TC/G	FA
1980	KC	A	0	0	–	0.00	1	0	0	1	0	0	2	0	0	0	0	0	0	0	–	0	0	0	0	0.0	–

Jimmy Pattison

PATTISON, JAMES WELLS
B. Dec. 18, 1908, New York, N. Y.   BL TL 6'   185 lbs.

Year	Team		W	L	PCT	ERA	G	GS	CG	IP	H	BB	SO	ShO	W	L	SV	AB	H	HR	BA	PO	A	E	DP	TC/G	FA
1929	BKN	N	0	1	.000	4.63	6	0	0	11.2	9	4	5	0	0	1	0	2	1	0	.500	0	2	0	0	0.3	1.000

Harry Patton

PATTON, HARRY CLAUDE
B. June 29, 1884, Gillespie, Ill.   D. June 9, 1930, St. Louis, Mo.

Year	Team		W	L	PCT	ERA	G	GS	CG	IP	H	BB	SO	ShO	W	L	SV	AB	H	HR	BA	PO	A	E	DP	TC/G	FA
1910	STL	N	0	0	–	2.25	1	0	0	4	4	2	2	0	0	0	0	0	0	0	–	0	3	0	0	3.0	1.000

Mike Paul

PAUL, MICHAEL GEORGE
B. Apr. 18, 1945, Detroit, Mich.   BL TL 6'   175 lbs.

Year	Team		W	L	PCT	ERA	G	GS	CG	IP	H	BB	SO	ShO	W	L	SV	AB	H	HR	BA	PO	A	E	DP	TC/G	FA
1968	CLE	A	5	8	.385	3.93	36	7	0	91.2	72	35	87	0	2	5	3	24	4	0	.167	3	9	1	0	0.4	.923
1969			5	10	.333	3.61	47	12	0	117.1	104	54	98	0	4	3	2	27	0	0	.000	1	14	1	1	0.3	.938
1970			2	8	.200	4.81	30	15	1	88	91	45	70	0	0	1	0	26	4	0	.154	2	6	1	1	0.3	.889
1971			2	7	.222	5.95	17	12	1	62	78	14	33	0	0	0	0	19	1	0	.053	2	6	0	0	0.5	1.000
1972	TEX	A	8	9	.471	2.17	49	20	2	162	149	52	108	1	1	1	1	48	8	0	.167	7	19	0	3	0.5	1.000
1973	2 teams		TEX A	(36G 5–4)		CHI N	(11G 0–1)																				
"	total		5	5	.500	4.71	47	11	1	105	121	45	55	0	1	1	2	4	0	0	.000	4	22	1	2	0.6	.963
1974	CHI	N	0	1	.000	36.00	2	0	0	1	4	1	1	0	0	0	0	0	0	0	–	0	0	0	0	0.0	–
7 yrs.			27	48	.360	3.92	228	77	5	627	619	246	452	1	8	12	8	148	17	0	.115	19	76	4	7	0.4	.960

Gene Paulette

PAULETTE, EUGENE EDWARD
B. May 26, 1891, Centralia, Ill.   D. Feb. 8, 1966, Little Rock, Ark.   BR TR 6'   150 lbs.

Year	Team		W	L	PCT	ERA	G	GS	CG	IP	H	BB	SO	ShO	W	L	SV	AB	H	HR	BA	PO	A	E	DP	TC/G	FA
1918	STL	N	0	0	–	0.00	1	0	0	.1	1	0	0	0	0	0	0	*				0	1	0	0	1.0	1.000

Gil Paulsen

PAULSEN, GUILFORD PAUL HANS
B. Nov. 14, 1902, Graettinger, Iowa   BR TR 6'2½"   190 lbs.

Year	Team		W	L	PCT	ERA	G	GS	CG	IP	H	BB	SO	ShO	W	L	SV	AB	H	HR	BA	PO	A	E	DP	TC/G	FA
1925	STL	N	0	0	–	0.00	1	0	0	2	1	0	1	0	0	0	0	0	0	0	–	0	0	0	0	1.0	1.000

John Pawlowski

PAWLOWSKI, JOHN
B. Sept. 6, 1963, Johnson City, N. Y.   BR TR 6'2"   175 lbs.

Year	Team		W	L	PCT	ERA	G	GS	CG	IP	H	BB	SO	ShO	W	L	SV	AB	H	HR	BA	PO	A	E	DP	TC/G	FA
1987	CHI	A	0	0	–	4.91	2	0	0	3.2	7	3	2	0	0	0	0	0	0	0	–	0	0	0	0	0.0	–
1988			1	0	1.000	8.36	6	0	0	14	20	3	10	0	1	0	0	0	0	0	–	1	2	0	0	0.5	1.000
2 yrs.			1	0	1.000	7.64	8	0	0	17.2	27	6	12	0	1	0	0	0	0	0	–	1	2	0	0	0.4	1.000

Mike Paxton

PAXTON, MICHAEL DeWAYNE
B. Sept. 3, 1953, Memphis, Tenn.   BR TR 5'11"   190 lbs.

Year	Team		W	L	PCT	ERA	G	GS	CG	IP	H	BB	SO	ShO	W	L	SV	AB	H	HR	BA	PO	A	E	DP	TC/G	FA
1977	BOS	A	10	5	.667	3.83	29	12	2	108	134	25	58	1	4	0	0	0	0	0	–	4	15	0	1	0.7	1.000
1978	CLE	A	12	11	.522	3.86	33	27	5	191	179	63	96	2	1	1	1	0	0	0	–	17	20	1	2	1.2	.974
1979			8	8	.500	5.91	33	24	3	160	210	52	70	0	0	0	0	0	0	0	–	16	20	0	3	1.1	1.000
1980			0	0	–	12.38	4	0	0	8	13	6	6	0	0	0	0	0	0	0	–	2	0	0	0	0.5	1.000
4 yrs.			30	24	.556	4.70	99	63	10	467	536	146	230	3	5	2	1	0	0	0	–	39	55	1	6	1.0	.989

George Payne

PAYNE, GEORGE WASHINGTON
B. May 23, 1890, Mt. Vernon, Ky.   D. Jan. 24, 1959, Bellflower, Calif.   BR TR 5'11"   172 lbs.

Year	Team		W	L	PCT	ERA	G	GS	CG	IP	H	BB	SO	ShO	W	L	SV	AB	H	HR	BA	PO	A	E	DP	TC/G	FA
1920	CHI	A	1	1	.500	5.46	12	0	0	29.2	39	9	9	0	1	1	0	8	1	0	.125	1	3	0	0	0.3	1.000

Year	Team		W	L	PCT	ERA	G	GS	CG	IP	H	BB	SO	ShO	Relief Pitching W	L	SV	Batting AB	H	HR	BA	PO	A	E	DP	TC/G	FA

Harley Payne

PAYNE, HARLEY FENWICK (Lady)
B. Jan. 9, 1868, Windsor, Ont., Canada   D. Dec. 29, 1935, Orwell, Ohio   BB TL 6'   160 lbs.

Year	Team		W	L	PCT	ERA	G	GS	CG	IP	H	BB	SO	ShO	W	L	SV	AB	H	HR	BA	PO	A	E	DP	TC/G	FA
1896	BKN	N	14	16	.467	3.39	34	28	24	241.2	284	58	52	2	2	2	0	98	21	0	.214	12	76	7	1	2.8	.926
1897			14	16	.467	4.63	40	38	30	280	350	71	86	1	0	0	0	110	26	0	.236	11	68	5	1	2.1	.940
1898			1	0	1.000	4.00	1	1	1	9	11	3	2	0	0	0	0	4	3	0	.750	0	4	0	0	4.0	1.000
1899	PIT	N	1	3	.250	3.76	5	5	2	26.1	33	4	8	0	0	0	0	10	1	0	.100	0	18	2	0	4.0	.900
4 yrs.			30	35	.462	4.04	80	72	57	557	678	136	148	3	2	2	0	222	51	0	.230	23	166	14	2	2.5	.931

Mike Payne

PAYNE, MICHAEL EARL
B. Nov. 15, 1961, Woonsocket, R. I.   BR TR 5'11"   165 lbs.

Year	Team		W	L	PCT	ERA	G	GS	CG	IP	H	BB	SO	ShO	W	L	SV	AB	H	HR	BA	PO	A	E	DP	TC/G	FA
1984	ATL	N	0	1	.000	6.35	3	1	0	5.2	7	3	3	0	0	0	0	1	0	0	.000	0	1	0	0	0.3	1.000

Mike Pazik

PAZIK, MICHAEL JOSEPH
B. Jan. 26, 1950, Lynn, Mass.   BL TL 6'2"   195 lbs.

Year	Team		W	L	PCT	ERA	G	GS	CG	IP	H	BB	SO	ShO	W	L	SV	AB	H	HR	BA	PO	A	E	DP	TC/G	FA
1975	MIN	A	0	4	.000	8.24	5	3	0	19.2	28	10	8	0	0	0	1	0	0	0	–	0	0	0	0	0.0	–
1976			0	0	–	7.00	5	0	0	9	13	4	6	0	0	0	0	0	0	0	–	0	0	0	0	0.0	–
1977			1	0	1.000	2.50	3	3	0	18	18	6	6	0	0	0	0	0	0	0	–	2	3	0	0	1.7	1.000
3 yrs.			1	4	.200	5.79	13	6	0	46.2	59	20	20	0	0	0	1	0	0	0	–	2	3	0	0	0.4	1.000

Frank Pearce

PEARCE, FRANK
B. Louisville, Ky.

Year	Team		W	L	PCT	ERA	G	GS	CG	IP	H	BB	SO	ShO	W	L	SV	AB	H	HR	BA	PO	A	E	DP	TC/G	FA
1876	LOU	N	0	0	–	4.50	1	0	0	4	5	1	1	0	0	0	0	2	0	0	.000	0	0	0	0	0.0	–

Frank Pearce

PEARCE, FRANKLIN THOMAS
B. Aug. 31, 1905, Middletown, Ky.   D. Sept. 3, 1950, Van Buren, N. Y.   BR TR 6'   170 lbs.

Year	Team		W	L	PCT	ERA	G	GS	CG	IP	H	BB	SO	ShO	W	L	SV	AB	H	HR	BA	PO	A	E	DP	TC/G	FA
1933	PHI	N	5	4	.556	3.62	20	7	3	82	78	29	18	1	2	2	0	26	5	0	.192	7	16	2	3	1.3	.920
1934			0	2	.000	7.20	7	1	0	20	25	5	4	0	0	1	0	3	2	0	.667	0	2	0	0	0.3	1.000
1935			0	0	–	8.31	5	0	0	13	22	6	7	0	0	0	0	4	2	0	.500	1	5	2	1	1.6	.750
3 yrs.			5	6	.455	4.77	32	8	3	115	125	40	29	1	2	3	0	33	9	0	.273	8	23	4	4	1.1	.886

George Pearce

PEARCE, GEORGE THOMAS
B. Jan. 10, 1888, Aurora, Ill.   D. Oct. 11, 1935, Joliet, Ill.   BL TL 5'10½"   175 lbs.

Year	Team		W	L	PCT	ERA	G	GS	CG	IP	H	BB	SO	ShO	W	L	SV	AB	H	HR	BA	PO	A	E	DP	TC/G	FA
1912	CHI	N	0	0	–	5.52	3	2	0	14.2	15	12	9	0	0	0	0	6	1	0	.167	0	7	0	0	2.3	1.000
1913			13	5	.722	2.31	25	21	14	163.1	137	59	73	3	1	0	0	55	4	0	.073	6	41	3	0	2.0	.940
1914			8	12	.400	3.51	30	16	4	141	122	65	78	0	2	3	1	45	4	0	.089	1	45	3	1	1.6	.939
1915			13	9	.591	3.32	36	20	8	176	158	77	96	2	4	1	0	56	11	0	.196	1	49	6	0	1.6	.893
1916			0	0	–	2.08	4	1	0	4.1	6	1	0	0	0	0	0	0	0	0	–	0	1	0	0	0.3	1.000
1917	STL	N	1	1	.500	3.48	5	0	0	10.1	7	3	4	0	1	1	0	4	0	0	.000	1	4	1	1	1.2	.833
6 yrs.			35	27	.565	3.11	103	60	26	509.2	445	217	260	5	8	5	1	166	20	0	.120	9	147	13	2	1.6	.923

Jim Pearce

PEARCE, JAMES MADISON
B. June 9, 1925, Zebulon, N. C.   BR TR 6'6"   180 lbs.

Year	Team		W	L	PCT	ERA	G	GS	CG	IP	H	BB	SO	ShO	W	L	SV	AB	H	HR	BA	PO	A	E	DP	TC/G	FA
1949	WAS	A	0	1	.000	8.44	2	1	0	5.1	9	5	1	0	0	0	0	2	0	0	.000	0	5	1	0	3.0	.833
1950			2	1	.667	6.04	20	3	0	56.2	58	37	18	0	1	1	0	13	2	0	.154	2	9	0	0	0.6	1.000
1953			0	1	.000	7.71	4	1	0	9.1	15	6	0	0	0	0	0	1	0	0	.000	0	1	1	0	0.5	.500
1954	CIN	N	1	0	1.000	0.00	2	1	1	11	7	5	3	0	0	0	0	3	0	0	.000	1	2	0	0	1.5	1.000
1955			0	1	.000	10.80	2	1	0	3.1	8	0	0	0	0	0	0	0	0	0	–	1	0	0	0	0.5	1.000
5 yrs.			3	4	.429	5.78	30	7	2	85.2	97	53	22	0	1	1	0	19	2	0	.105	4	17	2	0	0.8	.913

Frank Pears

PEARS, FRANK H.
B. Aug. 30, 1866, Kentucky   D. Nov. 29, 1923, St. Louis, Mo.   TR

Year	Team		W	L	PCT	ERA	G	GS	CG	IP	H	BB	SO	ShO	W	L	SV	AB	H	HR	BA	PO	A	E	DP	TC/G	FA
1889	KC	AA	0	2	.000	4.91	3	2	2	22	21	9	5	0	0	0	0	11	1	0	.091	0	3	0	0	1.0	1.000
1893	STL	N	0	0	–	13.50	1	0	0	4	9	2	0	0	0	0	0	2	0	0	.000	0	1	0	0	1.0	1.000
2 yrs.			0	2	.000	6.23	4	2	2	26	30	11	5	0	0	0	0	13	1	0	.077	0	4	0	0	1.0	1.000

Alex Pearson

PEARSON, ALEXANDER FRANKLIN
B. Mar. 9, 1877, Greensboro, Pa.   D. Oct. 30, 1966, Rochester, Pa.   BR TR 5'10½"   160 lbs.

Year	Team		W	L	PCT	ERA	G	GS	CG	IP	H	BB	SO	ShO	W	L	SV	AB	H	HR	BA	PO	A	E	DP	TC/G	FA
1902	STL	N	2	6	.250	3.95	11	10	8	82	90	22	24	0	0	0	0	34	9	0	.265	1	22	2	0	2.3	.920
1903	CLE	A	1	2	.333	3.56	4	3	2	30.1	34	3	12	0	0	0	0	12	1	0	.083	1	10	1	0	3.0	.917
2 yrs.			3	8	.273	3.85	15	13	10	112.1	124	25	36	0	0	0	0	46	10	0	.217	2	32	3	0	2.5	.919

Ike Pearson

PEARSON, ISSAC OVERTON
B. Mar. 1, 1917, Grenada, Miss.   D. Mar. 17, 1985, Sarasota, Fla.   BR TR 6'1"   180 lbs.

Year	Team		W	L	PCT	ERA	G	GS	CG	IP	H	BB	SO	ShO	W	L	SV	AB	H	HR	BA	PO	A	E	DP	TC/G	FA
1939	PHI	N	2	13	.133	5.76	26	13	4	125	144	56	29	0	0	2	0	37	2	0	.054	6	30	1	1	1.4	.973
1940			3	14	.176	5.45	29	20	5	145.1	160	57	43	0	0	1	1	44	9	0	.205	3	37	2	3	1.4	.952
1941			4	14	.222	3.57	46	10	0	136	139	70	38	0	4	4	6	40	5	0	.125	8	28	1	2	0.8	.973
1942			1	6	.143	4.54	35	7	0	85.1	87	50	21	0	1	1	0	23	1	0	.043	2	17	0	2	0.5	1.000
1946			1	0	1.000	3.77	5	2	1	14.1	19	8	6	1	0	0	0	5	1	1	.200	1	3	1	0	1.0	.800
1948	CHI	A	2	3	.400	4.92	23	2	0	53	62	27	12	0	1	2	1	10	2	0	.200	1	13	0	2	0.6	1.000
6 yrs.			13	50	.206	4.83	164	54	10	559	611	268	149	2	6	10	8	159	20	1	.126	21	128	5	10	0.9	.968

Monte Pearson

PEARSON, MONTGOMERY MARCELLUS
B. Sept. 2, 1909, Oakland, Calif.   D. Jan. 27, 1978, Fresno, Calif.   BR TR 6'   175 lbs.

Year	Team		W	L	PCT	ERA	G	GS	CG	IP	H	BB	SO	ShO	W	L	SV	AB	H	HR	BA	PO	A	E	DP	TC/G	FA
1932	CLE	A	0	0	–	10.13	8	0	0	8	10	11	5	0	0	0	0	–	0	0	–	0	6	0	0	0.8	1.000
1933			10	5	.667	2.33	19	16	10	135.1	111	55	54	0	0	0	0	50	13	0	.260	1	26	2	2	1.5	.931
1934			18	13	.581	4.52	39	33	19	254.2	257	130	140	0	2	1	2	92	25	1	.272	15	48	2	5	1.7	.969
1935			8	13	.381	4.90	30	24	10	181.2	199	103	90	1	1	0	0	62	11	0	.177	8	42	2	5	1.7	.962
1936	NY	A	19	7	.731	3.71	33	31	15	223	191	135	118	1	1	0	1	91	23	1	.253	12	39	1	3	1.6	.981
1937			9	3	.750	3.17	22	20	7	144.2	145	64	71	1	0	0	1	51	11	0	.216	5	23	1	3	1.3	.966
1938			16	7	.696	3.97	28	27	17	202	198	113	98	1	0	0	0	76	13	0	.171	11	40	2	8	1.9	.962
1939			12	5	.706	4.49	22	20	8	146.1	151	70	76	0	0	0	1	53	17	0	.321	3	29	0	5	1.5	1.000

Year	Team		W	L	PCT	ERA	G	GS	CG	IP	H	BB	SO	ShO	Relief Pitching W	L	SV	Batting AB	H	HR	BA	PO	A	E	DP	TC/G	FA

Monte Pearson *continued*

Year	Team		W	L	PCT	ERA	G	GS	CG	IP	H	BB	SO	ShO	W	L	SV	AB	H	HR	BA	PO	A	E	DP	TC/G	FA
1940			7	5	.583	3.69	16	16	7	109.2	108	44	43	1	0	0	0	33	4	0	.121	6	29	0	2	2.2	1.000
1941	CIN	N	1	3	.250	5.18	7	4	1	24.1	22	15	8	0	0	0	0	5	0	0	.000	1	3	0	0	0.6	1.000
10 yrs.			100	61	.621	4.00	224	191	94	1429.2	1392	740	703	5	5	3	4	513	117	2	.228	62	285	10	33	1.6	.972

WORLD SERIES

Year	Team		W	L	PCT	ERA	G	GS	CG	IP	H	BB	SO	ShO	W	L	SV	AB	H	HR	BA	PO	A	E	DP	TC/G	FA
1936	NY	A	1	0	1.000	2.00	1	1	1	9	7	2	7	0	0	0	0	4	2	0	.500	1	2	0	0	3.0	1.000
1937			1	0	1.000	1.04	1	1	0	8.2	5	2	4	0	0	0	0	3	0	0	.000	0	2	0	0	2.0	1.000
1938			1	0	1.000	1.00	1	1	1	9	5	2	9	0	0	0	0	3	1	0	.333	2	0	0	0	2.0	1.000
1939			1	0	1.000	0.00	1	1	1	9	2	1	8	0	0	0	0	2	0	0	.000	0	5	0	0	5.0	1.000
4 yrs.			4	0	1.000	1.01	4	4	3	35.2	19	7	28	0	0	0	0	12	3	0	.250	3	9	0	0	3.0	1.000
					1st	7th																					

Marv Peasley

PEASLEY, MARVIN WARREN
B. July 16, 1888, Jonesport, Me.   D. Dec. 27, 1948, San Francisco, Calif.
BL TL 6'1" 175 lbs.

Year	Team		W	L	PCT	ERA	G	GS	CG	IP	H	BB	SO	ShO	W	L	SV	AB	H	HR	BA	PO	A	E	DP	TC/G	FA
1910	DET	A	0	1	.000	8.10	2	1	0	10	13	11	4	0	0	0	0	3	0	0	.000	0	3	0	0	1.5	1.000

George Pechiney

PECHINEY, GEORGE ADOLPHE
B. Sept. 20, 1861, Cincinnati, Ohio   D. July 14, 1943, Cincinnati, Ohio
BR TR 5'9" 184 lbs.

Year	Team		W	L	PCT	ERA	G	GS	CG	IP	H	BB	SO	ShO	W	L	SV	AB	H	HR	BA	PO	A	E	DP	TC/G	FA
1885	CIN	AA	7	4	.636	2.02	11	11	11	98	95	30	49	1	0	0	0	40	6	0	.150	4	20	4	0	2.5	.857
1886			15	21	.417	4.14	40	40	35	330.1	355	133	110	2	0	0	0	144	30	1	.208	17	45	8	2	1.8	.886
1887	CLE	AA	1	9	.100	7.12	10	10	10	86	118	44	24	0	0	0	0	36	9	0	.250	0	23	5	1	2.8	.821
3 yrs.			23	34	.404	4.23	61	61	56	514.1	568	207	183	3	0	0	0	220	45	1	.205	21	88	17	3	2.1	.865

Steve Peek

PEEK, STEPHEN GEORGE
B. July 30, 1914, Springfield, Mass.
BB TR 6'2" 195 lbs.

Year	Team		W	L	PCT	ERA	G	GS	CG	IP	H	BB	SO	ShO	W	L	SV	AB	H	HR	BA	PO	A	E	DP	TC/G	FA
1941	NY	A	4	2	.667	5.06	17	8	2	80	85	39	18	0	0	0	0	28	1	0	.036	3	18	2	0	1.4	.913

Red Peery

PEERY, GEORGE ALLAN
B. Aug. 15, 1906, Payson, Utah   D. May 6, 1985, Salt Lake City, Utah
BL TL 5'11" 160 lbs.

Year	Team		W	L	PCT	ERA	G	GS	CG	IP	H	BB	SO	ShO	W	L	SV	AB	H	HR	BA	PO	A	E	DP	TC/G	FA
1927	PIT	N	0	0	–	0.00	1	0	0	1	0	1	0	0	0	0	0	0	0	0	–	0	1	0	0	1.0	1.000
1929	BOS	N	0	1	.000	5.11	9	1	0	44	53	9	3	0	0	0	0	14	3	0	.214	1	10	0	0	1.2	1.000
2 yrs.			0	1	.000	5.00	10	1	0	45	53	10	3	0	0	0	0	14	3	0	.214	1	11	0	0	1.2	1.000

Heinie Peitz

PEITZ, HENRY CLEMENT
Brother of Joe Peitz.
B. Nov. 28, 1870, St. Louis, Mo.   D. Oct. 23, 1943, Cincinnati, Ohio
BR TR 5'11" 165 lbs.

Year	Team		W	L	PCT	ERA	G	GS	CG	IP	H	BB	SO	ShO	W	L	SV	AB	H	HR	BA	PO	A	E	DP	TC/G	FA
1894	STL	N	0	0	–	9.00	1	0	0	3	7	2	0	0	0	0	0	338	89	3	.263	0	0	0	0	0.0	–
1897	CIN	N	0	1	.000	7.88	2	1	1	8	9	4	0	0	0	0	0	266	78	1	.293	1	5	0	0	3.0	1.000
1899			0	0	–	5.40	1	0	0	5	6	1	3	0	0	0	0	290	79	1	.272	2	2	0	0	4.0	1.000
3 yrs.			0	1	.000	7.31	4	1	1	16	22	7	3	0	0	0	0	*				3	7	0	0	2.5	1.000

Barney Pelty

PELTY, BARNEY
Born Barney Peltheimer.
B. Sept. 10, 1880, Farmington, Mo.   D. May 24, 1939, Farmington, Mo.
BR TR 5'9" 175 lbs.

Year	Team		W	L	PCT	ERA	G	GS	CG	IP	H	BB	SO	ShO	W	L	SV	AB	H	HR	BA	PO	A	E	DP	TC/G	FA
1903	STL	A	3	3	.500	2.40	7	6	5	48.2	49	15	20	0	0	0	1	20	3	0	.150	3	11	3	0	2.4	.824
1904			15	18	.455	2.84	39	35	31	301	270	77	126	2	2	0	0	118	15	0	.127	22	92	9	3	3.2	.927
1905			14	14	.500	2.75	31	28	26	258.2	222	68	114	1	1	0	0	98	15	0	.153	15	92	6	3	3.6	.947
1906			16	11	.593	1.59	34	30	25	260.2	189	59	92	4	1	0	2	95	16	0	.168	21	107	13	0	4.1	.908
1907			12	21	.364	2.57	36	31	29	273	234	64	85	5	0	3	1	95	16	0	.168	25	91	7	5	3.4	.943
1908			7	4	.636	1.99	20	13	7	122	104	32	36	1	0	0	0	42	5	0	.119	6	43	1	2	2.5	.980
1909			11	11	.500	2.30	27	23	17	199.1	158	53	88	5	0	2	0	91	15	0	.165	17	74	6	6	3.6	.938
1910			5	11	.313	3.48	27	18	12	165.1	157	70	48	3	1	1	0	56	5	0	.089	8	73	5	4	3.2	.942
1911			7	15	.318	2.83	28	22	18	207	197	69	59	1	0	2	0	65	9	0	.138	9	61	2	1	2.6	.972
1912	2 teams		STL A	(6G 1–5)		WAS A	(11G 1–4)																					
"	total		2	9	.182	4.37	17	10	3	82.1	83	25	25	0	1	2	0	21	2	0	.095	3	21	1	2	1.5	.960
10 yrs.			92	117	.440	2.62	266	216	173	1918	1663	532	693	22	7	11	4	701	101	0	.144	129	665	53	26	3.2	.937

Alejandro Pena

PENA, ALEJANDRO
Born Alejandro Pena y Vasquez.
B. June 25, 1959, Cambiaso Puerto Plata, Dominican Republic
BR TR 6'3" 200 lbs.

Year	Team		W	L	PCT	ERA	G	GS	CG	IP	H	BB	SO	ShO	W	L	SV	AB	H	HR	BA	PO	A	E	DP	TC/G	FA
1981	LA	N	1	1	.500	2.88	14	0	0	25	25	11	14	0	1	1	2	6	0	0	.000	1	5	1	0	0.5	.857
1982			0	2	.000	4.79	29	0	0	35.2	37	21	20	0	0	2	0	0	0	0	–	3	11	2	1	0.6	.875
1983			12	9	.571	2.75	34	26	4	177	152	51	120	3	2	1	1	60	6	1	.100	13	32	4	4	1.4	.918
1984			12	6	.667	2.48	28	28	8	199.1	186	46	135	4	0	0	0	66	8	0	.121	17	21	4	1	1.5	.905
1985			0	1	.000	8.31	2	1	0	4.1	7	3	2	0	0	1	0	1	0	0	.000	0	1	1	0	1.0	.500
1986			1	2	.333	4.89	24	10	0	70	74	30	46	0	0	1	1	17	3	0	.176	1	8	0	0	0.4	1.000
1987			2	7	.222	3.50	37	7	0	87.1	82	37	76	0	2	2	11	13	1	0	.077	4	1	1	0	0.2	.833
1988			6	7	.462	1.91	60	0	0	94.1	75	27	83	0	6	7	12	6	0	0	.000	9	10	2	1	0.4	.905
1989			4	3	.571	2.13	53	0	0	76	62	18	75	0	4	3	5	1	1	0	1.000	1	5	1	0	0.1	.857
9 yrs.			38	38	.500	2.93	281	72	12	769	693	244	571	7	15	18	32	170	19	1	.112	49	94	16	7	0.6	.899

LEAGUE CHAMPIONSHIP SERIES

Year	Team		W	L	PCT	ERA	G	GS	CG	IP	H	BB	SO	ShO	W	L	SV	AB	H	HR	BA	PO	A	E	DP	TC/G	FA
1981	LA	N	0	0	–	0.00	2	0	0	2.1	0	1	0	0	0	0	0	1	0	0	.000	0	0	0	0	0.0	–
1983			0	0	–	6.75	1	0	0	2.2	4	1	3	0	0	0	0	1	1	0	1.000	0	0	0	0	0.0	–
1988			1	1	.500	4.15	3	0	0	4.1	1	5	1	0	1	1	1	0	0	0	–	0	0	0	0	0.0	–
3 yrs.			1	1	.500	3.86	6	0	0	9.1	6	6	4	0	1	1	1	1	1	0	1.000	0	0	0	0	0.0	–

WORLD SERIES

Year	Team		W	L	PCT	ERA	G	GS	CG	IP	H	BB	SO	ShO	W	L	SV	AB	H	HR	BA	PO	A	E	DP	TC/G	FA
1988	LA	N	1	0	1.000	0.00	2	0	0	5	2	1	7	0	1	0	0	0	0	0	–	0	0	0	0	0.0	–

Year	Team		W	L	PCT	ERA	G	GS	CG	IP	H	BB	SO	ShO	Relief Pitching W	L	SV	Batting AB	H	HR	BA	PO	A	E	DP	TC/G	FA

Hipolito Pena

PENA, HIPOLITO
Born Hipolito Pena y Concepcion.
B. Jan. 30, 1964, Fantino, Dominican Republic

BL TL 6'3" 168 lbs.

Year	Team		W	L	PCT	ERA	G	GS	CG	IP	H	BB	SO	ShO	W	L	SV	AB	H	HR	BA	PO	A	E	DP	TC/G	FA
1986	PIT	N	0	3	.000	8.64	10	1	0	8.1	7	3	6	0	0	2	1	0	0	0	–	0	1	0	0	0.1	1.000
1987			0	3	.000	4.56	16	1	0	25.2	16	26	16	0	0	2	1	6	1	0	.167	1	4	0	0	0.3	1.000
1988	NY	A	1	1	.500	3.14	16	0	0	14.1	10	9	10	0	1	1	0	0	0	0	–	1	2	0	1	0.2	1.000
3 yrs.			1	7	.125	4.84	42	2	0	48.1	33	38	32	0	1	5	2	6	1	0	.167	2	7	0	1	0.2	1.000

Jose Pena

PENA, JOSE
Born Jose Pena y Gutierrez.
B. Dec. 3, 1942, Ciudad Juarez, Mexico

BR TR 6'2" 190 lbs.

Year	Team		W	L	PCT	ERA	G	GS	CG	IP	H	BB	SO	ShO	W	L	SV	AB	H	HR	BA	PO	A	E	DP	TC/G	FA
1969	CIN	N	1	1	.500	18.00	6	0	0	5	10	5	3	0	1	1	0	0	0	0	–	0	1	0	0	0.2	1.000
1970	LA	N	4	3	.571	4.42	29	0	0	57	51	29	31	0	4	3	4	8	1	0	.125	1	14	0	0	0.5	1.000
1971			2	0	1.000	3.56	21	0	0	43	32	18	44	0	2	0	1	3	2	0	.667	1	4	0	0	0.2	1.000
1972			0	0	–	8.59	5	0	0	7.1	13	6	4	0	0	0	0	0	0	0	–	1	0	0	0	0.2	1.000
4 yrs.			7	4	.636	4.97	61	0	0	112.1	106	58	82	0	7	4	5	11	3	0	.273	2	19	0	0	0.3	1.000

Orlando Pena

PENA, ORLANDO GREGORIO
Born Orlando Gregorio Pena y Quevara.
B. Nov. 17, 1933, Victoria de las Tunas, Cuba

BR TR 5'11" 154 lbs.

Year	Team		W	L	PCT	ERA	G	GS	CG	IP	H	BB	SO	ShO	W	L	SV	AB	H	HR	BA	PO	A	E	DP	TC/G	FA
1958	CIN	N	1	0	1.000	0.60	9	0	0	15	10	4	11	0	1	0	3	0	0	0	–	1	1	0	0	0.2	1.000
1959			5	9	.357	4.76	46	8	1	136	150	39	76	0	2	4	5	34	3	0	.088	12	16	1	1	0.6	.966
1960			0	1	.000	2.89	4	0	0	9.1	8	3	9	0	0	1	0	1	0	0	.000	0	0	0	0	0.0	–
1962	KC	A	6	4	.600	3.01	13	12	6	89.2	71	27	56	1	0	0	0	31	5	0	.161	5	9	1	0	1.2	.933
1963			12	20	.375	3.69	35	33	9	217	218	53	128	3	1	0	0	62	9	1	.145	11	26	0	0	1.1	1.000
1964			12	14	.462	4.43	40	32	5	219.1	231	73	184	0	0	0	0	75	12	1	.160	6	27	7	2	1.0	.825
1965	2 teams	KC A (12G 0–6)	DET A (30G 4–6)																								
"	total		4	12	.250	4.18	42	1	0	92.2	96	33	79	0	4	7	4	17	3	0	.176	4	10	2	0	0.4	.875
1966	DET	A	4	2	.667	3.08	54	0	0	108	105	35	79	0	4	2	7	18	2	0	.111	8	26	1	0	0.6	.971
1967	2 teams	DET A (2G 0–1)	CLE A (48G 0–3)																								
"	total		0	4	.000	3.59	50	1	0	90.1	72	22	74	0	0	3	8	8	0	0	.000	7	11	2	0	0.4	.900
1970	PIT	N	2	1	.667	4.74	23	0	0	38	38	7	25	0	2	1	2	6	0	0	.000	4	8	3	1	0.7	.800
1971	BAL	A	0	1	.000	3.00	5	0	0	15	16	5	4	0	0	1	0	3	0	0	.000	0	3	1	1	0.8	.750
1973	2 teams	BAL A (11G 1–1)	STL N (42G 4–4)																								
"	total		5	5	.500	2.94	53	2	0	107	96	22	61	0	5	5	7	7	1	0	.143	4	19	1	0	0.5	.958
1974	2 teams	STL N (42G 5–2)	CAL A (4G 0–0)																								
"	total		5	2	.714	2.21	46	0	0	53	51	21	28	0	5	2	4	2	1	0	.500	2	7	0	4	0.2	1.000
1975	CAL	A	0	2	.000	2.13	7	0	0	12.2	13	4	8	0	0	2	0	0	0	0	–	0	0	0	0	0.0	–
14 yrs.			56	77	.421	3.70	427	93	21	1203	1175	352	818	4	24	28	40	264	36	2	.136	64	163	19	11	0.6	.923

Ramon Pena

PENA, RAMON ARTURO
Born Ramon Arturo Pena y Padillia. Brother of Tony Pena.
B. May 5, 1962, Santiago, Dominican Republic

BR TR 5'10" 155 lbs.

Year	Team		W	L	PCT	ERA	G	GS	CG	IP	H	BB	SO	ShO	W	L	SV	AB	H	HR	BA	PO	A	E	DP	TC/G	FA
1989	DET	A	0	0	–	6.00	8	0	0	18	26	8	12	0	0	0	0	0	0	0	–	1	5	0	1	0.8	1.000

Russ Pence

PENCE, RUSSELL WILLIAM
B. Mar. 11, 1900, Marine, Ill. D. Aug. 11, 1971, Hot Springs, Ark.

BR TR 6' 185 lbs.

Year	Team		W	L	PCT	ERA	G	GS	CG	IP	H	BB	SO	ShO	W	L	SV	AB	H	HR	BA	PO	A	E	DP	TC/G	FA
1921	CHI	A	0	0	–	8.44	4	0	0	5.1	6	7	2	0	0	0	0	1	0	0	.000	1	2	0	0	0.8	1.000

Ken Penner

PENNER, KENNETH WILLIAM
B. Apr. 24, 1896, Booneville, Ind. D. May 28, 1959, Sacramento, Calif.

BL TR 5'11½" 170 lbs.

Year	Team		W	L	PCT	ERA	G	GS	CG	IP	H	BB	SO	ShO	W	L	SV	AB	H	HR	BA	PO	A	E	DP	TC/G	FA
1916	CLE	A	1	0	1.000	4.26	4	2	0	12.2	14	4	5	0	0	0	0	2	0	0	.000	0	7	1	1	2.0	.875
1929	CHI	N	0	1	.000	2.84	5	0	0	12.2	14	6	3	0	0	1	0	4	1	0	.250	0	3	0	0	0.6	1.000
2 yrs.			1	1	.500	3.55	9	2	0	25.1	28	10	8	0	0	1	0	6	1	0	.167	0	10	1	1	1.2	.909

Kewpie Pennington

PENNINGTON, GEORGE LOUIS
B. Sept. 24, 1896, New York, N. Y. D. May 3, 1953, Newark, N. J.

BR TR 5'8½" 168 lbs.

Year	Team		W	L	PCT	ERA	G	GS	CG	IP	H	BB	SO	ShO	W	L	SV	AB	H	HR	BA	PO	A	E	DP	TC/G	FA
1917	STL	A	0	0	–	0.00	1	0	0	1	1	0	0	0	0	0	0	0	0	0	–	0	0	0	0	0.0	–

Herb Pennock

PENNOCK, HERBERT JEFFERIS (The Knight of Kennett Square)
B. Feb. 19, 1894, Kennett Square, Pa.
D. Jan. 30, 1948, New York, N. Y.
Hall of Fame 1948.

BB TL 6' 160 lbs.
BL 1934

Year	Team		W	L	PCT	ERA	G	GS	CG	IP	H	BB	SO	ShO	W	L	SV	AB	H	HR	BA	PO	A	E	DP	TC/G	FA
1912	PHI	A	1	2	.333	4.50	17			50	48	30	38	0	1	1	2	15	2	0	.133	2	15	1	0	1.1	.944
1913			2	1	.667	5.13	14	4	1	33.1	30	22	17	0	1	0	0	9	1	0	.111	0	9	0	0	0.6	1.000
1914			11	4	.733	2.79	28	14	8	151.2	136	65	90	3	2	2	3	56	12	0	.214	9	37	3	1	1.8	.939
1915	2 teams	PHI A (11G 3–6)	BOS A (5G 0–0)																								
"	total		3	6	.333	6.36	16	9	3	58	69	39	31	1	0	1	1	24	6	0	.250	2	15	2	1	1.2	.895
1916	BOS	A	0	2	.000	3.04	9	2	0	26.2	23	8	12	0	0	0	1	8	1	0	.125	3	4	0	0	0.8	1.000
1917			5	5	.500	3.31	24	5	4	100.2	90	23	35	1	2	3	1	24	4	0	.167	1	30	2	1	1.4	.939
1919			16	8	.667	2.71	32	26	16	219	223	48	70	5	1	0	0	75	13	0	.173	13	45	3	5	1.9	.967
1920			16	13	.552	3.68	37	31	19	242.1	244	61	68	4	3	0	0	77	20	0	.260	6	53	1	0	1.6	.983
1921			12	14	.462	4.04	32	32	15	222.2	268	59	91	1	0	0	0	85	18	1	.212	11	59	2	3	2.3	.972
1922			10	17	.370	4.32	32	26	15	202	230	74	59	1	1	1	1	65	9	0	.138	8	56	1	1	2.0	.985
1923	NY	A	19	6	.760	3.33	35	27	21	224.1	235	68	93	1	1	0	0	83	16	0	.193	4	66	1	4	2.0	.986
1924			21	9	.700	2.83	40	34	25	286.1	302	64	101	4	1	0	3	101	16	2	.158	10	61	0	5	1.8	1.000
1925			16	17	.485	2.96	47	31	21	277	267	71	88	2	1	2	2	99	20	0	.202	7	54	4	3	1.4	.938
1926			23	11	.676	3.62	40	33	19	266.1	294	43	78	1	2	1	2	85	18	0	.212	2	73	1	6	1.9	.987
1927			19	8	.704	3.00	34	26	18	209.2	225	48	51	1	2	0	1	69	15	0	.217	4	45	1	2	1.5	.980
1928			17	6	.739	2.56	28	24	19	211	215	40	53	5	0	0	3	74	15	0	.203	5	59	1	3	2.3	.985
1929			9	11	.450	4.90	27	23	8	158	205	28	49	1	0	1	2	51	9	0	.176	4	31	0	2	1.3	1.000
1930			11	7	.611	4.32	25	19	11	156.1	194	20	46	1	1	0	1	60	11	0	.183	3	36	1	1	1.6	.975

Year	Team		W	L	PCT	ERA	G	GS	CG	IP	H	BB	SO	ShO	Relief Pitching W	L	SV	Batting AB	H	HR	BA	PO	A	E	DP	TC/G	FA

Herb Pennock *continued*

Year	Team		W	L	PCT	ERA	G	GS	CG	IP	H	BB	SO	ShO	W	L	SV	AB	H	HR	BA	PO	A	E	DP	TC/G	FA
1931			11	6	.647	4.28	25	25	12	189.1	247	30	65	1	0	0	0	66	10	1	.152	1	37	1	4	1.6	.974
1932			9	5	.643	4.60	22	21	9	146.2	191	38	54	1	0	1	0	53	8	0	.151	4	29	1	1	1.5	.971
1933			7	4	.636	5.54	23	5	2	65	96	21	22	1	3	3	4	21	5	0	.238	2	12	1	1	0.7	.933
1934	BOS	A	2	0	1.000	3.05	30	2	1	62	68	16	16	1	1	0	1	14	3	0	.214	0	8	0	0	0.3	1.000
22 yrs.			240	162	.597	3.61	617	421	248	3558.1	3900	916	1227	35	23	17	33	1214	232	4	.191	101	834	26	45	1.6	.973

WORLD SERIES

Year	Team		W	L	PCT	ERA	G	GS	CG	IP	H	BB	SO	ShO	W	L	SV	AB	H	HR	BA	PO	A	E	DP	TC/G	FA
1914	PHI	A	0	0	–	0.00	1	1	0	3	2	2	3	0	0	0	0	1	0	0	.000	0	1	0	0	1.0	1.000
1923	NY	A	2	0	1.000	3.63	3	2	1	17.1	19	1	8	0	0	0	1	6	0	0	.000	0	2	0	0	0.7	1.000
1926			2	0	1.000	1.23	3	2	2	22	13	4	8	0	0	0	0	7	1	0	.143	4	6	0	0	2.0	1.000
1927			1	0	1.000	1.00	1	1	1	9	3	0	1	0	0	0	0	4	0	0	.000	1	1	0	0	2.0	1.000
1932			0	0		2.25	2	0	0	4	2	1	4	0	0	0	2	1	0	0	.000	0	1	0	0	0.5	1.000
5 yrs.			5	0	1.000	1.95	10	5	4	55.1	39	8	24	0	0	0	3	19	1	0	.053	1	11	0	0	1.2	1.000
				8th	1st											4th											

Paul Penson

PENSON, PAUL EUGENE
B. July 12, 1931, Kansas City, Kans.   BR TR 6'1"   185 lbs.

Year	Team		W	L	PCT	ERA	G	GS	CG	IP	H	BB	SO	ShO	W	L	SV	AB	H	HR	BA	PO	A	E	DP	TC/G	FA
1954	PHI	N	1	1	.500	4.50	5	3	0	16	14	14	3	0	0	0	0	7	0	0	.000	0	1	1	0	0.4	.500

Gene Pentz

PENTZ, EUGENE DAVID
B. June 21, 1953, Johnstown, Pa.   BR TR 6'1"   200 lbs.

Year	Team		W	L	PCT	ERA	G	GS	CG	IP	H	BB	SO	ShO	W	L	SV	AB	H	HR	BA	PO	A	E	DP	TC/G	FA
1975	DET	A	0	4	.000	3.20	13	0	0	25.1	27	20	21	0	0	4	0	0	0	0	–	2	2	0	0	0.5	.667
1976	HOU	N	3	3	.500	2.95	40	0	0	64	62	31	36	0	3	3	5	5	1	0	.200	3	12	0	2	0.4	1.000
1977			5	2	.714	3.83	41	4	0	87	76	44	51	0	4	0	2	13	0	0	.000	5	13	0	0	0.4	1.000
1978			0	0		6.00	10	0	0	15	12	13	8	0	0	0	0	1	0	0	.000	3	6	0	0	0.9	1.000
4 yrs.			8	9	.471	3.62	104	4	0	191.1	177	108	116	0	7	7	7	19	1	0	.053	13	33	2	2	0.5	.958

Jimmy Peoples

PEOPLES, JAMES ELSWORTH
B. Oct. 8, 1863, Big Beaver, Mich.   D. Aug. 29, 1920, Detroit, Mich.   TR 5'8"   200 lbs.

Year	Team		W	L	PCT	ERA	G	GS	CG	IP	H	BB	SO	ShO	W	L	SV	AB	H	HR	BA	PO	A	E	DP	TC/G	FA
1885	BKN	AA	0	2	.000	12.00	2	2	1	15	30	2	4	0	0	0	0	*				3	4	0	0	3.5	1.000

Bob Pepper

PEPPER, ROBERT ERNEST
B. May 3, 1895, Rosston, Pa.   D. Apr. 8, 1968, Fort Cliff, Pa.   BR TR 6'2"   178 lbs.

Year	Team		W	L	PCT	ERA	G	GS	CG	IP	H	BB	SO	ShO	W	L	SV	AB	H	HR	BA	PO	A	E	DP	TC/G	FA
1915	PHI	A	0	0	–	1.80	1	0	0	5	6	4	0	0	0	0	0	2	0	0	.000	1	1	0	0	2.0	1.000

George Pepper

Playing record listed under George Prentiss

Laurin Pepper

PEPPER, HUGH McLAURIN
B. Jan. 18, 1931, Vaughan, Miss.   BR TR 5'11"   190 lbs.

Year	Team		W	L	PCT	ERA	G	GS	CG	IP	H	BB	SO	ShO	W	L	SV	AB	H	HR	BA	PO	A	E	DP	TC/G	FA
1954	PIT	N	1	5	.167	7.99	14	8	0	50.2	63	43	17	0	0	0	0	17	4	0	.235	1	17	1	0	1.4	.947
1955			0	1	.000	10.35	14	1	0	20	30	25	7	0	0	0	0	2	0	0	.000	2	0	2	1	0.2	1.000
1956			1	1	.500	3.00	11	7	0	30	30	25	12	0	0	0	0	6	0	0	.000	2	2	0	0	0.4	1.000
1957			0	1	.000	8.00	5	1	0	9	11	5	4	0	0	1	0	0	0	0	–	1	0	0	0	0.2	1.000
4 yrs.			2	8	.200	7.06	44	17	0	109.2	134	98	40	0	0	1	0	25	4	0	.160	5	21	1	1	0.6	.963

Bill Peppers

PEPPERS, HARRISON
B. Sept., 1866, Ky.   D. Nov. 5, 1903, Webb City, Mo.   BL

Year	Team		W	L	PCT	ERA	G	GS	CG	IP	H	BB	SO	ShO	W	L	SV	AB	H	HR	BA	PO	A	E	DP	TC/G	FA
1894	LOU	N	0	1	.000	6.75	2	1	0	8	10	4	0	0	0	0	0	4	0	0	.000	0	1	0	0	0.5	1.000

Luis Peraza

PERAZA, LUIS
Born Luis Peraza y Rios.
B. June 17, 1942, Rio Piedras, Puerto Rico   BR TR 5'11"   185 lbs.

Year	Team		W	L	PCT	ERA	G	GS	CG	IP	H	BB	SO	ShO	W	L	SV	AB	H	HR	BA	PO	A	E	DP	TC/G	FA
1969	PHI	N	0	0	–	6.00	8	0	0	9	12	2	7	0	0	0	0	1	0	0	.000	0	1	0	0	0.1	1.000

Oswaldo Peraza

PERAZA, OSWALD JOSE
B. Oct. 19, 1962, Puerto Cabello, Venezuela   BR TR 6'4"   172 lbs.

Year	Team		W	L	PCT	ERA	G	GS	CG	IP	H	BB	SO	ShO	W	L	SV	AB	H	HR	BA	PO	A	E	DP	TC/G	FA
1988	BAL	A	5	7	.417	5.55	19	15	1	86	98	37	61	0	0	0	0	0	0	0	–	8	11	3	1	1.2	.864

Hub Perdue

PERDUE, HERBERT RODNEY (The Gallatin Squash)
B. June 7, 1882, Bethpage, Tenn.   D. Oct. 31, 1968, Gallatin, Tenn.   BR TR 5'10½" 192 lbs.

Year	Team		W	L	PCT	ERA	G	GS	CG	IP	H	BB	SO	ShO	W	L	SV	AB	H	HR	BA	PO	A	E	DP	TC/G	FA
1911	BOS	N	6	10	.375	4.98	24	19	9	137.1	180	41	40	0	0	0	1	48	10	0	.208	6	36	5	4	2.0	.894
1912			13	16	.448	3.80	37	30	20	249	295	54	101	1	0	2	3	87	12	0	.138	6	45	4	1	1.5	.927
1913			16	13	.552	3.26	38	32	16	212.1	201	39	91	3	2	0	1	67	7	0	.104	7	21	3	0	0.8	.903
1914	2 teams		BOS N	(9G 2–5)		STL N	(22G 8–8)																				
"	total		10	13	.435	3.57	31	28	14	204.1	220	46	56	0	0	0	0	62	9	0	.145	2	41	2	0	1.5	.956
1915	STL	N	6	12	.333	4.21	31	13	5	115.1	141	19	29	1	3	5	1	36	4	0	.111	1	32	1	0	1.1	.971
5 yrs.			51	64	.443	3.85	161	122	64	918.1	1037	199	317	5	5	7	7	300	42	0	.140	22	175	15	5	1.3	.929

George Perez

PEREZ, GEORGE THOMAS
B. Dec. 29, 1937, San Fernando, Calif.   BR TR 6'2½" 200 lbs.

Year	Team		W	L	PCT	ERA	G	GS	CG	IP	H	BB	SO	ShO	W	L	SV	AB	H	HR	BA	PO	A	E	DP	TC/G	FA
1958	PIT	N	0	1	.000	5.40	4	0	0	8.1	9	4	2	0	0	1	0	2	0	0	.000	0	0	0	0	0.0	–

Melido Perez

PEREZ, MELIDO TURPEN
Born Melido Turpen Gross y Perez.   Brother of Pascual Perez.
B. Feb. 15, 1966, San Cristobal, Dominican Republic   BR TR 6'4"   180 lbs.

Year	Team		W	L	PCT	ERA	G	GS	CG	IP	H	BB	SO	ShO	W	L	SV	AB	H	HR	BA	PO	A	E	DP	TC/G	FA
1987	KC	A	1	1	.500	7.84	3	3	0	10.1	18	5	5	0	0	0	0	0	0	0	–	0	0	1	0	0.3	–
1988	CHI	A	12	10	.545	3.79	32	32	3	197	186	72	138	0	0	0	0	0	0	0	–	8	18	1	1	0.8	.963

Year	Team		W	L	PCT	ERA	G	GS	CG	IP	H	BB	SO	ShO	Relief Pitching W	L	SV	Batting AB	H	HR	BA	PO	A	E	DP	TC/G	FA

Melido Perez *continued*

| 1989 | | | 11 | 14 | .440 | 5.01 | 31 | 31 | 2 | 183.1 | 187 | 90 | 141 | 0 | 0 | 0 | 0 | 0 | 0 | 0 | – | 9 | 19 | 1 | 3 | 0.9 | .966 |
| 3 yrs. | | | 24 | 25 | .490 | 4.47 | 66 | 66 | 5 | 390.2 | 391 | 167 | 284 | 1 | 0 | 0 | 0 | 0 | 0 | 0 | – | 17 | 37 | 3 | 4 | 0.9 | .947 |

Pascual Perez

PEREZ, PASCUAL　　　　　　　　　　　　　　　BR TR 6'2" 162 lbs.
Born Pascual Gross y Perez.　Brother of Melido Perez.
B. May 17, 1957, San Cristobal, Dominican Republic

1980	PIT	N	0	1	.000	3.75	2	2	0	12	15	2	7	0	0	0	0	4	1	0	.250	1	1	0	0	1.0	1.000
1981			2	7	.222	3.98	17	13	2	86	92	34	46	0	0	1	0	22	3	0	.136	7	13	1	0	1.2	.952
1982	ATL	N	4	4	.500	3.06	16	11	0	79.1	85	17	29	0	2	0	0	18	3	0	.167	9	11	1	2	1.3	.952
1983			15	8	.652	3.43	33	33	7	215.1	213	51	144	1	0	0	0	75	12	0	.160	24	33	4	2	1.8	.934
1984			14	8	.636	3.74	30	30	4	211.2	208	51	145	1	0	0	0	66	5	0	.076	19	40	1	1	2.0	.983
1985			1	13	.071	6.14	22	22	0	95.1	115	57	57	0	0	0	0	25	3	0	.120	7	9	1	0	0.8	.941
1987	MON	N	7	0	1.000	2.30	10	10	2	70.1	52	16	58	0	0	0	0	24	1	0	.042	6	17	3	0	2.6	.885
1988			12	8	.600	2.44	27	27	4	188	133	44	131	2	0	0	0	54	2	0	.037	13	38	0	2	1.9	1.000
1989			9	13	.409	3.31	33	28	2	198.1	178	45	152	0	1	1	0	54	11	0	.204	17	26	2	1	1.4	.956
9 yrs.			64	62	.508	3.48	190	176	21	1156.1	1091	317	769	4	3	2	0	342	41	0	.120	103	188	13	8	1.6	.957

LEAGUE CHAMPIONSHIP SERIES

| 1982 | ATL | N | 0 | 1 | .000 | 5.19 | 2 | 1 | 0 | 8.2 | 10 | 2 | 4 | 0 | 0 | 0 | 0 | 3 | 0 | 0 | .000 | 0 | 0 | 0 | 0 | 0.0 | – |

Cecil Perkins

PERKINS, CECIL BOYCE　　　　　　　　　　　　BR TR 6' 175 lbs.
B. Dec. 1, 1940, Baltimore, Md.

| 1967 | NY | A | 0 | 1 | .000 | 9.00 | 2 | 1 | 0 | 5 | 6 | 2 | 1 | 0 | 0 | 0 | 0 | 1 | 0 | 0 | .000 | 1 | 1 | 0 | 0 | 1.0 | 1.000 |

Charlie Perkins

PERKINS, CHARLES SULLIVAN (Lefty)　　　　　BR TL 6'1" 175 lbs.
B. Sept. 9, 1905, Ensley, Ala.　D. May 25, 1988, Salem, Ore.

1930	PHI	A	0	0	–	6.46	8	1	0	23.2	25	15	15	0	0	0	0	8	1	0	.125	1	5	1	0	0.9	.857
1934	BKN	N	0	3	.000	8.51	11	2	0	24.1	37	14	5	0	0	1	0	7	2	0	.286	1	3	2	0	0.5	.667
2 yrs.			0	3	.000	7.50	19	3	0	48	62	29	20	0	0	1	0	15	3	0	.200	2	8	3	0	0.7	.769

John Perkovich

PERKOVICH, JOHN JOSEPH　　　　　　　　　　BR TR 5'11" 175 lbs.
B. Mar. 10, 1924, Chicago, Ill.

| 1950 | CHI | A | 0 | 0 | – | 7.20 | 1 | 0 | 0 | 5 | 7 | 3 | 1 | 0 | 0 | 0 | 0 | 0 | 0 | 0 | .000 | 0 | 0 | 0 | 0 | 0.0 | – |

Harry Perkowski

PERKOWSKI, HARRY WALTER　　　　　　　　　BL TL 6'2½" 196 lbs.
B. Sept. 6, 1922, Dante, Va.

1947	CIN	N	0	0	–	3.68	3	1	0	7.1	12	3	2	0	0	0	0	1	0	0	.000	0	1	0	0	0.3	1.000
1949			1	1	.500	4.56	5	3	2	23.2	21	14	3	0	0	0	0	9	3	0	.333	0	2	0	0	0.4	1.000
1950			0	0	–	5.24	22	0	0	34.1	36	23	19	0	0	0	0	22	7	0	.318	2	11	0	1	0.6	1.000
1951			3	6	.333	2.82	35	7	1	102	96	46	56	0	0	2	1	25	1	0	.040	1	22	0	2	0.7	1.000
1952			12	10	.545	3.80	33	24	11	194	197	89	86	1	0	2	0	75	12	0	.160	6	43	1	3	1.5	.980
1953			12	11	.522	4.52	33	25	7	193	204	62	70	2	2	0	2	69	14	0	.203	9	35	0	1	1.3	1.000
1954			2	8	.200	6.11	28	12	3	95.2	100	62	32	1	0	2	0	25	4	1	.160	5	12	1	2	0.6	.944
1955	CHI	N	3	4	.429	5.29	25	4	0	47.2	53	25	28	0	3	1	2	13	2	0	.154	8	12	0	0	0.8	1.000
8 yrs.			33	40	.452	4.37	184	76	24	697.2	719	324	296	4	5	7	5	239	43	1	.180	31	138	2	8	0.9	.988

Jon Perlman

PERLMAN, JONATHAN SAMUEL　　　　　　　　BL TR 6'3" 185 lbs.
B. Dec. 13, 1956, Dallas, Tex.

1985	CHI	N	1	0	1.000	11.42	6	0	0	8.2	10	8	4	0	1	0	0	1	0	0	.000	0	2	0	0	0.3	1.000
1987	SF	N	0	0	–	3.97	10	0	0	11.1	11	4	3	0	0	0	0	0	0	0	–	2	1	1	0	0.4	.750
1988	CLE	A	0	2	.000	5.49	10	0	0	19.2	25	11	10	0	0	2	0	0	0	0	–	1	7	0	0	0.8	1.000
3 yrs.			1	2	.333	6.35	26	0	0	39.2	46	23	17	0	1	2	0	1	0	0	.000	3	10	1	0	0.5	.929

Len Perme

PERME, LEONARD JOHN　　　　　　　　　　　　BL TL 6' 170 lbs.
B. Nov. 25, 1917, Cleveland, Ohio

1942	CHI	A	0	1	.000	1.38	4	1	1	13	5	4	4	0	0	0	0	3	1	0	.333	0	2	0	1	0.5	1.000
1946			0	0	–	8.31	4	0	0	4.1	6	7	2	0	0	0	0	0	0	0	–	0	3	0	0	0.8	1.000
2 yrs.			0	1	.000	3.12	8	1	1	17.1	11	11	6	0	0	0	0	3	1	0	.333	0	5	0	1	0.6	1.000

Hub Pernoll

PERNOLL, HENRY HUBBARD　　　　　　　　　BR TL 5'8" 175 lbs.
B. Mar. 14, 1888, Grant's Pass, Ore.　D. Feb. 18, 1944, Grant's Pass, Ore.

1910	DET	A	4	3	.571	2.96	11	5	4	54.2	54	14	25	0	0	0	0	16	1	0	.063	4	31	1	1	3.3	.972
1912			0	0	–	6.00	3	0	0	9	9	4	3	0	0	0	0	3	0	0	.000	0	3	0	0	1.0	1.000
2 yrs.			4	3	.571	3.39	14	5	4	63.2	63	18	28	0	0	0	0	19	1	0	.053	4	34	1	1	2.8	.974

Ron Perranoski

PERRANOSKI, RONALD PETER　　　　　　　　BL TL 6' 180 lbs.
Born Ronald Peter Perzanowski.
B. Apr. 1, 1936, Paterson, N. J.

1961	LA	N	7	5	.583	2.65	53	0	0	91.2	82	41	56	0	7	5	6	12	1	0	.083	5	17	1	1	0.4	.957
1962			6	6	.500	2.85	70	0	0	107.1	103	36	68	0	6	6	20	14	1	0	.071	3	17	4	3	0.3	.833
1963			16	3	**.842**	1.67	69	0	0	129	112	43	75	0	**16**	3	21	24	3	0	.125	6	24	1	0	0.4	.968
1964			5	7	.417	3.09	72	0	0	125.1	128	46	79	0	5	7	14	19	2	0	.105	6	32	2	2	0.4	.950
1965			6	6	.500	2.24	59	0	0	104.2	85	40	53	0	6	6	17	19	3	0	.158	4	15	2	1	0.4	.905
1966			6	7	.462	3.18	55	0	0	82	82	31	50	0	6	7	7	8	2	0	.250	7	23	1	1	0.6	.968
1967			6	7	.462	2.45	70	0	0	110	97	45	75	0	6	7	16	10	1	0	.100	4	26	1	2	0.4	.968
1968	MIN	A	8	7	.533	3.10	66	0	0	87	86	38	65	0	8	7	6	7	0	0	.000	4	13	1	0	0.3	.944
1969			9	10	.474	2.11	75	0	0	119.2	85	52	62	0	9	10	**31**	24	2	0	.083	4	23	1	2	0.4	.964
1970			7	8	.467	2.43	67	0	0	111	108	42	55	0	7	8	**34**	24	1	0	.042	0	15	1	1	0.2	.938

Year	Team	W	L	PCT	ERA	G	GS	CG	IP	H	BB	SO	ShO	Relief Pitching W	L	SV	Batting AB	H	HR	BA	PO	A	E	DP	TC/G	FA

Ron Perranoski *continued*

Year	Team	W	L	PCT	ERA	G	GS	CG	IP	H	BB	SO	ShO	W	L	SV	AB	H	HR	BA	PO	A	E	DP	TC/G	FA
1971	2 teams	MIN A (36G 1–4)			DET A (11G 0–1)																					
"	total	1	5	.167	5.49	47	0	0	60.2	76	31	29	0	1	5	7	5	0	0	.000	1	10	3	0	0.3	.786
1972	2 teams	DET A (17G 0–1)			LA N (9G 2–0)																					
"	total	2	1	.667	5.30	26	0	0	35.2	42	16	15	0	2	1	0	1	0	0	.000	1	3	0	0	0.2	1.000
1973	CAL A	0	2	.000	4.09	8	0	0	11	11	7	5	0	0	2	0	0	0	0	.000	0	3	0	0	0.4	1.000
13 yrs.		79	74	.516	2.79	737	1	0	1175	1097	468	687	0	79	74	179	167	16	0	.096	45	221	18	12	0.4	.937

LEAGUE CHAMPIONSHIP SERIES

Year	Team	W	L	PCT	ERA	G	GS	CG	IP	H	BB	SO	ShO	W	L	SV	AB	H	HR	BA	PO	A	E	DP	TC/G	FA
1969	MIN A	0	1	.000	5.79	3	0	0	4.2	8	0	2	0	0	1	0	1	0	0	.000	0	0	0	0	0.0	–
1970		0	0	–	19.29	2	0	0	2.1	5	1	3	0	0	0	0	0	0	0	–	0	1	0	1	0.5	1.000
2 yrs.		0	1	.000	10.29	5	0	0	7	13	1	5	0	0	1	0	1	0	0	.000	0	1	0	1	0.2	1.000

WORLD SERIES

Year	Team	W	L	PCT	ERA	G	GS	CG	IP	H	BB	SO	ShO	W	L	SV	AB	H	HR	BA	PO	A	E	DP	TC/G	FA
1963	LA N	0	0	–	0.00	1	0	0	.2	1	0	1	0	0	0	1	0	0	0	–	0	0	0	0	0.0	–
1965		0	0	–	7.36	2	0	0	3.2	3	4	1	0	0	0	0	0	0	0	–	0	1	0	1	0.5	1.000
1966		0	0	–	5.40	2	0	0	3.1	4	1	2	0	0	0	0	0	0	0	–	0	2	1	0	1.5	.667
3 yrs.		0	0	–	5.87	5	0	0	7.2	8	5	4	0	0	0	1	0	0	0	–	0	3	1	1	0.8	.750

Bill Perrin

PERRIN, WILLIAM JOSEPH (Lefty)
B. June 23, 1910, New Orleans, La.   D. June 30, 1974, New Orleans, La.   BR TL 5'11" 172 lbs.

Year	Team	W	L	PCT	ERA	G	GS	CG	IP	H	BB	SO	ShO	W	L	SV	AB	H	HR	BA	PO	A	E	DP	TC/G	FA
1934	CLE A	0	1	.000	14.40	1	1	0	5	13	2	3	0	0	0	0	2	0	0	.000	0	2	0	0	2.0	1.000

George Perring

PERRING, GEORGE WILSON
B. Aug. 13, 1884, Sharon, Wis.   D. Aug. 20, 1960, Beloit, Wis.   BR TR 6' 190 lbs.

Year	Team	W	L	PCT	ERA	G	GS	CG	IP	H	BB	SO	ShO	W	L	SV	AB	H	HR	BA	PO	A	E	DP	TC/G	FA
1914	KC F	0	0	–	13.50	1	0	0	.2	2	1	0	0	0	0	0	*				0	0	0	0	0.0	–

Pol Perritt

PERRITT, WILLIAM DAYTON
B. Aug. 30, 1892, Arcadia, La.   D. Oct. 15, 1947, Shreveport, La.   BR TR 6'2" 168 lbs.

Year	Team	W	L	PCT	ERA	G	GS	CG	IP	H	BB	SO	ShO	W	L	SV	AB	H	HR	BA	PO	A	E	DP	TC/G	FA
1912	STL N	1	1	.500	3.19	6	3	1	31	25	10	13	0	3	0	0	9	2	0	.222	0	8	0	0	1.3	1.000
1913		6	14	.300	5.25	36	21	8	175	205	64	64	0	3	0	0	59	12	0	.203	10	46	3	1	1.6	.949
1914	NY N	16	13	.552	2.36	41	32	18	286	248	93	115	3	2	1	2	92	13	0	.141	8	67	9	1	2.0	.893
1915		12	18	.400	2.66	35	30	16	220	226	59	91	4	1	1	0	68	11	0	.162	7	40	8	0	1.6	.855
1916		18	11	.621	2.62	40	28	17	251	243	56	115	5	2	5	2	83	7	0	.084	12	55	4	2	1.8	.944
1917		17	7	.708	1.88	35	26	14	215	186	45	72	5	2	3	1	70	11	0	.157	11	63	2	4	2.2	.974
1918		18	13	.581	2.74	35	31	19	233	212	38	60	6	1	1	0	80	14	0	.175	12	54	3	1	2.0	.957
1919		1	1	.500	7.11	11	3	0	19	27	12	2	0	1	0	1	4	0	0	.000	0	8	0	0	0.7	1.000
1920		0	0	–	1.80	8	0	0	15	9	4	3	0	0	0	2	4	0	0	.000	1	5	0	0	0.8	1.000
1921	2 teams	NY N (5G 2–0)			DET A (4G 1–0)																					
"	total	3	0	1.000	4.38	9	3	0	24.2	35	9	8	0	2	0	0	8	2	0	.250	1	3	1	0	0.6	.800
10 yrs.		92	78	.541	2.89	256	177	93	1469.2	1416	390	543	23	14	11	8	477	72	0	.151	62	349	30	9	1.7	.932

WORLD SERIES

Year	Team	W	L	PCT	ERA	G	GS	CG	IP	H	BB	SO	ShO	W	L	SV	AB	H	HR	BA	PO	A	E	DP	TC/G	FA
1917	NY N	0	0	–	2.16	3	0	0	8.1	9	3	3	0	0	0	0	2	2	0	1.000	0	1	0	0	0.3	1.000

Gaylord Perry

PERRY, GAYLORD JACKSON
Brother of Jim Perry.
B. Sept. 15, 1938, Williamston, N. C.   BR TR 6'4" 205 lbs.

Year	Team	W	L	PCT	ERA	G	GS	CG	IP	H	BB	SO	ShO	W	L	SV	AB	H	HR	BA	PO	A	E	DP	TC/G	FA
1962	SF N	3	1	.750	5.23	13	7	1	43	54	14	20	0	0	0	0	13	3	0	.231	3	5	1	1	0.7	.889
1963		1	6	.143	4.03	31	4	0	76	84	29	52	0	1	5	2	18	4	0	.222	4	12	0	0	0.5	1.000
1964		12	11	.522	2.75	44	19	5	206.1	179	43	155	2	6	5	5	56	3	0	.054	12	26	0	3	0.9	1.000
1965		8	12	.400	4.19	47	26	6	195.2	194	70	170	0	0	1	1	64	10	0	.156	18	40	1	4	1.3	.983
1966		21	8	.724	2.99	36	35	13	255.2	242	40	201	3	1	0	0	86	16	0	.186	16	40	1	2	1.6	.982
1967		15	17	.469	2.61	39	37	18	293	231	84	230	3	0	1	1	91	13	0	.143	20	64	3	2	2.2	.966
1968		16	15	.516	2.45	39	38	19	290.2	240	59	173	3	0	0	0	97	11	0	.113	31	62	2	3	2.4	.979
1969		19	14	.576	2.49	40	39	26	325	290	91	233	3	0	0	0	117	14	1	.120	18	67	0	2	2.1	1.000
1970		**23**	13	.639	3.20	41	**41**	23	**329**	**292**	84	214	**5**	0	0	0	120	14	1	.117	30	67	4	5	2.5	.960
1971		16	12	.571	2.76	37	37	14	280	255	67	158	2	0	0	0	98	10	1	.102	21	41	5	5	1.8	.925
1972	CLE A	**24**	16	.600	1.92	41	40	**29**	343	253	82	234	5	0	0	0	110	17	1	.155	18	61	2	7	2.0	.975
1973		19	19	.500	3.38	41	41	**29**	344	315	115	238	7	0	0	0	0	0	0	–	19	55	0	1	1.8	1.000
1974		21	13	.618	2.52	37	37	28	322	230	99	216	4	0	0	0	0	0	0	–	26	45	3	4	2.0	.959
1975	2 teams	CLE A (15G 6–9)			TEX A (22G 12–8)																					
"	total	18	17	.514	3.24	37	37	25	305.2	277	70	233	5	0	0	0	0	0	0	–	19	43	1	3	1.7	.984
1976	TEX A	15	14	.517	3.24	32	32	21	250	232	52	143	2	0	0	0	0	0	0	–	11	24	2	1	1.2	.946
1977		15	12	.556	3.37	34	34	13	238	239	56	177	4	0	0	0	0	0	0	–	14	28	1	2	1.3	.977
1978	SD N	**21**	6	**.778**	2.72	37	37	5	261	241	66	154	2	0	0	0	87	8	0	.092	13	40	2	6	1.5	.964
1979		12	11	.522	3.05	32	32	10	233	225	67	140	0	0	0	0	71	6	0	.085	11	41	2	2	1.7	.963
1980	2 teams	TEX A (24G 6–9)			NY A (10G 4–4)																					
"	total	10	13	.435	3.67	34	32	6	206	224	64	135	2	1	0	0	0	0	0	–	13	32	1	3	1.4	.978
1981	ATL N	8	9	.471	3.93	23	23	3	151	**182**	24	60	0	0	0	0	48	12	1	.250	11	19	3	0	1.4	.909
1982	SEA A	10	12	.455	4.40	32	32	6	216.2	245	54	116	0	0	0	0	0	0	0	–	11	35	3	1	1.5	.939
1983	2 teams	SEA A (16G 3–10)			KC A (14G 4–4)																					
"	total	7	14	.333	4.64	30	30	3	186.1	214	49	82	1	0	0	0	0	0	0	–	10	30	1	1	1.4	.976
22 yrs.		314	265	.542	3.10	777	690	303	5351	4938	1379	3534	53	9	12	11	1076	141	6	.131	349	877	38	58	1.6	.970
				5th					5th			6th														

LEAGUE CHAMPIONSHIP SERIES

Year	Team	W	L	PCT	ERA	G	GS	CG	IP	H	BB	SO	ShO	W	L	SV	AB	H	HR	BA	PO	A	E	DP	TC/G	FA
1971	SF N	1	1	.500	6.14	2	2	0	14.2	19	3	11	0	0	0	0	4	1	0	.250	1	2	0	0	1.5	1.000

Jim Perry

PERRY, JAMES EVAN
Brother of Gaylord Perry.
B. Oct. 30, 1936, Williamston, N. C.   BB TR 6'4" 190 lbs.

Year	Team	W	L	PCT	ERA	G	GS	CG	IP	H	BB	SO	ShO	W	L	SV	AB	H	HR	BA	PO	A	E	DP	TC/G	FA
1959	CLE A	12	10	.545	2.65	44	13	8	153	122	55	79	2	5	4	4	50	15	0	.300	12	24	0	1	0.8	1.000
1960		**18**	10	**.643**	3.62	41	**36**	10	261.1	257	91	120	**4**	1	0	1	91	22	0	.242	23	40	2	4	1.6	.969

Year	Team		W	L	PCT	ERA	G	GS	CG	IP	H	BB	SO	ShO	W	L	SV	AB	H	HR	BA	PO	A	E	DP	TC/G	FA
															Relief Pitching			**Batting**									

Dan Petry

PETRY, DANIEL JOSEPH
B. Nov. 13, 1958, Palo Alto, Calif.   BR TR 6'4"   185 lbs.

Year	Team		W	L	PCT	ERA	G	GS	CG	IP	H	BB	SO	ShO	W	L	SV	AB	H	HR	BA	PO	A	E	DP	TC/G	FA
1979	DET	A	6	5	.545	3.95	15	15	2	98	90	33	43	0	0	0	0	0	0	0	–	9	11	2	0	1.5	.909
1980			10	9	.526	3.93	27	25	4	165	156	83	88	3	1	0	0	0	0	0	–	12	32	3	3	1.7	.936
1981			10	9	.526	3.00	23	22	7	141	115	57	79	2	0	0	0	0	0	0	–	14	26	1	6	1.8	.976
1982			15	9	.625	3.22	35	35	8	246	220	100	132	1	0	0	0	0	0	0	–	28	48	0	4	2.2	1.000
1983			19	11	.633	3.92	38	38	9	266.1	256	99	122	0	0	0	0	0	0	0	–	30	43	2	10	2.0	.973
1984			18	8	.692	3.24	35	35	7	233.1	231	66	144	2	0	0	0	0	0	0	–	38	34	1	4	2.1	.986
1985			15	13	.536	3.36	34	34	8	238.2	190	81	109	4	0	0	0	0	0	0	–	36	26	0	3	1.8	1.000
1986			5	10	.333	4.66	20	20	2	116	122	53	56	0	0	0	0	0	0	0	–	16	18	0	1	1.7	1.000
1987			9	7	.563	5.61	30	21	0	134.2	148	76	93	0	2	0	0	0	0	0	–	16	21	2	0	1.3	.949
1988	CAL	A	3	9	.250	4.38	22	22	4	139.2	139	59	64	1	0	0	0	0	0	0	–	20	25	0	2	2.0	1.000
1989			3	2	.600	5.47	19	4	0	51	53	23	21	0	2	0	0	0	0	0	–	5	7	0	0	0.6	1.000
11 yrs.			113	92	.551	3.85	298	271	51	1829.2	1720	730	951	11	5	0	0	0	0	0	–	224	291	11	33	1.8	.979
LEAGUE CHAMPIONSHIP SERIES																											
1984	DET	A	0	0	–	2.57	1	1	0	7	4	1	4	0	0	0	0	0	0	0	–	0	0	0	0	0.0	–
1987			0	0	–	0.00	1	0	0	3.1	1	0	1	0	0	0	0	0	0	0	–	0	1	0	0	1.0	1.000
2 yrs.			0	0	–	1.74	2	1	0	10.1	5	1	5	0	0	0	0	0	0	0	–	0	1	0	0	0.5	1.000
WORLD SERIES																											
1984	DET	A	0	1	.000	9.00	2	2	0	8	14	5	4	0	0	0	0	0	0	0	–	1	1	0	0	1.0	1.000

Jay Pettibone

PETTIBONE, HARRY JONATHAN
B. June 21, 1957, Mt. Clemens, Mich.   BR TR 6'4"   185 lbs.

Year	Team		W	L	PCT	ERA	G	GS	CG	IP	H	BB	SO	ShO	W	L	SV	AB	H	HR	BA	PO	A	E	DP	TC/G	FA
1983	MIN	A	0	4	.000	5.33	4	4	1	27	28	8	10	0	0	0	0	0	0	0	–	4	4	0	0	2.0	1.000

Bob Pettit

PETTIT, ROBERT HENRY
B. July 19, 1861, Williamstown, Mass.   D. Nov. 1, 1910, Derby, Conn.   BL TR 5'9"   160 lbs.

Year	Team		W	L	PCT	ERA	G	GS	CG	IP	H	BB	SO	ShO	W	L	SV	AB	H	HR	BA	PO	A	E	DP	TC/G	FA
1887	CHI	N	0	0	–	0.00	1	0	0	1	3	2	0	0	0	0	0	1	*			0	0	0	0	0.0	

Leon Pettit

PETTIT, LEON ARTHUR (Lefty)
B. June 23, 1902, Waynesburg, Pa.   D. Nov. 21, 1974, Columbia, Tenn.   BL TL 5'10½" 165 lbs.

Year	Team		W	L	PCT	ERA	G	GS	CG	IP	H	BB	SO	ShO	W	L	SV	AB	H	HR	BA	PO	A	E	DP	TC/G	FA
1935	WAS	A	8	5	.615	4.95	41	7	1	109	129	58	45	0	6	3	3	25	2	0	.080	9	19	3	0	0.8	.903
1937	PHI	N	0	1	.000	11.25	3	1	0	4	6	4	0	0	0	0	0	0	0	0	–	2	0	0	0	0.7	1.000
2 yrs.			8	6	.571	5.18	44	8	1	113	135	62	45	0	6	3	3	25	2	0	.080	11	19	3	0	0.8	.909

Paul Pettit

PETTIT, GEORGE WILLIAM PAUL (Lefty)
B. Nov. 29, 1931, Los Angeles, Calif.   BL TL 6'2"   195 lbs.

Year	Team		W	L	PCT	ERA	G	GS	CG	IP	H	BB	SO	ShO	W	L	SV	AB	H	HR	BA	PO	A	E	DP	TC/G	FA
1951	PIT	N	0	0	–	3.38	2	0	0	2.2	2	1	0	0	0	0	0	1	0	0	.000	0	0	0	0	0.0	–
1953			1	2	.333	7.71	10	5	0	28	33	20	14	0	0	0	0	8	2	0	.250	2	6	0	0	0.8	1.000
2 yrs.			1	2	.333	7.34	12	5	0	30.2	35	21	14	0	0	0	0	9	2	0	.222	2	6	0	0	0.7	1.000

Charlie Petty

PETTY, CHARLES E.
B. June 28, 1866, Nashville, Tenn.   Deceased.   TR

Year	Team		W	L	PCT	ERA	G	GS	CG	IP	H	BB	SO	ShO	W	L	SV	AB	H	HR	BA	PO	A	E	DP	TC/G	FA
1889	CIN	AA	2	3	.400	5.52	5	5	5	44	44	20	10	0	0	0	0	20	6	0	.300	1	9	0	0	2.0	1.000
1893	NY	N	5	2	.714	3.33	9	6	4	54	66	28	12	0	2	0	0	22	7	1	.318	2	11	2	0	1.7	.867
1894	2 teams						WAS N (16G 3–8)									CLE N (4G 0–2)												
"	total		3	10	.231	6.23	20	15	10	130	198	46	18	0	0	0	0	53	9	0	.170	8	18	6	0	1.6	.813
3 yrs.			10	15	.400	5.41	34	26	19	228	308	94	40	0	2	0	0	95	22	1	.232	11	38	8	0	1.7	.860

Jesse Petty

PETTY, JESSE LEE (The Silver Fox)
B. Nov. 23, 1894, Orr, Okla.   D. Oct. 23, 1971, St. Paul, Minn.   BR TL 6'   195 lbs.

Year	Team		W	L	PCT	ERA	G	GS	CG	IP	H	BB	SO	ShO	W	L	SV	AB	H	HR	BA	PO	A	E	DP	TC/G	FA
1921	CLE	A	0	0	–	2.00	4	0	0	9	10	4	0	0	0	0	0	2	0	0	.000	0	7	0	0	1.8	1.000
1925	BKN	N	9	9	.500	4.88	28	22	7	153	188	47	39	0	0	3	0	50	7	0	.140	6	30	5	1	1.5	.878
1926			17	17	.500	2.84	38	33	23	275.2	246	79	101	1	2	1	1	97	17	0	.175	8	51	7	0	1.7	.894
1927			13	18	.419	2.98	42	33	19	271.2	263	53	101	2	2	1	1	91	9	0	.099	7	47	6	3	1.4	.900
1928			15	15	.500	4.04	40	31	15	234	264	56	74	2	1	2	1	81	9	0	.111	4	34	1	4	1.0	.974
1929	PIT	N	11	10	.524	3.71	36	25	12	184.1	197	42	58	1	1	0	0	67	7	0	.104	1	36	0	0	1.1	.974
1930	2 teams						PIT N (10G 1–6)									CHI N (9G 1–3)												
"	total		2	9	.182	5.69	19	10	0	80.2	118	19	34	0	1	1	1	25	4	0	.160	0	16	0	0	0.8	1.000
7 yrs.			67	78	.462	3.68	207	154	76	1208.1	1286	296	407	6	10	5	4	413	53	0	.128	26	221	20	8	1.3	.925

Pretzels Pezzullo

PEZZULLO, JOHN
B. Dec. 10, 1910, Bridgeport, Conn.   BL TL 5'11½" 180 lbs.

Year	Team		W	L	PCT	ERA	G	GS	CG	IP	H	BB	SO	ShO	W	L	SV	AB	H	HR	BA	PO	A	E	DP	TC/G	FA
1935	PHI	N	3	5	.375	6.40	41	7	2	84.1	115	45	24	0	1	1	1	24	6	0	.250	2	9	1	0	0.3	.917
1936			0	0	–	4.50	1	0	0	2	1	6	0	0	0	0	0	0	0	0	–	0	0	0	0	0.0	–
2 yrs.			3	5	.375	6.36	42	7	2	86.1	116	51	24	0	1	1	1	24	6	0	.250	2	9	1	0	0.3	.917

Big Jeff Pfeffer

PFEFFER, FRANCIS XAVIER
Brother of Jeff Pfeffer.
B. Mar. 31, 1882, Champaign, Ill.   D. Dec. 19, 1954, Kankakee, Ill.   BR TR 6'   185 lbs.

Year	Team		W	L	PCT	ERA	G	GS	CG	IP	H	BB	SO	ShO	W	L	SV	AB	H	HR	BA	PO	A	E	DP	TC/G	FA
1905	CHI	N	4	5	.444	2.50	15	11	9	101	84	36	56	0	0	0	0	40	8	0	.200	4	24	0	0	1.9	1.000
1906	BOS	N	13	22	.371	2.95	35	35	33	302.1	270	114	158	4	0	0	0	158	31	1	.196	13	91	4	0	3.1	.963
1907			6	8	.429	3.00	19	16	12	144	129	61	65	1	0	0	0	60	15	0	.250	4	38	2	0	2.3	.955
1908			0	0	–	12.60	4	0	0	10	18	8	3	0	0	0	0	2	0	0	.000	0	1	0	0	0.3	1.000
1910	CHI	N	1	0	1.000	3.27	13	1	1	41.1	43	16	11	0	0	0	0	17	3	0	.176	0	10	0	0	0.8	1.000
1911	BOS	N	7	5	.583	4.73	26	6	4	97	116	57	24	0	4	2	2	46	9	1	.196	8	25	0	0	1.3	1.000
6 yrs.			31	40	.437	3.30	112	69	59	695.2	660	292	317	6	4	2	2	*				29	189	6	0	2.0	.973

Year	Team		W	L	PCT	ERA	G	GS	CG	IP	H	BB	SO	ShO	W	L	SV	AB	H	HR	BA	PO	A	E	DP	TC/G	FA

Fred Pfeffer

PFEFFER, NATHANIEL FREDERICK (Dandelion, Fritz)   BR TR 5'10½" 184 lbs.
B. Mar. 17, 1860, Louisville, Ky.   D. Apr. 10, 1932, Chicago, Ill.
Manager 1892.

Year	Team		W	L	PCT	ERA	G	GS	CG	IP	H	BB	SO	ShO	W	L	SV	AB	H	HR	BA	PO	A	E	DP	TC/G	FA
1884	CHI	N	0	0	–	9.00	1	0	0	1	3	1	0	0	0	0	0	467	135	25	.289	0	0	0	0	0.0	–
1885			2	1	.667	2.56	5	2	2	31.2	26	8	13	0	1	0	2	469	113	6	.241	1	6	0	0	1.4	1.000
1892	LOU	N	0	0	–	1.80	1	0	0	5	4	5	0	0	0	0	0	470	121	2	.257	1	1	0	0	2.0	1.000
1894			0	0	–	2.57	1	0	0	7	8	6	0	0	0	0	0	409	126	5	.308	1	0	0	0	1.0	1.000
4 yrs.			2	1	.667	2.62	8	2	2	44.2	41	20	13	0	1	0	2	*				3	7	0	0	1.3	1.000

Jeff Pfeffer

PFEFFER, EDWARD JOSEPH   BR TR 6'3" 210 lbs.
Brother of Big Jeff Pfeffer.
B. Mar. 4, 1888, Seymour, Ill.   D. Aug. 15, 1972, Chicago, Ill.

Year	Team		W	L	PCT	ERA	G	GS	CG	IP	H	BB	SO	ShO	W	L	SV	AB	H	HR	BA	PO	A	E	DP	TC/G	FA
1911	STL	A	0	0	–	7.20	2	0	0	10	11	4	4	0	0	0	0	4	0	0	.000	0	2	0	0	1.0	1.000
1913	BKN	N	0	1	.000	3.33	5	2	1	24.1	28	13	13	0	0	0	0	7	0	0	.000	2	6	0	1	1.6	1.000
1914			23	12	.657	1.97	43	34	27	315	264	91	135	3	0	2	4	116	23	0	.198	4	65	2	3	1.7	.972
1915			19	14	.576	2.10	40	34	26	291.2	243	76	84	6	1	2	3	106	27	0	.255	9	62	2	0	1.8	.973
1916			25	11	.694	1.92	41	37	30	328.2	274	63	128	6	1	0	1	122	34	0	.279	8	66	3	3	1.9	.961
1917			11	15	.423	2.23	30	30	24	266	225	66	115	3	0	0	0	100	13	0	.130	5	69	4	0	2.6	.949
1918			1	0	1.000	0.00	1	1	1	9	2	3	1	1	0	0	0	4	1	0	.250	1	4	0	0	5.0	1.000
1919			17	13	.567	2.66	30	30	26	267	270	49	92	4	0	0	0	97	20	0	.206	14	78	5	3	3.2	.948
1920			16	9	.640	3.01	30	28	20	215	225	45	80	2	1	0	0	74	18	0	.243	4	47	3	2	1.8	.944
1921	2 teams		BKN	N	(6G 1–5)		STL	N	(18G 9–3)																		
"	total		10	8	.556	4.35	24	19	9	130.1	151	37	30	1	2	3	0	40	4	0	.100	4	29	1	1	1.4	.971
1922	STL	N	19	12	.613	3.58	44	32	19	261.1	286	58	83	1	3	1	2	98	24	0	.245	4	65	1	3	1.6	.986
1923			8	9	.471	4.02	26	18	7	152.1	171	40	32	1	1	1	0	55	7	0	.127	3	31	1	2	1.3	.971
1924	2 teams		STL	N	(16G 4–5)		PIT	N	(15G 5–3)																		
"	total		9	8	.529	4.35	31	16	4	136.2	170	47	39	0	4	3	0	51	9	0	.176	0	25	1	3	0.8	.962
13 yrs.			158	112	.585	2.77	347	280	194	2407.1	2320	592	836	28	13	9	10	874	180	0	.206	58	549	23	21	1.8	.963

WORLD SERIES

Year	Team		W	L	PCT	ERA	G	GS	CG	IP	H	BB	SO	ShO	W	L	SV	AB	H	HR	BA	PO	A	E	DP	TC/G	FA
1916	BKN	N	0	1	.000	2.53	3	1	0	10.2	7	4	5	0	0	0	1	4	1	0	.250	0	2	0	0	0.7	1.000
1920			0	0	–	3.00	1	0	0	3	4	2	1	0	0	0	0	1	0	0	.000	0	0	0	0	0.0	–
2 yrs.			0	1	.000	2.63	4	1	0	13.2	11	6	6	0	0	0	1	5	1	0	.200	0	2	0	0	0.5	1.000

Jack Pfiester

PFIESTER, JOHN ALBERT (Jack the Giant Killer)   BR TL 5'11" 180 lbs.
Born John Albert Hagenbush.
B. May 24, 1878, Cincinnati, Ohio   D. Sept. 3, 1953, Loveland, Ohio

Year	Team		W	L	PCT	ERA	G	GS	CG	IP	H	BB	SO	ShO	W	L	SV	AB	H	HR	BA	PO	A	E	DP	TC/G	FA
1903	PIT	N	0	3	.000	6.16	3	3	2	19	26	10	15	0	0	0	0	6	0	0	.000	2	3	1	0	2.0	.833
1904			1	1	.500	7.20	3	2	1	20	28	9	6	0	0	0	0	7	2	0	.286	0	6	0	0	2.0	1.000
1906	CHI	N	20	8	.714	1.56	31	29	20	241.2	173	63	153	4	1	0	0	84	4	0	.048	21	62	7	1	2.9	.922
1907			15	9	.625	1.15	30	22	13	195	143	48	90	3	2	1	0	64	6	0	.094	8	44	7	0	2.0	.881
1908			12	10	.545	2.00	33	29	18	252	204	70	117	3	0	1	0	79	8	0	.101	13	56	2	2	2.2	.972
1909			17	6	.739	2.43	29	25	13	196.2	179	49	73	5	1	0	1	65	11	0	.169	6	69	2	1	2.7	.974
1910			6	3	.667	1.79	14	13	5	100.1	82	26	34	2	0	0	0	33	3	0	.091	8	25	3	0	2.6	.917
1911			0	4	.000	4.01	6	5	3	33.2	34	18	15	0	0	0	0	11	2	0	.182	1	13	1	1	2.5	.933
8 yrs.			71	44	.617	2.04	149	128	75	1058.1	869	293	503	17	4	2	0	349	36	0	.103	59	278	23	5	2.4	.936

WORLD SERIES

Year	Team		W	L	PCT	ERA	G	GS	CG	IP	H	BB	SO	ShO	W	L	SV	AB	H	HR	BA	PO	A	E	DP	TC/G	FA
1906	CHI	N	0	2	.000	6.10	2	1	1	10.1	7	3	11	0	0	0	0	2	0	0	.000	0	2	1	0	1.5	.667
1907			1	0	1.000	1.00	1	1	1	9	3	1	3	0	0	0	0	2	0	0	.000	0	0	0	0	0.0	–
1908			0	1	.000	7.88	1	1	0	8	10	3	1	0	0	0	0	2	0	0	.000	0	0	0	0	0.0	–
1910			0	0	–	0.00	1	0	0	6.2	9	1	1	0	0	0	0	2	0	0	.000	0	1	0	0	1.0	1.000
4 yrs.			1	3	.250	3.97	5	3	2	34	35	8	16	0	0	0	0	8	0	0	.000	0	3	1	0	0.8	.750

Dan Pfister

PFISTER, DANIEL ALBIN   BR TR 6' 187 lbs.
B. Dec. 20, 1936, Plainfield, N. J.

Year	Team		W	L	PCT	ERA	G	GS	CG	IP	H	BB	SO	ShO	W	L	SV	AB	H	HR	BA	PO	A	E	DP	TC/G	FA
1961	KC	A	0	0	–	15.43	2	0	0	2.1	5	4	3	0	0	0	0	0	0	0	–	0	0	0	0	0.0	–
1962			4	14	.222	4.54	41	25	2	196.1	175	106	123	0	0	1	1	65	12	0	.185	24	30	2	2	1.4	.964
1963			1	0	1.000	1.93	3	1	0	9.1	8	3	9	0	0	0	0	3	0	0	.000	0	3	0	0	1.0	1.000
1964			1	5	.167	6.53	19	3	0	41.1	50	29	21	0	1	3	0	6	0	0	.000	4	6	3	0	0.7	.769
4 yrs.			6	19	.240	4.87	65	29	2	249.1	238	142	156	0	1	4	1	74	12	0	.162	28	39	5	2	1.1	.931

Bill Pflann

PFLANN, WILLIAM F   6' 205 lbs.
B. Brooklyn, N. Y.   Deceased.

Year	Team		W	L	PCT	ERA	G	GS	CG	IP	H	BB	SO	ShO	W	L	SV	AB	H	HR	BA	PO	A	E	DP	TC/G	FA
1894	CIN	N	0	1	.000	27.00	1	1	0	3	10	4	0	0	0	0	0	1	0	0	.000	0	2	0	0	2.0	1.000

Lee Pfund

PFUND, LeROY HERBERT   BR TR 6'1" 185 lbs.
B. Oct. 18, 1918, Oak Park, Ill.

Year	Team		W	L	PCT	ERA	G	GS	CG	IP	H	BB	SO	ShO	W	L	SV	AB	H	HR	BA	PO	A	E	DP	TC/G	FA
1945	BKN	N	3	2	.600	5.20	15	10	2	62.1	69	35	27	0	0	0	0	22	4	0	.182	4	14	2	1	1.3	.900

Bill Phebus

PHEBUS, RAYMOND WILLIAM   BR TR 5'9" 170 lbs.
B. Aug. 9, 1909, Cherryvale, Kans.

Year	Team		W	L	PCT	ERA	G	GS	CG	IP	H	BB	SO	ShO	W	L	SV	AB	H	HR	BA	PO	A	E	DP	TC/G	FA
1936	WAS	A	0	0	–	2.45	2	1	0	7.1	4	4	4	0	0	0	0	1	0	0	.000	0	0	0	0	0.0	–
1937			3	2	.600	2.21	6	5	4	40.2	33	24	12	1	0	0	1	8	0	0	.000	1	4	1	0	1.0	.833
1938			0	0	–	11.37	5	0	0	6.1	9	7	2	0	0	0	1	1	0	0	.000	0	3	0	0	0.6	1.000
3 yrs.			3	2	.600	3.31	13	6	4	54.1	46	35	18	1	0	0	2	10	0	0	.000	1	7	1	0	0.7	.889

Ray Phelps

PHELPS, RAYMOND CLIFFORD   BR TR 6'2" 200 lbs.
B. Dec. 11, 1903, Dunlap, Tenn.   D. July 7, 1971, Fort Pierce, Fla.

Year	Team		W	L	PCT	ERA	G	GS	CG	IP	H	BB	SO	ShO	W	L	SV	AB	H	HR	BA	PO	A	E	DP	TC/G	FA
1930	BKN	N	14	7	.667	4.11	36	24	11	179.2	198	52	64	2	2	1	0	68	10	1	.147	10	43	0	4	1.5	1.000
1931			7	9	.438	5.00	28	26	3	149.1	184	44	50	2	0	0	0	51	8	0	.157	4	31	1	6	1.3	.972
1932			4	5	.444	5.90	20	8	4	79.1	101	27	21	1	1	3	0	23	2	0	.087	3	20	4	1	1.4	.852
1935	CHI	A	4	8	.333	4.82	27	17	4	125	126	55	38	0	0	1	1	41	5	0	.122	7	32	2	1	1.5	.951

Year	Team		W	L	PCT	ERA	G	GS	CG	IP	H	BB	SO	ShO	Relief Pitching W	L	SV	Batting AB	H	HR	BA	PO	A	E	DP	TC/G	FA

Ray Phelps *continued*

| 1936 | | | 4 | 6 | .400 | 6.03 | 15 | 4 | 2 | 68.2 | 91 | 42 | 17 | 0 | 3 | 3 | 0 | 26 | 6 | 0 | .231 | 3 | 18 | 1 | 1 | 1.5 | .955 |
| 5 yrs. | | | 33 | 35 | .485 | 4.93 | 126 | 79 | 24 | 602 | 700 | 220 | 190 | 5 | 6 | 8 | 1 | 209 | 31 | 1 | .148 | 27 | 144 | 8 | 13 | 1.4 | .955 |

Deacon Phillippe

PHILLIPPE, CHARLES LOUIS
B. May 23, 1872, Rural Retreat, Va.   D. Mar. 30, 1952, Avalon, Pa.   BR TR 6'½" 180 lbs.

1899	LOU	N	21	17	.553	3.17	42	38	33	321	331	64	68	1	3	0	1	128	26	0	.203	14	77	7	3	2.3	.929
1900	PIT	N	20	13	.606	2.84	38	33	29	279	274	42	75	1	2	0	0	105	19	0	.181	9	57	3	1	1.8	.957
1901			22	12	.647	2.22	37	32	30	296	274	38	103	1	1	1	2	113	26	1	.230	15	89	6	2	3.0	.945
1902			20	9	.690	2.05	31	30	29	272	265	26	122	5	0	0	0	113	25	1	.221	5	59	3	1	2.2	.955
1903			24	7	.774	2.43	36	33	31	289.1	269	29	123	4	0	0	2	124	26	0	.210	11	65	3	1	2.2	.962
1904			10	10	.500	3.24	21	19	17	166.2	183	26	82	3	1	0	1	65	8	0	.123	8	41	1	3	2.4	.980
1905			22	13	.629	2.19	38	33	25	279	235	48	133	5	3	0	0	97	9	0	.093	4	74	5	2	2.2	.940
1906			15	10	.600	2.47	33	24	19	218.2	216	26	90	3	2	1	0	82	20	0	.244	5	61	3	2	2.1	.957
1907			13	11	.542	2.61	35	26	17	214	214	36	61	1	3	0	2	65	12	0	.185	8	53	1	1	1.8	.984
1908			0	0	—	11.25	5	0	0	12	20	3	1	0	0	0	0	4	1	0	.250	0	1	0	0	0.2	1.000
1909			8	3	.727	2.32	22	12	7	131.2	121	14	38	1	2	0	0	42	3	0	.071	6	26	0	1	1.5	1.000
1910			14	2	.875	2.29	31	8	5	121.2	111	9	30	1	7	1	4	41	9	1	.220	8	18	1	0	0.9	.963
1911			0	0	—	7.50	3	0	0	6	5	2	3	0	0	0	0	1	1	0	1.000	0	3	0	0	1.0	1.000
13 yrs.			189	107	.639	2.59	372	288	242	2607	2518	363	929	27	24	4	12	980	185	3	.189	93	624	33	17	2.0	.956

WORLD SERIES

1903	PIT	N	3	2	.600	3.27	5	5	5	44	38	3	20	0	0	0	0	18	4	0	.222	2	9	1	0	2.4	.917
1909			0	0	—	0.00	2	0	0	6	2	1	2	0	0	0	0	1	0	0	.000	1	2	2	0	2.5	.600
2 yrs.			3	2	.600	2.88	7	5	5	50	40	4	22	0	0	0	0	19	4	0	.211	3	11	3	0	2.4	.824

10th

Bill Phillips

PHILLIPS, WILLIAM CORCORAN (Whoa Bill, Silver Bill)
B. Nov. 9, 1868, Allenport, Pa.   D. Oct. 25, 1941, Charleroi, Pa.   BR TR 5'11" 180 lbs.
Manager 1914-15.

1890	PIT	N	1	9	.100	7.57	10	10	9	82	123	29	25	0	0	0	0	46	11	0	.239	1	17	0	0	1.8	1.000
1895	CIN	N	6	7	.462	6.03	18	9	6	109	126	44	15	0	3	2	1	48	15	0	.313	16	24	3	0	2.4	.930
1899			17	9	.654	3.32	33	27	18	227.2	234	71	43	1	2	1	1	92	12	0	.130	20	51	11	4	2.5	.866
1900			9	11	.450	4.28	29	24	17	208.1	229	67	51	3	1	0	0	79	13	0	.165	13	76	5	7	3.2	.947
1901			14	20	.412	4.64	37	36	29	281.1	364	67	109	1	0	0	0	109	22	0	.202	11	100	8	3	3.2	.933
1902			16	15	.516	2.50	33	32	29	263	264	50	85	0	0	0	0	114	39	0	.342	18	80	6	3	3.2	.942
1903			8	6	.571	3.35	16	13	11	118.1	134	30	46	1	0	0	0	57	10	0	.175	3	45	5	0	3.3	.906
7 yrs.			71	77	.480	4.10	176	151	119	1289.2	1474	358	374	6	6	3	3	545	122	0	.224	82	393	38	17	2.9	.926

Buz Phillips

PHILLIPS, ALBERT ABERNATHY
B. May 25, 1904, Newton, N.C.   D. Nov. 6, 1964, Baltimore, Md.   BR TR 5'11½" 185 lbs.

| 1930 | PHI | N | 0 | 0 | — | 8.04 | 14 | 1 | 0 | 43.2 | 68 | 18 | 9 | 0 | 0 | 0 | 0 | 13 | 6 | 1 | .462 | 2 | 5 | 0 | 0 | 0.5 | 1.000 |

Ed Phillips

PHILLIPS, NORMAN EDWIN
B. Sept. 20, 1944, Ardmore, Okla.   BR TR 6'1" 190 lbs.

| 1970 | BOS | A | 0 | 2 | .000 | 5.25 | 18 | 0 | 0 | 24 | 27 | 10 | 23 | 0 | 0 | 2 | 0 | 3 | 0 | 0 | .000 | 0 | 1 | 0 | 1 | 0.1 | 1.000 |

Jack Phillips

PHILLIPS, JACK DORN (Stretch)
B. Sept. 6, 1921, Clarence, N.Y.   BR TR 6'4" 193 lbs.

| 1950 | PIT | N | 0 | 0 | — | 7.20 | 1 | 0 | 0 | 5 | 7 | 1 | 2 | 0 | 0 | 0 | 0 | * | | | | 0 | 2 | 0 | 0 | 2.0 | 1.000 |

John Phillips

PHILLIPS, JOHN STEPHEN
B. May 24, 1919, St. Louis, Mo.   D. June 16, 1958, St. Louis, Mo.   BR TR 6'1" 185 lbs.

| 1945 | NY | N | 0 | 0 | — | 10.38 | 1 | 0 | 0 | 4.1 | 5 | 4 | 0 | 0 | 0 | 0 | 0 | 2 | 1 | 0 | .500 | 1 | 0 | 0 | 0 | 1.0 | 1.000 |

Red Phillips

PHILLIPS, CLARENCE LEMUEL
B. Nov. 3, 1908, Pauls Valley, Okla.   D. Feb. 1, 1988, Wichita, Kans.   BR TR 6'3½" 195 lbs.

1934	DET	A	2	0	1.000	6.17	7	1	1	23.1	31	16	3	0	1	0	1	12	3	0	.250	1	1	0	1	0.3	1.000
1936			2	4	.333	6.49	22	6	3	87.1	124	22	15	0	1	1	0	33	10	0	.303	3	15	1	2	0.9	.947
2 yrs.			4	4	.500	6.42	29	7	4	110.2	155	38	18	0	2	1	1	45	13	0	.289	4	16	1	3	0.7	.952

Taylor Phillips

PHILLIPS, WILLIAM TAYLOR (Tay)
B. June 18, 1933, Atlanta, Ga.   BL TL 5'11" 185 lbs.

1956	MIL	N	5	3	.625	2.26	23	6	3	87.2	69	33	36	0	2	1	2	21	0	0	.000	9	23	0	2	1.4	1.000
1957			3	2	.600	5.55	27	6	0	73	82	40	36	0	2	1	2	20	2	0	.100	4	14	0	2	0.7	1.000
1958	CHI	N	7	10	.412	4.76	39	27	5	170.1	178	79	102	1	1	0	1	54	3	0	.056	7	35	5	3	1.2	.894
1959	2 teams		CHI N	(7G 0-2)		PHI N	(32G 1-4)																				
"	total		1	6	.143	5.54	39	1	0	79.2	94	42	40	0	1	0	0	15	1	0	.067	6	16	1	0	0.6	.917
1960	PHI	N	0	1	.000	8.36	10	1	0	14	21	4	6	0	0	0	0	1	0	0	.000	1	2	0	0	0.3	1.000
1963	CHI	A	0	0	—	10.29	9	0	0	14	16	13	13	0	0	0	0	2	0	0	.000	1	2	0	0	0.3	1.000
6 yrs.			16	22	.421	4.82	147	45	9	438.2	460	211	233	1	5	5	6	113	6	0	.053	28	92	7	8	0.9	.945

Tom Phillips

PHILLIPS, THOMAS GERARD
B. Apr. 5, 1889, Philipsburg, Pa.   D. Apr. 12, 1929, Philipsburg, Pa.   BR TR 6'2" 190 lbs.

1915	STL	A	1	3	.250	2.96	5	4	1	27.1	28	12	5	0	1	1	0	9	1	0	.111	2	5	3	0	2.0	.700
1919	CLE	A	3	2	.600	2.95	22	3	2	55	55	34	18	0	1	1	0	11	4	0	.364	1	11	1	0	0.6	.923
1921	WAS	A	1	0	1.000	2.00	1	1	1	9	9	3	2	0	0	0	0	3	0	0	.000	0	1	1	0	2.0	.500
1922			3	7	.300	4.89	17	7	2	70	72	22	19	1	2	0	0	20	3	0	.150	2	14	0	1	0.9	1.000
4 yrs.			8	12	.400	3.74	45	15	6	161.1	164	71	44	1	3	1	0	43	8	0	.186	5	31	5	1	0.9	.878

Year	Team	W	L	PCT	ERA	G	GS	CG	IP	H	BB	SO	ShO	Relief Pitching W	L	SV	Batting AB	H	HR	BA	PO	A	E	DP	TC/G	FA

Tom Phoebus

PHOEBUS, THOMAS HAROLD
B. Apr. 7, 1942, Baltimore, Md. BR TR 5'8" 185 lbs.

1966	BAL A	2	1	.667	1.23	3	3	2	22	16	6	17	2	0	0	0	6	1	0	.167	0	2	0	0	0.7	1.000
1967		14	9	.609	3.33	33	33	7	208	177	114	179	4	0	0	0	76	11	1	.145	12	22	1	0	1.1	.971
1968		15	15	.500	2.62	36	36	9	240.2	186	105	193	3	0	0	0	82	15	1	.183	20	29	1	2	1.4	.980
1969		14	7	.667	3.52	35	33	6	202	180	87	117	2	0	0	0	75	15	0	.200	18	22	0	1	1.1	1.000
1970		5	5	.500	3.07	27	21	3	135	106	62	72	0	0	0	0	43	7	0	.163	14	20	1	0	1.3	.971
1971	SD N	3	11	.214	4.47	29	21	2	133	144	64	80	0	0	0	0	36	6	0	.167	13	15	3	1	1.1	.903
1972	2 teams	SD N	(1G 0–1)		CHI N	(37G 3–3)																				
"	total	3	4	.429	4.04	38	2	0	89	79	51	67	0	3	2	6	17	2	0	.118	7	15	0	2	0.6	1.000
7 yrs.		56	52	.519	3.33	201	149	29	1029.2	888	489	725	11	3	2	6	335	57	2	.170	84	125	6	6	1.1	.972

WORLD SERIES

| 1970 | BAL A | 1 | 0 | 1.000 | 0.00 | 1 | 0 | 0 | 1.2 | 1 | 0 | 0 | 0 | 1 | 0 | 0 | 0 | 0 | 0 | – | 0 | 0 | 0 | 0 | 0.0 | – |

Bill Phyle

PHYLE, WILLIAM JOSEPH
B. June 25, 1875, Duluth, Minn. D. Aug. 6, 1953, Los Angeles, Calif. TR

1898	CHI N	2	1	.667	0.78	3	3	3	23	24	6	4	0	0	0	0	9	1	0	.111	0	4	1	0	1.7	.800
1899		1	8	.111	4.20	10	9	9	83.2	92	29	10	0	0	0	1	34	6	0	.176	6	23	2	1	3.1	.935
1901	NY N	7	10	.412	4.27	24	19	16	168.2	208	54	62	0	0	0	1	66	12	0	.182	17	48	7	0	3.0	.903
1906	STL N	0	0	–	0.00	0	0	0	0	0	0	0	0	0	0	0	73	13	0	.178	0	0	0	0	0.0	–
4 yrs.		10	19	.345	3.96	37	31	28	275.1	324	89	76	2	0	0	2	182	32	0	.176	23	75	10	1	2.9	.907

Wiley Piatt

PIATT, WILEY HAROLD (Iron Man)
B. July 13, 1874, Blue Creek, Ohio D. Sept. 20, 1946, Cincinnati, Ohio BL TL 5'10" 175 lbs.

1898	PHI N	24	14	.632	3.18	39	37	33	306	285	97	121	6	1	0	0	122	32	0	.262	9	66	15	2	2.3	.833
1899		23	15	.605	3.45	39	38	31	305	323	86	89	2	1	0	0	122	33	0	.270	3	53	4	1	1.5	.933
1900		9	10	.474	4.65	22	20	16	160.2	194	71	47	1	0	1	0	68	17	0	.250	2	30	8	0	1.8	.800
1901	2 teams	PHI A	(18G 5–12)		CHI A	(7G 4–2)																				
"	total	9	14	.391	4.13	25	22	19	191.2	218	74	64	1	1	1	1	75	15	0	.200	3	31	4	0	1.5	.895
1902	CHI A	12	12	.500	3.51	32	30	22	246	263	66	96	2	0	0	0	85	17	0	.200	8	57	13	1	2.4	.833
1903	BOS N	8	13	.381	3.18	25	23	18	181	198	61	100	0	0	1	0	71	16	0	.225	3	37	9	0	2.0	.816
6 yrs.		85	78	.521	3.60	182	170	139	1390.1	1481	455	517	12	3	3	1	543	130	0	.239	28	274	53	4	2.0	.851

Ron Piche

PICHE, RONALD JACQUES
B. May 22, 1935, Verdun, Que., Canada BR TR 5'11" 165 lbs.

1960	MIL N	3	5	.375	3.56	37	0	0	48	48	23	38	0	3	5	9	7	0	0	.000	4	4	1	0	0.2	.889
1961		2	2	.500	3.47	12	1	1	23.1	20	16	16	0	1	2	1	5	0	0	.000	0	6	0	1	0.5	1.000
1962		3	2	.600	4.85	14	8	2	52	54	29	28	0	0	0	0	18	1	0	.056	7	9	0	1	1.1	1.000
1963		1	1	.500	3.40	37	1	0	53	53	25	40	0	1	1	0	7	0	0	.000	8	13	0	0	0.6	1.000
1965	CAL A	0	3	.000	6.86	14	1	0	19.2	20	12	14	0	0	2	0	1	0	0	.000	2	3	0	0	0.4	1.000
1966	STL N	1	3	.250	4.26	20	0	0	25.1	21	18	21	0	1	3	2	4	0	0	.000	1	2	0	0	0.2	1.000
6 yrs.		10	16	.385	4.19	134	11	3	221.1	216	123	157	0	6	13	12	42	1	0	.024	22	37	1	3	0.4	.983

Charlie Pickett

PICKETT, CHARLES ALBERT
B. Mar. 1, 1883, Delaware, Ohio D. May 20, 1969, Springfield, Ohio BR TR 6'1" 175 lbs.

| 1910 | STL N | 0 | 0 | – | 1.50 | 2 | 0 | 0 | 6 | 7 | 2 | 2 | 0 | 0 | 0 | 0 | 0 | 0 | 0 | – | 0 | 2 | 1 | 0 | 1.5 | .667 |

Clarence Pickrel

PICKREL, CLARENCE DOUGLAS
B. Mar. 28, 1911, Gretna, Va. D. Nov. 4, 1983, Rocky Mount, Va. BR TR 6'1" 180 lbs.

1933	PHI N	1	0	1.000	3.95	9	0	0	13.2	20	3	6	0	1	0	0	1	0	0	.000	0	0	0	0	0.0	–
1934	BOS N	0	0	–	5.06	10	1	0	16	24	7	9	0	0	0	0	2	0	0	.000	1	0	0	0	0.1	1.000
2 yrs.		1	0	1.000	4.55	19	1	0	29.2	44	10	15	0	1	0	0	3	0	0	.000	1	0	0	0	0.1	1.000

Jeff Pico

PICO, JEFFREY MARK
B. Feb. 12, 1966, Antioch, Calif. BR TR 6'1" 180 lbs.

1988	CHI N	6	7	.462	4.15	29	13	3	112.2	108	37	57	2	2	1	1	34	5	0	.147	5	18	1	3	0.8	.958
1989		3	1	.750	3.77	53	5	0	90.2	99	31	38	0	2	0	2	10	1	0	.100	4	22	3	2	0.5	.897
2 yrs.		9	8	.529	3.98	82	18	3	203.1	207	68	95	2	4	1	3	44	6	0	.136	9	40	4	5	0.6	.925

Mario Picone

PICONE, MARIO PETER (Babe)
B. July 5, 1926, Brooklyn, N.Y. BR TR 5'11" 180 lbs.

1947	NY N	0	0	–	7.71	2	1	0	7	10	2	1	0	0	0	0	2	1	0	.500	0	2	0	0	1.0	1.000
1952		0	1	.000	7.00	2	1	0	9	11	5	3	0	0	0	0	2	0	0	.000	0	3	0	1	1.5	1.000
1954	2 teams	NY N	(5G 0–0)		CIN N	(4G 0–1)																				
"	total	0	1	.000	5.63	9	1	0	24	22	18	7	0	0	0	0	2	0	0	.000	2	5	0	0	0.8	1.000
3 yrs.		0	2	.000	6.30	13	3	0	40	43	25	11	0	0	0	0	6	1	0	.167	2	10	0	1	0.9	1.000

Al Piechota

PIECHOTA, ALOYSIUS EDWARD
B. Jan. 19, 1914, Chicago, Ill. BR TR 6' 195 lbs.

1940	BOS N	2	5	.286	5.75	21	8	2	61	68	41	18	0	1	0	0	20	4	0	.200	2	12	0	0	0.7	1.000
1941		0	0	–	0.00	1	0	0	1	0	1	0	0	0	0	0	0	0	0	–	0	0	0	0	0.0	–
2 yrs.		2	5	.286	5.66	22	8	2	62	68	42	18	0	1	1	0	20	4	0	.200	2	12	0	0	0.6	1.000

Cy Pieh

PIEH, EDWIN JOHN
B. Sept. 29, 1886, Waunakee, Wis. D. Sept. 12, 1945, Jacksonville, Fla. BR TR 6'2" 190 lbs.

1913	NY A	1	0	1.000	4.35	4	0	0	10.1	10	7	6	0	1	0	0	4	1	0	.250	0	8	0	1	2.0	1.000
1914		4	4	.500	5.05	18	4	1	62.1	68	29	24	0	3	2	0	17	2	0	.118	1	13	1	0	0.8	.933
1915		4	5	.444	2.87	21	8	3	94	78	39	46	2	2	0	0	30	2	0	.067	3	28	2	1	1.6	.939
3 yrs.		9	9	.500	3.78	43	12	4	166.2	156	75	76	2	6	2	0	51	5	0	.098	4	49	3	2	1.3	.946

Year	Team		W	L	PCT	ERA	G	GS	CG	IP	H	BB	SO	ShO	W	L	SV	AB	H	HR	BA	PO	A	E	DP	TC/G	FA

Billy Pierce — PIERCE, WALTER WILLIAM — B. Apr. 2, 1927, Detroit, Mich. — BL TL 5'10" 160 lbs.

Year	Team		W	L	PCT	ERA	G	GS	CG	IP	H	BB	SO	ShO	W	L	SV	AB	H	HR	BA	PO	A	E	DP	TC/G	FA
1945	DET	A	0	0	–	1.80	5	0	0	10	6	10	10	0	0	0	0	2	0	0	.000	0	2	0	0	0.4	1.000
1948			3	0	1.000	6.34	22	5	0	55.1	47	51	36	0	1	0	0	17	5	0	.294	2	9	0	0	0.5	1.000
1949	CHI	A	7	15	.318	3.88	32	26	8	171.2	145	112	95	0	1	0	0	51	9	0	.176	12	33	4	2	1.5	.918
1950			12	16	.429	3.98	33	29	15	219.1	189	137	118	1	1	0	1	77	20	0	.260	4	30	1	1	1.1	.971
1951			15	14	.517	3.03	33	28	18	240.1	237	73	113	1	0	3	2	79	16	0	.203	11	38	2	4	1.4	.961
1952			15	12	.556	2.57	33	32	14	255.1	214	79	144	4	0	0	0	91	17	0	.187	13	43	1	3	1.7	.982
1953			18	12	.600	2.72	40	33	19	271.1	216	102	186	7	3	0	3	87	11	0	.126	10	33	4	1	1.2	.915
1954			9	10	.474	3.48	36	26	12	188.2	179	86	148	4	0	0	3	57	11	0	.193	7	19	1	1	0.8	.963
1955			15	10	.600	1.97	33	26	16	205.2	162	64	157	6	2	0	1	70	12	0	.171	7	25	0	1	1.0	1.000
1956			20	9	.690	3.32	35	33	21	276.1	261	100	192	1	0	1	1	102	16	0	.157	4	33	3	2	1.1	.925
1957			20	12	.625	3.26	37	34	16	257	228	71	171	4	0	0	2	99	17	0	.172	8	45	2	2	1.5	.964
1958			17	11	.607	2.68	35	32	19	245	204	66	144	3	0	0	2	83	17	0	.205	11	26	1	3	1.1	.974
1959			14	15	.483	3.62	34	33	12	224	217	62	114	2	0	0	0	68	13	0	.191	11	40	2	4	1.6	.962
1960			14	7	.667	3.62	32	30	8	196.1	201	46	108	1	1	0	0	67	12	0	.179	7	29	2	2	1.2	.947
1961			10	9	.526	3.80	39	28	5	180	190	54	106	1	3	0	3	56	8	0	.143	7	31	3	1	1.1	.927
1962	SF	N	16	6	.727	3.49	30	23	7	162.1	147	35	76	2	0	0	0	56	12	0	.214	4	24	1	3	1.0	.966
1963			3	11	.214	4.27	38	13	3	99	106	20	52	1	0	5	8	31	4	0	.129	4	20	0	2	0.6	1.000
1964			3	0	1.000	2.20	34	1	0	49	40	10	29	0	2	0	4	9	3	0	.333	1	7	1	0	0.3	.889
18 yrs.			211	169	.555	3.27	585	432	193	3306.2	2989	1178	1999	38	14	10	32	1102	203	0	.184	123	487	28	32	1.1	.956

WORLD SERIES

Year	Team		W	L	PCT	ERA	G	GS	CG	IP	H	BB	SO	ShO	W	L	SV	AB	H	HR	BA	PO	A	E	DP	TC/G	FA
1959	CHI	A	0	0	–	0.00	3	0	0	4	2	2	3	0	0	0	0	0	0	0	–	0	0	1	0	0.3	–
1962	SF	N	1	1	.500	2.40	2	2	1	15	8	2	5	0	0	0	0	5	0	0	.000	1	0	0	1	0.5	1.000
2 yrs.			1	1	.500	1.89	5	2	1	19	10	4	8	0	0	0	0	5	0	0	.000	1	0	1	0	0.4	.500

Ray Pierce — PIERCE, RAYMOND LESTER (Lefty) — B. June 6, 1897, Emporia, Kans. D. May 4, 1963, Denver, Colo. — BL TL 5'7" 156 lbs.

Year	Team		W	L	PCT	ERA	G	GS	CG	IP	H	BB	SO	ShO	W	L	SV	AB	H	HR	BA	PO	A	E	DP	TC/G	FA
1924	CHI	N	0	0	–	7.36	6	0	0	7.1	7	4	2	0	0	0	0	0	0	0	–	0	1	0	1	0.2	1.000
1925	PHI	N	5	4	.556	5.50	23	8	4	90	134	24	18	0	1	1	0	28	5	0	.179	4	22	0	2	1.1	1.000
1926			2	7	.222	5.63	37	7	1	84.2	128	35	18	0	2	0	0	24	3	0	.125	2	18	1	2	0.6	.952
3 yrs.			7	11	.389	5.64	66	15	5	182	269	63	38	0	3	1	0	52	8	0	.154	6	41	1	4	0.7	.979

Tony Pierce — PIERCE, TONY MICHAEL — B. Jan. 29, 1946, Brunswick, Ga. — BR TL 6'1" 190 lbs.

Year	Team		W	L	PCT	ERA	G	GS	CG	IP	H	BB	SO	ShO	W	L	SV	AB	H	HR	BA	PO	A	E	DP	TC/G	FA
1967	KC	A	3	4	.429	3.04	49	6	0	97.2	79	30	61	0	2	0	7	20	0	0	.000	9	9	0	0	0.4	1.000
1968	OAK	A	1	2	.333	3.86	17	3	0	32.2	39	10	16	0	0	0	1	6	0	0	.000	1	8	0	0	0.5	1.000
2 yrs.			4	6	.400	3.25	66	9	0	130.1	118	40	77	0	2	1	8	26	0	0	.000	10	17	0	1	0.4	1.000

Bill Piercy — PIERCY, WILLIAM BENTON (Wild Bill) — B. May 2, 1896, El Monte, Calif. D. Aug. 28, 1951, Long Beach, Calif. — BR TR 6'1½" 170 lbs.

Year	Team		W	L	PCT	ERA	G	GS	CG	IP	H	BB	SO	ShO	W	L	SV	AB	H	HR	BA	PO	A	E	DP	TC/G	FA
1917	NY	A	0	1	.000	3.00	1	1	1	9	9	2	4	0	0	0	0	2	0	0	.000	0	3	1	0	4.0	.750
1921			5	4	.556	2.98	14	10	5	81.2	82	28	35	1	1	1	0	28	6	0	.214	3	20	4	2	1.9	.852
1922	BOS	A	3	9	.250	4.67	29	12	7	121.1	140	62	24	1	0	1	0	34	5	0	.147	4	42	0	2	1.6	1.000
1923			8	17	.320	3.41	30	24	11	187.1	193	73	51	0	0	0	0	53	7	0	.132	10	65	4	3	2.6	.949
1924			5	7	.417	6.20	22	17	3	114.2	147	64	20	0	0	0	0	36	5	0	.139	4	35	4	0	1.9	.907
1926	CHI	N	6	5	.545	4.48	19	5	1	90.1	96	37	31	0	4	3	0	35	9	0	.257	5	23	3	1	1.6	.903
6 yrs.			27	43	.386	4.29	115	69	28	604.1	667	266	165	2	5	9	0	188	32	0	.170	26	188	16	8	2.0	.930

WORLD SERIES

Year	Team		W	L	PCT	ERA	G	GS	CG	IP	H	BB	SO	ShO	W	L	SV	AB	H	HR	BA	PO	A	E	DP	TC/G	FA
1921	NY	A	0	0	–	0.00	1	0	0	1	0	2	2	0	0	0	0	0	0	0	–	0	0	0	0	0.0	–

Marino Pieretti — PIERETTI, MARINO PAUL (Chick) — B. Sept. 23, 1920, Lucca, Italy D. Jan. 30, 1981, San Francisco, Calif. — BR TR 5'7" 153 lbs.

Year	Team		W	L	PCT	ERA	G	GS	CG	IP	H	BB	SO	ShO	W	L	SV	AB	H	HR	BA	PO	A	E	DP	TC/G	FA
1945	WAS	A	14	13	.519	3.32	44	27	14	233.1	235	91	66	3	1	1	2	81	18	0	.222	17	52	3	2	1.6	.958
1946			2	2	.500	5.95	30	2	1	62	70	40	20	0	1	1	0	14	3	0	.214	4	14	1	0	0.7	.952
1947			2	4	.333	4.21	23	10	2	83.1	97	47	32	1	0	1	0	26	6	0	.231	4	14	5	0	1.0	.783
1948	2 teams	WAS A	(8G 0-2)			CHI A	(21G 8-10)																				
"	total		8	12	.400	5.47	29	19	4	131.2	135	59	34	0	0	0	0	41	7	0	.171	6	31	1	1	1.3	.974
1949	CHI	A	4	6	.400	5.51	39	9	0	116	131	54	25	0	2	1	4	38	9	0	.237	7	31	2	1	1.0	.950
1950	CLE	A	0	1	.000	4.18	29	1	0	47.1	45	30	11	0	0	1	1	7	2	0	.286	5	12	2	1	0.7	.895
6 yrs.			30	38	.441	4.53	194	68	21	673.2	713	321	188	4	5	6	8	207	45	0	.217	45	154	14	5	1.1	.934

Al Pierotti — PIEROTTI, ALBERT FELIX — B. Oct. 24, 1895, Boston, Mass. D. Feb. 12, 1964, Everett, Mass. — BR TR 5'10½" 195 lbs.

Year	Team		W	L	PCT	ERA	G	GS	CG	IP	H	BB	SO	ShO	W	L	SV	AB	H	HR	BA	PO	A	E	DP	TC/G	FA
1920	BOS	N	1	1	.500	2.88	6	2	2	25	23	9	12	0	0	0	0	8	2	0	.250	1	5	0	0	1.0	1.000
1921			0	1	.000	21.60	2	0	0	1.2	3	3	1	0	0	0	1	1	0	0	.000	0	1	1	0	1.0	.500
2 yrs.			1	2	.333	4.05	8	2	2	26.2	26	12	13	0	0	0	1	9	2	0	.222	1	6	1	0	1.0	.875

Bill Pierro — PIERRO, WILLIAM LEONARD (Wild Bill) — B. Apr. 15, 1926, Brooklyn, N. Y. — BR TR 6'1" 155 lbs.

Year	Team		W	L	PCT	ERA	G	GS	CG	IP	H	BB	SO	ShO	W	L	SV	AB	H	HR	BA	PO	A	E	DP	TC/G	FA
1950	PIT	N	0	2	.000	10.55	12	3	0	29	33	28	13	0	0	0	0	9	2	0	.222	0	3	0	0	0.3	1.000

Bill Pierson — PIERSON, WILLIAM MORRIS (Wild Bill) — B. June 14, 1899, Atlantic City, N. J. D. Feb. 20, 1959, Atlantic City, N. J. — BL TL 6'2" 180 lbs.

Year	Team		W	L	PCT	ERA	G	GS	CG	IP	H	BB	SO	ShO	W	L	SV	AB	H	HR	BA	PO	A	E	DP	TC/G	FA
1918	PHI	A	0	1	.000	3.32	8	1	0	21.2	20	20	6	0	0	0	0	4	1	0	.250	1	2	1	0	0.5	.750
1919			0	0	–	3.52	2	1	0	7.2	9	8	4	0	0	0	0	3	1	0	.333	0	4	0	0	2.0	1.000
1924			0	0	–	3.38	1	0	0	2.2	3	3	0	0	0	0	0	0	0	0	–	0	1	0	0	1.0	1.000
3 yrs.			0	1	.000	3.38	11	2	0	32	32	31	10	0	0	0	0	7	2	0	.286	1	7	1	0	0.8	.889

Year	Team		W	L	PCT	ERA	G	GS	CG	IP	H	BB	SO	ShO	W	L	SV	AB	H	HR	BA	PO	A	E	DP	TC/G	FA
															Relief Pitching			Batting									

Dave Pierson

PIERSON, DAVID P.
Brother of Dick Pierson.
B. Aug. 20, 1855, Wilkes-Barre, Pa.   D. Nov. 11, 1922, Trenton, N. J.

BR TR 5'7"   142 lbs.

Year	Team		W	L	PCT	ERA	G	GS	CG	IP	H	BB	SO	ShO	W	L	SV	AB	H	HR	BA	PO	A	E	DP	TC/G	FA
1876	CIN	N	0	1	.000	∞	1	1	0	2	0	0	0	0	0	0	0	*				0	0	0	0	0.0	–

George Piktuzis

PIKTUZIS, GEORGE RICHARD
B. Jan. 3, 1932, Chicago, Ill.

BR TL 6'2"   200 lbs.

Year	Team		W	L	PCT	ERA	G	GS	CG	IP	H	BB	SO	ShO	W	L	SV	AB	H	HR	BA	PO	A	E	DP	TC/G	FA
1956	CHI	N	0	0	–	7.20	2	0	0	5	6	2	3	0	0	0	0	0	0	0	–	0	0	0	0	0.0	–

Duane Pillette

PILLETTE, DUANE XAVIER (Dee)
Son of Herman Pillette.
B. July 24, 1922, Detroit, Mich.

BR TR 6'3"   195 lbs.

Year	Team		W	L	PCT	ERA	G	GS	CG	IP	H	BB	SO	ShO	W	L	SV	AB	H	HR	BA	PO	A	E	DP	TC/G	FA
1949	NY	A	2	4	.333	4.34	12	3	2	37.1	43	19	9	0	1	2	0	11	0	0	.000	4	9	0	2	1.1	1.000
1950	2 teams	NY A (4G 0–0)				STL A	(24G 3–5)																				
"	total		3	5	.375	6.58	28	7	1	80.2	113	47	22	0	1	4	2	22	3	0	.136	3	14	4	2	0.8	.810
1951	STL	A	6	14	.300	4.99	35	24	6	191	205	115	65	1	1	1	0	59	8	0	.136	19	25	1	1	1.3	.978
1952			10	13	.435	3.59	30	30	9	205.1	222	55	62	1	0	0	0	66	12	0	.182	14	25	0	4	1.3	1.000
1953			7	13	.350	4.48	31	25	5	166.2	181	62	58	1	0	1	1	53	7	1	.132	14	20	2	3	1.2	.944
1954	BAL	A	10	14	.417	3.12	25	25	11	179	158	67	66	1	0	0	0	53	7	0	.132	12	43	2	4	2.3	.965
1955			0	3	.000	6.53	7	5	0	20.2	31	14	13	0	0	0	0	6	1	0	.167	0	5	1	0	0.9	.833
1956	PHI	N	0	0	–	6.56	20	0	0	23.1	32	12	10	0	0	0	0	1	0	0	.000	1	3	0	0	0.2	1.000
8 yrs.			38	66	.365	4.40	188	119	34	904	985	391	305	4	3	8	2	271	38	1	.140	67	144	10	16	1.2	.955

Herman Pillette

PILLETTE, HERMAN POLYCARP (Old Folks)
Father of Duane Pillette.
B. Dec. 26, 1895, St. Paul, Ore.   D. Apr. 30, 1960, Sacramento, Calif.

BR TR 6'2"   190 lbs.

Year	Team		W	L	PCT	ERA	G	GS	CG	IP	H	BB	SO	ShO	W	L	SV	AB	H	HR	BA	PO	A	E	DP	TC/G	FA
1917	CIN	N	0	0	–	18.00	1	0	0	1	4	0	0	0	0	0	0	0	0	0	–	0	0	0	0	0.0	–
1922	DET	A	19	12	.613	2.85	40	37	18	274.2	270	95	71	4	1	0	1	99	17	0	.172	11	82	4	5	2.4	.959
1923			14	19	.424	3.85	47	37	14	250.1	280	83	64	0	3	2	1	85	21	0	.247	17	86	11	2	2.4	.904
1924			1	1	.500	4.78	19	3	1	37.2	46	14	13	0	0	0	1	11	4	0	.364	2	11	1	0	0.7	.929
4 yrs.			34	32	.515	3.45	107	77	33	563.2	600	192	148	4	4	2	3	195	42	0	.215	30	179	16	7	2.1	.929

Squiz Pillion

PILLION, CECIL RANDOLPH
B. Apr. 13, 1894, Hartford, Conn.   D. Sept. 30, 1962, Pittsburgh, Pa.

BL TL 6'   178 lbs.

Year	Team		W	L	PCT	ERA	G	GS	CG	IP	H	BB	SO	ShO	W	L	SV	AB	H	HR	BA	PO	A	E	DP	TC/G	FA
1915	PHI	A	0	0	–	6.75	2	0	0	5.1	10	2	0	0	0	0	0	1	0	0	.000	0	2	0	0	1.0	1.000

Horacio Pina

PINA, HORACIO
Born Horacio Pina y Garcia.
B. Mar. 12, 1945, Coahuila, Mexico

BR TR 6'2"   177 lbs.

Year	Team		W	L	PCT	ERA	G	GS	CG	IP	H	BB	SO	ShO	W	L	SV	AB	H	HR	BA	PO	A	E	DP	TC/G	FA
1968	CLE	A	1	1	.500	1.72	12	3	0	31.1	24	15	24	0	0	0	2	6	0	0	.000	1	4	0	1	0.4	1.000
1969			4	2	.667	5.21	31	4	0	46.2	44	27	32	0	3	1	1	6	3	0	.500	3	8	0	1	0.4	1.000
1970	WAS	A	5	3	.625	2.79	61	0	0	71	66	35	41	0	5	3	6	3	0	0	.000	5	15	1	0	0.3	.952
1971			1	1	.500	3.57	56	0	0	58	47	31	38	0	1	1	2	1	0	0	.000	3	14	0	2	0.3	1.000
1972	TEX	A	2	7	.222	3.20	60	0	0	76	61	43	60	0	2	7	15	5	1	0	.200	5	22	2	4	0.5	.931
1973	OAK	A	6	3	.667	2.76	47	0	0	88	58	34	41	0	6	3	8	0	0	0	.000	0	26	0	4	0.7	1.000
1974	2 teams	CHI N (34G 3–4)				CAL A	(11G 1–2)																				
"	total		4	6	.400	3.66	45	0	0	59	58	31	38	0	4	6	4	5	1	0	.200	4	15	1	0	0.5	.950
1978	PHI	N	0	0	–	0.00	2	0	0	2	0	0	4	0	0	0	0	1	0	0	.000	1	0	0	0	0.5	1.000
8 yrs.			23	23	.500	3.25	314	7	0	432	358	216	278	0	21	21	38	27	5	0	.185	28	104	4	12	0.4	.971

LEAGUE CHAMPIONSHIP SERIES

Year	Team		W	L	PCT	ERA	G	GS	CG	IP	H	BB	SO	ShO	W	L	SV	AB	H	HR	BA	PO	A	E	DP	TC/G	FA
1973	OAK	A	0	0	–	0.00	1	0	0	2	3	1	1	0	0	0	0	0	0	0	–	0	0	0	0	0.0	–

WORLD SERIES

Year	Team		W	L	PCT	ERA	G	GS	CG	IP	H	BB	SO	ShO	W	L	SV	AB	H	HR	BA	PO	A	E	DP	TC/G	FA
1973	OAK	A	0	0	–	0.00	2	0	0	6	3	6	2	0	0	0	0	0	0	0	–	0	0	0	0	0.0	–

George Pinckney

PINCKNEY, GEORGE BURTON
B. Jan. 11, 1862, Orange Prairie, Ill.   D. Nov. 10, 1926, Peoria, Ill.

BR TR 5'7"   160 lbs.

Year	Team		W	L	PCT	ERA	G	GS	CG	IP	H	BB	SO	ShO	W	L	SV	AB	H	HR	BA	PO	A	E	DP	TC/G	FA
1886	BKN	AA	0	0	–	4.50	1	0	0	2	2	0	0	0	0	0	0	*				0	0	0	0	0.0	–

Ed Pinnance

PINNANCE, EDWARD D.
B. Oct. 22, 1879, Walpole Island, Ont., Canada   D. Dec. 12, 1944, Walpole Island, Ont., Canada

BL TR 6'1"   180 lbs.

Year	Team		W	L	PCT	ERA	G	GS	CG	IP	H	BB	SO	ShO	W	L	SV	AB	H	HR	BA	PO	A	E	DP	TC/G	FA
1903	PHI	A	0	0	–	2.57	2	1	0	7	5	2	2	0	0	0	1	3	0	0	.000	1	1	0	0	1.0	1.000

Lerton Pinto

PINTO, WILLIAM LERTON
B. Apr. 8, 1899, Chillicothe, Ohio   D. May 13, 1983, Oxnard, Calif.

BL TL 6'   190 lbs.

Year	Team		W	L	PCT	ERA	G	GS	CG	IP	H	BB	SO	ShO	W	L	SV	AB	H	HR	BA	PO	A	E	DP	TC/G	FA
1922	PHI	N	0	1	.000	5.11	9	0	0	24.2	31	14	4	0	0	0	0	9	1	0	.111	0	5	2	0	0.8	.714
1924			0	0	–	9.00	3	0	0	4	7	0	1	0	0	0	0	1	0	0	.000	0	1	0	0	0.3	1.000
2 yrs.			0	1	.000	5.65	12	0	0	28.2	38	14	5	0	0	0	0	10	1	0	.100	0	6	2	0	0.7	.750

Ed Pipgras

PIPGRAS, EDWARD JOHN
Brother of George Pipgras.
B. June 15, 1904, Schleswig, Iowa   D. Apr. 13, 1964, Currie, Minn.

BR TR 6'2½"   175 lbs.

Year	Team		W	L	PCT	ERA	G	GS	CG	IP	H	BB	SO	ShO	W	L	SV	AB	H	HR	BA	PO	A	E	DP	TC/G	FA
1932	BKN	N	0	1	.000	5.40	5	1	0	10	16	6	5	0	0	0	0	2	0	0	.000	2	1	0	0	0.6	1.000

George Pipgras

PIPGRAS, GEORGE WILLIAM
Brother of Ed Pipgras.
B. Dec. 20, 1899, Ida Grove, Iowa   D. Oct. 19, 1986, Gainesville, Fla.

BR TR 6'1½"   185 lbs.

Year	Team		W	L	PCT	ERA	G	GS	CG	IP	H	BB	SO	ShO	W	L	SV	AB	H	HR	BA	PO	A	E	DP	TC/G	FA
1923	NY	A	1	3	.250	5.94	8	2	2	33.1	34	25	12	0	0	0	0	9	0	0	.000	1	8	0	0	1.0	1.000
1924			0	1	.000	9.98	9	1	0	15.1	20	18	4	0	0	0	1	3	1	0	.333	1	9	0	0	1.1	1.000

Year	Team	W	L	PCT	ERA	G	GS	CG	IP	H	BB	SO	ShO	W	L	SV	AB	H	HR	BA	PO	A	E	DP	TC/G	FA

George Pipgras *continued*

Year	Team	W	L	PCT	ERA	G	GS	CG	IP	H	BB	SO	ShO	W	L	SV	AB	H	HR	BA	PO	A	E	DP	TC/G	FA
1927		10	3	.769	4.11	29	21	9	166.1	148	77	81	1	0	0	0	67	16	1	.239	6	33	1	1	1.4	.975
1928		**24**	13	.649	3.38	46	**38**	22	**300.2**	314	103	139	4	0	1	3	115	18	0	.157	7	49	4	2	1.3	.933
1929		18	12	.600	4.23	39	33	13	225.1	229	95	125	3	2	1	0	84	12	0	.143	4	30	1	2	0.9	.971
1930		15	15	.500	4.11	44	30	15	221	230	70	111	**3**	1	2	4	80	12	1	.150	12	30	5	1	1.1	.894
1931		7	6	.538	3.79	36	14	6	137.2	134	58	59	0	3	2	3	41	1	0	.024	2	20	2	0	0.7	.917
1932		16	9	.640	4.19	32	27	14	219	235	87	111	2	1	2	0	82	18	0	.220	9	35	7	1	1.6	.863
1933	2 teams	NY A	(4G 2–2)		BOS A	(22G 9–8)																				
"	total	11	10	.524	3.90	26	21	12	161.1	172	57	70	2	1	0	0	57	10	0	.175	8	25	2	3	1.3	.943
1934	BOS A	0	0	–	8.10	2	1	0	3.1	4	3	0	0	0	0	0	1	0	0	.000	0	2	0	0	1.0	1.000
1935		0	1	.000	14.40	5	1	0	5	9	5	2	0	0	0	0	0	0	0	–	0	1	0	0	0.2	1.000
11 yrs.		102	73	.583	4.09	276	189	93	1488.1	1529	598	714	15	8	12	12	539	88	2	.163	49	242	22	10	1.1	.930

WORLD SERIES

Year	Team	W	L	PCT	ERA	G	GS	CG	IP	H	BB	SO	ShO	W	L	SV	AB	H	HR	BA	PO	A	E	DP	TC/G	FA
1927	NY A	1	0	1.000	2.00	1	1	1	9	7	1	2	0	0	0	0	3	1	0	.333	1	2	0	0	3.0	1.000
1928		1	0	1.000	2.00	1	1	1	9	4	4	8	0	0	0	0	2	0	0	.000	0	1	0	0	1.0	1.000
1932		1	0	1.000	4.50	1	1	0	8	9	3	1	0	0	0	0	5	0	0	.000	0	0	0	0	0.0	–
3 yrs.		3	0	1.000	2.77	3	3	2	26	20	8	11	0	0	0	0	10	1	0	.100	1	3	0	0	1.3	1.000
					1st																					

Cotton Pippen

PIPPEN, HENRY HAROLD
B. Apr. 2, 1911, Cisco, Tex.   D. Feb. 15, 1981, Williams, Calif.   BR TR 6'2"   180 lbs.

Year	Team	W	L	PCT	ERA	G	GS	CG	IP	H	BB	SO	ShO	W	L	SV	AB	H	HR	BA	PO	A	E	DP	TC/G	FA
1936	STL N	0	2	.000	7.71	6	3	0	21	37	8	8	0	0	0	0	6	1	0	.167	2	8	0	0	1.7	1.000
1939	2 teams	PHI A	(25G 4–11)		DET A	(3G 0–1)																				
"	total	4	12	.250	6.11	28	19	5	132.2	187	46	38	0	0	1	1	40	5	0	.125	10	26	3	4	1.4	.923
1940	DET A	1	2	.333	6.75	4	3	0	21.1	29	10	9	0	0	0	0	8	0	0	.000	2	4	0	0	1.5	1.000
3 yrs.		5	16	.238	6.38	38	25	5	175	253	64	55	0	0	1	1	54	6	0	.111	14	38	3	4	1.4	.945

Gerry Pirtle

PIRTLE, GERALD EUGENE
B. Dec. 3, 1947, Tulsa, Okla.   BR TR 6'1"   185 lbs.

Year	Team	W	L	PCT	ERA	G	GS	CG	IP	H	BB	SO	ShO	W	L	SV	AB	H	HR	BA	PO	A	E	DP	TC/G	FA
1978	MON N	0	2	.000	5.88	19	0	0	26	33	23	14	0	0	2	0	0	0	0	–	2	4	1	0	0.4	.857

Skip Pitlock

PITLOCK, LEE PATRICK THOMAS
B. Nov. 6, 1947, Hillside, Ill.   BL TL 6'2"   180 lbs.

Year	Team	W	L	PCT	ERA	G	GS	CG	IP	H	BB	SO	ShO	W	L	SV	AB	H	HR	BA	PO	A	E	DP	TC/G	FA
1970	SF N	5	5	.500	4.66	18	15	1	87	92	48	56	0	0	0	0	25	2	1	.080	3	15	0	0	1.0	1.000
1974	CHI A	3	3	.500	4.42	40	5	0	106	103	55	68	0	2	2	1	0	0	0	–	5	10	4	2	0.5	.789
1975		0	0	–	0.00	1	0	0	1	0	0	0	0	0	0	0	0	0	0	–	0	0	0	0	0.0	–
3 yrs.		8	8	.500	4.52	59	20	1	193	196	103	124	0	2	2	1	25	2	1	.080	8	25	4	2	0.6	.892

Togie Pittinger

PITTINGER, CHARLES RENO
B. 1871, Greencastle, Pa.   D. Jan. 14, 1909, Greencastle, Pa.   BL TR 6'2"   175 lbs.

Year	Team	W	L	PCT	ERA	G	GS	CG	IP	H	BB	SO	ShO	W	L	SV	AB	H	HR	BA	PO	A	E	DP	TC/G	FA
1900	BOS N	2	9	.182	5.13	18	18	8	114	135	54	27	0	0	0	0	46	6	0	.130	9	23	5	2	2.1	.865
1901		13	16	.448	3.01	34	33	27	281.1	288	76	129	1	0	0	0	100	11	0	.110	8	86	4	4	2.9	.959
1902		27	16	.628	2.52	46	40	36	389.1	360	**128**	174	7	**2**	3	0	147	20	0	.136	20	83	6	2	2.4	.945
1903		19	**23**	.452	3.48	44	39	35	351.2	**396**	143	140	2	2	1	0	128	14	1	.109	14	84	15	1	2.6	.867
1904		15	21	.417	2.66	38	38	35	335.1	298	144	146	5	0	0	0	121	13	0	.107	22	114	12	2	3.9	.919
1905	PHI N	23	14	.622	3.10	**46**	37	29	337	311	104	136	4	3	2	2	122	19	0	.156	9	82	5	2	2.1	.948
1906		8	10	.444	3.40	20	16	9	129.2	128	50	43	1	0	0	0	44	4	0	.091	7	31	2	0	2.0	.950
1907		9	5	.643	3.00	16	12	8	102	101	35	37	1	2	0	0	36	5	0	.139	4	25	0	0	1.8	1.000
8 yrs.		116	114	.504	3.10	262	228	187	2040.1	2017	734	832	22	10	7	2	744	92	1	.124	93	528	49	13	2.6	.927

Stan Pitula

PITULA, STANLEY
B. Mar. 23, 1931, Hackensack, N. J.   D. Aug. 15, 1965, Hackensack, N. J.   BR TR 5'10"   170 lbs.

Year	Team	W	L	PCT	ERA	G	GS	CG	IP	H	BB	SO	ShO	W	L	SV	AB	H	HR	BA	PO	A	E	DP	TC/G	FA
1957	CLE A	2	2	.500	4.98	23	5	1	59.2	67	32	17	0	0	0	0	15	3	0	.200	2	9	0	1	0.5	1.000

Juan Pizarro

PIZARRO, JUAN ROMAN
Born Juan Roman Pizarro y Cordova.
B. Feb. 7, 1937, Santurce, Puerto Rico   BL TL 5'11"   170 lbs.

Year	Team	W	L	PCT	ERA	G	GS	CG	IP	H	BB	SO	ShO	W	L	SV	AB	H	HR	BA	PO	A	E	DP	TC/G	FA
1957	MIL N	5	6	.455	4.62	24	10	3	99.1	99	51	68	0	3	1	0	36	9	1	.250	0	15	1	1	0.7	.938
1958		6	4	.600	2.70	16	10	7	96.2	75	47	84	1	1	1	1	32	8	0	.250	3	16	0	2	1.2	1.000
1959		6	2	.750	3.77	29	14	0	133.2	117	70	126	0	0	0	0	41	5	0	.122	7	18	0	0	0.9	1.000
1960	CHI A	6	7	.462	4.55	21	17	3	114.2	105	72	88	0	0	1	0	40	11	0	.275	1	17	2	0	0.9	.900
1961		14	7	.667	3.05	39	25	12	194.2	164	89	188	1	0	0	0	69	17	0	.246	8	23	3	1	0.8	.909
1962		12	14	.462	3.81	36	32	9	203.1	182	97	173	1	3	0	1	69	11	0	.159	10	23	1	1	0.9	.971
1963		16	8	.667	2.39	32	28	10	214.2	177	63	163	3	2	0	1	73	13	2	.178	8	22	0	1	0.9	1.000
1964		19	9	.679	2.56	33	33	11	239	193	55	162	4	0	0	0	90	19	3	.211	8	32	0	2	1.2	1.000
1965		6	3	.667	3.43	18	18	2	97	96	37	65	1	0	0	0	34	8	1	.235	3	17	1	2	1.2	.952
1966		8	6	.571	3.76	34	9	1	88.2	91	39	42	0	4	2	3	26	4	0	.154	1	18	0	1	0.7	1.000
1967	PIT N	8	10	.444	3.95	50	9	1	107	99	52	96	1	7	5	9	27	7	0	.259	1	13	1	0	0.3	.933
1968	2 teams	PIT N	(12G 1–1)		BOS A	(19G 6–8)																				
"	total	7	9	.438	3.56	31	12	6	118.2	111	54	90	1	0	2	3	33	5	0	.152	7	23	1	3	1.0	.968
1969	3 teams	BOS A	(6G 0–1)		CLE A	(48G 3–3)		OAK A	(3G 1–1)																	
"	total	4	5	.444	3.35	57	4	1	99.1	84	58	52	0	3	5	7	20	5	0	.250	6	18	1	0	0.4	.960
1970	CHI N	0	0	–	4.50	12	0	0	16	16	9	14	0	0	0	0	3	0	0	.000	0	3	0	0	0.2	1.000
1971		7	6	.538	3.48	16	14	6	101	78	40	67	3	0	0	0	34	6	1	.176	4	16	0	0	1.3	1.000
1972		4	5	.444	3.97	16	7	1	59	66	32	24	1	0	0	0	21	3	0	.143	2	15	0	0	1.1	1.000
1973	2 teams	CHI N	(2G 0–1)		HOU N	(15G 2–2)																				
"	total	2	3	.400	7.24	17	1	0	27.1	34	12	13	0	0	0	0	4	0	0	.000	2	7	1	0	0.6	.900
1974	PIT N	1	1	.500	1.88	16	1	0	24	20	11	7	0	0	0	0	6	2	0	.333	1	3	0	0	0.6	1.000
18 yrs.		131	105	.555	3.43	488	245	79	2034	1807	888	1522	17	31	20	28	658	133	8	.202	74	299	12	15	0.8	.969

LEAGUE CHAMPIONSHIP SERIES

Year	Team	W	L	PCT	ERA	G	GS	CG	IP	H	BB	SO	ShO	W	L	SV	AB	H	HR	BA	PO	A	E	DP	TC/G	FA
1974	PIT N	0	0	–	0.00	1	0	0	.2	0	1	0	0	0	0	0	0	0	0	–	0	0	0	0	0.0	–

Year	Team		W	L	PCT	ERA	G	GS	CG	IP	H	BB	SO	ShO	W	L	SV	AB	H	HR	BA	PO	A	E	DP	TC/G	FA

Juan Pizarro *continued*
WORLD SERIES

Year	Team		W	L	PCT	ERA	G	GS	CG	IP	H	BB	SO	ShO	W	L	SV	AB	H	HR	BA	PO	A	E	DP	TC/G	FA
1957	MIL	N	0	0	–	10.80	1	0	0	1.2	3	2	1	0	0	0	0	1	0	0	.000	0	0	0	0	0.0	–
1958			0	0	–	5.40	1	0	0	1.2	2	1	3	0	0	0	0	0	0	0	–	0	1	0	0	1.0	1.000
2 yrs.			0	0	–	8.10	2	0	0	3.1	5	3	4	0	0	0	0	1	0	0	.000	0	1	0	0	0.5	1.000

Gordon Pladson
PLADSON, GORDON CECIL   BR TR 6'4"   210 lbs.
B. July 31, 1956, New Westminster, B. C., Canada

Year	Team		W	L	PCT	ERA	G	GS	CG	IP	H	BB	SO	ShO	W	L	SV	AB	H	HR	BA	PO	A	E	DP	TC/G	FA
1979	HOU	N	0	0	–	4.50	4	0	0	4	9	2	2	0	0	0	0	0	0	0	–	0	0	0	0	0.0	–
1980			0	4	.000	4.39	12	6	0	41	38	16	13	0	0	0	0	10	0	0	.000	3	9	2	0	1.2	.857
1981			0	0	–	9.00	2	0	0	4	9	3	3	0	0	0	0	0	0	0	–	0	0	0	0	0.0	–
1982			0	0	–	54.00	2	0	0	1.1	10	2	0	0	0	0	0	0	0	0	–	0	0	0	0	0.0	–
4 yrs.			0	4	.000	6.08	20	6	0	50.1	66	23	18	0	0	0	0	10	0	0	.000	3	9	2	0	0.7	.857

Emil Planeta
PLANETA, EMIL JOSEPH   BR TR 6'   190 lbs.
B. Jan. 13, 1909, Higganum, Conn.   D. Feb. 2, 1963, Rocky Hill, Conn.

Year	Team		W	L	PCT	ERA	G	GS	CG	IP	H	BB	SO	ShO	W	L	SV	AB	H	HR	BA	PO	A	E	DP	TC/G	FA
1931	NY	N	0	0	–	10.13	2	0	0	5.1	7	4	0	0	0	0	0	1	0	0	.000	0	0	0	0	0.0	–

Eddie Plank
PLANK, EDWARD ARTHUR   BR TR 6'1"   205 lbs.
B. Apr. 9, 1952, Chicago, Ill.

Year	Team		W	L	PCT	ERA	G	GS	CG	IP	H	BB	SO	ShO	W	L	SV	AB	H	HR	BA	PO	A	E	DP	TC/G	FA
1978	SF	N	0	0	–	3.86	5	0	0	7	6	2	1	0	0	0	0	0	0	0	–	0	0	0	0	0.0	–
1979			0	0	–	6.75	4	0	0	4	9	2	1	0	0	0	0	0	0	0	–	1	0	1	0	0.5	.500
2 yrs.			0	0	–	4.91	9	0	0	11	15	4	2	0	0	0	0	0	0	0	–	1	0	1	0	0.2	.500

Eddie Plank
PLANK, EDWARD STEWART (Hank)   BL TL 5'11½" 175 lbs.
B. Aug. 31, 1875, Gettysburg, Pa.   D. Feb. 24, 1926, Gettysburg, Pa.
Hall of Fame 1946.

Year	Team		W	L	PCT	ERA	G	GS	CG	IP	H	BB	SO	ShO	W	L	SV	AB	H	HR	BA	PO	A	E	DP	TC/G	FA
1901	PHI	A	17	13	.567	3.31	33	32	28	260.2	254	68	90	1	0	0	0	99	18	0	.182	6	63	5	2	2.2	.932
1902			20	15	.571	3.30	36	32	31	300	319	61	107	1	2	1	0	120	35	0	.292	18	74	5	2	2.7	.948
1903			23	16	.590	2.38	43	40	33	336	317	65	176	3	1	1	0	134	25	1	.187	23	85	4	1	2.6	.964
1904			26	16	.619	2.14	43	43	37	357	309	86	201	7	0	0	0	129	31	0	.240	22	103	3	4	3.0	.977
1905			25	12	.676	2.26	41	41	36	346.2	287	75	210	4	0	0	0	126	29	0	.230	24	82	6	0	2.7	.946
1906			19	6	**.760**	2.25	26	25	21	211.2	173	51	108	5	0	1	0	73	17	0	.233	16	46	2	2	2.5	.969
1907			24	16	.600	2.20	43	40	33	343.2	282	85	183	8	1	0	0	123	26	1	.211	33	88	2	4	2.9	.984
1908			14	16	.467	2.17	34	28	21	244.2	202	46	135	4	2	2	1	89	16	0	.180	17	45	2	1	1.9	.969
1909			19	10	.655	1.70	34	33	24	275.1	215	62	132	3	0	0	0	96	21	1	.219	11	82	1	3	2.8	.989
1910			16	10	.615	2.01	38	32	22	250.1	218	55	123	1	0	0	2	86	11	0	.128	9	64	1	1	1.9	.986
1911			23	8	.742	2.10	40	30	24	256.2	237	77	149	6	3	1	4	94	18	0	.191	7	71	2	2	2.0	.975
1912			26	6	.813	2.22	37	30	24	259.2	234	83	110	5	5	0	2	90	24	0	.267	6	68	0	1	2.0	1.000
1913			18	10	.643	2.60	41	29	18	242.2	211	57	151	7	4	0	4	75	8	0	.107	6	59	2	2	1.6	.970
1914			15	7	.682	2.87	34	22	12	185.1	178	42	110	4	4	1	3	60	9	0	.150	7	36	1	2	1.3	.977
1915	STL	F	21	11	.656	2.08	42	31	23	268.1	212	54	147	6	2	3	3	93	24	0	.258	13	58	1	4	1.7	.986
1916	STL	A	16	15	.516	2.33	37	26	17	235.2	203	67	88	3	3	3	3	81	15	0	.185	6	51	2	6	1.6	.966
1917			5	6	.455	1.79	20	13	8	131	105	38	26	1	0	1	1	38	4	0	.105	5	33	1	0	2.0	.974
17 yrs.			327	193	.629	2.34	622	527	412	4505.1	3956	1072	2246	69	27	14	23	1606	331	3	.206	229	1108	40	37	2.2	.971
					10th									5th													

WORLD SERIES

Year	Team		W	L	PCT	ERA	G	GS	CG	IP	H	BB	SO	ShO	W	L	SV	AB	H	HR	BA	PO	A	E	DP	TC/G	FA
1905	PHI	A	0	2	.000	1.59	2	2	2	17	14	4	11	0	0	0	0	6	1	0	.167	1	6	0	0	3.5	1.000
1911			1	1	.500	1.86	2	1	1	9.2	6	0	8	0	0	0	0	3	0	0	.000	0	2	0	0	1.0	1.000
1913			1	1	.500	0.95	2	2	2	19	9	3	7	0	0	0	0	7	1	0	.143	1	3	1	0	2.5	.800
1914			0	1	.000	1.00	1	1	1	9	7	4	6	0	0	0	0	2	0	0	.000	0	1	0	0	1.0	1.000
4 yrs.			2	5	.286	1.32	7	6	6	54.2	36	11	32	0	0	0	0	18	2	0	.111	2	12	1	0	2.1	.933
					2nd									10th			6th										

Bill Pleis
PLEIS, WILLIAM   BL TL 5'10"   170 lbs.
B. Aug. 5, 1937, St. Louis, Mo.

Year	Team		W	L	PCT	ERA	G	GS	CG	IP	H	BB	SO	ShO	W	L	SV	AB	H	HR	BA	PO	A	E	DP	TC/G	FA
1961	MIN	A	4	2	.667	4.95	37	0	0	56.1	59	34	32	0	4	2	2	9	1	0	.111	3	3	1	0	0.2	.857
1962			2	5	.286	4.40	21	4	0	45	46	14	31	0	2	3	3	14	4	0	.286	4	4	1	0	0.4	.889
1963			6	2	.750	4.37	36	4	0	68	67	16	37	0	4	1	0	16	2	0	.125	3	10	0	1	0.4	1.000
1964			4	1	.800	3.91	47	0	0	50.2	43	31	42	0	4	1	4	4	1	0	.250	6	6	0	1	0.3	1.000
1965			4	4	.500	2.98	41	2	0	51.1	49	27	33	0	4	2	4	7	0	0	.000	1	7	0	1	0.2	1.000
1966			1	2	.333	1.93	8	0	0	9.1	5	4	9	0	1	2	0	0	0	0	–	0	1	1	0	0.3	.500
6 yrs.			21	16	.568	4.07	190	10	1	280.2	269	126	184	0	19	10	13	50	8	0	.160	17	31	3	3	0.3	.941

WORLD SERIES

Year	Team		W	L	PCT	ERA	G	GS	CG	IP	H	BB	SO	ShO	W	L	SV	AB	H	HR	BA	PO	A	E	DP	TC/G	FA
1965	MIN	A	0	0	–	9.00	1	0	0	1	2	0	0	0	0	0	0	0	0	0	–	0	1	0	0	1.0	1.000

Dan Plesac
PLESAC, DANIEL THOMAS   BL TL 6'5"   205 lbs.
B. Feb. 4, 1962, Gary, Ind.

Year	Team		W	L	PCT	ERA	G	GS	CG	IP	H	BB	SO	ShO	W	L	SV	AB	H	HR	BA	PO	A	E	DP	TC/G	FA
1986	MIL	A	10	7	.588	2.97	51	0	0	91	81	29	75	0	10	7	14	0	0	0	–	1	11	0	0	0.2	1.000
1987			5	6	.455	2.61	57	0	0	79.1	63	23	89	0	5	6	23	0	0	0	–	0	12	2	1	0.2	.857
1988			1	2	.333	2.41	50	0	0	52.1	46	12	52	0	1	2	30	0	0	0	–	0	6	0	0	0.1	1.000
1989			3	4	.429	2.35	52	0	0	61.1	47	17	52	0	3	4	33	0	0	0	–	2	8	0	0	0.2	1.000
4 yrs.			19	19	.500	2.63	210	0	0	284	237	81	268	0	19	19	100	0	0	0	–	3	37	2	1	0.2	.952

Norman Plitt
PLITT, NORMAN WILLIAM (Duke)   BR TR 5'11"   180 lbs.
B. Feb. 21, 1893, York, Pa.   D. Feb. 1, 1954, New York, N. Y.

Year	Team		W	L	PCT	ERA	G	GS	CG	IP	H	BB	SO	ShO	W	L	SV	AB	H	HR	BA	PO	A	E	DP	TC/G	FA
1918	BKN	N	0	0	–	4.50	1	0	0	2	3	1	0	0	0	0	0	1	1	0	1.000	0	0	0	0	0.0	–

Year	Team	W	L	PCT	ERA	G	GS	CG	IP	H	BB	SO	ShO	Relief Pitching W	L	SV	Batting AB	H	HR	BA	PO	A	E	DP	TC/G	FA

Norman Plitt *continued*

Year	Team	W	L	PCT	ERA	G	GS	CG	IP	H	BB	SO	ShO	W	L	SV	AB	H	HR	BA	PO	A	E	DP	TC/G	FA
1927	2 teams	BKN N	(19G 2–6)		NY N	(3G 1–0)																				
"	total	3	6	.333	4.78	22	8	1	69.2	82	37	9	0	2	1	0	19	4	0	.211	4	19	2	1	1.1	.920
2 yrs.		3	6	.333	4.77	23	8	1	71.2	85	38	9	0	2	1	0	20	5	0	.250	4	19	2	1	1.1	.920

Tim Plodinec

PLODINEC, TIMOTHY ALFRED
B. Jan. 27, 1947, Aliquippa, Pa. BR TR 6'4" 190 lbs.

Year	Team	W	L	PCT	ERA	G	GS	CG	IP	H	BB	SO	ShO	W	L	SV	AB	H	HR	BA	PO	A	E	DP	TC/G	FA
1972	STL N	0	0	–	27.00	1	0	0	.1	3	0	0	0	0	0	0	0	0	0	–	0	0	0	0	0.0	–

Eric Plunk

PLUNK, ERIC VAUGHN
B. Sept. 3, 1963, Wilmington, Calif. BR TR 6'5" 210 lbs.

Year	Team	W	L	PCT	ERA	G	GS	CG	IP	H	BB	SO	ShO	W	L	SV	AB	H	HR	BA	PO	A	E	DP	TC/G	FA
1986	OAK A	4	7	.364	5.31	26	15	0	120.1	91	102	98	0	0	1	0	0	0	0	–	3	6	1	0	0.4	.900
1987		4	6	.400	4.74	32	11	0	95	91	62	90	0	3	2	2	0	0	0	–	1	9	0	0	0.3	1.000
1988		7	2	.778	3.00	49	0	0	78	62	39	79	0	7	2	5	0	0	0	–	2	5	1	0	0.2	.875
1989	2 teams	OAK A	(23G 1–1)		NY A	(27G 7–5)																				
"	total	8	6	.571	3.28	50	7	0	104.1	82	64	85	0	4	3	1	0	0	0	–	2	7	1	0	0.2	.900
4 yrs.		23	21	.523	4.19	157	33	0	397.2	326	267	352	0	14	8	8	0	0	0	–	8	27	3	0	0.2	.921

LEAGUE CHAMPIONSHIP SERIES

Year	Team	W	L	PCT	ERA	G	GS	CG	IP	H	BB	SO	ShO	W	L	SV	AB	H	HR	BA	PO	A	E	DP	TC/G	FA
1988	OAK A	0	0	–	0.00	1	0	0	.1	1	0	1	0	0	0	0	0	0	0	–	0	0	0	0	0.0	–

WORLD SERIES

Year	Team	W	L	PCT	ERA	G	GS	CG	IP	H	BB	SO	ShO	W	L	SV	AB	H	HR	BA	PO	A	E	DP	TC/G	FA
1988	OAK A	0	0	–	0.00	2	0	0	1.2	0	0	3	0	0	0	0	0	0	0	–	0	0	0	0	0.0	–

Ray Poat

POAT, RAYMOND WILLIS
B. Dec. 19, 1917, Chicago, Ill. BR TR 6'2" 200 lbs.

Year	Team	W	L	PCT	ERA	G	GS	CG	IP	H	BB	SO	ShO	W	L	SV	AB	H	HR	BA	PO	A	E	DP	TC/G	FA
1942	CLE A	1	3	.250	5.40	4	4	1	18.1	24	9	8	0	0	0	0	5	0	0	.000	1	3	0	1	1.0	1.000
1943		2	5	.286	4.40	17	4	1	45	44	20	31	0	0	4	0	13	2	0	.154	1	8	0	0	0.5	1.000
1944		4	8	.333	5.13	36	6	1	80.2	82	37	40	0	3	4	1	17	0	0	.000	6	11	1	3	0.5	1.000
1947	NY N	4	3	.571	2.55	7	7	5	60	53	13	25	0	0	0	0	21	4	1	.190	5	8	0	1	1.9	1.000
1948		11	10	.524	4.34	39	24	7	157.2	162	67	57	3	2	3	0	56	7	0	.125	2	20	1	5	0.6	.957
1949	2 teams	NY N	(2G 0–0)		PIT N	(11G 0–1)																				
"	total	0	1	.000	7.04	13	2	0	38.1	60	16	17	0	0	0	0	10	1	0	.100	1	6	1	0	0.6	.875
6 yrs.		22	30	.423	4.55	116	47	15	400	425	162	178	4	5	11	2	122	14	1	.115	16	56	3	10	0.6	.960

Bud Podbielan

PODBIELAN, CLARENCE ANTHONY
B. Mar. 6, 1924, Curlew, Wash. D. Oct. 26, 1982, Syracuse, N. Y. BR TR 6'1½" 170 lbs.

Year	Team	W	L	PCT	ERA	G	GS	CG	IP	H	BB	SO	ShO	W	L	SV	AB	H	HR	BA	PO	A	E	DP	TC/G	FA
1949	BKN N	0	1	.000	3.65	7	1	0	12.1	9	9	5	0	0	1	0	3	0	0	.000	0	5	0	0	0.7	1.000
1950		5	4	.556	5.33	20	10	2	72.2	93	29	28	0	1	2	1	28	3	0	.107	4	17	0	0	1.1	1.000
1951		2	2	.500	3.50	27	5	1	79.2	67	36	26	0	2	1	0	23	7	0	.304	6	16	0	0	0.8	1.000
1952	2 teams	BKN N	(3G 0–0)		CIN N	(24G 4–5)																				
"	total	4	5	.444	3.15	27	7	4	88.2	82	29	23	1	1	1	1	25	4	0	.160	7	11	2	2	0.7	.900
1953	CIN N	6	16	.273	4.73	36	24	8	186.1	214	67	74	1	1	1	1	56	7	0	.125	11	29	1	5	1.1	.976
1954		7	10	.412	5.36	27	24	4	131	157	58	42	0	0	0	0	42	6	0	.143	12	13	0	1	0.9	1.000
1955		1	2	.333	3.21	17	2	0	42	36	11	26	0	1	0	0	5	2	0	.400	0	9	0	0	0.5	1.000
1957		0	1	.000	6.19	5	3	1	16	18	4	13	0	0	0	0	0	0	0	.000	0	0	0	0	0.0	–
1959	CLE A	0	1	.000	5.84	6	0	0	12.1	17	2	5	0	0	1	0	1	0	0	.000	1	3	0	0	0.7	1.000
9 yrs.		25	42	.373	4.49	172	76	20	641	693	245	242	2	6	7	3	188	29	0	.154	41	103	3	8	0.9	.980

Johnny Podgajny

PODGAJNY, JOHN SIGMUND (Specs)
B. June 10, 1920, Chester, Pa. D. Mar. 2, 1971, Chester, Pa. BR TR 6'2" 173 lbs.

Year	Team	W	L	PCT	ERA	G	GS	CG	IP	H	BB	SO	ShO	W	L	SV	AB	H	HR	BA	PO	A	E	DP	TC/G	FA
1940	PHI N	1	3	.250	2.83	4	4	3	35	33	9	12	0	0	0	0	12	2	0	.167	2	9	1	0	3.0	.917
1941		9	12	.429	4.62	34	24	8	181.1	191	70	53	0	1	0	0	62	8	0	.129	10	40	2	4	1.5	.962
1942		6	14	.300	3.91	43	23	6	186.2	191	63	40	0	1	0	1	60	11	0	.183	6	39	3	2	1.1	.938
1943	2 teams	PHI N	(13G 4–4)		PIT N	(15G 0–4)																				
"	total	4	8	.333	4.39	28	10	3	98.1	114	29	20	0	1	2	0	27	6	0	.222	7	35	5	0	1.7	.894
1946	CLE A	0	0	–	5.00	6	0	0	9	13	2	4	0	0	1	0	0	0	0	–	2	1	0	0	0.5	1.000
5 yrs.		20	37	.351	4.20	115	61	20	510.1	542	165	129	0	2	3	0	161	27	0	.168	27	124	11	6	1.4	.932

Johnny Podres

PODRES, JOHN JOSEPH
B. Sept. 30, 1932, Witherbee, N. Y. BL TL 5'11" 170 lbs.

Year	Team	W	L	PCT	ERA	G	GS	CG	IP	H	BB	SO	ShO	W	L	SV	AB	H	HR	BA	PO	A	E	DP	TC/G	FA
1953	BKN N	9	4	.692	4.23	33	18	3	115	126	64	82	1	4	0	0	36	11	0	.306	6	17	1	0	0.7	.958
1954		11	7	.611	4.27	29	21	6	151.2	147	53	79	2	1	0	0	60	17	0	.283	11	15	1	0	0.9	.963
1955		9	10	.474	3.95	27	24	5	159.1	160	57	114	2	0	0	0	60	11	0	.183	7	21	1	2	1.1	.966
1957		12	9	.571	2.66	31	27	10	196	168	44	109	6	1	1	3	72	15	0	.208	9	32	1	3	1.4	.976
1958	LA N	13	15	.464	3.72	39	31	10	210.1	208	78	143	2	0	1	1	71	9	0	.127	7	25	2	3	0.9	.941
1959		14	9	.609	4.11	34	29	6	195	192	74	145	2	1	0	0	65	16	0	.246	6	37	2	5	1.3	.956
1960		14	12	.538	3.08	34	33	8	227.2	217	71	159	1	1	0	0	66	9	0	.136	8	30	1	4	1.1	.974
1961		18	5	.783	3.74	32	29	6	182.2	192	51	124	1	2	0	0	69	16	0	.232	6	26	1	2	1.0	.970
1962		15	13	.536	3.81	40	40	8	255	270	71	178	0	0	0	0	88	14	1	.159	4	31	0	1	1.0	.854
1963		14	12	.538	3.54	37	34	10	198.1	196	64	134	5	0	0	1	64	9	1	.141	2	33	0	1	0.9	1.000
1964		0	2	.000	16.88	2	2	0	2.2	5	3	0	0	0	0	0	0	0	0	–	0	0	0	0	0.0	–
1965		7	6	.538	3.43	27	22	3	134	126	39	63	1	0	1	0	45	8	0	.178	3	15	1	1	0.7	.947
1966	2 teams	LA N	(1G 0–0)		DET A	(36G 4–5)																				
"	total	4	5	.444	3.38	37	13	2	109.1	108	35	54	1	2	1	4	30	7	0	.233	7	15	1	1	0.6	.957
1967	DET A	3	1	.750	3.84	21	8	0	63.1	58	11	34	0	1	0	0	20	2	0	.100	4	7	0	0	0.5	1.000
1969	SD N	5	6	.455	4.29	17	9	0	65	66	28	17	0	0	0	0	16	1	0	.063	1	9	0	0	0.6	1.000
15 yrs.		148	116	.561	3.67	440	340	77	2265.1	2239	743	1435	24	13	4	11	762	145	2	.190	80	313	18	24	0.9	.956

WORLD SERIES

Year	Team	W	L	PCT	ERA	G	GS	CG	IP	H	BB	SO	ShO	W	L	SV	AB	H	HR	BA	PO	A	E	DP	TC/G	FA
1953	BKN N	0	1	.000	3.38	1	1	0	2.2	1	2	1	0	0	0	0	1	1	0	1.000	0	1	0	0	1.0	1.000
1955		2	0	1.000	1.00	2	2	2	18	15	4	10	1	0	0	0	7	1	0	.143	0	2	0	0	1.0	1.000
1959	LA N	1	0	1.000	4.82	2	2	0	9.1	7	6	4	0	0	0	0	4	2	0	.500	0	1	0	1	0.5	1.000

Year	Team	W	L	PCT	ERA	G	GS	CG	IP	H	BB	SO	ShO	W	L	SV	AB	H	HR	BA	PO	A	E	DP	TC/G	FA

Johnny Podres *continued*

Year	Team	W	L	PCT	ERA	G	GS	CG	IP	H	BB	SO	ShO	W	L	SV	AB	H	HR	BA	PO	A	E	DP	TC/G	FA
1963		1	0	1.000	1.08	1	1	0	8.1	6	1	4	0	0	0	0	4	1	0	.250	0	2	1	0	3.0	.667
4 yrs.		4	1	.800	2.11	6	6	2	38.1	29	13	18	1	0	0	0	16	5	0	.313	0	6	1	1	1.2	.857

Joe Poetz

POETZ, JOSEPH FRANK
B. June 22, 1900, St. Louis, Mo.   D. Feb. 7, 1942, St. Louis, Mo.   BR TR 5'10½" 185 lbs.

Year	Team	W	L	PCT	ERA	G	GS	CG	IP	H	BB	SO	ShO	W	L	SV	AB	H	HR	BA	PO	A	E	DP	TC/G	FA
1926	NY N	0	1	.000	3.38	2	1	0	8	5	8	0	0	0	0	0	1	0	0	.000	1	2	0	0	1.5	1.000

Boots Poffenberger

POFFENBERGER, CLETUS ELWOOD
B. July 1, 1915, Williamsport, Md.   BR TR 5'10" 178 lbs.

Year	Team	W	L	PCT	ERA	G	GS	CG	IP	H	BB	SO	ShO	W	L	SV	AB	H	HR	BA	PO	A	E	DP	TC/G	FA
1937	DET A	10	5	.667	4.65	29	16	5	137.1	147	79	35	0	3	1	3	51	11	0	.216	8	32	1	3	1.4	.976
1938		6	7	.462	4.82	25	15	8	125	147	66	28	0	0	2	1	44	8	0	.182	5	17	1	1	0.9	.957
1939	BKN N	0	0	—	5.40	3	1	0	5	7	4	2	0	0	0	0	1	0	0	.000	0	2	0	0	0.7	1.000
3 yrs.		16	12	.571	4.75	57	32	13	267.1	301	149	65	0	3	3	4	96	19	0	.198	13	51	2	4	1.2	.970

Tom Poholsky

POHOLSKY, THOMAS GEORGE
B. Aug. 26, 1929, Detroit, Mich.   BR TR 6'3" 205 lbs.

Year	Team	W	L	PCT	ERA	G	GS	CG	IP	H	BB	SO	ShO	W	L	SV	AB	H	HR	BA	PO	A	E	DP	TC/G	FA
1950	STL N	0	0	—	3.68	5	1	0	14.2	16	3	2	0	0	0	0	2	0	0	.000	0	2	0	0	0.4	1.000
1951		7	13	.350	4.43	38	26	10	195	204	68	70	1	1	2	1	67	14	0	.209	10	43	3	2	1.5	.946
1954		5	7	.417	3.06	25	13	4	106	101	20	55	0	0	2	0	27	4	0	.148	8	18	0	2	1.0	1.000
1955		9	11	.450	3.81	30	24	8	151	143	35	66	2	0	0	0	44	8	0	.182	14	20	0	0	1.1	1.000
1956		9	14	.391	3.59	33	29	7	203	210	44	95	2	0	0	0	69	11	0	.159	12	35	0	3	1.4	1.000
1957	CHI N	1	7	.125	4.93	28	11	1	84	117	22	28	0	0	0	0	19	2	0	.105	8	16	1	1	0.9	.960
6 yrs.		31	52	.373	3.93	159	104	30	753.2	791	192	316	5	1	4	1	228	39	0	.171	52	134	4	8	1.2	.979

Jennings Poindexter

POINDEXTER, CHESTER JENNINGS (Jinx)
B. Sept. 30, 1910, Pauls Valley, Okla.   D. Mar. 3, 1983, Norman, Okla.   BL TL 5'10" 165 lbs.

Year	Team	W	L	PCT	ERA	G	GS	CG	IP	H	BB	SO	ShO	W	L	SV	AB	H	HR	BA	PO	A	E	DP	TC/G	FA
1936	BOS A	0	2	.000	6.75	3	3	0	10.2	13	16	2	0	0	0	0	4	0	0	.000	0	2	0	0	0.7	1.000
1939	PHI N	0	0	—	4.15	11	1	0	30.1	29	15	12	0	0	0	0	10	2	0	.200	1	5	0	0	0.5	1.000
2 yrs.		0	2	.000	4.83	14	4	0	41	42	31	14	0	0	0	0	14	2	0	.143	1	7	0	0	0.6	1.000

Lou Polchow

POLCHOW, LOUIS WILLIAM
B. Mar. 14, 1881, Mankato, Minn.   D. Aug. 15, 1912, Good Thunder, Minn.   5'9"

Year	Team	W	L	PCT	ERA	G	GS	CG	IP	H	BB	SO	ShO	W	L	SV	AB	H	HR	BA	PO	A	E	DP	TC/G	FA
1902	CLE A	0	1	.000	5.63	1	1	1	8	9	4	2	0	0	0	0	4	0	0	.000	0	2	0	0	2.0	1.000

Dick Pole

POLE, RICHARD HENRY
B. Oct. 13, 1950, Trout Creek, Mich.   BR TR 6'3" 200 lbs.

Year	Team	W	L	PCT	ERA	G	GS	CG	IP	H	BB	SO	ShO	W	L	SV	AB	H	HR	BA	PO	A	E	DP	TC/G	FA
1973	BOS A	3	2	.600	5.56	12	7	0	55	70	18	24	0	0	0	0	0	0	0	—	3	7	0	0	0.8	1.000
1974		1	1	.500	4.20	15	2	0	45	55	13	32	0	1	0	1	0	0	0	—	5	8	1	0	0.9	.929
1975		4	6	.400	4.42	18	11	2	89.2	102	32	42	1	1	0	0	0	0	0	—	4	15	1	1	1.1	.950
1976		6	5	.545	4.31	31	15	1	121	131	48	49	0	1	0	1	1	0	0	.000	6	13	1	0	0.6	.950
1977	SEA A	7	12	.368	5.16	25	24	3	122	127	57	51	0	0	0	0	0	0	0	—	2	9	1	0	0.5	.917
1978		4	11	.267	6.48	21	18	2	98.2	122	41	41	0	0	0	1	0	0	0	—	10	9	0	0	0.9	1.000
6 yrs.		25	37	.403	5.05	122	77	8	531.1	607	209	239	1	3	2	1	1	0	0	.000	30	61	4	1	0.8	.958

WORLD SERIES

Year	Team	W	L	PCT	ERA	G	GS	CG	IP	H	BB	SO	ShO	W	L	SV	AB	H	HR	BA	PO	A	E	DP	TC/G	FA
1975	BOS A	0	0	—	∞	1	0	0	0	2	0	0	0	0	0	0	0	0	0	—	0	0	0	0	0.0	—

Ken Polivka

POLIVKA, KENNETH LYLE (Soup)
B. Jan. 21, 1921, Chicago, Ill.   D. July 23, 1988, Aurora, Ill.   BL TL 5'10½" 183 lbs.

Year	Team	W	L	PCT	ERA	G	GS	CG	IP	H	BB	SO	ShO	W	L	SV	AB	H	HR	BA	PO	A	E	DP	TC/G	FA
1947	CIN N	0	0	—	3.00	2	0	0	3	3	3	1	0	0	0	0	0	0	0	—	0	0	0	0	0.0	—

Howie Pollet

POLLET, HOWARD JOSEPH
B. June 26, 1921, New Orleans, La.   D. Aug. 8, 1974, Houston, Tex.   BL TL 6'1½" 175 lbs.

Year	Team	W	L	PCT	ERA	G	GS	CG	IP	H	BB	SO	ShO	W	L	SV	AB	H	HR	BA	PO	A	E	DP	TC/G	FA
1941	STL N	5	2	.714	1.93	9	8	6	70	55	27	37	2	0	0	0	28	5	0	.179	0	18	0	0	2.0	1.000
1942		7	5	.583	2.88	27	13	5	109.1	102	39	42	2	1	1	0	31	7	0	.226	4	16	2	1	0.8	.909
1943		8	4	.667	1.75	16	14	12	118.1	83	32	61	5	0	0	0	43	7	0	.163	1	17	0	0	1.1	1.000
1946		21	10	.677	2.10	40	32	22	266	228	86	107	4	0	0	5	87	14	0	.161	8	59	4	9	1.8	.944
1947		9	11	.450	4.34	37	24	9	176.1	195	87	73	0	1	0	2	65	15	0	.231	5	33	0	5	1.0	1.000
1948		13	8	.619	4.54	36	26	11	186.1	216	67	80	0	2	0	0	68	8	0	.118	5	44	2	2	1.4	.961
1949		20	9	.690	2.77	39	28	17	230.2	228	59	108	5	3	1	1	82	16	0	.195	9	33	2	2	1.1	.955
1950		14	13	.519	3.29	37	30	14	232.1	228	68	117	2	1	1	2	84	12	0	.143	13	40	4	5	1.5	.930
1951	2 teams			STL N	(6G 0–3)			PIT N	(21G 6–10)																	
"	total	6	13	.316	4.98	27	23	4	141	159	59	57	1	0	2	1	37	5	0	.135	5	26	0	2	1.1	1.000
1952	PIT N	7	16	.304	4.12	31	30	9	214	217	71	90	1	0	0	0	68	13	0	.191	7	48	3	2	1.9	.948
1953	2 teams			PIT N	(5G 1–1)			CHI N	(25G 5–6)																	
"	total	6	7	.462	4.79	30	18	2	124	147	50	53	0	0	0	1	34	5	0	.147	8	15	3	2	0.9	.885
1954	CHI N	8	10	.444	3.58	20	20	4	128.1	131	54	58	0	2	0	0	47	13	0	.277	6	22	0	1	1.4	1.000
1955		4	3	.571	5.61	24	7	1	61	62	27	27	1	3	0	5	15	6	0	.400	7	15	0	1	0.9	1.000
1956	2 teams			CHI A	(11G 3–1)			PIT N	(19G 0–4)																	
"	total	3	5	.375	3.62	30	4	0	49.2	45	19	24	0	3	4	3	9	3	0	.333	4	10	0	0	0.5	1.000
14 yrs.		131	116	.530	3.51	403	277	116	2107.1	2096	745	934	25	14	10	20	698	129	0	.185	82	396	20	32	1.2	.960

WORLD SERIES

Year	Team	W	L	PCT	ERA	G	GS	CG	IP	H	BB	SO	ShO	W	L	SV	AB	H	HR	BA	PO	A	E	DP	TC/G	FA
1942	STL N	0	0	—	0.00	1	0	0	.1	0	0	0	0	0	0	0	0	0	0	—	0	0	0	0	0.0	—
1946		0	1	.000	3.48	2	2	1	10.1	12	4	3	0	0	0	0	4	0	0	.000	0	0	0	0	0.0	—
2 yrs.		0	1	.000	3.38	3	2	1	10.2	12	4	3	0	0	0	0	4	0	0	.000	0	0	0	0	0.0	—

Lou Polli

POLLI, LOUIS AMERICO (Crip)
B. July 9, 1901, Barre, Vt.   BR TR 5'10½" 165 lbs.

Year	Team	W	L	PCT	ERA	G	GS	CG	IP	H	BB	SO	ShO	W	L	SV	AB	H	HR	BA	PO	A	E	DP	TC/G	FA
1932	STL A	0	0	—	5.40	5	0	0	6.2	13	3	5	0	0	0	0	2	1	0	.500	0	0	1	0	0.2	—

Year	Team		W	L	PCT	ERA	G	GS	CG	IP	H	BB	SO	ShO	Relief Pitching W	L	SV	Batting AB	H	HR	BA	PO	A	E	DP	TC/G	FA

Lou Polli *continued*

| 1944 | NY | N | 0 | 2 | .000 | 4.54 | 19 | 0 | 0 | 35.2 | 42 | 20 | 6 | 0 | 0 | 2 | 3 | 6 | 0 | 0 | .000 | 0 | 7 | 0 | 0 | 0.4 | 1.000 |
| 2 yrs. | | | 0 | 2 | .000 | 4.68 | 24 | 0 | 0 | 42.1 | 55 | 23 | 11 | 0 | 0 | 2 | 3 | 8 | 1 | 0 | .125 | 0 | 7 | 1 | 0 | 0.3 | .875 |

John Poloni

POLONI, JOHN PAUL
B. Feb. 28, 1954, Dearborn, Mich.   BL TL 6'5"   210 lbs.

| 1977 | TEX | A | 1 | 0 | 1.000 | 6.43 | 2 | 1 | 0 | 7 | 8 | 1 | 5 | 0 | 0 | 0 | 0 | 0 | 0 | 0 | — | 0 | 0 | 0 | 0 | 0.0 | — |

John Pomorski

POMORSKI, JOHN LEON
B. Dec. 30, 1905, Brooklyn, N.Y.   D. Dec. 6, 1977, Brampton, Ont., Canada   BR TR 6'   178 lbs.

| 1934 | CHI | A | 0 | 0 | — | 5.40 | 3 | 0 | 0 | 1.2 | 1 | 2 | 0 | 0 | 0 | 0 | 0 | 0 | 0 | 0 | — | 1 | 0 | 0 | 0 | 0.3 | 1.000 |

Arlie Pond

POND, ERASMUS ARLINGTON
B. Jan. 19, 1872, Rutland, Vt.   D. Sept. 19, 1930, Cebu, Philippines   BR TR 5'10"   160 lbs.

1895	BAL	N	0	1	.000	5.93	6	1	1	13.2	10	12	13	0	0	0	2	6	2	0	.333	0	3	0	1	0.5	1.000
1896			16	8	.667	3.49	28	26	21	214.1	232	57	80	2	0	0	0	81	19	0	.235	3	46	5	0	1.9	.907
1897			18	9	.667	3.52	32	28	23	248	267	72	59	0	0	0	0	90	22	0	.244	16	52	6	2	2.3	.919
1898			1	1	.500	0.45	3	2	1	20	8	9	4	1	0	0	0	7	2	0	.286	0	2	0	0	0.7	1.000
4 yrs.			35	19	.648	3.45	69	57	46	496	517	150	156	3	0	2	0	184	45	0	.245	19	103	11	3	1.9	.917

Elmer Ponder

PONDER, CHARLES ELMER
B. June 26, 1893, Reed, Okla.   D. Apr. 20, 1974, Albuquerque, N. M.   BR TR 6'   178 lbs.

1917	PIT	N	1	1	.500	1.69	3	2	1	21.1	12	6	11	0	0	0	0	7	0	0	.000	0	1	0	0	0.3	1.000
1919			0	5	.000	3.99	9	5	0	47.1	55	6	6	0	0	0	0	15	2	0	.133	1	12	3	0	1.8	.813
1920			11	15	.423	2.62	33	23	13	196	182	40	62	3	0	3	0	59	7	0	.119	13	55	3	2	2.2	.958
1921	2 teams	PIT N (8G 2–0)				CHI N				(16G 3–6)																	
"	total		5	6	.455	4.18	24	12	6	114	146	20	34	0	4	0	0	43	4	0	.093	3	38	2	3	1.8	.953
4 yrs.			17	27	.386	3.21	69	42	20	378.2	395	72	113	3	4	3	0	124	13	0	.105	17	106	8	5	1.9	.939

Ed Poole

POOLE, EDWARD T.
B. Sept. 7, 1874, Canton, Ohio   D. Mar. 11, 1919, Malvern, Ohio   BR TR 5'10"   175 lbs.

1900	PIT	N	1	0	1.000	1.29	1	0	0	7	4	0	3	0	1	0	0	4	2	1	.500	1	3	0	0	4.0	1.000
1901			5	4	.556	3.60	12	10	8	80	78	30	26	1	0	0	0	78	16	0	.205	7	21	2	1	2.5	.933
1902	2 teams	PIT N (1G 0–0)				CIN N				(16G 12–4)																	
"	total		12	4	.750	2.10	17	16	16	146	136	57	57	2	0	0	0	65	8	0	.123	5	35	1	1	2.4	.976
1903	CIN	N	8	13	.381	3.28	25	21	18	184	188	77	73	1	0	1	0	70	17	0	.243	3	62	5	3	2.8	.929
1904	BKN	N	8	13	.381	3.39	25	23	19	178	178	74	67	1	0	1	1	62	8	0	.129	6	65	2	2	2.9	.973
5 yrs.			34	34	.500	3.04	80	70	61	595	584	238	226	5	2	0	2	279	51	2	.183	22	186	10	7	2.7	.954

Tom Poorman

POORMAN, THOMAS IVERSON
B. Oct. 14, 1857, Lock Haven, Pa.   D. Feb. 18, 1905, Lock Haven, Pa.   BL TR 5'10½" 170 lbs.

1880	2 teams	BUF N (11G 1–8)				CHI N				(2G 2–0)																	
"	total		3	8	.273	3.87	13	10	9	100	129	27	13	0	1	0	0	95	16	0	.168	5	24	4	0	2.5	.879
1884	TOL	AA	0	1	.000	3.00	1	1	1	9	13	2	1	0	0	0	0	382	89	0	.233	1	2	1	0	4.0	.750
1887	PHI	AA	0	0	—	40.50	1	0	0	.2	5	1	1	0	0	0	0	585	155	4	.265	0	0	0	0	0.0	—
3 yrs.			3	9	.250	4.02	15	11	10	109.2	147	30	14	0	1	0	1	*					6	26	5	0	2.5	.865

Bill Popp

POPP, WILLIAM PETER
B. June 7, 1877, St. Louis, Mo.   D. Sept. 5, 1909, St. Louis, Mo.   TR 5'10½" 170 lbs.

| 1902 | STL | N | 2 | 6 | .250 | 4.92 | 9 | 7 | 5 | 60.1 | 87 | 26 | 20 | 0 | 0 | 1 | 0 | 21 | 1 | 0 | .048 | 2 | 19 | 2 | 0 | 2.6 | .913 |

Ed Porray

PORRAY, EDMUND JOSEPH
B. Dec. 5, 1888, Atlantic Ocean   D. July 13, 1954, Lackawaxen, Pa.   BR TR 5'11" 170 lbs.

| 1914 | BUF | F | 1 | 1 | .500 | 4.35 | 3 | 3 | 0 | 10.1 | 18 | 7 | 0 | 0 | 0 | 0 | 0 | 4 | 0 | 0 | .000 | 0 | 7 | 2 | 0 | 3.0 | .778 |

Chuck Porter

PORTER, CHARLES WILLIAM
B. Jan. 12, 1955, Baltimore, Md.   BR TR 6'3"   188 lbs.

1981	MIL	A	0	0	—	4.50	3	0	0	4	6	1	1	0	0	0	0	0	0	0	—	0	0	0	0	0.0	—
1982			0	0	—	4.91	3	0	0	3.2	3	1	3	0	0	0	0	0	0	0	—	0	0	0	0	0.0	—
1983			7	9	.438	4.50	25	21	6	134	162	38	76	1	0	1	0	0	0	0	—	11	18	0	2	1.2	1.000
1984			6	4	.600	3.87	17	12	1	81.1	92	12	48	0	0	0	0	0	0	0	—	7	10	1	2	1.1	.944
1985			0	0	—	1.98	6	1	0	13.2	15	2	8	0	0	0	0	0	0	0	—	2	0	1	0	0.5	.667
5 yrs.			13	13	.500	4.15	54	34	7	236.2	278	54	136	1	0	1	0	0	0	0	—	20	28	2	4	0.9	.960

Henry Porter

PORTER, HENRY
B. June, 1858, Vergennes, Vt.   D. Dec. 30, 1906, Brockton, Mass.   BR TR

1884	MIL	U	3	3	.500	3.00	6	6	6	51	32	9	71	1	0	0	0	40	11	0	.275	1	10	0	0	1.8	1.000
1885	BKN	AA	33	21	.611	2.78	54	54	53	481.2	427	107	197	0	0	0	0	195	40	0	.205	13	93	7	0	2.1	.938
1886			27	19	.587	3.42	48	48	48	424	489	120	163	1	0	0	0	184	33	0	.179	17	70	15	0	2.1	.853
1887	KC	AA	15	24	.385	4.21	40	40	38	339.2	416	96	74	1	0	0	0	146	29	1	.199	8	66	12	1	2.2	.860
1888	KC	AA	18	37	.327	4.16	55	54	53	474	527	120	145	4	1	0	0	195	28	0	.144	11	133	16	3	2.9	.900
1889			0	3	.000	12.52	4	4	3	23	42	14	9	0	0	0	0	10	1	0	.100	0	9	2	0	2.8	.818
6 yrs.			96	107	.473	3.70	207	206	201	1793.1	1893	466	659	9	1	0	0	770	142	1	.184	50	381	52	4	2.3	.892

Jim Porter

PORTER, ODIE OSCAR
B. May 24, 1877, Borden, Ind.   D. May 2, 1903, Borden, Ind.

| 1902 | PHI | A | 0 | 1 | .000 | 3.38 | 1 | 1 | 1 | 8 | 12 | 5 | 2 | 0 | 0 | 0 | 0 | 3 | 0 | 0 | .000 | 0 | 4 | 1 | 0 | 5.0 | .800 |

Year	Team	W	L	PCT	ERA	G	GS	CG	IP	H	BB	SO	ShO	Relief Pitching W	L	SV	Batting AB	H	HR	BA	PO	A	E	DP	TC/G	FA

Ned Porter

PORTER, NED SWINDELL
B. May 6, 1905, Apalachicola, Fla.   D. June 30, 1968, Gainesville, Fla.

BR TR 6'   173 lbs.

Year	Team	W	L	PCT	ERA	G	GS	CG	IP	H	BB	SO	ShO	RW	RL	SV	AB	H	HR	BA	PO	A	E	DP	TC/G	FA
1926	NY N	0	0	–	4.50	2	0	0	2	2	0	1	0	0	0	0	0	0	0	–	0	0	0	0	0.0	–
1927		0	0	–	0.00	1	0	0	2	3	1	0	0	0	0	0	0	0	0	–	0	0	1	0	1.0	–
2 yrs.		0	0	–	2.25	3	0	0	4	5	1	1	0	0	0	0	0	0	0	–	0	0	1	0	0.3	–

Bob Porterfield

PORTERFIELD, ERWIN COOLEDGE
B. Aug. 10, 1923, Newport, Va.   D. Apr. 28, 1980, Charlotte, N. C.

BR TR 6'   190 lbs.

Year	Team	W	L	PCT	ERA	G	GS	CG	IP	H	BB	SO	ShO	RW	RL	SV	AB	H	HR	BA	PO	A	E	DP	TC/G	FA
1948	NY A	5	3	.625	4.50	16	12	2	78	85	34	30	1	1	0	0	24	6	0	.250	4	8	0	0	0.8	1.000
1949		2	5	.286	4.06	12	8	3	57.2	53	29	25	0	0	2	0	19	1	0	.053	1	10	3	1	1.2	.786
1950		1	1	.500	8.69	10	2	0	19.2	28	8	9	0	1	0	1	3	1	0	.333	1	3	0	0	0.4	1.000
1951	2 teams			NY A	(2G 0-0)				WAS A	(19G 9-8)																
"	total	9	8	.529	3.50	21	19	10	136.1	114	57	55	3	0	0	0	46	6	0	.130	8	24	2	0	1.6	.941
1952	WAS A	13	14	.481	2.72	31	29	15	231.1	222	85	80	3	1	0	0	79	15	0	.190	4	34	0	0	1.2	1.000
1953		22	10	.688	3.35	34	32	24	255	243	73	77	9	1	0	0	98	25	3	.255	16	50	0	4	1.9	1.000
1954		13	15	.464	3.32	32	31	21	244	249	77	82	2	1	0	0	88	9	1	.102	10	61	3	4	2.3	.959
1955		10	17	.370	4.45	30	27	8	178	197	55	74	2	0	1	0	63	12	0	.190	8	28	1	2	1.2	.973
1956	BOS A	3	12	.200	5.14	25	18	4	126	127	64	53	1	0	2	0	43	14	1	.326	8	14	2	1	1.0	.917
1957		4	4	.500	4.05	28	9	3	102.1	107	30	28	1	1	1	0	29	5	0	.172	7	23	3	1	1.2	.909
1958	2 teams			BOS A	(2G 0-0)				PIT N	(37G 4-6)																
"	total	4	6	.400	3.34	39	6	2	91.2	81	19	40	1	2	3	5	20	1	1	.050	8	13	0	0	0.5	1.000
1959	2 teams			PIT N	(36G 1-2)				CHI N	(4G 0-0)																
"	total	1	2	.333	5.29	40	0	0	47.2	65	22	19	0	1	2	1	4	0	0	.000	5	12	1	2	0.5	.944
12 yrs.		87	97	.473	3.79	318	193	92	1567.2	1571	553	572	23	9	10	8	516	95	6	.184	80	280	15	15	1.2	.960

Al Porto

PORTO, ALFRED (Lefty)
B. June 27, 1926, Heilwood, Pa.

BL TL 5'11"   176 lbs.

Year	Team	W	L	PCT	ERA	G	GS	CG	IP	H	BB	SO	ShO	RW	RL	SV	AB	H	HR	BA	PO	A	E	DP	TC/G	FA
1948	PHI N	0	0	–	0.00	3	0	0	4	2	1	1	0	0	0	0	0	0	0	–	0	0	0	0	0.0	–

Arnie Portocarrero

PORTOCARRERO, ARNOLD MARIO
B. July 5, 1931, New York, N.Y.   D. July 21, 1986, Kansas City, Kans.

BR TR 6'3"   196 lbs.

Year	Team	W	L	PCT	ERA	G	GS	CG	IP	H	BB	SO	ShO	RW	RL	SV	AB	H	HR	BA	PO	A	E	DP	TC/G	FA
1954	PHI A	9	18	.333	4.06	34	33	16	248	233	114	132	1	0	0	0	75	8	1	.107	15	22	4	0	1.2	.902
1955	KC A	5	9	.357	4.77	24	20	4	111.1	109	67	34	1	0	0	0	37	4	1	.108	7	15	1	0	1.0	.957
1956		0	1	.000	10.13	3	1	0	8	9	7	2	0	0	0	0	1	0	0	.000	0	1	0	0	0.3	1.000
1957		4	9	.308	3.92	33	17	1	114.2	103	34	42	0	2	0	0	28	3	0	.107	6	16	1	1	0.7	.957
1958	BAL A	15	11	.577	3.25	32	27	10	204.2	173	57	90	3	0	1	2	67	11	1	.164	7	21	0	3	0.9	1.000
1959		2	7	.222	6.80	27	14	2	90	107	32	23	0	0	0	0	21	0	0	.000	6	20	1	0	1.0	.963
1960		3	2	.600	4.43	13	5	0	40.2	44	9	15	0	1	1	0	11	0	0	.000	2	3	0	0	0.4	1.000
7 yrs.		38	57	.400	4.32	166	117	33	817.1	778	320	338	5	3	2	2	240	26	3	.108	43	98	7	4	0.9	.953

Mark Portugal

PORTUGAL, MARK STEVEN
B. Oct. 30, 1962, Los Angeles, Calif.

BR TR 6'   170 lbs.

Year	Team	W	L	PCT	ERA	G	GS	CG	IP	H	BB	SO	ShO	RW	RL	SV	AB	H	HR	BA	PO	A	E	DP	TC/G	FA
1985	MIN A	1	3	.250	5.55	6	4	0	24.1	24	14	12	0	0	0	0	0	0	0	–	4	7	1	1	2.0	.917
1986		6	10	.375	4.31	27	15	3	112.2	112	50	67	0	2	4	1	0	0	0	–	5	14	1	3	0.7	.950
1987		1	3	.250	7.77	13	7	0	44	58	24	28	0	0	1	0	0	0	0	–	1	6	0	2	0.5	1.000
1988		3	3	.500	4.53	26	0	0	57.2	60	17	31	0	3	3	3	0	0	0	–	2	1	1	0	0.2	.750
1989	HOU N	7	1	.875	2.75	20	15	2	108	91	37	86	0	0	0	0	34	7	1	.206	11	15	2	0	1.4	.929
5 yrs.		18	20	.474	4.39	92	41	5	346.2	345	142	224	1	5	8	4	34	7	1	.206	23	43	5	6	0.8	.930

Bill Posedel

POSEDEL, WILLIAM JOHN (Sailor Bill)
B. Aug. 2, 1906, San Francisco, Calif.   D. Nov. 28, 1989, Livermore, Calif.

BR TR 5'11"   175 lbs.

Year	Team	W	L	PCT	ERA	G	GS	CG	IP	H	BB	SO	ShO	RW	RL	SV	AB	H	HR	BA	PO	A	E	DP	TC/G	FA
1938	BKN N	8	9	.471	5.66	33	17	6	140	178	46	49	1	0	3	0	44	10	0	.227	5	23	2	2	0.9	.933
1939	BOS N	15	13	.536	3.92	33	29	18	220.2	221	78	73	5	1	0	0	73	8	0	.110	10	40	4	0	1.6	.926
1940		12	17	.414	4.13	35	32	18	233	263	81	86	0	1	0	1	82	14	0	.171	17	42	3	1	1.8	.952
1941		4	4	.500	4.87	18	9	3	57.1	61	30	10	0	1	0	0	25	8	0	.320	3	11	1	2	0.8	.933
1946		2	0	1.000	6.99	19	0	0	28.1	34	13	9	0	2	0	4	3	0	0	.000	1	4	0	0	0.3	1.000
5 yrs.		41	43	.488	4.56	138	87	45	679.1	757	248	227	6	5	3	6	227	40	0	.176	36	120	10	7	1.2	.940

Bob Poser

POSER, JOHN FALK
B. Mar. 16, 1910, Columbus, Wis.

BL TR 6'   173 lbs.

Year	Team	W	L	PCT	ERA	G	GS	CG	IP	H	BB	SO	ShO	RW	RL	SV	AB	H	HR	BA	PO	A	E	DP	TC/G	FA
1932	CHI A	0	0	–	27.00	1	0	0	2	3	2	1	0	0	0	0	3	0	0	.000	0	0	0	0	0.0	–
1935	STL A	1	1	.500	9.22	4	1	0	13.2	26	4	1	0	1	0	0	4	1	0	.250	0	1	0	0	0.3	1.000
2 yrs.		1	1	.500	10.05	5	1	0	14.1	29	6	2	0	1	0	0	7	1	0	.143	0	1	0	0	0.2	1.000

Lou Possehl

POSSEHL, LOUIS THOMAS
B. Apr. 12, 1926, Chicago, Ill.

BR TR 6'2"   180 lbs.

Year	Team	W	L	PCT	ERA	G	GS	CG	IP	H	BB	SO	ShO	RW	RL	SV	AB	H	HR	BA	PO	A	E	DP	TC/G	FA
1946	PHI N	1	2	.333	5.93	4	4	0	13.2	19	10	4	0	0	0	0	3	0	0	.000	1	3	0	0	1.0	1.000
1947		0	0	–	4.15	2	0	0	4.1	5	0	1	0	0	0	0	0	0	0	–	0	3	0	0	1.5	1.000
1948		1	1	.500	4.91	3	2	1	14.2	17	4	7	0	0	0	0	4	1	0	.250	1	2	0	1	1.0	1.000
1951		0	1	.000	6.00	2	1	0	6	9	3	6	0	0	0	0	1	0	0	.000	1	1	0	0	1.0	1.000
1952		0	1	.000	4.97	4	1	0	12.2	12	7	4	0	0	0	0	2	0	0	.000	0	1	0	0	0.3	1.000
5 yrs.		2	5	.286	5.26	15	8	1	51.1	62	24	22	0	0	0	0	10	1	0	.100	3	10	0	1	0.9	1.000

Nellie Pott

POTT, NELSON ADOLPH (Lefty)
B. July 16, 1899, Cincinnati, Ohio   D. Dec. 3, 1963, Cincinnati, Ohio

BL TL 6'   185 lbs.

Year	Team	W	L	PCT	ERA	G	GS	CG	IP	H	BB	SO	ShO	RW	RL	SV	AB	H	HR	BA	PO	A	E	DP	TC/G	FA
1922	CLE A	0	0	–	31.50	2	0	0	2	7	2	0	0	0	0	0	0	0	0	–	0	0	0	0	0.0	–

Dykes Potter

POTTER, MARYLAND DYKES
Brother of Squire Potter.
B. Sept. 7, 1910, Ashland, Ky.

BR TR 6'   185 lbs.

Year	Team	W	L	PCT	ERA	G	GS	CG	IP	H	BB	SO	ShO	RW	RL	SV	AB	H	HR	BA	PO	A	E	DP	TC/G	FA
1938	BKN N	0	0	–	4.50	2	0	0	2	4	0	1	0	0	0	0	0	0	0	–	0	0	0	0	0.0	–

Year	Team	W	L	PCT	ERA	G	GS	CG	IP	H	BB	SO	ShO	Relief Pitching W	L	SV	Batting AB	H	HR	BA	PO	A	E	DP	TC/G	FA

Nels Potter

POTTER, NELSON THOMAS
B. Aug. 23, 1911, Mt. Morris, Ill.
BL TR 5'11" 180 lbs.

Year	Team	W	L	PCT	ERA	G	GS	CG	IP	H	BB	SO	ShO	W	L	SV	AB	H	HR	BA	PO	A	E	DP	TC/G	FA
1936	STL N	0	0	–	0.00	1	0	0	1	1	0	0	0	0	0	0	0	0	0	–	0	0	0	0	0.0	–
1938	PHI A	2	12	.143	6.47	35	9	4	111.1	139	49	43	0	1	3	5	39	10	0	.256	8	16	1	0	0.7	.960
1939		8	12	.400	6.60	41	25	9	196.1	258	88	60	0	2	2	2	67	12	0	.179	8	34	1	0	1.0	.977
1940		9	14	.391	4.44	31	25	13	200.2	213	71	73	0	1	1	0	71	18	0	.254	17	30	0	2	1.5	1.000
1941	2 teams			PHI A (10G 1-1)		BOS A (10G 2-0)																				
"	total	3	1	.750	7.06	20	3	1	43.1	56	32	13	0	2	0	2	9	1	0	.111	5	6	1	1	0.6	.917
1943	STL A	10	5	.667	2.78	33	13	8	168.1	146	54	80	0	2	0	1	55	8	0	.145	10	36	1	2	1.4	.979
1944		19	7	.731	2.83	32	29	16	232	211	70	91	3	0	2	0	82	13	0	.159	11	52	3	3	2.1	.955
1945		15	11	.577	2.47	32	32	21	255.1	212	68	129	3	0	0	0	92	28	0	.304	13	43	3	4	1.8	.949
1946		8	9	.471	3.72	23	19	10	145	152	59	72	0	0	0	0	52	12	0	.231	11	18	1	3	1.3	.967
1947		4	10	.286	4.04	32	16	10	122.2	130	44	65	0	2	2	2	35	9	0	.257	6	27	3	1	1.1	.917
1948	3 teams			STL A (2G 1-1)		PHI A (8G 2-2)		10 3		BOS N (18G 5-2)																
"	total	8	5	.615	2.86	28	9	3	113.1	105	17	64	0	3	2	3	37	14	0	.378	7	25	3	1	1.3	.914
1949	BOS N	6	11	.353	4.19	41	3	1	96.2	99	30	57	0	5	11	7	23	3	0	.130	2	20	1	1	0.6	.957
12 yrs.		92	97	.487	3.99	349	177	89	1686	1721	582	747	6	16	23	22	562	128	0	.228	98	307	18	18	1.2	.957

WORLD SERIES

Year	Team	W	L	PCT	ERA	G	GS	CG	IP	H	BB	SO	ShO	W	L	SV	AB	H	HR	BA	PO	A	E	DP	TC/G	FA
1944	STL A	0	1	.000	0.93	2	2	0	9.2	10	3	6	0	0	0	0	4	0	0	.000	2	2	2	0	3.0	.667
1948	BOS N	0	0	–	8.44	2	1	0	5.1	6	2	1	0	0	0	0	2	1	0	.500	1	0	0	0	0.5	1.000
2 yrs.		0	1	.000	3.60	4	3	0	15	16	5	7	0	0	0	0	6	1	0	.167	3	2	2	0	1.8	.714

Squire Potter

POTTER, SQUIRE
Brother of Dykes Potter.
B. Mar. 18, 1902, Flatwoods, Ky.   D. Jan. 27, 1983, Ashland, Ky.
BR TR 6'1" 185 lbs.

Year	Team	W	L	PCT	ERA	G	GS	CG	IP	H	BB	SO	ShO	W	L	SV	AB	H	HR	BA	PO	A	E	DP	TC/G	FA
1923	WAS A	0	0	–	21.00	1	0	0	3	11	4	1	0	0	0	0	0	0	0	–	0	0	0	0	0.0	–

Bill Pounds

POUNDS, JEARED WELLS
B. Mar. 11, 1878, Paterson, N. J.   D. July 7, 1936, Paterson, N. J.
BR TR 5'10½" 178 lbs.

Year	Team	W	L	PCT	ERA	G	GS	CG	IP	H	BB	SO	ShO	W	L	SV	AB	H	HR	BA	PO	A	E	DP	TC/G	FA
1903	2 teams			CLE A (1G 0-0)		BKN N (1G 0-0)																				
"	total	0	0	–	8.18	2	0	0	11	16	2	4	0	0	0	0	5	3	0	.600	0	4	0	0	2.0	1.000

Abner Powell

POWELL, CHARLES ABNER
B. Dec. 15, 1860, Shenandoah, Pa.   D. Aug. 7, 1953, New Orleans, La.
BR TR 5'7" 160 lbs.

Year	Team	W	L	PCT	ERA	G	GS	CG	IP	H	BB	SO	ShO	W	L	SV	AB	H	HR	BA	PO	A	E	DP	TC/G	FA
1884	WAS U	6	12	.333	3.43	18	17	14	134	135	19	78	1	1	0	0	191	54	0	.283	10	38	9	0	3.2	.842
1886	2 teams			BAL AA (7G 2-5)		CIN AA (4G 0-1)																				
"	total	2	6	.250	5.02	11	8	8	75.1	82	35	19	0	0	0	0	113	24	0	.212	5	22	3	2	2.7	.900
2 yrs.		8	18	.308	4.00	29	25	22	209.1	217	54	97	1	1	0	0	*				15	60	12	2	3.0	.862

Bill Powell

POWELL, WILLIAM BURRIS
B. May 8, 1885, Richmond, Va.   D. Sept. 28, 1967, East Liverpool, Ohio
BR TR 6'2½" 182 lbs.

Year	Team	W	L	PCT	ERA	G	GS	CG	IP	H	BB	SO	ShO	W	L	SV	AB	H	HR	BA	PO	A	E	DP	TC/G	FA
1909	PIT N	0	1	.000	3.68	3	1	0	7.1	7	6	2	0	0	0	0	4	1	0	.250	0	2	0	1	0.7	1.000
1910		4	6	.400	2.40	12	9	4	75	65	34	23	2	1	0	0	23	6	0	.261	6	27	1	1	2.8	.971
1912	CHI N	0	0	–	9.00	1	0	0	2	2	1	0	0	0	0	0	0	0	0	–	0	1	0	0	1.0	1.000
1913	CIN N	0	1	.000	54.00	1	1	0	.1	2	2	0	0	0	0	0	0	0	0	–	0	0	0	0	0.0	–
4 yrs.		4	8	.333	2.87	17	11	4	84.2	76	43	25	2	1	0	0	27	7	0	.259	6	30	1	2	2.2	.973

Dennis Powell

POWELL, DENNIS CLAY
B. Aug. 13, 1963, Moultrie, Ga.
BR TL 6'3" 175 lbs.

Year	Team	W	L	PCT	ERA	G	GS	CG	IP	H	BB	SO	ShO	W	L	SV	AB	H	HR	BA	PO	A	E	DP	TC/G	FA
1985	LA N	1	1	.500	5.22	16	2	0	29.1	30	13	19	0	1	0	1	3	0	0	.000	0	6	0	2	0.4	1.000
1986		2	7	.222	4.27	27	6	0	65.1	65	25	31	0	1	2	0	14	3	0	.214	7	6	1	1	0.5	.929
1987	SEA A	1	3	.250	3.15	16	3	0	34.1	32	15	17	0	1	2	0	0	0	0	–	0	5	0	0	0.5	1.000
1988		1	3	.250	8.68	12	2	0	18.2	29	11	15	0	1	2	0	0	0	0	–	1	3	0	0	0.3	1.000
1989		2	2	.500	5.00	43	1	0	45	49	21	27	0	2	1	2	0	0	0	–	2	11	0	0	0.3	1.000
5 yrs.		7	16	.304	4.81	114	14	0	192.2	205	85	109	0	6	7	3	17	3	0	.176	12	32	1	3	0.4	.978

Grover Powell

POWELL, GROVER DAVID
B. Oct. 10, 1940, Sayre, Pa.   D. May 21, 1985, Raleigh, N. C.
BL TL 5'10" 175 lbs.

Year	Team	W	L	PCT	ERA	G	GS	CG	IP	H	BB	SO	ShO	W	L	SV	AB	H	HR	BA	PO	A	E	DP	TC/G	FA
1963	NY N	1	1	.500	2.72	20	4	1	49.2	37	32	39	1	0	0	0	10	2	0	.200	7	7	2	1	0.8	.875

Jack Powell

POWELL, JOHN JOSEPH
B. July 9, 1874, Bloomington, Ill.   D. Oct. 17, 1944, Chicago, Ill.
BR TR 5'11" 195 lbs.

Year	Team	W	L	PCT	ERA	G	GS	CG	IP	H	BB	SO	ShO	W	L	SV	AB	H	HR	BA	PO	A	E	DP	TC/G	FA
1897	CLE N	15	10	.600	3.16	27	26	24	225	245	62	61	2	0	0	0	97	20	0	.206	7	45	4	2	2.1	.929
1898		23	15	.605	3.00	42	41	36	342	328	112	93	6	0	1	0	136	18	0	.132	11	70	3	2	2.0	.964
1899	STL N	23	21	.523	3.52	48	43	40	373	433	85	87	2	2	0	0	134	27	0	.201	12	78	6	2	2.0	.938
1900		17	17	.500	4.44	38	37	28	287.2	325	77	77	3	1	0	0	109	31	1	.284	11	70	6	2	2.3	.931
1901		19	19	.500	3.54	45	37	33	338.1	351	50	133	2	2	2	3	119	21	2	.176	15	64	7	4	1.9	.919
1902	STL A	22	17	.564	3.21	42	39	36	328.1	320	93	137	3	1	0	2	127	26	1	.205	16	63	6	5	2.0	.929
1903		15	19	.441	2.91	38	34	33	306.1	294	58	169	4	1	0	2	120	25	0	.208	10	85	6	1	2.7	.941
1904	NY A	23	19	.548	2.44	47	45	38	390.1	340	92	202	3	1	0	0	146	26	0	.178	9	100	4	3	2.4	.965
1905	2 teams			NY A (36G 8-13)		STL A (3G 2-1)																				
"	total	10	14	.417	3.29	39	26	16	230	236	62	96	1	2	3	1	75	13	0	.173	2	40	2	1	1.1	.955
1906	STL A	13	14	.481	1.77	28	26	25	244	196	55	132	3	1	0	1	94	22	1	.234	8	53	3	3	2.3	.953
1907		13	16	.448	2.68	32	31	27	255.2	229	62	96	4	0	0	0	91	12	0	.132	2	69	4	2	2.3	.947
1908		16	13	.552	2.11	33	32	23	256	208	47	85	6	0	0	0	89	21	0	.236	3	56	3	0	1.8	.951
1909		12	16	.429	2.11	34	27	18	239	221	42	82	0	1	1	0	78	14	0	.179	9	58	4	0	2.1	.944
1910		7	11	.389	2.30	21	18	8	129.1	121	28	52	3	1	0	0	43	7	0	.163	5	25	3	1	1.6	.909
1911		8	19	.296	3.29	31	27	18	207.2	224	44	52	1	1	0	0	73	12	0	.164	5	40	6	1	1.6	.882
1912		9	16	.360	3.10	32	28	19	235.1	248	52	67	0	0	0	0	82	15	1	.183	3	52	5	4	1.9	.917
16 yrs.		245	256	.489	2.97	577	517	422	4388	4319	1021	1621	47	15	9	15	1613	310	7	.192	127	968	72	34	2.0	.938
	7th																									

Year	Team		W	L	PCT	ERA	G	GS	CG	IP	H	BB	SO	ShO	Relief Pitching W	L	SV	Batting AB	H	HR	BA	PO	A	E	DP	TC/G	FA

Jack Powell

POWELL, REGINALD BERTRAND
B. Aug. 17, 1891, Holcomb, Mo. D. Mar. 12, 1930
TR 6'2"

| 1913 | STL | A | 0 | 0 | – | 0.00 | 2 | 0 | 0 | 2 | 1 | 2 | 0 | 0 | 0 | 0 | 0 | 0 | 0 | 0 | – | 0 | 3 | 0 | 0 | 1.5 | 1.000 |

Ted Power

POWER, TED HENRY
B. Jan. 31, 1955, Guthrie, Okla.
BR TR 6'4" 220 lbs.

1981	LA	N	1	3	.250	3.21	5	2	0	14	16	7	7	0	1	0	0	3	0	0	.000	1	0	1	0	0.4	.500
1982			1	1	.500	6.68	12	4	0	33.2	38	23	15	0	0	0	0	6	0	0	.000	3	5	0	0	0.7	1.000
1983	CIN	N	5	6	.455	4.54	49	6	1	111	120	49	57	0	4	3	2	16	0	0	.000	4	8	0	1	0.2	1.000
1984			9	7	.563	2.82	78	0	0	108.2	93	46	81	0	9	7	11	5	0	0	.000	6	16	1	3	0.3	.957
1985			8	6	.571	2.70	64	0	0	80	65	45	42	0	8	6	27	0	0	0	–	3	4	1	0	0.1	.875
1986			10	6	.625	3.70	56	10	0	129	115	52	95	0	4	5	1	24	3	0	.125	7	18	1	1	0.5	.962
1987			10	13	.435	4.50	34	34	2	204	213	71	133	0	0	0	0	59	7	1	.119	9	17	2	0	0.8	.929
1988	2 teams		KC A		(22G 5–6)		DET A		(4G 1–1)																		
"	total		6	7	.462	5.91	26	14	2	99	121	38	57	2	3	2	0	0	0	0	–	8	10	1	1	0.7	.947
1989	STL	N	7	7	.500	3.71	23	15	0	97	96	21	43	0	2	0	0	33	3	0	.091	5	8	0	0	0.6	1.000
9 yrs.			57	56	.504	4.15	347	85	5	876.1	877	352	530	3	31	24	41	146	13	1	.089	46	86	7	6	0.4	.950

Ike Powers

POWERS, JOHN LLOYD
B. Mar. 13, 1906, Hancock, Md. D. Dec. 22, 1968, Hancock, Md.
BR TR 6'½" 188 lbs.

1927	PHI	A	1	1	.500	4.50	11	1	0	26	26	7	3	0	1	0	0	5	2	0	.400	2	6	1	0	0.8	.889
1928			1	0	1.000	4.50	9	0	0	12	8	10	4	0	1	0	2	0	0	0	–	2	4	0	1	0.7	1.000
2 yrs.			2	1	.667	4.50	20	1	0	38	34	17	7	0	2	0	2	5	2	0	.400	4	10	1	1	0.8	.933

Jim Powers

POWERS, JAMES T.
B. 1868, New York, N. Y. D. Feb. 13, 1943, New York, N. Y.
5'10" 150 lbs.

| 1890 | BKN | AA | 1 | 2 | .333 | 5.70 | 4 | 2 | 2 | 30 | 38 | 16 | 3 | 0 | 1 | 0 | 0 | 13 | 2 | 0 | .154 | 0 | 5 | 0 | 0 | 1.3 | 1.000 |

Willie Prall

PRALL, WILFRED ANTHONY
B. Apr. 20, 1950, Hackensack, N. J.
BL TL 6'3" 200 lbs.

| 1975 | CHI | N | 0 | 2 | .000 | 8.40 | 3 | 3 | 0 | 15 | 21 | 8 | 7 | 0 | 0 | 0 | 0 | 4 | 0 | 0 | .000 | 0 | 3 | 0 | 0 | 1.0 | 1.000 |

John Pregenzer

PREGENZER, JOHN ARTHUR
B. Aug. 2, 1935, Burlington, Wis.
BR TR 6'5" 220 lbs.

1963	SF	N	0	0	–	4.82	6	0	0	9.1	8	8	5	0	0	0	1	0	0	0	–	0	2	0	1	0.3	1.000
1964			2	0	1.000	4.91	13	0	0	18.1	21	11	8	0	2	0	0	0	0	0	–	2	2	0	0	0.3	1.000
2 yrs.			2	0	1.000	4.88	19	0	0	27.2	29	19	13	0	2	0	1	0	0	0	–	2	4	0	1	0.3	1.000

Jim Prendergast

PRENDERGAST, JAMES BARTHOLOMEW
B. Aug. 23, 1917, Brooklyn, N. Y.
BL TL 6'1" 208 lbs.

| 1948 | BOS | N | 1 | 1 | .500 | 10.26 | 10 | 2 | 0 | 16.2 | 30 | 5 | 3 | 0 | 0 | 0 | 1 | 5 | 0 | 0 | .000 | 4 | 4 | 0 | 0 | 0.8 | 1.000 |

Mike Prendergast

PRENDERGAST, MICHAEL THOMAS (Iron Mike)
B. Dec. 15, 1888, Arlington, Ill. D. Nov. 18, 1967, Omaha, Neb.
BR TR 5'9½" 165 lbs.

1914	CHI	F	5	9	.357	2.38	30	19	7	136	131	40	71	1	0	1	0	37	4	0	.108	1	32	1	0	1.1	.971
1915			14	12	.538	2.48	42	30	16	253.2	220	67	95	3	2	3	0	80	6	0	.075	3	68	3	3	1.8	.959
1916	CHI	N	6	11	.353	2.31	35	10	4	152	127	23	56	2	3	4	2	46	7	0	.152	2	40	2	1	1.3	.955
1917			3	6	.333	3.35	35	8	1	99.1	112	21	43	0	1	1	1	28	7	0	.250	3	25	2	2	0.9	.933
1918	PHI	N	13	14	.481	2.89	33	30	20	252.1	257	46	41	0	0	0	1	85	7	0	.082	6	70	3	3	2.4	.962
1919			0	1	.000	8.40	5	0	0	15	20	10	5	0	0	1	0	3	1	0	.333	1	5	1	1	1.4	.857
6 yrs.			41	53	.436	2.74	180	97	48	908.1	867	207	311	6	6	10	4	279	32	0	.115	16	240	12	10	1.5	.955

George Prentiss

PRENTISS, GEORGE PEPPER (Kitten)
Played as George Pepper Wilson In 1901. Also known as George Pepper Wilson.
B. June 10, 1876, Wilmington, Del. D. Sept. 8, 1902, Wilmington, Del.
BB TR 5'11" 175 lbs.

1901	BOS	A	1	0	1.000	1.80	2	1	1	10	7	6	0	0	0	0	0	3	1	0	.333	0	3	0	0	1.5	1.000
1902	2 teams		BOS A		(7G 2–2)		BAL A		(2G 0–1)																		
"	total		2	3	.400	6.04	9	6	3	47.2	69	15	10	0	0	0	0	20	5	0	.250	1	13	0	0	1.6	1.000
2 yrs.			3	3	.500	5.31	11	7	4	57.2	76	21	10	0	0	0	0	23	6	0	.261	1	16	0	0	1.5	1.000

Joe Presko

PRESKO, JOSEPH EDWARD (Little Joe)
B. Oct. 7, 1928, Kansas City, Mo.
BR TR 5'9½" 165 lbs.

1951	STL	N	7	4	.636	3.45	15	12	5	88.2	86	20	38	0	1	0	2	37	6	0	.162	4	11	1	0	1.1	.938
1952			7	10	.412	4.05	28	18	5	146.2	140	57	63	1	2	1	0	43	4	0	.093	6	24	2	3	1.1	.938
1953			6	13	.316	5.01	34	25	4	161.2	165	65	56	0	0	0	1	59	13	0	.220	13	21	1	2	1.0	.971
1954			4	9	.308	6.91	37	6	1	71.2	97	41	36	1	3	5	0	16	4	0	.250	5	9	0	2	0.4	1.000
1957	DET	A	1	1	.500	1.64	7	0	0	11	10	4	3	0	1	1	0	1	0	0	.000	0	1	0	0	0.1	1.000
1958			0	0	–	3.38	7	0	0	10.2	13	1	6	0	0	0	2	0	0	0	–	1	1	0	0	0.3	1.000
6 yrs.			25	37	.403	4.61	128	61	15	490.1	511	188	202	2	7	7	5	156	27	0	.173	29	67	4	7	0.8	.960

Tot Pressnell

PRESSNELL, FOREST CHARLES
B. Aug. 8, 1906, Findlay, Ohio
BR TR 5'10½" 175 lbs.

1938	BKN	N	11	14	.440	3.56	43	19	6	192	209	56	57	1	4	3	3	63	9	0	.143	10	36	2	0	1.1	.958
1939			9	7	.563	4.02	31	18	10	156.2	171	33	43	2	0	0	2	51	10	0	.196	5	36	3	2	1.4	.932
1940			6	5	.545	3.69	24	4	1	68.1	58	17	21	1	4	4	2	17	0	0	.000	4	9	1	0	0.6	.929
1941	CHI	N	5	3	.625	3.09	29	1	0	70	69	23	27	0	5	3	4	15	3	0	.200	0	13	1	1	0.5	.929
1942			1	1	.500	5.49	27	0	0	39.1	40	5	9	0	1	0	1	3	2	0	.667	2	7	0	0	0.3	1.000
5 yrs.			32	30	.516	3.80	154	42	17	526.1	547	134	157	4	14	10	12	149	24	0	.161	21	101	7	3	0.8	.946

Year	Team		W	L	PCT	ERA	G	GS	CG	IP	H	BB	SO	ShO	Relief Pitching			Batting				PO	A	E	DP	TC/G	FA
															W	L	SV	AB	H	HR	BA						

Bill Price

PRICE, WILLIAM
B. Philadelphia, Pa.   Deceased.

| 1890 | PHI | AA | 1 | 0 | 1.000 | 2.00 | 1 | 1 | 1 | 9 | 6 | 7 | 1 | 0 | 0 | 0 | 0 | 4 | 1 | 0 | .250 | 0 | 2 | 0 | 0 | 2.0 | 1.000 |

Joe Price

PRICE, JOSEPH WALTER   BR TL 6'4"   220 lbs.
B. Nov. 29, 1956, Inglewood, Calif.

1980	CIN	N	7	3	.700	3.57	24	13	2	111	95	37	44	0	2	0	0	39	5	0	.128	3	16	2	0	0.9	.905
1981			6	1	.857	2.50	41	0	0	54	42	18	41	0	6	1	4	3	0	0	.000	1	13	2	0	0.4	.875
1982			3	4	.429	2.85	59	1	0	72.2	73	32	71	0	3	3	3	3	1	0	.333	1	8	2	0	0.2	.818
1983			10	6	.625	2.88	21	21	5	144	118	46	83	0	0	0	0	41	4	0	.098	8	21	4	3	1.6	.879
1984			7	13	.350	4.19	30	30	3	171.2	176	61	129	1	0	0	0	48	7	0	.146	4	14	0	0	0.6	1.000
1985			2	2	.500	3.90	26	8	0	64.2	59	23	52	0	0	0	1	14	0	0	.000	1	4	0	1	0.2	1.000
1986			1	2	.333	5.40	25	2	0	41.2	49	22	30	0	1	1	0	7	1	0	.143	2	2	0	0	0.2	1.000
1987	SF	N	2	2	.500	2.57	20	0	0	35	19	13	42	0	2	2	1	6	1	0	.167	1	2	0	0	0.2	1.000
1988			1	6	.143	3.94	38	3	0	61.2	59	27	49	0	1	6	4	8	0	0	.000	1	8	0	0	0.3	1.000
1989	2 teams	SF N	(7G 1–1)			BOS A	(31G 2–5)																				
"	total		3	6	.333	4.59	38	6	0	84.1	87	34	62	0	1	0	0	2	0	0	.000	1	8	0	1	0.3	1.000
10 yrs.			42	45	.483	3.65	322	84	10	840.2	777	313	603	1	16	16	13	171	19	0	.111	26	96	10	5	0.4	.924

LEAGUE CHAMPIONSHIP SERIES

| 1987 | SF | N | 1 | 0 | 1.000 | 0.00 | 2 | 0 | 0 | 5.2 | 3 | 1 | 7 | 0 | 1 | 0 | 0 | 1 | 0 | 0 | .000 | 0 | 0 | 0 | 0 | 0.0 | – |

Bob Priddy

PRIDDY, ROBERT SIMPSON   BR TR 6'1"   200 lbs.
B. Dec. 10, 1939, Pittsburgh, Pa.

1962	PIT	N	1	0	1.000	3.00	2	0	0	3	4	1	1	0	1	0	0	0	0	0	–	0	0	0	0	0.0	–
1964			1	2	.333	3.93	19	0	0	34.1	35	15	23	0	1	2	1	3	0	0	.000	3	1	0	0	0.2	1.000
1965	SF	N	1	0	1.000	1.74	8	0	0	10.1	6	2	7	0	1	0	0	1	0	0	.000	1	2	0	0	0.4	1.000
1966			6	3	.667	3.96	38	3	0	91	88	28	51	0	6	0	1	17	3	0	.176	4	10	3	2	0.4	.824
1967	WAS	A	3	7	.300	3.44	46	8	1	110	98	33	57	0	0	3	4	22	4	0	.182	13	21	1	0	0.8	.971
1968	CHI	A	3	11	.214	3.63	35	18	2	114	106	41	66	0	0	2	0	24	1	0	.042	5	10	1	0	0.5	.938
1969	3 teams	CHI A	(4G 0–0)			CAL A	(15G 0–1)			ATL N	(1G 0–0)																
"	total		0	1	.000	4.46	20	0	0	36.1	35	10	21	0	0	1	0	2	0	0	.000	3	5	0	1	0.4	1.000
1970	ATL	N	5	5	.500	5.42	41	0	0	73	75	24	32	0	5	5	8	15	3	0	.200	7	14	1	0	0.5	.955
1971			4	9	.308	4.22	40	0	0	64	71	44	36	0	4	9	4	11	2	0	.182	6	11	1	2	0.5	.944
9 yrs.			24	38	.387	4.00	249	29	3	536	518	198	294	0	18	22	18	95	13	1	.137	42	74	7	5	0.5	.943

Ray Prim

PRIM, RAYMOND LEE (Pop)   BR TL 6'   178 lbs.
B. Dec. 30, 1906, Salitpa, Ala.

1933	WAS	A	0	1	.000	3.14	2	1	0	14.1	13	2	6	0	0	0	0	5	0	0	.000	1	7	0	0	4.0	1.000
1934			0	2	.000	6.75	8	1	0	14.2	19	8	3	0	0	1	0	3	0	0	.000	0	5	1	1	0.8	.833
1935	PHI	N	3	4	.429	5.77	29	6	1	73.1	110	15	27	0	3	1	0	24	2	0	.083	4	13	0	2	0.6	1.000
1943	CHI	N	4	3	.571	2.55	29	5	0	60	67	14	27	0	2	1	1	12	2	0	.167	3	21	1	1	0.9	.960
1945			13	8	.619	2.40	34	19	9	165.1	142	23	88	2	3	2	2	51	13	0	.255	7	25	1	2	1.0	.970
1946			2	3	.400	5.79	14	2	0	23.1	28	10	10	0	0	1	1	5	1	0	.200	1	8	1	0	0.6	1.000
6 yrs.			22	21	.512	3.56	116	34	10	351	379	72	161	2	8	5	4	100	18	0	.180	16	79	3	6	0.8	.969

WORLD SERIES

| 1945 | CHI | N | 0 | 1 | .000 | 9.00 | 2 | 0 | 0 | 4 | 4 | 1 | 1 | 0 | 0 | 1 | 0 | 0 | 0 | 0 | – | 0 | 1 | 0 | 0 | 0.5 | 1.000 |

Don Prince

PRINCE, DONALD MARK   BR TR 6'4"   200 lbs.
B. Apr. 5, 1938, Clarkton, N. C.

| 1962 | CHI | N | 0 | 0 | – | 0.00 | 1 | 0 | 0 | 1 | 0 | 1 | 0 | 0 | 0 | 0 | 0 | 0 | 0 | 0 | – | 0 | 1 | 0 | 1 | 1.0 | 1.000 |

Jim Proctor

PROCTOR, JAMES ARTHUR   BR TR 6'   165 lbs.
B. Sept. 9, 1935, Brandywine, Md.

| 1959 | DET | A | 0 | 1 | .000 | 16.88 | 2 | 0 | 0 | 2.2 | 8 | 3 | 0 | 0 | 0 | 0 | 0 | 0 | 0 | 0 | – | 0 | 1 | 0 | 0 | 0.5 | 1.000 |

Red Proctor

PROCTOR, NOAH RICHARD   BR TR 6'1"   165 lbs.
B. Oct. 27, 1900, Williamsburg, Va.   D. Dec. 17, 1954, Richmond, Va.

| 1923 | CHI | A | 0 | 0 | – | 13.50 | 2 | 0 | 0 | 4 | 11 | 2 | 0 | 0 | 0 | 0 | 0 | 0 | 0 | 0 | – | 0 | 0 | 0 | 0 | 0.0 | – |

George Proeser

PROESER, GEORGE (White Wings)   BL TL 5'10"   190 lbs.
B. May 30, 1864, Cincinnati, Ohio   D. Oct. 14, 1941, New Burlington, Ohio

| 1888 | CLE | AA | 3 | 4 | .429 | 3.81 | 7 | 7 | 7 | 59 | 53 | 30 | 20 | 1 | 0 | 0 | 0 | * | | | | 0 | 11 | 2 | 0 | 1.9 | .846 |

Mike Proly

PROLY, MICHAEL JAMES   BR TR 6'   185 lbs.
B. Dec. 15, 1950, Jamaica, N. Y.

1976	STL	N	1	0	1.000	3.71	14	0	0	17	21	6	4	0	1	0	0	0	0	0	–	3	3	0	0	0.4	1.000
1978	CHI	A	5	2	.714	2.74	14	6	2	65.2	63	12	19	0	0	0	1	0	0	0	–	1	10	1	0	0.9	.917
1979			3	6	.273	3.89	38	6	0	88	89	40	32	0	3	4	9	0	0	0	–	5	17	1	2	0.6	.957
1980			5	10	.333	3.06	62	3	0	147	136	58	56	0	4	8	8	0	0	0	–	10	29	2	2	0.6	1.000
1981	PHI	N	2	1	.667	3.86	35	2	0	63	66	19	19	0	2	1	2	7	0	0	.000	9	14	1	0	0.7	.958
1982	CHI	N	5	3	.625	2.30	44	1	0	82	77	22	24	0	4	3	1	14	4	0	.286	1	18	0	1	0.4	1.000
1983			1	5	.167	3.58	60	0	0	83	79	38	31	0	1	5	1	11	1	0	.091	6	14	1	0	0.4	.952
7 yrs.			22	29	.431	3.23	267	18	2	545.2	531	195	185	0	15	17	22	32	5	0	.156	35	105	4	5	0.5	.972

Bill Prough

PROUGH, HERSCHEL CLINTON   BR TR 6'3"   185 lbs.
B. Nov. 28, 1887, Martle, Ind.   D. Dec. 29, 1936, Richmond, Ind.

| 1912 | CIN | N | 0 | 0 | – | 6.00 | 1 | 0 | 0 | 3 | 7 | 1 | 1 | 0 | 0 | 0 | 0 | 0 | 0 | 0 | .000 | 0 | 0 | 0 | 0 | 0.0 | – |

Year	Team		W	L	PCT	ERA	G	GS	CG	IP	H	BB	SO	ShO	Relief Pitching W	L	SV	Batting AB	H	HR	BA	PO	A	E	DP	TC/G	FA

Augie Prudhomme

PRUDHOMME, JOHN OLGUS
B. Nov. 20, 1902, Frierson, La.
BR TR 6'2" 186 lbs.

| 1929 | DET | A | 1 | 6 | .143 | 6.22 | 34 | 6 | 2 | 94 | 119 | 53 | 26 | 0 | 0 | 3 | 1 | 21 | 5 | 0 | .238 | 3 | 24 | 1 | 3 | 0.8 | .964 |

Hub Pruett

PRUETT, HUBERT SHELBY (Shucks)
B. Sept. 1, 1900, Malden, Mo.   D. Jan. 28, 1982, Ladue, Mo.
BL TL 5'10½" 165 lbs.

1922	STL	A	7	7	.500	2.33	39	8	4	119.2	99	59	70	0	4	4	7	34	5	0	.147	7	37	1	1	1.2	.978
1923			4	7	.364	4.31	32	8	3	104.1	109	64	59	0	1	1	2	23	3	0	.130	2	30	1	1	1.0	.970
1924			3	4	.429	4.57	33	1	0	65	64	42	27	0	3	3	0	15	3	0	.200	6	16	1	0	0.7	.957
1927	PHI	N	7	17	.292	6.05	31	28	12	186	238	89	90	1	0	0	1	60	13	0	.217	9	55	7	1	2.3	.901
1928			2	4	.333	4.54	13	9	4	71.1	78	49	35	0	0	0	0	24	5	0	.208	5	16	3	1	1.8	.875
1930	NY	N	5	4	.556	4.78	45	8	1	135.2	152	63	49	0	4	0	3	37	5	0	.135	7	30	1	1	0.8	.974
1932	BOS	N	1	5	.167	5.14	18	7	4	63	76	30	27	0	0	0	0	19	2	0	.105	5	21	1	0	1.5	.963
7 yrs.			29	48	.377	4.63	211	69	28	745	816	396	357	1	12	8	13	212	36	0	.170	41	205	15	5	1.2	.943

Tex Pruiett

PRUIETT, CHARLES LeROY
B. Apr. 10, 1883, Osgood, Ind.   D. Mar. 6, 1953, Ventura, Calif.
BL TR

1907	BOS	A	3	11	.214	3.11	35	17	6	173.2	166	59	54	2	0	1	3	51	8	0	.157	7	64	7	3	2.2	.910
1908			1	7	.125	1.99	13	6	1	58.2	55	21	28	1	0	2	2	16	1	0	.063	2	21	3	0	2.0	.885
2 yrs.			4	18	.182	2.83	48	23	7	232.1	221	80	82	3	0	3	5	67	9	0	.134	9	85	10	3	2.2	.904

Troy Puckett

PUCKETT, TROY LEVI
B. Dec. 10, 1889, Winchester, Ind.   D. Apr. 13, 1971, Winchester, Ind.
BL TR 6'2" 186 lbs.

| 1911 | PHI | N | 0 | 0 | — | 13.50 | 1 | 0 | 0 | 2 | 4 | 2 | 1 | 0 | 0 | 0 | 0 | 0 | 0 | 0 | — | 0 | 1 | 0 | 0 | 1.0 | 1.000 |

Miguel Puente

PUENTE, MIGUEL ANTONIO
Born Miguel Antonio Puente y Aguilar.
B. May 8, 1948, San Luis Potosi, Mexico
BR TR 6' 160 lbs.

| 1970 | SF | N | 1 | 3 | .250 | 8.05 | 6 | 4 | 1 | 19 | 25 | 11 | 14 | 0 | 0 | 1 | 0 | 7 | 0 | 0 | .000 | 1 | 4 | 1 | 0 | 1.0 | .833 |

Charlie Puleo

PULEO, CHARLES MICHAEL
B. Feb. 7, 1955, Glen Ridge, N. J.
BR TR 6'2" 190 lbs.

1981	NY	N	0	0	—	0.00	4	1	0	13	8	8	8	0	0	0	0	2	0	0	.000	1	2	0	0	0.8	1.000
1982			9	9	.500	4.47	36	24	1	171	179	90	98	1	2	1	1	48	6	0	.125	9	43	5	5	1.6	.912
1983	CIN	N	6	12	.333	4.89	27	24	0	143.2	145	91	71	0	0	0	0	50	5	0	.100	11	14	2	1	1.0	.926
1984			1	2	.333	5.73	5	4	0	22	27	15	6	0	0	0	0	5	1	0	.200	0	1	0	0	0.2	1.000
1986	ATL	N	1	2	.333	2.96	5	3	1	24.1	13	12	18	0	0	0	0	6	2	0	.333	0	3	0	0	0.6	1.000
1987			6	8	.429	4.23	35	16	1	123.1	122	40	99	0	2	0	0	28	5	1	.179	6	10	0	0	0.5	1.000
1988			5	5	.500	3.47	53	0	0	106.1	101	47	70	0	5	3	1	13	3	0	.231	5	16	1	0	0.4	.955
1989			1	1	.500	4.66	15	1	0	29	26	16	17	0	1	1	0	1	0	0	.000	2	0	0	0	0.2	1.000
8 yrs.			29	39	.426	4.25	180	76	3	632.2	621	319	387	1	10	5	2	153	22	1	.144	34	90	8	6	0.7	.939

Alfonso Pulido

PULIDO, ALFONSO
Born Alfonso Pulido y Manzo.
B. Jan. 23, 1957, Veracruz, Mexico
BL TL 5'11" 170 lbs.

1983	PIT	N	0	0	—	9.00	1	1	0	4	4	1	1	0	0	0	0	0	0	0	—	0	0	0	0	0.0	—
1984			0	0	—	9.00	1	0	0	2	3	1	2	0	0	0	0	0	0	0	—	0	0	0	0	0.0	—
1986	NY	A	1	1	.500	4.70	10	3	0	30.2	38	9	13	0	0	0	0	0	0	0	—	1	4	0	1	0.5	1.000
3 yrs.			1	1	.500	5.19	12	4	0	34.2	45	11	16	0	0	0	0	0	0	0	—	1	4	0	1	0.4	1.000

Spence Pumpelly

PUMPELLY, SPENCER ARMSTRONG
B. Apr. 11, 1893, Owego, N. Y.   D. Dec. 5, 1973, Sayre, Pa.

| 1925 | WAS | A | 0 | 0 | — | 9.00 | 1 | 0 | 0 | 1 | 1 | 1 | 0 | 0 | 0 | 0 | 0 | 0 | 0 | 0 | — | 0 | 0 | 0 | 0 | 0.0 | — |

Blondie Purcell

PURCELL, WILLIAM ALOYSIUS
B. Mar. 16, 1854, Paterson, N. J.   D. Feb. 20, 1912, Trenton N. J.,
Manager 1883.
BR TR 5'9½" 159 lbs.

1879	2 teams	SYR N (22G 4-15)				CIN N	(2G 0-2)																				
"	total		4	17	.190	3.78	24	19	17	197.2	272	21	31	0	1	0	0	327	83	0	.254	11	33	6	0	2.1	.880
1880	CIN	N	3	17	.150	3.21	25	21	21	196	235	32	47	0	0	0	0	325	95	1	.292	10	37	3	0	2.0	.940
1881	BUF	N	4	1	.800	2.77	9	5	5	61.2	62	9	15	0	0	0	0	193	47	0	.244	2	16	2	0	2.2	.900
1882			2	1	.667	4.94	6	3	2	31	44	4	9	0	0	0	0	380	105	2	.276	0	10	1	0	1.8	.909
1883	PHI	N	2	6	.250	4.39	11	9	7	80	110	12	30	0	0	0	0	425	114	1	.268	4	21	3	0	2.5	.893
1884			0	0	—	2.25	1			4	3	0	1	0	0	0	0	428	108	1	.252	0	0	0	0	0.0	—
1885	2 teams	PHI AA (1G 0-1)				BOS N	(0G 0-0)																				
"	total		0	1	.000	6.00	1	0	0	6	11	2	3	0	0	0	0	391	109	0	.279	0	1	0	0	1.0	1.000
1886	BAL	AA	0	0	—	9.00	1	0	0	1	1	0	0	0	0	0	0	85	19	0	.224	0	0	0	0	0.0	—
1887			0	0	—	15.75	1	0	0	4	8	4	2	0	0	0	0	567	142	0	.250	0	0	0	0	0.0	—
9 yrs.			15	43	.259	3.73	79	57	52	581.1	746	84	138	0	1	2	0	*				27	118	15	0	2.0	.906

John Purdin

PURDIN, JOHN NOLAN
B. July 16, 1942, Lynx, Ohio
BR TR 6'2" 185 lbs.

1964	LA	N	2	0	1.000	0.56	3	2	1	16	6	6	8	1	0	0	0	5	1	0	.200	2	0	0	0	0.7	1.000
1965			2	1	.667	6.75	11	2	0	22.2	26	13	16	0	2	0	0	3	0	0	.000	1	0	0	0	0.1	1.000
1968			2	3	.400	3.07	35	1	0	55.2	42	21	38	0	2	3	2	6	3	0	.500	2	8	0	0	0.3	1.000
1969			0	0	—	6.19	9	0	0	16	19	12	6	0	0	0	0	2	0	0	.000	1	3	0	0	0.4	1.000
4 yrs.			6	4	.600	3.92	58	5	1	110.1	93	52	68	1	4	3	2	16	4	0	.250	4	13	0	0	0.3	1.000

Year	Team		W	L	PCT	ERA	G	GS	CG	IP	H	BB	SO	ShO	W	L	SV	AB	H	HR	BA	PO	A	E	DP	TC/G	FA
															Relief Pitching			**Batting**									

Bob Purkey

PURKEY, ROBERT THOMAS
B. July 14, 1929, Pittsburgh, Pa.   BR TR 6'2"   175 lbs.

Year	Team		W	L	PCT	ERA	G	GS	CG	IP	H	BB	SO	ShO	W	L	SV	AB	H	HR	BA	PO	A	E	DP	TC/G	FA
1954	PIT	N	3	8	.273	5.07	36	11	0	131.1	145	62	38	0	1	1	0	26	2	0	.077	16	40	0	6	1.6	1.000
1955			2	7	.222	5.32	14	10	2	67.2	77	25	24	0	0	0	1	19	6	1	.316	2	16	1	0	1.4	.947
1956			0	0	–	2.25	2	0	0	4	2	0	1	0	0	0	0	0	0	0	–	0	1	0	0	0.5	1.000
1957			11	14	.440	3.86	48	21	6	179.2	194	38	51	1	5	3	2	45	5	0	.111	13	30	3	3	1.0	.935
1958	CIN	N	17	11	.607	3.60	37	34	17	250	259	49	70	3	0	0	0	81	9	1	.111	10	56	1	2	1.8	.985
1959			13	18	.419	4.25	38	33	9	218	241	43	78	1	2	1	1	66	11	0	.167	19	35	2	1	1.5	.964
1960			17	11	.607	3.60	41	33	11	252.2	259	59	97	1	0	0	0	83	11	0	.133	30	47	1	5	1.9	.987
1961			16	12	.571	3.73	36	34	13	246.1	245	51	116	1	0	0	0	80	8	1	.100	29	69	2	2	2.8	.980
1962			23	5	**.821**	2.81	37	37	18	288.1	260	64	141	2	0	0	0	107	11	2	.103	25	59	4	7	2.4	.955
1963			6	10	.375	3.55	21	21	4	137	143	33	55	1	0	0	0	41	4	0	.098	15	29	3	0	2.2	.936
1964			11	9	.550	3.04	34	25	9	195.2	181	49	78	2	1	1	1	58	3	0	.052	17	44	4	4	1.9	.938
1965	STL	N	10	9	.526	5.79	32	17	3	124.1	148	33	39	1	3	2	2	35	1	0	.029	8	28	1	1	1.2	.973
1966	PIT	N	0	1	.000	1.37	10	0	0	19.2	16	4	5	0	0	1	1	4	0	0	.000	0	10	1	1	1.1	.909
13 yrs.			129	115	.529	3.79	386	276	92	2114.2	2170	510	793	13	12	9	9	645	71	6	.110	184	464	23	32	1.7	.966

WORLD SERIES

| 1961 | CIN | N | 0 | 1 | .000 | 1.64 | 2 | 1 | 1 | 11 | 6 | 3 | 5 | 0 | 0 | 0 | 0 | 3 | 0 | 0 | .000 | 4 | 3 | 1 | 0 | 4.0 | .875 |

Oscar Purner

PURNER, OSCAR E.
B. 1873, Washington, D. C.

| 1895 | WAS | N | 0 | 0 | – | 9.00 | 1 | 0 | 0 | 2 | 4 | 3 | 0 | 0 | 0 | 0 | 0 | 1 | 0 | 0 | .000 | 0 | 0 | 0 | 0 | 0.0 | – |

Ambrose Puttmann

PUTTMANN, AMBROSE NICHOLAS (Putt)
B. Sept. 9, 1880, Cincinnati, Ohio   D. June 21, 1936, Jamaica, N. Y.   TL 6'4"   185 lbs.

1903	NY	A	2	0	1.000	0.95	3	1	0	19	16	4	8	0	0	0	0	7	1	0	.143	0	12	2	0	4.7	.857
1904			2	0	1.000	2.74	9	3	2	49.1	40	17	26	1	0	0	0	18	5	0	.278	2	17	1	0	2.2	.950
1905			2	7	.222	4.27	17	9	5	86.1	79	37	39	1	1	0	1	32	10	0	.313	3	28	5	0	2.1	.861
1906	STL	N	1	2	.333	5.30	4	4	0	18.2	23	9	12	0	0	0	0	6	2	0	.333	1	6	0	0	1.8	1.000
4 yrs.			7	9	.438	3.58	33	18	8	173.1	158	67	85	2	1	0	1	63	18	0	.286	6	63	8	0	2.3	.896

John Pyecha

PYECHA, JOHN NICHOLAS
B. Nov. 25, 1931, Aliquippa, Pa.   BR TR 6'5"   200 lbs.

| 1954 | CHI | N | 0 | 1 | .000 | 10.13 | 1 | 0 | 0 | 2.2 | 4 | 2 | 2 | 0 | 0 | 1 | 0 | 1 | 0 | 0 | .000 | 0 | 0 | 0 | 0 | 0.0 | – |

Ewald Pyle

PYLE, HERBERT EWALD (Lefty)
B. Aug. 27, 1910, St. Louis, Mo.   BL TL 6'½"   175 lbs.

1939	STL	A	0	2	.000	12.96	6	1	0	8.1	17	11	5	0	0	1	0	2	0	0	.000	1	3	0	1	0.7	1.000
1942			0	0	–	6.75	2	0	0	5.1	6	4	1	0	0	0	0	3	0	0	.000	0	0	0	0	0.0	–
1943	WAS	A	4	8	.333	4.09	18	11	2	72.2	70	45	25	1	0	2	1	20	2	0	.100	3	13	2	0	1.0	.889
1944	NY	N	7	10	.412	4.34	31	21	3	164	152	68	79	0	1	1	0	51	8	0	.157	10	28	1	2	1.3	.974
1945	2 teams		NY N	(6G 0–0)		BOS N	(4G 0–1)																					
"	total		0	1	.000	10.35	10	3	0	20	32	22	12	0	0	0	0	8	2	0	.250	0	5	0	1	0.5	1.000
5 yrs.			11	21	.344	5.03	67	36	5	270.1	277	150	122	1	1	5	1	84	12	0	.143	14	49	3	4	1.0	.955

Harlan Pyle

PYLE, HARLAN ALBERT (Firpo)
B. Nov. 29, 1905, Burchard, Neb.   BR TR 6'2"   180 lbs.

| 1928 | CIN | N | 0 | 0 | – | 20.25 | 2 | 1 | 0 | 1.1 | 1 | 4 | 1 | 0 | 0 | 0 | 0 | 1 | 0 | 0 | .000 | 0 | 0 | 0 | 0 | 0.0 | – |

Shadow Pyle

PYLE, HARRY THOMAS
B. Oct. 30, 1861, Reading, Pa.   D. Nov. 26, 1908, Reading, Pa.   5'8"   136 lbs.

1884	PHI	N	0	1	.000	4.00	1	1	1	9	9	6	4	0	0	0	0	4	0	0	.000	0	1	0	0	1.0	1.000
1887	CHI	N	1	3	.250	4.73	4	4	3	26.2	32	21	5	0	0	0	0	16	3	1	.188	1	9	0	0	2.5	1.000
2 yrs.			1	4	.200	4.54	5	5	4	35.2	41	27	9	0	0	0	0	20	3	1	.150	1	10	0	0	2.2	1.000

Tom Qualters

QUALTERS, THOMAS FRANCIS (Money Bags)
B. Apr. 1, 1935, McKeesport, Pa.   BR TR 6'½"   190 lbs.

1953	PHI	N	0	0	–	162.00	1	0	0	.1	4	1	0	0	0	0	0	0	0	0	–	0	0	0	0	0.0	–
1957			0	0	–	8.10	6	0	0	6.2	12	4	6	0	0	0	0	0	0	0	–	1	2	0	1	0.5	1.000
1958	2 teams		PHI N	(1G 0–0)		CHI A	(26G 0–0)																					
"	total		0	0	–	4.20	27	0	0	45	47	21	14	0	0	0	0	2	0	0	.000	2	11	0	2	0.5	1.000
3 yrs.			0	0	–	5.71	34	0	0	52	63	26	20	0	0	0	0	2	0	0	.000	3	13	0	3	0.5	1.000

Bill Quarles

QUARLES, WILLIAM H.
B. 1869, Petersburg, Va.   D. Mar. 25, 1897, Petersburg, Va.   6'3"

1891	WAS	AA	1	1	.500	8.18	3	2	2	22	32	12	10	0	0	0	0	11	0	0	.000	2	2	0	0	1.3	1.000
1893	BOS	N	2	1	.667	4.67	3	3	3	27	31	5	6	0	0	0	0	9	2	0	.222	0	6	1	0	2.3	.857
2 yrs.			3	2	.600	6.24	6	5	5	49	63	17	16	0	0	0	0	20	2	0	.100	2	8	1	0	1.8	.909

Mel Queen

QUEEN, MELVIN DOUGLAS
Son of Mel Queen.
B. Mar. 26, 1942, Johnson City, N. Y.   BL TR 6'1"   189 lbs.

1964	CIN	N	0	0	–	0.00	0	0	0	0	0	0	0	0	0	0	0	95	19	2	.200	0	0	0	0	0.0	–
1965			0	0	–	0.00	0	0	0	0	0	0	0	0	0	0	0	3	0	0	.000	0	0	0	0	0.0	–
1966			0	0	–	6.43	7	0	0	7	11	6	9	0	0	0	0	55	7	0	.127	0	1	0	0	0.1	1.000
1967			14	8	.636	2.76	31	24	6	195.2	155	52	154	2	3	1	0	81	17	0	.210	15	17	2	2	1.1	.941
1968			0	1	.000	5.89	5	4	0	18.1	25	6	20	0	0	0	0	8	1	0	.125	0	4	0	0	0.8	1.000
1969			1	0	1.000	2.25	2	2	0	12	7	3	7	0	0	0	0	6	1	0	.167	0	1	0	0	0.5	1.000
1970	CAL	A	3	6	.333	4.20	34	3	0	60	58	28	44	0	2	5	4	16	4	0	.250	1	5	0	0	0.2	.900
1971			2	2	.500	1.77	44	0	0	66	49	29	53	0	2	2	4	8	0	0	.000	1	8	1	0	0.2	.900

Year	Team		W	L	PCT	ERA	G	GS	CG	IP	H	BB	SO	ShO	W	L	SV	AB	H	HR	BA	PO	A	E	DP	TC/G	FA
															Relief Pitching			**Batting**									

Mel Queen *continued*

Year	Team		W	L	PCT	ERA	G	GS	CG	IP	H	BB	SO	ShO	W	L	SV	AB	H	HR	BA	PO	A	E	DP	TC/G	FA
1972			0	0	–	4.35	17	0	0	31	31	19	19	0	0	0	0	2	0	0	.000	1	4	0	0	0.3	1.000
9 yrs.			20	17	.541	3.14	140	33	6	390	336	143	306	2	7	8	14	*				18	40	3	2	0.4	.951

Mel Queen

QUEEN, MELVIN JOSEPH
Father of Mel Queen.
B. Mar. 4, 1918, Maxwell, Pa. D. Apr. 4, 1982, Fort Smith, Ark.

BR TR 6'½" 204 lbs.

Year	Team		W	L	PCT	ERA	G	GS	CG	IP	H	BB	SO	ShO	W	L	SV	AB	H	HR	BA	PO	A	E	DP	TC/G	FA
1942	NY	A	1	0	1.000	0.00	4	0	0	5.2	6	3	0	0	1	0	0	0	0	0	–	0	2	0	0	0.5	1.000
1944			6	3	.667	3.31	10	10	4	81.2	68	34	30	1	0	0	0	31	6	0	.194	1	7	0	0	0.8	1.000
1946			1	1	.500	6.53	14	3	1	30.1	40	21	26	0	0	0	0	7	1	0	.143	2	2	0	0	0.3	1.000
1947	2 teams		NY A	(5G 0–0)		PIT N	(14G 3–7)																				
"	total		3	7	.300	4.46	19	12	2	80.2	79	55	36	0	0	0	0	27	2	0	.074	5	7	1	1	0.7	.923
1948	PIT	N	4	4	.500	6.65	25	8	0	66.1	82	40	34	0	2	0	1	17	1	0	.059	6	8	1	0	0.6	.933
1950			5	14	.263	5.98	33	21	4	120.1	135	73	76	0	0	0	0	35	2	0	.057	9	13	0	0	0.7	1.000
1951			7	9	.438	4.44	39	21	4	168.1	149	99	123	1	0	1	0	47	5	0	.106	4	12	1	2	0.4	.941
1952			0	2	.000	29.70	2	2	0	3.1	8	4	3	0	0	0	0	0	0	0	–	0	0	0	0	0.0	–
8 yrs.			27	40	.403	5.09	146	77	15	556.2	567	329	328	3	3	1	1	164	17	0	.104	27	51	3	3	0.6	.963

Ed Quick

QUICK, EDWIN S.
Born Edwin S. Stillwell.
B. Baltimore, Md. D. June 19, 1913, Rocky Ford, Colo.

TR 5'11"

Year	Team		W	L	PCT	ERA	G	GS	CG	IP	H	BB	SO	ShO	W	L	SV	AB	H	HR	BA	PO	A	E	DP	TC/G	FA
1903	NY	A	0	0	–	9.00	1	1	0	2	5	1	0	0	0	0	0	1	0	0	.000	0	1	0	0	1.0	1.000

Frank Quinn

QUINN, FRANK WILLIAM
B. Nov. 27, 1927, Springfield, Mass.

BR TR 6'2" 180 lbs.

Year	Team		W	L	PCT	ERA	G	GS	CG	IP	H	BB	SO	ShO	W	L	SV	AB	H	HR	BA	PO	A	E	DP	TC/G	FA
1949	BOS	A	0	0	–	2.86	8	0	0	22	18	9	4	0	0	0	0	6	1	0	.167	3	3	0	0	0.8	1.000
1950			0	0	–	9.00	1	0	0	2	2	1	0	0	0	0	0	0	0	0	–	1	1	0	0	2.0	1.000
2 yrs.			0	0	–	3.38	9	0	0	24	20	10	4	0	0	0	0	6	1	0	.167	4	4	0	0	0.9	1.000

Jack Quinn

QUINN, JOHN PICUS
Born John Quinn Picus.
B. July 5, 1883, Jeanesville, Pa. D. Apr. 17, 1946, Pottsville, Pa.

BR TR 6' 196 lbs.

Year	Team		W	L	PCT	ERA	G	GS	CG	IP	H	BB	SO	ShO	W	L	SV	AB	H	HR	BA	PO	A	E	DP	TC/G	FA
1909	NY	A	9	5	.643	1.97	23	11	8	118.2	110	24	36	0	4	0	1	45	7	0	.156	5	52	2	3	2.6	.966
1910			18	12	.600	2.36	35	31	20	236.2	214	58	82	0	3	0	0	82	19	0	.232	8	111	3	5	3.5	.975
1911			8	10	.444	3.76	40	16	7	174.2	203	41	71	0	4	2	2	61	10	1	.164	4	65	2	2	1.8	.972
1912			5	7	.417	5.79	18	11	7	102.2	139	23	47	0	2	0	0	39	8	0	.205	4	39	1	0	2.4	.977
1913	BOS	N	4	3	.571	2.40	8	7	6	56.1	55	7	33	1	0	0	0	20	4	0	.200	0	24	0	1	3.0	1.000
1914	BAL	F	26	14	.650	2.60	46	42	27	342.2	335	65	164	4	2	1	1	121	33	2	.273	14	104	8	1	2.7	.937
1915	CHI		9	22	.290	3.45	44	31	21	273.2	289	63	118	0	2	2	1	110	29	0	.264	10	98	3	1	2.5	.973
1918	CHI		5	1	.833	2.29	6	5	5	51	38	7	22	0	1	0	0	18	4	0	.222	30	13	0	1	7.2	1.000
1919	NY	A	15	14	.517	2.63	38	31	18	264	242	65	97	4	3	1	0	91	19	0	.209	6	79	4	2	2.3	.955
1920			18	10	.643	3.20	41	31	16	253.1	271	48	101	2	1	0	3	88	8	2	.091	14	75	5	1	2.3	.947
1921			8	7	.533	3.48	33	13	6	129.1	158	32	44	0	3	2	0	41	9	1	.220	2	33	1	2	1.1	.972
1922	BOS		13	15	.464	3.48	40	32	16	256	263	59	67	4	1	3	0	91	9	1	.099	12	89	1	2	2.6	.990
1923			13	17	.433	3.89	42	28	16	243	302	53	71	1	2	2	7	80	18	0	.225	11	59	3	1	1.7	.959
1924			12	13	.480	3.20	43	25	13	227.2	237	51	64	2	3	0	7	77	14	0	.182	9	73	3	3	2.0	.965
1925	2 teams		BOS A	(19G 7–8)		PHI A	(18G 6–3)																				
"	total		13	11	.542	4.13	37	29	12	204.2	259	42	43	0	1	2	0	63	6	0	.095	12	67	2	3	2.2	.975
1926	PHI	A	10	11	.476	3.41	31	21	8	163.2	191	36	58	3	1	2	1	46	8	0	.174	8	47	4	3	1.9	.932
1927			15	10	.600	3.17	34	25	11	207.1	211	37	43	3	1	2	1	66	6	0	.091	4	47	0	2	1.5	1.000
1928			18	7	.720	2.90	31	28	18	211.1	239	34	43	4	0	0	1	79	13	0	.165	7	55	1	2	2.0	.984
1929			11	9	.550	3.97	35	17	8	161	182	39	41	0	4	2	2	60	8	0	.133	3	38	1	1	1.2	.976
1930			9	7	.563	4.42	35	7	0	89.2	109	22	28	0	8	5	9	34	9	1	.265	1	29	0	2	0.9	1.000
1931	BKN	N	5	4	.556	2.66	39	1	0	64.1	65	24	25	0	5	3	15	15	3	0	.200	0	17	1	2	0.5	.944
1932			3	7	.300	3.30	42	0	0	87.1	102	24	28	0	3	7	8	20	4	0	.200	1	20	0	0	0.5	1.000
1933	CIN	N	0	1	.000	4.02	14	0	0	15.2	20	5	3	0	0	1	1	1	0	0	.000	1	6	0	0	0.5	1.000
23 yrs.			247	217	.532	3.27	755	443	242	3934.2	4234	859	1329	28	54	35	57	1348	248	8	.184	166	1240	45	40	1.9	.969

WORLD SERIES

Year	Team		W	L	PCT	ERA	G	GS	CG	IP	H	BB	SO	ShO	W	L	SV	AB	H	HR	BA	PO	A	E	DP	TC/G	FA
1921	NY	A	0	1	.000	9.82	1	0	0	3.2	8	2	2	0	1	0	0	2	0	0	.000	0	1	0	1	1.0	1.000
1929	PHI	A	0	0	–	9.00	1	1	0	5	7	2	2	0	0	0	0	2	0	0	.000	0	0	0	0	–	–
1930			0	0	–	4.50	1	0	0	2	3	0	1	0	0	0	0	0	0	0	–	0	1	0	0	1.0	1.000
3 yrs.			0	1	.000	8.44	3	1	0	10.2	18	4	5	0	1	0	0	4	0	0	.000	0	2	0	1	0.7	1.000

Tad Quinn

QUINN, CLARENCE CARR
B. Sept. 21, 1882, Torrington, Conn. D. Aug. 7, 1946, Westbury, Conn.

TR 6'1"

Year	Team		W	L	PCT	ERA	G	GS	CG	IP	H	BB	SO	ShO	W	L	SV	AB	H	HR	BA	PO	A	E	DP	TC/G	FA
1902	PHI	A	0	1	.000	4.50	1	1	1	8	12	1	3	0	0	0	0	3	0	0	.000	0	1	1	0	2.0	.500
1903			0	0	–	5.00	2	0	0	9	11	5	1	0	0	0	0	3	2	0	.667	1	5	0	0	3.0	1.000
2 yrs.			0	1	.000	4.76	3	1	1	17	23	6	4	0	0	0	0	6	2	0	.333	1	6	1	0	2.7	.875

Wimpy Quinn

QUINN, WELLINGTON HUNT
B. May 12, 1918, Birmingham, Ala. D. Sept. 1, 1954, Santa Monica, Calif.

BR TR 6'2" 187 lbs.

Year	Team		W	L	PCT	ERA	G	GS	CG	IP	H	BB	SO	ShO	W	L	SV	AB	H	HR	BA	PO	A	E	DP	TC/G	FA
1941	CHI	N	0	0	–	7.20	3	0	0	5	3	3	2	0	0	0	0	2	1	0	.500	1	0	0	0	0.3	1.000

Luis Quintana

QUINTANA, LUIS JOAQUIN
Born Luis Joaquin Quintana y Santos.
B. Dec. 25, 1951, Vega Baja, Puerto Rico

BL TL 6'2" 175 lbs.

Year	Team		W	L	PCT	ERA	G	GS	CG	IP	H	BB	SO	ShO	W	L	SV	AB	H	HR	BA	PO	A	E	DP	TC/G	FA
1974	CAL	A	2	1	.667	4.15	18	0	0	13	17	14	11	0	2	1	0	0	0	0	–	0	1	0	0	0.1	1.000
1975			0	2	.000	6.43	4	0	0	7	13	6	5	0	0	2	0	0	0	0	–	0	0	0	0	0.0	–
2 yrs.			2	3	.400	4.95	22	0	0	20	30	20	16	0	2	3	0	0	0	0	–	0	1	0	0	0.0	1.000

Year	Team		W	L	PCT	ERA	G	GS	CG	IP	H	BB	SO	ShO	Relief Pitching			Batting				PO	A	E	DP	TC/G	FA
															W	L	SV	AB	H	HR	BA						

Art Quirk

QUIRK, ARTHUR LINCOLN
B. Apr. 11, 1938, Providence, R. I.   BR TL 5'11"   170 lbs.

Year	Team		W	L	PCT	ERA	G	GS	CG	IP	H	BB	SO	ShO	W	L	SV	AB	H	HR	BA	PO	A	E	DP	TC/G	FA
1962	BAL	A	2	2	.500	5.93	7	5	0	27.1	36	18	18	0	0	0	0	7	1	0	.143	2	7	0	0	1.3	1.000
1963	WAS	A	1	0	1.000	4.29	7	3	0	21	23	8	12	0	0	0	0	4	1	0	.250	1	3	1	0	0.7	.800
2 yrs.			3	2	.600	5.21	14	8	0	48.1	59	26	30	0	0	0	0	11	2	0	.182	3	10	1	0	1.0	.929

Dan Quisenberry

QUISENBERRY, DANIEL RAYMOND (Quiz)
B. Feb. 7, 1953, Santa Monica, Calif.   BR TR 6'2"   170 lbs.

Year	Team		W	L	PCT	ERA	G	GS	CG	IP	H	BB	SO	ShO	W	L	SV	AB	H	HR	BA	PO	A	E	DP	TC/G	FA
1979	KC	A	3	2	.600	3.15	32	0	0	40	42	7	13	0	3	2	5	0	0	0	—	0	10	1	2	0.3	.909
1980			12	7	.632	3.09	75	0	0	128	129	27	37	0	12	7	33	0	0	0	—	17	29	2	4	0.6	.958
1981			1	4	.200	1.74	40	0	0	62	59	15	20	0	1	4	18	0	0	0	—	8	23	1	1	0.8	.969
1982			9	7	.563	2.57	72	0	0	136.2	126	12	46	0	9	7	35	0	0	0	—	18	46	2	3	0.9	.970
1983			5	3	.625	1.94	69	0	0	139	118	11	48	0	5	3	45	0	0	0	—	8	30	3	1	0.6	.927
1984			6	3	.667	2.64	72	0	0	129.1	121	12	41	0	6	3	44	0	0	0	—	15	29	0	1	0.6	1.000
1985			8	9	.471	2.37	84	0	0	129	142	16	54	0	8	9	37	0	0	0	—	8	24	2	2	0.4	.941
1986			3	7	.300	2.77	62	0	0	81.1	92	24	36	0	3	7	12	0	0	0	—	9	19	1	3	0.5	.966
1987			4	1	.800	2.76	47	0	0	49	58	10	17	0	4	1	8	0	0	0	—	6	13	0	3	0.4	1.000
1988	2 teams	KC A (20G 0–1)				STL N	(33G 2–0)																				
"	total		2	1	.667	5.12	53	0	0	63.1	86	11	28	0	2	1	1	1	0	0	.000	1	18	1	1	0.4	.950
1989	STL	N	3	1	.750	2.64	63	0	0	78.1	78	14	37	0	3	1	6	4	1	0	.250	7	22	0	1	0.5	1.000
11 yrs.			56	45	.554	2.69	669	0	0	1036	1051	159	377	0	56	45	244	5	1	0	.200	97	263	13	22	0.6	.965
																	5th										

DIVISIONAL PLAYOFF SERIES

| 1981 | KC | A | 0 | 0 | — | 0.00 | 1 | 0 | 0 | 1 | 1 | 0 | 0 | 0 | 0 | 0 | 0 | 0 | 0 | 0 | — | 0 | 0 | 0 | 0 | 0.0 | — |

LEAGUE CHAMPIONSHIP SERIES

1980	KC	A	1	0	1.000	0.00	2	0	0	4.2	4	2	1	0	1	0	1	0	0	0	—	1	1	0	0	0.5	1.000
1984			0	1	.000	3.00	1	0	0	3	2	1	1	0	0	1	0	0	0	0	—	1	1	0	0	2.0	1.000
1985			0	1	.000	3.86	4	0	0	4.2	7	0	3	0	0	1	1	0	0	0	—	1	0	0	0	0.5	1.000
3 yrs.			1	2	.333	2.19	7	0	0	12.1	13	3	5	0	1	2	2	0	0	0	—	3	2	0	0	0.7	1.000

WORLD SERIES

1980	KC	A	1	2	.333	5.23	6	0	0	10.1	10	3	0	0	1	2	0	0	0	0	—	1	1	0	0	0.3	1.000
1985			1	0	1.000	2.08	4	0	0	4.1	5	3	3	0	1	0	1	0	0	0	—	1	1	0	0	0.5	1.000
2 yrs.			2	2	.500	4.30	10	0	0	14.2	15	6	3	0	2	2	1	0	0	0	—	2	2	0	0	0.4	1.000
															2nd	2nd											

Charlie Rabe

RABE, CHARLES HENRY
B. May 6, 1932, Boyce, Tex.   BL TL 6'1"   180 lbs.

Year	Team		W	L	PCT	ERA	G	GS	CG	IP	H	BB	SO	ShO	W	L	SV	AB	H	HR	BA	PO	A	E	DP	TC/G	FA
1957	CIN	N	0	1	.000	2.16	2	1	0	8.1	5	0	6	0	0	0	0	2	0	0	.000	0	0	0	0	0.0	—
1958			0	3	.000	4.34	9	1	0	18.2	25	9	10	0	0	2	0	4	0	0	.000	1	5	0	0	0.7	1.000
2 yrs.			0	4	.000	3.67	11	2	0	27	30	9	16	0	0	2	0	6	0	0	.000	1	5	0	0	0.5	1.000

Steve Rachunok

RACHUNOK, STEPHEN STEPANOVICH (The Mad Russian)
B. Dec. 5, 1916, Rittman, Ohio   BR TR 6'3½"   200 lbs.

Year	Team		W	L	PCT	ERA	G	GS	CG	IP	H	BB	SO	ShO	W	L	SV	AB	H	HR	BA	PO	A	E	DP	TC/G	FA
1940	BKN	N	0	1	.000	4.50	2	1	0	9	9	5	10	0	0	0	0	2	0	0	.000	0	3	0	0	1.5	1.000

Dick Radatz

RADATZ, RICHARD RAYMOND (The Monster)
B. Apr. 2, 1937, Detroit, Mich.   BR TR 6'6"   230 lbs.

Year	Team		W	L	PCT	ERA	G	GS	CG	IP	H	BB	SO	ShO	W	L	SV	AB	H	HR	BA	PO	A	E	DP	TC/G	FA
1962	BOS	A	9	6	.600	2.24	62	0	0	124.2	95	40	144	0	9	6	24	31	3	0	.097	5	8	1	0	0.2	.929
1963			15	6	.714	1.97	66	0	0	132.1	94	51	162	0	15	6	25	29	2	0	.069	4	9	2	0	0.2	.867
1964			16	9	.640	2.29	79	0	0	157	103	58	181	0	16	9	29	37	6	0	.162	5	11	2	0	0.2	.889
1965			9	11	.450	3.91	63	0	0	124.1	104	53	121	0	9	11	22	27	5	1	.185	5	14	1	1	0.3	.950
1966	2 teams	BOS A (16G 0–2)				CLE A	(39G 0–3)																				
"	total		0	5	.000	4.64	55	0	0	75.2	73	45	68	0	0	5	14	11	1	0	.091	1	5	1	0	0.1	.857
1967	2 teams	CLE A (3G 0–0)				CHI N	(20G 1–0)																				
"	total		1	0	1.000	6.49	23	0	0	26.1	17	26	19	0	1	0	5	4	1	0	.250	2	2	0	0	0.2	1.000
1969	2 teams	DET A (11G 2–2)				MON	N (22G 0–4)																				
"	total		2	6	.250	4.89	33	0	0	53.1	46	23	50	0	2	6	3	6	1	0	.167	3	6	0	0	0.3	1.000
7 yrs.			52	43	.547	3.13	381	0	0	693.2	532	296	745	0	52	43	122	145	19	1	.131	25	55	7	1	0.2	.920

George Radbourn

RADBOURN, GEORGE B. (Dordy)
Brother of Old Hoss Radbourn.
B. Apr. 8, 1856, Bloomington, Ill.   D. Jan. 1, 1904, Bloomington, Ill.

Year	Team		W	L	PCT	ERA	G	GS	CG	IP	H	BB	SO	ShO	W	L	SV	AB	H	HR	BA	PO	A	E	DP	TC/G	FA
1883	DET	N	1	2	.333	6.55	3	3	2	22	38	7	2	0	0	0	0	12	2	0	.167	1	4	0	0	1.7	1.000

Old Hoss Radbourn

RADBOURN, CHARLES GARDNER
Brother of George Radbourn.
B. Dec. 11, 1854, Rochester, N. Y.   D. Feb. 5, 1897, Bloomington, Ill.
Hall of Fame 1939.   BB TR 5'9"   168 lbs.

Year	Team		W	L	PCT	ERA	G	GS	CG	IP	H	BB	SO	ShO	W	L	SV	AB	H	HR	BA	PO	A	E	DP	TC/G	FA
1880	BUF	N	0	0	—	0.00									0	0	0	21	3	0	.143	0	0	0	0	0.0	—
1881	PRO	N	25	11	.694	2.43	41	36	34	325.1	309	64	117	3	1	1	0	270	59	0	.219	14	43	9	6	1.6	.864
1882			33	19	.635	2.09	55	52	51	474	429	51	201	6	1	0	0	326	78	1	.239	22	92	11	3	2.3	.912
1883			49	25	.662	2.05	76	68	66	632.1	563	56	315	4	3	2	1	381	108	3	.283	33	139	15	3	2.5	.920
1884			60	12	.833	1.38	75	73	73	678.2	528	98	441	11	1	1	0	361	83	1	.230	21	119	17	1	2.1	.892
1885			28	21	.571	2.20	49	49	49	445.2	423	83	154	2	0	0	0	249	58	0	.233	18	115	9	7	2.9	.937
1886	BOS	N	27	31	.466	3.00	58	58	57	509.1	521	111	218	3	0	0	0	253	60	2	.237	39	107	12	8	2.7	.924
1887			24	23	.511	4.55	50	50	48	425	505	133	87	1	0	0	0	175	40	1	.229	15	69	15	3	2.0	.848
1888			7	16	.304	2.87	24	24	24	207	187	45	64	1	0	0	0	79	17	0	.215	14	37	6	1	2.4	.895
1889			20	11	.645	3.67	33	31	28	277	282	72	99	1	0	0	0	122	23	1	.189	19	58	2	6	2.4	.975
1890	BOS	P	27	12	.692	3.31	41	38	36	343	352	100	80	1	1	1	0	154	39	0	.253	16	99	8	4	3.0	.935

Year	Team		W	L	PCT	ERA	G	GS	CG	IP	H	BB	SO	ShO	W	L	SV	AB	H	HR	BA	PO	A	E	DP	TC/G	FA

Old Hoss Radbourn *continued*

1891	CIN	N	11	13	.458	4.25	26	24	23	218	236	62	54	2	0	1	0	96	17	0	.177	8	36	6	1	1.9	.880
12 yrs.			311	194	.616	2.67	528	503	489	4535.1	4335	875	1830	35	8	5	2	*				219	914	110	43	2.4	.912
									7th																		

Roy Radebaugh

RADEBAUGH, ROY
B. Feb. 22, 1884, Champaign, Ill. D. Jan. 17, 1945, Cedar Rapids, Iowa
BR TR 5'7" 160 lbs.

| 1911 | STL | N | 0 | 0 | — | 2.70 | 2 | 1 | 0 | 10 | 6 | 4 | 1 | 0 | 0 | 0 | 0 | 3 | 0 | 0 | .000 | 0 | 4 | 0 | 0 | 2.0 | 1.000 |

Drew Rader

RADER, DREW LEON (Lefty)
B. May 14, 1901, Elmira, N. Y. D. June 5, 1975, Catskill, N. Y.
BR TL 6' 190 lbs.

| 1921 | PIT | N | 0 | 0 | — | 0.00 | 1 | 0 | 0 | 2 | 2 | 0 | 0 | 0 | 0 | 0 | 0 | 1 | 0 | 0 | .000 | 0 | 0 | 0 | 0 | 0.0 | — |

Paul Radford

RADFORD, PAUL REVERE
B. Oct. 14, 1861, Roxbury, Mass. D. Feb. 21, 1945, Boston, Mass.
BR TR 5'6" 148 lbs.

1884	PRO	N	0	2	.000	7.62	2	2	1	13	27	3	2	0	0	0	0	355	70	1	.197	0	3	1	0	2.0	.750
1885			0	2	.000	7.85	3	2	2	18.1	34	8	3	0	0	0	0	371	90	0	.243	1	4	0	0	1.7	1.000
1887	NY	AA	0	0	—	18.00	2	0	0	5	15	3	4	0	0	0	0	486	129	4	.265	0	0	0	0	0.0	—
1890	CLE	P	0	0	—	3.60	1	0	0	5	7	1	3	0	0	0	0	466	136	2	.292	1	5	1	0	7.0	.857
1891	BOS	AA	0	0	—	0.00	1	0	0	1	0	0	0	0	0	0	0	456	118	0	.259	0	0	0	0	0.0	—
1893	WAS	N	0	0	—	18.00	1	0	0	1	2	2	1	0	0	0	0	464	106	2	.228	0	0	0	0	0.0	—
6 yrs.			0	4	.000	8.52	10	4	3	43.1	85	17	13	0	0	0	0	*				2	12	2	0	1.6	.875

Hal Raether

RAETHER, HAROLD HERMAN (Bud)
B. Oct. 10, 1932, Lake Mills, Wis.
BR TR 6'1" 185 lbs.

1954	PHI	A	0	0	—	4.50	1	0	0	2	1	4	0	0	0	0	0	0	0	0	—	0	1	0	1	1.0	1.000
1957	KC	A	0	0	—	9.00	1	0	0	2	2	0	0	0	0	0	0	0	0	0	—	0	0	0	0	0.0	—
2 yrs.			0	0	—	6.75	2	0	0	4	3	4	0	0	0	0	0	0	0	0	—	0	1	0	1	0.5	1.000

Ken Raffensberger

RAFFENSBERGER, KENNETH DAVID
B. Aug. 8, 1917, York, Pa.
BR TL 6'2" 185 lbs.

1939	STL	N	0	0	—	0.00	1	0	0	1	2	0	1	0	0	0	0	—			—	0	0	0	0	0.0	—
1940	CHI	N	7	9	.438	3.38	43	10	3	114.2	120	29	55	0	4	4	3	30	5	0	.167	6	18	0	2	0.6	1.000
1941			0	1	.000	4.50	10	1	0	18	17	7	5	0	0	1	0	5	0	0	.000	2	7	0	1	0.9	1.000
1943	PHI	N	0	1	.000	1.13	1	1	1	8	7	2	3	0	0	0	0	3	0	0	.000	0	2	1	0	3.0	.667
1944			13	20	.394	3.06	37	31	18	258.2	257	45	136	3	1	2	0	80	11	0	.138	10	33	2	1	1.2	.956
1945			0	3	.000	4.44	5	4	1	24.1	28	14	6	0	0	0	0	8	0	0	.000	1	6	1	0	1.6	.875
1946			8	15	.348	3.63	39	23	14	196	203	39	73	2	0	0	6	60	10	0	.167	7	26	0	0	0.8	1.000
1947	2 teams		PHI N	(10G 2–6)		CHI N	(19G 6–5)																				
"	total		8	11	.421	4.51	29	22	10	147.2	182	37	54	1	1	2	1	52	10	0	.192	7	28	2	4	1.3	.946
1948	CIN	N	11	12	.478	3.84	40	24	7	180.1	187	37	57	4	3	0	0	62	7	0	.113	4	28	3	0	0.9	.914
1949			18	17	.514	3.39	41	38	20	284	289	80	103	5	1	1	0	90	16	1	.178	6	41	1	2	1.2	.979
1950			14	19	.424	4.26	38	35	18	239	271	40	87	4	0	0	0	82	11	1	.134	7	36	1	0	1.2	.977
1951			16	17	.485	3.44	42	33	14	248.2	232	38	81	5	2	2	5	82	10	0	.122	5	33	1	1	0.9	.923
1952			17	13	.567	2.81	38	33	18	247	247	45	93	6	0	2	1	75	8	1	.107	9	38	1	2	1.3	.979
1953			7	14	.333	3.93	26	26	9	174	200	33	47	1	0	0	0	57	8	1	.140	7	41	2	3	1.9	.960
1954			0	2	.000	7.84	6	1	0	10.1	15	3	5	0	0	2	0	2	1	0	.500	0	0	0	0	0.0	—
15 yrs.			119	154	.436	3.60	396	282	133	2151.2	2257	449	806	31	12	16	16	688	97	4	.141	71	335	17	16	1.1	.960

Al Raffo

RAFFO, ALBERT MARTIN
B. Nov. 27, 1941, San Francisco, Calif.
BR TR 6'5" 210 lbs.

| 1969 | PHI | N | 1 | 3 | .250 | 4.13 | 45 | 0 | 0 | 72 | 81 | 25 | 38 | 0 | 1 | 3 | 1 | 6 | 1 | 0 | .167 | 5 | 14 | 0 | 0 | 0.4 | 1.000 |

Pat Ragan

RAGAN, DON CARLOS PATRICK
B. Nov. 15, 1888, Blanchard, Iowa D. Sept. 4, 1956, Los Angeles, Calif.
BR TR 5'10½" 185 lbs.

1909	2 teams		CIN N	(2G 0–1)		CHI N	(2G 0–0)																				
"	total		0	1	.000	3.09	4	0	0	11.2	11	5	4	0	0	1	0	4	1	0	.250	1	1	0	0	0.5	1.000
1911	BKN	N	4	3	.571	2.11	22	7	5	93.2	81	31	39	2	0	0	1	29	4	0	.138	4	21	2	1	1.2	.926
1912			7	18	.280	3.63	36	26	12	208	211	65	101	1	1	2	1	67	4	0	.060	11	40	3	3	1.5	.944
1913			15	18	.455	3.77	44	32	14	264.2	284	64	109	0	3	3	0	91	15	0	.165	7	76	3	3	2.0	.965
1914			10	15	.400	2.98	38	26	14	208.1	214	85	106	1	1	2	3	75	10	0	.133	8	51	3	3	1.6	.952
1915	2 teams		BKN N	(5G 1–0)		BOS N	(33G 15–12)																				
"	total		16	12	.571	2.34	38	26	13	246.2	219	67	88	3	4	1	0	86	13	0	.151	8	56	3	2	1.8	.955
1916	BOS	N	9	9	.500	2.08	28	23	14	182	143	47	94	3	0	0	0	60	13	0	.217	3	52	2	2	2.0	.965
1917			6	9	.400	2.93	30	13	5	147.2	138	35	61	1	3	2	1	48	6	1	.125	6	42	1	1	1.6	.980
1918			8	17	.320	3.23	30	25	15	206.1	212	54	68	2	0	2	0	71	13	0	.183	6	60	2	1	2.3	.971
1919	3 teams		BOS N	(4G 0–2)		NY N	(7G 1–0)		CHI A	(1G 0–0)																	
"	total		1	2	.333	3.44	12	4	1	36.2	36	17	10	0	0	0	0	11	4	0	.364	2	12	1	0	1.3	.933
1923	PHI	N	0	0	—	6.00	1	0	0	3	6	0	0	0	0	0	0	2	1	0	.500	0	0	0	0	0.0	—
11 yrs.			76	104	.422	2.99	283	182	93	1608.2	1555	470	680	13	12	13	6	544	84	1	.154	56	411	20	16	1.7	.959

Frank Ragland

RAGLAND, FRANK ROLAND
B. May 26, 1904, Water Valley, Miss. D. July 28, 1959, Paris, Miss.
BR TR 6'1" 186 lbs.

1932	WAS	A	1	0	1.000	7.41	12	1	0	37.2	54	21	11	0	1	0	0	11	3	0	.273	3	8	0	1	0.9	1.000
1933	PHI	N	0	4	.000	6.81	11	5	0	38.1	51	10	4	0	0	1	0	10	2	0	.200	4	11	0	0	1.4	1.000
2 yrs.			1	4	.200	7.11	23	6	0	76	105	31	15	0	1	1	0	21	5	0	.238	7	19	0	1	1.1	1.000

Eric Raich

RAICH, ERIC JAMES
B. Nov. 1, 1951, Detroit, Mich.
BR TR 6'4" 225 lbs.

| 1975 | CLE | A | 7 | 8 | .467 | 5.54 | 18 | 17 | 2 | 92.2 | 118 | 31 | 34 | 0 | 1 | 0 | 0 | 0 | 0 | 0 | — | 5 | 11 | 1 | 0 | 0.9 | .941 |

Year	Team		W	L	PCT	ERA	G	GS	CG	IP	H	BB	SO	ShO	W	L	SV	AB	H	HR	BA	PO	A	E	DP	TC/G	FA

Eric Raich *continued*

Year	Team		W	L	PCT	ERA	G	GS	CG	IP	H	BB	SO	ShO	W	L	SV	AB	H	HR	BA	PO	A	E	DP	TC/G	FA
1976			0	0	–	15.00	1	0	0	3	7	0	1	0	0	0	0	0	0	0	–	0	0	0	0	0.0	–
	2 yrs.		7	8	.467	5.83	19	17	2	95.2	125	31	35	0	1	0	0	0	0	0	–	5	11	1	0	0.9	.941

Chuck Rainey

RAINEY, CHARLES DAVID
B. July 14, 1954, San Diego, Calif.
BR TR 5'11" 220 lbs.

Year	Team		W	L	PCT	ERA	G	GS	CG	IP	H	BB	SO	ShO	W	L	SV	AB	H	HR	BA	PO	A	E	DP	TC/G	FA
1979	BOS	A	8	5	.615	3.81	20	16	4	104	97	41	41	1	0	0	1	0	0	0	–	10	18	1	2	1.5	.966
1980			8	3	.727	4.86	16	13	2	87	92	41	43	1	0	0	0	0	0	0	–	4	10	2	2	1.0	.875
1981			0	1	.000	2.70	11	2	0	40	39	13	20	0	0	0	0	0	0	0	–	5	9	2	0	1.5	.875
1982			7	5	.583	5.02	27	25	3	129	146	63	57	3	0	0	0	0	0	0	–	17	19	1	0	1.4	.973
1983	CHI	N	14	13	.519	4.48	34	34	1	191	219	74	84	1	0	0	0	56	9	0	.161	28	38	7	2	2.1	.904
1984	2 teams		CHI N (17G 5–7)			OAK A (16G 1–1)																					
"	total		6	8	.429	4.92	33	16	0	119	145	55	55	0	1	1	1	31	3	0	.097	13	17	0	1	0.9	1.000
	6 yrs.		43	35	.551	4.50	141	106	10	670	738	287	300	6	1	1	2	87	12	0	.138	77	111	13	7	1.4	.935

Dave Rajsich

RAJSICH, DAVID CHRISTOPHER
Brother of Gary Rajsich.
B. Sept. 28, 1951, Youngstown, Ohio
BL TL 6'5" 175 lbs.

Year	Team		W	L	PCT	ERA	G	GS	CG	IP	H	BB	SO	ShO	W	L	SV	AB	H	HR	BA	PO	A	E	DP	TC/G	FA
1978	NY	A	0	0	–	4.05	4	2	0	13.1	16	6	9	0	0	0	0	0	0	0	–	0	1	0	0	0.3	1.000
1979	TEX	A	1	3	.250	3.50	27	3	0	54	56	18	32	0	1	1	0	0	0	0	–	1	13	0	0	0.5	1.000
1980			2	1	.667	6.00	24	1	0	48	56	22	35	0	0	0	2	0	0	0	–	0	7	0	1	0.3	1.000
	3 yrs.		3	4	.429	4.60	55	6	0	115.1	128	46	76	0	1	1	2	0	0	0	–	1	21	0	1	0.4	1.000

Ed Rakow

RAKOW, EDWARD CHARLES (Rock)
B. May 30, 1936, Pittsburgh, Pa.
BB TR 5'11" 178 lbs.
BR 1960-61

Year	Team		W	L	PCT	ERA	G	GS	CG	IP	H	BB	SO	ShO	W	L	SV	AB	H	HR	BA	PO	A	E	DP	TC/G	FA
1960	LA	N	0	1	.000	7.36	9	2	0	22	30	11	9	0	0	0	0	6	2	0	.333	1	4	0	0	0.6	1.000
1961	KC	A	2	8	.200	4.76	45	11	1	124.2	131	49	81	0	1	3	1	29	3	0	.103	12	19	1	3	0.7	.969
1962			14	17	.452	4.25	42	35	11	235.1	232	98	159	2	1	2	1	82	8	0	.098	17	45	5	3	1.6	.925
1963			9	10	.474	3.92	34	26	7	174.1	173	61	104	1	0	0	0	57	6	0	.105	15	30	1	3	1.4	1.000
1964	DET	A	8	9	.471	3.72	42	13	1	152.1	155	59	96	0	5	1	3	39	0	0	.000	16	28	0	2	1.0	1.000
1965			0	0	–	6.08	6	0	0	13.1	14	11	10	0	0	0	0	3	0	0	.000	0	0	1	0	0.2	–
1967	ATL	N	3	2	.600	5.26	17	3	0	39.1	36	15	25	0	1	2	0	10	0	0	.000	1	5	1	0	0.4	.857
	7 yrs.		36	47	.434	4.33	195	90	20	761.1	771	304	484	3	8	8	5	226	19	0	.084	62	131	9	11	1.0	.955

John Raleigh

RALEIGH, JOHN AUSTIN
B. Apr. 21, 1890, Elkhorn, Wis.   D. Aug. 24, 1955, Escondido, Calif.
BR TL

Year	Team		W	L	PCT	ERA	G	GS	CG	IP	H	BB	SO	ShO	W	L	SV	AB	H	HR	BA	PO	A	E	DP	TC/G	FA
1909	STL	N	1	10	.091	3.79	15	10	3	80.2	85	21	26	0	0	0	0	23	2	0	.087	4	24	3	0	2.1	.903
1910			0	0	–	9.00	3	1	0	5	8	0	2	0	0	0	0	1	0	0	.000	0	2	0	0	0.7	1.000
	2 yrs.		1	10	.091	4.10	18	11	3	85.2	93	21	28	0	0	0	0	24	2	0	.083	4	26	3	0	1.8	.909

Pep Rambert

RAMBERT, ELMER DONALD
B. Aug. 1, 1916, Cleveland, Ohio   D. Nov. 16, 1974, West Palm Beach, Fla.
BR TR 6' 195 lbs.

Year	Team		W	L	PCT	ERA	G	GS	CG	IP	H	BB	SO	ShO	W	L	SV	AB	H	HR	BA	PO	A	E	DP	TC/G	FA
1939	PIT	N	0	0	–	9.82	2	0	0	3.2	7	1	4	0	0	0	0	0	0	0	–	0	1	0	0	0.5	1.000
1940			0	1	.000	7.56	3	1	0	8.1	12	4	0	0	0	0	0	2	0	0	.000	0	2	0	0	0.7	1.000
	2 yrs.		0	1	.000	8.25	5	1	0	12	19	5	4	0	0	0	0	2	0	0	.000	0	3	0	0	0.6	1.000

Pete Rambo

RAMBO, WARREN DAWSON
B. Nov. 1, 1906, Thoroughfare, N. J.
BR TR 5'9" 150 lbs.

Year	Team		W	L	PCT	ERA	G	GS	CG	IP	H	BB	SO	ShO	W	L	SV	AB	H	HR	BA	PO	A	E	DP	TC/G	FA
1926	PHI	N	0	0	–	14.73	1	0	0	3.2	6	4	4	0	0	0	0	1	1	0	1.000	0	1	0	0	1.0	1.000

Allan Ramirez

RAMIREZ, DANIEL ALLAN
B. May 1, 1957, Victoria, Tex.
BR TR 5'10" 190 lbs.

Year	Team		W	L	PCT	ERA	G	GS	CG	IP	H	BB	SO	ShO	W	L	SV	AB	H	HR	BA	PO	A	E	DP	TC/G	FA
1983	BAL	A	4	4	.500	3.47	11	10	1	57	46	30	20	0	0	0	0	0	0	0	–	6	9	0	0	1.4	1.000

Pedro Ramos

RAMOS, PEDRO (Pete)
Born Pedro Ramos y Guerra.
B. Apr. 28, 1935, Pinar del Rio, Cuba
BR TR 6' 175 lbs.
BB 1960-61,1965-67

Year	Team		W	L	PCT	ERA	G	GS	CG	IP	H	BB	SO	ShO	W	L	SV	AB	H	HR	BA	PO	A	E	DP	TC/G	FA
1955	WAS	A	5	11	.313	3.88	45	9	3	130	121	39	34	1	3	4	5	38	3	0	.079	7	20	1	1	0.6	.964
1956			12	10	.545	5.27	37	18	4	152	178	76	54	0	6	2	0	44	9	0	.205	9	23	0	2	0.9	1.000
1957			12	16	.429	4.79	43	30	7	231	251	69	91	1	4	2	0	76	13	1	.171	8	41	0	4	1.1	1.000
1958			14	18	.438	4.23	43	37	10	259.1	277	77	132	4	0	0	3	88	21	0	.239	20	34	1	7	1.3	.982
1959			13	19	.406	4.16	37	35	11	233.2	233	52	95	0	1	1	0	75	11	1	.147	20	32	0	8	1.4	1.000
1960			11	18	.379	3.45	43	36	14	274	254	99	160	1	1	0	2	86	10	2	.116	16	44	0	2	1.4	1.000
1961	MIN	A	11	20	.355	3.95	42	34	9	264.1	265	79	174	3	1	2	2	93	16	3	.172	14	28	2	2	1.0	.955
1962	CLE	A	10	12	.455	3.71	37	27	7	201.1	189	85	96	2	0	1	1	68	10	3	.147	21	30	2	3	1.4	.962
1963			9	8	.529	3.12	36	22	5	184.2	156	41	169	3	0	2	1	55	6	3	.109	7	19	1	2	0.8	.963
1964	2 teams		CLE A	(36G 7–10)		NY A	(13G 1–0)																				
"	total		8	10	.444	4.60	49	19	0	154.2	157	26	119	0	4	4	8	44	7	2	.159	8	16	1	0	0.5	.960
1965	NY	A	5	5	.500	2.92	65	0	0	92.1	80	27	68	0	5	5	19	12	1	0	.083	6	11	2	0	0.3	.895
1966			3	9	.250	3.61	52	1	0	89.2	98	18	58	0	3	8	13	13	2	0	.154	7	13	1	0	0.4	.952
1967	PHI	N	0	0	–	9.00	6	0	0	8	14	8	1	0	0	0	0	1	0	0	.000	1	4	0	1	0.8	1.000
1969	2 teams		PIT N	(5G 0–1)		CIN N	(38G 4–3)																				
"	total		4	4	.500	5.23	43	0	0	72.1	81	24	44	0	4	4	2	9	0	0	.000	2	12	0	1	0.3	1.000
1970	WAS	A	0	0	–	7.88	4	0	0	8	10	4	10	0	0	0	0	1	0	0	.000	1	0	0	0	0.3	1.000
	15 yrs.		117	160	.422	4.08	582	268	73	2355.1	2364	724	1305	13	35	31	55	703	109	15	.155	146	328	11	33	0.8	.977

Willie Ramsdell

RAMSDELL, JAMES WILLARD (Willie the Knuck)
B. Apr. 4, 1916, Williamsburg, Kans.   D. Oct. 8, 1969, Wichita, Kans.
BR TR 5'11" 165 lbs.

Year	Team		W	L	PCT	ERA	G	GS	CG	IP	H	BB	SO	ShO	W	L	SV	AB	H	HR	BA	PO	A	E	DP	TC/G	FA
1947	BKN	N	1	1	.500	6.75	2	0	0	2.2	4	3	3	0	1	1	0	1	1	0	1.000	1	0	0	0	1.0	1.000
1948			4	4	.500	5.19	27	1	0	50.1	48	41	34	0	4	3	4	11	1	0	.091	4	13	0	0	0.6	1.000

Year	Team		W	L	PCT	ERA	G	GS	CG	IP	H	BB	SO	ShO	Relief Pitching W	L	SV	Batting AB	H	HR	BA	PO	A	E	DP	TC/G	FA

Willie Ramsdell *continued*

1950	2 teams	BKN N (5G 1–2)				CIN N	(27G 7–12)																				
"	total		8	14	.364	3.68	32	22	8	163.2	158	77	85	1	1	3	1	53	10	0	.189	8	24	1	0	1.0	.970
1951	CIN	N	9	17	.346	4.04	31	31	10	196	204	70	88	1	0	0	0	58	9	0	.155	7	29	3	3	1.3	.923
1952	CHI	N	2	3	.400	2.42	19	4	0	67	41	24	30	0	2	0	0	18	1	0	.056	6	10	4	1	1.1	.800
5 yrs.			24	39	.381	3.83	111	58	18	479.2	455	215	240	2	8	7	5	141	22	0	.156	26	77	8	4	1.0	.928

Toad Ramsey

RAMSEY, THOMAS A.
B. Aug. 8, 1864, Indianapolis, Ind.   D. Mar. 27, 1906, Indianapolis, Ind.   BR TL

1885	LOU	AA	3	6	.333	*1.94*	9	9	9	79	44	28	83	0	0	0	0	31	4	0	.129	1	11	5	1	1.9	.706
1886			38	27	.585	*2.45*	67	67	66	**588.2**	447	**207**	499	3	0	0	0	241	58	0	.241	14	78	23	1	1.7	.800
1887			37	27	.578	*3.43*	65	64	61	561	544	167	**355**	0	1	0	0	225	43	0	.191	7	88	31	0	1.9	.754
1888			8	30	.211	3.42	40	40	37	342.1	362	86	228	1	0	0	0	142	17	0	.120	8	57	18	1	2.1	.783
1889	2 teams	LOU AA (18G 1–16)				STL AA	(5G 3–1)																				
"	total		4	17	.190	5.22	23	21	18	181	219	81	93	0	1	0	0	74	20	0	.270	2	36	14	0	2.3	.731
1890	STL	AA	24	17	.585	3.69	44	40	34	348.2	325	102	257	1	2	1	0	145	33	0	.228	12	31	16	2	1.3	.729
6 yrs.			114	124	.479	3.29	248	241	225	2100.2	1941	671	1515	5	4	1	0	858	175	0	.204	44	301	107	5	1.8	.763

Ribs Raney

RANEY, FRANK ROBERT DONALD
Born Frank Robert Donald Raniszewski.
B. Feb. 16, 1923, Detroit, Mich.   BR TR 6'4"   190 lbs.

1949	STL	A	1	2	.333	7.71	3	3	1	16.1	23	12	5	0	0	0	0	6	0	0	.000	1	2	0	1	1.0	1.000
1950			0	1	.000	4.50	1	0	0	2	2	2	2	0	0	1	0	1	0	0	.000	0	1	0	0	1.0	1.000
2 yrs.			1	3	.250	7.36	4	3	1	18.1	25	14	7	0	0	1	0	7	0	0	.000	1	3	0	1	1.0	1.000

Vic Raschi

RASCHI, VICTOR JOHN ANGELO (The Springfield Rifle)
B. Mar. 28, 1919, West Springfield, Mass.   D. Oct. 14, 1988, Groveland, N. J.   BR TR 6'1"   205 lbs.

1946	NY	A	2	0	1.000	3.94	2	2	2	16	14	5	11	0	0	0	0	4	1	0	.250	1	3	0	0	2.0	1.000
1947			7	2	.778	3.87	15	14	6	104.2	89	38	51	1	0	0	0	40	10	0	.250	4	15	0	1	1.3	1.000
1948			19	8	.704	3.84	36	31	18	222.2	208	74	124	6	0	1	1	81	19	0	.235	12	28	0	3	1.1	1.000
1949			21	10	.677	3.34	38	**37**	21	274.2	247	138	124	3	1	0	0	83	13	0	.157	12	53	1	3	1.7	.985
1950			21	8	**.724**	4.00	33	32	17	256.2	232	116	155	2	0	0	1	86	17	1	.198	10	29	1	3	1.2	.975
1951			21	10	.677	3.27	35	**34**	15	258.1	233	103	**164**	4	0	0	0	85	15	0	.176	8	30	2	1	1.1	.950
1952			16	6	.727	2.78	31	31	13	223	174	91	127	4	0	0	0	69	13	0	.188	6	22	1	3	0.9	.966
1953			13	6	.684	3.33	28	26	7	181	150	55	76	4	1	0	1	63	9	0	.143	5	23	1	2	1.0	.966
1954	STL	N	8	9	.471	4.73	30	29	6	179	182	71	73	2	0	0	0	64	9	0	.141	16	35	1	3	1.7	.981
1955	2 teams	STL N (1G 0–1)				KC A	(20G 4–6)																				
"	total		4	7	.364	5.68	21	19	1	103	137	36	39	0	0	0	0	33	6	0	.182	10	21	1	1	1.5	.969
10 yrs.			132	66	.667	3.72	269	255	106	1819	1666	727	944	26	2	1	3	608	112	1	.184	84	259	8	20	1.3	.977
						5th																					

WORLD SERIES

1947	NY	A	0	0	—	6.75	2	0	0	1.1	2	0	1	0	0	0	0	0	0	0	—	0	0	0	0	0.0	—
1949			1	1	.500	4.30	2	2	0	14.2	15	5	11	0	0	0	0	5	1	0	.200	0	0	0	0	0.0	—
1950			1	0	1.000	0.00	1	1	1	9	2	1	5	1	0	0	0	3	1	0	.333	0	3	0	0	3.0	1.000
1951			1	1	.500	0.87	2	2	0	10.1	12	8	4	0	0	0	0	2	0	0	.000	0	0	0	0	0.0	—
1952			2	0	1.000	1.59	3	2	1	17	12	8	18	0	0	0	0	6	1	0	.167	0	1	0	0	0.3	1.000
1953			0	1	.000	3.38	1	1	1	8	9	3	4	0	0	0	0	2	0	0	.000	1	1	0	0	2.0	1.000
6 yrs.			5	3	.625	2.24	11	8	3	60.1	52	25	43	1	0	0	0	18	3	0	.167	1	5	0	0	0.5	1.000
			8th							10th	10th			10th													

Dennis Rasmussen

RASMUSSEN, DENNIS LEE
B. Apr. 18, 1959, Los Angeles, Calif.   BL TL 6'7"   230 lbs.

1983	SD	N	0	0	—	1.98	4	1	0	13.2	10	8	13	0	0	0	0	3	0	0	.000	0	4	0	1	1.0	1.000
1984	NY	A	9	6	.600	4.57	24	24	1	147.2	127	60	110	0	0	0	0	0	0	0	—	7	14	2	1	1.0	.913
1985			3	5	.375	3.98	22	16	2	101.2	97	42	63	0	0	0	0	0	0	0	—	7	13	0	2	0.9	1.000
1986			18	6	.750	3.88	31	31	3	202	160	74	131	1	0	0	0	0	0	0	—	6	26	0	0	1.0	1.000
1987	2 teams	NY A (26G 9–7)				CIN N	(7G 4–1)																				
"	total		13	8	.619	4.56	33	32	2	191.1	184	67	128	0	0	0	0	15	1	0	.067	6	30	2	0	1.2	.947
1988	2 teams	CIN N (11G 2–6)				SD N	(20G 14–4)																				
"	total		16	10	.615	3.43	31	31	7	204.2	199	58	112	1	0	0	0	70	14	0	.200	3	45	0	1	1.5	1.000
1989	SD	N	10	10	.500	4.26	33	33	1	183.2	190	72	87	0	0	0	0	65	11	0	.169	6	27	0	3	1.0	1.000
7 yrs.			69	45	.605	4.07	178	168	16	1044.2	967	381	644	2	0	0	0	153	26	0	.170	35	159	4	8	1.1	.980

Eric Rasmussen

RASMUSSEN, ERIC RALPH
Born Harold Ralph Rasmussen.
B. Mar. 22, 1952, Racine, Wis.   BR TR 6'3"   205 lbs.

1975	STL	N	5	5	.500	3.78	14	13	2	81	86	20	59	1	0	0	0	26	4	0	.154	2	11	0	0	0.9	1.000
1976			6	12	.333	3.53	43	17	2	150.1	139	54	76	1	3	5	0	38	4	0	.105	15	34	1	2	1.2	.980
1977			11	17	.393	3.48	34	34	11	233	223	63	120	3	0	0	0	72	10	0	.139	8	30	1	4	1.1	.974
1978	2 teams	STL N (10G 2–5)				SD N	(27G 12–10)																				
"	total		14	15	.483	4.09	37	34	5	206.2	215	63	91	3	0	0	0	64	9	0	.141	14	37	2	3	1.4	.962
1979	SD	N	6	9	.400	3.27	45	20	5	157	142	42	54	3	1	2	0	36	2	0	.056	8	24	1	1	0.7	.968
1980			4	11	.267	4.38	40	14	0	111	130	33	50	0	3	2	1	21	2	0	.095	8	15	2	2	0.6	.920
1982	STL	N	1	2	.333	4.42	8	3	0	18.1	21	8	15	0	1	0	0	3	0	0	.000	0	4	0	0	0.5	1.000
1983	2 teams	STL N (6G 0–0)				KC A	(11G 3–6)																				
"	total		3	6	.333	5.67	17	9	2	60.1	77	26	24	1	0	0	1	0	0	0	—	2	8	0	2	0.6	1.000
8 yrs.			50	77	.394	3.85	238	144	27	1017.2	1033	309	489	12	7	7	5	260	31	0	.119	55	163	7	14	0.9	.969

Hans Rasmussen

RASMUSSEN, HENRY FLORIAN
B. Apr. 18, 1895, Chicago, Ill.   D. Jan. 1, 1949, Chicago, Ill.   BR TR 6'6"   220 lbs.

| 1915 | CHI | F | 0 | 0 | — | 13.50 | 2 | 0 | 0 | 2 | 3 | 2 | 2 | 0 | 0 | 0 | 0 | 1 | 0 | 0 | .000 | 0 | 2 | 0 | 0 | 1.0 | 1.000 |

Year	Team	W	L	PCT	ERA	G	GS	CG	IP	H	BB	SO	ShO	W	L	SV	AB	H	HR	BA	PO	A	E	DP	TC/G	FA
														Relief Pitching			**Batting**									

Fred Rath

RATH, FREDERICK HELSHER
B. Sept. 1, 1943, Little Rock, Ark.

BR TR 6'3" 200 lbs.

Year	Team	W	L	PCT	ERA	G	GS	CG	IP	H	BB	SO	ShO	W	L	SV	AB	H	HR	BA	PO	A	E	DP	TC/G	FA
1968	CHI A	0	0	–	1.59	5	0	0	11.1	8	3	3	0	0	0	0	0	0	0		0	3	1	0	0.8	.750
1969		0	2	.000	7.71	3	2	0	11.2	11	8	4	0	0	0	0	3	0	0	.000	2	2	0	0	1.3	1.000
2 yrs.		0	2	.000	4.70	8	2	0	23	19	11	7	0	0	0	0	3	0	0	.000	2	5	1	0	1.0	.875

Steve Ratzer

RATZER, STEPHEN WAYNE
B. Sept. 9, 1953, Paterson, N. J.

BR TR 6' 180 lbs.

Year	Team	W	L	PCT	ERA	G	GS	CG	IP	H	BB	SO	ShO	W	L	SV	AB	H	HR	BA	PO	A	E	DP	TC/G	FA
1980	MON N	0	0	–	11.25	1	1	0	4	9	2	0	0	0	0	0	1	0	0	.000	1	2	0	0	3.0	1.000
1981		1	1	.500	6.35	12	0	0	17	23	7	4	0	1	1	0	2	0	0	.000	1	6	0	0	0.6	1.000
2 yrs.		1	1	.500	7.29	13	1	0	21	32	9	4	0	1	1	0	3	0	0	.000	2	8	0	0	0.8	1.000

Doug Rau

RAU, DOUGLAS JAMES
B. Dec. 15, 1948, Columbus, Tex.

BL TL 6'2" 175 lbs.

Year	Team	W	L	PCT	ERA	G	GS	CG	IP	H	BB	SO	ShO	W	L	SV	AB	H	HR	BA	PO	A	E	DP	TC/G	FA
1972	LA N	2	2	.500	2.20	7	3	2	32.2	18	11	19	0	1	0	0	7	1	0	.143	0	6	0	1	0.9	1.000
1973		4	2	.667	3.96	31	3	0	63.2	64	28	51	0	4	1	3	11	1	0	.091	1	8	0	0	0.3	1.000
1974		13	11	.542	3.73	36	35	3	198	191	70	126	0	1	0	0	64	9	0	.141	8	27	0	3	1.0	1.000
1975		15	9	.625	3.10	38	38	8	258	227	61	151	2	0	0	0	87	17	0	.195	6	40	5	1	1.3	.902
1976		16	12	.571	2.57	34	32	8	231	221	69	98	3	0	1	0	60	9	0	.150	5	39	1	1	1.3	.978
1977		14	8	.636	3.44	32	32	4	212	232	49	126	2	0	0	0	71	10	0	.141	3	30	0	1	1.0	1.000
1978		15	9	.625	3.26	30	30	7	199	219	68	95	2	0	0	0	63	9	0	.143	3	24	1	2	0.9	.964
1979		1	5	.167	5.30	11	11	1	56	73	22	28	1	0	0	0	14	2	0	.143	2	10	0	0	1.1	1.000
1981	CAL A	1	2	.333	9.00	3	3	0	10	14	4	3	0	0	0	0	0	0	0	–	2	0	0	0	0.3	1.000
9 yrs.		81	60	.574	3.35	222	187	33	1260.1	1259	382	697	11	5	2	3	377	58	0	.154	29	184	7	8	1.0	.968

LEAGUE CHAMPIONSHIP SERIES

Year	Team	W	L	PCT	ERA	G	GS	CG	IP	H	BB	SO	ShO	W	L	SV	AB	H	HR	BA	PO	A	E	DP	TC/G	FA
1974	LA N	0	1	.000	40.50	1	1	0	.2	3	1	0	0	0	0	0	0	0	0	–	0	0	0	0	0.0	–
1977		0	0	–	0.00	1	0	0	1	0	0	1	0	0	0	0	0	0	0	–	0	0	0	0	0.0	–
1978		0	0	–	3.60	1	1	0	5	5	2	1	0	0	0	0	1	0	0	.000	1	0	0	0	1.0	1.000
3 yrs.		0	1	.000	6.75	3	2	0	6.2	8	3	2	0	0	0	0	1	0	0	.000	1	0	0	0	0.3	1.000

WORLD SERIES

Year	Team	W	L	PCT	ERA	G	GS	CG	IP	H	BB	SO	ShO	W	L	SV	AB	H	HR	BA	PO	A	E	DP	TC/G	FA
1977	LA N	0	1	.000	11.57	2	1	0	2.1	4	0	1	0	0	0	0	0	0	0	–	0	1	0	0	1.0	–
1978		0	0	–	0.00	1	0	0	2	1	0	3	0	0	0	0	0	0	0	–	0	0	0	0	0.0	–
2 yrs.		0	1	.000	6.23	3	1	0	4.1	5	0	4	0	0	0	0	0	0	0	–	0	1	0	0	0.3	1.000

Bob Rauch

RAUCH, ROBERT JOHN
B. June 16, 1949, Brookings, S. D.

BR TR 6'4" 200 lbs.

Year	Team	W	L	PCT	ERA	G	GS	CG	IP	H	BB	SO	ShO	W	L	SV	AB	H	HR	BA	PO	A	E	DP	TC/G	FA
1972	NY N	0	1	.000	5.00	19	0	0	27	27	21	23	0	0	1	1	3	0	0	.000	1	5	0	0	0.3	1.000

Lance Rautzhan

RAUTZHAN, CLARENCE GEORGE
B. Aug. 20, 1952, Pottsville, Pa.

BR TL 6'1" 195 lbs.

Year	Team	W	L	PCT	ERA	G	GS	CG	IP	H	BB	SO	ShO	W	L	SV	AB	H	HR	BA	PO	A	E	DP	TC/G	FA
1977	LA N	4	1	.800	4.29	25	0	0	21	25	7	13	0	4	1	2	1	0	0	.000	0	5	1	1	0.2	.833
1978		2	1	.667	2.95	43	0	0	61	61	19	25	0	2	1	4	4	0	0	.000	9	15	1	0	0.6	.960
1979	2 teams	LA N	(12G 0–2)		MIL A	(3G 0–0)																				
"	total	0	2	.000	7.62	15	0	0	13	12	21	7	0	0	2	1	0	0	0	–	4	3	0	0	0.5	1.000
3 yrs.		6	4	.600	3.88	83	0	0	95	98	47	45	0	6	4	7	5	0	0	.000	13	23	2	1	0.5	.947

LEAGUE CHAMPIONSHIP SERIES

Year	Team	W	L	PCT	ERA	G	GS	CG	IP	H	BB	SO	ShO	W	L	SV	AB	H	HR	BA	PO	A	E	DP	TC/G	FA
1977	LA N	1	0	1.000	0.00	1	0	0	.1	0	0	0	0	1	0	0	0	0	0	–	0	0	0	0	0.0	–
1978		0	0	–	6.75	1	0	0	1.1	3	2	0	0	0	0	0	0	0	0	–	0	1	0	0	1.0	1.000
2 yrs.		1	0	1.000	5.40	2	0	0	1.2	3	2	0	0	1	0	0	0	0	0	–	0	1	0	0	0.5	1.000

WORLD SERIES

Year	Team	W	L	PCT	ERA	G	GS	CG	IP	H	BB	SO	ShO	W	L	SV	AB	H	HR	BA	PO	A	E	DP	TC/G	FA
1977	LA N	0	0	–	0.00	1	0	0	.1	0	0	0	0	0	0	0	0	0	0	–	0	1	0	0	1.0	1.000
1978		0	0	–	13.50	2	0	0	2	4	2	0	0	0	0	0	0	0	0	–	0	0	0	0	0.0	–
2 yrs.		0	0	–	11.57	3	0	0	2.1	4	2	0	0	0	0	0	0	0	0	–	0	1	0	0	0.3	1.000

Shane Rawley

RAWLEY, SHANE WILLIAM
B. July 27, 1955, Racine, Wis.

BR TL 6' 170 lbs.

Year	Team	W	L	PCT	ERA	G	GS	CG	IP	H	BB	SO	ShO	W	L	SV	AB	H	HR	BA	PO	A	E	DP	TC/G	FA
1978	SEA A	4	9	.308	4.12	52	2	0	111.1	114	51	66	0	4	7	4	0	0	0	–	8	20	1	1	0.6	.966
1979		5	9	.357	3.86	48	3	0	84	88	40	48	0	5	9	11	0	0	0	–	4	15	0	1	0.4	1.000
1980		7	7	.500	3.32	59	0	0	114	103	63	68	0	7	7	13	0	0	0	–	4	28	1	3	0.6	.970
1981		4	6	.400	3.97	46	0	0	68	64	38	35	0	4	6	8	0	0	0	–	1	15	0	1	0.3	1.000
1982	NY A	11	10	.524	4.06	47	17	3	164	165	54	111	0	4	5	3	0	0	0	–	5	29	1	1	0.7	.971
1983		14	14	.500	3.78	34	33	13	238.1	246	79	124	2	0	0	1	0	0	0	–	14	33	2	3	1.4	.959
1984	2 teams	NY A	(11G 2–3)		PHI N	(18G 10–6)																				
"	total	12	9	.571	4.44	29	28	3	162.1	163	54	82	0	0	0	0	43	5	0	.116	9	17	1	1	1.0	.929
1985	PHI N	13	8	.619	3.31	36	31	6	198.2	188	81	106	2	1	0	0	58	8	0	.138	12	36	1	2	1.4	.980
1986		11	7	.611	3.54	23	23	7	157.2	166	50	73	1	0	0	0	52	9	0	.173	4	28	0	2	1.6	.889
1987		17	11	.607	4.39	36	36	4	229.2	250	86	123	1	0	0	0	79	12	0	.152	6	34	1	2	1.1	.976
1988		8	16	.333	4.18	32	32	4	198	220	78	87	1	0	0	0	57	6	0	.105	9	33	2	2	1.4	.955
1989	MIN A	5	12	.294	5.21	27	25	1	145	167	60	68	0	0	0	0	0	0	0	–	4	20	2	1	1.0	.923
12 yrs.		111	118	.485	4.02	469	230	41	1871	1934	734	991	7	25	34	40	289	40	0	.138	80	308	17	22	0.9	.958

Carl Ray

RAY, CARL GRADY
B. Jan. 31, 1889, Danbury, N. C. D. Apr. 3, 1970, Walnut Cove, N. C.

BL TL 5'11" 170 lbs.

Year	Team	W	L	PCT	ERA	G	GS	CG	IP	H	BB	SO	ShO	W	L	SV	AB	H	HR	BA	PO	A	E	DP	TC/G	FA
1915	PHI A	0	1	.000	4.91	2	1	0	7.1	11	6	6	0	0	0	0	2	0	0	.000	0	0	0	0	0.0	–
1916		0	1	.000	4.82	3	1	0	9.1	9	14	5	0	0	0	0	3	0	0	.000	1	1	0	0	0.7	1.000
2 yrs.		0	2	.000	4.86	5	2	0	16.2	20	20	11	0	0	0	0	5	0	0	.000	1	1	0	0	0.4	1.000

Year	Team		W	L	PCT	ERA	G	GS	CG	IP	H	BB	SO	ShO	Relief Pitching			Batting			BA	PO	A	E	DP	TC/G	FA
															W	L	SV	AB	H	HR							

Farmer Ray

RAY, ROBERT HENRY
B. Sept. 17, 1886, Ft. Lyon, Colo.   D. Mar. 11, 1963, Electra, Tex.
BL TR 5'11" 160 lbs.

Year	Team		W	L	PCT	ERA	G	GS	CG	IP	H	BB	SO	ShO	W	L	SV	AB	H	HR	BA	PO	A	E	DP	TC/G	FA
1910	STL	A	4	10	.286	3.58	21	16	11	140.2	146	49	35	0	0	0	0	40	7	0	.175	4	34	5	1	2.0	.884

Jim Ray

RAY, JAMES FRANCIS (Sting)
B. Dec. 1, 1944, Rock Hill, S. C.
BR TR 6'1" 185 lbs.

Year	Team		W	L	PCT	ERA	G	GS	CG	IP	H	BB	SO	ShO	W	L	SV	AB	H	HR	BA	PO	A	E	DP	TC/G	FA
1965	HOU	N	0	2	.000	10.57	3	2	0	7.2	11	6	7	0	0	0	0	2	0	0	.000	1	2	0	0	1.0	1.000
1966			0	0	—	∞	1	0	0	0	1	0	0	0	0	0	0	0	0	0	—	0	0	0	0	0.0	—
1968			2	3	.400	2.67	41	2	1	81	65	25	71	0	1	2	1	15	1	0	.067	2	9	1	0	0.3	.917
1969			8	2	.800	3.91	40	13	0	115	105	48	115	0	4	0	0	26	3	0	.115	5	11	0	0	0.4	1.000
1970			6	3	.667	3.26	52	2	0	105	97	49	67	0	6	2	5	27	5	0	.185	4	17	1	1	0.4	.955
1971			10	4	.714	2.11	47	1	0	98	72	31	46	0	10	3	3	18	3	0	.167	2	7	0	0	0.2	1.000
1972			10	9	.526	4.30	54	0	0	90	77	44	50	0	10	9	8	16	1	0	.063	6	6	0	0	0.2	1.000
1973			6	4	.600	4.43	42	0	0	69	65	38	25	0	6	4	6	13	3	0	.231	4	9	0	0	0.3	1.000
1974	DET	A	1	3	.250	4.50	28	0	0	52	49	29	26	0	1	3	2	0	0	0	—	2	9	0	0	0.4	1.000
9 yrs.			43	30	.589	3.61	308	20	1	617.2	541	271	407	0	38	23	25	117	16	0	.137	26	70	2	1	0.3	.980

Curt Raydon

RAYDON, CURTIS LOWELL
B. Nov. 18, 1933, Bloomington, Ill.
BR TR 6'4" 190 lbs.

Year	Team		W	L	PCT	ERA	G	GS	CG	IP	H	BB	SO	ShO	W	L	SV	AB	H	HR	BA	PO	A	E	DP	TC/G	FA
1958	PIT	N	8	4	.667	3.62	31	20	2	134.1	118	61	85	1	0	1	1	38	1	0	.026	8	9	2	0	0.6	.895

Bugs Raymond

RAYMOND, ARTHUR LAWRENCE
B. Feb. 24, 1882, Chicago, Ill.   D. Sept. 7, 1912, Chicago, Ill.
BR TR 5'10" 180 lbs.

Year	Team		W	L	PCT	ERA	G	GS	CG	IP	H	BB	SO	ShO	W	L	SV	AB	H	HR	BA	PO	A	E	DP	TC/G	FA
1904	DET	A	0	1	.000	3.07	5	2	1	14.2	14	6	7	0	0	0	0	5	0	0	.000	3	10	0	0	2.6	1.000
1907	STL	N	2	4	.333	1.67	8	6	6	64.2	56	21	34	1	0	0	0	22	2	0	.091	5	16	1	2	2.8	.955
1908			15	25	.375	2.03	48	37	23	324.1	236	95	145	5	2	1	2	90	17	0	.189	12	108	8	1	2.7	.938
1909	NY	N	18	12	.600	2.47	39	31	18	270	239	87	121	2	3	1	0	89	13	0	.146	8	86	9	2	2.6	.913
1910			4	11	.267	3.81	19	11	6	99.1	106	40	55	0	1	2	0	32	5	0	.156	3	36	1	3	2.1	.975
1911			6	4	.600	3.31	17	9	4	81.2	73	33	39	1	2	1	0	25	5	0	.200	6	23	1	0	1.8	.967
6 yrs.			45	57	.441	2.49	136	96	58	854.2	724	282	401	9	8	5	2	263	42	0	.160	37	279	20	8	2.5	.940

Claude Raymond

RAYMOND, JEAN CLAUDE MARC (Frenchy)
B. May 7, 1937, St. Jean, Que., Canada
BR TR 5'10" 175 lbs.

Year	Team		W	L	PCT	ERA	G	GS	CG	IP	H	BB	SO	ShO	W	L	SV	AB	H	HR	BA	PO	A	E	DP	TC/G	FA
1959	CHI	A	0	0	—	9.00	3	0	0	4	5	2	1	0	0	0	0	—	0	0	0	1	0	0	1	0.3	1.000
1961	MIL	N	1	0	1.000	3.98	13	0	0	20.1	22	9	13	0	1	0	2	3	0	0	.000	2	5	0	0	0.5	1.000
1962			5	5	.500	2.74	26	0	0	42.2	37	15	40	0	5	5	10	8	0	0	.000	2	3	0	0	0.2	1.000
1963			4	6	.400	5.40	45	0	0	53.1	57	27	44	0	4	6	5	4	2	0	.500	4	12	0	1	0.4	1.000
1964	HOU	N	5	5	.500	2.82	38	0	0	79.2	64	22	56	0	5	5	0	14	1	0	.071	4	20	1	3	0.7	.960
1965			7	4	.636	2.90	33	7	2	96.1	87	16	79	0	3	2	5	26	3	0	.115	5	15	3	0	0.7	.870
1966			7	5	.583	3.13	62	0	0	92	85	25	73	0	7	5	16	9	1	0	.111	7	4	1	0	0.2	.917
1967	2 teams						HOU N	(21G 0–4)				ATL N	(28G 4–1)														
"	total		4	5	.444	2.89	49	0	0	65.1	64	18	31	0	4	5	10	7	1	0	.143	4	10	0	0	0.3	1.000
1968	ATL	N	3	5	.375	2.83	36	0	0	60.1	56	18	37	0	3	5	10	7	1	0	.143	4	12	2	0	0.5	.889
1969	2 teams						ATL N	(33G 2–2)				MON N	(15G 1–2)														
"	total		3	4	.429	4.89	48	0	0	70	77	21	26	0	3	4	2	11	2	0	.182	7	11	3	2	0.4	.857
1970	MON	N	6	7	.462	4.45	59	0	0	83	76	27	68	0	6	7	23	11	0	0	.000	6	7	4	0	0.3	.765
1971			1	7	.125	4.67	37	0	0	54	81	25	29	0	1	7	0	1	0	0	.000	4	13	0	0	0.5	1.000
12 yrs.			46	53	.465	3.66	449	7	2	721	711	225	497	0	42	51	83	101	11	0	.109	49	113	14	8	0.4	.920

Harry Raymond

RAYMOND, HARRY H.
Also known as Harry H. Truman.
B. Feb. 20, 1862, Utica, N. Y.   D. Mar. 21, 1925, San Diego, Calif.
5'9" 179 lbs.

Year	Team		W	L	PCT	ERA	G	GS	CG	IP	H	BB	SO	ShO	W	L	SV	AB	H	HR	BA	PO	A	E	DP	TC/G	FA
1889	LOU	AA	1	0	1.000	1.00	1	1	1	9	8	11	1	0	0	0	0	*				0	0	0	0	0.0	—

Barry Raziano

RAZIANO, BARRY JOHN
B. Feb. 5, 1947, New Orleans, La.
BB TR 5'10" 175 lbs.

Year	Team		W	L	PCT	ERA	G	GS	CG	IP	H	BB	SO	ShO	W	L	SV	AB	H	HR	BA	PO	A	E	DP	TC/G	FA
1973	KC	A	0	0	—	5.40	2	0	0	5	6	1	0	0	0	0	0	0	0	0	—	2	0	0	0	1.0	1.000
1974	CAL	A	1	2	.333	6.35	13	0	0	17	15	8	9	0	1	2	1	0	0	0	—	1	1	0	0	0.2	1.000
2 yrs.			1	2	.333	6.14	15	0	0	22	21	9	9	0	1	2	1	0	0	0	—	1	3	0	0	0.3	1.000

Rip Reagan

REAGAN, ARTHUR EDGAR
Born Arthur Edgar Ragan.
B. June 5, 1878, Lincoln, Ill.   D. June 8, 1953, Kansas City, Mo.
BR TR 5'11" 170 lbs.

Year	Team		W	L	PCT	ERA	G	GS	CG	IP	H	BB	SO	ShO	W	L	SV	AB	H	HR	BA	PO	A	E	DP	TC/G	FA
1903	CIN	N	0	2	.000	6.00	3	2	2	18	40	7	7	0	0	0	0	8	2	0	.250	1	4	0	0	1.7	1.000

Jeff Reardon

REARDON, JEFFREY JAMES
B. Oct. 1, 1955, Pittsfield, Mass.
BR TR 6' 190 lbs.

Year	Team		W	L	PCT	ERA	G	GS	CG	IP	H	BB	SO	ShO	W	L	SV	AB	H	HR	BA	PO	A	E	DP	TC/G	FA
1979	NY	N	1	2	.333	1.71	18	0	0	21	12	9	10	0	1	2	2	0	0	0	—	1	1	0	1	0.1	1.000
1980			8	7	.533	2.62	61	0	0	110	96	47	101	0	8	7	6	8	0	0	.000	1	7	4	0	0.2	.667
1981	2 teams						NY N	(18G 1–0)				MON N	(25G 2–0)														
"	total		3	0	1.000	2.18	43	0	0	70.1	48	21	49	0	3	0	8	5	0	0	.000	0	2	0	0	0.0	1.000
1982	MON	N	7	4	.636	2.06	75	0	0	109	87	36	86	0	7	4	26	10	1	0	.100	6	9	1	0	0.2	.938
1983			7	9	.438	3.03	66	0	0	92	87	44	78	0	7	9	21	8	1	0	.125	3	4	2	0	0.1	.778
1984			7	7	.500	2.90	68	0	0	87	70	37	79	0	7	7	23	9	0	0	.000	2	5	1	0	0.1	.875
1985			2	8	.200	3.18	63	0	0	87.2	68	26	67	0	2	8	41	7	2	0	.286	8	8	0	0	0.3	1.000
1986			7	9	.438	3.94	62	0	0	89	83	26	67	0	7	9	35	8	1	0	.125	8	10	1	0	0.3	1.000
1987	MIN	A	8	8	.500	4.48	63	0	0	80.1	70	28	83	0	8	8	31	0	0	0	—	2	6	0	1	0.1	1.000
1988			2	4	.333	2.47	63	0	0	73	68	15	56	0	2	4	42	0	0	0	—	1	2	0	0	0.0	1.000
1989			5	4	.556	4.07	65	0	0	73	68	12	46	0	5	4	31	0	0	0	—	1	1	0	0	0.1	1.000
11 yrs.			57	62	.479	3.03	647	0	0	892.1	757	301	722	0	57	62	266	55	5	0	.091	34	57	8	3	0.2	.919
																					4th						

Year	Team	W	L	PCT	ERA	G	GS	CG	IP	H	BB	SO	ShO	W	L	SV	AB	H	HR	BA	PO	A	E	DP	TC/G	FA
														Relief Pitching			Batting									

Jeff Reardon *continued*

DIVISIONAL PLAYOFF SERIES

| 1981 | MON N | 0 | 1 | .000 | 2.08 | 3 | 0 | 0 | 4.1 | 1 | 1 | 2 | 0 | 0 | 1 | 2 | 1 | 0 | 0 | .000 | 0 | 0 | 0 | 0 | 0.0 | – |

LEAGUE CHAMPIONSHIP SERIES

1981	MON N	0	0	–	27.00	1	0	0	1	3	0	0	0	0	0	0	0	0	0	–	0	0	0	0	0.0	–
1987	MIN A	1	1	.500	5.06	4	0	0	5.1	7	3	5	0	1	1	2	0	0	0	–	0	1	0	0	0.3	1.000
	2 yrs.	1	1	.500	8.53	5	0	0	6.1	10	3	5	0	1	1	2	0	0	0	–	0	1	0	0	0.2	1.000

WORLD SERIES

| 1987 | MIN A | 0 | 0 | – | 0.00 | 4 | 0 | 0 | 4.2 | 5 | 0 | 3 | 0 | 0 | 0 | 1 | 0 | 0 | 0 | – | 0 | 0 | 0 | 0 | 0.0 | – |

Jerry Reardon

REARDON, JEREMIAH
B. 1866, St. Louis, Mo.   D. Feb. 25, 1891, Deceased

| 1886 | 2 teams | | | STL N (1G 0–1) | | | | CIN AA (1G 0–1) | | | | | | | | | | | | | | | | | | |
| " | total | 0 | 2 | .000 | 9.00 | 2 | 2 | 1 | 10 | 15 | 9 | 0 | 0 | 0 | 0 | 0 | 7 | 1 | 0 | .143 | 0 | 1 | 0 | 0 | 0.5 | 1.000 |

Frank Reberger

REBERGER, FRANK BEALL (Crane)
B. June 7, 1944, Caldwell, Ida.   BL TR 6'5"   200 lbs.

1968	CHI N	0	1	.000	4.50	3	1	0	6	9	2	3	0	0	1	0	0	0	0	–	0	2	0	0	0.7	1.000
1969	SD N	1	2	.333	3.58	67	0	0	88	83	41	65	0	1	2	6	5	1	0	.200	6	23	1	0	0.4	.967
1970	SF N	7	8	.467	5.57	45	18	3	152	178	98	117	0	1	2	2	47	11	0	.234	15	19	4	1	0.8	.895
1971		3	0	1.000	3.89	13	7	0	44	37	19	21	0	0	0	0	13	3	0	.231	6	6	0	3	0.9	1.000
1972		3	4	.429	4.00	20	11	2	99	97	37	52	0	0	0	0	35	8	0	.229	4	22	1	0	1.4	.963
	5 yrs.	14	15	.483	4.51	148	37	5	389	404	197	258	0	2	5	8	100	23	0	.230	31	72	6	4	0.7	.945

John Reccius

RECCIUS, JOHN
Brother of Phil Reccius.   5'6½"
B. June 7, 1862, Louisville, Ky.   D. Sept. 1, 1930, Louisville, Ky.

1882	LOU AA	4	6	.400	3.03	13	10	9	95	106	22	31	1	0	0	0	266	63	1	.237	4	25	6	0	2.7	.829
1883		0	0	–	2.25	1	0	0	4	10	0	0	0	0	0	0	63	9	0	.143	1	2	0	0	3.0	1.000
	2 yrs.	4	6	.400	3.00	14	10	9	99	116	22	31	1	0	0	0	*				5	27	6	0	2.7	.842

Phil Reccius

RECCIUS, PHILIP
Brother of John Reccius.   5'9"   163 lbs.
B. June 7, 1862, Louisville, Ky.   D. Feb. 15, 1903, Louisville, Ky.

1884	LOU AA	6	7	.462	2.71	18	11	11	129.1	118	19	46	0	2	0	0	263	63	3	.240	10	24	1	0	1.9	.971
1885		0	4	.000	3.83	7	5	4	40	46	11	10	0	0	0	1	402	97	1	.241	2	10	0	1	1.7	1.000
1886		0	1	.000	9.00	1	1	0	3	7	3	0	0	0	0	0	13	4	0	.308	0	0	0	0	0.0	–
1887	CLE AA	0	0	–	7.71	1	0	0	7	8	5	0	0	0	0	0	266	56	0	.211	0	3	1	0	4.0	.750
	4 yrs.	6	12	.333	3.26	27	17	15	179.1	179	38	56	0	2	0	1	*				12	37	2	1	1.9	.961

Phil Redding

REDDING, PHILIP HAYDEN
B. Jan. 25, 1890, Crystal Springs, Miss.   D. Mar. 31, 1929, Greenwood, Miss.   BL TR 5'11½" 190 lbs.

1912	STL N	2	1	.667	4.97	3	3	2	25.1	31	11	9	0	0	0	0	8	0	0	.000	1	4	0	1	1.7	1.000
1913		0	0	–	6.75	1	0	0	2.2	2	1	1	0	0	0	0	1	0	0	.000	0	1	0	0	1.0	1.000
	2 yrs.	2	1	.667	5.14	4	3	2	28	33	12	10	0	0	0	0	9	0	0	.000	1	5	0	1	1.5	1.000

Pete Redfern

REDFERN, PETER IRVINE
B. Aug. 25, 1954, Glendale, Calif.   BR TR 6'2"   195 lbs.

1976	MIN A	8	8	.500	3.51	23	23	1	118	105	63	74	1	0	0	0	0	0	0	–	8	14	3	1	1.1	.880
1977		6	9	.400	5.19	30	28	1	137	164	66	73	0	1	0	0	0	0	0	–	11	23	1	1	1.2	.971
1978		0	2	.000	6.52	3	2	0	9.2	10	6	4	0	0	0	0	0	0	0	–	0	3	0	0	1.0	1.000
1979		7	3	.700	3.50	40	6	0	108	106	35	85	0	4	3	1	0	0	0	–	7	9	1	2	0.4	.941
1980		7	7	.500	4.54	23	16	2	105	117	33	73	0	1	1	2	0	0	0	–	9	10	2	0	0.9	.905
1981		9	8	.529	4.06	24	23	3	142	140	52	77	0	0	0	0	0	0	0	–	6	18	0	1	1.0	1.000
1982		5	11	.313	6.58	27	13	2	94.1	122	51	40	0	2	3	0	0	0	0	–	8	13	0	2	0.8	1.000
	7 yrs.	42	48	.467	4.54	170	111	9	714	764	306	426	1	8	7	3	0	0	0	–	49	90	7	6	0.9	.952

Bob Reed

REED, ROBERT EDWARD
B. Jan. 12, 1945, Boston, Mass.   BR TR 5'10"   175 lbs.

1969	DET A	0	0	–	1.84	8	1	0	14.2	9	8	9	0	0	0	0	2	1	0	.500	1	3	0	0	0.5	1.000
1970		2	4	.333	4.89	16	4	0	46	54	14	26	0	1	2	2	12	1	0	.083	2	4	0	0	0.4	1.000
	2 yrs.	2	4	.333	4.15	24	5	0	60.2	63	22	35	0	1	2	2	14	2	0	.143	3	7	0	0	0.4	1.000

Howie Reed

REED, HOWARD DEAN (Diz)
B. Dec. 21, 1936, Dallas, Tex.   D. Dec. 7, 1984, Corpus Christi, Tex.   BR TR 6'1"   195 lbs.

1958	KC A	1	0	1.000	0.87	3	1	1	10.1	5	4	5	0	0	0	0	2	0	0	.000	0	0	0	0	0.3	1.000
1959		0	3	.000	7.40	6	3	0	20.2	26	10	11	0	0	1	0	3	0	0	.000	0	2	1	0	0.5	.667
1960		0	0	–	0.00	1	0	0	1.2	2	0	1	0	0	0	0	0	0	0	–	0	0	0	0	0.0	–
1964	LA N	3	4	.429	3.20	26	7	0	90	79	36	52	0	0	1	1	20	2	0	.100	5	20	1	2	1.0	.962
1965		7	5	.583	3.12	38	5	0	78	73	27	47	0	6	3	1	12	0	0	.000	3	18	2	1	0.6	.913
1966	2 teams			LA N (1G 0–0)				CAL A (19G 0–1)																		
"	total	0	1	.000	2.82	20	1	0	44.2	40	15	17	0	0	0	1	7	0	0	.000	4	6	0	0	0.5	1.000
1967	HOU N	1	1	.500	3.44	4	2	0	18.1	19	2	9	0	0	0	0	4	0	0	.000	0	5	0	0	1.2	1.000
1969	MON N	6	7	.462	4.84	31	15	2	106	119	50	59	1	0	0	1	32	4	1	.125	10	27	0	1	1.2	1.000
1970		6	5	.545	3.13	57	1	0	89	81	40	42	0	6	4	5	10	0	0	.000	7	13	0	2	0.4	1.000
1971		2	3	.400	4.26	43	0	0	57	66	24	25	0	2	3	4	1	0	0	.000	3	9	0	0	0.3	1.000
	10 yrs.	26	29	.473	3.72	229	35	3	515.2	510	208	268	1	15	12	9	91	6	1	.066	32	98	4	8	0.6	.970

WORLD SERIES

| 1965 | LA N | 0 | 0 | – | 8.10 | 2 | 0 | 0 | 3.1 | 2 | 2 | 4 | 0 | 0 | 0 | 0 | 0 | 0 | 0 | – | 1 | 0 | 0 | 0 | 0.5 | 1.000 |

Year	Team	W	L	PCT	ERA	G	GS	CG	IP	H	BB	SO	ShO	Relief Pitching W	L	SV	Batting AB	H	HR	BA	PO	A	E	DP	TC/G	FA

Jerry Reed

REED, JERRY MAXWELL
B. Oct. 8, 1955, Bryson City, N. C.
BR TR 6'1" 190 lbs.

Year	Team	W	L	PCT	ERA	G	GS	CG	IP	H	BB	SO	ShO	W	L	SV	AB	H	HR	BA	PO	A	E	DP	TC/G	FA
1981	PHI N	0	1	.000	7.20	4	0	0	5	7	6	5	0	0	1	0	0	0	0	–	3	0	0	0	0.8	1.000
1982	2 teams	PHI N	(7G 1–0)		CLE A	(6G 1–1)																				
"	total	2	1	.667	4.07	13	1	0	24.1	26	6	11	0	2	0	0	0	0	0	–	1	3	1	0	0.4	.800
1983	CLE A	0	0	–	7.17	7	0	0	21.1	26	9	11	0	0	0	0	0	0	0	–	3	8	1	0	1.7	.917
1985		3	5	.375	4.11	33	5	0	72.1	67	19	37	0	3	2	8	0	0	0	–	13	8	0	1	0.6	1.000
1986	SEA A	4	0	1.000	3.12	11	4	0	34.2	38	13	16	0	1	0	0	0	0	0	–	4	3	0	0	0.6	1.000
1987		1	2	.333	3.42	39	1	0	81.2	79	24	51	0	1	2	7	0	0	0	–	10	8	0	1	0.5	1.000
1988		1	1	.500	3.96	46	0	0	86.1	82	33	48	0	1	1	1	0	0	0	–	6	14	1	2	0.5	.952
1989		7	7	.500	3.19	52	1	0	101.2	89	43	50	0	7	6	0	0	0	0	–	10	12	0	1	0.4	1.000
8 yrs.		18	17	.514	3.83	205	12	0	427.1	414	153	229	0	15	12	16	0	0	0	–	50	56	3	5	0.5	.972

Rick Reed

REED, RICHARD ALLEN
B. Aug. 16, 1964, Huntington, W. Va.
BR TR 6' 195 lbs.

Year	Team	W	L	PCT	ERA	G	GS	CG	IP	H	BB	SO	ShO	W	L	SV	AB	H	HR	BA	PO	A	E	DP	TC/G	FA
1988	PIT N	1	0	1.000	3.00	2	2	0	12	10	2	6	0	0	0	0	4	0	0	.000	0	3	0	1	1.5	1.000
1989		1	4	.200	5.60	15	7	0	54.2	62	11	34	0	0	0	0	13	1	0	.077	6	5	0	0	0.7	1.000
2 yrs.		2	4	.333	5.13	17	9	0	66.2	72	13	40	0	0	0	0	17	1	0	.059	6	8	0	1	0.8	1.000

Ron Reed

REED, RONALD LEE
B. Nov. 2, 1942, La Porte, Ind.
BR TR 6'6" 215 lbs.

Year	Team	W	L	PCT	ERA	G	GS	CG	IP	H	BB	SO	ShO	W	L	SV	AB	H	HR	BA	PO	A	E	DP	TC/G	FA
1966	ATL N	1	1	.500	2.16	2	2	0	8.1	7	4	6	0	0	0	0	2	0	0	.000	0	0	0	0	0.0	–
1967		1	1	.500	2.95	3	3	0	21.1	21	3	11	0	0	0	0	8	0	0	.000	1	7	0	0	2.7	1.000
1968		11	10	.524	3.35	35	28	6	201.2	189	49	111	1	0	0	0	62	10	0	.161	16	32	1	3	1.4	.980
1969		18	10	.643	3.47	36	33	7	241	227	56	160	1	0	0	0	80	10	0	.125	20	30	2	3	1.4	.962
1970		7	10	.412	4.40	21	18	6	135	140	39	68	0	0	1	0	44	4	0	.091	10	24	1	2	1.7	.971
1971		13	14	.481	3.73	32	32	8	222	221	54	129	1	0	0	0	74	11	0	.149	19	27	0	1	1.4	1.000
1972		11	15	.423	3.93	31	30	11	213	222	60	111	1	0	0	0	73	13	0	.178	15	36	3	3	1.7	.944
1973		4	11	.267	4.42	20	19	2	116	133	31	64	0	0	0	1	45	9	0	.200	15	20	1	1	1.8	.972
1974		10	11	.476	3.39	28	28	6	186	171	41	78	2	0	0	0	57	6	0	.105	11	21	0	2	1.1	1.000
1975	2 teams	ATL N	(10G 4–5)		STL N	(24G 9–8)																				
"	total	13	13	.500	3.52	34	34	8	250.1	274	53	139	2	0	0	0	82	15	0	.183	15	33	1	0	1.4	.980
1976	PHI N	8	7	.533	2.46	59	4	1	128	88	32	96	0	6	7	14	24	4	0	.167	7	13	2	1	0.4	.909
1977		7	5	.583	2.76	60	3	0	124	101	37	84	0	7	5	15	18	2	0	.111	6	16	0	0	0.4	1.000
1978		3	4	.429	2.23	66	0	0	109	87	23	85	0	3	4	17	6	0	0	.000	6	8	1	0	0.2	.933
1979		13	8	.619	4.15	61	0	0	102	110	32	58	0	13	8	5	10	3	0	.300	3	13	0	3	0.3	1.000
1980		7	5	.583	4.05	55	0	0	91	88	30	54	0	7	5	9	10	3	0	.300	14	15	0	1	0.5	1.000
1981		5	3	.625	3.10	39	0	0	61	54	17	40	0	5	3	8	6	3	0	.500	0	8	0	0	0.2	1.000
1982		5	5	.500	2.66	57	2	0	98	85	24	57	0	4	4	14	12	4	0	.333	8	21	0	2	0.5	1.000
1983		9	1	.900	3.48	61	0	0	95.2	89	34	73	0	9	1	8	6	1	0	.167	2	7	0	0	0.1	1.000
1984	CHI A	0	6	.000	3.08	51	0	0	73	67	14	57	0	0	6	12	1	0	0	.000	2	11	1	3	0.3	.929
19 yrs.		146	140	.510	3.46	751	236	55	2476.1	2374	633	1481	8	54	44	103	620	98	0	.158	170	342	13	25	0.7	.975

DIVISIONAL PLAYOFF SERIES

Year	Team	W	L	PCT	ERA	G	GS	CG	IP	H	BB	SO	ShO	W	L	SV	AB	H	HR	BA	PO	A	E	DP	TC/G	FA
1981	PHI N	0	0	–	3.00	4	0	0	6	5	3	4	0	0	0	0	0	0	0	–	0	0	0	0	0.0	–

LEAGUE CHAMPIONSHIP SERIES

Year	Team	W	L	PCT	ERA	G	GS	CG	IP	H	BB	SO	ShO	W	L	SV	AB	H	HR	BA	PO	A	E	DP	TC/G	FA
1969	ATL N	0	1	.000	21.60	1	1	0	1.2	5	3	3	0	0	0	0	0	0	0	–	0	1	0	0	1.0	1.000
1976	PHI N	0	0	–	7.71	2	0	0	4.2	6	2	2	0	0	0	0	1	0	0	.000	0	0	0	0	0.0	–
1977		0	0	–	1.80	3	0	0	5	3	2	5	0	0	0	0	0	0	0	–	0	0	0	0	0.0	–
1978		0	0	–	2.25	2	0	0	4	6	0	2	0	0	0	0	0	0	0	–	0	0	0	0	0.0	–
1980		0	1	.000	18.00	3	0	0	2	3	1	1	0	0	1	0	0	0	0	–	1	0	0	0	0.3	1.000
1983		0	0	–	2.70	2	0	0	3.1	4	1	3	0	0	0	0	0	0	0	–	0	1	0	0	0.5	1.000
6 yrs.		0	2	.000	6.53	13	1	0	20.2	27	9	16	0	0	1	0	1	0	0	.000	1	2	0	0	0.2	1.000

WORLD SERIES

Year	Team	W	L	PCT	ERA	G	GS	CG	IP	H	BB	SO	ShO	W	L	SV	AB	H	HR	BA	PO	A	E	DP	TC/G	FA
1980	PHI N	0	0	–	0.00	2	0	0	2	2	0	2	0	0	0	0	0	0	0	–	0	0	0	0	0.0	–
1983		0	0	–	2.70	3	0	0	3.1	4	2	4	0	0	0	1	0	0	0	–	0	0	0	0	0.0	–
2 yrs.		0	0	–	1.69	5	0	0	5.1	6	2	6	0	0	0	1	0	0	0	–	0	0	0	0	0.0	–

Bill Reeder

REEDER, WILLIAM EDGAR
B. Feb. 20, 1922, Dike, Tex.
BR TR 6'5" 205 lbs.

Year	Team	W	L	PCT	ERA	G	GS	CG	IP	H	BB	SO	ShO	W	L	SV	AB	H	HR	BA	PO	A	E	DP	TC/G	FA
1949	STL N	1	1	.500	5.08	21	1	0	33.2	33	30	21	0	1	0	0	3	0	0	.000	1	6	1	0	0.4	.875

Stan Rees

REES, STANLEY MILTON
B. Feb. 25, 1899, Cynthiana, Ky. D. Aug. 30, 1937, Lexington, Ky.
BL TL 6'3" 190 lbs.

Year	Team	W	L	PCT	ERA	G	GS	CG	IP	H	BB	SO	ShO	W	L	SV	AB	H	HR	BA	PO	A	E	DP	TC/G	FA
1918	WAS A	1	0	1.000	0.00	2	0	0	3	3	4	1	0	1	0	0	0	0	0	–	0	1	0	0	0.5	1.000

Bobby Reeves

REEVES, ROBERT EDWIN (Gunner)
B. June 24, 1904, Hill City, Tenn.
BR TR 5'11" 170 lbs.

Year	Team	W	L	PCT	ERA	G	GS	CG	IP	H	BB	SO	ShO	W	L	SV	AB	H	HR	BA	PO	A	E	DP	TC/G	FA
1931	BOS A	0	0	–	3.68	1	0	0	7.1	6	1	0	0	0	0	0	*				1	2	0	0	3.0	1.000

Mike Regan

REGAN, MICHAEL JOSEPH
B. Nov. 19, 1887, Phoenix, N. Y. D. May 22, 1961, Albany, N. Y.
BR TR 5'11" 165 lbs.

Year	Team	W	L	PCT	ERA	G	GS	CG	IP	H	BB	SO	ShO	W	L	SV	AB	H	HR	BA	PO	A	E	DP	TC/G	FA
1917	CIN N	11	10	.524	2.71	32	26	16	216	228	41	50	1	0	0	0	75	15	0	.200	10	77	4	1	2.8	.956
1918		5	5	.500	3.26	22	6	4	80	77	29	15	3	3	2	2	27	8	0	.296	6	21	3	0	1.4	.900
1919		0	0	–	0.00	1	0	0	2.1	1	0	1	0	0	0	0	1	0	0	.000	0	0	0	0	0.0	–
3 yrs.		16	15	.516	2.84	55	32	20	298.1	306	70	66	4	3	2	2	103	23	0	.223	16	98	7	1	2.2	.942

Phil Regan

REGAN, PHILIP RAYMOND (The Vulture)
B. Apr. 6, 1937, Ostego, Mich.
BR TR 6'3" 200 lbs.

Year	Team	W	L	PCT	ERA	G	GS	CG	IP	H	BB	SO	ShO	W	L	SV	AB	H	HR	BA	PO	A	E	DP	TC/G	FA
1960	DET A	0	4	.000	4.50	17	7	0	68	70	25	38	0	0	0	1	17	1	0	.059	1	8	0	1	0.5	1.000

Year	Team		W	L	PCT	ERA	G	GS	CG	IP	H	BB	SO	ShO	Relief Pitching W	L	SV	Batting AB	H	HR	BA	PO	A	E	DP	TC/G	FA

Phil Regan *continued*

Year	Team		W	L	PCT	ERA	G	GS	CG	IP	H	BB	SO	ShO	W	L	SV	AB	H	HR	BA	PO	A	E	DP	TC/G	FA
1961			10	7	.588	5.25	32	16	6	120	134	41	46	0	2	2	2	40	3	0	.075	7	8	0	0	0.5	1.000
1962			11	9	.550	4.04	35	23	6	171.1	169	64	87	0	1	2	0	63	13	0	.206	15	17	0	1	0.9	1.000
1963			15	9	.625	3.86	38	27	5	189	179	59	115	1	2	1	1	63	9	1	.143	6	20	1	0	0.7	.963
1964			5	10	.333	5.03	32	21	2	146.2	162	49	91	0	1	0	1	41	13	0	.317	13	20	0	1	1.0	1.000
1965			1	5	.167	5.05	16	7	1	51.2	57	20	37	0	0	0	0	12	1	0	.083	3	5	0	3	0.5	1.000
1966	LA	N	14	1	.933	1.62	65	0	0	116.2	85	24	88	0	14	1	21	21	3	0	.143	12	17	0	1	0.4	1.000
1967			6	9	.400	2.99	55	3	0	96.1	108	32	53	0	5	7	6	10	1	0	.100	3	23	2	1	0.5	.929
1968	2 teams	LA N	(5G 2-0)			CHI N	(68G 10-5)																				
"	total		12	5	.706	2.27	73	0	0	134.2	119	25	67	0	12	5	25	21	3	0	.143	9	23	2	1	0.5	.941
1969	CHI	N	12	6	.667	3.70	71	0	0	112	120	35	56	0	12	6	17	15	1	0	.067	8	20	0	1	0.4	1.000
1970			5	9	.357	4.74	54	0	0	76	81	32	31	0	5	9	12	9	0	0	.000	7	18	0	3	0.5	.920
1971			5	5	.500	3.95	48	1	0	73	84	33	28	0	4	5	6	8	0	0	.000	5	18	2	1	0.5	.920
1972	2 teams	CHI N	(5G 0-1)			CHI A	(10G 0-1)																				
"	total		0	2	.000	3.63	15	0	0	17.1	24	8	6	0	0	2	1	1	0	0	1.000	0	3	0	1	0.3	1.000
	13 yrs.		96	81	.542	3.84	551	105	20	1372.2	1392	447	743	1	58	40	92	321	49	1	.153	90	200	7	15	0.5	.976

WORLD SERIES

Year	Team		W	L	PCT	ERA	G	GS	CG	IP	H	BB	SO	ShO	W	L	SV	AB	H	HR	BA	PO	A	E	DP	TC/G	FA
1966	LA	N	0	0	—	0.00	2	0	0	1.2	0	1	2	0	0	0	0	0	0	0	—	0	1	0	0	0.5	1.000

Earl Reid

REID, EARL PERCY
B. June 8, 1913, Bangor, Ala. D. May 11, 1984, Cullman, Ala.   BL TR 6'3'' 190 lbs.

Year	Team		W	L	PCT	ERA	G	GS	CG	IP	H	BB	SO	ShO	W	L	SV	AB	H	HR	BA	PO	A	E	DP	TC/G	FA
1946	BOS	N	1	0	1.000	3.00	2	0	0	3	4	3	2	0	1	0	0	0	0	0	—	0	0	0	0	0.0	—

Bill Reidy

REIDY, WILLIAM JOSEPH (Wee Willie)
B. Oct. 9, 1873, Cleveland, Ohio D. Oct. 14, 1915, Cleveland, Ohio   BR TR 5'10'' 175 lbs.

Year	Team		W	L	PCT	ERA	G	GS	CG	IP	H	BB	SO	ShO	W	L	SV	AB	H	HR	BA	PO	A	E	DP	TC/G	FA
1896	NY	N	0	1	.000	7.62	2	1	1	13	24	2	1	0	0	0	0	5	0	0	.000	1	3	0	0	2.0	1.000
1899	BKN	N	1	0	1.000	2.57	1	1	1	7	9	2	2	0	0	0	1	3	0	0	.000	2	2	0	0	2.0	1.000
1901	MIL	A	16	20	.444	4.21	37	33	28	301.1	364	62	50	2	2	2	0	112	16	0	.143	10	72	4	2	2.3	.953
1902	STL	A	3	4	.429	4.45	12	9	7	95	111	13	16	0	0	1	0	41	8	0	.195	9	30	2	3	3.4	.951
1903	2 teams	STL A	(5G 1-4)			BKN N	(15G 7-6)																				
"	total		8	10	.444	3.61	20	18	16	147	183	21	29	1	0	0	0	52	10	0	.192	3	33	2	2	1.9	.947
1904	BKN	N	0	4	.000	4.46	6	4	2	38.1	49	6	11	0	0	0	0	32	5	0	.156	2	9	2	0	2.2	.846
	6 yrs.		28	39	.418	4.17	79	66	55	601.2	740	106	109	3	2	4	2	245	39	0	.159	27	149	10	7	2.4	.946

Art Reinhart

REINHART, ARTHUR CONRAD
B. May 29, 1899, Ackley, Iowa D. Nov. 11, 1946, Houston, Tex.   BL TL 6'1'' 170 lbs.

Year	Team		W	L	PCT	ERA	G	GS	CG	IP	H	BB	SO	ShO	W	L	SV	AB	H	HR	BA	PO	A	E	DP	TC/G	FA
1919	STL	N	0	0	—	0.00	1	0	0	0	0	0	0	0	0	0	0	0	0	0	—	0	0	0	0	0.0	—
1925			11	5	.688	3.05	20	16	15	144.2	149	47	26	1	0	0	0	67	22	0	.328	5	35	2	0	2.1	.952
1926			10	5	.667	4.22	27	11	9	143	159	47	26	0	2	2	0	63	20	0	.317	5	40	0	4	1.7	1.000
1927			5	2	.714	4.19	21	9	4	81.2	82	36	15	2	0	0	1	32	10	0	.313	2	13	0	3	0.7	1.000
1928			4	6	.400	2.87	23	9	3	75.1	80	27	12	1	2	2	2	24	4	0	.167	5	15	0	0	0.9	1.000
	5 yrs.		30	18	.625	3.60	92	45	31	444.2	470	157	79	4	4	4	3	186	56	0	.301	17	103	2	7	1.3	.984

WORLD SERIES

Year	Team		W	L	PCT	ERA	G	GS	CG	IP	H	BB	SO	ShO	W	L	SV	AB	H	HR	BA	PO	A	E	DP	TC/G	FA
1926	STL	N	0	1	.000	∞	1	0	0		1	4	0	0	0	0	0	0	0	0	—	0	0	0	0	0.0	—

Bobby Reis

REIS, ROBERT JOSEPH THOMAS
B. Jan. 2, 1909, Woodside, N. Y. D. May 1, 1973, St. Paul, Minn.   BR TR 6'1'' 175 lbs.

Year	Team		W	L	PCT	ERA	G	GS	CG	IP	H	BB	SO	ShO	W	L	SV	AB	H	HR	BA	PO	A	E	DP	TC/G	FA
1935	BKN	N	3	2	.600	2.83	14	2	1	41.1	46	24	7	0	1	2	2	85	21	0	.247	2	12	0	1	1.0	1.000
1936	BOS	N	6	5	.545	4.48	35	5	3	138.2	152	74	25	0	5	1	0	60	13	0	.217	10	47	0	2	1.6	1.000
1937			0	0	—	1.80	4	0	0	5	3	5	0	0	0	0	0	86	21	0	.244	0	1	0	0	0.3	1.000
1938			1	6	.143	4.99	16	2	1	57.2	61	41	20	0	1	4	0	49	9	0	.184	1	15	0	0	1.0	1.000
	4 yrs.		10	13	.435	4.27	69	9	5	242.2	262	144	52	0	7	7	2	*				13	75	0	3	1.3	1.000

Jack Reis

REIS, HARRIE CRANE
B. June 14, 1890, Cincinnati, Ohio D. July 20, 1939, Cincinnati, Ohio   BR TR 5'10½'' 160 lbs.

Year	Team		W	L	PCT	ERA	G	GS	CG	IP	H	BB	SO	ShO	W	L	SV	AB	H	HR	BA	PO	A	E	DP	TC/G	FA
1911	STL	N	0	0	—	0.96	3	0	0	9.1	5	8	4	0	0	0	0	2	0	0	.000	1	3	0	0	1.3	1.000

Laurie Reis

REIS, LAWRENCE P.
B. Nov. 20, 1858, Chicago, Ill. D. Jan. 24, 1921, Chicago, Ill.   BR TR   160 lbs.

Year	Team		W	L	PCT	ERA	G	GS	CG	IP	H	BB	SO	ShO	W	L	SV	AB	H	HR	BA	PO	A	E	DP	TC/G	FA
1877	CHI	N	3	1	.750	0.75	4	4	4	36	29	6	11	1	0	0	0	16	2	0	.125	1	4	0	0	1.3	1.000
1878			1	3	.250	3.25	4	4	4	36	55	4	8	0	0	0	0	20	3	0	.150	1	3	4	0	2.0	.500
	2 yrs.		4	4	.500	2.00	8	8	8	72	84	10	19	1	0	0	0	36	5	0	.139	2	7	4	0	1.6	.692

Tommy Reis

REIS, THOMAS EDWARD
B. Aug. 6, 1914, Newport, Ky.   BR TR 6'2'' 180 lbs.

Year	Team		W	L	PCT	ERA	G	GS	CG	IP	H	BB	SO	ShO	W	L	SV	AB	H	HR	BA	PO	A	E	DP	TC/G	FA
1938	2 teams	PHI N	(4G 0-1)			BOS N	(4G 0-0)																				
"	total		0	1	.000	12.27	8	0	0	11	16	9	6	0	0	1	0	2	0	0	.000	1	1	0	0	0.3	1.000

Bugs Reisigl

REISIGL, JACOB
B. Dec. 12, 1887, Brooklyn, N. Y. D. Feb. 24, 1957, Amsterdam, N. Y.   BR TR 5'10½'' 175 lbs.

Year	Team		W	L	PCT	ERA	G	GS	CG	IP	H	BB	SO	ShO	W	L	SV	AB	H	HR	BA	PO	A	E	DP	TC/G	FA
1911	CLE	A	0	1	.000	6.23	2	1	1	13	13	3	6	0	0	0	0	5	0	0	.000	0	3	0	0	1.5	1.000

Doc Reisling

REISLING, FRANK CARL
B. July 25, 1874, Martin's Ferry, Ohio D. Mar. 4, 1955, Tulsa, Okla.   BR TR 5'10'' 180 lbs.

Year	Team		W	L	PCT	ERA	G	GS	CG	IP	H	BB	SO	ShO	W	L	SV	AB	H	HR	BA	PO	A	E	DP	TC/G	FA
1904	BKN	N	3	4	.429	2.12	7	7	6	51	45	10	19	1	0	0	0	13	2	0	.154	5	14	2	1	3.0	.905
1905			0	1	.000	3.00	2	0	0	3	3	4	2	0	0	0	0	1	0	0	.000	0	1	0	0	0.5	1.000
1909	WAS	A	2	4	.333	2.43	10	6	6	66.2	70	17	22	1	0	0	0	24	4	0	.167	3	14	0	0	1.7	1.000
1910			10	10	.500	2.54	30	20	13	191	185	44	57	2	1	1	0	60	12	0	.200	7	65	3	1	2.5	.960
	4 yrs.		15	19	.441	2.45	49	33	25	311.2	303	75	100	4	1	1	0	98	18	0	.184	15	94	5	2	2.3	.956

Year	Team	W	L	PCT	ERA	G	GS	CG	IP	H	BB	SO	ShO	Relief Pitching W	L	SV	Batting AB	H	HR	BA	PO	A	E	DP	TC/G	FA

Win Remmerswaal

REMMERSWAAL, WILHELMUS ABRAHAM
B. Mar. 8, 1954, The Hague, Netherlands   BR TR 6'2"   160 lbs.

Year	Team	W	L	PCT	ERA	G	GS	CG	IP	H	BB	SO	ShO	W	L	SV	AB	H	HR	BA	PO	A	E	DP	TC/G	FA
1979	BOS A	1	0	1.000	7.20	8	0	0	20	26	12	16	0	1	0	0	0	0	0	–	1	1	0	0	0.3	1.000
1980		2	1	.667	4.63	14	0	0	35	39	9	20	0	2	1	0	0	0	0	–	1	1	0	0	0.1	1.000
2 yrs.		3	1	.750	5.56	22	0	0	55	65	21	36	0	3	1	0	0	0	0	–	2	2	0	0	0.2	1.000

Alex Remneas

REMNEAS, ALEXANDER NORMAN
B. Feb. 21, 1886, Minneapolis, Minn. D. Aug. 27, 1975, Phoenix, Ariz.   BR TR 6'1"   180 lbs.

Year	Team	W	L	PCT	ERA	G	GS	CG	IP	H	BB	SO	ShO	W	L	SV	AB	H	HR	BA	PO	A	E	DP	TC/G	FA
1912	DET A	0	0	–	27.00	1	0	0	1.2	5	0	0	0	0	0	0	0	0	0	–	0	1	0	0	1.0	1.000
1915	STL A	0	0	–	1.50	2	0	0	6	3	3	5	0	0	0	0	1	0	0	.000	0	2	0	0	1.0	1.000
2 yrs.		0	0	–	7.04	3	0	0	7.2	8	3	5	0	0	0	0	1	0	0	.000	0	3	0	0	1.0	1.000

Erwin Renfer

RENFER, ERWIN ARTHUR
B. Dec. 11, 1895, Elgin, Ill. D. Oct. 26, 1958, Sycamore, Ill.   BR TR 6'   180 lbs.

Year	Team	W	L	PCT	ERA	G	GS	CG	IP	H	BB	SO	ShO	W	L	SV	AB	H	HR	BA	PO	A	E	DP	TC/G	FA
1913	DET A	0	1	.000	6.00	1	1	0	6	5	3	1	0	0	0	0	2	0	0	.000	0	2	0	1	2.0	1.000

Marshall Renfroe

RENFROE, MARSHALL DANIEL
B. May 25, 1936, Century, Fla. D. Dec. 10, 1970, Pensacola, Fla.   BL TL 6'   180 lbs.

Year	Team	W	L	PCT	ERA	G	GS	CG	IP	H	BB	SO	ShO	W	L	SV	AB	H	HR	BA	PO	A	E	DP	TC/G	FA
1959	SF N	0	0	–	27.00	1	1	0	2	3	2	3	0	0	0	0	1	0	0	.000	0	0	0	0	0.0	–

Hal Reniff

RENIFF, HAROLD EUGENE (Porky)
B. July 2, 1938, Warren, Ohio   BR TR 6'   215 lbs.

Year	Team	W	L	PCT	ERA	G	GS	CG	IP	H	BB	SO	ShO	W	L	SV	AB	H	HR	BA	PO	A	E	DP	TC/G	FA
1961	NY A	2	0	1.000	2.58	25	0	0	45.1	31	31	21	0	2	0	2	5	0	0	.000	3	5	1	0	0.4	.889
1962		0	0	–	7.36	2	0	0	3.2	6	5	1	0	0	0	0	0	0	0	–	0	0	0	0	0.0	–
1963		4	3	.571	2.62	48	0	0	89.1	63	42	56	0	4	3	18	15	0	0	.000	8	25	2	2	0.7	.943
1964		6	4	.600	3.12	41	0	0	69.1	47	30	38	0	6	4	9	10	1	0	.100	4	13	1	1	0.4	.944
1965		3	4	.429	3.80	51	0	0	85.1	74	48	74	0	3	4	3	2	0	0	.000	11	8	0	0	0.4	1.000
1966		3	7	.300	3.21	56	0	0	95.1	80	49	79	0	3	7	9	14	4	0	.286	12	6	0	1	0.3	1.000
1967	2 teams	NY A (24G 0-2)			NY N	(29G 3-3)																				
"	total	3	5	.375	3.80	53	0	0	83	82	37	45	0	3	5	4	6	0	0	.000	6	7	0	1	0.2	1.000
7 yrs.		21	23	.477	3.27	276	0	0	471.1	383	242	314	0	21	23	45	52	5	0	.096	44	64	4	5	0.4	.964

WORLD SERIES

Year	Team	W	L	PCT	ERA	G	GS	CG	IP	H	BB	SO	ShO	W	L	SV	AB	H	HR	BA	PO	A	E	DP	TC/G	FA
1963	NY A	0	0	–	0.00	3	0	0	3	0	1	1	0	0	0	0	0	0	0	–	1	1	0	0	0.7	1.000
1964		0	0	–	0.00	1	0	0	.1	2	0	0	0	0	0	0	0	0	0	–	0	0	0	0	0.0	–
2 yrs.		0	0	–	0.00	4	0	0	3.1	2	1	1	0	0	0	0	0	0	0	–	1	1	0	0	0.5	1.000

Jim Reninger

RENINGER, JAMES DAVID
B. Mar. 7, 1913, Aurora, Ill.   BR TR 6'3"   210 lbs.

Year	Team	W	L	PCT	ERA	G	GS	CG	IP	H	BB	SO	ShO	W	L	SV	AB	H	HR	BA	PO	A	E	DP	TC/G	FA
1938	PHI A	0	2	.000	6.85	4	4	1	23.2	28	14	9	0	0	0	0	7	0	0	.000	0	6	0	0	1.5	1.000
1939		0	2	.000	7.71	4	2	0	16.1	24	12	3	0	0	0	0	6	1	0	.167	3	2	0	0	1.3	1.000
2 yrs.		0	4	.000	7.20	8	6	1	40	52	26	12	0	0	0	0	13	1	0	.077	3	8	0	0	1.4	1.000

Steve Renko

RENKO, STEVEN
B. Dec. 10, 1944, Kansas City, Kans.   BR TR 6'5"   230 lbs.

Year	Team	W	L	PCT	ERA	G	GS	CG	IP	H	BB	SO	ShO	W	L	SV	AB	H	HR	BA	PO	A	E	DP	TC/G	FA
1969	MON N	6	7	.462	4.02	18	15	4	103	94	50	68	0	0	0	0	36	6	1	.167	7	13	1	0	1.2	.952
1970		13	11	.542	4.32	41	33	7	223	203	104	142	1	0	0	1	80	16	1	.200	17	31	7	3	1.3	.873
1971		15	14	.517	3.75	40	37	9	276	256	135	129	3	0	0	0	100	21	2	.210	17	36	3	2	1.4	.946
1972		1	10	.091	5.20	30	12	0	97	96	67	66	0	0	0	0	24	7	0	.292	4	17	1	1	0.7	.955
1973		15	11	.577	2.81	36	34	9	249.2	201	108	164	0	0	0	1	88	24	0	.273	13	28	1	0	1.2	.976
1974		12	16	.429	4.03	37	35	8	228	222	81	138	1	0	0	0	81	17	1	.210	20	46	2	2	1.8	.971
1975		6	12	.333	4.08	31	25	3	170	175	76	99	0	0	0	1	54	15	1	.278	13	24	3	0	1.3	.925
1976	2 teams	MON N (5G 0-1)			CHI N	(28G 8-11)																				
"	total	8	12	.400	3.98	33	28	4	176.1	179	46	116	0	0	0	0	56	6	0	.107	9	17	1	1	0.8	.963
1977	2 teams	CHI N (13G 2-2)			CHI A	(8G 5-0)																				
"	total	7	2	.778	4.07	21	16	0	104	106	38	70	0	0	0	1	12	2	0	.167	9	8	1	0	0.9	.944
1978	OAK A	6	12	.333	4.29	27	25	3	151	152	67	89	1	0	0	0	0	0	0	–	5	22	1	3	1.0	.964
1979	BOS A	11	9	.550	4.11	27	27	4	171	174	53	99	1	0	0	0	0	0	0	–	14	20	2	0	1.3	.944
1980		9	9	.500	4.20	32	23	1	165	180	56	90	0	2	0	0	0	0	0	–	14	17	0	1	1.0	1.000
1981	CAL A	8	4	.667	3.44	22	15	0	102	93	42	50	0	1	0	1	0	0	0	–	2	10	0	0	0.5	1.000
1982	KC A	11	6	.647	4.44	31	23	4	156	163	51	81	0	3	0	0	0	0	0	–	9	14	3	4	0.8	.885
1983		6	11	.353	4.30	25	17	1	121.1	144	36	54	0	0	3	1	0	0	0	–	8	13	0	1	0.8	1.000
15 yrs.		134	146	.479	4.00	451	365	57	2493.1	2438	1010	1455	8	6	4	6	531	114	6	.215	161	316	26	18	1.1	.948

Andy Replogle

REPLOGLE, ANDREW DAVID
B. Oct. 7, 1953, South Bend, Ind.   BR TR 6'5"   205 lbs.

Year	Team	W	L	PCT	ERA	G	GS	CG	IP	H	BB	SO	ShO	W	L	SV	AB	H	HR	BA	PO	A	E	DP	TC/G	FA
1978	MIL A	9	5	.643	3.92	32	18	3	149.1	177	47	41	2	3	0	0	0	0	0	–	11	12	2	1	0.8	.920
1979		0	0	–	5.63	3	0	0	8	13	2	2	0	0	0	0	0	0	0	–	0	2	0	0	0.7	1.000
2 yrs.		9	5	.643	4.00	35	18	3	157.1	190	49	43	2	3	0	0	0	0	0	–	11	14	2	1	0.8	.926

Xavier Rescigno

RESCIGNO, XAVIER FREDERICK (Mr. X)
B. Oct. 13, 1913, New York, N. Y.   BR TR 5'10½"   175 lbs.

Year	Team	W	L	PCT	ERA	G	GS	CG	IP	H	BB	SO	ShO	W	L	SV	AB	H	HR	BA	PO	A	E	DP	TC/G	FA
1943	PIT N	6	9	.400	3.05	37	14	5	132.2	125	45	41	1	3	3	2	35	5	0	.143	8	16	3	1	0.7	.889
1944		10	8	.556	4.35	48	6	2	124	146	34	45	0	8	5	5	22	2	0	.091	7	21	1	2	0.6	.966
1945		3	5	.375	5.72	44	1	0	78.2	95	34	29	0	3	4	9	15	2	0	.133	4	14	0	0	0.4	1.000
3 yrs.		19	22	.463	4.16	129	21	7	335.1	366	113	115	1	14	12	16	72	9	0	.125	19	51	4	3	0.6	.946

George Rettger

RETTGER, GEORGE EDWARD
B. July 29, 1868, Cleveland, Ohio D. June 6, 1921, Lakewood, Ohio   BR TR 5'11"   175 lbs.

Year	Team	W	L	PCT	ERA	G	GS	CG	IP	H	BB	SO	ShO	W	L	SV	AB	H	HR	BA	PO	A	E	DP	TC/G	FA
1891	STL AA	7	3	.700	3.40	14	12	10	92.2	85	51	49	1	1	0	1	42	3	1	.071	5	17	2	0	1.7	.917

Year	Team	W	L	PCT	ERA	G	GS	CG	IP	H	BB	SO	ShO	Relief Pitching W	L	SV	Batting AB	H	HR	BA	PO	A	E	DP	TC/G	FA

George Rettger *continued*

Year	Team	W	L	PCT	ERA	G	GS	CG	IP	H	BB	SO	ShO	W	L	SV	AB	H	HR	BA	PO	A	E	DP	TC/G	FA
1892	2 teams	CLE N	(6G 1–3)		CIN N	(1G 1–0)																				
"	total	2	3	.400	4.21	7	6	4	47	40	41	13	0	0	0	0	23	3	0	.130	3	9	2	0	2.0	.857
2 yrs.		9	6	.600	3.67	21	18	14	139.2	125	92	62	1	1	0	1	65	6	1	.092	8	26	4	0	1.8	.895

Otto Rettig

RETTIG, ADOLPH JOHN BR TR 5'11" 165 lbs.
B. Jan. 29, 1894, New York, N.Y. D. June 16, 1977, Stuart, Fla.

Year	Team	W	L	PCT	ERA	G	GS	CG	IP	H	BB	SO	ShO	W	L	SV	AB	H	HR	BA	PO	A	E	DP	TC/G	FA
1922	PHI A	1	2	.333	4.91	4	4	1	18.1	18	12	3	0	0	0	0	6	0	0	.000	1	5	0	0	1.5	1.000

Ed Reulbach

REULBACH, EDWARD MARVIN (Big Ed) BR TR 6'1" 190 lbs.
B. Dec. 1, 1882, Detroit, Mich. D. July 17, 1961, Glens Falls, N.Y.

Year	Team	W	L	PCT	ERA	G	GS	CG	IP	H	BB	SO	ShO	W	L	SV	AB	H	HR	BA	PO	A	E	DP	TC/G	FA
1905	CHI N	18	13	.581	1.42	34	29	28	292	208	73	152	5	1	2	1	110	14	0	.127	14	71	4	4	2.6	.955
1906		19	4	.826	1.65	33	24	20	218	129	92	94	6	1	0	2	83	13	0	.157	17	74	3	3	2.8	.968
1907		17	4	.810	1.69	27	22	16	192	147	64	96	4	2	0	0	63	11	1	.175	13	53	5	3	2.6	.930
1908		24	7	.774	2.03	46	35	25	297.2	227	106	133	7	3	0	1	99	23	0	.232	15	77	7	7	2.2	.929
1909		19	10	.655	1.78	35	32	23	262.2	194	82	105	6	0	1	0	86	12	0	.140	15	91	5	4	3.2	.955
1910		12	8	.600	3.12	24	23	13	173.1	161	49	55	1	0	1	0	56	6	0	.107	8	53	4	1	2.6	.937
1911		16	9	.640	2.96	33	29	15	221.2	191	103	79	2	1	0	0	67	6	0	.090	5	77	5	2	2.6	.943
1912		10	6	.625	3.78	39	19	8	169	161	60	75	0	3	1	3	55	6	0	.109	8	60	3	4	1.8	.958
1913	2 teams	CHI N	(9G 1–3)		BKN N	(15G 7–6)																				
"	total	8	9	.471	2.66	24	14	9	148.2	118	55	56	2	1	0	0	41	6	0	.146	9	35	3	1	2.0	.936
1914	BKN N	11	18	.379	2.64	44	29	14	256	228	83	119	3	1	3	3	74	9	0	.122	11	71	6	2	2.0	.932
1915	NWK F	20	10	.667	2.23	33	30	23	270	233	69	117	4	1	0	1	92	18	0	.196	11	90	7	2	3.3	.935
1916	BOS N	7	6	.538	2.47	21	11	6	109.1	99	41	47	0	2	1	0	33	3	0	.091	11	55	1	1	3.0	.984
1917		0	1	.000	2.82	5	2	0	22.1	21	15	9	0	0	0	0	3	0	0	.000	1	12	1	1	2.8	.929
13 yrs.		181	105	.633	2.28	398	299	200	2632.2	2117	892	1137	40	17	8	11	862	127	1	.147	136	814	54	37	2.5	.946

WORLD SERIES

Year	Team	W	L	PCT	ERA	G	GS	CG	IP	H	BB	SO	ShO	W	L	SV	AB	H	HR	BA	PO	A	E	DP	TC/G	FA
1906	CHI N	1	0	1.000	2.45	2	2	1	11	6	8	4	0	0	0	0	3	0	0	.000	0	4	0	0	2.0	1.000
1907		1	0	1.000	0.75	2	1	1	12	6	3	4	0	0	0	0	5	1	0	.200	1	2	0	0	1.5	1.000
1908		0	0	–	4.70	2	1	0	7.2	9	1	5	0	0	0	0	3	0	0	.000	0	5	0	0	2.5	1.000
1910		0	0	–	13.50	1	1	0	2	3	2	0	0	0	0	0	0	0	0	–	0	1	0	0	1.0	1.000
4 yrs.		2	0	1.000 **1st**	3.03	7	5	2	32.2	24	14	13	0	0	0	0	11	1	0	.091	1	12	0	0	1.9	1.000

Paul Reuschel

REUSCHEL, PAUL RICHARD BR TR 6'4" 225 lbs.
Brother of Rick Reuschel.
B. Jan. 12, 1947, Quincy, Ill.

Year	Team	W	L	PCT	ERA	G	GS	CG	IP	H	BB	SO	ShO	W	L	SV	AB	H	HR	BA	PO	A	E	DP	TC/G	FA
1975	CHI N	1	3	.250	3.50	28	0	0	36	44	13	12	0	1	3	5	4	0	0	.000	1	7	1	0	0.3	.889
1976		4	2	.667	4.55	50	2	0	87	94	33	55	0	4	1	3	13	2	0	.154	4	19	1	2	0.5	.958
1977		5	6	.455	4.37	69	0	0	107	105	40	62	0	5	6	4	11	0	0	.000	7	25	1	5	0.5	.970
1978	2 teams	CHI N	(16G 2–0)		CLE A	(18G 2–4)																				
"	total	4	4	.500	3.59	34	6	1	117.2	124	35	37	0	4	0	0	4	0	0	.000	7	20	0	4	0.8	1.000
1979	CLE A	2	1	.667	8.00	17	1	0	45	73	11	22	0	2	1	1	0	0	0	–	2	10	1	2	0.8	.923
5 yrs.		16	16	.500	4.52	198	9	1	392.2	440	132	188	0	16	11	13	32	2	0	.063	21	81	4	13	0.5	.962

Rick Reuschel

REUSCHEL, RICKEY EUGENE (Big Daddy) BR TR 6'3" 215 lbs.
Brother of Paul Reuschel.
B. May 16, 1949, Quincy, Ill.

Year	Team	W	L	PCT	ERA	G	GS	CG	IP	H	BB	SO	ShO	W	L	SV	AB	H	HR	BA	PO	A	E	DP	TC/G	FA
1972	CHI N	10	8	.556	2.93	21	18	5	129	127	29	87	4	1	0	0	44	6	1	.136	9	15	1	1	1.2	.960
1973		14	15	.483	3.00	36	36	7	237	244	62	168	3	0	0	0	73	9	0	.123	24	49	3	0	2.1	.961
1974		13	12	.520	4.29	41	38	8	241	262	83	160	2	1	0	0	86	19	0	.221	28	51	5	4	2.0	.940
1975		11	17	.393	3.73	38	37	6	234	244	67	155	0	0	0	1	77	16	1	.208	23	39	0	5	1.6	1.000
1976		14	12	.538	3.46	38	37	9	260	260	64	146	2	0	0	1	83	19	0	.229	23	53	4	0	2.1	.950
1977		20	10	.667	2.79	39	37	8	252	233	74	166	4	1	0	1	87	18	0	.207	27	45	1	4	1.9	.986
1978		14	15	.483	3.41	35	35	9	243	235	54	115	1	0	0	0	73	10	0	.137	24	44	2	1	2.0	.971
1979		18	12	.600	3.62	36	36	5	239	251	75	125	1	0	0	0	79	13	0	.165	27	49	3	9	2.2	.962
1980		11	13	.458	3.40	38	38	6	257	281	76	140	0	0	0	0	82	13	0	.159	28	56	2	5	2.3	.977
1981	2 teams	CHI N	(13G 4–7)		NY A	(12G 4–4)																				
"	total	8	11	.421	3.10	25	24	4	157	162	33	75	0	0	0	0	25	2	0	.080	4	21	2	2	1.1	.926
1983	CHI N	1	1	.500	3.92	4	4	0	20.2	18	10	9	0	0	0	0	7	1	0	.143	4	7	0	0	2.8	1.000
1984		5	5	.500	5.17	19	14	1	92.1	123	23	43	0	1	0	0	29	7	0	.241	6	20	1	1	1.4	.963
1985	PIT N	14	8	.636	2.27	31	26	9	194	153	52	138	1	2	0	1	59	10	1	.169	24	40	0	2	2.1	1.000
1986		9	16	.360	3.96	35	34	4	215.2	232	57	125	2	0	0	0	70	11	0	.157	24	44	2	0	2.0	.971
1987	2 teams	PIT N	(25G 8–6)		SF N	(9G 5–3)																				
"	total	13	9	.591	3.09	34	33	12	227	207	42	107	4	0	0	0	79	11	0	.139	25	38	2	2	1.9	.969
1988	SF N	19	11	.633	3.12	36	36	7	245	242	42	92	2	0	0	0	73	8	0	.110	12	32	0	0	1.2	1.000
1989		17	8	.680	2.94	32	32	2	208.1	195	54	111	0	0	0	0	61	10	0	.164	8	33	0	0	1.3	1.000
17 yrs.		211	183	.536	3.36	538	515	102	3452	3469	897	1962	26	6	0	4	1087	183	4	.168	320	636	28	38	1.8	.972

DIVISIONAL PLAYOFF SERIES

Year	Team	W	L	PCT	ERA	G	GS	CG	IP	H	BB	SO	ShO	W	L	SV	AB	H	HR	BA	PO	A	E	DP	TC/G	FA
1981	NY A	0	1	.000	3.00	1	1	0	6	4	1	3	0	0	0	0	0	0	0	–	0	0	0	0	0.0	–

LEAGUE CHAMPIONSHIP SERIES

Year	Team	W	L	PCT	ERA	G	GS	CG	IP	H	BB	SO	ShO	W	L	SV	AB	H	HR	BA	PO	A	E	DP	TC/G	FA
1987	SF N	0	1	.000	6.30	2	2	0	10	15	2	2	0	0	0	0	2	0	0	.000	0	3	1	0	2.0	.750
1989		1	1	.500	5.19	2	2	0	8.2	12	2	5	0	0	0	0	2	0	0	.000	1	3	0	0	1.5	1.000
2 yrs.		1	2	.333	5.79	4	4	0	18.2	27	4	7	0	0	0	0	4	0	0	.000	1	6	1	0	1.8	.857

WORLD SERIES

Year	Team	W	L	PCT	ERA	G	GS	CG	IP	H	BB	SO	ShO	W	L	SV	AB	H	HR	BA	PO	A	E	DP	TC/G	FA
1981	NY A	0	0	–	4.91	2	1	0	3.2	7	3	2	0	0	0	0	2	0	0	.000	0	0	0	0	0.0	–
1989	SF N	0	1	.000	11.25	1	1	0	4	5	4	2	0	0	0	0	0	0	0	–	0	0	0	0	0.0	–
2 yrs.		0	1	.000	8.22	3	2	0	7.2	12	7	4	0	0	0	0	2	0	0	.000	0	0	0	0	0.0	–

Year	Team	W	L	PCT	ERA	G	GS	CG	IP	H	BB	SO	ShO	Relief W	Relief L	Relief SV	AB	H	HR	BA	PO	A	E	DP	TC/G	FA

Jerry Reuss

REUSS, JERRY
B. June 19, 1949, St. Louis, Mo. BL TL 6'5" 200 lbs.

Year	Team	W	L	PCT	ERA	G	GS	CG	IP	H	BB	SO	ShO	Rel W	Rel L	Rel SV	AB	H	HR	BA	PO	A	E	DP	TC/G	FA
1969	STL N	1	0	1.000	0.00	1	1	0	7	2	3	3	0	0	0	0	3	1	0	.333	0	2	0	0	2.0	1.000
1970		7	8	.467	4.11	20	20	5	127	132	49	74	2	0	0	0	40	2	0	.050	8	18	1	0	1.4	.963
1971		14	14	.500	4.78	36	35	7	211	228	109	131	2	0	0	0	65	8	0	.123	6	26	2	0	0.9	.941
1972	HOU N	9	13	.409	4.17	33	30	4	192	177	83	174	1	0	0	1	66	7	0	.106	4	25	4	0	1.0	.879
1973		16	13	.552	3.74	41	40	12	279.1	271	117	177	3	1	0	0	95	13	0	.137	4	37	3	2	1.1	.932
1974	PIT N	16	11	.593	3.50	35	35	14	260	259	101	105	1	0	0	0	86	13	0	.151	11	37	5	1	1.5	.906
1975		18	11	.621	2.54	32	32	15	237	224	78	131	6	0	0	0	71	14	0	.197	6	48	0	1	1.7	1.000
1976		14	9	.609	3.53	31	29	11	209.1	209	51	108	3	0	0	2	66	16	0	.242	8	26	2	2	1.2	.944
1977		10	13	.435	4.11	33	33	8	208	225	71	116	2	0	0	0	70	12	0	.171	7	40	3	2	1.5	.940
1978		3	2	.600	4.88	23	12	3	83	97	23	42	1	0	0	0	27	5	0	.185	4	10	0	4	0.6	1.000
1979	LA N	7	14	.333	3.54	39	21	4	160	178	60	83	1	2	4	3	42	7	0	.167	2	35	3	1	1.0	.925
1980		18	6	.750	2.52	37	29	10	229	193	40	111	6	3	0	3	68	6	1	.088	18	40	5	5	1.7	.921
1981		10	4	.714	2.29	22	22	8	153	138	27	51	2	0	0	0	51	10	0	.196	10	38	1	4	2.2	.980
1982		18	11	.621	3.11	39	37	8	254.2	232	50	138	4	1	0	0	77	17	0	.221	21	46	3	4	1.8	.957
1983		12	11	.522	2.94	32	31	7	223.1	233	50	143	3	0	0	0	71	20	0	.282	17	52	4	4	2.3	.945
1984		5	7	.417	3.82	30	15	2	99	102	31	44	0	0	2	1	24	4	0	.167	4	16	1	0	0.7	.952
1985		14	10	.583	2.92	34	33	5	212.2	210	58	84	3	0	0	0	74	10	0	.135	12	27	3	0	1.2	.929
1986		2	6	.250	5.84	19	13	0	74	96	17	29	0	0	0	1	20	5	0	.250	5	16	0	1	1.1	1.000
1987	3 teams	LA N (1G 0–0)			CIN N	(7G 0–5)			CAL A	(17G 4–5)																
"	total	4	10	.286	5.97	25	23	1	119	166	29	49	1	0	0	0	8	1	0	.125	8	21	1	4	1.2	.967
1988	CHI A	13	9	.591	3.44	32	29	2	183	183	43	73	0	0	0	0	0	0	0	–	10	27	1	2	1.2	.974
1989	2 teams	CHI A (23G 8–5)			MIL A	(7G 1–4)																				
"	total	9	9	.500	5.13	30	26	1	140.1	171	34	40	1	0	0	0	0	0	0	–	4	14	0	1	0.6	1.000
21 yrs.		220	191	.535	3.64	624	546	127	3661.2	3726	1124	1906	39	7	6	11	1024	171	1	.167	169	601	42	38	1.3	.948

DIVISIONAL PLAYOFF SERIES

Year	Team	W	L	PCT	ERA	G	GS	CG	IP	H	BB	SO	ShO	Rel W	Rel L	Rel SV	AB	H	HR	BA	PO	A	E	DP	TC/G	FA
1981	LA N	1	0	1.000	0.00	2	2	1	18	10	5	7	1	0	0	0	8	0	0	.000	0	0	0	0	0.0	–

LEAGUE CHAMPIONSHIP SERIES

Year	Team	W	L	PCT	ERA	G	GS	CG	IP	H	BB	SO	ShO	Rel W	Rel L	Rel SV	AB	H	HR	BA	PO	A	E	DP	TC/G	FA
1974	PIT N	0	2	.000	3.72	2	2	0	9.2	7	8	3	0	0	0	0	2	0	0	.000	0	0	0	0	0.0	–
1975		0	1	.000	13.50	1	1	0	2.2	4	4	1	0	0	0	0	1	0	0	.000	0	1	0	0	1.0	1.000
1981	LA N	0	1	.000	5.14	1	1	0	7	7	1	2	0	0	0	0	2	0	0	.000	0	0	0	0	0.0	–
1983		0	2	.000	4.50	2	2	0	12	14	3	4	0	0	0	0	3	0	0	.000	0	1	0	0	0.5	1.000
1985		0	1	.000	10.80	1	1	0	1.2	5	1	0	0	0	0	0	0	0	0	–	0	1	0	0	1.0	–
5 yrs.		0	7	.000	5.45	7	7	0	33	37	17	10	0	0	0	0	8	0	0	.000	0	2	1	0	0.4	.667

WORLD SERIES

Year	Team	W	L	PCT	ERA	G	GS	CG	IP	H	BB	SO	ShO	Rel W	Rel L	Rel SV	AB	H	HR	BA	PO	A	E	DP	TC/G	FA
1981	LA N	1	1	.500	3.86	2	2	0	11.2	10	3	8	0	0	0	0	3	0	0	.000	1	3	0	0	2.0	1.000

Allie Reynolds

REYNOLDS, ALLIE PIERCE (Superchief)
B. Feb. 10, 1915, Bethany, Okla. BR TR 6' 195 lbs.

Year	Team	W	L	PCT	ERA	G	GS	CG	IP	H	BB	SO	ShO	Rel W	Rel L	Rel SV	AB	H	HR	BA	PO	A	E	DP	TC/G	FA
1942	CLE A	0	0	–	0.00	2	0	0	5	5	4	2	0	0	0	0	2	0	0	.000	0	0	0	0	0.0	–
1943		11	12	.478	2.99	34	21	11	198.2	140	109	151	3	1	6	3	67	10	0	.149	5	35	2	3	1.2	.952
1944		11	8	.579	3.30	28	21	5	158	141	91	84	1	0	3	1	57	7	0	.123	8	21	1	3	1.1	.967
1945		18	12	.600	3.20	44	30	16	247.1	227	130	112	2	2	1	4	85	8	0	.094	11	44	5	3	1.4	.917
1946		11	15	.423	3.88	31	28	9	183.1	180	108	107	3	0	0	0	63	14	0	.222	8	27	5	1	1.3	.875
1947	NY A	19	8	.704	3.20	34	30	17	241.2	207	123	129	4	1	1	1	89	13	0	.146	9	31	2	1	1.2	.952
1948		16	7	.696	3.77	39	31	11	236.1	240	111	101	1	0	0	3	83	16	1	.193	10	27	1	1	1.0	.974
1949		17	6	.739	4.00	35	31	4	213.2	200	123	105	2	2	0	1	78	17	0	.218	7	39	2	3	1.3	.958
1950		16	12	.571	3.74	35	29	14	240.2	215	138	160	2	1	3	2	81	15	0	.185	8	36	3	1	1.3	.936
1951		17	8	.680	3.05	40	26	16	221	171	100	126	7	1	2	7	76	14	0	.184	17	19	5	2	1.0	.878
1952		20	8	.714	2.06	35	29	24	244.1	194	97	160	6	0	0	6	85	13	0	.153	13	35	2	1	1.4	.960
1953		13	7	.650	3.41	41	15	5	145	140	61	86	1	7	1	13	41	5	0	.122	7	13	4	1	0.6	.833
1954		13	4	.765	3.32	36	18	5	157.1	133	66	100	4	3	2	7	50	8	0	.160	8	22	0	2	0.8	1.000
13 yrs.		182	107	.630	3.30	434	309	137	2492.1	2193	1261	1423	36	18	19	49	857	140	1	.163	111	349	32	22	1.1	.935

WORLD SERIES

Year	Team	W	L	PCT	ERA	G	GS	CG	IP	H	BB	SO	ShO	Rel W	Rel L	Rel SV	AB	H	HR	BA	PO	A	E	DP	TC/G	FA
1947	NY A	1	0	1.000	4.76	2	2	1	11.1	15	3	6	0	0	0	0	4	2	0	.500	0	1	0	0	0.5	1.000
1949		1	0	1.000	0.00	2	1	1	12.1	2	4	14	1	0	0	1	4	2	0	.500	0	1	0	0	0.5	1.000
1950		1	0	1.000	0.87	2	1	1	10.1	7	4	7	0	0	0	1	3	1	0	.333	1	2	0	0	1.5	1.000
1951		1	1	.500	4.20	2	2	1	15	16	11	8	0	0	0	0	6	2	0	.333	0	5	0	2	2.5	1.000
1952		2	1	.667	1.77	4	2	1	20.1	12	6	18	1	1	0	1	7	0	0	.000	2	1	2	0	1.3	.600
1953		1	0	1.000	6.75	3	1	0	8	9	4	9	0	1	0	0	2	1	0	.500	0	0	0	0	0.0	–
6 yrs.		7	2	.778	2.79	15	9	5	77.1	61	32	62	2	2	0	4	26	8	0	.308	4	9	2	3	1.0	.867
		2nd				3rd	6th	10th			8th	6th		2nd	3rd	4th				2nd						

Archie Reynolds

REYNOLDS, ARCHIE EDWARD
B. Jan. 3, 1946, Glendale, Calif. BR TR 6'2" 205 lbs.

Year	Team	W	L	PCT	ERA	G	GS	CG	IP	H	BB	SO	ShO	Rel W	Rel L	Rel SV	AB	H	HR	BA	PO	A	E	DP	TC/G	FA
1968	CHI N	0	1	.000	6.75	7	1	0	13.1	14	7	6	0	0	0	0	2	1	0	.500	1	0	0	0	0.1	1.000
1969		0	1	.000	2.57	2	2	0	7	11	7	4	0	0	0	0	1	0	0	.000	1	1	0	1	1.0	1.000
1970		0	2	.000	6.60	7	1	0	15	17	9	9	0	0	0	0	2	0	0	.000	1	0	0	1	0.1	1.000
1971	CAL A	0	3	.000	4.67	15	1	0	27	32	18	15	0	0	0	3	2	0	0	.000	3	5	0	1	0.5	1.000
1972	MIL A	0	1	.000	7.11	5	2	0	19	26	8	13	0	0	1	0	4	2	0	.500	0	2	0	1	0.2	1.000
5 yrs.		0	8	.000	5.75	36	7	0	81.1	100	49	47	0	0	6	0	11	3	0	.273	6	7	0	3	0.4	1.000

Bob Reynolds

REYNOLDS, ROBERT ALLEN
B. Jan. 21, 1947, Seattle, Wash. BR TR 6' 205 lbs.

Year	Team	W	L	PCT	ERA	G	GS	CG	IP	H	BB	SO	ShO	Rel W	Rel L	Rel SV	AB	H	HR	BA	PO	A	E	DP	TC/G	FA
1969	MON N	0	0	–	20.25	1	1	0	1.1	3	3	2	0	0	0	0	0	0	0	–	0	0	0	0	0.0	–
1971	2 teams	MIL A (3G 0–1)			STL N	(4G 0–0)																				
"	total	0	1	.000	6.92	7	0	0	13	19	9	8	0	0	1	0	2	0	0	.000	0	2	0	0	0.3	1.000
1972	BAL A	0	0	–	1.80	3	0	0	10	8	7	5	0	0	0	0	2	0	0	.000	0	1	0	0	0.3	1.000
1973		7	5	.583	1.95	42	1	0	111	88	31	77	0	7	5	9	0	0	0	–	5	7	5	1	0.4	.706
1974		7	5	.583	2.74	54	0	0	69	75	14	43	0	7	5	7	0	0	0	–	4	8	0	0	0.2	1.000

Year	Team		W	L	PCT	ERA	G	GS	CG	IP	H	BB	SO	ShO	Relief Pitching			Batting			BA	PO	A	E	DP	TC/G	FA
															W	L	SV	AB	H	HR							

Bob Reynolds *continued*

1975	3 teams	BAL A (7G 0–1)				DET A (21G 0–2)				CLE A (5G 0–2)																	
"	total		0	5	.000	5.19	33	0	0	50.1	62	18	32	0	0	5	5	0	0	0	–	4	6	0	0	0.3	1.000
6 yrs.			14	16	.467	3.15	140	2	0	254.2	255	82	167	0	14	16	21	4	0	0	.000	13	24	5	1	0.3	.881

LEAGUE CHAMPIONSHIP SERIES

1973	BAL	A	0	0	–	3.18	2	0	0	5.2	5	3	5	0	0	0	0	0	0	0	–	1	0	0	0	0.5	1.000
1974			0	0	–	0.00	1	0	0	1.1	0	3	1	0	0	0	0	0	0	0	–	0	0	0	0	0.0	–
2 yrs.			0	0	–	2.57	3	0	0	7	5	6	6	0	0	0	0	0	0	0	–	1	0	0	0	0.3	1.000

Charlie Reynolds

REYNOLDS, CHARLES E.
B. July 31, 1857, Allegany, N. Y. D. May 1, 1913, Buffalo, N. Y.

| 1882 | PHI | AA | 1 | 1 | .500 | *5.25* | 2 | 2 | 1 | 12 | 18 | 3 | 4 | 0 | 0 | 0 | 0 | 8 | 1 | 0 | .125 | 1 | 1 | 1 | 0 | 1.5 | .667 |

Craig Reynolds

REYNOLDS, GORDON CRAIG
B. Dec. 27, 1952, Houston, Tex.   BL TR 6'1"   175 lbs.

1986	HOU	N	0	0	–	27.00	1	0	0	1	3	2	1	0	0	0	0	313	78	6	.249	0	0	0	0	0.0	–
1989			0	0	–	27.00	1	0	0	1	3	1	0	0	0	0	0	189	38	2	.201	0	0	0	0	0.0	–
2 yrs.			0	0	–	27.00	2	0	0	2	6	3	1	0	0	0	0	*				0	0	0	0	0.0	–

Ken Reynolds

REYNOLDS, KENNETH LEE
B. Jan. 4, 1947, Trevose, Pa.   BL TL 6'   180 lbs.

1970	PHI	N	0	0	–	0.00	4	0	0	2	3	4	1	0	0	0	0	0	0	0	–	1	1	0	0	0.8	.667
1971			5	9	.357	4.50	35	25	2	162	163	82	81	1	0	0	0	50	10	0	.200	5	25	2	1	0.9	.938
1972			2	15	.118	4.26	33	23	2	154.1	149	60	87	0	0	1	0	40	8	0	.200	4	23	1	1	0.8	.964
1973	MIL	A	0	1	.000	7.36	2	1	0	7.1	5	10	3	0	0	0	0	0	0	0	–	0	3	0	2	1.5	1.000
1975	STL	N	0	1	.000	1.59	10	0	0	17	12	11	7	0	0	1	0	2	0	0	.000	4	6	0	0	1.0	1.000
1976	SD	N	0	3	.000	6.40	19	2	0	32.1	38	29	18	0	0	2	1	5	0	0	.000	2	3	1	0	0.3	.833
6 yrs.			7	29	.194	4.46	103	51	4	375	370	196	197	1	0	4	1	97	18	0	.186	16	61	5	4	0.8	.939

Ross Reynolds

REYNOLDS, ROSS ERNEST
B. Aug. 20, 1887, Barksdale, Tex. D. June 23, 1970, Ada, Okla.   BR TR 6'2"   175 lbs.

1914	DET	A	5	3	.625	2.08	26	7	3	78	62	39	31	1	1	1	0	21	1	0	.048	5	19	4	0	1.1	.857
1915			0	1	.000	6.35	4	2	0	11.1	17	5	2	0	0	0	0	3	0	0	.000	1	5	0	0	1.5	1.000
2 yrs.			5	4	.556	2.62	30	9	3	89.1	79	44	33	1	1	1	0	24	1	0	.042	6	24	4	0	1.1	.882

Flint Rhem

RHEM, CHARLES FLINT (Shad)
B. Jan. 24, 1901, Rhems, S. C. D. July 30, 1969, Columbia, S. C.   BR TR 6'2"   180 lbs.

1924	STL	N	2	2	.500	4.45	6	3	3	32.1	31	17	20	0	0	1	1	12	2	0	.167	0	9	0	0	1.5	1.000
1925			8	13	.381	4.92	30	23	8	170	204	58	66	1	0	0	1	59	14	1	.237	9	38	5	3	1.7	.904
1926			**20**	7	.741	3.21	34	34	20	258	241	75	72	1	0	0	0	96	18	1	.188	1	76	6	6	2.4	.928
1927			10	12	.455	4.41	27	26	9	169.1	189	54	51	2	0	0	0	59	4	0	.068	2	27	1	0	1.1	.967
1928			11	8	.579	4.14	28	22	9	169.2	199	71	47	0	0	0	3	67	11	1	.164	3	48	0	5	1.8	1.000
1930			12	8	.600	4.45	26	19	9	139.2	173	37	47	0	1	4	0	52	12	0	.231	1	19	4	1	0.9	.833
1931			11	10	.524	3.56	33	26	10	207.1	214	60	72	2	1	0	1	69	9	0	.130	4	38	3	4	1.4	.933
1932	2 teams	STL N (6G 4–2)					PHI N (26G 11–7)																				
"	total		15	9	.625	3.58	32	26	15	218.2	225	59	53	1	1	0	1	78	10	0	.128	6	49	3	1	1.8	.948
1933	PHI	N	5	14	.263	6.57	28	19	3	126	182	33	27	0	1	2	2	46	4	0	.087	2	30	2	1	1.2	.941
1934	2 teams	STL N (5G 1–0)					BOS N (25G 8–8)																				
"	total		9	8	.529	3.69	30	21	5	168.1	190	45	62	1	3	0	1	54	3	0	.056	3	42	1	2	1.5	.978
1935	BOS	N	0	5	.000	5.31	10	6	0	40.2	61	11	10	0	0	0	0	10	0	0	.000	1	10	0	0	1.1	1.000
1936	STL	N	2	1	.667	6.75	10	4	0	26.2	49	49	9	0	0	0	0	8	1	0	.125	1	3	0	1	0.4	1.000
12 yrs.			105	97	.520	4.20	294	229	91	1726.2	1958	569	536	8	8	7	10	610	88	3	.144	33	389	25	24	1.5	.944

WORLD SERIES

1926	STL	N	0	0	–	6.75	1	1	0	4	7	2	4	0	0	0	0	1	0	0	.000	0	1	0	0	1.0	1.000
1928			0	0	–	0.00	1	0	0	2	0	1	1	0	0	0	0	0	0	0	–	0	0	0	0	0.0	–
1930			0	1	.000	10.80	1	1	0	3.1	7	2	3	0	0	0	0	1	0	0	.000	0	0	1	0	1.0	–
1931			0	0	–	0.00	1	0	0	1	1	0	1	0	0	0	0	0	0	0	–	0	0	0	0	0.0	–
4 yrs.			0	1	.000	6.10	4	2	0	10.1	15	4	9	0	0	0	0	2	0	0	.000	0	1	1	0	0.5	.500

Billy Rhines

RHINES, WILLIAM PEARL
B. Mar. 14, 1869, Ridgway, Pa. D. Jan. 30, 1922, Ridgway, Pa.   BR TR 5'11"   168 lbs.

1890	CIN	N	28	17	.622	**1.95**	46	45	45	401.1	337	113	182	6	0	0	0	154	29	0	.188	23	77	7	3	2.3	.935
1891			17	24	.415	2.87	48	43	40	372.2	364	124	138	1	2	0	1	148	18	0	.122	8	95	7	3	2.3	.935
1892			4	7	.364	5.06	12	10	8	83.2	113	36	12	0	1	0	0	30	5	1	.167	3	14	2	1	1.6	.895
1893	LOU	N	1	4	.200	8.71	5	5	3	31	49	19	0	0	1	0	0	11	1	0	.091	0	8	0	0	1.6	1.000
1895	CIN	N	19	10	.655	4.81	38	33	25	267.2	322	76	72	0	1	0	0	113	25	0	.221	17	56	9	3	2.0	.890
1896			8	6	.571	**2.45**	19	17	11	143	128	48	32	3	0	1	0	52	10	0	.192	8	35	3	2	2.4	.935
1897			21	15	.583	4.08	41	32	26	288.2	311	86	65	1	5	0	0	107	17	0	.159	16	53	8	2	1.9	.896
1898	PIT	N	12	16	.429	3.52	31	29	27	258	289	61	48	0	0	0	0	100	15	0	.150	11	88	3	0	3.3	.971
1899			4	4	.500	6.00	9	4	4	54	59	13	6	0	0	0	0	23	10	0	.435	2	7	0	1	1.0	1.000
9 yrs.			114	103	.525	3.47	249	223	189	1900	1972	576	555	13	9	1	1	738	130	1	.176	88	433	39	15	2.2	.930

Bob Rhoads

RHOADS, ROBERT BARTON (Dusty)
B. Oct. 4, 1879, Wooster, Ohio D. Feb. 12, 1967, San Bernardino, Calif.   BR TR 6'1"   215 lbs.

1902	CHI	N	4	8	.333	3.20	16	12	12	118	131	42	43	1	0	0	1	45	10	0	.222	7	28	3	0	2.4	.921
1903	2 teams	STL N (17G 5–8)					CLE A (5G 2–3)																				
"	total		7	11	.389	4.76	22	18	17	170	209	50	73	1	0	0	0	67	9	0	.134	4	40	4	1	2.2	.917
1904	CLE	A	10	9	.526	2.87	22	19	18	175.1	175	48	72	0	0	0	0	92	18	0	.196	10	52	3	4	3.0	.954
1905			16	9	.640	2.83	28	26	24	235	219	55	61	4	0	0	0	95	21	1	.221	6	78	1	3	3.0	.988
1906			22	10	.688	1.80	38	34	31	315	259	92	89	7	1	0	0	118	19	0	.161	17	88	4	5	2.9	.963
1907			15	14	.517	2.29	35	31	23	275	258	84	76	5	1	0	1	92	17	0	.185	13	83	5	6	2.9	.950

Year	Team	W	L	PCT	ERA	G	GS	CG	IP	H	BB	SO	ShO	Relief Pitching W	L	SV	Batting AB	H	HR	BA	PO	A	E	DP	TC/G	FA

Bob Rhoads *continued*

Year	Team	W	L	PCT	ERA	G	GS	CG	IP	H	BB	SO	ShO	W	L	SV	AB	H	HR	BA	PO	A	E	DP	TC/G	FA
1908		18	12	.600	1.77	37	30	20	270	229	73	62	1	2	2	0	90	20	0	.222	18	96	2	2	3.1	.983
1909		5	9	.357	2.90	20	15	9	133.1	124	50	46	2	0	1	0	43	7	0	.163	6	44	4	2	2.7	.926
8 yrs.		97	82	.542	2.61	218	185	154	1691.2	1604	494	522	21	5	3	2	642	121	2	.188	81	509	26	23	2.8	.958

Rick Rhoden

RHODEN, RICHARD ALAN
B. May 16, 1953, Boynton Beach, Fla.   BR TR 6'3"   195 lbs.

Year	Team	W	L	PCT	ERA	G	GS	CG	IP	H	BB	SO	ShO	W	L	SV	AB	H	HR	BA	PO	A	E	DP	TC/G	FA
1974	LA N	1	0	1.000	2.00	4	0	0	9	5	4	7	0	1	0	0	2	1	0	.500	0	1	0	0	0.3	1.000
1975		3	3	.500	3.09	26	11	1	99	94	32	40	0	0	1	0	28	2	0	.071	5	16	1	1	0.8	.955
1976		12	3	.800	2.98	27	26	10	181	165	53	77	3	0	0	0	65	20	1	.308	9	20	1	0	1.1	.967
1977		16	10	.615	3.75	31	31	4	216	223	63	122	1	0	0	0	78	18	3	.231	8	22	0	1	1.0	1.000
1978		10	8	.556	3.65	30	23	6	165	160	51	79	3	0	2	0	52	7	0	.135	2	23	0	0	0.9	1.000
1979	PIT N	0	1	.000	7.20	1	1	0	5	5	2	2	0	0	0	0	1	1	0	1.000	1	1	0	0	2.0	1.000
1980		7	5	.583	3.83	20	19	2	127	133	40	70	0	0	0	0	40	15	1	.375	6	22	1	1	1.5	.966
1981		9	4	.692	3.90	21	21	4	136	147	53	76	2	0	0	0	48	9	0	.188	8	25	0	4	1.6	1.000
1982		11	14	.440	4.14	35	35	6	230.1	239	70	128	1	0	0	0	83	22	3	.265	21	44	0	1	1.9	1.000
1983		13	13	.500	3.09	36	35	7	244.1	256	68	153	2	0	0	1	86	13	0	.151	14	38	0	4	1.4	1.000
1984		14	9	.609	2.72	33	33	6	238.1	216	62	136	3	0	0	0	84	28	0	.333	14	44	2	2	1.8	.967
1985		10	15	.400	4.47	35	34	4	213.1	254	69	128	0	0	0	0	74	14	0	.189	13	30	0	1	1.2	1.000
1986		15	12	.556	2.84	34	34	12	253.2	211	76	159	1	0	0	0	90	25	1	.278	32	34	0	4	1.9	1.000
1987	NY A	16	10	.615	3.86	30	29	4	181.2	184	61	107	0	0	0	0	0	0	0	–	14	24	1	2	1.3	.974
1988		12	12	.500	4.29	30	30	5	197	206	56	94	1	0	0	0	1	0	0	.000	17	22	0	2	1.3	1.000
1989	HOU N	2	6	.250	4.28	20	17	0	96.2	108	41	41	0	0	0	0	29	6	0	.207	6	20	0	0	1.3	1.000
16 yrs.		151	125	.547	3.60	413	380	69	2593.1	2606	801	1419	17	1	3	1	761	181	9	.238	173	386	6	23	1.4	.989

LEAGUE CHAMPIONSHIP SERIES

Year	Team	W	L	PCT	ERA	G	GS	CG	IP	H	BB	SO	ShO	W	L	SV	AB	H	HR	BA	PO	A	E	DP	TC/G	FA
1977	LA N	0	0	–	0.00	1	0	0	4.1	2	2	0	0	0	0	0	1	0	0	.000	0	0	0	0	0.0	–
1978		0	0	–	2.25	1	0	0	4	2	1	3	0	0	0	0	1	0	0	.000	0	2	0	0	2.0	1.000
2 yrs.		0	0	–	1.08	2	0	0	8.1	4	3	3	0	0	0	0	2	0	0	.000	0	2	0	0	1.0	1.000

WORLD SERIES

Year	Team	W	L	PCT	ERA	G	GS	CG	IP	H	BB	SO	ShO	W	L	SV	AB	H	HR	BA	PO	A	E	DP	TC/G	FA
1977	LA N	0	1	.000	2.57	2	0	0	7	4	1	5	0	0	0	0	2	1	0	.500	1	1	0	0	1.0	1.000

Bill Rhodes

RHODES, WILLIAM CLARENCE (Dusty)
B. Pottstown, Pa.   Deceased.

Year	Team	W	L	PCT	ERA	G	GS	CG	IP	H	BB	SO	ShO	W	L	SV	AB	H	HR	BA	PO	A	E	DP	TC/G	FA
1893	LOU N	5	12	.294	7.60	20	19	17	151.2	244	66	22	0	0	0	0	70	9	0	.129	3	26	5	0	1.7	.853

Charlie Rhodes

RHODES, CHARLES ANDERSON
B. Apr. 7, 1885, Caney, Kans.   D. Oct. 26, 1918, Caney, Kans.   BR TR 5'7"   180 lbs.

Year	Team	W	L	PCT	ERA	G	GS	CG	IP	H	BB	SO	ShO	W	L	SV	AB	H	HR	BA	PO	A	E	DP	TC/G	FA
1906	STL N	3	4	.429	3.40	9	6	3	45	37	20	32	0	1	0	0	16	3	0	.188	2	14	2	0	2.0	.889
1908	2 teams			CIN N	(1G 0–0)			STL N	(4G 1–2)																		
"	total	1	2	.333	2.68	5	4	3	37	24	14	19	0	0	0	0	13	3	0	.231	2	16	1	0	3.8	.947
1909	STL N	3	5	.375	3.98	12	10	4	61	55	33	25	0	1	0	0	19	4	0	.211	2	28	3	0	2.8	.909
3 yrs.		7	11	.389	3.46	26	20	10	143	116	67	76	0	2	0	0	48	10	0	.208	6	58	6	0	2.7	.914

Gordon Rhodes

RHODES, JOHN GORDON (Dusty)
B. Aug. 11, 1907, Winnemucca, Nev.   D. Mar. 24, 1960, Long Beach, Calif.   BR TR 6'   187 lbs.

Year	Team	W	L	PCT	ERA	G	GS	CG	IP	H	BB	SO	ShO	W	L	SV	AB	H	HR	BA	PO	A	E	DP	TC/G	FA
1929	NY A	0	4	.000	4.85	10	4	0	42.2	57	16	13	0	0	0	0	10	3	0	.300	2	7	2	0	1.1	.818
1930		0	0	–	9.00	3	0	0	2	3	4	1	0	0	0	0	0	0	0	–	0	0	0	0	0.3	1.000
1931		6	3	.667	3.41	18	11	4	87	82	52	36	0	1	0	0	28	6	0	.214	2	20	3	0	1.4	.880
1932	2 teams			NY A	(10G 1–2)			BOS A	(12G 1–8)																		
"	total	2	10	.167	5.75	22	13	5	103.1	104	52	27	0	0	2	0	34	4	0	.118	7	26	1	0	1.5	.971
1933	BOS A	12	15	.444	4.03	34	29	14	232	242	93	85	0	1	1	0	86	23	1	.267	8	46	4	2	1.7	.931
1934		12	12	.500	4.56	44	31	10	219	247	98	79	0	3	1	2	75	10	1	.133	5	47	0	1	1.2	1.000
1935		2	10	.167	5.41	34	19	1	146.1	195	60	44	0	0	1	2	48	7	0	.146	6	28	4	1	1.1	.895
1936	PHI A	9	20	.310	5.74	35	28	13	216.1	266	102	61	1	2	0	1	75	16	0	.213	4	29	3	1	1.0	.917
8 yrs.		43	74	.368	4.85	200	135	47	1048.2	1196	477	346	1	7	5	5	356	69	2	.194	34	204	17	6	1.3	.933

Dennis Ribant

RIBANT, DENNIS JOSEPH
B. Sept. 20, 1941, Detroit, Mich.   BR TR 5'11"   165 lbs.

Year	Team	W	L	PCT	ERA	G	GS	CG	IP	H	BB	SO	ShO	W	L	SV	AB	H	HR	BA	PO	A	E	DP	TC/G	FA
1964	NY N	1	5	.167	5.15	14	7	1	57.2	65	9	35	1	0	0	1	20	2	0	.100	2	7	0	0	0.6	1.000
1965		1	3	.250	3.82	19	1	0	35.1	29	6	13	0	1	3	3	6	0	0	.000	0	3	0	0	0.3	1.000
1966		11	9	.550	3.20	39	26	10	188.1	184	40	84	1	0	0	3	61	12	0	.197	12	34	2	1	1.2	.958
1967	PIT N	9	8	.529	4.08	38	22	2	172	186	40	75	0	3	2	0	60	16	0	.267	18	34	1	3	1.4	.981
1968	2 teams			DET A	(14G 2–2)			CHI A	(17G 0–2)																		
"	total	2	4	.333	4.37	31	0	0	55.2	62	27	27	0	2	4	2	12	1	0	.083	6	8	3	0	0.5	.824
1969	2 teams			STL N	(1G 0–0)			CIN N	(7G 0–0)																		
"	total	0	0	–	2.79	8	0	0	9.2	10	4	7	0	0	0	0	0	0	0	–	1	0	1	0	0.3	.500
6 yrs.		24	29	.453	3.87	149	56	13	518.2	536	126	241	2	6	9	9	159	31	0	.195	39	88	7	5	0.9	.948

Frank Riccelli

RICCELLI, FRANK JOSEPH
B. Feb. 24, 1953, Syracuse, N.Y.   BL TL 6'3"   205 lbs.

Year	Team	W	L	PCT	ERA	G	GS	CG	IP	H	BB	SO	ShO	W	L	SV	AB	H	HR	BA	PO	A	E	DP	TC/G	FA
1976	SF N	1	1	.500	5.63	4	3	0	16	16	5	11	0	0	0	0	6	1	0	.167	0	1	0	1	0.3	1.000
1978	HOU N	0	0	–	0.00	2	0	0	3	1	0	1	0	0	0	0	0	0	0	–	0	0	0	0	0.0	–
1979		2	2	.500	4.09	11	2	0	22	22	18	20	0	1	1	0	6	2	0	.333	0	6	0	0	0.5	1.000
3 yrs.		3	3	.500	4.39	17	5	0	41	39	23	32	0	1	1	0	12	3	0	.250	0	7	0	1	0.4	1.000

Sam Rice

RICE, EDGAR CHARLES
B. Feb. 20, 1890, Morocco, Ind.   D. Oct. 13, 1974, Rossmor, Md.   BL TR 5'9"   150 lbs.
Hall of Fame 1963.

Year	Team	W	L	PCT	ERA	G	GS	CG	IP	H	BB	SO	ShO	W	L	SV	AB	H	HR	BA	PO	A	E	DP	TC/G	FA
1915	WAS A	1	0	1.000	2.00	4	2	1	18	13	9	9	0	0	0	0	8	3	0	.375	1	7	1	1	2.3	.889

Year	Team		W	L	PCT	ERA	G	GS	CG	IP	H	BB	SO	ShO	Relief Pitching W	L	SV	Batting AB	H	HR	BA	PO	A	E	DP	TC/G	FA

Sam Rice *continued*

| 1916 | | | 0 | 1 | .000 | 2.95 | 5 | 1 | 0 | 21.1 | 18 | 10 | 3 | 0 | 0 | 1 | 0 | 197 | 59 | 1 | .299 | 0 | 6 | 0 | 0 | 1.2 | 1.000 |
| 2 yrs. | | | 1 | 1 | .500 | 2.52 | 9 | 3 | 1 | 39.1 | 31 | 19 | 12 | 0 | 0 | 1 | 0 | * | | | | 1 | 13 | 1 | 1 | 1.7 | .933 |

Woody Rich

RICH, WOODROW EARL
B. Mar. 9, 1916, Morganton, N. C.   D. Apr. 18, 1983, Morganton, N. C.   BL TR 6'2"   185 lbs.

1939	BOS	A	4	3	.571	4.91	21	12	3	77	78	35	24	0	0	0	1	27	7	0	.259	3	22	3	0	1.3	.893
1940			1	0	1.000	0.77	3	1	1	11.2	9	1	8	0	0	0	0	4	0	0	.000	0	1	0	0	0.3	1.000
1941			0	0	—	17.18	2	1	0	3.2	8	2	4	0	0	0	0	0	0	0	—	0	2	0	0	1.0	1.000
1944	BOS	N	1	1	.500	5.76	7	2	1	25	32	12	6	0	0	0	0	8	1	0	.125	1	5	0	1	0.9	1.000
4 yrs.			6	4	.600	5.06	33	16	5	117.1	127	50	42	0	0	0	1	39	8	0	.205	4	30	3	1	1.1	.919

J. R. Richard

RICHARD, JAMES RODNEY
B. Mar. 7, 1950, Vienna, La.   BR TR 6'8"   222 lbs.

1971	HOU	N	2	1	.667	3.43	4	4	1	21	17	16	29	0	0	0	0	7	0	0	.000	1	3	0	0	1.0	1.000
1972			1	0	1.000	13.50	4	1	0	6	10	8	8	0	1	0	0	0	0	0	—	0	2	0	1	0.5	1.000
1973			6	2	.750	4.00	16	10	2	72	54	38	75	1	0	1	0	28	5	0	.179	5	3	1	0	0.6	.889
1974			2	3	.400	4.15	15	9	0	65	58	36	42	0	0	0	0	21	3	1	.143	5	5	0	0	0.7	1.000
1975			12	10	.545	4.39	33	31	7	203	178	138	176	1	1	0	0	74	15	1	.203	8	19	1	0	0.8	.964
1976			20	15	.571	2.75	39	39	14	291	221	151	214	3	0	0	0	100	14	2	.140	19	39	10	2	1.7	.853
1977			18	12	.600	2.97	36	36	13	267	212	104	214	3	0	0	0	87	20	2	.230	26	44	0	2	1.9	1.000
1978			18	11	.621	3.11	36	36	16	275	192	141	303	3	0	0	0	101	18	1	.178	29	38	3	0	1.9	.957
1979			18	13	.581	2.71	38	38	19	292	220	98	313	4	0	0	0	95	12	2	.126	14	32	5	0	1.3	.902
1980			10	4	.714	1.89	17	17	4	114	65	40	119	4	0	0	0	39	6	1	.154	6	10	0	1	0.9	1.000
10 yrs.			107	71	.601	3.15	238	221	76	1606	1227	770	1493	19	2	1	0	552	93	10	.168	113	195	20	6	1.4	.939

Duane Richards

RICHARDS, DUANE LEE
B. Dec. 16, 1936, Spartanburg, Ind.   BR TR 6'3"   200 lbs.

| 1960 | CIN | N | 0 | 0 | — | 9.00 | 2 | 0 | 0 | 3 | 5 | 2 | 2 | 0 | 0 | 0 | 0 | 0 | 0 | 0 | — | 0 | 1 | 0 | 0 | 0.5 | 1.000 |

Rusty Richards

RICHARDS, RUSSELL EARL
B. Jan. 27, 1965, Houston, Tex.   BL TR 6'4"   200 lbs.

| 1989 | ATL | N | 0 | 0 | — | 4.82 | 2 | 2 | 0 | 9.1 | 10 | 6 | 4 | 0 | 0 | 0 | 0 | 3 | 0 | 0 | .000 | 1 | 3 | 0 | 0 | 2.0 | 1.000 |

Danny Richardson

RICHARDSON, DANIEL
B. Jan. 25, 1863, Elmira, N. Y.   D. Sept. 12, 1926, New York, N. Y.
Manager 1892.   BR TR 5'8"   165 lbs.

1885	NY	N	7	1	.875	2.40	9	8	7	75	58	18	21	1	1	0	0	198	52	0	.263	2	12	0	0	1.6	1.000
1886			0	2	.000	5.76	5	1	1	25	33	11	17	0	1	0	0	237	55	1	.232	3	8	0	1	2.2	1.000
1887			0	0	—	0.00	1	0	0	1	0	1	0	0	0	0	0	450	125	3	.278	0	0	0	0	0.0	—
3 yrs.			7	3	.700	3.24	15	9	8	100	91	30	38	1	2	0	0	*				5	20	0	1	1.7	1.000

Gordie Richardson

RICHARDSON, GORDON CLARK
B. July 19, 1939, Colquitt, Ga.   BR TL 6'   185 lbs.

1964	STL	N	4	2	.667	2.30	19	6	1	47	40	15	28	0	1	0	1	13	1	0	.077	1	3	0	0	0.2	1.000
1965	NY	N	2	2	.500	3.78	35	0	0	52.1	41	16	43	0	2	2	2	7	0	0	.000	4	6	1	0	0.3	.909
1966			0	2	.000	9.16	15	1	0	18.2	24	6	15	0	0	1	1	1	0	0	.000	2	2	0	0	0.3	1.000
3 yrs.			6	6	.500	4.04	69	7	1	118	105	37	86	0	3	3	4	21	1	0	.048	7	11	1	0	0.3	.947

WORLD SERIES

| 1964 | STL | N | 0 | 0 | — | 40.50 | 2 | 0 | 0 | .2 | 3 | 2 | 0 | 0 | 0 | 0 | 0 | 0 | 0 | 0 | — | 0 | 0 | 0 | 0 | 0.0 | — |

Hardy Richardson

RICHARDSON, ABRAM HARDING (Old True Blue)
B. Apr. 21, 1855, Clarksboro, N. J.   D. Jan. 14, 1931, Utica, N. Y.   BR TR 5'9½"   170 lbs.

1885	BUF	N	0	0	—	2.25	1	0	0	4	5	3	1	0	0	0	0	426	136	6	.319	0	2	0	0	2.0	1.000
1886	DET	N	3	0	1.000	4.50	4	0	0	12	11	10	5	0	2	0	0	538	189	11	.351	0	2	0	0	0.5	1.000
2 yrs.			3	0	1.000	3.94	5	0	0	16	16	13	6	0	2	0	0	*				0	4	0	0	0.8	1.000

Jack Richardson

RICHARDSON, JOHN WILLIAMSON
B. Oct. 3, 1891, Central City, Ill.   D. Jan. 18, 1970, Marion, Ill.   BB TR 6'3"   197 lbs.

1915	PHI	A	0	1	.000	2.63	3	3	2	24	21	14	11	0	0	0	0	8	0	0	.000	0	7	1	0	2.7	.875
1916			0	0	—	40.50	1	0	0	.2	2	1	1	0	0	0	0	0	0	0	—	0	0	0	0	0.0	—
2 yrs.			0	1	.000	3.65	4	3	2	24.2	23	15	12	0	0	0	0	8	0	0	.000	0	7	1	0	2.0	.875

Pete Richert

RICHERT, PETER GERARD
B. Oct. 29, 1939, Floral Park, N. Y.   BL TL 5'11"   165 lbs.

1962	LA	N	5	4	.556	3.87	19	12	1	81.1	77	45	75	0	1	1	0	25	2	0	.080	2	16	1	2	1.0	.947
1963			5	3	.625	4.50	20	12	1	78	80	28	54	0	1	1	0	22	4	0	.182	3	8	0	0	0.6	1.000
1964			2	3	.400	4.15	8	6	1	34.2	38	18	25	1	0	0	0	11	1	0	.091	2	9	2	1	1.6	.846
1965	WAS	A	15	12	.556	2.60	34	29	6	194	146	84	161	0	0	0	0	64	10	0	.156	5	30	1	1	1.1	.972
1966			14	14	.500	3.37	36	34	7	245.2	196	69	195	0	0	0	0	86	14	1	.163	13	29	5	0	1.3	.894
1967	2 teams	WAS A	(11G 2–6)				BAL A	(26G 7–10)																				
"	total		9	16	.360	3.47	37	29	6	186.2	156	56	131	2	2	2	0	54	5	0	.093	8	28	3	2	1.1	.923
1968	BAL	A	6	3	.667	3.47	36	0	0	62.1	51	12	47	0	6	3	6	10	2	0	.200	4	12	1	1	0.5	.941
1969			7	4	.636	2.20	44	0	0	57.1	42	14	54	0	7	4	12	8	1	0	.125	3	5	0	0	0.2	1.000
1970			7	2	.778	1.96	50	0	0	55	36	24	66	0	7	2	13	4	0	0	.000	0	8	0	0	0.2	1.000
1971			3	5	.375	3.50	35	0	0	36	26	22	35	0	3	5	4	2	0	0	.000	4	5	1	1	0.3	.900
1972	LA	N	2	3	.400	2.25	37	0	0	52	42	18	38	0	2	3	6	6	3	0	.500	3	5	2	0	0.3	.800
1973			3	3	.500	3.18	39	0	0	51	44	19	31	0	3	3	7	5	1	0	.200	4	10	0	2	0.4	1.000

Year	Team		W	L	PCT	ERA	G	GS	CG	IP	H	BB	SO	ShO	W	L	SV	AB	H	HR	BA	PO	A	E	DP	TC/G	FA
															Relief Pitching			**Batting**									

Pete Richert *continued*

Year	Team		W	L	PCT	ERA	G	GS	CG	IP	H	BB	SO	ShO	W	L	SV	AB	H	HR	BA	PO	A	E	DP	TC/G	FA
1974	2 teams	STL N (13G 0-0)	PHI N	(21G 2-1)																							
"	total		2	1	.667	2.27	34	0	0	31.2	25	15	13	0	2	1	0	0	0	0	–	2	3	2	0	0.2	.714
13 yrs.			80	73	.523	3.19	429	122	22	1165.2	959	424	925	3	35	23	51	297	43	1	.145	53	168	18	14	0.6	.925

LEAGUE CHAMPIONSHIP SERIES

Year	Team		W	L	PCT	ERA	G	GS	CG	IP	H	BB	SO	ShO	W	L	SV	AB	H	HR	BA	PO	A	E	DP	TC/G	FA
1969	BAL A		0	0	–	0.00	1	0	0	1	0	2	2	0	0	0	0	0	0	0	–	0	0	0	0	0.0	–

WORLD SERIES

Year	Team		W	L	PCT	ERA	G	GS	CG	IP	H	BB	SO	ShO	W	L	SV	AB	H	HR	BA	PO	A	E	DP	TC/G	FA
1969	BAL A		0	0	–	0.00	1	0	0	1	0	0	0	0	0	0	0	0	0	0	–	0	1	0	0	1.0	–
1970			0	0	–	0.00	1	0	0	.1	0	0	0	0	0	0	0	0	0	0	–	0	0	0	0	0.0	–
1971			0	0	–	0.00	1	0	0	.2	0	0	1	0	0	0	1	0	0	0	–	0	0	0	0	0.0	–
3 yrs.			0	0	–	0.00	3	0	0	1	0	0	1	0	0	0	1	0	0	0	–	0	1	0	0	0.3	–

Lew Richie

RICHIE, LEWIS A.
B. Aug. 23, 1883, Ambler, Pa.   D. Aug. 15, 1936, Ambler, Pa.
BR TR 5'8"   165 lbs.

Year	Team		W	L	PCT	ERA	G	GS	CG	IP	H	BB	SO	ShO	W	L	SV	AB	H	HR	BA	PO	A	E	DP	TC/G	FA
1906	PHI N		9	11	.450	2.41	33	22	14	205.2	170	79	65	3	0	1	0	60	3	0	.050	10	44	0	0	1.6	1.000
1907			6	6	.500	1.77	25	12	9	117	88	38	40	2	2	0	0	43	7	0	.163	7	26	2	0	1.4	.943
1908			7	10	.412	1.83	25	15	13	157.2	125	49	58	2	1	1	0	52	11	0	.212	7	40	6	4	2.1	.887
1909	2 teams	PHI N (11G 1-1)	BOS N	(22G 7-7)																							
"	total		8	8	.500	2.24	33	14	9	176.2	158	62	53	2	3	2	3	60	9	0	.150	8	31	4	2	1.3	.907
1910	2 teams	BOS N (4G 0-3)	CHI N	(30G 11-4)																							
"	total		11	7	.611	2.71	34	13	8	146.1	137	60	60	3	5	2	3	44	9	0	.205	8	45	3	2	1.6	.946
1911	CHI N		15	11	.577	2.31	36	28	18	253	213	103	78	4	0	1	1	91	14	0	.154	13	70	3	2	2.4	.965
1912			16	8	.667	2.95	39	27	15	238	222	74	69	4	2	2	0	76	10	0	.132	2	57	5	0	1.6	.922
1913			2	4	.333	5.82	16	6	1	65	77	30	15	0	1	0	1	17	2	0	.118	2	14	3	0	1.2	.842
8 yrs.			74	65	.532	2.54	241	137	87	1359.1	1190	495	438	20	13	10	8	443	65	0	.147	57	327	26	10	1.7	.937

WORLD SERIES

Year	Team		W	L	PCT	ERA	G	GS	CG	IP	H	BB	SO	ShO	W	L	SV	AB	H	HR	BA	PO	A	E	DP	TC/G	FA
1910	CHI N		0	0	–	0.00	1	0	0	1	1	0	0	0	0	0	0	0	0	0	–	0	0	0	0	0.0	–

Beryl Richmond

RICHMOND, BERYL JUSTICE
B. Aug. 24, 1907, Glen Easton, W. Va.
D. Apr. 24, 1980, Cameron, W. Va.
BB TL 6'1"   185 lbs.
BR 1933

Year	Team		W	L	PCT	ERA	G	GS	CG	IP	H	BB	SO	ShO	W	L	SV	AB	H	HR	BA	PO	A	E	DP	TC/G	FA
1933	CHI N		0	0	–	1.93	4	0	0	4.2	10	2	2	0	0	0	0	1	0	0	.000	0	0	0	0	0.0	–
1934	CIN N		1	2	.333	3.72	6	2	1	19.1	23	10	9	0	0	1	0	5	0	0	.000	0	3	0	0	0.5	1.000
2 yrs.			1	2	.333	3.38	10	2	1	24	33	12	11	0	0	1	0	6	0	0	.000	0	3	0	0	0.3	1.000

Lee Richmond

RICHMOND, J. LEE
B. May 5, 1857, Sheffield, Ohio   D. Oct. 1, 1929, Toledo, Ohio
TL 5'10"   142 lbs.

Year	Team		W	L	PCT	ERA	G	GS	CG	IP	H	BB	SO	ShO	W	L	SV	AB	H	HR	BA	PO	A	E	DP	TC/G	FA
1879	BOS N		1	0	1.000	2.00	1	1	1	9	4	1	11	0	0	0	0	6	2	0	.333	0	2	0	0	2.0	1.000
1880	WOR N		32	32	.500	2.15	**74**	66	57	590.2	541	74	243	5	1	0	3	309	70	0	.227	13	97	23	1	1.8	.827
1881			25	26	.490	3.39	53	52	50	462.1	547	68	156	3	0	0	0	252	63	0	.250	18	100	8	3	2.4	.937
1882			14	33	.298	3.74	48	46	44	411	525	88	123	0	1	0	0	228	64	2	.281	15	97	14	2	2.6	.889
1883	PRO N		3	7	.300	3.33	12	12	8	92	122	27	13	0	0	0	0	194	55	1	.284	2	19	2	0	1.9	.913
1886	CIN AA		0	2	.000	8.00	3	2	1	18	24	11	6	0	0	0	0	29	8	0	.276	2	2	0	0	1.3	1.000
6 yrs.			75	100	.429	3.06	191	179	161	1583	1763	269	552	8	2	0	3	*				50	317	47	6	2.2	.886

Ray Richmond

RICHMOND, RAYMOND SINCLAIR (Bud)
B. June 5, 1896, Fillmore, Ill.   D. Dec. 21, 1969, DeSoto, Mo.
BR TR 6'   175 lbs.

Year	Team		W	L	PCT	ERA	G	GS	CG	IP	H	BB	SO	ShO	W	L	SV	AB	H	HR	BA	PO	A	E	DP	TC/G	FA
1920	STL A		2	0	1.000	6.35	2	2	1	17	18	9	4	0	0	0	0	6	1	0	.167	3	4	0	0	3.5	1.000
1921			0	1	.000	11.66	7	1	0	14.2	23	14	7	0	0	1	0	4	0	0	.000	3	2	0	0	0.7	1.000
2 yrs.			2	1	.667	8.81	9	3	1	31.2	41	23	11	0	0	1	0	10	1	0	.100	6	6	0	0	1.3	1.000

Reggie Richter

RICHTER, EMIL HENRY
B. Sept. 14, 1888, Dusseldorf, Germany   D. Aug. 2, 1934, Winfield, Ill.
BR TR 6'2"   180 lbs.

Year	Team		W	L	PCT	ERA	G	GS	CG	IP	H	BB	SO	ShO	W	L	SV	AB	H	HR	BA	PO	A	E	DP	TC/G	FA
1911	CHI N		1	3	.250	3.13	22	5	0	54.2	62	20	34	0	0	1	0	10	1	0	.100	3	11	1	2	0.7	.933

Dick Ricketts

RICKETTS, RICHARD JAMES
Brother of Dave Ricketts.
B. Dec. 4, 1933, Pottstown, Pa.   D. Mar. 6, 1988, Rochester, N. Y.
BL TR 6'7"   215 lbs.

Year	Team		W	L	PCT	ERA	G	GS	CG	IP	H	BB	SO	ShO	W	L	SV	AB	H	HR	BA	PO	A	E	DP	TC/G	FA
1959	STL N		1	6	.143	5.82	12	9	0	55.2	68	30	25	0	0	0	0	18	1	0	.056	2	2	3	0	0.6	.571

Elmer Riddle

RIDDLE, ELMER RAY
Brother of Johnny Riddle.
B. July 31, 1914, Columbus, Ga.   D. May 14, 1984, Columbus, Ga.
BR TR 5'11½"   170 lbs.

Year	Team		W	L	PCT	ERA	G	GS	CG	IP	H	BB	SO	ShO	W	L	SV	AB	H	HR	BA	PO	A	E	DP	TC/G	FA
1939	CIN N		0	0	–	0.00	1	0	0	2	1	0	0	0	0	0	0	0	0	0	–	0	0	0	0	0.0	–
1940			1	2	.333	1.87	15	1	1	33.2	30	17	9	0	1	1	2	7	1	0	.143	0	7	0	2	0.5	1.000
1941			19	4	**.826**	2.24	33	22	15	216.2	180	59	80	4	3	0	1	71	16	0	.225	7	43	0	2	1.5	1.000
1942			7	11	.389	3.69	29	19	7	158.1	157	79	78	1	1	2	0	58	15	0	.259	7	28	0	3	1.2	1.000
1943			21	11	.656	2.63	36	33	19	260.1	235	107	69	5	0	0	3	93	18	0	.194	16	48	1	4	1.8	.985
1944			2	2	.500	4.05	4	4	2	26.2	25	12	6	0	0	0	0	8	1	0	.125	2	8	0	0	2.5	1.000
1945			1	4	.200	8.19	12	3	0	29.2	39	27	5	0	1	1	0	11	3	0	.273	1	7	0	1	0.7	1.000
1947			1	0	1.000	8.31	16	3	0	30.1	42	31	8	0	0	0	0	5	0	0	.000	1	2	0	0	0.2	1.000
1948	PIT N		12	10	.545	3.49	28	27	12	191	184	81	63	3	0	0	0	64	12	1	.188	9	39	2	3	1.7	.958
1949			1	8	.111	5.33	16	12	0	74.1	81	45	24	0	0	1	1	22	3	0	.136	6	4	0	0	0.6	1.000
10 yrs.			65	52	.556	3.40	190	124	57	1023	974	458	342	13	6	5	8	339	69	1	.204	49	184	3	15	1.2	.987

WORLD SERIES

Year	Team		W	L	PCT	ERA	G	GS	CG	IP	H	BB	SO	ShO	W	L	SV	AB	H	HR	BA	PO	A	E	DP	TC/G	FA
1940	CIN N		0	0	–	0.00	1	0	0	1	0	2	0	0	0	0	0	0	0	0	–	0	0	0	0	0.0	–

Year	Team	W	L	PCT	ERA	G	GS	CG	IP	H	BB	SO	ShO	Relief Pitching W	L	SV	Batting AB	H	HR	BA	PO	A	E	DP	TC/G	FA

Denny Riddleberger

RIDDLEBERGER, DENNIS MICHAEL
B. Nov. 22, 1945, Clifton Forge, Va.   BR TL 6'3"   195 lbs.

Year	Team	W	L	PCT	ERA	G	GS	CG	IP	H	BB	SO	ShO	W	L	SV	AB	H	HR	BA	PO	A	E	DP	TC/G	FA
1970	WAS A	0	0	–	1.00	8	0	0	9	7	2	5	0	0	0	0	0	0	0	–	0	0	0	0	0.0	
1971		3	1	.750	3.21	57	0	0	70	67	32	56	0	3	1	1	4	0	0	.000	6	8	0	1	0.2	1.000
1972	CLE A	1	3	.250	2.50	38	0	0	54	45	22	34	0	1	3	0	4	0	0	.000	0	9	0	0	0.2	1.000
3 yrs.		4	4	.500	2.77	103	0	0	133	119	56	95	0	4	4	1	8	0	0	.000	6	17	0	1	0.2	1.000

Dorsey Riddlemoser

RIDDLEMOSER, DORSEY LEE
B. Mar. 25, 1875, Frederick, Md.   D. May 11, 1954, Frederick, Md.   BR TR

Year	Team	W	L	PCT	ERA	G	GS	CG	IP	H	BB	SO	ShO	W	L	SV	AB	H	HR	BA	PO	A	E	DP	TC/G	FA
1899	WAS N	0	0	–	18.00	1	0	0	2	7	2	0	0	0	0	0	1	0	0	.000	0	1	0	0	1.0	1.000

Jack Ridgway

RIDGWAY, JACOB AUGUSTUS
B. July 23, 1888, Philadelphia, Pa.   D. Feb. 23, 1928, Philadelphia, Pa.   BL TR 5'11"   174 lbs.

Year	Team	W	L	PCT	ERA	G	GS	CG	IP	H	BB	SO	ShO	W	L	SV	AB	H	HR	BA	PO	A	E	DP	TC/G	FA
1914	BAL F	0	1	.000	11.00	4	1	0	9	20	3	2	0	0	0	0	1	0	0	.000	0	3	0	1	0.8	1.000

Steve Ridzik

RIDZIK, STEPHEN GEORGE
B. Apr. 29, 1929, Yonkers, N. Y.   BR TR 5'11"   170 lbs.

Year	Team	W	L	PCT	ERA	G	GS	CG	IP	H	BB	SO	ShO	W	L	SV	AB	H	HR	BA	PO	A	E	DP	TC/G	FA
1950	PHI N	0	0	–	6.00	1	0	0	3	3	1	2	0	0	0	0	0	0	0	–	0	0	0	0	0.0	–
1952		4	2	.667	3.01	24	9	2	92.2	74	37	43	0	2	0	0	22	3	0	.136	4	7	1	1	0.5	.917
1953		9	6	.600	3.77	42	12	1	124	119	48	53	0	7	1	0	36	7	1	.194	7	17	0	4	0.6	1.000
1954		4	5	.444	4.13	35	6	0	80.2	72	44	45	0	4	1	0	22	5	0	.227	6	13	0	0	0.5	1.000
1955	2 teams			PHI N	(3G 0–1)			CIN N	(13G 0–3)																	
"	total	0	4	.000	3.95	16	3	0	41	42	22	12	0	0	3	0	10	1	0	.100	3	5	2	0	0.6	.800
1956	NY N	6	2	.750	3.80	41	5	1	92.1	80	65	53	1	3	1	0	28	7	0	.250	8	12	2	1	0.5	.909
1957		0	2	.000	4.73	15	0	0	26.2	19	19	13	0	0	2	0	5	1	0	.200	0	3	0	0	0.5	1.000
1958	CLE A	0	2	.000	2.08	6	0	0	8.2	9	5	6	0	0	2	0	1	0	0	.000	0	3	0	0	0.5	1.000
1963	WAS A	5	6	.455	4.82	20	10	0	89.2	82	35	47	0	2	1	1	29	5	0	.172	9	13	1	0	1.2	.957
1964		5	5	.500	2.89	49	3	0	112	96	31	60	0	5	3	2	27	6	0	.222	7	13	2	2	0.4	.909
1965		6	4	.600	4.02	63	0	0	109.2	108	43	72	0	6	4	8	18	3	0	.167	5	19	1	3	0.4	.960
1966	PHI N	0	0	–	7.71	2	0	0	2.1	5	1	0	0	0	0	0	0	0	0	–	0	0	0	0	0.0	–
12 yrs.		39	38	.506	3.79	314	48	4	782.2	709	351	406	1	29	17	11	198	38	1	.192	51	107	9	13	0.5	.946

Elmer Rieger

RIEGER, ELMER JAY
B. Feb. 25, 1889, Perris, Calif.   D. Oct. 21, 1959, Los Angeles, Calif.   BB TR 6'   175 lbs.

Year	Team	W	L	PCT	ERA	G	GS	CG	IP	H	BB	SO	ShO	W	L	SV	AB	H	HR	BA	PO	A	E	DP	TC/G	FA
1910	STL N	0	2	.000	5.48	13	2	0	21.1	26	7	9	0	0	1	0	3	0	0	.000	0	7	1	0	0.6	.875

Dave Righetti

RIGHETTI, DAVID ALLAN (Rags)
B. Nov. 28, 1958, San Jose, Calif.   BL TL 6'2"   170 lbs.

Year	Team	W	L	PCT	ERA	G	GS	CG	IP	H	BB	SO	ShO	W	L	SV	AB	H	HR	BA	PO	A	E	DP	TC/G	FA
1979	NY A	0	1	.000	3.71	3	3	0	17	10	10	13	0	0	0	0	0	0	0	–	1	3	0	1	1.3	1.000
1981		8	4	.667	2.06	15	15	2	105	75	38	89	0	0	0	0	0	0	0	–	6	9	1	0	1.1	.938
1982		11	10	.524	3.79	33	27	4	183	155	**108**	163	0	0	0	1	0	0	0	–	5	18	3	1	0.8	.885
1983		14	8	.636	3.44	31	31	7	217	194	67	169	2	0	0	0	0	0	0	–	3	24	1	2	0.9	.964
1984		5	6	.455	2.34	64	0	0	96.1	79	37	90	0	5	6	31	0	0	0	–	2	13	2	0	0.3	.882
1985		12	7	.632	2.78	74	0	0	107	96	45	92	0	**12**	7	29	0	0	0	–	1	12	1	2	0.2	.929
1986		8	8	.500	2.45	74	0	0	106.2	88	35	83	0	8	8	46[1]	0	0	0	–	1	10	2	1	0.1	1.000
1987		8	6	.571	3.51	60	0	0	95	95	44	77	0	8	6	31	0	0	0	–	3	12	1	0	0.3	.938
1988		5	4	.556	3.52	60	0	0	87	86	37	70	0	5	4	25	0	0	0	–	2	8	0	0	0.2	1.000
1989		2	6	.250	3.00	55	0	0	69	73	26	51	0	2	6	25	0	0	0	–	0	9	0	0	0.2	1.000
10 yrs.		73	60	.549	3.09	469	76	13	1083	951	447	897	2	40	37	188	0	0	0	–	24	118	9	8	0.3	.940

DIVISIONAL PLAYOFF SERIES

Year	Team	W	L	PCT	ERA	G	GS	CG	IP	H	BB	SO	ShO	W	L	SV	AB	H	HR	BA	PO	A	E	DP	TC/G	FA
1981	NY A	2	0	1.000	1.00	2	1	0	9	8	3	13	0	1	0	0	0	0	0	–	0	0	0	0	0.0	–

LEAGUE CHAMPIONSHIP SERIES

Year	Team	W	L	PCT	ERA	G	GS	CG	IP	H	BB	SO	ShO	W	L	SV	AB	H	HR	BA	PO	A	E	DP	TC/G	FA
1981	NY A	1	0	1.000	0.00	1	1	0	6	4	2	4	0	0	0	0	0	0	0	–	0	0	0	0	0.0	–

WORLD SERIES

Year	Team	W	L	PCT	ERA	G	GS	CG	IP	H	BB	SO	ShO	W	L	SV	AB	H	HR	BA	PO	A	E	DP	TC/G	FA
1981	NY A	0	0	–	13.50	1	1	0	2	5	2	1	0	0	0	0	0	0	0	.000	0	0	0	0	0.0	–

Johnny Rigney

RIGNEY, JOHN DUNGAN
B. Oct. 28, 1914, Oak Park, Ill.   D. Oct. 21, 1984, Lombard, Ill.   BR TR 6'2"   190 lbs.

Year	Team	W	L	PCT	ERA	G	GS	CG	IP	H	BB	SO	ShO	W	L	SV	AB	H	HR	BA	PO	A	E	DP	TC/G	FA
1937	CHI A	2	5	.286	4.96	22	4	0	90.2	107	46	38	0	2	2	1	30	5	0	.167	3	14	2	0	0.9	.895
1938		9	9	.500	3.56	38	12	7	167	164	72	84	1	5	3	1	55	8	0	.145	4	32	2	4	1.0	.947
1939		15	8	.652	3.70	35	29	11	218.2	208	84	119	2	0	0	0	80	16	0	.200	3	30	3	1	1.0	.917
1940		14	18	.438	3.11	39	33	19	280.2	240	90	141	2	2	1	3	93	20	0	.215	4	46	0	2	1.3	1.000
1941		13	13	.500	3.84	30	29	18	237	224	92	119	3	0	0	0	84	17	0	.202	13	42	3	2	1.9	.948
1942		3	3	.500	3.20	7	7	6	59	40	16	34	0	0	0	0	19	1	0	.053	1	12	0	1	1.9	1.000
1946		5	5	.500	4.03	15	11	3	82.2	76	35	51	0	0	0	0	26	4	0	.154	2	11	0	0	0.9	1.000
1947		2	3	.400	1.95	11	7	2	50.2	42	15	19	0	0	1	0	14	0	0	.000	2	15	1	2	1.6	.944
8 yrs.		63	64	.496	3.59	197	132	66	1186.1	1101	450	605	10	9	7	5	401	71	0	.177	32	202	11	12	1.2	.955

Jose Rijo

RIJO, JOSE ANTONIO
Born Jose Antonio Rijo y Abreu.
B. May 13, 1965, San Cristobal, Dominican Republic   BR TR 6'1"   200 lbs.

Year	Team	W	L	PCT	ERA	G	GS	CG	IP	H	BB	SO	ShO	W	L	SV	AB	H	HR	BA	PO	A	E	DP	TC/G	FA
1984	NY A	2	8	.200	4.76	24	5	0	62.1	74	33	47	0	2	4	2	0	0	0	–	2	12	1	0	0.6	.933
1985	OAK A	6	4	.600	3.53	12	9	0	63.2	57	28	65	0	1	0	0	0	0	0	–	2	5	0	0	0.6	1.000
1986		9	11	.450	4.65	39	26	4	193.2	172	108	176	0	0	4	0	0	0	0	–	13	18	3	0	0.9	.912
1987		2	7	.222	5.90	21	14	1	82.1	106	41	67	0	0	0	0	0	0	0	–	10	10	1	0	1.0	.952
1988	CIN N	13	8	.619	2.39	49	19	0	162	120	63	160	1	6	1	0	37	2	0	.054	7	23	1	1	0.6	.968
1989		7	6	.538	2.84	19	19	1	111	101	48	86	1	0	0	0	38	8	0	.211	6	14	0	0	1.1	1.000
6 yrs.		39	44	.470	3.87	164	92	6	675	630	321	601	1	10	10	3	75	10	1	.133	40	82	6	1	0.8	.953

Year	Team		W	L	PCT	ERA	G	GS	CG	IP	H	BB	SO	ShO	Relief Pitching W	L	SV	Batting AB	H	HR	BA	PO	A	E	DP	TC/G	FA

George Riley

RILEY, GEORGE MICHAEL
B. Oct. 6, 1956, Philadelphia, Pa.
BL TL 6'2" 210 lbs.

Year	Team		W	L	PCT	ERA	G	GS	CG	IP	H	BB	SO	ShO	W	L	SV	AB	H	HR	BA	PO	A	E	DP	TC/G	FA
1979	CHI	N	0	1	.000	5.54	4	1	0	13	16	6	5	0	0	0	0	2	0	0	.000	1	3	0	0	1.0	1.000
1980	SF	N	0	4	.000	5.75	22	0	0	36	41	20	18	0	0	4	0	1	0	0	.000	1	12	2	1	0.7	.867
1984	SF	N	1	0	1.000	3.99	5	4	0	29.1	39	7	12	0	0	0	0	10	1	0	.100	1	4	0	0	1.0	1.000
1986	MON	N	0	0	–	4.15	10	0	0	8.2	7	8	5	0	0	0	0	0	0	0		0	0	0	0	0.0	
4 yrs.			1	5	.167	4.97	41	5	0	87	103	41	40	0	0	4	0	13	1	0	.077	3	19	2	1	0.6	.917

Andy Rincon

RINCON, ANDREW JOHN
B. Mar. 5, 1959, Monterey Park, Calif.
BR TR 6'3" 195 lbs.

Year	Team		W	L	PCT	ERA	G	GS	CG	IP	H	BB	SO	ShO	W	L	SV	AB	H	HR	BA	PO	A	E	DP	TC/G	FA
1980	STL	N	3	1	.750	2.61	4	4	1	31	23	7	22	0	0	0	0	12	3	0	.250	3	5	0	1	2.0	1.000
1981			3	1	.750	1.75	5	5	1	36	27	5	13	1	0	0	0	13	3	0	.231	2	5	0	0	1.4	1.000
1982			2	3	.400	4.73	11	6	1	40	35	25	11	0	1	0	0	10	1	0	.100	5	3	0	1	0.7	1.000
3 yrs.			8	5	.615	3.11	20	15	3	107	85	37	46	1	1	0	0	35	7	0	.200	10	13	0	2	1.2	1.000

Jeff Rineer

RINEER, JEFFREY ALAN
B. July 3, 1955, Lancaster, Pa.
BL TL 6'4" 205 lbs.

Year	Team		W	L	PCT	ERA	G	GS	CG	IP	H	BB	SO	ShO	W	L	SV	AB	H	HR	BA	PO	A	E	DP	TC/G	FA
1979	BAL	A	0	0	–	0.00	1	0	0	1	0	0	0	0	0	0	0	0	0	0	–	0	0	0	0	0.0	–

Jimmy Ring

RING, JAMES JOSEPH
B. Feb. 15, 1895, Brooklyn, N. Y. D. July 6, 1965, New York, N. Y.
BR TR 6'1" 170 lbs.

Year	Team		W	L	PCT	ERA	G	GS	CG	IP	H	BB	SO	ShO	W	L	SV	AB	H	HR	BA	PO	A	E	DP	TC/G	FA
1917	CIN	N	3	7	.300	4.40	24	7	3	88	90	35	33	0	0	3	2	26	2	0	.077	2	27	0	1	1.2	1.000
1918			9	5	.643	2.85	21	18	13	142.1	130	48	26	4	0	0	0	50	6	0	.120	2	29	3	1	1.6	.912
1919			10	9	.526	2.26	32	18	12	183	150	51	61	2	1	1	3	62	6	0	.097	7	64	0	5	2.2	1.000
1920			17	16	.515	3.23	42	33	18	292.2	268	92	73	1	2	1	1	96	19	0	.198	10	80	3	2	2.2	.968
1921	PHI	N	10	19	.345	4.24	34	30	21	246	258	88	88	0	1	1	1	83	12	0	.145	6	76	3	4	2.5	.965
1922			12	18	.400	4.58	40	33	17	249.1	292	103	116	0	2	1	1	88	13	1	.148	6	75	2	2	2.1	.964
1923			18	16	.529	3.76	39	36	23	313.1	336	115	112	0	1	2	0	113	12	1	.106	11	83	2	2	2.5	.979
1924			10	12	.455	3.97	32	31	16	215.1	236	108	72	1	0	0	0	74	17	0	.230	10	61	3	4	2.3	.959
1925			14	16	.467	4.37	38	37	21	270	325	119	93	1	1	0	0	101	11	2	.109	11	71	4	3	2.3	.953
1926	NY	N	11	10	.524	4.57	39	23	5	183.1	207	74	76	0	2	0	2	56	8	0	.143	5	37	2	3	1.1	.955
1927	STL	N	0	4	.000	6.55	13	3	1	33	39	17	13	0	0	2	0	8	3	0	.375	2	12	2	1	1.2	.875
1928	PHI	N	4	17	.190	6.40	35	25	4	173	214	103	72	0	0	1	0	60	11	0	.183	6	44	0	0	1.4	1.000
12 yrs.			118	149	.442	4.06	389	294	154	2389.1	2545	953	835	9	9	11	11	817	120	4	.147	78	659	25	30	2.0	.967

WORLD SERIES

Year	Team		W	L	PCT	ERA	G	GS	CG	IP	H	BB	SO	ShO	W	L	SV	AB	H	HR	BA	PO	A	E	DP	TC/G	FA
1919	CIN	N	1	1	.500	0.64	2	1	1	14	7	6	4	1	0	1	0	5	0	0	.000	1	3	0	0	2.0	1.000

Allen Ripley

RIPLEY, ALLEN STEVENS
Son of Walt Ripley.
B. Oct. 18, 1952, Norwood, Mass.
BR TR 6'3" 190 lbs.

Year	Team		W	L	PCT	ERA	G	GS	CG	IP	H	BB	SO	ShO	W	L	SV	AB	H	HR	BA	PO	A	E	DP	TC/G	FA
1978	BOS	A	2	5	.286	5.55	15	11	1	73	92	22	26	0	0	0	0	0	0	0	–	3	8	0	0	0.7	1.000
1979			3	1	.750	5.12	16	3	0	65	77	25	34	0	2	0	1	0	0	0	–	2	5	1	0	0.5	.875
1980	SF	N	9	10	.474	4.14	23	20	2	113	119	36	65	0	1	1	0	40	6	0	.150	9	19	2	0	1.3	.933
1981			4	4	.500	4.05	19	14	1	91	103	27	47	0	0	0	0	30	4	0	.133	6	18	1	1	1.3	.960
1982	CHI	N	5	7	.417	4.26	28	19	0	122.2	130	38	57	0	0	1	0	38	5	0	.132	12	22	3	0	1.3	.919
5 yrs.			23	27	.460	4.51	101	67	4	464.2	521	148	229	0	3	2	1	108	15	0	.139	32	72	7	1	1.1	.937

Walt Ripley

RIPLEY, WALTER FRANKLIN
Father of Allen Ripley.
B. Nov. 26, 1916, Worcester, Mass.
BR TR 6' 168 lbs.

Year	Team		W	L	PCT	ERA	G	GS	CG	IP	H	BB	SO	ShO	W	L	SV	AB	H	HR	BA	PO	A	E	DP	TC/G	FA
1935	BOS	A	0	0	–	9.00	2	0	0	4	7	3	0	0	0	0	0	0	0	0	–	0	0	0	0	0.0	–

Ray Rippelmeyer

RIPPELMEYER, RAYMOND ROY
B. July 9, 1933, Valmeyer, Ill.
BR TR 6'3" 200 lbs.

Year	Team		W	L	PCT	ERA	G	GS	CG	IP	H	BB	SO	ShO	W	L	SV	AB	H	HR	BA	PO	A	E	DP	TC/G	FA
1962	WAS	A	1	2	.333	5.49	18	1	0	39.1	47	17	17	0	1	1	0	6	3	1	.500	3	15	1	1	1.1	.947

Charlie Ripple

RIPPLE, CHARLES DAWSON
B. Dec. 1, 1921, Bolton, N. C. D. May 6, 1979, Wilmington, N. C.
BL TL 6'2" 210 lbs.

Year	Team		W	L	PCT	ERA	G	GS	CG	IP	H	BB	SO	ShO	W	L	SV	AB	H	HR	BA	PO	A	E	DP	TC/G	FA
1944	PHI	N	0	0	–	15.43	1	1	0	2.1	6	4	2	0	0	0	0	1	1	0	1.000	0	0	0	0	0.0	–
1945			0	1	.000	7.04	4	0	0	7.2	7	10	5	0	0	1	0	1	0	0	.000	0	1	0	0	0.3	1.000
1946			1	0	1.000	10.80	6	0	0	3.1	5	6	3	0	1	0	0	0	0	0	–	0	0	0	0	0.0	–
3 yrs.			1	1	.500	9.45	11	1	0	13.1	18	20	10	0	1	1	0	2	1	0	.500	0	1	0	0	0.1	1.000

Jay Ritchie

RITCHIE, JAY SEAY
B. Nov. 20, 1936, Salisbury, N. C.
BR TR 6'4" 175 lbs.

Year	Team		W	L	PCT	ERA	G	GS	CG	IP	H	BB	SO	ShO	W	L	SV	AB	H	HR	BA	PO	A	E	DP	TC/G	FA
1964	BOS	A	1	1	.500	2.74	21	0	0	46	43	14	35	0	1	1	0	9	1	0	.111	1	7	0	0	0.4	1.000
1965			1	2	.333	3.17	44	0	0	71	83	26	55	0	1	2	2	5	1	0	.200	4	12	2	1	0.4	.889
1966	ATL	N	0	1	.000	4.08	22	0	0	35.1	32	12	33	0	0	1	4	2	1	0	.500	2	6	0	0	0.4	1.000
1967			4	6	.400	3.17	52	0	0	82.1	75	29	57	0	4	6	1	10	3	0	.300	8	16	2	1	0.5	.923
1968	CIN	N	2	3	.400	4.61	28	2	0	56.2	68	13	32	0	2	1	0	7	0	0	.000	0	7	0	0	0.3	1.000
5 yrs.			8	13	.381	3.49	167	2	0	291.1	301	94	212	0	8	11	8	35	7	0	.200	15	48	4	2	0.4	.940

Wally Ritchie

RITCHIE, WALLACE REID
B. July 12, 1965, Glendale, Calif.
BL TL 6'2" 180 lbs.

Year	Team		W	L	PCT	ERA	G	GS	CG	IP	H	BB	SO	ShO	W	L	SV	AB	H	HR	BA	PO	A	E	DP	TC/G	FA
1987	PHI	N	3	2	.600	3.75	49	0	0	62.1	60	29	45	0	3	2	3	4	1	0	.250	1	9	0	0	0.2	1.000
1988			0	0	–	3.12	19	0	0	26	19	17	8	0	0	0	0	0	0	0		0	4	0	0	0.2	1.000
2 yrs.			3	2	.600	3.57	68	0	0	88.1	79	46	53	0	3	2	3	4	1	0	.250	1	13	0	0	0.2	1.000

Year	Team		W	L	PCT	ERA	G	GS	CG	IP	H	BB	SO	ShO	W	L	SV	AB	H	HR	BA	PO	A	E	DP	TC/G	FA
															Relief Pitching			**Batting**									

Hank Ritter

RITTER, WILLIAM HERBERT
B. Oct. 12, 1893, McCoysville, Pa.   D. Sept. 3, 1964, Akron, Ohio   BR TR 6' 180 lbs.

Year	Team		W	L	PCT	ERA	G	GS	CG	IP	H	BB	SO	ShO	W	L	SV	AB	H	HR	BA	PO	A	E	DP	TC/G	FA
1912	PHI	N	0	0	–	4.50	3	0	0	6	5	5	1	0	0	0	0	1	0	0	.000	0	0	0	0	0.0	–
1914	NY	N	1	0	1.000	1.13	1	0	0	8	4	4	4	0	1	0	0	3	0	0	.000	0	1	0	0	1.0	1.000
1915			2	1	.667	4.63	22	2	0	58.1	66	15	35	0	1	0	1	16	2	0	.125	2	13	2	0	0.8	.882
1916			1	0	1.000	0.00	3	0	0	5	3	0	3	0	1	0	0	0	0	0	–	0	2	0	0	0.7	1.000
4 yrs.			4	1	.800	3.96	29	2	0	77.1	78	24	43	0	3	0	1	20	2	0	.100	2	16	2	0	0.7	.900

Reggie Ritter

RITTER, REGGIE BLAKE
B. Jan. 23, 1960, Malvern, Ark.   BL TR 6'2" 195 lbs.

Year	Team		W	L	PCT	ERA	G	GS	CG	IP	H	BB	SO	ShO	W	L	SV	AB	H	HR	BA	PO	A	E	DP	TC/G	FA
1986	CLE	A	0	0	–	6.30	5	0	0	10	14	4	6	0	0	0	0	0	0	0	–	3	2	0	0	1.0	1.000
1987			1	1	.500	6.08	14	0	0	26.2	33	16	11	0	1	1	0	0	0	0	–	4	5	1	0	0.7	.900
2 yrs.			1	1	.500	6.14	19	0	0	36.2	47	20	17	0	1	1	0	0	0	0	–	7	7	1	0	0.8	.933

Jim Rittwage

RITTWAGE, JAMES MICHAEL
B. Oct. 23, 1944, Cleveland, Ohio   BR TR 6'3" 190 lbs.

Year	Team		W	L	PCT	ERA	G	GS	CG	IP	H	BB	SO	ShO	W	L	SV	AB	H	HR	BA	PO	A	E	DP	TC/G	FA
1970	CLE	A	1	1	.500	4.15	8	3	1	26	18	21	16	0	0	0	0	8	3	0	.375	2	4	0	1	0.8	1.000

Kevin Ritz

RITZ, KEVIN D.
B. June 8, 1965, Eatontown, N. J.   BR TR 6'4" 195 lbs.

Year	Team		W	L	PCT	ERA	G	GS	CG	IP	H	BB	SO	ShO	W	L	SV	AB	H	HR	BA	PO	A	E	DP	TC/G	FA
1989	DET	A	4	6	.400	4.38	12	12	1	74	75	44	56	0	0	0	0	0	0	0	–	4	10	0	0	1.2	1.000

Tink Riviere

RIVIERE, ARTHUR BERNARD
B. Aug. 2, 1899, Liberty, Tex.   D. Sept. 27, 1965, Liberty, Tex.   BR TR 5'10" 167 lbs.

Year	Team		W	L	PCT	ERA	G	GS	CG	IP	H	BB	SO	ShO	W	L	SV	AB	H	HR	BA	PO	A	E	DP	TC/G	FA
1921	STL	N	1	0	1.000	6.10	18	2	0	38.1	45	20	15	0	1	0	0	8	3	0	.375	1	1	2	0	0.2	.500
1925	CHI	A	0	0	–	13.50	3	0	0	4.2	6	7	1	0	0	0	0	1	0	0	.000	1	4	0	0	1.7	1.000
2 yrs.			1	0	1.000	6.91	21	2	0	43	51	27	16	0	1	0	0	9	3	0	.333	2	5	2	0	0.4	.778

Eppa Rixey

RIXEY, EPPA (Eppa Jephtha)
B. May 3, 1891, Culpeper, Va.   D. Feb. 28, 1963, Terrace Park, Ohio   BR TL 6'5" 210 lbs.
Hall of Fame 1963.

Year	Team		W	L	PCT	ERA	G	GS	CG	IP	H	BB	SO	ShO	W	L	SV	AB	H	HR	BA	PO	A	E	DP	TC/G	FA
1912	PHI	N	10	10	.500	2.50	23	20	10	162	147	54	59	3	1	0	0	53	9	0	.170	4	35	0	2	1.7	1.000
1913			9	5	.643	3.12	35	19	9	155.2	148	56	75	2	0	0	2	47	9	0	.191	1	39	0	1	1.1	1.000
1914			2	11	.154	4.37	24	15	2	103	124	45	41	0	0	2	0	26	1	0	.038	3	29	6	4	1.7	.850
1915			11	12	.478	2.39	29	22	10	176.2	163	64	88	2	1	1	1	55	9	0	.164	7	47	4	3	2.0	.931
1916			22	10	.688	1.85	38	33	20	287	239	74	134	3	2	0	0	97	15	0	.155	5	90	1	4	2.5	.990
1917			16	21	.432	2.27	39	36	23	281.1	249	67	121	4	1	0	1	94	18	0	.191	15	93	0	3	2.8	1.000
1919			6	12	.333	3.97	23	18	11	154	160	50	63	1	0	1	0	47	7	0	.149	5	51	1	3	2.5	.982
1920			11	22	.333	3.48	41	33	25	284.1	288	69	109	1	0	2	2	101	25	1	.248	13	90	4	4	2.6	.963
1921	CIN	N	19	18	.514	2.78	40	36	21	301	324	66	76	2	1	1	1	101	13	0	.129	4	97	2	4	2.6	.981
1922			25	13	.658	3.53	40	38	26	313.1	337	45	80	2	1	0	0	109	21	0	.193	10	72	2	3	2.1	.976
1923			20	15	.571	2.80	42	37	23	309	334	65	97	3	2	0	0	107	17	0	.159	12	78	1	4	2.2	.989
1924			15	14	.517	2.76	35	29	15	238.1	219	47	57	4	2	1	1	84	18	1	.214	7	58	3	4	1.9	.956
1925			21	11	.656	2.88	39	36	22	287.1	302	47	69	2	1	1	1	103	22	0	.214	4	64	1	3	1.8	.986
1926			14	8	.636	3.40	37	29	14	233	231	58	61	3	0	0	0	84	19	0	.226	3	52	1	3	1.5	.982
1927			12	10	.545	3.48	34	29	11	219.2	240	43	42	1	0	0	0	81	20	0	.247	4	50	1	1	1.6	.982
1928			19	18	.514	3.43	43	37	17	291.1	317	67	58	3	4	0	2	104	18	1	.173	10	69	1	3	1.9	.988
1929			10	13	.435	4.16	35	24	11	201	235	60	37	0	2	1	1	65	15	0	.231	6	43	0	1	1.4	1.000
1930			9	13	.409	5.10	32	21	5	164	207	47	37	0	1	0	0	55	11	0	.200	7	34	0	1	1.3	1.000
1931			4	7	.364	3.91	22	17	4	126.2	143	30	22	0	0	0	0	40	6	0	.150	3	45	0	2	2.2	1.000
1932			5	5	.500	2.66	25	11	6	111.2	108	16	14	2	1	3	0	34	9	0	.265	4	29	1	0	1.4	.971
1933			6	3	.667	3.15	16	12	5	94.1	118	12	10	1	0	0	0	35	9	0	.257	1	30	1	2	2.0	.969
21 yrs.			266	251	.515	3.15	692	552	290	4494.2	4633	1082	1350	39	20	17	14	1522	291	3	.191	131	1195	30	55	2.0	.978
					9th																						

WORLD SERIES

Year	Team		W	L	PCT	ERA	G	GS	CG	IP	H	BB	SO	ShO	W	L	SV	AB	H	HR	BA	PO	A	E	DP	TC/G	FA
1915	PHI	N	0	1	.000	4.05	1	0	0	6.2	4	2	2	0	0	1	0	2	1	0	.500	0	1	0	0	1.0	1.000

John Roach

ROACH, JOHN F.
B. Farrensville, Pa.   D. Mar. 1, 1915, Sandusky, Ohio   TL 5'9" 175 lbs.

Year	Team		W	L	PCT	ERA	G	GS	CG	IP	H	BB	SO	ShO	W	L	SV	AB	H	HR	BA	PO	A	E	DP	TC/G	FA
1887	NY	N	0	1	.000	11.25	1	1	1	8	18	4	3	0	0	0	0	4	1	0	.250	2	0	0	0	2.0	1.000

Skel Roach

ROACH, SKEL
Born Rudolph C. Weichbrodt.
B. Oct. 20, 1871, Germany   D. Mar. 9, 1958, Oak Park, Ill.   BR TR

Year	Team		W	L	PCT	ERA	G	GS	CG	IP	H	BB	SO	ShO	W	L	SV	AB	H	HR	BA	PO	A	E	DP	TC/G	FA
1899	CHI	N	1	0	1.000	3.00	1	1	1	9	13	1	0	0	0	0	0	4	0	0	.000	0	1	0	0	1.0	1.000

Bruce Robbins

ROBBINS, BRUCE DUANE
B. Sept. 10, 1959, Portland, Ind.   BL TL 6'1" 190 lbs.

Year	Team		W	L	PCT	ERA	G	GS	CG	IP	H	BB	SO	ShO	W	L	SV	AB	H	HR	BA	PO	A	E	DP	TC/G	FA
1979	DET	A	3	3	.500	3.91	10	8	0	46	45	21	22	0	0	0	0	0	0	0	–	1	5	0	1	0.6	1.000
1980			4	2	.667	6.58	15	6	0	52	60	28	23	0	2	0	0	0	0	0	–	2	9	0	0	0.7	1.000
2 yrs.			7	5	.583	5.33	25	14	0	98	105	49	45	0	2	0	0	0	0	0	–	3	14	0	1	0.7	1.000

Bert Roberge

ROBERGE, BERTRAND ROLAND
B. Oct. 3, 1954, Lewiston, Me.   BR TR 6'4" 190 lbs.

Year	Team		W	L	PCT	ERA	G	GS	CG	IP	H	BB	SO	ShO	W	L	SV	AB	H	HR	BA	PO	A	E	DP	TC/G	FA
1979	HOU	N	3	0	1.000	1.69	26	0	0	32	20	17	13	0	3	0	4	0	0	0	.000	3	3	0	0	0.2	1.000
1980			2	0	1.000	6.00	14	0	0	24	24	10	9	0	2	0	0	3	0	0	.000	2	5	0	0	0.5	1.000
1982			1	2	.333	4.21	22	0	0	25.2	29	6	18	0	1	2	3	1	0	0	.000	2	4	0	0	0.3	1.000
1984	CHI	A	3	3	.500	3.76	21	0	0	40.2	36	15	25	0	3	3	2	0	0	0	–	5	9	0	0	0.7	1.000
1985	MON	N	3	3	.500	3.44	42	0	0	68	58	22	34	0	3	3	1	0	0	0	–	5	12	0	0	0.4	1.000

Year	Team	W	L	PCT	ERA	G	GS	CG	IP	H	BB	SO	ShO	Relief Pitching W	L	SV	Batting AB	H	HR	BA	PO	A	E	DP	TC/G	FA

Bert Roberge *continued*

Year	Team	W	L	PCT	ERA	G	GS	CG	IP	H	BB	SO	ShO	W	L	SV	AB	H	HR	BA	PO	A	E	DP	TC/G	FA
1986		0	4	.000	6.28	21	0	0	28.2	33	10	20	0	0	4	1	2	0	0	.000	3	3	0	0	0.3	1.000
6 yrs.		12	12	.500	3.99	146	0	0	219	200	80	119	0	12	12	10	9	0	0	.000	20	36	0	1	0.4	1.000

Dale Roberts

ROBERTS, DALE (Mountain Man)
B. Apr. 12, 1942, Owenton, Ky.

BR TL 6'4" 180 lbs.

Year	Team	W	L	PCT	ERA	G	GS	CG	IP	H	BB	SO	ShO	W	L	SV	AB	H	HR	BA	PO	A	E	DP	TC/G	FA
1967	NY A	0	0	–	9.00	2	0	0	2	3	2	0	0	0	0	0	0	0	0	–	0	1	0	0	0.5	1.000

Dave Roberts

ROBERTS, DAVID ARTHUR
B. Sept. 11, 1944, Gallipolis, Ohio

BL TL 6'3" 195 lbs.

Year	Team	W	L	PCT	ERA	G	GS	CG	IP	H	BB	SO	ShO	W	L	SV	AB	H	HR	BA	PO	A	E	DP	TC/G	FA
1969	SD N	0	3	.000	4.78	22	5	0	49	65	19	19	0	0	0	1	15	4	0	.267	5	9	0	0	0.6	1.000
1970		8	14	.364	3.81	43	21	3	182	182	43	102	2	4	0	1	59	9	2	.153	5	29	1	3	0.8	.971
1971		14	17	.452	2.10	37	34	0	270	238	61	135	2	0	1	0	86	19	0	.221	10	47	1	2	1.6	.983
1972	HOU N	12	7	.632	4.50	35	28	7	192	227	57	111	3	1	0	2	67	16	2	.239	0	31	1	0	0.9	.969
1973		17	11	.607	2.85	39	36	12	249.1	264	62	119	6	0	0	0	85	11	0	.129	9	39	1	1	1.3	.980
1974		10	12	.455	3.40	34	30	8	204	216	65	72	2	1	0	1	73	16	1	.219	15	43	3	5	1.8	.951
1975		8	14	.364	4.27	32	27	7	198	182	73	101	1	0	2	0	63	9	0	.143	13	36	0	0	1.5	1.000
1976	DET A	16	17	.485	4.00	36	36	18	252	254	63	79	4	0	0	0	0	0	0	–	6	53	4	6	1.8	.937
1977	2 teams			DET A (22G 4–10)				CHI N (17G 1–1)																		
"	total	5	11	.313	4.60	39	28	6	182	198	53	69	1	0	0	0	17	1	0	.059	7	39	1	1	1.2	.979
1978	CHI N	6	8	.429	5.26	35	20	2	142	159	56	54	1	1	0	1	52	17	2	.327	8	29	0	2	1.1	1.000
1979	2 teams			SF N (26G 0–2)				PIT N (21G 5–2)																		
"	total	5	4	.556	2.90	47	4	0	80.2	89	30	38	0	5	2	4	10	0	0	.000	1	9	1	1	0.2	.909
1980	2 teams			PIT N (2G 0–1)				SEA A (37G 2–3)																		
"	total	2	4	.333	4.39	39	4	0	82	88	28	48	0	2	3	0	0	0	0	–	3	6	1	0	0.3	.900
1981	NY N	0	3	.000	9.60	7	4	0	15	26	5	10	0	0	0	0	4	1	0	.250	0	4	1	0	0.7	.800
13 yrs.		103	125	.452	3.78	445	277	77	2098	2188	615	957	20	14	5	15	531	103	7	.194	82	374	15	22	1.1	.968

LEAGUE CHAMPIONSHIP SERIES

Year	Team	W	L	PCT	ERA	G	GS	CG	IP	H	BB	SO	ShO	W	L	SV	AB	H	HR	BA	PO	A	E	DP	TC/G	FA
1979	PIT N	0	0	–	0.00	1	0	0	0	0	1	0	0	0	0	0	0	0	0	–	0	0	0	0	0.0	–

Jim Roberts

ROBERTS, JAMES NEWSON (Big Jim)
B. Oct. 13, 1895, Artesia, Miss. D. June 24, 1984, Columbus, Miss.

BR TR 6'3" 205 lbs.

Year	Team	W	L	PCT	ERA	G	GS	CG	IP	H	BB	SO	ShO	W	L	SV	AB	H	HR	BA	PO	A	E	DP	TC/G	FA
1924	BKN N	0	3	.000	7.46	11	5	0	25.1	41	8	10	0	0	0	0	7	1	0	.143	0	6	0	0	0.5	1.000
1925		0	0	–		1	0	0	1	1	0	0	0	0	0	0	0	0	0	–	0	1	1	0	2.0	.500
2 yrs.		0	3	.000	7.18	12	5	0	26.1	42	8	10	0	0	0	0	7	1	0	.143	0	7	1	0	0.7	.875

Leon Roberts

ROBERTS, LEON KAUFFMAN
B. Jan. 22, 1951, Vicksburg, Mich.

BR TR 6'3" 200 lbs.

Year	Team	W	L	PCT	ERA	G	GS	CG	IP	H	BB	SO	ShO	W	L	SV	AB	H	HR	BA	PO	A	E	DP	TC/G	FA
1984	KC A	0	0	–	27.00	1	0	0	1	4	1	1	0	0	0	0	*				0	0	0	0	0.0	–

Ray Roberts

ROBERTS, RAYMOND
B. Aug. 24, 1895, Cruger, Miss. D. Jan. 30, 1962, Cruger, Miss.

BL TR 5'11" 180 lbs.

Year	Team	W	L	PCT	ERA	G	GS	CG	IP	H	BB	SO	ShO	W	L	SV	AB	H	HR	BA	PO	A	E	DP	TC/G	FA
1919	PHI A	0	2	.000	7.71	3	2	0	14	21	3	2	0	0	0	0	4	1	0	.250	1	2	0	0	1.0	1.000

Robin Roberts

ROBERTS, ROBIN EVAN
B. Sept. 30, 1926, Springfield, Ill.
Hall of Fame 1976.

BB TR 6' 190 lbs.

BL 1948-52

Year	Team	W	L	PCT	ERA	G	GS	CG	IP	H	BB	SO	ShO	W	L	SV	AB	H	HR	BA	PO	A	E	DP	TC/G	FA
1948	PHI N	7	9	.438	3.19	20	20	9	146.2	148	61	84	0	0	0	0	44	11	1	.250	2	17	2	1	1.1	.905
1949		15	15	.500	3.69	43	31	11	226.2	229	75	95	3	3	2	4	67	5	0	.075	10	23	1	4	0.8	.971
1950		20	11	.645	3.02	40	39	21	304.1	282	77	146	5	0	0	1	102	12	0	.118	22	50	2	6	1.9	.973
1951		21	15	.583	3.03	44	39	22	315	284	64	127	6	0	1	2	87	15	0	.172	24	37	2	3	1.4	.968
1952		28	7	.800	2.59	39	37	30	330	292	45	148	3	0	0	0	112	14	0	.125	26	44	1	1	1.8	.986
1953		23	16	.590	2.75	44	41	33	346.2	324	61	198	5	0	0	0	123	22	1	.179	16	51	3	7	1.6	.957
1954		23	15	.605	2.97	45	38	29	336.2	289	56	185	4	3	0	4	122	15	0	.123	15	38	1	3	1.2	.981
1955		23	14	.622	3.28	41	38	26	305	292	53	160	1	0	0	3	107	27	2	.252	19	26	2	1	1.1	.957
1956		19	18	.514	4.45	43	37	22	297.1	328	40	157	1	2	0	3	100	20	1	.200	12	50	2	4	1.5	.969
1957		10	22	.313	4.07	39	32	14	249.2	246	43	128	2	1	2	2	80	13	0	.163	26	38	0	1	1.6	1.000
1958		17	14	.548	3.24	35	34	21	269.2	270	51	130	1	0	0	0	99	20	0	.202	17	34	0	0	1.5	1.000
1959		15	17	.469	4.27	35	35	19	257.1	267	35	137	2	0	0	0	89	17	0	.191	22	38	1	2	1.7	.984
1960		12	16	.429	4.02	35	33	13	237.1	256	34	122	2	0	0	0	79	12	0	.152	21	24	2	1	1.3	.957
1961		1	10	.091	5.85	26	18	2	117	154	23	54	0	0	0	0	33	3	0	.091	6	15	0	1	0.8	1.000
1962	BAL A	10	9	.526	2.78	27	25	6	191.1	176	41	102	0	0	0	0	52	10	0	.192	24	21	2	4	1.7	.957
1963		14	13	.519	3.33	35	35	9	251.1	230	40	124	2	0	0	0	79	16	0	.203	24	31	3	1	1.7	.948
1964		13	7	.650	2.91	31	31	8	204	203	52	109	4	0	0	0	68	9	0	.132	9	26	1	2	1.2	.972
1965	2 teams			BAL A (20G 5–7)				HOU N (10G 5–2)																		
"	total	10	9	.526	2.78	30	25	8	190.2	171	30	97	3	0	0	0	56	11	0	.196	14	21	4	1	1.3	.897
1966	2 teams			HOU N (13G 3–5)				CHI N (11G 2–3)																		
"	total	5	8	.385	4.82	24	21	2	112	141	21	54	1	1	0	1	26	3	0	.115	7	17	2	1	1.1	.923
19 yrs.		286	245	.539	3.41	676	609	305	4688.2	4582	902	2357	45	11	5	25	1525	255	5	.167	316	601	31	45	1.4	.967
			10th																								

WORLD SERIES

Year	Team	W	L	PCT	ERA	G	GS	CG	IP	H	BB	SO	ShO	W	L	SV	AB	H	HR	BA	PO	A	E	DP	TC/G	FA
1950	PHI N	0	1	.000	1.64	2	1	1	11	11	3	5	0	0	0	0	2	0	0	.000	0	0	0	0	0.0	–

Charlie Robertson

ROBERTSON, CHARLES CULBERTSON
B. Jan. 31, 1896, Dexter, Tex. D. Aug. 23, 1984, Fort Worth, Tex.

BL TR 6' 175 lbs.

Year	Team	W	L	PCT	ERA	G	GS	CG	IP	H	BB	SO	ShO	W	L	SV	AB	H	HR	BA	PO	A	E	DP	TC/G	FA
1919	CHI A	0	1	.000	9.00	1	1	0	2	5	0	1	0	0	0	0	0	0	0	–	0	0	0	0	0.0	–
1922		14	15	.483	3.64	37	34	21	272	294	89	83	3	1	1	0	87	16	0	.184	6	48	1	1	1.5	.982
1923		13	18	.419	3.81	38	34	18	255	262	104	91	1	0	3	0	85	21	0	.247	8	54	0	2	1.6	1.000
1924		4	10	.286	4.99	17	14	5	97.1	108	54	29	0	2	0	0	33	6	0	.182	0	15	2	1	1.0	.882
1925		8	12	.400	5.26	24	23	6	137	181	47	27	2	0	0	0	45	10	0	.222	6	28	1	0	1.5	.971

Year	Team		W	L	PCT	ERA	G	GS	CG	IP	H	BB	SO	ShO	Relief Pitching W	L	SV	Batting AB	H	HR	BA	PO	A	E	DP	TC/G	FA

Charlie Robertson *continued*

Year	Team		W	L	PCT	ERA	G	GS	CG	IP	H	BB	SO	ShO	W	L	SV	AB	H	HR	BA	PO	A	E	DP	TC/G	FA
1926	STL	A	1	2	.333	8.36	8	7	1	28	38	21	13	0	0	0	0	10	3	0	.300	6	2	0	0	1.0	1.000
1927	BOS	N	7	17	.292	4.72	28	22	6	154.1	188	46	49	0	1	1	0	50	12	0	.240	3	28	1	1	1.1	.969
1928			2	5	.286	5.31	13	7	3	59.1	73	16	17	0	0	1	1	17	0	0	.000	0	11	0	0	0.9	1.000
8 yrs.			49	80	.380	4.44	166	142	60	1005	1149	377	310	6	4	6	1	327	68	0	.208	30	186	5	5	1.3	.977

Dick Robertson

ROBERTSON, PRESTON
B. 1891, Washington, D. C. D. Oct. 2, 1944, New Orleans, La.

BR TR 5'9'' 160 lbs.

Year	Team		W	L	PCT	ERA	G	GS	CG	IP	H	BB	SO	ShO	W	L	SV	AB	H	HR	BA	PO	A	E	DP	TC/G	FA
1913	CIN	N	0	1	.000	7.20	2	1	1	10	13	9	1	0	0	0	0	3	0	0	.000	0	1	0	0	0.5	1.000
1918	BKN	N	3	6	.333	2.59	13	9	7	87	87	28	18	1	1	0	0	30	9	0	.300	4	24	1	1	2.2	.966
1919	WAS	A	0	1	.000	2.28	7	4	0	27.2	25	9	7	0	0	0	0	7	0	0	.000	3	8	0	1	1.6	1.000
3 yrs.			3	8	.273	2.89	22	14	8	124.2	125	46	26	1	1	0	0	40	9	0	.225	7	33	1	1	1.9	.976

Jerry Robertson

ROBERTSON, JERRY LEE
B. Oct. 13, 1943, Winchester, Kans.

BB TR 6'2'' 205 lbs.

Year	Team		W	L	PCT	ERA	G	GS	CG	IP	H	BB	SO	ShO	W	L	SV	AB	H	HR	BA	PO	A	E	DP	TC/G	FA
1969	MON	N	5	16	.238	3.96	38	27	3	179.2	186	81	133	0	0	0	1	56	5	0	.089	8	16	1	0	0.7	.960
1970	DET	A	0	0	–	3.60	11	0	0	15	19	5	11	0	0	0	0	0	0	0	–	0	1	1	0	0.2	.500
2 yrs.			5	16	.238	3.93	49	27	3	194.2	205	86	144	0	0	0	1	56	5	0	.089	8	17	2	0	0.6	.926

Rich Robertson

ROBERTSON, RICHARD PAUL
B. Oct. 14, 1944, Albany, Calif.

BR TR 6'2'' 210 lbs.

Year	Team		W	L	PCT	ERA	G	GS	CG	IP	H	BB	SO	ShO	W	L	SV	AB	H	HR	BA	PO	A	E	DP	TC/G	FA
1966	SF	N	0	0	–	7.71	1	0	0	2.1	3	2	2	0	0	0	0	0	0	0	–	0	0	0	0	0.0	
1967			0	0	–	4.50	1	0	0	2	3	0	1	0	0	0	0	0	0	0	–	1	0	0	0	1.0	1.000
1968			2	0	1.000	6.00	3	1	0	9	9	3	8	0	1	0	0	2	1	0	.500	0	3	0	0	1.0	1.000
1969			1	3	.250	5.52	17	7	1	44	53	21	20	1	0	0	0	10	0	0	.000	0	10	1	1	0.6	.909
1970			8	9	.471	4.84	41	26	6	184	199	96	121	0	1	1	1	59	6	2	.102	14	23	2	3	0.9	.949
1971			2	2	.500	4.57	23	6	1	61	66	31	32	0	1	0	1	15	1	0	.067	5	5	2	0	0.5	.833
6 yrs.			13	14	.481	4.94	86	40	8	302.1	333	153	184	1	3	1	2	86	8	2	.093	20	41	5	4	0.8	.924

Bill Robinson

ROBINSON, WILLIAM
Born William Anderson.
B. Taylorsville, Ky. Deceased.

Year	Team		W	L	PCT	ERA	G	GS	CG	IP	H	BB	SO	ShO	W	L	SV	AB	H	HR	BA	PO	A	E	DP	TC/G	FA
1889	LOU	AA	0	1	.000	10.13	1	1	1	8	10	6	2	0	0	0	0	3	1	0	.333	0	2	0	0	2.0	1.000

Dewey Robinson

ROBINSON, DEWEY EVERETT
B. Apr. 28, 1955, Evanston, Ill.

BR TR 6' 180 lbs.

Year	Team		W	L	PCT	ERA	G	GS	CG	IP	H	BB	SO	ShO	W	L	SV	AB	H	HR	BA	PO	A	E	DP	TC/G	FA
1979	CHI	A	0	1	.000	6.43	11	0	0	14	11	9	5	0	0	1	0	0	0	0	–	0	1	0	0	0.1	1.000
1980			1	1	.500	3.09	15	0	0	35	26	16	28	0	1	1	0	0	0	0	–	3	4	0	0	0.5	1.000
1981			1	0	1.000	4.50	4	0	0	4	5	3	2	0	1	0	0	0	0	0	–	1	0	0	0	0.3	1.000
3 yrs.			2	2	.500	4.08	30	0	0	53	42	28	35	0	2	2	0	0	0	0	–	4	5	0	0	0.3	1.000

Don Robinson

ROBINSON, DON ALLEN
B. June 8, 1957, Ashland, Ky.

BR TR 6'4'' 225 lbs.

Year	Team		W	L	PCT	ERA	G	GS	CG	IP	H	BB	SO	ShO	W	L	SV	AB	H	HR	BA	PO	A	E	DP	TC/G	FA
1978	PIT	N	14	6	.700	3.47	35	32	9	228	203	57	135	1	0	0	0	85	20	0	.235	10	32	1	1	1.2	.977
1979			8	8	.500	3.86	29	25	3	161	171	52	96	0	0	0	1	49	10	0	.204	7	10	2	1	0.7	.895
1980			7	10	.412	3.99	29	24	3	160	157	45	103	2	0	0	1	57	19	1	.333	13	23	2	2	1.3	.947
1981			0	3	.000	5.92	16	2	0	38	47	23	17	0	0	2	2	12	3	0	.250	7	8	0	1	0.9	1.000
1982			15	13	.536	4.28	38	30	6	227	213	103	165	0	2	0	0	85	24	2	.282	14	25	4	0	1.1	.907
1983			2	2	.500	4.46	9	6	0	36.1	43	21	28	0	1	0	0	13	2	1	.154	1	6	0	1	0.8	1.000
1984			5	6	.455	3.02	51	0	0	122	99	49	110	0	5	5	10	31	9	1	.290	8	18	0	0	0.5	1.000
1985			5	11	.313	3.87	44	6	0	95.1	95	42	65	0	4	7	3	21	5	1	.238	7	11	0	2	0.4	1.000
1986			3	4	.429	3.38	50	0	0	69.1	61	27	53	0	3	4	14	6	4	0	.667	6	0	0	0	0.3	1.000
1987	2 teams	PIT N	(42G 6–6)			SF N	(25G 5–1)																				
"	total		11	7	.611	3.42	67	0	0	108	105	40	79	0	11	7	19	18	4	1	.222	8	12	0	0	0.3	1.000
1988	SF	N	10	5	.667	2.45	51	19	3	176.2	152	49	122	2	2	1	6	52	9	1	.173	12	19	3	1	0.7	.912
1989			12	11	.522	3.43	34	32	5	197	184	37	96	1	0	1	0	81	15	3	.185	6	12	0	1	0.5	1.000
12 yrs.			92	86	.517	3.62	453	177	30	1618.2	1530	545	1069	6	28	28	56	510	124	11	.243	99	185	12	10	0.7	.959

LEAGUE CHAMPIONSHIP SERIES

Year	Team		W	L	PCT	ERA	G	GS	CG	IP	H	BB	SO	ShO	W	L	SV	AB	H	HR	BA	PO	A	E	DP	TC/G	FA
1979	PIT	N	1	0	1.000	0.00	2	0	0	2	0	1	3	0	1	0	1	0	0	0	–	0	0	0	0	0.0	–
1987	SF	N	0	1	.000	9.00	3	0	0	3	3	0	3	0	0	1	0	0	0	0	–	0	0	0	0	0.0	–
1989			1	0	1.000	0.00	1	0	0	1.2	3	0	0	0	1	0	1	0	0	0	–	0	0	0	0	0.0	–
3 yrs.			2	1	.667	4.05	6	0	0	6.2	6	1	6	0	2	1	2	0	0	0	–	0	0	0	0	0.0	–

WORLD SERIES

Year	Team		W	L	PCT	ERA	G	GS	CG	IP	H	BB	SO	ShO	W	L	SV	AB	H	HR	BA	PO	A	E	DP	TC/G	FA
1979	PIT	N	1	0	1.000	5.40	4	0	0	5	4	6	3	0	1	0	0	0	0	0	–	0	1	0	0	0.3	1.000
1989	SF	N	0	1	.000	21.60	1	1	0	1.2	4	1	0	0	0	1	0	0	0	0	–	0	0	0	0	0.0	–
2 yrs.			1	1	.500	9.45	5	1	0	6.2	8	7	3	0	1	1	0	0	0	0	–	0	1	0	0	0.2	1.000

Hank Robinson

ROBINSON, JOHN HENRY (Rube)
Born John Henry Roberson.
B. Aug. 16, 1889, Floyd, Ark. D. July 3, 1965, North Little Rock, Ark.

BR TL 5'11½'' 160 lbs.

Year	Team		W	L	PCT	ERA	G	GS	CG	IP	H	BB	SO	ShO	W	L	SV	AB	H	HR	BA	PO	A	E	DP	TC/G	FA
1911	PIT	N	0	1	.000	2.77	5	0	0	13	13	5	8	0	0	1	0	3	0	0	.000	0	5	0	2	1.0	1.000
1912			12	7	.632	2.26	33	16	11	175	146	30	79	0	3	1	2	59	15	0	.254	5	40	0	1	1.4	1.000
1913			14	9	.609	2.38	43	23	8	196.1	184	41	50	1	4	4	0	61	11	0	.180	5	45	1	2	1.2	.980
1914	STL	N	6	8	.429	3.00	26	16	6	126	128	32	30	1	2	1	0	35	6	0	.171	1	47	1	0	1.9	1.000
1915			7	8	.467	2.45	32	15	6	143	128	35	57	1	3	3	0	47	5	0	.106	3	43	0	4	1.4	1.000
1918	NY	A	2	4	.333	3.00	11	3	1	48	47	16	14	0	1	3	0	13	0	0	.000	1	13	0	0	1.3	1.000
6 yrs.			41	37	.526	2.53	150	73	32	701.1	646	159	238	3	13	14	2	218	37	0	.170	15	193	2	9	1.4	.990

Year	Team		W	L	PCT	ERA	G	GS	CG	IP	H	BB	SO	ShO	Relief Pitching W	L	SV	Batting AB	H	HR	BA	PO	A	E	DP	TC/G	FA

Humberto Robinson

ROBINSON, HUMBERTO VALENTINO
B. June 25, 1930, Colon, Panama — BR TR 6'1" 155 lbs.

Year	Team		W	L	PCT	ERA	G	GS	CG	IP	H	BB	SO	ShO	W	L	SV	AB	H	HR	BA	PO	A	E	DP	TC/G	FA
1955	MIL	N	3	1	.750	3.08	13	2	1	38	31	25	19	0	2	0	2	13	1	0	.077	1	7	0	1	0.6	1.000
1956			0	0	–	0.00	1	0	0	2	1	2	0	0	0	0	0	0	0	0	–	1	1	0	0	2.0	1.000
1958			2	4	.333	3.02	19	0	0	41.2	30	13	26	0	2	4	1	6	1	0	.167	4	9	0	1	0.7	1.000
1959	2 teams	CLE A (5G 1–0)					PHI N		(31G 2–4)																		
"	total		3	4	.429	3.42	36	4	1	81.2	79	28	38	0	2	2	1	13	3	0	.231	3	18	2	0	0.6	.913
1960	PHI	N	0	4	.000	3.44	33	1	0	49.2	48	22	31	0	0	3	0	6	1	0	.167	5	8	1	0	0.4	.929
5 yrs.			8	13	.381	3.25	102	7	2	213	189	90	114	0	6	9	4	38	6	0	.158	14	43	3	2	0.6	.950

Jack Robinson

ROBINSON, JOHN EDWARD
B. Feb. 20, 1921, Orange, N. J. — BR TR 6' 175 lbs.

Year	Team		W	L	PCT	ERA	G	GS	CG	IP	H	BB	SO	ShO	W	L	SV	AB	H	HR	BA	PO	A	E	DP	TC/G	FA
1949	BOS	A	0	0	–	2.25	3	0	0	4	4	1	1	0	0	0	0	0	0	0	–	1	2	0	0	1.0	1.000

Jeff Robinson

ROBINSON, JEFFREY DANIEL
B. Dec. 13, 1960, Santa Ana, Calif. — BR TR 6'4" 195 lbs.

Year	Team		W	L	PCT	ERA	G	GS	CG	IP	H	BB	SO	ShO	W	L	SV	AB	H	HR	BA	PO	A	E	DP	TC/G	FA
1984	SF	N	7	15	.318	4.56	34	33	1	171.2	195	52	102	1	0	0	0	61	7	0	.115	14	24	1	1	1.1	.974
1985			0	0	–	5.11	8	0	0	12.1	16	10	8	0	0	0	0	0	0	0	–	0	0	0	0	0.0	–
1986			6	3	.667	3.36	64	1	0	104.1	92	32	90	0	6	3	8	15	1	0	.067	10	11	1	1	0.3	.952
1987	2 teams	SF N (63G 6–8)					PIT N		(18G 2–1)																		
"	total		8	9	.471	2.85	81	0	0	123.1	89	54	101	0	8	9	14	22	3	1	.136	14	18	0	6	0.4	1.000
1988	PIT	N	11	5	.688	3.03	75	0	0	124.2	113	39	87	0	11	5	9	16	3	0	.188	13	17	0	0	0.4	1.000
1989			7	13	.350	4.58	50	19	0	141.1	161	59	95	0	2	6	4	35	8	1	.229	13	26	5	2	0.9	.886
6 yrs.			39	45	.464	3.80	312	53	1	677.2	666	246	483	1	27	23	35	149	22	2	.148	64	95	7	10	0.7	.958

Jeff Robinson

ROBINSON, JEFFREY MARK
B. Dec. 14, 1961, Ventura, Calif. — BR TR 6'6" 210 lbs.

Year	Team		W	L	PCT	ERA	G	GS	CG	IP	H	BB	SO	ShO	W	L	SV	AB	H	HR	BA	PO	A	E	DP	TC/G	FA
1987	DET	A	9	6	.600	5.37	29	21	2	127.1	132	54	98	1	1	1	0	0	0	0	–	14	9	2	2	0.9	.920
1988			13	6	.684	2.98	24	23	6	172	121	72	114	2	0	0	0	0	0	0	–	16	19	1	1	1.5	.972
1989			4	5	.444	4.73	16	16	1	78	76	46	40	1	0	0	0	0	0	0	–	3	6	0	1	0.6	1.000
3 yrs.			26	17	.605	4.15	69	60	9	377.1	329	172	252	4	1	1	0	0	0	0	–	33	34	3	4	1.0	.957

LEAGUE CHAMPIONSHIP SERIES

Year	Team		W	L	PCT	ERA	G	GS	CG	IP	H	BB	SO	ShO	W	L	SV	AB	H	HR	BA	PO	A	E	DP	TC/G	FA
1987	DET	A	0	0	–	0.00	1	0	0	.1	1	0	0	0	0	0	0	0	0	0	–	0	1	0	0	1.0	1.000

Ron Robinson

ROBINSON, RONALD DEAN
B. Mar. 24, 1962, Exeter, Calif. — BR TR 6'4" 235 lbs.

Year	Team		W	L	PCT	ERA	G	GS	CG	IP	H	BB	SO	ShO	W	L	SV	AB	H	HR	BA	PO	A	E	DP	TC/G	FA
1984	CIN	N	1	2	.333	2.72	12	5	1	39.2	35	13	24	0	0	0	0	8	0	0	.000	1	7	0	0	0.7	1.000
1985			7	7	.500	3.99	33	12	0	108.1	107	32	76	0	3	1	1	22	2	0	.091	9	17	2	4	0.8	.929
1986			10	3	.769	3.24	70	0	0	116.2	110	43	117	0	10	3	14	14	1	0	.071	8	20	0	2	0.4	1.000
1987			7	5	.583	3.68	48	18	0	154	148	43	99	0	1	2	4	36	7	0	.194	5	18	5	1	0.6	.821
1988			3	7	.300	4.12	17	16	0	78.2	88	26	38	0	0	0	0	25	5	0	.200	10	11	3	0	1.4	.875
1989			5	3	.625	3.35	15	15	0	83.1	80	28	36	0	0	0	0	28	6	0	.214	4	13	1	0	1.2	.944
6 yrs.			33	27	.550	3.60	195	66	1	580.2	568	185	390	0	14	6	19	133	21	0	.158	37	86	11	7	0.7	.918

Yank Robinson

ROBINSON, WILLIAM H.
B. Sept. 19, 1859, Philadelphia, Pa. D. Aug. 25, 1894, St. Louis, Mo. — BR TR 5'6½" 170 lbs.

Year	Team		W	L	PCT	ERA	G	GS	CG	IP	H	BB	SO	ShO	W	L	SV	AB	H	HR	BA	PO	A	E	DP	TC/G	FA
1882	DET	N	0	0	–	0.00	1	0	0	2	0	1	0	0	0	0	0	39	7	0	.179	0	1	0	0	1.0	1.000
1884	BAL	U	3	3	.500	3.48	11	3	3	75	96	18	61	0	2	1	0	415	111	2	.267	3	4	4	0	1.0	.636
1886	STL	AA	0	1	.000	3.00	1	1	1	9	10	7	1	0	0	0	0	481	132	3	.274	0	1	0	0	1.0	1.000
1887			0	0	–	3.00	1	0	0	3	3	3	0	0	0	0	1	430	131	1	.305	0	0	0	0	0.0	–
4 yrs.			3	4	.429	3.34	14	4	4	89	109	29	62	0	2	1	1	*				3	6	4	1	0.9	.692

Chick Robitaille

ROBITAILLE, JOSEPH ANTHONY
B. Mar. 2, 1879, Whitehall, N. Y. D. July 30, 1947, Waterford, N. Y. — BR TR 5'8" 150 lbs.

Year	Team		W	L	PCT	ERA	G	GS	CG	IP	H	BB	SO	ShO	W	L	SV	AB	H	HR	BA	PO	A	E	DP	TC/G	FA
1904	PIT	N	4	3	.571	1.91	9	8	8	66	52	13	34	0	0	0	0	21	2	0	.095	4	10	0	0	1.6	1.000
1905			8	5	.615	2.93	17	12	10	120	126	28	32	0	2	0	0	45	6	0	.133	3	35	0	1	2.2	1.000
2 yrs.			12	8	.600	2.56	26	20	18	186	178	41	66	0	2	0	0	66	8	0	.121	7	45	0	1	2.0	1.000

Armando Roche

ROCHE, ARMANDO BAEZ
Born Armando Roche y Baez.
B. Dec. 7, 1926, Havana, Cuba — BR TR 6' 190 lbs.

Year	Team		W	L	PCT	ERA	G	GS	CG	IP	H	BB	SO	ShO	W	L	SV	AB	H	HR	BA	PO	A	E	DP	TC/G	FA
1945	WAS	A	0	0	–	6.00	2	0	0	6	10	2	0	0	0	0	0	1	0	0	.000	0	3	0	0	1.5	1.000

Mike Rochford

ROCHFORD, MICHAEL JOSEPH
B. Mar. 14, 1963, Methuen, Mass. — BL TL 6'4" 205 lbs.

Year	Team		W	L	PCT	ERA	G	GS	CG	IP	H	BB	SO	ShO	W	L	SV	AB	H	HR	BA	PO	A	E	DP	TC/G	FA
1988	BOS	A	0	0	–	0.00	2	0	0	2.1	4	1	1	0	0	0	0	0	0	0	–	1	2	0	0	1.5	1.000
1989			0	0	–	6.75	4	0	0	4	4	4	1	0	0	0	0	0	0	0	–	0	0	0	0	0.0	–
2 yrs.			0	0	–	4.26	6	0	0	6.1	8	5	2	0	0	0	0	0	0	0	–	1	2	0	0	0.5	1.000

Rich Rodas

RODAS, RICHARD MARTIN
B. Nov. 7, 1959, Roseville, Calif. — BL TL 6'2" 180 lbs.

Year	Team		W	L	PCT	ERA	G	GS	CG	IP	H	BB	SO	ShO	W	L	SV	AB	H	HR	BA	PO	A	E	DP	TC/G	FA
1983	LA	N	0	0	–	1.93	7	0	0	4.2	4	3	5	0	0	0	0	0	0	0	–	1	0	0	0	0.1	1.000
1984			0	0	–	5.40	3	0	0	5	5	1	1	0	0	0	0	1	0	0	.000	1	1	0	0	0.7	1.000
2 yrs.			0	0	–	3.72	10	0	0	9.2	9	4	6	0	0	0	0	1	0	0	.000	2	1	0	0	0.3	1.000

Ed Rodriguez

RODRIGUEZ, EDUARDO
Born Eduardo Rodriguez y Reyes.
B. Mar. 6, 1952, Barceloneta, Puerto Rico — BR TR 6' 180 lbs.

Year	Team		W	L	PCT	ERA	G	GS	CG	IP	H	BB	SO	ShO	W	L	SV	AB	H	HR	BA	PO	A	E	DP	TC/G	FA
1973	MIL	A	9	7	.563	3.30	30	6	2	76.1	71	47	49	0	6	6	5	1	1	0	1.000	5	9	1	2	0.5	.933
1974			7	4	.636	3.62	43	6	0	112	97	51	58	0	6	1	4	0	0	0	–	9	15	1	1	0.6	.960

Year	Team		W	L	PCT	ERA	G	GS	CG	IP	H	BB	SO	ShO	Relief Pitching W	L	SV	Batting AB	H	HR	BA	PO	A	E	DP	TC/G	FA

Ed Rodriguez *continued*

Year	Team		W	L	PCT	ERA	G	GS	CG	IP	H	BB	SO	ShO	W	L	SV	AB	H	HR	BA	PO	A	E	DP	TC/G	FA
1975			7	0	1.000	3.49	43	1	0	87.2	77	44	65	0	7	0	7	0	0	0	–	4	6	3	0	0.3	.769
1976			5	13	.278	3.64	45	12	3	136	124	65	77	0	2	6	8	0	0	0	–	8	16	4	2	0.6	.857
1977			5	6	.455	4.34	42	5	1	143	126	56	104	1	4	3	4	0	0	0	–	11	14	1	1	0.6	.962
1978			5	5	.500	3.93	32	8	0	105.1	107	26	51	0	2	3	2	0	0	0	–	10	12	0	0	0.7	1.000
1979	KC	A	4	1	.800	4.86	29	1	1	74	79	34	26	0	3	1	2	0	0	0	–	0	8	1	0	0.3	.889
7 yrs.			42	36	.538	3.89	264	39	7	734.1	681	323	430	1	30	20	32	1	1	0	1.000	47	80	11	6	0.5	.920

Freddy Rodriguez

RODRIGUEZ, FERNANDO PEDRO
Born Fernando Pedro Rodriguez y Borrego.
B. Apr. 29, 1924, Havana, Cuba

BR TR 6' 180 lbs.

Year	Team		W	L	PCT	ERA	G	GS	CG	IP	H	BB	SO	ShO	W	L	SV	AB	H	HR	BA	PO	A	E	DP	TC/G	FA
1958	CHI	N	0	0	–	7.36	7	0	0	7.1	8	5	5	0	0	0	2	1	0	0	.000	0	0	0	0	0.0	–
1959	PHI	N	0	0	–	13.50	1	0	0	2	4	0	1	0	0	0	0	0	0	0	–	0	0	0	0	0.0	–
2 yrs.			0	0		8.68	8	0	0	9.1	12	5	6	0	0	0	2	1	0	0	.000	0	0	0	0	0.0	–

Rick Rodriguez

RODRIGUEZ, RICARDO
B. Sept. 21, 1960, Oakland, Calif.

BR TR 6'3" 190 lbs.

Year	Team		W	L	PCT	ERA	G	GS	CG	IP	H	BB	SO	ShO	W	L	SV	AB	H	HR	BA	PO	A	E	DP	TC/G	FA
1986	OAK	A	1	2	.333	6.61	3	3	0	16.1	17	7	2	0	0	0	0	0	0	0	–	1	4	0	0	1.7	1.000
1987			1	0	1.000	2.96	15	0	0	24.1	32	15	9	0	1	0	0	0	0	0	–	2	6	0	1	0.5	1.000
1988	CLE	A	1	2	.333	7.09	10	5	0	33	43	17	9	0	0	0	0	0	0	0	–	4	8	0	1	1.2	1.000
3 yrs.			3	4	.429	5.62	28	8	0	73.2	92	39	20	0	1	0	0	0	0	0	–	7	18	0	2	0.9	1.000

Roberto Rodriguez

RODRIGUEZ, ROBERTO (Bobby)
Born Roberto Rodriguez y Munoz.
B. Nov. 29, 1941, Caracas, Venezuela

BR TR 6'3" 185 lbs.

Year	Team		W	L	PCT	ERA	G	GS	CG	IP	H	BB	SO	ShO	W	L	SV	AB	H	HR	BA	PO	A	E	DP	TC/G	FA
1967	KC	A	1	1	.500	3.57	15	5	0	40.1	42	14	29	0	0	0	2	9	0	0	.000	0	5	0	0	0.3	1.000
1970	3 teams		OAK A (6G 0–0)			SD N (10G 0–0)				CHI N (26G 3–2)																	
"	total		3	2	.600	5.53	42	0	0	71.2	86	23	62	0	3	2	5	12	1	1	.083	3	9	0	0	0.3	1.000
2 yrs.			4	3	.571	4.82	57	5	0	112	128	37	91	0	3	2	7	21	1	1	.048	3	14	0	0	0.3	1.000

Rosario Rodriguez

RODRIGUEZ, ROSARIO ISABEL
Born Rosario Isabel Rodriguez y Echavarria.
B. July 8, 1969, Los Mochis, Mexico

BR TL 6' 185 lbs.

Year	Team		W	L	PCT	ERA	G	GS	CG	IP	H	BB	SO	ShO	W	L	SV	AB	H	HR	BA	PO	A	E	DP	TC/G	FA
1989	CIN	N	1	1	.500	4.15	7	0	0	4.1	3	3	0	0	1	1	0	0	0	0	–	1	1	0	0	0.3	1.000

Clay Roe

ROE, JAMES CLAY (Shad)
B. Jan. 7, 1904, Green Briar, Tenn. D. Apr. 3, 1956, Cleveland, Miss.

BL TL 6'1" 180 lbs.

Year	Team		W	L	PCT	ERA	G	GS	CG	IP	H	BB	SO	ShO	W	L	SV	AB	H	HR	BA	PO	A	E	DP	TC/G	FA
1923	WAS	A	0	1	.000	0.00	1	1	0	1.2	0	6	2	0	0	0	0	0	0	0	–	0	0	0	0	0.0	–

Preacher Roe

ROE, ELWIN CHARLES
B. Feb. 26, 1915, Ashflat, Ark.

BR TL 6'2" 170 lbs.

Year	Team		W	L	PCT	ERA	G	GS	CG	IP	H	BB	SO	ShO	W	L	SV	AB	H	HR	BA	PO	A	E	DP	TC/G	FA
1938	STL	N	0	0	–	13.50	1	0	0	2.2	4	2	1	0	0	0	0	1	0	0	.000	0	0	0	0	0.0	–
1944	PIT	N	13	11	.542	3.11	39	25	7	185.1	182	59	88	1	5	1	1	53	7	0	.132	11	27	2	0	1.0	.950
1945			14	13	.519	2.87	33	31	15	235	228	46	148	3	0	0	1	75	8	0	.107	16	40	0	3	1.7	1.000
1946			3	8	.273	5.14	21	10	1	70	83	25	28	0	1	2	0	15	1	0	.067	4	13	1	1	0.9	.944
1947			4	15	.211	5.25	38	22	4	144	156	63	59	1	1	0	2	40	5	0	.125	6	20	1	2	0.7	.963
1948	BKN	N	12	8	.600	2.63	34	22	8	177.2	156	33	86	2	2	0	2	51	5	0	.098	4	30	0	0	1.0	1.000
1949			15	6	.714	2.79	30	27	13	212.2	201	44	109	1	1	0	1	70	8	0	.114	5	29	2	4	1.2	.944
1950			19	11	.633	3.30	36	32	16	250.2	245	66	125	2	2	0	1	91	14	0	.154	12	34	1	3	1.3	.979
1951			22	3	.880	3.04	34	33	19	257.2	247	64	113	2	1	0	0	89	10	0	.112	18	39	3	6	1.8	.950
1952			11	2	.846	3.12	27	25	8	158.2	163	39	83	2	1	0	0	57	4	0	.070	9	23	0	1	1.2	1.000
1953			11	3	.786	4.36	25	24	9	157	171	40	85	1	1	0	0	57	3	0	.053	4	30	0	1	1.4	1.000
1954			3	4	.429	5.00	15	10	1	63	69	23	31	0	0	0	0	21	3	0	.143	1	10	0	1	0.7	1.000
12 yrs.			127	84	.602	3.43	333	261	101	1914.1	1907	504	956	17	14	3	10	620	68	1	.110	90	295	10	26	1.2	.975

WORLD SERIES

Year	Team		W	L	PCT	ERA	G	GS	CG	IP	H	BB	SO	ShO	W	L	SV	AB	H	HR	BA	PO	A	E	DP	TC/G	FA
1949	BKN	N	1	0	1.000	0.00	1	1	1	9	6	0	3	1	0	0	0	3	0	0	.000	1	1	0	0	3.0	.667
1952			1	0	1.000	3.18	3	1	1	11.1	9	6	7	0	0	0	0	2	0	0	.000	1	0	0	0	0.3	1.000
1953			0	1	.000	4.50	1	1	1	8	5	4	4	0	0	0	0	3	0	0	.000	1	1	0	0	2.0	1.000
3 yrs.			2	1	.667	2.54	5	3	3	28.1	20	10	14	1	0	0	0	8	0	0	.000	3	2	1	0	1.2	.833

Ed Roebuck

ROEBUCK, EDWARD JACK
B. July 3, 1931, East Millsboro, Pa.

BR TR 6'2" 185 lbs.

Year	Team		W	L	PCT	ERA	G	GS	CG	IP	H	BB	SO	ShO	W	L	SV	AB	H	HR	BA	PO	A	E	DP	TC/G	FA
1955	BKN	N	5	6	.455	4.71	47	0	0	84	96	24	33	0	5	6	12	18	2	0	.111	7	20	2	0	0.6	.931
1956			5	4	.556	3.93	43	0	0	89.1	83	29	60	0	5	4	1	18	6	0	.333	6	17	0	1	0.5	1.000
1957			8	2	.800	2.71	44	1	0	96.1	70	46	73	0	8	1	8	21	5	2	.238	8	26	3	2	0.8	.919
1958	LA	N	0	1	.000	3.48	32	0	0	44	45	15	26	0	0	1	5	4	2	0	.500	4	6	1	0	0.3	.909
1960			8	3	.727	2.78	58	0	0	116.2	109	38	77	0	8	3	8	24	4	0	.167	8	28	1	3	0.6	.973
1961			2	0	1.000	5.00	5	0	0	9	12	2	9	0	2	0	0	2	0	0	.000	2	1	1	0	0.8	.750
1962			10	2	.833	3.09	64	0	0	119.1	102	54	72	0	10	2	9	28	6	0	.214	7	22	1	2	0.5	.967
1963	2 teams		LA N (29G 2–4)			WAS A (26G 2–1)																					
"	total		4	5	.444	3.69	55	0	0	97.2	117	50	51	0	4	5	4	15	3	0	.200	3	24	0	1	0.5	.964
1964	2 teams		WAS A (2G 0–0)			PHI N (60G 5–3)																					
"	total		5	3	.625	2.30	62	0	0	78.1	55	27	42	0	5	3	12	6	0	0	.000	6	19	3	1	0.4	.893
1965	PHI	N	5	3	.625	3.40	44	0	0	50.1	55	15	29	0	5	3	3	1	0	0	.000	1	3	1	0	0.1	.800
1966			0	2	.000	6.00	6	0	0	6	9	2	5	0	0	2	0	0	0	0	–	0	0	0	0	0.0	–
11 yrs.			52	31	.627	3.35	460	1	0	791	753	302	477	0	52	30	62	137	28	2	.204	52	166	14	10	0.5	.940

WORLD SERIES

Year	Team		W	L	PCT	ERA	G	GS	CG	IP	H	BB	SO	ShO	W	L	SV	AB	H	HR	BA	PO	A	E	DP	TC/G	FA
1955	BKN	N	0	0	–	0.00	1	0	0	2	1	0	1	0	0	0	0	0	0	0	–	2	0	0	0	2.0	1.000

Year	Team	W	L	PCT	ERA	G	GS	CG	IP	H	BB	SO	ShO	Relief Pitching W	L	SV	Batting AB	H	HR	BA	PO	A	E	DP	TC/G	FA

Ed Roebuck *continued*

| 1956 | | 0 | 0 | – | 2.08 | 3 | 0 | 0 | 4.1 | 1 | 0 | 5 | 0 | 0 | 0 | 0 | 0 | 0 | 0 | – | 0 | 0 | 0 | 0 | 0.0 | – |
| 2 yrs. | | 0 | 0 | – | 1.42 | 4 | 0 | 0 | 6.1 | 2 | 0 | 5 | 0 | 0 | 0 | 0 | 0 | 0 | 0 | – | 2 | 0 | 0 | 0 | 0.5 | 1.000 |

Mike Roesler

ROESLER, MICHAEL JOSEPH
B. Sept. 12, 1963, Fort Wayne, Ind.　　BR TR 6'5" 195 lbs.

| 1989 | CIN N | 0 | 1 | .000 | 3.96 | 17 | 0 | 0 | 25 | 22 | 9 | 14 | 0 | 0 | 1 | 0 | 0 | 0 | 0 | – | 0 | 1 | 0 | 0 | 0.1 | 1.000 |

Oscar Roettger

ROETTGER, OSCAR FREDERICK LOUIS
Brother of Wally Roettger.
B. Feb. 19, 1900, St. Louis, Mo.　D. July 4, 1986, St. Louis, Mo.　　BR TR 6' 170 lbs.

1923	NY A	0	0	–	8.49	5	0	0	11.2	16	12	7	0	0	0	1	2	0	0	.000	3	2	0	0	1.0	1.000
1924		0	0	–	0.00	1	0	0	1	1	2	0	0	0	0	0	0	0	0	–	0	0	0	0	0.0	–
2 yrs.		0	0	–	8.49	6	0	0	11.2	17	14	7	0	0	0	1				*	3	2	0	0	0.8	1.000

Joe Rogalski

ROGALSKI, JOSEPH ANTHONY
B. July 15, 1912, Ashland, Wis.　D. Nov. 20, 1951, Ashland, Wis.　　BR TR 6'2" 187 lbs.

| 1938 | DET A | 0 | 0 | – | 2.57 | 2 | 0 | 0 | 7 | 12 | 0 | 2 | 0 | 0 | 0 | 0 | 2 | 0 | 0 | .000 | 1 | 0 | 0 | 0 | 0.5 | 1.000 |

Buck Rogers

ROGERS, ORLIN WOODROW (Lefty)
B. Nov. 5, 1912, Spring Garden, Va.　　BR TL 5'8½" 164 lbs.

| 1935 | WAS A | 0 | 1 | .000 | 7.20 | 2 | 1 | 0 | 10 | 16 | 6 | 7 | 0 | 0 | 0 | 0 | 3 | 0 | 0 | .000 | 0 | 0 | 0 | 0 | 0.0 | – |

Kenny Rogers

ROGERS, KENNETH SCOTT
B. Nov. 10, 1964, Savannah, Ga.　　BL TL 6'1" 200 lbs.

| 1989 | TEX A | 3 | 4 | .429 | 2.93 | 73 | 0 | 0 | 73.2 | 60 | 42 | 63 | 0 | 3 | 4 | 2 | 0 | 0 | 0 | – | 1 | 22 | 0 | 0 | 0.3 | 1.000 |

Lee Rogers

ROGERS, LEE OTIS (Buck, Lefty)
B. Oct. 8, 1913, Tuscaloosa, Ala.　　BR TL 5'11" 170 lbs.

| 1938 | 2 teams | BOS A | (14G 1–1) | | BKN N | (12G 0–2) | | | | | | | | | | | | | | | | | | | | |
| " | total | 1 | 3 | .250 | 6.14 | 26 | 4 | 0 | 51.1 | 55 | 28 | 18 | 0 | 0 | 0 | 0 | 7 | 0 | 0 | .000 | 6 | 19 | 2 | 1 | 1.0 | .926 |

Steve Rogers

ROGERS, STEPHEN DOUGLAS
B. Oct. 26, 1949, Jefferson City, Mo.　　BR TR 6'2" 175 lbs.

1973	MON N	10	5	.667	1.54	17	17	7	134	93	49	64	3	0	0	0	41	4	0	.098	14	22	1	2	2.2	.973
1974		15	22	.405	4.46	38	38	11	254	255	80	154	1	0	0	0	79	11	0	.139	30	40	1	4	1.9	.986
1975		11	12	.478	3.29	35	35	12	252	248	88	137	3	0	0	0	77	13	0	.169	18	41	7	2	1.9	.894
1976		7	17	.292	3.21	33	32	8	230	212	69	150	4	0	0	1	74	11	0	.149	26	50	3	3	2.4	.962
1977		17	16	.515	3.10	40	40	17	302	272	81	206	4	0	0	0	96	10	0	.104	20	63	7	5	2.3	.922
1978		13	10	.565	2.47	30	29	11	219	186	64	126	1	0	0	1	71	8	0	.113	16	38	1	1	1.8	.982
1979		13	12	.520	3.00	37	37	13	249	232	78	143	5	0	0	0	77	12	0	.156	14	46	3	7	1.7	.952
1980		16	11	.593	2.98	37	37	14	281	247	85	147	4	0	0	0	81	13	0	.160	21	37	3	3	1.6	.951
1981		12	8	.600	3.41	22	22	7	161	149	41	87	3	0	0	0	55	8	0	.145	10	20	0	1	1.4	1.000
1982		19	8	.704	2.40	35	35	14	277	245	65	179	4	0	0	0	85	11	0	.129	18	41	1	3	1.7	.983
1983		17	12	.586	3.23	36	36	13	273	258	78	146	5	0	0	0	82	12	0	.146	28	28	0	1	1.6	1.000
1984		6	15	.286	4.31	31	28	1	169.1	171	78	64	0	0	0	0	49	7	0	.143	17	25	3	5	1.5	.933
1985		2	4	.333	5.68	8	7	1	38	51	20	18	0	0	0	0	14	2	0	.143	5	11	1	0	2.1	.941
13 yrs.		158	152	.510	3.17	399	393	129	2839.1	2619	876	1621	37	0	0	2	881	122	0	.138	237	462	31	37	1.8	.958

DIVISIONAL PLAYOFF SERIES

| 1981 | MON N | 2 | 0 | 1.000 | 0.51 | 2 | 2 | 1 | 17.2 | 16 | 3 | 5 | 0 | 0 | 0 | 0 | 5 | 2 | 0 | .400 | 0 | 0 | 0 | 0 | 0.0 | – |

LEAGUE CHAMPIONSHIP SERIES

| 1981 | MON N | 1 | 1 | .500 | 1.80 | 2 | 1 | 1 | 10 | 8 | 1 | 6 | 0 | 0 | 0 | 0 | 2 | 0 | 0 | .000 | 0 | 0 | 0 | 0 | 0.0 | – |

Tom Rogers

ROGERS, THOMAS ANDREW (Shotgun)
B. Feb. 12, 1892, Sparta, Tenn.　D. Mar. 7, 1936, Nashville, Tenn.　　BR TR 6'½" 180 lbs.

1917	STL A	3	6	.333	3.89	24	8	3	108.2	112	44	27	0	1	0	0	29	5	0	.172	1	34	3	0	1.6	.921
1918		8	10	.444	3.27	29	16	11	154	148	49	29	0	3	1	2	53	13	0	.245	8	52	3	1	2.2	.952
1919	2 teams	STL A	(2G 0–1)		PHI A	(23G 4–12)																				
"	total	4	13	.235	4.47	25	18	7	141	159	60	38	1	0	1	0	49	11	1	.224	13	52	4	11	2.8	.942
1921	NY A	0	1	.000	7.36	5	0	0	11	12	9	0	0	0	1	1	3	1	0	.333	0	6	0	1	1.2	1.000
4 yrs.		15	30	.333	3.95	83	42	21	414.2	431	162	94	1	4	3	3	134	30	1	.224	22	144	10	13	2.1	.943

WORLD SERIES

| 1921 | NY A | 0 | 0 | – | 6.75 | 1 | 0 | 0 | 1.1 | 3 | 0 | 1 | 0 | 0 | 0 | 0 | 0 | 0 | 0 | – | 0 | 1 | 0 | 0 | 1.0 | 1.000 |

Clint Rogge

ROGGE, FRANCIS CLINTON
B. July 19, 1889, Memphis, Mich.　D. Jan. 6, 1969, Mount Clemens, Mich.　　BL TR 5'10" 185 lbs.

1915	PIT F	17	12	.586	2.55	37	31	17	254.1	240	93	93	5	2	1	0	81	14	0	.173	8	85	4	2	2.6	.959
1921	CIN N	1	2	.333	4.08	6	3	0	35.1	43	9	12	0	0	0	0	10	1	0	.100	0	10	0	0	1.7	1.000
2 yrs.		18	14	.563	2.73	43	34	17	289.2	283	102	105	5	2	1	0	91	15	0	.165	8	95	4	2	2.5	.963

Garry Roggenburk

ROGGENBURK, GARRY EARL
B. Apr. 16, 1940, Cleveland, Ohio　　BR TL 6'6" 195 lbs.

| 1963 | MIN A | 2 | 4 | .333 | 2.16 | 36 | 2 | 0 | 50 | 47 | 22 | 24 | 0 | 2 | 4 | 4 | 7 | 1 | 0 | .143 | 3 | 12 | 1 | 0 | 0.4 | .938 |
| 1965 | | 1 | 0 | 1.000 | 3.43 | 12 | 0 | 0 | 21 | 21 | 12 | 6 | 0 | 1 | 0 | 2 | 3 | 0 | 0 | .000 | 0 | 3 | 1 | 0 | 0.3 | .750 |

Year	Team	W	L	PCT	ERA	G	GS	CG	IP	H	BB	SO	ShO	Relief Pitching W	L	SV	Batting AB	H	HR	BA	PO	A	E	DP	TC/G	FA

Garry Roggenburk *continued*

Year	Team	W	L	PCT	ERA	G	GS	CG	IP	H	BB	SO	ShO	W	L	SV	AB	H	HR	BA	PO	A	E	DP	TC/G	FA
1966	2 teams	MIN A	(12G 1–2)		BOS A	(1G 0–0)																				
"	total	1	2	.333	5.68	13	0	0	12.2	15	11	3	0	1	2	1	0	0	0	–	1	2	0	0	0.2	1.000
1968	BOS A	0	0	–	2.16	4	0	0	8.1	9	3	4	0	0	0	0	0	0	0	–	1	0	0	0	0.3	1.000
1969	2 teams	BOS A	(7G 0–1)		SEA A	(7G 2–2)																				
"	total	2	3	.400	5.56	14	4	1	34	40	16	19	0	0	1	0	10	1	0	.100	3	5	0	0	0.6	1.000
	5 yrs.	6	9	.400	3.64	79	6	1	126	132	64	56	0	4	5	7	20	2	0	.100	8	22	2	0	0.4	.938

Saul Rogovin

ROGOVIN, SAUL WALTER
B. Oct. 10, 1923, Brooklyn, N. Y.

BR TR 6'2" 205 lbs.

Year	Team	W	L	PCT	ERA	G	GS	CG	IP	H	BB	SO	ShO	W	L	SV	AB	H	HR	BA	PO	A	E	DP	TC/G	FA
1949	DET A	0	1	.000	14.29	5	0	0	5.2	13	7	2	0	0	1	0	0	0	0	–	1	0	0	0	0.2	1.000
1950		2	1	.667	4.50	11	5	1	40	39	26	11	0	1	0	0	16	3	1	.188	1	5	1	1	0.6	.857
1951	2 teams	DET A	(5G 1–1)		CHI A	(22G 11–7)																				
"	total	12	8	.600	**2.78**	27	26	17	216.2	189	74	82	3	1	0	0	81	17	0	.210	16	35	3	4	2.0	.944
1952	CHI A	14	9	.609	3.85	33	30	12	231.2	224	79	121	3	0	0	1	84	17	1	.202	11	39	2	4	1.6	.962
1953		7	12	.368	5.22	22	19	4	131	151	48	62	1	1	0	1	37	5	0	.135	10	20	3	1	1.5	.909
1955	2 teams	BAL A	(14G 1–8)		PHI N	(12G 5–3)																				
"	total	6	11	.353	3.81	26	23	6	144	139	44	62	2	0	0	0	46	8	1	.174	6	20	3	2	1.1	.897
1956	PHI N	7	6	.538	4.98	22	18	3	106.2	122	27	48	0	0	0	0	36	4	0	.111	10	12	1	1	1.0	.957
1957		0	0	–	9.00	4	0	0	8	11	3	0	0	0	0	0	2	0	0	–	0	0	0	0	0.8	.667
	8 yrs.	48	48	.500	4.06	150	121	43	883.2	888	308	388	9	3	1	2	300	54	3	.180	57	131	14	14	1.3	.931

Billy Rohr

ROHR, WILLIAM JOSEPH
B. July 1, 1945, San Diego, Calif.

BL TL 6'3" 170 lbs.

Year	Team	W	L	PCT	ERA	G	GS	CG	IP	H	BB	SO	ShO	W	L	SV	AB	H	HR	BA	PO	A	E	DP	TC/G	FA
1967	BOS A	2	3	.400	5.10	10	8	2	42.1	43	22	16	1	0	0	0	10	0	0	.000	1	7	1	0	0.9	.889
1968	CLE A	1	0	1.000	6.87	17	0	0	18.1	18	10	5	0	1	0	1	1	0	0	.000	1	4	1	0	0.4	.833
	2 yrs.	3	3	.500	5.64	27	8	2	60.2	61	32	21	1	1	0	1	11	0	0	.000	2	11	2	0	0.6	.867

Les Rohr

ROHR, LESLIE NORVIN
B. Mar. 5, 1946, Lowestoft, England

BL TL 6'5" 205 lbs.

Year	Team	W	L	PCT	ERA	G	GS	CG	IP	H	BB	SO	ShO	W	L	SV	AB	H	HR	BA	PO	A	E	DP	TC/G	FA
1967	NY N	2	1	.667	2.12	3	3	0	17	13	9	15	0	0	0	0	6	0	0	.000	0	2	0	0	1.0	.333
1968		0	2	.000	4.50	2	1	0	6	9	7	5	0	0	0	0	0	0	0	–	0	1	0	0	0.5	1.000
1969		0	0	–	20.25	1	0	0	1.1	5	1	0	0	0	0	0	0	0	0	–	0	0	0	0	0.0	–
	3 yrs.	2	3	.400	3.70	6	4	0	24.1	27	17	20	0	0	0	0	6	0	0	.000	0	2	0	0	0.7	.500

Cookie Rojas

ROJAS, OCTAVIO VICTOR
Born Octavio Victor Rojas y Rivas.
B. Mar. 6, 1939, Havana, Cuba
Manager 1988.

BR TR 5'10" 160 lbs.

Year	Team	W	L	PCT	ERA	G	GS	CG	IP	H	BB	SO	ShO	W	L	SV	AB	H	HR	BA	PO	A	E	DP	TC/G	FA
1967	PHI N	0	0	–	0.00	1	0	0	1	1	0	0	0	0	0	0	*				0	0	0	0	0.0	–

Minnie Rojas

ROJAS, MINERVINO ALEJANDRO
Born Minervino Alejandro Rojas y Landin.
B. Nov. 26, 1938, Remedios Las Villas, Cuba

BR TR 6'1" 170 lbs.

Year	Team	W	L	PCT	ERA	G	GS	CG	IP	H	BB	SO	ShO	W	L	SV	AB	H	HR	BA	PO	A	E	DP	TC/G	FA
1966	CAL A	7	4	.636	2.88	47	2	0	84.1	83	15	37	0	5	4	10	14	1	0	.071	2	10	0	2	0.3	1.000
1967		12	9	.571	2.52	72	0	0	121.2	106	38	83	0	**12**	9	**27**	17	1	0	.059	1	13	0	0	0.2	1.000
1968		4	3	.571	4.25	38	0	0	55	55	15	33	0	4	3	6	10	1	0	.100	2	5	1	0	0.2	.875
	3 yrs.	23	16	.590	3.00	157	2	0	261	244	68	153	0	21	16	43	41	3	0	.073	5	28	1	2	0.2	.971

Jim Roland

ROLAND, JAMES IVAN
B. Dec. 14, 1942, Franklin, N. C.

BR TL 6'3" 175 lbs.

Year	Team	W	L	PCT	ERA	G	GS	CG	IP	H	BB	SO	ShO	W	L	SV	AB	H	HR	BA	PO	A	E	DP	TC/G	FA
1962	MIN A	0	0	–	0.00	1	0	0	2	1	0	1	0	0	0	0	–				0	0	0	0	0.0	–
1963		4	1	.800	2.57	10	7	2	49	32	27	34	1	1	0	0	15	0	0	.000	4	9	1	0	1.4	.929
1964		2	6	.250	4.10	30	13	1	94.1	76	55	63	0	0	0	3	27	4	0	.148	1	11	0	1	0.4	1.000
1966		0	0	–	0.00	1	0	0	2	0	1	0	0	0	0	0	0	0	0	–	0	0	0	0	0.0	–
1967		0	1	.000	3.03	25	0	0	35.2	33	17	16	0	0	1	2	3	0	0	.000	0	4	0	0	0.3	1.000
1968		4	1	.800	3.50	28	4	1	61.2	55	24	36	0	2	0	0	8	0	0	.000	2	14	1	1	0.6	.941
1969	OAK A	5	1	.833	2.19	39	3	2	86.1	59	46	48	0	2	1	1	21	2	0	.095	4	13	0	3	0.4	1.000
1970		3	3	.500	2.72	28	2	0	43	28	23	26	0	3	2	1	3	0	0	.000	3	9	0	0	0.4	1.000
1971		1	3	.250	3.20	31	0	0	45	34	19	30	0	1	3	1	3	0	0	.000	0	6	0	0	0.2	1.000
1972	3 teams	OAK A	(2G 0–0)		NY A	(16G 0–1)			TEX A	(5G 0–0)																
"	total	0	1	.000	5.28	23	0	0	30.2	39	18	17	0	0	0	1	0	0	0	.000	0	4	1	1	0.3	.833
	10 yrs.	19	17	.528	3.22	216	29	6	449.2	357	229	272	1	9	8	9	84	6	0	.071	19	70	3	6	0.4	.967

Jose Roman

ROMAN, JOSE RAFAEL
Born Jose Rafael Roman y Sarita.
B. May 21, 1963, Puerto Plata, Dominican Republic

BR TR 6' 175 lbs.

Year	Team	W	L	PCT	ERA	G	GS	CG	IP	H	BB	SO	ShO	W	L	SV	AB	H	HR	BA	PO	A	E	DP	TC/G	FA
1984	CLE A	0	2	.000	18.00	3	2	0	6	9	11	3	0	0	0	0	0	0	0	–	0	0	0	0	0.0	–
1985		0	4	.000	6.61	5	3	0	16.1	13	14	12	0	0	0	0	0	0	0	–	3	1	1	0	1.0	.800
1986		1	2	.333	6.55	6	5	0	22	23	17	9	0	0	0	0	0	0	0	–	2	1	1	0	0.5	.667
	3 yrs.	1	8	.111	8.12	14	10	0	44.1	45	42	24	0	0	0	0	0	0	0	–	5	1	2	1	0.6	.750

Ron Romanick

ROMANICK, RONALD JAMES
B. Nov. 6, 1960, Burley, Ida.

BR TR 6'4" 195 lbs.

Year	Team	W	L	PCT	ERA	G	GS	CG	IP	H	BB	SO	ShO	W	L	SV	AB	H	HR	BA	PO	A	E	DP	TC/G	FA
1984	CAL A	12	12	.500	3.76	33	33	8	229.2	240	61	87	2	0	0	0	0	0	0	–	18	24	6	3	1.5	.875
1985		14	9	.609	4.11	31	31	6	195	210	62	64	1	0	0	0	0	0	0	–	10	18	1	0	0.9	.966
1986		5	8	.385	5.50	18	18	1	106.1	124	44	38	1	0	0	0	0	0	0	–	13	8	0	1	1.2	1.000
	3 yrs.	31	29	.517	4.24	82	82	15	531	574	167	189	4	0	0	0	0	0	0	–	41	50	7	4	1.2	.929

Year	Team		W	L	PCT	ERA	G	GS	CG	IP	H	BB	SO	ShO	Relief Pitching W	L	SV	Batting AB	H	HR	BA	PO	A	E	DP	TC/G	FA

Jim Romano

ROMANO, JAMES KING
B. Apr. 6, 1927, Brooklyn, N. Y.
BR TR 6'4" 190 lbs.

| 1950 | BKN | N | 0 | 0 | – | 5.68 | 3 | 1 | 0 | 6.1 | 8 | 2 | 8 | 0 | 0 | 0 | 0 | 1 | 0 | 0 | .000 | 0 | 3 | 0 | 0 | 1.0 | 1.000 |

Dutch Romberger

ROMBERGER, ALLEN ISAIAH
B. May 26, 1927, Klingerstown, Pa. D. May 26, 1983, Weikert, Pa.
BR TR 6' 185 lbs.

| 1954 | PHI | A | 1 | 1 | .500 | 11.49 | 10 | 0 | 0 | 15.2 | 28 | 12 | 6 | 0 | 1 | 1 | 0 | 2 | 0 | 0 | .000 | 0 | 2 | 0 | 0 | 0.2 | 1.000 |

Ramon Romero

ROMERO, RAMON
Born Ramon Romero y De Los Santos.
B. Jan. 8, 1959, San Pedro de Macoris, Dominican Republic
BL TL 6'4" 170 lbs.

1984	CLE	A	0	0	–	0.00	1	0	0	3	0	0	3	0	0	0	0	0	0	0	–	0	0	0	0	0.0	–
1985			2	3	.400	6.58	19	10	0	64.1	69	38	38	0	0	0	0	0	0	0	–	0	6	0	0	0.3	1.000
2 yrs.			2	3	.400	6.28	20	10	0	67.1	69	38	41	0	0	0	0	0	0	0	–	0	6	0	0	0.3	1.000

Eddie Rommel

ROMMEL, EDWIN AMERICUS
B. Sept. 13, 1897, Baltimore, Md. D. Aug. 26, 1970, Baltimore, Md.
BR TR 6'2" 197 lbs.

1920	PHI	A	7	7	.500	2.85	33	12	8	173.2	165	43	43	2	3	1	1	51	11	0	.216	13	66	1	4	2.4	.988
1921			16	23	.410	3.94	46	32	20	285.1	312	87	71	0	4	7	3	94	18	0	.191	12	92	7	5	2.4	.937
1922			27	13	.675	3.28	51	33	22	294	294	63	54	3	8	1	2	94	17	0	.181	12	92	5	5	2.1	.954
1923			18	19	.486	3.27	56	31	19	297.2	306	108	76	3	3	4	5	101	24	0	.238	17	109	7	4	2.4	.947
1924			18	15	.545	3.95	43	34	21	278	302	94	72	3	1	1	1	95	15	0	.158	20	97	3	12	2.8	.975
1925			21	10	.677	3.69	52	28	14	261	285	95	67	1	7	2	3	81	15	1	.185	21	86	2	4	2.1	.982
1926			11	11	.500	3.08	37	26	12	219	225	54	52	3	2	1	0	61	6	0	.098	15	67	3	1	2.3	.965
1927			11	3	.786	4.36	30	17	8	146.2	166	48	33	2	0	1	1	51	8	0	.157	16	44	0	5	2.0	1.000
1928			13	5	.722	3.06	43	11	6	173.2	177	26	37	0	8	1	4	47	12	0	.255	8	51	0	5	1.4	1.000
1929			12	2	.857	2.85	32	6	4	113.2	135	34	25	0	8	2	4	39	8	0	.205	9	26	1	3	1.1	.972
1930			9	4	.692	4.28	35	9	5	130.1	142	27	35	0	5	3	3	38	10	0	.263	8	32	0	1	1.1	1.000
1931			7	5	.583	2.97	25	10	8	118	136	27	18	1	1	0	0	54	14	0	.259	5	25	2	1	1.3	.938
1932			1	2	.333	5.51	17	0	0	65.1	84	18	16	0	1	2	2	20	6	0	.300	3	23	1	1	1.6	.963
13 yrs.			171	119	.590	3.54	500	249	147	2556.1	2729	724	599	18	51	26	29	826	164	1	.199	159	810	32	51	2.0	.968

WORLD SERIES

1929	PHI	A	1	0	1.000	9.00	1	0	0	1	2	1	0	1	0	1	0	0	0	0	–	0	0	0	0	0.0	–
1931			0	0	–	9.00	1	0	0	1	3	0	0	0	0	0	0	0	0	0	–	0	0	0	0	0.0	–
2 yrs.			1	0	1.000	9.00	2	0	0	2	5	1	0	1	0	1	0	0	0	0	–	0	0	0	0	0.0	–

Enrique Romo

ROMO, ENRIQUE
Born Enrique Romo y Rivera. Brother of Vicente Romo.
B. July 15, 1947, Santa Rosalia, Mexico
BR TR 5'11" 185 lbs.

1977	SEA	A	8	10	.444	2.84	58	3	0	114	93	39	105	0	8	9	16	0	0	0	–	5	19	1	3	0.4	.960
1978			11	7	.611	3.69	56	0	0	107.1	88	39	62	0	11	7	10	0	0	0	–	6	9	0	1	0.3	1.000
1979	PIT	N	10	5	.667	3.00	84	0	0	129	122	43	106	0	10	5	5	12	2	0	.167	10	25	1	3	0.4	.972
1980			5	5	.500	3.27	74	0	0	124	117	28	82	0	5	5	11	11	5	1	.455	10	20	1	1	0.4	.968
1981			1	3	.250	4.50	33	0	0	42	47	18	23	0	1	3	9	4	0	0	.000	5	3	0	1	0.2	1.000
1982			9	3	.750	4.36	45	0	0	86.2	81	36	58	0	9	3	1	10	3	0	.300	7	10	0	0	0.4	1.000
6 yrs.			44	33	.571	3.45	350	3	0	603	548	203	436	0	44	32	52	37	10	1	.270	43	86	3	9	0.4	.977

LEAGUE CHAMPIONSHIP SERIES

| 1979 | PIT | N | 0 | 0 | – | 0.00 | 2 | 0 | 0 | .1 | 3 | 1 | 1 | 0 | 0 | 0 | 0 | 0 | 0 | 0 | – | 0 | 0 | 0 | 0 | 0.0 | – |

WORLD SERIES

| 1979 | PIT | N | 0 | 0 | – | 3.86 | 2 | 0 | 0 | 4.2 | 5 | 3 | 4 | 0 | 0 | 0 | 0 | 1 | 0 | 0 | .000 | 0 | 1 | 0 | 0 | 0.5 | 1.000 |

Vicente Romo

ROMO, VICENTE (Huevo)
Born Vicente Romo y Navarro. Brother of Enrique Romo.
B. Apr. 12, 1943, Santa Rosalia, Mexico
BR TR 6'1" 180 lbs.

1968	2 teams		LA N (1G 0–0)			CLE A	(40G 5–3)																				
"	total		5	3	.625	1.60	41	1	0	84.1	44	32	54	0	5	2	12	14	2	0	.143	6	11	1	1	0.4	.944
1969	2 teams		CLE A (3G 1–1)			BOS A	(52G 7–9)																				
"	total		8	10	.444	3.13	55	11	4	135.1	123	53	96	1	3	8	11	33	5	0	.152	4	22	1	1	0.5	.963
1970	BOS	A	7	3	.700	4.08	48	10	0	108	115	43	71	0	6	0	6	27	4	1	.148	7	20	3	1	0.6	.900
1971	CHI	A	1	7	.125	3.38	45	2	0	72	52	37	48	0	1	5	5	11	4	0	.364	0	19	0	1	0.4	1.000
1972			3	0	1.000	3.31	28	0	0	51.2	47	18	46	0	3	0	1	9	0	0	.000	3	11	1	1	0.5	.933
1973	SD	N	2	3	.400	3.70	49	1	0	87.2	85	46	51	0	2	2	7	16	2	0	.125	5	15	2	1	0.4	.909
1974			5	5	.500	4.56	54	1	0	71	78	37	26	0	5	5	4	6	0	0	.000	2	21	2	1	0.5	.920
1982	LA	N	1	2	.333	3.03	15	6	0	35.2	25	14	24	0	0	1	1	5	1	0	.200	2	8	0	0	0.7	1.000
8 yrs.			32	33	.492	3.36	335	32	4	645.2	569	280	416	1	25	23	52	121	18	1	.149	29	127	10	7	0.5	.940

John Romonosky

ROMONOSKY, JOHN
B. July 7, 1929, Harrisburg, Ill.
BR TR 6'2" 195 lbs.

1953	STL	N	0	0	–	4.70	2	2	0	7.2	9	4	3	0	0	0	0	2	0	0	.000	0	0	0	0	0.0	–
1958	WAS	A	2	4	.333	6.51	18	5	1	55.1	52	28	38	0	1	0	0	13	4	1	.308	2	10	0	0	0.7	1.000
1959			1	0	1.000	3.29	12	2	0	38.1	36	19	22	0	0	0	0	11	2	0	.182	1	6	0	1	0.6	1.000
3 yrs.			3	4	.429	5.15	32	9	1	101.1	97	51	63	0	1	0	0	26	6	1	.231	3	16	0	1	0.6	1.000

Gil Rondon

RONDON, GILBERT
B. Nov. 18, 1953, Bronx, N. Y.
BR TR 6'2" 200 lbs.

1976	HOU	N	2	2	.500	5.67	19	7	0	54	70	39	21	0	0	0	0	14	4	0	.286	5	4	0	0	0.5	1.000
1979	CHI	A	0	0	–	3.60	4	0	0	10	11	6	3	0	0	0	0	0	0	0	–	0	1	0	0	0.3	1.000
2 yrs.			2	2	.500	5.34	23	7	0	64	81	45	24	0	0	0	0	14	4	0	.286	5	5	0	0	0.4	1.000

Year	Team	W	L	PCT	ERA	G	GS	CG	IP	H	BB	SO	ShO	Relief Pitching W	L	SV	Batting AB	H	HR	BA	PO	A	E	DP	TC/G	FA

Jim Rooker
ROOKER, JAMES PHILLIP
B. Sept. 23, 1941, Lakeview, Ore. BR TL 6' 195 lbs.

Year	Team	W	L	PCT	ERA	G	GS	CG	IP	H	BB	SO	ShO	W	L	SV	AB	H	HR	BA	PO	A	E	DP	TC/G	FA
1968	DET A	0	0	–	3.86	2	0	0	4.2	4	1	4	0	0	0	0	2	0	0	.000	0	2	0	0	1.0	1.000
1969	KC A	4	16	.200	3.75	28	22	8	158.1	136	73	108	1	0	1	0	57	16	4	.281	3	24	4	0	1.1	.871
1970		10	15	.400	3.53	38	29	6	204	190	102	117	3	0	0	1	70	14	1	.200	6	32	2	4	1.1	.950
1971		2	7	.222	5.33	20	7	1	54	59	24	31	1	0	1	0	10	0	0	.000	1	5	1	1	0.4	.857
1972		5	6	.455	4.38	18	10	4	72	78	24	44	2	1	0	0	20	2	0	.100	3	16	0	1	1.1	1.000
1973	PIT N	10	6	.625	2.85	41	18	6	170.1	143	52	122	3	1	1	5	49	12	0	.245	6	29	2	3	0.9	.946
1974		15	11	.577	2.77	33	33	15	263	228	83	139	1	0	0	0	95	29	0	.305	14	45	1	3	1.8	.983
1975		13	11	.542	2.97	28	28	7	197	177	76	102	1	0	0	0	63	6	0	.095	10	32	4	1	1.6	.913
1976		15	8	.652	3.35	30	29	10	198.2	201	72	92	1	0	0	1	74	16	1	.216	8	29	2	1	1.3	.949
1977		14	9	.609	3.09	30	30	7	204	196	64	89	0	0	0	0	70	13	0	.186	6	27	2	2	1.2	.943
1978		9	11	.450	4.25	28	28	1	163	160	81	76	0	0	0	0	56	9	0	.161	14	24	0	5	1.4	1.000
1979		4	7	.364	4.59	19	17	1	104	106	39	44	0	0	0	0	33	4	0	.121	8	13	2	1	1.2	.913
1980		2	2	.500	3.50	4	4	0	18	16	12	8	0	0	0	0	7	1	1	.143	1	4	0	0	1.3	1.000
13 yrs.		103	109	.486	3.46	319	255	66	1811	1694	703	976	15	2	4	7	606	122	7	.201	80	282	20	22	1.2	.948

LEAGUE CHAMPIONSHIP SERIES

Year	Team	W	L	PCT	ERA	G	GS	CG	IP	H	BB	SO	ShO	W	L	SV	AB	H	HR	BA	PO	A	E	DP	TC/G	FA
1974	PIT N	0	0	–	2.57	1	1	0	7	6	5	4	0	0	0	0	2	1	0	.500	0	3	0	0	4.0	.750
1975		0	1	.000	9.00	1	1	0	4	7	0	5	0	0	0	0	1	0	0	.000	0	0	0	0	0.0	–
2 yrs.		0	1	.000	4.91	2	2	0	11	13	5	9	0	0	0	0	3	1	0	.333	0	3	0	0	2.0	.750

WORLD SERIES

Year	Team	W	L	PCT	ERA	G	GS	CG	IP	H	BB	SO	ShO	W	L	SV	AB	H	HR	BA	PO	A	E	DP	TC/G	FA
1979	PIT N	0	0	–	1.04	1	0	0	8.2	5	3	4	0	0	0	0	2	0	0	.000	1	0	0	0	1.5	1.000

Charlie Root
ROOT, CHARLES HENRY (Chinski)
B. Mar. 17, 1899, Middletown, Ohio D. Nov. 5, 1970, Hollister, Calif. BR TR 5'10½" 190 lbs.

Year	Team	W	L	PCT	ERA	G	GS	CG	IP	H	BB	SO	ShO	W	L	SV	AB	H	HR	BA	PO	A	E	DP	TC/G	FA
1923	STL A	0	4	.000	5.70	27	2	0	60	68	18	27	0	0	2	0	13	1	0	.077	1	13	0	0	0.5	1.000
1926	CHI N	18	17	.514	2.82	42	32	21	271.1	267	62	127	2	2	3	2	91	13	1	.143	8	58	4	4	1.7	.943
1927		26	15	.634	3.76	48	36	21	309	296	117	145	4	5	2	4	122	27	0	.221	6	49	2	2	1.2	.965
1928		14	18	.438	3.57	40	30	13	237	214	73	122	1	1	2	2	73	13	0	.178	6	39	1	2	1.2	.978
1929		19	6	.760	3.47	43	31	19	272	286	83	124	4	2	0	5	96	15	1	.156	12	35	1	2	1.1	.979
1930		16	14	.533	4.33	37	30	15	220.1	247	63	124	4	0	1	3	80	21	1	.263	9	27	0	1	1.0	1.000
1931		17	14	.548	3.48	39	31	19	251	240	71	131	3	2	1	2	90	20	1	.222	3	38	1	0	1.1	.976
1932		15	10	.600	3.58	39	23	11	216.1	211	55	96	0	3	2	3	76	13	1	.171	8	32	0	0	1.0	1.000
1933		15	10	.600	2.60	35	30	20	242.1	232	61	86	2	1	0	0	85	8	0	.094	11	36	1	4	1.4	.979
1934		4	7	.364	4.28	34	9	2	117.2	141	53	46	0	3	2	0	40	7	2	.175	2	23	0	1	0.7	1.000
1935		15	8	.652	3.08	38	18	11	201.1	193	47	94	1	5	3	2	69	14	1	.203	7	27	1	0	0.9	.971
1936		3	6	.333	4.15	33	4	0	73.2	81	20	32	0	2	5	1	15	5	0	.333	2	10	1	0	0.4	1.000
1937		13	5	.722	3.38	43	15	5	178.2	173	32	74	0	8	0	5	67	12	1	.179	8	36	1	2	1.0	.978
1938		8	7	.533	2.86	44	11	5	160.2	163	30	70	0	4	1	8	48	8	0	.167	5	23	1	0	0.7	.966
1939		8	8	.500	4.03	35	16	8	167.1	189	34	65	0	1	1	4	57	10	2	.175	2	22	2	0	0.7	.923
1940		2	4	.333	3.82	36	8	1	113	118	33	50	0	0	3	0	31	4	0	.129	3	22	0	0	0.7	1.000
1941		8	7	.533	5.40	19	15	6	106.2	133	37	46	0	1	0	0	33	5	1	.152	2	16	0	2	0.9	1.000
17 yrs.		201	160	.557	3.58	632	341	177	3198.1	3252	889	1459	21	42	26	40	1086	196	11	.180	95	506	15	21	1.0	.976

WORLD SERIES

Year	Team	W	L	PCT	ERA	G	GS	CG	IP	H	BB	SO	ShO	W	L	SV	AB	H	HR	BA	PO	A	E	DP	TC/G	FA
1929	CHI N	0	1	.000	4.73	2	2	0	13.1	12	2	8	0	0	0	0	5	0	0	.000	0	0	0	0	0.0	–
1932		0	1	.000	10.38	1	1	0	4.1	6	3	4	0	0	0	0	2	0	0	.000	0	0	0	0	0.0	–
1935		0	1	.000	18.00	2	1	0	2	5	1	2	0	0	0	0	0	0	0	–	0	1	0	0	0.5	1.000
1938		0	0	–	3.00	1	0	0	3	3	0	1	0	0	0	0	0	0	0	–	0	0	0	0	0.0	–
4 yrs.		0	3	.000	6.75	6	4	0	22.2	26	6	15	0	0	0	0	7	0	0	.000	0	1	0	0	0.2	1.000

Chuck Rose
ROSE, CHARLES ALFRED
B. Sept. 1, 1885, Macon, Mo. D. Aug. 4, 1961, Salina, Kans. BL TL 5'8½" 158 lbs.

Year	Team	W	L	PCT	ERA	G	GS	CG	IP	H	BB	SO	ShO	W	L	SV	AB	H	HR	BA	PO	A	E	DP	TC/G	FA
1909	STL A	1	2	.333	5.40	3	3	3	25	32	7	6	0	0	0	0	7	1	1	.143	1	4	2	0	2.3	.714

Don Rose
ROSE, DONALD GARY
B. Mar. 19, 1947, Covina, Calif. BR TR 6'3" 195 lbs.

Year	Team	W	L	PCT	ERA	G	GS	CG	IP	H	BB	SO	ShO	W	L	SV	AB	H	HR	BA	PO	A	E	DP	TC/G	FA
1971	NY N	0	0	–	0.00	1	0	0	2	2	0	1	0	0	0	0	0	0	0	–	0	0	0	0	0.0	–
1972	CAL N	1	4	.200	4.19	16	4	0	43	49	19	39	0	0	0	2	10	2	0	.200	3	3	0	0	0.4	1.000
1974	SF N	0	0	–	9.00	2	0	0	1	4	1	0	0	0	0	0	0	0	0	–	0	0	0	0	0.0	–
3 yrs.		1	4	.200	4.11	19	4	0	46	55	20	40	0	0	0	2	10	2	0	.200	3	3	0	0	0.3	1.000

Zeke Rosebraugh
ROSEBRAUGH, ELI ETHELBERT
B. Aug. 8, 1870, Charleston, Ill. D. July 16, 1930, Fresno, Calif. TL

Year	Team	W	L	PCT	ERA	G	GS	CG	IP	H	BB	SO	ShO	W	L	SV	AB	H	HR	BA	PO	A	E	DP	TC/G	FA
1898	PIT N	0	2	.000	3.32	4	2	0	21.2	23	9	6	0	0	0	0	8	3	0	.375	1	4	0	0	1.3	1.000
1899		0	1	.000	9.00	2	2	0	6	14	3	2	0	0	0	0	2	0	0	.000	0	1	0	0	0.5	1.000
2 yrs.		0	3	.000	4.55	6	4	0	27.2	37	12	8	0	0	0	0	10	3	0	.300	1	5	0	0	1.0	1.000

Chief Roseman
ROSEMAN, JAMES JOHN
B. July 4, 1856, Brooklyn, N.Y. D. July 4, 1938, Brooklyn, N.Y.
Manager 1890. BR TR 5'7" 167 lbs.

Year	Team	W	L	PCT	ERA	G	GS	CG	IP	H	BB	SO	ShO	W	L	SV	AB	H	HR	BA	PO	A	E	DP	TC/G	FA
1885	NY AA	0	1	.000	27.00	1	1	0	1	3	2	0	0	0	0	0	410	114	3	.278	0	0	0	0	0.0	–
1886		0	0	–	5.14	1	0	0	7	6	0	0	0	0	0	0	559	127	5	.227	0	2	0	0	2.0	1.000
1887	BKN AA	0	0	–	7.88	2	0	0	8	11	5	1	0	0	0	0	317	72	2	.227	0	1	0	0	0.5	1.000
3 yrs.		0	1	.000	7.88	4	1	0	16	20	7	1	0	0	0	0	*	1	2	0	0	0.8	1.000

Steve Rosenberg
ROSENBERG, STEVEN ALLEN
B. Oct. 31, 1964, Brooklyn, N.Y. BL TL 6' 186 lbs.

Year	Team	W	L	PCT	ERA	G	GS	CG	IP	H	BB	SO	ShO	W	L	SV	AB	H	HR	BA	PO	A	E	DP	TC/G	FA
1988	CHI A	0	1	.000	4.30	33	0	0	46	53	19	28	0	0	1	1	0	0	0	–	0	6	0	0	0.2	1.000

Year	Team		W	L	PCT	ERA	G	GS	CG	IP	H	BB	SO	ShO	Relief Pitching			Batting			BA	PO	A	E	DP	TC/G	FA
															W	L	SV	AB	H	HR							

Steve Rosenberg *continued*

Year	Team		W	L	PCT	ERA	G	GS	CG	IP	H	BB	SO	ShO	W	L	SV	AB	H	HR	BA	PO	A	E	DP	TC/G	FA
1989			4	13	.235	4.94	38	21	2	142	148	58	77	0	1	2	0	0	0	0	–	8	20	3	5	0.8	.903
2 yrs.			4	14	.222	4.79	71	21	2	188	201	77	105	0	1	3	1	0	0	0	–	8	26	3	5	0.5	.919

Steve Roser

ROSER, EMERSON COREY
B. Jan. 25, 1918, Rome, N. Y.   BR TR 6'4"   220 lbs.

Year	Team		W	L	PCT	ERA	G	GS	CG	IP	H	BB	SO	ShO	W	L	SV	AB	H	HR	BA	PO	A	E	DP	TC/G	FA
1944	NY	A	4	3	.571	3.86	16	6	1	84	80	34	34	0	2	1	1	30	3	0	.100	4	13	1	1	1.1	.944
1945			0	0	–	3.67	11	0	0	27	27	8	11	0	0	0	0	8	1	0	.125	2	6	0	0	0.7	1.000
1946	2 teams				NY A (4G 1–1)					BOS N (14G 1–1)																	
"	total		2	2	.500	4.70	18	2	0	38.1	40	22	19	0	2	0	1	5	0	0	.000	2	6	0	0	0.4	1.000
3 yrs.			6	5	.545	4.04	45	8	1	149.1	147	64	64	0	4	1	2	43	4	0	.093	8	25	1	1	0.8	.971

Bob Ross

ROSS, FLOYD ROBERT
B. Nov. 2, 1928, Fullerton, Calif.   BR TL 6'   165 lbs.

Year	Team		W	L	PCT	ERA	G	GS	CG	IP	H	BB	SO	ShO	W	L	SV	AB	H	HR	BA	PO	A	E	DP	TC/G	FA
1950	WAS	A	0	1	.000	8.53	6	2	0	12.2	15	15	2	0	0	0	0	3	0	0	.000	0	4	0	0	0.7	1.000
1951			0	1	.000	6.54	11	1	0	31.2	36	21	23	0	0	0	0	9	1	0	.111	0	2	1	0	0.3	.667
1956	PHI	N	0	0	–	8.10	3	0	0	3.1	4	2	4	0	0	0	0	0	0	0	–	0	2	0	0	0.7	1.000
3 yrs.			0	2	.000	7.17	20	3	0	47.2	55	38	29	0	0	0	0	12	1	0	.083	0	8	1	0	0.5	.889

Buck Ross

ROSS, LEE RAVON
B. Feb. 2, 1915, Norwood, N. C.   D. Nov. 23, 1978, Charlotte, N. C.   BR TR 6'2"   170 lbs.

Year	Team		W	L	PCT	ERA	G	GS	CG	IP	H	BB	SO	ShO	W	L	SV	AB	H	HR	BA	PO	A	E	DP	TC/G	FA
1936	PHI	A	9	14	.391	5.83	30	27	12	200.2	253	83	47	1	0	0	0	71	12	0	.169	6	30	3	4	1.3	.923
1937			5	10	.333	4.89	28	22	7	147.1	183	63	37	1	0	0	0	49	5	0	.102	7	28	1	2	1.3	.972
1938			9	16	.360	5.32	29	28	10	184.1	218	80	54	0	0	0	0	63	12	1	.190	5	36	2	2	1.5	.953
1939			6	14	.300	6.00	29	28	6	174	216	95	43	1	0	0	0	58	12	0	.207	9	20	2	1	1.1	.935
1940			5	10	.333	4.38	24	19	10	156.1	160	60	43	0	0	0	1	53	7	1	.132	12	32	3	0	1.6	.921
1941	2 teams				PHI A (1G 0–1)					CHI A (20G 3–8)																	
"	total		3	9	.250	3.69	21	12	7	112.1	109	45	30	0	1	0	0	33	7	0	.212	4	15	2	2	1.0	.905
1942	CHI	A	5	7	.417	5.00	22	14	4	113.1	118	39	37	2	0	2	1	38	6	0	.158	4	12	0	0	0.7	1.000
1943			11	7	.611	3.19	21	21	7	149.1	140	56	41	1	0	0	0	46	4	1	.087	5	26	0	1	1.5	1.000
1944			2	7	.222	5.18	20	9	2	90.1	97	35	20	0	1	3	0	26	2	0	.077	1	8	0	1	0.5	1.000
1945			1	1	.500	5.79	13	2	0	37.1	51	17	8	0	1	0	0	11	2	0	.182	0	2	0	0	0.2	1.000
10 yrs.			56	95	.371	4.94	237	182	65	1365.1	1545	573	360	6	3	5	2	448	69	3	.154	53	204	13	12	1.1	.952

Buster Ross

ROSS, CHESTER FRANKLIN
B. Mar. 11, 1903, Kuttawa, Ky.   D. Apr. 24, 1982, Mayfield, Ky.   BL TL 6'1"   195 lbs.

Year	Team		W	L	PCT	ERA	G	GS	CG	IP	H	BB	SO	ShO	W	L	SV	AB	H	HR	BA	PO	A	E	DP	TC/G	FA
1924	BOS	A	4	3	.571	3.47	30	2	1	93.1	109	30	16	1	3	2	1	25	5	0	.200	4	16	0	0	0.7	1.000
1925			3	8	.273	6.20	33	8	0	94.1	119	40	15	0	2	2	0	24	3	0	.125	1	24	5	0	0.9	.833
1926			0	1	.000	16.88	1	0	0	2.2	5	4	0	0	0	1	0	1	0	0	.000	0	1	0	0	1.0	1.000
3 yrs.			7	12	.368	5.01	64	10	1	190.1	233	74	31	1	5	5	1	50	8	0	.160	5	41	5	0	0.8	.902

Cliff Ross

ROSS, CLIFFORD DAVIS
B. Aug. 3, 1928, Philadelphia, Pa.   BL TL 6'4"   195 lbs.

Year	Team		W	L	PCT	ERA	G	GS	CG	IP	H	BB	SO	ShO	W	L	SV	AB	H	HR	BA	PO	A	E	DP	TC/G	FA
1954	CIN	N	0	0	–	0.00	4	0	0	2.2	0	2	0	1	0	0	0	1	0	0	–	0	1	0	0	0.3	1.000

Ernie Ross

ROSS, ERNEST BERTRAM (Curly)
B. Mar. 31, 1880, Toronto, Ont., Canada   D. Mar. 28, 1950, Toronto, Ont., Canada   BL TL 5'8"   150 lbs.

Year	Team		W	L	PCT	ERA	G	GS	CG	IP	H	BB	SO	ShO	W	L	SV	AB	H	HR	BA	PO	A	E	DP	TC/G	FA
1902	BAL	A	1	1	.500	7.41	2	2	2	17	20	12	2	0	0	0	0	8	0	0	.000	1	2	0	0	2.0	.500

Gary Ross

ROSS, GARY DOUGLAS
B. Sept. 16, 1947, McKeesport, Pa.   BR TR 6'1"   185 lbs.

Year	Team		W	L	PCT	ERA	G	GS	CG	IP	H	BB	SO	ShO	W	L	SV	AB	H	HR	BA	PO	A	E	DP	TC/G	FA
1968	CHI	N	1	1	.500	4.17	13	5	1	41	44	25	31	0	0	0	0	11	1	0	.091	2	7	0	0	0.7	1.000
1969	2 teams				CHI N (2G 0–0)					SD N (46G 3–12)																	
"	total		3	12	.200	4.35	48	8	0	111.2	105	58	60	0	0	0	3	23	0	0	.000	6	27	2	2	0.7	.943
1970	SD	N	2	3	.400	5.23	33	2	0	62	72	36	39	0	2	3	1	8	4	0	.500	3	12	0	1	0.5	1.000
1971			1	3	.250	3.00	13	0	0	24	27	11	13	0	1	3	0	1	0	0	.000	3	3	0	0	0.5	1.000
1972			4	3	.571	2.45	60	2	0	91.2	87	49	46	0	4	3	3	13	2	0	.154	10	16	1	3	0.5	.963
1973			4	4	.500	5.42	58	0	0	76.1	93	33	44	0	4	4	0	4	0	0	.000	8	10	0	2	0.3	1.000
1974			0	0	–	4.50	9	0	0	18	23	6	11	0	0	0	0	1	0	0	.000	1	4	0	0	0.6	1.000
1975	CAL	A	0	1	.000	5.40	1	1	0	5	6	1	4	0	0	0	0	0	0	0	–	0	0	0	0	0.0	–
1976			8	16	.333	3.00	34	31	7	225	224	58	100	0	0	0	0	0	0	0	–	23	55	1	1	2.3	.987
1977			2	4	.333	5.59	14	12	0	58	83	11	30	0	0	0	0	0	0	0	–	9	10	2	1	1.5	.905
10 yrs.			25	47	.347	3.93	283	59	8	712.2	764	288	378	2	11	13	7	61	7	0	.115	65	144	6	9	0.8	.972

George Ross

ROSS, GEORGE SIDNEY
B. June 27, 1892, San Rafael, Calif.   D. Apr. 22, 1935, Amityville, N. Y.   BL TL 5'10½"   175 lbs.

Year	Team		W	L	PCT	ERA	G	GS	CG	IP	H	BB	SO	ShO	W	L	SV	AB	H	HR	BA	PO	A	E	DP	TC/G	FA
1918	NY	N	0	0	–	0.00	1	0	0	2.1	2	3	2	0	0	0	0	1	0	0	.000	1	1	0	0	2.0	1.000

Mark Ross

ROSS, MARK JOSEPH
B. Aug. 8, 1954, Galveston, Tex.   BR TR 6'   195 lbs.

Year	Team		W	L	PCT	ERA	G	GS	CG	IP	H	BB	SO	ShO	W	L	SV	AB	H	HR	BA	PO	A	E	DP	TC/G	FA
1982	HOU	N	0	0	–	1.50	4	0	0	6	3	0	4	0	0	0	0	0	0	0	–	0	1	0	0	0.3	1.000
1984			1	0	1.000	0.00	2	0	0	2.1	1	0	1	0	1	0	0	0	0	0	–	0	0	0	0	0.0	–
1985			0	2	.000	4.85	8	0	0	13	12	2	3	0	0	2	1	1	0	0	.000	2	2	0	0	0.5	1.000
1987	PIT	N	0	0	–	9.00	1	0	0	1	1	0	0	0	0	0	0	0	0	0	–	0	1	0	0	1.0	1.000
1988	TOR	A	0	0	–	4.91	3	0	0	7.1	5	4	4	0	0	0	0	0	0	0	–	0	0	0	0	0.0	–
5 yrs.			1	2	.333	3.94	18	0	0	29.2	22	6	12	0	1	2	1	1	0	0	.000	2	4	0	0	0.3	1.000

Frank Rosso

ROSSO, FRANCIS JAMES
B. Mar. 1, 1921, Agawam, Mass.   D. Jan. 26, 1980, Springfield, Mass.   BR TR 5'11"   180 lbs.

Year	Team		W	L	PCT	ERA	G	GS	CG	IP	H	BB	SO	ShO	W	L	SV	AB	H	HR	BA	PO	A	E	DP	TC/G	FA
1944	NY	N	0	0	–	9.00	2	0	0	4	11	3	1	0	0	0	0	0	0	0	–	0	3	0	0	1.5	1.000

Year	Team		W	L	PCT	ERA	G	GS	CG	IP	H	BB	SO	ShO	W	L	SV	AB	H	HR	BA	PO	A	E	DP	TC/G	FA
															Relief Pitching			**Batting**									

Marv Rotblatt — ROTBLATT, MARVIN (Rotty) · B. Oct. 18, 1927, Chicago, Ill. · BB TL 5'7" 160 lbs.

Year	Team	W	L	PCT	ERA	G	GS	CG	IP	H	BB	SO	ShO	W	L	SV	AB	H	HR	BA	PO	A	E	DP	TC/G	FA
1948	CHI A	0	1	.000	7.85	7	2	0	18.1	19	23	4	0	0	0	0	4	0	0	.000	0	1	0	0	0.1	1.000
1950		0	0	–	6.23	2	0	0	8.2	11	5	6	0	0	0	0	2	0	0	.000	1	3	0	0	2.0	1.000
1951		4	2	.667	3.40	26	2	0	47.2	44	23	20	0	3	2	2	9	0	0	.000	5	11	0	1	0.6	1.000
3 yrs.		4	3	.571	4.82	35	4	0	74.2	74	51	30	0	3	2	2	15	0	0	.000	6	15	0	1	0.6	1.000

Jack Rothrock — ROTHROCK, JOHN HOUSTON · B. Mar. 14, 1905, Long Beach, Calif. · D. Feb. 2, 1980, San Bernardino, Calif. · BB TR 5'11½" 165 lbs. · BR 1925-27

Year	Team	W	L	PCT	ERA	G	GS	CG	IP	H	BB	SO	ShO	W	L	SV	AB	H	HR	BA	PO	A	E	DP	TC/G	FA
1928	BOS A	0	0	–	0.00	1	0	0	1	0	0	0	0	0	0	0	*				0	2	0	0	2.0	1.000

Larry Rothschild — ROTHSCHILD, LAWRENCE LEE · B. Mar. 12, 1954, Chicago, Ill. · BL TR 6'2" 180 lbs.

Year	Team	W	L	PCT	ERA	G	GS	CG	IP	H	BB	SO	ShO	W	L	SV	AB	H	HR	BA	PO	A	E	DP	TC/G	FA
1981	DET A	0	0	–	1.50	5	0	0	6	4	6	1	0	0	0	1	0	0	0	–	1	3	0	0	0.8	1.000
1982		0	0	–	13.50	2	0	0	2.2	4	2	0	0	0	0	0	0	0	0	–	0	0	0	0	0.0	–
2 yrs.		0	0	–	5.19	7	0	0	8.2	8	8	1	0	0	0	1	0	0	0	–	1	3	0	0	0.6	1.000

Virle Rounsaville — ROUNSAVILLE, VIRLE GENE · B. Sept. 27, 1944, Konawa, Okla. · BR TR 6'3" 205 lbs.

Year	Team	W	L	PCT	ERA	G	GS	CG	IP	H	BB	SO	ShO	W	L	SV	AB	H	HR	BA	PO	A	E	DP	TC/G	FA
1970	CHI A	0	1	.000	10.50	8	0	0	6	10	2	3	0	0	1	0	0	0	0	–	0	1	1	0	0.3	.500

Jack Rowan — ROWAN, JOHN ALBERT · B. June 16, 1887, New Castle, Pa. · D. Sept. 29, 1966, Dayton, Ohio · BR TR 6'1" 210 lbs.

Year	Team		W	L	PCT	ERA	G	GS	CG	IP	H	BB	SO	ShO	W	L	SV	AB	H	HR	BA	PO	A	E	DP	TC/G	FA
1906	DET A		0	1	.000	11.00	1	1	1	9	15	6	0	0	0	0	0	4	1	0	.250	1	1	0	0	2.0	1.000
1908	CIN N		3	3	.500	1.82	8	7	4	46	46	16	24	1	0	0	0	14	1	0	.071	1	17	1	0	2.4	.947
1909			11	12	.478	2.79	38	23	14	225.2	185	104	81	0	3	0	0	65	6	0	.092	7	40	3	2	1.3	.940
1910			14	13	.519	2.93	42	30	18	261	242	105	108	4	3	3	1	83	19	0	.229	3	56	6	1	1.5	.908
1911	2 teams	PHI N (12G 2–4)				CHI N (1G 0–0)																					
"	total		2	4	.333	4.72	13	6	2	47.2	60	22	17	0	0	0	0	14	1	0	.071	0	17	0	1	1.3	1.000
1913	CIN N		0	4	.000	3.00	5	5	5	39	37	9	21	0	0	0	0	11	2	0	.182	0	9	1	0	2.0	.900
1914			1	3	.250	3.46	12	2	0	39	38	10	16	0	1	1	1	8	0	0	.000	1	8	0	0	0.7	1.000
7 yrs.			31	40	.437	3.07	119	74	44	670.2	623	272	267	5	8	5	2	199	30	0	.151	12	148	11	4	1.4	.936

Dave Rowe — ROWE, DAVID (Eli) · Brother of Jack Rowe. · B. Feb., 1856, Jacksonville, Ill. Deceased. · Manager 1886, 1888. · BR TR 5'9" 180 lbs.

Year	Team		W	L	PCT	ERA	G	GS	CG	IP	H	BB	SO	ShO	W	L	SV	AB	H	HR	BA	PO	A	E	DP	TC/G	FA
1877	CHI N		0	1	.000	18.00	1	1	0	1	3	2	0	0	0	0	0	7	2	0	.286	0	0	0	0	0.0	
1882	CLE N		0	1	.000	12.00	1	1	1	9	29	7	0	0	0	0	0	97	25	1	.258	0	1	0	0	1.0	1.000
1883	BAL AA		0	0	–	20.25	1	0	0	4	12	2	1	0	0	0	0	256	80	0	.313	0	0	0	0	0.0	
1884	STL U		1	0	1.000	2.00	1	1	1	9	10	0	2	0	0	0	0	485	142	3	**.293**	0	4	0	0	4.0	1.000
4 yrs.			1	2	.333	9.78	4	3	2	23	54	11	3	0	0	0	0	*				0	5	0	0	1.3	1.000

Don Rowe — ROWE, DONALD HOWARD · B. Apr. 3, 1936, Brawley, Calif. · BL TL 6' 180 lbs.

Year	Team	W	L	PCT	ERA	G	GS	CG	IP	H	BB	SO	ShO	W	L	SV	AB	H	HR	BA	PO	A	E	DP	TC/G	FA
1963	NY N	0	0	–	4.28	26	1	0	54.2	59	21	27	0	0	0	0	13	3	0	.231	3	5	2	1	0.4	.800

Ken Rowe — ROWE, KENNETH DARRELL · B. Dec. 31, 1933, Ferndale, Mich. · BR TR 6'2" 185 lbs.

Year	Team	W	L	PCT	ERA	G	GS	CG	IP	H	BB	SO	ShO	W	L	SV	AB	H	HR	BA	PO	A	E	DP	TC/G	FA
1963	LA N	1	1	.500	2.93	14	0	0	27.2	28	11	12	0	1	1	1	5	0	0	.000	0	6	3	1	0.6	.667
1964	BAL A	1	0	1.000	8.31	6	0	0	4.1	10	1	4	0	1	0	0	0	0	0	–	1	2	1	0	0.7	.750
1965		0	0	–	3.38	6	0	0	13.1	17	2	3	0	0	0	0	1	1	0	1.000	0	0	1	0	0.2	–
3 yrs.		2	1	.667	3.57	26	0	0	45.1	55	14	19	0	2	1	1	6	1	0	.167	1	8	5	1	0.5	.643

Schoolboy Rowe — ROWE, LYNWOOD THOMAS · B. Jan. 11, 1910, Waco, Tex. · D. Jan. 8, 1961, El Dorado, Ark. · BR TR 6'4½" 210 lbs.

Year	Team		W	L	PCT	ERA	G	GS	CG	IP	H	BB	SO	ShO	W	L	SV	AB	H	HR	BA	PO	A	E	DP	TC/G	FA
1933	DET A		7	4	.636	3.58	19	15	8	123.1	129	31	75	1	1	0	0	50	11	0	.220	1	33	0	1	1.8	1.000
1934			24	8	.750	3.45	45	30	20	266	259	81	149	4	6	1	1	109	33	2	.303	9	46	0	3	1.2	1.000
1935			19	13	.594	3.69	42	34	21	275.2	272	68	140	6	3	0	3	109	34	3	.312	11	42	1	1	1.3	.981
1936			19	10	.655	4.51	41	35	19	245.1	266	64	115	4	1	0	3	90	23	1	.256	10	50	1	3	1.5	.984
1937			1	4	.200	8.62	10	2	1	31.1	49	9	6	0	1	2	0	10	2	0	.200	6	6	0	0	1.2	1.000
1938			0	2	.000	3.00	4	3	0	21	20	11	4	0	0	0	0	6	1	0	.167	0	8	1	0	2.3	.889
1939			10	12	.455	4.99	28	24	8	164	192	61	51	1	1	1	0	61	15	1	.246	9	27	2	5	1.4	.947
1940			16	3	**.842**	3.46	27	23	11	169	170	43	61	1	1	0	0	67	18	1	.269	10	28	0	2	1.4	1.000
1941			8	6	.571	4.14	27	14	4	139	155	33	54	0	4	2	1	55	15	1	.273	9	29	3	2	1.5	.927
1942	2 teams	DET A (2G 1–0)				BKN N (9G 1–0)																					
"	total		2	0	1.000	3.98	11	3	0	40.2	45	14	13	0	0	0	0	23	4	0	.174	2	11	0	0	1.2	1.000
1943	PHI N		14	8	.636	2.94	27	25	11	199	194	29	52	3	0	0	1	120	36	4	.300	9	42	1	4	1.9	.981
1946			11	4	.733	2.12	17	16	9	136	112	21	51	0	0	0	0	61	11	1	.180	2	20	0	0	1.3	1.000
1947			14	10	.583	4.32	31	28	15	195.2	232	45	74	1	0	0	1	79	22	2	.278	6	32	1	0	1.3	.974
1948			10	10	.500	4.07	30	20	8	148	167	31	46	0	1	2	2	52	10	1	.192	9	31	1	0	1.4	.976
1949			3	7	.300	4.82	23	6	2	65.1	68	17	22	0	3	0	0	17	4	1	.235	4	16	3	1	1.0	.870
15 yrs.			158	101	.610	3.87	382	278	137	2219.1	2330	558	913	23	22	10	12	*				97	421	14	22	1.4	.974

WORLD SERIES

Year	Team	W	L	PCT	ERA	G	GS	CG	IP	H	BB	SO	ShO	W	L	SV	AB	H	HR	BA	PO	A	E	DP	TC/G	FA
1934	DET A	1	1	.500	2.95	3	2	2	21.1	19	0	12	0	0	0	0	7	0	0	.000	1	1	0	0	0.7	1.000
1935		1	2	.333	2.57	3	2	2	21	19	1	14	0	1	0	0	8	2	0	.250	3	5	1	0	3.0	.889
1940		0	2	.000	17.18	2	2	0	3.2	12	1	1	0	0	0	0	1	0	0	.000	0	1	0	0	0.5	1.000
3 yrs.		2	5	.286	3.91	8	6	4	46	50	2	27	0	1	0	0	16	2	0	.125	4	7	1	0	1.5	.917
				2nd																						

Year	Team		W	L	PCT	ERA	G	GS	CG	IP	H	BB	SO	ShO	W	L	SV	AB	H	HR	BA	PO	A	E	DP	TC/G	FA
															Relief Pitching			**Batting**									

Mike Rowland

ROWLAND, MICHAEL EVAN
B. Jan. 31, 1953, Chicago, Ill.　　　　　　　　　　　BR TR 6'3"　205 lbs.

Year	Team		W	L	PCT	ERA	G	GS	CG	IP	H	BB	SO	ShO	W	L	SV	AB	H	HR	BA	PO	A	E	DP	TC/G	FA
1980	SF	N	1	1	.500	2.33	19	0	0	27	20	8	8	0	1	1	0	0	0	0	–	1	4	0	0	0.3	1.000
1981			0	1	.000	3.38	9	1	0	16	13	6	8	0	0	0	0	1	1	0	1.000	1	2	0	0	0.3	1.000
2 yrs.			1	2	.333	2.72	28	1	0	43	33	14	16	0	1	1	0	1	1	0	1.000	2	6	0	0	0.3	1.000

Charlie Roy

ROY, CHARLES ROBERT
Brother of Luther Roy.
B. June 22, 1884, Beaulieu, Minn.　D. Feb. 10, 1950, Blackfoot, Ida.　　　　BR TR 5'10"　190 lbs.

Year	Team		W	L	PCT	ERA	G	GS	CG	IP	H	BB	SO	ShO	W	L	SV	AB	H	HR	BA	PO	A	E	DP	TC/G	FA
1906	PHI	N	0	1	.000	4.91	7	1	0	18.1	24	5	6	0	0	0	0	7	0	0	.000	0	5	1	0	0.9	.833

Emile Roy

ROY, EMILE ARTHUR
B. May 26, 1907, Brighton, Mass.　　　　　　　　　BR TR 5'11"　180 lbs.

Year	Team		W	L	PCT	ERA	G	GS	CG	IP	H	BB	SO	ShO	W	L	SV	AB	H	HR	BA	PO	A	E	DP	TC/G	FA
1933	PHI	A	0	1	.000	27.00	1	1	0	2.1	4	4	3	0	0	0	0	0	0	0	–	1	0	1	0	2.0	.500

Jean Pierre Roy

ROY, JEAN-PIERRE
B. June 26, 1920, Montreal, Que., Canada　　　　　BB TR 5'10"　160 lbs.

Year	Team		W	L	PCT	ERA	G	GS	CG	IP	H	BB	SO	ShO	W	L	SV	AB	H	HR	BA	PO	A	E	DP	TC/G	FA
1946	BKN	N	0	0	–	9.95	3	1	0	6.1	5	5	6	0	0	0	0	2	0	0	.000	0	0	0	0	0.0	–

Luther Roy

ROY, LUTHER FRANKLIN
Brother of Charlie Roy.
B. July 29, 1902, Ooltewah, Tenn.　D. July 24, 1963, Grand Rapids, Mich.　　　BR TR 5'10½"　161 lbs.

Year	Team		W	L	PCT	ERA	G	GS	CG	IP	H	BB	SO	ShO	W	L	SV	AB	H	HR	BA	PO	A	E	DP	TC/G	FA
1924	CLE	A	0	5	.000	7.77	16	5	2	48.2	62	31	14	0	0	1	0	15	4	0	.267	5	12	0	1	1.1	1.000
1925			0	0	–	3.60	6	1	0	10	14	11	1	0	0	0	0	2	0	0	.000	0	1	0	0	0.2	1.000
1927	CHI	N	3	1	.750	2.29	11	0	0	19.2	14	11	5	0	3	1	0	3	1	0	.333	0	6	2	1	0.7	.750
1929	2 teams		PHI	N	(21G 3–6)				BKN	N	(2G 0–0)																	
"	total		3	6	.333	8.29	23	12	1	92.1	141	39	16	0	1	1	0	33	9	0	.273	3	25	0	2	1.2	1.000
4 yrs.			6	12	.333	7.17	56	18	3	170.2	231	92	36	0	4	3	0	53	14	0	.264	8	44	2	4	1.0	.963

Norm Roy

ROY, NORMAN BROOKS (Jumbo)
B. Nov. 15, 1928, Newton, Mass.　　　　　　　　　BR TR 6'　200 lbs.

Year	Team		W	L	PCT	ERA	G	GS	CG	IP	H	BB	SO	ShO	W	L	SV	AB	H	HR	BA	PO	A	E	DP	TC/G	FA
1950	BOS	N	4	3	.571	5.13	19	6	2	59.2	72	39	25	0	1	0	0	18	3	0	.167	3	0	0	0	0.2	1.000

Dick Rozek

ROZEK, RICHARD LOUIS
B. Mar. 27, 1927, Cedar Rapids, Iowa　　　　　　　BL TL 6'½"　190 lbs.

Year	Team		W	L	PCT	ERA	G	GS	CG	IP	H	BB	SO	ShO	W	L	SV	AB	H	HR	BA	PO	A	E	DP	TC/G	FA
1950	CLE	A	0	0	–	4.97	12	2	0	25.1	28	19	14	0	0	0	0	5	0	0	.000	0	2	0	0	0.2	1.000
1951			0	0	–	2.93	7	1	0	15.1	11	18	5	0	0	0	0	3	1	0	.333	0	1	1	0	0.3	.500
1952			1	0	1.000	4.97	10	1	0	12.2	11	13	5	0	0	0	0	2	0	0	.000	0	2	0	0	0.2	1.000
1953	PHI	A	0	0	–	5.06	2	0	0	10.2	8	9	2	0	0	0	0	2	0	0	.000	0	1	0	0	0.5	1.000
1954			0	0	–	6.75	2	0	0	1.1	3	0	0	0	0	0	0	0	0	0	–	0	0	0	0	0.0	–
5 yrs.			1	0	1.000	4.55	33	4	0	65.1	65	55	26	0	0	0	0	12	1	0	.083	0	6	1	0	0.2	.857

Dave Rozema

ROZEMA, DAVID SCOTT
B. Aug. 5, 1956, Grand Rapids, Mich.　　　　　　　BR TR 6'4"　185 lbs.

Year	Team		W	L	PCT	ERA	G	GS	CG	IP	H	BB	SO	ShO	W	L	SV	AB	H	HR	BA	PO	A	E	DP	TC/G	FA
1977	DET	A	15	7	.682	3.10	28	28	16	218	222	34	92	1	0	0	0	0	0	0	–	24	33	3	2	2.1	.950
1978			9	12	.429	3.14	28	28	11	209.1	205	41	57	2	0	0	0	0	0	0	–	17	29	0	0	1.6	1.000
1979			4	4	.500	3.53	16	16	4	97	101	30	33	1	0	0	0	0	0	0	–	7	17	1	1	1.6	.960
1980			6	9	.400	3.91	42	13	2	145	152	49	49	1	2	4	4	0	0	0	–	17	21	1	2	0.9	.974
1981			5	5	.500	3.63	28	9	2	104	99	25	46	2	3	0	3	0	0	0	–	5	15	1	1	0.8	.952
1982			3	0	1.000	1.63	8	2	0	27.2	7	7	15	0	2	0	1	0	0	0	–	7	5	0	0	1.5	1.000
1983			8	3	.727	3.43	29	16	1	105	100	29	63	0	1	0	2	0	0	0	–	12	17	2	1	1.1	.935
1984			7	6	.538	3.74	29	16	0	101	110	18	48	0	0	1	0	0	0	0	–	17	10	0	3	0.9	1.000
1985	TEX	A	3	7	.300	4.19	34	4	0	88	100	22	42	0	1	5	7	0	0	0	–	2	18	0	0	0.6	1.000
1986			0	0	–	5.91	6	0	0	10.2	19	3	3	0	0	0	0	0	0	0	–	0	3	0	0	0.5	1.000
10 yrs.			60	53	.531	3.47	248	132	36	1105.2	1125	258	448	7	9	10	17	0	0	0	–	108	168	8	10	1.1	.972

Jorge Rubio

RUBIO, JORGE JESUS CHAVEZ
Born Jorge Jesus Rubio y Chavez.
B. Apr. 23, 1945, Mexicali, Mexico　　　　　　　　BR TR 6'3"　200 lbs.

Year	Team		W	L	PCT	ERA	G	GS	CG	IP	H	BB	SO	ShO	W	L	SV	AB	H	HR	BA	PO	A	E	DP	TC/G	FA
1966	CAL	A	2	1	.667	2.96	7	4	1	27.1	22	16	27	1	0	0	0	8	0	0	.000	3	1	0	0	0.6	1.000
1967			0	2	.000	3.60	3	3	0	15	18	9	4	0	0	0	0	3	1	0	.333	1	3	0	0	1.3	1.000
2 yrs.			2	3	.400	3.19	10	7	1	42.1	40	25	31	1	0	0	0	11	1	0	.091	4	4	0	0	0.8	1.000

Dave Rucker

RUCKER, DAVID MICHAEL
B. Sept. 1, 1957, San Bernardino, Calif.　　　　　BL TL 6'1"　185 lbs.

Year	Team		W	L	PCT	ERA	G	GS	CG	IP	H	BB	SO	ShO	W	L	SV	AB	H	HR	BA	PO	A	E	DP	TC/G	FA
1981	DET	A	0	0	–	6.75	2	0	0	4	3	1	2	0	0	0	0	0	0	0	–	1	0	0	0	0.5	1.000
1982			5	6	.455	3.38	27	4	1	64	62	23	31	0	4	4	0	0	0	0	–	4	10	3	2	0.6	.824
1983	2 teams		DET	A	(4G 1–2)				STL	N	(34G 5–3)																	
"	total		6	5	.545	5.28	38	3	0	46	54	26	28	0	5	4	0	4	0	0	.000	6	8	1	1	0.4	.933
1984	STL	N	2	3	.400	2.10	50	0	0	73	62	34	38	0	2	3	0	7	1	0	.143	4	10	5	1	0.4	.737
1985	PHI	N	3	2	.600	4.31	39	3	0	79.1	83	40	41	0	2	1	1	12	4	0	.333	1	14	0	1	0.5	1.000
1986			0	2	.000	5.76	19	0	0	25	34	14	14	0	0	2	0	1	0	0	.000	1	5	0	1	0.3	1.000
1988	PIT	N	0	2	.000	4.76	31	0	0	28.1	39	9	16	0	0	2	0	2	0	0	.000	1	4	1	0	0.2	.833
7 yrs.			16	20	.444	3.94	206	10	1	319.2	337	147	170	0	13	16	1	26	5	0	.192	22	51	10	6	0.4	.880

Nap Rucker

RUCKER, GEORGE NAPOLEON
B. Sept. 30, 1884, Crabapple, Ga.　D. Dec. 19, 1970, Alpharetta, Ga.　　　BR TL 5'11"　190 lbs.

Year	Team		W	L	PCT	ERA	G	GS	CG	IP	H	BB	SO	ShO	W	L	SV	AB	H	HR	BA	PO	A	E	DP	TC/G	FA
1907	BKN	N	15	13	.536	2.06	37	36	26	275.1	242	80	131	4	1	0	0	97	15	0	.155	5	73	7	4	2.3	.918
1908			17	19	.472	2.08	42	35	30	333.1	265	125	199	6	1	1	0	117	21	0	.179	13	109	4	1	3.0	.968
1909			13	19	.406	2.24	38	33	28	309.1	245	101	201	6	0	2	1	101	12	0	.119	3	67	4	3	1.9	.946

Year	Team		W	L	PCT	ERA	G	GS	CG	IP	H	BB	SO	ShO	Relief Pitching W	L	SV	Batting AB	H	HR	BA	PO	A	E	DP	TC/G	FA

Nap Rucker *continued*

Year	Team		W	L	PCT	ERA	G	GS	CG	IP	H	BB	SO	ShO	W	L	SV	AB	H	HR	BA	PO	A	E	DP	TC/G	FA
1910			17	18	.486	2.58	41	39	27	320.1	293	84	147	6	1	0	0	110	23	0	.209	6	80	2	0	2.1	.977
1911			22	18	.550	2.71	48	33	23	315.2	255	110	190	5	5	4	4	104	21	1	.202	7	88	3	1	2.0	.969
1912			18	21	.462	2.21	45	34	23	297.2	272	72	151	6	3	4	4	102	25	0	.245	5	82	1	3	2.0	.989
1913			14	15	.483	2.87	41	33	16	260	236	67	111	4	1	1	3	87	21	0	.241	4	50	2	1	1.4	.965
1914			7	6	.538	3.39	16	16	5	103.2	113	27	35	0	0	0	0	34	9	0	.265	4	29	0	1	2.1	1.000
1915			9	4	.692	2.42	19	15	7	122.2	134	28	38	1	2	0	1	42	9	0	.214	6	40	1	2	2.5	.979
1916			2	1	.667	1.69	9	4	1	37.1	34	7	14	0	1	0	0	11	1	0	.091	1	9	0	2	1.1	1.000
10 yrs.			134	134	.500	2.42	336	272	186	2375.1	2089	701	1217	38	15	12	13	805	157	1	.195	55	627	24	18	2.1	.966

WORLD SERIES

Year	Team		W	L	PCT	ERA	G	GS	CG	IP	H	BB	SO	ShO	W	L	SV	AB	H	HR	BA	PO	A	E	DP	TC/G	FA
1916	BKN	N	0	0	—	0.00	1	0	0	2	1	0	3	0	0	0	0	0	0	0	—	0	0	0	0	0.0	—

Dick Rudolph

RUDOLPH, RICHARD (Baldy)
B. Aug. 25, 1887, New York, N. Y.
D. Oct. 20, 1949, Bronx, N. Y.
Manager 1924.

BB TR 5'9½" 160 lbs.
BR 1927

Year	Team		W	L	PCT	ERA	G	GS	CG	IP	H	BB	SO	ShO	W	L	SV	AB	H	HR	BA	PO	A	E	DP	TC/G	FA
1910	NY	N	0	1	.000	7.50	3	1	1	12	21	2	9	0	0	0	2	4	1	0	.250	1	1	0	0	0.7	1.000
1911			0	0	—	9.00	1	0	0	2	2	0	0	0	0	0	0	1	1	0	1.000	0	0	0	0	0.0	—
1913	BOS	N	14	13	.519	2.92	33	22	17	249.1	258	59	109	1	3	3	0	88	21	0	.239	16	81	2	2	3.0	.980
1914			27	10	.730	2.35	42	36	31	336.1	288	61	138	6	2	2	0	120	15	0	.125	13	96	3	5	2.7	.973
1915			22	19	.537	2.37	44	43	30	341.1	304	64	147	3	0	0	1	116	23	1	.198	8	92	3	6	2.3	.971
1916			19	12	.613	2.16	41	38	27	312	285	38	133	5	0	0	3	101	16	0	.158	6	113	5	3	3.0	.960
1917			13	13	.500	3.41	32	30	22	242.2	252	54	96	5	0	0	0	87	20	0	.230	7	75	5	0	2.7	.943
1918			9	10	.474	2.57	21	20	15	154	144	30	48	3	0	0	0	54	10	0	.185	8	49	1	3	2.8	.983
1919			13	18	.419	2.17	37	32	24	273.2	282	54	76	2	0	0	2	88	17	1	.193	15	81	3	0	2.7	.970
1920			4	8	.333	4.04	18	12	3	89	104	24	24	0	2	1	0	27	5	0	.185	4	26	0	0	1.7	1.000
1922			0	2	.000	5.06	3	3	1	16	22	5	3	0	0	0	0	5	2	0	.400	0	4	0	0	1.3	1.000
1923			1	2	.333	3.72	4	4	1	19.1	27	10	3	1	0	0	0	7	0	0	.000	1	6	0	1	1.8	1.000
1927			0	0	—	0.00	1	0	0	1.1	1	1	0	0	0	0	0	0	0	0	—	0	0	0	0	0.0	—
13 yrs.			122	108	.530	2.66	280	241	172	2049	1971	402	786	26	7	8	8	698	131	2	.188	79	624	22	19	2.6	.970

WORLD SERIES

Year	Team		W	L	PCT	ERA	G	GS	CG	IP	H	BB	SO	ShO	W	L	SV	AB	H	HR	BA	PO	A	E	DP	TC/G	FA
1914	BOS	N	2	0	1.000	0.50	2	2	2	18	12	4	15	0	0	0	0	6	2	0	.333	0	3	0	0	1.5	1.000

Don Rudolph

RUDOLPH, FREDERICK DONALD
B. Aug. 16, 1931, Baltimore, Md.   D. Sept. 12, 1968, Granada Hills, Calif.

BL TL 5'11" 195 lbs.

Year	Team		W	L	PCT	ERA	G	GS	CG	IP	H	BB	SO	ShO	W	L	SV	AB	H	HR	BA	PO	A	E	DP	TC/G	FA
1957	CHI	A	1	0	1.000	2.25	5	0	0	12	6	2	2	0	1	0	0				.500	1	0	0	0	0.2	1.000
1958			1	0	1.000	2.57	7	0	0	7	4	5	2	0	1	0	1	0	0	0	—	0	3	0	1	0.4	1.000
1959	2 teams		CHI A	(4G 0–0)		CIN N	(5G 0–0)																					
"	total		0	0	—	3.48	9	0	0	10.1	17	5	8	0	0	0	0				.000	1	2	0	1	0.3	1.000
1962	2 teams		CLE A	(1G 0–0)		WAS A	(37G 8–10)																					
"	total		8	10	.444	3.62	38	23	6	176.2	188	42	68	2	0	0	0	57	10	0	.175	6	32	2	0	1.1	.950
1963	WAS	A	7	19	.269	4.55	37	26	4	174	189	36	70	0	0	2	1	45	8	1	.178	9	27	0	2	1.0	1.000
1964			1	3	.250	4.09	28	8	0	70.1	81	12	32	0	0	0	1	15	1	0	.067	4	10	0	0	0.5	1.000
6 yrs.			18	32	.360	4.00	124	57	10	450.1	485	102	182	2	2	4	3	120	20	1	.167	20	75	2	4	0.8	.979

Ernie Rudolph

RUDOLPH, ERNEST WILLIAM
B. Feb. 13, 1910, Black River Falls, Wis.

BL TR 5'8" 165 lbs.

Year	Team		W	L	PCT	ERA	G	GS	CG	IP	H	BB	SO	ShO	W	L	SV	AB	H	HR	BA	PO	A	E	DP	TC/G	FA
1945	BKN	N	1	0	1.000	5.19	7	0	0	8.2	12	7	3	0	1	0	0	0	0	0	—	0	2	0	0	0.3	1.000

Dutch Ruether

RUETHER, WALTER HENRY
B. Sept. 13, 1893, Alameda, Calif.   D. May 16, 1970, Phoenix, Ariz.

BL TL 6'1½" 180 lbs.

Year	Team		W	L	PCT	ERA	G	GS	CG	IP	H	BB	SO	ShO	W	L	SV	AB	H	HR	BA	PO	A	E	DP	TC/G	FA
1917	2 teams		CHI N	(10G 2–0)		CIN N	(7G 1–2)																					
"	total		3	2	.600	3.00	17	8	2	72	80	26	35	1	0	0	0	68	17	0	.250	2	21	2	1	1.5	.920
1918	CIN	N	0	1	.000	2.70	2	2	1	10	10	3	10	0	0	0	0	3	0	0	.000	0	2	0	0	1.0	1.000
1919			19	6	.760	1.82	33	29	20	242.2	195	83	99	3	0	0	0	92	24	0	.261	10	57	2	1	2.1	.971
1920			16	12	.571	2.47	37	33	23	265.2	235	96	99	5	0	1	3	104	20	0	.192	5	74	4	6	2.2	.952
1921	BKN	N	10	13	.435	4.26	36	27	12	211.1	247	67	78	1	0	0	2	97	34	2	.351	6	51	2	3	1.6	.966
1922			21	12	.636	3.53	35	35	26	267.1	290	92	89	2	0	0	0	125	26	2	.208	9	56	0	6	1.9	1.000
1923			15	14	.517	4.22	34	34	20	275	308	86	87	0	0	0	0	117	32	0	.274	7	53	2	7	1.8	.968
1924			8	13	.381	3.94	30	21	13	166.2	189	45	65	2	1	1	3	62	15	0	.242	5	46	1	3	1.7	.981
1925	WAS	A	18	7	.720	3.87	30	29	16	223.1	241	105	68	1	0	1	0	108	36	1	.333	5	46	2	0	1.8	.962
1926	2 teams		WAS A	(23G 12–6)		NY A	(5G 2–3)																					
"	total		14	9	.609	4.60	28	28	14	205.1	246	84	56	0	0	0	0	113	25	1	.221	2	38	1	2	1.5	.976
1927	NY	A	13	6	.684	3.38	27	26	12	184	202	52	45	3	0	0	0	80	21	1	.263	7	47	0	2	2.0	1.000
11 yrs.			137	95	.591	3.50	309	272	155	2123.1	2243	739	710	18	1	3	8	*				58	491	16	32	1.8	.972

WORLD SERIES

Year	Team		W	L	PCT	ERA	G	GS	CG	IP	H	BB	SO	ShO	W	L	SV	AB	H	HR	BA	PO	A	E	DP	TC/G	FA
1919	CIN	N	1	0	1.000	2.57	2	2	1	14	12	4	1	0	0	0	0	6	4	0	.667	0	2	0	0	1.0	1.000
1926	NY	A	0	1	.000	8.31	1	1	0	4.1	7	2	1	0	0	0	0	4	0	0	.000	0	2	0	0	2.0	1.000
2 yrs.			1	1	.500	3.93	3	3	1	18.1	19	6	2	0	0	0	0	11	4	0	.364	0	4	0	0	1.3	1.000

Bruce Ruffin

RUFFIN, BRUCE WAYNE
B. Oct. 4, 1963, Lubbock, Tex.

BR TL 6'2" 205 lbs.

Year	Team		W	L	PCT	ERA	G	GS	CG	IP	H	BB	SO	ShO	W	L	SV	AB	H	HR	BA	PO	A	E	DP	TC/G	FA
1986	PHI	N	9	4	.692	2.46	21	21	6	146.1	138	44	70	0	0	0	0	55	4	0	.073	8	20	1	0	1.4	.966
1987			11	14	.440	4.35	35	35	3	204.2	236	73	93	1	0	0	0	73	4	0	.055	7	32	2	3	1.2	.951
1988			6	10	.375	4.43	55	15	3	144.1	151	80	82	0	2	4	3	33	4	0	.121	11	25	2	0	0.7	.947
1989			6	10	.375	4.44	24	23	1	125.2	152	62	70	0	0	0	0	34	6	0	.176	3	34	4	0	1.7	.902
4 yrs.			32	38	.457	3.94	135	94	13	621	677	259	315	1	2	4	3	195	18	0	.092	29	111	9	5	1.1	.940

Year	Team	W	L	PCT	ERA	G	GS	CG	IP	H	BB	SO	ShO	Relief Pitching W	L	SV	Batting AB	H	HR	BA	PO	A	E	DP	TC/G	FA

Red Ruffing

RUFFING, CHARLES HERBERT
B. May 3, 1904, Granville, Ill. D. Feb. 17, 1986, Mayfield Heights, Ohio
Hall of Fame 1967.

BR TR 6'1½" 205 lbs.

Year	Team	W	L	PCT	ERA	G	GS	CG	IP	H	BB	SO	ShO	W	L	SV	AB	H	HR	BA	PO	A	E	DP	TC/G	FA
1924	BOS A	0	0	–	6.65	8	2	0	23	29	9	10	0	0	0	0	7	1	0	.143	0	3	0	0	0.4	1.000
1925		9	18	.333	5.01	37	27	13	217.1	253	75	64	3	1	1	1	79	17	0	.215	7	50	1	3	1.6	.983
1926		6	15	.286	4.39	37	22	6	166	169	68	58	0	1	2	2	51	10	1	.196	8	42	0	3	1.4	1.000
1927		5	13	.278	4.66	26	18	10	158.1	160	87	77	0	1	1	2	55	14	0	.255	8	36	1	1	1.7	.978
1928		10	25	.286	3.89	42	34	25	289.1	303	96	118	1	0	2	2	121	38	2	.314	7	51	3	4	1.5	.951
1929		9	22	.290	4.86	35	30	18	244.1	280	118	109	2	0	3	1	114	35	2	.307	6	46	3	1	1.6	.945
1930	2 teams	BOS A	(4G 0–3)			NY A	(34G 15–5)																			
"	total	15	8	.652	4.38	38	28	13	221.2	242	68	131	2	2	1	2	110	40	4	.364	3	29	3	0	0.9	.914
1931	NY A	16	14	.533	4.41	37	30	19	237	240	87	132	1	1	2	2	109	36	3	.330	4	32	0	1	1.0	1.000
1932		18	7	.720	3.09	35	29	22	259	219	115	190	3	1	1	2	124	38	3	.306	4	38	2	4	1.3	.955
1933		9	14	.391	3.91	35	28	18	235	230	93	122	0	1	0	3	115	29	2	.252	8	45	2	5	1.6	.964
1934		19	11	.633	3.93	36	31	19	256.1	232	104	149	5	1	1	0	113	28	2	.248	10	32	3	2	1.3	.933
1935		16	11	.593	3.12	30	29	19	222	201	76	81	2	0	1	0	109	37	2	.339	17	26	0	3	1.4	1.000
1936		20	12	.625	3.85	33	33	25	271	274	90	102	3	0	0	0	127	37	5	.291	13	56	1	6	2.1	.986
1937		20	7	.741	2.98	31	31	22	256.1	242	68	131	5	0	0	0	129	26	1	.202	9	28	1	2	1.2	.974
1938		21	7	.750	3.31	31	31	22	247.1	246	82	127	4	0	0	0	107	24	3	.224	11	34	0	2	1.5	1.000
1939		21	7	.750	2.93	28	28	22	233.1	211	75	95	5	0	0	0	114	35	1	.307	8	32	2	2	1.5	.952
1940		15	12	.556	3.38	30	30	20	226	218	76	97	3	0	0	0	89	11	1	.124	6	30	2	2	1.3	.947
1941		15	6	.714	3.54	23	23	13	185.2	177	54	60	2	0	0	0	89	27	2	.303	7	21	0	3	1.2	1.000
1942		14	7	.667	3.21	24	24	16	193.2	183	41	80	4	0	0	0	80	20	1	.250	8	30	1	5	1.6	.974
1945		7	3	.700	2.89	11	11	8	87.1	85	20	24	1	0	0	0	46	10	1	.217	2	11	1	1	1.3	.929
1946		5	1	.833	1.77	8	8	4	61	37	23	19	2	0	0	0	25	3	0	.120	2	5	0	0	0.9	1.000
1947	CHI A	3	5	.375	6.11	9	9	1	53	63	16	11	0	0	0	0	24	5	0	.208	2	7	0	0	1.0	1.000
22 yrs.		273	225	.548	3.80	624	536	335	4344	4294	1541	1987	48	9	15	16	*				150	684	26	51	1.4	.970
												9th														

WORLD SERIES

Year	Team	W	L	PCT	ERA	G	GS	CG	IP	H	BB	SO	ShO	W	L	SV	AB	H	HR	BA	PO	A	E	DP	TC/G	FA
1932	NY A	1	0	1.000	4.00	1	1	1	9	10	6	10	0	0	0	0	4	0	0	.000	1	3	0	0	4.0	1.000
1936		0	1	.000	4.50	2	2	0	14	16	5	12	0	0	0	0	5	0	0	.000	1	3	0	0	2.0	1.000
1937		1	0	1.000	1.00	1	1	1	9	7	3	8	0	0	0	0	4	2	0	.500	0	0	0	0	0.0	–
1938		2	0	1.000	1.50	2	2	2	18	17	2	11	0	0	0	0	6	1	0	.167	2	4	0	0	3.0	1.000
1939		1	0	1.000	1.00	1	1	1	9	4	1	4	0	0	0	0	3	1	0	.333	0	3	0	1	3.0	1.000
1941		1	0	1.000	1.00	1	1	1	9	6	3	5	0	0	0	0	3	0	0	.000	0	0	0	0	0.0	–
1942		1	1	.500	4.08	2	2	1	17.2	14	7	11	0	0	0	0	9	2	0	.222	1	1	0	0	0.5	1.000
7 yrs.		7	2	.778	2.63	10	10	7	85.2	74	27	61	0	0	0	0	34	6	0	.176	4	14	0	1	1.8	1.000
			2nd				4th	4th		3rd	4th	6th	4th														

Vern Ruhle

RUHLE, VERNON GERALD
B. Jan. 25, 1951, Coleman, Mich.

BR TR 6'1" 185 lbs.

Year	Team	W	L	PCT	ERA	G	GS	CG	IP	H	BB	SO	ShO	W	L	SV	AB	H	HR	BA	PO	A	E	DP	TC/G	FA
1974	DET A	2	0	1.000	2.73	5	3	1	33	35	6	10	0	0	0	0	0	0	0	–	4	1	0	0	1.0	1.000
1975		11	12	.478	4.03	32	31	8	190	199	65	67	3	0	0	0	0	0	0	–	15	19	5	1	1.2	.872
1976		9	12	.429	3.92	32	32	5	200	227	59	88	1	0	0	0	0	0	0	–	14	28	0	1	1.3	1.000
1977		3	5	.375	5.73	14	10	0	66	83	15	27	0	0	0	1	0	0	0	–	5	7	1	1	0.9	.923
1978	HOU N	3	3	.500	2.12	13	10	2	68	57	20	27	2	0	0	0	18	1	0	.056	4	7	0	0	0.8	1.000
1979		0	0	.250	4.09	13	10	2	66	64	8	33	0	0	0	1	19	1	0	.053	3	5	0	0	0.6	1.000
1980		12	4	.750	2.38	28	22	6	159	148	29	55	2	0	0	0	49	12	0	.245	15	17	2	2	1.2	.941
1981		4	6	.400	2.91	20	15	1	102	97	20	39	0	0	1	1	24	6	0	.250	4	9	0	2	0.7	1.000
1982		9	13	.409	3.93	31	21	3	149	169	24	56	2	3	0	1	41	4	0	.098	9	23	2	1	1.1	.941
1983		8	5	.615	3.69	41	9	0	114.2	107	36	43	0	7	3	3	19	2	0	.105	12	19	0	0	0.8	1.000
1984		1	9	.100	4.58	40	6	0	90.1	112	29	60	0	0	5	2	12	1	0	.083	4	18	2	1	0.6	.917
1985	CLE A	2	10	.167	4.32	42	16	1	125	139	30	54	0	0	3	3	0	0	0	–	15	13	0	0	0.7	1.000
1986	CAL A	1	3	.250	4.15	16	3	0	47.2	46	7	23	0	0	1	1	0	0	0	–	7	8	1	1	1.0	.938
13 yrs.		67	88	.432	3.73	327	188	29	1410.2	1483	348	582	12	10	15	11	182	27	0	.148	111	174	13	10	0.9	.956

DIVISIONAL PLAYOFF SERIES

Year	Team	W	L	PCT	ERA	G	GS	CG	IP	H	BB	SO	ShO	W	L	SV	AB	H	HR	BA	PO	A	E	DP	TC/G	FA
1981	HOU N	0	1	.000	2.25	1	1	1	8	4	2	1	0	0	0	0	1	0	0	.000	0	0	0	0	0.0	–

LEAGUE CHAMPIONSHIP SERIES

Year	Team	W	L	PCT	ERA	G	GS	CG	IP	H	BB	SO	ShO	W	L	SV	AB	H	HR	BA	PO	A	E	DP	TC/G	FA
1980	HOU N	0	0	–	3.86	1	1	0	7	8	1	3	0	0	0	0	3	0	0	.000	1	1	0	1	2.0	1.000
1986	CAL A	0	0	–	13.50	1	0	0	.2	2	0	0	0	0	0	0	0	0	0	–	0	0	0	0	0.0	–
2 yrs.		0	0	–	4.70	2	1	0	7.2	10	1	3	0	0	0	0	3	0	0	.000	1	1	0	1	1.0	1.000

Andy Rush

RUSH, JESSE HOWARD
B. Dec. 26, 1889, Longton, Kans. D. Mar. 16, 1969, Fresno, Calif.

BR TR 6'3" 180 lbs.

Year	Team	W	L	PCT	ERA	G	GS	CG	IP	H	BB	SO	ShO	W	L	SV	AB	H	HR	BA	PO	A	E	DP	TC/G	FA
1925	BKN N	0	1	.000	9.31	4	2	0	9.2	16	5	4	0	0	0	0	3	0	0	.000	1	2	0	0	0.8	1.000

Bob Rush

RUSH, ROBERT RANSOM
B. Dec. 21, 1925, Battle Creek, Mich.

BR TR 6'4" 205 lbs.

Year	Team	W	L	PCT	ERA	G	GS	CG	IP	H	BB	SO	ShO	W	L	SV	AB	H	HR	BA	PO	A	E	DP	TC/G	FA
1948	CHI N	5	11	.313	3.92	36	16	4	133.1	153	37	72	0	2	0	0	39	5	0	.128	3	31	3	0	1.0	.919
1949		10	18	.357	4.07	35	27	9	201	197	79	80	1	2	0	4	63	2	0	.032	17	37	2	1	1.6	.964
1950		13	20	.394	3.71	39	34	19	254.2	261	93	93	1	0	2	1	90	15	1	.167	24	51	1	4	1.9	.987
1951		11	12	.478	3.83	37	29	12	211.1	212	68	129	2	0	0	0	68	13	0	.191	18	39	5	2	1.7	.919
1952		17	13	.567	2.70	34	32	17	250.1	205	81	157	4	0	0	2	96	28	0	.292	13	54	4	5	2.1	.944
1953		9	14	.391	4.54	29	28	8	166.2	177	66	84	1	0	0	0	54	6	0	.111	13	28	0	3	1.4	1.000
1954		13	15	.464	3.77	33	32	11	236.1	213	103	124	0	0	0	2	83	23	2	.277	15	54	3	4	2.2	.958
1955		13	11	.542	3.50	33	33	14	234	204	73	130	3	0	0	0	82	9	1	.110	16	43	1	1	1.8	.983
1956		13	10	.565	3.19	33	32	13	239.2	210	59	104	1	0	0	0	82	8	0	.098	14	34	2	2	1.6	.960
1957		6	16	.273	4.38	31	29	5	205.1	211	66	103	1	0	0	0	69	14	0	.203	15	25	3	1	1.4	.930
1958	MIL N	10	6	.625	3.42	28	20	5	147.1	142	31	84	2	3	0	0	45	9	0	.200	12	14	1	1	1.0	.963
1959		5	6	.455	2.40	31	9	1	101.1	102	23	64	1	3	2	0	32	6	0	.188	9	13	3	0	0.8	.880

Year	Team	W	L	PCT	ERA	G	GS	CG	IP	H	BB	SO	ShO	Relief Pitching W	L	SV	Batting AB	H	HR	BA	PO	A	E	DP	TC/G	FA

Bob Rush *continued*

Year	Team	W	L	PCT	ERA	G	GS	CG	IP	H	BB	SO	ShO	W	L	SV	AB	H	HR	BA	PO	A	E	DP	TC/G	FA
1960	2 teams	MIL N	(10G 2–0)		CHI A	(9G 0–0)																				
"	total	2	0	1.000	4.91	19	0	0	29.1	40	10	20	0	2	0	1	4	2	0	.500	2	5	0	1	0.4	1.000
13 yrs.		127	152	.455	3.65	417	321	118	2410.2	2327	789	1244	16	14	7	8	807	140	4	.173	171	428	28	25	1.5	.955

WORLD SERIES

Year	Team	W	L	PCT	ERA	G	GS	CG	IP	H	BB	SO	ShO	W	L	SV	AB	H	HR	BA	PO	A	E	DP	TC/G	FA
1958	MIL N	0	1	.000	3.00	1	1	0	6	3	5	2	0	0	0	0	2	0	0	.000	0	3	0	0	3.0	1.000

Amos Rusie

RUSIE, AMOS WILSON (The Hoosier Thunderbolt)   BR TR 6'1"   210 lbs.
B. May 30, 1871, Mooresville, Ind.   D. Dec. 6, 1942, Seattle, Wash.
Hall of Fame 1977.

Year	Team	W	L	PCT	ERA	G	GS	CG	IP	H	BB	SO	ShO	W	L	SV	AB	H	HR	BA	PO	A	E	DP	TC/G	FA
1889	IND N	12	10	.545	5.32	33	22	19	225	246	116	109	1	2	0	0	103	18	0	.175	9	32	6	2	1.4	.872
1890	NY N	29	34	.460	2.56	67	63	56	548.2	436	289	341	4	1	1	1	284	79	0	.278	25	129	20	5	2.6	.885
1891		33	20	.623	2.55	61	57	52	500.1	391	262	337	6	2	1	1	220	54	0	.245	10	106	14	4	2.1	.892
1892		32	31	.508	2.88	64	61	58	532	405	267	288	2	0	2	0	252	53	1	.210	27	132	21	5	2.8	.883
1893		33	21	.611	3.23	56	52[1]	50[1]	482 [1]	451	218[1]	208	4	2	1	1	212	57	3	.269	23	114	15	5	2.7	.901
1894		36	13	.735	2.78	54	50	45	444	426	200	195	3	2	0	1	186	52	3	.280	28	113	14	4	2.9	.910
1895		23	23	.500	3.73	49	47	42	393.1	384	159	201	4	1	1	0	179	44	1	.246	19	93	11	4	2.5	.911
1897		28	10	.737	2.54	38	37	35	322.1	314	87	135	2	0	1	0	144	40	0	.278	19	77	8	3	2.7	.923
1898		20	11	.645	3.03	37	36	33	300	288	103	114	4	0	0	1	138	29	0	.210	16	68	11	3	2.6	.884
1901	CIN N	0	1	.000	8.59	3	2	2	22	43	14	6	0	0	0	0	8	1	0	.125	1	8	1	0	3.3	.900
10 yrs.		246	174	.586	3.07	462	427	392	3769.2	3384	1704 7th	1934	30	10	7	5	*				177	872	121	35	2.5	.897

Russ

RUSS,
B. Louisville, Ky.   Deceased.

Year	Team	W	L	PCT	ERA	G	GS	CG	IP	H	BB	SO	ShO	W	L	SV	AB	H	HR	BA	PO	A	E	DP	TC/G	FA
1882	BAL AA	0	1	.000	7.20	1	1	0	5	10	1	0	0	0	0	0	3	1	0	.333	0	1	0	0	1.0	1.000

Allen Russell

RUSSELL, ALLEN E.   BR TR 5'11"   165 lbs.
Brother of Lefty Russell.
B. July 31, 1893, Baltimore, Md.   D. Oct. 20, 1972, Baltimore, Md.

Year	Team	W	L	PCT	ERA	G	GS	CG	IP	H	BB	SO	ShO	W	L	SV	AB	H	HR	BA	PO	A	E	DP	TC/G	FA
1915	NY A	1	2	.333	2.67	5	3	1	27	21	21	21	0	0	0	0	8	2	0	.250	1	6	1	0	1.6	.875
1916		6	10	.375	3.20	34	18	8	171.1	138	75	104	1	1	0	6	45	2	0	.044	4	49	3	1	1.6	.946
1917		7	8	.467	2.24	25	10	6	104.1	89	39	55	0	4	2	2	31	10	0	.323	3	26	5	1	1.4	.853
1918		7	11	.389	3.26	27	18	7	141	139	73	54	2	0	3	4	42	7	0	.167	6	33	2	0	1.5	.951
1919	2 teams	NY A	(23G 5–5)		BOS A	(21G 10–4)																				
"	total	15	9	.625	2.94	44	20	13	211	194	71	113	2	5	1	5	71	12	0	.169	9	53	6	1	1.5	.912
1920	BOS A	5	6	.455	3.01	16	10	7	107.2	100	38	53	0	1	1	1	41	5	0	.122	3	34	4	2	2.6	.902
1921		7	11	.389	4.11	39	14	8	173	204	77	60	0	4	2	3	57	7	0	.123	12	44	5	1	1.6	.918
1922		6	7	.462	5.01	34	11	1	125.2	152	57	34	0	3	2	2	38	3	0	.079	6	41	0	1	1.4	1.000
1923	WAS A	10	8	.556	3.03	52	6	3	181.1	177	77	67	0	9	7	9	50	10	0	.200	5	34	3	2	0.8	.929
1924		5	1	.833	4.37	37	0	0	82.1	83	45	17	0	5	1	8	18	5	0	.278	2	20	3	0	0.7	.880
1925		2	4	.333	5.77	32	2	0	68.2	85	37	25	0	2	2	2	14	2	0	.143	5	24	2	2	1.0	.935
11 yrs.		71	77	.480	3.52	345	112	54	1393.1	1382	610	603	5	34	21	42	415	65	0	.157	56	364	34	11	1.3	.925

WORLD SERIES

Year	Team	W	L	PCT	ERA	G	GS	CG	IP	H	BB	SO	ShO	W	L	SV	AB	H	HR	BA	PO	A	E	DP	TC/G	FA
1924	WAS A	0	0	–	3.00	1	0	0	3	4	0	0	0	0	0	0	0	0	0	–	0	1	0	0	1.0	1.000

Jack Russell

RUSSELL, JACK ERWIN   BR TR 6'1½"   178 lbs.
B. Oct. 24, 1905, Paris, Tex.

Year	Team	W	L	PCT	ERA	G	GS	CG	IP	H	BB	SO	ShO	W	L	SV	AB	H	HR	BA	PO	A	E	DP	TC/G	FA
1926	BOS A	0	5	.000	3.58	36	5	1	98	94	24	17	0	0	2	0	21	4	0	.190	10	34	1	2	1.3	.978
1927		4	9	.308	4.10	34	15	4	147	172	40	25	1	1	1	0	48	6	0	.125	13	44	6	1	1.9	.905
1928		11	14	.440	3.84	32	26	10	201.1	233	41	27	2	1	0	0	62	13	0	.210	13	50	4	6	2.1	.940
1929		6	18	.250	3.94	35	32	13	226.1	263	40	37	0	0	0	0	70	9	0	.129	15	69	0	1	2.4	1.000
1930		9	20	.310	5.45	35	30	15	229.2	302	53	35	0	0	0	0	79	14	1	.177	11	59	4	3	2.1	.946
1931		10	18	.357	5.16	36	31	13	232	298	65	45	0	0	1	0	82	16	0	.195	16	63	2	1	2.3	.975
1932	2 teams	BOS A	(11G 1–7)		CLE A	(18G 5–7)																				
"	total	6	14	.300	5.25	29	17	7	152.2	207	42	34	0	0	3	1	51	13	0	.255	13	39	4	1	1.9	.929
1933	WAS A	12	6	.667	2.69	50	3	2	124	119	32	28	0	11	4	13	34	5	0	.147	6	46	0	5	1.0	1.000
1934		5	10	.333	4.17	54	9	3	157.2	179	56	38	0	2	7	7	44	7	0	.159	8	44	2	3	1.0	.963
1935		4	9	.308	5.71	43	7	2	126	170	37	30	0	4	5	3	35	7	0	.200	4	39	2	2	1.1	.957
1936	2 teams	WAS A	(18G 3–2)		BOS A	(23G 0–3)																				
"	total	3	5	.375	6.02	41	7	1	89.2	123	41	15	0	1	4	3	22	2	0	.091	3	32	1	0	0.9	.946
1937	DET A	2	5	.286	7.59	25	0	0	40.1	63	20	10	0	2	5	4	7	0	0	.000	1	13	0	0	0.6	1.000
1938	CHI N	6	1	.857	3.34	42	0	0	102.1	100	30	29	0	6	1	3	32	7	0	.219	12	32	1	1	1.1	.978
1939		4	3	.571	3.67	39	0	0	68.2	78	24	32	0	4	3	3	17	0	0	.000	3	23	1	0	0.7	.963
1940	STL N	3	4	.429	2.50	26	0	0	54	53	26	16	0	3	4	1	13	0	0	.000	4	15	0	2	0.7	1.000
15 yrs.		85	141	.376	4.47	557	182	71	2049.2	2454	571	418	3	35	40	38	617	103	1	.167	134	602	29	29	1.4	.962

WORLD SERIES

Year	Team	W	L	PCT	ERA	G	GS	CG	IP	H	BB	SO	ShO	W	L	SV	AB	H	HR	BA	PO	A	E	DP	TC/G	FA
1933	WAS A	0	1	.000	0.87	3	0	0	10.1	8	0	7	0	0	1	0	2	0	0	.000	2	3	0	0	1.7	1.000
1938	CHI N	0	0	–	0.00	2	0	0	1.2	1	1	0	0	0	0	0	0	0	0	–	0	0	0	0	0.0	–
2 yrs.		0	1	.000	0.75	5	0	0	12	9	1	7	0	0	1	0	2	0	0	.000	2	3	0	0	1.0	1.000

Jeff Russell

RUSSELL, JEFFREY LEE   BR TR 6'4"   200 lbs.
B. Sept. 2, 1961, Cincinnati, Ohio

Year	Team	W	L	PCT	ERA	G	GS	CG	IP	H	BB	SO	ShO	W	L	SV	AB	H	HR	BA	PO	A	E	DP	TC/G	FA
1983	CIN N	4	5	.444	3.03	10	10	2	68.1	58	22	40	0	0	0	0	21	3	0	.143	2	10	1	0	1.3	.923
1984		6	18	.250	4.26	33	30	4	181.2	186	65	101	2	0	0	0	57	8	0	.140	7	34	2	4	1.3	.953
1985	TEX A	3	6	.333	7.55	13	13	0	62	85	27	44	0	0	0	0	0	0	0	–	6	10	0	1	1.2	1.000
1986		5	2	.714	3.40	37	0	0	82	74	31	54	0	5	2	2	0	0	0	–	6	17	0	3	0.6	1.000
1987		5	4	.556	4.44	52	2	0	97.1	109	52	56	0	5	3	3	0	0	0	–	11	17	0	2	0.5	1.000
1988		10	9	.526	3.82	34	24	5	188.2	183	66	88	0	1	0	0	1	0	0	.000	12	37	5	3	1.6	.907

Year	Team		W	L	PCT	ERA	G	GS	CG	IP	H	BB	SO	ShO	Relief Pitching			Batting				PO	A	E	DP	TC/G	FA
															W	L	SV	AB	H	HR	BA						

Jeff Russell *continued*

| 1989 | | | 6 | 4 | .600 | 1.98 | 71 | 0 | 0 | 72.2 | 45 | 24 | 77 | 0 | 6 | 4 | **38** | 0 | 0 | 0 | – | 6 | 14 | 0 | 3 | 0.3 | 1.000 |
| 7 yrs. | | | 39 | 48 | .448 | 4.02 | 250 | 79 | 11 | 752.2 | 740 | 287 | 460 | 2 | 17 | 9 | 43 | 79 | 11 | 1 | .139 | 50 | 139 | 8 | 16 | 0.8 | .959 |

John Russell

RUSSELL, JOHN ALBERT
B. Oct. 20, 1895, San Mateo, Calif. D. Nov. 19, 1930, Ely, Nev.   BL TL 6'2" 195 lbs.

1917	BKN	N	0	1	.000	4.50	5	1	1	16	12	6	1	0	0	0	0	4	1	0	.250	1	3	0	0	0.8	1.000
1918			0	0	–	18.00	1	0	0	1	2	1	0	0	0	0	0	0	0	0	–	0	0	0	0	0.0	–
1921	CHI	A	2	5	.286	5.29	11	8	4	66.1	82	35	15	0	0	0	0	25	10	0	.400	3	14	0	0	1.5	1.000
1922			0	1	.000	6.75	4	1	0	6.2	7	4	3	0	0	0	1	1	0	0	.000	1	2	0	0	0.8	1.000
4 yrs.			2	7	.222	5.40	21	10	5	90	103	46	19	0	0	0	1	30	11	0	.367	5	19	0	0	1.1	1.000

John Russell

RUSSELL, JOHN WILLIAM
B. Jan. 5, 1961, Oklahoma City, Okla.   BR TR 6' 195 lbs.

| 1989 | ATL | N | 0 | 0 | – | 0.00 | 1 | 0 | 0 | .1 | 0 | 0 | 0 | 0 | 0 | 0 | 0 | * | | | | 0 | 0 | 0 | 0 | 0.0 | – |

Lefty Russell

RUSSELL, CLARENCE DICKSON
Brother of Allen Russell.
B. July 8, 1890, Baltimore, Md. D. Jan. 22, 1962, Baltimore, Md.   BL TL 6'1" 165 lbs.

1910	PHI	A	1	0	1.000	0.00	1	1	1	9	8	2	5	0	0	0	0	3	0	0	.000	1	3	1	0	5.0	.800
1911			0	3	.000	7.67	7	2	0	31.2	45	18	7	0	0	0	1	13	5	0	.385	7	11	0	1	2.6	1.000
1912			0	2	.000	7.27	5	2	2	17.1	18	14	9	0	0	0	1	4	0	0	.000	0	5	0	0	1.0	1.000
3 yrs.			1	5	.167	6.36	13	5	3	58	71	34	21	1	0	2	0	20	5	0	.250	8	19	1	1	2.2	.964

Reb Russell

RUSSELL, EWELL ALBERT
B. Apr. 12, 1889, Jackson, Miss. D. Sept. 30, 1973, Indianapolis, Ind.   BL TL 5'11" 185 lbs.

1913	CHI	A	22	16	.579	1.91	**51**	36	26	316	249	79	122	8	3	1	4	106	20	0	.189	10	71	4	3	1.7	.953
1914			8	12	.400	2.90	38	23	8	167.1	168	33	79	1	1	0	1	64	17	0	.266	3	50	3	0	1.5	.946
1915			11	10	.524	2.59	41	25	10	229.1	215	47	90	3	1	1	2	86	21	0	.244	11	56	2	1	1.7	.971
1916			18	11	.621	2.42	56	25	16	264.1	207	42	112	5	5	1	3	91	13	0	.143	4	71	2	2	1.4	.974
1917			15	5	**.750**	1.95	35	24	11	189.1	170	32	54	5	2	1	3	68	19	0	.279	11	51	1	2	1.8	.984
1918			7	5	.583	2.60	19	14	10	124.2	117	33	38	2	0	0	0	50	7	0	.140	2	28	0	1	1.6	1.000
1919			0	0	–	0.00	1	0	0		1	1	0	0	0	0	0				–	0	0	0	0	0.0	–
1922	PIT	N	0	0	–	0.00	0	0	0	0	0	0	0	0	0	0	0	220	81	12	.368	0	0	0	0	0.0	–
1923			0	0	–	0.00	0	0	0	0	0	0	0	0	0	0	0	291	84	9	.289	0	0	0	0	0.0	–
9 yrs.			81	59	.579	2.34	241	147	81	1291	1127	267	495	24	12	4	13	*				41	327	12	9	1.6	.968

WORLD SERIES

| 1917 | CHI | A | 0 | 0 | – | ∞ | 1 | 1 | 0 | | 2 | 1 | 0 | 0 | 0 | 0 | 0 | 0 | 0 | 0 | – | 0 | 0 | 0 | 0 | 0.0 | – |

Marius Russo

RUSSO, MARIUS UGO (Lefty)
B. July 19, 1914, Brooklyn, N. Y.   BR TL 6'1" 190 lbs.

1939	NY	A	8	3	.727	2.41	21	11	9	116	86	41	55	2	0	1	2	41	10	0	.244	7	26	1	6	1.6	.971
1940			14	8	.636	3.28	30	24	15	189.1	181	55	87	0	0	0	1	64	12	0	.188	9	48	0	4	1.9	1.000
1941			14	10	.583	3.09	28	27	17	209.2	195	87	105	3	0	0	1	78	18	0	.231	14	42	4	2	2.1	.933
1942			4	1	.800	2.78	9	5	2	45.1	41	14	15	0	1	0	0	17	4	0	.235	3	9	0	1	1.3	1.000
1943			5	10	.333	3.72	24	14	5	101.2	89	45	42	1	1	2	1	31	6	0	.194	2	24	2	7	1.2	.929
1946			0	2	.000	4.34	8	3	0	18.2	26	11	7	0	0	0	0	4	0	0	.000	2	6	0	1	1.0	1.000
6 yrs.			45	34	.570	3.13	120	84	48	680.2	618	253	311	6	2	3	5	235	50	0	.213	37	155	7	22	1.7	.965

WORLD SERIES

1941	NY	A	1	0	1.000	1.00	1	1	1	9	4	2	5	0	0	0	0	4	0	0	.000	0	4	0	0	4.0	1.000
1943			1	0	1.000	0.00	1	1	1	9	7	1	2	0	0	0	0	3	2	0	.667	0	2	0	0	2.0	1.000
2 yrs.			2	0	1.000	0.50	2	2	2	18	11	3	7	0	0	0	0	7	2	0	.286	0	6	0	0	3.0	1.000

Dick Rusteck

RUSTECK, RICHARD FRANK
B. July 12, 1941, Chicago, Ill.   BR TL 6'1" 175 lbs.

| 1966 | NY | N | 1 | 2 | .333 | 3.00 | 8 | 3 | 1 | 24 | 24 | 8 | 9 | 1 | 0 | 0 | 0 | 5 | 0 | 0 | .000 | 1 | 4 | 1 | 0 | 0.8 | .833 |

Babe Ruth

RUTH, GEORGE HERMAN (The Sultan of Swat, The Bambino)
B. Feb. 6, 1895, Baltimore, Md.
D. Aug. 16, 1948, New York, N. Y.
Hall of Fame 1936.   BL TL 6'2" 215 lbs. BB 1923

1914	BOS	A	2	1	.667	3.91	4	3	1	23	21	7	3	0	0	0	0	10	2	0	.200	0	7	0	0	1.8	1.000
1915			18	8	.692	2.44	32	28	16	217.2	166	85	112	1	0	0	0	92	29	4	.315	17	63	2	3	2.6	.976
1916			23	12	.657	**1.75**	44	**41**	23	323.2	230	118	170	**9**	0	1	1	136	37	3	.272	24	83	3	6	2.5	.973
1917			24	13	.649	2.01	41	38	**35**	326.1	244	108	128	6	0	0	2	123	40	2	.325	19	101	2	4	3.0	.984
1918			13	7	.650	2.22	20	19	18	166.1	125	49	40	1	0	0	0	317	95	11	.300	19	58	6	5	4.2	.928
1919			9	5	.643	2.97	17	15	12	133.1	148	58	30	0	1	0	1	432	139	**29**	.322	13	35	2	1	2.9	.960
1920	NY	A	1	0	1.000	4.50	1	1	0	4	3	2	0	0	0	0	0	458	172	**54**	.376	1	0	0	0	1.0	1.000
1921			2	0	1.000	9.00	2	1	0	9	14	9	2	0	1	0	0	540	204	**59**	.378	1	2	0	0	1.5	1.000
1930			1	0	1.000	3.00	1	1	1	9	11	2	3	0	0	0	0	518	186	49	.359	1	4	0	0	4.0	1.000
1933			1	0	1.000	5.00	1	1	1	9	12	3	0	0	0	0	0	459	138	34	.301	1	0	0	0	2.0	1.000
10 yrs.			94	46	.671	2.28	163	148	107	1221.1	974	441	488	17	2	2	4	*				95	354	15	19	2.8	.968

WORLD SERIES

1916	BOS	A	1	0	1.000	0.64	1	1	1	14	6	3	4	0	0	0	0	5	0	0	.000	2	4	0	0	6.0	1.000
1918			2	0	1.000	1.06	2	2	1	17	13	7	4	1	0	0	0	5	1	0	.200	0	0	0	0	0.0	–
2 yrs.			3	0	1.000	0.87	3	3	2	31	19	10	8	1	0	0	0	129	42	15	.326	2	4	0	0	2.0	1.000
					1st	3rd																					

Year	Team		W	L	PCT	ERA	G	GS	CG	IP	H	BB	SO	ShO	Relief Pitching W	L	SV	Batting AB	H	HR	BA	PO	A	E	DP	TC/G	FA

Johnny Rutherford

RUTHERFORD, JOHN WILLIAM (Doc)
B. May 5, 1925, Belleville, Ont., Canada   BL TR 5'10½" 170 lbs.

Year	Team		W	L	PCT	ERA	G	GS	CG	IP	H	BB	SO	ShO	W	L	SV	AB	H	HR	BA	PO	A	E	DP	TC/G	FA
1952	BKN	N	7	7	.500	4.25	22	11	4	97.1	97	29	29	0	2	2	2	31	9	0	.290	3	24	0	1	1.2	1.000

WORLD SERIES

| 1952 | BKN | N | 0 | 0 | — | 9.00 | 1 | 0 | 0 | 1 | 1 | 1 | 1 | 0 | 0 | 0 | 0 | 0 | 0 | 0 | — | 0 | 0 | 0 | 0 | 0.0 | — |

Dick Ruthven

RUTHVEN, RICHARD DAVID
B. Mar. 27, 1951, Sacramento, Calif.   BR TR 6'3" 190 lbs.

Year	Team		W	L	PCT	ERA	G	GS	CG	IP	H	BB	SO	ShO	W	L	SV	AB	H	HR	BA	PO	A	E	DP	TC/G	FA
1973	PHI	N	6	9	.400	4.21	25	23	3	128.1	125	75	98	1	0	1	0	38	5	0	.132	6	23	6	2	1.4	.829
1974			9	13	.409	4.01	35	35	6	213	182	116	153	0	0	0	0	68	13	0	.191	7	30	7	2	1.3	.841
1975			2	2	.500	4.17	11	7	0	41	37	22	26	0	0	0	0	13	2	0	.154	2	5	2	1	0.8	.778
1976	ATL	N	14	17	.452	4.20	36	36	8	240	255	90	142	4	0	0	0	76	13	0	.171	18	44	1	2	1.8	.984
1977			7	13	.350	4.23	25	23	6	151	158	62	84	2	0	0	0	45	12	1	.267	10	16	5	1	1.2	.839
1978	2 teams	ATL N (13G 2–6)								PHI N (20G 13–5)																	
"	total		15	11	.577	3.38	33	33	11	231.2	214	56	120	3	0	0	0	77	17	0	.221	17	36	8	0	1.8	.869
1979	PHI	N	7	5	.583	4.28	20	20	3	122	121	37	58	2	0	0	0	41	6	0	.146	6	9	1	1	0.8	.938
1980			17	10	.630	3.55	33	33	6	223	241	74	86	1	0	0	0	68	16	0	.235	21	33	6	3	1.8	.900
1981			12	7	.632	5.14	23	22	5	147	162	54	80	0	0	0	0	50	7	0	.140	11	20	1	0	1.4	.969
1982			11	11	.500	3.79	33	31	8	204.1	189	59	115	2	0	0	0	64	7	0	.109	22	16	1	1	1.2	.974
1983	2 teams	PHI N (7G 1–3)								CHI N (25G 12–9)																	
"	total		13	12	.520	4.38	32	32	5	183	202	38	99	2	0	0	0	62	13	0	.210	16	35	2	4	1.7	.962
1984	CHI	N	6	10	.375	5.04	23	22	0	126.2	154	41	55	0	0	0	0	44	7	0	.159	8	19	0	1	1.2	1.000
1985			4	7	.364	4.53	20	15	0	87.1	103	37	26	0	0	0	0	24	5	0	.208	5	11	1	1	0.9	.941
1986			0	0	—	5.06	6	0	0	10.2	12	6	3	0	0	0	0	1	0	0	.000	0	1	0	0	0.2	1.000
14 yrs.			123	127	.492	4.14	355	332	61	2109	2155	767	1145	17	1	0	1	671	123	1	.183	149	298	41	19	1.4	.916

DIVISIONAL PLAYOFF SERIES

| 1981 | PHI | N | 0 | 1 | .000 | 4.50 | 1 | 1 | 0 | 4 | 3 | 1 | 0 | 0 | 0 | 0 | 0 | 1 | 0 | 0 | .000 | 0 | 0 | 0 | 0 | 0.0 | — |

LEAGUE CHAMPIONSHIP SERIES

1978	PHI	N	0	1	.000	5.79	1	1	0	4.2	6	0	3	0	0	0	0	1	0	0	.000	0	0	0	0	0.0	—
1980			1	0	1.000	2.00	2	1	0	9	3	5	4	0	1	0	0	2	0	0	.000	2	0	0	0	1.0	1.000
2 yrs.			1	1	.500	3.29	3	2	0	13.2	9	5	7	0	1	0	0	3	0	0	.000	2	0	0	0	0.7	1.000

WORLD SERIES

| 1980 | PHI | N | 0 | 0 | — | 3.00 | 1 | 0 | 0 | 9 | 9 | 0 | 7 | 0 | 0 | 0 | 0 | 0 | 0 | 0 | — | 0 | 0 | 0 | 0 | 0.0 | — |

Cyclone Ryan

RYAN, DANIEL R.
B. 1866, Capperwhite, Ireland   D. Jan. 30, 1917, Medfield, Mass.   TR 6'

Year	Team		W	L	PCT	ERA	G	GS	CG	IP	H	BB	SO	ShO	W	L	SV	AB	H	HR	BA	PO	A	E	DP	TC/G	FA
1887	NY	AA	0	1	.000	23.14	2	1	0	2.1	5	6	0	0	0	0	0	32	7	0	.219	0	0	0	0	0.0	—
1891	BOS	N	0	0	—	0.00	1	0	0	3	2	1	0	0	0	0	0	1	0	0	.000	0	1	0	0	1.0	1.000
2 yrs.			0	1	.000	10.13	3	1	0	5.1	7	7	0	0	0	0	0	*				0	1	0	0	0.3	1.000

Jack Ryan

RYAN, JACK (Gulfport)
B. Sept. 19, 1884, Lawrenceville, Ill.   D. Oct. 16, 1949, Mondsboro, Miss.   BR TR 5'10" 165 lbs.

Year	Team		W	L	PCT	ERA	G	GS	CG	IP	H	BB	SO	ShO	W	L	SV	AB	H	HR	BA	PO	A	E	DP	TC/G	FA
1908	CLE	A	1	1	.500	2.27	8	1	0	35.2	27	2	7	0	1	0	1	11	1	0	.091	0	12	0	1	1.5	1.000
1909	BOS	A	4	3	.571	3.23	13	8	2	61.1	65	20	24	0	1	0	0	19	4	0	.211	2	17	1	0	1.5	.950
1911	BKN	N	0	1	.000	3.00	3	1	0	6	9	4	1	0	0	0	0	1	0	0	.000	0	3	0	0	1.0	1.000
3 yrs.			5	5	.500	2.88	24	10	3	103	101	26	32	0	1	1	1	31	5	0	.161	2	32	1	1	1.5	.971

Jimmy Ryan

RYAN, JAMES EDWARD (Pony)
B. Feb. 11, 1863, Clinton, Mass.   D. Oct. 26, 1923, Chicago, Ill.   BR TL 5'9" 162 lbs.

Year	Team		W	L	PCT	ERA	G	GS	CG	IP	H	BB	SO	ShO	W	L	SV	AB	H	HR	BA	PO	A	E	DP	TC/G	FA
1886	CHI	N	0	0	—	4.63	5	0	0	23.1	19	13	15	0	0	0	0	327	100	4	.306	0	7	1	0	1.6	.875
1887			2	1	.667	4.20	8	3	2	45	53	17	14	0	1	0	0	508	145	16	.285	4	17	3	0	3.0	.875
1888			4	0	1.000	3.05	8	2	1	38.1	47	12	11	0	3	0	0	549	182	16	.332	2	9	3	1	1.8	.786
1891			0	0	—	1.59	2	0	0	5.2	11	2	2	0	0	0	0	505	140	9	.277	0	0	0	0	0.0	—
1893			0	0	—	0.00	1	0	0	4.2	3	0	1	0	0	0	0	341	102	3	.299	0	2	0	0	2.0	1.000
5 yrs.			6	1	.857	3.62	24	5	3	117	133	44	43	0	4	0	2	*				6	35	7	1	2.0	.854

John Ryan

RYAN, JOHN BERNARD (Jack)
B. Nov. 12, 1868, Haverhill, Mass.   D. Aug. 21, 1952, Boston, Mass.   BR TR 5'10½" 165 lbs.

Year	Team		W	L	PCT	ERA	G	GS	CG	IP	H	BB	SO	ShO	W	L	SV	AB	H	HR	BA	PO	A	E	DP	TC/G	FA
1902	STL	N	1	0	1.000	0.00	1	1	1	7	3	4	1	1	0	0	0	*				1	0	0	0	1.0	1.000

John Ryan

RYAN, JOHN M.
B. Hamilton, Ont.   Deceased.

Year	Team		W	L	PCT	ERA	G	GS	CG	IP	H	BB	SO	ShO	W	L	SV	AB	H	HR	BA	PO	A	E	DP	TC/G	FA
1884	BAL	U	3	2	.600	3.35	6	6	5	51	61	16	33	0	0	0	0	25	2	0	.080	2	12	4	1	3.0	.778

Johnny Ryan

RYAN, JOHN JOSEPH
B. Oct., 1853, Philadelphia, Pa.   D. Mar. 22, 1902, Philadelphia, Pa.   5'7½" 150 lbs.

Year	Team		W	L	PCT	ERA	G	GS	CG	IP	H	BB	SO	ShO	W	L	SV	AB	H	HR	BA	PO	A	E	DP	TC/G	FA
1876	LOU	N	0	0	—	5.63	1	0	0	8	22	0	1	0	0	0	0	*				1	1	0	0	2.0	1.000

Nolan Ryan

RYAN, LYNN NOLAN (The Express)
B. Jan. 31, 1947, Refugio, Tex.   BR TR 6'2" 170 lbs.

Year	Team		W	L	PCT	ERA	G	GS	CG	IP	H	BB	SO	ShO	W	L	SV	AB	H	HR	BA	PO	A	E	DP	TC/G	FA
1966	NY	N	0	1	.000	15.00	2	1	0	3	5	3	6	0	0	0	0	0	0	0	—	1	0	0	0	0.5	1.000
1968			6	9	.400	3.09	21	18	3	134	93	75	133	0	0	0	0	44	5	0	.114	5	11	4	0	1.0	.800
1969			6	3	.667	3.53	25	10	2	89.1	60	53	92	0	3	0	1	29	3	0	.103	0	4	1	0	0.2	.800
1970			7	11	.389	3.41	27	19	5	132	86	97	125	2	0	1	0	45	8	0	.178	11	10	4	2	0.9	.840
1971			10	14	.417	3.97	30	26	3	152	125	116	137	0	1	0	0	47	6	0	.128	6	15	3	2	0.8	.875
1972	CAL	A	19	16	.543	2.28	39	39	20	284	166	157	329	9	0	0	0	96	13	0	.135	7	28	6	2	1.1	.854
1973			21	16	.568	2.87	41	39	26	326	238	162	383	4	0	0	0	0	0	0	—	10	27	2	1	1.0	.949
1974			22	16	.579	2.89	42	41	26	333	221	202	367	3	1	0	0	0	0	0	—	12	48	6	1	1.6	.909
1975			14	12	.538	3.45	28	28	10	198	152	132	186	5	0	0	0	0	0	0	—	12	18	7	3	1.3	.811

Year	Team		W	L	PCT	ERA	G	GS	CG	IP	H	BB	SO	ShO	W	L	SV	AB	H	HR	BA	PO	A	E	DP	TC/G	FA
															Relief Pitching			**Batting**									

Nolan Ryan *continued*

Year	Team		W	L	PCT	ERA	G	GS	CG	IP	H	BB	SO	ShO	W	L	SV	AB	H	HR	BA	PO	A	E	DP	TC/G	FA
1976			17	**18**	.486	3.36	39	39	21	284	193	**183**	**327**	7	0	0	0	0	0	0	–	14	34	7	1	1.4	.873
1977			19	16	.543	2.77	37	37	**22**	299	198	**204**	**341**	4	0	0	0	0	0	0	–	20	35	8	1	1.7	.873
1978			10	13	.435	3.71	31	31	14	235	183	148	**260**	3	0	0	0	0	0	0	–	13	33	8	3	1.7	.852
1979			16	14	.533	3.59	34	34	17	223	169	114	223	5	0	0	0	0	0	0	–	8	29	4	1	1.2	.902
1980	HOU	N	11	10	.524	3.35	35	35	4	234	205	**98**	200	2	0	0	0	70	6	1	.086	13	27	5	0	1.3	.889
1981			11	5	.688	**1.69**	21	21	5	149	99	68	140	3	0	0	0	51	11	0	.216	5	16	1	3	1.0	.955
1982			16	12	.571	3.16	35	35	10	250.1	196	**109**	245	3	0	0	0	83	10	0	.120	9	33	2	1	1.3	.955
1983			14	9	.609	2.98	29	29	5	196.1	134	101	183	2	0	0	0	69	5	0	.072	4	28	2	0	1.2	.941
1984			12	11	.522	3.04	30	30	5	183.2	143	69	197	2	0	0	0	61	6	0	.098	7	11	2	0	0.7	.900
1985			10	12	.455	3.80	35	35	4	232	205	95	209	0	0	0	0	63	7	0	.111	4	23	2	0	0.8	.929
1986			12	8	.600	3.34	30	30	1	178	119	82	194	0	0	0	0	59	6	0	.102	10	17	2	2	0.9	.931
1987			8	16	.333	**2.76**	34	34	0	211.2	154	87	**270**	0	0	0	0	65	4	1	.062	11	18	1	1	0.9	.967
1988			12	11	.522	3.52	33	33	4	220	186	87	**228**	1	0	0	0	70	4	0	.057	8	18	4	0	0.9	.867
1989	TEX	A	16	10	.615	3.20	32	32	6	239.1	162	98	**301**	2	0	0	0	0	0	0	–	11	19	3	0	1.0	.909
23 yrs.			289	263	.524	3.15	710	676	213	4786.2	3492	2540	5076	57	5	0	3	852	94	2	.110	202	499	84	24	1.1	.893
				6th								**1st**	**1st**	10th													

DIVISIONAL PLAYOFF SERIES

Year	Team		W	L	PCT	ERA	G	GS	CG	IP	H	BB	SO	ShO	W	L	SV	AB	H	HR	BA	PO	A	E	DP	TC/G	FA
1981	HOU	N	1	1	.500	1.80	2	2	1	15	6	3	14	0	0	0	0	4	1	0	.250	0	0	0	0	0.0	–

LEAGUE CHAMPIONSHIP SERIES

Year	Team		W	L	PCT	ERA	G	GS	CG	IP	H	BB	SO	ShO	W	L	SV	AB	H	HR	BA	PO	A	E	DP	TC/G	FA
1969	NY	N	1	0	1.000	2.57	1	0	0	7	3	2	7	0	1	0	0	4	2	0	.500	1	0	0	0	1.0	1.000
1979	CAL	A	0	0	–	1.29	1	1	0	7	4	3	8	0	0	0	0	0	0	0	–	0	0	0	0	0.0	–
1980	HOU	N	0	0	–	5.40	2	2	0	13.1	16	3	14	0	0	0	0	4	0	0	.000	1	3	0	0	2.0	1.000
1986			0	1	.000	3.86	2	2	0	14	9	1	17	0	0	0	0	4	0	0	.000	0	0	0	0	0.0	–
4 yrs.			1	1	.500	3.70	6	5	0	41.1	32	9	46	0	1	0	0	12	2	0	.167	2	3	0	0	0.8	1.000

WORLD SERIES

Year	Team		W	L	PCT	ERA	G	GS	CG	IP	H	BB	SO	ShO	W	L	SV	AB	H	HR	BA	PO	A	E	DP	TC/G	FA
1969	NY	N	0	0	–	0.00	1	0	0	2.1	1	2	3	0	0	0	1	0	0	0	–	0	0	0	0	–	–

Rosy Ryan

RYAN, WILFRED PATRICK DOLAN
B. Mar. 15, 1898, Worcester, Mass.   D. Dec. 10, 1980, Scottsdale, Ariz.

BL TR 6'   185 lbs.

Year	Team		W	L	PCT	ERA	G	GS	CG	IP	H	BB	SO	ShO	W	L	SV	AB	H	HR	BA	PO	A	E	DP	TC/G	FA
1919	NY	N	1	2	.333	3.10	4	3	1	20.1	20	9	7	0	1	0	0	6	0	0	.000	1	3	0	0	1.0	1.000
1920			0	1	.000	1.76	3	1	1	15.1	14	4	5	0	0	0	0	5	0	0	.000	0	5	0	0	1.7	1.000
1921			7	10	.412	3.73	36	16	5	147.1	140	32	58	0	1	4	3	45	9	0	.200	5	33	0	1	1.1	1.000
1922			17	12	.586	**3.01**	46	20	8	191.2	194	74	75	1	**7**	3	3	62	12	0	.194	9	35	1	3	1.0	.978
1923			16	5	.762	3.49	**45**	15	7	172.2	169	46	58	0	**9**	2	4	53	11	0	.208	8	40	1	2	1.1	.980
1924			8	6	.571	4.26	37	9	2	124.2	137	37	36	0	6	2	5	36	5	0	.139	8	21	0	0	0.8	1.000
1925	BOS	N	2	8	.200	6.31	37	7	1	122.2	152	52	48	0	2	**5**	2	39	11	1	.282	4	25	5	0	0.9	.853
1926			0	2	.000	7.58	7	2	0	19	29	7	1	0	0	0	0	5	1	0	.200	1	5	0	0	0.7	1.000
1928	NY	A	0	0	–	16.50	3	0	0	6	17	1	5	0	0	0	0	4	0	0	.000	0	0	0	0	0.0	–
1933	BKN	N	1	1	.500	4.55	30	0	0	61.1	69	16	22	0	1	1	2	13	2	0	.154	1	12	0	0	0.4	1.000
10 yrs.			52	47	.525	4.14	248	73	29	881	941	278	315	1	27	17	19	268	51	1	.190	37	178	7	6	0.9	.968

WORLD SERIES

Year	Team		W	L	PCT	ERA	G	GS	CG	IP	H	BB	SO	ShO	W	L	SV	AB	H	HR	BA	PO	A	E	DP	TC/G	FA
1922	NY	N	1	0	1.000	0.00	1	0	0	2	1	0	2	0	1	0	0	0	0	0	–	0	0	0	0	0.0	–
1923			1	0	1.000	0.96	3	0	0	9.1	11	3	3	0	1	0	0	2	0	0	.000	1	2	0	1	1.0	1.000
1924			1	0	1.000	3.18	2	0	0	5.2	7	4	3	0	1	0	1	2	1	0	.500	0	1	0	0	0.5	1.000
3 yrs.			3	0	1.000	1.59	6	0	0	17	19	7	8	0	3	0	1	4	1	0	.250	1	3	0	1	0.7	1.000
															1st													

Mike Ryba

RYBA, DOMINIC JOSEPH
B. June 9, 1903, DeLancey, Pa.   D. Dec. 13, 1971, Brookline Station, Mo.

BR TR 5'11½" 190 lbs.

Year	Team		W	L	PCT	ERA	G	GS	CG	IP	H	BB	SO	ShO	W	L	SV	AB	H	HR	BA	PO	A	E	DP	TC/G	FA
1935	STL	N	1	1	.500	3.38	2	2	1	16	15	1	6	0	0	0	0	5	2	0	.400	1	4	0	0	2.5	1.000
1936			5	1	.833	5.40	14	0	0	45	55	16	25	0	5	1	0	18	3	0	.167	0	5	0	0	0.4	1.000
1937			9	6	.600	4.13	38	8	5	135	152	40	57	0	6	3	0	48	15	0	.313	5	31	1	1	1.0	.973
1938			1	1	.500	5.40	3	0	0	5	8	1	0	0	1	1	0	0	0	0	–	0	1	0	0	0.3	1.000
1941	BOS	A	7	3	.700	4.46	40	3	0	121	143	42	54	0	6	2	6	37	8	0	.216	10	30	2	3	1.1	.952
1942			3	3	.500	3.86	18	0	0	44.1	49	13	16	0	3	3	3	17	5	0	.294	0	14	0	0	0.8	1.000
1943			7	5	.583	3.26	40	8	4	143.2	142	57	50	1	4	4	2	43	8	0	.186	9	25	1	1	0.9	.971
1944			12	7	.632	3.33	42	7	2	138	119	39	50	0	9	5	2	41	6	0	.146	8	38	3	3	1.2	.939
1945			7	6	.538	2.49	34	9	4	123	122	33	44	1	4	2	2	36	9	0	.250	8	19	0	2	0.8	1.000
1946			0	1	.000	3.55	9	0	0	12.2	12	5	5	0	0	1	1	2	2	0	1.000	0	1	0	0	0.1	1.000
10 yrs.			52	34	.605	3.66	240	36	16	783.2	817	247	307	2	39	22	16	247	58	0	.235	41	168	7	11	0.9	.968

WORLD SERIES

Year	Team		W	L	PCT	ERA	G	GS	CG	IP	H	BB	SO	ShO	W	L	SV	AB	H	HR	BA	PO	A	E	DP	TC/G	FA
1946	BOS	A	0	0	–	13.50	1	0	0	.2	2	1	0	0	0	0	0	0	0	0	–	0	0	1	0	1.0	–

Gary Ryerson

RYERSON, GARY LAWRENCE
B. June 7, 1948, Los Angeles, Calif.

BL TL 6'1" 175 lbs.

Year	Team		W	L	PCT	ERA	G	GS	CG	IP	H	BB	SO	ShO	W	L	SV	AB	H	HR	BA	PO	A	E	DP	TC/G	FA
1972	MIL	A	3	8	.273	3.62	20	14	4	102	119	21	45	1	0	0	0	24	1	0	.042	2	15	4	0	1.1	.810
1973			0	1	.000	7.83	9	4	0	23	32	7	10	0	0	0	0	0	0	0	–	1	5	2	0	0.9	.750
2 yrs.			3	9	.250	4.39	29	18	4	125	151	28	55	1	0	0	0	24	1	0	.042	3	20	6	0	1.0	.793

Bret Saberhagen

SABERHAGEN, BRET WILLIAM
B. Apr. 11, 1964, Chicago Heights, Ill.

BR TR 6'1" 160 lbs.

Year	Team		W	L	PCT	ERA	G	GS	CG	IP	H	BB	SO	ShO	W	L	SV	AB	H	HR	BA	PO	A	E	DP	TC/G	FA
1984	KC	A	10	11	.476	3.48	38	18	2	157.2	138	36	73	1	1	4	1	0	0	0	–	15	22	1	1	1.0	.974
1985			20	6	.769	2.87	32	32	10	235.1	211	38	158	1	0	0	0	0	0	0	–	22	38	2	4	1.9	.968
1986			7	12	.368	4.15	30	25	4	156	165	29	112	2	1	0	0	0	0	0	–	14	26	2	0	1.4	.952
1987			18	10	.643	3.36	33	33	15	257	246	53	163	4	0	0	0	0	0	0	–	21	34	2	5	1.7	.965
1988			14	16	.467	3.80	35	35	9	260.2	271	59	171	0	0	0	0	0	0	0	–	15	34	3	3	1.5	.942

Year	Team	W	L	PCT	ERA	G	GS	CG	IP	H	BB	SO	ShO	W	L	SV	AB	H	HR	BA	PO	A	E	DP	TC/G	FA

Bret Saberhagen *continued*

Year	Team	W	L	PCT	ERA	G	GS	CG	IP	H	BB	SO	ShO	W	L	SV	AB	H	HR	BA	PO	A	E	DP	TC/G	FA
1989		**23**	6	.793	2.16	36	35	12	**262.1**	209	43	193	4	0	1	0	0	0	0	–	21	36	4	1	1.7	.934
6 yrs.		92	61	.601	3.23	204	178	52	1329	1240	258	870	12	5	2	1	0	0	0	–	108	190	14	14	1.5	.955

LEAGUE CHAMPIONSHIP SERIES

Year	Team	W	L	PCT	ERA	G	GS	CG	IP	H	BB	SO	ShO	W	L	SV	AB	H	HR	BA	PO	A	E	DP	TC/G	FA
1984	KC A	0	0	–	2.25	1	1	0	8	6	1	5	0	0	0	0	0	0	0	–	1	1	1	0	3.0	.667
1985		0	0	–	6.14	2	2	0	7.1	12	2	6	0	0	0	0	0	0	0	–	2	1	0	0	1.5	1.000
2 yrs.		0	0	–	4.11	3	3	0	15.1	18	3	11	0	0	0	0	0	0	0	–	3	2	1	0	2.0	.833

WORLD SERIES

Year	Team	W	L	PCT	ERA	G	GS	CG	IP	H	BB	SO	ShO	W	L	SV	AB	H	HR	BA	PO	A	E	DP	TC/G	FA
1985	KC A	2	0	1.000	0.50	2	2	2	18	11	1	10	1	0	0	0	7	0	0	.000	0	0	0	0	0.0	–

Ray Sadecki

SADECKI, RAYMOND MICHAEL   BL TL 5'11" 180 lbs.
B. Dec. 26, 1940, Kansas City, Kans.

Year	Team	W	L	PCT	ERA	G	GS	CG	IP	H	BB	SO	ShO	W	L	SV	AB	H	HR	BA	PO	A	E	DP	TC/G	FA
1960	STL N	9	9	.500	3.78	26	26	7	157.1	148	86	95	0	0	0	0	57	12	0	.211	6	19	2	3	1.0	.926
1961		14	10	.583	3.72	31	31	13	222.2	196	102	114	0	0	0	0	87	22	0	.253	3	24	7	1	1.1	.794
1962		6	8	.429	5.54	22	17	4	102.1	121	43	50	0	1	0	0	37	3	1	.081	2	13	5	2	0.9	.750
1963		10	10	.500	4.10	36	28	4	193.1	198	78	136	1	0	1	0	64	9	0	.141	3	22	4	4	0.8	.926
1964		20	11	.645	3.68	37	32	9	220	232	60	119	2	0	2	1	75	12	0	.160	1	34	5	2	1.1	.875
1965		6	15	.286	5.21	36	28	4	172.2	192	64	122	0	0	0	0	55	11	0	.200	5	22	3	2	0.8	.900
1966	2 teams	STL N	(5G 2–1)		SF N	(26G 3–7)																				
"	total	5	8	.385	4.80	31	22	4	129.1	141	48	83	1	0	0	0	41	14	3	.341	4	14	0	0	0.6	1.000
1967	SF N	12	6	.667	2.78	35	24	10	188	165	58	145	2	1	0	0	73	18	0	.247	7	30	5	3	1.2	.881
1968		12	**18**	.400	2.91	38	36	13	253.2	225	70	206	6	0	0	0	85	8	0	.094	5	34	6	1	1.2	.867
1969		5	8	.385	4.24	29	17	4	138	137	53	104	3	0	0	0	40	5	1	.125	9	29	2	1	1.4	.950
1970	NY N	8	4	.667	3.88	28	19	4	139	134	52	89	0	0	0	0	39	8	0	.205	3	13	4	0	0.7	.800
1971		7	7	.500	2.93	34	20	5	163	139	44	120	1	1	0	0	50	10	0	.200	5	17	1	1	0.7	.957
1972		2	1	.667	3.09	34	2	0	75.2	73	31	38	0	1	0	0	13	2	0	.154	1	8	2	0	0.3	.818
1973		5	4	.556	3.39	31	11	1	116.2	109	41	87	0	1	0	1	31	7	0	.226	1	7	1	0	0.3	.889
1974		8	8	.500	3.48	34	10	3	101	107	35	46	1	4	3	0	27	7	0	.259	3	16	3	3	0.6	.864
1975	3 teams	STL N	(8G 1–0)		ATL N	(25G 2–3)		KC A	(5G 1–0)																	
"	total	4	3	.571	4.03	38	5	0	80.1	91	31	32	0	3	1	1	15	3	0	.200	3	8	2	0	0.3	.846
1976	2 teams	KC A	(3G 0–0)		MIL A	(36G 2–0)																				
"	total	2	0	1.000	3.86	39	0	0	42	45	23	28	0	2	0	0	0	0	0	–	1	2	0	0	0.1	.600
1977	NY N	0	1	.000	6.00	4	0	0	3	3	3	3	0	0	1	0	0	0	0	–	0	0	0	0	0.0	–
18 yrs.		135	131	.508	3.79	563	328	85	2498	2456	922	1614	20	15	7	7	789	151	5	.191	62	312	52	23	0.8	.878

WORLD SERIES

Year	Team	W	L	PCT	ERA	G	GS	CG	IP	H	BB	SO	ShO	W	L	SV	AB	H	HR	BA	PO	A	E	DP	TC/G	FA
1964	STL N	1	0	1.000	8.53	2	2	0	6.1	12	5	2	0	0	0	0	0	0	0	.500	0	1	0	0	0.5	1.000
1973	NY N	0	0	–	1.93	4	0	0	4.2	5	1	6	0	0	0	1	0	0	0	–	0	1	0	0	0.3	1.000
2 yrs.		1	0	1.000	5.73	6	2	0	11	17	6	8	0	0	0	1	2	1	0	.500	0	2	0	0	0.3	1.000

Bob Sadowski

SADOWSKI, ROBERT   BR TR 6'2" 195 lbs.
Brother of Eddie Sadowski. Brother of Ted Sadowski.
B. Feb. 19, 1938, Pittsburgh, Pa.

Year	Team	W	L	PCT	ERA	G	GS	CG	IP	H	BB	SO	ShO	W	L	SV	AB	H	HR	BA	PO	A	E	DP	TC/G	FA
1963	MIL N	5	7	.417	2.62	19	18	5	116.2	99	30	72	1	0	0	0	35	2	0	.057	7	23	0	2	1.6	1.000
1964		9	10	.474	4.10	51	18	5	166.2	159	56	96	0	3	2	5	52	8	0	.154	9	43	1	1	1.0	.981
1965		5	9	.357	4.32	34	13	3	123	117	35	78	0	2	1	3	35	3	0	.086	4	17	0	1	0.6	1.000
1966	BOS A	1	1	.500	5.40	11	5	0	33.1	41	9	11	0	0	0	0	7	0	0	.000	1	7	3	1	1.0	.727
4 yrs.		20	27	.426	3.87	115	54	13	439.2	416	130	257	1	5	3	8	129	13	0	.101	21	90	4	5	1.0	.965

Jim Sadowski

SADOWSKI, JAMES MICHAEL   BR TR 6'3" 195 lbs.
B. Aug. 7, 1951, Pittsburgh, Pa.

Year	Team	W	L	PCT	ERA	G	GS	CG	IP	H	BB	SO	ShO	W	L	SV	AB	H	HR	BA	PO	A	E	DP	TC/G	FA
1974	PIT N	0	1	.000	6.00	4	0	0	9	7	9	1	0	0	1	0	1	0	0	.000	2	4	0	0	1.5	1.000

Ted Sadowski

SADOWSKI, THEODORE   BR TR 6'1½" 190 lbs.
Brother of Eddie Sadowski. Brother of Bob Sadowski.
B. Apr. 1, 1936, Pittsburgh, Pa.

Year	Team	W	L	PCT	ERA	G	GS	CG	IP	H	BB	SO	ShO	W	L	SV	AB	H	HR	BA	PO	A	E	DP	TC/G	FA
1960	WAS A	1	0	1.000	5.19	9	1	0	17.1	17	9	12	0	1	0	1	3	0	0	.000	0	2	0	0	0.2	1.000
1961	MIN A	0	2	.000	6.82	15	1	0	33	49	11	12	0	0	1	0	6	0	0	.000	1	9	0	0	0.7	1.000
1962		1	1	.500	5.03	19	0	0	34	37	11	15	0	1	1	0	4	2	0	.500	2	7	0	0	0.5	1.000
3 yrs.		2	3	.400	5.76	43	2	0	84.1	103	31	39	0	2	2	1	13	2	0	.154	3	18	0	0	0.5	1.000

Johnny Sain

SAIN, JOHN FRANKLIN   BR TR 6'2" 185 lbs.
B. Sept. 25, 1917, Havana, Ark.

Year	Team	W	L	PCT	ERA	G	GS	CG	IP	H	BB	SO	ShO	W	L	SV	AB	H	HR	BA	PO	A	E	DP	TC/G	FA
1942	BOS N	4	7	.364	3.90	40	3	0	97	79	63	68	0	3	**6**	6	27	2	0	.074	1	25	0	0	0.7	1.000
1946		20	14	.588	2.21	37	34	24	265	225	87	129	1	0	0	2	94	28	0	.298	20	61	1	0	2.2	.988
1947		21	12	.636	3.52	38	35	22	266	**265**	79	132	3	0	0	1	107	37	0	.346	11	55	5	1	1.8	.957
1948		**24**	15	.615	2.60	42	**39**	28	314.2	297	83	137	4	0	0	1	115	25	0	.217	21	48	2	3	1.7	.972
1949		10	17	.370	4.81	37	36	16	243	285	75	73	1	0	0	0	97	20	0	.206	14	35	3	2	1.4	.942
1950		20	13	.606	3.94	37	37	25	278.1	294	70	96	3	0	0	0	102	21	1	.206	14	42	4	3	1.6	.933
1951	2 teams	BOS N	(26G 5–13)		NY A	(7G 2–1)																				
"	total	7	14	.333	4.20	33	26	7	197.1	236	53	84	1	0	0	2	66	15	1	.227	13	28	1	3	1.3	.976
1952	NY A	11	6	.647	3.46	35	16	8	148.1	149	38	57	1	0	3	7	71	19	1	.268	15	18	3	0	1.0	.917
1953		14	7	.667	3.00	40	19	10	189	189	45	84	1	4	1	9	68	17	0	.250	8	32	2	1	1.0	.952
1954		6	6	.500	3.16	45	1	0	77	66	15	33	0	4	6	**22**	17	6	0	.353	6	11	0	0	0.4	1.000
1955	2 teams	NY A	(3G 0–0)		KC A	(25G 2–5)																				
"	total	2	5	.286	5.58	28	0	0	50	60	11	17	0	2	5	1	10	0	0	.000	3	6	0	0	0.3	1.000
11 yrs.		139	116	.545	3.49	412	245	140	2125.2	2145	619	910	16	20	19	51	774	190	3	.245	126	361	19	13	1.2	.962

WORLD SERIES

Year	Team	W	L	PCT	ERA	G	GS	CG	IP	H	BB	SO	ShO	W	L	SV	AB	H	HR	BA	PO	A	E	DP	TC/G	FA
1948	BOS N	1	1	.500	1.06	2	2	2	17	9	0	9	1	0	0	0	5	1	0	.200	2	2	0	0	2.0	1.000
1951	NY A	0	0	–	9.00	1	0	0	2	4	2	1	0	0	0	0	1	0	0	.000	0	0	0	0	0.0	–
1952		0	1	.000	3.00	1	0	0	6	6	3	3	0	0	1	0	3	0	0	.000	0	2	0	0	2.0	1.000

Year	Team	W	L	PCT	ERA	G	GS	CG	IP	H	BB	SO	ShO	Relief Pitching W	L	SV	Batting AB	H	HR	BA	PO	A	E	DP	TC/G	FA

Johnny Sain *continued*

| 1953 | | 1 | 0 | 1.000 | 4.76 | 2 | 0 | 0 | 5.2 | 8 | 1 | 1 | 0 | 1 | 0 | 0 | 2 | 1 | 0 | .500 | 0 | 0 | 0 | 0 | 0.0 | — |
| 4 yrs. | | 2 | 2 | .500 | 2.64 | 6 | 2 | 2 | 30.2 | 27 | 6 | 15 | 1 | 1 | 1 | 0 | 11 | 2 | 0 | .182 | 2 | 4 | 0 | 0 | 1.0 | 1.000 |

Randy St. Claire

ST. CLAIRE, RANDY ANTHONY
Son of Ebba St. Claire.
B. Aug. 23, 1960, Glens Falls, N. Y.

BR TR 6'3" 180 lbs.

1984	MON N	0	0	—	4.50	4	0	0	8	11	2	4	0	0	0	0	0	0	0	—	0	1	0	0	0.3	1.000
1985		5	3	.625	3.93	42	0	0	68.2	69	26	25	0	5	3	0	5	1	0	.200	4	13	0	2	0.4	1.000
1986		2	0	1.000	2.37	11	0	0	19	13	6	21	0	2	0	1	1	0	0	.000	1	5	0	0	0.5	1.000
1987		3	3	.500	4.03	44	0	0	67	64	20	43	0	3	3	7	6	2	0	.333	1	9	0	2	0.2	1.000
1988	2 teams	MON N	(6G 0–0)		CIN N	(10G 1–0)																				
"	total	1	0	1.000	3.86	16	0	0	21	24	10	14	0	1	0	0	1	0	0	.000	1	3	0	0	0.3	1.000
1989	MIN A	1	0	1.000	5.24	14	0	0	22.1	19	10	14	0	1	0	1	0	0	0	—	4	2	0	1	0.4	1.000
6 yrs.		12	6	.667	3.98	131	0	0	206	200	74	121	0	12	6	9	13	3	0	.231	11	33	0	5	0.3	1.000

Jim St. Vrain

ST. VRAIN, JAMES MARCELLIN
B. June 6, 1871, Ralls County, Mo.   D. June 12, 1937, Butte, Mont.

BR TL 5'9" 175 lbs.

| 1902 | CHI N | 4 | 6 | .400 | 2.08 | 12 | 11 | 10 | 95 | 88 | 25 | 51 | 1 | 0 | 0 | 0 | 31 | 3 | 0 | .097 | 3 | 25 | 3 | 3 | 2.6 | .903 |

Luis Salazar

SALAZAR, LUIS ERNESTO
Born Luis Ernesto Salazar y Garacia.
B. May 19, 1956, Barcelona, Venezuela

BR TR 6' 185 lbs.

| 1987 | SD N | 0 | 0 | — | 4.50 | 2 | 0 | 0 | 2 | 2 | 1 | 0 | 0 | 0 | 0 | 0 | * | | | | 0 | 1 | 0 | 0 | 0.5 | 1.000 |

Freddy Sale

SALE, FREDERICK LINK
B. May 2, 1902, Chester, S. C.   D. May 27, 1956, Hermosa Beach, Calif.

BR TR 5'9" 160 lbs.

| 1924 | PIT N | 0 | 0 | — | 0.00 | 1 | 0 | 0 | 1 | 2 | 0 | 0 | 0 | 0 | 0 | 0 | 0 | 0 | 0 | — | 0 | 0 | 0 | 0 | 0.0 | — |

Harry Salisbury

SALISBURY, HENRY H.
B. May 15, 1855, Providence, R. I.   D. Mar. 29, 1933, Chicago, Ill.

BL

1879	TRO N	4	6	.400	2.22	10	10	9	89	103	11	31	0	0	0	0	36	2	0	.056	3	27	2	0	3.2	.938
1882	PIT AA	20	18	.526	2.63	38	38	38	335	315	37	135	1	0	0	0	145	22	0	.152	10	96	11	1	3.1	.906
2 yrs.		24	24	.500	2.55	48	48	47	424	418	48	166	1	0	0	0	181	24	0	.133	13	123	13	1	3.1	.913

Solly Salisbury

SALISBURY, WILLIAM ANSEL
B. Nov. 12, 1876, Algona, Iowa   D. Jan. 17, 1952, Rowena, Ore.

BR TR 6' 180 lbs.

| 1902 | PHI N | 0 | 0 | — | 13.50 | 2 | 1 | 0 | 6 | 15 | 2 | 0 | 0 | 0 | 0 | 0 | 1 | 0 | 0 | .000 | 0 | 0 | 1 | 0 | 0.5 | — |

Slim Sallee

SALLEE, HARRY FRANKLIN
B. Feb. 3, 1885, Higginsport, Ohio   D. Mar. 22, 1950, Higginsport, Ohio

BL TL 6'3" 180 lbs.

1908	STL N	3	8	.273	3.15	25	12	7	128.2	144	36	39	1	1	0	0	41	2	0	.049	5	37	1	0	1.7	.977
1909		10	11	.476	2.42	32	27	12	219	223	59	55	1	0	2	0	71	8	0	.113	7	63	3	2	2.3	.959
1910		7	8	.467	2.97	18	13	9	115	112	24	46	1	1	1	2	37	4	0	.108	2	34	0	1	2.0	1.000
1911		15	9	.625	2.76	36	30	18	245	234	64	74	1	1	1	2	89	15	0	.169	7	55	2	0	1.8	.969
1912		16	17	.485	2.60	48	32	20	294	289	72	108	3	4	3	6	103	14	0	.136	17	61	3	0	1.7	.963
1913		18	15	.545	2.70	49	31	17	273	254	59	105	3	2	1	5	94	19	2	.202	12	72	2	1	1.8	.977
1914		18	17	.514	2.10	46	30	18	282.1	252	72	105	3	2	5	6	91	21	0	.231	3	71	2	2	1.7	.974
1915		13	17	.433	2.84	46	33	17	275.1	245	57	91	2	1	1	0	92	11	0	.120	7	74	4	1	1.8	.953
1916	2 teams	STL N	(16G 5–5)		NY N	(15G 9–4)																				
"	total	14	9	.609	2.18	31	18	11	181.2	171	33	63	4	4	1	1	53	12	0	.226	5	28	0	3	1.1	1.000
1917	NY N	18	7	.720	2.17	34	24	18	215.2	199	34	54	1	2	3	4	77	17	0	.221	4	46	0	5	1.5	1.000
1918		8	8	.500	2.25	18	16	12	132	122	12	33	1	0	0	0	41	5	0	.122	9	28	0	0	2.1	1.000
1919	CIN N	21	7	.750	2.06	29	28	22	227.2	221	20	24	4	1	0	0	74	14	0	.189	3	50	2	2	1.9	.964
1920	2 teams	CIN N	(21G 5–6)		NY N	(5G 1–0)																				
"	total	6	6	.500	3.11	26	13	7	133	145	16	15	0	0	1	2	38	7	0	.184	1	25	2	0	1.1	.929
1921	NY N	6	4	.600	3.64	37	0	0	96.1	115	14	23	0	6	4	2	22	8	0	.364	4	17	0	1	0.6	1.000
14 yrs.		173	143	.547	2.56	475	307	188	2818.2	2726	572	835	25	24	24	35	923	157	2	.170	86	661	21	17	1.6	.973

WORLD SERIES

1917	NY N	0	0	.000	4.70	2	2	1	15.1	20	4	4	0	0	0	0	6	1	0	.167	0	8	0	0	4.0	1.000
1919	CIN N	1	1	.500	1.35	2	2	1	13.1	19	1	2	0	0	0	0	4	0	0	.000	1	4	0	0	2.5	1.000
2 yrs.		1	3	.250	3.14	4	4	2	28.2	39	5	6	0	0	0	0	10	1	0	.100	1	12	0	0	3.3	1.000

Roger Salmon

SALMON, ROGER ELLIOTT
B. May 11, 1891, Newark, N. J.   D. June 17, 1974, Belfast, Me.

BL TL 6'2" 170 lbs.

| 1912 | PHI A | 1 | 0 | 1.000 | 9.00 | 2 | 1 | 0 | 5 | 7 | 4 | 5 | 0 | 0 | 0 | 0 | 1 | 0 | 0 | .000 | 0 | 0 | 0 | 0 | 0.0 | — |

Gus Salve

SALVE, AUGUSTUS WILLIAM
B. Dec. 29, 1885, Boston, Mass.   D. Mar. 29, 1971, Providence, R. I.

BL TL 6' 190 lbs.

| 1908 | PHI A | 0 | 1 | .000 | 1.93 | 1 | 1 | 1 | 9.1 | 9 | 8 | 5 | 0 | 0 | 0 | 0 | 4 | 0 | 0 | .000 | 1 | 1 | 0 | 0 | 2.0 | 1.000 |

Jack Salveson

SALVESON, JOHN THEODORE
B. Jan. 5, 1914, Fullerton, Calif.   D. Dec. 28, 1974, Norwalk, Calif.

BR TR 6'½" 180 lbs.

1933	NY N	0	2	.000	3.82	8	2	0	30.2	30	14	8	0	0	2	0	9	1	0	.111	5	7	1	0	1.6	.923
1934		3	1	.750	3.52	12	4	0	38.1	43	13	18	0	2	0	0	10	3	0	.300	5	8	0	1	1.1	1.000
1935	2 teams	PIT N	(5G 0–1)		CHI A	(20G 1–2)																				
"	total	1	3	.250	5.25	25	2	0	73.2	90	28	24	0	1	3	1	22	6	0	.273	3	15	1	1	0.8	.947
1943	CLE A	5	3	.625	3.35	23	11	4	86	87	26	24	3	1	1	3	26	6	1	.231	2	19	0	4	0.9	1.000

Year	Team	W	L	PCT	ERA	G	GS	CG	IP	H	BB	SO	ShO	W	L	SV	AB	H	HR	BA	PO	A	E	DP	TC/G	FA

Relief Pitching: W L SV ; Batting: AB H HR

Jack Salveson *continued*

| 1945 | | 0 | 0 | – | 3.68 | 19 | 0 | 0 | 44 | 52 | 6 | 11 | 0 | 0 | 0 | 0 | 10 | 4 | 1 | .400 | 4 | 13 | 0 | 0 | 0.9 | 1.000 |
| | 5 yrs. | 9 | 9 | .500 | 3.99 | 87 | 19 | 8 | 272.2 | 302 | 87 | 85 | 3 | 4 | 4 | 4 | 77 | 20 | 3 | .260 | 19 | 62 | 2 | 5 | 1.0 | .976 |

Manny Salvo
SALVO, MANUEL (Gyp)
B. June 30, 1913, Sacramento, Calif.
BR TR 6'4" 210 lbs.

1939	NY N	4	10	.286	4.63	32	18	4	136	150	76	69	0	1	0	0	41	4	1	.098	8	31	3	2	1.3	.929
1940	BOS N	10	9	.526	3.08	21	20	14	160.2	151	43	60	5	0	0	0	58	6	0	.103	7	26	2	1	1.7	.943
1941		7	16	.304	4.06	35	27	11	195	192	93	67	2	1	1	0	62	7	0	.113	11	37	1	2	1.4	.980
1942		7	8	.467	3.03	25	14	6	130.2	129	41	25	1	2	1	0	41	5	0	.122	6	26	2	0	1.4	.941
1943	3 teams	BOS N	(1G 0–1)		PHI N	(1G 0–0)		BOS N	(20G 5–6)																	
"	total	5	7	.417	3.55	22	14	5	99	101	32	26	1	0	0	0	30	8	0	.267	6	17	2	2	1.1	.920
	5 yrs.	33	50	.398	3.69	135	93	40	721.1	723	285	247	9	4	2	1	232	30	1	.129	38	137	10	7	1.4	.946

Joe Sambito
SAMBITO, JOSEPH CHARLES
B. June 28, 1952, Brooklyn, N. Y.
BL TL 6'1" 185 lbs.

1976	HOU N	3	2	.600	3.57	20	4	1	53	45	14	26	1	1	0	1	9	2	0	.222	4	10	0	1	0.7	1.000
1977		5	5	.500	2.33	54	1	0	89	77	24	67	0	5	4	7	13	2	0	.154	4	17	2	1	0.4	.913
1978		4	9	.308	3.07	62	0	0	88	85	32	96	0	4	9	11	6	1	0	.167	6	16	2	3	0.4	.917
1979		8	7	.533	1.78	63	0	0	91	86	23	83	0	8	7	22	7	2	0	.286	5	14	2	2	0.3	.905
1980		8	4	.667	2.20	64	0	0	90	65	22	75	0	8	4	17	9	0	0	.000	7	13	2	2	0.3	.909
1981		5	5	.500	1.83	49	0	0	64	43	22	41	0	5	5	10	5	0	0	.000	5	12	0	2	0.3	1.000
1982		0	0	–	0.71	9	0	0	12.2	7	2	7	0	0	0	4	1	0	0	.000	1	4	1	1	0.6	.800
1984		0	0	–	3.02	32	0	0	47.2	39	16	26	0	0	0	0	2	0	0	.000	1	3	0	0	0.1	1.000
1985	NY N	0	0	–	12.66	8	0	0	10.2	21	8	3	0	0	0	0	0	0	0	–	1	3	0	0	0.5	1.000
1986	BOS A	2	0	1.000	4.84	53	0	0	44.2	54	16	30	0	2	0	12	0	0	0	–	1	4	0	1	0.1	1.000
1987		2	6	.250	6.93	47	0	0	37.2	46	16	35	0	2	6	0	0	0	0	–	1	4	0	1	0.1	1.000
	11 yrs.	37	38	.493	3.04	461	5	1	628.1	562	195	489	1	35	35	84	52	7	0	.135	35	104	9	13	0.3	.939

DIVISIONAL PLAYOFF SERIES

| 1981 | HOU N | 1 | 0 | 1.000 | 16.20 | 2 | 0 | 0 | 1.2 | 5 | 2 | 2 | 0 | 1 | 0 | 0 | 0 | 0 | 0 | – | 0 | 0 | 0 | 0 | 0.0 | |

LEAGUE CHAMPIONSHIP SERIES

1980	HOU N	0	1	.000	4.91	3	0	0	3.2	4	2	6	0	0	1	0	0	0	0	–	0	0	0	0	0.0	
1986	BOS A	0	0	–	0.00	3	0	0	.2	1	1	0	0	0	0	0	0	0	0	–	0	0	0	0	0.0	–
	2 yrs.	0	1	.000	4.15	6	0	0	4.1	5	3	6	0	0	1	0	0	0	0	–	0	0	0	0	0.0	

WORLD SERIES

| 1986 | BOS A | 0 | 0 | – | 27.00 | 2 | 0 | 0 | .1 | 2 | 2 | 0 | 0 | 0 | 0 | 0 | 0 | 0 | 0 | – | 0 | 0 | 0 | 0 | 0.0 | |

Joe Samuels
SAMUELS, JOSEPH JONAS (Skabotch)
B. Mar. 21, 1905, Scranton, Pa.
BR TR 6'1½" 196 lbs.

| 1930 | DET A | 0 | 0 | – | 16.50 | 2 | 0 | 0 | 6 | 10 | 6 | 1 | 0 | 0 | 0 | 0 | 1 | 0 | 0 | .000 | 1 | 0 | 0 | 0 | 0.5 | 1.000 |

Roger Samuels
SAMUELS, ROGER HOWARD
B. Jan. 5, 1961, San Jose, Calif.
BL TL 6'5" 210 lbs.

1988	SF N	1	2	.333	3.47	15	0	0	23.1	17	7	22	0	1	2	0	3	0	0	.000	1	4	0	0	0.3	1.000
1989	PIT N	0	0	–	9.82	5	0	0	3.2	9	4	2	0	0	0	0	0	0	0	–	0	0	0	0	0.0	
	2 yrs.	1	2	.333	4.33	20	0	0	27	26	11	24	0	1	2	0	3	0	0	.000	1	4	0	0	0.3	1.000

Alex Sanchez
SANCHEZ, ALEX ANTHONY
B. Apr. 8, 1966, Concord, Calif.
BR TR 6'2" 185 lbs.

| 1989 | TOR A | 0 | 1 | .000 | 10.03 | 4 | 3 | 0 | 11.2 | 16 | 14 | 4 | 0 | 0 | 0 | 0 | 0 | 0 | 0 | – | 1 | 6 | 0 | 1 | 1.8 | 1.000 |

Israel Sanchez
SANCHEZ, ISRAEL
Born Israel Sanchez y Matos.
B. Aug. 20, 1963, Falcon Lasvias, Cuba
BL TL 5'9" 170 lbs.

| 1988 | KC A | 3 | 2 | .600 | 4.54 | 19 | 1 | 0 | 35.2 | 36 | 18 | 14 | 0 | 3 | 2 | 1 | 0 | 0 | 0 | – | 2 | 7 | 1 | 0 | 0.5 | .900 |

Luis Sanchez
SANCHEZ, LUIS MERCEDES
Born Luis Mercedes Escoba y Sanchez.
B. Aug. 24, 1953, Cariaco, Venezuela
BR TR 6'2" 170 lbs.

1981	CAL A	0	2	.000	2.91	17	0	0	34	39	11	13	0	0	2	2	0	0	0	–	1	6	2	0	0.5	.778
1982		7	4	.636	3.21	46	0	0	92.2	89	34	58	0	7	4	5	0	0	0	–	1	19	1	1	0.5	.952
1983		10	8	.556	3.66	56	1	0	98.1	92	40	49	0	10	7	7	0	0	0	–	1	24	0	2	0.4	1.000
1984		9	7	.563	3.33	49	0	0	83.2	84	33	62	0	9	7	11	0	0	0	–	3	10	2	2	0.3	.867
1985		2	0	1.000	5.72	26	0	0	61.1	67	27	34	0	2	0	2	0	0	0	–	3	11	1	1	0.6	.933
	5 yrs.	28	21	.571	3.75	194	1	0	370	371	145	216	0	28	20	27	0	0	0	–	9	70	6	6	0.4	.929

LEAGUE CHAMPIONSHIP SERIES

| 1982 | CAL A | 0 | 1 | .000 | 6.75 | 2 | 0 | 0 | 2.2 | 4 | 1 | 1 | 0 | 0 | 1 | 0 | 0 | 0 | 0 | – | 0 | 0 | 0 | 0 | 0.0 | |

Raul Sanchez
SANCHEZ, RAUL GUADALUPE
Born Raul Guadalupe Sanchez y Rodriguez.
B. Dec. 12, 1930, Marianao, Cuba
BR TR 6' 150 lbs.

1952	WAS A	1	1	.500	3.55	3	2	1	12.2	13	7	6	1	0	0	0	5	0	0	.000	1	2	0	0	1.0	1.000
1957	CIN N	3	2	.600	4.76	38	0	0	62.1	61	25	37	0	3	2	5	7	2	0	.286	6	12	3	2	0.6	.857
1960		1	0	1.000	4.91	8	0	0	14.2	12	11	5	0	1	0	0	2	1	0	.500	2	3	0	0	0.6	1.000
	3 yrs.	5	3	.625	4.62	49	2	1	89.2	86	43	48	1	4	2	5	14	3	0	.214	9	17	3	2	0.6	.897

Year	Team		W	L	PCT	ERA	G	GS	CG	IP	H	BB	SO	ShO	W	L	SV	AB	H	HR	BA	PO	A	E	DP	TC/G	FA
															Relief Pitching			Batting									

Ben Sanders

SANDERS, ALEXANDER BENNETT
B. Feb. 16, 1865, Catharpin, Va.   D. Aug. 29, 1930, Memphis, Tenn.   BR TR 6'   210 lbs.

Year	Team		W	L	PCT	ERA	G	GS	CG	IP	H	BB	SO	ShO	W	L	SV	AB	H	HR	BA	PO	A	E	DP	TC/G	FA
1888	PHI	N	19	10	.655	1.90	31	29	28	275.1	240	33	121	4	0	1	0	236	58	1	.246	17	74	7	1	3.2	.929
1889			19	18	.514	3.55	44	39	34	349.2	406	96	123	1	0	1	1	169	47	0	.278	22	58	11	1	2.1	.879
1890	PHI	P	20	17	.541	3.76	43	40	37	346.2	412	69	107	2	0	0	1	189	59	0	.312	17	93	9	5	2.8	.924
1891	PHI	AA	11	5	.688	3.79	19	18	15	145	157	37	40	0	0	0	0	156	39	1	.250	6	31	3	1	2.1	.925
1892	LOU	N	12	19	.387	3.22	31	31	30	268.1	281	62	77	3	0	0	0	198	54	3	.273	12	54	5	3	2.3	.930
5 yrs.			81	69	.540	3.24	168	157	144	1385	1496	297	468	10	1	1	2	*				74	310	35	11	2.5	.916

Dee Sanders

SANDERS, DEE WILMA
B. Apr. 8, 1921, Quitman, Tex.   BR TR 6'3"   195 lbs.

Year	Team		W	L	PCT	ERA	G	GS	CG	IP	H	BB	SO	ShO	W	L	SV	AB	H	HR	BA	PO	A	E	DP	TC/G	FA
1945	STL	A	0	0	–	40.50	2	0	0	1.1	7	1	1	0	0	0	0	0	0	0	–	0	1	0	0	0.5	1.000

Ken Sanders

SANDERS, KENNETH GEORGE (Daffy)
B. July 8, 1941, St. Louis, Mo.   BR TR 5'11"   168 lbs.

Year	Team		W	L	PCT	ERA	G	GS	CG	IP	H	BB	SO	ShO	W	L	SV	AB	H	HR	BA	PO	A	E	DP	TC/G	FA
1964	KC	A	0	2	.000	3.67	21	0	0	27	23	17	18	0	0	2	1	0	0	0	–	2	7	1	2	0.5	.900
1966	2 teams		BOS A	(24G 3–6)		KC A	(38G 3–4)																				
"	total		6	10	.375	3.75	62	1	0	112.2	95	76	74	0	6	10	1	14	2	0	.143	8	20	3	2	0.5	.903
1968	OAK	A	0	1	.000	3.38	7	0	0	10.2	8	8	6	0	0	1	0	0	0	0	–	0	2	0	0	0.3	1.000
1970	MIL	A	5	2	.714	1.76	50	0	0	92	64	25	64	0	5	2	13	13	3	0	.231	5	19	1	1	0.5	.960
1971			7	12	.368	1.92	83	0	0	136	111	34	80	0	7	12	31	14	0	0	.000	12	30	1	1	0.5	.977
1972			2	9	.182	3.13	62	0	0	92	88	31	51	0	2	9	17	7	1	0	.143	7	18	1	1	0.4	.962
1973	2 teams		MIN A	(27G 2–4)		CLE A	(15G 5–1)																				
"	total		7	5	.583	4.40	42	0	0	71.2	71	30	33	0	7	5	13	0	0	0	–	5	13	1	1	0.5	.947
1974	2 teams		CLE A	(9G 0–1)		CAL A	(9G 0–0)																				
"	total		0	1	.000	6.53	18	0	0	20.2	31	8	8	0	0	1	2	0	0	0	–	0	7	0	0	0.4	1.000
1975	NY	N	1	1	.500	2.30	29	0	0	43	31	14	8	0	1	1	5	2	0	0	.000	7	5	0	0	0.4	1.000
1976	2 teams		NY N	(31G 1–2)		KC A	(3G 0–0)																				
"	total		1	2	.333	2.70	34	0	0	50	42	15	18	0	1	2	1	2	0	0	.000	8	8	0	1	0.5	1.000
10 yrs.			29	45	.392	2.98	408	1	0	655.2	564	258	360	0	29	45	86	52	6	0	.115	54	129	8	8	0.5	.958

Roy Sanders

SANDERS, ROY GARVIN (Butch, Pep)
B. Aug. 1, 1892, Stafford, Kans.   D. Jan. 17, 1950, Kansas City, Mo.   BR TR 6'½"   195 lbs.

Year	Team		W	L	PCT	ERA	G	GS	CG	IP	H	BB	SO	ShO	W	L	SV	AB	H	HR	BA	PO	A	E	DP	TC/G	FA
1917	CIN	N	0	1	.000	4.50	2	2	1	14	12	16	3	0	0	0	0	6	0	0	.000	1	6	0	1	3.5	1.000
1918	PIT	N	7	9	.438	2.60	28	14	6	156	135	52	55	1	3	3	1	53	8	0	.151	5	51	2	5	2.1	.966
2 yrs.			7	10	.412	2.75	30	16	7	170	147	68	58	1	3	3	1	59	8	0	.136	6	57	2	6	2.2	.969

Roy Sanders

SANDERS, ROY L. (Simon)
B. 1894   BR TR 6'   185 lbs.

Year	Team		W	L	PCT	ERA	G	GS	CG	IP	H	BB	SO	ShO	W	L	SV	AB	H	HR	BA	PO	A	E	DP	TC/G	FA
1918	NY	A	0	2	.000	4.21	6	2	0	25.2	28	16	8	0	0	0	0	7	0	0	.000	0	5	2	0	1.2	.714
1920	STL	A	1	1	.500	5.19	8	1	0	17.1	20	17	2	0	1	0	0	4	0	0	.000	0	2	0	0	0.3	1.000
2 yrs.			1	3	.250	4.60	14	3	0	43	48	33	10	0	1	0	0	11	0	0	.000	0	7	2	0	0.6	.778

War Sanders

SANDERS, WARREN WILLIAMS
B. Aug. 2, 1877, Maynardville, Tenn.   D. Aug. 3, 1962, Chattanooga, Tenn.   BR TL 5'10"   160 lbs.

Year	Team		W	L	PCT	ERA	G	GS	CG	IP	H	BB	SO	ShO	W	L	SV	AB	H	HR	BA	PO	A	E	DP	TC/G	FA
1903	STL	N	1	5	.167	6.08	8	6	3	40	48	21	9	0	0	1	0	15	1	0	.067	1	9	1	0	1.4	.909
1904			1	2	.333	4.74	4	3	1	19	25	1	11	0	0	0	0	6	0	0	.000	2	6	0	0	2.0	1.000
2 yrs.			2	7	.222	5.64	12	9	4	59	73	22	20	0	0	1	0	21	1	0	.048	3	15	1	0	1.6	.947

Scott Sanderson

SANDERSON, SCOTT DOUGLAS
B. July 22, 1956, Dearborn, Mich.   BR TR 6'5"   195 lbs.

Year	Team		W	L	PCT	ERA	G	GS	CG	IP	H	BB	SO	ShO	W	L	SV	AB	H	HR	BA	PO	A	E	DP	TC/G	FA
1978	MON	N	4	2	.667	2.51	10	9	1	61	52	21	50	1	0	0	0	19	2	0	.105	2	6	1	0	0.9	.889
1979			9	8	.529	3.43	34	24	5	168	148	54	138	3	1	1	1	50	8	0	.160	9	13	1	1	0.7	.957
1980			16	11	.593	3.11	33	33	7	211	206	56	125	3	0	0	0	64	5	0	.078	14	21	1	0	1.1	.972
1981			9	7	.563	2.96	22	22	4	137	122	31	77	0	0	0	0	35	4	0	.114	6	14	0	0	1.0	1.000
1982			12	12	.500	3.46	32	32	7	224	212	58	158	0	0	0	0	57	8	1	.140	13	16	1	1	0.9	.967
1983			6	7	.462	4.65	18	16	0	81.1	98	20	55	0	0	0	0	28	4	0	.143	4	6	2	0	0.7	.833
1984	CHI	N	8	5	.615	3.14	24	24	3	140.2	140	24	76	0	0	0	0	42	5	0	.119	11	24	1	0	1.5	.972
1985			5	6	.455	3.12	19	19	2	121	100	27	80	0	0	0	0	31	2	0	.065	11	21	0	2	1.7	1.000
1986			9	11	.450	4.19	37	28	1	169.2	165	37	124	1	0	0	0	51	3	0	.059	11	20	2	3	0.9	.939
1987			8	9	.471	4.29	32	22	0	144.2	156	50	106	0	1	2	2	40	3	1	.075	10	14	2	3	0.8	.923
1988			1	2	.333	5.28	11	0	0	15.1	13	3	6	0	1	2	0	0	0	0	–	0	1	0	0	0.1	1.000
1989			11	9	.550	3.94	37	23	2	146.1	155	31	86	0	1	2	0	43	2	0	.047	10	12	0	1	0.6	1.000
12 yrs.			98	89	.524	3.55	309	252	32	1620	1567	412	1081	9	6	7	5	460	46	0	.100	101	168	11	11	0.9	.961

DIVISIONAL PLAYOFF SERIES

Year	Team		W	L	PCT	ERA	G	GS	CG	IP	H	BB	SO	ShO	W	L	SV	AB	H	HR	BA	PO	A	E	DP	TC/G	FA
1981	MON	N	0	0	–	6.75	1	1	0	2.2	4	2	2	0	0	0	0	1	0	0	.000	0	0	0	0	0.0	–

LEAGUE CHAMPIONSHIP SERIES

Year	Team		W	L	PCT	ERA	G	GS	CG	IP	H	BB	SO	ShO	W	L	SV	AB	H	HR	BA	PO	A	E	DP	TC/G	FA
1984	CHI	N	0	0	–	5.79	1	1	0	4.2	6	1	2	0	0	0	0	2	0	0	.000	0	1	0	0	1.0	1.000
1989			0	0	–	0.00	1	0	0	2	2	0	1	0	0	0	0	0	0	0	–	0	0	0	0	0.0	–
2 yrs.			0	0	–	4.05	2	1	0	6.2	8	1	3	0	0	0	0	2	0	0	.000	0	1	0	0	0.5	1.000

Fred Sanford

SANFORD, JOHN FREDERICK
B. Aug. 9, 1919, Garfield, Utah   BB TR 6'1"   200 lbs.
BR 1948

Year	Team		W	L	PCT	ERA	G	GS	CG	IP	H	BB	SO	ShO	W	L	SV	AB	H	HR	BA	PO	A	E	DP	TC/G	FA
1943	STL	A	0	0	–	1.93	3	0	0	9.1	7	4	2	0	0	0	0	0	0	0	–	0	3	0	0	1.0	1.000
1946			2	1	.667	2.05	3	3	2	22	19	9	8	2	0	0	0	7	2	0	.286	1	3	0	1	1.3	1.000
1947			7	16	.304	3.71	34	23	9	186.2	186	76	62	0	0	2	4	54	11	0	.204	7	26	1	0	1.0	.971
1948			12	21	.364	4.64	42	33	9	227	250	91	79	1	2	2	2	73	11	1	.151	9	46	4	1	1.4	.932
1949	NY	A	7	3	.700	3.87	29	11	3	95.1	100	57	51	0	2	0	0	34	4	0	.118	2	17	2	1	0.7	.905
1950			5	4	.556	4.55	26	12	2	112.2	103	79	54	0	1	1	0	35	8	0	.229	9	30	0	5	1.5	1.000

Year	Team	W	L	PCT	ERA	G	GS	CG	IP	H	BB	SO	ShO	Relief Pitching W	L	SV	Batting AB	H	HR	BA	PO	A	E	DP	TC/G	FA

Fred Sanford *continued*

Year	Team	W	L	PCT	ERA	G	GS	CG	IP	H	BB	SO	ShO	W	L	SV	AB	H	HR	BA	PO	A	E	DP	TC/G	FA
1951	3 teams NY A (11G 0–3) WAS A (7G 2–3) STL A (9G 2–4)																									
"	total	4	10	.286	6.82	27	16	1	91	103	75	29	0	0	1	0	26	3	0	.115	5	15	0	0	0.7	1.000
7 yrs.		37	55	.402	4.45	164	98	26	744	768	391	285	3	5	6	6	229	39	1	.170	33	140	7	8	1.1	.961

Jack Sanford

SANFORD, JOHN STANLEY
B. May 18, 1929, Wellesley Hills, Mass.

BR TR 6' 190 lbs.

Year	Team	W	L	PCT	ERA	G	GS	CG	IP	H	BB	SO	ShO	W	L	SV	AB	H	HR	BA	PO	A	E	DP	TC/G	FA
1956	PHI N	1	0	1.000	1.38	3	1	0	13	7	13	6	0	0	0	0	3	1	0	.333	0	2	0	1	0.7	1.000
1957		19	8	.704	3.08	33	33	15	236.2	194	94	188	3	0	0	0	89	15	0	.169	15	30	2	2	1.4	.957
1958		10	13	.435	4.44	38	27	7	186.1	197	81	106	2	0	0	0	59	10	0	.169	12	23	2	0	1.0	.946
1959	SF N	15	12	.556	3.16	36	31	10	222.1	198	70	132	0	0	1	1	72	8	0	.111	10	31	1	1	1.2	.976
1960		12	14	.462	3.82	37	34	11	219	199	99	125	6	0	1	0	74	13	0	.176	13	33	1	3	1.3	.979
1961		13	9	.591	4.22	38	33	6	217.1	203	87	112	0	0	0	0	74	16	3	.216	9	41	3	1	1.4	.943
1962		24	7	.774	3.43	39	38	13	265.1	233	92	147	2	0	0	0	98	15	0	.153	21	52	4	4	2.0	.948
1963		16	13	.552	3.51	42	42	11	284.1	273	76	158	0	0	0	0	94	13	0	.138	16	65	2	4	2.0	.976
1964		5	7	.417	3.30	18	17	3	106.1	91	37	64	1	0	0	1	30	4	0	.133	8	22	2	0	1.8	.938
1965	2 teams SF N (23G 4–5) CAL A (9G 1–2)																									
"	total	5	7	.417	4.11	32	21	0	120.1	127	40	56	0	0	0	3	32	4	0	.125	7	23	1	0	1.0	.938
1966	CAL A	13	7	.650	3.83	50	6	0	108	108	27	54	0	12	4	5	22	3	0	.136	7	23	1	0	0.6	.938
1967	2 teams CAL A (12G 3–2) KC A (10G 1–2)																									
"	total	4	4	.500	5.12	22	10	0	70.1	77	21	34	0	1	1	1	18	3	0	.167	4	20	0	1	1.1	1.000
12 yrs.		137	101	.576	3.69	388	293	76	2049.1	1907	737	1182	14	15	8	11	665	105	3	.158	122	365	21	19	1.3	.959

WORLD SERIES

Year	Team	W	L	PCT	ERA	G	GS	CG	IP	H	BB	SO	ShO	W	L	SV	AB	H	HR	BA	PO	A	E	DP	TC/G	FA
1962	SF N	1	2	.333	1.93	3	3	0	23.1	16	8	19	1	0	0	0	7	3	0	.429	3	3	0	1	2.0	1.000

Jose Santiago

SANTIAGO, JOSE GUILLERMO (Pants)
Born Jose Guillermo Santiago y Guzman.
B. Sept. 4, 1928, Coamo, Puerto Rico

BR TR 5'10'' 175 lbs.

Year	Team	W	L	PCT	ERA	G	GS	CG	IP	H	BB	SO	ShO	W	L	SV	AB	H	HR	BA	PO	A	E	DP	TC/G	FA
1954	CLE A	0	0	–	0.00	1	0	0	1.2	0	2	1	0	0	0	0	0	0	0	–	0	0	1	0	1.0	–
1955		2	0	1.000	2.48	17	0	0	32.2	31	14	19	0	2	0	0	4	2	0	.500	1	6	1	0	0.5	.875
1956	KC A	1	2	.333	8.31	9	5	0	21.2	36	17	9	0	0	0	0	5	2	0	.400	1	5	0	1	0.7	1.000
3 yrs.		3	2	.600	4.66	27	5	0	56	67	33	29	0	2	0	0	9	4	0	.444	2	11	2	1	0.6	.867

Jose Santiago

SANTIAGO, JOSE RAFAEL
Born Jose Rafael Santiago y Alfonso.
B. Aug. 15, 1940, Juana Diaz, Puerto Rico

BR TR 6'2'' 185 lbs.

Year	Team	W	L	PCT	ERA	G	GS	CG	IP	H	BB	SO	ShO	W	L	SV	AB	H	HR	BA	PO	A	E	DP	TC/G	FA
1963	KC A	1	0	1.000	9.00	4	0	0	7	8	2	6	0	1	0	0	0	0	0	–	2	1	0	0	0.8	1.000
1964		0	6	.000	4.73	34	8	0	83.2	84	35	64	0	0	1	0	18	0	0	.000	10	9	4	0	0.7	.826
1965		0	0	–	9.00	4	0	0	5	8	4	8	0	0	0	0	0	0	0	–	1	0	0	0	0.3	1.000
1966	BOS A	12	13	.480	3.66	35	28	7	172	155	58	119	1	0	1	2	56	11	0	.196	9	22	0	1	0.9	1.000
1967		12	4	.750	3.59	50	11	0	145.1	138	47	109	0	8	3	5	42	8	1	.190	9	22	0	2	0.6	1.000
1968		9	4	.692	2.25	18	18	7	124	96	42	86	2	0	0	0	43	7	0	.163	7	16	1	2	1.3	.958
1969		0	0	–	3.52	10	0	0	7.2	11	4	4	0	0	0	0	0	0	0	–	0	0	0	0	0.0	–
1970		0	2	.000	10.64	8	0	0	11	18	8	8	0	0	2	1	3	2	0	.667	2	0	0	0	0.3	1.000
8 yrs.		34	29	.540	3.74	163	65	16	555.2	518	200	404	3	9	7	8	162	28	1	.173	39	71	5	5	0.7	.957

WORLD SERIES

Year	Team	W	L	PCT	ERA	G	GS	CG	IP	H	BB	SO	ShO	W	L	SV	AB	H	HR	BA	PO	A	E	DP	TC/G	FA
1967	BOS A	0	2	.000	5.59	3	2	0	9.2	16	3	6	0	0	0	0	2	1	0	.500	1	1	0	0	0.0	–

Al Santorini

SANTORINI, ALAN JOEL
B. May 19, 1948, Irvington, N. J.

BR TR 6' 190 lbs.

Year	Team	W	L	PCT	ERA	G	GS	CG	IP	H	BB	SO	ShO	W	L	SV	AB	H	HR	BA	PO	A	E	DP	TC/G	FA
1968	ATL N	0	1	.000	0.00	1	1	0	3	4	0	0	0	0	0	0	0	0	0	–	0	1	1	0	2.0	.500
1969	SD N	8	14	.364	3.94	32	30	2	185	194	73	111	1	0	0	0	63	7	1	.111	9	34	2	1	1.4	.956
1970		1	8	.111	6.04	21	12	0	76	91	43	41	0	0	0	1	18	0	0	.000	2	7	0	1	0.4	1.000
1971	2 teams SD N (18G 0–2) STL N (19G 0–2)																									
"	total	0	4	.000	3.78	37	8	0	88	94	30	42	0	0	0	0	15	5	0	.333	6	9	3	0	0.5	.833
1972	STL N	8	11	.421	4.11	30	19	3	133.2	136	46	72	3	2	3	0	40	3	0	.075	10	12	1	1	0.8	.957
1973		0	0	–	5.40	6	0	0	8.1	14	2	2	0	0	0	0	1	0	0	.000	1	0	0	0	0.2	1.000
6 yrs.		17	38	.309	4.28	127	70	5	494	533	194	268	4	2	3	2	137	15	1	.109	28	63	7	4	0.8	.929

Manny Sarmiento

SARMIENTO, MANUEL EDUARDO
Born Manuel Eduardo Sarmiento y Aponte.
B. Feb. 2, 1956, Cagua, Venezuela

BR TR 6' 170 lbs.

Year	Team	W	L	PCT	ERA	G	GS	CG	IP	H	BB	SO	ShO	W	L	SV	AB	H	HR	BA	PO	A	E	DP	TC/G	FA
1976	CIN N	5	1	.833	2.05	22	0	0	44	36	12	20	0	5	1	0	7	0	0	.000	2	2	0	0	0.2	1.000
1977		0	0	–	2.48	24	0	0	40	28	11	23	0	0	0	1	1	0	0	.000	0	2	0	0	0.1	1.000
1978		9	7	.563	4.39	63	4	0	127	109	54	72	0	7	5	5	16	0	0	.000	10	15	0	1	0.4	1.000
1979		0	4	.000	4.62	23	1	0	39	47	7	23	0	0	0	0	6	0	0	.000	1	4	0	0	0.2	1.000
1980	SEA A	0	1	.000	3.60	9	0	0	15	14	6	15	0	0	1	1	0	0	0	–	1	1	0	0	0.1	1.000
1982	PIT N	9	4	.692	3.39	35	17	4	164.2	153	46	81	0	2	0	1	47	9	0	.191	8	17	2	3	0.8	.926
1983		3	5	.375	2.99	52	0	0	84.1	74	36	49	0	3	5	4	10	0	0	.000	4	9	0	0	0.3	1.000
7 yrs.		26	22	.542	3.48	228	22	4	514	461	172	283	0	17	15	12	87	9	0	.103	27	49	2	4	0.3	.974

LEAGUE CHAMPIONSHIP SERIES

Year	Team	W	L	PCT	ERA	G	GS	CG	IP	H	BB	SO	ShO	W	L	SV	AB	H	HR	BA	PO	A	E	DP	TC/G	FA
1976	CIN N	0	0	–	18.00	1	0	0	1	2	1	0	0	0	0	0	1	0	0	.000	0	0	0	0	0.0	–

Kevin Saucier

SAUCIER, KEVIN ANDREW (Hot Sauce)
B. Aug. 9, 1956, Pensacola, Fla.

BL TL 6'1'' 190 lbs.

Year	Team	W	L	PCT	ERA	G	GS	CG	IP	H	BB	SO	ShO	W	L	SV	AB	H	HR	BA	PO	A	E	DP	TC/G	FA
1978	PHI N	0	1	.000	18.00	2	0	0	2	4	1	2	0	0	1	0	0	0	0	–	0	0	0	0	0.0	–
1979		1	4	.200	4.21	29	2	0	62	68	33	21	0	1	2	1	10	1	0	.100	2	12	1	1	0.5	.933
1980		7	3	.700	3.42	40	0	0	50	50	20	25	0	7	3	0	8	0	0	.000	3	10	1	0	0.4	.929
1981	DET A	4	2	.667	1.65	38	0	0	49	26	21	23	0	4	2	13	0	0	0	–	3	10	2	1	0.4	.867

Year	Team		W	L	PCT	ERA	G	GS	CG	IP	H	BB	SO	ShO	Relief Pitching W	L	SV	Batting AB	H	HR	BA	PO	A	E	DP	TC/G	FA

Kevin Saucier *continued*

Year	Team		W	L	PCT	ERA	G	GS	CG	IP	H	BB	SO	ShO	W	L	SV	AB	H	HR	BA	PO	A	E	DP	TC/G	FA
1982			3	1	.750	3.12	31	1	0	40.1	35	29	23	0	3	1	5	0	0	0	–	6	4	2	4	0.4	.833
5 yrs.			15	11	.577	3.32	139	3	0	203.1	183	104	94	0	15	9	19	18	1	0	.056	14	36	6	6	0.4	.893

LEAGUE CHAMPIONSHIP SERIES

| 1980 | PHI | N | 0 | 0 | – | 0.00 | 2 | 0 | 0 | .2 | 1 | 2 | 0 | 0 | 0 | 0 | 0 | 0 | 0 | 0 | – | 0 | 0 | 0 | 0 | 0.0 | – |

WORLD SERIES

| 1980 | PHI | N | 0 | 0 | – | 0.00 | 1 | 0 | 0 | .2 | 0 | 2 | 0 | 0 | 0 | 0 | 0 | 0 | 0 | 0 | – | 0 | 0 | 0 | 0 | 0.0 | – |

Dennis Saunders

SAUNDERS, DENNIS JAMES
B. Jan. 4, 1949, Alhambra, Calif. BB TR 6'3" 195 lbs.

| 1970 | DET | A | 1 | 1 | .500 | 3.21 | 8 | 0 | 0 | 14 | 16 | 5 | 8 | 0 | 1 | 1 | 1 | 5 | 0 | 0 | .000 | 2 | 5 | 0 | 0 | 0.9 | 1.000 |

Rich Sauveur

SAUVEUR, RICHARD DANIEL
B. Nov. 23, 1963, Arlington, Va. BL TL 6'4" 163 lbs.

1986	PIT	N	0	0	–	6.00	3	3	0	12	17	6	6	0	0	0	0	3	1	0	.333	1	5	0	1	2.0	1.000
1988	MON	N	0	0	–	6.00	4	0	0	3	3	2	3	0	0	0	0	0	0	0	–	0	1	0	0	0.3	1.000
2 yrs.			0	0	–	6.00	7	3	0	15	20	8	9	0	0	0	0	3	1	0	.333	1	6	0	1	1.0	1.000

Bob Savage

SAVAGE, JOHN ROBERT
B. Dec. 1, 1921, Manchester, N. H. BR TR 6'2" 180 lbs.

1942	PHI	A	0	1	.000	3.23	8	3	0	30.2	24	31	10	0	0	0	0	9	1	0	.111	4	4	0	0	1.0	1.000
1946			3	15	.167	4.06	40	19	7	164	164	93	78	1	0	1	2	41	5	0	.122	4	14	1	1	0.5	.947
1947			8	10	.444	3.76	44	8	2	146	135	55	56	1	6	7	2	40	2	0	.050	6	16	2	0	0.5	.917
1948			5	1	.833	6.21	33	1	1	75.1	98	33	26	0	5	0	5	13	1	0	.077	1	11	0	0	0.4	1.000
1949	STL	A	0	0	–	6.43	4	0	0	7	12	3	1	0	0	0	0	1	0	0	.000	0	2	0	0	0.5	1.000
5 yrs.			16	27	.372	4.32	129	31	10	423	433	215	171	2	11	8	9	104	9	0	.087	15	47	3	1	0.5	.954

Jack Savage

SAVAGE, JOHN JOSEPH
B. Apr. 22, 1964, Louisville, Ky. BR TR 6'3" 190 lbs.

| 1987 | LA | N | 0 | 0 | – | 2.70 | 3 | 0 | 0 | 3.1 | 4 | 0 | 0 | 0 | 0 | 0 | 0 | 0 | 0 | 0 | – | 0 | 0 | 0 | 0 | 0.0 | – |

Don Savidge

SAVIDGE, DONALD SNYDER
Son of Ralph Savidge.
B. Aug. 28, 1908, Berwick, Pa. D. Mar. 22, 1983, Santa Barbara, Calif. BR TR 6'1" 180 lbs.

| 1929 | WAS | A | 0 | 0 | – | 9.00 | 3 | 0 | 0 | 6 | 12 | 2 | 2 | 0 | 0 | 0 | 0 | 0 | 0 | 0 | – | 0 | 2 | 0 | 0 | 0.7 | 1.000 |

Ralph Savidge

SAVIDGE, RALPH AUSTIN (The Human Whipcord)
Father of Don Savidge.
B. Feb. 3, 1879, Jerseytown, Pa. D. July 22, 1959, Berwick, Pa. BR TR 6'2" 210 lbs.

1908	CIN	N	0	1	.000	2.57	4	1	1	21	18	8	7	0	0	0	0	7	0	0	.000	0	3	0	0	0.8	1.000
1909			0	0	–	22.50	1	0	0	4	10	3	2	0	0	0	0	1	0	0	.000	0	2	1	0	3.0	.667
2 yrs.			0	1	.000	5.76	5	1	1	25	28	11	9	0	0	0	0	8	0	0	.000	0	5	1	0	1.2	.833

Moe Savransky

SAVRANSKY, MORRIS
B. Jan. 13, 1929, Cleveland, Ohio BL TL 5'11" 175 lbs.

| 1954 | CIN | N | 0 | 2 | .000 | 4.88 | 16 | 0 | 0 | 24 | 23 | 8 | 7 | 0 | 0 | 0 | 2 | 2 | 1 | 0 | .500 | 2 | 7 | 0 | 1 | 0.6 | 1.000 |

Rick Sawyer

SAWYER, RICHARD CLYDE
B. Apr. 7, 1948, Bakersfield, Calif. BR TR 6'2" 205 lbs.

1974	NY	A	0	0	–	13.50	1	0	0	2	2	1	1	0	0	0	0	0	0	0	–	0	2	0	0	2.0	1.000
1975			0	0	–	3.00	4	0	0	6	7	2	3	0	0	0	0	0	0	0	–	0	0	0	0	0.0	–
1976	SD	N	5	3	.625	2.53	13	11	4	81.2	84	38	33	2	0	0	1	24	5	0	.208	3	12	0	1	1.2	1.000
1977			7	6	.538	5.84	56	9	0	111	136	55	45	0	6	2	0	20	3	0	.150	3	24	2	2	0.5	.931
4 yrs.			12	9	.571	4.49	74	20	4	200.2	229	96	82	2	6	3	0	44	8	0	.182	6	38	2	2	0.6	.957

Will Sawyer

SAWYER, WILLARD NEWTON
B. July 29, 1864, Brimfield, Ohio D. Jan. 5, 1936, Kent, Ohio BL TL

| 1883 | CLE | N | 4 | 10 | .286 | 2.36 | 17 | 15 | 15 | 141 | 119 | 47 | 76 | 0 | 0 | 0 | 0 | 47 | 1 | 0 | .021 | 6 | 11 | 4 | 0 | 1.2 | .810 |

Bill Sayles

SAYLES, WILLIAM NISBETH
B. July 27, 1917, Portland, Ore. BR TR 6'2" 175 lbs.

1939	BOS	A	0	0	–	7.07	5	0	0	14	14	13	9	0	0	0	0	7	1	0	.143	0	3	0	0	0.6	1.000
1943	2 teams	NY N	(18G 1–3)			BKN N	(5G 0–0)																					
"	total		1	3	.250	5.29	23	3	1	64.2	73	33	43	0	0	0	0	15	5	0	.333	3	10	2	0	0.7	.867
2 yrs.			1	3	.250	5.61	28	3	1	78.2	87	46	52	0	0	0	0	22	6	0	.273	3	13	2	0	0.6	.889

Phil Saylor

SAYLOR, PHILIP ANDREW (Lefty)
B. Jan. 2, 1871, Van Wert County, Ohio D. July 23, 1937, West Alexandria, Ohio TL

| 1891 | PHI | N | 0 | 0 | – | 6.00 | 1 | 0 | 0 | 3 | 2 | 0 | 0 | 0 | 0 | 0 | 0 | 1 | 0 | 0 | .000 | 0 | 0 | 0 | 0 | 0.0 | – |

Doc Scanlan

SCANLAN, WILLIAM DENNIS
Brother of Frank Scanlan.
B. Mar. 7, 1881, Syracuse, N. Y. D. May 29, 1949, Brooklyn, N. Y. BL TR 5'8" 165 lbs.

| 1903 | PIT | N | 0 | 1 | .000 | 4.00 | 1 | 1 | 1 | 9 | 5 | 6 | 0 | 0 | 0 | 0 | 0 | 2 | 0 | 0 | .000 | 0 | 1 | 0 | 0 | 1.0 | 1.000 |

Year	Team	W	L	PCT	ERA	G	GS	CG	IP	H	BB	SO	ShO	W	L	SV	AB	H	HR	BA	PO	A	E	DP	TC/G	FA

(Header spanning: **Relief Pitching** over W L SV; **Batting** over AB H HR)

Doc Scanlan *continued*

Year	Team	W	L	PCT	ERA	G	GS	CG	IP	H	BB	SO	ShO	W	L	SV	AB	H	HR	BA	PO	A	E	DP	TC/G	FA
1904	2 teams	PIT N	(4G 1–3)						BKN N	(13G 7–6)																
"	total	8	9	.471	2.64	17	15	12	126	115	60	50	3	0	1	0	41	5	0	.122	11	20	1	1	1.9	.969
1905	BKN N	14	12	.538	2.92	33	28	22	250	220	104	135	2	0	2	0	96	16	0	.167	6	57	5	3	2.1	.926
1906		18	13	.581	3.19	38	33	28	288	230	**127**	120	6	1	0	1	97	18	0	.186	5	50	5	0	1.6	.917
1907		6	8	.429	3.20	17	15	10	107	90	61	59	2	0	0	0	34	9	0	.265	1	21	3	2	1.5	.880
1909		8	7	.533	2.93	19	17	12	141.1	125	65	72	2	0	0	0	44	12	0	.273	0	33	1	2	1.8	.971
1910		9	11	.450	2.61	34	25	14	217.1	175	116	103	2	0	0	2	69	14	0	.203	4	49	0	1	1.6	1.000
1911		3	10	.231	3.64	22	15	3	113.2	101	69	45	0	1	1	1	33	4	0	.121	1	31	4	1	1.6	.889
8 yrs.		66	71	.482	3.00	181	149	102	1252.1	1061	608	584	15	2	4	4	416	78	0	.188	28	262	19	10	1.7	.939

Frank Scanlan

SCANLAN, FRANK ALOYSIUS (Dreamy)
Brother of Doc Scanlan.
B. Apr. 28, 1890, Syracuse, N. Y. D. Apr. 9, 1969, Brooklyn, N. Y.

BL TL 6'1½" 175 lbs.

Year	Team	W	L	PCT	ERA	G	GS	CG	IP	H	BB	SO	ShO	W	L	SV	AB	H	HR	BA	PO	A	E	DP	TC/G	FA
1909	PHI N	0	0	–	1.64	6	0	0	11	8	5	5	0	0	0	1	4	0	0	.000	1	1	0	1	0.3	1.000

Pat Scantlebury

SCANTLEBURY, PATRICIO ATHELSTAN
B. Nov. 11, 1925, Gatun, Canal Zone

BL TL 6'1" 180 lbs.

Year	Team	W	L	PCT	ERA	G	GS	CG	IP	H	BB	SO	ShO	W	L	SV	AB	H	HR	BA	PO	A	E	DP	TC/G	FA
1956	CIN N	0	1	.000	6.63	6	2	0	19	24	5	10	0	0	0	0	3	0	0	.000	1	3	0	0	0.7	1.000

Randy Scarbery

SCARBERY, RANDY JAMES
B. June 22, 1952, Fresno, Calif.

BB TR 6'1" 185 lbs.

Year	Team	W	L	PCT	ERA	G	GS	CG	IP	H	BB	SO	ShO	W	L	SV	AB	H	HR	BA	PO	A	E	DP	TC/G	FA
1979	CHI A	2	8	.200	4.63	45	5	0	101	102	34	45	0	2	3	4	0	0	0	–	5	17	2	1	0.5	.917
1980		1	2	.333	4.03	15	0	0	29	24	7	18	0	1	2	2	0	0	0	–	2	2	0	0	0.3	1.000
2 yrs.		3	10	.231	4.50	60	5	0	130	126	41	63	0	3	5	6	0	0	0	–	7	19	2	1	0.5	.929

Ray Scarborough

SCARBOROUGH, RAE WILSON
B. July 23, 1917, Mt. Gilead, N. C. D. July 1, 1982, Mount Olive, N. C.

BR TR 6' 185 lbs.

Year	Team	W	L	PCT	ERA	G	GS	CG	IP	H	BB	SO	ShO	W	L	SV	AB	H	HR	BA	PO	A	E	DP	TC/G	FA
1942	WAS A	2	1	.667	4.12	17	5	1	63.1	68	32	16	0	0	0	0	21	4	0	.190	6	15	0	1	1.2	1.000
1943		4	4	.500	2.83	24	6	2	86	93	46	43	0	2	3	0	24	8	0	.333	3	18	2	1	1.0	.913
1946		7	11	.389	4.05	32	20	6	155.2	176	74	46	1	3	1	1	50	7	0	.140	13	35	3	5	1.6	.941
1947		6	13	.316	3.41	33	18	8	161	165	67	63	2	1	2	0	50	6	0	.120	7	24	2	3	1.0	.939
1948		15	8	.652	2.82	31	26	9	185.1	166	72	76	1	1	1	1	64	14	0	.219	13	35	3	3	1.6	.941
1949		13	11	.542	4.60	34	27	11	199.2	204	88	81	1	0	0	0	67	13	0	.194	11	41	5	3	1.7	.912
1950	2 teams	WAS A	(8G 3–5)						CHI A	(27G 10–13)																
"	total	13	18	.419	4.94	35	31	12	207.2	222	84	94	3	1	1	1	66	10	0	.152	13	33	4	4	1.4	.920
1951	BOS A	12	9	.571	5.09	37	22	8	184	201	61	71	0	2	2	0	68	13	0	.191	18	30	1	4	1.3	.980
1952	2 teams	BOS A	(28G 1–5)						NY A	(9G 5–1)																
"	total	6	6	.500	4.23	37	12	2	110.2	106	50	42	1	2	1	4	32	9	0	.281	13	17	1	0	0.8	.968
1953	2 teams	NY A	(25G 0–2)						DET A	(13G 0–2)																
"	total	2	4	.333	4.66	38	1	0	75.1	86	37	32	0	1	0	0	14	1	0	.071	3	15	4	0	0.6	.818
10 yrs.		80	85	.485	4.13	318	168	59	1428.2	1487	611	564	9	16	14	14	456	85	1	.186	100	263	25	24	1.2	.936

WORLD SERIES

Year	Team	W	L	PCT	ERA	G	GS	CG	IP	H	BB	SO	ShO	W	L	SV	AB	H	HR	BA	PO	A	E	DP	TC/G	FA
1952	NY A	0	0	–	9.00	1	0	0	1	1	0	1	0	0	1	0	0	0	0	–	1	0	0	0	1.0	1.000

Mac Scarce

SCARCE, GUERRAND McCURDY
B. Apr. 8, 1949, Danville, Va.

BL TL 6'3" 180 lbs.

Year	Team	W	L	PCT	ERA	G	GS	CG	IP	H	BB	SO	ShO	W	L	SV	AB	H	HR	BA	PO	A	E	DP	TC/G	FA
1972	PHI N	1	2	.333	3.44	31	0	0	36.2	30	20	40	0	1	2	4	6	0	0	.000	2	7	0	1	0.3	1.000
1973		1	8	.111	2.42	52	0	0	70.2	54	47	57	0	1	8	12	5	0	0	.000	2	6	1	0	0.2	.889
1974		3	8	.273	5.01	58	0	0	70	72	35	50	0	3	8	5	6	0	0	.000	2	4	0	0	0.1	1.000
1975	NY N	0	0	–	0.00	1	0	0	1	1	0	0	0	0	0	0	0	0	0	–	0	0	0	0	0.0	–
1978	MIN A	1	1	.500	3.94	17	0	0	32	35	15	17	0	1	1	0	0	0	0	–	0	2	1	0	0.2	.667
5 yrs.		6	19	.240	3.70	159	0	0	209.1	192	117	164	0	6	19	21	17	0	0	.000	6	19	2	1	0.2	.926

Al Schacht

SCHACHT, ALEXANDER (The Clown Prince of Baseball)
B. Nov. 11, 1892, New York, N. Y. D. July 14, 1984, Waterbury, Conn.

BR TR 5'11" 142 lbs.

Year	Team	W	L	PCT	ERA	G	GS	CG	IP	H	BB	SO	ShO	W	L	SV	AB	H	HR	BA	PO	A	E	DP	TC/G	FA
1919	WAS A	2	0	1.000	2.40	2	2	1	15	14	4	4	0	0	0	0	3	0	0	.000	2	1	0	0	2.0	1.000
1920		6	4	.600	4.44	22	11	5	99.1	130	30	19	1	0	2	1	26	5	0	.192	8	33	2	2	2.0	.953
1921		6	6	.500	4.90	29	5	2	82.2	110	27	15	0	4	4	1	23	5	0	.217	3	7	2	0	0.4	.833
3 yrs.		14	10	.583	4.48	53	18	8	197	254	61	38	1	4	6	2	52	10	0	.192	13	42	4	2	1.1	.932

Sid Schacht

SCHACHT, SIDNEY
B. Feb. 3, 1918, Bogota, N. J.

BR TR 5'11" 170 lbs.

Year	Team	W	L	PCT	ERA	G	GS	CG	IP	H	BB	SO	ShO	W	L	SV	AB	H	HR	BA	PO	A	E	DP	TC/G	FA
1950	STL A	0	0	–	16.03	8	1	0	10.2	24	14	7	0	0	0	0	2	0	0	.000	2	0	0	0	0.3	1.000
1951	2 teams	STL A	(6G 0–0)						BOS N	(5G 0–2)																
"	total	0	2	.000	12.66	11	0	0	10.2	20	7	5	0	0	2	0	0	0	0	–	0	0	0	0	0.0	–
2 yrs.		0	2	.000	14.34	19	1	0	21.1	44	21	12	0	0	2	0	2	0	0	.000	2	0	0	0	0.1	1.000

Hal Schacker

SCHACKER, HAROLD
B. Apr. 6, 1925, Brooklyn, N. Y.

BR TR 6' 190 lbs.

Year	Team	W	L	PCT	ERA	G	GS	CG	IP	H	BB	SO	ShO	W	L	SV	AB	H	HR	BA	PO	A	E	DP	TC/G	FA
1945	BOS N	0	1	.000	5.28	6	0	0	15.1	14	9	6	0	0	0	1	2	0	0	.000	0	2	1	0	0.5	.667

Germany Schaefer

SCHAEFER, HERMAN A.
B. Feb. 4, 1877, Chicago, Ill. D. May 16, 1919, Saranac Lake, N. Y.

BR TR 5'9" 175 lbs.

Year	Team	W	L	PCT	ERA	G	GS	CG	IP	H	BB	SO	ShO	W	L	SV	AB	H	HR	BA	PO	A	E	DP	TC/G	FA
1912	WAS A	0	0	–	0.00	1	0	0	.2	1	0	0	0	0	0	0	166	41	0	.247	0	0	0	0	0.0	–
1913		0	0	–	54.00	1	0	0	.1	3	0	0	0	0	0	0	100	32	0	.320	0	1	0	0	1.0	1.000
2 yrs.		0	0	–	18.00	2	0	0	1	3	0	0	0	0	0	0	*				0	1	0	0	0.5	1.000

Year	Team	W	L	PCT	ERA	G	GS	CG	IP	H	BB	SO	ShO	W	L	SV	AB	H	HR	BA	PO	A	E	DP	TC/G	FA

Harry Schaeffer SCHAEFFER, HARRY EDWARD (Lefty) B. June 23, 1924, Reading, Pa. BL TL 6'2½" 175 lbs.

| 1952 | NY A | 0 | 1 | .000 | 5.29 | 5 | 2 | 0 | 17 | 18 | 18 | 15 | 0 | 0 | 0 | 0 | 3 | 0 | 0 | .000 | 0 | 5 | 0 | 0 | 1.0 | 1.000 |

Mark Schaeffer SCHAEFFER, MARK PHILIP B. June 5, 1948, Santa Monica, Calif. BL TL 6'5" 215 lbs.

| 1972 | SD N | 2 | 0 | 1.000 | 4.61 | 41 | 0 | 0 | 41 | 52 | 28 | 25 | 0 | 2 | 0 | 1 | 3 | 0 | 0 | .000 | 5 | 6 | 0 | 3 | 0.3 | 1.000 |

Joe Schaffernoth SCHAFFERNOTH, JOSEPH ARTHUR B. Aug. 6, 1937, Trenton, N. J. BR TR 6'4½" 195 lbs.

1959	CHI N	1	0	1.000	8.22	5	1	0	7.2	11	4	3	0	1	0	0	3	0	0	.000	0	1	0	0	0.2	1.000
1960		2	3	.400	2.78	33	0	0	55	46	17	33	0	2	3	3	7	2	0	.286	4	10	0	2	0.4	1.000
1961	2 teams					CHI N	(21G 0–4)			CLE A	(15G 0–1)																
"	total	0	5	.000	5.86	36	0	0	55.1	59	32	32	0	0	5	0	6	0	0	.000	1	14	1	0	0.4	.938
3 yrs.		3	8	.273	4.58	74	1	0	118	116	53	68	0	3	8	3	16	2	0	.125	5	25	1	2	0.4	.968

Art Schallock SCHALLOCK, ARTHUR LAWRENCE B. Apr. 25, 1924, Mill Valley, Calif. BL TL 5'9" 160 lbs.

1951	NY A	3	1	.750	3.88	11	6	1	46.1	50	20	19	0	0	0	0	17	5	0	.294	3	9	1	1	1.2	.923
1952		0	0	–	9.00	2	0	0	2	3	2	1	0	0	0	0	0	0	0	–	0	0	0	0	0.0	–
1953		0	0	–	2.95	7	1	0	21.1	30	15	13	0	0	0	0	6	2	0	.333	1	2	0	1	0.4	1.000
1954		0	1	.000	4.15	6	1	1	17.1	20	11	9	0	0	0	0	3	0	0	.000	0	1	0	0	0.2	1.000
1955	2 teams					NY A	(2G 0–0)			BAL A	(30G 3–5)																
"	total	3	5	.375	4.21	32	6	1	83.1	96	43	35	0	2	1	0	19	2	0	.105	11	8	2	0	0.7	.905
5 yrs.		6	7	.462	4.02	58	14	3	170.1	199	91	77	0	2	1	1	45	9	0	.200	15	20	3	2	0.7	.921

WORLD SERIES

| 1953 | NY A | 0 | 0 | – | 4.50 | 1 | 0 | 0 | 2 | 2 | 1 | 1 | 0 | 0 | 0 | 0 | 0 | 0 | 0 | – | 0 | 1 | 0 | 0 | 1.0 | 1.000 |

Charley Schanz SCHANZ, CHARLEY MURRELL B. June 8, 1919, Anacortes, Wash. BR TR 6'3½" 215 lbs.

1944	PHI N	13	16	.448	3.32	40	30	13	241.1	231	103	84	2	4	0	3	81	12	1	.148	10	47	5	4	1.6	.919
1945		4	15	.211	4.35	35	21	5	144.2	165	87	56	1	0	0	5	39	6	0	.154	4	34	6	1	1.2	.905
1946		6	6	.500	5.80	32	15	4	116.1	130	71	47	0	1	1	4	36	3	0	.083	4	28	3	0	1.1	.914
1947		2	4	.333	4.16	34	6	1	101.2	107	47	42	0	1	3	2	27	4	0	.148	5	19	1	0	0.7	.960
1950	BOS A	3	2	.600	8.34	14	0	0	22.2	25	24	14	0	3	2	0	11	1	0	.091	0	5	1	0	0.4	.833
5 yrs.		28	43	.394	4.34	155	72	23	626.2	658	332	243	3	9	6	14	194	26	1	.134	23	133	14	4	1.1	.918

Jack Schappert SCHAPPERT, JOHN B. Brooklyn, N. Y. D. July 29, 1916, Rockaway Beach, N. Y. BR TR 5'10" 170 lbs.

| 1882 | STL AA | 8 | 7 | .533 | 3.52 | 15 | 14 | 13 | 128 | 131 | 32 | 38 | 0 | 0 | 1 | 0 | 50 | 9 | 0 | .180 | 5 | 31 | 7 | 1 | 2.9 | .837 |

Bill Schardt SCHARDT, WILBURT (Big Bill) B. Jan. 20, 1886, Cleveland, Ohio D. July 20, 1964, Vermilion, Ohio BR TR 6'4" 210 lbs.

1911	BKN N	5	15	.250	3.59	39	22	10	195.1	190	91	77	1	2	0	4	59	10	0	.169	7	57	7	0	1.8	.901
1912		0	1	.000	4.35	7	0	0	20.2	25	6	7	0	0	1	1	6	0	0	.000	1	15	0	1	2.3	1.000
2 yrs.		5	16	.238	3.67	46	22	10	216	215	97	84	1	2	1	5	65	10	0	.154	8	72	7	1	1.9	.920

Jeff Schattinger SCHATTINGER, JEFFREY CHARLES B. Oct. 25, 1955, Fresno, Calif. BL TR 6'5" 200 lbs.

| 1981 | KC A | 0 | 0 | – | 0.00 | 1 | 0 | 0 | 3 | 2 | 1 | 1 | 0 | 0 | 0 | 0 | 0 | 0 | 0 | – | 0 | 0 | 0 | 0 | 0.0 | – |

Dan Schatzeder SCHATZEDER, DANIEL ERNEST B. Dec. 1, 1954, Elmhurst, Ill. BL TL 6' 185 lbs.

1977	MON N	2	1	.667	2.45	6	3	1	22	16	13	14	1	0	0	0	6	2	0	.333	1	3	0	0	0.7	1.000
1978		7	7	.500	3.06	29	18	2	144	108	68	69	0	2	0	0	45	10	1	.222	4	17	2	0	0.8	.913
1979		10	5	.667	2.83	32	21	3	162	136	59	106	0	1	1	1	51	11	1	.216	5	13	4	0	0.7	.818
1980	DET A	11	13	.458	4.01	32	26	9	193	178	58	94	2	2	0	0	0	0	0	–	7	21	3	3	1.0	.903
1981		6	8	.429	6.08	17	14	1	71	74	29	20	0	0	0	0	0	0	0	–	6	12	3	0	1.2	.857
1982	2 teams					SF N	(13G 1–4)			MON N	(26G 0–2)																
"	total	1	6	.143	5.32	39	4	0	69.1	84	24	33	0	1	3	0	13	3	0	.231	3	11	1	2	0.4	.933
1983	MON N	5	2	.714	3.21	58	2	0	87	88	25	48	0	4	1	2	10	2	0	.200	9	8	1	0	0.3	.944
1984		7	7	.500	2.71	36	14	1	136	112	36	89	1	1	1	1	35	11	0	.314	9	8	5	0	0.6	.773
1985		3	5	.375	3.80	24	15	1	104.1	101	31	64	0	0	0	0	31	6	2	.194	3	20	4	1	1.1	.852
1986	2 teams					MON N	(30G 3–2)			PHI N	(25G 3–3)																
"	total	6	5	.545	3.26	55	1	0	88.1	81	35	47	0	6	5	2	26	10	1	.385	3	9	0	0	0.2	1.000
1987	2 teams					PHI N	(26G 3–1)			MIN A	(30G 3–1)																
"	total	6	2	.750	5.31	56	1	0	81.1	104	32	58	0	6	2	0	12	2	0	.167	3	3	1	0	0.1	.857
1988	2 teams					CLE A	(15G 0–2)			MIN A	(10G 0–1)																
"	total	0	3	.000	6.49	25	0	0	26.1	34	7	17	0	0	3	0	–	2	9	2	1	0.4	.846			
1989	HOU N	4	1	.800	4.45	36	0	0	56.2	64	28	46	0	4	1	1	9	0	0	.000	2	9	2	1	0.4	.846
13 yrs.		68	65	.511	3.80	445	119	18	1241.1	1180	445	705	4	27	17	10	238	57	5	.239	58	135	26	7	0.5	.881

LEAGUE CHAMPIONSHIP SERIES

| 1987 | MIN A | 0 | 0 | – | 0.00 | 2 | 0 | 0 | 4.1 | 2 | 0 | 5 | 0 | 0 | 0 | 0 | 0 | 0 | 0 | – | 0 | 1 | 0 | 0 | 1.0 | 1.000 |

WORLD SERIES

| 1987 | MIN A | 1 | 0 | 1.000 | 6.23 | 3 | 0 | 0 | 4.1 | 4 | 3 | 3 | 0 | 1 | 0 | 0 | 0 | 0 | 0 | – | 0 | 0 | 0 | 0 | 0.0 | – |

Rube Schauer SCHAUER, ALEXANDER JOHN Born Dimitri Ivanovich Dimitrihoff. B. Mar. 19, 1891, Odessa, Russia D. Apr. 15, 1957, Minneapolis, Minn. BR TR 6'2" 192 lbs.

Year	Team		W	L	PCT	ERA	G	GS	CG	IP	H	BB	SO	ShO	Relief Pitching W	L	SV	Batting AB	H	HR	BA	PO	A	E	DP	TC/G	FA

Rube Schauer *continued*

Year	Team		W	L	PCT	ERA	G	GS	CG	IP	H	BB	SO	ShO	W	L	SV	AB	H	HR	BA	PO	A	E	DP	TC/G	FA
1913	NY	N	0	1	.000	7.50	3	1	1	12	14	9	7	0	0	0	0	3	0	0	.000	0	3	0		1.0	1.000
1914			0	0	–	3.22	6	0	0	22.1	16	8	6	0	0	0	0	7	1	0	.143	1	4	1	0	1.0	.833
1915			2	8	.200	3.50	32	7	4	105.1	101	35	65	0	2	3	0	26	2	0	.077	4	24	2	0	0.9	.933
1916			1	4	.200	2.96	19	3	1	45.2	44	16	24	0	1	2	0	9	2	0	.222	1	11	2	0	0.7	.857
1917	PHI	A	7	16	.304	3.14	33	21	10	215	209	69	62	0	3	2	1	76	11	0	.145	14	62	0	0	2.3	1.000
5 yrs.			10	29	.256	3.35	93	32	16	400.1	384	137	164	0	6	7	1	121	16	0	.132	20	104	5	0	1.4	.961

Owen Scheetz

SCHEETZ, OWEN FRANKLIN
B. Dec. 24, 1913, New Bedford, Ohio

BR TR 6' 190 lbs.

Year	Team		W	L	PCT	ERA	G	GS	CG	IP	H	BB	SO	ShO	W	L	SV	AB	H	HR	BA	PO	A	E	DP	TC/G	FA
1943	WAS	A	0	0	–	7.00	6	0	0	9	16	4	5	0	0	0	1	2	0	0	.000	0	3	0	0	0.5	1.000

Lefty Schegg

SCHEGG, GILBERT EUGENE
Born Gilbert Eugene Price.
B. Aug. 29, 1889, Leesville, Ohio D. Feb. 27, 1963, Niles, Ohio

BL TL 5'11" 180 lbs.

Year	Team		W	L	PCT	ERA	G	GS	CG	IP	H	BB	SO	ShO	W	L	SV	AB	H	HR	BA	PO	A	E	DP	TC/G	FA
1912	WAS	A	0	0	–	3.38	2	1	0	5.1	7	4	3	0	0	0	0	2	0	0	.000	0	0	2	0	1.0	–

Carl Scheib

SCHEIB, CARL ALVIN
B. Jan. 1, 1927, Gratz, Pa.

BR TR 6'1" 192 lbs.

Year	Team		W	L	PCT	ERA	G	GS	CG	IP	H	BB	SO	ShO	W	L	SV	AB	H	HR	BA	PO	A	E	DP	TC/G	FA
1943	PHI	A	0	1	.000	4.34	6	0	0	18.2	24	3	3	0	0	1	0	5	0	0	.000	1	1	0	0	0.3	1.000
1944			0	0	–	4.10	15	0	0	37.1	36	11	13	0	0	0	0	10	3	0	.300	0	13	0	0	0.9	1.000
1945			0	0	–	3.12	4	0	0	8.2	6	4	2	0	0	0	0	2	0	0	.000	1	2	0	0	0.8	1.000
1947			4	6	.400	5.04	21	12	6	116	121	55	26	2	1	0	0	45	6	0	.133	3	13	1	2	0.8	.941
1948			14	8	.636	3.94	32	24	15	198.2	219	76	44	1	3	1	0	104	31	2	.298	14	36	1	5	1.6	.980
1949			9	12	.429	5.12	38	23	11	182.2	191	118	43	2	2	2	0	72	17	0	.236	6	24	3	3	0.9	.909
1950			3	10	.231	7.22	43	8	1	106	138	70	37	0	1	9	9	52	13	1	.250	3	16	0	2	0.4	1.000
1951			1	12	.077	4.47	46	11	3	143	132	71	49	0	1	3	10	53	21	2	.396	14	43	1	3	1.3	.983
1952			11	7	.611	4.39	30	19	8	158	153	50	42	1	2	3	2	82	18	0	.220	19	26	2	3	1.6	.957
1953			3	7	.300	4.88	28	8	3	96	99	29	25	0	1	3	2	41	8	0	.195	4	16	1	1	0.8	.952
1954	2 teams		PHI A	(1G 0–1)		STL N	(3G 0–1)																					
"	total		0	2	.000	14.85	4	2	0	6.2	11	6	6	0	0	0	0	2	0	0	.000	1	1	0	0	0.5	1.000
11 yrs.			45	65	.409	4.88	267	107	47	1071.2	1130	493	290	6	11	22	17	*					66	191	9	19	1.0	.966

Frank Scheibeck

SCHEIBECK, FRANK S. (Archer)
B. June 28, 1865, Detroit, Mich. D. Oct. 22, 1956, Detroit, Mich.

BR TR 5'7" 145 lbs.

Year	Team		W	L	PCT	ERA	G	GS	CG	IP	H	BB	SO	ShO	W	L	SV	AB	H	HR	BA	PO	A	E	DP	TC/G	FA
1887	CLE	AA	0	1	.000	12.00	1	1	1	9	17	4	3	0	0	0	0	*				0	0	0	0	0.0	–

John Scheible

SCHEIBLE, JOHN G.
B. Feb. 16, 1866, Youngstown, Ohio D. Aug. 9, 1897, Youngstown, Ohio

TL

Year	Team		W	L	PCT	ERA	G	GS	CG	IP	H	BB	SO	ShO	W	L	SV	AB	H	HR	BA	PO	A	E	DP	TC/G	FA
1893	CLE	N	1	1	.500	2.00	2	2	2	18	15	11	1	1	0	0	0	7	1	0	.143	4	2	1	1	3.5	.857
1894	PHI	N	0	1	.000	189.00	1	1	0	.1	6	2	0	0	0	0	0	0	0	0	–	0	0	1	0	1.0	–
2 yrs.			1	2	.333	5.40	3	3	2	18.1	21	13	1	1	0	0	0	7	1	0	.143	4	2	2	1	2.7	.750

Jim Schelle

SCHELLE, GERARD ANTHONY
B. Apr. 13, 1917, Baltimore, Md.

BR TR 6'3" 190 lbs.

Year	Team		W	L	PCT	ERA	G	GS	CG	IP	H	BB	SO	ShO	W	L	SV	AB	H	HR	BA	PO	A	E	DP	TC/G	FA
1939	PHI	A	0	0	–	∞	1	0	0		1	3	0	0	0	0	0	0	0	0	–	0	0	0	0	0.0	–

Fred Schemanske

SCHEMANSKE, FREDERICK GEORGE (Buck)
B. Apr. 28, 1903, Detroit, Mich. D. Feb. 18, 1960, Detroit, Mich.

BR TR 6'2" 190 lbs.

Year	Team		W	L	PCT	ERA	G	GS	CG	IP	H	BB	SO	ShO	W	L	SV	AB	H	HR	BA	PO	A	E	DP	TC/G	FA
1923	WAS	A	0	0	–	27.00	1	0	0	1	3	0	0	0	0	0	0	2	2	0	1.000	0	0	0	0	0.0	–

Bill Schenck

SCHENCK, WILLIAM G.
B. Brooklyn, N. Y. Deceased.

5'7" 171 lbs.

Year	Team		W	L	PCT	ERA	G	GS	CG	IP	H	BB	SO	ShO	W	L	SV	AB	H	HR	BA	PO	A	E	DP	TC/G	FA
1882	LOU	AA	1	0	1.000	0.90	2	1	1	10	6	1	4	0	0	0	0	*				0	0	0	0	0.5	1.000

John Scheneberg

SCHENEBERG, JOHN BLUFORD
B. Nov. 20, 1887, Guyandotte, W. Va. D. Sept. 26, 1950, Huntington, W. Va.

BB TR 6'1" 180 lbs.

Year	Team		W	L	PCT	ERA	G	GS	CG	IP	H	BB	SO	ShO	W	L	SV	AB	H	HR	BA	PO	A	E	DP	TC/G	FA
1913	PIT	N	0	1	.000	6.00	1	1	0	6	10	2	1	0	0	0	0	2	1	0	.500	1	3	1	0	5.0	.800
1920	STL	A	0	0	–	27.00	1	0	0	2	7	1	0	0	0	0	0	0	0	0	–	0	0	0	0	0.0	–
2 yrs.			0	1	.000	11.25	2	1	0	8	17	3	1	0	0	0	0	2	1	0	.500	1	3	1	0	2.5	.800

Fred Scherman

SCHERMAN, FREDERICK JOHN
B. July 25, 1944, Dayton, Ohio

BL TL 6'1" 195 lbs.

Year	Team		W	L	PCT	ERA	G	GS	CG	IP	H	BB	SO	ShO	W	L	SV	AB	H	HR	BA	PO	A	E	DP	TC/G	FA
1969	DET	A	1	0	1.000	6.75	4	0	0	4	6	0	3	0	1	0	0	0	0	0	–	0	1	0	0	0.3	1.000
1970			4	4	.500	3.21	48	0	0	70	61	28	58	0	4	4	1	12	2	0	.167	8	7	1	2	0.3	.938
1971			11	6	.647	2.71	69	1	1	113	91	49	46	0	10	6	20	24	5	0	.208	7	23	0	1	0.4	1.000
1972			7	3	.700	3.64	57	3	0	94	91	53	53	0	7	1	12	22	2	0	.091	5	12	2	1	0.3	.895
1973			2	2	.500	4.21	34	0	0	62	59	30	28	0	2	2	1	0	0	0	–	2	5	0	0	0.2	1.000
1974	HOU	N	2	5	.286	4.13	53	0	0	61	67	26	35	0	2	5	4	3	0	0	.000	6	7	1	0	0.3	.929
1975	2 teams		HOU N	(16G 0–1)		MON N	(34G 4–3)																					
"	total		4	4	.500	3.79	50	7	0	92.2	105	45	56	0	4	4	0	17	1	0	.059	5	16	0	2	0.4	1.000
1976	MON	N	2	2	.500	4.95	31	0	0	40	42	14	18	0	2	2	1	4	1	0	.250	2	4	0	0	0.2	1.000
8 yrs.			33	26	.559	3.66	346	11	1	536.2	522	245	297	0	32	21	39	82	11	0	.134	35	75	4	6	0.3	.965

LEAGUE CHAMPIONSHIP SERIES

Year	Team		W	L	PCT	ERA	G	GS	CG	IP	H	BB	SO	ShO	W	L	SV	AB	H	HR	BA	PO	A	E	DP	TC/G	FA
1972	DET	A	0	0	–	0.00	1	0	0	.2	1	0	1	0	0	0	0	0	0	0	–	0	0	0	0	0.0	–

Year	Team	W	L	PCT	ERA	G	GS	CG	IP	H	BB	SO	ShO	W	L	SV	AB	H	HR	BA	PO	A	E	DP	TC/G	FA
														Relief Pitching			Batting									

Bill Scherrer

SCHERRER, WILLIAM JOSEPH
B. Jan. 20, 1958, Tonawanda, N. Y.   BL TL 6'4"   180 lbs.

Year	Team	W	L	PCT	ERA	G	GS	CG	IP	H	BB	SO	ShO	W	L	SV	AB	H	HR	BA	PO	A	E	DP	TC/G	FA
1982	CIN N	0	1	.000	2.60	5	2	0	17.1	17	0	7	0	0	0	0	2	1	0	.500	0	3	1	0	0.8	.750
1983		2	3	.400	2.74	73	0	0	92	73	33	57	0	2	3	10	11	1	0	.091	2	18	0	1	0.3	1.000
1984	2 teams			CIN N	(36G 1–1)				DET A	(18G 1–0)																
"	total	2	1	.667	4.16	54	0	0	71.1	78	23	51	0	2	1	1	3	0	0	.000	1	13	1	0	0.3	.933
1985	DET A	3	2	.600	4.36	48	0	0	66	62	41	46	0	3	2	0	0	0	0	–	7	11	2	2	0.4	.900
1986	CIN N	0	1	.000	7.29	13	0	0	21	19	22	16	0	0	1	0	0	0	0	–	1	3	0	0	0.3	1.000
1987	CIN N	1	1	.500	4.36	23	0	0	33	43	16	24	0	1	1	0	0	0	0	.000	3	3	0	0	0.3	1.000
1988	2 teams			BAL A	(4G 0–1)				PHI N	(8G 0–0)																
"	total	0	1	.000	8.44	12	0	0	10.2	15	5	6	0	0	1	0	0	0	0	–	0	1	0	1	0.1	1.000
7 yrs.		8	10	.444	4.08	228	2	0	311.1	307	140	207	0	8	9	11	17	2	0	.118	14	52	4	4	0.3	.943

WORLD SERIES

1984	DET A	0	0	–	3.00	3	0	0	3	5	0	0	0	0	0	0	0	0	0	–	0	2	0	0	0.7	1.000

Dutch Schesler

SCHESLER, CHARLES
B. June 1, 1900, Frankfurt, Germany   D. Nov. 19, 1953, Harrisburg, Pa.   BR TR 6'2"   180 lbs.

1931	PHI N	0	0	–	7.28	17	0	0	38.1	65	18	14	0	0	0	0	9	1	0	.111	0	11	1	0	0.7	.917

Lou Schettler

SCHETTLER, LOUIS MARTIN
B. June 12, 1886, Pittsburgh, Pa.   D. May 1, 1960, Youngstown, Ohio   BR TR 5'11"   160 lbs.

1910	PHI N	2	6	.250	3.20	27	7	3	107	96	51	62	0	1	2	1	41	7	0	.171	4	24	5	0	1.2	.848

Curt Schilling

SCHILLING, CURTIS MONTAGUE
B. Nov. 14, 1966, Anchorage, Alaska   BR TR 6'5"   205 lbs.

1988	BAL A	0	3	.000	9.82	4	4	0	14.2	22	10	4	0	0	0	0	0	0	0	–	0	0	1	0	0.3	–
1989		0	1	.000	6.23	5	1	0	8.2	10	3	6	0	0	0	0	0	0	0	–	1	0	0	0	0.2	1.000
2 yrs.		0	4	.000	8.49	9	5	0	23.1	32	13	10	0	0	0	0	0	0	0	–	1	0	1	0	0.2	.500

Red Schillings

SCHILLINGS, ELBERT ISAIAH
B. Mar. 29, 1900, Deport, Tex.   D. Jan. 7, 1954, Oklahoma City, Okla.   BR TR 5'10"   180 lbs.

1922	PHI A	0	0	–	6.75	4	0	0	8	10	11	4	0	0	0	0	2	0	0	.000	0	1	0	0	0.3	1.000

Calvin Schiraldi

SCHIRALDI, CALVIN DREW
B. June 16, 1962, Houston, Tex.   BR TR 6'5"   215 lbs.

Year	Team	W	L	PCT	ERA	G	GS	CG	IP	H	BB	SO	ShO	W	L	SV	AB	H	HR	BA	PO	A	E	DP	TC/G	FA
1984	NY N	0	2	.000	5.71	5	3	0	17.1	20	10	16	0	0	0	0	3	0	0	.000	0	3	0	1	0.6	1.000
1985		2	1	.667	8.89	10	4	0	26.1	43	11	21	0	0	0	0	8	1	0	.125	2	3	0	2	0.5	1.000
1986	BOS A	4	2	.667	1.41	25	0	0	51	36	15	55	0	4	2	9	0	0	0	–	2	3	0	0	0.2	1.000
1987		8	5	.615	4.41	62	1	0	83.2	75	40	93	0	8	5	6	0	0	0	–	3	10	1	0	0.2	.929
1988	CHI N	9	13	.409	4.38	29	27	2	166.1	166	63	140	1	0	0	1	60	6	0	.100	13	12	4	0	1.0	.862
1989	2 teams			CHI N	(54G 3–6)				SD N	(5G 3–1)																
"	total	6	7	.462	3.51	59	4	0	100	72	63	71	0	3	7	4	16	1	1	.063	9	5	0	0	0.2	1.000
6 yrs.		29	30	.492	4.17	190	39	2	444.2	412	202	396	1	15	14	20	87	8	1	.092	29	36	5	3	0.4	.929

LEAGUE CHAMPIONSHIP SERIES

1986	BOS A	0	1	.000	1.50	4	0	0	6	5	3	9	0	0	1	1	0	0	0	–	0	0	0	0	0.0	–

WORLD SERIES

1986	BOS A	0	2	.000	13.50	3	0	0	4	7	3	2	0	0	2	1	1	0	0	.000	0	1	0	0	0.3	1.000
												2nd														

Biff Schlitzer

SCHLITZER, VICTOR JOSEPH
B. Dec. 4, 1884, Rochester, N. Y.   D. Jan. 4, 1948, Wellesley Hills, Mass.   BR TR 5'11"   175 lbs.

1908	PHI A	6	8	.429	3.16	24	18	11	131	110	45	57	2	0	0	0	46	9	0	.196	2	31	1	0	1.4	.971
1909	2 teams			PHI A	(4G 0–3)				BOS A	(13G 4–4)																
"	total	4	7	.364	3.54	17	11	5	89	94	26	30	0	1	1	1	33	6	0	.182	6	37	6	0	2.9	.878
1914	BUF F	0	0	–	16.20	3	0	0	3.1	7	2	1	0	0	0	0	1	1	0	1.000	0	1	0	0	0.3	1.000
3 yrs.		10	15	.400	3.51	44	29	16	223.1	211	73	88	2	1	1	1	80	16	0	.200	8	69	7	0	1.9	.917

George Schmees

SCHMEES, GEORGE EDWARD (Rocky)
B. Sept. 6, 1924, Cincinnati, Ohio   BL TL 6'   190 lbs.

1952	BOS A	0	0	–	3.00	2	1	0	6	9	2	2	0	0	0	0	*				0	4	0	1	2.0	1.000

Al Schmelz

SCHMELZ, ALAN GEORGE
B. Nov. 12, 1943, Whittier, Calif.   BR TR 6'4"   210 lbs.

1967	NY N	0	0	–	3.00	2	0	0	3	4	1	2	0	0	0	0	0	0	0	–	1	1	0	1	1.0	1.000

Butch Schmidt

SCHMIDT, CHARLES JOHN
B. July 19, 1886, Baltimore, Md.   D. Sept. 4, 1952, Baltimore, Md.   BL TL 6'1½"   200 lbs.

1909	NY A	0	0	–	7.20	1	0	0	5	10	1	2	0	0	0	0	*				1	0	1	0	2.0	.500

Dave Schmidt

SCHMIDT, DAVID JOSEPH
B. Apr. 22, 1957, Niles, Mich.   BR TR 6'1"   185 lbs.

Year	Team	W	L	PCT	ERA	G	GS	CG	IP	H	BB	SO	ShO	W	L	SV	AB	H	HR	BA	PO	A	E	DP	TC/G	FA
1981	TEX A	0	1	.000	3.09	14	1	0	32	31	11	13	0	0	1	0	0	0	0	–	1	6	0	0	0.5	1.000
1982		4	6	.400	3.20	33	8	0	109.2	118	25	69	0	3	1	6	0	0	0	–	2	16	2	2	0.6	.900
1983		3	3	.500	3.88	31	0	0	46.1	42	14	29	0	3	3	2	0	0	0	–	6	4	0	1	0.3	1.000
1984		6	6	.500	2.56	43	0	0	70.1	69	20	46	0	6	6	12	0	0	0	–	6	13	1	2	0.5	.950
1985		7	6	.538	3.15	51	4	1	85.2	81	22	46	1	5	4	5	0	0	0	–	3	19	3	3	0.5	.880
1986	CHI A	3	6	.333	3.31	49	1	0	92.1	94	27	67	0	3	5	8	0	0	0	–	7	7	3	0	0.3	.824
1987	BAL A	10	5	.667	3.77	35	14	2	124	128	26	70	2	6	1	1	0	0	0	–	6	14	1	2	0.6	.952

Year	Team		W	L	PCT	ERA	G	GS	CG	IP	H	BB	SO	ShO	Relief Pitching W	L	SV	Batting AB	H	HR	BA	PO	A	E	DP	TC/G	FA

Dave Schmidt *continued*

1988			8	5	.615	3.40	41	9	0	129.2	129	38	67	0	3	3	2	0	0	0	–	18	20	1	2	1.0	.974
1989			10	13	.435	5.69	38	26	2	156.2	196	36	46	0	1	0	0	0	0	0	–	18	28	3	2	1.3	.939
9 yrs.			51	51	.500	3.76	335	63	5	846.2	888	219	453	3	30	23	37	0	0	0	–	67	127	14	14	0.6	.933

Freddy Schmidt SCHMIDT, FREDERICK ALBERT BR TR 6'1" 185 lbs.
B. Feb. 9, 1916, Hartford, Conn.

1944	STL	N	7	3	.700	3.15	37	9	3	114.1	94	58	58	2	3	0	5	34	7	0	.206	3	17	0	2	0.5	1.000
1946			1	0	1.000	3.29	16	0	0	27.1	27	15	14	0	1	0	0	1	0	0	.000	1	7	0	0	0.5	1.000
1947	3 teams		STL N	(2G 0–0)		PHI N	(29G 5–8)			CHI N	(1G 0–0)																
"	total		5	8	.385	4.73	32	6	0	83.2	85	49	26	0	5	4	0	22	1	0	.045	1	13	1	1	0.5	.933
3 yrs.			13	11	.542	3.75	85	15	3	225.1	206	122	98	2	9	4	5	57	8	0	.140	5	37	1	3	0.5	.977

WORLD SERIES

| 1944 | STL | N | 0 | 0 | – | 0.00 | 1 | 0 | 0 | 3.1 | 1 | 1 | 1 | 0 | 0 | 0 | 0 | 1 | 0 | 0 | .000 | 0 | 0 | 0 | 0 | 0.0 | – |

Henry Schmidt SCHMIDT, HENRY MARTIN BR TR 5'11" 170 lbs.
B. June 26, 1873, Brownsville, Tex. D. Apr. 23, 1926, Nashville, Tenn.

| 1903 | BKN | N | 21 | 13 | .618 | 3.83 | 40 | 36 | 29 | 301 | 321 | 120 | 96 | 5 | 1 | 0 | 2 | 107 | 21 | 1 | .196 | 14 | 109 | 4 | 5 | 3.2 | .969 |

Pete Schmidt SCHMIDT, FREDERICH CHRISTOPH HERMAN BR TR 5'11" 175 lbs.
B. July 23, 1890, Lowden, Iowa D. Mar. 11, 1973, Pembroke, Ont., Canada

| 1913 | STL | A | 0 | 0 | – | 4.50 | 1 | 0 | 0 | 2 | 3 | 2 | 0 | 0 | 0 | 0 | 0 | 0 | 0 | 0 | – | 0 | 0 | 0 | 0 | 0.0 | – |

Willard Schmidt SCHMIDT, WILLARD RAYMOND BR TR 6'1" 187 lbs.
B. May 29, 1928, Hays, Kans.

1952	STL	N	2	3	.400	5.19	18	3	0	34.2	36	18	30	0	1	1	1	8	1	0	.125	2	11	1	0	0.8	.929
1953			0	2	.000	9.17	6	2	0	17.2	21	13	11	0	0	0	0	4	0	0	.000	2	2	0	0	0.7	1.000
1955			7	6	.538	2.78	20	15	8	129.2	89	57	86	1	0	0	0	42	5	0	.119	12	20	2	5	1.7	.941
1956			6	8	.429	3.84	33	21	2	147.2	131	78	52	0	0	0	0	43	10	0	.233	6	34	0	3	1.2	1.000
1957			10	3	.769	4.78	40	8	1	116.2	146	49	63	0	5	3	0	33	7	0	.212	8	22	1	1	0.8	.968
1958	CIN	N	3	5	.375	2.86	41	2	0	69.1	60	33	41	0	3	5	0	11	1	0	.091	5	17	2	0	0.6	.917
1959			3	2	.600	3.95	36	4	0	70.2	80	30	40	0	2	0	0	12	1	0	.083	5	16	0	2	0.6	1.000
7 yrs.			31	29	.517	3.93	194	55	11	586.1	563	278	323	1	11	9	2	153	25	0	.163	40	122	6	11	0.9	.964

Crazy Schmit SCHMIT, FREDERICK M. (Germany) BL TL 5'10½" 165 lbs.
B. Feb. 13, 1866, Chicago, Ill. D. Oct. 5, 1940, Chicago, Ill.

1890	PIT	N	1	9	.100	5.83	11	10	9	83.1	108	42	35	1	0	1	0	33	2	0	.061	2	16	5	1	2.1	.783
1892	BAL	N	1	4	.200	3.23	6	6	6	47.1	37	26	17	0	0	0	0	19	2	0	.105	0	15	1	0	2.7	.938
1893	2 teams		BAL N	(9G 3–2)		NY N	(4G 0–2)																				
"	total		3	4	.429	6.85	13	10	5	69.2	97	39	15	0	0	0	0	30	9	0	.300	0	14	3	0	1.3	.824
1899	CLE	N	2	17	.105	5.86	20	19	16	138.1	197	62	24	0	0	0	0	70	11	0	.157	7	43	6	0	2.8	.893
1901	BAL	A	0	2	.000	1.99	4	3	1	22.2	25	16	2	0	0	0	0	9	2	0	.222	0	11	0	0	2.8	1.000
5 yrs.			7	36	.163	5.45	54	48	37	361.1	464	185	93	1	0	1	0	161	26	0	.161	9	99	15	1	2.3	.878

Johnny Schmitz SCHMITZ, JOHN ALBERT (Bear Tracks) BR TL 6' 170 lbs.
B. Nov. 27, 1920, Wausau, Wis.

1941	CHI	N	2	0	1.000	1.31	5	3	1	20.2	12	9	11	0	1	0	0	7	4	0	.571	0	10	0	1	2.0	1.000
1942			3	7	.300	3.43	23	10	1	86.2	70	45	51	0	1	0	2	26	4	0	.154	5	38	1	2	1.9	.977
1946			11	11	.500	2.61	41	31	14	224.1	184	94	135	3	1	1	2	70	9	1	.129	12	49	0	2	1.5	1.000
1947			13	18	.419	3.22	38	28	10	207	209	80	97	3	1	3	4	68	9	0	.132	12	45	2	2	1.6	.966
1948			18	13	.581	2.64	34	30	18	242	186	97	100	2	3	0	1	84	11	0	.131	17	68	4	3	2.6	.955
1949			11	13	.458	4.35	36	31	9	207	227	92	75	3	1	1	3	70	10	0	.143	13	59	4	8	2.1	.947
1950			10	16	.385	4.99	39	27	8	193	217	91	75	3	0	1	0	67	8	0	.119	14	61	6	5	2.1	.926
1951	2 teams		CHI N	(8G 1–2)		BKN N	(16G 1–4)																				
"	total		2	6	.250	5.99	24	10	0	73.2	77	43	26	0	0	2	0	24	5	1	.208	8	23	0	2	1.3	1.000
1952	3 teams		BKN N	(10G 1–1)		NY N	(5G 1–1)			CIN N	(3G 1–0)																
"	total		3	2	.600	3.71	18	5	2	53.1	47	30	17	0	1	1	1	13	4	0	.308	3	18	0	1	1.2	1.000
1953	2 teams		NY A	(3G 0–0)		WAS A	(24G 2–7)																				
"	total		2	7	.222	3.62	27	13	5	112	120	40	39	0	1	1	4	34	2	0	.059	5	22	3	4	1.1	.900
1954	WAS	A	11	8	.579	2.91	29	23	12	185.1	176	64	56	2	0	1	1	60	7	0	.117	12	40	2	9	1.9	.963
1955			7	10	.412	3.71	32	21	6	165	187	54	49	1	0	0	1	54	10	0	.185	8	40	0	3	1.5	1.000
1956	2 teams		BOS A	(2G 0–0)		BAL A	(18G 0–3)																				
"	total		0	3	.000	3.59	20	3	0	42.2	54	18	15	0	0	0	0	10	0	0	.000	4	10	1	1	0.8	.933
13 yrs.			93	114	.449	3.55	366	235	86	1812.2	1766	757	746	17	11	12	19	587	83	2	.141	113	483	23	43	1.7	.963

Charlie Schmutz SCHMUTZ, CHARLES OTTO (King) BR TR 6'1½" 195 lbs.
B. Jan. 1, 1890, San Diego, Calif. D. June 27, 1962, Seattle, Wash.

1914	BKN	N	1	3	.250	3.30	18	5	1	57.1	57	13	21	0	1	0	1	16	3	0	.188	2	15	1	2	1.0	.944
1915			0	0	–	6.75	1	0	0	4	7	1	1	0	0	0	0	1	0	0	.000	0	3	0	0	3.0	1.000
2 yrs.			1	3	.250	3.52	19	5	1	61.1	64	14	22	0	1	0	1	17	3	0	.176	2	18	1	2	1.1	.952

Frank Schneiberg SCHNEIBERG, FRANK FREDERICK TR
B. Mar. 12, 1882, Milwaukee, Wis. D. May 18, 1948, Milwaukee, Wis.

| 1910 | BKN | N | 0 | 0 | – | 63.00 | 1 | 0 | 0 | 1 | 5 | 4 | 0 | 0 | 0 | 0 | 0 | 0 | 0 | 0 | – | 0 | 0 | 0 | 0 | 0.0 | – |

Dan Schneider SCHNEIDER, DANIEL LOUIS BL TL 6'3" 170 lbs.
B. Aug. 29, 1942, Evansville, Ind.

1963	MIL	N	1	0	1.000	3.09	30	0	0	43.2	36	20	19	0	0	0	0	7	0	0	.000	4	3	1	0	0.3	.875
1964			1	2	.333	5.45	13	5	0	36.1	38	13	14	0	1	1	0	8	0	0	.000	3	11	0	0	1.1	1.000
1966	ATL	N	0	0	–	3.42	14	0	0	26.1	35	5	11	0	0	0	0	8	4	0	.500	0	4	1	0	0.4	.800

Year	Team		W	L	PCT	ERA	G	GS	CG	IP	H	BB	SO	ShO	Relief Pitching W	L	SV	Batting AB	H	HR	BA	PO	A	E	DP	TC/G	FA

Dan Schneider *continued*

1967	HOU	N	0	2	.000	4.96	54	0	0	52.2	60	27	39	0	0	2	2	5	1	0	.200	4	14	0	1	0.3	1.000
1969			0	1	.000	14.14	6	0	0	7	16	5	3	0	0	1	0	1	0	0	.000	0	3	1	0	0.7	.750
5 yrs.			2	5	.286	4.72	117	8	0	166	185	70	86	0	1	4	2	29	5	0	.172	11	35	3	1	0.4	.939

Jeff Schneider

SCHNEIDER, JEFFREY THEODORE
B. Dec. 6, 1952, Bremerton, Wash.   BB TL 6'3"   195 lbs.

| 1981 | BAL | A | 0 | 0 | – | 4.88 | 11 | 0 | 0 | 24 | 27 | 12 | 17 | 0 | 0 | 0 | 1 | 0 | 0 | 0 | – | 2 | 2 | 2 | 0 | 0.5 | .667 |

Pete Schneider

SCHNEIDER, PETER JOSEPH
B. Aug. 20, 1895, Los Angeles, Calif.   D. June 1, 1957, Los Angeles, Calif.   BR TR 6'1"   194 lbs.

1914	CIN	N	5	13	.278	2.81	29	20	11	144.1	143	56	62	1	1	3	1	45	8	1	.178	6	32	4	4	1.4	.905
1915			13	19	.406	2.48	48	35	16	275.2	254	104	108	5	2	0	2	94	23	2	.245	7	75	8	3	1.9	.911
1916			10	19	.345	2.69	44	31	16	274.1	259	82	117	3	2	2	1	89	21	0	.236	4	63	3	0	1.6	.957
1917			20	19	.513	1.98	46	42	25	341.2	316	119	142	0	1	0	0	114	19	1	.167	14	67	3	4	1.8	.964
1918			10	15	.400	3.51	33	30	17	217.2	213	117	51	2	0	0	0	83	24	1	.289	4	54	6	1	1.9	.906
1919	NY	A	0	1	.000	3.41	7	4	0	29	19	22	11	0	0	0	0	9	1	0	.111	0	5	2	0	1.0	.714
6 yrs.			58	86	.403	2.62	207	162	85	1282.2	1204	500	491	11	6	5	4	434	96	5	.221	35	296	26	12	1.7	.927

Karl Schnell

SCHNELL, KARL OTTO
B. Sept. 20, 1899, Los Angeles, Calif.   BR TR 6'1"   176 lbs.

1922	CIN	N	0	0	–	2.70	10	0	0	20	21	18	5	0	0	0	0	4	1	0	.250	0	6	1	0	0.7	.857
1923			0	0	–	36.00	1	0	0	1	2	2	0	0	0	0	0	0	0	0	–	0	0	0	0	0.0	–
2 yrs.			0	0	–	4.29	11	0	0	21	23	20	5	0	0	0	0	4	1	0	.250	0	6	1	0	0.6	.857

Gerry Schoen

SCHOEN, GERALD THOMAS
B. Jan. 15, 1947, New Orleans, La.   BR TR 6'3"   215 lbs.

| 1968 | WAS | A | 0 | 1 | .000 | 7.36 | 1 | 1 | 0 | 3.2 | 6 | 1 | 1 | 0 | 0 | 0 | 0 | 1 | 0 | 0 | .000 | 0 | 0 | 0 | 0 | 0.0 | – |

Jumbo Schoeneck

SCHOENECK, LEWIS W. (Lon)
B. Mar. 3, 1862, Chicago, Ill.   D. Jan. 20, 1930, Chicago, Ill.   BR TR 6'2"   223 lbs.

| 1888 | IND | N | 0 | 0 | – | 0.00 | 2 | 0 | 0 | 4.1 | 5 | 1 | 1 | 0 | 0 | 0 | 0 | * | | | | 0 | 0 | 0 | 0 | 0.0 | – |

Mike Schooler

SCHOOLER, MICHAEL RALPH
B. Aug. 10, 1962, Anaheim, Calif.   BR TR 6'3"   220 lbs.

1988	SEA	A	5	8	.385	3.54	40	0	0	48.1	45	24	54	0	5	8	15	0	0	0	–	2	4	0	0	0.2	1.000
1989			1	7	.125	2.81	67	0	0	77	81	19	69	0	1	7	33	0	0	0	–	4	14	0	3	0.3	1.000
2 yrs.			6	15	.286	3.09	107	0	0	125.1	126	43	123	0	6	15	48	0	0	0	–	6	18	0	3	0.2	1.000

Ed Schorr

SCHORR, EDWARD WALTER
B. Feb. 14, 1891, Bremen, Ohio   D. Sept. 12, 1969, Atlantic City, N. J.   BR TR 6'2½"   180 lbs.

| 1915 | CHI | N | 0 | 0 | – | 7.50 | 2 | 0 | 0 | 6 | 9 | 5 | 3 | 0 | 0 | 0 | 0 | 2 | 1 | 0 | .500 | 1 | 1 | 0 | 0 | 1.0 | 1.000 |

Gene Schott

SCHOTT, EUGENE ARTHUR
B. July 14, 1913, Batavia, Ohio   BR TR 6'2"   185 lbs.

1935	CIN	N	8	11	.421	3.91	33	19	9	159	153	64	49	1	0	1	0	60	12	0	.200	6	49	2	0	1.7	.965
1936			11	11	.500	3.80	31	22	8	180	184	73	65	0	3	1	1	60	18	1	.300	10	44	3	3	1.8	.947
1937			4	13	.235	2.97	37	17	7	154.1	150	48	56	2	0	3	1	49	7	0	.143	9	40	2	1	1.4	.961
1938			5	5	.500	4.45	31	4	0	83	89	32	21	0	4	3	2	24	3	0	.125	5	21	0	2	0.8	1.000
1939	2 teams				PHI N	(4G 0–1)				BKN N	(0G 0–0)																
"	total		0	1	.000	4.91	4	0	0	11	14	5	1	0	0	1	0	6	2	0	.333	1	0	1	0	0.5	.500
5 yrs.			28	41	.406	3.72	136	62	24	587.1	590	222	192	3	7	9	4	199	42	1	.211	31	154	8	6	1.4	.959

Barney Schreiber

SCHREIBER, DAVID HENRY
B. May 8, 1882, Waverly, Ohio   D. Oct. 6, 1964, Chillicothe, Ohio   BL TL 6'   185 lbs.

| 1911 | CIN | N | 0 | 0 | – | 5.40 | 3 | 0 | 0 | 10 | 19 | 2 | 5 | 0 | 0 | 0 | 0 | 3 | 0 | 0 | .000 | 0 | 1 | 0 | 0 | 0.3 | 1.000 |

Paul Schreiber

SCHREIBER, PAUL FREDERICK (Von)
B. Oct. 8, 1902, Jacksonville, Fla.   D. Jan. 28, 1982, Sarasota, Fla.   BR TR 6'2"   180 lbs.

1922	BKN	N	0	0	–	0.00	1	0	0	1	2	0	0	0	0	0	0	0	0	0	–	1	1	0	0	2.0	1.000
1923			0	0	–	4.20	9	0	0	15	16	8	4	0	0	0	1	2	0	0	.000	0	3	1	0	0.4	.750
1945	NY	A	0	0	–	4.15	2	0	0	4.1	4	2	1	0	0	0	0	1	0	0	.000	0	4	0	1	2.0	1.000
3 yrs.			0	0	–	3.98	12	0	0	20.1	22	10	5	0	0	0	1	3	0	0	.000	1	8	1	1	0.8	.900

Al Schroll

SCHROLL, ALBERT BRINGHURST (Bull)
B. Mar. 22, 1932, New Orleans, La.   BR TR 6'2"   210 lbs.

1958	BOS	A	0	0	–	4.50	5	0	0	10	6	4	7	0	0	0	0	1	1	0	1.000	0	3	0	0	0.6	1.000
1959	2 teams				PHI N	(3G 1–1)				BOS A	(14G 1–4)																
"	total		2	5	.286	5.37	17	5	1	55.1	59	28	30	0	1	2	0	13	2	0	.154	0	9	1	0	0.6	.900
1960	CHI	N	0	0	–	10.13	2	0	0	2.2	3	5	2	0	0	0	0	1	1	0	1.000	0	0	0	0	0.0	–
1961	MIN	A	4	4	.500	5.22	11	8	2	50	53	27	24	0	1	0	0	18	5	1	.278	2	8	0	0	0.9	1.000
4 yrs.			6	9	.400	5.34	35	13	3	118	121	64	63	0	2	2	0	33	9	1	.273	2	20	1	0	0.7	.957

Ken Schrom

SCHROM, KENNETH MARVIN
B. Nov. 23, 1954, Grangeville, Ida.   BR TR 6'2"   195 lbs.

1980	TOR	A	1	0	1.000	5.23	17	0	0	31	32	19	13	0	1	0	1	0	0	0	–	3	6	0	0	0.5	1.000
1982			1	0	1.000	5.87	6	0	0	15.1	13	8	8	0	1	0	0	0	0	0	–	0	0	0	0	0.0	–
1983	MIN	A	15	8	.652	3.71	33	28	6	196.1	196	80	80	1	1	0	0	0	0	0	–	8	15	2	1	0.8	.920
1984			5	11	.313	4.47	25	21	3	137	156	41	49	0	0	0	0	0	0	0	–	8	9	1	0	0.7	.944

Year	Team		W	L	PCT	ERA	G	GS	CG	IP	H	BB	SO	ShO	Relief Pitching W	L	SV	Batting AB	H	HR	BA	PO	A	E	DP	TC/G	FA

Ken Schrom *continued*

Year	Team		W	L	PCT	ERA	G	GS	CG	IP	H	BB	SO	ShO	W	L	SV	AB	H	HR	BA	PO	A	E	DP	TC/G	FA
1985			9	12	.429	4.99	29	26	6	160.2	164	59	74	0	0	0	0	0	0	0	–	23	20	3	3	1.6	.935
1986	CLE	A	14	7	.667	4.54	34	33	3	206	217	49	87	1	0	0	0	0	0	0	–	16	15	4	1	1.0	.886
1987			6	13	.316	6.50	32	29	4	153.2	185	57	61	1	0	0	0	0	0	0	–	11	13	1	1	0.8	.960
7 yrs.			51	51	.500	4.81	176	137	22	900	963	320	372	3	3	0	1	0	0	0	–	69	78	11	6	0.9	.930

Ron Schueler

SCHUELER, RONALD RICHARD
B. Apr. 18, 1948, Catherine, Kans.   BR TR 6'4"   205 lbs.

Year	Team		W	L	PCT	ERA	G	GS	CG	IP	H	BB	SO	ShO	W	L	SV	AB	H	HR	BA	PO	A	E	DP	TC/G	FA
1972	ATL	N	5	8	.385	3.66	37	18	3	145	122	60	96	0	3	0	1	42	8	0	.190	14	11	0	1	0.7	1.000
1973			8	7	.533	3.86	39	20	4	186.1	179	66	124	2	2	3	2	62	11	0	.177	11	23	1	1	0.9	.971
1974	PHI	N	11	16	.407	3.72	44	27	5	203	202	98	109	0	4	2	1	51	6	0	.118	16	18	3	0	0.8	.919
1975			4	4	.500	5.23	46	6	1	93	88	40	69	0	2	1	0	13	2	0	.154	11	14	2	3	0.6	.926
1976			1	0	1.000	2.90	35	0	0	49.2	44	16	43	0	1	0	3	2	0	0	.000	2	5	1	0	0.2	.875
1977	MIN	A	8	7	.533	4.40	52	7	0	135	131	61	77	0	7	6	3	0	0	0	–	11	26	0	1	0.7	1.000
1978	CHI	A	3	5	.375	4.30	30	7	0	81.2	76	39	39	0	1	1	0	0	0	0	–	5	13	1	1	0.6	.947
1979			0	1	.000	7.20	8	1	0	20	19	13	6	0	0	0	0	0	0	0	–	0	3	0	0	0.4	1.000
8 yrs.			40	48	.455	4.08	291	86	13	913.2	861	393	563	2	20	13	11	170	27	0	.159	70	113	8	7	0.7	.958

Dave Schuler

SCHULER, DAVID PAUL
B. Oct. 4, 1953, Framingham, Mass.   BR TL 6'4"   210 lbs.

Year	Team		W	L	PCT	ERA	G	GS	CG	IP	H	BB	SO	ShO	W	L	SV	AB	H	HR	BA	PO	A	E	DP	TC/G	FA
1979	CAL	A	0	0	–	9.00	1	0	0	2	0	0	0	0	0	0	0	0	0	0	–	0	0	0	0	0.0	–
1980			0	1	.000	3.46	8	0	0	13	13	2	7	0	0	1	0	0	0	0	–	0	1	0	0	0.1	1.000
1985	ATL	N	0	0	–	6.75	9	0	0	10.2	19	3	10	0	0	0	0	0	0	0	–	1	0	0	0	0.1	1.000
3 yrs.			0	1	.000	5.26	18	0	0	25.2	34	5	17	0	0	1	0	0	0	0	–	1	1	0	0	0.1	1.000

Barney Schultz

SCHULTZ, GEORGE WARREN
B. Aug. 15, 1926, Beverly, N. J.   BR TR 6'2"   200 lbs.

Year	Team		W	L	PCT	ERA	G	GS	CG	IP	H	BB	SO	ShO	W	L	SV	AB	H	HR	BA	PO	A	E	DP	TC/G	FA
1955	STL	N	1	2	.333	7.89	19	0	0	29.2	28	15	19	0	1	2	4	4	0	0	.000	6	7	0	0	0.7	1.000
1959	DET	A	1	2	.333	4.42	13	0	0	18.1	17	14	17	0	1	2	0	2	2	0	1.000	1	2	2	0	0.4	.600
1961	CHI	N	7	6	.538	2.70	41	0	0	66.2	57	25	59	0	7	6	7	10	1	0	.100	4	9	0	0	0.3	1.000
1962			5	5	.500	3.82	51	0	0	77.2	66	23	58	0	5	5	5	5	0	0	.000	5	12	1	2	0.4	.944
1963	2 teams		CHI N	(15G 1–0)				STL N		(24G 2–0)																	
"	total		3	0	1.000	3.59	39	0	0	62.2	61	17	44	0	3	0	3	4	0	0	.000	4	11	0	0	0.4	1.000
1964	STL	N	1	3	.250	1.64	30	0	0	49.1	35	11	29	0	1	3	14	6	1	0	.167	0	7	1	0	0.3	.875
1965			2	2	.500	3.83	34	0	0	42.1	39	11	38	0	2	2	2	2	0	0	.000	1	8	0	0	0.3	1.000
7 yrs.			20	20	.500	3.63	227	0	0	346.2	303	116	264	0	20	20	35	33	4	0	.121	21	56	4	2	0.4	.951

WORLD SERIES

Year	Team		W	L	PCT	ERA	G	GS	CG	IP	H	BB	SO	ShO	W	L	SV	AB	H	HR	BA	PO	A	E	DP	TC/G	FA
1964	STL	N	0	1	.000	18.00	4	0	0	4	9	3	1	0	0	1	1	1	0	0	.000	0	0	0	0	0.0	

Bob Schultz

SCHULTZ, ROBERT DUFFY (Bill)
B. Nov. 27, 1923, Louisville, Ky.   D. Mar. 31, 1979, Nashville, Tenn.   BR TL 6'3"   200 lbs.

Year	Team		W	L	PCT	ERA	G	GS	CG	IP	H	BB	SO	ShO	W	L	SV	AB	H	HR	BA	PO	A	E	DP	TC/G	FA
1951	CHI	N	3	6	.333	5.24	17	10	2	77.1	75	51	27	0	1	0	0	29	4	0	.138	5	11	3	0	1.1	.842
1952			6	3	.667	4.01	29	5	1	74	63	51	31	0	4	0	0	18	4	0	.222	3	5	1	0	0.3	.889
1953	2 teams		CHI N	(7G 0–2)				PIT N		(11G 0–2)																	
"	total		0	4	.000	7.12	18	4	0	30.1	39	21	9	0	0	0	0	5	0	0	.000	1	2	1	0	0.2	.750
1955	DET	A	0	0	–	20.25	1	0	0	1.1	2	2	0	0	0	0	0	0	0	0	–	0	0	0	0	0.0	–
4 yrs.			9	13	.409	5.16	65	19	3	183	179	125	67	0	5	0	0	52	8	0	.154	9	18	5	0	0.5	.844

Buddy Schultz

SCHULTZ, CHARLES BUDD
B. Sept. 19, 1950, Cleveland, Ohio   BR TL 6'   170 lbs.

Year	Team		W	L	PCT	ERA	G	GS	CG	IP	H	BB	SO	ShO	W	L	SV	AB	H	HR	BA	PO	A	E	DP	TC/G	FA
1975	CHI	N	2	0	1.000	6.00	6	0	0	6	11	5	4	0	2	0	0	0	0	0	–	1	0	0	0	0.2	1.000
1976			1	1	.500	6.00	29	0	0	24	37	9	15	0	1	1	2	4	0	0	.000	5	4	0	0	0.3	1.000
1977	STL	N	6	1	.857	2.33	40	3	0	85	76	24	66	0	5	1	1	12	2	0	.167	3	10	1	1	0.4	.929
1978			2	4	.333	3.80	62	0	0	83	68	36	70	0	2	4	6	5	1	0	.200	4	6	0	1	0.2	1.000
1979			4	3	.571	4.50	31	0	0	42	40	14	38	0	4	3	3	4	0	0	.000	1	5	0	0	0.2	1.000
5 yrs.			15	9	.625	3.68	168	3	0	240	232	88	193	0	14	9	12	25	3	0	.120	14	25	1	2	0.2	.975

Mike Schultz

SCHULTZ, WILLIAM MICHAEL
B. Dec. 17, 1920, Syracuse, N. Y.   BL TL 6'1"   175 lbs.

Year	Team		W	L	PCT	ERA	G	GS	CG	IP	H	BB	SO	ShO	W	L	SV	AB	H	HR	BA	PO	A	E	DP	TC/G	FA
1947	CIN	N	0	0	–	4.50	1	0	0	2	4	2	0	0	0	0	0	0	0	0	–	0	0	0	0	0.0	–

Webb Schultz

SCHULTZ, WEBB CARL
B. Jan. 31, 1898, Wautoma, Wis.   D. July 26, 1986, Delevan, Wis.   BR TR 5'11"   172 lbs.

Year	Team		W	L	PCT	ERA	G	GS	CG	IP	H	BB	SO	ShO	W	L	SV	AB	H	HR	BA	PO	A	E	DP	TC/G	FA
1924	CHI	A	0	0	–	9.00	1	0	0	1	0	0	0	0	0	0	0	0	0	0	–	0	0	0	0	0.0	–

John Schultze

SCHULTZE, JOHN F.
B. Burlington, N. J.   Deceased.   6'½"   165 lbs.

Year	Team		W	L	PCT	ERA	G	GS	CG	IP	H	BB	SO	ShO	W	L	SV	AB	H	HR	BA	PO	A	E	DP	TC/G	FA
1891	PHI	N	0	1	.000	6.60	6	1	0	15	18	11	4	0	0	0	0	6	1	0	.167	0	1	0	0	0.2	1.000

Al Schulz

SCHULZ, ALBERT CHRISTOPHER (Lefty)
B. May 12, 1889, Toledo, Ohio   D. Dec. 13, 1931, Gallipolis, Ohio   BR TL 6'   182 lbs.

Year	Team		W	L	PCT	ERA	G	GS	CG	IP	H	BB	SO	ShO	W	L	SV	AB	H	HR	BA	PO	A	E	DP	TC/G	FA
1912	NY	A	1	1	.500	2.20	3	1	1	16.1	11	11	8	0	1	0	0	5	0	0	.000	3	7	1	0	3.7	.909
1913			7	13	.350	3.73	38	22	9	193	197	69	77	0	1	0	0	63	11	0	.175	8	52	4	2	1.7	.938
1914	2 teams		NY A	(6G 1–3)				BUF F		(27G 10–11)																	
"	total		11	14	.440	3.57	33	27	11	199.1	187	87	105	0	3	0	0	63	10	1	.159	14	66	5	1	2.6	.941
1915	BUF	F	21	14	.600	3.08	42	38	25	309.2	264	149	160	5	0	0	0	109	18	0	.165	10	94	2	3	2.5	.981
1916	CIN	N	8	19	.296	3.14	44	22	10	215	208	93	95	0	4	4	2	64	8	0	.125	10	57	3	2	1.6	.957
5 yrs.			48	61	.440	3.32	160	110	56	933.1	867	409	445	5	9	4	3	304	47	1	.155	45	276	15	8	2.1	.955

Year	Team		W	L	PCT	ERA	G	GS	CG	IP	H	BB	SO	ShO	Relief Pitching W	L	SV	Batting AB	H	HR	BA	PO	A	E	DP	TC/G	FA

Walt Schulz

SCHULZ, WALTER FREDERICK
B. Apr. 16, 1900, St. Louis, Mo.   D. Feb. 27, 1928, Prescott, Ariz.
BR TR 6'   170 lbs.

Year	Team		W	L	PCT	ERA	G	GS	CG	IP	H	BB	SO	ShO	W	L	SV	AB	H	HR	BA	PO	A	E	DP	TC/G	FA
1920	STL	N	0	0	–	6.00	2	0	0	6	10	2	0	0	0	0	0	2	0	0	.000	0	3	0	0	1.5	1.000

Don Schulze

SCHULZE, DONALD ARTHUR
B. Sept. 27, 1962, Roselle, Ill.
BR TR 6'3"   215 lbs.

Year	Team		W	L	PCT	ERA	G	GS	CG	IP	H	BB	SO	ShO	W	L	SV	AB	H	HR	BA	PO	A	E	DP	TC/G	FA
1983	CHI	N	0	1	.000	7.07	4	3	0	14	19	7	8	0	0	0	0	1	0	0	.000	1	2	0	0	0.8	1.000
1984	2 teams	CHI N (1G 0–0)				CLE A	(19G 3–6)																				
"	total		3	6	.333	5.08	20	15	2	88.2	113	28	41	0	0	0	0	0	0	0	–	10	9	0	0	1.0	1.000
1985	CLE	A	4	10	.286	6.01	19	18	1	94.1	128	19	37	0	0	0	0	0	0	0	–	8	16	2	2	1.4	.923
1986			4	4	.500	5.00	19	13	1	84.2	88	34	33	0	1	0	0	0	0	0	–	7	7	0	0	0.7	1.000
1987	NY	N	1	2	.333	6.23	5	4	0	21.2	24	6	5	0	0	0	0	2	0	0	.000	6	6	0	0	2.4	1.000
1989	2 teams	NY A (2G 1–1)				SD N	(7G 2–1)																				
"	total		3	2	.600	5.09	9	6	0	35.1	50	11	20	0	0	0	0	4	0	0	.000	5	6	1	0	1.3	.917
6 yrs.			15	25	.375	5.47	76	59	4	338.2	422	105	144	0	1	0	0	7	0	0	.000	37	46	3	2	1.1	.965

Hal Schumacher

SCHUMACHER, HAROLD HENRY (Prince Hal)
B. Nov. 23, 1910, Hinckley, N. Y.
BR TR 6'   190 lbs.

Year	Team		W	L	PCT	ERA	G	GS	CG	IP	H	BB	SO	ShO	W	L	SV	AB	H	HR	BA	PO	A	E	DP	TC/G	FA
1931	NY	N	1	0	1.000	10.80	8	2	1	18.1	31	14	11	0	0	1	0	7	1	0	.143	2	7	1	1	1.3	.900
1932			5	6	.455	3.55	27	13	2	101.1	119	39	38	1	0	1	0	31	7	0	.226	9	31	3	1	1.6	.930
1933			19	12	.613	2.16	35	33	21	258.2	199	84	96	7	0	1	1	98	21	0	.214	15	70	1	3	2.5	.988
1934			23	10	.697	3.18	41	36	18	297	299	89	112	4	2	2	0	117	28	6	.239	21	71	3	4	2.3	.968
1935			19	9	.679	2.89	33	33	19	261.2	235	70	79	3	0	0	1	107	21	2	.196	14	89	0	4	3.1	1.000
1936			11	13	.458	3.49	35	30	9	214.1	234	69	75	3	0	0	1	74	16	1	.216	12	63	4	6	2.3	.949
1937			13	12	.520	3.60	38	29	10	217.2	222	89	100	1	2	1	1	81	18	2	.222	17	46	2	2	1.7	.969
1938			13	8	.619	3.50	28	28	12	185	178	50	54	4	0	0	0	67	16	2	.239	4	49	2	1	2.1	.967
1939			13	10	.565	4.81	29	27	8	181.2	199	89	58	1	0	0	0	69	14	0	.203	4	37	3	4	1.5	.932
1940			13	13	.500	3.25	34	30	12	227	218	96	123	1	1	1	0	78	15	1	.192	14	61	1	2	2.2	.987
1941			12	10	.545	3.36	30	26	12	206	187	79	63	3	1	1	1	66	10	0	.152	12	39	2	2	1.8	.962
1942			12	13	.480	3.04	29	29	12	216	208	82	49	3	0	0	0	75	13	1	.173	13	56	1	3	2.4	.986
1946			4	4	.500	3.91	24	13	2	96.2	95	52	48	0	0	0	0	26	1	0	.038	12	27	1	1	1.7	.975
13 yrs.			158	120	.568	3.36	391	329	138	2481.1	2424	902	906	29	6	6	7	896	181	15	.202	154	646	24	34	2.1	.971

WORLD SERIES

Year	Team		W	L	PCT	ERA	G	GS	CG	IP	H	BB	SO	ShO	W	L	SV	AB	H	HR	BA	PO	A	E	DP	TC/G	FA
1933	NY	N	1	0	1.000	2.45	2	2	1	14.2	13	5	3	0	0	0	0	7	2	0	.286	0	2	0	0	1.0	1.000
1936			1	1	.500	5.25	2	2	1	12	13	10	11	0	0	0	0	4	0	0	.000	0	2	0	1	1.0	1.000
1937			0	1	.000	6.00	1	1	0	6	9	4	3	0	0	0	0	1	0	0	.000	0	1	0	0	1.0	1.000
3 yrs.			2	2	.500	4.13	5	5	2	32.2	35	19	17	0	0	0	0	12	2	0	.167	0	5	0	1	1.0	1.000

Hack Schumann

SCHUMANN, CARL J.
B. Aug. 13, 1884, Buffalo, N. Y.   D. Mar. 25, 1946, Millgrove, N. Y.
TR 6'2"   230 lbs.

Year	Team		W	L	PCT	ERA	G	GS	CG	IP	H	BB	SO	ShO	W	L	SV	AB	H	HR	BA	PO	A	E	DP	TC/G	FA
1906	PHI	A	0	2	.000	4.00	4	2	1	18	21	8	9	0	0	0	0	6	0	0	.000	0	4	0	0	1.0	1.000

Ferdie Schupp

SCHUPP, FERDINAND MAURICE
B. Jan. 16, 1891, Louisville, Ky.   D. Dec. 16, 1971, Los Angeles, Calif.
BB TL 5'10"   150 lbs.

Year	Team		W	L	PCT	ERA	G	GS	CG	IP	H	BB	SO	ShO	W	L	SV	AB	H	HR	BA	PO	A	E	DP	TC/G	FA
1913	NY	N	0	0	–	0.75	5	1	0	12	10	3	2	0	0	0	0	3	1	0	.333	2	2	0	0	0.8	1.000
1914			0	0	–	5.82	8	0	0	17	19	9	9	0	0	0	1	2	0	0	.000	0	4	1	0	0.6	.800
1915			1	0	1.000	5.10	23	1	0	54.2	57	29	28	0	1	0	0	10	2	0	.200	1	15	0	0	0.7	1.000
1916			9	3	.750	0.90	30	11	8	140.1	79	37	86	4	2	1	1	41	4	0	.098	1	24	4	0	1.0	.862
1917			21	7	**.750**	1.95	36	32	25	272	202	70	147	6	1	0	1	93	15	0	.161	6	60	3	3	1.9	.957
1918			0	1	.000	7.56	10	2	1	33.1	42	27	22	0	0	0	0	9	1	0	.111	1	9	1	0	1.1	.909
1919	2 teams	NY N (9G 1–3)				STL N	(10G 4–4)																				
"	total		5	7	.417	4.34	19	13	6	101.2	87	48	54	0	1	0	1	26	3	1	.115	5	19	2	0	1.4	.923
1920	STL	N	16	13	.552	3.52	38	37	17	250.2	246	127	119	0	0	0	0	86	22	0	.256	5	57	3	4	1.7	.954
1921	2 teams	STL N (9G 2–0)				BKN N	(20G 3–4)																				
"	total		5	4	.556	4.39	29	11	2	98.1	117	48	48	1	3	0	3	26	5	0	.192	1	23	0	1	0.8	1.000
1922	CHI	A	4	4	.500	6.08	18	12	3	74	79	66	38	1	0	0	0	25	5	0	.200	1	18	1	0	1.1	.950
10 yrs.			61	39	.610	3.32	216	120	62	1054	938	464	553	11	8	2	6	321	58	1	.181	23	231	15	8	1.2	.944

WORLD SERIES

Year	Team		W	L	PCT	ERA	G	GS	CG	IP	H	BB	SO	ShO	W	L	SV	AB	H	HR	BA	PO	A	E	DP	TC/G	FA
1917	NY	N	1	0	1.000	1.74	2	2	1	10.1	11	2	9	1	0	0	0	4	1	0	.250	1	4	0	2	2.5	1.000

Wayne Schurr

SCHURR, WAYNE ALLEN
B. Aug. 6, 1937, Garrett, Ind.
BR TR 6'4"   185 lbs.

Year	Team		W	L	PCT	ERA	G	GS	CG	IP	H	BB	SO	ShO	W	L	SV	AB	H	HR	BA	PO	A	E	DP	TC/G	FA
1964	CHI	N	0	0	–	3.72	26	0	0	48.1	57	11	29	0	0	0	0	5	0	0	.000	2	7	0	0	0.3	1.000

Mike Schwabe

SCHWABE, MICHAEL SCOTT
B. July 12, 1964, Fort Dodge, Iowa
BR TR 6'4"   200 lbs.

Year	Team		W	L	PCT	ERA	G	GS	CG	IP	H	BB	SO	ShO	W	L	SV	AB	H	HR	BA	PO	A	E	DP	TC/G	FA
1989	DET	A	2	4	.333	6.04	13	4	0	44.2	58	16	13	0	0	1	0	0	0	0	–	7	8	0	1	1.2	1.000

Don Schwall

SCHWALL, DONALD BERNARD
B. Mar. 2, 1936, Wilkes-Barre, Pa.
BR TR 6'6"   200 lbs.

Year	Team		W	L	PCT	ERA	G	GS	CG	IP	H	BB	SO	ShO	W	L	SV	AB	H	HR	BA	PO	A	E	DP	TC/G	FA
1961	BOS	A	15	7	.682	3.22	25	25	10	178.2	167	110	91	2	0	0	0	61	11	0	.180	8	33	3	4	1.8	.932
1962			9	15	.375	4.94	33	32	5	182.1	180	121	89	1	0	0	0	66	9	0	.136	8	34	2	4	1.3	.955
1963	PIT	N	6	12	.333	3.33	33	24	3	167.2	158	74	86	2	0	2	0	50	8	0	.160	15	35	1	3	1.5	.980
1964			4	3	.571	4.35	15	9	0	49.2	53	15	36	0	0	0	0	19	5	0	.263	2	10	1	0	0.9	.923
1965			9	6	.600	2.92	43	1	0	77	77	30	55	0	9	5	4	15	0	0	.000	8	16	0	5	0.6	1.000
1966	2 teams	PIT N (11G 3–2)				ATL N	(11G 3–3)																				
"	total		6	5	.545	3.31	22	12	0	87	75	40	51	0	1	2	0	23	1	0	.043	11	9	0	2	0.9	1.000
1967	ATL	N	0	0	–	0.00	1	0	0	.2	0	1	0	0	0	0	0	0	0	0	–	0	0	0	0	0.0	–
7 yrs.			49	48	.505	3.72	172	103	18	743	710	391	408	5	12	8	4	234	34	0	.145	52	137	7	18	1.1	.964

Year	Team	W	L	PCT	ERA	G	GS	CG	IP	H	BB	SO	ShO	Relief Pitching W	L	SV	Batting AB	H	HR	BA	PO	A	E	DP	TC/G	FA

Blackie Schwamb
SCHWAMB, RALPH RICHARD
B. Aug. 6, 1926, Los Angeles, Calif.
BR TR 6'5½" 198 lbs.

Year	Team	W	L	PCT	ERA	G	GS	CG	IP	H	BB	SO	ShO	W	L	SV	AB	H	HR	BA	PO	A	E	DP	TC/G	FA
1948	STL A	1	1	.500	8.53	12	5	0	31.2	44	21	7	0	0	0	0	10	3	0	.300	2	8	0	0	0.8	1.000

Rudy Schwenck
SCHWENCK, RUDOLPH CHRISTIAN
B. Apr. 6, 1884, Louisville, Ky. D. Nov. 27, 1941, Anchorage, Ky.
BL TL 6' 174 lbs.

Year	Team	W	L	PCT	ERA	G	GS	CG	IP	H	BB	SO	ShO	W	L	SV	AB	H	HR	BA	PO	A	E	DP	TC/G	FA
1909	CHI N	1	1	.500	13.50	3	2	0	16	3	3	0	0	0	0	4	1	0	.250	2	5	0	1	2.3	1.000

Hal Schwenk
SCHWENK, HAROLD EDWARD
B. Aug. 23, 1890, Schuylkill Haven, Pa. D. Sept. 3, 1955, Kansas City, Mo.
BL TL 6' 185 lbs.

Year	Team	W	L	PCT	ERA	G	GS	CG	IP	H	BB	SO	ShO	W	L	SV	AB	H	HR	BA	PO	A	E	DP	TC/G	FA
1913	STL A	1	0	1.000	3.27	1	1	1	11	12	4	3	0	0	0	0	3	1	0	.333	1	2	0	0	3.0	1.000

Jim Scoggins
SCOGGINS, LYNN J. (Lefty)
B. July 19, 1891, Killeen, Tex. D. Aug. 16, 1923, Columbia, S. C.
BL TL 5'11" 165 lbs.

Year	Team	W	L	PCT	ERA	G	GS	CG	IP	H	BB	SO	ShO	W	L	SV	AB	H	HR	BA	PO	A	E	DP	TC/G	FA
1913	CHI A	0	1	.000	0.00	1	1	0	0	1	0	0	0	0	0	0	0	0	0	—	0	0	0	0	0.0	—

Herb Score
SCORE, HERBERT JUDE
B. June 7, 1933, Rosedale, N. Y.
BL TL 6'2" 185 lbs.

Year	Team	W	L	PCT	ERA	G	GS	CG	IP	H	BB	SO	ShO	W	L	SV	AB	H	HR	BA	PO	A	E	DP	TC/G	FA
1955	CLE A	16	10	.615	2.85	33	32	11	227.1	158	154	**245**	2	0	0	0	84	10	0	.119	4	15	4	2	0.7	.826
1956		20	9	.690	2.53	35	33	16	249.1	162	129	**263**	5	0	0	0	87	16	1	.184	1	19	2	0	0.6	.909
1957		2	1	.667	2.00	5	5	3	36	18	26	39	1	0	0	0	11	1	0	.091	0	6	1	0	1.4	.857
1958		2	3	.400	3.95	12	5	2	41	29	34	48	1	1	1	3	11	1	0	.091	0	2	3	0	0.4	.400
1959		9	11	.450	4.71	30	25	9	160.2	123	115	147	1	0	0	0	52	5	0	.096	1	15	5	1	0.7	.762
1960	CHI A	5	10	.333	3.72	23	22	5	113.2	91	87	78	1	0	0	0	30	3	0	.100	1	16	0	0	0.7	1.000
1961		1	2	.333	6.66	8	5	1	24.1	22	24	14	0	0	0	0	6	0	0	.000	1	5	0	0	0.8	1.000
1962		0	0	—	4.50	4	0	0	6	6	4	3	0	0	0	0	0	0	0	—	0	2	0	0	0.5	1.000
8 yrs.		55	46	.545	3.36	150	127	47	858.1	609	573	837	11	1	1	3	281	36	1	.128	8	80	15	3	0.7	.854

Dick Scott
SCOTT, AMOS RICHARD
B. Feb. 5, 1883, Bethel, Ohio D. Jan. 18, 1911, Chicago, Ill.
BR TR 6' 180 lbs.

Year	Team	W	L	PCT	ERA	G	GS	CG	IP	H	BB	SO	ShO	W	L	SV	AB	H	HR	BA	PO	A	E	DP	TC/G	FA
1901	CIN N	0	2	.000	5.14	3	2	2	21	26	9	7	0	0	0	0	9	0	0	.000	1	3	2	0	2.0	.667

Dick Scott
SCOTT, RICHARD LEWIS
B. Mar. 15, 1933, Portsmouth, N. H.
BR TL 6'2" 185 lbs.

Year	Team	W	L	PCT	ERA	G	GS	CG	IP	H	BB	SO	ShO	W	L	SV	AB	H	HR	BA	PO	A	E	DP	TC/G	FA
1963	LA N	0	0	—	6.75	9	0	0	12	17	3	6	0	0	0	2	0	0	0	—	0	3	0	0	0.3	1.000
1964	CHI N	0	0	—	12.46	3	0	0	4.1	10	1	1	0	0	0	0	0	0	0	—	0	2	0	0	0.7	1.000
2 yrs.		0	0	—	8.27	12	0	0	16.1	27	4	7	0	0	0	2	0	0	0	—	0	5	0	0	0.4	1.000

Ed Scott
SCOTT, EDWARD
B. Aug. 12, 1870, Walbridge, Ohio D. Nov. 1, 1933, Toledo, Ohio
BR TR 6'3"

Year	Team	W	L	PCT	ERA	G	GS	CG	IP	H	BB	SO	ShO	W	L	SV	AB	H	HR	BA	PO	A	E	DP	TC/G	FA
1900	CIN N	17	21	.447	3.82	43	36	32	323	380	66	92	0	1	2	1	127	20	1	.157	21	120	14	7	3.6	.910
1901	CLE A	7	6	.538	4.40	17	16	11	124.2	149	38	23	0	0	0	1	48	10	1	.208	5	43	2	1	2.9	.960
2 yrs.		24	27	.471	3.98	60	52	43	447.2	529	104	115	0	1	2	2	175	30	2	.171	26	163	16	8	3.4	.922

George Scott
SCOTT, GEORGE WILLIAM
B. Nov. 17, 1896, Trenton, Mo.
BR TR 6'1" 175 lbs.

Year	Team	W	L	PCT	ERA	G	GS	CG	IP	H	BB	SO	ShO	W	L	SV	AB	H	HR	BA	PO	A	E	DP	TC/G	FA
1920	STL N	0	0	—	4.50	2	0	0	6	4	3	1	0	0	0	0	1	0	0	.000	0	0	0	0	0.0	—

Jack Scott
SCOTT, JOHN WILLIAM
B. Apr. 18, 1892, Ridgeway, N. C. D. Nov. 30, 1959, Durham, N. C.
BL TR 6'2½" 199 lbs.

Year	Team	W	L	PCT	ERA	G	GS	CG	IP	H	BB	SO	ShO	W	L	SV	AB	H	HR	BA	PO	A	E	DP	TC/G	FA
1916	PIT N	0	0	—	10.80	1	0	0	5	5	3	4	0	0	0	0	2	0	0	.000	1	1	0	0	2.0	1.000
1917	BOS N	1	2	.333	1.82	7	3	3	39.2	36	5	21	0	1	0	0	16	2	0	.125	1	8	1	0	1.4	.900
1919		6	6	.500	3.13	19	12	7	103.2	109	39	44	0	1	1	1	40	7	0	.175	3	16	1	0	1.1	.950
1920		10	21	.323	3.53	44	32	22	291	308	85	94	3	0	1	1	99	21	0	.212	8	65	6	1	1.8	.924
1921		15	13	.536	3.70	47	29	16	233.2	258	57	83	2	1	2	3	88	30	1	.341	4	56	3	2	1.3	.952
1922	2 teams					CIN N	(1G 0–0)		NY N	(17G 8–2)																	
"	total	8	2	.800	4.46	18	10	5	80.2	85	24	37	0	1	1	2	31	8	0	.258	0	14	1	0	0.8	.933
1923	NY N	16	7	.696	3.89	40	25	9	220	223	65	79	3	3	2	1	79	25	1	.316	6	43	2	1	1.3	.961
1925		14	15	.483	3.15	36	28	18	239.2	251	55	87	2	1	2	3	87	21	1	.241	11	63	1	3	2.1	.987
1926		13	15	.464	4.34	**50**	22	13	226	242	53	82	0	5	3	5	83	28	1	.337	12	49	2	4	1.3	.968
1927	PHI N	9	**21**	.300	5.09	**48**	25	17	233.1	304	69	69	1	2	**7**	1	114	33	1	.289	7	51	3	1	1.3	.951
1928	NY N	4	1	.800	3.58	16	3	3	50.1	59	11	17	0	1	1	2	15	4	0	.267	3	11	1	2	0.9	.933
1929		7	6	.538	3.53	30	6	2	91.2	89	27	40	0	4	4	1	26	8	0	.308	6	22	0	1	0.9	1.000
12 yrs.		103	109	.486	3.85	356	195	115	1814.2	1969	493	657	11	19	24	19	*				62	399	21	15	1.4	.956

WORLD SERIES

Year	Team	W	L	PCT	ERA	G	GS	CG	IP	H	BB	SO	ShO	W	L	SV	AB	H	HR	BA	PO	A	E	DP	TC/G	FA
1922	NY N	1	0	1.000	0.00	1	1	1	9	4	1	2	1	0	0	0	4	1	0	.250	1	1	0	0	2.0	1.000
1923		0	1	.000	12.00	2	1	0	3	9	1	2	0	0	0	0	1	0	0	.000	0	1	0	0	0.5	1.000
2 yrs.		1	1	.500	3.00	3	2	1	12	13	2	4	1	0	0	0	5	1	0	.200	1	2	0	0	1.0	1.000

Jim Scott
SCOTT, JAMES (Death Valley Jim)
B. Apr. 23, 1888, Deadwood, S. D. D. Apr. 7, 1957, Palm Springs, Calif.
BR TR 6'1" 235 lbs.

Year	Team	W	L	PCT	ERA	G	GS	CG	IP	H	BB	SO	ShO	W	L	SV	AB	H	HR	BA	PO	A	E	DP	TC/G	FA
1909	CHI A	12	12	.500	2.30	36	29	19	250.1	194	93	135	4	1	0	0	85	9	0	.106	6	70	4	2	2.2	.950
1910		8	18	.308	2.43	41	23	14	229.2	182	86	135	2	2	4	1	74	15	0	.203	11	84	3	4	2.4	.969
1911		14	11	.560	2.63	39	26	14	202	195	81	128	3	4	2	0	71	11	0	.155	7	43	8	3	1.5	.862
1912		2	2	.500	2.15	6	4	2	37.2	36	15	23	1	1	0	0	12	0	0	.000	0	11	1	0	2.0	.917
1913		20	**20**	.500	1.90	48	**38**	25	312.1	252	86	158	4	1	4	1	97	7	1	.072	7	90	9	2	2.2	.956
1914		14	18	.438	2.84	43	33	12	253.1	228	75	138	2	2	3	1	86	14	0	.163	6	87	7	1	2.3	.930
1915		24	11	.686	2.03	48	35	23	296.1	256	78	120	**7**	4	1	2	95	12	0	.126	6	103	5	2	2.4	.956
1916		7	14	.333	2.72	32	21	8	165.1	155	53	71	1	4	3		52	6	0	.115	4	45	1	3	1.6	.980

Year	Team	W	L	PCT	ERA	G	GS	CG	IP	H	BB	SO	ShO	W	L	SV	AB	H	HR	BA	PO	A	E	DP	TC/G	FA

Jim Scott *continued*

Year	Team	W	L	PCT	ERA	G	GS	CG	IP	H	BB	SO	ShO	W	L	SV	AB	H	HR	BA	PO	A	E	DP	TC/G	FA
1917		6	7	.462	1.87	24	17	6	125	126	42	37	2	2	2	1	42	5	0	.119	7	37	2	1	1.9	.957
9 yrs.		107	113	.486	2.32	317	226	123	1872	1624	609	945	26	17	21	9	614	79	1	.129	54	570	40	18	2.1	.940

Lefty Scott SCOTT, MARSHALL
B. July 15, 1915, Roswell, N. M. D. Mar. 3, 1964, Houston, Tex. BR TL 6'½" 165 lbs.

Year	Team	W	L	PCT	ERA	G	GS	CG	IP	H	BB	SO	ShO	W	L	SV	AB	H	HR	BA	PO	A	E	DP	TC/G	FA
1945	PHI N	0	2	.000	4.43	8	2	0	22.1	29	12	5	0	0	0	0	3	0	0	.000	1	2	0	0	0.4	1.000

Mickey Scott SCOTT, RALPH ROBERT
B. July 25, 1947, Weimar, Germany BL TL 6'1" 155 lbs.

Year	Team	W	L	PCT	ERA	G	GS	CG	IP	H	BB	SO	ShO	W	L	SV	AB	H	HR	BA	PO	A	E	DP	TC/G	FA
1972	BAL A	0	1	.000	2.74	15	0	0	23	23	5	11	0	0	1	0	1	0	0	.000	3	1	0	0	0.3	1.000
1973	2 teams		BAL A	(1G 0–0)		MON N	(22G 1–2)																				
"	total	1	2	.333	5.19	23	0	0	26	29	11	13	0	1	2	0	3	0	0	.000	2	4	0	0	0.3	1.000
1975	CAL A	4	2	.667	3.29	50	0	0	68.1	59	18	31	0	4	2	1	0	0	0	–	2	9	0	0	0.2	1.000
1976		3	0	1.000	3.23	33	0	0	39	47	12	10	0	3	0	3	0	0	0	–	2	4	0	0	0.2	1.000
1977		0	2	.000	5.63	12	0	0	16	19	4	5	0	0	2	0	0	0	0	–	1	4	0	0	0.4	1.000
5 yrs.		8	7	.533	3.71	133	0	0	172.1	177	50	70	0	8	7	4	4	0	0	.000	10	22	0	0	0.2	1.000

Mike Scott SCOTT, MICHAEL WARREN
B. Apr. 26, 1955, Santa Monica, Calif. BR TR 6'2" 210 lbs.

Year	Team	W	L	PCT	ERA	G	GS	CG	IP	H	BB	SO	ShO	W	L	SV	AB	H	HR	BA	PO	A	E	DP	TC/G	FA
1979	NY N	1	3	.250	5.37	18	9	0	52	59	20	21	0	0	0	0	12	0	0	.000	3	7	2	0	0.7	.833
1980		1	1	.500	4.34	6	6	1	29	40	8	13	1	0	0	0	9	1	0	.111	1	5	2	1	1.3	.750
1981		5	10	.333	3.90	23	23	1	136	130	34	54	0	0	0	0	41	3	0	.073	14	35	1	2	2.2	.980
1982		7	13	.350	5.14	37	22	1	147	185	60	63	0	1	3	3	48	7	0	.146	7	43	4	3	1.5	.926
1983	HOU N	10	6	.625	3.72	24	24	2	145	143	46	73	2	0	0	0	48	8	0	.167	20	20	2	0	1.8	.952
1984		5	11	.313	4.68	31	29	0	154	179	43	83	0	0	0	0	47	6	0	.128	10	23	1	1	1.1	.971
1985		18	8	.692	3.29	36	35	4	221.2	194	80	137	2	0	0	0	72	11	1	.153	21	22	2	1	1.3	.956
1986		18	10	.643	2.22	37	37	7	275.1	182	72	306	5	0	0	0	95	12	0	.126	24	39	2	2	1.8	.969
1987		16	13	.552	3.23	36	36	8	247.2	199	79	233	3	0	0	0	80	10	0	.125	17	32	2	2	1.4	.961
1988		14	8	.636	2.92	32	32	8	218.2	162	53	190	5	0	0	0	71	6	0	.085	14	27	0	0	1.3	1.000
1989		20	10	.667	3.10	33	32	9	229	180	62	172	2	1	0	0	75	10	1	.133	15	25	4	0	1.3	.909
11 yrs.		115	93	.553	3.47	313	285	41	1855.1	1653	557	1345	20	2	3	3	598	74	2	.124	146	278	22	12	1.4	.951

LEAGUE CHAMPIONSHIP SERIES

Year	Team	W	L	PCT	ERA	G	GS	CG	IP	H	BB	SO	ShO	W	L	SV	AB	H	HR	BA	PO	A	E	DP	TC/G	FA
1986	HOU N	2	0	1.000	0.50	2	2	2	18	8	1	19	1	0	0	0	6	0	0	.000	0	0	1	0	0.5	–

Milt Scott SCOTT, MILTON PARKER (Mikado Milt)
B. Jan. 17, 1866, Chicago, Ill. D. Nov. 3, 1938, Baltimore, Md. 5'9" 160 lbs.

Year	Team	W	L	PCT	ERA	G	GS	CG	IP	H	BB	SO	ShO	W	L	SV	AB	H	HR	BA	PO	A	E	DP	TC/G	FA
1886	BAL AA	0	0	–	3.00	1	0	0	3	2	2	0	0	0	0	0	*				0	0	0	0	0.0	–

Scott Scudder SCUDDER, WILLIAM SCOTT
B. Feb. 14, 1968, Paris, Tex. BR TR 6'2" 180 lbs.

Year	Team	W	L	PCT	ERA	G	GS	CG	IP	H	BB	SO	ShO	W	L	SV	AB	H	HR	BA	PO	A	E	DP	TC/G	FA
1989	CIN N	4	9	.308	4.49	23	17	0	100.1	91	61	66	0	0	0	0	24	4	0	.167	5	9	1	0	0.7	.933

Rod Scurry SCURRY, RODNEY GRANT
B. Mar. 17, 1956, Sacramento, Calif. BL TL 6'2" 180 lbs.

Year	Team	W	L	PCT	ERA	G	GS	CG	IP	H	BB	SO	ShO	W	L	SV	AB	H	HR	BA	PO	A	E	DP	TC/G	FA
1980	PIT N	0	2	.000	2.13	20	0	0	38	23	17	28	0	0	2	0	4	1	0	.250	2	5	0	0	0.4	1.000
1981		4	5	.444	3.77	27	7	0	74	74	40	65	0	1	2	7	19	3	0	.158	1	8	0	1	0.3	1.000
1982		4	5	.444	1.74	76	0	0	103.2	79	64	94	0	4	5	14	21	5	0	.238	11	9	0	0	0.3	1.000
1983		4	9	.308	5.56	61	0	0	68	63	53	67	0	4	9	7	5	0	0	.000	2	8	0	0	0.2	1.000
1984		5	6	.455	2.53	43	0	0	46.1	28	22	48	0	5	6	4	2	0	0	.000	0	9	1	0	0.2	.900
1985	2 teams		PIT N	(30G 0–1)		NY A	(5G 1–0)																				
"	total	1	1	.500	3.13	35	0	0	60.1	47	38	60	0	1	1	3	4	0	0	.000	1	10	0	0	0.3	1.000
1986	NY A	1	2	.333	3.66	31	0	0	39.1	38	22	36	0	1	2	2	0	0	0	–	4	5	0	1	0.3	1.000
1988	SEA A	0	2	.000	4.02	39	0	0	31.1	32	18	33	0	0	2	2	0	0	0	–	4	4	1	0	0.2	.889
8 yrs.		19	32	.373	3.24	332	7	0	461	384	274	431	0	16	29	39	55	9	0	.164	24	58	2	2	0.3	.976

Johnnie Seale SEALE, JOHNNY RAY (Durango Kid)
B. Nov. 14, 1938, Edgewater, Colo. BL TL 5'10" 155 lbs.

Year	Team	W	L	PCT	ERA	G	GS	CG	IP	H	BB	SO	ShO	W	L	SV	AB	H	HR	BA	PO	A	E	DP	TC/G	FA
1964	DET A	1	0	1.000	3.60	4	0	0	10	6	4	5	0	1	0	0	1	0	0	.000	0	4	0	1	1.0	1.000
1965		0	0	–	12.00	4	0	0	3	7	2	3	0	0	0	0	0	0	0	–	0	0	0	0	0.0	–
2 yrs.		1	0	1.000	5.54	8	0	0	13	13	6	8	0	1	0	0	1	0	0	.000	0	4	0	1	0.5	1.000

Kim Seaman SEAMAN, KIM MICHAEL
B. May 6, 1957, Pascagoula, Miss. BL TL 6'4" 205 lbs.

Year	Team	W	L	PCT	ERA	G	GS	CG	IP	H	BB	SO	ShO	W	L	SV	AB	H	HR	BA	PO	A	E	DP	TC/G	FA
1979	STL N	0	0	–	0.00	1	0	0	2	0	2	3	0	0	0	0	–				0	0	0	0	0.0	–
1980		3	2	.600	3.38	26	0	0	24	16	13	10	0	3	2	4	1	0	0	.000	1	3	0	0	0.2	1.000
2 yrs.		3	2	.600	3.12	27	0	0	26	16	15	13	0	3	2	4	1	0	0	.000	1	3	0	0	0.1	1.000

Rudy Seanez SEANEZ, RUDY CABALLERO
B. Oct. 20, 1968, Brawley, Calif. BR TR 6' 170 lbs.

Year	Team	W	L	PCT	ERA	G	GS	CG	IP	H	BB	SO	ShO	W	L	SV	AB	H	HR	BA	PO	A	E	DP	TC/G	FA
1989	CLE A	0	0	–	3.60	5	0	0	5	1	4	7	0	0	0	0	0	0	0	–	0	0	0	0	0.0	–

Ray Searage SEARAGE, RAYMOND MARK
B. May 1, 1955, Freeport, N. Y. BL TL 6'1" 180 lbs.

Year	Team	W	L	PCT	ERA	G	GS	CG	IP	H	BB	SO	ShO	W	L	SV	AB	H	HR	BA	PO	A	E	DP	TC/G	FA
1981	NY N	1	0	1.000	3.65	26	0	0	37	34	17	16	0	1	0	1	1	1	0	1.000	2	5	0	0	0.3	1.000
1984	MIL A	2	1	.667	0.70	21	0	0	38.1	20	16	29	0	2	1	6	0	0	0	–	1	5	1	0	0.3	.857
1985		1	4	.200	5.92	33	0	0	38	54	24	36	0	1	4	1	0	0	0	–	1	2	1	0	0.1	.750

Year	Team		W	L	PCT	ERA	G	GS	CG	IP	H	BB	SO	ShO	Relief Pitching			Batting			BA	PO	A	E	DP	TC/G	FA
															W	L	SV	AB	H	HR							

Ray Searage *continued*

1986	2 teams	MIL A (17G 0–1)			CHI A	(29G 1–0)																					
"	total		1	1	.500	3.35	46	0	0	51	44	28	36	0	1	1	1	0	0	0	–	3	8	0	0	0.2	1.000
1987	CHI	A	2	3	.400	4.20	58	0	0	55.2	56	24	33	0	2	3	2	0	0	0	–	1	9	0	0	0.2	1.000
1989	LA	N	3	4	.429	3.53	41	0	0	35.2	29	18	24	0	3	4	0	0	0	0	–	5	8	1	0	0.3	.929
6 yrs.			10	13	.435	3.59	225	0	0	255.2	237	127	174	0	10	13	11	1	1	0	1.000	13	37	3	0	0.2	.943

Steve Searcy

SEARCY, WILLIAM STEVEN
B. June 4, 1964, Knoxville, Tenn.

BL TL 6'1" 190 lbs.

1988	DET	A	0	2	.000	5.63	2	2	0	8	8	4	5	0	0	0	0	0	0	0	–	0	1	0	0	0.5	1.000
1989			1	1	.500	6.04	8	2	0	22.1	27	12	11	0	0	0	1	0	0	0	–	2	2	1	0	0.6	.800
2 yrs.			1	3	.250	5.93	10	4	0	30.1	35	16	16	0	0	0	1	0	0	0	–	2	3	1	0	0.6	.833

Tom Seaton

SEATON, THOMAS GORDON
B. Aug. 30, 1887, Blair, Neb. D. Apr. 10, 1940, El Paso, Tex.

BB TR 6' 175 lbs.

1912	PHI	N	16	12	.571	3.28	44	27	16	255	246	106	118	2	3	1	2	83	18	0	.217	9	55	5	2	1.6	.928
1913			27	12	.692	2.60	52	35	21	322.1	262	136	168	2	6	5	1	110	12	1	.109	18	86	2	1	2.0	.981
1914	BKN	F	25	13	.658	3.03	44	38	26	302.2	299	102	172	7	2	0	2	107	22	1	.206	18	84	8	3	2.5	.927
1915	2 teams	BKN F (32G 12–11)			NWK F	(12G 3–6)																					
"	total		15	17	.469	3.92	44	33	20	264.1	260	120	114	0	1	1	4	92	20	2	.217	5	92	3	4	2.3	.970
1916	CHI	N	6	6	.500	3.27	31	14	4	121	108	43	45	0	3	2	1	38	7	0	.184	5	36	1	0	1.4	.976
1917			5	4	.556	2.53	16	9	3	74.2	60	23	27	1	1	1	1	21	5	0	.238	2	25	1	0	1.8	.964
6 yrs.			94	64	.595	3.14	231	156	90	1340	1235	530	644	16	15	10	11	451	84	4	.186	54	378	20	10	2.0	.956

Tom Seats

SEATS, THOMAS EDWARD
B. Sept. 24, 1911, Farmington, N. C.

BR TL 5'11" 190 lbs.
BB 1940

1940	DET	A	2	2	.500	4.69	26	2	0	55.2	67	21	25	0	2	1	1	12	1	0	.083	4	11	0	0	0.6	1.000
1945	BKN	N	10	7	.588	4.36	31	18	6	121.2	127	37	44	2	2	1	0	43	9	0	.209	5	25	2	0	1.0	.938
2 yrs.			12	9	.571	4.47	57	20	6	177.1	194	58	69	2	4	2	1	55	10	0	.182	9	36	2	0	0.8	.957

Tom Seaver

SEAVER, GEORGE THOMAS (Tom Terrific)
B. Nov. 17, 1944, Fresno, Calif.

BR TR 6'1" 195 lbs.

1967	NY	N	16	13	.552	2.76	35	34	18	251	224	78	170	2	0	0	0	77	11	0	.143	17	38	1	3	1.6	.982
1968			16	12	.571	2.20	36	35	14	278	224	48	205	5	0	0	1	95	15	0	.158	21	48	1	4	1.9	.986
1969			25	7	.781	2.21	36	35	18	273.1	202	82	208	5	0	0	0	91	11	0	.121	18	48	2	7	1.9	.971
1970			18	12	.600	2.81	37	36	19	291	230	83	283	2	0	0	0	95	17	1	.179	19	46	3	3	1.8	.956
1971			20	10	.667	1.76	36	35	21	286	210	61	289	4	0	1	0	92	18	1	.196	17	38	1	3	1.6	.982
1972			21	12	.636	2.92	35	35	13	262	215	77	249	3	0	0	0	89	13	3	.146	17	40	3	3	1.7	.950
1973			19	10	.655	2.08	36	36	18	290	219	64	251	3	0	0	0	93	15	1	.161	26	35	5	1	1.8	.924
1974			11	11	.500	3.20	32	32	12	236	199	75	201	5	0	0	0	71	7	0	.099	9	42	1	7	1.6	.981
1975			22	9	.710	2.38	36	36	15	280	217	88	243	5	0	0	0	95	17	0	.179	21	43	4	6	1.9	.941
1976			14	11	.560	2.59	35	34	13	271	211	77	235	5	0	0	0	82	7	0	.085	12	41	1	3	1.5	.981
1977	2 teams	NY N (13G 7–3)			CIN N	(20G 14–3)																					
"	total		21	6	.778	2.58	33	33	19	261.1	199	66	196	7	0	0	0	86	17	3	.198	13	33	1	3	1.4	.979
1978	CIN	N	16	14	.533	2.87	36	36	8	260	218	89	226	1	0	0	0	74	9	0	.122	15	28	6	2	1.4	.878
1979			16	6	.727	3.14	32	32	9	215	187	61	131	5	0	0	0	76	12	2	.158	22	26	2	2	1.6	.960
1980			10	8	.556	3.64	26	26	5	168	140	59	101	1	0	0	0	46	6	0	.130	16	26	0	1	1.6	1.000
1981			14	2	.875	2.55	23	23	6	166	120	66	87	1	0	0	0	55	11	1	.200	8	22	1	1	1.3	.968
1982			5	13	.278	5.50	21	21	0	111.1	136	44	62	0	0	0	0	34	6	0	.176	7	11	2	1	1.0	.900
1983	NY	N	9	14	.391	3.55	34	34	5	231	201	86	135	2	0	0	0	64	10	0	.156	22	28	4	0	1.6	.926
1984	CHI	A	15	11	.577	3.95	34	33	10	236.2	216	61	131	4	1	0	0	0	0	0	–	11	40	0	2	1.5	1.000
1985			16	11	.593	3.17	35	33	6	238.2	223	69	134	1	0	0	0	0	0	0	–	20	43	2	2	1.9	.969
1986	2 teams	CHI A (12G 2–6)			BOS A	(16G 5–7)																					
"	total		7	13	.350	4.03	28	28	2	176.1	180	56	103	0	0	0	0	0	0	0	–	17	16	2	1	1.3	.943
20 yrs.			311	205	.603	2.86	656	647	231	4782.2	3971	1390	3640	61	1	2	1	1315	202	12	.154	328	692	42	54	1.6	.960
														3rd	7th												

LEAGUE CHAMPIONSHIP SERIES

1969	NY	N	1	0	1.000	6.43	1	1	0	7	8	3	2	0	0	0	0	3	0	0	.000	1	1	0	0	2.0	1.000
1973			1	1	.500	1.62	2	2	1	16.2	13	5	17	0	0	0	0	6	2	0	.333	0	3	0	0	1.5	1.000
1979	CIN	N	0	0	–	2.25	1	1	0	8	5	2	5	0	0	0	0	2	0	0	.000	0	0	0	0	0.0	–
3 yrs.			2	1	.667	2.84	4	4	1	31.2	26	10	24	0	0	0	0	11	2	0	.182	1	4	0	0	1.3	1.000

WORLD SERIES

1969	NY	N	1	1	.500	3.00	2	2	1	15	12	3	9	0	0	0	0	4	0	0	.000	1	1	0	0	1.5	1.000
1973			0	1	.000	2.40	2	2	0	15	13	3	18	0	0	0	0	5	0	0	.000	0	2	0	0	1.0	1.000
2 yrs.			1	2	.333	2.70	4	4	1	30	25	6	27	0	0	0	0	9	0	0	.000	2	3	0	0	1.3	1.000

Bob Sebra

SEBRA, ROBERT BUSH
B. Dec. 11, 1961, Ridgewood, N. J.

BR TR 6'2" 200 lbs.

1985	TEX	A	0	2	.000	7.52	7	4	0	20.1	26	14	13	0	0	0	0	0	0	0	–	1	1	0	1	0.3	1.000
1986	MON	N	5	5	.500	3.55	17	13	3	91.1	82	25	66	1	1	1	0	29	6	0	.207	8	8	0	2	0.9	1.000
1987			6	15	.286	4.42	36	27	4	177.1	184	67	156	1	0	0	0	51	8	0	.157	11	21	2	0	0.9	.941
1988	PHI	N	1	2	.333	7.94	3	3	0	11.1	15	10	7	0	0	0	0	5	0	0	.000	0	1	0	0	0.3	1.000
1989	2 teams	PHI N (6G 2–3)			CIN N	(15G 0–0)																					
"	total		2	3	.400	5.20	21	5	0	55.1	65	28	35	0	0	1	1	11	0	0	.000	2	8	3	0	0.6	.769
5 yrs.			14	27	.341	4.61	84	52	7	355.2	372	144	277	2	1	2	1	96	14	0	.146	22	39	5	3	0.8	.924

Doc Sechrist

SECHRIST, THEODORE O'HARA
B. Feb. 10, 1876, Williamstown, Ky. D. Apr. 2, 1950, Louisville, Ky.

BR TR 5'9" 160 lbs.

| 1899 | NY | N | 0 | 0 | – | 0.00 | 1 | 0 | 0 | 0 | 2 | 0 | 0 | 0 | 0 | 0 | 0 | 0 | 0 | 0 | – | 0 | 0 | 0 | 0 | 0.0 | – |

Year	Team		W	L	PCT	ERA	G	GS	CG	IP	H	BB	SO	ShO	Relief Pitching W	L	SV	Batting AB	H	HR	BA	PO	A	E	DP	TC/G	FA

Don Secrist

SECRIST, DONALD LAVERNE
B. Feb. 26, 1944, Seattle, Wash.

BL TL 6'2" 195 lbs.

Year	Team		W	L	PCT	ERA	G	GS	CG	IP	H	BB	SO	ShO	W	L	SV	AB	H	HR	BA	PO	A	E	DP	TC/G	FA
1969	CHI	A	0	1	.000	6.08	19	0	0	40	35	14	23	0	0	1	0	7	1	0	.143	2	7	1	0	0.5	.900
1970			0	0	–	5.40	9	0	0	15	19	12	9	0	0	0	0	0	0	0	–	0	2	0	0	0.2	1.000
2 yrs.			0	1	.000	5.89	28	0	0	55	54	26	32	0	0	1	0	7	1	0	.143	2	9	1	0	0.4	.917

Duke Sedgwick

SEDGWICK, HENRY KENNETH
B. June 1, 1898, Martin's Ferry, Ohio D. Nov. 4, 1982, Clearwater, Fla.

BR TR 6' 175 lbs.

Year	Team		W	L	PCT	ERA	G	GS	CG	IP	H	BB	SO	ShO	W	L	SV	AB	H	HR	BA	PO	A	E	DP	TC/G	FA
1921	PHI	N	1	3	.250	4.92	16	5	1	71.1	81	32	21	0	0	0	0	24	5	0	.208	2	14	3	0	1.2	.842
1923	WAS	A	0	1	.000	7.88	5	2	1	16	27	6	4	0	0	0	0	5	0	0	.000	0	8	1	1	1.8	.889
2 yrs.			1	4	.200	5.46	21	7	2	87.1	108	38	25	0	0	0	0	29	5	0	.172	2	22	4	1	1.3	.857

Charlie See

SEE, CHARLES HENRY (Chad)
B. Oct. 13, 1896, Pleasantville, N. Y. D. July 19, 1948, Bridgeport, Conn.

BL TR 5'10½" 175 lbs.

Year	Team		W	L	PCT	ERA	G	GS	CG	IP	H	BB	SO	ShO	W	L	SV	AB	H	HR	BA	PO	A	E	DP	TC/G	FA
1920	CIN	N	0	0	–	6.00	1	0	0	6	6	4	3	0	0	0	0	*				0	2	2	0	4.0	.500

Chuck Seelbach

SEELBACH, CHARLES FREDERICK III
B. Mar. 20, 1948, Lakewood, Ohio

BR TR 6' 180 lbs.

Year	Team		W	L	PCT	ERA	G	GS	CG	IP	H	BB	SO	ShO	W	L	SV	AB	H	HR	BA	PO	A	E	DP	TC/G	FA
1971	DET	A	0	0	–	13.50	5	0	0	4	6	7	1	0	0	0	0	0	0	0	–	0	0	0	0	0.0	–
1972			9	8	.529	2.89	61	3	0	112	96	39	76	0	9	5	14	21	3	0	.143	1	17	3	1	0.3	.857
1973			1	0	1.000	3.86	5	0	0	7	7	2	2	0	1	0	0	0	0	0	–	1	4	0	0	1.0	1.000
1974			0	0	–	4.50	4	0	0	8	9	3	0	0	0	0	0	0	0	0	–	0	1	0	0	0.3	1.000
4 yrs.			10	8	.556	3.37	75	3	0	131	118	51	79	0	10	5	14	21	3	0	.143	2	22	3	1	0.4	.889

LEAGUE CHAMPIONSHIP SERIES

Year	Team		W	L	PCT	ERA	G	GS	CG	IP	H	BB	SO	ShO	W	L	SV	AB	H	HR	BA	PO	A	E	DP	TC/G	FA
1972	DET	A	0	0	–	18.00	2	0	0	1	4	0	0	0	0	0	0	0	0	0	–	0	0	0	0	0.0	–

Emmett Seery

SEERY, JOHN EMMETT
B. Feb. 13, 1861, Princeville, Ill. Deceased.

BL TR

Year	Team		W	L	PCT	ERA	G	GS	CG	IP	H	BB	SO	ShO	W	L	SV	AB	H	HR	BA	PO	A	E	DP	TC/G	FA
1886	STL	N	0	0	–	7.71	2	0	0	7	8	3	2	0	0	0	0	*				0	1	1	0	1.0	.500

Herman Segelke

SEGELKE, HERMAN NEILS
B. Apr. 24, 1958, San Mateo, Calif.

BR TR 6'4" 215 lbs.

Year	Team		W	L	PCT	ERA	G	GS	CG	IP	H	BB	SO	ShO	W	L	SV	AB	H	HR	BA	PO	A	E	DP	TC/G	FA
1982	CHI	N	0	0	–	8.31	3	0	0	4.1	6	6	4	0	0	0	0	0	0	0	–	1	0	0	0	0.3	1.000

Diego Segui

SEGUI, DIEGO PABLO
Born Diego Pablo Segui y Gonzalez.
B. Aug. 17, 1937, Holguin, Cuba

BR TR 6' 190 lbs.

Year	Team		W	L	PCT	ERA	G	GS	CG	IP	H	BB	SO	ShO	W	L	SV	AB	H	HR	BA	PO	A	E	DP	TC/G	FA
1962	KC	A	8	5	.615	3.86	37	13	2	116.2	89	46	71	0	3	2	6	34	8	1	.235	11	17	1	2	0.8	.966
1963			9	6	.600	3.77	38	23	4	167	173	73	116	1	1	0	0	55	12	0	.218	7	33	6	1	1.2	.870
1964			8	17	.320	4.56	40	35	5	217	219	94	155	2	0	0	0	71	11	1	.155	24	38	2	0	1.6	.969
1965			5	15	.250	4.64	40	25	5	163	166	67	119	1	0	2	0	47	9	1	.191	13	20	1	1	0.9	.971
1966	WAS	A	3	7	.300	5.00	21	13	1	72	82	24	54	1	1	0	0	18	2	0	.111	6	8	1	0	0.7	.933
1967	KC	A	3	4	.429	3.09	36	3	0	70	62	31	52	0	3	1	1	9	0	0	.000	5	8	0	0	0.4	1.000
1968	OAK	A	6	5	.545	2.39	52	0	0	83	51	32	72	0	6	5	6	9	1	0	.111	4	8	0	0	0.2	1.000
1969	SEA	A	12	6	.667	3.35	66	8	2	142.1	127	61	113	0	8	4	12	27	4	0	.148	8	23	0	0	0.5	1.000
1970	OAK	A	10	10	.500	2.56	47	19	3	162	130	68	95	2	2	3	2	43	5	0	.116	17	14	2	2	0.7	.939
1971			10	8	.556	3.14	26	21	5	146	122	63	81	0	1	0	0	47	4	1	.085	11	21	1	0	1.2	.969
1972	2 teams	OAK A (7G 0–1)				STL N (33G 3–1)																					
"	total		3	2	.600	3.20	40	3	0	78.2	72	39	65	0	3	2	9	14	2	0	.143	5	12	1	1	0.5	.895
1973	STL	N	7	6	.538	2.78	65	0	0	100.1	78	53	93	0	7	6	17	10	0	0	.000	4	8	1	0	0.2	.923
1974	BOS	A	6	8	.429	4.00	58	0	0	108	106	49	76	0	6	8	10	0	0	0	–	5	12	0	1	0.3	1.000
1975			2	5	.286	4.82	33	1	1	71	71	43	45	0	2	4	6	0	0	0	–	2	8	0	1	0.3	1.000
1977	SEA	A	0	7	.000	5.68	40	7	0	111	108	43	91	0	0	3	2	0	0	0	–	6	14	0	2	0.5	1.000
15 yrs.			92	111	.453	3.81	639	171	28	1808	1656	786	1298	7	43	40	71	384	58	4	.151	128	243	17	11	0.6	.956

LEAGUE CHAMPIONSHIP SERIES

Year	Team		W	L	PCT	ERA	G	GS	CG	IP	H	BB	SO	ShO	W	L	SV	AB	H	HR	BA	PO	A	E	DP	TC/G	FA
1971	OAK	A	0	1	.000	5.79	1	1	0	4.2	6	6	4	0	0	0	0	2	0	0	.000	0	0	0	0	0.0	–

WORLD SERIES

Year	Team		W	L	PCT	ERA	G	GS	CG	IP	H	BB	SO	ShO	W	L	SV	AB	H	HR	BA	PO	A	E	DP	TC/G	FA
1975	BOS	A	0	0	–	0.00	1	0	0	1	0	2	0	0	0	0	0	0	0	0	–	0	0	0	0	0.0	–

Jose Segura

SEGURA, JOSE ALTAGRACIA
Born Jose Altagracia Segura y Mota.
B. Jan. 26, 1963, Fundacion, Dominican Republic

BR TR 5'11" 180 lbs.

Year	Team		W	L	PCT	ERA	G	GS	CG	IP	H	BB	SO	ShO	W	L	SV	AB	H	HR	BA	PO	A	E	DP	TC/G	FA
1988	CHI	A	0	0	–	13.50	4	0	0	8.2	19	8	2	0	0	0	0	–				0	3	0	0	0.8	1.000
1989			0	1	.000	15.00	7	0	0	6	13	3	4	0	0	1	0	–				0	2	0	0	0.3	1.000
2 yrs.			0	1	.000	14.11	11	0	0	14.2	32	11	6	0	0	1	0	–				0	5	0	0	0.5	1.000

Socks Seibold

SEIBOLD, HARRY
B. Apr. 3, 1896, Philadelphia, Pa. D. Sept. 21, 1965, Philadelphia, Pa.

BR TR 5'8½" 162 lbs.

Year	Team		W	L	PCT	ERA	G	GS	CG	IP	H	BB	SO	ShO	W	L	SV	AB	H	HR	BA	PO	A	E	DP	TC/G	FA
1915	PHI	A	0	0	–	0.00	0	0	0	0	0	0	0	0	0	0	0	26	3	0	.115	0	0	0	0	0.0	–
1916			1	2	.333	4.15	3	2	1	21.2	22	9	5	1	0	0	0	12	2	0	.167	4	10	0	0	4.7	1.000
1917			4	16	.200	3.94	33	15	9	160	141	85	55	1	1	5	1	59	13	0	.220	3	41	1	2	1.4	.978
1919			2	3	.400	5.32	14	4	1	45.2	58	26	19	0	1	0	0	13	2	0	.154	5	11	1	1	1.2	.941
1929	BOS	N	12	17	.414	4.73	33	27	16	205.2	228	80	54	1	1	1	1	70	20	0	.286	11	40	0	3	1.5	1.000
1930			15	16	.484	4.12	36	33	20	251	288	85	70	0	1	1	1	90	19	1	.211	10	38	3	3	1.4	.941
1931			10	18	.357	4.67	33	29	10	206.1	226	65	50	3	1	1	0	70	9	0	.129	5	44	0	5	1.5	1.000
1932			3	10	.231	4.68	28	20	6	136.2	173	41	33	1	0	1	1	46	7	0	.152	12	36	0	4	1.7	1.000
1933			1	4	.200	3.68	11	5	1	36.2	43	14	10	0	0	1	1	9	1	0	.111	1	9	0	0	1.0	1.000
9 yrs.			48	86	.358	4.43	191	135	64	1063.2	1179	405	296	8	4	11	5	395	76	1	.192	51	229	5	18	1.5	.982

Year	Team		W	L	PCT	ERA	G	GS	CG	IP	H	BB	SO	ShO	Relief Pitching W	L	SV	Batting AB	H	HR	BA	PO	A	E	DP	TC/G	FA

Epp Sell

SELL, LESTER ELWOOD BR TR 6' 175 lbs.
B. Apr. 26, 1897, Llewellyn, Pa. D. Feb. 19, 1961, Reading, Pa.

Year	Team		W	L	PCT	ERA	G	GS	CG	IP	H	BB	SO	ShO	W	L	SV	AB	H	HR	BA	PO	A	E	DP	TC/G	FA
1922	STL	N	4	2	.667	6.82	7	5	0	33	47	6	5	0	2	0	0	12	4	0	.333	0	11	0	0	1.6	1.000
1923			0	1	.000	6.00	5	1	0	15	16	8	2	0	0	1	0	7	0	0	.000	0	3	0	0	0.6	1.000
2 yrs.			4	3	.571	6.56	12	6	0	48	63	14	7	0	2	1	0	19	4	0	.211	0	14	0	0	1.2	1.000

Jeff Sellers

SELLERS, JEFFREY DOYLE BR TR 6'1" 195 lbs.
B. May 11, 1964, Compton, Calif.

Year	Team		W	L	PCT	ERA	G	GS	CG	IP	H	BB	SO	ShO	W	L	SV	AB	H	HR	BA	PO	A	E	DP	TC/G	FA
1985	BOS	A	2	0	1.000	3.63	4	4	1	22.1	24	7	6	0	0	0	0	0	0	0	–	2	4	2	0	2.0	.750
1986			3	7	.300	4.94	14	13	1	82	90	40	51	0	0	0	0	0	0	0	–	9	9	0	1	1.3	1.000
1987			7	8	.467	5.28	25	22	4	139.2	161	61	99	2	0	0	0	0	0	0	–	13	20	2	0	1.4	.943
1988			1	7	.125	4.83	18	12	1	85.2	89	56	70	0	1	0	0	0	0	0	–	4	10	1	0	0.8	.933
4 yrs.			13	22	.371	4.97	61	51	7	329.2	364	164	226	2	1	0	0	0	0	0	–	28	43	5	1	1.2	.934

Dave Sells

SELLS, DAVID WAYNE BR TR 5'11" 175 lbs.
B. Sept. 18, 1946, Vacaville, Calif.

Year	Team		W	L	PCT	ERA	G	GS	CG	IP	H	BB	SO	ShO	W	L	SV	AB	H	HR	BA	PO	A	E	DP	TC/G	FA
1972	CAL	A	2	0	1.000	2.81	10	0	0	16	11	6	5	0	2	0	0	0	0	0	–	2	4	0	0	0.6	1.000
1973			7	2	.778	3.71	51	0	0	68	72	35	25	0	7	2	10	0	0	0	–	1	13	1	1	0.3	.933
1974			2	3	.400	3.69	20	0	0	39	48	16	14	0	2	3	2	0	0	0	–	2	8	1	1	0.6	.909
1975	2 teams	CAL A (4G 0–0)													LA N	(5G 0–2)											
"	total		0	2	.000	6.46	9	0	0	15.1	15	11	8	0	0	2	0	1	1	0	1.000	1	3	0	0	0.4	1.000
4 yrs.			11	7	.611	3.90	90	0	0	138.1	146	67	49	0	11	7	12	1	1	0	1.000	6	28	2	2	0.4	.944

Dick Selma

SELMA, RICHARD JAY BR TR 5'11" 160 lbs.
B. Nov. 4, 1943, Santa Ana, Calif. BB 1966

Year	Team		W	L	PCT	ERA	G	GS	CG	IP	H	BB	SO	ShO	W	L	SV	AB	H	HR	BA	PO	A	E	DP	TC/G	FA
1965	NY	N	2	1	.667	3.71	4	4	1	26.2	22	9	26	0	0	0	0	9	2	0	.222	4	5	0	0	2.3	1.000
1966			4	6	.400	4.24	30	7	0	80.2	84	39	58	0	4	2	1	14	1	0	.071	4	20	1	1	0.8	.960
1967			2	4	.333	2.77	38	4	0	81.1	71	36	52	0	2	3	2	22	2	0	.091	7	16	1	1	0.6	.958
1968			9	10	.474	2.75	33	23	4	170.1	148	54	117	3	0	0	0	58	12	0	.207	12	35	1	0	1.5	.979
1969	2 teams	SD N (4G 1–0)													CHI N	(36G 10–8)											
"	total		12	10	.545	3.68	40	28	5	190.2	156	81	181	2	3	1	1	59	10	0	.169	8	25	2	2	0.9	.943
1970	PHI	N	8	9	.471	2.75	73	0	0	134	108	59	153	0	8	9	22	20	3	0	.150	8	24	1	3	0.5	.970
1971			0	2	.000	3.24	17	0	0	25	21	8	15	0	0	2	0	1	1	0	1.000	2	5	1	0	0.5	.875
1972			2	9	.182	5.56	46	10	1	98.2	91	73	58	0	1	0	3	20	4	0	.200	3	18	0	1	0.5	1.000
1973			1	1	.500	5.63	6	0	0	8	6	5	4	0	1	1	0	0	0	0	–	2	3	0	0	0.8	1.000
1974	2 teams	CAL A (18G 2–2)													MIL A	(2G 0–0)											
"	total		2	2	.500	6.48	20	0	0	25	27	17	17	0	2	2	1	0	0	0	–	2	6	0	1	0.4	1.000
10 yrs.			42	54	.438	3.62	307	76	11	840.1	734	381	681	6	21	20	31	203	35	0	.172	52	157	7	9	0.7	.968

Carroll Sembera

SEMBERA, CARROLL WILLIAM BR TR 6' 155 lbs.
B. July 26, 1941, Shiner, Tex.

Year	Team		W	L	PCT	ERA	G	GS	CG	IP	H	BB	SO	ShO	W	L	SV	AB	H	HR	BA	PO	A	E	DP	TC/G	FA
1965	HOU	N	0	1	.000	3.68	2	1	0	7.1	5	3	4	0	0	0	0	1	0	0	.000	2	0	0	0	1.0	1.000
1966			1	2	.333	3.00	24	0	0	33	36	16	21	0	1	2	1	3	0	0	.000	3	6	0	0	0.4	1.000
1967			2	6	.250	4.83	45	0	0	59.2	66	19	48	0	2	6	3	7	1	0	.143	2	15	0	0	0.4	1.000
1969	MON	N	0	2	.000	3.55	23	0	0	33	28	24	15	0	0	2	2	4	1	0	.250	0	6	1	1	0.3	.857
1970			0	0	–	18.00	5	0	0	7	14	11	6	0	0	0	0	0	0	0	–	0	1	0	0	0.2	1.000
5 yrs.			3	11	.214	4.69	99	1	0	140	149	73	94	0	3	10	6	15	2	0	.133	5	30	1	1	0.4	.972

Ray Semproch

SEMPROCH, ROMAN ANTHONY (Baby) BR TR 5'11" 180 lbs.
B. Jan. 7, 1931, Cleveland, Ohio

Year	Team		W	L	PCT	ERA	G	GS	CG	IP	H	BB	SO	ShO	W	L	SV	AB	H	HR	BA	PO	A	E	DP	TC/G	FA
1958	PHI	N	13	11	.542	3.92	36	30	12	204.1	211	89	92	2	2	2	0	74	7	0	.095	13	31	0	0	1.2	1.000
1959			3	10	.231	5.40	30	18	2	111.2	119	59	54	0	1	0	3	34	6	0	.176	6	21	1	4	0.9	.964
1960	DET	A	3	0	1.000	4.00	17	0	0	27	29	16	9	0	3	0	0	4	0	0	.000	0	11	2	1	0.8	.846
1961	LA	A	0	0	–	9.00	2	0	0	1	1	3	1	0	0	0	0	0	0	0	–	0	1	0	0	0.5	1.000
4 yrs.			19	21	.475	4.42	85	48	14	344	360	136	156	2	6	2	3	112	13	0	.116	19	64	3	5	1.0	.965

Steve Senteney

SENTENEY, STEPHEN LEONARD BR TR 6'2" 205 lbs.
B. Aug. 7, 1955, Indianapolis, Ind. D. June 19, 1989, Colusa, Calif.

Year	Team		W	L	PCT	ERA	G	GS	CG	IP	H	BB	SO	ShO	W	L	SV	AB	H	HR	BA	PO	A	E	DP	TC/G	FA
1982	TOR	A	0	0	–	4.91	11	0	0	22	23	6	20	0	0	0	0	0	0	0	–	1	1	0	0	0.2	1.000

Manny Seoane

SEOANE, MANUEL MODESTO BR TR 6'3" 187 lbs.
B. June 26, 1955, Tampa, Fla.

Year	Team		W	L	PCT	ERA	G	GS	CG	IP	H	BB	SO	ShO	W	L	SV	AB	H	HR	BA	PO	A	E	DP	TC/G	FA
1977	PHI	N	0	0	–	6.00	2	1	0	6	11	3	4	0	0	0	0	2	1	0	.500	0	0	0	0	0.0	–
1978	CHI	N	1	0	1.000	5.63	7	1	0	8	11	6	5	0	1	0	0	0	0	0	–	0	0	0	0	0.0	–
2 yrs.			1	0	1.000	5.79	9	2	0	14	22	9	9	0	1	0	0	2	1	0	.500	0	0	0	0	0.0	–

Billy Serad

SERAD, WILLIAM I. BR TR 5'7" 156 lbs.
B. 1863, Philadelphia, Pa. D. Nov. 1, 1925, Chester, Pa.

Year	Team		W	L	PCT	ERA	G	GS	CG	IP	H	BB	SO	ShO	W	L	SV	AB	H	HR	BA	PO	A	E	DP	TC/G	FA
1884	BUF	N	16	20	.444	4.27	37	37	34	308	373	111	150	2	0	0	0	137	24	0	.175	4	57	14	1	2.0	.813
1885			7	21	.250	4.10	30	29	27	241.1	299	80	90	0	0	0	0	104	16	0	.154	9	38	9	2	1.9	.839
1887	CIN	AA	10	11	.476	4.08	22	21	20	187.1	201	80	34	2	0	0	0	79	14	0	.177	7	37	6	1	2.3	.880
1888			2	3	.400	3.55	6	5	5	50.2	62	19	4	0	1	0	0	23	3	0	.130	2	10	3	1	2.5	.800
4 yrs.			35	55	.389	4.13	95	92	86	787.1	935	290	278	4	1	0	0	343	57	0	.166	22	142	32	5	2.1	.837

Gary Serum

SERUM, GARY WAYNE BR TR 6'1" 180 lbs.
B. Oct. 24, 1956, Fargo, N. D.

Year	Team		W	L	PCT	ERA	G	GS	CG	IP	H	BB	SO	ShO	W	L	SV	AB	H	HR	BA	PO	A	E	DP	TC/G	FA
1977	MIN	A	0	0	–	4.30	8	0	0	23	22	10	14	0	0	0	0	0	0	0	–	0	2	0	0	0.3	1.000
1978			9	9	.500	4.10	34	23	6	184.1	188	44	80	1	1	1	1	0	0	0	–	17	25	0	2	1.2	1.000
1979			1	3	.250	6.61	20	5	0	64	93	20	31	0	1	0	0	0	0	0	–	5	10	1	0	0.8	.938
3 yrs.			10	12	.455	4.71	62	28	6	271.1	303	74	125	1	2	1	1	0	0	0	–	22	37	1	2	1.0	.983

Year	Team		W	L	PCT	ERA	G	GS	CG	IP	H	BB	SO	ShO	Relief Pitching W	L	SV	Batting AB	H	HR	BA	PO	A	E	DP	TC/G	FA

Scott Service

SERVICE, DAVID SCOTT
B. Feb. 26, 1967, Cincinnati, Ohio
BR TR 6'6" 225 lbs.

| 1988 | PHI | N | 0 | 0 | – | 1.69 | 5 | 0 | 0 | 5.1 | 7 | 1 | 6 | 0 | 0 | 0 | 0 | 0 | 0 | 0 | – | 0 | 0 | 0 | 0 | 0.0 | – |

Merle Settlemire

SETTLEMIRE, EDGAR MERLE (Lefty)
B. Jan. 19, 1903, Santa Fe, Ohio   D. June 12, 1988, Russells Point, Ohio
BL TL 5'9" 156 lbs.

| 1928 | BOS | A | 0 | 6 | .000 | 5.47 | 30 | 9 | 0 | 82.1 | 116 | 34 | 12 | 0 | 0 | 5 | 0 | 17 | 3 | 0 | .176 | 1 | 30 | 2 | 3 | 1.1 | .939 |

Al Severinsen

SEVERINSEN, ALBERT HENRY
B. Nov. 9, 1944, Brooklyn, N. Y.
BR TR 6'3" 220 lbs.

1969	BAL	A	1	1	.500	2.29	12	0	0	19.2	14	10	13	0	1	1	0	3	1	0	.333	2	4	0	1	0.5	1.000
1971	SD	N	2	5	.286	3.47	59	0	0	70	77	30	31	0	2	5	8	1	0	0	.000	5	17	0	2	0.4	1.000
1972			0	1	.000	2.53	17	0	0	21.1	13	7	9	0	0	1	1	1	0	0	.000	0	5	0	0	0.3	1.000
3 yrs.			3	7	.300	3.08	88	0	0	111	104	47	53	0	3	7	9	5	1	0	.200	7	26	0	3	0.4	1.000

Ed Seward

SEWARD, EDWARD WILLIAM
Born Edward William Sourhardt.
B. June 29, 1867, Cleveland, Ohio   D. July 30, 1947, Cleveland, Ohio
TR 5'7" 175 lbs.

1885	PRO	N	0	0	–	0.00	1	0	0	6	2	0	1	0	0	0	0	3	0	0	.000	0	4	0	0	4.0	1.000
1887	PHI	AA	25	25	.500	4.13	55	52	52	470.2	445	140	155	3	1	0	0	266	50	5	.188	21	79	11	1	2.0	.901
1888			35	19	.648	2.01	57	57	57	518.2	388	127	272	6	0	0	0	225	32	2	.142	24	125	19	4	2.9	.887
1889			21	15	.583	3.97	39	38	35	320	353	101	102	3	0	0	0	143	31	2	.217	13	67	9	1	2.3	.899
1890			6	12	.333	4.73	21	19	15	154	165	72	55	1	0	1	0	72	10	0	.139	17	26	10	2	2.5	.811
1891	CLE	N	2	1	.667	3.86	3	3	0	16.1	16	11	4	0	0	0	0	19	4	0	.211	0	1	0	0	0.3	1.000
6 yrs.			89	72	.553	3.40	176	169	159	1485.2	1369	451	589	13	1	1	0	*				75	302	49	8	2.4	.885

Frank Seward

SEWARD, FRANK MARTIN
B. Apr. 7, 1921, Pennsauken, N. J.
BR TR 6'3" 200 lbs.

1943	NY	N	0	1	.000	3.00	1	1	1	9	12	5	2	0	0	0	0	4	0	0	.000	0	2	0	0	2.0	1.000
1944			3	2	.600	5.40	25	7	2	78.1	98	32	16	0	2	2	0	24	2	0	.083	5	8	0	0	0.5	1.000
2 yrs.			3	3	.500	5.15	26	8	3	87.1	110	37	18	0	2	2	0	28	2	0	.071	5	10	0	0	0.6	1.000

Rip Sewell

SEWELL, TRUETT BANKS
B. May 11, 1907, Decatur, Ala.   D. Sept. 3, 1989, Plant City, Fla.
BR TR 6'1" 180 lbs.

1932	DET	A	0	0	–	12.66	5	0	0	10.2	19	8	2	0	0	0	0	2	1	0	.500	1	3	0	0	0.8	1.000
1938	PIT	N	0	1	.000	4.23	17	0	0	38.1	41	21	17	0	0	1	1	12	1	0	.083	0	13	1	3	0.8	.929
1939			10	9	.526	4.08	52	12	5	176.1	177	73	69	1	4	3	2	55	11	1	.200	9	47	1	3	1.1	.982
1940			16	5	.762	2.80	33	23	14	189.2	169	67	60	2	3	1	1	73	14	1	.192	17	46	5	0	2.1	.926
1941			14	17	.452	3.72	39	32	18	249	225	84	76	2	2	0	2	92	16	1	.174	21	56	2	6	2.0	.975
1942			17	15	.531	3.41	40	33	18	248	259	72	69	5	2	2	2	87	13	0	.149	19	51	3	3	1.8	.959
1943			21	9	.700	2.54	35	31	25	265.1	267	75	65	2	0	1	3	105	30	0	.286	13	60	4	4	2.2	.948
1944			21	12	.636	3.18	38	33	24	286	263	99	87	3	3	0	2	112	25	1	.223	21	49	4	1	1.9	.946
1945			11	9	.550	4.07	33	24	9	188	212	91	60	1	2	1	1	64	20	0	.313	10	35	1	2	1.4	.978
1946			8	12	.400	3.68	25	20	11	149.1	140	53	33	2	1	1	0	50	9	0	.180	8	26	3	1	1.4	.944
1947			6	4	.600	3.57	24	12	4	121	121	36	36	1	2	0	1	40	5	1	.125	10	26	1	3	1.5	.973
1948			13	3	.813	3.48	21	17	7	121.2	126	37	36	1	0	2	0	42	6	1	.143	10	21	3	1	1.6	.912
1949			6	1	.857	3.91	28	6	2	76	82	32	26	1	4	1	1	16	1	0	.063	3	12	2	0	0.6	.882
13 yrs.			143	97	.596	3.48	390	243	137	2119.1	2101	748	636	20	25	11	15	750	152	6	.203	142	445	29	27	1.6	.953

Elmer Sexauer

SEXAUER, ELMER GEORGE
B. May 21, 1926, St. Louis County, Mo.
BR TR 6'4" 220 lbs.

| 1948 | BKN | N | 0 | 0 | – | 13.50 | 2 | 0 | 0 | .2 | 0 | 2 | 0 | 0 | 0 | 0 | 0 | 0 | 0 | 0 | – | 0 | 0 | 0 | 0 | 0.0 | – |

Frank Sexton

SEXTON, FRANK JOSEPH
B. July 8, 1872, Brockton, Mass.   D. Jan. 4, 1938, Brighton, Mass.

| 1895 | BOS | N | 1 | 5 | .167 | 5.69 | 7 | 5 | 4 | 49 | 59 | 22 | 14 | 0 | 0 | 1 | 0 | 22 | 5 | 0 | .227 | 2 | 8 | 0 | 0 | 1.4 | 1.000 |

Gordon Seyfried

SEYFRIED, GORDON CLAY
B. July 4, 1937, Long Beach, Calif.
BR TR 6' 185 lbs.

1963	CLE	A	0	1	.000	1.23	3	1	0	7.1	9	3	1	0	0	0	0	2	0	0	.000	1	3	0	0	1.3	1.000
1964			0	0	–	0.00	2	0	0	2.1	4	0	0	0	0	0	0	0	0	0	–	0	0	0	0	0.0	–
2 yrs.			0	1	.000	0.93	5	1	0	9.2	13	3	1	0	0	0	0	2	0	0	.000	1	3	0	0	0.8	1.000

Cy Seymour

SEYMOUR, JAMES BENTLEY
B. Dec. 9, 1872, Albany, N. Y.   D. Sept. 20, 1919, New York, N. Y.
BL TL 6' 200 lbs.

1896	NY	N	2	4	.333	6.40	11	8	4	70.1	75	51	33	0	0	0	0	32	7	0	.219	5	19	4	1	2.5	.857
1897			20	14	.588	3.21	38	33	28	292	254	164	149	2	1	1	0	137	33	2	.241	15	98	20	5	3.5	.850
1898			25	19	.568	3.18	45	43	39	356.2	313	213	239	4	2	0	0	297	82	4	.276	22	112	17	7	3.4	.887
1899			14	18	.438	3.56	32	32	31	268.1	247	170	142	0	0	0	0	159	52	2	.327	16	88	20	1	3.9	.839
1900			2	2	.500	6.63	13	7	3	57	60	60	19	0	0	0	0	40	12	0	.300	4	20	5	0	2.2	.828
1902	2 teams		BAL A		(0G 0–0)		CIN N	(1G 0–0)																				
"	total		0	0	–	9.00	3	0	0	4	3	4	3	0	0	0	0	515	157	5	.305	0	0	0	0	0.0	–
6 yrs.			63	57	.525	3.70	140	123	105	1047.1	953	661	584	6	3	1	1	*				62	337	66	14	3.3	.858

Jake Seymour

SEYMOUR, JACOB
Born Jacob Semer.
B. 1854, Pittsburgh, Pa.   D. Aug. 1, 1897, Allegheny, Pa.

| 1882 | PIT | AA | 0 | 1 | .000 | 7.88 | 1 | 1 | 1 | 8 | 16 | 2 | 2 | 0 | 0 | 0 | 0 | 4 | 0 | 0 | .000 | 1 | 2 | 1 | 0 | 4.0 | .750 |

Year	Team		W	L	PCT	ERA	G	GS	CG	IP	H	BB	SO	ShO	Relief Pitching W	L	SV	Batting AB	H	HR	BA	PO	A	E	DP	TC/G	FA

John Shaffer

SHAFFER, JOHN W. (Cannon Ball)
B. Feb. 18, 1864, Lock Haven, Pa.   D. Nov. 21, 1926, Endicott, N. Y.

Year	Team		W	L	PCT	ERA	G	GS	CG	IP	H	BB	SO	ShO	W	L	SV	AB	H	HR	BA	PO	A	E	DP	TC/G	FA
1886	NY	AA	5	3	.625	1.96	8	8	8	69	40	29	36	1	0	0	0	25	6	0	.240	2	7	2	1	1.4	.818
1887			2	11	.154	6.19	13	13	13	112	148	53	22	0	0	0	0	48	8	0	.167	7	33	4	0	3.4	.909
2 yrs.			7	14	.333	4.57	21	21	21	181	188	82	58	1	0	0	0	73	14	0	.192	9	40	6	1	2.6	.891

Gus Shallix

SHALLIX, AUGUST
Born August Schallick.
B. Mar. 29, 1858, Paderborn, Germany   D. Oct. 28, 1937, Cincinnati, Ohio

BR TR 5'11"   165 lbs.

Year	Team		W	L	PCT	ERA	G	GS	CG	IP	H	BB	SO	ShO	W	L	SV	AB	H	HR	BA	PO	A	E	DP	TC/G	FA
1884	CIN	AA	11	10	.524	3.70	23	23	23	199.2	163	53	78	0	0	0	0	84	3	0	.036	13	42	4	2	2.6	.932
1885			6	4	.600	3.25	13	12	7	91.1	95	33	15	0	1	0	0	39	5	0	.128	4	28	4	3	2.8	.889
2 yrs.			17	14	.548	3.56	36	35	30	291	258	86	93	0	1	0	0	123	8	0	.065	17	70	8	5	2.6	.916

Greg Shanahan

SHANAHAN, PAUL GREGORY JR.
B. Dec. 11, 1947, Eureka, Calif.

BR TR 6'2"   190 lbs.

Year	Team		W	L	PCT	ERA	G	GS	CG	IP	H	BB	SO	ShO	W	L	SV	AB	H	HR	BA	PO	A	E	DP	TC/G	FA
1973	LA	N	0	0	–	3.45	7	0	0	15.2	14	4	11	0	0	0	1	1	0	0	.000	1	2	0	0	0.4	1.000
1974			0	0	–	3.86	4	0	0	7	7	5	2	0	0	0	0	0	0	0	–	0	2	0	0	0.5	1.000
2 yrs.			0	0	–	3.57	11	0	0	22.2	21	9	13	0	0	0	1	1	0	0	.000	1	4	0	0	0.5	1.000

Harvey Shank

SHANK, HARVEY TILLMAN
B. July 29, 1946, Toronto, Ont., Canada

BR TR 6'4"   220 lbs.

Year	Team		W	L	PCT	ERA	G	GS	CG	IP	H	BB	SO	ShO	W	L	SV	AB	H	HR	BA	PO	A	E	DP	TC/G	FA
1970	CAL	A	0	0	–	0.00	1	0	0	3	2	2	1	0	0	0	0	0	0	0	–	0	0	0	0	0.0	–

Bill Shanner

SHANNER, WILFRED WILLIAM
B. Nov. 4, 1894, Oakland City, Ind.   D. Dec. 18, 1986, Evansville, Ind.

BL TR

Year	Team		W	L	PCT	ERA	G	GS	CG	IP	H	BB	SO	ShO	W	L	SV	AB	H	HR	BA	PO	A	E	DP	TC/G	FA
1920	PHI	A	0	0	–	6.75	1	0	0	4	6	1	1	0	0	0	0	1	0	0	.000	0	1	0	0	1.0	1.000

Bobby Shantz

SHANTZ, ROBERT CLAYTON
Brother of Billy Shantz.
B. Sept. 26, 1925, Pottstown, Pa.

BR TL 5'6"   139 lbs.

Year	Team		W	L	PCT	ERA	G	GS	CG	IP	H	BB	SO	ShO	W	L	SV	AB	H	HR	BA	PO	A	E	DP	TC/G	FA
1949	PHI	A	6	8	.429	3.40	33	7	4	127	100	74	58	1	3	4	2	37	7	0	.189	12	36	0	5	1.5	1.000
1950			8	14	.364	4.61	36	23	6	214.2	251	85	93	1	2	0	0	66	11	1	.167	13	52	2	6	1.9	.970
1951			18	10	.643	3.94	32	25	13	205.1	213	70	77	4	2	1	0	72	18	0	.250	20	44	2	7	2.1	.970
1952			24	7	.774	2.48	33	33	27	279.2	230	63	152	5	0	0	0	96	19	0	.198	29	49	0	3	2.4	1.000
1953			5	9	.357	4.09	16	16	6	105.2	107	26	58	0	0	0	0	38	9	0	.237	10	21	1	3	2.0	.969
1954			1	0	1.000	7.88	2	1	0	8	12	3	3	0	0	0	0	3	1	0	.333	1	2	1	0	2.0	.750
1955	KC	A	5	10	.333	4.54	23	17	4	125	124	66	58	1	2	0	0	41	6	0	.146	9	26	2	1	1.6	.946
1956			2	7	.222	4.35	45	2	1	101.1	95	37	67	0	1	6	9	22	2	0	.091	10	20	2	2	0.8	.938
1957	NY	A	11	5	.688	2.45	30	21	9	173	157	40	72	1	1	0	5	56	10	0	.179	14	57	1	8	2.4	.986
1958			7	6	.538	3.36	33	13	3	126	127	35	80	0	5	5	0	35	8	0	.229	6	35	0	1	1.2	1.000
1959			7	3	.700	2.38	33	4	2	94.2	64	33	66	2	5	1	3	23	5	0	.217	8	20	2	1	0.9	.933
1960			5	4	.556	2.79	42	0	0	67.2	57	24	54	0	5	4	11	10	1	0	.100	4	13	0	1	0.4	1.000
1961	PIT	N	6	3	.667	3.32	43	6	2	89.1	91	26	61	1	3	1	2	16	7	0	.438	13	18	0	2	0.7	1.000
1962	2 teams		HOU N (3G 1–1)			STL N (28G 5–3)																					
"	total		6	4	.600	1.95	31	3	1	78.1	60	25	61	0	5	3	4	21	2	0	.095	10	25	1	2	1.2	.972
1963	STL	N	6	4	.600	2.61	55	0	0	79.1	55	17	70	0	4	4	11	7	1	0	.143	9	22	1	2	0.6	.969
1964	3 teams		STL N (16G 0–1)			CHI N (20G 0–1)			PHI N (14G 1–1)																		
"	total		2	5	.286	3.12	50	0	0	60.2	52	19	42	0	2	5	1	5	0	0	.000	6	28	1	0	0.7	.971
16 yrs.			119	99	.546	3.38	537	171	78	1935.2	1795	643	1072	16	42	34	48	548	107	1	.195	174	468	16	48	1.2	.976

WORLD SERIES

Year	Team		W	L	PCT	ERA	G	GS	CG	IP	H	BB	SO	ShO	W	L	SV	AB	H	HR	BA	PO	A	E	DP	TC/G	FA
1957	NY	A	0	1	.000	4.05	3	1	0	6.2	8	2	7	0	0	1	0	1	0	0	.000	0	1	0	0	0.3	1.000
1960			0	0	–	4.26	3	0	0	6.1	4	1	1	0	0	0	0	3	1	0	.333	3	2	0	1	1.7	1.000
2 yrs.			0	1	.000	4.15	6	1	0	13	12	3	8	0	0	1	0	4	1	0	.250	3	3	0	1	1.0	1.000

George Sharrott

SHARROTT, GEORGE OSCAR
B. Nov. 2, 1869, West New Brighton, N. Y.   D. Jan. 6, 1932, Jamaica, N. Y.

BL TL

Year	Team		W	L	PCT	ERA	G	GS	CG	IP	H	BB	SO	ShO	W	L	SV	AB	H	HR	BA	PO	A	E	DP	TC/G	FA
1893	BKN	N	4	6	.400	5.87	13	10	10	95	114	58	24	0	0	0	0	39	9	1	.231	5	17	4	1	2.0	.846
1894			0	1	.000	7.00	2	2	1	9	7	5	2	0	0	0	0	3	1	0	.333	0	1	0	0	0.5	1.000
2 yrs.			4	7	.364	5.97	15	12	11	104	121	63	26	0	0	0	0	42	10	1	.238	5	18	4	1	1.8	.852

John Sharrott

SHARROTT, JOHN HENRY
B. Aug. 13, 1869, Bangor, Me.   D. Dec. 31, 1927, Los Angeles, Calif.

BL TL 5'9"   165 lbs.

Year	Team		W	L	PCT	ERA	G	GS	CG	IP	H	BB	SO	ShO	W	L	SV	AB	H	HR	BA	PO	A	E	DP	TC/G	FA
1890	NY	N	11	10	.524	2.89	25	20	18	184	162	88	84	0	1	1	0	109	22	0	.202	7	46	9	0	2.5	.855
1891			4	5	.444	2.60	10	9	6	69.1	47	35	41	0	0	0	0	30	10	1	.333	4	15	1	0	2.0	.950
1892			0	0	–	4.50	1	0	0	2	2	1	1	0	0	0	0	8	1	0	.125	0	0	0	0	0.0	–
1893	PHI	N	4	2	.667	4.50	12	4	2	56	53	33	11	0	4	0	0	152	38	1	.250	1	14	2	0	1.4	.882
4 yrs.			19	17	.528	3.12	48	33	26	311.1	264	157	137	0	5	1	0	299	71	2	.237	12	75	12	0	2.1	.879

Joe Shaute

SHAUTE, JOSEPH BENJAMIN (Lefty)
B. Aug. 1, 1899, Peckville, Pa.   D. Feb. 21, 1970, Scranton, Pa.

BL TL 6'   190 lbs.

Year	Team		W	L	PCT	ERA	G	GS	CG	IP	H	BB	SO	ShO	W	L	SV	AB	H	HR	BA	PO	A	E	DP	TC/G	FA
1922	CLE	A	0	0	–	19.64	2	0	0	3.2	7	3	3	0	0	0	0	5	0	0	.000	0	0	0	0	0.0	–
1923			10	8	.556	3.51	33	16	7	172	176	53	61	0	2	2	0	68	11	0	.162	6	37	2	2	1.4	.956
1924			20	17	.541	3.75	46	34	21	283	317	83	68	2	3	2	2	107	34	1	.318	12	59	5	1	1.7	.934
1925			4	12	.250	5.43	26	17	10	131	160	44	34	1	0	2	4	53	16	0	.302	4	26	0	1	1.2	1.000
1926			14	10	.583	3.53	34	25	15	206.2	215	65	47	2	1	0	0	73	20	0	.274	7	30	0	0	1.1	1.000
1927			9	16	.360	4.22	45	28	14	230.1	255	75	63	0	1	0	2	83	27	0	.325	15	45	0	2	1.3	1.000
1928			13	17	.433	4.04	36	32	21	253.2	295	68	81	1	1	0	1	92	21	0	.228	16	60	2	3	2.2	.974
1929			8	8	.500	4.28	26	24	8	162	211	52	43	0	0	0	0	58	17	0	.293	9	23	3	1	1.3	.914
1930			0	0	–	15.43	4	0	0	4.2	16	4	2	0	0	0	0	1	0	0	.000	0	1	0	0	0.5	1.000
1931	BKN	N	11	8	.579	4.83	25	19	6	128.2	162	32	50	0	4	3	2	45	8	0	.178	7	27	1	1	1.4	.971

Year	Team	W	L	PCT	ERA	G	GS	CG	IP	H	BB	SO	ShO	W	L	SV	AB	H	HR	BA	PO	A	E	DP	TC/G	FA
														Relief Pitching			Batting									

Joe Shaute continued

Year	Team	W	L	PCT	ERA	G	GS	CG	IP	H	BB	SO	ShO	W	L	SV	AB	H	HR	BA	PO	A	E	DP	TC/G	FA
1932		7	7	.500	4.62	34	9	1	117	147	21	32	0	6	4	4	45	9	0	.200	6	18	2	1	0.8	.923
1933		3	4	.429	3.49	41	4	0	108.1	125	31	26	0	3	2	2	27	6	0	.222	5	28	2	0	0.9	.943
1934	CIN N	0	2	.000	4.15	8	1	0	17.1	19	3	2	0	0	1	1	4	1	0	.250	0	1	0	0	0.1	1.000
13 yrs.		99	109	.476	4.15	360	209	103	1818.1	2097	534	512	5	20	14	18	660	170	1	.258	87	356	17	12	1.3	.963

Jeff Shaver

SHAVER, JEFFREY THOMAS
B. July 30, 1963, Beaver, Pa.

BR TR 6'3" 195 lbs.

Year	Team	W	L	PCT	ERA	G	GS	CG	IP	H	BB	SO	ShO	W	L	SV	AB	H	HR	BA	PO	A	E	DP	TC/G	FA
1988	OAK A	0	0	–	0.00	1	0	0	1	0	0	0	0	0	0	0	0	0	0	–	0	0	0	0	0.0	–

Bob Shaw

SHAW, ROBERT JOHN
B. June 29, 1933, Bronx, N. Y.

BR TR 6'2" 195 lbs.

Year	Team	W	L	PCT	ERA	G	GS	CG	IP	H	BB	SO	ShO	W	L	SV	AB	H	HR	BA	PO	A	E	DP	TC/G	FA
1957	DET A	0	1	.000	7.45	7	0	0	9.2	11	7	4	0	0	1	0	2	0	0	.000	1	1	0	0	0.3	1.000
1958	2 teams			DET A	(11G 1-2)				CHI A	(29G 4-2)																
"	total	5	4	.556	4.76	40	5	0	90.2	99	41	35	0	5	1	1	22	3	0	.136	1	29	1	2	0.8	.968
1959	CHI A	18	6	.750	2.69	47	26	8	230.2	217	54	89	3	2	0	3	73	9	0	.123	17	46	2	3	1.4	.969
1960		13	13	.500	4.06	36	32	7	192.2	221	62	46	1	1	1	0	58	8	0	.138	14	33	5	0	1.4	.904
1961	2 teams			CHI A	(14G 3-4)				KC A	(26G 9-10)																
"	total	12	14	.462	4.14	40	34	9	221.2	250	78	91	0	1	0	0	73	11	0	.151	19	35	3	2	1.4	.947
1962	MIL N	15	9	.625	2.80	38	29	12	225	223	44	124	3	1	0	2	73	10	0	.137	16	38	5	0	1.6	.915
1963		7	11	.389	2.66	48	16	3	159	144	55	105	3	3	5	13	41	5	0	.122	8	20	2	3	0.6	.933
1964	SF N	7	6	.538	3.76	61	1	0	93.1	105	31	57	0	7	5	11	13	0	0	.000	4	10	0	1	0.2	1.000
1965		16	9	.640	2.64	42	33	6	235	213	53	148	1	1	1	2	79	8	0	.101	15	45	4	1	1.5	.938
1966	2 teams			SF N	(13G 1-4)				NY N	(26G 11-10)																
"	total	12	14	.462	4.29	39	31	7	199.1	216	49	125	2	0	1	0	56	13	0	.232	12	31	0	3	1.1	1.000
1967	2 teams			NY N	(23G 3-9)				CHI N	(9G 0-2)																
"	total	3	11	.214	4.61	32	16	3	121	138	37	56	1	1	2	0	29	2	0	.069	7	11	2	1	0.6	.900
11 yrs.		108	98	.524	3.52	430	223	55	1778	1837	511	880	14	22	17	32	519	69	0	.133	114	299	24	16	1.0	.945

WORLD SERIES

Year	Team	W	L	PCT	ERA	G	GS	CG	IP	H	BB	SO	ShO	W	L	SV	AB	H	HR	BA	PO	A	E	DP	TC/G	FA
1959	CHI A	1	1	.500	2.57	2	2	0	14	17	2	2	0	0	0	0	4	1	0	.250	0	4	0	0	2.0	1.000

Don Shaw

SHAW, DONALD WELLINGTON
B. Feb. 23, 1944, Pittsburgh, Pa.

BL TL 6' 180 lbs.

Year	Team	W	L	PCT	ERA	G	GS	CG	IP	H	BB	SO	ShO	W	L	SV	AB	H	HR	BA	PO	A	E	DP	TC/G	FA
1967	NY N	4	5	.444	2.98	40	0	0	51.1	40	23	44	0	4	5	3	3	0	0	.000	3	5	0	0	0.2	1.000
1968		0	0	–	0.75	7	0	0	12	13	2	5	11	0	0	0	0	0	0	0	–	1	2	0	0	0.4	1.000
1969	MON N	2	5	.286	5.21	35	1	0	65.2	61	37	45	0	2	4	0	10	0	0	.000	2	15	1	0	0.5	.944
1971	STL N	7	2	.778	2.65	45	0	0	51	45	31	19	0	7	2	2	1	0	0	.000	3	8	2	0	0.3	.846
1972	2 teams			STL N	(8G 0-1)				OAK A	(3G 0-1)																
"	total	0	2	.000	14.63	11	0	0	8	17	5	4	0	0	2	0	1	0	0	.000	0	0	0	0	0.0	–
5 yrs.		13	14	.481	4.02	138	1	0	188	166	101	123	0	13	13	5	15	0	0	.000	9	30	3	0	0.3	.929

Dupee Shaw

SHAW, FREDERICK LANDER
B. May 31, 1859, Charlestown, Mass.   D. June 11, 1938, Everett, Mass.

BL TL 5'8" 165 lbs.

Year	Team	W	L	PCT	ERA	G	GS	CG	IP	H	BB	SO	ShO	W	L	SV	AB	H	HR	BA	PO	A	E	DP	TC/G	FA
1883	DET N	10	15	.400	2.50	26	25	23	227	238	44	73	1	0	0	0	141	29	0	.206	7	44	2	4	2.0	.962
1884	2 teams			DET N	(28G 9-18)				BOS U	(39G 21-15)																
"	total	30	33	.476	2.30	67	66	60	543.1	446	109	451	5	0	0	0	289	63	1	.218	28	114	28	3	2.5	.835
1885	PRO N	23	26	.469	2.57	49	49	47	399.2	343	99	194	6	0	0	0	165	22	0	.133	11	76	8	2	1.9	.916
1886	WAS N	13	31	.295	3.34	45	44	43	385.2	384	91	177	1	0	0	0	148	13	0	.088	13	70	3	1	1.9	.965
1887		7	13	.350	6.45	21	20	20	181.1	263	46	47	0	0	0	0	70	13	0	.186	4	24	2	0	1.4	.933
1888		0	3	.000	6.48	3	3	3	25	36	7	8	0	0	0	0	10	0	0	.000	0	2	0	0	0.7	1.000
6 yrs.		83	121	.407	3.10	211	207	196	1762	1710	396	950	13	1	0	0	*				63	330	43	10	2.1	.901

Jim Shaw

SHAW, JAMES ALOYSIUS (Grunting Jim)
B. Aug. 13, 1893, Pittsburgh, Pa.   D. Jan. 27, 1962, Washington, D. C.

BR TR 6' 180 lbs.

Year	Team	W	L	PCT	ERA	G	GS	CG	IP	H	BB	SO	ShO	W	L	SV	AB	H	HR	BA	PO	A	E	DP	TC/G	FA
1913	WAS A	0	1	.000	2.08	2	1	1	13	8	7	14	0	0	0	0	2	0	0	.000	0	8	0	0	4.0	1.000
1914		15	17	.469	2.70	48	31	15	257	198	137	164	5	2	3	4	85	10	1	.118	18	72	9	4	2.1	.909
1915		6	11	.353	2.50	25	18	7	133	102	76	78	1	1	1	1	43	10	0	.233	5	32	3	2	1.6	.925
1916		3	8	.273	2.62	26	9	5	106.1	86	50	44	2	1	2	1	32	5	0	.156	4	16	3	2	0.9	.870
1917		15	14	.517	3.21	47	31	15	266.1	233	123	118	2	1	1	1	91	14	0	.154	16	54	3	6	1.6	.959
1918		16	12	.571	2.42	41	30	14	241.1	201	90	129	4	2	1	0	83	11	0	.133	10	41	6	2	1.4	.895
1919		16	17	.485	2.73	45	38	23	306.2	274	101	128	3	0	1	0	106	17	3	.160	9	53	3	1	1.4	.954
1920		11	18	.379	4.27	38	32	17	236.1	285	87	88	0	0	3	1	74	14	0	.189	7	42	1	1	1.3	.980
1921		1	0	1.000	7.36	15	4	0	40.1	59	17	4	0	0	0	3	12	5	0	.417	2	1	2	0	1.0	.933
9 yrs.		83	98	.459	3.07	287	194	96	1600.1	1446	688	767	17	7	12	16	528	86	4	.163	71	330	29	18	1.5	.933

Sam Shaw

SHAW, SAMUEL E.
B. 1863, Baltimore, Md.   Deceased.

BR TR 5'5" 140 lbs.

Year	Team	W	L	PCT	ERA	G	GS	CG	IP	H	BB	SO	ShO	W	L	SV	AB	H	HR	BA	PO	A	E	DP	TC/G	FA
1888	BAL AA	2	4	.333	3.40	6	6	6	53	65	15	22	0	0	0	0	20	3	0	.150	2	10	5	0	2.8	.706
1893	CHI N	1	0	1.000	5.63	2	2	1	16	12	13	1	0	0	0	0	7	2	0	.286	0	3	0	0	1.5	1.000
2 yrs.		3	4	.429	3.91	8	8	7	69	77	28	23	0	0	0	0	27	5	0	.185	2	13	5	0	2.5	.750

Bob Shawkey

SHAWKEY, JAMES ROBERT
B. Dec. 4, 1890, Sigel, Pa.   D. Dec. 31, 1980, Syracuse, N. Y.
Manager 1930.

BR TR 5'11" 168 lbs.

Year	Team	W	L	PCT	ERA	G	GS	CG	IP	H	BB	SO	ShO	W	L	SV	AB	H	HR	BA	PO	A	E	DP	TC/G	FA
1913	PHI A	6	5	.545	2.34	18	15	8	111.1	92	50	52	1	1	0	0	44	6	0	.136	3	40	4	0	2.6	.915
1914		16	8	.667	2.73	38	31	18	237	223	75	89	5	0	0	2	83	17	0	.205	6	63	5	1	1.9	.932
1915	2 teams			PHI A	(17G 6-6)				NY A	(16G 4-7)																
"	total	10	13	.435	3.68	33	22	12	185.2	181	73	87	2	2	1	0	60	11	0	.183	5	49	3	3	1.7	.947
1916	NY A	24	14	.632	2.21	53	27	21	276.2	204	81	122	4	7	4	8	93	17	0	.183	12	79	3	2	1.8	.968
1917		13	15	.464	2.44	32	26	16	236.1	207	72	97	2	2	0	0	84	16	0	.190	18	79	4	5	3.2	.960
1918		1	1	.500	1.13	3	2	1	16	7	10	3	1	0	0	0	4	3	0	.750	6	4	0	0	3.3	1.000
1919		20	11	.645	2.72	41	27	22	261.1	218	92	122	3	4	1	0	94	22	0	.234	22	59	4	1	2.1	.953

Year	Team	W	L	PCT	ERA	G	GS	CG	IP	H	BB	SO	ShO	W	L	SV	AB	H	HR	BA	PO	A	E	DP	TC/G	FA
														Relief Pitching			**Batting**									

Bob Shawkey *continued*

Year	Team	W	L	PCT	ERA	G	GS	CG	IP	H	BB	SO	ShO	W	L	SV	AB	H	HR	BA	PO	A	E	DP	TC/G	FA
1920		20	13	.606	**2.45**	38	31	20	267.2	246	85	126	5	1	0	2	100	23	0	.230	15	48	1	0	1.7	.984
1921		18	12	.600	4.08	38	31	18	245	245	86	126	3	1	3	2	90	27	1	.300	14	35	3	1	1.4	.942
1922		20	12	.625	2.91	39	33	19	299.2	286	98	130	3	1	0	1	115	21	1	.183	13	70	4	4	2.2	.954
1923		16	11	.593	3.51	36	31	17	258.2	232	102	125	1	0	0	1	99	20	0	.202	9	61	2	3	2.0	.972
1924		16	11	.593	4.12	38	25	10	207.2	226	74	114	1	2	4	0	69	22	1	.319	11	39	6	1	1.5	.893
1925		6	14	.300	4.11	33	20	9	186	209	67	81	1	1	2	0	68	10	0	.147	7	37	0	1	1.3	1.000
1926		8	7	.533	3.62	29	10	3	104.1	102	37	63	1	4	3	3	35	9	0	.257	2	23	1	0	0.9	.962
1927		2	3	.400	2.89	19	2	0	43.2	44	16	23	0	2	2	4	11	1	0	.091	3	11	1	0	0.8	.933
15 yrs.		196	150	.566	3.09	488	333	194	2937	2722	1018	1360	33	28	22	27	1049	225	3	.214	146	697	41	22	1.8	.954

WORLD SERIES

Year	Team		W	L	PCT	ERA	G	GS	CG	IP	H	BB	SO	ShO	W	L	SV	AB	H	HR	BA	PO	A	E	DP	TC/G	FA
1914	PHI	A	0	1	.000	5.40	1	1	0	5	4	2	0	0	0	0	0	2	1	0	.500	0	3	0	0	3.0	1.000
1921	NY	A	0	1	.000	7.00	2	1	0	9	13	6	5	0	0	1	0	4	2	0	.500	0	0	0	0	0.0	—
1922			0	0	—	2.70	1	1	1	10	8	2	4	0	0	0	0	4	0	0	.000	0	2	0	1	2.0	1.000
1923			1	0	1.000	3.52	1	1	0	7.2	12	4	2	0	0	0	0	3	1	0	.333	1	2	0	1	3.0	1.000
1926			0	1	.000	5.40	3	1	0	10	8	2	7	0	0	1	0	2	0	0	.000	0	1	0	0	1.1	1.000
5 yrs.			1	3	.250	4.75	8	5	1	41.2	45	16	18	0	0	0	1	15	4	0	.267	1	8	0	1	1.1	1.000

John Shea

SHEA, JOHN MICHAEL JOSEPH
B. Dec. 27, 1904, Everett, Mass. D. Nov. 30, 1956, Malden, Mass.

BL TL 5'10½" 171 lbs.

Year	Team		W	L	PCT	ERA	G	GS	CG	IP	H	BB	SO	ShO	W	L	SV	AB	H	HR	BA	PO	A	E	DP	TC/G	FA
1928	BOS	A	0	0	—	18.00	1	0	0	1	1	1	0	0	0	0	0	0	0	0	—	0	1	0	0	1.0	1.000

Mike Shea

SHEA, MICHAEL J.
B. Mar. 10, 1867, New Orleans, La. Deceased.

TR 5'10" 170 lbs.

Year	Team		W	L	PCT	ERA	G	GS	CG	IP	H	BB	SO	ShO	W	L	SV	AB	H	HR	BA	PO	A	E	DP	TC/G	FA
1887	CIN	AA	1	1	.500	7.02	2	2	2	16.2	26	10	0	0	0	0	0	8	2	0	.250	1	8	2	0	5.5	.818

Red Shea

SHEA, PATRICK HENRY
B. Nov. 29, 1898, Ware, Mass. D. Nov. 17, 1981, Stafford Springs, Conn.

BR TR 6' 160 lbs.

Year	Team		W	L	PCT	ERA	G	GS	CG	IP	H	BB	SO	ShO	W	L	SV	AB	H	HR	BA	PO	A	E	DP	TC/G	FA
1918	PHI	A	0	0	—	4.00	3	0	0	9	14	2	2	0	0	0	0	3	0	0	.000	0	1	0	0	0.3	1.000
1921	NY	N	5	2	.714	3.09	9	2	1	32	28	2	10	0	4	1	0	9	1	0	.111	2	5	1	0	0.9	.875
1922			0	3	.000	4.70	11	2	0	23	22	11	5	0	0	2	0	7	0	0	.000	0	10	0	0	0.9	1.000
3 yrs.			5	5	.500	3.80	23	4	1	64	64	15	17	0	4	3	0	19	1	0	.053	2	16	1	0	0.8	.947

Spec Shea

SHEA, FRANCIS JOSEPH (The Naugatuck Nugget)
Born Francis Joseph O'Shea.
B. Oct. 2, 1920, Naugatuck, Conn.

BR TR 6' 195 lbs.

Year	Team		W	L	PCT	ERA	G	GS	CG	IP	H	BB	SO	ShO	W	L	SV	AB	H	HR	BA	PO	A	E	DP	TC/G	FA
1947	NY	A	14	5	.737	3.07	27	23	13	178.2	127	89	89	3	0	1	1	56	11	0	.196	9	14	0	0	0.9	1.000
1948			9	10	.474	3.41	28	22	8	155.2	117	87	71	3	1	1	1	47	7	0	.149	4	17	1	0	0.8	.955
1949			1	1	.500	5.33	20	3	0	52.1	48	43	22	0	1	0	1	12	3	0	.250	2	9	1	1	0.6	.917
1951			5	5	.500	4.33	25	11	2	95.2	112	50	38	2	2	2	0	28	6	1	.214	7	14	1	3	0.9	.955
1952	WAS	A	11	7	.611	2.93	22	21	12	169	144	92	65	2	0	0	0	63	15	0	.238	14	23	0	1	1.7	1.000
1953			12	7	.632	3.94	23	23	11	164.2	151	75	38	0	0	0	0	62	11	0	.177	5	24	0	2	1.3	1.000
1954			2	9	.182	6.18	23	11	1	71.1	97	34	22	0	1	1	0	20	1	0	.050	5	17	1	1	1.0	.957
1955			2	2	.500	3.99	27	4	1	56.1	53	27	16	1	1	2	0	10	4	0	.400	3	2	2	0	0.4	.833
8 yrs.			56	46	.549	3.80	195	118	48	943.2	849	497	361	12	6	5	5	298	58	1	.195	49	125	6	8	0.9	.967

WORLD SERIES

Year	Team		W	L	PCT	ERA	G	GS	CG	IP	H	BB	SO	ShO	W	L	SV	AB	H	HR	BA	PO	A	E	DP	TC/G	FA
1947	NY	A	2	0	1.000	2.35	3	3	1	15.1	10	8	10	0	0	0	0	5	2	0	.400	1	3	0	0	1.3	1.000

Steve Shea

SHEA, STEVEN FRANCIS
B. Dec. 5, 1942, Worcester, Mass.

BR TR 6'3" 215 lbs.

Year	Team		W	L	PCT	ERA	G	GS	CG	IP	H	BB	SO	ShO	W	L	SV	AB	H	HR	BA	PO	A	E	DP	TC/G	FA
1968	HOU	N	4	4	.500	3.38	30	0	0	34.2	27	11	15	0	4	4	1	6	0	0	.000	2	9	0	1	0.4	1.000
1969	MON	N	0	0	—	2.87	10	0	0	15.2	18	8	11	0	0	0	0	0	0	0	—	1	2	0	1	0.3	1.000
2 yrs.			4	4	.500	3.22	40	0	0	50.1	45	19	26	0	4	4	1	6	0	0	.000	3	11	0	2	0.4	1.000

Al Shealy

SHEALY, ALBERT BERLY
B. May 20, 1900, Chapin, S. C. D. Mar. 7, 1967, Hagerstown, Md.

BR TR 5'11" 175 lbs.

Year	Team		W	L	PCT	ERA	G	GS	CG	IP	H	BB	SO	ShO	W	L	SV	AB	H	HR	BA	PO	A	E	DP	TC/G	FA
1928	NY	A	8	6	.571	5.06	23	12	3	96	124	42	39	0	2	1	2	38	9	1	.237	4	22	1	0	1.2	.963
1930	CHI	N	0	0	—	8.00	24	0	0	27	37	14	14	0	0	0	0	5	3	0	.600	1	4	0	0	0.2	1.000
2 yrs.			8	6	.571	5.71	47	12	3	123	161	56	53	0	2	1	2	43	12	1	.279	5	26	1	0	0.7	.969

John Shearon

SHEARON, JOHN M.
B. 1870, Pittsburgh, Pa. D. Feb. 1, 1923, Bradford, Pa.

Year	Team		W	L	PCT	ERA	G	GS	CG	IP	H	BB	SO	ShO	W	L	SV	AB	H	HR	BA	PO	A	E	DP	TC/G	FA
1891	CLE	N	1	3	.250	3.52	6	5	4	46	57	24	19	0	0	0	0	*				2	8	0	1	1.7	1.000

George Shears

SHEARS, GEORGE PENFIELD
B. Apr. 13, 1890, Marshall, Mo. D. Nov. 12, 1978, Loveland, Colo.

BR TL 6'3" 180 lbs.

Year	Team		W	L	PCT	ERA	G	GS	CG	IP	H	BB	SO	ShO	W	L	SV	AB	H	HR	BA	PO	A	E	DP	TC/G	FA
1912	NY	A	0	0	—	5.40	4	0	0	15	24	11	9	0	0	0	0	6	1	0	.167	0	5	0	0	1.3	1.000

Tom Sheehan

SHEEHAN, THOMAS CLANCY
B. Mar. 31, 1894, Grand Ridge, Ill. D. Oct. 29, 1982, Chillicothe, Ohio
Manager 1960.

BR TR 6'2½" 190 lbs.

Year	Team		W	L	PCT	ERA	G	GS	CG	IP	H	BB	SO	ShO	W	L	SV	AB	H	HR	BA	PO	A	E	DP	TC/G	FA
1915	PHI	A	4	9	.308	4.15	15	13	8	102	131	38	22	1	0	0	0	34	4	0	.118	2	30	3	0	2.3	.914
1916			1	16	.059	3.69	38	17	8	188	197	94	54	0	1	2	0	56	7	0	.125	10	71	6	3	2.3	.931
1921	NY	A	1	0	1.000	5.45	12	1	0	33	43	19	7	0	0	0	1	8	5	0	.625	2	16	0	0	1.5	1.000
1924	CIN	N	9	11	.450	3.24	39	16	8	166.2	170	54	52	2	5	4	1	58	18	0	.310	7	31	1	1	1.0	.974
1925	2 teams		CIN N	(10G 1–0)		PIT N	(23G 1–1)																				
"	total		2	1	.667	4.48	33	3	1	86.1	100	25	18	0	1	1	3	25	4	0	.160	8	15	1	2	0.7	.958

Year	Team	W	L	PCT	ERA	G	GS	CG	IP	H	BB	SO	ShO	Relief Pitching W	L	SV	Batting AB	H	HR	BA	PO	A	E	DP	TC/G	FA

Tom Sheehan *continued*

| 1926 | PIT N | 0 | 2 | .000 | 6.68 | 9 | 4 | 1 | 31 | 36 | 12 | 16 | 0 | 0 | 0 | 0 | 9 | 1 | 0 | .111 | 0 | 7 | 1 | 0 | 0.9 | .875 |
| 6 yrs. | | 17 | 39 | .304 | 4.00 | 146 | 54 | 26 | 607 | 677 | 242 | 169 | 3 | 7 | 7 | 5 | 190 | 39 | 0 | .205 | 29 | 170 | 12 | 6 | 1.4 | .943 |

Rollie Sheldon

SHELDON, ROLAND FRANK
B. Dec. 17, 1936, Putnam, Conn. — BR TR 6'4" 185 lbs.

1961	NY A	11	5	.688	3.60	35	21	6	162.2	149	55	84	2	2	0	0	56	7	0	.125	11	30	0	3	1.2	1.000
1962		7	8	.467	5.49	34	16	2	118	136	28	54	0	3	1	1	26	2	0	.077	7	10	1	1	0.5	.944
1964		5	2	.714	3.61	19	12	3	102.1	92	18	57	0	0	0	1	34	3	0	.088	7	20	0	2	1.4	1.000
1965	2 teams	NY A	(3G 0–0)		KC A	(32G 10–8)																				
"	total	10	8	.556	3.86	35	29	4	193.1	185	57	112	1	0	0	0	52	4	0	.077	14	31	2	4	1.3	.957
1966	2 teams	KC A	(14G 4–7)		BOS A	(23G 1–6)																				
"	total	5	13	.278	4.12	37	23	2	148.2	179	49	64	1	0	2	0	41	4	0	.098	9	28	0	2	1.0	1.000
5 yrs.		38	36	.514	4.08	160	101	17	725	741	207	371	4	5	3	2	209	20	0	.096	48	119	3	12	1.1	.982

WORLD SERIES

| 1964 | NY A | 0 | 0 | — | 0.00 | 2 | 0 | 0 | 2.2 | 0 | 2 | 2 | 0 | 0 | 0 | 0 | 0 | 0 | 0 | — | 1 | 1 | 0 | 1 | 1.0 | 1.000 |

Frank Shellenback

SHELLENBACK, FRANK VICTOR
B. Dec. 16, 1898, Joplin, Mo. D. Aug. 17, 1969, Newton, Mass. — BR TR 6'2" 192 lbs.

1918	CHI A	9	12	.429	2.66	28	20	10	182.2	180	74	47	2	3	0	2	54	7	0	.130	5	28	3	0	1.3	.917
1919		1	3	.250	5.14	8	4	2	35	40	16	10	0	0	1	0	11	1	0	.091	1	9	0	0	1.3	1.000
2 yrs.		10	15	.400	3.06	36	24	12	217.2	220	90	57	2	3	1	2	65	8	0	.123	6	37	3	0	1.3	.935

Jim Shellenback

SHELLENBACK, JAMES PHILIP
B. Nov. 18, 1943, Riverside, Calif. — BL TL 6'2" 200 lbs.

1966	PIT N	0	0	—	9.00	2	0	0	3	3	3	0	0	0	0	0	0	0	0	—	0	2	0	0	1.0	1.000
1967		1	1	.500	2.70	6	2	1	23.1	23	12	11	0	0	0	0	6	1	0	.167	1	4	0	0	0.8	1.000
1969	2 teams	PIT N	(8G 0–0)		WAS A	(30G 4–7)																				
"	total	4	7	.364	3.90	38	11	2	101.2	101	52	57	0	0	3	1	28	5	0	.179	6	33	2	1	1.1	.951
1970	WAS A	6	7	.462	3.69	39	14	2	117	107	51	57	1	3	1	0	30	2	0	.067	5	16	1	1	0.6	.955
1971		3	11	.214	3.53	40	15	3	120	123	49	47	1	0	1	0	30	5	0	.167	2	26	2	4	0.8	.933
1972	TEX A	2	4	.333	3.47	22	6	0	57	46	16	30	0	1	1	1	10	1	0	.100	4	5	0	0	0.4	1.000
1973		0	0	—	0.00	2	0	0	2	0	0	3	0	0	0	0	0	0	0	—	0	1	0	0	0.5	1.000
1974		0	0	—	5.76	11	0	0	25	30	12	14	0	0	0	0	0	0	0	—	1	4	0	0	0.5	1.000
1977	MIN A	0	0	—	7.50	5	0	0	6	10	5	3	0	0	0	0	0	0	0	—	2	0	0	0	0.4	1.000
9 yrs.		16	30	.348	3.80	165	48	8	455	443	200	222	2	4	6	2	104	14	0	.135	21	91	5	6	0.7	.957

Bert Shepard

SHEPARD, ROBERT EARL
B. June 28, 1920, Dana, Ind. — BL TL 5'11" 185 lbs.

| 1945 | WAS A | 0 | 0 | — | 1.69 | 1 | 0 | 0 | 5.1 | 3 | 1 | 2 | 0 | 0 | 0 | 0 | 3 | 0 | 0 | .000 | 0 | 2 | 0 | 0 | 2.0 | 1.000 |

Bill Sherdel

SHERDEL, WILLIAM HENRY (Wee Willie)
B. Aug. 15, 1896, McSherrystown, Pa. D. Nov. 14, 1968, McSherrystown, Pa. — BL TL 5'10" 160 lbs.

1918	STL N	6	12	.333	2.71	35	17	9	182.1	174	49	40	1	1	4	1	62	15	1	.242	6	46	0	2	1.5	1.000
1919		5	9	.357	3.47	36	10	7	137.1	137	42	52	0	3	1	1	48	13	0	.271	5	45	4	0	1.5	.926
1920		11	10	.524	3.28	43	7	4	170	183	40	74	0	8	8	6	63	14	1	.222	7	50	1	4	1.3	.983
1921		9	8	.529	3.18	38	8	5	144.1	137	38	57	1	4	6	1	44	5	0	.114	5	40	3	0	1.1	.938
1922		17	13	.567	3.88	47	31	16	241.1	298	62	79	3	2	1	2	88	17	1	.193	5	41	5	1	1.1	.902
1923		15	13	.536	4.32	39	26	14	225	270	59	78	0	3	2	2	83	28	1	.337	6	41	5	3	1.3	.904
1924		8	9	.471	3.42	35	10	6	168.2	188	38	57	0	6	3	1	75	15	0	.200	6	30	0	2	1.0	1.000
1925		15	6	.714	3.11	32	21	17	200	216	42	53	2	0	0	1	73	15	1	.205	6	42	0	4	1.5	1.000
1926		16	12	.571	3.49	34	29	17	234.2	255	49	59	3	3	0	6	90	22	1	.244	3	44	1	0	1.6	.981
1927		17	12	.586	3.53	39	28	18	232.1	241	48	59	1	0	3	0	72	14	1	.194	3	36	5	5	1.1	.886
1928		21	10	.677	2.86	38	27	20	248.2	251	56	72	0	3	2	5	84	19	1	.226	6	36	2	1	1.2	.955
1929		10	15	.400	5.93	33	22	11	195.2	278	58	69	1	3	2	0	70	16	1	.229	1	36	1	0	1.2	.974
1930	2 teams	STL N	(13G 3–2)		BOS N	(21G 6–5)																				
"	total	9	7	.563	4.71	34	21	8	183.1	217	43	55	0	1	0	1	61	6	0	.098	7	31	2	4	1.2	.950
1931	BOS N	6	10	.375	4.25	27	16	8	137.2	163	35	34	0	1	1	0	46	14	0	.304	4	20	0	1	0.9	1.000
1932	2 teams	BOS N	(1G 0–0)		STL N	(3G 0–0)																				
"	total	0	0	—	3.68	4	0	0	7.1	10	2	1	0	0	0	0	1	1	0	1.000	1	2	0	0	0.8	1.000
15 yrs.		165	146	.531	3.72	514	273	159	2708.2	3018	661	839	12	39	32	26	960	214	9	.223	77	540	29	26	1.3	.955

WORLD SERIES

1926	STL N	0	2	.000	2.12	2	2	1	17	15	8	3	0	0	0	0	5	0	0	.000	2	5	0	0	3.5	1.000
1928		0	2	.000	4.73	2	2	0	13.1	15	3	3	0	0	0	0	5	0	0	.000	0	3	0	0	1.5	1.000
2 yrs.		0	4	.000	3.26	4	4	1	30.1	30	11	6	0	0	0	0	10	0	0	.000	2	8	0	0	2.5	1.000
			7th																							

Roy Sherid

SHERID, ROYDEN RICHARD
B. Jan. 25, 1907, Norristown, Pa. D. Feb. 28, 1982, Parker Ford, Pa. — BR TR 6'2" 185 lbs.

1929	NY A	6	6	.500	3.49	33	15	9	159.2	165	55	51	0	0	0	1	50	9	0	.180	8	29	3	3	1.2	.925
1930		12	13	.480	5.23	37	21	8	184	214	87	59	0	2	3	4	69	7	0	.101	11	30	2	4	1.2	.953
1931		5	5	.500	5.69	17	8	3	74.1	94	24	39	0	1	3	2	30	10	0	.333	3	14	0	0	1.0	1.000
3 yrs.		23	24	.489	4.65	87	44	20	418	473	166	149	0	3	6	7	149	26	0	.174	22	73	5	7	1.1	.950

Babe Sherman

SHERMAN, LESTER DANIEL (General)
B. May 9, 1890, Hubbardsville, N.Y. D. Sept. 16, 1955, Highland Park, Mich. — BR TR 5'6" 145 lbs.

| 1914 | CHI F | 0 | 1 | .000 | 0.00 | 1 | 1 | 0 | 1 | 0 | 1 | 2 | 0 | 0 | 0 | 0 | 0 | 0 | 0 | — | 0 | 0 | 0 | 0 | 0.0 | — |

Year	Team		W	L	PCT	ERA	G	GS	CG	IP	H	BB	SO	ShO	Relief Pitching W	L	SV	Batting AB	H	HR	BA	PO	A	E	DP	TC/G	FA

Joe Sherman

SHERMAN, JOEL POWERS
B. Nov. 4, 1890, Yarmouth, Mass.   D. Dec. 21, 1987, Cape Coral, Fla.
BR TR 6'   165 lbs.

| 1915 | PHI | A | 1 | 0 | 1.000 | 2.40 | 2 | 1 | 1 | 15 | 15 | 1 | 5 | 0 | 0 | 0 | 0 | 6 | 2 | 0 | .333 | 0 | 3 | 0 | 0 | 1.5 | 1.000 |

Fred Sherry

SHERRY, FRED PETER
Born Fred Peter Schuerholz.
B. June 13, 1889, Honesdale, Pa.   D. July 27, 1975, Honesdale, Pa.
BR TR 6'   170 lbs.

| 1911 | WAS | A | 0 | 4 | .000 | 4.30 | 10 | 3 | 2 | 52.1 | 63 | 19 | 20 | 0 | 0 | 1 | 0 | 19 | 3 | 0 | .158 | 3 | 15 | 2 | 1 | 2.0 | .900 |

Larry Sherry

SHERRY, LAWRENCE
Brother of Norm Sherry.
B. July 25, 1935, Los Angeles, Calif.
BR TR 6'2"   180 lbs.

1958	LA	N	0	0	—	12.46	5	0	0	4.1	10	7	2	0	0	0	0	0	0	0	—	0	1	0	0	0.2	1.000
1959			7	2	.778	2.19	23	9	1	94.1	75	43	72	1	2	0	3	32	7	2	.219	3	11	1	1	0.7	.933
1960			14	10	.583	3.79	57	3	1	142.1	125	82	114	0	13	8	7	37	6	1	.162	18	21	0	0	0.7	1.000
1961			4	4	.500	3.90	53	1	0	94.2	90	39	79	0	4	3	15	13	2	0	.154	8	5	3	0	0.3	.813
1962			7	3	.700	3.20	58	0	0	90	81	44	71	0	7	3	11	17	2	0	.118	2	13	0	1	0.3	1.000
1963			2	6	.250	3.73	36	3	0	79.2	82	24	47	0	2	4	3	9	1	0	.111	4	15	1	1	0.5	.941
1964	DET	A	7	5	.583	3.66	38	0	0	66.1	52	37	58	0	7	5	11	14	0	0	.000	4	9	4	2	0.4	.765
1965			3	6	.333	3.10	39	0	0	78.1	71	40	46	0	3	6	5	10	3	0	.300	4	15	0	1	0.5	1.000
1966			8	5	.615	3.82	55	0	0	77.2	66	36	63	0	8	5	20	10	4	0	.400	4	9	2	2	0.3	.867
1967	2 teams	DET A	(20G 0–1)			HOU N	(29G 1–2)																					
"	total		1	3	.250	5.50	49	0	0	68.2	88	20	52	0	1	3	7	6	0	0	.000	7	14	2	1	0.5	.913
1968	CAL	A	0	0	—	6.00	3	0	0	3	7	2	2	0	0	0	0	0	0	0	—	0	0	0	0	0.0	—
	11 yrs.		53	44	.546	3.67	416	16	2	799.1	747	374	606	1	47	37	82	148	25	3	.169	51	113	13	9	0.4	.927

WORLD SERIES

| 1959 | LA | N | 2 | 0 | 1.000 | 0.71 | 4 | 0 | 0 | 12.2 | 8 | 2 | 5 | 0 | 2 | 0 | 2 | 4 | 2 | 0 | .500 | 1 | 3 | 0 | 0 | 1.0 | 1.000 |

2nd

Ben Shields

SHIELDS, BENJAMIN COWAN (Lefty, Big Ben)
B. June 17, 1903, Huntersville, N. C.
D. Jan. 24, 1982, Woodruff, S. C.
BB TL 6'1½"   195 lbs.
BL 1931

1924	NY	A	0	0	—	27.00	2	0	0	2	6	2	3	0	0	0	0	0	0	0	—	0	0	0	0	0.0	—
1925			3	0	1.000	4.88	4	2	2	24	24	12	5	0	1	0	0	8	1	0	.125	2	3	0	0	1.3	1.000
1930	BOS	A	0	0	—	9.00	3	0	0	10	16	6	1	0	0	0	0	3	0	0	.000	0	3	0	0	1.0	1.000
1931	PHI	N	1	0	1.000	15.19	4	0	0	5.1	9	7	0	0	1	0	0	2	0	0	.000	0	1	0	0	0.3	1.000
	4 yrs.		4	0	1.000	8.27	13	2	2	41.1	55	27	9	0	2	0	0	13	1	0	.077	2	7	0	0	0.7	1.000

Charlie Shields

SHIELDS, CHARLES JESSAMINE
B. Dec. 10, 1879, Jackson, Tenn.   D. Aug. 27, 1953, Memphis, Tenn.
BL TL

1902	2 teams	BAL A	(23G 4–11)			STL A	(4G 3–0)																					
"	total		7	11	.389	4.07	27	19	13	172.1	238	39	34	1	1	1	1	61	14	0	.230	4	30	6	2	1.5	.850
1907	STL	N	0	2	.000	9.45	3	2	0	6.2	12	7	1	0	0	0	0	2	0	0	.000	0	3	0	0	1.0	1.000
	2 yrs.		7	13	.350	4.27	30	21	13	179	250	46	35	1	1	1	1	63	14	0	.222	4	33	6	2	1.4	.860

Steve Shields

SHIELDS, STEPHEN MACK
B. Nov. 30, 1958, Gadsden, Ala.
BR TR 6'5"   220 lbs.

1985	ATL	N	1	2	.333	5.16	23	6	0	68	86	32	29	0	0	0	0	18	2	0	.111	6	6	1	0	0.6	.923
1986	2 teams	ATL N	(6G 0–0)			KC A	(3G 0–0)																					
"	total		0	0	—	5.06	9	0	0	21.1	16	11	8	0	0	0	0	1	0	0	.000	1	2	0	0	0.4	1.000
1987	SEA	A	2	0	1.000	6.60	20	0	0	30	43	12	22	0	2	0	3	0	0	0	—	1	5	0	0	0.3	1.000
1988	NY	A	5	5	.500	4.37	39	0	0	82.1	96	30	55	0	5	5	0	0	0	0	—	9	8	1	2	0.5	.944
1989	MIN	A	0	1	.000	7.79	11	0	0	17.1	28	6	12	0	0	0	0	0	0	0	—	1	3	1	1	0.3	.955
	5 yrs.		8	8	.500	5.26	102	6	0	219	269	91	126	0	7	5	3	19	2	0	.105	18	24	3	3	0.4	.955

Vince Shields

SHIELDS, VINCENT WILLIAM
B. Nov. 18, 1900, Fredericton, N. B., Canada   D. Oct. 17, 1952, Plaster Rock, N. B., Canada
BL TR 5'11"   185 lbs.

| 1924 | STL | N | 1 | 1 | .500 | 3.00 | 2 | 1 | 0 | 12 | 10 | 3 | 4 | 0 | 1 | 0 | 0 | 5 | 2 | 0 | .400 | 0 | 1 | 1 | 0 | 1.0 | .500 |

Garland Shifflett

SHIFFLETT, GARLAND JESSIE (Duck)
B. Mar. 28, 1935, Elkton, Va.
BR TR 5'10½"   165 lbs.

1957	WAS	A	0	0	—	10.13	6	1	0	8	6	10	2	0	0	0	0	0	0	0	—	0	1	0	0	0.2	1.000
1964	MIN	A	0	2	.000	4.58	10	0	0	17.2	22	7	8	0	0	2	1	4	0	0	.000	0	5	1	2	0.6	.833
	2 yrs.		0	2	.000	6.31	16	1	0	25.2	28	17	10	0	0	2	1	4	0	0	.000	0	6	1	2	0.4	.857

Razor Shines

SHINES, ANTHONY RAYMOND
B. July 18, 1956, Durham, N. C.
BB TR 6'1"   210 lbs.

| 1985 | MON | N | 0 | 0 | — | 0.00 | 1 | 0 | 0 | 1 | 1 | 0 | 0 | 0 | 0 | 0 | 0 | * | | | | 0 | 0 | 0 | 0 | 0.0 | — |

Dave Shipanoff

SHIPANOFF, DAVID NOEL
B. Nov. 13, 1959, Edmonton, Alta., Canada
BR TR 6'2"   185 lbs.

| 1985 | PHI | N | 1 | 2 | .333 | 3.22 | 26 | 0 | 0 | 36.1 | 33 | 16 | 26 | 0 | 1 | 2 | 3 | 0 | 0 | 0 | .000 | 2 | 1 | 0 | 0 | 0.2 | .800 |

Joe Shipley

SHIPLEY, JOSEPH CLARK (Moses)
B. May 9, 1935, Morristown, Tenn.
BR TR 6'4"   210 lbs.

1958	SF	N	0	0	—	33.75	1	0	0	1.1	3	3	0	0	0	0	0	0	0	0	—	0	0	0	0	0.0	—
1959			0	0	—	4.50	10	1	0	18	16	17	11	0	0	0	0	3	0	0	.000	0	2	1	0	0.3	.667
1960			0	0	—	5.40	15	0	0	20	20	9	9	0	0	0	0	0	0	0	—	0	7	0	0	0.5	1.000

Year	Team		W	L	PCT	ERA	G	GS	CG	IP	H	BB	SO	ShO	Relief Pitching W	L	SV	Batting AB	H	HR	BA	PO	A	E	DP	TC/G	FA

Joe Shipley *continued*

| 1963 | CHI | A | 0 | 1 | .000 | 5.79 | 3 | 0 | 0 | 4.2 | 9 | 6 | 3 | 0 | 0 | 1 | 0 | 2 | 0 | 0 | .000 | 0 | 1 | 0 | 0 | 0.3 | 1.000 |
| | 4 yrs. | | 0 | 1 | .000 | 5.93 | 29 | 1 | 0 | 44 | 48 | 35 | 23 | 0 | 0 | 1 | 0 | 5 | 0 | 0 | .000 | 0 | 10 | 1 | 0 | 0.4 | .909 |

Duke Shirey

SHIREY, CLAIR LEE
B. June 20, 1898, Jersey Shore, Pa. D. Sept. 1, 1962, Hagerstown, Md.
BR TR 6'1" 175 lbs.

| 1920 | WAS | A | 0 | 1 | .000 | 6.75 | 2 | 1 | 0 | 4 | 5 | 2 | 0 | 0 | 0 | 0 | 0 | 1 | 0 | 0 | .000 | 0 | 0 | 0 | 0 | 0.0 | — |

Bob Shirley

SHIRLEY, ROBERT CHARLES
B. June 25, 1954, Cushing, Okla.
BR TL 5'11" 180 lbs.

1977	SD	N	12	18	.400	3.70	39	35	1	214	215	100	146	0	0	0	1	74	9	0	.122	10	37	3	2	1.3	.940
1978			8	11	.421	3.69	50	20	2	166	164	61	102	0	1	2	5	40	5	0	.125	6	35	0	1	0.8	1.000
1979			8	16	.333	3.38	49	25	4	205	196	59	117	1	2	4	5	55	5	0	.091	13	30	1	1	0.9	.977
1980			11	12	.478	3.55	59	12	3	137	143	54	67	0	7	6	7	30	1	0	.033	7	32	1	1	0.7	.975
1981	STL	N	6	4	.600	4.10	28	11	1	79	78	34	36	0	1	0	1	22	3	0	.136	1	10	0	0	0.4	1.000
1982	CIN	N	8	13	.381	3.60	41	20	1	152.2	138	73	89	0	2	3	0	42	6	0	.143	4	31	2	1	0.9	.946
1983	NY	A	5	8	.385	5.08	25	17	1	108	122	36	53	1	1	0	0	0	0	0	—	5	20	0	1	1.0	1.000
1984			3	3	.500	3.38	41	7	1	114.1	119	38	48	0	1	1	0	0	0	0	—	6	16	1	4	0.6	.957
1985			5	5	.500	2.64	48	8	2	109	103	26	55	0	3	2	2	0	0	0	—	4	15	3	1	0.5	.864
1986			0	4	.000	5.04	39	6	0	105.1	108	40	64	0	0	1	3	0	0	0	—	4	20	1	1	0.6	.960
1987	2 teams		NY A	(12G 1–0)		KC A	(3G 0–0)																					
"	total		1	0	1.000	6.31	15	1	0	41.1	46	22	13	0	0	0	0	0	0	0	—	2	3	0	0	0.3	1.000
	11 yrs.		67	94	.416	3.82	434	162	16	1431.2	1432	543	790	2	18	19	18	263	29	0	.110	62	249	12	13	0.7	.963

Steve Shirley

SHIRLEY, STEVEN BRIAN
B. Oct. 12, 1956, San Francisco, Calif.
BL TL 6' 185 lbs.

| 1982 | LA | N | 1 | 1 | .500 | 4.26 | 11 | 0 | 0 | 12.2 | 15 | 7 | 8 | 0 | 1 | 1 | 0 | 1 | 1 | 0 | 1.000 | 0 | 4 | 0 | 0 | 0.4 | 1.000 |

Tex Shirley

SHIRLEY, ALVIS NEWMAN
B. Apr. 25, 1918, Birthright, Tex.
BB TR 6'1" 175 lbs.
BR 1941

1941	PHI	A	0	1	.000	2.45	5	0	0	7.1	8	6	1	0	0	1	1	1	0	0	.000	0	0	0	0	0.6	1.000
1942			0	1	.000	5.30	15	1	0	35.2	37	22	10	0	0	2	0	9	0	0	.000	1	5	0	0	0.4	1.000
1944	STL	A	5	4	.556	4.15	23	11	2	80.1	59	64	35	1	2	0	0	28	4	0	.143	6	7	2	1	0.7	.867
1945			8	12	.400	3.63	32	24	10	183.2	191	93	77	2	0	2	0	70	20	0	.286	8	31	3	3	1.3	.951
1946			6	12	.333	4.96	27	18	7	139.2	148	105	45	0	1	2	0	51	10	0	.196	6	23	2	1	1.1	.935
	5 yrs.		19	30	.388	4.25	102	54	19	446.2	443	290	168	3	3	5	2	159	34	0	.214	21	69	6	5	0.9	.938

WORLD SERIES

| 1944 | STL | A | 0 | 0 | — | 0.00 | 1 | 0 | 0 | 2 | 2 | 1 | 1 | 0 | 0 | 0 | 0 | 0 | 0 | 0 | — | 0 | 1 | 0 | 0 | 1.0 | 1.000 |

George Shoch

SHOCH, GEORGE QUINTUS
B. Jan. 6, 1859, Philadelphia, Pa. D. Sept. 30, 1937, Philadelphia, Pa.
BR TR

| 1888 | WAS | N | 0 | 0 | — | 0.00 | 1 | 0 | 0 | 3 | 2 | 1 | 0 | 0 | 0 | 0 | 0 | * | | | | 0 | 0 | 0 | 0 | 0.0 | — |

Urban Shocker

SHOCKER, URBAN JAMES
Born Urbain Jacques Shookcor.
B. Aug. 22, 1890, Cleveland, Ohio D. Sept. 9, 1928, Denver, Colo.
BR TR 5'10" 170 lbs.

1916	NY	A	4	3	.571	2.62	12	9	4	82.1	67	32	43	1	0	0	0	21	4	0	.190	9	18	1	0	2.3	.964
1917			8	5	.615	2.61	26	13	7	145	124	46	68	0	1	1	1	45	8	0	.178	6	50	2	2	2.2	.966
1918	STL	A	6	5	.545	1.81	14	9	7	94.2	69	40	33	0	2	0	2	34	11	0	.324	8	25	0	3	2.4	1.000
1919			13	11	.542	2.69	30	25	13	211	193	55	86	5	1	1	0	58	8	0	.138	11	48	3	2	2.1	.952
1920			20	10	.667	2.71	38	28	22	245.2	224	70	107	5	2	1	5	80	18	0	.225	13	58	1	0	1.9	.986
1921			27	12	.692	3.55	47	39	31	326.2	345	86	132	4	2	2	4	104	27	0	.260	21	91	2	1	2.4	.982
1922			24	17	.585	2.97	48	38	29	348	265	59	149	2	4	1	3	115	22	1	.191	33	59	1	1	1.9	.989
1923			20	12	.625	3.41	43	35	24	277.1	292	49	109	3	0	0	5	80	16	0	.200	11	56	3	3	1.6	.957
1924			16	13	.552	4.17	39	32	17	239.1	262	49	84	4	2	0	1	66	15	0	.227	11	42	0	3	1.4	1.000
1925	NY	A	12	12	.500	3.65	41	30	15	244.1	278	58	74	2	0	1	0	64	11	0	.172	11	50	0	5	1.5	1.000
1926			19	11	.633	3.38	41	33	19	258.1	272	71	59	0	1	0	2	76	13	0	.171	11	59	1	0	1.7	.986
1927			18	6	.750	2.84	31	27	13	200	207	41	35	2	1	0	0	54	13	0	.241	10	42	1	2	1.7	.981
1928			0	0	—	0.00	2	0	0	2	3	0	0	0	0	0	0	0	0	0	—	0	0	0	0	0.0	—
	13 yrs.		187	117	.615	3.17	411	318	201	2674.2	2601	656	979	28	16	8	25	797	166	1	.208	155	598	15	22	1.8	.980

WORLD SERIES

| 1926 | NY | A | 0 | 1 | .000 | 5.87 | 2 | 1 | 0 | 7.2 | 13 | 0 | 3 | 0 | 0 | 0 | 0 | 2 | 0 | 0 | .000 | 0 | 2 | 0 | 0 | 1.0 | 1.000 |

Milt Shoffner

SHOFFNER, MILBURN JAMES
B. Nov. 13, 1905, Sherman, Tex. D. Jan. 19, 1978, Madison, Ohio
BL TL 6'1½" 184 lbs.

1929	CLE	A	2	3	.400	5.04	11	3	1	44.2	46	22	15	0	2	0	0	15	0	0	.000	1	10	0	1	1.0	1.000
1930			3	4	.429	7.97	24	10	1	84.2	129	50	17	0	1	1	0	33	7	1	.212	3	17	2	2	0.9	.909
1931			2	3	.400	7.24	12	4	1	41	55	26	12	0	1	0	0	13	1	0	.077	2	10	0	0	0.8	1.000
1937	BOS	N	3	1	.750	2.53	6	5	3	42.2	38	9	13	1	0	0	1	16	2	1	.125	2	12	0	1	2.3	1.000
1938			8	7	.533	3.54	26	15	9	139.2	147	36	49	1	2	1	0	57	12	0	.211	8	19	2	0	1.1	.931
1939	2 teams		BOS N	(25G 4–6)		CIN N	(10G 2–2)																					
"	total		6	8	.429	3.18	35	14	7	170	176	53	57	0	3	0	1	55	8	0	.145	3	37	2	2	1.2	.952
1940	CIN	N	1	0	1.000	5.63	20	0	0	54.1	56	18	17	0	1	0	0	16	2	0	.125	0	7	0	0	0.5	1.000
	7 yrs.		25	26	.490	4.59	134	51	22	577	647	214	180	2	10	2	3	205	32	3	.156	20	112	6	4	1.0	.957

Ernie Shore

SHORE, ERNEST GRADY
B. Mar. 24, 1891, East Bend, N. C. D. Sept. 24, 1980, Winston-Salem, N. C.
BR TR 6'4" 220 lbs.

| 1912 | NY | N | 0 | 0 | — | 27.00 | 1 | 0 | 0 | 1 | 8 | 1 | 0 | 0 | 0 | 0 | 0 | 0 | 0 | 0 | — | 0 | 0 | 0 | 0 | 1.0 | — |
| 1914 | BOS | A | 10 | 4 | .714 | 1.89 | 20 | 17 | 10 | 147.2 | 111 | 38 | 53 | 1 | 1 | 0 | 1 | 49 | 5 | 0 | .102 | 2 | 52 | 2 | 1 | 2.8 | .964 |

Year	Team	W	L	PCT	ERA	G	GS	CG	IP	H	BB	SO	ShO	W	L	SV	AB	H	HR	BA	PO	A	E	DP	TC/G	FA

Ernie Shore *continued*

Year	Team	W	L	PCT	ERA	G	GS	CG	IP	H	BB	SO	ShO	W	L	SV	AB	H	HR	BA	PO	A	E	DP	TC/G	FA
1915		19	8	.704	1.64	38	32	17	247	207	66	102	4	2	0	0	79	8	0	.101	10	95	7	3	2.9	.938
1916		16	10	.615	2.63	38	28	10	225.2	221	49	62	3	2	2	1	77	7	0	.091	18	90	5	2	3.0	.956
1917		13	10	.565	2.22	29	27	14	226.2	201	55	57	1	1	0	1	78	13	0	.167	19	77	4	5	3.4	.960
1919	NY A	5	8	.385	4.17	20	13	3	95	105	44	24	0	2	1	0	28	4	0	.143	5	27	0	0	1.6	1.000
1920		2	2	.500	4.87	14	5	2	44.1	61	21	12	0	1	0	1	11	2	0	.182	1	16	1	0	1.3	.944
7 yrs.		65	42	.607	2.45	160	122	56	987.1	914	274	311	9	8	3	5	322	39	0	.121	55	357	20	11	2.7	.954

WORLD SERIES

Year	Team	W	L	PCT	ERA	G	GS	CG	IP	H	BB	SO	ShO	W	L	SV	AB	H	HR	BA	PO	A	E	DP	TC/G	FA
1915	BOS A	1	1	.500	2.12	2	2	2	17	12	8	6	0	0	0	0	5	1	0	.200	0	5	1	0	3.0	.833
1916		2	0	1.000	1.53	2	2	1	17.2	12	4	9	0	0	0	0	7	0	0	.000	2	6	0	1	4.0	1.000
2 yrs.		3	1	.750	1.82	4	4	3	34.2	24	12	15	0	0	0	0	12	1	0	.083	2	11	1	1	3.5	.929

Ray Shore

SHORE, RAYMOND EVERETT
B. June 9, 1921, Cincinnati, Ohio

BR TR 6'3" 210 lbs.

Year	Team	W	L	PCT	ERA	G	GS	CG	IP	H	BB	SO	ShO	W	L	SV	AB	H	HR	BA	PO	A	E	DP	TC/G	FA
1946	STL A	0	0	—	18.00	1	0	0	1	3	1	1	0	0	0	0	0	0	0	—	0	0	0	0	0.0	—
1948		1	2	.333	6.39	17	4	0	38	40	35	12	0	1	0	0	9	0	0	.000	2	8	0	0	0.6	1.000
1949		0	1	.000	10.80	13	0	0	23.1	27	31	13	0	0	1	0	5	0	0	.000	0	7	0	0	0.5	1.000
3 yrs.		1	3	.250	8.23	31	4	0	62.1	70	67	26	0	1	1	0	14	0	0	.000	2	15	0	0	0.5	1.000

Bill Shores

SHORES, WILLIAM DAVID
B. May 26, 1904, Abilene, Tex. D. Feb. 19, 1984, Purcell, Okla.

BR TR 6' 210 lbs.

Year	Team	W	L	PCT	ERA	G	GS	CG	IP	H	BB	SO	ShO	W	L	SV	AB	H	HR	BA	PO	A	E	DP	TC/G	FA
1928	PHI A	1	1	.500	3.21	3	2	1	14	13	7	5	0	0	0	0	5	0	0	.000	0	2	0	0	0.7	1.000
1929		11	6	.647	3.60	39	13	5	152.2	150	59	49	1	6	2	7	40	5	0	.125	7	28	3	2	1.0	.921
1930		12	4	.750	4.19	31	19	7	159	169	70	48	1	2	0	0	57	11	0	.193	8	35	3	1	1.5	.935
1931		0	3	.000	5.06	6	2	0	16	26	10	2	0	0	2	0	3	1	0	.333	3	4	1	0	1.0	.833
1933	NY N	2	1	.667	3.93	8	3	1	36.2	41	14	20	0	0	0	0	11	3	0	.273	2	13	0	0	1.9	1.000
1936	CHI A	0	0	—	9.53	9	0	0	17	26	8	5	0	0	0	0	5	1	0	.200	0	4	0	0	0.7	1.000
6 yrs.		26	15	.634	4.17	96	39	14	395.1	425	168	129	2	8	4	7	121	21	0	.174	20	86	7	3	1.2	.938

WORLD SERIES

Year	Team	W	L	PCT	ERA	G	GS	CG	IP	H	BB	SO	ShO	W	L	SV	AB	H	HR	BA	PO	A	E	DP	TC/G	FA
1930	PHI A	0	0	—	13.50	1	0	0	1.1	3	0	0	0	0	0	0	0	0	0	—	0	0	0	0	0.0	—

Bill Short

SHORT, WILLIAM ROSS
B. Nov. 27, 1937, Kingston, N. Y.

BL TL 5'9" 170 lbs.

Year	Team	W	L	PCT	ERA	G	GS	CG	IP	H	BB	SO	ShO	W	L	SV	AB	H	HR	BA	PO	A	E	DP	TC/G	FA
1960	NY A	3	5	.375	4.79	10	10	2	47	49	30	14	0	0	0	0	15	3	0	.200	7	4	1	1	1.2	.917
1962	BAL A	0	0	—	15.75	5	0	0	4	8	6	3	0	0	0	0	1	0	0	.000	0	1	0	0	0.2	1.000
1966	2 teams	BAL A	(6G 2–3)		BOS A	(8G 0–0)																				
"	total	2	3	.400	3.13	14	6	1	46	44	12	29	1	0	0	0	12	1	0	.083	4	11	0	0	1.1	1.000
1967	PIT N	0	0	—	3.86	6	0	0	2.1	1	1	1	0	0	0	0	1	0	0	.000	2	1	0	0	0.5	1.000
1968	NY N	0	3	.000	4.85	34	0	0	29.2	24	14	24	0	0	3	1	2	0	0	.000	0	0	0	0	0.0	—
1969	CIN N	0	0	—	15.43	4	0	0	2.1	4	1	0	0	0	0	0	1	0	0	.000	0	0	0	0	0.0	—
6 yrs.		5	11	.313	4.73	73	16	3	131.1	130	64	71	1	0	3	2	32	4	0	.125	15	26	1	1	0.6	.976

Chris Short

SHORT, CHRISTOPHER JOSEPH
B. Sept. 19, 1937, Milford, Del.

BR TL 6'4" 205 lbs.

Year	Team	W	L	PCT	ERA	G	GS	CG	IP	H	BB	SO	ShO	W	L	SV	AB	H	HR	BA	PO	A	E	DP	TC/G	FA
1959	PHI N	0	0	—	8.16	3	2	0	14.1	19	10	8	0	0	0	0	6	0	0	.000	0	2	0	0	0.7	1.000
1960		6	9	.400	3.94	42	10	2	107.1	101	52	54	0	4	1	3	25	4	0	.000	8	18	1	2	0.6	.963
1961		6	12	.333	5.94	39	16	1	127.1	157	71	80	0	3	4	1	37	6	0	.162	6	20	1	0	0.7	.963
1962		11	9	.550	3.42	47	12	4	142	149	56	91	0	5	4	3	36	8	0	.222	11	22	1	2	0.7	.971
1963		9	12	.429	2.95	38	27	6	198	185	69	160	3	1	1	0	66	7	0	.106	15	46	3	3	1.6	1.000
1964		17	9	.654	2.20	42	31	12	220.2	174	51	181	4	0	0	2	65	7	0	.108	9	39	4	3	1.1	.923
1965		18	11	.621	2.82	47	40	15	297.1	237	89	237	4	0	0	0	99	13	0	.131	9	39	4	3	1.1	.923
1966		20	10	.667	3.54	42	39	19	272	257	68	177	4	1	0	0	106	22	0	.208	14	45	2	3	1.5	.967
1967		9	11	.450	2.39	29	26	8	199.1	163	74	142	2	0	1	0	66	6	0	.091	11	38	2	4	1.4	.961
1968		19	13	.594	2.94	42	36	9	269.2	236	81	202	3	0	1	0	79	12	0	.152	11	38	2	4	1.2	.961
1969		0	0	—	7.20	2	2	0	10	11	4	5	0	0	0	0	3	0	0	.000	2	1	0	0	1.5	1.000
1970		9	16	.360	4.30	36	34	7	199	211	66	133	2	0	0	0	61	3	0	.049	10	18	1	0	0.8	.966
1971		7	14	.333	3.85	31	26	5	173	182	63	95	0	0	0	0	48	4	0	.083	10	26	3	0	1.3	.923
1972		1	1	.500	3.91	19	0	0	23	24	8	24	0	1	1	1	0	0	0	—	1	2	1	0	0.2	.750
1973	MIL A	3	5	.375	5.13	42	7	0	72	86	44	44	0	2	4	2	0	0	0	—	1	11	0	0	0.3	1.000
15 yrs.		135	132	.506	3.43	501	308	88	2325	2215	806	1629	24	20	15	18	697	88	0	.126	112	358	17	22	1.0	.965

Clyde Shoun

SHOUN, CLYDE MITCHELL (Hardrock)
B. Mar. 20, 1912, Mountain City, Tenn. D. Mar. 20, 1968, Mountain Home, Tenn.

BL TL 6'1" 188 lbs.

Year	Team	W	L	PCT	ERA	G	GS	CG	IP	H	BB	SO	ShO	W	L	SV	AB	H	HR	BA	PO	A	E	DP	TC/G	FA
1935	CHI N	1	0	1.000	2.84	5	1	0	12.2	14	5	5	0	0	0	0	3	0	0	.000	0	1	0	0	0.2	1.000
1936		0	0	—	12.46	4	0	0	4.1	9	3	6	0	0	0	0	0	0	0	—	0	2	0	0	0.5	1.000
1937		7	7	.500	5.61	37	9	2	93	118	45	43	0	3	3	0	29	4	0	.138	3	18	2	0	0.6	.913
1938	STL N	6	6	.500	4.14	40	12	3	117.1	130	43	37	0	2	2	1	31	8	0	.258	5	19	1	1	0.6	.960
1939		3	1	.750	3.76	53	2	0	103	98	42	50	0	3	1	9	26	3	0	.115	2	19	1	0	0.4	.955
1940		13	11	.542	3.92	54	19	13	197.1	193	46	82	1	3	4	5	63	12	0	.190	11	36	1	3	0.9	.979
1941		3	5	.375	5.66	26	6	0	70	98	20	34	0	3	1	1	22	4	0	.182	1	20	2	2	0.9	.913
1942	2 teams	STL N	(2G 0–0)		CIN N	(34G 1–3)																				
"	total	1	3	.250	2.18	36	2	0	74.1	56	24	32	0	1	3	0	13	4	0	.308	3	21	0	0	0.7	.960
1943	CIN N	14	5	.737	3.06	45	5	2	147	131	46	61	0	13	3	7	42	13	0	.310	6	32	2	5	0.9	.950
1944		13	10	.565	3.02	38	21	12	202.2	193	42	55	1	3	3	2	67	15	0	.224	3	29	1	1	0.9	.970
1946		1	6	.143	4.10	27	5	0	79	87	26	20	0	1	3	0	21	2	0	.095	0	7	0	0	0.3	1.000
1947	2 teams	CIN N	(10G 0–0)		BOS N	(26G 5–3)																				
"	total	5	3	.625	4.50	36	3	1	88	89	26	30	0	4	1	4	19	3	0	.158	3	12	0	0	0.4	1.000
1948	BOS N	5	1	.833	4.01	36	2	1	74	77	20	25	0	4	1	4	21	4	0	.190	5	4	3	1	0.3	.750
1949	2 teams	BOS N	(1G 0–0)		CHI A	(16G 1–1)																				
"	total	1	1	.500	5.55	17	0	0	24.1	38	13	8	0	1	1	0	5	1	0	.200	1	5	0	0	0.4	1.000
14 yrs.		73	59	.553	3.91	454	85	34	1287	1325	404	483	3	41	25	29	362	73	0	.202	43	225	14	13	0.6	.950

Year	Team		W	L	PCT	ERA	G	GS	CG	IP	H	BB	SO	ShO	Relief Pitching W	L	SV	Batting AB	H	HR	BA	PO	A	E	DP	TC/G	FA

Eric Show
SHOW, ERIC VAUGHN
B. May 19, 1956, Riverside, Calif.
BR TR 6'1" 185 lbs.

Year	Team		W	L	PCT	ERA	G	GS	CG	IP	H	BB	SO	ShO	W	L	SV	AB	H	HR	BA	PO	A	E	DP	TC/G	FA
1981	SD	N	1	3	.250	3.13	15	0	0	23	17	9	22	0	1	3	3	0	0	0	–	0	4	1	0	0.3	.800
1982			10	6	.625	2.64	47	14	2	150	117	48	88	2	6	3	3	41	6	0	.146	4	35	3	1	0.9	.929
1983			15	12	.556	4.17	35	33	4	200.2	201	74	120	2	0	0	0	64	11	0	.172	7	27	4	0	1.1	.895
1984			15	9	.625	3.40	32	32	3	206.2	175	88	104	1	0	0	0	69	17	3	.246	14	28	2	2	1.4	.955
1985			12	11	.522	3.09	35	35	5	233	212	87	141	2	0	0	0	79	10	1	.127	14	24	4	2	1.2	.905
1986			9	5	.643	2.97	24	22	2	136.1	109	69	94	0	1	0	0	43	7	0	.163	6	14	1	1	0.9	.952
1987			8	16	.333	3.84	34	34	5	206.1	188	85	117	3	0	0	0	70	5	0	.071	10	27	3	2	1.2	.925
1988			16	11	.593	3.26	32	32	13	234.2	201	53	144	1	0	0	0	81	12	0	.148	5	21	1	0	0.8	.963
1989			8	6	.571	4.23	16	16	1	106.1	113	39	66	0	0	0	0	34	8	0	.235	4	10	1	1	0.9	.933
9 yrs.			94	79	.543	3.43	270	218	35	1497	1333	552	896	11	8	6	6	481	76	4	.158	64	190	20	9	1.0	.927

LEAGUE CHAMPIONSHIP SERIES
| 1984 | SD | N | 0 | 1 | .000 | 13.50 | 2 | 2 | 0 | 5.1 | 8 | 4 | 2 | 0 | 0 | 0 | 0 | 1 | 0 | 0 | .000 | 0 | 0 | 0 | 0 | 0.0 | – |

WORLD SERIES
| 1984 | SD | N | 0 | 1 | .000 | 10.13 | 1 | 1 | 0 | 2.2 | 4 | 1 | 2 | 0 | 0 | 0 | 0 | 0 | 0 | 0 | – | 0 | 0 | 0 | 0 | 0.0 | – |

Lev Shreve
SHREVE, LEVEN LAWRENCE
B. Jan. 14, 1869, Louisville, Ky. D. Oct. 18, 1942, Detroit, Mich.
BR TR 5'11" 150 lbs.

Year	Team		W	L	PCT	ERA	G	GS	CG	IP	H	BB	SO	ShO	W	L	SV	AB	H	HR	BA	PO	A	E	DP	TC/G	FA
1887	2 teams	BAL AA (5G 3–1)								IND N	(14G 5–9)																
"	total		8	10	.444	4.50	19	19	18	160	174	84	35	2	0	0	0	73	17	0	.233	4	25	5	0	1.8	.853
1888	IND	N	11	24	.314	4.63	35	35	34	297.2	352	93	101	1	0	0	0	115	21	0	.183	7	74	16	0	2.8	.835
1889			0	3	.000	13.79	3	3	1	15.2	25	12	5	0	0	0	0	7	0	0	.000	1	5	0	0	2.0	1.000
3 yrs.			19	37	.339	4.89	57	57	53	473.1	551	189	141	3	0	0	0	195	38	0	.195	12	104	21	0	2.4	.847

Harry Shriver
SHRIVER, HARRY GRAYDON (Pop)
B. Sept. 2, 1896, Wadestown, W. Va. D. Jan. 21, 1970, Morgantown, W. Va.
BR TR 6'2" 180 lbs.

Year	Team		W	L	PCT	ERA	G	GS	CG	IP	H	BB	SO	ShO	W	L	SV	AB	H	HR	BA	PO	A	E	DP	TC/G	FA
1922	BKN	N	4	6	.400	2.99	25	14	4	108.1	114	48	38	2	0	0	0	27	1	0	.037	4	13	1	0	0.7	.944
1923			0	0	–	6.75	1	1	0	4	8	0	1	0	0	0	0	1	0	0	.000	0	0	0	0	0.0	–
2 yrs.			4	6	.400	3.12	26	15	4	112.1	122	48	39	2	0	0	0	28	1	0	.036	4	13	1	0	0.7	.944

Toots Shultz
SHULTZ, WALLACE LUTHER
B. Oct. 10, 1888, Homestead, Pa. D. Jan. 30, 1959, McKeesport, Pa.
BR TR 5'10" 175 lbs.

Year	Team		W	L	PCT	ERA	G	GS	CG	IP	H	BB	SO	ShO	W	L	SV	AB	H	HR	BA	PO	A	E	DP	TC/G	FA
1911	PHI	N	0	3	.000	9.36	5	3	2	25	30	15	9	0	0	0	0	8	2	0	.250	0	9	1	1	2.0	.900
1912			1	4	.200	4.58	22	4	1	59	75	35	20	0	1	2	1	21	5	0	.238	4	17	4	0	1.1	.840
2 yrs.			1	7	.125	6.00	27	7	3	84	105	50	29	0	1	2	1	29	7	0	.241	4	26	5	1	1.3	.857

Harry Shuman
SHUMAN, HARRY
B. Mar. 5, 1916, Philadelphia, Pa.
BR TR 6'2" 195 lbs.

Year	Team		W	L	PCT	ERA	G	GS	CG	IP	H	BB	SO	ShO	W	L	SV	AB	H	HR	BA	PO	A	E	DP	TC/G	FA
1942	PIT	N	0	0	–	0.00	1	0	0	2	0	1	1	0	0	0	0	0	0	0	–	0	0	0	0	0.0	–
1943			0	0	–	5.32	11	0	0	22	30	8	5	0	0	0	0	2	0	0	.000	0	7	0	1	0.6	1.000
1944	PHI	N	0	0	–	4.05	18	0	0	26.2	26	11	4	0	0	0	0	1	0	0	.000	0	8	3	0	0.6	.727
3 yrs.			0	0	–	4.44	30	0	0	50.2	56	20	10	0	0	0	0	3	0	0	.000	0	15	3	1	0.6	.833

Paul Siebert
SIEBERT, PAUL EDWARD
Son of Dick Siebert.
B. June 5, 1953, Minneapolis, Minn.
BL TL 6'2" 205 lbs.

Year	Team		W	L	PCT	ERA	G	GS	CG	IP	H	BB	SO	ShO	W	L	SV	AB	H	HR	BA	PO	A	E	DP	TC/G	FA
1974	HOU	N	1	1	.500	3.60	5	5	0	25	21	11	10	1	0	0	0	6	0	0	.000	1	9	0	0	2.0	1.000
1975			0	2	.000	3.00	7	2	0	18	20	6	4	0	0	1	2	3	0	0	.000	3	4	0	0	1.0	1.000
1976			0	2	.000	3.12	19	0	0	26	29	18	10	0	0	2	0	2	0	0	.000	3	1	0	0	0.3	.800
1977	2 teams	SD N (4G 0–0)								NY N	(25G 2–1)																
"	total		2	1	.667	3.69	29	0	0	31.2	30	17	21	0	2	1	0	3	0	0	.000	3	2	0	0	0.2	1.000
1978	NY	N	0	2	.000	5.14	27	0	0	28	30	21	12	0	0	2	1	1	0	0	.000	3	5	0	0	0.3	1.000
5 yrs.			3	8	.273	3.78	87	7	1	128.2	130	73	59	1	2	6	3	13	0	0	.000	13	21	1	0	0.4	.971

Sonny Siebert
SIEBERT, WILFRED CHARLES
B. Jan. 14, 1937, St. Mary's, Mo.
BR TR 6'3" 190 lbs.

Year	Team		W	L	PCT	ERA	G	GS	CG	IP	H	BB	SO	ShO	W	L	SV	AB	H	HR	BA	PO	A	E	DP	TC/G	FA
1964	CLE	A	7	9	.438	3.23	41	14	3	156	142	57	144	1	1	2	3	49	13	2	.265	6	16	3	1	0.6	.880
1965			16	8	.667	2.43	39	27	4	188.2	139	46	191	1	4	0	1	66	7	1	.106	15	29	2	4	1.2	.957
1966			16	8	**.667**	2.80	34	32	11	241	193	62	163	1	0	0	1	85	11	0	.129	19	46	4	4	2.0	.942
1967			10	12	.455	2.38	34	26	7	185.1	136	54	136	1	1	1	1	52	7	1	.135	8	21	2	2	0.9	.935
1968			12	10	.545	2.97	31	30	8	206	145	88	146	4	0	0	0	70	11	0	.157	18	33	4	2	1.8	.927
1969	2 teams	CLE A (2G 0–1)								BOS A	(43G 14–10)																
"	total		14	11	.560	3.76	45	24	2	177.1	161	76	133	0	5	1	5	57	9	1	.158	6	36	1	6	1.0	.977
1970	BOS	A	15	8	.652	3.43	33	33	7	223	207	60	142	2	0	0	0	77	10	0	.130	25	26	2	3	1.6	.962
1971			16	10	.615	2.91	32	32	12	235	220	60	131	4	0	0	0	79	21	6	.266	15	42	4	1	1.9	.934
1972			12	12	.500	3.80	32	30	7	196.1	204	59	123	3	0	0	0	72	17	1	.236	24	30	2	2	1.8	.964
1973	2 teams	BOS A (2G 0–1)								TEX A	(25G 7–11)																
"	total		7	12	.368	4.06	27	20	1	122	125	38	81	1	0	2	0	0	0	0	–	13	25	0	0	1.4	1.000
1974	STL	N	8	8	.500	3.83	28	20	5	134	150	51	68	3	1	0	0	44	5	0	.114	6	16	0	3	0.8	1.000
1975	2 teams	SD N (6G 3–2)								OAK A	(17G 4–4)																
"	total		7	6	.538	3.89	23	19	0	88	97	41	54	0	0	0	0	9	3	0	.333	4	9	2	1	0.7	.867
12 yrs.			140	114	.551	3.21	399	307	67	2152.2	1919	692	1512	21	12	6	16	660	114	12	.173	159	329	26	28	1.3	.949

Dwight Siebler
SIEBLER, DWIGHT LEROY
B. Aug. 5, 1937, Columbus, Neb.
BR TR 6'2" 184 lbs.

Year	Team		W	L	PCT	ERA	G	GS	CG	IP	H	BB	SO	ShO	W	L	SV	AB	H	HR	BA	PO	A	E	DP	TC/G	FA
1963	MIN	A	2	1	.667	2.79	7	5	2	38.2	25	12	22	0	0	0	0	15	2	0	.133	2	2	0	0	0.6	1.000
1964			0	0	–	4.91	9	0	0	11	10	6	10	0	0	0	0	0	0	0	–	0	1	0	0	0.1	1.000
1965			0	0	–	4.20	7	1	0	15	11	11	15	0	0	0	0	1	0	0	.000	0	4	0	0	0.4	1.000
1966			2	2	.500	3.44	23	0	0	49.2	47	14	24	0	2	2	1	11	0	0	.000	3	5	1	0	0.4	.889

Year	Team	W	L	PCT	ERA	G	GS	CG	IP	H	BB	SO	ShO	W	L	SV	AB	H	HR	BA	PO	A	E	DP	TC/G	FA
														Relief Pitching			Batting									

Dwight Siebler *continued*

Year	Team	W	L	PCT	ERA	G	GS	CG	IP	H	BB	SO	ShO	W	L	SV	AB	H	HR	BA	PO	A	E	DP	TC/G	FA
1967		0	0	–	3.00	2	0	0	3	4	1	0	0	0	0	0	0	0	0	–	0	0	0	0	0.0	–
5 yrs.		4	3	.571	3.45	48	8	2	117.1	97	44	71	0	2	2	1	27	2	0	.074	6	10	1	0	0.4	.941

Candy Sierra

SIERRA, ULISES
Born Ulises Sierra y Pizarro.
B. Mar. 27, 1967, Rio Piedras, Puerto Rico

BR TR 6'2" 190 lbs.

Year	Team	W	L	PCT	ERA	G	GS	CG	IP	H	BB	SO	ShO	W	L	SV	AB	H	HR	BA	PO	A	E	DP	TC/G	FA
1988	2 teams	SD N	(15G 0–1)		CIN N	(1G 0–0)																				
"	total	0	1	.000	5.53	16	0	0	27.2	41	12	24	0	0	1	0	4	0	0	.000	1	3	0	0	0.3	1.000

Ed Siever

SIEVER, EDWARD T.
B. Apr. 2, 1877, Goodard, Kans. D. Feb. 5, 1920, Detroit, Mich.

BL TL 5'11½" 190 lbs.

Year	Team	W	L	PCT	ERA	G	GS	CG	IP	H	BB	SO	ShO	W	L	SV	AB	H	HR	BA	PO	A	E	DP	TC/G	FA
1901	DET A	18	15	.545	3.24	38	33	30	288.2	334	65	85	2	1	1	0	107	18	0	.168	16	74	9	5	2.6	.909
1902		8	11	.421	1.91	25	23	17	188.1	166	32	36	4	0	0	1	66	10	0	.152	5	40	8	1	2.1	.849
1903	STL A	13	14	.481	2.48	31	27	24	254	245	39	90	1	1	0	0	93	13	0	.140	17	87	8	3	3.6	.929
1904		10	15	.400	2.65	29	24	19	217	235	65	77	2	1	1	0	71	11	0	.155	11	77	4	2	3.2	.957
1906	DET A	14	11	.560	2.71	30	25	20	222.2	240	45	71	1	1	0	0	77	12	0	.156	7	59	1	0	2.2	.985
1907		18	11	.621	2.16	39	33	22	274.2	256	52	88	3	1	1	0	91	14	0	.154	11	69	3	2	2.1	.964
1908		2	6	.250	3.50	11	9	4	61.2	74	13	23	0	1	0	1	18	3	0	.167	5	16	2	0	2.1	.913
7 yrs.		83	83	.500	2.60	203	174	136	1507	1550	311	470	14	5	3	2	523	81	0	.155	72	422	35	13	2.6	.934

WORLD SERIES

Year	Team	W	L	PCT	ERA	G	GS	CG	IP	H	BB	SO	ShO	W	L	SV	AB	H	HR	BA	PO	A	E	DP	TC/G	FA
1907	DET A	0	1	.000	4.50	1	1	0	4	7	0	1	0	0	0	0	0	0	0	.000	1	0	0	0	1.0	1.000

Walter Signer

SIGNER, WALTER DONALD ALOYSIUS
B. Oct. 12, 1910, New York, N. Y. D. July 23, 1974, Greenwich, Conn.

BR TR 6' 165 lbs.

Year	Team	W	L	PCT	ERA	G	GS	CG	IP	H	BB	SO	ShO	W	L	SV	AB	H	HR	BA	PO	A	E	DP	TC/G	FA
1943	CHI N	2	1	.667	2.88	4	2	1	25	24	4	5	1	0	0	0	8	2	0	.250	2	4	0	1	1.5	1.000
1945		0	0	–	3.38	6	0	0	8	11	5	0	0	0	0	1	1	0	0	.000	0	1	0	0	0.2	1.000
2 yrs.		2	1	.667	3.00	10	2	1	33	35	9	5	1	0	0	1	9	2	0	.222	2	5	0	1	0.7	1.000

Seth Sigsby

SIGSBY, SETH DeWITT
Born Seth DeWitt.
B. Apr. 30, 1874, Cobleskill, N. Y. D. Sept. 15, 1953, Schenectady, N. Y.

6' 175 lbs.

Year	Team	W	L	PCT	ERA	G	GS	CG	IP	H	BB	SO	ShO	W	L	SV	AB	H	HR	BA	PO	A	E	DP	TC/G	FA
1893	NY N	0	0	–	9.00	1	0	0	3	1	4	2	0	0	0	0	1	0	0	.000	0	0	0	0	0.0	–

Al Sima

SIMA, ALBERT
B. Oct. 7, 1922, Mahwah, N. J.

BR TL 6' 187 lbs.

Year	Team	W	L	PCT	ERA	G	GS	CG	IP	H	BB	SO	ShO	W	L	SV	AB	H	HR	BA	PO	A	E	DP	TC/G	FA
1950	WAS A	4	5	.444	4.79	17	9	1	77	89	26	23	0	1	0	0	26	3	0	.115	1	10	0	0	0.6	1.000
1951		3	7	.300	4.79	18	8	1	77	79	41	26	0	1	2	0	17	3	1	.176	1	14	2	0	0.9	.882
1953		2	3	.400	3.42	31	5	1	68.1	63	31	25	0	2	0	1	17	2	0	.118	3	15	0	2	0.6	1.000
1954	2 teams	CHI A	(5G 0–1)		PHI A	(29G 2–5)																				
"	total	2	6	.250	5.21	34	8	1	86.1	112	34	37	0	1	1	3	22	1	0	.045	2	13	2	0	0.5	.882
4 yrs.		11	21	.344	4.61	100	30	4	308.2	343	132	111	0	5	3	4	82	9	1	.110	7	52	4	2	0.6	.937

Curt Simmons

SIMMONS, CURTIS THOMAS
B. May 19, 1929, Egypt, Pa.

BL TL 5'11" 175 lbs.

Year	Team	W	L	PCT	ERA	G	GS	CG	IP	H	BB	SO	ShO	W	L	SV	AB	H	HR	BA	PO	A	E	DP	TC/G	FA
1947	PHI N	1	0	1.000	1.00	1	1	1	9	5	6	9	0	0	0	0	2	1	0	.500	0	0	0	0	0.0	–
1948		7	12	.368	4.87	31	23	7	170	169	108	86	0	0	0	0	51	7	0	.137	4	34	2	4	1.3	.950
1949		4	10	.286	4.59	38	14	2	131.1	133	55	83	0	1	3	1	41	7	0	.171	5	22	2	0	0.8	.931
1950		17	8	.680	3.40	31	27	11	214.2	178	88	146	2	2	0	1	77	12	0	.156	12	32	0	2	1.4	1.000
1952		14	8	.636	2.82	28	28	15	201.1	170	70	141	6	0	0	0	67	11	1	.164	3	25	0	0	1.0	1.000
1953		16	13	.552	3.21	32	30	19	238	211	82	138	4	0	0	0	93	13	0	.140	3	30	2	1	1.1	.943
1954		14	15	.483	2.81	34	33	21	253	226	98	125	3	0	0	0	91	16	0	.176	6	33	3	1	1.2	.929
1955		8	8	.500	4.92	25	23	3	130	148	50	58	0	1	1	0	46	8	0	.174	8	17	1	1	1.0	.962
1956		15	10	.600	3.36	33	27	14	198	186	65	88	2	0	0	0	72	17	0	.236	4	35	1	3	1.1	.975
1957		12	11	.522	3.44	32	29	9	212	214	50	92	2	0	0	0	71	17	0	.239	8	26	0	0	1.1	1.000
1958		7	14	.333	4.38	29	27	7	168.1	196	40	78	1	0	0	0	59	12	0	.203	14	21	2	1	1.3	.946
1959		0	0	–	4.50	7	0	0	10	16	0	4	0	0	0	0	0	0	0	–	0	2	0	0	0.3	1.000
1960	2 teams	PHI N	(4G 0–0)		STL N	(23G 7–4)																				
"	total	7	4	.636	3.06	27	19	3	156	162	37	67	1	0	0	0	47	10	0	.213	7	30	1	5	1.4	.974
1961	STL N	9	10	.474	3.13	30	29	6	195.2	203	64	99	2	0	0	0	66	20	0	.303	6	36	1	4	1.4	.977
1962		10	10	.500	3.51	31	22	9	154	167	32	74	4	0	3	0	50	8	0	.160	6	26	1	1	1.1	.970
1963		15	9	.625	2.48	32	32	11	232.2	209	48	127	6	0	0	0	81	13	0	.160	12	23	0	0	1.1	1.000
1964		18	9	.667	3.43	34	34	12	244	233	49	104	3	0	0	0	94	10	0	.106	12	45	2	0	1.7	.966
1965		9	15	.375	4.08	34	32	5	203	229	54	96	0	0	0	0	64	3	0	.047	8	32	1	0	1.2	.976
1966	2 teams	STL N	(10G 1–1)		CHI N	(19G 4–7)																				
"	total	5	8	.385	4.23	29	15	4	110.2	114	35	38	1	2	0	0	26	3	0	.115	5	26	2	0	1.1	.939
1967	2 teams	CHI N	(17G 3–7)		CAL A	(14G 2–1)																				
"	total	5	8	.385	4.24	31	18	4	116.2	144	32	44	1	1	0	1	37	6	0	.162	4	19	2	1	0.8	.920
20 yrs.		193	182	.515	3.54	569	462	163	3348.1	3313	1063	1697	36	8	9	5	1135	194	1	.171	127	514	23	26	1.2	.965

WORLD SERIES

Year	Team	W	L	PCT	ERA	G	GS	CG	IP	H	BB	SO	ShO	W	L	SV	AB	H	HR	BA	PO	A	E	DP	TC/G	FA
1964	STL N	0	1	.000	2.51	2	2	0	14.1	11	3	8	0	0	0	0	4	2	0	.500	2	1	0	0	1.5	1.000

Pat Simmons

SIMMONS, PATRICK CLEMENT
Born Patrick Clement Simoni.
B. Nov. 29, 1908, Watervliet, N. Y. D. July 3, 1968, Albany, N. Y.

BR TR 5'11" 172 lbs.

Year	Team	W	L	PCT	ERA	G	GS	CG	IP	H	BB	SO	ShO	W	L	SV	AB	H	HR	BA	PO	A	E	DP	TC/G	FA
1928	BOS A	0	2	.000	4.04	31	3	0	69	69	38	16	0	0	0	1	15	2	0	.133	3	15	1	0	0.6	.947
1929		0	0	–	0.00	2	0	0	7	6	3	2	0	0	0	0	1	0	0	.000	1	0	0	0	0.5	1.000
2 yrs.		0	2	.000	3.67	33	3	0	76	75	41	18	0	0	0	1	16	2	0	.125	4	15	1	0	0.6	.950

Year	Team		W	L	PCT	ERA	G	GS	CG	IP	H	BB	SO	ShO	Relief Pitching W	L	SV	Batting AB	H	HR	BA	PO	A	E	DP	TC/G	FA

Duke Simpson

SIMPSON, THOMAS LEO
B. Sept. 15, 1927, Columbus, Ohio
BR TR 6'1½" 190 lbs.

| 1953 | CHI | N | 1 | 2 | .333 | 8.00 | 30 | 1 | 0 | 45 | 60 | 25 | 21 | 0 | 1 | 1 | 0 | 8 | 2 | 0 | .250 | 4 | 6 | 0 | 2 | 0.3 | 1.000 |

Joe Simpson

SIMPSON, JOE ALLEN
B. Dec. 31, 1951, Purcell, Okla.
BL TL 6'3" 175 lbs.

| 1983 | KC | A | 0 | 0 | — | 3.00 | 2 | 0 | 0 | 3 | 4 | 2 | 1 | 0 | 0 | 0 | 0 | * | | | | 0 | 0 | 0 | 0 | 0.0 | — |

Steve Simpson

SIMPSON, STEVEN EDWARD
B. Aug. 30, 1948, St. Joseph, Mo.
BR TR 6'3" 200 lbs.

| 1972 | SD | N | 0 | 2 | .000 | 4.76 | 9 | 0 | 0 | 11.1 | 10 | 8 | 9 | 0 | 0 | 2 | 2 | 0 | 0 | 0 | — | 0 | 1 | 0 | 0 | 0.1 | 1.000 |

Wayne Simpson

SIMPSON, WAYNE KIRBY
B. Dec. 2, 1948, Los Angeles, Calif.
BR TR 6'3" 220 lbs.

1970	CIN	N	14	3	.824	3.02	26	26	10	176	125	81	119	2	0	0	0	64	6	0	.094	22	30	2	2	2.1	.963
1971			4	7	.364	4.77	22	21	1	117	106	77	61	0	0	0	0	32	1	0	.031	4	30	1	0	1.6	.971
1972			8	5	.615	4.14	24	22	1	130.1	124	49	70	0	0	0	0	48	3	0	.063	3	8	1	1	0.5	.917
1973	KC	A	3	4	.429	5.70	16	10	1	60	66	35	29	0	0	0	0	0	0	0	—	6	7	1	0	0.9	.929
1975	PHI	N	1	0	1.000	3.19	7	5	0	31	31	11	19	0	0	0	0	9	2	0	.222	6	4	0	0	1.4	1.000
1977	CAL	A	6	12	.333	5.83	27	23	0	122	154	62	55	0	0	1	0	0	0	0	—	7	13	1	1	0.8	.952
6 yrs.			36	31	.537	4.37	122	107	13	636.1	606	315	353	2	0	1	0	153	12	0	.078	48	92	6	4	1.2	.959

Pete Sims

SIMS, CLARENCE
B. May 24, 1891, Crown City, Ohio D. Dec. 2, 1968, Dallas, Tex.
BR TR 5'11½" 165 lbs.

| 1915 | STL | A | 1 | 0 | 1.000 | 4.32 | 3 | 2 | 0 | 8.1 | 6 | 6 | 4 | 0 | 0 | 0 | 0 | 1 | 1 | 0 | 1.000 | 2 | 1 | 2 | 0 | 1.7 | .600 |

Bert Sincock

SINCOCK, HERBERT SYLVESTER
B. Sept. 8, 1887, Barkerville, B. C., Canada D. Aug. 1, 1946, Houghton, Mich.
BL TL 5'10½" 165 lbs.

| 1908 | CIN | N | 0 | 0 | — | 3.86 | 1 | 0 | 0 | 4.2 | 3 | 0 | 1 | 0 | 0 | 0 | 0 | 2 | 0 | 0 | .000 | 0 | 1 | 0 | 0 | 1.0 | 1.000 |

Bill Singer

SINGER, WILLIAM ROBERT (The Singer Throwing Machine)
B. Apr. 24, 1944, Los Angeles, Calif.
BR TR 6'4" 184 lbs.

1964	LA	N	0	1	.000	3.21	2	2	0	14	11	12	3	0	0	0	0	6	1	0	.167	0	3	0	0	1.5	1.000
1965			0	0	—	0.00	2	0	0	1	2	2	1	0	0	0	0	0	0	0	—	0	0	0	0	0.0	—
1966			0	0	—	0.00	3	0	0	4	4	2	4	0	0	0	0	0	0	0	—	0	1	0	0	0.3	1.000
1967			12	8	.600	2.64	32	29	7	204.1	185	61	169	3	0	1	0	67	6	0	.090	10	37	5	0	1.6	.904
1968			13	17	.433	2.88	37	36	12	256.1	227	78	227	6	0	1	0	81	12	0	.148	13	41	7	0	1.6	.885
1969			20	12	.625	2.34	41	40	16	316	244	74	247	2	0	0	1	108	11	0	.102	14	41	2	0	1.4	.965
1970			8	5	.615	3.14	16	16	5	106	79	32	93	3	0	0	0	38	5	0	.132	8	12	3	0	1.4	.870
1971			10	17	.370	4.17	31	31	8	203	195	71	144	1	0	0	0	58	6	0	.103	8	24	1	2	1.1	.970
1972			6	16	.273	3.67	26	25	4	169.1	148	60	101	3	0	1	0	55	4	0	.073	7	28	2	2	1.4	.946
1973	CAL	A	20	14	.588	3.22	40	40	19	315.2	280	130	241	2	0	0	0	0	0	0	—	13	38	5	1	1.4	.911
1974			7	4	.636	2.97	14	14	8	109	102	43	77	0	0	0	0	0	0	0	—	6	16	1	0	1.6	.957
1975			7	15	.318	4.98	29	27	8	179	171	81	78	0	0	0	1	0	0	0	—	7	28	3	1	1.3	.921
1976	2 teams		TEX A		(10G 4–1)	MIN A			(26G 9–9)																		
"	total		13	10	.565	3.69	36	36	7	236.2	233	96	97	4	0	0	0	0	0	0	—	7	31	3	0	1.1	.927
1977	TOR	A	2	8	.200	6.75	13	12	0	60	71	39	33	0	0	0	0	0	0	0	—	10	2	10	1	1.1	.857
14 yrs.			118	127	.482	3.39	322	308	94	2174.1	1952	781	1515	24	0	3	2	413	45	0	.109	95	310	34	16	1.4	.923

Elmer Singleton

SINGLETON, BERT ELMER (Smoky)
B. June 26, 1918, Ogden, Utah
BR TR 6'2" 174 lbs.
BB 1957-58

1945	BOS	N	1	4	.200	4.82	7	5	1	37.1	35	14	14	0	0	0	0	11	0	0	.000	0	8	1	0	1.3	.889
1946			0	1	.000	3.74	15	2	1	33.2	27	21	17	0	0	0	1	4	0	0	.000	3	6	0	0	0.6	1.000
1947	PIT		2	2	.500	6.31	36	3	0	67	70	39	24	0	2	0	1	13	4	0	.308	9	11	1	1	0.6	.952
1948			4	6	.400	4.97	38	5	1	92.1	90	40	53	0	3	4	2	23	2	0	.087	13	18	0	1	0.8	1.000
1950	WAS	A	1	2	.333	5.20	21	1	0	36.1	39	17	19	0	1	2	0	7	3	0	.429	5	7	0	1	0.6	1.000
1957	CHI	N	0	1	.000	6.75	5	2	0	13.1	20	2	6	0	0	1	0	3	0	0	.000	2	4	2	1	1.6	.750
1958			1	0	1.000	0.00	2	0	0	4.2	1	1	2	0	1	0	0	1	0	0	.000	1	0	0	0	0.5	1.000
1959			2	1	.667	2.72	21	1	0	43	40	12	25	0	1	1	0	6	0	0	.000	5	10	1	1	0.8	.938
8 yrs.			11	17	.393	4.83	145	19	2	327.2	322	146	160	0	8	8	4	68	9	0	.132	38	64	5	5	0.7	.953

John Singleton

SINGLETON, JOHN EDWARD (Sheriff)
B. Nov. 27, 1896, Gallipolis, Ohio D. Oct. 23, 1937, Dayton, Ohio
BR TR 5'11" 171 lbs.

| 1922 | PHI | N | 1 | 10 | .091 | 5.90 | 22 | 9 | 3 | 93 | 127 | 38 | 27 | 1 | 0 | 3 | 0 | 36 | 5 | 0 | .139 | 2 | 19 | 3 | 1 | 1.1 | .875 |

Doug Sisk

SISK, DOUGLAS RANDALL
B. Sept. 26, 1957, Renton, Wash.
BR TR 6'2" 210 lbs.

1982	NY	N	0	1	.000	1.04	8	0	0	8.2	5	4	4	0	0	1	1	0	0	0	—	0	2	0	0	0.3	1.000
1983			5	4	.556	2.24	67	0	0	104.1	88	59	33	0	5	4	11	6	3	0	.500	7	14	1	1	0.3	.955
1984			1	3	.250	2.09	50	0	0	77.2	57	54	32	0	1	3	15	11	1	0	.091	5	13	1	1	0.4	.947
1985			4	5	.444	5.30	42	0	0	73	86	40	26	0	4	5	2	12	0	0	.000	3	15	0	0	0.4	1.000
1986			4	2	.667	3.06	41	0	0	70.2	77	31	31	0	4	2	1	4	0	0	.000	10	6	0	0	0.4	1.000
1987			3	1	.750	3.46	55	0	0	78	83	22	37	0	3	1	3	5	0	0	.000	9	21	3	0	0.4	1.000
1988	BAL	A	3	3	.500	3.72	52	0	0	94.1	109	45	26	0	3	3	0	0	0	0	—	9	16	3	1	0.5	.893
7 yrs.			20	19	.513	3.22	315	0	0	506.2	505	255	189	0	20	19	33	38	4	0	.105	39	85	5	3	0.4	.961

LEAGUE CHAMPIONSHIP SERIES

| 1986 | NY | N | 0 | 0 | — | 0.00 | 1 | 0 | 0 | 1 | 1 | 1 | 0 | 0 | 0 | 0 | 0 | 0 | 0 | 0 | — | 0 | 0 | 0 | 0 | 0.0 | — |

WORLD SERIES

| 1986 | NY | N | 0 | 0 | — | 0.00 | 1 | 0 | 0 | .2 | 0 | 1 | 0 | 0 | 0 | 0 | 0 | 0 | 0 | 0 | — | 0 | 0 | 0 | 0 | 0.0 | — |

Year	Team		W	L	PCT	ERA	G	GS	CG	IP	H	BB	SO	ShO	W	L	SV	AB	H	HR	BA	PO	A	E	DP	TC/G	FA

Tommie Sisk

SISK, TOMMIE WAYNE
B. Apr. 12, 1942, Ardmore, Okla.

BR TR 6'3" 195 lbs.

Year	Team		W	L	PCT	ERA	G	GS	CG	IP	H	BB	SO	ShO	W	L	SV	AB	H	HR	BA	PO	A	E	DP	TC/G	FA
1962	PIT	N	0	2	.000	4.08	5	3	1	17.2	18	8	6	0	0	0	0	5	1	0	.200	1	2	1	0	0.8	.750
1963			1	3	.250	2.92	57	4	1	108	85	45	73	0	1	1	1	16	1	0	.063	3	24	1	2	0.5	.964
1964			1	4	.200	6.16	42	1	0	61.1	91	29	35	0	1	4	0	8	0	0	.000	7	17	0	0	0.6	1.000
1965			7	3	.700	3.40	38	12	1	111.1	103	50	66	1	3	0	0	33	2	0	.061	4	17	1	0	0.6	.955
1966			10	5	.667	4.14	34	23	4	150	146	52	60	1	2	0	1	51	5	0	.098	9	27	2	3	1.1	.947
1967			13	13	.500	3.34	37	31	11	207.2	196	78	85	2	0	0	1	69	7	0	.101	18	38	2	4	1.6	.966
1968			5	5	.500	3.28	33	11	0	96	101	35	41	0	3	1	1	24	2	0	.083	11	16	3	3	0.9	.900
1969	SD	N	2	13	.133	4.78	53	13	1	143	160	48	59	0	0	0	6	25	3	0	.120	15	24	0	0	0.7	1.000
1970	CHI	A	1	1	.500	5.45	17	1	0	33	37	13	16	0	1	1	0	4	1	0	.250	1	8	1	1	0.6	.900
9 yrs.			40	49	.449	3.92	316	99	19	928	937	358	441	4	11	7	10	235	22	0	.094	69	173	11	13	0.8	.957

Dave Sisler

SISLER, DAVID MICHAEL
Son of George Sisler. Brother of Dick Sisler.
B. Oct. 16, 1931, St. Louis, Mo.

BR TR 6'4" 200 lbs.

Year	Team		W	L	PCT	ERA	G	GS	CG	IP	H	BB	SO	ShO	W	L	SV	AB	H	HR	BA	PO	A	E	DP	TC/G	FA
1956	BOS	A	9	8	.529	4.62	39	14	3	142.1	120	72	93	0	3	3	3	42	5	0	.119	9	22	0	0	0.8	1.000
1957			7	8	.467	4.71	22	19	5	122.1	135	61	55	0	0	0	1	42	7	0	.167	13	22	1	3	1.6	.972
1958			8	9	.471	4.94	30	25	4	149.1	157	79	71	1	1	1	0	46	9	0	.196	7	22	2	1	1.0	.935
1959	2 teams		BOS A	(3G 0–0)		DET A	(32G 1–3)																					
"	total		1	3	.250	4.32	35	0	0	58.1	55	37	32	0	1	3	7	7	2	0	.286	1	7	0	0	0.2	1.000
1960	DET	A	7	5	.583	2.48	41	0	0	80	54	45	47	0	7	5	6	16	2	0	.125	5	18	1	2	0.6	.958
1961	WAS	A	2	8	.200	4.18	45	1	0	60.1	55	48	30	0	2	7	11	6	0	0	.000	4	11	0	1	0.3	1.000
1962	CIN	N	4	3	.571	3.92	35	0	0	43.2	44	26	27	0	4	3	1	0	0	0	–	3	5	0	0	0.2	1.000
7 yrs.			38	44	.463	4.33	247	59	12	656.1	622	368	355	1	18	22	29	159	25	0	.157	42	107	4	7	0.6	.974

George Sisler

SISLER, GEORGE HAROLD (Gorgeous George)
Father of Dick Sisler. Father of Dave Sisler.
B. Mar. 24, 1893, Manchester, Ohio D. Mar. 26, 1973, Richmond Heights, Mo.
Manager 1924-26.
Hall of Fame 1939.

BL TL 5'11" 170 lbs.

Year	Team		W	L	PCT	ERA	G	GS	CG	IP	H	BB	SO	ShO	W	L	SV	AB	H	HR	BA	PO	A	E	DP	TC/G	FA
1915	STL	A	4	4	.500	2.83	15	8	6	70	62	38	41	0	1	1	0	274	78	3	.285	5	18	0	1	1.5	1.000
1916			1	2	.333	1.00	3	3	3	27	18	6	12	1	0	0	0	580	177	4	.305	3	9	0	0	4.0	1.000
1918			0	0	–	4.50	2	1	0	8	10	4	4	0	0	0	0	452	154	2	.341	0	2	0	1	1.0	1.000
1920			0	0	–	0.00	1	0	0	1	0	0	2	0	0	0	1	631	257	19	.407	0	0	0	0	0.0	–
1925			0	0	–	0.00	1	0	0	2	1	1	1	0	0	0	0	649	224	12	.345	0	2	0	0	2.0	1.000
1926			0	0	–	0.00	1	0	0	2	0	2	3	0	0	0	1	613	178	7	.290	0	1	0	0	1.0	1.000
1928	WAS	A	0	0	–	0.00	1	0	0	1	0	1	0	0	0	0	0	540	179	4	.331	0	0	0	0	0.0	–
7 yrs.			5	6	.455	2.35	24	12	9	111	91	52	63	1	1	1	3	*				8	32	0	2	1.7	1.000

Carl Sitton

SITTON, CARL VETTER
B. Sept. 22, 1882, Pendleton, S. C. D. Sept. 11, 1931, Valdosta, Ga.

BR TR 5'10½" 170 lbs.

Year	Team		W	L	PCT	ERA	G	GS	CG	IP	H	BB	SO	ShO	W	L	SV	AB	H	HR	BA	PO	A	E	DP	TC/G	FA
1909	CLE	A	3	2	.600	2.88	14	5	3	50	50	16	16	0	0	0	0	13	2	0	.154	3	11	1	1	1.1	.933

Pete Sivess

SIVESS, PETER
B. Sept. 23, 1913, South River, N. J.

BR TR 6'3½" 195 lbs.

Year	Team		W	L	PCT	ERA	G	GS	CG	IP	H	BB	SO	ShO	W	L	SV	AB	H	HR	BA	PO	A	E	DP	TC/G	FA
1936	PHI	N	3	4	.429	4.57	17	6	2	65	84	36	22	0	1	0	0	25	3	0	.120	3	6	0	1	0.5	1.000
1937			1	1	.500	8.10	6	2	1	20	30	11	4	0	0	0	0	6	0	0	.000	1	2	0	0	0.5	1.000
1938			3	6	.333	5.51	39	8	2	116	143	69	32	0	2	1	3	32	6	0	.188	5	21	2	2	0.7	.929
3 yrs.			7	11	.389	5.46	62	16	5	201	257	116	58	0	3	1	3	63	9	0	.143	9	29	2	3	0.6	.950

Jim Siwy

SIWY, JAMES GERARD
B. Sept. 20, 1958, Pawtucket, R. I.

BR TR 6'4" 200 lbs.

Year	Team		W	L	PCT	ERA	G	GS	CG	IP	H	BB	SO	ShO	W	L	SV	AB	H	HR	BA	PO	A	E	DP	TC/G	FA
1982	CHI	A	0	0	–	10.29	2	1	0	7	10	5	3	0	0	0	0	0	0	0	–	0	0	0	0	0.0	–
1984			0	0	–	2.08	1	0	0	4.1	3	2	1	0	0	0	0	0	0	0	–	0	1	0	0	1.0	1.000
2 yrs.			0	0	–	7.15	3	1	0	11.1	13	7	4	0	0	0	0	0	0	0	–	0	1	0	0	0.3	1.000

Joe Skalski

SKALSKI, JOSEPH DOUGLAS
B. Sept. 26, 1964, Chicago, Ill.

BR TR 6'3" 190 lbs.

Year	Team		W	L	PCT	ERA	G	GS	CG	IP	H	BB	SO	ShO	W	L	SV	AB	H	HR	BA	PO	A	E	DP	TC/G	FA
1989	CLE	A	0	2	.000	6.75	2	1	0	6.2	7	4	3	0	0	1	0	0	0	0	–	1	0	0	0	0.5	1.000

Dave Skaugstad

SKAUGSTAD, DAVID WENDELL
B. Jan. 10, 1940, Algona, Iowa

BL TL 6'1" 179 lbs.

Year	Team		W	L	PCT	ERA	G	GS	CG	IP	H	BB	SO	ShO	W	L	SV	AB	H	HR	BA	PO	A	E	DP	TC/G	FA
1957	CIN	N	0	0	–	1.59	2	0	0	5.2	4	6	4	0	0	0	0	1	0	0	.000	1	2	0	0	1.5	1.000

Dave Skeels

SKEELS, DAVID
B. Dec. 29, 1892, Wash. D. Dec. 3, 1926, Spokane, Wash.

BL TR 6'1" 187 lbs.

Year	Team		W	L	PCT	ERA	G	GS	CG	IP	H	BB	SO	ShO	W	L	SV	AB	H	HR	BA	PO	A	E	DP	TC/G	FA
1910	DET	A	0	0	–	12.00	1	1	0	6	9	4	2	0	0	0	0	3	0	0	.000	0	4	0	0	4.0	1.000

Craig Skok

SKOK, CRAIG RICHARD
B. Sept. 1, 1947, Dobbs Ferry, N. Y.

BB TL 6' 190 lbs.

Year	Team		W	L	PCT	ERA	G	GS	CG	IP	H	BB	SO	ShO	W	L	SV	AB	H	HR	BA	PO	A	E	DP	TC/G	FA
1973	BOS	A	0	1	.000	6.21	11	0	0	29	35	11	22	0	0	1	1	0	0	0	–	1	2	0	0	0.3	1.000
1976	TEX	A	0	1	.000	12.60	9	0	0	5	13	3	5	0	0	1	0	0	0	0	–	0	1	0	0	0.1	1.000
1978	ATL	N	3	2	.600	4.35	43	0	0	62	64	27	28	0	3	2	2	8	2	0	.250	3	9	0	0	0.3	1.000
1979			1	3	.250	4.00	44	0	0	54	58	17	30	0	1	2	2	3	0	0	.000	1	10	0	1	0.2	1.000
4 yrs.			4	7	.364	4.86	107	0	0	150	170	58	85	0	4	6	5	11	2	0	.182	4	22	0	1	0.2	1.000

John Skopec

SKOPEC, JOHN S. (Buckshot)
B. May 8, 1880, Chicago, Ill. D. Oct. 12, 1912, Chicago, Ill.

BR TL 5'10" 190 lbs.

Year	Team		W	L	PCT	ERA	G	GS	CG	IP	H	BB	SO	ShO	W	L	SV	AB	H	HR	BA	PO	A	E	DP	TC/G	FA
1901	CHI	A	6	3	.667	3.16	9	9	6	68.1	62	45	24	0	0	0	0	30	10	1	.333	3	32	3	1	4.2	.921

Year	Team		W	L	PCT	ERA	G	GS	CG	IP	H	BB	SO	ShO	Relief Pitching W	L	SV	Batting AB	H	HR	BA	PO	A	E	DP	TC/G	FA

John Skopec *continued*

Year	Team		W	L	PCT	ERA	G	GS	CG	IP	H	BB	SO	ShO	W	L	SV	AB	H	HR	BA	PO	A	E	DP	TC/G	FA
1903	DET	A	2	2	.500	3.43	6	5	3	39.1	46	13	14	0	0	0	0	13	2	0	.154	0	14	2	0	2.7	.875
2 yrs.			8	5	.615	3.26	15	14	9	107.2	108	58	38	0	0	0	0	43	12	1	.279	3	46	5	1	3.6	.907

John Slagle

SLAGLE, JOHN A.
B. Lawrence, Ind. — BL TR

| 1891 | CIN | AA | 0 | 0 | – | 0.00 | 1 | 0 | 0 | 1.1 | 3 | 1 | 1 | 0 | 0 | 0 | 1 | 1 | 0 | 0 | .000 | 0 | 0 | 0 | 0 | 0.0 | – |

Roger Slagle

SLAGLE, ROGER LEE
B. Nov. 4, 1953, Wichita., Kans. — BR TR 6'3" 190 lbs.

| 1979 | NY | A | 0 | 0 | – | 0.00 | 1 | 0 | 0 | 2 | 0 | 2 | 0 | 0 | 0 | 0 | 0 | 0 | 0 | 0 | – | 1 | 0 | 0 | 0 | 1.0 | 1.000 |

Walt Slagle

SLAGLE, WALTER JENNINGS
B. Dec. 15, 1878, Kenton, Ohio   D. June 17, 1974, San Gabriel, Calif. — BR TR 6' 165 lbs.

| 1910 | CIN | N | 0 | 0 | – | 9.00 | 1 | 0 | 0 | 1 | 0 | 3 | 0 | 0 | 0 | 0 | 0 | 0 | 0 | 0 | – | 0 | 0 | 0 | 0 | 0.0 | – |

Cy Slapnicka

SLAPNICKA, CYRIL CHARLES
B. Mar. 23, 1886, Cedar Rapids, Iowa   D. Oct. 20, 1979, Cedar Rapids, Iowa — BB TR 5'10" 165 lbs.

1911	CHI	N	0	2	.000	3.38	3	2	1	24	21	7	10	0	0	0	0	9	2	0	.222	5	9	0	0	4.7	1.000
1918	PIT	N	1	4	.200	4.74	7	6	4	49.1	50	22	3	0	0	0	1	14	1	0	.071	3	14	2	0	2.7	.895
2 yrs.			1	6	.143	4.30	10	8	5	73.1	71	29	13	0	0	0	1	23	3	0	.130	8	23	2	0	3.3	.939

John Slappey

SLAPPEY, JOHN HENRY
B. Aug. 8, 1898, Albany, Ga.   D. June 10, 1957, Marietta, Ga. — BL TL 6'4" 170 lbs.

| 1920 | PHI | A | 0 | 1 | .000 | 7.11 | 3 | 1 | 0 | 6.1 | 15 | 4 | 1 | 0 | 0 | 0 | 0 | 2 | 1 | 0 | .500 | 0 | 1 | 0 | 0 | 0.3 | 1.000 |

Jim Slaton

SLATON, JAMES MICHAEL
B. June 19, 1950, Long Beach, Calif. — BR TR 6' 185 lbs.

1971	MIL	A	10	8	.556	3.77	26	23	5	148	140	71	63	4	0	0	0	46	5	0	.109	12	12	2	1	1.0	.923
1972			1	6	.143	5.52	9	8	0	44	50	21	17	0	0	1	0	11	1	0	.091	1	11	0	0	1.3	1.000
1973			13	15	.464	3.71	38	38	13	276.1	266	99	134	3	0	0	0	0	0	0	–	19	27	6	4	1.4	.885
1974			13	16	.448	3.92	40	35	10	250	255	102	126	3	1	0	0	0	0	0	–	16	36	1	3	1.3	.981
1975			11	18	.379	4.52	37	33	10	217	238	90	119	3	0	0	0	0	0	0	–	16	34	4	3	1.5	.926
1976			14	15	.483	3.44	38	38	12	292.2	287	94	138	2	0	0	0	0	0	0	–	18	43	3	2	1.7	.953
1977			10	14	.417	3.58	32	31	7	221	223	77	104	1	1	0	0	0	0	0	–	21	34	4	1	1.8	.932
1978	DET	A	17	11	.607	4.12	35	34	11	233.2	235	85	92	2	0	1	0	0	0	0	–	9	32	2	6	1.2	.953
1979	MIL	A	15	9	.625	3.63	32	31	12	213	229	54	80	3	0	0	0	0	0	0	–	16	35	1	3	1.6	.981
1980			1	1	.500	4.50	3	3	0	16	17	5	4	0	0	0	0	0	0	0	–	0	3	0	0	1.0	1.000
1981			5	7	.417	4.38	24	21	0	117	120	50	47	0	0	0	0	0	0	0	–	14	14	0	3	1.2	1.000
1982			10	6	.625	3.29	39	7	0	117.2	117	41	59	0	7	4	6	0	0	0	–	6	16	0	0	0.6	1.000
1983			14	6	.700	4.33	46	0	0	112.1	112	56	38	0	14	6	5	0	0	0	–	4	16	0	1	0.4	1.000
1984	CAL	A	7	10	.412	4.97	32	22	5	163	192	56	67	1	1	0	0	0	0	0	–	9	25	3	1	1.1	1.000
1985			6	10	.375	4.37	29	24	1	148.1	162	63	60	0	0	0	1	0	0	0	–	6	22	1	4	0.9	.966
1986	2 teams		CAL A	(14G 4–6)		DET A	(22G 0–0)																					
"	total		4	6	.400	5.08	36	12	0	113.1	130	40	43	0	0	0	2	0	0	0	–	13	18	0	2	0.9	1.000
16 yrs.			151	158	.489	4.03	496	360	86	2683.1	2773	1004	1191	22	25	12	14	57	6	0	.105	180	378	24	36	1.2	.959

DIVISIONAL PLAYOFF SERIES

| 1981 | MIL | A | 0 | 0 | – | 3.00 | 4 | 0 | 0 | 6 | 6 | 0 | 2 | 0 | 0 | 0 | 0 | 0 | 0 | 0 | – | 0 | 0 | 0 | 0 | 0.0 | – |

LEAGUE CHAMPIONSHIP SERIES

| 1982 | MIL | A | 0 | 0 | – | 1.93 | 2 | 0 | 0 | 4.2 | 3 | 1 | 3 | 0 | 0 | 0 | 0 | 0 | 0 | 0 | – | 0 | 0 | 0 | 0 | 0.0 | – |

WORLD SERIES

| 1982 | MIL | A | 1 | 0 | 1.000 | 0.00 | 2 | 0 | 0 | 2.2 | 2 | 2 | 1 | 0 | 0 | 0 | 0 | 0 | 0 | 0 | – | 0 | 0 | 0 | 0 | 0.0 | – |

Phil Slattery

SLATTERY, PHILIP RYAN
B. Feb. 25, 1893, Harper, Iowa   D. Mar. 10, 1968, Long Beach, Calif. — BR TL 5'11" 160 lbs.

| 1915 | PIT | N | 0 | 0 | – | 0.00 | 3 | 0 | 0 | 8 | 5 | 1 | 1 | 0 | 0 | 0 | 0 | 1 | 0 | 0 | .000 | 0 | 0 | 0 | 0 | 0.0 | – |

Barney Slaughter

SLAUGHTER, BYRON ATKINS
B. Oct. 6, 1884, Smyrna, Del.   D. May 17, 1961, Philadelphia, Pa. — BR TR 5'11½" 165 lbs.

| 1910 | PHI | N | 0 | 1 | .000 | 5.50 | 8 | 1 | 0 | 18 | 21 | 11 | 7 | 0 | 0 | 1 | 0 | 5 | 1 | 0 | .200 | 0 | 6 | 0 | 0 | 0.8 | 1.000 |

Sterling Slaughter

SLAUGHTER, STERLING FEORE
B. Nov. 18, 1941, Danville, Ill. — BR TR 5'11" 165 lbs.

| 1964 | CHI | N | 2 | 4 | .333 | 5.75 | 20 | 6 | 1 | 51.2 | 64 | 32 | 32 | 0 | 0 | 2 | 0 | 12 | 1 | 0 | .083 | 3 | 3 | 0 | 0 | 0.3 | 1.000 |

Bill Slayback

SLAYBACK, WILLIAM GROVER
B. Feb. 21, 1948, Hollywood, Calif. — BR TR 6'4" 200 lbs.

1972	DET	A	5	6	.455	3.18	23	13	3	82	74	25	65	1	1	0	0	23	4	0	.174	5	15	2	0	1.0	.909
1973			0	0	–	4.50	3	0	0	2	5	0	1	0	0	0	0	0	0	0	–	0	0	0	0	0.0	–
1974			1	3	.250	4.75	16	4	0	55	57	26	23	0	0	0	0	0	0	0	–	1	8	1	0	0.6	.900
3 yrs.			6	9	.400	3.82	42	17	3	139	136	51	89	1	1	0	0	23	4	0	.174	6	23	3	0	0.8	.906

Steve Slayton

SLAYTON, FOSTER HERBERT
B. Apr. 26, 1902, Barre, Vt.   D. Dec. 20, 1984, Manchester, N. H. — BR TR 6' 163 lbs.

| 1928 | BOS | A | 0 | 0 | – | 3.86 | 3 | 0 | 0 | 7 | 6 | 3 | 2 | 0 | 0 | 0 | 0 | 2 | 0 | 0 | .000 | 0 | 1 | 0 | 0 | 0.3 | 1.000 |

Year	Team	W	L	PCT	ERA	G	GS	CG	IP	H	BB	SO	ShO	W	L	SV	AB	H	HR	BA	PO	A	E	DP	TC/G	FA
														Relief Pitching			Batting									

Lou Sleater

SLEATER, LOUIS MORTIMER
B. Sept. 8, 1926, St. Louis, Mo.
BL TL 5'10'' 185 lbs.

Year	Team		W	L	PCT	ERA	G	GS	CG	IP	H	BB	SO	ShO	W	L	SV	AB	H	HR	BA	PO	A	E	DP	TC/G	FA
1950	STL	A	0	0	–	0.00	1	0	0	1	0	0	1	0	0	0	0	0	0	0	–	0	0	0	0	0.0	–
1951			1	9	.100	5.11	20	8	4	81	88	53	33	0	1	1	1	31	7	0	.226	2	10	1	1	0.7	.923
1952	2 teams			STL A	(4G 0–1)			WAS A	(14G 4–2)																		
"	total		4	3	.571	4.11	18	11	3	65.2	65	35	23	1	1	0	0	22	1	0	.045	0	8	1	0	0.5	.889
1955	KC	A	1	1	.500	7.71	16	1	0	25.2	33	21	11	0	1	0	0	13	2	0	.154	2	3	0	0	0.3	1.000
1956	MIL	N	2	2	.500	3.15	25	1	0	45.2	42	27	32	0	2	2	2	10	5	0	.500	4	11	0	0	0.6	1.000
1957	DET	A	3	3	.500	3.76	41	0	0	69.1	61	28	43	0	3	3	2	20	5	3	.250	2	11	3	2	0.4	.813
1958	2 teams			DET A	(4G 0–0)			BAL A	(6G 1–0)																		
"	total		1	0	1.000	10.22	10	0	0	12.1	17	8	9	0	1	0	0	7	1	0	.143	1	4	1	0	0.6	.833
	7 yrs.		12	18	.400	4.70	131	21	7	300.2	306	172	152	1	9	6	5	103	21	4	.204	11	47	6	3	0.5	.906

Dwain Sloat

SLOAT, DWAIN CLIFFORD (Lefty)
B. Dec. 1, 1918, Nokomis, Ill.
BR TL 6' 168 lbs.

Year	Team		W	L	PCT	ERA	G	GS	CG	IP	H	BB	SO	ShO	W	L	SV	AB	H	HR	BA	PO	A	E	DP	TC/G	FA
1948	BKN	N	0	1	.000	6.14	4	1	0	7.1	7	8	1	0	0	0	0	1	0	0	.000	3	3	0	0	1.5	1.000
1949	CHI	N	0	0	–	7.00	5	1	0	9	14	3	3	0	0	0	0	0	0	0	–	0	2	0	0	0.4	1.000
	2 yrs.		0	1	.000	6.61	9	2	0	16.1	21	11	4	0	0	0	0	1	0	0	.000	3	5	0	0	0.9	1.000

Walt Smallwood

SMALLWOOD, WALTER CLAYTON
B. Apr. 24, 1893, Dayton, Md. D. Apr. 29, 1967, Baltimore, Md.
BR TR 6'2'' 190 lbs.

Year	Team		W	L	PCT	ERA	G	GS	CG	IP	H	BB	SO	ShO	W	L	SV	AB	H	HR	BA	PO	A	E	DP	TC/G	FA
1917	NY	A	0	0	–	0.00	2	0	0	2	1	1	1	0	0	0	0	0	0	0	–	0	1	0	0	0.5	1.000
1919			0	0	–	4.98	6	0	0	21.2	20	9	6	0	0	0	0	5	0	0	.000	1	4	0	1	0.8	1.000
	2 yrs.		0	0	–	4.56	8	0	0	23.2	21	10	7	0	0	0	0	5	0	0	.000	1	5	0	1	0.8	1.000

John Smiley

SMILEY, JOHN PATRICK
B. Mar. 17, 1965, Phoenixville, Pa.
BL TL 6'4'' 180 lbs.

Year	Team		W	L	PCT	ERA	G	GS	CG	IP	H	BB	SO	ShO	W	L	SV	AB	H	HR	BA	PO	A	E	DP	TC/G	FA
1986	PIT	N	1	0	1.000	3.86	12	0	0	11.2	4	4	9	0	1	0	0	0	0	0	–	1	2	0	0	0.3	1.000
1987			5	5	.500	5.76	63	0	0	75	69	50	58	0	5	5	4	7	1	0	.143	7	9	0	2	0.3	1.000
1988			13	11	.542	3.25	34	32	5	205	185	46	129	1	0	0	0	63	5	0	.079	14	27	0	3	1.2	1.000
1989			12	8	.600	2.81	28	28	8	205.1	174	49	123	1	0	0	0	65	9	0	.138	7	23	4	2	1.2	.882
	4 yrs.		31	24	.564	3.46	137	60	13	497	432	149	319	2	6	5	4	135	15	0	.111	29	61	4	7	0.7	.957

Al Smith

SMITH, ALFRED JOHN
B. Oct. 12, 1907, Belleville, Ill. D. Apr. 28, 1977, Brownsville, Tex.
BL TL 5'11'' 180 lbs.

Year	Team		W	L	PCT	ERA	G	GS	CG	IP	H	BB	SO	ShO	W	L	SV	AB	H	HR	BA	PO	A	E	DP	TC/G	FA
1934	NY	N	3	5	.375	4.32	30	5	0	66.2	70	21	27	0	3	1	5	14	4	0	.286	1	14	1	2	0.5	.938
1935			10	8	.556	3.41	40	10	4	124	125	32	44	1	5	4	5	34	4	1	.118	5	24	2	2	0.8	.935
1936			14	13	.519	3.78	43	30	9	209.1	217	69	89	4	4	1	2	73	10	0	.137	4	44	5	4	1.2	.906
1937			5	4	.556	4.20	33	9	2	85.2	91	30	41	0	3	2	0	25	3	0	.120	3	15	0	1	0.5	1.000
1938	PHI	N	1	4	.200	6.28	37	1	0	86	115	40	46	0	0	4	1	21	0	0	.000	5	16	1	1	0.6	.955
1939			0	0	–	4.00	5	0	0	9	11	5	2	0	0	0	0	2	0	0	.000	1	2	0	0	0.6	1.000
1940	CLE	A	15	7	.682	3.44	31	24	11	183	187	55	46	1	1	1	2	62	19	0	.306	6	44	0	5	1.6	1.000
1941			12	13	.480	3.83	29	27	13	206.2	204	75	76	2	0	0	0	71	11	1	.155	9	46	3	5	2.0	.948
1942			10	15	.400	3.96	30	24	7	168.1	163	71	66	1	2	2	0	60	15	0	.250	5	34	1	0	1.3	.975
1943			17	7	.708	2.55	29	27	14	208.1	186	72	72	3	0	0	1	68	14	0	.206	6	45	2	1	1.8	.962
1944			7	13	.350	3.42	28	26	7	181.2	197	69	44	1	1	1	0	64	10	0	.156	4	46	1	2	1.8	.980
1945			5	12	.294	3.84	21	19	8	133.2	141	48	34	3	0	0	1	41	12	0	.293	6	37	1	3	2.1	.977
	12 yrs.		99	101	.495	3.72	356	202	75	1662.1	1707	587	587	16	19	16	17	535	102	2	.191	55	367	17	26	1.2	.961

WORLD SERIES

Year	Team		W	L	PCT	ERA	G	GS	CG	IP	H	BB	SO	ShO	W	L	SV	AB	H	HR	BA	PO	A	E	DP	TC/G	FA
1936	NY	N	0	0	–	81.00	1	0	0	.1	2	1	0	0	0	0	0	0	0	0	–	0	0	0	0	0.0	–
1937			0	0	–	3.00	2	0	0	3	2	0	1	0	0	0	0	0	0	0	–	0	1	0	0	0.5	1.000
	2 yrs.		0	0	–	10.80	3	0	0	3.1	4	1	1	0	0	0	0	0	0	0	–	0	1	0	0	0.3	1.000

Al Smith

SMITH, ALFRED KENDRICKS
B. Dec. 13, 1903, Norristown, Pa.
BR TR 6' 170 lbs.

Year	Team		W	L	PCT	ERA	G	GS	CG	IP	H	BB	SO	ShO	W	L	SV	AB	H	HR	BA	PO	A	E	DP	TC/G	FA
1926	NY	N	0	0	–	9.00	1	0	0	2	4	2	0	0	0	0	0	0	0	0	–	0	0	0	0	0.0	–

Art Smith

SMITH, ARTHUR LAIRD
B. June 21, 1906, Boston, Mass.
BR TR 6' 175 lbs.

Year	Team		W	L	PCT	ERA	G	GS	CG	IP	H	BB	SO	ShO	W	L	SV	AB	H	HR	BA	PO	A	E	DP	TC/G	FA
1932	CHI	A	0	1	.000	11.57	3	2	0	7	17	4	1	0	0	0	0	1	0	0	.000	1	4	0	0	1.7	1.000

Bill Smith

SMITH, WILLIAM
B. 1851 D. Oct. 27, 1897, Guelph, Ont., Canada
151 lbs.

Year	Team		W	L	PCT	ERA	G	GS	CG	IP	H	BB	SO	ShO	W	L	SV	AB	H	HR	BA	PO	A	E	DP	TC/G	FA
1886	DET	N	5	4	.556	4.09	9	9	9	77	81	30	36	0	0	0	0	38	7	0	.184	4	12	3	0	2.1	.842

Bill Smith

SMITH, WILLIAM GARLAND
B. June 8, 1934, Washington, D. C.
BL TL 6' 190 lbs.

Year	Team		W	L	PCT	ERA	G	GS	CG	IP	H	BB	SO	ShO	W	L	SV	AB	H	HR	BA	PO	A	E	DP	TC/G	FA
1958	STL	N	0	1	.000	6.52	2	1	0	9.2	12	4	4	0	0	0	0	2	0	0	.000	1	2	0	0	1.5	1.000
1959			0	0	–	1.08	6	0	0	8.1	11	3	4	0	0	0	0	1	0	0	.000	0	1	0	0	0.2	1.000
1962	PHI	N	1	5	.167	4.29	24	5	0	50.1	59	10	26	0	1	1	1	11	2	0	.182	6	6	2	1	0.6	.857
	3 yrs.		1	6	.143	4.21	32	6	0	68.1	82	17	34	0	1	1	1	14	2	0	.143	7	9	2	1	0.6	.889

Billy Smith

SMITH, BILLY LAVERN
B. Sept. 13, 1954, La Marque, Tex.
BR TR 6'7'' 200 lbs.

Year	Team		W	L	PCT	ERA	G	GS	CG	IP	H	BB	SO	ShO	W	L	SV	AB	H	HR	BA	PO	A	E	DP	TC/G	FA
1981	HOU	N	1	1	.500	3.00	10	1	0	21	20	3	3	0	0	1	1	2	0	0	.000	2	3	0	1	0.5	1.000

DIVISIONAL PLAYOFF SERIES

Year	Team		W	L	PCT	ERA	G	GS	CG	IP	H	BB	SO	ShO	W	L	SV	AB	H	HR	BA	PO	A	E	DP	TC/G	FA
1981	HOU	N	0	0	–	0.00	1	0	0	.1	0	0	0	0	0	0	0	0	0	0	–	0	0	0	0	0.0	–

Year	Team		W	L	PCT	ERA	G	GS	CG	IP	H	BB	SO	ShO	W	L	SV	AB	H	HR	BA	PO	A	E	DP	TC/G	FA
															Relief Pitching			**Batting**									

Bob Smith

SMITH, ROBERT ASHLEY
B. July 19, 1891, Hardwick, Vt.

BR TR 5'11" 160 lbs.

Year	Team		W	L	PCT	ERA	G	GS	CG	IP	H	BB	SO	ShO	W	L	SV	AB	H	HR	BA	PO	A	E	DP	TC/G	FA
1913	CHI	A	0	0	–	13.50	1	0	0	2	3	3	1	0	0	0	0	0	0	0	–	0	0	0	0	0.0	
1915	BUF	F	0	0	–	18.00	1	0	0	1	1	2	0	0	0	0	0	0	0	0	–	0	1	0	0	1.0	1.000
2 yrs.			0	0	–	15.00	2	0	0	3	4	5	1	0	0	0	0	0	0	0	–	0	1	0	0	0.5	1.000

Bob Smith

SMITH, ROBERT ELDRIDGE
B. Apr. 22, 1895, Rogersville, Tenn.   D. July 19, 1987, Waycross, Ga.

BR TR 5'10" 175 lbs.

Year	Team		W	L	PCT	ERA	G	GS	CG	IP	H	BB	SO	ShO	W	L	SV	AB	H	HR	BA	PO	A	E	DP	TC/G	FA
1923	BOS	N	0	0	–	0.00	0	0	0	0	0	0	0	0	0	0	0	375	94	0	.251	0	0	0	0	0.0	–
1924			0	0	–	0.00	0	0	0	0	0	0	0	0	0	0	0	347	79	2	.228	0	0	0	0	0.0	–
1925			5	3	.625	4.47	13	10	6	92.2	110	36	19	0	0	1	0	174	49	0	.282	1	23	0	1	1.8	.960
1926			10	13	.435	3.91	33	23	14	193.1	199	75	44	4	2	0	1	84	25	0	.298	9	60	2	6	2.2	.972
1927			10	18	.357	3.76	41	32	16	260.2	297	75	81	1	2	2	3	109	27	1	.248	22	63	3	3	2.1	.966
1928			13	17	.433	3.87	38	25	14	244.1	274	74	59	0	2	2	2	92	23	1	.250	16	66	3	3	2.2	.965
1929			11	17	.393	4.68	34	29	19	231	256	71	65	1	0	1	3	99	17	1	.172	12	56	1	3	2.0	.986
1930			10	14	.417	4.26	38	24	14	219.2	247	85	84	2	2	0	5	81	19	0	.235	16	47	1	3	1.7	.984
1931	CHI	N	15	12	.556	3.22	36	29	18	240.1	239	62	63	2	0	2	0	87	19	0	.218	8	55	0	4	1.8	1.000
1932			4	3	.571	4.61	34	11	4	119	148	36	35	1	0	1	2	42	10	0	.238	7	26	0	3	1.0	1.000
1933	2 teams					CIN N	(16G 4–4)			BOS N	(14G 4–3)																
"	total		8	7	.533	2.65	30	10	7	132.1	143	18	34	1	3	2	1	45	9	0	.200	1	34	2	4	1.2	.946
1934	BOS	N	6	9	.400	4.66	39	5	3	121.2	133	36	26	0	4	6	5	36	9	0	.250	7	30	2	0	0.9	1.000
1935			8	18	.308	3.94	46	20	8	203.1	232	61	58	2	3	3	5	63	17	0	.270	10	39	1	1	1.1	.980
1936			6	7	.462	3.77	35	11	5	136	142	35	36	2	2	1	8	45	10	0	.222	8	34	0	2	1.2	1.000
1937			0	1	.000	4.09	18	0	0	44	52	6	14	0	0	1	3	10	2	0	.200	1	6	0	0	0.4	1.000
15 yrs.			106	139	.433	3.95	435	229	128	2238.1	2472	670	618	16	20	20	40	*				118	539	13	37	1.5	.981

WORLD SERIES

1932	CHI	N	0	0	–	9.00	1	0	0	1	2	0	1	0	0	0	0	0	0	0	–	0	0	0	0	0.0	–

Bob Smith

SMITH, ROBERT GILCHRIST
B. Feb. 1, 1931, Woodsville, N. H.

BR TL 6'1½" 190 lbs.

Year	Team		W	L	PCT	ERA	G	GS	CG	IP	H	BB	SO	ShO	W	L	SV	AB	H	HR	BA	PO	A	E	DP	TC/G	FA
1955	BOS	A	0	0	–	0.00	1	0	0	1.2	1	1	1	0	0	0	0	0	0	0	–	0	0	0	0	0.0	–
1957	2 teams					STL N	(6G 0–0)			PIT N	(20G 2–4)																
"	total		2	4	.333	3.34	26	4	2	64.2	60	31	46	0	0	3	1	15	1	0	.067	3	7	1	0	0.4	.909
1958	PIT	N	2	2	.500	4.43	35	4	0	61	61	31	24	0	2	0	1	11	1	0	.091	5	14	2	1	0.6	.905
1959	2 teams					PIT N	(20G 0–0)			DET A	(9G 0–3)																
"	total		0	3	.000	4.81	29	0	0	39.1	52	20	22	0	0	3	0	3	0	0	.000	1	6	1	0	0.3	.875
4 yrs.			4	9	.308	4.05	91	8	2	166.2	174	83	93	0	2	6	2	29	2	0	.069	9	27	4	1	0.4	.900

Bryn Smith

SMITH, BRYN NELSON
B. Aug. 11, 1955, Marietta, Ga.

BR TR 6'2" 200 lbs.

Year	Team		W	L	PCT	ERA	G	GS	CG	IP	H	BB	SO	ShO	W	L	SV	AB	H	HR	BA	PO	A	E	DP	TC/G	FA
1981	MON	N	1	0	1.000	2.77	7	0	0	13	14	3	9	0	1	0	0	1	0	0	.000	0	1	0	0	0.3	.500
1982			2	4	.333	4.20	47	1	0	79.1	81	23	50	0	2	3	3	8	0	0	.000	2	15	1	0	0.4	.944
1983			6	11	.353	2.49	49	12	5	155.1	142	43	101	3	1	4	3	30	5	0	.167	10	22	0	3	0.7	1.000
1984			12	13	.480	3.32	28	28	4	179	178	51	101	2	0	0	0	53	7	0	.132	25	28	4	3	2.0	.930
1985			18	5	.783	2.91	32	32	4	222.1	193	41	127	2	0	0	0	72	14	1	.194	24	27	5	2	1.8	.911
1986			10	8	.556	3.94	30	30	1	187.1	182	63	105	0	0	0	0	58	8	1	.138	11	44	2	5	1.9	.965
1987			10	9	.526	4.37	26	26	2	150.1	164	31	94	0	0	0	0	44	6	0	.136	10	21	1	2	1.2	.969
1988			12	10	.545	3.00	32	32	1	198	179	32	122	0	0	0	0	55	6	0	.109	7	26	2	1	1.1	.943
1989			10	11	.476	2.84	33	32	3	215.2	177	54	129	1	0	0	0	62	4	0	.065	16	42	1	2	1.8	.983
9 yrs.			81	71	.533	3.28	284	193	20	1400.1	1310	341	838	8	4	7	6	383	50	2	.131	105	226	17	18	1.2	.951

Charlie Smith

SMITH, CHARLES EDWIN
Brother of Fred Smith.
B. Apr. 20, 1880, Cleveland, Ohio   D. Jan. 3, 1929, Wickliffe, Ohio

BR TR 6'1" 185 lbs.

Year	Team		W	L	PCT	ERA	G	GS	CG	IP	H	BB	SO	ShO	W	L	SV	AB	H	HR	BA	PO	A	E	DP	TC/G	FA
1902	CLE	A	2	1	.667	4.05	3	3	2	20	23	5	5	1	0	0	0	8	1	0	.125	0	6	0	0	2.0	1.000
1906	WAS	A	9	16	.360	2.91	33	22	17	235.1	250	75	105	2	3	2	0	87	16	1	.184	5	60	5	0	2.1	.929
1907			10	20	.333	2.61	36	31	21	258.2	254	51	119	3	0	3	0	84	12	0	.143	10	95	6	2	3.1	.946
1908			9	13	.409	2.40	26	22	13	184	166	60	83	1	0	1	1	65	8	0	.123	2	53	1	2	2.2	.982
1909	2 teams					WAS A	(23G 3–12)			BOS A	(3G 3–0)																
"	total		6	12	.333	3.11	26	18	9	170.2	163	39	83	1	0	0	0	55	10	0	.182	6	56	2	0	2.5	.969
1910	BOS	A	11	6	.647	2.30	24	18	11	156.1	141	35	53	0	1	1	1	44	5	0	.114	5	44	7	1	2.3	.875
1911	2 teams					BOS A	(1G 0–0)			CHI N	(7G 3–2)																
"	total		3	2	.600	3.86	8	6	3	40	33	8	11	1	0	0	0	13	1	0	.077	4	9	2	0	1.9	.867
1912	CHI	N	7	4	.636	4.21	21	5	1	94	92	31	47	0	6	1	1	35	9	0	.257	2	29	0	2	1.5	1.000
1913			7	9	.438	2.55	20	17	8	137.2	138	34	47	1	1	0	0	45	4	0	.089	1	38	1	0	2.0	.975
1914			2	4	.333	3.86	16	5	1	53.2	49	15	17	0	1	0	0	11	1	0	.091	1	10	0	0	0.7	1.000
10 yrs.			66	87	.431	2.81	213	147	86	1350.1	1309	353	570	10	12	10	3	447	67	1	.150	36	400	24	7	2.2	.948

Chick Smith

SMITH, JOHN WILLIAM
Born Jan Smadt.
B. Dec. 2, 1892, Dayton, Ky.   D. Oct. 11, 1935, Dayton, Ky.

BL TL 5'8" 165 lbs.

Year	Team		W	L	PCT	ERA	G	GS	CG	IP	H	BB	SO	ShO	W	L	SV	AB	H	HR	BA	PO	A	E	DP	TC/G	FA
1913	CIN	N	0	1	.000	3.57	5	1	0	17.2	15	11	11	0	0	0	0	4	0	0	.000	0	5	0	0	1.0	1.000

Clay Smith

SMITH, CLAY JAMIESON
B. Sept. 11, 1914, Cambridge, Kans.

BR TR 6'2" 190 lbs.

Year	Team		W	L	PCT	ERA	G	GS	CG	IP	H	BB	SO	ShO	W	L	SV	AB	H	HR	BA	PO	A	E	DP	TC/G	FA
1938	CLE	A	0	0	–	6.55	4	0	0	11	18	2	3	0	0	0	0	4	0	0	.000	1	2	0	0	0.8	1.000
1940	DET	A	1	1	.500	5.08	14	1	0	28.1	32	13	14	0	1	0	0	7	0	0	.000	1	10	0	0	0.8	1.000
2 yrs.			1	1	.500	5.49	18	1	0	39.1	50	15	17	0	1	0	0	11	0	0	.000	2	12	0	0	0.8	1.000

WORLD SERIES

1940	DET	A	0	0	–	2.25	1	0	0	4	3	1	1	0	0	0	0	0	0	0	.000	0	1	0	0	1.0	1.000

Year	Team		W	L	PCT	ERA	G	GS	CG	IP	H	BB	SO	ShO	Relief Pitching W	L	SV	Batting AB	H	HR	BA	PO	A	E	DP	TC/G	FA

Dave Smith — SMITH, DAVID MERWIN
B. Dec. 17, 1914, Sellers, S. C.   BR TR 5'10" 170 lbs.

Year	Team		W	L	PCT	ERA	G	GS	CG	IP	H	BB	SO	ShO	W	L	SV	AB	H	HR	BA	PO	A	E	DP	TC/G	FA
1938	PHI	A	2	1	.667	5.08	21	0	0	44.1	50	28	13	0	2	1	0	12	0	0	.000	2	8	0	0	0.5	1.000
1939			0	0	—	0.00	1	0	0		1	2	0	0	0	0	0	0	0	0	—	0	0	0	0	0.0	—
2 yrs.			2	1	.667	5.08	22	0	0	44.1	51	30	13	0	2	1	0	12	0	0	.000	2	8	0	0	0.5	1.000

Dave Smith — SMITH, DAVID STANLEY
B. Jan. 21, 1955, Richmond, Calif.   BR TR 6'1" 195 lbs.

Year	Team		W	L	PCT	ERA	G	GS	CG	IP	H	BB	SO	ShO	W	L	SV	AB	H	HR	BA	PO	A	E	DP	TC/G	FA
1980	HOU	N	7	5	.583	1.92	57	0	0	103	90	32	85	0	7	5	10	12	0	0	.000	3	11	1	0	0.3	.933
1981			5	3	.625	2.76	42	0	0	75	54	23	52	0	5	3	8	8	2	0	.250	3	11	1	0	0.4	.933
1982			5	4	.556	3.84	49	1	0	63.1	69	31	28	0	5	4	11	2	0	0	.000	3	7	2	2	0.2	.833
1983			3	1	.750	3.10	42	0	0	72.2	72	36	41	0	3	1	6	5	0	0	.000	3	4	2	0	0.2	.778
1984			5	4	.556	2.21	53	0	0	77.1	60	20	45	0	5	4	5	4	0	0	.000	5	9	1	1	0.3	.933
1985			9	5	.643	2.27	64	0	0	79.1	69	17	40	0	9	5	27	3	0	0	.000	4	7	3	1	0.2	.786
1986			4	7	.364	2.73	54	0	0	56	39	22	46	0	4	7	33	2	0	0	.000	7	6	0	0	0.2	1.000
1987			2	3	.400	1.65	50	0	0	60	39	21	73	0	2	3	24	2	1	0	.500	4	4	0	0	0.2	1.000
1988			4	5	.444	2.67	51	0	0	57.1	60	19	38	0	4	5	27	2	0	0	.000	6	4	0	1	0.2	1.000
1989			3	4	.429	2.64	52	0	0	58	49	19	31	0	3	4	25	1	0	0	.000	6	10	0	1	0.3	1.000
10 yrs.			47	41	.534	2.54	514	1	0	702	601	240	479	0	47	41	176	41	3	0	.073	41	77	10	5	0.2	.922

DIVISIONAL PLAYOFF SERIES

Year	Team		W	L	PCT	ERA	G	GS	CG	IP	H	BB	SO	ShO	W	L	SV	AB	H	HR	BA	PO	A	E	DP	TC/G	FA
1981	HOU	N	0	0	—	3.86	2	0	0	2.1	2	0	4	0	0	0	0	0	0	0	—	0	0	0	0	0.0	—

LEAGUE CHAMPIONSHIP SERIES

Year	Team		W	L	PCT	ERA	G	GS	CG	IP	H	BB	SO	ShO	W	L	SV	AB	H	HR	BA	PO	A	E	DP	TC/G	FA
1980	HOU	N	1	0	1.000	3.86	3	0	0	2.1	4	2	4	0	1	0	0	0	0	0	—	0	0	0	0	0.0	—
1986			0	1	.000	9.00	2	0	0	2	2	3	2	0	0	1	0	0	0	0	—	0	0	0	0	0.0	—
2 yrs.			1	1	.500	6.23	5	0	0	4.1	6	5	6	0	1	1	0	0	0	0	—	0	0	0	0	0.0	—

Dave Smith — SMITH, DAVID WAYNE
B. Aug. 30, 1957, Tomball, Tex.   BR TR 6'1" 190 lbs.

Year	Team		W	L	PCT	ERA	G	GS	CG	IP	H	BB	SO	ShO	W	L	SV	AB	H	HR	BA	PO	A	E	DP	TC/G	FA
1984	CAL	A	0	0	—	18.00	1	0	0	1	4	0	0	0	0	0	0	0	0	0	—	0	0	0	0	0.0	—
1985			0	0	—	7.20	4	0	0	5	5	1	3	0	0	0	0	0	0	0	—	1	0	0	0	0.3	1.000
2 yrs.			0	0	—	9.00	5	0	0	6	9	1	3	0	0	0	0	0	0	0	—	1	0	0	0	0.2	1.000

Doug Smith — SMITH, DOUGLASS WELDON
B. May 25, 1892, Miller's Falls, Mass. D. Sept. 18, 1973, Greenfield, Mass.   BL TL 5'10" 168 lbs.

Year	Team		W	L	PCT	ERA	G	GS	CG	IP	H	BB	SO	ShO	W	L	SV	AB	H	HR	BA	PO	A	E	DP	TC/G	FA
1912	BOS	A	0	0	—	3.00	1	0	0	3	4	0	1	0	0	0	0	0	0	0	—	0	0	0	0	0.0	—

Ed Smith — SMITH, RHESA EDWARD
B. Feb. 21, 1879, Mentone, Ind. D. Mar. 20, 1955, Tarpon Springs, Fla.   BR TR 5'11" 170 lbs.

Year	Team		W	L	PCT	ERA	G	GS	CG	IP	H	BB	SO	ShO	W	L	SV	AB	H	HR	BA	PO	A	E	DP	TC/G	FA
1906	STL	A	8	11	.421	3.72	19	18	13	154.2	153	53	45	0	1	0	0	54	11	0	.204	7	54	6	2	3.5	.910

Eddie Smith — SMITH, EDGAR
B. Dec. 14, 1913, Columbus, N. J.   BB TL 5'10" 174 lbs.

Year	Team		W	L	PCT	ERA	G	GS	CG	IP	H	BB	SO	ShO	W	L	SV	AB	H	HR	BA	PO	A	E	DP	TC/G	FA
1936	PHI	A	1	1	.500	1.89	2	2	2	19	22	8	7	0	0	0	0	8	1	0	.125	0	4	0	0	2.0	1.000
1937			4	17	.190	3.94	38	23	14	196.2	178	90	79	1	0	1	5	73	17	0	.233	6	28	0	1	0.9	1.000
1938			3	10	.231	5.92	43	7	0	130.2	151	76	78	0	0	5	4	42	12	0	.286	10	20	1	1	0.7	.968
1939	2 teams	PHI A (3G 1–0)						CHI A	(29G 9–11)																		
"	total		10	11	.476	3.79	32	22	7	180.1	168	92	70	1	2	0		52	6	0	.115	7	23	3	1	1.0	.909
1940	CHI	A	14	9	.609	3.21	32	28	12	207.1	179	95	119	0	0	1	0	69	15	0	.217	6	32	2	2	1.3	.950
1941			13	17	.433	3.18	34	33	21	263.1	243	114	111	0	0	0	1	88	19	0	.216	10	51	1	3	1.8	.984
1942			7	20	.259	3.98	29	28	18	215	223	86	78	2	0	0	0	73	9	0	.123	7	55	2	3	2.2	.969
1943			11	11	.500	3.69	25	25	14	187.2	197	76	66	2	0	0	0	69	11	1	.159	6	43	1	4	2.0	.980
1946			8	11	.421	2.85	24	21	3	145.1	135	60	59	1	1	0	0	45	8	0	.178	2	29	6	1	1.5	.838
1947	2 teams	CHI A (15G 1–3)						BOS A	(8G 1–3)																		
"	total		2	6	.250	7.33	23	8	0	50.1	58	42	27	0	0	0	0	12	2	0	.167	2	5	3	0	0.4	.700
10 yrs.			73	113	.392	3.82	282	197	91	1595.2	1554	739	694	8	3	8	12	531	100	1	.188	56	290	19	16	1.3	.948

Edgar Smith — SMITH, EDGAR EUGENE
B. June 12, 1862, Providence, R. I. D. Nov. 3, 1892, Providence, R. I.   BR TR 5'10" 160 lbs.

Year	Team		W	L	PCT	ERA	G	GS	CG	IP	H	BB	SO	ShO	W	L	SV	AB	H	HR	BA	PO	A	E	DP	TC/G	FA
1883	PHI	N	0	1	.000	15.43	1	1	0	7	18	3	2	0	0	0	0	13	5	0	.385	0	0	1	0	1.0	—
1884	WAS	AA	0	2	.000	4.91	3	2	2	22	27	5	4	0	0	0	0	57	5	0	.088	1	5	2	0	2.7	.750
1885	PRO	N	1	0	1.000	1.00	1	1	1	9	9	0	1	0	0	0	0	4	1	0	.250	0	3	1	0	4.0	.750
1890	CLE	N	1	4	.200	4.30	6	6	5	44	42	10	11	0	0	0	0	24	7	0	.292	0	14	2	0	2.7	.875
4 yrs.			2	7	.222	5.05	11	10	8	82	96	18	18	0	0	0	0	*				1	22	6	0	2.6	.793

Elmer Smith — SMITH, ELMER ELLSWORTH
B. Mar. 23, 1868, Pittsburgh, Pa. D. Nov. 3, 1945, Pittsburgh, Pa.   BL TL 5'11" 178 lbs.

Year	Team		W	L	PCT	ERA	G	GS	CG	IP	H	BB	SO	ShO	W	L	SV	AB	H	HR	BA	PO	A	E	DP	TC/G	FA
1886	CIN	AA	4	5	.444	3.75	10	10	9	81.2	65	54	41	0	0	0	0	32	9	0	.281	0	4	2	0	0.6	.667
1887			34	18	.654	2.94	52	52	49	447.1	400	126	176	3	0	0	0	186	47	0	.253	7	67	13	2	1.7	.851
1888			22	17	.564	2.74	40	40	37	348.1	309	89	154	5	0	0	0	129	29	0	.225	4	58	12	0	1.9	.838
1889			9	12	.429	4.88	29	22	16	203	253	101	104	0	2	0	0	83	23	2	.277	2	21	5	0	1.0	.821
1892	PIT	N	6	7	.462	3.63	17	13	12	134	140	58	51	1	0	1	0	511	140	4	.274	9	23	6	0	2.2	.842
1894			0	0	—	4.50	1	0	0	4	6	1	0	0	0	0	0	489	174	6	.356	0	0	0	0	0.0	—
1898	CIN	N	0	0	—	18.00	1	0	0	1	2	3	0	0	0	0	0	486	166	1	.342	0	0	0	0	0.0	—
7 yrs.			75	59	.560	3.35	150	137	123	1219.1	1175	432	526	9	2	1	0	*				22	173	38	2	1.6	.837

Frank Smith — SMITH, FRANK ELMER (Piano Mover)
Born Frank Elmer Schmidt.
B. Oct. 28, 1879, Pittsburgh, Pa. D. Nov. 3, 1952, Pittsburgh, Pa.   BR TR 5'10½" 194 lbs.

Year	Team		W	L	PCT	ERA	G	GS	CG	IP	H	BB	SO	ShO	W	L	SV	AB	H	HR	BA	PO	A	E	DP	TC/G	FA
1904	CHI	A	16	9	.640	2.09	26	23	22	202.1	157	58	107	4	2	0	0	72	18	0	.250	15	53	7	2	2.9	.907
1905			19	13	.594	2.13	39	31	27	291.2	215	107	171	4	2	1	0	106	24	1	.226	27	77	3	3	2.7	.972

Year	Team	W	L	PCT	ERA	G	GS	CG	IP	H	BB	SO	ShO	Relief Pitching W	L	SV	Batting AB	H	HR	BA	PO	A	E	DP	TC/G	FA

Frank Smith *continued*

Year	Team		W	L	PCT	ERA	G	GS	CG	IP	H	BB	SO	ShO	W	L	SV	AB	H	HR	BA	PO	A	E	DP	TC/G	FA
1906			5	5	.500	3.39	20	13	8	122	124	37	53	1	0	0	1	41	12	0	.293	6	42	2	1	2.5	.960
1907			23	10	.697	2.47	41	37	29	310	280	111	139	3	0	0	0	92	18	0	.196	20	109	5	2	3.3	.963
1908			16	17	.485	2.03	41	35	24	297.2	213	73	129	3	1	1	1	106	20	0	.189	23	101	2	4	3.1	.984
1909			25	17	.595	1.80	51	41	37	365	278	70	177	7	3	2	1	127	22	0	.173	26	154	4	3	3.6	.978
1910	2 teams	CHI A (19G 4–9)								BOS A	(4G 1–2)																
"	total		5	11	.313	2.53	23	18	11	156.2	113	51	58	3	0	0	0	52	9	0	.173	14	68	4	0	3.7	.953
1911	2 teams	BOS A (1G 0–0)								CIN N	(34G 10–14)																
"	total		10	14	.417	4.13	35	19	10	178.2	204	58	68	0	4	5	1	56	12	0	.214	16	68	6	4	2.6	.933
1912	CIN N		1	1	.500	6.35	7	3	1	22.2	34	15	5	0	1	0	0	6	0	0	.000	3	3	1	1	1.0	.857
1914	BAL F		10	8	.556	2.99	39	22	9	174.2	180	47	83	1	1	2	2	59	12	0	.203	10	57	2	1	1.8	.971
1915	2 teams	BAL F (17G 4–4)								BKN F	(15G 5–2)																
"	total		9	6	.600	4.04	32	14	6	151.2	177	49	61	1	3	0	0	49	9	1	.184	7	50	1	0	1.8	.983
11 yrs.			139	111	.556	2.59	354	256	184	2273	1975	676	1051	27	17	11	6	766	156	2	.204	167	782	37	22	2.8	.962

Frank Smith

SMITH, FRANK THOMAS
B. Apr. 4, 1928, Pierrepont Manor, N. Y.   BR TR 6'3"   195 lbs.

Year	Team	W	L	PCT	ERA	G	GS	CG	IP	H	BB	SO	ShO	W	L	SV	AB	H	HR	BA	PO	A	E	DP	TC/G	FA
1950	CIN N	2	7	.222	3.87	38	4	0	90.2	73	39	55	0	2	4	3	21	2	0	.095	0	14	0	0	0.4	.875
1951		5	5	.500	3.20	50	0	0	76	65	22	34	0	5	5	11	10	0	0	.000	3	17	1	0	0.4	.952
1952		12	11	.522	3.75	53	2	1	122.1	109	41	77	0	12	9	7	29	5	0	.172	1	16	3	2	0.4	.850
1953		8	1	.889	5.49	50	1	0	83.2	89	25	42	0	8	1	2	13	2	0	.154	1	19	2	2	0.4	.909
1954		5	8	.385	2.67	50	1	0	81	60	29	51	0	5	8	20	10	1	0	.100	1	15	0	0	0.3	1.000
1955	STL N	3	1	.750	3.23	28	0	0	39	27	23	17	0	3	1	1	4	0	0	.000	1	7	1	0	0.3	.889
1956	CIN N	0	0	–	12.00	2	0	0	3	3	3	1	0	0	0	0	0	0	0	–	0	0	0	0	0.0	–
7 yrs.		35	33	.515	3.81	271	7	1	495.2	426	181	277	0	35	28	44	87	10	0	.115	7	88	9	4	0.4	.913

Fred Smith

SMITH, FREDERICK
B. Nov. 24, 1878, New Diggins, Wis.   D. Feb. 4, 1964, Los Angeles, Calif.   BR TR 6'   186 lbs.

Year	Team	W	L	PCT	ERA	G	GS	CG	IP	H	BB	SO	ShO	W	L	SV	AB	H	HR	BA	PO	A	E	DP	TC/G	FA
1907	CIN N	2	7	.222	2.85	18	9	5	85.1	90	24	19	0	0	3	1	28	3	0	.107	6	25	2	0	1.8	.939

Fred Smith

SMITH, FREDERICK C.
B. Mar. 25, 1863, Greene, N. Y.   D. Jan. 9, 1941, Syracuse, N. Y.   BL TR 5'11"   156 lbs.

Year	Team	W	L	PCT	ERA	G	GS	CG	IP	H	BB	SO	ShO	W	L	SV	AB	H	HR	BA	PO	A	E	DP	TC/G	FA
1890	TOL AA	19	13	.594	3.27	35	34	31	286	273	90	116	3	0	0	0	126	21	0	.167	13	69	5	1	2.5	.943

George Smith

SMITH, GEORGE ALLEN (Columbia George)
B. May 31, 1892, Byram, Conn.   D. Jan. 7, 1965, Greenwich, Conn.   BR TR 5'11"   156 lbs.

Year	Team		W	L	PCT	ERA	G	GS	CG	IP	H	BB	SO	ShO	W	L	SV	AB	H	HR	BA	PO	A	E	DP	TC/G	FA
1916	NY N		1	0	1.000	2.61	9	1	0	20.2	14	6	9	0	0	0	0	2	0	0	.000	1	8	1	0	1.1	.900
1917			0	3	.000	2.84	14	1	1	38	38	11	16	0	0	2	0	9	0	0	.000	2	10	0	0	0.9	1.000
1918	3 teams	CIN N (10G 2–3)				NY N	(5G 2–3)				BKN N	(8G 4–1)															
"	total		8	7	.533	3.41	31	18	9	132	140	22	41	1	2	1	0	40	5	0	.125	2	40	1	1	1.9	.977
1919	2 teams	NY N (3G 0–2)								PHI N	(31G 5–11)																
"	total		5	13	.278	3.36	34	22	11	195.2	212	50	42	1	1	1	0	63	8	0	.127	9	55	4	0	2.0	.941
1920	PHI N		13	18	.419	3.81	43	28	10	250.2	265	51	51	2	3	5	2	72	7	0	.097	8	65	4	1	1.8	.948
1921			4	20	.167	4.76	39	28	12	221.1	303	52	45	1	1	1	1	71	4	0	.056	5	54	4	0	1.6	.937
1922			5	14	.263	4.78	42	18	6	194	250	35	44	1	3	0	0	66	5	0	.076	4	41	4	1	1.2	.918
1923	BKN N		3	6	.333	3.66	25	7	3	91	99	28	15	0	0	3	1	26	5	0	.192	2	13	1	0	0.6	.938
8 yrs.			39	81	.325	3.89	229	118	52	1143.1	1321	255	263	6	8	16	4	349	34	0	.097	33	286	19	3	1.5	.944

George Smith

SMITH, GEORGE SHELBY
B. Oct. 27, 1901, Louisville, Ky.   D. May 26, 1981, Richmond, Va.   BR TR 6'1"   175 lbs.

Year	Team	W	L	PCT	ERA	G	GS	CG	IP	H	BB	SO	ShO	W	L	SV	AB	H	HR	BA	PO	A	E	DP	TC/G	FA
1926	DET A	1	2	.333	6.95	23	4	0	44	55	33	15	0	1	1	0	5	0	0	.000	5	6	2	0	0.6	.846
1927		4	1	.800	3.91	29	0	0	71.1	62	50	32	0	4	1	0	19	7	2	.368	4	15	3	0	0.8	.864
1928		1	1	.500	4.42	39	2	0	106	103	50	54	0	0	1	3	27	3	0	.111	8	13	2	0	0.6	.913
1929		3	2	.600	5.80	14	1	0	35.2	42	36	13	0	2	2	0	12	5	0	.417	3	11	3	2	1.2	.824
1930	BOS A	1	2	.333	6.84	27	2	0	73.2	92	49	21	0	1	2	0	24	8	0	.333	5	15	1	1	0.8	.952
5 yrs.		10	8	.556	5.33	132	7	1	330.2	354	218	135	0	8	7	3	87	23	2	.264	25	60	11	3	0.7	.885

Germany Smith

SMITH, GEORGE J.
B. Apr. 21, 1863, Pittsburgh, Pa.   D. Dec. 1, 1927, Altoona, Pa.   BR TR 6'   175 lbs.

Year	Team	W	L	PCT	ERA	G	GS	CG	IP	H	BB	SO	ShO	W	L	SV	AB	H	HR	BA	PO	A	E	DP	TC/G	FA
1884	CLE N	0	0	–	9.00	1	0	1	6	6	2	3	0	0	0	0	*				0	0	0	0	0.0	–

Hal Smith

SMITH, HAROLD LAVERNE
B. June 30, 1902, Creston, Iowa   BR TR 6'3"   195 lbs.

Year	Team	W	L	PCT	ERA	G	GS	CG	IP	H	BB	SO	ShO	W	L	SV	AB	H	HR	BA	PO	A	E	DP	TC/G	FA
1932	PIT N	1	0	1.000	0.75	2	1	1	12	9	2	4	1	0	0	0	3	0	0	.000	0	3	0	0	1.5	1.000
1933		8	7	.533	2.86	28	19	8	145	149	31	40	2	1	0	1	47	6	0	.128	3	25	2	1	1.1	.933
1934		3	4	.429	7.20	20	5	1	50	72	18	15	0	1	2	0	17	1	0	.059	1	10	1	0	0.6	.917
1935		0	0	–	3.00	1	0	0	3	2	1	0	0	0	0	0	0	0	0	–	0	0	0	0	0.0	–
4 yrs.		12	11	.522	3.77	51	25	10	210	232	52	59	3	2	2	1	67	7	0	.104	4	38	3	1	0.9	.933

Harry Smith

SMITH, HARRISON MORTON
B. Aug. 15, 1889, Union, Neb.   D. July 26, 1964, Dunbar, Neb.   BR TR 5'9"   160 lbs.

Year	Team	W	L	PCT	ERA	G	GS	CG	IP	H	BB	SO	ShO	W	L	SV	AB	H	HR	BA	PO	A	E	DP	TC/G	FA
1912	CHI A	1	0	1.000	1.80	1	1	0	5	6	0	1	0	0	0	0	0	0	0	.000	0	1	0	0	1.0	1.000

Heinie Smith

SMITH, GEORGE HENRY
B. Oct. 24, 1871, Pittsburgh, Pa.   D. June 25, 1939, Buffalo, N. Y.   BR TR 5'9½"   160 lbs.
Manager 1902.

Year	Team	W	L	PCT	ERA	G	GS	CG	IP	H	BB	SO	ShO	W	L	SV	AB	H	HR	BA	PO	A	E	DP	TC/G	FA
1901	NY N	0	1	.000	8.10	2	1	1	13.1	24	5	5	0	0	0	0	*				0	2	0	0	1.0	1.000

Year	Team		W	L	PCT	ERA	G	GS	CG	IP	H	BB	SO	ShO	Relief Pitching W	L	SV	Batting AB	H	HR	BA	PO	A	E	DP	TC/G	FA

Jack Smith
SMITH, JACK HATFIELD
B. Nov. 15, 1935, Pikeville, Ky.   BR TR 6'   185 lbs.

Year	Team		W	L	PCT	ERA	G	GS	CG	IP	H	BB	SO	ShO	W	L	SV	AB	H	HR	BA	PO	A	E	DP	TC/G	FA
1962	LA	N	0	0	–	4.50	8	0	0	10	10	4	7	0	0	0	1	1	0	0	.000	0	0	0	0	0.0	–
1963			0	0	–	7.56	4	0	0	8.1	10	2	5	0	0	0	0	2	0	0	.000	0	3	0	0	0.8	1.000
1964	MIL	N	2	2	.500	3.77	22	0	0	31	28	11	19	0	2	2	0	3	1	0	.333	1	11	1	1	0.6	.923
3 yrs.			2	2	.500	4.56	34	0	0	49.1	48	17	31	0	2	2	1	6	1	0	.167	1	14	1	1	0.5	.938

Jake Smith
SMITH, JACOB
Born Jacob Schmidt.
B. June 10, 1887, Dravosburg, Pa.   D. Nov. 7, 1948, East McKeesport, Pa.   BB TL 6'5"   200 lbs.

Year	Team		W	L	PCT	ERA	G	GS	CG	IP	H	BB	SO	ShO	W	L	SV	AB	H	HR	BA	PO	A	E	DP	TC/G	FA
1911	PHI	N	0	0	–	0.00	2	0	0	5	3	2	1	0	0	0	0	3	0	0	.000	0	2	0	0	1.0	1.000

Lee Smith
SMITH, LEE ARTHUR JR.
B. Dec. 4, 1957, Jamestown, La.   BR TR 6'5"   220 lbs.

Year	Team		W	L	PCT	ERA	G	GS	CG	IP	H	BB	SO	ShO	W	L	SV	AB	H	HR	BA	PO	A	E	DP	TC/G	FA
1980	CHI	N	2	0	1.000	2.86	18	0	0	22	21	14	17	0	2	0	0	0	0	0	–	0	3	0	0	0.2	1.000
1981			3	6	.333	3.49	40	1	0	67	57	31	50	0	3	5	1	9	0	0	.000	3	9	0	0	0.3	1.000
1982			2	5	.286	2.69	72	5	0	117	105	37	99	0	2	1	17	16	1	1	.063	9	10	1	2	0.3	.950
1983			4	10	.286	1.65	66	0	0	103.1	70	41	91	0	4	10	**29**	9	1	0	.111	8	9	0	0	0.3	1.000
1984			9	7	.563	3.65	69	0	0	101	98	35	86	0	9	7	33	13	1	0	.077	6	13	0	2	0.3	1.000
1985			7	4	.636	3.04	65	0	0	97.2	87	32	112	0	7	4	33	6	0	0	.000	3	9	0	1	0.2	1.000
1986			9	9	.500	3.09	66	0	0	90.1	69	42	93	0	9	9	31	5	0	0	.000	1	12	0	2	0.2	1.000
1987			4	10	.286	3.12	62	0	0	83.2	84	32	96	0	4	10	36	2	0	0	.000	3	8	0	0	0.2	1.000
1988	BOS	A	4	5	.444	2.80	64	0	0	83.2	72	37	96	0	4	5	29	0	0	0	–	5	4	1	0	0.2	.900
1989			6	1	.857	3.57	64	0	0	70.2	53	33	96	0	6	1	25	0	0	0	–	1	1	0	0	0.1	1.000
10 yrs.			50	57	.467	2.96	586	6	0	836.1	716	334	836	0	50	52	234 7th	60	3	1	.050	39	78	2	7	0.2	.983

LEAGUE CHAMPIONSHIP SERIES

Year	Team		W	L	PCT	ERA	G	GS	CG	IP	H	BB	SO	ShO	W	L	SV	AB	H	HR	BA	PO	A	E	DP	TC/G	FA
1984	CHI	N	0	1	.000	9.00	2	0	0	2	3	0	3	0	0	1	1	0	0	0	–	0	0	0	0	0.0	–
1988	BOS	A	0	1	.000	8.10	2	0	0	3.1	6	1	4	0	0	1	0	0	0	0	–	0	0	0	0	0.0	–
2 yrs.			0	2	.000	8.44	4	0	0	5.1	9	1	7	0	0	2	1	0	0	0	–	0	0	0	0	0.0	–

Mark Smith
SMITH, MARK CHRISTOPHER
B. Nov. 23, 1955, Alexandria, Va.   BL TR 6'2"   215 lbs.

Year	Team		W	L	PCT	ERA	G	GS	CG	IP	H	BB	SO	ShO	W	L	SV	AB	H	HR	BA	PO	A	E	DP	TC/G	FA
1983	OAK	A	1	0	1.000	6.75	8	1	0	14.2	24	6	10	0	1	0	0	0	0	0	–	1	0	0	0	0.1	1.000

Mike Smith
SMITH, MICHAEL ANTHONY
B. Feb. 23, 1961, Hinds, Miss.   BB TR 6'1"   195 lbs.

Year	Team		W	L	PCT	ERA	G	GS	CG	IP	H	BB	SO	ShO	W	L	SV	AB	H	HR	BA	PO	A	E	DP	TC/G	FA
1984	CIN	N	1	0	1.000	5.23	8	1	0	10.1	12	5	7	0	1	0	0	0	0	0	–	1	0	0	0	0.1	1.000
1985			0	0	–	5.40	2	0	0	3.1	2	1	2	0	0	0	0	0	0	0	–	0	1	0	0	0.5	1.000
1986			0	0	–	13.50	2	1	0	3.1	7	1	1	0	0	0	0	0	0	0	–	0	0	0	0	0.0	–
1988	MON	N	0	0	–	3.12	5	0	0	8.2	6	5	4	0	0	0	1	2	0	0	.000	0	1	0	0	0.2	1.000
1989	PIT	N	0	1	.000	3.75	16	0	0	24	28	10	12	0	0	1	0	3	0	0	.000	2	8	0	0	0.6	1.000
5 yrs.			1	1	.500	4.71	33	1	0	49.2	55	22	26	0	1	1	1	5	0	0	.000	3	10	0	0	0.4	1.000

Mike Smith
SMITH, MICHAEL ANTHONY
B. Oct. 31, 1963, San Antonio, Tex.   BR TR 6'3"   180 lbs.

Year	Team		W	L	PCT	ERA	G	GS	CG	IP	H	BB	SO	ShO	W	L	SV	AB	H	HR	BA	PO	A	E	DP	TC/G	FA
1989	BAL	A	2	0	1.000	7.65	13	1	0	20	25	14	12	0	2	0	0	0	0	0	–	1	4	0	0	0.4	1.000

Pete Smith
SMITH, PETER JOHN
B. Feb. 27, 1966, Abington, Mass.   BR TR 6'2"   185 lbs.

Year	Team		W	L	PCT	ERA	G	GS	CG	IP	H	BB	SO	ShO	W	L	SV	AB	H	HR	BA	PO	A	E	DP	TC/G	FA
1987	ATL	N	1	2	.333	4.83	6	6	0	31.2	39	14	11	0	0	0	0	11	1	0	.091	1	2	1	0	0.7	.750
1988			7	15	.318	3.69	32	32	5	195.1	183	88	124	3	0	0	0	53	6	0	.113	12	19	3	0	1.1	.912
1989			5	14	.263	4.75	28	27	1	142	144	57	115	0	0	0	0	41	4	0	.098	11	11	1	2	0.8	.957
3 yrs.			13	31	.295	4.20	66	65	6	369	366	159	250	3	0	0	0	105	11	0	.105	24	32	5	2	0.9	.918

Pete Smith
SMITH, PETER LUKE
B. Mar. 19, 1940, Natick, Mass.   BR TR 6'2"   190 lbs.

Year	Team		W	L	PCT	ERA	G	GS	CG	IP	H	BB	SO	ShO	W	L	SV	AB	H	HR	BA	PO	A	E	DP	TC/G	FA
1962	BOS	A	0	1	.000	19.64	1	1	0	3.2	7	2	1	0	0	0	0	1	0	0	.000	0	1	0	0	1.0	1.000
1963			0	0	–	3.60	6	1	0	15	11	6	6	0	0	0	0	2	0	0	.000	1	3	0	0	0.7	1.000
2 yrs.			0	1	.000	6.75	7	2	0	18.2	18	8	7	0	0	0	0	3	0	0	.000	1	4	0	0	0.7	1.000

Phenomenal Smith
SMITH, JOHN FRANCIS
Born John Francis Gammon.
B. Dec. 12, 1864, Philadelphia, Pa.   D. Apr. 3, 1952, Manchester, N. H.   BL TL 5'6½"   161 lbs.

Year	Team		W	L	PCT	ERA	G	GS	CG	IP	H	BB	SO	ShO	W	L	SV	AB	H	HR	BA	PO	A	E	DP	TC/G	FA
1884	3 teams		BAL U (10G 3–4)			PHI AA (1G 0–1)			PIT AA (1G 0–1)																		
"	total		3	6	.333	4.45	12	11	7	85	123	22	22	0	0	0	0	47	7	0	.149	6	14	6	1	2.2	.769
1885	2 teams		BKN AA (1G 0–1)			PHI AA (1G 0–1)																					
"	total		0	2	.000	11.25	2	2	1	12	19	10	9	0	0	0	0	5	1	0	.200	3	3	1	0	3.5	.857
1886	DET	N	1	1	.500	2.16	3	3	3	25	16	8	5	0	0	0	0	9	1	0	.111	1	2	0	0	1.0	1.000
1887	BAL	AA	25	30	.455	3.79	58	55	54	491.1	526	176	206	1	0	2	0	205	48	1	.234	9	108	20	1	2.4	.854
1888	2 teams		BAL AA (35G 14–19)			PHI AA (3G 2–1)																					
"	total		16	20	.444	3.55	38	35	34	314	270	147	171	0	1	0	0	118	30	1	.254	8	51	17	1	2.0	.776
1889	PHI	AA	2	3	.400	4.40	5	5	5	43	53	25	12	0	0	0	0	16	3	0	.188	0	4	1	1	1.0	.800
1890	2 teams		PHI N (24G 8–12)			PIT N (5G 1–3)																					
"	total		9	15	.375	4.06	29	25	24	248	248	102	96	1	1	0	0	103	31	0	.301	8	32	5	5	1.6	.889
1891	PHI	N	1	1	.500	4.26	3	2	0	19	20	8	3	0	0	0	0	8	3	0	.375	1	0	1	0	0.7	.500
8 yrs.			57	78	.422	3.90	150	138	128	1237.1	1275	498	534	2	2	2	0	511	124	2	.243	36	214	51	9	2.0	.831

Year	Team		W	L	PCT	ERA	G	GS	CG	IP	H	BB	SO	ShO	Relief Pitching W	L	SV	Batting AB	H	HR	BA	PO	A	E	DP	TC/G	FA

Pop Smith

SMITH, CHARLES MARVIN
B. Oct. 12, 1856, Digby, N. S., Canada   D. Apr. 18, 1927, Boston, Mass.
BR TR 5'11" 170 lbs.

| 1883 | COL AA | 0 | 0 | – | 6.35 | 3 | 0 | 0 | 5.2 | 10 | 0 | 0 | 0 | 0 | 0 | 0 | * | | | | 1 | 0 | 0 | 0 | 0.3 | 1.000 |

Pop Boy Smith

SMITH, CLARENCE OSSIE
B. May 23, 1892, Newport, Tenn.   D. Feb. 16, 1924, Sweetwater, Tex.
BR TR 6'1" 176 lbs.

1913	CHI A	0	1	.000	3.38	15	2	0	32	31	11	13	0	0	0	0	5	0	0	.000	2	15	0	0	1.1	1.000
1916	CLE A	1	2	.333	3.86	5	3	0	25.2	25	11	4	0	0	1	1	7	2	0	.286	4	5	1	0	2.0	.900
1917		0	1	.000	8.31	6	0	0	8.2	14	4	3	0	0	1	0	1	0	0	.000	0	9	0	0	1.5	1.000
3 yrs.		1	4	.200	4.21	26	5	0	66.1	70	26	20	0	0	2	1	13	2	0	.154	6	29	1	0	1.4	.972

Reggie Smith

SMITH, REGINALD
B. Louisville, Ky.   Deceased.

| 1886 | PHI AA | 0 | 1 | .000 | 7.00 | 1 | 1 | 1 | 9 | 15 | 5 | 4 | 0 | 0 | 0 | 0 | 4 | 0 | 0 | .000 | 1 | 1 | 1 | 0 | 3.0 | .667 |

Riverboat Smith

SMITH, ROBERT WALKAY
B. May 13, 1928, Clarence, Mo.
BL TL 6' 185 lbs.
BB 1959

1958	BOS A	4	3	.571	3.78	17	7	1	66.2	61	45	43	0	1	1	0	19	2	0	.105	3	14	1	1	1.1	.944
1959	2 teams	CHI N	(1G 0–0)	CLE A	(12G 0–1)																					
"	total	0	1	.000	6.90	13	3	0	30	36	14	17	0	0	0	0	6	0	0	.000	1	6	0	2	0.5	1.000
2 yrs.		4	4	.500	4.75	30	10	1	96.2	97	59	60	0	1	1	0	25	2	0	.080	4	20	1	3	0.8	.960

Roy Smith

SMITH, LEROY PURDY III
B. Sept. 6, 1961, Mt. Vernon, N. Y.
BR TR 6'3" 205 lbs.

1984	CLE A	5	5	.500	4.59	22	14	0	86.1	91	40	55	0	0	0	0	0	0	0	–	4	6	3	0	0.6	.769
1985		1	4	.200	5.34	12	11	1	62.1	84	17	28	0	0	0	0	0	0	0	–	6	3	0	0	0.8	1.000
1986	MIN A	0	2	.000	6.97	5	0	0	10.1	13	5	8	0	0	2	0	0	0	0	–	0	1	0	0	0.2	1.000
1987		1	0	1.000	4.96	7	1	0	16.1	20	6	8	0	0	1	0	0	0	0	–	0	2	0	0	0.3	1.000
1988		3	0	1.000	2.68	9	4	0	37	29	12	17	0	1	0	0	0	0	0	–	3	2	0	0	0.6	1.000
1989		10	6	.625	3.92	32	26	2	172.1	180	51	92	0	0	0	1	0	0	0	–	9	13	0	1	0.7	1.000
6 yrs.		20	17	.541	4.31	87	56	3	384.2	417	131	208	0	1	2	1	0	0	0	–	22	27	3	1	0.6	.942

Rufus Smith

SMITH, RUFUS FRAZIER
B. Jan. 24, 1905, Guilford College, N. C.   D. Aug. 22, 1984, Aiken, S. C.
BR TL 5'8" 165 lbs.

| 1927 | DET A | 0 | 0 | – | 3.38 | 1 | 1 | 0 | 8 | 8 | 3 | 2 | 0 | 0 | 0 | 0 | 3 | 0 | 0 | .000 | 0 | 1 | 0 | 0 | 1.0 | 1.000 |

Sherry Smith

SMITH, SHERROD MALONE
B. Feb. 18, 1891, Monticello, Ga.   D. Sept. 12, 1949, Reidsville, Ga.
BR TL 6'1" 170 lbs.

1911	PIT N	0	0	–	54.00	1	0	0	.2	4	1	0	0	0	0	0	0	0	0	–	0	0	0	0	0.0	–
1912		0	0	–	6.75	3	0	0	4	6	1	3	0	0	0	0	0	0	0	–	0	0	0	0	0.0	–
1915	BKN N	14	8	.636	2.59	29	20	11	173.2	169	42	52	2	3	1	2	57	14	0	.246	5	49	3	1	2.0	.947
1916		14	10	.583	2.34	36	23	15	219	193	45	67	4	2	4	1	77	21	0	.273	3	67	4	0	2.1	.946
1917		12	12	.500	3.32	38	23	15	211.1	210	51	58	0	2	1	3	77	15	0	.195	6	81	3	2	2.4	.967
1919		7	12	.368	2.24	30	19	13	173	181	29	40	2	0	1	1	54	8	0	.148	5	66	2	3	2.4	.973
1920		11	9	.550	1.85	33	12	6	136.1	134	27	33	2	6	3	3	43	10	0	.233	10	63	3	3	2.3	.961
1921		7	11	.389	3.90	35	17	9	175.1	232	34	36	0	1	2	4	57	13	1	.228	8	70	3	1	2.3	.963
1922	2 teams	BKN N	(28G 4–8)	CLE A	(2G 1–0)																					
"	total	5	8	.385	4.42	30	11	4	124.1	146	38	19	1	2	3	2	41	11	0	.268	6	40	4	2	1.7	.920
1923	CLE A	9	6	.600	3.27	30	16	10	124	129	37	23	1	1	0	1	45	11	1	.244	4	42	0	5	1.5	1.000
1924		12	14	.462	3.02	39	27	20	247.2	267	42	34	2	2	0	1	89	18	1	.202	21	72	7	4	2.6	.930
1925		11	14	.440	4.86	31	30	22	237	296	48	30	1	0	0	0	92	28	1	.304	8	64	3	1	2.4	.960
1926		11	10	.524	3.73	27	24	16	188.1	214	31	25	2	1	0	0	65	14	1	.215	10	62	0	6	2.7	1.000
1927		1	4	.200	5.45	11	2	1	38	53	14	8	0	1	1	0	12	2	0	.167	5	10	1	0	1.5	.938
14 yrs.		114	118	.491	3.32	373	224	142	2052.2	2234	440	428	17	21	17	20	709	165	6	.233	91	686	33	28	2.2	.959

WORLD SERIES

1916	BKN N	0	1	.000	1.35	1	1	1	13.1	7	6	2	0	0	0	0	5	1	0	.200	1	7	0	0	8.0	1.000
1920		1	1	.500	0.53	2	2	2	17	10	3	3	0	0	0	0	6	0	0	.000	2	4	0	0	3.0	1.000
2 yrs.		1	2	.333	0.89	3	3	3	30.1	17	9	5	0	0	0	0	11	1	0	.091	3	11	0	0	4.7	1.000
				4th																						

Tom Smith

SMITH, THOMAS E.
B. Dec. 5, 1871, Boston, Mass.   D. Mar. 2, 1929, Dorchester, Mass.
BR TR 180 lbs.

1894	BOS N	0	0	–	15.00	2	0	0	6	8	6	2	0	0	0	0	2	0	0	.000	0	0	0	0	0.0	–
1895	PHI N	2	3	.400	6.88	11	7	4	68	76	53	21	0	0	0	0	33	8	0	.242	1	11	1	0	1.2	.923
1896	LOU N	2	3	.400	5.40	11	5	4	55	73	25	14	0	1	0	0	39	8	0	.205	2	18	0	0	1.8	1.000
1898	STL N	0	1	.000	2.00	1	1	1	9	9	5	1	0	0	0	0	2	1	0	.500	0	3	0	0	3.0	1.000
4 yrs.		4	7	.364	6.33	25	13	9	138	166	89	38	0	1	0	0	76	17	0	.224	3	32	1	0	1.4	.972

Willie Smith

SMITH, WILLIE (Wonderful Willie)
B. Feb. 11, 1939, Anniston, Ala.
BL TL 6' 182 lbs.

1963	DET A	1	0	1.000	4.57	11	2	0	21.2	24	13	16	0	1	0	2	8	1	0	.125	1	4	0	0	0.5	1.000
1964	LA A	1	4	.200	2.84	15	1	0	31.2	34	10	20	0	1	4	0	359	108	11	.301	1	6	0	1	0.5	1.000
1968	2 teams	CLE A	(2G 0–0)	CHI N	(1G 0–0)																					
"	total	0	0	–	0.00	3	0	0	7.2	2	1	3	0	0	0	0	184	45	5	.245	3	2	0	1	1.7	1.000
3 yrs.		2	4	.333	3.10	29	3	0	61	60	24	39	0	2	4	2	*				5	12	0	2	0.6	1.000

Zane Smith

SMITH, ZANE WILLIAM
B. Dec. 28, 1960, Madison, Wis.
BL TL 6'2" 195 lbs.

1984	ATL N	1	0	1.000	2.25	3	3	0	20	16	13	16	0	0	0	0	9	5	0	.556	2	3	1	1	2.0	.833
1985		9	10	.474	3.80	42	18	2	147	135	80	85	2	3	4	0	37	6	0	.162	7	35	3	2	1.1	.933
1986		8	16	.333	4.05	38	32	3	204.2	209	105	139	1	1	0	1	59	5	0	.085	7	45	1	4	1.4	.981

Year	Team		W	L	PCT	ERA	G	GS	CG	IP	H	BB	SO	ShO	Relief Pitching W	L	SV	Batting AB	H	HR	BA	PO	A	E	DP	TC/G	FA

Zane Smith *continued*

1987			15	10	.600	4.09	36	**36**	9	242	245	91	130	3	0	0	0	76	10	0	.132	15	43	0	4	1.6	1.000
1988			5	10	.333	4.30	23	22	3	140.1	159	44	59	0	0	0	0	42	7	0	.167	16	33	1	6	2.2	.980
1989	2 teams	ATL N (17G 1–12)				MON N	(31G 0–1)																				
"	total		1	13	.071	3.49	48	17	0	147	141	52	93	0	0	1	2	32	6	0	.188	7	39	3	0	1.0	.939
6 yrs.			39	59	.398	3.93	190	128	17	901	905	385	522	6	4	5	3	255	39	0	.153	54	198	9	17	1.4	.966

Mike Smithson

SMITHSON, BILLY MIKE
B. Jan. 21, 1955, Centerville, Tenn.
BL TR 6'8" 200 lbs.

1982	TEX	A	3	4	.429	5.01	8	8	3	46.2	51	13	24	0	0	0	0	0	0	0	–	2	3	0	0	0.6	1.000
1983			10	14	.417	3.91	33	33	10	223.1	233	71	135	0	0	0	0	0	0	0	–	19	33	2	3	1.6	.963
1984	MIN	A	15	13	.536	3.68	36	**36**	10	252	246	54	144	1	0	0	0	0	0	0	–	17	29	2	2	1.3	.958
1985			15	14	.517	4.34	37	**37**	8	257	264	78	127	3	0	0	0	0	0	0	–	16	28	2	4	1.2	.957
1986			13	14	.481	4.77	34	33	8	198	234	57	114	1	0	0	0	0	0	0	–	10	32	2	4	1.3	.955
1987			4	7	.364	5.94	21	20	0	109	126	38	53	0	0	0	0	0	0	0	–	6	11	0	1	0.8	1.000
1988	BOS	A	9	6	.600	5.97	31	18	1	126.2	149	37	73	0	1	1	0	0	0	0	–	7	13	3	0	0.7	.870
1989			7	14	.333	4.95	40	19	1	143.2	170	35	61	1	1	4	2	0	0	0	–	9	19	1	3	0.7	.966
8 yrs.			76	86	.469	4.58	240	204	41	1356.1	1473	383	731	6	2	6	2	0	0	0	–	86	168	12	17	1.1	.955

LEAGUE CHAMPIONSHIP SERIES

| 1988 | BOS | A | 0 | 0 | – | 0.00 | 1 | 0 | 0 | 2.1 | 3 | 0 | 1 | 0 | 0 | 0 | 0 | 0 | 0 | 0 | – | 0 | 0 | 0 | 0 | 0.0 | |

Lefty Smoll

SMOLL, CLYDE HETRICK
B. Apr. 17, 1914, Quakertown, Pa. D. Aug. 31, 1985, Quakertown, Pa.
BB TL 5'10" 175 lbs.

| 1940 | PHI | N | 2 | 8 | .200 | 5.37 | 33 | 9 | 0 | 109 | 145 | 36 | 31 | 0 | 2 | 0 | 0 | 31 | 5 | 0 | .161 | 3 | 17 | 4 | 1 | 0.7 | .833 |

John Smoltz

SMOLTZ, JOHN ANDREW
B. May 15, 1967, Detroit, Mich.
BR TR 6'3" 210 lbs.

1988	ATL	N	2	7	.222	5.48	12	12	0	64	74	33	37	0	0	0	0	17	2	0	.118	4	6	0	1	0.8	1.000
1989			12	11	.522	2.94	29	29	5	208	160	72	168	0	0	0	0	62	7	1	.113	23	32	7	2	2.1	.887
2 yrs.			14	18	.438	3.54	41	41	5	272	234	105	205	0	0	0	0	79	9	1	.114	27	38	7	3	1.8	.903

Harry Smythe

SMYTHE, WILLIAM HENRY
B. Oct. 24, 1904, Augusta, Ga. D. Aug. 28, 1980, Augusta, Ga.
BL TL 5'10½" 179 lbs.

1929	PHI	N	4	6	.400	5.24	19	7	2	68.2	94	15	12	0	4	1	1	26	5	0	.192	4	23	0	0	1.4	1.000
1930			0	3	.000	7.79	25	3	0	49.2	84	31	9	0	0	1	2	14	4	0	.286	2	9	2	0	0.5	.846
1934	2 teams	NY A (8G 0–2)					BKN N	(8G 1–1)																			
"	total		1	3	.250	6.69	16	0	0	36.1	54	16	12	0	1	3	1	14	4	0	.286	2	14	2	1	1.1	.889
3 yrs.			5	12	.294	6.40	60	10	2	154.2	232	62	33	0	5	5	4	54	13	0	.241	8	46	4	1	1.0	.931

Nate Snell

SNELL, NATHANIEL
B. Sept. 2, 1952, Orangeburg, S. C.
BR TR 6'4" 190 lbs.

1984	BAL	A	1	1	.500	2.35	5	0	0	7.2	8	1	7	0	1	1	0	0	0	0	–	1	0	0	0	0.2	1.000
1985			3	2	.600	2.69	43	0	0	100.1	100	30	41	0	3	2	5	0	0	0	–	6	21	2	3	0.7	.931
1986			2	1	.667	3.86	34	0	0	72.1	69	22	29	0	2	1	0	0	0	0	–	5	14	0	1	0.6	1.000
1987	DET	A	1	2	.333	3.96	22	2	0	38.2	39	19	19	0	1	1	0	0	0	0	–	6	1	0	0	0.3	1.000
4 yrs.			7	6	.538	3.29	104	2	0	219	216	72	96	0	7	5	5	0	0	0	–	18	36	2	4	0.5	.964

Frank Snook

SNOOK, FRANK WALTER JR.
B. Mar. 28, 1949, Somerville, N. J.
BR TR 6'2" 180 lbs.

| 1973 | SD | N | 0 | 2 | .000 | 3.62 | 18 | 0 | 0 | 27.1 | 19 | 18 | 13 | 0 | 0 | 2 | 1 | 2 | 0 | 0 | .000 | 2 | 7 | 0 | 0 | 0.5 | 1.000 |

Colonel Snover

SNOVER, COLONEL LESTER (Bosco)
B. May 16, 1895, Hallstead, Pa. D. Apr. 30, 1969, Rochester, N. Y.
BL TL 6'½" 200 lbs.

| 1919 | NY | N | 0 | 1 | .000 | 1.00 | 2 | 1 | 0 | 9 | 7 | 3 | 4 | 0 | 0 | 1 | 0 | 2 | 0 | 0 | .000 | 0 | 2 | 1 | 0 | 1.5 | .667 |

Bill Snyder

SNYDER, WILLIAM NICHOLAS
B. Jan. 28, 1898, Mansfield, Ohio D. Oct. 8, 1934, Vicksburg, Mich.
BR TR

1919	WAS	A	0	1	.000	1.13	2	1	0	8	6	3	5	0	0	0	0	2	0	0	.000	0	1	0	0	0.5	1.000
1920			2	1	.667	4.17	16	4	1	54	59	28	17	0	1	1	1	19	6	0	.316	0	11	2	0	0.8	.846
2 yrs.			2	2	.500	3.77	18	5	1	62	65	31	22	0	1	1	1	21	6	0	.286	0	12	2	0	0.8	.857

Brian Snyder

SNYDER, BRIAN ROBERT
B. Feb. 20, 1958, Flemington, N. J.
BL TL 6'3" 185 lbs.

1985	SEA	A	1	2	.333	6.37	15	6	0	35.1	44	19	23	0	1	0	1	0	0	0	–	4	7	0	0	0.7	1.000
1989	OAK	A	0	0	–	27.00	2	0	0	.2	2	2	1	0	0	0	0	0	0	0	–	0	0	0	0	0.0	
2 yrs.			1	2	.333	6.75	17	6	0	36	46	21	24	0	1	0	1	0	0	0	–	4	7	0	0	0.6	1.000

Gene Snyder

SNYDER, GENE WALTER
B. Mar. 31, 1931, York, Pa.
BR TL 5'11" 175 lbs.

| 1959 | LA | N | 1 | 1 | .500 | 5.47 | 11 | 2 | 0 | 26.1 | 32 | 20 | 20 | 0 | 1 | 0 | 0 | 6 | 0 | 0 | .000 | 1 | 2 | 1 | 1 | 0.4 | .750 |

George Snyder

SNYDER, GEORGE T.
B. 1849, Philadelphia, Pa. D. Aug. 2, 1905, Philadelphia, Pa.

| 1882 | PHI | AA | 1 | 0 | 1.000 | 0.00 | 1 | 1 | 1 | 9 | 4 | 2 | 0 | 0 | 0 | 0 | 0 | 3 | 1 | 0 | .333 | 1 | 3 | 0 | 0 | 4.0 | 1.000 |

Ray Soff

SOFF, RAYMOND JOHN
B. Oct. 31, 1958, Adrian, Mich.
BR TR 6' 185 lbs.

| 1986 | STL | N | 4 | 2 | .667 | 3.29 | 30 | 0 | 0 | 38.1 | 37 | 13 | 22 | 0 | 4 | 2 | 0 | 2 | 0 | 0 | .000 | 6 | 7 | 1 | 0 | 0.5 | .929 |

Year	Team	W	L	PCT	ERA	G	GS	CG	IP	H	BB	SO	ShO	Relief Pitching W	L	SV	Batting AB	H	HR	BA	PO	A	E	DP	TC/G	FA

Ray Soff *continued*

Year	Team	W	L	PCT	ERA	G	GS	CG	IP	H	BB	SO	ShO	W	L	SV	AB	H	HR	BA	PO	A	E	DP	TC/G	FA
1987		1	0	1.000	6.46	12	0	0	15.1	18	5	9	0	1	0	0	1	0	0	.000	1	2	0	0	0.3	1.000
2 yrs.		5	2	.714	4.19	42	0	0	53.2	55	18	31	0	5	2	0	3	0	0	.000	7	9	1	0	0.4	.941

Julio Solano

SOLANO, JULIO CESAR
Born Julio Cesar Mercado y Solano.
B. Jan. 8, 1960, Aqua Blanca, Dominican Republic

BR TR 6'1" 157 lbs.

Year	Team		W	L	PCT	ERA	G	GS	CG	IP	H	BB	SO	ShO	W	L	SV	AB	H	HR	BA	PO	A	E	DP	TC/G	FA
1983	HOU	N	0	2	.000	6.00	4	0	0	6	5	4	3	0	0	2	0	0	0	0	—	0	1	0	0	0.3	1.000
1984			1	3	.250	1.95	31	0	0	50.2	31	18	33	0	1	3	0	3	1	0	.333	5	3	2	0	0.3	.800
1985			2	2	.500	3.48	20	0	0	33.2	34	13	17	0	2	2	0	2	0	0	.000	0	2	0	0	0.1	1.000
1986			3	1	.750	7.59	16	1	0	32	39	22	21	0	3	0	0	6	0	0	.000	2	4	1	0	0.4	.857
1987			0	0	—	7.65	11	0	0	20	25	9	12	0	0	0	0	2	0	0	.000	1	3	0	0	0.4	1.000
1988	SEA	A	0	0	—	4.09	17	0	0	22	22	12	10	0	0	0	3	0	0	0	—	1	5	0	0	0.4	1.000
1989			0	0	—	5.59	7	0	0	9.2	6	4	6	0	0	0	0	0	0	0	—	1	3	0	0	0.6	1.000
7 yrs.			6	8	.429	4.55	106	1	0	174	162	82	102	0	6	7	3	13	1	0	.077	10	21	3	0	0.3	.912

Marcelino Solis

SOLIS, MARCELINO
B. July 19, 1930, San Luis Potosi, Mexico

BL TL 6'1" 185 lbs.

Year	Team		W	L	PCT	ERA	G	GS	CG	IP	H	BB	SO	ShO	W	L	SV	AB	H	HR	BA	PO	A	E	DP	TC/G	FA
1958	CHI	N	3	3	.500	6.06	15	4	0	52	74	20	15	0	3	1	0	20	5	0	.250	5	8	0	0	0.9	1.000

Eddie Solomon

SOLOMON, EDDIE, JR. (Buddy)
B. Feb. 9, 1951, Perry, Ga.   D. Jan. 12, 1986, Macon, Ga.

BR TR 6'3½" 198 lbs.

Year	Team		W	L	PCT	ERA	G	GS	CG	IP	H	BB	SO	ShO	W	L	SV	AB	H	HR	BA	PO	A	E	DP	TC/G	FA
1973	LA	N	0	0	—	7.11	4	0	0	6.1	10	4	6	0	0	0	0	1	0	0	.000	1	0	0	0	0.3	1.000
1974			0	0	—	1.35	4	0	0	6.2	5	2	2	0	0	0	0	0	0	0	—	0	3	0	0	0.8	1.000
1975	CHI	N	0	0	—	1.29	6	0	0	7	7	6	3	0	0	0	0	0	0	0	—	0	2	0	0	0.3	1.000
1976	STL	N	1	1	.500	4.86	26	2	0	37	45	16	19	0	0	1	0	5	2	0	.400	2	11	1	1	0.5	.929
1977	ATL	N	6	6	.500	4.55	18	16	0	89	110	34	54	0	0	0	0	31	4	0	.129	5	12	1	0	1.0	.944
1978			4	6	.400	4.08	37	8	0	106	98	50	64	0	1	3	2	29	4	0	.138	5	16	2	1	0.6	.913
1979			7	14	.333	4.21	31	30	4	186	184	51	96	0	0	0	0	64	13	0	.203	12	22	4	0	1.2	.895
1980	PIT	N	7	3	.700	2.70	26	12	2	100	96	37	35	0	2	0	0	32	7	0	.219	9	14	3	2	1.0	.885
1981			8	6	.571	3.12	22	17	2	127	133	27	38	0	1	1	1	43	7	0	.163	6	19	1	1	1.2	.962
1982	2 teams		PIT N	(11G 2-6)			CHI A	(6G 1-0)																			
"	total		3	6	.333	6.33	17	10	0	54	76	20	20	0	2	0	0	15	2	0	.133	0	3	2	0	0.3	.600
10 yrs.			36	42	.462	3.99	191	95	8	719	764	247	337	0	6	5	4	220	39	0	.177	40	102	14	5	0.8	.910

LEAGUE CHAMPIONSHIP SERIES

Year	Team		W	L	PCT	ERA	G	GS	CG	IP	H	BB	SO	ShO	W	L	SV	AB	H	HR	BA	PO	A	E	DP	TC/G	FA
1974	LA	N	0	0	—	0.00	1	0	0	2	2	1	1	0	0	0	0	0	0	0	—	0	0	0	0	0.0	—

Joe Sommer

SOMMER, JOSEPH JOHN
B. Nov. 20, 1858, Covington, Ky.   D. Jan. 16, 1938, Cincinnati, Ohio

BR TR

Year	Team		W	L	PCT	ERA	G	GS	CG	IP	H	BB	SO	ShO	W	L	SV	AB	H	HR	BA	PO	A	E	DP	TC/G	FA
1883	CIN	AA	0	0	—	5.40	1	0	0	5	9	1	2	0	0	0	0	413	115	3	.278	0	0	0	0	0.0	—
1885	BAL	AA	0	0	—	9.00	2	0	0	3	6	0	0	0	0	0	1	471	118	1	.251	0	0	0	0	0.0	—
1886			0	0	—	18.00	1	0	0	4	14	3	1	0	0	0	0	560	117	1	.209	0	1	1	0	2.0	.500
1887	CLE	N	0	0	—	9.00	1	0	0	1	2	1	0	0	0	0	0	463	123	0	.266	0	0	0	0	0.0	—
1890			0	0	—	0.00	1	0	0	1	2	2	0	0	0	0	0	164	41	0	.250	0	0	0	0	1.0	—
5 yrs.			0	0	—	9.64	6	0	0	14	33	7	3	0	0	0	1	*				0	1	2	0	0.5	.333

Rudy Sommers

SOMMERS, RUDOLPH
B. Oct. 30, 1888, Cincinnati, Ohio   D. Mar. 18, 1949, Louisville, Ky.

BB TL 5'11" 165 lbs.

Year	Team		W	L	PCT	ERA	G	GS	CG	IP	H	BB	SO	ShO	W	L	SV	AB	H	HR	BA	PO	A	E	DP	TC/G	FA
1912	CHI	N	0	1	.000	3.00	1	1	0	3	4	2	1	0	0	0	0	0	0	0	—	0	0	0	0	0.0	—
1914	BKN	F	4	7	.364	4.06	23	8	2	82	88	34	40	0	3	0	0	24	6	0	.250	2	22	3	0	1.2	.889
1926	BOS	A	0	0	—	13.50	2	0	0	2	3	3	1	0	0	0	0	0	0	0	—	0	1	0	0	0.5	1.000
1927			0	0	—	8.36	7	0	0	14	18	14	2	0	0	1	0	2	1	0	.500	0	7	0	0	1.0	1.000
4 yrs.			4	8	.333	4.81	33	8	2	101	113	53	44	0	3	1	0	26	7	0	.269	2	30	3	0	1.1	.914

Andy Sommerville

SOMMERVILLE, ANDREW HENRY
Born Henry Travers Summersgill.
B. Feb. 6, 1876, Brooklyn, N. Y.   D. June 16, 1931, Richmond Hill, N. Y.

Year	Team		W	L	PCT	ERA	G	GS	CG	IP	H	BB	SO	ShO	W	L	SV	AB	H	HR	BA	PO	A	E	DP	TC/G	FA
1894	BKN	N	0	1	.000	162.00	1	1	0	.1	1	5	0	0	0	0	0	0	0	0	—	0	0	0	0	0.0	—

Don Songer

SONGER, DONALD C.
B. Jan. 31, 1900, Walnut, Kans.   D. Oct. 3, 1962, Kansas City, Mo.

BL TL 6' 165 lbs.

Year	Team		W	L	PCT	ERA	G	GS	CG	IP	H	BB	SO	ShO	W	L	SV	AB	H	HR	BA	PO	A	E	DP	TC/G	FA
1924	PIT	N	0	0	—	6.75	4	1	0	9.1	14	3	3	0	0	0	1	2	0	0	.000	1	3	0	0	1.0	1.000
1925			0	1	.000	2.31	8	0	0	11.2	14	8	4	0	0	1	0	2	0	0	.000	0	3	1	0	0.5	.750
1926			7	8	.467	3.13	35	15	5	126.1	118	52	27	1	0	2	2	38	4	0	.105	1	36	2	2	1.1	.949
1927	2 teams		PIT N	(2G 0-0)			NY N	(22G 3-5)																			
"	total		3	5	.375	3.60	24	1	0	55	58	35	10	0	3	4	1	11	3	0	.273	6	15	0	1	0.9	1.000
4 yrs.			10	14	.417	3.38	71	17	5	202.1	204	98	44	1	3	7	4	53	7	0	.132	8	57	3	3	1.0	.956

Lary Sorensen

SORENSEN, LARY ALAN
B. Oct. 4, 1955, Detroit, Mich.

BR TR 6'2" 200 lbs.

Year	Team		W	L	PCT	ERA	G	GS	CG	IP	H	BB	SO	ShO	W	L	SV	AB	H	HR	BA	PO	A	E	DP	TC/G	FA
1977	MIL	A	7	10	.412	4.37	23	20	9	142	147	36	57	0	0	1	0	0	0	0	—	15	23	1	4	1.7	.974
1978			18	12	.600	3.21	37	36	17	280.2	277	50	78	3	0	0	1	0	0	0	—	28	44	3	1	2.0	.960
1979			15	14	.517	3.98	34	34	16	235	250	42	63	2	0	0	0	0	0	0	—	23	39	6	3	2.0	.912
1980			12	10	.545	3.67	35	29	8	196	242	45	54	2	0	1	0	0	0	0	—	18	30	0	5	1.4	1.000
1981	STL	N	7	7	.500	3.28	23	23	3	140	149	26	52	1	0	0	0	46	3	0	.065	15	21	2	3	1.7	.947
1982	CLE	A	10	15	.400	5.61	32	30	6	189.1	251	55	62	1	0	0	0	0	0	0	—	10	28	4	2	1.3	.905
1983			12	11	.522	4.24	36	34	8	222.2	238	65	76	1	0	0	0	0	0	0	—	20	39	2	1	1.7	.967
1984	OAK	A	6	13	.316	4.91	46	21	2	183.1	240	44	63	0	1	2	1	0	0	0	—	15	18	1	3	0.7	.971
1985	CHI	N	3	7	.300	4.26	45	3	0	82.1	86	24	34	0	3	5	0	6	0	0	.000	4	14	2	1	0.4	.900
1987	MON	N	3	4	.429	4.72	23	5	0	47.2	56	12	21	0	1	1	1	8	0	0	.000	3	5	1	0	0.4	.889

Year	Team	W	L	PCT	ERA	G	GS	CG	IP	H	BB	SO	ShO	Relief Pitching W	L	SV	Batting AB	H	HR	BA	PO	A	E	DP	TC/G	FA

Lary Sorensen *continued*

Year	Team	W	L	PCT	ERA	G	GS	CG	IP	H	BB	SO	ShO	W	L	SV	AB	H	HR	BA	PO	A	E	DP	TC/G	FA
1988	SF N	0	0	–	4.86	12	0	0	16.2	24	3	9	0	0	0	2	1	0	0	.000	0	2	0	0	0.2	1.000
11 yrs.		93	103	.474	4.15	346	235	69	1735.2	1960	402	569	10	5	10	6	61	3	0	.049	151	263	22	23	1.3	.950

Vic Sorrell

SORRELL, VICTOR GARLAND
B. Apr. 9, 1901, Morrisville, N. C. D. May 4, 1972, Raleigh, N. C.

BR TR 5'10" 180 lbs.

Year	Team	W	L	PCT	ERA	G	GS	CG	IP	H	BB	SO	ShO	W	L	SV	AB	H	HR	BA	PO	A	E	DP	TC/G	FA
1928	DET A	8	11	.421	4.79	29	23	8	171	182	83	67	0				55	6	0	.109	3	28	6	2	1.3	.838
1929		14	15	.483	5.18	36	31	13	226	270	106	81	1	2	0	1	83	12	0	.145	7	41	0	2	1.3	1.000
1930		16	11	.593	3.86	35	30	14	233.1	245	106	97	2	2	1	1	80	15	0	.188	3	33	1	2	1.1	.973
1931		13	14	.481	4.12	35	32	19	247	267	114	99	1	0	0	1	88	14	0	.159	12	52	3	4	1.9	.955
1932		14	14	.500	4.03	32	31	13	234.1	234	77	84	1	1	0	0	76	9	0	.118	9	40	1	0	1.6	.980
1933		11	15	.423	3.79	36	28	13	232.2	233	78	75	2	2	1	1	74	11	0	.149	14	48	2	1	1.8	.969
1934		6	9	.400	4.79	28	19	6	129.2	146	45	46	0	0	2	2	37	4	0	.108	7	34	3	2	1.6	.932
1935		4	3	.571	4.03	12	6	4	51.1	65	25	22	0	2	2	0	18	0	0	.000	3	11	0	0	1.2	1.000
1936		6	7	.462	5.28	30	14	5	131.1	153	64	37	1	2	3	3	39	6	0	.154	9	31	0	4	1.3	1.000
1937		0	2	.000	9.00	7	2	0	17	25	8	11	0	0	0	1	3	0	0	.000	1	3	1	0	0.7	.800
10 yrs.		92	101	.477	4.43	280	216	95	1673.2	1820	706	619	8	9	9	10	553	77	0	.139	68	321	17	17	1.5	.958

Elias Sosa

SOSA, ELIAS
Born Elias Sosa y Martinez.
B. June 10, 1950, La Vega, Dominican Republic

BR TR 6'2" 186 lbs.

Year	Team	W	L	PCT	ERA	G	GS	CG	IP	H	BB	SO	ShO	W	L	SV	AB	H	HR	BA	PO	A	E	DP	TC/G	FA
1972	SF N	0	1	.000	2.25	8	0	0	16	10	12	10	0	0	1	3	4	0	0	.000	0	2	0	0	0.3	1.000
1973		10	4	.714	3.28	71	1	0	107	95	41	70	0	10	3	18	14	1	0	.071	7	12	0	0	0.3	1.000
1974		9	7	.563	3.48	68	0	0	101	94	45	48	0	9	7	6	15	1	0	.067	4	14	3	2	0.3	.857
1975	2 teams	STL N	(14G 0–3)		ATL N	(43G 2–2)																				
"	total	2	5	.286	4.32	57	1	0	89.2	92	43	46	0	2	4	4	15	2	0	.133	3	14	2	1	0.3	.895
1976	2 teams	ATL N	(21G 4–4)		LA N	(24G 2–4)																				
"	total	6	8	.429	4.43	45	0	0	69	71	25	52	0	6	8	4	7	1	0	.143	1	10	2	0	0.3	.846
1977	LA N	2	2	.500	1.97	44	0	0	64	42	12	47	0	2	2	1	4	1	0	.250	3	9	0	0	0.3	1.000
1978	OAK A	8	2	.800	2.64	68	0	0	109	106	44	61	0	8	2	14	0	0	0	–	9	15	0	1	0.4	1.000
1979	MON N	8	7	.533	1.95	62	0	0	97	77	37	59	0	8	7	18	13	2	0	.154	8	8	2	0	0.3	.889
1980		9	6	.600	3.06	67	0	0	94	104	19	58	0	9	6	9	11	1	0	.091	4	13	1	0	0.3	.944
1981		1	2	.333	3.69	32	0	0	39	46	8	18	0	1	2	3	2	2	0	1.000	3	8	0	0	0.3	1.000
1982	DET A	3	3	.500	4.43	38	0	0	61	64	28	24	0	3	3	4	0	0	0	–	3	13	0	0	0.4	1.000
1983	SD N	1	4	.200	4.35	41	1	0	72.1	72	30	45	0	1	4	1	7	1	0	.143	5	5	0	0	0.3	1.000
12 yrs.		59	51	.536	3.32	601	3	0	919	873	334	538	0	59	49	83	92	12	0	.130	52	123	10	4	0.3	.946

DIVISIONAL PLAYOFF SERIES

| 1981 | MON N | 0 | 0 | – | 3.00 | 2 | 0 | 0 | 3 | 4 | 0 | 1 | 0 | 0 | 0 | 0 | 0 | 0 | 0 | – | 0 | 0 | 1 | 0 | 0.5 | – |

LEAGUE CHAMPIONSHIP SERIES

1977	LA N	0	1	.000	10.13	2	0	0	2.2	5	0	0	0	0	1	0	0	0	0	.000	0	1	0	0	0.5	1.000
1981	MON N	0	0	–	0.00	1	0	0	.1	1	1	0	0	0	0	0	0	0	0	–	0	0	0	0	0.0	–
2 yrs.		0	1	.000	9.00	3	0	0	3	6	1	0	0	0	1	0	1	0	0	.000	0	1	0	0	0.3	1.000

WORLD SERIES

| 1977 | LA N | 0 | 0 | – | 11.57 | 2 | 0 | 0 | 2.1 | 3 | 1 | 1 | 0 | 0 | 0 | 0 | 0 | 0 | 0 | – | 0 | 0 | 0 | 0 | 0.0 | – |

Jose Sosa

SOSA, JOSE
Born Jose Ynocencio y Sosa.
B. Dec. 28, 1952, Santo Domingo, Dominican Republic

BR TR 5'11" 158 lbs.

Year	Team	W	L	PCT	ERA	G	GS	CG	IP	H	BB	SO	ShO	W	L	SV	AB	H	HR	BA	PO	A	E	DP	TC/G	FA
1975	HOU N	1	3	.250	4.02	25	2	0	47	51	23	31	0	1	3	1	9	3	0	.333	1	1	0	0	0.1	1.000
1976		0	0	–	6.75	9	0	0	12	16	6	5	0	0	0	0	0	0	0	–	2	5	0	0	0.8	1.000
2 yrs.		1	3	.250	4.58	34	2	0	59	67	29	36	0	1	3	1	9	3	1	.333	3	6	0	0	0.3	1.000

Allen Sothoron

SOTHORON, ALLEN SUTTON
B. Apr. 27, 1893, Bradford, Ohio
D. June 17, 1939, St. Louis, Mo.
Manager 1933.

BB TR 5'11" 182 lbs.
BR 1924-26

Year	Team	W	L	PCT	ERA	G	GS	CG	IP	H	BB	SO	ShO	W	L	SV	AB	H	HR	BA	PO	A	E	DP	TC/G	FA
1914	STL A	0	0	–	6.00	1	0	0	6	6	4	3	0				2	0	0	.000	0	1	0	0	1.0	1.000
1915		0	1	.000	7.36	3	1	0	3.2	8	5	2	0	0	0	0	1	0	0	.000	0	3	0	0	1.0	1.000
1917		14	19	.424	2.83	48	33	17	276.2	259	96	85	3	2	3	4	91	19	0	.209	13	81	11	0	2.2	.895
1918		12	12	.500	1.94	29	24	14	209	152	67	71	2	0	1	0	63	10	0	.159	10	43	8	2	2.1	.869
1919		20	13	.606	2.20	40	30	21	270	256	87	106	3	5	0	3	97	17	0	.175	17	39	13	2	1.7	.812
1920		8	15	.348	4.70	36	26	12	218.1	263	89	81	1	0	1	2	72	16	0	.222	12	49	14	0	2.1	.813
1921	3 teams	STL A	(5G 1–2)		BOS A	(2G 0–2)		CLE A	(22G 12–4)																	
"	total	13	8	.619	3.89	29	22	11	178.1	194	71	72	1	2	0	0	69	18	0	.261	8	34	4	0	1.6	.913
1922	CLE A	1	3	.250	6.39	6	4	2	25.1	26	14	8	0	0	1	0	9	4	0	.444	0	5	1	0	1.0	.833
1924	STL N	10	16	.385	3.57	29	28	16	196.2	209	84	62	4	0	1	0	72	14	0	.194	2	35	0	1	1.3	1.000
1925		10	10	.500	4.05	28	23	8	155.2	173	63	67	2	1	1	0	56	11	0	.196	4	15	3	0	0.8	.864
1926		3	3	.500	4.22	15	4	1	42.2	37	16	19	0	2	2	0	13	3	0	.231	0	7	2	0	0.6	.778
11 yrs.		91	100	.476	3.31	264	195	102	1582.1	1583	596	576	17	12	10	9	545	112	0	.206	66	312	56	3	1.6	.871

Mario Soto

SOTO, MARIO MELVIN
B. July 12, 1956, Bani, Dominican Republic

BR TR 6' 174 lbs.

Year	Team	W	L	PCT	ERA	G	GS	CG	IP	H	BB	SO	ShO	W	L	SV	AB	H	HR	BA	PO	A	E	DP	TC/G	FA
1977	CIN N	2	6	.250	5.31	12	10	2	61	60	26	44	1	0	0	0	13	1	0	.077	5	9	0	1	1.2	1.000
1978		1	0	1.000	2.50	5	1	0	18	13	13	13	0	1	0	0	2	0	0	.000	1	0	0	0	0.2	1.000
1979		3	2	.600	5.35	25	0	0	37	33	30	32	0	3	2	0	7	4	0	.571	1	2	0	0	0.1	1.000
1980		10	8	.556	3.08	53	12	0	190	126	84	182	1	3	8	4	46	2	0	.043	12	25	3	2	0.8	.925
1981		12	9	.571	3.29	25	25	10	175	142	61	151	0	0	0	0	59	4	0	.068	10	19	2	1	1.2	.935
1982		14	13	.519	2.79	35	34	13	257.2	202	71	274	2	1	0	0	84	14	0	.167	10	29	3	1	1.2	.929
1983		17	13	.567	2.70	34	34	18	273.2	207	95	242	3	0	0	0	88	11	0	.125	22	28	5	1	1.6	.909
1984		18	7	**.720**	3.53	33	33	13	237.1	181	87	185	0	0	0	0	87	18	1	.207	12	22	3	1	1.1	.919

Year	Team		W	L	PCT	ERA	G	GS	CG	IP	H	BB	SO	ShO	Relief Pitching W	L	SV	Batting AB	H	HR	BA	PO	A	E	DP	TC/G	FA

Mario Soto *continued*

Year	Team		W	L	PCT	ERA	G	GS	CG	IP	H	BB	SO	ShO	W	L	SV	AB	H	HR	BA	PO	A	E	DP	TC/G	FA
1985			12	15	.444	3.58	36	36	9	256.2	196	104	214	1	0	0	0	83	11	0	.133	13	34	2	0	1.4	.959
1986			5	10	.333	4.71	19	19	1	105	113	46	67	1	0	0	0	27	3	0	.111	3	16	1	1	1.1	.950
1987			3	2	.600	5.12	6	6	0	31.2	34	12	11	0	0	0	0	12	1	0	.083	2	6	0	0	1.3	1.000
1988			3	7	.300	4.66	14	14	3	87	88	28	34	1	0	0	0	22	1	0	.045	5	12	3	1	1.4	.850
12 yrs.			100	92	.521	3.47	297	224	72	1730	1395	657	1449	13	8	10	4	530	70	1	.132	95	203	22	9	1.1	.931

LEAGUE CHAMPIONSHIP SERIES

1979	CIN	N	0	0	–	0.00	1	0	0	2	0	0	1	0	0	0	0	0	0	0	–	0	0	0	0	0.0	–

Mark Souza

SOUZA, KENNETH MARK
B. Feb. 1, 1954, Redwood City, Calif.
BL TL 6' 180 lbs.

1980	OAK	A	0	0	–	7.71	5	0	0	7	9	5	2	0	0	0	0	0	0	0	–	1	0	0	0	0.2	1.000

Bill Sowders

SOWDERS, WILLIAM JEFFERSON
Brother of Len Sowders. Brother of John Sowders.
B. Nov. 29, 1864, Louisville, Ky. D. Feb. 2, 1951, Indianapolis, Ind.
BR TR 6'

1888	BOS	N	19	15	.559	2.07	36	35	34	317	278	73	132	2	0	0	0	122	18	0	.148	23	69	8	1	2.8	.920
1889	2 teams						BOS N	(7G 1–2)			PIT N	(13G 6–5)															
"	total		7	7	.500	6.37	20	15	12	94.2	147	52	43	0	2	0	2	65	17	0	.262	11	30	3	0	2.2	.932
1890	PIT	N	3	8	.273	4.42	15	11	9	106	117	24	30	0	1	1	0	50	9	0	.180	7	9	3	0	1.3	.842
3 yrs.			29	30	.492	3.34	71	61	55	517.2	542	149	205	2	3	1	2	237	44	0	.186	41	108	14	1	2.3	.914

John Sowders

SOWDERS, JOHN
Brother of Len Sowders. Brother of Bill Sowders.
B. Dec. 10, 1866, Louisville, Ky. D. July 29, 1908, Indianapolis, Ind.
BR TL 6'

1887	IND	N	0	0	–	21.00	1	0	0	3	11	5	0	0	0	0	0	2	0	0	.000	0	0	2	0	2.0	–
1889	KC	AA	6	16	.273	4.82	25	23	20	185	204	105	104	0	0	0	1	87	19	0	.218	5	27	6	0	1.5	.842
1890	BKN	P	19	16	.543	3.82	39	37	28	309	358	161	91	1	0	0	0	132	25	1	.189	7	75	7	1	2.3	.921
3 yrs.			25	32	.439	4.29	65	60	48	497	573	271	195	1	0	0	1	221	44	1	.199	12	102	15	1	2.0	.884

Bob Spade

SPADE, ROBERT
B. Jan. 4, 1877, Akron, Ohio D. Sept. 7, 1924, Cincinnati, Ohio
BR TR 5'10" 190 lbs.

1907	CIN	N	1	2	.333	1.00	3	3	3	27	21	9	7	1	0	0	0	7	2	0	.286	0	5	1	1	2.0	.833
1908			17	12	.586	2.74	35	28	22	249.1	230	85	74	2	1	1	1	87	17	0	.195	4	57	6	2	1.9	.910
1909			5	5	.500	2.85	14	13	8	98	91	39	31	0	1	0	0	34	10	0	.294	2	9	2	0	0.9	.846
1910	2 teams						CIN N	(3G 1–2)			STL A	(7G 1–3)															
"	total		2	5	.286	5.19	10	8	3	52	69	26	9	1	0	0	0	16	3	0	.188	1	14	0	0	1.5	1.000
4 yrs.			25	24	.510	2.96	62	52	36	426.1	411	159	121	4	2	1	1	144	32	0	.222	7	85	9	3	1.6	.911

Warren Spahn

SPAHN, WARREN EDWARD
B. Apr. 23, 1921, Buffalo, N. Y.
Hall of Fame 1973.
BL TL 6' 172 lbs.

1942	BOS	N	0	0	–	5.74	4	2	1	15.2	25	11	7	0	0	0	0	6	1	0	.167	1	2	0	0	0.8	1.000
1946			8	5	.615	2.94	24	16	8	125.2	107	36	67	0	0	1	1	43	7	0	.163	2	16	2	0	0.8	.900
1947			21	10	.677	2.33	40	35	22	289.2	245	84	123	7	0	0	3	98	16	0	.163	5	48	1	1	1.4	.981
1948			15	12	.556	3.71	36	35	16	257	237	77	114	3	0	0	1	90	15	1	.167	4	52	1	3	1.6	.982
1949			21	14	.600	3.07	38	38	25	302.1	283	86	151	4	0	0	2	111	18	2	.162	14	41	4	2	1.6	.932
1950			21	17	.553	3.16	41	39	25	293	248	111	191	1	0	1	1	106	23	1	.217	9	55	8	3	1.8	.889
1951			22	14	.611	2.98	39	36	26	310.2	278	109	164	7	0	3	0	116	22	1	.190	7	50	3	1	1.5	.950
1952			14	19	.424	2.98	40	35	19	290	263	73	183	5	0	1	3	112	18	2	.161	18	56	5	4	2.0	.937
1953	MIL	N	23	7	.767	2.10	35	32	24	265.2	211	70	148	5	0	0	3	105	23	2	.219	12	53	4	7	2.0	.942
1954			21	12	.636	3.14	39	34	23	283.1	262	86	136	1	1	1	3	101	21	1	.208	12	57	4	4	1.9	.945
1955			17	14	.548	3.26	39	32	16	245.2	249	65	110	1	0	3	1	81	17	4	.210	13	44	3	4	1.5	.950
1956			20	11	.645	2.78	39	35	20	281.1	249	52	128	3	0	0	3	105	22	3	.210	16	41	1	7	1.5	.983
1957			21	11	.656	2.69	39	35	18	271	241	78	111	4	0	1	3	94	13	2	.138	18	47	0	4	1.7	1.000
1958			22	11	.667	3.07	38	36	23	290	257	76	150	2	0	1	1	108	36	2	.333	11	67	2	7	2.1	.975
1959			21	15	.583	2.96	40	36	21	292	282	70	143	4	0	3	0	104	24	2	.231	14	45	3	4	1.6	.952
1960			21	10	.677	3.50	40	33	18	267.2	254	74	154	4	2	2	0	95	14	3	.147	14	59	3	7	1.9	.961
1961			21	13	.618	3.02	38	34	21	262.2	236	64	115	4	1	3	0	94	21	4	.223	16	63	2	7	2.1	.975
1962			18	14	.563	3.04	34	34	22	269.1	248	55	118	0	0	0	0	98	18	2	.184	13	55	1	5	2.0	.986
1963			23	7	.767	2.60	33	33	22	259.2	241	49	102	7	0	0	0	90	16	2	.178	11	71	3	8	2.6	.965
1964			6	13	.316	5.29	38	25	4	173.2	204	52	78	1	0	0	4	59	11	1	.186	4	36	6	2	1.2	.870
1965	2 teams						NY N	(20G 4–12)			SF N	(16G 3–4)															
"	total		7	16	.304	4.01	36	30	8	197.2	210	56	90	0	0	0	0	56	7	0	.125	8	41	2	2	1.4	.961
21 yrs.			363	245	.597	3.09	750	665	382	5243.2	4830	1434	2583	63	5	18	29	1872	363	35	.194	222	999	58	82	1.7	.955
			5th	10th						7th				6th													

WORLD SERIES

1948	BOS	N	1	1	.500	3.00	3	1	0	12	10	3	12	1	0	0	0	4	0	0	.000	0	3	0	0	1.0	1.000
1957	MIL	N	1	1	.500	4.70	2	2	1	15.1	18	2	2	0	0	0	0	4	0	0	.000	1	3	0	0	2.0	1.000
1958			2	1	.667	2.20	3	3	2	28.2	19	8	18	1	0	0	0	12	4	0	.333	2	6	0	0	2.7	1.000
3 yrs.			4	3	.571	3.05	8	6	3	56	47	13	32	1	0	0	0	20	4	0	.200	3	12	0	0	1.9	1.000

Al Spalding

SPALDING, ALBERT GOODWILL
B. Sept. 2, 1850, Byron, Ill. D. Sept. 9, 1915, San Diego, Calif.
Manager 1876–77.
Hall of Fame 1939.
BR TR 6'1" 170 lbs.

1876	CHI	N	47	13	.783	1.75	61	60	53	528.2	542	26	39	8	0	0	0	292	91	0	.312	45	92	7	7	2.4	.951
1877			1	0	1.000	3.27	4	1	0	11	17	0	2	0	1	0	1	254	65	0	.256	2	6	1	0	2.3	.889
1878			0	0	–	0.00	0	0	0	0	0	0	0	0	0	0	0	4	2	0	.500	0	0	0	0	0.0	–
3 yrs.			48	13	.787	1.78	65	61	53	539.2	559	26	41	8	1	0	1	*				47	98	8	7	2.4	.948

Year	Team		W	L	PCT	ERA	G	GS	CG	IP	H	BB	SO	ShO	Relief Pitching W	L	SV	Batting AB	H	HR	BA	PO	A	E	DP	TC/G	FA

Bill Spanswick

SPANSWICK, WILLIAM HENRY
B. July 8, 1938, Springfield, Mass.   BL TL 6'3"   195 lbs.

| 1964 | BOS | A | 2 | 3 | .400 | 6.89 | 29 | 7 | 0 | 65.1 | 75 | 44 | 55 | 0 | 1 | 0 | 0 | 14 | 4 | 0 | .286 | 3 | 13 | 0 | 1 | 0.6 | 1.000 |

Tully Sparks

SPARKS, THOMAS FRANK
B. Dec. 12, 1874, Aetna, Ga.   D. July 15, 1937, Anniston, Ala.   BR TR

1897	PHI	N	0	1	.000	10.13	1	1	1	8	12	4	0	0	0	0	0	3	0	0	.000	0	3	0	0	3.0	1.000
1899	PIT	N	8	6	.571	3.86	28	17	8	170	180	82	53	0	2	1	0	62	8	0	.129	5	41	8	1	1.9	.852
1901	MIL	A	7	16	.304	3.51	29	26	18	210	228	93	62	0	0	0	0	71	12	0	.169	9	60	8	1	2.7	.896
1902	2 teams	NY N	(15G 4–10)			BOS A	(17G 7–9)																				
"	total		11	19	.367	3.60	32	28	26	257.2	274	80	77	1	1	1	1	89	13	0	.146	13	84	5	4	3.2	.951
1903	PHI	N	11	15	.423	2.72	28	28	27	248	248	56	88	0	0	0	0	92	10	0	.109	14	59	8	0	2.9	.901
1904			7	18	.280	2.65	26	25	19	200.2	208	43	67	3	0	1	0	76	8	0	.105	11	35	4	3	1.9	.920
1905			14	11	.560	2.18	34	26	20	260	217	73	98	1	1	1	0	94	12	0	.128	9	45	0	3	1.6	1.000
1906			19	16	.543	2.16	42	37	29	316.2	244	62	114	6	1	0	3	104	16	0	.154	20	66	3	4	2.1	.966
1907			22	8	.733	2.00	33	31	24	265	221	51	90	3	1	0	1	89	3	0	.034	10	50	4	1	1.9	.938
1908			16	15	.516	2.60	33	31	24	263.1	251	51	85	2	0	0	2	77	4	0	.052	15	65	6	3	2.6	.930
1909			6	11	.353	2.96	24	16	6	121.2	126	32	40	1	2	0	0	36	5	0	.139	4	31	0	1	1.5	1.000
1910			0	2	.000	6.00	3	3	0	15	22	2	4	0	0	0	0	5	0	0	.000	0	5	0	0	1.7	1.000
12 yrs.			121	138	.467	2.79	313	269	202	2336	2231	629	778	19	8	4	8	798	91	0	.114	110	544	46	20	2.2	.934

Joe Sparma

SPARMA, JOSEPH BLASE
B. Feb. 4, 1942, Massillon, Ohio   D. May 14, 1986, Columbus, Ohio   BR TR 6'1"   190 lbs.

1964	DET	A	5	6	.455	3.00	21	11	3	84	62	45	71	2	1	1	0	25	4	0	.160	5	16	1	2	1.0	.955
1965			13	8	.619	3.18	30	28	6	167	142	75	127	0	1	0	0	52	7	0	.135	11	25	6	1	1.4	.857
1966			2	7	.222	5.30	29	13	0	91.2	103	52	61	0	0	0	0	23	5	0	.217	5	8	2	1	0.5	.867
1967			16	9	.640	3.76	37	37	11	217.2	186	85	153	5	0	0	0	74	4	0	.054	16	20	2	1	0.9	.947
1968			10	10	.500	3.70	34	31	7	182.1	169	77	110	1	1	0	0	60	8	0	.133	9	19	2	0	0.9	.933
1969			6	8	.429	4.76	23	16	3	92.2	78	77	41	2	0	1	0	29	4	0	.138	9	7	0	2	0.7	1.000
1970	MON	N	0	4	.000	7.14	9	6	1	29	34	25	23	0	0	0	0	6	0	0	.000	2	3	2	0	0.8	.714
7 yrs.			52	52	.500	3.95	183	142	31	864.1	774	436	586	10	3	2	0	269	32	0	.119	57	98	15	7	0.9	.912

WORLD SERIES

| 1968 | DET | A | 0 | 0 | – | 54.00 | 1 | 0 | 0 | .1 | 2 | 0 | 0 | 0 | 0 | 0 | 0 | 0 | 0 | 0 | – | 0 | 0 | 0 | 0 | 0.0 | – |

Tris Speaker

SPEAKER, TRISTRAM E (The Grey Eagle, Spoke)
B. Apr. 4, 1888, Hubbard, Tex.   D. Dec. 8, 1958, Lake Whitney, Tex.   BL TL 5'11½" 193 lbs.
Manager 1919-26.
Hall of Fame 1937.

| 1914 | BOS | A | 0 | 0 | – | 9.00 | 1 | 0 | 0 | 1 | 2 | 0 | 0 | 0 | 0 | 0 | 0 | * | | | | 0 | 1 | 0 | 1 | 1.0 | 1.000 |

Cliff Speck

SPECK, ROBERT CLIFFORD
B. Aug. 8, 1956, Portland, Ore.   BR TR 6'4"   196 lbs.

| 1986 | ATL | N | 2 | 1 | .667 | 4.13 | 13 | 1 | 0 | 28.1 | 25 | 15 | 21 | 0 | 1 | 1 | 0 | 3 | 0 | 0 | .000 | 1 | 5 | 0 | 0 | 0.5 | 1.000 |

Byron Speece

SPEECE, BYRON FRANKLIN
B. Jan. 6, 1897, West Baden, Ind.   D. Sept. 29, 1974, Elgin, Ore.   BR TR 5'11" 170 lbs.

1924	WAS	A	2	1	.667	2.65	21	1	0	54.1	60	27	15	0	2	0	0	20	3	0	.150	2	19	1	0	1.0	.955
1925	CLE	A	3	5	.375	4.28	28	3	3	90.1	106	28	26	0	2	3	1	31	5	0	.161	4	23	1	2	1.0	.964
1926			0	0	–	0.00	2	0	0	3	1	2	1	0	0	0	0	0	0	0	–	0	2	0	1	1.0	1.000
1930	PHI	N	0	0	–	13.27	11	0	0	19.2	41	4	9	0	0	0	0	3	1	0	.333	2	3	0	0	0.5	1.000
4 yrs.			5	6	.455	4.73	62	4	3	167.1	208	61	51	0	4	3	1	54	9	0	.167	8	47	2	3	0.9	.965

WORLD SERIES

| 1924 | WAS | A | 0 | 0 | – | 9.00 | 1 | 0 | 0 | 1 | 1 | 0 | 0 | 0 | 0 | 0 | 0 | 0 | 0 | 0 | – | 0 | 2 | 0 | 0 | 2.0 | 1.000 |

Floyd Speer

SPEER, FLOYD VERNIE
B. Jan. 27, 1913, Booneville, Ark.   D. Mar. 22, 1969, Little Rock, Ark.   BR TR 6'   180 lbs.

1943	CHI	A	0	0	–	9.00	1	0	0	1	1	2	1	0	0	0	0	0	0	0	–	0	1	0	0	1.0	1.000
1944			0	0	–	9.00	2	0	0	2	4	0	1	0	0	0	0	0	0	0	–	0	0	0	0	0.0	
2 yrs.			0	0	–	9.00	3	0	0	3	5	2	2	0	0	0	0	0	0	0	–	0	1	0	0	0.3	1.000

Kid Speer

SPEER, GEORGE NATHAN
B. June 16, 1886, Corning Mo.,   D. Jan. 13, 1946, Edmonton, Alta., Canada   BL TL

| 1909 | DET | A | 4 | 4 | .500 | 2.83 | 12 | 8 | 4 | 76.1 | 88 | 13 | 12 | 1 | 1 | 1 | 1 | 25 | 3 | 0 | .120 | 4 | 30 | 2 | 2 | 3.0 | .944 |

George Spencer

SPENCER, GEORGE ELWELL
B. July 7, 1926, Columbus, Ohio   BR TR 6'1"   215 lbs.

1950	NY	N	1	0	1.000	2.49	10	1	1	25.1	12	7	5	0	0	0	0	4	0	0	.000	0	6	0	0	0.6	1.000
1951			10	4	.714	3.75	57	4	2	132	125	56	36	0	8	2	6	32	4	0	.125	13	29	4	2	0.8	.913
1952			3	5	.375	5.55	35	4	0	60	57	21	27	0	3	4	3	10	2	0	.200	5	10	1	1	0.5	.938
1953			0	0	–	7.71	1	0	0	2.1	3	2	1	0	0	0	0	0	0	0	–	0	0	0	0	0.0	–
1954			1	0	1.000	3.65	6	0	0	12.1	9	8	4	0	1	0	0	3	0	0	.000	2	4	0	1	1.0	1.000
1955			0	0	–	5.40	1	0	0	1.2	1	3	0	0	0	0	0	0	0	0	–	0	1	0	0	1.0	1.000
1958	DET	A	1	0	1.000	2.70	7	0	0	10	11	4	5	0	1	0	0	0	0	0	–	0	3	0	0	0.4	1.000
1960			0	1	.000	3.52	5	0	0	7.2	10	5	4	0	0	1	0	0	0	0	.000	0	1	0	0	0.2	1.000
8 yrs.			16	10	.615	4.05	122	9	3	251.1	228	106	82	0	13	7	9	50	6	0	.120	20	54	5	4	0.6	.937

WORLD SERIES

| 1951 | NY | N | 0 | 0 | – | 18.90 | 2 | 0 | 0 | 3.1 | 6 | 3 | 0 | 0 | 0 | 0 | 0 | 0 | 0 | 0 | – | 0 | 1 | 0 | 0 | 0.5 | 1.000 |

Year	Team		W	L	PCT	ERA	G	GS	CG	IP	H	BB	SO	ShO	Relief Pitching			Batting			BA	PO	A	E	DP	TC/G	FA
															W	L	SV	AB	H	HR							

Glenn Spencer

SPENCER, GLENN EDWARD
B. Sept. 11, 1905, Corning, N. Y.   D. Dec. 30, 1958, Binghamton, N. Y.   BR TR 5'11" 155 lbs.

Year	Team		W	L	PCT	ERA	G	GS	CG	IP	H	BB	SO	ShO	W	L	SV	AB	H	HR	BA	PO	A	E	DP	TC/G	FA
1928	PIT	N	0	0	–	1.59	4	0	0	5.2	4	3	2	0	0	0	0	1	0	0	.000	0	0	1	0	0.3	–
1930			8	9	.471	5.40	41	10	5	156.2	185	63	60	0	3	5	4	53	6	0	.113	4	25	3	1	0.8	.906
1931			11	12	.478	3.42	38	18	11	186.2	180	65	51	1	3	3	3	52	5	0	.096	7	39	3	2	1.3	.939
1932			4	8	.333	4.97	39	13	5	137.2	167	44	35	1	2	1	1	37	6	0	.162	4	25	2	2	0.8	.935
1933	NY	N	0	2	.000	5.13	17	3	1	47.1	52	26	14	0	0	0	0	12	2	0	.167	5	10	0	2	0.9	1.000
5 yrs.			23	31	.426	4.53	139	44	22	534	588	201	162	2	8	9	8	155	19	0	.123	20	99	9	7	0.9	.930

Hack Spencer

SPENCER, FRED CALVIN
B. Apr. 25, 1885, Minneapolis, Minn.   D. Feb. 5, 1969, St. Anthony, Minn.   BR TR 5'10½" 172 lbs.

Year	Team		W	L	PCT	ERA	G	GS	CG	IP	H	BB	SO	ShO	W	L	SV	AB	H	HR	BA	PO	A	E	DP	TC/G	FA
1912	STL	A	0	0	–	0.00	1	0	0	1.2	2	0	0	0	0	0	0	0	0	0	–	0	1	0	0	1.0	1.000

Bob Spicer

SPICER, ROBERT OBERTON
B. Apr. 11, 1925, Richmond, Va.   BL TR 5'10" 173 lbs.

Year	Team		W	L	PCT	ERA	G	GS	CG	IP	H	BB	SO	ShO	W	L	SV	AB	H	HR	BA	PO	A	E	DP	TC/G	FA
1955	KC	A	0	0	–	33.75	2	0	0	2.2	9	4	2	0	0	0	0	1	0	0	.000	0	0	0	0	0.0	–
1956			0	0	–	19.29	2	0	0	2.1	6	1	0	0	0	0	0	0	0	0	–	0	1	0	0	0.5	1.000
2 yrs.			0	0	–	27.00	4	0	0	5	15	5	2	0	0	0	0	1	0	0	.000	0	1	0	0	0.3	1.000

Dan Spillner

SPILLNER, DANIEL RAY
B. Nov. 27, 1951, Casper, Wyo.   BR TR 6'1" 190 lbs.

Year	Team		W	L	PCT	ERA	G	GS	CG	IP	H	BB	SO	ShO	W	L	SV	AB	H	HR	BA	PO	A	E	DP	TC/G	FA
1974	SD	N	9	11	.450	4.01	30	25	5	148	153	70	95	2	0	0	0	43	1	0	.023	6	16	0	0	0.7	1.000
1975			5	13	.278	4.26	37	25	3	167	194	63	104	0	0	0	1	45	6	0	.133	13	21	3	2	1.0	.919
1976			2	11	.154	5.06	32	14	0	106.2	120	55	57	0	1	1	0	25	1	0	.040	7	21	3	3	1.0	.903
1977			7	6	.538	3.73	76	0	0	123	130	60	74	0	7	6	6	17	2	0	.118	5	9	1	1	0.2	.933
1978	2 teams	SD N (17G 1–0)				CLE A (36G 3–1)																					
"	total		4	1	.800	3.94	53	0	0	82.1	86	28	64	0	4	1	3	0	0	0	–	1	6	0	1	0.1	1.000
1979	CLE	A	9	5	.643	4.61	49	13	3	158	153	64	97	0	3	3	1	0	0	0	–	9	18	0	0	0.6	1.000
1980			16	11	.593	5.29	34	30	7	194	225	74	100	1	1	0	0	0	0	0	–	9	17	0	2	0.8	1.000
1981			4	4	.500	3.15	32	5	1	97	86	39	59	0	3	0	7	0	0	0	–	6	16	1	1	0.7	.957
1982			12	10	.545	2.49	65	0	0	133.2	117	45	90	0	12	10	21	0	0	0	–	6	7	1	0	0.2	.929
1983			2	9	.182	5.07	60	0	0	92.1	117	38	48	0	2	9	8	0	0	0	–	4	8	1	0	0.2	.923
1984	2 teams	CLE A (14G 0–5)				CHI A (22G 1–0)																					
"	total		1	5	.167	4.89	36	8	0	99.1	121	36	49	0	1	0	2	0	0	0	–	11	16	0	0	0.8	1.000
1985	CHI	A	4	3	.571	3.44	52	3	0	91.2	83	33	41	0	4	3	0	0	0	0	–	4	2	1	0	0.1	.857
12 yrs.			75	89	.457	4.21	556	123	19	1493	1585	605	878	3	39	33	50	130	10	0	.077	81	157	11	10	0.4	.956

Scipio Spinks

SPINKS, SCIPIO RONALD
B. July 12, 1947, Chicago, Ill.   BR TR 6'1" 183 lbs.

Year	Team		W	L	PCT	ERA	G	GS	CG	IP	H	BB	SO	ShO	W	L	SV	AB	H	HR	BA	PO	A	E	DP	TC/G	FA
1969	HOU	N	0	0	–	0.00	1	0	0	2	1	1	4	0	0	0	0	0	0	0	–	0	0	0	0	0.0	–
1970			0	1	.000	9.64	5	2	0	14	17	9	6	0	0	0	0	3	0	0	.000	0	0	0	0	0.0	–
1971			1	0	1.000	3.72	5	3	1	29	22	13	26	0	0	0	0	9	2	0	.222	1	4	0	0	1.0	1.000
1972	STL	N	5	5	.500	2.67	16	16	6	118	96	59	93	0	0	0	0	42	7	0	.167	2	21	1	1	1.5	.958
1973			1	5	.167	4.89	8	8	0	38.2	39	25	25	0	0	0	0	11	2	1	.182	5	7	0	0	1.5	1.000
5 yrs.			7	11	.389	3.70	35	29	7	201.2	175	107	154	0	0	0	0	65	11	1	.169	8	32	1	1	1.2	.976

Paul Splittorff

SPLITTORFF, PAUL WILLIAM JR
B. Oct. 8, 1946, Evansville, Ind.   BL TL 6'3" 205 lbs.

Year	Team		W	L	PCT	ERA	G	GS	CG	IP	H	BB	SO	ShO	W	L	SV	AB	H	HR	BA	PO	A	E	DP	TC/G	FA
1970	KC	A	0	1	.000	7.00	2	1	0	9	16	5	10	0	0	0	0	2	1	0	.500	0	0	0	1	0.5	1.000
1971			8	9	.471	2.69	22	22	6	144	129	35	80	3	0	0	0	48	5	0	.104	7	32	2	3	1.9	.951
1972			12	12	.500	3.12	35	33	12	216.1	189	67	140	2	0	0	0	71	16	0	.225	6	51	0	5	1.6	1.000
1973			20	11	.645	3.99	38	38	12	261.2	279	78	110	3	0	0	0	0	0	0	–	9	46	1	7	1.5	.982
1974			13	19	.406	4.10	36	36	8	226	252	75	90	1	0	0	0	0	0	0	–	8	39	2	2	1.4	.959
1975			9	10	.474	3.17	35	23	6	159	156	56	76	3	1	0	1	0	0	0	–	10	33	1	4	1.3	.977
1976			11	8	.579	3.96	26	23	5	159	169	59	59	1	0	0	0	0	0	0	–	9	30	0	5	1.5	1.000
1977			16	6	.727	3.69	37	37	6	229	243	83	99	2	0	0	0	0	0	0	–	9	38	2	3	1.3	.959
1978			19	13	.594	3.40	39	38	13	262	244	60	76	2	0	0	0	0	0	0	–	18	45	2	4	1.7	.969
1979			15	17	.469	4.24	36	35	11	240	248	77	77	0	0	0	0	0	0	0	–	15	27	3	3	1.3	.933
1980			14	11	.560	4.15	34	33	4	204	236	43	53	0	0	0	0	0	0	0	–	14	30	0	1	1.3	1.000
1981			5	5	.500	4.36	21	15	1	99	111	23	48	0	1	0	0	0	0	0	–	2	22	0	2	1.1	1.000
1982			10	10	.500	4.28	29	28	0	162	166	57	74	0	0	0	0	0	0	0	–	7	24	1	4	1.1	.969
1983			13	8	.619	3.63	27	27	4	156	159	52	61	0	0	0	0	0	0	0	–	9	23	1	2	1.2	.970
1984			1	3	.250	7.71	12	3	0	28	47	10	4	0	1	0	0	0	0	0	–	2	9	0	0	0.9	1.000
15 yrs.			166	143	.537	3.81	429	392	88	2555	2644	780	1057	17	3	0	1	121	22	0	.182	125	450	15	49	1.4	.975

LEAGUE CHAMPIONSHIP SERIES

Year	Team		W	L	PCT	ERA	G	GS	CG	IP	H	BB	SO	ShO	W	L	SV	AB	H	HR	BA	PO	A	E	DP	TC/G	FA
1976	KC	A	1	0	1.000	1.93	2	2	0	9.1	7	5	2	0	0	0	0	0	0	0	–	0	1	0	0	0.5	1.000
1977			1	0	1.000	2.40	2	2	0	15	14	3	4	0	0	0	0	0	0	0	–	0	3	0	0	1.5	1.000
1978			0	0	–	4.91	1	1	0	7.1	9	2	2	0	0	0	0	0	0	0	–	0	0	0	0	0.0	–
1980			0	0	–	1.69	1	1	0	5.1	5	2	3	0	0	0	0	0	0	0	–	1	0	0	1	1.0	1.000
4 yrs.			2	0	1.000	2.68	6	4	0	37	35	10	11	0	0	0	0	0	0	0	–	0	4	0	1	0.8	1.000

WORLD SERIES

Year	Team		W	L	PCT	ERA	G	GS	CG	IP	H	BB	SO	ShO	W	L	SV	AB	H	HR	BA	PO	A	E	DP	TC/G	FA
1980	KC	A	0	0	–	5.40	1	0	0	1.2	4	0	0	0	0	0	0	0	0	0	–	0	1	0	1	1.0	1.000

Carl Spongberg

SPONGBERG, CARL GUSTAV
B. May 21, 1884, Idaho Falls, Ida.   D. July 21, 1938, Los Angeles, Calif.   BR TR 6'2" 208 lbs.

Year	Team		W	L	PCT	ERA	G	GS	CG	IP	H	BB	SO	ShO	W	L	SV	AB	H	HR	BA	PO	A	E	DP	TC/G	FA
1908	CHI	N	0	0	–	9.00	1	0	0	7	9	6	4	0	0	0	0	3	2	0	.667	0	3	0	0	3.0	1.000

Karl Spooner

SPOONER, KARL BENJAMIN
B. June 23, 1931, Oriskany Falls, N. Y.   D. Apr. 10, 1984, Vero Beach, Fla.   BR TL 6' 185 lbs.

Year	Team		W	L	PCT	ERA	G	GS	CG	IP	H	BB	SO	ShO	W	L	SV	AB	H	HR	BA	PO	A	E	DP	TC/G	FA
1954	BKN	N	2	0	1.000	0.00	2	2	2	18	7	6	27	2	0	0	0	6	1	0	.167	1	0	0	0	0.5	1.000

Year	Team		W	L	PCT	ERA	G	GS	CG	IP	H	BB	SO	ShO	Relief Pitching W	L	SV	Batting AB	H	HR	BA	PO	A	E	DP	TC/G	FA

Karl Spooner *continued*

1955			8	6	.571	3.65	29	14	2	98.2	79	41	78	1	5	1	2	28	8	0	.286	9	11	0	0	0.7	1.000
2 yrs.			10	6	.625	3.09	31	16	4	116.2	86	47	105	3	5	1	2	34	9	0	.265	10	11	0	0	0.7	1.000
WORLD SERIES																											
1955	BKN	N	0	1	.000	13.50	2	1	0	3.1	4	3	6	0	0	0	0	0	0	0	—	0	1	0	0	0.5	1.000

Homer Spragins

SPRAGINS, HOMER FRANKLIN
B. Nov. 9, 1920, Grenada, Miss.   BR TR 6'1" 190 lbs.

| 1947 | PHI | N | 0 | 0 | — | 6.75 | 4 | 0 | 0 | 5.1 | 3 | 3 | 3 | 0 | 0 | 0 | 0 | 0 | 0 | 0 | — | 2 | 0 | 0 | 0 | 0.5 | 1.000 |

Charlie Sprague

SPRAGUE, CHARLES WELLINGTON
B. Oct. 10, 1864, Cleveland, Ohio   D. Dec. 31, 1912, Des Moines, Iowa   BL TL 5'11" 150 lbs.

1887	CHI	N	1	0	1.000	4.91	3	3	2	22	24	13	9	0	0	0	0	13	2	0	.154	0	2	1	0	1.0	.667
1889	CLE	N	0	2	.000	8.47	2	2	2	17	27	10	8	0	0	0	0	7	1	0	.143	0	6	1	1	3.5	.857
1890	TOL	AA	9	5	.643	3.89	19	12	9	122.2	111	78	59	0	1	2	0	199	47	1	.236	7	13	1	0	1.1	.952
3 yrs.			10	7	.588	4.51	24	17	13	161.2	162	101	76	0	1	2	0	*				7	21	3	1	1.3	.903

Ed Sprague

SPRAGUE, EDWARD NELSON
B. Sept. 16, 1945, Boston, Mass.   BR TR 6'4" 195 lbs.

1968	OAK	A	3	4	.429	3.28	47	1	0	68.2	51	34	34	0	3	3	4	7	0	0	.000	8	15	2	0	0.5	.920
1969			1	1	.500	4.47	27	0	0	46.1	47	31	20	0	1	1	2	5	1	0	.200	5	17	1	1	0.9	.957
1971	CIN	N	1	0	1.000	0.00	7	0	0	11	8	1	7	0	1	0	0	1	0	0	.000	0	1	0	0	0.1	—
1972			3	3	.500	4.13	33	1	0	56.2	55	26	25	0	2	3	0	7	0	0	.000	2	6	1	1	0.3	.889
1973	3 teams	CIN N (28G 1–3)				STL N	(8G 0–0)			MIL A		(7G 0–1)															
"	total		1	4	.200	5.43	43	0	0	56.1	56	40	24	0	1	4	2	2	0	0	.000	6	11	2	1	0.4	.895
1974	MIL	A	7	2	.778	2.39	20	10	3	94	94	31	57	0	0	0	0	0	0	0	—	8	9	2	2	1.0	.895
1975			1	7	.125	4.68	18	11	0	67.1	81	40	21	0	0	2	1	0	0	0	—	7	8	3	0	1.0	.833
1976			0	2	.000	6.75	3	0	0	8	14	3	0	0	0	0	0	0	0	0	—	0	4	0	1	1.3	1.000
8 yrs.			17	23	.425	3.84	198	23	3	408.1	406	206	188	0	8	15	9	22	1	0	.045	36	70	12	6	0.6	.898

Jack Spring

SPRING, JACK RUSSELL
B. Mar. 11, 1933, Spokane, Wash.   BR TL 6'1" 175 lbs.

1955	PHI	N	0	1	.000	6.75	2	0	0	2.2	2	1	2	0	1	0	0	1	0	0	.000	0	0	0	0	0.0	—
1957	BOS	A	0	0	—	0.00	1	0	0	1	0	0	2	0	0	0	0	0	0	0	—	0	0	0	0	0.0	—
1958	WAS	A	0	0	—	14.14	3	1	0	7	16	7	1	0	0	0	0	2	0	0	.000	0	1	0	1	0.3	1.000
1961	LA	A	3	0	1.000	4.26	18	4	0	38	35	15	27	0	1	0	0	8	0	0	.000	2	6	1	0	0.5	.889
1962			4	2	.667	4.02	57	0	0	65	66	30	31	0	4	2	6	11	1	0	.091	4	16	2	2	0.4	.909
1963			3	0	1.000	3.05	45	0	0	38.1	40	9	13	0	3	0	2	3	1	0	.333	2	10	0	0	0.3	1.000
1964	3 teams	LA A (6G 1–0)				CHI N	(7G 0–0)			STL N	(2G 0–0)																
"	total		1	0	1.000	4.38	15	0	0	12.1	15	6	1	0	1	0	0	0	0	0	—	0	4	1	1	0.3	.800
1965	CLE	A	1	2	.333	3.74	14	0	0	21.2	21	10	9	0	1	2	0	3	1	0	.333	1	2	0	0	0.2	1.000
8 yrs.			12	5	.706	4.26	155	5	0	186	195	78	86	0	9	5	8	28	3	0	.107	9	39	4	4	0.3	.923

Brad Springer

SPRINGER, BRADFORD LOUIS
B. May 9, 1904, Detroit, Mich.   D. Jan. 4, 1970, Birmingham, Mich.   BL TL 6' 155 lbs.

1925	STL	A	0	0	—	3.00	2	0	0	3	1	7	0	0	0	0	0	0	0	0	—	2	0	0	0	1.0	1.000
1926	CIN	N	0	0	—	6.75	1	0	0	1.1	2	2	1	0	0	0	0	0	0	0	.000	0	0	0	0	0.0	—
2 yrs.			0	0	—	4.15	3	0	0	4.1	3	9	1	0	0	0	0	1	0	0	.000	2	0	0	0	0.7	1.000

Ed Springer

SPRINGER, EDWARD H.
B. Feb. 8, 1861, California   D. Apr. 24, 1926, Los Angeles, Calif.   6'2" 187 lbs.

| 1889 | LOU | AA | 0 | 1 | .000 | 9.00 | 1 | 1 | 1 | 5 | 8 | 2 | 1 | 0 | 0 | 0 | 0 | 2 | 0 | 0 | .000 | 1 | 0 | 2 | 0 | 3.0 | .333 |

Charlie Sproull

SPROULL, CHARLES WILLIAM
B. Jan. 9, 1919, Taylorsville, Ga.   D. Jan. 13, 1980, Rockford, Ill.   BR TR 6'3" 185 lbs.

| 1945 | PHI | N | 4 | 10 | .286 | 5.94 | 34 | 19 | 2 | 130.1 | 158 | 80 | 47 | 0 | 1 | 0 | 1 | 35 | 5 | 0 | .143 | 7 | 21 | 3 | 1 | 0.9 | .903 |

Bob Sprout

SPROUT, ROBERT SAMUEL
B. Dec. 5, 1941, Florian, Pa.   BL TL 6' 165 lbs.

| 1961 | LA | A | 0 | 0 | — | 4.50 | 1 | 1 | 0 | 4 | 4 | 3 | 2 | 0 | 0 | 0 | 0 | 0 | 0 | 0 | — | 0 | 0 | 1 | 0 | 1.0 | — |

Bobby Sprowl

SPROWL, ROBERT JOHN, JR.
B. Apr. 14, 1956, Sandusky, Ohio   BL TL 6'2" 190 lbs.

1978	BOS	A	0	2	.000	6.39	3	3	0	12.2	12	10	10	0	0	0	0	0	0	0	—	0	1	0	0	0.3	1.000
1979	HOU	N	0	0	—	0.00	3	0	0	3	2	2	3	0	0	0	0	0	0	0	—	0	0	0	0	0.0	—
1980			0	0	—	0.00	1	0	0	1	1	1	3	0	0	0	0	0	0	0	—	0	0	0	0	0.0	—
1981			0	1	.000	5.90	15	1	0	29	40	14	18	0	0	1	0	6	1	0	.167	2	3	0	0	0.3	1.000
4 yrs.			0	3	.000	5.40	22	4	0	46.2	54	27	34	0	0	1	0	6	1	0	.167	2	4	0	0	0.3	1.000

Mike Squires

SQUIRES, MICHAEL LYNN
B. Mar. 5, 1952, Kalamazoo, Mich.   BL TL 5'11" 185 lbs.

| 1984 | CHI | A | 0 | 0 | — | 0.00 | 1 | 0 | 0 | .1 | 0 | 0 | 0 | 0 | 0 | 0 | 0 | * | | | | 0 | 0 | 0 | 0 | 0.0 | — |

George Stablein

STABLEIN, GEORGE CHARLES
B. Oct. 29, 1957, Inglewood, Calif.   BR TR 6'4" 185 lbs.

| 1980 | SD | N | 0 | 1 | .000 | 3.00 | 4 | 2 | 0 | 12 | 16 | 3 | 4 | 0 | 0 | 0 | 0 | 3 | 0 | 0 | .000 | 1 | 0 | 0 | 0 | 0.5 | 1.000 |

Year	Team		W	L	PCT	ERA	G	GS	CG	IP	H	BB	SO	ShO	Relief Pitching W	L	SV	Batting AB	H	HR	BA	PO	A	E	DP	TC/G	FA

Eddie Stack

STACK, WILLIAM EDWARD
B. Oct. 24, 1887, Chicago, Ill. D. Aug. 28, 1958, Chicago, Ill.
BR TR 6' 175 lbs.

Year	Team		W	L	PCT	ERA	G	GS	CG	IP	H	BB	SO	ShO	W	L	SV	AB	H	HR	BA	PO	A	E	DP	TC/G	FA
1910	PHI	N	6	7	.462	4.00	20	16	7	117	115	34	48	1	0	0	0	36	3	0	.083	3	27	2	0	1.6	.938
1911			5	5	.500	3.59	13	10	5	77.2	67	41	36	0	0	0	0	24	2	0	.083	1	24	1	0	2.0	.962
1912	BKN	N	7	5	.583	3.36	28	17	4	142	139	55	45	0	2	1	1	52	7	0	.135	2	34	2	1	1.4	.947
1913	2 teams		BKN	N	(23G 4–4)			CHI	N	(11G 4–2)																	
"	total		8	6	.571	3.07	34	16	7	138	135	47	62	2	0	1	1	41	5	0	.122	3	22	0	0	0.8	.926
1914	CHI	N	0	1	.000	4.96	7	1	0	16.1	13	11	9	0	0	0	0	4	0	0	.000	0	6	0	0	0.9	1.000
5 yrs.			26	24	.520	3.52	102	60	23	491	469	188	200	3	2	2	2	157	17	0	.108	9	113	7	1	1.3	.946

Bill Stafford

STAFFORD, WILLIAM CHARLES
B. Aug. 13, 1939, Catskill, N. Y.
BR TR 6'1" 188 lbs.

Year	Team		W	L	PCT	ERA	G	GS	CG	IP	H	BB	SO	ShO	W	L	SV	AB	H	HR	BA	PO	A	E	DP	TC/G	FA
1960	NY	A	3	1	.750	2.25	11	8	2	60	50	18	36	1	0	0	0	22	1	0	.045	7	10	0	2	1.5	1.000
1961			14	9	.609	2.68	36	25	8	195	168	59	101	3	0	2	2	67	12	0	.179	7	29	1	5	1.0	.973
1962			14	9	.609	3.67	35	33	7	213.1	188	77	109	2	0	1	0	78	17	0	.218	12	33	0	1	1.3	1.000
1963			4	8	.333	6.02	28	14	0	89.2	104	42	52	0	2	1	3	24	7	0	.292	5	12	0	1	0.6	1.000
1964			5	0	1.000	2.67	31	1	0	60.2	50	22	39	0	5	0	4	13	1	0	.077	3	10	0	2	0.4	1.000
1965			3	8	.273	3.56	22	15	1	111.1	93	31	71	0	0	0	0	29	0	0	.000	10	16	1	2	1.2	.963
1966	KC	A	0	4	.000	4.99	9	8	0	39.2	42	12	31	0	0	0	0	11	0	0	.000	0	4	0	0	0.4	1.000
1967			0	1	.000	1.69	14	0	0	16	12	9	10	0	0	1	0	1	0	0	.000	1	3	0	0	0.3	1.000
8 yrs.			43	40	.518	3.52	186	104	18	785.2	707	270	449	6	7	6	9	245	38	0	.155	45	117	2	13	0.9	.988

WORLD SERIES

Year	Team		W	L	PCT	ERA	G	GS	CG	IP	H	BB	SO	ShO	W	L	SV	AB	H	HR	BA	PO	A	E	DP	TC/G	FA
1960	NY	A	0	0	–	1.50	2	0	0	6	5	1	2	0	0	0	0	1	0	0	.000	0	2	0	0	1.0	1.000
1961			0	0	–	2.70	1	1	0	6.2	7	2	5	0	0	0	0	2	0	0	.000	1	0	1	0	2.0	.500
1962			1	0	1.000	2.00	1	1	1	9	4	2	5	0	0	0	0	3	0	0	.000	0	1	0	0	1.0	1.000
3 yrs.			1	0	1.000	2.08	4	2	1	21.2	16	5	12	0	0	0	0	6	0	0	.000	1	3	1	2	1.3	.800

General Stafford

STAFFORD, JAMES JOSEPH
Brother of John Stafford.
B. July 9, 1868, Webster, Mass. D. Sept. 11, 1923, Webster, Mass.
BR TR 5'8" 165 lbs.

Year	Team		W	L	PCT	ERA	G	GS	CG	IP	H	BB	SO	ShO	W	L	SV	AB	H	HR	BA	PO	A	E	DP	TC/G	FA
1890	BUF	P	3	9	.250	5.14	12	12	11	98	123	43	21	0	0	0	0	*				4	21	3	2	2.3	.893

John Stafford

STAFFORD, JOHN HENRY (Doc)
Brother of Bob Stafford.
B. Apr. 8, 1870, Dudley, Mass. D. July 3, 1940, Worcester, Mass.
BR TR 5'10" 170 lbs.

Year	Team		W	L	PCT	ERA	G	GS	CG	IP	H	BB	SO	ShO	W	L	SV	AB	H	HR	BA	PO	A	E	DP	TC/G	FA
1893	CLE	N	0	1	.000	14.14	2	0	0	7	12	7	4	0	0	1	0	4	0	0	.000	0	1	2	0	1.5	.333

Chick Stahl

STAHL, CHARLES SYLVESTER
B. Jan. 10, 1873, Avila, Ind. D. Mar. 28, 1907, West Baden, Ind.
Manager 1906.
BL TL 5'10" 160 lbs.

Year	Team		W	L	PCT	ERA	G	GS	CG	IP	H	BB	SO	ShO	W	L	SV	AB	H	HR	BA	PO	A	E	DP	TC/G	FA
1899	BOS	N	0	0	–	9.00	1	0	0	2	2	3	0	0	0	0	0	*				0	1	1	0	2.0	.500

Gerry Staley

STALEY, GERALD LEE
B. Aug. 21, 1920, Brush Prairie, Wash.
BR TR 6' 195 lbs.

Year	Team		W	L	PCT	ERA	G	GS	CG	IP	H	BB	SO	ShO	W	L	SV	AB	H	HR	BA	PO	A	E	DP	TC/G	FA
1947	STL	N	1	0	1.000	2.76	18	1	1	29.1	33	8	14	0	0	0	0	6	0	0	.000	0	10	0	1	0.6	1.000
1948			4	4	.500	6.92	31	3	0	52	61	21	23	0	4	3	0	9	2	1	.222	0	15	1	1	0.5	.938
1949			10	10	.500	2.73	45	17	5	171.1	154	41	55	2	4	2	6	41	5	0	.122	11	46	1	2	1.3	.983
1950			13	13	.500	4.99	42	22	7	169.2	201	61	62	1	6	1	0	55	8	0	.145	10	46	0	4	1.3	1.000
1951			19	13	.594	3.81	42	30	10	227	244	74	67	4	6	1	3	81	13	0	.160	14	54	1	2	1.6	.986
1952			17	14	.548	3.27	35	33	15	239.2	238	52	93	3	0	0	0	85	13	0	.153	27	55	2	5	2.4	.976
1953			18	9	.667	3.99	40	32	10	230	243	54	88	1	0	0	0	78	8	0	.103	13	52	4	2	1.7	.942
1954			7	13	.350	5.26	48	20	3	155.2	198	47	50	1	3	6	2	36	5	0	.139	26	32	1	2	1.2	.983
1955	2 teams		CIN	N	(30G 5–8)				NY	A	(2G 0–0)																	
"	total		5	8	.385	4.81	32	18	2	121.2	151	29	40	0	0	0	0	36	2	0	.056	9	25	3	2	1.2	.919
1956	2 teams		NY	A	(1G 0–0)				CHI	A	(26G 8–3)																	
"	total		8	3	.727	3.26	27	0	0	102	102	20	26	0	1	0	0	33	3	0	.091	4	23	0	2	1.0	1.000
1957	CHI	A	5	1	.833	2.06	47	0	0	105	95	27	44	0	5	1	7	22	1	0	.045	5	31	2	0	0.8	.947
1958			4	5	.444	3.16	50	0	0	85.1	81	24	27	0	4	5	8	11	0	0	.000	6	28	0	3	0.7	1.000
1959			8	5	.615	2.24	67	0	0	116.1	111	25	54	0	8	5	14	13	2	0	.154	7	19	2	3	0.4	.929
1960			13	8	.619	2.42	64	0	0	115.1	94	25	52	0	13	8	10	17	4	0	.235	10	31	2	1	0.7	.953
1961	3 teams		CHI	A	(16G 0–3)				KC	A	(23G 1–1)				DET	A	(13G 1–1)										
"	total		2	5	.286	3.96	52	0	0	61.1	64	21	32	0	2	5	4	2	0	0	.000	4	14	0	2	0.3	1.000
15 yrs.			134	111	.547	3.70	640	186	58	1981.2	2070	529	727	9	56	41	61	525	66	1	.126	146	481	19	33	1.0	.971

WORLD SERIES

Year	Team		W	L	PCT	ERA	G	GS	CG	IP	H	BB	SO	ShO	W	L	SV	AB	H	HR	BA	PO	A	E	DP	TC/G	FA
1959	CHI	A	0	1	.000	2.16	4	0	0	8.1	8	0	3	0	0	1	1	1	0	0	.000	1	1	0	0	0.5	1.000

Harry Staley

STALEY, HENRY E.
B. Nov. 3, 1866, Jacksonville, Ill. D. Jan. 12, 1910, Battle Creek, Mich.
BR TR 5'10" 175 lbs.

Year	Team		W	L	PCT	ERA	G	GS	CG	IP	H	BB	SO	ShO	W	L	SV	AB	H	HR	BA	PO	A	E	DP	TC/G	FA
1888	PIT	N	12	12	.500	2.69	25	24	24	207.1	185	53	89	2	0	0	0	85	11	0	.129	8	41	5	0	2.2	.907
1889			21	26	.447	3.51	49	47	46	420	433	116	159	1	0	0	1	186	30	0	.161	19	89	5	3	2.3	.956
1890	PIT	P	21	25	.457	3.23	46	46	44	387.2	392	74	145	3	0	0	0	164	34	1	.207	11	86	6	5	2.2	.942
1891	2 teams		PIT	N	(9G 4–5)				BOS	N	(31G 20–8)																	
"	total		24	13	.649	2.58	40	37	32	324	313	80	139	1	2	1	0	133	24	1	.180	9	61	5	2	1.9	.933
1892	BOS	N	22	10	.688	3.03	37	35	31	299.2	273	97	93	3	0	0	0	122	16	1	.131	0	63	3	5	1.8	.955
1893			18	10	.643	5.13	36	31	23	263	344	81	61	0	2	0	0	113	30	2	.265	3	60	9	2	2.0	.875
1894			13	10	.565	6.81	27	21	18	208.2	305	61	32	0	1	3	0	85	20	2	.235	5	28	6	1	1.4	.846
1895	STL	N	6	13	.316	5.22	23	16	13	158.2	223	39	28	1	2	1	0	67	9	0	.134	1	27	1	0	1.3	.966
8 yrs.			137	119	.535	3.80	283	257	231	2269	2468	601	746	10	7	5	1	955	174	7	.182	56	455	40	17	1.9	.927

Year	Team	W	L	PCT	ERA	G	GS	CG	IP	H	BB	SO	ShO	Relief Pitching W	L	SV	Batting AB	H	HR	BA	PO	A	E	DP	TC/G	FA

Tracy Stallard
STALLARD, EVAN TRACY
B. Aug. 31, 1937, Coeburn, Va.   BR TR 6'5"   204 lbs.

Year	Team	W	L	PCT	ERA	G	GS	CG	IP	H	BB	SO	ShO	W	L	SV	AB	H	HR	BA	PO	A	E	DP	TC/G	FA
1960	BOS A	0	0	–	0.00	4	0	0	4	0	2	6	0	0	0	0	0	0	0	–	1	0	0	0	0.3	1.000
1961		2	7	.222	4.88	43	14	1	132.2	110	96	109	0	0	0	2	36	3	0	.083	3	14	0	0	0.4	1.000
1962		0	0	–	0.00	1	0	0	1	0	0	0	0	0	0	0	0	0	0	–	0	0	0	0	0.0	–
1963	NY N	6	17	.261	4.71	39	23	5	154.2	156	77	110	0	0	3	1	48	3	0	.063	12	20	0	0	0.8	1.000
1964		10	20	.333	3.79	36	34	11	225.2	213	73	118	2	0	1	0	79	15	0	.190	18	29	3	0	1.4	.940
1965	STL N	11	8	.579	3.38	40	26	4	194.1	172	70	99	1	0	0	0	68	6	0	.088	12	26	1	1	1.0	.974
1966		1	5	.167	5.68	20	7	0	52.1	65	25	35	0	0	2	1	14	0	0	.000	5	8	1	0	0.7	.929
7 yrs.		30	57	.345	4.17	183	104	21	764.2	716	343	477	3	0	6	4	245	27	0	.110	51	97	5	1	0.8	.967

Charley Stanceu
STANCEU, CHARLES
B. Jan. 9, 1916, Canton, Ohio   D. Apr. 3, 1969, Canton, Ohio   BR TR 6'2"   190 lbs.

Year	Team	W	L	PCT	ERA	G	GS	CG	IP	H	BB	SO	ShO	W	L	SV	AB	H	HR	BA	PO	A	E	DP	TC/G	FA
1941	NY A	3	3	.500	5.63	22	2	0	48	58	35	21	0	1	1	0	12	0	0	.000	1	5	0	0	0.3	1.000
1946	2 teams					NY A	(3G 0–0)			PHI N	(14G 2–4)																
"	total	2	4	.333	4.48	17	11	1	74.1	77	44	26	0	0	0	0	19	0	0	.000	1	12	0	0	0.8	1.000
2 yrs.		5	7	.417	4.93	39	13	1	122.1	135	79	47	0	0	0	0	31	0	0	.000	2	17	0	0	0.5	1.000

Pete Standridge
STANDRIDGE, ALFRED PETER
B. Apr. 25, 1891, Black Diamond, Wash.   D. Aug. 2, 1963, San Francisco, Calif.   BR TR 5'10½" 165 lbs.

Year	Team	W	L	PCT	ERA	G	GS	CG	IP	H	BB	SO	ShO	W	L	SV	AB	H	HR	BA	PO	A	E	DP	TC/G	FA
1911	STL N	0	0	–	9.64	2	0	0	4.2	10	4	3	0	0	0	0	1	0	0	.000	0	2	0	0	1.0	1.000
1915	CHI N	4	1	.800	3.61	29	3	2	112.1	120	36	42	0	2	1	0	40	9	0	.225	2	33	2	1	1.3	.946
2 yrs.		4	1	.800	3.85	31	3	2	117	130	40	45	0	2	1	0	41	9	0	.220	2	35	2	1	1.3	.949

Al Stanek
STANEK, ALBERT WILFRED (Lefty)
B. Dec. 24, 1943, Springfield, Mass.   BL TL 5'11½" 190 lbs.

Year	Team	W	L	PCT	ERA	G	GS	CG	IP	H	BB	SO	ShO	W	L	SV	AB	H	HR	BA	PO	A	E	DP	TC/G	FA
1963	SF N	0	0	–	4.73	11	0	0	13.1	10	12	5	0	0	0	0	1	0	0	.000	1	6	0	1	0.6	1.000

Kevin Stanfield
STANFIELD, KEVIN BRUCE
B. Dec. 19, 1955, Huron, S. D.   BL TL 6'   190 lbs.

Year	Team	W	L	PCT	ERA	G	GS	CG	IP	H	BB	SO	ShO	W	L	SV	AB	H	HR	BA	PO	A	E	DP	TC/G	FA
1979	MIN A	0	0	–	6.00	3	0	0	3	2	0	0	0	0	0	0	0	0	0	–	1	0	0	0	0.3	1.000

Lee Stange
STANGE, ALBERT LEE
B. Oct. 27, 1936, Chicago, Ill.   BR TR 5'10"   165 lbs.

Year	Team	W	L	PCT	ERA	G	GS	CG	IP	H	BB	SO	ShO	W	L	SV	AB	H	HR	BA	PO	A	E	DP	TC/G	FA
1961	MIN A	1	0	1.000	2.92	7	0	0	12.1	15	10	10	0	0	0	0	1	0	0	.000	1	2	0	0	0.4	1.000
1962		4	3	.571	4.45	44	6	1	95	98	39	70	0	2	3	3	17	1	0	.059	7	14	2	0	0.5	.913
1963		12	5	.706	2.62	32	20	7	164.2	145	43	100	2	0	0	0	52	5	0	.096	14	22	1	2	1.2	.973
1964	2 teams					MIN A	(14G 3–6)			CLE A	(23G 4–8)																
"	total	7	14	.333	4.41	37	25	2	171.1	176	50	132	0	0	3	0	50	3	0	.060	10	27	2	2	1.1	.949
1965	CLE A	8	4	.667	3.34	41	12	4	132	122	26	80	2	2	1	0	28	3	0	.107	5	14	1	0	0.5	.950
1966	2 teams					CLE A	(8G 1–0)			BOS A	(28G 7–9)																
"	total	8	9	.471	3.30	36	21	9	169.1	157	46	85	2	0	2	1	52	4	0	.077	12	21	0	0	0.9	1.000
1967	BOS A	8	10	.444	2.77	35	24	6	181.2	171	32	101	2	0	2	1	49	3	0	.061	13	17	1	1	0.9	.968
1968		5	5	.500	3.93	50	2	1	103	89	25	53	0	5	3	12	15	2	0	.133	3	12	2	0	0.3	.882
1969		6	9	.400	3.68	41	15	2	137	137	56	59	0	2	1	3	35	3	0	.086	12	12	0	2	0.6	1.000
1970	2 teams					BOS A	(20G 2–2)			CHI A	(16G 1–0)																
"	total	3	2	.600	5.44	36	0	0	49.2	62	17	28	0	3	2	2	6	0	0	.000	4	7	2	0	0.4	.846
10 yrs.		62	61	.504	3.56	359	125	32	1216	1172	344	718	8	15	17	21	305	24	0	.079	81	148	11	7	0.7	.954

WORLD SERIES

Year	Team	W	L	PCT	ERA	G	GS	CG	IP	H	BB	SO	ShO	W	L	SV	AB	H	HR	BA	PO	A	E	DP	TC/G	FA
1967	BOS A	0	0	–	0.00	1	0	0	2	3	0	0	0	0	0	0	0	0	0	–	0	0	1	0	1.0	–

Don Stanhouse
STANHOUSE, DONALD JOSEPH (Stan, The Man Unusual)
B. Feb. 12, 1951, DuQuoin, Ill.   BR TR 6'2½"   185 lbs.

Year	Team	W	L	PCT	ERA	G	GS	CG	IP	H	BB	SO	ShO	W	L	SV	AB	H	HR	BA	PO	A	E	DP	TC/G	FA
1972	TEX A	2	9	.182	3.77	24	16	1	105	83	73	78	0	0	0	0	31	4	0	.129	8	23	2	1	1.4	.939
1973		1	7	.125	4.76	21	5	1	70	70	44	42	0	1	3	1	0	0	0	–	11	18	1	2	1.4	.967
1974		1	1	.500	4.94	18	0	0	31	38	17	26	0	1	1	0	0	0	0	–	0	7	1	2	0.4	.875
1975	MON N	0	0	–	8.31	4	3	0	13	19	11	5	0	0	0	0	3	1	0	.333	2	1	0	0	0.8	1.000
1976		9	12	.429	3.77	34	26	8	184	182	92	79	1	2	0	1	52	11	0	.212	24	33	1	4	1.7	.983
1977		10	10	.500	3.42	47	16	1	158	147	84	89	1	6	6	10	47	9	1	.191	7	21	2	1	0.6	.933
1978	BAL A	6	9	.400	2.89	56	0	0	74.2	60	52	42	0	6	9	24	0	0	0	–	6	11	2	2	0.3	.895
1979		7	3	.700	2.84	52	0	0	73	49	51	34	0	7	3	21	0	0	0	–	3	16	1	2	0.4	.950
1980	LA N	2	2	.500	5.04	21	0	0	25	30	16	5	0	2	2	7	0	0	0	.000	2	6	0	0	0.4	1.000
1982	BAL A	0	1	.000	5.40	17	0	0	26.2	29	15	8	0	0	1	0	0	0	0	–	2	5	0	1	0.4	1.000
10 yrs.		38	54	.413	3.84	294	66	11	760.1	707	455	408	2	25	21	64	135	25	1	.185	65	142	10	17	0.7	.954

LEAGUE CHAMPIONSHIP SERIES

Year	Team	W	L	PCT	ERA	G	GS	CG	IP	H	BB	SO	ShO	W	L	SV	AB	H	HR	BA	PO	A	E	DP	TC/G	FA
1979	BAL A	1	1	.500	6.00	3	0	0	3	5	3	0	0	1	1	0	0	0	0	–	0	0	0	0	0.0	–

WORLD SERIES

Year	Team	W	L	PCT	ERA	G	GS	CG	IP	H	BB	SO	ShO	W	L	SV	AB	H	HR	BA	PO	A	E	DP	TC/G	FA
1979	BAL A	0	1	.000	13.50	3	0	0	2	6	3	0	0	0	1	0	0	0	0	–	0	1	0	0	0.3	–

Joe Stanka
STANKA, JOE DONALD
B. July 23, 1931, Hammon, Okla.   BR TR 6'5"   201 lbs.

Year	Team	W	L	PCT	ERA	G	GS	CG	IP	H	BB	SO	ShO	W	L	SV	AB	H	HR	BA	PO	A	E	DP	TC/G	FA
1959	CHI A	1	0	1.000	3.38	2	0	0	5.1	2	4	3	0	1	0	0	3	1	0	.333	0	0	0	0	0.0	–

Bob Stanley
STANLEY, ROBERT WILLIAM (Bigfoot)
B. Nov. 10, 1954, Portland, Me.   BR TR 6'4"   210 lbs.

Year	Team	W	L	PCT	ERA	G	GS	CG	IP	H	BB	SO	ShO	W	L	SV	AB	H	HR	BA	PO	A	E	DP	TC/G	FA
1977	BOS A	8	7	.533	3.99	41	13	3	151	176	43	44	1	3	2	3	0	0	0	–	6	43	2	6	1.2	.961
1978		15	2	.882	2.60	52	3	0	141.2	142	34	38	0	13	2	10	0	0	0	–	10	34	1	2	0.9	.978
1979		16	12	.571	3.98	40	30	9	217	250	44	56	4	3	1	1	0	0	0	–	19	43	3	2	1.6	.954
1980		10	8	.556	3.39	52	17	5	175	186	52	71	1	4	2	14	0	0	0	–	9	42	2	8	1.0	.962

Year	Team	W	L	PCT	ERA	G	GS	CG	IP	H	BB	SO	ShO	Relief Pitching W	L	SV	Batting AB	H	HR	BA	PO	A	E	DP	TC/G	FA

Bob Stanley *continued*

Year	Team	W	L	PCT	ERA	G	GS	CG	IP	H	BB	SO	ShO	W	L	SV	AB	H	HR	BA	PO	A	E	DP	TC/G	FA
1981		10	8	.556	3.82	35	1	0	99	110	38	28	0	10	7	0	0	0	0	–	10	29	2	6	1.2	.951
1982		12	7	.632	3.10	48	0	0	168.1	161	50	83	0	12	7	14	0	0	0	–	13	43	2	4	1.2	.966
1983		8	10	.444	2.85	64	0	0	145.1	145	38	65	0	8	10	33	0	0	0	–	9	18	3	3	0.5	.900
1984		9	10	.474	3.54	57	0	0	106.2	113	23	52	0	9	10	22	0	0	0	–	7	28	2	0	0.6	.946
1985		6	6	.500	2.87	48	0	0	87.2	76	30	46	0	6	6	10	0	0	0	–	8	12	1	1	0.4	.952
1986		6	6	.500	4.37	66	1	0	82.1	109	22	54	0	6	5	16	0	0	0	–	6	14	2	0	0.3	.909
1987		4	15	.211	5.01	34	20	4	152.2	198	42	67	1	0	3	0	0	0	0	–	15	22	1	4	1.1	.974
1988		6	4	.600	3.19	57	0	0	101.2	90	29	57	0	6	4	5	0	0	0	–	7	12	2	2	0.4	.905
1989		5	2	.714	4.88	43	0	0	79.1	102	26	32	0	5	2	4	0	0	0	–	3	17	1	0	0.5	.952
13 yrs.		115	97	.542	3.64	637	85	21	1707.2	1858	471	693	7	85	61	132	0	0	0	–	122	357	24	38	0.8	.952

LEAGUE CHAMPIONSHIP SERIES

Year	Team	W	L	PCT	ERA	G	GS	CG	IP	H	BB	SO	ShO	W	L	SV	AB	H	HR	BA	PO	A	E	DP	TC/G	FA
1986	BOS A	0	0	–	4.76	3	0	0	5.2	7	3	1	0	0	0	0	0	0	0	–	0	1	0	0	0.3	1.000
1988		0	0	–	9.00	2	0	0	1	2	1	0	0	0	0	0	0	0	0	–	0	0	0	0	0.0	–
2 yrs.		0	0	–	5.40	5	0	0	6.2	9	4	1	0	0	0	0	0	0	0	–	0	1	0	0	0.2	1.000

WORLD SERIES

Year	Team	W	L	PCT	ERA	G	GS	CG	IP	H	BB	SO	ShO	W	L	SV	AB	H	HR	BA	PO	A	E	DP	TC/G	FA
1986	BOS A	0	0	–	0.00	5	0	0	6.1	5	1	4	0	0	0	1	1	0	0	.000	1	2	0	0	0.6	1.000

Buck Stanley

STANLEY, JOHN LEONARD
Brother of Joe Stanley.
B. Nov. 13, 1889, Washington, D. C. D. Aug. 13, 1940, Norfolk, Va.

BL TL 5'10" 160 lbs.

Year	Team	W	L	PCT	ERA	G	GS	CG	IP	H	BB	SO	ShO	W	L	SV	AB	H	HR	BA	PO	A	E	DP	TC/G	FA
1911	PHI N	0	0	–	6.35	4	0	0	11.1	14	9	5	0	0	0	0	4	0	0	.000	1	0	1	0	0.5	.500

Joe Stanley

STANLEY, JOSEPH BERNARD
Brother of Buck Stanley.
B. Apr. 2, 1881, Washington, D. C. D. Sept. 13, 1967, Detroit, Mich.

BB TR 5'9½" 150 lbs.

Year	Team	W	L	PCT	ERA	G	GS	CG	IP	H	BB	SO	ShO	W	L	SV	AB	H	HR	BA	PO	A	E	DP	TC/G	FA
1897	WAS N	0	0	–	0.00	1	0	0	.2	0	0	0	0	0	0	0	1	0	0	.000	0	0	0	0	0.0	–
1903	BOS N	0	0	–	9.00	1	0	0	4	4	4	4	0	0	0	0	308	77	1	.250	0	0	0	0	0.0	–
1906	WAS A	0	0	–	12.00	1	0	0	3	3	1	0	0	0	0	0	221	36	0	.163	0	0	0	0	0.0	–
3 yrs.		0	0	–	9.39	3	0	0	7.2	7	5	4	0	0	0	0	*				0	0	0	0	0.0	–

Mike Stanton

STANTON, MICHAEL THOMAS
B. Sept. 25, 1952, Phenix City, Ala.

BB TR 6'2" 205 lbs.

Year	Team	W	L	PCT	ERA	G	GS	CG	IP	H	BB	SO	ShO	W	L	SV	AB	H	HR	BA	PO	A	E	DP	TC/G	FA
1975	HOU N	0	2	.000	7.41	7	2	0	17	20	20	16	0	0	0	1	4	1	0	.250	2	3	0	0	0.7	1.000
1980	CLE A	1	3	.250	5.44	51	0	0	86	98	44	74	0	1	3	5	0	0	0	–	4	15	0	2	0.4	1.000
1981		3	3	.500	4.40	24	0	0	43	43	18	34	0	3	3	2	0	0	0	–	3	3	0	0	0.3	1.000
1982	SEA A	2	4	.333	4.16	56	1	0	71.1	70	21	49	0	2	3	7	0	0	0	–	10	13	2	1	0.4	.920
1983		2	3	.400	3.32	50	0	0	65	65	28	47	0	2	3	7	0	0	0	–	1	7	0	1	0.2	1.000
1984		4	4	.500	3.54	54	0	0	61	55	22	55	0	4	4	8	0	0	0	–	4	4	1	0	0.2	.889
1985	2 teams			SEA A	(24G 1–2)				CHI A	(11G 0–1)																
"	total	1	3	.250	6.42	35	0	0	40.2	47	29	29	0	1	3	1	0	0	0	–	4	7	1	1	0.3	.917
7 yrs.		13	22	.371	4.62	277	3	0	384	398	182	304	0	13	19	31	4	1	0	.250	28	52	4	5	0.3	.952

Mike Stanton

STANTON, WILLIAM MICHAEL
B. June 2, 1967, Galena Park, Tex.

BL TL 6'1" 190 lbs.

Year	Team	W	L	PCT	ERA	G	GS	CG	IP	H	BB	SO	ShO	W	L	SV	AB	H	HR	BA	PO	A	E	DP	TC/G	FA
1989	ATL N	0	1	.000	1.50	20	0	0	24	17	8	27	0	0	1	7	0	0	0	–	1	2	1	0	0.2	.750

Dave Stapleton

STAPLETON, DAVID EARL
B. Oct. 16, 1961, Miami, Ariz.

BL TL 6'1" 185 lbs.

Year	Team	W	L	PCT	ERA	G	GS	CG	IP	H	BB	SO	ShO	W	L	SV	AB	H	HR	BA	PO	A	E	DP	TC/G	FA
1987	MIL A	2	0	1.000	1.84	4	0	0	14.2	13	3	14	0	2	0	0	0	0	0	–	0	2	0	0	0.5	1.000
1988		0	0	–	5.93	6	0	0	13.2	20	9	6	0	0	0	0	0	0	0	–	0	2	0	0	0.3	1.000
2 yrs.		2	0	1.000	3.81	10	0	0	28.1	33	12	20	0	2	0	0	0	0	0	–	0	4	0	0	0.4	1.000

Con Starkell

STARKELL, CONRAD
B. Nov. 16, 1880, Germany D. Jan. 19, 1933, Tacoma, Wash.

BR TR 6' 200 lbs.

Year	Team	W	L	PCT	ERA	G	GS	CG	IP	H	BB	SO	ShO	W	L	SV	AB	H	HR	BA	PO	A	E	DP	TC/G	FA
1906	WAS A	0	0	–	18.00	1	0	0	3	7	2	1	0	0	0	0	0	0	0	–	0	1	0	0	1.0	1.000

Dick Starr

STARR, RICHARD EUGENE
B. Mar. 2, 1921, Kittanning, Pa.

BR TR 6'3" 190 lbs.

Year	Team	W	L	PCT	ERA	G	GS	CG	IP	H	BB	SO	ShO	W	L	SV	AB	H	HR	BA	PO	A	E	DP	TC/G	FA
1947	NY A	1	0	1.000	1.46	4	1	1	12.1	12	8	1	0	0	0	0	3	1	0	.333	1	2	0	0	0.8	1.000
1948		0	0	–	4.50	1	0	0	2	2	2	2	0	0	0	0	0	0	0	–	0	0	0	0	0.0	–
1949	STL A	1	7	.125	4.32	30	8	1	83.1	96	48	44	1	0	1	0	23	2	0	.087	3	9	0	1	0.4	1.000
1950		7	5	.583	5.02	32	16	4	123.2	140	74	30	0	1	0	2	36	5	0	.139	2	21	3	3	0.8	.885
1951	2 teams			STL A	(15G 2–5)				WAS A	(11G 1–7)																
"	total	3	12	.200	6.49	26	20	1	123.1	142	66	43	0	0	0	0	35	7	0	.200	7	11	0	1	0.7	1.000
5 yrs.		12	24	.333	5.25	93	45	7	344.2	390	198	120	2	1	1	2	97	15	0	.155	13	43	3	5	0.6	.949

Ray Starr

STARR, RAYMOND FRANCIS (Iron Man)
B. Apr. 23, 1906, Nowata, Okla. D. Feb. 9, 1963, Baylis, Ill.

BR TR 6'1" 178 lbs.

Year	Team	W	L	PCT	ERA	G	GS	CG	IP	H	BB	SO	ShO	W	L	SV	AB	H	HR	BA	PO	A	E	DP	TC/G	FA
1932	STL N	1	1	.500	2.70	3	2	1	20	19	10	6	1	0	0	0	4	1	0	.250	2	6	1	0	3.0	.889
1933	2 teams			NY N	(6G 0–1)				BOS N	(9G 0–1)																
"	total	0	2	.000	4.35	15	3	0	41.1	51	19	17	0	0	0	0	10	1	0	.100	4	8	0	0	0.9	1.000
1941	CIN N	3	2	.600	2.65	7	4	3	34	28	6	11	2	1	1	0	11	2	0	.182	2	8	1	0	1.6	.909
1942		15	13	.536	2.67	37	33	17	276.2	228	106	83	4	0	0	0	88	8	0	.091	12	55	1	3	1.8	.985
1943		11	10	.524	3.64	36	33	9	217.1	201	91	42	2	1	0	1	74	9	0	.122	4	50	1	2	1.5	.982
1944	PIT N	6	5	.545	5.02	27	12	5	89.2	116	36	25	0	2	2	3	22	3	0	.136	1	16	1	0	0.7	.944
1945	2 teams			PIT N	(4G 0–2)				CHI N	(9G 1–0)																
"	total	1	2	.333	8.10	13	1	0	20	27	11	5	0	1	2	0	3	2	0	.667	0	6	0	0	0.5	1.000
7 yrs.		37	35	.514	3.53	138	88	35	699	670	279	189	9	5	6	4	212	26	0	.123	25	150	5	5	1.3	.972

Year	Team		W	L	PCT	ERA	G	GS	CG	IP	H	BB	SO	ShO	W	L	SV	AB	H	HR	BA	PO	A	E	DP	TC/G	FA

Herm Starrette

STARRETTE, HERMAN PAUL
B. Nov. 20, 1938, Statesville, N. C.   BR TR 6'   175 lbs.

Year	Team		W	L	PCT	ERA	G	GS	CG	IP	H	BB	SO	ShO	W	L	SV	AB	H	HR	BA	PO	A	E	DP	TC/G	FA
1963	BAL	A	0	1	.000	3.46	18	0	0	26	26	7	13	0	0	1	0	1	0	0	.000	2	7	0	0	0.5	1.000
1964			1	0	1.000	1.64	5	0	0	11	9	6	5	0	1	0	0	3	0	0	.000	0	1	0	0	0.2	1.000
1965			0	0	–	1.00	4	0	0	9	8	3	3	0	0	0	0	1	0	0	.000	0	4	1	0	1.3	.800
3 yrs.			1	1	.500	2.54	27	0	0	46	43	16	21	0	1	1	0	5	0	0	.000	2	12	1	0	0.6	.933

Ed Stauffer

STAUFFER, CHARLES EDWARD
B. Jan. 10, 1898, Emsworth, Pa.   D. July 2, 1979, St. Petersburg, Fla.   BR TR 5'11"   185 lbs.

Year	Team		W	L	PCT	ERA	G	GS	CG	IP	H	BB	SO	ShO	W	L	SV	AB	H	HR	BA	PO	A	E	DP	TC/G	FA
1923	CHI	N	0	0	–	13.50	1	0	0	2	5	0	0	0	0	0	0	0	0	0	–	0	1	0	0	1.0	1.000
1925	STL	A	0	1	.000	5.34	20	1	0	30.1	34	21	13	0	0	0	0	4	1	0	.250	2	1	0	1	0.2	1.000
2 yrs.			0	1	.000	5.85	21	1	0	32.1	39	22	13	0	0	0	0	4	1	0	.250	2	2	0	1	0.2	1.000

Charlie Stecher

STECHER, CHARLES
B. Bordentown, N. J.   Deceased.

Year	Team		W	L	PCT	ERA	G	GS	CG	IP	H	BB	SO	ShO	W	L	SV	AB	H	HR	BA	PO	A	E	DP	TC/G	FA
1890	PHI	AA	0	10	.000	10.32	10	10	9	68	111	60	18	0	0	0	0	29	7	0	.241	3	23	3	0	2.9	.897

Bill Steele

STEELE, WILLIAM MITCHELL (Big Bill)
B. Oct. 5, 1885, Milford, Pa.   D. Oct. 19, 1949, Overland, Pa.   BR TR 5'11"   200 lbs.

Year	Team		W	L	PCT	ERA	G	GS	CG	IP	H	BB	SO	ShO	W	L	SV	AB	H	HR	BA	PO	A	E	DP	TC/G	FA
1910	STL	N	4	4	.500	3.27	9	8	8	71.2	71	24	25	0	0	0	1	31	8	0	.258	2	24	0	0	2.9	1.000
1911			18	19	.486	3.73	43	34	23	287.1	287	113	115	1	2	2	3	101	21	0	.208	14	88	2	5	2.4	.981
1912			9	13	.409	4.69	40	25	7	194	245	66	67	0	4	2	1	61	11	0	.180	10	66	2	2	2.0	.974
1913			4	4	.500	5.00	12	9	2	54	58	18	10	0	0	0	0	18	1	0	.056	5	9	0	2	1.2	1.000
1914	2 teams	STL N	(17G 2-2)			BKN N	(8G 0-1)																					
"	total		2	3	.400	3.36	25	3	0	69.2	72	14	19	0	2	3	0	20	6	0	.300	1	24	2	0	1.1	.926
5 yrs.			37	43	.463	4.02	129	79	40	676.2	733	235	236	1	8	7	5	231	47	0	.203	32	211	6	9	1.9	.976

Bob Steele

STEELE, ROBERT WESLEY
B. Mar. 29, 1894, Cassburn, Ont., Canada   D. Jan. 27, 1962, Ocala, Fla.   BB TL 5'10½"   175 lbs.

Year	Team		W	L	PCT	ERA	G	GS	CG	IP	H	BB	SO	ShO	W	L	SV	AB	H	HR	BA	PO	A	E	DP	TC/G	FA
1916	STL	N	5	15	.250	3.41	29	22	7	148	156	42	67	1	0	0	0	51	10	0	.196	3	26	3	0	1.1	.906
1917	2 teams	STL N	(12G 1-3)			PIT N	(27G 5-11)																					
"	total		6	14	.300	2.84	39	25	14	221.2	191	72	105	1	2	1	1	89	22	0	.247	5	52	7	3	1.6	.891
1918	2 teams	PIT N	(10G 2-3)			NY N	(12G 3-5)																					
"	total		5	8	.385	2.90	22	11	7	115	100	28	45	2	1	2	2	37	8	0	.216	2	21	2	0	1.1	.920
1919	NY	N	0	1	.000	6.00	1	0	0	3	3	2	0	0	0	1	0	1	0	0	.000	0	0	0	0	0.0	–
4 yrs.			16	38	.296	3.05	91	58	28	487.2	450	144	217	4	3	6	3	178	40	0	.225	10	99	12	3	1.3	.901

Elmer Steele

STEELE, ELMER RAE
B. May 17, 1884, Muitzeskill, N. Y.   D. Mar. 9, 1966, Rhinebeck, N. Y.   BB TR 5'11"   200 lbs.

Year	Team		W	L	PCT	ERA	G	GS	CG	IP	H	BB	SO	ShO	W	L	SV	AB	H	HR	BA	PO	A	E	DP	TC/G	FA
1907	BOS	A	0	1	.000	1.59	4	1	0	11.1	11	1	10	0	0	0	0	4	0	0	.000	0	4	0	0	1.0	1.000
1908			5	7	.417	1.83	16	13	9	118	85	13	37	1	1	0	0	39	2	0	.051	11	30	2	1	2.7	.953
1909			4	4	.500	2.85	16	8	2	75.2	75	15	32	0	1	0	1	24	6	0	.250	4	27	2	0	2.1	.939
1910	PIT	N	0	3	.000	2.25	3	3	2	24	19	3	7	0	0	0	0	7	0	0	.000	3	11	0	0	4.7	1.000
1911	2 teams	PIT N	(31G 9-9)			BKN N	(5G 0-0)																					
"	total		9	9	.500	2.67	36	18	7	189	177	36	61	2	3	2	2	70	11	0	.157	11	61	3	1	2.1	.960
5 yrs.			18	24	.429	2.41	75	43	20	418	367	68	147	3	5	2	3	144	19	0	.132	29	133	7	2	2.3	.959

Bill Steen

STEEN, WILLIAM JOHN
B. Nov. 11, 1887, Pittsburgh, Pa.   D. Mar. 13, 1979, Signal Hill, Calif.   BR TR 6'½"   180 lbs.

Year	Team		W	L	PCT	ERA	G	GS	CG	IP	H	BB	SO	ShO	W	L	SV	AB	H	HR	BA	PO	A	E	DP	TC/G	FA
1912	CLE	A	9	8	.529	3.77	26	16	6	143.1	163	45	61	1	1	2	0	49	13	0	.265	7	36	2	0	1.7	.956
1913			4	5	.444	2.45	22	13	8	128.1	113	49	57	2	0	1	2	41	7	0	.171	3	38	5	0	2.1	.891
1914			9	14	.391	2.60	30	22	13	200.2	201	68	97	1	2	2	0	70	14	0	.200	8	54	8	2	2.3	.886
1915	2 teams	CLE A	(10G 1-4)			DET A	(20G 5-1)																					
"	total		6	5	.545	3.54	30	14	5	124.2	134	37	50	0	1	1	1	44	8	0	.182	8	54	3	0	2.2	.954
4 yrs.			28	32	.467	3.05	108	65	32	597	611	199	265	4	3	6	3	204	42	0	.206	26	182	18	2	2.1	.920

Milt Steengrafe

STEENGRAFE, MILTON HENRY
B. May 26, 1900, San Francisco, Calif.   D. June 2, 1977, Oklahoma City, Okla.   BR TR 6'   170 lbs.

Year	Team		W	L	PCT	ERA	G	GS	CG	IP	H	BB	SO	ShO	W	L	SV	AB	H	HR	BA	PO	A	E	DP	TC/G	FA
1924	CHI	A	0	0	–	12.71	3	0	0	5.2	15	4	3	0	0	0	0	1	0	0	.000	1	1	0	0	0.7	1.000
1926			1	1	.500	3.99	13	1	0	38.1	43	19	10	0	1	1	0	14	0	0	.000	2	7	2	1	0.8	.818
2 yrs.			1	1	.500	5.11	16	1	0	44	58	23	13	0	1	1	0	15	0	0	.000	3	8	2	2	0.8	.846

Morrie Steevens

STEEVENS, MORRIS DALE
B. Oct. 7, 1940, Salem, Ill.   BL TL 6'2"   175 lbs.

Year	Team		W	L	PCT	ERA	G	GS	CG	IP	H	BB	SO	ShO	W	L	SV	AB	H	HR	BA	PO	A	E	DP	TC/G	FA
1962	CHI	N	0	1	.000	2.40	12	0	0	15	10	11	5	0	0	1	0	1	0	0	.000	0	5	1	0	0.5	.833
1964	PHI	N	0	0	–	3.38	4	0	0	2.2	5	1	3	0	0	0	0	0	0	0	–	0	1	0	0	0.3	1.000
1965			0	1	.000	16.88	6	0	0	2.2	5	4	3	0	0	0	0	0	0	0		0	0	0	0	0.0	–
3 yrs.			0	2	.000	4.43	22	0	0	20.1	20	16	11	0	0	1	0	1	0	0	.000	0	6	1	0	0.3	.857

Ed Stein

STEIN, EDWARD F.
B. Sept. 5, 1869, Detroit, Mich.   D. May 10, 1928, Detroit, Mich.   BR TR 5'11"   170 lbs.

Year	Team		W	L	PCT	ERA	G	GS	CG	IP	H	BB	SO	ShO	W	L	SV	AB	H	HR	BA	PO	A	E	DP	TC/G	FA
1890	CHI	N	12	6	.667	3.81	20	18	14	160.2	147	83	65	1	0	1	0	59	9	0	.153	3	21	2	0	1.3	.923
1891			7	6	.538	3.74	14	10	9	101	99	57	38	1	2	1	0	43	7	0	.163	10	27	3	2	2.9	.925
1892	BKN	N	27	16	.628	2.84	48	42	38	377.1	310	150	190	6	3	0	1	144	31	0	.215	36	78	5	2	2.5	.958
1893			19	15	.559	3.77	37	34	28	298.1	294	119	81	1	2	0	0	118	25	0	.212	25	67	6	2	2.6	.939
1894			27	14	.659	4.54	45	41	38	359	396	171	84	2	2	0	1	146	38	2	.260	20	64	7	1	2.0	.923
1895			15	13	.536	4.72	32	27	24	255.1	282	93	55	1	1	0	1	104	26	0	.250	12	62	2	1	2.4	.974
1896			3	6	.333	4.88	17	10	6	90.1	130	51	16	0	1	0	0	39	10	0	.256	3	24	2	0	1.7	.931
1898			0	2	.000	5.48	3	2	2	23	39	9	6	0	0	0	0	10	4	0	.400	1	4	1	0	2.0	.833
8 yrs.			110	78	.585	3.96	216	184	159	1665	1697	733	535	12	11	2	3	663	150	2	.226	110	347	28	8	2.2	.942

Year	Team	W	L	PCT	ERA	G	GS	CG	IP	H	BB	SO	ShO	Relief Pitching W	L	SV	Batting AB	H	HR	BA	PO	A	E	DP	TC/G	FA

Irv Stein

STEIN, IRVIN MICHAEL
B. May 21, 1911, Madisonville, La.   D. Jan. 7, 1981, Covington, La.   BR TR 6'2"   170 lbs.

Year	Team	W	L	PCT	ERA	G	GS	CG	IP	H	BB	SO	ShO	W	L	SV	AB	H	HR	BA	PO	A	E	DP	TC/G	FA
1932	PHI A	0	0	—	12.00	1	0	0	3	7	1	0	0	0	0	0	1	0	0	.000	0	2	0	0	2.0	1.000

Randy Stein

STEIN, WILLIAM RANDOLPH
B. Mar. 7, 1953, Pomona, Calif.   BR TR 6'4"   210 lbs.

Year	Team	W	L	PCT	ERA	G	GS	CG	IP	H	BB	SO	ShO	W	L	SV	AB	H	HR	BA	PO	A	E	DP	TC/G	FA
1978	MIL A	3	2	.600	5.33	31	1	0	72.2	78	39	42	0	3	1	1	0	0	0	—	9	10	3	0	0.7	.864
1979	SEA A	2	3	.400	5.93	23	1	0	41	48	27	39	0	2	2	0	0	0	0	—	1	3	1	0	0.2	.800
1981		0	1	.000	11.00	5	0	0	9	18	8	6	0	0	1	0	0	0	0	—	0	2	0	1	0.4	1.000
1982	CHI N	0	0	—	3.48	6	0	0	10.1	7	7	6	0	0	0	0	0	0	0	—	1	0	0	0	0.2	1.000
4 yrs.		5	6	.455	5.75	65	2	0	133	151	81	93	0	5	4	1	0	0	0	—	11	15	4	1	0.5	.867

Ray Steineder

STEINEDER, RAYMOND
B. Nov. 13, 1895, Salem, N. J.   D. Aug. 25, 1982, Vineland, N. J.   BR TR 6'½"   160 lbs.

Year	Team	W	L	PCT	ERA	G	GS	CG	IP	H	BB	SO	ShO	W	L	SV	AB	H	HR	BA	PO	A	E	DP	TC/G	FA
1923	PIT N	2	0	1.000	4.75	15	2	1	55	58	18	23	0	1	0	0	15	7	0	.467	1	8	1	0	0.7	.900
1924	2 teams	PIT N	(5G 0–1)		PHI N	(9G 1–1)																				
"	total	1	2	.333	5.17	14	0	0	31.1	37	21	11	0	1	2	0	10	3	0	.300	1	9	0	0	0.7	1.000
2 yrs.		3	2	.600	4.90	29	2	1	86.1	95	39	34	0	2	2	0	25	10	0	.400	2	17	1	0	0.7	.950

Ricky Steirer

STEIRER, RICKY FRANCIS
B. Aug. 27, 1956, Baltimore, Md.   BR TR 6'4"   200 lbs.

Year	Team	W	L	PCT	ERA	G	GS	CG	IP	H	BB	SO	ShO	W	L	SV	AB	H	HR	BA	PO	A	E	DP	TC/G	FA
1982	CAL A	1	0	1.000	3.76	10	1	0	26.1	25	11	14	0	1	0	0	0	0	0	—	2	5	0	0	0.7	1.000
1983		3	2	.600	4.82	19	5	0	61.2	77	18	25	0	2	1	0	0	0	0	—	5	11	1	1	0.9	.941
1984		0	1	.000	16.88	1	1	0	2.2	6	2	2	0	0	0	0	0	0	0	—	1	0	0	1	1.0	1.000
3 yrs.		4	3	.571	4.86	30	7	0	90.2	108	31	41	0	3	1	0	0	0	0	—	8	16	1	2	0.8	.960

Bill Stellberger

STELLBERGER, WILLIAM F.
B. Apr. 22, 1865, Detroit, Mich.   D. Nov. 9, 1936, Detroit, Mich.   BL TL

Year	Team	W	L	PCT	ERA	G	GS	CG	IP	H	BB	SO	ShO	W	L	SV	AB	H	HR	BA	PO	A	E	DP	TC/G	FA
1885	PRO N	0	1	.000	7.88	1	1	1	8	14	4	0	0	0	0	0	4	0	0	.000	0	4	0	0	4.0	1.000

Jeff Stember

STEMBER, JEFFREY ALAN
B. Mar. 2, 1958, Elizabeth, N. J.   BR TR 6'5"   220 lbs.

Year	Team	W	L	PCT	ERA	G	GS	CG	IP	H	BB	SO	ShO	W	L	SV	AB	H	HR	BA	PO	A	E	DP	TC/G	FA
1980	SF N	0	0	—	3.00	1	1	0	3	2	2	0	0	0	0	0	1	0	0	.000	0	0	0	0	0.0	—

Bill Stemmeyer

STEMMEYER, WILLIAM (Cannon Ball Bill)
B. May 6, 1865, Cleveland, Ohio   D. May 3, 1945, Cleveland, Ohio   BR TR 6'2"   190 lbs.

Year	Team	W	L	PCT	ERA	G	GS	CG	IP	H	BB	SO	ShO	W	L	SV	AB	H	HR	BA	PO	A	E	DP	TC/G	FA
1885	BOS N	1	1	.500	0.00	2	2	2	11	7	11	8	0	0	0	0	7	3	0	.429	0	4	0	0	2.0	1.000
1886		22	18	.550	3.02	41	41	41	348.2	300	144	239	0	0	0	0	148	41	0	.277	6	61	17	0	2.0	.798
1887		6	8	.429	5.20	15	14	14	119.1	138	41	41	0	0	0	1	47	12	1	.255	1	16	3	0	1.3	.850
1888	CLE AA	0	2	.000	9.00	2	2	2	16	37	9	7	0	0	0	0	10	4	0	.400	0	3	2	0	2.5	.600
4 yrs.		29	29	.500	3.67	60	59	59	495	482	205	295	1	0	0	1	212	60	1	.283	7	84	22	0	1.9	.805

Dave Stenhouse

STENHOUSE, DAVID ROTCHFORD
Father of Mike Stenhouse.
B. Sept. 12, 1933, Westerly, R. I.   BR TR 6'   195 lbs.

Year	Team	W	L	PCT	ERA	G	GS	CG	IP	H	BB	SO	ShO	W	L	SV	AB	H	HR	BA	PO	A	E	DP	TC/G	FA
1962	WAS A	11	12	.478	3.65	34	26	9	197	169	90	123	2	0	1	0	58	3	0	.052	21	33	0	3	1.6	1.000
1963		3	9	.250	4.55	16	16	2	87	90	45	47	1	0	0	0	25	2	0	.080	4	14	0	2	1.1	1.000
1964		2	7	.222	4.81	26	14	1	88	80	39	44	0	0	1	1	20	6	0	.300	7	13	1	0	0.8	.952
3 yrs.		16	28	.364	4.14	76	56	12	372	339	174	214	3	0	2	1	103	11	0	.107	32	60	1	5	1.2	.989

Buzz Stephen

STEPHEN, LOUIS ROBERTS
B. July 13, 1944, Porterville, Calif.   BR TR 6'4"   205 lbs.

Year	Team	W	L	PCT	ERA	G	GS	CG	IP	H	BB	SO	ShO	W	L	SV	AB	H	HR	BA	PO	A	E	DP	TC/G	FA
1968	MIN A	1	1	.500	4.76	2	2	0	11.1	11	7	4	0	0	0	0	3	0	0	.000	1	2	1	0	2.0	.750

Bryan Stephens

STEPHENS, BRYAN MARIS
B. July 14, 1920, Fayetteville, Ark.   BR TR 6'4"   175 lbs.

Year	Team	W	L	PCT	ERA	G	GS	CG	IP	H	BB	SO	ShO	W	L	SV	AB	H	HR	BA	PO	A	E	DP	TC/G	FA
1947	CLE A	5	10	.333	4.01	31	5	1	92	79	39	34	0	4	6	1	27	3	0	.111	5	10	1	0	0.5	.938
1948	STL A	3	6	.333	6.02	43	12	2	122.2	141	67	35	0	2	1	3	32	4	0	.125	2	22	2	2	0.6	.923
2 yrs.		8	16	.333	5.16	74	17	3	214.2	220	106	69	0	6	7	4	59	7	0	.119	7	32	3	2	0.6	.929

Clarence Stephens

STEPHENS, CLARENCE WRIGHT
B. Aug. 19, 1863, Cincinnati, Ohio   D. Feb. 28, 1945, Cincinnati, Ohio   TR

Year	Team	W	L	PCT	ERA	G	GS	CG	IP	H	BB	SO	ShO	W	L	SV	AB	H	HR	BA	PO	A	E	DP	TC/G	FA
1886	CIN AA	1	0	1.000	5.63	1	1	1	8	9	5	6	0	0	0	0	5	3	0	.600	0	3	0	0	3.0	1.000
1891	CIN N	0	1	.000	7.88	1	1	1	8	9	3	3	0	0	0	0	3	0	0	.000	0	0	0	0	0.0	—
1892		0	1	.000	1.29	1	1	0	7	12	4	1	0	0	0	0	2	0	0	.000	0	4	0	0	4.0	1.000
3 yrs.		1	2	.333	5.09	3	3	2	23	30	12	10	0	0	0	0	10	3	0	.300	0	7	0	0	2.3	1.000

George Stephens

STEPHENS, GEORGE BENJAMIN
B. Sept. 28, 1867, Romeo, Mich.   D. Aug. 5, 1896, Armada, Mich.   5'10½"   170 lbs.

Year	Team	W	L	PCT	ERA	G	GS	CG	IP	H	BB	SO	ShO	W	L	SV	AB	H	HR	BA	PO	A	E	DP	TC/G	FA
1892	BAL N	1	1	.500	2.79	5	2	2	29	37	9	7	0	0	0	0	13	0	0	.000	2	6	1	0	2.0	.800
1893	WAS N	0	6	.000	5.80	9	6	6	63.2	83	31	14	0	0	0	0	29	3	0	.103	2	17	2	1	2.3	.905
1894		0	1	.000	4.91	3	2	1	11	19	8	1	0	0	0	0	4	1	0	.250	1	3	1	0	1.7	.800
3 yrs.		1	8	.111	4.86	17	10	9	103.2	139	48	22	1	0	0	0	46	4	0	.087	5	26	5	1	2.1	.861

Earl Stephenson

STEPHENSON, CHESTER EARL
B. July 31, 1947, Benson, N. C.   BL TL 6'3"   175 lbs.

Year	Team	W	L	PCT	ERA	G	GS	CG	IP	H	BB	SO	ShO	W	L	SV	AB	H	HR	BA	PO	A	E	DP	TC/G	FA
1971	CHI N	1	0	1.000	4.50	16	0	0	20	24	11	11	0	1	0	0	2	0	0	.000	2	4	0	1	0.4	1.000
1972	MIL A	3	5	.375	3.26	35	8	1	80	79	33	33	0	1	0	0	18	0	0	.000	4	14	1	0	0.5	.947
1977	BAL A	0	0	—	9.00	1	0	0	3	5	3	0	0	0	0	0	0	0	0							

Year	Team		W	L	PCT	ERA	G	GS	CG	IP	H	BB	SO	ShO	Relief Pitching W	L	SV	Batting AB	H	HR	BA	PO	A	E	DP	TC/G	FA

Earl Stephenson *continued*

| 1978 | | | 0 | 0 | – | 2.79 | 2 | 0 | 0 | 9.2 | 10 | 5 | 4 | 0 | 0 | 0 | 0 | 0 | 0 | 0 | – | 0 | 0 | 0 | 0 | 0.0 | – |
| 4 yrs. | | | 4 | 5 | .444 | 3.59 | 54 | 8 | 1 | 112.2 | 118 | 49 | 50 | 0 | 2 | 0 | 1 | 20 | 0 | 0 | .000 | 6 | 18 | 1 | 1 | 0.5 | .960 |

Jerry Stephenson

STEPHENSON, JERRY JOSEPH
Son of Joe Stephenson.
B. Oct. 6, 1943, Detroit, Mich.

BL TR 6'2" 185 lbs.

1963	BOS	A	0	0	–	7.71	1	1	0	2.1	5	2	3	0	0	0	0	1	0	0	.000	0	0	0	0	0.0	–
1965			1	5	.167	6.23	15	8	0	52	62	33	49	0	0	0	0	13	3	0	.231	3	9	0	0	0.8	1.000
1966			2	5	.286	5.83	15	11	1	66.1	68	44	50	0	0	0	0	17	2	0	.118	3	11	1	0	1.0	.933
1967			3	1	.750	3.86	8	6	0	39.2	32	16	24	0	0	0	1	16	4	0	.250	1	7	0	1	1.0	1.000
1968			2	8	.200	5.64	23	7	2	68.2	81	42	51	0	0	3	0	17	6	0	.353	2	15	1	0	0.8	.944
1969	SEA	A	0	0	–	10.13	2	0	0	2.2	6	3	1	0	0	0	0	0	0	0	.000	0	1	0	0	0.5	1.000
1970	LA	N	0	0	–	9.00	3	0	0	7	11	5	6	0	0	0	0	1	0	0	.000	0	0	0	0	0.0	–
7 yrs.			8	19	.296	5.69	67	33	3	238.2	265	145	184	0	0	3	1	65	15	0	.231	9	43	2	1	0.8	.963

WORLD SERIES

| 1967 | BOS | A | 0 | 0 | – | 9.00 | 1 | 0 | 0 | 2 | 3 | 1 | 0 | 0 | 0 | 0 | 0 | 0 | 0 | 0 | – | 0 | 0 | 0 | 0 | 0.0 | – |

John Sterling

STERLING, JOHN A.
B. Philadelphia, Pa. Deceased.

| 1890 | PHI | AA | 0 | 1 | .000 | 21.60 | 1 | 1 | 1 | 5 | 16 | 4 | 1 | 0 | 0 | 0 | 0 | 2 | 0 | 0 | .000 | 0 | 0 | 0 | 0 | 0.0 | – |

Randy Sterling

STERLING, RANDALL WAYNE
B. Apr. 21, 1951, Key West, Fla.

BB TR 6'2" 195 lbs.

| 1974 | NY | N | 1 | 1 | .500 | 5.00 | 3 | 2 | 0 | 9 | 13 | 3 | 2 | 0 | 0 | 0 | 0 | 2 | 0 | 0 | .000 | 0 | 2 | 0 | 0 | 0.7 | 1.000 |

Jim Stevens

STEVENS, JAMES ARTHUR (Harry)
B. Aug. 25, 1889, Williamsburg, Md. D. Sept. 25, 1966, Baltimore, Md.

BR TR 5'11" 180 lbs.

| 1914 | WAS | A | 0 | 0 | – | 9.00 | 2 | 0 | 0 | 3 | 4 | 2 | 0 | 0 | 0 | 0 | 0 | 1 | 0 | 0 | .000 | 0 | 0 | 0 | 0 | 0.0 | – |

Bunky Stewart

STEWART, VESTON GOFF
B. Jan. 7, 1931, Jasper, N. C.

BL TL 6' 154 lbs.

1952	WAS	A	0	0	–	18.00	1	0	0	1	2	1	1	0	0	0	0	0	0	0	–	0	1	0	0	1.0	1.000
1953			0	2	.000	4.70	2	2	1	15.1	17	11	3	0	0	0	0	5	1	0	.200	0	1	0	0	0.5	1.000
1954			0	2	.000	7.64	29	2	0	50.2	67	27	27	0	0	1	1	3	0	0	.000	1	15	2	1	0.6	.889
1955			0	0	–	4.11	7	1	0	15.1	18	6	10	0	0	0	0	2	0	0	.000	0	3	0	1	0.4	1.000
1956			5	7	.417	5.57	33	9	1	105	111	82	36	0	4	2	2	28	7	0	.250	5	22	2	2	0.9	.931
5 yrs.			5	11	.313	6.01	72	14	2	187.1	215	127	77	0	4	3	3	38	8	0	.211	6	42	4	4	0.7	.923

Dave Stewart

STEWART, DAVID KEITH
B. Feb. 19, 1957, Oakland, Calif.

BR TR 6'2" 200 lbs.

1978	LA	N	0	0	–	0.00	1	0	0	2	1	0	1	0	0	0	0	0	0	0	–	0	0	0	0	0.0	–
1981			4	3	.571	2.51	32	0	0	43	40	14	29	0	4	3	6	5	2	0	.400	4	7	0	0	0.3	1.000
1982			9	8	.529	3.81	45	14	0	146.1	137	49	80	0	6	3	1	39	7	0	.179	15	16	3	2	0.8	.912
1983	2 teams	LA N (46G 5–2)				TEX A	(8G 5–2)																				
"	total		10	4	.714	2.60	54	9	0	135	117	50	78	0	5	2	8	7	1	0	.143	9	17	1	2	0.5	.963
1984	TEX	A	7	14	.333	4.73	32	27	3	192.1	193	87	119	0	0	1	0	0	0	0	–	11	19	3	2	1.0	.909
1985	2 teams	TEX A (42G 0–6)				PHI N	(4G 0–0)																				
"	total		0	6	.000	5.46	46	5	0	85.2	91	41	66	0	0	4	4	0	0	0	–	6	10	3	2	0.4	.842
1986	2 teams	PHI N (8G 0–0)				OAK A	(29G 9–5)																				
"	total		9	5	.643	3.95	37	17	4	161.2	152	69	111	1	0	0	0	0	0	0	–	10	18	1	2	0.8	.966
1987	OAK	A	20	13	.606	3.68	37	37	8	261.1	224	105	205	1	0	0	0	0	0	0	–	18	20	1	0	1.1	.974
1988			21	12	.636	3.23	37	37	14	275.2	240	110	192	2	0	0	0	0	0	0	–	26	16	5	2	1.3	.894
1989			21	9	.700	3.32	36	36	8	257.2	260	69	155	0	0	0	0	0	0	0	–	22	28	4	4	1.5	.926
10 yrs.			101	74	.577	3.68	357	182	39	1560.2	1455	594	1036	4	15	13	19	51	10	0	.196	121	151	21	16	0.8	.928

DIVISIONAL PLAYOFF SERIES

| 1981 | LA | N | 0 | 2 | .000 | 40.50 | 2 | 0 | 0 | .2 | 4 | 0 | 1 | 0 | 2 | 0 | 0 | 0 | 0 | 0 | – | 0 | 0 | 0 | 0 | 0.0 | – |

LEAGUE CHAMPIONSHIP SERIES

1988	OAK	A	1	0	1.000	1.35	2	2	0	13.1	9	6	11	0	0	0	0	0	0	0	–	0	2	0	0	1.0	1.000
1989			2	0	1.000	2.81	2	2	0	16	13	3	9	0	0	0	0	0	0	0	–	0	1	0	0	0.5	1.000
2 yrs.			3	0	1.000	2.15	4	4	0	29.1	22	9	20	0	0	0	0	0	0	0	–	0	3	0	0	0.8	1.000

WORLD SERIES

1981	LA	N	0	0	–	0.00	2	0	0	1.2	2	1	0	0	0	0	0	0	0	0	–	0	1	0	1	0.5	–
1988	OAK	A	0	1	.000	3.14	2	2	0	14.1	12	5	5	0	0	0	0	3	0	0	.000	0	1	0	0	0.5	1.000
1989			2	0	1.000	1.69	2	2	1	16	10	2	14	1	0	0	0	3	0	0	.000	3	0	1	0	2.0	.750
3 yrs.			2	1	.667	2.25	6	4	1	32	23	9	20	1	0	0	0	6	0	0	.000	3	2	1	1	1.0	.667

Frank Stewart

STEWART, FRANK (Stewy)
B. Sept. 8, 1906, Minneapolis, Minn.

BR TR 6'1½" 180 lbs.

| 1927 | CHI | A | 0 | 1 | .000 | 9.00 | 1 | 1 | 0 | 4 | 5 | 4 | 0 | 0 | 0 | 0 | 0 | 1 | 0 | 0 | .000 | 1 | 3 | 0 | 0 | 4.0 | 1.000 |

Joe Stewart

STEWART, JOSEPH LAWRENCE
B. Mar. 11, 1879, Monroe, N. C. D. Feb. 9, 1913, Youngstown, Ohio

TR 5'11" 175 lbs.

| 1904 | BOS | N | 0 | 0 | – | 9.64 | 2 | 0 | 0 | 9.1 | 12 | 4 | 1 | 0 | 0 | 0 | 0 | 5 | 1 | 0 | .200 | 1 | 1 | 0 | 0 | 1.0 | 1.000 |

Lefty Stewart

STEWART, WALTER CLEVELAND
B. Sept. 23, 1900, Sparta, Tenn. D. Sept. 26, 1974, Knoxville, Tenn.

BR TL 5'10" 160 lbs.

| 1921 | DET | A | 0 | 0 | – | 12.00 | 5 | 0 | 0 | 9 | 20 | 5 | 4 | 0 | 0 | 0 | 1 | 1 | 0 | 0 | .000 | 1 | 3 | 0 | 0 | 0.8 | 1.000 |

Lefty Stewart *continued*

Year	Team	W	L	PCT	ERA	G	GS	CG	IP	H	BB	SO	ShO	Relief Pitching			Batting				PO	A	E	DP	TC/G	FA
														W	L	SV	AB	H	HR	BA						
1927	STL A	8	11	.421	4.28	27	19	11	155.2	187	43	43	0	0	1	1	49	15	0	.306	7	45	0	2	1.9	1.000
1928		7	9	.438	4.67	29	17	7	142.2	173	32	25	1	2	0	3	51	14	0	.275	3	33	0	2	1.2	1.000
1929		9	6	.600	3.25	23	18	8	149.1	137	49	47	1	1	1	0	51	6	0	.118	8	30	2	1	1.7	.950
1930		20	12	.625	3.45	35	33	23	271	281	70	79	1	1	1	0	90	22	0	.244	13	56	2	3	2.0	.972
1931		14	17	.452	4.40	36	33	20	258	287	85	89	1	1	1	0	88	22	0	.250	17	52	3	3	2.0	.958
1932		14	19	.424	4.61	41	32	18	259.2	269	99	86	2	0	3	1	82	12	0	.146	8	50	0	3	1.4	1.000
1933	WAS A	15	6	.714	3.82	34	31	11	230.2	227	60	69	1	0	0	0	77	11	0	.143	5	56	1	2	1.8	.984
1934		7	11	.389	4.03	24	22	7	152	184	36	36	1	0	1	0	45	7	0	.156	4	30	1	2	1.5	.971
1935	2 teams			WAS A	(1G 0–1)			CLE A	(24G 6–6)																	
"	total	6	7	.462	5.67	25	11	2	93.2	130	19	25	1	2	2	2	31	6	0	.194	2	15	3	0	0.8	.850
10 yrs.		100	98	.505	4.19	279	216	107	1721.2	1895	498	503	9	7	10	8	565	115	0	.204	68	370	12	18	1.6	.973

WORLD SERIES

Year	Team	W	L	PCT	ERA	G	GS	CG	IP	H	BB	SO	ShO	W	L	SV	AB	H	HR	BA	PO	A	E	DP	TC/G	FA
1933	WAS A	0	1	.000	9.00	1	1	0	2	6	0	0	0	0	0	0	1	0	0	.000	0	0	0	0	0.0	—

Mack Stewart

STEWART, WILLIAM MACKLIN
B. Sept. 23, 1914, Stevenson, Ala.   D. Mar. 21, 1960, Macon, Ga.   BR TR 6'   167 lbs.

Year	Team	W	L	PCT	ERA	G	GS	CG	IP	H	BB	SO	ShO	W	L	SV	AB	H	HR	BA	PO	A	E	DP	TC/G	FA
1944	CHI N	0	0	—	1.46	8	0	0	12.1	11	4	3	0	0	0	0	1	0	0	.000	0	1	0	0	0.1	1.000
1945		0	1	.000	4.76	16	1	0	28.1	37	14	9	0	0	0	0	3	1	0	.333	1	6	0	1	0.4	1.000
2 yrs.		0	1	.000	3.76	24	1	0	40.2	48	18	12	0	0	0	0	4	1	0	.250	1	7	0	1	0.3	1.000

Sammy Stewart

STEWART, SAMUEL LEE
B. Oct. 28, 1954, Asheville, N. C.   BR TR 6'3"   200 lbs.

Year	Team	W	L	PCT	ERA	G	GS	CG	IP	H	BB	SO	ShO	W	L	SV	AB	H	HR	BA	PO	A	E	DP	TC/G	FA
1978	BAL A	1	1	.500	3.18	2	2	0	11.1	10	3	11	0	0	0	0	0	0	0	—	1	2	1	0	2.0	.750
1979		8	5	.615	3.51	31	3	1	118	96	71	71	0	6	4	1	0	0	0	—	10	27	1	3	1.2	.974
1980		7	7	.500	3.55	33	3	2	119	103	60	78	0	6	6	3	0	0	0	—	5	16	2	1	0.7	.913
1981		4	8	.333	2.33	29	3	0	112	89	57	57	0	4	5	4	0	0	0	—	12	14	1	3	0.9	.963
1982		10	9	.526	4.14	38	12	1	139	140	62	69	1	7	4	5	0	0	0	—	10	21	1	3	0.8	.969
1983		9	4	.692	3.62	58	1	0	144.1	138	67	95	0	9	3	7	0	0	0	—	6	17	0	1	0.4	1.000
1984		7	4	.636	3.29	60	0	0	93	81	47	56	0	7	4	13	0	0	0	—	2	14	0	0	0.3	1.000
1985		5	7	.417	3.61	56	1	0	129.2	117	66	77	0	5	6	9	0	0	0	—	12	13	0	0	0.4	1.000
1986	BOS A	4	1	.800	4.38	27	0	0	63.2	64	48	47	0	4	1	0	0	0	0	—	6	5	0	0	0.4	1.000
1987	CLE A	4	2	.667	5.67	25	0	0	27	25	21	25	0	4	3	3	0	0	0	—	1	3	0	2	0.2	1.000
10 yrs.		59	48	.551	3.59	359	25	4	957	863	502	586	1	52	35	45	0	0	0	—	65	132	6	13	0.6	.970

LEAGUE CHAMPIONSHIP SERIES

Year	Team	W	L	PCT	ERA	G	GS	CG	IP	H	BB	SO	ShO	W	L	SV	AB	H	HR	BA	PO	A	E	DP	TC/G	FA
1983	BAL A	0	0	—	0.00	1	0	0	4.1	2	1	2	0	0	0	1	0	0	0	—	0	1	0	0	1.0	1.000

WORLD SERIES

Year	Team	W	L	PCT	ERA	G	GS	CG	IP	H	BB	SO	ShO	W	L	SV	AB	H	HR	BA	PO	A	E	DP	TC/G	FA
1979	BAL A	0	0	—	0.00	1	0	0	2.2	4	1	0	0	0	0	0	1	0	0	.000	1	2	0	0	3.0	1.000
1983		0	0	—	0.00	3	0	0	5	2	2	6	0	0	0	0	2	0	0	.000	0	0	0	0	0.0	—
2 yrs.		0	0	—	0.00	4	0	0	7.2	6	3	6	0	0	0	0	3	0	0	.000	1	2	0	0	0.8	1.000

Dave Stieb

STIEB, DAVID ANDREW
B. July 22, 1957, Santa Ana, Calif.   BR TR 6'   185 lbs.

Year	Team	W	L	PCT	ERA	G	GS	CG	IP	H	BB	SO	ShO	W	L	SV	AB	H	HR	BA	PO	A	E	DP	TC/G	FA
1979	TOR A	8	8	.500	4.33	18	18	7	129	139	48	52	0	0	0	0	0	0	0	—	12	31	1	1	2.4	.977
1980		12	15	.444	3.70	34	32	14	243	232	83	108	4	0	0	0	1	0	0	.000	20	58	1	8	2.3	.987
1981		11	10	.524	3.18	25	25	11	184	148	61	89	2	0	0	0	0	0	0	—	11	38	1	3	2.0	.980
1982		17	14	.548	3.25	38	38	19	288.1	271	75	141	5	0	0	0	0	0	0	—	27	53	2	6	2.2	.976
1983		17	12	.586	3.04	36	36	14	278	223	93	187	4	0	0	0	0	0	0	—	28	33	2	1	1.8	.968
1984		16	8	.667	2.83	35	35	11	267	215	88	198	2	0	0	0	0	0	0	—	22	34	1	4	1.6	.982
1985		14	13	.519	2.48	36	36	8	265	206	96	167	2	0	0	0	0	0	0	—	34	53	5	5	2.6	.946
1986		7	12	.368	4.74	37	34	1	205	239	87	127	1	0	1	0	0	0	0	—	15	33	1	4	1.3	.980
1987		13	9	.591	4.09	33	31	3	185	164	87	115	1	0	0	0	0	0	0	—	24	25	2	2	1.5	.961
1988		16	8	.667	3.04	32	31	8	207.1	157	79	147	4	0	0	0	0	0	0	—	19	26	0	3	1.4	1.000
1989		17	8	.680	3.35	33	33	3	206.2	164	76	101	2	0	0	0	0	0	0	—	18	29	0	1	1.4	.976
11 yrs.		148	117	.558	3.37	357	349	99	2458.1	2158	873	1432	28	0	0	1	1	0	0	.000	230	413	16	38	1.8	.976

LEAGUE CHAMPIONSHIP SERIES

Year	Team	W	L	PCT	ERA	G	GS	CG	IP	H	BB	SO	ShO	W	L	SV	AB	H	HR	BA	PO	A	E	DP	TC/G	FA
1985	TOR A	1	1	.500	3.10	3	3	0	20.1	11	10	18	0	0	0	0	0	0	0	—	1	3	0	0	1.3	1.000
1989		0	2	.000	6.35	2	2	0	11.1	12	6	10	0	0	0	0	0	0	0	—	0	1	0	0	0.5	1.000
2 yrs.		1	3	.250	4.26	5	5	0	31.2	23	16	28	0	0	0	0	0	0	0	—	1	4	0	0	1.0	1.000

Fred Stiely

STIELY, FRED WARREN
B. June 1, 1901, Pillow, Pa.   D. Jan. 6, 1981, Valley View, Pa.   BB TL 5'8"   170 lbs.

Year	Team	W	L	PCT	ERA	G	GS	CG	IP	H	BB	SO	ShO	W	L	SV	AB	H	HR	BA	PO	A	E	DP	TC/G	FA
1929	STL A	1	0	1.000	0.00	1	1	1	9	11	3	2	0	0	0	0	3	2	0	.667	1	1	0	1	2.0	1.000
1930		0	1	.000	8.53	4	2	1	19	27	8	5	0	0	0	0	7	3	0	.429	0	3	0	0	0.8	1.000
1931		0	0	—	6.75	4	0	0	6.2	7	3	2	0	0	0	0	0	0	0	—	1	0	0	0	0.3	1.000
3 yrs.		1	1	.500	5.97	9	3	2	34.2	45	14	9	0	0	0	0	10	5	0	.500	2	4	0	1	0.7	1.000

Dick Stigman

STIGMAN, RICHARD LEWIS
B. Jan. 24, 1936, Nimrod, Minn.   BR TL 6'3"   200 lbs.

Year	Team	W	L	PCT	ERA	G	GS	CG	IP	H	BB	SO	ShO	W	L	SV	AB	H	HR	BA	PO	A	E	DP	TC/G	FA
1960	CLE A	5	11	.313	4.51	41	18	3	133.2	118	87	104	0	2	3	9	36	8	0	.222	8	11	0	0	0.5	1.000
1961		2	5	.286	4.62	22	6	0	64.1	65	25	48	0	1	1	0	16	2	0	.125	2	12	0	0	0.6	1.000
1962	MIN A	12	5	.706	3.66	40	15	6	142.2	122	64	116	0	3	2	3	45	2	0	.044	5	12	0	0	0.4	1.000
1963		15	15	.500	3.25	33	33	15	241	210	81	193	3	0	0	0	84	9	0	.107	6	17	0	0	0.7	1.000
1964		6	15	.286	4.03	32	29	5	190	160	70	159	1	1	0	0	69	7	0	.101	5	14	4	2	0.8	.846
1965		4	2	.667	4.37	33	8	0	70	59	33	70	0	4	2	4	15	2	0	.133	1	8	1	0	0.3	.900
1966	BOS A	2	1	.667	5.44	34	10	0	81	85	46	65	1	1	0	0	17	2	0	.118	0	9	2	1	0.3	.818
7 yrs.		46	54	.460	4.03	235	119	30	922.2	819	406	755	5	12	8	16	282	32	0	.113	27	86	7	3	0.5	.942

Year	Team	W	L	PCT	ERA	G	GS	CG	IP	H	BB	SO	ShO	Relief Pitching W	L	SV	Batting AB	H	HR	BA	PO	A	E	DP	TC/G	FA

Rollie Stiles
STILES, ROLLAND MAYS
B. Nov. 17, 1906, Ratcliff, Ark. BR TR 6'1½" 180 lbs.

Year	Team	W	L	PCT	ERA	G	GS	CG	IP	H	BB	SO	ShO	W	L	SV	AB	H	HR	BA	PO	A	E	DP	TC/G	FA
1930	STL A	3	6	.333	5.89	20	7	3	102.1	136	41	25	0	1	3	0	37	10	0	.270	5	18	1	0	1.2	.958
1931		3	1	.750	7.22	34	2	0	81	112	60	32	0	2	0	0	22	1	0	.045	3	16	2	1	0.6	.905
1933		3	7	.300	5.01	31	9	6	115	154	47	29	1	1	3	1	33	2	0	.061	5	22	3	0	1.0	.900
3 yrs.		9	14	.391	5.91	85	18	9	298.1	402	148	86	1	4	6	1	92	13	0	.141	13	56	6	1	0.9	.920

Archie Stimmel
STIMMEL, ARCHIBALD RAY (Lumbago)
B. May 30, 1873, Woodsboro, Md. D. Aug. 18, 1958, Frederick, Md. BR TR 6' 175 lbs.

Year	Team	W	L	PCT	ERA	G	GS	CG	IP	H	BB	SO	ShO	W	L	SV	AB	H	HR	BA	PO	A	E	DP	TC/G	FA
1900	CIN N	1	1	.500	6.92	2	1	1	13	18	4	2	0	1	0	0	5	1	0	.200	0	2	0	0	1.0	1.000
1901		4	14	.222	4.11	20	18	14	153.1	170	44	55	1	0	0	0	62	5	0	.081	2	28	2	2	1.6	.938
1902		0	4	.000	3.46	4	3	3	26	37	12	7	0	0	1	0	10	2	0	.200	0	6	1	0	1.8	.857
3 yrs.		5	19	.208	4.21	26	22	18	192.1	225	60	64	1	1	1	0	77	8	0	.104	2	36	3	2	1.6	.927

Carl Stimson
STIMSON, CARL REMUS
B. July 18, 1894, Hamburg, Iowa D. Nov. 9, 1936, Omaha, Neb. BB TR 6'5" 190 lbs.

Year	Team	W	L	PCT	ERA	G	GS	CG	IP	H	BB	SO	ShO	W	L	SV	AB	H	HR	BA	PO	A	E	DP	TC/G	FA
1923	BOS A	0	0	–	22.50	2	0	0	4	12	5	1	0	0	0	0	2	0	0	.000	0	2	0	1	1.0	1.000

Harry Stine
STINE, HARRY C.
B. Feb. 20, 1864, Shenandoah, Pa. D. June 5, 1924, Niagara Falls, N. Y. TL 5'6" 150 lbs.

Year	Team	W	L	PCT	ERA	G	GS	CG	IP	H	BB	SO	ShO	W	L	SV	AB	H	HR	BA	PO	A	E	DP	TC/G	FA
1890	PHI AA	0	1	.000	9.00	1	1	1	8	17	4	1	0	0	0	0	3	0	0	.000	0	0	0	0	0.0	–

Lee Stine
STINE, LEE ELBERT
B. Nov. 17, 1913, Stillwater, Okla. BR TR 5'11" 185 lbs.

Year	Team	W	L	PCT	ERA	G	GS	CG	IP	H	BB	SO	ShO	W	L	SV	AB	H	HR	BA	PO	A	E	DP	TC/G	FA
1934	CHI A	0	0	–	8.18	4	0	0	11	11	10	8	0	0	0	0	1	0	0	.000	1	0	0	0	0.3	1.000
1935		0	0	–	9.00	1	0	0	2	3	3	1	0	0	0	0	0	0	0	–	0	3	0	1	3.0	1.000
1936	CIN N	3	8	.273	5.03	40	13	5	121.2	157	41	26	1	0	1	2	27	8	0	.296	8	33	0	1	1.0	1.000
1938	NY A	0	0	–	1.04	4	0	0	8.2	9	1	4	0	0	0	0	2	1	0	.500	0	1	0	0	0.3	1.000
4 yrs.		3	8	.273	5.09	49	13	5	143.1	179	55	39	1	0	1	2	30	9	0	.300	9	37	0	2	0.9	1.000

Jack Stivetts
STIVETTS, JOHN ELMER (Happy Jack)
B. Mar. 31, 1868, Ashland, Pa. D. Apr. 18, 1930, Ashland, Pa. BR TR 6'2" 185 lbs.

Year	Team	W	L	PCT	ERA	G	GS	CG	IP	H	BB	SO	ShO	W	L	SV	AB	H	HR	BA	PO	A	E	DP	TC/G	FA
1889	STL AA	13	7	.650	**2.25**	26	20	18	191.2	153	68	143	2	3	1	1	79	18	0	.228	12	43	5	0	2.3	.917
1890		29	20	.592	3.52	54	46	41	419.1	399	179	289	3	3	2	0	226	65	7	.288	24	86	13	3	2.3	.894
1891		33	22	.600	2.86	**64**	56	40	440	357	**232**	**259**	3	4	1	1	302	92	7	.305	22	110	15	2	2.3	.898
1892	BOS N	35	16	.686	3.04	53	48	45	414.2	346	171	180	3	2	1	1	240	71	3	.296	17	96	12	5	2.4	.904
1893		20	12	.625	4.41	38	34	29	283.2	315	115	61	1	2	0	1	172	51	3	.297	13	50	3	2	1.7	.955
1894		25	14	.641	4.90	45	39	30	338	429	127	76	0	3	1	0	244	80	8	.328	19	47	4	1	1.6	.943
1895		17	17	.500	4.64	38	34	30	291	341	89	111	0	1	0	0	158	30	0	.190	24	50	3	1	2.0	.961
1896		21	14	.600	4.10	42	36	31	329	353	99	71	2	0	1	0	221	76	3	.344	30	57	5	3	2.2	.946
1897		11	4	.733	3.41	18	15	10	129.1	147	43	27	0	1	0	0	199	73	2	.367	3	36	2	0	2.3	.951
1898		0	1	.000	8.25	2	1	1	12	17	7	1	0	0	0	0	111	28	2	.252	0	5	0	0	2.5	1.000
1899	CLE N	0	4	.000	5.68	7	4	3	38	48	25	5	0	0	0	0	39	8	0	.205	2	16	0	0	2.6	1.000
11 yrs.		204	131	.609	3.74	387	333	278	2886.2	2905	1155	1223	14	19	7	4	*				166	596	62	17	2.1	.925

Chuck Stobbs
STOBBS, CHARLES KLEIN
B. July 2, 1929, Wheeling, W. Va. BL TL 6'1" 185 lbs.

Year	Team	W	L	PCT	ERA	G	GS	CG	IP	H	BB	SO	ShO	W	L	SV	AB	H	HR	BA	PO	A	E	DP	TC/G	FA
1947	BOS A	0	1	.000	6.00	4	1	0	9	10	10	5	0	0	0	0	1	0	0	.000	1	0	0	0	0.3	1.000
1948		0	0	–	6.43	6	0	0	7	9	7	4	0	0	0	0	1	0	0	.000	0	3	0	0	0.5	1.000
1949		11	6	.647	4.03	26	19	10	152	145	75	70	0	0	2	0	53	11	0	.208	5	25	3	4	1.3	.909
1950		12	7	.632	5.10	32	21	6	169.1	158	88	78	0	1	1	1	57	14	0	.246	12	33	0	0	1.4	1.000
1951		10	9	.526	4.76	34	25	6	170	180	74	75	0	0	0	0	61	11	0	.180	9	20	1	1	0.9	.967
1952	CHI A	7	12	.368	3.13	38	17	2	135	118	72	73	0	3	1	1	38	3	0	.079	8	26	1	2	0.9	.971
1953	WAS A	11	8	.579	3.29	27	20	8	153	146	44	67	0	0	0	0	44	10	0	.227	12	21	1	0	1.3	.971
1954		11	11	.500	4.10	31	24	10	182	189	67	67	3	1	0	0	51	7	0	.137	8	35	2	5	1.5	.956
1955		4	14	.222	5.00	41	16	2	140.1	169	57	60	0	3	3	3	35	6	0	.171	12	28	1	0	1.0	1.000
1956		15	15	.500	3.60	37	33	15	240	264	54	97	1	1	0	1	84	15	0	.179	19	39	1	5	1.6	.983
1957		8	20	.286	5.36	42	31	5	211.2	235	80	114	2	1	2	1	76	16	0	.211	9	24	0	1	0.8	1.000
1958	2 teams		WAS A	(19G 2–6)		STL N	(17G 1–3)																				
"	total	3	9	.250	5.04	36	8	0	96.1	127	30	48	0	2	3	0	16	1	0	.063	8	19	1	0	0.8	.964
1959	WAS A	1	8	.111	2.98	41	7	0	90.2	82	24	50	0	0	3	7	19	2	0	.105	6	14	0	1	0.5	1.000
1960		12	7	.632	3.32	40	13	1	119.1	115	38	72	1	6	2	2	34	3	0	.088	4	11	0	1	0.4	1.000
1961	MIN A	2	3	.400	7.46	24	3	0	44.2	56	15	17	0	2	1	2	8	3	0	.375	3	3	0	0	0.3	1.000
15 yrs.		107	130	.451	4.29	459	238	65	1920.1	2003	735	897	7	20	18	19	578	102	0	.176	116	301	10	21	0.9	.977

Wes Stock
STOCK, WESLEY GAY
B. Apr. 10, 1934, Longview, Wash. BR TR 6'2" 188 lbs.

Year	Team	W	L	PCT	ERA	G	GS	CG	IP	H	BB	SO	ShO	W	L	SV	AB	H	HR	BA	PO	A	E	DP	TC/G	FA
1959	BAL A	0	0	–	3.55	7	0	0	12.2	16	2	8	0	0	0	1	2	0	0	.000	0	2	1	0	0.4	.667
1960		2	2	.500	2.88	17	0	0	34.1	26	14	23	0	2	2	2	6	0	0	.000	1	8	0	1	0.5	1.000
1961		5	0	1.000	3.01	35	1	0	71.2	58	27	47	0	5	0	3	11	0	0	.000	5	22	0	1	0.8	1.000
1962		3	2	.600	4.43	53	0	0	65	50	36	34	0	3	2	3	3	0	0	.000	4	23	0	4	0.5	1.000
1963		7	0	1.000	3.94	47	0	0	75.1	69	31	55	0	7	0	1	10	0	0	.000	6	13	1	1	0.4	.950
1964	2 teams		BAL A	(14G 2–0)		KC A	(50G 6–3)																				
"	total	8	3	.727	2.30	64	0	0	113.2	86	42	115	0	8	3	5	19	3	0	.158	8	12	0	0	0.3	1.000
1965	KC A	0	4	.000	5.24	62	2	0	99.2	96	40	52	0	0	3	4	6	0	0	.000	9	25	1	0	0.6	.971
1966		2	2	.500	2.66	35	0	0	44	30	21	31	0	2	2	3	2	0	0	.000	1	5	0	1	0.2	1.000
1967		0	0	–	18.00	1	0	0	1	3	2	0	0	0	0	0	0	0	0	–	0	1	0	0	1.0	1.000
9 yrs.		27	13	.675	3.60	321	3	0	517.1	434	215	365	0	27	12	22	59	3	0	.051	34	111	3	8	0.5	.980

Otis Stocksdale
STOCKSDALE, OTIS HINKLEY
B. Aug. 7, 1871, Acadia, Md. D. Mar. 15, 1933, Pennsville, N. J. BL TR 5'10½" 180 lbs.

Year	Team	W	L	PCT	ERA	G	GS	CG	IP	H	BB	SO	ShO	W	L	SV	AB	H	HR	BA	PO	A	E	DP	TC/G	FA
1893	WAS N	2	8	.200	8.22	11	11	7	69	111	32	12	0	0	0	0	40	12	0	.300	9	16	1	0	2.4	.962

Year	Team	W	L	PCT	ERA	G	GS	CG	IP	H	BB	SO	ShO	Relief Pitching W	L	SV	Batting AB	H	HR	BA	PO	A	E	DP	TC/G	FA

Otis Stocksdale *continued*

Year	Team	W	L	PCT	ERA	G	GS	CG	IP	H	BB	SO	ShO	W	L	SV	AB	H	HR	BA	PO	A	E	DP	TC/G	FA
1894		5	9	.357	5.06	18	14	11	117.1	176	42	10	0	0	1	0	71	23	0	.324	8	24	1	0	1.8	.970
1895	2 teams	WAS N	(20G 6–11)			BOS N	(4G 2–2)																			
"	total	8	13	.381	6.06	24	21	12	159	230	60	25	0	0	0	1	89	27	0	.303	15	30	4	2	2.0	.918
1896	BAL N	0	1	.000	16.20	1	0	0	1.2	4	2	1	0	0	1	0	3	1	0	.333	0	0	0	0	0.0	—
4 yrs.		15	31	.326	6.20	54	46	30	347	521	136	48	0	0	2	1	203	63	0	.310	32	70	6	2	2.0	.944

Bob Stoddard

STODDARD, ROBERT LYLE
B. Mar. 8, 1957, San Jose, Calif.

BR TR 6'1" 190 lbs.

Year	Team	W	L	PCT	ERA	G	GS	CG	IP	H	BB	SO	ShO	W	L	SV	AB	H	HR	BA	PO	A	E	DP	TC/G	FA
1981	SEA A	2	1	.667	2.57	5	5	1	35	35	9	22	0	0	0	0	0	0	0	—	0	6	0	0	1.2	1.000
1982		3	3	.500	2.41	9	9	2	67.1	48	18	24	1	0	0	0	0	0	0	—	0	14	0	1	1.6	1.000
1983		9	17	.346	4.41	35	23	2	175.2	182	58	87	1	1	4	0	0	0	0	—	15	36	2	2	1.5	.962
1984		2	3	.400	5.13	27	6	0	79	86	37	39	0	2	1	0	0	0	0	—	3	14	0	1	0.6	1.000
1985	DET A	0	0	—	6.75	8	0	0	13.1	15	5	11	0	0	0	1	0	0	0	—	2	3	0	1	0.6	1.000
1986	SD N	1	0	1.000	2.31	18	0	0	23.1	20	11	17	0	1	0	1	1	0	0	.000	0	3	0	0	0.2	1.000
1987	KC A	1	3	.250	4.28	17	2	0	40	51	22	23	0	1	2	1	0	0	0	—	4	10	0	1	0.8	1.000
7 yrs.		18	27	.400	4.03	119	45	5	433.2	437	160	223	2	5	7	3	1	0	0	.000	24	86	2	6	0.9	.982

Tim Stoddard

STODDARD, TIMOTHY PAUL
B. Jan. 24, 1953, East Chicago, Ind.

BR TR 6'7" 230 lbs.

Year	Team	W	L	PCT	ERA	G	GS	CG	IP	H	BB	SO	ShO	W	L	SV	AB	H	HR	BA	PO	A	E	DP	TC/G	FA
1975	CHI A	0	0	—	9.00	1	0	0	1	2	0	0	0	0	0	0	0	0	0	—	1	0	0	0	1.0	1.000
1978	BAL A	0	1	.000	6.00	8	0	0	18	22	8	14	0	0	1	0	0	0	0	—	0	3	0	0	0.4	1.000
1979		3	1	.750	1.71	29	0	0	58	44	19	47	0	3	1	3	0	0	0	—	9	5	1	0	0.5	.933
1980		5	3	.625	2.51	64	0	0	86	72	38	64	0	5	3	26	0	0	0	—	4	9	0	0	0.2	1.000
1981		4	2	.667	3.89	31	0	0	37	38	18	32	0	4	2	7	0	0	0	—	4	3	0	1	0.2	1.000
1982		3	4	.429	4.02	50	0	0	56	53	29	42	0	3	4	12	0	0	0	—	2	6	1	0	0.2	.889
1983		4	3	.571	6.09	47	0	0	57.2	65	29	50	0	4	3	9	0	0	0	—	3	7	0	1	0.2	1.000
1984	CHI N	10	6	.625	3.82	58	0	0	92	77	57	87	0	10	6	7	11	1	0	.091	4	8	1	0	0.2	.923
1985	SD N	1	6	.143	4.65	44	0	0	60	63	37	42	0	1	6	1	5	0	0	.000	3	5	0	0	0.2	1.000
1986	2 teams	SD N	(30G 1–3)			NY A	(24G 4–1)																			
"	total	5	4	.556	3.80	54	0	0	94.2	74	57	81	0	5	4	4	4	1	1	.250	3	14	2	2	0.4	.895
1987	NY A	4	3	.571	3.50	57	0	0	92.2	83	30	78	0	4	3	8	0	0	0	—	8	8	1	0	0.3	.941
1988		2	2	.500	6.38	28	0	0	55	62	27	33	0	2	0	0	0	0	0	—	4	7	0	2	0.4	1.000
1989	CLE A	0	0	—	2.95	14	0	0	21.1	25	7	12	0	0	0	0	0	0	0	—	0	4	0	0	0.3	1.000
13 yrs.		41	35	.539	3.95	485	0	0	729.1	680	356	582	0	41	35	76	20	2	1	.100	44	80	6	6	0.3	.954

LEAGUE CHAMPIONSHIP SERIES

Year	Team	W	L	PCT	ERA	G	GS	CG	IP	H	BB	SO	ShO	W	L	SV	AB	H	HR	BA	PO	A	E	DP	TC/G	FA
1984	CHI N	0	0	—	4.50	2	0	0	2	1	2	2	0	0	0	0	0	0	0	—	1	1	0	0	1.0	1.000

WORLD SERIES

Year	Team	W	L	PCT	ERA	G	GS	CG	IP	H	BB	SO	ShO	W	L	SV	AB	H	HR	BA	PO	A	E	DP	TC/G	FA
1979	BAL A	1	0	1.000	5.40	4	0	0	5	6	1	3	0	1	0	0	1	1	0	1.000	1	4	1	0	1.5	.833

Art Stokes

STOKES, ARTHUR MILTON
B. Sept. 13, 1896, Emmitsburg, Md. D. June 3, 1962, Titusville, Pa.

BR TR 5'10½" 155 lbs.

Year	Team	W	L	PCT	ERA	G	GS	CG	IP	H	BB	SO	ShO	W	L	SV	AB	H	HR	BA	PO	A	E	DP	TC/G	FA
1925	PHI A	1	1	.500	4.07	12	0	0	24.1	24	10	7	0	1	1	0	4	0	0	.000	1	6	2	0	0.8	.778

Arnie Stone

STONE, EDWIN ARNOLD
B. Dec. 19, 1892, North Creek, N. Y. D. July 29, 1948, Hudson Falls, N. Y.

BR TL 6' 180 lbs.

Year	Team	W	L	PCT	ERA	G	GS	CG	IP	H	BB	SO	ShO	W	L	SV	AB	H	HR	BA	PO	A	E	DP	TC/G	FA
1923	PIT N	0	1	.000	8.03	9	0	0	12.1	19	4	2	0	0	1	0	1	0	0	.000	0	1	1	0	0.2	.500
1924		4	2	.667	2.95	26	2	1	64	57	15	7	0	3	1	0	15	2	0	.133	1	18	0	0	0.7	1.000
2 yrs.		4	3	.571	3.77	35	2	1	76.1	76	19	9	0	3	2	0	16	2	0	.125	1	19	1	0	0.6	.952

Dean Stone

STONE, DARRAGH DEAN
B. Sept. 1, 1930, Moline, Ill.

BL TL 6'4" 205 lbs.

Year	Team	W	L	PCT	ERA	G	GS	CG	IP	H	BB	SO	ShO	W	L	SV	AB	H	HR	BA	PO	A	E	DP	TC/G	FA
1953	WAS A	0	1	.000	8.31	3	1	0	8.2	13	5	5	0	0	0	0	2	0	0	.000	2	0	0	0	0.7	1.000
1954		12	10	.545	3.22	31	23	10	178.2	161	69	87	2	1	0	0	52	5	0	.096	5	17	0	3	0.7	1.000
1955		6	13	.316	4.15	43	24	5	180	180	114	84	1	0	2	1	46	2	0	.043	4	23	0	2	0.6	1.000
1956		5	7	.417	6.27	41	21	2	132	148	93	86	0	1	3	3	34	3	0	.088	4	20	5	2	0.7	.828
1957	2 teams	WAS A	(3G 0–0)			BOS A	(17G 1–3)																			
"	total	1	3	.250	5.27	20	8	0	54.2	61	37	35	0	0	0	0	14	0	0	.000	2	11	0	1	0.7	1.000
1959	STL N	0	1	.000	4.20	18	1	0	30	30	16	17	0	0	1	0	4	0	0	.000	2	4	1	0	0.4	.857
1962	2 teams	HOU N	(15G 3–2)			CHI A	(27G 1–0)																			
"	total	4	2	.667	4.03	42	7	2	82.2	89	29	54	2	2	0	5	18	5	0	.278	5	13	1	0	0.5	.947
1963	BAL A	1	2	.333	5.12	17	0	0	19.1	23	10	12	0	1	2	1	0	0	0	—	1	5	0	0	0.4	1.000
8 yrs.		29	39	.426	4.47	215	85	19	686	705	373	380	5	4	5	12	170	15	1	.088	25	93	7	8	0.6	.944

Dick Stone

STONE, CHARLES RICHARD
B. Dec. 5, 1911, Oklahoma City, Okla. D. Feb. 18, 1980, Oklahoma City, Okla.

BL TL 5'9" 153 lbs.

Year	Team	W	L	PCT	ERA	G	GS	CG	IP	H	BB	SO	ShO	W	L	SV	AB	H	HR	BA	PO	A	E	DP	TC/G	FA
1945	WAS A	0	0	—	0.00	3	0	0	5	6	1	0	0	0	0	0	0	0	0	—	0	1	0	1	0.3	1.000

Dwight Stone

STONE, DWIGHT ELY
B. Aug. 2, 1886, Holt County, Neb. D. July 3, 1976, Glendale, Calif.

BR TR 6'1½" 170 lbs.

Year	Team	W	L	PCT	ERA	G	GS	CG	IP	H	BB	SO	ShO	W	L	SV	AB	H	HR	BA	PO	A	E	DP	TC/G	FA
1913	STL A	2	6	.250	3.56	18	7	4	91	94	46	37	1	1	0	0	33	9	0	.273	4	33	1	1	2.1	.974
1914	KC F	7	14	.333	4.34	39	22	6	186.2	205	77	88	0	2	1	0	58	7	1	.121	9	57	4	4	1.8	.943
2 yrs.		9	20	.310	4.08	57	29	10	277.2	299	123	125	1	3	1	0	91	16	1	.176	13	90	5	5	1.9	.954

George Stone

STONE, GEORGE HEARD
B. July 9, 1946, Ruston, La.

BL TL 6'3" 205 lbs.

Year	Team	W	L	PCT	ERA	G	GS	CG	IP	H	BB	SO	ShO	W	L	SV	AB	H	HR	BA	PO	A	E	DP	TC/G	FA
1967	ATL N	0	0	—	4.91	2	1	0	7.1	8	1	5	0	0	0	0	2	0	0	.000	1	1	0	0	1.0	1.000
1968		7	4	.636	2.76	17	10	2	75	63	19	52	0	1	1	0	27	9	0	.333	4	6	2	1	0.7	.833
1969		13	10	.565	3.65	36	20	3	165	166	48	102	0	0	3	0	59	11	0	.186	7	24	0	3	0.9	1.000
1970		11	11	.500	3.87	35	30	9	207	218	50	131	2	0	0	0	72	17	0	.236	14	42	3	3	1.7	.949

George Stone *continued*

Year	Team		W	L	PCT	ERA	G	GS	CG	IP	H	BB	SO	ShO	RW	RL	SV	AB	H	HR	BA	PO	A	E	DP	TC/G	FA
1971			6	8	.429	3.59	27	24	4	173	186	35	110	2	0	0	0	62	11	0	.177	5	26	1	4	1.2	.969
1972			6	11	.353	5.51	31	16	2	111	143	44	63	1	2	2	1	25	5	0	.200	3	23	1	2	0.9	.963
1973	NY	N	12	3	.800	2.80	27	20	2	148	157	31	77	0	1	0	1	48	13	0	.271	6	27	0	2	1.2	1.000
1974			2	7	.222	5.03	15	13	1	77	103	21	29	0	0	0	0	26	3	0	.115	6	13	1	1	1.3	.950
1975			3	3	.500	5.05	13	11	1	57	75	21	21	0	0	0	0	18	3	0	.167	1	15	0	1	1.2	1.000
9 yrs.			60	57	.513	3.89	203	145	24	1020.1	1119	270	590	5	4	3	5	339	72	1	.212	47	177	8	17	1.1	.966

LEAGUE CHAMPIONSHIP SERIES

Year	Team		W	L	PCT	ERA	G	GS	CG	IP	H	BB	SO	ShO	RW	RL	SV	AB	H	HR	BA	PO	A	E	DP	TC/G	FA
1969	ATL	N	0	0	—	9.00	1	0	0	1	2	0	0	0	0	0	0	1	0	0	.000	1	0	0	0	1.0	1.000
1973	NY	N	0	0	—	1.35	1	1	0	6.2	3	2	4	0	0	0	0	1	0	0	.000	1	2	0	0	3.0	1.000
2 yrs.			0	0	—	2.35	2	1	0	7.2	5	2	4	0	0	0	0	2	0	0	.000	2	3	0	0	2.5	1.000

WORLD SERIES

Year	Team		W	L	PCT	ERA	G	GS	CG	IP	H	BB	SO	ShO	RW	RL	SV	AB	H	HR	BA	PO	A	E	DP	TC/G	FA
1973	NY	N	0	0	—	0.00	2	0	0	3	4	1	3	0	0	0	0	0	0	0	—	0	0	0	0	0.0	—

Rocky Stone

STONE, JOHN VERNON B. Aug. 23, 1918, Redding, Calif. D. Nov. 12, 1986, Fountain Valley, Calif. BR TR 6' 200 lbs.

Year	Team		W	L	PCT	ERA	G	GS	CG	IP	H	BB	SO	ShO	RW	RL	SV	AB	H	HR	BA	PO	A	E	DP	TC/G	FA
1943	CIN	N	0	1	.000	4.38	13	0	0	24.2	23	8	11	0	0	1	0	4	1	0	.250	1	3	1	0	0.4	.800

Steve Stone

STONE, STEVEN MICHAEL B. July 14, 1947, Euclid, Ohio BR TR 5'10" 175 lbs.

Year	Team		W	L	PCT	ERA	G	GS	CG	IP	H	BB	SO	ShO	RW	RL	SV	AB	H	HR	BA	PO	A	E	DP	TC/G	FA
1971	SF	N	5	9	.357	4.14	24	19		111	110	55	63	2	0	0	0	34	0	0	.000	12	21	1	2	1.4	.971
1972			6	8	.429	2.98	27	16	4	124	97	49	85	1	1	0	0	34	4	0	.118	6	21	3	0	1.1	.900
1973	CHI	A	6	11	.353	4.24	36	22	3	176.1	163	82	138	0	1	0	1	0	0	0	—	13	24	2	2	1.1	.949
1974	CHI	N	8	6	.571	4.13	38	23	1	170	185	64	90	0	1	1	0	58	7	0	.121	15	30	3	0	1.3	.938
1975			12	8	.600	3.95	33	32	6	214	198	80	139	1	0	0	0	72	8	0	.111	21	27	3	1	1.5	.941
1976			3	6	.333	4.08	17	15	1	75	70	21	33	1	0	0	0	21	3	0	.143	3	6	1	1	0.6	.900
1977	CHI	A	15	12	.556	4.52	31	31	8	207	228	80	124	0	0	0	0	0	0	0	—	5	34	2	2	1.3	.951
1978			12	12	.500	4.37	30	30	6	212	196	84	118	0	0	0	0	0	0	0	—	12	28	4	1	1.5	.909
1979	BAL	A	11	7	.611	3.77	32	32	3	186	173	73	96	0	0	0	0	0	0	0	—	21	27	1	3	1.5	.980
1980			**25**	7	**.781**	3.23	37	37	9	251	224	101	149	1	0	0	0	0	0	0	—	14	26	2	1	1.1	.952
1981			4	7	.364	4.57	15	12	0	63	63	27	30	0	0	0	0	0	0	0	—	3	10	0	0	0.9	1.000
11 yrs.			107	93	.535	3.96	320	269	43	1789.1	1707	716	1065	7	2	3	1	219	22	0	.100	125	254	22	13	1.3	.945

WORLD SERIES

Year	Team		W	L	PCT	ERA	G	GS	CG	IP	H	BB	SO	ShO	RW	RL	SV	AB	H	HR	BA	PO	A	E	DP	TC/G	FA
1979	BAL	A	0	0	—	9.00	1	0	0	2	4	2	2	0	0	0	0	0	0	0	—	0	0	0	0	0.0	—

Tige Stone

STONE, WILLIAM ARTHUR B. Sept. 18, 1901, Macon, Ga. D. Jan. 1, 1960, Jacksonville, Fla. BR TR 5'8" 145 lbs.

Year	Team		W	L	PCT	ERA	G	GS	CG	IP	H	BB	SO	ShO	RW	RL	SV	AB	H	HR	BA	PO	A	E	DP	TC/G	FA
1923	STL	N	0	0	—	12.00	1	0	0	3	5	3	1	0	0	0	0	*				0	2	0	0	2.0	1.000

Bill Stoneman

STONEMAN, WILLIAM HAMBLY B. Apr. 7, 1944, Oak Park, Ill. BR TR 5'10" 170 lbs.

Year	Team		W	L	PCT	ERA	G	GS	CG	IP	H	BB	SO	ShO	RW	RL	SV	AB	H	HR	BA	PO	A	E	DP	TC/G	FA
1967	CHI	N	2	4	.333	3.29	28	2	0	63	51	22	52	0	2	4	4	13	0	0	.000	2	5	0	0	0.3	1.000
1968			0	1	.000	5.52	18	0	0	29.1	35	14	18	0	0	1	0	4	0	0	.000	2	4	1	0	0.4	.857
1969	MON	N	11	19	.367	4.39	42	36	8	235.2	233	**123**	185	5	0	0	0	73	4	0	.055	22	26	1	3	1.2	.980
1970			7	15	.318	4.59	40	30	5	208	209	109	176	3	0	0	0	60	6	0	.100	10	22	0	1	0.8	1.000
1971			17	16	.515	3.14	39	**39**	20	295	243	**146**	251	5	0	0	0	93	12	0	.129	18	39	1	2	1.5	.983
1972			12	14	.462	2.98	36	35	13	250.2	213	102	171	4	0	0	0	75	6	0	.080	20	32	3	2	1.5	.945
1973			4	8	.333	6.80	29	17	0	96.2	120	55	48	0	1	0	1	20	1	0	.050	5	16	1	0	0.8	.955
1974	CAL	A	1	8	.111	6.10	13	11	0	59	78	31	33	0	0	0	0	0	0	0	—	3	9	0	0	0.9	1.000
8 yrs.			54	85	.388	4.08	245	170	46	1237.1	1182	602	934	15	3	5	5	338	29	0	.086	82	153	7	8	1.0	.971

Lil Stoner

STONER, ULYSSES SIMPSON GRANT B. Feb. 28, 1899, Bowie, Tex. D. June 26, 1966, Enid, Okla. BR TR 5'9½" 180 lbs.

Year	Team		W	L	PCT	ERA	G	GS	CG	IP	H	BB	SO	ShO	RW	RL	SV	AB	H	HR	BA	PO	A	E	DP	TC/G	FA
1922	DET	A	4	4	.500	7.04	17	7	2	62.2	76	35	18	0	1	0	0	20	2	0	.100	1	23	2	1	1.5	.923
1924			11	11	.500	4.72	36	25	10	215.2	271	65	66	1	1	2	0	77	15	2	.195	5	50	3	2	1.6	.948
1925			10	9	.526	4.26	34	18	8	152	166	53	51	0	1	3	1	55	16	0	.291	1	24	1	0	0.8	.962
1926			7	10	.412	5.47	32	22	7	159.2	179	63	57	0	2	1	0	53	9	0	.170	7	36	0	2	1.3	.945
1927			10	13	.435	3.98	38	24	13	215	251	77	63	0	1	2	5	74	8	0	.108	5	47	3	2	1.4	.945
1928			5	8	.385	4.35	36	11	2	126.1	151	42	29	0	0	1	4	39	7	0	.179	4	19	3	2	0.7	.885
1929			3	3	.500	5.26	24	3	1	53	57	31	12	0	0	1	4	15	1	0	.067	3	20	2	1	1.0	.920
1930	PIT	N	0	0	—	4.76	5	0	0	5.2	7	3	7	0	0	0	0	0	0	0	—	0	3	0	0	0.6	1.000
1931	PHI	N	0	0	—	6.59	7	1	0	13.2	22	5	2	0	0	0	0	5	0	0	.000	0	3	0	0	0.4	1.000
9 yrs.			50	58	.463	4.76	229	111	45	1003.2	1180	374	299	1	9	10	14	338	58	2	.172	26	225	14	11	1.2	.947

Mel Stottlemyre

STOTTLEMYRE, MELVIN LEON Father of Todd Stottlemyre. B. Nov. 13, 1941, Hazelton, Mo. BR TR 6'1" 178 lbs.

Year	Team		W	L	PCT	ERA	G	GS	CG	IP	H	BB	SO	ShO	RW	RL	SV	AB	H	HR	BA	PO	A	E	DP	TC/G	FA
1964	NY	A	9	3	.750	2.06	13	12	5	96	77	35	49	2	0	0	0	37	9	0	.243	7	20	2	3	2.2	.931
1965			20	9	.690	2.63	37	37	**18**	**291**	250	88	155	4	0	0	0	99	13	2	.131	30	74	1	3	2.8	.990
1966			12	**20**	.375	3.80	37	35	9	251	239	82	146	3	0	1	1	80	11	1	.138	27	54	3	5	2.3	.964
1967			15	15	.500	2.96	36	36	10	255	239	88	151	4	0	0	0	82	8	0	.098	36	60	5	4	2.8	.950
1968			21	12	.636	2.45	36	36	19	278.2	**243**	65	140	6	0	0	0	91	13	0	.143	20	54	0	0	2.1	1.000
1969			20	14	.588	2.82	39	39	**24**	303	267	97	113	3	0	0	0	101	18	1	.178	24	88	5	3	3.0	.957
1970			15	13	.536	3.09	37	37	14	271	262	84	126	0	0	0	0	85	16	2	.188	22	51	1	3	2.0	.986
1971			16	12	.571	2.87	35	35	19	270	234	69	132	7	0	0	0	94	16	1	.170	23	55	4	6	2.3	.951
1972			14	**18**	.438	3.22	36	36	9	260	250	85	110	7	0	0	0	80	16	0	.200	19	52	0	7	2.0	1.000
1973			16	16	.500	3.07	38	38	19	273	259	79	95	4	0	0	0	0	0	0	—	27	48	5	4	2.1	.938
1974			6	7	.462	3.58	16	15	6	113	119	37	40	0	0	0	0	0	0	0	—	7	14	0	1	1.3	1.000
11 yrs.			164	139	.541	2.97	360	356	152	2661.2	2435	809	1257	40	0	1	1	749	120	7	.160	242	570	26	38	2.3	.969

Year	Team	W	L	PCT	ERA	G	GS	CG	IP	H	BB	SO	ShO	W	L	SV	AB	H	HR	BA	PO	A	E	DP	TC/G	FA
														Relief Pitching			Batting									

Mel Stottlemyre *continued*
WORLD SERIES

Year	Team	W	L	PCT	ERA	G	GS	CG	IP	H	BB	SO	ShO	W	L	SV	AB	H	HR	BA	PO	A	E	DP	TC/G	FA
1964	NY A	1	1	.500	3.15	3	3	1	20	18	6	12	0	0	0	0	8	1	0	.125	2	5	0	0	2.3	1.000

Todd Stottlemyre
STOTTLEMYRE, TODD VERNON
Son of Mel Stottlemyre.
B. May 20, 1965, Sunnyside, Wash.
BL TR 6'3" 195 lbs.

Year	Team	W	L	PCT	ERA	G	GS	CG	IP	H	BB	SO	ShO	W	L	SV	AB	H	HR	BA	PO	A	E	DP	TC/G	FA
1988	TOR A	4	8	.333	5.69	28	16	0	98	109	46	67	0	2	1	0	0	0	0	–	7	11	0	0	0.6	1.000
1989		7	7	.500	3.88	27	18	0	127.2	137	44	63	0	0	1	0	0	0	0	–	7	16	5	1	1.0	.821
2 yrs.		11	15	.423	4.67	55	34	0	225.2	246	90	130	0	2	2	0	0	0	0	–	14	27	5	1	0.8	.891

LEAGUE CHAMPIONSHIP SERIES

| 1989 | TOR A | 0 | 1 | .000 | 7.20 | 1 | 1 | 0 | 5 | 7 | 2 | 3 | 0 | 0 | 0 | 0 | 0 | 0 | 0 | – | 0 | 0 | 0 | 0 | 0.0 | – |

Allyn Stout
STOUT, ALLYN McCLELLAND (Fish Hook)
B. Oct. 31, 1904, Peoria, Ill. D. Dec. 22, 1974, Sikeston, Mo.
BR TR 5'10" 167 lbs.

Year	Team	W	L	PCT	ERA	G	GS	CG	IP	H	BB	SO	ShO	W	L	SV	AB	H	HR	BA	PO	A	E	DP	TC/G	FA
1931	STL N	6	0	1.000	4.21	30	3	1	72.2	87	34	40	0	4	0	3	19	2	0	.105	1	18	0	4	0.6	1.000
1932		4	5	.444	4.40	36	3	1	73.2	87	28	32	0	4	3	1	20	2	0	.100	6	16	1	2	0.6	.957
1933	2 teams				STL N	(1G 0–0)					CIN N	(23G 2–3)														
"	total	2	3	.400	3.68	24	5	2	73.1	86	27	30	0	1	0	0	22	4	0	.182	4	13	3	1	0.8	.850
1934	CIN N	6	8	.429	4.86	41	16	4	140.2	170	47	51	0	1	3	1	43	8	0	.186	4	29	1	0	0.8	.971
1935	NY N	1	4	.200	4.91	40	2	0	88	99	37	29	0	1	4	5	15	2	1	.133	6	12	1	1	0.5	.947
1943	BOS N	1	0	1.000	6.75	9	0	0	9.1	17	4	3	0	1	0	1	2	0	0	.000	1	1	0	0	0.2	1.000
6 yrs.		20	20	.500	4.54	180	29	8	457.2	546	177	185	0	11	10	11	121	18	1	.149	22	89	6	8	0.7	.949

Jesse Stovall
STOVALL, JESSE CRAMER (Scout)
Brother of George Stovall.
B. July 24, 1875, Independence, Mo. D. July 12, 1955, San Diego, Calif.
BL TR 6' 175 lbs.

Year	Team	W	L	PCT	ERA	G	GS	CG	IP	H	BB	SO	ShO	W	L	SV	AB	H	HR	BA	PO	A	E	DP	TC/G	FA
1903	CLE A	5	1	.833	2.05	6	6	6	57	44	21	12	2	0	0	0	22	1	0	.045	4	15	1	1	3.3	.950
1904	DET A	3	13	.188	4.42	22	17	13	146.2	170	45	41	1	0	1	0	56	11	0	.196	9	51	3	1	2.9	.952
2 yrs.		8	14	.364	3.76	28	23	19	203.2	214	66	53	3	0	1	0	78	12	0	.154	13	66	4	2	3.0	.952

Harry Stovey
STOVEY, HARRY DUFFIELD
Born Harry Duffield Stowe.
B. Dec. 20, 1856, Philadelphia, Pa. D. Sept. 20, 1937, New Bedford, Mass.
Manager 1881, 1885.
BR TR 5'11½" 180 lbs.

Year	Team	W	L	PCT	ERA	G	GS	CG	IP	H	BB	SO	ShO	W	L	SV	AB	H	HR	BA	PO	A	E	DP	TC/G	FA
1880	WOR N	0	0	–	4.50	2	0	0	6	8	3	3	0	0	0	0	355	94	6	.265	0	0	0	0	0.0	–
1883	PHI AA	0	0	–	9.00	1	0	0	3	5	0	4	0	0	0	0	421	127	14	.302	0	0	0	0	0.0	–
1886		0	0	–	27.00	1	0	0	.1	2	0	0	0	0	0	0	489	144	7	.294	0	0	0	0	0.0	–
3 yrs.		0	0	–	6.75	4	0	0	9.1	15	3	7	0	0	0	0	*				0	0	0	0	0.0	–

Hal Stowe
STOWE, HAROLD RUDOLPH (Rudy)
B. Aug. 29, 1937, Gastonia, N. C.
BL TL 6' 170 lbs.

Year	Team	W	L	PCT	ERA	G	GS	CG	IP	H	BB	SO	ShO	W	L	SV	AB	H	HR	BA	PO	A	E	DP	TC/G	FA
1960	NY A	0	0	–	9.00	1	0	0	1	0	1	0	0	0	0	0	0	0	0	–	0	0	0	0	0.0	–

Mike Strahler
STRAHLER, MICHAEL WAYNE
B. Mar. 14, 1947, Chicago, Ill.
BR TR 6'4" 180 lbs.

Year	Team	W	L	PCT	ERA	G	GS	CG	IP	H	BB	SO	ShO	W	L	SV	AB	H	HR	BA	PO	A	E	DP	TC/G	FA
1970	LA N	1	1	.500	1.42	6	0	0	19	13	10	11	0	1	1	1	8	2	0	.250	3	2	0	0	0.8	1.000
1971		0	0	–	2.77	6	0	0	13	10	8	7	0	0	0	0	1	0	0	.000	1	1	0	0	0.3	1.000
1972		1	2	.333	3.26	19	2	1	47	42	22	25	0	0	1	0	11	2	0	.182	3	6	2	0	0.6	.818
1973	DET A	4	5	.444	4.39	22	11	1	80	84	39	37	0	0	1	0	0	0	0	–	3	9	0	1	0.5	1.000
4 yrs.		6	8	.429	3.57	53	13	2	159	149	79	80	0	1	3	1	20	4	0	.200	10	18	2	1	0.6	.933

Dick Strahs
STRAHS, RICHARD BERNARD
B. Dec. 4, 1924, Evanston, Ill.
BL TR 6' 192 lbs.

Year	Team	W	L	PCT	ERA	G	GS	CG	IP	H	BB	SO	ShO	W	L	SV	AB	H	HR	BA	PO	A	E	DP	TC/G	FA
1954	CHI A	0	0	–	5.65	9	0	0	14.1	16	8	8	0	0	0	0	1	0	0	.000	0	4	0	0	0.4	1.000

Les Straker
STRAKER, LESTER PAUL
Born Lester Paul Straker y Bolnalda.
B. Oct. 10, 1959, Ciudad Bolivar, Venezuela
BR TR 6'1" 193 lbs.

Year	Team	W	L	PCT	ERA	G	GS	CG	IP	H	BB	SO	ShO	W	L	SV	AB	H	HR	BA	PO	A	E	DP	TC/G	FA
1987	MIN A	8	10	.444	4.37	31	26	1	154.1	150	59	76	0	0	0	0	0	0	0	–	5	18	0	0	0.8	.958
1988		2	5	.286	3.92	16	14	0	82.2	86	25	23	1	0	0	1	0	0	0	–	9	13	1	1	1.4	.957
2 yrs.		10	15	.400	4.22	47	40	2	237	236	84	99	1	0	1	1	0	0	0	–	14	31	2	1	1.0	.957

LEAGUE CHAMPIONSHIP SERIES

| 1987 | MIN A | 0 | 0 | – | 16.88 | 1 | 1 | 0 | 2.2 | 3 | 4 | 1 | 0 | 0 | 0 | 0 | 0 | 0 | 0 | – | 0 | 2 | 0 | 0 | 2.0 | 1.000 |

WORLD SERIES

| 1987 | MIN A | 0 | 0 | – | 4.00 | 2 | 2 | 0 | 9 | 9 | 3 | 6 | 0 | 0 | 0 | 0 | 2 | 0 | 0 | .000 | 1 | 0 | 0 | 0 | 0.5 | 1.000 |

Bob Strampe
STRAMPE, ROBERT EDWIN
B. June 13, 1950, Janesville, Wis.
BB TR 6'1" 185 lbs.

Year	Team	W	L	PCT	ERA	G	GS	CG	IP	H	BB	SO	ShO	W	L	SV	AB	H	HR	BA	PO	A	E	DP	TC/G	FA
1972	DET A	0	0	–	10.80	7	0	0	5	6	7	4	0	0	0	0	0	0	0	–	0	0	0	0	0.0	–

Paul Strand
STRAND, PAUL EDWARD
B. Dec. 19, 1893, Carbonado, Wash. D. July 2, 1974, Salt Lake City, Utah
BR TL 6'½" 190 lbs.

Year	Team	W	L	PCT	ERA	G	GS	CG	IP	H	BB	SO	ShO	W	L	SV	AB	H	HR	BA	PO	A	E	DP	TC/G	FA
1913	BOS N	0	0	–	2.12	7	0	0	17	22	12	6	0	0	0	0	6	1	0	.167	1	6	1	0	1.1	.875
1914		6	2	.750	2.44	16	3	1	55.1	47	23	33	0	5	1	0	19	2	0	.105	0	13	3	1	1.0	.813

Year	Team		W	L	PCT	ERA	G	GS	CG	IP	H	BB	SO	ShO	Relief Pitching W	L	SV	Batting AB	H	HR	BA	PO	A	E	DP	TC/G	FA

Paul Strand *continued*

| 1915 | | | 1 | 1 | .500 | 2.38 | 6 | 2 | 2 | 22.2 | 26 | 3 | 13 | 0 | 0 | 0 | 1 | 22 | 2 | 0 | .091 | 1 | 2 | 1 | 0 | 0.7 | .750 |
| 3 yrs. | | | 7 | 3 | .700 | 2.37 | 29 | 5 | 3 | 95 | 95 | 38 | 52 | 0 | 5 | 1 | 1 | * | | | | 2 | 21 | 5 | 1 | 1.0 | .821 |

Monty Stratton

STRATTON, MONTY FRANKLIN PIERCE (Gander)
B. May 21, 1912, Celeste, Tex.   D. Sept. 29, 1982, Greenville, Tex.   BR TR 6'5''   180 lbs.

1934	CHI	A	0	0	–	5.40	1	0	0	3.1	4	1	0	0	0	0	0	2	0	0	.000	0	0	0	0	0.0	–
1935			1	2	.333	4.03	5	5	2	38	40	9	8	0	0	0	0	14	2	0	.143	1	9	0	0	2.0	1.000
1936			5	7	.417	5.21	16	14	3	95	117	46	37	0	0	1	0	37	8	1	.216	3	25	1	1	1.8	.966
1937			15	5	.750	2.40	22	21	14	164.2	142	37	69	5	0	0	0	60	12	1	.200	4	35	0	2	1.8	1.000
1938			15	9	.625	4.01	26	22	17	186.1	186	56	82	0	1	1	2	79	21	2	.266	6	36	2	1	1.7	.955
5 yrs.			36	23	.610	3.71	70	62	36	487.1	489	149	196	5	1	2	2	192	43	4	.224	14	105	3	4	1.7	.975

Scott Stratton

STRATTON, C. SCOTT
B. Oct. 2, 1869, Campbellsburg, Ky.   D. Mar. 8, 1939, Louisville, Ky.   BL TR 6'   180 lbs.

1888	LOU	AA	10	17	.370	3.64	33	28	28	269.2	287	53	97	2	0	0	0	249	64	1	.257	26	51	7	1	2.5	.917
1889			3	13	.188	3.23	19	17	13	133.2	157	42	42	0	0	1	1	229	66	4	.288	7	38	6	3	2.7	.882
1890			34	14	**.708**	**2.36**	50	49	44	431	398	61	207	4	0	0	0	189	61	3	.323	18	111	3	2	2.6	.977
1891	2 teams		PIT N	(2G 0–2)		LOU AA	(20G 6–13)																				
"	total		6	15	.286	3.92	22	22	22	190.1	220	39	57	1	0	0	0	123	28	0	.228	7	64	5	5	3.5	.934
1892	LOU	N	21	19	.525	2.92	42	40	39	351.2	342	70	93	2	0	0	0	219	56	0	.256	22	86	10	4	2.8	.915
1893			12	24	.333	5.45	38	36	35	323.2	451	104	44	1	0	0	0	221	50	0	.226	25	92	3	2	3.2	.975
1894	2 teams		LOU N	(7G 1–5)		CHI N	(15G 8–5)																				
"	total		9	10	.474	6.65	22	17	15	162.1	270	53	26	0	2	1	0	133	48	3	.361	10	31	3	2	2.0	.932
1895	CHI	N	2	3	.400	9.60	5	5	3	30	51	14	4	0	0	0	0	24	7	0	.292	5	10	3	0	3.6	.833
8 yrs.			97	115	.458	3.88	231	214	199	1892.1	2176	436	570	10	2	2	1	*				120	483	40	19	2.8	.938

Joe Strauss

STRAUSS, JOSEF (The Socker)
B. Mar. 17, 1844, Gecse, Hungary   D. June 25, 1906, Cincinnati, Ohio   BR TR

| 1886 | BKN | AA | 0 | 0 | – | 4.50 | 2 | 0 | 0 | 4 | 6 | 3 | 0 | 0 | 0 | 0 | 1 | * | | | | 0 | 0 | 0 | 0 | 0.0 | – |

Oscar Streit

STREIT, OSCAR WILLIAM
B. July 7, 1873, Florence, Ala.   D. Oct. 10, 1935, Birmingham, Ala.   BL TL 6'5''   190 lbs.

1899	BOS	N	1	0	1.000	6.75	2	1	1	14.2	15	15	0	0	0	0	0	7	0	0	.000	0	5	0	0	2.5	1.000
1902	CLE	A	0	7	.000	5.23	8	7	4	51.2	72	25	10	0	0	0	0	19	4	0	.211	1	13	4	0	2.3	.778
2 yrs.			1	7	.125	5.56	10	8	5	66.1	87	40	10	0	0	0	0	26	4	0	.154	1	18	4	0	2.3	.826

Ed Strelecki

STRELECKI, EDWARD HENRY
B. Apr. 10, 1908, Newark, N. J.   D. Jan. 9, 1968, Newark, N. J.   BR TR 5'11½'' 180 lbs.

1928	STL	A	0	2	.000	4.29	22	2	1	50.1	49	17	8	0	0	0	0	10	2	0	.200	0	13	1	0	0.6	.929
1929			1	1	.500	4.91	7	0	0	11	12	6	2	0	1	1	0	2	0	0	.000	1	3	0	0	0.6	1.000
1931	CIN	N	0	0	–	9.25	13	0	0	24.1	37	9	3	0	0	0	1	5	1	0	.200	1	8	1	0	0.8	.900
3 yrs.			1	3	.250	5.78	42	2	1	85.2	98	32	13	0	1	1	1	17	3	0	.176	2	24	2	0	0.7	.929

Phil Stremmel

STREMMEL, PHILIP
B. Apr. 16, 1880, Zanesville, Ohio   D. Dec. 26, 1947, Chicago, Ill.   BR TR 6'   175 lbs.

1909	STL	A	0	2	.000	4.50	2	2	2	18	20	4	6	0	0	0	0	6	0	0	.000	2	7	0	0	4.5	1.000
1910			0	2	.000	3.72	5	2	2	29	31	16	7	0	0	0	0	8	1	0	.125	4	17	1	1	4.4	.955
2 yrs.			0	4	.000	4.02	7	4	4	47	51	20	13	0	0	0	0	14	1	0	.071	6	24	1	1	4.4	.968

Cub Stricker

STRICKER, JOHN A.
Born John A. Streaker.
B. June 8, 1859, Philadelphia, Pa.   D. Nov. 19, 1937, Philadelphia, Pa.   BR TR 5'3''   133 lbs.
Manager 1892.

1882	PHI	AA	1	0	1.000	1.29	2	0	0	7	3	1	2	0	1	0	0	272	59	0	.217	0	1	0	0	0.5	1.000
1884			0	0	–	6.00	2	0	0	3	6	1	1	0	0	0	0	399	92	1	.231	0	0	1	0	1.0	–
1887	CLE	AA	0	0	–	3.18	3	0	0	5.2	5	7	2	0	0	0	0	534	141	2	.264	1	3	2	0	2.0	.667
1888			1	0	1.000	4.50	2	0	0	12	16	2	5	0	1	0	0	493	115	1	.233	0	2	0	0	1.0	1.000
4 yrs.			2	0	1.000	3.58	8	0	0	27.2	30	11	10	0	2	0	1	*				1	6	3	0	1.3	.700

Bill Strickland

STRICKLAND, WILLIAM GOSS
B. Mar. 29, 1908, Nashville, Ga.   BR TR 6'2''   170 lbs.

| 1937 | STL | A | 0 | 0 | – | 5.91 | 9 | 0 | 0 | 21.1 | 28 | 15 | 6 | 0 | 0 | 0 | 0 | 6 | 1 | 0 | .167 | 1 | 3 | 0 | 0 | 0.4 | 1.000 |

Jim Strickland

STRICKLAND, JAMES MICHAEL
B. June 12, 1946, Los Angeles, Calif.   BL TL 6'   175 lbs.

1971	MIN	A	1	0	1.000	1.45	24	0	0	31	20	18	21	0	1	0	1	1	0	0	.000	4	5	1	0	0.4	.900
1972			3	1	.750	2.50	25	0	0	36	28	19	30	0	3	1	3	3	1	0	.333	3	6	2	1	0.4	.818
1973			0	1	.000	11.81	7	0	0	5.1	11	5	6	0	0	0	0	0	0	0	–	0	1	0	0	0.1	1.000
1975	CLE	A	0	0	–	1.93	4	0	0	4.2	4	2	3	0	0	0	0	0	0	0	–	0	0	0	0	0.0	–
4 yrs.			4	2	.667	2.69	60	0	0	77	63	44	60	0	4	2	4	4	1	0	.250	7	12	3	1	0.4	.864

Elmer Stricklett

STRICKLETT, ELMER GRIFFIN
B. Aug. 29, 1876, Glasco, Kans.   D. June 7, 1964, Santa Cruz, Calif.   BR TR 5'6''   140 lbs.

1904	CHI	A	0	1	.000	10.29	1	1	0	7	12	2	3	0	0	0	0	3	0	0	.000	0	3	0	0	3.0	1.000
1905	BKN	N	9	18	.333	3.34	33	28	25	237	259	71	77	1	0	0	1	88	13	0	.148	13	112	10	4	4.1	.926
1906			14	18	.438	2.72	41	35	28	291.2	273	77	88	5	0	1	5	97	20	0	.206	22	128	5	2	3.8	.968
1907			12	14	.462	2.27	29	26	25	229.2	211	65	69	4	1	0	0	81	12	0	.148	17	95	2	4	3.9	.958
4 yrs.			35	51	.407	2.85	104	90	78	765.1	755	215	237	10	1	2	6	269	45	0	.167	52	338	17	10	3.9	.958

Year	Team		W	L	PCT	ERA	G	GS	CG	IP	H	BB	SO	ShO	W	L	SV	AB	H	HR	BA	PO	A	E	DP	TC/G	FA

John Strike

STRIKE, JOHN
B. 1865, Philadelphia, Pa. Deceased.

Year	Team		W	L	PCT	ERA	G	GS	CG	IP	H	BB	SO	ShO	W	L	SV	AB	H	HR	BA	PO	A	E	DP	TC/G	FA
1886	PHI	N	1	1	.500	4.80	2	2	1	15	19	7	11	0	0	0	0	*				0	0	0	0	0.0	–

Jake Striker

STRIKER, WILBUR SCOTT
B. Oct. 23, 1933, New Washington, Ohio
BL TL 6'2" 200 lbs.

Year	Team		W	L	PCT	ERA	G	GS	CG	IP	H	BB	SO	ShO	W	L	SV	AB	H	HR	BA	PO	A	E	DP	TC/G	FA
1959	CLE	A	1	0	1.000	2.70	1	1	0	6.2	8	4	5	0	0	0	0	1	0	0	.000	1	1	0	0	2.0	1.000
1960	CHI	A	0	0	–	4.91	2	0	0	3.2	5	1	1	0	0	0	0	0	0	0	–	0	0	0	0	0.0	
2 yrs.			1	0	1.000	3.48	3	1	0	10.1	13	5	6	0	0	0	0	1	0	0	.000	1	1	0	0	0.7	1.000

Nick Strincevich

STRINCEVICH, NICHOLAS MIHAILOVICH (Jumbo)
B. Mar. 1, 1915, Gary, Ind.
BR TR 6'1" 180 lbs.

Year	Team		W	L	PCT	ERA	G	GS	CG	IP	H	BB	SO	ShO	W	L	SV	AB	H	HR	BA	PO	A	E	DP	TC/G	FA
1940	BOS	N	4	8	.333	5.53	32	14	5	128.2	142	63	54	0	0	1	1	43	5	0	.116	11	14	1	1	0.8	.962
1941	2 teams		BOS N	(3G 0–0)		PIT N	(12G 1–2)																					
"	total		1	2	.333	5.77	15	3	0	34.1	42	19	13	0	1	0	0	7	3	0	.429	3	8	2	0	0.9	.846
1942	PIT	N	0	0	–	2.82	7	1	0	22.1	19	9	10	0	0	0	0	4	0	0	.000	4	3	1	0	1.1	.875
1944			14	7	.667	3.08	40	26	11	190	190	37	47	0	2	0	2	57	9	0	.158	19	60	2	2	2.0	.975
1945			16	10	.615	3.31	36	29	18	228.1	235	49	74	1	0	0	2	84	17	0	.202	14	36	2	1	1.4	.962
1946			10	15	.400	3.58	32	22	11	176	185	44	49	3	0	3	1	52	8	0	.154	14	25	1	0	1.3	.975
1947			1	6	.143	5.26	32	7	1	89	111	37	22	0	0	1	0	21	1	0	.048	2	17	0	1	0.6	1.000
1948	2 teams		PIT N	(3G 0–0)		PHI N	(6G 0–1)																					
"	total		0	1	.000	9.00	9	1	0	21	34	12	5	0	0	0	0	4	0	0	.000	1	3	1	0	0.6	.800
8 yrs.			46	49	.484	4.05	203	103	46	889.2	958	270	274	4	3	5	6	272	43	0	.158	68	166	10	5	1.2	.959

John Strohmayer

STROHMAYER, JOHN EMERY
B. Oct. 13, 1946, Belle Fourche, S. D.
BR TR 6'1" 181 lbs.

Year	Team		W	L	PCT	ERA	G	GS	CG	IP	H	BB	SO	ShO	W	L	SV	AB	H	HR	BA	PO	A	E	DP	TC/G	FA
1970	MON	N	3	1	.750	4.86	42	0	0	76	85	39	74	0	3	1	0	6	1	0	.167	7	7	0	0	0.3	1.000
1971			7	5	.583	4.34	27	14	2	114	124	31	56	0	1	1	1	35	8	0	.229	12	12	1	0	0.9	.960
1972			1	2	.333	3.52	48	0	0	76.2	73	31	50	0	1	2	3	4	0	0	.000	1	16	0	2	0.4	1.000
1973	2 teams		MON N	(17G 0–1)		NY N	(7G 0–0)																					
"	total		0	1	.000	5.84	24	3	0	44.2	47	26	20	0	0	1	0	5	1	0	.200	3	6	0	0	0.4	1.000
1974	NY	N	0	0	–	0.00	1	0	0	1	0	1	0	0	0	0	0	0	0	0	–	0	0	0	0	0.0	–
5 yrs.			11	9	.550	4.47	142	17	2	312.1	329	128	200	0	5	4	4	50	10	0	.200	23	41	1	2	0.5	.985

Brent Strom

STROM, BRENT TERRY
B. Oct. 14, 1948, San Diego, Calif.
BR TL 6'3" 189 lbs.

Year	Team		W	L	PCT	ERA	G	GS	CG	IP	H	BB	SO	ShO	W	L	SV	AB	H	HR	BA	PO	A	E	DP	TC/G	FA
1972	NY	N	0	3	.000	6.82	11	5	0	30.1	34	15	20	0	0	0	0	6	0	0	.000	0	2	0	0	0.2	1.000
1973	CLE	A	2	10	.167	4.61	27	18	2	123	134	47	91	0	0	1	0	0	0	0	–	2	23	1	1	1.0	.962
1975	SD	N	8	8	.500	2.55	18	16	6	120	103	33	56	2	0	0	0	30	3	0	.100	8	19	1	2	1.6	.964
1976			12	16	.429	3.29	36	33	8	210.2	188	73	103	1	0	0	0	63	4	0	.063	13	32	3	3	1.3	.938
1977			0	2	.000	12.18	8	3	0	17	23	12	8	0	0	0	0	3	1	0	.333	1	2	0	0	0.4	1.000
5 yrs.			22	39	.361	3.95	100	75	16	501	482	180	278	3	0	1	0	102	8	0	.078	24	78	5	6	1.1	.953

Floyd Stromme

STROMME, FLOYD MARVIN (Rock)
B. Aug. 1, 1916, Cooperstown, N. D.
BR TR 5'11" 170 lbs.

Year	Team		W	L	PCT	ERA	G	GS	CG	IP	H	BB	SO	ShO	W	L	SV	AB	H	HR	BA	PO	A	E	DP	TC/G	FA
1939	CLE	A	0	1	.000	4.85	5	0	0	13	13	13	4	0	0	1	0	3	1	0	.333	0	2	1	0	0.6	.667

Sailor Stroud

STROUD, RALPH VIVIAN
B. May 15, 1885, Ironia, N. J. D. Apr. 11, 1970, Stockton, Calif.
BR TR 6' 160 lbs.

Year	Team		W	L	PCT	ERA	G	GS	CG	IP	H	BB	SO	ShO	W	L	SV	AB	H	HR	BA	PO	A	E	DP	TC/G	FA
1910	DET	A	5	9	.357	3.25	28	15	7	130.1	123	41	63	3	0	0	1	39	1	0	.026	6	21	1	0	1.0	.964
1915	NY	N	11	9	.550	2.79	32	22	8	184	194	35	62	0	1	2	1	56	9	0	.161	6	53	3	0	1.9	.952
1916			1	2	.333	2.70	10	4	0	46.2	47	9	16	0	1	1	1	14	1	0	.071	0	12	0	0	1.2	1.000
3 yrs.			17	20	.459	2.94	70	41	15	361	364	85	141	3	2	3	3	109	11	0	.101	12	86	4	0	1.5	.961

Steamboat Struss

STRUSS, CLARENCE HERBERT
B. Feb. 24, 1909, Riverdale, Ill. D. Sept. 12, 1985, Grand Rapids, Mich.
BR TR 5'11" 163 lbs.

Year	Team		W	L	PCT	ERA	G	GS	CG	IP	H	BB	SO	ShO	W	L	SV	AB	H	HR	BA	PO	A	E	DP	TC/G	FA
1934	PIT	N	0	1	.000	6.43	1	1	0	7	7	6	3	0	0	0	0	3	1	0	.333	0	2	0	0	2.0	1.000

Dutch Stryker

STRYKER, STERLING ALPA
B. July 29, 1895, Atlantic Highlands, N. J. D. Nov. 5, 1964, Red Bank, N. J.
BR TR 5'11½" 180 lbs.

Year	Team		W	L	PCT	ERA	G	GS	CG	IP	H	BB	SO	ShO	W	L	SV	AB	H	HR	BA	PO	A	E	DP	TC/G	FA
1924	BOS	N	3	8	.273	6.01	20	10	2	73.1	90	22	22	0	2	2	0	23	5	0	.217	0	30	1	1	1.6	.968
1926	BKN	N	0	0	–	27.00	2	0	0	2	8	1	0	0	0	0	0	0	0	0	–	0	0	0	0	0.0	–
2 yrs.			3	8	.273	6.57	22	10	2	75.1	98	23	22	0	2	2	0	23	5	0	.217	0	30	1	1	1.4	.968

Johnny Stuart

STUART, JOHN DAVIS (Stud)
B. Apr. 27, 1901, Clinton, Tenn. D. May 13, 1970, Charleston, W. Va.
BR TR 5'11" 170 lbs.

Year	Team		W	L	PCT	ERA	G	GS	CG	IP	H	BB	SO	ShO	W	L	SV	AB	H	HR	BA	PO	A	E	DP	TC/G	FA
1922	STL	N	0	0	–	9.00	2	1	0	2	2	2	1	0	0	0	0	0	0	0	–	0	0	0	0	0.0	–
1923			9	5	.643	4.27	37	10	7	149.2	139	70	55	1	2	3	3	57	14	0	.246	6	29	3	2	1.0	.921
1924			9	11	.450	4.75	28	22	13	159	167	60	54	0	0	1	0	54	11	0	.204	3	23	0	1	0.9	1.000
1925			2	2	.500	6.13	15	1	1	47	52	24	14	0	1	2	0	16	4	0	.250	2	10	1	0	0.9	.923
4 yrs.			20	18	.526	4.76	82	34	21	357.2	360	156	124	1	3	6	3	127	29	0	.228	11	62	4	3	0.9	.948

Marlin Stuart

STUART, MARLIN HENRY
B. Aug. 8, 1918, Paragould, Ark.
BL TR 6'2" 185 lbs.

Year	Team		W	L	PCT	ERA	G	GS	CG	IP	H	BB	SO	ShO	W	L	SV	AB	H	HR	BA	PO	A	E	DP	TC/G	FA
1949	DET	A	0	2	.000	9.10	14	2	0	29.2	39	35	14	0	0	1	0	6	2	0	.333	0	7	0	0	0.5	1.000
1950			3	1	.750	5.56	19	1	0	43.2	59	22	19	0	3	0	2	12	1	0	.083	2	8	0	0	0.5	1.000
1951			4	6	.400	3.77	29	15	5	124	119	71	46	0	0	0	0	43	10	1	.233	6	25	1	0	1.1	.969
1952	2 teams		DET A	(30G 3–2)		STL A	(12G 1–2)																					
"	total		4	4	.500	4.76	42	11	2	117.1	117	57	45	0	0	0	0	29	2	0	.069	9	17	6	0	0.8	.813
1953	STL	A	8	2	.800	3.94	60	2	0	114.1	136	44	46	0	8	1	7	26	5	0	.192	9	15	1	2	0.4	.960

Year	Team	W	L	PCT	ERA	G	GS	CG	IP	H	BB	SO	ShO	Relief Pitching W	L	SV	Batting AB	H	HR	BA	PO	A	E	DP	TC/G	FA

Marlin Stuart *continued*

1954	2 teams	BAL A	(22G 1–2)		NY A	(10G 3–0)																				
"	total	4	2	.667	4.76	32	0	0	56.2	74	27	15	0	4	2	3	9	2	0	.222	5	13	1	2	0.6	.947
	6 yrs.	23	17	.575	4.65	196	31	7	485.2	544	256	185	0	17	5	15	125	22	1	.176	31	85	9	4	0.6	.928

George Stueland

STUELAND, GEORGE ANTON
B. Mar. 2, 1899, Algona, Iowa
D. Sept. 9, 1964, Onawa, Iowa

BB TR 6'1½" 174 lbs.
BR 1925

1921	CHI N	0	1	.000	5.73	2	1	0	11	11	7	4	0	0	0	0	3	1	0	.333	0	3	0	0	1.5	1.000
1922		9	4	.692	5.92	35	12	4	111	129	48	43	0	3	1	0	31	4	0	.129	3	20	0	0	0.7	1.000
1923		0	1	.000	5.63	6	0	0	8	11	5	2	0	0	1	0	0	0	0	—	0	3	0	0	0.5	1.000
1925		0	0	—	3.00	2	0	0	3	2	3	2	0	0	0	0	1	1	0	1.000	0	1	0	1	0.5	1.000
	4 yrs.	9	6	.600	5.82	45	13	4	133	153	63	51	0	3	2	0	35	6	0	.171	3	27	0	1	0.7	1.000

Paul Stuffel

STUFFEL, PAUL HARRINGTON (Stu)
B. Mar. 22, 1927, Canton, Ohio

BR TR 6'2" 185 lbs.

1950	PHI N	0	0	—	1.80	3	0	0	5	4	1	3	0	0	0	0	0	0	0	—	0	1	0	0	0.3	1.000
1952		1	0	1.000	3.00	2	1	0	6	5	7	3	0	0	0	0	2	0	0	.000	0	3	0	0	1.5	1.000
1953		0	0	—	∞	2	0	0	0	0	4	0	0	0	0	0	0	0	0	—	0	0	0	0	0.0	—
	3 yrs.	1	0	1.000	5.73	7	1	0	11	9	12	6	0	0	0	0	2	0	0	.000	0	4	0	0	0.6	1.000

George Stultz

STULTZ, GEORGE IRVIN
B. June 30, 1873, Louisville, Ky. D. Mar. 19, 1955, Louisville, Ky.

5'10" 150 lbs.

| 1894 | BOS N | 1 | 0 | 1.000 | 0.00 | 1 | 1 | 1 | 9 | 4 | 5 | 1 | 0 | 0 | 0 | 0 | 3 | 1 | 0 | .333 | 0 | 5 | 0 | 0 | 5.0 | 1.000 |

Jim Stump

STUMP, JAMES GILBERT
B. Feb. 10, 1932, Lansing, Mich.

BR TR 6' 188 lbs.

1957	DET A	1	0	1.000	2.03	6	0	0	13.1	11	8	2	0	1	0	0	2	1	0	.500	2	3	0	0	0.8	1.000
1959		0	0	—	2.38	5	0	0	11.1	12	4	6	0	0	0	0	1	1	0	1.000	1	2	0	0	0.6	1.000
	2 yrs.	1	0	1.000	2.19	11	0	0	24.2	23	12	8	0	1	0	0	3	2	0	.667	3	5	0	0	0.7	1.000

John Stuper

STUPER, JOHN ANTON
B. May 9, 1957, Butler, Pa.

BR TR 6'2" 200 lbs.

1982	STL N	9	7	.563	3.36	23	21	2	136.2	137	55	53	0	0	0	0	42	5	0	.119	7	10	1	1	0.8	.944
1983		12	11	.522	3.68	40	30	6	198	202	71	81	1	1	1	1	59	8	0	.136	17	24	4	2	1.1	.911
1984		3	5	.375	5.28	15	12	0	61.1	73	20	19	0	0	0	0	16	1	0	.063	5	12	1	0	1.2	.944
1985	CIN N	8	5	.615	4.55	33	13	1	99	116	37	38	0	2	0	0	17	1	0	.059	12	14	0	0	0.8	1.000
	4 yrs.	32	28	.533	3.96	111	76	9	495	528	183	191	1	3	1	1	134	15	0	.112	41	60	6	3	1.0	.944

LEAGUE CHAMPIONSHIP SERIES

| 1982 | STL N | 0 | 0 | — | 3.00 | 1 | 1 | 0 | 6 | 4 | 1 | 4 | 0 | 0 | 0 | 0 | 1 | 0 | 0 | .000 | 0 | 0 | 0 | 0 | 0.0 | — |

WORLD SERIES

| 1982 | STL N | 1 | 0 | 1.000 | 3.46 | 2 | 2 | 1 | 13 | 10 | 5 | 5 | 0 | 0 | 0 | 0 | 0 | 0 | 0 | — | 1 | 1 | 0 | 0 | 1.0 | 1.000 |

Tom Sturdivant

STURDIVANT, THOMAS VIRGIL (Snake)
B. Apr. 28, 1930, Gordon, Kans.

BL TR 6'½" 170 lbs.

1955	NY A	1	3	.250	3.16	33	1	0	68.1	48	42	48	0	1	1	0	12	1	0	.083	4	8	0	2	0.4	1.000
1956		16	8	.667	3.30	32	17	6	158.1	134	52	110	2	6	2	5	64	20	0	.313	11	13	2	1	0.8	.923
1957		16	6	**.727**	2.54	28	28	7	201.2	170	80	118	2	0	0	0	71	13	0	.183	8	26	2	4	1.3	.944
1958		3	6	.333	4.20	15	10	0	70.2	77	38	41	0	0	0	0	21	4	0	.190	3	4	1	1	0.5	.875
1959	2 teams	NY A	(7G 0–2)		KC A	(36G 2–6)																				
"	total	2	8	.200	4.73	43	6	0	97	90	43	73	0	2	4	5	23	1	0	.043	9	21	3	2	0.8	.909
1960	BOS A	3	3	.500	4.97	40	3	0	101.1	106	45	67	0	0	1	1	22	4	0	.182	7	14	1	0	0.6	.955
1961	2 teams	WAS A	(15G 2–6)		PIT N	(13G 5–2)																				
"	total	7	8	.467	3.69	28	21	7	165.2	148	57	84	2	0	0	0	58	10	0	.172	11	29	0	0	1.4	1.000
1962	PIT N	9	5	.643	3.73	49	12	2	125.1	120	39	76	1	3	1	2	33	6	0	.182	10	23	3	0	0.7	.917
1963	3 teams	PIT N	(3G 0–0)		DET A	(28G 1–2)		KC A	(17G 1–2)																	
"	total	2	4	.333	3.95	48	2	0	116.1	98	45	68	0	2	3	4	22	0	0	.000	8	21	0	1	0.6	1.000
1964	2 teams	KC A	(3G 0–0)		NY N	(16G 0–0)																				
"	total	0	0	—	6.40	19	0	0	32.1	38	8	19	0	0	1	0	2	1	0	.500	1	4	1	0	0.3	.833
	10 yrs.	59	51	.536	3.74	335	101	22	1137	1029	449	704	7	14	15	17	328	60	0	.183	72	163	13	11	0.7	.948

WORLD SERIES

1955	NY A	0	0	—	6.00	2	0	0	3	5	2	0	0	0	0	0	0	0	0	—	0	1	0	0	0.5	1.000
1956		1	0	1.000	2.79	2	1	1	9.2	8	8	9	0	0	0	0	3	1	0	.333	2	0	0	0	1.0	1.000
1957		0	0	—	6.00	2	1	0	6	6	1	2	0	0	0	0	1	0	0	.000	0	1	0	0	0.5	1.000
	3 yrs.	1	0	1.000	4.34	6	2	1	18.2	19	11	11	0	0	0	0	4	1	0	.250	2	2	0	0	0.7	1.000

Dick Such

SUCH, RICHARD STANLEY
B. Oct. 15, 1944, Sanford, N. C.

BL TR 6'4" 190 lbs.

| 1970 | WAS A | 1 | 5 | .167 | 7.56 | 21 | 5 | 0 | 50 | 48 | 45 | 41 | 0 | 1 | 0 | 0 | 13 | 3 | 0 | .231 | 1 | 7 | 0 | 1 | 0.4 | 1.000 |

Charley Suche

SUCHE, CHARLES MORRIS
B. Aug. 5, 1915, Cranes Mill, Tex. D. Feb. 11, 1984, San Antonio, Tex.

BR TL 6'2" 190 lbs.

| 1938 | CLE A | 0 | 0 | — | 27.00 | 2 | 0 | 0 | 1.1 | 4 | 3 | 1 | 0 | 0 | 0 | 0 | 1 | 1 | 0 | 1.000 | 0 | 0 | 0 | 0 | 0.0 | — |

Jim Suchecki

SUCHECKI, JAMES JOSEPH
B. Aug. 25, 1927, Chicago, Ill.

BR TR 6' 200 lbs.

| 1950 | BOS A | 0 | 0 | — | 4.50 | 4 | 0 | 0 | 4 | 3 | 4 | 3 | 0 | 0 | 0 | 0 | 0 | 0 | 0 | — | 0 | 0 | 0 | 0 | 0.0 | — |
| 1951 | STL A | 0 | 6 | .000 | 5.42 | 29 | 6 | 0 | 89.2 | 113 | 42 | 47 | 0 | 0 | 1 | 0 | 20 | 2 | 0 | .100 | 4 | 11 | 1 | 1 | 0.6 | .938 |

Year	Team		W	L	PCT	ERA	G	GS	CG	IP	H	BB	SO	ShO	W	L	SV	AB	H	HR	BA	PO	A	E	DP	TC/G	FA
															Relief Pitching			Batting									

Jim Suchecki *continued*

Year	Team		W	L	PCT	ERA	G	GS	CG	IP	H	BB	SO	ShO	W	L	SV	AB	H	HR	BA	PO	A	E	DP	TC/G	FA
1952	PIT	N	0	0	—	5.40	5	0	0	10	14	4	6	0	0	0	0	2	0	0	.000	0	2	1	0	0.6	.667
3 yrs.			0	6	.000	5.38	38	6	0	103.2	130	50	56	0	0	1	0	22	2	0	.091	4	13	2	1	0.5	.895

Willie Sudhoff

SUDHOFF, JOHN WILLIAM (Wee Willie)
B. Sept. 17, 1874, St. Louis, Mo. D. May 25, 1917, St. Louis, Mo. — BR TR 5'7" 165 lbs.

Year	Team		W	L	PCT	ERA	G	GS	CG	IP	H	BB	SO	ShO	W	L	SV	AB	H	HR	BA	PO	A	E	DP	TC/G	FA
1897	STL	N	1	8	.111	4.47	11	9	9	92.2	126	21	19	0	0	0	0	42	10	0	.238	8	29	3	2	3.6	.925
1898			11	27	.289	4.34	41	38	35	315	355	102	65	0	1	0	1	120	19	0	.158	15	114	12	5	3.4	.915
1899	2 teams					CLE N (11G 3–8)				STL N (26G 13–10)																	
"	total		16	18	.471	4.67	37	34	26	275.2	334	92	43	0	0	0	0	99	16	0	.162	11	99	11	3	3.3	.909
1900	STL	N	6	8	.429	2.76	16	14	13	127	128	37	29	2	0	1	0	106	20	0	.189	5	35	4	0	2.8	.909
1901			17	11	.607	3.52	38	26	25	276.1	281	92	78	1	1	0	2	108	19	1	.176	14	84	5	4	2.7	.951
1902	STL	A	13	13	.500	2.86	30	25	20	220	213	67	42	1	2	1	0	77	13	0	.169	8	84	10	4	3.4	.902
1903			21	15	.583	2.27	38	35	30	293.2	262	56	104	5	2	1	0	110	20	0	.182	15	104	5	0	3.3	.960
1904			8	15	.348	3.76	27	24	20	222.1	232	54	63	1	2	1	0	85	14	0	.165	9	104	2	4	4.3	.983
1905			10	19	.345	2.99	32	30	23	244	222	78	70	1	1	0	0	86	16	0	.186	20	96	4	5	3.8	.967
1906	WAS	A	0	2	.000	9.15	9	5	0	19.2	30	9	7	0	0	0	0	7	3	0	.429	1	11	1	0	1.4	.923
10 yrs.			103	136	.431	3.56	279	240	201	2086.1	2183	608	520	11	11	4	3	*					106	760	57	22	3.3	.938

Joe Sugden

SUGDEN, JOSEPH
B. July 31, 1870, Philadelphia, Pa. D. June 28, 1959, Philadelphia, Pa. — BB TR 5'10" 180 lbs.

Year	Team		W	L	PCT	ERA	G	GS	CG	IP	H	BB	SO	ShO	W	L	SV	AB	H	HR	BA	PO	A	E	DP	TC/G	FA
1902	STL	A	0	0	—	0.00	1	0	1	1	1	0	0	0	0	0	0	*					0	1	0	0	1.0	1.000

George Suggs

SUGGS, GEORGE FRANKLIN
B. July 7, 1882, Kinston, N. C. D. Apr. 4, 1949, Kinston, N. C. — BR TR 5'7½" 168 lbs.

Year	Team		W	L	PCT	ERA	G	GS	CG	IP	H	BB	SO	ShO	W	L	SV	AB	H	HR	BA	PO	A	E	DP	TC/G	FA
1908	DET	A	1	1	.500	1.67	6	1	1	27	32	2	8	0	0	1	0	10	2	0	.200	0	4	0	1	0.7	1.000
1909			1	3	.250	2.03	9	4	2	44.1	34	10	18	0	0	1	1	15	1	0	.067	1	12	0	0	1.4	1.000
1910	CIN	N	19	11	.633	2.40	35	30	23	266	248	48	91	2	2	0	3	85	14	0	.165	8	81	4	4	2.7	.957
1911			15	13	.536	3.00	36	29	17	260.2	258	79	91	1	2	1	0	90	23	0	.256	13	83	3	9	2.8	.970
1912			19	16	.543	2.94	42	36	25	303	320	56	104	5	2	1	3	106	17	1	.160	14	82	4	0	2.4	.960
1913			8	15	.348	4.03	36	22	9	199	220	35	73	2	2	2	2	67	17	0	.254	8	64	1	1	2.0	.986
1914	BAL	F	24	14	.632	2.90	46	38	26	319.1	322	57	132	6	3	3	3	99	21	0	.212	23	114	3	4	3.0	.979
1915			13	17	.433	4.14	35	25	12	232.2	288	68	71	0	3	2	1	77	17	0	.221	7	81	2	1	2.6	.978
8 yrs.			100	90	.526	3.11	245	185	115	1652	1722	355	588	16	14	10	14	549	112	1	.204	74	521	17	20	2.5	.972

Ed Sukla

SUKLA, EDWARD ANTHONY
B. Mar. 3, 1943, Long Beach, Calif. — BR TR 5'11" 170 lbs.

Year	Team		W	L	PCT	ERA	G	GS	CG	IP	H	BB	SO	ShO	W	L	SV	AB	H	HR	BA	PO	A	E	DP	TC/G	FA
1964	LA	A	0	1	.000	6.75	2	0	0	2.2	2	1	3	0	0	1	0	0	0	0	—	1	0	0	0	0.5	1.000
1965	CAL	A	2	3	.400	4.50	25	0	0	32	32	10	15	0	2	3	3	0	0	0	—	2	9	0	1	0.4	1.000
1966			1	1	.500	6.48	12	0	0	16.2	18	6	8	0	1	1	1	1	0	0	.000	0	1	0	0	0.1	1.000
3 yrs.			3	5	.375	5.26	39	0	0	51.1	52	17	26	0	3	5	4	1	0	0	.000	3	10	0	1	0.3	1.000

Bill Sullivan

SULLIVAN, WILLIAM T.
Deceased.

Year	Team		W	L	PCT	ERA	G	GS	CG	IP	H	BB	SO	ShO	W	L	SV	AB	H	HR	BA	PO	A	E	DP	TC/G	FA
1890	SYR	AA	1	4	.200	7.93	6	6	4	42	51	27	13	0	0	0	0	22	2	0	.091	0	8	0	0	1.3	1.000

Charlie Sullivan

SULLIVAN, CHARLES EDWARD
B. May 23, 1903, Yadkin Valley, N. C. D. May 28, 1935, Maiden, N. C. — BL TR 6'1" 185 lbs.

Year	Team		W	L	PCT	ERA	G	GS	CG	IP	H	BB	SO	ShO	W	L	SV	AB	H	HR	BA	PO	A	E	DP	TC/G	FA
1928	DET	A	0	2	.000	6.57	3	2	0	12.1	18	6	2	0	0	0	0	4	0	0	.000	0	3	1	1	1.3	.750
1930			1	5	.167	6.53	40	3	2	93.2	112	53	38	0	1	2	5	24	7	0	.292	6	20	4	1	0.7	.866
1931			3	2	.600	4.73	31	4	2	99	109	46	28	0	1	0	0	24	4	0	.167	2	20	2	0	0.8	.917
3 yrs.			4	9	.308	5.66	74	9	4	205	239	105	68	0	2	2	5	52	11	0	.212	8	43	3	5	0.7	.944

Fleury Sullivan

SULLIVAN, FLORENCE P.
B. 1862, East St. Louis, Ill. D. Feb. 15, 1897, East St. Louis, Ill.

Year	Team		W	L	PCT	ERA	G	GS	CG	IP	H	BB	SO	ShO	W	L	SV	AB	H	HR	BA	PO	A	E	DP	TC/G	FA
1884	PIT	AA	16	35	.314	4.20	51	51	51	441	496	96	189	2	0	0	0	189	29	0	.153	24	90	24	2	2.7	.826

Frank Sullivan

SULLIVAN, FRANKLIN LEAL
B. Jan. 23, 1930, Hollywood, Calif. — BR TR 6'6½" 215 lbs.

Year	Team		W	L	PCT	ERA	G	GS	CG	IP	H	BB	SO	ShO	W	L	SV	AB	H	HR	BA	PO	A	E	DP	TC/G	FA
1953	BOS	A	1	1	.500	5.61	14	0	0	25.2	24	11	17	0	1	1	0	4	1	0	.250	4	2	0	0	0.4	1.000
1954			15	12	.556	3.14	36	26	11	206.1	185	66	124	3	1	3	1	68	7	0	.103	12	36	2	5	1.4	.960
1955			18	13	.581	2.91	35	35	16	260	235	100	129	3	0	0	0	89	10	0	.112	21	41	1	5	1.8	.984
1956			14	7	.667	3.42	34	33	12	242	253	82	116	1	1	0	0	85	12	0	.141	16	37	1	5	1.6	.981
1957			14	11	.560	2.73	31	30	14	240.2	206	48	127	3	0	0	0	79	13	0	.165	17	48	1	5	2.1	.985
1958			13	9	.591	3.57	32	29	10	199.1	216	49	103	2	0	0	3	67	11	0	.164	13	26	0	5	1.2	1.000
1959			9	11	.450	3.95	30	26	5	177.2	172	67	107	2	0	0	0	60	12	0	.200	15	20	2	4	1.2	.946
1960			6	16	.273	5.10	40	22	4	153.2	164	52	98	0	2	3	1	40	5	0	.125	6	17	0	1	0.6	1.000
1961	PHI	N	3	16	.158	4.29	49	18	1	159.1	161	55	114	1	1	4	6	33	5	0	.152	10	34	2	0	0.9	.957
1962	2 teams		PHI N (19G 0–2)			MIN A (21G 4–1)																					
"	total		4	3	.571	4.47	40	7	0	56.1	71	25	22	0	4	3	4	4	0	0	.000	6	10	0	0	0.4	1.000
1963	MIN	A	0	1	.000	5.73	10	0	0	11	15	4	2	0	0	1	1	0	0	0	—	0	4	0	0	0.4	1.000
11 yrs.			97	100	.492	3.60	351	219	73	1732	1702	559	959	15	10	15	18	529	76	0	.144	121	275	9	30	1.2	.978

Harry Sullivan

SULLIVAN, HARRY ANDREW
B. Apr. 12, 1888, Rockford, Ill. D. Sept. 22, 1919, Rockford, Ill. — BL TL

Year	Team		W	L	PCT	ERA	G	GS	CG	IP	H	BB	SO	ShO	W	L	SV	AB	H	HR	BA	PO	A	E	DP	TC/G	FA
1909	STL	N	0	0	—	36.00	2	1	0	1	4	2	1	0	0	0	0	1	0	0	.000	0	0	1	0	0.5	—

Jim Sullivan

SULLIVAN, JAMES E.
B. Apr. 25, 1869, Charlestown, Mass. D. Nov. 30, 1901, Roxbury, Mass. — BR TR 5'10" 155 lbs.

Year	Team		W	L	PCT	ERA	G	GS	CG	IP	H	BB	SO	ShO	Relief Pitching W	L	SV	Batting AB	H	HR	BA	PO	A	E	DP	TC/G	FA

Jim Sullivan *continued*

1891	2 teams	BOS N (1G 0–0)		COL AA (1G 0–1)																								
"	total		0	1	.000	7.00	2	1	1	9	12	10	1	0	0	0	0	4	0	0	.000	0	6	2	0	4.0	.750
1895	BOS	N	11	9	.550	4.82	21	19	16	179.1	236	58	46	0	1	0	0	85	15	0	.176	5	31	5	1	2.0	.878
1896			11	12	.478	4.03	31	26	21	225.1	268	68	33	1	0	0	1	88	19	1	.216	7	43	5	2	1.8	.909
1897			4	5	.444	3.94	13	9	8	89	91	26	17	1	0	1	2	33	6	0	.182	4	16	2	1	1.7	.909
4 yrs.			26	27	.491	4.35	67	55	46	502.2	607	162	97	2	1	1	3	210	40	1	.190	16	96	14	4	1.9	.889

Jim Sullivan

SULLIVAN, JAMES RICHARD
B. Apr. 5, 1894, Mine Run, Va. D. Feb. 12, 1972, Burtonville, Md.

BR TR 5'11" 165 lbs.

1921	PHI	A	0	2	.000	3.18	2	2	1	17	20	7	4	0	0	0	0	6	0	0	.000	0	4	0	0	2.0	1.000
1922			0	2	.000	5.44	20	2	1	51.1	76	25	15	0	0	0	0	11	1	0	.091	2	12	3	0	0.9	.824
1923	CLE	A	0	1	.000	14.40	3	0	0	5	10	5	4	0	0	0	1	2	0	0	.000	0	1	0	0	0.3	1.000
3 yrs.			0	5	.000	5.52	25	4	3	73.1	106	37	27	0	0	0	1	19	1	0	.053	2	17	3	0	0.9	.864

Joe Sullivan

SULLIVAN, JOE
B. Sept. 26, 1910, Mason City, Ill. D. Apr. 8, 1985, Sequim, Wash.

BL TL 5'11" 175 lbs.

1935	DET	A	6	6	.500	3.51	25	12	6	125.2	119	71	53	0	2	1	0	43	7	0	.163	7	20	4	5	1.2	.871
1936			2	5	.286	6.78	26	4	1	79.2	111	40	32	0	1	3	1	28	5	0	.179	3	12	1	0	0.6	.938
1939	BOS	N	6	9	.400	3.64	31	11	7	113.2	114	50	46	0	2	5	2	40	12	0	.300	6	23	0	0	0.9	1.000
1940			10	14	.417	3.55	36	22	7	177.1	157	89	64	0	3	3	1	71	14	0	.197	8	38	3	1	1.4	.939
1941	2 teams	BOS N (16G 2–2)		PIT N (16G 4–1)																								
"	total		6	3	.667	3.63	32	6	0	91.2	100	48	21	0	4	1	1	26	5	0	.192	7	22	0	1	0.9	1.000
5 yrs.			30	37	.448	4.01	150	55	20	588	601	298	216	0	12	13	5	208	43	0	.207	31	115	8	7	1.0	.948

John Sullivan

SULLIVAN, JOHN JEREMIAH (Lefty)
B. May 31, 1894, Chicago, Ill. D. July 7, 1958, Chicago, Ill.

BL TL 5'11" 165 lbs.

| 1919 | CHI | A | 0 | 1 | .000 | 4.20 | 4 | 2 | 1 | 15 | 24 | 8 | 9 | 0 | 0 | 0 | 0 | 3 | 0 | 0 | .000 | 0 | 2 | 3 | 1 | 1.3 | .400 |

Lefty Sullivan

SULLIVAN, PAUL THOMAS
B. Sept. 7, 1916, Nashville, Tenn. D. Nov. 1, 1988, Scottsdale, Ariz.

BL TL 6'3" 204 lbs.

| 1939 | CLE | A | 0 | 1 | .000 | 4.26 | 7 | 1 | 0 | 12.2 | 9 | 9 | 4 | 0 | 0 | 0 | 0 | 3 | 0 | 0 | .000 | 0 | 1 | 0 | 0 | 0.1 | — |

Marty Sullivan

SULLIVAN, MARTIN C.
B. Oct. 20, 1862, Lowell, Mass. D. Jan. 6, 1894, Lowell, Mass.

BR TR

| 1887 | CHI | N | 0 | 0 | — | 7.71 | 1 | 0 | 0 | 2.1 | 6 | 1 | 1 | 0 | 0 | 0 | 0 | * | | | | 0 | 0 | 0 | 0 | 0.0 | — |

Mike Sullivan

SULLIVAN, MICHAEL JOSEPH (Big Mike)
B. Oct. 23, 1866, Boston, Mass. D. June 14, 1906, Boston, Mass.

BL 6'1" 210 lbs.

1889	WAS	N	0	3	.000	7.24	9	3	3	41	47	32	15	0	0	0	0	19	1	0	.053	3	7	4	0	1.6	.714
1890	CHI	N	5	6	.455	4.59	12	12	10	96	108	58	33	0	0	0	0	40	5	0	.125	6	11	1	2	1.5	.944
1891	2 teams	PHI AA (2G 0–2)		NY N (3G 1–2)																								
"	total		1	4	.200	3.43	5	5	5	42	41	18	18	0	0	0	0	17	2	0	.118	1	8	2	0	2.2	.818
1892	CIN	N	12	4	.750	3.08	21	16	15	166.1	169	74	56	0	2	0	0	74	13	0	.176	3	31	6	1	1.9	.850
1893			8	11	.421	5.05	27	18	14	183.2	200	103	40	0	2	2	1	79	16	1	.203	11	40	10	4	2.3	.836
1894	2 teams	WAS N (20G 2–10)		CLE N (13G 6–5)																								
"	total		8	15	.348	6.48	33	23	20	208.1	294	121	40	0	2	1	0	101	22	1	.218	8	35	5	0	1.5	.896
1895	CLE	N	1	2	.333	8.42	4	3	1	31	42	16	5	0	0	0	0	15	2	0	.133	1	5	1	0	1.8	.857
1896	NY	N	10	13	.435	4.66	25	22	18	185.1	188	71	42	0	3	0	0	77	16	0	.208	8	45	6	2	2.4	.898
1897			8	7	.533	5.09	23	16	11	148.2	183	71	35	1	1	2	2	66	18	0	.273	4	39	6	2	2.1	.878
1898	BOS	N	0	1	.000	12.00	3	2	0	12	19	9	1	0	0	0	0	3	1	0	.333	0	3	2	0	1.7	.600
1899			1	0	1.000	5.00	1	1	1	9	10	4	1	0	0	0	0	3	1	0	.333	1	0	0	0	1.0	1.000
11 yrs.			54	66	.450	5.11	163	121	99	1123.1	1311	577	286	1	9	5	4	494	97	2	.196	46	224	43	11	1.9	.863

Pat Sullivan

SULLIVAN, PATRICK B.
B. Dec. 22, 1862, Milwaukee, Wis. D. Mar. 29, 1886, West Roxbury, Mass.

TR 5'11" 165 lbs.

| 1884 | KC | U | 0 | 1 | .000 | 11.57 | 1 | 1 | 0 | 7 | 15 | 5 | 1 | 0 | 0 | 0 | 0 | * | | | | 0 | 1 | 1 | 0 | 2.0 | .500 |

Sleeper Sullivan

SULLIVAN, THOMAS JEFFERSON
B. St. Louis, Mo. D. Sept. 25, 1899, Camden, N. J.

BR TR 175 lbs.

1882	STL	AA	0	1	.000	8.00	1	1	1	9	15	1	0	0	0	0	0	188	34	0	.181	1	0	3	0	4.0	.250
1884	STL	U	1	0	1.000	4.50	1	1	1	6	10	0	3	0	0	0	0	9	1	0	.111	3	0	1	0	4.0	.750
2 yrs.			1	1	.500	6.60	2	2	1	15	25	1	3	0	0	0	0	*				4	0	4	0	4.0	.500

Suter Sullivan

SULLIVAN, SUTER G.
B. Oct. 14, 1872, Baltimore, Md. D. Apr. 19, 1925, Baltimore, Md.

| 1898 | STL | N | 0 | 0 | — | 1.50 | 1 | 0 | 0 | 6 | 10 | 4 | 3 | 0 | 0 | 0 | 0 | * | | | | 0 | 0 | 0 | 0 | 0.0 | — |

Tom Sullivan

SULLIVAN, THOMAS
B. Mar. 1, 1860, New York, N. Y. D. Apr. 12, 1947, Boston, Mass.

1884	COL	AA	2	2	.500	4.06	4	4	4	31	42	3	12	0	0	0	0	11	1	0	.091	0	3	0	0	0.8	1.000
1886	LOU	AA	2	7	.222	3.96	9	9	8	75	94	33	27	0	0	0	0	27	3	0	.111	6	13	2	0	2.3	.905
1888	KC	AA	8	16	.333	3.40	24	24	24	214.2	227	68	84	0	0	0	0	92	10	0	.109	17	68	4	2	3.7	.955
1889			2	8	.200	5.67	10	10	10	87.1	111	48	24	0	0	0	0	33	5	0	.152	3	16	5	0	2.4	.792
4 yrs.			14	33	.298	4.04	47	47	46	408	474	152	147	0	0	0	0	163	19	0	.117	26	100	11	2	2.9	.920

Tom Sullivan

SULLIVAN, THOMAS AUGUSTIN
B. Oct. 18, 1895, Boston, Mass. D. Sept. 23, 1962, Boston, Mass.

BL TL 5'11" 178 lbs.

| 1922 | PHI | N | 0 | 0 | — | 11.25 | 3 | 0 | 0 | 8 | 16 | 5 | 2 | 0 | 0 | 0 | 0 | 4 | 1 | 1 | .250 | 0 | 2 | 0 | 1 | 0.7 | 1.000 |

Year	Team	W	L	PCT	ERA	G	GS	CG	IP	H	BB	SO	ShO	Relief Pitching W	L	SV	Batting AB	H	HR	BA	PO	A	E	DP	TC/G	FA

Ed Summers

SUMMERS, ORON EDGAR (Kickapoo Chief) — BB TR 6'2" 180 lbs.
B. Dec. 5, 1884, Ladoga, Ind. D. May 12, 1953, Indianapolis, Ind.

Year	Team	W	L	PCT	ERA	G	GS	CG	IP	H	BB	SO	ShO	W	L	SV	AB	H	HR	BA	PO	A	E	DP	TC/G	FA
1908	DET A	24	12	.667	1.64	40	32	24	301	271	55	103	5	5	0	1	113	14	0	.124	20	90	7	2	2.9	.940
1909		19	9	.679	2.24	35	32	24	281.2	243	52	107	3	0	1	0	94	10	0	.106	14	89	3	8	3.0	.972
1910		13	12	.520	2.53	30	25	18	220.1	211	60	82	1	1	1	0	76	14	2	.184	14	74	3	1	3.0	.967
1911		11	11	.500	3.66	30	20	13	179.1	189	51	65	0	3	2	0	63	16	0	.254	5	46	1	1	1.7	.981
1912		1	1	.500	4.86	3	3	1	16.2	16	3	5	0	0	0	0	6	3	0	.500	1	5	0	0	2.0	1.000
5 yrs.		68	45	.602	2.42	138	112	80	999	930	221	362	9	9	3	2	352	57	2	.162	54	304	14	12	2.7	.962

WORLD SERIES

Year	Team	W	L	PCT	ERA	G	GS	CG	IP	H	BB	SO	ShO	W	L	SV	AB	H	HR	BA	PO	A	E	DP	TC/G	FA
1908	DET A	0	2	.000	4.30	2	1	0	14.2	18	4	7	0	0	1	0	5	1	0	.200	0	7	0	0	3.5	1.000
1909		0	2	.000	8.59	2	2	0	7.1	13	4	4	0	0	0	0	3	0	0	.000	0	2	0	0	1.0	1.000
2 yrs.		0	4	.000	5.73	4	3	0	22	31	8	11	0	0	1	0	8	1	0	.125	0	9	0	0	2.3	1.000
	7th																									

Billy Sunday

SUNDAY, WILLIAM ASHLEY (The Evangelist) — BL TR 5'10" 160 lbs.
B. Nov. 19, 1862, Ames, Iowa D. Nov. 6, 1935, Chicago, Ill.

Year	Team	W	L	PCT	ERA	G	GS	CG	IP	H	BB	SO	ShO	W	L	SV	AB	H	HR	BA	PO	A	E	DP	TC/G	FA
1890	PHI N	0	0	—	∞	1	0	0	2	0	0	0	0	0	0	0	*				0	0	0	0	0.0	—

Gordie Sundin

SUNDIN, GORDON VINCENT — BR TR 6'4" 215 lbs.
B. Oct. 10, 1937, Minneapolis, Minn.

Year	Team	W	L	PCT	ERA	G	GS	CG	IP	H	BB	SO	ShO	W	L	SV	AB	H	HR	BA	PO	A	E	DP	TC/G	FA
1956	BAL A	0	0	—	∞	1	0	0	2	0	0	0	0	0	0	0	0	0	0	—	0	0	0	0	0.0	—

Steve Sundra

SUNDRA, STEPHEN RICHARD (Smokey) — BB TR 6'2" 190 lbs. BR 1941-43
B. Mar. 27, 1910, Luxor, Pa.
D. Mar. 23, 1952, Cleveland, Ohio

Year	Team	W	L	PCT	ERA	G	GS	CG	IP	H	BB	SO	ShO	W	L	SV	AB	H	HR	BA	PO	A	E	DP	TC/G	FA
1936	NY A	0	0	—	0.00	1	0	0	2	2	2	1	0	0	0	0	1	0	0	.000	0	0	0	0	0.0	—
1938		6	4	.600	4.80	25	8	3	93.2	107	43	33	0	3	2	0	33	6	1	.182	0	25	1	2	1.0	.962
1939		11	1	.917	2.76	24	11	8	120.2	110	56	27	1	3	0	0	49	13	0	.265	2	27	0	1	1.2	1.000
1940		4	6	.400	5.53	27	8	2	99.1	121	42	26	0	2	2	2	29	4	0	.138	3	22	2	1	1.0	.926
1941	WAS A	9	13	.409	5.29	28	23	11	168.1	203	61	50	0	1	0	0	60	13	0	.217	12	29	3	0	1.6	.932
1942	2 teams	WAS A	(6G 1–3)		STL A	(20G 8-3)																				
"	total	9	6	.600	4.24	26	17	8	144.1	165	44	31	0	0	1	0	52	11	1	.212	11	28	2	3	1.6	.951
1943	STL A	15	11	.577	3.25	32	29	13	208	212	66	44	3	0	1	0	73	16	0	.219	10	47	4	2	1.9	.934
1944		2	0	1.000	1.42	3	3	2	19	15	4	1	0	0	0	0	5	0	0	.000	0	3	0	0	1.0	1.000
1946		0	0	—	11.25	2	0	0	4	9	3	1	0	0	0	0	0	0	0	—	0	1	0	0	0.5	1.000
9 yrs.		56	41	.577	4.17	168	99	47	859.1	944	321	214	4	9	5	2	302	63	2	.209	38	182	12	9	1.4	.948

WORLD SERIES

Year	Team	W	L	PCT	ERA	G	GS	CG	IP	H	BB	SO	ShO	W	L	SV	AB	H	HR	BA	PO	A	E	DP	TC/G	FA
1939	NY A	0	0	—	0.00	1	0	0	2.2	4	1	2	0	0	0	0	0	0	0	—	0	0	0	0	0.0	—

Tom Sunkel

SUNKEL, THOMAS JACOB (Lefty) — BL TL 6'1" 190 lbs.
B. Aug. 9, 1912, Paris, Ill.

Year	Team	W	L	PCT	ERA	G	GS	CG	IP	H	BB	SO	ShO	W	L	SV	AB	H	HR	BA	PO	A	E	DP	TC/G	FA
1937	STL N	0	0	—	2.06	9	1	0	39.1	24	11	9	0	0	0	1	9	1	0	.111	2	5	0	0	0.8	1.000
1939		4	4	.500	4.22	20	11	2	85.1	79	56	54	1	0	0	0	28	9	0	.321	2	9	1	2	0.6	.917
1941	NY N	1	1	.500	2.93	2	2	1	15.1	7	12	14	1	0	0	0	6	2	0	.333	1	1	0	0	1.0	1.000
1942		3	6	.333	4.81	19	11	3	63.2	65	41	29	0	0	0	0	19	2	0	.105	1	5	0	0	0.3	1.000
1943		0	1	.000	10.13	1	1	0	2.2	4	2	1	0	0	0	0	0	0	0	—	0	0	0	0	0.2	
1944	BKN N	1	3	.250	7.50	12	3	0	24	39	10	6	0	1	1	1	4	0	0	.000	1	0	1	0	0.2	.500
6 yrs.		9	15	.375	4.34	63	29	6	230.1	218	133	112	2	1	1	2	66	14	0	.212	7	20	2	2	0.5	.931

Rick Surhoff

SURHOFF, RICHARD CLIFFORD — BR TR 6'3" 210 lbs.
Brother of B. J. Surhoff.
B. Oct. 3, 1962, Bronx, N. Y.

Year	Team	W	L	PCT	ERA	G	GS	CG	IP	H	BB	SO	ShO	W	L	SV	AB	H	HR	BA	PO	A	E	DP	TC/G	FA
1985	2 teams	PHI N	(2G 1–0)		TEX A	(7G 0-1)																				
"	total	1	1	.500	6.75	9	0	0	9.1	14	3	9	0	1	1	2	0	0	0	—	0	0	0	0	0.0	—

Max Surkont

SURKONT, MATTHEW CONSTANTINE — BR TR 6'1" 195 lbs.
B. June 16, 1922, Central Falls, R. I. D. Oct. 8, 1986, Largo, Fla.

Year	Team	W	L	PCT	ERA	G	GS	CG	IP	H	BB	SO	ShO	W	L	SV	AB	H	HR	BA	PO	A	E	DP	TC/G	FA
1949	CHI A	3	5	.375	4.78	44	2	0	96	92	60	38	0	3	4	4	22	1	0	.045	4	13	0	0	0.4	1.000
1950	BOS N	5	2	.714	3.23	9	6	2	55.2	63	20	21	0	2	0	0	23	10	1	.435	1	9	0	0	1.1	1.000
1951		12	16	.429	3.99	37	33	11	237	230	89	110	2	0	0	1	73	11	0	.151	11	31	2	1	1.2	.955
1952		12	13	.480	3.77	31	29	12	215	201	76	125	3	0	0	0	63	7	0	.111	9	38	5	3	1.7	.904
1953	MIL N	11	5	.688	4.18	28	24	11	170	168	64	83	2	0	0	0	56	16	0	.286	11	32	2	3	1.6	.956
1954	PIT N	9	18	.333	4.41	33	29	11	208.1	216	74	78	0	1	0	0	60	10	0	.167	8	40	1	1	1.5	.980
1955		7	14	.333	5.57	35	22	5	166.1	194	78	84	0	1	1	2	50	7	0	.140	8	21	2	0	0.9	.935
1956	3 teams	PIT N	(1G 0–0)		STL N	(5G 0–0)		NY N	(8G 2-2)																	
"	total	2	2	.500	5.45	14	4	1	39.2	36	14	24	0	0	0	1	10	1	0	.100	0	5	0	0	0.4	1.000
1957	NY N	0	1	.000	9.95	5	0	0	6.1	9	6	8	0	0	1	0	0	0	0	—	0	1	0	0	0.2	1.000
9 yrs.		61	76	.445	4.38	236	149	53	1194.1	1209	481	571	7	8	6	8	357	63	1	.176	52	190	12	9	1.1	.953

George Susce

SUSCE, GEORGE DANIEL — BR TR 6'1" 180 lbs.
Son of George Susce.
B. Sept. 13, 1931, Pittsburgh, Pa.

Year	Team	W	L	PCT	ERA	G	GS	CG	IP	H	BB	SO	ShO	W	L	SV	AB	H	HR	BA	PO	A	E	DP	TC/G	FA
1955	BOS A	9	7	.563	3.06	29	15	6	144.1	123	49	60	1	2	1	1	49	7	0	.143	9	22	0	2	1.1	1.000
1956		2	4	.333	6.20	21	6	0	69.2	71	44	26	0	2	1	0	18	4	0	.222	3	11	1	1	0.7	.933
1957		7	3	.700	4.28	29	5	0	88.1	93	41	40	0	6	1	1	25	3	0	.120	4	11	1	0	0.6	.938
1958	2 teams	BOS A	(2G 0–0)		DET A	(27G 4-3)																				
"	total	4	3	.571	3.98	29	10	2	92.2	96	27	42	0	3	2	1	24	3	0	.125	6	6	1	1	0.4	.923
1959	DET A	0	0	—	12.89	9	0	0	14.2	24	9	9	0	0	0	0	1	0	0	.000	2	1	0	0	0.3	1.000
5 yrs.		22	17	.564	4.42	117	36	8	409.2	407	170	177	1	13	5	3	117	17	0	.145	24	51	3	5	0.7	.962

Year	Team		W	L	PCT	ERA	G	GS	CG	IP	H	BB	SO	ShO	Relief Pitching			Batting			BA	PO	A	E	DP	TC/G	FA
															W	L	SV	AB	H	HR							

Rick Sutcliffe

SUTCLIFFE, RICHARD LEE
B. June 21, 1956, Independence, Mo.　　　　　　　　　BL TR 6'7"　215 lbs.

Year	Team		W	L	PCT	ERA	G	GS	CG	IP	H	BB	SO	ShO	W	L	SV	AB	H	HR	BA	PO	A	E	DP	TC/G	FA
1976	LA	N	0	0	–	0.00	1	1	0	5	2	1	3	0	0	0	0	1	0	0	.000	0	0	0	0	0.0	–
1978			0	0	–	0.00	2	0	0	2	1	1	0	0	0	0	0	0	0	0	–	0	1	0	1	0.5	1.000
1979			17	10	.630	3.46	39	30	5	242	217	97	117	1	1	2	0	85	21	1	.247	18	24	0	1	1.1	1.000
1980			3	9	.250	5.56	42	10	1	110	122	55	59	1	2	5	5	27	4	0	.148	6	13	0	0	0.5	1.000
1981			2	2	.500	4.02	14	6	0	47	41	20	16	0	0	0	0	11	2	0	.182	6	8	0	0	1.0	1.000
1982	CLE	A	14	8	.636	**2.96**	34	27	6	216	174	98	142	1	2	1	1	0	0	0	–	14	32	1	1	1.4	.979
1983			17	11	.607	4.29	36	35	10	243.1	251	102	160	2	1	0	0	0	0	0	–	36	29	0	1	1.8	1.000
1984	2 teams		CLE A	(15G 4–5)		CHI N	(20G 16–1)																				
"	total		20	6	.769	3.64	35	35	9	244.2	234	85	213	3	0	0	0	56	14	0	.250	19	35	2	1	1.6	.964
1985	CHI	N	8	8	.500	3.18	20	20	6	130	119	44	102	3	0	0	0	43	10	1	.233	12	23	1	0	1.8	.972
1986			5	14	.263	4.64	28	27	4	176.2	166	96	122	1	0	0	0	53	11	1	.208	8	30	1	4	1.4	.974
1987			**18**	10	.643	3.68	34	34	6	237.1	223	106	174	1	0	0	0	81	12	0	.148	12	54	4	4	2.1	.943
1988			13	14	.481	3.86	32	32	12	226	232	70	144	2	0	0	0	75	12	0	.160	21	37	3	2	1.9	.951
1989			16	11	.593	3.66	35	34	5	229	202	69	153	1	0	0	0	70	10	0	.143	22	31	1	3	1.5	.981
	13 yrs.		133	103	.564	3.81	352	291	64	2109	1985	844	1405	16	6	8	6	502	96	4	.191	174	317	13	18	1.4	.974

LEAGUE CHAMPIONSHIP SERIES

Year	Team		W	L	PCT	ERA	G	GS	CG	IP	H	BB	SO	ShO	W	L	SV	AB	H	HR	BA	PO	A	E	DP	TC/G	FA
1984	CHI	N	1	1	.500	3.38	2	2	0	13.1	9	8	10	0	0	0	0	6	3	1	.500	0	0	0	0	0.0	–
1989			0	0	–	4.50	1	1	0	6	5	4	2	0	0	0	0	2	1	0	.500	0	2	0	0	2.0	1.000
	2 yrs.		1	1	.500	3.72	3	3	0	19.1	14	12	12	0	0	0	0	8	4	1	.500	0	2	0	0	0.7	1.000

Rube Suter

SUTER, HARRY RICHARD
B. Sept. 15, 1887, Independence, Mo.　D. July 24, 1971, Topeka, Kans.　　　　BL TL 5'10"　190 lbs.

Year	Team		W	L	PCT	ERA	G	GS	CG	IP	H	BB	SO	ShO	W	L	SV	AB	H	HR	BA	PO	A	E	DP	TC/G	FA
1909	CHI	A	2	3	.400	2.47	18	6	3	87.1	72	28	53	1	0	0	1	32	3	0	.094	6	19	0	2	1.4	1.000

Darrell Sutherland

SUTHERLAND, DARRELL WAYNE
Brother of Gary Sutherland.
B. Nov. 14, 1941, Glendale, Calif.　　　　　　　　BR TR 6'4"　169 lbs.

Year	Team		W	L	PCT	ERA	G	GS	CG	IP	H	BB	SO	ShO	W	L	SV	AB	H	HR	BA	PO	A	E	DP	TC/G	FA
1964	NY	N	0	3	.000	7.76	10	4	0	26.2	32	12	9	0	0	0	0	5	1	0	.200	4	9	1	1	1.4	.929
1965			3	1	.750	2.81	18	2	0	48	33	17	16	0	3	0	0	13	2	0	.154	4	17	1	1	1.2	.955
1966			2	0	1.000	4.87	31	0	0	44.1	60	25	23	0	2	0	1	3	2	0	.667	4	11	0	1	0.5	1.000
1968	CLE	A	0	0	–	8.10	3	0	0	3.1	6	4	2	0	0	0	0	0	0	0	–	0	0	0	0	0.0	–
	4 yrs.		5	4	.556	4.78	62	6	0	122.1	131	58	50	0	5	0	1	21	5	0	.238	12	37	2	3	0.8	.961

Dizzy Sutherland

SUTHERLAND, HOWARD ALVIN
B. Apr. 9, 1923, Washington, D. C.　D. Aug. 21, 1979, Washington, D. C.　　BL TL 6'　200 lbs.

Year	Team		W	L	PCT	ERA	G	GS	CG	IP	H	BB	SO	ShO	W	L	SV	AB	H	HR	BA	PO	A	E	DP	TC/G	FA
1949	WAS	A	0	1	.000	45.00	1	1	0	1	2	6	0	0	0	0	0	0	0	0	–	0	1	0	0	1.0	1.000

Suds Sutherland

SUTHERLAND, HARVEY SCOTT
B. Feb. 20, 1894, Beaverton, Ore.　D. May 11, 1972, Portland, Ore.　　　BR TR 6'　180 lbs.

Year	Team		W	L	PCT	ERA	G	GS	CG	IP	H	BB	SO	ShO	W	L	SV	AB	H	HR	BA	PO	A	E	DP	TC/G	FA
1921	DET	A	6	2	.750	4.97	13	8	3	58	80	18	18	0	2	0	0	27	11	0	.407	2	24	0	1	2.0	1.000

Bruce Sutter

SUTTER, HOWARD BRUCE
B. Jan. 8, 1953, Lancaster, Pa.　　　　　　　　　BR TR 6'2"　190 lbs.

Year	Team		W	L	PCT	ERA	G	GS	CG	IP	H	BB	SO	ShO	W	L	SV	AB	H	HR	BA	PO	A	E	DP	TC/G	FA
1976	CHI	N	6	3	.667	2.71	52	0	0	83	63	26	73	0	6	3	10	8	0	0	.000	6	9	1	1	0.3	.938
1977			7	3	.700	1.35	62	0	0	107	69	23	129	0	7	3	31	20	3	0	.150	11	14	0	0	0.4	1.000
1978			8	10	.444	3.18	64	0	0	99	82	34	106	0	8	10	27	13	1	0	.077	12	9	0	0	0.3	1.000
1979			6	6	.500	2.23	62	0	0	101	67	32	110	0	6	6	**37**	12	3	0	.250	9	15	3	0	0.4	.889
1980			5	8	.385	2.65	60	0	0	102	90	34	76	0	5	8	**28**	9	1	0	.111	6	14	0	0	0.3	1.000
1981	STL	N	3	5	.375	2.63	48	0	0	82	64	24	57	0	3	5	**25**	9	0	0	.000	7	8	0	0	0.3	1.000
1982			9	8	.529	2.90	70	0	0	102.1	88	34	61	0	9	8	**36**	8	1	0	.125	6	15	1	5	0.3	.955
1983			9	10	.474	4.23	60	0	0	89.1	90	30	64	0	9	10	21	7	0	0	.000	11	19	2	1	0.5	.938
1984			5	7	.417	1.54	71	0	0	122.2	109	23	77	0	5	7	**45**	10	0	0	.000	14	19	0	2	0.5	1.000
1985	ATL	N	7	7	.500	4.48	58	0	0	88.1	91	29	52	0	7	7	23	4	0	0	.000	5	13	0	0	0.3	1.000
1986			2	0	1.000	4.34	16	0	0	18.2	17	9	16	0	2	0	3	1	0	0	.000	1	3	0	0	0.3	1.000
1988			1	4	.200	4.76	38	0	0	45.1	49	11	40	0	1	4	14	1	0	0	.000	2	7	2	0	0.3	.818
	12 yrs.		68	71	.489	2.84	661	0	0	1040.2	879	309	861	0	68	71	300 **3rd**	102	9	0	.088	90	145	9	9	0.4	.963

LEAGUE CHAMPIONSHIP SERIES

Year	Team		W	L	PCT	ERA	G	GS	CG	IP	H	BB	SO	ShO	W	L	SV	AB	H	HR	BA	PO	A	E	DP	TC/G	FA
1982	STL	N	1	0	1.000	0.00	2	0	0	4.1	0	1	1	0	1	0	1	1	0	0	.000	0	0	0	0	0.0	–

WORLD SERIES

Year	Team		W	L	PCT	ERA	G	GS	CG	IP	H	BB	SO	ShO	W	L	SV	AB	H	HR	BA	PO	A	E	DP	TC/G	FA
1982	STL	N	1	0	1.000	4.70	4	0	0	7.2	6	3	6	0	1	0	2	0	0	0	–	0	1	0	0	0.3	1.000

Jack Sutthoff

SUTTHOFF, JOHN GERHARD (Sunny Jack)
B. June 29, 1873, Cincinnati, Ohio　D. Aug. 3, 1942, Cincinnati, Ohio　　BL TR 5'9"　175 lbs.

Year	Team		W	L	PCT	ERA	G	GS	CG	IP	H	BB	SO	ShO	W	L	SV	AB	H	HR	BA	PO	A	E	DP	TC/G	FA
1898	WAS	N	0	0	–	12.96	2	2	0	8.1	16	8	3	0	0	0	0	3	1	0	.333	0	2	0	0	1.0	1.000
1899	STL	N	1	1	.500	10.38	2	2	1	13	19	10	4	0	0	0	0	6	0	0	.000	1	6	1	0	4.0	.875
1901	CIN	N	1	3	.250	5.50	10	4	1	70.1	82	39	12	0	0	0	0	28	3	0	.107	4	15	5	0	2.4	.792
1903			16	10	.615	2.80	30	27	21	224.2	207	79	76	3	0	0	0	84	12	0	.143	10	54	3	2	2.2	.955
1904	2 teams		CIN N	(12G 5–6)		PHI N	(19G 6–13)																				
"	total		11	19	.367	3.19	31	28	25	253.2	255	114	73	0	2	1	0	94	16	0	.170	11	57	9	6	2.5	.883
1905	PHI	N	3	4	.429	3.81	13	6	4	78	82	36	26	1	0	1	0	25	2	0	.080	3	23	1	0	2.1	.963
	6 yrs.		32	37	.464	3.65	88	68	55	648	661	286	194	4	2	2	0	240	34	0	.142	29	157	19	8	2.3	.907

Don Sutton

SUTTON, DONALD HOWARD
B. Apr. 2, 1945, Clio, Ala.　　　　　　　　　BR TR 6'1"　185 lbs.

Year	Team		W	L	PCT	ERA	G	GS	CG	IP	H	BB	SO	ShO	W	L	SV	AB	H	HR	BA	PO	A	E	DP	TC/G	FA
1966	LA	N	12	12	.500	2.99	37	35	6	225.2	192	52	209	2	0	0	0	82	15	0	.183	8	32	2	3	1.1	.952
1967			11	15	.423	3.95	37	34	11	232.2	223	57	169	3	0	1	0	75	10	0	.133	7	31	1	2	1.1	.974
1968			11	15	.423	2.60	35	27	7	207.2	179	59	162	2	1	1	1	62	11	0	.177	12	25	1	0	1.1	.974

Year	Team	W	L	PCT	ERA	G	GS	CG	IP	H	BB	SO	ShO	Relief Pitching W	L	SV	Batting AB	H	HR	BA	PO	A	E	DP	TC/G	FA

Don Sutton *continued*

Year	Team	W	L	PCT	ERA	G	GS	CG	IP	H	BB	SO	ShO	W	L	SV	AB	H	HR	BA	PO	A	E	DP	TC/G	FA
1969		17	18	.486	3.47	41	41	11	293	269	91	217	4	0	0	0	98	15	0	.153	19	43	1	3	1.5	.984
1970		15	13	.536	4.08	38	38	10	260	251	78	201	4	0	0	0	84	13	0	.155	21	28	3	1	1.4	.942
1971		17	12	.586	2.55	38	37	12	265	231	55	194	4	0	0	1	88	19	0	.216	27	26	2	5	1.4	.964
1972		19	9	.679	2.08	33	33	18	272.2	186	63	207	9	0	0	0	91	13	0	.143	18	34	1	2	1.6	.981
1973		18	10	.643	2.42	33	33	14	256.1	196	56	200	3	0	0	0	84	10	0	.119	12	34	1	2	1.4	.979
1974		19	9	.679	3.23	40	**40**	10	276	241	80	179	5	0	0	0	98	18	0	.184	17	33	0	1	1.3	1.000
1975		16	13	.552	2.87	35	35	11	254	202	62	175	4	0	0	0	80	11	0	.138	24	25	2	0	1.5	.961
1976		21	10	.677	3.06	35	34	15	267.2	231	82	161	4	1	0	0	84	7	0	.083	5	31	1	2	1.1	.973
1977		14	8	.636	3.19	33	33	9	240	207	69	150	3	0	0	0	73	11	0	.151	15	29	1	3	1.4	.978
1978		15	11	.577	3.55	34	34	12	238	228	54	154	2	0	0	0	72	6	0	.083	13	23	0	2	1.1	1.000
1979		12	15	.444	3.82	33	32	6	226	201	61	146	1	0	0	1	77	11	0	.143	16	24	1	2	1.2	.976
1980		13	5	.722	**2.21**	32	31	4	212	163	47	128	2	0	0	1	64	5	0	.078	24	25	2	3	1.6	.961
1981	HOU N	11	9	.550	2.60	23	23	6	159	132	29	104	3	0	0	0	51	7	0	.137	11	24	2	1	1.6	.946
1982	2 teams	HOU N	(27G 13–8)	MIL A	(7G 4–1)																					
"	total	17	9	.654	3.06	34	34	6	249.2	224	64	175	1	0	0	0	68	11	0	.162	16	20	1	2	1.1	.973
1983	MIL A	8	13	.381	4.08	31	31	4	220.1	209	54	134	0	0	0	0	0	0	0	–	13	23	1	1	1.2	.973
1984		14	12	.538	3.77	33	33	1	212.2	224	51	143	0	0	0	0	0	0	0	–	11	19	1	1	0.9	.968
1985	2 teams	OAK A	(29G 13–8)	CAL A	(5G 2–2)																					
"	total	15	10	.600	3.86	34	34	1	226	221	59	107	1	0	0	0	0	0	0	–	8	32	4	1	1.3	.909
1986	CAL A	15	11	.577	3.74	34	34	3	207	192	49	116	1	0	0	0	0	0	0	–	18	14	2	1	1.0	.941
1987		11	11	.500	4.70	35	34	1	191.2	199	41	99	0	1	0	0	0	0	0	–	8	18	0	1	0.7	1.000
1988	LA N	3	6	.333	3.92	16	16	0	87.1	91	30	44	0	0	0	0	23	2	0	.087	5	12	1	0	1.1	.944
23 yrs.		324	256	.559	3.26	774	756	178	5280.1	4692	1343	3574	58	3	3	5	1354	195	0	.144	328	605	31	41	1.2	.968
				7th					6th			4th	9th													

LEAGUE CHAMPIONSHIP SERIES

Year	Team	W	L	PCT	ERA	G	GS	CG	IP	H	BB	SO	ShO	W	L	SV	AB	H	HR	BA	PO	A	E	DP	TC/G	FA
1974	LA N	2	0	1.000	0.53	2	2	1	17	7	2	13	1	0	0	0	7	2	0	.286	2	3	0	1	2.5	1.000
1977		1	0	1.000	1.00	1	1	1	9	9	0	4	0	0	0	0	3	0	0	.000	0	2	0	0	2.0	1.000
1978		0	1	.000	6.35	1	1	0	5.2	7	2	0	0	0	0	0	2	0	0	.000	0	1	0	0	1.0	1.000
1982	MIL A	1	0	1.000	3.52	1	1	0	7.2	8	2	9	0	0	0	0	0	0	0	–	0	0	0	0	0.0	–
1986	CAL A	0	0	–	1.86	2	1	0	9.2	6	1	4	0	0	0	0	0	0	0	–	0	0	0	0	0.0	–
5 yrs.		4	1	.800	2.02	7	6	2	49	37	7	30	1	0	0	0	12	2	0	.167	2	6	0	1	1.1	1.000

WORLD SERIES

Year	Team	W	L	PCT	ERA	G	GS	CG	IP	H	BB	SO	ShO	W	L	SV	AB	H	HR	BA	PO	A	E	DP	TC/G	FA
1974	LA N	1	0	1.000	2.77	2	2	0	13	9	3	12	0	0	0	0	3	0	0	.000	0	2	0	0	1.0	1.000
1977		1	0	1.000	3.94	2	2	1	16	17	1	6	0	0	0	0	6	0	0	.000	1	1	0	0	1.0	1.000
1978		0	2	.000	7.50	2	2	0	12	17	4	8	0	0	0	0	0	0	0	–	0	0	0	0	0.0	–
1982	MIL A	0	1	.000	7.84	2	2	0	10.1	12	1	6	0	0	0	0	0	0	0	–	1	2	0	0	1.5	1.000
4 yrs.		2	3	.400	5.26	8	8	1	51.1	55	9	31	0	0	0	0	9	0	0	.000	2	5	0	0	0.9	1.000
					10th					9th																	

Johnny Sutton

SUTTON, JOHNNY IKE
B. Nov. 13, 1952, Dallas, Tex.
BR TR 5'11" 185 lbs.

Year	Team	W	L	PCT	ERA	G	GS	CG	IP	H	BB	SO	ShO	W	L	SV	AB	H	HR	BA	PO	A	E	DP	TC/G	FA
1977	STL N	2	1	.667	2.63	14	0	0	24	28	9	9	0	2	1	0	1	0	0	.000	1	5	0	2	0.4	1.000
1978	MIN A	0	0	–	3.48	17	0	0	44	46	15	18	0	0	0	0	0	0	0	–	2	6	2	0	0.6	.800
2 yrs.		2	1	.667	3.18	31	0	0	68	74	24	27	0	2	1	0	1	0	0	.000	3	11	2	2	0.5	.875

Bill Swabach

SWABACH, WILLIAM
Deceased.

Year	Team	W	L	PCT	ERA	G	GS	CG	IP	H	BB	SO	ShO	W	L	SV	AB	H	HR	BA	PO	A	E	DP	TC/G	FA
1887	NY N	0	2	.000	5.06	2	2	2	16	27	6	6	0	0	0	0	7	0	0	.000	0	3	0	0	1.5	1.000

Bill Swaggerty

SWAGGERTY, WILLIAM DAVID
B. Dec. 5, 1956, Sanford, Fla.
BR TR 6'2" 190 lbs.

Year	Team	W	L	PCT	ERA	G	GS	CG	IP	H	BB	SO	ShO	W	L	SV	AB	H	HR	BA	PO	A	E	DP	TC/G	FA
1983	BAL A	1	1	.500	2.91	7	2	0	21.2	23	6	7	0	1	1	0	0	0	0	–	4	7	0	0	1.6	1.000
1984		3	2	.600	5.21	23	6	0	57	68	21	18	0	2	0	0	0	0	0	–	3	6	2	1	0.5	.818
1985		0	0	–	5.40	1	0	0	1.2	3	2	2	0	0	0	0	0	0	0	–	0	0	0	0	0.0	–
1986		0	0	–	18.00	1	0	0	1	6	1	1	0	0	0	0	0	0	0	–	0	0	0	0	0.0	–
4 yrs.		4	3	.571	4.76	32	8	0	81.1	100	30	28	0	3	1	0	0	0	0	–	7	13	2	1	0.7	.909

Cy Swaim

SWAIM, JOHN HILLARY
B. Mar. 11, 1874, Cadwallader, Ohio D. Nov. 8, 1918, Oakland, Calif.
6'6" 180 lbs.

Year	Team	W	L	PCT	ERA	G	GS	CG	IP	H	BB	SO	ShO	W	L	SV	AB	H	HR	BA	PO	A	E	DP	TC/G	FA
1897	WAS N	10	11	.476	4.41	27	20	16	194	227	61	55	0	0	0	0	75	17	0	.227	12	25	6	1	1.6	.860
1898		3	11	.214	4.26	16	13	9	101.1	119	28	30	0	0	1	1	35	5	0	.143	4	18	4	1	1.6	.846
2 yrs.		13	22	.371	4.36	43	33	25	295.1	346	89	85	0	1	1	1	110	22	0	.200	16	43	10	2	1.6	.855

Craig Swan

SWAN, CRAIG STEVEN
B. Nov. 30, 1950, Van Nuys, Calif.
BR TR 6'3" 215 lbs.

Year	Team	W	L	PCT	ERA	G	GS	CG	IP	H	BB	SO	ShO	W	L	SV	AB	H	HR	BA	PO	A	E	DP	TC/G	FA
1973	NY N	0	1	.000	8.64	3	1	0	8.1	16	2	4	0	0	0	0	2	0	0	.000	0	1	1	0	0.7	.500
1974		1	3	.250	4.50	7	5	0	30	28	21	10	0	0	0	0	11	4	0	.364	0	7	1	0	1.1	.875
1975		1	3	.250	6.39	6	6	0	31	38	13	19	0	0	0	0	7	0	0	.000	1	1	0	0	0.3	1.000
1976		6	9	.400	3.55	23	22	2	132	129	44	89	1	0	0	0	39	4	0	.103	6	17	2	1	1.1	.920
1977		9	10	.474	4.22	26	24	2	147	153	56	71	1	0	0	0	48	9	0	.188	13	10	2	0	1.0	.920
1978		9	6	.600	**2.43**	29	28	5	207	164	58	125	1	0	0	0	65	10	0	.154	17	30	2	5	1.7	.959
1979		14	13	.519	3.30	35	35	10	251	241	57	145	3	0	0	0	81	10	0	.123	17	29	0	3	1.3	1.000
1980		5	9	.357	3.59	21	21	4	128	117	30	79	1	0	0	0	32	7	0	.219	4	10	3	0	0.8	.824
1981		0	2	.000	3.21	5	3	0	14	10	1	9	0	0	0	0	3	0	0	.000	0	2	0	0	0.4	1.000
1982		11	7	.611	3.35	37	21	2	166.1	165	37	67	0	2	0	0	44	8	1	.182	16	18	0	0	0.9	1.000
1983		2	8	.200	5.51	27	18	0	96.1	112	42	43	0	0	0	1	26	2	0	.077	4	10	0	0	0.5	1.000
1984	2 teams	NY N	(10G 1–0)	CAL A	(2G 0–1)																					
"	total	1	1	.500	8.75	12	0	0	23.2	26	7	12	0	1	0	0	0	0	0	–	1	3	0	0	0.3	1.000
12 yrs.		59	72	.450	3.75	231	185	25	1234.2	1199	368	673	7	3	1	2	358	54	1	.151	79	138	11	8	1.0	.952

Year	Team		W	L	PCT	ERA	G	GS	CG	IP	H	BB	SO	ShO	Relief Pitching W	L	SV	Batting AB	H	HR	BA	PO	A	E	DP	TC/G	FA

Ducky Swan

SWAN, HARRY GORDON
B. Aug. 11, 1887, Lancaster, Pa. D. May 9, 1946, Pittsburgh, Pa.

BR TR 5'10" 165 lbs.

| 1914 | KC | F | 0 | 0 | — | 0.00 | 1 | 0 | 0 | 1 | 0 | 1 | 1 | 0 | 0 | 0 | 0 | 0 | 0 | 0 | — | 0 | 0 | 0 | 0 | 0.0 | — |

Russ Swan

SWAN, RUSSELL HOWARD
B. Jan. 3, 1964, Fremont, Calif.

BL TL 6'4" 210 lbs.

| 1989 | SF | N | 0 | 2 | .000 | 10.80 | 2 | 2 | 0 | 6.2 | 11 | 4 | 2 | 0 | 0 | 0 | 0 | 2 | 0 | 0 | .000 | 1 | 1 | 0 | 0 | 1.0 | 1.000 |

Red Swanson

SWANSON, ARTHUR LEONARD
B. Oct. 15, 1936, Baton Rouge, La.

BR TR 6'1½" 175 lbs.

1955	PIT	N	0	0	—	18.00	1	0	0	2	2	3	0	0	0	0	0	0	0	0	—	0	0	0	0	0.0	—
1956			0	0	—	10.03	9	0	0	11.2	21	8	5	0	0	0	0	0	0	0	—	1	5	0	0	0.7	1.000
1957			3	3	.500	3.72	32	8	1	72.2	68	31	29	0	0	0	0	13	0	0	.000	4	8	0	1	0.4	1.000
3 yrs.			3	3	.500	4.90	42	8	1	86.1	91	42	34	0	0	0	0	13	0	0	.000	5	13	0	1	0.4	1.000

Ed Swartwood

SWARTWOOD, CYRUS EDWARD
B. Jan. 12, 1859, Rockford, Ill. D. May 15, 1924, Pittsburgh, Pa.

BL TR 198 lbs.

1884	PIT	AA	0	0	—	11.57	1	0	0	2.1	6	1	0	0	0	0	0	399	115	0	.288	0	0	0	0	0.0	—
1890	TOL	AA	0	0	—	3.00	1	0	0	3	2	0	1	0	0	0	0	462	151	3	.327	0	0	0	0	0.0	—
2 yrs.			0	0	—	6.75	2	0	0	5.1	8	1	1	0	0	0	0	*				0	0	0	0	0.0	—

Bud Swartz

SWARTZ, SHERWIN MERLE
B. June 13, 1929, Tulsa, Okla.

BL TL 6'2½" 180 lbs.

| 1947 | STL | A | 0 | 0 | — | 6.75 | 5 | 0 | 0 | 5.1 | 9 | 7 | 1 | 0 | 0 | 0 | 0 | 1 | 1 | 0 | 1.000 | 0 | 0 | 0 | 0 | 0.0 | — |

Dazzy Swartz

SWARTZ, VERNON MONROE (Monty)
B. Jan. 1, 1897, Farmersville, Ohio D. Jan. 13, 1980, Germantown, Ohio

BR TR 5'11" 182 lbs.

| 1920 | CIN | N | 0 | 1 | .000 | 4.50 | 1 | 1 | 1 | 12 | 17 | 2 | 2 | 0 | 0 | 0 | 0 | 4 | 2 | 0 | .500 | 0 | 4 | 0 | 0 | 4.0 | 1.000 |

Park Swartzel

SWARTZEL, PARKE B.
B. Nov. 21, 1865, Knightstown, Ind. D. Jan. 3, 1940, Los Angeles, Calif.

BR TR

| 1889 | KC | AA | 19 | 27 | .413 | 4.32 | 48 | 47 | 45 | 410.1 | 481 | 117 | 147 | 0 | 0 | 0 | 1 | 174 | 25 | 0 | .144 | 19 | 145 | 11 | 6 | 3.6 | .937 |

Bill Sweeney

SWEENEY, WILLIAM J.
B. 1858, Philadelphia, Pa. D. Aug. 2, 1903, Philadelphia, Pa.

TR

1882	PHI	AA	9	11	.450	2.91	20	20	18	170	178	42	48	0	0	0	0	88	14	0	.159	9	51	6	0	3.3	.909
1884	BAL	U	40	21	.656	2.59	62	60	58	538	522	74	374	4	1	1	0	296	71	0	.240	25	133	34	3	3.1	.823
2 yrs.			49	32	.605	2.67	82	80	76	708	700	116	422	4	1	1	0	384	85	0	.221	34	184	40	3	3.1	.845

Charlie Sweeney

SWEENEY, CHARLES J.
B. Apr. 13, 1863, San Francisco, Calif. D. Apr. 4, 1902, San Francisco, Calif.

BR TR 5'10½" 160 lbs.

1882	PRO	N	0	0	—	0.00	0	0	0	0	0	0	0	0	0	0	0	4	0	0	.000	0	0	0	0	0.0	—
1883			7	7	.500	3.13	20	18	14	146.2	142	28	48	0	0	0	0	87	19	0	.218	7	37	7	1	2.6	.863
1884	2 teams				PRO N	(27G 17–8)				STL U	(33G 24–7)																
"	total		41	15	.732	1.70	60	56	53	492	360	42	337	6	1	2	1	339	104	2	.307	39	123	10	5	2.9	.942
1885	STL	N	11	21	.344	3.93	35	35	32	275	276	50	84	2	0	0	0	267	55	0	.206	19	62	13	2	2.7	.862
1886			5	6	.455	4.16	11	11	11	93	108	39	28	0	0	0	0	64	16	0	.250	6	20	2	1	2.5	.941
1887	CLE	AA	0	3	.000	8.25	3	3	3	24	42	13	8	0	0	0	0	133	30	0	.226	2	4	0	0	2.0	1.000
6 yrs.			64	52	.552	2.87	129	123	113	1030.2	928	172	505	8	1	2	1	*				73	246	32	9	2.7	.909

Leo Sweetland

SWEETLAND, LEO (Sugar)
B. Aug. 15, 1901, St. Ignace, Mich.
D. Mar. 4, 1974, Melbourne, Fla.

BB TL 5'11½" 155 lbs.
BL 1927,
BR 1928-29

1927	PHI	N	2	10	.167	6.16	21	13	6	103.2	147	53	21	0	0	1	0	38	12	0	.316	7	43	1	3	2.4	.980
1928			3	15	.167	6.58	37	18	6	135.1	163	97	23	0	1	3	2	47	9	0	.191	8	44	4	3	1.5	.929
1929			13	11	.542	5.11	43	25	10	204.1	255	87	47	2	2	0	2	89	26	0	.292	14	64	3	1	1.9	.963
1930			7	15	.318	7.71	34	25	8	167	271	60	36	1	0	2	0	57	16	0	.281	10	38	3	2	1.5	.941
1931	CHI	N	8	7	.533	5.04	26	14	9	130.1	156	61	32	0	1	1	0	56	15	0	.268	5	30	4	0	1.5	.897
5 yrs.			33	58	.363	6.10	161	95	38	740.2	992	358	159	3	4	7	4	287	78	0	.272	44	219	15	9	1.7	.946

Steve Swetonic

SWETONIC, STEPHEN ALBERT
B. Aug. 13, 1903, Mt. Pleasant, Pa. D. Apr. 22, 1974, Canonsburg, Pa.

BR TR 5'11" 185 lbs.

1929	PIT	N	8	10	.444	4.82	41	12	3	143.2	172	50	35	0	5	5	5	48	13	0	.271	7	41	2	0	1.2	.960
1930			6	6	.500	4.47	23	6	3	96.2	107	27	35	1	4	2	5	36	4	0	.111	3	16	0	3	0.8	1.000
1931			0	2	.000	3.90	14	0	0	27.2	28	16	8	0	0	2	1	7	1	0	.143	1	5	0	0	0.4	1.000
1932			11	6	.647	2.82	24	19	11	162.2	134	55	39	4	0	0	0	54	5	0	.093	3	31	0	0	1.4	1.000
1933			12	12	.500	3.50	31	21	8	164.2	166	64	37	3	3	3	0	55	11	0	.200	4	34	2	2	1.3	.950
1935			0	0	—	0.00	0	0	0	0	0	0	0	0	0	0	0	0	0	0	—	0	0	0	0	0.0	—
6 yrs.			37	36	.507	3.81	133	58	25	595.1	607	212	154	8	12	12	11	200	34	0	.170	18	127	4	5	1.1	.973

Bill Swift

SWIFT, WILLIAM CHARLES
B. Oct. 27, 1961, Portland, Me.

BR TR 6' 170 lbs.

1985	SEA	A	6	10	.375	4.77	23	21	0	120.2	131	48	55	0	1	0	0	0	0	0	—	10	18	1	1	1.3	.966
1986			2	9	.182	5.46	29	17	1	115.1	148	55	55	0	0	0	0	0	0	0	—	13	21	1	1	1.2	.971
1988			8	12	.400	4.59	38	24	6	174.2	199	65	47	1	3	0	1	0	0	0	—	19	33	4	3	1.5	.929
1989			7	3	.700	4.43	37	16	0	130	140	38	45	0	2	0	1	0	0	0	—	18	39	2	5	1.6	.966
4 yrs.			23	34	.404	4.78	127	78	7	540.2	618	206	202	1	6	1	1	0	0	0	—	60	111	8	10	1.4	.955

Year	Team		W	L	PCT	ERA	G	GS	CG	IP	H	BB	SO	ShO	W	L	SV	AB	H	HR	BA	PO	A	E	DP	TC/G	FA
															Relief Pitching			**Batting**									

Bill Swift

SWIFT, WILLIAM VINCENT
B. Jan. 10, 1908, Elmira, N. Y. D. Feb. 23, 1969, Bartow, Fla.　　　　BR TR 6'1½" 192 lbs.

Year	Team		W	L	PCT	ERA	G	GS	CG	IP	H	BB	SO	ShO	W	L	SV	AB	H	HR	BA	PO	A	E	DP	TC/G	FA
1932	PIT	N	14	10	.583	3.61	39	23	11	214.1	205	26	64	0	6	1	4	78	15	0	.192	8	27	2	1	0.9	.946
1933			14	10	.583	3.13	37	29	13	218.1	214	36	64	2	2	0	0	82	20	0	.244	11	39	2	1	1.4	.962
1934			11	13	.458	3.98	37	24	13	212.2	244	46	81	1	1	2	0	84	18	0	.214	8	38	2	0	1.3	.958
1935			15	8	.652	2.70	39	21	11	203.2	193	37	74	3	3	4	1	78	19	0	.244	4	23	0	2	0.7	1.000
1936			16	16	.500	4.01	45	31	17	262.1	275	63	92	0	4	1	2	105	31	2	.295	4	36	2	3	0.9	.952
1937			9	10	.474	3.95	36	17	9	164	160	34	84	0	2	2	3	54	9	0	.167	4	36	2	1	1.2	.952
1938			7	5	.583	3.24	36	9	2	150	155	40	77	0	5	2	4	50	10	1	.200	1	26	2	1	0.8	.931
1939			5	7	.417	3.89	36	8	2	129.2	150	28	56	1	2	4	4	42	10	0	.238	2	14	0	0	0.4	1.000
1940	BOS	N	1	1	.500	2.89	4	0	0	9.1	12	7	7	0	1	1	1	3	0	0	.000	0	2	0	0	0.5	1.000
1941	BKN	N	3	0	1.000	3.27	9	0	0	22	26	7	9	0	3	0	1	5	1	0	.200	0	3	0	0	0.3	1.000
1943	CHI	A	0	2	.000	4.21	18	1	0	51.1	48	27	28	0	0	1	0	10	1	0	.100	0	2	1	0	0.2	.750
11 yrs.			95	82	.537	3.58	336	163	78	1637.2	1682	351	636	7	29	18	20	591	134	3	.227	43	246	13	9	0.9	.957

Oad Swigart

SWIGART, OADIS VAUGHN
B. Feb. 13, 1915, Archie, Mo.　　　　BL TR 6' 175 lbs.

Year	Team		W	L	PCT	ERA	G	GS	CG	IP	H	BB	SO	ShO	W	L	SV	AB	H	HR	BA	PO	A	E	DP	TC/G	FA
1939	PIT	N	1	1	.500	4.44	3	3	1	24.1	27	6	8	1	0	0	0	8	2	0	.250	2	3	0	1	1.7	1.000
1940			0	2	.000	4.43	7	2	0	22.1	27	10	9	0	0	1	0	5	1	0	.200	0	6	0	0	0.9	1.000
2 yrs.			1	3	.250	4.44	10	5	1	46.2	54	16	17	1	0	1	0	13	3	0	.231	2	9	0	1	1.1	1.000

Ad Swigler

SWIGLER, ADAM WILLIAM
B. Sept. 21, 1895, Philadelphia, Pa. D. Feb. 5, 1975, Philadelphia, Pa.　　　　BR TR 5'10" 180 lbs.

Year	Team		W	L	PCT	ERA	G	GS	CG	IP	H	BB	SO	ShO	W	L	SV	AB	H	HR	BA	PO	A	E	DP	TC/G	FA
1917	NY	N	0	1	.000	6.00	1	1	0	6	7	8	4	0	0	0	0	2	0	0	.000	0	2	0	0	2.0	1.000

Greg Swindell

SWINDELL, FORREST GREGORY
B. Jan. 2, 1965, Houston, Tex.　　　　BR TL 6'2" 225 lbs.

Year	Team		W	L	PCT	ERA	G	GS	CG	IP	H	BB	SO	ShO	W	L	SV	AB	H	HR	BA	PO	A	E	DP	TC/G	FA
1986	CLE	A	5	2	.714	4.23	9	9	1	61.2	57	15	46	0	0	0	0	0	0	0	—	2	12	0	1	1.6	1.000
1987			3	8	.273	5.10	16	15	4	102.1	112	37	97	1	0	0	0	0	0	0	—	0	13	1	1	0.9	.929
1988			18	14	.563	3.20	33	33	12	242	234	45	180	4	0	0	0	0	0	0	—	8	29	1	0	1.2	.974
1989			13	6	.684	3.37	28	28	5	184.1	170	51	129	2	0	0	0	0	0	0	—	7	25	0	1	1.1	1.000
4 yrs.			39	30	.565	3.69	86	85	22	590.1	573	148	452	7	0	0	0	0	0	0	—	17	79	2	3	1.1	.980

Josh Swindell

SWINDELL, JOSHUA ERNEST
B. July 5, 1885, Rose Hill, Kans. D. Mar. 19, 1969, Fruita, Colo.　　　　BR TR 6' 180 lbs.

Year	Team		W	L	PCT	ERA	G	GS	CG	IP	H	BB	SO	ShO	W	L	SV	AB	H	HR	BA	PO	A	E	DP	TC/G	FA
1911	CLE	A	0	1	.000	2.08	4	1	1	17.1	19	4	6	0	0	0	0	4	1	0	.250	1	3	1	0	1.3	.800
1913			0	0	—	0.00	0	0	0	0	0	0	0	0	0	0	0	0	0	0	—	0	0	0	0	0.0	—
2 yrs.			0	1	.000	2.08	4	1	1	17.1	19	4	6	0	0	0	0	4	1	0	.250	1	3	1	0	1.3	.800

Len Swormstedt

SWORMSTEDT, LEONARD JORDAN
B. Oct. 6, 1878, Cincinnati, Ohio D. July 19, 1964, Salem, Mass.　　　　BR TR 5'11½" 165 lbs.

Year	Team		W	L	PCT	ERA	G	GS	CG	IP	H	BB	SO	ShO	W	L	SV	AB	H	HR	BA	PO	A	E	DP	TC/G	FA
1901	CIN	N	2	1	.667	1.73	3	3	3	26	19	5	13	0	0	0	0	9	0	0	.000	2	6	0	0	2.7	1.000
1902			0	2	.000	4.00	2	2	2	18	22	5	3	0	0	0	0	6	0	0	.000	1	3	0	0	2.0	1.000
1906	BOS	A	1	1	.500	1.29	3	2	2	21	17	0	6	0	0	0	0	8	1	0	.125	1	4	1	0	2.0	.833
3 yrs.			3	4	.429	2.22	8	7	7	65	58	10	22	0	0	0	0	23	1	0	.043	4	13	1	0	2.3	.944

Bob Sykes

SYKES, ROBERT JOSEPH
B. Dec. 11, 1954, Neptune, N. J.　　　　BB TL 6'1" 195 lbs.

Year	Team		W	L	PCT	ERA	G	GS	CG	IP	H	BB	SO	ShO	W	L	SV	AB	H	HR	BA	PO	A	E	DP	TC/G	FA
1977	DET	A	5	7	.417	4.40	32	20	3	133	141	50	58	0	0	0	0	0	0	0	—	6	20	2	3	0.9	.929
1978			6	6	.500	3.94	22	10	3	93.2	99	34	58	2	3	1	2	0	0	0	—	1	7	1	0	0.4	.889
1979	STL	N	4	3	.571	6.18	13	11	0	67	86	34	35	0	0	0	0	21	2	0	.095	0	7	0	0	0.5	1.000
1980			6	10	.375	4.64	27	19	4	126	134	54	50	3	0	3	0	39	4	0	.103	4	14	1	2	0.7	.947
1981			2	0	1.000	4.62	22	1	0	37	37	18	14	0	2	1	0	2	0	0	.000	4	8	0	1	0.5	1.000
5 yrs.			23	26	.469	4.65	116	61	10	456.2	497	190	215	5	5	5	2	62	6	0	.097	15	56	4	6	0.6	.947

Lou Sylvester

SYLVESTER, LOUIS J.
B. Feb. 14, 1855, Springfield, Ill. Deceased.　　　　BR TR 5'3" 165 lbs.

Year	Team		W	L	PCT	ERA	G	GS	CG	IP	H	BB	SO	ShO	W	L	SV	AB	H	HR	BA	PO	A	E	DP	TC/G	FA
1884	CIN	U	0	1	.000	*3.58*	6	1	1	32.2	32	6	7	0	0	0	1	*				1	5	1	0	1.2	.857

John Taber

TABER, JOHN PARDON
B. June 28, 1868, Acushnet, Mass. D. Feb. 21, 1940, Boston, Mass.　　　　BR TR 5'8"

Year	Team		W	L	PCT	ERA	G	GS	CG	IP	H	BB	SO	ShO	W	L	SV	AB	H	HR	BA	PO	A	E	DP	TC/G	FA
1890	BOS	N	0	1	.000	4.15	2	1	1	13	11	8	3	0	0	0	1	6	0	0	.000	0	4	0	0	2.0	1.000

Lefty Taber

TABER, EDWARD TIMOTHY
B. Jan. 11, 1900, Rock Island, Ill. D. Nov. 5, 1983, Lincoln, Neb.　　　　BL TL 6' 180 lbs.

Year	Team		W	L	PCT	ERA	G	GS	CG	IP	H	BB	SO	ShO	W	L	SV	AB	H	HR	BA	PO	A	E	DP	TC/G	FA
1926	PHI	N	0	0	—	7.56	6	0	0	8.1	8	5	0	0	0	0	0	1	0	0	.000	0	2	0	0	0.3	1.000
1927			0	1	.000	18.90	3	1	0	3.1	8	5	0	0	0	0	0	1	0	0	.000	1	0	0	0	0.7	1.000
2 yrs.			0	1	.000	10.80	9	1	0	11.2	16	10	0	0	0	0	0	2	0	0	.000	1	2	0	0	0.4	1.000

John Taff

TAFF, JOHN GALLATIN
B. June 3, 1890, Austin, Tex. D. May 15, 1961, Houston, Tex.　　　　BR TR 6' 170 lbs.

Year	Team		W	L	PCT	ERA	G	GS	CG	IP	H	BB	SO	ShO	W	L	SV	AB	H	HR	BA	PO	A	E	DP	TC/G	FA
1913	PHI	A	0	1	.000	6.62	7	1	0	17.2	22	5	9	0	0	0	1	5	1	0	.200	0	6	0	0	0.9	1.000

Doug Taitt

TAITT, DOUGLAS JOHN (Poco)
B. Aug. 3, 1902, Bay City, Mich. D. Dec. 12, 1970, Portland, Ore.　　　　BL TR 6' 176 lbs.

Year	Team		W	L	PCT	ERA	G	GS	CG	IP	H	BB	SO	ShO	W	L	SV	AB	H	HR	BA	PO	A	E	DP	TC/G	FA
1928	BOS	A	0	0	—	27.00	1	0	0	1	2	2	1	0	0	0	0	*				1	0	0	0	1.0	1.000

Year	Team	W	L	PCT	ERA	G	GS	CG	IP	H	BB	SO	ShO	W	L	SV	AB	H	HR	BA	PO	A	E	DP	TC/G	FA
														Relief Pitching			Batting									

Fred Talbot

TALBOT, FREDERICK LEALAND (Bubby)
B. June 28, 1941, Washington, D. C.   BR TR 6'2"   195 lbs.

Year	Team	W	L	PCT	ERA	G	GS	CG	IP	H	BB	SO	ShO	W	L	SV	AB	H	HR	BA	PO	A	E	DP	TC/G	FA
1963	CHI A	0	0	–	3.00	1	0	0	3	2	4	2	0	0	0	0	1	0	0	.000	1	1	0	1	2.0	1.000
1964		4	5	.444	3.70	17	12	3	75.1	83	20	34	2	1	1	0	19	5	0	.263	4	9	0	0	0.8	1.000
1965	KC A	10	12	.455	4.14	39	33	2	198	188	86	117	1	0	1	0	70	14	0	.200	15	30	4	3	1.3	.918
1966	2 teams	KC A	(11G 4–4)		NY A	(23G 7–7)																				
"	total	11	11	.500	4.36	34	30	3	192	188	73	85	0	0	0	0	55	8	0	.145	17	30	2	1	1.4	.959
1967	NY A	6	8	.429	4.22	29	22	2	138.2	132	54	61	0	1	1	0	38	6	1	.158	14	34	1	0	1.7	.980
1968		1	9	.100	3.36	29	11	1	99	89	42	67	0	1	1	0	17	2	1	.118	8	16	0	2	0.8	1.000
1969	3 teams	NY A	(8G 0–0)		SEA A	(25G 5–8)		OAK A	(12G 1–2)																	
"	total	6	10	.375	4.38	45	18	1	146	160	54	83	1	2	3	0	41	7	2	.171	10	22	2	3	0.8	.941
1970	OAK A	0	1	.000	9.00	1	0	0	2	2	1	2	0	0	0	0	0	0	0	–	0	1	0	0	1.0	1.000
8 yrs.		38	56	.404	4.12	195	126	12	854	844	334	449	4	5	7	1	241	42	4	.174	69	143	9	10	1.1	.959

Roy Talcott

TALCOTT, LeROY EVERETT
B. Jan. 16, 1920, Brookline, Mass.   BR TR 6'1½"   180 lbs.

Year	Team	W	L	PCT	ERA	G	GS	CG	IP	H	BB	SO	ShO	W	L	SV	AB	H	HR	BA	PO	A	E	DP	TC/G	FA
1943	BOS N	0	0	–	27.00	1	0	0	.2	1	2	0	0	0	0	0	0	0	0	–	0	1	0	0	1.0	1.000

Vito Tamulis

TAMULIS, VITAUTRIS CASIMIRUS
B. July 11, 1911, Cambridge, Mass.   D. May 5, 1974, Nashville, Tenn.   BL TL 5'9"   170 lbs.

Year	Team	W	L	PCT	ERA	G	GS	CG	IP	H	BB	SO	ShO	W	L	SV	AB	H	HR	BA	PO	A	E	DP	TC/G	FA
1934	NY A	1	0	1.000	0.00	1	1	1	9	7	1	5	1	0	0	0	4	1	0	.250	2	1	0	0	3.0	1.000
1935		10	5	.667	4.09	30	19	9	160.2	178	55	57	3	2	1	0	57	14	1	.246	7	29	1	0	1.2	.973
1938	2 teams	STL A	(3G 0–3)		BKN N	(38G 12–6)																				
"	total	12	9	.571	4.17	41	20	9	175	207	50	81	0	3	3	2	60	9	0	.150	3	28	1	1	0.8	.969
1939	BKN N	9	8	.529	4.37	39	17	8	158.2	177	45	83	1	1	1	4	55	10	0	.182	5	31	0	5	0.9	1.000
1940		8	5	.615	3.09	41	12	4	154.1	147	34	55	1	3	5	2	46	6	0	.130	4	28	2	3	0.8	.941
1941	2 teams	PHI N	(6G 0–1)		BKN N	(12G 0–0)																				
"	total	0	1	.000	5.56	18	1	0	34	42	17	13	0	0	0	1	7	0	0	.000	2	8	0	0	0.6	1.000
6 yrs.		40	28	.588	3.97	170	70	31	691.2	758	202	294	6	9	9	10	229	40	1	.175	23	125	4	9	0.9	.974

Frank Tanana

TANANA, FRANK DARYL
B. July 3, 1953, Detroit, Mich.   BL TL 6'2"   180 lbs.

Year	Team	W	L	PCT	ERA	G	GS	CG	IP	H	BB	SO	ShO	W	L	SV	AB	H	HR	BA	PO	A	E	DP	TC/G	FA
1973	CAL A	2	2	.500	3.08	4	4	2	26.1	20	8	22	1	0	0	0	0	0	0	–	0	5	0	0	1.3	1.000
1974		14	19	.424	3.11	39	35	12	269	262	77	180	4	2	0	0	0	0	0	–	9	39	1	4	1.3	.980
1975		16	9	.640	2.62	34	33	16	257.1	211	73	269	5	0	0	0	0	0	0	–	9	44	2	5	1.6	.964
1976		19	10	.655	2.44	34	34	23	288	212	73	261	2	0	0	0	0	0	0	–	12	45	1	1	1.7	.983
1977		15	9	.625	2.54	31	31	20	241.1	201	61	205	7	0	0	0	0	0	0	–	15	37	1	2	1.7	.981
1978		18	12	.600	3.65	33	33	10	239	239	60	137	4	0	0	0	0	0	0	–	8	25	0	2	1.0	1.000
1979		7	5	.583	3.90	18	17	2	90	93	25	46	1	0	0	0	0	0	0	–	3	12	1	1	0.9	.938
1980		11	12	.478	4.15	32	31	7	204	223	45	113	0	0	0	0	0	0	0	–	12	24	0	1	1.1	1.000
1981	BOS A	4	10	.286	4.02	24	23	5	141	142	43	78	1	0	0	0	0	0	0	–	9	25	1	2	1.5	.971
1982	TEX A	7	18	.280	4.21	30	30	7	194.1	199	55	87	0	0	0	0	0	0	0	–	8	30	1	0	1.3	.974
1983		7	9	.438	3.16	29	22	3	159.1	144	49	108	0	1	0	0	0	0	0	–	9	37	2	0	1.7	.958
1984		15	15	.500	3.25	35	35	9	246.1	234	81	141	1	0	0	0	0	0	0	–	18	35	0	2	1.5	1.000
1985	2 teams	TEX A	(13G 2–7)		DET A	(20G 10–7)																				
"	total	12	14	.462	4.27	33	33	4	215	220	57	159	0	0	0	0	0	0	0	–	14	31	1	2	1.4	.978
1986	DET A	12	9	.571	4.16	32	31	3	188.1	196	65	119	1	0	0	0	0	0	0	–	19	26	2	5	1.5	.957
1987		15	10	.600	3.91	34	34	5	218.2	216	56	146	3	0	0	0	0	0	0	–	14	35	0	0	1.4	1.000
1988		14	11	.560	4.21	32	32	2	203	213	64	127	0	0	0	0	0	0	0	–	11	31	1	4	1.3	.977
1989		10	14	.417	3.58	33	33	6	223.2	227	74	147	1	0	0	0	0	0	0	–	16	41	0	2	1.7	1.000
17 yrs.		198	188	.513	3.49	507	491	136	3404.2	3252	966	2345	32	3	0	0	0	0	0	–	186	522	14	35	1.4	.981

LEAGUE CHAMPIONSHIP SERIES

Year	Team	W	L	PCT	ERA	G	GS	CG	IP	H	BB	SO	ShO	W	L	SV	AB	H	HR	BA	PO	A	E	DP	TC/G	FA
1979	CAL A	0	0	–	3.60	1	1	0	5	6	2	3	0	0	0	0	0	0	0	–	0	0	0	0	0.0	–
1987	DET A	0	1	.000	5.06	1	1	0	5.1	6	4	1	0	0	0	0	0	0	0	–	0	1	0	0	1.0	1.000
2 yrs.		0	1	.000	4.35	2	2	0	10.1	12	6	4	0	0	0	0	0	0	0	–	0	1	0	0	0.5	1.000

Jesse Tannehill

TANNEHILL, JESSE NILES (Tanny)
Brother of Lee Tannehill.
B. July 14, 1874, Dayton, Ky.   D. Sept. 22, 1956, Dayton, Ky.   BB TL 5'8"   150 lbs.
BL 1903

Year	Team	W	L	PCT	ERA	G	GS	CG	IP	H	BB	SO	ShO	W	L	SV	AB	H	HR	BA	PO	A	E	DP	TC/G	FA
1894	CIN N	1	0	1.000	7.14	5			29	37	16		0				11	0	0	.000	1	2	2	0	1.0	.600
1897	PIT N	9	9	.500	4.25	21	16	11	142	172	24	40	1	1	2	1	184	49	0	.266	7	45	3	1	2.6	.945
1898		25	13	.658	2.95	43	38	34	326.2	338	63	93	5	1	0	2	152	44	1	.289	14	94	5	2	2.6	.956
1899		24	14	.632	2.57	41	35	32	333	354	51	64	3	3	1	1	132	34	0	.258	9	95	5	7	2.7	.954
1900		20	6	.769	2.88	29	27	23	234	247	43	50	2	0	0	0	110	37	0	.336	9	64	6	0	2.7	.924
1901		18	10	.643	2.18	32	30	25	252.1	240	36	118	4	0	0	1	135	33	1	.244	5	50	5	0	1.9	.917
1902		20	6	.769	1.95	26	24	23	231	203	25	100	2	2	0	0	148	43	1	.291	6	56	2	3	2.5	.969
1903	NY A	15	15	.500	3.27	32	31	22	239.2	258	34	106	2	0	0	0	111	26	1	.234	10	83	3	2	3.0	.969
1904	BOS A	21	11	.656	2.04	33	31	30	281.2	256	33	116	4	2	0	0	122	24	0	.197	9	107	1	4	3.5	.991
1905		22	9	.710	2.48	37	31	27	271.2	238	59	113	6	3	1	0	93	21	1	.226	9	97	6	3	3.0	.946
1906		13	11	.542	3.16	27	26	18	196.1	207	39	82	2	0	0	0	79	22	0	.278	15	58	4	1	2.9	.948
1907		6	7	.462	2.47	18	16	10	131	131	20	29	2	0	0	0	51	10	0	.196	9	42	1	3	2.9	.981
1908	2 teams	BOS A	(1G 0–0)		WAS A	(10G 2–4)																				
"	total	2	4	.333	3.76	11	10	7	76.2	81	26	16	0	0	0	0	45	12	0	.267	5	34	4	2	3.9	.907
1909	WAS A	1	1	.500	3.43	3	2	2	21	19	5	8	1	0	0	0	36	6	0	.167	2	9	0	1	3.7	1.000
1911	CIN N	0	0	–	6.23	1	0	0	4.1	6	3	1	0	0	0	0	0	0	0	.000	0	1	0	0	1.0	1.000
15 yrs.		197	116	.629	2.77	359	318	263	2770.1	2787	477	943	34	12	4	7	*				110	837	47	29	2.8	.953

Bruce Tanner

TANNER, BRUCE MATTHEW
Son of Chuck Tanner.
B. Dec. 9, 1961, New Castle, Pa.   BL TR 6'3"   220 lbs.

Year	Team	W	L	PCT	ERA	G	GS	CG	IP	H	BB	SO	ShO	W	L	SV	AB	H	HR	BA	PO	A	E	DP	TC/G	FA
1985	CHI A	1	2	.333	5.33	10	4	0	27	34	13	9	0	0	0	0	0	0	0	–	3	7	1	1	1.1	.909

Year	Team	W	L	PCT	ERA	G	GS	CG	IP	H	BB	SO	ShO	W	L	SV	AB	H	HR	BA	PO	A	E	DP	TC/G	FA

Kevin Tapani
TAPANI, KEVIN RAY
B. Feb. 18, 1964, Des Moines, Iowa
BR TR 6' 180 lbs.

Year	Team	W	L	PCT	ERA	G	GS	CG	IP	H	BB	SO	ShO	W	L	SV	AB	H	HR	BA	PO	A	E	DP	TC/G	FA
1989	2 teams	NY N (3G 0–0)			MIN A (5G 2–2)																					
"	total	2	2	.500	3.83	8	5	0	40	39	12	23	0	0	0	0	2	0	0	.000	4	4	0	1	1.0	1.000

Al Tate
TATE, ALVIN WALTER
B. July 1, 1918, Coleman, Okla.
BR TR 6' 180 lbs.

Year	Team	W	L	PCT	ERA	G	GS	CG	IP	H	BB	SO	ShO	W	L	SV	AB	H	HR	BA	PO	A	E	DP	TC/G	FA
1946	PIT N	0	1	.000	5.00	2	1	1	9	8	7	2	0	0	0	0	3	1	0	.333	0	3	0	0	1.5	1.000

Randy Tate
TATE, RANDALL LEE
B. Oct. 23, 1952, Florence, Ala.
BR TR 6'3" 190 lbs.

Year	Team	W	L	PCT	ERA	G	GS	CG	IP	H	BB	SO	ShO	W	L	SV	AB	H	HR	BA	PO	A	E	DP	TC/G	FA
1975	NY N	5	13	.278	4.43	26	23	2	138	121	86	99	0	0	0	0	41	0	0	.000	11	19	2	0	1.2	.938

Stu Tate
TATE, STUART DOUGLAS
B. June 17, 1962, Huntsville, Ala.
BR TR 6'3" 205 lbs.

Year	Team	W	L	PCT	ERA	G	GS	CG	IP	H	BB	SO	ShO	W	L	SV	AB	H	HR	BA	PO	A	E	DP	TC/G	FA
1989	SF N	0	0	–	3.38	2	0	0	2.2	3	0	4	0	0	0	0	0	0	0	–	0	0	0	0	0.0	–

Ken Tatum
TATUM, KENNETH RAY
B. Apr. 25, 1944, Alexandria, La.
BR TR 6'2" 205 lbs.

Year	Team	W	L	PCT	ERA	G	GS	CG	IP	H	BB	SO	ShO	W	L	SV	AB	H	HR	BA	PO	A	E	DP	TC/G	FA
1969	CAL A	7	2	.778	1.36	45	0	0	86.1	51	39	65	0	7	2	22	21	6	2	.286	1	12	0	0	0.3	1.000
1970		7	4	.636	2.93	62	0	0	89	68	26	50	0	7	4	17	11	2	1	.182	4	15	1	0	0.3	.950
1971	BOS A	2	4	.333	4.17	36	1	0	54	50	25	21	0	2	3	9	10	3	1	.300	2	11	0	2	0.4	1.000
1972		0	2	.000	3.10	22	0	0	29	32	15	15	0	0	2	4	2	0	0	.000	1	4	1	0	0.3	.833
1973		0	0	–	9.00	1	0	0	4	6	3	0	0	0	0	0	0	0	0	–	0	0	0	0	0.0	–
1974	CHI A	0	0	–	4.71	10	1	0	21	23	9	5	0	0	0	0	1	0	0	.000	2	5	0	1	0.7	1.000
6 yrs.		16	12	.571	2.92	176	2	0	283.1	230	117	156	0	16	11	52	45	11	4	.244	10	47	2	3	0.3	.966

Walt Tauscher
TAUSCHER, WALTER EDWARD
B. Nov. 22, 1901, LaSalle, Ill.
BR TR 6'1" 186 lbs.

Year	Team	W	L	PCT	ERA	G	GS	CG	IP	H	BB	SO	ShO	W	L	SV	AB	H	HR	BA	PO	A	E	DP	TC/G	FA
1928	PIT N	0	0	–	4.91	17	0	0	29.1	28	12	7	0	0	0	1	6	1	0	.167	1	6	0	0	0.4	1.000
1931	WAS A	1	0	1.000	7.50	6	0	0	12	24	4	5	0	1	0	0	0	0	0	–	1	9	1	2	1.8	.909
2 yrs.		1	0	1.000	5.66	23	0	0	41.1	52	16	12	0	1	0	1	6	1	0	.167	2	15	1	2	0.8	.944

Arlas Taylor
TAYLOR, ARLAS WALTER (Lefty, Foxy)
B. Mar. 16, 1896, Warrick County, Ind. D. Sept. 10, 1968, Dade City, Fla.
BR TL 5'11"

Year	Team	W	L	PCT	ERA	G	GS	CG	IP	H	BB	SO	ShO	W	L	SV	AB	H	HR	BA	PO	A	E	DP	TC/G	FA
1921	PHI A	0	1	.000	22.50	1	1	0	2	7	2	1	0	0	0	0	0	0	0	–	0	0	0	0	0.0	–

Ben Taylor
TAYLOR, BENJAMIN HARRISON
B. Apr. 2, 1889, Paoli, Ind. D. Nov. 3, 1946, Martin County, Ind.
TR 5'11" 163 lbs.

Year	Team	W	L	PCT	ERA	G	GS	CG	IP	H	BB	SO	ShO	W	L	SV	AB	H	HR	BA	PO	A	E	DP	TC/G	FA
1912	CIN N	0	0	–	3.18	2	0	0	5.2	9	3	2	0	0	0	0	2	0	0	.000	0	1	0	0	0.5	1.000

Billy Taylor
TAYLOR, WILLIAM HENRY (Bollicky)
B. 1855, Washington, D. C. D. May 14, 1900, Jacksonville, Fla.
BR TR 5'11½" 204 lbs.

Year	Team	W	L	PCT	ERA	G	GS	CG	IP	H	BB	SO	ShO	W	L	SV	AB	H	HR	BA	PO	A	E	DP	TC/G	FA
1881	3 teams	WOR N (1G 0–1)			DET N (0G 0–0)				CLE N (1G 0–0)																	
"	total	0	1	.000	5.73	2	1	1	11	15	7	2	0	0	0	0	135	30	0	.222	1	1	0	0	1.0	1.000
1882	PIT AA	0	1	.000	16.20	1	0	0	5	11	4	1	0	0	0	1	299	84	4	.281	0	0	0	0	0.0	–
1883		4	7	.364	5.39	19	9	8	127	166	34	41	0	1	1	0	369	96	0	.260	8	15	3	0	1.4	.885
1884	2 teams	STL U (33G 25–4)			PHI AA (30G 18–12)																					
"	total	43	16	.729	2.10	63	59	59	523	454	84	284	3	0	0	4	297	96	3	.323	29	115	31	3	2.8	.823
1885	PHI AA	1	5	.167	3.27	6	6	6	52.1	68	9	11	0	0	0	0	21	4	0	.190	0	5	4	0	1.5	.556
1886	BAL AA	1	6	.143	5.72	8	8	8	72.1	87	20	37	0	0	0	0	39	12	0	.308	0	13	3	0	1.9	.800
1887	PHI AA	1	0	1.000	3.00	1	1	1	9	10	7	0	0	0	0	0	4	1	0	.250	1	1	0	0	1.0	1.000
7 yrs.		50	36	.581	3.17	100	84	83	799.2	811	165	376	3	1	2	4	*				38	149	41	3	2.3	.820

Bruce Taylor
TAYLOR, BRUCE BELL
B. Apr. 16, 1953, Holden, Mass.
BR TR 6' 178 lbs.

Year	Team	W	L	PCT	ERA	G	GS	CG	IP	H	BB	SO	ShO	W	L	SV	AB	H	HR	BA	PO	A	E	DP	TC/G	FA
1977	DET A	1	0	1.000	3.41	19	0	0	29	23	10	19	0	1	0	2	0	0	0	–	2	4	0	0	0.3	1.000
1978		0	0	–	0.00	1	0	0	1	0	0	0	0	0	0	0	0	0	0	–	0	0	0	0	0.0	–
1979		1	2	.333	4.74	10	0	0	19	16	7	8	0	1	2	0	0	0	0	–	2	3	1	1	0.6	.833
3 yrs.		2	2	.500	3.86	30	0	0	49	39	17	27	0	2	2	2	0	0	0	–	4	7	1	1	0.4	.917

Chuck Taylor
TAYLOR, CHARLES GILBERT
B. Apr. 18, 1942, Shelbyville, Tenn.
BR TR 6'2" 195 lbs.

Year	Team	W	L	PCT	ERA	G	GS	CG	IP	H	BB	SO	ShO	W	L	SV	AB	H	HR	BA	PO	A	E	DP	TC/G	FA
1969	STL N	7	5	.583	2.55	27	13	5	127	108	30	62	1	0	0	0	39	7	0	.179	3	15	0	1	0.7	1.000
1970		6	7	.462	3.12	56	7	1	124	116	31	64	1	3	5	8	26	3	0	.115	7	23	0	1	0.5	1.000
1971		3	1	.750	3.55	43	1	0	71	72	25	46	0	3	1	3	12	2	0	.167	4	11	1	0	0.4	.938
1972	2 teams	NY N (20G 0–0)			MIL A (5G 0–0)																					
"	total	0	0	–	4.40	25	0	0	43	52	12	14	0	0	0	3	5	1	0	.200	5	11	0	2	0.6	1.000
1973	MON N	2	0	1.000	1.77	8	0	0	20.1	17	2	10	0	2	0	0	4	0	0	.000	1	6	0	1	0.9	1.000
1974		6	2	.750	2.17	61	0	0	108	101	25	43	0	6	2	11	10	3	0	.300	8	15	1	2	0.4	.958
1975		2	2	.500	3.53	54	0	0	74	72	24	29	0	2	2	6	2	0	0	.000	2	11	0	0	0.3	1.000
1976		2	3	.400	4.50	31	0	0	40	38	13	14	0	2	3	0	2	0	0	.000	2	5	0	1	0.2	1.000
8 yrs.		28	20	.583	3.07	305	21	6	607.1	576	162	282	2	18	14	31	101	16	0	.158	36	97	2	8	0.4	.985

Dorn Taylor
TAYLOR, DONALD CLYDE
B. Aug. 11, 1958, Abington, Pa.
BR TR 6'2" 180 lbs.

Year	Team	W	L	PCT	ERA	G	GS	CG	IP	H	BB	SO	ShO	W	L	SV	AB	H	HR	BA	PO	A	E	DP	TC/G	FA
1987	PIT N	2	3	.400	5.74	14	8	0	53.1	48	28	37	0	1	0	0	18	3	0	.167	3	5	2	3	0.7	.800
1989		1	1	.500	5.06	9	0	0	10.2	14	5	3	0	1	1	0	1	0	0	.000	0	1	0	0	0.1	1.000
2 yrs.		3	4	.429	5.63	23	8	0	64	62	33	40	0	2	1	0	19	3	0	.158	3	6	2	3	0.5	.818

Year	Team	W	L	PCT	ERA	G	GS	CG	IP	H	BB	SO	ShO	W	L	SV	AB	H	HR	BA	PO	A	E	DP	TC/G	FA

Dummy Taylor
TAYLOR, LUTHER HADEN
B. Feb. 21, 1875, Oskaloosa, Kans. D. Aug. 22, 1958, Jacksonville, Ill. BR TR 6'1" 160 lbs.

Year	Team	W	L	PCT	ERA	G	GS	CG	IP	H	BB	SO	ShO	W	L	SV	AB	H	HR	BA	PO	A	E	DP	TC/G	FA
1900	NY N	4	3	.571	2.45	11	7	6	62.1	74	24	16	0	0	0	0	22	3	0	.136	0	9	2	0	1.0	.818
1901		18	27	.400	3.18	45	43	37	353.1	377	112	136	4	1	1	0	136	18	0	.132	19	92	6	2	2.6	.949
1902	2 teams	CLE A	(4G 1–3)		NY N	(26G 7–15)																				
"	total	8	18	.308	2.19	30	29	22	234.2	231	63	95	1	0	0	0	75	7	0	.093	7	63	5	0	2.5	.933
1903	NY N	13	13	.500	4.23	33	31	18	244.2	306	89	94	1	0	1	0	82	12	0	.146	10	62	4	2	2.3	.947
1904		21	15	.583	2.34	37	36	29	296.1	231	75	138	5	0	1	0	102	16	0	.157	20	87	1	7	2.9	.991
1905		15	9	.625	2.66	32	28	18	213	200	51	91	4	0	0	0	69	9	0	.130	13	62	5	1	2.5	.938
1906		17	9	.654	2.20	31	27	13	213	186	57	91	2	0	2	0	76	14	0	.184	10	54	4	2	2.2	.941
1907		11	7	.611	2.42	28	21	11	171	145	46	56	3	2	0	1	48	6	0	.125	8	45	4	0	2.0	.930
1908		8	5	.615	2.33	27	15	6	127.2	127	34	50	1	2	0	2	35	8	0	.229	8	35	4	1	1.7	.915
9 yrs.		115	106	.520	2.75	274	237	160	1916	1877	551	767	21	5	5	3	645	93	0	.144	95	509	35	15	2.3	.945

Gary Taylor
TAYLOR, GARY WILLIAM
B. Oct. 19, 1945, Detroit, Mich. BR TR 6'2" 190 lbs.

Year	Team	W	L	PCT	ERA	G	GS	CG	IP	H	BB	SO	ShO	W	L	SV	AB	H	HR	BA	PO	A	E	DP	TC/G	FA
1969	DET A	0	1	.000	5.23	7	0	0	10.1	10	6	3	0	0	1	0	1	0	0	.000	0	2	0	0	0.3	1.000

Harry Taylor
TAYLOR, HARRY EVANS
B. Dec. 2, 1935, San Angelo, Tex. BR TR 6' 185 lbs.

Year	Team	W	L	PCT	ERA	G	GS	CG	IP	H	BB	SO	ShO	W	L	SV	AB	H	HR	BA	PO	A	E	DP	TC/G	FA
1957	KC A	0	0	–	3.12	2	0	0	8.2	11	4	4	0	0	0	0	4	1	0	.250	0	1	1	0	1.0	.500

Harry Taylor
TAYLOR, JAMES HARRY
B. May 20, 1919, East Glenn, Ind. BR TR 6'1" 175 lbs.

Year	Team	W	L	PCT	ERA	G	GS	CG	IP	H	BB	SO	ShO	W	L	SV	AB	H	HR	BA	PO	A	E	DP	TC/G	FA
1946	BKN N	0	0	–	3.86	4	0	0	4.2	5	1	6	0	0	0	0	0	0	0	–	0	1	0	0	0.3	1.000
1947		10	5	.667	3.11	33	20	10	162	130	83	58	2	0	0	1	62	8	0	.129	5	35	1	4	1.2	.976
1948		2	7	.222	5.36	17	13	2	80.2	90	61	32	0	0	1	0	22	6	0	.273	9	19	4	1	1.6	.966
1950	BOS A	2	0	1.000	1.42	3	2	2	19	13	8	8	1	0	0	0	7	2	0	.286	3	3	0	0	2.0	1.000
1951		4	9	.308	5.75	31	8	1	81.1	100	42	22	0	2	5	2	29	3	0	.103	6	20	0	3	0.8	1.000
1952		1	0	1.000	1.80	2	1	1	10	6	6	1	0	0	0	0	4	1	0	.250	1	2	0	0	1.5	1.000
6 yrs.		19	21	.475	4.10	90	44	16	357.2	344	201	127	3	2	6	4	124	20	0	.161	24	80	5	8	1.2	.990

WORLD SERIES

Year	Team	W	L	PCT	ERA	G	GS	CG	IP	H	BB	SO	ShO	W	L	SV	AB	H	HR	BA	PO	A	E	DP	TC/G	FA
1947	BKN N	0	0	–	0.00	1	1	0	2	1	0	0	0	0	0	0	–	0	0	0	0	0.0

Jack Taylor
TAYLOR, JOHN BUDD (Brewery Jack)
B. May 23, 1873, West New Brighton, N. Y. D. Feb. 7, 1900, Staten Island, N. Y. BR TR 6'1" 190 lbs.

Year	Team	W	L	PCT	ERA	G	GS	CG	IP	H	BB	SO	ShO	W	L	SV	AB	H	HR	BA	PO	A	E	DP	TC/G	FA
1891	NY N	0	1	.000	1.13	1	1	1	8	4	3	3	0	0	0	0	2	0	0	.000	1	0	0	0	1.0	1.000
1892	PHI N	1	0	1.000	1.38	3	3	2	26	28	10	7	0	0	0	0	12	2	0	.167	0	3	5	0	2.7	.375
1893		10	9	.526	4.24	25	16	14	170	189	77	41	0	3	2	1	93	20	0	.215	13	42	2	4	2.3	.965
1894		23	13	.639	4.08	41	34	31	298	347	96	76	1	1	2	1	144	48	0	.333	13	68	12	3	2.3	.871
1895		26	14	.650	4.49	41	37	33	335	403	83	93	1	1	2	1	155	45	3	.290	19	89	5	3	2.8	.956
1896		20	21	.488	4.79	45	41	35	359	459	112	97	1	0	1	1	157	29	0	.185	19	107	11	3	3.0	.920
1897		16	20	.444	4.23	40	37	35	317.1	376	76	88	2	0	1	2	139	35	1	.252	12	89	16	2	2.9	.863
1898	STL N	15	29	.341	3.90	50	47	42	397.1	465	83	89	0	0	0	1	157	38	1	.242	18	144	22	3	3.7	.880
1899	CIN N	9	10	.474	4.12	24	18	15	168.1	197	41	34	1	1	1	2	68	17	0	.250	6	37	4	2	2.0	.915
9 yrs.		120	117	.506	4.23	270	234	208	2079	2468	581	528	7	6	9	9	927	234	5	.252	101	579	77	19	2.8	.898

Jack Taylor
TAYLOR, JOHN W.
B. Jan. 14, 1874, New Straightsville, Ohio D. Mar. 4, 1938, Columbus, Ohio BR TR 5'10" 170 lbs.

Year	Team	W	L	PCT	ERA	G	GS	CG	IP	H	BB	SO	ShO	W	L	SV	AB	H	HR	BA	PO	A	E	DP	TC/G	FA
1898	CHI N	5	0	1.000	2.20	5	5	5	41	32	10	11	0	0	0	0	15	3	0	.200	0	9	0	1	1.8	1.000
1899		18	21	.462	3.76	41	39	39	354.2	380	84	67	1	1	0	0	139	37	0	.266	24	88	8	8	2.9	.933
1900		10	17	.370	2.55	28	26	25	222.1	226	58	57	2	1	0	0	81	19	1	.235	10	42	7	2	2.1	.881
1901		13	19	.406	3.36	33	31	30	275.2	341	44	68	2	1	0	0	106	23	0	.217	24	78	6	3	3.3	.944
1902		22	11	.667	1.33	36	33	33	324.2	271	43	83	8	1	0	1	186	44	0	.237	13	106	5	3	3.4	.960
1903		21	14	.600	2.45	37	33	33	312.1	277	57	83	1	1	1	1	126	28	0	.222	14	91	6	2	3.0	.946
1904	STL N	21	19	.525	2.22	41	40	39	352	297	82	103	4	0	1	0	133	28	1	.211	14	109	6	1	3.1	.953
1905		15	21	.417	3.44	37	34	34	309	302	85	102	3	1	1	0	121	23	0	.190	10	80	2	1	2.5	.978
1906	2 teams	STL N	(17G 8–9)		CHI N	(17G 12–3)																				
"	total	20	12	.625	1.99	34	33	32	302.1	249	86	61	3	0	0	0	106	22	0	.208	12	95	2	2	3.2	.982
1907	CHI N	6	5	.545	3.29	18	13	8	123	127	33	22	0	1	0	0	47	9	0	.191	6	40	0	1	2.6	1.000
10 yrs.		151	139	.521	2.66	310	287	278	2617	2502	582	657	20	7	5	5	*				127	738	42	24	2.9	.954

Pete Taylor
TAYLOR, VERNON CHARLES
B. Nov. 26, 1927, Severn, Md. BR TR 6'1" 170 lbs.

Year	Team	W	L	PCT	ERA	G	GS	CG	IP	H	BB	SO	ShO	W	L	SV	AB	H	HR	BA	PO	A	E	DP	TC/G	FA
1952	STL A	0	0	–	13.50	1	0	0	2	4	3	0	0	0	0	0	0	0	0	–	0	1	0	1	1.0	1.000

Ron Taylor
TAYLOR, RONALD WESLEY
B. Dec. 13, 1937, Toronto, Ont., Canada BR TR 6'1" 195 lbs.

Year	Team	W	L	PCT	ERA	G	GS	CG	IP	H	BB	SO	ShO	W	L	SV	AB	H	HR	BA	PO	A	E	DP	TC/G	FA
1962	CLE A	2	2	.500	5.94	8	4	1	33.1	36	13	15	0	1	0	0	11	3	0	.273	0	5	0	0	0.6	1.000
1963	STL N	9	7	.563	2.84	54	9	2	133.1	119	30	91	0	7	3	11	32	1	0	.031	2	13	0	0	0.3	1.000
1964		8	4	.667	4.62	63	2	0	101.1	109	33	69	0	8	2	7	15	2	0	.133	2	27	1	3	0.5	.967
1965	2 teams	STL N	(25G 2–1)		HOU N	(32G 1–5)																				
"	total	3	6	.333	5.60	57	1	0	101.1	111	31	63	0	2	1	5	18	2	0	.111	5	15	0	0	0.4	1.000
1966	HOU N	2	3	.400	5.71	36	1	0	64.2	89	10	29	0	2	3	0	12	2	0	.167	5	13	0	0	0.2	1.000
1967	NY N	4	6	.400	2.34	50	0	0	73	60	23	46	0	4	6	8	7	0	0	.000	7	11	1	1	0.4	.947
1968		1	5	.167	2.70	58	0	0	76.2	64	18	49	0	1	5	13	9	0	0	.000	9	14	1	1	0.4	.958
1969		9	4	.692	2.72	59	0	0	76	61	24	42	0	4	4	13	4	1	0	.250	6	13	0	1	0.3	1.000
1970		5	4	.556	3.95	57	0	0	66	65	16	28	0	5	4	13	4	0	0	.000	5	11	0	0	0.3	1.000
1971		2	2	.500	3.65	45	0	0	69	71	11	32	0	2	2	8	4	1	0	.250	1	10	0	0	0.3	1.000

Year	Team		W	L	PCT	ERA	G	GS	CG	IP	H	BB	SO	ShO	Relief Pitching W	L	SV	Batting AB	H	HR	BA	PO	A	E	DP	TC/G	FA

Ron Taylor *continued*

Year	Team		W	L	PCT	ERA	G	GS	CG	IP	H	BB	SO	ShO	W	L	SV	AB	H	HR	BA	PO	A	E	DP	TC/G	FA
1972	SD	N	0	0	–	12.60	4	0	0	5	9	0	0	0	0	0	0	0	0	0	–	0	1	0	0	0.3	1.000
11 yrs.			45	43	.511	3.93	491	17	3	799.2	794	209	464	0	41	30	72	116	12	0	.103	37	129	3	6	0.3	.982

LEAGUE CHAMPIONSHIP SERIES

| 1969 | NY | N | 1 | 0 | 1.000 | 0.00 | 2 | 0 | 0 | 3.1 | 3 | 0 | 4 | 0 | 1 | 0 | 1 | 0 | 0 | 0 | – | 1 | 0 | 0 | 0 | 0.5 | 1.000 |

WORLD SERIES

1964	STL	N	0	0	–	0.00	2	0	0	4.2	0	1	2	0	0	0	1	1	0	0	.000	0	2	0	0	1.0	1.000
1969	NY	N	0	0	–	0.00	2	0	0	2.1	0	1	3	0	0	0	1	0	0	0	–	0	1	0	0	0.5	1.000
2 yrs.			0	0	–	0.00	4	0	0	7	0	2	5	0	0	0	2	1	0	0	.000	0	3	0	0	0.8	1.000

Rube Taylor

TAYLOR, EDGAR RUBEN
B. Mar. 23, 1877, Palestine, Tex. D. Jan. 31, 1912, Dallas, Tex. TL

| 1903 | STL | N | 0 | 0 | – | 0.00 | 1 | 0 | 0 | 3 | 0 | 0 | 1 | 0 | 0 | 0 | 0 | 1 | 0 | 0 | .000 | 0 | 1 | 0 | 0 | 1.0 | 1.000 |

Terry Taylor

TAYLOR, TERRY DERRELL
B. July 28, 1964, Crestview, Fla. BR TR 6'1" 180 lbs.

| 1988 | SEA | A | 0 | 1 | .000 | 6.26 | 5 | 5 | 0 | 23 | 26 | 11 | 9 | 0 | 0 | 0 | 0 | 0 | 0 | 0 | – | 1 | 0 | 0 | 0 | 0.2 | 1.000 |

Wiley Taylor

TAYLOR, PHILIP WILEY
B. Mar. 18, 1888, Wamego, Kans. D. July 8, 1954, Westmoreland, Kans. BR TR 6'1" 175 lbs.

1911	DET	A	0	2	.000	3.79	3	2	1	19	18	10	9	0	0	0	0	6	0	0	.000	0	3	0	0	1.0	1.000
1912	CHI	A	0	1	.000	4.95	3	3	0	20	21	14	4	0	0	0	0	5	0	0	.000	1	6	0	0	2.3	1.000
1913	STL	A	0	2	.000	4.83	5	4	1	31.2	33	16	12	0	0	0	0	10	0	0	.000	1	12	2	0	3.0	.867
1914			2	5	.286	3.42	16	8	2	50	41	25	20	1	0	1	0	12	2	0	.167	1	15	3	1	1.2	.842
4 yrs.			2	10	.167	4.10	27	17	4	120.2	113	65	45	1	0	1	0	33	2	0	.061	3	36	5	1	1.6	.886

Bud Teachout

TEACHOUT, ARTHUR JOHN
B. Feb. 27, 1904, Los Angeles, Calif. D. May 11, 1985, Laguna Beach, Calif. BR TL 6'2" 183 lbs.

1930	CHI	N	11	4	.733	4.06	40	16	6	153	178	48	59	0	4	1	0	63	17	0	.270	10	27	3	2	1.0	.925
1931			1	2	.333	5.72	27	3	1	61.1	79	28	14	0	1	0	0	21	5	0	.238	2	19	2	0	0.9	.913
1932	STL	N	0	0	–	0.00	1	0	0	1	2	0	0	0	0	0	0	0	0	0	–	0	0	0	0	0.0	–
3 yrs.			12	6	.667	4.51	68	19	7	215.1	259	76	73	0	5	1	0	84	22	0	.262	12	46	5	2	0.9	.921

Patsy Tebeau

TEBEAU, OLIVER WENDELL
Brother of White Wings Tebeau.
B. Dec. 5, 1864, St. Louis, Mo. D. May 15, 1918, St. Louis, Mo. BR TR 5'8" 163 lbs.
Manager 1890-1900.

| 1896 | CLE | N | 0 | 0 | – | 0.00 | 1 | 0 | 0 | 1 | 0 | 0 | 0 | 0 | 0 | 0 | 0 | * | | | | 0 | 0 | 0 | 0 | 0.0 | – |

White Wings Tebeau

TEBEAU, GEORGE E. (Hard Call)
Brother of Patsy Tebeau.
B. Dec. 26, 1861, St. Louis, Mo. D. Feb. 4, 1923, Denver, Colo. BR TR 5'9" 175 lbs.

1887	CIN	AA	0	1	.000	13.50	1	1	1	8	21	3	1	0	0	0	0	318	94	4	.296	1	3	0	0	4.0	1.000
1890	TOL	AA	0	0	–	9.00	1	0	0	5	9	5	0	0	0	0	0	381	102	1	.268	0	0	0	0	0.0	–
2 yrs.			0	1	.000	11.77	2	1	1	13	30	8	1	0	0	0	0	*				1	3	0	0	2.0	1.000

Al Tedrow

TEDROW, ALLEN SEYMOUR
B. Dec. 14, 1891, Westerville, Ohio D. Jan. 23, 1958, Westerville, Ohio BR TL 6' 180 lbs.

| 1914 | CLE | A | 1 | 2 | .333 | 1.21 | 4 | 3 | 1 | 22.1 | 19 | 14 | 4 | 0 | 0 | 0 | 0 | 6 | 1 | 0 | .167 | 0 | 7 | 1 | 0 | 2.0 | .875 |

Kent Tekulve

TEKULVE, KENTON CHARLES
B. Mar. 5, 1947, Cincinnati, Ohio BR TR 6'4" 180 lbs.

1974	PIT	N	1	1	.500	6.00	8	0	0	9	12	5	6	0	1	1	0	0	0	0	–	2	3	0	0	0.6	1.000
1975			1	2	.333	2.25	34	0	0	56	43	23	28	0	1	2	5	11	1	0	.091	5	17	1	1	0.7	.957
1976			5	3	.625	2.45	64	0	0	102.2	91	25	68	0	5	3	9	9	0	0	.000	6	24	1	0	0.5	.968
1977			10	1	.909	3.06	72	0	0	103	89	33	59	0	10	1	7	12	3	0	.250	7	32	0	1	0.5	1.000
1978			8	7	.533	2.33	91	0	0	135	115	55	77	0	8	7	31	21	2	0	.095	8	38	4	1	0.5	.920
1979			10	8	.556	2.75	94	0	0	134	109	49	75	0	10	8	31	15	2	0	.133	7	28	1	0	0.4	.972
1980			8	12	.400	3.39	78	0	0	93	96	40	47	0	8	12	21	9	0	0	.000	5	18	1	1	0.3	.958
1981			5	5	.500	2.49	45	0	0	65	61	17	34	0	5	5	3	2	0	0	.000	4	16	0	2	0.4	1.000
1982			12	8	.600	2.87	85	0	0	128.2	113	46	66	0	12	8	20	14	1	0	.071	11	27	1	2	0.5	.974
1983			7	5	.583	1.64	76	0	0	99	78	36	52	0	7	5	18	8	0	0	.000	3	20	0	2	0.3	1.000
1984			3	9	.250	2.66	72	0	0	88	86	33	36	0	3	9	13	7	0	0	.000	6	25	0	3	0.4	1.000
1985	2 teams	PIT N (3G 0-0)								PHI N (58G 4-10)																	
"	total		4	10	.286	3.57	61	0	0	75.2	74	30	40	0	4	10	14	3	0	0	.000	4	14	0	1	0.3	1.000
1986	PHI	N	11	5	.688	2.54	73	0	0	110	99	25	57	0	11	5	4	5	0	0	.000	4	22	3	2	0.4	.897
1987			6	4	.600	3.09	90	0	0	105	96	29	60	0	6	4	3	1	0	0	.000	11	20	1	0	0.4	.969
1988			3	7	.300	3.60	70	0	0	80	87	22	43	0	3	7	4	2	0	0	.000	7	14	0	1	0.3	1.000
1989	CIN	N	0	3	.000	5.02	37	0	0	52	56	23	31	0	0	3	1	2	1	0	.500	2	9	0	1	0.3	1.000
16 yrs.			94	90	.511	2.85	1050	0	0	1436	1305	491	779	0	94	90	184	121	10	0	.083	92	327	13	17	0.4	.970
							2nd										7th										

LEAGUE CHAMPIONSHIP SERIES

1975	PIT	N	0	0	–	6.75	2	0	0	1.1	3	1	2	0	0	0	0	0	0	0	–	0	0	0	0	0.0	–
1979			0	0	–	3.00	2	0	0	3	2	2	2	0	0	0	0	1	0	0	.000	0	1	0	0	0.5	1.000
2 yrs.			0	0	–	4.15	4	0	0	4.1	5	3	4	0	0	0	0	1	0	0	.000	0	1	0	0	0.3	1.000

WORLD SERIES

| 1979 | PIT | N | 0 | 1 | .000 | 2.89 | 5 | 0 | 0 | 9.1 | 4 | 3 | 10 | 0 | 0 | 1 | 3 | 2 | 0 | 0 | .000 | 1 | 0 | 0 | 0 | 0.2 | 1.000 |
| | | | | | | | 4th | | | | | | | | | | | | | | | | | | | | |

Year	Team		W	L	PCT	ERA	G	GS	CG	IP	H	BB	SO	ShO	W	L	SV	AB	H	HR	BA	PO	A	E	DP	TC/G	FA
															Relief Pitching			**Batting**									

Tom Tellmann

TELLMANN, THOMAS JOHN
B. Mar. 29, 1954, Warren, Pa.
BR TR 6'3" 195 lbs.

Year	Team		W	L	PCT	ERA	G	GS	CG	IP	H	BB	SO	ShO	W	L	SV	AB	H	HR	BA	PO	A	E	DP	TC/G	FA
1979	SD	N	0	0	–	15.00	1	0	0	3	7	0	1	0	0	0	0	1	0	0	.000	1	1	0	0	2.0	1.000
1980			3	0	1.000	1.64	6	2	2	22	23	8	9	0	1	0	1	8	1	0	.125	1	4	0	1	0.8	1.000
1983	MIL	A	9	4	.692	2.80	44	0	0	99.2	95	35	48	0	9	4	8	0	0	0	–	9	26	0	0	0.8	1.000
1984			6	3	.667	2.78	50	0	0	81	82	31	28	0	6	3	4	0	0	0	–	4	15	0	0	0.4	1.000
1985	OAK	A	0	0	–	5.06	11	0	0	21.1	33	9	8	0	0	0	0	0	0	0	–	0	4	0	0	0.4	1.000
5 yrs.			18	7	.720	3.05	112	2	2	227	240	83	94	0	16	7	13	9	1	0	.111	15	50	0	1	0.6	1.000

Chuck Templeton

TEMPLETON, CHARLES SHERMAN
B. June 1, 1932, Detroit, Mich.
BR TL 6'3" 210 lbs.

Year	Team		W	L	PCT	ERA	G	GS	CG	IP	H	BB	SO	ShO	W	L	SV	AB	H	HR	BA	PO	A	E	DP	TC/G	FA
1955	BKN	N	0	1	.000	11.57	4	0	0	4.2	5	5	3	0	0	1	0	0	0	0	–	1	0	0	0	0.3	1.000
1956			0	1	.000	6.61	6	2	0	16.1	20	10	8	0	0	0	0	3	0	0	.000	1	1	1	0	0.5	.667
2 yrs.			0	2	.000	7.71	10	2	0	21	25	15	11	0	0	1	0	3	0	0	.000	1	2	1	0	0.4	.750

John Tener

TENER, JOHN KINLEY
B. July 25, 1863, County Tyrone, Ireland   D. May 19, 1946, Pittsburgh, Pa.
BR TR 6'4" 180 lbs.

Year	Team		W	L	PCT	ERA	G	GS	CG	IP	H	BB	SO	ShO	W	L	SV	AB	H	HR	BA	PO	A	E	DP	TC/G	FA
1885	BAL	AA	0	0	–	0.00	0	0	0	0	0	0	0	0	0	0	0	4	0	0	.000	0	0	0	0	0.0	–
1888	CHI	N	7	5	.583	2.74	12	12	11	102	90	25	39	1	0	0	0	46	9	0	.196	9	24	4	0	3.1	.892
1889			15	15	.500	3.64	35	30	28	287	302	105	105	1	1	0	2	0	150	41	1	.273	22	69	7	1	2.8	.929
1890	PIT	P	3	11	.214	7.31	14	14	13	117	160	70	30	0	0	0	0	63	12	2	.190	12	45	2	2	4.2	.966
4 yrs.			25	31	.446	4.30	61	56	52	506	552	200	174	2	1	2	0	263	62	3	.236	43	138	13	3	3.2	.933

Jim Tennant

TENNANT, JAMES McDONNELL
B. Mar. 3, 1907, Shepherdstown, W. Va.   D. Apr. 16, 1967, Trumbull, Conn.
BR TR 6'1" 190 lbs.

Year	Team		W	L	PCT	ERA	G	GS	CG	IP	H	BB	SO	ShO	W	L	SV	AB	H	HR	BA	PO	A	E	DP	TC/G	FA
1929	NY	N	0	0	–	0.00	1	0	0	1	0	1	0	0	0	0	0	0	0	0	–	0	0	0	0	0.0	–

Fred Tenney

TENNEY, FRED CLAY
B. July 9, 1859, Marlborough, N. H.   D. June 15, 1919, Fall River, Mass.

Year	Team		W	L	PCT	ERA	G	GS	CG	IP	H	BB	SO	ShO	W	L	SV	AB	H	HR	BA	PO	A	E	DP	TC/G	FA
1884	2 teams		N	(0G 0–0)		BOS	U	(4G 3–1)																				
"	total		3	2	.600	2.09	5	5	5	43	37	9	28	0	0	0	0	*				2	5	2	1	1.8	.778

Fred Tenney

TENNEY, FREDERICK
B. Nov. 26, 1871, Georgetown, Mass.   D. July 3, 1952, Boston, Mass.
Manager 1905-07, 1911.
BL TL 5'9" 155 lbs.

Year	Team		W	L	PCT	ERA	G	GS	CG	IP	H	BB	SO	ShO	W	L	SV	AB	H	HR	BA	PO	A	E	DP	TC/G	FA
1905	BOS	N	0	0		4.50	1	0	0	2	5	1	0	0	0	0	0	*				1	0	0	0	1.0	1.000

Bob Terlecki

TERLECKI, ROBERT JOSEPH (Terk)
B. Feb. 14, 1945, Trenton, N. J.
BR TR 5'8" 185 lbs.

Year	Team		W	L	PCT	ERA	G	GS	CG	IP	H	BB	SO	ShO	W	L	SV	AB	H	HR	BA	PO	A	E	DP	TC/G	FA
1972	PHI	N	0	0		4.73	9	0	0	13.1	16	10	5	0	0	0	0	0	0	0	–	1	3	1	0	0.6	.800

Greg Terlecky

TERLECKY, GREGORY JOHN
B. Mar. 20, 1952, Culver City, Calif.
BR TR 6'3" 200 lbs.

Year	Team		W	L	PCT	ERA	G	GS	CG	IP	H	BB	SO	ShO	W	L	SV	AB	H	HR	BA	PO	A	E	DP	TC/G	FA
1975	STL	N	0	1	.000	4.50	20	0	0	30	38	12	13	0	0	1	0	3	1	0	.333	2	5	0	0	0.4	1.000

Jeff Terpko

TERPKO, JEFFREY MICHAEL
B. Oct. 16, 1950, Sayre, Pa.
BR TR 6' 180 lbs.

Year	Team		W	L	PCT	ERA	G	GS	CG	IP	H	BB	SO	ShO	W	L	SV	AB	H	HR	BA	PO	A	E	DP	TC/G	FA
1974	TEX	A	0	0	–	1.29	3	0	0	7	6	4	3	0	0	0	0	0	0	0	–	0	0	0	0	0.0	–
1976			3	3	.500	2.38	32	0	0	53	42	29	24	0	3	3	0	0	0	0	–	2	8	0	0	0.3	1.000
1977	MON	N	0	1	.000	5.57	13	0	0	21	28	15	14	0	0	1	0	1	0	0	.000	0	2	2	1	0.3	.500
3 yrs.			3	4	.429	3.11	48	0	0	81	76	48	41	0	3	4	0	1	0	0	.000	2	10	2	1	0.3	.857

Jerry Terrell

TERRELL, JERRY WAYNE
B. July 13, 1946, Waseca, Minn.
BR TR 5'11" 165 lbs.

Year	Team		W	L	PCT	ERA	G	GS	CG	IP	H	BB	SO	ShO	W	L	SV	AB	H	HR	BA	PO	A	E	DP	TC/G	FA
1979	KC	A	0	0	–	0.00	1	0	0	1	0	0	0	0	0	0	0	40	12	1	.300	0	0	0	0	0.0	–
1980			0	0	–	0.00	1	0	0	1	1	1	0	0	0	0	0	16	1	0	.063	0	1	0	0	1.0	1.000
2 yrs.			0	0	–	0.00	2	0	0	2	1	1	0	0	0	0	0	*				0	1	0	0	0.5	1.000

Walt Terrell

TERRELL, CHARLES WALTER
B. May 11, 1958, Jeffersonville, Ind.
BL TR 6'2" 205 lbs.

Year	Team		W	L	PCT	ERA	G	GS	CG	IP	H	BB	SO	ShO	W	L	SV	AB	H	HR	BA	PO	A	E	DP	TC/G	FA
1982	NY	N	0	3	.000	3.43	3	3	0	21	22	14	8	0	0	0	0	5	2	0	.400	16	2	0	1	1.3	1.000
1983			8	8	.500	3.57	21	20	4	133.2	123	55	59	2	0	0	0	44	8	3	.182	16	15	0	2	1.5	1.000
1984			11	12	.478	3.52	33	33	3	215	232	80	114	1	0	0	0	75	6	0	.080	16	32	5	5	1.5	.960
1985	DET	A	15	10	.600	3.85	34	34	5	229	221	95	130	3	0	0	0	0	0	0	–	21	43	2	8	1.9	.970
1986			15	12	.556	4.56	34	33	9	217.1	199	98	93	2	0	0	0	0	0	0	–	30	29	0	0	1.7	1.000
1987			17	10	.630	4.05	35	35	10	244.2	254	94	143	1	0	0	0	0	0	0	–	24	25	3	3	1.5	.961
1988			7	16	.304	3.97	29	29	11	206.1	199	78	84	1	0	0	0	0	0	0	–	22	29	3	3	1.8	.962
1989	2 teams		SD	N	(19G 5–13)		NY	A	(13G 6–5)																			
"	total		11	18	.379	4.49	32	32	3	206.1	236	50	93	1	0	0	0	40	4	0	.100	19	41	0	4	1.9	1.000
8 yrs.			84	89	.486	4.01	221	219	47	1473.1	1486	564	724	12	0	0	0	164	20	3	.122	150	216	8	25	1.7	.979

LEAGUE CHAMPIONSHIP SERIES

Year	Team		W	L	PCT	ERA	G	GS	CG	IP	H	BB	SO	ShO	W	L	SV	AB	H	HR	BA	PO	A	E	DP	TC/G	FA
1987	DET	A	0	0	–	9.00	1	1	0	6	7	4	4	0	0	0	0	0	0	0	–	0	1	0	0	1.0	1.000

Adonis Terry

TERRY, WILLIAM H
B. Aug. 7, 1864, Westfield, Mass.   D. Feb. 24, 1915, Milwaukee, Wis.
BR TR 5'11½" 168 lbs.

Year	Team		W	L	PCT	ERA	G	GS	CG	IP	H	BB	SO	ShO	W	L	SV	AB	H	HR	BA	PO	A	E	DP	TC/G	FA
1884	BKN	AA	20	35	.364	3.49	57	56	55	485	487	75	233	3	0	0	0	240	56	0	.233	32	81	34	0	2.6	.769
1885			6	17	.261	4.26	25	23	23	209	213	42	96	0	0	0	1	264	45	1	.170	16	36	2	0	2.2	.963
1886			18	16	.529	3.09	34	34	32	288.1	263	115	162	5	0	0	0	299	71	2	.237	22	68	6	2	3.8	.938
1887			16	16	.500	4.02	40	35	35	318	331	99	138	1	0	0	3	352	103	3	.293	35	81	12	0	3.2	.906

Adonis Terry *continued*

Year	Team		W	L	PCT	ERA	G	GS	CG	IP	H	BB	SO	ShO	Relief Pitching W	Relief Pitching L	Relief Pitching SV	Batting AB	Batting H	Batting HR	BA	PO	A	E	DP	TC/G	FA
1888			13	8	.619	2.03	23	23	20	195	145	67	138	2	0	0	0	115	29	0	.252	10	40	5	2	2.4	.909
1889			22	15	.595	3.29	41	39	35	326	285	126	186	2	0	0	0	160	48	2	.300	24	86	4	2	2.8	.965
1890	BKN	N	26	16	.619	2.94	46	44	38	370	362	133	185	1	0	0	0	363	101	4	.278	20	75	11	3	2.3	.896
1891			6	16	.273	4.22	25	22	18	194	207	80	65	1	0	0	1	91	19	0	.209	10	34	2	1	1.8	.957
1892	2 teams	BAL N (1G 0–1)	PIT N (30G 17–7)																								
"	total		17	8	.680	2.57	31	27	25	249	192	113	98	2	0	0	1	104	16	2	.154	27	51	5	0	2.7	.940
1893	PIT	N	12	8	.600	4.45	26	19	14	170	177	99	52	0	2	1	0	71	18	0	.254	9	37	4	2	1.9	.920
1894	2 teams	PIT N (1G 0–1)	CHI N (23G 5–11)																								
"	total		5	12	.294	6.09	24	22	16	164	234	127	39	0	0	0	0	95	33	0	.347	9	26	5	0	1.7	.875
1895	CHI	N	21	14	.600	4.80	38	34	31	311.1	346	131	88	0	2	0	0	137	30	1	.219	13	81	11	3	2.8	.895
1896			15	13	.536	4.28	30	28	25	235.1	268	88	74	1	1	1	0	99	26	0	.263	18	43	2	0	2.1	.968
1897			0	1	.000	10.13	1	1	1	8	11	6	1	0	0	0	0	3	0	0	.000	0	3	1	0	4.0	.750
14 yrs.			197	195	.503	3.72	441	407	368	3523	3521	1301	1555	18	5	2	6	*				245	742	104	15	2.5	.905

John Terry

TERRY, JOHN BUCHARD
B. Nov. 1, 1879, Waterbury, Conn. D. Apr. 27, 1933, Kansas City, Mo.

Year	Team		W	L	PCT	ERA	G	GS	CG	IP	H	BB	SO	ShO	Relief W	Relief L	Relief SV	AB	H	HR	BA	PO	A	E	DP	TC/G	FA
1902	DET	A	0	1	.000	3.60	1	1	1	5	8	1	0	0	0	0	0	2	0	0	.000	0	0	0	0	0.0	–
1903	STL	A	1	1	.500	2.55	3	1	1	17.2	21	4	2	0	0	1	0	9	0	0	.000	1	5	2	0	2.7	.750
2 yrs.			1	2	.333	2.78	4	2	2	22.2	29	5	2	0	0	1	0	11	0	0	.000	1	5	2	0	2.0	.750

Ralph Terry

TERRY, RALPH WILLARD BR TR 6'3" 195 lbs.
B. Jan. 9, 1936, Big Cabin, Okla.

Year	Team		W	L	PCT	ERA	G	GS	CG	IP	H	BB	SO	ShO	Relief W	Relief L	Relief SV	AB	H	HR	BA	PO	A	E	DP	TC/G	FA
1956	NY	A	1	2	.333	9.45	3	3	0	13.1	17	11	8	0	0	0	0	6	1	0	.167	0	1	0	0	0.3	1.000
1957	2 teams	NY A (7G 1–1)	KC A (21G 4–11)																								
"	total		5	12	.294	3.33	28	21	4	151.1	137	55	87	2	0	1	0	46	7	0	.152	13	24	2	2	1.4	.949
1958	KC	A	11	13	.458	4.24	40	33	8	216.2	217	61	134	3	0	0	2	71	14	0	.197	13	24	4	3	1.0	.902
1959	2 teams	KC A (9G 2–4)	NY A (24G 3–7)																								
"	total		5	11	.313	3.89	33	23	7	173.2	186	49	90	1	0	0	0	58	7	0	.121	14	29	3	4	1.4	.935
1960	NY	A	10	8	.556	3.40	35	23	7	166.2	149	52	92	3	1	1	1	49	6	0	.122	12	24	0	3	1.0	1.000
1961			16	3	.842	3.15	31	27	9	188.1	162	42	86	2	1	0	0	66	15	0	.227	20	30	0	1	1.6	1.000
1962			**23**	12	.657	3.19	43	**39**	14	**298.2**	257	57	176	3	1	0	2	106	20	0	.189	21	31	1	0	1.2	.981
1963			17	15	.531	3.22	40	**37**	**18**	268	246	39	114	3	0	0	1	87	7	0	.080	31	32	1	2	1.6	.984
1964			7	11	.389	4.54	27	14	2	115	130	31	77	1	2	3	4	35	7	0	.200	10	16	0	0	1.0	1.000
1965	CLE	A	11	6	.647	3.69	30	26	6	165.2	154	23	84	2	0	0	0	49	7	1	.143	11	12	1	1	0.8	.958
1966	2 teams	KC A (15G 1–5)	NY N (11G 0–1)																								
"	total		1	6	.143	4.06	26	11	0	88.2	92	26	47	0	0	1	1	20	4	0	.200	5	11	1	0	0.7	.941
1967	NY	N	0	0	–	0.00	2	0	0	3.1	1	0	5	0	0	0	0	0	0	0	–	0	1	0	0	0.5	1.000
12 yrs.			107	99	.519	3.62	338	257	75	1849.1	1748	446	1000	20	5	6	11	593	95	1	.160	150	235	13	16	1.2	.967

WORLD SERIES

Year	Team		W	L	PCT	ERA	G	GS	CG	IP	H	BB	SO	ShO	Relief W	Relief L	Relief SV	AB	H	HR	BA	PO	A	E	DP	TC/G	FA
1960	NY	A	0	2	.000	5.40	2	1	0	6.2	7	1	5	0	0	1	0	2	0	0	.000	0	3	0	0	1.5	1.000
1961			0	1	.000	4.82	2	2	0	9.1	12	2	7	0	0	0	0	3	0	0	.000	1	2	0	0	1.5	1.000
1962			2	1	.667	1.80	3	3	2	25	17	2	16	1	0	0	0	8	1	0	.125	3	2	0	0	1.7	1.000
1963			0	0	–	3.00	1	1	0	3	3	1	0	0	0	0	0	0	0	0	–	1	1	0	1	2.0	1.000
1964			0	0	–	0.00	1	0	0	2	2	0	3	0	0	0	0	0	0	0	–	0	0	0	0	0.0	–
5 yrs.			2	4 7th	.333	2.93	9	6	2	46	41	6	31	1	0	1	0	13	1	0	.077	5	8	0	1	1.4	1.000

Scott Terry

TERRY, SCOTT RAY BR TR 5'11" 195 lbs.
B. Nov. 21, 1959, Hobbs, N. M.

Year	Team		W	L	PCT	ERA	G	GS	CG	IP	H	BB	SO	ShO	Relief W	Relief L	Relief SV	AB	H	HR	BA	PO	A	E	DP	TC/G	FA
1986	CIN	N	1	2	.333	6.14	28	3	0	55.2	66	32	32	0	1	1	0	4	1	0	.250	2	9	1	2	0.4	.917
1987	STL	N	0	0	–	3.38	11	0	0	13.1	13	8	9	0	0	0	0	2	0	0	.000	0	4	0	0	0.4	1.000
1988			9	6	.600	2.92	51	11	1	129.1	119	34	65	0	2	3	3	28	7	0	.250	7	22	0	1	0.6	1.000
1989			8	10	.444	3.57	31	24	1	148.2	142	43	69	0	0	0	2	45	7	2	.156	6	33	2	2	1.3	.951
4 yrs.			18	18	.500	3.73	121	38	2	347	340	117	175	0	3	4	5	79	15	2	.190	15	68	3	5	0.7	.965

Yank Terry

TERRY, LANCELOT YANK BR TR 6'1" 180 lbs.
B. Feb. 11, 1911, Bedford, Ind. D. Nov. 4, 1979, Bloomington, Ind.

Year	Team		W	L	PCT	ERA	G	GS	CG	IP	H	BB	SO	ShO	Relief W	Relief L	Relief SV	AB	H	HR	BA	PO	A	E	DP	TC/G	FA
1940	BOS	A	1	0	1.000	8.84	4	1	0	19.1	24	11	9	0	0	0	0	8	2	0	.250	0	4	0	0	1.0	1.000
1942			6	5	.545	3.92	20	11	3	85	82	43	37	0	1	1	1	27	3	0	.111	3	16	1	1	1.0	.950
1943			7	9	.438	3.52	30	22	7	163.2	147	63	63	0	1	1	1	45	3	0	.067	8	37	2	0	1.6	.957
1944			6	10	.375	4.21	27	17	3	132.2	142	65	30	0	2	1	0	47	11	0	.234	2	28	0	2	1.1	1.000
1945			0	4	.000	4.13	12	4	1	56.2	68	14	28	0	0	1	0	18	2	0	.111	0	9	0	0	0.8	1.000
5 yrs.			20	28	.417	4.09	93	55	14	457.1	463	196	167	0	4	4	2	145	21	0	.145	13	94	3	3	1.2	.973

Dick Terwilliger

TERWILLIGER, RICHARD MARTIN BR TR 5'11" 178 lbs.
B. June 27, 1906, Sand Lake, Mich. D. Jan. 21, 1969, Greenville, Mich.

Year	Team		W	L	PCT	ERA	G	GS	CG	IP	H	BB	SO	ShO	Relief W	Relief L	Relief SV	AB	H	HR	BA	PO	A	E	DP	TC/G	FA
1932	STL	N	0	0	–	0.00	1	0	0	3	1	2	2	0	0	0	0	1	0	0	.000	0	2	0	0	2.0	1.000

Jeff Tesreau

TESREAU, CHARLES MONROE BR TR 6'2½" 218 lbs.
B. Mar. 5, 1889, Silvermine, Mo. D. Sept. 24, 1946, Hanover, N. H.

Year	Team		W	L	PCT	ERA	G	GS	CG	IP	H	BB	SO	ShO	Relief W	Relief L	Relief SV	AB	H	HR	BA	PO	A	E	DP	TC/G	FA
1912	NY	N	17	7	.708	**1.96**	36	28	19	243	177	106	119	3	0	0	1	82	12	0	.146	9	63	5	2	2.1	.935
1913			22	13	.629	2.17	41	**38**	17	282	222	119	167	1	1	2	0	95	21	0	.221	3	73	2	2	1.9	.974
1914			26	10	.722	2.37	42	**40**	26	322.1	238	128	189	**8**	1	0	1	117	28	0	.239	8	71	6	5	2.0	.929
1915			19	16	.543	2.29	43	38	24	306	235	75	176	8	1	0	3	103	24	1	.233	13	80	4	5	2.3	.959
1916			18	14	.563	2.92	40	33	23	268.1	249	65	113	5	1	0	1	94	18	1	.191	12	67	1	2	2.0	.988
1917			13	8	.619	3.09	33	20	11	183.2	168	58	85	1	4	2	2	61	14	0	.230	6	60	5	2	2.2	.930
1918			4	4	.500	2.32	12	9	3	73.2	61	21	31	1	1	1	0	22	7	0	.318	1	26	0	1	2.3	1.000
7 yrs.			119	72	.623	2.43	247	206	123	1679	1350	572	880	27	9	5	8	574	124	2	.216	52	440	23	19	2.1	.955

WORLD SERIES

Year	Team		W	L	PCT	ERA	G	GS	CG	IP	H	BB	SO	ShO	Relief W	Relief L	Relief SV	AB	H	HR	BA	PO	A	E	DP	TC/G	FA
1912	NY	N	1	2	.333	3.13	3	3	1	23	19	11	15	0	0	0	0	8	3	0	.375	0	10	0	0	3.3	1.000
1913			0	1	.000	5.40	2	1	0	8.1	11	1	4	0	0	0	0	2	0	0	.000	0	1	0	0	0.5	1.000

Year	Team	W	L	PCT	ERA	G	GS	CG	IP	H	BB	SO	ShO	Relief Pitching W	L	SV	Batting AB	H	HR	BA	PO	A	E	DP	TC/G	FA

Jeff Tesreau *continued*

Year	Team	W	L	PCT	ERA	G	GS	CG	IP	H	BB	SO	ShO	W	L	SV	AB	H	HR	BA	PO	A	E	DP	TC/G	FA
1917		0	0	–	0.00	1	0	0	1	0	1	1	0	0	0	0	0	0	0	–	0	0	0	0	0.0	
3 yrs.		1	3	.250	3.62	6	4	1	32.1	30	13	20	0	0	0	0	10	3	0	.300	0	11	0	0	1.8	1.000

Bob Tewksbury

TEWKSBURY, ROBERT ALAN
B. Nov. 30, 1960, Concord, N. H.   BR TR 6'4" 200 lbs.

Year	Team	W	L	PCT	ERA	G	GS	CG	IP	H	BB	SO	ShO	W	L	SV	AB	H	HR	BA	PO	A	E	DP	TC/G	FA
1986	NY A	9	5	.643	3.31	23	20	2	130.1	144	31	49	0	0	0	0	0	0	0	–	7	29	1	2	1.6	.973
1987	2 teams NY A (8G 1–4) CHI N (7G 0–4)																									
"	total	1	8	.111	6.66	15	9	0	51.1	79	20	22	0	0	1	0	5	0	0	.000	3	6	1	1	0.7	.900
1988	CHI N	0	0	–	8.10	1	1	0	3.1	6	2	1	0	0	0	0	2	0	0	.000	0	1	0	0	1.0	1.000
1989	STL N	1	0	1.000	3.30	7	4	1	30	25	10	17	1	0	0	0	9	1	0	.111	1	3	0	0	0.6	1.000
4 yrs.		11	13	.458	4.19	46	34	3	215	254	63	89	1	0	1	0	16	1	0	.063	11	39	2	3	1.1	.962

Grant Thatcher

THATCHER, ULYSSES GRANT
B. Feb. 23, 1877, Maytown, Pa.   D. Mar. 17, 1936, Lancaster, Pa.   TR 5'10½" 180 lbs.

Year	Team	W	L	PCT	ERA	G	GS	CG	IP	H	BB	SO	ShO	W	L	SV	AB	H	HR	BA	PO	A	E	DP	TC/G	FA
1903	BKN N	3	1	.750	2.89	4	4	4	28	33	7	9	0	0	0	0	11	2	0	.182	0	8	1	0	2.3	.889
1904		1	0	1.000	4.00	1	0	0	9	9	2	4	0	1	0	0	4	1	0	.250	0	1	0	0	1.0	1.000
2 yrs.		4	1	.800	3.16	5	4	4	37	42	9	13	0	1	0	0	15	3	0	.200	0	9	1	0	2.0	.900

Greg Thayer

THAYER, GREGORY ALLEN
B. Oct. 23, 1949, Cedar Rapids, Iowa   BR TR 5'11" 182 lbs.

Year	Team	W	L	PCT	ERA	G	GS	CG	IP	H	BB	SO	ShO	W	L	SV	AB	H	HR	BA	PO	A	E	DP	TC/G	FA
1978	MIN A	1	1	.500	3.80	20	0	0	45	40	30	30	0	1	0	1	0	0	0	–	0	7	0	0	0.4	1.000

Jack Theis

THEIS, JOHN LOUIS
B. July 23, 1891, Georgetown, Ohio   D. July 6, 1941, Georgetown, Ohio   BR TR 6' 190 lbs.

Year	Team	W	L	PCT	ERA	G	GS	CG	IP	H	BB	SO	ShO	W	L	SV	AB	H	HR	BA	PO	A	E	DP	TC/G	FA
1920	CIN N	0	0	–	0.00	1	0	0	2	1	3	0	0	0	0	0	0	0	0	–	0	0	0	0	0.0	

Duane Theiss

THEISS, DUANE CHARLES
B. Nov. 20, 1953, Zanesville, Ohio   BR TR 6'3" 185 lbs.

Year	Team	W	L	PCT	ERA	G	GS	CG	IP	H	BB	SO	ShO	W	L	SV	AB	H	HR	BA	PO	A	E	DP	TC/G	FA
1977	ATL N	1	1	.500	6.43	17	0	0	21	26	16	7	0	1	1	0	1	0	0	.000	2	3	0	0	0.3	1.000
1978		0	0	–	1.50	3	0	0	6	3	3	3	0	0	0	0	1	0	0	.000	2	0	0	0	0.7	1.000
2 yrs.		1	1	.500	5.33	20	0	0	27	29	19	10	0	1	1	0	2	0	0	.000	4	3	0	0	0.4	1.000

Jug Thesenga

THESENGA, ARNOLD JOSEPH
B. Apr. 27, 1914, Jefferson, S. D.   BR TR 6' 200 lbs.

Year	Team	W	L	PCT	ERA	G	GS	CG	IP	H	BB	SO	ShO	W	L	SV	AB	H	HR	BA	PO	A	E	DP	TC/G	FA
1944	WAS A	0	0	–	5.11	5	1	0	12.1	18	12	2	0	0	0	0	2	0	0	.000	0	3	0	1	0.6	1.000

Bert Thiel

THIEL, MAYNARD BERT
B. May 4, 1926, Marion, Wis.   BR TR 5'10" 185 lbs.

Year	Team	W	L	PCT	ERA	G	GS	CG	IP	H	BB	SO	ShO	W	L	SV	AB	H	HR	BA	PO	A	E	DP	TC/G	FA
1952	BOS N	1	1	.500	7.71	4	0	0	7	11	4	6	0	1	1	0	0	0	0	–	0	1	0	0	0.3	1.000

Henry Thielman

THIELMAN, HENRY JOSEPH
Brother of Jake Thielman.
B. Oct. 30, 1880, St. Cloud, Minn.   D. Sept. 2, 1942, New York, N. Y.   BR TR 5'11" 175 lbs.

Year	Team	W	L	PCT	ERA	G	GS	CG	IP	H	BB	SO	ShO	W	L	SV	AB	H	HR	BA	PO	A	E	DP	TC/G	FA
1902	2 teams NY N (2G 0–1) CIN N (25G 8–15)																									
"	total	8	16	.333	3.19	27	25	22	217	209	84	54	0	0	0	1	104	13	0	.125	8	57	7	2	2.7	.903
1903	BKN N	0	3	.000	4.66	4	3	3	29	31	14	10	0	0	0	0	23	5	1	.217	3	10	0	1	3.3	1.000
2 yrs.		8	19	.296	3.37	31	28	25	246	240	98	64	0	0	0	1	127	18	1	.142	11	67	7	3	2.7	.918

Jake Thielman

THIELMAN, JOHN PETER
Brother of Henry Thielman.
B. Mar. 20, 1879, St. Cloud, Minn.   D. Jan. 28, 1928, Minneapolis, Minn.   BR TR 5'11" 175 lbs.

Year	Team	W	L	PCT	ERA	G	GS	CG	IP	H	BB	SO	ShO	W	L	SV	AB	H	HR	BA	PO	A	E	DP	TC/G	FA
1905	STL N	15	16	.484	3.50	32	29	26	242	265	62	87	0	1	1	0	91	21	0	.231	9	84	3	3	3.0	.969
1906		0	1	.000	3.60	1	1	0	5	5	2	0	0	0	0	0	2	1	0	.500	0	2	1	0	3.0	.667
1907	CLE A	11	8	.579	2.33	20	18	18	166	151	34	56	3	1	0	0	59	12	0	.203	7	41	4	1	2.6	.923
1908	2 teams CLE A (11G 4–3) BOS A (1G 0–0)																									
"	total	4	3	.571	4.04	12	8	5	62.1	62	9	15	0	0	0	0	23	8	0	.348	1	28	0	2	2.4	1.000
4 yrs.		30	28	.517	3.16	65	56	49	475.1	483	107	158	3	2	1	0	175	42	0	.240	17	155	8	6	2.8	.956

Dave Thies

THIES, DAVID ROBERT
B. Mar. 21, 1937, Minneapolis, Minn.   BR TR 6'4" 205 lbs.

Year	Team	W	L	PCT	ERA	G	GS	CG	IP	H	BB	SO	ShO	W	L	SV	AB	H	HR	BA	PO	A	E	DP	TC/G	FA
1963	KC A	0	1	.000	4.62	9	2	0	25.1	26	12	9	0	0	0	0	6	2	0	.333	0	6	0	0	0.7	1.000

Jake Thies

THIES, VERNON ARTHUR
B. Apr. 1, 1926, St. Louis, Mo.   BR TR 5'11" 170 lbs.

Year	Team	W	L	PCT	ERA	G	GS	CG	IP	H	BB	SO	ShO	W	L	SV	AB	H	HR	BA	PO	A	E	DP	TC/G	FA
1954	PIT N	3	9	.250	3.87	33	18	3	130.1	120	49	57	1	0	0	0	33	1	0	.030	8	24	4	0	1.1	.889
1955		0	1	.000	4.91	1	1	0	3.2	5	3	0	0	0	0	0	0	0	0	–	0	0	0	0	0.0	
2 yrs.		3	10	.231	3.90	34	19	3	134	125	52	57	1	0	0	0	33	1	0	.030	8	24	4	0	1.1	.889

Bobby Thigpen

THIGPEN, ROBERT THOMAS
B. July 17, 1963, Tallahassee, Fla.   BR TR 6'3" 195 lbs.

Year	Team	W	L	PCT	ERA	G	GS	CG	IP	H	BB	SO	ShO	W	L	SV	AB	H	HR	BA	PO	A	E	DP	TC/G	FA
1986	CHI A	2	0	1.000	1.77	20	0	0	35.2	26	12	20	0	2	0	7	0	0	0	–	2	4	0	1	0.3	1.000
1987		7	5	.583	2.73	51	0	0	89	86	24	52	0	7	5	16	0	0	0	–	8	14	2	1	0.5	.917
1988		5	8	.385	3.30	68	0	0	90	96	33	62	0	5	8	34	0	0	0	–	5	11	0	2	0.2	1.000
1989		2	6	.250	3.76	61	0	0	79	62	40	47	0	2	6	34	0	0	0	–	7	7	0	0	0.2	1.000
4 yrs.		16	19	.457	3.06	200	0	0	293.2	270	109	181	0	16	19	91	0	0	0	–	22	36	2	4	0.3	.967

Year	Team	W	L	PCT	ERA	G	GS	CG	IP	H	BB	SO	ShO	Relief Pitching W	L	SV	Batting AB	H	HR	BA	PO	A	E	DP	TC/G	FA

Dick Thoenen
THOENEN, RICHARD CRISPIN
B. Jan. 9, 1944, Mexico, Mo.
BR TR 6'6" 215 lbs.

Year	Team	W	L	PCT	ERA	G	GS	CG	IP	H	BB	SO	ShO	W	L	SV	AB	H	HR	BA	PO	A	E	DP	TC/G	FA
1967	PHI N	0	0	–	9.00	1	0	0	1	2	0	0	0	0	0	0	0	0	0	–	0	2	0	0	2.0	1.000

Blaine Thomas
THOMAS, BLAINE M.
B. 1888, Glendora, Calif. D. Aug. 21, 1915, Glendora, Calif.
BR TR 5'10" 165 lbs.

Year	Team	W	L	PCT	ERA	G	GS	CG	IP	H	BB	SO	ShO	W	L	SV	AB	H	HR	BA	PO	A	E	DP	TC/G	FA
1911	BOS A	0	0	–	0.00	2	2	0	4.2	3	7	0	0	0	0	0	2	1	0	.500	0	3	1	0	2.0	.750

Bud Thomas
THOMAS, LUTHER BAXTER
B. Sept. 9, 1910, Faber, Va.
BR TR 6' 180 lbs.

Year	Team	W	L	PCT	ERA	G	GS	CG	IP	H	BB	SO	ShO	W	L	SV	AB	H	HR	BA	PO	A	E	DP	TC/G	FA
1932	WAS A	0	0	–	0.00	2	0	0	3	1	2	1	0	0	0	0	0	0	0	–	0	0	0	0	0.0	–
1933		0	0	–	15.75	2	0	0	4	11	2	1	0	0	0	0	1	0	0	.000	0	3	0	0	1.5	1.000
1937	PHI A	8	15	.348	4.99	35	26	6	169.2	208	52	54	1	1	1	0	47	6	1	.128	7	17	0	0	0.7	1.000
1938		9	14	.391	4.92	42	29	7	212.1	259	62	48	0	0	0	0	69	9	0	.130	7	39	2	1	1.1	.958
1939	3 teams	PHI A	(2G 0–1)		WAS A	(4G 0–0)		DET A	(27G 7–0)																		
"	total	7	1	.875	5.22	33	2	0	60.1	64	23	14	0	7	0	1	14	1	0	.071	2	13	0	0	0.5	1.000
1940	DET A	0	1	.000	9.00	3	0	0	4	8	3	0	0	0	0	0	0	0	0	–	0	4	0	0	1.3	1.000
1941		1	3	.250	4.21	26	1	0	72.2	74	22	17	0	1	2	2	19	2	0	.105	6	22	0	0	1.1	1.000
7 yrs.		25	34	.424	4.96	143	58	13	526	625	166	135	1	9	4	3	150	18	1	.120	22	98	2	1	0.9	.984

Carl Thomas
THOMAS, CARL LESLIE
B. May 28, 1932, Minneapolis, Minn.
BR TR 6'5" 245 lbs.

Year	Team	W	L	PCT	ERA	G	GS	CG	IP	H	BB	SO	ShO	W	L	SV	AB	H	HR	BA	PO	A	E	DP	TC/G	FA
1960	CLE A	1	0	1.000	7.45	4	0	0	9.2	8	10	5	0	1	0	0	3	1	0	.333	2	1	0	0	0.8	1.000

Claude Thomas
THOMAS, CLAUDE ALFRED (Lefty)
B. May 15, 1890, Stanberry, Mo. D. Mar. 6, 1946, Sulphur, Okla.
BL TL 6'1" 180 lbs.

Year	Team	W	L	PCT	ERA	G	GS	CG	IP	H	BB	SO	ShO	W	L	SV	AB	H	HR	BA	PO	A	E	DP	TC/G	FA
1916	WAS A	1	2	.333	4.13	7	4	1	28.1	27	12	7	1	0	0	0	10	1	0	.100	2	7	1	0	1.4	.900

Fay Thomas
THOMAS, FAY WESLEY (Scow)
B. Oct. 10, 1904, Holyrood, Kans.
BR TR 6'2" 195 lbs.

Year	Team	W	L	PCT	ERA	G	GS	CG	IP	H	BB	SO	ShO	W	L	SV	AB	H	HR	BA	PO	A	E	DP	TC/G	FA
1927	NY N	0	0	–	3.31	9	0	0	16.1	19	4	11	0	0	0	0	2	0	0	.000	0	1	0	0	0.1	1.000
1931	CLE A	2	4	.333	5.18	16	2	1	48.2	63	32	25	0	1	3	0	13	2	0	.154	1	6	1	0	0.5	.875
1932	BKN N	0	1	.000	7.41	7	2	0	17	22	8	9	0	0	0	0	3	0	0	.000	1	4	0	0	0.7	1.000
1935	STL A	7	15	.318	4.78	49	19	4	147	165	89	67	0	5	2	1	38	4	0	.105	5	41	3	1	1.0	.939
4 yrs.		9	20	.310	4.95	81	23	5	229	269	133	112	0	6	5	1	56	6	0	.107	7	52	4	1	0.8	.937

Frosty Thomas
THOMAS, FORREST
B. May 23, 1881, Faucett, Mo. D. Mar. 18, 1970, St. Joseph, Mo.
BR TR 6' 185 lbs.

Year	Team	W	L	PCT	ERA	G	GS	CG	IP	H	BB	SO	ShO	W	L	SV	AB	H	HR	BA	PO	A	E	DP	TC/G	FA
1905	DET A	0	1	.000	7.50	2	1	0	6	10	3	5	0	0	0	0	2	0	0	.000	0	2	0	0	1.0	1.000

Lefty Thomas
THOMAS, CLARENCE FLETCHER
B. Oct. 4, 1903, Glade Springs, Va. D. Mar. 21, 1952, Charlottesville, Va.
BL TL 6' 183 lbs.

Year	Team	W	L	PCT	ERA	G	GS	CG	IP	H	BB	SO	ShO	W	L	SV	AB	H	HR	BA	PO	A	E	DP	TC/G	FA
1925	WAS A	0	2	.000	2.08	2	2	1	13	14	7	10	0	0	0	0	5	0	0	.000	0	3	0	0	1.5	1.000
1926		0	0	–	5.19	6	0	0	8.2	8	10	3	0	0	0	0	2	0	0	.000	0	0	0	0	0.0	–
2 yrs.		0	2	.000	3.32	8	2	1	21.2	22	17	13	0	0	0	0	7	0	0	.000	0	3	0	0	0.4	1.000

Myles Thomas
THOMAS, MYLES LEWIS
B. Oct. 22, 1897, State College, Pa. D. Dec. 12, 1963, Toledo, Ohio.
BR TR 5'9½" 170 lbs.

Year	Team	W	L	PCT	ERA	G	GS	CG	IP	H	BB	SO	ShO	W	L	SV	AB	H	HR	BA	PO	A	E	DP	TC/G	FA
1926	NY A	6	6	.500	4.23	33	13	3	140.1	140	65	38	0	0	2	0	43	5	0	.116	7	39	2	1	1.5	.958
1927		7	4	.636	4.87	21	9	0	88.2	111	43	25	0	4	1	0	27	9	0	.333	4	22	1	2	1.3	.963
1928		1	0	1.000	3.41	12	1	0	31.2	33	9	10	0	0	0	0	10	4	0	.400	2	7	1	0	0.8	.900
1929	2 teams	NY A	(5G 0–2)		WAS A	(22G 7–8)																				
"	total	7	10	.412	4.30	27	15	7	140.1	166	57	36	0	0	2	2	55	15	0	.273	6	34	1	1	1.5	.976
1930	WAS A	2	2	.500	8.29	12	2	0	33.2	49	15	12	0	2	0	0	11	2	0	.182	1	4	1	0	0.5	.833
5 yrs.		23	22	.511	4.64	105	40	11	434.2	499	189	121	0	6	5	2	146	35	0	.240	20	106	6	4	1.3	.955

WORLD SERIES

Year	Team	W	L	PCT	ERA	G	GS	CG	IP	H	BB	SO	ShO	W	L	SV	AB	H	HR	BA	PO	A	E	DP	TC/G	FA
1926	NY A	0	0	–	3.00	2	0	0	3	3	0	0	0	0	0	0	0	0	0	–	0	2	0	0	1.0	1.000

Roy Thomas
THOMAS, ROY ALLEN
Brother of Bill Thomas.
B. Mar. 24, 1874, Norristown, Pa. D. Nov. 20, 1959, Norristown, Pa.
BL TL 5'11" 150 lbs.

Year	Team	W	L	PCT	ERA	G	GS	CG	IP	H	BB	SO	ShO	W	L	SV	AB	H	HR	BA	PO	A	E	DP	TC/G	FA
1900	PHI N	0	0	–	3.38	1	0	0	2.2	4	0	0	0	0	0	0	*				0	0	0	0	0.0	–

Roy Thomas
THOMAS, ROY JUSTIN
B. June 22, 1953, Quantico, Va.
BR TR 6'5" 215 lbs.

Year	Team	W	L	PCT	ERA	G	GS	CG	IP	H	BB	SO	ShO	W	L	SV	AB	H	HR	BA	PO	A	E	DP	TC/G	FA
1977	HOU N	0	0	–	3.00	4	0	0	6	5	3	4	0	0	0	0	0	0	0	–	0	1	0	0	0.3	1.000
1978	STL N	1	1	.500	3.86	16	1	0	28	21	16	16	0	1	0	3	4	1	0	.250	0	7	0	0	0.5	1.000
1979		3	4	.429	2.92	26	6	0	77	66	24	44	0	2	2	1	17	1	0	.059	10	13	0	1	0.9	1.000
1980		2	3	.400	4.75	24	6	0	55	59	25	22	0	0	2	0	13	2	0	.154	7	10	0	1	0.7	1.000
1983	SEA A	3	1	.750	3.45	43	0	0	88.2	95	32	77	0	3	1	1	0	0	0	–	7	8	0	1	0.3	1.000
1984		3	2	.600	5.26	21	1	0	49.2	52	37	42	0	3	1	0	0	0	0	–	4	7	0	1	0.5	1.000
1985		7	0	1.000	3.36	40	0	0	93.2	91	48	70	0	7	0	1	0	0	0	–	7	7	0	0	0.4	1.000
1987		1	0	1.000	5.23	8	0	0	20.2	23	11	14	0	1	0	0	0	0	0	–	1	1	0	0	0.1	1.000
8 yrs.		20	11	.645	3.83	182	13	0	418.2	387	196	289	0	17	6	7	34	4	0	.118	36	54	0	4	0.5	1.000

Stan Thomas
THOMAS, STANLEY BROWN
B. July 11, 1949, Rumford, Me.
BR TR 6'2" 185 lbs.

Year	Team	W	L	PCT	ERA	G	GS	CG	IP	H	BB	SO	ShO	W	L	SV	AB	H	HR	BA	PO	A	E	DP	TC/G	FA
1974	TEX A	0	0	–	6.43	12	0	0	14	22	6	8	0	0	0	0	0	0	0	–	1	3	0	0	0.3	1.000
1975		4	4	.500	3.10	46	1	0	81.1	72	34	46	0	4	3	3	0	0	0	–	6	13	0	1	0.4	1.000

Year	Team	W	L	PCT	ERA	G	GS	CG	IP	H	BB	SO	ShO	Relief Pitching W	L	SV	Batting AB	H	HR	BA	PO	A	E	DP	TC/G	FA

Stan Thomas *continued*

Year	Team	W	L	PCT	ERA	G	GS	CG	IP	H	BB	SO	ShO	W	L	SV	AB	H	HR	BA	PO	A	E	DP	TC/G	FA
1976	CLE A	4	4	.500	2.29	37	7	2	106	88	41	54	0	1	2	6	0	0	0	–	12	26	1	2	1.1	.974
1977	2 teams	SEA A	(13G 2–6)		NY A	(3G 1–0)																				
"	total	3	6	.333	6.12	16	9	1	64.2	81	29	15	0	2	1	0	0	0	0	–	3	10	2	1	0.9	.867
4 yrs.		11	14	.440	3.69	111	17	3	266	263	110	123	0	7	6	9	0	0	0	–	22	52	3	4	0.7	.961

Tom Thomas

THOMAS, THOMAS R. (Savage Tom)
B. Dec. 27, 1873, Shawnee, Ohio D. Sept. 23, 1942, Shawnee, Ohio

BR TR 6'4" 195 lbs.

Year	Team	W	L	PCT	ERA	G	GS	CG	IP	H	BB	SO	ShO	W	L	SV	AB	H	HR	BA	PO	A	E	DP	TC/G	FA
1899	STL N	1	1	.500	2.52	4	2	2	25	22	4	8	0	0	0	0	12	3	0	.250	0	7	2	0	2.3	.778
1900		1	1	.500	3.76	5	1	1	26.1	38	4	7	0	1	0	0	11	1	0	.091	0	3	1	0	0.8	.750
2 yrs.		2	2	.500	3.16	9	3	3	51.1	60	8	15	0	1	0	0	23	4	0	.174	0	10	3	0	1.4	.769

Tommy Thomas

THOMAS, ALPHONSE
B. Dec. 23, 1899, Baltimore, Md. D. Apr. 27, 1988, Dallastown, Pa.

BR TR 5'10" 175 lbs.

Year	Team	W	L	PCT	ERA	G	GS	CG	IP	H	BB	SO	ShO	W	L	SV	AB	H	HR	BA	PO	A	E	DP	TC/G	FA
1926	CHI A	15	12	.556	3.80	44	32	13	249	225	110	127	2	3	2	1	86	16	0	.186	8	44	0	3	1.2	1.000
1927		19	16	.543	2.98	40	36	24	307.2	271	94	107	3	1	0	1	95	14	1	.147	6	55	2	4	1.6	.968
1928		17	16	.515	3.08	36	32	24	283	277	76	129	3	1	0	0	96	21	2	.219	9	48	1	2	1.6	.983
1929		14	18	.438	3.19	36	31	24	259.2	270	60	62	2	1	0	1	98	25	0	.255	8	44	2	2	1.5	.963
1930		5	13	.278	5.22	34	27	7	169	229	44	58	0	0	0	0	56	7	0	.125	8	34	2	2	1.3	.955
1931		10	14	.417	4.80	42	36	11	242	296	69	71	2	0	0	2	87	21	0	.241	8	47	1	3	1.3	.982
1932	2 teams	CHI A	(12G 3–3)		WAS A	(18G 8–7)																				
"	total	11	10	.524	4.26	30	17	8	160.2	169	61	47	1	4	1	0	55	11	0	.200	2	24	1	2	0.9	.963
1933	WAS A	7	7	.500	4.80	35	14	2	135	149	49	35	0	4	3	1	42	10	0	.238	3	22	1	1	0.7	.962
1934		8	9	.471	5.47	33	18	7	133.1	154	58	42	1	2	2	1	38	7	0	.184	1	20	1	1	0.7	.955
1935	2 teams	WAS A	(1G 0–0)		PHI N	(4G 0–1)																				
"	total	0	1	.000	6.57	5	1	0	12.1	18	5	3	0	0	1	0	3	0	0	.000	0	2	0	0	0.4	1.000
1936	STL A	11	9	.550	5.26	36	21	8	179.2	219	72	40	1	2	0	0	58	8	0	.138	2	24	0	1	0.7	1.000
1937	2 teams	STL A	(17G 0–1)		BOS A	(9G 0–2)																				
"	total	0	3	.000	6.26	26	2	0	41.2	62	14	14	0	0	0	0	8	1	0	.125	1	8	0	0	0.3	1.000
12 yrs.		117	128	.478	4.12	397	267	128	2173	2339	712	735	15	18	12	12	722	141	3	.195	56	372	11	21	1.1	.975

WORLD SERIES

Year	Team	W	L	PCT	ERA	G	GS	CG	IP	H	BB	SO	ShO	W	L	SV	AB	H	HR	BA	PO	A	E	DP	TC/G	FA
1933	WAS A	0	0	–	0.00	2	0	0	1.1	1	0	2	0	0	0	0	0	0	0	–	0	0	0	0	0.0	–

Erskine Thomason

THOMASON, MELVIN ERSKINE
B. Aug. 13, 1948, Laurens, S. C.

BR TR 6'1" 190 lbs.

Year	Team	W	L	PCT	ERA	G	GS	CG	IP	H	BB	SO	ShO	W	L	SV	AB	H	HR	BA	PO	A	E	DP	TC/G	FA
1974	PHI N	0	0	–	0.00	1	0	0	1	0	0	1	0	0	0	0	0	0	0	–	0	0	0	0	0.0	–

Art Thompson

THOMPSON, ARTHUR J.
Deceased.

Year	Team	W	L	PCT	ERA	G	GS	CG	IP	H	BB	SO	ShO	W	L	SV	AB	H	HR	BA	PO	A	E	DP	TC/G	FA
1884	WAS U	0	1	.000	6.75	1	1	1	8	10	3	8	0	0	0	0	3	0	0	.000	0	3	0	0	3.0	1.000

Bill Thompson

THOMPSON, WILL McLAIN
B. Aug. 30, 1870, Pittsburgh, Pa. D. June 9, 1962, Pittsburgh, Pa.

BR TR 5'11½" 190 lbs.

Year	Team	W	L	PCT	ERA	G	GS	CG	IP	H	BB	SO	ShO	W	L	SV	AB	H	HR	BA	PO	A	E	DP	TC/G	FA
1892	PIT N	0	1	.000	3.00	1	1	0	3	3	5	0	0	0	0	0	0	0	0	–	0	1	0	0	1.0	1.000

Dave Thompson

THOMPSON, DAVID FORREST
B. Mar. 3, 1918, Mooresville, N. C. D. Feb. 26, 1979, Charlotte, N. C.

BL TL 5'11" 195 lbs.

Year	Team	W	L	PCT	ERA	G	GS	CG	IP	H	BB	SO	ShO	W	L	SV	AB	H	HR	BA	PO	A	E	DP	TC/G	FA
1948	WAS A	6	10	.375	3.84	46	7	0	131.1	134	54	40	0	5	4	4	35	10	0	.286	7	22	2	1	0.7	.935
1949		1	3	.250	4.41	9	1	1	16.1	22	9	8	0	1	2	0	5	3	0	.600	0	3	1	1	0.4	.750
2 yrs.		7	13	.350	3.90	55	8	1	147.2	156	63	48	0	6	4	4	40	13	0	.325	7	25	3	2	0.6	.914

Fuller Thompson

THOMPSON, FULLER WEIDNER
B. May 1, 1889, Los Angeles, Calif. D. Feb. 19, 1972, Los Angeles, Calif.

BR TR 5'11½" 164 lbs.

Year	Team	W	L	PCT	ERA	G	GS	CG	IP	H	BB	SO	ShO	W	L	SV	AB	H	HR	BA	PO	A	E	DP	TC/G	FA
1911	BOS N	0	0	–	3.86	3	0	0	4.2	5	2	0	0	0	0	0	0	0	0	–	0	2	0	1	0.7	1.000

Gus Thompson

THOMPSON, JOHN GUSTAV
B. June 22, 1877, Humboldt, Iowa D. Mar. 28, 1958, Kalispell, Mont.

BR TR 6'2" 185 lbs.

Year	Team	W	L	PCT	ERA	G	GS	CG	IP	H	BB	SO	ShO	W	L	SV	AB	H	HR	BA	PO	A	E	DP	TC/G	FA
1903	PIT N	2	3	.400	3.56	5	4	3	43	52	16	22	0	0	1	0	16	4	0	.250	2	8	3	0	2.6	.769
1906	STL N	2	11	.154	4.28	17	12	8	103	111	25	36	0	0	3	0	34	6	0	.176	1	36	1	1	2.2	.974
2 yrs.		4	14	.222	4.07	22	16	11	146	163	41	58	0	0	4	0	50	10	0	.200	3	44	4	1	2.3	.922

WORLD SERIES

Year	Team	W	L	PCT	ERA	G	GS	CG	IP	H	BB	SO	ShO	W	L	SV	AB	H	HR	BA	PO	A	E	DP	TC/G	FA
1903	PIT N	0	0	–	4.50	1	0	0	2	3	1	0	0	0	0	0	1	0	0	.000	0	1	0	0	1.0	1.000

Harry Thompson

THOMPSON, HAROLD
B. Sept. 9, 1889, Nanticoke, Pa. D. Feb. 14, 1951, Reno, Nev.

BL TL 5'8" 150 lbs.

Year	Team	W	L	PCT	ERA	G	GS	CG	IP	H	BB	SO	ShO	W	L	SV	AB	H	HR	BA	PO	A	E	DP	TC/G	FA
1919	2 teams	WAS A	(12G 0–3)		PHI A	(3G 0–1)																				
"	total	0	4	.000	4.23	15	2	0	55.1	64	11	11	0	0	2	1	38	8	0	.211	5	16	0	1	1.4	1.000

Jocko Thompson

THOMPSON, JOHN SAMUEL
B. Jan. 17, 1917, Beverly, Mass. D. Feb. 3, 1988, Olney, Md.

BL TL 6' 185 lbs.

Year	Team	W	L	PCT	ERA	G	GS	CG	IP	H	BB	SO	ShO	W	L	SV	AB	H	HR	BA	PO	A	E	DP	TC/G	FA
1948	PHI N	1	0	1.000	2.77	2	2	1	13	10	9	7	0	0	0	0	3	0	0	.000	0	1	0	0	0.5	1.000
1949		1	3	.250	6.89	8	5	1	31.1	38	11	12	0	0	0	0	11	2	0	.182	0	5	0	1	0.6	1.000
1950		0	0	–	0.00	2	0	0	4	1	4	2	0	0	0	0	1	0	0	–	0	1	0	0	0.5	1.000
1951		4	8	.333	3.85	29	14	3	119.1	102	59	60	2	0	1	1	39	4	0	.103	9	16	3	2	1.0	.893
4 yrs.		6	11	.353	4.24	41	21	5	167.2	151	83	81	2	0	1	1	53	6	0	.113	9	23	3	3	0.9	.914

Year	Team		W	L	PCT	ERA	G	GS	CG	IP	H	BB	SO	ShO	W	L	SV	AB	H	HR	BA	PO	A	E	DP	TC/G	FA
															Relief Pitching			Batting									

Junior Thompson

THOMPSON, EUGENE EARL
B. June 7, 1917, Latham, Ill. — BR TR 6'1" 185 lbs.

Year	Team		W	L	PCT	ERA	G	GS	CG	IP	H	BB	SO	ShO	W	L	SV	AB	H	HR	BA	PO	A	E	DP	TC/G	FA
1939	CIN	N	13	5	.722	2.54	42	11	5	152.1	130	55	87	3	8	1	2	48	11	0	.229	3	25	3	0	0.7	.903
1940			16	9	.640	3.32	33	31	17	225.1	197	96	103	3	1	0	0	79	18	0	.228	12	40	4	1	1.7	.929
1941			6	6	.500	4.87	27	15	4	109	117	57	46	0	2	0	1	30	7	0	.233	6	32	2	0	1.5	.950
1942			4	7	.364	3.36	29	10	1	101.2	86	53	35	0	1	3	0	30	8	0	.267	9	39	4	4	1.8	.923
1946	NY	N	4	6	.400	1.29	39	1	0	62.2	36	40	31	0	4	5	4	7	1	0	.143	5	18	0	1	0.6	1.000
1947			4	2	.667	4.29	15	0	0	35.2	36	27	13	0	4	2	0	6	0	0	.000	5	9	0	1	0.9	1.000
6 yrs.			47	35	.573	3.26	185	68	27	686.2	602	328	315	6	20	11	7	200	45	0	.225	40	163	13	6	1.2	.940
WORLD SERIES																											
1939	CIN	N	0	1	.000	13.50	1	1	0	4.2	5	4	3	0	0	0	0	1	1	0	1.000	0	0	0	0	0.0	–
1940			0	1	.000	16.20	1	1	0	3.1	8	4	2	0	0	0	0	1	0	0	.000	0	1	0	0	1.0	1.000
2 yrs.			0	2	.000	14.63	2	2	0	8	13	8	5	0	0	0	0	2	1	0	.500	0	1	0	0	0.5	1.000

Lee Thompson

THOMPSON, JOHN DUDLEY (Lefty)
B. Feb. 26, 1898, Smithfield, Utah D. Feb. 17, 1963, Santa Barbara, Calif. — BL TL 6'1" 185 lbs.

Year	Team		W	L	PCT	ERA	G	GS	CG	IP	H	BB	SO	ShO	W	L	SV	AB	H	HR	BA	PO	A	E	DP	TC/G	FA
1921	CHI	A	0	3	.000	8.27	4	4	0	20.2	32	6	4	0	0	0	0	7	2	0	.286	1	2	0	0	0.8	1.000

Mike Thompson

THOMPSON, MICHAEL WAYNE
B. Sept. 6, 1949, Denver, Colo. — BR TR 6'3" 190 lbs.

Year	Team		W	L	PCT	ERA	G	GS	CG	IP	H	BB	SO	ShO	W	L	SV	AB	H	HR	BA	PO	A	E	DP	TC/G	FA
1971	WAS	A	1	6	.143	4.84	16	12	0	67	53	54	41	0	0	0	0	17	2	0	.118	6	12	1	0	1.2	.947
1973	STL	N	0	0	–	0.00	2	2	0	4	1	5	3	0	0	0	0	1	0	0	.000	0	0	0	0	0.0	–
1974	2 teams		STL N (19G 0-3)				ATL N (1G 0-0)																				
"	total		0	3	.000	5.53	20	5	0	42.1	44	37	27	0	0	0	0	9	1	0	.111	4	6	0	1	0.5	1.000
1975	ATL	N	0	6	.000	4.67	16	10	0	52	60	32	42	0	0	0	0	14	1	0	.071	3	9	0	0	0.8	1.000
4 yrs.			1	15	.063	4.84	54	29	0	165.1	158	128	113	0	0	0	0	41	4	0	.098	13	27	1	1	0.8	.976

Rich Thompson

THOMPSON, RICHARD NEIL
B. Nov. 1, 1958, New York, N. Y. — BB TR 6'3" 225 lbs.

Year	Team		W	L	PCT	ERA	G	GS	CG	IP	H	BB	SO	ShO	W	L	SV	AB	H	HR	BA	PO	A	E	DP	TC/G	FA
1985	CLE	A	3	8	.273	6.30	57	0	0	80	95	48	30	0	3	8	5	0	0	0	–	2	7	3	1	0.2	.750
1989	MON	N	0	2	.000	2.18	19	0	0	33	27	11	15	0	0	1	0	2	0	0	.000	0	4	0	0	0.2	1.000
2 yrs.			3	10	.231	5.10	76	1	0	113	122	59	45	0	3	9	5	2	0	0	.000	2	11	3	1	0.2	.813

Tommy Thompson

THOMPSON, THOMAS CARL
Brother of Homer Thompson.
B. Nov. 7, 1889, Spring City, Tenn. D. Jan. 16, 1963, La Jolla, Calif. — BR TR 5'9½" 170 lbs.

Year	Team		W	L	PCT	ERA	G	GS	CG	IP	H	BB	SO	ShO	W	L	SV	AB	H	HR	BA	PO	A	E	DP	TC/G	FA
1912	NY	A	0	2	.000	6.06	7	2	1	32.2	43	13	15	0	0	0	0	10	3	0	.300	0	7	1	0	1.1	.875

Hank Thormahlen

THORMAHLEN, HERBERT EHLER (Lefty)
B. July 5, 1896, Jersey City, N. J. D. Feb. 6, 1955, Los Angeles, Calif. — BL TL 6' 180 lbs.

Year	Team		W	L	PCT	ERA	G	GS	CG	IP	H	BB	SO	ShO	W	L	SV	AB	H	HR	BA	PO	A	E	DP	TC/G	FA
1917	NY	A	0	1	.000	2.25	1	1	0	8	9	4	5	0	0	0	0	2	0	0	.000	1	1	1	1	2.0	.500
1918			7	3	.700	2.48	16	12	5	112.2	85	52	22	2	1	1	0	39	3	0	.077	1	34	0	3	2.2	1.000
1919			12	10	.545	2.62	30	25	13	188.2	155	61	62	2	0	1	1	59	11	0	.186	7	47	2	0	1.9	.964
1920			9	6	.600	4.14	29	14	5	143.1	178	43	35	0	3	0	1	45	10	0	.222	6	45	4	1	1.9	.927
1921	BOS	A	1	7	.125	4.48	23	9	3	96.1	101	34	17	0	0	0	0	23	4	0	.174	1	26	1	2	1.2	.964
1925	BKN	N	0	3	.000	3.94	5	2	0	16	22	9	7	0	0	1	0	5	1	0	.200	2	6	2	0	2.0	.800
6 yrs.			29	30	.492	3.33	104	63	26	565	550	203	148	4	4	3	2	173	29	0	.168	17	159	10	7	1.8	.946

Paul Thormodsgard

THORMODSGARD, PAUL GAYTON
B. Nov. 10, 1953, San Francisco, Calif. — BR TR 6'2" 190 lbs.

Year	Team		W	L	PCT	ERA	G	GS	CG	IP	H	BB	SO	ShO	W	L	SV	AB	H	HR	BA	PO	A	E	DP	TC/G	FA
1977	MIN	A	11	15	.423	4.62	37	37	8	218	236	65	94	1	0	0	0	0	0	0	–	8	31	2	2	1.1	.951
1978			1	6	.143	5.05	12	12	1	66	81	17	23	0	0	0	0	0	0	0	–	3	9	2	0	1.2	.857
1979			0	0	–	9.00	1	0	0	1	3	0	1	0	0	0	0	0	0	0	–	0	0	0	0	0.0	–
3 yrs.			12	21	.364	4.74	50	49	9	285	320	82	118	1	0	0	0	0	0	0	–	11	40	4	2	1.1	.927

John Thornton

THORNTON, JOHN
B. 1870, Washington, D. C. D. Aug. 31, 1893, Pensacola, Fla. — 5'10½" 175 lbs.

Year	Team		W	L	PCT	ERA	G	GS	CG	IP	H	BB	SO	ShO	W	L	SV	AB	H	HR	BA	PO	A	E	DP	TC/G	FA
1889	WAS	N	0	1	.000	5.00	1	1	1	9	8	7	3	0	0	0	0	4	0	0	.000	0	1	0	0	1.0	1.000
1891	PHI	N	15	16	.484	3.68	37	32	23	269	268	115	52	1	0	0	2	123	17	0	.138	28	61	12	4	2.7	.881
1892			0	2	.000	12.75	3	2	1	12	16	17	2	0	0	0	0	16	5	0	.313	2	4	1	0	2.3	.857
3 yrs.			15	19	.441	4.10	41	35	25	290	292	139	57	1	0	0	2	143	22	0	.154	30	66	13	4	2.7	.881

Walter Thornton

THORNTON, WALTER MILLER
B. Feb. 18, 1875, Lewiston, Me. D. July 14, 1960, Los Angeles, Calif. — TL 6'1" 180 lbs.

Year	Team		W	L	PCT	ERA	G	GS	CG	IP	H	BB	SO	ShO	W	L	SV	AB	H	HR	BA	PO	A	E	DP	TC/G	FA
1895	CHI	N	2	0	1.000	6.08	7	2	2	40	58	31	13	0	0	0	0	22	7	1	.318	4	5	1	0	1.4	.900
1896			2	1	.667	5.70	5	5	2	23.2	30	13	10	0	0	0	0	22	8	0	.364	1	3	1	0	1.0	.800
1897			6	7	.462	4.70	16	16	15	130.1	164	51	55	0	0	0	0	265	85	0	.321	11	25	1	1	2.3	.973
1898			13	10	.565	3.34	28	25	21	215.1	226	56	56	2	0	0	0	210	62	0	.295	8	48	7	3	2.3	.889
4 yrs.			23	18	.561	4.18	56	48	40	409.1	478	151	134	2	0	0	1	*				24	81	10	4	2.1	.913

Bob Thorpe

THORPE, ROBERT JOSEPH
B. Jan. 12, 1935, San Diego, Calif. D. Mar. 17, 1960, San Diego, Calif. — BR TR 6'1" 170 lbs.

Year	Team		W	L	PCT	ERA	G	GS	CG	IP	H	BB	SO	ShO	W	L	SV	AB	H	HR	BA	PO	A	E	DP	TC/G	FA
1955	CHI	N	0	0	–	3.00	2	0	0	3	4	0	0	0	0	0	0	0	0	0	–	0	2	0	0	1.0	1.000

George Throop

THROOP, GEORGE LYNFORD III
B. Nov. 24, 1950, Pasadena, Calif. — BR TR 6'7" 205 lbs.

Year	Team		W	L	PCT	ERA	G	GS	CG	IP	H	BB	SO	ShO	W	L	SV	AB	H	HR	BA	PO	A	E	DP	TC/G	FA
1975	KC	A	0	0	–	4.00	7	0	0	9	8	2	8	0	0	0	2	0	0	0	–	1	2	0	0	0.4	1.000
1977			0	0	–	3.60	4	0	0	5	1	4	1	0	0	0	0	0	0	0	–	1	2	0	0	0.8	1.000
1978			1	0	1.000	0.00	1	0	0	3	2	3	0	0	1	0	0	0	0	0	–	0	1	0	0	1.0	1.000

Year	Team	W	L	PCT	ERA	G	GS	CG	IP	H	BB	SO	ShO	W	L	SV	AB	H	HR	BA	PO	A	E	DP	TC/G	FA
														Relief Pitching			**Batting**									

George Throop *continued*

Year	Team	W	L	PCT	ERA	G	GS	CG	IP	H	BB	SO	ShO	W	L	SV	AB	H	HR	BA	PO	A	E	DP	TC/G	FA
1979	2 teams	KC A		(4G 0–0)		HOU N		(14G 1–0)																		
"	total	1	0	1.000	4.32	18	0	0	25	30	16	16	0	1	0	0	3	0	0	.000	1	2	0	0	0.2	1.000
4 yrs.		2	0	1.000	3.86	30	0	0	42	41	25	27	0	2	0	3	3	0	0	.000	3	7	0	0	0.3	1.000

Lou Thuman

THUMAN, LOUIS CHARLES FRANK
B. Dec. 13, 1916, Baltimore, Md.
BR TR 6'2" 185 lbs.

Year	Team	W	L	PCT	ERA	G	GS	CG	IP	H	BB	SO	ShO	W	L	SV	AB	H	HR	BA	PO	A	E	DP	TC/G	FA
1939	WAS A	0	0	–	9.00	3	0	0	4	5	2	1	0	0	0	0	0	0	0	–	2	2	0	0	1.3	1.000
1940		0	1	.000	14.40	2	0	0	5	10	7	0	0	0	1	0	2	0	0	.000	1	1	1	0	1.5	.667
2 yrs.		0	1	.000	12.00	5	0	0	9	15	9	1	0	0	1	0	2	0	0	.000	3	3	1	0	1.4	.857

Mark Thurmond

THURMOND, MARK ANTHONY
B. Sept. 12, 1956, Houston, Tex.
BL TL 6' 190 lbs.

Year	Team	W	L	PCT	ERA	G	GS	CG	IP	H	BB	SO	ShO	W	L	SV	AB	H	HR	BA	PO	A	E	DP	TC/G	FA
1983	SD N	7	3	.700	2.65	21	18	2	115.1	104	33	49	0	0	0	0	37	2	0	.054	7	22	0	0	1.4	1.000
1984		14	8	.636	2.97	32	29	1	178.2	174	55	57	1	0	1	0	58	11	0	.190	11	38	0	3	1.5	1.000
1985		7	11	.389	3.97	36	23	1	138.1	154	44	57	1	1	1	2	34	3	0	.088	8	27	1	2	1.0	.972
1986	2 teams	SD N		(17G 3–7)		DET A		(25G 4–1)																		
"	total	7	8	.467	4.56	42	19	2	122.1	140	44	49	1	2	0	3	24	6	0	.250	10	15	0	0	0.6	1.000
1987	DET A	0	1	.000	4.23	48	0	0	61.2	83	24	21	0	1	0	5	0	0	0	–	2	9	0	0	0.2	1.000
1988	BAL A	1	8	.111	4.58	43	6	0	74.2	80	27	29	0	1	2	3	0	0	0	–	3	8	1	0	0.3	.917
1989		2	4	.333	3.90	49	2	0	90	102	17	34	0	2	3	4	0	0	0	–	4	10	0	0	0.3	1.000
7 yrs.		38	43	.469	3.71	271	97	6	781	837	244	296	3	6	8	17	153	22	0	.144	45	129	2	5	0.6	.989

LEAGUE CHAMPIONSHIP SERIES

Year	Team	W	L	PCT	ERA	G	GS	CG	IP	H	BB	SO	ShO	W	L	SV	AB	H	HR	BA	PO	A	E	DP	TC/G	FA
1984	SD N	0	1	.000	9.82	1	1	0	3.2	7	2	1	0	0	0	0	1	1	0	1.000	0	1	0	0	1.0	1.000
1987	DET A	0	0	–	0.00	1	0	0	.1	0	0	0	0	0	0	0	0	0	0	–	0	0	0	0	0.0	–
2 yrs.		0	1	.000	9.00	2	1	0	4	7	2	1	0	0	0	0	1	1	0	1.000	0	1	0	0	0.5	1.000

WORLD SERIES

Year	Team	W	L	PCT	ERA	G	GS	CG	IP	H	BB	SO	ShO	W	L	SV	AB	H	HR	BA	PO	A	E	DP	TC/G	FA
1984	SD N	0	1	.000	10.13	2	2	0	5.1	12	3	2	0	0	0	0	0	0	0	–	0	2	0	0	1.0	1.000

Sloppy Thurston

THURSTON, HOLLIS JOHN
B. June 2, 1899, Fremont, Neb. D. Sept. 14, 1973, Los Angeles, Calif.
BR TR 5'11" 165 lbs.

Year	Team	W	L	PCT	ERA	G	GS	CG	IP	H	BB	SO	ShO	W	L	SV	AB	H	HR	BA	PO	A	E	DP	TC/G	FA
1923	2 teams	STL A		(2G 0–0)		CHI A		(44G 7–8)																		
"	total	7	8	.467	3.13	46	13	8	195.2	231	38	55	0	4	3	4	79	25	0	.316	6	50	2	2	1.3	.966
1924	CHI A	20	14	.588	3.80	38	36	28	291	330	60	37	1	0	1	1	122	31	1	.254	15	75	3	1	2.4	.968
1925		10	14	.417	6.17	36	25	9	175	250	47	35	0	1	4	1	84	24	0	.286	15	55	2	4	2.0	.972
1926		6	8	.429	5.02	31	13	6	134.1	164	36	35	1	2	3	3	61	19	0	.311	4	30	1	1	1.1	.971
1927	WAS A	13	13	.500	4.47	29	28	13	205.1	254	60	38	2	0	1	0	92	29	2	.315	12	46	4	4	2.1	.935
1930	BKN N	6	4	.600	3.40	24	11	5	106	110	17	26	2	1	0	0	50	10	1	.200	3	30	0	0	1.4	1.000
1931		9	9	.500	3.97	24	17	11	143	175	39	23	1	0	3	0	60	13	1	.217	3	30	2	3	1.5	.943
1932		12	8	.600	4.06	28	20	10	153	174	38	35	1	1	1	0	56	17	0	.304	10	34	0	2	1.6	1.000
1933		6	8	.429	4.52	32	15	5	131.1	171	34	22	0	3	1	3	44	7	0	.159	3	40	1	0	1.4	.977
9 yrs.		89	86	.509	4.26	288	178	95	1534.2	1859	369	306	8	13	17	13	*				71	390	15	17	1.7	.968

Luis Tiant

TIANT, LUIS CLEMENTE
Born Luis Clemente Tiant y Vega.
B. Nov. 23, 1940, Marianao, Cuba
BR TR 6' 180 lbs.

Year	Team	W	L	PCT	ERA	G	GS	CG	IP	H	BB	SO	ShO	W	L	SV	AB	H	HR	BA	PO	A	E	DP	TC/G	FA
1964	CLE A	10	4	.714	2.83	19	16	9	127	94	47	105	3	1	1	1	45	5	1	.111	3	21	1	2	1.3	.960
1965		11	11	.500	3.53	41	30	10	196.1	166	66	152	1	2	0	1	68	6	1	.088	17	27	1	2	1.1	.978
1966		12	11	.522	2.79	46	16	7	155	121	50	145	5	4	6	8	36	4	0	.111	9	20	4	0	0.7	.879
1967		12	9	.571	2.74	33	29	9	213.2	177	67	219	1	0	0	2	71	18	1	.254	13	17	4	3	1.0	.882
1968		21	9	.700	**1.60**	34	32	19	258.1	152	73	264	**9**	0	1	0	87	7	0	.080	15	19	1	2	1.0	.971
1969		9	**20**	.310	3.71	38	37	9	249.2	229	**129**	156	1	0	0	0	81	19	2	.235	22	31	4	1	1.5	.930
1970	MIN A	7	3	.700	3.39	18	17	2	93	84	41	50	1	0	0	0	32	13	0	.406	3	14	1	2	1.0	.944
1971	BOS A	1	7	.125	4.88	21	10	1	72	73	32	59	0	1	1	0	19	3	0	.158	5	9	1	0	0.7	.933
1972		15	6	.714	**1.91**	43	19	12	179	128	65	123	6	3	1	3	56	6	0	.107	7	24	1	1	0.7	.969
1973		20	13	.606	3.34	35	35	23	272	217	78	206	0	0	0	0	0	0	0	–	17	31	1	4	1.4	.980
1974		22	13	.629	2.92	38	38	25	311	281	82	176	**7**	0	0	0	0	0	0	–	22	31	4	1	1.5	.930
1975		18	14	.563	4.02	35	35	18	260	262	72	142	2	0	0	0	0	0	0	.000	16	22	4	2	1.2	.905
1976		21	12	.636	3.06	38	38	19	279	274	64	131	3	0	0	0	1	0	0	.000	12	34	4	4	1.3	.920
1977		12	8	.600	4.53	32	32	3	188.2	210	51	124	3	0	0	0	0	0	0	–	16	16	0	0	1.0	1.000
1978		13	8	.619	3.31	32	31	12	212.1	185	57	114	5	1	0	0	0	0	0	–	14	12	0	0	1.1	1.000
1979	NY A	13	8	.619	3.90	30	30	5	196	190	53	104	0	0	0	0	0	0	0	–	13	27	2	4	1.4	.952
1980		8	9	.471	4.90	25	25	3	136	139	50	84	0	0	0	0	0	0	0	–	13	21	2	3	1.4	.944
1981	PIT N	2	5	.286	3.95	9	9	1	57	54	19	32	0	0	0	0	16	3	0	.188	3	5	0	0	0.9	1.000
1982	CAL A	2	2	.500	5.76	6	5	0	29.2	39	8	30	0	0	0	0	0	0	0	–	1	0	0	0	0.2	1.000
19 yrs.		229	172	.571	3.30	573	484	187	3485.2	3075	1104	2416	49	10	11	15	513	84	5	.164	221	389	35	31	1.1	.946

LEAGUE CHAMPIONSHIP SERIES

Year	Team	W	L	PCT	ERA	G	GS	CG	IP	H	BB	SO	ShO	W	L	SV	AB	H	HR	BA	PO	A	E	DP	TC/G	FA
1970	MIN A	0	0	–	13.50	1	1	0	.2	1	0	0	0	0	0	0	0	0	0	–	0	0	0	0	0.0	–
1975	BOS A	1	0	1.000	0.00	1	1	1	9	3	3	8	1	0	0	0	0	0	0	–	0	1	0	0	1.0	1.000
2 yrs.		1	0	1.000	0.93	2	2	1	9.2	4	3	8	1	0	0	0	0	0	0	–	0	1	0	0	0.5	1.000

WORLD SERIES

Year	Team	W	L	PCT	ERA	G	GS	CG	IP	H	BB	SO	ShO	W	L	SV	AB	H	HR	BA	PO	A	E	DP	TC/G	FA
1975	BOS A	2	0	1.000	3.60	3	3	2	25	25	8	12	1	0	0	0	8	2	0	.250	0	4	0	0	1.3	1.000
				1st																						

Jay Tibbs

TIBBS, JAY LINDSEY
B. Jan. 4, 1962, Birmingham, Ala.
BR TR 6'3" 185 lbs.

Year	Team	W	L	PCT	ERA	G	GS	CG	IP	H	BB	SO	ShO	W	L	SV	AB	H	HR	BA	PO	A	E	DP	TC/G	FA
1984	CIN N	6	2	.750	2.86	14	14	3	100.2	87	33	40	1	0	0	0	36	5	0	.139	6	10	1	1	1.2	.941
1985		10	16	.385	3.92	35	34	5	218	216	63	98	2	0	1	0	65	6	0	.092	15	40	3	4	1.7	.948
1986	MON N	7	9	.438	3.97	35	31	3	190.1	181	70	117	2	0	0	0	54	7	0	.130	14	24	0	2	1.1	1.000
1987		4	5	.444	4.99	19	12	0	83	95	34	54	0	0	0	0	25	3	0	.120	7	8	0	1	0.8	1.000

Year	Team		W	L	PCT	ERA	G	GS	CG	IP	H	BB	SO	ShO	W	L	SV	AB	H	HR	BA	PO	A	E	DP	TC/G	FA
															Relief Pitching			**Batting**									

Jay Tibbs *continued*

Year	Team		W	L	PCT	ERA	G	GS	CG	IP	H	BB	SO	ShO	W	L	SV	AB	H	HR	BA	PO	A	E	DP	TC/G	FA
1988	BAL	A	4	15	.211	5.39	30	24	1	158.2	184	63	82	0	0	1	0	0	0	0	–	17	18	0	0	1.2	1.000
1989			5	0	1.000	2.82	10	8	1	54.1	62	20	30	0	0	0	0	0	0	0	–	5	5	0	0	1.0	1.000
6 yrs.			36	47	.434	4.13	143	123	13	805	825	303	421	5	0	2	0	180	21	0	.117	64	105	4	8	1.2	.977

Dick Tidrow

TIDROW, RICHARD WILLIAM (Dirt)
B. May 14, 1947, San Francisco, Calif. BR TR 6'4" 210 lbs.

Year	Team		W	L	PCT	ERA	G	GS	CG	IP	H	BB	SO	ShO	W	L	SV	AB	H	HR	BA	PO	A	E	DP	TC/G	FA
1972	CLE	A	14	15	.483	2.77	39	34	10	237	200	70	123	3	1	0	0	70	7	0	.100	10	23	1	0	0.9	.971
1973			14	16	.467	4.42	42	40	13	274.2	289	95	138	2	0	0	0	0	0	0	–	17	34	2	3	1.3	.962
1974	2 teams		CLE A	(4G 1–3)		NY A	(33G 11–9)																					
"	total		12	12	.500	4.16	37	29	5	210	226	66	108	0	2	0	0	0	0	0	–	8	27	3	2	1.0	.921
1975	NY	A	6	3	.667	3.13	37	0	0	69	65	31	38	0	6	3	5	0	0	0	–	3	6	0	1	0.2	1.000
1976			4	5	.444	2.63	47	2	0	92.1	80	24	65	0	3	5	10	0	0	0	–	2	9	1	0	0.3	.917
1977			11	4	.733	3.16	49	7	0	151	143	41	83	0	6	4	5	0	0	0	–	13	18	2	2	0.7	.939
1978			7	11	.389	3.84	31	25	4	185.1	191	53	73	0	0	1	0	0	0	0	–	12	18	0	0	1.0	1.000
1979	2 teams		NY A	(14G 2–1)		CHI N	(63G 11–5)																					
"	total		13	6	.684	3.64	77	0	0	126	124	46	75	0	13	6	6	10	2	0	.200	9	28	0	2	0.5	1.000
1980	CHI	N	6	5	.545	2.79	84	0	0	116	97	53	97	0	6	5	6	4	0	0	.000	7	13	1	0	0.3	.952
1981			3	10	.231	5.04	51	0	0	75	73	30	39	0	3	10	9	5	0	0	.000	4	10	1	1	0.2	.909
1982			8	3	.727	3.39	65	0	0	103.2	106	29	62	0	8	3	6	6	0	0	.000	6	7	0	0	0.2	1.000
1983	CHI	A	2	4	.333	4.22	50	1	0	91.2	86	34	66	0	2	4	7	0	0	0	–	7	16	1	0	0.5	.958
1984	NY	N	0	0	–	9.19	11	0	0	15.2	25	7	8	0	0	0	0	0	0	0	–	3	3	0	0	0.5	1.000
13 yrs.			100	94	.515	3.68	620	138	32	1747.1	1705	579	975	5	50	41	55	95	9	0	.095	97	212	12	10	0.5	.963

LEAGUE CHAMPIONSHIP SERIES

Year	Team		W	L	PCT	ERA	G	GS	CG	IP	H	BB	SO	ShO	W	L	SV	AB	H	HR	BA	PO	A	E	DP	TC/G	FA
1976	NY	A	1	0	1.000	3.68	3	0	0	7.1	6	4	0	0	1	0	0	0	0	0	–	1	0	0	0	0.3	1.000
1977			0	0	–	3.86	2	0	0	7	6	3	3	0	0	0	0	0	0	0	–	1	2	0	0	1.5	1.000
1978			0	0	–	4.76	1	0	0	5.2	8	2	1	0	0	0	0	0	0	0	–	0	2	0	0	2.0	1.000
1983	CHI	A	0	0	–	3.00	1	0	0	3	1	3	3	0	0	0	0	0	0	0	–	0	0	0	0	0.0	–
4 yrs.			1	0	1.000	3.91	7	0	0	23	21	12	7	0	1	0	0	0	0	0	–	2	4	0	0	0.9	1.000

WORLD SERIES

Year	Team		W	L	PCT	ERA	G	GS	CG	IP	H	BB	SO	ShO	W	L	SV	AB	H	HR	BA	PO	A	E	DP	TC/G	FA
1976	NY	A	0	0	–	7.71	2	0	0	2.1	5	1	1	0	0	0	0	0	0	0	–	0	0	0	0	0.0	–
1977			0	0	–	4.91	2	0	0	3.2	5	0	1	0	0	0	0	1	0	0	.000	0	1	0	0	0.5	1.000
1978			0	0	–	1.93	2	0	0	4.2	4	0	5	0	0	0	0	0	0	0	–	0	0	0	0	0.0	–
3 yrs.			0	0	–	4.22	6	0	0	10.2	14	1	7	0	0	0	0	1	0	0	.000	0	1	0	0	0.2	1.000

Bobby Tiefenauer

TIEFENAUER, BOBBY GENE
B. Oct. 10, 1929, Desloge, Mo. BR TR 6'2" 185 lbs.

Year	Team		W	L	PCT	ERA	G	GS	CG	IP	H	BB	SO	ShO	W	L	SV	AB	H	HR	BA	PO	A	E	DP	TC/G	FA
1952	STL	N	0	0	–	7.88	6	0	0	8	12	7	3	0	0	0	0	1	0	0	.000	0	3	0	0	0.5	1.000
1955			1	4	.200	4.41	18	0	0	32.2	31	10	16	0	1	4	0	5	0	0	.000	3	7	0	0	0.6	1.000
1960	CLE	A	0	1	.000	2.00	6	0	0	9	8	3	2	0	0	1	0	1	0	0	.000	0	1	0	1	0.2	1.000
1961	STL	N	0	0	–	6.23	3	0	0	4.1	9	4	3	0	0	0	0	0	0	0	–	0	0	0	0	0.0	–
1962	HOU	N	2	4	.333	4.34	43	0	0	85	91	21	60	0	2	4	1	9	1	0	.111	6	6	0	0	0.3	.857
1963	MIL	N	1	1	.500	1.21	12	0	0	29.2	20	4	22	0	1	1	2	5	0	0	.000	4	8	0	0	1.0	1.000
1964			4	6	.400	3.21	46	0	0	73	61	15	48	0	4	6	13	14	0	0	.000	4	9	1	0	0.3	.929
1965	3 teams		MIL N	(6G 0–1)		NY A	(10G 1–1)		CLE A	(15G 0–5)																		
"	total		1	7	.125	4.71	31	0	0	49.2	51	18	35	0	1	7	6	3	0	0	.000	5	6	0	0	0.4	1.000
1967	CLE	A	0	1	.000	0.79	5	0	0	11.1	9	3	6	0	0	1	0	0	0	0	–	0	1	0	0	0.2	–
1968	CHI	N	0	1	.000	6.08	9	0	0	13.1	20	2	9	0	0	1	1	1	0	0	.000	1	0	0	0	0.2	1.000
10 yrs.			9	25	.265	3.84	179	0	0	316	312	87	204	0	9	25	23	39	1	0	.026	23	41	4	1	0.4	.941

Verle Tiefenthaler

TIEFENTHALER, VERLE MATTHEW
B. July 11, 1937, Breda, Iowa BL TR 6'1" 190 lbs.

Year	Team		W	L	PCT	ERA	G	GS	CG	IP	H	BB	SO	ShO	W	L	SV	AB	H	HR	BA	PO	A	E	DP	TC/G	FA
1962	CHI	A	0	0	–	9.82	3	0	0	3.2	6	7	1	0	0	0	0	0	0	0	–	0	0	0	0	0.0	–

Eddie Tiemeyer

TIEMEYER, EDWARD CARL
B. May 9, 1885, Cincinnati, Ohio D. Sept. 27, 1946, Cincinnati, Ohio BR TR 5'11½" 185 lbs.

Year	Team		W	L	PCT	ERA	G	GS	CG	IP	H	BB	SO	ShO	W	L	SV	AB	H	HR	BA	PO	A	E	DP	TC/G	FA
1906	CIN	N	0	0	–	0.00	1	0	0	1	1	1	1	0	0	0	0	*				0	0	0	0	0.0	–

Mike Tiernan

TIERNAN, MICHAEL JOSEPH (Silent Mike)
B. Jan. 21, 1867, Trenton, N. J. D. Nov. 9, 1918, New York, N. Y. BL TL 5'11" 165 lbs.

Year	Team		W	L	PCT	ERA	G	GS	CG	IP	H	BB	SO	ShO	W	L	SV	AB	H	HR	BA	PO	A	E	DP	TC/G	FA
1887	NY	N	1	2	.333	8.69	5	0	0	19.2	33	7	3	0	1	2	1	*				0	3	0	0	0.6	1.000

Les Tietje

TIETJE, LESLIE WILLIAM (Toots)
B. Sept. 11, 1911, Summer, Iowa BR TR 6'½" 178 lbs.

Year	Team		W	L	PCT	ERA	G	GS	CG	IP	H	BB	SO	ShO	W	L	SV	AB	H	HR	BA	PO	A	E	DP	TC/G	FA
1933	CHI	A	2	0	1.000	2.42	3	3	1	22.1	16	15	9	0	0	0	0	8	1	0	.125	1	5	0	1	2.0	1.000
1934			5	14	.263	4.81	34	22	6	176	174	96	81	1	1	0	0	59	1	0	.017	3	43	0	1	1.4	1.000
1935			9	15	.375	4.30	30	21	9	169.2	184	81	64	1	1	5	0	61	12	0	.197	4	26	1	0	1.0	.968
1936	2 teams		CHI A	(2G 0–0)		STL A	(14G 3–5)																					
"	total		3	5	.375	7.52	16	7	2	52.2	71	35	19	0	1	0	0	15	1	0	.067	1	14	1	0	1.0	.938
1937	STL	A	1	2	.333	4.20	5	4	2	30	32	17	5	0	0	0	0	10	0	0	.000	0	3	0	1	0.6	1.000
1938			2	5	.286	7.55	17	8	2	62	83	38	15	1	0	1	0	18	2	0	.111	5	10	0	0	0.9	1.000
6 yrs.			22	41	.349	5.11	105	65	22	512.2	560	282	193	3	3	6	0	171	17	0	.099	14	101	2	3	1.1	.983

Ray Tift

TIFT, RAYMOND FRANK
B. June 21, 1884, Fitchburg, Mass. D. Mar. 29, 1945, Verona, N. J. TR

Year	Team		W	L	PCT	ERA	G	GS	CG	IP	H	BB	SO	ShO	W	L	SV	AB	H	HR	BA	PO	A	E	DP	TC/G	FA
1907	NY	A	0	0	–	4.74	4	1	0	19	33	4	6	0	0	0	0	5	0	0	.000	0	4	0	0	1.0	1.000

Johnny Tillman

TILLMAN, JOHN LAWRENCE
B. Oct. 6, 1893, Bridgeport, Conn. D. Apr. 7, 1964, Harrisburg, Pa. BB TR 5'11" 170 lbs.

Year	Team		W	L	PCT	ERA	G	GS	CG	IP	H	BB	SO	ShO	W	L	SV	AB	H	HR	BA	PO	A	E	DP	TC/G	FA
1915	STL	A	1	0	1.000	0.90	2	1	0	10	6	4	6	0	0	0	0	3	0	0	.000	0	3	0	0	1.5	1.000

Year	Team	W	L	PCT	ERA	G	GS	CG	IP	H	BB	SO	ShO	Relief Pitching W	L	SV	Batting AB	H	HR	BA	PO	A	E	DP	TC/G	FA

Thad Tillotson

TILLOTSON, THADDEUS ASA
B. Dec. 20, 1940, Merced, Calif.
BR TR 6'2½" 195 lbs.

Year	Team	W	L	PCT	ERA	G	GS	CG	IP	H	BB	SO	ShO	W	L	SV	AB	H	HR	BA	PO	A	E	DP	TC/G	FA
1967	NY A	3	9	.250	4.03	43	5	1	98.1	99	39	62	0	1	6	2	16	1	0	.063	12	14	0	0	0.6	1.000
1968		1	0	1.000	4.35	7	0	0	10.1	11	7	1	0	1	0	0	1	0	0	.000	0	4	0	0	0.6	1.000
2 yrs.		4	9	.308	4.06	50	5	1	108.2	110	46	63	0	2	6	2	17	1	0	.059	12	18	0	0	0.6	1.000

Gary Timberlake

TIMBERLAKE, GARY DALE
B. Aug. 9, 1948, Laconia, Ind.
BR TL 6'2" 205 lbs.

Year	Team	W	L	PCT	ERA	G	GS	CG	IP	H	BB	SO	ShO	W	L	SV	AB	H	HR	BA	PO	A	E	DP	TC/G	FA
1969	SEA A	0	0	–	7.50	2	2	0	6	7	9	4	0	0	0	0	1	0	0	.000	0	0	0	0	0.0	–

Tom Timmerman

TIMMERMAN, THOMAS HENRY
B. May 12, 1940, Breese, Ill.
BR TR 6'4" 215 lbs.

Year	Team	W	L	PCT	ERA	G	GS	CG	IP	H	BB	SO	ShO	W	L	SV	AB	H	HR	BA	PO	A	E	DP	TC/G	FA
1969	DET A	4	3	.571	2.75	31	1	1	55.2	50	26	42	0	3	3	1	9	1	0	.111	2	5	0	0	0.2	1.000
1970		6	7	.462	4.13	61	0	0	85	90	34	49	0	6	7	27	16	0	0	.000	7	10	1	0	0.3	.944
1971		7	6	.538	3.86	52	2	0	84	82	37	51	0	6	5	4	19	1	0	.053	4	14	0	2	0.3	1.000
1972		8	10	.444	2.89	34	25	3	149.2	121	41	88	2	0	0	0	44	6	0	.136	7	16	3	2	0.8	.885
1973	2 teams	DET A	(17G 1–1)		CLE A		(29G 8–7)																			
"	total	9	8	.529	4.63	46	16	4	163.1	156	65	83	0	2	1	3	0	0	0	–	10	22	3	2	0.8	.914
1974	CLE A	1	1	.500	5.40	4	0	0	10	9	5	2	0	1	1	0	0	0	0	–	0	5	0	0	1.3	1.000
6 yrs.		35	35	.500	3.78	228	44	8	547.2	508	208	315	2	18	17	35	88	8	0	.091	30	72	7	6	0.5	.936

Ben Tincup

TINCUP, AUSTIN BEN
B. Dec. 14, 1890, Adair, Okla. D. July 5, 1980, Claremore, Okla.
BL TR 6'1" 180 lbs.

Year	Team	W	L	PCT	ERA	G	GS	CG	IP	H	BB	SO	ShO	W	L	SV	AB	H	HR	BA	PO	A	E	DP	TC/G	FA
1914	PHI N	7	10	.412	2.61	28	17	9	155	165	62	108	3	2	1	1	53	9	0	.170	10	40	4	1	1.9	.926
1915		0	0	–	2.03	10	0	0	31	26	9	10	0	0	0	0	9	0	0	.000	0	11	0	0	1.1	1.000
1916		0	0	–	0.00	0	0	0	0	0	0	0	0	0	0	0	1	0	0	.000	0	0	0	0	0.0	–
1918		0	1	.000	7.56	8	1	0	16.2	24	6	6	0	0	0	0	8	1	0	.125	3	9	3	1	1.9	.800
1928	CHI N	0	0	–	7.00	2	0	0	9	14	1	3	0	0	0	0	3	0	0	.000	1	3	0	0	2.0	1.000
5 yrs.		7	11	.389	3.10	48	18	9	211.2	229	78	127	3	2	1	1	74	10	0	.135	14	63	7	2	1.8	.917

Bud Tinning

TINNING, LYLE FORREST
B. Mar. 12, 1906, Pilger, Neb.
D. Jan. 17, 1961, Evansville, Ind.
BB TR 6' 198 lbs.
BR 1934-35

Year	Team	W	L	PCT	ERA	G	GS	CG	IP	H	BB	SO	ShO	W	L	SV	AB	H	HR	BA	PO	A	E	DP	TC/G	FA
1932	CHI N	5	3	.625	2.80	24	7	2	93.1	93	24	30	0	4	0	0	23	2	0	.087	9	20	5	0	1.4	.853
1933		13	6	.684	3.18	32	21	10	175.1	169	60	59	3	1	0	1	67	14	0	.209	3	28	2	3	1.0	.939
1934		4	6	.400	3.34	39	7	1	129.1	134	46	44	1	3	1	3	39	7	0	.179	4	23	2	0	0.7	.931
1935	STL N	0	0	–	5.87	4	0	0	7.2	9	5	2	0	0	0	0	1	0	0	.000	2	1	0	0	0.8	1.000
4 yrs.		22	15	.595	3.19	99	35	13	405.2	405	135	135	4	8	1	4	130	23	0	.177	18	72	9	3	1.0	.909

WORLD SERIES

Year	Team	W	L	PCT	ERA	G	GS	CG	IP	H	BB	SO	ShO	W	L	SV	AB	H	HR	BA	PO	A	E	DP	TC/G	FA
1932	CHI N	0	0	–	0.00	2	0	0	2.1	0	0	3	0	0	0	0	0	0	0	–	0	1	0	0	0.5	1.000

Dan Tipple

TIPPLE, DANIEL E. (Rusty, Big Dan)
B. Feb. 13, 1890, Rockford, Ill. D. Mar. 26, 1960, Omaha, Neb.
BR TR 6' 176 lbs.

Year	Team	W	L	PCT	ERA	G	GS	CG	IP	H	BB	SO	ShO	W	L	SV	AB	H	HR	BA	PO	A	E	DP	TC/G	FA
1915	NY A	1	1	.500	2.84	3	2	1	19	14	11	14	0	0	0	0	6	0	0	.000	1	1	1	0	1.0	.667

Jack Tising

TISING, JOHNNIE JOSEPH
B. Oct. 9, 1903, High Point, Mo. D. Sept. 5, 1967, Leadville, Colo.
BL TR 6'2" 180 lbs.

Year	Team	W	L	PCT	ERA	G	GS	CG	IP	H	BB	SO	ShO	W	L	SV	AB	H	HR	BA	PO	A	E	DP	TC/G	FA
1936	PIT N	1	3	.250	4.21	10	6	1	47	52	24	27	0	0	0	0	11	3	0	.273	2	10	4	0	1.6	.750

Cannonball Titcomb

TITCOMB, LEDELL
B. Aug. 21, 1866, W. Baldwin, Me. D. June 8, 1950, Kingston, N. H.
BL TL 5'6" 157 lbs.

Year	Team	W	L	PCT	ERA	G	GS	CG	IP	H	BB	SO	ShO	W	L	SV	AB	H	HR	BA	PO	A	E	DP	TC/G	FA
1886	PHI N	0	5	.000	3.73	5	5	5	41	43	24	24	0	0	0	0	16	1	0	.063	0	13	2	0	3.0	.867
1887	2 teams	PHI AA	(3G 1–2)		NY N		(9G 4–3)																			
"	total	5	5	.500	4.59	12	12	12	96	99	56	50	0	0	0	0	39	2	0	.051	0	9	1	1	0.8	.900
1888	NY N	14	8	.636	2.24	23	23	22	197	149	46	129	4	0	0	0	82	10	0	.122	1	24	8	0	1.4	.758
1889		1	2	.333	6.58	3	3	3	26	27	16	7	0	0	0	0	12	1	0	.083	1	3	0	0	1.3	1.000
1890	ROC AA	10	9	.526	3.74	20	19	19	168.2	168	97	73	1	1	0	0	75	8	0	.107	5	22	6	0	1.7	.818
5 yrs.		30	29	.508	3.47	63	62	61	528.2	486	239	283	5	1	0	0	224	22	0	.098	7	71	17	1	1.5	.821

Dave Tobik

TOBIK, DAVID VANCE
B. Mar. 2, 1953, Euclid, Ohio
BR TR 6'1" 190 lbs.

Year	Team	W	L	PCT	ERA	G	GS	CG	IP	H	BB	SO	ShO	W	L	SV	AB	H	HR	BA	PO	A	E	DP	TC/G	FA
1978	DET A	0	0	–	3.75	5	0	0	12	12	3	11	0	0	0	0	0	0	0	–	0	1	0	0	0.2	1.000
1979		3	5	.375	4.30	37	0	0	69	59	25	48	0	3	5	3	0	0	0	–	5	5	0	1	0.3	1.000
1980		1	0	1.000	3.98	17	1	0	61	61	21	34	0	0	0	0	0	0	0	–	4	7	0	1	0.6	1.000
1981		2	2	.500	2.70	27	0	0	60	47	33	32	0	2	2	1	0	0	0	–	2	3	0	0	0.2	1.000
1982		4	9	.308	3.56	51	1	0	98.2	86	38	63	0	4	8	9	0	0	0	–	8	8	1	1	0.3	.941
1983	TEX A	2	1	.667	3.68	27	0	0	44	36	13	30	0	2	1	9	0	0	0	–	6	4	0	1	0.4	1.000
1984		1	6	.143	3.61	24	0	0	42.1	44	17	30	0	1	6	5	0	0	0	–	3	7	0	1	0.4	1.000
1985	SEA A	1	0	1.000	6.00	8	0	0	9	10	3	8	0	1	0	1	0	0	0	–	1	0	0	0	0.1	1.000
8 yrs.		14	23	.378	3.70	196	2	0	396	355	153	256	0	13	23	28	0	0	0	–	29	35	1	4	0.3	.985

Jim Tobin

TOBIN, JAMES ANTHONY (Abba Dabba)
Brother of Johnny Tobin.
B. Dec. 27, 1912, Oakland, Calif. D. May 19, 1969, Oakland, Calif.
BR TR 6' 185 lbs.

Year	Team	W	L	PCT	ERA	G	GS	CG	IP	H	BB	SO	ShO	W	L	SV	AB	H	HR	BA	PO	A	E	DP	TC/G	FA
1937	PIT N	6	3	.667	3.00	20	8	7	87	74	28	37	0	1	0	1	34	15	0	.441	5	10	1	0	0.8	.938
1938		14	12	.538	3.47	40	33	14	241.1	254	66	70	2	4	1	0	103	25	0	.243	11	41	0	1	1.3	1.000
1939		9	9	.500	4.52	25	19	8	145.1	194	33	43	0	2	1	0	74	18	2	.243	2	26	0	2	1.1	1.000
1940	BOS N	7	3	.700	3.83	15	11	9	96.1	102	24	29	0	1	0	0	43	12	0	.279	6	16	1	1	1.5	.957
1941		12	12	.500	3.10	33	26	20	238	229	60	61	3	0	1	0	103	19	0	.184	15	71	3	4	2.7	.966
1942		12	21	.364	3.97	37	33	28	287.2	283	96	71	1	0	1	0	114	28	6	.246	14	93	6	6	3.1	.947

Year	Team	W	L	PCT	ERA	G	GS	CG	IP	H	BB	SO	ShO	Relief Pitching W	L	SV	Batting AB	H	HR	BA	PO	A	E	DP	TC/G	FA

Jim Tobin *continued*

1943		14	14	.500	2.66	33	30	24	250	241	69	52	1	0	1	0	107	30	2	.280	10	66	6	6	2.5	.927
1944		18	19	.486	3.01	43	36	**28**	299.1	271	97	83	5	0	2	3	116	22	2	.190	13	93	3	4	2.5	.972
1945	2 teams	BOS N	(27G 9–14)		DET A	(14G 4–5)																				
"	total	13	19	.406	3.78	41	31	18	255	281	84	52	0	2	2	1	102	14	5	.137	17	48	0	5	1.6	1.000
9 yrs.		105	112	.484	3.44	287	227	156	1900	1929	557	498	12	10	11	5	*				93	464	20	29	2.0	.965

WORLD SERIES

| 1945 | DET A | 0 | 0 | – | 6.00 | 1 | 0 | 0 | 3 | 4 | 1 | 0 | 0 | 0 | 0 | 0 | 1 | 0 | 0 | .000 | 0 | 1 | 0 | 0 | 1.0 | 1.000 |

Pat Tobin

TOBIN, MARION BROOKS
B. Jan. 28, 1916, Hermitage, Ark. D. Jan. 21, 1975, Shreveport, La. BR TR 6'1" 198 lbs.

| 1941 | PHI A | 0 | 0 | – | 36.00 | 1 | 0 | 0 | 1 | 4 | 2 | 0 | 0 | 0 | 0 | 0 | 0 | 0 | 0 | – | 0 | 1 | 0 | 0 | 1.0 | 1.000 |

Frank Todd

TODD, GEORGE FRANKLIN
Also known as George Franklin Todd.
B. Oct. 18, 1869, Aberdeen, Md. D. Aug. 11, 1919, Havre de Grace, Md. TL

| 1898 | LOU N | 0 | 2 | .000 | 13.91 | 4 | 2 | 0 | 11 | 23 | 8 | 5 | 0 | 0 | 0 | 0 | 5 | 1 | 0 | .200 | 0 | 0 | 1 | 0 | 0.3 | – |

Jackson Todd

TODD, JACKSON A.
B. Sept. 20, 1951, Tulsa, Okla. BR TR 6'2" 180 lbs.

1977	NY N	3	6	.333	4.75	19	10	0	72	78	20	39	0	1	0	0	17	1	0	.059	7	10	1	0	0.9	.944
1979	TOR A	0	1	.000	5.91	12	0	0	32	40	7	14	0	0	0	0	0	0	0	–	6	3	0	0	0.8	1.000
1980		5	2	.714	4.02	12	12	4	85	90	30	44	0	0	0	0	0	0	0	–	7	16	2	3	2.1	.920
1981		2	7	.222	3.95	21	13	3	98	94	31	41	0	0	0	0	0	0	0	–	11	20	1	0	1.5	.969
4 yrs.		10	16	.385	4.39	64	36	7	287	302	88	138	0	1	0	0	17	1	0	.059	31	49	4	3	1.3	.952

Jim Todd

TODD, JAMES RICHARD JR.
B. Sept. 21, 1947, Lancaster, Pa. BL TR 6'2" 190 lbs.

1974	CHI N	4	2	.667	3.89	43	6	0	88	82	41	42	0	3	0	3	16	1	0	.063	8	15	0	1	0.5	1.000
1975	OAK A	8	3	.727	2.29	58	0	0	122	104	33	50	0	8	3	12	0	0	0	–	6	37	2	4	0.8	.956
1976		7	8	.467	3.80	49	0	0	83	87	34	22	0	7	8	4	0	0	0	–	7	22	2	1	0.6	.935
1977	CHI N	1	1	.500	9.00	20	0	0	31	47	19	17	0	1	1	0	1	0	0	.000	4	5	0	1	0.5	1.000
1978	SEA A	3	4	.429	3.88	49	2	0	106.2	113	61	37	0	3	3	3	0	0	0	–	11	17	2	0	0.6	.933
1979	OAK A	2	5	.286	6.56	51	0	0	81	108	51	26	0	2	5	2	0	0	0	–	5	14	0	2	0.4	1.000
6 yrs.		25	23	.521	4.22	270	8	0	511.2	541	239	194	0	24	20	24	17	1	0	.059	41	110	6	9	0.6	.962

LEAGUE CHAMPIONSHIP SERIES

| 1975 | OAK A | 0 | 0 | – | 9.00 | 3 | 0 | 0 | 1 | 3 | 0 | 0 | 0 | 0 | 0 | 0 | 0 | 0 | 0 | – | 0 | 0 | 0 | 0 | 0.0 | – |

Hal Toenes

TOENES, WILLIAM HARREL
B. Oct. 8, 1917, Mobile, Ala. BR TR 5'11½" 175 lbs.

| 1947 | WAS A | 0 | 1 | .000 | 6.75 | 3 | 1 | 0 | 6.2 | 11 | 2 | 5 | 0 | 0 | 0 | 0 | 1 | 0 | 0 | .000 | 0 | 0 | 0 | 0 | 0.0 | – |

Fred Toliver

TOLIVER, FREDDIE LEE
B. Feb. 3, 1961, Natchez, Miss. BR TR 6'1" 170 lbs.

1984	CIN N	0	0	–	0.90	3	1	0	10	7	7	4	0	0	0	0	1	0	0	.000	0	1	0	0	0.3	1.000
1985	PHI N	0	4	.000	4.68	11	3	0	25	27	17	23	0	0	1	1	4	2	0	.500	4	1	0	0	0.5	.800
1986		0	2	.000	3.51	5	5	0	25.2	28	11	20	0	0	0	0	6	0	0	.000	1	4	0	1	1.0	1.000
1987		1	1	.500	5.64	10	4	0	30.1	34	17	25	0	0	0	0	5	0	0	.000	1	6	0	0	0.7	1.000
1988	MIN A	7	6	.538	4.24	21	19	0	114.2	116	52	69	0	0	0	0	0	0	0	–	1	19	2	2	1.0	.909
1989	2 teams	MIN A	(7G 1–3)		SD N	(9G 0–0)																				
"	total	1	3	.250	7.53	16	5	0	43	56	24	25	0	1	0	0	–				4	12	0	0	1.0	1.000
6 yrs.		9	16	.360	4.81	66	37	0	248.2	268	128	166	0	1	1	1	16	2	0	.125	7	46	3	3	0.8	.946

Dick Tomanek

TOMANEK, RICHARD CARL (Bones)
B. Jan. 6, 1931, Avon Lake, Ohio BL TL 6'1" 175 lbs.

1953	CLE A	1	0	1.000	2.00	1	1	1	9	6	6	6	0	0	0	0	5	0	0	.000	0	0	1	0	1.0	–
1954		0	0	–	5.40	1	0	0	1.2	1	1	0	0	0	0	0	0	0	0	–	0	1	0	0	1.0	1.000
1957		2	1	.667	5.68	34	2	0	69.2	67	37	55	0	2	1	0	13	3	0	.231	5	11	0	2	0.5	1.000
1958	2 teams	CLE A	(18G 2–3)		KC A	(36G 5–5)																				
"	total	7	8	.467	4.50	54	8	3	130	130	56	92	0	6	5	5	30	5	1	.167	5	20	1	3	0.5	.962
1959	KC A	0	1	.000	6.53	16	0	0	20.2	27	12	13	0	0	1	2	2	1	0	.500	0	6	0	0	0.4	1.000
5 yrs.		10	10	.500	4.95	106	11	4	231	231	112	166	0	8	7	7	50	9	1	.180	10	38	2	5	0.5	.960

Andy Tomasic

TOMASIC, ANDREW JOHN
B. Dec. 10, 1919, Hokendauqua, Pa. BR TR 6' 175 lbs.

| 1949 | NY N | 0 | 1 | .000 | 18.00 | 2 | 0 | 0 | 5 | 9 | 5 | 2 | 0 | 0 | 1 | 0 | 1 | 0 | 0 | .000 | 0 | 0 | 0 | 0 | 0.0 | – |

Dave Tomlin

TOMLIN, DAVID ALLEN
B. June 22, 1949, Maysville, Ky. BL TL 6'2" 180 lbs.

1972	CIN N	0	0	–	9.00	3	0	0	4	7	1	2	0	0	0	0	0	0	0	–	0	1	0	0	0.3	1.000
1973		1	2	.333	4.88	16	0	0	27.2	24	15	20	0	1	2	1	3	0	0	.000	2	4	0	0	0.4	1.000
1974	SD N	2	0	1.000	4.34	47	0	0	58	59	30	29	0	2	0	2	4	0	0	.000	5	11	0	1	0.3	1.000
1975		4	2	.667	3.25	67	0	0	83	87	31	48	0	4	2	1	5	1	0	.200	7	27	3	3	0.6	.919
1976		0	1	.000	2.84	49	0	0	73	62	20	43	0	0	1	0	8	0	0	.000	8	21	2	1	0.6	.935
1977		4	4	.500	3.00	76	0	0	102	98	32	55	0	4	4	3	7	2	0	.286	7	21	0	2	0.4	1.000
1978	CIN N	9	1	.900	5.81	57	0	0	62	88	30	32	0	9	1	4	5	1	0	.200	5	13	3	0	0.4	.857
1979		2	2	.500	2.64	53	0	0	58	59	18	30	0	2	2	1	2	1	0	.500	4	10	3	1	0.3	.824
1980		3	0	1.000	5.54	27	0	0	26	38	11	6	0	3	0	0	1	0	0	–	1	7	0	0	0.3	1.000
1982	MON N	0	0	–	4.50	1	0	0	2	1	1	2	0	0	0	0	0	0	0	–	0	0	0	0	0.0	–

Year	Team		W	L	PCT	ERA	G	GS	CG	IP	H	BB	SO	ShO	Relief Pitching W	L	SV	Batting AB	H	HR	BA	PO	A	E	DP	TC/G	FA

Dave Tomlin *continued*

Year	Team		W	L	PCT	ERA	G	GS	CG	IP	H	BB	SO	ShO	W	L	SV	AB	H	HR	BA	PO	A	E	DP	TC/G	FA
1983	PIT	N	0	0	–	6.75	5	0	0	4	6	1	5	0	0	0	0	0	0	0	–	0	0	0	0	0.0	–
1985			0	0	–	0.00	1	0	0	1	1	1	0	0	0	0	0	0	0	0	–	0	0	0	0	0.0	–
1986	MON	N	0	0	–	5.23	7	0	0	10.1	13	7	6	0	0	0	0	0	0	0	–	0	4	0	0	0.6	1.000
13 yrs.			25	12	.676	3.82	409	1	0	511	543	198	278	0	25	11	12	34	5	0	.147	39	119	11	8	0.4	.935

LEAGUE CHAMPIONSHIP SERIES

Year	Team		W	L	PCT	ERA	G	GS	CG	IP	H	BB	SO	ShO	W	L	SV	AB	H	HR	BA	PO	A	E	DP	TC/G	FA
1973	CIN	N	0	0	–	16.20	1	0	0	1.2	5	1	1	0	0	0	0	0	0	0	–	0	0	0	0	0.0	–
1979			0	0	–	0.00	3	0	0	3	3	2	3	0	0	0	0	0	0	0	–	1	1	0	0	0.7	1.000
2 yrs.			0	0	–	5.79	4	0	0	4.2	8	3	4	0	0	0	0	0	0	0	–	1	1	0	0	0.5	1.000

Chuck Tompkins

TOMPKINS, CHARLES HERBERT
B. Sept. 1, 1889, Prescott, Ark. D. Sept. 20, 1975, Prescott, Ark.　　BR TR 6'　185 lbs.

Year	Team		W	L	PCT	ERA	G	GS	CG	IP	H	BB	SO	ShO	W	L	SV	AB	H	HR	BA	PO	A	E	DP	TC/G	FA
1912	CIN	N	0	0	–	0.00	1	0	0	3	5	0	1	0	0	0	0	1	1	0	1.000	0	1	1	0	2.0	.500

Ron Tompkins

TOMPKINS, RONALD EVERETT (Stretch)
B. Nov. 27, 1944, San Diego, Calif.　　BR TR 6'4"　198 lbs.

Year	Team		W	L	PCT	ERA	G	GS	CG	IP	H	BB	SO	ShO	W	L	SV	AB	H	HR	BA	PO	A	E	DP	TC/G	FA
1965	KC	A	0	0	–	3.48	5	1	0	10.1	9	3	4	0	0	0	0	1	0	0	.000	1	2	0	0	0.6	1.000
1971	CHI	N	0	2	.000	4.05	35	0	0	40	31	21	20	0	0	2	3	0	0	0	–	2	12	0	0	0.4	1.000
2 yrs.			0	2	.000	3.93	40	1	0	50.1	40	24	24	0	0	2	3	1	0	0	.000	3	14	0	0	0.4	1.000

Tommy Toms

TOMS, THOMAS HOWARD
B. Oct. 15, 1951, Charlottesville, Va.　　BR TR 6'4"　195 lbs.

Year	Team		W	L	PCT	ERA	G	GS	CG	IP	H	BB	SO	ShO	W	L	SV	AB	H	HR	BA	PO	A	E	DP	TC/G	FA
1975	SF	N	0	1	.000	6.30	7	0	0	10	13	6	6	0	0	1	0	0	0	0	–	2	0	0	0	0.3	1.000
1976			0	1	.000	6.23	7	0	0	8.2	13	1	4	0	0	1	1	0	0	0	–	1	1	0	0	0.3	1.000
1977			0	1	.000	2.25	4	0	0	4	7	2	2	0	0	1	0	0	0	0	–	0	0	0	0	0.0	–
3 yrs.			0	3	.000	5.56	18	0	0	22.2	33	9	12	0	0	3	1	0	0	0	–	3	1	0	0	0.2	1.000

Fred Toney

TONEY, FRED ALEXANDRA
B. Dec. 11, 1888, Nashville, Tenn. D. Mar. 11, 1953, Nashville, Tenn.　　BR TR 6'6"　245 lbs.

Year	Team		W	L	PCT	ERA	G	GS	CG	IP	H	BB	SO	ShO	W	L	SV	AB	H	HR	BA	PO	A	E	DP	TC/G	FA
1911	CHI	N	1	1	.500	2.42	18	4	1	67	55	35	27	0	0	0	0	18	2	0	.111	0	23	2	0	1.4	.920
1912			1	2	.333	5.25	9	2	0	24	21	11	9	0	1	0	0	5	0	0	.000	0	4	1	0	0.6	.800
1913			2	2	.500	6.00	7	5	2	39	52	22	12	0	0	0	0	12	3	0	.250	1	11	0	0	1.7	1.000
1915	CIN	N	15	6	.714	1.58	36	23	18	222.2	160	73	108	6	1	1	2	74	7	0	.095	6	63	1	2	1.9	.986
1916			14	17	.452	2.28	41	38	21	300	247	78	146	3	0	0	0	99	12	0	.121	7	59	2	2	1.7	.971
1917			24	16	.600	2.20	43	42	31	339.2	300	77	123	7	0	0	1	116	13	0	.112	13	76	7	1	2.2	.927
1918	2 teams		CIN N (21G 6–10)			NY N (11G 6–2)																					
"	total		12	12	.500	2.43	32	28	16	222	203	38	51	2	0	0	3	74	15	0	.203	6	67	4	3	2.4	.948
1919	NY	N	13	6	.684	1.84	24	20	14	181	157	35	40	4	0	1	1	66	15	0	.227	5	39	1	0	1.9	.978
1920			21	11	.656	2.65	42	37	17	278.1	266	57	81	4	2	0	1	96	23	0	.240	6	72	3	0	1.9	.963
1921			18	11	.621	3.61	42	32	16	249.1	274	65	63	1	3	0	3	86	18	3	.209	4	63	2	3	1.6	.971
1922			5	6	.455	4.17	13	12	6	86.1	91	31	10	0	0	0	0	30	2	0	.067	0	15	1	0	1.2	.938
1923	STL	N	11	12	.478	3.84	29	28	16	196.2	211	61	48	1	0	0	0	69	8	0	.116	9	63	2	3	2.6	.973
12 yrs.			137	102	.573	2.69	336	271	158	2206	2037	583	718	28	7	2	12	745	118	3	.158	57	555	26	14	1.9	.959

WORLD SERIES

Year	Team		W	L	PCT	ERA	G	GS	CG	IP	H	BB	SO	ShO	W	L	SV	AB	H	HR	BA	PO	A	E	DP	TC/G	FA
1921	NY	N	0	0	–	23.63	2	2	0	2.2	7	3	1	0	0	0	0	0	0	0	–	0	1	0	0	0.5	1.000

Doc Tonkin

TONKIN, HARRY GLENVILLE
B. Aug. 11, 1881, Concord, N. H. D. May 30, 1959, Miami, Fla.　　BL TL 5'9"　165 lbs.

Year	Team		W	L	PCT	ERA	G	GS	CG	IP	H	BB	SO	ShO	W	L	SV	AB	H	HR	BA	PO	A	E	DP	TC/G	FA
1907	WAS	A	0	0	–	6.75	1	0	0	2.2	6	5	0	0	0	0	0	2	2	0	1.000	0	2	0	0	2.0	1.000

Steve Toole

TOOLE, STEPHEN JOHN
B. Apr. 9, 1859, New Orleans, La. D. Mar. 28, 1919, Pittsburgh, Pa.　　BL TL 6'　170 lbs.

Year	Team		W	L	PCT	ERA	G	GS	CG	IP	H	BB	SO	ShO	W	L	SV	AB	H	HR	BA	PO	A	E	DP	TC/G	FA
1886	BKN	AA	6	6	.500	4.41	13	12	11	104	100	64	48	0	0	0	0	57	20	0	.351	8	24	5	1	2.8	.865
1887			14	10	.583	4.31	24	24	22	194	186	106	48	1	0	0	0	103	24	1	.233	17	32	10	1	2.5	.831
1888	KC	AA	5	6	.455	6.68	12	10	10	91.2	124	50	35	0	1	0	0	48	10	0	.208	8	20	1	0	2.4	.966
1890	BKN	AA	2	4	.333	4.08	6	6	6	53	47	39	10	0	0	0	0	20	6	0	.300	5	13	3	1	3.5	.857
4 yrs.			27	26	.509	4.80	55	52	49	442.2	457	259	141	1	1	0	0	228	60	1	.263	38	89	19	3	2.7	.870

Rupe Toppin

TOPPIN, RUPERTO
B. Dec. 7, 1941, Panama City, Panama　　BR TR 6'　185 lbs.

Year	Team		W	L	PCT	ERA	G	GS	CG	IP	H	BB	SO	ShO	W	L	SV	AB	H	HR	BA	PO	A	E	DP	TC/G	FA
1962	KC	A	0	0	–	13.50	2	0	0	2	1	5	1	0	0	0	0	1	1	0	1.000	0	0	0	0	0.0	–

Red Torkelson

TORKELSON, CHESTER LeROY
B. Mar. 19, 1894, Chicago, Ill. D. Sept. 22, 1964, Chicago, Ill.　　BR TR 6'　175 lbs.

Year	Team		W	L	PCT	ERA	G	GS	CG	IP	H	BB	SO	ShO	W	L	SV	AB	H	HR	BA	PO	A	E	DP	TC/G	FA
1917	CLE	A	2	1	.667	7.66	4	3	0	22.1	33	13	10	0	0	0	0	9	2	0	.222	1	9	4	0	3.5	.714

Pablo Torrealba

TORREALBA, PABLO ARNOLDO
Born Pablo Arnoldo Torrealba y Torrealba.
B. Apr. 28, 1948, Barquisimento, Venezuela　　BL TL 5'10"　173 lbs.

Year	Team		W	L	PCT	ERA	G	GS	CG	IP	H	BB	SO	ShO	W	L	SV	AB	H	HR	BA	PO	A	E	DP	TC/G	FA
1975	ATL	N	0	1	.000	1.29	6	0	0	7	3	5	3	0	0	1	0	1	1	0	1.000	1	3	0	0	0.7	1.000
1976			0	2	.000	3.57	36	0	0	53	67	22	33	0	0	2	2	4	0	0	.000	1	13	0	2	0.4	1.000
1977	OAK	A	4	6	.400	2.62	41	10	3	117	127	38	51	0	4	1	3	0	0	0	–	11	26	4	1	1.0	.902
1978	CHI	A	2	4	.333	4.71	25	3	1	57.1	69	39	23	1	1	3	1	0	0	0	–	2	4	1	0	0.3	.857
1979			0	0	–	1.50	3	0	0	6	5	2	1	0	0	0	0	0	0	0	–	0	1	0	0	0.3	1.000
5 yrs.			6	13	.316	3.26	111	13	4	240.1	275	104	113	1	5	7	5	5	1	0	.200	15	47	5	3	0.6	.925

Angel Torres

TORRES, ANGEL RAFAEL
Born Angel Rafael Torres y Ruiz.
B. Oct. 24, 1952, Las Ciengas Azua, Dominican Republic　　BL TL 5'11"　168 lbs.

Year	Team		W	L	PCT	ERA	G	GS	CG	IP	H	BB	SO	ShO	Relief Pitching W	L	SV	Batting AB	H	HR	BA	PO	A	E	DP	TC/G	FA

Angel Torres *continued*

| 1977 | CIN | N | 0 | 0 | – | 2.25 | 5 | 0 | 0 | 8 | 7 | 8 | 8 | 0 | 0 | 0 | 0 | 0 | 0 | 0 | – | 0 | 1 | 0 | 0 | 0.2 | 1.000 |

Gil Torres

TORRES, DON GILBERTO
Born Don Gilberto Torres y Nunez. Son of Ricardo Torres.
B. Aug. 23, 1915, Regla, Cuba D. Jan. 11, 1983, Regla, Cuba

BR TR 6'   155 lbs.

1940	WAS	A	0	0	–	0.00	2	0	0	2.2	3	0	1	0	0	0	0	0	0	0	–	0	1	0	0	0.5	1.000
1946			0	0	–	7.71	3	0	0	7	9	3	2	0	0	0	1	185	47	0	.254	1	0	0	0	0.3	1.000
2 yrs.			0	0	–	5.59	5	0	0	9.2	12	3	3	0	0	0	1	*				1	1	0	0	0.4	1.000

Hector Torres

TORRES, HECTOR EPITACIO
Born Hector Epitacio Torres y Marroquin.
B. Sept. 16, 1945, Monterrey, Mexico

BR TR 6'   175 lbs.

| 1972 | MON | N | 0 | 0 | – | 27.00 | 1 | 0 | 0 | .2 | 5 | 0 | 0 | 0 | 0 | 0 | 0 | * | | | | 0 | 0 | 0 | 0 | 0.0 | – |

Mike Torrez

TORREZ, MICHAEL AUGUSTINE
B. Aug. 28, 1946, Topeka, Kans.

BR TR 6'5"   220 lbs.

1967	STL	N	0	1	.000	3.18	3	1	0	5.2	5	1	5	0	0	1	0	1	0	0	.000	0	0	0	0	0.0	–
1968			2	1	.667	2.84	5	2	0	19	20	12	6	0	1	0	0	7	2	0	.286	2	4	1	0	1.4	.857
1969			10	4	.714	3.58	24	15	3	108	96	62	61	0	0	0	0	41	3	0	.073	11	17	0	2	1.2	1.000
1970			8	10	.444	4.22	30	28	5	179	168	103	100	1	0	0	0	63	17	0	.270	7	27	1	2	1.2	.971
1971	2 teams				STL N	(9G 1-2)				MON N	(1G 0-0)																
"	total		1	2	.333	5.54	10	6	0	39	45	31	10	0	0	0	0	7	1	0	.143	4	9	1	0	1.4	.929
1972	MON	N	16	12	.571	3.33	34	33	13	243.1	215	103	112	0	0	0	0	85	15	0	.176	15	48	1	2	1.9	.984
1973			9	12	.429	4.46	35	34	3	208	207	115	90	1	0	0	0	69	12	0	.174	13	41	2	1	1.6	.964
1974			15	8	.652	3.58	32	30	6	186	184	84	92	1	0	0	0	64	8	0	.125	19	48	2	4	2.2	.971
1975	BAL	A	20	9	.690	3.06	36	36	16	270.2	238	133	119	2	0	0	0	0	0	0	–	19	46	5	3	1.9	.929
1976	OAK	A	16	12	.571	2.50	39	39	13	266	231	87	115	4	0	0	0	0	0	0	–	19	37	6	4	1.6	.903
1977	2 teams				OAK A	(4G 3-1)				NY A	(31G 14-12)																
"	total		17	13	.567	3.92	35	35	17	243.1	235	86	102	2	0	0	0	0	0	0	–	5	4	0	0	0.3	1.000
1978	BOS	A	16	13	.552	3.96	36	36	15	250	272	99	120	2	0	0	0	0	0	0	–	12	29	2	3	1.2	.953
1979			16	13	.552	4.50	36	36	12	252	254	121	125	1	0	0	0	0	0	0	–	19	35	4	3	1.6	.931
1980			9	16	.360	5.09	36	32	6	207	256	75	97	1	0	2	0	0	0	0	–	20	36	6	4	1.7	.903
1981			10	3	.769	3.69	22	22	2	127	130	51	54	0	0	0	0	0	0	0	–	12	13	3	2	1.3	.893
1982			9	9	.500	5.23	31	31	1	175.2	196	74	84	0	0	0	0	0	0	0	–	12	14	1	0	0.9	.963
1983	NY	N	10	17	.370	4.37	39	34	5	222.1	227	113	94	0	0	0	0	65	3	0	.046	20	33	2	4	1.4	.964
1984	2 teams				NY N	(9G 1-5)				OAK A	(2G 0-0)																
"	total		1	5	.167	6.30	11	8	0	40	64	21	18	0	0	0	0	10	3	0	.300	2	6	1	2	0.8	.889
18 yrs.			185	160	.536	3.97	494	458	117	3042	3043	1371	1404	15	1	3	0	412	64	0	.155	211	447	38	36	1.4	.945

LEAGUE CHAMPIONSHIP SERIES

| 1977 | NY | A | 0 | 1 | .000 | 4.09 | 2 | 1 | 0 | 11 | 11 | 5 | 5 | 0 | 0 | 0 | 0 | 0 | 0 | 0 | – | 2 | 1 | 0 | 0 | 1.5 | 1.000 |

WORLD SERIES

| 1977 | NY | A | 2 | 0 | 1.000 | 2.50 | 2 | 2 | 2 | 18 | 16 | 5 | 15 | 0 | 0 | 0 | 0 | 6 | 0 | 0 | .000 | 2 | 3 | 0 | 0 | 2.5 | 1.000 |

Lou Tost

TOST, LOUIS EUGENE
B. June 1, 1911, Cumberland, Wash. D. Feb. 22, 1967, Santa Clara, Calif.

BL TL 6'   175 lbs.

1942	BOS	N	10	10	.500	3.53	35	22	5	147.2	146	52	43	1	3	2	0	51	9	0	.176	4	27	2	2	0.9	.939
1943			0	1	.000	5.40	3	1	0	6.2	10	4	3	0	0	0	0	1	0	0	.000	0	2	0	0	0.7	1.000
1947	PIT	N	0	0	–	9.00	1	0	0	1	3	0	0	0	0	0	0	0	0	0	–	0	1	0	0	1.0	1.000
3 yrs.			10	11	.476	3.65	39	23	5	155.1	159	56	46	1	3	2	0	52	9	0	.173	4	30	2	2	0.9	.944

Paul Toth

TOTH, PAUL LOUIS
B. June 30, 1935, McRoberts, Ky.

BR TR 6'1"   175 lbs.

1962	2 teams				STL N	(6G 1-0)				CHI N	(6G 3-1)																
"	total		4	1	.800	4.62	12	5	2	50.2	47	14	16	0	0	0	0	16	4	0	.250	4	7	2	0	1.1	.846
1963	CHI	N	5	9	.357	3.10	27	14	3	130.2	115	35	66	2	1	3	0	39	1	0	.026	5	18	1	2	0.9	.958
1964			0	2	.000	8.44	4	2	0	10.2	15	5	0	0	0	0	0	3	1	0	.333	2	5	0	0	1.8	1.000
3 yrs.			9	12	.429	3.80	43	21	5	192	177	54	82	2	1	3	0	58	6	0	.103	11	30	3	2	1.0	.932

Clay Touchstone

TOUCHSTONE, CLAYLAND MAFFITT
B. Jan. 24, 1903, Moore, Pa. D. Apr. 28, 1949, Beaumont, Tex.

BR TR 5'11½" 175 lbs.

1928	BOS	N	0	0	–	4.50	5	0	0	8	15	2	1	0	0	0	0	2	0	0	.000	0	3	0	0	0.6	1.000
1929			0	0	–	16.88	1	0	0	2.2	6	0	1	0	0	0	0	1	1	0	1.000	0	0	0	0	0.0	–
1945	CHI	A	0	0	–	5.40	6	0	0	10	14	6	4	0	0	0	0	1	0	0	.000	1	2	0	0	0.5	1.000
3 yrs.			0	0	–	6.53	12	0	0	20.2	35	8	6	0	0	0	0	4	1	0	.250	1	5	0	0	0.5	1.000

Cesar Tovar

TOVAR, CESAR LEONARDO (Pepito)
Born Cesar Leonardo Perez y Tovar.
B. July 3, 1940, Caracas, Venezuela

BR TR 5'9"   155 lbs.

| 1968 | MIN | A | 0 | 0 | – | 0.00 | 1 | 0 | 0 | 1 | 0 | 0 | 1 | 0 | 0 | 0 | 0 | * | | | | 0 | 0 | 0 | 0 | 0.0 | – |

Ira Townsend

TOWNSEND, IRA DANCE (Pat)
B. Jan. 9, 1894, Weimar, Tex. D. July 21, 1965, Schulenburg, Tex.

BR TR 6'1"   180 lbs.

1920	BOS	N	0	0	–	1.35	4	1	0	6.2	10	2	1	0	0	0	0	2	0	0	.000	0	2	1	0	0.8	.667
1921			0	0	–	6.14	4	0	0	7.1	11	4	0	0	0	0	0	2	0	0	.000	0	4	0	0	1.0	1.000
2 yrs.			0	0	–	3.86	8	1	0	14	21	6	1	0	0	0	0	4	0	0	.000	0	6	1	0	0.9	.857

Year	Team	W	L	PCT	ERA	G	GS	CG	IP	H	BB	SO	ShO	W	L	SV	AB	H	HR	BA	PO	A	E	DP	TC/G	FA

Jack Townsend
TOWNSEND, JOHN (Happy)
B. Apr. 9, 1879, Townsend, Del.   D. Dec. 21, 1963, Wilmington, Del.
BR TR 6'   190 lbs.

Year	Team	W	L	PCT	ERA	G	GS	CG	IP	H	BB	SO	ShO	W	L	SV	AB	H	HR	BA	PO	A	E	DP	TC/G	FA
1901	PHI	N	9	6	.600	3.45	19	16	14	143.2	118	64	72	2	0	0	0	64	7	0	.109	5	25	3	2	1.7	.909
1902	WAS	A	9	16	.360	4.45	27	26	22	220.1	233	89	71	0	0	0	0	87	23	0	.264	12	57	6	1	2.8	.920
1903			2	11	.154	4.76	20	13	10	126.2	145	48	54	0	0	1	0	44	2	0	.045	6	37	0	2	2.2	1.000
1904			5	26	.161	3.58	36	34	31	291.1	319	100	143	2	0	0	0	119	20	1	.168	15	81	4	8	2.8	.960
1905			7	16	.304	2.63	34	24	22	263	247	84	102	0	1	1	0	83	15	0	.181	21	64	5	1	2.6	.944
1906	CLE	A	3	7	.300	2.91	17	12	8	92.2	92	31	31	1	0	1	0	30	4	0	.133	2	31	3	0	2.1	.917
6 yrs.			35	82	.299	3.59	153	125	107	1137.2	1154	416	473	5	1	3	0	427	71	1	.166	61	295	21	14	2.5	.944

Leo Townsend
TOWNSEND, LEO ALPHONSE (Lefty)
B. Jan. 15, 1891, Mobile, Ala.   D. Dec. 3, 1976, Mobile, Ala.
BL TL 5'10"   160 lbs.

Year	Team	W	L	PCT	ERA	G	GS	CG	IP	H	BB	SO	ShO	W	L	SV	AB	H	HR	BA	PO	A	E	DP	TC/G	FA
1920	BOS	N	2	2	.500	1.48	7	1	1	24.1	18	2	0	0	0	0	0	6	1	0	.167	0	8	0	0	1.1	1.000
1921			0	1	.000	27.00	1	1	0	1.1	2	3	0	0	0	0	0	0	0	0	–	1	1	0	1	2.0	1.000
2 yrs.			2	3	.400	2.81	8	2	1	25.2	20	5	0	0	0	0	0	6	1	0	.167	1	9	0	1	1.3	1.000

Bill Tozer
TOZER, WILLIAM LOUIS
B. July 3, 1882, St. Louis, Mo.   D. Feb. 23, 1955, Belmont, Calif.
BR TR 6'   200 lbs.

Year	Team	W	L	PCT	ERA	G	GS	CG	IP	H	BB	SO	ShO	W	L	SV	AB	H	HR	BA	PO	A	E	DP	TC/G	FA
1908	CIN	N	0	0	–	1.69	4	0	0	10.2	11	4	5	0	0	0	0	2	0	0	.000	1	4	1	0	1.5	.833

Fred Trautman
TRAUTMAN, FREDERICK ORLANDO
B. Mar. 24, 1892, Bucyrus, Ohio   D. Feb. 15, 1964, Bucyrus, Ohio
BR TR 6'1"   175 lbs.

Year	Team	W	L	PCT	ERA	G	GS	CG	IP	H	BB	SO	ShO	W	L	SV	AB	H	HR	BA	PO	A	E	DP	TC/G	FA
1915	NWK	F	0	0	–	6.00	1	0	0	3	4	1	2	0	0	0	0	1	0	0	.000	0	0	0	0	0.0	–

John Trautwein
TRAUTWEIN, JOHN HOWARD
B. Aug. 7, 1962, Lafayette Hills, Pa.
BR TR 6'3"   205 lbs.

Year	Team	W	L	PCT	ERA	G	GS	CG	IP	H	BB	SO	ShO	W	L	SV	AB	H	HR	BA	PO	A	E	DP	TC/G	FA
1988	BOS	A	0	1	.000	9.00	9	0	0	26	26	9	8	0	0	1	0	0	0	0	–	2	1	0	0	0.3	1.000

Al Travers
TRAVERS, ALOYSIUS JOSEPH
B. May 7, 1892, Philadelphia, Pa.   D. Apr. 19, 1968, Philadelphia, Pa.
BR TR 6'1"   180 lbs.

Year	Team	W	L	PCT	ERA	G	GS	CG	IP	H	BB	SO	ShO	W	L	SV	AB	H	HR	BA	PO	A	E	DP	TC/G	FA
1912	DET	A	0	1	.000	15.75	1	1	1	8	26	7	1	0	0	0	0	3	0	0	.000	0	7	0	0	7.0	1.000

Bill Travers
TRAVERS, WILLIAM EDWARD
B. Oct. 27, 1952, Norwood, Mass.
BL TL 6'4"   187 lbs.

Year	Team	W	L	PCT	ERA	G	GS	CG	IP	H	BB	SO	ShO	W	L	SV	AB	H	HR	BA	PO	A	E	DP	TC/G	FA
1974	MIL	A	2	3	.400	4.92	23	1	0	53	59	30	31	0	2	3	0	0	0	0	–	2	8	0	0	0.4	1.000
1975			6	11	.353	4.29	28	23	5	136.1	130	60	57	0	0	0	1	0	0	0	–	2	19	2	5	0.8	.913
1976			15	16	.484	2.81	34	34	15	240	211	95	120	3	0	0	0	0	0	0	–	13	31	1	4	1.3	.978
1977			4	12	.250	5.24	19	19	2	122	140	57	49	1	0	0	0	0	0	0	–	6	21	2	3	1.5	.931
1978			12	11	.522	4.41	28	28	8	175.2	184	58	66	3	0	0	0	0	0	0	–	5	36	3	1	1.6	.932
1979			14	8	.636	3.90	30	27	9	187	196	45	74	2	2	0	0	0	0	0	–	7	25	2	0	1.1	.941
1980			12	6	.667	3.92	29	25	7	154	147	47	62	1	0	0	0	0	0	0	–	12	18	1	2	1.1	.968
1981	CAL	A	0	1	.000	8.10	4	4	0	10	14	4	5	0	0	0	0	0	0	0	–	1	1	0	0	0.5	1.000
1983			0	3	.000	5.91	10	7	0	42.2	58	19	24	0	0	0	0	0	0	0	–	0	8	1	1	0.9	.889
9 yrs.			65	71	.478	4.10	205	168	46	1120.2	1139	415	488	10	4	3	1	0	0	0	–	48	167	12	16	1.1	.947

Harry Trekell
TREKELL, HARRY ROY
B. Nov. 18, 1892, Breda, Ill.   D. Nov. 4, 1965, Spokane, Wash.
BR TR 6'1½"   170 lbs.

Year	Team	W	L	PCT	ERA	G	GS	CG	IP	H	BB	SO	ShO	W	L	SV	AB	H	HR	BA	PO	A	E	DP	TC/G	FA
1913	STL	N	0	1	.000	4.50	7	1	1	30	25	8	15	0	0	0	0	9	1	0	.111	2	6	2	0	1.4	.800

Bill Tremel
TREMEL, WILLIAM LEONARD (Mumbles)
B. July 4, 1929, Lilly, Pa.
BR TR 5'11"   180 lbs.

Year	Team	W	L	PCT	ERA	G	GS	CG	IP	H	BB	SO	ShO	W	L	SV	AB	H	HR	BA	PO	A	E	DP	TC/G	FA
1954	CHI	N	1	2	.333	4.21	33	0	0	51.1	45	28	21	0	1	2	4	8	2	0	.250	1	5	1	0	0.2	.857
1955			3	0	1.000	3.72	23	0	0	38.2	33	18	13	0	3	0	2	7	2	0	.286	2	5	2	0	0.4	.778
1956			0	0	–	13.50	1	0	0	.2	3	0	0	0	0	0	0	0	0	0	–	0	0	0	0	0.0	–
3 yrs.			4	2	.667	4.07	57	0	0	90.2	81	46	34	0	4	2	6	15	4	0	.267	3	10	3	0	0.3	.813

Bob Trice
TRICE, ROBERT LEE
B. Aug. 28, 1926, Newton, Ga.
BR TR 6'3"   190 lbs.

Year	Team	W	L	PCT	ERA	G	GS	CG	IP	H	BB	SO	ShO	W	L	SV	AB	H	HR	BA	PO	A	E	DP	TC/G	FA
1953	PHI	A	2	1	.667	5.48	3	3	1	23	25	6	4	0	0	0	0	7	1	0	.143	2	8	0	2	3.3	1.000
1954			7	8	.467	5.60	19	18	8	119	146	48	22	1	0	1	0	42	12	1	.286	11	21	3	4	1.8	.914
1955	KC	A	0	0	–	9.00	4	0	0	10	14	6	2	0	0	0	0	3	2	0	.667	3	4	0	0	1.8	1.000
3 yrs.			9	9	.500	5.80	26	21	9	152	185	60	28	1	0	1	0	52	15	1	.288	16	33	3	6	2.0	.942

Joe Trimble
TRIMBLE, JOSEPH GERARD
B. Oct. 12, 1930, Providence, R. I.
BR TR 6'1"   190 lbs.

Year	Team	W	L	PCT	ERA	G	GS	CG	IP	H	BB	SO	ShO	W	L	SV	AB	H	HR	BA	PO	A	E	DP	TC/G	FA
1955	BOS	A	0	0	–	0.00	2	0	0	2	0	3	1	0	0	0	0	0	0	0	–	0	1	0	0	0.5	1.000
1957	PIT	N	0	2	.000	8.24	5	4	0	19.2	23	13	9	0	0	0	0	7	1	0	.143	1	5	1	1	1.4	.857
2 yrs.			0	2	.000	7.48	7	4	0	21.2	23	16	10	0	0	0	0	7	1	0	.143	1	6	1	1	1.1	.875

Ken Trinkle
TRINKLE, KENNETH WAYNE
B. Dec. 15, 1919, Paoli, Ind.   D. May 10, 1976, Paoli, Ind.
BR TR 6'1½"   175 lbs.

Year	Team	W	L	PCT	ERA	G	GS	CG	IP	H	BB	SO	ShO	W	L	SV	AB	H	HR	BA	PO	A	E	DP	TC/G	FA
1943	NY	N	1	5	.167	3.74	11	6	1	45.2	51	15	10	0	0	0	0	12	3	0	.250	5	16	1	0	2.0	.955
1946			7	14	.333	3.87	48	13	2	151	146	74	49	0	3	5	2	38	3	0	.079	6	30	1	1	0.8	.973
1947			8	4	.667	3.75	62	0	0	93.2	100	48	37	0	8	4	10	16	3	0	.188	4	27	0	2	0.5	1.000
1948			4	5	.444	3.18	53	0	0	70.2	66	41	20	0	5	4	7	8	2	0	.250	4	18	0	1	0.4	1.000
1949	PHI	N	1	1	.500	4.00	42	0	0	74.1	79	30	14	0	0	3	2	6	0	0	.000	7	20	1	0	0.7	.964
5 yrs.			21	29	.420	3.74	216	19	3	435.1	442	208	130	0	16	16	21	80	11	0	.138	26	111	3	4	0.7	.979

Year	Team	W	L	PCT	ERA	G	GS	CG	IP	H	BB	SO	ShO	Relief Pitching W	L	SV	Batting AB	H	HR	BA	PO	A	E	DP	TC/G	FA

Rich Troedson

TROEDSON, RICHARD LAMONTE
B. May 1, 1950, Palo Alto, Calif.   BL TL 6'1"   170 lbs.

Year	Team	W	L	PCT	ERA	G	GS	CG	IP	H	BB	SO	ShO	W	L	SV	AB	H	HR	BA	PO	A	E	DP	TC/G	FA
1973	SD N	7	9	.438	4.25	50	18	2	152.1	167	59	81	0	2	0	1	40	7	0	.175	5	34	0	0	0.8	1.000
1974		1	1	.500	8.53	15	1	0	19	24	8	11	0	1	0	1	1	0	0	.000	1	5	1	0	0.5	.857
2 yrs.		8	10	.444	4.73	65	19	2	171.1	191	67	92	0	3	0	2	41	7	0	.171	6	39	1	0	0.7	.978

Hal Trosky

TROSKY, HAROLD ARTHUR, JR. (Hoot)
Born Harold Arthur Troyavesky, Jr.   Son of Hal Trosky.
B. Sept. 29, 1936, Cleveland, Ohio   BR TR 6'3"   205 lbs.

Year	Team	W	L	PCT	ERA	G	GS	CG	IP	H	BB	SO	ShO	W	L	SV	AB	H	HR	BA	PO	A	E	DP	TC/G	FA
1958	CHI A	1	0	1.000	6.00	2	0	0	3	5	2	1	0	1	0	0	0	0	0	—	0	1	0	0	0.5	1.000

Bill Trotter

TROTTER, WILLIAM FELIX
B. Aug. 10, 1908, Cisne, Ill.   D. Aug. 26, 1984, Arlington, Mass.   BR TR 6'2"   195 lbs.

Year	Team	W	L	PCT	ERA	G	GS	CG	IP	H	BB	SO	ShO	W	L	SV	AB	H	HR	BA	PO	A	E	DP	TC/G	FA
1937	STL A	2	9	.182	5.81	34	12	3	122.1	150	50	37	0	0	2	1	33	1	0	.030	2	18	3	0	0.7	.870
1938		0	1	.000	5.63	1	1	1	8	8	0	1	0	0	0	0	2	0	0	.000	0	5	0	0	5.0	1.000
1939		6	13	.316	5.34	41	13	4	156.2	205	54	61	0	3	2	0	37	4	0	.108	9	29	0	1	0.9	1.000
1940		7	6	.538	3.77	36	4	1	98	117	31	29	0	6	3	2	22	1	0	.045	2	21	0	3	0.6	1.000
1941		4	2	.667	5.98	29	0	0	49.2	68	19	17	0	4	2	0	6	0	0	.000	0	13	0	1	0.4	1.000
1942	2 teams	STL A	(3G 0–1)		WAS A	(17G 3–1)																				
"	total	3	2	.600	6.33	20	0	0	42.2	57	16	13	0	3	2	0	8	0	0	.000	2	12	1	0	0.8	.933
1944	STL N	0	1	.000	13.50	2	1	0	6	14	4	0	0	0	0	0	1	0	0	.000	0	2	0	0	1.0	1.000
7 yrs.		22	34	.393	5.40	163	31	9	483.1	619	174	158	0	16	11	3	109	6	0	.055	15	100	4	7	0.7	.966

Dizzy Trout

TROUT, PAUL HOWARD
Father of Steve Trout.
B. June 29, 1915, Sandcut, Ind.   D. Feb. 28, 1972, Harvey, Ill.   BR TR 6'2½"   195 lbs.

Year	Team	W	L	PCT	ERA	G	GS	CG	IP	H	BB	SO	ShO	W	L	SV	AB	H	HR	BA	PO	A	E	DP	TC/G	FA
1939	DET A	9	10	.474	3.61	33	22	6	162	168	74	72	0	0	0	2	57	12	0	.211	3	23	4	1	0.9	.867
1940		3	7	.300	4.47	33	10	1	100.2	125	54	64	0	1	2	2	31	4	0	.129	5	25	2	1	1.0	.938
1941		9	9	.500	3.74	37	18	6	151.2	144	84	88	1	2	2	2	50	9	0	.180	7	30	2	3	1.1	.949
1942		12	18	.400	3.43	35	29	13	223	214	89	91	1	2	1	0	75	16	1	.213	24	56	6	6	2.5	.930
1943		20	12	.625	2.48	44	30	18	246.2	204	101	111	5	3	1	6	91	20	1	.220	20	67	4	1	2.1	.956
1944		27	14	.659	2.12	49	40	33	352.1	314	83	144	7	3	0	0	133	36	5	.271	21	94	4	8	2.4	.966
1945		18	15	.545	3.14	41	31	18	246.1	252	79	97	4	2	0	2	102	25	2	.245	13	65	9	9	2.1	.897
1946		17	13	.567	2.34	38	32	23	276.1	244	97	151	5	0	0	3	103	20	3	.194	17	64	5	6	2.3	.942
1947		10	11	.476	3.48	32	26	9	186.1	186	65	74	2	0	0	2	68	11	3	.162	22	40	3	4	2.0	.954
1948		10	14	.417	3.43	32	23	11	183.2	193	73	91	2	1	1	2	69	15	1	.217	11	37	5	7	1.7	.906
1949		3	6	.333	4.40	33	0	0	59.1	68	21	19	0	3	6	3	14	2	1	.143	4	19	3	4	0.8	.885
1950		13	5	.722	3.75	34	20	11	184.2	190	64	88	1	1	0	4	63	12	1	.190	15	43	0	5	1.7	1.000
1951		9	14	.391	4.04	42	22	7	191.2	172	75	89	1	3	1	5	52	14	1	.269	18	47	1	6	1.6	.985
1952	2 teams	DET A	(10G 1–5)		BOS A	(26G 9–8)																				
"	total	10	13	.435	3.92	36	19	2	160.2	163	87	77	0	4	3	2	53	9	1	.170	13	35	2	2	1.4	.960
1957	BAL A	0	0	—	81.00	2	0	0	.1	4	0	0	0	0	0	0	0	0	0	—	0	0	0	0	0.0	—
15 yrs.		170	161	.514	3.23	521	322	158	2725.2	2641	1046	1256	28	25	17	35	961	205	20	.213	193	645	50	63	1.7	.944

WORLD SERIES

Year	Team	W	L	PCT	ERA	G	GS	CG	IP	H	BB	SO	ShO	W	L	SV	AB	H	HR	BA	PO	A	E	DP	TC/G	FA
1940	DET A	0	1	.000	9.00	1	1	0	2	6	1	1	0	0	0	0	1	0	0	.000	0	1	0	0	1.0	1.000
1945		1	1	.500	0.66	2	1	1	13.2	9	3	9	0	0	1	0	6	1	0	.167	2	5	0	0	3.5	1.000
2 yrs.		1	2	.333	1.72	3	2	1	15.2	15	4	10	0	0	1	0	7	1	0	.143	2	6	0	0	2.7	1.000

Steve Trout

TROUT, STEVEN RUSSELL (Rainbow)
Son of Dizzy Trout.
B. July 30, 1957, Detroit, Mich.   BL TL 6'4"   195 lbs.

Year	Team	W	L	PCT	ERA	G	GS	CG	IP	H	BB	SO	ShO	W	L	SV	AB	H	HR	BA	PO	A	E	DP	TC/G	FA
1978	CHI A	3	0	1.000	4.03	4	3	1	22.1	19	11	11	0	0	0	0	0	0	0	—	0	3	0	1	0.8	1.000
1979		11	8	.579	3.89	34	18	6	155	165	59	76	2	1	2	4	0	0	0	—	6	33	3	2	1.2	.929
1980		9	16	.360	3.69	32	30	7	200	229	49	89	2	0	0	0	0	0	0	—	11	42	2	3	1.7	.964
1981		8	7	.533	3.46	20	18	3	125	122	38	54	0	0	0	0	0	0	0	—	3	23	2	5	1.4	.929
1982		6	9	.400	4.26	25	19	2	120.1	130	50	62	0	0	0	0	0	0	0	—	9	18	4	2	1.2	.871
1983	CHI N	10	14	.417	4.65	34	32	1	180	217	59	80	1	0	0	0	62	12	0	.194	8	40	2	3	1.5	.960
1984		13	7	.650	3.41	32	31	6	190	205	59	81	2	0	0	1	61	8	0	.131	13	48	4	3	2.0	.938
1985		9	7	.563	3.39	24	24	3	140.2	132	63	44	1	0	0	0	46	5	0	.109	6	38	2	0	1.9	.957
1986		5	7	.417	4.75	37	25	0	161	184	78	69	0	1	0	0	43	9	0	.209	7	31	1	3	1.1	.974
1987	2 teams	CHI N	(11G 6–3)		NY A	(14G 0–4)																				
"	total	6	7	.462	4.38	25	20	3	121.1	123	64	59	2	0	0	0	26	4	0	.154	7	21	0	1	1.1	1.000
1988	SEA A	4	7	.364	7.83	15	13	0	56.1	86	31	14	0	0	0	0	0	0	0	—	5	8	2	1	1.0	.867
1989		4	3	.571	6.60	19	3	0	30	43	17	17	0	3	2	0	0	0	0	—	2	5	0	1	0.4	1.000
12 yrs.		88	92	.489	4.18	301	236	32	1502	1665	578	656	9	7	5	4	238	38	0	.160	77	310	22	28	1.4	.946

LEAGUE CHAMPIONSHIP SERIES

Year	Team	W	L	PCT	ERA	G	GS	CG	IP	H	BB	SO	ShO	W	L	SV	AB	H	HR	BA	PO	A	E	DP	TC/G	FA
1984	CHI N	1	0	1.000	2.00	2	1	0	9	5	3	3	0	0	0	0	2	1	0	.500	0	1	0	0	1.0	.500

Bob Trowbridge

TROWBRIDGE, ROBERT MICHAEL
B. June 27, 1930, Hudson, N.Y.   D. Apr. 3, 1980, Hudson, N.Y.   BR TR 6'1"   180 lbs.

Year	Team	W	L	PCT	ERA	G	GS	CG	IP	H	BB	SO	ShO	W	L	SV	AB	H	HR	BA	PO	A	E	DP	TC/G	FA
1956	MIL N	3	2	.600	2.66	19	4	1	50.2	38	34	40	1	1	2	0	7	0	0	.000	0	11	1	1	0.6	.917
1957		7	5	.583	3.64	32	16	3	126	118	56	75	1	2	0	1	39	4	0	.103	13	15	0	1	0.9	1.000
1958		1	3	.250	3.93	27	4	0	55	53	26	31	0	1	2	1	9	1	0	.111	1	5	1	3	0.3	.857
1959		1	0	1.000	5.93	16	0	0	30.1	45	10	22	0	1	0	1	4	0	0	.000	0	4	0	0	0.3	1.000
1960	KC A	1	3	.250	4.61	22	1	0	68.1	70	34	33	0	1	3	2	18	1	0	.056	4	13	0	0	0.8	1.000
5 yrs.		13	13	.500	3.95	116	25	4	330.1	324	156	201	1	6	7	5	77	6	0	.078	18	48	2	5	0.6	.971

WORLD SERIES

Year	Team	W	L	PCT	ERA	G	GS	CG	IP	H	BB	SO	ShO	W	L	SV	AB	H	HR	BA	PO	A	E	DP	TC/G	FA
1957	MIL N	0	0	—	45.00	1	0	0	1	2	3	1	0	0	0	0	0	0	0	—	0	0	0	0	0.0	—

Year	Team		W	L	PCT	ERA	G	GS	CG	IP	H	BB	SO	ShO	Relief Pitching W	L	SV	Batting AB	H	HR	BA	PO	A	E	DP	TC/G	FA

Bun Troy

TROY, ROBERT
B. Aug. 22, 1888, Germany   D. Oct. 7, 1918, Meuse, France
BR TR 6'4"   195 lbs.

| 1912 | DET | A | 0 | 1 | .000 | 5.40 | 1 | 1 | 0 | 6.2 | 9 | 3 | 1 | 0 | 0 | 0 | 0 | 2 | 0 | 0 | .000 | 0 | 1 | 0 | 0 | 1.0 | 1.000 |

Virgil Trucks

TRUCKS, VIRGIL OLIVER (Fire)
B. Apr. 26, 1919, Birmingham, Ala.
BR TR 5'11"   198 lbs.

1941	DET	A	0	0	–	9.00	1	0	0	2	4	3	0	3	0	0	0	0	0	0	–	1	0	0	0	1.0	1.000
1942			14	8	.636	2.74	28	20	8	167.2	147	74	91	2	4	1	0	65	8	0	.123	5	28	3	0	1.3	.917
1943			16	10	.615	2.84	33	25	10	202.2	170	52	118	3	2	1	2	72	13	0	.181	16	24	0	0	1.2	1.000
1945			0	0	–	1.69	1	1	0	5.1	3	2	3	0	0	0	0	2	0	0	.000	1	1	0	0	2.0	1.000
1946			14	9	.609	3.23	32	29	15	236.2	217	75	161	3	1	1	0	95	17	0	.179	11	33	3	1	1.5	.936
1947			10	12	.455	4.53	36	26	8	180.2	186	79	108	2	0	2	2	70	19	0	.271	13	22	2	0	1.0	.946
1948			14	13	.519	3.78	43	26	7	211.2	190	85	123	0	4	2	2	79	13	0	.165	13	28	0	1	1.0	1.000
1949			19	11	.633	2.81	41	32	17	275	209	124	153	6	2	0	4	100	12	0	.120	13	33	2	2	1.2	.958
1950			3	1	.750	3.54	7	7	2	48.1	45	21	25	1	0	0	0	20	3	0	.150	2	13	1	1	2.3	.938
1951			13	8	.619	4.33	37	18	6	153.2	153	75	89	1	4	2	1	55	13	0	.236	11	32	3	2	1.2	.935
1952			5	19	.208	3.97	35	29	8	197	190	82	129	3	0	1	1	64	12	1	.188	21	37	2	1	1.7	.967
1953	2 teams	STL A	(16G 5–4)			CHI A	(24G 15–6)																				
"	total		20	10	.667	2.93	40	33	17	264.1	234	99	149	5	0	1	3	88	19	1	.216	14	42	6	1	1.6	.903
1954	CHI	A	19	12	.613	2.79	40	33	16	264.2	224	95	152	5	3	1	3	93	17	0	.183	10	48	0	1	1.5	1.000
1955			13	8	.619	3.96	32	26	7	175	176	61	91	3	1	0	0	64	8	0	.125	4	33	0	1	1.2	1.000
1956	DET	A	6	5	.545	3.83	22	16	3	120	104	63	43	1	0	1	1	45	11	0	.244	6	18	3	1	1.2	.889
1957	KC	A	9	7	.563	3.03	48	7	0	116	106	62	55	0	8	3	7	28	4	0	.143	8	21	1	0	0.6	.967
1958	2 teams	KC A	(16G 0–1)			NY A	(25G 2–1)																				
"	total		2	2	.500	3.65	41	0	0	61.2	58	39	41	0	2	2	4	9	2	0	.222	7	7	1	0	0.4	.933
	17 yrs.		177	135	.567	3.39	517	328	124	2682.1	2416	1088	1534	35	31	18	30	949	171	2	.180	156	420	27	14	1.2	.955

WORLD SERIES

| 1945 | DET | A | 1 | 0 | 1.000 | 3.38 | 2 | 2 | 1 | 13.1 | 14 | 5 | 7 | 0 | 0 | 0 | 0 | 4 | 0 | 0 | .000 | 1 | 1 | 0 | 0 | 1.0 | 1.000 |

Mike Trujillo

TRUJILLO, MICHAEL ANDREW
B. Jan. 12, 1960, Denver, Colo.
BR TR 6'1"   180 lbs.

1985	BOS	A	4	4	.500	4.82	27	7	1	84	112	23	19	0	2	1	1	0	0	0	–	11	20	2	1	1.2	.939
1986	2 teams	BOS A	(3G 0–0)			SEA A	(11G 3–2)																				
"	total		3	2	.600	3.26	14	4	1	47	39	21	23	1	1	1	1	0	0	0	–	5	8	0	0	0.9	1.000
1987	SEA	A	4	4	.500	6.17	28	7	0	65.2	70	26	36	0	2	1	1	0	0	0	–	5	3	0	2	0.3	1.000
1988	DET	A	0	0	–	5.11	6	0	0	12.1	11	5	5	0	0	0	0	0	0	0	–	1	3	0	0	0.7	1.000
1989			1	2	.333	5.96	8	4	1	25.2	35	13	13	0	0	0	0	0	0	0	–	0	5	0	0	0.6	1.000
	5 yrs.		12	12	.500	5.02	83	22	3	234.2	267	88	96	1	5	3	3	0	0	0	–	22	39	2	3	0.8	.968

Ed Trumbull

TRUMBULL, EDWARD J.
Born Edward J. Trembly.
B. Nov. 3, 1860, Chicopee, Mass.   Deceased.

| 1884 | WAS | AA | 1 | 9 | .100 | 4.71 | 10 | 10 | 10 | 84 | 108 | 31 | 43 | 0 | 0 | 0 | 0 | * | | | | 4 | 20 | 9 | 0 | 3.3 | .727 |

John Tsitouris

TSITOURIS, JOHN PHILIP
B. May 4, 1936, Monroe, N. C.
BR TR 6'   175 lbs.

1957	DET	A	1	0	1.000	8.10	2	0	0	3.1	8	2	2	0	1	0	0	1	0	0	.000	1	0	0	0	0.5	1.000
1958	KC	A	0	0	–	3.00	1	1	0	3	2	2	1	0	0	0	0	1	0	0	.000	1	0	0	0	1.0	1.000
1959			4	3	.571	4.97	24	10	0	83.1	90	35	50	0	2	0	0	20	3	0	.150	3	13	2	0	0.8	.889
1960			0	2	.000	6.55	14	2	0	33	38	21	12	0	0	1	0	6	0	0	.000	2	6	0	0	0.6	1.000
1962	CIN	N	1	0	1.000	0.84	2	1	0	21.1	13	7	7	1	0	0	0	5	0	0	.000	1	3	0	0	1.0	1.000
1963			12	8	.600	3.16	30	21	8	191	167	38	113	3	0	0	0	62	5	0	.081	13	16	1	0	1.0	.967
1964			9	13	.409	3.80	37	24	6	175.1	178	75	146	1	0	1	2	58	11	0	.190	14	23	0	1	1.0	1.000
1965			6	9	.400	4.95	31	20	3	131	134	65	91	0	1	0	1	43	3	0	.070	5	19	2	0	0.8	.923
1966			0	0	–	18.00	1	0	0	1	3	1	0	0	0	0	0	0	0	0	–	0	0	0	0	0.0	–
1967			1	0	1.000	3.38	2	1	0	8	4	6	4	0	0	0	0	2	0	0	.000	2	1	0	0	1.5	1.000
1968			0	3	.000	7.11	3	3	0	12.2	16	8	6	0	0	0	0	2	0	0	.000	0	3	0	0	1.0	1.000
	11 yrs.		34	38	.472	4.13	149	84	18	663	653	260	432	5	4	3	3	198	22	0	.111	41	85	5	1	0.9	.962

Tommy Tucker

TUCKER, THOMAS JOSEPH
B. Oct. 28, 1863, Holyoke, Mass.   D. Oct. 22, 1935, Montague, Mass.
BB TR 5'11"   165 lbs.

1888	BAL	AA	0	0	–	3.86	1	0	0	2.1	4	0	2	0	0	0	0	520	149	6	.287	0	0	0	0	0.0	–
1891	BOS	N	0	0	–	9.00	1	0	0	1	3	0	0	0	0	0	0	548	148	2	.270	0	0	0	0	0.0	–
	2 yrs.		0	0	–	5.40	2	0	0	3.1	7	0	2	0	0	0	0	*				0	0	0	0	0.0	–

Tom Tuckey

TUCKEY, THOMAS H.
B. Oct. 7, 1883, Birmingham, Conn.   D. Oct. 17, 1950, New York, N. Y.
TL 6'3"

1908	BOS	N	3	3	.500	2.50	8	8	3	72	60	20	26	1	0	0	0	20	1	0	.050	4	22	1	1	3.4	.963
1909			0	9	.000	4.27	17	10	4	90.2	104	22	16	0	0	0	1	29	4	0	.138	11	28	3	1	2.5	.929
	2 yrs.		3	12	.200	3.49	25	18	7	162.2	164	42	42	1	0	0	1	49	5	0	.102	15	50	4	2	2.8	.942

John Tudor

TUDOR, JOHN THOMAS
B. Feb. 2, 1954, Schenectady, N. Y.
BL TL 6'   185 lbs.

1979	BOS	A	1	2	.333	6.43	6	6	1	28	39	9	11	0	0	0	0	0	0	0	–	1	7	0	0	1.3	1.000
1980			8	5	.615	3.03	16	13	5	92	81	31	45	0	0	1	0	0	0	0	–	5	24	1	1	1.9	.967
1981			4	3	.571	4.56	18	11	2	79	74	28	44	0	1	1	1	0	0	0	–	2	17	0	1	1.1	1.000
1982			13	10	.565	3.63	32	30	6	195.2	215	59	146	1	0	0	0	0	0	0	–	5	39	2	4	1.4	.957
1983			13	12	.520	4.09	34	34	7	242	236	81	136	2	0	0	0	0	0	0	–	12	26	2	4	1.2	.950
1984	PIT	N	12	11	.522	3.27	32	32	6	212	200	56	117	0	0	0	0	76	16	0	.211	11	31	0	0	1.3	1.000
1985	STL	N	21	8	.724	1.93	36	36	14	275	209	49	169	10	0	0	0	94	13	0	.138	18	45	3	4	1.8	.955
1986			13	7	.650	2.92	30	30	3	219	197	53	107	1	0	0	0	72	11	0	.153	10	41	2	4	1.8	.962

Year	Team	W	L	PCT	ERA	G	GS	CG	IP	H	BB	SO	ShO	Relief Pitching W	L	SV	Batting AB	H	HR	BA	PO	A	E	DP	TC/G	FA

John Tudor *continued*

Year	Team	W	L	PCT	ERA	G	GS	CG	IP	H	BB	SO	ShO	W	L	SV	AB	H	HR	BA	PO	A	E	DP	TC/G	FA
1987		10	2	.833	3.84	16	16	0	96	100	32	54	0	0	0	0	35	7	0	.200	4	20	0	2	1.5	1.000
1988	2 teams	STL N	(21G 6–5)			LA N	(9G 4–3)																			
"	total	10	8	.556	2.32	30	30	5	197.2	189	41	87	1	0	0	0	59	5	0	.085	6	32	0	4	1.3	1.000
1989	LA N	0	0	–	3.14	6	3	0	14.1	17	6	9	0	0	0	0	2	0	0	.000	0	3	0	0	0.5	1.000
11 yrs.		105	68	.607	3.18	256	241	49	1650.2	1557	445	925	15	1	2	1	338	52	0	.154	74	285	10	25	1.4	.973

LEAGUE CHAMPIONSHIP SERIES

Year	Team	W	L	PCT	ERA	G	GS	CG	IP	H	BB	SO	ShO	W	L	SV	AB	H	HR	BA	PO	A	E	DP	TC/G	FA
1985	STL N	1	1	.500	2.84	2	2	0	12.2	10	3	8	0	0	0	0	4	0	0	.000	0	1	0	0	0.5	1.000
1987		1	1	.500	1.76	2	2	0	15.1	16	5	12	0	0	0	0	4	0	0	.000	0	4	0	0	2.0	1.000
1988	LA N	0	0	–	7.20	1	1	0	5	8	1	1	0	0	0	0	2	0	0	.000	1	2	0	0	3.0	1.000
3 yrs.		2	2	.500	3.00	5	5	0	33	34	9	21	0	0	0	0	10	0	0	.000	1	7	0	0	1.6	1.000

WORLD SERIES

Year	Team	W	L	PCT	ERA	G	GS	CG	IP	H	BB	SO	ShO	W	L	SV	AB	H	HR	BA	PO	A	E	DP	TC/G	FA
1985	STL N	2	1	.667	3.00	3	3	0	18	15	7	14	1	0	0	0	5	0	0	.000	0	3	0	0	1.0	1.000
1987		1	1	.500	5.73	2	2	0	11	15	3	8	0	0	0	0	2	0	0	.000	0	4	0	0	2.0	1.000
1988	LA N	0	0	–	0.00	1	1	0	1.1	0	0	1	0	0	0	0	0	0	0	–	0	0	0	0	0.0	–
3 yrs.		3	2	.600	3.86	6	6	1	30.1	30	10	23	1	0	0	0	7	0	0	.000	0	7	0	0	1.2	1.000

Oscar Tuero

TUERO, OSCAR BR TR 5'8½" 158 lbs.
Born Oscar Monzon y Tuero.
B. Dec. 17, 1898, Havana, Cuba   D. Oct. 21, 1960, Houston, Tex.

Year	Team	W	L	PCT	ERA	G	GS	CG	IP	H	BB	SO	ShO	W	L	SV	AB	H	HR	BA	PO	A	E	DP	TC/G	FA
1918	STL N	1	2	.333	1.02	11	3	2	44.1	32	10	13	0	0	0	0	12	3	0	.250	4	10	1	0	1.4	.933
1919		5	7	.417	3.20	45	17	4	154.2	137	42	45	0	1	1	4	39	8	0	.205	3	44	2	1	1.1	.959
1920		0	0	–	54.00	2	0	0	.2	5	1	0	0	0	0	0	0	0	0	–	0	0	0	0	0.0	–
3 yrs.		6	9	.400	2.88	58	20	6	199.2	174	53	58	0	1	1	4	51	11	0	.216	7	54	3	1	1.1	.953

Bob Tufts

TUFTS, ROBERT MALCOLM BL TL 6'5" 215 lbs.
B. Nov. 2, 1955, Medford, Mass.

Year	Team	W	L	PCT	ERA	G	GS	CG	IP	H	BB	SO	ShO	W	L	SV	AB	H	HR	BA	PO	A	E	DP	TC/G	FA
1981	SF N	0	0	–	3.60	11	0	0	15	20	6	12	0	0	0	0	1	0	0	.000	3	4	0	0	0.6	1.000
1982	KC A	2	0	1.000	4.50	10	0	0	20	24	3	13	0	2	0	2	0	0	0	–	1	0	0	0	0.1	1.000
1983		0	0	–	8.10	6	0	0	6.2	16	5	3	0	0	0	0	0	0	0	–	0	2	0	0	0.3	1.000
3 yrs.		2	0	1.000	4.75	27	0	0	41.2	60	14	28	0	2	0	2	1	0	0	.000	4	6	0	0	0.4	1.000

Lee Tunnell

TUNNELL, BYRON LEE BR TR 6'1" 180 lbs.
B. Oct. 30, 1960, Tyler, Tex.

Year	Team	W	L	PCT	ERA	G	GS	CG	IP	H	BB	SO	ShO	W	L	SV	AB	H	HR	BA	PO	A	E	DP	TC/G	FA
1982	PIT N	1	1	.500	3.93	5	3	0	18.1	17	5	4	0	0	1	0	4	0	0	.000	1	4	0	0	1.0	1.000
1983		11	6	.647	3.65	35	25	5	177.2	167	58	95	3	1	0	0	58	7	0	.121	11	35	0	6	1.3	1.000
1984		1	7	.125	5.27	26	6	0	68.1	81	40	51	0	0	5	1	12	1	0	.083	8	14	1	1	0.9	.957
1985		4	10	.286	4.01	24	23	0	132.1	126	57	74	0	0	1	0	47	4	0	.085	7	23	0	1	1.3	1.000
1987	STL N	4	4	.500	4.84	32	9	0	74.1	90	34	49	0	2	2	0	17	4	0	.235	6	12	0	1	0.6	1.000
1989	MIN A	1	0	1.000	6.00	10	0	0	12	18	6	7	0	1	0	0	0	0	0	–	0	0	0	0	0.0	–
6 yrs.		22	28	.440	4.23	132	66	5	483	499	200	280	3	4	9	1	138	16	0	.116	33	88	1	9	0.9	.992

WORLD SERIES

Year	Team	W	L	PCT	ERA	G	GS	CG	IP	H	BB	SO	ShO	W	L	SV	AB	H	HR	BA	PO	A	E	DP	TC/G	FA
1987	STL N	0	0	–	2.08	2	0	0	4.1	4	2	1	0	0	0	0	0	0	0	–	0	1	0	0	0.5	1.000

George Turbeville

TURBEVILLE, GEORGE ELKINS BR TL 6'1" 175 lbs.
B. Aug. 24, 1914, Turbeville, S. C.   D. Oct. 5, 1983, Salisbury, N. C.

Year	Team	W	L	PCT	ERA	G	GS	CG	IP	H	BB	SO	ShO	W	L	SV	AB	H	HR	BA	PO	A	E	DP	TC/G	FA
1935	PHI A	0	3	.000	7.63	19	6	2	63.2	74	69	20	0	0	0	0	19	2	0	.105	2	11	2	0	0.8	.867
1936		2	5	.286	6.39	12	6	2	43.2	42	32	10	0	1	0	0	14	2	0	.143	2	7	1	0	0.8	.900
1937		0	4	.000	4.77	31	3	0	77.1	80	56	17	0	0	2	0	26	6	0	.231	2	14	5	0	0.7	.762
3 yrs.		2	12	.143	6.14	62	15	4	184.2	196	157	47	0	1	2	0	59	10	0	.169	6	32	8	0	0.7	.826

Lucas Turk

TURK, LUCAS NEWTON (Chief) BR TR 6' 165 lbs.
B. May 2, 1898, Homer, Ga.

Year	Team	W	L	PCT	ERA	G	GS	CG	IP	H	BB	SO	ShO	W	L	SV	AB	H	HR	BA	PO	A	E	DP	TC/G	FA
1922	WAS A	0	0	–	6.94	5	0	0	11.2	16	5	1	0	0	0	0	4	1	0	.250	0	0	0	0	0.0	–

Bob Turley

TURLEY, ROBERT LEE (Bullet Bob) BR TR 6'2" 215 lbs.
B. Sept. 19, 1930, Troy, Ill.

Year	Team	W	L	PCT	ERA	G	GS	CG	IP	H	BB	SO	ShO	W	L	SV	AB	H	HR	BA	PO	A	E	DP	TC/G	FA
1951	STL A	0	1	.000	7.36	1	1	0	7.1	11	3	5	0	0	0	0	2	0	0	.000	1	1	0	1	2.0	1.000
1953		2	6	.250	3.28	10	7	3	60.1	39	44	61	1	1	1	0	18	5	1	.278	4	3	0	2	0.7	1.000
1954	BAL A	14	15	.483	3.46	35	35	14	247.1	178	181	185	0	0	0	0	81	11	0	.136	7	35	1	1	1.2	.977
1955	NY A	17	13	.567	3.06	36	34	13	246.2	168	177	210	6	0	0	1	82	11	0	.134	6	30	4	2	1.1	.900
1956		8	4	.667	5.05	27	21	5	132	138	103	91	1	0	0	1	46	8	0	.174	3	18	1	2	0.8	.955
1957		13	6	.684	2.71	32	23	9	176.1	120	85	152	4	1	0	3	57	5	0	.088	13	22	2	1	1.2	.946
1958		21	7	.750	2.97	33	31	19	245.1	178	128	168	6	0	0	1	88	12	2	.136	17	26	0	4	1.3	1.000
1959		8	11	.421	4.32	33	22	7	154.1	141	83	111	3	0	0	0	46	4	0	.087	11	18	1	0	0.9	.967
1960		9	3	.750	3.27	34	24	4	173.1	138	87	87	1	1	0	5	55	4	0	.073	10	21	0	1	0.9	1.000
1961		3	5	.375	5.75	15	12	1	72	74	51	48	0	0	0	0	21	2	0	.095	4	8	0	0	0.8	1.000
1962		3	3	.500	4.57	24	8	0	69	68	47	42	0	3	0	1	12	0	0	.000	3	15	0	0	0.8	1.000
1963	2 teams	LA A	(19G 2–7)			BOS A	(11G 1–4)																			
"	total	3	11	.214	4.20	30	19	3	128.2	113	79	105	2	0	0	0	39	7	0	.179	9	14	0	1	0.8	1.000
12 yrs.		101	85	.543	3.64	310	237	78	1712.2	1366	1068	1265	24	6	2	12	547	69	4	.126	88	211	9	16	1.0	.971

WORLD SERIES

Year	Team	W	L	PCT	ERA	G	GS	CG	IP	H	BB	SO	ShO	W	L	SV	AB	H	HR	BA	PO	A	E	DP	TC/G	FA
1955	NY A	0	1	.000	8.44	3	1	0	5.1	7	4	7	0	0	0	0	1	0	0	.000	0	1	0	0	0.3	1.000
1956		0	1	.000	0.82	3	1	1	11	4	8	14	0	0	0	0	4	0	0	.000	0	2	0	0	0.7	1.000
1957		1	0	1.000	2.31	3	2	1	11.2	7	6	12	0	0	0	0	4	0	0	.000	2	4	0	1	1.3	1.000
1958		2	1	.667	2.76	4	2	1	16.1	10	7	13	1	1	0	1	5	1	0	.200	0	1	0	0	0.3	1.000
1960		1	0	1.000	4.82	2	2	0	9.1	15	4	0	0	0	0	0	4	1	0	.250	2	8	0	1	1.0	1.000
5 yrs.		4	3	.571	3.19	15	8	3	53.2	43	29	46	1	1	0	1	18	2	0	.111	2	8	0	1	0.7	1.000

3rd 10th   5th 10th

Year	Team		W	L	PCT	ERA	G	GS	CG	IP	H	BB	SO	ShO	W	L	SV	AB	H	HR	BA	PO	A	E	DP	TC/G	FA
															Relief Pitching			**Batting**									

Jim Turner

TURNER, JAMES RILEY (Milkman Jim)   BL TR 6'   185 lbs.
B. Aug. 6, 1903, Antioch, Tenn.

Year	Team		W	L	PCT	ERA	G	GS	CG	IP	H	BB	SO	ShO	W	L	SV	AB	H	HR	BA	PO	A	E	DP	TC/G	FA
1937	BOS	N	20	11	.645	**2.38**	33	30	**24**	256.2	228	52	69	**5**	0	1	1	96	24	0	.250	12	59	4	3	2.3	.947
1938			14	18	.438	3.46	35	34	22	268	267	54	71	3	0	0	0	96	22	0	.229	17	72	0	4	2.5	1.000
1939			4	11	.267	4.28	25	22	9	157.2	181	51	50	0	0	0	0	55	13	1	.236	8	38	2	0	1.9	.958
1940	CIN	N	14	7	.667	2.89	24	23	11	187	181	32	53	0	1	0	0	75	18	0	.240	8	35	1	1	1.8	.977
1941			6	4	.600	3.11	23	10	3	113	120	24	34	0	1	0	0	41	6	0	.146	0	33	1	4	1.5	.971
1942	2 teams		CIN N	(3G 0–0)		NY A	(5G 1–1)																					
"	total		1	1	.500	4.35	8	0	0	10.1	9	4	2	0	1	1	1	2	0	0	.000	2	1	0	0	0.4	1.000
1943	NY	A	3	0	1.000	3.53	18	0	0	43.1	44	13	15	0	3	0	1	13	1	0	.077	3	8	1	0	0.7	.917
1944			4	4	.500	3.46	35	0	0	41.2	42	22	13	0	4	4	7	10	2	0	.200	2	6	2	0	0.3	.800
1945			3	4	.429	3.64	30	0	0	54.1	45	31	22	0	3	4	**10**	11	1	0	.091	3	14	1	2	0.6	.944
9 yrs.			69	60	.535	3.22	231	119	69	1132	1117	283	329	8	13	10	20	399	87	1	.218	55	266	12	14	1.4	.964

WORLD SERIES

Year	Team		W	L	PCT	ERA	G	GS	CG	IP	H	BB	SO	ShO	W	L	SV	AB	H	HR	BA	PO	A	E	DP	TC/G	FA
1940	CIN	N	0	1	.000	7.50	1	1	0	6	8	0	4	0	0	0	0	2	0	0	.000	0	1	0	0	1.0	1.000
1942	NY	A	0	0	–	0.00	1	0	0	1	0	1	0	0	0	0	0	0	0	0	–	0	0	0	0	0.0	–
2 yrs.			0	1	.000	6.43	2	1	0	7	8	1	4	0	0	0	0	2	0	0	.000	0	1	0	0	0.5	1.000

Ken Turner

TURNER, KENNETH CHARLES   BR TL 6'2"   190 lbs.
B. Aug. 17, 1943, Framingham, Mass.

Year	Team		W	L	PCT	ERA	G	GS	CG	IP	H	BB	SO	ShO	W	L	SV	AB	H	HR	BA	PO	A	E	DP	TC/G	FA
1967	CAL	A	1	2	.333	4.15	13	1	0	17.1	16	4	6	0	1	0	1	4	0	0	.000	1	4	0	0	0.4	1.000

Ted Turner

TURNER, THEODORE HOLHOT   BR TR 6'   180 lbs.
B. May 4, 1892, Lawrenceburg, Ky.   D. Feb. 4, 1958, Lexington, Ky.

Year	Team		W	L	PCT	ERA	G	GS	CG	IP	H	BB	SO	ShO	W	L	SV	AB	H	HR	BA	PO	A	E	DP	TC/G	FA
1920	CHI	N	0	0	–	13.50	1	0	0	1.1	2	1	0	0	0	0	0	0	0	0	.000	0	0	0	0	0.0	–

Tink Turner

TURNER, THOMAS LOVATT   BR TR 6'1"   190 lbs.
B. Feb. 20, 1890, Swarthmore, Pa.   D. Feb. 25, 1962, Philadelphia, Pa.

Year	Team		W	L	PCT	ERA	G	GS	CG	IP	H	BB	SO	ShO	W	L	SV	AB	H	HR	BA	PO	A	E	DP	TC/G	FA
1915	PHI	A	0	1	.000	22.50	1	1	0	2	5	3	0	0	0	0	0	0	0	0	–	0	1	0	0	1.0	1.000

Tuck Turner

TURNER, GEORGE A.   BB TL
B. Feb. 13, 1873, West Brighton, N. Y.   D. July 16, 1945, Staten Island, N. Y.

Year	Team		W	L	PCT	ERA	G	GS	CG	IP	H	BB	SO	ShO	W	L	SV	AB	H	HR	BA	PO	A	E	DP	TC/G	FA
1894	PHI	N	0	0	–	7.50	1	0	0	6	9	2	3	0	0	0	0	*					0	0	0	0	0.0	–

Elmer Tutwiler

TUTWILER, ELMER STRANGE   BR TR 5'11"   158 lbs.
B. Nov. 19, 1905, Carbon Hill, Ala.   D. May 3, 1976, Pensacola, Fla.

Year	Team		W	L	PCT	ERA	G	GS	CG	IP	H	BB	SO	ShO	W	L	SV	AB	H	HR	BA	PO	A	E	DP	TC/G	FA
1928	PIT	N	0	0	–	4.91	2	0	0	3.2	4	0	1	0	0	0	0	1	0	0	.000	1	0	0	0	0.5	1.000

Twink Twining

TWINING, HOWARD EARLE (Doc)   BR TR 6'   168 lbs.
B. May 30, 1894, Horsham, Pa.   D. June 14, 1973, Lansdale, Pa.

Year	Team		W	L	PCT	ERA	G	GS	CG	IP	H	BB	SO	ShO	W	L	SV	AB	H	HR	BA	PO	A	E	DP	TC/G	FA
1916	CIN	N	0	0	–	13.50	1	0	0	2	4	1	0	0	0	0	0	0	0	0	–	0	0	0	0	1.0	1.000

Larry Twitchell

TWITCHELL, LAWRENCE GRANT   BR TR 6'   185 lbs.
B. Feb. 18, 1864, Cleveland, Ohio   D. Aug. 23, 1930, Cleveland, Ohio

Year	Team		W	L	PCT	ERA	G	GS	CG	IP	H	BB	SO	ShO	W	L	SV	AB	H	HR	BA	PO	A	E	DP	TC/G	FA
1886	DET	N	0	2	.000	6.48	4	4	2	25	35	12	6	0	0	0	0	16	1	0	.063	1	8	0	1	2.3	1.000
1887			11	1	.917	4.33	15	12	11	112.1	120	36	24	0	1	0	1	264	88	0	.333	5	12	1	1	1.1	1.000
1888			0	0	–	6.75	2	0	0	4	6	1	3	0	0	0	0	524	128	5	.244	0	2	1	0	1.5	.667
1889	CLE	N	0	0	–	0.00	1	0	0	1	0	1	0	0	0	0	0	549	151	4	.275	0	0	0	0	0.0	–
1890	BUF	P	5	7	.417	4.57	12	12	12	104.1	112	72	29	0	0	0	0	405	90	4	.222	7	34	3	0	3.7	.932
1891	COL	AA	1	1	.500	4.06	6	1	1	31	29	13	8	0	1	0	0	224	62	2	.277	3	6	0	0	1.5	1.000
1894	LOU	N	0	0	–	6.00	1	0	0	3	5	1	0	0	0	0	0	210	56	2	.267	0	2	0	0	2.0	1.000
7 yrs.			17	11	.607	4.62	41	29	26	280.2	307	135	70	0	2	0	2	*				16	64	4	2	2.0	.952

Wayne Twitchell

TWITCHELL, WAYNE LEE   BR TR 6'6"   215 lbs.
B. Mar. 10, 1948, Portland, Ore.

Year	Team		W	L	PCT	ERA	G	GS	CG	IP	H	BB	SO	ShO	W	L	SV	AB	H	HR	BA	PO	A	E	DP	TC/G	FA
1970	MIL	A	0	0	–	9.00	2	0	0	2	3	1	5	0	0	0	0	0	0	0	–	0	0	0	0	0.0	–
1971	PHI	N	1	0	1.000	0.00	6	1	0	16	8	10	15	0	1	0	0	3	0	0	.000	0	2	0	0	0.3	1.000
1972			5	9	.357	4.06	49	15	1	139.2	138	56	112	1	2	1	1	28	2	0	.071	8	14	4	1	0.5	.846
1973			13	9	.591	2.50	34	28	10	223.1	172	99	169	5	0	0	0	72	7	0	.097	12	17	4	0	1.0	.879
1974			6	9	.400	5.22	25	18	2	112	122	65	72	0	1	1	0	35	6	0	.171	4	11	3	1	0.7	.833
1975			5	10	.333	4.43	36	20	0	134	132	78	101	0	0	0	0	34	3	0	.088	7	6	4	0	0.5	.765
1976			3	1	.750	1.75	26	2	0	61.2	55	18	67	0	2	0	1	6	1	0	.167	1	9	1	1	0.4	.909
1977	2 teams		PHI N	(12G 0–5)		MON N	(22G 6–5)																					
"	total		6	10	.375	4.29	34	30	2	184.2	166	74	130	0	0	0	0	50	9	0	.180	10	24	0	3	1.0	1.000
1978	MON	N	4	12	.250	5.38	33	15	0	112	121	71	69	0	1	4	0	24	2	0	.083	2	15	3	1	0.6	.850
1979	2 teams		NY N	(33G 5–3)		SEA A	(4G 0–2)																					
"	total		5	5	.500	5.19	37	4	0	78	66	65	49	0	5	0	4	8	3	0	.375	2	10	1	1	0.4	.923
10 yrs.			48	65	.425	3.98	282	133	15	1063.1	983	537	789	6	12	9	2	260	33	0	.127	46	108	20	8	0.6	.885

Jeff Twitty

TWITTY, JEFFREY DEAN   BL TL 6'2"   185 lbs.
B. Nov. 10, 1957, Lancaster, S. C.

Year	Team		W	L	PCT	ERA	G	GS	CG	IP	H	BB	SO	ShO	W	L	SV	AB	H	HR	BA	PO	A	E	DP	TC/G	FA
1980	KC	A	2	1	.667	6.14	13	0	0	22	33	7	9	0	2	1	0	0	0	0	–	0	5	0	0	0.4	1.000

Cy Twombly

TWOMBLY, EDWIN PARKER   BR TR 5'10½"   170 lbs.
B. June 15, 1897, Groveland, Mass.   D. Dec. 3, 1974, Savannah, Ga.

Year	Team		W	L	PCT	ERA	G	GS	CG	IP	H	BB	SO	ShO	W	L	SV	AB	H	HR	BA	PO	A	E	DP	TC/G	FA
1921	CHI	A	1	2	.333	5.86	7	4	0	27.2	26	25	7	0	0	0	0	10	0	0	.000	0	10	0	2	1.4	1.000

Year	Team	W	L	PCT	ERA	G	GS	CG	IP	H	BB	SO	ShO	Relief Pitching W	L	SV	Batting AB	H	HR	BA	PO	A	E	DP	TC/G	FA

Lefty Tyler

TYLER, GEORGE ALBERT Brother of Fred Tyler. B. Dec. 14, 1889, Derry, N. H. D. Sept. 29, 1953, Lowell, Mass. BL TL 6' 175 lbs.

Year	Team	W	L	PCT	ERA	G	GS	CG	IP	H	BB	SO	ShO	W	L	SV	AB	H	HR	BA	PO	A	E	DP	TC/G	FA
1910	BOS N	0	0	–	2.38	2	0	0	11.1	11	6	6	0	0	0	0	4	2	0	.500	0	2	0	0	1.0	1.000
1911		7	10	.412	5.06	28	20	10	165.1	150	109	90	1	1	0	0	61	10	0	.164	8	58	8	2	2.6	.892
1912		12	22	.353	4.18	42	31	29	256.1	262	126	144	1	2	3	0	96	19	0	.198	15	75	5	3	2.3	.947
1913		16	17	.485	2.79	39	34	28	290.1	245	108	143	4	1	0	2	102	19	0	.206	13	107	9	1	3.3	.930
1914		16	14	.533	2.69	38	34	21	271.1	247	101	140	6	0	1	2	94	19	0	.202	16	57	5	3	2.1	.936
1915		10	9	.526	2.86	32	24	15	204.2	182	84	89	1	0	0	0	88	23	1	.261	6	50	1	1	1.8	.982
1916		17	10	.630	2.02	34	28	21	249.1	200	58	117	6	2	1	1	93	19	3	.204	9	72	3	3	2.5	.964
1917		14	12	.538	2.52	32	28	22	239	203	86	98	4	1	1	1	134	31	0	.231	14	76	2	4	2.9	.978
1918	CHI N	19	9	.679	2.00	33	30	22	269.1	218	67	102	8	1	1	1	100	21	0	.210	17	88	3	3	3.3	.972
1919		2	2	.500	2.10	6	5	3	30	20	13	9	0	0	0	0	7	1	0	.143	1	13	0	1	2.3	1.000
1920		11	12	.478	3.31	27	27	18	193	193	57	57	2	0	0	0	65	17	0	.262	15	64	2	3	3.0	.975
1921		3	2	.600	3.24	10	6	4	50	59	14	8	0	1	0	0	26	6	0	.231	3	10	0	1	1.3	1.000
12 yrs.		127	119	.516	2.95	323	267	193	2230	1990	829	1003	33	9	7	7	*				117	672	38	25	2.6	.954

WORLD SERIES

Year	Team	W	L	PCT	ERA	G	GS	CG	IP	H	BB	SO	ShO	W	L	SV	AB	H	HR	BA	PO	A	E	DP	TC/G	FA
1914	BOS N	0	0	–	3.60	1	1	0	10	8	3	4	0	0	0	0	3	0	0	.000	1	5	0	0	6.0	1.000
1918	CHI N	1	1	.500	1.17	3	3	1	23	14	11	4	0	0	0	0	5	1	0	.200	2	9	1	0	4.0	.917
2 yrs.		1	1	.500	1.91	4	4	1	33	22	14	8	0	0	0	0	8	1	0	.125	3	14	1	0	4.5	.944

Jim Tyng

TYNG, JAMES ALEXANDER B. Mar. 27, 1856, Philadelphia, Pa. D. Oct. 30, 1931, New York, N. Y. 5'9" 155 lbs.

Year	Team	W	L	PCT	ERA	G	GS	CG	IP	H	BB	SO	ShO	W	L	SV	AB	H	HR	BA	PO	A	E	DP	TC/G	FA
1879	BOS N	1	2	.333	5.00	3	3	3	27	35	6	7	0	0	0	0	14	5	0	.357	2	6	0	0	2.7	1.000
1888	PHI N	0	0	–	4.50	1	0	0	4	8	2	2	0	0	0	1	1	0	0	.000	0	2	0	0	2.0	1.000
2 yrs.		1	2	.333	4.94	4	3	3	31	43	8	9	0	0	0	1	15	5	0	.333	2	8	0	0	2.5	1.000

Dave Tyriver

TYRIVER, DAVID BURTON B. Oct. 31, 1937, Oshkosh, Wis. D. Oct. 28, 1988, Oshkosh, Wis. BR TR 6' 175 lbs.

Year	Team	W	L	PCT	ERA	G	GS	CG	IP	H	BB	SO	ShO	W	L	SV	AB	H	HR	BA	PO	A	E	DP	TC/G	FA
1962	CLE A	0	0	–	4.22	4	0	0	10.2	10	7	7	0	0	0	0	3	0	0	.000	1	2	0	0	0.8	1.000

Jimmy Uchrinsko

UCHRINSKO, JAMES EMERSON B. Oct. 20, 1900, West Newton, Pa. BL TR 6' 180 lbs.

Year	Team	W	L	PCT	ERA	G	GS	CG	IP	H	BB	SO	ShO	W	L	SV	AB	H	HR	BA	PO	A	E	DP	TC/G	FA
1926	WAS A	0	0	–	10.13	3	0	0	8	13	8	0	0	0	0	0	2	0	0	.000	1	2	0	1	1.0	1.000

Bob Uhle

UHLE, ROBERT ELLWOOD (Lefty) B. Sept. 17, 1913, San Francisco, Calif. BB TL 5'11" 175 lbs.

Year	Team	W	L	PCT	ERA	G	GS	CG	IP	H	BB	SO	ShO	W	L	SV	AB	H	HR	BA	PO	A	E	DP	TC/G	FA
1938	CHI A	0	0	–	0.00	1	0	0	2	1	0	0	0	0	0	0	0	0	0	–	0	0	0	0	0.0	–
1940	DET A	0	0	–	∞	1	0	0	0	4	2	0	0	0	0	0	0	0	0	–	0	0	0	0	0.0	–
2 yrs.		0	0	–	18.00	2	0	0	2	5	2	0	0	0	0	0	0	0	0	–	0	0	0	0	0.0	–

George Uhle

UHLE, GEORGE ERNEST (The Bull) B. Sept. 18, 1898, Cleveland, Ohio D. Feb. 26, 1985, Lakewood, Ohio BR TR 6' 190 lbs.

Year	Team	W	L	PCT	ERA	G	GS	CG	IP	H	BB	SO	ShO	W	L	SV	AB	H	HR	BA	PO	A	E	DP	TC/G	FA
1919	CLE A	10	5	.667	2.91	26	12	7	127	129	43	50	1	2	2	0	43	13	0	.302	10	33	4	1	1.8	.915
1920		4	5	.444	5.21	27	6	2	84.2	98	29	27	0	4	1	1	32	11	0	.344	6	21	0	0	1.0	1.000
1921		16	13	.552	4.01	41	28	13	238	288	62	63	2	2	2	2	94	23	1	.245	15	46	4	2	1.6	.938
1922		22	16	.579	4.07	50	40	23	287.1	328	89	82	5	1	1	3	109	29	0	.266	16	53	5	5	1.5	.932
1923		26	16	.619	3.77	54	44	29	357.2	378	102	109	1	1	0	5	144	52	0	.361	18	89	2	9	2.0	.982
1924		9	15	.375	4.77	28	25	15	196.1	238	75	57	0	1	1	1	107	33	1	.308	19	42	0	5	2.2	1.000
1925		13	11	.542	4.10	29	26	17	210.2	218	78	68	1	1	1	0	104	29	0	.279	12	39	3	2	1.9	.944
1926		27	11	.711	2.83	39	36	32	318.1	300	118	159	3	1	1	1	132	30	1	.227	30	67	7	3	2.7	.933
1927		8	9	.471	4.34	25	22	10	153.1	187	59	69	1	0	1	1	79	21	0	.266	6	31	1	3	1.5	.974
1928		12	17	.414	4.07	31	28	18	214.1	252	48	74	1	1	1	1	98	28	1	.286	10	59	2	4	2.3	.972
1929	DET A	15	11	.577	4.08	32	30	23	249	283	58	100	1	1	0	0	108	37	0	.343	13	39	4	2	1.8	.929
1930		12	12	.500	3.65	33	29	18	239	239	75	117	0	0	0	3	117	36	2	.308	10	29	1	2	1.2	.975
1931		11	12	.478	3.50	29	18	15	193	190	49	63	2	4	3	2	90	22	2	.244	3	38	0	1	1.4	1.000
1932		6	6	.500	4.48	33	15	6	146.2	152	42	51	1	1	2	5	55	10	0	.182	5	25	0	2	0.9	1.000
1933	3 teams	DET A	(1G 0–0)		NY N	(6G 1–1)			NY A	(12G 6–1)																
"	total	7	2	.778	5.85	19	7	4	75.1	81	26	31	0	2	0	0	25	8	0	.320	1	13	0	1	0.7	1.000
1934	NY A	2	4	.333	9.92	10	2	0	16.1	30	7	10	0	2	2	0	5	3	0	.600	1	0	0	1	0.2	1.000
1936	CLE A	0	1	.000	8.53	7	0	0	12.2	26	5	5	0	0	1	0	21	8	0	.381	0	0	0	0	0.0	–
17 yrs.		200	166	.546	3.99	513	368	232	3119.2	3417	965	1135	21	24	19	25	*				175	625	33	42	1.6	.960

WORLD SERIES

Year	Team	W	L	PCT	ERA	G	GS	CG	IP	H	BB	SO	ShO	W	L	SV	AB	H	HR	BA	PO	A	E	DP	TC/G	FA
1920	CLE A	0	0	–	0.00	1	0	0	3	1	0	3	0	0	0	0	0	0	0	–	0	1	0	0	1.0	1.000

Jerry Ujdur

UJDUR, GERALD RAYMOND B. Mar. 5, 1957, Duluth, Minn. BR TR 6'1" 195 lbs.

Year	Team	W	L	PCT	ERA	G	GS	CG	IP	H	BB	SO	ShO	W	L	SV	AB	H	HR	BA	PO	A	E	DP	TC/G	FA
1980	DET A	1	0	1.000	7.71	9	2	0	21	36	10	8	0	0	0	0	–				0	0	0	0	0.1	1.000
1981		0	0	–	6.43	4	4	0	14	19	5	5	0	0	0	0	–				1	3	0	0	1.0	1.000
1982		10	10	.500	3.69	25	25	7	178	150	69	86	0	0	0	0	–				11	21	2	2	1.4	.941
1983		0	4	.000	7.15	11	6	0	34	41	20	13	0	0	0	0	–				3	1	1	0	0.5	.800
1984	CLE A	1	2	.333	6.91	4	3	0	14.1	22	6	6	0	1	0	0	–				0	1	0	0	0.3	–
5 yrs.		12	16	.429	4.79	53	40	7	261.1	268	110	118	0	1	0	0	–				15	26	4	2	0.8	.911

Sandy Ullrich

ULLRICH, CARLOS SANTIAGO Born Carlos Santiago Ullrich y Castello. B. July 25, 1921, Havana, Cuba BR TR 6'½" 175 lbs.

Year	Team	W	L	PCT	ERA	G	GS	CG	IP	H	BB	SO	ShO	W	L	SV	AB	H	HR	BA	PO	A	E	DP	TC/G	FA
1944	WAS A	0	0	–	9.31	3	0	0	9.2	17	4	2	0	0	0	0	3	1	0	.333	1	2	0	0	1.0	1.000

Year	Team		W	L	PCT	ERA	G	GS	CG	IP	H	BB	SO	ShO	Relief Pitching W	L	SV	Batting AB	H	HR	BA	PO	A	E	DP	TC/G	FA

Sandy Ullrich *continued*

| 1945 | | | 3 | 3 | .500 | 4.54 | 28 | 6 | 0 | 81.1 | 91 | 34 | 26 | 0 | 3 | 1 | 1 | 22 | 6 | 0 | .273 | 2 | 24 | 0 | 1 | 0.9 | 1.000 |
| 2 yrs. | | | 3 | 3 | .500 | 5.04 | 31 | 6 | 0 | 91 | 108 | 38 | 28 | 0 | 3 | 1 | 1 | 25 | 7 | 0 | .280 | 3 | 26 | 0 | 1 | 0.9 | 1.000 |

Dutch Ulrich

ULRICH, FRANK W.   BR TR 6'2"   195 lbs.
B. Nov. 18, 1899, Baltimore, Md.   D. Feb. 11, 1929, Baltimore, Md.

1925	PHI	N	3	3	.500	3.05	21	4	2	65	73	12	29	1	2	0	0	16	2	0	.125	2	18	0	2	1.0	1.000
1926			8	13	.381	4.08	45	17	8	147.2	178	37	52	1	1	4	1	49	12	0	.245	7	33	2	3	0.9	.952
1927			8	11	.421	3.17	32	18	14	193.1	201	40	42	1	1	1	1	73	9	0	.123	12	29	0	1	1.3	1.000
3 yrs.			19	27	.413	3.48	98	39	24	406	452	89	123	3	4	5	2	138	23	0	.167	21	80	2	6	1.1	.981

Arnie Umbach

UMBACH, ARNOLD WILLIAM   BR TR 6'1"   180 lbs.
B. Dec. 6, 1942, Williamsburg, Va.

1964	MIL	N	1	0	1.000	3.24	1	1	0	8.1	11	4	7	0	0	0	0	3	0	0	.000	0	1	0	0	1.0	1.000
1966	ATL	N	0	2	.000	3.10	22	3	0	40.2	40	18	23	0	0	1	0	5	1	0	.200	4	5	1	0	0.5	.900
2 yrs.			1	2	.333	3.12	23	4	0	49	51	22	30	0	0	1	0	8	1	0	.125	4	6	1	0	0.5	.909

Jim Umbarger

UMBARGER, JAMES HAROLD   BL TL 6'6"   200 lbs.
B. Feb. 17, 1953, Burbank, Calif.

1975	TEX	A	8	7	.533	4.12	56	12	3	131	134	59	50	2	3	2	2	0	0	0	—	8	26	1	2	0.6	.971
1976			10	12	.455	3.15	30	30	10	197	208	54	105	3	0	0	0	0	0	0	—	4	30	1	3	1.2	.971
1977	2 teams	OAK A (12G 1–5)		TEX A	(3G 1–1)																						
"	total		2	6	.250	6.32	15	10	1	57	76	32	29	0	0	0	0	0	0	0	—	0	11	1	1	0.8	.917
1978	TEX	A	5	8	.385	4.88	32	9	0	97.2	116	36	60	0	2	3	1	0	0	0	—	1	21	2	0	0.8	.917
4 yrs.			25	33	.431	4.14	133	61	15	482.2	534	181	244	5	5	6	3	0	0	0	—	13	88	5	6	0.8	.953

Jim Umbricht

UMBRICHT, JAMES   BR TR 6'4"   215 lbs.
B. Sept. 17, 1930, Chicago, Ill.   D. Apr. 8, 1964, Houston, Tex.

1959	PIT	N	0	0	—	6.43	1	1	0	7	7	4	3	0	0	0	0	3	0	0	.000	1	1	0	0	2.0	1.000
1960			1	2	.333	5.09	17	3	0	40.2	40	27	26	0	1	1	0	6	2	0	.333	1	4	2	1	0.4	.714
1961			0	0	—	2.70	9	0	0	3.1	5	2	1	0	0	0	0	1	1	0	1.000	1	0	0	0	0.2	1.000
1962	HOU	N	4	0	1.000	2.01	34	0	0	67	51	17	55	0	4	0	2	9	1	0	.111	0	14	0	0	0.4	1.000
1963			4	3	.571	2.61	35	3	0	76	52	21	48	0	4	1	0	9	1	0	.111	7	14	0	2	0.6	1.000
5 yrs.			9	5	.643	3.06	88	7	0	194	155	71	133	0	9	1	3	28	5	0	.179	10	33	2	3	0.5	.956

Willie Underhill

UNDERHILL, WILLIE VERN   BR TR 6'2"   185 lbs.
B. Sept. 6, 1904, Yowell, Tex.   D. Oct. 26, 1970, Bay City, Tex.

1927	CLE	A	0	2	.000	9.72	4	1	0	8.1	12	11	4	0	0	1	0	1	0	0	.000	0	2	0	0	0.5	1.000
1928			1	2	.333	4.50	11	3	1	28	33	20	16	0	1	0	0	11	4	0	.364	1	6	0	0	0.6	1.000
2 yrs.			1	4	.200	5.70	15	4	1	36.1	45	31	20	0	1	1	0	12	4	0	.333	1	8	0	0	0.6	1.000

Fred Underwood

UNDERWOOD, FREDERICK THEODORE
B. Oct. 14, 1868, St. Louis County, Mo.   D. Jan. 26, 1906, Kansas City, Mo.

| 1894 | BKN | N | 2 | 4 | .333 | 7.85 | 7 | 6 | 5 | 47 | 80 | 30 | 10 | 0 | 0 | 0 | 0 | 18 | 7 | 0 | .389 | 2 | 7 | 1 | 0 | 1.4 | .900 |

Pat Underwood

UNDERWOOD, PATRICK JOHN   BL TL 6'   175 lbs.
Brother of Tom Underwood.
B. Feb. 9, 1957, Kokomo, Ind.

1979	DET	A	6	4	.600	4.57	27	15	0	122	126	29	83	0	0	0	0	0	0	0	—	1	15	1	0	0.6	.941
1980			3	6	.333	3.58	49	7	0	113	121	35	60	0	1	4	5	0	0	0	—	7	16	0	0	0.5	1.000
1982			4	8	.333	4.73	33	12	2	99	108	22	43	0	1	1	3	0	0	0	—	1	21	1	1	0.7	.957
1983			0	0	—	8.71	4	0	0	10.1	11	6	2	0	0	0	0	0	0	0	—	1	0	0	0	0.3	1.000
4 yrs.			13	18	.419	4.42	113	34	3	344.1	366	92	188	0	2	5	8	0	0	0	—	10	52	2	1	0.6	.969

Tom Underwood

UNDERWOOD, THOMAS GERALD   BR TL 5'11"   170 lbs.
Brother of Pat Underwood.
B. Dec. 22, 1953, Kokomo, Ind.

1974	PHI	N	1	0	1.000	4.85	7	0	0	13	15	5	8	0	1	0	0	1	0	0	.000	0	0	0	0	0.0	—
1975			14	13	.519	4.15	35	35	7	219	221	84	123	2	0	0	0	74	9	0	.122	3	21	4	1	0.8	.852
1976			10	5	.667	3.53	33	25	0	155.2	154	63	94	0	1	0	2	46	5	0	.109	3	17	1	1	0.6	.952
1977	2 teams	PHI N (14G 3–2)		STL N	(19G 6–9)																						
"	total		9	11	.450	5.01	33	17	1	133	148	75	86	0	3	3	1	33	4	0	.121	4	14	3	2	0.6	.857
1978	TOR	A	6	14	.300	4.10	31	30	7	197.2	201	87	139	1	0	1	0	0	0	0	—	5	19	5	0	0.9	.828
1979			9	16	.360	3.69	33	32	12	227	213	95	127	1	0	0	0	0	0	0	—	6	36	5	2	1.4	.894
1980	NY	A	13	9	.591	3.66	38	27	2	187	163	66	116	2	0	0	0	0	0	0	—	10	26	2	2	1.0	.947
1981	2 teams	NY A (9G 1–4)		OAK A	(16G 3–2)																						
"	total		4	6	.400	3.64	25	11	1	84	69	38	75	0	2	2	1	0	0	0	—	2	13	2	1	0.7	.882
1982	OAK	A	10	6	.625	3.29	56	10	2	153	136	68	79	0	5	3	7	0	0	0	—	9	11	2	0	0.4	.909
1983			9	7	.563	4.04	51	15	0	144.2	156	50	62	0	4	2	4	0	0	0	—	3	11	2	2	0.3	.875
1984	BAL	A	1	0	1.000	3.52	37	1	0	71.2	78	31	39	0	1	0	1	0	0	0	—	5	12	0	2	0.5	1.000
11 yrs.			86	87	.497	3.89	379	203	35	1585.2	1554	662	948	6	19	13	18	154	18	0	.117	49	180	26	13	0.7	.898

DIVISIONAL PLAYOFF SERIES

| 1981 | OAK | A | 0 | 0 | — | 0.00 | 1 | 0 | 0 | .1 | 0 | 0 | 1 | 0 | 0 | 0 | 0 | 0 | 0 | 0 | — | 0 | 0 | 0 | 0 | 0.0 | — |

LEAGUE CHAMPIONSHIP SERIES

1976	PHI	N	0	0	—	0.00	1	0	0	.1	1	2	0	0	0	0	0	0	0	0	—	0	0	0	0	0.0	—
1980	NY	A	0	0	—	0.00	2	0	0	3	3	0	3	0	0	0	0	0	0	0	—	0	2	0	0	1.0	1.000
1981	OAK	A	0	0	—	13.50	2	0	0	1.1	4	2	2	0	0	0	0	0	0	0	—	0	0	0	0	0.0	—
3 yrs.			0	0	—	3.86	5	0	0	4.2	8	4	5	0	0	0	0	0	0	0	—	0	2	0	0	0.4	1.000

Year	Team	W	L	PCT	ERA	G	GS	CG	IP	H	BB	SO	ShO	Relief Pitching W	L	SV	Batting AB	H	HR	BA	PO	A	E	DP	TC/G	FA

Woody Upchurch

UPCHURCH, JEFFERSON WOODROW BR TL 6' 180 lbs.
B. Apr. 13, 1911, Buies Creek, N. C. D. Oct. 23, 1971, Buies Creek, N. C.

Year	Team	W	L	PCT	ERA	G	GS	CG	IP	H	BB	SO	ShO	W	L	SV	AB	H	HR	BA	PO	A	E	DP	TC/G	FA
1935	PHI A	0	2	.000	5.06	3	3	1	21.1	23	12	2	0	0	0	0	7	2	0	.286	0	4	1	0	1.7	.800
1936		0	2	.000	9.67	7	2	1	22.1	36	14	6	0	0	0	0	7	1	0	.143	0	1	0	0	0.1	1.000
2 yrs.		0	4	.000	7.42	10	5	2	43.2	59	26	8	0	0	0	0	14	3	0	.214	0	5	1	0	0.6	.833

Bill Upham

UPHAM, WILLIAM LAWRENCE BB TR 6' 178 lbs.
B. Apr. 4, 1888, Akron, Ohio D. Sept. 14, 1959, Newark, N. J.

1915	BKN F	7	8	.467	3.05	33	11	4	121	129	40	46	2	3	2	4	36	4	0	.111	5	48	3	3	1.7	.946
1918	BOS N	1	1	.500	5.23	3	2	2	20.2	28	1	8	0	0	0	0	9	2	0	.222	0	6	0	0	2.0	1.000
2 yrs.		8	9	.471	3.37	36	13	6	141.2	157	41	54	2	3	2	4	45	6	0	.133	5	54	3	3	1.7	.952

John Upham

UPHAM, JOHN LESLIE BL TL 6' 180 lbs.
B. Dec. 29, 1941, Windsor, Ont., Canada

1967	CHI N	0	1	.000	33.75	5	0	0	1.1	4	2	2	0	0	1	0	3	2	0	.667	0	0	0	0	0.0	—
1968		0	0	—	0.00	2	0	0	7	2	3	2	0	0	0	0	10	2	0	.200	0	3	0	0	1.5	1.000
2 yrs.		0	1	.000	5.40	7	0	0	8.1	6	5	4	0	0	1	0	*				0	3	0	0	0.4	1.000

Jerry Upp

UPP, GEORGE HENRY TL
B. Dec. 10, 1883, Sandusky, Ohio D. June 30, 1937, Sandusky, Ohio

1909	CLE A	2	1	.667	1.69	7	4	2	26.2	26	12	13	0	0	0	0	9	2	0	.222	3	11	1	0	2.1	.933

Cecil Upshaw

UPSHAW, CECIL LEE BR TR 6'6" 205 lbs.
B. Oct. 22, 1942, Spearsville, La.

1966	ATL N	0	0	—	0.00	1	0	0	3	3	0	2	0	0	0	0	1	1	0	1.000	0	0	0	0	0.0	—
1967		2	3	.400	2.58	30	0	0	45.1	42	8	31	0	2	3	8	6	1	0	.167	2	8	1	0	0.4	.909
1968		8	7	.533	2.47	52	0	0	116.2	98	24	74	0	8	7	13	23	4	0	.174	6	19	1	0	0.5	.962
1969		6	4	.600	2.91	62	0	0	105	102	29	57	0	6	4	27	21	5	1	.238	6	21	1	1	0.5	.964
1971		11	6	.647	3.51	49	0	0	82	95	28	56	0	11	6	17	15	0	0	.000	3	11	1	0	0.3	.933
1972		3	5	.375	3.67	42	0	0	54	50	19	23	0	3	5	13	7	1	0	.143	2	11	1	0	0.4	.933
1973	2 teams	ATL N	(5G 0–1)		HOU N	(35G 2–3)																				
"	total	2	4	.333	4.93	40	0	0	42	46	17	24	0	2	4	1	2	0	0	.000	3	10	0	0	0.3	1.000
1974	2 teams	CLE A	(7G 0–1)		NY A	(36G 1–5)																				
"	total	1	6	.143	3.04	43	0	0	68	63	28	34	0	1	6	6	0	0	0	—	6	13	3	1	0.5	.864
1975	CHI A	1	1	.500	3.23	29	0	0	47.1	49	21	22	0	1	1	1	0	0	0	—	0	8	2	1	0.3	.800
9 yrs.		34	36	.486	3.13	348	0	0	563.1	545	177	323	0	34	36	86	75	12	1	.160	28	102	10	3	0.4	.929

LEAGUE CHAMPIONSHIP SERIES

1969	ATL N	0	0	—	2.84	3	0	0	6.1	5	1	4	0	0	0	0	1	0	0	.000	0	1	0	0	0.3	1.000

Bill Upton

UPTON, WILLIAM RAY BR TR 6' 167 lbs.
Brother of Tom Upton.
B. June 18, 1929, Esther, Mo.

1954	PHI A	0	0	—	1.80	2	0	0	5	6	1	2	0	0	0	1	0	0	0	—	0	1	0	0	0.5	1.000

Jack Urban

URBAN, JACK ELMER BR TR 5'8" 155 lbs.
B. Dec. 5, 1928, Omaha, Neb.

1957	KC A	7	4	.636	3.34	31	13	3	129.1	111	45	55	0	1	0	0	39	11	0	.282	12	27	1	2	1.3	.975
1958		8	11	.421	5.93	30	24	5	132	150	51	54	1	0	0	1	46	7	0	.152	13	14	2	2	1.0	.931
1959	STL N	0	0	—	9.28	8	0	0	10.2	18	7	4	0	0	0	0	1	0	0	.000	0	1	0	0	0.1	1.000
3 yrs.		15	15	.500	4.83	69	37	8	272	279	103	113	1	1	0	1	86	18	0	.209	25	42	3	4	1.0	.957

John Urrea

URREA, JOHN GODOY BR TR 6'3" 200 lbs.
B. Feb. 9, 1955, Los Angeles, Calif.

1977	STL N	7	6	.538	3.15	41	12	2	140	126	35	81	1	2	3	4	29	4	0	.138	7	24	2	2	0.8	.939
1978		4	9	.308	5.36	27	12	1	99	108	47	61	0	0	2	0	24	3	0	.125	3	18	2	0	0.9	.913
1979		0	0	—	4.09	3	2	0	11	13	9	5	0	0	0	0	4	1	0	.250	2	1	0	0	1.0	1.000
1980		4	1	.800	3.46	30	1	0	65	57	41	36	0	3	1	3	13	3	0	.231	2	6	2	0	0.3	.800
1981	SD N	2	2	.500	2.39	38	0	0	49	43	28	19	0	2	2	2	4	1	0	.250	2	6	1	0	0.2	.857
5 yrs.		17	18	.486	3.73	139	27	3	364	347	160	202	1	7	8	9	74	12	0	.162	14	55	7	2	0.5	.908

Bob Vail

VAIL, ROBERT GARFIELD (Doc) BR TR 5'10" 165 lbs.
B. Sept. 24, 1881, Linneus, Me. D. May 28, 1948, Pittsburgh, Pa.

1908	PIT N	1	2	.333	6.00	4	1	0	15	15	7	9	0	1	1	0	3	1	0	.333	0	0	0	0	0.0	—

Rene Valdez

VALDEZ, RENE (Latigo) BR TR 6'3" 175 lbs.
Born Rene Valdez y Gutierrez.
B. June 2, 1929, Guanabacoa, Cuba

1957	BKN N	1	1	.500	5.54	5	1	0	13	13	7	10	0	1	1	0	3	0	0	.000	0	1	1	0	0.4	.500

Sergio Valdez

VALDEZ, SERGIO BR TR 6' 165 lbs.
Born Sergio Sanchez y Valdez.
B. Sept. 7, 1964, Elias Pina, Dominican Republic

1986	MON N	0	4	.000	6.84	5	5	0	25	39	11	20	0	0	0	0	8	1	0	.125	3	1	1	1	1.0	.800
1989	ATL N	1	2	.333	6.06	19	1	0	32.2	31	17	26	0	1	1	0	1	1	0	1.000	2	2	0	0	0.2	1.000
2 yrs.		1	6	.143	6.40	24	6	0	57.2	70	28	46	0	1	1	0	9	2	0	.222	5	3	1	1	0.4	.889

Corky Valentine

VALENTINE, HAROLD LEWIS BR TR 6'1" 203 lbs.
B. Jan. 4, 1929, Troy, Ohio

1954	CIN N	12	11	.522	4.45	36	28	7	194.1	211	60	73	3	2	1	1	65	9	0	.138	9	25	1	6	1.0	.971

Year	Team	W	L	PCT	ERA	G	GS	CG	IP	H	BB	SO	ShO	W	L	SV	AB	H	HR	BA	PO	A	E	DP	TC/G	FA

Corky Valentine *continued*

Year	Team	W	L	PCT	ERA	G	GS	CG	IP	H	BB	SO	ShO	W	L	SV	AB	H	HR	BA	PO	A	E	DP	TC/G	FA
1955		2	1	.667	7.43	10	5	0	26.2	29	16	14	0	2	0	0	7	0	0	.000	2	9	1	0	1.2	.917
2 yrs.		14	12	.538	4.81	46	33	7	221	240	76	87	3	4	1	1	72	9	0	.125	11	34	2	6	1.0	.957

John Valentine

VALENTINE, JOHN GILL
B. Nov. 21, 1855, Brooklyn, N. Y. D. Oct. 10, 1903, Central Islip, N. Y.

Year	Team	W	L	PCT	ERA	G	GS	CG	IP	H	BB	SO	ShO	W	L	SV	AB	H	HR	BA	PO	A	E	DP	TC/G	FA
1883	COL AA	2	10	.167	*3.53*	13	12	11	102	130	17	13	0	0	0	0	60	17	0	.283	9	24	7	1	3.1	.825

Vito Valentinetti

VALENTINETTI, VITO JOHN
B. Sept. 16, 1928, West New York, N. J.   BR TR 6'   195 lbs.

Year	Team	W	L	PCT	ERA	G	GS	CG	IP	H	BB	SO	ShO	W	L	SV	AB	H	HR	BA	PO	A	E	DP	TC/G	FA
1954	CHI A	0	0	–	54.00	1	0	0	1	4	2	1	0	0	0	0	0	0	0	–	0	0	0	0	0.0	–
1956	CHI N	6	4	.600	3.78	42	2	0	95.1	84	36	26	0	6	3	1	20	2	0	.100	4	12	1	0	0.4	.941
1957	2 teams	CHI N	(9G 0–0)		CLE A	(11G 2–2)																				
"	total	2	2	.500	4.04	20	2	1	35.2	38	20	17	0	2	2	0	7	1	0	.143	2	6	0	0	0.4	1.000
1958	2 teams	DET A	(15G 1–0)		WAS A	(23G 4–6)																				
"	total	5	6	.455	4.80	38	10	2	114.1	124	54	43	0	1	1	2	28	9	0	.321	8	23	1	5	0.8	.969
1959	WAS A	0	2	.000	10.13	7	1	0	10.2	16	10	7	0	0	0	0	0	0	0	–	2	3	0	0	0.7	1.000
5 yrs.		13	14	.481	4.73	108	15	3	257	266	122	94	0	8	7	3	55	12	0	.218	16	44	2	5	0.6	.968

Fernando Valenzuela

VALENZUELA, FERNANDO
Born Fernando Valenzuela y Anguamea.
B. Nov. 1, 1960, Navajoa, Mexico   BL TL 5'11"   180 lbs.

Year	Team	W	L	PCT	ERA	G	GS	CG	IP	H	BB	SO	ShO	W	L	SV	AB	H	HR	BA	PO	A	E	DP	TC/G	FA
1980	LA N	2	0	1.000	0.00	10	0	0	18	8	5	16	0	2	0	1	1	0	0	.000	0	3	0	1	0.3	1.000
1981		13	7	.650	2.48	25	25	11	192	140	61	180	8	0	0	0	64	16	0	.250	12	33	3	2	1.9	.938
1982		19	13	.594	2.87	37	37	18	285	247	83	199	4	0	0	0	95	16	1	.168	20	64	2	4	2.3	.977
1983		15	10	.600	3.75	35	35	9	257	245	99	189	4	0	0	0	91	17	1	.187	20	54	2	5	2.2	.974
1984		12	17	.414	3.03	34	34	12	261	218	106	240	2	0	0	0	79	15	3	.190	21	48	2	4	2.1	.972
1985		17	10	.630	2.45	35	35	14	272.1	211	101	208	5	0	0	0	97	21	1	.216	18	45	0	0	1.8	1.000
1986		21	11	.656	3.14	34	34	20	269.1	226	85	242	3	0	0	0	109	24	0	.220	29	47	1	2	2.3	.987
1987		14	14	.500	3.98	34	34	12	251	254	124	190	1	0	0	0	92	13	1	.141	15	53	4	2	2.1	.944
1988		5	8	.385	4.24	23	22	3	142.1	142	76	64	0	0	0	1	44	8	0	.182	6	38	1	2	2.0	.978
1989		10	13	.435	3.43	31	31	3	196.2	185	98	116	0	0	0	0	66	12	0	.182	18	35	5	4	1.9	.914
10 yrs.		128	103	.554	3.19	298	287	102	2144.2	1876	838	1644	27	2	0	2	738	142	7	.192	159	420	20	26	2.0	.967

DIVISIONAL PLAYOFF SERIES

Year	Team	W	L	PCT	ERA	G	GS	CG	IP	H	BB	SO	ShO	W	L	SV	AB	H	HR	BA	PO	A	E	DP	TC/G	FA
1981	LA N	1	0	1.000	1.06	2	2	1	17	10	3	10	0	0	0	0	4	0	0	.000	0	0	0	0	0.0	–

LEAGUE CHAMPIONSHIP SERIES

Year	Team	W	L	PCT	ERA	G	GS	CG	IP	H	BB	SO	ShO	W	L	SV	AB	H	HR	BA	PO	A	E	DP	TC/G	FA
1981	LA N	1	1	.500	2.45	2	2	0	14.2	10	5	10	0	0	0	0	5	0	0	.000	0	0	0	0	0.0	–
1983		1	0	1.000	1.13	1	1	0	8	7	4	5	0	0	0	0	3	0	0	.000	1	0	0	0	1.0	1.000
1985		1	0	1.000	1.88	2	2	0	14.1	11	10	13	0	0	0	0	5	1	0	.200	1	3	1	0	2.5	.800
3 yrs.		3	1	.750	1.95	5	5	0	37	28	19	28	0	0	0	0	13	1	0	.077	2	3	1	0	1.2	.833

WORLD SERIES

Year	Team	W	L	PCT	ERA	G	GS	CG	IP	H	BB	SO	ShO	W	L	SV	AB	H	HR	BA	PO	A	E	DP	TC/G	FA
1981	LA N	1	0	1.000	4.00	1	1	1	9	9	7	6	0	0	0	0	3	0	0	.000	0	1	0	0	1.0	1.000

Clay Van Alstyne

VAN ALSTYNE, CLAYTON EMORY (Spike)
B. May 24, 1900, Stuyvesant, N. Y. D. Jan. 5, 1960, Hudson, N. Y.   BR TR 5'11"   180 lbs.

Year	Team	W	L	PCT	ERA	G	GS	CG	IP	H	BB	SO	ShO	W	L	SV	AB	H	HR	BA	PO	A	E	DP	TC/G	FA
1927	WAS A	0	0	–	3.00	2	0	0	3	3	0	0	0	0	0	0	0	0	0	–	0	0	0	0	0.0	–
1928		0	0	–	5.48	4	0	0	21.1	26	13	5	0	0	0	0	8	2	1	.250	0	9	0	1	2.3	1.000
2 yrs.		0	0	–	5.18	6	0	0	24.1	29	13	5	0	0	0	0	8	2	1	.250	0	9	0	1	1.5	1.000

Russ Van Atta

VAN ATTA, RUSSELL (Sheriff)
B. June 21, 1906, Augusta, N. J. D. Oct. 10, 1986, Andover, N. J.   BL TL 6'   184 lbs.

Year	Team	W	L	PCT	ERA	G	GS	CG	IP	H	BB	SO	ShO	W	L	SV	AB	H	HR	BA	PO	A	E	DP	TC/G	FA
1933	NY A	12	4	.750	4.18	26	22	10	157	160	63	76	2	0	0	0	60	17	0	.283	7	32	1	1	1.5	.975
1934		3	5	.375	6.34	28	9	1	88	107	46	39	0	2	0	0	29	6	1	.207	3	13	1	0	0.6	.941
1935	2 teams	NY A	(5G 0–1)		STL A	(53G 9–16)																				
"	total	9	16	.360	5.30	58	17	1	175	206	90	90	0	6	4	3	43	9	0	.209	2	28	5	1	0.6	.857
1936	STL A	4	7	.364	6.60	52	9	2	122.2	164	68	59	0	4	2	2	29	5	0	.172	3	28	1	0	0.6	.969
1937		1	2	.333	5.52	16	6	1	58.2	74	32	34	0	1	0	0	13	6	1	.462	2	14	2	1	1.1	.889
1938		4	7	.364	6.06	25	12	3	104	118	61	35	1	1	0	0	30	4	0	.133	3	21	2	3	1.0	.923
1939		0	0	–	11.57	2	1	0	7	9	7	6	0	0	0	0	2	0	0	.000	0	0	0	0	0.0	–
7 yrs.		33	41	.446	5.60	207	76	17	712.1	838	367	339	3	13	6	6	206	47	2	.228	20	136	12	5	0.8	.929

Ozzie Van Brabant

VAN BRABANT, CAMILLE OSCAR
B. Sept. 28, 1926, Kingsville, Ont., Canada   BR TR 6'1"   165 lbs.

Year	Team	W	L	PCT	ERA	G	GS	CG	IP	H	BB	SO	ShO	W	L	SV	AB	H	HR	BA	PO	A	E	DP	TC/G	FA
1954	PHI A	0	2	.000	7.09	9	2	0	26.2	35	18	10	0	0	0	0	5	1	0	.200	1	8	0	0	1.0	1.000
1955	KC A	0	0	–	18.00	2	0	0	2	4	2	1	0	0	0	0	0	0	0	–	0	0	0	0	0.0	–
2 yrs.		0	2	.000	7.85	11	2	0	28.2	39	20	11	0	0	0	0	5	1	0	.200	1	8	0	0	0.8	1.000

Dazzy Vance

VANCE, CLARENCE ARTHUR
B. Mar. 4, 1891, Orient, Iowa D. Feb. 16, 1961, Homosassa Springs, Fla.   BR TR 6'2"   200 lbs.
Hall of Fame 1955.

Year	Team	W	L	PCT	ERA	G	GS	CG	IP	H	BB	SO	ShO	W	L	SV	AB	H	HR	BA	PO	A	E	DP	TC/G	FA
1915	2 teams	PIT N	(1G 0–1)		NY A	(8G 0–3)																				
"	total	0	4	.000	4.11	9	4	1	30.2	26	21	18	0	0	0	0	4	2	0	.500	1	9	2	1	1.3	.833
1918	NY A	0	0	–	15.43	2	0	0	2.1	9	2	0	0	0	0	0	0	0	0	–	0	0	0	0	0.0	–
1922	BKN N	18	12	.600	3.70	36	30	16	245.2	259	94	134	5	0	0	0	89	20	0	.225	10	51	0	2	1.7	1.000
1923		18	15	.545	3.50	37	35	21	280.1	263	100	197	3	2	0	0	83	7	1	.084	12	54	2	3	1.8	.971
1924		28	6	.824	2.16	35	34	30	308.2	238	77	262	3	1	0	0	106	16	2	.151	16	58	1	3	2.1	.987
1925		22	9	.710	3.53	31	31	26	265.1	247	66	221	4	1	0	0	98	14	3	.143	10	55	1	1	2.3	.985
1926		9	10	.474	3.89	24	22	12	169	172	58	140	0	1	0	0	55	10	0	.182	5	41	1	2	2.0	.979
1927		16	15	.516	2.70	34	32	25	273.1	242	69	184	2	0	0	1	90	15	0	.167	14	42	3	2	1.7	.949

Year	Team		W	L	PCT	ERA	G	GS	CG	IP	H	BB	SO	ShO	Relief Pitching W	L	SV	Batting AB	H	HR	BA	PO	A	E	DP	TC/G	FA

Dazzy Vance *continued*

Year	Team		W	L	PCT	ERA	G	GS	CG	IP	H	BB	SO	ShO	W	L	SV	AB	H	HR	BA	PO	A	E	DP	TC/G	FA
1928			22	10	.688	**2.09**	38	32	24	280.1	226	72	**200**	4	1	1	2	96	17	0	.177	17	55	0	6	1.9	1.000
1929			14	13	.519	3.89	31	26	17	231.1	244	47	126	1	1	2	0	74	10	0	.135	13	49	0	1	2.0	1.000
1930			17	15	.531	**2.61**	35	31	20	258.2	241	55	173	4	1	1	0	89	12	0	.135	5	44	5	0	1.5	.907
1931			11	13	.458	3.38	30	29	12	218.2	221	53	150	2	1	0	0	67	9	0	.134	4	46	0	0	1.7	1.000
1932			12	11	.522	4.20	27	24	9	175.2	171	57	103	1	1	0	1	56	5	0	.089	7	32	1	3	1.5	.975
1933	STL	N	6	2	.750	3.55	28	11	2	99	105	28	67	0	3	0	3	28	5	0	.179	5	14	2	0	0.8	.905
1934	2 teams		STL N	(19G 1-1)		CIN N	(6G 0-2)																					
"	total		1	3	.250	4.56	25	6	1	77	90	25	42	0	0	0	1	19	3	1	.158	4	12	0	3	0.6	1.000
1935	BKN	N	3	2	.600	4.41	20	0	0	51	55	16	28	0	3	2	2	17	1	0	.059	3	8	0	1	0.6	1.000
16 yrs.			197	140	.585	3.24	442	347	216	2967	2809	840	2045	30	14	7	11	971	146	7	.150	126	570	18	28	1.6	.975

WORLD SERIES

Year	Team		W	L	PCT	ERA	G	GS	CG	IP	H	BB	SO	ShO	W	L	SV	AB	H	HR	BA	PO	A	E	DP	TC/G	FA
1934	STL	N	0	0	–	0.00	1	0	0	1.1	2	1	3	0	0	0	0	0	0	0	–	0	0	0	0	0.0	–

Joe Vance

VANCE, JOSEPH ALBERT (Sandy)
B. Sept. 16, 1905, Devine, Tex.   D. July 4, 1978, Devine, Tex.

BR TR 6'1½"   190 lbs.

Year	Team		W	L	PCT	ERA	G	GS	CG	IP	H	BB	SO	ShO	W	L	SV	AB	H	HR	BA	PO	A	E	DP	TC/G	FA
1935	CHI	A	2	2	.500	6.68	10	0	0	31	36	21	12	0	2	2	0	11	2	0	.182	0	9	1	1	1.0	.900
1937	NY	A	1	0	1.000	3.00	2	2	0	15	11	9	3	0	0	0	0	5	0	0	.000	4	4	0	1	4.0	1.000
1938			0	0	–	7.15	3	1	0	11.1	20	4	2	0	0	0	0	4	3	0	.750	0	3	0	0	1.0	1.000
3 yrs.			3	2	.600	5.81	15	3	0	57.1	67	34	17	0	2	2	0	20	5	0	.250	4	16	1	2	1.4	.952

Sandy Vance

VANCE, GENE COVINGTON
B. Jan. 5, 1947, Lamar, Colo.

BR TR 6'2"   180 lbs.

Year	Team		W	L	PCT	ERA	G	GS	CG	IP	H	BB	SO	ShO	W	L	SV	AB	H	HR	BA	PO	A	E	DP	TC/G	FA
1970	LA	N	7	7	.500	3.13	20	18	0	115	109	37	45	0	0	0	0	37	7	0	.189	6	8	2	0	0.8	.875
1971			2	1	.667	6.92	10	3	0	26	38	9	11	0	1	1	0	5	0	0	.000	2	2	0	0	0.4	1.000
2 yrs.			9	8	.529	3.83	30	21	2	141	147	46	56	0	1	1	0	42	7	0	.167	8	10	2	0	0.7	.900

Chris Van Cuyk

VAN CUYK, CHRISTIAN GERALD
Brother of Johnny Van Cuyk.
B. Mar. 1, 1927, Kimberly, Wis.

BL TL 6'6"   215 lbs.

Year	Team		W	L	PCT	ERA	G	GS	CG	IP	H	BB	SO	ShO	W	L	SV	AB	H	HR	BA	PO	A	E	DP	TC/G	FA
1950	BKN	N	1	3	.250	4.86	12	4	1	33.1	33	12	21	0	0	1	0	10	1	0	.100	1	3	0	0	0.3	1.000
1951			1	2	.333	5.52	9	6	0	29.1	33	11	16	0	0	0	0	8	2	0	.250	2	4	1	2	0.8	.857
1952			5	6	.455	5.16	23	16	4	97.2	104	40	66	0	0	1	1	33	8	0	.242	4	13	1	0	0.8	.944
3 yrs.			7	11	.389	5.16	44	26	5	160.1	170	63	103	0	0	2	1	51	11	0	.216	7	20	2	2	0.7	.931

Johnny Van Cuyk

VAN CUYK, JOHN HENRY
Brother of Chris Van Cuyk.
B. July 7, 1921, Little Chute, Wis.

BL TL 6'1"   190 lbs.

Year	Team		W	L	PCT	ERA	G	GS	CG	IP	H	BB	SO	ShO	W	L	SV	AB	H	HR	BA	PO	A	E	DP	TC/G	FA
1947	BKN	N	0	0	–	5.40	2	0	0	3.1	5	1	2	0	0	0	0	0	0	0	–	0	1	0	0	0.5	1.000
1948			0	0	–	3.60	3	0	0	5	4	1	1	0	0	0	0	0	0	0	–	0	2	0	0	0.7	1.000
1949			0	0	–	9.00	2	0	0	2	3	1	0	0	0	0	0	0	0	0	–	0	0	0	0	0.0	–
3 yrs.			0	0	–	5.23	7	0	0	10.1	12	3	3	0	0	0	0	0	0	0	–	0	3	0	0	0.4	1.000

Ed Vande Berg

VANDE BERG, EDWARD JOHN
B. Oct. 26, 1958, Redlands, Calif.

BR TL 6'2"   175 lbs.

Year	Team		W	L	PCT	ERA	G	GS	CG	IP	H	BB	SO	ShO	W	L	SV	AB	H	HR	BA	PO	A	E	DP	TC/G	FA
1982	SEA	A	9	4	.692	2.37	**78**	0	0	76	54	32	60	0	9	4	5	0	0	0	–	5	19	1	3	0.3	.960
1983			2	4	.333	3.36	68	0	0	64.1	59	22	49	0	2	4	5	0	0	0	–	3	9	2	0	0.2	.857
1984			8	12	.400	4.76	50	17	2	130.1	165	50	71	0	3	1	7	0	0	0	–	4	42	4	2	0.5	.920
1985			2	1	.667	3.72	76	0	0	67.2	71	31	34	0	2	1	3	0	0	0	–	8	11	0	1	0.3	1.000
1986	LA	N	1	5	.167	3.41	60	0	0	71.1	83	33	42	0	1	5	0	1	0	0	.000	5	16	2	0	0.4	.913
1987	CLE	A	1	0	1.000	5.10	55	0	0	72.1	96	21	40	0	1	0	0	0	0	0	–	7	11	1	1	0.3	.947
1988	TEX	A	2	2	.500	4.14	26	0	0	37	44	11	18	0	2	2	2	0	0	0	–	1	4	1	0	0.2	.833
7 yrs.			25	28	.472	3.92	413	17	2	519	572	200	314	0	20	17	22	1	0	0	.000	32	90	9	5	0.3	.931

Hy Vandenburg

VANDENBURG, HAROLD HARRIS
B. Mar. 17, 1907, Abilene, Kans.

BR TR 6'2½"   195 lbs.

Year	Team		W	L	PCT	ERA	G	GS	CG	IP	H	BB	SO	ShO	W	L	SV	AB	H	HR	BA	PO	A	E	DP	TC/G	FA
1935	BOS	A	0	0	–	20.25	3	0	0	5.1	15	4	2	0	0	0	0	1	1	0	1.000	0	1	0	0	0.3	1.000
1937	NY	N	0	1	.000	7.88	1	1	1	8	10	6	2	0	0	0	0	4	0	0	.000	1	4	0	0	5.0	1.000
1938			0	1	.000	7.50	6	1	0	18	28	12	7	0	0	1	0	4	0	0	.000	2	8	0	1	1.7	1.000
1939			0	0	–	5.68	2	1	0	6.1	10	6	3	0	0	0	0	2	0	0	.000	0	2	0	0	1.0	1.000
1940			1	1	.500	3.90	13	3	1	32.1	27	16	17	0	0	0	1	8	1	0	.125	0	4	0	1	0.3	1.000
1944	CHI	N	7	4	.636	3.63	35	9	2	126.1	123	51	54	0	4	2	2	38	9	0	.237	4	24	1	1	0.8	.966
1945			6	3	.667	3.49	30	7	3	95.1	91	33	35	1	2	2	2	32	4	0	.125	7	18	2	1	0.9	.926
7 yrs.			14	10	.583	4.32	90	22	7	291.2	304	128	120	1	6	5	5	89	15	0	.169	14	61	3	4	0.9	.962

WORLD SERIES

Year	Team		W	L	PCT	ERA	G	GS	CG	IP	H	BB	SO	ShO	W	L	SV	AB	H	HR	BA	PO	A	E	DP	TC/G	FA
1945	CHI	N	0	0	–	0.00	3	0	0	6	1	3	3	0	0	0	0	1	0	0	.000	1	2	0	0	1.0	1.000

Johnny Vander Meer

VANDER MEER, JOHN SAMUEL (The Dutch Master)
B. Nov. 2, 1914, Prospect Park, N. J.

BR TL 6'1"   190 lbs.
BB 1937-42

Year	Team		W	L	PCT	ERA	G	GS	CG	IP	H	BB	SO	ShO	W	L	SV	AB	H	HR	BA	PO	A	E	DP	TC/G	FA
1937	CIN	N	3	5	.375	3.84	19	9	4	84.1	63	69	52	0	0	0	0	23	5	0	.217	7	23	0	1	1.6	1.000
1938			15	10	.600	3.12	32	29	16	225.1	177	103	125	3	0	0	0	83	15	0	.181	8	38	3	0	1.5	.939
1939			5	9	.357	4.67	30	21	8	129	128	95	102	0	0	0	2	36	4	0	.111	5	16	3	5	0.8	.875
1940			3	1	.750	3.75	10	7	2	48	38	41	41	0	0	0	1	20	6	0	.300	0	9	0	0	0.9	1.000
1941			16	13	.552	2.82	33	32	18	226.1	172	126	**202**	6	0	0	0	76	10	0	.132	10	42	2	3	1.8	.966
1942			18	12	.600	2.43	33	33	21	244	188	102	**186**	3	0	0	0	75	11	0	.147	6	51	2	4	1.8	.966
1943			15	16	.484	2.87	36	**36**	21	289	228	162	**174**	3	0	0	0	95	13	0	.137	11	67	4	7	2.3	.951
1946			10	12	.455	3.17	29	25	11	204.1	175	78	94	5	0	0	0	73	18	0	.247	6	33	3	1	1.4	.929
1947			9	14	.391	4.40	30	29	9	186	186	87	79	3	0	0	0	57	5	0	.088	6	37	2	1	1.4	.951
1948			17	14	.548	3.41	33	33	14	232	204	**124**	120	3	0	0	0	78	11	1	.141	11	39	5	3	1.7	.909
1949			5	10	.333	4.90	28	24	7	159.2	172	85	76	3	0	0	0	52	4	0	.077	6	33	2	4	1.5	.951

Year	Team		W	L	PCT	ERA	G	GS	CG	IP	H	BB	SO	ShO	Relief Pitching W	L	SV	Batting AB	H	HR	BA	PO	A	E	DP	TC/G	FA

Johnny Vander Meer *continued*

1950	CHI	N	3	4	.429	3.79	32	6	0	73.2	60	59	41	0	3	1	1	16	2	0	.125	4	14	3	0	0.7	.857
1951	CLE	A	0	1	.000	18.00	1	1	0	3	8	1	2	0	0	0	0	1	0	0	.000	0	3	0	0	3.0	1.000
13 yrs.			119	121	.496	3.44	346	285	131	2104.2	1799	1132	1294	30	4	3	2	685	104	1	.152	82	404	29	30	1.5	.944

WORLD SERIES

| 1940 | CIN | N | 0 | 0 | — | 0.00 | 1 | 0 | 0 | 3 | 2 | 3 | 2 | 0 | 0 | 0 | 0 | 0 | 0 | 0 | — | 0 | 0 | 0 | 0 | 0.0 | — |

Ben Van Dyke   VAN DYKE, BENJAMIN HARRISON   BR TL 6'1"   150 lbs.
B. Aug. 15, 1888, Clintonville, Pa.   D. Oct. 22, 1973, Sarasota, Fla.

1909	PHI	N	0	0	—	3.68	2	0	0	7.1	7	4	5	0	0	0	0	3	0	0	.000	0	0	0	0	0.0	—
1912	BOS	A	0	0	—	3.14	3	1	0	14.1	13	7	8	0	0	0	0	4	1	0	.250	2	1	1	0	1.3	.750
2 yrs.			0	0	—	3.32	5	1	0	21.2	20	11	13	0	0	0	0	7	1	0	.143	2	1	1	0	0.8	.750

Elam Vangilder   VANGILDER, ELAM RUSSELL   BR TR 6'1"   192 lbs.
B. Apr. 23, 1896, Cape Girardeau, Mo.   D. Apr. 30, 1977, Cape Girardeau, Mo.

1919	STL	A	1	0	1.000	2.08	3	3	1	13	15	3	6	0	0	0	0	3	2	0	.667	1	6	0	0	2.3	1.000
1920			3	8	.273	5.50	24	13	4	104.2	131	40	25	0	0	2	0	30	4	0	.133	1	28	2	2	1.3	.935
1921			11	12	.478	3.94	31	21	10	180.1	196	67	48	1	1	1	0	65	13	1	.200	3	47	0	2	1.6	1.000
1922			19	13	.594	3.42	43	30	19	245	248	48	63	3	3	4	1	93	32	2	.344	14	47	1	3	1.6	.984
1923			16	17	.485	3.06	41	35	20	282.1	276	120	74	4	1	2	1	110	24	1	.218	4	61	1	4	1.6	.985
1924			5	10	.333	5.76	43	18	5	145.1	183	55	49	0	2	2	1	44	13	1	.295	8	38	3	6	1.1	.939
1925			14	8	.636	4.70	52	16	4	193.1	225	92	61	1	11	4	6	71	13	0	.183	11	44	2	3	1.1	.965
1926			9	11	.450	5.17	42	19	8	181	196	98	40	1	3	2	1	58	11	0	.190	5	38	3	1	1.1	.935
1927			10	12	.455	4.79	44	23	12	203	245	102	62	3	0	2	1	68	19	1	.279	9	32	2	0	1.0	.953
1928	DET	A	11	10	.524	3.91	38	11	7	156.1	163	68	43	0	4	5	2	58	15	2	.259	8	37	4	3	1.3	.918
1929			0	1	.000	6.35	6	0	0	11.1	16	7	3	0	0	0	1	1	0	0	.000	3	6	0	0	1.5	1.000
11 yrs.			99	102	.493	4.29	367	187	90	1715.2	1894	700	474	13	25	26	19	601	146	8	.243	67	384	18	24	1.3	.962

George Van Haltren   VAN HALTREN, GEORGE EDWARD MARTIN   BL TL 5'11"   170 lbs.
B. Mar. 30, 1866, St. Louis, Mo.   D. Sept. 29, 1945, Oakland, Calif.
Manager 1891-92.

1887	CHI	N	11	7	.611	3.86	20	18	18	161	177	66	76	1	0	0	1	172	35	3	.203	10	25	5	1	2.0	.875
1888			13	13	.500	3.52	30	24	24	245.2	263	60	139	4	0	2	1	318	90	4	.283	25	53	5	0	2.8	.940
1890	BKN	P	15	10	.600	4.28	28	25	23	223	272	89	48	0	0	0	0	376	126	5	.335	25	68	6	5	3.5	.939
1891	BAL	AA	0	1	.000	5.09	6	1	0	23	38	10	7	0	0	0	0	566	180	5	.318	3	5	2	0	1.7	.800
1892	BAL	N	0	0	—	9.20	4	0	0	14.2	28	7	5	0	0	0	0	611	179	7	.293	0	5	1	1	1.5	.833
1895	NY	N	0	0	—	12.60	1	0	0	5	13	2	1	0	0	0	0	521	177	8	.340	1	1	1	0	2.0	.500
1896			1	0	1.000	2.25	2	0	0	8	5	1	3	0	0	0	0	562	197	5	.351	1	1	0	0	1.0	1.000
1900			0	0	—	0.00	1	0	0	3	1	3	0	0	0	0	0	571	180	1	.315	0	0	0	0	0.0	—
1901			0	0	—	3.00	1	0	0	6	12	6	2	0	0	0	0	544	186	1	.342	0	4	0	0	4.0	1.000
9 yrs.			40	31	.563	4.05	93	68	65	689.1	809	244	281	5	1	2	4	*				64	162	20	7	2.6	.919

Ike Van Zandt   VAN ZANDT, CHARLES ISAAC   BL
B. 1877, Brooklyn, N. Y.   D. Sept. 14, 1908, Nashua, N. H.

1901	NY	N	0	0	—	7.11	2	0	0	12.2	16	8	4	0	0	0	0	6	1	0	.167	1	2	0	0	1.5	.333
1905	STL	A	0	0	—	0.00	1	0	0	6.2	2	2	3	0	0	0	0	322	75	1	.233	1	2	0	0	3.0	1.000
2 yrs.			0	0	—	4.66	3	0	0	19.1	18	10	5	0	0	0	0	*				2	2	0	0	2.0	.667

Andy Varga   VARGA, ANDREW WILLIAM   BR TL 6'4"   187 lbs.
B. Dec. 11, 1930, Chicago, Ill.

1950	CHI	N	0	0	—	0.00	1	0	0	1	0	1	0	0	0	0	0	—	0	0	—	0	0	0	0	0.0	—
1951			0	0	—	3.00	2	0	0	3	2	6	1	0	0	0	0	0	0	0	—	0	0	0	0	0.0	—
2 yrs.			0	0	—	2.25	3	0	0	4	2	7	1	0	0	0	0	0	0	0	—	0	0	0	0	0.0	—

Roberto Vargas   VARGAS, ROBERTO ENRIQUE   BL TL 5'11"   170 lbs.
B. May 29, 1929, Santurce, Puerto Rico

| 1955 | MIL | N | 0 | 0 | — | 8.76 | 25 | 0 | 0 | 24.2 | 39 | 14 | 13 | 0 | 0 | 0 | 2 | 2 | 1 | 0 | .500 | 4 | 8 | 0 | 0 | 0.5 | 1.000 |

Bill Vargus   VARGUS, WILLIAM FAY   BL TL 6'   165 lbs.
B. Nov. 11, 1899, N. Scituate, Mass.   D. Feb. 12, 1979, Cape Cod, Mass.

1925	BOS	N	1	1	.500	3.96	11	2	1	36.1	45	13	5	0	0	0	0	12	3	0	.250	0	11	2	0	1.2	.846
1926			0	0	—	3.00	4	0	0	3	4	1	0	0	0	0	0	0	0	0	—	0	1	0	0	0.3	1.000
2 yrs.			1	1	.500	3.89	15	2	1	39.1	49	14	5	0	0	0	0	12	3	0	.250	0	12	2	0	0.9	.857

Dike Varney   VARNEY, LAWRENCE DELANO   BL TL 6'   165 lbs.
B. Aug. 9, 1880, Dover, N. H.   D. Apr. 23, 1950, Long Island City, N. Y.

| 1902 | CLE | A | 1 | 1 | .500 | 6.14 | 3 | 3 | 0 | 14.2 | 14 | 12 | 7 | 0 | 0 | 0 | 0 | 6 | 1 | 0 | .167 | 0 | 5 | 1 | 0 | 2.0 | .833 |

Moses Vasbinder   VASBINDER, MOSES CALHOUN   BR TR 6'2"
B. July 19, 1880, Scio, Ohio   D. Dec. 22, 1950, Cadiz, Ohio

| 1902 | CLE | A | 0 | 0 | — | 9.00 | 2 | 0 | 0 | 5 | 5 | 8 | 2 | 0 | 0 | 0 | 0 | 2 | 1 | 0 | .500 | 0 | 2 | 0 | 0 | 1.0 | 1.000 |

Rafael Vasquez   VASQUEZ, RAFAEL   BR TR 6'   160 lbs.
Born Rafael Vasquez y Santiago.
B. June 28, 1958, La Romana, Dominican Republic

| 1979 | SEA | A | 1 | 0 | 1.000 | 5.06 | 9 | 0 | 0 | 16 | 23 | 6 | 9 | 0 | 1 | 0 | 0 | 0 | 0 | 0 | — | 0 | 1 | 0 | 0 | 0.1 | 1.000 |

Year	Team		W	L	PCT	ERA	G	GS	CG	IP	H	BB	SO	ShO	W	L	SV	AB	H	HR	BA	PO	A	E	DP	TC/G	FA

Charlie Vaughan

VAUGHAN, CHARLES WAYNE   BR TL 6'1½" 185 lbs.
B. Oct. 6, 1947, Mercedes, Tex.

Year	Team		W	L	PCT	ERA	G	GS	CG	IP	H	BB	SO	ShO	W	L	SV	AB	H	HR	BA	PO	A	E	DP	TC/G	FA
1966	ATL	N	1	0	1.000	2.57	1	1	0	7	8	3	6	0	0	0	0	4	1	0	.250	0	1	0	0	1.0	1.000
1969			0	0	–	18.00	1	0	0	1	1	3	1	0	0	0	0	0	0	0	–	0	1	0	0	1.0	1.000
2 yrs.			1	0	1.000	4.50	2	1	0	8	9	6	7	0	0	0	0	4	1	0	.250	0	2	0	0	1.0	1.000

Porter Vaughan

VAUGHAN, CECIL PORTER (Lefty)   BR TL 6'1" 178 lbs.
B. May 11, 1919, Stevensville, Va.

Year	Team		W	L	PCT	ERA	G	GS	CG	IP	H	BB	SO	ShO	W	L	SV	AB	H	HR	BA	PO	A	E	DP	TC/G	FA
1940	PHI	A	2	9	.182	5.35	18	15	5	99.1	104	61	46	0	0	0	2	34	8	0	.235	2	16	3	0	1.2	.857
1941			0	2	.000	7.94	5	3	1	22.2	32	12	6	0	0	0	0	7	1	0	.143	2	3	1	0	1.2	.833
1946			0	0	–	0.00	1	0	0		1	1	0	0	0	0	0	0	0	0	–	0	0	0	0	0.0	–
3 yrs.			2	11	.154	5.83	24	18	6	122	137	74	52	0	0	0	2	41	9	0	.220	4	19	4	0	1.1	.852

Clarence Vaughn

VAUGHN, CLARENCE LeROY   BB TR 6'½" 178 lbs.
B. Sept. 4, 1911, Sedalia, Mo. D. Mar. 1, 1937, Martinsville, Va.

Year	Team		W	L	PCT	ERA	G	GS	CG	IP	H	BB	SO	ShO	W	L	SV	AB	H	HR	BA	PO	A	E	DP	TC/G	FA
1934	PHI	A	0	0	–	2.08	2	0	0	4.1	3	3	1	0	0	0	0	2	0	0	.000	0	0	0	0	0.0	–

DeWayne Vaughn

VAUGHN, DeWAYNE MATHEW   BR TR 6'1" 175 lbs.
B. July 22, 1959, Oklahoma City, Okla.

Year	Team		W	L	PCT	ERA	G	GS	CG	IP	H	BB	SO	ShO	W	L	SV	AB	H	HR	BA	PO	A	E	DP	TC/G	FA
1988	TEX	A	0	0	–	7.63	8	0	0	15.1	24	4	8	0	0	0	0	0	0	0	–	0	0	0	0	0.0	–

Farmer Vaughn

VAUGHN, HENRY FRANCIS   BR TR 6'3" 177 lbs.
B. Mar. 1, 1864, Rural Dale, Ohio D. Feb. 21, 1914, Cincinnati, Ohio

Year	Team		W	L	PCT	ERA	G	GS	CG	IP	H	BB	SO	ShO	W	L	SV	AB	H	HR	BA	PO	A	E	DP	TC/G	FA
1891	CIN	AA	0	0	–	3.86	1	0	0	7	12	1	0	0	0	0	0	*				0	1	0	0	1.0	1.000

Hippo Vaughn

VAUGHN, JAMES LESLIE   BB TL 6'4" 215 lbs.
B. Apr. 9, 1888, Weatherford, Tex. D. May 29, 1966, Chicago, Ill.

Year	Team		W	L	PCT	ERA	G	GS	CG	IP	H	BB	SO	ShO	W	L	SV	AB	H	HR	BA	PO	A	E	DP	TC/G	FA
1908	NY	A	0	0	–	3.86	2	0	0	2.1	1	4	2	0	0	0	0	1	0	0	.000	0	2	0	0	1.0	1.000
1910			13	11	.542	1.83	30	25	18	221.2	190	58	107	5	4	0	1	75	10	0	.133	5	73	8	2	2.9	.907
1911			8	10	.444	4.39	26	18	11	145.2	158	54	74	1	2	0	0	49	7	0	.143	9	41	4	1	2.1	.926
1912	2 teams	NY A (15G 2–8)				WAS A	(12G 4–3)																				
"	total		6	11	.353	3.88	27	18	9	144	141	80	95	1	1	2	0	51	8	0	.157	5	53	4	0	2.3	.935
1913	CHI	N	5	1	.833	1.45	7	6	5	56	37	27	36	2	0	0	0	21	4	0	.190	3	13	2	1	2.6	.889
1914			21	13	.618	2.05	42	35	23	293.2	236	109	165	4	0	1	1	97	14	1	.144	11	75	13	1	2.4	.869
1915			20	12	.625	2.87	41	34	18	269.2	240	77	148	4	4	1	1	86	14	0	.163	5	70	8	1	2.0	.904
1916			17	15	.531	2.20	44	35	21	294	269	67	144	4	1	2	1	104	14	0	.135	6	82	4	0	2.1	.957
1917			23	13	.639	2.01	41	39	27	295.2	255	91	195	5	0	0	0	100	16	0	.160	14	89	7	2	2.7	.936
1918			22	10	.688	1.74	35	33	27	290.1	216	76	148	8	0	0	0	96	23	0	.240	14	73	3	2	2.6	.967
1919			21	14	.600	1.79	38	37	25	306.2	264	62	141	4	0	0	1	98	17	0	.173	10	74	9	3	2.4	.903
1920			19	16	.543	2.54	40	38	24	301	301	81	131	4	0	0	0	102	22	1	.216	9	71	10	4	2.3	.889
1921			3	11	.214	6.01	17	14	7	109.1	153	31	30	0	0	2	0	41	10	1	.244	1	24	2	0	1.6	.926
13 yrs.			178	137	.565	2.49	390	332	215	2730	2461	817	1416	41	11	12	5	921	159	3	.173	92	740	74	17	2.3	.918

WORLD SERIES

Year	Team		W	L	PCT	ERA	G	GS	CG	IP	H	BB	SO	ShO	W	L	SV	AB	H	HR	BA	PO	A	E	DP	TC/G	FA
1918	CHI	N	1	2	.333	1.00 6th	3	3	3	27	17	5	17	1	0	0	0	10	0	0	.000	6	11	0	1	5.7	1.000

Al Veach

VEACH, ALVIS LINDELL   BR TR 5'11" 178 lbs.
B. Aug. 6, 1909, Maylene, Ala.

Year	Team		W	L	PCT	ERA	G	GS	CG	IP	H	BB	SO	ShO	W	L	SV	AB	H	HR	BA	PO	A	E	DP	TC/G	FA
1935	PHI	A	0	2	.000	11.70	2	2	1	10	20	9	3	0	0	0	0	4	0	0	.000	2	1	0	1	1.5	1.000

Bobby Veach

VEACH, ROBERT HAYES   BL TR 5'11" 160 lbs.
B. June 29, 1888, Island, Ky. D. Aug. 7, 1945, Detroit, Mich.

Year	Team		W	L	PCT	ERA	G	GS	CG	IP	H	BB	SO	ShO	W	L	SV	AB	H	HR	BA	PO	A	E	DP	TC/G	FA
1918	DET	A	0	0	–	4.50	1	0	0	2	2	2	0	0	0	0	1	*				0	0	0	0	0.0	–

Peek-A-Boo Veach

VEACH, WILLIAM WALTER
B. June 15, 1862, Indianapolis, Ind. D. Nov. 12, 1937, Indianapolis, Ind.

Year	Team		W	L	PCT	ERA	G	GS	CG	IP	H	BB	SO	ShO	W	L	SV	AB	H	HR	BA	PO	A	E	DP	TC/G	FA
1884	KC	U	3	9	.250	2.42	12	12	12	104	95	10	62	0	0	0	0	82	11	1	.134	6	25	3	3	2.8	.912
1887	LOU	AA	0	1	.000	4.00	1	1	1	9	5	8	2	0	0	0	0	3	0	0	.000	2	1	1	0	4.0	.750
2 yrs.			3	10	.231	2.55	13	13	13	113	100	18	64	0	0	0	0	*				8	26	4	3	2.9	.895

Bob Veale

VEALE, ROBERT ANDREW   BB TL 6'6" 212 lbs.
B. Oct. 28, 1935, Birmingham, Ala.

Year	Team		W	L	PCT	ERA	G	GS	CG	IP	H	BB	SO	ShO	W	L	SV	AB	H	HR	BA	PO	A	E	DP	TC/G	FA
1962	PIT	N	2	2	.500	3.74	11	6	2	45.2	39	25	42	0	0	0	1	16	4	0	.250	0	6	0	0	0.5	1.000
1963			5	2	.714	1.04	34	7	3	77.2	59	40	68	2	1	0	3	23	2	0	.087	1	14	2	0	0.5	.882
1964			18	12	.600	2.74	40	38	14	279.2	222	124	250	1	0	0	0	96	15	0	.156	14	39	2	4	1.4	.964
1965			17	12	.586	2.84	39	37	14	266	221	119	276	7	0	0	0	93	8	0	.086	3	36	2	1	1.1	.951
1966			16	12	.571	3.02	38	37	12	268.1	228	102	229	3	0	0	0	94	13	0	.138	2	34	3	5	1.0	.923
1967			16	8	.667	3.64	33	31	6	203	184	119	179	1	0	0	0	69	3	0	.043	6	36	1	3	1.3	.977
1968			13	14	.481	2.05	36	33	13	245.1	187	94	171	4	0	1	0	82	9	0	.110	4	37	3	0	1.2	.932
1969			13	14	.481	3.23	34	34	9	226	232	91	213	1	0	0	0	79	4	0	.051	6	33	1	2	1.2	.975
1970			10	15	.400	3.92	34	32	5	202	189	94	178	1	0	0	0	67	11	0	.164	0	23	3	1	0.8	.885
1971			6	0	1.000	7.04	37	0	0	46	59	24	40	0	6	0	2	9	3	0	.333	1	3	0	0	0.1	.400
1972	2 teams	PIT N (5G 0–0)				BOS A	(6G 2–0)																				
"	total		2	0	1.000	3.18	11	0	0	17	12	10	16	0	2	0	2	2	0	0	.000	2	1	0	0	0.3	.667
1973	BOS	A	2	3	.400	3.50	32	0	0	36	37	12	25	0	2	3	11	0	0	0	–	0	9	0	1	0.3	1.000
1974			0	1	.000	5.54	18	0	0	13	15	4	16	0	0	1	2	0	0	0	–	0	0	0	0	0.0	–
13 yrs.			120	95	.558	3.08	397	255	78	1925.2	1684	858	1703	20	11	5	21	630	72	0	.114	37	270	21	19	0.8	.936

WORLD SERIES

Year	Team		W	L	PCT	ERA	G	GS	CG	IP	H	BB	SO	ShO	W	L	SV	AB	H	HR	BA	PO	A	E	DP	TC/G	FA
1971	PIT	N	0	0	–	13.50	1	0	0	.2	1	2	0	0	0	0	0	0	0	0	–	0	1	0	0	1.0	1.000

Year	Team	W	L	PCT	ERA	G	GS	CG	IP	H	BB	SO	ShO	Relief Pitching W	L	SV	Batting AB	H	HR	BA	PO	A	E	DP	TC/G	FA

Lou Vedder
VEDDER, LOUIS EDWARD
B. Apr. 20, 1897, Oakville, Mich.   BR TR 5'10½" 175 lbs.

Year	Team	W	L	PCT	ERA	G	GS	CG	IP	H	BB	SO	ShO	W	L	SV	AB	H	HR	BA	PO	A	E	DP	TC/G	FA
1920	DET A	0	0	–	0.00	1	0	0	2	2	0	0	1	0	0	0	0	0	0	–	0	2	0	0	2.0	1.000

Al Veigel
VEIGEL, ALLEN FRANCIS
B. Jan. 30, 1917, Dover, Ohio   BR TR 6'1" 180 lbs.

Year	Team	W	L	PCT	ERA	G	GS	CG	IP	H	BB	SO	ShO	W	L	SV	AB	H	HR	BA	PO	A	E	DP	TC/G	FA
1939	BOS N	0	1	.000	6.75	2	2	0	2.2	3	5	1	0	0	0	0	1	0	0	.000	0	0	1	0	0.5	

Bucky Veil
VEIL, FREDERICK WILLIAM
B. Aug. 2, 1881, Tyrone, Pa. D. Apr. 16, 1931, Altoona, Pa.   BR TR 5'10½" 165 lbs.

Year	Team	W	L	PCT	ERA	G	GS	CG	IP	H	BB	SO	ShO	W	L	SV	AB	H	HR	BA	PO	A	E	DP	TC/G	FA
1903	PIT N	5	4	.556	3.82	12	6	4	70.2	70	36	20	0	2	0	0	29	6	0	.207	4	17	0	0	1.8	1.000
1904		0	0	–	5.79	1	1	0	4.2	4	4	1	0	0	0	0	1	1	0	1.000	0	2	0	0	2.0	1.000
2 yrs.		5	4	.556	3.94	13	7	4	75.1	74	40	21	0	2	0	0	30	7	0	.233	4	19	0	0	1.8	1.000
WORLD SERIES																										
1903	PIT N	0	0	–	1.29	1	0	0	7	6	4	1	0	0	0	0	2	0	0	.000	0	0	1	0	1.0	–

Carlos Velasquez
VELASQUEZ, CARLOS
Born Carlos Velasquez y Quinones.
B. Mar. 22, 1948, Loiza, Puerto Rico   BR TR 5'11" 180 lbs.

Year	Team	W	L	PCT	ERA	G	GS	CG	IP	H	BB	SO	ShO	W	L	SV	AB	H	HR	BA	PO	A	E	DP	TC/G	FA
1973	MIL A	2	2	.500	2.58	18	0	0	38.1	46	10	12	0	2	2	2	0	0	0	–	2	7	0	0	0.5	1.000

Joe Verbanic
VERBANIC, JOSEPH MICHAEL
B. Apr. 24, 1943, Washington, Pa.   BR TR 6' 155 lbs.

Year	Team	W	L	PCT	ERA	G	GS	CG	IP	H	BB	SO	ShO	W	L	SV	AB	H	HR	BA	PO	A	E	DP	TC/G	FA
1966	PHI N	1	1	.500	5.14	17	0	0	14	12	10	7	0	1	1	0	0	0	0	–	1	2	1	0	0.2	.750
1967	NY A	4	3	.571	2.80	28	6	0	80.1	74	21	39	1	1	1	2	18	2	0	.111	9	19	2	1	1.0	.900
1968		6	7	.462	3.15	40	11	2	97	104	41	40	1	3	3	4	25	2	0	.080	6	21	3	4	0.8	.900
1970		1	0	1.000	4.50	7	0	0	16	20	12	8	0	1	0	0	3	1	0	.333	2	7	0	0	1.3	1.000
4 yrs.		12	11	.522	3.26	92	17	3	207.1	210	84	94	2	6	5	6	46	5	0	.109	18	49	4	6	0.8	.944

Al Verdel
VERDEL, ALBERT ALFRED (Stumpy)
B. June 10, 1921, Punxsutawney, Pa.   BR TR 5'9½" 186 lbs.

Year	Team	W	L	PCT	ERA	G	GS	CG	IP	H	BB	SO	ShO	W	L	SV	AB	H	HR	BA	PO	A	E	DP	TC/G	FA
1944	PHI N	0	0	–	0.00	1	0	0	1	0	0	0	0	0	0	0	0	0	0	–	0	0	0	0	0.0	–

Tommy Vereker
VEREKER, JOHN JAMES
B. Dec. 2, 1893, Baltimore, Md. D. Apr. 2, 1974, Baltimore, Md.   5'10" 185 lbs.

Year	Team	W	L	PCT	ERA	G	GS	CG	IP	H	BB	SO	ShO	W	L	SV	AB	H	HR	BA	PO	A	E	DP	TC/G	FA
1915	BAL F	0	0	–	15.00	2	0	0	3	3	2	1	0	0	0	0	0	0	0	–	0	1	0	0	0.5	1.000

Randy Veres
VERES, RANDOLF RUHLAND
B. Nov. 25, 1965, San Francisco, Calif.   BR TR 6'3" 190 lbs.

Year	Team	W	L	PCT	ERA	G	GS	CG	IP	H	BB	SO	ShO	W	L	SV	AB	H	HR	BA	PO	A	E	DP	TC/G	FA
1989	MIL A	0	1	.000	4.32	3	1	0	8.1	9	4	8	0	0	0	0	0	0	0	–	0	1	0	0	0.3	1.000

John Verhoeven
VERHOEVEN, JOHN C.
B. July 3, 1953, Long Beach, Calif.   BR TR 6'5" 200 lbs.

Year	Team	W	L	PCT	ERA	G	GS	CG	IP	H	BB	SO	ShO	W	L	SV	AB	H	HR	BA	PO	A	E	DP	TC/G	FA
1976	CAL A	0	2	.000	3.41	21	0	0	37	35	14	23	0	0	2	4	0	0	0	–	4	10	0	0	0.7	1.000
1977	2 teams CAL A (3G 0–2)									CHI A (6G 0–0)																
"	total	0	2	.000	2.40	9	0	0	15	13	6	9	0	0	2	0	1	0	0	.000	1	6	0	0	0.8	1.000
1980	MIN A	3	4	.429	3.96	44	0	0	100	109	29	42	0	3	4	0	0	0	0	–	4	17	3	2	0.5	.875
1981		0	0	–	3.98	25	0	0	52	57	14	16	0	0	0	0	0	0	0	–	0	11	0	1	0.4	1.000
4 yrs.		3	8	.273	3.75	99	0	0	204	214	63	90	0	3	8	4	0	0	0	–	9	44	3	3	0.6	.946

Joe Vernon
VERNON, JOSEPH HENRY
B. Nov. 25, 1889, Mansfield, Mass. D. Mar. 13, 1955, Philadelphia, Pa.   BR TR 5'11" 160 lbs.

Year	Team	W	L	PCT	ERA	G	GS	CG	IP	H	BB	SO	ShO	W	L	SV	AB	H	HR	BA	PO	A	E	DP	TC/G	FA
1912	CHI N	0	0	–	11.25	1	0	0	4	4	6	1	0	0	0	0	2	0	0	.000	0	0	0	0		
1914	BKN F	0	0	–	10.80	1	1	0	3.1	4	5	0	0	0	0	0	1	0	0	.000	0	1	0	0	1.0	1.000
2 yrs.		0	0	–	11.05	2	1	0	7.1	8	11	1	0	0	0	0	3	0	0	.000	0	1	0	0	0.5	1.000

Bob Veselic
VESELIC, ROBERT MITCHELL
B. Sept. 27, 1955, Pittsburgh, Pa.   BR TR 6' 175 lbs.

Year	Team	W	L	PCT	ERA	G	GS	CG	IP	H	BB	SO	ShO	W	L	SV	AB	H	HR	BA	PO	A	E	DP	TC/G	FA
1980	MIN A	0	0	–	4.50	1	0	0	4	3	1	2	0	0	0	0	0	0	0	–	0	0	0	0	0.0	
1981		1	1	.500	3.13	5	0	0	23	22	12	13	0	1	1	0	0	0	0	–	1	1	0	0	0.4	1.000
2 yrs.		1	1	.500	3.33	6	0	0	27	25	13	15	0	1	1	0	0	0	0	–	1	1	0	0	0.3	1.000

Lee Viau
VIAU, LEON A.
B. July 5, 1866, Corinth, Vt. D. Dec. 17, 1947, Hopewell, N. J.   BR TR 5'4" 160 lbs.

Year	Team	W	L	PCT	ERA	G	GS	CG	IP	H	BB	SO	ShO	W	L	SV	AB	H	HR	BA	PO	A	E	DP	TC/G	FA
1888	CIN AA	27	14	.659	2.65	42	42	42	387.2	331	110	164	1	0	0	0	149	13	0	.087	18	78	9	0	2.5	.914
1889		22	20	.524	3.79	47	42	38	373	379	136	152	1	1	1	0	147	21	0	.143	9	61	4	2	1.6	.946
1890	2 teams CIN N (13G 7–5)									CLE N (13G 4–9)																
"	total	11	14	.440	3.88	26	23	20	197	198	81	71	2	2	0	0	79	12	0	.152	6	51	7	0	2.5	.891
1891	CLE N	18	17	.514	3.01	45	38	31	343.2	367	138	130	0	2	1	0	144	23	0	.160	12	79	14	2	2.3	.867
1892	3 teams CLE N (1G 0–1)									LOU N (16G 4–11)					BOS N (1G 1–0)											
"	total	5	12	.294	3.97	18	17	15	140.2	166	61	37	1	0	0	0	69	13	0	.188	10	41	4	4	3.1	.927
5 yrs.		83	77	.519	3.33	178	162	146	1442	1441	526	554	5	5	1	0	588	82	0	.139	55	310	38	8	2.3	.906

Rube Vickers
VICKERS, HARRY PORTER
B. May 17, 1878, St. Mary's Ont., Canada D. Dec. 9, 1958, Belleville, Mich.   BL TR 6'2" 225 lbs.

Year	Team	W	L	PCT	ERA	G	GS	CG	IP	H	BB	SO	ShO	W	L	SV	AB	H	HR	BA	PO	A	E	DP	TC/G	FA
1902	CIN N	0	3	.000	6.00	3	3	3	21	31	8	6	0	0	0	0	11	4	0	.364	0	3	0	0	1.0	1.000
1903	BKN N	0	1	.000	10.93	4	1	1	14	27	9	5	0	0	0	0	10	1	0	.100	0	10	1	0	2.8	.909
1907	PHI A	2	2	.500	3.40	10	4	3	50.1	44	12	21	1	0	0	0	20	3	0	.150	2	17	1	1	2.0	.950

Year	Team		W	L	PCT	ERA	G	GS	CG	IP	H	BB	SO	ShO	W	L	SV	AB	H	HR	BA	PO	A	E	DP	TC/G	FA
															Relief Pitching			**Batting**									

Rube Vickers *continued*

Year	Team	W	L	PCT	ERA	G	GS	CG	IP	H	BB	SO	ShO	W	L	SV	AB	H	HR	BA	PO	A	E	DP	TC/G	FA
1908		18	19	.486	2.34	53	33	21	300	264	71	156	6	6	2	1	106	17	0	.160	10	83	7	0	1.9	.930
1909		2	2	.500	3.40	18	3	1	55.2	60	19	25	0	1	1	1	16	1	0	.063	3	11	1	0	0.8	.933
5 yrs.		22	27	.449	3.04	88	44	29	441	426	119	213	7	8	3	2	163	26	0	.160	15	124	10	1	1.7	.933

Tom Vickery

VICKERY, THOMAS GILL
B. May 5, 1867, Milford, N. J.   D. Mar. 21, 1921, Bulington, N. J.

6'   170 lbs.

Year	Team		W	L	PCT	ERA	G	GS	CG	IP	H	BB	SO	ShO	W	L	SV	AB	H	HR	BA	PO	A	E	DP	TC/G	FA
1890	PHI	N	24	22	.522	3.44	46	46	41	382	405	184	162	1	0	0	0	159	33	0	.208	17	71	20	3	2.3	.815
1891	CHI	N	5	5	.500	4.07	14	12	7	79.2	72	44	39	0	0	0	0	39	7	0	.179	5	19	2	0	1.9	.923
1892	BAL	N	8	10	.444	3.53	24	21	17	176	189	87	49	0	0	0	0	74	18	0	.243	11	30	5	1	1.9	.891
1893	PHI	N	4	5	.444	5.40	13	11	7	80	100	37	15	0	1	1	0	35	11	0	.314	6	28	2	3	2.8	.944
4 yrs.			41	42	.494	3.75	97	90	72	717.2	766	352	265	1	1	1	0	307	69	0	.225	39	148	29	7	2.2	.866

Bob Vines

VINES, ROBERT EARL
B. Feb. 25, 1897, Waxahachie, Tex.   D. Oct. 18, 1982, Orlando, Fla.

BR TR 6'4"   184 lbs.

Year	Team		W	L	PCT	ERA	G	GS	CG	IP	H	BB	SO	ShO	W	L	SV	AB	H	HR	BA	PO	A	E	DP	TC/G	FA
1924	STL	N	0	0	–	9.28	2	0	0	10.2	23	0	0	0	0	0	0	4	0	0	.000	0	2	0	0	1.0	1.000
1925	PHI	N	0	0	–	11.25	3	0	0	4	9	3	0	0	0	0	0	0	0	0	–	0	1	0	0	0.3	1.000
2 yrs.			0	0	–	9.82	5	0	0	14.2	32	3	0	0	0	0	0	4	0	0	.000	0	3	0	0	0.6	1.000

Dave Vineyard

VINEYARD, DAVID KENT
B. Feb. 25, 1941, Clay, W. Va.

BR TR 6'3"   195 lbs.

Year	Team		W	L	PCT	ERA	G	GS	CG	IP	H	BB	SO	ShO	W	L	SV	AB	H	HR	BA	PO	A	E	DP	TC/G	FA
1964	BAL	A	2	5	.286	4.17	19	6	1	54	57	27	50	0	0	1	0	12	2	0	.167	2	5	0	0	0.4	1.000

Bill Vinton

VINTON, WILLIAM MILLER
B. Apr. 27, 1865, Winthrop, Mass.   D. Sept. 3, 1893, Pawtucket, R. I.

BR TR 6'1"   170 lbs.

Year	Team		W	L	PCT	ERA	G	GS	CG	IP	H	BB	SO	ShO	W	L	SV	AB	H	HR	BA	PO	A	E	DP	TC/G	FA
1884	PHI	N	10	10	.500	2.23	21	21	20	182	166	35	105	1	0	0	0	78	9	0	.115	8	50	5	1	3.0	.921
1885	2 teams						PHI N	(9G 3–6)		PHI AA	(7G 4–3)																
"	total		7	9	.438	2.80	16	16	14	132	136	38	55	2	0	0	0	56	6	0	.107	4	30	11	0	2.8	.756
2 yrs.			17	19	.472	2.46	37	37	34	314	302	73	160	3	0	0	0	134	15	0	.112	12	80	16	1	2.9	.852

Frank Viola

VIOLA, FRANK JOHN, JR. (Sweet Music)
B. Apr. 19, 1960, Hempstead, N. Y.

BL TL 6'4"   195 lbs.

Year	Team		W	L	PCT	ERA	G	GS	CG	IP	H	BB	SO	ShO	W	L	SV	AB	H	HR	BA	PO	A	E	DP	TC/G	FA
1982	MIN	A	4	10	.286	5.21	22	22	3	126	152	38	84	1	0	0	0	–	1	15	2	0	0.8	.889			
1983			7	15	.318	5.49	35	34	4	210	242	92	127	0	0	0	0	–	7	23	1	2	0.9	.968			
1984			18	12	.600	3.21	35	35	10	257.2	225	73	149	4	0	0	0	–	6	26	1	1	0.9	.970			
1985			18	14	.563	4.09	36	36	9	250.2	262	68	135	0	0	0	0	–	6	33	5	0	1.2	.886			
1986			16	13	.552	4.51	37	37	7	245.2	257	83	191	1	0	0	0	–	8	21	3	1	0.9	.906			
1987			17	10	.630	2.90	36	36	7	251.2	230	66	197	1	0	0	0	–	6	34	3	1	1.2	.930			
1988			24	7	.774	2.64	35	35	7	255.1	236	54	193	2	0	0	0	–	5	30	2	1	1.1	.946			
1989	2 teams		MIN A	(24G 8–12)			NY N	(12G 5–5)																			
"	total		13	17	.433	3.66	36	36	9	261	246	74	211	2	0	0	0	23	3	0	.130	10	35	4	3	1.4	.918
8 yrs.			117	98	.544	3.84	272	271	56	1858	1850	548	1287	11	0	0	0	23	3	0	.130	49	217	21	9	1.1	.927

LEAGUE CHAMPIONSHIP SERIES

Year	Team		W	L	PCT	ERA	G	GS	CG	IP	H	BB	SO	ShO	W	L	SV	AB	H	HR	BA	PO	A	E	DP	TC/G	FA
1987	MIN	A	1	0	1.000	5.25	2	2	0	12	14	5	9	0	0	0	0	–	0	1	0	0	0.5	1.000			

WORLD SERIES

Year	Team		W	L	PCT	ERA	G	GS	CG	IP	H	BB	SO	ShO	W	L	SV	AB	H	HR	BA	PO	A	E	DP	TC/G	FA
1987	MIN	A	2	1	.667	3.72	3	3	0	19.1	17	3	16	0	0	0	0	1	0	0	.000	1	5	0	0	2.0	1.000

Jake Virtue

VIRTUE, JACOB KITCHLINE
B. Mar. 2, 1865, Philadelphia, Pa.   D. Feb. 3, 1943, Camden, N. J.

BB TR 5'9½"   165 lbs.

Year	Team		W	L	PCT	ERA	G	GS	CG	IP	H	BB	SO	ShO	W	L	SV	AB	H	HR	BA	PO	A	E	DP	TC/G	FA
1893	CLE	N	0	0	–	1.80	1	0	0	5	3	3	2	0	0	0	0	378	100	1	.265	0	0	0	0	0.0	–
1894			0	0	–	0.00	1	0	0	0	0	1	0	0	0	0	0	89	23	0	.258	0	0	0	0	0.0	–
2 yrs.			0	0	–	1.80	2	0	0	5	3	4	2	0	0	0	0	*				0	0	0	0	0.0	–

Joe Vitelli

VITELLI, ANTONIO JOSEPH
B. Apr. 12, 1908, McKees Rocks, Pa.   D. Feb. 7, 1967, Pittsburgh, Pa.

BR TR 6'1"   195 lbs.

Year	Team		W	L	PCT	ERA	G	GS	CG	IP	H	BB	SO	ShO	W	L	SV	AB	H	HR	BA	PO	A	E	DP	TC/G	FA
1944	PIT	N	0	0	–	2.57	4	0	0	7	5	7	2	0	0	0	0	3	0	0	.000	1	2	1	0	1.0	.750
1945			0	0	–	0.00	0	0	0	0	0	0	0	0	0	0	0	0	0	0	–	0	0	0	0	0.0	–
2 yrs.			0	0	–	2.57	4	0	0	7	5	7	2	0	0	0	0	3	0	0	.000	1	2	1	0	1.0	.750

Ollie Voigt

VOIGT, OLEN EDWARD
B. Jan. 29, 1900, Wheaton, Ill.   D. Apr. 7, 1970, Scottsdale, Ariz.

BR TR 6'1"   170 lbs.

Year	Team		W	L	PCT	ERA	G	GS	CG	IP	H	BB	SO	ShO	W	L	SV	AB	H	HR	BA	PO	A	E	DP	TC/G	FA
1924	STL	A	1	0	1.000	5.51	8	1	0	16.1	21	13	4	0	1	0	0	4	1	0	.250	0	9	2	0	1.4	.818

Bill Voiselle

VOISELLE, WILLIAM SYMMES (Big Bill, Ninety-Six)
B. Jan. 29, 1919, Greenwood, S. C.

BR TR 6'4"   200 lbs.

Year	Team		W	L	PCT	ERA	G	GS	CG	IP	H	BB	SO	ShO	W	L	SV	AB	H	HR	BA	PO	A	E	DP	TC/G	FA
1942	NY	N	0	1	.000	2.00	2	1	0	9	6	4	5	0	0	0	0	2	0	0	.000	1	3	0	0	2.0	1.000
1943			1	2	.333	2.03	4	4	3	31	18	14	19	0	0	0	0	9	1	0	.111	2	2	1	0	1.3	.800
1944			21	16	.568	3.02	43	41	25	312.2	276	118	161	1	1	0	0	105	22	0	.210	9	42	6	4	1.3	.895
1945			14	14	.500	4.49	41	35	14	232.1	249	97	115	0	0	0	0	79	10	0	.127	11	41	1	3	1.3	.981
1946			9	15	.375	3.74	36	25	10	178	171	85	89	2	1	1	0	55	9	0	.164	14	29	3	3	1.3	.935
1947	2 teams		NY N	(11G 1–4)			BOS N	(22G 8–7)																			
"	total		9	11	.450	4.40	33	25	8	174	190	73	71	0	1	1	0	68	11	0	.162	6	34	1	0	1.2	.976
1948	BOS	N	13	13	.500	3.63	37	30	9	215.2	226	90	89	2	2	0	2	72	7	0	.097	6	33	5	0	1.2	.886
1949			7	8	.467	4.04	30	22	5	169.1	170	78	63	4	1	0	1	61	7	0	.115	7	34	2	2	1.4	.953
1950	CHI	N	0	4	–	5.79	19	7	0	51.1	64	29	25	0	0	0	1	13	1	0	.077	3	6	1	0	0.5	.900
9 yrs.			74	84	.468	3.83	245	190	74	1373.1	1370	588	637	13	7	2	3	464	68	0	.147	59	224	20	16	1.2	.934

WORLD SERIES

Year	Team		W	L	PCT	ERA	G	GS	CG	IP	H	BB	SO	ShO	W	L	SV	AB	H	HR	BA	PO	A	E	DP	TC/G	FA
1948	BOS	N	0	1	.000	2.53	2	1	0	10.2	8	2	6	0	0	0	0	2	0	0	.000	1	0	0	0	0.5	1.000

Year	Team	W	L	PCT	ERA	G	GS	CG	IP	H	BB	SO	ShO	W	L	SV	AB	H	HR	BA	PO	A	E	DP	TC/G	FA
														Relief Pitching			Batting									

Jake Volz

VOLZ, JACOB PHILLIP (Silent Jake)
B. Apr. 4, 1878, San Antonio, Tex.   D. Aug. 11, 1962, San Antonio, Tex.   BR TR 5'10"   175 lbs.

Year	Team	W	L	PCT	ERA	G	GS	CG	IP	H	BB	SO	ShO	W	L	SV	AB	H	HR	BA	PO	A	E	DP	TC/G	FA
1901	BOS A	1	0	1.000	9.00	1	1	1	7	6	9	5	0	0	0	0	4	0	0	.000	0	0	2	0	2.0	—
1905	BOS N	0	2	.000	10.38	3	2	0	8.2	12	8	1	0	0	0	0	2	0	0	.000	0	0	0	0	0.0	—
1908	CIN N	1	2	.333	3.57	7	4	1	22.2	16	12	6	0	0	0	0	4	1	0	.250	0	2	0	0	0.3	1.000
3 yrs.		2	4	.333	6.10	11	7	2	38.1	34	29	12	0	0	0	0	10	1	0	.100	0	2	2	0	0.4	.500

Hon Von Fricken

VON FRICKEN, ANTHONY
B. May 30, 1870, Brooklyn, N. Y.   D. Mar. 22, 1947, Troy, N. Y.   BB TR 5'11½"   160 lbs.

Year	Team	W	L	PCT	ERA	G	GS	CG	IP	H	BB	SO	ShO	W	L	SV	AB	H	HR	BA	PO	A	E	DP	TC/G	FA
1890	BOS N	0	1	.000	10.13	1	1	1	8	23	8	2	0	0	0	0	3	0	0	.000	0	2	2	0	4.0	.500

Bruce Von Hoff

VON HOFF, BRUCE FREDERICK
B. Nov. 17, 1943, Oakland, Calif.   BR TR 6'   187 lbs.

Year	Team	W	L	PCT	ERA	G	GS	CG	IP	H	BB	SO	ShO	W	L	SV	AB	H	HR	BA	PO	A	E	DP	TC/G	FA
1965	HOU N	0	0	—	9.00	3	0	0	3	3	2	1	0	0	0	0	0	0	0	—	0	0	0	0	0.0	—
1967		0	3	.000	4.83	10	10	0	50.1	52	28	22	0	0	0	0	15	1	0	.067	1	5	0	0	0.6	1.000
2 yrs.		0	3	.000	5.06	13	10	0	53.1	55	30	23	0	0	0	0	15	1	0	.067	1	5	0	0	0.5	1.000

Dave Von Ohlen

VON OHLEN, DAVID
B. Oct. 25, 1958, Flushing, N. Y.   BL TL 6'2"   200 lbs.

Year	Team	W	L	PCT	ERA	G	GS	CG	IP	H	BB	SO	ShO	W	L	SV	AB	H	HR	BA	PO	A	E	DP	TC/G	FA
1983	STL N	3	2	.600	3.29	46	0	0	68.1	71	25	21	0	3	2	2	7	1	0	.143	2	11	1	1	0.3	.929
1984		1	0	1.000	3.12	27	0	0	34.2	39	8	19	0	1	0	1	1	1	0	1.000	2	10	0	2	0.4	1.000
1985	CLE A	3	2	.600	2.91	26	0	0	43.1	47	20	12	0	3	2	0	0	0	0	—	2	9	0	1	0.4	1.000
1986	OAK A	0	3	.000	3.52	24	0	0	15.1	18	7	4	0	0	3	1	0	0	0	—	0	5	0	0	0.2	1.000
1987		0	0	—	7.50	4	0	0	6	10	1	3	0	0	0	0	0	0	0	—	0	0	0	0	0.0	—
5 yrs.		7	7	.500	3.33	127	0	0	167.2	185	61	59	0	7	7	4	8	2	0	.250	6	35	1	4	0.3	.976

Cy Vorhees

VORHEES, HENRY BERT
B. Sept. 30, 1874, Lodi, Ohio   D. Feb. 8, 1910, Perry, Ohio   6'3"   200 lbs.

Year	Team	W	L	PCT	ERA	G	GS	CG	IP	H	BB	SO	ShO	W	L	SV	AB	H	HR	BA	PO	A	E	DP	TC/G	FA
1902	2 teams			PHI N	(10G 3–3)				WAS A	(1G 0–1)																
"	total	3	4	.429	3.94	11	5	4	61.2	73	22	25	1	1	1	0	23	9	0	.391	2	12	3	0	1.5	.824

Ed Vosberg

VOSBERG, EDWARD JOHN
B. Sept. 28, 1961, Tucson, Ariz.   BL TL 6'1"   190 lbs.

Year	Team	W	L	PCT	ERA	G	GS	CG	IP	H	BB	SO	ShO	W	L	SV	AB	H	HR	BA	PO	A	E	DP	TC/G	FA
1986	SD N	0	1	.000	6.59	5	3	0	13.2	17	9	8	0	0	0	0	2	0	0	.000	0	1	1	0	0.4	.500

Alex Voss

VOSS, ALEXANDER
B. 1855, Atlanta, Ga.   D. Aug. 31, 1906, Cincinnati, Ohio   BR TR 6'1"   180 lbs.

Year	Team	W	L	PCT	ERA	G	GS	CG	IP	H	BB	SO	ShO	W	L	SV	AB	H	HR	BA	PO	A	E	DP	TC/G	FA
1884	2 teams			WAS U	(27G 5–14)				KC U	(7G 0–6)																
"	total	5	20	.200	3.72	34	26	24	239.1	280	39	129	0	0	1	0	*					17	68	14	3	2.9	.859

Rip Vowinkel

VOWINKEL, JOHN HENRY
B. Nov. 18, 1884, Oswego, N. Y.   D. July 13, 1966, Oswego, N. Y.   BR TR 5'10"   195 lbs.

Year	Team	W	L	PCT	ERA	G	GS	CG	IP	H	BB	SO	ShO	W	L	SV	AB	H	HR	BA	PO	A	E	DP	TC/G	FA
1905	CIN N	3	3	.500	4.20	6	6	4	45	52	10	7	0	0	0	0	14	1	0	.071	1	6	1	0	1.3	.875

Pete Vuckovich

VUCKOVICH, PETER DENNIS
B. Oct. 27, 1952, Johnstown, Pa.   BR TR 6'4"   215 lbs.

Year	Team	W	L	PCT	ERA	G	GS	CG	IP	H	BB	SO	ShO	W	L	SV	AB	H	HR	BA	PO	A	E	DP	TC/G	FA
1975	CHI A	0	1	.000	13.06	4	2	0	10.1	17	7	5	0	0	0	0	0	0	0	—	1	2	0	0	0.8	1.000
1976		7	4	.636	4.66	33	7	1	110	122	60	62	0	2	2	0	0	0	0	—	3	19	3	0	0.8	.880
1977	TOR A	7	7	.500	3.47	53	8	3	148	143	59	123	1	5	3	8	0	0	0	—	9	23	5	3	0.7	.865
1978	STL N	12	12	.500	2.55	45	23	6	198	187	59	149	2	1	1	4	58	8	0	.138	12	34	2	4	1.1	.958
1979		15	10	.600	3.59	34	32	9	233	229	64	145	0	1	0	0	79	12	0	.152	14	28	5	2	1.4	.894
1980		12	9	.571	3.41	32	30	7	222	203	68	132	3	0	0	1	71	13	0	.183	16	28	1	3	1.4	.978
1981	MIL A	14	4	.778	3.54	24	23	2	150	137	57	84	1	0	0	0	0	0	0	—	11	27	0	1	1.6	1.000
1982		18	6	.750	3.34	30	30	9	223.2	234	102	105	1	0	0	0	0	0	0	—	13	39	4	1	1.9	.929
1983		0	2	.000	4.91	3	3	0	14.2	15	10	10	0	0	0	0	0	0	0	—	0	1	0	0	0.7	1.000
1985		6	10	.375	5.51	22	16	0	112.2	134	48	55	0	0	0	0	0	0	0	—	5	14	1	1	0.9	.950
1986		2	4	.333	3.06	6	6	0	32.1	33	11	12	0	0	0	0	0	0	0	—	2	7	0	0	1.5	1.000
11 yrs.		93	69	.574	3.66	286	186	38	1454.2	1454	545	882	8	8	10	10	208	33	0	.159	87	222	21	15	1.2	.936

DIVISIONAL PLAYOFF SERIES

Year	Team	W	L	PCT	ERA	G	GS	CG	IP	H	BB	SO	ShO	W	L	SV	AB	H	HR	BA	PO	A	E	DP	TC/G	FA
1981	MIL A	1	0	1.000	0.00	2	1	0	5.1	2	3	4	0	0	0	0	0	0	0	—	0	0	0	0	0.0	—

LEAGUE CHAMPIONSHIP SERIES

Year	Team	W	L	PCT	ERA	G	GS	CG	IP	H	BB	SO	ShO	W	L	SV	AB	H	HR	BA	PO	A	E	DP	TC/G	FA
1982	MIL A	0	1	.000	4.40	2	1	1	14.1	15	7	8	0	0	0	0	0	0	0	—	0	0	0	0	0.0	—

WORLD SERIES

Year	Team	W	L	PCT	ERA	G	GS	CG	IP	H	BB	SO	ShO	W	L	SV	AB	H	HR	BA	PO	A	E	DP	TC/G	FA
1982	MIL A	0	1	.000	4.50	2	2	0	14	16	5	4	0	0	0	0	0	0	0	—	0	2	0	0	1.0	1.000

Paul Wachtel

WACHTEL, PAUL HORINE
B. Apr. 30, 1888, Myersville, Md.   D. Dec. 15, 1964, San Antonio, Tex.   BR TR 5'11"   175 lbs.

Year	Team	W	L	PCT	ERA	G	GS	CG	IP	H	BB	SO	ShO	W	L	SV	AB	H	HR	BA	PO	A	E	DP	TC/G	FA
1917	BKN N	0	0	—	10.50	2	0	0	6	9	4	3	0	0	0	0	3	1	0	.333	0	0	0	0	0.0	—

Charlie Wacker

WACKER, CHARLES JAMES
B. Dec. 8, 1883, Jeffersonville, Ind.   D. Aug. 7, 1948, Evansville, Ind.   BL TL 5'9"

Year	Team	W	L	PCT	ERA	G	GS	CG	IP	H	BB	SO	ShO	W	L	SV	AB	H	HR	BA	PO	A	E	DP	TC/G	FA
1909	PIT N	0	0	—	0.00	1	0	0	2	2	1	0	0	0	0	0	0	0	0	—	0	1	0	0	1.0	1.000

Rube Waddell

WADDELL, GEORGE EDWARD
B. Oct. 13, 1876, Bradford, Pa.   D. Apr. 1, 1914, San Antonio, Tex.   BR TL 6'1½"   196 lbs.
Hall of Fame 1946.

Year	Team	W	L	PCT	ERA	G	GS	CG	IP	H	BB	SO	ShO	W	L	SV	AB	H	HR	BA	PO	A	E	DP	TC/G	FA
1897	LOU N	0	1	.000	3.21	2	1	1	14	17	6	5	0	0	0	0	6	0	0	.000	0	4	0	0	2.0	1.000

Year	Team	W	L	PCT	ERA	G	GS	CG	IP	H	BB	SO	ShO	W	L	SV	AB	H	HR	BA	PO	A	E	DP	TC/G	FA
														Relief Pitching			Batting									

Rube Waddell *continued*

Year	Team	W	L	PCT	ERA	G	GS	CG	IP	H	BB	SO	ShO	W	L	SV	AB	H	HR	BA	PO	A	E	DP	TC/G	FA
1899		7	2	.778	3.08	10	9	9	79	69	14	44	1	0	0	1	34	8	0	.235	4	14	2	1	2.0	.900
1900	PIT N	8	13	.381	2.37	29	22	16	208.2	176	55	130	2	0	3	0	81	14	0	.173	12	49	5	1	2.3	.924
1901	2 teams			PIT N	(2G 0–2)		CHI N	(29G 13–15)																		
"	total	13	17	.433	3.01	31	30	26	251.1	249	75	172	0	0	1	0	101	25	2	.248	32	66	5	0	3.3	.951
1902	PHI A	24	7	.774	2.05	33	27	26	276.1	224	64	210	3	5	0	0	112	32	1	.286	15	64	7	1	2.6	.919
1903		21	16	.568	2.44	39	38	34	324	274	85	302	4	0	0	0	115	14	0	.122	17	77	7	3	2.6	.931
1904		25	19	.568	1.62	46	46	39	383	307	91	349	8	0	0	0	139	17	0	.122	27	105	9	2	3.1	.936
1905		26	11	.703	1.48	46	34	27	328.2	231	90	287	7	8	0	0	116	20	0	.172	13	89	15	3	2.5	.872
1906		15	17	.469	2.21	43	34	22	272.2	221	92	196	8	2	0	0	86	14	0	.163	15	64	6	0	2.0	.929
1907		19	13	.594	2.15	44	33	20	284.2	234	73	232	7	3	0	0	97	12	0	.124	16	67	12	3	2.2	.874
1908	STL A	19	14	.576	1.89	43	36	25	285.2	223	90	232	5	1	1	3	91	10	0	.110	5	79	10	1	2.2	.894
1909		11	14	.440	2.37	31	28	16	220.1	204	57	141	5	1	0	0	75	5	0	.067	13	56	11	1	2.6	.863
1910		3	1	.750	3.55	10	2	0	33	31	11	16	0	2	1	1	9	1	0	.111	0	6	2	0	0.8	.750
13 yrs.		191	145	.568	2.16 6th	407	340	261	2961.1	2460	803	2316	50	22	6	5	1062	172	4	.162	169	740	91	16	2.5	.909

Tom Waddell

WADDELL, THOMAS DAVID
B. Sept. 17, 1958, Dundee, Scotland
BR TR 6'1" 185 lbs.

Year	Team	W	L	PCT	ERA	G	GS	CG	IP	H	BB	SO	ShO	W	L	SV	AB	H	HR	BA	PO	A	E	DP	TC/G	FA
1984	CLE A	7	4	.636	3.06	58	0	0	97	68	37	59	0	7	4	6	0	0	0	–	8	9	0	1	0.3	1.000
1985		8	6	.571	4.87	49	9	1	112.2	104	39	53	0	4	5	9	0	0	0	–	10	15	0	0	0.5	1.000
1987		0	1	.000	14.29	6	0	0	5.2	7	7	6	0	0	1	0	0	0	0	–	0	0	0	0	0.0	–
3 yrs.		15	11	.577	4.30	113	9	1	215.1	179	83	118	0	11	10	15	0	0	0	–	18	24	0	1	0.4	1.000

Ben Wade

WADE, BENJAMIN STYRON
Brother of Jake Wade.
B. Nov. 26, 1922, Morehead City, N. C.
BR TR 6'3" 195 lbs.

Year	Team	W	L	PCT	ERA	G	GS	CG	IP	H	BB	SO	ShO	W	L	SV	AB	H	HR	BA	PO	A	E	DP	TC/G	FA
1948	CHI N	0	1	.000	7.20	2	0	0	5	4	4	1	0	0	1	0	2	0	0	.000	1	1	0	0	1.0	1.000
1952	BKN N	11	9	.550	3.60	37	24	5	180	166	94	118	1	2	0	3	60	7	3	.117	12	20	1	1	0.9	.970
1953		7	5	.583	3.79	32	0	0	90.1	79	33	65	0	7	5	3	24	4	1	.167	4	4	1	2	0.3	.889
1954	2 teams			BKN N	(23G 1–1)		STL N	(13G 0–0)																		
"	total	1	1	.500	7.28	36	0	0	68	89	36	44	0	1	1	3	8	0	0	.000	6	8	2	1	0.4	.875
1955	PIT N	0	1	.000	3.21	11	1	0	28	26	14	7	0	0	1	1	4	0	0	.000	4	3	0	0	0.6	1.000
5 yrs.		19	17	.528	4.34	118	25	5	371.1	364	181	235	1	10	8	10	98	11	4	.112	27	36	4	4	0.6	.940

WORLD SERIES

Year	Team	W	L	PCT	ERA	G	GS	CG	IP	H	BB	SO	ShO	W	L	SV	AB	H	HR	BA	PO	A	E	DP	TC/G	FA
1953	BKN N	0	0	–	15.43	2	0	0	2.1	4	1	2	0	0	0	0	0	0	0	–	0	0	0	0	0.0	–

Jake Wade

WADE, JACOB FIELDS (Whistlin' Jake)
Brother of Ben Wade.
B. Apr. 1, 1912, Morehead City, N. C.
BL TL 6'2" 175 lbs.

Year	Team	W	L	PCT	ERA	G	GS	CG	IP	H	BB	SO	ShO	W	L	SV	AB	H	HR	BA	PO	A	E	DP	TC/G	FA
1936	DET A	4	5	.444	5.29	13	11	4	78.1	93	52	30	1	0	0	0	29	5	0	.172	1	14	4	0	1.5	.789
1937		7	10	.412	5.39	33	25	7	165.1	160	107	69	1	0	1	0	59	11	0	.186	6	33	0	1	1.2	1.000
1938		3	2	.600	6.56	27	2	0	70	73	48	23	0	3	0	0	21	1	0	.048	2	14	1	1	0.6	.941
1939	2 teams			BOS A	(20G 1–4)		STL A	(4G 0–2)																		
"	total	1	6	.143	7.45	24	8	2	64	94	56	30	0	1	0	0	17	0	0	.000	0	12	0	0	0.5	1.000
1942	CHI A	5	5	.500	4.10	15	10	3	85.2	84	56	32	0	1	0	0	29	7	0	.241	6	23	2	3	2.1	.935
1943		3	7	.300	3.01	21	9	3	83.2	66	54	41	1	0	1	0	27	4	0	.148	2	11	1	2	0.7	.929
1944		2	4	.333	4.82	19	5	1	74.2	75	41	35	0	1	1	2	24	7	0	.292	1	4	1	1	0.3	.833
1946	2 teams			NY A	(13G 2–1)		WAS A	(6G 0–0)																		
"	total	2	1	.667	2.89	19	1	0	46.2	45	26	31	0	2	0	1	10	1	0	.100	4	9	0	0	0.7	1.000
8 yrs.		27	40	.403	5.00	171	71	20	668.1	690	440	291	3	8	4	3	216	36	0	.167	22	120	9	8	0.9	.940

Jack Wadsworth

WADSWORTH, JOHN L.
B. Dec. 17, 1867, Wellington, Ohio D. July 8, 1941, Elyria, Ohio
BL TR 180 lbs.

Year	Team	W	L	PCT	ERA	G	GS	CG	IP	H	BB	SO	ShO	W	L	SV	AB	H	HR	BA	PO	A	E	DP	TC/G	FA
1890	CLE N	2	16	.111	5.20	20	19	19	169.2	202	81	26	0	0	0	0	68	12	0	.176	5	35	4	0	2.2	.909
1893	BAL N	0	3	.000	11.25	3	3	0	16	37	8	2	0	0	0	0	7	3	0	.429	3	0	1	0	1.3	.750
1894	LOU N	4	18	.182	7.60	22	22	20	173	261	103	57	0	0	0	0	74	19	0	.257	14	25	2	1	1.9	.951
1895		0	1	.000	16.00	2	0	0	9	24	7	2	0	0	1	0	4	1	0	.250	0	3	0	1	1.5	1.000
4 yrs.		6	38	.136	6.85	47	44	39	367.2	524	199	87	0	0	1	0	153	35	0	.229	22	63	7	3	2.0	.924

Bull Wagner

WAGNER, WILLIAM GEORGE
B. Jan. 1, 1888, Lillie, Mich. D. Oct. 2, 1967, Muskegon, Mich.
BR TR 6'½" 225 lbs.

Year	Team	W	L	PCT	ERA	G	GS	CG	IP	H	BB	SO	ShO	W	L	SV	AB	H	HR	BA	PO	A	E	DP	TC/G	FA
1913	BKN N	4	2	.667	5.48	18	1	0	70.2	77	30	11	0	4	2	0	26	6	0	.231	4	12	1	0	0.9	.941
1914		0	1	.000	6.57	6	0	0	12.1	14	12	4	0	0	1	0	1	0	0	.000	0	3	0	0	0.5	1.000
2 yrs.		4	3	.571	5.64	24	1	0	83	91	42	15	0	4	3	0	27	6	0	.222	4	15	1	0	0.8	.950

Charlie Wagner

WAGNER, CHARLES THOMAS (Broadway)
B. Dec. 3, 1912, Reading, Pa.
BR TR 5'11" 170 lbs.

Year	Team	W	L	PCT	ERA	G	GS	CG	IP	H	BB	SO	ShO	W	L	SV	AB	H	HR	BA	PO	A	E	DP	TC/G	FA
1938	BOS A	1	3	.250	8.35	13	6	1	36.2	47	24	14	0	0	1	0	12	2	0	.167	2	4	0	0	0.5	1.000
1939		3	1	.750	4.23	9	5	0	38.1	49	14	13	0	0	0	0	14	1	0	.071	2	6	0	0	0.9	1.000
1940		1	0	1.000	5.52	12	1	0	29.1	45	8	13	0	1	0	0	5	1	0	.200	1	5	0	0	0.5	1.000
1941		12	8	.600	3.07	29	25	12	187.1	175	85	51	3	2	0	0	63	10	0	.159	13	33	1	3	1.6	.979
1942		14	11	.560	3.29	29	26	17	205.1	184	95	52	2	2	0	0	65	5	0	.077	9	46	0	3	1.9	1.000
1946		1	0	1.000	5.87	8	4	0	30.2	32	19	14	0	0	0	0	11	1	0	.091	0	5	0	0	0.6	1.000
6 yrs.		32	23	.582	3.91	100	67	30	527.2	532	245	157	5	5	1	0	170	20	0	.118	27	99	1	6	1.3	.992

Gary Wagner

WAGNER, GARY EDWARD
B. June 28, 1940, Bridgeport, Ill.
BR TR 6'4" 185 lbs.

Year	Team	W	L	PCT	ERA	G	GS	CG	IP	H	BB	SO	ShO	W	L	SV	AB	H	HR	BA	PO	A	E	DP	TC/G	FA
1965	PHI N	7	7	.500	3.00	59	0	0	105	87	49	91	0	7	7	7	13	1	0	.077	9	21	2	1	0.5	.938
1966		0	1	.000	8.53	5	1	0	6.1	9	8	5	0	0	1	0	0	0	0	–	0	0	0	0	0.0	–
1967		0	0	–	0.00	1	0	0	2	1	0	1	0	0	0	0	0	0	0	–	0	1	0	0	1.0	1.000
1968		4	4	.500	3.00	44	0	0	78	69	31	43	0	4	4	8	12	1	0	.083	11	15	2	1	0.6	.929

Year	Team	W	L	PCT	ERA	G	GS	CG	IP	H	BB	SO	ShO	W	L	SV	AB	H	HR	BA	PO	A	E	DP	TC/G	FA

Gary Wagner *continued*

Year	Team	W	L	PCT	ERA	G	GS	CG	IP	H	BB	SO	ShO	W	L	SV	AB	H	HR	BA	PO	A	E	DP	TC/G	FA
1969	**2 teams**	PHI N	(9G 0–3)		BOS A	(6G 1–3)																				
"	total	1	6	.143	7.13	15	3	0	35.1	49	22	17	0	1	2	0	6	0	0	.000	0	5	3	0	0.5	.625
1970	BOS A	3	1	.750	3.38	38	0	0	40	36	19	20	0	3	1	7	6	1	0	.167	5	3	1	0	0.2	.889
6 yrs.		15	19	.441	3.71	162	4	0	266.2	250	126	174	0	15	15	22	37	3	0	.081	25	45	8	2	0.5	.897

Honus Wagner

WAGNER, JOHN PETER (The Flying Dutchman)   BR TR 5'11" 200 lbs.
Brother of Butts Wagner.
B. Feb. 24, 1874, Mansfield, Pa.   D. Dec. 6, 1955, Carnegie, Pa.
Manager 1917.
Hall of Fame 1936.

Year	Team	W	L	PCT	ERA	G	GS	CG	IP	H	BB	SO	ShO	W	L	SV	AB	H	HR	BA	PO	A	E	DP	TC/G	FA
1900	PIT N	0	0	–	0.00	1	0	0	3	3	4	1	0	0	0	0	527	201	4	.381	0	0	0	0	0.0	–
1902		0	0	–	0.00	1	0	0	5.1	4	2	5	0	0	0	0	538	177	3	.329	1	0	0	0	1.0	1.000
2 yrs.		0	0	–	0.00	2	0	0	8.1	7	6	6	0	0	0	0	*				1	0	0	0	0.5	1.000

Mark Wagner

WAGNER, MARK DUANE   BR TR 6' 165 lbs.
B. Mar. 4, 1954, Conneaut, Ohio

Year	Team	W	L	PCT	ERA	G	GS	CG	IP	H	BB	SO	ShO	W	L	SV	AB	H	HR	BA	PO	A	E	DP	TC/G	FA
1984	OAK A	0	0	–	0.00	1	0	0	1.2	2	1	1	0	0	0	0	*				0	0	0	0	0.0	

Rick Waits

WAITS, MICHAEL RICHARD   BB TL 6'3" 194 lbs.
B. May 15, 1952, Atlanta, Ga.

Year	Team	W	L	PCT	ERA	G	GS	CG	IP	H	BB	SO	ShO	W	L	SV	AB	H	HR	BA	PO	A	E	DP	TC/G	FA
1973	TEX A	0	0	–	9.00	1	0	0	1	1	1	0	0	0	0	1	0	0	0	–	0	0	0	0	0.0	
1975	CLE A	6	2	.750	2.94	16	7	3	70.1	57	25	34	0	2	0	1	0	0	0	–	5	12	1	1	1.1	.944
1976		7	9	.438	3.99	26	22	4	124	143	54	65	2	0	0	0	0	0	0	–	10	20	2	2	1.2	.938
1977		9	7	.563	4.00	37	16	1	135	132	64	62	0	3	2	2	0	0	0	–	4	24	2	0	0.8	.933
1978		13	15	.464	3.20	34	33	15	230.1	206	86	97	2	0	0	0	0	0	0	–	19	49	1	1	2.0	.986
1979		16	13	.552	4.44	34	34	8	231	230	91	91	3	0	0	0	0	0	0	–	15	43	0	2	1.7	1.000
1980		13	14	.481	4.46	33	33	9	224	231	82	109	0	0	0	0	0	0	0	–	10	30	1	0	1.2	.976
1981		8	10	.444	4.93	22	21	5	126	173	44	51	0	0	0	0	0	0	0	–	12	28	0	2	1.8	1.000
1982		2	13	.133	5.40	25	21	2	115	128	57	44	0	0	0	0	0	0	0	–	6	23	0	1	1.2	1.000
1983	**2 teams**	CLE A	(8G 0–1)		MIL A	(10G 0–2)																				
"	total	0	3	.000	4.89	18	2	0	49.2	62	20	33	0	0	0	0	0	0	0	–	0	7	1	0	0.4	.875
1984	MIL A	2	4	.333	3.58	47	1	0	73	84	24	49	0	2	3	3	0	0	0	–	2	12	0	0	0.3	1.000
1985		3	2	.600	6.51	24	0	0	47	67	20	24	0	3	2	1	1	0	0	.000	8	4	0	0	0.5	1.000
12 yrs.		79	92	.462	4.25	317	190	47	1426.1	1514	568	659	10	11	10	8	1	0	0	.000	91	252	8	9	1.1	.977

Bill Wakefield

WAKEFIELD, WILLIAM SUMNER   BR TR 6' 175 lbs.
B. May 24, 1941, Kansas City, Mo.

Year	Team	W	L	PCT	ERA	G	GS	CG	IP	H	BB	SO	ShO	W	L	SV	AB	H	HR	BA	PO	A	E	DP	TC/G	FA
1964	NY N	3	5	.375	3.61	62	4	0	119.2	103	61	61	0	3	2	2	24	4	0	.167	4	23	0	2	0.4	1.000

Rube Walberg

WALBERG, GEORGE ELVIN   BL TL 6'1½" 190 lbs.
B. July 27, 1896, Pine City, Minn.   D. Oct. 27, 1978, Tempe, Ariz.

Year	Team	W	L	PCT	ERA	G	GS	CG	IP	H	BB	SO	ShO	W	L	SV	AB	H	HR	BA	PO	A	E	DP	TC/G	FA
1923	**2 teams**	NY N	(2G 0–0)		PHI A	(26G 4–8)																				
"	total	4	8	.333	5.18	28	10	4	120	126	61	39	0	3	1	0	42	13	0	.310	2	35	3	2	1.4	.925
1924	PHI A	0	0	–	12.86	6	2	0	7	10	10	3	0	0	0	0	2	1	0	.500	0	2	0	0	0.3	1.000
1925		8	14	.364	3.99	53	20	7	191.2	197	77	82	0	3	4	7	64	10	0	.156	10	51	2	0	1.2	.968
1926		12	10	.545	2.80	40	19	5	151	168	60	72	2	3	1	2	46	7	0	.152	4	35	4	2	1.1	.907
1927		16	12	.571	3.97	46	34	15	249.1	257	91	136	0	2	2	4	87	18	2	.207	2	62	6	0	1.5	.914
1928		17	12	.586	3.55	38	30	15	235.2	236	64	112	3	3	1	1	86	18	1	.209	9	56	4	3	1.8	.942
1929		18	11	.621	3.60	40	33	20	267.2	256	99	94	3	1	1	4	103	23	1	.223	11	49	0	1	1.5	1.000
1930		13	12	.520	4.69	38	30	12	205.1	207	85	100	2	4	1	4	73	12	0	.164	7	34	3	1	1.2	.932
1931		20	12	.625	3.74	44	35	19	291	298	109	106	1	1	0	3	105	13	0	.124	13	52	0	1	1.5	1.000
1932		17	10	.630	4.73	41	34	19	272	305	103	96	3	0	0	1	94	16	0	.170	14	55	4	2	1.8	.945
1933		9	13	.409	4.88	40	20	10	201	224	95	68	1	3	3	4	68	9	0	.132	14	45	2	1	1.5	.967
1934	BOS A	6	7	.462	4.04	30	10	2	104.2	118	41	38	0	4	2	1	32	6	0	.188	5	25	2	0	1.1	.938
1935		5	9	.357	3.91	44	10	4	142.2	152	54	44	0	4	3	3	37	6	0	.162	8	23	2	0	0.8	.939
1936		5	4	.556	4.40	24	9	5	100.1	98	36	49	0	0	1	1	32	5	0	.156	8	17	1	2	1.1	.962
1937		5	7	.417	5.59	32	11	3	104.2	143	46	46	0	2	1	1	34	5	0	.147	6	17	4	3	0.8	.852
15 yrs.		155	141	.524	4.17	544	307	140	2644	2795	1031	1085	15	34	23	32	905	162	4	.179	113	558	37	18	1.3	.948

WORLD SERIES

Year	Team	W	L	PCT	ERA	G	GS	CG	IP	H	BB	SO	ShO	W	L	SV	AB	H	HR	BA	PO	A	E	DP	TC/G	FA
1929	PHI A	1	0	1.000	0.00	2	0	0	6.1	3	0	8	0	0	0	0	1	0	0	.000	0	1	1	0	1.0	.500
1930		0	1	.000	3.86	1	1	0	4.2	4	1	3	0	0	0	0	2	0	0	.000	0	0	0	0	0.0	–
1931		0	0	–	3.00	2	0	0	3	3	2	4	0	0	0	0	0	0	0	–	0	0	0	0	0.0	–
3 yrs.		1	1	.500	1.93	5	1	0	14	10	3	15	0	1	0	0	3	0	0	.000	0	1	1	0	0.4	.500

Doc Waldbauer

WALDBAUER, ALBERT CHARLES   BR TR 6' 172 lbs.
B. Feb. 22, 1892, Richmond, Va.   D. July 16, 1969, Yakima, Wash.

Year	Team	W	L	PCT	ERA	G	GS	CG	IP	H	BB	SO	ShO	W	L	SV	AB	H	HR	BA	PO	A	E	DP	TC/G	FA
1917	WAS A	0	0	–	7.20	2	0	0	5	10	2	2	0	0	0	1	1	0	0	.000	0	3	0	0	1.5	1.000

Bob Walk

WALK, ROBERT VERNON (Whirlybird)   BR TR 6'3" 185 lbs.
B. Nov. 26, 1956, Van Nuys, Calif.

Year	Team	W	L	PCT	ERA	G	GS	CG	IP	H	BB	SO	ShO	W	L	SV	AB	H	HR	BA	PO	A	E	DP	TC/G	FA
1980	PHI N	11	7	.611	4.56	27	27	2	152	163	71	94	0	0	0	0	50	7	0	.140	17	15	1	2	1.2	.970
1981	ATL N	1	4	.200	4.60	12	8	0	43	41	23	16	0	0	0	0	7	1	0	.143	3	4	0	0	0.6	1.000
1982		11	9	.550	4.87	32	27	3	164.1	179	59	84	1	0	0	0	51	10	0	.196	12	17	6	2	1.1	.829
1983		0	0	–	7.36	1	1	0	3.2	7	2	4	0	0	0	0	1	0	0	.000	0	2	0	0	2.0	1.000
1984	PIT N	1	1	.500	2.61	2	2	0	10.1	8	4	10	0	0	0	0	3	0	0	.000	0	0	0	0	0.0	–
1985		2	3	.400	3.68	9	9	1	58.2	60	18	40	1	0	0	0	17	0	0	.000	7	2	0	1	1.0	1.000
1986		7	8	.467	3.75	44	15	1	141.2	129	64	78	1	2	3	2	39	6	0	.154	21	28	3	4	1.2	.942
1987		8	2	.800	3.31	39	12	1	117	107	51	78	1	2	1	0	26	6	0	.231	9	22	2	0	0.8	.939
1988		12	10	.545	2.71	32	32	1	212.2	183	65	81	1	0	0	0	69	6	0	.087	23	34	3	3	1.9	.950

Year	Team	W	L	PCT	ERA	G	GS	CG	IP	H	BB	SO	ShO	W	L	SV	AB	H	HR	BA	PO	A	E	DP	TC/G	FA
														Relief Pitching			Batting									

Bob Walk *continued*

Year	Team	W	L	PCT	ERA	G	GS	CG	IP	H	BB	SO	ShO	W	L	SV	AB	H	HR	BA	PO	A	E	DP	TC/G	FA
1989		13	10	.565	4.41	33	31	2	196	208	65	83	0	0	0	0	70	13	0	.186	19	31	3	3	1.6	.943
10 yrs.		66	54	.550	3.93	231	164	11	1099.1	1085	422	568	5	4	4	2	333	49	0	.147	111	155	18	16	1.2	.937

LEAGUE CHAMPIONSHIP SERIES

Year	Team	W	L	PCT	ERA	G	GS	CG	IP	H	BB	SO	ShO	W	L	SV	AB	H	HR	BA	PO	A	E	DP	TC/G	FA
1982	ATL N	0	0	—	9.00	1	0	0	1	2	1	1	0	0	0	0	0	0	0	—	0	0	0	0	0.0	—

WORLD SERIES

Year	Team	W	L	PCT	ERA	G	GS	CG	IP	H	BB	SO	ShO	W	L	SV	AB	H	HR	BA	PO	A	E	DP	TC/G	FA
1980	PHI N	1	0	1.000	7.71	1	1	0	7	8	3	3	0	0	0	0	0	0	0	—	2	0	0	0	2.0	1.000

Bill Walker

WALKER, WILLIAM HENRY   BR TL 6'   175 lbs.
B. Oct. 7, 1903, East St. Louis, Ill.   D. June 14, 1966, East St. Louis, Ill.

Year	Team	W	L	PCT	ERA	G	GS	CG	IP	H	BB	SO	ShO	W	L	SV	AB	H	HR	BA	PO	A	E	DP	TC/G	FA
1927	NY N	0	0	—	9.00	3	0	0	4	6	5	4	0	0	0	0	0	0	0	—	0	0	0	0	0.0	—
1928		3	6	.333	4.72	22	8	1	76.1	79	31	39	0	1	1	0	22	2	0	.091	0	17	1	0	0.8	.944
1929		14	7	.667	3.09	29	23	13	177.2	188	57	65	1	1	1	0	61	7	1	.115	10	23	3	1	1.2	.917
1930		17	15	.531	3.93	39	34	13	245.1	258	88	105	2	2	1	1	86	16	2	.186	8	44	4	1	1.5	.931
1931		17	9	.654	2.26	37	28	19	239.1	212	64	121	6	1	0	3	77	5	0	.065	8	31	4	1	1.2	.907
1932		8	12	.400	4.14	31	22	9	163	177	55	74	0	1	1	2	52	7	0	.135	10	39	2	1	1.6	.961
1933	STL N	9	10	.474	3.42	29	20	6	158	168	67	41	2	3	1	1	53	7	1	.132	11	40	4	0	1.9	.927
1934		12	4	.750	3.12	24	19	10	153	160	66	76	1	0	0	0	54	5	0	.093	8	23	1	2	1.3	.969
1935		13	8	.619	3.82	37	25	8	193.1	222	78	79	2	4	1	1	59	6	0	.102	4	42	4	0	1.4	.920
1936		5	6	.455	5.87	21	13	4	79.2	106	27	22	1	1	1	1	25	7	0	.280	3	23	1	1	1.3	.963
10 yrs.		98	77	.560	3.59	272	192	83	1489.2	1576	538	626	15	14	7	8	489	62	4	.127	64	282	24	7	1.4	.935

WORLD SERIES

Year	Team	W	L	PCT	ERA	G	GS	CG	IP	H	BB	SO	ShO	W	L	SV	AB	H	HR	BA	PO	A	E	DP	TC/G	FA
1934	STL N	0	2	.000	7.11	2	0	0	6.1	6	6	2	0	0	2	0	2	0	0	.000	0	1	1	0	1.0	.500

2nd

Dixie Walker

WALKER, EWART GLADSTONE   BL TR 6'   192 lbs.
Father of Harry Walker.   Father of Dixie Walker.
Brother of Ernie Walker.
B. June 1, 1887, Brownsville, Pa.   D. Nov. 14, 1965, Leeds, Ala.

Year	Team	W	L	PCT	ERA	G	GS	CG	IP	H	BB	SO	ShO	W	L	SV	AB	H	HR	BA	PO	A	E	DP	TC/G	FA
1909	WAS A	3	1	.750	2.50	4	4	4	36	31	6	25	0	0	0	0	13	2	0	.154	1	10	2	1	3.3	.846
1910		11	11	.500	3.30	29	26	16	199.1	167	68	85	3	0	0	0	69	9	0	.130	4	60	4	1	2.3	.941
1911		8	13	.381	3.39	32	24	15	185.2	205	50	65	2	1	2	0	66	20	0	.303	11	45	4	0	1.9	.933
1912		3	6	.333	5.25	9	8	5	60	72	18	29	0	1	0	0	16	2	0	.125	5	18	6	0	3.2	.793
4 yrs.		25	31	.446	3.52	74	62	40	481	475	142	204	5	2	2	0	164	33	0	.201	21	133	16	2	2.3	.906

Ed Walker

WALKER, EDWARD HARRISON   BL TL 6'5"   242 lbs.
B. Aug. 11, 1874, Cambois, England   D. Sept. 29, 1947, Akron, Ohio

Year	Team	W	L	PCT	ERA	G	GS	CG	IP	H	BB	SO	ShO	W	L	SV	AB	H	HR	BA	PO	A	E	DP	TC/G	FA
1902	CLE A	0	1	.000	3.38	1	1	1	8	11	3	1	0	0	0	0	3	1	0	.333	0	3	1	0	4.0	.750
1903		0	0	—	5.25	3	3	0	12	13	10	4	0	0	0	0	3	0	0	.000	0	1	0	0	0.3	1.000
2 yrs.		0	1	.000	4.50	4	4	1	20	24	13	5	0	0	0	0	6	1	0	.167	0	4	1	0	1.3	.800

George Walker

WALKER, GEORGE A.   5'9"   184 lbs.
B. Hamilton, Ont., Canada   Deceased.

Year	Team	W	L	PCT	ERA	G	GS	CG	IP	H	BB	SO	ShO	W	L	SV	AB	H	HR	BA	PO	A	E	DP	TC/G	FA
1888	BAL AA	1	3	.250	5.91	4	4	4	35	36	14	18	1	0	0	0	13	1	0	.077	0	7	1	0	2.0	.875

Jerry Walker

WALKER, JERRY ALLEN   BB TR 6'1"   195 lbs.
B. Feb. 12, 1939, Ada, Okla.   BR 1963-64

Year	Team	W	L	PCT	ERA	G	GS	CG	IP	H	BB	SO	ShO	W	L	SV	AB	H	HR	BA	PO	A	E	DP	TC/G	FA
1957	BAL A	1	0	1.000	2.93	13	3	1	27.2	24	14	13	1	0	0	1	5	0	0	.000	0	5	0	0	0.4	1.000
1958		0	0	—	6.97	6	0	0	10.1	16	5	6	0	0	0	0	2	0	0	.000	2	0	0	0	0.3	1.000
1959		11	10	.524	2.92	30	22	7	182	160	52	100	2	0	1	4	65	11	1	.169	5	32	0	2	1.2	1.000
1960		3	4	.429	3.74	29	18	1	118	107	56	48	0	0	0	0	38	14	0	.368	5	23	0	1	1.0	1.000
1961	KC A	8	14	.364	4.82	36	24	4	168	161	96	56	0	2	1	2	64	16	0	.250	9	31	0	4	1.1	1.000
1962		8	9	.471	5.90	31	21	3	143.1	165	78	57	0	1	0	0	57	15	3	.263	15	27	0	3	1.4	1.000
1963	CLE A	6	6	.500	4.91	39	2	0	88	92	36	41	0	6	4	1	19	2	0	.105	7	14	2	0	0.6	.913
1964		0	1	.000	4.66	6	0	0	9.2	9	4	5	0	0	0	0	2	0	0	.000	0	1	0	0	0.2	1.000
8 yrs.		37	44	.457	4.36	190	90	16	747	734	341	326	4	8	8	13	252	58	4	.230	43	133	2	10	0.9	.989

Luke Walker

WALKER, JAMES LUKE   BL TL 6'2"   190 lbs.
B. Sept. 2, 1943, DeKalb, Tex.

Year	Team	W	L	PCT	ERA	G	GS	CG	IP	H	BB	SO	ShO	W	L	SV	AB	H	HR	BA	PO	A	E	DP	TC/G	FA
1965	PIT N	0	0	—	0.00	2	0	0	5	2	1	5	0	0	0	0	0	0	0	—	0	1	0	0	0.5	1.000
1966		0	1	.000	4.50	10	1	0	10	8	15	7	0	0	1	0	2	0	0	.000	1	1	1	0	0.3	.667
1968		0	3	.000	2.02	39	2	0	62.1	42	39	66	0	0	2	3	8	0	0	.000	3	12	0	0	0.4	1.000
1969		4	6	.400	3.63	31	15	3	119	98	57	96	1	0	0	0	32	0	0	.000	2	24	2	0	0.9	.929
1970		15	6	.714	3.04	42	19	5	163	129	89	124	3	3	1	3	46	6	0	.130	3	24	1	3	0.7	.964
1971		10	8	.556	3.54	28	24	4	160	157	53	86	2	2	0	0	46	1	0	.022	3	8	1	3	0.8	.955
1972		4	6	.400	3.40	26	12	2	92.2	98	34	48	0	0	1	2	24	2	0	.083	3	13	3	3	0.7	.842
1973		7	12	.368	4.65	37	18	2	122	129	66	74	1	0	2	1	30	2	0	.067	4	16	2	1	0.6	.909
1974	DET A	5	5	.500	4.99	28	9	0	92	100	54	52	0	2	0	0	0	0	0	—	6	11	1	0	0.6	.944
9 yrs.		45	47	.489	3.64	243	100	16	826	763	408	558	7	7	7	9	188	11	0	.059	25	120	11	10	0.6	.929

LEAGUE CHAMPIONSHIP SERIES

Year	Team	W	L	PCT	ERA	G	GS	CG	IP	H	BB	SO	ShO	W	L	SV	AB	H	HR	BA	PO	A	E	DP	TC/G	FA
1970	PIT N	0	1	.000	1.29	1	1	0	7	5	1	5	0	0	0	0	2	0	0	.000	0	1	0	0	1.0	—
1972		0	0	—	18.00	1	0	0	1	3	0	0	0	0	0	0	0	0	0	—	0	0	0	0	0.0	—
2 yrs.		0	1	.000	3.38	2	1	0	8	8	1	5	0	0	0	0	2	0	0	.000	0	1	0	0	0.5	—

WORLD SERIES

Year	Team	W	L	PCT	ERA	G	GS	CG	IP	H	BB	SO	ShO	W	L	SV	AB	H	HR	BA	PO	A	E	DP	TC/G	FA
1971	PIT N	0	0	—	40.50	1	1	0	.2	3	1	0	0	0	0	0	0	0	0	—	0	0	0	0	0.0	—

Year	Team		W	L	PCT	ERA	G	GS	CG	IP	H	BB	SO	ShO	Relief Pitching			Batting				PO	A	E	DP	TC/G	FA
															W	L	SV	AB	H	HR	BA						

Marty Walker

WALKER, MARTIN VAN BUREN (Buddy) — BL TL 6' 170 lbs.
B. Mar. 27, 1899, Philadelphia, Pa. D. Apr. 24, 1978, Philadelphia, Pa.

Year	Team		W	L	PCT	ERA	G	GS	CG	IP	H	BB	SO	ShO	W	L	SV	AB	H	HR	BA	PO	A	E	DP	TC/G	FA
1928	PHI	N	0	1	.000	∞	1	1	0	2	3	0	0	0	0	0	0	0	0	0	–	0	0	0	0	0.0	–

Mike Walker

WALKER, MICHAEL CHARLES — BR TR 6'1" 175 lbs.
B. Oct. 4, 1966, Chicago, Ill.

Year	Team		W	L	PCT	ERA	G	GS	CG	IP	H	BB	SO	ShO	W	L	SV	AB	H	HR	BA	PO	A	E	DP	TC/G	FA
1988	CLE	A	0	1	.000	7.27	3	1	0	8.2	8	10	7	0	0	0	0	0	0	0	–	0	3	0	0	1.0	1.000

Mysterious Walker

WALKER, FREDERICK MITCHELL — BR TR 5'10½" 185 lbs.
B. Mar. 21, 1884, Utica, Neb. D. Feb. 1, 1958, Oak Park, Ill.

Year	Team		W	L	PCT	ERA	G	GS	CG	IP	H	BB	SO	ShO	W	L	SV	AB	H	HR	BA	PO	A	E	DP	TC/G	FA
1910	CIN	N	0	0	–	3.00	1	0	0	3	4	4	1	0	0	0	0	1	0	0	.000	0	3	0	0	3.0	1.000
1913	BKN	N	1	3	.250	3.55	11	8	3	58.1	44	35	35	0	0	0	0	18	3	0	.167	1	22	0	0	2.1	1.000
1914	PIT	F	3	16	.158	4.31	35	21	12	169.1	197	74	79	0	1	1	0	53	6	0	.113	10	64	7	3	2.3	.914
1915	BKN	F	2	4	.333	3.70	13	7	2	65.2	61	22	28	0	0	1	1	27	6	0	.222	1	28	1	0	2.3	.967
4 yrs.			6	23	.207	4.01	60	36	17	296.1	306	135	143	0	1	2	1	99	15	0	.152	12	117	8	3	2.3	.942

Roy Walker

WALKER, JAMES ROY (Dixie) — BR TR 6'1½" 180 lbs.
B. Apr. 13, 1893, Lawrenceburg, Tenn. BB 1922
D. Feb. 10, 1962, New Orleans, La.

Year	Team		W	L	PCT	ERA	G	GS	CG	IP	H	BB	SO	ShO	W	L	SV	AB	H	HR	BA	PO	A	E	DP	TC/G	FA
1912	CLE	A	0	0	–	0.00	2	0	0	3	0	3	1	0	0	0	0	0	0	0	–	0	0	0	0	0.0	–
1915			4	9	.308	3.98	25	15	4	131	122	65	57	0	0	1	1	38	5	0	.132	6	25	1	1	1.3	.969
1917	CHI	N	0	1	.000	3.86	2	1	0	7	8	5	4	0	0	0	0	1	0	0	.000	0	1	0	0	0.5	1.000
1918			1	3	.250	2.70	13	7	2	43.1	50	15	20	0	0	0	1	11	0	0	.000	1	12	0	1	1.0	1.000
1921	STL	N	11	12	.478	4.22	38	24	11	170.2	194	53	52	0	2	0	3	54	11	0	.204	6	38	3	1	1.2	.936
1922			1	2	.333	4.78	12	2	0	32	34	15	14	0	1	0	0	7	1	0	.143	1	1	2	0	0.3	.500
6 yrs.			17	27	.386	3.98	92	49	17	387	408	156	148	0	3	2	5	111	17	0	.153	14	77	6	3	1.1	.938

Tom Walker

WALKER, ROBERT THOMAS — BR TR 6'1" 188 lbs.
B. Nov. 7, 1948, Tampa, Fla.

Year	Team		W	L	PCT	ERA	G	GS	CG	IP	H	BB	SO	ShO	W	L	SV	AB	H	HR	BA	PO	A	E	DP	TC/G	FA
1972	MON	N	2	2	.500	2.89	46	0	0	74.2	71	22	42	0	2	2	2	3	0	0	.000	6	10	3	1	0.4	.842
1973			7	5	.583	3.63	54	0	0	91.2	95	42	68	0	7	5	4	7	0	0	.000	5	12	1	0	0.3	.944
1974			4	5	.444	3.82	33	8	1	92	96	28	70	0	2	1	2	16	3	0	.188	5	9	1	0	0.4	1.000
1975	DET	A	3	8	.273	4.45	36	9	1	115.1	116	40	60	0	1	3	0	0	0	0	–	3	12	2	0	0.5	.882
1976	STL	N	1	2	.333	4.12	10	0	0	19.2	22	3	11	0	1	2	3	5	2	0	.400	1	0	0	0	0.1	1.000
1977	2 teams	MON N (11G 1–1)					CAL A (1G 0–0)																				
"	total		1	1	.500	5.14	12	0	0	21	18	7	11	0	1	1	0	2	0	0	.000	1	2	0	0	0.3	1.000
6 yrs.			18	23	.439	3.87	191	17	2	414.1	418	142	262	0	14	14	11	33	5	0	.152	21	45	6	2	0.4	.917

Tom Walker

WALKER, THOMAS WILLIAM — BR TR 5'11" 170 lbs.
B. Aug. 1, 1881, Philadelphia, Pa. D. July 10, 1944, Woodbury Heights, N. J.

Year	Team		W	L	PCT	ERA	G	GS	CG	IP	H	BB	SO	ShO	W	L	SV	AB	H	HR	BA	PO	A	E	DP	TC/G	FA
1902	PHI	A	0	1	.000	5.63	1	1	0	8	10	1	2	0	0	0	0	4	1	0	.250	1	5	0	0	6.0	1.000
1904	CIN	N	15	8	.652	2.24	24	24	22	217	196	53	64	2	0	0	0	77	9	0	.117	9	55	3	1	2.8	.955
1905			9	7	.563	3.23	23	19	12	145	171	44	28	1	0	0	0	51	7	0	.137	5	41	0	1	2.0	1.000
3 yrs.			24	16	.600	2.70	48	44	35	370	377	97	94	3	0	0	0	132	17	0	.129	15	101	3	2	2.5	.975

Jim Walkup

WALKUP, JAMES ELTON — BR TR 6'1" 170 lbs.
B. Dec. 14, 1909, Havana, Ark.

Year	Team		W	L	PCT	ERA	G	GS	CG	IP	H	BB	SO	ShO	W	L	SV	AB	H	HR	BA	PO	A	E	DP	TC/G	FA
1934	STL	A	0	0	–	2.16	3	0	0	8.1	6	5	6	0	0	0	0	3	1	0	.333	0	0	0	0	0.0	–
1935			6	9	.400	6.25	55	20	4	181.1	226	104	44	1	1	1	0	47	6	0	.128	11	28	2	2	0.7	.951
1936			0	3	.000	8.04	5	2	0	15.2	20	6	5	0	0	1	0	4	0	0	.000	1	6	0	1	1.4	1.000
1937			9	12	.429	7.36	27	18	6	150.1	218	83	46	0	2	3	0	58	14	0	.241	7	37	2	1	1.7	.957
1938			1	12	.077	6.80	18	13	1	94	127	53	28	0	1	2	0	29	4	0	.138	3	19	0	2	1.2	1.000
1939	2 teams	STL A (1G 0–1)					DET A (7G 0–1)																				
"	total		0	2	.000	7.11	8	0	0	12.2	17	9	5	0	0	2	0	2	1	0	.500	1	2	0	0	0.4	1.000
6 yrs.			16	38	.296	6.74	116	53	11	462.1	614	260	134	1	4	9	0	143	26	0	.182	23	92	4	6	1.0	.966

Jim Walkup

WALKUP, JAMES HUEY — BR TL 5'8" 150 lbs.
B. Nov. 3, 1895, Havana, Ark.

Year	Team		W	L	PCT	ERA	G	GS	CG	IP	H	BB	SO	ShO	W	L	SV	AB	H	HR	BA	PO	A	E	DP	TC/G	FA
1927	DET	A	0	0	–	5.40	2	0	0	1.2	3	1	0	0	0	0	0	1	0	0	.000	0	1	0	0	0.5	1.000

Murray Wall

WALL, MURRAY WESLEY (Tex) — BR TR 6'3" 185 lbs.
B. Sept. 19, 1926, Dallas, Tex. D. Oct. 8, 1971, Lone Oak, Tex.

Year	Team		W	L	PCT	ERA	G	GS	CG	IP	H	BB	SO	ShO	W	L	SV	AB	H	HR	BA	PO	A	E	DP	TC/G	FA
1950	BOS	N	0	0	–	9.00	4	0	0	4	6	2	2	0	0	0	0	0	0	0	.000	0	1	0	0	1.0	–
1957	BOS	A	3	0	1.000	3.33	11	0	0	24.1	21	2	13	0	3	0	1	6	2	0	.333	4	8	0	1	1.1	1.000
1958			8	9	.471	3.62	52	1	0	114.1	109	33	53	0	8	8	10	28	3	0	.107	9	32	0	2	0.8	1.000
1959	3 teams	BOS A (15G 1–4)					WAS A (1G 0–0)					BOS A (11G 1–1)														
"	total		2	5	.286	5.54	27	0	0	50.1	60	26	14	0	2	5	3	11	0	0	.000	4	14	2	0	0.7	.900
4 yrs.			13	14	.481	4.20	91	1	0	193	196	63	82	0	13	13	14	46	5	0	.109	17	54	3	3	0.8	.959

Stan Wall

WALL, STANLEY ARTHUR — BL TL 6'1" 175 lbs.
B. June 16, 1951, Butler, Mo.

Year	Team		W	L	PCT	ERA	G	GS	CG	IP	H	BB	SO	ShO	W	L	SV	AB	H	HR	BA	PO	A	E	DP	TC/G	FA
1975	LA	N	0	1	.000	1.69	10	0	0	16	12	7	6	0	0	1	0	0	0	0	–	0	3	0	0	0.3	1.000
1976			2	2	.500	3.60	31	0	0	50	50	15	27	0	2	1	1	4	0	0	.000	0	6	0	1	0.2	1.000
1977			2	3	.400	5.34	25	0	0	32	36	13	22	0	2	3	0	1	0	0	.000	0	3	1	0	0.2	.750
3 yrs.			4	6	.400	3.86	66	0	0	98	98	35	55	0	4	6	1	5	0	0	.000	0	12	1	1	0.2	.923

Bobby Wallace

WALLACE, RHODERICK JOHN (Rhody) — BR TR 5'8" 170 lbs.
B. Nov. 4, 1873, Pittsburgh, Pa. D. Nov. 3, 1960, Torrance, Calif.
Manager 1911-12, 1937.
Hall of Fame 1953.

Year	Team		W	L	PCT	ERA	G	GS	CG	IP	H	BB	SO	ShO	W	L	SV	AB	H	HR	BA	PO	A	E	DP	TC/G	FA
1894	CLE	N	2	1	.667	5.47	4	3	3	26.1	28	22	10	0	0	0	0	13	2	0	.154	3	9	0	0	3.0	1.000

Year	Team	W	L	PCT	ERA	G	GS	CG	IP	H	BB	SO	ShO	Relief Pitching W	L	SV	Batting AB	H	HR	BA	PO	A	E	DP	TC/G	FA

Bobby Wallace *continued*

1895		12	14	.462	4.09	30	28	22	228.2	271	87	63	1	0	1	1	98	21	0	.214	15	66	8	2	3.0	.910
1896		10	7	.588	3.34	22	16	13	145.1	167	49	46	2	1	1	0	149	35	1	.235	7	32	3	4	1.9	.929
1902	STL A	0	0		0.00	1	1	0	2	3	0	1	0	0	0	0	495	142	1	.287	0	1	0	0	1.0	1.000
4 yrs.		24	22	.522	3.89	57	48	38	402.1	469	158	120	3	1	2	1	*				25	108	11	6	2.5	.924

Dave Wallace

WALLACE, DAVID WILLIAM — BR TR 5'10" 185 lbs.
B. Sept. 7, 1947, Waterbury, Conn.

1973	PHI N	0	0		22.09	4	0	0	3.2	13	2	2	0	0	0	0	0	0	0	–	0	2	0	0	0.5	1.000
1974		0	1	.000	9.00	3	0	0	3	4	3	3	0	0	1	0	0	0	0	–	0	1	0	0	0.3	1.000
1978	TOR A	0	0		3.86	6	0	0	14	12	11	7	0	0	0	0	0	0	0	–	1	1	0	0	0.3	1.000
3 yrs.		0	1	.000	7.84	13	0	0	20.2	29	16	12	0	0	1	0	0	0	0	–	1	4	0	0	0.4	1.000

Huck Wallace

WALLACE, HARRY CLINTON (Lefty) — BL TL 5'6" 160 lbs.
B. July 27, 1882, Richmond, Ind.   D. July 6, 1951, Cleveland, Ohio

| 1912 | PHI N | 0 | 0 | | 0.00 | 4 | 0 | 0 | 4.2 | 7 | 4 | 4 | 0 | 0 | 0 | 0 | 0 | 0 | 0 | – | 0 | 1 | 0 | 0 | 0.3 | 1.000 |

Lefty Wallace

WALLACE, JAMES HAROLD — BL TL 5'11" 160 lbs.
B. Aug. 12, 1921, Evansville, Ind.   D. July 28, 1982, Evansville, Ind.

1942	BOS N	1	3	.250	3.83	19	3	1	49.1	39	24	20	0	0	0	0	14	2	0	.143	0	7	0	0	0.4	1.000
1945		1	0	1.000	4.50	5	3	1	20	18	9	4	0	0	0	0	6	0	0	.000	2	4	0	1	1.2	1.000
1946		3	3	.500	4.18	27	8	2	75.1	76	31	27	0	1	1	0	18	1	0	.056	7	21	0	0	1.0	1.000
3 yrs.		5	6	.455	4.11	51	14	4	144.2	133	64	51	0	1	2	0	38	3	0	.079	9	32	0	1	0.8	1.000

Mike Wallace

WALLACE, MICHAEL SHERMAN — BL TL 6'2" 190 lbs.
B. Feb. 3, 1951, Gastonia, N. C.

1973	PHI N	1	1	.500	3.78	20	3	1	33.1	38	15	20	0	0	0	1	4	0	0	.000	2	3	0	0	0.3	1.000
1974	2 teams	PHI N	(8G 1–0)			NY A	(23G 6–0)																			
"	total	7	0	1.000	2.85	31	1	0	60	54	37	35	0	6	0	0	0	0	0	–	4	3	1	0	0.3	.875
1975	2 teams	NY A	(3G 0–0)			STL N	(9G 0–0)																			
"	total	0	0		6.23	12	0	0	13	20	6	8	0	0	0	0	0	0	0	–	2	2	0	0	0.3	1.000
1976	STL N	3	2	.600	4.07	49	0	0	66.1	66	39	40	0	3	2	2	3	1	0	.333	1	12	1	2	0.3	.929
1977	TEX A	0	0		7.88	5	0	0	8	10	10	2	0	0	0	0	0	0	0	–	0	3	0	0	0.6	1.000
5 yrs.		11	3	.786	3.94	117	4	1	180.2	188	107	105	0	9	2	3	7	1	0	.143	9	23	2	2	0.3	.941

Tim Wallach

WALLACH, TIMOTHY CHARLES — BR TR 6'3" 220 lbs.
B. Sept. 14, 1957, Huntington Park, Calif.

1987	MON N	0	0		0.00	1	0	0	1	1	0	0	0	0	0	0	593	177	26	.298	0	0	0	0	0.0	–
1989		0	0		9.00	1	0	0	1	2	0	0	0	0	0	0	573	159	13	.277	0	0	0	0	0.0	–
2 yrs.		0	0		4.50	2	0	0	2	3	0	0	0	0	0	0	*				0	0	0	0	0.0	–

Red Waller

WALLER, JOHN FRANCIS
B. June 16, 1883, Washington, D. C.   D. Feb. 9, 1915, Secaucus, N. J.

| 1909 | NY N | 0 | 0 | | 0.00 | 1 | 0 | 0 | 1 | 3 | 0 | 1 | 0 | 1 | 0 | 0 | 0 | 0 | 0 | – | 0 | 1 | 0 | 1 | 1.0 | 1.000 |

Augie Walsh

WALSH, AUGUST SOTHLEY — BR TR 6' 175 lbs.
B. Aug. 9, 1904, Wilmington, Del.   D. Nov. 12, 1985, San Rafael, Calif.

1927	PHI N	0	1	.000	4.50	1	1	1	10	12	5	0	0	0	0	0	4	1	0	.250	0	1	0	1	1.0	1.000
1928		4	9	.308	6.18	38	11	2	122.1	160	40	38	0	2	1	2	39	10	1	.256	2	20	0	2	0.6	1.000
2 yrs.		4	10	.286	6.05	39	12	3	132.1	172	45	38	0	2	1	2	43	11	1	.256	2	21	0	3	0.6	1.000

Connie Walsh

WALSH, CORNELIUS R.
B. Apr. 23, 1882, St. Louis, Mo.   D. Apr. 5, 1953, St. Louis, Mo.

| 1907 | PIT N | 0 | 0 | | 9.00 | 1 | 0 | 0 | 1 | 1 | 1 | 0 | 0 | 0 | 0 | 0 | 0 | 0 | 0 | – | 0 | 0 | 0 | 0 | 0.0 | – |

Dee Walsh

WALSH, LEO THOMAS — BB TR 5'9½" 165 lbs.
B. Mar. 28, 1890, St. Louis, Mo.   D. July 14, 1971, St. Louis, Mo.

| 1915 | STL A | 0 | 0 | | 13.50 | 1 | 0 | 0 | 2 | 2 | 2 | 0 | 0 | 0 | 0 | 0 | * | | | | 1 | 0 | 1 | 0 | 2.0 | .500 |

Ed Walsh

WALSH, EDWARD ARTHUR — BR TR 6'1" 180 lbs.
Son of Ed Walsh.
B. Feb. 11, 1905, Meriden, Conn.   D. Oct. 31, 1937, Meriden, Conn.

1928	CHI A	4	7	.364	4.96	14	10	3	78	86	42	32	0	1	0	0	27	3	0	.111	0	14	0	1	1.0	1.000
1929		6	11	.353	5.65	24	20	7	129	156	64	31	0	0	1	0	43	10	0	.233	5	31	1	2	1.5	.973
1930		1	4	.200	5.38	37	4	4	103.2	131	30	37	0	1	3	0	34	9	0	.265	5	25	1	1	0.8	.968
1932		0	2	.000	8.41	4	4	1	20.1	26	13	7	0	0	0	0	7	2	0	.286	2	3	0	0	1.3	1.000
4 yrs.		11	24	.314	5.57	79	38	15	331	399	149	107	0	2	4	0	111	24	0	.216	12	73	2	4	1.1	.977

Ed Walsh

WALSH, EDWARD AUGUSTINE (Big Ed) — BR TR 6'1" 193 lbs.
Father of Ed Walsh.
B. May 14, 1881, Plains, Pa.   D. May 26, 1959, Pompano Beach, Fla.
Manager 1924.
Hall of Fame 1946.

1904	CHI A	6	3	.667	2.60	18	8	6	110.2	90	32	57	1	2	0	1	41	9	1	.220	8	35	1	2	2.4	.977
1905		8	3	.727	2.17	22	13	9	136.2	121	29	71	1	1	0	0	58	9	0	.155	9	41	1	1	2.3	.980
1906		17	13	.567	1.88	41	31	24	278.1	215	58	171	10	1	1	1	99	14	0	.141	30	108	6	2	3.5	.958
1907		24	18	.571	1.60	56	46	37	422.1	341	87	206	5	0	1	4	154	25	1	.162	35	227	4	2	4.8	.985
1908		40	15	.727	1.42	66	49	42	464	343	56	269	11	5	1	6	157	27	1	.172	41	190	6	9	3.6	.975
1909		15	11	.577	1.41	31	28	20	230.1	166	50	127	8	0	1	2	84	18	0	.214	23	93	1	2	3.8	.991

Year	Team	W	L	PCT	ERA	G	GS	CG	IP	H	BB	SO	ShO	W	L	SV	AB	H	HR	BA	PO	A	E	DP	TC/G	FA
														Relief Pitching			Batting									

Ed Walsh *continued*

Year	Team	W	L	PCT	ERA	G	GS	CG	IP	H	BB	SO	ShO	W	L	SV	AB	H	HR	BA	PO	A	E	DP	TC/G	FA
1910		18	20	.474	1.27	45	36	33	369.2	242	61	258	7	2	2	5	138	30	0	.217	21	154	9	5	4.1	.951
1911		27	18	.600	2.22	56	37	33	368.2	327	72	255	5	7	5	4	155	32	0	.206	27	159	8	5	3.5	.959
1912		27	17	.614	2.15	62	41	32	393	332	94	254	6	4	2	10	136	33	0	.243	22	143	15	3	2.9	.917
1913		8	3	.727	2.58	16	14	7	97.2	91	39	34	1	0	0	1	32	5	0	.156	6	32	3	1	2.6	.927
1914		2	3	.400	2.82	8	5	3	44.2	33	20	15	1	0	0	0	16	1	0	.063	7	15	1	0	2.9	.957
1915		3	0	1.000	1.33	3	3	3	27	19	7	12	1	0	0	0	11	4	0	.364	3	4	0	0	2.3	1.000
1916		0	1	.000	2.70	2	1	0	3.1	4	3	3	0	0	0	0	0	0	0	—	0	2	0	0	1.0	1.000
1917	BOS N	0	1	.000	3.50	4	3	1	18	22	9	4	0	0	0	0	4	1	0	.250	1	7	1	0	2.3	.889
14 yrs.		195	126	.607	1.82 1st	430	315	250	2964.1	2346	617	1736	57 10th	22	13	34	*				233	1210	56	32	3.5	.963

WORLD SERIES

Year	Team	W	L	PCT	ERA	G	GS	CG	IP	H	BB	SO	ShO	W	L	SV	AB	H	HR	BA	PO	A	E	DP	TC/G	FA
1906	CHI A	2	0	1.000	1.80	2	2	1	15	7	6	17	1	0	0	0	4	0	0	.000	0	5	1	0	3.0	.833

Jim Walsh

WALSH, JAMES THOMAS
B. July 10, 1894, Roxbury, Mass. D. May 13, 1967, Boston, Mass.
BL TL 5'11" 175 lbs.

Year	Team	W	L	PCT	ERA	G	GS	CG	IP	H	BB	SO	ShO	W	L	SV	AB	H	HR	BA	PO	A	E	DP	TC/G	FA
1921	DET A	0	0	—	2.25	3	0	0	4	2	1	3	0	0	0	0	0	0	0	—	0	0	1	0	0.3	

Jimmy Walsh

WALSH, MICHAEL TIMOTHY (Runt)
B. Mar. 25, 1886, Lima, Ohio D. Jan. 21, 1947, Baltimore, Md.
BR TR 5'9" 174 lbs.

Year	Team	W	L	PCT	ERA	G	GS	CG	IP	H	BB	SO	ShO	W	L	SV	AB	H	HR	BA	PO	A	E	DP	TC/G	FA
1911	PHI N	0	1	.000	13.50	1	0	0	2.2	7	1	1	0	0	0	0	*				0	0	0	0	0.0	

Junior Walsh

WALSH, JAMES GERALD
B. Mar. 7, 1919, Newark, N. J.
BR TR 5'11" 185 lbs.

Year	Team	W	L	PCT	ERA	G	GS	CG	IP	H	BB	SO	ShO	W	L	SV	AB	H	HR	BA	PO	A	E	DP	TC/G	FA
1946	PIT N	0	1	.000	5.23	4	2	0	10.1	9	10	2	0	0	0	0	4	0	0	.000	0	2	0	0	0.5	1.000
1948		1	0	1.000	10.38	2	0	0	4.1	4	5	0	0	0	0	0	2	0	0	.000	0	2	0	0	1.0	1.000
1949		1	4	.200	5.06	9	7	1	42.2	40	16	24	1	0	0	0	12	0	0	.000	2	5	2	0	1.0	.778
1950		1	1	.500	5.05	38	2	0	62.1	56	34	33	0	1	1	2	6	1	0	.167	4	11	1	1	0.4	.938
1951		1	4	.200	6.87	36	1	0	73.1	92	46	32	0	2	3	0	7	1	0	.143	6	13	2	0	0.6	.905
5 yrs.		4	10	.286	5.88	89	12	1	193	201	111	91	1	3	4	2	31	2	0	.065	12	33	5	1	0.6	.900

Bernie Walter

WALTER, JAMES BERNARD
B. Aug. 15, 1908, Dover, Tenn. D. Oct. 30, 1988, Nashville, Tenn.
BR TR 6'1" 175 lbs.

Year	Team	W	L	PCT	ERA	G	GS	CG	IP	H	BB	SO	ShO	W	L	SV	AB	H	HR	BA	PO	A	E	DP	TC/G	FA
1930	PIT N	0	0	—	0.00	1	0	0	1	0	0	1	0	0	0	0	0	0	0	—	0	1	0	0	1.0	1.000

Gene Walter

WALTER, GENE WINSTON
B. Nov. 22, 1960, Chicago, Ill.
BL TL 6'4" 200 lbs.

Year	Team	W	L	PCT	ERA	G	GS	CG	IP	H	BB	SO	ShO	W	L	SV	AB	H	HR	BA	PO	A	E	DP	TC/G	FA
1985	SD N	0	2	.000	2.05	15	0	0	22	12	8	18	0	0	2	3	1	0	0	.000	1	4	0	0	0.3	1.000
1986		2	2	.500	3.86	57	0	0	98	89	49	84	0	2	2	1	10	2	0	.200	8	17	1	1	0.5	.962
1987	NY N	1	2	.333	3.20	21	0	0	19.2	18	13	11	0	1	0	0	2	1	0	.500	2	2	1	1	0.2	.800
1988	2 teams			NY N	(19G 0–1)			SEA A	(16G 1–0)																	
"	total	1	1	.500	4.60	35	0	0	43	42	26	27	0	1	0	0	2	0	0	—	2	3	0	0	0.1	1.000
4 yrs.		4	7	.364	3.74	128	0	0	182.2	161	96	140	0	4	7	4	12	2	0	.167	13	26	2	2	0.3	.951

Bucky Walters

WALTERS, WILLIAM HENRY
B. Apr. 19, 1909, Philadelphia, Pa.
Manager 1948-49.
BR TR 6'1" 180 lbs.

Year	Team	W	L	PCT	ERA	G	GS	CG	IP	H	BB	SO	ShO	W	L	SV	AB	H	HR	BA	PO	A	E	DP	TC/G	FA
1931	BOS N	0	0	—	0.00	0	0	0	0	0	0	0	0	0	0	0	38	8	0	.211	0	0	0	0	0.0	—
1932		0	0	—	0.00	0	0	0	0	0	0	0	0	0	0	0	75	14	0	.187	0	0	0	0	0.0	—
1933	BOS A	0	0	—	0.00	0	0	0	0	0	0	0	0	0	0	0	195	50	4	.256	0	0	0	0	0.0	—
1934		0	0	—	1.29	2	1	0	7	8	2	7	0	0	0	0	388	97	8	.250	0	3	0	0	1.5	1.000
1935	PHI N	9	9	.500	4.17	24	22	8	151	168	68	40	2	0	1	0	96	24	0	.250	7	40	0	4	2.0	1.000
1936		11	21	.344	4.26	40	33	15	258	284	115	66	4	1	1	0	121	29	1	.240	15	96	3	6	2.9	.974
1937		14	15	.483	4.75	37	34	15	246.1	292	86	87	3	0	1	0	137	38	1	.277	7	76	1	7	2.3	.988
1938	2 teams			PHI N	(12G 4–8)			CIN N	(27G 11–6)																	
"	total	15	14	.517	4.20	39	34	20	251	259	108	93	3	1	0	1	99	19	1	.192	6	66	2	5	1.9	.973
1939	CIN N	27	11	.711	2.29	39	36	31	319	250	109	137	2	1	0	3	120	39	1	.325	16	77	2	10	2.4	.979
1940		22	10	.688	2.48	36	36	29	305	241	92	115	3	0	0	0	117	24	1	.205	13	56	4	7	2.0	.945
1941		19	15	.559	2.83	37	35	27	302	292	88	129	5	0	0	2	106	20	0	.189	18	68	2	6	2.4	.977
1942		15	14	.517	2.66	34	32	21	253.2	223	73	109	2	0	0	1	99	24	2	.242	13	60	3	6	2.2	.961
1943		15	15	.500	3.54	34	34	21	246.1	244	109	80	5	0	0	0	90	24	0	.267	19	49	2	7	2.1	.971
1944		23	8	.742	2.40	34	32	27	285	233	87	77	6	1	0	1	107	30	0	.280	15	55	0	7	2.1	1.000
1945		10	10	.500	2.68	22	22	12	168	166	51	45	3	0	0	0	61	14	0	.230	6	33	1	3	1.8	.975
1946		10	7	.588	2.56	22	22	10	151.1	146	64	60	2	0	0	0	55	7	0	.127	10	37	3	7	2.3	.940
1947		8	8	.500	5.75	20	20	5	122	137	49	43	0	0	0	0	45	12	0	.267	6	19	1	0	1.3	.962
1948		0	3	.000	4.63	7	5	1	35	42	18	19	0	0	0	0	15	4	0	.267	1	11	0	0	1.7	1.000
1950	BOS N	0	0	—	4.50	1	0	0	4	3	5	2	0	0	0	0	2	0	0	.000	0	2	0	0	1.0	1.000
19 yrs.		198	160	.553	3.30	428	398	242	3104.2	2990	1121	1107	42	3	7	4	*				153	746	24	76	2.2	.974

WORLD SERIES

Year	Team	W	L	PCT	ERA	G	GS	CG	IP	H	BB	SO	ShO	W	L	SV	AB	H	HR	BA	PO	A	E	DP	TC/G	FA
1939	CIN N	0	2	.000	4.91	2	1	1	11	13	1	6	0	0	0	0	3	0	0	.000	0	3	0	1	1.5	1.000
1940		2	0	1.000	1.50	2	2	2	18	8	6	6	1	0	0	0	7	2	1	.286	0	4	0	0	2.0	1.000
2 yrs.		2	2	.500	2.79	4	3	3	29	21	7	12	1	0	0	0	10	2	1	.200	0	7	0	1	1.8	1.000

Charley Walters

WALTERS, CHARLES LEONARD
B. Feb. 21, 1947, Minneapolis, Minn.
BR TR 6'4" 190 lbs.

Year	Team	W	L	PCT	ERA	G	GS	CG	IP	H	BB	SO	ShO	W	L	SV	AB	H	HR	BA	PO	A	E	DP	TC/G	FA
1969	MIN A	0	0	—	5.40	6	0	0	6.2	6	3	2	0	0	0	0	0	0	0	—	0	1	0	0	0.2	1.000

Year	Team	W	L	PCT	ERA	G	GS	CG	IP	H	BB	SO	ShO	W	L	SV	AB	H	HR	BA	PO	A	E	DP	TC/G	FA
														Relief Pitching			**Batting**									

Mike Walters

WALTERS, MICHAEL CHARLES
B. Oct. 18, 1957, St. Louis, Mo.

BR TR 6'5" 195 lbs.

Year	Team	W	L	PCT	ERA	G	GS	CG	IP	H	BB	SO	ShO	W	L	SV	AB	H	HR	BA	PO	A	E	DP	TC/G	FA
1983	MIN A	1	1	.500	4.12	23	0	0	59	52	20	21	0	1	1	2	0	0	0	–	3	10	0	1	0.6	1.000
1984		0	3	.000	3.72	23	0	0	29	31	14	10	0	0	3	2	0	0	0	–	1	2	0	1	0.1	1.000
2 yrs.		1	4	.200	3.99	46	0	0	88	83	34	31	0	1	4	4	0	0	0	–	4	12	0	2	0.3	1.000

Zach Walton

Playing record listed under Tom Zachary

Dick Wantz

WANTZ, RICHARD CARTER
B. Apr. 11, 1940, South Gate, Calif.   D. May 13, 1965, Inglewood, Calif.

BR TR 6'5" 175 lbs.

Year	Team	W	L	PCT	ERA	G	GS	CG	IP	H	BB	SO	ShO	W	L	SV	AB	H	HR	BA	PO	A	E	DP	TC/G	FA
1965	CAL A	0	0	–	18.00	1	0	0	1	3	0	2	0	0	0	0	0	0	0	–	0	0	0	0	0.0	–

Colin Ward

WARD, COLIN NORVAL
B. Nov. 22, 1960, Los Angeles, Calif.

BL TL 6'3" 190 lbs.

Year	Team	W	L	PCT	ERA	G	GS	CG	IP	H	BB	SO	ShO	W	L	SV	AB	H	HR	BA	PO	A	E	DP	TC/G	FA
1985	SF N	0	0	–	4.38	6	2	0	12.1	10	7	8	0	0	0	0	2	0	0	.000	0	2	0	0	0.3	1.000

Dick Ward

WARD, RICHARD O. (Ole)
B. May 21, 1909, Herrick, S. D.   D. May 30, 1966, Freeland, Wash.

BR TR 6'1" 198 lbs.

Year	Team	W	L	PCT	ERA	G	GS	CG	IP	H	BB	SO	ShO	W	L	SV	AB	H	HR	BA	PO	A	E	DP	TC/G	FA
1934	CHI N	0	0	–	3.18	3	0	0	5.2	9	2	1	0	0	0	0	1	0	0	.000	0	1	0	0	0.3	1.000
1935	STL N	0	0	–	0.00	1	0	0	0	0	1	0	0	0	0	0	0	0	0	–	0	0	0	0	0.0	–
2 yrs.		0	0	–	3.18	4	0	0	5.2	9	3	1	0	0	0	0	1	0	0	.000	0	1	0	0	0.3	1.000

Duane Ward

WARD, ROY DUANE
B. May 28, 1964, Park View, N. M.

BR TR 6'4" 185 lbs.

Year	Team	W	L	PCT	ERA	G	GS	CG	IP	H	BB	SO	ShO	W	L	SV	AB	H	HR	BA	PO	A	E	DP	TC/G	FA
1986	2 teams					ATL N	(10G 0–1)				TOR A	(2G 0–1)														
"	total	0	2	.000	8.00	12	1	0	18	25	12	9	0	0	1	0	1	0	0	.000	1	6	0	0	0.6	1.000
1987	TOR A	1	0	1.000	6.94	12	1	0	11.2	14	12	10	0	1	0	0	0	0	0	–	2	2	0	0	0.3	1.000
1988		9	3	.750	3.30	64	0	0	111.2	101	60	91	0	9	3	15	0	0	0	–	6	12	1	0	0.3	.947
1989		4	10	.286	3.77	66	0	0	114.2	94	58	122	0	4	10	15	0	0	0	–	5	21	1	2	0.4	.963
4 yrs.		14	15	.483	4.01	154	2	0	256	234	142	232	0	14	14	30	1	0	0	.000	14	41	2	2	0.4	.965

LEAGUE CHAMPIONSHIP SERIES

Year	Team	W	L	PCT	ERA	G	GS	CG	IP	H	BB	SO	ShO	W	L	SV	AB	H	HR	BA	PO	A	E	DP	TC/G	FA
1989	TOR A	0	0	–	7.36	2	0	0	3.2	6	3	5	0	0	0	0	0	0	0	–	1	0	0	0	0.5	1.000

John Ward

WARD, JOHN E.
B. Washington, D. C.   Deceased.

Year	Team	W	L	PCT	ERA	G	GS	CG	IP	H	BB	SO	ShO	W	L	SV	AB	H	HR	BA	PO	A	E	DP	TC/G	FA
1885	PRO N	0	1	.000	4.50	1	1	1	8	10	1	3	0	0	0	0	3	0	0	.000	0	1	1	0	2.0	.500

Monte Ward

WARD, JOHN MONTGOMERY
B. Mar. 3, 1860, Bellefonte, Pa.
D. Mar. 4, 1925, Augusta, Ga.
Manager 1880, 1884, 1890-94.
Hall of Fame 1964.

BL TR 5'9" 165 lbs.
BB 1888

Year	Team	W	L	PCT	ERA	G	GS	CG	IP	H	BB	SO	ShO	W	L	SV	AB	H	HR	BA	PO	A	E	DP	TC/G	FA
1878	PRO N	22	13	.629	**1.51**	37	37	37	334	308	34	116	6	0	0	0	138	27	1	.196	23	74	15	4	3.0	.866
1879		**47**	17	**.734**	2.15	70	60	58	587	571	36	**239**	2	5	1	1	364	104	2	.286	31	134	11	2	2.5	.938
1880		40	23	.635	1.74	70	67	59	595	501	45	230	9	1	1	1	356	81	0	.228	43	133	3	1	2.6	.983
1881		18	18	.500	2.13	39	35	32	330	326	53	119	3	1	1	0	357	87	0	.244	26	77	7	7	2.8	.936
1882		19	13	.594	2.59	33	32	29	278	261	36	72	4	0	0	1	355	87	0	.245	18	73	6	4	2.9	.938
1883	NY N	16	13	.552	2.70	33	25	24	277	278	31	121	1	4	1	0	380	97	7	.255	25	67	10	2	3.1	.902
1884		3	3	.500	3.41	9	5	5	60.2	72	18	23	0	0	1	0	482	122	2	.253	3	16	2	0	2.3	.905
7 yrs.		165	100	.623	2.10 4th	291	261	244	2461.2	2317	253	920	25	11	5	3	*				169	574	54	20	2.7	.932

Jon Warden

WARDEN, JONATHAN EDGAR (Warbler)
B. Oct. 1, 1946, Columbus, Ohio

BB TL 6' 205 lbs.

Year	Team	W	L	PCT	ERA	G	GS	CG	IP	H	BB	SO	ShO	W	L	SV	AB	H	HR	BA	PO	A	E	DP	TC/G	FA
1968	DET A	4	1	.800	3.62	28	0	0	37.1	30	15	25	0	4	1	3	2	0	0	.000	0	2	1	0	0.1	.667

Curt Wardle

WARDLE, CURTIS RAY
B. Nov. 16, 1960, Downey, Calif.

BL TL 6'5" 220 lbs.

Year	Team	W	L	PCT	ERA	G	GS	CG	IP	H	BB	SO	ShO	W	L	SV	AB	H	HR	BA	PO	A	E	DP	TC/G	FA
1984	MIN A	0	0	–	4.50	2	0	0	4	3	0	5	0	0	0	0	0	0	0	–	0	1	0	0	0.5	1.000
1985	2 teams			MIN A	(35G 1–3)				CLE A	(15G 7–6)																
"	total	8	9	.471	6.18	50	12	0	115	127	62	84	0	2	3	1	0	0	0	–	5	15	1	1	0.4	.952
2 yrs.		8	9	.471	6.13	52	12	0	119	130	62	89	0	2	3	1	0	0	0	–	5	16	1	1	0.4	.955

Jack Warhop

WARHOP, JOHN MILTON (Crab, Chief)
Born John Milton Wauhop.
B. July 4, 1884, Hinton, W. Va.   D. Oct. 4, 1960, Freeport, Ill.

BR TR 5'9½" 168 lbs.

Year	Team	W	L	PCT	ERA	G	GS	CG	IP	H	BB	SO	ShO	W	L	SV	AB	H	HR	BA	PO	A	E	DP	TC/G	FA
1908	NY A	1	2	.333	4.46	5	4	3	36.1	40	8	11	0	0	0	0	16	1	0	.063	0	14	1	0	3.0	.933
1909		13	15	.464	2.40	36	23	21	243.1	197	81	95	3	4	2	2	86	11	0	.128	15	67	7	2	2.8	.931
1910		14	14	.500	2.87	37	27	20	254	219	79	75	0	3	2	2	79	14	0	.177	15	65	11	0	2.5	.879
1911		12	13	.480	4.16	31	25	17	209.2	239	44	71	1	1	2	0	77	12	0	.156	7	53	4	1	2.1	.938
1912		10	19	.345	2.86	39	22	16	258	256	59	110	0	4	3	0	92	19	0	.207	3	64	7	1	1.9	.905
1913		4	6	.400	3.75	15	7	1	62.1	69	33	11	0	0	2	0	23	3	0	.130	0	12	4	2	1.1	.750
1914		8	15	.348	2.37	37	23	15	216.2	182	44	56	0	0	3	0	71	10	0	.141	5	60	7	3	1.9	.903
1915		7	9	.438	3.96	21	19	12	143.1	164	52	34	0	1	0	0	51	7	0	.137	4	34	3	1	2.0	.927
8 yrs.		69	93	.426	3.09	221	150	105	1423.2	1366	400	463	4	13	15	7	495	77	0	.156	49	382	44	10	2.1	.907

Year	Team		W	L	PCT	ERA	G	GS	CG	IP	H	BB	SO	ShO	Relief Pitching W	L	SV	Batting AB	H	HR	BA	PO	A	E	DP	TC/G	FA

Cy Warmoth

WARMOTH, WALLACE WALTER
B. Feb. 2, 1893, Bone Gap, Ill. D. June 20, 1957, Mt. Carmel, Ill.   BL TL 5'11" 158 lbs.

1916	STL	N	0	0	–	14.40	3	0	0	5	12	4	1	0	0	0	0	2	0	0	.000	1	0	0	0	0.3	1.000
1922	WAS	A	1	0	1.000	1.42	5	1	1	19	15	9	8	0	1	0	0	7	1	0	.143	2	3	0	0	1.0	1.000
1923			7	4	.636	4.29	21	13	4	105	103	76	45	0	1	0	0	36	8	0	.222	8	25	1	2	1.6	.971
3 yrs.			8	4	.667	4.26	29	14	5	129	130	89	54	0	2	0	0	45	9	0	.200	11	28	1	2	1.4	.975

Lon Warneke

WARNEKE, LONNIE (The Arkansas Humming Bird)
B. Mar. 28, 1909, Mt. Ida, Ark. D. June 23, 1976, Hot Springs, Ark.   BR TR 6'2" 185 lbs.

1930	CHI	N	0	0	–	33.75	1	0	0	1.1	2	5	0	0	0	0	0	0	0	0	–	0	1	0	0	1.0	1.000
1931			2	4	.333	3.22	20	7	3	64.1	67	37	27	0	0	1	0	19	5	0	.263	1	8	1	0	0.5	.900
1932			**22**	6	**.786**	**2.37**	35	32	25	277	247	64	106	**4**	0	0	0	99	19	0	.192	11	55	1	1	1.9	.985
1933			18	13	.581	2.00	36	34	**26**	287.1	262	75	133	4	0	1	0	100	30	2	.300	8	72	0	7	2.2	1.000
1934			22	10	.688	3.21	43	35	23	291.1	273	66	143	3	2	1	3	113	22	0	.195	15	58	0	1	1.7	1.000
1935			20	13	.606	3.06	42	30	20	261.2	257	50	120	1	4	3	4	91	20	0	.220	15	47	1	1	1.5	.984
1936			16	13	.552	3.44	40	29	13	240.2	246	76	113	**4**	1	5	1	84	17	1	.202	15	44	1	1	1.5	.983
1937	STL	N	18	11	.621	4.53	36	33	18	238.2	280	69	87	2	0	0	0	80	21	0	.263	10	40	2	0	1.4	.962
1938			13	8	.619	3.97	31	26	12	197	199	64	89	4	2	0	0	71	23	0	.324	4	34	2	0	1.3	.950
1939			13	7	.650	3.78	34	21	6	162	160	49	59	3	3	1	2	52	10	0	.192	9	28	0	4	1.1	1.000
1940			16	10	.615	3.14	33	31	17	232	235	47	85	1	0	0	0	86	18	1	.209	10	50	0	5	1.8	1.000
1941			17	9	.654	3.15	37	30	12	246	227	82	83	4	3	1	0	77	9	0	.117	8	43	0	3	1.4	1.000
1942	2 teams	STL N (12G 6–4)				CHI N (15G 5–7)																					
" total			11	11	.500	2.73	27	24	13	181	173	36	59	1	0	0	2	62	16	0	.258	14	33	0	1	1.7	1.000
1943	CHI	N	4	5	.444	3.16	21	10	4	88.1	82	18	30	0	1	0	0	26	5	0	.192	3	22	0	2	1.2	1.000
1945			1	1	.500	3.86	9	1	0	14	16	1	6	0	1	0	0	2	0	0	.000	3	3	0	0	0.7	1.000
15 yrs.			193	121	.615	3.18	445	343	192	2782.2	2726	739	1140	31	17	12	13	962	215	4	.223	126	538	8	25	1.5	.988

WORLD SERIES

1932	CHI	N	0	1	.000	5.91	2	1	1	10.2	15	5	8	0	0	0	0	4	0	0	.000	1	2	0	1	1.5	1.000
1935			2	0	1.000	0.54	3	2	1	16.2	9	4	5	1	0	0	0	5	1	0	.200	2	9	0	0	3.7	1.000
2 yrs.			2	1	.667	2.63	5	3	2	27.1	24	9	13	1	0	0	0	9	1	0	.111	3	11	0	1	2.8	1.000

Ed Warner

WARNER, EDWARD EMORY
B. June 20, 1889, Fitchburg, Mass. D. Feb. 2, 1954, Fitchburg, Mass.   BR TL 5'10½" 165 lbs.

| 1912 | PIT | N | 1 | 1 | .500 | 3.60 | 11 | 3 | 1 | 45 | 40 | 18 | 13 | 1 | 0 | 1 | 0 | 15 | 2 | 0 | .133 | 2 | 15 | 2 | 0 | 1.7 | .895 |

Jack Warner

WARNER, JACK DYER
B. July 12, 1940, Brandywine, W. Va.   BR TR 5'11" 190 lbs.

1962	CHI	N	0	0	–	7.71	7	0	0	7	9	0	3	0	0	0	0	0	0	0	–	0	3	0	0	0.4	1.000
1963			0	1	.000	2.78	8	0	0	22.2	21	8	7	0	0	1	0	4	1	0	.250	0	4	0	0	0.5	1.000
1964			0	0	–	2.89	7	0	0	9.1	12	4	6	0	0	0	1	0	0	0	–	2	3	0	0	0.7	1.000
1965			0	1	.000	8.62	11	0	0	15.2	22	9	7	0	0	1	0	1	0	0	.000	1	3	0	0	0.4	1.000
4 yrs.			0	2	.000	5.10	33	0	0	54.2	64	21	23	0	0	2	0	5	1	0	.200	3	13	0	0	0.5	1.000

Mike Warren

WARREN, MICHAEL BRUCE
B. Mar. 26, 1961, Inglewood, Calif.   BR TR 6'1" 175 lbs.

1983	OAK	A	5	3	.625	4.11	12	9	3	65.2	51	18	30	1	0	0	0	0	0	0	–	2	7	1	1	0.8	.900
1984			3	6	.333	4.90	24	12	0	90	104	44	61	0	0	0	0	0	0	0	–	1	4	2	0	0.3	.714
1985			1	4	.200	6.61	16	6	0	49	52	38	48	0	1	0	0	0	0	0	–	2	1	1	1	0.3	.750
3 yrs.			9	13	.409	5.06	52	27	3	204.2	207	100	139	1	1	0	0	0	0	0	–	5	12	4	2	0.4	.810

Tommy Warren

WARREN, THOMAS GENTRY
B. July 5, 1922, Tulsa, Okla. D. Jan. 2, 1968, Tulsa, Okla.   BL TR 6'1" 180 lbs.

| 1944 | BKN | N | 1 | 4 | .200 | 4.98 | 22 | 4 | 2 | 68.2 | 74 | 40 | 18 | 0 | 1 | 0 | 0 | 43 | 11 | 0 | .256 | 6 | 14 | 2 | 0 | 1.0 | .909 |

Dan Warthen

WARTHEN, DANIEL DEAN
B. Dec. 1, 1952, Omaha, Neb.   BB TL 6' 200 lbs.

1975	MON	N	8	6	.571	3.11	40	18	2	168	130	87	128	0	4	1	3	51	6	0	.118	6	26	1	3	0.8	.970
1976			2	10	.167	5.30	23	16	2	90	76	66	67	1	0	0	0	27	0	0	.000	3	13	0	0	0.7	1.000
1977	2 teams	MON N (12G 2–3)				PHI N (3G 0–1)																					
" total			2	4	.333	7.22	15	6	1	38.2	37	43	27	0	1	0	0	9	1	0	.111	1	8	1	2	0.7	.900
1978	HOU	N	0	1	.000	4.09	5	1	0	11	10	2	2	0	0	1	0	2	0	0	.000	1	1	0	0	0.4	1.000
4 yrs.			12	21	.364	4.30	83	41	5	307.2	253	198	224	1	5	2	3	89	7	0	.079	11	48	2	5	0.7	.967

George Washburn

WASHBURN, GEORGE EDWARD
B. Oct. 6, 1914, Solon, Me. D. Jan. 5, 1979, Baton Rouge, La.   BL TR 6'1" 175 lbs.

| 1941 | NY | A | 0 | 1 | .000 | 13.50 | 1 | 1 | 0 | 2 | 2 | 5 | 1 | 0 | 0 | 0 | 0 | 1 | 0 | 0 | .000 | 1 | 0 | 0 | 0 | 1.0 | 1.000 |

Greg Washburn

WASHBURN, GREGORY JAMES
B. Dec. 3, 1946, Coal City, Ill.   BR TR 6' 190 lbs.

| 1969 | CAL | A | 0 | 2 | .000 | 7.94 | 8 | 2 | 0 | 11.1 | 21 | 5 | 4 | 0 | 0 | 0 | 0 | 0 | 0 | 0 | – | 2 | 2 | 0 | 0 | 0.5 | 1.000 |

Libe Washburn

WASHBURN, LIBEUS
B. June 16, 1874, Lynn, N. H. D. Mar. 22, 1940, Malone, N. Y.   BB TL 5'10" 180 lbs.

| 1903 | PHI | N | 0 | 4 | .000 | 4.37 | 4 | 4 | 4 | 35 | 44 | 11 | 9 | 0 | 0 | 0 | 0 | * | | | | 1 | 7 | 0 | 0 | 2.0 | 1.000 |

Ray Washburn

WASHBURN, RAY CLARK
B. May 31, 1938, Pasco, Wash.   BR TR 6'1" 205 lbs.

| 1961 | STL | N | 1 | 1 | .500 | 1.77 | 3 | 2 | 1 | 20.1 | 10 | 7 | 12 | 0 | 0 | 0 | 0 | 8 | 1 | 0 | .125 | 0 | 5 | 0 | 0 | 1.7 | 1.000 |

Year	Team		W	L	PCT	ERA	G	GS	CG	IP	H	BB	SO	ShO	W	L	SV	AB	H	HR	BA	PO	A	E	DP	TC/G	FA
															Relief Pitching			**Batting**									

Ray Washburn *continued*

Year	Team		W	L	PCT	ERA	G	GS	CG	IP	H	BB	SO	ShO	W	L	SV	AB	H	HR	BA	PO	A	E	DP	TC/G	FA
1962			12	9	.571	4.10	34	25	2	175.2	187	58	109	1	1	2	0	56	10	0	.179	9	34	2	1	1.3	.956
1963			5	3	.625	3.08	11	11	4	64.1	50	14	47	2	0	0	0	19	1	0	.053	5	15	0	0	1.8	1.000
1964			3	4	.429	4.05	15	10	0	60	60	17	28	0	0	0	2	15	2	0	.133	4	14	0	3	1.2	1.000
1965			9	11	.450	3.62	28	16	1	119.1	114	28	67	1	5	0	2	33	5	0	.152	7	19	1	0	1.0	.963
1966			11	9	.550	3.76	27	26	4	170	183	44	98	1	0	0	0	54	5	1	.093	10	33	3	2	1.7	.935
1967			10	7	.588	3.53	27	27	3	186.1	190	42	98	1	0	0	0	66	6	0	.091	14	40	2	4	2.1	.964
1968			14	8	.636	2.26	31	30	8	215.1	191	47	124	4	1	0	0	60	5	0	.083	24	20	1	2	1.5	.978
1969			3	8	.273	3.07	28	16	2	132	133	49	80	0	0	0	1	37	3	0	.081	11	23	2	2	1.3	.944
1970	CIN	N	4	4	.500	6.95	35	3	0	66	90	48	37	0	4	2	0	13	0	0	.000	7	13	2	2	0.6	.909
10 yrs.			72	64	.529	3.54	239	166	25	1209.1	1208	354	700	10	11	4	5	361	38	1	.105	91	216	13	16	1.3	.959

WORLD SERIES

Year	Team		W	L	PCT	ERA	G	GS	CG	IP	H	BB	SO	ShO	W	L	SV	AB	H	HR	BA	PO	A	E	DP	TC/G	FA
1967	STL	N	0	0	–	0.00	2	0	0	2.1	1	1	2	0	0	0	0	0	0	0	–	0	1	0	0	0.5	1.000
1968			1	1	.500	9.82	2	2	0	7.1	7	7	6	0	0	0	0	3	0	0	.000	0	1	0	0	0.5	1.000
1970	CIN	N	0	0	–	13.50	1	0	0	1.1	2	2	0	0	0	0	0	0	0	0	–	1	3	0	0	4.0	1.000
3 yrs.			1	1	.500	8.18	5	2	0	11	10	10	8	0	0	0	0	3	0	0	.000	1	5	0	0	1.2	1.000

Buck Washer

WASHER, WILLIAM   BR TR 5'10"   175 lbs.
B. Oct. 11, 1882, Akron, Ohio   D. Dec. 8, 1955, Akron, Ohio

Year	Team		W	L	PCT	ERA	G	GS	CG	IP	H	BB	SO	ShO	W	L	SV	AB	H	HR	BA	PO	A	E	DP	TC/G	FA
1905	PHI	N	0	0	–	6.00	1	0	0	3	4	5	0	0	0	0	0	1	0	0	.000	1	0	0	0	1.000

Gary Waslewski

WASLEWSKI, GARY LEE   BR TR 6'4"   190 lbs.
B. July 21, 1941, Meriden, Conn.

Year	Team		W	L	PCT	ERA	G	GS	CG	IP	H	BB	SO	ShO	W	L	SV	AB	H	HR	BA	PO	A	E	DP	TC/G	FA
1967	BOS	A	2	2	.500	3.21	12	8	0	42	34	20	20	0	0	0	0	11	1	0	.091	5	7	0	1	1.0	1.000
1968			4	7	.364	3.67	34	11	2	105.1	108	40	59	0	1	1	2	26	1	0	.038	9	23	0	2	0.9	1.000
1969	2 teams		STL N	(12G 0–2)			MON N	(30G 3–7)																				
"	total		3	9	.250	3.39	42	14	3	130	121	71	79	1	0	2	2	31	1	0	.032	10	24	1	3	0.8	.971
1970	2 teams		MON N	(6G 0–2)			NY A	(26G 2–2)																				
"	total		2	4	.333	3.71	32	9	0	80	65	42	46	0	1	0	0	16	1	0	.063	9	15	1	1	0.8	.960
1971	NY	A	0	1	.000	3.25	24	0	0	36	28	16	17	0	0	1	0	1	0	0	.000	3	5	0	0	0.3	1.000
1972	OAK	A	0	3	.000	2.00	8	0	0	18	12	8	8	0	0	3	0	3	0	0	.000	2	4	0	0	0.8	1.000
6 yrs.			11	26	.297	3.44	152	42	5	411.1	368	197	229	1	2	7	5	88	4	0	.045	38	78	2	7	0.8	.983

WORLD SERIES

Year	Team		W	L	PCT	ERA	G	GS	CG	IP	H	BB	SO	ShO	W	L	SV	AB	H	HR	BA	PO	A	E	DP	TC/G	FA
1967	BOS	A	0	0	–	2.16	2	1	0	8.1	4	2	7	0	0	0	0	1	0	0	.000	0	0	0	0	1.0	1.000

Steve Waterbury

WATERBURY, STEVEN CRAIG   BR TR 6'5"   190 lbs.
B. Apr. 6, 1952, Carbondale, Ill.

Year	Team		W	L	PCT	ERA	G	GS	CG	IP	H	BB	SO	ShO	W	L	SV	AB	H	HR	BA	PO	A	E	DP	TC/G	FA
1976	STL	N	0	0	–	6.00	5	0	0	6	7	3	4	0	0	0	0	0	0	0	–	1	0	0	0	0.2	1.000

Fred Waters

WATERS, FRED WARREN   BL TL 5'11"   185 lbs.
B. Feb. 2, 1927, Benton, Miss.   D. Aug. 28, 1989, Pensacola, Fla.

Year	Team		W	L	PCT	ERA	G	GS	CG	IP	H	BB	SO	ShO	W	L	SV	AB	H	HR	BA	PO	A	E	DP	TC/G	FA
1955	PIT	N	0	0	–	3.60	2	0	0	5	7	2	0	0	0	0	0	1	0	0	.000	0	1	0	0	0.5	1.000
1956			2	2	.500	2.82	23	5	1	51	48	30	14	0	0	1	0	20	1	0	.050	2	3	0	0	0.2	1.000
2 yrs.			2	2	.500	2.89	25	5	1	56	55	32	14	0	0	1	0	21	1	0	.048	2	4	0	0	0.2	1.000

Bob Watkins

WATKINS, ROBERT CECIL   BR TR 6'1"   170 lbs.
B. Mar. 12, 1948, San Francisco, Calif.

Year	Team		W	L	PCT	ERA	G	GS	CG	IP	H	BB	SO	ShO	W	L	SV	AB	H	HR	BA	PO	A	E	DP	TC/G	FA
1969	HOU	N	0	0	–	5.06	5	0	0	16	13	13	11	0	0	0	0	2	0	0	.000	0	1	0	0	0.2	1.000

Doc Watson

WATSON, CHARLES JOHN   BL TL 6'   170 lbs.
B. Jan. 30, 1886, Carroll County, Ohio   D. Dec. 30, 1949, San Diego, Calif.

Year	Team		W	L	PCT	ERA	G	GS	CG	IP	H	BB	SO	ShO	W	L	SV	AB	H	HR	BA	PO	A	E	DP	TC/G	FA
1913	CHI	N	1	0	1.000	1.00	1	1	1	9	8	6	1	0	0	0	0	2	0	0	.000	0	0	0	0	0.0	–
1914	2 teams		CHI F	(26G 9–11)			STL F	(9G 3–4)																				
"	total		12	15	.444	2.01	35	25	14	228	186	73	87	5	1	3	1	70	7	0	.100	7	60	2	0	2.0	.971
1915	STL	F	9	9	.500	3.98	33	20	6	135.2	132	58	45	0	2	0	0	40	5	0	.125	2	24	2	1	0.8	.929
3 yrs.			22	24	.478	2.70	69	46	21	372.2	326	137	133	5	3	3	1	112	12	0	.107	9	84	4	1	1.4	.959

Milt Watson

WATSON, MILTON WILSON (Mule)   BR TR 6'1"   180 lbs.
B. Jan. 10, 1890, Flovilla, Ga.   D. Apr. 20, 1962, Pine Bluff, Ark.

Year	Team		W	L	PCT	ERA	G	GS	CG	IP	H	BB	SO	ShO	W	L	SV	AB	H	HR	BA	PO	A	E	DP	TC/G	FA
1916	STL	N	4	6	.400	3.06	18	13	5	103	109	33	27	2	0	0	0	32	7	0	.219	4	26	5	1	1.9	.857
1917			10	13	.435	3.51	41	20	5	161.1	149	51	45	3	3	3	0	51	5	0	.098	3	55	2	2	1.5	.967
1918	PHI	N	5	7	.417	3.43	23	11	6	112.2	126	36	29	0	2	1	0	40	3	0	.075	0	31	2	1	1.4	.939
1919			2	4	.333	5.17	8	4	3	47	51	19	12	0	1	1	0	16	1	0	.063	0	17	1	0	2.3	.944
4 yrs.			21	30	.412	3.57	90	48	19	424	435	139	113	5	6	5	0	139	16	0	.115	7	129	10	4	1.6	.932

Mother Watson

WATSON, WALTER L.   5'9"   145 lbs.
B. Jan. 27, 1865, Middleport, Ohio   D. Nov. 23, 1898, Middleport, Ohio

Year	Team		W	L	PCT	ERA	G	GS	CG	IP	H	BB	SO	ShO	W	L	SV	AB	H	HR	BA	PO	A	E	DP	TC/G	FA
1887	CIN	AA	0	1	.000	5.79	2	2	2	14	22	6	1	0	0	0	0	8	1	0	.125	0	1	2	0	1.5	.333

Mule Watson

WATSON, JOHN REEVES   BR TR 6'1½"   185 lbs.
B. Oct. 15, 1896, Homer, La.   D. Aug. 25, 1949, Shreveport, La.

Year	Team		W	L	PCT	ERA	G	GS	CG	IP	H	BB	SO	ShO	W	L	SV	AB	H	HR	BA	PO	A	E	DP	TC/G	FA
1918	PHI	A	7	10	.412	3.37	21	19	11	141.2	139	44	30	3	0	0	0	52	7	0	.135	5	30	3	3	1.8	.921
1919			0	1	.000	6.91	4	2	0	14.1	17	7	6	0	0	0	0	6	0	0	.000	0	9	0	0	2.3	1.000
1920	2 teams		BOS N	(13G 5–4)			PIT N	(5G 0–0)																				
"	total		5	4	.556	4.29	18	10	4	86	94	24	17	2	0	0	1	27	3	0	.111	0	26	1	1	1.5	.963
1921	BOS	N	14	13	.519	3.85	44	31	15	259.1	269	57	48	1	2	1	2	87	12	0	.138	7	72	6	1	1.9	.929
1922			8	14	.364	4.70	41	29	8	201	262	59	53	1	1	0	1	66	13	0	.197	4	47	3	1	1.3	.944

Year	Team		W	L	PCT	ERA	G	GS	CG	IP	H	BB	SO	ShO	Relief Pitching W	L	SV	Batting AB	H	HR	BA	PO	A	E	DP	TC/G	FA

Mule Watson *continued*

1923	2 teams	BOS N (11G 1–2)				NY N	(17G 8–5)																				
"	total		9	7	.563	3.84	28	19	9	138.1	159	41	36	0	1	0	1	54	10	0	.185	5	29	1	0	1.3	.971
1924	NY	N	7	4	.636	3.79	22	16	6	99.2	122	24	18	1	1	0	0	35	9	2	.257	1	22	1	3	1.1	.958
7 yrs.			50	53	.485	4.04	178	126	53	940.1	1062	256	208	8	5	2	4	327	54	2	.165	22	235	15	9	1.5	.945

WORLD SERIES

1923	NY	N	0	0	–	13.50	1	1	0	2	4	1	1	0	0	0	0	0	0	0	–	0	0	1	0	1.0	–
1924			0	0	–	0.00	1	0	0	.2	0	0	0	0	0	0	1	0	0	0	–	0	0	0	0	0.0	–
2 yrs.			0	0	–	10.13	2	1	0	2.2	4	1	1	0	0	0	1	0	0	0	–	0	0	1	0	0.5	–

Eddie Watt

WATT, EDWARD DEAN
B. Apr. 4, 1942, Lamonie, Iowa

BR TR 5'10" 183 lbs.

1966	BAL	A	9	7	.563	3.83	43	13	1	145.2	123	44	102	0	7	4	0	46	14	2	.304	7	14	1	0	0.5	.955
1967			3	5	.375	2.26	49	0	0	103.2	67	37	93	0	3	5	8	22	4	1	.182	6	15	0	1	0.4	1.000
1968			5	5	.500	2.27	59	0	0	83.1	63	35	72	0	5	5	11	8	0	0	.000	1	14	1	1	0.3	.938
1969			5	2	.714	1.65	56	0	0	71	49	26	46	0	5	2	16	8	0	0	.000	4	10	0	0	0.3	1.000
1970			7	7	.500	3.27	53	0	0	55	44	29	33	0	7	7	12	8	1	0	.125	2	10	0	1	0.2	1.000
1971			3	1	.750	1.80	35	0	0	40	39	8	26	0	3	1	11	5	0	0	.000	2	4	0	0	0.2	1.000
1972			2	3	.400	2.15	38	0	0	46	30	20	23	0	2	3	7	2	0	0	.000	2	7	0	0	0.2	1.000
1973			3	4	.429	3.30	30	0	0	71	62	21	38	0	3	4	5	0	0	0	–	3	6	1	0	0.3	.900
1974	PHI	N	1	1	.500	4.03	42	0	0	38	39	26	23	0	1	1	6	1	0	0	.000	0	6	1	2	0.2	.857
1975	CHI	N	0	1	.000	13.50	6	0	0	6	14	8	6	0	0	1	0	0	0	0	–	1	0	0	0	0.2	1.000
10 yrs.			38	36	.514	2.91	411	13	1	659.2	530	254	462	0	36	31	80	100	19	3	.190	27	87	4	5	0.3	.966

LEAGUE CHAMPIONSHIP SERIES

1969	BAL	A	0	0	–	0.00	1	0	0	2	0	0	2	0	0	0	0	0	0	0	–	0	0	0	0	0.0	–
1971			0	0	–	0.00	1	0	0	2	2	0	1	0	0	0	1	0	0	0	–	0	1	0	0	1.0	1.000
1973			0	0	–	0.00	1	0	0	.1	0	0	0	0	0	0	0	0	0	0	–	0	1	0	0	1.0	1.000
3 yrs.			0	0	–	0.00	3	0	0	4.1	2	0	3	0	0	0	1	0	0	0	–	0	2	0	0	0.7	1.000

WORLD SERIES

1969	BAL	A	0	1	.000	3.00	2	0	0	3	4	0	3	0	0	1	0	0	0	0	–	0	0	0	0	0.5	–
1970			0	1	.000	9.00	1	0	0	1	2	1	3	0	0	1	0	0	0	0	–	0	0	0	0	0.0	–
1971			0	1	.000	3.86	2	0	0	2.1	4	0	2	0	0	0	0	0	0	0	–	0	0	0	0	0.0	–
3 yrs.			0	3	.000	4.26	5	0	0	6.1	10	1	8	0	0	2	0	0	0	0	–	0	0	1	0	0.2	–

2nd

Frank Watt

WATT, FRANK MARION (Kilo)
Brother of Allie Watt.
B. Dec. 15, 1902, Washington, D. C. D. Aug. 31, 1956, Glen Cove, Md.

BR TR 6'1" 205 lbs.

| 1931 | PHI | N | 5 | 5 | .500 | 4.84 | 38 | 12 | 5 | 122.2 | 147 | 49 | 25 | 0 | 1 | 0 | 2 | 39 | 8 | 0 | .205 | 7 | 19 | 4 | 1 | 0.8 | .867 |

Jim Waugh

WAUGH, JAMES ELDEN
B. Nov. 25, 1933, Lancaster, Ohio

BR TR 6'3" 185 lbs.

1952	PIT	N	1	6	.143	6.36	17	7	1	52.1	61	32	18	0	0	1	0	10	1	0	.100	0	11	1	1	0.7	.917
1953			4	5	.444	6.48	29	11	1	90.1	108	56	23	0	0	0	0	22	5	0	.227	5	13	1	1	0.7	.947
2 yrs.			5	11	.313	6.43	46	18	2	142.2	169	88	41	0	0	1	0	32	6	0	.188	5	24	2	2	0.7	.935

Frank Wayenberg

WAYENBERG, FRANK
B. Aug. 27, 1898, Franklin, Kans. D. Apr. 16, 1975, Zanesville, Ohio

BR TR 6'½" 172 lbs.

| 1924 | CLE | A | 0 | 0 | – | 5.40 | 2 | 1 | 0 | 6.2 | 7 | 5 | 3 | 0 | 0 | 0 | 0 | 2 | 1 | 0 | .500 | 0 | 1 | 0 | 0 | 0.5 | 1.000 |

Gary Wayne

WAYNE, GARY ANTHONY
B. Nov. 30, 1962, Dearborn, Mich.

BL TL 6'3" 185 lbs.

| 1989 | MIN | A | 3 | 4 | .429 | 3.30 | 60 | 0 | 0 | 71 | 55 | 36 | 41 | 0 | 3 | 4 | 1 | 0 | 0 | 0 | – | 2 | 11 | 1 | 1 | 0.2 | .929 |

Hal Weafer

WEAFER, KENNETH ALBERT (Al)
B. Feb. 6, 1914, Woburn, Mass.

BR TR 6'½" 183 lbs.

| 1936 | BOS | N | 0 | 0 | – | 12.00 | 1 | 0 | 0 | 3 | 6 | 3 | 0 | 0 | 0 | 0 | 0 | 1 | 0 | 0 | .000 | 0 | 0 | 0 | 0 | 0.0 | – |

Floyd Weaver

WEAVER, DAVID FLOYD
B. May 12, 1941, Ben Franklin, Tex.

BR TR 6'4" 195 lbs.

1962	CLE	A	1	0	1.000	1.80	1	1	0	5	3	0	8	0	0	0	0	2	1	0	.500	0	0	0	0	0.0	–
1965			2	2	.500	5.43	32	1	0	61.1	61	24	37	0	2	2	1	11	1	0	.091	6	9	0	0	0.5	1.000
1970	CHI	A	1	2	.333	4.35	31	3	0	62	52	31	51	0	1	2	0	7	0	0	.000	4	4	2	0	0.3	.800
1971	MIL	A	0	1	.000	7.33	21	0	0	27	33	18	12	0	0	1	0	0	0	0	–	1	6	0	1	0.3	1.000
4 yrs.			4	5	.444	5.21	85	5	0	155.1	149	73	108	0	3	5	1	20	2	0	.100	11	19	2	1	0.4	.938

Harry Weaver

WEAVER, HARRY ABRAHAM
B. Feb. 26, 1892, Clarendon, Pa. D. May 30, 1983, Rochester, N. Y.

BR TR 5'11" 160 lbs.

1915	PHI	A	0	2	.000	3.00	3	2	2	18	18	10	1	0	0	0	0	6	1	0	.167	2	11	0	0	6.5	1.000
1916			0	0	–	10.13	3	0	0	8	14	5	2	0	0	0	0	2	1	0	.500	1	2	0	0	1.0	1.000
1917	CHI	N	1	1	.500	2.75	4	2	1	19.2	17	7	8	0	0	1	0	5	1	0	.200	0	10	1	0	2.8	.909
1918			2	2	.500	2.20	8	3	1	32.2	27	7	9	1	1	0	1	8	2	0	.250	2	13	0	1	1.9	1.000
1919			0	1	.000	10.80	2	1	0	3.1	6	2	1	0	0	0	0	1	0	0	.000	0	0	0	0	0.0	–
5 yrs.			3	6	.333	3.64	19	8	4	81.2	82	31	21	1	1	1	1	22	5	0	.227	5	36	1	1	2.2	.976

Jim Weaver

WEAVER, JAMES BRIAN (Fluss)
B. Feb. 19, 1939, Lancaster, Pa.

BL TL 6' 178 lbs.

| 1967 | CAL | A | 3 | 0 | 1.000 | 2.67 | 13 | 2 | 0 | 30.1 | 26 | 9 | 20 | 0 | 1 | 0 | 1 | 6 | 0 | 0 | .000 | 7 | 9 | 0 | 2 | 1.2 | 1.000 |

Year	Team	W	L	PCT	ERA	G	GS	CG	IP	H	BB	SO	ShO	W	L	SV	AB	H	HR	BA	PO	A	E	DP	TC/G	FA
														Relief Pitching			**Batting**									

Jim Weaver *continued*

Year	Team	W	L	PCT	ERA	G	GS	CG	IP	H	BB	SO	ShO	W	L	SV	AB	H	HR	BA	PO	A	E	DP	TC/G	FA
1968		0	1	.000	2.38	14	0	0	22.2	22	10	8	0	0	1	0	1	0	0	.000	0	2	1	0	0.2	.667
2 yrs.		3	1	.750	2.55	27	2	0	53	48	19	28	0	1	1	1	7	0	0	.000	7	11	1	2	0.7	.947

Jim Weaver

WEAVER, JAMES DEMENT (Big Jim)
B. Nov. 25, 1903, Obion County, Tenn. D. Dec. 12, 1983, Lakeland, Fla.
BR TR 6'6" 230 lbs.

Year	Team	W	L	PCT	ERA	G	GS	CG	IP	H	BB	SO	ShO	W	L	SV	AB	H	HR	BA	PO	A	E	DP	TC/G	FA
1928	WAS A	0	0	–	1.50	3	0	0	6	2	6	2	0	0	0	0	1	0	0	.000	0	2	1	0	1.0	.667
1931	NY A	2	1	.667	5.31	17	5	2	57.2	66	29	28	0	0	1	0	20	1	0	.050	0	13	1	3	0.8	.929
1934	2 teams			STL A	(5G 2–0)				CHI N	(27G 11–9)																
"	total	13	9	.591	4.18	32	25	10	178.2	180	74	109	1	2	0	0	59	4	0	.068	10	33	2	1	1.4	.956
1935	PIT N	14	8	.636	3.42	33	22	11	176.1	177	58	87	4	2	0	0	56	4	0	.071	4	40	2	2	1.4	.957
1936		14	8	.636	4.31	38	31	11	225.2	239	74	108	1	0	0	0	79	8	0	.101	7	38	4	1	1.3	.918
1937		8	5	.615	3.20	32	9	2	109.2	106	31	44	1	5	4	0	27	4	0	.148	3	16	2	1	0.7	.905
1938	2 teams			STL A	(1G 0–1)				CIN N	(30G 6–4)																
"	total	6	5	.545	3.43	31	16	2	136.1	118	63	68	0	1	0	3	46	9	0	.196	5	25	4	1	1.1	.882
1939	CIN N	0	0	–	3.00	3	0	0	3	3	3	3	0	0	0	0	0	0	0	.000	0	2	0	0	0.7	1.000
8 yrs.		57	36	.613	3.88	189	108	38	893.1	891	336	449	7	10	5	3	289	30	0	.104	29	169	16	9	1.1	.925

Monte Weaver

WEAVER, MONTGOMERY MORTON (Prof)
B. June 15, 1906, Hilton, N. C.
BL TR 6' 170 lbs.

Year	Team	W	L	PCT	ERA	G	GS	CG	IP	H	BB	SO	ShO	W	L	SV	AB	H	HR	BA	PO	A	E	DP	TC/G	FA
1931	WAS A	1	0	1.000	4.50	3	1	1	10	11	6	6	0	0	0	0	3	0	0	.000	0	4	0	0	1.3	1.000
1932		22	10	.688	4.08	43	30	13	234	236	112	83	1	2	2	2	94	27	0	.287	8	37	1	3	1.1	.978
1933		10	5	.667	3.25	23	21	12	152.1	147	53	45	1	0	0	0	56	7	0	.125	2	30	1	4	1.4	.970
1934		11	15	.423	4.79	31	31	11	204.2	255	63	51	0	0	0	0	80	13	0	.163	3	37	5	0	1.5	.889
1935		1	1	.500	5.25	5	2	0	12	16	6	4	0	1	0	0	3	1	0	.333	0	3	1	1	0.8	.750
1936		6	4	.600	4.35	26	5	3	91	92	38	15	0	4	1	1	25	5	0	.200	5	15	1	1	0.8	.952
1937		12	9	.571	4.20	30	26	9	188.2	197	70	44	0	2	1	0	68	14	0	.206	3	45	4	3	1.7	.923
1938		7	6	.538	5.24	31	18	7	139	157	74	43	0	2	1	0	45	12	0	.267	6	25	2	0	1.1	.939
1939	BOS A	1	0	1.000	6.64	9	1	1	20.1	26	13	6	0	0	0	1	4	0	0	.000	1	0	0	0	0.1	1.000
9 yrs.		71	50	.587	4.36	201	135	57	1052	1137	435	297	2	11	5	4	378	79	0	.209	28	196	15	12	1.2	.937

WORLD SERIES

Year	Team	W	L	PCT	ERA	G	GS	CG	IP	H	BB	SO	ShO	W	L	SV	AB	H	HR	BA	PO	A	E	DP	TC/G	FA
1933	WAS A	0	1	.000	1.74	1	1	0	10.1	11	4	3	0	0	0	0	4	0	0	.000	0	6	0	0	6.0	1.000

Orlie Weaver

WEAVER, ORVILLE FOREST
B. June 4, 1886, Newport, Ky. D. Nov. 28, 1970, New Orleans, La.
BR TR 6' 180 lbs.

Year	Team	W	L	PCT	ERA	G	GS	CG	IP	H	BB	SO	ShO	W	L	SV	AB	H	HR	BA	PO	A	E	DP	TC/G	FA
1910	CHI N	1	2	.333	3.66	7	2	2	32	34	15	22	0	0	0	0	13	2	0	.154	1	3	0	1	0.6	1.000
1911	2 teams			CHI N	(6G 3–2)				BOS N	(27G 3–12)																
"	total	6	14	.300	5.30	33	21	5	164.2	169	101	70	1	1	0	0	58	6	0	.103	3	34	5	0	1.3	.881
2 yrs.		7	16	.304	5.03	40	23	7	196.2	203	116	92	1	1	2	0	71	8	0	.113	4	37	5	1	1.2	.891

Roger Weaver

WEAVER, ROGER EDWARD
B. Oct. 6, 1954, Amsterdam, N. Y.
BR TR 6'3" 190 lbs.

Year	Team	W	L	PCT	ERA	G	GS	CG	IP	H	BB	SO	ShO	W	L	SV	AB	H	HR	BA	PO	A	E	DP	TC/G	FA
1980	DET A	3	4	.429	4.08	19	6	0	64	56	34	42	0	2	0	0				–	8	9	2	1	1.0	.895

Sam Weaver

WEAVER, SAMUEL H.
B. July 10, 1855, Philadelphia, Pa. D. Feb. 1, 1914, Philadelphia, Pa.
BR TR 185 lbs.

Year	Team	W	L	PCT	ERA	G	GS	CG	IP	H	BB	SO	ShO	W	L	SV	AB	H	HR	BA	PO	A	E	DP	TC/G	FA
1878	MIL N	12	31	.279	1.95	45	43	39	383	371	21	95	1	1	0	0	170	34	0	.200	31	78	16	1	2.8	.872
1882	PHI AA	26	15	.634	2.74	42	41	41	371	374	35	104	2	0	0	0	155	36	0	.232	16	127	9	1	3.6	.941
1883	LOU AA	24	20	.545	3.70	46	44	43	418.2	468	38	116	4	0	0	0	203	39	0	.192	21	81	6	3	2.3	.944
1884	PHI U	5	12	.294	5.76	17	17	14	136	206	11	40	0	0	0	0	84	18	0	.214	13	29	9	0	3.0	.824
1886	PHI AA	0	2	.000	14.73	2	2	1	11	30	2	2	0	0	0	0	7	1	0	.143	4	1	0	0	2.5	1.000
5 yrs.		67	80	.456	3.23	152	147	138	1319.2	1449	107	357	7	1	0	0	619	128	0	.207	85	316	40	5	2.9	.909

Bill Webb

WEBB, WILLIAM FREDERICK
B. Dec. 12, 1913, Atlanta, Ga.
BR TR 6'2" 180 lbs.

Year	Team	W	L	PCT	ERA	G	GS	CG	IP	H	BB	SO	ShO	W	L	SV	AB	H	HR	BA	PO	A	E	DP	TC/G	FA
1943	PHI N	0	0	–	9.00	1	0	0	1	1	1	0	0	0	0	0	0	0	0	–	0	0	0	0	0.0	–

Hank Webb

WEBB, HENRY GAYLON MATTHEW
B. May 21, 1950, Copiague, N. Y.
BR TR 6'3" 175 lbs.

Year	Team	W	L	PCT	ERA	G	GS	CG	IP	H	BB	SO	ShO	W	L	SV	AB	H	HR	BA	PO	A	E	DP	TC/G	FA
1972	NY N	0	0	–	4.42	6	2	0	18.1	18	9	15	0	0	0	0	5	0	0	.000	3	4	0	0	1.2	1.000
1973		0	0	–	10.80	2	0	0	1.2	2	1	0	0	0	0	0	0	0	0	–	0	0	0	0	0.0	–
1974		0	2	.000	7.20	9	0	0	10	15	10	8	0	0	1	0	3	0	0	.000	2	1	0	0	1.0	.667
1975		7	6	.538	4.07	29	15	3	115	102	62	38	1	2	0	0	31	8	0	.258	11	10	0	2	0.7	1.000
1976		0	1	.000	4.50	8	0	0	16	17	7	7	0	0	1	0	1	0	0	.000	0	3	0	0	0.4	1.000
1977	LA N	0	0	–	2.25	5	0	0	8	5	1	2	0	0	0	0	0	0	0	–	0	1	0	0	0.2	1.000
6 yrs.		7	9	.438	4.31	53	19	3	169	159	91	71	1	2	2	0	40	8	0	.200	16	18	1	2	0.7	.971

Lefty Webb

WEBB, CLEON EARL
B. Mar. 1, 1885, Mt. Gilead, Ohio D. Jan. 12, 1958, Circleville, Ohio
BB TL 5'11" 165 lbs.

Year	Team	W	L	PCT	ERA	G	GS	CG	IP	H	BB	SO	ShO	W	L	SV	AB	H	HR	BA	PO	A	E	DP	TC/G	FA
1910	PIT N	2	1	.667	5.67	7	3	2	27	29	9	6	0	0	0	0	10	2	0	.200	1	8	2	1	1.6	.818

Red Webb

WEBB, SAMUEL HENRY
B. Sept. 25, 1924, Washington, D. C.
BL TR 6' 175 lbs.

Year	Team	W	L	PCT	ERA	G	GS	CG	IP	H	BB	SO	ShO	W	L	SV	AB	H	HR	BA	PO	A	E	DP	TC/G	FA
1948	NY N	2	1	.667	3.21	5	3	2	28	27	10	9	0	0	0	0	9	2	0	.222	3	5	0	1	1.6	1.000
1949		1	1	.500	4.03	20	0	0	44.2	41	21	9	0	1	1	0	10	4	0	.400	3	18	2	2	1.2	.913
2 yrs.		3	2	.600	3.72	25	3	2	72.2	68	31	18	0	1	1	0	19	6	0	.316	6	23	2	3	1.2	.935

Les Webber

WEBBER, LESTER ELMER
B. May 6, 1915, Lakeport, Calif. D. Nov. 13, 1986, Santa Maria, Calif.
BR TR 6'½" 185 lbs.

Year	Team	W	L	PCT	ERA	G	GS	CG	IP	H	BB	SO	ShO	W	L	SV	AB	H	HR	BA	PO	A	E	DP	TC/G	FA
1942	BKN N	3	2	.600	2.96	19	3	1	51.2	46	22	23	0	1	2	1	14	1	0	.071	2	14	0	1	0.8	1.000

Year	Team	W	L	PCT	ERA	G	GS	CG	IP	H	BB	SO	ShO	W	L	SV	AB	H	HR	BA	PO	A	E	DP	TC/G	FA

Les Webber *continued*

Year	Team	W	L	PCT	ERA	G	GS	CG	IP	H	BB	SO	ShO	W	L	SV	AB	H	HR	BA	PO	A	E	DP	TC/G	FA
1943		2	2	.500	3.81	54	0	0	115.2	112	69	24	0	2	2	**10**	25	3	0	.120	11	34	2	1	0.9	.957
1944		7	8	.467	4.94	48	9	1	140.1	157	64	42	0	7	2	3	39	8	1	.205	10	43	1	0	1.1	.981
1945		7	3	.700	3.58	17	7	5	75.1	69	25	30	0	2	1	0	22	2	0	.091	6	7	0	0	0.8	1.000
1946	2 teams	BKN N	(11G 3–3)		CLE A	(4G 1–1)																				
"	total	4	4	.500	4.66	15	6	0	48.1	47	20	21	0	2	1	0	11	1	0	.091	3	8	0	0	0.7	1.000
1948	CLE A	0	0	–	40.50	1	0	0	.2	3	1	1	0	0	0	0	0	0	0	–	0	0	0	0	0.0	–
6 yrs.		23	19	.548	4.19	154	25	7	432	434	201	141	0	14	8	14	111	15	1	.135	32	106	3	2	0.9	.979

Charlie Weber

WEBER, CHARLES P.
B. Oct. 22, 1868, Cincinnati, Ohio   D. June 13, 1914, Beaumont, Tex.

Year	Team	W	L	PCT	ERA	G	GS	CG	IP	H	BB	SO	ShO	W	L	SV	AB	H	HR	BA	PO	A	E	DP	TC/G	FA
1898	WAS N	0	1	.000	15.75	1	1	0	4	9	1	0	0	0	0	0	2	0	0	.000	0	1	1	0	2.0	.500

Mike Wegener

WEGENER, MICHAEL DENIS
B. Oct. 8, 1946, Denver, Colo.   BR TR 6'4"   215 lbs.

Year	Team	W	L	PCT	ERA	G	GS	CG	IP	H	BB	SO	ShO	W	L	SV	AB	H	HR	BA	PO	A	E	DP	TC/G	FA
1969	MON N	5	14	.263	4.40	32	26	4	165.2	150	96	124	1	0	0	0	54	13	0	.241	11	31	1	1	1.3	.977
1970		3	6	.333	5.28	25	16	1	104	100	56	35	0	0	0	0	34	4	0	.118	7	14	0	0	0.8	1.000
2 yrs.		8	20	.286	4.74	57	42	5	269.2	250	152	159	1	0	0	0	88	17	0	.193	18	45	1	1	1.1	.984

Bill Wegman

WEGMAN, WILLIAM EDWARD
B. Dec. 19, 1962, Cincinnati, Ohio   BR TR 6'5"   200 lbs.

Year	Team	W	L	PCT	ERA	G	GS	CG	IP	H	BB	SO	ShO	W	L	SV	AB	H	HR	BA	PO	A	E	DP	TC/G	FA
1985	MIL A	2	0	1.000	3.57	3	3	0	17.2	17	3	6	0	0	0	0	0	0	0	–	3	0	0	0	1.0	1.000
1986		5	12	.294	5.13	35	32	2	198.1	217	43	82	0	0	0	0	0	0	0	–	20	19	1	4	1.1	.975
1987		12	11	.522	4.24	34	33	7	225	229	53	102	0	0	0	0	0	0	0	–	29	27	2	2	1.7	.966
1988		13	13	.500	4.12	32	31	4	199	207	50	84	1	0	0	0	0	0	0	–	14	24	3	3	1.3	.927
1989		2	6	.250	6.71	11	8	0	51	69	21	27	0	0	0	0	0	0	0	–	3	11	0	0	1.3	1.000
5 yrs.		34	42	.447	4.62	115	107	13	691	739	170	301	1	0	2	0	0	0	0	–	69	81	6	9	1.4	.962

Biggs Wehde

WEHDE, WILBUR
B. Nov. 23, 1906, Holstein, Iowa   D. Sept. 21, 1970, Sioux Falls, S. D.   BR TR 5'10½" 180 lbs.

Year	Team	W	L	PCT	ERA	G	GS	CG	IP	H	BB	SO	ShO	W	L	SV	AB	H	HR	BA	PO	A	E	DP	TC/G	FA
1930	CHI A	0	0	–	9.95	4	0	0	6.1	7	7	3	0	0	0	0	1	0	0	.000	0	5	0	0	1.3	1.000
1931		1	0	1.000	6.75	8	0	0	16	19	10	3	0	1	0	0	3	0	0	.000	1	6	0	0	0.9	1.000
2 yrs.		1	0	1.000	7.66	12	0	0	22.1	26	17	6	0	1	0	0	4	0	0	.000	1	11	0	0	1.0	1.000

Herm Wehmeier

WEHMEIER, HERMAN RALPH
B. Feb. 18, 1927, Cincinnati, Ohio   D. May 21, 1973, Dallas, Tex.   BR TR 6'2"   185 lbs.

Year	Team	W	L	PCT	ERA	G	GS	CG	IP	H	BB	SO	ShO	W	L	SV	AB	H	HR	BA	PO	A	E	DP	TC/G	FA
1945	CIN N	0	1	.000	12.60	2	2	0	5	10	4	0	0	0	0	0	1	0	0	.000	0	2	0	0	1.0	1.000
1947		0	0	–	0.00	1	0	0	1	0	0	0	0	0	0	0	0	0	0	–	0	0	0	0	0.0	–
1948		11	8	.579	5.86	33	24	6	147.1	179	75	56	0	1	1	0	55	5	0	.091	4	29	3	1	1.1	.917
1949		11	12	.478	4.68	33	29	11	213.1	202	117	80	1	1	1	0	78	20	0	.256	3	31	3	2	1.1	.944
1950		10	18	.357	5.67	41	32	12	230	255	135	121	0	0	0	4	92	14	0	.152	9	27	5	1	1.0	.878
1951		7	10	.412	3.70	39	22	10	184.2	167	89	93	2	0	0	2	59	17	0	.288	14	23	4	3	1.1	.902
1952		9	11	.450	5.15	33	26	6	190.1	197	103	83	1	0	0	0	64	12	1	.188	8	18	3	2	0.9	.897
1953		1	6	.143	7.16	28	10	2	81.2	100	47	32	0	0	0	0	20	4	0	.200	2	10	0	0	0.4	1.000
1954	2 teams	CIN N	(12G 0–3)		PHI N	(25G 10–8)																				
"	total	10	11	.476	4.40	37	20	10	171.2	153	72	62	0	0	0	2	59	6	0	.102	7	37	3	2	1.3	.936
1955	PHI N	10	12	.455	4.41	31	29	10	193.2	176	67	85	1	0	0	0	72	20	0	.278	6	29	3	2	1.2	.921
1956	2 teams	PHI N	(3G 0–2)		STL N	(34G 12–9)																				
"	total	12	11	.522	3.73	37	22	7	190.2	168	82	76	2	5	0	1	66	13	2	.197	16	24	2	1	1.1	.952
1957	STL N	10	7	.588	4.31	36	18	5	165	165	54	91	0	2	2	0	59	12	0	.203	18	24	1	0	1.2	.977
1958	2 teams	STL N	(3G 0–1)		DET A	(7G 1–0)																				
"	total	1	1	.500	4.71	10	6	0	28.2	34	7	15	0	0	0	0	8	1	0	.125	0	5	0	0	0.5	1.000
13 yrs.		92	108	.460	4.80	361	240	79	1803	1806	852	794	9	10	7	9	633	124	3	.196	87	259	26	16	1.0	.930

Dave Wehrmeister

WEHRMEISTER, DAVID THOMAS
B. Nov. 9, 1952, Berwyn, Ill.   BR TR 6'4"   195 lbs.

Year	Team	W	L	PCT	ERA	G	GS	CG	IP	H	BB	SO	ShO	W	L	SV	AB	H	HR	BA	PO	A	E	DP	TC/G	FA
1976	SD N	0	4	.000	7.45	7	4	0	19.1	27	11	10	0	0	0	0	6	0	0	.000	1	4	0	1	0.7	1.000
1977		1	3	.250	6.04	30	6	0	70	81	44	32	0	1	2	0	12	2	0	.167	7	9	2	1	0.6	.889
1978		1	0	1.000	6.43	4	0	0	7	8	5	2	0	1	0	0	0	0	0	–	0	0	0	0	0.0	–
1981	NY A	0	0	–	5.14	5	0	0	7	6	7	7	0	0	0	0	0	0	0	–	1	2	0	0	0.6	1.000
1984	PHI N	0	0	–	7.20	7	0	0	15	18	7	13	0	0	0	0	2	0	0	.000	1	3	0	1	0.6	1.000
1985	CHI A	2	2	.500	3.43	23	0	0	39.1	35	10	32	0	2	2	2	0	0	0	–	3	2	0	2	0.2	1.000
6 yrs.		4	9	.308	5.65	76	10	0	157.2	175	84	96	0	4	4	2	20	2	0	.100	13	20	2	5	0.5	.943

Stump Weidman

WEIDMAN, GEORGE EDWARD
B. Feb. 17, 1861, Rochester, N. Y.   D. Mar. 3, 1905, New York, N. Y.   BR TR

Year	Team	W	L	PCT	ERA	G	GS	CG	IP	H	BB	SO	ShO	W	L	SV	AB	H	HR	BA	PO	A	E	DP	TC/G	FA
1880	BUF N	0	9	.000	3.40	17	13	9	113.2	141	9	26	0	0	0	0	78	8	0	.103	7	18	3	0	1.6	.893
1881	DET N	8	5	.615	**1.80**	13	13	13	115	108	12	26	1	0	0	0	47	12	0	.255	3	15	0	0	1.4	1.000
1882		25	20	.556	2.63	46	45	43	411	391	39	161	4	0	0	0	193	42	0	.218	35	71	11	2	2.5	.906
1883		20	24	.455	*3.53*	52	47	41	402.1	435	72	183	3	0	0	2	313	58	1	.185	28	72	10	1	2.1	.909
1884		4	21	.160	*3.72*	26	26	24	212.2	257	57	96	0	0	0	0	300	49	0	.163	12	45	17	1	2.8	.770
1885		14	24	.368	*3.14*	38	38	37	330	343	63	149	3	0	0	0	153	24	1	.157	5	2	6	1	0.3	.538
1886	KC N	12	**36**	.250	*4.52*	51	51	48	427.2	549	112	168	1	0	0	0	179	30	0	.168	25	106	9	5	2.7	.936
1887	3 teams	DET N	(21G 13–7)		NY AA	(12G 4–8)		NY N	(1G 0–1)																	
"	total	17	16	.515	*5.00*	34	34	32	288	353	87	97	1	0	0	0	131	25	0	.191	15	57	13	0	2.5	.847
1888	NY N	0	1	.000	3.50	2	2	2	18	17	8	5	0	0	0	0	22	0	0	.000	3	2	2	0	3.5	.714
9 yrs.		100	156	.391	3.61	279	269	249	2318.1	2594	459	910	13	0	0	2	*				133	388	71	10	2.1	.880

Dick Weik

WEIK, RICHARD HENRY (Legs)
B. Nov. 17, 1927, Waterloo, Iowa   BR TR 6'3½" 184 lbs.

Year	Team	W	L	PCT	ERA	G	GS	CG	IP	H	BB	SO	ShO	W	L	SV	AB	H	HR	BA	PO	A	E	DP	TC/G	FA
1948	WAS A	1	2	.333	5.68	3	3	0	12.2	14	22	8	0	0	0	0	4	3	0	.750	0	2	0	0	0.7	1.000
1949		3	12	.200	5.38	27	14	2	95.1	78	103	58	2	1	1	1	28	5	0	.179	5	22	1	0	1.0	.964

Year	Team	W	L	PCT	ERA	G	GS	CG	IP	H	BB	SO	ShO	W	L	SV	AB	H	HR	BA	PO	A	E	DP	TC/G	FA

Dick Weik *continued*

Year	Team	W	L	PCT	ERA	G	GS	CG	IP	H	BB	SO	ShO	W	L	SV	AB	H	HR	BA	PO	A	E	DP	TC/G	FA
1950	2 teams	WAS A	(14G 1-3)		CLE A	(11G 1-3)																				
"	total	2	6	.250	4.11	25	7	1	70	56	73	42	0	1	1	0	18	3	0	.167	1	9	0	1	0.4	1.000
1953	2 teams	CLE A	(0G 0-0)		DET A	(12G 0-1)																				
"	total	0	1	.000	13.97	12	1	0	19.1	32	23	6	0	0	1	0	2	1	0	.500	3	3	0	1	0.5	1.000
1954	DET A	0	1	.000	7.16	9	1	0	16.1	23	16	9	0	0	1	0	1	0	0	.000	0	1	0	0	0.2	.500
5 yrs.		6	22	.214	5.90	76	26	3	213.2	203	237	123	2	2	4	1	53	12	0	.226	9	37	2	2	0.6	.958

Bob Weiland

WEILAND, ROBERT GEORGE (Lefty)
Brother of Ed Weiland.
B. Dec. 14, 1905, Chicago, Ill.   D. Nov. 9, 1988, Chicago, Ill.

BL TL 6'4"   215 lbs.

Year	Team	W	L	PCT	ERA	G	GS	CG	IP	H	BB	SO	ShO	W	L	SV	AB	H	HR	BA	PO	A	E	DP	TC/G	FA
1928	CHI A	1	0	1.000	0.00	1	1	1	9	7	5	9	1	0	0	0	3	1	0	.333	1	1	0	0	2.0	1.000
1929		2	4	.333	5.81	15	9	1	62	62	43	25	0	0	0	1	18	2	0	.111	1	8	0	0	0.6	1.000
1930		0	4	.000	6.61	14	3	0	32.2	38	21	15	0	0	0	0	8	0	0	.000	0	6	0	0	0.4	1.000
1931		2	7	.222	5.16	15	8	3	75	75	46	38	0	0	1	0	22	4	0	.182	2	18	0	0	1.3	1.000
1932	BOS A	6	16	.273	4.51	43	27	7	195.2	231	97	63	0	0	1	1	61	9	0	.148	14	49	3	7	1.5	.955
1933		8	14	.364	3.87	39	27	12	216.1	197	100	97	0	0	0	3	65	7	0	.108	5	38	2	3	1.2	.956
1934	2 teams	BOS A	(11G 1-5)		CLE A	(16G 1-5)																				
"	total	2	10	.167	4.73	27	14	4	125.2	134	57	71	0	0	0	0	43	5	0	.116	4	22	1	2	1.0	.963
1935	STL A	0	2	.000	9.56	14	4	0	32	39	31	11	0	0	0	0	8	0	0	.000	0	4	1	0	0.4	.800
1937	STL N	15	14	.517	3.54	41	34	21	264.1	283	94	105	0	2	0	2	89	15	2	.169	6	54	4	2	1.6	.938
1938		16	11	.593	3.59	35	29	11	228.1	248	67	117	1	0	0	1	80	11	0	.138	7	41	3	1	1.5	.941
1939		10	12	.455	3.57	32	23	6	146.1	146	50	63	3	2	1	1	46	3	0	.065	4	24	1	2	0.9	.966
1940		0	0	–	40.50	1	0	0	.2	3	3	0	0	0	0	0	0	0	0	–	0	0	0	0	0.0	–
12 yrs.		62	94	.397	4.24	277	179	66	1388	1463	611	614	7	6	2	6	7	443	57	3	.129	44	265	15	19	1.2	.954

Ed Weiland

WEILAND, EDWIN NICHOLAS
Brother of Bob Weiland.
B. Nov. 26, 1914, Evanston, Ill.   D. July 12, 1971, Chicago, Ill.

BL TR 5'11"   180 lbs.

Year	Team	W	L	PCT	ERA	G	GS	CG	IP	H	BB	SO	ShO	W	L	SV	AB	H	HR	BA	PO	A	E	DP	TC/G	FA
1940	CHI A	0	0	–	8.79	5	0	0	14.1	15	7	3	0	0	0	0	5	1	0	.200	0	1	0	0	0.2	1.000
1942		0	0	–	7.45	5	0	0	9.2	18	3	4	0	0	0	0	2	0	0	.000	0	1	0	0	0.2	1.000
2 yrs.		0	0	–	8.25	10	0	0	24	33	10	7	0	0	0	0	7	1	0	.143	0	2	0	0	0.2	1.000

Carl Weilman

WEILMAN, CARL WOOLWORTH (Zeke)
Born Carl Woolworth Weilenmann.
B. Nov. 29, 1889, Hamilton, Ohio.   D. May 25, 1924, Hamilton, Ohio

BL TL 6'5½"   187 lbs.

Year	Team	W	L	PCT	ERA	G	GS	CG	IP	H	BB	SO	ShO	W	L	SV	AB	H	HR	BA	PO	A	E	DP	TC/G	FA
1912	STL A	2	4	.333	2.79	9	6	5	48.1	42	3	24	2	0	0	1	17	2	0	.118	2	15	0	0	1.9	1.000
1913		10	20	.333	3.40	39	28	17	251.2	262	60	79	2	2	2	0	82	12	0	.146	8	83	8	3	2.5	.919
1914		18	13	.581	2.08	44	36	20	299	260	84	119	3	2	1	1	101	15	0	.149	15	88	3	4	2.4	.972
1915		18	19	.486	2.34	47	31	19	295.2	240	83	125	3	5	2	4	100	23	0	.230	8	85	5	2	2.1	.949
1916		17	18	.486	2.15	46	31	19	276	237	76	91	1	5	4	2	91	14	0	.154	7	69	7	6	1.8	.916
1917		1	2	.333	1.89	5	3	0	19	19	6	9	0	0	0	0	4	0	0	.000	0	10	1	1	2.2	.909
1919		10	6	.625	2.07	20	20	12	148	133	45	44	3	0	0	0	47	9	0	.191	3	40	0	2	2.2	1.000
1920		9	13	.409	4.47	30	24	13	183.1	201	61	45	1	0	0	2	63	11	0	.175	16	52	4	1	2.4	.944
8 yrs.		85	95	.472	2.67	240	179	105	1521	1394	418	536	15	14	9	10	505	86	0	.170	59	442	28	19	2.2	.947

Jake Weimer

WEIMER, JACOB (Tornado Jake)
B. Nov. 29, 1873, Ottumwa, Iowa   D. June 19, 1928, Chicago, Ill.

BR TL 5'11"   175 lbs.

Year	Team	W	L	PCT	ERA	G	GS	CG	IP	H	BB	SO	ShO	W	L	SV	AB	H	HR	BA	PO	A	E	DP	TC/G	FA
1903	CHI N	21	9	.700	2.30	35	33	27	282	241	104	128	3	0	0	0	107	21	0	.196	20	66	9	2	2.7	.905
1904		20	14	.588	1.91	37	37	31	307	229	97	177	5	0	0	0	115	21	0	.183	37	81	5	0	3.3	.959
1905		18	12	.600	2.27	33	30	26	250	212	80	107	2	1	1	1	92	19	0	.207	18	65	7	2	2.7	.922
1906	CIN N	20	14	.588	2.22	41	39	31	304.2	263	99	141	7	1	0	1	108	29	0	.269	18	87	4	1	2.7	.963
1907		11	14	.440	2.41	29	26	19	209	165	63	67	3	2	1	0	72	14	1	.194	21	66	7	1	3.2	.926
1908		8	7	.533	2.39	15	15	9	116.2	110	50	36	1	0	0	0	45	11	0	.244	7	37	0	2	2.9	1.000
1909	NY N	0	0	–	9.00	1	0	0	3	7	0	1	0	0	0	0	1	0	0	.000	1	0	0	0	1.0	1.000
7 yrs.		98	70	.583	2.23	191	180	143	1472.1	1227	493	657	22	4	2	2	540	115	1	.213	122	402	32	8	2.9	.942

Lefty Weinert

WEINERT, PHILIP WALTER
B. Apr. 21, 1902, Philadelphia, Pa.   D. Apr. 17, 1973, Rockledge, Fla.

BL TL 6'1"   195 lbs.

Year	Team	W	L	PCT	ERA	G	GS	CG	IP	H	BB	SO	ShO	W	L	SV	AB	H	HR	BA	PO	A	E	DP	TC/G	FA
1919	PHI N	0	0	–	18.00	1	0	0	4	11	2	0	0	0	0	0	2	2	0	1.000	2	1	0	0	3.0	1.000
1920		1	1	.500	6.14	10	2	0	22	27	19	10	0	1	0	0	5	0	0	.000	1	5	0	0	0.6	1.000
1921		1	0	1.000	1.46	8	0	0	12.1	8	5	2	0	1	0	0	1	1	0	1.000	0	1	1	0	0.3	.500
1922		8	11	.421	3.40	34	22	10	166.2	189	70	58	0	3	1	1	58	14	0	.241	3	31	2	1	1.1	.944
1923		4	17	.190	5.42	38	20	8	156	207	81	46	0	0	1	0	59	19	0	.322	1	26	2	1	0.8	.931
1924		0	1	.000	2.45	8	1	0	14.2	10	11	7	0	0	0	0	4	0	0	.000	1	4	1	0	0.8	.833
1927	CHI N	1	1	.500	4.58	5	3	1	19.2	21	7	5	0	0	0	1	5	1	0	.200	3	2	1	0	1.2	.833
1928		1	0	1.000	5.29	10	1	0	17	24	9	8	0	1	0	0	2	0	0	.000	0	0	0	0	0.0	–
1931	NY A	2	2	.500	6.20	17	0	0	24.2	31	19	24	0	1	2	0	6	0	0	.000	1	4	0	1	0.2	1.000
9 yrs.		18	33	.353	4.59	131	49	19	437	528	222	160	0	8	5	2	142	37	0	.261	10	75	7	3	0.7	.924

Roy Weir

WEIR, WILLIAM FRANKLIN (Bill)
B. Feb. 25, 1911, Portland, Me.

BL TL 5'8½"   170 lbs.

Year	Team	W	L	PCT	ERA	G	GS	CG	IP	H	BB	SO	ShO	W	L	SV	AB	H	HR	BA	PO	A	E	DP	TC/G	FA
1936	BOS N	4	3	.571	2.83	12	7	2	57.1	53	24	29	2	1	0	0	18	5	0	.278	3	14	0	2	1.4	1.000
1937		1	1	.500	3.82	10	4	1	33	27	19	8	0	0	0	0	10	0	0	.000	0	0	0	0	0.0	–
1938		1	0	1.000	6.75	5	0	0	13.1	14	6	3	0	1	0	0	3	1	0	.333	0	5	0	0	1.0	1.000
1939		0	0	–	0.00	2	0	0	2.2	1	1	2	0	0	0	0	1	0	0	.000	1	1	0	0	1.0	1.000
4 yrs.		6	4	.600	3.55	29	11	3	106.1	95	50	42	2	2	0	0	32	6	0	.188	4	20	0	2	0.8	1.000

Bob Welch

WELCH, ROBERT LYNN
B. Nov. 3, 1956, Detroit, Mich.

BR TR 6'3"   190 lbs.

Year	Team	W	L	PCT	ERA	G	GS	CG	IP	H	BB	SO	ShO	W	L	SV	AB	H	HR	BA	PO	A	E	DP	TC/G	FA
1978	LA N	7	4	.636	2.03	23	13	0	111	92	26	66	3	1	0	3	29	5	0	.172	6	12	1	0	0.8	.947

Year	Team	W	L	PCT	ERA	G	GS	CG	IP	H	BB	SO	ShO	Relief Pitching W	L	SV	Batting AB	H	HR	BA	PO	A	E	DP	TC/G	FA

Bob Welch *continued*

Year	Team	W	L	PCT	ERA	G	GS	CG	IP	H	BB	SO	ShO	W	L	SV	AB	H	HR	BA	PO	A	E	DP	TC/G	FA
1979		5	6	.455	4.00	25	12	1	81	82	32	64	0	3	1	5	19	3	0	.158	2	8	3	3	0.5	.769
1980		14	9	.609	3.28	32	32	3	214	190	79	141	2	0	0	0	70	17	0	.243	15	26	1	3	1.3	.976
1981		9	5	.643	3.45	23	23	2	141	141	41	88	1	0	0	0	45	10	0	.222	4	18	0	1	1.0	1.000
1982		16	11	.593	3.36	36	36	9	235.2	199	81	176	3	0	0	0	85	12	0	.141	19	26	2	0	1.3	.957
1983		15	12	.556	2.65	31	31	4	204	164	72	156	3	0	0	0	73	7	1	.096	14	27	3	1	1.4	.932
1984		13	13	.500	3.78	31	29	3	178.2	191	58	126	1	0	0	0	51	4	0	.078	20	28	2	5	1.6	.960
1985		14	4	.778	2.31	23	23	8	167.1	141	35	96	3	0	0	0	50	9	0	.180	15	27	3	1	2.0	.933
1986		7	13	.350	3.28	33	33	7	235.2	227	55	183	3	0	0	0	76	8	1	.105	21	26	2	2	1.5	.959
1987		15	9	.625	3.22	35	35	6	251.2	204	86	196	4	0	0	0	83	13	0	.157	25	38	0	3	1.8	1.000
1988	OAK A	17	9	.654	3.64	36	36	4	244.2	237	81	158	2	0	0	0	16	32	1	2	1.4	.980
1989		17	8	.680	3.00	33	33	1	209.2	191	78	137	0	0	0	0	0	0	0	—	26	21	4	3	1.5	.922
12 yrs.		149	103	.591	3.18	361	336	52	2274.1	2059	724	1587	25	4	1	8	581	88	2	.151	183	289	22	24	1.4	.955

DIVISIONAL PLAYOFF SERIES

Year	Team	W	L	PCT	ERA	G	GS	CG	IP	H	BB	SO	ShO	W	L	SV	AB	H	HR	BA	PO	A	E	DP	TC/G	FA
1981	LA N	0	0	—	0.00	1	0	0	1	0	1	0	0	0	0	0	0	0	0	—	0	0	0	0	0.0	—

LEAGUE CHAMPIONSHIP SERIES

Year	Team	W	L	PCT	ERA	G	GS	CG	IP	H	BB	SO	ShO	W	L	SV	AB	H	HR	BA	PO	A	E	DP	TC/G	FA
1978	LA N	1	0	1.000	2.08	1	0	0	4.1	2	0	5	0	0	0	0	2	0	0	.000	0	1	0	0	1.0	1.000
1981		0	0	—	5.40	3	0	0	1.2	2	0	2	0	0	0	1	0	0	0	—	0	0	0	0	0.0	—
1983		0	1	.000	6.75	1	1	0	1.1	0	2	0	0	0	0	0	0	0	0	—	0	0	0	0	0.0	—
1985		0	1	.000	6.75	1	1	0	2.2	5	6	2	0	0	0	0	1	0	0	.000	0	0	0	0	0.0	—
1988	OAK A	0	0	—	27.00	1	1	0	1.2	6	2	0	0	0	0	0	0	0	0	—	1	0	0	0	1.0	1.000
1989		1	0	1.000	3.18	1	1	0	5.2	8	1	4	0	0	0	0	0	0	0	—	1	0	0	0	1.0	1.000
6 yrs.		2	2	.500	6.23	8	4	0	17.1	23	11	13	0	0	1	1	3	0	0	.000	2	1	0	0	0.5	.750

WORLD SERIES

Year	Team	W	L	PCT	ERA	G	GS	CG	IP	H	BB	SO	ShO	W	L	SV	AB	H	HR	BA	PO	A	E	DP	TC/G	FA
1978	LA N	0	1	.000	6.23	3	0	0	4.1	4	2	6	0	0	0	1	0	0	0	—	0	0	0	0	0.0	—
1981		0	0	—	∞	1	1	0	0	3	1	0	0	0	0	0	0	0	0	—	0	0	0	0	0.0	—
1988	OAK A	0	0	—	1.80	1	1	0	5	6	3	8	0	0	0	0	0	0	0	—	1	1	0	0	2.0	1.000
3 yrs.		0	1	.000	5.79	5	2	0	9.1	13	6	14	0	0	0	1	0	0	0	—	1	1	0	0	0.4	1.000

Curt Welch

WELCH, CURTIS BENTON   BR TR 5'10" 175 lbs.
B. Feb. 11, 1862, East Liverpool, Ohio   D. Aug. 29, 1896, East Liverpool, Ohio

Year	Team	W	L	PCT	ERA	G	GS	CG	IP	H	BB	SO	ShO	W	L	SV	AB	H	HR	BA	PO	A	E	DP	TC/G	FA
1884	TOL AA	1	0	1.000	0.00	1	1	1	9	5	0	5	1	0	0	0	425	95	0	.224	1	0	0	0	2.0	1.000
1890	BAL AA	0	0	—	54.00	1	0	0	1	6	0	1	0	0	0	0	464	115	2	.248	0	2	0	0	2.0	1.000
2 yrs.		1	0	1.000	5.40	2	1	1	10	11	0	6	1	0	0	0	*				1	2	0	0	1.5	1.000

Johnny Welch

WELCH, JOHN VERNON   BL TR 6'3" 184 lbs.
B. Dec. 2, 1906, Washington, D. C.   D. Sept. 2, 1940, St. Louis, Mo.

Year	Team	W	L	PCT	ERA	G	GS	CG	IP	H	BB	SO	ShO	W	L	SV	AB	H	HR	BA	PO	A	E	DP	TC/G	FA
1926	CHI N	0	0	—	2.08	3	0	0	4.1	5	1	0	0	0	0	0	1	1	0	1.000	0	0	0	0	0.0	—
1927		0	0	—	9.00	1	0	0	1	0	3	1	0	0	0	0	0	0	0	—	0	0	0	0	0.0	—
1928		0	0	—	15.75	3	0	0	4	13	0	2	0	0	0	0	0	0	0	—	0	1	0	0	0.3	1.000
1931		2	1	.667	3.74	8	3	1	33.2	39	10	7	0	1	1	0	12	5	0	.417	2	7	0	0	1.1	1.000
1932	BOS A	4	6	.400	5.23	20	8	3	72.1	93	38	26	1	1	1	0	36	9	1	.250	1	17	1	0	1.0	.947
1933		4	9	.308	4.60	47	7	1	129	142	67	68	0	3	5	3	37	6	0	.162	1	33	1	0	0.7	.971
1934		13	15	.464	4.49	41	24	8	206.1	223	76	91	1	3	6	0	74	15	0	.203	9	40	0	3	1.2	1.000
1935		10	9	.526	4.47	31	19	10	143	155	53	48	1	0	1	2	50	9	0	.180	5	27	1	2	1.1	.970
1936	2 teams	BOS A	(9G 2–1)			PIT N	(9G 0–0)																			
"	total	2	1	.667	5.10	18	4	1	54.2	65	14	14	0	0	0	1	18	5	0	.278	2	10	1	0	0.7	.923
9 yrs.		35	41	.461	4.66	172	63	24	648.1	735	262	257	3	10	13	6	228	50	1	.219	20	135	4	5	0.9	.975

Mickey Welch

WELCH, MICHAEL FRANCIS (Smiling Mickey)   BR TR 5'8" 160 lbs.
B. July 4, 1859, Brooklyn, N. Y.   D. July 30, 1941, Concord, N. H.
Hall of Fame 1973.

Year	Team	W	L	PCT	ERA	G	GS	CG	IP	H	BB	SO	ShO	W	L	SV	AB	H	HR	BA	PO	A	E	DP	TC/G	FA
1880	TRO N	34	30	.531	2.54	65	64	64	574	575	80	123	4	0	0	0	251	72	0	.287	35	86	21	4	2.2	.852
1881		21	18	.538	2.67	40	40	40	368	371	78	104	3	0	0	0	148	30	0	.203	20	39	7	3	1.7	.894
1882		14	16	.467	3.46	33	33	30	281	334	62	53	5	0	0	0	151	37	1	.245	10	46	10	4	2.0	.848
1883	NY N	25	23	.521	2.73	54	52	46	426	431	66	144	4	1	1	0	320	75	3	.234	29	54	21	2	1.9	.798
1884		39	21	.650	2.50	65	65	62	557.1	528	146	345	4	0	0	0	249	60	3	.241	25	78	14	6	1.8	.880
1885		44	11	.800	1.66	56	55	55	492	372	131	258	7	0	0	0	199	41	2	.206	16	70	14	0	1.8	.860
1886		33	22	.600	2.99	59	59	56	500	514	163	272	1	0	0	0	213	46	0	.216	19	82	5	0	1.8	.953
1887		22	15	.595	3.36	40	40	39	346	339	91	115	2	0	0	0	148	36	2	.243	17	51	12	0	2.0	.850
1888		26	19	.578	1.93	47	47	47	425.1	328	108	167	5	0	0	0	169	32	2	.189	16	75	17	1	2.0	.843
1889		27	12	.692	3.02	45	41	39	375	340	149	125	3	0	0	2	156	30	0	.192	13	59	4	2	1.7	.947
1890		17	13	.567	2.99	37	37	33	292.1	268	122	97	2	0	0	0	123	22	0	.179	10	43	4	1	1.5	.930
1891		6	9	.400	4.28	22	15	14	160	176	97	46	0	2	1	1	71	10	0	.141	7	21	4	0	1.5	.875
1892		0	0	—	14.40	1	1	0	5	11	4	1	0	0	0	0	3	1	0	.333	0	1	0	0	1.0	1.000
13 yrs.		308	209	.596	2.71	564	549	525	4802	4587	1297	1850	40	3	2	4	*				217	705	133	23	1.9	.874
				6th																						

Ted Welch

WELCH, FLOYD JOHN   BL TR 5'9½" 160 lbs.
B. Oct. 17, 1892, Coyville, Kans.   D. Jan. 6, 1943, Great Bend, Kans.

Year	Team	W	L	PCT	ERA	G	GS	CG	IP	H	BB	SO	ShO	W	L	SV	AB	H	HR	BA	PO	A	E	DP	TC/G	FA
1914	STL F	0	0	—	6.00	3	0	0	6	6	3	2	0	0	0	0	1	0	0	.000	1	1	0	0	0.7	1.000

Don Welchel

WELCHEL, DONALD RAY   BR TR 6'4" 205 lbs.
B. Feb. 3, 1957, Atlanta, Tex.

Year	Team	W	L	PCT	ERA	G	GS	CG	IP	H	BB	SO	ShO	W	L	SV	AB	H	HR	BA	PO	A	E	DP	TC/G	FA
1982	BAL A	1	0	1.000	8.31	2	0	0	4.1	6	2	3	0	1	0	0	0	0	0	—	0	0	0	0	0.0	—
1983		0	2	.000	5.40	11	0	0	26.2	33	10	16	0	0	2	0	0	0	0	—	2	3	1	0	0.5	.833
2 yrs.		1	2	.333	5.81	13	0	0	31	39	12	19	0	1	2	0	0	0	0	—	2	3	1	0	0.5	.833

Year	Team		W	L	PCT	ERA	G	GS	CG	IP	H	BB	SO	ShO	Relief Pitching W	L	SV	Batting AB	H	HR	BA	PO	A	E	DP	TC/G	FA

David Wells

WELLS, DAVID LEE
B. May 20, 1963, Torrance, Calif.   BL TL 6'3" 187 lbs.

Year	Team		W	L	PCT	ERA	G	GS	CG	IP	H	BB	SO	ShO	W	L	SV	AB	H	HR	BA	PO	A	E	DP	TC/G	FA
1987	TOR	A	4	3	.571	3.99	18	2	0	29.1	37	12	32	0	4	1	1	0	0	0	–	2	4	0	1	0.3	1.000
1988			3	5	.375	4.62	41	0	0	64.1	65	31	56	0	3	5	4	0	0	0	–	5	5	0	1	0.2	1.000
1989			7	4	.636	2.40	54	0	0	86.1	66	28	78	0	7	4	2	0	0	0	–	9	11	1	0	0.4	.952
3 yrs.			14	12	.538	3.45	113	2	0	180	168	71	166	0	14	10	7	0	0	0	–	16	20	1	2	0.3	.973

LEAGUE CHAMPIONSHIP SERIES

Year	Team		W	L	PCT	ERA	G	GS	CG	IP	H	BB	SO	ShO	W	L	SV	AB	H	HR	BA	PO	A	E	DP	TC/G	FA
1989	TOR	A	0	0	–	0.00	1	0	0	1	0	2	1	0	0	0	0	0	0	0	–	0	0	0	0	0.0	–

Ed Wells

WELLS, EDWIN LEE
B. June 7, 1900, Ashland, Ohio   D. May 1, 1986, Birmingham, Ala.   BL TL 6'1½" 183 lbs.

Year	Team		W	L	PCT	ERA	G	GS	CG	IP	H	BB	SO	ShO	W	L	SV	AB	H	HR	BA	PO	A	E	DP	TC/G	FA
1923	DET	A	0	0	–	5.40	7	0	0	10	11	6	6	0	0	0	0	1	0	0	.000	1	1	0	0	0.3	1.000
1924			6	8	.429	4.06	29	15	5	102	117	42	33	0	1	1	4	33	7	0	.212	4	30	1	1	1.2	.971
1925			6	9	.400	6.23	35	14	5	134.1	190	62	45	0	2	3	2	43	12	0	.279	8	34	1	1	1.2	.977
1926			12	10	.545	4.15	36	26	9	178	201	76	58	4	2	2	0	73	15	0	.205	9	30	3	3	1.2	.929
1927			0	1	.000	6.75	8	1	0	20	28	5	5	0	0	0	1	7	2	0	.286	1	8	1	0	1.3	.900
1929	NY	A	13	9	.591	4.33	31	23	10	193.1	179	81	78	0	3	0	0	74	17	0	.230	5	21	2	2	0.9	.929
1930			12	3	.800	5.20	27	21	7	150.2	185	49	46	0	1	1	0	58	15	0	.259	6	21	1	1	1.0	.964
1931			9	5	.643	4.32	27	10	6	116.2	130	37	34	0	2	4	2	45	10	0	.222	6	17	2	1	0.9	.920
1932			3	3	.500	4.26	22	0	0	31.2	38	12	13	0	3	3	2	6	0	0	.000	1	6	0	0	0.3	1.000
1933	STL	A	6	14	.300	4.20	36	22	10	203.2	230	63	58	0	2	3	1	71	14	0	.197	11	31	2	0	1.2	.955
1934			1	7	.125	4.79	33	8	2	92	108	35	27	0	1	3	1	22	1	0	.045	5	23	0	2	0.8	1.000
11 yrs.			68	69	.496	4.65	291	140	54	1232.1	1417	468	403	7	14	20	13	433	93	0	.215	57	222	13	11	1.0	.955

John Wells

WELLS, JOHN FREDERICK
B. Nov. 25, 1922, Junction City, Kans.   BR TR 5'11½" 180 lbs.

Year	Team		W	L	PCT	ERA	G	GS	CG	IP	H	BB	SO	ShO	W	L	SV	AB	H	HR	BA	PO	A	E	DP	TC/G	FA
1944	BKN	N	0	2	.000	5.40	4	2	0	15	18	11	7	0	0	1	0	4	1	0	.250	0	1	0	1	0.5	1.000

Chris Welsh

WELSH, CHRISTOPHER CHARLES
B. Apr. 14, 1955, Wilmington, Del.   BL TL 6'2" 185 lbs.

Year	Team		W	L	PCT	ERA	G	GS	CG	IP	H	BB	SO	ShO	W	L	SV	AB	H	HR	BA	PO	A	E	DP	TC/G	FA
1981	SD	N	6	7	.462	3.77	22	19	4	124	122	41	51	2	0	0	0	41	6	0	.146	3	30	0	0	1.5	1.000
1982			8	8	.500	4.91	28	20	3	139.1	146	63	48	1	1	2	0	42	11	0	.262	7	29	2	0	1.4	.947
1983	2 teams		SD N	(7G 0-1)		MON N	(16G 0-1)																				
"	total		0	2	.000	4.42	23	6	0	59	59	20	22	0	0	1	0	18	4	0	.222	3	15	2	2	0.9	.900
1985	TEX	A	2	5	.286	4.13	25	6	0	76.1	101	25	31	0	1	1	0	0	0	0	–	1	10	0	1	0.4	1.000
1986	CIN	N	6	9	.400	4.78	24	24	1	139.1	163	40	40	0	0	0	0	42	5	1	.119	7	23	0	1	1.3	1.000
5 yrs.			22	31	.415	4.45	122	75	8	538	591	189	192	3	2	4	0	143	26	1	.182	21	107	4	4	1.1	.970

Dick Welteroth

WELTEROTH, RICHARD JOHN
B. Aug. 3, 1927, Williamsport, Pa.   BR TR 5'11" 165 lbs.

Year	Team		W	L	PCT	ERA	G	GS	CG	IP	H	BB	SO	ShO	W	L	SV	AB	H	HR	BA	PO	A	E	DP	TC/G	FA
1948	WAS	A	2	1	.667	5.51	33	2	0	65.1	73	50	16	0	1	1	1	10	1	0	.100	1	11	0	1	0.4	1.000
1949			2	5	.286	7.36	52	2	0	95.1	107	89	37	0	2	3	2	17	1	0	.059	3	18	0	1	0.4	1.000
1950			0	0	–	3.00	5	0	0	6	5	6	2	0	0	0	0	0	0	0	–	0	2	0	0	0.4	1.000
3 yrs.			4	6	.400	6.48	90	4	0	166.2	185	145	55	0	3	4	3	27	2	0	.074	4	31	0	1	0.4	1.000

Tony Welzer

WELZER, ANTON FRANK
B. Apr. 5, 1899, Germany   D. Mar. 18, 1971, Milwaukee, Wis.   BR TR 5'11" 160 lbs.

Year	Team		W	L	PCT	ERA	G	GS	CG	IP	H	BB	SO	ShO	W	L	SV	AB	H	HR	BA	PO	A	E	DP	TC/G	FA
1926	BOS	A	4	3	.571	4.79	40	6	1	141	167	57	30	1	2	1	0	38	8	0	.211	7	55	1	1	1.6	.984
1927			6	11	.353	4.46	37	19	8	181.2	214	71	56	0	1	2	1	42	4	0	.095	3	45	2	4	1.4	.960
2 yrs.			10	14	.417	4.60	77	25	9	322.2	381	128	86	1	3	3	1	80	12	0	.150	10	100	3	5	1.5	.973

Butch Wensloff

WENSLOFF, CHARLES WILLIAM
B. Dec. 3, 1915, Sausalito, Calif.   BR TR 5'11" 185 lbs.

Year	Team		W	L	PCT	ERA	G	GS	CG	IP	H	BB	SO	ShO	W	L	SV	AB	H	HR	BA	PO	A	E	DP	TC/G	FA
1943	NY	A	13	11	.542	2.54	29	27	18	223.1	179	70	105	1	0	0	1	79	14	0	.177	4	46	4	0	1.9	.926
1947			3	1	.750	2.61	11	5	1	51.2	41	22	18	0	0	1	0	19	5	0	.263	3	4	0	0	0.6	1.000
1948	CLE	A	0	1	.000	10.80	1	0	0	1.2	2	3	2	0	0	1	0	0	0	0	–	0	0	0	0	0.0	–
3 yrs.			16	13	.552	2.60	41	32	19	276.2	222	95	125	1	0	2	1	98	19	0	.194	7	50	4	2	1.5	.934

WORLD SERIES

Year	Team		W	L	PCT	ERA	G	GS	CG	IP	H	BB	SO	ShO	W	L	SV	AB	H	HR	BA	PO	A	E	DP	TC/G	FA
1947	NY	A	0	0	–	0.00	1	0	0	2	0	0	0	0	0	0	0	0	0	0	–	0	1	0	0	1.0	1.000

Fred Wenz

WENZ, FREDERICK CHARLES (Fireball)
B. Aug. 26, 1941, Bound Brook, N. J.   BR TR 6'3" 214 lbs.

Year	Team		W	L	PCT	ERA	G	GS	CG	IP	H	BB	SO	ShO	W	L	SV	AB	H	HR	BA	PO	A	E	DP	TC/G	FA
1968	BOS	A	0	0	–	0.00	1	0	0	1	0	2	3	0	0	0	0	0	0	0	–	0	0	0	0	0.0	–
1969			1	0	1.000	5.73	8	0	0	11	9	10	11	0	1	0	0	0	0	0	–	1	1	0	0	0.3	1.000
1970	PHI	N	2	0	1.000	4.50	22	0	0	30	27	13	24	0	2	0	1	5	0	0	.000	1	1	0	0	0.1	1.000
3 yrs.			3	0	1.000	4.71	31	0	0	42	36	25	38	0	3	0	1	5	0	0	.000	2	2	0	0	0.1	1.000

Perry Werden

WERDEN, PERCIVAL WHERITT (Moose)
B. July 21, 1865, St. Louis, Mo.   D. Jan. 9, 1934, Minneapolis, Minn.   BR TR 6'2" 220 lbs.

Year	Team		W	L	PCT	ERA	G	GS	CG	IP	H	BB	SO	ShO	W	L	SV	AB	H	HR	BA	PO	A	E	DP	TC/G	FA
1884	STL	U	12	1	.923	1.97	16	16	12	141.1	113	22	51	1	0	0	0	*				14	36	6	1	3.5	.893

Bill Werle

WERLE, WILLIAM GEORGE (Bugs)
B. Dec. 21, 1920, Oakland, Calif.   BL TL 6'2½" 182 lbs.

Year	Team		W	L	PCT	ERA	G	GS	CG	IP	H	BB	SO	ShO	W	L	SV	AB	H	HR	BA	PO	A	E	DP	TC/G	FA
1949	PIT	N	12	13	.480	4.24	35	29	10	221	243	51	106	2	2	1	0	77	9	0	.117	7	43	2	3	1.5	.962
1950			8	16	.333	4.60	48	22	6	215.1	249	65	78	0	2	5	8	67	13	0	.194	11	58	2	4	1.5	.972
1951			8	6	.571	5.65	59	9	2	149.2	181	51	59	0	4	2	6	40	12	0	.300	10	42	0	3	0.9	1.000
1952	2 teams		PIT N	(5G 0-0)		STL N	(19G 1-2)																				
"	total		1	2	.333	5.23	24	0	0	43	49	16	24	0	1	2	1	9	1	0	.111	4	14	2	3	0.8	.900
1953	BOS	A	0	1	.000	1.54	5	0	0	11.2	7	1	4	0	0	1	0	2	0	0	.000	0	6	0	1	1.2	1.000

Year	Team		W	L	PCT	ERA	G	GS	CG	IP	H	BB	SO	ShO	W	L	SV	AB	H	HR	BA	PO	A	E	DP	TC/G	FA
															Relief Pitching			Batting									

Bill Werle *continued*

Year	Team		W	L	PCT	ERA	G	GS	CG	IP	H	BB	SO	ShO	W	L	SV	AB	H	HR	BA	PO	A	E	DP	TC/G	FA
1954			0	1	.000	4.38	14	0	0	24.2	41	10	14	0	0	1	0	4	0	0	.000	0	4	0	0	0.3	1.000
6 yrs.			29	39	.426	4.69	185	60	18	665.1	770	194	285	2	9	12	15	199	35	0	.176	32	167	6	14	1.1	.971

George Werley
WERLEY, GEORGE WILLIAM B. Sept. 8, 1938, St. Louis, Mo. BR TR 6'2" 196 lbs.

Year	Team		W	L	PCT	ERA	G	GS	CG	IP	H	BB	SO	ShO	W	L	SV	AB	H	HR	BA	PO	A	E	DP	TC/G	FA
1956	BAL	A	0	0	—	9.00	1	0	0	1	1	2	0	0	0	0	0	0	0	0	—	1	0	0	0	1.0	1.000

Johnny Wertz
WERTZ, HENRY LEVI B. Apr. 20, 1898, Pomaria, S. C. BR TR 5'10" 180 lbs.

Year	Team		W	L	PCT	ERA	G	GS	CG	IP	H	BB	SO	ShO	W	L	SV	AB	H	HR	BA	PO	A	E	DP	TC/G	FA
1926	BOS	N	11	9	.550	3.28	32	23	7	189.1	212	47	65	1	3	0	0	64	17	1	.266	14	54	2	2	2.2	.971
1927			4	10	.286	4.55	42	15	4	164.1	204	52	39	0	1	3	1	43	7	0	.163	8	32	3	1	1.0	.930
1928			0	2	.000	10.31	10	2	0	18.1	31	8	5	0	0	0	0	3	1	0	.333	1	5	0	0	0.6	1.000
1929			0	0	—	10.50	4	0	0	6	13	4	2	0	0	0	0	1	1	0	1.000	0	1	0	0	0.3	1.000
4 yrs.			15	21	.417	4.29	88	40	11	378	460	111	111	1	4	3	2	111	26	1	.234	23	92	5	3	1.4	.958

David West
WEST, DAVID LEE B. Sept. 1, 1964, Memphis, Tenn. BL TL 6'6" 205 lbs.

Year	Team		W	L	PCT	ERA	G	GS	CG	IP	H	BB	SO	ShO	W	L	SV	AB	H	HR	BA	PO	A	E	DP	TC/G	FA
1988	NY	N	1	0	1.000	3.00	2	1	0	6	6	3	3	0	0	0	0	2	2	0	1.000	1	0	0	0	0.5	1.000
1989	2 teams	NY N (11G 0–2)				MIN A (10G 3–2)																					
"	total		3	4	.429	6.79	21	7	0	63.2	73	33	50	0	0	0	0	2	1	0	.200	2	1	0	0	0.2	.800
2 yrs.			4	4	.500	6.46	23	8	0	69.2	79	36	53	0	0	0	0	7	3	0	.429	3	2	1	0	0.3	.833

Frank West
WEST, FRANK B. 1873, Wilmerding, Pa. Deceased.

Year	Team		W	L	PCT	ERA	G	GS	CG	IP	H	BB	SO	ShO	W	L	SV	AB	H	HR	BA	PO	A	E	DP	TC/G	FA
1894	BOS	N	0	0	—	9.00	1	0	0	3	5	2	1	0	0	0	0	1	0	0	.000	0	0	0	0	0.0	—

Hi West
WEST, JAMES HIRAM B. Aug. 8, 1884, Roseville, Ill. D. May 25, 1963, Los Angeles, Calif. BR TR 6' 185 lbs.

Year	Team		W	L	PCT	ERA	G	GS	CG	IP	H	BB	SO	ShO	W	L	SV	AB	H	HR	BA	PO	A	E	DP	TC/G	FA
1905	CLE	A	2	2	.500	4.09	6	4	4	33	43	10	15	1	0	0	0	13	1	0	.077	0	3	1	0	0.7	.750
1911			3	4	.429	3.76	13	8	3	64.2	84	18	17	0	0	0	1	23	3	0	.130	3	13	1	1	1.3	.941
2 yrs.			5	6	.455	3.87	19	12	7	97.2	127	28	32	1	0	0	1	36	4	0	.111	3	16	2	1	1.1	.905

Lefty West
WEST, WELDON EDISON B. Sept. 3, 1915, Gibsonville, N. C. D. July 23, 1979, Hendersonville, N. C. BR TL 6' 165 lbs.

Year	Team		W	L	PCT	ERA	G	GS	CG	IP	H	BB	SO	ShO	W	L	SV	AB	H	HR	BA	PO	A	E	DP	TC/G	FA
1944	STL	A	0	0	—	6.29	11	0	0	24.1	34	19	11	0	0	0	0	7	1	0	.143	0	3	0	0	0.3	1.000
1945			3	4	.429	3.63	24	8	1	74.1	71	31	38	0	1	0	0	27	2	0	.074	2	7	0	0	0.4	1.000
2 yrs.			3	4	.429	4.29	35	8	1	98.2	105	50	49	0	1	0	0	34	3	0	.088	2	10	0	0	0.3	1.000

Huyler Westervelt
WESTERVELT, HUYLER B. Oct. 1, 1870, Piermont, N. Y. Deceased.

Year	Team		W	L	PCT	ERA	G	GS	CG	IP	H	BB	SO	ShO	W	L	SV	AB	H	HR	BA	PO	A	E	DP	TC/G	FA
1894	NY	N	7	10	.412	5.04	23	18	11	141	170	76	35	1	1	0	0	56	8	0	.143	13	24	6	3	1.9	.860

Mickey Weston
WESTON, MICHAEL LEE B. Mar. 26, 1961, Flint, Mich. BR TR 6'1" 180 lbs.

Year	Team		W	L	PCT	ERA	G	GS	CG	IP	H	BB	SO	ShO	W	L	SV	AB	H	HR	BA	PO	A	E	DP	TC/G	FA
1989	BAL	A	1	0	1.000	5.54	7	0	0	13	18	2	7	0	1	0	0	0	0	0	—	0	1	0	0	0.1	1.000

John Wetteland
WETTELAND, JOHN KARL B. Aug. 22, 1966, San Mateo, Calif. BR TR 6'2" 195 lbs.

Year	Team		W	L	PCT	ERA	G	GS	CG	IP	H	BB	SO	ShO	W	L	SV	AB	H	HR	BA	PO	A	E	DP	TC/G	FA
1989	LA	N	5	8	.385	3.77	31	12	0	102.2	81	34	96	0	3	2	1	21	3	0	.143	5	8	2	0	0.5	.867

Buzz Wetzel
WETZEL, CHARLES EDWARD B. Aug. 25, 1894, Jay, Okla. D. Mar. 7, 1941, Globe, Ariz. BR TR 6'1" 162 lbs.

Year	Team		W	L	PCT	ERA	G	GS	CG	IP	H	BB	SO	ShO	W	L	SV	AB	H	HR	BA	PO	A	E	DP	TC/G	FA
1927	PHI	A	0	0	—	7.71	2	1	0	4.2	8	5	0	0	0	0	0	1	1	0	1.000	0	2	0	0	1.0	1.000

Shorty Wetzel
WETZEL, GEORGE WILLIAM B. 1868, Philadelphia, Pa. D. Feb. 25, 1899, Dayton, Ohio

Year	Team		W	L	PCT	ERA	G	GS	CG	IP	H	BB	SO	ShO	W	L	SV	AB	H	HR	BA	PO	A	E	DP	TC/G	FA
1885	BAL	AA	0	2	.000	8.00	2	2	2	18	27	9	6	0	0	0	0	7	0	0	.000	4	6	0	1	5.0	1.000

Stefan Wever
WEVER, STEFAN MATTHEW B. Apr. 22, 1958, Marburg, West Germany BR TR 6'8" 245 lbs.

Year	Team		W	L	PCT	ERA	G	GS	CG	IP	H	BB	SO	ShO	W	L	SV	AB	H	HR	BA	PO	A	E	DP	TC/G	FA
1982	NY	A	0	1	.000	27.00	1	1	0	2.2	6	3	2	0	0	0	0	0	0	0	—	0	0	0	0	0.0	—

Gus Weyhing
WEYHING, AUGUST (Rubber Arm Gus) Brother of John Weyhing. B. Sept. 29, 1866, Louisville, Ky. D. Sept. 4, 1955, Louisville, Ky. BR TR 5'10" 145 lbs.

Year	Team		W	L	PCT	ERA	G	GS	CG	IP	H	BB	SO	ShO	W	L	SV	AB	H	HR	BA	PO	A	E	DP	TC/G	FA
1887	PHI	AA	26	28	.481	4.27	55	55	53	466.1	465	167	193	2	0	0	0	209	42	0	.201	18	88	24	5	2.4	.815
1888			28	18	.609	2.25	47	47	45	404	314	111	204	3	0	0	0	184	40	1	.217	22	93	17	1	2.8	.871
1889			30	21	.588	2.95	54	53	50	449	382	212	213	4	0	0	0	191	25	0	.131	12	71	8	2	1.7	.912
1890	BKN	P	30	16	.652	3.60	49	46	38	390	419	179	177	3	1	1	0	165	27	1	.164	12	55	12	2	1.6	.848
1891	PHI	AA	31	20	.608	3.18	52	51	51	450	428	161	219	3	0	0	0	198	22	0	.111	27	73	8	2	2.1	.926
1892	PHI	N	32	21	.604	2.66	59	49	46	469.2	411	168	202	6	4	0	3	214	29	0	.136	20	63	20	2	1.7	.806
1893			23	16	.590	4.74	42	40	33	345.1	399	145	101	2	1	1	0	147	22	0	.150	31	56	5	3	2.2	.946
1894			16	14	.533	5.81	38	34	25	266.1	365	116	81	2	1	0	1	115	20	0	.174	15	33	4	1	1.4	.923
1895	3 teams	PHI N (2G 0–2)				PIT N (1G 1–0)					LOU N (28G 7–19)																	
"	total		8	21	.276	5.81	31	28	23	231	318	84	61	1	1	0	0	97	21	1	.216	13	54	7	3	2.4	.905
1896	LOU	N	2	3	.400	6.64	5	5	4	42	62	15	9	0	1	0	0	15	2	0	.133	2	17	2	1	4.2	.905
1898	WAS	N	15	26	.366	4.51	45	42	39	361	428	84	92	0	0	1	0	141	25	0	.177	16	73	8	2	2.2	.918

Year	Team	W	L	PCT	ERA	G	GS	CG	IP	H	BB	SO	ShO	W	L	SV	AB	H	HR	BA	PO	A	E	DP	TC/G	FA
														Relief Pitching			Batting									

Gus Weyhing *continued*

Year	Team	W	L	PCT	ERA	G	GS	CG	IP	H	BB	SO	ShO	W	L	SV	AB	H	HR	BA	PO	A	E	DP	TC/G	FA
1899		17	23	.425	4.54	43	38	34	334.2	414	76	96	2	1	0	0	126	26	0	.206	7	50	10	2	1.6	.851
1900	**2 teams**		STL N	(7G 3–4)		BKN N	(8G 3–3)																			
"	total	6	7	.462	4.47	15	13	6	94.2	126	41	14	0	1	0	0	39	6	0	.154	6	16	3	1	1.7	.880
1901	**2 teams**		CLE A	(2G 0–0)		CIN N	(1G 0–1)																			
"	total	0	1	.000	5.75	3	2	1	20.1	31	7	3	0	0	0	0	0	0	0	.000	0	4	0	0	1.3	1.000
14 yrs.		264	235	.529	3.89	538	503	448	4324.1	4562	1566	1665	28	10	3	4	1849	307	3	.166	201	746	128	27	2.0	.881
											8th															

John Weyhing

WEYHING, JOHN
Brother of Gus Weyhing.
B. June 24, 1869, Louisville, Ky. D. June 20, 1890, Louisville, Ky.

BL TL 6'2" 185 lbs.

Year	Team	W	L	PCT	ERA	G	GS	CG	IP	H	BB	SO	ShO	W	L	SV	AB	H	HR	BA	PO	A	E	DP	TC/G	FA
1888	CIN AA	3	4	.429	1.23	8	8	7	65.2	52	17	30	0	0	0	0	23	3	0	.130	6	9	1	0	2.0	.938
1889	COL AA	0	0	–	27.00	1	0	0	1	4	4	0	0	0	0	0	0	0	0	–	0	0	0	0	0.0	–
2 yrs.		3	4	.429	1.62	9	8	7	66.2	53	21	30	0	0	0	0	23	3	0	.130	6	9	1	0	1.8	.938

Lee Wheat

WHEAT, LEROY WILLIAM
B. Sept. 15, 1929, Edwardsville, Ill.

BR TR 6'4" 200 lbs.

Year	Team	W	L	PCT	ERA	G	GS	CG	IP	H	BB	SO	ShO	W	L	SV	AB	H	HR	BA	PO	A	E	DP	TC/G	FA
1954	PHI A	0	2	.000	5.72	8	3	1	28.1	38	9	7	0	0	2	0	8	1	0	.125	3	3	0	1	0.8	1.000
1955	KC A	0	0	–	22.50	3	0	0	2	8	3	1	0	0	0	0	0	0	0	–	0	1	0	0	0.3	1.000
2 yrs.		0	2	.000	6.82	11	3	1	30.1	46	12	8	0	0	2	0	8	1	0	.125	3	4	0	1	0.6	1.000

Charlie Wheatley

WHEATLEY, CHARLES
B. June 27, 1893, Rosedale, Kans. D. Dec. 10, 1982, Tulsa, Okla.

BR TR 5'11" 174 lbs.

Year	Team	W	L	PCT	ERA	G	GS	CG	IP	H	BB	SO	ShO	W	L	SV	AB	H	HR	BA	PO	A	E	DP	TC/G	FA
1912	DET A	1	4	.200	6.17	5	5	2	35	45	17	14	0	0	0	0	12	0	0	.000	1	13	1	0	3.0	.933

Woody Wheaton

WHEATON, ELWOOD PIERCE
B. Oct. 3, 1914, Philadelphia, Pa.

BL TL 5'8½" 160 lbs.

Year	Team	W	L	PCT	ERA	G	GS	CG	IP	H	BB	SO	ShO	W	L	SV	AB	H	HR	BA	PO	A	E	DP	TC/G	FA
1944	PHI A	0	1	.000	3.55	11	1	1	38	36	20	15	0	0	0	0	*				0	4	0	0	0.4	1.000

George Wheeler

WHEELER, GEORGE L.
Born George L. Heroux.
B. Aug. 3, 1869, Methuen, Mass. D. Mar. 23, 1946, Santa Ana, Calif.

BB TB

Year	Team	W	L	PCT	ERA	G	GS	CG	IP	H	BB	SO	ShO	W	L	SV	AB	H	HR	BA	PO	A	E	DP	TC/G	FA
1896	PHI N	1	1	.500	3.86	3	2	2	16.1	18	5	5	0	0	0	0	9	1	0	.111	0	6	0	0	2.0	1.000
1897		11	10	.524	3.96	26	19	17	191	229	62	35	0	3	0	0	79	16	0	.203	10	48	3	3	2.3	.951
1898		6	8	.429	4.17	15	13	10	112.1	155	36	20	0	1	0	0	43	8	0	.186	8	41	6	0	3.7	.891
1899		3	1	.750	6.00	6	5	3	39	44	13	3	0	0	0	0	17	4	1	.235	1	11	1	0	2.2	.923
4 yrs.		21	20	.512	4.24	50	39	32	358.2	446	116	60	0	4	0	0	148	29	1	.196	19	106	10	3	2.7	.926

Harry Wheeler

WHEELER, HARRY EUGENE
B. Mar. 3, 1858, Versailles, Ind. D. Oct. 9, 1900, Cincinnati, Ohio
Manager 1884.

BR TR 5'11" 165 lbs.

Year	Team	W	L	PCT	ERA	G	GS	CG	IP	H	BB	SO	ShO	W	L	SV	AB	H	HR	BA	PO	A	E	DP	TC/G	FA
1878	PRO N	6	1	.857	3.48	7	6	6	62	70	25	25	0	1	0	0	27	4	0	.148	2	5	1	0	1.1	.875
1879	CIN N	0	1	.000	81.00	1	1	0	1	6	4	0	0	0	0	0	3	0	0	.000	0	0	0	0	0.0	–
1882	CIN AA	1	2	.333	5.40	4	1	1	21.2	21	12	10	0	1	1	0	344	86	1	.250	1	5	0	0	1.5	1.000
1883	COL AA	1	0	.000	7.20	1	1	0	5	13	2	0	0	0	0	0	371	84	1	.226	0	2	3	0	5.0	.400
1884	**3 teams**		STL AA	(0G 0–0)		KC U	(1G 0–1)		U	(0G 0–0)																
"	total	0	1	.000	1.13	1	1	1	8	7	0	6	0	0	0	0	308	75	1	.244	1	2	0	0	3.0	1.000
5 yrs.		7	6	.538	4.70	14	10	8	97.2	117	43	41	0	2	1	0	*				4	14	4	0	1.6	.818

Rip Wheeler

WHEELER, FLOYD CLARK
B. Mar. 2, 1898, Marion, Ky. D. Sept. 18, 1968, Marion, Ky.

BR TR 6' 180 lbs.

Year	Team	W	L	PCT	ERA	G	GS	CG	IP	H	BB	SO	ShO	W	L	SV	AB	H	HR	BA	PO	A	E	DP	TC/G	FA
1921	PIT N	0	0	–	9.00	1	0	0	3	6	1	0	0	0	0	0	1	0	0	.000	0	2	0	0	2.0	1.000
1922		0	0	–	0.00	1	0	0	1	2	0	0	0	0	0	0	0	0	0	–	0	1	0	0	1.0	1.000
1923	CHI N	1	2	.333	4.88	3	3	1	24	28	5	5	0	0	0	0	9	1	0	.111	2	10	0	1	4.0	1.000
1924		3	6	.333	3.91	29	4	0	101.1	103	21	16	0	2	3	0	32	7	0	.219	4	28	0	0	1.1	1.000
4 yrs.		4	8	.333	4.18	34	7	1	129.1	138	29	21	0	2	3	0	42	8	0	.190	6	41	0	1	1.4	1.000

Gary Wheelock

WHEELOCK, GARY RICHARD
B. Nov. 29, 1951, Bakersfield, Calif.

BR TR 6'3" 205 lbs.

Year	Team	W	L	PCT	ERA	G	GS	CG	IP	H	BB	SO	ShO	W	L	SV	AB	H	HR	BA	PO	A	E	DP	TC/G	FA
1976	CAL A	0	0	–	27.00	2	0	0	2	6	1	2	0	0	0	0	0	0	0	–	0	0	0	0	0.0	–
1977	SEA A	6	9	.400	4.91	17	17	2	88	94	26	47	0	0	0	0	0	0	0	–	10	9	2	0	1.2	.905
1980		0	0	–	6.00	1	1	0	3	4	1	1	0	0	0	0	0	0	0	–	0	1	0	0	1.0	1.000
3 yrs.		6	9	.400	5.42	20	18	2	93	104	28	50	0	0	0	0	0	0	0	–	10	10	2	0	1.1	.909

Jack Whillock

WHILLOCK, JACK FRANKLIN
B. Nov. 4, 1942, Clinton, Ark.

BR TR 6'3" 195 lbs.

Year	Team	W	L	PCT	ERA	G	GS	CG	IP	H	BB	SO	ShO	W	L	SV	AB	H	HR	BA	PO	A	E	DP	TC/G	FA
1971	DET A	0	2	.000	5.63	7	0	0	8	10	2	6	0	0	2	1	1	0	0	.000	0	2	0	0	0.3	1.000

Pat Whitaker

WHITAKER, WILLIAM H.
B. 1865, St. Louis, Mo. D. July 15, 1902, St. Louis, Mo.

TR

Year	Team	W	L	PCT	ERA	G	GS	CG	IP	H	BB	SO	ShO	W	L	SV	AB	H	HR	BA	PO	A	E	DP	TC/G	FA
1888	BAL AA	1	1	.500	5.14	2	2	2	14	13	6	5	0	0	0	0	6	0	0	.000	0	11	0	0	5.5	1.000
1889		1	0	1.000	2.00	1	1	1	9	10	4	1	0	0	0	0	4	1	0	.250	1	3	0	0	4.0	1.000
2 yrs.		2	1	.667	3.91	3	3	3	23	23	10	6	0	0	0	0	10	1	0	.100	1	14	0	0	5.0	1.000

Bill Whitby

WHITBY, WILLIAM EDWARD
B. July 29, 1943, Crewe, Va.

BR TR 6'1" 190 lbs.

Year	Team	W	L	PCT	ERA	G	GS	CG	IP	H	BB	SO	ShO	W	L	SV	AB	H	HR	BA	PO	A	E	DP	TC/G	FA
1964	MIN A	0	0	–	8.53	4	0	0	6.1	8	1	2	0	0	0	0	1	0	0	.000	0	1	0	0	0.3	1.000

Year	Team		W	L	PCT	ERA	G	GS	CG	IP	H	BB	SO	ShO	Relief Pitching W	L	SV	Batting AB	H	HR	BA	PO	A	E	DP	TC/G	FA

Bob Whitcher

WHITCHER, ROBERT ARTHUR
B. Apr. 29, 1917, Berlin, N. H.

BL TL 5'8" 165 lbs.

| 1945 | BOS | N | 0 | 2 | .000 | 2.87 | 6 | 3 | 0 | 15.2 | 12 | 12 | 6 | 0 | 0 | 0 | 0 | 3 | 1 | 0 | .333 | 1 | 2 | 0 | 1 | 0.5 | 1.000 |

Ade White

WHITE, ADEL
B. May 16, 1904, Winder, Ga. D. Oct. 1, 1978, Atlanta, Ga.

BR TL 6' 185 lbs.

| 1937 | STL | N | 0 | 1 | .000 | 6.75 | 5 | 0 | 0 | 9.1 | 14 | 3 | 2 | 0 | 1 | 0 | 0 | 1 | 1 | 0 | 1.000 | 0 | 2 | 0 | 0 | 0.4 | 1.000 |

Bill White

WHITE, WILLIAM DIGHTON
B. May 1, 1860, Bridgeport, Ohio   D. Dec. 31, 1924, Bellaire, Ohio

| 1886 | LOU | AA | 0 | 0 | – | 9.00 | 1 | 0 | 0 | 1 | 2 | 2 | 1 | 0 | 0 | 0 | 0 | * | | | | | 0 | 1 | 0 | 2.0 | .500 |

Deacon White

WHITE, JAMES LAURIE
Brother of Will White.
B. Dec. 7, 1847, Caton, N. Y.   D. July 7, 1939, Aurora, Ill.
Manager 1872, 1879.

BL TR 5'11" 175 lbs.

1876	CHI	N	0	0	–	0.00	1	0	0	2	1	0	3	0	0	0	1	303	104	1	.343	0	1	0	0	1.0	1.000
1890	BUF	P	0	0	–	9.00	1	0	0	8	18	2	0	0	0	0	0	439	114	0	.260	0	0	0	0	0.0	–
2 yrs.			0	0		7.20	2	0	0	10	19	2	3	0	0	0	1	*				0	1	0	0	0.5	1.000

Deke White

WHITE, GEORGE FREDERICK
B. Sept. 8, 1872, Albany, N. Y. D. Nov. 27, 1957, Albany, N. Y.

BB TL

| 1895 | PHI | N | 1 | 0 | 1.000 | 9.87 | 3 | 1 | 0 | 17.1 | 17 | 13 | 6 | 0 | 1 | 0 | 0 | 8 | 1 | 0 | .125 | 1 | 2 | 0 | 0 | 1.0 | 1.000 |

Doc White

WHITE, GUY HARRIS
B. Apr. 9, 1879, Washington, D. C. D. Feb. 19, 1969, Silver Springs, Md.

BL TL 6'1" 165 lbs.

1901	PHI	N	14	13	.519	3.19	31	27	22	236.2	241	56	132	1	0	1	0	95	26	1	.274	6	72	4	0	2.6	.951
1902			16	20	.444	2.53	36	35	34	306	277	72	185	3	0	1	0	179	47	1	.263	11	83	7	0	2.8	.931
1903	CHI	A	17	16	.515	2.13	37	36	29	300	258	69	114	3	0	0	0	99	20	0	.202	25	98	4	5	3.4	.969
1904			16	12	.571	1.78	30	30	23	228	201	68	115	7	0	0	0	76	12	0	.158	29	68	5	2	3.4	.951
1905			18	14	.563	1.76	36	33	25	260.1	204	58	120	4	1	0	0	86	14	0	.163	20	75	4	2	2.8	.960
1906			18	6	.750	1.52	28	24	20	219.1	160	38	95	7	2	1	0	65	12	0	.185	16	77	8	1	3.6	.921
1907			27	13	.675	2.26	46	35	24	291	270	38	141	7	5	1	1	90	20	0	.222	33	103	2	1	3.0	.986
1908			18	13	.581	2.55	41	37	24	296	267	69	126	5	0	0	0	109	25	0	.229	28	116	2	7	3.6	.986
1909			11	9	.550	1.72	24	21	14	177.2	149	31	77	3	1	0	0	192	45	0	.234	15	47	3	0	2.7	.954
1910			15	13	.536	2.56	33	29	20	245.2	219	50	111	2	1	0	1	126	25	0	.198	30	76	3	4	3.3	.972
1911			10	14	.417	2.98	34	29	16	214.1	219	35	72	4	1	0	2	78	20	0	.256	11	57	6	2	2.2	.919
1912			8	10	.444	3.24	32	19	9	172	172	47	57	1	2	2	0	56	7	0	.125	5	46	0	1	1.6	1.000
1913			2	4	.333	3.50	19	8	2	103	106	39	39	0	1	0	0	25	3	0	.120	2	44	2	0	2.5	.958
13 yrs.			190	157	.548	2.38	427	363	262	3050	2743	670	1384	46	14	6	5	*				231	962	50	25	2.9	.960

WORLD SERIES

| 1906 | CHI | A | 1 | 1 | .500 | 1.80 | 3 | 2 | 1 | 15 | 12 | 7 | 4 | 0 | 0 | 0 | 1 | 3 | 0 | 0 | .000 | 1 | 3 | 0 | 0 | 1.3 | 1.000 |

Ernie White

WHITE, ERNEST DANIEL
B. Sept. 5, 1916, Pacolet Mills, S. C. D. May 22, 1974, Augusta, Ga.

BR TL 5'11½" 175 lbs.

1940	STL	N	1	1	.500	4.15	8	1	1	21.2	29	14	15	0	1	0	0	7	3	0	.429	1	7	0	1	1.0	1.000
1941			17	7	.708	2.40	32	25	12	210	169	70	117	3	3	0	2	79	15	0	.190	10	25	3	0	1.2	.921
1942			7	5	.583	2.52	26	19	7	128.1	113	41	67	1	1	0	2	41	8	0	.195	3	16	1	1	0.8	.950
1943			5	5	.500	3.78	14	10	5	78.2	78	33	28	1	0	1	0	28	6	0	.214	3	12	0	1	1.1	1.000
1946	BOS	N	0	1	.000	4.18	12	1	0	23.2	22	12	8	0	0	0	0	4	1	0	.250	2	1	0	0	0.3	1.000
1947			0	0	–	0.00	1	1	0	4	1	1	1	0	0	0	0	1	1	0	1.000	0	0	0	0	0.3	–
1948			0	2	.000	1.96	15	0	0	23	13	17	8	0	0	2	2	3	0	0	.000	0	2	2	0	0.3	.500
7 yrs.			30	21	.588	2.78	108	57	24	489.1	425	188	244	5	5	3	6	163	34	0	.209	19	63	6	2	0.8	.932

WORLD SERIES

| 1942 | STL | N | 1 | 0 | 1.000 | 0.00 | 1 | 1 | 1 | 9 | 6 | 1 | 6 | 1 | 0 | 0 | 0 | 2 | 0 | 0 | .000 | 0 | 0 | 0 | 0 | 0.0 | – |

Hal White

WHITE, HAROLD GEORGE
B. Mar. 18, 1919, Utica, N. Y.

BL TR 5'10" 165 lbs.

1941	DET	A	0	0	–	6.00	4	0	0	9	11	6	2	0	0	0	0	2	0	0	.000	2	0	0	0	0.8	1.000
1942			12	12	.500	2.91	34	25	12	216.2	212	82	93	4	1	3	1	77	13	0	.169	20	41	6	6	2.0	.910
1943			7	12	.368	3.39	32	24	7	177.2	150	71	58	2	0	2	2	57	8	0	.140	12	38	1	0	1.6	.980
1946			1	1	.500	5.60	11	1	1	27.1	34	15	12	0	1	0	0	7	0	0	.000	3	6	0	1	0.8	1.000
1947			4	5	.444	3.61	35	5	0	84.2	91	47	33	0	2	2	4	18	3	0	.167	4	22	3	0	0.8	.897
1948			2	1	.667	6.12	27	0	0	42.2	46	26	17	0	2	1	1	13	2	0	.154	2	4	0	0	0.2	1.000
1949			1	0	1.000	0.00	9	0	0	12	5	4	4	0	1	0	2	3	1	0	.333	1	5	0	0	0.7	1.000
1950			9	6	.600	4.54	42	8	3	111	96	65	53	1	6	4	4	33	4	0	.121	8	19	1	1	0.7	.964
1951			3	4	.429	4.74	38	4	0	76	74	49	23	0	2	1	4	16	4	0	.250	5	21	2	2	0.7	.929
1952			1	8	.111	3.69	41	0	0	63.1	53	39	18	0	1	8	5	11	2	0	.182	3	18	0	0	0.5	1.000
1953	2 teams		STL A	(10G 0–0)		STL N	(49G 6–5)																				
"	total		6	5	.545	2.94	59	0	0	95	92	42	34	0	6	3	7	17	0	0	.000	8	21	2	1	0.5	.935
1954	STL	N	0	0	–	19.80	4	0	0	5	11	4	2	0	0	0	0	1	0	0	.000	1	0	0	0	0.3	1.000
12 yrs.			46	54	.460	3.78	336	67	23	920.1	875	450	349	7	23	26	25	255	37	0	.145	68	197	15	13	0.8	.946

Kirby White

WHITE, OLIVER KIRBY (Redbuck, Buck)
B. Jan. 3, 1884, Hillsboro, Ohio D. Apr. 22, 1943, Hillsboro, Ohio

BL TR 6' 190 lbs.

| 1909 | BOS | N | 6 | 13 | .316 | 3.22 | 23 | 19 | 11 | 148.1 | 134 | 80 | 53 | 0 | 1 | 0 | 0 | 50 | 8 | 0 | .160 | 6 | 37 | 6 | 1 | 2.1 | .878 |

Year	Team	W	L	PCT	ERA	G	GS	CG	IP	H	BB	SO	ShO	W	L	SV	AB	H	HR	BA	PO	A	E	DP	TC/G	FA

Kirby White *continued*

Year	Team	W	L	PCT	ERA	G	GS	CG	IP	H	BB	SO	ShO	W	L	SV	AB	H	HR	BA	PO	A	E	DP	TC/G	FA
1910	2 teams	BOS N	(3G 1–2)		PIT N	(30G 10–9)																				
"	total	11	11	.500	3.16	33	24	10	179.1	157	87	48	3	2	1	2	52	14	0	.269	5	41	6	1	1.6	.885
1911	PIT N	0	1	.000	9.00	2	1	0	3	3	1	1	0	0	0	0	1	0	0	.000	0	1	0	0	0.5	1.000
3 yrs.		17	25	.405	3.24	58	44	21	330.2	294	168	102	3	3	1	2	103	22	0	.214	11	79	12	2	1.8	.882

Larry White

WHITE, LARRY DAVID
B. Sept. 25, 1958, San Fernando, Calif.
BR TR 6'5" 190 lbs.

Year	Team	W	L	PCT	ERA	G	GS	CG	IP	H	BB	SO	ShO	W	L	SV	AB	H	HR	BA	PO	A	E	DP	TC/G	FA
1983	LA N	0	0	–	1.29	4	0	0	7	4	3	5	0	0	0	0	–	1	0	–	1	1	0	0	0.5	1.000
1984		0	1	.000	3.00	7	1	0	12	9	6	10	0	0	1	0	1	0	0	.000	1	1	1	0	0.4	.667
2 yrs.		0	1	.000	2.37	11	1	0	19	13	9	15	0	0	1	0	1	0	0	.000	2	2	1	0	0.5	.800

Steve White

WHITE, STEPHEN VINCENT
B. Dec. 21, 1884, Dorchester, Mass. D. Jan. 29, 1975, Braintree, Mass.
BR TR 5'10" 160 lbs.

Year	Team	W	L	PCT	ERA	G	GS	CG	IP	H	BB	SO	ShO	W	L	SV	AB	H	HR	BA	PO	A	E	DP	TC/G	FA
1912	2 teams	WAS A	(1G 0–0)		BOS N	(3G 0–0)																				
"	total	0	0	–	5.40	4	0	0	6.2	11	5	3	0	0	0	0	3	0	0	.000	0	2	1	0	0.8	.667

Will White

WHITE, WILLIAM HENRY (Whoop-La)
Brother of Deacon White.
B. Oct. 11, 1854, Caton, N. Y. D. Aug. 31, 1911, Port Carling, Ont., Canada
Manager 1884.
BB TR 5'9½" 175 lbs.

Year	Team	W	L	PCT	ERA	G	GS	CG	IP	H	BB	SO	ShO	W	L	SV	AB	H	HR	BA	PO	A	E	DP	TC/G	FA
1877	BOS N	2	1	.667	3.00	3	3	3	27	27	2	7	1	0	0	0	15	3	0	.200	3	1	1	0	1.7	.800
1878	CIN N	30	21	.588	1.79	52	52	52	468	477	45	169	5	0	0	0	197	28	0	.142	13	90	15	2	2.3	.873
1879		43	31	.581	1.99	76	75	75	680	676	68	232	4	0	0	0	294	40	0	.136	20	114	20	0	2.0	.870
1880		18	42	.300	2.14	62	62	58	517.1	550	56	161	3	0	0	0	207	35	0	.169	17	68	10	2	1.5	.895
1881	DET N	0	2	.000	5.00	2	2	2	18	24	2	5	0	0	0	0	7	0	0	.000	0	1	0	0	0.5	1.000
1882	CIN AA	40	12	.769	1.54	54	54	52	480	411	71	122	8	0	0	0	207	55	0	.266	23	223	11	3	4.8	.957
1883		43	22	.662	2.09	65	64	64	577	473	104	141	6	0	0	1	240	54	0	.225	23	106	23	1	2.3	.849
1884		34	18	.654	3.32	52	52	52	456	479	74	118	4	0	0	0	184	35	1	.190	8	72	18	2	1.9	.816
1885		18	15	.545	3.53	34	34	33	293.1	295	64	80	2	0	0	0	118	20	0	.169	10	35	6	0	1.5	.882
1886		1	2	.333	4.15	3	3	3	26	28	10	6	0	0	0	0	9	1	0	.111	0	5	2	0	2.3	.714
10 yrs.		229	166	.580	2.28 10th	403	401	394	3542.2	3440	496	1041	36	0	0	1	1478	271	1	.183	117	715	106	10	2.3	.887

John Whitehead

WHITEHEAD, JOHN HENDERSON (Silent John)
B. Apr. 27, 1909, Coleman, Tex. D. Oct. 20, 1964, Bonham, Tex.
BR TR 6'2" 195 lbs.

Year	Team	W	L	PCT	ERA	G	GS	CG	IP	H	BB	SO	ShO	W	L	SV	AB	H	HR	BA	PO	A	E	DP	TC/G	FA
1935	CHI A	13	13	.500	3.72	28	27	18	222.1	209	101	72	1	0	0	0	82	12	0	.146	7	56	1	6	2.3	.984
1936		13	13	.500	4.64	34	32	15	230.2	254	98	70	1	0	0	1	87	21	0	.241	10	60	5	4	2.2	.933
1937		11	8	.579	4.07	26	24	8	165.2	191	56	45	4	0	0	0	58	13	0	.224	6	27	1	1	1.3	.971
1938		10	11	.476	4.76	32	24	10	183.1	218	80	38	2	1	0	2	60	6	0	.100	4	35	1	3	1.3	.975
1939	2 teams	CHI A	(7G 0–3)		STL A	(26G 1–3)																				
"	total	1	6	.143	6.61	33	8	0	98	148	22	18	0	1	1	1	26	1	0	.038	7	20	0	2	0.8	1.000
1940	STL A	1	3	.250	5.40	15	4	1	40	46	14	11	0	1	0	0	12	2	0	.167	1	6	1	0	0.5	.875
1942		0	0	–	6.75	4	0	0	4	8	1	0	0	0	0	0	0	0	0	–	0	2	0	0	0.5	1.000
7 yrs.		49	54	.476	4.60	172	119	52	944	1074	372	254	9	2	3	4	325	55	0	.169	35	206	9	16	1.5	.964

Milt Whitehead

WHITEHEAD, MILTON P.
B. 1862, Canada D. Aug. 15, 1901, Highland, Calif.

Year	Team	W	L	PCT	ERA	G	GS	CG	IP	H	BB	SO	ShO	W	L	SV	AB	H	HR	BA	PO	A	E	DP	TC/G	FA
1884	2 teams	STL U	(1G 0–1)		KC U	(0G 0–0)																				
"	total	0	1	.000	9.00	1	1	1	8	14	2	2	0	0	0	0	*				0	2	0	0	2.0	1.000

Earl Whitehill

WHITEHILL, EARL OLIVER
B. Feb. 7, 1900, Cedar Rapids, Iowa D. Oct. 22, 1954, Omaha, Neb.
BL TL 5'9½" 174 lbs.

Year	Team	W	L	PCT	ERA	G	GS	CG	IP	H	BB	SO	ShO	W	L	SV	AB	H	HR	BA	PO	A	E	DP	TC/G	FA
1923	DET A	2	0	1.000	2.73	8	3	2	33	22	15	19	1	2	0	0	11	4	0	.364	1	7	2	0	1.3	.800
1924		17	9	.654	3.86	35	32	16	233	260	79	65	2	1	0	2	89	19	0	.213	14	53	4	3	2.0	.944
1925		11	11	.500	4.66	35	33	15	239.1	267	88	83	1	0	0	2	87	19	0	.218	13	52	5	2	2.0	.929
1926		16	13	.552	3.99	36	34	13	252.1	271	79	109	0	2	0	0	91	23	0	.253	12	54	2	2	1.9	.971
1927		16	14	.533	3.36	41	31	17	236	238	105	95	3	3	3	3	78	16	0	.205	5	47	7	3	1.4	.881
1928		11	16	.407	4.31	31	30	12	196.1	214	78	93	1	0	0	0	67	13	0	.194	17	40	1	3	1.9	.983
1929		14	15	.483	4.62	38	28	18	245.1	267	96	103	1	4	1	1	90	23	3	.256	15	49	4	0	1.8	.941
1930		17	13	.567	4.24	34	31	16	220.2	248	80	109	0	1	0	1	83	16	0	.193	8	32	1	1	1.2	.976
1931		13	16	.448	4.06	34	34	22	272.1	287	118	81	0	0	0	0	97	15	0	.155	20	62	2	5	2.5	.882
1932		16	12	.571	4.54	33	31	17	244	255	93	81	3	1	0	0	90	22	0	.244	9	44	2	1	1.7	.964
1933	WAS A	22	8	.733	3.33	39	37	19	270	271	100	96	2	0	0	1	108	24	0	.222	8	51	7	2	1.7	.894
1934		14	11	.560	4.52	32	31	15	235	269	94	96	0	0	0	0	85	17	1	.200	2	47	1	2	1.6	.980
1935		14	13	.519	4.29	34	34	19	279.1	318	104	102	1	0	0	0	104	19	0	.183	13	60	3	4	2.2	.961
1936		14	11	.560	4.87	28	28	14	212.1	252	89	63	0	0	0	0	77	13	0	.169	10	35	2	0	1.7	.957
1937	CLE A	8	8	.500	6.49	33	22	6	147	189	80	53	1	0	0	0	49	11	0	.224	9	33	2	0	1.3	.955
1938		9	8	.529	5.56	26	23	4	160.1	187	83	60	0	1	0	0	56	7	0	.125	9	21	2	3	1.2	.938
1939	CHI N	4	7	.364	5.14	24	11	2	89.1	102	50	42	1	0	1	1	29	3	0	.103	1	14	0	0	0.6	1.000
17 yrs.		218	185	.541	4.36	541	473	227	3565.2	3917	1431	1350	17	14	6	11	1291	264	4	.204	166	701	47	31	1.7	.949

WORLD SERIES

Year	Team	W	L	PCT	ERA	G	GS	CG	IP	H	BB	SO	ShO	W	L	SV	AB	H	HR	BA	PO	A	E	DP	TC/G	FA
1933	WAS A	1	0	1.000	0.00	1	1	1	9	5	2	2	1	0	0	0	3	0	0	.000	0	4	0	0	4.0	1.000

Charlie Whitehouse

WHITEHOUSE, CHARLES EVIS (Lefty)
B. Jan. 25, 1894, Charleston, Ill. D. July 19, 1960, Indianapolis, Ind.
BB TL 6' 152 lbs.

Year	Team	W	L	PCT	ERA	G	GS	CG	IP	H	BB	SO	ShO	W	L	SV	AB	H	HR	BA	PO	A	E	DP	TC/G	FA
1914	IND F	2	0	1.000	4.85	8	2	2	26	34	5	10	0	0	0	0	8	0	0	.000	0	8	0	0	1.0	1.000
1915	NWK F	2	2	.500	4.31	11	3	1	39.2	46	17	18	0	1	0	0	10	0	0	.000	0	10	1	0	1.0	.909
1919	WAS A	0	1	.000	4.50	6	1	0	12	13	6	5	0	0	1	0	1	0	0	.000	0	2	0	0	0.3	1.000
3 yrs.		4	3	.571	4.52	25	6	3	77.2	93	28	33	0	1	0	0	19	0	0	.000	0	20	1	0	0.8	.952

Year	Team		W	L	PCT	ERA	G	GS	CG	IP	H	BB	SO	ShO	Relief Pitching W	L	SV	Batting AB	H	HR	BA	PO	A	E	DP	TC/G	FA

Gil Whitehouse

WHITEHOUSE, GILBERT ARTHUR
B. Oct. 15, 1893, Somerville, Mass. D. Feb. 14, 1926, Brewer, Me.
BB TR 5'10½" 170 lbs.

| 1915 | NWK | F | 0 | 0 | – | 0.00 | 1 | 0 | 0 | 1 | 0 | 1 | 0 | 0 | 0 | 0 | 0 | * | | | | 0 | 0 | 0 | 0 | 0.0 | – |

Len Whitehouse

WHITEHOUSE, LEONARD JOSEPH
B. Sept. 10, 1957, Burlington, Vt.
BL TL 5'11" 175 lbs.

1981	TEX	A	0	1	.000	18.00	2	1	0	3	8	2	2	0	0	0	0	0	0	0	–	0	0	0	0	0.0	–
1983	MIN	A	7	1	.875	4.15	60	0	0	73.2	70	44	44	0	7	1	2	0	0	0	–	3	6	0	0	0.2	1.000
1984			2	2	.500	3.16	30	0	0	31.1	29	17	18	0	2	2	1	0	0	0	–	2	3	0	0	0.2	1.000
1985			0	0	–	11.05	5	0	0	7.1	12	2	4	0	0	0	1	0	0	0	–	1	0	0	0	0.2	1.000
4 yrs.			9	4	.692	4.68	97	1	0	115.1	119	65	68	0	9	3	4	0	0	0	–	6	9	0	0	0.2	1.000

Wally Whitehurst

WHITEHURST, WALTER RICHARD
B. Apr. 11, 1964, Shreveport, La.
BR TR 6'3" 180 lbs.

| 1989 | NY | N | 0 | 1 | .000 | 4.50 | 9 | 1 | 0 | 14 | 17 | 5 | 9 | 0 | 0 | 0 | 0 | 1 | 0 | 0 | .000 | 1 | 1 | 0 | 0 | 0.2 | 1.000 |

Jesse Whiting

WHITING, JESSE W.
B. May 30, 1879, Philadelphia, Pa. D. Oct. 28, 1937, Philadelphia, Pa.

1902	PHI	N	0	1	.000	5.00	1	1	1	9	13	6	0	0	0	0	0	3	1	0	.333	0	4	0	0	4.0	1.000
1906	BKN	N	1	1	.500	2.92	3	2	2	24.2	26	6	7	1	0	0	0	10	3	0	.300	1	11	0	0	4.0	1.000
1907			0	0	–	12.00	1	0	0	3	3	3	2	0	0	0	0	2	0	0	.000	0	1	0	0	1.0	1.000
3 yrs.			1	2	.333	4.17	5	3	3	36.2	42	15	9	1	0	0	0	15	4	0	.267	1	16	0	0	3.4	1.000

Art Whitney

WHITNEY, ARTHUR WILSON
Brother of Frank Whitney.
B. Jan. 16, 1858, Brockton, Mass. D. Aug. 15, 1943, Lowell, Mass.
BR TR 5'8" 155 lbs.

1882	DET	N	0	1	.000	6.00	3	2	1	18	31	8	11	0	0	0	0	155	24	0	.155	0	1	0	0	0.3	1.000
1886	PIT	AA	0	0	–	3.00	1	0	0	6	7	3	2	0	0	0	0	511	122	0	.239	0	0	0	0	0.0	–
1889	NY	N	0	1	.000	3.00	1	0	0	6	7	3	3	0	0	1	0	473	103	1	.218	0	0	0	0	0.0	–
3 yrs.			0	2	.000	4.80	5	2	1	30	45	14	16	0	0	1	0	*				0	1	0	0	0.2	1.000

Jim Whitney

WHITNEY, JAMES EVANS (Grasshopper Jim)
B. Nov. 10, 1857, Conklin, N. Y. D. May 21, 1891, Binghamton, N. Y.
BL TR 6'2" 172 lbs.

1881	BOS	N	31	33	.484	2.48	66	63	57	552.1	548	90	162	6	0	1	0	282	72	0	.255	19	99	28	3	2.2	.808
1882			24	21	.533	2.64	49	48	46	420	404	41	180	3	0	0	0	251	81	5	.323	13	88	13	3	2.3	.886
1883			37	21	.638	2.24	62	56	54	514	492	35	345	1	3	0	2	409	115	5	.281	12	93	9	2	1.8	.921
1884			23	14	.622	2.09	41	40	35	336	272	27	270	6	0	1	0	270	70	3	.259	8	78	0	2	2.1	1.000
1885			18	32	.360	2.98	51	50	50	441.1	503	37	200	2	0	0	0	290	68	0	.234	18	128	16	1	3.2	.901
1886	KC	N	12	32	.273	4.49	46	44	42	393	465	55	167	3	0	0	0	247	59	2	.239	20	107	10	5	3.0	.927
1887	WAS	N	24	21	.533	3.22	47	47	46	404.2	430	42	146	3	0	0	0	201	53	2	.264	13	92	11	5	2.5	.905
1888			18	21	.462	3.05	39	39	37	325	317	54	79	2	0	0	0	141	24	1	.170	15	67	11	2	2.4	.882
1889	IND	N	2	7	.222	6.81	9	8	7	70	106	19	16	0	0	1	0	32	12	0	.375	4	9	0	0	1.4	1.000
1890	PHI	AA	2	2	.500	5.18	6	4	3	40	61	11	6	0	0	0	0	21	5	0	.238	1	8	1	1	1.7	.900
10 yrs.			191	204	.484	2.97	416	399	377	3496.1	3598	411	1571	26	3	3	2	*				123	769	99	24	2.4	.900

Bill Whitrock

WHITROCK, WILLIAM FRANKLIN
B. Mar. 4, 1870, Cincinnati, Ohio D. July 26, 1935, Derby, Conn.
TR 5'7½" 170 lbs.

1890	STL	AA	5	6	.455	3.51	16	11	10	105	104	40	39	0	0	0	1	48	7	0	.146	6	23	5	0	2.1	.853
1893	LOU	N	2	4	.333	7.88	6	6	4	37.2	54	14	7	0	0	0	0	21	6	0	.286	2	10	2	1	2.3	.857
1894	2 teams	LOU N (1G 0–1)	CIN N (10G 2–6)																								
"	total		2	7	.222	6.78	11	9	8	74.1	118	41	9	0	0	0	0	62	13	0	.210	3	15	0	0	1.6	1.000
1896	PHI	N	0	1	.000	3.00	2	1	1	9	10	3	1	0	0	0	0	3	0	0	.000	0	1	0	0	0.5	1.000
4 yrs.			9	18	.333	5.30	35	27	23	226	286	98	56	0	0	0	1	134	26	0	.194	11	49	7	1	1.9	.896

Ed Whitson

WHITSON, EDDIE LEE
B. May 19, 1955, Johnson City, Tenn.
BR TR 6'3" 195 lbs.

1977	PIT	N	1	0	1.000	3.38	5	2	0	16	11	9	10	0	1	0	0	4	0	0	.000	0	2	0	0	0.4	1.000
1978			5	6	.455	3.28	43	0	0	74	66	37	64	0	5	6	4	11	2	0	.182	3	8	1	0	0.3	.917
1979	2 teams	PIT N (19G 2–3)	SF N (18G 5–8)																								
"	total		7	11	.389	4.10	37	24	2	158	151	75	93	0	0	3	1	45	5	0	.111	4	21	2	2	0.7	.926
1980	SF	N	11	13	.458	3.10	34	34	6	212	222	56	90	0	0	0	0	66	6	0	.091	8	27	3	0	1.1	.921
1981			6	9	.400	4.02	22	22	2	123	130	47	65	1	0	0	0	33	3	0	.091	10	11	3	1	1.1	.875
1982	CLE	A	4	2	.667	3.26	40	9	1	107.2	91	58	61	1	2	1	2	0	0	0	–	4	8	0	0	0.3	1.000
1983	SD	N	5	7	.417	4.30	31	21	2	144.1	143	50	81	0	0	1	0	44	8	0	.182	4	6	0	0	0.3	1.000
1984			14	8	.636	3.24	31	31	3	189	181	42	103	0	0	0	0	61	3	0	.049	11	35	0	3	1.5	1.000
1985	NY	A	10	8	.556	4.88	30	30	2	158.2	201	43	89	2	0	0	0	0	0	0	–	8	16	3	3	0.9	.889
1986	2 teams	NY A (14G 5–2)	SD N (17G 1–7)																								
"	total		6	9	.400	6.23	31	16	0	112.2	139	60	73	0	4	0	4	18	3	0	.167	7	18	2	1	0.9	.926
1987	SD	N	10	13	.435	4.73	36	34	3	205.2	197	64	135	1	0	0	0	65	8	0	.123	14	19	1	0	0.9	.971
1988			13	11	.542	3.77	34	33	3	205.1	202	45	118	1	1	0	0	66	11	0	.167	10	30	4	2	1.3	.909
1989			16	11	.593	2.66	33	33	5	227	198	48	117	1	0	0	0	72	10	0	.139	17	22	2	1	1.2	.951
13 yrs.			108	108	.500	3.88	407	289	27	1933.1	1932	634	1099	9	13	10	8	485	59	0	.122	100	223	21	13	0.8	.939

LEAGUE CHAMPIONSHIP SERIES

| 1984 | SD | N | 1 | 0 | 1.000 | 1.13 | 1 | 1 | 0 | 8 | 5 | 2 | 6 | 0 | 0 | 0 | 0 | 3 | 0 | 0 | .000 | 1 | 0 | 0 | 0 | 1.0 | 1.000 |

WORLD SERIES

| 1984 | SD | N | 0 | 0 | – | 40.50 | 1 | 1 | 0 | .2 | 5 | 4 | 0 | 0 | 0 | 0 | 0 | 0 | 0 | 0 | – | 0 | 0 | 0 | 0 | 0.0 | – |

Walt Whittaker

WHITTAKER, WALTER ELTON (Doc)
B. June 11, 1894, Chelsea, Mass. D. Aug. 7, 1965, Pembroke, Mass.
BL TR 5'9½" 165 lbs.

| 1916 | PHI | A | 0 | 0 | – | 4.50 | 1 | 0 | 0 | 2 | 3 | 2 | 0 | 0 | 0 | 0 | 0 | 0 | 0 | 0 | – | 0 | 1 | 0 | 0 | 1.0 | 1.000 |

Year	Team		W	L	PCT	ERA	G	GS	CG	IP	H	BB	SO	ShO	Relief Pitching W	L	SV	Batting AB	H	HR	BA	PO	A	E	DP	TC/G	FA

Kevin Wickander

WICKANDER, KEVIN DEAN
B. Jan. 4, 1965, Fort Dodge, Iowa. BL TL 6'2" 202 lbs.

Year	Team	W	L	PCT	ERA	G	GS	CG	IP	H	BB	SO	ShO	W	L	SV	AB	H	HR	BA	PO	A	E	DP	TC/G	FA
1989	CLE A	0	0	—	3.38	2	0	0	2.2	6	2	0	0	0	0	0	0	0	0	—	0	0	0	0	0.0	—

Bob Wicker

WICKER, ROBERT KITRIDGE
B. May 24, 1878, Bedford, Ind. D. Jan. 22, 1955, Evanston, Ill. BR TR 6'2" 180 lbs.

Year	Team	W	L	PCT	ERA	G	GS	CG	IP	H	BB	SO	ShO	W	L	SV	AB	H	HR	BA	PO	A	E	DP	TC/G	FA
1901	STL N	0	0	—	0.00	1	0	0	3	4	1	2	0	0	0	0	3	1	0	.333	0	0	0	0	0.0	—
1902		5	13	.278	3.19	22	16	14	152.1	159	45	78	1	1	2	0	77	18	0	.234	15	47	9	3	3.2	.873
1903	2 teams				STL N (1G 0-0)				CHI N (32G 19-10)																	
"	total	19	10	.655	2.96	33	27	24	252	240	77	113	1	1	1	1	100	24	0	.240	13	45	9	2	2.0	.866
1904	CHI N	17	8	.680	2.67	30	27	23	229	201	58	99	4	0	1	0	155	34	0	.219	18	33	5	1	1.9	.911
1905		13	7	.650	2.02	22	22	17	178	139	47	86	0	0	0	0	72	10	0	.139	3	36	2	3	1.9	.951
1906	2 teams				CHI N (10G 3-5)				CIN N (20G 6-14)																	
"	total	9	19	.321	2.79	30	25	19	222.1	220	65	94	0	1	3	0	70	11	0	.157	13	38	6	2	1.9	.895
6 yrs.		63	57	.525	2.73	138	117	97	1036.2	963	293	472	10	3	7	1	*				62	199	31	11	2.1	.894

Kemp Wicker

WICKER, KEMP CASWELL
Born Kemp Caswell Whicker.
B. Aug. 13, 1906, Kernersville, N. C. D. June 11, 1973, Kernersville, N. C. BR TL 5'11" 182 lbs.

Year	Team	W	L	PCT	ERA	G	GS	CG	IP	H	BB	SO	ShO	W	L	SV	AB	H	HR	BA	PO	A	E	DP	TC/G	FA
1936	NY A	1	2	.333	7.65	7	0	0	20	31	11	5	0	1	2	0	7	1	0	.143	0	5	0	0	0.7	1.000
1937		7	3	.700	4.40	16	10	6	88	107	26	14	1	1	0	0	35	4	0	.114	0	9	1	0	0.6	.900
1938		1	0	1.000	0.00	1	0	0	1	0	1	0	0	1	0	0	0	0	0	—	0	0	0	0	0.0	—
1941	BKN N	1	2	.333	3.66	16	2	0	32	30	14	8	0	1	1	1	4	1	0	.250	0	7	0	0	0.4	1.000
4 yrs.		10	7	.588	4.66	40	12	6	141	168	52	27	1	4	3	1	46	6	0	.130	0	21	1	0	0.6	.955

WORLD SERIES

Year	Team	W	L	PCT	ERA	G	GS	CG	IP	H	BB	SO	ShO	W	L	SV	AB	H	HR	BA	PO	A	E	DP	TC/G	FA
1937	NY A	0	0	—	0.00	1	0	0	1	0	0	0	0	0	0	0	0	0	0	—	0	0	0	0	0.0	—

Dave Wickersham

WICKERSHAM, DAVID CLIFFORD
B. Sept. 27, 1935, Erie, Pa. BR TR 6'3" 188 lbs.

Year	Team	W	L	PCT	ERA	G	GS	CG	IP	H	BB	SO	ShO	W	L	SV	AB	H	HR	BA	PO	A	E	DP	TC/G	FA
1960	KC A	0	0	—	1.08	5	0	0	8.1	4	1	3	0	0	0	2	1	0	0	.000	2	0	0	0	0.4	1.000
1961		2	1	.667	5.14	17	0	0	21	25	5	10	0	2	1	2	3	2	0	.667	0	5	1	0	0.4	.833
1962		11	4	.733	4.17	30	9	3	110	105	43	61	0	5	2	1	35	2	0	.057	7	22	0	1	1.0	1.000
1963		12	15	.444	4.09	38	34	4	237.2	244	79	118	1	1	0	1	80	11	0	.138	15	43	2	2	1.6	.967
1964	DET A	19	12	.613	3.44	40	36	11	254	224	81	164	1	0	1	1	82	6	0	.073	22	35	2	2	1.5	.966
1965		9	14	.391	3.78	34	27	8	195.1	179	61	109	3	1	0	0	58	4	0	.069	15	37	2	0	1.6	.963
1966		8	3	.727	3.20	38	14	0	140.2	139	54	93	0	4	1	1	45	2	0	.044	11	24	0	2	0.9	1.000
1967		4	5	.444	2.74	36	4	0	85.1	72	33	44	0	4	1	4	15	0	0	.000	8	18	2	1	0.8	.929
1968	PIT N	1	0	1.000	3.48	11	0	0	20.2	21	13	9	0	1	0	1	3	1	0	.333	1	2	0	0	0.4	1.000
1969	KC A	2	3	.400	3.96	34	0	0	50	58	14	27	0	2	3	5	2	0	0	.000	2	10	1	0	0.4	.923
10 yrs.		68	57	.544	3.66	283	124	29	1123	1071	384	638	5	20	9	18	324	28	0	.086	80	200	10	9	1.0	.966

Al Widmar

WIDMAR, ALBERT JOSEPH
B. Mar. 20, 1925, Cleveland, Ohio. BR TR 6'3" 185 lbs.

Year	Team	W	L	PCT	ERA	G	GS	CG	IP	H	BB	SO	ShO	W	L	SV	AB	H	HR	BA	PO	A	E	DP	TC/G	FA
1947	BOS A	0	0	—	13.50	2	0	0	1.1	1	2	1	0	0	0	0	0	0	0	—	0	0	0	0	0.0	—
1948	STL A	2	6	.250	4.46	49	0	0	82.2	88	48	34	0	2	6	1	10	3	0	.300	4	22	0	0	0.5	1.000
1950		7	15	.318	4.76	36	26	8	194.2	211	74	78	1	0	1	4	67	10	0	.149	17	32	0	3	1.4	1.000
1951		4	9	.308	6.52	26	16	4	107.2	157	52	28	0	1	0	0	30	5	0	.167	10	22	1	3	1.3	.970
1952	CHI A	0	0	—	4.50	1	0	0	2	4	0	2	0	0	0	0	0	0	0	—	0	0	0	0	0.0	—
5 yrs.		13	30	.302	5.21	114	42	12	388.1	461	176	143	1	3	8	5	107	18	0	.168	31	76	1	6	0.9	.991

Wild Bill Widner

WIDNER, WILLIAM WATERFIELD
B. June 3, 1867, Cincinnati, Ohio D. Dec. 10, 1908, Cincinnati, Ohio. BR TR 6' 180 lbs.

Year	Team	W	L	PCT	ERA	G	GS	CG	IP	H	BB	SO	ShO	W	L	SV	AB	H	HR	BA	PO	A	E	DP	TC/G	FA
1887	CIN AA	1	0	1.000	5.00	1	1	1	9	11	4	2	0	0	0	0	4	1	0	.250	0	3	0	0	3.0	1.000
1888	WAS N	5	7	.417	2.82	13	13	13	115	111	22	33	0	0	0	0	60	12	0	.200	13	21	5	0	3.0	.872
1889	COL AA	12	20	.375	5.20	41	34	25	294	368	85	63	2	1	1	1	133	28	2	.211	18	63	9	3	2.2	.900
1890		4	8	.333	3.28	13	10	8	96	103	24	14	1	0	2	0	41	8	0	.195	7	30	3	2	3.1	.925
1891	CIN AA	0	1	.000	7.88	1	1	1	8	13	4	0	0	0	0	0	4	1	0	.250	0	2	0	0	2.0	1.000
5 yrs.		22	36	.379	4.36	69	59	48	522	606	137	110	3	1	3	1	242	50	2	.207	38	119	17	5	2.5	.902

Ted Wieand

WIEAND, FRANKLIN DELANO ROOSEVELT
B. Apr. 4, 1933, Walnutport, Pa. BR TR 6'2" 195 lbs.

Year	Team	W	L	PCT	ERA	G	GS	CG	IP	H	BB	SO	ShO	W	L	SV	AB	H	HR	BA	PO	A	E	DP	TC/G	FA
1958	CIN N	0	0	—	9.00	1	0	0	2	4	0	4	0	0	0	0	0	0	0	—	0	0	0	0	0.0	—
1960		0	1	.000	10.38	5	0	0	4.1	4	5	3	0	0	1	0	0	0	0	—	0	1	0	1	0.2	1.000
2 yrs.		0	1	.000	9.95	6	0	0	6.1	8	5	5	0	0	1	0	0	0	0	—	0	1	0	1	0.2	1.000

Charlie Wiedemeyer

WIEDEMEYER, CHARLES JOHN
B. Jan. 31, 1914, Chicago, Ill. D. Oct. 27, 1979, Lake Geneva, Fla. BL TL 6'3" 180 lbs.

Year	Team	W	L	PCT	ERA	G	GS	CG	IP	H	BB	SO	ShO	W	L	SV	AB	H	HR	BA	PO	A	E	DP	TC/G	FA
1934	CHI N	0	0	—	9.72	4	0	0	8.1	16	8	4	0	0	0	0	1	0	0	.000	0	2	0	0	0.5	1.000

Jack Wieneke

WIENEKE, JOHN
B. Mar. 10, 1894, Saltsburg, Pa. D. Mar. 16, 1933, Pleasant Ridge, Mich. BR TL 6' 182 lbs.

Year	Team	W	L	PCT	ERA	G	GS	CG	IP	H	BB	SO	ShO	W	L	SV	AB	H	HR	BA	PO	A	E	DP	TC/G	FA
1921	CHI A	0	1	.000	8.17	10	3	0	25.1	39	17	10	0	0	0	0	9	1	0	.111	0	8	0	0	0.8	1.000

Bob Wiesler

WIESLER, ROBERT GEORGE
B. Aug. 13, 1930, St. Louis, Mo. BB TL 6'3" 188 lbs.

Year	Team	W	L	PCT	ERA	G	GS	CG	IP	H	BB	SO	ShO	W	L	SV	AB	H	HR	BA	PO	A	E	DP	TC/G	FA
1951	NY A	0	2	.000	13.50	4	2	0	9.1	13	11	3	0	0	0	0	3	0	0	.000	0	3	0	0	0.8	1.000
1954		3	2	.600	4.15	6	5	0	30.1	28	30	25	0	0	0	0	11	3	0	.273	1	2	0	0	0.5	1.000
1955		0	2	.000	3.91	16	7	0	53	39	49	22	0	0	0	0	14	2	0	.143	2	13	0	1	0.9	1.000
1956	WAS A	3	12	.200	6.44	37	21	3	123	141	112	49	0	0	0	0	33	3	0	.091	12	24	3	5	1.1	.923
1957		1	1	.500	4.41	3	2	1	16.1	15	11	9	0	0	0	0	6	1	0	.167	2	3	0	0	1.7	1.000

Year	Team		W	L	PCT	ERA	G	GS	CG	IP	H	BB	SO	ShO	Relief Pitching W	L	SV	Batting AB	H	HR	BA	PO	A	E	DP	TC/G	FA

Bob Wiesler *continued*

Year	Team	W	L	PCT	ERA	G	GS	CG	IP	H	BB	SO	ShO	W	L	SV	AB	H	HR	BA	PO	A	E	DP	TC/G	FA
1958		0	0	–	6.75	4	0	0	9.1	14	5	5	0	0	0	0	2	0	0	.000	0	4	0	1	1.0	1.000
6 yrs.		7	19	.269	5.74	70	38	4	241.1	250	218	113	0	0	0	0	69	9	0	.130	17	49	3	8	1.0	.957

Whitey Wietelmann

WIETELMANN, WILLIAM FREDERICK
B. Mar. 15, 1919, Zanesville, Ohio

BB TR 6' 170 lbs.
BR 1939-40,1942,
BL 1943,1945

Year	Team		W	L	PCT	ERA	G	GS	CG	IP	H	BB	SO	ShO	W	L	SV	AB	H	HR	BA	PO	A	E	DP	TC/G	FA
1945	BOS	N	0	0	–	54.00	1	0	0	1	6	2	0	0	0	0	0	428	116	4	.271	0	0	0	0	0.0	–
1946			0	0	–	8.10	3	0	0	6.2	9	4	2	0	0	0	0	78	16	0	.205	2	0	1	0	1.0	.667
2 yrs.			0	0	–	14.09	4	0	0	7.2	15	6	2	0	0	0	0	*				2	0	1	0	0.8	.667

Jimmy Wiggs

WIGGS, JAMES ALVIN (Big Jim)
B. Sept. 1, 1876, Trondhjem, Norway   D. Jan. 20, 1963, Xenia, Ohio

BB TR 6'4" 200 lbs.

Year	Team		W	L	PCT	ERA	G	GS	CG	IP	H	BB	SO	ShO	W	L	SV	AB	H	HR	BA	PO	A	E	DP	TC/G	FA
1903	CIN	N	0	1	.000	5.40	2	1	0	5	12	2	0	0	0	0	0	1	0	0	.000	0	1	0	0	0.5	1.000
1905	DET	A	3	3	.500	3.27	7	7	4	41.1	30	29	37	0	0	0	0	15	2	0	.133	1	11	3	0	2.1	.800
1906			0	0	–	5.23	4	1	0	10.1	11	7	7	0	0	0	0	3	1	0	.333	0	5	1	0	1.5	.833
3 yrs.			3	4	.429	3.81	13	9	4	56.2	53	38	46	0	0	0	0	19	3	0	.158	1	17	4	0	1.7	.818

Bill Wight

WIGHT, WILLIAM ROBERT (Lefty)
B. Apr. 12, 1922, Rio Vista, Calif.

BL TL 6'1" 180 lbs.

Year	Team		W	L	PCT	ERA	G	GS	CG	IP	H	BB	SO	ShO	W	L	SV	AB	H	HR	BA	PO	A	E	DP	TC/G	FA
1946	NY	A	2	2	.500	4.46	14	4	1	40.1	44	30	11	0	0	0	0	9	0	0	.000	1	11	3	0	1.1	.800
1947			1	0	1.000	1.00	1	1	1	9	8	2	3	0	0	0	0	2	0	0	.000	1	3	0	0	4.0	1.000
1948	CHI	A	9	20	.310	4.80	34	32	7	223.1	238	135	68	1	0	0	1	73	6	0	.082	4	47	3	2	1.6	.944
1949			15	13	.536	3.31	35	33	14	245	254	96	78	3	0	0	1	85	14	0	.165	10	50	5	3	1.9	.923
1950			10	16	.385	3.58	30	28	13	206	213	79	62	0	0	1	0	61	0	0	.000	5	49	6	2	2.0	.900
1951	BOS	A	7	7	.500	5.10	34	17	4	118.1	128	63	38	2	2	0	0	41	3	0	.073	1	29	3	2	1.0	.909
1952	2 teams				BOS A	(10G 2–1)			DET A	(23G 5–9)																	
"	total		7	10	.412	3.75	33	21	8	168	181	69	70	3	1	0	0	57	12	0	.211	7	44	4	1	1.7	.927
1953	2 teams				DET A	(13G 0–3)			CLE A	(20G 2–1)																	
"	total		2	4	.333	6.23	33	4	0	52	64	30	24	0	2	2	1	12	3	0	.250	1	9	4	1	0.4	.714
1955	2 teams				CLE A	(17G 0–0)			BAL A	(19G 6–8)																	
"	total		6	8	.429	2.48	36	14	8	141.1	135	48	63	2	0	1	3	36	3	0	.083	3	49	3	1	1.5	.945
1956	BAL	A	9	12	.429	4.02	35	26	7	174.2	198	72	84	1	1	0	0	60	12	0	.200	6	27	4	1	1.1	.892
1957			6	6	.500	3.64	27	17	2	121	122	54	50	0	1	0	0	34	1	0	.029	5	21	3	1	1.1	.897
1958	2 teams				CIN N	(7G 0–1)			STL N	(28G 3–0)																	
"	total		3	1	.750	4.92	35	1	0	64	71	36	23	0	2	1	2	10	1	0	.100	3	16	2	0	0.6	.905
12 yrs.			77	99	.438	3.95	347	198	66	1563	1656	714	574	15	8	5	8	480	55	0	.115	47	355	40	16	1.3	.910

Fred Wigington

WIGINGTON, FRED THOMAS
B. Dec. 16, 1897, Rogers, Neb.   D. May 8, 1980, Mesa, Ariz.

BR TR 5'10" 168 lbs.

Year	Team		W	L	PCT	ERA	G	GS	CG	IP	H	BB	SO	ShO	W	L	SV	AB	H	HR	BA	PO	A	E	DP	TC/G	FA
1923	STL	N	0	0	–	3.24	4	0	0	8.1	11	5	2	0	0	0	0	1	0	0	.000	0	5	2	0	1.8	.714

Sandy Wihtol

WIHTOL, ALEXANDER AMES
B. June 1, 1955, Palo Alto, Calif.

BR TR 6'1" 195 lbs.

Year	Team		W	L	PCT	ERA	G	GS	CG	IP	H	BB	SO	ShO	W	L	SV	AB	H	HR	BA	PO	A	E	DP	TC/G	FA
1979	CLE	A	0	0	–	3.27	5	0	0	11	10	3	6	0	0	0	0	0	0	0	–	2	2	0	0	0.8	1.000
1980			1	0	1.000	3.60	17	0	0	35	35	14	20	0	1	0	1	0	0	0	–	1	2	0	0	0.2	1.000
1982			0	0	–	4.63	6	0	0	11.2	9	7	8	0	0	0	0	0	0	0	–	0	1	0	0	0.2	1.000
3 yrs.			1	0	1.000	3.75	28	0	0	57.2	54	24	34	0	1	0	1	0	0	0	–	3	5	0	0	0.3	1.000

Milt Wilcox

WILCOX, MILTON EDWARD
B. Apr. 20, 1950, Honolulu, Hawaii

BR TR 6'2" 185 lbs.

Year	Team		W	L	PCT	ERA	G	GS	CG	IP	H	BB	SO	ShO	W	L	SV	AB	H	HR	BA	PO	A	E	DP	TC/G	FA
1970	CIN	N	3	1	.750	2.45	5	2	1	22	19	7	13	1	1	1	1	5	1	0	.200	1	5	0	0	1.2	1.000
1971			2	2	.500	3.35	18	3	0	43	43	17	21	0	2	1	1	9	0	0	.000	1	9	0	0	0.6	1.000
1972	CLE	A	7	14	.333	3.40	32	27	4	156	145	72	90	2	0	1	0	45	9	0	.200	9	14	5	1	0.9	.821
1973			8	10	.444	5.83	26	19	4	134.1	143	68	82	0	0	1	0	0	0	0	–	6	26	1	0	1.3	.970
1974			2	2	.500	4.69	41	2	1	71	74	24	33	0	1	1	4	0	0	0	–	5	14	3	1	0.5	.864
1975	CHI	N	0	1	.000	5.68	25	0	0	38	50	17	21	0	0	1	0	3	1	0	.333	0	8	1	0	0.4	.889
1977	DET	A	6	2	.750	3.65	20	13	1	106	96	37	82	0	1	0	0	0	0	0	–	4	14	2	2	1.0	.900
1978			13	12	.520	3.76	29	27	16	215.1	208	68	132	2	0	1	0	0	0	0	–	10	36	1	0	1.6	.979
1979			12	10	.545	4.36	33	29	7	196	201	73	109	0	1	0	0	0	0	0	–	10	41	0	7	1.5	1.000
1980			13	11	.542	4.48	32	31	13	199	201	68	97	1	0	0	0	0	0	0	–	14	36	4	1	1.7	.926
1981			12	9	.571	3.04	24	24	8	166	152	52	79	1	0	0	0	0	0	0	–	5	33	2	1	1.7	.950
1982			12	10	.545	3.62	29	29	9	193.2	187	85	112	1	0	0	0	0	0	0	–	11	38	2	5	1.8	.961
1983			11	10	.524	3.97	26	26	9	186	164	74	101	2	0	0	0	0	0	0	–	19	34	1	3	2.1	.981
1984			17	8	.680	4.00	33	33	0	193.2	183	66	119	0	0	0	0	0	0	0	–	20	28	3	4	1.5	.941
1985			1	3	.250	4.85	8	8	0	39	51	14	20	0	0	0	0	0	0	0	–	3	12	2	2	2.1	.882
1986	SEA	A	0	8	.000	5.50	13	10	0	55.2	74	28	26	0	0	0	0	0	0	0	–	4	9	0	0	1.0	1.000
16 yrs.			119	113	.513	4.08	394	283	73	2014.2	1991	770	1137	10	7	8	6	62	11	0	.177	122	357	27	28	1.3	.947

LEAGUE CHAMPIONSHIP SERIES

Year	Team		W	L	PCT	ERA	G	GS	CG	IP	H	BB	SO	ShO	W	L	SV	AB	H	HR	BA	PO	A	E	DP	TC/G	FA
1970	CIN	N	1	0	1.000	0.00	1	0	0	3	1	2	5	0	0	0	0	0	0	0	–	0	1	0	0	1.0	1.000
1984	DET	A	1	0	1.000	0.00	1	1	0	8	2	2	8	0	0	0	0	0	0	0	–	2	0	0	0	2.0	1.000
2 yrs.			2	0	1.000	0.00	2	1	0	11	3	4	13	0	0	0	0	0	0	0	–	2	1	0	0	1.5	1.000

WORLD SERIES

Year	Team		W	L	PCT	ERA	G	GS	CG	IP	H	BB	SO	ShO	W	L	SV	AB	H	HR	BA	PO	A	E	DP	TC/G	FA
1970	CIN	N	0	1	.000	9.00	2	0	0	2	3	2	0	0	0	0	0	0	0	0	–	0	1	0	0	0.5	1.000
1984	DET	A	1	0	1.000	1.50	1	1	0	6	7	2	6	0	0	1	0	0	0	0	–	1	1	0	0	2.0	1.000
2 yrs.			1	1	.500	3.38	3	1	0	8	10	2	6	0	0	1	0	0	0	0	–	1	2	0	0	1.0	1.000

Randy Wiles

WILES, RANDALL E.
B. Sept. 10, 1951, Ft. Belvoir, Va.

BL TL 6'1" 185 lbs.

Year	Team		W	L	PCT	ERA	G	GS	CG	IP	H	BB	SO	ShO	W	L	SV	AB	H	HR	BA	PO	A	E	DP	TC/G	FA
1977	CHI	A	1	1	.500	9.00	5	0	0	3	5	3	0	0	1	1	0	0	0	0	–	0	1	0	0	0.2	1.000

Year	Team		W	L	PCT	ERA	G	GS	CG	IP	H	BB	SO	ShO	Relief Pitching W	L	SV	Batting AB	H	HR	BA	PO	A	E	DP	TC/G	FA

Mark Wiley

WILEY, MARK EUGENE
B. Feb. 28, 1948, National City, Calif.

BR TR 6'1"   200 lbs.

Year	Team		W	L	PCT	ERA	G	GS	CG	IP	H	BB	SO	ShO	W	L	SV	AB	H	HR	BA	PO	A	E	DP	TC/G	FA
1975	MIN	A	1	3	.250	6.05	15	3	1	38.2	50	13	15	0	0	1	2	0	0	0	–	3	3	1	1	0.5	.857
1978	2 teams	SD N (4G 1-0)				TOR A (2G 0-0)																					
"	total		1	0	1.000	5.91	6	1	0	10.2	14	2	3	0	0	0	0	2	0	0	.000	0	1	0	0	0.2	1.000
2 yrs.			2	3	.400	6.02	21	4	1	49.1	64	15	18	0	0	1	2	2	0	0	.000	3	4	1	1	0.4	.875

Harry Wilhelm

WILHELM, HARRY LESTER
B. Apr. 7, 1874, Uniontown, Pa.   D. Feb. 20, 1944, Republic, Pa.

BR TR 5'7"   155 lbs.

Year	Team		W	L	PCT	ERA	G	GS	CG	IP	H	BB	SO	ShO	W	L	SV	AB	H	HR	BA	PO	A	E	DP	TC/G	FA
1899	LOU	N	1	1	.500	6.12	5	3	2	25	36	3	6	0	0	0	0	12	3	1	.250	1	8	0	0	1.8	1.000

Hoyt Wilhelm

WILHELM, JAMES HOYT
B. July 26, 1923, Huntersville, N. C.
Hall of Fame 1985.

BR TR 6'   190 lbs.

Year	Team		W	L	PCT	ERA	G	GS	CG	IP	H	BB	SO	ShO	W	L	SV	AB	H	HR	BA	PO	A	E	DP	TC/G	FA
1952	NY	N	15	3	.833	2.43	71	0	0	159.1	127	57	108	0	15	3	11	38	6	1	.158	9	32	2	0	0.6	.953
1953			7	8	.467	3.04	68	0	0	145	127	77	71	0	7	8	15	33	5	0	.152	11	19	1	1	0.5	.968
1954			12	4	.750	2.10	57	0	0	111.1	77	52	64	0	12	4	7	21	1	0	.048	5	25	0	0	0.5	1.000
1955			4	1	.800	3.93	59	0	0	103	104	40	71	0	4	1	0	19	3	0	.158	4	28	1	2	0.6	.971
1956			4	9	.308	3.83	64	0	0	89.1	97	43	71	0	4	9	8	9	2	0	.222	4	20	0	2	0.4	1.000
1957	2 teams	STL N (40G 1-4)				CLE A (2G 1-0)																					
"	total		2	4	.333	4.14	42	0	0	58.2	54	22	29	0	2	4	12	6	0	0	.000	3	8	0	0	0.3	1.000
1958	2 teams	CLE A (30G 2-7)				BAL A (9G 1-3)																					
"	total		3	10	.231	2.34	39	10	4	131	95	45	92	1	2	5	5	32	3	0	.094	9	22	0	0	0.8	1.000
1959	BAL	A	15	11	.577	2.19	32	27	13	226	178	77	139	3	0	2	0	76	4	0	.053	13	32	0	1	1.4	1.000
1960			11	8	.579	3.31	41	11	3	147	125	39	107	1	8	4	7	42	3	0	.071	4	28	1	2	0.8	.970
1961			9	7	.563	2.30	51	1	0	109.2	89	41	87	0	9	7	18	20	1	0	.050	6	22	2	1	0.6	.933
1962			7	10	.412	1.94	52	0	0	93	64	34	90	0	7	10	15	16	2	0	.125	10	12	0	0	0.4	1.000
1963	CHI	A	5	8	.385	2.64	55	3	0	136.1	106	30	111	0	5	7	21	29	2	0	.069	4	24	1	1	0.5	.966
1964			12	9	.571	1.99	73	0	0	131.1	94	30	95	0	12	9	27	21	3	0	.143	5	16	0	2	0.3	1.000
1965			7	7	.500	1.81	66	0	0	144	88	32	106	0	7	7	20	22	0	0	.000	7	20	0	2	0.4	1.000
1966			5	2	.714	1.66	46	0	0	81.1	50	17	61	0	5	2	6	8	1	0	.125	2	10	0	1	0.3	1.000
1967			8	3	.727	1.31	49	0	0	89	58	34	76	0	8	3	12	13	1	0	.077	3	11	1	1	0.3	.929
1968			4	4	.500	1.73	72	0	0	93.2	69	24	72	0	4	4	12	3	0	0	.000	3	10	0	1	0.3	1.000
1969	2 teams	CAL A (44G 5-7)				ATL N (8G 2-0)																					
"	total		7	7	.500	2.20	52	0	0	77.2	50	22	67	0	7	7	14	9	0	0	.000	3	10	0	0	0.3	.929
1970	2 teams	ATL N (50G 6-4)				CHI N (3G 0-1)																					
"	total		6	5	.545	3.40	53	0	0	82	73	42	68	0	6	5	13	11	1	0	.091	4	16	1	0	0.4	.952
1971	2 teams	ATL N (3G 0-0)				LA N (9G 0-1)																					
"	total		0	1	.000	2.70	12	0	0	20	12	5	16	0	0	1	3	3	0	0	.000	1	3	0	0	0.3	1.000
1972	LA	N	0	1	.000	4.62	16	0	0	25.1	20	15	9	0	0	1	1	1	0	0	.000	3	5	0	0	0.5	1.000
21 yrs.			143	122	.540	2.52	1070	52	20	2254	1757	778	1610	5	124	103	227	432	38	1	.088	114	373	11	17	0.5	.978
						1st									1st		8th										

WORLD SERIES

Year	Team		W	L	PCT	ERA	G	GS	CG	IP	H	BB	SO	ShO	W	L	SV	AB	H	HR	BA	PO	A	E	DP	TC/G	FA
1954	NY	N	0	0	–	0.00	2	0	0	2.1	1	0	3	0	0	0	1	1	0	0	.000	0	1	1	0	1.0	.500

Kaiser Wilhelm

WILHELM, IRVIN KEY
B. Jan. 26, 1874, Wooster Ohio   D. May 21, 1936, Rochester, N. Y.
Manager 1921-22.

BR TR 6'   162 lbs.

Year	Team		W	L	PCT	ERA	G	GS	CG	IP	H	BB	SO	ShO	W	L	SV	AB	H	HR	BA	PO	A	E	DP	TC/G	FA
1903	PIT	N	5	4	.556	3.24	12	9	7	86	88	25	20	1	0	0	0	34	3	0	.088	1	33	2	2	3.0	.944
1904	BOS	N	14	22	.389	3.69	39	36	30	288	316	74	73	3	0	1	0	100	7	0	.070	10	90	7	3	2.7	.935
1905			4	23	.148	4.54	34	27	23	242	287	75	76	0	1	0	0	100	16	0	.160	17	77	6	2	2.9	.940
1908	BKN	N	16	22	.421	1.87	42	36	33	332	266	83	99	6	1	2	0	111	12	0	.108	17	109	6	3	3.1	.955
1909			3	13	.188	3.26	22	17	14	163	176	59	45	1	0	0	0	57	13	0	.228	3	56	6	0	3.0	.908
1910			3	7	.300	4.74	15	5	0	68.1	88	18	17	0	3	1	0	19	6	0	.316	2	24	1	0	1.8	.963
1914	BAL	F	12	17	.414	4.03	47	27	11	243.2	263	81	113	1	5	4	4	84	21	0	.250	14	82	4	1	2.1	.960
1915			0	0	–	0.00	1	0	0	1	0	0	0	0	0	0	0	0	0	0	–	0	0	0	0	0.0	–
1921	PHI	N	0	0	–	3.38	4	0	0	8	11	3	1	0	0	0	0	2	0	0	.000	1	1	0	0	0.5	1.000
9 yrs.			57	108	.345	3.44	216	157	118	1432	1495	418	444	12	10	6	4	507	78	0	.154	65	472	32	11	2.6	.944

Lefty Wilkie

WILKIE, ALDON JAY
B. Oct. 30, 1914, Zealandia, Sask., Canada

BL TL 5'11½" 175 lbs.

Year	Team		W	L	PCT	ERA	G	GS	CG	IP	H	BB	SO	ShO	W	L	SV	AB	H	HR	BA	PO	A	E	DP	TC/G	FA
1941	PIT	N	2	4	.333	4.56	26	6	2	79	90	40	16	1	2	4	2	24	7	0	.292	2	22	0	1	0.9	1.000
1942			6	7	.462	4.19	35	6	3	107.1	112	37	18	0	3	4	1	38	10	0	.263	3	36	1	0	1.1	.975
1946			0	0	–	10.57	7	0	0	7.2	13	3	3	0	0	0	0	0	0	0	–	0	1	0	0	0.1	1.000
3 yrs.			8	11	.421	4.59	68	12	5	194	215	80	37	1	5	8	3	62	17	0	.274	5	59	1	1	1.0	.985

Dean Wilkins

WILKINS, DEAN ALLAN
B. Aug. 24, 1966, Blue Island, Ill.

BR TR 6'1"   170 lbs.

Year	Team		W	L	PCT	ERA	G	GS	CG	IP	H	BB	SO	ShO	W	L	SV	AB	H	HR	BA	PO	A	E	DP	TC/G	FA
1989	CHI	N	1	0	1.000	5.17	11	0	0	15.2	13	9	14	0	1	0	0	1	0	0	.000	1	3	0	0	0.4	1.000

Eric Wilkins

WILKINS, ERIC LAMOINE
B. Dec. 9, 1956, St. Louis, Mo.

BR TR 6'1"   190 lbs.

Year	Team		W	L	PCT	ERA	G	GS	CG	IP	H	BB	SO	ShO	W	L	SV	AB	H	HR	BA	PO	A	E	DP	TC/G	FA
1979	CLE	A	2	4	.333	4.37	16	14	0	70	77	38	52	0	1	0	0	0	0	0	–	4	12	6	2	1.4	.727

Bill Wilkinson

WILKINSON, WILLIAM CARL
B. Aug. 10, 1964, Greybull, Wyo.

BR TL 5'10"   160 lbs.

Year	Team		W	L	PCT	ERA	G	GS	CG	IP	H	BB	SO	ShO	W	L	SV	AB	H	HR	BA	PO	A	E	DP	TC/G	FA
1985	SEA	A	0	2	.000	13.50	2	2	0	6	9	8	5	0	0	0	0	0	0	0	–	2	0	0	0	1.0	1.000
1987			3	4	.429	3.66	56	0	0	76.1	61	21	73	0	3	4	10	0	0	0	–	1	6	1	0	0.1	.875
1988			2	2	.500	3.48	30	0	0	31	28	15	25	0	2	2	2	0	0	0	–	1	1	1	1	0.1	1.000
3 yrs.			5	8	.385	4.13	88	2	0	113.1	97	42	103	0	5	6	12	0	0	0	–	2	9	1	1	0.1	.917

Year	Team	W	L	PCT	ERA	G	GS	CG	IP	H	BB	SO	ShO	Relief Pitching W	L	SV	Batting AB	H	HR	BA	PO	A	E	DP	TC/G	FA

Roy Wilkinson

WILKINSON, ROY HAMILTON
B. May 8, 1894, Canandaigua, N. Y. D. July 2, 1956, Louisville, Ky. BR TR 6'1" 170 lbs.

Year	Team	W	L	PCT	ERA	G	GS	CG	IP	H	BB	SO	ShO	W	L	SV	AB	H	HR	BA	PO	A	E	DP	TC/G	FA
1918	CLE A	0	0	—	0.00	1	0	0	1	0	0	0	0	0	0	0	0	0	0	—	0	0	0	0	0.0	
1919	CHI A	1	1	.500	2.05	4	1	1	22	21	10	5	1	0	1	0	8	3	0	.375	0	11	0	1	2.8	1.000
1920		7	9	.438	4.03	34	11	9	145	162	48	30	0	5	2	0	48	7	0	.146	3	27	1	1	0.9	.968
1921		4	20	.167	5.13	36	22	11	198.1	259	78	50	0	0	3	3	65	8	0	.123	12	76	1	1	2.5	.989
1922		0	1	.000	8.79	4	1	0	14.1	24	6	3	0	0	0	1	3	0	0	.000	1	3	0	0	1.0	1.000
5 yrs.		12	31	.279	4.66	79	35	21	380.2	466	142	88	1	5	4	6	124	18	0	.145	16	117	2	3	1.7	.985

WORLD SERIES

| 1919 | CHI A | 0 | 0 | — | 3.68 | 2 | 0 | 0 | 7.1 | 9 | 4 | 3 | 0 | 0 | 0 | 0 | 2 | 0 | 0 | .000 | 0 | 2 | 0 | 0 | 1.0 | 1.000 |

Ted Wilks

WILKS, THEODORE (Cork)
B. Nov. 13, 1915, Fulton, N. Y. D. Aug. 21, 1989, Houston, Tex. BR TR 5'9½" 178 lbs.

Year	Team	W	L	PCT	ERA	G	GS	CG	IP	H	BB	SO	ShO	W	L	SV	AB	H	HR	BA	PO	A	E	DP	TC/G	FA
1944	STL N	17	4	.810	2.65	36	21	16	207.1	173	49	70	4	2	1	0	64	9	0	.141	6	20	0	3	0.7	1.000
1945		4	7	.364	2.93	18	16	4	98.1	103	29	28	1	0	0	0	30	4	0	.133	1	12	1	0	0.8	.929
1946		8	0	1.000	3.41	40	4	0	95	88	38	40	0	6	0	1	24	5	0	.208	2	16	1	3	0.5	.947
1947		4	0	1.000	5.01	37	0	0	50.1	57	11	28	0	4	0	5	6	1	0	.167	2	9	1	0	0.3	.917
1948		6	6	.500	2.62	57	2	1	130.2	113	39	71	0	4	6	13	30	5	0	.167	6	19	0	1	0.4	1.000
1949		10	3	.769	3.73	59	0	0	118.1	105	38	71	0	10	3	9	27	1	0	.037	4	10	4	0	0.3	.778
1950		2	0	1.000	6.66	18	0	0	24.1	27	9	15	0	2	0	0	4	0	0	.000	1	4	0	0	0.3	1.000
1951	2 teams	STL N	(17G 0–0)		PIT N	(48G 3–5)																				
"	total	3	5	.375	2.86	65	1	1	100.2	88	29	48	1	2	5	13	13	1	0	.077	5	18	0	1	0.4	1.000
1952	2 teams	PIT N	(44G 5–5)		CLE A	(7G 0–0)																				
"	total	5	5	.500	3.64	51	0	0	84	73	38	30	0	5	5	5	8	1	0	.125	3	12	1	1	0.3	.938
1953	CLE A	0	0	—	7.36	4	0	0	3.2	5	3	2	0	0	0	0	0	0	0	—	0	0	0	0	0.0	
10 yrs.		59	30	.663	3.26	385	44	22	912.2	832	283	403	5	35	18	46	206	27	0	.131	30	120	8	9	0.4	.949

WORLD SERIES

1944	STL N	0	1	.000	5.68	2	1	0	6.1	5	3	7	0	0	0	0	2	0	0	.000	0	1	0	0	0.5	1.000
1946		0	0	—	0.00	1	0	0	1	2	0	0	0	0	0	0	0	0	0	—	0	1	0	0	1.0	1.000
2 yrs.		0	1	.000	4.91	3	1	0	7.1	7	3	7	0	0	0	1	2	0	0	.000	0	2	0	0	0.7	1.000

Ed Willett

WILLETT, ROBERT EDGAR
B. Mar. 7, 1884, Norfolk, Va. D. May 10, 1934, Wellington, Kans. BR TR 6' 183 lbs.

Year	Team	W	L	PCT	ERA	G	GS	CG	IP	H	BB	SO	ShO	W	L	SV	AB	H	HR	BA	PO	A	E	DP	TC/G	FA
1906	DET A	0	3	.000	3.96	3	3	3	25	24	8	16	0	0	0	0	9	0	0	.000	3	9	0	0	4.0	1.000
1907		1	5	.167	3.70	10	6	1	48.2	47	20	27	0	0	0	0	13	1	0	.077	3	18	1	0	2.2	.955
1908		15	8	.652	2.28	30	22	18	197.1	186	60	77	2	0	0	1	67	11	0	.164	14	81	4	3	3.3	.960
1909		21	10	.677	2.34	41	34	25	292.2	239	76	89	3	0	2	1	112	22	0	.196	12	92	8	2	2.7	.929
1910		16	11	.593	3.60	37	25	18	147.1	175	74	65	4	1	2	0	83	11	0	.133	6	113	7	2	3.4	.944
1911		13	14	.481	3.66	38	27	15	231.1	261	80	86	2	2	3	1	82	22	1	.268	5	84	3	2	2.4	.967
1912		17	15	.531	3.29	37	31	28	284.1	281	84	89	1	2	1	0	115	19	2	.165	12	113	7	2	3.6	.947
1913		13	14	.481	3.09	34	30	19	242	237	89	59	0	0	1	0	92	26	1	.283	8	93	5	3	3.1	.953
1914	STL F	4	16	.200	4.22	27	21	14	175	208	56	73	0	0	1	0	64	15	1	.234	6	76	4	2	3.2	.953
1915		2	3	.400	4.61	17	2	1	52.2	61	18	19	0	1	3	2	15	3	0	.200	2	17	3	2	1.3	.864
10 yrs.		102	99	.507	3.22	274	201	142	1696.1	1719	565	600	12	7	14	5	652	130	6	.199	71	696	42	18	3.0	.948

WORLD SERIES

| 1909 | DET A | 0 | 0 | — | 0.00 | 2 | 0 | 0 | 7.2 | 3 | 0 | 1 | 0 | 0 | 0 | 0 | 2 | 0 | 0 | .000 | 1 | 3 | 1 | 0 | 2.5 | .800 |

Carl Willey

WILLEY, CARLTON FRANCIS
B. June 6, 1931, Cherryfield, Me. BR TR 6' 175 lbs.

Year	Team	W	L	PCT	ERA	G	GS	CG	IP	H	BB	SO	ShO	W	L	SV	AB	H	HR	BA	PO	A	E	DP	TC/G	FA
1958	MIL N	9	7	.563	2.70	23	19	9	140	110	53	74	4	0	1	0	48	5	0	.104	6	15	0	1	0.9	1.000
1959		5	9	.357	4.15	26	15	5	117	126	31	51	2	0	1	0	39	4	0	.103	5	17	1	0	0.9	.957
1960		6	7	.462	4.35	28	21	2	144.2	136	65	109	1	1	0	0	48	7	1	.146	8	18	2	0	1.0	.929
1961		6	12	.333	3.83	35	22	4	159.2	147	65	91	0	2	1	0	54	1	0	.019	9	42	0	3	1.5	1.000
1962		2	5	.286	5.40	30	6	0	73.1	95	20	40	0	2	2	1	11	3	0	.273	3	12	1	0	0.5	.938
1963	NY N	9	14	.391	3.10	30	28	9	183	149	69	101	4	0	0	0	54	6	1	.111	20	29	2	0	1.7	.961
1964		0	2	.000	3.60	14	3	0	30	37	8	14	0	0	0	0	4	0	0	.000	3	0	1	0	0.3	.750
1965		1	2	.333	4.18	13	3	1	28	30	15	13	0	0	0	0	5	0	0	.000	3	2	1	0	0.6	.750
8 yrs.		38	58	.396	3.76	199	117	28	875.2	830	326	493	11	5	6	1	263	26	2	.099	55	138	9	5	1.0	.955

WORLD SERIES

| 1958 | MIL N | 0 | 0 | — | 0.00 | 1 | 0 | 0 | 1 | 0 | 0 | 2 | 0 | 0 | 0 | 0 | 0 | 0 | 0 | — | 0 | 0 | 0 | 0 | 0.0 | |

Nick Willhite

WILLHITE, JON NICHOLAS
B. Jan. 27, 1941, Tulsa, Okla. BL TL 6'2" 190 lbs.

Year	Team	W	L	PCT	ERA	G	GS	CG	IP	H	BB	SO	ShO	W	L	SV	AB	H	HR	BA	PO	A	E	DP	TC/G	FA
1963	LA N	2	3	.400	3.79	8	8	1	38	44	10	28	1	0	0	0	10	3	0	.300	1	3	1	0	0.6	.800
1964		2	4	.333	3.71	10	7	2	43.2	43	13	24	0	0	0	0	11	0	0	.000	3	12	0	1	1.5	1.000
1965	2 teams	WAS A	(5G 0–0)		LA N	(15G 2–2)																				
"	total	2	2	.500	5.59	20	6	0	48.1	57	26	31	0	0	0	0	10	4	0	.400	0	9	0	0	0.5	1.000
1966	LA N	0	0	—	2.08	6	0	0	4.1	3	5	4	0	0	2	1	0	0	0	—	0	2	0	0	0.3	1.000
1967	2 teams	CAL A	(10G 0–2)		NY N	(4G 0–1)																				
"	total	0	3	.000	5.10	14	8	0	47.2	48	21	31	0	0	0	0	12	0	0	.000	1	9	0	1	0.7	1.000
5 yrs.		6	12	.333	4.55	58	29	3	182	195	75	118	1	0	2	1	43	7	0	.163	5	35	1	2	0.7	.976

Ace Williams

WILLIAMS, ROBERT FULTON
B. Mar. 18, 1917, Montclair, N. J. BR TL 6'2" 174 lbs.

Year	Team	W	L	PCT	ERA	G	GS	CG	IP	H	BB	SO	ShO	W	L	SV	AB	H	HR	BA	PO	A	E	DP	TC/G	FA
1940	BOS N	0	0	—	16.00	5	0	0	9	21	12	5	0	0	0	0	2	0	0	.000	0	4	0	0	0.8	1.000
1946		0	0	—	0.00	1	0	0	1	1	1	0	0	0	0	0	0	0	0	—	0	0	0	0	0.0	
2 yrs.		0	0	—	16.00	6	0	0	9	22	13	5	0	0	0	0	2	0	0	.000	0	4	0	0	0.7	1.000

Year	Team	W	L	PCT	ERA	G	GS	CG	IP	H	BB	SO	ShO	Relief Pitching W	L	SV	Batting AB	H	HR	BA	PO	A	E	DP	TC/G	FA

Al Williams

WILLIAMS, ALBERT HAMILTON
Born Albert Hamilton Williams y DeSouza.
B. May 6, 1954, Pearl Lagoon, Nicaragua
BR TR 6'4" 190 lbs.

Year	Team	W	L	PCT	ERA	G	GS	CG	IP	H	BB	SO	ShO	W	L	SV	AB	H	HR	BA	PO	A	E	DP	TC/G	FA
1980	MIN A	6	2	.750	3.51	18	9	3	77	73	30	35	0	1	2	1	0	0	0	–	5	9	2	1	0.9	.875
1981		6	10	.375	4.08	23	22	4	150	160	52	76	0	0	0	0	0	0	0	–	9	13	3	2	1.1	.880
1982		9	7	.563	4.22	26	26	3	153.2	166	55	61	0	0	0	0	0	0	0	–	14	23	3	0	1.5	.925
1983		11	14	.440	4.14	36	29	4	193.1	196	68	68	1	1	2	1	0	0	0	–	11	22	3	1	1.0	.917
1984		3	5	.375	5.77	17	11	1	68.2	75	22	22	0	1	0	0	0	0	0	–	4	10	0	1	0.8	1.000
5 yrs.		35	38	.479	4.24	120	97	15	642.2	670	227	262	1	3	4	2	0	0	0	–	43	77	11	5	1.1	.916

Al Williams

WILLIAMS, ALMON EDWARD
B. May 11, 1914, Valhermosa Springs, Ala. D. July 19, 1969, Groves, Tex.
BR TR 6'3" 200 lbs.

Year	Team	W	L	PCT	ERA	G	GS	CG	IP	H	BB	SO	ShO	W	L	SV	AB	H	HR	BA	PO	A	E	DP	TC/G	FA
1937	PHI A	4	1	.800	5.38	16	8	2	75.1	88	49	27	0	0	1	0	24	2	0	.083	2	14	1	5	1.1	.941
1938		0	7	.000	6.94	30	8	1	93.1	128	54	25	0	0	0	1	25	1	0	.040	4	18	2	0	0.8	.917
2 yrs.		4	8	.333	6.24	46	16	3	168.2	216	103	52	0	0	1	1	49	3	0	.061	6	32	3	5	0.9	.927

Charlie Williams

WILLIAMS, CHARLES PROSEK
B. Oct. 11, 1947, Flushing, N. Y.
BR TR 6'2" 200 lbs.

Year	Team	W	L	PCT	ERA	G	GS	CG	IP	H	BB	SO	ShO	W	L	SV	AB	H	HR	BA	PO	A	E	DP	TC/G	FA
1971	NY N	5	6	.455	4.80	31	9	0	90	92	41	53	0	2	0	0	23	2	0	.087	6	7	2	1	0.5	.867
1972	SF N	0	2	.000	9.00	3	2	0	9	14	3	3	0	0	0	0	2	0	0	.000	0	0	1	0	0.3	–
1973		3	0	1.000	6.65	12	2	0	23	32	7	11	0	3	0	0	3	1	0	.333	2	5	0	0	0.6	1.000
1974		1	3	.250	2.79	39	7	0	100	93	31	48	0	1	0	0	22	3	0	.136	5	27	0	2	0.8	1.000
1975		5	3	.625	3.49	55	2	0	98	94	66	45	0	5	2	3	16	2	0	.125	12	18	1	5	0.6	.968
1976		2	0	1.000	2.96	48	2	0	85	80	39	34	0	1	0	1	8	1	0	.125	1	19	3	2	0.5	.870
1977		6	5	.545	4.01	55	8	1	119	116	60	41	0	4	2	0	18	4	0	.222	6	18	1	2	0.5	.960
1978		1	3	.250	5.44	25	1	0	48	60	28	22	0	1	3	0	5	0	0	.000	2	8	0	0	0.4	1.000
8 yrs.		23	22	.511	3.98	268	33	2	572	581	275	257	0	17	9	4	97	13	0	.134	34	102	8	12	0.5	.944

Dale Williams

WILLIAMS, ELISHA ALPHONSO
B. Oct. 6, 1855, Ludlow, Ky. D. Oct. 22, 1939, Covington, Ky.
BR TR 5'9" 175 lbs.

Year	Team	W	L	PCT	ERA	G	GS	CG	IP	H	BB	SO	ShO	W	L	SV	AB	H	HR	BA	PO	A	E	DP	TC/G	FA
1876	CIN N	1	8	.111	4.23	9	9	9	83	123	4	9	0	0	0	0	35	7	0	.200	10	8	0	0	2.0	1.000

Dave Williams

WILLIAMS, DAVID OWEN
B. 1879, Scranton, Pa. D. Apr. 25, 1918, Hot Springs, Ark.
BR TL

Year	Team	W	L	PCT	ERA	G	GS	CG	IP	H	BB	SO	ShO	W	L	SV	AB	H	HR	BA	PO	A	E	DP	TC/G	FA
1902	BOS A	0	0	–	5.30	3	0	0	18.2	22	11	7	0	0	0	0	9	3	0	.333	0	2	0	0	0.7	1.000

Don Williams

WILLIAMS, DONALD FRED
B. Sept. 14, 1931, Floyd, Va.
BR TR 6'2" 180 lbs.

Year	Team	W	L	PCT	ERA	G	GS	CG	IP	H	BB	SO	ShO	W	L	SV	AB	H	HR	BA	PO	A	E	DP	TC/G	FA
1958	PIT N	0	0	–	6.75	2	0	0	4	6	1	3	0	0	0	0	0	0	0	–	1	0	0	0	0.5	1.000
1959		0	0	–	6.75	6	0	0	12	17	3	3	0	0	0	0	3	1	0	.333	0	0	0	0	0.0	–
1962	KC A	0	0	–	9.00	3	0	0	4	6	0	1	0	0	0	0	1	0	0	.000	1	0	0	0	0.3	1.000
3 yrs.		0	0	–	7.20	11	0	0	20	29	4	7	0	0	0	0	4	1	0	.250	2	0	0	0	0.2	1.000

Don Williams

WILLIAMS, DONALD REID (Dino)
B. Sept. 2, 1935, Los Angeles, Calif.
BR TR 6'5" 218 lbs.

Year	Team	W	L	PCT	ERA	G	GS	CG	IP	H	BB	SO	ShO	W	L	SV	AB	H	HR	BA	PO	A	E	DP	TC/G	FA
1963	MIN A	0	0	–	10.38	3	0	0	4.1	8	6	2	0	0	0	0	0	0	0	–	2	0	0	0	1.3	1.000

Frank Williams

WILLIAMS, FRANK LEE
B. Feb. 13, 1958, Seattle, Wash.
BR TR 6'1" 180 lbs.

Year	Team	W	L	PCT	ERA	G	GS	CG	IP	H	BB	SO	ShO	W	L	SV	AB	H	HR	BA	PO	A	E	DP	TC/G	FA
1984	SF N	9	4	.692	3.55	61	1	1	106.1	88	51	91	1	8	4	3	18	4	0	.222	4	35	4	2	0.7	.907
1985		2	4	.333	4.19	49	0	0	73	65	35	54	0	2	4	0	3	0	0	.000	4	12	4	2	0.4	.800
1986		3	1	.750	1.20	36	0	0	52.1	35	21	33	0	3	1	1	2	1	0	.500	1	10	0	3	0.3	1.000
1987	CIN N	4	0	1.000	2.30	85	0	0	105.2	101	39	60	0	4	0	2	5	0	0	.000	8	19	2	5	0.3	.931
1988		3	2	.600	2.59	60	0	0	62.2	59	35	43	0	3	2	1	0	0	0	.000	2	13	4	1	0.3	.789
1989	DET A	3	3	.500	3.64	42	0	0	71.2	70	46	33	0	3	3	1	0	0	0	–	3	10	0	0	0.3	1.000
6 yrs.		24	14	.632	3.00	333	1	1	471.2	418	227	314	1	23	14	8	29	5	0	.172	22	99	14	13	0.4	.896

Gus Williams

WILLIAMS, AUGUSTINE H.
B. 1870, New York, N. Y. D. Oct. 14, 1890, New York, N. Y.
5'11" 170 lbs.

Year	Team	W	L	PCT	ERA	G	GS	CG	IP	H	BB	SO	ShO	W	L	SV	AB	H	HR	BA	PO	A	E	DP	TC/G	FA
1890	BKN AA	0	1	.000	7.50	2	2	1	12	13	12	2	0	0	0	0	4	2	0	.500	0	0	1	0	0.5	–

Johnny Williams

WILLIAMS, JOHN BRODIE (Honolulu Johnny)
B. July 16, 1889, Honolulu, Hawaii D. Sept. 8, 1963, Long Beach, Calif.
BR TR 6' 180 lbs.

Year	Team	W	L	PCT	ERA	G	GS	CG	IP	H	BB	SO	ShO	W	L	SV	AB	H	HR	BA	PO	A	E	DP	TC/G	FA
1914	DET A	0	2	.000	6.35	4	3	1	11.1	17	5	4	0	0	0	0	3	0	0	.000	0	2	1	0	0.8	.667

Lefty Williams

WILLIAMS, CLAUDE PRESTON
B. Mar. 9, 1893, Aurora, Mo. D. Nov. 4, 1959, Laguna Beach, Calif.
BR TL 5'9" 160 lbs.

Year	Team	W	L	PCT	ERA	G	GS	CG	IP	H	BB	SO	ShO	W	L	SV	AB	H	HR	BA	PO	A	E	DP	TC/G	FA
1913	DET A	1	3	.250	4.97	5	4	3	29	34	4	9	0	0	0	0	10	1	0	.100	1	3	0	0	0.6	1.000
1914		0	1	.000	0.00	1	1	0	1	3	2	0	0	0	0	0	0	0	0	–	0	0	0	0	0.0	–
1916	CHI A	13	7	.650	2.89	43	26	10	224.1	220	65	138	2	1	1	1	74	10	0	.135	9	37	0	0	1.1	1.000
1917		17	8	.680	2.97	45	29	8	230	221	81	85	1	4	2	1	67	6	0	.090	8	46	4	2	1.3	.931
1918		6	4	.600	2.73	15	14	7	105.2	76	47	30	2	0	0	1	38	5	0	.132	3	20	2	0	1.7	.920
1919		23	11	.676	2.64	41	**40**	27	297	265	58	125	5	0	0	1	94	17	0	.181	8	54	3	1	1.6	.954
1920		22	14	.611	3.91	39	38	26	299	302	90	128	1	0	1	0	101	22	0	.218	8	57	3	5	1.7	.956
7 yrs.		82	48	.631	3.13	189	152	81	1186	1121	347	515	10	6	3	5	384	61	0	.159	36	217	12	8	1.4	.955

WORLD SERIES

Year	Team	W	L	PCT	ERA	G	GS	CG	IP	H	BB	SO	ShO	W	L	SV	AB	H	HR	BA	PO	A	E	DP	TC/G	FA
1917	CHI A	0	0	–	9.00	1	0	0	1	2	0	0	0	0	0	0	0	0	0	–	0	1	0	0	1.0	–

Year	Team		W	L	PCT	ERA	G	GS	CG	IP	H	BB	SO	ShO	Relief Pitching			Batting			BA	PO	A	E	DP	TC/G	FA
															W	L	SV	AB	H	HR							

Lefty Williams *continued*

Year	Team		W	L	PCT	ERA	G	GS	CG	IP	H	BB	SO	ShO	W	L	SV	AB	H	HR	BA	PO	A	E	DP	TC/G	FA
1919			0	3	.000	6.61	3	3	1	16.1	12	8	4	0	0	0	0	5	1	0	.200	1	2	0	0	1.0	1.000
2 yrs.			0	3	.000	6.75	4	3	1	17.1	14	8	7	0	0	0	0	5	1	0	.200	1	2	1	0	1.0	.750

Leon Williams

WILLIAMS, LEON THEO
B. Dec. 2, 1905, Macon, Ga.

BL TL 5'10½" 154 lbs.

Year	Team		W	L	PCT	ERA	G	GS	CG	IP	H	BB	SO	ShO	W	L	SV	AB	H	HR	BA	PO	A	E	DP	TC/G	FA
1926	BKN	N	0	0	—	5.40	8	0	0	8.1	16	2	3	0	0	0	0	5	1	0	.200	0	5	0	0	0.6	1.000

Marsh Williams

WILLIAMS, MARSHALL McDIARMID (Cap)
B. Feb. 21, 1893, Fairson, N. C.   D. Feb. 22, 1935, Tucson, Ariz.

BR TR 6'   180 lbs.

Year	Team		W	L	PCT	ERA	G	GS	CG	IP	H	BB	SO	ShO	W	L	SV	AB	H	HR	BA	PO	A	E	DP	TC/G	FA
1916	PHI	A	0	6	.000	7.89	10	4	3	51.1	71	31	17	0	0	2	0	19	2	0	.105	2	11	2	1	1.5	.867

Matt Williams

WILLIAMS, MATTHEW EVAN
B. July 25, 1959, Houston, Tex.

BR TR 6'1"   200 lbs.

Year	Team		W	L	PCT	ERA	G	GS	CG	IP	H	BB	SO	ShO	W	L	SV	AB	H	HR	BA	PO	A	E	DP	TC/G	FA
1983	TOR	A	1	1	.500	14.63	4	3	0	8	13	7	5	0	0	0	0	0	0	0	—	0	3	0	0	0.8	1.000
1985	TEX	A	2	1	.667	2.42	6	3	0	26	20	10	22	0	1	0	0	0	0	0	—	0	1	0	0	0.3	.500
2 yrs.			3	2	.600	5.29	10	6	0	34	33	17	27	0	1	0	0	0	0	0	—	0	4	0	0	0.5	.800

Mitch Williams

WILLIAMS, MITCHELL STEVEN (Wild Thing)
B. Nov. 17, 1964, Santa Ana, Calif.

BL TL 6'3"   180 lbs.

Year	Team		W	L	PCT	ERA	G	GS	CG	IP	H	BB	SO	ShO	W	L	SV	AB	H	HR	BA	PO	A	E	DP	TC/G	FA
1986	TEX	A	8	6	.571	3.58	**80**	0	0	98	69	79	90	0	8	6	8	0	0	0	—	1	10	2	1	0.2	.846
1987			8	6	.571	3.23	85	1	0	108.2	63	94	129	0	8	5	6	0	0	0	—	5	15	3	3	0.3	.870
1988			2	7	.222	4.63	67	0	0	68	48	47	61	0	2	7	18	0	0	0	—	3	10	1	0	0.2	.929
1989	CHI	N	4	4	.500	2.64	**76**	0	0	81.2	71	52	67	0	4	4	36	5	1	1	.200	0	11	3	0	0.2	.786
4 yrs.			22	23	.489	3.46	308	1	0	356.1	251	272	347	0	22	22	68	5	1	1	.200	9	46	9	4	0.2	.859

LEAGUE CHAMPIONSHIP SERIES

Year	Team		W	L	PCT	ERA	G	GS	CG	IP	H	BB	SO	ShO	W	L	SV	AB	H	HR	BA	PO	A	E	DP	TC/G	FA
1989	CHI	N	0	0	—	0.00	2	0	0	1	1	0	2	0	0	0	0	0	0	0	—	0	0	0	0	0.0	—

Mutt Williams

WILLIAMS, DAVID CARTER
B. July 31, 1891, Ozark, Ark.   D. Mar. 30, 1962, Fayetteville, Ark.

BR TR 6'3½"   195 lbs.

Year	Team		W	L	PCT	ERA	G	GS	CG	IP	H	BB	SO	ShO	W	L	SV	AB	H	HR	BA	PO	A	E	DP	TC/G	FA
1913	WAS	A	1	0	1.000	4.50	1	1	0	4	4	2	1	0	0	0	0	2	1	0	.500	1	2	1	0	4.0	.750
1914			0	0	—	5.14	5	0	0	7	5	4	3	0	0	0	1	0	0	0	—	0	0	0	0	0.0	—
2 yrs.			1	0	1.000	4.91	6	1	0	11	9	6	4	0	0	0	1	2	1	0	.500	1	2	1	0	0.7	.750

Pop Williams

WILLIAMS, WALTER MERRILL
B. May 19, 1874, Bowdoinham, Me.   D. Aug. 4, 1959, Topsham, Me.

BL TL 5'11"   190 lbs.

Year	Team		W	L	PCT	ERA	G	GS	CG	IP	H	BB	SO	ShO	W	L	SV	AB	H	HR	BA	PO	A	E	DP	TC/G	FA
1898	WAS	N	0	2	.000	8.47	2	2	2	17	32	7	3	0	0	0	0	8	3	0	.375	0	2	1	0	1.5	.667
1902	CHI	N	12	16	.429	2.51	31	31	26	254.1	259	63	94	1	0	0	0	116	23	0	.198	12	78	4	1	3.0	.957
1903	**3 teams**							CHI N	(1G 0–1)		PHI N	(2G 1–1)		BOS N	(10G 4–5)												
"	total		5	7	.417	3.99	13	13	12	106	127	43	30	1	0	0	0	51	12	0	.235	7	28	3	2	2.9	.921
3 yrs.			17	25	.405	3.20	46	46	40	377.1	418	113	127	2	0	0	0	175	38	0	.217	19	108	8	3	2.9	.941

Rick Williams

WILLIAMS, RICHARD ALLEN
B. Nov. 9, 1952, Merced, Calif.

BR TR 6'1"   180 lbs.

Year	Team		W	L	PCT	ERA	G	GS	CG	IP	H	BB	SO	ShO	W	L	SV	AB	H	HR	BA	PO	A	E	DP	TC/G	FA
1978	HOU	N	1	2	.333	4.63	17	1	0	35	43	10	17	0	1	0	0	5	0	0	.000	1	7	1	0	0.5	.889
1979			4	7	.364	3.27	31	16	2	121	122	30	37	2	0	0	0	31	8	0	.258	3	23	1	2	0.9	.963
2 yrs.			5	9	.357	3.58	48	17	2	156	165	40	54	2	1	1	0	36	8	0	.222	4	30	2	2	0.8	.944

Stan Williams

WILLIAMS, STANLEY WILSON
B. Sept. 14, 1936, Enfield, N. H.

BR TR 6'5"   230 lbs.

Year	Team		W	L	PCT	ERA	G	GS	CG	IP	H	BB	SO	ShO	W	L	SV	AB	H	HR	BA	PO	A	E	DP	TC/G	FA
1958	LA	N	9	7	.563	4.01	27	21	3	119	99	65	80	2	1	1	0	40	2	1	.050	10	16	1	1	1.0	.963
1959			5	5	.500	3.97	35	15	2	124.2	102	86	89	0	2	2	0	36	7	0	.194	6	21	0	1	0.8	1.000
1960			14	10	.583	3.00	38	30	9	207.1	162	72	175	2	0	0	1	64	9	2	.141	15	33	1	2	1.3	.980
1961			15	12	.556	3.90	41	35	6	235.1	213	108	205	2	1	0	0	78	13	0	.167	12	37	7	3	1.4	.875
1962			14	12	.538	4.46	40	28	4	185.2	184	98	108	1	1	1	1	66	5	2	.076	8	28	2	3	1.0	.947
1963	NY	A	9	8	.529	3.20	29	21	6	146.1	137	57	98	1	2	2	0	49	5	0	.102	9	25	2	2	1.2	.944
1964			1	5	.167	3.84	21	10	1	82	76	38	54	0	1	1	0	21	3	0	.143	8	15	2	1	1.2	.920
1965	CLE	A	0	0	—	6.23	3	0	0	4.1	6	3	1	0	0	0	0	0	0	0	—	0	1	0	0	0.3	1.000
1967			6	4	.600	2.62	16	8	0	79	64	24	75	1	3	0	1	22	2	0	.091	4	4	1	0	0.6	.889
1968			13	11	.542	2.50	44	24	0	194.1	163	51	147	2	2	0	9	56	9	0	.161	7	27	1	2	0.8	.971
1969			6	14	.300	3.94	61	15	0	178.1	155	67	139	0	4	4	0	40	4	0	.100	15	19	3	1	0.6	.919
1970	MIN	A	10	1	.909	1.99	68	0	0	113	85	32	76	0	**10**	1	15	19	0	0	.000	8	8	0	0	0.2	1.000
1971	**2 teams**							MIN A	(46G 4–5)		STL N	(10G 3–0)																
"	total		7	5	.583	3.76	56	1	0	91	76	46	55	0	7	5	4	11	0	0	.000	7	11	1	2	0.3	.947
1972	BOS	A	0	0	—	6.75	3	0	0	4	5	1	3	0	0	0	0	0	0	0	—	0	0	0	0	0.3	1.000
14 yrs.			109	94	.537	3.48	482	208	42	1764.1	1527	748	1305	11	32	22	43	502	59	5	.118	109	246	21	17	0.8	.944

LEAGUE CHAMPIONSHIP SERIES

Year	Team		W	L	PCT	ERA	G	GS	CG	IP	H	BB	SO	ShO	W	L	SV	AB	H	HR	BA	PO	A	E	DP	TC/G	FA
1970	MIN	A	0	0	—	0.00	2	0	0	6	2	1	2	0	0	0	0	0	0	0	—	0	0	0	0	0.0	—

WORLD SERIES

Year	Team		W	L	PCT	ERA	G	GS	CG	IP	H	BB	SO	ShO	W	L	SV	AB	H	HR	BA	PO	A	E	DP	TC/G	FA
1959	LA	N	0	0	—	0.00	1	0	0	2	0	2	1	0	0	0	0	0	0	0	—	0	0	0	0	0.0	—
1963	NY	A	0	0	—	0.00	1	0	0	3	1	0	5	0	0	0	0	0	0	0	—	0	0	0	0	0.0	—
2 yrs.			0	0	—	0.00	2	0	0	5	1	2	6	0	0	0	0	0	0	0	—	0	0	0	0	0.0	—

Steamboat Williams

WILLIAMS, REES GEPHARDT
B. Jan. 31, 1892, Cascade, Mont.   D. June 29, 1979, Deer River, Minn.

BL TR 5'11"   170 lbs.

Year	Team		W	L	PCT	ERA	G	GS	CG	IP	H	BB	SO	ShO	W	L	SV	AB	H	HR	BA	PO	A	E	DP	TC/G	FA
1914	STL	N	0	1	.000	6.55	5	1	0	11	13	6	2	0	0	0	0	1	0	0	.000	0	3	0	0	0.6	1.000

Year	Team		W	L	PCT	ERA	G	GS	CG	IP	H	BB	SO	ShO	Relief Pitching W	L	SV	Batting AB	H	HR	BA	PO	A	E	DP	TC/G	FA

Steamboat Williams *continued*

| 1916 | | | 6 | 7 | .462 | 4.20 | 36 | 8 | 5 | 105 | 121 | 27 | 25 | 0 | 4 | 2 | 1 | 24 | 5 | 0 | .208 | 1 | 31 | 5 | 1 | 1.0 | .865 |
| 2 yrs. | | | 6 | 8 | .429 | 4.42 | 41 | 9 | 5 | 116 | 134 | 33 | 27 | 0 | 4 | 2 | 1 | 25 | 5 | 0 | .200 | 1 | 34 | 5 | 1 | 1.0 | .875 |

Ted Williams

WILLIAMS, THEODORE SAMUEL (The Splendid Splinter, The Thumper)   BL TR 6'3"   205 lbs.
B. Aug. 30, 1918, San Diego, Calif.
Manager 1969-72.
Hall of Fame 1966.

| 1940 | BOS | A | 0 | 0 | – | 4.50 | 1 | 0 | 0 | 2 | 3 | 0 | 1 | 0 | 0 | 0 | 0 | * | | | | 0 | 2 | 0 | 0 | 2.0 | 1.000 |

Tom Williams

WILLIAMS, THOMAS C.
B. Aug. 19, 1870, Minersville, Ohio   D. July 27, 1940, Columbus, Ohio

1892	CLE	N	1	0	1.000	3.00	2	1	1	9	9	1	3	0	0	0	0	10	1	0	.100	0	2	1	0	1.5	.667
1893			1	1	.500	4.88	5	2	2	24	33	10	6	0	0	0	0	18	5	0	.278	0	7	3	0	2.0	.700
2 yrs.			2	1	.667	4.36	7	3	3	33	42	11	9	0	0	0	0	28	6	0	.214	0	9	4	0	1.9	.692

Wash Williams

WILLIAMS, WASHINGTON J.   5'11"   180 lbs.
B. Philadelphia, Pa.   D. Aug. 9, 1892, Philadelphia, Pa.

| 1885 | CHI | N | 0 | 0 | – | 13.50 | 1 | 1 | 0 | 2 | 2 | 5 | 0 | 0 | 0 | 0 | 0 | * | | | | 0 | 1 | 0 | 0 | 1.0 | 1.000 |

Al Williamson

WILLIAMSON, SILAS ALBERT   BR TR 5'11"   160 lbs.
B. Feb. 20, 1900, Buckville, Ark.   D. Nov. 29, 1978, Hot Springs, Ark.

| 1928 | CHI | A | 0 | 0 | – | 0.00 | 1 | 0 | 0 | 2 | 1 | 0 | 0 | 0 | 0 | 0 | 0 | 0 | 0 | 0 | – | 1 | 0 | 0 | 0 | 1.0 | 1.000 |

Mark Williamson

WILLIAMSON, MARK ALAN   BR TR 6'   155 lbs.
B. July 21, 1959, Corpus Christi, Tex.

1987	BAL	A	8	9	.471	4.03	61	2	0	125	122	41	73	0	8	8	3	0	0	0	–	20	17	2	1	0.6	.949
1988			5	8	.385	4.90	37	10	2	117.2	125	40	69	0	4	2	2	0	0	0	–	9	14	1	0	0.6	.958
1989			10	5	.667	2.93	65	0	0	107.1	105	30	55	0	10	5	9	0	0	0	–	9	10	0	1	0.3	1.000
3 yrs.			23	22	.511	3.99	163	12	2	350	352	111	197	0	22	15	14	0	0	0	–	38	41	3	2	0.5	.963

Ned Williamson

WILLIAMSON, EDWARD NAGLE   BR TR 5'11"   170 lbs.
B. Oct. 24, 1857, Philadelphia, Pa.   D. Mar. 3, 1894, Willow Springs, Ark.

1881	CHI	N	1	1	.500	2.00	3	1	1	18	14	0	2	0	0	0	0	343	92	1	.268	1	2	0	0	1.0	1.000
1882			0	0	–	6.00	1	0	0	3	9	1	0	0	0	0	0	348	98	3	.282	0	1	0	0	1.0	1.000
1883			0	0	–	9.00	1	0	0	1	1	1	1	0	0	0	0	402	111	2	.276	0	0	0	0	0.0	–
1884			0	0	–	18.00	2	0	0	2	8	2	0	0	0	0	0	417	116	27	.278	0	0	0	0	0.5	1.000
1885			0	0	–	0.00	2	0	0	6	2	0	3	0	0	0	2	407	97	3	.238	0	0	0	0	1.5	1.000
1886			0	0	–	0.00	2	0	0	3	2	0	1	0	0	0	0	430	93	6	.216	0	0	0	0	0.0	–
1887			0	0	–	9.00	1	0	0	2	2	1	0	0	0	0	0	439	117	9	.267	0	1	0	0	1.0	1.000
7 yrs.			1	1	.500	3.34	12	1	1	35	38	5	7	0	0	0	3	*				2	7	0	0	0.8	1.000

Carl Willis

WILLIS, CARL BLAKE   BL TR 6'4"   210 lbs.
B. Dec. 28, 1960, Danville, Va.

1984	**2 teams**	DET A (10G 0–2)	CIN N	(7G 0–1)																							
"	total		0	3	.000	5.96	17	2	0	25.2	33	7	7	0	0	2	1	0	0	0	–	1	5	0	1	0.4	1.000
1985	CIN	N	1	0	1.000	9.22	11	0	0	13.2	21	5	6	0	1	0	1	1	0	0	.000	0	1	1	0	0.2	.500
1986			1	3	.250	4.47	29	0	0	52.1	54	32	24	0	1	3	0	3	1	0	.333	4	10	0	3	0.5	1.000
1988	CHI	A	0	0	–	8.25	6	0	0	12	17	7	6	0	0	0	0	0	0	0	–	3	0	0	0	0.5	1.000
4 yrs.			2	6	.250	5.90	63	2	0	103.2	125	51	43	0	2	5	2	4	1	0	.250	8	16	1	4	0.4	.960

Dale Willis

WILLIS, DALE JEROME   BR TR 5'11"   165 lbs.
B. May 29, 1938, Calhoun, Ga.

| 1963 | KC | A | 0 | 2 | .000 | 5.04 | 25 | 0 | 0 | 44.2 | 46 | 25 | 47 | 0 | 0 | 2 | 1 | 6 | 1 | 0 | .167 | 4 | 8 | 1 | 0 | 0.5 | .923 |

Jim Willis

WILLIS, JAMES GLADDEN   BL TR 6'3"   175 lbs.
B. Mar. 20, 1927, Doyline, La.

1953	CHI	N	2	1	.667	3.12	13	3	2	43.1	37	17	15	0	0	0	0	9	0	0	.000	4	12	0	0	1.2	1.000
1954			0	1	.000	3.91	14	1	0	23	22	18	5	0	0	0	0	5	0	0	.000	0	8	0	1	0.6	1.000
2 yrs.			2	2	.500	3.39	27	4	2	66.1	59	35	20	0	0	0	0	14	0	0	.000	4	20	0	1	0.9	1.000

Joe Willis

WILLIS, JOSEPH DANK (Big Joe)   BR TL 6'1"   185 lbs.
B. Apr. 9, 1890, Coal Grove, Ohio   D. Dec. 4, 1966, Ironton, Ohio

1911	**2 teams**	STL A (1G 0–1)	STL N	(2G 0–1)																							
"	total		0	2	.000	4.50	3	3	1	22	21	7	5	0	0	0	0	7	0	0	.000	0	5	0	0	1.7	1.000
1912	STL	N	4	9	.308	4.44	31	17	4	129.2	143	62	55	0	1	2	2	38	6	0	.158	3	26	0	4	0.9	1.000
1913			0	0	–	7.45	7	0	0	9.2	9	11	6	0	0	0	0	3	0	0	.000	0	2	0	0	0.3	1.000
3 yrs.			4	11	.267	4.63	41	20	5	161.1	173	80	66	0	1	2	3	48	6	0	.125	3	33	0	4	0.9	1.000

Lefty Willis

WILLIS, CHARLES WILLIAM   BL TL 6'1"   175 lbs.
B. Nov. 4, 1905, Leetown, W. Va.   BR 1925
D. May 10, 1962, Bethesda, Md.

1925	PHI	A	0	0	–	10.80	1	1	0	5	9	2	3	0	0	0	0	3	0	0	.000	0	2	0	0	2.0	1.000
1926			0	0	–	1.39	13	1	0	32.1	31	12	13	0	0	0	0	9	2	0	.222	1	6	1	1	0.6	.875
1927			3	1	.750	5.67	15	2	1	27	32	11	7	0	2	0	0	6	0	0	.000	2	11	0	0	0.9	1.000
3 yrs.			3	1	.750	3.92	29	4	1	64.1	72	25	23	0	2	0	1	18	2	0	.111	3	19	1	1	0.8	.957

Year	Team		W	L	PCT	ERA	G	GS	CG	IP	H	BB	SO	ShO	Relief Pitching W	L	SV	Batting AB	H	HR	BA	PO	A	E	DP	TC/G	FA

Les Willis

WILLIS, LESTER EVANS (Lefty, Wimpy)
B. Jan. 17, 1908, Nacogdoches, Tex. D. Jan. 22, 1982, Jasper, Tex.

BL TL 5'9½" 195 lbs.

Year	Team		W	L	PCT	ERA	G	GS	CG	IP	H	BB	SO	ShO	W	L	SV	AB	H	HR	BA	PO	A	E	DP	TC/G	FA
1947	CLE	A	0	2	.000	3.48	22	2	0	44	58	24	10	0	0	1	1	11	1	0	.091	2	4	0	1	0.3	1.000

Mike Willis

WILLIS, MICHAEL HENRY
B. Dec. 26, 1950, Oklahoma City, Okla.

BL TL 6'2" 205 lbs.

Year	Team		W	L	PCT	ERA	G	GS	CG	IP	H	BB	SO	ShO	W	L	SV	AB	H	HR	BA	PO	A	E	DP	TC/G	FA
1977	TOR	A	2	6	.250	3.95	43	3	0	107	105	38	59	0	2	5	5	0	0	0	–	6	19	1	1	0.6	.962
1978			3	7	.300	4.56	44	2	1	100.2	104	39	52	0	2	6	7	0	0	0	–	4	18	1	0	0.5	.957
1979			0	3	.000	8.33	17	1	0	27	35	16	8	0	0	2	0	0	0	0	–	1	5	0	0	0.4	1.000
1980			2	1	.667	1.73	20	0	0	26	25	11	14	0	2	1	3	0	0	0	–	5	2	0	0	0.4	1.000
1981			0	4	.000	5.91	20	0	0	35	43	20	16	0	0	4	0	0	0	0	–	3	5	0	1	0.4	1.000
5 yrs.			7	21	.250	4.60	144	6	1	295.2	312	124	149	0	6	18	15	0	0	0	–	19	49	2	2	0.5	.971

Ron Willis

WILLIS, RONALD EARL
B. July 12, 1943, Willisville, Tenn. D. Nov. 21, 1977, Memphis, Tenn.

BR TR 6'2" 185 lbs.

Year	Team		W	L	PCT	ERA	G	GS	CG	IP	H	BB	SO	ShO	W	L	SV	AB	H	HR	BA	PO	A	E	DP	TC/G	FA
1966	STL	N	0	0	–	0.00	4	0	0	3	1	1	2	0	0	0	1	0	0	0	–	0	0	0	0	0.0	–
1967			6	5	.545	2.67	65	0	0	81	76	43	42	0	6	5	10	8	3	0	.375	8	20	0	5	0.4	1.000
1968			2	3	.400	3.39	48	0	0	63.2	50	28	39	0	2	3	4	11	0	0	.000	2	15	0	0	0.4	1.000
1969	2 teams		STL N	(26G 1–2)		HOU N	(3G 0–0)																				
"	total		1	2	.333	3.89	29	0	0	34.2	29	19	25	0	1	2	0	1	1	0	1.000	1	6	0	0	0.2	1.000
1970	SD	N	2	2	.500	4.02	42	0	0	56	53	28	20	0	2	2	4	5	0	0	.000	9	13	0	1	0.5	1.000
5 yrs.			11	12	.478	3.32	188	0	0	238.1	209	119	128	0	11	12	19	25	4	0	.160	24	56	0	6	0.4	1.000

WORLD SERIES

Year	Team		W	L	PCT	ERA	G	GS	CG	IP	H	BB	SO	ShO	W	L	SV	AB	H	HR	BA	PO	A	E	DP	TC/G	FA
1967	STL	N	0	0	–	27.00	3	0	0	1	2	4	1	0	0	0	0	0	0	0	–	0	0	0	0	0.0	–
1968			0	0	–	8.31	3	0	0	4.1	2	4	3	0	0	0	0	0	0	0	–	1	0	0	0	0.3	1.000
2 yrs.			0	0	–	11.81	6	0	0	5.1	4	8	4	0	0	0	0	0	0	0	–	1	0	0	0	0.2	1.000

Vic Willis

WILLIS, VICTOR GAZAWAY
B. Apr. 12, 1876, Cecil County, Md. D. Aug. 3, 1947, Elkton, Md.

BR TR 6'2" 185 lbs.

Year	Team		W	L	PCT	ERA	G	GS	CG	IP	H	BB	SO	ShO	W	L	SV	AB	H	HR	BA	PO	A	E	DP	TC/G	FA
1898	BOS	N	25	13	.658	2.84	41	38	29	311	264	148	160	1	1	1	0	117	17	0	.145	19	67	11	1	2.4	.887
1899			27	8	.771	2.50	41	38	35	342.2	277	117	120	5	0	0	2	134	29	0	.216	17	81	8	2	2.6	.925
1900			10	17	.370	4.19	32	29	22	236	258	106	53	0	1	0	0	88	12	0	.136	10	49	2	0	1.9	.967
1901			20	17	.541	2.36	38	35	33	305.1	262	78	133	6	2	0	0	107	20	1	.187	22	66	3	2	2.4	.967
1902			27	19	.587	2.20	51	46	45	410	372	101	225	4	1	1	3	150	23	0	.153	37	105	4	5	2.9	.973
1903			12	18	.400	2.98	33	32	29	278	256	88	125	2	0	0	0	128	24	0	.188	13	84	4	1	3.1	.960
1904			18	25	.419	2.85	43	43	39	350	357	109	196	2	0	0	0	148	27	0	.182	39	110	1	5	3.5	.993
1905			11	29	.275	3.21	41	41	36	342	340	107	149	4	0	0	0	131	20	0	.153	37	115	7	3	3.9	.956
1906	PIT	N	22	13	.629	1.73	41	36	32	322	295	76	124	6	0	1	0	115	20	0	.174	22	117	8	5	3.6	.946
1907			22	11	.667	2.34	39	37	27	292.2	234	69	107	6	1	0	1	103	14	0	.136	17	87	3	2	2.7	.972
1908			23	11	.676	2.07	41	38	25	304.2	239	69	97	7	1	0	0	103	17	0	.165	11	87	1	2	2.4	.990
1909			22	11	.667	2.24	41	35	24	289.2	243	83	95	4	1	0	0	103	14	0	.136	16	85	5	1	2.7	.953
1910	STL	N	9	12	.429	3.35	33	23	12	212	224	61	67	1	3	0	3	66	11	0	.167	11	71	4	0	2.6	.953
13 yrs.			248	204	.549	2.63	513	471	388	3996	3621	1212	1651	50	13	3	10	1493	248	1	.166	271	1124	61	29	2.8	.958

WORLD SERIES

Year	Team		W	L	PCT	ERA	G	GS	CG	IP	H	BB	SO	ShO	W	L	SV	AB	H	HR	BA	PO	A	E	DP	TC/G	FA
1909	PIT	N	0	1	.000	4.76	2	1	0	11.1	10	8	3	0	0	0	0	4	0	0	.000	1	2	0	0	1.5	1.000

Claude Willoughby

WILLOUGHBY, CLAUDE WILLIAM (Weeping Willie, Flunky)
B. Nov. 14, 1898, Fredonia, Kans. D. Aug. 14, 1973, McPherson, Kans.

BR TR 5'9½" 165 lbs.

Year	Team		W	L	PCT	ERA	G	GS	CG	IP	H	BB	SO	ShO	W	L	SV	AB	H	HR	BA	PO	A	E	DP	TC/G	FA
1925	PHI	N	2	1	.667	1.96	3	3	1	23	26	11	6	0	0	0	0	8	0	0	.000	1	3	0	0	1.3	1.000
1926			8	12	.400	5.95	47	18	6	168	218	71	37	0	4	1	1	52	11	0	.212	6	54	2	4	1.3	.968
1927			3	7	.300	6.54	35	6	1	97.2	126	53	14	1	2	3	2	26	2	0	.077	4	19	1	2	0.7	.958
1928			6	5	.545	5.30	35	13	5	130.2	180	83	26	1	2	1	1	40	6	0	.150	9	25	2	6	1.0	.944
1929			15	14	.517	4.99	49	34	14	243.1	288	108	50	1	0	2	4	91	13	0	.143	8	76	2	6	1.8	.977
1930			4	17	.190	7.59	41	24	5	153	241	68	38	1	0	1	1	48	5	0	.104	3	41	0	7	1.1	1.000
1931	PIT	N	0	2	.000	6.31	9	2	1	25.2	32	12	4	0	0	0	0	7	2	0	.286	0	8	1	0	1.0	.889
7 yrs.			38	58	.396	5.84	219	100	33	841.1	1111	406	175	4	8	9	9	272	39	0	.143	31	226	8	25	1.2	.970

Jim Willoughby

WILLOUGHBY, JAMES ARTHUR
B. Jan. 31, 1949, Salinas, Calif.

BR TR 6'2" 185 lbs.

Year	Team		W	L	PCT	ERA	G	GS	CG	IP	H	BB	SO	ShO	W	L	SV	AB	H	HR	BA	PO	A	E	DP	TC/G	FA
1971	SF	N	0	1	.000	9.00	2	1	0	4	8	1	3	0	0	0	0	1	0	0	.000	0	2	0	0	1.0	1.000
1972			6	4	.600	2.35	11	11	7	88	72	14	40	0	0	0	0	27	5	0	.185	8	12	1	1	1.9	.952
1973			4	5	.444	4.70	39	12	1	122.2	138	37	60	1	1	2	1	28	4	1	.143	7	15	0	1	0.6	1.000
1974			1	4	.200	4.61	18	4	0	41	51	9	12	0	1	4	0	10	1	0	.100	6	10	0	0	0.9	1.000
1975	BOS	A	5	2	.714	3.54	24	0	0	48.1	46	16	29	0	5	2	8	0	0	0	–	3	7	0	0	0.4	1.000
1976			3	12	.200	2.82	54	0	0	99	94	31	37	0	3	12	10	1	0	0	.000	7	22	2	1	0.6	.935
1977			6	2	.750	4.94	31	0	0	54.2	54	18	33	0	6	2	2	0	0	0	–	12	10	1	1	0.7	.957
1978	CHI	A	1	6	.143	3.86	59	0	0	93.1	95	19	36	0	1	6	13	0	0	0	–	11	19	1	3	0.5	.968
8 yrs.			26	36	.419	3.79	238	28	8	551	558	145	250	1	16	25	34	67	10	1	.149	54	97	5	7	0.7	.968

WORLD SERIES

Year	Team		W	L	PCT	ERA	G	GS	CG	IP	H	BB	SO	ShO	W	L	SV	AB	H	HR	BA	PO	A	E	DP	TC/G	FA
1975	BOS	A	0	1	.000	0.00	3	0	0	6.1	3	0	2	0	0	1	0	0	0	0	–	1	0	0	0	0.3	1.000

Frank Wills

WILLS, FRANK LEE, JR.
B. Oct. 26, 1958, New Orleans, La.

BR TR 6'2" 200 lbs.

Year	Team		W	L	PCT	ERA	G	GS	CG	IP	H	BB	SO	ShO	W	L	SV	AB	H	HR	BA	PO	A	E	DP	TC/G	FA
1983	KC	A	2	1	.667	4.15	6	4	0	34.2	35	15	23	0	0	0	0	0	0	0	–	1	3	1	1	0.8	.800
1984			2	3	.400	5.11	10	5	0	37	39	13	21	0	1	0	0	0	0	0	–	3	2	2	0	0.7	.714
1985	SEA	A	5	11	.313	6.00	24	18	1	123	122	68	67	0	0	0	0	0	0	0	–	9	17	0	1	1.1	1.000
1986	CLE	A	4	4	.500	4.91	26	0	0	40.1	43	16	32	0	4	4	1	0	0	0	–	3	6	1	0	0.4	.900
1987			0	1	.000	5.06	6	0	0	5.1	7	4	7	0	0	1	0	0	0	0	–	1	0	0	0	0.3	1.000
1988	TOR	A	0	0	–	5.23	10	0	0	20.2	22	6	19	0	0	0	0	0	0	0	–	1	5	0	0	0.6	1.000

Year	Team	W	L	PCT	ERA	G	GS	CG	IP	H	BB	SO	ShO	Relief Pitching W	L	SV	Batting AB	H	HR	BA	PO	A	E	DP	TC/G	FA

Frank Wills *continued*

Year	Team	W	L	PCT	ERA	G	GS	CG	IP	H	BB	SO	ShO	W	L	SV	AB	H	HR	BA	PO	A	E	DP	TC/G	FA
1989		3	1	.750	3.66	24	4	0	71.1	65	30	41	0	3	0	0	0	0	0	–	5	10	0	0	0.6	1.000
7 yrs.		16	21	.432	5.01	106	31	1	332.1	329	155	207	0	8	5	6	0	0	0	–	22	45	4	2	0.7	.944

Ted Wills

WILLS, THEODORE CARL
B. Feb. 9, 1934, Fresno, Calif.
BL TL 6'2" 200 lbs.

Year	Team	W	L	PCT	ERA	G	GS	CG	IP	H	BB	SO	ShO	W	L	SV	AB	H	HR	BA	PO	A	E	DP	TC/G	FA
1959	BOS A	2	6	.250	5.27	9	8	0	56.1	68	24	24	0	0	0	0	16	4	0	.250	1	9	0	1	1.1	1.000
1960		1	1	.500	7.42	15	0	0	30.1	38	16	28	0	1	1	1	8	2	0	.250	1	7	0	0	0.5	1.000
1961		3	2	.600	5.95	17	0	0	19.2	24	19	11	0	3	2	0	2	0	0	.000	1	4	1	1	0.4	.833
1962	2 teams	BOS A	(1G 0–0)		CIN N	(26G 0–2)																				
"	total	0	2	.000	5.46	27	5	0	61	63	24	58	0	0	1	3	16	5	0	.313	3	8	2	2	0.5	.846
1965	CHI A	2	0	1.000	2.84	15	0	0	19	17	14	12	0	2	0	1	2	0	0	.000	1	6	1	0	0.5	.875
5 yrs.		8	11	.421	5.51	83	13	2	186.1	210	97	133	0	6	4	5	44	11	0	.250	7	34	4	4	0.5	.911

Paul Wilmet

WILMET, PAUL RICHARD
B. Nov. 8, 1958, Green Bay, Wis.
BR TR 5'11" 170 lbs.

Year	Team	W	L	PCT	ERA	G	GS	CG	IP	H	BB	SO	ShO	W	L	SV	AB	H	HR	BA	PO	A	E	DP	TC/G	FA
1989	TEX A	0	0	–	15.43	3	0	0	2.1	5	2	1	0	0	0	0	0	0	0	–	0	1	0	0	0.3	1.000

Whitey Wilshere

WILSHERE, VERNON SPRAGUE
B. Aug. 3, 1912, Poplar Ridge, N. Y. D. May 23, 1985, Cooperstown, N. Y.
BL TL 6' 180 lbs.

Year	Team	W	L	PCT	ERA	G	GS	CG	IP	H	BB	SO	ShO	W	L	SV	AB	H	HR	BA	PO	A	E	DP	TC/G	FA
1934	PHI A	0	1	.000	12.05	9	2	0	21.2	39	15	19	0	0	0	0	3	0	0	.000	0	0	0	0	0.0	–
1935		9	9	.500	4.05	27	18	7	142.1	136	78	80	3	2	1	1	43	4	0	.093	2	25	0	1	1.0	1.000
1936		1	2	.333	6.87	5	3	0	18.1	21	19	4	0	0	0	0	4	0	0	.000	1	3	1	0	1.0	.800
3 yrs.		10	12	.455	5.28	41	23	7	182.1	196	112	103	3	2	1	1	50	4	0	.080	3	28	1	1	0.8	.969

Terry Wilshusen

WILSHUSEN, TERRY WAYNE
B. Mar. 22, 1949, Atascadero, Calif.
BR TR 6'2" 210 lbs.

Year	Team	W	L	PCT	ERA	G	GS	CG	IP	H	BB	SO	ShO	W	L	SV	AB	H	HR	BA	PO	A	E	DP	TC/G	FA
1973	CAL A	0	0	–	81.00	1	0	0	.1	0	2	0	0	0	0	0	0	0	0	–	0	0	0	0	0.0	–

Bill Wilson

WILSON, WILLIAM DONALD
B. Nov. 6, 1928, Central City, Neb.
BR TR 6'2" 200 lbs.

Year	Team	W	L	PCT	ERA	G	GS	CG	IP	H	BB	SO	ShO	W	L	SV	AB	H	HR	BA	PO	A	E	DP	TC/G	FA
1955	KC A	0	0	–	0.00	1	0	0	1	1	1	1	0	0	0	0	*				0	0	0	0	0.0	–

Billy Wilson

WILSON, WILLIAM HARLAN
B. Sept. 21, 1942, Pomeroy, Ohio
BR TR 6'2" 195 lbs.

Year	Team	W	L	PCT	ERA	G	GS	CG	IP	H	BB	SO	ShO	W	L	SV	AB	H	HR	BA	PO	A	E	DP	TC/G	FA
1969	PHI N	2	5	.286	3.34	37	0	0	62	53	36	48	0	2	5	6	6	0	0	.000	2	6	0	0	0.2	1.000
1970		1	0	1.000	4.81	37	0	0	58	57	33	41	0	1	0	0	4	1	0	.250	0	9	1	1	0.3	.900
1971		4	6	.400	3.05	38	0	0	59	39	22	40	0	4	6	7	10	1	0	.100	5	16	1	0	0.6	.955
1972		1	1	.500	3.30	23	0	0	30	26	11	18	0	1	1	0	0	0	0	–	4	4	0	0	0.3	1.000
1973		1	3	.250	6.66	44	0	0	48.2	54	29	24	0	1	3	4	4	0	0	.000	2	6	0	0	0.2	1.000
5 yrs.		9	15	.375	4.23	179	0	0	257.2	229	131	171	0	9	15	17	24	2	0	.083	13	41	2	1	0.3	.964

Chink Wilson

WILSON, WILLIAM
B. Jan. 7, 1884, Columbus, Ohio D. Oct. 28, 1925, Seattle, Wash.
BR TR

Year	Team	W	L	PCT	ERA	G	GS	CG	IP	H	BB	SO	ShO	W	L	SV	AB	H	HR	BA	PO	A	E	DP	TC/G	FA
1906	WAS A	0	1	.000	2.57	1	1	1	7	3	2	1	0	0	0	0	2	0	0	.000	0	3	0	0	3.0	1.000

Don Wilson

WILSON, DONALD EDWARD
B. Feb. 12, 1945, Monroe, La. D. Jan. 5, 1975, Houston, Tex.
BR TR 6'2½" *195 lbs.

Year	Team	W	L	PCT	ERA	G	GS	CG	IP	H	BB	SO	ShO	W	L	SV	AB	H	HR	BA	PO	A	E	DP	TC/G	FA
1966	HOU N	1	0	1.000	3.00	1	0	0	6	5	1	7	0	1	0	0	2	1	0	.500	0	1	0	1	1.0	1.000
1967		10	9	.526	2.79	31	28	7	184	141	69	159	3	0	2	0	66	6	0	.091	9	17	2	0	0.9	.929
1968		13	16	.448	3.28	33	30	9	208.2	187	70	175	3	0	2	0	70	15	1	.214	16	22	4	0	1.3	.905
1969		16	12	.571	4.00	34	34	13	225	210	97	235	1	0	0	0	81	8	0	.099	19	25	3	0	1.4	.936
1970		11	6	.647	3.91	29	27	3	184	188	66	94	0	0	0	0	69	8	0	.116	6	17	2	2	0.9	.920
1971		16	10	.615	2.45	35	34	18	268	195	79	180	3	0	0	0	91	14	0	.154	9	26	2	4	1.1	.946
1972		15	10	.600	2.68	33	33	13	228.1	196	66	172	3	0	0	0	76	8	0	.105	8	37	2	1	1.4	.957
1973		11	16	.407	3.20	37	32	10	239.1	187	92	149	3	0	0	2	79	14	0	.177	15	25	4	3	1.2	.909
1974		11	13	.458	3.07	33	27	5	205	170	100	112	4	1	0	0	63	13	0	.206	11	21	5	1	1.1	.865
9 yrs.		104	92	.531	3.15	266	245	78	1748.1	1479	640	1283	20	3	4	2	597	87	1	.146	93	191	24	12	1.2	.922

Duane Wilson

WILSON, DUANE LEWIS
B. June 29, 1934, Wichita, Kans.
BL TL 6'1" 185 lbs.

Year	Team	W	L	PCT	ERA	G	GS	CG	IP	H	BB	SO	ShO	W	L	SV	AB	H	HR	BA	PO	A	E	DP	TC/G	FA
1958	BOS A	0	0	–	5.68	2	2	0	6.1	10	7	3	0	0	0	0	1	0	0	.000	0	2	0	0	1.0	1.000

Earl Wilson

WILSON, EARL LAWRENCE
B. Oct. 2, 1934, Ponchatoula, La.
BR TR 6'3" 216 lbs.

Year	Team	W	L	PCT	ERA	G	GS	CG	IP	H	BB	SO	ShO	W	L	SV	AB	H	HR	BA	PO	A	E	DP	TC/G	FA
1959	BOS A	1	1	.500	6.08	9	4	0	23.2	21	31	17	0	1	0	0	8	4	0	.500	2	5	1	0	0.9	.875
1960		3	2	.600	4.71	13	9	2	65	61	48	40	0	0	0	0	23	4	0	.174	6	10	1	1	1.3	.941
1962		12	8	.600	3.90	31	28	4	191.1	163	111	137	1	0	0	0	69	12	3	.174	19	22	3	2	1.4	.932
1963		11	16	.407	3.76	37	34	6	210.2	184	**105**	123	3	0	0	0	72	15	1	.208	17	36	3	1	1.5	.946
1964		11	12	.478	4.49	33	31	5	202.1	213	73	166	0	0	0	0	73	15	4	.205	14	29	2	0	1.4	.956
1965		13	14	.481	3.98	36	36	8	230.2	221	77	164	0	0	0	0	79	14	6	.177	24	26	3	2	1.5	.943
1966	2 teams	BOS A	(15G 5–5)		DET A	(23G 13–6)																				
"	total	18	11	.621	3.07	38	37	13	264	214	74	200	3	0	0	0	96	23	7	.240	36	39	5	4	2.1	.938
1967	DET A	22	11	.667	3.27	39	38	12	264	214	92	184	0	0	0	0	108	20	4	.185	26	42	0	2	1.7	1.000
1968		13	12	.520	2.85	34	33	10	224.1	192	65	168	4	0	0	0	88	20	7	.227	26	30	4	3	1.8	.933
1969		12	10	.545	3.31	35	35	5	214.2	209	69	150	1	0	0	0	76	10	0	.132	8	38	4	3	1.4	.920
1970	2 teams	DET A	(18G 4–6)		SD N	(15G 1–6)																				
"	total	5	12	.294	4.58	33	25	4	161	169	51	103	1	1	0	0	48	7	2	.146	7	18	2	1	0.8	.926
11 yrs.		121	109	.526	3.69	338	310	69	2051.2	1863	796	1452	13	2	1	0	740	144	35	.195	185	295	28	19	1.5	.945

Year	Team		W	L	PCT	ERA	G	GS	CG	IP	H	BB	SO	ShO	W	L	SV	AB	H	HR	BA	PO	A	E	DP	TC/G	FA
															Relief Pitching			**Batting**									

Earl Wilson *continued*

WORLD SERIES

Year	Team		W	L	PCT	ERA	G	GS	CG	IP	H	BB	SO	ShO	W	L	SV	AB	H	HR	BA	PO	A	E	DP	TC/G	FA
1968	DET	A	0	1	.000	6.23	1	1	0	4.1	4	6	3	0	0	0	0	1	0	0	.000	0	2	0	0	2.0	1.000

Fin Wilson

WILSON, FINIS ELBERT
B. Dec. 9, 1889, East Fork, Ky. D. Mar. 9, 1959, Coral Gables, Fla.   BL TL 6'1"   194 lbs.

Year	Team		W	L	PCT	ERA	G	GS	CG	IP	H	BB	SO	ShO	W	L	SV	AB	H	HR	BA	PO	A	E	DP	TC/G	FA
1914	BKN	F	0	1	.000	7.71	2	1	1	7	7	11	4	0	0	0	0	2	1	0	.500	0	0	0	0	0.0	–
1915			1	7	.125	3.78	18	11	5	102.1	85	53	47	0	0	0	0	35	11	0	.314	6	29	2	2	2.1	.946
2 yrs.			1	8	.111	4.03	20	12	6	109.1	92	64	51	0	0	0	0	37	12	0	.324	6	29	2	2	1.9	.946

Gary Wilson

WILSON, GARY STEVEN
B. Nov. 21, 1954, Camden, Ark.   BR TR 6'2"   185 lbs.

Year	Team		W	L	PCT	ERA	G	GS	CG	IP	H	BB	SO	ShO	W	L	SV	AB	H	HR	BA	PO	A	E	DP	TC/G	FA
1979	HOU	N	0	0	–	12.86	6	0	0	7	15	6	6	0	0	0	0	0	0	0	–	0	0	0	0	0.0	–

Glenn Wilson

WILSON, GLENN DWIGHT
B. Dec. 22, 1958, Baytown, Tex.   BR TR 6'1"   190 lbs.

Year	Team		W	L	PCT	ERA	G	GS	CG	IP	H	BB	SO	ShO	W	L	SV	AB	H	HR	BA	PO	A	E	DP	TC/G	FA
1987	PHI	N	0	0	–	0.00	1	0	0	1	0	1	0	0	0	0	0	*				0	1	0	0	1.0	1.000

Highball Wilson

WILSON, HOWARD PAUL
B. Aug. 9, 1878, Philadelphia, Pa. D. Oct. 16, 1934, Havre de Grace, Md.   TR

Year	Team		W	L	PCT	ERA	G	GS	CG	IP	H	BB	SO	ShO	W	L	SV	AB	H	HR	BA	PO	A	E	DP	TC/G	FA
1899	CLE	N	0	1	.000	9.00	1	1	1	8	12	5	1	0	0	0	0	3	1	0	.333	1	1	0	0	2.0	1.000
1902	PHI	A	7	5	.583	2.43	13	10	8	96.1	103	19	18	0	1	1	0	35	6	0	.171	5	21	0	1	2.0	1.000
1903	WAS	A	7	18	.280	3.31	30	28	25	242.1	269	43	56	1	0	0	0	85	17	0	.200	11	58	2	0	2.4	.972
1904			0	3	.000	4.68	3	3	3	25	33	4	11	0	0	0	0	9	2	0	.222	2	8	1	0	3.7	.909
4 yrs.			14	27	.341	3.29	47	42	37	371.2	417	71	86	1	1	1	0	132	26	0	.197	19	88	3	1	2.3	.973

Jack Wilson

WILSON, JOHN FRANCIS (Black Jack)
B. Apr. 12, 1912, Portland, Ore.   BR TR 5'11"   210 lbs.

Year	Team		W	L	PCT	ERA	G	GS	CG	IP	H	BB	SO	ShO	W	L	SV	AB	H	HR	BA	PO	A	E	DP	TC/G	FA
1934	PHI	A	0	1	.000	12.00	2	2	1	9	15	9	2	0	0	0	0	3	0	0	.000	1	1	0	0	1.0	1.000
1935	BOS	A	3	4	.429	4.22	23	6	2	64	72	36	19	0	1	0	1	16	5	1	.313	4	19	2	0	1.1	.920
1936			6	8	.429	4.42	43	9	2	136.1	152	86	74	0	5	3	3	50	11	0	.220	9	21	1	1	0.7	.968
1937			16	10	.615	3.70	51	21	14	221.1	209	119	137	1	5	4	7	85	14	0	.165	9	41	2	3	1.0	.962
1938			15	15	.500	4.30	37	27	11	194.2	200	91	96	3	6	2	1	68	15	0	.221	15	27	3	2	1.2	.933
1939			11	11	.500	4.67	36	22	6	177.1	198	75	80	0	3	0	2	63	10	0	.159	14	25	1	1	1.1	.975
1940			12	6	.667	5.08	41	16	9	157.2	170	87	102	0	4	4	5	66	18	2	.273	14	12	0	1	0.6	1.000
1941			4	13	.235	5.03	27	12	4	116.1	140	70	55	1	2	4	1	44	7	0	.159	15	26	2	4	1.6	.953
1942	2 teams		WAS A		(12G 1–4)		DET A		(9G 0–0)																		
"	total		1	4	.200	6.22	21	6	1	55	77	28	25	0	0	1	0	18	2	0	.111	2	10	1	1	0.6	.923
9 yrs.			68	72	.486	4.59	281	121	50	1131.2	1233	601	590	5	26	18	20	413	82	3	.199	83	182	12	13	1.0	.957

Jim Wilson

WILSON, JAMES ALGER
B. Feb. 20, 1922, San Diego, Calif. D. Sept. 2, 1986, Newport Beach, Calif.   BR TR 6'1½"   200 lbs.

Year	Team		W	L	PCT	ERA	G	GS	CG	IP	H	BB	SO	ShO	W	L	SV	AB	H	HR	BA	PO	A	E	DP	TC/G	FA
1945	BOS	A	6	8	.429	3.30	23	21	8	144.1	121	88	50	2	0	0	0	53	13	0	.245	4	19	1	0	1.0	.958
1946			0	0	–	27.00	1	0	0	.2	2	0	0	0	0	0	0	0	0	0	–	0	0	0	0	0.0	–
1948	STL	A	0	0	–	13.50	4	0	0	2.2	5	5	1	0	0	0	0	0	0	0	–	0	2	0	0	0.5	1.000
1949	PHI	A	0	0	–	14.40	2	0	0	5	7	5	2	0	0	0	0	3	0	0	.000	0	0	0	0	0.0	–
1951	BOS	N	7	7	.500	5.40	20	15	5	110	131	40	33	0	1	0	1	39	7	0	.179	4	16	0	2	1.0	1.000
1952			12	14	.462	4.23	33	33	14	234	234	90	104	0	0	0	0	86	14	0	.163	21	32	1	4	1.6	.981
1953	MIL	N	4	9	.308	4.34	20	18	5	114	107	43	71	0	0	0	0	36	6	1	.167	10	23	0	1	1.7	1.000
1954			8	2	.800	3.52	27	19	6	127.2	129	36	52	4	0	0	0	44	7	0	.159	7	26	0	2	1.2	1.000
1955	BAL	A	12	18	.400	3.44	34	31	14	235.1	200	87	96	4	0	0	0	89	15	0	.169	15	39	2	0	1.6	.964
1956	2 teams		BAL A		(7G 4–2)		CHI A		(28G 9–12)																		
"	total		13	14	.481	4.28	35	28	7	208	198	86	113	3	2	1	0	77	23	1	.299	10	33	0	3	1.2	1.000
1957	CHI	A	15	8	.652	3.48	30	29	12	201.2	189	65	100	5	0	1	0	68	10	0	.147	14	26	0	0	1.3	1.000
1958			9	9	.500	4.10	28	23	4	155.2	156	63	70	1	1	2	1	51	4	0	.078	9	19	0	1	1.0	1.000
12 yrs.			86	89	.491	4.01	257	217	75	1539	1479	608	692	19	4	5	2	546	99	2	.181	94	235	4	13	1.3	.988

John Wilson

WILSON, JOHN NICODEMUS (Lefty)
B. June 15, 1890, Boonsboro, Md. D. Sept. 23, 1954, Annapolis, Md.   BR TL 6'1"   185 lbs.

Year	Team		W	L	PCT	ERA	G	GS	CG	IP	H	BB	SO	ShO	W	L	SV	AB	H	HR	BA	PO	A	E	DP	TC/G	FA
1913	WAS	A	0	0	–	4.50	3	0	0	4	3	1	0	0	0	0	0	0	0	0	–	0	2	0	1	0.7	1.000

John Wilson

WILSON, JOHN SAMUEL
B. Apr. 25, 1905, Coal City, Ala. D. Aug. 27, 1980, Chattanooga, Tenn.   BR TR 6'2"   164 lbs.

Year	Team		W	L	PCT	ERA	G	GS	CG	IP	H	BB	SO	ShO	W	L	SV	AB	H	HR	BA	PO	A	E	DP	TC/G	FA
1927	BOS	A	0	2	.000	3.55	5	2	2	25.1	31	13	8	0	0	0	0	9	1	0	.111	0	5	1	0	1.2	.833
1928			0	0	–	9.00	2	0	0	5	6	6	1	0	0	0	0	1	0	0	.000	0	2	0	0	1.0	1.000
2 yrs.			0	2	.000	4.45	7	2	2	30.1	37	19	9	0	0	0	0	10	1	0	.100	0	7	1	0	1.1	.875

Maxie Wilson

WILSON, MAX
B. June 3, 1916, Haw River, N. C. D. Jan. 2, 1977, Greensboro, N. C.   BL TL 5'7"   150 lbs.

Year	Team		W	L	PCT	ERA	G	GS	CG	IP	H	BB	SO	ShO	W	L	SV	AB	H	HR	BA	PO	A	E	DP	TC/G	FA
1940	PHI	N	0	0	–	12.86	3	0	0	7	16	2	3	0	0	0	0	2	0	0	.000	0	2	0	0	0.7	1.000
1946	WAS	A	0	1	.000	7.11	9	0	0	12.2	16	9	8	0	0	1	0	2	0	0	.000	1	1	0	0	0.2	1.000
2 yrs.			0	1	.000	9.15	12	0	0	19.2	32	11	11	0	0	1	0	4	0	0	.000	1	3	0	0	0.3	1.000

Mutt Wilson

WILSON, WILLIAM CLARENCE
B. July 20, 1896, Kiser, N. C. D. Aug. 31, 1962, Wildwood, Fla.   BR TR 6'3"   167 lbs.

Year	Team		W	L	PCT	ERA	G	GS	CG	IP	H	BB	SO	ShO	W	L	SV	AB	H	HR	BA	PO	A	E	DP	TC/G	FA
1920	DET	A	1	1	.500	3.46	3	2	1	13	12	5	4	0	0	0	0	4	1	0	.250	0	0	0	0	0.0	–

Year	Team	W	L	PCT	ERA	G	GS	CG	IP	H	BB	SO	ShO	Relief Pitching W	L	SV	Batting AB	H	HR	BA	PO	A	E	DP	TC/G	FA

Pete Wilson

WILSON, PETER ALEX TL
B. Oct. 9, 1885, Springfield, Mass. D. June 5, 1957, St. Petersburg, Fla.

Year	Team	W	L	PCT	ERA	G	GS	CG	IP	H	BB	SO	ShO	W	L	SV	AB	H	HR	BA	PO	A	E	DP	TC/G	FA
1908	NY A	3	3	.500	3.46	6	6	4	39	27	33	28	1	0	0	0	13	1	0	.077	1	9	1	1	1.8	.909
1909		6	5	.545	3.17	14	12	7	93.2	82	43	44	1	0	0	0	34	4	0	.118	2	27	4	0	2.4	.879
2 yrs.		9	8	.529	3.26	20	18	11	132.2	109	76	72	2	0	0	0	47	5	0	.106	3	36	5	1	2.2	.886

Roy Wilson

WILSON, ROY EDWARD (Lefty) BL TL 6' 175 lbs.
B. Sept. 13, 1896, Foster, Iowa D. Dec. 3, 1969, Clarion, Iowa

Year	Team	W	L	PCT	ERA	G	GS	CG	IP	H	BB	SO	ShO	W	L	SV	AB	H	HR	BA	PO	A	E	DP	TC/G	FA
1928	CHI A	0	0	–	0.00	1	0	0	3.1	2	3	2	0	0	0	0	0	0	0	.000	0	2	0	0	2.0	1.000

Steve Wilson

WILSON, STEPHEN DOUGLAS BL TL 6'4" 205 lbs.
B. Dec. 13, 1964, Victoria, B. C., Canada

Year	Team	W	L	PCT	ERA	G	GS	CG	IP	H	BB	SO	ShO	W	L	SV	AB	H	HR	BA	PO	A	E	DP	TC/G	FA
1988	TEX A	0	0	–	5.87	3	0	0	7.2	7	4	1	0	0	0	0	0	0	0	–	0	0	0	0	0.0	–
1989	CHI N	6	4	.600	4.20	53	8	0	85.2	83	31	65	0	3	2	2	16	1	0	.063	6	14	2	0	0.4	.909
2 yrs.		6	4	.600	4.34	56	8	0	93.1	90	35	66	0	3	2	2	16	1	0	.063	6	14	2	0	0.4	.909

LEAGUE CHAMPIONSHIP SERIES

Year	Team	W	L	PCT	ERA	G	GS	CG	IP	H	BB	SO	ShO	W	L	SV	AB	H	HR	BA	PO	A	E	DP	TC/G	FA
1989	CHI N	0	1	.000	4.91	2	0	0	3.2	3	1	4	0	0	1	0	0	0	0	–	0	1	0	0	0.5	1.000

Tex Wilson

WILSON, GOMER RUSSELL BR TL 5'10" 170 lbs.
B. July 8, 1901, Trenton, Tex. D. Sept. 15, 1946, Sulphur Springs, Tex.

Year	Team	W	L	PCT	ERA	G	GS	CG	IP	H	BB	SO	ShO	W	L	SV	AB	H	HR	BA	PO	A	E	DP	TC/G	FA
1924	BKN N	0	0	–	14.73	2	0	0	3.2	7	1	0	0	0	0	0	1	0	0	.000	0	2	0	0	1.0	1.000

Trevor Wilson

WILSON, TREVOR KIRK BL TL 6' 185 lbs.
B. June 7, 1966, Torrance, Calif.

Year	Team	W	L	PCT	ERA	G	GS	CG	IP	H	BB	SO	ShO	W	L	SV	AB	H	HR	BA	PO	A	E	DP	TC/G	FA
1988	SF N	0	2	.000	4.09	4	4	0	22	25	8	15	0	0	0	0	7	2	0	.286	0	5	0	0	0.5	1.000
1989		2	3	.400	4.35	14	4	0	39.1	28	24	22	0	1	1	0	8	2	0	.250	0	7	1	0	0.6	.875
2 yrs.		2	5	.286	4.26	18	8	0	61.1	53	32	37	0	1	1	0	15	4	0	.267	1	8	1	0	0.6	.900

Walter Wilson

WILSON, WALTER WOOD BL TR 6'4" 190 lbs.
B. Nov. 24, 1913, Glenn, Ga.

Year	Team	W	L	PCT	ERA	G	GS	CG	IP	H	BB	SO	ShO	W	L	SV	AB	H	HR	BA	PO	A	E	DP	TC/G	FA
1945	DET A	1	3	.250	4.61	25	4	1	70.1	76	35	28	0	0	1	0	19	1	0	.053	3	20	0	2	0.9	1.000

Zeke Wilson

WILSON, FRANK EALTON BR TR 5'10"
B. Dec. 24, 1869, Benton, Ala. D. Apr. 26, 1928, Montgomery, Ala.

Year	Team	W	L	PCT	ERA	G	GS	CG	IP	H	BB	SO	ShO	W	L	SV	AB	H	HR	BA	PO	A	E	DP	TC/G	FA
1895	2 teams	BOS N (6G 2–4)				CLE N	(8G 3–1)																				
"	total	5	5	.500	4.72	14	13	7	89.2	117	47	21	0	1	0	0	37	8	1	.216	4	25	0	0	2.1	1.000
1896	CLE N	17	9	.654	4.01	33	29	20	240	265	81	56	1	1	0	1	100	27	0	.270	23	85	8	3	3.5	.931
1897		16	11	.593	4.16	34	30	26	263.2	323	83	69	0	0	0	0	116	26	0	.224	19	59	4	2	2.4	.951
1898		13	18	.419	3.60	33	31	28	254.2	307	51	45	1	0	0	0	118	21	0	.178	11	83	5	1	3.0	.949
1899	STL N	1	1	.500	4.50	5	2	2	26	30	4	3	0	0	0	0	10	0	0	.000	3	12	1	0	3.2	.938
5 yrs.		52	44	.542	4.03	119	105	83	874	1042	266	194	3	2	0	1	381	82	1	.215	60	264	18	6	2.9	.947

Hal Wiltse

WILTSE, HAROLD JAMES (Whitey) BL TL 5'9" 168 lbs.
B. Aug. 6, 1903, Clay City, Ill. D. Nov. 2, 1983, Bunkie, La.

Year	Team	W	L	PCT	ERA	G	GS	CG	IP	H	BB	SO	ShO	W	L	SV	AB	H	HR	BA	PO	A	E	DP	TC/G	FA
1926	BOS A	8	15	.348	4.22	37	29	9	196.1	201	99	59	1	1	1	0	59	5	0	.085	5	53	5	4	1.7	.921
1927		10	18	.357	5.10	36	29	13	219	276	76	47	1	1	1	1	77	16	0	.208	12	63	5	1	2.2	.938
1928	2 teams	BOS A (2G 0–2)				STL A	(26G 2–5)																				
"	total	2	7	.222	5.79	28	7	1	84	109	36	28	0	2	0	0	26	5	0	.192	4	19	1	0	0.9	.958
1931	PHI N	0	0	–	9.00	1	0	0	1	3	0	0	0	0	0	0	0	0	0	–	0	1	0	0	1.0	1.000
4 yrs.		20	40	.333	4.87	102	65	23	500.1	589	211	134	2	4	1	1	162	26	0	.160	21	136	11	5	1.6	.935

Hooks Wiltse

WILTSE, GEORGE LeROY BR TL 6' 185 lbs.
Brother of Snake Wiltse.
B. Sept. 7, 1880, Hamilton, N. Y. D. Jan. 21, 1959, Long Beach, N. Y.

Year	Team	W	L	PCT	ERA	G	GS	CG	IP	H	BB	SO	ShO	W	L	SV	AB	H	HR	BA	PO	A	E	DP	TC/G	FA
1904	NY N	13	3	.813	2.84	24	16	14	164.2	150	61	105	2	0	0	3	67	15	1	.224	11	54	5	2	2.9	.929
1905		15	6	.714	2.47	32	19	18	197	158	61	120	1	2	0	0	72	20	0	.278	19	71	3	3	2.9	.968
1906		16	11	.593	2.27	38	26	21	249.1	227	58	125	4	4	0	5	94	18	0	.191	12	65	3	1	2.1	.963
1907		13	12	.520	2.18	33	21	14	190.1	171	48	79	3	2	2	1	67	9	0	.134	11	59	2	2	2.2	.972
1908		23	14	.622	2.24	44	38	30	330	266	73	118	7	0	2	2	110	26	0	.236	28	89	2	1	2.7	.983
1909		20	11	.645	2.00	37	30	22	269.1	228	51	119	4	1	1	3	95	19	1	.200	9	62	2	2	2.0	.973
1910		14	12	.538	2.72	36	30	18	235.1	232	52	88	2	2	1	1	74	13	0	.176	8	52	9	4	1.9	.870
1911		12	9	.571	3.27	30	24	11	187.1	177	39	92	4	2	2	0	69	13	0	.188	19	44	4	2	2.2	.940
1912		9	6	.600	3.16	28	17	5	134	140	28	58	0	2	1	2	46	15	0	.326	5	40	0	2	1.6	1.000
1913		0	0	–	1.56	17	2	0	57.2	53	8	25	0	0	0	3	24	5	0	.208	0	18	1	0	1.1	.947
1914		1	1	.500	2.84	20	0	0	38	41	12	19	1	1	1	0	3	2	0	.667	2	10	1	0	0.7	.923
1915	BKN F	3	5	.375	2.28	18	3	1	59.1	49	7	17	0	3	2	5	22	1	0	.045	2	15	3	0	1.1	.850
12 yrs.		139	90	.607	2.47	357	226	154	2112.1	1892	498	965	27	19	13	29	743	156	2	.210	126	579	35	19	2.1	.953

WORLD SERIES

Year	Team	W	L	PCT	ERA	G	GS	CG	IP	H	BB	SO	ShO	W	L	SV	AB	H	HR	BA	PO	A	E	DP	TC/G	FA
1911	NY N	0	0	–	18.90	2	0	0	3.1	8	0	2	0	0	0	0	1	0	0	.000	0	1	0	0	0.5	1.000

Snake Wiltse

WILTSE, LEWIS DeWITT BR TL
Brother of Hooks Wiltse.
B. Dec. 5, 1871, Bouckville, N. Y. D. Aug. 25, 1928, Harrisburg, Pa.

Year	Team	W	L	PCT	ERA	G	GS	CG	IP	H	BB	SO	ShO	W	L	SV	AB	H	HR	BA	PO	A	E	DP	TC/G	FA
1901	2 teams	PIT N (7G 1–4)				PHI A	(19G 13–5)																				
"	total	14	9	.609	3.72	26	24	21	210.1	242	48	50	2	0	0	0	86	28	0	.326	11	68	6	2	3.3	.929
1902	2 teams	PHI A (19G 8–8)				BAL A	(19G 7–11)																				
"	total	15	19	.441	5.13	38	35	31	302	397	92	65	0	1	1	1	189	49	2	.259	38	69	8	7	3.0	.930

Year	Team		W	L	PCT	ERA	G	GS	CG	IP	H	BB	SO	ShO	Relief Pitching W	L	SV	Batting AB	H	HR	BA	PO	A	E	DP	TC/G	FA

Snake Wiltse *continued*

| 1903 | NY | A | 1 | 3 | .250 | 5.40 | 4 | 3 | 2 | 25 | 35 | 6 | 6 | 0 | 0 | 0 | 1 | 9 | 2 | 0 | .222 | 2 | 6 | 0 | 0 | 2.0 | 1.000 |
| 3 yrs. | | | 30 | 31 | .492 | 4.59 | 68 | 62 | 54 | 537.1 | 674 | 146 | 121 | 2 | 1 | 1 | 2 | 284 | 79 | 2 | .278 | 51 | 143 | 14 | 9 | 3.1 | .933 |

Fred Winchell

WINCHELL, FREDERICK RUSSELL   TL 5'8"
Born Frederick Russell Cook.
B. Jan. 23, 1882, Arlington, Mass.   D. Aug. 8, 1958, Toronto, Ontario, Canada

| 1909 | CLE | A | 0 | 3 | .000 | 6.28 | 4 | 3 | 0 | 14.1 | 16 | 2 | 7 | 0 | 0 | 0 | 1 | 5 | 1 | 0 | .200 | 1 | 2 | 0 | 0 | 0.8 | 1.000 |

Ed Wineapple

WINEAPPLE, EDWARD (Lefty)   BL TL 6'   210 lbs.
B. Aug. 10, 1905, Boston, Mass.

| 1929 | WAS | A | 0 | 0 | — | 4.50 | 1 | 0 | 0 | 4 | 7 | 3 | 1 | 0 | 0 | 0 | 0 | 2 | 0 | 0 | .000 | 0 | 1 | 2 | 0 | 3.0 | .333 |

Ralph Winegarner

WINEGARNER, RALPH LEE   BR TR 6'   182 lbs.
B. Oct. 29, 1909, Benton, Kans.   D. Apr. 14, 1988, Wichita, Kans.

1930	CLE	A	0	0	—	0.00	0	0	0	0	0	0	0	0	0	0	0	22	10	0	.455	0	0	0	0	0.0	—
1932			1	0	1.000	1.04	5	1	1	17.1	7	13	5	0	0	0	0	7	1	0	.143	0	3	1	1	0.8	.750
1934			5	4	.556	5.51	22	6	4	78.1	91	39	32	0	2	1	0	51	10	1	.196	1	16	0	0	0.8	1.000
1935			2	2	.500	5.75	25	4	2	67.1	89	29	41	0	1	1	0	84	26	3	.310	3	14	1	0	0.7	.944
1936			0	0	—	4.91	9	0	0	14.2	18	6	3	0	0	0	0	16	2	0	.125	0	1	0	0	0.1	1.000
1949	STL	A	0	0	—	7.56	9	0	0	16.2	24	2	8	0	0	0	0	5	2	1	.400	1	1	0	0	0.2	1.000
6 yrs.			8	6	.571	5.33	70	11	7	194.1	229	89	89	0	3	2	0	*				5	35	2	1	0.6	.952

Jim Winford

WINFORD, JAMES HEAD (Cowboy)   BR TR 6'1"   180 lbs.
B. Oct. 9, 1909, Shelbyville, Tenn.   D. Dec. 16, 1970, Miami, Okla.

1932	STL	N	1	1	.500	6.48	4	1	0	8.1	9	5	4	0	0	0	0	3	2	0	.667	0	2	0	0	0.5	1.000
1934			0	2	.000	7.82	5	1	0	12.2	17	6	3	0	0	1	0	1	0	0	.000	0	3	0	1	0.6	1.000
1935			0	0	—	3.97	2	1	0	11.1	13	5	7	0	0	0	0	2	0	0	.000	0	0	0	0	0.0	—
1936			11	10	.524	3.80	39	23	10	192	203	68	72	1	1	2	3	59	5	0	.085	5	23	2	0	0.8	.933
1937			2	4	.333	5.83	16	4	0	46.1	56	27	19	0	2	0	0	8	1	0	.125	1	8	0	1	0.6	1.000
1938	BKN	N	0	1	.000	11.12	2	1	0	5.2	9	4	4	0	0	0	0	1	0	0	.000	0	0	0	0	0.0	—
6 yrs.			14	18	.438	4.56	68	31	10	276.1	307	115	109	1	4	3	3	74	8	0	.108	6	36	2	2	0.6	.955

Ernie Wingard

WINGARD, ERNEST JAMES (Jim)   BL TL 6'2"   176 lbs.
B. Oct. 17, 1900, Prattville, Ala.   D. Jan. 17, 1977, Prattville, Ala.

1924	STL	A	13	12	.520	3.51	36	26	14	218	215	85	23	0	2	0	1	76	17	3	.224	10	42	3	1	1.5	.945
1925			9	10	.474	5.06	32	18	8	153	184	77	20	0	2	4	0	52	15	1	.288	6	49	5	3	1.9	.917
1926			5	8	.385	3.57	39	16	7	169	188	76	30	0	1	2	3	61	14	0	.230	10	58	3	3	1.8	.958
1927			2	13	.133	6.56	38	17	7	156.1	213	79	28	0	0	2	0	56	10	3	.179	14	45	3	1	1.6	.952
4 yrs.			29	43	.403	4.55	145	77	36	696.1	800	317	101	0	5	8	4	245	56	7	.229	40	194	14	8	1.7	.944

Ted Wingfield

WINGFIELD, FREDERICK DAVIS   BR TR 5'11"   168 lbs.
B. Aug. 7, 1899, Bedford, Va.   D. July 18, 1975, Johnson City, Tenn.

1923	WAS	A	0	0	—	0.00	1	0	0	1	0	0	0	1	0	0	0	0	0	0	—	0	0	0	0	0.0	—
1924	2 teams		WAS A	(4G 0–0)		BOS A	(4G 0–2)																				
"	total		0	2	.000	2.48	8	3	2	32.2	32	12	6	0	0	0	0	11	3	0	.273	4	7	2	0	1.6	.846
1925	BOS	A	12	19	.387	3.96	41	26	18	254.1	267	92	30	2	2	4	2	94	23	1	.245	19	94	2	6	2.8	.983
1926			11	16	.407	4.44	43	20	9	190.2	220	50	30	1	5	3	3	69	15	0	.217	13	56	2	3	1.7	.972
1927			1	7	.125	5.06	20	8	2	74.2	105	27	1	0	0	1	0	18	4	0	.222	6	30	1	3	1.9	.973
5 yrs.			24	44	.353	4.18	113	57	31	553.1	624	181	68	3	7	8	5	192	45	1	.234	42	187	7	12	2.1	.970

Lave Winham

WINHAM, LAFAYETTE SHARKEY   BL TL 5'11"   200 lbs.
B. Oct. 23, 1881, Brooklyn, N. Y.   D. Sept. 12, 1951, Brooklyn, N. Y.

1902	BKN	N	0	0	—	0.00	1	0	0	3	4	2	1	0	0	0	0	2	0	0	.000	0	3	0	0	3.0	1.000
1903	PIT	N	3	1	.750	2.25	5	4	3	36	33	21	22	1	0	0	0	14	1	0	.071	3	5	4	0	2.4	.667
2 yrs.			3	1	.750	2.08	6	4	3	39	37	23	23	1	0	0	0	16	1	0	.063	3	8	4	0	2.5	.733

George Winkelman

WINKELMAN, GEORGE EDWARD   BL TL
B. June 14, 1861, Philadelphia, Pa.   D. May 19, 1960, Washington, D. C.

| 1886 | WAS | N | 0 | 1 | .000 | 10.50 | 1 | 1 | 0 | 6 | 12 | 5 | 4 | 0 | 0 | 0 | 0 | * | | | | 0 | 0 | 0 | 0 | 0.0 | — |

George Winn

WINN, GEORGE BENJAMIN (Breezy, Lefty)   BL TL 5'11"   170 lbs.
B. Oct. 26, 1897, Perry, Ga.   D. Nov. 1, 1969, Roberta, Ga.

1919	BOS	A	0	0	—	7.71	3	0	0	4.2	6	1	0	0	0	0	0	1	0	0	.000	0	0	0	0	0.0	—
1922	CLE	A	1	2	.333	4.54	8	3	1	33.2	44	5	7	0	1	0	0	9	3	0	.333	1	9	0	1	1.3	1.000
1923			0	0	—	0.00	1	0	0	2	0	1	0	0	0	0	0	0	0	0	—	0	0	0	0	0.0	—
3 yrs.			1	2	.333	4.69	12	3	1	40.1	50	7	7	0	1	0	0	10	3	0	.300	1	9	0	1	0.8	1.000

Jim Winn

WINN, JAMES FRANCIS   BR TR 6'3"   190 lbs.
B. Sept. 23, 1959, Stockton, Calif.

1983	PIT	N	0	0	—	7.36	7	0	0	11	12	6	3	0	0	0	0	0	0	0	—	1	2	0	0	0.4	1.000
1984			1	0	1.000	3.86	9	0	0	18.2	19	9	11	0	1	0	0	1	0	0	.000	1	3	0	1	0.4	1.000
1985			3	6	.333	5.23	30	7	0	75.2	77	31	22	0	1	4	0	18	2	0	.111	4	21	0	1	0.8	1.000
1986			3	5	.375	3.58	50	3	0	88	85	38	70	0	3	3	3	16	1	0	.063	8	15	1	1	0.5	.958
1987	CHI	A	4	6	.400	4.79	56	0	0	94	95	62	44	0	4	6	6	0	0	0	—	4	28	1	5	0.6	.970
1988	MIN	A	1	0	1.000	6.00	9	0	0	21	33	10	9	0	1	0	1	0	0	0	—	2	4	1	0	0.8	.857
6 yrs.			12	17	.414	4.67	161	10	0	308.1	321	156	159	0	10	13	10	35	3	0	.086	20	73	3	8	0.6	.969

Year	Team		W	L	PCT	ERA	G	GS	CG	IP	H	BB	SO	ShO	Relief Pitching W	L	SV	Batting AB	H	HR	BA	PO	A	E	DP	TC/G	FA

Tom Winsett

WINSETT, JOHN THOMAS (Long Tom)
B. Nov. 24, 1909, McKenzie, Tenn. BL TR 6'2" 190 lbs.

| 1937 | BKN | N | 0 | 0 | – | 18.00 | 1 | 0 | 0 | 1 | 3 | 2 | 0 | 0 | 0 | 0 | 0 | * | | | | 0 | 0 | 0 | 0 | 0.0 | – |

Hank Winston

WINSTON, HENRY RUDOLPH
B. June 15, 1904, Youngsville, N. C. D. Feb. 4, 1974, Jacksonville, Fla. BL TR 6'3½" 226 lbs.

1933	PHI	A	0	0	–	6.75	1	0	0	6.2	7	6	2	0	0	0	0	3	0	0	.000	0	3	0	0	3.0	1.000
1936	BKN	N	1	3	.250	6.12	14	0	0	32.1	40	16	8	0	1	3	0	11	1	0	.091	0	7	0	0	0.5	1.000
2 yrs.			1	3	.250	6.23	15	0	0	39	47	22	10	0	1	3	0	14	1	0	.071	0	10	0	0	0.7	1.000

George Winter

WINTER, GEORGE LOVINGTON (Sassafras)
B. Apr. 27, 1878, New Providence, Pa. D. May 26, 1951, Ramsey, N. J. TR 5'8" 155 lbs.

1901	BOS	A	16	12	.571	2.80	28	28	26	241	234	66	63	1	0	0	0	100	19	1	.190	15	64	8	4	3.1	.908
1902			11	9	.550	2.99	20	20	18	168.1	149	53	51	0	0	0	0	61	10	0	.164	4	50	5	1	3.0	.915
1903			9	8	.529	3.08	24	19	14	178.1	182	37	64	0	0	0	0	66	7	0	.106	19	47	4	0	2.9	.943
1904			8	4	.667	2.32	20	16	12	135.2	126	27	31	1	0	0	0	43	5	0	.116	7	43	6	1	2.8	.893
1905			16	16	.500	2.96	35	27	24	264.1	249	54	119	2	4	2	0	89	24	0	.270	14	81	6	4	2.9	.941
1906			6	18	.250	4.12	29	22	18	207.2	215	38	72	1	0	2	2	69	17	0	.246	13	59	2	4	2.6	.973
1907			12	15	.444	2.07	35	27	21	256.2	198	61	88	4	2	1	1	94	21	0	.223	6	77	5	5	2.5	.943
1908	2 teams		BOS A	(22G 4–14)		DET A	(7G 1–5)																				
"	total		5	19	.208	2.65	29	23	13	204	199	43	80	0	1	1	0	67	11	0	.164	16	67	10	2	3.2	.892
8 yrs.			83	101	.451	2.87	220	182	146	1656	1552	379	568	9	7	6	4	589	114	1	.194	94	488	46	21	2.9	.927

WORLD SERIES

| 1908 | DET | A | 0 | 0 | – | 0.00 | 1 | 0 | 0 | 1 | 1 | 1 | 0 | 0 | 0 | 0 | 0 | 0 | 0 | 0 | – | 0 | 0 | 0 | 0 | 0.0 | – |

Clarence Winters

WINTERS, CLARENCE JOHN
B. Sept. 7, 1898, Detroit, Mich. D. June 29, 1945, Detroit, Mich.

| 1924 | BOS | A | 0 | 1 | .000 | 20.57 | 4 | 2 | 0 | 7 | 22 | 4 | 3 | 0 | 0 | 0 | 0 | 3 | 1 | 0 | .333 | 0 | 0 | 0 | 0 | 0.0 | – |

Jesse Winters

WINTERS, JESSE FRANKLIN (T-Bone)
B. Dec. 22, 1893, Stephenville, Tex. D. June 5, 1986, Abilene, Tex. BR TR 6'1" 165 lbs.

1919	NY	N	1	2	.333	5.46	16	2	0	28	39	13	6	0	1	1	3	3	0	0	.000	0	8	1	0	0.6	.889
1920			0	0	–	3.50	21	0	0	46.1	37	28	14	0	0	0	0	7	0	0	.000	0	18	1	0	0.9	.947
1921	PHI	N	5	10	.333	3.63	18	14	10	114	142	28	22	0	0	1	0	39	5	0	.128	6	37	1	3	2.4	.977
1922			6	6	.500	5.33	34	9	4	138.1	176	56	29	0	4	1	2	43	11	0	.256	5	36	3	2	1.3	.932
1923			1	6	.143	7.35	21	6	1	78.1	116	39	23	0	1	1	1	25	4	0	.160	3	17	4	1	1.1	.833
5 yrs.			13	24	.351	5.04	110	31	15	405	510	164	94	0	6	4	6	117	20	0	.171	14	116	10	6	1.3	.929

Alan Wirth

WIRTH, ALAN LEE
B. Dec. 8, 1956, Mesa, Ariz. BR TR 6'4" 190 lbs.

1978	OAK	A	5	6	.455	3.43	16	14	2	81.1	72	34	31	1	1	0	0	0	0	0	–	2	9	0	2	0.7	1.000
1979			1	0	1.000	6.00	5	1	0	12	14	8	7	0	0	0	0	0	0	0	–	0	3	0	0	0.6	1.000
1980			0	0	–	4.50	2	0	0	2	3	0	1	0	0	0	0	0	0	0	–	0	0	0	0	0.0	–
3 yrs.			6	6	.500	3.78	23	15	2	95.1	89	42	39	1	1	0	0	0	0	0	–	2	12	0	2	0.6	1.000

Archie Wise

WISE, ARCHIBALD EDWIN
B. July 31, 1912, Waxahachie, Tex. D. Feb. 2, 1978, Dallas, Tex. BR TR 6' 165 lbs.

| 1932 | CHI | A | 0 | 0 | – | 4.91 | 2 | 0 | 0 | 7.1 | 8 | 5 | 2 | 0 | 0 | 0 | 0 | 4 | 0 | 0 | .000 | 0 | 2 | 0 | 0 | 1.0 | 1.000 |

Bill Wise

WISE, WILLIAM E.
B. Mar. 15, 1861, Washington, D. C. D. May 5, 1940, Washington, D. C.

1882	BAL	AA	1	2	.333	2.77	3	3	3	26	30	4	9	0	0	0	0	20	2	0	.100	2	6	1	0	3.0	.889
1884	WAS	U	23	18	.561	3.04	50	41	34	364.1	383	60	268	4	0	2	0	339	79	2	.233	25	98	22	1	2.9	.848
1886	WAS	N	0	1	.000	9.00	1	1	0	3	6	2	0	0	0	0	0	3	0	0	.000	0	0	0	0	0.0	–
3 yrs.			24	21	.533	3.07	54	45	37	393.1	419	66	277	4	0	2	0	*				27	104	23	1	2.9	.851

Rick Wise

WISE, RICHARD CHARLES
B. Sept. 13, 1945, Jackson, Mich. BR TR 6'1" 180 lbs.

1964	PHI	N	5	3	.625	4.04	25	8	3	69	78	25	39	0	1	1	0	17	5	0	.294	2	7	1	0	0.4	.900
1966			5	6	.455	3.71	22	13	3	99.1	100	24	58	0	0	2	0	30	0	0	.000	3	14	0	1	0.8	1.000
1967			11	11	.500	3.28	36	25	6	181.1	177	45	111	3	2	0	1	53	11	0	.208	11	32	0	4	1.2	1.000
1968			9	15	.375	4.54	30	30	7	182.1	210	37	97	1	0	0	0	58	14	2	.241	13	32	0	3	1.5	1.000
1969			15	13	.536	3.23	33	31	14	220	215	61	144	4	0	0	0	74	20	1	.270	7	43	0	3	1.5	1.000
1970			13	14	.481	4.17	35	34	5	220	253	65	113	1	0	0	0	75	15	2	.200	17	35	1	3	1.5	.981
1971			17	14	.548	2.88	38	37	17	272	261	70	155	4	0	0	0	97	23	6	.237	23	36	0	7	1.6	1.000
1972	STL	N	16	16	.500	3.11	35	35	20	269	250	71	142	2	0	0	0	93	16	1	.172	15	48	1	7	1.8	.984
1973			16	12	.571	3.37	35	34	14	259	259	59	144	4	1	0	0	88	17	3	.193	19	34	1	3	1.5	.981
1974	BOS	A	3	4	.429	3.86	9	9	1	49	47	16	25	0	0	0	0	0	0	0	–	3	4	0	2	0.8	1.000
1975			19	12	.613	3.95	35	35	17	255.1	262	72	141	1	0	0	0	0	0	0	–	16	32	4	3	1.5	.923
1976			14	11	.560	3.54	34	34	11	224	218	48	93	4	0	0	0	0	0	0	–	15	39	0	5	1.6	1.000
1977			11	5	.688	4.78	26	20	4	128	151	28	85	2	2	0	0	0	0	0	–	8	23	0	1	1.2	1.000
1978	CLE	A	9	19	.321	4.32	33	31	9	212.2	226	59	106	1	0	0	0	0	0	0	–	15	29	2	2	1.4	.957
1979			15	10	.600	3.72	34	34	9	232	229	68	108	2	0	0	0	0	0	0	–	23	53	2	2	2.3	.974
1980	SD	N	6	8	.429	3.68	27	27	1	154	172	37	59	0	0	0	0	58	8	0	.138	11	22	1	0	1.3	.971
1981			4	8	.333	3.77	18	18	0	98	116	19	27	0	0	0	0	25	1	0	.040	3	21	0	0	1.3	1.000
1982			0	0	–	9.00	2	0	0	2	3	2	0	0	0	0	0	0	0	0	–	0	2	0	0	2.0	1.000
18 yrs.			188	181	.509	3.69	506	455	138	3127	3227	804	1647	30	6	3	0	668	130	15	.195	206	504	13	46	1.4	.982

LEAGUE CHAMPIONSHIP SERIES

| 1975 | BOS | A | 1 | 0 | 1.000 | 2.45 | 1 | 1 | 0 | 7.1 | 6 | 3 | 2 | 0 | 0 | 0 | 0 | 0 | 0 | 0 | – | 2 | 3 | 0 | 0 | 5.0 | 1.000 |

Year	Team		W	L	PCT	ERA	G	GS	CG	IP	H	BB	SO	ShO	W	L	SV	AB	H	HR	BA	PO	A	E	DP	TC/G	FA

Rick Wise *continued*

WORLD SERIES

Year	Team		W	L	PCT	ERA	G	GS	CG	IP	H	BB	SO	ShO	W	L	SV	AB	H	HR	BA	PO	A	E	DP	TC/G	FA
1975	BOS	A	1	0	1.000	8.44	2	1	0	5.1	6	2	2	0	1	0	0	2	0	0	.000	0	0	0	0	0.0	–

Roy Wise

WISE, ROY OGDEN   BB TR 6'2" 170 lbs.
B. Nov. 18, 1924, Springfield, Ill.

Year	Team		W	L	PCT	ERA	G	GS	CG	IP	H	BB	SO	ShO	W	L	SV	AB	H	HR	BA	PO	A	E	DP	TC/G	FA
1944	PIT	N	0	0	–	9.00	2	0	0	3	4	3	1	0	0	0	0	0	0	0	–	0	0	0	0	0.0	–

John Wisner

WISNER, JOHN HENRY   BR TR 6'3" 195 lbs.
B. Nov. 5, 1899, Grand Rapids, Mich.   D. Dec. 15, 1981, Jackson, Mich.

Year	Team		W	L	PCT	ERA	G	GS	CG	IP	H	BB	SO	ShO	W	L	SV	AB	H	HR	BA	PO	A	E	DP	TC/G	FA
1919	PIT	N	1	0	1.000	0.96	4	1	1	18.2	12	7	4	0	0	0	0	7	0	0	.000	1	6	2	0	2.3	.778
1920			1	3	.250	3.43	17	2	1	44.2	46	10	13	0	1	1	0	7	0	0	.000	5	15	0	1	1.2	1.000
1925	NY	N	0	0	–	3.79	25	0	0	40.1	33	14	13	0	0	1	0	7	0	0	.000	5	9	1	0	0.6	.933
1926			2	2	.500	3.54	5	3	2	28	21	10	5	0	0	1	0	10	2	0	.200	2	6	0	1	1.6	1.000
4 yrs.			4	5	.444	3.21	51	6	4	131.2	112	41	35	0	1	2	0	31	2	0	.065	13	36	3	1	1.0	.942

Whitey Wistert

WISTERT, FRANCIS MICHAEL   BR TR 6'4" 210 lbs.
B. Feb. 20, 1912, Chicago, Ill.   D. Apr. 23, 1985, Painesville, Ohio

Year	Team		W	L	PCT	ERA	G	GS	CG	IP	H	BB	SO	ShO	W	L	SV	AB	H	HR	BA	PO	A	E	DP	TC/G	FA
1934	CIN	N	0	1	.000	1.13	2	1	0	8	5	5	1	0	0	0	0	3	0	0	.000	0	1	0	0	0.5	1.000

Roy Witherup

WITHERUP, FOSTER LeROY   BR TR 6' 185 lbs.
B. July 26, 1886, N. Washington, Pa.   D. Dec. 23, 1941, New Bethlehem, Pa.

Year	Team		W	L	PCT	ERA	G	GS	CG	IP	H	BB	SO	ShO	W	L	SV	AB	H	HR	BA	PO	A	E	DP	TC/G	FA
1906	BOS	N	0	3	.000	6.26	8	3	3	46	59	19	14	0	0	0	0	15	2	0	.133	0	12	3	1	1.9	.800
1908	WAS	A	2	4	.333	2.98	6	6	4	48.1	51	8	31	0	0	0	0	18	3	0	.167	1	15	0	0	2.7	1.000
1909			1	5	.167	4.24	12	8	5	68	79	20	26	0	0	0	0	19	1	0	.053	0	15	1	0	1.3	.938
3 yrs.			3	12	.200	4.44	26	17	12	162.1	189	47	71	0	0	0	0	52	6	0	.115	1	42	4	1	1.8	.915

Bobby Witt

WITT, ROBERT ANDREW   BR TR 6'2" 190 lbs.
B. May 11, 1964, Arlington, Mass.

Year	Team		W	L	PCT	ERA	G	GS	CG	IP	H	BB	SO	ShO	W	L	SV	AB	H	HR	BA	PO	A	E	DP	TC/G	FA
1986	TEX	A	11	9	.550	5.48	31	31	0	157.2	130	**143**	174	0	0	0	0	0	0	0	–	8	20	3	1	1.0	.903
1987			8	10	.444	4.91	26	25	1	143	114	**140**	160	0	0	0	0	1	0	0	.000	8	17	0	1	1.0	1.000
1988			8	10	.444	3.92	22	22	13	174.1	134	101	148	2	0	0	0	0	0	0	–	15	15	4	2	1.5	.882
1989			12	13	.480	5.14	31	31	5	194.1	182	**114**	166	1	0	0	0	0	0	0	–	13	22	1	1	1.2	.972
4 yrs.			39	42	.481	4.85	110	109	19	669.1	560	498	648	3	0	0	0	1	0	0	.000	44	74	8	5	1.1	.937

George Witt

WITT, GEORGE ADRIAN (Red)   BR TR 6'3" 185 lbs.
B. Nov. 9, 1933, Long Beach, Calif.

Year	Team		W	L	PCT	ERA	G	GS	CG	IP	H	BB	SO	ShO	W	L	SV	AB	H	HR	BA	PO	A	E	DP	TC/G	FA
1957	PIT	N	0	1	.000	40.50	1	1	0	1.1	4	5	1	0	0	0	0	0	0	0	–	0	0	0	0	0.0	–
1958			9	2	.818	1.61	18	15	5	106	78	59	81	3	0	0	0	39	6	0	.154	4	14	1	1	1.1	.947
1959			0	7	.000	6.93	15	11	0	50.2	58	32	30	0	0	0	0	12	0	0	.000	2	7	1	1	0.7	.900
1960			1	2	.333	4.20	10	6	0	30	33	12	15	0	0	0	0	9	0	0	.000	1	4	0	0	0.5	1.000
1961			0	1	.000	6.32	9	1	0	15.2	17	5	9	0	0	0	0	2	1	0	.500	0	1	0	0	0.1	1.000
1962	2 teams	LA A (5G 1–1)				HOU N	(8G 0–2)																					
"	total		1	3	.250	7.46	13	4	0	25.1	35	14	20	0	1	0	0	7	2	0	.286	1	4	0	0	0.4	1.000
6 yrs.			11	16	.407	4.32	66	38	5	229	225	127	156	3	1	0	0	69	9	0	.130	8	30	2	2	0.6	.950

WORLD SERIES

Year	Team		W	L	PCT	ERA	G	GS	CG	IP	H	BB	SO	ShO	W	L	SV	AB	H	HR	BA	PO	A	E	DP	TC/G	FA
1960	PIT	N	0	0	–	0.00	3	0	0	2.2	5	2	1	0	0	0	0	0	0	0	–	0	0	0	0	0.0	–

Mike Witt

WITT, MICHAEL ATWATER   BR TR 6'7" 185 lbs.
B. July 20, 1960, Fullerton, Calif.

Year	Team		W	L	PCT	ERA	G	GS	CG	IP	H	BB	SO	ShO	W	L	SV	AB	H	HR	BA	PO	A	E	DP	TC/G	FA
1981	CAL	A	8	9	.471	3.28	22	21	7	129	123	47	75	1	0	1	0	0	0	0	–	7	16	3	0	1.2	.885
1982			8	6	.571	3.51	33	26	5	179.2	177	47	85	1	0	1	0	0	0	0	–	14	24	4	3	1.3	.905
1983			7	14	.333	4.91	43	19	2	154	173	75	77	0	3	3	5	0	0	0	–	6	24	1	2	0.7	.968
1984			15	11	.577	3.47	34	34	9	246.2	227	84	196	2	0	0	0	0	0	0	–	16	27	2	0	1.3	.955
1985			15	9	.625	3.56	35	35	6	250	228	98	180	1	0	0	0	0	0	0	–	16	33	2	2	1.5	.961
1986			18	10	.643	2.84	34	34	14	269	218	73	208	3	0	0	0	0	0	0	–	22	39	1	5	1.8	.984
1987			16	14	.533	4.01	36	36	10	247	252	84	192	0	0	0	0	0	0	0	–	18	29	3	2	1.4	.940
1988			13	16	.448	4.15	34	34	12	249.2	263	87	133	0	0	0	0	0	0	0	–	19	32	2	2	1.6	.962
1989			9	15	.375	4.54	33	33	5	220	252	48	123	0	0	0	0	0	0	0	–	18	49	4	4	2.2	.944
9 yrs.			109	104	.512	3.78	304	272	70	1945	1913	643	1269	10	3	5	5	0	0	0	–	136	273	22	20	1.4	.949

LEAGUE CHAMPIONSHIP SERIES

Year	Team		W	L	PCT	ERA	G	GS	CG	IP	H	BB	SO	ShO	W	L	SV	AB	H	HR	BA	PO	A	E	DP	TC/G	FA
1982	CAL	A	0	0	–	6.00	1	0	0	3	2	2	3	0	0	0	0	0	0	0	–	0	0	0	0	0.0	–
1986			1	0	1.000	2.55	2	2	1	17.2	13	2	8	0	0	0	0	0	0	0	–	2	4	0	0	3.0	1.000
2 yrs.			1	0	1.000	3.05	3	2	1	20.2	15	4	11	0	0	0	0	0	0	0	–	2	4	0	0	2.0	1.000

Johnnie Wittig

WITTIG, JOHN CARL (Hans)   BR TR 6' 180 lbs.
B. June 16, 1914, Baltimore, Md.

Year	Team		W	L	PCT	ERA	G	GS	CG	IP	H	BB	SO	ShO	W	L	SV	AB	H	HR	BA	PO	A	E	DP	TC/G	FA
1938	NY	N	2	3	.400	4.81	13	6	2	39.1	41	26	14	0	1	0	0	10	0	0	.000	0	1	0	1	0.1	1.000
1939			0	2	.000	7.56	5	2	1	16.2	18	14	4	0	0	0	0	5	0	0	.000	0	4	0	0	0.8	1.000
1941			3	5	.375	5.59	25	9	0	85.1	111	45	47	0	0	1	0	25	5	0	.200	0	10	0	1	0.4	1.000
1943			5	15	.250	4.23	40	22	4	164	77	76	56	1	0	1	4	51	5	0	.098	3	22	1	1	0.7	.962
1949	BOS	A	0	0	–	9.00	1	0	0	2	2	2	0	0	1	0	0	0	0	0	–	0	1	0	0	1.0	1.000
5 yrs.			10	25	.286	4.89	84	39	7	307.1	249	163	121	1	2	2	4	91	10	0	.110	3	38	1	3	0.5	.976

Pete Wojey

WOJEY, PETER PAUL   BR TR 5'11" 185 lbs.
B. Dec. 1, 1919, Stowe, Pa.

Year	Team		W	L	PCT	ERA	G	GS	CG	IP	H	BB	SO	ShO	W	L	SV	AB	H	HR	BA	PO	A	E	DP	TC/G	FA
1954	BKN	N	1	1	.500	3.25	14	0	0	27.2	24	14	21	0	1	1	0	3	0	0	.000	1	8	0	0	0.6	1.000
1956	DET	A	0	0	–	2.25	2	0	0	4	2	1	1	0	0	0	0	0	0	0	–	0	2	0	0	1.0	1.000

Year	Team	W	L	PCT	ERA	G	GS	CG	IP	H	BB	SO	ShO	Relief Pitching W	L	SV	Batting AB	H	HR	BA	PO	A	E	DP	TC/G	FA

Pete Wojey *continued*

Year	Team	W	L	PCT	ERA	G	GS	CG	IP	H	BB	SO	ShO	W	L	SV	AB	H	HR	BA	PO	A	E	DP	TC/G	FA
1957		0	0	–	0.00	2	0	0	1.1	1	0	0	0	0	0	0	0	0	0	–	0	1	0	0	0.5	1.000
3 yrs.		1	1	.500	3.00	18	1	0	33	27	15	22	0	0	0	1	3	0	0	.000	1	11	0	0	0.7	1.000

Ed Wojna

WOJNA, EDWARD DAVID
B. Aug. 20, 1960, Bridgeport, Conn.   BR TR 6'1"   195 lbs.

Year	Team	W	L	PCT	ERA	G	GS	CG	IP	H	BB	SO	ShO	W	L	SV	AB	H	HR	BA	PO	A	E	DP	TC/G	FA
1985	SD N	2	4	.333	5.79	15	7	0	42	53	19	18	0	1	1	0	12	2	0	.167	4	8	3	1	1.0	.800
1986		2	2	.500	3.23	7	7	1	39	42	16	19	0	0	0	0	14	2	0	.143	1	5	2	0	1.1	.750
1987		0	3	.000	5.89	5	3	0	18.1	25	6	13	0	0	0	0	5	0	0	.000	3	5	0	0	1.6	1.000
1989	CLE A	0	1	.000	4.09	9	3	0	33	31	14	10	0	0	0	0	0	0	0	–	4	7	0	1	1.2	1.000
4 yrs.		4	10	.286	4.62	36	20	1	132.1	151	55	60	0	1	1	0	31	4	0	.129	12	25	5	2	1.2	.881

Chicken Wolf

WOLF, WILLIAM VAN WINKLE
B. May 12, 1862, Louisville, Ky.   D. May 16, 1903, Louisville, Ky.   BR TR 5'9"   190 lbs.
Manager 1889.

Year	Team	W	L	PCT	ERA	G	GS	CG	IP	H	BB	SO	ShO	W	L	SV	AB	H	HR	BA	PO	A	E	DP	TC/G	FA
1882	LOU AA	0	0	–	9.00	1	0	0	6	11	3	1	0	0	0	0	318	95	0	.299	0	0	0	0	0.0	–
1885		0	0	–	9.00	1	0	0	1	1	0	1	0	0	0	0	483	141	1	.292	1	0	0	0	1.0	1.000
1886		0	0	–	15.00	1	0	0	3	7	0	0	0	0	0	0	545	148	3	.272	0	2	1	0	3.0	.667
3 yrs.		0	0	–	10.80	3	0	0	10	19	3	2	0	0	0	0	*				1	2	1	0	1.3	.750

Ernie Wolf

WOLF, ERNEST ADOLPH
B. Feb. 2, 1889, Newark, N. J.   D. May 23, 1964, Atlantic Highlands, N. J.   BR TR 5'11"   174 lbs.

Year	Team	W	L	PCT	ERA	G	GS	CG	IP	H	BB	SO	ShO	W	L	SV	AB	H	HR	BA	PO	A	E	DP	TC/G	FA
1912	CLE A	0	0	–	6.35	1	0	0	5.2	8	4	1	0	0	0	0	2	0	0	.000	0	0	0	0	0.0	–

Lefty Wolf

WOLF, WALTER FRANCIS
B. June 10, 1900, Hartford, Conn.   D. Sept. 25, 1971, New Orleans, La.   BR TL 5'10"   163 lbs.

Year	Team	W	L	PCT	ERA	G	GS	CG	IP	H	BB	SO	ShO	W	L	SV	AB	H	HR	BA	PO	A	E	DP	TC/G	FA
1921	PHI A	0	0	–	7.20	8	0	0	15	15	16	12	0	0	0	0	4	1	0	.250	1	3	2	0	0.8	.667

Wally Wolf

WOLF, WALTER BECK
B. Jan. 5, 1942, South Gate, Calif.   BR TR 6'½"   191 lbs.

Year	Team	W	L	PCT	ERA	G	GS	CG	IP	H	BB	SO	ShO	W	L	SV	AB	H	HR	BA	PO	A	E	DP	TC/G	FA
1969	CAL A	0	0	–	11.57	2	0	0	2.1	3	3	2	0	0	0	0	0	0	0	–	0	0	0	0	0.0	–
1970		0	0	–	5.40	4	0	0	5	3	4	5	0	0	0	0	0	0	0	–	0	0	0	0	0.0	–
2 yrs.		0	0	–	7.36	6	0	0	7.1	6	7	7	0	0	0	0	0	0	0	–	0	0	0	0	0.0	–

Bill Wolfe

WOLFE, WILBERT OTTO (Barney)
B. June 7, 1876, Independence, Pa.   D. Feb. 27, 1953, Gibsontown, Pa.   BR TR 6'1"

Year	Team	W	L	PCT	ERA	G	GS	CG	IP	H	BB	SO	ShO	W	L	SV	AB	H	HR	BA	PO	A	E	DP	TC/G	FA
1903	NY A	6	9	.400	2.97	20	12	12	148.1	143	26	48	1	0	1	0	53	4	0	.075	6	45	2	1	2.7	.962
1904	2 teams	NY A		(7G 0–3)		WAS A		(17G 6–9)																		
"	total	6	12	.333	3.26	24	19	15	160.1	162	26	52	2	0	1	0	52	5	0	.096	10	44	2	1	2.3	.964
1905	WAS A	8	14	.364	2.57	28	24	17	182	162	37	52	1	1	0	2	60	8	1	.133	10	48	3	1	2.2	.951
1906		0	3	.000	4.05	4	3	2	20	17	10	8	0	0	0	0	7	2	0	.286	0	7	1	0	2.0	.875
4 yrs.		20	38	.345	2.96	76	62	46	510.2	484	99	160	4	1	2	2	172	19	1	.110	26	144	8	3	2.3	.955

Bill Wolfe

WOLFE, WILLIAM F.
B. Jersey City, N. J.

Year	Team	W	L	PCT	ERA	G	GS	CG	IP	H	BB	SO	ShO	W	L	SV	AB	H	HR	BA	PO	A	E	DP	TC/G	FA
1902	PHI N	0	1	.000	4.00	1	1	1	9	11	4	3	0	0	0	0	3	1	0	.333	0	3	0	0	3.0	1.000

Chuck Wolfe

WOLFE, CHARLES HUNT
B. Feb. 15, 1897, Wolfsburg, Pa.   D. Nov. 27, 1957, Schellsburg, Pa.   BL TR 5'7"   175 lbs.

Year	Team	W	L	PCT	ERA	G	GS	CG	IP	H	BB	SO	ShO	W	L	SV	AB	H	HR	BA	PO	A	E	DP	TC/G	FA
1923	PHI A	0	0	–	3.72	3	0	0	9.2	6	8	1	0	0	0	0	3	1	0	.333	0	2	0	0	0.7	1.000

Ed Wolfe

WOLFE, EDWARD ANTHONY
B. Jan. 2, 1929, Los Angeles, Calif.   BR TR 6'3"   185 lbs.

Year	Team	W	L	PCT	ERA	G	GS	CG	IP	H	BB	SO	ShO	W	L	SV	AB	H	HR	BA	PO	A	E	DP	TC/G	FA
1952	PIT N	0	0	–	7.36	3	0	0	3.2	7	5	1	0	0	0	0	0	0	0	–	1	1	0	1	0.7	1.000

Roger Wolff

WOLFF, ROGER FRANCIS
B. Apr. 10, 1911, Evansville, Ill.   BR TR 6'½"   208 lbs.

Year	Team	W	L	PCT	ERA	G	GS	CG	IP	H	BB	SO	ShO	W	L	SV	AB	H	HR	BA	PO	A	E	DP	TC/G	FA
1941	PHI A	0	2	.000	3.18	2	2	2	17	15	4	2	0	0	0	0	5	1	0	.200	1	2	0	0	1.5	1.000
1942		12	15	.444	3.32	32	25	15	214.1	206	69	94	2	2	2	3	68	6	0	.088	17	38	2	5	1.8	.965
1943		10	15	.400	3.54	41	26	13	221	232	72	91	2	2	2	6	74	9	0	.122	12	30	1	0	1.0	.977
1944	WAS A	4	15	.211	4.99	33	21	5	155	186	60	73	0	1	1	0	55	12	0	.218	8	37	0	2	1.4	1.000
1945		20	10	.667	2.12	33	29	21	250	200	53	108	4	0	0	2	84	9	0	.107	6	45	1	2	1.6	.981
1946		5	8	.385	2.58	21	17	6	122	115	30	50	0	1	0	0	39	4	0	.103	9	17	1	0	1.3	.963
1947	2 teams	CLE A		(7G 0–0)		PIT N		(13G 1–4)																		
"	total	1	4	.200	7.04	20	8	1	46	64	28	12	0	0	0	0	12	0	0	.000	4	8	0	1	0.6	1.000
7 yrs.		52	69	.430	3.41	182	128	63	1025.1	1018	316	430	8	6	11	13	337	41	0	.122	57	177	5	10	1.3	.979

Mellie Wolfgang

WOLFGANG, MELDON JOHN (Red)
B. Mar. 20, 1890, Albany, N. Y.   D. June 30, 1947, Albany, N. Y.   BR TR 5'9"   160 lbs.

Year	Team	W	L	PCT	ERA	G	GS	CG	IP	H	BB	SO	ShO	W	L	SV	AB	H	HR	BA	PO	A	E	DP	TC/G	FA
1914	CHI A	9	5	.643	1.89	24	11	9	119.1	96	32	50	2	4	0	0	40	7	0	.175	7	53	2	1	2.6	.968
1915		2	2	.500	1.84	17	2	0	53.2	39	12	21	1	2	1	0	17	2	0	.118	1	13	3	0	1.0	.824
1916		4	6	.400	1.98	27	14	6	127	103	42	36	1	0	2	0	40	9	0	.225	5	46	4	1	2.0	.927
1917		0	0	–	5.09	5	0	0	17.2	18	6	3	0	0	0	0	4	0	0	.000	0	5	1	0	1.2	.833
1918		0	1	.000	5.40	4	0	0	8.1	12	3	1	0	0	1	0	2	1	0	.500	1	4	0	0	1.3	1.000
5 yrs.		15	14	.517	2.18	77	27	15	326	268	95	111	3	6	4	0	103	19	0	.184	14	121	10	2	1.9	.931

Harry Wolter

WOLTER, HARRY MEIGS
B. July 11, 1884, Monterey, Calif.   D. July 7, 1970, Palo Alto, Calif.   BL TL 5'10"   175 lbs.

Year	Team	W	L	PCT	ERA	G	GS	CG	IP	H	BB	SO	ShO	Relief Pitching W	L	SV	Batting AB	H	HR	BA	PO	A	E	DP	TC/G	FA

Harry Wolter *continued*

Year	Team	W	L	PCT	ERA	G	GS	CG	IP	H	BB	SO	ShO	W	L	SV	AB	H	HR	BA	PO	A	E	DP	TC/G	FA
1907	**3 teams**				CIN N		(0G 0–0)			PIT N		(1G 0–0)		STL N		(3G 1–2)										
"	total	1	2	.333	4.32	4	3	1	25	30	20	8	0	0	0	0	63	18	0	.286	1	3	1	0	1.3	.800
1909	BOS A	4	4	.500	3.91	10	6	0	53	53	28	20	0	1	1	0	119	29	2	.244	3	13	1	1	1.6	1.000
2 yrs.		5	6	.455	4.04	14	9	1	78	83	48	28	0	1	1	0	*				4	16	1	1	1.5	.952

Dooley Womack

WOMACK, HORACE GUY
B. Aug. 25, 1939, Columbia, S. C.   BL TR 6'   170 lbs.

Year	Team	W	L	PCT	ERA	G	GS	CG	IP	H	BB	SO	ShO	W	L	SV	AB	H	HR	BA	PO	A	E	DP	TC/G	FA
1966	NY A	7	3	.700	2.64	42	0	0	75	52	23	50	0	7	2	4	5	1	0	.200	7	21	1	2	0.7	.966
1967		5	6	.455	2.41	65	0	0	97	80	35	57	0	5	6	18	14	4	0	.286	13	33	2	3	0.7	.958
1968		3	7	.300	3.21	45	0	0	61.2	53	29	27	0	3	7	2	5	1	0	.200	6	19	0	1	0.6	1.000
1969	**2 teams**				HOU N		(30G 2–1)			SEA A		(9G 2–1)														
"	total	4	2	.667	3.31	39	0	0	65.1	64	23	40	0	4	2	0	7	1	0	.143	9	20	1	0	0.8	.967
1970	OAK A	0	0	–	15.00	2	0	0	3	4	1	3	0	0	0	0	0	0	0	–	0	1	0	0	0.5	1.000
5 yrs.		19	18	.514	2.95	193	1	0	302	253	111	177	0	19	17	24	31	7	0	.226	35	94	4	6	0.7	.970

George Wood

WOOD, GEORGE A. (Dandy)
B. Nov. 9, 1858, Boston, Mass.   D. Apr. 4, 1924, Harrisburg, Pa.
Manager 1891.   BL TR 5'10½" 175 lbs.

Year	Team	W	L	PCT	ERA	G	GS	CG	IP	H	BB	SO	ShO	W	L	SV	AB	H	HR	BA	PO	A	E	DP	TC/G	FA
1883	DET N	0	0	–	7.20	1	1	0	5	8	3	0	0	0	0	0	441	133	5	.302	0	3	0	0	3.0	1.000
1885		0	0	–	0.00	1	0	0	4	5	1	1	0	0	0	0	362	105	5	.290	0	0	0	0	0.0	
1888	PHI N	0	0	–	4.50	2	0	0	2	3	1	0	0	0	0	2	433	99	5	.229	0	1	0	0	0.5	1.000
1889		0	0	–	18.00	1	0	0	1	2	0	2	0	0	0	0	432	108	5	.250	0	0	0	0	0.0	
4 yrs.		0	0	–	5.25	5	0	0	12	18	5	3	0	0	0	2	*				0	4	0	0	0.8	1.000

Joe Wood

WOOD, JOSEPH FRANK
Son of Smoky Joe Wood.
B. May 20, 1916, Shohola, Pa.   BR TR 6'   190 lbs.

Year	Team	W	L	PCT	ERA	G	GS	CG	IP	H	BB	SO	ShO	W	L	SV	AB	H	HR	BA	PO	A	E	DP	TC/G	FA
1944	BOS A	0	1	.000	6.52	3	1	0	9.2	13	3	5	0	0	0	0	2	0	0	.000	3	1	0	1	1.3	1.000

John Wood

WOOD, JOHN B.
B. 1871   Deceased.   5'7"   142 lbs.

Year	Team	W	L	PCT	ERA	G	GS	CG	IP	H	BB	SO	ShO	W	L	SV	AB	H	HR	BA	PO	A	E	DP	TC/G	FA
1896	STL N	0	0	–	∞	1	0	0		1	2	0	0	0	0	0	0	0	0	–	0	0	0	0	0.0	

Pete Wood

WOOD, PETER BURKE
Brother of Fred Wood.
B. Feb. 1, 1857, Hamilton, Ont., Canada   D. Mar. 15, 1923, Chicago, Ill.   TR 5'7"   185 lbs.

Year	Team	W	L	PCT	ERA	G	GS	CG	IP	H	BB	SO	ShO	W	L	SV	AB	H	HR	BA	PO	A	E	DP	TC/G	FA
1885	BUF N	8	15	.348	4.44	24	22	21	198.2	235	66	38	0	0	1	0	104	23	0	.221	8	43	9	0	2.5	.850
1889	PHI N	1	1	.500	5.21	3	2	2	19	28	3	8	0	0	0	0	8	0	0	.000	0	4	2	1	2.0	.667
2 yrs.		9	16	.360	4.51	27	24	23	217.2	263	69	46	0	0	1	0	112	23	0	.205	8	47	11	1	2.4	.833

Smoky Joe Wood

WOOD, JOE (Smoky Joe)
Born Howard Ellsworth Wood.   Father of Joe Wood.
B. Oct. 25, 1889, Kansas City, Mo.   D. July 27, 1985, West Haven, Conn.   BR TR 5'11"   180 lbs.

Year	Team	W	L	PCT	ERA	G	GS	CG	IP	H	BB	SO	ShO	W	L	SV	AB	H	HR	BA	PO	A	E	DP	TC/G	FA
1908	BOS A	1	1	.500	2.38	6	2	1	22.2	14	16	11	1	0	0	0	7	0	0	.000	3	5	1	1	1.5	.889
1909		11	7	.611	2.21	24	19	13	158.2	121	43	88	4	2	0	0	55	9	0	.164	7	27	1	0	1.5	.971
1910		12	13	.480	1.68	35	17	14	197.2	155	56	145	3	6	3	0	69	18	0	.261	17	62	2	3	2.3	.975
1911		23	17	.575	2.02	44	33	25	276.2	226	76	231	5	6	2	3	88	23	2	.261	23	67	5	3	2.2	.947
1912		**34**	5	.872	1.91	43	38	35	344	267	82	258	**10**	1	0	1	124	36	1	.290	41	110	4	2	3.6	.974
1913		11	5	.688	2.29	23	18	12	145.2	120	61	123	1	1	1	2	56	15	0	.268	9	55	3	1	2.9	.955
1914		9	3	.750	2.62	18	14	11	113.1	94	34	67	1	0	0	1	43	6	0	.140	13	28	0	2	2.3	1.000
1915		15	5	.750	1.49	25	16	10	157.1	120	44	63	3	3	2	2	54	14	1	.259	8	41	1	6	2.3	.982
1917	CLE A	0	1	.000	3.45	5	1	0	15.2	17	7	2	0	0	1	0	6	0	0	.000	2	5	0	0	1.4	1.000
1919		0	0	–	0.00	1	0	0	.2	0	0	0	0	0	0	0	192	49	1	.255	0	1	0	0	1.0	1.000
1920		0	0	–	22.50	1	0	0	2	4	2	1	0	0	0	0	137	37	1	.270	0	0	0	0	0.0	
11 yrs.		116	57	.671	2.03	225	158	121	1434.1	1138	421	989	28	19	8	11	*				123	408	17	16	2.4	.969

WORLD SERIES

Year	Team	W	L	PCT	ERA	G	GS	CG	IP	H	BB	SO	ShO	W	L	SV	AB	H	HR	BA	PO	A	E	DP	TC/G	FA
1912	BOS A	3	1	.750	3.68	4	3	2	22	27	3	21	0	1	0	0	7	2	0	.286	1	6	0	1	1.8	1.000

Spades Wood

WOOD, CHARLES ASHER
B. Jan. 13, 1909, Spartanburg, S. C.   D. May 18, 1986, Wichita, Kans.   BL TL 5'10½" 150 lbs.

Year	Team	W	L	PCT	ERA	G	GS	CG	IP	H	BB	SO	ShO	W	L	SV	AB	H	HR	BA	PO	A	E	DP	TC/G	FA
1930	PIT N	4	3	.571	5.12	9	7	4	58	61	32	23	2	0	0	0	20	5	0	.250	1	4	0	1	0.6	1.000
1931		2	6	.250	6.05	15	10	2	64	69	46	33	0	0	0	0	22	5	0	.227	1	13	1	0	1.0	.933
2 yrs.		6	9	.400	5.61	24	17	6	122	130	78	56	2	0	0	0	42	10	0	.238	2	17	1	1	0.8	.950

Wilbur Wood

WOOD, WILBUR FORRESTER
B. Oct. 22, 1941, Cambridge, Mass.   BR TL 6'   180 lbs.

Year	Team	W	L	PCT	ERA	G	GS	CG	IP	H	BB	SO	ShO	W	L	SV	AB	H	HR	BA	PO	A	E	DP	TC/G	FA
1961	BOS A	0	0	–	5.54	6	1	0	13	14	7	7	0	0	0	0	3	0	0	.000	2	0	0	0	0.3	1.000
1962		0	0	–	3.52	1	1	0	7.2	6	3	3	0	0	0	0	3	0	0	.000	0	3	0	0	3.0	1.000
1963		0	5	.000	3.76	25	6	0	64.2	67	13	28	0	0	1	0	12	0	0	.000	2	10	1	0	0.5	.923
1964	**2 teams**				BOS A		(4G 0–0)			PIT N		(3G 0–2)														
"	total	0	2	.000	7.04	7	2	1	23	29	14	12	0	0	0	0	6	0	0	.000	1	3	0	0	0.6	1.000
1965	PIT N	1	1	.500	3.16	34	1	0	51.1	44	16	29	0	1	0	0	6	0	0	.000	2	6	0	0	0.2	1.000
1967	CHI A	4	2	.667	2.45	51	8	0	95.1	95	28	47	0	4	2	0	16	1	0	.063	7	13	2	2	0.4	.909
1968		13	12	.520	1.87	**88**	2	0	159	127	33	74	0	12	11	16	22	2	0	.091	7	25	0	1	0.4	1.000
1969		10	11	.476	3.01	**76**	0	0	119.2	113	40	73	0	10	11	15	15	0	0	.000	5	22	1	0	0.4	.964
1970		9	13	.409	2.80	**77**	0	0	122	118	36	85	0	9	13	21	18	2	0	.111	7	27	0	3	0.4	1.000
1971		22	13	.629	1.91	44	42	22	334	272	62	210	7	0	0	0	96	5	0	.052	11	65	1	3	1.8	.987
1972		**24**	17	.585	2.51	49	**49**	20	376.2	325	74	193	8	0	0	0	125	17	0	.136	9	82	4	8	1.9	.958
1973		**24**	20	.545	3.46	49	**48**	21	359.1	381	91	199	4	1	0	0	0	0	0	–	9	62	1	3	1.5	.986

Year	Team		W	L	PCT	ERA	G	GS	CG	IP	H	BB	SO	ShO	Relief Pitching W	L	SV	Batting AB	H	HR	BA	PO	A	E	DP	TC/G	FA

Wilbur Wood *continued*

Year	Team		W	L	PCT	ERA	G	GS	CG	IP	H	BB	SO	ShO	W	L	SV	AB	H	HR	BA	PO	A	E	DP	TC/G	FA
1974			20	19	.513	3.60	42	**42**	22	320	305	80	169	1	0	0	0	0	0	0	—	8	67	3	1	1.9	.962
1975			16	**20**	.444	4.11	43	**43**	14	291.1	309	92	140	2	0	0	0	0	0	0	—	8	53	1	3	1.4	.984
1976			4	3	.571	2.25	7	7	5	56	51	11	31	1	0	0	0	0	0	0	—	1	12	0	1	1.9	1.000
1977			7	8	.467	4.98	24	18	5	123	139	50	42	1	0	0	0	0	0	0	—	3	33	0	1	1.5	1.000
1978			10	10	.500	5.20	28	27	4	168	187	74	69	0	0	0	0	0	0	0	—	2	40	0	1	1.5	1.000
17 yrs.			164	156	.513	3.24	651	297	114	2684	2582	724	1411	24	33	36	57	322	27	0	.084	84	523	14	26	1.0	.977

Gene Woodburn

WOODBURN, EUGENE STEWART
B. Aug. 20, 1886, Bellaire, Ohio   D. Jan. 18, 1961, Sandusky, Ohio

BR TR 6'   175 lbs.

Year	Team		W	L	PCT	ERA	G	GS	CG	IP	H	BB	SO	ShO	W	L	SV	AB	H	HR	BA	PO	A	E	DP	TC/G	FA
1911	STL	N	1	5	.167	5.40	11	6	1	38.1	22	40	23	0	0	1	0	6	1	0	.167	1	13	5	1	1.4	.933
1912			1	4	.200	5.59	20	5	1	48.1	60	42	25	0	1	0	0	13	0	0	.000	2	10	5	0	0.9	.706
2 yrs.			2	9	.182	5.50	31	11	2	86.2	82	82	48	0	1	1	0	19	1	0	.053	3	23	6	1	1.0	.813

Fred Woodcock

WOODCOCK, FRED WAYLAND
B. May 17, 1868, Winchendon, Mass.   D. Aug. 11, 1943, Ashburnham, Mass.

BL TL 6'2"   190 lbs.

Year	Team		W	L	PCT	ERA	G	GS	CG	IP	H	BB	SO	ShO	W	L	SV	AB	H	HR	BA	PO	A	E	DP	TC/G	FA
1892	PIT	N	1	2	.333	3.55	5	4	3	33	42	17	8	0	0	0	0	15	3	0	.200	2	6	0	2	1.6	1.000

George Woodend

WOODEND, GEORGE ANTHONY
B. Dec. 9, 1917, Hartford, Conn.   D. May 1, 1980, Hartford, Conn.

BR TR 6'   200 lbs.

Year	Team		W	L	PCT	ERA	G	GS	CG	IP	H	BB	SO	ShO	W	L	SV	AB	H	HR	BA	PO	A	E	DP	TC/G	FA
1944	BOS	N	0	0	—	13.50	3	0	0	2	5	5	0	0	0	0	0	0	0	0	—	0	1	0	0	0.3	1.000

Hal Woodeshick

WOODESHICK, HAROLD JOSEPH
B. Aug. 24, 1932, Wilkes-Barre, Pa.

BR TL 6'3"   200 lbs.

Year	Team		W	L	PCT	ERA	G	GS	CG	IP	H	BB	SO	ShO	W	L	SV	AB	H	HR	BA	PO	A	E	DP	TC/G	FA
1956	DET	A	0	2	.000	13.50	2	2	0	5.1	12	3	1	0	0	0	0	0	0	0	—	1	1	0	0	1.0	1.000
1958	CLE	A	6	6	.500	3.64	14	9	3	71.2	72	25	27	0	3	0	0	24	4	0	.167	4	26	4	4	2.4	.882
1959	WAS	A	2	4	.333	3.69	31	3	0	61	58	36	30	0	2	1	0	8	0	0	.000	1	16	2	0	0.6	.895
1960			4	5	.444	4.70	41	14	1	115	131	60	46	0	2	1	4	29	2	0	.069	4	33	4	1	1.0	.902
1961	2 teams	WAS A (7G 3–2)						DET A	(12G 1–1)																		
"	total		4	3	.571	5.22	19	8	1	58.2	63	41	37	0	1	0	0	20	2	0	.100	6	19	3	0	1.5	.893
1962	HOU	N	5	16	.238	4.39	31	26	2	139.1	161	54	82	1	1	0	0	37	3	0	.081	7	26	3	0	1.2	.917
1963			11	9	.550	1.97	55	0	0	114	75	42	94	0	11	9	10	23	3	0	.130	6	33	3	1	0.8	.929
1964			2	9	.182	2.76	61	0	0	78.1	73	32	58	0	2	9	23	10	0	0	.000	5	23	5	0	0.5	.848
1965	2 teams	HOU N (27G 3–4)						STL N	(51G 3–2)																		
"	total		6	6	.500	2.25	78	0	0	92	74	45	59	0	6	6	18	14	1	0	.071	11	24	1	1	0.5	.972
1966	STL	N	2	1	.667	1.92	59	0	0	70.1	57	23	30	0	2	1	4	5	1	0	.200	7	26	0	1	0.6	1.000
1967			2	1	.667	5.18	36	0	0	41.2	41	28	20	0	2	1	2	4	0	0	.000	2	12	2	1	0.4	.875
11 yrs.			44	62	.415	3.56	427	62	7	847.1	816	389	484	1	31	29	61	174	16	0	.092	54	239	27	9	0.7	.916

WORLD SERIES

Year	Team		W	L	PCT	ERA	G	GS	CG	IP	H	BB	SO	ShO	W	L	SV	AB	H	HR	BA	PO	A	E	DP	TC/G	FA
1967	STL	N	0	0	—	0.00	1	0	0	1	1	0	0	0	0	0	0	0	0	0	—	0	1	0	0	1.0	1.000

Dan Woodman

WOODMAN, DANIEL COURTENAY (Cocoa)
B. July 8, 1893, Danvers, Mass.   D. Dec. 14, 1962, Danvers, Mass.

BR TR 5'8"   160 lbs.

Year	Team		W	L	PCT	ERA	G	GS	CG	IP	H	BB	SO	ShO	W	L	SV	AB	H	HR	BA	PO	A	E	DP	TC/G	FA
1914	BUF	F	0	0	—	2.41	13	0	0	33.2	30	11	13	0	0	0	1	7	1	0	.143	1	7	2	0	0.8	.800
1915			0	0	—	4.11	5	1	0	15.1	14	9	1	0	0	0	0	4	1	0	.250	1	10	0	0	2.2	1.000
2 yrs.			0	0	—	2.94	18	1	0	49	44	20	14	0	0	0	1	11	2	0	.182	2	17	2	0	1.2	.905

Clarence Woods

WOODS, CLARENCE COFIELD
B. June 11, 1892, Woods Ridge, Ind.   D. July 2, 1969, Rising Sun, Ind.

BR TR 6'5½"   230 lbs.

Year	Team		W	L	PCT	ERA	G	GS	CG	IP	H	BB	SO	ShO	W	L	SV	AB	H	HR	BA	PO	A	E	DP	TC/G	FA
1914	IND	F	0	0	—	4.50	2	0	0	2	1	2	1	0	0	0	1	0	0	0	—	0	1	0	0	0.5	1.000

John Woods

WOODS, JOHN FULTON (Abe)
B. Jan. 18, 1898, Princeton, W. Va.   D. Oct. 4, 1946, Norfolk, Va.

BR TR 5'11"   150 lbs.

Year	Team		W	L	PCT	ERA	G	GS	CG	IP	H	BB	SO	ShO	W	L	SV	AB	H	HR	BA	PO	A	E	DP	TC/G	FA
1924	BOS	A	0	0	—	0.00	1	0	0	1	0	3	0	0	0	0	0	0	0	0	—	0	0	0	0	0.0	—

Pinky Woods

WOODS, GEORGE ROWLAND
B. May 22, 1915, Waterbury, Conn.   D. Oct. 30, 1982, Los Angeles, Calif.

BR TR 6'5"   225 lbs.

Year	Team		W	L	PCT	ERA	G	GS	CG	IP	H	BB	SO	ShO	W	L	SV	AB	H	HR	BA	PO	A	E	DP	TC/G	FA
1943	BOS	A	5	6	.455	4.92	23	12	2	100.2	109	55	32	0	1	0	1	36	8	0	.222	9	20	2	1	1.3	.935
1944			4	8	.333	3.27	38	20	5	170.2	171	88	56	1	0	1	0	48	7	0	.146	13	37	1	3	1.3	.980
1945			4	7	.364	4.19	24	12	3	107.1	108	63	36	0	1	1	2	42	9	0	.214	8	25	0	3	1.4	1.000
3 yrs.			13	21	.382	3.97	85	44	10	378.2	388	206	124	1	2	2	3	126	24	0	.190	30	82	3	7	1.4	.974

Walt Woods

WOODS, WALTER SYDNEY
B. Apr. 28, 1875, Rye, N. H.   D. Oct. 30, 1951, Portsmouth, N. H.

BR TR 5'9½"   165 lbs.

Year	Team		W	L	PCT	ERA	G	GS	CG	IP	H	BB	SO	ShO	W	L	SV	AB	H	HR	BA	PO	A	E	DP	TC/G	FA
1898	CHI	N	9	13	.409	3.14	27	22	18	215	224	59	26	3	0	0	0	154	27	0	.175	19	56	5	1	3.0	.938
1899	LOU	N	9	13	.409	3.28	26	21	17	186.1	216	37	21	0	2	1	0	126	19	1	.151	10	68	2	1	3.1	.975
1900	PIT	N	0	0	—	21.00	1	0	0	3	9	1	1	0	0	0	0	1	0	0	.000	0	0	0	0	0.0	—
3 yrs.			18	26	.409	3.34	54	43	35	404.1	449	97	48	3	2	2	0	*				29	124	7	2	3.0	.956

Dick Woodson

WOODSON, RICHARD LEE
B. Mar. 30, 1945, Oelwein, Iowa

BR TR 6'5"   205 lbs.

Year	Team		W	L	PCT	ERA	G	GS	CG	IP	H	BB	SO	ShO	W	L	SV	AB	H	HR	BA	PO	A	E	DP	TC/G	FA
1969	MIN	A	7	5	.583	3.67	44	10	2	110.1	99	49	66	0	3	2	1	27	2	0	.074	3	22	0	3	0.6	1.000
1970			1	2	.333	3.77	21	0	0	31	19	22	22	0	1	2	1	2	0	0	.000	1	6	2	1	0.4	.778
1972			14	14	.500	2.71	36	36	9	252	193	101	150	3	0	0	0	88	7	0	.080	17	43	4	1	1.8	.938
1973			10	8	.556	3.95	23	23	4	141.1	137	68	53	2	0	0	0	0	0	0	—	10	14	1	0	1.1	.960
1974	2 teams	MIN A (5G 1–1)						NY A	(8G 1–2)																		
"	total		2	3	.400	5.07	13	12	0	55	64	16	24	0	1	0	0	0	0	0	—	4	8	1	0	1.0	.923
5 yrs.			34	32	.515	3.46	137	76	15	589.2	522	253	315	5	5	4	2	117	9	0	.077	35	93	8	5	1.0	.941

Year	Team		W	L	PCT	ERA	G	GS	CG	IP	H	BB	SO	ShO	Relief Pitching W	L	SV	Batting AB	H	HR	BA	PO	A	E	DP	TC/G	FA

Dick Woodson *continued*

LEAGUE CHAMPIONSHIP SERIES

Year	Team		W	L	PCT	ERA	G	GS	CG	IP	H	BB	SO	ShO	W	L	SV	AB	H	HR	BA	PO	A	E	DP	TC/G	FA
1969	MIN	A	0	0	–	10.80	1	0	0	1.2	3	3	2	0	0	0	0	1	1	0	1.000	0	0	0	0	0.0	–
1970			0	0	–	9.00	1	0	0	1	2	1	0	0	0	0	0	0	0	0	–	0	0	0	0	0.0	–
2 yrs.			0	0	–	10.13	2	0	0	2.2	5	4	2	0	0	0	0	1	1	0	1.000	0	0	0	0	0.0	–

Frank Woodward

WOODWARD, FRANK RUSSELL
B. May 17, 1894, New Haven, Conn. D. June 11, 1961, New Haven, Conn.   BR TR 5'10" 175 lbs.

Year	Team		W	L	PCT	ERA	G	GS	CG	IP	H	BB	SO	ShO	W	L	SV	AB	H	HR	BA	PO	A	E	DP	TC/G	FA
1918	PHI	N	0	0	–	6.00	2	0	0	6	6	4	4	0	0	0	0	3	1	0	.333	0	1	0	0	0.5	1.000
1919	2 teams		PHI N	(17G 6–9)		STL N	(17G 3–5)																					
"	total		9	14	.391	3.86	34	19	8	172.2	174	63	45	0	3	2	1	50	7	0	.140	9	39	4	2	1.5	.923
1921	WAS	A	0	0	–	5.91	3	1	0	10.2	11	3	4	0	0	0	0	3	1	0	.333	0	4	0	0	1.3	1.000
1922			0	0	–	11.57	1	0	0	2.1	3	3	2	0	0	0	0	1	0	0	.000	0	1	0	0	1.0	1.000
1923	CHI	A	0	1	.000	13.50	2	1	0	2	5	1	0	0	0	0	0	0	0	0	–	0	2	0	0	1.0	1.000
5 yrs.			9	15	.375	4.23	42	21	8	193.2	199	74	55	0	3	2	1	57	9	0	.158	9	47	4	2	1.4	.933

Rob Woodward

WOODWARD, ROBERT JOHN
B. Sept. 28, 1962, Hanover, N. H.   BR TR 6'3" 185 lbs.

Year	Team		W	L	PCT	ERA	G	GS	CG	IP	H	BB	SO	ShO	W	L	SV	AB	H	HR	BA	PO	A	E	DP	TC/G	FA
1985	BOS	A	1	0	1.000	1.69	5	2	0	26.2	17	9	16	0	0	0	0	0	0	0	–	5	0	2	0	1.4	.714
1986			2	3	.400	5.30	9	6	0	35.2	46	11	14	0	1	0	0	0	0	0	–	5	6	0	0	1.2	1.000
1987			1	1	.500	7.05	9	6	0	37	53	15	15	0	0	0	0	0	0	0	–	2	1	0	0	0.3	1.000
1988			0	0	–	13.50	1	0	0	.2	2	1	0	0	0	0	0	0	0	0	–	0	0	0	0	0.0	–
4 yrs.			4	4	.500	5.04	24	14	0	100	118	36	45	0	1	0	0	0	0	0	–	12	7	2	0	0.9	.905

Floyd Wooldridge

WOOLDRIDGE, FLOYD LEWIS
B. Aug. 25, 1928, Jerico Springs, Mo.   BR TR 6'1" 185 lbs.

Year	Team		W	L	PCT	ERA	G	GS	CG	IP	H	BB	SO	ShO	W	L	SV	AB	H	HR	BA	PO	A	E	DP	TC/G	FA
1955	STL	N	2	4	.333	4.84	18	8	2	57.2	64	27	14	0	0	1	0	18	4	0	.222	2	5	0	0	0.4	1.000

Earl Wooten

WOOTEN, EARL HAZWELL (Junior)
B. Jan. 16, 1924, Pelzer, S. C.   BR TL 5'11" 160 lbs.

Year	Team		W	L	PCT	ERA	G	GS	CG	IP	H	BB	SO	ShO	W	L	SV	AB	H	HR	BA	PO	A	E	DP	TC/G	FA
1948	WAS	A	0	0	–	9.00	1	0	0	2	2	2	1	0	0	0	0	*				0	1	0	0	1.0	1.000

Fred Worden

WORDEN, FREDERICK BAMFORD
B. Sept. 4, 1894, St. Louis, Mo. D. Nov. 9, 1941, St. Louis, Mo.   BR TR

Year	Team		W	L	PCT	ERA	G	GS	CG	IP	H	BB	SO	ShO	W	L	SV	AB	H	HR	BA	PO	A	E	DP	TC/G	FA
1914	PHI	A	0	0	–	18.00	1	0	0	2	8	0	1	0	0	0	0	1	0	0	.000	0	1	0	0	1.0	1.000

Hoge Workman

WORKMAN, HARRY HALL
B. Sept. 25, 1899, Huntington, W. Va. D. May 20, 1972, Fort Myers, Fla.   BR TR 5'11" 170 lbs.

Year	Team		W	L	PCT	ERA	G	GS	CG	IP	H	BB	SO	ShO	W	L	SV	AB	H	HR	BA	PO	A	E	DP	TC/G	FA
1924	BOS	A	0	0	–	8.50	11	0	0	18	25	11	7	0	0	0	0	2	0	0	.000	2	4	0	0	0.5	1.000

Ralph Works

WORKS, RALPH TALMADGE (Judge)
B. Mar. 16, 1888, Payson, Ill. D. Aug. 8, 1941, Pasadena, Calif.   BL TR 6'2½" 185 lbs.

Year	Team		W	L	PCT	ERA	G	GS	CG	IP	H	BB	SO	ShO	W	L	SV	AB	H	HR	BA	PO	A	E	DP	TC/G	FA
1909	DET	A	4	1	.800	1.97	16	4	4	64	62	17	31	0	1	0	2	17	1	0	.059	2	16	2	1	1.3	.900
1910			3	6	.333	3.57	18	10	5	85.2	73	39	36	0	0	1	1	30	8	0	.267	4	26	5	1	1.9	.857
1911			11	5	.688	3.87	30	15	9	167.1	173	67	68	3	4	0	1	61	9	0	.148	3	28	4	1	1.2	.886
1912	2 teams		DET A	(27G 5–10)		CIN N	(3G 1–1)																					
"	total		6	11	.353	4.16	30	18	10	166.2	189	71	69	1	1	1	1	61	9	0	.148	2	52	6	0	2.0	.900
1913	CIN	N	0	1	.000	7.80	5	2	0	15	15	8	4	0	0	0	0	6	1	0	.167	0	6	0	0	1.2	1.000
5 yrs.			24	24	.500	3.79	99	49	28	498.2	512	202	208	4	6	2	5	175	28	0	.160	11	128	17	3	1.6	.891

WORLD SERIES

Year	Team		W	L	PCT	ERA	G	GS	CG	IP	H	BB	SO	ShO	W	L	SV	AB	H	HR	BA	PO	A	E	DP	TC/G	FA
1909	DET	A	0	0	–	9.00	1	0	0	2	2	0	2	0	0	0	0	0	0	0	–	0	1	0	0	1.0	1.000

Todd Worrell

WORRELL, TODD ROLAND
B. Sept. 28, 1959, Arcadia, Calif.   BR TR 6'5" 215 lbs.

Year	Team		W	L	PCT	ERA	G	GS	CG	IP	H	BB	SO	ShO	W	L	SV	AB	H	HR	BA	PO	A	E	DP	TC/G	FA
1985	STL	N	3	0	1.000	2.91	17	0	0	21.2	17	7	17	0	3	0	5	1	0	0	.000	3	5	0	0	0.2	1.000
1986			9	10	.474	2.08	74	0	0	103.2	86	41	73	0	9	10	36	7	1	0	.143	5	8	2	0	0.2	.867
1987			8	6	.571	2.66	75	0	0	94.2	86	34	92	0	8	6	33	10	1	0	.100	0	17	0	0	0.2	1.000
1988			5	9	.357	3.00	68	0	0	90	69	34	78	0	5	9	32	6	0	0	.000	3	10	0	4	0.2	1.000
1989			3	5	.375	2.96	47	0	0	51.2	42	26	41	0	3	5	20	1	0	0	.000	0	11	0	1	0.2	1.000
5 yrs.			28	30	.483	2.64	281	0	0	361.2	300	142	301	0	28	30	126	25	2	0	.080	11	46	2	5	0.2	.966

LEAGUE CHAMPIONSHIP SERIES

Year	Team		W	L	PCT	ERA	G	GS	CG	IP	H	BB	SO	ShO	W	L	SV	AB	H	HR	BA	PO	A	E	DP	TC/G	FA
1985	STL	N	1	0	1.000	1.42	4	0	0	6.1	4	2	3	0	1	0	0	0	0	0	–	0	1	0	0	0.3	1.000
1987			0	0	–	2.08	3	0	0	4.1	4	1	6	0	0	0	1	0	0	0	–	0	0	0	0	0.0	–
2 yrs.			1	0	1.000	1.69	7	0	0	10.2	8	3	9	0	1	0	1	0	0	0	–	0	1	0	0	0.1	1.000

WORLD SERIES

Year	Team		W	L	PCT	ERA	G	GS	CG	IP	H	BB	SO	ShO	W	L	SV	AB	H	HR	BA	PO	A	E	DP	TC/G	FA
1985	STL	N	0	1	.000	3.86	3	0	0	4.2	4	2	6	0	0	1	1	1	0	0	.000	0	1	0	0	0.3	1.000
1987			0	0	–	1.29	4	0	0	7	6	4	3	0	0	0	2	0	0	0	–	0	0	0	0	0.0	1.000
2 yrs.			0	1	.000	2.31	7	0	0	11.2	10	6	9	0	0	1	3	1	0	0	.000	0	1	0	0	0.1	1.000

4th

Rich Wortham

WORTHAM, RICHARD COOPER (Tex)
B. Oct. 22, 1953, Odessa, Tex.   BR TL 6' 185 lbs.

Year	Team		W	L	PCT	ERA	G	GS	CG	IP	H	BB	SO	ShO	W	L	SV	AB	H	HR	BA	PO	A	E	DP	TC/G	FA
1978	CHI	A	3	2	.600	3.05	8	8	2	59	59	23	25	0	0	0	0	0	0	0	–	0	9	0	0	1.1	1.000
1979			14	14	.500	4.90	34	33	5	204	195	100	119	0	0	0	0	0	0	0	–	7	27	5	0	1.1	.872
1980			4	7	.364	5.97	41	10	0	92	102	58	45	0	2	2	1	0	0	0	–	7	18	5	1	0.7	.833
1983	OAK	A	0	0	–	∞	1	0	0	0	3	1	0	0	0	0	0	0	0	0	–	0	0	0	0	0.0	–
4 yrs.			21	23	.477	4.89	84	51	7	355	359	182	189	0	2	2	1	0	0	0	–	14	54	10	1	0.9	.872

Year	Team	W	L	PCT	ERA	G	GS	CG	IP	H	BB	SO	ShO	Relief Pitching W	L	SV	Batting AB	H	HR	BA	PO	A	E	DP	TC/G	FA

Al Worthington

WORTHINGTON, ALLAN FULTON (Red)
B. Feb. 5, 1929, Birmingham, Ala.   BR TR 6'2" 195 lbs.

Year	Team		W	L	PCT	ERA	G	GS	CG	IP	H	BB	SO	ShO	W	L	SV	AB	H	HR	BA	PO	A	E	DP	TC/G	FA
1953	NY	N	4	8	.333	3.44	20	17	5	102	103	54	52	2	0	0	0	31	2	0	.065	12	16	2	1	1.5	.933
1954			0	2	.000	3.50	10	1	0	18	21	15	8	0	0	0	0	4	0	0	.000	0	4	1	0	0.5	.800
1956			7	14	.333	3.97	28	24	4	165.2	158	74	95	0	0	1	0	51	12	1	.235	9	35	4	6	1.7	.917
1957			8	11	.421	4.22	55	12	1	157.2	140	56	90	1	7	5	4	40	4	0	.100	10	26	0	0	0.7	1.000
1958	SF	N	11	7	.611	3.63	54	12	1	151.1	152	57	76	0	3	4	6	44	8	0	.182	9	26	2	0	0.7	.946
1959			2	3	.400	3.68	42	3	0	73.1	68	37	45	0	1	2	2	13	1	0	.077	5	15	0	0	0.5	1.000
1960	2 teams	BOS A	(6G 0–1)			CHI A	(4G 1–1)																				
"	total		1	2	.333	6.35	10	0	0	17	20	15	8	0	1	2	0	3	2	0	.667	2	3	0	0	0.5	1.000
1963	CIN	N	4	4	.500	2.99	50	0	0	81.1	75	31	55	0	4	4	10	12	1	0	.083	5	22	0	3	0.5	1.000
1964	2 teams	CIN N	(6G 1–0)			MIN A	(41G 5–6)																				
"	total		6	6	.500	2.16	47	0	0	79.1	61	30	65	0	6	6	14	16	1	0	.063	8	14	4	0	0.6	.846
1965	MIN	A	10	7	.588	2.13	62	0	0	80.1	57	41	59	0	10	7	21	10	1	0	.100	3	24	1	0	0.5	.964
1966			6	3	.667	2.46	65	0	0	91.1	66	27	93	0	6	3	16	11	3	0	.273	8	14	2	0	0.4	.917
1967			8	9	.471	2.84	59	0	0	92	77	38	80	0	8	9	16	8	0	0	.000	4	13	0	1	0.3	1.000
1968			4	5	.444	2.71	54	0	0	76.1	67	32	57	0	4	5	18	7	0	0	.000	5	11	1	0	0.3	.941
1969			4	1	.800	4.57	46	0	0	61	65	20	51	0	4	1	3	5	0	0	.000	2	6	0	1	0.2	1.000
14 yrs.			75	82	.478	3.39	602	69	11	1246.2	1130	527	834	3	54	50	110	255	35	1	.137	82	229	17	12	0.5	.948

LEAGUE CHAMPIONSHIP SERIES

| 1969 | MIN | A | 0 | 0 | – | 6.75 | 1 | 0 | 0 | 1.1 | 3 | 0 | 1 | 0 | 0 | 0 | 0 | 0 | 0 | 0 | – | 0 | 0 | 0 | 0 | 0.0 | – |

WORLD SERIES

| 1965 | MIN | A | 0 | 0 | – | 0.00 | 2 | 0 | 0 | 4 | 2 | 2 | 2 | 0 | 0 | 0 | 0 | 0 | 0 | 0 | – | 1 | 1 | 1 | 0 | 1.5 | .667 |

Bob Wright

WRIGHT, ROBERT CASSIUS
B. Dec. 13, 1891, Greensburg, Ind.   BR TR 6'1½" 175 lbs.

| 1915 | CHI | N | 0 | 0 | – | 2.25 | 2 | 0 | 0 | 4 | 6 | 3 | 0 | 0 | 0 | 0 | 0 | 0 | 0 | 0 | – | 0 | 0 | 0 | 0 | 0.5 | 1.000 |

Clarence Wright

WRIGHT, CLARENCE EUGENE
B. Dec. 11, 1878, Cleveland, Ohio D. Oct. 29, 1930, Barberton, Ohio   BR TR 6'2½" 190 lbs.

1901	BKN	N	1	0	1.000	1.00	1	1	1	9	6	1	6	0	0	0	0	3	1	0	.333	0	1	0	0	1.0	1.000
1902	CLE	A	7	11	.389	3.95	21	18	15	148	150	75	52	1	0	1	0	70	10	1	.143	2	35	1	0	1.8	.974
1903	2 teams	CLE A	(15G 3–9)			STL A	(8G 3–5)																				
"	total		6	14	.300	4.98	23	20	15	162.2	195	74	79	1	0	0	0	64	12	0	.188	5	61	3	3	3.0	.957
1904	STL	A	0	1	.000	13.50	1	1	0	4	10	2	3	0	0	0	0	1	0	0	.000	0	4	0	0	4.0	1.000
4 yrs.			14	26	.350	4.50	46	40	31	323.2	361	152	140	2	0	2	1	138	23	1	.167	7	101	4	3	2.4	.964

Clyde Wright

WRIGHT, CLYDE
B. Feb. 20, 1941, Jefferson City, Tenn.   BR TL 6'1" 180 lbs.

1966	CAL	A	4	7	.364	3.74	20	13	3	91.1	92	25	37	1	1	1	0	29	3	0	.103	7	17	1	1	1.3	.960
1967			5	5	.500	3.26	20	11	1	77.1	76	24	35	0	1	0	0	22	6	0	.273	7	13	0	1	1.0	1.000
1968			10	6	.625	3.94	41	13	2	125.2	123	44	71	1	6	0	3	37	8	0	.216	8	14	0	1	0.5	1.000
1969			1	8	.111	4.10	37	5	0	63.2	66	30	31	0	1	3	0	11	2	0	.182	1	12	0	1	0.4	1.000
1970			22	12	.647	2.83	39	39	7	261	226	88	110	2	0	0	0	105	18	2	.171	18	33	3	1	1.4	.944
1971			16	17	.485	2.99	37	37	10	277	225	82	135	2	0	0	0	91	14	0	.154	18	67	2	6	2.4	.977
1972			18	11	.621	2.98	35	35	15	251	229	80	87	2	0	0	0	83	18	2	.217	8	61	4	4	2.1	.920
1973			11	19	.367	3.68	37	36	13	257	273	76	65	1	0	0	0	0	0	0	–	16	63	3	9	2.2	.963
1974	MIL	A	9	20	.310	4.42	38	32	15	232	264	54	64	0	1	1	0	0	0	0	–	18	42	1	4	1.6	.984
1975	TEX	A	4	6	.400	4.44	25	14	1	93.1	105	47	32	0	1	0	0	0	0	0	–	7	22	2	2	1.2	.935
10 yrs.			100	111	.474	3.50	329	235	67	1729.1	1679	550	667	9	11	5	3	378	69	4	.183	108	344	18	30	1.4	.962

Dave Wright

WRIGHT, DAVID WILLIAM
B. Aug. 27, 1875, Dennison, Ohio D. Jan. 18, 1946, Dennison, Ohio   BR TR 6' 185 lbs.

1895	PIT	N	0	0	–	27.00	1	0	0	2	6	1	0	0	0	0	0	0	0	0	.000	0	1	1	0	2.0	.500
1897	CHI	N	1	0	1.000	15.43	1	1	1	7	17	2	4	0	0	0	0	3	1	0	.333	0	2	1	0	3.0	.667
2 yrs.			1	0	1.000	18.00	2	1	1	9	23	3	4	0	0	0	0	4	1	0	.250	0	3	2	0	2.5	.600

Ed Wright

WRIGHT, HENDERSON EDWARD
B. May 15, 1919, Dyersburg, Tenn.   BR TR 6'1" 180 lbs.

1945	BOS	N	8	3	.727	2.51	15	12	7	111.1	104	33	24	1	0	0	0	39	5	0	.128	2	20	1	1	1.5	.957
1946			12	9	.571	3.52	36	21	9	176.1	164	71	44	2	2	0	0	59	18	0	.305	12	35	1	0	1.3	.979
1947			3	3	.500	6.40	23	6	1	64.2	80	35	14	0	1	0	0	23	3	0	.130	4	10	0	1	0.6	1.000
1948			0	0	–	1.93	3	0	0	4.2	9	2	2	0	0	0	0	0	0	0	–	0	1	0	0	0.3	1.000
1952	PHI	A	2	1	.667	6.53	24	0	0	41.1	55	20	9	0	2	1	1	7	1	0	.143	1	6	0	1	0.3	1.000
5 yrs.			25	16	.610	4.00	101	39	17	398.1	412	161	93	3	5	1	1	128	27	0	.211	19	72	2	3	0.9	.978

George Wright

WRIGHT, GEORGE
Brother of Harry Wright. Brother of Sam Wright.
B. Jan. 28, 1847, Yonkers, N.Y. D. Aug. 21, 1937, Boston, Mass.
Manager 1879.
Hall of Fame 1937.   BR TR 5'9½" 150 lbs.

| 1876 | BOS | N | 0 | 0 | – | 0.00 | 1 | 0 | 0 | 1 | 1 | 0 | 1 | 0 | 0 | 0 | 0 | 0 | 0 | 0 | * | 0 | 0 | 0 | 0 | 0.0 | – |

Jim Wright

WRIGHT, JAMES
B. Sept. 19, 1900, Hyde, England D. Apr. 10, 1963, Oakland, Calif.   BR TR 6'4" 195 lbs.

1927	STL	A	1	0	1.000	4.50	2	1	1	12	8	4	4	0	0	0	0	4	0	0	.000	1	1	0	0	1.0	1.000
1928			0	0	–	13.50	2	0	0	2	3	2	2	0	0	0	0	0	0	0	–	0	2	0	0	1.0	1.000
2 yrs.			1	0	1.000	5.79	4	1	1	14	11	6	6	0	0	0	0	4	0	0	.000	1	3	0	0	1.0	1.000

Year	Team		W	L	PCT	ERA	G	GS	CG	IP	H	BB	SO	ShO	W	L	SV	AB	H	HR	BA	PO	A	E	DP	TC/G	FA

Jim Wright
WRIGHT, JAMES CLIFTON
B. Dec. 21, 1950, Reed City, Mich.
BR TR 6'1" 165 lbs.

1978	BOS	A	8	4	.667	3.57	24	16	5	116	122	24	56	3	0	0	0	0	0	0	–	4	12	1	0	0.7	.941
1979			1	0	1.000	5.09	11	1	0	23	19	7	15	0	0	0	0	0	0	0	–	2	1	0	0	0.3	1.000
2 yrs.			9	4	.692	3.82	35	17	5	139	141	31	71	3	0	0	0	0	0	0	–	6	13	1	0	0.6	.950

Jim Wright
WRIGHT, JAMES LEON, JR.
B. Mar. 3, 1955, St. Joseph, Mo.
BR TR 6'5" 205 lbs.

1981	KC	A	2	3	.400	3.46	17	4	0	52	57	21	27	0	1	1	0	0	0	0	–	2	6	0	0	0.5	1.000
1982			0	0	–	5.32	7	0	0	23.2	32	6	9	0	0	0	0	0	0	0	–	1	2	1	0	0.6	.750
2 yrs.			2	3	.400	4.04	24	4	0	75.2	89	27	36	0	1	1	0	0	0	0	–	3	8	1	0	0.5	.917

Ken Wright
WRIGHT, KENNETH WARREN
B. Sept. 4, 1946, Pensacola, Fla.
BR TR 6'2" 210 lbs.

1970	KC	A	1	2	.333	5.26	47	0	0	53	49	29	30	0	1	2	3	4	0	0	.000	1	8	1	0	0.2	.900
1971			3	6	.333	3.69	21	12	1	78	66	47	56	0	0	0	1	22	2	0	.091	1	16	1	2	0.9	.944
1972			1	2	.333	5.00	17	0	0	18	15	15	18	0	1	2	4	2	0	0	.000	1	2	0	0	0.2	1.000
1973			6	5	.545	4.89	25	12	1	81	60	82	75	0	1	0	0	0	0	0	–	1	6	2	0	0.4	.778
1974	NY	A	0	0	–	3.00	3	0	0	6	5	7	2	0	0	0	0	0	0	0	–	2	1	0	0	1.0	1.000
5 yrs.			11	15	.423	4.54	113	24	2	236	195	180	181	0	3	4	8	28	2	0	.071	6	33	4	2	0.4	.907

Lucky Wright
WRIGHT, WILLIAM SIMMONS (William The Red, Deacon)
B. Feb. 21, 1880, Tontogany, Ohio D. July 6, 1941, Tontogany, Ohio
BR TR 6' 178 lbs.

| 1909 | CLE | A | 0 | 4 | .000 | 3.97 | 5 | 4 | 3 | 22.2 | 20 | 8 | 6 | 0 | 0 | 0 | 0 | 7 | 0 | 0 | .000 | 0 | 10 | 1 | 0 | 2.2 | .909 |

Mel Wright
WRIGHT, MELVIN JAMES
B. May 11, 1928, Manila, Ark. D. May 16, 1983, Montreal, Quebec, Canada
BR TR 6'3" 210 lbs.

1954	STL	N	0	0	–	10.45	9	0	0	10.1	16	11	4	0	0	0	0	1	0	0	.000	2	1	0	1	0.3	1.000
1955			2	2	.500	6.19	29	0	0	36.1	44	9	18	0	2	2	1	6	0	0	.000	5	6	0	0	0.4	1.000
1960	CHI	N	0	1	.000	4.96	9	0	0	16.1	17	3	8	0	0	1	0	2	0	0	.000	2	0	0	0	0.2	1.000
1961			0	1	.000	10.71	11	0	0	21	42	4	6	0	0	1	2	2	0	0	.000	3	7	0	1	0.9	1.000
4 yrs.			2	4	.333	7.61	58	0	0	84	119	27	36	0	2	4	3	11	0	0	.000	12	14	0	2	0.4	1.000

Rasty Wright
WRIGHT, WAYNE BROMLEY
B. Nov. 5, 1895, Ceredo, W. Va. D. June 12, 1948, Columbus, Ohio
BR TR 5'11" 160 lbs.

1917	STL	A	0	1	.000	5.45	16	1	0	39.2	48	10	5	0	0	0	0	10	2	0	.200	3	13	0	1	1.0	1.000
1918			8	2	.800	2.51	18	13	6	111.1	99	18	25	1	0	0	0	34	10	0	.294	8	25	1	0	1.9	.971
1919			0	5	.000	5.54	24	5	2	63.1	79	20	14	0	0	0	0	12	1	0	.083	4	18	0	0	0.9	1.000
1922			9	7	.563	2.92	31	16	5	154	148	50	44	0	3	2	5	50	7	0	.140	6	40	1	4	1.5	.979
1923			7	4	.636	6.42	20	8	4	82.2	107	34	26	0	4	1	0	27	6	0	.222	4	23	2	1	1.5	.931
5 yrs.			24	19	.558	4.05	109	43	17	451	481	132	114	1	7	3	5	133	26	0	.195	25	119	4	5	1.4	.973

Ricky Wright
WRIGHT, JAMES RICHARD
B. Nov. 22, 1958, Paris, Tex.
BL TL 6'3" 175 lbs.

1982	LA	N	2	1	.667	3.03	14	5	0	32.2	28	20	24	0	1	1	0	8	1	0	.125	3	6	0	0	0.6	1.000
1983	2 teams	LA N (6G 0–0)					TEX A	(1G 0–0)																			
"	total		0	0	–	2.16	7	0	0	8.1	5	3	7	0	0	0	0	0	0	0	–	0	0	1	0	0.1	–
1984	TEX	A	0	2	.000	6.14	8	1	0	14.2	20	11	6	0	0	0	0	0	0	0	–	1	4	0	0	0.6	1.000
1985			0	0	–	4.70	5	0	0	7.2	5	5	7	0	0	0	0	0	0	0	–	0	1	0	0	0.2	1.000
1986			1	0	1.000	5.03	21	1	0	39.1	44	21	23	0	1	0	0	0	0	0	–	3	7	1	1	0.5	1.000
5 yrs.			3	3	.500	4.30	55	7	0	102.2	102	60	67	0	2	3	0	8	1	0	.125	7	18	1	1	0.5	.962

Roy Wright
WRIGHT, ROY EARL
B. Sept. 26, 1933, Buchtel, Ohio
BR TR 6'2" 170 lbs.

| 1956 | NY | N | 0 | 1 | .000 | 16.88 | 1 | 1 | 0 | 2.2 | 8 | 2 | 0 | 0 | 0 | 0 | 0 | 1 | 0 | 0 | .000 | 1 | 0 | 0 | 0 | 1.0 | 1.000 |

Frank Wurm
WURM, FRANK JAMES
B. Apr. 27, 1924, Cambridge, N. Y.
BB TL 6'1" 175 lbs.

| 1944 | BKN | N | 0 | 0 | – | 108.00 | 1 | 1 | 0 | .1 | 1 | 5 | 1 | 0 | 0 | 0 | 0 | 0 | 0 | 0 | – | 0 | 0 | 0 | 0 | 0.0 | – |

John Wyatt
WYATT, JOHN THOMAS
B. Apr. 19, 1935, Chicago, Ill.
BR TR 5'11½" 200 lbs.

1961	KC	A	0	0	–	2.45	5	0	0	7.1	8	4	6	0	0	0	1	0	0	0	–	0	2	1	0	0.6	.667
1962			10	7	.588	4.46	59	9	0	125	121	80	106	0	7	4	11	29	3	0	.103	8	14	3	0	0.4	.880
1963			6	4	.600	3.13	63	0	0	92	83	43	81	0	6	4	21	9	0	0	.000	3	12	2	1	0.3	.882
1964			9	8	.529	3.59	81	0	0	128	111	52	74	0	9	8	20	14	0	0	.000	8	16	1	0	0.3	.960
1965			2	6	.250	3.25	65	0	0	88.2	78	53	70	0	2	6	18	4	0	0	.000	2	16	0	0	0.3	1.000
1966	2 teams	KC A (19G 0–3)					BOS A	(42G 3–4)																			
"	total		3	7	.300	3.68	61	0	0	95.1	78	43	88	0	3	7	10	11	0	0	.000	3	11	1	0	0.2	.933
1967	BOS	A	10	7	.588	2.60	60	0	0	93.1	71	39	68	0	10	7	20	12	1	0	.083	1	21	0	0	0.4	1.000
1968	3 teams	BOS A (8G 1–2)					NY A	(7G 0–2)		DET A	(22G 1–0)															
"	total		2	4	.333	2.74	37	0	0	49.1	42	26	42	0	2	4	2	5	0	0	.000	2	7	1	1	0.4	.923
1969	OAK	A	0	1	.000	5.40	4	0	0	8.1	8	6	5	0	0	1	0	1	0	0	.000	0	1	0	0	0.3	1.000
9 yrs.			42	44	.488	3.47	435	9	0	687.1	600	346	540	0	39	41	103	83	4	0	.048	30	100	9	2	0.3	.935

WORLD SERIES

| 1967 | BOS | A | 1 | 0 | 1.000 | 4.91 | 2 | 0 | 0 | 3.2 | 1 | 3 | 1 | 0 | 0 | 0 | 0 | 0 | 0 | 0 | – | 0 | 0 | 0 | 0 | 0.0 | – |

Whit Wyatt
WYATT, JOHN WHITLOW
B. Sept. 27, 1907, Kensington, Ga.
BR TR 6'1" 185 lbs.

| 1929 | DET | A | 0 | 1 | .000 | 6.75 | 4 | 4 | 1 | 25.1 | 30 | 18 | 14 | 0 | 0 | 0 | 0 | 10 | 1 | 0 | .100 | 0 | 8 | 1 | 2 | 2.3 | .889 |

Year	Team	W	L	PCT	ERA	G	GS	CG	IP	H	BB	SO	ShO	Relief Pitching W	L	SV	Batting AB	H	HR	BA	PO	A	E	DP	TC/G	FA

Whit Wyatt *continued*

Year	Team	W	L	PCT	ERA	G	GS	CG	IP	H	BB	SO	ShO	W	L	SV	AB	H	HR	BA	PO	A	E	DP	TC/G	FA
1930		4	5	.444	3.57	21	7	2	85.2	76	35	68	0	3	2	2	34	12	1	.353	4	15	1	0	1.0	.950
1931		0	2	.000	8.44	4	1	1	21.1	30	12	8	0	0	0	1	7	2	0	.286	0	1	1	0	0.5	.500
1932		9	13	.409	5.03	43	22	10	205.2	228	102	82	0	3	3	1	78	15	2	.192	7	35	1	3	1.0	.977
1933	2 teams	DET A	(10G 0–1)		CHI A	(26G 3–4)																				
"	total	3	5	.375	4.56	36	7	2	104.2	111	54	40	0	1	2	1	30	6	0	.200	3	23	0	0	0.7	1.000
1934	CHI A	4	11	.267	7.18	23	6	2	67.2	83	37	36	0	3	6	2	26	6	0	.231	3	14	3	2	0.9	.850
1935		4	3	.571	6.75	30	1	0	52	65	25	22	0	4	3	5	13	3	0	.231	2	13	0	0	0.5	1.000
1936		0	0	–	0.00	3	0	0	3	3	0	0	0	0	0	0	0	0	0	–	0	0	0	0	0.0	–
1937	CLE A	2	3	.400	4.44	29	4	2	73	67	40	52	0	2	2	0	18	7	0	.389	2	12	1	1	0.5	.933
1939	BKN N	8	3	.727	2.31	16	14	6	109	88	39	52	2	1	0	0	36	6	0	.167	5	28	3	1	2.3	.917
1940		15	14	.517	3.46	37	34	16	239.1	233	62	124	5	1	1	0	80	14	1	.175	8	37	1	0	1.2	.978
1941		22	10	.688	2.34	38	35	23	288.1	223	82	176	7	0	1	1	109	26	3	.239	11	47	2	5	1.6	.967
1942		19	7	.731	2.73	31	30	16	217.1	185	63	104	0	1	0	0	77	14	0	.182	11	39	3	1	1.7	.943
1943		14	5	.737	2.49	26	26	13	180.2	139	43	80	3	0	0	0	60	17	0	.283	9	27	1	0	1.4	.973
1944		2	6	.250	7.17	9	9	1	37.2	51	16	4	0	0	0	0	13	2	0	.154	4	5	0	1	1.0	1.000
1945	PHI N	0	7	.000	5.26	10	10	2	51.1	72	14	10	0	0	0	0	16	2	0	.125	5	12	0	0	1.7	1.000
16 yrs.		106	95	.527	3.78	360	210	97	1762	1684	642	872	17	20	19	13	607	133	7	.219	74	316	18	16	1.1	.956

WORLD SERIES

| 1941 | BKN N | 1 | 1 | .500 | 2.50 | 2 | 2 | 2 | 18 | 15 | 10 | 14 | 0 | 0 | 0 | 0 | 6 | 1 | 0 | .167 | 1 | 2 | 0 | 0 | 1.5 | 1.000 |

John Wyckoff

WYCKOFF, JOHN WELDON   BR TR 6'1" 175 lbs.
B. Feb. 19, 1892, Williamsport, Pa.   D. May 8, 1961, Sheboygan Falls, Wis.

Year	Team	W	L	PCT	ERA	G	GS	CG	IP	H	BB	SO	ShO	W	L	SV	AB	H	HR	BA	PO	A	E	DP	TC/G	FA
1913	PHI A	2	4	.333	4.38	17	7	3	61.2	56	46	31	0	1	1	0	21	4	0	.190	3	19	1	0	1.4	.957
1914		11	7	.611	3.02	32	20	11	185	153	103	86	0	1	1	2	75	11	1	.147	4	34	4	0	1.3	.905
1915		10	22	.313	3.52	43	34	20	276	238	165	157	1	1	1	0	96	12	0	.125	11	85	10	2	2.5	.906
1916	2 teams	PHI A	(7G 0–1)		BOS A	(8G 0–0)																				
"	total	0	1	.000	5.11	15	2	1	44	39	38	22	0	0	0	0	14	4	0	.286	0	9	0	1	0.6	1.000
1917	BOS A	0	0	–	1.80	1	0	0	5	4	4	1	0	0	0	0	1	0	0	.000	0	3	0	0	3.0	1.000
1918		0	0	–	0.00	1	0	0	2	4	1	2	0	0	0	0	1	0	0	.000	0	0	0	0	0.0	–
6 yrs.		23	34	.404	3.55	109	63	35	573.2	494	357	299	1	2	3	3	208	31	1	.149	18	150	15	3	1.7	.918

WORLD SERIES

| 1914 | PHI A | 0 | 0 | – | 2.45 | 1 | 0 | 0 | 3.2 | 3 | 1 | 2 | 0 | 0 | 0 | 0 | 1 | 1 | 0 | 1.000 | 1 | 0 | 0 | 0 | 1.0 | 1.000 |

Frank Wyman

WYMAN, FRANK C.
B. May 10, 1862, Haverhill, Mass.   D. Feb. 4, 1916, Everett, Mass.

Year	Team	W	L	PCT	ERA	G	GS	CG	IP	H	BB	SO	ShO	W	L	SV	AB	H	HR	BA	PO	A	E	DP	TC/G	FA
1884	CHI U	0	1	.000	6.86	3	1	1	21	37	3	9	0	0	0	0	*				1	3	2	0	2.0	.667

Early Wynn

WYNN, EARLY (Gus)   BB TR 6' 190 lbs.
B. Jan. 6, 1920, Hartford, Ala.
Hall of Fame 1972.   BR 1939-44

Year	Team	W	L	PCT	ERA	G	GS	CG	IP	H	BB	SO	ShO	W	L	SV	AB	H	HR	BA	PO	A	E	DP	TC/G	FA
1939	WAS A	0	2	.000	5.75	3	3	1	20.1	26	10	1	0	0	0	0	6	1	0	.167	1	0	0	0	0.3	1.000
1941		3	1	.750	1.58	5	5	4	40	35	10	15	0	0	0	0	15	2	0	.133	2	9	1	1	2.4	.917
1942		10	16	.385	5.12	30	28	10	190	246	73	58	1	0	2	0	69	15	0	.217	5	36	2	3	1.4	.953
1943		18	12	.600	2.91	37	33	12	256.2	232	83	89	3	2	0	0	98	29	1	.296	5	49	3	3	1.5	.947
1944		8	17	.320	3.38	33	25	19	207.2	221	67	65	2	0	2	2	92	19	1	.207	4	31	1	4	1.1	.972
1946		8	5	.615	3.11	17	12	9	107	112	33	36	0	1	0	0	47	15	1	.319	7	18	1	2	1.5	.962
1947		17	15	.531	3.64	33	31	22	247	251	90	73	2	1	0	0	120	33	2	.275	15	33	1	3	1.5	.980
1948		8	19	.296	5.82	33	31	15	198	236	94	49	1	0	0	0	106	23	0	.217	6	32	2	1	1.2	.950
1949	CLE A	11	7	.611	4.15	26	23	6	164.2	186	57	62	0	1	0	0	70	10	1	.143	16	31	0	3	1.8	1.000
1950		18	8	.692	3.20	32	28	14	213.2	166	101	143	2	1	0	0	77	18	2	.234	5	36	3	5	1.4	.932
1951		20	13	.606	3.02	37	34	21	274.1	227	107	133	3	1	0	1	108	20	1	.185	13	42	1	2	1.5	.982
1952		23	12	.657	2.90	42	33	19	285.2	239	132	153	4	3	0	3	99	22	0	.222	20	46	4	2	1.7	.943
1953		17	12	.586	3.93	36	34	16	251.2	234	107	138	1	2	0	0	91	25	3	.275	11	36	0	2	1.3	1.000
1954		23	11	.676	2.73	40	36	20	270.2	225	83	155	3	0	0	2	93	17	0	.183	17	27	2	1	1.2	.957
1955		17	11	.607	2.82	32	31	16	230	207	80	122	6	0	0	0	84	15	1	.179	7	27	2	0	1.1	.944
1956		20	9	.690	2.72	38	35	18	277.2	233	91	158	4	0	0	2	101	23	0	.228	15	48	3	3	1.7	.955
1957	CHI A	14	17	.452	4.31	40	37	13	263	270	104	184	1	0	0	1	86	10	0	.116	10	38	0	5	1.2	1.000
1958		14	16	.467	4.13	40	34	11	239.2	214	104	179	4	0	0	2	75	15	0	.200	12	25	0	2	0.9	1.000
1959		22	10	.688	3.17	37	37	14	255.2	202	119	179	5	0	0	0	90	22	2	.244	6	39	2	2	1.3	.957
1960		13	12	.520	3.49	36	35	4	237.1	220	112	158	4	0	0	0	75	15	1	.200	7	28	1	1	0.9	.972
1961		8	2	.800	3.51	17	16	5	110.1	88	47	64	0	0	0	0	37	6	0	.162	4	11	0	0	0.9	1.000
1962		7	15	.318	4.46	27	26	11	167.2	171	56	91	3	0	0	0	54	7	0	.130	3	20	0	0	0.9	1.000
1963	CLE A	1	2	.333	2.28	20	5	1	55.1	50	15	29	0	0	1	1	11	3	0	.273	2	8	0	0	0.5	1.000
23 yrs.		300	244	.551	3.54	691	612	290	4564	4291	1775	2334	49	11	12	15	*				193	670	29	47	1.3	.967
								4th																		

WORLD SERIES

1954	CLE A	0	1	.000	3.86	1	1	0	7	4	2	5	0	0	0	0	2	1	0	.500	1	1	0	0	2.0	1.000
1959	CHI A	1	1	.500	5.54	3	3	0	13	19	4	10	0	0	0	0	5	1	0	.200	1	3	0	0	1.3	1.000
2 yrs.		1	2	.333	4.95	4	4	0	20	23	6	15	0	0	0	0	7	2	0	.286	2	4	0	0	1.5	1.000

Bill Wynne

WYNNE, WILLIAM ANDREW   BR TR 5'11½" 161 lbs.
B. Mar. 27, 1869, Neuse, N. C.   D. Aug. 7, 1951, Raleigh, N. C.

Year	Team	W	L	PCT	ERA	G	GS	CG	IP	H	BB	SO	ShO	W	L	SV	AB	H	HR	BA	PO	A	E	DP	TC/G	FA
1894	WAS N	0	1	.000	6.75	1	1	1	8	10	8	2	0	0	0	0	3	0	0	.000	0	1	0	0	1.0	1.000

Billy Wynne

WYNNE, BILLY VERNON   BR TR 6'3" 205 lbs.
B. July 31, 1943, Williamston, N. C.   BB 1967

Year	Team	W	L	PCT	ERA	G	GS	CG	IP	H	BB	SO	ShO	W	L	SV	AB	H	HR	BA	PO	A	E	DP	TC/G	FA
1967	NY N	0	0	–	3.12	6	1	0	8.2	12	2	4	0	0	0	0	1	0	0	.000	1	0	0	0	0.2	1.000
1968	CHI A	0	0	–	4.50	1	0	0	2	0	1	0	0	0	0	0	0	0	0	–	0	0	0	0	0.0	–
1969		7	7	.500	4.06	20	20	6	128.2	143	50	67	1	0	0	0	41	5	0	.122	11	19	0	2	1.5	1.000

Year	Team	W	L	PCT	ERA	G	GS	CG	IP	H	BB	SO	ShO	Relief Pitching W	L	SV	Batting AB	H	HR	BA	PO	A	E	DP	TC/G	FA

Billy Wynne *continued*

Year	Team	W	L	PCT	ERA	G	GS	CG	IP	H	BB	SO	ShO	W	L	SV	AB	H	HR	BA	PO	A	E	DP	TC/G	FA
1970		1	4	.200	5.32	12	9	0	44	54	22	19	0	0	0	0	13	1	0	.077	1	11	1	1	1.1	.923
1971	CAL A	0	0	—	4.50	3	0	0	4	6	2	6	0	0	0	0	0	0	0	—	0	1	0	0	0.3	1.000
5 yrs.		8	11	.421	4.32	42	30	6	187.1	217	78	97	1	0	0	0	55	6	0	.109	13	31	1	3	1.1	.978

Hank Wyse

WYSE, HENRY WASHINGTON (Hooks)
B. Mar. 1, 1918, Lunsford, Ark.   BR TR 5'11½" 185 lbs.

Year	Team	W	L	PCT	ERA	G	GS	CG	IP	H	BB	SO	ShO	W	L	SV	AB	H	HR	BA	PO	A	E	DP	TC/G	FA
1942	CHI N	2	1	.667	1.93	4	4	1	28	33	6	8	1	0	0	0	8	1	0	.125	0	5	0	0	1.3	1.000
1943		9	7	.563	2.94	38	15	8	156	160	34	45	2	1	2	5	50	4	0	.080	9	47	1	4	1.5	.982
1944		16	15	.516	3.15	41	34	14	257.1	**277**	57	86	3	2	1	1	90	16	0	.178	7	51	1	3	1.4	.983
1945		22	10	.688	2.68	38	34	23	278.1	272	55	77	2	1	0	0	101	17	0	.168	10	67	2	5	2.1	.975
1946		14	12	.538	2.68	40	27	12	201.1	206	52	52	2	0	0	1	74	18	0	.243	9	50	1	4	1.5	.983
1947		6	9	.400	4.31	37	19	5	142	158	64	53	1	1	0	1	45	5	0	.111	7	33	5	5	1.2	.889
1950	PHI A	9	14	.391	5.85	41	23	4	170.2	192	87	33	0	1	4	0	59	9	0	.153	13	34	5	1	1.3	.904
1951	2 teams			PHI A	(9G 1–2)			WAS A	(3G 0–0)																	
"	total	1	2	.333	8.63	12	3	0	24	41	18	8	0	1	1	0	8	1	0	.125	1	4	0	1	0.4	1.000
8 yrs.		79	70	.530	3.52	251	159	67	1257.2	1339	373	362	11	7	8	8	435	71	0	.163	56	291	15	24	1.4	.959

WORLD SERIES

Year	Team	W	L	PCT	ERA	G	GS	CG	IP	H	BB	SO	ShO	W	L	SV	AB	H	HR	BA	PO	A	E	DP	TC/G	FA
1945	CHI N	0	1	.000	7.04	3	1	0	7.2	8	4	1	0	0	0	0	3	0	0	.000	0	0	0	0	0.0	—

Biff Wysong

WYSONG, HARLIN
B. Apr. 13, 1905, Clarksville, Ohio   D. Aug. 8, 1951, Xenia, Ohio   BL TL 6'3" 195 lbs.

Year	Team	W	L	PCT	ERA	G	GS	CG	IP	H	BB	SO	ShO	W	L	SV	AB	H	HR	BA	PO	A	E	DP	TC/G	FA
1930	CIN N	0	1	.000	19.29	1	1	0	2.1	6	3	1	0	0	0	0	0	0	0	—	0	0	0	0	0.0	—
1931		0	2	.000	7.89	12	2	0	21.2	25	23	5	0	0	0	0	4	1	0	.250	0	3	1	0	0.3	.750
1932		1	0	1.000	3.65	7	0	0	12.1	13	8	5	0	1	0	0	2	0	0	.000	1	3	1	1	0.7	.800
3 yrs.		1	3	.250	7.18	20	3	0	36.1	44	34	11	0	1	0	0	6	1	0	.167	1	6	2	1	0.5	.778

Rusty Yarnall

YARNALL, WALDO WILLIAM
B. Oct. 22, 1902, Chicago, Ill.   D. Oct. 9, 1985, Lowell, Mass.   BR TR 6' 175 lbs.

Year	Team	W	L	PCT	ERA	G	GS	CG	IP	H	BB	SO	ShO	W	L	SV	AB	H	HR	BA	PO	A	E	DP	TC/G	FA
1926	PHI N	0	1	.000	18.00	1	0	0	3	3	1	0	0	0	1	0	1	0	0	.000	0	1	0	0	1.0	1.000

Rube Yarrison

YARRISON, BYRON WARDSWORTH
B. Mar. 9, 1896, Montgomery, Pa.   D. Apr. 22, 1977, Williamsport, Pa.   BR TR 5'11" 165 lbs.

Year	Team	W	L	PCT	ERA	G	GS	CG	IP	H	BB	SO	ShO	W	L	SV	AB	H	HR	BA	PO	A	E	DP	TC/G	FA
1922	PHI A	1	2	.333	8.29	18	1	0	33.2	50	12	10	0	1	1	0	6	1	0	.167	8	0	1	0	0.4	1.000
1924	BKN N	0	2	.000	6.55	3	2	0	11	12	3	2	0	0	0	0	2	0	0	.000	0	5	1	0	2.0	.833
2 yrs.		1	4	.200	7.86	21	3	0	44.2	62	15	12	0	1	1	0	8	1	0	.125	0	13	1	1	0.7	.929

Emil Yde

YDE, EMIL OGDEN
B. Jan. 28, 1900, Great Lakes, Ill.
D. Dec. 4, 1968, Leesburg, Fla.   BB TL 5'11" 165 lbs.   BL 1925

Year	Team	W	L	PCT	ERA	G	GS	CG	IP	H	BB	SO	ShO	W	L	SV	AB	H	HR	BA	PO	A	E	DP	TC/G	FA
1924	PIT N	16	3	**.842**	2.83	33	22	14	194	171	62	53	4	1	0	0	88	21	1	.239	5	57	6	4	2.1	.912
1925		17	9	.654	4.13	33	28	13	207	254	75	41	0	2	0	0	89	17	0	.191	8	46	4	8	1.8	.931
1926		8	7	.533	3.65	37	22	12	187.1	181	81	34	1	0	0	0	74	17	0	.230	10	47	4	3	1.6	.934
1927		1	3	.250	9.71	9	2	0	29.2	45	15	9	0	1	0	0	18	3	0	.167	2	11	1	0	1.6	.929
1929	DET A	7	3	.700	5.30	29	6	4	86.2	100	63	23	1	3	1	0	48	16	0	.333	5	16	2	0	0.8	.913
5 yrs.		49	25	.662	4.02	141	80	43	704.2	751	296	160	6	7	2	0	*				30	177	17	15	1.6	.924

WORLD SERIES

Year	Team	W	L	PCT	ERA	G	GS	CG	IP	H	BB	SO	ShO	W	L	SV	AB	H	HR	BA	PO	A	E	DP	TC/G	FA
1925	PIT N	0	1	.000	11.57	1	1	0	2.1	5	3	1	0	0	0	0	1	0	0	.000	0	0	0	0	0.0	—

Joe Yeager

YEAGER, JOSEPH F. (Little Joe)
B. Aug. 28, 1875, Philadelphia, Pa.   D. July 2, 1937, Detroit, Mich.   TR

Year	Team	W	L	PCT	ERA	G	GS	CG	IP	H	BB	SO	ShO	W	L	SV	AB	H	HR	BA	PO	A	E	DP	TC/G	FA
1898	BKN N	12	22	.353	3.65	36	33	32	291.1	333	80	70	1	2	0	134	23	0	.172	10	99	11	3	3.3	.908
1899		2	2	.500	4.72	10	4	2	47.2	56	16	6	1	1	1	1	47	9	0	.191	3	13	0	2	1.6	1.000
1900		1	1	.500	6.88	2	2	2	17	21	5	2	0	0	0	0	9	3	0	.333	0	3	0	0	1.5	1.000
1901	DET A	12	11	.522	2.61	26	25	22	199.2	209	46	38	3	0	0	1	125	37	2	.296	13	66	7	4	3.3	.919
1902		6	12	.333	4.82	19	15	14	140	171	41	28	0	1	2	0	161	39	1	.242	14	52	3	1	3.6	.957
1903		0	1	.000	4.00	1	1	1	9	15	0	1	0	0	0	0	402	103	0	.256	3	3	0	0	6.0	1.000
6 yrs.		33	49	.402	3.74	94	80	73	704.2	805	188	145	4	3	5	2	*				43	236	21	10	3.2	.930

Jim Yeargin

YEARGIN, JAMES ALMOND (Grapefruit)
B. Oct. 16, 1901, Mauldin, S. C.   D. May 8, 1937, Greenville, S. C.   BR TR 5'11" 170 lbs.

Year	Team	W	L	PCT	ERA	G	GS	CG	IP	H	BB	SO	ShO	W	L	SV	AB	H	HR	BA	PO	A	E	DP	TC/G	FA
1922	BOS N	0	1	.000	1.29	1	1	1	7	5	2	1	0	0	0	0	3	0	0	.000	0	2	0	0	2.0	1.000
1924		1	11	.083	5.09	32	12	6	141.1	162	42	34	0	0	0	1	42	6	0	.143	11	50	2	2	2.0	.968
2 yrs.		1	12	.077	4.91	33	13	7	148.1	167	44	35	0	0	0	1	45	6	0	.133	11	52	2	2	2.0	.969

Larry Yellen

YELLEN, LAWRENCE ALAN
B. Jan. 4, 1943, Brooklyn, N. Y.   BR TR 5'11" 190 lbs.

Year	Team	W	L	PCT	ERA	G	GS	CG	IP	H	BB	SO	ShO	W	L	SV	AB	H	HR	BA	PO	A	E	DP	TC/G	FA
1963	HOU N	0	0	—	3.60	1	1	0	5	7	1	3	0	0	0	0	2	0	0	.000	0	2	0	0	2.0	1.000
1964		0	0	—	6.86	13	1	0	21	27	10	9	0	0	0	0	3	0	0	.000	0	4	0	0	0.3	1.000
2 yrs.		0	0	—	6.23	14	2	0	26	34	11	12	0	0	0	0	5	0	0	.000	0	6	0	0	0.4	1.000

Chief Yellowhorse

YELLOWHORSE, MOSES J.
B. Jan. 28, 1898, Pawnee, Okla.   D. Apr. 10, 1964, Pawnee, Okla.   BR TR 5'10" 180 lbs.

Year	Team	W	L	PCT	ERA	G	GS	CG	IP	H	BB	SO	ShO	W	L	SV	AB	H	HR	BA	PO	A	E	DP	TC/G	FA
1921	PIT N	5	3	.625	2.98	10	4	1	48.1	45	13	19	0	3	0	1	17	0	0	.000	1	3	1	0	0.5	.800
1922		3	1	.750	4.52	28	5	2	77.2	92	20	24	0	2	0	0	19	6	0	.316	4	15	1	0	0.7	.950
2 yrs.		8	4	.667	3.93	38	9	3	126	137	33	43	0	5	0	1	36	6	0	.167	5	18	2	0	0.7	.920

Year	Team		W	L	PCT	ERA	G	GS	CG	IP	H	BB	SO	ShO	W	L	SV	AB	H	HR	BA	PO	A	E	DP	TC/G	FA
															Relief Pitching			Batting									

Carroll Yerkes

YERKES, CHARLES CARROLL (Lefty) — BR TL 5'11" 180 lbs.
B. June 13, 1903, McSherrystown, Pa. D. Dec. 20, 1950, Oakland, Calif.

Year	Team	W	L	PCT	ERA	G	GS	CG	IP	H	BB	SO	ShO	W	L	SV	AB	H	HR	BA	PO	A	E	DP	TC/G	FA
1927	PHI A	0	0	–	0.00	1	0	0	1	1	0	1	0	0	0	0	0	0	0	–	0	2	0	0	2.0	1.000
1928		0	1	.000	2.08	2	1	1	8.2	7	2	1	0	0	0	0	3	0	0	.000	0	5	0	1	2.5	1.000
1929		1	0	1.000	4.58	19	2	0	37.1	47	13	11	0	1	0	1	10	0	0	.000	3	18	0	3	1.1	1.000
1932	CHI N	0	0	–	3.00	2	0	0	9	5	3	4	0	0	0	0	3	1	0	.333	0	1	0	0	0.0	–
1933		0	0	–	4.50	1	0	0	2	2	1	0	0	0	0	0	0	0	0	–	0	1	0	0	1.0	1.000
5 yrs.		1	1	.500	3.88	25	3	1	58	61	20	16	0	1	0	1	16	1	0	.063	3	26	0	4	1.2	1.000

Stan Yerkes

YERKES, STANLEY LEWIS — 5'10"
B. Nov. 28, 1874, Cheltenham, Pa. D. July 28, 1940, Boston, Mass.

Year	Team	W	L	PCT	ERA	G	GS	CG	IP	H	BB	SO	ShO	W	L	SV	AB	H	HR	BA	PO	A	E	DP	TC/G	FA
1901	2 teams			BAL A (1G 0–1)			STL N	(4G 3–1)																		
"	total	3	2	.600	3.86	5	5	5	42	47	8	19	0	0	0	0	15	2	0	.133	0	10	0	0	2.0	1.000
1902	STL N	11	20	.355	3.66	39	37	27	272.2	341	79	81	1	0	0	0	91	12	0	.132	11	61	7	0	2.0	.911
1903		0	1	.000	1.80	1	1	0	5	8	0	3	0	0	0	0	2	0	0	.000	0	0	0	0	0.0	–
3 yrs.		14	23	.378	3.66	45	43	32	319.2	396	87	103	1	0	0	0	108	14	0	.130	11	71	7	0	2.0	.921

Rich Yett

YETT, RICHARD MARTIN — BR TR 6'2" 187 lbs.
B. Oct. 6, 1962, Pomona, Calif.

Year	Team	W	L	PCT	ERA	G	GS	CG	IP	H	BB	SO	ShO	W	L	SV	AB	H	HR	BA	PO	A	E	DP	TC/G	FA
1985	MIN A	0	0	–	27.00	1	1	0	.1	1	2	0	0	0	0	0	0	0	0	–	0	0	0	0	0.0	–
1986	CLE A	5	3	.625	5.15	39	3	1	78.2	84	37	50	1	4	2	1	0	0	0	–	2	7	0	0	0.2	1.000
1987		3	9	.250	5.25	37	11	2	97.2	96	49	59	0	1	5	1	0	0	0	–	6	9	0	0	0.4	1.000
1988		9	6	.600	4.62	23	22	0	134.1	146	55	71	0	0	0	0	0	0	0	–	8	9	0	1	0.7	1.000
1989		5	6	.455	5.00	32	12	1	99	111	47	47	0	1	1	0	0	0	0	–	9	7	0	0	0.5	1.000
5 yrs.		22	24	.478	4.98	132	49	4	410	438	190	227	1	6	8	2	0	0	0	–	25	32	0	1	0.4	1.000

Earl Yingling

YINGLING, EARL HERSHEY (Chink) — BL TL 5'11½" 180 lbs.
B. Oct. 29, 1888, Chillicothe, Ohio D. Oct. 2, 1962, Columbus, Ohio

Year	Team	W	L	PCT	ERA	G	GS	CG	IP	H	BB	SO	ShO	W	L	SV	AB	H	HR	BA	PO	A	E	DP	TC/G	FA
1911	CLE A	1	0	1.000	4.43	4	3	1	22.1	30	9	6	0	0	0	0	11	3	0	.273	2	6	0	1	2.0	1.000
1912	BKN N	6	11	.353	3.59	25	16	12	163	186	56	51	0	1	3	0	64	16	0	.250	7	36	5	0	1.9	.896
1913		8	8	.500	2.58	26	13	8	146.2	158	10	40	2	3	3	0	60	23	0	.383	8	34	4	2	1.8	.913
1914	CIN N	8	13	.381	3.45	34	27	8	198	207	54	80	3	0	0	0	120	23	1	.192	6	44	5	1	1.6	.909
1918	WAS A	1	2	.333	2.13	5	2	2	38	30	12	15	0	1	0	0	15	7	0	.467	4	12	0	3	3.2	1.000
5 yrs.		24	34	.414	3.22	94	61	31	568	611	141	192	5	5	6	0	*				27	132	14	7	1.8	.919

Joe Yingling

YINGLING, JOSEPH GRANVILLE — BR TL 5'7½" 145 lbs.
B. July 23, 1866, Baltimore, Md. D. Oct. 24, 1946, Baltimore, Md.

Year	Team	W	L	PCT	ERA	G	GS	CG	IP	H	BB	SO	ShO	W	L	SV	AB	H	HR	BA	PO	A	E	DP	TC/G	FA
1886	WAS N	0	0	–	12.00	1	0	0	3	7	1	1	0	0	0	0	2	0	0	.000	0	1	1	1	2.0	.500

Len Yochim

YOCHIM, LEONARD JOSEPH — BL TL 6'2" 200 lbs.
Brother of Ray Yochim.
B. Oct. 16, 1928, New Orleans, La.

Year	Team	W	L	PCT	ERA	G	GS	CG	IP	H	BB	SO	ShO	W	L	SV	AB	H	HR	BA	PO	A	E	DP	TC/G	FA
1951	PIT N	1	1	.500	8.31	2	2	0	8.2	10	11	5	0	0	0	0	3	0	0	.000	2	1	0	0	1.5	1.000
1954		0	1	.000	7.32	10	1	0	19.2	30	8	7	0	0	0	0	2	1	0	.500	4	6	1	0	1.1	.909
2 yrs.		1	2	.333	7.62	12	3	0	28.1	40	19	12	0	0	0	0	5	1	0	.200	6	7	1	0	1.2	.929

Ray Yochim

YOCHIM, RAYMOND AUSTIN ALOYSIUS — BR TR 6'1" 170 lbs.
Brother of Len Yochim.
B. July 19, 1922, New Orleans, La.

Year	Team	W	L	PCT	ERA	G	GS	CG	IP	H	BB	SO	ShO	W	L	SV	AB	H	HR	BA	PO	A	E	DP	TC/G	FA
1948	STL N	0	0	–	0.00	1	0	0	1	0	3	1	0	0	0	0	0	0	0	–	0	0	0	0	0.0	–
1949		0	0	–	15.43	3	0	0	2.1	3	4	3	0	0	0	0	0	0	0	–	1	0	1	0	0.7	.500
2 yrs.		0	0	–	10.80	4	0	0	3.1	3	7	4	0	0	0	0	0	0	0	–	1	0	1	0	0.5	.500

Jim York

YORK, JAMES HARLAN — BR TR 6'3" 200 lbs.
B. Aug. 27, 1947, Maywood, Calif.

Year	Team	W	L	PCT	ERA	G	GS	CG	IP	H	BB	SO	ShO	W	L	SV	AB	H	HR	BA	PO	A	E	DP	TC/G	FA
1970	KC A	1	1	.500	3.38	4	0	0	8	5	2	6	0	1	1	0	2	0	0	.000	0	0	0	0	0.0	–
1971		5	5	.500	2.90	53	0	0	93	70	44	103	0	5	5	3	17	2	1	.118	6	10	2	1	0.3	.889
1972	HOU N	0	1	.000	5.25	26	0	0	36	45	18	25	0	0	1	0	1	0	0	.000	0	6	0	0	0.2	1.000
1973		3	4	.429	4.42	41	0	0	53	65	20	22	0	3	4	6	5	0	0	.000	1	12	2	0	0.4	.867
1974		2	2	.500	3.32	28	0	0	38	48	19	15	0	2	2	1	4	0	0	.000	4	6	0	0	0.3	1.000
1975		4	4	.500	3.83	19	4	0	47	43	25	17	0	1	3	0	11	1	0	.091	3	2	1	0	0.3	.833
1976	NY A	1	0	1.000	5.59	3	0	0	9.2	14	4	6	0	1	0	0	0	0	0	–	0	1	0	0	0.3	1.000
7 yrs.		16	17	.485	3.79	174	4	0	284.2	290	132	194	0	13	16	10	40	3	1	.075	14	37	5	1	0.3	.911

Lefty York

YORK, JAMES EDWARD — BL TL 5'10" 185 lbs.
B. Nov. 1, 1892, West Fork, Ark. D. Apr. 9, 1961, York, Pa.

Year	Team	W	L	PCT	ERA	G	GS	CG	IP	H	BB	SO	ShO	W	L	SV	AB	H	HR	BA	PO	A	E	DP	TC/G	FA
1919	PHI A	0	2	.000	24.92	2	2	0	4.1	13	5	2	0	0	0	0	1	0	0	.000	0	1	0	0	0.5	1.000
1921	CHI N	5	9	.357	4.73	40	10	4	139	170	63	57	1	4	0	1	39	5	0	.128	1	22	4	0	0.7	.852
2 yrs.		5	11	.313	5.34	42	12	4	143.1	183	68	59	1	4	0	1	40	5	0	.125	1	23	4	0	0.7	.857

Gus Yost

YOST, AUGUST — 6'5"

Year	Team	W	L	PCT	ERA	G	GS	CG	IP	H	BB	SO	ShO	W	L	SV	AB	H	HR	BA	PO	A	E	DP	TC/G	FA
1893	CHI N	0	1	.000	13.50	1	1	0	2.2	3	8	1	0	0	0	0	1	0	0	.000	1	1	0	1	2.0	1.000

Floyd Youmans

YOUMANS, FLOYD EVERETT — BR TR 6'2" 180 lbs.
B. May 11, 1964, Tampa, Fla.

Year	Team	W	L	PCT	ERA	G	GS	CG	IP	H	BB	SO	ShO	W	L	SV	AB	H	HR	BA	PO	A	E	DP	TC/G	FA
1985	MON N	4	3	.571	2.45	14	12	0	77	57	49	54	0	1	0	0	19	1	0	.053	6	1	0	0	0.5	1.000
1986		13	12	.520	3.53	33	32	6	219	145	118	202	2	0	0	0	75	12	1	.160	11	16	3	0	0.9	.900
1987		9	8	.529	4.64	23	23	3	116.1	112	47	94	3	0	0	0	40	6	1	.150	16	10	0	1	1.1	1.000
1988		3	6	.333	3.21	14	13	1	84	64	41	54	1	0	0	0	26	4	0	.154	7	10	1	0	1.3	.944

Year	Team	W	L	PCT	ERA	G	GS	CG	IP	H	BB	SO	ShO	Relief Pitching W	L	SV	Batting AB	H	HR	BA	PO	A	E	DP	TC/G	FA

Floyd Youmans *continued*

Year	Team	W	L	PCT	ERA	G	GS	CG	IP	H	BB	SO	ShO	W	L	SV	AB	H	HR	BA	PO	A	E	DP	TC/G	FA
1989	PHI N	1	5	.167	5.70	10	10	0	42.2	50	25	20	0	0	0	0	13	1	0	.077	4	6	0	1	1.0	1.000
5 yrs.		30	34	.469	3.74	94	90	10	539	428	280	424	6	1	1	0	173	24	2	.139	44	43	4	3	1.0	.956

Charlie Young

YOUNG, CHARLES (Cy)
B. Jan. 12, 1893, Philadelphia, Pa. D. May 12, 1952, Riverside, N. J.   BB TR 5'10½" 155 lbs.

Year	Team	W	L	PCT	ERA	G	GS	CG	IP	H	BB	SO	ShO	W	L	SV	AB	H	HR	BA	PO	A	E	DP	TC/G	FA
1915	BAL F	1	3	.250	5.91	9	5	1	35	39	21	13	0	0	0	0	9	2	0	.222	3	17	0	2	2.2	1.000

Curt Young

YOUNG, CURTIS ALLEN
B. Apr. 16, 1960, Saginaw, Mich.   BR TL 6' 175 lbs.

Year	Team	W	L	PCT	ERA	G	GS	CG	IP	H	BB	SO	ShO	W	L	SV	AB	H	HR	BA	PO	A	E	DP	TC/G	FA
1983	OAK A	0	1	.000	16.00	8	2	0	9	17	5	5	0	0	0	0	0	0	0	–	0	0	0	0	0.0	
1984		9	4	.692	4.06	20	17	2	108.2	118	31	41	0	0	0	0	0	0	0	–	6	13	0	1	1.0	1.000
1985		0	4	.000	7.24	19	7	0	46	57	22	19	0	0	0	0	0	0	0	–	4	4	0	0	0.4	1.000
1986		13	9	.591	3.45	29	27	5	198	176	57	116	2	1	0	0	0	0	0	–	9	32	4	1	1.6	.911
1987		13	7	.650	4.08	31	31	6	203	194	44	124	0	0	0	0	1	0	0	.000	15	28	1	2	1.4	.977
1988		11	8	.579	4.14	26	26	1	156.1	162	50	69	0	0	0	0	0	0	0	–	11	16	0	0	1.0	1.000
1989		5	9	.357	3.73	25	20	1	111	117	47	55	0	0	0	0	0	0	0	–	2	14	0	0	0.6	1.000
7 yrs.		51	42	.548	4.20	158	130	15	832	841	256	429	3	1	0	0	1	0	0	.000	47	107	5	4	1.0	.969

LEAGUE CHAMPIONSHIP SERIES

Year	Team	W	L	PCT	ERA	G	GS	CG	IP	H	BB	SO	ShO	W	L	SV	AB	H	HR	BA	PO	A	E	DP	TC/G	FA
1988	OAK A	0	0	–	0.00	1	0	0	1.1	1	0	2	0	0	0	0	0	0	0	–	0	0	0	0	0.0	

WORLD SERIES

Year	Team	W	L	PCT	ERA	G	GS	CG	IP	H	BB	SO	ShO	W	L	SV	AB	H	HR	BA	PO	A	E	DP	TC/G	FA
1988	OAK A	0	0	–	0.00	1	0	0	1	1	1	0	0	0	0	0	0	0	0	–	0	1	0	0	1.0	1.000

Cy Young

YOUNG, DENTON TRUE (Foxy Grandpa)
B. Mar. 29, 1867, Gilmore, Ohio D. Nov. 4, 1955, Newcomerstown, Ohio   BR TR 6'2" 210 lbs.
Manager 1907.
Hall of Fame 1937.

Year	Team	W	L	PCT	ERA	G	GS	CG	IP	H	BB	SO	ShO	W	L	SV	AB	H	HR	BA	PO	A	E	DP	TC/G	FA
1890	CLE N	9	6	.600	3.47	17	16	16	147.2	145	30	39	0	0	0	0	65	8	0	.123	6	39	5	0	2.9	.900
1891		27	22	.551	2.85	55	46	43	423.2	431	140	147	0	1	3	2	174	29	1	.167	10	89	9	0	2.0	.917
1892		36	12	**.750**	**1.93**	53	49	48	453	363	118	168	**9**	1	0	0	196	31	0	.158	19	122	8	7	2.8	.946
1893		34	16	.680	3.36	53	46	42	422.2	442	103	102	1	4	0	1	187	44	1	.235	27	112	8	1	2.8	.946
1894		26	21	.553	3.94	52	47	44	408.2	488	106	101	2	1	1	1	186	40	2	.215	16	108	7	4	2.5	.947
1895		**35**	10	.778	3.24	47	40	36	369.2	363	75	121	4	**7**	0	0	140	30	0	.214	15	120	6	2	3.0	.957
1896		28	15	.651	3.24	51	46	42	414.1	**477**	62	**140**	5	0	1	3	180	52	3	.289	8	145	12	3	3.2	.927
1897		21	19	.525	3.79	**46**	38	35	335	391	49	88	2	1	4	0	153	34	0	.222	16	88	9	2	2.5	.920
1898		25	13	.658	2.53	46	41	40	377.2	387	41	101	1	0	0	0	154	39	2	.253	12	122	4	0	3.0	.971
1899	STL N	26	16	.619	2.58	44	42	40	369.1	368	44	111	4	0	0	1	148	32	1	.216	13	117	9	0	3.2	.935
1900		19	19	.500	3.00	41	35	32	321.1	337	36	115	4	2	0	0	124	22	1	.177	12	79	11	1	2.5	.892
1901	BOS A	**33**	10	.767	**1.62**	43	41	38	371.1	324	37	**158**	5	2	0	0	153	32	0	.209	12	105	3	3	2.8	.975
1902		**32**	11	.744	2.15	**45**	43	41	384.2	350	53	160	3	0	0	0	148	34	1	.230	10	82	7	4	2.2	.929
1903		28	9	**.757**	2.08	40	35	34	341.2	294	37	176	**7**	2	1	2	137	44	1	.321	6	86	5	4	2.4	.948
1904		26	16	.619	1.97	43	41	40	380	327	29	200	**10**	0	1	1	148	33	1	.223	7	103	7	0	2.7	.940
1905		18	19	.486	1.82	38	33	32	320.2	248	30	210	4	5	0	0	120	18	2	.150	2	87	3	1	2.4	.967
1906		13	**21**	.382	3.19	39	34	28	287.2	288	25	140	0	0	0	2	104	16	0	.154	8	81	6	1	2.4	.937
1907		21	15	.583	1.99	43	37	33	343.1	286	51	147	6	3	0	1	125	27	1	.216	5	83	6	2	2.2	.936
1908		21	11	.656	1.26	36	33	30	299	230	37	150	3	0	0	2	115	26	0	.226	5	62	3	2	1.9	.957
1909	CLE A	19	15	.559	2.26	35	34	30	295	267	59	109	3	0	0	0	107	21	0	.196	10	88	5	0	3.1	.907
1910		7	10	.412	2.53	21	20	14	163.1	149	27	58	1	0	0	0	55	8	0	.145	6	62	6	0	3.5	.919
1911	2 teams	CLE A (7G 3–4)				BOS N (11G 4–5)																				
"	total	7	9	.438	3.78	18	18	12	126.1	137	28	55	2	0	0	0	41	3	0	.073	4	33	2	2	2.2	.949
22 yrs.		511	315	.619	2.63	906	815	750	7356	7092	1217	2796	76	30	18	16	2960	623	18	.210	229	2013	146	40	2.6	.939
		1st	1st			6th			1st	1st			4th													

WORLD SERIES

Year	Team	W	L	PCT	ERA	G	GS	CG	IP	H	BB	SO	ShO	W	L	SV	AB	H	HR	BA	PO	A	E	DP	TC/G	FA
1903	BOS A	2	1	.667	1.59	4	3	3	34	31	4	17	0	0	0	0	15	2	0	.133	0	7	1	0	2.0	.875

Harley Young

YOUNG, HARLAN EDWARD (Cy The Third)
B. Sept. 28, 1883, Portland, Ind. D. Mar. 26, 1975, Jacksonville, Fla.   BR TR 6'2"

Year	Team	W	L	PCT	ERA	G	GS	CG	IP	H	BB	SO	ShO	W	L	SV	AB	H	HR	BA	PO	A	E	DP	TC/G	FA
1908	2 teams	PIT N (8G 0–2)				BOS N (6G 0–1)																				
"	total	0	3	.000	2.62	14	5	1	75.2	69	14	29	0	0	0	0	22	3	0	.136	2	27	4	1	2.4	.879

Irv Young

YOUNG, IRVING MELROSE (Young Cy, Cy the Second)
B. July 21, 1877, Columbia Falls, Me. D. Jan. 14, 1935, Brewer, Me.   BL TL 5'10" 170 lbs.

Year	Team	W	L	PCT	ERA	G	GS	CG	IP	H	BB	SO	ShO	W	L	SV	AB	H	HR	BA	PO	A	E	DP	TC/G	FA
1905	BOS N	20	21	.488	2.90	43	**42**	**41**	**378**	337	71	156	7	0	0	0	136	14	0	.103	33	115	3	1	3.5	.980
1906		16	25	.390	2.91	43	**41**	37	358.1	**349**	83	151	4	0	1	0	125	12	0	.096	27	108	8	5	3.3	.944
1907		10	23	.303	3.96	40	32	22	245.1	287	58	86	3	2	1	1	80	13	0	.163	20	69	3	4	2.3	.967
1908	2 teams	BOS N (16G 4–8)				PIT N (16G 4–3)																				
"	total	8	11	.421	2.42	32	18	10	174.2	167	40	63	2	1	2	1	62	11	0	.177	10	42	7	2	1.8	.881
1910	CHI A	4	8	.333	2.72	27	17	8	135.2	122	39	64	1	0	0	0	44	5	0	.114	11	38	0	1	1.8	1.000
1911		5	6	.455	4.37	24	11	3	92.2	99	25	40	1	2	0	2	28	5	0	.179	4	28	1	1	1.4	.970
6 yrs.		63	94	.401	3.11	209	161	120	1384.2	1361	316	560	21	5	4	4	475	60	0	.126	105	400	22	14	2.5	.958

Joe Young

YOUNG, JOSEPH B.
B. June, 1857, Mt. Carmel, Pa. Deceased.

Year	Team	W	L	PCT	ERA	G	GS	CG	IP	H	BB	SO	ShO	W	L	SV	AB	H	HR	BA	PO	A	E	DP	TC/G	FA
1892	STL N	0	0	–	22.50	1	0	0	2	9	2	1	0	0	0	0	1	0	0	.000	0	0	0	0	0.0	–

Kip Young

YOUNG, KIP LANE
B. Oct. 29, 1954, Georgetown, Ohio   BR TR 5'11" 175 lbs.

Year	Team	W	L	PCT	ERA	G	GS	CG	IP	H	BB	SO	ShO	W	L	SV	AB	H	HR	BA	PO	A	E	DP	TC/G	FA
1978	DET A	6	7	.462	2.81	14	13	7	105.2	94	30	49	0	0	0	0	0	0	0	–	4	10	1	1	1.1	.933

Year	Team		W	L	PCT	ERA	G	GS	CG	IP	H	BB	SO	ShO	Relief Pitching W	L	SV	Batting AB	H	HR	BA	PO	A	E	DP	TC/G	FA

Kip Young *continued*

Year	Team		W	L	PCT	ERA	G	GS	CG	IP	H	BB	SO	ShO	W	L	SV	AB	H	HR	BA	PO	A	E	DP	TC/G	FA
1979			2	2	.500	6.34	13	7	0	44	60	11	22	0	0	1	0	0	0	0	–	3	10	0	0	1.0	1.000
2 yrs.			8	9	.471	3.85	27	20	7	149.2	154	41	71	0	0	2	0	0	0	0	–	7	20	1	1	1.0	.964

Matt Young

YOUNG, MATTHEW JOHN   BL TL 6'3"   205 lbs.
B. Aug. 9, 1958, Pasadena, Calif.

Year	Team		W	L	PCT	ERA	G	GS	CG	IP	H	BB	SO	ShO	W	L	SV	AB	H	HR	BA	PO	A	E	DP	TC/G	FA
1983	SEA	A	11	15	.423	3.27	33	32	5	203.2	178	79	130	2	0	0	0	0	0	0	–	9	39	1	1.5		1.5	.941
1984			6	8	.429	5.72	22	22	1	113.1	141	57	73	0	0	0	0	0	0	0	–	3	21	2	3	1.2	.923
1985			12	19	.387	4.91	37	35	5	218.1	242	76	136	2	0	0	1	0	0	0	–	6	24	1	1	0.8	.968
1986			8	6	.571	3.82	65	5	1	103.2	108	46	82	0	6	3	13	0	0	0	–	4	9	4	0	0.3	.765
1987	LA	N	5	8	.385	4.47	47	0	0	54.1	62	17	42	0	5	8	11	3	0	0	.000	3	1	2	0	0.1	.667
1989	OAK	A	1	4	.200	6.75	26	4	0	37.1	42	31	27	0	1	2	0	0	0	0	–	3	6	0	0	0.3	1.000
6 yrs.			43	60	.417	4.48	230	98	12	730.2	773	306	490	4	12	13	25	3	0	0	.000	28	100	12	4	0.6	.914

LEAGUE CHAMPIONSHIP SERIES

| 1989 | OAK | A | 0 | 0 | – | 0.00 | 1 | 0 | 0 | .1 | 0 | 2 | 0 | 0 | 0 | 0 | 0 | 0 | 0 | 0 | – | 0 | 0 | 0 | 0 | 0.0 | – |

Chief Youngblood

YOUNGBLOOD, ARTHUR CLYDE   BL TR 6'3"   202 lbs.
B. June 13, 1900, Hillsboro, Tex.   D. July 6, 1968, Amarillo, Tex.

Year	Team		W	L	PCT	ERA	G	GS	CG	IP	H	BB	SO	ShO	W	L	SV	AB	H	HR	BA	PO	A	E	DP	TC/G	FA
1922	WAS	A	0	0	–	14.54	2	0	0	4.1	9	7	0	0	0	0	0	2	0	0	.000	0	1	0	0	0.5	1.000

Ducky Yount

YOUNT, HENRY MACON (Hub)   BR TR 6'2"   178 lbs.
B. Dec. 7, 1885, Iredell County, N. C.   D. May 9, 1970, Winston-Salem, N. C.

Year	Team		W	L	PCT	ERA	G	GS	CG	IP	H	BB	SO	ShO	W	L	SV	AB	H	HR	BA	PO	A	E	DP	TC/G	FA
1914	BAL	F	1	1	.500	4.14	13	1	1	41.1	44	19	19	0	1	0	0	12	1	0	.083	2	15	2	1	1.5	.895

Larry Yount

YOUNT, LAWRENCE KING   BR TR 6'2"   185 lbs.
Brother of Robin Yount.
B. Feb. 15, 1950, Houston, Tex.

Year	Team		W	L	PCT	ERA	G	GS	CG	IP	H	BB	SO	ShO	W	L	SV	AB	H	HR	BA	PO	A	E	DP	TC/G	FA
1971	HOU	N	0	0	–	0.00	1	0	0	0	0	0	0	0	0	0	0	0	0	0	–	0	0	0	0	0.0	–

Carl Yowell

YOWELL, CARL COLUMBUS (Sundown)   BL TL 6'4"   180 lbs.
B. Dec. 20, 1902, Madison, Va.   D. July 27, 1985, Jacksonville, Tex.

Year	Team		W	L	PCT	ERA	G	GS	CG	IP	H	BB	SO	ShO	W	L	SV	AB	H	HR	BA	PO	A	E	DP	TC/G	FA
1924	CLE	A	1	1	.500	6.67	4	2	2	27	37	13	8	0	0	0	0	11	2	0	.182	2	4	0	0	1.5	1.000
1925			2	3	.400	4.46	12	4	1	36.1	40	17	12	0	1	0	0	8	1	0	.125	1	11	0	0	1.0	1.000
2 yrs.			3	4	.429	5.40	16	6	3	63.1	77	30	20	0	1	0	0	19	3	0	.158	3	15	0	0	1.1	1.000

Eddie Yuhas

YUHAS, JOHN EDWARD   BR TR 6'1"   180 lbs.
B. Aug. 5, 1924, Youngstown, Ohio   D. July 6, 1986, Winston-Salem, N. C.

Year	Team		W	L	PCT	ERA	G	GS	CG	IP	H	BB	SO	ShO	W	L	SV	AB	H	HR	BA	PO	A	E	DP	TC/G	FA
1952	STL	N	12	2	.857	2.72	54	2	0	99.1	90	35	39	0	11	1	6	21	4	0	.190	3	15	1	1	0.4	.947
1953			0	0	–	18.00	2	0	0	1	3	0	0	0	0	0	0	0	0	0	–	0	0	0	0	0.0	–
2 yrs.			12	2	.857	2.87	56	2	0	100.1	93	35	39	0	11	1	6	21	4	0	.190	3	15	1	1	0.3	.947

Adrian Zabala

ZABALA, ADRIAN   BL TL 5'11"   165 lbs.
Born Adrian Zabala y Rodriguez.
B. Aug. 26, 1916, San Antonio de los Banos, Cuba

Year	Team		W	L	PCT	ERA	G	GS	CG	IP	H	BB	SO	ShO	W	L	SV	AB	H	HR	BA	PO	A	E	DP	TC/G	FA
1945	NY	N	2	4	.333	4.78	11	5	1	43.1	46	20	14	0	1	1	0	13	3	0	.231	3	8	1	1	1.1	.917
1949			2	3	.400	5.27	15	4	2	41	44	10	13	1	0	2	1	13	1	0	.077	0	2	1	1	0.2	.667
2 yrs.			4	7	.364	5.02	26	9	3	84.1	90	30	27	1	1	3	1	26	4	0	.154	3	10	2	2	0.6	.867

Zip Zabel

ZABEL, GEORGE WASHINGTON   BR TR 6'1½"   185 lbs.
B. Feb. 18, 1891, Wetmore, Kans.   D. May 31, 1970, Beloit, Wis.

Year	Team		W	L	PCT	ERA	G	GS	CG	IP	H	BB	SO	ShO	W	L	SV	AB	H	HR	BA	PO	A	E	DP	TC/G	FA
1913	CHI	N	1	0	1.000	0.00	1	1	0	5	3	1	0	0	0	0	0	2	0	0	.000	0	2	0	0	2.0	1.000
1914			4	4	.500	2.18	29	7	2	128	104	45	50	0	2	0	1	38	7	0	.184	5	29	2	0	1.2	.944
1915			7	10	.412	3.20	36	17	8	163	124	84	60	3	2	2	0	54	4	0	.074	6	62	4	1	2.0	.944
3 yrs.			12	14	.462	2.71	66	25	10	296	231	130	110	3	4	2	1	94	11	0	.117	11	93	6	1	1.7	.945

Chink Zachary

ZACHARY, ALBERT MYRON   BR TR 5'11"   182 lbs.
Born Albert Myron Zarski.
B. Oct. 19, 1917, Brooklyn, N. Y.

Year	Team		W	L	PCT	ERA	G	GS	CG	IP	H	BB	SO	ShO	W	L	SV	AB	H	HR	BA	PO	A	E	DP	TC/G	FA
1944	BKN	N	0	2	.000	9.58	4	2	0	10.1	10	7	3	0	0	2	0	3	0	0	.000	0	1	0	0	0.3	1.000

Chris Zachary

ZACHARY, WILLIAM CHRISTOPHER   BL TR 6'2"   200 lbs.
B. Feb. 19, 1944, Knoxville, Tenn.

Year	Team		W	L	PCT	ERA	G	GS	CG	IP	H	BB	SO	ShO	W	L	SV	AB	H	HR	BA	PO	A	E	DP	TC/G	FA
1963	HOU	N	2	2	.500	4.89	22	7	0	57	62	22	42	0	0	0	0	13	0	0	.000	3	14	0	0	0.8	1.000
1964			0	1	.000	9.00	1	1	0	4	6	1	2	0	0	0	0	1	0	0	.000	0	2	0	0	2.0	1.000
1965			0	2	.000	4.22	9	1	0	10.2	12	6	4	0	0	0	0	2	0	0	.000	2	1	0	0	0.8	1.000
1966			3	5	.375	3.44	10	8	0	55	44	32	37	0	0	1	0	18	4	0	.222	5	6	2	0	1.3	.846
1967			1	6	.143	5.70	9	7	0	36.1	42	12	18	0	0	0	0	10	1	0	.100	2	5	2	1	1.0	.778
1969	KC	A	0	1	.000	7.85	8	2	0	18.1	27	7	6	0	0	0	0	2	1	0	.500	0	3	0	0	0.3	1.000
1971	STL	N	3	10	.231	5.30	23	12	1	90	114	26	48	1	1	2	0	33	8	0	.242	4	14	1	2	0.8	.947
1972	DET	A	1	1	.500	1.42	25	1	0	38	27	15	21	0	1	0	1	2	1	0	.500	2	3	0	0	0.3	1.000
1973	PIT	N	0	1	.000	3.00	6	0	0	12	10	1	6	0	0	1	1	2	0	0	.000	1	0	0	0	0.2	1.000
9 yrs.			10	29	.256	4.57	108	40	1	321.1	344	122	184	1	2	4	2	83	15	0	.181	19	49	5	3	0.7	.932

LEAGUE CHAMPIONSHIP SERIES

| 1972 | DET | A | 0 | 0 | – | ∞ | 1 | 0 | 0 | 0 | 1 | 0 | 1 | 0 | 0 | 0 | 0 | 0 | 0 | 0 | – | 0 | 0 | 0 | 0 | 0.0 | – |

Tom Zachary

ZACHARY, JONATHAN THOMPSON WALTON
Played as Zach Walton in 1918.
B. May 7, 1896, Graham, N. C. D. Jan. 24, 1969, Burlington, N. C.
BL TL 6'1" 187 lbs.

Year	Team	W	L	PCT	ERA	G	GS	CG	IP	H	BB	SO	ShO	RP W	RP L	SV	AB	H	HR	BA	PO	A	E	DP	TC/G	FA
1918	PHI A	2	0	1.000	5.63	2	2	0	8	9	7	1	0	0	0	0	4	2	0	.500	1	2	1	0	2.0	.750
1919	WAS A	1	5	.167	2.92	17	7	0	61.2	68	20	9	0	0	0	0	15	5	0	.333	3	15	0	1	1.1	1.000
1920		15	16	.484	3.77	44	30	18	262.2	289	78	53	3	3	0	2	111	29	0	.261	5	74	2	2	1.8	.975
1921		18	16	.529	3.96	39	31	17	250	314	59	53	2	3	3	1	90	23	0	.256	6	68	5	1	2.0	.937
1922		15	10	.600	3.12	32	25	13	184.2	190	43	37	1	1	1	1	71	21	1	.296	4	48	0	2	1.6	1.000
1923		10	16	.385	4.49	35	29	10	204.1	270	63	40	0	1	2	0	78	15	0	.192	9	50	0	3	1.7	1.000
1924		15	9	.625	2.75	33	27	13	202.2	198	53	45	1	1	0	2	72	22	0	.306	3	58	0	0	1.8	1.000
1925		12	15	.444	3.85	38	33	11	217.2	247	74	58	1	1	2	2	69	12	1	.174	17	50	1	1	1.8	.985
1926	STL A	14	15	.483	3.60	34	31	18	247.1	264	97	53	3	0	3	0	86	23	1	.267	5	80	5	4	2.6	.944
1927	2 teams	STL A (13G 4–6)			WAS A (15G 4–7)																					
"	total	8	13	.381	3.96	28	26	11	188.2	236	57	26	1	0	2	0	64	8	0	.125	3	32	2	3	1.3	.946
1928	2 teams	WAS A (20G 6–9)			NY A (7G 3–3)																					
"	total	9	12	.429	4.98	27	20	8	148.1	184	55	26	1	0	1	1	48	12	1	.250	2	33	1	2	1.3	.972
1929	NY A	12	0	1.000	2.48	26	11	7	119.2	131	30	35	1	2	3	0	42	10	0	.238	2	15	2	1	0.7	.895
1930	2 teams	NY A (3G 1–1)			BOS N (24G 11–5)																					
"	total	12	6	.667	4.77	27	25	10	168	210	59	58	1	1	0	0	62	15	2	.242	5	31	3	2	1.4	.923
1931	BOS N	11	15	.423	3.10	33	28	16	229	243	53	64	3	0	3	2	84	14	0	.167	2	65	2	1	2.1	.971
1932		12	11	.522	3.10	32	24	12	212	231	55	67	1	2	1	0	77	21	0	.273	4	39	1	1	1.4	.977
1933		7	9	.438	3.53	26	20	6	125	134	35	22	2	0	0	2	42	5	0	.119	1	32	0	1	1.3	1.000
1934	2 teams	BOS N (5G 1–2)			BKN N (22G 5–6)																					
"	total	6	8	.429	4.23	27	16	6	125.2	149	29	32	1	1	1	2	46	7	0	.152	5	23	2	0	1.1	.933
1935	BKN N	7	12	.368	3.59	25	21	9	158	193	35	33	1	0	0	4	52	7	0	.135	5	38	2	2	1.8	.956
1936	2 teams	BKN N (1G 0–0)			PHI N (7G 0–3)																					
"	total	0	3	.000	8.71	8	2	0	20.2	30	12	8	0	0	0	1	9	3	0	.333	0	5	0	0	0.6	1.000
19 yrs.		186	191	.493	3.72	533	408	185	3134	3590	914	720	24	17	20	22	1122	254	6	.226	82	758	29	27	1.6	.967

WORLD SERIES

Year	Team	W	L	PCT	ERA	G	GS	CG	IP	H	BB	SO	ShO	RP W	RP L	SV	AB	H	HR	BA	PO	A	E	DP	TC/G	FA
1924	WAS A	2	0	1.000	2.04	2	2	1	17.2	13	3	3	0	0	0	0	5	0	0	.000	1	4	0	0	2.5	1.000
1925		0	0	–	10.80	1	0	0	1.2	3	1	0	0	0	0	0	0	0	0	–	0	0	0	0	0.0	–
1928	NY A	1	0	1.000	3.00	1	1	1	9	9	1	7	0	0	0	0	4	0	0	.000	0	1	0	0	1.0	1.000
3 yrs.		3	0	1.000	2.86	4	3	2	28.1	25	5	10	0	0	0	0	9	0	0	.000	1	5	0	0	1.5	1.000
				1st																						

Pat Zachry

ZACHRY, PATRICK PAUL
B. Apr. 24, 1952, Richmond, Tex.
BR TR 6'5" 180 lbs.

Year	Team	W	L	PCT	ERA	G	GS	CG	IP	H	BB	SO	ShO	RP W	RP L	SV	AB	H	HR	BA	PO	A	E	DP	TC/G	FA
1976	CIN N	14	7	.667	2.74	38	28	6	204	170	83	143	1	2	0	0	62	7	0	.113	13	20	1	2	0.9	.971
1977	2 teams	CIN N (12G 3–7)			NY N (19G 7–6)																					
"	total	10	13	.435	4.25	31	31	5	194.2	207	77	99	2	0	0	0	64	9	0	.141	6	30	1	4	1.2	.973
1978	NY N	10	6	.625	3.33	21	21	5	138	120	60	78	2	0	0	0	43	3	0	.070	9	24	2	4	1.7	.943
1979		5	1	.833	3.56	7	7	0	43	44	21	17	0	0	0	0	16	2	0	.125	3	7	0	0	1.4	1.000
1980		6	10	.375	3.00	28	26	7	165	145	58	88	3	0	1	0	46	2	0	.043	5	20	1	1	0.9	.962
1981		7	14	.333	4.14	24	24	3	139	151	56	76	0	0	0	0	38	6	0	.158	4	26	3	4	1.4	.909
1982		6	9	.400	4.05	36	16	2	137.2	149	57	69	0	2	3	1	38	3	0	.079	10	19	1	1	0.8	.967
1983	LA N	6	1	.857	2.49	40	1	0	61.1	63	21	36	0	5	1	0	4	2	0	.500	6	9	2	1	0.4	.882
1984		5	6	.455	3.81	58	0	0	82.2	84	51	55	0	5	6	2	6	2	0	.333	4	16	2	2	0.4	.909
1985	PHI N	0	0	–	4.26	10	0	0	12.2	14	11	8	0	0	0	0	1	0	0	.000	0	3	1	0	0.5	.909
10 yrs.		69	67	.507	3.52	293	154	29	1178	1147	495	669	8	14	11	3	318	36	0	.113	60	176	13	19	0.8	.948

LEAGUE CHAMPIONSHIP SERIES

Year	Team	W	L	PCT	ERA	G	GS	CG	IP	H	BB	SO	ShO	RP W	RP L	SV	AB	H	HR	BA	PO	A	E	DP	TC/G	FA
1976	CIN N	1	0	1.000	3.60	1	1	0	5	3	3	3	0	0	0	0	1	0	0	.000	1	3	0	0	4.0	1.000
1983	LA N	0	0	–	2.25	2	0	0	4	4	2	2	0	0	0	0	0	0	0	–	1	0	0	0	0.5	1.000
2 yrs.		1	0	1.000	3.00	3	1	0	9	10	5	5	0	0	0	0	1	0	0	.000	2	3	0	0	1.7	1.000

WORLD SERIES

Year	Team	W	L	PCT	ERA	G	GS	CG	IP	H	BB	SO	ShO	RP W	RP L	SV	AB	H	HR	BA	PO	A	E	DP	TC/G	FA
1976	CIN N	1	0	1.000	2.70	1	1	1	6.2	6	5	6	0	0	0	0	0	0	0	–	0	2	1	0	3.0	.667

George Zackert

ZACKERT, GEORGE CARL (Zeke)
B. Dec. 24, 1884, Buchanan County, Mo. D. Feb. 18, 1977, Burlington, Iowa
BL TL 6' 177 lbs.

Year	Team	W	L	PCT	ERA	G	GS	CG	IP	H	BB	SO	ShO	RP W	RP L	SV	AB	H	HR	BA	PO	A	E	DP	TC/G	FA
1911	STL N	0	2	.000	11.05	4	1	0	7.1	17	6	6	0	0	0	1	1	0	0	.000	0	4	0	0	1.0	1.000
1912		0	0	–	18.00	1	0	0	1	2	1	0	0	0	0	0	1	0	0	.000	0	1	0	0	1.0	1.000
2 yrs.		0	2	.000	11.88	5	1	0	8.1	19	7	6	0	0	0	1	2	0	0	.000	0	5	0	0	1.0	1.000

Geoff Zahn

ZAHN, GEOFFREY CLAYTON
B. Dec. 19, 1945, Baltimore, Md.
BL TL 6'1" 180 lbs.

Year	Team	W	L	PCT	ERA	G	GS	CG	IP	H	BB	SO	ShO	RP W	RP L	SV	AB	H	HR	BA	PO	A	E	DP	TC/G	FA
1973	LA N	1	0	1.000	1.35	6	1	0	13.1	5	2	9	0	0	0	0	2	0	0	.000	0	4	1	0	0.8	.800
1974		3	5	.375	2.03	21	10	1	80	78	16	33	0	1	0	0	23	4	0	.174	2	15	2	1	0.9	.895
1975	2 teams	LA N (2G 0–1)			CHI N (16G 2–7)																					
"	total	2	8	.200	4.66	18	10	0	65.2	69	31	22	0	2	1	1	15	2	0	.133	6	16	2	0	1.3	.917
1976	CHI N	0	1	.000	11.25	3	2	0	8	16	2	4	0	0	0	0	3	0	0	.000	1	3	1	0	1.3	.750
1977	MIN A	12	14	.462	4.68	34	32	7	198	234	66	88	0	1	2	0				–	16	40	2	5	1.7	.966
1978		14	14	.500	3.03	35	35	12	252.1	260	81	106	2	0	0	0				–	9	41	2	2	1.5	.962
1979		13	7	.650	3.57	26	24	4	169	181	41	58	0	0	0	0				–	8	37	4	2	1.9	.918
1980		14	18	.438	4.40	38	35	13	233	273	66	96	5	0	0	0				–	12	37	1	3	1.3	.980
1981	CAL A	10	11	.476	4.42	25	25	9	161	181	43	52	0	0	0	0				–	7	31	3	2	1.6	.927
1982		18	8	.692	3.73	34	34	12	229.1	225	65	81	4	0	0	0				–	3	35	2	1	1.2	.950
1983		9	11	.450	3.33	29	28	11	203	212	51	81	0	0	0	0				–	5	25	3	2	1.3	.919
1984		13	10	.565	3.12	28	27	9	199.1	200	48	61	5	0	0	0				–	14	33	1	1	1.7	.919
1985		2	2	.500	4.38	7	7	1	37	44	14	14	1	0	0	0				–	1	9	0	0	1.4	1.000
13 yrs.		111	109	.505	3.74	304	270	79	1849	1978	526	705	20	4	3	1	43	6	0	.140	87	326	24	19	1.4	.945

LEAGUE CHAMPIONSHIP SERIES

Year	Team	W	L	PCT	ERA	G	GS	CG	IP	H	BB	SO	ShO	RP W	RP L	SV	AB	H	HR	BA	PO	A	E	DP	TC/G	FA
1982	CAL A	0	1	.000	7.36	1	1	0	3.2	4	1	2	0	0	0	0				–	0	0	0	0	0.0	–

Year	Team		W	L	PCT	ERA	G	GS	CG	IP	H	BB	SO	ShO	W	L	SV	AB	H	HR	BA	PO	A	E	DP	TC/G	FA

Paul Zahniser ZAHNISER, PAUL VERNON BR TR 5'10½" 170 lbs.
B. Sept. 6, 1896, Sac City, Iowa D. Sept. 26, 1964, Klamath Falls, Ore.

Year	Team		W	L	PCT	ERA	G	GS	CG	IP	H	BB	SO	ShO	W	L	SV	AB	H	HR	BA	PO	A	E	DP	TC/G	FA
1923	WAS	A	9	10	.474	3.86	33	21	10	177	201	76	52	1	2	2	0	52	5	0	.096	8	38	3	1	1.5	.939
1924			5	7	.417	4.40	24	14	5	92	98	49	28	1	1	0	0	30	4	0	.133	4	14	0	0	0.8	1.000
1925	BOS	A	5	12	.294	5.15	37	21	7	176.2	232	89	30	1	1	0	1	58	8	0	.138	6	34	0	0	1.1	1.000
1926			6	18	.250	4.97	30	24	7	172	213	69	35	1	0	2	0	49	8	0	.163	11	57	2	1	2.3	.971
1929	CIN	N	0	0	–	27.00	1	0	0	1	2	1	0	0	0	0	0	0	0	0	–	0	0	0	0	0.0	–
5 yrs.			25	47	.347	4.66	125	80	29	618.2	746	284	145	4	4	4	1	189	25	0	.132	29	143	5	2	1.4	.972

Carl Zamloch ZAMLOCH, CARL EUGENE BR TR 6'1" 176 lbs.
B. Oct. 6, 1889, Oakland, Calif. D. Aug. 19, 1963, Santa Barbara, Calif.

| 1913 | DET | A | 1 | 6 | .143 | 2.45 | 17 | 5 | 3 | 69.2 | 66 | 23 | 28 | 1 | 1 | 2 | 0 | 22 | 4 | 0 | .182 | 3 | 16 | 2 | 1 | 1.2 | .905 |

Oscar Zamora ZAMORA, OSCAR JOSE BR TR 5'10" 178 lbs.
Born Oscar Jose Zamora y Sosa.
B. Sept. 23, 1944, Camaguey, Cuba

1974	CHI	N	3	9	.250	3.11	56	0	0	84	82	19	38	0	3	9	10	11	2	0	.182	5	13	1	0	0.3	.947
1975			5	2	.714	5.07	52	0	0	71	84	15	28	0	5	2	10	6	1	0	.167	3	10	1	0	0.3	.929
1976			5	3	.625	5.24	40	2	0	55	70	17	27	0	5	2	3	9	0	0	.000	1	7	2	0	0.3	.800
1978	HOU	N	0	0	–	7.20	10	0	0	15	20	7	6	0	0	0	0	2	0	0	.000	1	2	0	1	0.3	1.000
4 yrs.			13	14	.481	4.52	158	2	0	225	256	58	99	0	13	13	23	28	3	0	.107	10	32	4	1	0.3	.913

Dom Zanni ZANNI, DOMINICK THOMAS BR TR 5'11" 180 lbs.
B. Mar. 1, 1932, Bronx, N. Y.

1958	SF	N	1	0	1.000	2.25	1	0	0	4	7	1	3	0	1	0	0	2	0	0	.000	0	0	0	0	0.0	–
1959			0	0	–	6.55	9	0	0	11	12	8	11	0	0	0	0	0	0	0	–	3	5	0	1	0.9	1.000
1961			1	0	1.000	3.95	8	0	0	13.2	13	12	11	0	1	0	0	0	0	0	–	0	3	0	0	0.4	1.000
1962	CHI	A	6	5	.545	3.75	44	2	0	86.1	67	31	66	0	6	3	5	18	5	0	.278	6	22	0	1	0.6	1.000
1963	2 teams		CHI A	(5G 0–0)			CIN N	(31G 1–1)																			
"	total		1	1	.500	4.56	36	1	0	47.1	44	25	42	0	1	1	5	3	1	0	.333	6	10	1	1	0.5	.941
1965	CIN	N	0	0	–	1.35	8	0	0	13.1	7	5	10	0	0	0	0	1	0	0	.000	1	2	0	0	0.4	1.000
1966			0	0	–	0.00	5	0	0	7.1	5	3	5	0	0	0	0	1	1	0	1.000	0	0	0	0	0.0	–
7 yrs.			9	6	.600	3.79	111	3	0	183	155	85	148	0	9	4	10	25	7	0	.280	16	42	1	3	0.5	.983

Jeff Zaske ZASKE, LLOYD JEFFREY BR TR 6'5" 180 lbs.
B. Oct. 6, 1960, Seattle, Wash.

| 1984 | PIT | N | 0 | 0 | – | 0.00 | 3 | 0 | 0 | 5 | 4 | 1 | 2 | 0 | 0 | 0 | 0 | 0 | 0 | 0 | – | 0 | 2 | 0 | 0 | 0.7 | 1.000 |

Clint Zavaras ZAVARAS, CLINTON WAYNE BR TR 6'1" 175 lbs.
B. Jan. 4, 1967, Denver, Colo.

| 1989 | SEA | A | 1 | 6 | .143 | 5.19 | 10 | 10 | 0 | 52 | 49 | 30 | 31 | 0 | 0 | 0 | 0 | 0 | 0 | 0 | – | 0 | 8 | 1 | 0 | 0.9 | .889 |

Zay ZAY,
B. Pittsburgh, Pa.

| 1886 | BAL | AA | 0 | 1 | .000 | 9.00 | 1 | 1 | 0 | 2 | 4 | 4 | 2 | 0 | 0 | 0 | 0 | 1 | 0 | 0 | .000 | 1 | 0 | 1 | 0 | 2.0 | .500 |

Matt Zeiser ZEISER, MATTHEW J. BR TR 5'10" 170 lbs.
B. Sept. 25, 1888, Chicago, Ill. D. June 10, 1942, Norwood Park, Ill.

| 1914 | BOS | A | 0 | 0 | – | 1.80 | 2 | 0 | 0 | 10 | 9 | 8 | 0 | 0 | 0 | 0 | 0 | 3 | 0 | 0 | .000 | 1 | 1 | 1 | 0 | 1.5 | .667 |

Bill Zepp ZEPP, WILLIAM CLINTON BR TR 6'2" 185 lbs.
B. July 22, 1946, Detroit, Mich.

1969	MIN	A	0	0	–	6.75	4	0	0	5.1	6	4	2	0	0	0	0	1	0	0	.000	1	0	0	0	0.3	1.000
1970			9	4	.692	3.22	43	20	1	151	154	51	64	1	3	0	2	44	6	0	.136	8	17	2	1	0.6	.926
1971	DET	A	1	1	.500	5.06	16	4	0	32	41	17	15	0	0	0	2	4	0	0	.000	3	6	0	0	0.6	1.000
3 yrs.			10	5	.667	3.63	63	24	1	188.1	201	72	81	1	3	0	4	49	6	0	.122	12	23	2	1	0.6	.946

LEAGUE CHAMPIONSHIP SERIES

| 1970 | MIN | A | 0 | 0 | – | 6.75 | 2 | 0 | 0 | 1.1 | 2 | 2 | 2 | 0 | 0 | 0 | 0 | 0 | 0 | 0 | – | 0 | 0 | 0 | 0 | 0.0 | – |

George Zettlein ZETTLEIN, GEORGE (The Charmer) BR TR 5'9" 162 lbs.
B. July 18, 1844, Brooklyn, N. Y. D. May 23, 1905, Patchogue, N. Y.

| 1876 | PHI | N | 4 | 20 | .167 | 3.88 | 28 | 25 | 23 | 234 | 358 | 6 | 10 | 1 | 0 | 0 | 2 | 128 | 27 | 0 | .211 | 7 | 36 | 5 | 2 | 1.7 | .896 |

Bob Zick ZICK, ROBERT GEORGE BL TR 6' 168 lbs.
B. Apr. 26, 1927, Chicago, Ill.

| 1954 | CHI | N | 0 | 0 | – | 8.27 | 8 | 0 | 0 | 16.1 | 23 | 7 | 9 | 0 | 0 | 0 | 0 | 4 | 1 | 0 | .250 | 1 | 2 | 1 | 0 | 0.5 | .750 |

George Ziegler ZIEGLER, GEORGE J.
B. 1872, Chicago, Ill. D. July 22, 1916, Kankakee, Ill.

| 1890 | PIT | N | 0 | 1 | .000 | 10.50 | 1 | 1 | 0 | 6 | 12 | 0 | 1 | 0 | 0 | 0 | 0 | 2 | 0 | 0 | .000 | 0 | 1 | 0 | 0 | 1.0 | 1.000 |

Steve Ziem ZIEM, STEPHEN GRAELING BR TR 6'2" 210 lbs.
B. Oct. 24, 1961, Milwaukee, Wis.

| 1987 | ATL | N | 0 | 1 | .000 | 7.71 | 2 | 0 | 0 | 2.1 | 4 | 1 | 0 | 0 | 0 | 1 | 0 | 0 | 0 | 0 | – | 0 | 0 | 0 | 0 | 0.0 | – |

Walt Zink ZINK, WALTER NOBLE BR TR 6' 165 lbs.
B. Nov. 21, 1899, Pittsfield, Mass. D. June 12, 1964, Quincy, Mass.

| 1921 | NY | N | 0 | 0 | – | 2.25 | 2 | 0 | 0 | 4 | 4 | 3 | 1 | 0 | 0 | 0 | 0 | 1 | 0 | 0 | .000 | 0 | 0 | 0 | 0 | 0.0 | – |

Year	Team	W	L	PCT	ERA	G	GS	CG	IP	H	BB	SO	ShO	Relief Pitching W	L	SV	Batting AB	H	HR	BA	PO	A	E	DP	TC/G	FA

Jimmy Zinn

ZINN, JAMES EDWARD
B. Jan. 21, 1895, Benton, Ark. — BL TR 6'½" 195 lbs. — BR 1929

Year	Team	W	L	PCT	ERA	G	GS	CG	IP	H	BB	SO	ShO	W	L	SV	AB	H	HR	BA	PO	A	E	DP	TC/G	FA
1919	PHI A	1	3	.250	6.31	5	3	2	25.2	38	10	9	0	0	1	0	13	4	1	.308	0	7	0	0	1.4	1.000
1920	PIT N	1	1	.500	3.48	6	3	2	31	32	5	18	0	0	0	0	15	3	0	.200	2	6	0	0	1.3	1.000
1921		7	6	.538	3.68	32	9	5	127.1	159	30	49	1	3	1	4	49	11	0	.224	4	26	3	1	1.0	.909
1922		0	0	—	1.86	5	0	0	9.2	11	2	3	0	0	0	1	1	0	0	.000	1	1	1	0	0.6	.667
1929	CLE A	4	6	.400	5.04	18	11	6	105.1	150	33	29	1	0	1	2	42	16	1	.381	11	19	3	2	1.8	.909
5 yrs.		13	16	.448	4.30	66	26	15	299	390	80	108	2	3	3	7	120	34	2	.283	18	59	7	3	1.3	.917

Bill Zinser

ZINSER, WILLIAM FRANCIS
B. Jan. 6, 1918, Astoria, N. Y. — BR TR 6'1" 185 lbs.

Year	Team	W	L	PCT	ERA	G	GS	CG	IP	H	BB	SO	ShO	W	L	SV	AB	H	HR	BA	PO	A	E	DP	TC/G	FA
1944	WAS A	0	0	—	27.00	2	0	0	.2	1	5	1	0	0	0	0	0	0	0	—	0	0	0	0	0.0	—

Ed Zmich

ZMICH, EDWARD ALBERT (Ike)
B. Oct. 1, 1884, Cleveland, Ohio D. Aug. 20, 1950, Cleveland, Ohio — BL TL 6' 180 lbs.

Year	Team	W	L	PCT	ERA	G	GS	CG	IP	H	BB	SO	ShO	W	L	SV	AB	H	HR	BA	PO	A	E	DP	TC/G	FA
1910	STL N	0	5	.000	6.25	9	6	2	36	38	29	19	0	0	0	0	13	1	0	.077	2	13	0	0	1.7	1.000
1911		1	0	1.000	2.13	4	0	0	12.2	8	8	4	0	1	0	0	4	0	0	.000	0	0	0	0	0.0	—
2 yrs.		1	5	.167	5.18	13	6	2	48.2	46	37	23	0	1	0	0	17	1	0	.059	2	13	0	0	1.2	1.000

Sam Zoldak

ZOLDAK, SAMUEL WALTER (Sad Sam)
B. Dec. 8, 1918, Brooklyn, N. Y. D. Aug. 25, 1966, New Hyde Park, N. Y. — BL TL 5'11½" 185 lbs.

Year	Team	W	L	PCT	ERA	G	GS	CG	IP	H	BB	SO	ShO	W	L	SV	AB	H	HR	BA	PO	A	E	DP	TC/G	FA
1944	STL A	0	0	—	3.72	18	0	0	38.2	49	19	15	0	0	0	0	6	2	0	.333	0	8	0	2	0.4	1.000
1945		3	2	.600	3.36	26	1	1	69.2	74	18	19	0	2	2	0	20	1	0	.050	3	9	1	0	0.5	.923
1946		9	11	.450	3.43	35	21	9	170.1	166	57	51	2	1	1	2	52	9	0	.173	10	32	1	3	1.2	.977
1947		9	10	.474	3.47	35	19	6	171	162	76	36	1	2	1	1	58	10	0	.172	6	44	1	2	1.5	.980
1948	2 teams	STL A	(11G 2-4)	CLE A	(23G 9-6)																					
"	total	11	10	.524	3.44	34	21	4	159.2	168	43	30	1	4	2	4	58	11	0	.190	7	39	1	4	1.4	.979
1949	CLE A	1	2	.333	4.25	27	0	0	53	60	18	11	0	1	2	0	8	3	0	.375	12	19	0	1	1.1	1.000
1950		4	2	.667	3.96	33	2	0	63.2	64	21	15	0	4	0	0	16	3	0	.188	4	10	0	0	0.4	1.000
1951	PHI A	6	10	.375	3.16	26	18	8	128	127	24	18	1	0	1	0	45	7	0	.156	6	17	0	0	0.9	1.000
1952		0	6	.000	4.06	16	10	2	75.1	86	25	12	0	0	0	0	23	4	0	.174	6	22	0	2	1.8	1.000
9 yrs.		43	53	.448	3.54	250	93	30	929.1	956	301	207	5	14	9	8	286	50	0	.175	54	200	4	14	1.0	.984

Bill Zuber

ZUBER, WILLIAM HENRY (Goober)
B. Mar. 26, 1913, Middle Amana, Iowa D. Nov. 2, 1982, Cedar Rapids, Iowa — BR TR 6'2" 195 lbs.

Year	Team	W	L	PCT	ERA	G	GS	CG	IP	H	BB	SO	ShO	W	L	SV	AB	H	HR	BA	PO	A	E	DP	TC/G	FA
1936	CLE A	1	1	.500	6.59	2	1	1	13.2	14	15	5	0	0	0	0	5	1	0	.200	0	2	0	1	1.0	1.000
1938		0	3	.000	5.02	15	0	0	28.2	33	20	14	0	0	3	1	7	0	0	.000	2	3	1	1	0.4	.833
1939		2	0	1.000	5.97	16	1	0	31.2	41	19	16	0	2	0	1	5	1	0	.200	1	9	0	1	0.6	1.000
1940		1	1	.500	5.63	17	0	0	24	25	14	12	0	1	1	0	3	1	0	.333	1	2	0	0	0.2	1.000
1941	WAS A	6	4	.600	5.42	36	7	1	96.1	110	61	51	0	1	2	2	26	0	0	.000	5	10	1	0	0.4	.938
1942		9	9	.500	3.84	37	7	3	126.2	115	82	64	0	8	5	5	39	6	0	.154	6	11	1	3	0.5	.944
1943	NY A	8	4	.667	3.89	20	13	7	118	100	74	57	0	1	1	1	38	7	0	.184	1	18	0	1	1.0	1.000
1944		5	7	.417	4.21	22	13	2	107	101	54	59	0	1	1	0	31	4	0	.129	6	16	1	0	1.0	.957
1945		5	11	.313	3.19	21	14	7	127	121	56	50	0	2	0	1	42	7	0	.167	3	19	1	2	1.1	.957
1946	2 teams	NY A	(3G 0-1)	BOS A	(15G 5-1)																					
"	total	5	2	.714	3.47	18	7	2	62.1	47	42	32	1	1	1	0	20	2	0	.100	0	0	0	0	0.0	—
1947	BOS A	1	0	1.000	5.33	20	1	0	50.2	60	31	23	0	1	0	0	13	2	0	.154	2	7	0	0	0.5	1.000
11 yrs.		43	42	.506	4.28	224	65	23	786	767	468	383	1	18	14	6	229	31	0	.135	26	97	5	9	0.6	.961

WORLD SERIES

Year	Team	W	L	PCT	ERA	G	GS	CG	IP	H	BB	SO	ShO	W	L	SV	AB	H	HR	BA	PO	A	E	DP	TC/G	FA
1946	BOS A	0	0	—	4.50	1	0	0	2	3	1	1	0	0	0	0	0	0	0	—	0	0	0	0	0.0	—

George Zuverink

ZUVERINK, GEORGE
B. Aug. 20, 1924, Holland, Mich. — BR TR 6'4" 195 lbs.

Year	Team	W	L	PCT	ERA	G	GS	CG	IP	H	BB	SO	ShO	W	L	SV	AB	H	HR	BA	PO	A	E	DP	TC/G	FA
1951	CLE A	0	0	—	5.33	16	0	0	25.1	24	13	14	0	0	0	0	0	0	0	—	1	7	1	0	0.6	.889
1952		0	0	—	0.00	1	1	0	1.1	1	0	1	0	0	0	0	0	0	0	—	0	1	0	0	1.0	1.000
1954	2 teams	CIN N	(2G 0-0)	DET A	(35G 9-13)																					
"	total	9	13	.409	3.75	37	25	9	209	211	63	72	2	0	0	4	66	9	0	.136	18	46	3	3	1.8	.955
1955	2 teams	DET A	(14G 0-5)	BAL A	(28G 4-3)																					
"	total	4	8	.333	3.38	42	6	0	114.2	118	31	44	0	3	6	4	27	5	0	.185	9	25	3	2	0.9	.919
1956	BAL A	7	6	.538	4.16	62	0	0	97.1	112	34	33	0	7	6	16	17	2	0	.118	8	17	0	2	0.4	1.000
1957		10	6	.625	2.48	56	0	0	112.2	105	39	36	0	10	6	9	23	3	0	.130	5	26	0	2	0.6	1.000
1958		2	2	.500	3.39	45	0	0	69	74	17	22	0	2	2	7	9	2	0	.222	4	19	0	1	0.5	1.000
1959		0	1	.000	4.15	6	0	0	13	15	6	1	0	0	1	0	0	0	0	—	0	4	0	0	0.7	1.000
8 yrs.		32	36	.471	3.54	265	31	9	642.1	660	203	223	2	22	21	40	142	21	0	.148	45	145	7	10	0.7	.964

PART NINE

Trades

Chronological Listing by Player
Of Every Trade, Sale,
Or Re-Entry Free Agent Signing

Trades

The Trades section is a listing, for each player, of every trade, sale, or free agent signing he was involved in during the course of his career. Players are listed alphabetically, with no separation of pitchers and non-pitchers. At present, trades and sales are included from 1900 through January 1, 1990.

Date	Traded To		Traded With	Traded By		In Exchange For
Doyle Alexander						
Dec. 2, 1971	BAL	A	Bob O'Brien Sergio Robles Royle Stillman	LA	N	Frank Robinson Pete Richert
June 15, 1976	NY	A	——	BAL	A	*See Tippy Martinez*
Nov. 23, 1976	TEX	A	——	NY	A	No compensation (free agent signing)

The name given for each player is the shortened version of his full name which will be most familiar to fans. This is the same name as that used in the Player and Pitcher registers. If more specific biographical information is needed, consult those registers.

For each player, all trades in which he was involved are listed chronologically. Player-for-player, player-for-cash, and re-entry free agent signings are listed; the movement of a player from one team to another following his outright release is not listed. Selection of a player by a new expansion franchise in a stocking draft, or by an existing club in a minor league free agent draft, is also not included in his record. Dollar amounts, where known, are included for player sales; if the dollar amount is not known, "cash" or "waiver price" is listed.

Players to Be Named Later. Transactions involving "a player to be named later" have, for the most part, been rewritten to reflect the players who were ultimately exchanged (or cash, in those cases where money was accepted in lieu of a player). If there was an unusually long delay between the announcement of a trade and the final transfer of players, that fact has been noted in an explanatory note.

See John Doe. For many particularly large transactions (generally involving six or more players), the entire transaction is listed under the primary players only. Minor players involved in the deal are listed with the date of the trade, the teams involved, and the notation *"See Player X"* in italic type. The entire deal will be listed under that player on the appropriate date.

Three-Team Trades. Three-team or four-team trades have been rewritten as a series of two-team transactions: a player from Team A is traded to Team B, and then traded on to Team C in a separate transaction on the same date. In any such series, each step is noted with the explanatory comment, "Part of a three-team trade involving Team A, Team B, and Team C."

Minor League Players. Any player involved in a transaction who never played in the major leagues (or has not through the 1989 season) is listed in the "Traded With" or "In Exchange For" columns but does not have a separate entry in this section. Minor leaguers are so noted in the listing, along with their primary positions. (Players involved in a transaction who later played in the major leagues are simply listed by name, with no "minor league" reference.)

Date	Traded To	Traded With	Traded By	In Exchange For

Hank Aaron

Date	Traded To	Traded With	Traded By	In Exchange For
Nov 2, 1974	MIL A	——	ATL N	Dave May minor league P Roger Alexander

Don Aase

Date	Traded To	Traded With	Traded By	In Exchange For
Dec 8, 1977	CAL A	Cash	BOS A	Jerry Remy
Dec 13, 1984	BAL A	——	CAL A	No compensation (free agent signing)

Ed Abbaticchio

Date	Traded To	Traded With	Traded By	In Exchange For
Dec 1906	PIT N	——	BOS N	Ginger Beaumont Claude Ritchey Patsy Flaherty
May 1910	BOS N	——	PIT N	Cash

Glenn Abbott

Date	Traded To	Traded With	Traded By	In Exchange For
Aug 23, 1983	DET A	——	SEA A	$100,000.

Al Aber

Date	Traded To	Traded With	Traded By	In Exchange For
June 15, 1953	DET A	*See Ray Boone*	CLE A	——
Aug 27, 1957	KC A	——	DET A	Waiver price

Ted Abernathy

Date	Traded To	Traded With	Traded By	In Exchange For
April 14, 1965	CHI N	——	CLE A	Cash
May 28, 1966	ATL N	——	CHI N	Lee Thomas
Jan 9, 1969	CHI N	——	CIN N	Bill Plummer Clarence Jones minor league P Ken Myette
May 29, 1970	STL N	——	CHI N	Phil Gagliano
July 1, 1970	KC A	——	STL N	Chris Zachary

Shawn Abner

Date	Traded To	Traded With	Traded By	In Exchange For
Dec 11, 1986	SD N	——	NY N	*See Kevin McReynolds*

Cal Abrams

Date	Traded To	Traded With	Traded By	In Exchange For
June 9, 1952	CIN N	——	BKN N	Rudy Rufer and cash
Oct 14, 1952	PIT N	Joe Rossi Gail Henley	CIN N	Gus Bell
May 25, 1954	BAL A	——	PIT N	Dick Littlefield
Oct 18, 1955	CHI A	——	BAL A	Bobby Adams

Bill Abstein

Date	Traded To	Traded With	Traded By	In Exchange For
Jan 1910	STL A	——	PIT N	Cash

Jim Acker

Date	Traded To	Traded With	Traded By	In Exchange For
July 6, 1986	ATL N	——	TOR A	Joe Johnson
Aug 24, 1989	TOR A	——	ATL N	Tony Castillo Francisco Cabrera

(Atlanta received Cabrera on Aug. 29, 1989.)

Tom Acker

Date	Traded To	Traded With	Traded By	In Exchange For
Nov 21, 1959	KC A	——	CIN N	Frank House

Fritz Ackley

Date	Traded To	Traded With	Traded By	In Exchange For
Nov 24, 1964	STL N	——	CHI A	Cash

Cy Acosta

Date	Traded To	Traded With	Traded By	In Exchange For
March 17, 1975	PHI N	——	CHI A	Cash

Ed Acosta

Date	Traded To	Traded With	Traded By	In Exchange For
Aug 10, 1971	SD N	John Jeter	PIT N	Bob Miller

Jose Acosta

Date	Traded To	Traded With	Traded By	In Exchange For
Jan 10, 1922	PHI A	Bing Miller	WAS A	Joe Dugan

(Part of three-team trade involving Boston, Philadelphia, and Washington.)

Date	Traded To	Traded With	Traded By	In Exchange For
Feb 4, 1922	CHI A	——	PHI A	Cash

Merito Acosta

Date	Traded To	Traded With	Traded By	In Exchange For
May 25, 1918	PHI A	——	WAS A	Cash

Jerry Adair

Date	Traded To	Traded With	Traded By	In Exchange For
June 12, 1966	CHI A	minor league OF Johnny Riddle	BAL A	Eddie Fisher
June 3, 1967	BOS A	——	CHI A	Don McMahon minor league P Bob Snow

Babe Adams

Date	Traded To	Traded With	Traded By	In Exchange For
Oct 1907	PIT N	——	STL N	Cash

Bert Adams

Date	Traded To	Traded With	Traded By	In Exchange For
Jan 1915	PHI N	Al Demaree Milt Stock	NY N	Hans Lobert

Bob Adams

Date	Traded To	Traded With	Traded By	In Exchange For
March 29, 1971	MIN A	minor league P Art Clifford	DET A	Bill Zepp

Bobby Adams

Date	Traded To	Traded With	Traded By	In Exchange For
July 26, 1955	CHI A	——	CIN N	Cash
Oct 18, 1955	BAL A	——	CHI A	Cal Abrams

Buster Adams

Date	Traded To	Traded With	Traded By	In Exchange For
June 1, 1943	PHI N	Coaker Triplett Dain Clay	STL N	Danny Litwhiler Earl Naylor
May 8, 1945	STL N	——	PHI N	John Antonelli Glenn Crawford
March 21, 1947	PHI N	——	STL N	Cash

Glenn Adams

Date	Traded To	Traded With	Traded By	In Exchange For
Dec 6, 1976	MIN A	——	SF N	Cash

Herb Adams

Date	Traded To	Traded With	Traded By	In Exchange For
Sept 11, 1950	CLE A	——	CHI A	Waiver price

Mike Adams

Date	Traded To	Traded With	Traded By	In Exchange For
April 1, 1978	OAK A	——	CHI N	Cash

Sparky Adams

Date	Traded To	Traded With	Traded By	In Exchange For
Nov 28, 1927	PIT N	Pete Scott	CHI N	Kiki Cuyler
Nov 1929	STL N	——	PIT N	Cash
May 7, 1933	CIN N	Paul Derringer Allyn Stout	STL N	Leo Durocher Dutch Henry Jack Ogden

Spencer Adams

Date	Traded To	Traded With	Traded By	In Exchange For
Jan 20, 1926	NY A	——	WAS A	Cash

Date	Traded To		Traded With	Traded By		In Exchange For

Joe Adcock

Date	Traded To		Traded With	Traded By		In Exchange For
Feb 16, 1953	MIL	N	———	CIN	N	Rocky Bridges and cash

(Part of four-team trade involving Milwaukee Braves, Philadelphia Phillies, Brooklyn, and Cincinnati.)

Nov 27, 1962	CLE	A	Jack Curtis	MIL	N	Ty Cline Don Dillard Frank Funk
Dec 2, 1963	LA	A	Barry Latman	CLE	A	Leon Wagner

Bob Addis

Date	Traded To		Traded With	Traded By		In Exchange For
Oct 11, 1951	CHI	N	———	BOS	N	Jack Cusick
June 4, 1953	PIT	N	———	CHI	N	See Ralph Kiner

Jim Adduci

Date	Traded To		Traded With	Traded By		In Exchange For
Oct 3, 1984	MIL	A	Paul Householder	STL	N	Minor leaguers P Rich Buonantony C Jim Koontz IF Ron Koenigsfeld

Dave Adlesh

Date	Traded To		Traded With	Traded By		In Exchange For
Oct 11, 1968	STL	N	Dave Giusti	HOU	N	Johnny Edwards minor league C Tommy Smith
March 25, 1969	ATL	N	———	STL	N	Bob Johnson

Troy Afenir

Date	Traded To		Traded With	Traded By		In Exchange For
April 6, 1989	OAK	A	———	HOU	N	Matt Sinatro

Tommie Agee

Date	Traded To		Traded With	Traded By		In Exchange For
Jan 20, 1965	CHI	A	Tommy John Johnny Romano	CLE	A	Rocky Colavito Camilo Carreon

(Part of three-team trade involving Kansas City, Cleveland, and Chicago White Sox.)

Dec 15, 1967	NY	N	Al Weis	CHI	A	Tommy Davis Jack Fisher Billy Wynne Buddy Booker
Nov 27, 1972	HOU	N	———	NY	N	Rich Chiles Buddy Harris
Aug 18, 1973	STL	N	———	HOU	N	Dave Campbell and cash
Dec 5, 1973	LA	N	———	STL	N	Pete Richert

Joe Agler

Date	Traded To		Traded With	Traded By		In Exchange For
May 1915	BAL	F	———	BUF	F	Cash

Sam Agnew

Date	Traded To		Traded With	Traded By		In Exchange For
Dec 1915	BOS	A	———	STL	A	Cash
Jan 1919	WAS	A	———	BOS	A	Cash

Juan Agosto

Date	Traded To		Traded With	Traded By		In Exchange For
April 30, 1986	MIN	A	———	CHI	A	Cash

Luis Aguayo

Date	Traded To		Traded With	Traded By		In Exchange For
July 15, 1988	NY	A	———	PHI	N	Minor league P Amalio Carreno
Dec 2, 1988	CLE	A	———	NY	A	No compensation (free agent signing)

Rick Aguilera

Date	Traded To		Traded With	Traded By		In Exchange For
July 31, 1989	MIN	A	David West Tim Drummond Kevin Tapani Jack Savage	NY	N	Frank Viola

(Minnesota received Savage on Oct. 16, 1989.)

Hank Aguirre

Date	Traded To		Traded With	Traded By		In Exchange For
Feb 18, 1958	DET	A	Jim Hegan	CLE	A	Hal Woodeshick J. W. Porter
April 3, 1968	LA	N	———	DET	A	Minor league IF Fred Moulder

Willie Aikens

Date	Traded To		Traded With	Traded By		In Exchange For
Dec 6, 1979	KC	A	Rance Mulliniks	CAL	A	Al Cowens Todd Cruz Craig Eaton
Dec 20, 1983	TOR	A	———	KC	A	Jorge Orta

Eddie Ainsmith

Date	Traded To		Traded With	Traded By		In Exchange For
Jan 17, 1919	BOS	A	George Dumont	WAS	A	Hal Janvrin and cash
Jan 17, 1919	DET	A	Chick Shorten Slim Love	BOS	A	Ossie Vitt

Jack Aker

Date	Traded To		Traded With	Traded By		In Exchange For
May 20, 1969	NY	A	———	SEA	A	Fred Talbot
Jan 20, 1972	CHI	N	———	NY	A	Johnny Callison

(Chicago received Aker on May 17, 1972.)

June 14, 1974	NY	N	———	ATL	N	Cash

Darrel Akerfelds

Date	Traded To		Traded With	Traded By		In Exchange For
Nov 21, 1983	OAK	A	See Bill Caudill	SEA	A	———
July 15, 1987	CLE	A	Brian Dorsett	OAK	A	Tony Bernazard

Butch Alberts

Date	Traded To		Traded With	Traded By		In Exchange For
Dec 8, 1977	TOR	A	Dale Kelly	CAL	A	Ron Fairly

Santo Alcala

Date	Traded To		Traded With	Traded By		In Exchange For
May 21, 1977	MON	N	———	CIN	N	Shane Rawley Angel Torres
March 23, 1978	SEA	A	———	MON	N	Cash

(Alcala was returned to Montreal before the start of the 1979 season.)

Luis Alcaraz

Date	Traded To		Traded With	Traded By		In Exchange For
March 24, 1971	CHI	A	Cash	KC	A	Bobby Knoop

Mike Aldrete

Date	Traded To		Traded With	Traded By		In Exchange For
Dec 8, 1988	MON	N	———	SF	N	Tracy Jones

Jay Aldrich

Date	Traded To		Traded With	Traded By		In Exchange For
Aug 23, 1989	ATL	N	———	MIL	A	Ed Romero

Vic Aldridge

Date	Traded To		Traded With	Traded By		In Exchange For
Oct 27, 1924	PIT	N	George Grantham Al Niehaus	CHI	N	Charlie Grimm Rabbit Maranville Wilbur Cooper
Feb 11, 1928	NY	N	———	PIT	N	Burleigh Grimes
Dec 9, 1928	BKN	N	———	NY	N	Waiver price

(Aldridge refused to report and retired.)

Dale Alexander

Date	Traded To		Traded With	Traded By		In Exchange For
June 12, 1932	BOS	A	Roy Johnson	DET	A	Earl Webb

Doyle Alexander

Date	Traded To		Traded With	Traded By		In Exchange For
Dec 2, 1971	BAL	A	Bob O'Brien Sergio Robles Royle Stillman	LA	N	Frank Robinson Pete Richert
June 15, 1976	NY	A	———	BAL	A	See Tippy Martinez

Date	Traded To		Traded With	Traded By		In Exchange For

Doyle Alexander *continued*

Date	Traded To		Traded With	Traded By		In Exchange For
Nov 23, 1976	TEX	A	———	NY	A	No compensation (free agent signing)
Dec 6, 1979	ATL	N	Larvell Blanks and $50,000.	TEX	A	Adrian Devine Pepe Frias
Dec 12, 1980	SF	N	———	ATL	N	John Montefusco minor league OF Craig Landis
March 30, 1982	NY	A	———	SF	N	Andy McGaffigan Ted Wilborn
July 6, 1986	ATL	N	———	TOR	A	Duane Ward
Aug 12, 1987	DET	A	———	ATL	N	John Smoltz

Gary Alexander

Date	Traded To		Traded With	Traded By		In Exchange For
March 15, 1978	OAK	A	Gary Thomasson Dave Heaverlo Alan Wirth John Henry Johnson Phil Huffman Mario Guerrero and $390,000.	SF	N	Vida Blue
June 15, 1978	CLE	A	———	OAK	A	Joe Wallis
Dec 9, 1980	PIT	N	Victor Cruz Rafael Vasquez Bob Owchinko	CLE	A	Bert Blyleven Manny Sanguillen

Grover Alexander

Date	Traded To		Traded With	Traded By		In Exchange For
Dec 11, 1917	CHI	N	Bill Killefer	PHI	N	Mike Prendergast Pickles Dillhoefer and $55,000.
June 22, 1926	STL	N	———	CHI	N	Waiver price
Dec 11, 1929	PHI	N	Harry McCurdy	STL	N	Homer Peel Bob McGraw

Matt Alexander

Date	Traded To		Traded With	Traded By		In Exchange For
April 28, 1975	OAK	A	———	CHI	N	Minor league P Howell Copeland

Walt Alexander

Date	Traded To		Traded With	Traded By		In Exchange For
July 30, 1915	NY	A	———	STL	A	Cash

Brian Allard

Date	Traded To		Traded With	Traded By		In Exchange For
Dec 12, 1980	SEA	A	———	TEX	A	*See Rick Honeycutt*

Bernie Allen

Date	Traded To		Traded With	Traded By		In Exchange For
Dec 3, 1966	WAS	A	Camilo Pascual	MIN	A	Ron Kline
Dec 2, 1971	NY	A	———	TEX	A	Gary Jones Terry Ley
Aug 13, 1973	MON	N	———	NY	A	Cash

Bob Allen

Date	Traded To		Traded With	Traded By		In Exchange For
Dec 14, 1963	PIT	N	———	CLE	A	Cash

Dick Allen

Date	Traded To		Traded With	Traded By		In Exchange For
Oct 7, 1969	STL	N	Cookie Rojas Jerry Johnson	PHI	N	Curt Flood Tim McCarver Joe Hoerner Byron Browne

(Flood refused to report to the Philadelphia Phillies, and the Cardinals sent Willie Montanez and Bob Browning on April 8, 1970 to complete the trade.)

Date	Traded To		Traded With	Traded By		In Exchange For
Oct 5, 1970	LA	N	———	STL	N	Ted Sizemore Bob Stinson
Dec 2, 1971	CHI	A	———	LA	N	Tommy John Steve Huntz
Dec 3, 1974	ATL	N	———	CHI	A	Jim Essian and cash

(Chicago received Essian on May 15, 1975.)

Date	Traded To		Traded With	Traded By		In Exchange For
May 7, 1975	PHI	N	Johnny Oates	ATL	N	Jim Essian Barry Bonnell and cash

Dick Allen *continued*

Date	Traded To		Traded With	Traded By		In Exchange For
March 15, 1977	OAK	A	———	PHI	N	No compensation (free agent signing)

Ethan Allen

Date	Traded To		Traded With	Traded By		In Exchange For
May 27, 1930	NY	N	Pete Donohue	CIN	N	Pat Crawford
Oct 10, 1932	STL	N	Bob O'Farrell Bill Walker Jim Mooney	NY	N	Gus Mancuso Ray Starr
Jan 1934	PHI	N	———	STL	N	Cash
May 21, 1936	CHI	N	Curt Davis	PHI	N	Chuck Klein Fabian Kowalik
Dec 2, 1936	STL	A	———	CHI	N	Cash

Frank Allen

Date	Traded To		Traded With	Traded By		In Exchange For
Sept 1914	PIT	F		BKN	F	Cash
Feb 10, 1916	BOS	N	Elmer Knetzer	PIT	F	Cash

Hank Allen

Date	Traded To		Traded With	Traded By		In Exchange For
May 11, 1970	MIL	A	Ron Theobald	WAS	A	Wayne Comer
Dec 2, 1970	ATL	N	minor leaguers P Paul Click and IF John Ryan	MIL	A	Bob Tillman

Johnny Allen

Date	Traded To		Traded With	Traded By		In Exchange For
Dec 11, 1935	CLE	A	———	NY	A	Monte Pearson Steve Sundra
Dec 24, 1940	STL	A	———	CLE	A	$20,000.
July 30, 1941	BKN	N	———	STL	A	Waiver price
Dec 12, 1942	PHI	N	$30,000.	BKN	N	Rube Melton
April 22, 1943	BKN	N	George Washburn	PHI	N	Cash
July 31, 1943	NY	N	Dolf Camilli	BKN	N	Bill Lohrman Bill Sayles Joe Orengo

(Camilli refused to report to New York and retired.)

Lloyd Allen

Date	Traded To		Traded With	Traded By		In Exchange For
May 20, 1973	TEX	A	———	CAL	A	*See Mike Epstein*
July 1, 1974	CHI	A	———	TEX	A	Cash
Aug 1, 1975	STL	N	———	CHI	A	Cash

Neil Allen

Date	Traded To		Traded With	Traded By		In Exchange For
June 15, 1983	STL	N	Rick Ownbey	NY	N	Keith Hernandez
July 16, 1985	NY	A	———	STL	N	Cash

Nick Allen

Date	Traded To		Traded With	Traded By		In Exchange For
Feb 10, 1916	CHI	N	———	BUF	F	Cash

Rod Allen

Date	Traded To		Traded With	Traded By		In Exchange For
Dec 11, 1981	SEA	A	Todd Cruz Jim Essian	CHI	A	Tom Paciorek

Gary Allenson

Date	Traded To		Traded With	Traded By		In Exchange For
Feb 25, 1985	TOR	A	———	BOS	A	No compensation (free agent signing)

Mel Almada

Date	Traded To		Traded With	Traded By		In Exchange For
June 11, 1937	WAS	A	Wes Ferrell Rick Ferrell	BOS	A	Ben Chapman Bobo Newsom
June 15, 1938	STL	A	———	WAS	A	Sammy West
June 15, 1939	BKN	N	———	STL	A	$25,000.

Bill Almon

Date	Traded To		Traded With	Traded By		In Exchange For
Nov 27, 1979	MON	N	Dan Briggs	SD	N	Dave Cash

Date	Traded To	Traded With	Traded By	In Exchange For

Bill Almon *continued*

Date	Traded To	Traded With	Traded By	In Exchange For
July 11, 1980	NY N	———	MON N	No compensation (free agent signing)

(Almon became a free agent after refusing to accept demotion to Montreal's Denver farm club.)

Date	Traded To	Traded With	Traded By	In Exchange For
Jan 18, 1983	OAK A	———	CHI A	No compensation (free agent signing)
April 8, 1985	PIT N	———	OAK A	No compensation (free agent signing)
May 29, 1987	NY N	———	PIT N	Al Pedrique / Scott Little
March 21, 1988	PHI N	———	NY N	Minor league P Shawn Barton / Minor league P Vladimir Perez

Sandy Alomar

Date	Traded To	Traded With	Traded By	In Exchange For
Dec 31, 1966	HOU N	Eddie Mathews / Arnie Umbach	ATL N	Dave Nicholson / Bob Bruce
March 24, 1967	NY N	———	HOU N	Derrell Griffith
Aug 15, 1967	CHI A	———	NY N	Cash
May 14, 1969	CAL A	Bob Priddy	CHI A	Bobby Knoop
July 8, 1974	NY A	———	CAL A	Cash
Feb 17, 1977	TEX A	———	NY A	Greg Pryor / Brian Doyle / and cash

Sandy Alomar

Date	Traded To	Traded With	Traded By	In Exchange For
Dec 6, 1989	CLE A	Chris James / Minor league 3B Carlos Baerga	SD N	Joe Carter

Felipe Alou

Date	Traded To	Traded With	Traded By	In Exchange For
Dec 3, 1963	MIL N	Billy Hoeft / Ed Bailey / Ernie Bowman	SF N	Del Crandall / Bob Shaw / Bob Hendley
Dec 3, 1969	OAK A	———	ATL N	Jim Nash
April 9, 1971	NY A	———	OAK A	Ron Klimkowski / Rob Gardner
Sept 6, 1973	MON N	———	NY A	Cash
Dec 7, 1973	MIL A	———	MON N	Cash

Jesus Alou

Date	Traded To	Traded With	Traded By	In Exchange For
Jan 22, 1969	HOU N	Donn Clendenon / Jack Billingham / Skip Guinn / and $100,000.	MON N	Rusty Staub

(Clendenon refused to report, and Houston sent Billingham, Guinn, and Cash on April 8, 1969.)

Date	Traded To	Traded With	Traded By	In Exchange For
July 31, 1973	OAK A	———	HOU N	Cash

Matty Alou

Date	Traded To	Traded With	Traded By	In Exchange For
Oct 1, 1965	PIT N	———	SF N	Joe Gibbon / Ozzie Virgil
Jan 29, 1971	STL N	George Brunet	PIT N	Nellie Briles / Vic Davalillo
Aug 27, 1972	OAK A	———	STL N	Bill Voss / minor league P Steve Easton
Nov 24, 1972	NY A	———	OAK A	Rob Gardner / Rich McKinney
Sept 6, 1973	STL N	———	NY A	Cash
Oct 25, 1973	SD N	———	STL N	Cash

Dell Alston

Date	Traded To	Traded With	Traded By	In Exchange For
June 15, 1978	OAK A	Mickey Klutts / and $50,000.	NY A	Gary Thomasson

Porfi Altamirano

Date	Traded To	Traded With	Traded By	In Exchange For
March 26, 1984	CHI N	Gary Matthews / Bob Dernier	PHI N	Bill Campbell / Mike Diaz

Porfi Altamirano *continued*

Date	Traded To	Traded With	Traded By	In Exchange For
Dec 4, 1984	NY A	Henry Cotto / Ron Hassey / Rich Bordi	CHI N	Ray Fontenot / Brian Dayett

Dave Altizer

Date	Traded To	Traded With	Traded By	In Exchange For
Aug 1908	CLE A	Cy Falkenberg	WAS A	Cash

George Altman

Date	Traded To	Traded With	Traded By	In Exchange For
Oct 17, 1962	STL N	Don Cardwell / Moe Thacker	CHI N	Larry Jackson / Jimmie Schaffer / Lindy McDaniel
Nov 4, 1963	NY N	Bill Wakefield	STL N	Roger Craig
Jan 15, 1965	CHI N	———	NY N	Billy Cowan

Nick Altrock

Date	Traded To	Traded With	Traded By	In Exchange For
April 1903	CHI A	———	BOS A	Cash
May 16, 1909	WAS A	Gavvy Cravath / Jiggs Donahue	CHI A	Bill Burns

George Alusik

Date	Traded To	Traded With	Traded By	In Exchange For
May 7, 1962	KC A	———	DET A	Cash

Luis Alvarado

Date	Traded To	Traded With	Traded By	In Exchange For
Dec 1, 1970	CHI A	Mike Andrews	BOS A	Luis Aparicio
April 27, 1974	STL N	———	CHI A	Ken Tatum
June 1, 1974	CLE A	Ed Crosby	STL N	Jack Heidemann
Sept 30, 1975	STL N	———	CLE A	Doug Howard
Nov 6, 1976	DET A	———	STL N	Cash
Feb 25, 1977	NY N	———	DET A	Cash

(Alvarado was returned to Detroit on April 27, 1977.)

Jose Alvarez

Date	Traded To	Traded With	Traded By	In Exchange For
Feb 14, 1984	HOU N	———	ATL N	Ron Meredith

Orlando Alvarez

Date	Traded To	Traded With	Traded By	In Exchange For
March 21, 1976	CAL A	Cash	LA N	Ellie Rodriguez

Ossie Alvarez

Date	Traded To	Traded With	Traded By	In Exchange For
Oct 27, 1958	CLE A	———	WAS A	J. W. Porter
Nov 20, 1958	DET A	Don Mossi / Ray Narleski	CLE A	Billy Martin / Al Cicotte

Rogelio Alvarez

Date	Traded To	Traded With	Traded By	In Exchange For
Nov 24, 1962	WAS A	———	CIN N	Harry Bright

Wilson Alvarez

Date	Traded To	Traded With	Traded By	In Exchange For
July 29, 1989	CHI A	Scott Fletcher / Sammy Sosa	TEX A	Harold Baines / Fred Manrique

Max Alvis

Date	Traded To	Traded With	Traded By	In Exchange For
April 4, 1970	MIL A	Russ Snyder	CLE A	Roy Foster / Frank Coggins / and cash

Brant Alyea

Date	Traded To	Traded With	Traded By	In Exchange For
March 21, 1970	MIN A	———	WAS A	Joe Grzenda / Charley Walters
May 18, 1972	STL N	———	OAK A	Marty Martinez

(Alyea was returned to Oakland on July 23.)

Date	Traded To	Traded With	Traded By	In Exchange For
Oct 30, 1972	TEX A	Bill McNulty	OAK A	Paul Lindblad

Date	Traded To	Traded With	Traded By	In Exchange For

Joey Amalfitano

Date	Traded To	Traded With	Traded By	In Exchange For
Nov 30, 1962	SF N	—	HOU N	Dick LeMay Manny Mota

Ruben Amaro

Date	Traded To	Traded With	Traded By	In Exchange For
Dec 3, 1958	PHI N	—	STL N	Chuck Essegian
Nov 29, 1965	NY A	—	PHI N	Phil Linz
Nov 6, 1968	CAL A	—	NY A	Cash

Red Ames

Date	Traded To	Traded With	Traded By	In Exchange For
May 22, 1913	CIN N	Heinie Groh Josh Devore and $20,000.	NY N	Art Fromme Eddie Grant
July 24, 1915	STL N	—	CIN N	Cash
Sept 5, 1919	PHI N	—	STL N	Cash

(Ames was returned to St. Louis in October.)

Sandy Amoros

Date	Traded To	Traded With	Traded By	In Exchange For
May 7, 1960	DET A	—	LA N	Gail Harris

Larry Andersen

Date	Traded To	Traded With	Traded By	In Exchange For
Dec 21, 1979	PIT N	—	CLE A	Larry Littleton and minor league P John Burden
April 1, 1980	SEA A	Cash	PIT N	Odell Jones
July 29, 1983	PHI N	—	SEA A	Cash

Bob Anderson

Date	Traded To	Traded With	Traded By	In Exchange For
Nov 28, 1962	DET A	—	CHI N	Steve Boros
Nov 18, 1963	KC A	*See Rocky Colavito*	DET A	—

Brady Anderson

Date	Traded To	Traded With	Traded By	In Exchange For
July 29, 1988	BAL A	Curt Schilling	BOS A	Mike Boddicker

Bud Anderson

Date	Traded To	Traded With	Traded By	In Exchange For
Dec 6, 1979	CLE A	Rafael Vasquez and minor league P Bob Pietroburgo	SEA A	Ted Cox

Dave Anderson

Date	Traded To	Traded With	Traded By	In Exchange For
Nov 28, 1989	SF N	—	LA N	No compensation (free agent signing)

Dwain Anderson

Date	Traded To	Traded With	Traded By	In Exchange For
May 15, 1972	STL N	—	OAK A	Don Shaw
June 7, 1973	SD N	—	STL N	Dave Campbell

Fred Anderson

Date	Traded To	Traded With	Traded By	In Exchange For
Feb 10, 1916	NY N	—	BUF F	Cash

Harry Anderson

Date	Traded To	Traded With	Traded By	In Exchange For
June 15, 1960	CIN N	Wally Post minor league 1B Fred Hopke	PHI N	Tony Gonzalez Lee Walls

Jim Anderson

Date	Traded To	Traded With	Traded By	In Exchange For
Aug 29, 1979	SEA A	—	CAL A	John Montague
Nov 2, 1985	MON N	—	TEX A	*See Pete Incaviglia*

John Anderson

Date	Traded To	Traded With	Traded By	In Exchange For
May 7, 1962	HOU N	Carl Warwick	STL N	Bobby Shantz

John Anderson

Date	Traded To	Traded With	Traded By	In Exchange For
Oct 26, 1903	NY A	—	STL A	Jack O'Connor
Feb 1904	NY A	—	STL A	Cash
June 3, 1905	WAS A	—	NY A	Waiver price
Jan 1908	CHI A	—	WAS A	Cash

Larry Anderson

Date	Traded To	Traded With	Traded By	In Exchange For
Aug 18, 1977	CHI N	Cash	CHI A	Steve Renko

Mike Anderson

Date	Traded To	Traded With	Traded By	In Exchange For
Dec 9, 1975	STL N	—	PHI N	Ron Reed

Rick Anderson

Date	Traded To	Traded With	Traded By	In Exchange For
March 27, 1987	KC A	Ed Hearn Mauro Gozzo	NY N	David Cone Minor league C Chris Jelic

Rick Anderson

Date	Traded To	Traded With	Traded By	In Exchange For
Nov 1, 1979	SEA A	*See Jim Beattie*	NY A	—

Sparky Anderson

Date	Traded To	Traded With	Traded By	In Exchange For
Dec 23, 1958	PHI N	—	LA N	Rip Repulski Jim Golden Gene Snyder

Fred Andrews

Date	Traded To	Traded With	Traded By	In Exchange For
March 24, 1978	NY N	Cash	PHI N	Bud Harrelson

Ivy Andrews

Date	Traded To	Traded With	Traded By	In Exchange For
June 5, 1932	BOS A	Hank Johnson and $50,000.	NY A	Danny MacFayden
Dec 14, 1933	STL A	Smead Jolley and cash	BOS A	Carl Reynolds
Jan 17, 1937	CLE A	Lyn Lary Moose Solters	STL A	Bill Knickerbocker Joe Vosmik Oral Hildebrand
Aug 14, 1937	NY A	—	CLE A	$7,500.

John Andrews

Date	Traded To	Traded With	Traded By	In Exchange For
Dec 6, 1973	CAL A	—	STL N	Jeff Torborg

Mike Andrews

Date	Traded To	Traded With	Traded By	In Exchange For
Dec 1, 1970	CHI A	Luis Alvarado	BOS A	Luis Aparicio

Nate Andrews

Date	Traded To	Traded With	Traded By	In Exchange For
Sept 25, 1939	STL A	—	STL N	Cash
June 10, 1940	CLE A	—	STL A	Cash
Dec 4, 1942	BOS N	Eddie Joost and $25,000.	CIN N	Eddie Miller
Aug 22, 1945	CIN N	—	BOS N	Cash

Rob Andrews

Date	Traded To	Traded With	Traded By	In Exchange For
Dec 3, 1974	HOU N	Enos Cabell	BAL A	Lee May Jay Schlueter
March 26, 1977	SF N	Cash	HOU N	Willie Crawford Rob Sperring

Joaquin Andujar

Date	Traded To	Traded With	Traded By	In Exchange For
Oct 24, 1975	HOU N	—	CIN N	Luis Sanchez minor league P Carlos Alfonso
June 7, 1981	STL N	—	HOU N	Tony Scott
Dec 10, 1985	OAK A	—	STL N	Mike Heath Tim Conroy

Date	Traded To	Traded With	Traded By	In Exchange For

Joaquin Andujar *continued*

Date	Traded To	Traded With	Traded By	In Exchange For
Jan 8, 1988	HOU N	——	OAK A	No compensation (free agent signing)

Norm Angelini

Date	Traded To	Traded With	Traded By	In Exchange For
June 30, 1975	ATL N	Bruce Dal Canton Al Autry	KC A	Ray Sadecki and cash

(Atlanta received Angelini and Autry on September 4.)

John Antonelli

Date	Traded To	Traded With	Traded By	In Exchange For
May 8, 1945	PHI N	Glenn Crawford	STL N	Buster Adams

Johnny Antonelli

Date	Traded To	Traded With	Traded By	In Exchange For
Feb 1, 1954	NY N	Don Liddle Ebba St. Claire Billy Klaus and $50,000.	MIL N	Bobby Thomson Sammy Calderone
Dec 3, 1960	CLE A	Willie Kirkland	SF N	Harvey Kuenn
July 4, 1961	MIL N	——	CLE A	Cash
Oct 11, 1961	NY N	Ken MacKenzie	MIL N	Cash

Luis Aparicio

Date	Traded To	Traded With	Traded By	In Exchange For
Jan 14, 1963	BAL A	Al Smith	CHI A	Hoyt Wilhelm Pete Ward Ron Hansen Dave Nicholson
Nov 29, 1967	CHI A	Russ Snyder John Matias	BAL A	Don Buford Bruce Howard Roger Nelson
Dec 1, 1970	BOS A	——	CHI A	Mike Andrews Luis Alvarado

Luis Aponte

Date	Traded To	Traded With	Traded By	In Exchange For
March 24, 1984	CLE A		BOS A	Minor league Ps Mike Poindexter and Paul Perry

Pete Appleton

Date	Traded To	Traded With	Traded By	In Exchange For
June 10, 1932	BOS A	——	CLE A	Jack Russell
Dec 8, 1939	CHI A	Taffy Wright	WAS A	Gee Walker

Luis Aquino

Date	Traded To	Traded With	Traded By	In Exchange For
July 15, 1987	KC A	——	TOR A	Juan Beniquez

Jim Archer

Date	Traded To	Traded With	Traded By	In Exchange For
Jan 24, 1961	KC A		BAL A	*See Russ Snyder*

Jimmy Archer

Date	Traded To	Traded With	Traded By	In Exchange For
Dec 1917	PIT N	——	CHI N	Cash
Sept 1918	CIN N	——	BKN N	Cash

George Archie

Date	Traded To	Traded With	Traded By	In Exchange For
Sept 10, 1941	STL A		WAS A	Bobby Estalella

Steve Arlin

Date	Traded To	Traded With	Traded By	In Exchange For
June 15, 1974	CLE A		SD N	Brent Strom minor league P Jerry Lee

Tony Armas

Date	Traded To	Traded With	Traded By	In Exchange For
March 15, 1977	OAK A	Dave Giusti Doc Medich Doug Bair Rick Langford Mitchell Page	PIT N	Phil Garner Tommy Helms Chris Batton
Dec 6, 1982	BOS A	Jeff Newman	OAK A	Carney Lansford Garry Hancock minor league P Jerry King

Ed Armbrister

Date	Traded To	Traded With	Traded By	In Exchange For
Nov 29, 1971	CIN N	*See Joe Morgan*	HOU N	——

Charlie Armbruster

Date	Traded To	Traded With	Traded By	In Exchange For
Sept 1, 1907	CHI A	——	BOS A	Cash

Mike Armstrong

Date	Traded To	Traded With	Traded By	In Exchange For
April 4, 1982	KC A	——	SD N	Cash
Dec 7, 1983	NY A	minor league C Duane Dewey	KC A	Steve Balboni Roger Erickson

Harry Arndt

Date	Traded To	Traded With	Traded By	In Exchange For
May 1902	BAL A	——	DET A	Cash

Morrie Arnovich

Date	Traded To	Traded With	Traded By	In Exchange For
June 15, 1940	CIN N	——	PHI N	Johnny Rizzo
Dec 10, 1940	NY N	——	CIN N	Cash

Brad Arnsberg

Date	Traded To	Traded With	Traded By	In Exchange For
Nov 2, 1987	TEX A	——	NY A	Don Slaught

Jerry Arrigo

Date	Traded To	Traded With	Traded By	In Exchange For
Dec 4, 1964	CIN N	——	MIN A	Cesar Tovar
May 20, 1966	NY N	——	CIN N	Cash
Aug 16, 1966	CIN N	——	NY N	Cash
Dec 15, 1969	CHI A	——	CIN N	Angel Bravo

Fernando Arroyo

Date	Traded To	Traded With	Traded By	In Exchange For
Dec 5, 1979	MIN A	——	DET A	Jeff Holly

Luis Arroyo

Date	Traded To	Traded With	Traded By	In Exchange For
May 5, 1956	PIT N	——	STL N	Max Surkont

Rudy Arroyo

Date	Traded To	Traded With	Traded By	In Exchange For
Oct 26, 1972	LA N	minor league P Greg Millikan	STL N	Larry Hisle

Randy Asadoor

Date	Traded To	Traded With	Traded By	In Exchange For
April 6, 1985	SD N	——	TEX A	Mitch Williams

Richie Ashburn

Date	Traded To	Traded With	Traded By	In Exchange For
Jan 11, 1960	CHI N	——	PHI N	John Buzhardt Alvin Dark Jim Woods
Dec 8, 1961	NY N	——	CHI N	Cash

Alan Ashby

Date	Traded To	Traded With	Traded By	In Exchange For
Nov 5, 1976	TOR A	Doug Howard	CLE A	Al Fitzmorris
Nov 27, 1978	HOU N	——	TOR A	Joe Cannon Pedro Hernandez Mark Lemongello

Date	Traded To		Traded With		Traded By		In Exchange For

Tucker Ashford

Date	Traded To		Traded With		Traded By		In Exchange For
Feb 15, 1980	TEX	A	Gaylord Perry minor league P Joe Carroll		SD	N	Willie Montanez
Oct 24, 1980	NY	A	Cash		TEX	A	Roger Holt
Oct 27, 1982	TOR	A	———		NY	A	Cash

(Ashford was returned to the Yankees on April 5, 1983.)

| April 18, 1983 | NY | N | ——— | | NY | A | Minor leaguers P Steve Ray and IF Felix Perdomo |
| April 1, 1984 | KC | A | ——— | | NY | N | Tom Edens |

Bob Aspromonte

| Dec 4, 1968 | ATL | N | ——— | | HOU | N | Marty Martinez |
| Dec 1, 1970 | NY | N | ——— | | ATL | N | Ron Herbel |

Ken Aspromonte

May 1, 1958	WAS	A	———		BOS	A	Lou Berberet
May 15, 1960	CLE	A	———		WAS	A	Pete Whisenant
July 3, 1961	CLE	A	———		LA	A	Waiver price
June 24, 1962	MIL	N	Cash		CLE	A	Bob Hartman
Dec 3, 1962	CHI	N	———		MIL	N	Jim McKnight

Paul Assenmacher

| Aug 24, 1989 | CHI | N | ——— | | ATL | N | Rick Luecken Minor league P Pat Gomez |

Keith Atherton

| May 20, 1986 | MIN | A | ——— | | OAK | A | Cash and player to be named |

(Oakland received P Eric Broersma on May 23, 1985.)

| March 26, 1989 | CLE | A | ——— | | MIN | A | Carmen Castillo |

Bill Atkinson

| Dec 12, 1979 | CHI | A | ——— | | MON | N | Cash |

Toby Atwell

| June 4, 1953 | PIT | N | ——— | | CHI | N | *See Ralph Kiner* |

Rick Auerbach

Oct 27, 1973	LA	N	———		MIL	A	Cash
Feb 7, 1977	NY	N	———		LA	N	Hank Webb minor league P Dick Sander
April 26, 1977	TEX	A	Cash		NY	N	Lenny Randle
June 15, 1977	CIN	N	———		TEX	A	Cash
July 19, 1980	TEX	A	———		CIN	N	Cash

(Auerbach refused to report and was suspended.)

| Dec 12, 1980 | SEA | A | ——— | | TEX | A | *See Rick Honeycutt* |

Don August

| Aug 19, 1986 | MIL | A | Mark Knudson | | HOU | N | Danny Darwin |

Eldon Auker

| Dec 15, 1938 | BOS | A | Jake Wade Chet Morgan | | DET | A | Pinky Higgins Archie McKain |
| Feb 8, 1940 | STL | A | ——— | | BOS | A | Cash |

Jimmy Austin

| Jan 1911 | STL | A | Frank LaPorte | | NY | A | Roy Hartzell |

Al Autry

Date	Traded To		Traded With		Traded By		In Exchange For
June 30, 1975	ATL	N	Bruce Dal Canton Norm Angelini		KC	A	Ray Sadecki and cash

(Atlanta received Angelini and Autry on September 4.)

Chick Autry

| May 1909 | BOS | N | ——— | | CIN | N | Bill Chappelle |
| June 10, 1909 | BOS | N | ——— | | CIN | N | Cash |

Martin Autry

| Feb 28, 1929 | CHI | A | ——— | | CLE | A | Bibb Falk |

Earl Averill

Jan 23, 1959	CHI	N	———		CLE	A	Johnny Briggs Jim Bolger
Aug 13, 1960	CHI	A	———		CHI	N	Minor league C Don Prohovich and cash
Dec 11, 1962	PHI	N	———		LA	A	Jacke Davis

Earl Averill

| June 14, 1939 | DET | A | ——— | | CLE | A | Harry Eisenstat and cash |

Bobby Avila

Dec 2, 1958	BAL	A	———		CLE	A	Russ Heman and $30,000.
May 21, 1959	BOS	A	———		BAL	A	Waiver price
July 21, 1959	MIL	N	———		BOS	A	Waiver price

Ramon Aviles

| April 5, 1978 | PHI | N | ——— | | BOS | A | Cash |
| Oct 20, 1981 | TEX | A | ——— | | PHI | N | Dave Rajsich |

Benny Ayala

| March 30, 1977 | STL | N | ——— | | NY | N | Doug Clarey |
| April 19, 1985 | CLE | A | ——— | | BAL | A | No compensation (free agent signing) |

Doc Ayers

| July 5, 1919 | DET | A | ——— | | WAS | A | Eric Erickson |

Joe Azcue

Dec 15, 1961	KC	A	Ed Charles Manny Jimenez		MIL	N	Bob Shaw Lou Klimchock
May 25, 1963	CLE	A	Dick Howser		KC	A	Doc Edwards and $100,000.
April 19, 1969	BOS	A	———		CLE	A	*See Ken Harrelson*
June 15, 1969	CAL	A	———		BOS	A	Tom Satriano
July 28, 1972	MIL	A	Syd O'Brien		CAL	A	Paul Ratliff Ron Clark

Charlie Babb

| Dec 12, 1903 | NY | N | John Cronin | | BKN | N | Bill Dahlen |

Bob Babcock

| Jan 27, 1983 | SEA | A | ——— | | TEX | A | Vance McHenry |

Loren Babe

| April 27, 1953 | PHI | A | ——— | | NY | A | Cash |
| Dec 16, 1953 | NY | A | *See Harry Byrd* | | PHI | A | ——— |

Date	Traded To		Traded With	Traded By		In Exchange For

Johnny Babich

| Feb 6, 1936 | BOS | N | Gene Moore | BKN | N | Fred Frankhouse |
| Aug 10, 1938 | CIN | N | Tommy Reis Gil English Johnny Riddle Vince DiMaggio and Cash | BOS | N | Eddie Miller |

Wally Backman

| Dec 7, 1988 | MIN | A | Minor league P Mike Santiago | NY | N | Minor league Ps Jeff Bumgarner Steve Gasser Toby Nivens |

Mike Bacsik

| Dec 13, 1978 | MIN | A | —— | TEX | A | Mac Scarce |
| Dec 19, 1980 | SEA | A | —— | MIN | A | Steve Stroughter |

Fred Baczewski

| June 12, 1953 | CIN | N | Bob Kelly | CHI | N | Bubba Church |

Jose Baez

| Oct 22, 1976 | SEA | A | —— | LA | N | Cash |
| June 26, 1978 | STL | N | —— | SEA | A | Mike Potter |

Jim Bagby

| Nov 5, 1922 | PIT | N | —— | CLE | A | Waiver price |

Jim Bagby

Dec 12, 1940	CLE	A	Gene Desautels Gee Walker	BOS	A	Frankie Pytlak Odell Hale Joe Dobson
Dec 12, 1945	BOS	A	——	CLE	A	Vic Johnson and cash
Feb 10, 1947	PIT	N	——	BOS	A	Cash

Stan Bahnsen

Dec 2, 1971	CHI	A	——	NY	A	Rich McKinney
June 15, 1975	OAK	A	Skip Pitlock	CHI	A	Dave Hamilton Chet Lemon
May 22, 1977	MON	N	——	OAK	A	Mike Jorgensen

Scott Bailes

| May 30, 1985 | CLE | A | —— | PIT | N | Johnnie LeMaster |

(Cleveland received Bailes on July 3, 1985.)

Bill Bailey

| Sept 1915 | CHI | F | —— | BAL | F | Jimmy Smith Adam Johnson |

Bob Bailey

Dec 1, 1966	LA	N	Gene Michael	PIT	N	Maury Wills
Oct 21, 1968	MON	N	——	LA	N	Cash
Dec 12, 1975	CIN	N	——	MON	N	Clay Kirby
Sept 19, 1977	BOS	A	——	CIN	N	Minor league P Frank Newcomer and cash

Ed Bailey

April 27, 1961	SF	N	——	CIN	N	Bob Schmidt Don Blasingame Sherman Jones
Dec 3, 1963	MIL	N	See Felipe Alou	SF	N	
Feb 1, 1965	SF	N	——	MIL	N	Billy O'Dell

Ed Bailey continued

| May 29, 1965 | CHI | N | Harvey Kuenn Bob Hendley | SF | N | Dick Bertell Len Gabrielson |
| Feb 15, 1966 | CAL | A | —— | CHI | N | Cash |

Gene Bailey

| May 1920 | BOS | A | —— | BOS | N | Cash |

Mark Bailey

| July 23, 1988 | MON | N | —— | HOU | N | Casey Candaele |
| March 28, 1989 | NY | N | Tom O'Malley | MON | N | Steve Frey |

Sweetbreads Bailey

| May 1921 | BKN | N | —— | CHI | N | Cash |

Bob Bailor

| Dec 12, 1980 | NY | N | —— | TOR | A | Roy Lee Jackson |
| Dec 8, 1983 | LA | N | Carlos Diaz | NY | N | Sid Fernandez Ross Jones |

Harold Baines

| July 29, 1989 | TEX | A | Fred Manrique | CHI | A | Scott Fletcher Sammy Sosa Wilson Alvarez |

Doug Bair

March 15, 1977	OAK	A	——	PIT	N	See Phil Garner
Feb 25, 1978	CIN	N	——	OAK	A	Dave Revering and cash
Sept 10, 1981	STL	N	——	CIN	N	Neil Fiala Joe Edelen
June 22, 1983	DET	A	——	STL	N	Dave Rucker

Doug Baird

June 14, 1917	STL	N	——	PIT	N	Bob Steele
Jan 21, 1919	PHI	N	Stuffy Stewart Gene Packard	STL	N	Milt Stock Pickles Dillhoefer Dixie Davis
July 14, 1919	STL	N	Elmer Jacobs Frank Woodward	PHI	N	Lee Meadows Gene Paulette
Aug 1919	BKN	N	——	STL	N	Cash
July 27, 1920	NY	N	——	BKN	N	Cash

Bill Baker

| May 12, 1941 | PIT | N | —— | CIN | N | Cash |

Bock Baker

| April 23, 1901 | PHI | A | —— | CLE | A | Cash |

Chuck Baker

| Dec 8, 1980 | MIN | A | —— | SD | N | Dave Edwards |

Dave Baker

| Dec 10, 1982 | MIN | A | —— | TOR | A | Don Cooper |

Doug Baker

| Feb 24, 1988 | MIN | A | —— | DET | A | Minor league SS Julius McDougal |

Date	Traded To	Traded With	Traded By		In Exchange For

Dusty Baker

Date	Traded To		Traded With	Traded By		In Exchange For
Nov 17, 1975	LA	N	Ed Goodson	ATL	N	Jimmy Wynn
						Tom Paciorek
						Lee Lacy
						Jerry Royster
April 3, 1984	SF	N	——	LA	N	No compensation
						(free agent signing)
March 24, 1985	OAK	A	——	SF	N	Minor league
						P Ed Puikunas
						Minor league
						C Dan Winters

Floyd Baker

Date	Traded To		Traded With	Traded By		In Exchange For
Dec 30, 1944	CHI	A	——	STL	A	Cash
Oct 24, 1951	WAS	A	——	CHI	A	Willie Miranda
May 12, 1953	BOS	A	——	WAS	A	Cash
July 18, 1954	PHI	N	——	BOS	A	Cash

Frank Baker

Date	Traded To		Traded With	Traded By		In Exchange For
Oct 5, 1971	CAL	A	——	CLE	A	See Alex Johnson

Frank Baker

Date	Traded To		Traded With	Traded By		In Exchange For
April 5, 1973	BAL	A	——	NY	A	Tom Matchick

Frank Baker

Date	Traded To		Traded With	Traded By		In Exchange For
Feb 15, 1916	NY	A	——	PHI	A	$37,500.

Gene Baker

Date	Traded To		Traded With	Traded By		In Exchange For
May 1, 1957	PIT	N	Dee Fondy	CHI	N	Dale Long
						Lee Walls

Howard Baker

Date	Traded To		Traded With	Traded By		In Exchange For
July 1915	NY	N	——	CHI	A	Cash

Jack Baker

Date	Traded To		Traded With	Traded By		In Exchange For
Dec 9, 1977	CLE	A	——	BOS	A	Garry Hancock

Kirtley Baker

Date	Traded To		Traded With	Traded By		In Exchange For
Jan 10, 1900	BOS	N	Shad Barry	WAS	N	Cash
			Bill Dinneen			

Steve Baker

Date	Traded To		Traded With	Traded By		In Exchange For
Sept 2, 1983	STL	N	——	OAK	A	Minor league
						Ps Tom Dozier
						and Jim Strichek

Tom Baker

Date	Traded To		Traded With	Traded By		In Exchange For
June 11, 1937	NY	N	——	BKN	N	Freddie Fitzsimmons
Dec 11, 1938	WAS	A	Jim Carlin	NY	N	Zeke Bonura
			and $20,000.			

John Balaz

Date	Traded To		Traded With	Traded By		In Exchange For
March 3, 1976	BOS	A	Dick Sharon	CAL	A	Dick Drago
			Dave Machemer			

Steve Balboni

Date	Traded To		Traded With	Traded By		In Exchange For
Dec 7, 1983	KC	A	Roger Erickson	NY	A	Mike Armstrong
						minor league
						C Duane Dewey
March 27, 1989	NY	A	——	SEA	A	Minor league
						P Dana Ridenour

Jack Baldschun

Date	Traded To		Traded With	Traded By		In Exchange For
Dec 6, 1965	BAL	A	——	PHI	N	Jackie Brandt
						Darold Knowles
Dec 9, 1965	CIN	N	Milt Pappas	BAL	A	Frank Robinson
			Dick Simpson			

Billy Baldwin

Date	Traded To		Traded With	Traded By		In Exchange For
Dec 12, 1975	NY	N	Mickey Lolich	DET	A	Rusty Staub
						Bill Laxton

Dave Baldwin

Date	Traded To		Traded With	Traded By		In Exchange For
Dec 4, 1969	SEA	A	——	WAS	A	George Brunet

Reggie Baldwin

Date	Traded To		Traded With	Traded By		In Exchange For
Feb 20, 1980	NY	N	——	HOU	N	Minor league
						OF Keith Bodie

Lee Bales

Date	Traded To		Traded With	Traded By		In Exchange For
Oct 13, 1966	HOU	N	See Tom Dukes	ATL	N	——

Neal Ball

Date	Traded To		Traded With	Traded By		In Exchange For
May 1909	CLE	A	——	NY	A	Cash
May 1912	BOS	A	——	CLE	A	Cash

Jay Baller

Date	Traded To		Traded With	Traded By		In Exchange For
Dec 9, 1982	CLE	A	Manny Trillo	PHI	N	Von Hayes
			George Vukovich			
			Julio Franco			
			Jerry Willard			
April 1, 1985	CHI	N	——	CLE	A	Dan Rohn

Win Ballou

Date	Traded To		Traded With	Traded By		In Exchange For
Feb 1926	STL	A	Tom Zachary	WAS	A	Joe Bush
						Jack Tobin

Dave Bancroft

Date	Traded To		Traded With	Traded By		In Exchange For
June 8, 1920	NY	N	——	PHI	N	Art Fletcher
						Bill Hubbell
						and cash
Nov 12, 1923	BOS	N	Casey Stengel	NY	N	Billy Southworth
			Bill Cunningham			Joe Oeschger
			(Bancroft was named Boston manager.)			

Sal Bando

Date	Traded To		Traded With	Traded By		In Exchange For
Nov 19, 1976	MIL	A	——	OAK	A	No compensation
						(free agent signing)

Eddie Bane

Date	Traded To		Traded With	Traded By		In Exchange For
Jan 15, 1980	KC	A	——	CHI	A	Joe Zdeb

Dick Baney

Date	Traded To		Traded With	Traded By		In Exchange For
June 15, 1970	BAL	A	Buzz Stephen	MIL	A	Dave May

Scott Bankhead

Date	Traded To		Traded With	Traded By		In Exchange For
Dec 10, 1986	SEA	A	Mike Kingery	KC	A	Danny Tartabull
			Steve Shields			Rick Luecken

George Banks

Date	Traded To		Traded With	Traded By		In Exchange For
June 15, 1964	CLE	A	Lee Stange	MIN	A	Mudcat Grant

Date	Traded To		Traded With	Traded By		In Exchange For

Alan Bannister

Date	Traded To		Traded With	Traded By		In Exchange For
Dec 10, 1975	CHI	A	Dick Ruthven Roy Thomas	PHI	N	Jim Kaat Mike Buskey
June 13, 1980	CLE	A	———	CHI	A	Ron Pruitt
March 25, 1984	HOU	N	———	CLE	A	Cash
May 25, 1984	TEX	A	———	HOU	N	Mike Richardt

Floyd Bannister

Date	Traded To		Traded With	Traded By		In Exchange For
Dec 8, 1978	SEA	A	———	HOU	N	Craig Reynolds
Dec 13, 1982	CHI	A	———	SEA	A	No compensation (free agent signing)
Dec 10, 1987	KC	A	Dave Cochrane	CHI	A	Melido Perez John Davis Greg Hibbard Minor league P Chuck Mount

Walter Barbare

Date	Traded To		Traded With	Traded By		In Exchange For
Jan 1919	PIT	N	———	BOS	A	Cash
Feb 23, 1921	BOS	N	Billy Southworth Fred Nicholson and $15,000.	PIT	N	Rabbit Maranville

Jap Barbeau

Date	Traded To		Traded With	Traded By		In Exchange For
Aug 19, 1909	STL	N	Alan Storke	PIT	N	Bobby Byrne

Steve Barber

Date	Traded To		Traded With	Traded By		In Exchange For
July 5, 1967	NY	A	———	BAL	A	Ray Barker minor league IFs Chet Trail and Joe Brady and cash
Oct 22, 1973	MIL	A	Clyde Wright Ken Berry Art Kusnyer and cash	CAL	A	Ellie Rodriguez Skip Lockwood Gary Ryerson Ollie Brown Joe Lahoud

Turner Barber

Date	Traded To		Traded With	Traded By		In Exchange For
Jan 2, 1923	BKN	N	———	CHI	N	Cash

George Barclay

Date	Traded To		Traded With	Traded By		In Exchange For
Sept 11, 1904	BOS	N	———	STL	N	Cash

Ray Bare

Date	Traded To		Traded With	Traded By		In Exchange For
April 4, 1975	DET	A	———	STL	N	Cash

Jesse Barfield

Date	Traded To		Traded With	Traded By		In Exchange For
April 30, 1989	NY	A	———	TOR	A	Al Leiter

Len Barker

Date	Traded To		Traded With	Traded By		In Exchange For
Oct 3, 1978	CLE	A	Bobby Bonds	TEX	A	Jim Kern Larvell Blanks
Aug 28, 1983	ATL	N	———	CLE	A	Rick Behenna Brett Butler Brook Jacoby and $150,000.

(Butler and Jacoby were sent to Cleveland at the end of the season.)

Ray Barker

Date	Traded To		Traded With	Traded By		In Exchange For
Nov 16, 1961	CLE	A	Harry Chiti and minor leaguer Art Kay	BAL	A	Johnny Temple
May 10, 1965	NY	A	———	CLE	A	Pedro Gonzalez

Ray Barker continued

Date	Traded To		Traded With	Traded By		In Exchange For
July 5, 1967	BAL	A	minor league IFs Chet Trail and Joe Brady and cash	NY	A	Steve Barber

Mike Barlow

Date	Traded To		Traded With	Traded By		In Exchange For
May 18, 1975	STL	N	Minor league P Steve Staniland	OAK	A	Teddy Martinez
Sept 30, 1975	HOU	N	———	STL	N	Mike Easler
June 6, 1976	CAL	A	Terry Humphrey	HOU	N	Ed Herrmann

Frank Barnes

Date	Traded To		Traded With	Traded By		In Exchange For
May 19, 1960	CHI	A	———	STL	N	Cash
Dec 15, 1961	PHI	N	Andy Carey Cal McLish	CHI	A	Bob Sadowski Taylor Phillips minor league IF Lou Vassie

(Carey refused to report, and the Phillies received McLish in exchange for Vassie to complete the trade on March 24, 1962.)

Jesse Barnes

Date	Traded To		Traded With	Traded By		In Exchange For
Jan 8, 1918	NY	N	Larry Doyle	BOS	N	Buck Herzog
June 7, 1923	BOS	N	Earl Smith	NY	N	Hank Gowdy Mule Watson
Oct 7, 1925	BKN	N	Mickey O'Neil Gus Felix	BOS	N	Zack Taylor Jimmy Johnston Eddie Brown

Red Barnes

Date	Traded To		Traded With	Traded By		In Exchange For
June 13, 1930	CHI	A	———	WAS	A	Dave Harris

Rich Barnes

Date	Traded To		Traded With	Traded By		In Exchange For
Aug 25, 1983	CLE	A	———	CHI	A	Miguel Dilone

Skeeter Barnes

Date	Traded To		Traded With	Traded By		In Exchange For
April 26, 1985	MON	N	———	CIN	N	Max Venable
July 24, 1986	PHI	N	*See Dan Schatzeder*	MON	N	———

Virgil Barnes

Date	Traded To		Traded With	Traded By		In Exchange For
June 15, 1928	BOS	N	Ben Cantwell Al Spohrer Bill Clarkson	NY	N	Joe Genewich

Ed Barney

Date	Traded To		Traded With	Traded By		In Exchange For
Aug 19, 1915	PIT	N	———	NY	A	Waiver price

Salome Barojas

Date	Traded To		Traded With	Traded By		In Exchange For
June 29, 1984	SEA	A	———	CHI	A	Gene Nelson Jerry Don Gleaton

Jim Barr

Date	Traded To		Traded With	Traded By		In Exchange For
Dec 3, 1978	CAL	A	———	SF	N	No compensation (free agent signing)

Steve Barr

Date	Traded To		Traded With	Traded By		In Exchange For
Nov 17, 1975	TEX	A	Juan Beniquez Craig Skok	BOS	A	Ferguson Jenkins

Cuno Barragan

Date	Traded To		Traded With	Traded By		In Exchange For
Dec 13, 1963	LA	N	Jim Brewer	CHI	N	Dick Scott

Date	Traded To	Traded With	Traded By	In Exchange For

German Barranca

Date	Traded To	Traded With	Traded By	In Exchange For
Jan 21, 1981	CIN N	———	KC A	Cesar Geronimo
Sept 7, 1982	DET A	———	CIN N	Cash

Bill Barrett

Date	Traded To	Traded With	Traded By	In Exchange For
May 23, 1929	BOS A	———	CHI A	Doug Taitt
April 30, 1930	WAS A	———	BOS A	Earl Webb

Bob Barrett

Date	Traded To	Traded With	Traded By	In Exchange For
May 10, 1925	BKN N		CHI N	Tommy Griffith

Dick Barrett

Date	Traded To	Traded With	Traded By	In Exchange For
Dec 1933	BOS N	———	PHI A	Cash
July 1943	PHI N	———	CHI N	Cash

Jimmy Barrett

Date	Traded To	Traded With	Traded By	In Exchange For
Feb 1906	CIN N	———	DET A	Waiver price

Johnny Barrett

Date	Traded To	Traded With	Traded By	In Exchange For
June 12, 1946	BOS N	———	PIT N	Chuck Workman

Red Barrett

Date	Traded To	Traded With	Traded By	In Exchange For
May 23, 1945	STL N	$60,000.	BOS N	Mort Cooper
Dec 9, 1946	BOS N	———	STL N	Cash

Tom Barrett

Date	Traded To	Traded With	Traded By	In Exchange For
Dec 11, 1986	PHI N	———	NY A	See Charles Hudson

Jack Barry

Date	Traded To	Traded With	Traded By	In Exchange For
July 2, 1915	BOS A	———	PHI A	$8,000.
June 27, 1919	PHI A	Amos Strunk	BOS A	Braggo Roth / Red Shannon

(Barry refused to report, and retired.)

Shad Barry

Date	Traded To	Traded With	Traded By	In Exchange For
Jan 10, 1900	BOS N	Kirtley Baker / Bill Dinneen	WAS N	Cash
June 1901	PHI N	———	BOS N	Jimmy Slagle
July 20, 1904	CHI N	———	PHI N	Frank Corridon / Jack Sutthoff
May 20, 1905	CIN N	———	CHI N	Cash
July 25, 1906	STL N	Carl Druhot	CIN N	Homer Smoot
July 1908	NY N	———	STL N	Cash

Dick Bartell

Date	Traded To	Traded With	Traded By	In Exchange For
Nov 6, 1930	PHI N	———	PIT N	Tommy Thevenow / Claude Willoughby
Nov 1, 1934	NY N	———	PHI N	Pretzels Pezzullo / Blondy Ryan / Johnny Vergez / George Watkins / and cash
Dec 6, 1938	CHI N	Hank Leiber / Gus Mancuso	NY N	Frank Demaree / Bill Jurges / Ken O'Dea
Dec 6, 1939	DET A	———	CHI N	Billy Rogell

Bob Barton

Date	Traded To	Traded With	Traded By	In Exchange For
Dec 5, 1969	SD N	Ron Herbel / Bobby Etheridge	SF N	Frank Reberger
June 11, 1972	CIN N	———	SD N	Pat Corrales

Eddie Basinski

Date	Traded To	Traded With	Traded By	In Exchange For
Dec 5, 1946	PIT N	———	BKN N	Al Gerheauser

Kevin Bass

Date	Traded To	Traded With	Traded By	In Exchange For
Aug 30, 1982	HOU N	Frank DiPino / Mike Madden / and cash	MIL A	Don Sutton
Nov 16, 1989	SF N	———	HOU N	No compensation (free agent signing)

Randy Bass

Date	Traded To	Traded With	Traded By	In Exchange For
Aug 11, 1980	SD N	———	MON N	John D'Acquisto / and cash
May 17, 1982	TEX A	———	SD N	Cash

John Bateman

Date	Traded To	Traded With	Traded By	In Exchange For
June 14, 1972	PHI N	———	MON N	Tim McCarver

Bud Bates

Date	Traded To	Traded With	Traded By	In Exchange For
Dec 5, 1939	BOS N	———	PHI N	Waiver price

Johnny Bates

Date	Traded To	Traded With	Traded By	In Exchange For
July 16, 1909	PHI N	Charlie Starr	BOS N	Buster Brown / Lew Richie / Dave Shean
Feb 1911	CIN N	———	PHI N	See Dode Paskert
Aug 1914	CHI N	———	CIN N	Elmer Koestner

Kevin Batiste

Date	Traded To	Traded With	Traded By	In Exchange For
Dec 17, 1989	ATL N	Ernie Whitt	TOR A	Minor league P Rick Trlicek

Earl Battey

Date	Traded To	Traded With	Traded By	In Exchange For
April 4, 1960	WAS A	Don Mincher / and $150,000.	CHI A	Roy Sievers

Chris Batton

Date	Traded To	Traded With	Traded By	In Exchange For
March 15, 1977	PIT N	See Phil Garner	OAK A	———

Matt Batts

Date	Traded To	Traded With	Traded By	In Exchange For
May 17, 1951	STL A	Jim Suchecki / Jim McDonald / and $100,000.	BOS A	Les Moss
May 29, 1954	CHI A	———	DET A	Red Wilson
Dec 6, 1954	BAL A	———	CHI A	See Clint Courtney

Hank Bauer

Date	Traded To	Traded With	Traded By	In Exchange For
Dec 11, 1959	KC A	Don Larsen / Norm Siebern / Marv Throneberry	NY A	Roger Maris / Joe DeMaestri / Kent Hadley

Frank Baumann

Date	Traded To	Traded With	Traded By	In Exchange For
Nov 3, 1959	CHI A	———	BOS A	Ron Jackson
Dec 1, 1964	CHI N	———	CHI A	Jimmie Schaffer

Jim Baumer

Date	Traded To	Traded With	Traded By	In Exchange For
May 10, 1961	DET A	———	CIN N	Dick Gernert

Ross Baumgarten

Date	Traded To	Traded With	Traded By	In Exchange For
March 21, 1982	PIT N	Butch Edge	CHI A	Vance Law / Ernie Camacho

Frankie Baumholtz

Date	Traded To	Traded With	Traded By	In Exchange For
June 15, 1949	CHI N	Hank Sauer	CIN N	Harry Walker / Peanuts Lowrey
Dec 9, 1955	PHI N	———	CHI N	Cash

Date	Traded To		Traded With	Traded By		In Exchange For

Ed Bauta

Date	Traded To		Traded With	Traded By		In Exchange For
May 28, 1960	STL	N	Julian Javier	PIT	N	Vinegar Bend Mizell Dick Gray
Aug 5, 1963	NY	N	———	STL	N	Ken MacKenzie

Mike Baxes

Date	Traded To		Traded With	Traded By		In Exchange For
April 12, 1959	NY	A	Bob Martyn	KC	A	Russ Snyder Tommy Carroll

Don Baylor

Date	Traded To		Traded With	Traded By		In Exchange For
April 2, 1976	OAK	A	Mike Torrez Paul Mitchell	BAL	A	Reggie Jackson Ken Holtzman minor leaguer Bill Van Bommell
Nov 16, 1976	CAL	A	———	OAK	A	No compensation (free agent signing)
Dec 1, 1982	NY	A	———	CAL	A	No compensation (free agent signing)
March 28, 1986	BOS	A	———	NY	A	Mike Easler
Sept 1, 1987	MIN	A	———	BOS	A	Minor league Enrique Rios

Bill Bayne

Date	Traded To		Traded With	Traded By		In Exchange For
Nov 22, 1928	BOS	A	———	CLE	A	Cash

Bob Beall

Date	Traded To		Traded With	Traded By		In Exchange For
Dec 4, 1973	ATL	N	———	PHI	N	Gil Garrido

Belve Bean

Date	Traded To		Traded With	Traded By		In Exchange For
May 14, 1935	WAS	A	———	CLE	A	Lefty Stewart

Billy Bean

Date	Traded To		Traded With	Traded By		In Exchange For
July 17, 1989	LA	N	———	DET	A	Minor league OF Steve Green Minor league 1B-OF Domingo Michel

Billy Beane

Date	Traded To		Traded With	Traded By		In Exchange For
Jan 16, 1986	MIN	A	Bill Latham Joe Klink	NY	N	Tim Teufel Minor league OF Pat Crosby
March 24, 1988	DET	A	———	MIN	A	Balvino Galvez

Dave Beard

Date	Traded To		Traded With	Traded By		In Exchange For
Nov 21, 1983	SEA	A	Bob Kearney	OAK	A	Bill Caudill Darrel Akerfelds

Gene Bearden

Date	Traded To		Traded With	Traded By		In Exchange For
Dec 20, 1946	CLE	A	Hal Peck Al Gettel	NY	A	Sherm Lollar Ray Mack
Aug 2, 1950	WAS	A	———	CLE	A	Waiver price
April 26, 1951	DET	A	———	WAS	A	Waiver price
Feb 14, 1952	STL	A	Bob Cain Dick Kryhoski	DET	A	Dick Littlefield Ben Taylor Cliff Mapes
March 18, 1953	CHI	A	———	STL	A	Waiver price

Gary Beare

Date	Traded To		Traded With	Traded By		In Exchange For
March 28, 1979	PHI	N	———	MIL	A	Danny Boitano

Jim Beattie

Date	Traded To		Traded With	Traded By		In Exchange For
Nov 1, 1979	SEA	A	Rick Anderson Juan Beniquez Jerry Narron	NY	A	Ruppert Jones Jim Lewis

Blaine Beatty

Date	Traded To		Traded With	Traded By		In Exchange For
Dec 8, 1987	NY	N	Minor league P Greg Talamantez	BAL	A	Doug Sisk

Jim Beauchamp

Date	Traded To		Traded With	Traded By		In Exchange For
Feb 17, 1964	HOU	N	Chuck Taylor	STL	N	Carl Warwick
May 13, 1965	MIL	N	Ken Johnson	HOU	N	Lee Maye
Oct 10, 1967	CIN	N	Mack Jones Jay Ritchie	ATL	N	Deron Johnson
June 13, 1970	STL	N	Leon McFadden	HOU	N	George Culver
Oct 18, 1971	NY	N	———	STL	N	See Jim Bibby

Ginger Beaumont

Date	Traded To		Traded With	Traded By		In Exchange For
Dec 1906	BOS	N	Claude Ritchey Patsy Flaherty	PIT	N	Ed Abbaticchio
Feb 1910	CHI	N	———	BOS	N	Fred Liese

Johnny Beazley

Date	Traded To		Traded With	Traded By		In Exchange For
April 18, 1947	BOS	N	———	STL	N	Cash

Clyde Beck

Date	Traded To		Traded With	Traded By		In Exchange For
Jan 1931	CIN	N	———	CHI	N	Waiver price

Fred Beck

Date	Traded To		Traded With	Traded By		In Exchange For
March 1911	CIN	N	———	BOS	N	Cash
July 15, 1911	PHI	N	Bill Burns	CIN	N	Bert Humphries

Heinie Beckendorf

Date	Traded To		Traded With	Traded By		In Exchange For
April 1910	WAS	A	———	DET	A	Cash

Beals Becker

Date	Traded To		Traded With	Traded By		In Exchange For
June 1908	BOS	N	———	PIT	N	Cash
Dec 1909	NY	N	———	BOS	N	Buck Herzog
June 5, 1913	PHI	N	Josh Devore	CIN	N	John Dodge Red Nelson

Heinz Becker

Date	Traded To		Traded With	Traded By		In Exchange For
May 1946	CLE	A	———	CHI	N	Mickey Rocco

Glenn Beckert

Date	Traded To		Traded With	Traded By		In Exchange For
Nov 7, 1973	SD	N	Bobby Fenwick	CHI	N	Jerry Morales

Jake Beckley

Date	Traded To		Traded With	Traded By		In Exchange For
Feb 1904	STL	N	———	CIN	N	Cash

Joe Beckwith

Date	Traded To		Traded With	Traded By		In Exchange For
Dec 7, 1983	KC	A	———	LA	N	Minor leaguers C Joe Szekely P Jose Torres and P John Serritella

Steve Bedrosian

Date	Traded To		Traded With	Traded By		In Exchange For
Dec 10, 1985	PHI	N	Milt Thompson	ATL	N	Ozzie Virgil Pete Smith
June 18, 1989	SF	N	Minor league IF Rick Parker	PHI	N	Dennis Cook Terry Mulholland Charlie Hayes

Fred Beebe

Date	Traded To		Traded With	Traded By		In Exchange For
July 1, 1906	STL	N	Pete Noonan and cash	CHI	N	Jack Taylor

Date	Traded To		Traded With	Traded By		In Exchange For

Fred Beebe *continued*

Date	Traded To		Traded With	Traded By		In Exchange For
Feb 1910	CIN	N	Alan Storke	STL	N	Miller Huggins
						Rebel Oakes
						Frank Corridon
Feb 1911	PHI	N	*See Dode Paskert*	CIN	N	——

Fred Beene

| Dec 1, 1970 | SD | N | —— | BAL | A | *See Pat Dobson* |
| April 27, 1974 | CLE | A | —— | NY | A | *See Chris Chambliss* |

Joe Beggs

| Jan 4, 1940 | CIN | N | —— | NY | A | Lee Grissom |
| June 7, 1947 | NY | N | —— | CIN | N | Babe Young |

Rick Behenna

Aug 28, 1983	CLE	A	Brett Butler	ATL	N	Len Barker
			Brook Jacoby			
			and $150,000.			

(Butler and Jacoby were sent to Cleveland at the end of the season.)

Mel Behney

| March 27, 1973 | BOS | A | —— | CIN | N | Phil Gagliano |
| | | | | | | Andy Kosco |

Hank Behrman

May 3, 1947	PIT	N	Kirby Higbe	BKN	N	Al Gionfriddo
			Cal McLish			and $100,000.
			Gene Mauch			
			Dixie Howell			
June 14, 1947	BKN	N	——	PIT	N	Cash
Feb 26, 1949	NY	N	——	BKN	N	Cash

Mark Belanger

| Dec 11, 1981 | LA | N | —— | BAL | A | No compensation |
| | | | | | | (free agent signing) |

Wayne Belardi

June 9, 1954	DET	A	——	BKN	N	Charlie Kress
						Johnny Bucha
						Ernie Nevel
						and cash
Dec 5, 1956	KC	A	*See Ned Garver*	DET	A	——
Feb 19, 1957	NY	A	——	KC	A	*See Billy Hunter*

Tim Belcher

| Aug 30, 1987 | LA | N | —— | OAK | A | Rick Honeycutt |

Bo Belinsky

| Dec 3, 1964 | PHI | N | —— | LA | A | Costen Shockley |
| | | | | | | Rudy May |

Beau Bell

May 13, 1939	DET	A	Bobo Newsom	STL	A	Vern Kennedy
			Red Kress			Bob Harris
			Jim Walkup			George Gill
						Roxie Lawson
						Chet Laabs
						Mark Christman
Jan 20, 1940	CLE	A	——	DET	A	Bruce Campbell

Buddy Bell

Dec 8, 1978	TEX	A	——	CLE	A	Toby Harrah
July 19, 1985	CIN	N	——	TEX	A	Jeff Russell
						Duane Walker

Buddy Bell *continued*

| June 19, 1988 | HOU | N | —— | CIN | N | player to be named |

(Cincinnati received P Carl Grovam on October 20, 1988.)

Gary Bell

June 4, 1967	BOS	A	——	CLE	A	Tony Horton
						Don Demeter
June 8, 1969	CHI	A	——	SEA	A	Bob Locker

Gus Bell

Oct 14, 1952	CIN	N	——	PIT	N	Cal Abrams
						Joe Rossi
						Gail Henley
Nov 28, 1961	MIL	N	Cash	NY	N	Frank Thomas

(Milwaukee received Bell on May 21, 1962.)

Jay Bell

| March 25, 1989 | PIT | N | —— | CLE | A | Felix Fermin |
| | | | | | | Denny Gonzalez |

(Completion of deal in which Cleveland acquired Gonzalez on November 28, 1988 for a player to be named.)

Juan Bell

| Dec 4, 1988 | BAL | A | Brian Holton | LA | N | Eddie Murray |
| | | | Ken Howell | | | |

Kevin Bell

March 27, 1981	OAK	A	Tony Phillips	SD	N	Bob Lacey
			minor league			minor league
			P Eric Mustard			P Ray Moretti

Les Bell

March 25, 1928	BOS	N	——	STL	N	Andy High
						and $25,000.
Oct 29, 1929	CHI	N	——	BOS	N	Waiver price

Terry Bell

| May 21, 1986 | KC | A | —— | SEA | A | Mark Huismann |
| Aug 30, 1987 | ATL | N | —— | KC | A | Gene Garber |

Zeke Bella

| Aug 22, 1958 | KC | A | Cash | NY | A | Murry Dickson |

Bob Belloir

| June 7, 1975 | ATL | N | Blue Moon Odom | CLE | A | Roric Harrison |

Chief Bender

| Feb 10, 1916 | PHI | N | —— | BAL | F | Cash |

Ray Benge

Dec 15, 1932	BKN	N	$15,000.	PHI	N	Cy Moore
						Mickey Finn
						Jack Warner
Dec 12, 1935	BOS	N	Tony Cuccinello	BKN	N	Ed Brandt
			Al Lopez			Randy Moore
			Bobby Reis			
Aug 4, 1936	PHI	N	——	BOS	N	Fabian Kowalik

Juan Beniquez

Nov 17, 1975	TEX	A	Steve Barr	BOS	A	Ferguson Jenkins
			Craig Skok			
Nov 10, 1978	NY	A	*See Dave Righetti*	TEX	A	——

Date	Traded To	Traded With	Traded By	In Exchange For

Juan Beniquez *continued*

Date	Traded To	Traded With	Traded By	In Exchange For
Nov 1, 1979	SEA A	Jim Beattie Rick Anderson Jerry Narron	NY A	Ruppert Jones Jim Lewis
Dec 29, 1980	CAL A	——	SEA A	No compensation (free agent signing)
Jan 28, 1986	BAL A	——	CAL A	No compensation (free agent signing)
Dec 17, 1986	KC A	——	BAL A	Minor league SS Joe Jarrell Minor league P Jimmy Daniels
July 15, 1987	TOR A	——	KC A	Luis Aquino

Dennis Bennett

Date	Traded To	Traded With	Traded By	In Exchange For
Nov 29, 1964	BOS A	——	PHI N	Dick Stuart
June 24, 1967	NY N	——	BOS A	Al Yates and cash

Joe Bennett

Date	Traded To	Traded With	Traded By	In Exchange For
May 1921	STL A	——	CHI A	Cash

Jack Bentley

Date	Traded To	Traded With	Traded By	In Exchange For
Dec 30, 1925	PHI N	Wayland Dean	NY N	Jimmy Ring
Sept 15, 1926	NY N	——	PHI N	Waiver price

Al Benton

Date	Traded To	Traded With	Traded By	In Exchange For
Jan 1938	DET A	——	PHI A	Cash
April 20, 1949	CLE A	——	DET A	Cash

Butch Benton

Date	Traded To	Traded With	Traded By	In Exchange For
April 6, 1981	CHI N	——	NY N	Cash

Larry Benton

Date	Traded To	Traded With	Traded By	In Exchange For
July 30, 1922	BOS N	Fred Toney and $100,000.	NY N	Hugh McQuillan

(Toney refused to report and remained Giants' property.)

Date	Traded To	Traded With	Traded By	In Exchange For
June 12, 1927	NY N	Zack Taylor Herb Thomas	BOS N	Hugh McQuillan Kent Greenfield Doc Farrell
May 21, 1930	CIN N	——	NY N	Hughie Critz

Rube Benton

Date	Traded To	Traded With	Traded By	In Exchange For
Aug 19, 1915	NY N	——	CIN N	$3,000.
July 30, 1922	CIN N	——	NY N	Cash

Todd Benzinger

Date	Traded To	Traded With	Traded By	In Exchange For
Dec 13, 1988	CIN N	Jeff Sellers player to be named	BOS A	Nick Esasky Rob Murphy

(Cincinnati received P Luis Vasquez on January 12, 1989.)

Johnny Berardino

Date	Traded To	Traded With	Traded By	In Exchange For
Nov 22, 1947	WAS A	——	STL A	Gerry Priddy

(Berardino announced his retirement to go into movies. Commissioner Chandler cancelled the trade. Berardino then unretired.)

Date	Traded To	Traded With	Traded By	In Exchange For
Dec 9, 1947	CLE A	——	STL A	Catfish Metkovich and $50,000.

(Metkovich was returned to Cleveland because of a broken finger and the St. Louis Browns received another $15,000 to complete the trade.)

Date	Traded To	Traded With	Traded By	In Exchange For
Aug 18, 1952	PIT N	minor league P Charlie Sipple and $50,000.	CLE A	George Strickland Ted Wilks

Lou Berberet

Date	Traded To	Traded With	Traded By	In Exchange For
Feb 8, 1956	WAS A	*See Whitey Herzog*	NY A	——
May 1, 1958	BOS A	——	WAS A	Ken Aspromonte

Lou Berberet *continued*

Date	Traded To	Traded With	Traded By	In Exchange For
Dec 2, 1958	DET A	——	BOS A	Herb Moford

Juan Berenguer

Date	Traded To	Traded With	Traded By	In Exchange For
March 31, 1981	KC A	——	NY N	Marvell Wynne minor league P John Skinner
Aug 8, 1981	TOR A	——	KC A	Cash
Oct 7, 1985	SF N	Bob Melvin Scott Medvin	DET A	Dave LaPoint Matt Nokes Eric King

(San Francisco received Medvin on Dec. 11, 1985.)

Date	Traded To	Traded With	Traded By	In Exchange For
Jan 11, 1987	MIN A	——	SF N	No compensation (free agent signing)

Bruce Berenyi

Date	Traded To	Traded With	Traded By	In Exchange For
June 15, 1984	NY N	——	CIN N	Jay Tibbs Eddie Williams Minor league P Matt Bullinger

Moe Berg

Date	Traded To	Traded With	Traded By	In Exchange For
Aug 1925	CHI A	——	BKN N	Cash
April 2, 1931	CLE A	——	CHI A	Waiver price

Bill Bergen

Date	Traded To	Traded With	Traded By	In Exchange For
Feb 1904	BKN N	——	CIN N	Cash

Boze Berger

Date	Traded To	Traded With	Traded By	In Exchange For
April 1937	CHI A	——	CLE A	Cash
Dec 21, 1938	BOS A	——	CHI A	Eric McNair
Dec 26, 1939	BKN N	——	BOS A	Waiver price

Wally Berger

Date	Traded To	Traded With	Traded By	In Exchange For
June 15, 1937	NY N	——	BOS N	Frank Gabler and $35,000.
June 6, 1938	CIN N	——	NY N	Alex Kampouris

Dave Bergman

Date	Traded To	Traded With	Traded By	In Exchange For
June 15, 1977	HOU N	Randy Niemann Mike Fischlin	NY A	Cliff Johnson

(Houston received Bergman on November 23.)

Date	Traded To	Traded With	Traded By	In Exchange For
April 20, 1981	SF N	Jeffrey Leonard	HOU N	Mike Ivie
March 24, 1984	PHI N	——	SF N	Alejandro Sanchez
March 24, 1984	DET A	Guillermo Hernandez	PHI N	John Wockenfuss Glenn Wilson

Dwight Bernard

Date	Traded To	Traded With	Traded By	In Exchange For
Oct 26, 1979	MIL A	——	NY N	Mark Bomback

Tony Bernazard

Date	Traded To	Traded With	Traded By	In Exchange For
Dec 12, 1980	CHI A	——	MON N	Rich Wortham
June 15, 1983	SEA A	——	CHI A	Julio Cruz
Dec 7, 1983	CLE A	——	SEA A	Gorman Thomas Jack Perconte
July 15, 1987	OAK A	——	CLE A	Darrel Akerfelds Brian Dorsett

Bill Bernhard

Date	Traded To	Traded With	Traded By	In Exchange For
June 1902	CLE A	——	PHI A	Ossee Schreckengost Frank Bonner

Juan Bernhardt

Date	Traded To	Traded With	Traded By	In Exchange For
July 6, 1979	CHI A	——	SEA A	Rich Hinton

Date	Traded To		Traded With	Traded By		In Exchange For

Dale Berra

Date	Traded To		Traded With	Traded By		In Exchange For
Dec 20, 1984	NY	A	Jay Buhner	PIT	N	Steve Kemp Tim Foli and $400,000.

Ray Berres

Date	Traded To		Traded With	Traded By		In Exchange For
June 14, 1940	BOS	N	$40,000.	PIT	N	Al Lopez
Feb 6, 1942	NY	N	——	BOS	N	Cash

Charlie Berry

Date	Traded To		Traded With	Traded By		In Exchange For
April 29, 1932	CHI	A	——	BOS	A	Bennie Tate Smead Jolley Cliff Watwood
Dec 12, 1933	PHI	A	$20,000.	CHI	A	George Earnshaw Johnny Pasek

Joe Berry

Date	Traded To		Traded With	Traded By		In Exchange For
May 1946	CLE	A	——	PHI	A	Cash

Ken Berry

Date	Traded To		Traded With	Traded By		In Exchange For
Nov 30, 1970	CAL	A	Syd O'Brien Billy Wynne	CHI	A	Jay Johnstone Tom Egan Tom Bradley
Oct 22, 1973	MIL	A	Clyde Wright Steve Barber Art Kusnyer and cash	CAL	A	Ellie Rodriguez Skip Lockwood Gary Ryerson Ollie Brown Joe Lahoud

Neil Berry

Date	Traded To		Traded With	Traded By		In Exchange For
Oct 27, 1952	STL	A	Cliff Mapes and $25,000.	DET	A	Rufus Crawford
Sept 1, 1953	CHI	A	——	STL	A	Waiver price
Feb 5, 1954	BAL	A	Sam Mele	CHI	A	Johnny Groth Johnny Lipon

Frank Bertaina

Date	Traded To		Traded With	Traded By		In Exchange For
May 29, 1967	WAS	A	Mike Epstein	BAL	A	Pete Richert
June 16, 1969	BAL	A	——	WAS	A	Minor league P Paul Campbell
Aug 14, 1970	STL	N	——	BAL	A	Cash

Dick Bertell

Date	Traded To		Traded With	Traded By		In Exchange For
May 29, 1965	SF	N	Len Gabrielson	CHI	N	Harvey Kuenn Ed Bailey Bob Hendley

Reno Bertoia

Date	Traded To		Traded With	Traded By		In Exchange For
Dec 6, 1958	WAS	A	——	DET	A	See Eddie Yost
June 1, 1961	KC	A	Paul Giel	MIN	A	Bill Tuttle
(Giel was returned to Minnesota for a cash payment.)					
Aug 2, 1961	DET	A	Gerry Staley	KC	A	Ozzie Virgil Bill Fischer

Bob Bescher

Date	Traded To		Traded With	Traded By		In Exchange For
Dec 12, 1913	NY	N	——	CIN	N	Buck Herzog Grover Hartley
(Hartley jumped to the Federal League and Herzog was made Cincinnati manager.)					

Karl Best

Date	Traded To		Traded With	Traded By		In Exchange For
June 22, 1987	DET	A	——	SEA	A	Bryan Kelly
March 28, 1988	MIN	A	——	DET	A	Don Schulze

Kurt Bevacqua

Date	Traded To		Traded With	Traded By		In Exchange For
May 8, 1971	CLE	A	——	CIN	N	Buddy Bradford

Kurt Bevacqua *continued*

Date	Traded To		Traded With	Traded By		In Exchange For
Nov 2, 1972	KC	A	——	CLE	A	Mike Hedlund
Dec 4, 1973	PIT	N	Ed Kirkpatrick minor league 1B Winston Cole	KC	A	Nellie Briles Fernando Gonzalez
July 8, 1974	KC	A	——	PIT	N	Minor league IF Cal Meier and cash
March 6, 1975	MIL	A	——	KC	A	Cash
Oct 22, 1976	SEA	A	——	MIL	A	Cash
Oct 25, 1978	SD	N	Mike Hargrove Bill Fahey	TEX	A	Oscar Gamble Dave Roberts and $300,000.
Aug 5, 1980	PIT	N	Mark Lee	SD	N	Rick Lancellotti Luis Salazar

Hal Bevan

Date	Traded To		Traded With	Traded By		In Exchange For
May 3, 1952	PHI	A	——	BOS	A	Waiver price

Bill Bevens

Date	Traded To		Traded With	Traded By		In Exchange For
Jan 17, 1949	CHI	A	——	NY	A	Cash
(Bevens was returned to New York Yankees on March 28, 1949.)					

Monte Beville

Date	Traded To		Traded With	Traded By		In Exchange For
July 25, 1904	DET	A	——	NY	A	Frank McManus

Buddy Biancalana

Date	Traded To		Traded With	Traded By		In Exchange For
July 26, 1987	HOU	N	——	KC	A	Minor league Mel Stottlemyre Jr.

Jim Bibby

Date	Traded To		Traded With	Traded By		In Exchange For
Oct 18, 1971	STL	N	Art Shamsky Rich Folkers Charles Hudson	NY	N	Jim Beauchamp Chuck Taylor Harry Parker Tom Coulter
June 6, 1973	TEX	A	——	STL	N	Mike Nagy John Wockenfuss
June 13, 1975	CLE	A	Jackie Brown Rick Waits and $100,000.	TEX	A	Gaylord Perry
March 15, 1978	PIT	N	——	CLE	A	No compensation (free agent signing)
Feb 7, 1984	TEX	A	——	PIT	N	No compensation (free agent signing)

Vern Bickford

Date	Traded To		Traded With	Traded By		In Exchange For
Feb 10, 1954	BAL	A	——	MIL	N	Charlie White and $10,000.

Mike Bielecki

Date	Traded To		Traded With	Traded By		In Exchange For
March 31, 1988	CHI	N	——	PIT	N	Minor league P Mike Curtis

Elliott Bigelow

Date	Traded To		Traded With	Traded By		In Exchange For
Dec 15, 1928	BOS	A	Milt Gaston Hod Lisenbee Bobby Reeves Grant Gillis	WAS	A	Buddy Myer

Larry Biittner

Date	Traded To		Traded With	Traded By		In Exchange For
Dec 20, 1973	MON	N	——	TEX	A	Pat Jarvis
May 17, 1976	CHI	N	Steve Renko	MON	N	Andre Thornton
Jan 8, 1981	CIN	N	——	CHI	N	No compensation (free agent signing)

Dann Bilardello

Date	Traded To		Traded With	Traded By		In Exchange For
Dec 19, 1985	MON	N	——	CIN	N	See Bill Gullickson

Date	Traded To	Traded With	Traded By	In Exchange For

Dann Bilardello *continued*

Date	Traded To	Traded With	Traded By	In Exchange For
July 23, 1987	KC A	——	PIT N	Cash

Steve Bilko

Date	Traded To	Traded With	Traded By	In Exchange For
April 30, 1954	CHI N	——	STL N	$12,500.
June 15, 1958	LA N	Johnny Klippstein	CIN N	Don Newcombe

Jack Billingham

Date	Traded To	Traded With	Traded By	In Exchange For
Jan 22, 1969	HOU N	Jesus Alou Donn Clendenon Skip Guinn and $100,000.	MON N	Rusty Staub

(Clendenon refused to report, and Houston sent Billingham, Guinn, and Cash on April 8, 1969.)

Date	Traded To	Traded With	Traded By	In Exchange For
Nov 29, 1971	CIN N	*See Joe Morgan*	HOU N	——
March 6, 1978	DET A	——	CIN N	George Cappuzzello minor league OF John Valle
May 12, 1980	BOS A	——	DET A	Cash

Dick Billings

Date	Traded To	Traded With	Traded By	In Exchange For
Aug 12, 1974	STL N	——	TEX A	Cash

Josh Billings

Date	Traded To	Traded With	Traded By	In Exchange For
March 1919	STL A	——	CLE A	Les Nunamaker

George Binks

Date	Traded To	Traded With	Traded By	In Exchange For
Feb 14, 1947	PHI A	——	WAS A	Lou Knerr
June 4, 1948	STL A	$20,000.	PHI A	Ray Coleman

Doug Bird

Date	Traded To	Traded With	Traded By	In Exchange For
April 3, 1979	PHI N	——	KC A	Todd Cruz
June 12, 1981	CHI N	Mike Griffin and $400,000.	NY A	Rick Reuschel
Dec 10, 1982	BOS A	——	CHI N	Chuck Rainey

Ralph Birkofer

Date	Traded To	Traded With	Traded By	In Exchange For
Dec 4, 1936	BKN N	Cookie Lavagetto	PIT N	Ed Brandt

Babe Birrer

Date	Traded To	Traded With	Traded By	In Exchange For
April 5, 1956	BAL A	——	DET A	Waiver price

Tim Birtsas

Date	Traded To	Traded With	Traded By	In Exchange For
Dec 8, 1984	OAK A	——	NY A	*See Rickey Henderson*
Dec 8, 1987	CIN N	——	OAK A	*See Dave Parker*

John Bischooff

Date	Traded To	Traded With	Traded By	In Exchange For
July 11, 1925	BOS A	——	CHI A	Cash

Max Bishop

Date	Traded To	Traded With	Traded By	In Exchange For
Dec 12, 1933	BOS A	Lefty Grove Rube Walberg	PHI A	Bob Kline Rabbit Warstler and $125,000.

Rivington Bisland

Date	Traded To	Traded With	Traded By	In Exchange For
March 1913	STL A	——	PIT N	Waiver price

Hi Bithorn

Date	Traded To	Traded With	Traded By	In Exchange For
Jan 25, 1947	PIT N	——	CHI N	Cash
March 22, 1947	CHI A	——	PIT N	Waiver price

Jeff Bittiger

Date	Traded To	Traded With	Traded By	In Exchange For
Jan 16, 1986	PHI N	*See Ronn Reynolds*	NY N	——
Nov 9, 1989	LA N	——	CHI A	Tracy Woodson

George Bjorkman

Date	Traded To	Traded With	Traded By	In Exchange For
March 16, 1983	HOU N	——	STL N	Minor league P Jeff Meadows
Feb 24, 1984	MON N	——	HOU N	Tom Wieghaus

(Montreal received Bjorkman on March 26, 1984.)

Bill Black

Date	Traded To	Traded With	Traded By	In Exchange For
Aug 14, 1952	DET A	——	STL A	*See Vic Wertz*

Bud Black

Date	Traded To	Traded With	Traded By	In Exchange For
Oct 23, 1981	KC A	——	SEA A	Manny Castillo
June 3, 1988	CLE A	——	KC A	Pat Tabler

Don Black

Date	Traded To	Traded With	Traded By	In Exchange For
Oct 2, 1945	CLE A	——	PHI A	Cash

Joe Black

Date	Traded To	Traded With	Traded By	In Exchange For
June 9, 1955	CIN N	——	BKN N	Bob Borkowski and cash

Earl Blackburn

Date	Traded To	Traded With	Traded By	In Exchange For
June 1912	CIN N	——	PIT N	Cash

Lena Blackburne

Date	Traded To	Traded With	Traded By	In Exchange For
Feb 1919	BOS N	——	CIN N	Wally Rehg
July 9, 1919	PHI N	——	BOS N	Cash

Ewell Blackwell

Date	Traded To	Traded With	Traded By	In Exchange For
Aug 28, 1952	NY A	——	CIN N	Jim Greengrass Johnny Schmitz Ernie Nevel Bob Marquis and $35,000.
March 30, 1955	KC A	Dick Kryhoski Tom Gorman	NY A	$50,000.

Tim Blackwell

Date	Traded To	Traded With	Traded By	In Exchange For
April 19, 1976	PHI N	——	BOS A	Cash
June 15, 1977	MON N	Wayne Twitchell	PHI N	Barry Foote Dan Warthen
Jan 14, 1982	MON N	——	CHI N	No compensation (free agent signing)

Rick Bladt

Date	Traded To	Traded With	Traded By	In Exchange For
Jan 20, 1977	BAL A	Elliott Maddox	NY A	Paul Blair

George Blaeholder

Date	Traded To	Traded With	Traded By	In Exchange For
May 21, 1935	PHI A	——	STL A	Ed Coleman Sugar Cain
Jan 27, 1936	CLE A	——	PHI A	Waiver price

Dennis Blair

Date	Traded To	Traded With	Traded By	In Exchange For
July 14, 1977	BAL A	——	MON N	Fred Holdsworth

Paul Blair

Date	Traded To	Traded With	Traded By	In Exchange For
Jan 20, 1977	NY A	——	BAL A	Elliott Maddox Rick Bladt

Date	Traded To	Traded With	Traded By	In Exchange For

Sheriff Blake

Date	Traded To		Traded With	Traded By		In Exchange For
July 27, 1931	PHI	N	——	CHI	N	Waiver price

Johnny Blanchard

| May 3, 1965 | KC | A | Rollie Sheldon | NY | A | Doc Edwards |
| Sept 9, 1965 | MIL | N | —— | KC | A | Cash |

Gil Blanco

| June 10, 1966 | KC | A | Roger Repoz | NY | A | Fred Talbot |
| | | | Bill Stafford | | | Billy Bryan |

Ossie Blanco

Nov 30, 1970	CHI	N	Jose Ortiz	CHI	A	Pat Jacquez
						Dave Lemonds
						Roe Skidmore

Kevin Blankenship

| Sept 29, 1988 | CHI | N | —— | ATL | N | *See Jody Davis* |

Larvell Blanks

Dec 12, 1975	CHI	A	Ralph Garr	ATL	N	Ken Henderson
						Dick Ruthven
						Danny Osborn
Dec 12, 1975	CLE	A	——	CHI	A	Jack Brohamer
Oct 3, 1978	TEX	A	Jim Kern	CLE	A	Bobby Bonds
						Len Barker
Dec 6, 1979	ATL	N	Doyle Alexander	TEX	A	Adrian Devine
			and $50,000.			Pepe Frias

Don Blasingame

Dec 15, 1959	SF	N	——	STL	N	Daryl Spencer
						Leon Wagner
April 27, 1961	CIN	N	Bob Schmidt	SF	N	Ed Bailey
			Sherman Jones			
July 1, 1963	WAS	A	——	CIN	N	Cash
Aug 22, 1966	KC	A	——	WAS	A	Cash

Wade Blasingame

| June 15, 1967 | HOU | N | —— | ATL | N | Claude Raymond |
| June 6, 1972 | NY | A | —— | HOU | N | Cash |

Steve Blateric

| Sept 16, 1972 | NY | A | —— | CIN | N | Cash |
| Dec 12, 1973 | CLE | A | —— | CIN | N | Roger Freed |

Johnny Blatnik

| April 27, 1950 | STL | N | —— | PHI | N | Ken Johnson |

Gary Blaylock

| July 26, 1959 | NY | A | —— | STL | N | Waiver price |

Curt Blefary

Dec 4, 1968	HOU	N	Minor leaguer	BAL	A	Mike Cuellar
			John Mason			Enzo Hernandez
						Minor League
						IF Elijah Johnson
Dec 4, 1969	NY	A	——	HOU	N	Joe Pepitone
May 26, 1971	OAK	A	——	NY	A	Rob Gardner
May 17, 1972	SD	N	Mike Kilkenny	OAK	A	Ollie Brown
			minor league			
			OF Greg Schubert			

Ron Blomberg

| Nov 17, 1977 | CHI | A | —— | NY | A | No compensation |
| | | | | | | (free agent signing) |

Jimmy Bloodworth

Dec 12, 1941	DET	A	Doc Cramer	WAS	A	Frank Croucher
						Bruce Campbell
Dec 12, 1946	PIT	N	——	DET	A	Cash
May 10, 1950	PHI	N	——	CIN	N	Cash

Mike Blowers

| Aug 29, 1989 | NY | A | —— | MON | N | John Candelaria |

Bert Blue

| July 1908 | PHI | A | —— | STL | A | Syd Smith |

Lu Blue

Dec 2, 1927	STL	A	Heinie Manush	DET	A	Chick Galloway
						Elam Vangilder
						Harry Rice
April 3, 1931	CHI	A	——	STL	A	$15,000.

Vida Blue

March 15, 1978	SF	N	——	OAK	A	Gary Alexander
						Gary Thomasson
						Dave Heaverlo
						Alan Wirth
						John Henry Johnson
						Phil Huffman
						Mario Guerrero
						and $390,000.
March 30, 1982	KC	A	Bob Tufts	SF	N	Renie Martin
						Craig Chamberlain
						Atlee Hammaker
						Brad Wellman

Otto Bluege

| Dec 20, 1933 | PHI | N | Irv Jeffries | CIN | N | Mark Koenig |

Jim Bluejacket

| Feb 10, 1916 | CIN | N | —— | BKN | F | Cash |

Bert Blyleven

June 1, 1976	TEX	A	Danny Thompson	MIN	A	Bill Singer
						Roy Smalley
						Mike Cubbage
						Jim Gideon
						and $250,000.
Dec 8, 1977	PIT	N	John Milner	TEX	A	Al Oliver
						Nelson Norman

(Part of four-team trade involving Texas, New York Mets, Pittsburgh, and Atlanta.)

Dec 9, 1980	CLE	A	Manny Sanguillen	PIT	N	Gary Alexander
						Victor Cruz
						Rafael Vasquez
						Bob Owchinko
Aug 1, 1985	MIN	A	——	CLE	A	Jim Weaver
						Curt Wardle
Nov 3, 1988	CAL	A	Minor league	MIN	A	Mike Cook
			P Kevin Trudeau			Paul Sorrento
						Minor league
						P Rob Wassenaar

Mike Blyzka

| Dec 1, 1954 | NY | A | *See Dick Kryhoski* | BAL | A | —— |

Date	Traded To		Traded With	Traded By		In Exchange For

Randy Bobb

Date	Traded To		Traded With	Traded By		In Exchange For
March 29, 1970	NY	N	——	CHI	N	J. C. Martin

John Boccabella

| April 1, 1974 | SF | N | —— | MON | N | Don Carrithers |

Bruce Bochte

| May 11, 1977 | CLE | A | Sid Monge and $250,000. | CAL | A | Dave LaRoche Dave Schuler |
| Dec 20, 1977 | SEA | A | —— | CLE | A | No compensation (free agent signing) |

Bruce Bochy

| Feb 11, 1981 | NY | N | —— | HOU | N | Minor leaguers C Stan Hough and IF Randy Rogers |

Eddie Bockman

| Oct 19, 1946 | CLE | A | Joe Gordon | NY | A | Allie Reynolds |
| Jan 16, 1948 | PIT | N | —— | CLE | A | Cash |

Mike Boddicker

| July 29, 1988 | BOS | A | —— | BAL | A | Brady Anderson Curt Schilling |

Ping Bodie

| March 8, 1918 | NY | A | —— | PHI | A | George Burns |

Tony Boeckel

| June 12, 1919 | BOS | N | —— | PIT | N | Waiver price |

Joe Boehling

| Aug 18, 1916 | CLE | A | Danny Moeller | WAS | A | Elmer Smith Joe Leonard |

Len Boehmer

| Sept 18, 1967 | NY | A | —— | CIN | N | Bill Henry |

Joe Boever

| July 23, 1987 | ATL | N | —— | STL | N | Randy O'Neal |

Tommy Boggs

| Dec 8, 1977 | ATL | N | Adrian Devine Eddie Miller | TEX | A | Willie Montanez |

(Part of four-team trade involving Texas, Atlanta, Pittsburgh, and New York Mets.)

Pat Bohen

| Jan 1914 | PIT | N | —— | PHI | A | Waiver price |

Sammy Bohne

| June 15, 1926 | BKN | N | —— | CIN | N | Cash |

Danny Boitano

March 28, 1979	MIL	A	——	PHI	N	Gary Beare
April 5, 1981	NY	N	——	MIL	A	Cash
Dec 11, 1981	TEX	A	Doug Flynn	NY	N	Jim Kern

Bob Boken

| May 12, 1934 | CHI | A | —— | WAS | A | Red Kress |

Joe Boley

| June 6, 1932 | CLE | A | —— | PHI | A | Cash |

Jim Bolger

Oct 1, 1954	CHI	N	Ted Tappe Harry Perkowski	CIN	N	Johnny Klippstein Jim Willis
Jan 23, 1959	CLE	A	Johnny Briggs	CHI	N	Earl Averill
June 6, 1959	PHI	N	Cash	CLE	A	Willie Jones
Nov 30, 1962	HOU	N	Connie Grob	MIL	N	Norm Larker

Bobby Bolin

| Dec 12, 1969 | SEA | A | —— | SF | N | Steve Whitaker Dick Simpson |
| Sept 10, 1970 | BOS | A | —— | MIL | A | Cash |

Frank Bolling

| Dec 7, 1960 | MIL | N | Neil Chrisley | DET | A | Bill Bruton Terry Fox Dick Brown Chuck Cottier |

Milt Bolling

April 29, 1957	WAS	A	Russ Kemmerer Faye Throneberry	BOS	A	Dean Stone Bob Chakales
Feb 25, 1958	CLE	A	——	WAS	A	Minor league P Pete Mesa
March 27, 1958	DET	A	Vito Valentinetti	CLE	A	Pete Wojey and $20,000.

Don Bollweg

| May 14, 1951 | NY | A | $15,000. | STL | N | Billy Johnson |
| Dec 16, 1953 | PHI | A | —— | NY | A | See Harry Byrd |

Cliff Bolton

| June 10, 1937 | DET | A | —— | WAS | A | Waiver price |

Mark Bomback

| Oct 26, 1979 | NY | N | —— | MIL | A | Dwight Bernard |
| April 6, 1981 | TOR | A | —— | NY | N | Charlie Puleo and cash |

Bobby Bonds

Oct 22, 1974	NY	A	——	SF	N	Bobby Murcer
Dec 11, 1975	CAL	A	——	NY	A	Mickey Rivers Ed Figueroa
Dec 5, 1977	CHI	A	Thad Bosley Richard Dotson	CAL	A	Brian Downing Chris Knapp Dave Frost
May 16, 1978	TEX	A	——	CHI	A	Claudell Washington Rusty Torres
Oct 3, 1978	CLE	A	Len Barker	TEX	A	Jim Kern Larvell Blanks
Dec 7, 1979	STL	N	——	CLE	A	Jerry Mumphrey John Denny
June 4, 1981	CHI	N	——	TEX	A	Cash

Bill Bonham

| Oct 31, 1977 | CIN | N | —— | CHI | N | Woodie Fryman Bill Caudill |

Ernie Bonham

| Oct 21, 1946 | PIT | N | —— | NY | A | Cookie Cuccurullo |

Bobby Bonilla

| July 23, 1986 | PIT | N | —— | CHI | A | Jose DeLeon |

Date	Traded To		Traded With	Traded By		In Exchange For

Juan Bonilla
Date	Traded To		Traded With	Traded By		In Exchange For
April 1, 1981	SD	N	———	CLE	A	Bob Lacey

Barry Bonnell
Date	Traded To		Traded With	Traded By		In Exchange For
May 7, 1975	ATL	N	Jim Essian and cash	PHI	N	Dick Allen Johnny Oates
Dec 5, 1979	TOR	A	Pat Rockett Joey McLaughlin	ATL	N	Chris Chambliss Luis Gomez
Dec 8, 1983	SEA	A		TOR	A	Bryan Clark

Frank Bonner
Date	Traded To		Traded With	Traded By		In Exchange For
June 1902	PHI	A	Ossee Schreckengost	CLE	A	Bill Bernhard

Zeke Bonura
Date	Traded To		Traded With	Traded By		In Exchange For
March 18, 1938	WAS	A	———	CHI	A	Joe Kuhel
Dec 11, 1938	NY	N	———	WAS	A	Jim Carlin Tom Baker and $20,000.
April 26, 1940	WAS	A	———	NY	N	$20,000.
July 22, 1940	CHI	N	———	WAS	A	Cash

Everitt Booe
Date	Traded To		Traded With	Traded By		In Exchange For
June 1914	BUF	F	———	IND	F	Cash

Buddy Booker
Date	Traded To		Traded With	Traded By		In Exchange For
Dec 15, 1967	CHI	A	———	NY	N	*See Tommie Agee*

Greg Booker
Date	Traded To		Traded With	Traded By		In Exchange For
June 29, 1989	MIN	A	———	SD	N	Fred Toliver

Al Bool
Date	Traded To		Traded With	Traded By		In Exchange For
Nov 12, 1930	BOS	N	———	PIT	N	Waiver price

Bob Boone
Date	Traded To		Traded With	Traded By		In Exchange For
Dec 6, 1981	CAL	A	———	PHI	N	Cash
Nov 30, 1988	KC	A	———	CAL	A	No compensation (free agent signing)

Danny Boone
Date	Traded To		Traded With	Traded By		In Exchange For
June 8, 1982	HOU	N	———	SD	N	Joe Pittman

Danny Boone
Date	Traded To		Traded With	Traded By		In Exchange For
Jan 7, 1924	BOS	A	Steve O'Neill Joe Connolly Bill Wambsganss	CLE	A	George Burns Roxy Walters Chick Fewster

Ray Boone
Date	Traded To		Traded With	Traded By		In Exchange For
June 15, 1953	DET	A	Al Aber Steve Gromek Dick Weik	CLE	A	Art Houtteman Owen Friend Bill Wight Joe Ginsberg
June 15, 1958	CHI	A	Bob Shaw	DET	A	Bill Fischer Tito Francona
May 2, 1959	KC	A	———	CHI	A	Harry Simpson
Aug 20, 1959	MIL	N	———	KC	A	Waiver price
May 17, 1960	BOS	A	———	MIL	N	Ron Jackson

Pedro Borbon
Date	Traded To		Traded With	Traded By		In Exchange For
Nov 25, 1969	CIN	N	Jim McGlothlin Vern Geishert	CAL	A	Alex Johnson Chico Ruiz
June 28, 1979	SF	N	———	CIN	N	Hector Cruz

Frenchy Bordagaray
Date	Traded To		Traded With	Traded By		In Exchange For
Dec 3, 1936	STL	N	Dutch Leonard Jimmy Jordan	BKN	N	Tom Winsett
Dec 8, 1938	CIN	N	———	STL	N	Dusty Cooke
April 4, 1942	BOS	N	———	NY	A	Cash

Rich Bordi
Date	Traded To		Traded With	Traded By		In Exchange For
Dec 9, 1981	SEA	A	———	OAK	A	Dan Meyer
Dec 9, 1982	CHI	N	———	SEA	A	Steve Henderson
Dec 4, 1984	NY	A	Henry Cotto Ron Hassey Porfi Altamirano	CHI	N	Ray Fontenot Brian Dayett
Dec 12, 1985	BAL	A	Rex Hudler	NY	A	Gary Roenicke Leo Hernandez

Glenn Borgmann
Date	Traded To		Traded With	Traded By		In Exchange For
Jan 29, 1980	CHI	A	———	MIN	A	No compensation (free agent signing)
March 24, 1981	CLE	A	———	CHI	A	No compensation (free agent signing)

Paul Boris
Date	Traded To		Traded With	Traded By		In Exchange For
April 10, 1982	MIN	A	Ron Davis Greg Gagne	NY	A	Roy Smalley

Bob Borkowski
Date	Traded To		Traded With	Traded By		In Exchange For
Oct 4, 1951	CIN	N	Smoky Burgess	CHI	N	Johnny Pramesa Bob Usher
June 9, 1955	BKN	N	Cash	CIN	N	Joe Black

Tom Borland
Date	Traded To		Traded With	Traded By		In Exchange For
March 24, 1962	HOU	N	———	BOS	A	Dave Philley

Steve Boros
Date	Traded To		Traded With	Traded By		In Exchange For
Nov 28, 1962	CHI	N	———	DET	A	Bob Anderson

Hank Borowy
Date	Traded To		Traded With	Traded By		In Exchange For
July 27, 1945	CHI	N	———	NY	A	$97,000.
Dec 14, 1948	PHI	N	Eddie Waitkus	CHI	N	Monk Dubiel Dutch Leonard
June 12, 1950	PIT	N	———	PHI	N	$10,000.
Aug 3, 1950	DET	A	———	PIT	N	$15,000.

Babe Borton
Date	Traded To		Traded With	Traded By		In Exchange For
June 1, 1913	NY	A	Rollie Zeider	CHI	A	Hal Chase
Feb 10, 1916	STL	A	*See Eddie Plank*	STL	F	———

Don Bosch
Date	Traded To		Traded With	Traded By		In Exchange For
Dec 6, 1966	NY	N	Don Cardwell	PIT	N	Dennis Ribant Gary Kolb
Oct 16, 1968	MON	N	———	NY	N	Cash

Rick Bosetti
Date	Traded To		Traded With	Traded By		In Exchange For
June 15, 1977	STL	N	Tom Underwood Dane Iorg	PHI	N	Bake McBride Steve Waterbury
March 15, 1978	TOR	A	———	STL	N	Cash
June 10, 1981	OAK	A	———	TOR	A	Cash

Thad Bosley
Date	Traded To		Traded With	Traded By		In Exchange For
Dec 5, 1977	CHI	A	———	CAL	A	*See Brian Downing*
April 1, 1981	MIL	A	———	CHI	A	John Poff
March 5, 1982	SEA	A	———	MIL	A	Mike Parrott
March 30, 1983	CHI	N	———	OAK	A	Cash
March 26, 1987	KC	A	Dave Gumpert	CHI	N	Jim Sundberg

Date	Traded To		Traded With	Traded By		In Exchange For

Dick Bosman
May 10, 1973	CLE	A	Ted Ford	TEX	A	Steve Dunning
May 20, 1975	OAK	A	Jim Perry	CLE	A	Blue Moon Odom and cash

Harley Boss
Dec 15, 1932	CLE	A	——	WAS	A	Jack Russell Bruce Connatser

Lyman Bostock
Nov 21, 1976	CAL	A	——	MIN	A	No compensation (free agent signing)

Ken Boswell
Oct 29, 1974	HOU	N	——	NY	N	Bob Gallagher

Derek Botelho
Feb 23, 1979	CHI	N	Barry Foote Ted Sizemore Jerry Martin minor league P Henry Mack	PHI	N	Manny Trillo Dave Rader Greg Gross
March 30, 1984	CHI	N	——	KC	A	Alan Hargesheimer

Jim Bottomley
Dec 17, 1932	CIN	N	——	STL	N	Estel Crabtree Ownie Carroll
March 21, 1936	STL	A	——	CIN	N	Johnny Burnett

Ed Bouchee
May 13, 1960	CHI	N	Don Cardwell	PHI	N	Tony Taylor Cal Neeman

Medric Boucher
Aug 1914	PIT	F	——	BAL	F	Doc Kerr

Carl Bouldin
July 13, 1964	CHI	A	Bill Skowron	WAS	A	Joe Cunningham Frank Kreutzer

Chris Bourjos
Dec 8, 1980	HOU	N	Bob Knepper	SF	N	Enos Cabell
April 1, 1981	BAL	A	Cash	HOU	N	Kiko Garcia

Pat Bourque
Aug 29, 1973	OAK	A	——	CHI	N	Gonzalo Marquez
Aug 19, 1974	MIN	A	——	OAK	A	Jim Holt
Oct 23, 1974	OAK	A	——	MIN	A	Dan Ford minor league P Denny Myers

Jim Bouton
Oct 21, 1968	SEA	A	——	NY	A	Cash
Aug 24, 1969	HOU	N	——	SEA	A	Dooley Womack Roric Harrison

Larry Bowa
Jan 27, 1982	CHI	N	Ryne Sandberg	PHI	N	Ivan DeJesus

Sam Bowens
Nov 28, 1967	WAS	A	——	BAL	A	Cash

Frank Bowerman
Feb 1900	NY	N	——	PIT	N	Cash
Dec 3, 1907	BOS	N	——	NY	N	See Fred Tenney

Bob Bowman
Dec 5, 1940	NY	N	——	STL	N	Cash
Dec 4, 1941	CHI	N	——	NY	N	Hank Leiber

Ernie Bowman
Dec 3, 1963	MIL	N	See Felipe Alou	SF	N	——

Joe Bowman
Dec 13, 1934	PHI	N	——	NY	N	Kiddo Davis
April 16, 1937	PIT	N	——	PHI	N	Earl Browne

Roger Bowman
May 12, 1953	PIT	N	——	NY	N	Waiver price

Ted Bowsfield
June 13, 1960	CLE	A	Marty Keough	BOS	A	Russ Nixon Carroll Hardy
July 23, 1962	KC	A	Gordie Windhorn	LA	A	Dan Osinski

(Kansas City received Bowsfield on November 30.)

Bob Boyd
Jan 24, 1961	KC	A	——	BAL	A	See Russ Snyder
June 10, 1961	MIL	N	——	KC	A	Cash

Oil Can Boyd
Dec 7, 1989	MON	N	——	BOS	A	No compensation (free agent signing)

Clete Boyer
Feb 19, 1957	NY	A	Art Ditmar Bobby Shantz Jack McMahan Wayne Belardi Curt Roberts	KC	A	Billy Hunter Rip Coleman Tom Morgan Mickey McDermott Milt Graff Irv Noren

(New York received Roberts on April 4, and Boyer on June 4, 1957.)

Nov 29, 1966	ATL	N	——	NY	A	Bill Robinson Chi Chi Olivo

Ken Boyer
Oct 20, 1965	NY	N	——	STL	N	Charley Smith Al Jackson
July 22, 1967	CHI	A	——	NY	N	J. C. Martin Bill Southworth

Doe Boyland
Dec 11, 1981	SF	N	——	PIT	N	Tom Griffin

Gene Brabender
March 31, 1969	SEA	A	Gordon Lund	BAL	A	Chico Salmon
Jan 28, 1971	CAL	A	——	MIL	A	Bill Voss

Gib Brack
July 11, 1938	PHI	N	——	BKN	N	Tuck Stainback

Buddy Bradford
June 15, 1970	CLE	A	——	CHI	A	Barry Moore Bob Miller

Date	Traded To	Traded With	Traded By	In Exchange For

Buddy Bradford *continued*

Date	Traded To		Traded With	Traded By		In Exchange For
May 8, 1971	CIN	N	——	CLE	A	Kurt Bevacqua
June 30, 1975	STL	N	——	CHI	A	Bill Parsons and cash
Dec 12, 1975	CHI	A	Greg Terlecky	STL	N	Lee Richard

Bert Bradley

Dec 8, 1984	NY	A	*See Rickey Henderson*	OAK	A	——

Fred Bradley

Feb 24, 1948	CHI	A	Aaron Robinson Bill Wight	NY	A	Ed Lopat

Hugh Bradley

Feb 1915	NWK	F	Larry Pratt Tom Seaton	BKN	F	Cy Falkenberg

Mark Bradley

March 29, 1983	NY	N	——	LA	N	Minor league Ps Steve Walker Jody Johnston and cash

Phil Bradley

Dec 9, 1987	PHI	N	Minor league P John Fortugno	SEA	A	Glenn Wilson Mike Jackson Minor league OF Dave Grundage
Dec 8, 1988	BAL	A	——	PHI	N	Ken Howell Gordon Dillard

Scott Bradley

June 26, 1986	SEA	A	——	CHI	A	Ivan Calderon

(Chicago received Calderon on July 1, 1986.)

Tom Bradley

Nov 30, 1970	CHI	A	——	CAL	A	*See Ken Berry*
Nov 28, 1972	SF	N	——	CHI	A	Ken Henderson Steve Stone

Bobby Bragan

March 24, 1943	BKN	N	——	PHI	N	Tex Kraus and cash

Dave Brain

July 4, 1905	PIT	N	——	STL	N	George McBride
Dec 15, 1905	BOS	N	Del Howard Vive Lindaman	PIT	N	Vic Willis
Feb 1908	CIN	N	——	BOS	N	Cash
July 1908	NY	N	——	CIN	N	Cash

Ralph Branca

July 10, 1953	DET	A	——	BKN	N	Waiver price

Harvey Branch

Sept 1, 1962	STL	N	——	CHI	N	Paul Toth

Darrell Brandon

Sept 14, 1965	BOS	A	——	HOU	N	Jack Lamabe
July 8, 1969	MIN	A	——	SEA	A	Cash

Ed Brandt

Dec 12, 1935	BKN	N	Randy Moore	BOS	N	Tony Cuccinello Al Lopez Ray Benge Bobby Reis
Dec 4, 1936	PIT	N	——	BKN	N	Cookie Lavagetto Ralph Birkofer

Jackie Brandt

June 14, 1956	NY	N	Red Schoendienst Bobby Stephenson Dick Littlefield Bill Sarni	STL	N	Alvin Dark Ray Katt Don Liddle Whitey Lockman
Nov 30, 1959	BAL	A	Gordon Jones Roger McCardell	SF	N	Billy O'Dell Billy Loes
Dec 6, 1965	PHI	N	Darold Knowles	BAL	A	Jack Baldschun
June 3, 1967	HOU	N	——	PHI	N	Cash

Kitty Bransfield

Dec 20, 1904	PHI	N	Otto Krueger Moose McCormick	PIT	N	Del Howard
Aug 9, 1911	CHI	N	——	PHI	N	Cash

Marshall Brant

April 1, 1980	NY	A	——	NY	N	Cash
June 15, 1983	OAK	A	Ben Callahan and cash	NY	A	Matt Keough

Steve Braun

June 1, 1978	KC	A	——	SEA	A	Jim Colborn

Angel Bravo

Dec 15, 1969	CIN	N	——	CHI	A	Jerry Arrigo
May 13, 1971	SD	N	——	CIN	N	Al Ferrara

Garland Braxton

Aug 27, 1926	WAS	A	Nick Cullop	NY	A	Dutch Ruether

(New York sent Braxton and Cullop to Washington on October 19, 1926.)

June 16, 1930	CHI	A	Bennie Tate	WAS	A	Art Shires
July 13, 1931	STL	A	——	CHI	A	Waiver price

Sid Bream

Aug 31, 1985	PIT	N	R. J. Reynolds Cecil Espy	LA	N	Bill Madlock

(Pittsburgh received Reynolds on Sept. 3 and Bream and Espy on September 9, 1985.)

Danny Breeden

Dec 3, 1968	SD	N	Ed Spiezio Ron Davis minor league P Phil Knuckles	STL	N	Dave Giusti
June 30, 1969	CIN	N	——	SD	N	Cash
Nov 30, 1970	CHI	N	——	CIN	N	Willie Smith
Nov 18, 1974	STL	N	Ed Brinkman	SD	N	Alan Foster Rich Folkers Sonny Siebert

(Part of three-team trade involving San Diego, Detroit, and St. Louis Cardinals.)

Hal Breeden

Nov 30, 1970	CHI	N	——	ATL	N	Hoyt Wilhelm
April 7, 1972	MON	N	Hector Torres	CHI	N	Dan McGinn

Date	Traded To	Traded With	Traded By	In Exchange For

Marv Breeding

Date	Traded To	Traded With	Traded By	In Exchange For
Dec 5, 1962	WAS A	Barry Shetrone and minor league P Art Quick	BAL A	Bob Johnson Pete Burnside
July 20, 1963	LA N	——	WAS A	Ed Roebuck

Fred Breining

Date	Traded To	Traded With	Traded By	In Exchange For
June 28, 1979	SF N	——	PIT N	*See Bill Madlock*
Feb 27, 1984	MON N	Max Venable Andy McGaffigan	SF N	Al Oliver

(San Francisco sent McGaffigan to Montreal on April 1, 1984, after Breining reported to the Expos with a sore arm.)

Bob Brenly

Date	Traded To	Traded With	Traded By	In Exchange For
Jan 18, 1989	TOR A	——	SF N	No compensation (free agent signing)

Ad Brennan

Date	Traded To	Traded With	Traded By	In Exchange For
Jan 20, 1910	PHI N	——	CIN N	Harry Coveleski
June 1918	CLE A	——	WAS A	Cash

Tom Brennan

Date	Traded To	Traded With	Traded By	In Exchange For
Jan 21, 1984	CHI A	——	CLE A	Player to be named later

Roger Bresnahan

Date	Traded To	Traded With	Traded By	In Exchange For
Dec 12, 1908	STL N	——	NY N	Admiral Schlei Bugs Raymond Red Murray
June 8, 1913	CHI N	——	STL N	Cash

Rube Bressler

Date	Traded To	Traded With	Traded By	In Exchange For
March 13, 1928	BKN N	——	CIN N	Waiver price
June 28, 1932	STL N	——	PHI N	Waiver price

Ed Bressoud

Date	Traded To	Traded With	Traded By	In Exchange For
Nov 26, 1961	BOS A	——	HOU N	Don Buddin
Nov 30, 1965	NY N	——	BOS A	Joe Christopher
April 1, 1967	STL N	Danny Napoleon and cash	NY N	Jerry Buchek Art Mahaffey Tony Martinez

Ken Brett

Date	Traded To	Traded With	Traded By	In Exchange For
Oct 11, 1971	MIL A	*See George Scott*	BOS A	——
Oct 31, 1972	PHI N	——	MIL A	*See Don Money*
Oct 18, 1973	PIT N	——	PHI N	Dave Cash
Dec 11, 1975	NY A	Willie Randolph Dock Ellis	PIT N	Doc Medich
May 18, 1976	CHI A	Rich Coggins	NY A	Carlos May
June 15, 1977	CAL A	——	CHI A	Don Kirkwood John Verhoeven John Flannery

Jim Brewer

Date	Traded To	Traded With	Traded By	In Exchange For
Dec 13, 1963	LA N	Cuno Barragan	CHI N	Dick Scott
July 15, 1975	CAL A	——	LA N	Cash

Mike Brewer

Date	Traded To	Traded With	Traded By	In Exchange For
April 4, 1985	CLE A	——	KC A	player to be named

(Brewer returned to Kansas City on Sept. 17, 1985.)

Charlie Brewster

Date	Traded To	Traded With	Traded By	In Exchange For
June 6, 1943	PHI N	——	CIN N	Dain Clay

Fred Brickell

Date	Traded To	Traded With	Traded By	In Exchange For
Aug 7, 1930	PHI N	——	PIT N	Denny Sothern

Fritzie Brickell

Date	Traded To	Traded With	Traded By	In Exchange For
April 4, 1961	LA A	——	NY A	Duke Maas

Jim Brideweser

Date	Traded To	Traded With	Traded By	In Exchange For
May 11, 1954	BAL A	——	NY A	Waiver price
Dec 6, 1954	CHI A	*See Clint Courtney*	BAL A	——
May 15, 1956	DET A	Harry Byrd Bob Kennedy	CHI A	Fred Hatfield Jim Delsing
Feb 8, 1957	BAL A	——	DET A	Cash
Oct 14, 1958	STL N	Art Ceccarelli	BAL A	Jim Finigan

Marshall Bridges

Date	Traded To	Traded With	Traded By	In Exchange For
Aug 2, 1960	CIN N	——	STL N	Waiver price
Nov 27, 1963	WAS A	——	NY A	Cash

Rocky Bridges

Date	Traded To	Traded With	Traded By	In Exchange For
Feb 16, 1953	MIL N	Jim Pendleton	BKN N	Russ Meyer

(Part of four-team trade involving Milwaukee, Philadelphia Phillies, Brooklyn, and Cincinnati.)

Date	Traded To	Traded With	Traded By	In Exchange For
Feb 16, 1953	CIN N	Cash	MIL N	Joe Adcock

(Part of four-team trade involving Milwaukee Braves, Philadelphia Phillies, Brooklyn, and Cincinnati.)

Date	Traded To	Traded With	Traded By	In Exchange For
May 20, 1957	WAS A	——	CIN N	Waiver price
Dec 6, 1958	DET A	Eddie Yost Neil Chrisley	WAS A	Reno Bertoia Ron Samford Jim Delsing
July 26, 1960	CLE A	Red Wilson	DET A	Hank Foiles
Sept 2, 1960	STL N	——	CLE A	Cash

Al Bridwell

Date	Traded To	Traded With	Traded By	In Exchange For
March 1906	BOS N	——	CIN N	Jim Delahanty Chick Fraser
Dec 3, 1907	NY N	Fred Tenney Tom Needham	BOS N	Dan McGann Frank Bowerman Bill Dahlen George Browne George Ferguson
July 22, 1911	BOS N	Hank Gowdy	NY N	Buck Herzog
Nov 1912	CHI N	——	BOS N	Cash

Buttons Briggs

Date	Traded To	Traded With	Traded By	In Exchange For
Dec 30, 1905	BKN N	Billy Maloney Jack McCarthy Doc Casey and $2,000.	CHI N	Jimmy Sheckard

Dan Briggs

Date	Traded To	Traded With	Traded By	In Exchange For
March 30, 1979	SD N	——	CLE A	Mike Champion
Nov 27, 1979	MON N	Bill Almon	SD N	Dave Cash
March 16, 1982	CHI N	——	MON N	Mike Griffin

John Briggs

Date	Traded To	Traded With	Traded By	In Exchange For
April 22, 1971	MIL A	——	PHI N	Ray Peters Pete Koegel
June 14, 1975	MIN A	——	MIL A	Bobby Darwin

Johnny Briggs

Date	Traded To	Traded With	Traded By	In Exchange For
Jan 23, 1959	CLE A	Jim Bolger	CHI N	Earl Averill
July 30, 1960	KC A	——	CLE A	Cash
Jan 25, 1961	CIN N	John Tsitouris	KC A	Joe Nuxhall

Date	Traded To	Traded With	Traded By	In Exchange For

Harry Bright
Dec 16, 1960	WAS A	Bennie Daniels R C Stevens	PIT N	Bobby Shantz
Nov 24, 1962	CIN N	——	WAS A	Rogelio Alvarez
April 21, 1963	NY A	——	CIN N	Cash

Nellie Briles
Jan 29, 1971	PIT N	Vic Davalillo	STL N	Matty Alou George Brunet
Dec 4, 1973	KC A	Fernando Gonzalez	PIT N	Ed Kirkpatrick Kurt Bevacqua minor league 1B Winston Cole
Nov 12, 1975	TEX A	——	KC A	Dave Nelson
Sept 19, 1977	BAL A	——	TEX A	Cash

Chuck Brinkman
| July 11, 1974 | PIT N | —— | CHI A | Cash |

Ed Brinkman
| Oct 9, 1970 | DET A | Joe Coleman Aurelio Rodriguez Jim Hannan | WAS A | Denny McLain Don Wert Norm McRae Elliott Maddox |
| Nov 18, 1974 | SD N | Bob Strampe Dick Sharon | DET A | Nate Colbert |

(Part of three-team trade involving San Diego, Detroit, and St. Louis Cardinals.)

| Nov 18, 1974 | STL N | Danny Breeden | SD N | Alan Foster Rich Folkers Sonny Siebert |

(Part of three-team trade involving San Diego, Detroit, and St. Louis Cardinals.)

| June 4, 1975 | TEX A | Tommy Moore | STL N | Willie Davis |
| June 13, 1975 | NY A | —— | TEX A | Cash |

Lou Brissie
| April 30, 1951 | CLE A | —— | PHI A | Sam Zoldak Ray Murray Minnie Minoso |

(Part of three-team trade involving Cleveland, Philadelphia A's, and Chicago White Sox.)

Jim Britton
| Dec 2, 1969 | MON N | minor league C Don Johnson | ATL N | Larry Jaster |

Johnny Broaca
| Nov 1938 | CLE A | —— | NY A | Waiver price |

Pete Broberg
Dec 5, 1974	MIL A	——	TEX A	Clyde Wright
April 20, 1977	CHI N	——	SEA A	Jim Todd
March 29, 1978	OAK A	——	CHI N	Rodney Scott and cash

Greg Brock
| Dec 10, 1986 | MIL A | —— | LA N | Tim Leary Tim Crews |

Lou Brock
| June 15, 1964 | STL N | Jack Spring Paul Toth | CHI N | Ernie Broglio Bobby Shantz Doug Clemens |

Dick Brodowski
| Nov 8, 1955 | WAS A | —— | BOS A | *See Mickey Vernon* |

Ernie Broglio
| Oct 8, 1958 | STL N | Marv Grissom | SF N | Hobie Landrith Billy Muffett Benny Valenzuela |
| June 15, 1964 | CHI N | Bobby Shantz Doug Clemens | STL N | Lou Brock Jack Spring Paul Toth |

Jack Brohamer
| Dec 12, 1975 | CHI A | —— | CLE A | Larvell Blanks |
| June 20, 1980 | CLE A | —— | BOS A | Cash |

Jim Bronstad
| March 21, 1963 | WAS A | —— | NY A | Cash |

Tom Brookens
| March 23, 1989 | NY A | —— | DET A | Charles Hudson |
| Dec 8, 1989 | CLE A | —— | NY A | No compensation (free agent signing) |

Hubie Brooks
| Dec 10, 1984 | MON N | Mike Fitzgerald Herm Winningham Floyd Youmans | NY N | Gary Carter |
| Dec 21, 1989 | LA N | —— | MON N | No compensation (free agent signing) |

Jim Brosnan
May 20, 1958	STL N	——	CHI N	Alvin Dark
June 8, 1959	CIN N	——	STL N	Hal Jeffcoat
May 5, 1963	CHI A	——	CIN N	Dom Zanni

Tony Brottem
| July 1921 | PIT N | —— | WAS A | Cash |

Bob Brower
| Dec 5, 1988 | NY A | —— | TEX A | Bobby Meacham |

Frank Brower
| Jan 8, 1923 | CLE A | —— | WAS A | Joe Evans |

Boardwalk Brown
| June 1914 | NY A | —— | PHI A | Cash |

Bobby Brown
June 14, 1978	NY A	Jay Johnstone	PHI N	Rawly Eastwick
March 25, 1979	TOR A	——	NY N	Cash
April 1, 1982	SEA A	Bill Caudill Gene Nelson	NY A	Shane Rawley

Buster Brown
| July 16, 1909 | BOS N | Lew Richie Dave Shean | PHI N | Johnny Bates Charlie Starr |

Charlie Brown
| June 10, 1907 | PHI N | —— | STL N | Johnny Lush |

Chris Brown
| July 4, 1987 | SD N | Mark Davis Keith Comstock Mark Grant | SF N | Kevin Mitchell Craig Lefferts Dave Dravecky |
| Oct 28, 1988 | DET A | Keith Moreland | SD N | Walt Terrell |

Date	Traded To		Traded With	Traded By		In Exchange For

Clint Brown

Date	Traded To		Traded With	Traded By		In Exchange For
April 11, 1936	CHI	A	——	CLE	A	Cash
Feb 7, 1941	CLE	A	——	CHI	A	John Humphries

Curt Brown

Date	Traded To		Traded With	Traded By		In Exchange For
Dec 19, 1983	NY	A	——	CAL	A	Minor league P Mike Browning
June 30, 1987	MIL	A	——	MON	N	player to be named

Darrell Brown

Date	Traded To		Traded With	Traded By		In Exchange For
March 1, 1982	OAK	A	minor league Ps Mark Fellows and Jack Smith	DET	A	Jeff Cox Scott Meyer

Dick Brown

Date	Traded To		Traded With	Traded By		In Exchange For
Dec 6, 1959	CHI	A	——	CLE	A	See Norm Cash
Nov 28, 1960	MIL	N	——	CHI	A	Cash
Dec 7, 1960	DET	A	See Bill Bruton	MIL	N	——
Nov 26, 1962	BAL	A	——	DET	A	Gus Triandos Whitey Herzog

Eddie Brown

Date	Traded To		Traded With	Traded By		In Exchange For
Oct 7, 1925	BOS	N	Zack Taylor Jimmy Johnston	BKN	N	Jesse Barnes Mickey O'Neil Gus Felix

Elmer Brown

Date	Traded To		Traded With	Traded By		In Exchange For
Nov 1912	BKN	N	——	STL	A	Cash

Hal Brown

Date	Traded To		Traded With	Traded By		In Exchange For
Feb 9, 1953	BOS	A	Marv Grissom Bill Kennedy	CHI	A	Vern Stephens
Sept 7, 1962	NY	A	——	BAL	A	Cash
April 21, 1963	HOU	N	——	NY	A	Cash

Jackie Brown

Date	Traded To		Traded With	Traded By		In Exchange For
June 13, 1975	CLE	A	Jim Bibby Rick Waits and $100,000.	TEX	A	Gaylord Perry
Dec 10, 1976	MON	N	——	CLE	A	Andre Thornton

Jake Brown

Date	Traded To		Traded With	Traded By		In Exchange For
June 13, 1976	ATL	N	——	SF	N	See Darrell Evans

Jimmy Brown

Date	Traded To		Traded With	Traded By		In Exchange For
Jan 5, 1946	PIT	N	——	STL	N	$30,000.

Jumbo Brown

Date	Traded To		Traded With	Traded By		In Exchange For
June 1937	NY	N	——	CIN	N	Cash

Larry Brown

Date	Traded To		Traded With	Traded By		In Exchange For
April 24, 1971	OAK	A	——	CLE	A	Cash

Leon Brown

Date	Traded To		Traded With	Traded By		In Exchange For
Dec 9, 1976	STL	N	Brock Pemberton	NY	N	Minor league 1B Ed Kurpiel

Lloyd Brown

Date	Traded To		Traded With	Traded By		In Exchange For
Dec 14, 1932	STL	A	Sammy West Carl Reynolds and $20,000.	WAS	A	Goose Goslin Fred Schulte Lefty Stewart

Lloyd Brown *continued*

Date	Traded To		Traded With	Traded By		In Exchange For
May 9, 1933	BOS	A	Rick Ferrell	STL	A	Merv Shea and cash
Oct 12, 1933	CLE	A	——	BOS	A	Bill Cissell

Mace Brown

Date	Traded To		Traded With	Traded By		In Exchange For
April 22, 1941	BKN	N	——	PIT	N	Cash
Dec 10, 1941	BOS	A	——	BKN	N	Cash

Mark Brown

Date	Traded To		Traded With	Traded By		In Exchange For
March 27, 1985	MIN	A	——	BAL	A	Brad Havens

Mike Brown

Date	Traded To		Traded With	Traded By		In Exchange For
Aug 2, 1985	PIT	N	Pat Clements Bob Kipper	CAL	A	John Candelaria Al Holland George Hendrick

(Pittsburgh received Kipper on Aug. 16, 1985.)

Mike Brown

Date	Traded To		Traded With	Traded By		In Exchange For
Aug 19, 1986	SEA	A	——	BOS	A	See Dave Henderson

Ollie Brown

Date	Traded To		Traded With	Traded By		In Exchange For
May 17, 1972	OAK	A	——	SD	N	Curt Blefary Mike Kilkenny minor league OF Greg Schubert
June 29, 1972	MIL	A	——	OAK	A	Cash
Oct 22, 1973	CAL	A	Ellie Rodriguez Skip Lockwood Gary Ryerson Joe Lahoud	MIL	A	Clyde Wright Steve Barber Ken Berry Art Kusnyer and cash
March 28, 1974	HOU	N	——	CAL	A	Cash
June 24, 1974	PHI	N	——	HOU	N	Cash

Scott Brown

Date	Traded To		Traded With	Traded By		In Exchange For
Dec 11, 1981	KC	A	——	CIN	N	Clint Hurdle

Three Finger Brown

Date	Traded To		Traded With	Traded By		In Exchange For
Dec 12, 1903	CHI	N	Jack O'Neill	STL	N	Jack Taylor Larry McLean
Feb 10, 1916	CHI	N	Clem Clemens Mickey Doolan Bill Fischer Max Flack Claude Hendrix Les Mann Dykes Potter Joe Tinker Rollie Zeider George McConnell	CHI	F	Cash

Tommy Brown

Date	Traded To		Traded With	Traded By		In Exchange For
June 8, 1951	PHI	N	——	BKN	N	Dick Whitman and cash
June 15, 1952	CHI	N	——	PHI	N	Cash

Byron Browne

Date	Traded To		Traded With	Traded By		In Exchange For
May 4, 1968	HOU	N	——	CHI	N	Aaron Pointer
Oct 7, 1969	PHI	N	See Curt Flood	STL	N	——

Earl Browne

Date	Traded To		Traded With	Traded By		In Exchange For
April 16, 1937	PHI	N	——	PIT	N	Joe Bowman

Date	Traded To	Traded With	Traded By	In Exchange For

George Browne

Date	Traded To		Traded With	Traded By		In Exchange For
July 1902	NY	N	———	PHI	N	Cash
Dec 3, 1907	BOS	N	Dan McGann Frank Bowerman Bill Dahlen George Ferguson	NY	N	Fred Tenney Al Bridwell Tom Needham
Sept 1908	CHI	N	———	BOS	N	Cash
May 21, 1909	WAS	A	———	CHI	N	Waiver price
May 1910	CHI	A	———	WAS	A	Cash

Jerry Browne

Date	Traded To		Traded With	Traded By		In Exchange For
Dec 6, 1988	CLE	A	———	TEX	A	See Julio Franco

Cal Browning

Date	Traded To		Traded With	Traded By		In Exchange For
Jan 26, 1961	LA	A	Leon Wagner Ellis Burton and cash	STL	N	Al Cicotte

Bob Bruce

Date	Traded To		Traded With	Traded By		In Exchange For
Dec 1, 1961	HOU	N	Manny Montejo	DET	A	Sam Jones
Dec 31, 1966	ATL	N	Dave Nicholson	HOU	N	Sandy Alomar Eddie Mathews Arnie Umbach

Frank Bruggy

Date	Traded To		Traded With	Traded By		In Exchange For
Dec 1921	PHI	A	———	PHI	N	Cash

Mike Bruhert

Date	Traded To		Traded With	Traded By		In Exchange For
June 15, 1979	TEX	A	Bob Myrick	NY	N	Dock Ellis

Mike Brumley

Date	Traded To		Traded With	Traded By		In Exchange For
May 25, 1984	CHI	N	———	BOS	A	See Bill Buckner
Feb 12, 1988	SD	N	———	CHI	N	See Goose Gossage
March 23, 1989	DET	A	———	SD	N	Luis Salazar

Mike Brumley

Date	Traded To		Traded With	Traded By		In Exchange For
Oct 14, 1963	WAS	A	———	LA	N	Cash

Tom Brunansky

Date	Traded To		Traded With	Traded By		In Exchange For
May 12, 1982	MIN	A	Mike Walters and $400,000.	CAL	A	Doug Corbett Rob Wilfong
April 22, 1988	STL	N	———	MIN	A	Tommy Herr

Jack Bruner

Date	Traded To		Traded With	Traded By		In Exchange For
July 1, 1950	STL	A	———	CHI	A	Cash

George Brunet

Date	Traded To		Traded With	Traded By		In Exchange For
May 11, 1960	MIL	N	———	KC	A	Bob Giggie
July 14, 1963	BAL	N	———	HOU	N	Cash
May 12, 1964	HOU	N	———	BAL	N	Cash
Aug 18, 1964	LA	A	———	HOU	N	Cash
July 31, 1969	SEA	A	———	CAL	A	Cash
Dec 4, 1969	WAS	A	———	SEA	A	Dave Baldwin
Aug 31, 1970	PIT	N	———	WAS	A	Denny Riddleberger and cash
Jan 29, 1971	STL	N	Matty Alou	PIT	N	Nellie Briles Vic Davalillo

Warren Brusstar

Date	Traded To		Traded With	Traded By		In Exchange For
Aug 30, 1982	CHI	A	———	PHI	N	Cash
Jan 25, 1983	CHI	N	Steve Trout	CHI	A	Scott Fletcher Pat Tabler Randy Martz Dick Tidrow

Bill Bruton

Date	Traded To		Traded With	Traded By		In Exchange For
Dec 7, 1960	DET	A	Terry Fox Dick Brown Chuck Cottier	MIL	N	Frank Bolling Neil Chrisley

Billy Bryan

Date	Traded To		Traded With	Traded By		In Exchange For
June 10, 1966	NY	A	Fred Talbot	KC	A	Gil Blanco Roger Repoz Bill Stafford

Don Bryant

Date	Traded To		Traded With	Traded By		In Exchange For
April 3, 1967	SF	N	———	CHI	N	Cash

Ron Bryant

Date	Traded To		Traded With	Traded By		In Exchange For
May 9, 1975	STL	N	———	SF	N	Larry Herndon minor league P Luis Gonzalez

Steve Brye

Date	Traded To		Traded With	Traded By		In Exchange For
March 21, 1977	MIL	A	———	MIN	A	Cash
Feb 7, 1979	SD	N	———	PIT	N	No compensation (free agent signing)

Johnny Bucha

Date	Traded To		Traded With	Traded By		In Exchange For
June 9, 1954	BKN	N	Charlie Kress Ernie Nevel and cash	DET	A	Wayne Belardi

Bob Buchanan

Date	Traded To		Traded With	Traded By		In Exchange For
Nov 11, 1985	CIN	N	———	SF	N	Colin Ward

Jerry Buchek

Date	Traded To		Traded With	Traded By		In Exchange For
April 1, 1967	NY	N	Art Mahaffey Tony Martinez	STL	N	Ed Bressoud Danny Napoleon and cash
April 3, 1969	PHI	N	Jim Hutto	STL	N	Bill White

Jim Bucher

Date	Traded To		Traded With	Traded By		In Exchange For
Oct 4, 1937	STL	N	Johnny Cooney Joe Stripp Roy Henshaw	BKN	N	Leo Durocher

Kevin Buckley

Date	Traded To		Traded With	Traded By		In Exchange For
April 4, 1985	CLE	A	———	TEX	A	Jeff Moronko
(Texas received Moronko on April 29, 1985.)						

Bill Buckner

Date	Traded To		Traded With	Traded By		In Exchange For
Jan 11, 1977	CHI	N	Ivan DeJesus minor league P Jeff Albert	LA	N	Rick Monday Mike Garman
May 25, 1984	BOS	A	———	CHI	N	Dennis Eckersley Mike Brumley

Don Buddin

Date	Traded To		Traded With	Traded By		In Exchange For
Nov 26, 1961	HOU	N	———	BOS	A	Ed Bressoud
July 20, 1962	DET	A	———	HOU	N	Cash

Fritz Buelow

Date	Traded To		Traded With	Traded By		In Exchange For
Aug 7, 1904	CLE	A	Charlie Carr	DET	A	Piano Legs Hickman
Dec 1906	STL	A	———	CLE	A	Pete O'Brien

Date	Traded To	Traded With	Traded By	In Exchange For

Don Buford

Date	Traded To	Traded With	Traded By	In Exchange For
Nov 29, 1967	BAL A	Bruce Howard Roger Nelson	CHI A	Luis Aparicio Russ Snyder John Matias

Bob Buhl

Date	Traded To	Traded With	Traded By	In Exchange For
April 30, 1962	CHI N	——	MIL N	Jack Curtis
April 21, 1966	PHI N	Larry Jackson	CHI N	Adolfo Phillips John Herrnstein Ferguson Jenkins

Jay Buhner

Date	Traded To	Traded With	Traded By	In Exchange For
Dec 20, 1984	NY A	Dale Berra	PIT N	Steve Kemp Tim Foli and $400,000.
July 21, 1988	SEA A	Minor league P Rich Balabon player to be named	NY A	Ken Phelps
(Seattle received P Troy Evers on October 12, 1988.)				

DeWayne Buice

Date	Traded To	Traded With	Traded By	In Exchange For
March 9, 1989	TOR A	——	CAL A	Minor league P Cliff Young

Terry Bulling

Date	Traded To	Traded With	Traded By	In Exchange For
March 29, 1979	SEA A	——	MIN A	Cash

Eric Bullock

Date	Traded To	Traded With	Traded By	In Exchange For
Oct 24, 1988	PHI N	*See Tommy Herr*	MIN A	——

Al Bumbry

Date	Traded To	Traded With	Traded By	In Exchange For
March 28, 1985	SD N	——	BAL A	No compensation (free agent signing)

Jim Bunning

Date	Traded To	Traded With	Traded By	In Exchange For
Dec 4, 1963	PHI N	Gus Triandos	DET A	Don Demeter Jack Hamilton
Dec 15, 1967	PIT N	——	PHI N	Don Money Woodie Fryman Bill Laxton minor league P Hal Clem
Aug 15, 1969	LA N	——	PIT N	Minor leaguers OF Ron Mitchell and IF Chuck Coggin and cash

Bill Burbach

Date	Traded To	Traded With	Traded By	In Exchange For
May 28, 1971	BAL A	——	NY A	Jim Hardin

Al Burch

Date	Traded To	Traded With	Traded By	In Exchange For
July 5, 1907	BKN N	——	STL N	Cash

Bob Burda

Date	Traded To	Traded With	Traded By	In Exchange For
Feb 11, 1965	SF N	Bob Priddy	PIT N	Del Crandall
June 9, 1970	MIL A	——	SF N	Cash
Feb 2, 1971	STL N	——	MIL A	Minor league P Fred Reahm
March 20, 1972	BOS A	——	STL N	Mike Fiore

Lew Burdette

Date	Traded To	Traded With	Traded By	In Exchange For
Aug 30, 1951	BOS N	$50,000.	NY A	Johnny Sain
June 15, 1963	STL N	——	MIL N	Gene Oliver Bob Sadowski
June 2, 1964	CHI N	——	STL N	Glen Hobbie

Lew Burdette *continued*

Date	Traded To	Traded With	Traded By	In Exchange For
May 30, 1965	PHI N	——	CHI N	Cash

Smoky Burgess

Date	Traded To	Traded With	Traded By	In Exchange For
Oct 4, 1951	CIN N	Bob Borkowski	CHI N	Johnny Pramesa Bob Usher
Dec 10, 1951	PHI N	Howie Fox Connie Ryan	CIN N	Andy Seminick Eddie Pellagrini Dick Sisler Niles Jordan
April 30, 1955	CIN N	Steve Ridzik Stan Palys	PHI N	Andy Seminick Glen Gorbous Jim Greengrass
Jan 30, 1959	PIT N	Harvey Haddix Don Hoak	CIN N	Whammy Douglas Jim Pendleton Frank Thomas Johnny Powers
Sept 12, 1964	CHI A	——	PIT N	Waiver price

Tom Burgmeier

Date	Traded To	Traded With	Traded By	In Exchange For
Oct 24, 1973	MIN A	——	KC A	Minor leaguer Ken Gill
Nov 15, 1982	OAK A	——	BOS A	No compensation (free agent signing)

Sandy Burk

Date	Traded To	Traded With	Traded By	In Exchange For
April 1912	STL N	——	BKN N	Cash

Glenn Burke

Date	Traded To	Traded With	Traded By	In Exchange For
May 17, 1978	OAK A	——	LA N	Billy North

Jimmy Burke

Date	Traded To	Traded With	Traded By	In Exchange For
July 1901	CHI A	——	MIL A	Cash
Sept 1901	PIT N	——	CHI A	Cash
Jan 1903	STL N	——	PIT N	Otto Krueger

Leo Burke

Date	Traded To	Traded With	Traded By	In Exchange For
Jan 4, 1961	LA A	——	WAS A	Cash
March 25, 1963	STL N	——	LA A	Cash
June 24, 1963	CHI N	——	STL N	Barney Schultz

Tim Burke

Date	Traded To	Traded With	Traded By	In Exchange For
Dec 22, 1982	NY A	Minor league P John Holland Minor league 1B Jose Rivera Minor league OF Don Aubin	PIT N	Lee Mazzilli
Dec 20, 1983	MON N	——	NY A	Pat Rooney

Jesse Burkett

Date	Traded To	Traded With	Traded By	In Exchange For
Jan 16, 1905	BOS A	——	STL A	George Stone

Ken Burkhart

Date	Traded To	Traded With	Traded By	In Exchange For
July 26, 1948	CIN N	——	STL N	Cash

Rick Burleson

Date	Traded To	Traded With	Traded By	In Exchange For
Dec 10, 1980	CAL A	Butch Hobson	BOS A	Carney Lansford Rick Miller Mark Clear
Jan 7, 1987	BAL A	——	CAL A	No compensation (free agent signing)

Johnny Burnett

Date	Traded To	Traded With	Traded By	In Exchange For
Nov 20, 1934	STL A	Bob Weiland and cash	CLE A	Bruce Campbell

Date	Traded To		Traded With	Traded By		In Exchange For

Johnny Burnett *continued*

Date	Traded To		Traded With	Traded By		In Exchange For
March 21, 1936	CIN	N	———	STL	A	Jim Bottomley

Bill Burns

May 16, 1909	CHI	A	———	WAS	A	Nick Altrock Gavvy Cravath Jiggs Donahue
June 7, 1910	CIN	N	———	CHI	A	Cash
July 15, 1911	PHI	N	Fred Beck	CIN	N	Bert Humphries

Britt Burns

Dec 12, 1985	NY	A	Minor league SS Mike Soper Minor league OF Glen Braxton	CHI	A	Joe Cowley Ron Hassey

George Burns

March 8, 1918	NY	A	———	DET	A	Cash
March 8, 1918	PHI	A	———	NY	A	Ping Bodie
May 29, 1920	CLE	A	———	PHI	A	Cash
Dec 24, 1921	BOS	A	Joe Harris Elmer Smith	CLE	A	Stuffy McInnis
Jan 7, 1924	CLE	A	Roxy Walters Chick Fewster	BOS	A	Danny Boone Steve O'Neill Joe Connolly Bill Wambsganss
June 19, 1929	PHI	A	———	NY	A	Cash

George Burns

Dec 6, 1921	CIN	N	Mike Gonzalez and $150,000.	NY	N	Heinie Groh
April 2, 1925	PHI	N	———	CIN	N	Waiver price

Jack Burns

April 30, 1936	DET	A	———	STL	A	Chief Hogsett

Pete Burnside

Oct 5, 1958	DET	A	———	SF	N	Cash
Dec 5, 1962	BAL	A	Bob Johnson	WAS	A	Barry Shetrone Marv Breeding and minor league P Art Quick

Sheldon Burnside

May 25, 1979	CIN	N	———	DET	A	Champ Summers

Larry Burright

Nov 30, 1962	NY	N	Tim Harkness	LA	N	Bob Miller

Ray Burris

May 23, 1979	NY	A	———	CHI	N	Dick Tidrow
Aug 20, 1979	NY	N	———	NY	A	Cash
Feb 18, 1981	MON	N	———	NY	N	No compensation (free agent signing)
Dec 7, 1983	OAK	A	———	MON	N	Rusty McNealy and cash
Dec 7, 1984	MIL	A	minor league P Eric Barry and a player to be named later	OAK	A	Don Sutton

Jeff Burroughs

Dec 9, 1976	ATL	N	———	TEX	A	Ken Henderson Dave May Carl Morton Roger Moret Adrian Devine and $250,000.
March 7, 1981	SEA	A	———	ATL	N	Carlos Diaz
April 7, 1982	OAK	A	———	SEA	A	No compensation (free agent signing)
Dec 22, 1984	TOR	A	———	OAK	A	Cash

Ellis Burton

Jan 26, 1961	LA	A	Leon Wagner Cal Browning and cash	STL	N	Al Cicotte
April 2, 1963	CLE	A	———	HOU	N	Cash

Jim Burton

March 29, 1978	NY	N	———	BOS	A	Leo Foster

Moe Burtschy

June 14, 1956	NY	A	Bill Renna and cash	KC	A	Lou Skizas Eddie Robinson

Jim Busby

May 3, 1952	WAS	A	Mel Hoderlein	CHI	A	Sam Mele
June 7, 1955	CHI	A	———	WAS	A	Bob Chakales Clint Courtney Johnny Groth
Oct 25, 1955	CLE	A	Chico Carrasquel	CHI	A	Larry Doby
June 13, 1957	BAL	A	———	CLE	A	Dick Williams
Dec 15, 1958	BOS	A	———	BAL	A	Billy Klaus

Donie Bush

Aug 20, 1921	WAS	A	———	DET	A	Waiver price

Guy Bush

Nov 22, 1934	PIT	N	Jim Weaver Babe Herman	CHI	N	Larry French Freddie Lindstrom
Feb 2, 1938	STL	N	———	BOS	N	Cash

Joe Bush

Dec 14, 1917	BOS	A	Amos Strunk Wally Schang	PHI	A	Vean Gregg Merlin Kopp Pinch Thomas and $60,000.
Dec 20, 1921	NY	A	Everett Scott Sad Sam Jones	BOS	A	Roger Peckinpaugh Jack Quinn Rip Collins Bill Piercy
Dec 17, 1924	STL	A	Milt Gaston Joe Giard	NY	A	Urban Shocker
Feb 1926	WAS	A	Jack Tobin	STL	A	Tom Zachary Win Ballou
July 1, 1926	PIT	N	———	WAS	A	Cash

Mike Buskey

Dec 10, 1975	PHI	N	Jim Kaat	CHI	A	Dick Ruthven Roy Thomas Alan Bannister
Sept 11, 1978	HOU	N	———	PHI	N	Cash

Tom Buskey

April 27, 1974	CLE	A	———	NY	A	*See Chris Chambliss*
Feb 28, 1978	TEX	A	John Lowenstein	CLE	A	Willie Horton David Clyde

Date	Traded To		Traded With	Traded By		In Exchange For

Ray Busse

Nov 28, 1972	STL	N	Bobby Fenwick	HOU	N	Skip Jutze
						Milt Ramirez
June 8, 1973	HOU	N	——	STL	N	Stan Papi

John Butcher

Dec 7, 1983	MIN	A	Mike Smithson	TEX	A	Gary Ward
			minor league			
			C Sam Sorce			
June 20, 1986	CLE	A	——	MIN	A	Neal Heaton

Max Butcher

| Aug 8, 1938 | PHI | N | | BKN | N | Wayne LaMaster |
| July 28, 1939 | PIT | N | | PHI | N | Gus Suhr |

Sal Butera

March 25, 1983	DET	A	——	MIN	A	Minor league
						C Stine Poole
						and cash
Dec 19, 1985	CIN	N	Bill Gullickson	MON	N	Jay Tibbs
						Andy McGaffigan
						Dann Bilardello
						John Stuper

Art Butler

| Jan 1912 | PIT | N | —— | BOS | N | Cash |
| Dec 12, 1913 | STL | N | —— | PIT | N | See Ed Konetchy |

Bill Butler

| July 11, 1972 | CLE | A | | KC | A | Cash |

Brett Butler

Aug 28, 1983	CLE	A	Rick Behenna	ATL	N	Len Barker
			Brook Jacoby			
			and $150,000.			
(Butler and Jacoby were sent to Cleveland at the end of the season.)						
Dec 1, 1987	SF	N	——	CLE	A	No compensation
						(free agent signing)

Johnny Butler

| Dec 1927 | CHI | N | —— | BKN | N | Howard Freigau |

John Buzhardt

Jan 11, 1960	PHI	N	Alvin Dark	CHI	N	Richie Ashburn
			Jim Woods			
Nov 28, 1961	CHI	A	Charley Smith	PHI	N	Roy Sievers
Aug 21, 1967	BAL	A	——	CHI	A	Cash
Sept 23, 1967	HOU	N	——	BAL	A	Cash

Bud Byerly

| June 15, 1952 | BKN | N | Cash | CIN | N | Bud Podbielan |
| June 24, 1958 | BOS | A | —— | WAS | A | Jack Spring |

Harry Byrd

Dec 16, 1953	NY	A	Eddie Robinson	PHI	A	Don Bollweg
			Tom Hamilton			John Gray
			Carmen Mauro			Jim Robertson
			Loren Babe			Jim Finigan
						Vic Power
						Bill Renna
Nov 18, 1954	BAL	A	——	NY	A	See Bob Turley
June 15, 1955	CHI	A	——	BAL	A	Waiver price
May 15, 1956	DET	A	Jim Brideweser	CHI	A	Fred Hatfield
			Bob Kennedy			Jim Delsing

Sammy Byrd

| Dec 19, 1934 | CIN | N | —— | NY | A | Cash |

Bobby Byrne

Aug 19, 1909	PIT	N		STL	N	Jap Barbeau
						Alan Storke
Aug 20, 1913	PHI	N	Howie Camnitz	PIT	N	Cozy Dolan
						and cash
Sept 1917	CHI	A	——	PHI	N	Waiver price

Tommy Byrne

June 15, 1951	STL	A	$25,000.	NY	A	Stubby Overmire
Oct 16, 1952	CHI	A	Joe DeMaestri	STL	A	Willie Miranda
						Hank Edwards
June 11, 1953	WAS	A	——	CHI	A	Cash

Marty Bystrom

| June 30, 1984 | NY | A | Keith Hughes | PHI | N | Shane Rawley |

Enos Cabell

Dec 3, 1974	HOU	N	Rob Andrews	BAL	A	Lee May
						Jay Schlueter
Dec 8, 1980	SF	N	——	HOU	N	Bob Knepper
						Chris Bourjos
March 4, 1982	DET	A	Cash	SF	N	Champ Summers
Feb 14, 1984	HOU	N	——	DET	A	No compensation
						(free agent signing)
July 10, 1985	LA	N	——	HOU	N	Rafael Montalvo
						German Rivera

Francisco Cabrera

| Aug 24, 1989 | ATL | N | Tony Castillo | TOR | A | Jim Acker |
| (Atlanta received Cabrera on Aug. 29, 1989.) | | | | | | |

Craig Cacek

| Dec 17, 1981 | CAL | A | —— | PIT | N | Cash |

Greg Cadaret

| June 21, 1989 | NY | A | Eric Plunk | OAK | A | Rickey Henderson |
| | | | Luis Polonia | | | |

Leon Cadore

| July 6, 1923 | CHI | A | —— | BKN | N | Waiver price |

Hick Cady

| Jan 10, 1918 | PHI | A | Larry Gardner | BOS | A | Stuffy McInnis |
| | | | Tilly Walker | | | |

Wayne Cage

| March 26, 1981 | SEA | A | —— | CLE | A | Rodney Craig |

Bob Cain

May 15, 1951	DET	A	——	CHI	A	Saul Rogovin
Feb 14, 1952	STL	A	Gene Bearden	DET	A	Dick Littlefield
			Dick Kryhoski			Ben Taylor
						Cliff Mapes
Dec 17, 1953	PHI	A	——	BAL	A	Frank Fanovich
						Joe Coleman

Sugar Cain

| May 21, 1935 | STL | A | Ed Coleman | PHI | A | George Blaeholder |
| May 5, 1936 | CHI | A | —— | STL | A | Les Tietje |

Date	Traded To		Traded With	Traded By		In Exchange For

Ivan Calderon

June 26, 1986	CHI	A	———	SEA	A	Scott Bradley

(Chicago received Calderon on July 1, 1986.)

Sammy Calderone

Feb 1, 1954	MIL	N	———	NY	N	*See Johnny Antonelli*

Mike Caldwell

Oct 25, 1973	SF	N	———	SD	N	Willie McCovey Bernie Williams
Oct 20, 1976	STL	N	John D'Acquisto Dave Rader	SF	N	Willie Crawford Vic Harris John Curtis
March 29, 1977	CIN	N	———	STL	N	Pat Darcy
June 15, 1977	MIL	A	———	CIN	N	Minor leaguers P Dick O'Keefe and IF Garry Pyka

Ray Caldwell

Dec 18, 1918	BOS	A	Frank Gilhooley Slim Love Roxy Walters and $15,000.	NY	A	Ernie Shore Duffy Lewis Dutch Leonard

Jeff Calhoun

April 2, 1987	PHI	N	———	HOU	N	Ronn Reynolds

Ben Callahan

June 15, 1983	OAK	A	Marshall Brant and cash	NY	A	Matt Keough

Johnny Callison

Dec 9, 1959	PHI	N	———	CHI	A	Gene Freese
Nov 17, 1969	CHI	N	———	PHI	N	Dick Selma Oscar Gamble
Jan 20, 1972	NY	A	———	CHI	N	Jack Aker

(Chicago received Aker on May 17, 1972.)

Paul Calvert

Feb 15, 1950	DET	A	———	WAS	A	Waiver price

Ernie Camacho

April 6, 1981	PIT	N	Cash	OAK	A	Bob Owchinko
March 21, 1982	CHI	A	Vance Law	PIT	N	Ross Baumgarten Butch Edge
June 6, 1983	CLE	A	Gorman Thomas Jamie Easterly	MIL	A	Rick Manning Rick Waits

Hank Camelli

Sept 30, 1946	BOS	N	Bob Elliott	PIT	N	Billy Herman Elmer Singleton Stan Wentzel Whitey Wietelmann

Dolf Camilli

June 11, 1934	PHI	N	———	CHI	N	Don Hurst
March 6, 1938	BKN	N	———	PHI	N	Eddie Morgan and $45,000.
July 31, 1943	NY	N	Johnny Allen	BKN	N	Bill Lohrman Bill Sayles Joe Orengo

(Camilli refused to report to New York and retired.)

Doug Camilli

Nov 30, 1964	WAS	A	———	LA	N	Cash

Howie Camnitz

Aug 20, 1913	PHI	N	Bobby Byrne	PIT	N	Cozy Dolan and cash

Bert Campaneris

Nov 17, 1976	TEX	A	———	OAK	A	No compensation (free agent signing)
May 4, 1979	CAL	A	———	TEX	A	Dave Chalk

Jim Campanis

Dec 15, 1968	KC	A	———	LA	N	Two minor leaguers
Dec 2, 1970	PIT	N	———	KC	A	*See Freddie Patek*

Bill Campbell

Nov 6, 1976	BOS	A	———	MIN	A	No compensation (free agent signing)
Dec 8, 1981	CHI	N	———	BOS	A	No compensation (free agent signing)
March 26, 1984	PHI	N	Mike Diaz	CHI	N	Gary Matthews Bob Dernier Porfi Altamirano
April 6, 1985	STL	N	Ivan DeJesus	PHI	N	Dave Rucker
Jan 31, 1986	DET	A	———	STL	N	No compensation (free agent signing)

Bruce Campbell

April 27, 1932	STL	A	Bump Hadley	CHI	A	Red Kress
Nov 20, 1934	CLE	A	———	STL	A	Johnny Burnett Bob Weiland and cash
Jan 20, 1940	DET	A	———	CLE	A	Beau Bell
Dec 12, 1941	WAS	A	Frank Croucher	DET	A	Jimmy Bloodworth Doc Cramer

Dave Campbell

March 31, 1979	MON	N	———	ATL	N	Pepe Frias

Dave Campbell

Dec 4, 1969	SD	N	Pat Dobson	DET	A	Joe Niekro
June 7, 1973	STL	N	———	SD	N	Dwain Anderson
Aug 18, 1973	HOU	N	Cash	STL	N	Tommie Agee

Jim Campbell

Oct 9, 1963	CIN	N	———	HOU	N	Cash

Jim Campbell

Oct 21, 1970	BOS	A	———	STL	N	Dick Schofield

Mike Campbell

May 25, 1989	MON	N	Mark Langston	SEA	A	Randy Johnson Brian Holman Gene Harris

(Montreal received Campbell on July 31, 1989.)

Ron Campbell

Jan 15, 1969	PIT	N	Chuck Hartenstein	CHI	N	Manny Jimenez

Vin Campbell

Jan 1910	PIT	N	———	CHI	N	Cash
Feb 1912	BOS	N	———	PIT	N	Mike Donlin

Card Camper

May 28, 1976	CLE	A	———	STL	N	Cash

Date	Traded To		Traded With		Traded By		In Exchange For

Sal Campisi

Date	Traded To		Traded With		Traded By		In Exchange For
Oct 20, 1970	MIN	A	Jim Kennedy		STL	N	Herman Hill / minor league OF Charlie Wissler

Casey Candaele

July 23, 1988	HOU	N	——		MON	N	Mark Bailey

John Candelaria

Aug 2, 1985	CAL	A	Al Holland / George Hendrick		PIT	N	Pat Clements / Mike Brown / Bob Kipper

(Pittsburgh received Kipper on Aug. 16, 1985.)

Sept 15, 1987	NY	N	——		CAL	A	Minor league P Shane Young / Minor league P Jeff Richardson
Jan 15, 1988	NY	A	——		NY	N	No compensation (free agent signing)
Aug 29, 1989	MON	N	——		NY	A	Mike Blowers

Milo Candini

Jan 29, 1943	WAS	A	Gerry Priddy		NY	A	Bill Zuber and cash

Chris Cannizzaro

Dec 7, 1966	NY	A	——		NY	N	Cash
Dec 19, 1966	DET	A	——		NY	A	Cash
Nov 29, 1967	PIT	N	——		DET	A	Cash
March 28, 1969	SD	N	Tommie Sisk		PIT	N	Ron Davis / Bobby Klaus
May 19, 1971	CHI	N	——		SD	N	Garry Jestadt
Dec 17, 1971	LA	N	——		CHI	N	Cash

Joe Cannon

Nov 27, 1978	TOR	A	Pedro Hernandez / Mark Lemongello		HOU	N	Alan Ashby

Ben Cantwell

June 15, 1928	BOS	N	Al Spohrer / Bill Clarkson / Virgil Barnes		NY	N	Joe Genewich
Jan 27, 1937	NY	N	Hal Lee		BOS	N	Cash
Aug 9, 1937	BKN	N	——		NY	N	Cash

Doug Capilla

June 15, 1977	CIN	N	——		STL	N	Rawly Eastwick
May 3, 1979	CHI	N	——		CIN	N	Minor league P Mark Gilbert
Dec 7, 1981	SF	N	——		CHI	N	Allen Ripley

George Cappuzzello

March 6, 1978	CIN	N	minor league OF John Valle		DET	A	Jack Billingham

Buzz Capra

March 26, 1974	ATL	N	——		NY	N	Cash

Ralph Capron

Jan 1913	PHI	N	——		PIT	N	Cash

Bernie Carbo

May 19, 1972	STL	N	——		CIN	N	Joe Hague
Oct 26, 1973	BOS	A	Rick Wise		STL	N	Reggie Smith / Ken Tatum

Bernie Carbo *continued*

June 3, 1976	MIL	A	——		BOS	A	Tom Murphy / Bobby Darwin
Dec 6, 1976	BOS	A	George Scott		MIL	A	Cecil Cooper
June 15, 1978	CLE	A	——		BOS	A	Cash
March 10, 1979	STL	N	——		BOS	A	No compensation (free agent signing)

Jose Cardenal

Nov 21, 1964	LA	A	——		SF	N	Jack Hiatt
Nov 29, 1967	CLE	A	——		CAL	A	Chuck Hinton
Nov 21, 1969	STL	N	——		CLE	A	Vada Pinson
July 29, 1971	MIL	A	Dick Schofield / Bob Reynolds		STL	N	Ted Kubiak / minor league P Charlie Loseth
Dec 3, 1971	CHI	N	——		MIL	A	Brock Davis / Jim Colborn / Earl Stephenson
Oct 25, 1977	PHI	N	——		CHI	N	Minor league P Manny Seoane
Aug 2, 1979	NY	N	——		PHI	N	Cash

Leo Cardenas

Nov 21, 1968	MIN	A	——		CIN	N	Jim Merritt
Nov 30, 1971	CAL	A	——		MIN	A	Dave LaRoche
April 2, 1973	CLE	A	——		CAL	A	Tom McCraw and minor league 2B Bob Marcano
Feb 12, 1974	TEX	A	——		CLE	A	Ken Suarez

Don Cardwell

May 13, 1960	CHI	N	Ed Bouchee		PHI	N	Tony Taylor / Cal Neeman
Oct 17, 1962	STL	N	George Altman / Moe Thacker		CHI	N	Larry Jackson / Jimmie Schaffer / Lindy McDaniel
Nov 19, 1962	PIT	N	Julio Gotay		STL	N	Dick Groat / Diomedes Olivo
Dec 6, 1966	NY	N	Don Bosch		PIT	N	Dennis Ribant / Gary Kolb
July 12, 1970	ATL	N	——		NY	N	Cash

Rod Carew

Feb 3, 1979	CAL	A	——		MIN	A	Ken Landreaux / Dave Engle / Paul Hartzell / Brad Havens

Andy Carey

May 19, 1960	KC	A	——		NY	A	Bob Cerv
June 10, 1961	CHI	A	——		KC	A	See Wes Covington
Dec 15, 1961	PHI	N	Frank Barnes / Cal McLish		CHI	A	Bob Sadowski / Taylor Phillips / minor league IF Lou Vassie

(Carey refused to report, and the Phillies received McLish in exchange for Vassie to complete the trade on March 24, 1962.)

March 24, 1962	LA	N	——		CHI	A	Minor leaguers IF Ramon Conde and 1B Jim Koranda

Max Carey

Aug 13, 1926	BKN	N	——		PIT	N	Waiver price

Tom Carey

Dec 6, 1938	BOS	A	——		STL	A	Johnny Marcum

Date	Traded To		Traded With	Traded By		In Exchange For

Tex Carleton

Date	Traded To		Traded With	Traded By		In Exchange For
Nov 21, 1934	CHI	N	——	STL	N	Bud Tinning Dick Ward and cash

Jim Carlin

Date	Traded To		Traded With	Traded By		In Exchange For
Dec 11, 1938	WAS	A	Tom Baker and $20,000.	NY	N	Zeke Bonura

Cisco Carlos

Date	Traded To		Traded With	Traded By		In Exchange For
Aug 25, 1969	WAS	A	——	CHI	A	Cash

Hal Carlson

Date	Traded To		Traded With	Traded By		In Exchange For
June 7, 1927	CHI	N	——	PHI	N	Jimmy Cooney Tony Kaufmann

Steve Carlton

Date	Traded To		Traded With	Traded By		In Exchange For
Feb 25, 1972	PHI	N	——	STL	N	Rick Wise
July 31, 1987	MIN	A	——	CLE	A	Minor league P Jeff Perry

Roy Carlyle

Date	Traded To		Traded With	Traded By		In Exchange For
April 26, 1925	BOS	A	Paul Zahniser	WAS	A	Joe Harris
June 15, 1926	NY	A	——	BOS	A	Waiver price

Duke Carmel

Date	Traded To		Traded With	Traded By		In Exchange For
July 29, 1963	NY	N	——	STL	N	Jacke Davis and cash

Eddie Carnett

Date	Traded To		Traded With	Traded By		In Exchange For
Dec 12, 1944	CLE	A	——	CHI	A	Oris Hockett

Charlie Carr

Date	Traded To		Traded With	Traded By		In Exchange For
Aug 7, 1904	CLE	A	Fritz Buelow	DET	A	Piano Legs Hickman
Feb 1906	CIN	N	——	CLE	A	Cash

Alex Carrasquel

Date	Traded To		Traded With	Traded By		In Exchange For
Jan 2, 1946	CHI	A	Fred Vaughn	WAS	A	Cash

Chico Carrasquel

Date	Traded To		Traded With	Traded By		In Exchange For
Oct 25, 1955	CLE	A	Jim Busby	CHI	A	Larry Doby
June 12, 1958	KC	A	——	CLE	A	Billy Hunter
Oct 2, 1958	BAL	A	——	KC	A	Dick Williams

Camilo Carreon

Date	Traded To		Traded With	Traded By		In Exchange For
Jan 20, 1965	CLE	A	Rocky Colavito	CHI	A	Tommy John Tommie Agee Johnny Romano

(Part of three-team trade involving Kansas City, Cleveland, and Chicago White Sox.)

Don Carrithers

Date	Traded To		Traded With	Traded By		In Exchange For
April 1, 1974	MON	N	——	SF	N	John Boccabella
April 6, 1977	MIN	A	——	MON	N	Cash

Clay Carroll

Date	Traded To		Traded With	Traded By		In Exchange For
June 11, 1968	CIN	N	Woody Woodward Tony Cloninger	ATL	N	Milt Pappas Ted Davidson Bob Johnson
Dec 12, 1975	CHI	A	——	CIN	N	Rich Hinton minor league C Jeff Sovern
March 23, 1977	STL	N	——	CHI	A	Lerrin LaGrow

Clay Carroll *continued*

Date	Traded To		Traded With	Traded By		In Exchange For
Aug 31, 1977	CHI	A	——	STL	N	Nyls Nyman Dave Hamilton Silvio Martinez

Ownie Carroll

Date	Traded To		Traded With	Traded By		In Exchange For
May 30, 1930	NY	A	Yats Wuestling Harry Rice	DET	A	Waite Hoyt Mark Koenig
Sept 13, 1930	CIN	N	——	NY	A	Cash
Dec 17, 1932	STL	N	Estel Crabtree	CIN	N	Jim Bottomley
Feb 1933	BKN	N	Jake Flowers	STL	N	Dazzy Vance Gordon Slade

Tom Carroll

Date	Traded To		Traded With	Traded By		In Exchange For
Nov 6, 1976	PIT	N	——	CIN	N	Jim Sadowski

Tommy Carroll

Date	Traded To		Traded With	Traded By		In Exchange For
April 12, 1959	KC	A	Russ Snyder	NY	A	Mike Baxes Bob Martyn

Gary Carter

Date	Traded To		Traded With	Traded By		In Exchange For
Dec 10, 1984	NY	N	——	MON	N	Hubie Brooks Mike Fitzgerald Herm Winningham Floyd Youmans

Joe Carter

Date	Traded To		Traded With	Traded By		In Exchange For
June 13, 1984	CLE	A	Mel Hall Don Schulze Minor league P Darryl Banks	CHI	N	Rick Sutcliffe George Frazier Ron Hassey
Dec 6, 1989	SD	N	——	CLE	A	Sandy Alomar Chris James Minor league 3B Carlos Baerga

Rico Carty

Date	Traded To		Traded With	Traded By		In Exchange For
Oct 27, 1972	TEX	A	——	ATL	N	Jim Panther
Aug 13, 1973	CHI	N	——	TEX	A	Cash
Sept 11, 1973	OAK	A	——	CHI	N	Cash
Dec 6, 1976	CLE	A	——	TOR	A	John Lowenstein Rick Cerone
March 15, 1978	TOR	A	——	CLE	A	Denny DeBarr
Aug 15, 1978	OAK	A	——	TOR	A	Willie Horton Phil Huffman
Oct 3, 1978	TOR	A	——	OAK	A	Cash

Chuck Cary

Date	Traded To		Traded With	Traded By		In Exchange For
Jan 27, 1987	ATL	N	——	DET	A	*See Terry Harper*

Jerry Casale

Date	Traded To		Traded With	Traded By		In Exchange For
June 7, 1961	DET	A	——	LA	A	Jim Donohue

Paul Casanova

Date	Traded To		Traded With	Traded By		In Exchange For
Dec 2, 1971	ATL	N	——	TEX	A	Hal King

Joe Cascarella

Date	Traded To		Traded With	Traded By		In Exchange For
June 30, 1935	BOS	A	——	PHI	A	Cash
June 13, 1936	WAS	A	——	BOS	A	Jack Russell
July 3, 1937	CIN	N	——	WAS	A	Cash

George Case

Date	Traded To		Traded With	Traded By		In Exchange For
Dec 14, 1945	CLE	A	——	WAS	A	Jeff Heath
March 4, 1947	WAS	A	——	CLE	A	Roger Wolff

Date	Traded To		Traded With	Traded By		In Exchange For

Doc Casey

Date	Traded To		Traded With	Traded By		In Exchange For
Dec 30, 1905	BKN	N	Billy Maloney / Jack McCarthy / Buttons Briggs / and $2,000.	CHI	N	Jimmy Sheckard

Dave Cash

Date	Traded To		Traded With	Traded By		In Exchange For
Oct 18, 1973	PHI	N	———	PIT	N	Ken Brett
Nov 17, 1976	MON	N	———	PHI	N	No compensation (free agent signing)
Nov 27, 1979	SD	N	———	MON	N	Bill Almon / Dan Briggs

Norm Cash

Date	Traded To		Traded With	Traded By		In Exchange For
Dec 6, 1959	CLE	A	Johnny Romano / Bubba Phillips	CHI	A	Dick Brown / Don Ferrarese / Jake Striker / Minnie Minoso
April 12, 1960	DET	A	———	CLE	A	Steve Demeter

Harry Cassady

Date	Traded To		Traded With	Traded By		In Exchange For
March 1905	WAS	A	———	PIT	N	Waiver price

George Caster

Date	Traded To		Traded With	Traded By		In Exchange For
Nov 16, 1940	STL	A	———	PHI	A	Waiver price
Aug 8, 1945	DET	A	———	STL	A	Waiver price

Pete Castiglione

Date	Traded To		Traded With	Traded By		In Exchange For
June 14, 1953	STL	N	———	PIT	N	Hal Rice / and cash

Bobby Castillo

Date	Traded To		Traded With	Traded By		In Exchange For
Jan 6, 1982	MIN	A	Bobby Mitchell	LA	N	Scotti Madison / Minor League P Paul Voight
Feb 11, 1985	LA	N	———	MIN	A	No compensation (free agent signing)

Carmen Castillo

Date	Traded To		Traded With	Traded By		In Exchange For
March 26, 1989	MIN	A	———	CLE	A	Keith Atherton

Manny Castillo

Date	Traded To		Traded With	Traded By		In Exchange For
Oct 23, 1981	SEA	A	———	KC	A	Bud Black

Tony Castillo

Date	Traded To		Traded With	Traded By		In Exchange For
Aug 24, 1989	ATL	N	Francisco Cabrera	TOR	A	Jim Acker

(Atlanta received Cabrera on Aug. 29, 1989.)

Foster Castleman

Date	Traded To		Traded With	Traded By		In Exchange For
March 24, 1958	BAL	A	———	SF	N	$30,000.

Bill Castro

Date	Traded To		Traded With	Traded By		In Exchange For
Feb 17, 1981	NY	A	———	MIL	A	No compensation (free agent signing)
March 24, 1982	CAL	A	———	NY	A	Butch Hobson

Danny Cater

Date	Traded To		Traded With	Traded By		In Exchange For
Dec 1, 1964	CHI	A	Lee Elia	PHI	N	Ray Herbert / Jeoff Long
May 27, 1966	KC	A	———	CHI	A	Wayne Causey
Dec 5, 1969	NY	A	Ossie Chavarria	OAK	A	Al Downing / Frank Fernandez
March 22, 1972	BOS	A	———	NY	A	Sparky Lyle
March 29, 1975	STL	N	———	BOS	A	Danny Godby

Ted Cather

Date	Traded To		Traded With	Traded By		In Exchange For
June 1914	BOS	N	Possum Whitted	STL	N	Hub Perdue

Keefe Cato

Date	Traded To		Traded With	Traded By		In Exchange For
Nov 1, 1984	SD	N	———	CIN	N	Minor league P Darren Burroughs

Bill Caudill

Date	Traded To		Traded With	Traded By		In Exchange For
March 28, 1977	CIN	N	———	STL	N	Joel Youngblood
Oct 31, 1977	CHI	N	Woodie Fryman	CIN	N	Bill Bonham
Aug 19, 1981	NY	A	Jay Howell	CHI	N	Pat Tabler

(New York received Caudill on April 1, 1982, and Howell on August 2, 1982.)

Date	Traded To		Traded With	Traded By		In Exchange For
April 1, 1982	SEA	A	Gene Nelson / Bobby Brown	NY	A	Shane Rawley
Nov 21, 1983	OAK	A	Darrel Akerfelds	SEA	A	Dave Beard / Bob Kearney
Dec 8, 1984	TOR	A	———	OAK	A	Alfredo Griffin / Dave Collins / and cash

Red Causey

Date	Traded To		Traded With	Traded By		In Exchange For
Aug 15, 1919	BOS	N	Joe Oeschger / Johnny Jones / Mickey O'Neil / and $55,000.	NY	N	Art Nehf
July 1, 1921	NY	N	Casey Stengel / Johnny Rawlings	PHI	N	Goldie Rapp / Lee King / Lance Richbourg

Wayne Causey

Date	Traded To		Traded With	Traded By		In Exchange For
Jan 24, 1961	KC	A	Jim Archer / Bob Boyd / Al Pilarcik	BAL	A	Whitey Herzog / Russ Snyder
May 27, 1966	CHI	A	———	KC	A	Danny Cater
July 20, 1968	CAL	A	———	CHI	A	Woodie Held
July 29, 1968	ATL	N	———	CAL	A	Cash

Art Ceccarelli

Date	Traded To		Traded With	Traded By		In Exchange For
Oct 11, 1956	BAL	A	Al Pilarcik	KC	A	Ryne Duren / Jim Pisoni
Oct 14, 1958	STL	N	Jim Brideweser	BAL	A	Jim Finigan
May 19, 1960	NY	A	minor league IF Ray Bellino	CHI	N	Mark Freeman

Cesar Cedeno

Date	Traded To		Traded With	Traded By		In Exchange For
Dec 18, 1981	CIN	N	———	HOU	N	Ray Knight
Aug 29, 1985	STL	N	———	CIN	N	Minor league OF Mark Jackson

Orlando Cepeda

Date	Traded To		Traded With	Traded By		In Exchange For
May 8, 1966	STL	N	———	SF	N	Ray Sadecki
March 17, 1969	ATL	N	———	STL	N	Joe Torre
June 29, 1972	OAK	A	———	ATL	N	Denny McLain

Rick Cerone

Date	Traded To		Traded With	Traded By		In Exchange For
Dec 6, 1976	TOR	A	John Lowenstein	CLE	A	Rico Carty
Nov 1, 1979	NY	A	Tom Underwood / Ted Wilborn	TOR	A	Chris Chambliss / Damaso Garcia / Paul Mirabella
Dec 5, 1984	ATL	N	———	NY	A	Brian Fisher
March 5, 1986	MIL	A	Minor league SS Flavio Alfaro	ATL	N	Ted Simmons
Dec 21, 1989	NY	A	———	BOS	A	No compensation (free agent signing)

Bob Cerv

Date	Traded To		Traded With	Traded By		In Exchange For
Oct 16, 1956	KC	A	———	NY	A	Cash
May 19, 1960	NY	A	———	KC	A	Andy Carey

Date	Traded To		Traded With	Traded By		In Exchange For
Bob Cerv *continued*						
May 8, 1961	NY	A	Tex Clevenger	LA	A	Lee Thomas
						Ryne Duren
						Johnny James
June 26, 1962	HOU	N	———	NY	A	Cash
Ron Cey						
Jan 20, 1983	CHI	N	———	LA	N	Vance Lovelace
						Minor leaguers
						P Vance Lovelace and
						Minor League
						OF Dan Cataline
						OF Dan Cataline
Jan 30, 1987	OAK	A	———	CHI	N	Luis Quinones
Elio Chacon						
Dec 7, 1964	STL	N	Tracy Stallard	NY	N	Johnny Lewis
						Gordie Richardson
Ray Chadwick						
Aug 2, 1989	BOS	A	———	CHI	A	Dana Williams
Leon Chagnon						
Dec 1934	NY	N	———	PIT	N	Cash
Bob Chakales						
June 1, 1954	BAL	A	———	CLE	A	Vic Wertz
Dec 6, 1954	CHI	A	*See Clint Courtney*	BAL	A	
June 7, 1955	WAS	A	Clint Courtney	CHI	A	Jim Busby
			Johnny Groth			
April 29, 1957	BOS	A	Dean Stone	WAS	A	Milt Bolling
						Russ Kemmerer
						Faye Throneberry
Dave Chalk						
May 4, 1979	TEX	A	———	CAL	A	Bert Campaneris
June 15, 1979	OAK	A	Mike Heath	TEX	A	John Henry Johnson
			and cash			
Feb 29, 1980	KC	A	———	OAK	A	No compensation
						(free agent signing)
Craig Chamberlain						
March 30, 1982	SF	N	———	KC	A	*See Vida Blue*
Icebox Chamberlain						
Jan 1900	PIT	N	*See Honus Wagner*	LOU	N	———
Cliff Chambers						
Dec 8, 1948	PIT	N	Clyde McCullough	CHI	N	Cal McLish
						Frankie Gustine
June 15, 1951	STL	N	———	PIT	N	*See Joe Garagiola*
Chris Chambliss						
April 27, 1974	NY	A	Dick Tidrow	CLE	A	Fritz Peterson
			Cecil Upshaw			Steve Kline
						Fred Beene
						Tom Buskey
Nov 1, 1979	TOR	A	Damaso Garcia	NY	A	Tom Underwood
			Paul Mirabella			Rick Cerone
						Ted Wilborn
Dec 5, 1979	ATL	N	Luis Gomez	TOR	A	Barry Bonnell
						Pat Rockett
						Joey McLaughlin
Billy Champion						
Oct 31, 1972	MIL	A	*See Don Money*	PHI	N	———

Date	Traded To		Traded With	Traded By		In Exchange For
Mike Champion						
March 30, 1979	CLE	A	———	SD	N	Dan Briggs
Bob Chance						
Dec 1, 1964	WAS	A	Woodie Held	CLE	A	Chuck Hinton
Dean Chance						
Dec 2, 1966	MIN	A	Jackie Hernandez	CAL	A	Jimmie Hall
						Don Mincher
						Pete Cimino
Dec 10, 1969	CLE	A	*See Graig Nettles*	MIN	A	
Sept 18, 1970	NY	N	———	CLE	A	Cash
March 30, 1971	DET	A	Bill Denehy	NY	N	Jerry Robertson
Darrel Chaney						
Dec 12, 1975	ATL	N	———	CIN	N	Mike Lum
Charlie Chant						
Oct 28, 1975	STL	N	———	OAK	A	Larry Lintz
Tiny Chaplin						
Jan 17, 1936	BOS	N	———	NY	N	Cash
Ben Chapman						
June 14, 1936	WAS	A	———	NY	A	Jake Powell
June 11, 1937	BOS	A	Bobo Newsom	WAS	A	Wes Ferrell
						Rick Ferrell
						Mel Almada
Dec 15, 1938	CLE	A	———	BOS	A	Denny Galehouse
						Tommy Irwin
Dec 24, 1940	WAS	A	———	CLE	A	Joe Krakauskas
June 15, 1945	PHI	N	———	BKN	N	Johnny Peacock
Harry Chapman						
Dec 15, 1912	CIN	N	*See Joe Tinker*	CHI	N	———
Feb 10, 1916	STL	A	*See Eddie Plank*	STL	F	———
Sam Chapman						
May 10, 1951	CLE	A	———	PHI	A	Allie Clark
						Lou Klein
Larry Chappell						
Aug 21, 1915	CLE	A	Braggo Roth	CHI	A	Joe Jackson
			Ed Klepfer			
			and $31,500.			
May 1916	BOS	N	———	CLE	A	Cash
Bill Chappelle						
May 24, 1909	CIN	N	———	BOS	N	Cash
May 1909	CIN	N	———	BOS	N	Chick Autry
Chappy Charles						
Aug 22, 1909	CIN	N	———	STL	N	Mike Mowrey
Ed Charles						
Dec 15, 1961	KC	A	Joe Azcue	MIL	N	Bob Shaw
			Manny Jimenez			Lou Klimchock
May 10, 1967	NY	N	———	KC	A	Larry Elliot
						and $50,000.

Date	Traded To	Traded With	Traded By	In Exchange For

Norm Charlton

Date	Traded To	Traded With	Traded By	In Exchange For
March 31, 1986	CIN N	Minor league 2B Tim Barker	MON N	Wayne Krenchicki

Mike Chartak

| June 7, 1942 | STL A | Steve Sundra | WAS A | Roy Cullenbine Bill Trotter |

Hal Chase

| June 1, 1913 | CHI A | —— | NY A | Rollie Zeider Babe Borton |
| Feb 2, 1919 | NY N | —— | CIN N | Bill Rariden |

Ken Chase

| Dec 13, 1941 | BOS A | Johnny Welaj | WAS A | Stan Spence Jack Wilson |

Ossie Chavarria

| Dec 5, 1969 | NY A | Danny Cater | OAK A | Al Downing Frank Fernandez |

Dave Cheadle

| June 7, 1973 | ATL N | Frank Tepedino Wayne Nordhagen Al Closter | NY A | Pat Dobson |

Charlie Chech

| Feb 18, 1909 | BOS A | Jack Ryan and $12,500. | CLE A | Cy Young |

Larry Cheney

Aug 1915	BKN N	——	CHI N	Joe Schultz and $3,000.
June 1919	BOS N	——	BKN N	Waiver price
Aug 1919	PHI N	——	BOS N	Waiver price

Tom Cheney

| Dec 21, 1959 | PIT N | Gino Cimoli | STL N | Ron Kline |
| June 29, 1961 | WAS A | —— | PIT N | Tom Sturdivant |

Jack Chesbro

| Jan 1900 | LOU N | —— | PIT N | *See Honus Wagner* |
| Sept 11, 1909 | BOS A | —— | NY A | Waiver price |

Floyd Chiffer

| Dec 7, 1984 | MIN A | —— | SD N | Ray Smith |

Rocky Childress

| Nov 16, 1986 | HOU N | —— | PHI N | Cash |

Cupid Childs

| Jan 1900 | CHI N | —— | STL N | Cash |

Rich Chiles

| Nov 27, 1972 | NY N | Buddy Harris | HOU N | Tommie Agee |

Lou Chiozza

| Dec 8, 1936 | NY N | —— | PHI N | George Scharein and cash |

Bob Chipman

| June 6, 1944 | CHI N | —— | BKN N | Eddie Stanky |
| April 18, 1950 | BOS N | —— | CHI N | Cash |

Tom Chism

| Dec 7, 1979 | MIN A | —— | BAL A | Dan Graham |

Harry Chiti

July 26, 1960	DET A	——	KC A	Cash
Nov 16, 1961	CLE A	Ray Barker and minor leaguer Art Kay	BAL A	Johnny Temple
April 26, 1962	NY N	——	CLE A	Cash

Nels Chittum

| March 15, 1959 | BOS A | —— | STL N | Dean Stone |
| May 6, 1960 | LA N | —— | BOS A | Rip Repulski |

Bob Chlupsa

| June 20, 1972 | SD N | Mike Fiore | STL N | Rafael Robles |

(Fiore was returned to St. Louis on July 3.)

Don Choate

| March 25, 1959 | SF N | Sam Jones | STL N | Bill White Ray Jablonski |

Mike Chris

| Dec 9, 1981 | SF N | Dan Schatzeder | DET A | Larry Herndon |
| Sept 30, 1983 | CHI N | —— | SF N | Cash |

Neil Chrisley

Nov 8, 1955	WAS A	——	BOS A	*See Mickey Vernon*
Dec 6, 1958	DET A	*See Eddie Yost*	WAS A	
Dec 7, 1960	MIL N	——	DET A	*See Bill Bruton*
Oct 16, 1961	NY N	——	MIL N	Cash

John Christensen

| Nov 13, 1985 | BOS A | Calvin Schiraldi Wes Gardner LaSchelle Tarver | NY N | Bob Ojeda John Mitchell Tom McCarthy Minor league P Chris Bayer |
| Aug 19, 1986 | SEA A | —— | BOS A | *See Dave Henderson* |

Bob Christian

| Sept 30, 1968 | CHI A | —— | DET A | Cash |

Mark Christman

| May 13, 1939 | STL A | —— | DET A | *See Beau Bell* |
| April 9, 1947 | WAS A | —— | STL A | Cash |

Steve Christmas

| Nov 21, 1983 | CHI A | —— | CIN N | Fran Mullins |

Joe Christopher

| Nov 30, 1965 | BOS A | —— | NY N | Ed Bressoud |
| June 14, 1966 | DET A | Earl Wilson | BOS A | Julio Navarro Don Demeter |

Russ Christopher

| April 3, 1948 | CLE A | —— | PHI A | Cash |

Date			Traded To	Traded With			Traded By	In Exchange For

Bubba Church

Date			Traded To	Traded With	Traded By		In Exchange For
May 23, 1952	CIN	N	——		PHI	N	Johnny Wyrostek Kent Peterson
June 12, 1953	CHI	N	——		CIN	N	Fred Baczewski Bob Kelly

Chuck Churn

March 26, 1958	CLE	A	——		BOS	A	Waiver price

Al Cicotte

May 14, 1958	WAS	A	——		NY	A	Cash
June 23, 1958	DET	A	——		WAS	A	Vito Valentinetti
Nov 20, 1958	CLE	A	Billy Martin		DET	A	Don Mossi Ray Narleski Ossie Alvarez
Jan 26, 1961	STL	N	——		LA	A	Leon Wagner Cal Browning Ellis Burton and cash
Oct 13, 1961	HOU	N	——		STL	N	Cash

Eddie Cicotte

July 22, 1912	CHI	A	——		BOS	A	Cash

Pete Cimino

Dec 2, 1966	CAL	A	——		MIN	A	*See Dean Chance*

Gino Cimoli

Dec 4, 1958	STL	N	——		LA	N	Wally Moon Phil Paine
Dec 21, 1959	PIT	N	Tom Cheney		STL	N	Ron Kline
June 15, 1961	MIL	N	——		PIT	N	Johnny Logan

Galen Cisco

Sept 7, 1962	NY	N	——		BOS	A	Waiver price

Bill Cissell

April 24, 1932	CLE	A	Jim Moore		CHI	A	Johnny Hodapp Bob Seeds
Oct 12, 1933	BOS	A	——		CLE	A	Lloyd Brown
March 1938	NY	N	——		PHI	A	Cash

Ralph Citarella

Jan 23, 1985	PHI	N	——		STL	N	Cash

Jim Clancy

Dec 16, 1988	HOU	N	——		TOR	A	No compensation (free agent signing)

Doug Clarey

March 30, 1977	NY	N	——		STL	N	Benny Ayala

Allie Clark

Oct 10, 1947	CLE	A	——		NY	A	Red Embree
May 10, 1951	PHI	A	Lou Klein		CLE	A	Sam Chapman
May 12, 1953	CHI	A	——		PHI	A	Waiver price

Bobby Clark

Dec 20, 1983	MIL	A	——		CAL	A	Jim Slaton

Bryan Clark

Dec 8, 1983	TOR	A	——		SEA	A	Barry Bonnell

Cap Clark

Dec 8, 1937	PHI	N	——		STL	A	Earl Grace

Danny Clark

Oct 30, 1922	BOS	A	Carl Holling Howard Ehmke Babe Herman and $25,000.		DET	A	Del Pratt Rip Collins

Dave Clark

Nov 20, 1989	CHI	N	——		CLE	A	Mitch Webster

Jack Clark

Feb 1, 1985	STL	N	——		SF	N	David Green Jose Uribe Dave LaPoint Gary Rajsich
Jan 6, 1988	NY	A	——		STL	N	No compensation (free agent signing)
Oct 24, 1988	SD	N	Pat Clements		NY	A	Lance McCullers Jimmy Jones Stan Jefferson

Jim Clark

July 10, 1972	KC	A	——		CLE	A	Tom Hilgendorf

Rickey Clark

Jan 29, 1973	PHI	N	——		CAL	A	Cash

Ron Clark

Jan 15, 1970	OAK	A	*See Don Mincher*		MIL	A	——
June 20, 1972	MIL	A	——		OAK	A	Bill Voss
July 28, 1972	CAL	A	Paul Ratliff		MIL	A	Syd O'Brien Joe Azcue

Watty Clark

June 16, 1933	NY	N	Lefty O'Doul		BKN	N	Sam Leslie

Fred Clarke

Jan 1900	PIT	N	*See Honus Wagner*		LOU	N	——

Horace Clarke

May 31, 1974	SD	N	——		NY	A	Cash

Nig Clarke

Aug 1, 1905	DET	A	——		CLE	A	Cash
Aug 11, 1905	CLE	A	——		DET	A	Cash
Oct 1910	STL	A	——		CLE	A	Art Griggs
Nov 1919	PIT	N	——		PHI	N	Waiver price

Tommy Clarke

April 28, 1918	NY	A	——		CIN	N	Lee Magee

Bill Clarkson

June 15, 1928	BOS	N	Ben Cantwell Al Spohrer Virgil Barnes		NY	N	Joe Genewich

Walter Clarkson

May 16, 1907	CLE	A	——		NY	A	Earl Moore

Date	Traded To		Traded With	Traded By		In Exchange For

Ellis Clary

Date	Traded To		Traded With	Traded By		In Exchange For
Aug 18, 1943	STL	A	Ox Miller and cash	WAS	A	Harlond Clift Johnny Niggeling

Dain Clay

Date	Traded To		Traded With	Traded By		In Exchange For
June 1, 1943	PHI	N	Buster Adams Coaker Triplett	STL	N	Danny Litwhiler Earl Naylor
June 6, 1943	CIN	N	——	PHI	N	Charlie Brewster

Ken Clay

Date	Traded To		Traded With	Traded By		In Exchange For
Aug 14, 1980	TEX	A	minor league OF Marvin Thompson	NY	A	Gaylord Perry
Dec 12, 1980	SEA	A	——	TEX	A	See Rick Honeycutt

Mark Clear

Date	Traded To		Traded With	Traded By		In Exchange For
Dec 10, 1980	BOS	A	Carney Lansford Rick Miller	CAL	A	Rick Burleson Butch Hobson
Dec 11, 1985	MIL	A	——	BOS	A	Ed Romero

Clem Clemens

Date	Traded To		Traded With	Traded By		In Exchange For
Feb 10, 1916	CHI	N	See Three Finger Brown	CHI	F	——

Doug Clemens

Date	Traded To		Traded With	Traded By		In Exchange For
June 15, 1964	CHI	N	——	STL	N	See Lou Brock
Jan 10, 1966	PHI	N	——	CHI	N	Wes Covington

Jack Clements

Date	Traded To		Traded With	Traded By		In Exchange For
Jan 1900	BOS	N		CLE	N	Cash

Pat Clements

Date	Traded To		Traded With	Traded By		In Exchange For
Aug 2, 1985	PIT	N		CAL	A	See John Candelaria
Nov 26, 1986	NY	A	See Rick Rhoden	PIT	N	
Oct 24, 1988	SD	N	Jack Clark	NY	A	Lance McCullers Jimmy Jones Stan Jefferson

Lance Clemons

Date	Traded To		Traded With	Traded By		In Exchange For
Dec 2, 1971	HOU	N	Jim York	KC	A	John Mayberry minor league IF Dave Grangaard
April 15, 1972	STL	N	Scipio Spinks	HOU	N	Jerry Reuss
Jan 24, 1973	BOS	A	——	STL	N	Mike Nagy

Donn Clendenon

Date	Traded To		Traded With	Traded By		In Exchange For
Jan 22, 1969	HOU	N	Jesus Alou Jack Billingham Skip Guinn and $100,000.	MON	N	Rusty Staub

(Clendenon refused to report, and Houston sent Billingham, Guinn, and Cash on April 8, 1969.)

Date	Traded To		Traded With	Traded By		In Exchange For
June 15, 1969	NY	N	——	MON	N	Steve Renko Kevin Collins minor league Ps Bill Carden and Dave Colon

Reggie Cleveland

Date	Traded To		Traded With	Traded By		In Exchange For
Dec 7, 1973	BOS	A	Diego Segui Terry Hughes	STL	N	Lynn McGlothen John Curtis Mike Garman
April 18, 1978	TEX	A	——	BOS	A	Cash
Dec 15, 1978	MIL	A	——	TEX	A	Ed Farmer Gary Holle and cash

Tex Clevenger

Date	Traded To		Traded With	Traded By		In Exchange For
Nov 8, 1955	WAS	A	——	BOS	A	See Mickey Vernon
May 8, 1961	NY	A	Bob Cerv	LA	A	Lee Thomas Ryne Duren Johnny James

Harlond Clift

Date	Traded To		Traded With	Traded By		In Exchange For
Aug 18, 1943	WAS	A	Johnny Niggeling	STL	A	Ellis Clary Ox Miller and cash

Ty Cline

Date	Traded To		Traded With	Traded By		In Exchange For
Nov 27, 1962	MIL	N	Don Dillard Frank Funk	CLE	A	Joe Adcock Jack Curtis
May 31, 1967	SF	N	——	ATL	N	Cash
June 15, 1970	CIN	N	——	MON	N	Clyde Mashore

Gene Clines

Date	Traded To		Traded With	Traded By		In Exchange For
Oct 22, 1974	NY	N	——	PIT	N	Duffy Dyer
Dec 12, 1975	TEX	A	——	NY	N	Joe Lovitto
Feb 5, 1977	CHI	N	Cash	TEX	A	Darold Knowles

Billy Clingman

Date	Traded To		Traded With	Traded By		In Exchange For
Jan 1900	CHI	N	——	WAS	N	Cash

Lu Clinton

Date	Traded To		Traded With	Traded By		In Exchange For
June 4, 1964	LA	A	——	BOS	A	Lee Thomas
Sept 9, 1965	CLE	A	——	CAL	A	Waiver price

(Clinton was claimed on waivers by Kansas City and played one game for them before Cleveland's claim was upheld.)

Date	Traded To		Traded With	Traded By		In Exchange For
Jan 14, 1966	NY	A	——	CLE	A	Doc Edwards

Tony Cloninger

Date	Traded To		Traded With	Traded By		In Exchange For
June 11, 1968	CIN	N	Woody Woodward Clay Carroll	ATL	N	Milt Pappas Ted Davidson Bob Johnson
March 24, 1972	STL	N	——	CIN	N	Julian Javier

Al Closter

Date	Traded To		Traded With	Traded By		In Exchange For
April 5, 1966	WAS	A	——	CLE	A	Cash
May 3, 1966	NY	A	——	WAS	A	Cash
June 7, 1973	ATL	N	Frank Tepedino Wayne Nordhagen Dave Cheadle	NY	A	Pat Dobson

David Clyde

Date	Traded To		Traded With	Traded By		In Exchange For
Feb 28, 1978	CLE	A	Willie Horton	TEX	A	Tom Buskey John Lowenstein
Jan 4, 1980	TEX	A	Jim Norris	CLE	A	Larry McCall Gary Gray minor league 3B-OF Mike Bucci

Otis Clymer

Date	Traded To		Traded With	Traded By		In Exchange For
June 26, 1907	WAS	A	——	PIT	N	Cash
July 1913	BOS	N	——	CHI	N	Cash

Andy Coakley

Date	Traded To		Traded With	Traded By		In Exchange For
Sept 1908	CHI	N	——	CIN	N	Cash

Gil Coan

Date	Traded To		Traded With	Traded By		In Exchange For
Feb 18, 1954	BAL	A	——	WAS	A	Roy Sievers
July 17, 1955	CHI	A	——	BAL	A	Waiver price
Aug 26, 1955	NY	N	——	CHI	A	Waiver price

Date	Traded To	Traded With	Traded By	In Exchange For

Jim Coates

Date	Traded To	Traded With	Traded By	In Exchange For
April 21, 1963	WAS A ———		NY A	Steve Hamilton

Dave Cochrane

Date	Traded To	Traded With	Traded By	In Exchange For
July 12, 1985	CHI A ———		NY N	Tom Paciorek
Dec 10, 1987	KC A	*See Floyd Bannister*	CHI A	———
Feb 3, 1988	SEA A ———		KC A	Minor league P Ken Spratke

Mickey Cochrane

Date	Traded To	Traded With	Traded By	In Exchange For
Dec 12, 1933	DET A ———		PHI A	Johnny Pasek and $100,000.

Jack Coffey

Date	Traded To	Traded With	Traded By	In Exchange For
July 1918	BOS A ———		DET A	Cash

Dick Coffman

Date	Traded To	Traded With	Traded By	In Exchange For
Oct 19, 1927	STL A	Earl McNeely	WAS A	Milt Gaston
June 9, 1932	WAS A ———		STL A	Carl Fischer
Dec 13, 1932	STL A ———		WAS A	Carl Fischer
Nov 14, 1935	NY N ———		STL A	Cash

Kevin Coffman

Date	Traded To	Traded With	Traded By	In Exchange For
Sept 29, 1988	CHI N	Kevin Blankenship	ATL N	Jody Davis

Frank Coggins

Date	Traded To	Traded With	Traded By	In Exchange For
April 4, 1970	CLE A	Roy Foster and cash	MIL A	Max Alvis Russ Snyder

Rich Coggins

Date	Traded To	Traded With	Traded By	In Exchange For
Dec 4, 1974	MON N	Dave McNally minor league P Bill Kirkpatrick	BAL A	Ken Singleton Mike Torrez
June 20, 1975	NY A ———		MON N	Cash
May 18, 1976	CHI A	Ken Brett	NY A	Carlos May
July 14, 1976	PHI N ———		CHI A	Wayne Nordhagen

Jimmie Coker

Date	Traded To	Traded With	Traded By	In Exchange For
Nov 21, 1962	BAL A ———		PHI N	Cash
Dec 15, 1962	SF N ———		BAL A	*See Mike McCormick*
Oct 1, 1963	STL N ———		SF N	Ken MacKenzie
April 9, 1964	MIL N	Gary Kolb	STL N	Bob Uecker

Rocky Colavito

Date	Traded To	Traded With	Traded By	In Exchange For
April 17, 1960	DET A ———		CLE A	Harvey Kuenn
Nov 18, 1963	KC A	Bob Anderson and $50,000.	DET A	Jerry Lumpe Ed Rakow Dave Wickersham
Jan 20, 1965	CHI A ———		KC A	Jim Landis Mike Hershberger Fred Talbot
(Part of three-team trade involving Kansas City, Cleveland, and the Chicago White Sox.)				
Jan 20, 1965	CLE A	Camilo Carreon	CHI A	Tommy John Tommie Agee Johnny Romano
(Part of three-team trade involving Kansas City, Cleveland, and Chicago White Sox.)				
July 29, 1967	CHI A ———		CLE A	Jim King Marv Staehle
March 26, 1968	LA N ———		CHI A	Cash

Nate Colbert

Date	Traded To	Traded With	Traded By	In Exchange For
Nov 18, 1974	DET A ———		SD N	Ed Brinkman Bob Strampe Dick Sharon
(Part of three-team trade involving San Diego, Detroit, and St. Louis Cardinals.)				
June 15, 1975	MON N ———		DET A	Cash

Vince Colbert

Date	Traded To	Traded With	Traded By	In Exchange For
Nov 30, 1972	TEX A ———		CLE A	Tom Ragland
March 8, 1973	CLE A	Rich Hinton	TEX A	Alex Johnson

Jim Colborn

Date	Traded To	Traded With	Traded By	In Exchange For
Dec 3, 1971	MIL A	Brock Davis Earl Stephenson	CHI N	Jose Cardenal
Dec 6, 1976	KC A	Darrell Porter	MIL A	Jim Wohlford Jamie Quirk Bob McClure
June 1, 1978	SEA A ———		KC A	Steve Braun

Bert Cole

Date	Traded To	Traded With	Traded By	In Exchange For
July 1925	CLE A ———		DET A	Cash

Dave Cole

Date	Traded To	Traded With	Traded By	In Exchange For
March 20, 1954	CHI N	Cash	MIL N	Roy Smalley
March 19, 1955	PHI N ———		CHI N	Cash

Dick Cole

Date	Traded To	Traded With	Traded By	In Exchange For
June 15, 1951	PIT N	*See Joe Garagiola*	STL N	———
April 3, 1957	MIL N ———		PIT N	Jim Pendleton

Ed Cole

Date	Traded To	Traded With	Traded By	In Exchange For
Feb 10, 1938	STL A	Roy Hughes Billy Sullivan	CLE A	Rollie Hemsley

King Cole

Date	Traded To	Traded With	Traded By	In Exchange For
June 22, 1912	PIT N	Solly Hofman	CHI N	Tommy Leach Lefty Leifield

Dave Coleman

Date	Traded To	Traded With	Traded By	In Exchange For
Feb 3, 1979	MIN A ———		BOS A	Larry Wolfe

Ed Coleman

Date	Traded To	Traded With	Traded By	In Exchange For
May 21, 1935	STL A	Sugar Cain	PHI A	George Blaeholder

Gordy Coleman

Date	Traded To	Traded With	Traded By	In Exchange For
Dec 15, 1959	CIN N	Cal McLish Billy Martin	CLE A	Johnny Temple

Joe Coleman

Date	Traded To	Traded With	Traded By	In Exchange For
Oct 9, 1970	DET A	Ed Brinkman Aurelio Rodriguez Jim Hannan	WAS A	Denny McLain Don Wert Norm McRae Elliott Maddox
June 8, 1976	CHI N ———		DET A	Cash
March 15, 1977	OAK A ———		CHI N	Jim Todd
May 22, 1978	TOR A ———		OAK A	Cash

Joe Coleman

Date	Traded To	Traded With	Traded By	In Exchange For
Dec 17, 1953	BAL A	Frank Fanovich	PHI A	Bob Cain

Date	Traded To		Traded With	Traded By		In Exchange For

Ray Coleman

Date	Traded To		Traded With	Traded By		In Exchange For
June 4, 1948	PHI	A	———	STL	A	George Binks and $20,000.
Dec 13, 1949	STL	A	Frankie Gustine Billy DeMars minor league OF Ray Ippolito and $100,000.	PHI	A	Bob Dillinger Paul Lehner
July 31, 1951	CHI	A	———	STL	A	Waiver price
July 28, 1952	STL	A	J. W. Porter	CHI	A	Jim Rivera Darrell Johnson
Oct 14, 1952	BKN	N	Bob Mahoney Stan Rojek and $90,000.	STL	A	Billy Hunter

Rip Coleman

Date	Traded To		Traded With	Traded By		In Exchange For
Feb 19, 1957	KC	A	*See Billy Hunter*	NY	A	———
Sept 6, 1959	BAL	A	———	KC	A	Waiver price

Darnell Coles

Date	Traded To		Traded With	Traded By		In Exchange For
Dec 12, 1985	DET	A	———	SEA	A	Rich Monteleone
Aug 9, 1987	PIT	N	Morris Madden	DET	A	Jim Morrison
July 22, 1988	SEA	A	———	PIT	N	Glenn Wilson

Chris Coletta

Date	Traded To		Traded With	Traded By		In Exchange For
Aug 15, 1972	CAL	A	———	BOS	A	Andy Kosco
Aug 14, 1973	PHI	N	Aurelio Monteagudo Billy Grabarkewitz	CAL	A	Denny Doyle

Bill Collins

Date	Traded To		Traded With	Traded By		In Exchange For
June 10, 1911	CHI	N	———	BOS	N	*See Johnny Kling*

Dave Collins

Date	Traded To		Traded With	Traded By		In Exchange For
Dec 9, 1977	CIN	N	———	SEA	A	Shane Rawley
Dec 23, 1981	NY	A	———	CIN	N	No compensation (free agent signing)
Dec 9, 1982	TOR	A	Mike Morgan Fred McGriff and $400,000.	NY	A	Dale Murray minor league OF Tom Dodd
Dec 8, 1984	OAK	A	Alfredo Griffin and cash	TOR	A	Bill Caudill
Nov 13, 1985	DET	A	———	OAK	A	Barbaro Garbey

Don Collins

Date	Traded To		Traded With	Traded By		In Exchange For
Feb 15, 1980	CLE	A	———	ATL	N	Minor league P Gary Melson

Eddie Collins

Date	Traded To		Traded With	Traded By		In Exchange For
Dec 8, 1914	CHI	A	———	PHI	A	$50,000.

Jimmy Collins

Date	Traded To		Traded With	Traded By		In Exchange For
June 7, 1907	PHI	A	———	BOS	A	Jack Knight

Joe Collins

Date	Traded To		Traded With	Traded By		In Exchange For
March 20, 1958	PHI	N	———	NY	A	Cash
			(Collins refused to report and retired.)			

Kevin Collins

Date	Traded To		Traded With	Traded By		In Exchange For
June 15, 1969	MON	N	Steve Renko minor league Ps Bill Carden and Dave Colon	NY	N	Donn Clendenon
June 15, 1973	CLE	A	Tom Timmerman	DET	A	Ed Farmer

Pat Collins

Date	Traded To		Traded With	Traded By		In Exchange For
Dec 13, 1928	BOS	N	———	NY	A	$7,500.

Phil Collins

Date	Traded To		Traded With	Traded By		In Exchange For
May 18, 1935	STL	N	———	PHI	N	Cash

Rip Collins

Date	Traded To		Traded With	Traded By		In Exchange For
Dec 20, 1921	BOS	A	Roger Peckinpaugh Jack Quinn Bill Piercy	NY	A	Everett Scott Joe Bush Sad Sam Jones
Oct 30, 1922	DET	A	Del Pratt	BOS	A	Carl Holling Howard Ehmke Danny Clark Babe Herman and $25,000.

Ripper Collins

Date	Traded To		Traded With	Traded By		In Exchange For
Oct 8, 1936	CHI	N	Roy Parmelee	STL	N	Lon Warneke

Shano Collins

Date	Traded To		Traded With	Traded By		In Exchange For
March 4, 1921	BOS	A	Nemo Leibold	CHI	A	Harry Hooper

Zip Collins

Date	Traded To		Traded With	Traded By		In Exchange For
Sept 3, 1915	BOS	N	———	PIT	N	Cash

Jackie Collum

Date	Traded To		Traded With	Traded By		In Exchange For
May 23, 1953	CIN	N	———	STL	N	Eddie Erautt
Jan 31, 1956	STL	N	———	CIN	N	Brooks Lawrence Sonny Senerchia
Dec 11, 1956	CHI	N	*See Tom Poholsky*	STL	N	———
May 23, 1957	CHI	N	Vito Valentinetti	BKN	N	Don Elston
Aug 20, 1962	CLE	A	Georges Maranda and cash	MIN	A	Ruben Gomez

Bob Coluccio

Date	Traded To		Traded With	Traded By		In Exchange For
May 8, 1975	CHI	A	———	MIL	A	Bill Sharp
June 8, 1978	STL	N	———	HOU	N	Frank Riccelli
Oct 2, 1978	NY	N	———	STL	N	Paul Siebert

Merrill Combs

Date	Traded To		Traded With	Traded By		In Exchange For
May 8, 1950	WAS	A	Tommy O'Brien	BOS	A	Clyde Vollmer
April 1, 1951	CLE	A	Snuffy Stirnweiss	STL	A	Freddie Marsh and $35,000.

Wayne Comer

Date	Traded To		Traded With	Traded By		In Exchange For
March 23, 1963	DET	A	———	WAS	A	Bobo Osborne
May 11, 1970	WAS	A	———	MIL	A	Hank Allen Ron Theobald

Adam Comorosky

Date	Traded To		Traded With	Traded By		In Exchange For
Nov 17, 1933	CIN	N	Tony Piet	PIT	N	Red Lucas Wally Roettger

Pete Compton

Date	Traded To		Traded With	Traded By		In Exchange For
June 1916	PIT	N	———	BOS	N	Cash
			(Pittsburgh returned Compton to Boston ten days later.)			

Keith Comstock

Date	Traded To		Traded With	Traded By		In Exchange For
July 4, 1987	SD	N	———	SF	N	*See Kevin Mitchell*

Date	Traded To	Traded With		Traded By		In Exchange For

David Cone
| March 27, 1987 | NY | N | Minor league
C Chris Jelic | KC | A | Ed Hearn
Rick Anderson
Mauro Gozzo |

Bunk Congalton
| May 20, 1907 | BOS | A | ——— | CLE | A | Cash |

Billy Conigliaro
| Oct 11, 1971 | MIL | A | *See George Scott* | BOS | A | ——— |
| Feb 14, 1973 | OAK | A | ——— | MIL | A | Cash |

Tony Conigliaro
| Oct 11, 1970 | CAL | A | Ray Jarvis
Gerry Moses | BOS | A | Ken Tatum
Jarvis Tatum
Doug Griffin |

Gene Conley
| March 31, 1959 | PHI | N | Joe Koppe
Harry Hanebrink | MIL | N | Stan Lopata
Ted Kazanski
Johnny O'Brien |
| Dec 15, 1960 | BOS | A | ——— | PHI | N | Frank Sullivan |

Fritz Connally
| Dec 7, 1983 | SD | N | Carmelo Martinez
Craig Lefferts | CHI | N | Scott Sanderson |

(Part of three-team trade involving Chicago Cubs, San Diego, and Montreal.)

| Feb 7, 1985 | BAL | A | ——— | SD | N | Vic Rodriguez |

Bruce Connatser
| Dec 15, 1932 | WAS | A | Jack Russell | CLE | A | Harley Boss |

Joe Connolly
| April 10, 1913 | BOS | N | ——— | WAS | A | Cash |

Joe Connolly
| Jan 7, 1924 | BOS | A | *See Bill Wambsganss* | CLE | A | ——— |

Bill Connors
| Aug 20, 1967 | NY | N | ——— | CHI | N | Cash |

Chuck Connors
| Oct 10, 1950 | CHI | N | Dee Fondy | BKN | N | Hank Edwards
and cash |

Tim Conroy
| Dec 10, 1985 | STL | N | ——— | OAK | A | *See Joaquin Andujar* |

Billy Consolo
| June 11, 1959 | WAS | A | Murray Wall | BOS | A | Dick Hyde
Herb Plews |

(Hyde was returned to Washington and Wall was returned to Boston.)

June 1, 1961	MIL	N	———	MIN	A	Billy Martin
May 8, 1962	LA	A	———	PHI	N	Cash
June 26, 1962	KC	A	———	LA	A	Cash

Jim Constable
| June 7, 1958 | CLE | A | ——— | SF | N | Waiver price |
| July 12, 1958 | WAS | A | ——— | CLE | A | Waiver price |

Sandy Consuegra
May 12, 1953	CHI	A	———	WAS	A	Cash
May 14, 1956	BAL	A	———	CHI	A	Cash
May 14, 1957	NY	N	———	BAL	A	Waiver price

Jack Conway
| Jan 16, 1948 | NY | N | ——— | CLE | A | Cash |

Cliff Cook
| May 7, 1962 | NY | N | Bob Miller | CIN | N | Don Zimmer |

Dennis Cook
| June 18, 1989 | PHI | N | Terry Mulholland
Charlie Hayes | SF | N | Steve Bedrosian
Minor league
IF Rick Parker |

Mike Cook
| Nov 3, 1988 | MIN | A | Paul Sorrento
Minor league
P Rob Wassenaar | CAL | A | Bert Blyleven
Minor league
P Kevin Trudeau |

Dusty Cooke
| Dec 8, 1938 | STL | N | ——— | CIN | N | Frenchy Bordagaray |

Duff Cooley
Feb 1900	PIT	N	———	PHI	N	Tully Sparks Heinie Reitz
May 1901	BOS	N	———	PIT	N	Cash
Oct 1904	DET	A	———	BOS	N	Waiver price
Dec 1905	DET	A	———	BOS	N	Cash

Danny Coombs
| Oct 22, 1969 | SD | N | ——— | HOU | N | Cash |

Jimmy Cooney
Dec 11, 1925	CHI	N	———	STL	N	Vic Keen
June 7, 1927	PHI	N	Tony Kaufmann	CHI	N	Hal Carlson
Dec 13, 1927	STL	N	Johnny Mokan Bubber Jonnard	PHI	N	Johnny Schulte Jimmy Ring
Feb 3, 1928	BOS	N	———	STL	N	Waiver price

Johnny Cooney
| Oct 4, 1937 | STL | N | Jim Bucher
Joe Stripp
Roy Henshaw | BKN | N | Leo Durocher |

Cecil Cooper
| Dec 6, 1976 | MIL | A | ——— | BOS | A | George Scott
Bernie Carbo |

Claude Cooper
| Feb 10, 1916 | PHI | N | ——— | BKN | F | Cash |

Don Cooper
| Dec 10, 1982 | TOR | A | ——— | MIN | A | Dave Baker |

Guy Cooper
| May 27, 1914 | BOS | A | ——— | NY | A | Cash |

Date	Traded To	Traded With	Traded By	In Exchange For

Mort Cooper

Date	Traded To		Traded With	Traded By		In Exchange For
May 23, 1945	BOS	N	——	STL	N	Red Barrett and $60,000.
June 13, 1947	NY	N	——	BOS	N	Bill Voiselle and cash

Walker Cooper

Date	Traded To		Traded With	Traded By		In Exchange For
Jan 5, 1946	NY	N	——	STL	N	$175,000.
June 13, 1949	CIN	N	——	NY	N	Ray Mueller
May 10, 1950	BOS	N	——	CIN	N	Connie Ryan
May 19, 1954	CHI	N	——	PIT	N	Waiver price

Wilbur Cooper

Date	Traded To		Traded With	Traded By		In Exchange For
Oct 27, 1924	CHI	N	Charlie Grimm Rabbit Maranville	PIT	N	Vic Aldridge George Grantham Al Niehaus
June 7, 1926	DET	A	——	CHI	N	Waiver price

Doug Corbett

Date	Traded To		Traded With	Traded By		In Exchange For
May 12, 1982	CAL	A	Rob Wilfong	MIN	A	Tom Brunansky Mike Walters and $400,000.

Claude Corbitt

Date	Traded To		Traded With	Traded By		In Exchange For
March 18, 1946	CIN	N	——	BKN	N	Cash

Tim Corcoran

Date	Traded To		Traded With	Traded By		In Exchange For
Aug 23, 1981	MIN	A	——	DET	A	Ron Jackson

Mardie Cornejo

Date	Traded To		Traded With	Traded By		In Exchange For
March 13, 1979	DET	A	——	NY	N	Ed Glynn

Pat Corrales

Date	Traded To		Traded With	Traded By		In Exchange For
Oct 27, 1965	STL	N	Art Mahaffey Alex Johnson	PHI	N	Bill White Dick Groat Bob Uecker
Feb 8, 1968	CIN	N	Jimy Williams	STL	N	Johnny Edwards
June 11, 1972	SD	N	——	CIN	N	Bob Barton

Ed Correa

Date	Traded To		Traded With	Traded By		In Exchange For
Nov 25, 1985	TEX	A	Scott Fletcher player to be named	CHI	A	Wayne Tolleson Dave Schmidt

(Texas received IF Jose Mota on Dec. 12, 1985.)

Vic Correll

Date	Traded To		Traded With	Traded By		In Exchange For
March 26, 1974	ATL	N	——	BOS	A	Chuck Goggin

Red Corriden

Date	Traded To		Traded With	Traded By		In Exchange For
Nov 16, 1912	CIN	N	——	DET	A	Cash
Dec 15, 1912	CHI	N	——	CIN	N	See Joe Tinker

Frank Corridon

Date	Traded To		Traded With	Traded By		In Exchange For
July 20, 1904	PHI	N	Jack Sutthoff	CHI	N	Shad Barry
Jan 20, 1910	CIN	N	——	PHI	N	Bob Ewing
Feb 1910	STL	N	Miller Huggins Rebel Oakes	CIN	N	Fred Beebe Alan Storke

Pete Coscarart

Date	Traded To		Traded With	Traded By		In Exchange For
Dec 12, 1941	PIT	N	Luke Hamlin Babe Phelps Jimmy Wasdell	BKN	N	Arky Vaughan

Dan Costello

Date	Traded To		Traded With	Traded By		In Exchange For
Jan 1914	PIT	N	——	NY	A	Waiver price

Dick Cotter

Date	Traded To		Traded With	Traded By		In Exchange For
Oct 1911	CHI	N	——	PHI	N	Peaches Graham

Chuck Cottier

Date	Traded To		Traded With	Traded By		In Exchange For
Dec 7, 1960	DET	A	Bill Bruton Terry Fox Dick Brown	MIL	N	Frank Bolling Neil Chrisley
June 5, 1961	WAS	A	——	DET	A	Hal Woodeshick
Feb 16, 1967	CAL	A	——	WAS	A	Cash

Henry Cotto

Date	Traded To		Traded With	Traded By		In Exchange For
Dec 4, 1984	NY	A	Ron Hassey Rich Bordi Porfi Altamirano	CHI	N	Ray Fontenot Brian Dayett
Dec 22, 1987	SEA	A	Steve Trout	NY	A	Lee Guetterman Clay Parker Minor league P Wade Taylor

Ensign Cottrell

Date	Traded To		Traded With	Traded By		In Exchange For
Jan 1912	CHI	N	——	PIT	N	Cash
April 18, 1915	NY	A	——	BOS	N	Cash

Johnny Couch

Date	Traded To		Traded With	Traded By		In Exchange For
Aug 2, 1923	PHI	N	——	CIN	N	Waiver price

Bill Coughlin

Date	Traded To		Traded With	Traded By		In Exchange For
Aug 10, 1904	DET	A	Lew Drill	WAS	A	$7,500.

Marlan Coughtry

Date	Traded To		Traded With	Traded By		In Exchange For
May 12, 1962	KC	A	——	LA	A	Gordie Windhorn
July 2, 1962	CLE	A	——	KC	A	Cash

Tom Coulter

Date	Traded To		Traded With	Traded By		In Exchange For
Oct 18, 1971	NY	N	——	STL	N	See Jim Bibby

Fritz Coumbe

Date	Traded To		Traded With	Traded By		In Exchange For
Aug 20, 1914	CLE	A	Adam Johnson Ben Egan	BOS	A	Vean Gregg

Clint Courtney

Date	Traded To		Traded With	Traded By		In Exchange For
Nov 23, 1951	STL	A	——	NY	A	Jim McDonald
Dec 6, 1954	CHI	A	Jim Brideweser Bob Chakales	BAL	A	Don Ferrarese Don Johnson Matt Batts Freddie Marsh
June 7, 1955	WAS	A	Bob Chakales Johnny Groth	CHI	A	Jim Busby
April 3, 1960	BAL	A	Ron Samford	WAS	A	Billy Gardner

Ernie Courtney

Date	Traded To		Traded With	Traded By		In Exchange For
June 10, 1903	DET	A	Herman Long	NY	A	Kid Elberfeld

Henry Courtney

Date	Traded To		Traded With	Traded By		In Exchange For
May 1922	CHI	A	——	WAS	A	Cash

Harry Coveleski

Date	Traded To		Traded With	Traded By		In Exchange For
Jan 20, 1910	CIN	N	——	PHI	N	Ad Brennan

Date	Traded To	Traded With	Traded By	In Exchange For

Stan Coveleski

Date	Traded To	Traded With	Traded By	In Exchange For
Dec 12, 1924	WAS A ——		CLE A	Byron Speece Carr Smith

Wes Covington

Date	Traded To	Traded With	Traded By	In Exchange For
May 10, 1961	CHI A ——		MIL N	Waiver price
June 10, 1961	KC A	Bob Shaw Gerry Staley Stan Johnson	CHI A	Ray Herbert Don Larsen Andy Carey Al Pilarcik
July 2, 1961	PHI N ——		KC A	Bobby Del Greco
Jan 10, 1966	CHI N ——		PHI N	Doug Clemens

Billy Cowan

Date	Traded To	Traded With	Traded By	In Exchange For
Jan 15, 1965	NY N ——		CHI N	George Altman
April 28, 1966	CHI N ——		ATL N	Cash
July 26, 1969	CAL A ——		NY A	Cash

Al Cowens

Date	Traded To	Traded With	Traded By	In Exchange For
Dec 6, 1979	CAL A	Todd Cruz Craig Eaton	KC A	Rance Mulliniks Willie Aikens
May 27, 1980	DET A ——		CAL A	Jason Thompson
March 28, 1982	SEA A ——		DET A	Cash

Joe Cowley

Date	Traded To	Traded With	Traded By	In Exchange For
Dec 12, 1985	CHI A	Ron Hassey	NY A	Britt Burns Minor league SS Mike Soper Minor league OF Glen Braxton
March 27, 1987	PHI N ——		CHI A	Gary Redus

Billy Cox

Date	Traded To	Traded With	Traded By	In Exchange For
June 11, 1938	STL A ——		CHI A	Jack Knott
Dec 8, 1947	BKN N	Preacher Roe Gene Mauch	PIT N	Dixie Walker Hal Gregg Vic Lombardi
Dec 13, 1954	BAL A	Preacher Roe	BKN N	Minor leaguers John Jancse and Harry Schwegeman and $50,000.

(Roe retired; Erv Palica trade of March 17, 1955 was additional compensation.)

Date	Traded To	Traded With	Traded By	In Exchange For
June 15, 1955	CLE A	Gene Woodling	BAL A	Dave Pope Wally Westlake

(Cox refused to report and announced retirement. Cleveland received $15,000 to complete trade.)

Bobby Cox

Date	Traded To	Traded With	Traded By	In Exchange For
Dec 7, 1967	NY A ——		ATL N	Bob Tillman Dale Roberts

Casey Cox

Date	Traded To	Traded With	Traded By	In Exchange For
Aug 30, 1972	NY A ——		TEX A	Jim Roland

Glenn Cox

Date	Traded To	Traded With	Traded By	In Exchange For
Sept 12, 1955	KC A ——		BKN N	Waiver price

Jeff Cox

Date	Traded To	Traded With	Traded By	In Exchange For
March 1, 1982	DET A	Scott Meyer	OAK A	Darrell Brown minor league Ps Mark Fellows and Jack Smith

Larry Cox

Date	Traded To	Traded With	Traded By	In Exchange For
Oct 24, 1975	MIN A ——		PHI N	Sergio Ferrer
Oct 22, 1976	SEA A ——		MIN A	Cash

Larry Cox *continued*

Date	Traded To	Traded With	Traded By	In Exchange For
Oct 25, 1977	CHI N ——		SEA A	Minor league P Steve Hamrick
March 20, 1979	SEA A ——		CHI N	Luis Delgado
Dec 12, 1980	TEX A	*See Rick Honeycutt*	SEA A ——	

Ted Cox

Date	Traded To	Traded With	Traded By	In Exchange For
March 30, 1978	CLE A ——		BOS A	*See Dennis Eckersley*
Dec 6, 1979	SEA A ——		CLE A	Rafael Vasquez Bud Anderson and minor league P Bob Pietroburgo

Jim Crabb

Date	Traded To	Traded With	Traded By	In Exchange For
May 1912	PHI A ——		CHI A	Cash

Estel Crabtree

Date	Traded To	Traded With	Traded By	In Exchange For
Dec 17, 1932	STL N	Ownie Carroll	CIN N	Jim Bottomley

Rodney Craig

Date	Traded To	Traded With	Traded By	In Exchange For
March 26, 1981	CLE A ——		SEA A	Wayne Cage

Roger Craig

Date	Traded To	Traded With	Traded By	In Exchange For
Nov 4, 1963	STL N ——		NY N	George Altman Bill Wakefield
Dec 14, 1964	CIN N	Charlie James	STL N	Bob Purkey

Doc Cramer

Date	Traded To	Traded With	Traded By	In Exchange For
Jan 4, 1936	BOS A	Eric McNair	PHI A	Hank Johnson Al Niemiec and $75,000.
Dec 12, 1940	WAS A ——		BOS A	Gee Walker
Dec 12, 1941	DET A	Jimmy Bloodworth	WAS A	Frank Croucher Bruce Campbell

Del Crandall

Date	Traded To	Traded With	Traded By	In Exchange For
Dec 3, 1963	SF N	Bob Shaw Bob Hendley	MIL N	Felipe Alou Billy Hoeft Ed Bailey Ernie Bowman
Feb 11, 1965	PIT N ——		SF N	Bob Priddy Bob Burda

Doc Crandall

Date	Traded To	Traded With	Traded By	In Exchange For
Aug 6, 1913	STL N ——		NY N	Larry McLean
Aug 13, 1913	NY N ——		STL N	Cash
Feb 10, 1916	STL A	*See Eddie Plank*	STL F ——	

Sam Crane

Date	Traded To	Traded With	Traded By	In Exchange For
Feb 3, 1917	WAS A ——		PHI A	Cash
Jan 24, 1922	BKN N ——		CIN N	Cash

Gavvy Cravath

Date	Traded To	Traded With	Traded By	In Exchange For
Aug 1908	CHI A ——		BOS A	Cash
May 16, 1909	WAS A	Nick Altrock Jiggs Donahue	CHI A	Bill Burns

Glenn Crawford

Date	Traded To	Traded With	Traded By	In Exchange For
May 8, 1945	PHI N	John Antonelli	STL N	Buster Adams

Jim Crawford

Date	Traded To	Traded With	Traded By	In Exchange For
Dec 6, 1975	DET A	*See Milt May*	HOU N ——	

Date	Traded To		Traded With	Traded By		In Exchange For

Pat Crawford

| May 27, 1930 | CIN | N | —— | NY | N | Ethan Allen |
| | | | | | | Pete Donohue |

Rufus Crawford

Oct 27, 1952	DET	A	——	STL	A	Neil Berry
						Cliff Mapes
						and $25,000.

Willie Crawford

March 2, 1976	STL	N	——	LA	N	Ted Sizemore
Oct 20, 1976	SF	N	Vic Harris	STL	N	John D'Acquisto
			John Curtis			Mike Caldwell
						Dave Rader
March 26, 1977	HOU	N	Rob Sperring	SF	N	Rob Andrews
						and cash
June 15, 1977	OAK	A	——	HOU	N	Denny Walling
						and cash

Birdie Cree

| March 1908 | NY | A | —— | PHI | A | Cash |

Keith Creel

| March 19, 1985 | CLE | A | —— | KC | A | player to be named |
| (Kansas City received OF Dwight Taylor on Oct. 3, 1985.) |

Tim Crews

| Dec 10, 1986 | LA | N | —— | MIL | A | See Greg Brock |

Lou Criger

| Dec 12, 1908 | STL | A | —— | BOS | A | Tubby Spencer |
| Dec 1909 | NY | A | —— | STL | A | Joe Lake |

Jack Crimian

| Dec 2, 1953 | CIN | N | $100,000. | STL | N | Alex Grammas |
| Dec 5, 1956 | DET | A | —— | KC | A | See Ned Garver |

Chris Cristante

| Dec 6, 1954 | DET | A | See Ferris Fain | CHI | A | —— |

Hughie Critz

| May 21, 1930 | NY | N | —— | CIN | N | Larry Benton |

Fred Crolius

| Feb 1902 | PIT | N | —— | BOS | N | Cash |

Ray Crone

| June 15, 1957 | NY | N | Danny O'Connell | MIL | N | Red Schoendienst |
| | | | Bobby Thomson | | | |

Joe Cronin

| Oct 26, 1934 | BOS | A | —— | WAS | A | Lyn Lary |
| | | | | | | and $225,000. |

John Cronin

| June 1902 | BAL | A | —— | DET | A | Cash |
| Dec 12, 1903 | NY | N | Charlie Babb | BKN | N | Bill Dahlen |

Ed Crosby

| July 27, 1973 | CIN | N | minor league | STL | N | Ed Sprague |
| | | | C Gene Dusan | | | Roe Skidmore |

Ed Crosby *continued*

| March 29, 1974 | STL | N | —— | PHI | N | Cash |
| June 1, 1974 | CLE | A | Luis Alvarado | STL | N | Jack Heidemann |

Ken Crosby

| Aug 7, 1973 | STL | N | Cash | NY | A | Wayne Granger |

Jeff Cross

| May 2, 1948 | CHI | N | —— | STL | N | Cash |

Lave Cross

| May 1900 | BKN | N | —— | STL | N | Cash |
| Jan 1905 | WAS | A | —— | PHI | A | Cash |

Bill Crouch

Nov 11, 1940	PHI	N	Vito Tamulis	BKN	N	Kirby Higbe
			Mickey Livingston			
			and $100,000.			

Jack Crouch

| Sept 1, 1933 | CIN | N | —— | STL | A | Waiver price |

Frank Croucher

| Dec 12, 1941 | WAS | A | Bruce Campbell | DET | A | Jimmy Bloodworth |
| | | | | | | Doc Cramer |

General Crowder

July 7, 1927	STL	A	——	WAS	A	Tom Zachary
June 13, 1930	WAS	A	Heinie Manush	STL	A	Goose Goslin
Aug 4, 1934	DET	A	——	WAS	A	Waiver price

George Crowe

April 9, 1956	CIN	N	——	MIL	N	Bob Hazle
						Corky Valentine
Oct 3, 1958	STL	N	Alex Kellner	CIN	N	Bob Mabe
			Alex Grammas			Eddie Kasko
						Del Ennis

Terry Crowley

Dec 6, 1973	TEX	A	——	BAL	A	Cash
March 19, 1974	CIN	N	——	TEX	A	Cash
April 7, 1976	ATL	N	——	CIN	N	Mike Thompson

Walt Cruise

| May 1919 | BOS | N | —— | STL | N | Cash |

Hector Cruz

Dec 8, 1977	CHI	N	Dave Rader	STL	N	Jerry Morales
						Steve Swisher
						and cash
June 15, 1978	SF	N	——	CHI	N	Lynn McGlothen
June 28, 1979	CIN	N	——	SF	N	Pedro Borbon
Dec 12, 1980	CHI	N	——	CIN	N	Mike Vail

Henry Cruz

| Sept 2, 1977 | CHI | A | —— | LA | N | Cash |

Jose Cruz

Oct 24, 1974	HOU	N	——	STL	N	Cash
Feb 25, 1988	NY	A	——	HOU	N	No compensation
						(free agent signing)

Date	Traded To	Traded With	Traded By	In Exchange For

Julio Cruz

Date				
June 15, 1983	CHI A	——	SEA A	Tony Bernazard

Todd Cruz

April 3, 1979	KC A	——	PHI N	Doug Bird
Dec 6, 1979	CAL A	Al Cowens Craig Eaton	KC A	Rance Mulliniks Willie Aikens
June 12, 1980	CHI A	——	CAL A	Randy Scarbery
Dec 11, 1981	SEA A	Jim Essian Rod Allen	CHI A	Tom Paciorek
June 30, 1983	BAL A	——	SEA A	Cash

Tommy Cruz

Date				
Oct 26, 1973	TEX A	Cash	STL N	Sonny Siebert
Dec 12, 1977	NY A	Jim Spencer minor league P Bob Polinsky	CHI A	Stan Thomas minor league P Ed Ricks

Victor Cruz

Date				
Dec 6, 1977	TOR A	Tom Underwood John Scott	STL N	Pete Vuckovich
Dec 5, 1978	CLE A	——	TOR A	Alfredo Griffin minor league 3B Phil Lansford
Dec 9, 1980	PIT N	Gary Alexander Rafael Vasquez Bob Owchinko	CLE A	Bert Blyleven Manny Sanguillen

Mike Cubbage

Date				
June 1, 1976	MIN A	*See Roy Smalley*	TEX A	——
Dec 19, 1980	NY N	——	MIN A	No compensation (free agent signing)

Tony Cuccinello

Date				
March 14, 1932	BKN N	Joe Stripp Clyde Sukeforth	CIN N	Babe Herman Wally Gilbert Ernie Lombardi
Dec 12, 1935	BOS N	Al Lopez Ray Benge Bobby Reis	BKN N	Ed Brandt Randy Moore
June 15, 1940	NY N	——	BOS N	Manny Salvo Al Glossop

Cookie Cuccurullo

Date				
Oct 21, 1946	NY A	——	PIT N	Ernie Bonham

Bobby Cuellar

Date				
Aug 31, 1978	CLE A	minor league OF Dave Rivera	TEX A	Johnny Grubb

Mike Cuellar

Date				
June 15, 1965	HOU N	Ron Taylor	STL N	Hal Woodeshick Chuck Taylor
Dec 4, 1968	BAL A	Enzo Hernandez Minor League IF Elijah Johnson	HOU N	Curt Blefary Minor leaguer John Mason

Leon Culberson

Date				
Dec 10, 1947	WAS A	Al Kozar	BOS A	Stan Spence
May 13, 1948	NY A	$15,000.	WAS A	Bud Stewart

Jack Cullen

Date				
April 3, 1967	LA N	John Miller and $25,000.	NY A	John Kennedy

Tim Cullen

Date				
Feb 13, 1968	CHI A	Buster Narum Bob Priddy	WAS A	Dennis Higgins Steve Jones Ron Hansen
Aug 2, 1968	WAS A	——	CHI A	Ron Hansen

Roy Cullenbine

Date				
May 27, 1940	STL A	——	BKN N	Joe Gallagher
June 7, 1942	WAS A	Bill Trotter	STL A	Mike Chartak Steve Sundra
Aug 31, 1942	NY A	——	WAS A	Waiver price
Dec 17, 1942	CLE A	Buddy Rosar	NY A	Roy Weatherly Oscar Grimes
April 27, 1945	DET A	——	CLE A	Don Ross Dutch Meyer

Dick Culler

Date				
March 1, 1948	CHI N	——	BOS N	Bobby Sturgeon

Nick Cullop

Date				
Aug 27, 1926	WAS A	Garland Braxton	NY A	Dutch Ruether
		(New York sent Braxton and Cullop to Washington on October 19, 1926.)		
Dec 2, 1931	STL N	Cash	CIN N	Andy High

Nick Cullop

Date				
Dec 23, 1915	NY A	——	KC F	Cash
Jan 22, 1918	STL A	——	NY A	*See Eddie Plank*

Wil Culmer

Sept 12, 1982	CLE A	Jerry Reed Roy Smith	PHI N	John Denny

Ray Culp

Date				
Dec 7, 1966	CHI N	Cash	PHI N	Dick Ellsworth
Nov 30, 1967	BOS A	——	CHI N	Rudy Schlesinger and cash

George Culver

Date				
Nov 21, 1967	CIN N	Fred Whitfield Bob Raudman	CLE A	Tommy Harper
Nov 5, 1969	STL N	——	CIN N	Ray Washburn
June 13, 1970	HOU N	——	STL N	Jim Beauchamp Leon McFadden
March 26, 1973	LA N	——	HOU N	Cash
Aug 10, 1973	PHI N	——	LA N	Cash

John Cumberland

Date				
July 20, 1970	SF N	——	NY A	Mike McCormick
June 16, 1972	STL N	——	SF N	Cash
Nov 29, 1972	MIN A	Larry Hisle	STL N	Wayne Granger

Jack Cummings

Date				
July 14, 1929	BOS N	——	NY N	Cash

Bert Cunningham

Date				
Jan 1900	CHI N	——	PIT N	Cash

Bill Cunningham

Date				
Nov 12, 1923	BOS N	Casey Stengel Dave Bancroft	NY N	Billy Southworth Joe Oeschger
		(Bancroft was named Boston manager.)		

Date	Traded To		Traded With	Traded By		In Exchange For

Bruce Cunningham

Date	Traded To		Traded With	Traded By		In Exchange For
Nov 7, 1928	BOS	N	Socks Seibold Percy Jones Lou Legett Freddie Maguire and $200,000.	CHI	N	Rogers Hornsby

Joe Cunningham

Date	Traded To		Traded With	Traded By		In Exchange For
Nov 27, 1961	CHI	A	———	STL	N	Minnie Minoso
July 13, 1964	WAS	A	Frank Kreutzer	CHI	A	Bill Skowron Carl Bouldin

Nig Cuppy

Date	Traded To		Traded With	Traded By		In Exchange For
Jan 1900	BOS	N	———	STL	N	Cash

Clarence Currie

Date	Traded To		Traded With	Traded By		In Exchange For
Aug 1902	STL	N	———	CIN	N	Cash
July 1903	CHI	N	———	STL	N	Cash

Tony Curry

Date	Traded To		Traded With	Traded By		In Exchange For
March 20, 1962	CLE	A	Ken Lehman	PHI	N	Mel Roach
July 19, 1966	HOU	N	———	CLE	A	Jim Gentile

Cliff Curtis

Date	Traded To		Traded With	Traded By		In Exchange For
June 10, 1911	CHI	N	———	BOS	N	See Johnny Kling
Aug 1911	PHI	N	———	CHI	N	Jack Rowan
May 1912	BKN	N	———	PHI	N	Cash

Jack Curtis

Date	Traded To		Traded With	Traded By		In Exchange For
April 30, 1962	MIL	N	———	CHI	N	Bob Buhl
Nov 27, 1962	CLE	A	Joe Adcock	MIL	N	Ty Cline Don Dillard Frank Funk

John Curtis

Date	Traded To		Traded With	Traded By		In Exchange For
Dec 7, 1973	STL	N	Lynn McGlothen Mike Garman	BOS	A	Reggie Cleveland Diego Segui Terry Hughes
Oct 20, 1976	SF	N	Willie Crawford Vic Harris	STL	N	John D'Acquisto Mike Caldwell Dave Rader
Nov 26, 1979	SD	N	———	SF	N	No compensation (free agent signing)
Aug 31, 1982	CAL	A	———	SD	N	Cash

Jack Cusick

Date	Traded To		Traded With	Traded By		In Exchange For
Oct 11, 1951	BOS	N	———	CHI	N	Bob Addis

George Cutshaw

Date	Traded To		Traded With	Traded By		In Exchange For
Jan 9, 1918	PIT	N	Casey Stengel	BKN	N	Chuck Ward Burleigh Grimes Al Mamaux
Dec 29, 1921	DET	A	———	PIT	N	Waiver price

Kiki Cuyler

Date	Traded To		Traded With	Traded By		In Exchange For
Nov 28, 1927	CHI	N	———	PIT	N	Sparky Adams Pete Scott

Mike Cvengros

Date	Traded To		Traded With	Traded By		In Exchange For
Dec 1927	CHI	N	———	PIT	N	Fred Fussell

John D'Acquisto

Date	Traded To		Traded With	Traded By		In Exchange For
Oct 20, 1976	STL	N	See Mike Caldwell	SF	N	———
May 17, 1977	SD	N	Pat Scanlon	STL	N	Butch Metzger

John D'Acquisto continued

Date	Traded To		Traded With	Traded By		In Exchange For
Aug 11, 1980	MON	N	Cash	SD	N	Randy Bass
Dec 11, 1980	CAL	A	———	MON	N	No compensation (free agent signing)

Paul Dade

Date	Traded To		Traded With	Traded By		In Exchange For
June 14, 1979	SD	N	———	CLE	A	Mike Hargrove

Bill Dahlen

Date	Traded To		Traded With	Traded By		In Exchange For
Dec 12, 1903	BKN	N	———	NY	N	John Cronin Charlie Babb
Dec 3, 1907	BOS	N	Dan McGann Frank Bowerman George Browne George Ferguson	NY	N	Fred Tenney Al Bridwell Tom Needham

Babe Dahlgren

Date	Traded To		Traded With	Traded By		In Exchange For
Feb 17, 1937	NY	A	———	BOS	A	Cash
Feb 25, 1941	BOS	N	———	NY	A	Cash
June 15, 1941	CHI	N	———	BOS	N	Cash
May 13, 1942	STL	A	———	CHI	N	Cash
(Ten-day conditional sale; Dahlgren was returned to the Cubs on May 19, 1940.)						
May 19, 1942	BKN	N	———	CHI	N	Cash
March 9, 1943	PHI	N	———	BKN	N	Lloyd Waner Al Glossop
Dec 30, 1943	PIT	N	———	PHI	N	Babe Phelps and cash
April 23, 1946	STL	A	———	PIT	N	Cash

Bill Dailey

Date	Traded To		Traded With	Traded By		In Exchange For
April 8, 1963	MIN	A	———	CLE	A	Cash

Bruce Dal Canton

Date	Traded To		Traded With	Traded By		In Exchange For
Dec 2, 1970	KC	A	See Freddie Patek	PIT	N	———
June 30, 1975	ATL	N	Norm Angelini Al Autry	KC	A	Ray Sadecki and cash
(Atlanta received Angelini and Autry on September 4.)						

Bud Daley

Date	Traded To		Traded With	Traded By		In Exchange For
April 1, 1958	BAL	A	Dick Williams Gene Woodling	CLE	A	Larry Doby Don Ferrarese
April 17, 1958	KC	A	———	BAL	A	Arnie Portocarrero
June 14, 1961	NY	A	———	KC	A	Art Ditmar Deron Johnson
Sept 5, 1964	CLE	A	Ralph Terry and $75,000.	NY	A	Pedro Ramos

Pete Daley

Date	Traded To		Traded With	Traded By		In Exchange For
Dec 3, 1959	KC	A	———	BOS	A	Tom Sturdivant

Tom Daley

Date	Traded To		Traded With	Traded By		In Exchange For
June 10, 1914	NY	A	———	PHI	A	Jimmy Walsh

Clay Dalrymple

Date	Traded To		Traded With	Traded By		In Exchange For
Jan 20, 1969	BAL	A	———	PHI	N	Ron Stone

Jack Dalton

Date	Traded To		Traded With	Traded By		In Exchange For
Feb 10, 1916	DET	A	Howard Ehmke	BUF	F	Cash

Tom Daly

Date	Traded To		Traded With	Traded By		In Exchange For
Dec 1915	CLE	A	———	CHI	A	Cash

Date	Traded To		Traded With	Traded By		In Exchange For

Tom Daly

| June 9, 1903 | CIN | N | Cozy Dolan | CHI | A | George Magoon |

Bennie Daniels

| Dec 16, 1960 | WAS | A | Harry Bright
R C Stevens | PIT | N | Bobby Shantz |

Bert Daniels

| Oct 1913 | CIN | N | ——— | NY | A | Cash |

Kal Daniels

| July 18, 1989 | LA | N | Mariano Duncan | CIN | N | Tim Leary
Lenny Harris |

Pat Darcy

| Feb 18, 1974 | CIN | N | Cash | HOU | N | Denis Menke |
| March 29, 1977 | STL | N | ——— | CIN | N | Mike Caldwell |

Alvin Dark

Dec 14, 1949	NY	N	Eddie Stanky	BOS	N	Sid Gordon Buddy Kerr Willard Marshall Red Webb
June 14, 1956	STL	N	Ray Katt Don Liddle Whitey Lockman	NY	N	Jackie Brandt Red Schoendienst Bobby Stephenson Dick Littlefield Bill Sarni
May 20, 1958	CHI	N	———	STL	N	Jim Brosnan
Jan 11, 1960	PHI	N	John Buzhardt Jim Woods	CHI	N	Richie Ashburn
June 23, 1960	MIL	N	———	PHI	N	Joe Morgan
Oct 31, 1960	SF	N	———	MIL	N	Andre Rodgers

Ron Darling

| April 1, 1982 | NY | N | Walt Terrell | TEX | A | Lee Mazzilli |

Bobby Darwin

Oct 22, 1971	MIN	A	———	LA	N	Paul Ray Powell
June 14, 1975	MIL	A	———	MIN	A	John Briggs
June 3, 1976	BOS	A	Tom Murphy	MIL	A	Bernie Carbo
May 28, 1977	CHI	N	———	BOS	A	Ramon Hernandez

Danny Darwin

| Jan 18, 1985 | MIL | A | Minor league
C Bill Hance | TEX | A | Don Slaught |

(Part of a four-team trade involving Texas, Milwaukee, Kansas City, and New York Mets.)

| Aug 19, 1986 | HOU | N | ——— | MIL | A | Don August
Mark Knudson |

Jake Daubert

| March 1919 | CIN | N | ——— | BKN | N | Tommy Griffith |

Jack Daugherty

| Sept 1, 1988 | TEX | A | ——— | MON | N | Tom O'Malley |

(Texas received Daugherty on Sept. 13, 1988.)

Vic Davalillo

June 15, 1968	CAL	A	———	CLE	A	Jimmie Hall
May 30, 1969	STL	N	———	CAL	A	Jim Hicks
Jan 29, 1971	PIT	N	Nellie Briles	STL	N	Matty Alou George Brunet
Aug 1, 1973	OAK	A	———	PIT	N	Cash

Jerry DaVanon

May 22, 1969	STL	N	Bill Davis	SD	N	John Sipin Sonny Ruberto
Nov 30, 1970	BAL	A	———	STL	N	Moe Drabowsky
June 10, 1972	CAL	A	———	BAL	A	Roger Repoz
Nov 23, 1976	STL	N	Larry Dierker	HOU	N	Joe Ferguson Bob Detherage

Mike Davey

| Feb 23, 1979 | SEA | A | ——— | ATL | N | Cash |

Mark Davidson

| May 16, 1989 | HOU | N | ——— | MIN | A | Player to be named |

(Minnesota received P Greg Johnson on September 6, 1989.)

Ted Davidson

| June 11, 1968 | ATL | N | *See Milt Pappas* | CIN | N | ——— |

Bill Davis

| Oct 21, 1968 | SD | N | ——— | CLE | A | Zoilo Versalles |
| May 22, 1969 | STL | N | Jerry DaVanon | SD | N | John Sipin
Sonny Ruberto |

Brock Davis

| Dec 3, 1971 | MIL | A | Jim Colborn
Earl Stephenson | CHI | N | Jose Cardenal |
| Feb 25, 1975 | CLE | A | Dave LaRoche | CHI | N | Milt Wilcox |

Curt Davis

May 21, 1936	CHI	N	Ethan Allen	PHI	N	Chuck Klein Fabian Kowalik
April 16, 1938	STL	N	Clyde Shoun Tuck Stainback and $185,000.	CHI	N	Dizzy Dean
June 12, 1940	BKN	N	Joe Medwick	STL	N	Ernie Koy Carl Doyle Sam Nahem Bert Haas and $125,000.

Dick Davis

March 1, 1981	PHI	N	———	MIL	A	Randy Lerch
June 15, 1982	TOR	A	———	PHI	N	Wayne Nordhagen
June 22, 1982	PIT	N	———	TOR	A	Wayne Nordhagen

Dixie Davis

| Jan 21, 1919 | STL | N | Milt Stock
Pickles Dillhoefer | PHI | N | Doug Baird
Stuffy Stewart
Gene Packard |

George Davis

| Dec 1912 | BOS | N | Guy Zinn | NY | A | Cash |

Jacke Davis

Dec 11, 1962	LA	A	———	PHI	N	Earl Averill
March 29, 1963	SF	N	———	LA	A	Charlie Dees
July 29, 1963	STL	N	Cash	NY	N	Duke Carmel

Jim Davis

| Dec 11, 1956 | STL | N | ——— | CHI | N | *See Tom Poholsky* |
| June 4, 1957 | NY | N | ——— | STL | N | Waiver price |

TRADES

Date	Traded To	Traded With	Traded By	In Exchange For

Jody Davis

Date	Traded To	Traded With	Traded By	In Exchange For
Sept 29, 1988	ATL N		CHI N	Kevin Coffman / Kevin Blankenship

Joel Davis

Date	Traded To	Traded With	Traded By	In Exchange For
Jan 23, 1989	CLE A		CHI A	See Eddie Williams

John Davis

Date	Traded To	Traded With	Traded By	In Exchange For
Dec 10, 1987	CHI A		KC A	See Floyd Bannister

Kiddo Davis

Date	Traded To	Traded With	Traded By	In Exchange For
Dec 12, 1932	NY N		PHI N	Gus Dugas / Chick Fullis

(Part of three-team trade involving New York, Philadelphia, and Pittsburgh.)

Date	Traded To	Traded With	Traded By	In Exchange For
Feb 1934	STL N		NY N	George Watkins
June 15, 1934	PHI N		STL N	Chick Fullis
Dec 13, 1934	NY N		PHI N	Joe Bowman
Aug 4, 1937	CIN N		NY N	Cash

Lefty Davis

Date	Traded To	Traded With	Traded By	In Exchange For
May 1901	PIT N		BKN N	Tom McCreery

Mark Davis

Date	Traded To	Traded With	Traded By	In Exchange For
Dec 14, 1982	SF N	Mike Krukow / minor league OF Charles Penigar	PHI N	Joe Morgan / Al Holland
July 4, 1987	SD N		SF N	See Kevin Mitchell
Dec 11, 1989	KC A		SD N	No compensation (free agent signing)

Mike Davis

Date	Traded To	Traded With	Traded By	In Exchange For
Dec 15, 1987	LA N		OAK A	No compensation (free agent signing)

Peaches Davis

Date	Traded To	Traded With	Traded By	In Exchange For
Aug 19, 1939	PHI N		CIN N	Cash

Ron Davis

Date	Traded To	Traded With	Traded By	In Exchange For
June 15, 1968	STL N		HOU N	Dick Simpson / Hal Gilson
Dec 3, 1968	SD N	Danny Breeden / Ed Spiezio / minor league P Phil Knuckles	STL N	Dave Giusti
March 28, 1969	PIT N	Bobby Klaus	SD N	Chris Cannizzaro / Tommie Sisk

Ron Davis

Date	Traded To	Traded With	Traded By	In Exchange For
June 10, 1978	NY A		CHI N	Ken Holtzman
April 10, 1982	MIN A	Paul Boris / Greg Gagne	NY A	Roy Smalley
Aug 13, 1986	CHI N	Minor league P Dewayne Coleman	MIN A	George Frazier / Ray Fontenot / Minor league SS Julius McDougal

Spud Davis

Date	Traded To	Traded With	Traded By	In Exchange For
May 11, 1928	PHI N	Homer Peel	STL N	Jimmie Wilson
Nov 15, 1933	STL N	Eddie Delker	PHI N	Jimmie Wilson

(Wilson was named manager of the Phillies.)

Date	Traded To	Traded With	Traded By	In Exchange For
Dec 2, 1936	CIN N		STL N	Cash
June 13, 1938	PHI N	Al Hollingsworth and $50,000.	CIN N	Bucky Walters
Oct 27, 1939	PIT N		PHI N	Cash

Steve Davis

Date	Traded To	Traded With	Traded By	In Exchange For
Dec 12, 1989	LA N		CLE A	Minor league IF Manny Francois / Minor league OF Joe Kesselmark

Storm Davis

Date	Traded To	Traded With	Traded By	In Exchange For
Oct 30, 1986	SD N		BAL A	Terry Kennedy / Mark Williamson
Aug 30, 1987	OAK A		SD N	Dave Leiper
Dec 7, 1989	KC A		OAK A	No compensation (free agent signing)

Tommy Davis

Date	Traded To	Traded With	Traded By	In Exchange For
Nov 29, 1966	NY N	Derrell Griffith	LA N	Ron Hunt / Jim Hickman
Dec 15, 1967	CHI A	Jack Fisher / Billy Wynne / Buddy Booker	NY N	Tommie Agee / Al Weis
Aug 30, 1969	HOU N		SEA A	Danny Walton / Sandy Valdespino
June 22, 1970	OAK A		HOU N	Cash
Sept 16, 1970	CHI N		OAK A	Cash
Aug 18, 1972	BAL A		CHI N	Ellie Hendricks
Sept 20, 1976	KC A		CAL A	Cash

Willie Davis

Date	Traded To	Traded With	Traded By	In Exchange For
Dec 5, 1973	MON N		LA N	Mike Marshall
Dec 5, 1974	TEX A		MON N	Don Stanhouse / Pete Mackanin
June 4, 1975	STL N		TEX A	Ed Brinkman / Tommy Moore
Oct 20, 1975	SD N		STL N	Dick Sharon

Bill Dawley

Date	Traded To	Traded With	Traded By	In Exchange For
March 31, 1983	HOU N	Tony Walker	CIN N	Alan Knicely
Dec 22, 1986	STL N		CHI A	Fred Manrique

Andre Dawson

Date	Traded To	Traded With	Traded By	In Exchange For
March 6, 1987	CHI N		MON N	No compensation (free agent signing)

Boots Day

Date	Traded To	Traded With	Traded By	In Exchange For
Dec 4, 1969	CHI N		STL N	Rich Nye
May 12, 1970	MON N		CHI N	Jack Hiatt

Brian Dayett

Date	Traded To	Traded With	Traded By	In Exchange For
Dec 4, 1984	CHI N	Ray Fontenot	NY A	Henry Cotto / Ron Hassey / Rich Bordi / Porfi Altamirano

Ken Dayley

Date	Traded To	Traded With	Traded By	In Exchange For
June 15, 1984	STL N	Mike Jorgensen	ATL N	Ken Oberkfell

Charlie Deal

Date	Traded To	Traded With	Traded By	In Exchange For
June 1913	BOS N		DET A	Cash
Feb 10, 1916	STL A	See Eddie Plank	STL F	
June 2, 1916	CHI N		STL A	Cash

Chubby Dean

Date	Traded To	Traded With	Traded By	In Exchange For
Aug 9, 1941	CLE A		PHI A	Waiver price

Date	Traded To		Traded With	Traded By		In Exchange For
Dizzy Dean						
April 16, 1938	CHI	N	——	STL	N	Curt Davis Clyde Shoun Tuck Stainback and $185,000.
Paul Dean						
May 14, 1941	STL	N	Harry Gumbert and cash	NY	N	Bill McGee
Feb 1, 1943	WAS	A	——	STL	A	Cash
Tommy Dean						
April 17, 1969	SD	N	Leon Everitt	LA	N	Al McBean
Wayland Dean						
Dec 30, 1925	PHI	N	Jack Bentley	NY	N	Jimmy Ring
June 14, 1927	CHI	N	——	PHI	N	Cash
Denny DeBarr						
March 15, 1978	CLE	A	——	TOR	A	Rico Carty
June 26, 1978	CHI	N	——	CLE	A	Paul Reuschel
Art Decatur						
May 1, 1925	PHI	N	——	BKN	N	Bill Hubbell
Doug DeCinces						
Jan 28, 1982	CAL	A	Jeff Schneider	BAL	A	Dan Ford
Joe Decker						
Nov 30, 1972	MIN	A	Bill Hands minor league P Bob Maneely	CHI	N	Dave LaRoche
Marty Decker						
Aug 31, 1983	SD	N	——	PHI	N	See Sixto Lezcano
Jeff Dedmon						
March 28, 1988	CLE	A	——	ATL	N	player to be named
(Atlanta received P Tommy Kurczewski on June 22, 1988.)						
Rob Deer						
Dec 17, 1985	MIL	A	——	SF	N	Minor league P Dean Freeland Minor league P Eric Pilkington
Charlie Dees						
March 29, 1963	LA	A	——	SF	N	Jacke Davis
Tony DeFate						
Sept 1917	DET	A	——	STL	N	Waiver price
Ivan DeJesus						
Jan 11, 1977	CHI	N	Bill Buckner minor league P Jeff Albert	LA	N	Rick Monday Mike Garman
Jan 27, 1982	PHI	N	——	CHI	N	Larry Bowa Ryne Sandberg
April 6, 1985	STL	N	Bill Campbell	PHI	N	Dave Rucker
Feb 4, 1986	MON	N	——	STL	N	No compensation (free agent signing)

Date	Traded To		Traded With	Traded By		In Exchange For
Frank Delahanty						
Nov 1907	NY	A	——	CLE	A	Cash
Aug 1914	PIT	F	——	BUF	F	Tex McDonald
Jim Delahanty						
Feb 1902	NY	N	Jack Doyle	CHI	N	Cash
March 1906	CIN	N	Chick Fraser	BOS	N	Al Bridwell
June 11, 1907	WAS	A	——	STL	A	$2,000.
Sept 1907	STL	A	——	CIN	N	Cash
Aug 13, 1909	DET	A	——	WAS	A	Germany Schaefer Red Killefer
Mike de la Hoz						
April 1, 1964	MIL	N	——	CLE	A	Chico Salmon
Jose DeLeon						
July 23, 1986	CHI	A	——	PIT	N	Bobby Bonilla
Feb 9, 1988	STL	N	——	CHI	A	Ricky Horton Lance Johnson and cash
Luis DeLeon						
Dec 10, 1981	SD	N	Sixto Lezcano Garry Templeton	STL	N	Ozzie Smith Steve Mura Al Olmsted
(Templeton and Smith were exchanged on February 11, 1982; Olmsted and DeLeon were exchanged on February 19.)						
Luis Delgado						
March 20, 1979	CHI	N	——	SEA	A	Larry Cox
Bobby Del Greco						
May 17, 1956	STL	N	Dick Littlefield	PIT	N	Bill Virdon
April 20, 1957	CHI	N	Ed Mayer	STL	N	Jim King
Sept 10, 1957	NY	A	——	CHI	N	Cash
July 2, 1961	KC	A	——	PHI	N	Wes Covington
Eddie Delker						
May 30, 1932	PHI	N	Flint Rhem	STL	N	Cash
Nov 15, 1933	STL	N	Spud Davis	PHI	N	Jimmie Wilson
(Wilson was named manager of the Phillies.)						
Garton Del Savio						
April 2, 1943	PHI	N	——	CIN	N	Cash
Jim Delsing						
Dec 14, 1948	NY	A	——	CHI	A	Steve Souchock
June 15, 1950	STL	A	Don Johnson Duane Pillette Snuffy Stirnweiss and $50,000.	NY	A	Tom Ferrick Joe Ostrowski Leo Thomas Sid Schacht
Aug 14, 1952	DET	A	——	STL	A	See Vic Wertz
May 15, 1956	CHI	A	Fred Hatfield	DET	A	Jim Brideweser Harry Byrd Bob Kennedy
Dec 6, 1958	WAS	A	——	DET	A	See Eddie Yost
Joe DeMaestri						
Nov 27, 1951	STL	A	Dick Littlefield Gus Niarhos Gordon Goldsberry Jim Rivera	CHI	A	Al Widmar Sherm Lollar Tom Upton
Oct 16, 1952	CHI	A	Tommy Byrne	STL	A	Willie Miranda Hank Edwards

Date	Traded To	Traded With	Traded By	In Exchange For

Joe DeMaestri *continued*

Date	Traded To		Traded With	Traded By		In Exchange For
Jan 27, 1953	PHI	A	Eddie Robinson Ed McGhee	CHI	A	Ferris Fain minor league 2B Bob Wilson
Dec 11, 1959	NY	A	*See Roger Maris*	KC	A	——

Al Demaree

Date	Traded To		Traded With	Traded By		In Exchange For
Jan 1915	PHI	N	Milt Stock Bert Adams	NY	N	Hans Lobert
Jan 16, 1917	CHI	N	——	PHI	N	Jimmy Lavender and $5,000.
July 31, 1917	NY	N	——	CHI	N	Pete Kilduff
Feb 1919	BOS	N	——	NY	N	Cash

Frank Demaree

Date	Traded To		Traded With	Traded By		In Exchange For
Dec 6, 1938	NY	N	Bill Jurges Ken O'Dea	CHI	N	Dick Bartell Hank Leiber Gus Mancuso
July 21, 1941	BOS	N	——	NY	N	Waiver price
Jan 1943	STL	N	——	BOS	N	Cash

Billy DeMars

Date	Traded To		Traded With	Traded By		In Exchange For
Dec 13, 1949	STL	A	Ray Coleman Frankie Gustine minor league OF Ray Ippolito and $100,000.	PHI	A	Bob Dillinger Paul Lehner

Larry Demery

Date	Traded To		Traded With	Traded By		In Exchange For
March 27, 1978	TOR	A	——	PIT	N	Cash

(Demery was returned on March 31.)

Don Demeter

Date	Traded To		Traded With	Traded By		In Exchange For
May 4, 1961	PHI	N	Charley Smith	LA	N	Dick Farrell Joe Koppe
Dec 4, 1963	DET	A	Jack Hamilton	PHI	N	Jim Bunning Gus Triandos
June 14, 1966	BOS	A	Julio Navarro	DET	A	Earl Wilson Joe Christopher
June 4, 1967	CLE	A	Tony Horton	BOS	A	Gary Bell

Steve Demeter

Date	Traded To		Traded With	Traded By		In Exchange For
April 12, 1960	CLE	A	——	DET	A	Norm Cash

Ray Demmitt

Date	Traded To		Traded With	Traded By		In Exchange For
April 1914	CHI	A	——	DET	A	Cash

Gene DeMontreville

Date	Traded To		Traded With	Traded By		In Exchange For
Jan 1900	BKN	N	——	BAL	N	Cash
Feb 1901	BOS	N	——	BKN	N	Cash

Rick Dempsey

Date	Traded To		Traded With	Traded By		In Exchange For
Oct 27, 1972	NY	A	——	MIN	A	Danny Walton
June 15, 1976	BAL	A	Rudy May Tippy Martinez Dave Pagan Scott McGregor	NY	A	Ken Holtzman Doyle Alexander Grant Jackson Ellie Hendricks Jimmy Freeman
Feb 3, 1987	CLE	A	——	BAL	A	No compensation (free agent signing)

Bill Denehy

Date	Traded To		Traded With	Traded By		In Exchange For
Nov 27, 1967	WAS	A	$100,000.	NY	N	Gil Hodges

(Hodges was named New York manager.)

Date	Traded To		Traded With	Traded By		In Exchange For
June 20, 1969	CLE	A	Cash	WAS	A	Lee Maye
March 30, 1971	DET	A	Dean Chance	NY	N	Jerry Robertson

Don Dennis

Date	Traded To		Traded With	Traded By		In Exchange For
Dec 14, 1966	CHI	A	Walt Williams	STL	N	Johnny Romano and minor league P Lee White

John Denny

Date	Traded To		Traded With	Traded By		In Exchange For
Dec 7, 1979	CLE	A	Jerry Mumphrey	STL	N	Bobby Bonds
Sept 12, 1982	PHI	N	——	CLE	A	Wil Culmer Jerry Reed Roy Smith
Dec 11, 1985	CIN	N	Jeff Gray	PHI	N	Gary Redus Tom Hume

Bucky Dent

Date	Traded To		Traded With	Traded By		In Exchange For
April 5, 1977	NY	A	——	CHI	A	Oscar Gamble LaMarr Hoyt minor league P Bob Polinsky and $200,000.
Aug 8, 1982	TEX	A	——	NY	A	Lee Mazzilli

Sam Dente

Date	Traded To		Traded With	Traded By		In Exchange For
Nov 18, 1947	STL	A	Clem Dreisewerd Bill Sommers and $65,000.	BOS	A	Ellis Kinder Billy Hitchcock
Oct 4, 1948	WAS	A	——	STL	A	Tom Ferrick John Sullivan and $25,000.
Nov 27, 1951	CHI	A	——	WAS	A	Tom Upton

Bob Dernier

Date	Traded To		Traded With	Traded By		In Exchange For
March 26, 1984	CHI	N	Gary Matthews Porfi Altamirano	PHI	N	Bill Campbell Mike Diaz

Claud Derrick

Date	Traded To		Traded With	Traded By		In Exchange For
Nov 1912	NY	A	——	PHI	A	Cash
July 20, 1914	CHI	N	——	CIN	N	Fritz Mollwitz

Paul Derringer

Date	Traded To		Traded With	Traded By		In Exchange For
May 7, 1933	CIN	N	Sparky Adams Allyn Stout	STL	N	Leo Durocher Dutch Henry Jack Ogden
Jan 27, 1943	CHI	N	——	CIN	N	Cash

Gene Desautels

Date	Traded To		Traded With	Traded By		In Exchange For
Dec 12, 1940	CLE	A	Jim Bagby Gee Walker	BOS	A	Frankie Pytlak Odell Hale Joe Dobson
Sept 17, 1945	PHI	A	——	CLE	A	Waiver price

Jim Deshaies

Date	Traded To		Traded With	Traded By		In Exchange For
Sept 15, 1985	HOU	N	Two players to be named	NY	A	Joe Niekro

(Houston received IF Neder Horta and P Dody Rather on Jan. 11, 1986.)

Jimmie DeShong

Date	Traded To		Traded With	Traded By		In Exchange For
Jan 17, 1936	WAS	A	Jesse Hill	NY	A	Bump Hadley Roy Johnson
June 20, 1939	NY	A	——	WAS	A	Waiver price

Orestes Destrade

Date	Traded To		Traded With	Traded By		In Exchange For
March 30, 1988	PIT	N	——	NY	A	Hipolito Pena

Date		Traded To	Traded With		Traded By	In Exchange For
Bob Detherage						
June 15, 1976	STL	N	Joe Ferguson minor league IF Fred Tisdale	LA	N	Reggie Smith
Nov 23, 1976	HOU	N	Joe Ferguson	STL	N	Larry Dierker Jerry DaVanon
Tom Dettore						
April 1, 1974	CHI	N	Cash	PIT	N	Paul Popovich
Mike Devereaux						
March 11, 1989	BAL	A	——	LA	N	Mike Morgan
Adrian Devine						
Dec 9, 1976	TEX	A	Ken Henderson Dave May Carl Morton Roger Moret and $250,000.	ATL	N	Jeff Burroughs
Dec 8, 1977	ATL	N	Tommy Boggs Eddie Miller	TEX	A	Willie Montanez
(Part of four-team trade involving Texas, Atlanta, Pittsburgh, and New York Mets.)						
Dec 6, 1979	TEX	A	Pepe Frias	ATL	N	Doyle Alexander Larvell Blanks and $50,000.
Art Devlin						
Dec 1911	BOS	N	——	NY	N	Cash
Josh Devore						
May 22, 1913	CIN	N	Red Ames Heinie Groh and $20,000.	NY	N	Art Fromme Eddie Grant
June 5, 1913	PHI	N	Beals Becker	CIN	N	John Dodge Red Nelson
July 3, 1914	BOS	N	——	PHI	N	Jack Martin
Al DeVormer						
Jan 3, 1923	BOS	A	Cash	NY	A	George Pipgras Harvey Hendrick
Charlie Dexter						
Jan 1900	CHI	N	——	LOU	N	Cash
July 1902	BOS	N	——	CHI	N	Bobby Lowe
Bo Diaz						
March 30, 1978	CLE	A	Rick Wise Mike Paxton Ted Cox	BOS	A	Dennis Eckersley Fred Kendall
Nov 20, 1981	PHI	N	——	CLE	A	Lonnie Smith Scott Munninghoff
(Part of three-team trade involving Cleveland, Philadelphia, and St. Louis.)						
Aug 8, 1985	CIN	N	Minor league P Greg Simpson	PHI	N	Tom Foley Alan Knicely Fred Toliver
(Philadelphia received Toliver on August 27, 1985.)						
Carlos Diaz						
March 7, 1981	ATL	N	——	SEA	A	Jeff Burroughs
Sept 10, 1982	NY	N	——	ATL	N	Tom Hausman
Dec 8, 1983	LA	N	Bob Bailor	NY	N	Sid Fernandez Ross Jones
Mike Diaz						
March 26, 1984	PHI	N	Bill Campbell	CHI	N	Gary Matthews Bob Dernier Porfi Altamirano

Date		Traded To	Traded With		Traded By	In Exchange For
Mike Diaz *continued*						
April 27, 1985	PIT	N	——	PHI	N	Minor league C Steve Herz
Leo Dickerman						
June 13, 1924	STL	N	——	BKN	N	Bill Doak
Johnny Dickshot						
Dec 16, 1938	BOS	N	Al Todd and cash	PIT	N	Ray Mueller
Jim Dickson						
Jan 20, 1964	CIN	N	Wally Wolf and cash	HOU	N	Eddie Kasko
Murry Dickson						
Jan 29, 1949	PIT	N	——	STL	N	$125,000.
Jan 13, 1954	PHI	N	——	PIT	N	Andy Hansen Lucky Lohrke and $70,000.
May 11, 1956	STL	N	Herm Wehmeier	PHI	N	Harvey Haddix Ben Flowers Stu Miller
Aug 22, 1958	NY	A	——	KC	A	Zeke Bella and cash
May 9, 1959	KC	A	——	NY	A	Cash
Bob Didier						
May 14, 1973	DET	A	——	ATL	N	Gene Lamont
March 26, 1974	BOS	A	——	DET	A	Cash
Chuck Diering						
Dec 11, 1951	NY	N	Max Lanier	STL	N	Eddie Stanky
(Stanky was named St. Louis manager.)						
Larry Dierker						
Nov 23, 1976	STL	N	Jerry DaVanon	HOU	N	Joe Ferguson Bob Detherage
Bill Dietrich						
July 1, 1936	WAS	A	——	PHI	A	Waiver price
July 20, 1936	CHI	A	——	WAS	A	Waiver price
Dick Dietz						
April 14, 1972	LA	N	——	SF	N	Cash
March 27, 1973	ATL	N	——	LA	N	Cash
Dutch Dietz						
Aug 1940	PIT	N	——	CIN	N	Cash
June 15, 1943	PHI	N	——	PIT	N	Johnny Podgajny
Don Dillard						
Nov 27, 1962	MIL	N	Ty Cline Frank Funk	CLE	A	Joe Adcock Jack Curtis
Gordon Dillard						
Dec 8, 1988	PHI	N	——	BAL	A	*See Phil Bradley*

Steve Dillard

Date	Traded To	Traded With	Traded By	In Exchange For
Jan 30, 1978	DET A ——		BOS A	Minor league Ps Mike Burns and Frank Harris and cash
March 20, 1979	CHI N ——		DET A	Ed Putman

Pickles Dillhoefer

Date	Traded To	Traded With	Traded By	In Exchange For
Dec 11, 1917	PHI N	Mike Prendergast and $55,000.	CHI N	Grover Alexander Bill Killefer
Jan 21, 1919	STL N	Milt Stock Dixie Davis	PHI N	Doug Baird Stuffy Stewart Gene Packard

Bob Dillinger

Date	Traded To	Traded With	Traded By	In Exchange For
Dec 13, 1949	PHI A	Paul Lehner	STL A	Ray Coleman Frankie Gustine Billy DeMars minor league OF Ray Ippolito and $100,000.
July 20, 1950	PIT N ——		PHI A	$35,000.
May 16, 1951	CHI A ——		PIT N	Cash

Bill Dillman

Date	Traded To	Traded With	Traded By	In Exchange For
Dec 5, 1969	STL N ——		BAL A	Cash

Pop Dillon

Date	Traded To	Traded With	Traded By	In Exchange For
Jan 1901	DET A ——		PIT N	Cash
July 1902	BAL A ——		DET A	Cash

Miguel Dilone

Date	Traded To	Traded With	Traded By	In Exchange For
April 4, 1978	OAK A	Elias Sosa Mike Edwards	PIT N	Manny Sanguillen
July 4, 1979	CHI N ——		OAK A	Cash
May 7, 1980	CLE A ——		CHI N	Cash
Aug 25, 1983	CHI A ——		CLE A	Rich Barnes
Sept 7, 1983	PIT N	minor league P Mike Maitland	CHI A	Randy Niemann
Jan 19, 1984	MON N ——		PIT N	No compensation (free agent signing)

Vince DiMaggio

Date	Traded To	Traded With	Traded By	In Exchange For
Aug 10, 1938	CIN N	Tommy Reis Johnny Babich Gil English Johnny Riddle and Cash	BOS N	Eddie Miller
May 8, 1940	PIT N ——		CIN N	Johnny Rizzo
March 31, 1945	PHI N ——		PIT N	Al Gerheauser
May 1, 1946	NY N ——		PHI N	Clyde Kluttz

Kerry Dineen

Date	Traded To	Traded With	Traded By	In Exchange For
March 26, 1977	PHI N ——		NY A	Sergio Ferrer

Bill Dinneen

Date	Traded To	Traded With	Traded By	In Exchange For
Jan 10, 1900	BOS N	Kirtley Baker Shad Barry	WAS N	Cash
June 22, 1907	STL A ——		BOS A	Beany Jacobson and $1,000.

Frank DiPino

Date	Traded To	Traded With	Traded By	In Exchange For
Aug 30, 1982	HOU N	Kevin Bass Mike Madden and cash	MIL A	Don Sutton
July 21, 1986	CHI N ——		HOU N	Davey Lopes
Dec 21, 1988	STL N ——		CHI N	No compensation (free agent signing)

Art Ditmar

Date	Traded To	Traded With	Traded By	In Exchange For
Feb 19, 1957	NY A	Bobby Shantz Jack McMahan Wayne Belardi Curt Roberts Clete Boyer	KC A	Billy Hunter Rip Coleman Tom Morgan Mickey McDermott Milt Graff Irv Noren

(New York received Roberts on April 4, and Boyer on June 4, 1957.)

Date	Traded To	Traded With	Traded By	In Exchange For
June 14, 1961	KC A	Deron Johnson	NY A	Bud Daley

Jack Dittmer

Date	Traded To	Traded With	Traded By	In Exchange For
Feb 12, 1957	DET A ——		MIL N	Charlie King Cash

Ken Dixon

Date	Traded To	Traded With	Traded By	In Exchange For
Dec 9, 1987	SEA A ——		BAL A	Mike Morgan

Sonny Dixon

Date	Traded To	Traded With	Traded By	In Exchange For
June 11, 1954	CHI A ——		WAS A	Gus Keriazakos
June 11, 1954	PHI A	Al Sima Bill Wilson and $20,000.	CHI A	Ed McGhee Morrie Martin
May 11, 1955	NY A	Cash	KC A	Johnny Sain Enos Slaughter

Bill Doak

Date	Traded To	Traded With	Traded By	In Exchange For
June 13, 1924	BKN N ——		STL N	Leo Dickerman

Dan Dobbek

Date	Traded To	Traded With	Traded By	In Exchange For
Jan 30, 1962	CIN N ——		MIN A	Jerry Zimmerman

John Dobbs

Date	Traded To	Traded With	Traded By	In Exchange For
July 1902	CHI N ——		CIN N	Cash
May 1903	BKN N ——		CHI N	Cash

Joe Dobson

Date	Traded To	Traded With	Traded By	In Exchange For
Dec 12, 1940	BOS A	Frankie Pytlak Odell Hale	CLE A	Gene Desautels Jim Bagby Gee Walker
Dec 10, 1950	CHI A	Dick Littlefield Al Zarilla	BOS A	Ray Scarborough Bill Wight

Pat Dobson

Date	Traded To	Traded With	Traded By	In Exchange For
Dec 4, 1969	SD N	Dave Campbell	DET A	Joe Niekro
Dec 1, 1970	BAL A	Tom Dukes	SD N	Tom Phoebus Al Severinsen Fred Beene Enzo Hernandez
Nov 30, 1972	ATL N	Roric Harrison Davey Johnson Johnny Oates	BAL A	Earl Williams Taylor Duncan
June 7, 1973	NY A ——		ATL N	Frank Tepedino Wayne Nordhagen Al Closter Dave Cheadle
Nov 22, 1975	CLE A ——		NY A	Oscar Gamble

Larry Doby

Date	Traded To	Traded With	Traded By	In Exchange For
Oct 25, 1955	CHI A ——		CLE A	Jim Busby Chico Carrasquel
Dec 3, 1957	BAL A	Jack Harshman Russ Heman Jim Marshall	CHI A	Tito Francona Ray Moore Billy Goodman
April 1, 1958	CLE A	Don Ferrarese	BAL A	Bud Daley Dick Williams Gene Woodling
March 21, 1959	DET A ——		CLE A	Tito Francona
May 13, 1959	CHI A ——		DET A	$30,000.

Date	Traded To		Traded With	Traded By		In Exchange For

John Dodge
Date	Traded To		Traded With	Traded By		In Exchange For
June 5, 1913	CIN	N	Red Nelson	PHI	N	Josh Devore
						Beals Becker

Ed Doheny
| June 1901 | PIT | N | —— | NY | N | Heinie Smith |

Cozy Dolan
May 1912	PHI	N	——	NY	A	Cash
Aug 20, 1913	PIT	N	Cash	PHI	N	Bobby Byrne
						Howie Camnitz
Dec 12, 1913	STL	N	——	PIT	N	See Ed Konetchy

Cozy Dolan
June 1901	BKN	N	——	CHI	N	Cash
June 9, 1903	CIN	N	Tom Daly	CHI	A	George Magoon
June 6, 1905	BOS	N	——	CIN	N	Cash

Joe Dolan
| May 1901 | PHI | A | —— | PHI | N | Cash |

Jiggs Donahue
April 1901	MIL	A	——	PIT	N	Cash
Aug 1908	WAS	A	——	CHI	A	Cash
May 16, 1909	WAS	A	Nick Altrock	CHI	A	Bill Burns
			Gavvy Cravath			

Pat Donahue
| May 1910 | PHI | A | —— | BOS | A | Cash |
| Sept 1910 | CLE | A | —— | PHI | A | Cash |

Red Donahue
June 1903	CLE	A	——	STL	A	Completes
						Charlie Hemphill
						May, 1902.
Dec 1905	DET	A	——	CLE	A	Cash

John Donaldson
June 14, 1969	SEA	A	——	OAK	A	Larry Haney
May 18, 1970	OAK	A	——	MIL	A	Roberto Pena
May 22, 1971	DET	A	——	OAK	A	Daryl Patterson

Mike Donlin
July 3, 1904	NY	N	——	CIN	N	Moose McCormick
Aug 1, 1911	BOS	N	——	NY	N	Cash
Feb 1912	PIT	N	——	BOS	N	Vin Campbell
Dec 1912	PHI	N	——	PIT	N	Waiver price

(Donlin refused to report and announced his retirement.)

Blix Donnelly
| July 6, 1946 | PHI | N | —— | STL | N | Cash |
| April 16, 1951 | BOS | N | —— | PHI | N | Waiver price |

Jim Donohue
June 15, 1960	LA	N	——	STL	N	John Glenn
June 7, 1961	LA	A	——	DET	A	Jerry Casale
May 29, 1962	MIN	A	——	LA	A	Don Lee

Pete Donohue
| May 27, 1930 | NY | N | Ethan Allen | CIN | N | Pat Crawford |

Dick Donovan
Date	Traded To		Traded With	Traded By		In Exchange For
Oct 5, 1961	CLE	A	Gene Green	WAS	A	Jimmy Piersall
			Jim Mahoney			

Mike Donovan
| Jan 1908 | NY | A | —— | CLE | A | Cash |

Patsy Donovan
| Jan 1900 | STL | N | —— | PIT | N | $1,000. |

Red Dooin
| Nov 1914 | CIN | N | —— | PHI | N | Bert Niehoff |
| July 6, 1915 | NY | N | —— | CIN | N | Waiver price |

Mickey Doolan
Feb 10, 1916	CHI	N	See Three Finger Brown	CHI	F	——
Aug 28, 1916	NY	N	Heinie Zimmerman	CHI	N	Larry Doyle
						Herb Hunter
						Merwin Jacobson

John Dopson
Dec 8, 1988	BOS	A	Luis Rivera	MON	N	Spike Owen
						Minor league
						P Dan Gakeler

Tom Doran
| May 18, 1905 | DET | A | —— | BOS | A | Waiver price |

Harry Dorish
May 9, 1950	STL	A	——	BOS	A	Cash
June 6, 1955	BAL	A	——	CHI	A	Les Moss
June 25, 1956	BOS	A	——	BAL	A	Cash

Gus Dorner
| May 13, 1906 | BOS | N | —— | CIN | N | Cash |

Brian Dorsett
July 15, 1987	CLE	A	——	OAK	A	See Tony Bernazard
June 7, 1988	CAL	A	——	CLE	A	Cash
Nov 17, 1988	NY	A	——	CAL	A	Minor league
						P Eric Schmidt

Jim Dorsey
| Jan 23, 1981 | BOS | A | Frank Tanana | CAL | A | Fred Lynn |
| | | | Joe Rudi | | | Steve Renko |

Jack Doscher
| June 1903 | BKN | N | —— | CHI | N | Cash |

Richard Dotson
Dec 5, 1977	CHI	A	Bobby Bonds	CAL	A	Brian Downing
			Thad Bosley			Chris Knapp
						Dave Frost
Nov 13, 1987	NY	A	Scott Nielsen	CHI	A	Dan Pasqua
						Mark Salas
						Steve Rosenberg
Dec 5, 1989	KC	A	——	CHI	A	No compensation
						(free agent signing)

Patsy Dougherty
| June 18, 1904 | NY | A | —— | BOS | A | Bob Unglaub |
| June 6, 1906 | CHI | A | —— | NY | A | Cash |

Date	Traded To	Traded With	Traded By	In Exchange For

Phil Douglas

Date	Traded To		Traded With	Traded By		In Exchange For
June 13, 1915	BKN	N	——	CIN	N	Cash
Sept 8, 1915	CHI	N	——	BKN	N	Cash
July 25, 1919	NY	N	——	CHI	N	Dave Robertson

Whammy Douglas

June 30, 1959	CIN	N	——	PIT	N	*See Harvey Haddix*

Jan 30, 1959 CIN N —— PIT N *See Harvey Haddix*

Taylor Douthit

June 15, 1931	CIN	N	——	STL	N	Wally Roettger
April 29, 1933	CHI	N	——	CIN	N	Waiver price

Snooks Dowd

April 1919	PHI	A	——	DET	A	Cash

Dave Dowling

May 11, 1965	CHI	N	——	STL	N	Waiver price
April 22, 1968	STL	N	Pete Mikkelsen	CHI	N	Jack Lamabe Ron Piche

Pete Dowling

May 1901	CLE	A	——	MIL	A	Cash

Tom Downey

Jan 18, 1909	CIN	N	Kid Durbin	CHI	N	John Kane
Aug 1912	CHI	N	——	PHI	N	Cash

Al Downing

Dec 5, 1969	OAK	A	Frank Fernandez	NY	A	Danny Cater Ossie Chavarria
June 11, 1970	MIL	A	Tito Francona	OAK	A	Steve Hovley
Feb 10, 1971	LA	N	——	MIL	A	Andy Kosco

Brian Downing

Dec 5, 1977	CAL	A	Chris Knapp Dave Frost	CHI	A	Bobby Bonds Thad Bosley Richard Dotson

Kelly Downs

Aug 20, 1984	SF	N	George Riley	PHI	N	Al Oliver Renie Martin

Red Downs

May 1912	CHI	N	——	BKN	N	Cash

Brian Doyle

Feb 17, 1977	NY	A	Greg Pryor and cash	TEX	A	Sandy Alomar
Nov 3, 1980	OAK	A	Fred Stanley	NY	A	Mike Morgan

Carl Doyle

June 12, 1940	STL	N	Ernie Koy Sam Nahem Bert Haas and $125,000.	BKN	N	Joe Medwick Curt Davis

Conny Doyle

Jan 1900	PIT	N	*See Honus Wagner*	LOU	N	——

Denny Doyle

Aug 14, 1973	CAL	A	——	PHI	N	Aurelio Monteagudo Chris Coletta Billy Grabarkewitz
June 14, 1975	BOS	A	——	CAL	A	Cash

(California also received minor league P Chuck Ross on March 5, 1976.)

Jack Doyle

Feb 1901	CHI	N	——	NY	N	Sammy Strang
Feb 1902	NY	N	Jim Delahanty	CHI	N	Cash
Jan 30, 1903	BKN	N	——	WAS	A	Cash
April 30, 1904	PHI	N	Deacon Van Buren	BKN	N	Cash

Larry Doyle

Aug 28, 1916	CHI	N	Herb Hunter Merwin Jacobson	NY	N	Heinie Zimmerman Mickey Doolan
Jan 4, 1918	BOS	N	Art Wilson and $15,000.	CHI	N	Lefty Tyler
Jan 8, 1918	NY	N	Jesse Barnes	BOS	N	Buck Herzog

Paul Doyle

Nov 27, 1969	CAL	A	——	ATL	N	Cash
Aug 25, 1970	SD	N	——	CAL	A	Cash

Slow Joe Doyle

May 1910	CIN	N	——	NY	A	Cash

Doug Drabek

July 17, 1984	NY	A	Kevin Hickey	CHI	A	Roy Smalley
Nov 26, 1986	PIT	N	Logan Easley Brian Fisher	NY	A	Rick Rhoden Cecilio Guante Pat Clements

Moe Drabowsky

March 31, 1961	MIL	N	Seth Morehead	CHI	N	Andre Rodgers Daryl Robertson
Aug 13, 1962	KC	A	——	CIN	N	Cash
June 15, 1970	BAL	A	——	KC	A	Bobby Floyd
Nov 30, 1970	STL	N	——	BAL	A	Jerry DaVanon

Dick Drago

Oct 24, 1973	BOS	A	——	KC	A	Marty Pattin
March 3, 1976	CAL	A	——	BOS	A	John Balaz Dick Sharon Dave Machemer
June 13, 1977	BAL	A	——	CAL	A	Dyar Miller
April 8, 1981	SEA	A	——	BOS	A	Manny Sarmiento

Solly Drake

June 9, 1959	PHI	N	——	LA	N	Waiver price

Dave Dravecky

July 4, 1987	SF	N	*See Kevin Mitchell*	SD	N	——

Clem Dreisewerd

Nov 18, 1947	STL	A	——	BOS	A	*See Ellis Kinder*

Rob Dressler

July 18, 1978	STL	N	——	SF	N	John Tamargo
June 7, 1979	SEA	A	——	STL	N	Cash

Karl Drews

Aug 9, 1948	STL	A	——	NY	A	Cash

Date	Traded To	Traded With	Traded By	In Exchange For

Karl Drews continued

Date	Traded To	Traded With	Traded By	In Exchange For
June 15, 1954	CIN N	——	PHI N	Cash

Dan Driessen

Date	Traded To	Traded With	Traded By	In Exchange For
July 26, 1984	MON N	——	CIN N	Andy McGaffigan minor league P Jim Jefferson
Aug 1, 1985	SF N	——	MON N	Scot Thompson player to be named

(Montreal returned Bill Laskey on Oct. 24 to complete deal.)

Lew Drill

Date	Traded To	Traded With	Traded By	In Exchange For
Sept 1902	WAS A	——	BAL A	Cash
Aug 10, 1904	DET A	Bill Coughlin	WAS A	$7,500.

Walt Dropo

Date	Traded To	Traded With	Traded By	In Exchange For
June 3, 1952	DET A	Bill Wight Fred Hatfield Johnny Pesky Don Lenhardt	BOS A	Dizzy Trout George Kell Johnny Lipon Hoot Evers
Dec 6, 1954	CHI A	Ted Gray Bob Nieman	DET A	Chris Cristante Ferris Fain Jack Phillips
June 24, 1958	CIN N	——	CHI A	Waiver price
June 23, 1959	BAL A	——	CIN N	Whitey Lockman

Carl Druhot

Date	Traded To	Traded With	Traded By	In Exchange For
July 25, 1906	STL N	Shad Barry	CIN N	Homer Smoot

Tim Drummond

Date	Traded To	Traded With	Traded By	In Exchange For
March 26, 1988	NY N	See Mackey Sasser	PIT N	——
July 31, 1989	MIN A	Rick Aguilera David West Kevin Tapani Jack Savage	NY N	Frank Viola

(Minnesota received Savage on Oct. 16, 1989.)

Keith Drumright

Date	Traded To	Traded With	Traded By	In Exchange For
April 27, 1979	KC A	——	HOU N	George Throop
Dec 11, 1980	OAK A	Cliff Johnson	CHI N	Minor league P Mike King

Monk Dubiel

Date	Traded To	Traded With	Traded By	In Exchange For
Dec 14, 1948	CHI N	Dutch Leonard	PHI N	Hank Borowy Eddie Waitkus
Dec 20, 1952	BOS N	——	CHI N	Sheldon Jones

Brian Dubois

Date	Traded To	Traded With	Traded By	In Exchange For
July 28, 1989	DET A	——	BAL A	Keith Moreland

Jim Duckworth

Date	Traded To	Traded With	Traded By	In Exchange For
June 23, 1966	KC A	——	WAS A	Ken Harrelson
July 30, 1966	WAS A	——	KC A	Diego Segui

Clise Dudley

Date	Traded To	Traded With	Traded By	In Exchange For
Oct 14, 1930	PHI N	Jumbo Elliott Hal Lee and cash	BKN N	Lefty O'Doul Fresco Thompson

Jim Duffalo

Date	Traded To	Traded With	Traded By	In Exchange For
May 4, 1965	CIN N	——	SF N	Bill Henry

Frank Duffy

Date	Traded To	Traded With	Traded By	In Exchange For
May 29, 1971	SF N	Vern Geishert	CIN N	George Foster

Frank Duffy continued

Date	Traded To	Traded With	Traded By	In Exchange For
Nov 29, 1971	CLE A	Gaylord Perry	SF N	Sam McDowell
March 24, 1978	BOS A	——	CLE A	Rick Kreuger

Joe Dugan

Date	Traded To	Traded With	Traded By	In Exchange For
Jan 10, 1922	WAS A	——	PHI A	Jose Acosta Bing Miller

(Part of three-team trade involving Boston, Philadelphia, and Washington.)

Date	Traded To	Traded With	Traded By	In Exchange For
Jan 10, 1922	BOS A	Frank O'Rourke	WAS A	Roger Peckinpaugh

(Part of three-team trade involving Boston, Philadelphia, and Washington.)

Date	Traded To	Traded With	Traded By	In Exchange For
July 23, 1922	NY A	Elmer Smith	BOS A	Chick Fewster Elmer Miller Johnny Mitchell Lefty O'Doul and $50,000.
Dec 29, 1928	BOS N	——	NY A	Waiver price

Gus Dugas

Date	Traded To	Traded With	Traded By	In Exchange For
Dec 12, 1932	NY N	Glenn Spencer	PIT N	Freddie Lindstrom

(Part of three-team trade involving New York, Philadelphia, and Pittsburgh.)

Date	Traded To	Traded With	Traded By	In Exchange For
Dec 12, 1932	PHI N	Chick Fullis	NY N	Kiddo Davis

(Part of three-team trade involving New York, Philadelphia, and Pittsburgh.)

Oscar Dugey

Date	Traded To	Traded With	Traded By	In Exchange For
Feb 10, 1915	PHI N	Possum Whitted	BOS N	Cash

Bill Duggleby

Date	Traded To	Traded With	Traded By	In Exchange For
July 15, 1907	PIT N	——	PHI N	Cash

Tom Dukes

Date	Traded To	Traded With	Traded By	In Exchange For
Oct 13, 1966	HOU N	Dan Schneider Lee Bales	ATL N	Gene Ratliff John Hoffman minor league IF Ed Pacheco
Dec 1, 1970	BAL A	See Pat Dobson	SD N	——

George Dumont

Date	Traded To	Traded With	Traded By	In Exchange For
Jan 17, 1919	BOS A	Eddie Ainsmith	WAS A	Hal Janvrin and cash

Dave Duncan

Date	Traded To	Traded With	Traded By	In Exchange For
March 24, 1973	CLE A	George Hendrick	OAK A	Ray Fosse Jack Heidemann
Feb 25, 1975	BAL A	minor league OF Al McGrew	CLE A	Boog Powell Don Hood
Nov 18, 1976	CHI A	——	BAL A	Pat Kelly

Mariano Duncan

Date	Traded To	Traded With	Traded By	In Exchange For
July 18, 1989	LA N	Kal Daniels	CIN N	Tim Leary Lenny Harris

Pat Duncan

Date	Traded To	Traded With	Traded By	In Exchange For
Oct 1924	WAS A	——	CIN N	Waiver price

Taylor Duncan

Date	Traded To	Traded With	Traded By	In Exchange For
Nov 30, 1972	BAL A	See Earl Williams	ATL N	——
Sept 7, 1977	STL N	——	BAL A	Cash

Davey Dunkle

Date	Traded To	Traded With	Traded By	In Exchange For
June 1903	WAS A	——	CHI A	Ducky Holmes

Jack Dunn

Date	Traded To	Traded With	Traded By	In Exchange For
June 1900	PHI N	——	BKN N	Cash

Date	Traded To		Traded With	Traded By		In Exchange For

Mike Dunne

Date	Traded To		Traded With	Traded By		In Exchange For
April 1, 1987	PIT	N	——	STL	N	*See Tony Pena*
April 21, 1989	SEA	A	Minor league OF Mark Merchant Minor league P Mike Walker	PIT	N	Rey Quinones Bill Wilkinson

Steve Dunning

Date	Traded To		Traded With	Traded By		In Exchange For
May 10, 1973	TEX	A	——	CLE	A	Dick Bosman Ted Ford
Feb 25, 1975	CHI	A	——	TEX	A	Stan Perzanowski
Dec 11, 1975	CAL	A	Bill Melton	CHI	A	Jim Spencer Morris Nettles
Nov 6, 1976	STL	N	Pat Scanlon Tony Scott	MON	N	Bill Greif Angel Torres Sam Mejias
Aug 12, 1977	OAK	A	——	STL	N	Randy Scarbery

Kid Durbin

Date	Traded To		Traded With	Traded By		In Exchange For
Jan 18, 1909	CIN	N	Tom Downey	CHI	N	John Kane
May 28, 1909	PIT	N	——	CIN	N	Ward Miller and cash

Ryne Duren

Date	Traded To		Traded With	Traded By		In Exchange For
Oct 11, 1956	KC	A	Jim Pisoni	BAL	A	Art Ceccarelli Al Pilarcik
June 15, 1957	NY	A	Jim Pisoni Milt Graff Harry Simpson	KC	A	Billy Martin Woodie Held Ralph Terry Bob Martyn
May 8, 1961	LA	A	Lee Thomas Johnny James	NY	A	Tex Clevenger Bob Cerv
March 14, 1963	PHI	N	——	LA	A	Cash
May 13, 1964	CIN	N	——	PHI	N	Cash

Don Durham

Date	Traded To		Traded With	Traded By		In Exchange For
July 16, 1973	TEX	A	——	STL	N	Jim Kremmel

Ed Durham

Date	Traded To		Traded With	Traded By		In Exchange For
Dec 15, 1932	CHI	A	Hal Rhyne	BOS	A	Johnny Hodapp Greg Mulleavy Bob Fothergill Bob Seeds

Leon Durham

Date	Traded To		Traded With	Traded By		In Exchange For
Dec 9, 1980	CHI	N	Ken Reitz Tye Waller	STL	N	Bruce Sutter
May 19, 1988	CIN	N	——	CHI	N	Pat Perry and cash

Leo Durocher

Date	Traded To		Traded With	Traded By		In Exchange For
Feb 2, 1930	CIN	N	——	NY	A	Waiver price
May 7, 1933	STL	N	Dutch Henry Jack Ogden	CIN	N	Paul Derringer Sparky Adams Allyn Stout
Oct 4, 1937	BKN	N	——	STL	N	Johnny Cooney Jim Bucher Joe Stripp Roy Henshaw

Cedric Durst

Date	Traded To		Traded With	Traded By		In Exchange For
Feb 8, 1927	NY	A	Joe Giard	STL	A	Sad Sam Jones
May 6, 1930	BOS	A	$50,000.	NY	A	Red Ruffing

Erv Dusak

Date	Traded To		Traded With	Traded By		In Exchange For
May 17, 1951	PIT	N	Rocky Nelson	STL	N	Stan Rojek

Jim Dwyer

Date	Traded To		Traded With	Traded By		In Exchange For
July 25, 1975	MON	N	——	STL	N	Larry Lintz
July 21, 1976	NY	N	Pepe Mangual	MON	N	Del Unser Wayne Garrett
Dec 8, 1976	CHI	N	——	NY	N	Sheldon Mallory
(Part of three-team trade involving Chicago Cubs, New York Mets, and Kansas City.)						
Oct 25, 1977	SF	N	——	STL	N	Frank Riccelli
(San Francisco received Dwyer on June 15, 1978.)						
March 15, 1979	BOS	A	——	SF	N	Cash
Dec 23, 1980	BAL	A	——	BOS	A	No compensation (free agent signing)
Aug 29, 1988	MIN	A	——	BAL	A	player to be named
(Baltimore received P Doug Cline on August 31, 1988.)						
Aug 28, 1989	MON	N	——	MIN	A	Alonzo Powell
(Minnesota received Powell on Sept. 15, 1989.)						

Jerry Dybzinski

Date	Traded To		Traded With	Traded By		In Exchange For
April 1, 1983	CHI	A	——	CLE	A	Pat Tabler

Jim Dyck

Date	Traded To		Traded With	Traded By		In Exchange For
April 17, 1954	CLE	A	——	BAL	A	Bob Kennedy
July 16, 1955	BAL	A	——	CLE	A	Cash
May 11, 1956	CIN	N	——	BAL	A	$25,000.

Duffy Dyer

Date	Traded To		Traded With	Traded By		In Exchange For
Oct 22, 1974	PIT	N	——	NY	N	Gene Clines
Nov 28, 1978	MON	N	——	PIT	N	No compensation (free agent signing)
March 15, 1980	DET	A	——	MON	N	Jerry Manuel

Jimmy Dykes

Date	Traded To		Traded With	Traded By		In Exchange For
Sept 28, 1932	CHI	A	Al Simmons Mule Haas	PHI	A	$100,000.
Aug 10, 1960	CLE	A	——	DET	A	Joe Gordon

Len Dykstra

Date	Traded To		Traded With	Traded By		In Exchange For
June 18, 1989	PHI	N	Roger McDowell Tom Edens	NY	N	Juan Samuel
(Philadelphia received Edens on July 26, 1989.)						

Arnie Earley

Date	Traded To		Traded With	Traded By		In Exchange For
Dec 15, 1965	MIL	N	Lee Thomas Jay Ritchie	BOS	A	Bob Sadowski Dan Osinski

Jake Early

Date	Traded To		Traded With	Traded By		In Exchange For
Dec 16, 1946	WAS	A	——	STL	A	Frank Mancuso
March 26, 1948	WAS	A	——	STL	A	Cash

George Earnshaw

Date	Traded To		Traded With	Traded By		In Exchange For
Dec 12, 1933	CHI	A	Johnny Pasek	PHI	A	Charlie Berry and $20,000.
May 16, 1935	BKN	N	——	CHI	A	Cash
July 1936	STL	N	——	BKN	N	Cash

Mike Easler

Date	Traded To		Traded With	Traded By		In Exchange For
Sept 30, 1975	STL	N	——	HOU	N	Mike Barlow
Sept 3, 1976	CAL	A	——	STL	N	Minor league IF Ron Farkas
April 4, 1977	PIT	N	——	CAL	A	Minor league P Randy Sealy
Oct 27, 1978	BOS	A	——	PIT	N	Cash
March 15, 1979	PIT	N	——	BOS	A	Minor league OF George Hill and P Martin Rivas and cash
Dec 6, 1983	BOS	A	——	PIT	N	John Tudor
March 28, 1986	NY	A	——	BOS	A	Don Baylor

2378

Date	Traded To	Traded With	Traded By	In Exchange For

Mike Easler continued

| Dec 11, 1986 | PHI N | Tom Barrett | NY A | Charles Hudson
Minor league
P Jeff Knox |
| June 10, 1987 | NY A | —— | PHI N | Keith Hughes
Shane Turner |

Logan Easley

| Nov 26, 1986 | PIT N | —— | NY A | See Rick Rhoden |

Mal Eason

| April 1902 | BOS N | —— | CHI N | Cash |

Jamie Easterly

Oct 19, 1979	MON N	——	ATL N	Cash
Sept 22, 1980	MIL A	——	MON N	Cash
June 6, 1983	CLE A	Gorman Thomas Ernie Camacho	MIL A	Rick Manning Rick Waits

Ted Easterly

| Jan 1912 | CHI A | —— | CLE A | Cash |

Rawly Eastwick

June 15, 1977	STL N	——	CIN N	Doug Capilla
Dec 12, 1977	NY A	——	STL N	No compensation (free agent signing)
June 14, 1978	PHI N	——	NY A	Jay Johnstone Bobby Brown

Craig Eaton

| Dec 6, 1979 | CAL A | Al Cowens
Todd Cruz | KC A | Rance Mulliniks
Willie Aikens |

Eddie Eayrs

| Aug 31, 1921 | BKN N | —— | BOS N | Cash |

Dennis Eckersley

March 30, 1978	BOS A	Fred Kendall	CLE A	Bo Diaz Rick Wise Mike Paxton Ted Cox
May 25, 1984	CHI N	Mike Brumley	BOS A	Bill Buckner
April 3, 1987	OAK A	Dan Rohn	CHI N	Minor league OF David Wilder Minor league IF Brian Guinn Minor league P Mark Leonette

Don Eddy

| July 9, 1972 | SD N | Cash | CHI A | Ed Spiezio |

Joe Edelen

| Sept 10, 1981 | CIN N | Neil Fiala | STL N | Doug Bair |

Mike Eden

| June 13, 1976 | ATL N | —— | SF N | See Darrell Evans |

Tom Edens

| April 1, 1984 | NY N | —— | KC A | Tucker Ashford |
| June 18, 1989 | PHI N | —— | NY N | See Juan Samuel |

Butch Edge

| March 21, 1982 | PIT N | Ross Baumgarten | CHI A | Vance Law
Ernie Camacho |

Bill Edgerton

| Feb 15, 1965 | CLE A | —— | KC A | Waiver price |
| April 9, 1965 | KC A | —— | CLE A | Waiver price |

Bruce Edwards

| June 15, 1951 | CHI N | —— | BKN N | See Andy Pafko |

Dave Edwards

| Dec 8, 1980 | SD N | —— | MIN A | Chuck Baker |

Doc Edwards

May 25, 1963	KC A	$100,000.	CLE A	Joe Azcue Dick Howser
May 3, 1965	NY A	——	KC A	Johnny Blanchard Rollie Sheldon
Jan 14, 1966	CLE A	——	NY A	Lu Clinton
Jan 4, 1967	HOU N	Jim Landis Jim Weaver	CLE A	Lee Maye Ken Retzer

Hank Edwards

May 7, 1949	CHI N	——	CLE A	Waiver price
Oct 10, 1950	BKN N	Cash	CHI N	Chuck Connors Dee Fondy
July 21, 1951	CIN N	——	BKN N	Waiver price
Sept 1, 1952	CHI A	——	CIN N	Howie Judson
		(Cincinnati received Judson on December 9.)		
Oct 16, 1952	STL A	Willie Miranda	CHI A	Joe DeMaestri Tommy Byrne

Jim Joe Edwards

| July 1925 | CHI A | —— | CLE A | Cash |

Johnny Edwards

| Feb 8, 1968 | STL N | —— | CIN N | Pat Corrales
Jimy Williams |
| Oct 11, 1968 | HOU N | minor league
C Tommy Smith | STL N | Dave Giusti
Dave Adlesh |

Mike Edwards

| April 4, 1978 | OAK A | Miguel Dilone
Elias Sosa | PIT N | Manny Sanguillen |

Ben Egan

| Aug 20, 1914 | CLE A | Adam Johnson
Fritz Coumbe | BOS A | Vean Gregg |

Dick Egan

Dec 1913	CIN N	$6,500.	BKN N	Joe Tinker
		(Tinker demanded $2,000 of the purchase price; when this was refused, he jumped to the Federal League and the deal was cancelled.)		
April 1914	BKN N	——	CIN N	Herbie Moran Earl Yingling
April 23, 1915	BOS N	——	BKN N	Cash

Dick Egan

| May 27, 1966 | LA N | minor league
IF John Butler | CAL A | Howie Reed |

Tom Egan

| Nov 30, 1970 | CHI A | —— | CAL A | See Ken Berry |

Date	Traded To		Traded With	Traded By		In Exchange For
Howard Ehmke						
Feb 10, 1916	DET	A	Jack Dalton	BUF	F	Cash
Oct 30, 1922	BOS	A	Carl Holling Danny Clark Babe Herman and $25,000.	DET	A	Del Pratt Rip Collins
June 15, 1926	PHI	A	Tom Jenkins	BOS	A	Fred Heimach Slim Harriss Baby Doll Jacobson
Rube Ehrhardt						
April 18, 1929	CIN	N	Johnny Gooch	BKN	N	Val Picinich
Juan Eichelberger						
Nov 18, 1982	CLE	A	Broderick Perkins	SD	N	Ed Whitson
Mark Eichhorn						
March 28, 1989	ATL	N	——	TOR	A	Cash
Dave Eilers						
Aug 18, 1965	NY	N	——	MIL	N	Cash
Harry Eisenstat						
June 14, 1939	CLE	A	Cash	DET	A	Earl Averill
Kid Elberfeld						
June 10, 1903	NY	A	——	DET	A	Herman Long Ernie Courtney
Dec 16, 1909	WAS	A	——	NY	A	$5,000.
Lee Elia						
Dec 1, 1964	CHI	A	Danny Cater	PHI	N	Ray Herbert Jeoff Long
April 19, 1969	NY	A	——	CHI	N	Nate Oliver
Frank Ellerbe						
May 31, 1921	STL	A	——	WAS	A	Earl Smith
June 3, 1924	CLE	A	——	STL	A	Cash
Bruce Ellingsen						
April 3, 1974	CLE	A	——	LA	N	Pedro Guerrero
Larry Elliot						
May 10, 1967	KC	A	$50,000.	NY	N	Ed Charles
Bob Elliott						
Sept 30, 1946	BOS	N	Hank Camelli	PIT	N	Billy Herman Elmer Singleton Stan Wentzel Whitey Wietelmann
April 8, 1952	NY	N	——	BOS	N	Sheldon Jones and $50,000.
June 13, 1953	CHI	A	Virgil Trucks	STL	A	Darrell Johnson Lou Kretlow and $75,000.
Claude Elliott						
Aug 1904	NY	N	——	CIN	N	Cash
Jumbo Elliott						
Oct 14, 1930	PHI	N	Clise Dudley Hal Lee and cash	BKN	N	Lefty O'Doul Fresco Thompson

Date	Traded To		Traded With	Traded By		In Exchange For
Jumbo Elliott *continued*						
May 16, 1934	BOS	N	——	PHI	N	Cash
Dock Ellis						
Dec 11, 1975	NY	A	Willie Randolph Ken Brett	PIT	N	Doc Medich
April 27, 1977	OAK	A	Marty Perez Larry Murray	NY	A	Mike Torrez
June 15, 1977	TEX	A	——	OAK	A	Cash
June 15, 1979	NY	N	——	TEX	A	Bob Myrick Mike Bruhert
Sept 21, 1979	PIT	N	——	NY	N	Cash
Jim Ellis						
April 23, 1968	LA	N	Ted Savage	CHI	N	Jim Hickman Phil Regan
Oct 20, 1970	MIL	A	Carl Taylor	STL	N	Jerry McNertney George Lauzerique minor league P Jesse Higgins
John Ellis						
Nov 27, 1972	CLE	A	Jerry Kenney Charlie Spikes Rusty Torres	NY	A	Graig Nettles Gerry Moses
Dec 9, 1975	TEX	A	——	CLE	A	Stan Thomas Ron Pruitt
Sammy Ellis						
Nov 29, 1967	CAL	A	——	CIN	N	Bill Kelso Jorge Rubio
Jan 20, 1969	CHI	A	——	CAL	N	Bill Voss minor league P Andy Rubicotta
June 13, 1969	CLE	A	——	CHI	A	Jack Hamilton
Dick Ellsworth						
Dec 7, 1966	PHI	N	——	CHI	N	Ray Culp and cash
Dec 15, 1967	BOS	A	Gene Oliver	PHI	N	Mike Ryan and cash
April 19, 1969	CLE	A	*See Ken Harrelson*	BOS	A	
Aug 7, 1970	MIL	A	——	CLE	A	Cash
Don Elston						
Dec 9, 1955	BKN	N	Randy Jackson	CHI	N	Don Hoak Russ Meyer Walt Moryn
May 23, 1957	BKN	N	——	CHI	N	Jackie Collum Vito Valentinetti
Red Embree						
Oct 10, 1947	NY	A	——	CLE	A	Allie Clark
Dec 13, 1948	STL	A	Sherm Lollar Dick Starr and $100,000.	NY	A	Fred Sanford Roy Partee
Steve Engel						
Dec 16, 1985	HOU	N	*See Billy Hatcher*	CHI	N	——
Clyde Engle						
May 10, 1910	BOS	A	——	NY	A	Harry Wolter
Feb 10, 1916	CLE	A	——	BUF	F	Cash

Date	Traded To		Traded With	Traded By		In Exchange For

Dave Engle

Date	Traded To		Traded With	Traded By		In Exchange For
Feb 3, 1979	MIN	A	Ken Landreaux Paul Hartzell Brad Havens	CAL	A	Rod Carew
Jan 18, 1986	DET	A	———	MIN	A	Chris Pittaro Alejandro Sanchez

Gil English

Date	Traded To		Traded With	Traded By		In Exchange For
June 1937	BOS	N	———	DET	A	Cash
Aug 10, 1938	CIN	N	Tommy Reis Johnny Babich Johnny Riddle Vince DiMaggio and Cash	BOS	N	Eddie Miller

Woody English

Date	Traded To		Traded With	Traded By		In Exchange For
Dec 5, 1936	BKN	N	Roy Henshaw	CHI	N	Lonny Frey
July 8, 1938	CIN	N		BKN	N	Cash

Del Ennis

Date	Traded To		Traded With	Traded By		In Exchange For
Nov 19, 1956	STL	N	———	PHI	N	Bobby Morgan Rip Repulski
Oct 3, 1958	CIN	N	Bob Mabe Eddie Kasko	STL	N	George Crowe Alex Kellner Alex Grammas
May 1, 1959	CHI	A	———	CIN	N	Don Rudolph Lou Skizas

Johnny Enzmann

Date	Traded To		Traded With	Traded By		In Exchange For
Dec 1919	PHI	N	———	CLE	A	Cash

Mike Epstein

Date	Traded To		Traded With	Traded By		In Exchange For
May 29, 1967	WAS	A	Frank Bertaina	BAL	A	Pete Richert
May 8, 1971	OAK	A	Darold Knowles	WAS	A	Frank Fernandez Don Mincher Paul Lindblad and cash
Nov 30, 1972	TEX	A	———	OAK	A	Horacio Pina
May 20, 1973	CAL	A	Rich Hand Rick Stelmaszek	TEX	A	Jim Spencer Lloyd Allen

Eddie Erautt

Date	Traded To		Traded With	Traded By		In Exchange For
May 23, 1953	STL	N	———	CIN	N	Jackie Collum

Eric Erickson

Date	Traded To		Traded With	Traded By		In Exchange For
July 5, 1919	WAS	A	———	DET	A	Doc Ayers

Paul Erickson

Date	Traded To		Traded With	Traded By		In Exchange For
May 20, 1948	PHI	N	———	CHI	N	Waiver price
July 1, 1948	NY	N	———	PHI	N	Waiver price
July 30, 1948	PIT	N	———	NY	N	Cash

Roger Erickson

Date	Traded To		Traded With	Traded By		In Exchange For
May 12, 1982	NY	A	Butch Wynegar	MIN	A	John Pacella Larry Milbourne Pete Filson and cash
Dec 7, 1983	KC	A	Steve Balboni	NY	A	Mike Armstrong minor league C Duane Dewey

Tex Erwin

Date	Traded To		Traded With	Traded By		In Exchange For
June 1914	CIN	N	———	BKN	N	Cash

Nick Esasky

Date	Traded To		Traded With	Traded By		In Exchange For
Dec 13, 1988	BOS	A	Rob Murphy	CIN	N	Todd Benzinger Jeff Sellers player to be named
			(Cincinnati received P Luis Vasquez on January 12, 1989.)			
Nov 17, 1989	ATL	N	———	BOS	A	No compensation (free agent signing)

Angel Escobar

Date	Traded To		Traded With	Traded By		In Exchange For
Nov 20, 1988	MON	N	———	SF	N	Wil Tejada

Juan Espino

Date	Traded To		Traded With	Traded By		In Exchange For
April 1, 1984	CLE	A	———	NY	A	Cash

Nino Espinosa

Date	Traded To		Traded With	Traded By		In Exchange For
March 27, 1979	PHI	N	———	NY	N	Richie Hebner Jose Moreno

Cecil Espy

Date	Traded To		Traded With	Traded By		In Exchange For
Aug 31, 1985	PIT	N	———	LA	N	*See Bill Madlock*

Chuck Essegian

Date	Traded To		Traded With	Traded By		In Exchange For
Dec 3, 1958	STL	N	———	PHI	N	Ruben Amaro
June 15, 1959	LA	N	Lloyd Merritt	STL	N	Dick Gray
April 12, 1961	KC	A	Jerry Walker	BAL	A	Dick Hall Dick Williams
May 3, 1961	CLE	A	———	KC	A	Cash
Feb 27, 1963	KC	A	———	CLE	A	Jerry Walker

Jim Essian

Date	Traded To		Traded With	Traded By		In Exchange For
Dec 3, 1974	CHI	A	Cash	ATL	N	Dick Allen
			(Chicago received Essian on May 15, 1975.)			
May 7, 1975	ATL	N	Barry Bonnell and cash	PHI	N	Dick Allen Johnny Oates
March 30, 1978	OAK	A	Steve Renko	CHI	A	Pablo Torrealba
Nov 20, 1980	CHI	A	———	OAK	A	No compensation (free agent signing)
Dec 11, 1981	SEA	A	Todd Cruz Rod Allen	CHI	A	Tom Paciorek
Jan 21, 1983	CLE	A	———	SEA	A	Cash
Dec 6, 1983	OAK	A	———	CLE	A	Luis Quinones

Bobby Estalella

Date	Traded To		Traded With	Traded By		In Exchange For
Sept 10, 1941	WAS	A	———	STL	A	George Archie
March 21, 1943	PHI	A	Cash	WAS	A	Bob Johnson

Francisco Estrada

Date	Traded To		Traded With	Traded By		In Exchange For
Dec 10, 1971	CAL	A	Nolan Ryan Don Rose Leroy Stanton	NY	N	Jim Fregosi
June 12, 1972	BAL	A	———	CAL	A	Cash
Oct 27, 1972	CHI	N	———	BAL	A	Ellie Hendricks

Andy Etchebarren

Date	Traded To		Traded With	Traded By		In Exchange For
June 15, 1975	CAL	A	———	BAL	A	Cash
Dec 15, 1977	MIL	A	———	CAL	A	Cash

Bobby Etheridge

Date	Traded To		Traded With	Traded By		In Exchange For
Dec 5, 1969	SD	N	Bob Barton Ron Herbel	SF	N	Frank Reberger

Date	Traded To	Traded With	Traded By	In Exchange For

Nick Etten

Jan 22, 1943	NY	A ———	PHI	N	Tom Padden Al Gerheauser Ed Levy Al Gettel and $10,000.

Al Evans

Feb 5, 1951	BOS	A ———	WAS	A	Waiver price

Barry Evans

Feb 22, 1982	NY	A ———	SD	N	Cash

Darrell Evans

June 13, 1976	SF	N	Marty Perez	ATL	N	Willie Montanez Craig Robinson Mike Eden Jake Brown
Dec 19, 1983	DET	A ———		SF	N	No compensation (free agent signing)
Dec 23, 1988	ATL	N ———		DET	A	No compensation (free agent signing)

Joe Evans

Jan 8, 1923	WAS	A ———	CLE	A	Frank Brower
Jan 1924	STL	A ———	WAS	A	Cash

Roy Evans

July 1902	BKN	N	Joe Wall	NY	N	Cash
July 1903	STL	A ———		BKN	N	Cash

Steve Evans

June 1915	BAL	F ———	BKN	F	Frank Smith

Leon Everitt

April 17, 1969	SD	N	Tommy Dean	LA	N	Al McBean

Hoot Evers

June 3, 1952	BOS	A	Dizzy Trout George Kell Johnny Lipon	DET	A	Walt Dropo Bill Wight Fred Hatfield Johnny Pesky Don Lenhardt
May 18, 1954	NY	N ———		BOS	A	Waiver price
July 29, 1954	DET	A ———		NY	N	Waiver price
Jan 3, 1955	BAL	A ———		DET	A	Cash
July 13, 1955	CLE	A ———		BAL	A	Bill Wight
May 13, 1956	BAL	A ———		CLE	A	Dave Pope

Johnny Evers

Feb 1914	BOS	N ———	CHI	N	Bill Sweeney and cash
July 12, 1917	PHI	N ———	BOS	N	Waiver price

Bob Ewing

Jan 20, 1910	PHI	N ———	CIN	N	Frank Corridon

Homer Ezzell

Dec 1923	BOS	A ———	STL	A	Norm McMillan
Dec 9, 1925	DET	A	Tex Vache	BOS	A	Fred Haney

Roy Face

Aug 31, 1968	DET	A ———	PIT	N	Cash

Bill Fahey

Oct 25, 1978	SD	N	Mike Hargrove Kurt Bevacqua	TEX	A	Oscar Gamble Dave Roberts and $300,000.
March 24, 1981	DET	A ———		SD	N	Cash

Ferris Fain

Jan 27, 1953	CHI	A	minor league 2B Bob Wilson	PHI	A	Joe DeMaestri Eddie Robinson Ed McGhee
Dec 6, 1954	DET	A	Chris Cristante Jack Phillips	CHI	A	Walt Dropo Ted Gray Bob Nieman

Ron Fairly

June 11, 1969	MON	N	Paul Popovich	LA	N	Maury Wills Manny Mota
Dec 6, 1974	STL	N ———		MON	N	Minor leaguers IF Rudy Kinard and 1B Ed Kurpiel
Sept 14, 1976	OAK	A ———		STL	N	Cash
Feb 24, 1977	TOR	A ———		OAK	A	Minor league IF Mike Weathers and cash
Dec 8, 1977	CAL	A ———		TOR	A	Dale Kelly Butch Alberts

Pete Falcone

Dec 8, 1975	STL	N ———	SF	N	Ken Reitz
Dec 5, 1978	NY	N ———	STL	N	Tom Grieve Kim Seaman
Jan 25, 1983	ATL	N ———	NY	N	No compensation (free agent signing)

Bibb Falk

Feb 28, 1929	CLE	A ———	CHI	A	Martin Autry

Cy Falkenberg

Aug 1908	CLE	A	Dave Altizer	WAS	A	Cash
Feb 1915	BKN	F ———		NWK	F	Hugh Bradley Larry Pratt Tom Seaton

Frank Fanovich

Dec 17, 1953	BAL	A	Joe Coleman	PHI	A	Bob Cain

Carmen Fanzone

Dec 3, 1970	CHI	N ———	BOS	A	Phil Gagliano

Bob Farley

Nov 30, 1961	CHI	A ———	SF	N	*See Billy Pierce*
June 25, 1962	DET	A ———	CHI	A	Charlie Maxwell

Ed Farmer

June 15, 1973	DET	A ———	CLE	A	Tom Timmerman Kevin Collins
March 19, 1974	NY	A	Rick Sawyer Walt Williams	DET	A	Gerry Moses
		(Part of three-team trade involving Detroit, New York Yankees, and Cleveland.)			
March 21, 1974	PHI	A ———	NY	A	Cash
Dec 3, 1974	MIL	A ———	PHI	N	Minor league IF Steve McCartney
Dec 15, 1978	TEX	A	Gary Holle and cash	MIL	A	Reggie Cleveland
June 15, 1979	CHI	A	Gary Holle	TEX	A	Eric Soderholm
Jan 28, 1982	PHI	N ———	CHI	A	
		(Chicago selected Joel Skinner of Pittsburgh from the compensation pool.)			

Date	Traded To		Traded With	Traded By		In Exchange For

Dick Farrell

Date	Traded To		Traded With	Traded By		In Exchange For
May 4, 1961	LA	N	Joe Koppe	PHI	N	Don Demeter Charley Smith
May 8, 1967	PHI	N	———	HOU	N	Cash

Doc Farrell

Date	Traded To		Traded With	Traded By		In Exchange For
June 12, 1927	BOS	N	Hugh McQuillan Kent Greenfield	NY	N	Zack Taylor Larry Benton Herb Thomas
June 14, 1929	NY	N	———	BOS	N	Jimmy Welsh
April 10, 1930	STL	N	Showboat Fisher	NY	N	Wally Roettger
June 29, 1930	CHI	N	———	STL	N	Waiver price

Bill Faul

Date	Traded To		Traded With	Traded By		In Exchange For
March 27, 1965	CHI	N	———	DET	A	Cash

Ernie Fazio

Date	Traded To		Traded With	Traded By		In Exchange For
June 4, 1965	KC	A	Jess Hickman and $100,000.	HOU	N	Jim Gentile

(Kansas City received Fazio on October 15.)

Gus Felix

Date	Traded To		Traded With	Traded By		In Exchange For
Oct 7, 1925	BKN	N	Jesse Barnes Mickey O'Neil	BOS	N	Zack Taylor Jimmy Johnston Eddie Brown

Bobby Fenwick

Date	Traded To		Traded With	Traded By		In Exchange For
Nov 28, 1972	STL	N	Ray Busse	HOU	N	Skip Jutze Milt Ramirez
Nov 7, 1973	SD	N	Glenn Beckert	CHI	N	Jerry Morales

Alex Ferguson

Date	Traded To		Traded With	Traded By		In Exchange For
Feb 24, 1922	BOS	A	———	NY	A	Waiver price
May 5, 1925	NY	A	Bobby Veach	BOS	A	Ray Francis and $9,000.
Aug 19, 1925	WAS	A	———	NY	A	Cash
Oct 1926	PHI	N	———	WAS	A	Cash
May 14, 1929	BKN	N	———	PHI	N	Cash

George Ferguson

Date	Traded To		Traded With	Traded By		In Exchange For
Dec 3, 1907	BOS	N	———	NY	N	*See Fred Tenney*

Joe Ferguson

Date	Traded To		Traded With	Traded By		In Exchange For
June 15, 1976	STL	N	Bob Detherage minor league IF Fred Tisdale	LA	N	Reggie Smith
Nov 23, 1976	HOU	N	Bob Detherage	STL	N	Larry Dierker Jerry DaVanon
July 1, 1978	LA	N	Cash	HOU	N	Rafael Landestoy Jeffrey Leonard

Felix Fermin

Date	Traded To		Traded With	Traded By		In Exchange For
March 25, 1989	CLE	A	Denny Gonzalez	PIT	N	Jay Bell

(Completion of deal in which Cleveland acquired Gonzalez on November 28, 1988 for a player to be named.)

Chico Fernandez

Date	Traded To		Traded With	Traded By		In Exchange For
April 5, 1957	PHI	N	———	BKN	N	Ron Negray Tim Harkness Elmer Valo Ben Flowers minor league SS Mel Geho
Dec 5, 1959	DET	A	Ray Semproch	PHI	N	Ken Walters Ted Lepcio minor league P Alex Cosmidis

Chico Fernandez *continued*

Date	Traded To		Traded With	Traded By		In Exchange For
May 8, 1963	MIL	N	———	DET	A	Lou Johnson and cash
May 8, 1963	NY	N	———	MIL	N	Larry Foss
April 23, 1964	CHI	A	minor league C Bobby Catton and cash	NY	N	Charley Smith

Frank Fernandez

Date	Traded To		Traded With	Traded By		In Exchange For
Dec 5, 1969	OAK	A	Al Downing	NY	A	Danny Cater Ossie Chavarria
May 8, 1971	WAS	A	Don Mincher Paul Lindblad and cash	OAK	A	Mike Epstein Darold Knowles
June 23, 1971	OAK	A	———	WAS	A	Cash
Aug 31, 1971	CHI	N	Bill McNulty	OAK	A	Adrian Garrett

Sid Fernandez

Date	Traded To		Traded With	Traded By		In Exchange For
Dec 8, 1983	NY	N	Ross Jones	LA	N	Carlos Diaz Bob Bailor

Al Ferrara

Date	Traded To		Traded With	Traded By		In Exchange For
May 13, 1971	CIN	N	———	SD	N	Angel Bravo

Don Ferrarese

Date	Traded To		Traded With	Traded By		In Exchange For
Dec 6, 1954	BAL	A	———	CHI	A	*See Clint Courtney*
April 1, 1958	CLE	A	Larry Doby	BAL	A	Bud Daley Dick Williams Gene Woodling
Dec 6, 1959	CHI	A	———	CLE	A	*See Norm Cash*
April 28, 1962	STL	N	———	PHI	N	Larry Locke and cash

Mike Ferraro

Date	Traded To		Traded With	Traded By		In Exchange For
April 30, 1969	BAL	A	Gerry Schoen	SEA	A	John O'Donoghue Tom Fisher and minor league P Lloyd Fourroux
March 27, 1973	MIN	A	———	MIL	A	Ken Reynolds

Tony Ferreira

Date	Traded To		Traded With	Traded By		In Exchange For
April 1, 1986	NY	N	———	KC	A	Angel Salazar

Rick Ferrell

Date	Traded To		Traded With	Traded By		In Exchange For
May 9, 1933	BOS	A	Lloyd Brown	STL	A	Merv Shea and cash
June 11, 1937	WAS	A	Wes Ferrell Mel Almada	BOS	A	Ben Chapman Bobo Newsom
May 15, 1941	STL	A	———	WAS	A	Vern Kennedy
March 1, 1944	WAS	A	———	STL	A	Tony Giuliani Gene Moore and cash

(Giuliani announced his retirement, and St. Louis received Moore to complete the trade.)

Wes Ferrell

Date	Traded To		Traded With	Traded By		In Exchange For
May 25, 1934	BOS	A	Dick Porter	CLE	A	Bob Weiland Bob Seeds and $25,000.
June 11, 1937	WAS	A	Rick Ferrell Mel Almada	BOS	A	Ben Chapman Bobo Newsom

Sergio Ferrer

Date	Traded To		Traded With	Traded By		In Exchange For
Oct 24, 1975	PHI	N	———	MIN	A	Larry Cox
March 26, 1977	NY	A	———	PHI	N	Kerry Dineen
Dec 9, 1977	NY	N	———	NY	A	Roy Staiger

Tom Ferrick

Date	Traded To		Traded With	Traded By		In Exchange For
Sept 22, 1941	CLE	A	———	PHI	A	Waiver price
June 24, 1946	STL	A	———	CLE	A	Cash
Jan 14, 1947	WAS	A	———	STL	A	Cash
Oct 4, 1948	STL	A	John Sullivan and $25,000.	WAS	A	Sam Dente
June 15, 1950	NY	A	Joe Ostrowski Leo Thomas Sid Schacht	STL	A	Jim Delsing Don Johnson Duane Pillette Snuffy Stirnweiss and $50,000.
June 15, 1951	WAS	A	Fred Sanford Bob Porterfield	NY	A	Bob Kuzava

Hobe Ferris

Date	Traded To		Traded With	Traded By		In Exchange For
Oct 1907	STL	A	———	BOS	A	Cash
Feb 1908	STL	A	Jimmy Williams Danny Hoffman	NY	A	Fred Glade Charlie Hemphill

Lou Fette

Date	Traded To		Traded With	Traded By		In Exchange For
July 1940	BKN	N	———	BOS	N	Cash

Chick Fewster

Date	Traded To		Traded With	Traded By		In Exchange For
July 23, 1922	BOS	A	Elmer Miller Johnny Mitchell Lefty O'Doul and $50,000.	NY	A	Joe Dugan Elmer Smith
Jan 7, 1924	CLE	A	———	BOS	A	See Bill Wambsganss
Jan 1926	BKN	N	———	CLE	A	Cash

Neil Fiala

Date	Traded To		Traded With	Traded By		In Exchange For
Sept 10, 1981	CIN	N	Joe Edelen	STL	N	Doug Bair

Cecil Fielder

Date	Traded To		Traded With	Traded By		In Exchange For
Feb 5, 1983	TOR	A	———	KC	A	Leon Roberts

Dan Fife

Date	Traded To		Traded With	Traded By		In Exchange For
March 27, 1973	MIN	A	Cash	DET	A	Jim Perry

Ed Figueroa

Date	Traded To		Traded With	Traded By		In Exchange For
Dec 11, 1975	NY	A	Mickey Rivers	CAL	A	Bobby Bonds
July 28, 1980	TEX	A	———	NY	A	Cash

Jesus Figueroa

Date	Traded To		Traded With	Traded By		In Exchange For
Dec 12, 1980	SF	N	Jerry Martin minor league IF Mike Turgeon	CHI	N	Joe Strain Phil Nastu

Tom Filer

Date	Traded To		Traded With	Traded By		In Exchange For
April 27, 1981	CHI	N	Cash	NY	A	Barry Foote

Pete Filson

Date	Traded To		Traded With	Traded By		In Exchange For
May 12, 1982	MIN	A	John Pacella Larry Milbourne and cash	NY	A	Butch Wynegar Roger Erickson
April 30, 1986	CHI	A	———	MIN	A	Minor league P Kurt Walker
Jan 5, 1987	NY	A	Randy Velarde	CHI	A	Scott Nielsen Minor league IF Mike Soper

Jack Fimple

Date	Traded To		Traded With	Traded By		In Exchange For
Dec 9, 1981	LA	N	Jorge Orta Larry White	CLE	A	Rick Sutcliffe Jack Perconte

Rollie Fingers

Date	Traded To		Traded With	Traded By		In Exchange For
Dec 14, 1976	SD	N	———	OAK	A	No compensation (free agent signing)
Dec 8, 1980	STL	N	Bob Shirley Gene Tenace minor league C Bob Geren	SD	N	Terry Kennedy Steve Swisher Mike Phillips John Littlefield John Urrea Kim Seaman Al Olmsted
Dec 12, 1980	MIL	A	Pete Vuckovich Ted Simmons	STL	N	Sixto Lezcano David Green Lary Sorensen Dave LaPoint

Jim Finigan

Date	Traded To		Traded With	Traded By		In Exchange For
Dec 16, 1953	PHI	A	Don Bollweg John Gray Jim Robertson Vic Power Bill Renna	NY	A	Harry Byrd Eddie Robinson Tom Hamilton Carmen Mauro Loren Babe
Dec 5, 1956	DET	A	Jack Crimian Bill Harrington Eddie Robinson	KC	A	Ned Garver Gene Host Virgil Trucks Wayne Belardi and $20,000.
Jan 28, 1958	SF	N	$25,000.	DET	A	Gail Harris Ozzie Virgil
Oct 14, 1958	BAL	A	———	STL	N	Jim Brideweser Art Ceccarelli

Mickey Finn

Date	Traded To		Traded With	Traded By		In Exchange For
Dec 15, 1932	PHI	N	Cy Moore Jack Warner	BKN	N	Ray Benge and $15,000.

Happy Finneran

Date	Traded To		Traded With	Traded By		In Exchange For
May 1918	NY	A	———	DET	A	Cash

Lou Finney

Date	Traded To		Traded With	Traded By		In Exchange For
May 8, 1939	BOS	A	———	PHI	A	Cash
July 27, 1945	STL	A	———	BOS	A	Cash

Mike Fiore

Date	Traded To		Traded With	Traded By		In Exchange For
May 28, 1970	BOS	A	———	KC	A	Tom Matchick
March 20, 1972	STL	N	———	BOS	A	Bob Burda
June 20, 1972	SD	N	Bob Chlupsa	STL	N	Rafael Robles

(Fiore was returned to St. Louis on July 3.)

Steve Fireovid

Date	Traded To		Traded With	Traded By		In Exchange For
Aug 31, 1983	PHI	N	See Sixto Lezcano	SD	N	———

Bill Fischer

Date	Traded To		Traded With	Traded By		In Exchange For
Feb 10, 1916	CHI	N	See Three Finger Brown	CHI	F	
July 29, 1916	PIT	N	Wildfire Schulte	CHI	N	Art Wilson Otto Knabe

Bill Fischer

Date	Traded To		Traded With	Traded By		In Exchange For
June 15, 1958	DET	A	Tito Francona	CHI	A	Ray Boone Bob Shaw
Sept 11, 1958	WAS	A	———	DET	A	Waiver price
July 22, 1960	DET	A	———	WAS	A	Tom Morgan
Aug 2, 1961	KC	A	Ozzie Virgil	DET	A	Gerry Staley Reno Bertoia

Carl Fischer

Date	Traded To		Traded With	Traded By		In Exchange For
June 9, 1932	STL	A	———	WAS	A	Dick Coffman
Dec 13, 1932	WAS	A	———	STL	A	Dick Coffman
Dec 14, 1932	DET	A	Firpo Marberry	WAS	A	Earl Whitehill

Date	Traded To	Traded With	Traded By	In Exchange For

Carl Fischer *continued*

Date	Traded To	Traded With	Traded By	In Exchange For
May 17, 1935	CHI A	——	DET A	Cash
May 1937	WAS A	——	CLE A	Cash

Hank Fischer

| June 15, 1966 | CIN N | —— | ATL N | Joey Jay |
| Aug 15, 1966 | BOS A | —— | CIN N | Dick Stigman
Rollie Sheldon |

(Cincinnati received Stigman and Sheldon on December 15, 1966.)

Jeff Fischer

| March 27, 1989 | LA N | —— | MON N | Gilberto Reyes |

Mike Fischlin

| June 15, 1977 | HOU N | Randy Niemann
Dave Bergman | NY A | Cliff Johnson |

(Houston received Bergman on November 23.)

| April 3, 1981 | CLE A | —— | HOU N | Jim Lentine
and cash |
| Dec 15, 1985 | NY A | —— | CLE A | Minor league
P Kevin Trudeau |

(Cleveland received Trudeau on Apr. 7, 1986.)

John Fishel

| Jan 10, 1989 | NY A | —— | HOU N | *See Rick Rhoden* |

Bob Fisher

| Jan 1916 | CIN N | —— | CHI N | Cash |

Brian Fisher

| Dec 5, 1984 | NY A | —— | ATL N | Rick Cerone |
| Nov 26, 1986 | PIT N | —— | NY A | *See Rick Rhoden* |

Chauncey Fisher

| May 1901 | STL N | —— | NY N | Bill Magee |

Eddie Fisher

Nov 30, 1961	CHI A	Dom Zanni Verle Tiefenthaler Bob Farley	SF N	Billy Pierce Don Larsen
June 12, 1966	BAL A	——	CHI A	Jerry Adair and minor league OF Johnny Riddle
Nov 28, 1967	CLE A	minor leaguers P Bob Scott and IF John Scruggs	BAL A	John O'Donoghue Gordon Lund
Oct 8, 1968	CAL A	——	CLE A	Jack Hamilton
Aug 17, 1972	CHI A	——	CAL A	Bruce Miller Bruce Kimm
Aug 29, 1973	STL N	——	CHI A	Cash

Gus Fisher

| March 1912 | NY A | —— | CLE A | Waiver price |

Jack Fisher

Dec 15, 1962	SF N	Jimmie Coker Billy Hoeft	BAL A	Mike McCormick Stu Miller John Orsino
Oct 10, 1963	NY N	——	SF N	$30,000.
Dec 15, 1967	CHI A	Tommy Davis Billy Wynne Buddy Booker	NY N	Tommie Agee Al Weis
Dec 5, 1968	CIN N	——	CHI A	Don Pavletich Don Secrist

Jack Fisher *continued*

| Jan 14, 1970 | CAL A | —— | CIN N | Bill Harrelson
minor league
IF Dan Loomer |

Ray Fisher

| March 15, 1919 | CIN N | —— | NY A | Waiver price |

Showboat Fisher

| April 10, 1930 | STL N | Doc Farrell | NY N | Wally Roettger |

Tom Fisher

| April 30, 1969 | SEA A | John O'Donoghue
and minor league
P Lloyd Fourroux | BAL A | Gerry Schoen
Mike Ferraro |

Carlton Fisk

| March 18, 1981 | CHI A | —— | BOS A | No compensation
(free agent signing) |

Ed Fitz Gerald

| May 13, 1953 | WAS A | —— | PIT N | Cash |
| May 25, 1959 | CLE A | —— | WAS A | Hal Woodeshick
Hal Naragon |

Mike Fitzgerald

| Dec 10, 1984 | MON N | Hubie Brooks
Herm Winningham
Floyd Youmans | NY N | Gary Carter |

Al Fitzmorris

| Nov 5, 1976 | CLE A | —— | TOR A | Alan Ashby
Doug Howard |

Freddie Fitzsimmons

| June 11, 1937 | BKN N | —— | NY N | Tom Baker |

Max Flack

| Feb 10, 1916 | CHI N | *See Three Finger Brown* | CHI F | —— |
| May 30, 1922 | STL N | —— | CHI N | Cliff Heathcote |

Ira Flagstead

April 20, 1923	BOS A	——	DET A	Cash
May 25, 1929	WAS A	——	BOS A	Waiver price
July 12, 1929	PIT N	——	WAS A	Waiver price

Patsy Flaherty

| Jan 1900 | PIT N | *See Honus Wagner* | LOU N | —— |
| Dec 1906 | BOS N | Ginger Beaumont
Claude Ritchey | PIT N | Ed Abbaticchio |

Mike Flanagan

| Aug 31, 1987 | TOR A | —— | BAL A | Oswaldo Peraza |

John Flannery

| June 15, 1977 | CHI A | Don Kirkwood
John Verhoeven | CAL A | Ken Brett |

Les Fleming

| Dec 4, 1947 | PIT N | —— | CLE A | Cash |

Date	Traded To		Traded With	Traded By		In Exchange For

Art Fletcher

Date	Traded To		Traded With	Traded By		In Exchange For
June 8, 1920	PHI	N	Bill Hubbell and cash	NY	N	Dave Bancroft

Elbie Fletcher

| June 15, 1939 | PIT | N | —— | BOS | N | Bill Schuster and cash |
| Dec 4, 1947 | CLE | A | —— | PIT | N | Cash |

Scott Fletcher

| Jan 25, 1983 | CHI | A | Pat Tabler Randy Martz Dick Tidrow | CHI | N | Steve Trout Warren Brusstar |
| Nov 25, 1985 | TEX | A | Ed Correa player to be named | CHI | A | Wayne Tolleson Dave Schmidt |

(Texas received IF Jose Mota on Dec. 12, 1985.)

| July 29, 1989 | CHI | A | Sammy Sosa Wilson Alvarez | TEX | A | Harold Baines Fred Manrique |

Elmer Flick

| May 16, 1902 | CLE | A | —— | PHI | A | Cash |

John Flinn

| Dec 6, 1979 | MIL | A | —— | BAL | A | Lenn Sakata |

Curt Flood

| Dec 5, 1957 | STL | N | Joe Taylor | CIN | N | Marty Kutyna Ted Wieand Willard Schmidt |
| Oct 7, 1969 | PHI | N | Tim McCarver Joe Hoerner Byron Browne | STL | N | Dick Allen Cookie Rojas Jerry Johnson |

(Flood refused to report to the Philadelphia Phillies, and the Cardinals sent Willie Montanez and Bob Browning on April 8, 1970 to complete the trade.)

| Nov 3, 1970 | WAS | A | —— | PHI | N | Greg Goossen Jeff Terpko Gene Martin |

Gil Flores

| July 28, 1978 | NY | N | —— | CAL | A | Cash |

Ben Flowers

Sept 8, 1955	STL	N	——	DET	A	Bobby Tiefenauer
May 11, 1956	PHI	N	Harvey Haddix Stu Miller	STL	N	Murry Dickson Herm Wehmeier
Oct 15, 1956	KC	A	——	PHI	N	Waiver price
April 5, 1957	BKN	N	——	PHI	N	See Chico Fernandez

Jake Flowers

May 1927	BKN	N	——	STL	N	Bob McGraw
June 15, 1931	STL	N	——	BKN	N	Waiver price
Feb 1933	BKN	N	Ownie Carroll	STL	N	Dazzy Vance Gordon Slade

Bobby Floyd

| June 15, 1970 | KC | A | —— | BAL | A | Moe Drabowsky |

Doug Flynn

June 15, 1977	NY	N	Pat Zachry Steve Henderson Dan Norman	CIN	N	Tom Seaver
Dec 11, 1981	TEX	A	Danny Boitano	NY	N	Jim Kern
Aug 2, 1982	MON	N	——	TEX	A	Cash

John Flynn

| Feb 1912 | WAS | A | —— | PIT | N | Waiver price |

Lee Fohl

| Oct 1903 | CIN | N | —— | PIT | N | Waiver price |

Hank Foiles

May 3, 1953	CLE	A	——	CIN	N	Cash
May 15, 1956	PIT	N	——	CLE	A	Preston Ward
Dec 15, 1959	KC	A	——	PIT	N	Cash
June 1, 1960	PIT	N	Cash	KC	A	Danny Kravitz
June 2, 1960	CLE	A	——	PIT	N	Johnny Powers
July 26, 1960	DET	A	——	CLE	A	Rocky Bridges Red Wilson
April 20, 1962	CIN	N	——	BAL	A	Cash

Tom Foley

| Aug 8, 1985 | PHI | N | Alan Knicely Fred Toliver | CIN | N | Bo Diaz Minor league P Greg Simpson |

(Philadelphia received Toliver on August 27, 1985.)

| July 24, 1986 | MON | N | Lary Sorensen | PHI | N | Dan Schatzeder Skeeter Barnes |

Tim Foli

April 5, 1972	MON	N	Ken Singleton Mike Jorgensen	NY	N	Rusty Staub
April 27, 1977	SF	N	——	MON	N	Chris Speier
Dec 7, 1977	NY	N	——	SF	N	Cash
April 19, 1979	PIT	N	minor league P Greg Field	NY	N	Frank Taveras
Dec 11, 1981	CAL	A	——	PIT	N	Brian Harper
Dec 7, 1983	NY	A	——	CAL	A	Curt Kaufman and cash
Dec 20, 1984	PIT	N	Steve Kemp and $400,000.	NY	A	Dale Berra Jay Buhner

Rich Folkers

| Oct 18, 1971 | STL | N | See Jim Bibby | NY | N | —— |
| Nov 18, 1974 | SD | N | Alan Foster Sonny Siebert | STL | N | Ed Brinkman Danny Breeden |

(Part of three-team trade involving San Diego, Detroit, and St. Louis Cardinals.)

| March 23, 1977 | MIL | A | —— | SD | N | Cash |
| Dec 9, 1977 | DET | A | Jim Slaton | MIL | A | Ben Oglivie |

Dee Fondy

Oct 10, 1950	CHI	N	Chuck Connors	BKN	N	Hank Edwards and cash
May 1, 1957	PIT	N	Gene Baker	CHI	N	Dale Long Lee Walls
Dec 28, 1957	CIN	N	——	PIT	N	Ted Kluszewski

Lew Fonseca

| March 30, 1925 | PHI | N | —— | CIN | N | Cash |
| May 17, 1931 | CHI | A | —— | CLE | A | Willie Kamm |

Ray Fontenot

Aug 1, 1979	NY	A	Oscar Gamble Gene Nelson minor league 3B Amos Lewis	TEX	A	Mickey Rivers minor league Ps Bob Polinsky Neil Mersch and Mark Softy
Dec 4, 1984	CHI	N	Brian Dayett	NY	A	Henry Cotto Ron Hassey Rich Bordi Porfi Altamirano
Aug 13, 1986	MIN	A	——	CHI	N	See Ron Davis

Date	Traded To		Traded With	Traded By		In Exchange For

Jim Foor

Date	Traded To		Traded With	Traded By		In Exchange For
Nov 30, 1972	PIT	N	Norm McRae	DET	A	Dick Sharon
March 28, 1974	KC	A	——	PIT	N	Wayne Simpson

Barry Foote

Date	Traded To		Traded With	Traded By		In Exchange For
June 15, 1977	PHI	N	Dan Warthen	MON	N	Wayne Twitchell / Tim Blackwell
Feb 23, 1979	CHI	N	Ted Sizemore / Jerry Martin / Derek Botelho / minor league / P Henry Mack	PHI	N	Manny Trillo / Dave Rader / Greg Gross
April 27, 1981	NY	A	——	CHI	N	Tom Filer / and cash

Curt Ford

Date	Traded To		Traded With	Traded By		In Exchange For
Dec 16, 1988	PHI	N	Steve Lake	STL	N	Milt Thompson

Dan Ford

Date	Traded To		Traded With	Traded By		In Exchange For
Oct 23, 1974	MIN	A	minor league / P Denny Myers	OAK	A	Pat Bourque
Dec 4, 1978	CAL	A	——	MIN	A	Ron Jackson / Danny Goodwin
Jan 28, 1982	BAL	A	——	CAL	A	Doug DeCinces / Jeff Schneider

Hod Ford

Date	Traded To		Traded With	Traded By		In Exchange For
Dec 15, 1923	PHI	N	Ray Powell	BOS	N	Cotton Tierney

(Powell announced his intention to retire after the 1924 season. He remained with Boston, and Philadelphia received cash instead.)

Date	Traded To		Traded With	Traded By		In Exchange For
May 16, 1925	BKN	N	——	PHI	N	Waiver price
Jan 26, 1932	STL	N	——	CIN	N	Cash

Ted Ford

Date	Traded To		Traded With	Traded By		In Exchange For
April 3, 1972	TEX	A	——	CLE	A	Roy Foster / Tom McCraw
May 10, 1973	CLE	A	Dick Bosman	TEX	A	Steve Dunning

Frank Foreman

Date	Traded To		Traded With	Traded By		In Exchange For
April 1901	BAL	A	——	BOS	A	Cash

Mike Fornieles

Date	Traded To		Traded With	Traded By		In Exchange For
Dec 10, 1952	CHI	A	——	WAS	A	Chuck Stobbs
May 21, 1956	BAL	A	Bob Nieman / Connie Johnson / George Kell	CHI	A	Jim Wilson / Dave Philley
June 14, 1957	BOS	A	——	BAL	A	Billy Goodman
June 14, 1963	MIN	A	——	BOS	A	Cash

Bob Forsch

Date	Traded To		Traded With	Traded By		In Exchange For
Aug 31, 1988	HOU	N	——	STL	N	Denny Walling

Ken Forsch

Date	Traded To		Traded With	Traded By		In Exchange For
April 1, 1981	CAL	A	——	HOU	N	Dickie Thon

Terry Forster

Date	Traded To		Traded With	Traded By		In Exchange For
Dec 10, 1976	PIT	N	Goose Gossage	CHI	A	Richie Zisk / Silvio Martinez
Nov 22, 1977	LA	N	——	PIT	N	No compensation / (free agent signing)
Dec 1, 1982	ATL	N	——	LA	N	No compensation / (free agent signing)

Larry Foss

Date	Traded To		Traded With	Traded By		In Exchange For
Sept 6, 1962	NY	N	——	PIT	N	Waiver price

Larry Foss continued

Date	Traded To		Traded With	Traded By		In Exchange For
May 8, 1963	MIL	N	——	NY	N	Chico Fernandez

Ray Fosse

Date	Traded To		Traded With	Traded By		In Exchange For
March 24, 1973	OAK	A	Jack Heidemann	CLE	A	George Hendrick / Dave Duncan
Dec 9, 1975	CLE	A	——	OAK	A	Cash
Sept 9, 1977	SEA	A	——	CLE	A	Bill Laxton / and cash

Alan Foster

Date	Traded To		Traded With	Traded By		In Exchange For
Dec 11, 1970	CLE	A	Ray Lamb	LA	N	Duke Sims
Oct 5, 1971	CAL	A	——	CLE	A	See Alex Johnson
April 5, 1973	STL	N	——	CAL	A	Cash
Nov 18, 1974	SD	N	Rich Folkers / Sonny Siebert	STL	N	Ed Brinkman / Danny Breeden

(Part of three-team trade involving San Diego, Detroit, and St. Louis Cardinals.)

Eddie Foster

Date	Traded To		Traded With	Traded By		In Exchange For
Jan 20, 1920	BOS	A	Mike Menosky / Harry Harper	WAS	A	Braggo Roth / Red Shannon
Aug 15, 1922	STL	A	——	BOS	A	Waiver price

George Foster

Date	Traded To		Traded With	Traded By		In Exchange For
May 29, 1971	CIN	N	——	SF	N	Frank Duffy / Vern Geishert
Feb 10, 1982	NY	N	——	CIN	N	Alex Trevino / Jim Kern / Greg Harris

Leo Foster

Date	Traded To		Traded With	Traded By		In Exchange For
March 29, 1978	BOS	A	——	NY	N	Jim Burton

Pop Foster

Date	Traded To		Traded With	Traded By		In Exchange For
Sept 1901	CHI	A	——	WAS	A	Cash

Roy Foster

Date	Traded To		Traded With	Traded By		In Exchange For
April 4, 1970	CLE	A	Frank Coggins / and cash	MIL	A	Max Alvis / Russ Snyder
Dec 2, 1971	TEX	A	——	CLE	A	See Del Unser
April 3, 1972	CLE	A	Tom McCraw	TEX	A	Ted Ford

Rube Foster

Date	Traded To		Traded With	Traded By		In Exchange For
April 1918	CIN	N	——	BOS	A	Dave Shean

(Foster refused to report to Cincinnati; Cincinnati received cash instead.)

Bob Fothergill

Date	Traded To		Traded With	Traded By		In Exchange For
July 18, 1930	CHI	A	——	DET	A	Waiver price
Dec 15, 1932	BOS	A	Johnny Hodapp / Greg Mulleavy / Bob Seeds	CHI	A	Ed Durham / Hal Rhyne

Steve Foucault

Date	Traded To		Traded With	Traded By		In Exchange For
April 12, 1977	DET	A	——	TEX	A	Willie Horton
Aug 16, 1978	KC	A	——	DET	A	Cash

Jack Fournier

Date	Traded To		Traded With	Traded By		In Exchange For
May 8, 1912	CHI	A	——	BOS	A	Cash
Feb 15, 1923	BKN	N	——	STL	N	Hy Myers / Ray Schmandt
Nov 5, 1926	BOS	N	——	BKN	N	Cash

Howie Fox

Date	Traded To	Traded With	Traded By	In Exchange For
Dec 10, 1951	PHI N	See Smoky Burgess	CIN N	——

Nellie Fox

Date	Traded To	Traded With	Traded By	In Exchange For
Oct 19, 1949	CHI A	——	PHI A	Joe Tipton
Dec 10, 1963	HOU N	——	CHI A	Jim Golden Danny Murphy and cash

Paddy Fox

Date	Traded To	Traded With	Traded By	In Exchange For
Jan 1900	LOU N	——	PIT N	See Honus Wagner

Pete Fox

Date	Traded To	Traded With	Traded By	In Exchange For
Dec 12, 1940	BOS A	——	DET A	Cash

Terry Fox

Date	Traded To	Traded With	Traded By	In Exchange For
Dec 7, 1960	DET A	See Bill Bruton	MIL N	——
May 10, 1966	PHI N	——	DET A	Cash

Bill Foxen

Date	Traded To	Traded With	Traded By	In Exchange For
July 1910	CHI N	——	PHI N	Fred Luderus

Jimmie Foxx

Date	Traded To	Traded With	Traded By	In Exchange For
Dec 10, 1935	BOS A	Johnny Marcum	PHI A	Gordon Rhodes minor league C George Savino and $150,000.
June 1, 1942	CHI N	——	BOS A	Waiver price

Joe Foy

Date	Traded To	Traded With	Traded By	In Exchange For
Dec 3, 1969	NY N	——	KC A	Amos Otis Bob Johnson

Paul Foytack

Date	Traded To	Traded With	Traded By	In Exchange For
June 15, 1963	LA A	Frank Kostro	DET A	George Thomas and cash

Ken Frailing

Date	Traded To	Traded With	Traded By	In Exchange For
Dec 11, 1973	CHI N	Steve Stone Steve Swisher Jim Kremmel	CHI A	Ron Santo

Ray Francis

Date	Traded To	Traded With	Traded By	In Exchange For
Nov 24, 1922	DET A	——	WAS A	Chick Gagnon
May 5, 1925	BOS A	$9,000.	NY A	Bobby Veach Alex Ferguson

John Franco

Date	Traded To	Traded With	Traded By	In Exchange For
May 9, 1983	CIN N	minor league P Brett Wise	LA N	Rafael Landestoy
Dec 6, 1989	NY N	Minor league OF Don Brown	CIN N	Randy Myers Minor league P Kip Gross

Julio Franco

Date	Traded To	Traded With	Traded By	In Exchange For
Dec 9, 1982	CLE A	Manny Trillo George Vukovich Jay Baller Jerry Willard	PHI N	Von Hayes
Dec 6, 1988	TEX A	——	CLE A	Pete O'Brien Oddibe McDowell Jerry Browne

Tito Francona

Date	Traded To	Traded With	Traded By	In Exchange For
Dec 3, 1957	CHI A	Ray Moore Billy Goodman	BAL A	Jack Harshman Russ Heman Jim Marshall Larry Doby
June 15, 1958	DET A	Bill Fischer	CHI A	Ray Boone Bob Shaw
March 21, 1959	CLE A	——	DET A	Larry Doby
Dec 15, 1964	STL N	——	CLE A	Cash
April 10, 1967	PHI N	——	STL N	Cash
June 12, 1967	ATL N	——	PHI N	Cash
Aug 22, 1969	OAK A	——	ATL N	Cash
June 11, 1970	MIL A	Al Downing	OAK A	Steve Hovley

Fred Frankhouse

Date	Traded To	Traded With	Traded By	In Exchange For
June 16, 1930	BOS N	Bill Sherdel	STL N	Burleigh Grimes
Feb 6, 1936	BKN N	——	BOS N	Johnny Babich Gene Moore
Dec 13, 1938	BOS N	——	BKN N	Joe Stripp

Herman Franks

Date	Traded To	Traded With	Traded By	In Exchange For
Feb 6, 1940	BKN N	——	STL N	Cash

Chick Fraser

Date	Traded To	Traded With	Traded By	In Exchange For
Dec 20, 1904	BOS N	Harry Wolverton	PHI N	Togie Pittinger
March 1906	CIN N	Jim Delahanty	BOS N	Al Bridwell
Oct 1906	CIN N	——	CHI N	Jack Harper

Vic Frasier

Date	Traded To	Traded With	Traded By	In Exchange For
June 2, 1933	DET A	——	CHI A	Whit Wyatt

George Frazier

Date	Traded To	Traded With	Traded By	In Exchange For
Dec 8, 1977	STL N	——	MIL A	Buck Martinez
June 7, 1981	NY A	——	STL N	Cash
Feb 5, 1984	CLE A	Otis Nixon Minor league P Guy Elston	NY A	Toby Harrah Minor league P Rick Browne
June 13, 1984	CHI N	Rick Sutcliffe Ron Hassey	CLE A	Mel Hall Joe Carter Don Schulze Minor league P Darryl Banks
Aug 13, 1986	MIN A	Ray Fontenot Minor league SS Julius McDougal	CHI N	Ron Davis Minor league P Dewayne Coleman

Joe Frazier

Date	Traded To	Traded With	Traded By	In Exchange For
Nov 20, 1947	STL A	Dick Kokos Bryan Stephens and $25,000.	CLE A	Bob Muncrief Walt Judnich
May 16, 1956	CIN N	Alex Grammas	STL N	Chuck Harmon
June 26, 1956	BAL A	——	CIN N	Cash

Roger Freed

Date	Traded To	Traded With	Traded By	In Exchange For
Dec 16, 1970	PHI N	——	BAL A	Grant Jackson Jim Hutto Sam Parrilla
Nov 30, 1972	CLE A	Oscar Gamble	PHI N	Del Unser minor league IF Terry Wedgewood
Dec 12, 1973	CIN N	——	CLE A	Steve Blateric

Hersh Freeman

Date	Traded To	Traded With	Traded By	In Exchange For
May 10, 1955	CIN N	——	BOS A	Cash
May 8, 1958	CHI N	——	CIN N	Turk Lown

Jimmy Freeman

Date	Traded To	Traded With	Traded By	In Exchange For
April 17, 1975	BAL A	$75,000.	ATL N	Earl Williams

Date	Traded To		Traded With	Traded By		In Exchange For
Jimmy Freeman *continued*						
June 15, 1976	NY	A		BAL	A	*See Tippy Martinez*
LaVel Freeman						
June 29, 1989	TEX	A	Minor league P Todd Simmons	MIL	A	Scott May Minor league OF Mike Wilson
Mark Freeman						
April 8, 1959	KC	A	———	NY	A	Jack Urban
(Freeman was returned to the Yankees on May 8, 1959.)						
May 19, 1960	CHI	N	———	NY	A	Art Ceccarelli minor league IF Ray Bellino
Gene Freese						
June 15, 1958	STL	N	Johnny O'Brien	PIT	N	Dick Schofield and cash
Sept 29, 1958	PHI	N	———	STL	N	Solly Hemus
(Hemus was named St. Louis manager.)						
Dec 9, 1959	CHI	A	———	PHI	N	Johnny Callison
Dec 15, 1960	CIN	N	———	CHI	A	Juan Pizarro Cal McLish
Nov 26, 1963	PIT	N	———	CIN	N	Cash
Aug 25, 1965	CHI	A	———	PIT	N	Cash
July 20, 1966	HOU	N	———	CHI	A	Jim Mahoney and cash
George Freese						
April 7, 1953	DET	A	———	STL	A	Cash
June 4, 1953	PIT	N	———	CHI	N	*See Ralph Kiner*
Jim Fregosi						
Dec 10, 1971	NY	N	———	CAL	A	Nolan Ryan Don Rose Leroy Stanton Francisco Estrada
July 11, 1973	TEX	A	———	NY	N	Cash
June 15, 1977	PIT	N	———	TEX	A	Ed Kirkpatrick
Howard Freigau						
May 23, 1925	CHI	N	Mike Gonzalez	STL	N	Bob O'Farrell
Dec 1927	BKN	N	———	CHI	N	Johnny Butler
June 23, 1928	BOS	N	———	BKN	N	Cash
Dave Freisleben						
June 22, 1978	CLE	A	———	SD	N	Bill Laxton
Nov 3, 1978	TOR	A	———	CLE	A	Sheldon Mallory
Tony Freitas						
Dec 1933	CIN	N	———	PHI	A	Cash
Charlie French						
May 1910	CHI	A	———	BOS	A	Cash
Larry French						
Nov 22, 1934	CHI	N	Freddie Lindstrom	PIT	N	Guy Bush Jim Weaver Babe Herman
Aug 20, 1941	BKN	N	———	CHI	N	Waiver price
Benny Frey						
April 11, 1932	STL	N	Harvey Hendrick and cash	CIN	N	Chick Hafey
May 10, 1932	CIN	N	———	STL	N	Cash

Date	Traded To		Traded With	Traded By		In Exchange For
Lonny Frey						
Dec 5, 1936	CHI	N	———	BKN	N	Roy Henshaw Woody English
Feb 4, 1938	CIN	N	———	CHI	N	Cash
April 16, 1947	CHI	N	———	CIN	N	Cash
June 25, 1947	NY	A	———	CHI	N	Cash
Steve Frey						
Dec 11, 1987	NY	N	Phil Lombardi Minor league OF Darren Reed	NY	A	Rafael Santana Minor league P Victor Garcia
March 28, 1989	MON	N	———	NY	N	Tom O'Malley Mark Bailey
Pepe Frias						
March 31, 1979	ATL	N	———	MON	N	Dave Campbell
Dec 6, 1979	TEX	A	Adrian Devine	ATL	N	Doyle Alexander Larvell Blanks and $50,000.
Sept 13, 1980	LA	N	———	TEX	A	Dennis Lewallyn
Barney Friberg						
June 15, 1925	PHI	N	———	CHI	N	Waiver price
Jan 7, 1932	BOS	A	———	PHI	N	Waiver price
Jan 7, 1933	BOS	A	———	PHI	N	Waiver price
Jim Fridley						
April 6, 1953	STL	A	———	CLE	A	Waiver price
Dec 1, 1954	NY	A	*See Dick Kryhoski*	BAL	A	
Bob Friend						
Dec 10, 1965	NY	A	———	PIT	N	Pete Mikkelsen and cash
June 15, 1966	NY	N	———	NY	A	Cash
Owen Friend						
Dec 4, 1952	DET	A	———	STL	A	*See Virgil Trucks*
June 15, 1953	CLE	A	———	DET	A	*See Ray Boone*
John Frill						
Jan 1912	CIN	N	———	STL	A	Waiver price
Charlie Frisbee						
Feb 17, 1900	NY	N	———	BOS	N	Cash
Frankie Frisch						
Dec 20, 1926	STL	N	Jimmy Ring	NY	N	Rogers Hornsby
Danny Frisella						
Nov 2, 1972	ATL	N	Gary Gentry	NY	N	Felix Millan George Stone
Nov 8, 1974	SD	N	———	ATL	N	Clarence Gaston
April 8, 1976	STL	N	———	SD	N	Ken Reynolds and minor leaguer Bob Stewart
June 7, 1976	MIL	A	———	STL	N	Sam Mejias
Sam Frock						
June 1, 1910	BOS	N	———	PIT	N	Kirby White
Art Fromme						
Dec 12, 1908	CIN	N	Ed Karger	STL	N	Admiral Schlei

Date	Traded To		Traded With	Traded By		In Exchange For

Art Fromme *continued*

Date	Traded To		Traded With	Traded By		In Exchange For
May 22, 1913	NY	N	Eddie Grant	CIN	N	Red Ames Heinie Groh Josh Devore and $20,000.

Dave Frost

Date	Traded To		Traded With	Traded By		In Exchange For
Dec 5, 1977	CAL	A	*See Brian Downing*	CHI	A	——
Feb 3, 1982	KC	A	——	CAL	A	No compensation (free agent signing)

Woodie Fryman

Date	Traded To		Traded With	Traded By		In Exchange For
Dec 15, 1967	PHI	N	Don Money Bill Laxton minor league P Hal Clem	PIT	N	Jim Bunning
Aug 2, 1972	DET	A	——	PHI	N	Cash
Dec 4, 1974	MON	N	——	DET	A	Tom Walker Terry Humphrey
Dec 16, 1976	CIN	N	Dale Murray	MON	N	Tony Perez Will McEnaney
Oct 31, 1977	CHI	N	Bill Caudill	CIN	N	Bill Bonham
June 9, 1978	MON	N	——	CHI	N	Jerry White

Tito Fuentes

Date	Traded To		Traded With	Traded By		In Exchange For
Dec 6, 1974	SD	N	Butch Metzger	SF	N	Derrel Thomas
Feb 23, 1977	DET	A	——	SD	N	No compensation (free agent signing)
Jan 30, 1978	MON	N	——	DET	A	Cash

Chick Fullis

Date	Traded To		Traded With	Traded By		In Exchange For
Dec 12, 1932	PHI	N	Gus Dugas	NY	N	Kiddo Davis
	(Part of three-team trade involving New York, Philadelphia, and Pittsburgh.)					
June 15, 1934	STL	N	——	PHI	N	Kiddo Davis

Dave Fultz

Date	Traded To		Traded With	Traded By		In Exchange For
March 1903	NY	A	——	PHI	A	Cash

Frank Funk

Date	Traded To		Traded With	Traded By		In Exchange For
Nov 27, 1962	MIL	N	Ty Cline Don Dillard	CLE	A	Joe Adcock Jack Curtis

Fred Fussell

Date	Traded To		Traded With	Traded By		In Exchange For
Dec 1927	PIT	N	——	CHI	N	Mike Cvengros

Frank Gabler

Date	Traded To		Traded With	Traded By		In Exchange For
June 15, 1937	BOS	N	$35,000.	NY	N	Wally Berger
May 2, 1938	CHI	A	——	BOS	N	Cash

Len Gabrielson

Date	Traded To		Traded With	Traded By		In Exchange For
June 3, 1964	CHI	N	——	MIL	N	Merritt Ranew and $40,000.
May 29, 1965	SF	N	Dick Bertell	CHI	N	Harvey Kuenn Ed Bailey Bob Hendley
Dec 14, 1966	CAL	A	——	SF	N	Norm Siebern
May 10, 1967	LA	N	——	CAL	A	Johnny Werhas

Phil Gagliano

Date	Traded To		Traded With	Traded By		In Exchange For
May 29, 1970	CHI	N	——	STL	N	Ted Abernathy
Dec 3, 1970	BOS	A	——	CHI	N	Carmen Fanzone
March 27, 1973	CIN	N	Andy Kosco	BOS	A	Mel Behney

Greg Gagne

Date	Traded To		Traded With	Traded By		In Exchange For
April 10, 1982	MIN	A	Ron Davis Paul Boris	NY	A	Roy Smalley

Ed Gagnier

Date	Traded To		Traded With	Traded By		In Exchange For
July 1915	BUF	F	Ed Lafitte	BKN	F	Fred Smith

Chick Gagnon

Date	Traded To		Traded With	Traded By		In Exchange For
Nov 24, 1922	WAS	A	——	DET	A	Ray Francis

Del Gainer

Date	Traded To		Traded With	Traded By		In Exchange For
June 2, 1911	BOS	A	——	DET	A	Waiver price
June 2, 1914	BOS	A	——	DET	A	Waiver price

Joe Gaines

Date	Traded To		Traded With	Traded By		In Exchange For
Dec 15, 1962	BAL	A	——	CIN	N	Dick Luebke minor league IF Willard Oplinger
June 15, 1964	HOU	N	——	BAL	A	Johnny Weekly and cash

Augie Galan

Date	Traded To		Traded With	Traded By		In Exchange For
Dec 4, 1946	CIN	N	——	BKN	N	Ed Heusser

Rich Gale

Date	Traded To		Traded With	Traded By		In Exchange For
Dec 11, 1981	SF	N	Bill Laskey	KC	A	Jerry Martin
Jan 5, 1983	CIN	N	——	SF	N	Mike Vail

Denny Galehouse

Date	Traded To		Traded With	Traded By		In Exchange For
Dec 15, 1938	BOS	A	Tommy Irwin	CLE	A	Ben Chapman
Dec 3, 1940	STL	A	——	BOS	A	Cash
June 20, 1947	BOS	A	——	STL	A	Cash

Al Gallagher

Date	Traded To		Traded With	Traded By		In Exchange For
April 14, 1973	CAL	A	——	SF	N	Bruce Miller

Bob Gallagher

Date	Traded To		Traded With	Traded By		In Exchange For
Oct 29, 1974	NY	N	——	HOU	N	Ken Boswell

Dave Gallagher

Date	Traded To		Traded With	Traded By		In Exchange For
May 12, 1987	SEA	A	——	CLE	A	Mark Huismann

Joe Gallagher

Date	Traded To		Traded With	Traded By		In Exchange For
June 13, 1939	STL	A	——	NY	A	Roy Hughes and cash
May 27, 1940	BKN	N	——	STL	A	Roy Cullenbine

Bert Gallia

Date	Traded To		Traded With	Traded By		In Exchange For
Dec 15, 1917	STL	A	$15,000.	WAS	A	Burt Shotton Doc Lavan
April 1920	PHI	N	——	STL	A	Cash

Chick Galloway

Date	Traded To		Traded With	Traded By		In Exchange For
Dec 2, 1927	STL	A	——	PHI	A	Cash
Dec 2, 1927	DET	A	Elam Vangilder Harry Rice	STL	A	Heinie Manush Lu Blue

Balvino Galvez

Date	Traded To		Traded With	Traded By		In Exchange For
March 24, 1988	MIN	A	——	DET	A	Billy Beane
March 20, 1989	NY	A	——	MIN	A	Steve Shields

Date	Traded To		Traded With	Traded By		In Exchange For

Oscar Gamble

Date	Traded To		Traded With	Traded By		In Exchange For
Nov 17, 1969	PHI	N	Dick Selma	CHI	N	Johnny Callison
Nov 30, 1972	CLE	A	Roger Freed	PHI	N	Del Unser minor league IF Terry Wedgewood
Nov 22, 1975	NY	A	——	CLE	A	Pat Dobson
April 5, 1977	CHI	A	LaMarr Hoyt minor league P Bob Polinsky and $200,000.	NY	A	Bucky Dent
Nov 29, 1977	SD	N	——	CHI	A	No compensation (free agent signing)
Oct 25, 1978	TEX	A	Dave Roberts and $300,000.	SD	N	Mike Hargrove Kurt Bevacqua Bill Fahey
Aug 1, 1979	NY	A	Ray Fontenot Gene Nelson minor league 3B Amos Lewis	TEX	A	Mickey Rivers minor league Ps Bob Polinsky Neil Mersch and Mark Softy
March 23, 1985	CHI	A	——	NY	A	No compensation (free agent signing)

Chick Gandil

Date	Traded To		Traded With	Traded By		In Exchange For
Feb 15, 1916	CLE	A	——	WAS	A	$7,500.
Feb 25, 1917	CHI	A	——	CLE	A	$3,500.

Bob Ganley

Date	Traded To		Traded With	Traded By		In Exchange For
Feb 1907	WAS	A	——	PIT	N	Cash
May 1909	PHI	A	——	WAS	A	Cash

John Ganzel

Date	Traded To		Traded With	Traded By		In Exchange For
Feb 1901	NY	N	——	CHI	N	Cash

Joe Garagiola

Date	Traded To		Traded With	Traded By		In Exchange For
June 15, 1951	PIT	N	Bill Howerton Howie Pollet Ted Wilks Dick Cole	STL	N	Cliff Chambers Wally Westlake
June 4, 1953	CHI	N	Ralph Kiner Howie Pollet Catfish Metkovich	PIT	N	Toby Atwell Bob Schultz Preston Ward George Freese Bob Addis Gene Hermanski $150,000.
Sept 8, 1954	NY	N	——	CHI	N	Waiver price

Gene Garber

Date	Traded To		Traded With	Traded By		In Exchange For
Oct 25, 1972	KC	A	——	PIT	N	Jim Rooker
June 15, 1978	ATL	N	——	PHI	N	Dick Ruthven
Aug 30, 1987	KC	A	——	ATL	N	Terry Bell

Barbaro Garbey

Date	Traded To		Traded With	Traded By		In Exchange For
Nov 13, 1985	OAK	A	——	DET	A	Dave Collins

Damaso Garcia

Date	Traded To		Traded With	Traded By		In Exchange For
Nov 1, 1979	TOR	A	Chris Chambliss Paul Mirabella	NY	A	Tom Underwood Rick Cerone Ted Wilborn
Feb 2, 1987	ATL	N	Luis Leal	TOR	A	Craig McMurtry
Dec 22, 1989	NY	A	——	MON	N	No compensation (free agent signing)

Kiko Garcia

Date	Traded To		Traded With	Traded By		In Exchange For
April 1, 1981	HOU	N	——	BAL	A	Chris Bourjos and cash

Leo Garcia

Date	Traded To		Traded With	Traded By		In Exchange For
Aug 23, 1982	CIN	N	——	CHI	A	See Jim Kern

Miguel Garcia

Date	Traded To		Traded With	Traded By		In Exchange For
Aug 29, 1987	PIT	N	Minor league IF Bill Merrifield	CAL	A	Johnny Ray

Pedro Garcia

Date	Traded To		Traded With	Traded By		In Exchange For
June 10, 1976	DET	A	——	MIL	A	Gary Sutherland

Ron Gardenhire

Date	Traded To		Traded With	Traded By		In Exchange For
Nov 12, 1986	MIN	A	——	NY	N	player to be named

Billy Gardner

Date	Traded To		Traded With	Traded By		In Exchange For
April 21, 1956	BAL	A	——	NY	N	$20,000.
April 3, 1960	WAS	A	——	BAL	A	Clint Courtney Ron Samford
June 14, 1961	NY	A	——	MIN	A	Danny McDevitt
June 12, 1962	BOS	A	——	NY	A	Tommy Umphlett and cash

Larry Gardner

Date	Traded To		Traded With	Traded By		In Exchange For
Jan 10, 1918	PHI	A	Tilly Walker Hick Cady	BOS	A	Stuffy McInnis
March 1, 1919	CLE	A	Elmer Myers Charlie Jamieson	PHI	A	Braggo Roth

Rob Gardner

Date	Traded To		Traded With	Traded By		In Exchange For
June 12, 1967	CHI	N	Johnny Stephenson	NY	N	Bob Hendley
March 30, 1968	CLE	A	——	CHI	N	Bobby Tiefenauer
April 9, 1971	OAK	A	Ron Klimkowski	NY	A	Felipe Alou
May 26, 1971	NY	A	——	OAK	A	Curt Blefary
Nov 24, 1972	OAK	A	Rich McKinney	NY	A	Matty Alou
May 31, 1973	MIL	A	——	OAK	A	Cash
(Deal was cancelled and Gardner was returned to Oakland on July 16.)						

Wes Gardner

Date	Traded To		Traded With	Traded By		In Exchange For
Nov 13, 1985	BOS	A	Calvin Schiraldi John Christensen LaSchelle Tarver	NY	N	Bob Ojeda John Mitchell Tom McCarthy Minor league P Chris Bayer

Wayne Garland

Date	Traded To		Traded With	Traded By		In Exchange For
Nov 19, 1976	CLE	A	——	BAL	A	No compensation (free agent signing)

Mike Garman

Date	Traded To		Traded With	Traded By		In Exchange For
Dec 7, 1973	STL	N	Lynn McGlothen John Curtis	BOS	A	Reggie Cleveland Diego Segui Terry Hughes
Oct 28, 1975	CHI	N	minor league IF Bobby Hrapmann	STL	N	Don Kessinger
Jan 11, 1977	LA	N	Rick Monday	CHI	N	Bill Buckner Ivan DeJesus minor league P Jeff Albert
May 20, 1978	MON	N	——	LA	N	Larry Landreth Gerald Hannahs

Debs Garms

Date	Traded To		Traded With	Traded By		In Exchange For
March 3, 1940	PIT	N	——	BOS	N	Cash

Date	Traded To		Traded With		Traded By		In Exchange For

Phil Garner

March 15, 1977	PIT	N	Tommy Helms Chris Batton	OAK	A	Dave Giusti Doc Medich Doug Bair Rick Langford Tony Armas Mitchell Page
Aug 31, 1981	HOU	N	——	PIT	N	Johnny Ray minor league OF Kevin Houston Randy Niemann
June 19, 1987	LA	N	——	HOU	N	Minor league P Jeff Edwards
Jan 28, 1988	SF	N	——	LA	N	No compensation (free agent signing)

Ralph Garr

| Dec 12, 1975 | CHI | A | Larvell Blanks | ATL | N | Ken Henderson
Dick Ruthven
Danny Osborn |
| Sept 20, 1979 | CAL | A | —— | CHI | A | Cash |

Adrian Garrett

May 8, 1964	MIL	N	Jay Hook	NY	N	Roy McMillan
Aug 31, 1971	OAK	A	——	CHI	N	Frank Fernandez Bill McNulty
July 31, 1975	CAL	A	——	CHI	N	Cash

Greg Garrett

| Dec 15, 1970 | CIN | N | —— | CAL | A | Jim Maloney |

Wayne Garrett

| July 21, 1976 | MON | N | Del Unser | NY | N | Jim Dwyer
Pepe Mangual |
| July 21, 1978 | STL | N | —— | MON | N | Cash |

Gil Garrido

| May 16, 1966 | ATL | N | —— | SF | N | Cash |
| Dec 4, 1973 | PHI | N | —— | ATL | N | Bob Beall |

Ford Garrison

| May 7, 1944 | PHI | A | —— | BOS | A | Hal Wagner |

Ned Garver

| Aug 14, 1952 | DET | A | Jim Delsing
Dave Madison
Bill Black | STL | A | Dick Littlefield
Marlin Stuart
Don Lenhardt
Vic Wertz |
| Dec 5, 1956 | KC | A | Gene Host
Virgil Trucks
Wayne Belardi
and $20,000. | DET | A | Jim Finigan
Jack Crimian
Bill Harrington
Eddie Robinson |

Steve Garvey

| Dec 21, 1982 | SD | N | —— | LA | N | No compensation
(free agent signing) |

Jerry Garvin

| Jan 18, 1983 | STL | N | —— | TOR | A | Cash |

Ned Garvin

| Sept 1904 | NY | A | —— | BKN | N | Waiver price |

Rod Gaspar

| Sept 1, 1970 | SD | N | —— | NY | N | Ron Herbel |

(San Diego received Gaspar on October 20.)

Clarence Gaston

| Nov 8, 1974 | ATL | N | —— | SD | N | Danny Frisella |
| Sept 22, 1978 | PIT | N | —— | ATL | N | Cash |

Milt Gaston

Dec 17, 1924	STL	A	Joe Bush Joe Giard	NY	A	Urban Shocker
Oct 19, 1927	WAS	A	——	STL	A	Dick Coffman Earl McNeely
Dec 15, 1928	BOS	A	Hod Lisenbee Bobby Reeves Grant Gillis Elliott Bigelow	WAS	A	Buddy Myer
Dec 2, 1931	CHI	A	——	BOS	A	Bob Weiland

Doc Gautreau

| July 1, 1925 | BOS | N | —— | PHI | A | Cash |

Dinty Gearin

| June 5, 1924 | BOS | N | —— | NY | N | Cash |

Joe Gedeon

| Jan 22, 1918 | STL | A | Les Nunamaker
Fritz Maisel
Nick Cullop
Urban Shocker | NY | A | Eddie Plank
Del Pratt
and $15,000. |

Johnny Gee

| June 12, 1944 | NY | N | —— | PIT | N | Cash |

Phil Geier

| June 1901 | MIL | A | —— | PHI | A | Tom Leahy |

Gary Geiger

| Dec 2, 1958 | BOS | A | Vic Wertz | CLE | A | Jimmy Piersall |

Dave Geisel

| Dec 28, 1981 | TOR | A | —— | CHI | N | Paul Mirabella |

Vern Geishert

| Nov 25, 1969 | CIN | N | Pedro Borbon
Jim McGlothlin | CAL | A | Alex Johnson
Chico Ruiz |
| May 29, 1971 | SF | N | Frank Duffy | CIN | N | George Foster |

Charley Gelbert

Dec 2, 1936	CIN	N	——	STL	N	Cash
July 9, 1937	DET	A	——	CIN	N	Waiver price
Aug 30, 1940	BOS	A	——	WAS	A	Waiver price

John Gelnar

Oct 18, 1968	KC	A	——	PIT	N	Cash
April 1, 1969	SEA	A	Steve Whitaker	KC	A	Lou Piniella
May 11, 1971	DET	A	Jose Herrera	MIL	A	Jim Hannan

Joe Genewich

| June 15, 1928 | NY | N | —— | BOS | N | Ben Cantwell
Al Spohrer
Bill Clarkson
Virgil Barnes |

Date	Traded To	Traded With	Traded By	In Exchange For

Jim Gentile

Date	Traded To		Traded With	Traded By		In Exchange For
Nov 27, 1963	KC	A	Cash	BAL	A	Norm Siebern
June 4, 1965	HOU	N	——	KC	A	Jess Hickman
						Ernie Fazio
						and $100,000.

(Kansas City received Fazio on October 15.)

| July 19, 1966 | CLE | A | —— | HOU | N | Tony Curry |

Gary Gentry

| Nov 2, 1972 | ATL | N | Danny Frisella | NY | N | Felix Millan |
| | | | | | | George Stone |

Lefty George

| Jan 1912 | CLE | A | —— | STL | A | George Stovall |

Dave Gerard

March 28, 1963	HOU	N	Danny Murphy	CHI	N	Merritt Ranew
						Hal Haydel
						Dick LeMay

Wally Gerber

| April 25, 1928 | BOS | A | —— | STL | A | Hal Wiltse |

Ken Gerhart

| March 24, 1989 | SF | N | —— | BAL | A | Francisco Melendez |

Al Gerheauser

Jan 22, 1943	PHI	N	Tom Padden	NY	A	Nick Etten
			Ed Levy			
			Al Gettel			
			and $10,000.			
March 31, 1945	PIT	N	——	PHI	N	Vince DiMaggio
Dec 5, 1946	BKN	N	——	PIT	N	Eddie Basinski

Dick Gernert

Nov 21, 1959	CHI	N	——	BOS	A	Dave Hillman
						Jim Marshall
Aug 31, 1960	DET	A	——	CHI	N	Cash
May 10, 1961	CIN	N	——	DET	A	Jim Baumer

Cesar Geronimo

Nov 29, 1971	CIN	N	Joe Morgan	HOU	N	Lee May
			Denis Menke			Tommy Helms
			Jack Billingham			Jimmy Stewart
			Ed Armbrister			
Jan 21, 1981	KC	A	——	CIN	N	German Barranca

Doc Gessler

| May 8, 1906 | CHI | N | —— | BKN | N | Cash |
| Sept 1909 | WAS | A | —— | BOS | A | Charlie Smith |

Al Gettel

Jan 22, 1943	PHI	N	Tom Padden	NY	A	Nick Etten
			Al Gerheauser			
			Ed Levy			
			and $10,000.			
Dec 20, 1946	CLE	A	Hal Peck	NY	A	Sherm Lollar
			Gene Bearden			Ray Mack
June 2, 1948	CHI	A	Pat Seerey	CLE	A	Bob Kennedy
July 12, 1949	WAS	A	——	CHI	A	Cash

Gus Getz

| June 1918 | PIT | N | —— | CLE | A | Waiver price |

Joe Giard

Dec 17, 1924	STL	A	Joe Bush	NY	A	Urban Shocker
			Milt Gaston			
Feb 8, 1927	NY	A	Cedric Durst	STL	A	Sad Sam Jones

Joe Gibbon

| Oct 1, 1965 | SF | N | Ozzie Virgil | PIT | N | Matty Alou |
| June 10, 1969 | PIT | N | —— | SF | N | Ron Kline |

John Gibbons

| April 1, 1988 | LA | N | —— | NY | N | Craig Shipley |

Frank Gibson

| Dec 15, 1927 | STL | N | —— | BOS | N | Cash |

George Gibson

| Aug 5, 1916 | NY | N | —— | PIT | N | Waiver price |
| Jan 1917 | NY | N | —— | PIT | N | Waiver price |

Kirk Gibson

| Jan 29, 1988 | LA | N | —— | DET | A | No compensation |
| | | | | | | (free agent signing) |

Russ Gibson

| April 4, 1970 | SF | N | —— | BOS | A | Cash |

Brett Gideon

| March 28, 1989 | MON | N | —— | PIT | N | Neal Heaton |

Jim Gideon

| June 1, 1976 | MIN | A | *See Roy Smalley* | TEX | A | —— |

Paul Giel

| April 13, 1959 | PIT | N | —— | SF | N | Waiver price |
| June 1, 1961 | KC | A | Reno Bertoia | MIN | A | Bill Tuttle |

(Giel was returned to Minnesota for a cash payment.)

Bob Giggie

| May 11, 1960 | KC | A | —— | MIL | N | George Brunet |

Gus Gil

| Oct 15, 1966 | CLE | A | —— | CIN | N | Cash |

Charlie Gilbert

May 6, 1941	CHI	N	Johnny Hudson	BKN	N	Billy Herman
			and $65,000.			
June 15, 1946	PHI	N	——	CHI	N	Cash

Wally Gilbert

March 14, 1932	CIN	N	Babe Herman	BKN	N	Tony Cuccinello
			Ernie Lombardi			Joe Stripp
						Clyde Sukeforth

Bill Gilbreth

| Sept 6, 1972 | CAL | A | —— | DET | A | Cash |
| Sept 12, 1974 | CLE | A | —— | CAL | A | Charles Hudson |

Frank Gilhooley

| Aug 25, 1913 | NY | A | —— | STL | N | Cash |

Date	Traded To	Traded With	Traded By	In Exchange For
Frank Gilhooley *continued*				
Dec 18, 1918	BOS A ————		NY A	*See Duffy Lewis*
George Gill				
May 13, 1939	STL A ————		DET A	*See Beau Bell*
Grant Gillis				
Dec 15, 1928	BOS A	Milt Gaston	WAS A	Buddy Myer
		Hod Lisenbee		
		Bobby Reeves		
		Elliott Bigelow		
Hal Gilson				
June 15, 1968	HOU N	Dick Simpson	STL N	Ron Davis
Joe Ginsberg				
June 15, 1953	CLE A ————		DET A	*See Ray Boone*
Aug 17, 1956	BAL A ————		KC A	Hal Smith
Al Gionfriddo				
May 3, 1947	BKN N	$100,000.	PIT N	Kirby Higbe
				Hank Behrman
				Cal McLish
				Gene Mauch
				Dixie Howell
Tony Giuliani				
March 24, 1938	WAS A ————		STL A	Cash
March 1, 1944	STL A	Gene Moore	WAS A	Rick Ferrell
		and cash		
(Giuliani announced his retirement, and St. Louis received Moore to complete the trade.)				
Dave Giusti				
Oct 11, 1968	STL N	Dave Adlesh	HOU N	Johnny Edwards
				minor league
				C Tommy Smith
Dec 3, 1968	STL N ————		SD N	Danny Breeden
				Ed Spiezio
				Ron Davis
				minor league
				P Phil Knuckles
Oct 21, 1969	PIT N	Dave Ricketts	STL N	Carl Taylor
				minor league
				OF Frank Vanzin
March 15, 1977	OAK A ————		PIT N	*See Phil Garner*
Aug 5, 1977	CHI N ————		OAK A	Cash
Dan Gladden				
March 31, 1987	MIN A	Minor league	SF N	Minor league
		P David Blakely		P Jose Dominguez
				Minor league
				P Ray Velasquez
				Minor league
				P Bryan Hickerson
Fred Gladding				
Aug 17, 1967	HOU N	Cash	DET A	Eddie Mathews
Fred Glade				
Feb 1908	NY A	Charlie Hemphill	STL A	Jimmy Williams
				Hobe Ferris
				Danny Hoffman
Tommy Glaviano				
Sept 30, 1952	PHI N ————		STL N	Waiver price

Date	Traded To	Traded With	Traded By	In Exchange For
Whitey Glazner				
May 22, 1923	PHI N	Cotton Tierney	PIT N	Lee Meadows
		and $50,000.		Johnny Rawlings
Jerry Don Gleaton				
Dec 12, 1980	SEA A ————		TEX A	*See Rick Honeycutt*
June 29, 1984	CHI A	Gene Nelson	SEA A	Salome Barojas
Jim Gleeson				
Jan 24, 1939	CHI N ————		NY A	$25,000.
Dec 4, 1940	CIN N	Bobby Mattick	CHI N	Billy Myers
Joe Glenn				
Oct 26, 1938	STL A	Myril Hoag	NY A	Oral Hildebrand
				Buster Mills
John Glenn				
June 15, 1960	STL N ————		LA N	Jim Donohue
Al Glossop				
June 15, 1940	BOS N	Manny Salvo	NY N	Tony Cuccinello
March 9, 1943	BKN N	Lloyd Waner	PHI N	Babe Dahlgren
Sept 28, 1943	CHI N ————		BKN N	Cash
Ed Glynn				
March 13, 1979	NY N ————		DET A	Mardie Cornejo
April 6, 1981	CLE A ————		NY N	Minor league
				P Dominick Bullinger
June 24, 1984	NY N ————		CLE A	Minor league
				P Rich Miles
Nov 9, 1984	BOS A ————		NY N	Cash
April 27, 1985	MON N ————		BOS A	Cash
Danny Godby				
March 29, 1975	BOS A ————		STL N	Danny Cater
Ed Goebel				
Feb 10, 1923	BOS A	Val Picinich	WAS A	Muddy Ruel
		Howard Shanks		Allen Russell
Chuck Goggin				
May 24, 1973	ATL N ————		PIT N	Cash
March 26, 1974	BOS A ————		ATL N	Vic Correll
Bill Gogolewski				
March 23, 1974	CLE A ————		TEX A	Steve Hargan
Jim Golden				
Dec 23, 1958	LA N	Rip Repulski	PHI N	Sparky Anderson
		Gene Snyder		
Dec 10, 1963	CHI A	Danny Murphy	HOU N	Nellie Fox
		and cash		
Gordon Goldsberry				
Nov 27, 1951	STL A ————		CHI A	*See Sherm Lollar*
Mike Goliat				
Sept 12, 1951	STL A ————		PHI N	Waiver price

Date	Traded To	Traded With	Traded By	In Exchange For

Dave Goltz
Nov 15, 1979	LA N ——		MIN A	No compensation (free agent signing)

Lefty Gomez
Jan 25, 1943	BOS N ——		NY A	Cash

Luis Gomez
Dec 5, 1979	ATL N	Chris Chambliss	TOR A	Barry Bonnell Pat Rockett Joey McLaughlin

Ruben Gomez
Dec 3, 1958	PHI N	Valmy Thomas	SF N	Jack Sanford
Aug 20, 1962	MIN A ——		CLE A	Georges Maranda Jackie Collum and cash

Jesse Gonder
July 1, 1963	NY N ——		CIN N	Charlie Neal Sammy Taylor
July 21, 1965	MIL N ——		NY N	Gary Kolb

Rene Gonzales
June 16, 1986	BAL A ——		MON N	Dennis Martinez

(Baltimore received Gonzales on Dec. 16, 1986.)

Dec 8, 1986	BAL A ——		MON N	John Stefero

(Baltimore received Gonzales on Dec. 16, 1986, also completing Dennis Martinez deal.)

Denny Gonzalez
March 25, 1989	CLE A	Felix Fermin	PIT N	Jay Bell

(Completion of deal in which Cleveland acquired Gonzalez on November 28, 1988 for a player to be named.)

Fernando Gonzalez
Dec 4, 1973	KC A	Nellie Briles	PIT N	Ed Kirkpatrick Kurt Bevacqua minor league 1B Winston Cole
May 5, 1974	NY A ——		KC A	Cash
June 5, 1978	SD N ——		PIT N	Cash

Julio Gonzalez
Dec 8, 1976	HOU N ——		CHI N	Greg Gross

Mike Gonzalez
April 8, 1915	STL N ——		CIN N	Ivy Wingo
May 1919	NY N ——		STL N	Waiver price
Dec 6, 1921	CIN N	George Burns and $150,000.	NY N	Heinie Groh
April 27, 1924	STL N ——		BKN N	Milt Stock
May 23, 1925	CHI N	Howard Freigau	STL N	Bob O'Farrell

Orlando Gonzalez
July 25, 1980	OAK A ——		PHI N	Cash

Pedro Gonzalez
May 10, 1965	CLE A ——		NY A	Ray Barker

Tony Gonzalez
June 15, 1960	PHI N	Lee Walls	CIN N	Harry Anderson Wally Post minor league 1B Fred Hopke
June 12, 1969	ATL N ——		SD N	Walt Hriniak Van Kelly minor league OF Andy Finlay
Aug 31, 1970	CAL A ——		ATL N	Cash

Johnny Gooch
June 8, 1928	BKN N	Joe Harris	PIT N	Charlie Hargreaves
April 18, 1929	CIN N	Rube Ehrhardt	BKN N	Val Picinich

Wilbur Good
June 10, 1911	CHI N	Cliff Curtis Bill Collins Peaches Graham	BOS N	Johnny Kling Al Kaiser Orlie Weaver Hank Griffin
Feb 3, 1916	PHI N ——		CHI N	Cash

Billy Goodman
June 14, 1957	BAL A ——		BOS A	Mike Fornieles
Dec 3, 1957	CHI A	Tito Francona Ray Moore	BAL A	Jack Harshman Russ Heman Jim Marshall Larry Doby

Ival Goodman
Nov 3, 1934	CIN N ——		STL N	$25,000.
Nov 14, 1942	CHI N ——		CIN N	Cash

Ed Goodson
June 11, 1975	ATL N ——		SF N	Craig Robinson
Nov 17, 1975	LA N	Dusty Baker	ATL N	Jimmy Wynn Tom Paciorek Lee Lacy Jerry Royster

Danny Goodwin
Dec 4, 1978	MIN A	Ron Jackson	CAL A	Dan Ford

Greg Goossen
Nov 3, 1970	PHI N	Jeff Terpko Gene Martin	WAS A	Curt Flood

Glen Gorbous
April 30, 1955	PHI N	*See Andy Seminick*	CIN N	
May 10, 1957	STL N ——		PHI N	Chuck Harmon

Joe Gordon
Oct 19, 1946	CLE A	Eddie Bockman	NY A	Allie Reynolds
Aug 10, 1960	DET A ——		CLE A	Jimmy Dykes

Sid Gordon
Dec 14, 1949	BOS N	Buddy Kerr Willard Marshall Red Webb	NY N	Eddie Stanky Alvin Dark
Dec 26, 1953	PIT N	Max Surkont Sam Jethroe Curt Raydon Fred Walters minor league P Larry Lasalle	MIL N	Danny O'Connell
May 23, 1955	NY N ——		PIT N	Cash

Date		Traded To	Traded With		Traded By	In Exchange For

Tom Gorman

| March 30, 1955 | KC | A | Dick Kryhoski Ewell Blackwell | NY | A | $50,000. |

Tom Gorman

| Aug 4, 1982 | NY | N | —— | MON | N | Joel Youngblood |

Hank Gornicki

| Sept 2, 1941 | CHI | N | —— | STL | N | Cash |

(Gornicki was returned to St. Louis after the season.)

| Dec 1, 1941 | PIT | N | —— | STL | N | Waiver price |

John Goryl

| April 8, 1960 | LA | N | Ron Perranoski minor league OF Lee Handley and $25,000. | CHI | N | Don Zimmer |

Jim Gosger

June 13, 1966	KC	A	Ken Sanders Guido Grilli	BOS	A	John Wyatt Rollie Sheldon Jose Tartabull
Dec 12, 1969	SF	N	Bob Heise	NY	N	Ray Sadecki Dave Marshall
April 20, 1970	MON	N	——	SF	N	Cash

Goose Goslin

June 13, 1930	STL	A	——	WAS	A	General Crowder Heinie Manush
Dec 14, 1932	WAS	A	Fred Schulte Lefty Stewart	STL	A	Sammy West Carl Reynolds Lloyd Brown and $20,000.
Dec 20, 1933	DET	A	——	WAS	A	John Stone

Howie Goss

| April 4, 1963 | HOU | N | Cash | PIT | N | Manny Mota |

Goose Gossage

Dec 10, 1976	PIT	N	Terry Forster	CHI	A	Richie Zisk Silvio Martinez
Nov 23, 1977	NY	A	——	PIT	N	No compensation (free agent signing)
Jan 12, 1984	SD	N	——	NY	N	No compensation (free agent signing)
Feb 12, 1988	CHI	N	Ray Hayward	SD	N	Keith Moreland Mike Brumley
Aug 11, 1989	NY	A	——	SF	N	Waiver price

Julio Gotay

| Nov 19, 1962 | PIT | N | Don Cardwell | STL | N | Dick Groat Diomedes Olivo |

Jim Gott

| Jan 26, 1985 | SF | N | Minor league IF Augie Schmidt Minor league Jack McKnight | TOR | A | Gary Lavelle |
| Dec 7, 1989 | LA | N | —— | PIT | N | No compensation (free agent signing) |

Hank Gowdy

| July 22, 1911 | BOS | N | Al Bridwell | NY | N | Buck Herzog |
| June 7, 1923 | NY | N | Mule Watson | BOS | N | Jesse Barnes Earl Smith |

Mauro Gozzo

| March 27, 1987 | KC | A | Ed Hearn Rick Anderson | NY | N | David Cone Minor league C Chris Jelic |

Billy Grabarkewitz

Nov 28, 1972	CAL	A	——	LA	N	See Andy Messersmith
Aug 14, 1973	PHI	N	Aurelio Monteagudo Chris Coletta	CAL	A	Denny Doyle
July 10, 1974	CHI	N	——	PHI	N	Cash

Johnny Grabowski

| Jan 13, 1927 | NY | A | Ray Morehart | CHI | A | Aaron Ward |

Earl Grace

June 13, 1931	PIT	N	——	CHI	N	Rollie Hemsley
Nov 21, 1935	PHI	N	Claude Passeau	PIT	N	Al Todd
Dec 8, 1937	STL	A	——	PHI	N	Cap Clark

Joe Grace

| June 15, 1946 | WAS | A | Al LaMacchia | STL | A | Jeff Heath |
| Dec 1947 | PIT | N | —— | WAS | A | Cash |

Milt Graff

| Feb 19, 1957 | KC | A | See Billy Hunter | NY | A | —— |
| June 15, 1957 | NY | A | —— | KC | A | See Ralph Terry |

Dan Graham

| Dec 7, 1979 | BAL | A | —— | MIN | A | Tom Chism |

Jack Graham

| May 1946 | NY | N | —— | BKN | N | Cash |

Peaches Graham

| June 10, 1911 | CHI | N | —— | BOS | N | See Johnny Kling |
| Oct 1911 | PHI | N | —— | CHI | N | Dick Cotter |

Wayne Graham

| Aug 7, 1964 | NY | N | Gary Kroll and cash | PHI | N | Frank Thomas |
| Feb 22, 1966 | PHI | N | Jimmie Schaffer Bobby Klaus | NY | N | Dick Stuart |

Alex Grammas

Dec 2, 1953	STL	N	——	CIN	N	Jack Crimian and $100,000.
May 16, 1956	CIN	N	Joe Frazier	STL	N	Chuck Harmon
Oct 3, 1958	STL	N	George Crowe Alex Kellner	CIN	N	Bob Mabe Eddie Kasko Del Ennis
June 5, 1962	CHI	N	Don Landrum	STL	N	Bobby Gene Smith Daryl Robertson

Wayne Granger

Oct 11, 1968	CIN	N	Bobby Tolan	STL	N	Vada Pinson
Dec 3, 1971	MIN	A	——	CIN	N	Tom Hall
Nov 29, 1972	STL	N	——	MIN	A	Larry Hisle John Cumberland
Aug 7, 1973	NY	A	——	STL	N	Ken Crosby and cash

Date	Traded To		Traded With	Traded By		In Exchange For

Eddie Grant

Date	Traded To		Traded With	Traded By		In Exchange For
Feb 1911	CIN	N	Johnny Bates George McQuillan Lew Moren	PHI	N	Fred Beebe Jack Rowan Dode Paskert Hans Lobert
May 22, 1913	NY	N	Art Fromme	CIN	N	Red Ames Heinie Groh Josh Devore and $20,000.
June 1913	NY	N		CIN	N	Cash

Jimmy Grant

Date	Traded To		Traded With	Traded By		In Exchange For
Aug 11, 1943	CLE	A	——	CHI	A	Cash

Mark Grant

Date	Traded To		Traded With	Traded By		In Exchange For
July 4, 1987	SD	N	——	SF	N	*See Kevin Mitchell*

Mudcat Grant

Date	Traded To		Traded With	Traded By		In Exchange For
June 15, 1964	MIN	A		CLE	A	George Banks Lee Stange
Nov 28, 1967	LA	N	Zoilo Versalles	MIN	A	Johnny Roseboro Ron Perranoski Bob Miller
June 3, 1969	STL	N		MON	N	Gary Waslewski
Dec 5, 1969	OAK	A	——	STL	N	Cash
Sept 14, 1970	PIT	N		OAK	A	Angel Mangual

(Oakland received Mangual on October 20.)

Date	Traded To		Traded With	Traded By		In Exchange For
Aug 10, 1971	OAK	A	——	PIT	N	Cash

George Grantham

Date	Traded To		Traded With	Traded By		In Exchange For
Oct 27, 1924	PIT	N	Vic Aldridge Al Niehaus	CHI	N	Charlie Grimm Rabbit Maranville Wilbur Cooper
Feb 4, 1932	CIN	N	——	PIT	N	Cash
Nov 15, 1933	NY	N	——	CIN	N	Glenn Spencer

Mickey Grasso

Date	Traded To		Traded With	Traded By		In Exchange For
Jan 20, 1954	CLE	A	——	WAS	A	Joe Tipton

Dick Gray

Date	Traded To		Traded With	Traded By		In Exchange For
June 15, 1959	STL	N	——	LA	N	Chuck Essegian Lloyd Merritt
May 28, 1960	PIT	N	Vinegar Bend Mizell	STL	N	Julian Javier Ed Bauta

Gary Gray

Date	Traded To		Traded With	Traded By		In Exchange For
Jan 4, 1980	CLE	A	Larry McCall minor league 3B-OF Mike Bucci	TEX	A	David Clyde Jim Norris
Feb 17, 1983	CAL	A	——	SEA	A	Cash

Jeff Gray

Date	Traded To		Traded With	Traded By		In Exchange For
Dec 11, 1985	CIN	N	*See John Denny*	PHI	N	——
July 13, 1989	PHI	N	——	CIN	N	Bob Sebra

(Philadelphia received Gray on Sept. 6, 1989.)

John Gray

Date	Traded To		Traded With	Traded By		In Exchange For
Dec 16, 1953	PHI	A		NY	A	*See Harry Byrd*

Sam Gray

Date	Traded To		Traded With	Traded By		In Exchange For
Dec 13, 1927	STL	A	——	PHI	A	Bing Miller

Ted Gray

Date	Traded To		Traded With	Traded By		In Exchange For
Dec 6, 1954	CHI	A	Walt Dropo Bob Nieman	DET	A	Chris Cristante Ferris Fain Jack Phillips

Dallas Green

Date	Traded To		Traded With	Traded By		In Exchange For
April 11, 1965	WAS	A	——	PHI	N	Cash

(Green was returned to Philadelphia on May 11.)

Date	Traded To		Traded With	Traded By		In Exchange For
July 22, 1966	NY	N	——	PHI	N	Cash

(Green was returned to Philadelphia on Aug. 10.)

David Green

Date	Traded To		Traded With	Traded By		In Exchange For
Dec 12, 1980	STL	N	Sixto Lezcano Lary Sorensen Dave LaPoint	MIL	A	Pete Vuckovich Rollie Fingers Ted Simmons
Feb 1, 1985	SF	N	Jose Uribe Dave LaPoint Gary Rajsich	STL	N	Jack Clark
Dec 4, 1985	MIL	A	——	SF	N	player to be named

(San Francisco received SS Hector Quinones on Dec. 11, 1985.)

Freddie Green

Date	Traded To		Traded With	Traded By		In Exchange For
Sept 25, 1961	WAS	A	——	PIT	N	Waiver price

Gene Green

Date	Traded To		Traded With	Traded By		In Exchange For
Dec 2, 1959	BAL	A	minor league C Charles Staniland	STL	N	Bob Nieman
Oct 5, 1961	CLE	A	Dick Donovan Jim Mahoney	WAS	A	Jimmy Piersall
Aug 1, 1963	CIN	N	——	CLE	A	Sammy Taylor

Lenny Green

Date	Traded To		Traded With	Traded By		In Exchange For
May 26, 1959	WAS	A	——	BAL	A	Albie Pearson
June 11, 1964	LA	A	Vic Power	MIN	A	Jerry Kindall Frank Kostro

(Part of three-team trade involving Los Angeles Angels, Minnesota, and Cleveland.)

Date	Traded To		Traded With	Traded By		In Exchange For
Sept 5, 1964	BAL	A	——	LA	A	Cash

Pumpsie Green

Date	Traded To		Traded With	Traded By		In Exchange For
Dec 11, 1962	NY	N	Tracy Stallard Al Moran	BOS	A	Felix Mantilla

Hank Greenberg

Date	Traded To		Traded With	Traded By		In Exchange For
Jan 18, 1947	PIT	N	——	DET	A	$75,000.

Al Greene

Date	Traded To		Traded With	Traded By		In Exchange For
June 2, 1980	STL	N	John Martin	DET	A	Jim Lentine

Kent Greenfield

Date	Traded To		Traded With	Traded By		In Exchange For
June 12, 1927	BOS	N	Hugh McQuillan Doc Farrell	NY	N	Zack Taylor Larry Benton Herb Thomas
July 4, 1929	BKN	N	——	BOS	N	Cash

Jim Greengrass

Date	Traded To		Traded With	Traded By		In Exchange For
Aug 28, 1952	CIN	N	Johnny Schmitz Ernie Nevel Bob Marquis and $35,000.	NY	A	Ewell Blackwell
April 30, 1955	PHI	N	*See Andy Seminick*	CIN	N	——

Hal Gregg

Date	Traded To		Traded With	Traded By		In Exchange For
Dec 8, 1947	PIT	N	Dixie Walker Vic Lombardi	BKN	N	Preacher Roe Billy Cox Gene Mauch

Date	Traded To		Traded With	Traded By		In Exchange For

Tommy Gregg

Date	Traded To		Traded With	Traded By		In Exchange For
Aug 28, 1988	ATL	N	———	PIT	N	Ken Oberkfell

(Atlanta received Gregg on September 1, 1988.)

Vean Gregg

Date	Traded To		Traded With	Traded By		In Exchange For
Aug 20, 1914	BOS	A	———	CLE	A	Adam Johnson Fritz Coumbe Ben Egan
Dec 14, 1917	PHI	A	Merlin Kopp Pinch Thomas and $60,000.	BOS	A	Amos Strunk Joe Bush Wally Schang

Bill Greif

Date	Traded To		Traded With	Traded By		In Exchange For
Dec 3, 1971	SD	N	Derrel Thomas Mark Schaeffer	HOU	N	Dave Roberts
May 19, 1976	STL	N	———	SD	N	Luis Melendez
Nov 6, 1976	MON	N	Angel Torres Sam Mejias	STL	N	Steve Dunning Pat Scanlon Tony Scott

Ed Gremminger

Date	Traded To		Traded With	Traded By		In Exchange For
July 24, 1904	DET	A	———	BOS	N	Cash

Bobby Grich

Date	Traded To		Traded With	Traded By		In Exchange For
Nov 24, 1976	CAL	A	———	BAL	A	No compensation (free agent signing)

Tom Grieve

Date	Traded To		Traded With	Traded By		In Exchange For
Dec 8, 1977	NY	N	Willie Montanez Ken Henderson	TEX	A	Jon Matlack John Milner

(Part of four-team trade involving Texas, New York Mets, Pittsburgh, and Atlanta.)

Date	Traded To		Traded With	Traded By		In Exchange For
Dec 5, 1978	STL	N	Kim Seaman	NY	N	Pete Falcone

Ken Griffey

Date	Traded To		Traded With	Traded By		In Exchange For
Nov 4, 1981	NY	A	———	CIN	N	Fred Toliver minor league P Bryan Ryder
June 29, 1986	ATL	N	Andre Robertson	NY	A	Claudell Washington Paul Zuvella

(Atlanta received Robertson on July 3, 1986.)

Alfredo Griffin

Date	Traded To		Traded With	Traded By		In Exchange For
Dec 5, 1978	TOR	A	minor league 3B Phil Lansford	CLE	A	Victor Cruz
Dec 8, 1984	OAK	A	Dave Collins and cash	TOR	A	Bill Caudill
Dec 11, 1987	LA	N	Jay Howell	OAK	A	Bob Welch Matt Young

(Part of three-team trade involving Oakland, Los Angeles and New York Mets.)

Doug Griffin

Date	Traded To		Traded With	Traded By		In Exchange For
Oct 11, 1970	BOS	A	———	CAL	A	See Tony Conigliaro

Hank Griffin

Date	Traded To		Traded With	Traded By		In Exchange For
June 10, 1911	BOS	N	See Johnny Kling	CHI	N	———

Mike Griffin

Date	Traded To		Traded With	Traded By		In Exchange For
Nov 10, 1978	NY	A	See Dave Righetti	TEX	A	———
June 12, 1981	CHI	N	Doug Bird and $400,000.	NY	A	Rick Reuschel
March 16, 1982	MON	N	———	CHI	N	Dan Briggs
June 8, 1982	SD	N	———	MON	N	Jerry Manuel

Tom Griffin

Date	Traded To		Traded With	Traded By		In Exchange For
Aug 3, 1976	SD	N	———	HOU	N	Cash

Tom Griffin continued

Date	Traded To		Traded With	Traded By		In Exchange For
Dec 11, 1981	PIT	N	———	SF	N	Doe Boyland

Bart Griffith

Date	Traded To		Traded With	Traded By		In Exchange For
Dec 1923	WAS	A	———	BKN	N	Bonnie Hollingsworth

Derrell Griffith

Date	Traded To		Traded With	Traded By		In Exchange For
Nov 29, 1966	NY	N	Tommy Davis	LA	N	Ron Hunt Jim Hickman
March 24, 1967	HOU	N	———	NY	N	Sandy Alomar

Tommy Griffith

Date	Traded To		Traded With	Traded By		In Exchange For
March 1919	BKN	N	———	CIN	N	Jake Daubert
May 10, 1925	CHI	N	———	BKN	N	Bob Barrett

Art Griggs

Date	Traded To		Traded With	Traded By		In Exchange For
Oct 1910	CLE	A	———	STL	A	Nig Clarke

Guido Grilli

Date	Traded To		Traded With	Traded By		In Exchange For
June 13, 1966	KC	A	———	BOS	A	See John Wyatt

Steve Grilli

Date	Traded To		Traded With	Traded By		In Exchange For
Feb 23, 1978	TOR	A	———	DET	A	Cash

Bob Grim

Date	Traded To		Traded With	Traded By		In Exchange For
June 15, 1958	KC	A	Harry Simpson	NY	A	Duke Maas Virgil Trucks
April 5, 1960	CLE	A	———	KC	A	Leo Kiely
May 18, 1960	CIN	N	———	CLE	A	Cash
July 29, 1960	STL	N	———	CIN	N	Cash

Burleigh Grimes

Date	Traded To		Traded With	Traded By		In Exchange For
Jan 9, 1918	BKN	N	Chuck Ward Al Mamaux	PIT	N	Casey Stengel George Cutshaw
Jan 9, 1927	NY	N	———	BKN	N	Butch Henline

(Part of three-team trade involving Brooklyn, New York, and Philadelphia.)

Date	Traded To		Traded With	Traded By		In Exchange For
Feb 11, 1928	PIT	N	———	NY	N	Vic Aldridge
April 9, 1930	BOS	N	———	PIT	N	Percy Jones and cash
June 16, 1930	STL	N	———	BOS	N	Fred Frankhouse Bill Sherdel
Dec 1931	CHI	N	———	STL	N	Bud Teachout Hack Wilson
Aug 4, 1933	STL	N	———	CHI	N	Waiver price
May 15, 1934	PIT	N	———	STL	N	Waiver price
May 26, 1934	NY	A	———	PIT	N	Cash

Oscar Grimes

Date	Traded To		Traded With	Traded By		In Exchange For
Dec 17, 1942	NY	A	Roy Weatherly	CLE	A	Roy Cullenbine Buddy Rosar

Charlie Grimm

Date	Traded To		Traded With	Traded By		In Exchange For
Oct 27, 1924	CHI	N	Rabbit Maranville Wilbur Cooper	PIT	N	Vic Aldridge George Grantham Al Niehaus

Ross Grimsley

Date	Traded To		Traded With	Traded By		In Exchange For
Dec 4, 1973	BAL	A	minor league C Wally Williams	CIN	N	Merv Rettenmund Junior Kennedy and minor league C Bill Wood
Dec 21, 1977	MON	N	———	BAL	A	No compensation (free agent signing)
July 11, 1980	CLE	A	———	MON	N	Dave Oliver

Date	Traded To	Traded With	Traded By	In Exchange For

Lee Grissom

Date	Traded To	Traded With	Traded By	In Exchange For
Jan 4, 1940	NY A	——	CIN N	Joe Beggs
May 15, 1940	BKN N	——	NY A	Waiver price
May 6, 1941	PHI N	——	BKN N	Vito Tamulis

Marv Grissom

Date	Traded To	Traded With	Traded By	In Exchange For
Feb 9, 1953	BOS A	Hal Brown Bill Kennedy	CHI A	Vern Stephens
July 1, 1953	NY N	——	BOS A	Waiver price
Oct 8, 1958	STL N	Ernie Broglio	SF N	Hobie Landrith Billy Muffett Benny Valenzuela

Dick Groat

Date	Traded To	Traded With	Traded By	In Exchange For
Nov 19, 1962	STL N	Diomedes Olivo	PIT N	Julio Gotay Don Cardwell
Oct 27, 1965	PHI N	Bill White Bob Uecker	STL N	Pat Corrales Art Mahaffey Alex Johnson
June 22, 1967	SF N	——	PHI N	Cash

Connie Grob

Date	Traded To	Traded With	Traded By	In Exchange For
Nov 30, 1962	HOU N	Jim Bolger	MIL N	Norm Larker

Heinie Groh

Date	Traded To	Traded With	Traded By	In Exchange For
May 22, 1913	CIN N	Red Ames Josh Devore and $20,000.	NY N	Art Fromme Eddie Grant
Dec 6, 1921	NY N	——	CIN N	Mike Gonzalez George Burns and $150,000.

Steve Gromek

Date	Traded To	Traded With	Traded By	In Exchange For
June 15, 1953	DET A	Ray Boone Al Aber Dick Weik	CLE A	Art Houtteman Owen Friend Bill Wight Joe Ginsberg

Bob Groom

Date	Traded To	Traded With	Traded By	In Exchange For
Feb 10, 1916	STL A	*See Eddie Plank*	STL F	——
Feb 15, 1918	CLE A	——	STL A	Waiver price

Don Gross

Date	Traded To	Traded With	Traded By	In Exchange For
Dec 9, 1957	PIT N	——	CIN N	Bob Purkey

Greg Gross

Date	Traded To	Traded With	Traded By	In Exchange For
Dec 8, 1976	CHI N	——	HOU N	Julio Gonzalez
Feb 23, 1979	PHI N	*See Manny Trillo*	CHI N	

Kevin Gross

Date	Traded To	Traded With	Traded By	In Exchange For
Dec 6, 1988	MON N	——	PHI N	Floyd Youmans Jeff Parrett

Wayne Gross

Date	Traded To	Traded With	Traded By	In Exchange For
Dec 8, 1983	BAL A	——	OAK A	Tim Stoddard

Jerry Grote

Date	Traded To	Traded With	Traded By	In Exchange For
Oct 19, 1965	NY N	——	HOU N	Tom Parsons and cash
Aug 31, 1977	LA N	——	NY N	Minor leaguers P Dan Smith and IF Randy Rogers
Feb 5, 1981	KC A	——	LA N	No compensation (free agent signing)

Ernie Groth

Date	Traded To	Traded With	Traded By	In Exchange For
Dec 2, 1948	CHI A	Bob Kuzava	CLE A	Frank Papish

Johnny Groth

Date	Traded To	Traded With	Traded By	In Exchange For
Dec 4, 1952	STL A	Virgil Trucks Hal White	DET A	Owen Friend Bob Nieman J. W. Porter
Feb 5, 1954	CHI A	Johnny Lipon	BAL A	Neil Berry Sam Mele
June 7, 1955	WAS A	Bob Chakales Clint Courtney	CHI A	Jim Busby
April 16, 1956	KC A	——	WAS A	Cash
Aug 1, 1957	DET A	——	KC A	Cash

Lefty Grove

Date	Traded To	Traded With	Traded By	In Exchange For
Dec 12, 1933	BOS A	Rube Walberg Max Bishop	PHI A	Bob Kline Rabbit Warstler and $125,000.

Roy Grover

Date	Traded To	Traded With	Traded By	In Exchange For
June 1919	WAS A	——	PHI A	Cash

Johnny Grubb

Date	Traded To	Traded With	Traded By	In Exchange For
Dec 8, 1976	CLE A	Fred Kendall Hector Torres	SD N	George Hendrick
Aug 31, 1978	TEX A	——	CLE A	Bobby Cuellar minor league OF Dave Rivera
March 24, 1983	DET A	——	TEX A	Dave Tobik

Frank Grube

Date	Traded To	Traded With	Traded By	In Exchange For
Dec 15, 1933	STL A	——	CHI A	Cash
Sept 20, 1935	CHI A	——	STL A	Cash

Joe Grzenda

Date	Traded To	Traded With	Traded By	In Exchange For
Aug 14, 1967	NY N	——	KC A	Cash
Nov 29, 1967	MIN A	——	NY N	Cash
March 21, 1970	WAS A	Charley Walters	MIN A	Brant Alyea
Nov 3, 1971	STL N	——	TEX A	Ted Kubiak

Cecilio Guante

Date	Traded To	Traded With	Traded By	In Exchange For
Nov 26, 1986	NY A	Rick Rhoden Pat Clements	PIT N	Doug Drabek Logan Easley Brian Fisher
Aug 30, 1988	TEX A	——	NY A	Dale Mohorcic
Nov 21, 1989	CLE A	——	TEX A	No compensation (free agent signing)

Mike Guerra

Date	Traded To	Traded With	Traded By	In Exchange For
Dec 2, 1946	PHI A	——	WAS A	Cash
Dec 13, 1950	BOS A	——	PHI A	Cash
May 7, 1951	WAS A	——	BOS A	Cash

Mario Guerrero

Date	Traded To	Traded With	Traded By	In Exchange For
April 4, 1975	STL N	——	BOS A	Jim Willoughby
May 29, 1976	CAL A	——	STL N	Minor leaguers C Ed Jordan and 1B Ed Kurpiel
March 15, 1978	OAK A	——	SF N	*See Vida Blue*
Dec 8, 1980	SEA A	——	OAK A	Cash

Pedro Guerrero

Date	Traded To	Traded With	Traded By	In Exchange For
April 3, 1974	LA N	——	CLE A	Bruce Ellingsen
Aug 16, 1988	STL N	——	LA N	John Tudor

Date	Traded To	Traded With	Traded By	In Exchange For

Lee Guetterman

Date					
Dec 22, 1987	NY	A	Clay Parker Minor league P Wade Taylor	SEA A	Steve Trout Henry Cotto

Ozzie Guillen

Dec 6, 1984	CHI	A	Tim Lollar Luis Salazar Bill Long	SD N	LaMarr Hoyt Minor league Ps Todd Simmons and Kevin Kristan

Skip Guinn

Jan 22, 1969	HOU	N	Jesus Alou Donn Clendenon Jack Billingham and $100,000.	MON N	Rusty Staub

(Clendenon refused to report, and Houston sent Billingham, Guinn, and Cash on April 8, 1969.)

Brad Gulden

Feb 15, 1979	NY	A	——	LA N	Gary Thomasson
Nov 18, 1980	SEA	A	$150,000.	NY A	Larry Milbourne
April 5, 1982	MON	N	——	NY A	Bobby Ramos
Oct 26, 1982	NY	A	——	MON N	Cash
June 12, 1985	HOU	N	——	CIN N	Cash

Don Gullett

Nov 18, 1976	NY	A	——	CIN N	No compensation (free agent signing)

Bill Gullickson

Dec 19, 1985	CIN	N	Sal Butera	MON N	Jay Tibbs Andy McGaffigan Dann Bilardello John Stuper
Aug 26, 1987	NY	A	——	CIN N	Dennis Rasmussen

Glenn Gulliver

July 5, 1984	STL	N	——	BAL A	A player to be named later

Harry Gumbert

May 14, 1941	STL	N	Paul Dean and cash	NY N	Bill McGee
June 15, 1944	CIN	N	——	STL N	Cash
July 27, 1949	PIT	N	——	CIN N	Waiver price

Dave Gumpert

March 26, 1987	KC	A	——	CHI N	See Jim Sundberg

Randy Gumpert

July 28, 1948	CHI	A	——	NY A	Cash
Nov 13, 1951	BOS	A	Don Lenhardt	CHI A	Mel Hoderlein Chuck Stobbs
June 10, 1952	WAS	A	Walt Masterson	BOS A	Sid Hudson

Larry Gura

Aug 31, 1973	TEX	A	——	CHI N	Mike Paul
May 8, 1974	NY	A	Cash	TEX A	Duke Sims
May 16, 1976	KC	A	——	NY A	Fran Healy

Frankie Gustine

Dec 8, 1948	CHI	N	Cal McLish	PIT N	Clyde McCullough Cliff Chambers
Sept 14, 1949	PHI	A	——	CHI N	Waiver price

Frankie Gustine *continued*

Dec 13, 1949	STL	A	Ray Coleman Billy DeMars minor league OF Ray Ippolito and $100,000.	PHI A	Bob Dillinger Paul Lehner

Cesar Gutierrez

Sept 2, 1969	DET	A	——	SF N	Cash
March 24, 1972	MON	N	——	DET A	Cash

Jackie Gutierrez

Dec 17, 1985	BAL	A	——	BOS A	Sammy Stewart

Don Gutteridge

March 26, 1948	PIT	N	——	BOS A	Cash

Doug Gwosdz

Dec 17, 1986	SEA	A	——	NY N	Ricky Nelson

Bert Haas

June 12, 1940	STL	N	Ernie Koy Carl Doyle Sam Nahem and $125,000.	BKN N	Joe Medwick Curt Davis
Dec 11, 1947	PHI	N	——	CIN N	Tommy Hughes

Eddie Haas

Dec 5, 1957	MIL	N	Don Kaiser Bob Rush	CHI N	Taylor Phillips Sammy Taylor

Moose Haas

March 30, 1986	OAK	A	——	MIL A	Steve Kiefer Charlie O'Brien Minor league P Mike Fulmer Minor league P Pete Kendrick

Mule Haas

Sept 28, 1932	CHI	A	Al Simmons Jimmy Dykes	PHI A	$100,000.

Bob Habenicht

Oct 1, 1952	STL	A	——	STL N	Waiver price

John Habyan

July 20, 1989	NY	A	——	BAL A	Stan Jefferson

Rich Hacker

March 31, 1971	MON	N	Ron Swoboda	NY N	Don Hahn

Warren Hacker

Nov 13, 1956	CIN	N	Don Hoak Pete Whisenant	CHI N	Elmer Singleton Ray Jablonski
June 26, 1957	PHI	N	——	CIN N	Waiver price

Harvey Haddix

May 11, 1956	PHI	N	Ben Flowers Stu Miller	STL N	Murry Dickson Herm Wehmeier
Dec 16, 1957	CIN	N	——	PHI N	Wally Post

Date	Traded To	Traded With	Traded By	In Exchange For

Harvey Haddix *continued*

Date	Traded To		Traded With	Traded By		In Exchange For
Jan 30, 1959	PIT	N	Smoky Burgess Don Hoak	CIN	N	Whammy Douglas Jim Pendleton Frank Thomas Johnny Powers
Dec 14, 1963	BAL	A	——	PIT	N	Minor league SS Dick Yencha and cash

Bump Hadley

Dec 4, 1931	CHI	A	Jackie Hayes Sad Sam Jones	WAS	A	Carl Reynolds John Kerr
April 27, 1932	STL	A	Bruce Campbell	CHI	A	Red Kress
Jan 22, 1935	WAS	A	——	STL	A	Luke Sewell
Jan 17, 1936	NY	A	Roy Johnson	WAS	A	Jimmie DeShong Jesse Hill
Jan 2, 1941	NY	N	——	NY	A	Cash
May 29, 1941	PHI	A	——	NY	N	Cash

Kent Hadley

Nov 20, 1957	KC	A	——	DET	A	*See Billy Martin*
Dec 11, 1959	NY	A	*See Roger Maris*	KC	A	——

Mickey Haefner

July 21, 1949	CHI	A	——	WAS	A	Cash
Aug 8, 1950	BOS	N	——	CHI	A	Cash

Bud Hafey

Aug 5, 1939	PHI	N	——	CIN	N	Cash

Chick Hafey

April 11, 1932	CIN	N	——	STL	N	Harvey Hendrick Benny Frey and cash

Casey Hageman

June 1914	BKN	N	——	STL	N	Joe Riggert
June 1914	CHI	N	——	BKN	N	Cash

Joe Hague

May 19, 1972	CIN	N	——	STL	N	Bernie Carbo

Don Hahn

March 31, 1971	NY	N	——	MON	N	Ron Swoboda Rich Hacker
Dec 3, 1974	PHI	N	Tug McGraw Dave Schneck	NY	N	Del Unser John Stearns Mac Scarce
June 24, 1975	SD	N	——	STL	N	Cash

Ed Hahn

May 9, 1906	CHI	A	——	NY	A	Cash

Noodles Hahn

April 1906	NY	A	——	CIN	N	Waiver price

Hal Haid

Jan 1931	BOS	N	——	STL	N	Waiver price

Jerry Hairston

June 13, 1977	PIT	N	——	CHI	A	Cash

Bob Hale

July 26, 1961	NY	A	——	CLE	A	Cash

John Hale

Sept 2, 1977	TOR	A	——	LA	N	Cash
Sept 14, 1977	SEA	A	——	TOR	A	Cash

Odell Hale

Dec 12, 1940	BOS	A	Frankie Pytlak Joe Dobson	CLE	A	Gene Desautels Jim Bagby Gee Walker
June 19, 1941	NY	N	——	BOS	A	Waiver price

Sammy Hale

Dec 11, 1929	STL	A	——	PHI	A	Wally Schang

Ray Haley

Sept 2, 1916	PHI	A	——	BOS	A	Jimmy Walsh

Ed Halicki

June 20, 1980	CAL	A	——	SF	N	Cash

Bob Hall

April 1905	BKN	N	——	NY	N	Cash

Dick Hall

Dec 15, 1959	KC	A	Ken Hamlin	PIT	N	Hal Smith
April 12, 1961	BAL	A	Dick Williams	KC	A	Jerry Walker Chuck Essegian
Dec 15, 1966	PHI	N	——	BAL	A	John Morris

Drew Hall

Dec 5, 1988	TEX	A	*See Rafael Palmeiro*	CHI	N	——

Jimmie Hall

Dec 2, 1966	CAL	A	Don Mincher Pete Cimino	MIN	A	Dean Chance Jackie Hernandez
June 15, 1968	CLE	A	——	CAL	A	Vic Davalillo
April 14, 1969	NY	A	——	CLE	A	Cash
Sept 11, 1969	CHI	N	——	NY	A	Minor league P Terry Bongiovanni and cash
June 29, 1970	ATL	N	——	CHI	N	Cash

Mel Hall

June 13, 1984	CLE	A	Joe Carter Don Schulze Minor league P Darryl Banks	CHI	N	Rick Sutcliffe George Frazier Ron Hassey
March 19, 1989	NY	A	——	CLE	A	Joel Skinner Minor league OF Turner Ward

Tom Hall

Dec 3, 1971	CIN	N	——	MIN	A	Wayne Granger
April 15, 1975	NY	N	——	CIN	N	Mac Scarce
May 7, 1976	KC	A	——	NY	N	Minor league IF Bryan Jones and cash

Bill Hallahan

May 31, 1936	CIN	N	——	STL	N	Cash

Date	Traded To	Traded With	Traded By	In Exchange For

Tom Haller

Date	Traded To		Traded With	Traded By		In Exchange For
Feb 13, 1968	LA	N	minor league P Frank Kasmeta	SF	N	Ron Hunt Nate Oliver
Dec 2, 1971	DET	A	———	LA	N	Minor league P Bernie Beckman and cash
Oct 25, 1972	PHI	N	Don Leshnock	DET	A	Cash

Jack Hallett

Dec 9, 1941	PHI	A	Mike Kreevich	CHI	A	Wally Moses

Dave Hamilton

June 15, 1975	CHI	A	Chet Lemon	OAK	A	Stan Bahnsen Skip Pitlock
Aug 31, 1977	STL	N	Nyls Nyman Silvio Martinez	CHI	A	Clay Carroll
May 28, 1978	PIT	N	———	STL	N	Cash

Earl Hamilton

May 30, 1916	DET	A	———	STL	A	Cash
June 22, 1916	STL	A	———	DET	A	Waiver price
Unknown	PIT	N	———	STL	A	Cash
Dec 1923	PHI	N	———	PIT	N	Waiver price

Jack Hamilton

Dec 4, 1963	DET	A	Don Demeter	PHI	N	Jim Bunning Gus Triandos
Oct 14, 1965	NY	N	———	DET	A	Cash
June 10, 1967	CAL	A	———	NY	N	Nick Willhite
Oct 8, 1968	CLE	A	———	CAL	A	Eddie Fisher
June 13, 1969	CHI	A	———	CLE	A	Sammy Ellis

Steve Hamilton

May 3, 1962	WAS	A	Don Rudolph	CLE	A	Willie Tasby
April 21, 1963	NY	A	———	WAS	A	Jim Coates
Sept 9, 1970	CHI	A	———	NY	A	Cash
March 23, 1971	SF	N	———	CHI	A	Steve Huntz

Tom Hamilton

Dec 16, 1953	NY	A	*See Harry Byrd*	PHI	A	———

Ken Hamlin

Dec 15, 1959	KC	A	Dick Hall	PIT	N	Hal Smith

Luke Hamlin

Dec 12, 1941	PIT	N	Pete Coscarart Babe Phelps Jimmy Wasdell	BKN	N	Arky Vaughan

Pete Hamm

Feb 5, 1972	CHI	A	———	MIN	A	Cash

Atlee Hammaker

March 30, 1982	SF	N	Renie Martin Craig Chamberlain Brad Wellman	KC	A	Vida Blue Bob Tufts

Jack Hammond

May 13, 1922	PIT	N	———	CLE	A	Cash

Steve Hammond

April 28, 1982	KC	A	———	ATL	N	Cash

Granny Hamner

May 16, 1959	CLE	A	———	PHI	N	Humberto Robinson

Ike Hampton

March 22, 1975	CAL	A	———	NY	N	Ken Sanders

Garry Hancock

Dec 9, 1977	BOS	A	———	CLE	A	Jack Baker
Dec 6, 1982	OAK	A	Carney Lansford minor league P Jerry King	BOS	A	Tony Armas Jeff Newman

Rich Hand

Dec 2, 1971	TEX	A	Roy Foster Ken Suarez Mike Paul	CLE	A	Del Unser Denny Riddleberger Gary Jones minor league P Terry Ley
May 20, 1973	CAL	A	Mike Epstein Rick Stelmaszek	TEX	A	Jim Spencer Lloyd Allen
Sept 5, 1974	STL	N	———	CAL	A	Orlando Pena

(St. Louis received Hand on October 15, 1974.)

Bill Hands

Dec 2, 1965	CHI	N	Randy Hundley	SF	N	Lindy McDaniel Don Landrum Jim Rittwage
Nov 30, 1972	MIN	A	Joe Decker minor league P Bob Maneely	CHI	N	Dave LaRoche
Sept 9, 1974	TEX	A	———	MIN	A	Cash
Feb 24, 1976	NY	N	———	TEX	A	George Stone

Harry Hanebrink

March 31, 1959	PHI	N	Gene Conley Joe Koppe	MIL	N	Stan Lopata Ted Kazanski Johnny O'Brien

Fred Haney

Dec 9, 1925	BOS	A	———	DET	A	Tex Vache Homer Ezzell
July 12, 1927	CHI	N	———	BOS	A	Cash

Larry Haney

June 14, 1969	OAK	A	———	SEA	A	John Donaldson
Sept 6, 1972	OAK	A	———	SD	N	Cash
Sept 1, 1973	STL	N	Lew Krausse	OAK	A	Cash
March 26, 1974	OAK	A	———	STL	N	Cash
Dec 6, 1976	MIL	A	———	OAK	A	Cash

Gerald Hannahs

May 20, 1978	LA	N	Larry Landreth	MON	N	Mike Garman

Jim Hannan

Oct 9, 1970	DET	A	———	WAS	A	*See Denny McLain*
May 11, 1971	MIL	A	———	DET	A	John Gelnar Jose Herrera

Jack Hannifin

June 1906	NY	N	———	PHI	A	Waiver price
April 1908	BOS	N	———	NY	N	Cash

Andy Hansen

Jan 13, 1954	PIT	N	Lucky Lohrke and $70,000.	PHI	N	Murry Dickson

Date	Traded To		Traded With	Traded By		In Exchange For

Ron Hansen

Date	Traded To		Traded With	Traded By		In Exchange For
Jan 14, 1963	CHI	A	Hoyt Wilhelm Pete Ward Dave Nicholson	BAL	A	Luis Aparicio Al Smith
Feb 13, 1968	WAS	A	Dennis Higgins Steve Jones	CHI	A	Tim Cullen Buster Narum Bob Priddy
Aug 2, 1968	CHI	A	——	WAS	A	Tim Cullen
Feb 28, 1970	NY	A	——	CHI	A	Cash

Snipe Hansen

Date	Traded To		Traded With	Traded By		In Exchange For
June 22, 1935	STL	A	——	PHI	N	Cash

Jim Hardin

Date	Traded To		Traded With	Traded By		In Exchange For
May 28, 1971	NY	A	——	BAL	A	Bill Burbach

Carroll Hardy

Date	Traded To		Traded With	Traded By		In Exchange For
June 13, 1960	BOS	A	Russ Nixon	CLE	A	Marty Keough Ted Bowsfield
Dec 10, 1962	HOU	N	——	BOS	A	Dick Williams

Larry Hardy

Date	Traded To		Traded With	Traded By		In Exchange For
Dec 11, 1975	HOU	N	Joe McIntosh	SD	N	Doug Rader

Steve Hargan

Date	Traded To		Traded With	Traded By		In Exchange For
March 23, 1974	TEX	A	——	CLE	A	Bill Gogolewski
May 9, 1977	TEX	A	Jim Mason and $200,000.	TOR	A	Roy Howell
June 15, 1977	ATL	N	——	TEX	A	Cash

Alan Hargesheimer

Date	Traded To		Traded With	Traded By		In Exchange For
Oct 15, 1982	CHI	N	——	SF	N	Herman Segelke
March 30, 1984	KC	A	——	CHI	N	Derek Botelho

Pinky Hargrave

Date	Traded To		Traded With	Traded By		In Exchange For
June 8, 1925	STL	A	George Mogridge	WAS	A	Hank Severeid
Jan 15, 1927	DET	A	Marty McManus Bobby LaMotte	STL	A	Lefty Stewart Frank O'Rourke Billy Mullen Otto Miller
Sept 10, 1930	WAS	A	——	DET	A	Cash
Dec 1931	BOS	N	——	WAS	A	Waiver price

Charlie Hargreaves

Date	Traded To		Traded With	Traded By		In Exchange For
June 8, 1928	PIT	N	——	BKN	N	Joe Harris Johnny Gooch

Mike Hargrove

Date	Traded To		Traded With	Traded By		In Exchange For
Oct 25, 1978	SD	N	Kurt Bevacqua Bill Fahey	TEX	A	Oscar Gamble Dave Roberts and $300,000.
June 14, 1979	CLE	A	——	SD	N	Paul Dade

Tim Harkness

Date	Traded To		Traded With	Traded By		In Exchange For
April 5, 1957	BKN	N	Ron Negray Elmer Valo Ben Flowers minor league SS Mel Geho	PHI	N	Chico Fernandez
Nov 30, 1962	NY	N	Larry Burright	LA	N	Bob Miller

Dick Harley

Date	Traded To		Traded With	Traded By		In Exchange For
April 1900	CIN	N	——	CLE	N	Cash

Larry Harlow

Date	Traded To		Traded With	Traded By		In Exchange For
June 5, 1979	CAL	A	——	BAL	A	Floyd Rayford and cash

Bob Harmon

Date	Traded To		Traded With	Traded By		In Exchange For
Dec 12, 1913	PIT	N	Ed Konetchy Mike Mowrey	STL	N	Art Butler Dots Miller Cozy Dolan Owen Wilson Hank Robinson

Chuck Harmon

Date	Traded To		Traded With	Traded By		In Exchange For
May 16, 1956	STL	N	——	CIN	N	Joe Frazier Alex Grammas
May 10, 1957	PHI	N	——	STL	N	Glen Gorbous

Brian Harper

Date	Traded To		Traded With	Traded By		In Exchange For
Dec 11, 1981	PIT	N	——	CAL	A	Tim Foli
Dec 12, 1984	STL	N	John Tudor	PIT	N	George Hendrick minor league C Steve Barnard

George Harper

Date	Traded To		Traded With	Traded By		In Exchange For
May 30, 1924	PHI	N	——	CIN	N	Curt Walker
Jan 9, 1927	NY	N	Butch Henline	PHI	N	Jack Scott Fresco Thompson
(Part of three-team trade involving Philadelphia, New York, and Brooklyn.)						
May 1, 1928	STL	N	——	NY	N	Bob O'Farrell
Dec 8, 1928	BOS	N	——	STL	N	Cash

Harry Harper

Date	Traded To		Traded With	Traded By		In Exchange For
Jan 20, 1920	BOS	A	Mike Menosky Eddie Foster	WAS	A	Braggo Roth Red Shannon
Dec 15, 1920	NY	A	*See Waite Hoyt*	BOS	A	——

Jack Harper

Date	Traded To		Traded With	Traded By		In Exchange For
Jan 1900	STL	N	Otto Krueger Joe Quinn Jim Hughey	CLE	N	Cash
Oct 1906	CHI	N	——	CIN	N	Chick Fraser

Terry Harper

Date	Traded To		Traded With	Traded By		In Exchange For
Jan 27, 1987	DET	A	Minor league OF Freedie Tiburco	ATL	N	Randy O'Neal Chuck Cary
June 28, 1987	PIT	N	——	DET	A	Shawn Holman Minor league IF Pete Rice

Tommy Harper

Date	Traded To		Traded With	Traded By		In Exchange For
Nov 21, 1967	CLE	A	——	CIN	N	George Culver Fred Whitfield Bob Raudman
Oct 11, 1971	BOS	A	Marty Pattin Lew Krausse Minor leaguer Pat Skrable	MIL	A	George Scott Billy Conigliaro Joe Lahoud Jim Lonborg Ken Brett Don Pavletich
Dec 2, 1974	CAL	A	——	BOS	A	Bob Heise
Aug 13, 1975	OAK	A	——	CAL	A	Cash

Toby Harrah

Date	Traded To		Traded With	Traded By		In Exchange For
Dec 8, 1978	CLE	A	——	TEX	A	Buddy Bell
Feb 5, 1984	NY	A	Minor league P Rick Browne	CLE	A	George Frazier Otis Nixon Minor league P Guy Elston

Date	Traded To	Traded With	Traded By	In Exchange For

Toby Harrah *continued*

Date	Traded To	Traded With	Traded By	In Exchange For
Feb 27, 1985	TEX A ———		NY A	Billy Sample player to be named

(New York received P Eric Dersin on July 14, 1985.)

Billy Harrell

Date	Traded To	Traded With	Traded By	In Exchange For
Feb 2, 1959	STL N ———		CLE A	Waiver price

Ray Harrell

Date	Traded To	Traded With	Traded By	In Exchange For
Dec 8, 1938	CHI N ———		STL N	Cash
May 29, 1939	PHI N	Joe Marty Kirby Higbe	CHI N	Claude Passeau
Jan 22, 1940	PIT N ———		PHI N	Waiver price

Bill Harrelson

Date	Traded To	Traded With	Traded By	In Exchange For
Jan 14, 1970	CIN N	minor league IF Dan Loomer	CAL A	Jack Fisher

Bud Harrelson

Date	Traded To	Traded With	Traded By	In Exchange For
March 24, 1978	PHI N ———		NY N	Fred Andrews and cash

Ken Harrelson

Date	Traded To	Traded With	Traded By	In Exchange For
June 23, 1966	WAS A ———		KC A	Jim Duckworth
June 9, 1967	KC A ———		WAS A	Cash
April 19, 1969	CLE A	Juan Pizarro Dick Ellsworth	BOS A	Sonny Siebert Joe Azcue Vicente Romo

Bill Harrington

Date	Traded To	Traded With	Traded By	In Exchange For
Dec 5, 1956	DET A ———		KC A	*See Ned Garver*

Bob Harris

Date	Traded To	Traded With	Traded By	In Exchange For
May 13, 1939	STL A ———		DET A	*See Beau Bell*
June 1, 1942	PHI A	Bob Swift	STL A	Frankie Hayes

Bucky Harris

Date	Traded To	Traded With	Traded By	In Exchange For
Dec 19, 1928	DET A ———		WAS A	Jack Warner

(Harris was named Detroit manager.)

Buddy Harris

Date	Traded To	Traded With	Traded By	In Exchange For
Nov 27, 1972	NY N	Rich Chiles	HOU N	Tommie Agee

Charlie Harris

Date	Traded To	Traded With	Traded By	In Exchange For
May 2, 1951	CLE A ———		PHI A	Cash

Dave Harris

Date	Traded To	Traded With	Traded By	In Exchange For
June 13, 1930	WAS A ———		CHI A	Red Barnes

Gail Harris

Date	Traded To	Traded With	Traded By	In Exchange For
Jan 28, 1958	DET A	Ozzie Virgil	SF N	Jim Finigan and $25,000.
May 7, 1960	LA N ———		DET A	Sandy Amoros

Gene Harris

Date	Traded To	Traded With	Traded By	In Exchange For
May 25, 1989	SEA A	Randy Johnson Brian Holman	MON N	Mark Langston Mike Campbell

(Montreal received Campbell on July 31, 1989.)

Greg Harris

Date	Traded To	Traded With	Traded By	In Exchange For
Feb 10, 1982	CIN N	Alex Trevino Jim Kern	NY N	George Foster
Sept 27, 1983	MON N ———		CIN N	Cash
Feb 13, 1985	TEX A ———		SD N	Cash
Aug 7, 1989	BOS A ———		PHI N	Waiver price

Joe Harris

Date	Traded To	Traded With	Traded By	In Exchange For
Dec 24, 1921	BOS A	George Burns Elmer Smith	CLE A	Stuffy McInnis
April 26, 1925	WAS A ———		BOS A	Paul Zahniser Roy Carlyle
Feb 4, 1927	PIT N ———		WAS A	Waiver price
June 8, 1928	BKN N	Johnny Gooch	PIT N	Charlie Hargreaves

John Harris

Date	Traded To	Traded With	Traded By	In Exchange For
Jan 10, 1983	CIN N ———		CAL A	Mike O'Berry

Lenny Harris

Date	Traded To	Traded With	Traded By	In Exchange For
July 18, 1989	CIN N	Tim Leary	LA N	Kal Daniels Mariano Duncan

Lum Harris

Date	Traded To	Traded With	Traded By	In Exchange For
Feb 14, 1947	WAS A ———		PHI A	Waiver price

Mickey Harris

Date	Traded To	Traded With	Traded By	In Exchange For
June 13, 1949	WAS A	Sam Mele	BOS A	Walt Masterson
April 22, 1952	CLE A ———		WAS A	Waiver price

Vic Harris

Date	Traded To	Traded With	Traded By	In Exchange For
July 20, 1972	TEX A	Marty Martinez Steve Lawson	OAK A	Don Mincher Ted Kubiak
Oct 25, 1973	CHI N	Bill Madlock	TEX A	Ferguson Jenkins
Dec 22, 1975	STL N ———		CHI N	Mick Kelleher
Oct 20, 1976	SF N ———		STL N	*See Mike Caldwell*

Chuck Harrison

Date	Traded To	Traded With	Traded By	In Exchange For
Oct 8, 1967	ATL N	Sonny Jackson	HOU N	Denny Lemaster Denis Menke
Oct 17, 1968	KC A ———		HOU N	Cash

Roric Harrison

Date	Traded To	Traded With	Traded By	In Exchange For
Aug 24, 1969	SEA A	Dooley Womack	HOU N	Jim Bouton
April 5, 1971	BAL A	minor leaguer Marion Jackson	MIL A	Marcelino Lopez
Nov 30, 1972	ATL N ———		BAL A	*See Earl Williams*
June 7, 1975	CLE A ———		ATL N	Blue Moon Odom Bob Belloir
April 7, 1976	STL N ———		CLE A	Harry Parker

Slim Harriss

Date	Traded To	Traded With	Traded By	In Exchange For
June 15, 1926	BOS A	Fred Heimach Baby Doll Jacobson	PHI A	Tom Jenkins Howard Ehmke

Earl Harrist

Date	Traded To	Traded With	Traded By	In Exchange For
June 9, 1948	WAS A ———		CHI A	Marino Pieretti
March 7, 1953	CHI A ———		STL A	Cash
May 23, 1953	DET A ———		CHI A	Waiver price

Jack Harshman

Date	Traded To	Traded With	Traded By	In Exchange For
Dec 3, 1957	BAL A	*See Larry Doby*	CHI A	———
June 15, 1959	BOS A ———		BAL A	Billy Hoeft
July 30, 1959	CLE A ———		BOS A	Waiver price

Date		Traded To	Traded With		Traded By		In Exchange For

Jim Ray Hart
April 17, 1973   NY   A   ——   SF   N   Cash

Mike Hart
Dec 8, 1978   TEX   A   ——   MON   N   Jim Mason

Chuck Hartenstein
Jan 15, 1969   PIT   N   Ron Campbell   CHI   N   Manny Jimenez
June 22, 1970   STL   N   ——   PIT   N   Cash
Nov 5, 1976   TOR   A   ——   SD   N   Cash

Grover Hartley
Dec 12, 1913   CIN   N   Buck Herzog   NY   N   Bob Bescher
    (Hartley jumped to the Federal League and Herzog was made Cincinnati manager.)
Feb 10, 1916   STL   A   *See Eddie Plank*   STL   F   ——
Dec 1927   CLE   A   ——   BOS   A   Waiver price

Bob Hartman
June 24, 1962   CLE   A   ——   MIL   N   Ken Aspromonte and cash

Topsy Hartsel
April 1901   CHI   N   Mike Kahoe   CIN   N   Cash

Roy Hartsfield
Jan 17, 1953   BKN   N $50,000.   MIL   N   Andy Pafko

Paul Hartzell
Feb 3, 1979   MIN   A   Ken Landreaux   CAL   A   Rod Carew
          Dave Engle
          Brad Havens

Roy Hartzell
Jan 1911   NY   A   ——   STL   A   Jimmy Austin
          Frank LaPorte

Ervin Harvey
May 1901   CLE   A   ——   CHI   A   Cash

Mickey Haslin
April 30, 1936   BOS   N   ——   PHI   N   Pinky Whitney
Dec 4, 1936   NY   N   ——   BOS   N   Eddie Mayo

Buddy Hassett
Jan 1936   BKN   N   ——   NY   A   Cash
Dec 13, 1938   BOS   N   Jimmy Outlaw   BKN   N   Gene Moore
          Ira Hutchinson
Feb 5, 1942   NY   A   Gene Moore   BOS   N   Tommy Holmes

Ron Hassey
June 13, 1984   CHI   N   *See Rick Sutcliffe*   CLE   A   ——
Dec 4, 1984   NY   A   Henry Cotto   CHI   N   Ray Fontenot
          Rich Bordi   Brian Dayett
          Porfi Altamirano
Dec 12, 1985   CHI   A   Joe Cowley   NY   A   Britt Burns
                      Minor league
                      SS Mike Soper
                      Minor league
                      OF Glen Braxton

Date		Traded To	Traded With		Traded By		In Exchange For

Ron Hassey *continued*
Feb 13, 1986   CHI   A   ——   NY   A   Minor league
                      C Chris Alvarez
                      Minor league
                      P Eric Schmidt
                      Minor league
                      OF Matt Winters
July 30, 1986   CHI   A   Carlos Martinez   NY   A   Ron Kittle
          Bill Lindsey   Joel Skinner
                      Wayne Tolleson
      (Chicago received Lindsey on Dec. 24, 1986.)

Andy Hassler
July 5, 1976   KC   A   ——   CAL   A   Cash
July 24, 1978   BOS   A   ——   KC   A   Cash
June 15, 1979   NY   N   ——   BOS   A   Cash
Nov 19, 1979   PIT   N   ——   NY   N   No compensation
                      (free agent signing)
June 10, 1980   CAL   A   ——   PIT   N   Cash

Billy Hatcher
Dec 16, 1985   HOU   N   Steve Engel   CHI   N   Jerry Mumphrey
Aug 18, 1989   PIT   N   ——   HOU   N   Glenn Wilson

Mickey Hatcher
March 30, 1981   MIN   A   minor leaguers   LA   N   Ken Landreaux
          P Matt Reeves and
          1B Kelly Snider

Fred Hatfield
June 3, 1952   DET   A   ——   BOS   A   *See George Kell*
May 15, 1956   CHI   A   Jim Delsing   DET   A   Jim Brideweser
                      Harry Byrd
                      Bob Kennedy
Dec 4, 1957   CLE   A   Minnie Minoso   CHI   A   Early Wynn
                      Al Smith
April 23, 1958   CIN   N   ——   CLE   A   Bob Kelly

Joe Hatten
June 15, 1951   CHI   N   Bruce Edwards   BKN   N   Johnny Schmitz
          Eddie Miksis   Rube Walker
          Gene Hermanski   Andy Pafko
                      Wayne Terwilliger

Grady Hatton
April 18, 1954   CHI   A   ——   CIN   N   Johnny Lipon
May 23, 1954   BOS   A $100,000.   CHI   A   George Kell
May 11, 1956   STL   N   ——   BOS   A   Cash
Aug 1, 1956   BAL   A   ——   STL   N   Cash

Phil Haugstad
May 25, 1952   CIN   N   ——   BKN   N   Waiver price

Joe Hauser
June 7, 1929   CLE   A   ——   PHI   A   Waiver price

Tom Hausman
Nov 21, 1977   NY   N   ——   MIL   A   No compensation
                      (free agent signing)
Sept 10, 1982   ATL   N   ——   NY   N   Carlos Diaz

Brad Havens
Feb 3, 1979   MIN   A   Ken Landreaux   CAL   A   Rod Carew
          Dave Engle
          Paul Hartzell
March 27, 1985   BAL   A   ——   MIN   A   Mark Brown
May 22, 1987   LA   N   *See John Shelby*   BAL   A   ——

Date	Traded To	Traded With	Traded By	In Exchange For

Andy Hawkins

| Dec 8, 1988 | NY | A | ——— | SD | N | No compensation (free agent signing) |

Wynn Hawkins

| Nov 27, 1962 | NY | N | ——— | CLE | A | Cash |

Pink Hawley

| Feb 27, 1900 | NY | N | ——— | CIN | N | Cash |

Hal Haydel

| March 28, 1963 | CHI | N | Merritt Ranew Dick LeMay | HOU | N | Dave Gerard Danny Murphy |

Charlie Hayes

| June 18, 1989 | PHI | N | ——— | SF | N | *See Steve Bedrosian* |

Frankie Hayes

June 1, 1942	STL	A	———	PHI	A	Bob Harris Bob Swift
Feb 17, 1944	PHI	A	———	STL	A	Sam Zoldak and minor league OF Barney Lutz
May 29, 1945	CLE	A	———	PHI	A	Buddy Rosar
June 1946	CHI	A	———	CLE	A	Tom Jordan

Jackie Hayes

| Dec 4, 1931 | CHI | A | Bump Hadley Sad Sam Jones | WAS | A | Carl Reynolds John Kerr |

Von Hayes

| Dec 9, 1982 | PHI | N | ——— | CLE | A | Manny Trillo George Vukovich Jay Baller Julio Franco Jerry Willard |

Joe Haynes

Jan 4, 1941	CHI	A	———	WAS	A	Cash
Nov 22, 1948	CLE	A	———	CHI	A	Joe Tipton
Dec 14, 1948	WAS	A	Eddie Klieman Eddie Robinson	CLE	A	Mickey Vernon Early Wynn

Ray Hayward

| Feb 12, 1988 | CHI | N | *See Goose Gossage* | SD | N | ——— |
| March 17, 1988 | TEX | A | ——— | CHI | N | Dave Meier Greg Tabor |

Ray Hayworth

| Sept 14, 1938 | BKN | N | ——— | DET | A | Waiver price |
| Aug 23, 1939 | NY | N | ——— | BKN | N | Jimmy Ripple |

Bob Hazle

| April 9, 1956 | MIL | N | Corky Valentine | CIN | N | George Crowe |
| May 24, 1958 | DET | A | ——— | MIL | N | Cash |

Fran Healy

| April 2, 1973 | KC | A | ——— | SF | N | Greg Minton |
| May 16, 1976 | NY | A | ——— | KC | A | Larry Gura |

Francis Healy

| May 4, 1934 | STL | N | ——— | NY | N | Cash |

Ed Hearn

| March 27, 1987 | KC | A | Rick Anderson Mauro Gozzo | NY | N | David Cone Minor league C Chris Jelic |

Jim Hearn

| July 10, 1950 | NY | N | ——— | STL | N | Cash |
| Oct 11, 1956 | PHI | N | ——— | NY | N | Stu Miller |

Bill Heath

Oct 15, 1964	CHI	A	minor league P Joel Gibson	PHI	N	Rudy May
Dec 1, 1965	HOU	N	Dave Nicholson	CHI	A	Jack Lamabe minor league P Ray Cordeiro and cash
May 8, 1967	DET	A	———	HOU	N	Cash

Jeff Heath

Dec 14, 1945	WAS	A	———	CLE	A	George Case
June 15, 1946	STL	A	———	WAS	A	Joe Grace Al LaMacchia
Dec 4, 1947	BOS	N	———	STL	A	Cash

Mickey Heath

| May 7, 1931 | BKN | N | ——— | CIN | N | Harvey Hendrick |

Mike Heath

Nov 10, 1978	TEX	A	———	NY	A	*See Dave Righetti*
June 15, 1979	OAK	A	Dave Chalk and cash	TEX	A	John Henry Johnson
Dec 10, 1985	STL	N	Tim Conroy	OAK	A	Joaquin Andujar
Aug 10, 1986	DET	A	———	STL	N	Mike Laga Ken Hill

(St. Louis received Laga on Sept. 2, 1986.)

Cliff Heathcote

May 30, 1922	CHI	N	———	STL	N	Max Flack
May 1931	CIN	N	———	CHI	N	Waiver price
June 25, 1932	PHI	N	———	CIN	N	Waiver price

Neal Heaton

June 20, 1986	MIN	A	———	CLE	A	John Butcher
Feb 3, 1987	MON	N	Jeff Reed Minor league P Yorkis Perez Minor league P Al Cardwood	MIN	A	Jeff Reardon Tom Nieto
March 28, 1989	PIT	N	———	MON	N	Brett Gideon

Dave Heaverlo

| March 15, 1978 | OAK | A | ——— | SF | N | *See Vida Blue* |
| April 9, 1980 | SEA | A | ——— | OAK | A | Cash |

Richie Hebner

Dec 15, 1976	PHI	N	———	PIT	N	No compensation (free agent signing)
March 27, 1979	NY	N	Jose Moreno	PHI	N	Nino Espinosa
Oct 31, 1979	DET	A	———	NY	N	Jerry Morales Phil Mankowski
Aug 16, 1982	PIT	N	———	DET	A	Cash
Jan 5, 1984	CHI	N	———	PIT	N	No compensation (free agent signing)

Mike Hechinger

| May 1913 | BKN | N | ——— | CHI | N | Waiver price |

Date	Traded To	Traded With	Traded By	In Exchange For

Mike Hedlund

Date	Traded To	Traded With	Traded By	In Exchange For
Nov 2, 1972	CLE A ——		KC A	Kurt Bevacqua

Danny Heep

Date	Traded To	Traded With	Traded By	In Exchange For
Dec 10, 1982	NY N ——		HOU N	Mike Scott
June 19, 1987	LA N ——		NY N	No compensation (free agent signing)

Bob Heffner

Date	Traded To	Traded With	Traded By	In Exchange For
Oct 15, 1966	NY N ——		CLE A	Cash

Don Heffner

Date	Traded To	Traded With	Traded By	In Exchange For
Feb 15, 1938	STL A $10,000.		NY A	Bill Knickerbocker
June 14, 1943	PHI A ——		STL A	Cash
Oct 11, 1943	DET A Bob Swift		PHI A	Rip Radcliff

Jim Hegan

Date	Traded To	Traded With	Traded By	In Exchange For
Feb 18, 1958	DET A Hank Aguirre		CLE A	Hal Woodeshick J. W. Porter
July 27, 1958	PHI N ——		DET A	Minor league OF John Turk and cash
June 14, 1959	SF N ——		PHI N	Cash

Mike Hegan

Date	Traded To	Traded With	Traded By	In Exchange For
June 14, 1968	SEA A ——		NY A	Cash
June 14, 1971	OAK A ——		MIL A	Cash
Aug 18, 1973	NY A ——		OAK A	Cash
May 13, 1974	MIL A ——		NY A	Cash

Jack Heidemann

Date	Traded To	Traded With	Traded By	In Exchange For
March 24, 1973	OAK A Ray Fosse		CLE A	George Hendrick Dave Duncan
March 25, 1974	CLE A ——		OAK A	Cash
June 1, 1974	STL N ——		CLE A	Luis Alvarado Ed Crosby
Dec 11, 1974	NY N Mike Vail		STL N	Teddy Martinez
June 22, 1976	MIL A ——		NY N	Minor league P Tom Deidel

Harry Heilmann

Date	Traded To	Traded With	Traded By	In Exchange For
Oct 14, 1929	CIN N ——		DET A	Cash

Fred Heimach

Date	Traded To	Traded With	Traded By	In Exchange For
June 15, 1926	BOS A Slim Harriss Baby Doll Jacobson		PHI A	Tom Jenkins Howard Ehmke

Ken Heintzelman

Date	Traded To	Traded With	Traded By	In Exchange For
May 9, 1947	PHI N ——		PIT N	Cash

Tom Heintzelman

Date	Traded To	Traded With	Traded By	In Exchange For
Oct 14, 1974	SF N ——		STL N	Jim Willoughby

Bob Heise

Date	Traded To	Traded With	Traded By	In Exchange For
Dec 12, 1969	SF N Jim Gosger		NY N	Ray Sadecki Dave Marshall
June 1, 1971	MIL A ——		SF N	Floyd Wicker
Dec 8, 1973	STL N ——		MIL A	Tom Murphy
July 31, 1974	CAL A ——		STL N	Doug Howard
Dec 2, 1974	BOS A ——		CAL A	Tommy Harper
Dec 6, 1976	KC A ——		BOS A	Cash

Woodie Held

Date	Traded To	Traded With	Traded By	In Exchange For
June 15, 1957	KC A See Ralph Terry		NY A	——

Woodie Held continued

Date	Traded To	Traded With	Traded By	In Exchange For
June 15, 1958	CLE A Vic Power		KC A	Roger Maris Dick Tomanek Preston Ward
Dec 1, 1964	WAS A Bob Chance		CLE A	Chuck Hinton
Oct 12, 1965	BAL A ——		WAS A	John Orsino
June 15, 1967	CAL A ——		BAL A	Marcelino Lopez and minor league P Tom Arruda
July 20, 1968	CHI A ——		CAL A	Wayne Causey

Tommy Helms

Date	Traded To	Traded With	Traded By	In Exchange For
Nov 29, 1971	HOU N ——		CIN N	See Joe Morgan
Dec 12, 1975	PIT N ——		HOU N	Art Howe
Nov 5, 1976	OAK A ——		PIT N	Cash
March 15, 1977	PIT N See Phil Garner		OAK A	——

Russ Heman

Date	Traded To	Traded With	Traded By	In Exchange For
Dec 3, 1957	BAL A See Larry Doby		CHI A	——
Dec 2, 1958	CLE A $30,000.		BAL A	Bobby Avila
June 5, 1961	LA A ——		CLE A	Cash

Charlie Hemphill

Date	Traded To	Traded With	Traded By	In Exchange For
May 30, 1902	STL A ——		CLE A	Player to be named later
	(Cleveland received P Red Donahue in June, 1903.)			
Feb 1908	NY A Fred Glade		STL A	Jimmy Williams Hobe Ferris Danny Hoffman

Rollie Hemsley

Date	Traded To	Traded With	Traded By	In Exchange For
June 13, 1931	CHI N ——		PIT N	Earl Grace
Nov 30, 1932	CIN N Bob Smith Johnny Moore Lance Richbourg		CHI N	Babe Herman
Aug 3, 1933	STL A ——		CIN N	Waiver price
Feb 10, 1938	CLE A ——		STL A	Ed Cole Roy Hughes Billy Sullivan
Dec 4, 1941	CIN N ——		CLE A	Cash
March 25, 1946	PHI N ——		NY A	Cash

Solly Hemus

Date	Traded To	Traded With	Traded By	In Exchange For
May 14, 1956	PHI N ——		STL N	Bobby Morgan
Sept 29, 1958	STL N ——		PHI N	Gene Freese
	(Hemus was named St. Louis manager.)			

Dave Henderson

Date	Traded To	Traded With	Traded By	In Exchange For
Aug 19, 1986	BOS A Spike Owen		SEA A	Rey Quinones Mike Trujillo John Christensen Mike Brown
Sept 1, 1987	SF N ——		BOS A	Randy Kutcher

Joe Henderson

Date	Traded To	Traded With	Traded By	In Exchange For
Oct 31, 1977	TOR A ——		CIN N	Cash

Ken Henderson

Date	Traded To	Traded With	Traded By	In Exchange For
Nov 28, 1972	CHI A Steve Stone		SF N	Tom Bradley
Dec 12, 1975	ATL N Dick Ruthven Danny Osborn		CHI A	Ralph Garr Larvell Blanks
Dec 9, 1976	TEX A Dave May Carl Morton Roger Moret Adrian Devine and $250,000.		ATL N	Jeff Burroughs

Date	Traded To		Traded With	Traded By		In Exchange For

Ken Henderson continued

Date	Traded To		Traded With	Traded By		In Exchange For
Dec 8, 1977	NY	N	Willie Montanez	TEX	A	Jon Matlack
			Tom Grieve			John Milner
(Part of four-team trade involving Texas, New York Mets, Pittsburgh, and Atlanta.)						
May 19, 1978	CIN	N	——	NY	N	Dale Murray
June 28, 1979	CHI	N	——	CIN	N	Cash

Rickey Henderson

Date	Traded To		Traded With	Traded By		In Exchange For
Dec 8, 1984	NY	A	Bert Bradley	OAK	A	Jay Howell
			and cash			Jose Rijo
						Stan Javier
						Tim Birtsas
						Eric Plunk
June 21, 1989	OAK	A	——	NY	A	Eric Plunk
						Greg Cadaret
						Luis Polonia

Steve Henderson

Date	Traded To		Traded With	Traded By		In Exchange For
June 15, 1977	NY	N	Pat Zachry	CIN	N	Tom Seaver
			Doug Flynn			
			Dan Norman			
Feb 28, 1981	CHI	N	Cash	NY	N	Dave Kingman
Dec 9, 1982	SEA	A	——	CHI	N	Rich Bordi
March 31, 1985	OAK	A	——	SEA	A	No compensation (free agent signing)
March 10, 1988	HOU	N	——	OAK	A	No compensation (free agent signing)

Bob Hendley

Date	Traded To		Traded With	Traded By		In Exchange For
Dec 3, 1963	SF	N	Del Crandall	MIL	N	Felipe Alou
			Bob Shaw			Billy Hoeft
						Ed Bailey
						Ernie Bowman
May 29, 1965	CHI	N	Harvey Kuenn	SF	N	Dick Bertell
			Ed Bailey			Len Gabrielson
June 12, 1967	NY	N	——	CHI	N	Johnny Stephenson
						Rob Gardner

George Hendrick

Date	Traded To		Traded With	Traded By		In Exchange For
March 24, 1973	CLE	A	Dave Duncan	OAK	A	Ray Fosse
						Jack Heidemann
Dec 8, 1976	SD	N	——	CLE	N	Johnny Grubb
						Fred Kendall
						Hector Torres
May 26, 1978	STL	N	——	SD	N	Eric Rasmussen
Dec 12, 1984	PIT	N	minor league	STL	N	John Tudor
			C Steve Barnard			Brian Harper
Aug 2, 1985	CAL	A	John Candelaria	PIT	N	Pat Clements
			Al Holland			Mike Brown
						Bob Kipper
(Pittsburgh received Kipper on Aug. 16, 1985.)						

Harvey Hendrick

Date	Traded To		Traded With	Traded By		In Exchange For
Jan 3, 1923	NY	A	George Pipgras	BOS	A	Al DeVormer
						and cash
May 7, 1931	CIN	N	——	BKN	N	Mickey Heath
April 11, 1932	STL	N	Benny Frey	CIN	N	Chick Hafey
			and cash			
June 5, 1932	CIN	N	——	STL	N	Cash
Nov 21, 1933	PHI	N	Ted Kleinhans	CHI	N	Chuck Klein
			Mark Koenig			
			and $65,000.			

Ellie Hendricks

Date	Traded To		Traded With	Traded By		In Exchange For
Aug 18, 1972	CHI	N	——	BAL	A	Tommy Davis
Oct 27, 1972	BAL	A	——	CHI	N	Francisco Estrada
June 15, 1976	NY	A	——	BAL	A	See Tippy Martinez

Jack Hendricks

Date	Traded To		Traded With	Traded By		In Exchange For
July 1902	CHI	N	——	NY	N	Hal O'Hagen

Claude Hendrix

Date	Traded To		Traded With	Traded By		In Exchange For
Feb 10, 1916	CHI	N	See Three Finger Brown	CHI	F	——

Tim Hendryx

Date	Traded To		Traded With	Traded By		In Exchange For
April 28, 1918	STL	A	——	NY	A	Lee Magee
Jan 1920	BOS	A	——	STL	A	Cash

Dave Hengel

Date	Traded To		Traded With	Traded By		In Exchange For
April 2, 1989	CLE	A	——	SEA	A	Paul Noce
						Minor League IF Chuck Baldwin

Tom Henke

Date	Traded To		Traded With	Traded By		In Exchange For
Jan 24, 1985	TOR	A	——	TEX	A	
(Claimed in compensation draft after Toronto lost free agent DH Cliff Johnson to Texas.)						

Gail Henley

Date	Traded To		Traded With	Traded By		In Exchange For
Oct 13, 1952	CIN	N	——	NY	N	Frank Hiller
Oct 14, 1952	PIT	N	Cal Abrams	CIN	N	Gus Bell
			Joe Rossi			

Butch Henline

Date	Traded To		Traded With	Traded By		In Exchange For
July 25, 1921	PHI	N	Curt Walker	NY	N	Irish Meusel
			Jesse Winters			
			and $30,000.			
Jan 9, 1927	NY	N	George Harper	PHI	N	Jack Scott
						Fresco Thompson
(Part of three-team trade involving Philadelphia, New York, and Brooklyn.)						
Jan 9, 1927	BKN	N	——	NY	N	Burleigh Grimes
(Part of three-team trade involving Brooklyn, New York, and Philadelphia.)						

Phil Hennigan

Date	Traded To		Traded With	Traded By		In Exchange For
Nov 27, 1972	NY	N	——	CLE	A	Brent Strom
						Bob Rauch

Bill Henry

Date	Traded To		Traded With	Traded By		In Exchange For
Sept 18, 1967	CIN	N	——	NY	A	Len Boehmer

Bill Henry

Date	Traded To		Traded With	Traded By		In Exchange For
Dec 6, 1959	CIN	N	Lou Jackson	CHI	N	Frank Thomas
			Lee Walls			
May 4, 1965	SF	N	——	CIN	N	Jim Duffalo
June 27, 1968	PIT	N	——	SF	N	Cash

Dutch Henry

Date	Traded To		Traded With	Traded By		In Exchange For
Sept 27, 1929	CHI	A	——	NY	N	Waiver price
May 7, 1933	STL	N	See Leo Durocher	CIN	N	——

Dwayne Henry

Date	Traded To		Traded With	Traded By		In Exchange For
July 1, 1984	CHI	N	minor league	TEX	A	Dickie Noles
			IF Jorge Gomez			
(The Cubs received Henry and Gomez on December 22.)						
March 30, 1989	ATL	N	——	TEX	A	Minor league P David Miller and cash

John Henry

Date	Traded To		Traded With	Traded By		In Exchange For
Feb 14, 1918	BOS	N	——	WAS	A	Cash

Roy Henshaw

Date	Traded To		Traded With	Traded By		In Exchange For
Dec 5, 1936	BKN	N	Woody English	CHI	N	Lonny Frey

Date	Traded To		Traded With	Traded By		In Exchange For

Roy Henshaw *continued*

Date	Traded To		Traded With	Traded By		In Exchange For
Oct 4, 1937	STL	N	Johnny Cooney Jim Bucher Joe Stripp	BKN	N	Leo Durocher

Ron Herbel

Date	Traded To		Traded With	Traded By		In Exchange For
Dec 5, 1969	SD	N	Bob Barton Bobby Etheridge	SF	N	Frank Reberger
Sept 1, 1970	NY	N	——	SD	N	Rod Gaspar
		(San Diego received Gaspar on October 20.)				
Dec 1, 1970	ATL	N	——	NY	N	Bob Aspromonte

Ray Herbert

Date	Traded To		Traded With	Traded By		In Exchange For
May 11, 1955	KC	A	——	DET	A	Cash
June 10, 1961	CHI	A	——	KC	A	*See Wes Covington*
Dec 1, 1964	PHI	N	Jeoff Long	CHI	A	Danny Cater Lee Elia

Babe Herman

Date	Traded To		Traded With	Traded By		In Exchange For
Oct 30, 1922	BOS	A	Carl Holling Howard Ehmke Danny Clark and $25,000.	DET	A	Del Pratt Rip Collins
March 14, 1932	CIN	N	Wally Gilbert Ernie Lombardi	BKN	N	Tony Cuccinello Joe Stripp Clyde Sukeforth
Nov 30, 1932	CHI	N	——	CIN	N	Bob Smith Rollie Hemsley Johnny Moore Lance Richbourg
Nov 22, 1934	PIT	N	Guy Bush Jim Weaver	CHI	N	Larry French Freddie Lindstrom
June 21, 1935	CIN	N	——	PIT	N	Cash
April 1, 1937	DET	A	——	CIN	N	Cash

Billy Herman

Date	Traded To		Traded With	Traded By		In Exchange For
May 6, 1941	BKN	N	——	CHI	N	Johnny Hudson Charlie Gilbert and $65,000.
June 15, 1946	BOS	N	——	BKN	N	Stew Hofferth
Sept 30, 1946	PIT	N	Elmer Singleton Stan Wentzel Whitey Wietelmann	BOS	N	Bob Elliott Hank Camelli

Gene Hermanski

Date	Traded To		Traded With	Traded By		In Exchange For
June 15, 1951	CHI	N	Bruce Edwards Joe Hatten Eddie Miksis	BKN	N	Johnny Schmitz Rube Walker Andy Pafko Wayne Terwilliger
June 4, 1953	PIT	N	——	CHI	N	*See Ralph Kiner*

Enzo Hernandez

Date	Traded To		Traded With	Traded By		In Exchange For
Dec 4, 1968	BAL	A	——	HOU	N	*See Curt Blefary*
Dec 1, 1970	SD	N	——	BAL	A	*See Pat Dobson*

Guillermo Hernandez

Date	Traded To		Traded With	Traded By		In Exchange For
May 22, 1983	PHI	N	——	CHI	N	Dick Ruthven Bill Johnson
March 24, 1984	DET	A	Dave Bergman	PHI	N	John Wockenfuss Glenn Wilson

Jackie Hernandez

Date	Traded To		Traded With	Traded By		In Exchange For
Dec 2, 1966	MIN	A	*See Dean Chance*	CAL	A	——
Dec 2, 1970	PIT	N	——	KC	A	*See Freddie Patek*
Jan 31, 1974	PHI	N	——	PIT	N	Mike Ryan

Keith Hernandez

Date	Traded To		Traded With	Traded By		In Exchange For
June 15, 1983	NY	N	——	STL	N	Neil Allen Rick Ownbey
Dec 7, 1989	CLE	A	——	NY	N	No compensation (free agent signing)

Leo Hernandez

Date	Traded To		Traded With	Traded By		In Exchange For
April 28, 1982	BAL	A	——	LA	N	Jose Morales
Dec 12, 1985	NY	A	*See Gary Roenicke*	BAL	A	——

Manny Hernandez

Date	Traded To		Traded With	Traded By		In Exchange For
Aug 1, 1989	NY	N	——	MIN	A	Cash

Pedro Hernandez

Date	Traded To		Traded With	Traded By		In Exchange For
Nov 27, 1978	TOR	A	Joe Cannon Mark Lemongello	HOU	N	Alan Ashby
Aug 23, 1982	NY	A	——	TOR	A	Cash

Ramon Hernandez

Date	Traded To		Traded With	Traded By		In Exchange For
Sept 8, 1976	CHI	N	——	PIT	N	Cash
May 28, 1977	BOS	A	——	CHI	N	Bobby Darwin

Larry Herndon

Date	Traded To		Traded With	Traded By		In Exchange For
May 9, 1975	SF	N	minor league P Luis Gonzalez	STL	N	Ron Bryant
Dec 9, 1981	DET	A	——	SF	N	Dan Schatzeder Mike Chris

Tommy Herr

Date	Traded To		Traded With	Traded By		In Exchange For
April 22, 1988	MIN	A	——	STL	N	Tom Brunansky
Oct 24, 1988	PHI	N	Tom Nieto Eric Bullock	MIN	A	Shane Rawley and cash

Jose Herrera

Date	Traded To		Traded With	Traded By		In Exchange For
May 11, 1971	DET	A	John Gelnar	MIL	A	Jim Hannan

Pancho Herrera

Date	Traded To		Traded With	Traded By		In Exchange For
Nov 28, 1962	PIT	N	Ted Savage	PHI	N	Don Hoak

Art Herring

Date	Traded To		Traded With	Traded By		In Exchange For
Dec 1933	BKN	N	——	DET	A	Cash
Oct 19, 1946	PIT	N	——	BKN	N	Cash

Ed Herrmann

Date	Traded To		Traded With	Traded By		In Exchange For
April 1, 1975	NY	A	——	CHI	A	Minor leaguers Ken Bennett Fred Anyzeski John Narron and cash
Feb 20, 1976	CAL	A	——	NY	A	Cash
June 6, 1976	HOU	N	——	CAL	A	Terry Humphrey Mike Barlow
June 9, 1978	MON	N	——	HOU	N	Cash

John Herrnstein

Date	Traded To		Traded With	Traded By		In Exchange For
April 21, 1966	CHI	N	Adolfo Phillips Ferguson Jenkins	PHI	N	Larry Jackson Bob Buhl
May 29, 1966	ATL	N	——	CHI	N	Marty Keough

Mike Hershberger

Date	Traded To		Traded With	Traded By		In Exchange For
Jan 20, 1965	KC	A	Jim Landis Fred Talbot	CHI	A	Rocky Colavito
	(Part of three-team trade involving Kansas City, Cleveland, and the Chicago White Sox.)					

Date	Traded To	Traded With	Traded By	In Exchange For

Mike Hershberger *continued*

Date	Traded To	Traded With	Traded By	In Exchange For
Jan 15, 1970	MIL A	Lew Krausse Phil Roof Ken Sanders	OAK A	Don Mincher Ron Clark

Buck Herzog

Date	Traded To	Traded With	Traded By	In Exchange For
Dec 1909	BOS N	——	NY N	Beals Becker
July 22, 1911	NY N	——	BOS N	Hank Gowdy Al Bridwell
Dec 12, 1913	CIN N	Grover Hartley	NY N	Bob Bescher
(Hartley jumped to the Federal League and Herzog was made Cincinnati manager.)				
July 20, 1916	NY N	Red Killefer	CIN N	Christy Mathewson Edd Roush Bill McKechnie
Jan 8, 1918	BOS N	——	NY N	Larry Doyle Jesse Barnes
Aug 1919	CHI N	——	BOS N	Les Mann Charlie Pick

Whitey Herzog

Date	Traded To	Traded With	Traded By	In Exchange For
Feb 8, 1956	WAS A	Lou Berberet Bob Wiesler Herb Plews Dick Tettelbach	NY A	Mickey McDermott Bobby Kline
May 14, 1958	KC A	——	WAS A	Cash
Jan 24, 1961	BAL A	Russ Snyder	KC A	Wayne Causey Jim Archer Bob Boyd Al Pilarcik
Nov 26, 1962	DET A	Gus Triandos	BAL A	Dick Brown

Ed Heusser

Date	Traded To	Traded With	Traded By	In Exchange For
Dec 4, 1946	BKN N	——	CIN N	Augie Galan

Joe Heving

Date	Traded To	Traded With	Traded By	In Exchange For
Aug 1938	BOS A	——	CLE A	Cash
Feb 3, 1941	CLE A	——	BOS A	Cash

Johnnie Heving

Date	Traded To	Traded With	Traded By	In Exchange For
Jan 1931	PHI A	——	BOS A	Waiver price

Jack Hiatt

Date	Traded To	Traded With	Traded By	In Exchange For
Nov 21, 1964	SF N	——	LA A	Jose Cardenal
April 6, 1970	MON N	——	SF N	Cash
May 12, 1970	CHI N	——	MON N	Boots Day
Dec 1, 1970	HOU N	——	CHI N	Cash
July 29, 1972	CAL A	——	HOU N	Cash

Kevin Hickey

Date	Traded To	Traded With	Traded By	In Exchange For
July 17, 1984	NY A	——	CHI A	*See Roy Smalley*

Jess Hickman

Date	Traded To	Traded With	Traded By	In Exchange For
June 4, 1965	KC A	Ernie Fazio and $100,000.	HOU N	Jim Gentile
(Kansas City received Fazio on October 15.)				

Jim Hickman

Date	Traded To	Traded With	Traded By	In Exchange For
Feb 10, 1916	BKN N	——	BAL F	Cash

Jim Hickman

Date	Traded To	Traded With	Traded By	In Exchange For
Nov 29, 1966	LA N	Ron Hunt	NY N	Tommy Davis Derrell Griffith
April 23, 1968	CHI N	Phil Regan	LA N	Ted Savage Jim Ellis
March 23, 1974	STL N	——	CHI N	Scipio Spinks

Piano Legs Hickman

Date	Traded To	Traded With	Traded By	In Exchange For
Feb 17, 1900	NY N	——	BOS N	Cash
May 30, 1902	CLE A	——	BOS A	Candy LaChance
Aug 7, 1904	DET A	——	CLE A	Charlie Carr Fritz Buelow
July 6, 1905	WAS A	——	DET A	Cash
Aug 1, 1907	CHI A	——	WAS A	Cash
Nov 1907	CLE A	——	CHI A	Cash

Jim Hicks

Date	Traded To	Traded With	Traded By	In Exchange For
Oct 13, 1967	STL N	——	CHI N	Cash
May 30, 1969	CAL A	——	STL N	Vic Davalillo

Kirby Higbe

Date	Traded To	Traded With	Traded By	In Exchange For
May 29, 1939	PHI N	Joe Marty Ray Harrell	CHI N	Claude Passeau
Nov 11, 1940	BKN N	——	PHI N	Vito Tamulis Bill Crouch Mickey Livingston and $100,000.
May 3, 1947	PIT N	Hank Behrman Cal McLish Gene Mauch Dixie Howell	BKN N	Al Gionfriddo and $100,000.
June 6, 1949	NY N	——	PIT N	Ray Poat Bobby Rhawn

Dennis Higgins

Date	Traded To	Traded With	Traded By	In Exchange For
Feb 13, 1968	WAS A	*See Ron Hansen*	CHI A	
Dec 5, 1969	CLE A	Barry Moore	WAS A	Dave Nelson Horacio Pina Ron Law
July 15, 1971	STL N	——	CLE A	Cash
Sept 1, 1972	SD N	——	STL N	Cash

Pinky Higgins

Date	Traded To	Traded With	Traded By	In Exchange For
Dec 9, 1936	BOS A	——	PHI A	Bill Werber
Dec 15, 1938	DET A	Archie McKain	BOS A	Eldon Auker Jake Wade Chet Morgan
May 19, 1946	BOS A	——	DET A	Cash

Andy High

Date	Traded To	Traded With	Traded By	In Exchange For
July 25, 1925	BOS N	——	BKN N	Waiver price
March 25, 1928	STL N	$25,000.	BOS N	Les Bell
Dec 2, 1931	CIN N	——	STL N	Nick Cullop and Cash

Hugh High

Date	Traded To	Traded With	Traded By	In Exchange For
Jan 7, 1915	NY A	——	DET A	Waiver price

Oral Hildebrand

Date	Traded To	Traded With	Traded By	In Exchange For
Jan 17, 1937	STL A	Bill Knickerbocker Joe Vosmik	CLE A	Ivy Andrews Lyn Lary Moose Solters
Oct 26, 1938	NY A	Buster Mills	STL A	Joe Glenn Myril Hoag

Tom Hilgendorf

Date	Traded To	Traded With	Traded By	In Exchange For
July 10, 1972	CLE A	——	KC A	Jim Clark
March 6, 1975	PHI N	——	CLE A	Minor league OF Nelson Garcia

Carmen Hill

Date	Traded To	Traded With	Traded By	In Exchange For
Aug 28, 1929	STL N	——	PIT N	Waiver price

Date	Traded To	Traded With	Traded By	In Exchange For

Donnie Hill

Date	Traded To		Traded With	Traded By		In Exchange For
Dec 11, 1986	CHI	A	——	OAK	A	Gene Nelson
						Bruce Tanner

(Oakland received Tanner on Dec. 18, 1986.)

Herman Hill

Date	Traded To		Traded With	Traded By		In Exchange For
Oct 20, 1970	STL	N	minor league	MIN	A	Sal Campisi
			OF Charlie Wissler			Jim Kennedy

Hunter Hill

Date	Traded To		Traded With	Traded By		In Exchange For
July 14, 1904	WAS	A	Frank Huelsman	STL	A	Charlie Moran

(Huelsmann went to Washington on loan.)

Jesse Hill

Date	Traded To		Traded With	Traded By		In Exchange For
Jan 17, 1936	WAS	A	Jimmie DeShong	NY	A	Bump Hadley
						Roy Johnson
July 13, 1937	PHI	A	——	WAS	A	Cash

Ken Hill

Date	Traded To		Traded With	Traded By		In Exchange For
Aug 10, 1986	STL	N	——	DET	A	*See Bill Campbell*

Marc Hill

Date	Traded To		Traded With	Traded By		In Exchange For
Oct 14, 1974	SF	N	——	STL	N	Elias Sosa
						Ken Rudolph
June 20, 1980	SEA	A	——	SF	N	Cash
Feb 12, 1981	CHI	A	——	SEA	A	No compensation
						(free agent signing)

Shawn Hillegas

Date	Traded To		Traded With	Traded By		In Exchange For
Aug 30, 1988	CHI	A	——	LA	N	Ricky Horton

(Chicago received Hillegas on September 1, 1988.)

Chuck Hiller

Date	Traded To		Traded With	Traded By		In Exchange For
May 12, 1965	NY	N	——	SF	N	Cash
July 11, 1967	PHI	N	——	NY	N	Phil Linz

Frank Hiller

Date	Traded To		Traded With	Traded By		In Exchange For
Jan 3, 1952	CIN	N	——	CHI	N	Willie Ramsdell
Oct 13, 1952	NY	N	——	CIN	N	Gail Henley

Dave Hillman

Date	Traded To		Traded With	Traded By		In Exchange For
Nov 21, 1959	BOS	A	Jim Marshall	CHI	N	Dick Gernert

Dave Hilton

Date	Traded To		Traded With	Traded By		In Exchange For
Nov 22, 1976	TOR	A	Dave Roberts	SD	N	Cash
			John Scott			

Chuck Hinton

Date	Traded To		Traded With	Traded By		In Exchange For
Dec 1, 1964	CLE	A	——	WAS	A	Bob Chance
						Woodie Held
Nov 29, 1967	CAL	A	——	CLE	A	Jose Cardenal
April 4, 1969	CLE	A	——	CAL	A	Lou Johnson

Rich Hinton

Date	Traded To		Traded With	Traded By		In Exchange For
Oct 13, 1971	NY	A	——	CHI	A	Jim Lyttle
Sept 6, 1972	TEX	A	——	NY	A	Cash
March 8, 1973	CLE	A	Vince Colbert	TEX	A	Alex Johnson
Dec 12, 1975	CIN	N	minor league	CHI	A	Clay Carroll
			C Jeff Sovern			
July 6, 1979	SEA	A	——	CHI	A	Juan Bernhardt

Larry Hisle

Date	Traded To		Traded With	Traded By		In Exchange For
Oct 21, 1971	LA	N	——	PHI	N	Tom Hutton
Oct 26, 1972	STL	N	——	LA	N	Rudy Arroyo
						minor league
						P Greg Millikan
Nov 29, 1972	MIN	A	John Cumberland	STL	N	Wayne Granger
Nov 17, 1977	MIL	A	——	MIN	A	No compensation
						(free agent signing)

Billy Hitchcock

Date	Traded To		Traded With	Traded By		In Exchange For
May 16, 1946	WAS	A	——	DET	A	Cash
Feb 8, 1947	STL	A	——	WAS	A	Cash
Nov 18, 1947	BOS	A	Ellis Kinder	STL	A	Sam Dente
						Clem Dreisewerd
						Bill Sommers
						and $65,000.
Oct 8, 1949	PHI	A	——	BOS	A	Buddy Rosar
Jan 29, 1953	DET	A	——	PHI	A	Don Kolloway

Myril Hoag

Date	Traded To		Traded With	Traded By		In Exchange For
Oct 26, 1938	STL	A	Joe Glenn	NY	A	Oral Hildebrand
						Buster Mills
April 30, 1940	CHI	A	——	STL	A	Cash
June 27, 1944	CLE	A	——	CHI	A	Cash

Don Hoak

Date	Traded To		Traded With	Traded By		In Exchange For
Dec 9, 1955	CHI	N	Russ Meyer	BKN	N	Randy Jackson
			Walt Moryn			Don Elston
Nov 13, 1956	CIN	N	Warren Hacker	CHI	N	Elmer Singleton
			Pete Whisenant			Ray Jablonski
Jan 30, 1959	PIT	N	Smoky Burgess	CIN	N	Whammy Douglas
			Harvey Haddix			Jim Pendleton
						Frank Thomas
						Johnny Powers
Nov 28, 1962	PHI	N	——	PIT	N	Pancho Herrera
						Ted Savage

Glen Hobbie

Date	Traded To		Traded With	Traded By		In Exchange For
June 2, 1964	STL	N	——	CHI	N	Lew Burdette

Dick Hoblitzell

Date	Traded To		Traded With	Traded By		In Exchange For
July 16, 1914	BOS	A	——	CIN	N	Waiver price

Butch Hobson

Date	Traded To		Traded With	Traded By		In Exchange For
Dec 10, 1980	CAL	A	Rick Burleson	BOS	A	Carney Lansford
						Rick Miller
						Mark Clear
March 24, 1982	NY	A	——	CAL	A	Bill Castro

Oris Hockett

Date	Traded To		Traded With	Traded By		In Exchange For
Dec 12, 1944	CHI	A	——	CLE	A	Eddie Carnett

Johnny Hodapp

Date	Traded To		Traded With	Traded By		In Exchange For
April 24, 1932	CHI	A	Bob Seeds	CLE	A	Bill Cissell
						Jim Moore
Dec 15, 1932	BOS	A	Greg Mulleavy	CHI	A	Ed Durham
			Bob Fothergill			Hal Rhyne
			Bob Seeds			

Mel Hoderlein

Date	Traded To		Traded With	Traded By		In Exchange For
Nov 13, 1951	CHI	A	Chuck Stobbs	BOS	A	Randy Gumpert
						Don Lenhardt
May 3, 1952	WAS	A	Jim Busby	CHI	A	Sam Mele
June 14, 1954	DET	A	——	WAS	A	Johnny Pesky

Date	Traded To		Traded With			Traded By		In Exchange For

Gil Hodges

May 23, 1963	WAS	A	———			NY	N	Jimmy Piersall

(Hodges was named Washington manager.)

Nov 27, 1967	NY	N	———			WAS	A	Bill Denehy

$100,000.

(Hodges was named New York manager.)

Billy Hoeft

May 2, 1959	BOS	A	———			DET	A	Dave Sisler
								Ted Lepcio
June 15, 1959	BAL	A	———			BOS	A	Jack Harshman
Dec 15, 1962	SF	N	Jack Fisher			BAL	A	Mike McCormick
			Jimmie Coker					Stu Miller
								John Orsino
Dec 3, 1963	MIL	N	Felipe Alou			SF	N	Del Crandall
			Ed Bailey					Bob Shaw
			Ernie Bowman					Bob Hendley

Joe Hoerner

Oct 7, 1969	PHI	N	*See Curt Flood*			STL	N	———
June 15, 1972	ATL	N	Andre Thornton			PHI	N	Jim Nash
								Gary Neibauer
July 18, 1973	KC	A	———			ATL	N	Cash

Bill Hoffer

Jan 1901	CLE	A	———			PIT	N	Cash

Stew Hofferth

June 15, 1946	BKN	N	———			BOS	N	Billy Herman

Danny Hoffman

May 11, 1906	NY	A	———			PHI	A	Cash
Feb 1908	STL	A	Jimmy Williams			NY	A	Fred Glade
			Hobe Ferris					Charlie Hemphill

Guy Hoffman

Feb 17, 1987	CIN	N	———			CHI	N	Wade Rowdon

(Chicago received Rowdon on Feb. 23, 1987.)

John Hoffman

Oct 13, 1966	ATL	N	———			HOU	N	*See Tom Dukes*

Solly Hofman

Jan 1904	CHI	N	———			PIT	N	Cash
June 22, 1912	PIT	N	King Cole			CHI	N	Tommy Leach
								Lefty Leifield

Happy Hogan

May 1911	STL	A	———			PHI	A	Cash

Shanty Hogan

Jan 10, 1928	NY	N	Jimmy Welsh			BOS	N	Rogers Hornsby
Dec 29, 1932	BOS	N	———			NY	N	$25,000.
Dec 1935	WAS	A	———			BOS	N	Cash

Chief Hogsett

April 30, 1936	STL	A	———			DET	A	Jack Burns
Dec 1, 1937	WAS	A	———			STL	A	Ed Linke

Bobby Hogue

May 14, 1951	STL	A	———			BOS	N	Waiver price

Bobby Hogue *continued*

July 31, 1951	NY	A	Kermit Wahl			STL	A	Cliff Mapes
			Tom Upton					
			Lou Sleater					
Aug 4, 1952	STL	A	———			NY	A	Waiver price

Chris Hoiles

Aug 31, 1988	BAL	A	Minor league			DET	A	Fred Lynn
			P Robinson Garces					
			Minor league					
			P Cesar Mejia					

Ken Holcombe

June 16, 1952	STL	A	———			CHI	A	Cash

Bill Holden

Aug 1914	CIN	N	———			NY	A	Waiver price

Fred Holdsworth

May 29, 1975	BAL	A	———			DET	A	Bob Reynolds
July 14, 1977	MON	N	———			BAL	A	Dennis Blair

Walter Holke

Feb 1919	BOS	N	———			NY	N	Jimmy Smith
Dec 1922	PHI	N	———			BOS	N	Cash
July 9, 1925	CIN	N	———			PHI	N	Waiver price

Al Holland

June 28, 1979	SF	N	Ed Whitson			PIT	N	Bill Madlock
			Fred Breining					Lenny Randle
								Dave Roberts
Dec 14, 1982	PHI	N	Joe Morgan			SF	N	Mike Krukow
								Mark Davis
								minor league
								OF Charles Penigar
April 20, 1985	PIT	N	Minor league			PHI	N	Kent Tekulve
			P Frankie Griffin					
Aug 2, 1985	CAL	A	John Candelaria			PIT	N	Pat Clements
			George Hendrick					Mike Brown
								Bob Kipper

(Pittsburgh received Kipper on Aug. 16, 1985.)

Feb 6, 1986	NY	A	———			CAL	A	No compensation

(free agent signing)

Gary Holle

Dec 15, 1978	TEX	A	Ed Farmer			MIL	A	Reggie Cleveland
			and cash					
June 15, 1979	CHI	A	Ed Farmer			TEX	A	Eric Soderholm
Oct 30, 1981	PHI	N	Dewey Robinson			CHI	A	Minor league
								IF Jose Castro

Ed Holley

July 12, 1934	PIT	N	———			PHI	N	Cash

Carl Holling

Oct 30, 1922	BOS	A	Howard Ehmke			DET	A	Del Pratt
			Danny Clark					Rip Collins
			Babe Herman					
			and $25,000.					

Al Hollingsworth

June 13, 1938	PHI	N	Spud Davis			CIN	N	Bucky Walters
			and $50,000.					
July 13, 1939	NY	A	———			PHI	N	Roy Hughes
Aug 12, 1939	BKN	N	———			NY	A	Cash
June 6, 1946	CHI	A	———			STL	A	Waiver price

Date	Traded To		Traded With	Traded By		In Exchange For

Bonnie Hollingsworth

| Dec 1923 | BKN | N | —— | WAS | A | Bart Griffith |

Ken Holloway

| Dec 11, 1928 | CLE | A | Jackie Tavener | DET | A | George Uhle |
| June 30, 1930 | NY | A | —— | CLE | A | Cash |

Jeff Holly

| Dec 5, 1979 | DET | A | —— | MIN | A | Fernando Arroyo |

Billy Holm

| Dec 1944 | BOS | A | —— | CHI | N | Cash |

Brian Holman

| May 25, 1989 | SEA | A | Randy Johnson Gene Harris | MON | N | Mark Langston Mike Campbell |

(Montreal received Campbell on July 31, 1989.)

Shawn Holman

| June 28, 1987 | DET | A | Minor league IF Pete Rice | PIT | N | Terry Harper |

Ducky Holmes

| Feb 1903 | WAS | A | —— | DET | A | Cash |
| June 1903 | CHI | A | —— | WAS | A | Davey Dunkle |

Tommy Holmes

| Feb 5, 1942 | BOS | N | —— | NY | A | Buddy Hassett Gene Moore |

Jim Holt

| Aug 19, 1974 | OAK | A | —— | MIN | A | Pat Bourque |

Roger Holt

| Oct 24, 1980 | TEX | A | —— | NY | A | Tucker Ashford and cash |

Brian Holton

| Dec 4, 1988 | BAL | A | Ken Howell Juan Bell | LA | N | Eddie Murray |

Ken Holtzman

Nov 29, 1971	OAK	A	——	CHI	N	Rick Monday
April 2, 1976	BAL	A	Reggie Jackson minor leaguer Bill Van Bommell	OAK	A	Don Baylor Mike Torrez Paul Mitchell
June 15, 1976	NY	A	Doyle Alexander Grant Jackson Ellie Hendricks Jimmy Freeman	BAL	A	Rudy May Tippy Martinez Dave Pagan Scott McGregor Rick Dempsey
June 10, 1978	CHI	N	——	NY	A	Ron Davis

Rick Honeycutt

| July 27, 1977 | SEA | A | —— | PIT | N | Dave Pagan |
| Dec 12, 1980 | TEX | A | Mario Mendoza Larry Cox Leon Roberts Willie Horton | SEA | A | Richie Zisk Rick Auerbach Ken Clay Jerry Don Gleaton Brian Allard Minor league P Steve Finch |

Rick Honeycutt continued

| Aug 19, 1983 | LA | N | —— | TEX | A | Dave Stewart Ricky Wright and $200,000. |
| Aug 30, 1987 | OAK | A | —— | LA | N | Tim Belcher |

Don Hood

Feb 25, 1975	CLE	A	Boog Powell	BAL	A	Dave Duncan and minor league OF Al McGrew
June 15, 1979	NY	A	——	CLE	A	Cliff Johnson
March 13, 1980	STL	N	——	NY	A	No compensation (free agent signing)

Wally Hood

| July 1920 | PIT | N | —— | BKN | N | Cash |

Jay Hook

| May 8, 1964 | MIL | N | Adrian Garrett | NY | N | Roy McMillan |

Bob Hooper

| Dec 19, 1952 | CLE | A | —— | PHI | A | Dick Rozek minor league 2B Bob Wilson |
| April 13, 1955 | CIN | N | —— | CLE | A | Cash |

Harry Hooper

| March 4, 1921 | CHI | A | —— | BOS | A | Shano Collins Nemo Leibold |

Burt Hooton

| May 2, 1975 | LA | N | —— | CHI | N | Geoff Zahn Eddie Solomon |
| Dec 20, 1984 | TEX | A | —— | LA | N | No compensation (free agent signing) |

Don Hopkins

| March 26, 1975 | OAK | A | —— | MON | N | Cash |

Gail Hopkins

| Oct 13, 1970 | KC | A | John Matias | CHI | A | Pat Kelly Don O'Riley |
| July 11, 1974 | LA | N | —— | SD | N | Cash |

Marty Hopkins

| June 27, 1934 | CHI | A | —— | PHI | N | Waiver price |

Paul Hopkins

| June 26, 1929 | STL | A | —— | WAS | A | Cash |

Johnny Hopp

Feb 5, 1946	BOS	N	——	STL	N	Eddie Joost and $40,000.
Nov 18, 1947	PIT	N	Danny Murtaugh	BOS	N	Jim Russell Bill Salkeld Al Lyons
May 18, 1949	BKN	N	$25,000.	PIT	N	Marv Rackley
(Trade was cancelled on June 7, 1949.)
Sept 5, 1950	NY	A	——	PIT	N	Cash

Bob Horner

| Jan 14, 1988 | STL | N | —— | ATL | N | No compensation (free agent signing) |

Date	Traded To	Traded With	Traded By	In Exchange For

Rogers Hornsby

Date	Traded To		Traded With	Traded By		In Exchange For
Dec 20, 1926	NY	N	——	STL	N	Frankie Frisch / Jimmy Ring
Jan 10, 1928	BOS	N	——	NY	N	Shanty Hogan / Jimmy Welsh
Nov 7, 1928	CHI	N	——	BOS	N	Socks Seibold / Percy Jones / Lou Legett / Freddie Maguire / Bruce Cunningham / and $200,000.

Ricky Horton

Date	Traded To		Traded With	Traded By		In Exchange For
Feb 9, 1988	CHI	A	Lance Johnson / and cash	STL	N	Jose DeLeon
Aug 30, 1988	LA	N	——	CHI	A	Shawn Hillegas

(Chicago received Hillegas on September 1, 1988.)

Tony Horton

Date	Traded To		Traded With	Traded By		In Exchange For
June 4, 1967	CLE	A	Don Demeter	BOS	A	Gary Bell

Willie Horton

Date	Traded To		Traded With	Traded By		In Exchange For
April 12, 1977	TEX	A	——	DET	A	Steve Foucault
Feb 28, 1978	CLE	A	David Clyde	TEX	A	Tom Buskey / John Lowenstein
Aug 15, 1978	TOR	A	Phil Huffman	OAK	A	Rico Carty
Jan 27, 1979	SEA	A	——	TOR	A	No compensation (free agent signing)
Dec 12, 1980	TEX	A	Rick Honeycutt / Mario Mendoza / Larry Cox / Leon Roberts	SEA	A	Richie Zisk / Rick Auerbach / Ken Clay / Jerry Don Gleaton / Brian Allard / Minor league / P Steve Finch

Tim Hosley

Date	Traded To		Traded With	Traded By		In Exchange For
April 19, 1976	OAK	A	——	CHI	N	Cash

Gene Host

Date	Traded To		Traded With	Traded By		In Exchange For
Dec 5, 1956	KC	A	*See Ned Garver*	DET	A	——

Dave Hostetler

Date	Traded To		Traded With	Traded By		In Exchange For
March 31, 1982	TEX	A	Larry Parrish	MON	N	Al Oliver
Nov 8, 1984	MON	N	——	TEX	A	Chris Welsh

Charlie Hough

Date	Traded To		Traded With	Traded By		In Exchange For
July 11, 1980	TEX	A	——	LA	N	Cash

Frank House

Date	Traded To		Traded With	Traded By		In Exchange For
Nov 20, 1957	KC	A	——	DET	A	*See Billy Martin*
Nov 21, 1959	CIN	N	——	KC	A	Tom Acker

Tom House

Date	Traded To		Traded With	Traded By		In Exchange For
Dec 12, 1975	BOS	A	——	ATL	N	Roger Moret
May 28, 1977	SEA	A	——	BOS	A	Cash

Paul Householder

Date	Traded To		Traded With	Traded By		In Exchange For
Sept 10, 1984	STL	N	——	CIN	N	John Stuper
Oct 3, 1984	MIL	A	Jim Adduci	STL	N	Minor leaguers / P Rich Buonantony / C Jim Koontz / IF Ron Koenigsfeld

Art Houtteman

Date	Traded To		Traded With	Traded By		In Exchange For
June 15, 1953	CLE	A	Owen Friend / Bill Wight / Joe Ginsberg	DET	A	Ray Boone / Al Aber / Steve Gromek / Dick Weik
May 20, 1957	BAL	A	——	CLE	A	Cash

Steve Hovley

Date	Traded To		Traded With	Traded By		In Exchange For
June 11, 1970	OAK	A	——	MIL	A	Al Downing / Tito Francona

Bruce Howard

Date	Traded To		Traded With	Traded By		In Exchange For
Nov 29, 1967	BAL	A	——	CHI	A	*See Luis Aparicio*
June 15, 1968	WAS	A	——	BAL	A	Fred Valentine

Del Howard

Date	Traded To		Traded With	Traded By		In Exchange For
Dec 20, 1904	PIT	N		PHI	N	Kitty Bransfield / Otto Krueger / Moose McCormick
Dec 15, 1905	BOS	N	Dave Brain / Vive Lindaman	PIT	N	Vic Willis
June 24, 1907	CHI	N		BOS	N	Bill Sweeney / Newt Randall

Doug Howard

Date	Traded To		Traded With	Traded By		In Exchange For
July 31, 1974	STL	N	——	CAL	A	Bob Heise
Sept 30, 1975	CLE	A	——	STL	N	Luis Alvarado
Nov 5, 1976	TOR	A	Alan Ashby	CLE	A	Al Fitzmorris

Elston Howard

Date	Traded To		Traded With	Traded By		In Exchange For
Aug 3, 1967	BOS	A	——	NY	A	Ron Klimkowski / Pete Magrini

Frank Howard

Date	Traded To		Traded With	Traded By		In Exchange For
Dec 4, 1964	WAS	A	Phil Ortega / Pete Richert / Dick Nen / Ken McMullen	LA	N	Claude Osteen / John Kennedy / and $100,000.
Aug 31, 1972	DET	A	——	TEX	A	Cash

Ivon Howard

Date	Traded To		Traded With	Traded By		In Exchange For
July 14, 1914	STL	A	——	DET	A	Waiver price
Jan 1916	CLE	A	——	STL	A	Cash

Larry Howard

Date	Traded To		Traded With	Traded By		In Exchange For
May 22, 1973	ATL	N	——	HOU	N	Minor league / C Tom Heierle

Art Howe

Date	Traded To		Traded With	Traded By		In Exchange For
Dec 12, 1975	HOU	N	——	PIT	N	Tommy Helms
Feb 22, 1984	STL	N	——	HOU	N	No compensation (free agent signing)

Dixie Howell

Date	Traded To		Traded With	Traded By		In Exchange For
May 3, 1947	PIT	N	Kirby Higbe / Hank Behrman / Cal McLish / Gene Mauch	BKN	N	Al Gionfriddo / and $100,000.

Harry Howell

Date	Traded To		Traded With	Traded By		In Exchange For
Jan 1900	BKN	N	Jimmy Sheckard / Jerry Nops / Broadway Aleck Smith / Frank Kitson / Joe McGinnity	BAL	N	Cash
Jan 1904	STL	A	Jack O'Connor	NY	A	Jack Powell

Date	Traded To	Traded With	Traded By	In Exchange For

Jay Howell

Date	Traded To	Traded With	Traded By	In Exchange For
Oct 17, 1980	CHI N	———	CIN N	Mike O'Berry
Aug 19, 1981	NY A	Bill Caudill	CHI N	Pat Tabler

(New York received Caudill on April 1, 1982, and Howell on August 2, 1982.)

| Dec 8, 1984 | OAK A | Jose Rijo
Stan Javier
Tim Birtsas
Eric Plunk | NY A | Rickey Henderson
Bert Bradley
and cash |
| Dec 11, 1987 | LA N | Alfredo Griffin | OAK A | Bob Welch
Matt Young |

(Part of three-team trade involving Oakland, Los Angeles and New York Mets.)

Ken Howell

Date	Traded To	Traded With	Traded By	In Exchange For
Dec 4, 1988	BAL A	Brian Holton Juan Bell	LA N	Eddie Murray
Dec 8, 1988	PHI N	Gordon Dillard	BAL A	Phil Bradley

Roy Howell

Date	Traded To	Traded With	Traded By	In Exchange For
May 9, 1977	TOR A	———	TEX A	Steve Hargan Jim Mason and $200,000.
Dec 23, 1980	MIL A	———	TOR A	No compensation (free agent signing)

Bill Howerton

Date	Traded To	Traded With	Traded By	In Exchange For
June 15, 1951	PIT N	See Joe Garagiola	STL N	———
May 7, 1952	NY N	———	PIT N	Waiver price

Dick Howser

Date	Traded To	Traded With	Traded By	In Exchange For
May 25, 1963	CLE A	Joe Azcue	KC A	Doc Edwards and $100,000.
Dec 20, 1966	NY A	———	CLE A	Minor league P Gil Downs

LaMarr Hoyt

Date	Traded To	Traded With	Traded By	In Exchange For
April 5, 1977	CHI A	Oscar Gamble minor league P Bob Polinsky and $200,000.	NY A	Bucky Dent
Dec 6, 1984	SD N	Minor league Ps Todd Simmons and Kevin Kristan	CHI A	Ozzie Guillen Tim Lollar Luis Salazar Bill Long

Waite Hoyt

Date	Traded To	Traded With	Traded By	In Exchange For
Dec 15, 1920	NY A	Harry Harper Wally Schang Mike McNally	BOS A	Muddy Ruel Del Pratt Sammy Vick Hank Thormahlen
May 30, 1930	DET A	Mark Koenig	NY A	Ownie Carroll Yats Wuestling Harry Rice
June 30, 1931	PHI A	———	DET A	Cash
Nov 1932	PIT N	———	NY N	Waiver price

Al Hrabosky

Date	Traded To	Traded With	Traded By	In Exchange For
Dec 8, 1977	KC A	———	STL N	Mark Littell Buck Martinez
Nov 20, 1979	ATL N	———	KC A	No compensation (free agent signing)

Walt Hriniak

Date	Traded To	Traded With	Traded By	In Exchange For
June 12, 1969	SD N	Van Kelly minor league OF Andy Finlay	ATL N	Tony Gonzalez

Glenn Hubbard

Date	Traded To	Traded With	Traded By	In Exchange For
Jan 11, 1988	OAK A	———	ATL N	No compensation (free agent signing)

Bill Hubbell

Date	Traded To	Traded With	Traded By	In Exchange For
June 8, 1920	PHI N	Art Fletcher and cash	NY N	Dave Bancroft
May 1, 1925	BKN N	———	PHI N	Art Decatur

Rex Hudler

Date	Traded To	Traded With	Traded By	In Exchange For
Dec 12, 1985	BAL A	Rich Bordi	NY A	Gary Roenicke Leo Hernandez

Charles Hudson

Date	Traded To	Traded With	Traded By	In Exchange For
Oct 18, 1971	STL N	See Jim Bibby	NY N	———
Feb 1, 1973	TEX A	Mike Nagy	STL N	Mike Thompson

(Thompson and Nagy were exchanged on March 31.)

| Sept 12, 1974 | CAL A | ——— | CLE A | Bill Gilbreth |

Charles Hudson

Date	Traded To	Traded With	Traded By	In Exchange For
Dec 11, 1986	NY A	Minor league P Jeff Knox	PHI N	Mike Easler Tom Barrett
March 23, 1989	DET A	———	NY A	Tom Brookens

Hal Hudson

Date	Traded To	Traded With	Traded By	In Exchange For
Aug 27, 1952	CHI A	———	STL A	Waiver price

Johnny Hudson

Date	Traded To	Traded With	Traded By	In Exchange For
May 6, 1941	CHI N	Charlie Gilbert and $65,000.	BKN N	Billy Herman

Sid Hudson

Date	Traded To	Traded With	Traded By	In Exchange For
June 10, 1952	BOS A	———	WAS A	Randy Gumpert Walt Masterson

Frank Huelsman

Date	Traded To	Traded With	Traded By	In Exchange For
May 30, 1904	DET A	———	CHI A	Cash
June 16, 1904	STL A	———	DET A	Cash
July 14, 1904	WAS A	Hunter Hill	STL A	Charlie Moran

(Huelsmann went to Washington on loan.)

| Jan 16, 1905 | WAS A | ——— | BOS A | See note |

(St. Louis reclaimed Huelsmann, who was with Washington on loan, and traded him to Boston. Boston then sent him to Washington as payment for George Stone.)

Phil Huffman

Date	Traded To	Traded With	Traded By	In Exchange For
March 15, 1978	OAK A	———	SF N	See Vida Blue
Aug 15, 1978	TOR A	Willie Horton	OAK A	Rico Carty
March 25, 1982	KC A	———	TOR A	Rance Mulliniks

Miller Huggins

Date	Traded To	Traded With	Traded By	In Exchange For
Feb 1910	STL N	Rebel Oakes Frank Corridon	CIN N	Fred Beebe Alan Storke

Jim Hughes

Date	Traded To	Traded With	Traded By	In Exchange For
May 15, 1956	CHI N	———	BKN N	Cash

Keith Hughes

Date	Traded To	Traded With	Traded By	In Exchange For
June 30, 1984	NY A	Marty Bystrom	PHI N	Shane Rawley
June 10, 1987	PHI N	Shane Turner	NY A	Mike Easler
March 21, 1988	BAL A	See Rick Schu	PHI N	———
Dec 5, 1989	NY N	Minor league P Cesar Mejia	BAL A	John Mitchell Minor league OF Joaquin Contreras

Date	Traded To	Traded With	Traded By	In Exchange For

Long Tom Hughes

July 1902	BOS A ———		BAL A	Cash
Dec 1903	NY A ———		BOS A	Jesse Tannehill
July 13, 1904	WAS A	Bill Wolfe	NY A	Al Orth

Roy Hughes

Feb 10, 1938	STL A	Ed Cole	CLE A	Rollie Hemsley
		Billy Sullivan		
June 13, 1939	NY A	Cash	STL A	Joe Gallagher
July 13, 1939	PHI N ———		NY A	Al Hollingsworth
Jan 21, 1946	PHI N ———		CHI N	Cash

Terry Hughes

| Dec 7, 1973 | BOS A | *See Reggie Cleveland* | STL N ——— | |
| Jan 9, 1976 | STL N ——— | | BOS A | Cash |

Tommy Hughes

| Dec 11, 1947 | CIN N ——— | | PHI N | Bert Haas |

Jim Hughey

Jan 1900	STL N	Jack Harper	CLE N	Cash
		Otto Krueger		
		Joe Quinn		

Emil Huhn

| Feb 10, 1916 | CIN N ——— | | NWK F | Cash |

Mark Huismann

| May 21, 1986 | SEA A ——— | | KC A | Terry Bell |
| May 12, 1987 | CLE A ——— | | SEA A | Dave Gallagher |

Rudy Hulswitt

| Dec 1908 | STL N ——— | | CIN N | Cash |

Tom Hume

| Dec 11, 1985 | PHI N | Gary Redus | CIN N | John Denny |
| | | | | Jeff Gray |

Terry Humphrey

Dec 4, 1974	DET A	Tom Walker	MON N	Woodie Fryman
Dec 6, 1975	HOU N	Leon Roberts	DET A	Milt May
		Gene Pentz		Dave Roberts
		Mark Lemongello		Jim Crawford
June 6, 1976	CAL A	Mike Barlow	HOU N	Ed Herrmann

Bob Humphreys

March 25, 1963	STL N ———		DET A	Cash
April 10, 1965	CHI N ———		STL N	Bobby Pfeil
				minor league
				P Hal Gibson
April 2, 1966	WAS A ———		CHI N	Ken Hunt
				and cash

Bert Humphries

July 15, 1911	CIN N ———		PHI N	Fred Beck
				Bill Burns
Dec 15, 1912	CHI N	Red Corriden	CIN N	Joe Tinker
		Pete Knisely		Grover Lowdermilk
		Art Phelan		Harry Chapman
		Mike Mitchell		
Aug 8, 1915	PHI N ———		CHI N	Cash

John Humphries

| Feb 7, 1941 | CHI A ——— | | CLE A | Clint Brown |

John Humphries *continued*

| Dec 7, 1945 | PHI N ——— | | CHI A | Cash |

Randy Hundley

Dec 2, 1965	CHI N	Bill Hands	SF N	Lindy McDaniel
				Don Landrum
				Jim Rittwage
Dec 6, 1973	MIN A ———		CHI N	George Mitterwald
April 13, 1976	CHI N ———		SD N	Cash

Bill Hunnefield

Nov 1930	CLE A ———		CHI A	Cash
May 28, 1931	BOS N ———		CLE A	Waiver price
June 30, 1931	NY N ———		BOS N	Waiver price

Ken Hunt

| Sept 12, 1963 | WAS A ——— | | LA A | Cash |
| April 2, 1966 | CHI N | Cash | WAS A | Bob Humphreys |

Randy Hunt

| Feb 27, 1986 | MON N ——— | | STL N | Cash |

Ron Hunt

Nov 29, 1966	LA N	Jim Hickman	NY N	Tommy Davis
				Derrell Griffith
Feb 13, 1968	SF N	Nate Oliver	LA N	Tom Haller
				minor league
				P Frank Kasmeta
Dec 30, 1970	MON N ———		SF N	Dave McDonald
Sept 5, 1974	STL N ———		MON N	Cash

Billy Hunter

Oct 14, 1952	STL A ———		BKN N	Bob Mahoney
				Stan Rojek
				Ray Coleman
				and $90,000.
Nov 18, 1954	NY A	*See Bob Turley*	BAL A ———	
Feb 19, 1957	KC A	Rip Coleman	NY A	Art Ditmar
		Tom Morgan		Bobby Shantz
		Mickey McDermott		Jack McMahan
		Milt Graff		Wayne Belardi
		Irv Noren		Curt Roberts
				Clete Boyer

(New York received Roberts on April 4, and Boyer on June 4, 1957.)

| June 12, 1958 | CLE A ——— | | KC A | Chico Carrasquel |

Buddy Hunter

| Dec 10, 1973 | KC A ——— | | BOS A | Cash |

Catfish Hunter

| Dec 31, 1974 | NY A ——— | | OAK A | No compensation |
| | | | | (free agent signing) |

Herb Hunter

| Aug 28, 1916 | CHI N | Larry Doyle | NY N | Heinie Zimmerman |
| | | Merwin Jacobson | | Mickey Doolan |

Steve Huntz

April 2, 1970	SD N ———		STL N	Billy McCool
Dec 4, 1970	SF N ———		SD N	Don Mason
				minor league
				P Bill Frost
March 23, 1971	CHI A ———		SF N	Steve Hamilton
Dec 2, 1971	LA N	Tommy John	CHI A	Dick Allen

Date	Traded To	Traded With	Traded By	In Exchange For

Walter Huntzinger
June 21, 1926	CHI N ——		STL N	Waiver price

Clint Hurdle
Dec 11, 1981	CIN N ——		KC A	Scott Brown

Bruce Hurst
Dec 8, 1988	SD N ——		BOS A	No compensation (free agent signing)

Don Hurst
June 11, 1934	CHI N ——		PHI N	Dolf Camilli

Bert Husting
June 1902	PHI A ——		BOS A	Cash

Johnny Hutchings
June 12, 1941	BOS N ——		CIN N	Lloyd Waner

Ira Hutchinson
Dec 13, 1938	BKN N	Gene Moore	BOS N	Jimmy Outlaw Buddy Hassett
June 13, 1940	STL N ——		BKN N	Cash

Jim Hutto
April 3, 1969	PHI N	Jerry Buchek	STL N	Bill White
Dec 16, 1970	BAL A	Grant Jackson Sam Parrilla	PHI N	Roger Freed

Tom Hutton
Oct 21, 1971	PHI N ——		LA N	Larry Hisle
Dec 8, 1977	TOR A ——		PHI N	Cash
July 20, 1978	MON N ——		TOR A	Cash

Ham Hyatt
Nov 10, 1914	STL N ——		PIT N	Waiver price
June 19, 1918	NY A ——		BOS N	Cash

Dick Hyde
June 11, 1959	BOS A	Herb Plews	WAS A	Billy Consolo Murray Wall

(Hyde was returned to Washington and Wall was returned to Boston.)

Pete Incaviglia
Nov 2, 1985	TEX A ——		MON N	Bob Sebra Jim Anderson

Alexis Infante
Nov 20, 1989	ATL N ——		TOR A	Cash

Scotty Ingerton
Jan 1911	BOS N	Big Jeff Pfeffer	CHI N	Dave Shean

Dane Iorg
June 15, 1977	STL N	Tom Underwood Rick Bosetti	PHI N	Bake McBride Steve Waterbury
May 10, 1984	KC A ——		STL N	Cash
Jan 28, 1986	SD N ——		KC A	No compensation (free agent signing)

Hooks Iott
April 9, 1952	PIT N ——		CIN N	Cash

Charlie Irwin
July 2, 1901	BKN N ——		CIN N	Cash

Tommy Irwin
Dec 15, 1938	BOS A	Denny Galehouse	CLE A	Ben Chapman

Mike Ivie
Feb 28, 1978	SF N ——		SD N	Derrel Thomas
April 20, 1981	HOU N ——		SF N	Dave Bergman Jeffrey Leonard

Ray Jablonski
Dec 8, 1954	CIN N	Gerry Staley	STL N	Frank Smith
Nov 13, 1956	CHI N	Elmer Singleton	CIN N	Don Hoak Warren Hacker Pete Whisenant
April 16, 1957	NY N	Ray Katt	CHI N	Dick Littlefield Bob Lennon
March 25, 1959	STL N	Bill White	SF N	Sam Jones Don Choate
Aug 20, 1959	KC A ——		STL N	Waiver price

Fred Jacklitsch
Feb 1903	BKN N ——		PHI N	Cash

Al Jackson
Oct 20, 1965	STL N	Charley Smith	NY N	Ken Boyer
July 16, 1967	NY N ——		STL N	Jack Lamabe
June 13, 1969	CIN N ——		NY N	Cash

Danny Jackson
Nov 6, 1987	CIN N	Angel Salazar	KC A	Ted Power Kurt Stillwell

Darrin Jackson
Aug 30, 1989	SD N	Calvin Schiraldi Phil Stephenson	CHI N	Marvell Wynne Luis Salazar

(San Diego Received Stephenson on Sept. 5, 1989).

Grant Jackson
Dec 16, 1970	BAL A	Jim Hutto Sam Parrilla	PHI N	Roger Freed
June 15, 1976	NY A ——		BAL A	See Tippy Martinez
Dec 7, 1976	PIT N ——		SEA A	Craig Reynolds Jimmy Sexton
Sept 1, 1981	MON N ——		PIT N	$50,000.
Jan 19, 1982	KC A ——		MON N	Ken Phelps

Joe Jackson
July 25, 1910	CLE A ——		PHI A	Bris Lord
Aug 21, 1915	CHI A ——		CLE A	Braggo Roth Larry Chappell Ed Klepfer and $31,500.

Larry Jackson
Oct 17, 1962	CHI N	Jimmie Schaffer Lindy McDaniel	STL N	George Altman Don Cardwell Moe Thacker
April 21, 1966	PHI N	Bob Buhl	CHI N	Adolfo Phillips John Herrnstein Ferguson Jenkins

Date	Traded To		Traded With	Traded By		In Exchange For

Lou Jackson

Date	Traded To		Traded With	Traded By		In Exchange For
Dec 6, 1959	CIN	N	Bill Henry Lee Walls	CHI	N	Frank Thomas

Mike Jackson

Date	Traded To		Traded With	Traded By		In Exchange For
Dec 9, 1987	SEA	A	——	PHI	N	See Phil Bradley

Mike Jackson

Date	Traded To		Traded With	Traded By		In Exchange For
Sept 6, 1969	PHI	N	——	BOS	A	Gary Wagner
Sept 13, 1971	STL	N	——	KC	A	Cash

Randy Jackson

Date	Traded To		Traded With	Traded By		In Exchange For
Dec 9, 1955	BKN	N	Don Elston	CHI	N	Don Hoak Russ Meyer Walt Moryn
Aug 4, 1958	CLE	A	——	LA	N	Cash
May 4, 1959	CHI	N	——	CLE	A	Riverboat Smith

Reggie Jackson

Date	Traded To		Traded With	Traded By		In Exchange For
April 2, 1976	BAL	A	Ken Holtzman minor leaguer Bill Van Bommell	OAK	A	Don Baylor Mike Torrez Paul Mitchell
Nov 29, 1976	NY	A	——	BAL	A	No compensation (free agent signing)
Jan 22, 1982	CAL	A	——	NY	A	No compensation (free agent signing)
Dec 24, 1986	OAK	A	——	CAL	A	No compensation (free agent signing)

Ron Jackson

Date	Traded To		Traded With	Traded By		In Exchange For
Nov 3, 1959	BOS	A	——	CHI	A	Frank Baumann
May 17, 1960	MIL	N	——	BOS	A	Ray Boone

Ron Jackson

Date	Traded To		Traded With	Traded By		In Exchange For
Dec 4, 1978	MIN	A	Danny Goodwin	CAL	A	Dan Ford
Aug 23, 1981	DET	A	——	MIN	A	Tim Corcoran
April 11, 1982	CAL	A	——	DET	A	No compensation (free agent signing)

Roy Lee Jackson

Date	Traded To		Traded With	Traded By		In Exchange For
Dec 12, 1980	TOR	A	——	NY	N	Bob Bailor
June 27, 1985	SD	N	player to be named	BAL	A	Alan Wiggins

(San Diego received P Rich Caldwell on Sept. 16, 1985.)

Sonny Jackson

Date	Traded To		Traded With	Traded By		In Exchange For
Oct 8, 1967	ATL	N	Chuck Harrison	HOU	N	Denny Lemaster Denis Menke

Elmer Jacobs

Date	Traded To		Traded With	Traded By		In Exchange For
Dec 1915	PIT	N	——	PHI	N	Cash
July 1, 1918	PHI	N	——	PIT	N	Erskine Mayer
July 14, 1919	STL	N	Frank Woodward Doug Baird	PHI	N	Lee Meadows Gene Paulette

Spook Jacobs

Date	Traded To		Traded With	Traded By		In Exchange For
June 23, 1956	PIT	N	——	KC	A	Jack McMahan

Baby Doll Jacobson

Date	Traded To		Traded With	Traded By		In Exchange For
Aug 18, 1915	STL	A	——	DET	A	Bill James Grover Lowdermilk
June 15, 1926	PHI	A	——	STL	A	Bing Miller
June 15, 1926	BOS	A	Fred Heimach Slim Harriss	PHI	A	Tom Jenkins Howard Ehmke
June 12, 1927	CLE	A	——	BOS	A	Cash
Aug 5, 1927	PHI	A	——	CLE	A	Waiver price

Beany Jacobson

Date	Traded To		Traded With	Traded By		In Exchange For
Dec 1905	STL	A	——	WAS	A	Willie Sudhoff
June 22, 1907	BOS	A	$1,000.	STL	A	Bill Dinneen

Merwin Jacobson

Date	Traded To		Traded With	Traded By		In Exchange For
Aug 28, 1916	CHI	N	Larry Doyle Herb Hunter	NY	N	Heinie Zimmerman Mickey Doolan

Brook Jacoby

Date	Traded To		Traded With	Traded By		In Exchange For
Aug 28, 1983	CLE	A	Rick Behenna Brett Butler and $150,000.	ATL	N	Len Barker

(Butler and Jacoby were sent to Cleveland at the end of the season.)

Pat Jacquez

Date	Traded To		Traded With	Traded By		In Exchange For
Nov 30, 1970	CHI	A	Dave Lemonds Roe Skidmore	CHI	N	Jose Ortiz Ossie Blanco
Nov 28, 1972	STL	N	——	CIN	N	Bill Voss

Art Jahn

Date	Traded To		Traded With	Traded By		In Exchange For
May 29, 1928	PHI	N	——	NY	N	Russ Wrightstone

Bill James

Date	Traded To		Traded With	Traded By		In Exchange For
Aug 18, 1915	DET	A	Grover Lowdermilk	STL	A	Baby Doll Jacobson
Aug 1919	BOS	A	——	DET	A	Cash
Aug 1919	CHI	A	——	BOS	A	Cash

Bob James

Date	Traded To		Traded With	Traded By		In Exchange For
May 4, 1983	MON	N	——	DET	A	Cash
Dec 7, 1984	CHI	A	Bryan Little	MON	N	Vance Law Bert Roberge

Charlie James

Date	Traded To		Traded With	Traded By		In Exchange For
Dec 14, 1964	CIN	N	Roger Craig	STL	N	Bob Purkey

Chris James

Date	Traded To		Traded With	Traded By		In Exchange For
June 2, 1989	SD	N	——	PHI	N	John Kruk Randy Ready
Dec 6, 1989	CLE	A	Sandy Alomar Minor league 3B Carlos Baerga	SD	N	Joe Carter

Dion James

Date	Traded To		Traded With	Traded By		In Exchange For
Jan 19, 1987	ATL	N	——	MIL	A	Brad Komminsk
July 2, 1989	CLE	A	——	ATL	N	Oddibe McDowell

Johnny James

Date	Traded To		Traded With	Traded By		In Exchange For
May 8, 1961	LA	A	Lee Thomas Ryne Duren	NY	A	Tex Clevenger Bob Cerv

Skip James

Date	Traded To		Traded With	Traded By		In Exchange For
March 27, 1979	MIL	A	——	SF	N	Cash

Charlie Jamieson

Date	Traded To		Traded With	Traded By		In Exchange For
July 17, 1917	PHI	A	——	WAS	A	Waiver price
March 1, 1919	CLE	A	Larry Gardner Elmer Myers	PHI	A	Braggo Roth

Date	Traded To	Traded With	Traded By	In Exchange For

Gerry Janeski

Date	Traded To	Traded With	Traded By	In Exchange For
Dec 13, 1969	CHI A	Syd O'Brien minor league P Billy Farmer	BOS A	Don Pavletich Gary Peters
	(Janeski replaced Farmer, who retired.)			
Feb 9, 1971	WAS A	——	CHI A	Rick Reichardt

Hal Janvrin

Date	Traded To	Traded With	Traded By	In Exchange For
Jan 17, 1919	WAS A	Cash	BOS A	Eddie Ainsmith George Dumont
Sept 10, 1919	STL N	——	WAS A	Waiver price
June 18, 1921	BKN N	Ferdie Schupp	STL N	Jeff Pfeffer

Pat Jarvis

Date	Traded To	Traded With	Traded By	In Exchange For
Feb 28, 1973	MON N	——	ATL N	Carl Morton
Dec 20, 1973	TEX A	——	MON N	Larry Biittner

Ray Jarvis

Date	Traded To	Traded With	Traded By	In Exchange For
Oct 11, 1970	CAL A	See Tony Conigliaro	BOS A	——

Larry Jaster

Date	Traded To	Traded With	Traded By	In Exchange For
Dec 2, 1969	ATL N	——	MON N	Jim Britton minor league C Don Johnson

Julian Javier

Date	Traded To	Traded With	Traded By	In Exchange For
May 28, 1960	STL N	Ed Bauta	PIT N	Vinegar Bend Mizell Dick Gray
March 24, 1972	CIN N	——	STL N	Tony Cloninger

Stan Javier

Date	Traded To	Traded With	Traded By	In Exchange For
Dec 8, 1984	OAK A	——	NY A	See Rickey Henderson

Joey Jay

Date	Traded To	Traded With	Traded By	In Exchange For
Dec 15, 1960	CIN N	Juan Pizarro	MIL N	Roy McMillan
June 15, 1966	ATL N	——	CIN N	Hank Fischer

Hal Jeffcoat

Date	Traded To	Traded With	Traded By	In Exchange For
Nov 28, 1955	CIN N	——	CHI N	Hobie Landrith
June 8, 1959	STL N	——	CIN N	Jim Brosnan

Mike Jeffcoat

Date	Traded To	Traded With	Traded By	In Exchange For
May 7, 1985	SF N	Luis Quinones	CLE A	Johnnie LeMaster

Jesse Jefferson

Date	Traded To	Traded With	Traded By	In Exchange For
June 15, 1975	CHI A	——	BAL A	Tony Muser
Sept 11, 1980	PIT N	——	TOR A	Cash
Jan 23, 1981	CAL A	——	PIT N	No compensation (free agent signing)
Feb 19, 1982	BAL A	——	TOR A	No compensation (free agent signing)

Stan Jefferson

Date	Traded To	Traded With	Traded By	In Exchange For
Dec 11, 1986	SD N	Kevin Mitchell Shawn Abner Minor league Ps Kevin Armstrong and Kevin Brown.	NY N	Kevin McReynolds Gene Walter Minor league IF Adam Ging
Oct 24, 1988	NY A	——	SD N	See Jack Clark
July 20, 1989	BAL A	——	NY A	John Habyan

Irv Jeffries

Date	Traded To	Traded With	Traded By	In Exchange For
Dec 20, 1933	PHI N	Otto Bluege	CIN N	Mark Koenig

Ferguson Jenkins

Date	Traded To	Traded With	Traded By	In Exchange For
April 21, 1966	CHI N	Adolfo Phillips John Herrnstein	PHI N	Larry Jackson Bob Buhl
Oct 25, 1973	TEX A	——	CHI N	Bill Madlock Vic Harris
Nov 17, 1975	BOS A	——	TEX A	Juan Beniquez Steve Barr Craig Skok
Dec 14, 1977	TEX A	——	BOS A	John Poloni and cash
Dec 8, 1981	CHI N	——	TEX A	No compensation (free agent signing)

Jack Jenkins

Date	Traded To	Traded With	Traded By	In Exchange For
Sept 1, 1969	LA N	——	WAS A	Cash

Tom Jenkins

Date	Traded To	Traded With	Traded By	In Exchange For
June 15, 1926	PHI A	Howard Ehmke	BOS A	Fred Heimach Slim Harriss Baby Doll Jacobson

Bill Jennings

Date	Traded To	Traded With	Traded By	In Exchange For
July 16, 1951	STL A	——	NY N	Waiver price

Hughie Jennings

Date	Traded To	Traded With	Traded By	In Exchange For
Feb 1901	PHI N	——	BKN N	$3,000.

Jackie Jensen

Date	Traded To	Traded With	Traded By	In Exchange For
May 3, 1952	WAS A	Spec Shea Jerry Snyder Archie Wilson	NY A	Irv Noren Tom Upton
Dec 9, 1953	BOS A	——	WAS A	Mickey McDermott Tommy Umphlett

Garry Jestadt

Date	Traded To	Traded With	Traded By	In Exchange For
May 19, 1971	SD N	——	CHI N	Chris Cannizzaro

John Jeter

Date	Traded To	Traded With	Traded By	In Exchange For
Aug 10, 1971	SD N	Ed Acosta	PIT N	Bob Miller
Oct 28, 1972	CHI A	——	SD N	Vicente Romo

Sam Jethroe

Date	Traded To	Traded With	Traded By	In Exchange For
Dec 26, 1953	PIT N	Sid Gordon Max Surkont Curt Raydon Fred Walters minor league P Larry Lasalle	MIL N	Danny O'Connell

Manny Jimenez

Date	Traded To	Traded With	Traded By	In Exchange For
Dec 15, 1961	KC A	——	MIL N	See Bob Shaw
Jan 15, 1969	CHI N	——	PIT N	Ron Campbell Chuck Hartenstein

Tommy John

Date	Traded To	Traded With	Traded By	In Exchange For
Jan 20, 1965	CHI A	Tommie Agee Johnny Romano	CLE A	Rocky Colavito Camilo Carreon
	(Part of three-team trade involving Kansas City, Cleveland, and Chicago White Sox.)			
Dec 2, 1971	LA N	Steve Huntz	CHI A	Dick Allen
Nov 21, 1978	NY A	——	LA N	No compensation (free agent signing)
Aug 31, 1982	CAL A	——	NY A	Dennis Rasmussen
May 2, 1986	NY A	——	OAK A	No compensation (free agent signing)

2419

Date	Traded To		Traded With	Traded By		In Exchange For

Adam Johnson

Date	Traded To		Traded With	Traded By		In Exchange For
Aug 20, 1914	CLE	A	Fritz Coumbe Ben Egan	BOS	A	Vean Gregg
Sept 1915	BAL	F	Jimmy Smith	CHI	F	Bill Bailey

Alex Johnson

Date	Traded To		Traded With	Traded By		In Exchange For
Oct 27, 1965	STL	N	Pat Corrales Art Mahaffey	PHI	N	Bill White Dick Groat Bob Uecker
Jan 11, 1968	CIN	N	——	STL	N	Dick Simpson
Nov 25, 1969	CAL	A	Chico Ruiz	CIN	N	Pedro Borbon Jim McGlothlin Vern Geishert
Oct 5, 1971	CLE	A	Gerry Moses	CAL	A	Vada Pinson Frank Baker Alan Foster
March 8, 1973	TEX	A	——	CLE	A	Rich Hinton Vince Colbert
Sept 9, 1974	NY	A	——	TEX	A	Cash

Ben Johnson

Date	Traded To		Traded With	Traded By		In Exchange For
Nov 10, 1957	CHI	N	Charlie King minor league OF Len Williams	MIL	N	Casey Wise

Bill Johnson

Date	Traded To		Traded With	Traded By		In Exchange For
May 22, 1983	CHI	N	Dick Ruthven	PHI	N	Guillermo Hernandez

Billy Johnson

Date	Traded To		Traded With	Traded By		In Exchange For
May 14, 1951	STL	N	——	NY	A	Don Bollweg and $15,000.

Bob Johnson

Date	Traded To		Traded With	Traded By		In Exchange For
Dec 3, 1969	KC	A	Amos Otis	NY	N	Joe Foy
Dec 2, 1970	PIT	N	——	KC	A	See Freddie Patek
Dec 7, 1973	CLE	A	——	PIT	N	Minor league OF Burnel Flowers
July 1, 1974	TEX	A	——	CLE	A	Cash

Bob Johnson

Date	Traded To		Traded With	Traded By		In Exchange For
March 21, 1943	WAS	A	——	PHI	A	Bobby Estalella and cash
Dec 4, 1943	BOS	A	——	WAS	A	Cash

Bob Johnson

Date	Traded To		Traded With	Traded By		In Exchange For
Dec 5, 1962	BAL	A	Pete Burnside	WAS	A	Barry Shetrone Marv Breeding and minor league P Art Quick
May 10, 1967	NY	N	——	BAL	A	Cash
Nov 8, 1967	CIN	N	——	NY	N	Art Shamsky
June 11, 1968	ATL	N	See Milt Pappas	CIN	N	——
March 25, 1969	STL	N	——	ATL	N	Dave Adlesh
July 12, 1969	OAK	N	——	STL	N	Joe Nossek

Cliff Johnson

Date	Traded To		Traded With	Traded By		In Exchange For
June 15, 1977	NY	A	——	HOU	N	Randy Niemann Mike Fischlin Dave Bergman

(Houston received Bergman on November 23.)

Date	Traded To		Traded With	Traded By		In Exchange For
June 15, 1979	CLE	A	——	NY	A	Don Hood
June 23, 1980	CHI	N	——	CLE	A	Karl Pagel and cash
Dec 11, 1980	OAK	A	Keith Drumright	CHI	N	Minor league P Mike King
Nov 5, 1982	TOR	A	——	OAK	A	Al Woods
Dec 4, 1984	TEX	A	——	TOR	A	Free agent signing

(Toronto selected Tom Henke from Texas as compensation.)

Cliff Johnson continued

Date	Traded To		Traded With	Traded By		In Exchange For
Aug 28, 1985	TOR	A	——	TEX	A	three players to be named

(Texas received Ps Matt Williams and Jeff Mays on August 29, and P Greg Ferlenda on November 14, 1985.)

Connie Johnson

Date	Traded To		Traded With	Traded By		In Exchange For
May 21, 1956	BAL	A	See George Kell	CHI	A	——

Darrell Johnson

Date	Traded To		Traded With	Traded By		In Exchange For
July 28, 1952	CHI	A	Jim Rivera	STL	A	J. W. Porter Ray Coleman
June 13, 1953	STL	A	Lou Kretlow and $75,000.	CHI	A	Virgil Trucks Bob Elliott
Dec 1, 1954	NY	A	See Dick Kryhoski	BAL	A	——
Aug 14, 1961	CIN	N	——	PHI	N	Cash

Dave Johnson

Date	Traded To		Traded With	Traded By		In Exchange For
Sept 29, 1976	SEA	A	——	BAL	A	Cash
May 2, 1977	MIN	A	——	SEA	A	Cash

Dave Johnson

Date	Traded To		Traded With	Traded By		In Exchange For
March 31, 1989	BAL	A	Minor league OF Victor Hithe	HOU	N	Carl Nichols

Davey Johnson

Date	Traded To		Traded With	Traded By		In Exchange For
Nov 30, 1972	ATL	N	Pat Dobson Roric Harrison Johnny Oates	BAL	A	Earl Williams Taylor Duncan
Aug 6, 1978	CHI	N	——	PHI	N	

Deron Johnson

Date	Traded To		Traded With	Traded By		In Exchange For
June 14, 1961	KC	A	Art Ditmar	NY	A	Bud Daley
Oct 10, 1967	ATL	N	——	CIN	N	Jim Beauchamp Mack Jones Jay Ritchie
Dec 3, 1968	PHI	N	——	ATL	N	Cash
May 2, 1973	OAK	A	——	PHI	N	Minor league UT Jack Bastable
June 24, 1974	MIL	A	——	OAK	A	Bill Parsons and cash
Sept 7, 1974	BOS	A	——	MIL	A	Cash
Sept 22, 1975	BOS	A	——	CHI	A	Minor league C Chuck Erickson and cash

Don Johnson

Date	Traded To		Traded With	Traded By		In Exchange For
June 15, 1950	STL	A	See Snuffy Stirnweiss	NY	A	——
May 29, 1951	WAS	A	——	STL	A	$12,500.
Dec 6, 1954	BAL	A	——	CHI	A	See Clint Courtney

Ernie Johnson

Date	Traded To		Traded With	Traded By		In Exchange For
Feb 10, 1916	STL	A	See Eddie Plank	STL	F	——
May 31, 1923	NY	A	——	CHI	A	Waiver price

Hank Johnson

Date	Traded To		Traded With	Traded By		In Exchange For
June 5, 1932	BOS	A	Ivy Andrews and $50,000.	NY	A	Danny MacFayden
Jan 4, 1936	PHI	A	Al Niemiec and $75,000.	BOS	A	Doc Cramer Eric McNair

Howard Johnson

Date	Traded To		Traded With	Traded By		In Exchange For
Dec 7, 1984	NY	N	——	DET	A	Walt Terrell

Date	Traded To	Traded With	Traded By	In Exchange For

Jerry Johnson

Date	Traded To		Traded With	Traded By		In Exchange For
Oct 7, 1969	STL	N	——	PHI	N	*See Curt Flood*
May 19, 1970	SF	N	——	STL	N	Frank Linzy
March 6, 1973	CLE	A	——	SF	N	Cash
Dec 3, 1973	HOU	N	——	CLE	A	Cecil Upshaw
Feb 16, 1977	TOR	A	——	SD	N	Dave Roberts

Joe Johnson

Date	Traded To		Traded With	Traded By		In Exchange For
July 6, 1986	TOR	A	——	ATL	N	Jim Acker

John Henry Johnson

Date	Traded To		Traded With	Traded By		In Exchange For
March 15, 1978	OAK	A	——	SF	N	*See Vida Blue*
June 15, 1979	TEX	A	——	OAK	A	Dave Chalk Mike Heath and cash
April 9, 1982	BOS	A	——	TEX	A	Mike Smithson

Johnny Johnson

Date	Traded To		Traded With	Traded By		In Exchange For
Dec 15, 1944	CHI	A	——	NY	A	Jake Wade

Ken Johnson

Date	Traded To		Traded With	Traded By		In Exchange For
July 21, 1961	CIN	N	——	KC	A	Cash
May 13, 1965	MIL	N	Jim Beauchamp	HOU	N	Lee Maye
June 10, 1969	NY	N	——	ATL	N	Cash
Aug 11, 1969	CHI	N	——	NY	A	Cash

Ken Johnson

Date	Traded To		Traded With	Traded By		In Exchange For
April 27, 1950	PHI	N	——	STL	N	Johnny Blatnik
March 21, 1952	DET	A	——	PHI	N	Waiver price

Lamar Johnson

Date	Traded To		Traded With	Traded By		In Exchange For
Jan 15, 1982	TEX	A	——	CHI	A	No compensation (free agent signing)

Lance Johnson

Date	Traded To		Traded With	Traded By		In Exchange For
Feb 9, 1988	CHI	A	Ricky Horton and cash	STL	N	Jose DeLeon

Lou Johnson

Date	Traded To		Traded With	Traded By		In Exchange For
April 1, 1961	LA	A	——	CHI	N	Jim McAnany
May 8, 1963	DET	A	Cash	MIL	N	Chico Fernandez
April 9, 1964	LA	N	$10,000.	DET	A	Larry Sherry
Nov 30, 1967	CHI	N	——	LA	N	Paul Popovich Jim Williams
June 28, 1968	CLE	A	——	CHI	N	Willie Smith
April 4, 1969	CAL	A	——	CLE	A	Chuck Hinton

Mike Johnson

Date	Traded To		Traded With	Traded By		In Exchange For
June 12, 1973	SD	N	Gene Locklear and cash	CIN	N	Fred Norman

Randy Johnson

Date	Traded To		Traded With	Traded By		In Exchange For
May 25, 1989	SEA	A	Brian Holman Gene Harris	MON	N	Mark Langston Mike Campbell

(Montreal received Campbell on July 31, 1989.)

Randy Johnson

Date	Traded To		Traded With	Traded By		In Exchange For
Aug 30, 1981	MIN	A	minor leaguers SS Ivan Mesa and 3B Ronnie Perry and cash	CHI	A	Jerry Koosman
Feb 19, 1985	CHI	A	Minor league OF Ron Scheer	MIN	A	Roy Smalley

Roy Johnson

Date	Traded To		Traded With	Traded By		In Exchange For
June 12, 1932	BOS	A	Dale Alexander	DET	A	Earl Webb
Dec 17, 1935	WAS	A	Carl Reynolds	BOS	A	Heinie Manush
Jan 17, 1936	NY	A	Bump Hadley	WAS	A	Jimmie DeShong Jesse Hill
May 11, 1937	BOS	N	——	NY	A	Waiver price

Si Johnson

Date	Traded To		Traded With	Traded By		In Exchange For
Aug 6, 1936	STL	N	——	CIN	N	Bill Walker
April 24, 1946	BOS	N	——	PHI	N	Cash

Stan Johnson

Date	Traded To		Traded With	Traded By		In Exchange For
June 10, 1961	KC	A	*See Wes Covington*	CHI	A	——

Syl Johnson

Date	Traded To		Traded With	Traded By		In Exchange For
Jan 11, 1934	CIN	N	Bob O'Farrell	STL	N	Glenn Spencer
	(O'Farrell was named Cincinnati manager.)					
May 16, 1934	PHI	N	Johnny Moore	CIN	N	Ted Kleinhans Wes Schulmerich Art Ruble

Tim Johnson

Date	Traded To		Traded With	Traded By		In Exchange For
April 24, 1973	MIL	A	——	LA	N	Cash
April 29, 1978	TOR	A	——	MIL	A	Tim Nordbrook

Vic Johnson

Date	Traded To		Traded With	Traded By		In Exchange For
Dec 12, 1945	CLE	A	Cash	BOS	A	Jim Bagby

Wallace Johnson

Date	Traded To		Traded With	Traded By		In Exchange For
May 25, 1983	SF	N	——	MON	N	Mike Vail

Doc Johnston

Date	Traded To		Traded With	Traded By		In Exchange For
Feb 22, 1915	PIT	N	——	CLE	A	$7,500.
Feb 16, 1922	PHI	A	——	CLE	A	Cash

Greg Johnston

Date	Traded To		Traded With	Traded By		In Exchange For
April 3, 1980	MIN	A	——	SF	N	Cash

Jimmy Johnston

Date	Traded To		Traded With	Traded By		In Exchange For
Oct 7, 1925	BOS	N	Zack Taylor Eddie Brown	BKN	N	Jesse Barnes Mickey O'Neil Gus Felix
July 1926	NY	N	——	BOS	N	Waiver price

Jay Johnstone

Date	Traded To		Traded With	Traded By		In Exchange For
Nov 30, 1970	CHI	A	Tom Egan Tom Bradley	CAL	A	Ken Berry Syd O'Brien Billy Wynne
Jan 9, 1974	STL	N	——	OAK	A	Cash
June 14, 1978	NY	A	Bobby Brown	PHI	N	Rawly Eastwick
June 15, 1979	SD	N	——	NY	A	Dave Wehrmeister
Dec 4, 1979	LA	N	——	SD	N	No compensation (free agent signing)

Stan Jok

Date	Traded To		Traded With	Traded By		In Exchange For
May 10, 1954	CHI	A	——	PHI	N	Waiver price

Smead Jolley

Date	Traded To		Traded With	Traded By		In Exchange For
April 29, 1932	BOS	A	Bennie Tate Cliff Watwood	CHI	A	Charlie Berry
Dec 14, 1933	STL	A	Ivy Andrews and cash	BOS	A	Carl Reynolds

Date	Traded To		Traded With	Traded By		In Exchange For

Dave Jolly

Date	Traded To		Traded With	Traded By		In Exchange For
Oct 15, 1957	NY	N	——	MIL	N	Waiver price

Al Jones

Date	Traded To		Traded With	Traded By		In Exchange For
July 23, 1986	MIL	A	——	CHI	A	*See Ray Searage*

Barry Jones

Date	Traded To		Traded With	Traded By		In Exchange For
Aug 13, 1988	CHI	A	——	PIT	N	Dave LaPoint
Aug 19, 1988	CHI	A	——	PIT	N	Gary Redus

Charlie Jones

Date	Traded To		Traded With	Traded By		In Exchange For
Oct 5, 1907	STL	A	——	WAS	A	Ollie Pickering

Clarence Jones

Date	Traded To		Traded With	Traded By		In Exchange For
Jan 9, 1969	CIN	N	Bill Plummer minor league P Ken Myette	CHI	N	Ted Abernathy

Dalton Jones

Date	Traded To		Traded With	Traded By		In Exchange For
Dec 13, 1969	DET	A	——	BOS	A	Tom Matchick
May 30, 1972	TEX	A	——	DET	A	Norm McRae

Davy Jones

Date	Traded To		Traded With	Traded By		In Exchange For
Dec 1912	CHI	A	——	DET	A	Cash

Gary Jones

Date	Traded To		Traded With	Traded By		In Exchange For
Dec 2, 1971	TEX	A	Terry Ley	NY	A	Bernie Allen
Dec 2, 1971	CLE	A	Del Unser Denny Riddleberger minor league P Terry Ley	TEX	A	Roy Foster Ken Suarez Mike Paul Rich Hand

Gordon Jones

Date	Traded To		Traded With	Traded By		In Exchange For
Oct 1, 1956	NY	N	——	STL	N	Cash
Nov 30, 1959	BAL	A	Jackie Brandt Roger McCardell	SF	N	Billy O'Dell Billy Loes

Jake Jones

Date	Traded To		Traded With	Traded By		In Exchange For
June 14, 1947	BOS	A	——	CHI	A	Rudy York

Jimmy Jones

Date	Traded To		Traded With	Traded By		In Exchange For
Oct 24, 1988	NY	A	Lance McCullers Stan Jefferson	SD	N	Jack Clark Pat Clements

Johnny Jones

Date	Traded To		Traded With	Traded By		In Exchange For
Aug 15, 1919	BOS	N	Joe Oeschger Red Causey Mickey O'Neil and $55,000.	NY	N	Art Nehf

Mack Jones

Date	Traded To		Traded With	Traded By		In Exchange For
Oct 10, 1967	CIN	N	Jim Beauchamp Jay Ritchie	ATL	N	Deron Johnson

Odell Jones

Date	Traded To		Traded With	Traded By		In Exchange For
Dec 5, 1978	SEA	A	Rafael Vasquez Mario Mendoza	PIT	N	Enrique Romo Rick Jones Tommy McMillan
April 1, 1980	PIT	N	——	SEA	A	Larry Andersen and cash

Percy Jones

Date	Traded To		Traded With	Traded By		In Exchange For
Nov 7, 1928	BOS	N	Socks Seibold Lou Legett Freddie Maguire Bruce Cunningham and $200,000.	CHI	N	Rogers Hornsby
April 9, 1930	PIT	N	Cash	BOS	N	Burleigh Grimes

Randy Jones

Date	Traded To		Traded With	Traded By		In Exchange For
Dec 15, 1980	NY	N	——	SD	N	John Pacella Jose Moreno

Rick Jones

Date	Traded To		Traded With	Traded By		In Exchange For
Dec 5, 1978	PIT	N	——	SEA	A	*See Mario Mendoza*

Ross Jones

Date	Traded To		Traded With	Traded By		In Exchange For
Dec 8, 1983	NY	N	Sid Fernandez	LA	N	Carlos Diaz Bob Bailor

Ruppert Jones

Date	Traded To		Traded With	Traded By		In Exchange For
Nov 1, 1979	NY	A	Jim Lewis	SEA	A	Jim Beattie Rick Anderson Juan Beniquez Jerry Narron
April 1, 1981	SD	N	Joe Lefebvre Tim Lollar Chris Welsh	NY	A	Jerry Mumphrey John Pacella
Jan 30, 1985	CAL	A	——	DET	A	No compensation (free agent signing)

Sad Sam Jones

Date	Traded To		Traded With	Traded By		In Exchange For
April 12, 1916	BOS	A	Fred Thomas and $55,000.	CLE	A	Tris Speaker
Dec 20, 1921	NY	A	Everett Scott Joe Bush	BOS	A	Roger Peckinpaugh Jack Quinn Rip Collins Bill Piercy
Feb 8, 1927	STL	A	——	NY	A	Cedric Durst Joe Giard
Sept 28, 1927	WAS	A	——	STL	A	Waiver price
Dec 4, 1931	CHI	A	Jackie Hayes Bump Hadley	WAS	A	Carl Reynolds John Kerr

Sam Jones

Date	Traded To		Traded With	Traded By		In Exchange For
Nov 16, 1954	CHI	N	Gale Wade and $60,000.	CLE	A	Ralph Kiner
Dec 11, 1956	STL	N	Hobie Landrith Jim Davis Eddie Miksis	CHI	N	Tom Poholsky Jackie Collum Ray Katt minor league P Wally Lammers
March 25, 1959	SF	N	Don Choate	STL	N	Bill White Ray Jablonski
Dec 1, 1961	DET	A	——	HOU	N	Bob Bruce Manny Montejo

Sheldon Jones

Date	Traded To		Traded With	Traded By		In Exchange For
April 8, 1952	BOS	N	$50,000.	NY	N	Bob Elliott
Dec 20, 1952	CHI	N	——	BOS	N	Monk Dubiel

Sherman Jones

Date	Traded To		Traded With	Traded By		In Exchange For
April 27, 1961	CIN	N	Bob Schmidt Don Blasingame	SF	N	Ed Bailey

Steve Jones

Date	Traded To		Traded With	Traded By		In Exchange For
Feb 13, 1968	WAS	A	*See Ron Hansen*	CHI	A	——

Date	Traded To	Traded With	Traded By	In Exchange For
Tim Jones				
March 29, 1978	MON N	——	PIT N	Will McEnaney
Tom Jones				
Aug 20, 1909	DET A	——	STL A	Claude Rossman
Tracy Jones				
July 13, 1988	MON N	Pat Pacillo	CIN N	Jeff Reed Herm Winningham Randy St. Claire
Dec 8, 1988	SF N	——	MON N	Mike Aldrete
June 16, 1989	DET A	——	SF N	Pat Sheridan
Willie Jones				
June 6, 1959	CLE A	——	PHI N	Jim Bolger and cash
July 1, 1959	CIN N	——	CLE A	Cash
Bubber Jonnard				
Dec 13, 1927	STL N	Johnny Mokan Jimmy Cooney	PHI N	Johnny Schulte Jimmy Ring
Eddie Joost				
Dec 4, 1942	BOS N	Nate Andrews and $25,000.	CIN N	Eddie Miller
Feb 5, 1946	STL N	$40,000.	BOS N	Johnny Hopp
Buck Jordan				
May 12, 1937	CIN N	——	BOS N	Cash
June 10, 1938	PHI N	——	CIN N	Justin Stein
Jimmy Jordan				
Dec 3, 1936	STL N	Frenchy Bordagaray Dutch Leonard	BKN N	Tom Winsett
Niles Jordan				
Dec 10, 1951	CIN N	——	PHI N	*See Smoky Burgess*
Tim Jordan				
May 1901	BAL A	——	WAS A	Cash
Tom Jordan				
June 1946	CLE A	——	CHI A	Frankie Hayes
Mike Jorgensen				
April 5, 1972	MON N	Tim Foli Ken Singleton	NY N	Rusty Staub
May 22, 1977	OAK A	——	MON N	Stan Bahnsen
Jan 21, 1978	TEX A	——	OAK A	No compensation (free agent signing)
Aug 12, 1979	NY N	Ed Lynch	TEX A	Willie Montanez
June 15, 1983	ATL N	——	NY N	$75,000.
June 15, 1984	STL N	Ken Dayley	ATL N	Ken Oberkfell
Duane Josephson				
March 31, 1971	BOS A	Danny Murphy	CHI A	Vicente Romo Tony Muser
Von Joshua				
Jan 29, 1975	SF N	——	LA N	Cash
June 2, 1976	MIL A	——	SF N	Cash
Dec 3, 1979	SD N	——	LA N	Cash

Date	Traded To	Traded With	Traded By	In Exchange For
Mike Joyce				
March 31, 1964	NY N	——	CHI A	Cash
Oscar Judd				
May 31, 1945	PHI N	——	BOS A	Waiver price
Ralph Judd				
May 15, 1930	STL N	——	NY N	Clarence Mitchell
Walt Judnich				
Jan 30, 1940	STL A	——	NY A	Cash
Nov 20, 1947	CLE A	Bob Muncrief	STL A	Dick Kokos Bryan Stephens Joe Frazier and $25,000.
Feb 9, 1949	PIT N	——	CLE A	Waiver price
Howie Judson				
Sept 1, 1952	CIN N	——	CHI A	Hank Edwards
(Cincinnati received Judson on December 9.)				
Bill Jurges				
Dec 6, 1938	NY N	Frank Demaree Ken O'Dea	CHI N	Dick Bartell Hank Leiber Gus Mancuso
Al Jurisich				
Feb 5, 1946	PHI N	——	STL N	Cash
Skip Jutze				
Nov 28, 1972	HOU N	Milt Ramirez	STL N	Ray Busse Bobby Fenwick
Jan 12, 1977	SEA A	——	HOU N	Minor league P Alan Griffin and cash
Jim Kaat				
Aug 15, 1973	CHI A	——	MIN A	Cash
Dec 10, 1975	PHI N	Mike Buskey	CHI A	Dick Ruthven Roy Thomas Alan Bannister
May 11, 1979	NY A	——	PHI N	Cash
April 30, 1980	STL N	——	NY A	Cash
Mike Kahoe				
April 1901	CHI N	Topsy Hartsel	CIN N	Cash
March 1905	PHI N	——	STL A	Cash
June 27, 1907	WAS A	——	CHI N	Cash
Al Kaiser				
June 10, 1911	BOS N	*See Johnny Kling*	CHI N	——
Don Kaiser				
Dec 5, 1957	MIL N	Eddie Haas Bob Rush	CHI N	Taylor Phillips Sammy Taylor
Oct 15, 1959	DET A	Mike Roarke Casey Wise	MIL N	Charlie Lau Don Lee
Jeff Kaiser				
Feb 23, 1987	CLE A	——	OAK A	Curt Wardle

2423

Date	Traded To		Traded With	Traded By		In Exchange For

Willie Kamm
| May 17, 1931 | CLE | A | ——— | CHI | A | Lew Fonseca |

Alex Kampouris
| June 6, 1938 | NY | N | ——— | CIN | N | Wally Berger |
| May 20, 1943 | WAS | A | ——— | BKN | N | Cash |

John Kane
| Jan 18, 1909 | CHI | N | ——— | CIN | N | Kid Durbin |
| | | | | | | Tom Downey |

Erv Kantlehner
| Sept 2, 1916 | PHI | N | ——— | PIT | N | Cash |

Ed Karger
June 3, 1906	STL	N	———	PIT	N	Cash
Dec 12, 1908	CIN	N	Art Fromme	STL	N	Admiral Schlei
June 1909	BOS	A	———	CIN	N	Waiver price

Andy Karl
| March 27, 1947 | BOS | N | ——— | PHI | N | Don Padgett |

Eddie Kasko
Oct 3, 1958	CIN	N	Bob Mabe	STL	N	George Crowe
			Del Ennis			Alex Kellner
						Alex Grammas
Jan 20, 1964	HOU	N	———	CIN	N	Jim Dickson
						Wally Wolf
						and cash
April 3, 1966	BOS	A	———	HOU	N	Felix Mantilla

John Katoll
| May 5, 1902 | BAL | A | Herm McFarland | CHI | A | Cash |

Ray Katt
June 14, 1956	STL	N	———	NY	N	*See Red Schoendienst*
Dec 11, 1956	CHI	N	*See Tom Poholsky*	STL	N	
April 16, 1957	NY	N	Ray Jablonski	CHI	N	Dick Littlefield
						Bob Lennon
April 2, 1958	STL	N	———	SF	N	Jim King

Benny Kauff
| Dec 23, 1915 | NY | N | ——— | BKN | F | $35,000. |

Curt Kaufman
| Dec 7, 1983 | CAL | A | Cash | NY | A | Tim Foli |

Tony Kaufmann
| June 7, 1927 | PHI | N | Jimmy Cooney | CHI | N | Hal Carlson |
| Sept 10, 1927 | STL | N | ——— | PHI | N | Cash |

Marty Kavanagh
May 1916	CLE	A	———	DET	A	Cash
June 1918	STL	A	———	CLE	A	Cash
Aug 1918	DET	A	———	STL	N	Cash

Eddie Kazak
| May 13, 1952 | CIN | N | Wally Westlake | STL | N | Dick Sisler |
| | | | | | | Virgil Stallcup |

Ted Kazanski
March 31, 1959	MIL	N	Stan Lopata	PHI	N	Gene Conley
			Johnny O'Brien			Joe Koppe
						Harry Hanebrink

Steve Kealey
| March 15, 1971 | CHI | A | ——— | CAL | A | Cash |
| Aug 29, 1973 | CIN | N | ——— | CHI | A | Jim McGlothlin |

Bob Kearney
| Nov 21, 1983 | SEA | A | Dave Beard | OAK | A | Bill Caudill |
| | | | | | | Darrel Akerfelds |

Ray Keating
| March 6, 1919 | BOS | N | ——— | NY | A | Cash |

Dave Keefe
| June 2, 1921 | CLE | A | ——— | PHI | A | Waiver price |

Vic Keen
| Dec 11, 1925 | STL | N | ——— | CHI | N | Jimmy Cooney |

Buster Keeton
| Oct 23, 1981 | HOU | N | ——— | MIL | A | Pete Ladd |

Bill Keister
| Feb 11, 1900 | STL | N | John McGraw | BAL | N | Cash |
| | | | Wilbert Robinson | | | |

Mike Kekich
| Dec 4, 1968 | NY | A | ——— | LA | N | Andy Kosco |
| June 12, 1973 | CLE | A | ——— | NY | A | Lowell Palmer |

George Kell
May 18, 1946	DET	A	———	PHI	A	Barney McCosky
June 3, 1952	BOS	A	Dizzy Trout	DET	A	Walt Dropo
			Johnny Lipon			Bill Wight
			Hoot Evers			Fred Hatfield
						Johnny Pesky
						Don Lenhardt
May 23, 1954	CHI	A	———	BOS	A	Grady Hatton
						and $100,000.
May 21, 1956	BAL	A	Bob Nieman	CHI	A	Jim Wilson
			Mike Fornieles			Dave Philley
			Connie Johnson			

Frankie Kelleher
| July 16, 1942 | CIN | N | ——— | NY | A | Jim Turner |

John Kelleher
| Dec 13, 1923 | BOS | N | ——— | CHI | N | Cash |

Mick Kelleher
Oct 23, 1973	HOU	N	———	STL	N	Cash
Dec 13, 1974	STL	N	———	HOU	N	Cash
Dec 22, 1975	CHI	N	———	STL	N	Vic Harris
April 1, 1981	DET	A	———	CHI	N	Cash
April 21, 1982	CAL	A	———	DET	A	Cash

Frank Kellert
| March 17, 1955 | BKN | N | Cash | BAL | A | Erv Palica |
| Oct 11, 1955 | CHI | N | ——— | BKN | N | Waiver price |

Date	Traded To	Traded With	Traded By	In Exchange For

Harry Kelley

Date	Traded To	Traded With	Traded By	In Exchange For
May 4, 1938	WAS A ———		PHI A	Waiver price

Alex Kellner

Date	Traded To	Traded With	Traded By	In Exchange For
June 23, 1958	CIN N		KC A	Waiver price
Oct 3, 1958	STL N	George Crowe Alex Grammas	CIN N	Bob Mabe Eddie Kasko Del Ennis

Win Kellum

Date	Traded To	Traded With	Traded By	In Exchange For
Feb 1905	STL N ———		CIN N	Cash

Bill Kelly

Date	Traded To	Traded With	Traded By	In Exchange For
Jan 1911	PIT N ———		STL N	Cash

Bob Kelly

Date	Traded To	Traded With	Traded By	In Exchange For
June 12, 1953	CIN N	Fred Baczewski	CHI N	Bubba Church
April 23, 1958	CLE A ———		CIN N	Fred Hatfield

Bryan Kelly

Date	Traded To	Traded With	Traded By	In Exchange For
June 22, 1987	SEA A ———		DET A	Karl Best

Dale Kelly

Date	Traded To	Traded With	Traded By	In Exchange For
Dec 8, 1977	TOR A	Butch Alberts	CAL A	Ron Fairly

George Kelly

Date	Traded To	Traded With	Traded By	In Exchange For
July 25, 1917	PIT N ———		NY N	Waiver price
Aug 4, 1917	NY N ———		PIT N	Waiver price
Feb 9, 1927	CIN N	Cash	NY N	Edd Roush

Joe Kelly

Date	Traded To	Traded With	Traded By	In Exchange For
Dec 14, 1916	BOS N ———		CHI N	Fred Mitchell

Mike Kelly

Date	Traded To	Traded With	Traded By	In Exchange For
Jan 1900	PIT N	See Honus Wagner	LOU N ———	

Pat Kelly

Date	Traded To	Traded With	Traded By	In Exchange For
Oct 13, 1970	CHI A	Don O'Riley	KC A	Gail Hopkins John Matias
Nov 18, 1976	BAL A ———		CHI A	Dave Duncan
Dec 29, 1980	CLE A ———		BAL A	No compensation (free agent signing)

Van Kelly

Date	Traded To	Traded With	Traded By	In Exchange For
June 12, 1969	SD N	Walt Hriniak minor league OF Andy Finlay	ATL N	Tony Gonzalez

Bill Kelso

Date	Traded To	Traded With	Traded By	In Exchange For
Nov 29, 1967	CIN N	Jorge Rubio	CAL A	Sammy Ellis
March 18, 1969	BOS A ———		CIN N	Cash
	(Kelso was returned to Cincinnati on March 29.)			

Russ Kemmerer

Date	Traded To	Traded With	Traded By	In Exchange For
April 29, 1957	WAS A	Milt Bolling Faye Throneberry	BOS A	Dean Stone Bob Chakales
May 18, 1960	CHI A ———		WAS A	Cash
June 22, 1962	HOU N ———		CHI A	Dean Stone

Steve Kemp

Date	Traded To	Traded With	Traded By	In Exchange For
Nov 27, 1981	CHI A ———		DET A	Chet Lemon

Steve Kemp *continued*

Date	Traded To	Traded With	Traded By	In Exchange For
Dec 9, 1982	NY A ———		CHI A	
	(Chicago claimed P Steve Mura from St. Louis as compensation.)			
Dec 20, 1984	PIT N	Tim Foli and $400,000.	NY A	Dale Berra Jay Buhner

Fred Kendall

Date	Traded To	Traded With	Traded By	In Exchange For
Dec 8, 1976	CLE A	Johnny Grubb Hector Torres	SD N	George Hendrick
March 30, 1978	BOS A	See Dennis Eckersley	CLE A ———	

Bill Kennedy

Date	Traded To	Traded With	Traded By	In Exchange For
June 15, 1948	STL A	$100,000.	CLE A	Sam Zoldak
March 13, 1952	CHI A ———		STL A	Cash
Feb 9, 1953	BOS A	Hal Brown Marv Grissom	CHI A	Vern Stephens

Bob Kennedy

Date	Traded To	Traded With	Traded By	In Exchange For
June 2, 1948	CLE A ———		CHI A	Al Gettel Pat Seerey
April 17, 1954	BAL A ———		CLE A	Jim Dyck
May 30, 1955	CHI A ———		BAL A	Cash
May 15, 1956	DET A	Jim Brideweser Harry Byrd	CHI A	Fred Hatfield Jim Delsing
May 20, 1957	BKN N ———		CHI A	Cash

Brickyard Kennedy

Date	Traded To	Traded With	Traded By	In Exchange For
Jan 1903	PIT N ———		NY N	Cash

Jim Kennedy

Date	Traded To	Traded With	Traded By	In Exchange For
Oct 20, 1970	MIN A	Sal Campisi	STL N	Herman Hill minor league OF Charlie Wissler

John Kennedy

Date	Traded To	Traded With	Traded By	In Exchange For
Dec 4, 1964	LA N ———		WAS A	See Frank Howard
April 3, 1967	NY A ———		LA N	Jack Cullen John Miller and $25,000.
Nov 13, 1968	SEA A ———		NY A	Cash
June 26, 1970	BOS A ———		MIL A	Cash

Junior Kennedy

Date	Traded To	Traded With	Traded By	In Exchange For
Dec 4, 1973	CIN N	Merv Rettenmund and minor league C Bill Wood	BAL A	Ross Grimsley and minor league C Wally Williams
Oct 20, 1977	CIN N ———		SF N	Cash
Oct 23, 1981	CHI N ———		CIN N	$50,000.

Terry Kennedy

Date	Traded To	Traded With	Traded By	In Exchange For
Dec 8, 1980	SD N	Steve Swisher Mike Phillips John Littlefield John Urrea Kim Seaman Al Olmsted	STL N	Rollie Fingers Bob Shirley Gene Tenace minor league C Bob Geren
Oct 30, 1986	BAL A	Mark Williamson	SD N	Storm Davis
Jan 24, 1989	SF N ———		BAL A	Bob Melvin

Vern Kennedy

Date	Traded To	Traded With	Traded By	In Exchange For
Dec 2, 1937	DET A	Tony Piet Dixie Walker	CHI A	Marv Owen Mike Tresh Gee Walker
May 13, 1939	STL A	Bob Harris George Gill Roxie Lawson Chet Laabs Mark Christman	DET A	Beau Bell Bobo Newsom Red Kress Jim Walkup

2425

Date	Traded To	Traded With	Traded By	In Exchange For

Vern Kennedy *continued*

Date	Traded To	Traded With	Traded By	In Exchange For
May 15, 1941	WAS A ———		STL A	Rick Ferrell
Dec 11, 1941	CLE A ———		WAS A	Cash
July 28, 1944	PHI N ———		CLE A	Cash

Jerry Kenney

Nov 27, 1972	CLE A ———		NY A	*See Graig Nettles*

Joe Keough

Feb 1, 1973	CHI A ———		KC A	Jim Lyttle

Marty Keough

June 13, 1960	CLE A	Ted Bowsfield	BOS A	Russ Nixon / Carroll Hardy
Dec 15, 1961	CIN N	Johnny Klippstein	WAS A	Dave Stenhouse / Bob Schmidt
April 4, 1966	ATL N ———		CIN N	Cash and minor league player to later
May 29, 1966	CHI N ———		ATL N	John Herrnstein

Matt Keough

June 15, 1983	NY A ———		OAK A	Ben Callahan / Marshall Brant / and cash
Feb 1, 1986	CHI N ———		STL N	No compensation (free agent signing)

Gus Keriazakos

June 11, 1954	WAS A ———		CHI A	Sonny Dixon

Bill Kerksieck

June 15, 1939	BOS N ———		PHI N	Cash

Jim Kern

Oct 3, 1978	TEX A	Larvell Blanks	CLE A	Bobby Bonds / Len Barker
Dec 11, 1981	NY N ———		TEX A	Doug Flynn / Danny Boitano
Feb 10, 1982	CIN N	Alex Trevino / Greg Harris	NY N	George Foster
Aug 23, 1982	CHI A ———		CIN N	Wade Rowdon / Leo Garcia

George Kernek

Oct 13, 1967	CHI A ———		STL N	Cash

Buddy Kerr

Dec 14, 1949	BOS N	Sid Gordon / Willard Marshall / Red Webb	NY N	Eddie Stanky / Alvin Dark

Doc Kerr

Aug 1914	BAL F ———		PIT F	Medric Boucher

John Kerr

Dec 4, 1931	WAS A	Carl Reynolds	CHI A	Jackie Hayes / Bump Hadley / Sad Sam Jones

Joe Kerrigan

Dec 7, 1977	BAL A	Don Stanhouse / Gary Roenicke	MON N	Rudy May / Randy Miller / Bryn Smith

Don Kessinger

Oct 28, 1975	STL N ———		CHI N	Mike Garman / minor league / IF Bobby Hrapmann
Aug 20, 1977	CHI A ———		STL N	Minor league / P Steve Staniland

Steve Kiefer

March 30, 1986	MIL A	Charlie O'Brien / Minor league / P Mike Fulmer / Minor league / P Pete Kendrick	OAK A	Moose Haas

Leo Kiely

Jan 8, 1960	CLE A ———		BOS A	Ray Webster
April 5, 1960	KC A ———		CLE A	Bob Grim

Pete Kilduff

July 31, 1917	CHI N ———		NY N	Al Demaree
June 2, 1919	BKN N ———		CHI N	Lee Magee

Paul Kilgus

Dec 5, 1988	CHI N	Mitch Williams / Steve Wilson / Curtis Wilkerson / Minor league / IF Luis Benitez / Minor league / OF Pablo Delgado	TEX A	Rafael Palmeiro / Jamie Moyer / Drew Hall
Dec 7, 1989	TOR A ———		CHI N	Jose Nunez

Mike Kilkenny

May 9, 1972	OAK A ———		DET A	Reggie Sanders
May 17, 1972	SD N	Curt Blefary / minor league / OF Greg Schubert	OAK A	Ollie Brown
June 11, 1972	CLE A ———		SD N	Fred Stanley

Bill Killefer

Dec 11, 1917	CHI N	Grover Alexander	PHI N	Mike Prendergast / Pickles Dillhoefer / and $55,000.

Red Killefer

Aug 13, 1909	WAS A	Germany Schaefer	DET A	Jim Delahanty
July 20, 1916	NY N	Buck Herzog	CIN N	Christy Mathewson / Edd Roush / Bill McKechnie

Frank Killen

Unknown	CHI N ———		BOS N	Cash

Ed Killian

Jan 1904	DET A	Jesse Stovall	CLE A	Billy Lush

Newt Kimball

Dec 8, 1939	BKN N	Gus Mancuso	CHI N	Al Todd
Sept 1940	STL N ———		BKN N	Cash
		(Sale was cancelled by Commissioner Landis.)		
May 20, 1943	PHI N ———		BKN N	Cash

Bruce Kimm

Aug 17, 1972	CAL A	Bruce Miller	CHI A	Eddie Fisher
Aug 30, 1979	CHI N ———		DET A	Cash

Date	Traded To	Traded With	Traded By	In Exchange For

Chad Kimsey

| Sept 9, 1932 | CHI | A | —— | STL | A | Cash |

Jerry Kindall

| Nov 27, 1961 | CLE | A | —— | CHI | N | Larry Locke |
| June 11, 1964 | LA | A | —— | CLE | A | Billy Moran |

(Part of three-team trade involving Los Angeles Angels, Cleveland, and Minnesota.)

| June 11, 1964 | MIN | A | Frank Kostro | LA | A | Lenny Green |
| | | | | | | Vic Power |

(Part of three-team trade involving Los Angeles Angels, Minnesota, and Cleveland.)

Ellis Kinder

Nov 18, 1947	BOS	A	Billy Hitchcock	STL	A	Sam Dente
						Clem Dreisewerd
						Bill Sommers
						and $65,000.
Dec 4, 1955	STL	N	——	BOS	A	Waiver price
July 11, 1956	CHI	A	——	STL	N	Waiver price

Ralph Kiner

June 4, 1953	CHI	N	Joe Garagiola	PIT	N	Toby Atwell
			Howie Pollet			Bob Schultz
			Catfish Metkovich			Preston Ward
						George Freese
						Bob Addis
						Gene Hermanski
						$150,000.
Nov 16, 1954	CLE	A	——	CHI	N	Sam Jones
						Gale Wade
						and $60,000.

Charlie King

Feb 12, 1957	MIL	N	Cash	DET	A	Jack Dittmer
Nov 10, 1957	CHI	N	Ben Johnson	MIL	N	Casey Wise
			minor league			
			OF Len Williams			
May 19, 1959	STL	N	——	CHI	N	Irv Noren

Clyde King

| Oct 10, 1952 | CIN | N | —— | BKN | N | Cash |

Eric King

| Oct 7, 1985 | DET | A | *See Dave LaPoint* | SF | N | —— |
| March 23, 1989 | CHI | A | —— | DET | A | Ken Williams |

Hal King

Dec 2, 1971	TEX	A	——	ATL	N	Paul Casanova
Dec 1, 1972	CIN	N	Minor leaguer	TEX	A	Jim Merritt
			Jim Driscoll			

Jim King

April 20, 1957	STL	N	——	CHI	N	Ed Mayer
						Bobby Del Greco
April 2, 1958	SF	N	——	STL	N	Ray Katt
June 15, 1967	CHI	A	——	WAS	A	Ed Stroud
July 29, 1967	CLE	A	Marv Staehle	CHI	A	Rocky Colavito

Lee King

July 1, 1921	PHI	N	Goldie Rapp	NY	N	Casey Stengel
			Lance Richbourg			Johnny Rawlings
						Red Causey
July 1921	PHI	N	——	NY	N	Waiver price

Lee King

| Jan 1919 | NY | N | —— | PIT | N | Cash |

Mike Kingery

| Dec 10, 1986 | SEA | A | Scott Bankhead | KC | A | Danny Tartabull |
| | | | Steve Shields | | | Rick Luecken |

Brian Kingman

| Jan 17, 1983 | BOS | A | —— | OAK | A | Cash |

Dave Kingman

Feb 28, 1975	NY	N	——	SF	N	$150,000.
June 15, 1977	SD	N	——	NY	N	Bobby Valentine
						Paul Siebert
Sept 6, 1977	CAL	A	——	SD	N	Cash
Sept 15, 1977	NY	A	——	CAL	A	Cash
Nov 30, 1977	CHI	N	——	NY	A	No compensation
						(free agent signing)
Feb 28, 1981	NY	N	——	CHI	N	Steve Henderson
						and cash

Dennis Kinney

| June 14, 1978 | SD | N | —— | CLE | A | Dan Spillner |
| Dec 12, 1980 | DET | A | —— | SD | N | Dave Stegman |

Mike Kinnunen

| Jan 7, 1985 | KC | A | Minor League | MON | N | Mike Young |
| | | | OF Ken Baker | | | |

Matt Kinzer

Dec 6, 1989	DET	A	Jim Lindeman	STL	N	Minor league
						2B Pat Austin
						Minor league
						C Bill Henderson
						Minor league
						P Marcos Betances

Fred Kipp

April 5, 1960	NY	A	——	LA	N	Gordie Windhorn
						minor league
						1B Dick Sanders

Bob Kipper

| Aug 2, 1985 | PIT | N | —— | CAL | A | *See John Candelaria* |

Clay Kirby

Nov 9, 1973	CIN	N	——	SD	N	Bobby Tolan
						Dave Tomlin
Dec 12, 1975	MON	N	——	CIN	N	Bob Bailey

Willie Kirkland

Dec 3, 1960	CLE	A	Johnny Antonelli	SF	N	Harvey Kuenn
Dec 4, 1963	BAL	A	——	CLE	A	Al Smith
						and $25,000.
Aug 12, 1964	WAS	A	——	BAL	A	Cash

Ed Kirkpatrick

Dec 12, 1968	KC	A	Dennis Paepke	CAL	A	Hoyt Wilhelm
Dec 4, 1973	PIT	N	Kurt Bevacqua	KC	A	Nellie Briles
			minor league			Fernando Gonzalez
			1B Winston Cole			
June 15, 1977	TEX	A	——	PIT	N	Jim Fregosi
Aug 20, 1977	MIL	A	——	TEX	A	Gorman Thomas

Don Kirkwood

June 15, 1977	CHI	A	John Verhoeven	CAL	A	Ken Brett
			John Flannery			
April 11, 1978	TOR	A	——	CHI	A	Cash

Bruce Kison

Date	Traded To		Traded With	Traded By		In Exchange For
Nov 16, 1979	CAL	A	———	PIT	N	No compensation (free agent signing)
Jan 14, 1985	BOS	A	———	CAL	A	No compensation (free agent signing)

Frank Kitson

Date	Traded To		Traded With	Traded By		In Exchange For
Jan 1900	BKN	N	Jimmy Sheckard, Jerry Nops, Broadway Aleck Smith, Harry Howell, Joe McGinnity	BAL	N	Cash
Dec 1905	WAS	A	———	DET	A	Cash
July 1907	NY	A	———	WAS	A	Cash

Ron Kittle

Date	Traded To		Traded With	Traded By		In Exchange For
July 30, 1986	NY	A	Joel Skinner, Wayne Tolleson	CHI	A	Ron Hassey, Carlos Martinez, Bill Lindsey

(Chicago received Lindsey on Dec. 24, 1986.)

Date	Traded To		Traded With	Traded By		In Exchange For
Feb 9, 1988	CLE	A	———	NY	A	No compensation (free agent signing)
Nov 26, 1988	CHI	A	———	CLE	A	No compensation (free agent signing)

Mal Kittridge

Date	Traded To		Traded With	Traded By		In Exchange For
June 1903	WAS	A	———	BOS	N	Cash
Aug 15, 1906	CLE	A	———	WAS	A	Cash

Billy Klaus

Date	Traded To		Traded With	Traded By		In Exchange For
Feb 1, 1954	NY	N	See Johnny Antonelli	MIL	N	———
Dec 14, 1954	BOS	A	———	NY	N	Del Wilber
Dec 15, 1958	BAL	A	———	BOS	A	Jim Busby
April 5, 1962	PHI	N	———	WAS	A	Cash

Bobby Klaus

Date	Traded To		Traded With	Traded By		In Exchange For
July 19, 1964	NY	N	———	CIN	N	Cash
Feb 22, 1966	PHI	N	Jimmie Schaffer, Wayne Graham	NY	N	Dick Stuart
March 28, 1969	PIT	N	Ron Davis	SD	N	Chris Cannizzaro, Tommie Sisk

Chuck Klein

Date	Traded To		Traded With	Traded By		In Exchange For
Nov 21, 1933	CHI	N	———	PHI	N	Ted Kleinhans, Mark Koenig, Harvey Hendrick and $65,000.
May 21, 1936	PHI	N	Fabian Kowalik	CHI	N	Ethan Allen, Curt Davis

Lou Klein

Date	Traded To		Traded With	Traded By		In Exchange For
Dec 14, 1949	CIN	N	Ron Northey	STL	N	Harry Walker
May 10, 1951	PHI	A	Allie Clark	CLE	A	Sam Chapman

Ted Kleinhans

Date	Traded To		Traded With	Traded By		In Exchange For
Nov 21, 1933	PHI	N	Mark Koenig, Harvey Hendrick and $65,000.	CHI	N	Chuck Klein
May 16, 1934	CIN	N	Wes Schulmerich, Art Ruble	PHI	N	Syl Johnson, Johnny Moore

Red Kleinow

Date	Traded To		Traded With	Traded By		In Exchange For
May 1910	BOS	A	———	NY	A	Cash
June 1911	PHI	N	———	BOS	A	Waiver price

Ed Klepfer

Date	Traded To		Traded With	Traded By		In Exchange For
Aug 21, 1915	CLE	A	Braggo Roth, Larry Chappell and $31,500.	CHI	A	Joe Jackson

Eddie Klieman

Date	Traded To		Traded With	Traded By		In Exchange For
Dec 14, 1948	WAS	A	Joe Haynes, Eddie Robinson	CLE	A	Mickey Vernon, Early Wynn
May 3, 1949	NY	A	———	WAS	A	Waiver price
May 16, 1949	CHI	A	———	NY	A	Cash
Dec 14, 1949	PHI	A	———	CHI	A	Hank Majeski

Lou Klimchock

Date	Traded To		Traded With	Traded By		In Exchange For
Dec 15, 1961	MIL	N	See Bob Shaw	KC	A	———

Ron Klimkowski

Date	Traded To		Traded With	Traded By		In Exchange For
Aug 3, 1967	NY	A	Pete Magrini	BOS	A	Elston Howard
April 9, 1971	OAK	A	Rob Gardner	NY	A	Felipe Alou

Bob Kline

Date	Traded To		Traded With	Traded By		In Exchange For
Dec 12, 1933	PHI	A	Rabbit Warstler and $125,000.	BOS	A	Lefty Grove, Rube Walberg, Max Bishop
June 23, 1934	WAS	A	———	PHI	A	Cash

Bobby Kline

Date	Traded To		Traded With	Traded By		In Exchange For
Feb 8, 1956	NY	A	———	WAS	A	See Whitey Herzog

Ron Kline

Date	Traded To		Traded With	Traded By		In Exchange For
Dec 21, 1959	STL	N	———	PIT	N	Gino Cimoli, Tom Cheney
April 10, 1961	LA	A	———	STL	N	Cash
Aug 10, 1961	DET	A	———	LA	A	Waiver price
March 18, 1963	WAS	A	———	DET	A	Cash
Dec 3, 1966	MIN	A	———	WAS	A	Bernie Allen, Camilo Pascual
Dec 2, 1967	PIT	N	———	MIN	A	Bob Oliver
June 10, 1969	SF	N	———	PIT	N	Joe Gibbon
July 5, 1969	BOS	A	———	SF	N	Cash

Steve Kline

Date	Traded To		Traded With	Traded By		In Exchange For
April 27, 1974	CLE	A	———	NY	A	See Chris Chambliss
Dec 13, 1976	ATL	N	———	CLE	A	Cash

Johnny Kling

Date	Traded To		Traded With	Traded By		In Exchange For
June 10, 1911	BOS	N	Al Kaiser, Orlie Weaver, Hank Griffin	CHI	N	Cliff Curtis, Wilbur Good, Bill Collins, Peaches Graham
Feb 1913	CIN	N	———	BOS	N	Cash

Joe Klink

Date	Traded To		Traded With	Traded By		In Exchange For
Jan 16, 1986	MIN	N	Billy Beane, Bill Latham	NY	N	Tim Teufel, Minor league OF Pat Crosby

Johnny Klippstein

Date	Traded To		Traded With	Traded By		In Exchange For
Oct 1, 1954	CIN	N	Jim Willis	CHI	N	Ted Tappe, Harry Perkowski, Jim Bolger
June 15, 1958	LA	N	Steve Bilko	CIN	N	Don Newcombe
April 11, 1960	CLE	A	———	LA	N	$25,000.
Dec 15, 1961	CIN	N	Marty Keough	WAS	A	Dave Stenhouse, Bob Schmidt
March 25, 1963	PHI	N	———	CIN	N	Cash
June 29, 1964	MIN	A	———	PHI	N	Cash

Date	Traded To		Traded With	Traded By		In Exchange For

Ted Kluszewski

Date	Traded To		Traded With	Traded By		In Exchange For
Dec 28, 1957	PIT	N	——	CIN	N	Dee Fondy
Aug 25, 1959	CHI	A	——	PIT	N	Harry Simpson minor league IF Bob Sagers

Mickey Klutts

Date	Traded To		Traded With	Traded By		In Exchange For
June 15, 1978	OAK	A	Dell Alston and $50,000.	NY	A	Gary Thomasson

Clyde Kluttz

Date	Traded To		Traded With	Traded By		In Exchange For
June 16, 1945	NY	N	——	BOS	N	Ewald Pyle Joe Medwick
May 1, 1946	PHI	N	——	NY	N	Vince DiMaggio
May 2, 1946	STL	N	——	PHI	N	Emil Verban
Dec 26, 1946	PIT	N	——	STL	N	Cash
June 12, 1951	WAS	A	——	STL	A	Waiver price

Otto Knabe

Date	Traded To		Traded With	Traded By		In Exchange For
Feb 10, 1916	PIT	N	Jimmy Smith	BAL	F	Cash
July 29, 1916	CHI	N	Art Wilson	PIT	N	Wildfire Schulte Bill Fischer

Chris Knapp

Date	Traded To		Traded With	Traded By		In Exchange For
Dec 5, 1977	CAL	A	*See Brian Downing*	CHI	A	——

Bob Knepper

Date	Traded To		Traded With	Traded By		In Exchange For
Dec 8, 1980	HOU	N	Chris Bourjos	SF	N	Enos Cabell

Lou Knerr

Date	Traded To		Traded With	Traded By		In Exchange For
Feb 14, 1947	WAS	A	——	PHI	A	George Binks

Elmer Knetzer

Date	Traded To		Traded With	Traded By		In Exchange For
Feb 10, 1916	BOS	N	Frank Allen	PIT	F	Cash
April 1916	CIN	N	——	BOS	N	Cash

Alan Knicely

Date	Traded To		Traded With	Traded By		In Exchange For
March 31, 1983	CIN	N	——	HOU	N	Bill Dawley Tony Walker
Aug 8, 1985	PHI	N	——	CIN	N	*See Bo Diaz*

Bill Knickerbocker

Date	Traded To		Traded With	Traded By		In Exchange For
Jan 17, 1937	STL	A	Joe Vosmik Oral Hildebrand	CLE	A	Ivy Andrews Lyn Lary Moose Solters
Feb 15, 1938	NY	A	——	STL	A	Don Heffner and $10,000.
Dec 31, 1940	CHI	A	——	NY	A	Ken Silvestri
April 3, 1942	PHI	A	——	CHI	A	Waiver price

Jack Knight

Date	Traded To		Traded With	Traded By		In Exchange For
June 7, 1907	BOS	A	——	PHI	A	Jimmy Collins

John Knight

Date	Traded To		Traded With	Traded By		In Exchange For
Feb 1909	NY	A	——	BOS	A	Waiver price
Dec 1911	WAS	A	Roxy Roach	NY	A	Gabby Street Jack Lelivelt
July 7, 1913	NY	A	——	WAS	A	Cash

Ray Knight

Date	Traded To		Traded With	Traded By		In Exchange For
Dec 18, 1981	HOU	N	——	CIN	N	Cesar Cedeno

Ray Knight *continued*

Date	Traded To		Traded With	Traded By		In Exchange For
Aug 28, 1984	NY	N	——	HOU	N	Gerald Young Manny Lee Minor league P Mitch Cook
Feb 11, 1987	BAL	A	——	NY	N	No compensation (free agent signing)
Feb 27, 1988	DET	A	——	BAL	A	Mark Thurmond

Pete Knisely

Date	Traded To		Traded With	Traded By		In Exchange For
Dec 15, 1912	CHI	N	——	CIN	N	*See Joe Tinker*

Bobby Knoop

Date	Traded To		Traded With	Traded By		In Exchange For
May 14, 1969	CHI	A	——	CAL	A	Sandy Alomar Bob Priddy
March 24, 1971	KC	A	——	CHI	A	Luis Alcaraz and cash

Fritz Knothe

Date	Traded To		Traded With	Traded By		In Exchange For
June 17, 1933	PHI	N	Wes Schulmerich and cash	BOS	N	Hal Lee Pinky Whitney

Jack Knott

Date	Traded To		Traded With	Traded By		In Exchange For
June 11, 1938	CHI	A	——	STL	A	Billy Cox
Dec 16, 1940	PHI	A	——	CHI	A	Dario Lodigiani

Darold Knowles

Date	Traded To		Traded With	Traded By		In Exchange For
Dec 6, 1965	PHI	N	Jackie Brandt	BAL	A	Jack Baldschun
Nov 30, 1966	WAS	A	Cash	PHI	N	Don Lock
May 8, 1971	OAK	A	Mike Epstein	WAS	A	Frank Fernandez Don Mincher Paul Lindblad and cash
Oct 23, 1974	CHI	N	Bob Locker Manny Trillo	OAK	A	Billy Williams
Feb 5, 1977	TEX	A	——	CHI	N	Gene Clines and cash
Nov 10, 1977	MON	N	——	TEX	A	Cash
Jan 16, 1979	STL	N	——	MON	N	No compensation (free agent signing)

Mark Knudson

Date	Traded To		Traded With	Traded By		In Exchange For
Aug 19, 1986	MIL	A	——	HOU	N	*See Danny Darwin*

Kevin Kobel

Date	Traded To		Traded With	Traded By		In Exchange For
June 17, 1980	KC	A	——	NY	N	Randy McGilberry

Alan Koch

Date	Traded To		Traded With	Traded By		In Exchange For
May 9, 1964	WAS	A	——	DET	A	Cash

Pete Koegel

Date	Traded To		Traded With	Traded By		In Exchange For
Aug 29, 1969	SEA	A	Bob Meyer	OAK	A	Fred Talbot
April 22, 1971	PHI	N	Ray Peters	MIL	A	John Briggs

Mark Koenig

Date	Traded To		Traded With	Traded By		In Exchange For
May 30, 1930	DET	A	Waite Hoyt	NY	A	Ownie Carroll Yats Wuestling Harry Rice
Nov 21, 1933	PHI	N	Ted Kleinhans Harvey Hendrick and $65,000.	CHI	N	Chuck Klein
Dec 20, 1933	CIN	N	——	PHI	N	Otto Bluege Irv Jeffries
Dec 14, 1934	NY	N	Allyn Stout	CIN	N	Billy Myers and cash

Date	Traded To	Traded With	Traded By	In Exchange For
Elmer Koestner				
Aug 1914	CIN N	———	CHI N	Johnny Bates
Dick Kokos				
Nov 20, 1947	STL A	Bryan Stephens Joe Frazier and $25,000.	CLE A	Bob Muncrief Walt Judnich
Gary Kolb				
April 9, 1964	MIL N	Jimmie Coker	STL N	Bob Uecker
July 21, 1965	NY N	———	MIL N	Jesse Gonder
Dec 6, 1966	PIT N	Dennis Ribant	NY N	Don Bosch Don Cardwell
Don Kolloway				
May 7, 1949	DET A	———	CHI A	Vern Rapp
Jan 29, 1953	PHI A	———	DET A	Billy Hitchcock
Fred Kommers				
Aug 1914	BAL F	———	STL F	Cash
Brad Komminsk				
Jan 19, 1987	MIL A	———	ATL N	Dion James
Ed Konetchy				
Dec 12, 1913	PIT N	Mike Mowrey Bob Harmon	STL N	Art Butler Dots Miller Cozy Dolan Owen Wilson Hank Robinson
Feb 10, 1916	BOS N	———	PIT N	Cash
April 14, 1919	BKN N	———	BOS N	Cash
July 4, 1921	PHI N	———	BKN N	Waiver price
Jim Konstanty				
April 18, 1946	BOS N	Cash	CIN N	Max West
Aug 22, 1954	NY A	———	PHI N	Cash
Cal Koonce				
Aug 2, 1967	NY N	———	CHI N	Cash
June 8, 1970	BOS A	———	NY N	Cash
Jerry Koosman				
Dec 8, 1978	MIN A	———	NY N	Jesse Orosco minor league P Greg Field
Aug 30, 1981	CHI A	———	MIN A	Randy Johnson minor leaguers SS Ivan Mesa and 3B Ronnie Perry and cash
Dec 5, 1983	PHI N	———	CHI A	Ron Reed
Larry Kopf				
Dec 1915	CIN N	———	PHI A	Cash
Feb 18, 1922	CIN N	Jack Scott	BOS N	Rube Marquard
Merlin Kopp				
Dec 14, 1917	PHI A	Vean Gregg Pinch Thomas and $60,000.	BOS A	Amos Strunk Joe Bush Wally Schang
Joe Koppe				
March 31, 1959	PHI N	Gene Conley Harry Hanebrink	MIL N	Stan Lopata Ted Kazanski Johnny O'Brien
May 4, 1961	LA N	Dick Farrell	PHI N	Don Demeter Charley Smith
Andy Kosco				
Dec 4, 1968	LA N	———	NY A	Mike Kekich
Feb 10, 1971	MIL A	———	LA N	Al Downing
Jan 26, 1972	CAL A	———	MIL A	Tommie Reynolds
Aug 15, 1972	BOS A	———	CAL A	Chris Coletta
March 27, 1973	CIN N	Phil Gagliano	BOS A	Mel Behney
Dave Koslo				
April 8, 1954	BAL A	———	NY N	Cash
Frank Kostro				
June 15, 1963	LA A	Paul Foytack	DET A	George Thomas and cash
June 11, 1964	MIN A	Jerry Kindall	LA A	Lenny Green Vic Power
(Part of three-team trade involving Los Angeles Angels, Minnesota, and Cleveland.)				
Lou Koupal				
July 24, 1929	PHI N	———	BKN N	Luther Roy
Fabian Kowalik				
May 21, 1936	PHI N	Chuck Klein	CHI N	Ethan Allen Curt Davis
Aug 4, 1936	BOS N	———	PHI N	Ray Benge
Ernie Koy				
April 15, 1938	BKN N	———	NY A	Cash
June 12, 1940	STL N	Carl Doyle Sam Nahem Bert Haas and $125,000.	BKN N	Joe Medwick Curt Davis
May 14, 1941	CIN N	———	STL N	Cash
May 2, 1942	PHI N	———	CIN N	Cash
Al Kozar				
Dec 10, 1947	WAS A	Leon Culberson	BOS A	Stan Spence
May 31, 1950	CHI A	*See Eddie Robinson*	WAS A	———
Joe Krakauskas				
Dec 24, 1940	CLE A	———	WAS A	Ben Chapman
Jack Kralick				
May 2, 1963	CLE A	———	MIN A	Jim Perry
May 1, 1967	NY N	———	CLE A	Cash
Jack Kramer				
Nov 17, 1947	BOS A	Vern Stephens	STL A	Roy Partee Jim Wilson Al Widmar Eddie Pellagrini Pete Layden Joe Ostrowski and $310,000.
March 26, 1950	NY N	———	BOS A	Cash
Tex Kraus				
March 24, 1943	PHI N	Cash	BKN N	Bobby Bragan

Date	Traded To		Traded With	Traded By		In Exchange For

Harry Krause
Date	Traded To		Traded With	Traded By		In Exchange For
July 1912	CLE	A	——	PHI	A	Cash

Lew Krausse
Date	Traded To		Traded With	Traded By		In Exchange For
Dec 13, 1938	CIN	N	Cash	BKN	N	Jimmy Outlaw

Lew Krausse
Date	Traded To		Traded With	Traded By		In Exchange For
Jan 15, 1970	MIL	A	——	OAK	A	*See Don Mincher*
Oct 11, 1971	BOS	A	——	MIL	A	*See George Scott*
Sept 1, 1973	STL	N	Larry Haney	OAK	A	Cash

Ken Kravec
Date	Traded To		Traded With	Traded By		In Exchange For
March 28, 1981	CHI	N	——	CHI	A	Dennis Lamp

Danny Kravitz
Date	Traded To		Traded With	Traded By		In Exchange For
June 1, 1960	KC	A	——	PIT	N	Hank Foiles Cash

Mike Kreevich
Date	Traded To		Traded With	Traded By		In Exchange For
Dec 9, 1941	PHI	A	Jack Hallett	CHI	A	Wally Moses
Aug 8, 1945	WAS	A	——	STL	A	Waiver price

Jim Kremmel
Date	Traded To		Traded With	Traded By		In Exchange For
July 16, 1973	STL	N	——	TEX	A	Don Durham
Oct 26, 1973	CHI	A	——	STL	N	Denny O'Toole
Dec 11, 1973	CHI	N	Steve Stone Ken Frailing Steve Swisher	CHI	A	Ron Santo

Wayne Krenchicki
Date	Traded To		Traded With	Traded By		In Exchange For
Feb 9, 1982	CIN	N	——	BAL	A	Paul Moskau
June 30, 1983	DET	A	——	CIN	N	Pat Underwood
Nov 21, 1983	CIN	N	——	DET	A	Cash
March 31, 1986	MON	N	——	CIN	N	Norm Charlton Minor league 2B Tim Barker

Charlie Kress
Date	Traded To		Traded With	Traded By		In Exchange For
June 8, 1949	CHI	A	——	CIN	N	Cash
June 9, 1954	BKN	N	Johnny Bucha Ernie Nevel and cash	DET	A	Wayne Belardi

Red Kress
Date	Traded To		Traded With	Traded By		In Exchange For
April 27, 1932	CHI	A	——	STL	A	Bruce Campbell Bump Hadley
May 12, 1934	WAS	A	——	CHI	A	Bob Boken
Dec 2, 1937	STL	A	Bobo Newsom Buster Mills	BOS	A	Joe Vosmik
May 13, 1939	DET	A	Beau Bell Bobo Newsom Jim Walkup	STL	A	Vern Kennedy Bob Harris George Gill Roxie Lawson Chet Laabs Mark Christman

Lou Kretlow
Date	Traded To		Traded With	Traded By		In Exchange For
Dec 14, 1949	STL	A	$100,000.	DET	A	Gerry Priddy
July 5, 1950	CHI	A	——	STL	A	Waiver price
June 13, 1953	STL	A	Darrell Johnson and $75,000.	CHI	A	Virgil Trucks Bob Elliott

Rick Kreuger
Date	Traded To		Traded With	Traded By		In Exchange For
March 24, 1978	CLE	A	——	BOS	A	Frank Duffy

Frank Kreutzer
Date	Traded To		Traded With	Traded By		In Exchange For
July 13, 1964	WAS	A	Joe Cunningham	CHI	A	Bill Skowron Carl Bouldin
May 17, 1969	PIT	N	——	WAS	A	Jim Shellenback

Gary Kroll
Date	Traded To		Traded With	Traded By		In Exchange For
Aug 7, 1964	NY	N	Wayne Graham and cash	PHI	N	Frank Thomas
Jan 6, 1966	HOU	N	——	NY	N	Johnny Weekly and cash
July 20, 1967	CLE	A	——	HOU	N	Cash

John Kroner
Date	Traded To		Traded With	Traded By		In Exchange For
Dec 1936	CLE	A	——	BOS	A	Cash

Rocky Krsnich
Date	Traded To		Traded With	Traded By		In Exchange For
Dec 10, 1953	CIN	N	Saul Rogovin Connie Ryan	CHI	A	Willard Marshall

Bill Krueger
Date	Traded To		Traded With	Traded By		In Exchange For
Oct 3, 1988	LA	N	——	PIT	N	Minor league P Jim Neidlinger

Ernie Krueger
Date	Traded To		Traded With	Traded By		In Exchange For
May 1917	BKN	N	——	NY	N	Waiver price
Feb 17, 1922	CIN	N	——	BKN	N	Cash

Otto Krueger
Date	Traded To		Traded With	Traded By		In Exchange For
Jan 1900	STL	N	Jack Harper Joe Quinn Jim Hughey	CLE	N	Cash
Jan 1903	PIT	N	——	STL	N	Jimmy Burke
Dec 20, 1904	PHI	N	Kitty Bransfield Moose McCormick	PIT	N	Del Howard
Jan 1905	PHI	N	——	PIT	N	Waiver price

Art Kruger
Date	Traded To		Traded With	Traded By		In Exchange For
Sept 1910	BOS	N	——	CLE	A	Cash

John Kruk
Date	Traded To		Traded With	Traded By		In Exchange For
June 2, 1989	PHI	N	Randy Ready	SD	N	Chris James

Mike Krukow
Date	Traded To		Traded With	Traded By		In Exchange For
Dec 8, 1981	PHI	N	Cash	CHI	N	Keith Moreland Dan Larson Dickie Noles
Dec 14, 1982	SF	N	Mark Davis minor league OF Charles Penigar	PHI	N	Joe Morgan Al Holland

Dick Kryhoski
Date	Traded To		Traded With	Traded By		In Exchange For
Dec 17, 1949	DET	A	——	NY	A	Dick Wakefield
Feb 14, 1952	STL	A	*See Gene Bearden*	DET	A	
Dec 1, 1954	NY	A	Mike Blyzka Darrell Johnson Jim Fridley	BAL	A	Bill Miller Kal Segrist Don Leppert minor league OF Ted Del Guercio and a player to be named later

(Second part of 18-player trade begun on November 18, 1954; see Bob Turley.)

Date	Traded To		Traded With	Traded By		In Exchange For
March 30, 1955	KC	A	Ewell Blackwell Tom Gorman	NY	A	$50,000.

Date	Traded To	Traded With	Traded By	In Exchange For

Ted Kubiak

Date	Traded To		Traded With	Traded By		In Exchange For
Dec 7, 1969	SEA	A	George Lauzerique	OAK	A	Diego Segui
						Ray Oyler
July 29, 1971	STL	N	minor league	MIL	A	Jose Cardenal
			P Charlie Loseth			Dick Schofield
						Bob Reynolds
Nov 3, 1971	TEX	A	——	STL	N	Joe Grzenda
July 20, 1972	OAK	A	Don Mincher	TEX	A	Marty Martinez
						Vic Harris
						Steve Lawson
May 16, 1975	SD	N	——	OAK	A	Sonny Siebert

Jack Kubiszyn

Date	Traded To		Traded With	Traded By		In Exchange For
Dec 15, 1962	STL	N	Ron Taylor	CLE	A	Fred Whitfield

Gil Kubski

Date	Traded To		Traded With	Traded By		In Exchange For
May 10, 1981	MIL	A	——	TOR	A	Buck Martinez

Jack Kucek

Date	Traded To		Traded With	Traded By		In Exchange For
April 13, 1979	PHI	N	——	CHI	A	Jim Morrison

Johnny Kucks

Date	Traded To		Traded With	Traded By		In Exchange For
May 26, 1959	KC	A	Tom Sturdivant	NY	A	Hector Lopez
			Jerry Lumpe			Ralph Terry
Oct 11, 1961	BAL	A	——	KC	A	Cash
Dec 1, 1961	STL	N	——	BAL	A	Minor leaguer
						Ron Kabbes

Harvey Kuenn

Date	Traded To		Traded With	Traded By		In Exchange For
April 17, 1960	CLE	A	——	DET	A	Rocky Colavito
Dec 3, 1960	SF	N	——	CLE	A	Johnny Antonelli
						Willie Kirkland
May 29, 1965	CHI	N	Ed Bailey	SF	N	Dick Bertell
			Bob Hendley			Len Gabrielson
April 23, 1966	PHI	N	——	CHI	N	Cash

Joe Kuhel

Date	Traded To		Traded With	Traded By		In Exchange For
March 18, 1938	CHI	A	——	WAS	A	Zeke Bonura
Nov 24, 1943	WAS	A	——	CHI	A	Cash
June 13, 1946	CHI	A	——	WAS	A	Cash

Duane Kuiper

Date	Traded To		Traded With	Traded By		In Exchange For
Nov 14, 1981	SF	N	——	CLE	A	Ed Whitson

Rusty Kuntz

Date	Traded To		Traded With	Traded By		In Exchange For
June 21, 1983	MIN	A	——	CHI	A	Minor league
						IF Mike Sodders
Dec 8, 1983	DET	A	——	MIN	A	Larry Pashnick

Craig Kusick

Date	Traded To		Traded With	Traded By		In Exchange For
July 25, 1979	TOR	A	——	MIN	A	Cash

Art Kusnyer

Date	Traded To		Traded With	Traded By		In Exchange For
Oct 22, 1973	MIL	A	See Clyde Wright	CAL	A	——

Randy Kutcher

Date	Traded To		Traded With	Traded By		In Exchange For
Sept 1, 1987	BOS	A	——	SF	N	Dave Henderson

Marty Kutyna

Date	Traded To		Traded With	Traded By		In Exchange For
Dec 5, 1957	CIN	N	Ted Wieand	STL	N	Curt Flood
			Willard Schmidt			Joe Taylor
Dec 29, 1960	WAS	A	Cash	KC	A	Haywood Sullivan

Bob Kuzava

Date	Traded To		Traded With	Traded By		In Exchange For
Dec 2, 1948	CHI	A	Ernie Groth	CLE	A	Frank Papish
May 31, 1950	WAS	A	Cass Michaels	CHI	A	Al Kozar
			John Ostrowski			Ray Scarborough
						Eddie Robinson
June 15, 1951	NY	A	——	WAS	A	Fred Sanford
						Tom Ferrick
						Bob Porterfield
Aug 7, 1954	BAL	A	——	NY	A	Waiver price
May 23, 1955	PHI	N	——	BAL	A	Waiver price

Chet Laabs

Date	Traded To		Traded With	Traded By		In Exchange For
May 13, 1939	STL	A	Vern Kennedy	DET	A	Beau Bell
			Bob Harris			Bobo Newsom
			George Gill			Red Kress
			Roxie Lawson			Jim Walkup
			Mark Christman			
April 9, 1947	PHI	A	——	STL	A	Cash

Clem Labine

Date	Traded To		Traded With	Traded By		In Exchange For
June 15, 1960	DET	A	——	LA	N	Ray Semproch
						and cash

Bob Lacey

Date	Traded To		Traded With	Traded By		In Exchange For
March 27, 1981	SD	N	minor league	OAK	A	Kevin Bell
			P Ray Moretti			Tony Phillips
						minor league
						P Eric Mustard
April 1, 1981	CLE	A	——	SD	N	Juan Bonilla
Sept 8, 1981	TEX	A	——	CLE	A	Cash

Candy LaChance

Date	Traded To		Traded With	Traded By		In Exchange For
May 30, 1902	BOS	A	——	CLE	A	Piano Legs Hickman

George LaClaire

Date	Traded To		Traded With	Traded By		In Exchange For
June 15, 1915	BUF	F	——	PIT	F	Cash
June 30, 1915	BAL	F	——	BUF	F	Cash

Pete LaCock

Date	Traded To		Traded With	Traded By		In Exchange For
Dec 8, 1976	KC	A	——	CHI	N	Sheldon Mallory

(Part of three-team trade involving Kansas City, Chicago Cubs, and New York Mets.)

Frank LaCorte

Date	Traded To		Traded With	Traded By		In Exchange For
May 25, 1979	HOU	N	——	ATL	N	Bo McLaughlin
Dec 8, 1983	CAL	A	——	HOU	N	No compensation
						(free agent signing)

Mike LaCoss

Date	Traded To		Traded With	Traded By		In Exchange For
April 6, 1982	HOU	N	——	CIN	N	Cash
Feb 19, 1985	KC	A	——	HOU	N	No compensation
						(free agent signing)

Lee Lacy

Date	Traded To		Traded With	Traded By		In Exchange For
Nov 17, 1975	ATL	N	Jimmy Wynn	LA	N	Dusty Baker
			Tom Paciorek			Ed Goodson
			Jerry Royster			
June 23, 1976	LA	N	Elias Sosa	ATL	N	Mike Marshall
Jan 18, 1979	PIT	N	——	LA	N	No compensation
						(free agent signing)
Dec 7, 1984	BAL	A	——	PIT	N	No compensation
						(free agent signing)

Pete Ladd

Date	Traded To		Traded With	Traded By		In Exchange For
June 13, 1979	HOU	N	Bobby Sprowl	BOS	A	Bob Watson
			and cash			
Oct 23, 1981	MIL	A	——	HOU	N	Buster Keeton

Date	Traded To		Traded With		Traded By		In Exchange For

Ed Lafitte

Date	Traded To		Traded With	Traded By		In Exchange For
July 1915	BUF	F	Ed Gagnier	BKN	F	Fred Smith

Mike Laga

Date	Traded To		Traded With	Traded By		In Exchange For
Aug 10, 1986	STL	N	Ken Hill	DET	A	Mike Heath

(St. Louis received Laga on Sept. 2, 1986.)

Lerrin LaGrow

Date	Traded To		Traded With	Traded By		In Exchange For
April 2, 1976	STL	N	——	DET	A	Cash
March 23, 1977	CHI	A	——	STL	N	Clay Carroll
May 11, 1979	LA	N	——	CHI	A	Cash
Jan 31, 1980	PHI	N	——	LA	N	No compensation (free agent signing)

Joe Lahoud

Date	Traded To		Traded With	Traded By		In Exchange For
Oct 11, 1971	MIL	A	See George Scott	BOS	A	——
Oct 22, 1973	CAL	A	——	MIL	A	See Clyde Wright
June 15, 1976	TEX	A	——	CAL	A	Cash

Jeff Lahti

Date	Traded To		Traded With	Traded By		In Exchange For
April 1, 1982	STL	N	minor league P Jose Brito	CIN	N	Bob Shirley

Nap Lajoie

Date	Traded To		Traded With	Traded By		In Exchange For
June 1902	CLE	A	——	PHI	A	Cash
Jan 1915	PHI	A	——	CLE	A	Waiver price

Eddie Lake

Date	Traded To		Traded With	Traded By		In Exchange For
Jan 3, 1946	DET	A	——	BOS	A	Rudy York

Joe Lake

Date	Traded To		Traded With	Traded By		In Exchange For
Dec 1909	STL	A	——	NY	A	Lou Criger
May 1912	DET	A	——	STL	A	Cash

Steve Lake

Date	Traded To		Traded With	Traded By		In Exchange For
April 1, 1983	CHI	N	——	MIL	A	Minor league P Rich Buonantony and cash
Dec 16, 1988	PHI	N	Curt Ford	STL	N	Milt Thompson

Al Lakeman

Date	Traded To		Traded With	Traded By		In Exchange For
June 14, 1947	PHI	N	——	CIN	N	Ken Raffensberger Hugh Poland

Jack Lamabe

Date	Traded To		Traded With	Traded By		In Exchange For
Nov 20, 1962	BOS	A	Dick Stuart	PIT	N	Jim Pagliaroni Don Schwall
Sept 14, 1965	HOU	N	——	BOS	A	Darrell Brandon
Dec 1, 1965	CHI	A	minor league P Ray Cordeiro and cash	HOU	N	Dave Nicholson Bill Heath
April 26, 1967	NY	N	——	CHI	A	Cash
July 16, 1967	STL	N	——	NY	N	Al Jackson
April 22, 1968	CHI	N	Ron Piche	STL	N	Pete Mikkelsen Dave Dowling
June 11, 1969	MON	N	Adolfo Phillips	CHI	N	Paul Popovich

Al LaMacchia

Date	Traded To		Traded With	Traded By		In Exchange For
June 15, 1946	WAS	A	Joe Grace	STL	A	Jeff Heath

Bill Lamar

Date	Traded To		Traded With	Traded By		In Exchange For
May 1919	BOS	A	——	NY	A	Cash
March 1920	BKN	N	——	BOS	A	Cash

Wayne LaMaster

Date	Traded To		Traded With	Traded By		In Exchange For
Aug 8, 1938	BKN	N	——	PHI	N	Max Butcher

Ray Lamb

Date	Traded To		Traded With	Traded By		In Exchange For
Dec 11, 1970	CLE	A	Alan Foster	LA	N	Duke Sims

Gene Lamont

Date	Traded To		Traded With	Traded By		In Exchange For
May 14, 1973	ATL	N	——	DET	A	Bob Didier

Bobby LaMotte

Date	Traded To		Traded With	Traded By		In Exchange For
Jan 15, 1927	DET	A	See Marty McManus	STL	A	——

Dennis Lamp

Date	Traded To		Traded With	Traded By		In Exchange For
March 28, 1981	CHI	A	——	CHI	N	Ken Kravec
Jan 10, 1984	TOR	A	——	CHI	N	Free agent signing

(Chicago selected Tom Seaver from the New York Mets as compensation.)

Date	Traded To		Traded With	Traded By		In Exchange For
Feb 5, 1987	CLE	A	——	TOR	A	No compensation (free agent signing)

Gary Lance

Date	Traded To		Traded With	Traded By		In Exchange For
June 5, 1978	SEA	A	——	KC	A	Minor league P Steve Hamrick

Rick Lancellotti

Date	Traded To		Traded With	Traded By		In Exchange For
Aug 5, 1980	SD	N	Luis Salazar	PIT	N	Kurt Bevacqua Mark Lee
Oct 7, 1982	MON	N	——	SD	N	Cash
March 31, 1985	NY	N	——	SD	N	Rusty Tillman

Rafael Landestoy

Date	Traded To		Traded With	Traded By		In Exchange For
July 1, 1978	HOU	N	Jeffrey Leonard	LA	N	Joe Ferguson and cash
June 8, 1981	CIN	N	——	HOU	N	Harry Spilman
May 9, 1983	LA	N	——	CIN	N	John Franco minor league P Brett Wise

Jim Landis

Date	Traded To		Traded With	Traded By		In Exchange For
Jan 20, 1965	KC	A	Mike Hershberger Fred Talbot	CHI	A	Rocky Colavito

(Part of three-team trade involving Kansas City, Cleveland, and the Chicago White Sox.)

Date	Traded To		Traded With	Traded By		In Exchange For
Dec 1, 1965	CLE	A	Jim Rittwage	KC	A	Phil Roof Joe Rudi
Jan 4, 1967	HOU	N	Jim Weaver Doc Edwards	CLE	A	Lee Maye Ken Retzer
June 29, 1967	DET	A	——	HOU	N	Larry Sherry

Ken Landreaux

Date	Traded To		Traded With	Traded By		In Exchange For
Feb 3, 1979	MIN	A	Dave Engle Paul Hartzell Brad Havens	CAL	A	Rod Carew
March 30, 1981	LA	N	——	MIN	A	Mickey Hatcher and minor leaguers P Matt Reeves and 1B Kelly Snider

Larry Landreth

Date	Traded To		Traded With	Traded By		In Exchange For
May 20, 1978	LA	N	Gerald Hannahs	MON	N	Mike Garman

Hobie Landrith

Date	Traded To		Traded With	Traded By		In Exchange For
Nov 28, 1955	CHI	N	——	CIN	N	Hal Jeffcoat
Dec 11, 1956	STL	N	——	CHI	N	See Tom Poholsky

Date	Traded To		Traded With	Traded By		In Exchange For

Hobie Landrith *continued*

Date	Traded To		Traded With	Traded By		In Exchange For
Oct 8, 1958	SF	N	Billy Muffett Benny Valenzuela	STL	N	Ernie Broglio Marv Grissom
May 9, 1962	BAL	A	Cash	NY	N	Marv Throneberry
May 8, 1963	WAS	A	———	BAL	A	Cash

Bill Landrum

April 1, 1988	CIN	N	———	CHI	N	Luis Quintana

Don Landrum

June 5, 1962	CHI	N	Alex Grammas	STL	N	Bobby Gene Smith Daryl Robertson
Dec 2, 1965	SF	N	———	CHI	N	*See Randy Hundley*

Tito Landrum

June 15, 1983	BAL	A	———	STL	N	Floyd Rayford
March 25, 1984	STL	N	———	BAL	A	Minor league P Jose Brito

Don Lang

Dec 30, 1940	NY	A	$20,000.	CIN	N	Monte Pearson

Rick Langford

March 15, 1977	OAK	A	———	PIT	N	*See Phil Garner*

Mark Langston

May 25, 1989	MON	N	Mike Campbell	SEA	A	Randy Johnson Brian Holman Gene Harris

(Montreal received Campbell on July 31, 1989.)

Dec 1, 1989	CAL	A	———	MON	N	No compensation (free agent signing)

Hal Lanier

Feb 2, 1972	NY	A	———	SF	N	Cash

Max Lanier

Dec 11, 1951	NY	N	Chuck Diering	STL	N	Eddie Stanky

(Stanky was named St. Louis manager.)

Johnny Lanning

Dec 6, 1939	PIT	N	———	BOS	N	Jim Tobin and cash

Carney Lansford

Dec 10, 1980	BOS	A	Rick Miller Mark Clear	CAL	A	Rick Burleson Butch Hobson
Dec 6, 1982	OAK	A	Garry Hancock minor league P Jerry King	BOS	A	Tony Armas Jeff Newman

Paul LaPalme

Jan 11, 1955	STL	N	———	PIT	N	Ben Wade and cash
May 1, 1956	CIN	N	———	STL	N	Milt Smith
June 22, 1956	CHI	A	———	CIN	N	Waiver price

Dave LaPoint

Dec 12, 1980	STL	N	Sixto Lezcano David Green Lary Sorensen	MIL	A	Pete Vuckovich Rollie Fingers Ted Simmons
Feb 1, 1985	SF	N	David Green Jose Uribe Gary Rajsich	STL	N	Jack Clark

Dave LaPoint *continued*

Date	Traded To		Traded With	Traded By		In Exchange For
Oct 7, 1985	DET	A	Matt Nokes Eric King	SF	N	Juan Berenguer Bob Melvin Scott Medvin

(San Francisco received Medvin on Dec. 11, 1985.)

July 9, 1986	SD	N	———	DET	A	Mark Thurmond
July 30, 1987	CHI	A	———	STL	N	Minor league P Bryce Hulstrom
Aug 13, 1988	PIT	N	———	CHI	A	Barry Jones
Dec 3, 1988	NY	A	———	PIT	N	No compensation (free agent signing)

Ralph LaPointe

April 7, 1948	STL	N	$30,000.	PHI	N	Dick Sisler

Frank LaPorte

Dec 1907	BOS	A	———	NY	A	Cash
Aug 17, 1908	NY	A	———	BOS	A	Harry Niles
Jan 1911	STL	A	Jimmy Austin	NY	A	Roy Hartzell
July 1912	WAS	A	———	STL	A	Cash

Jack Lapp

Jan 7, 1916	CHI	A	———	PHI	A	Cash

Norm Larker

Nov 30, 1962	MIL	N	———	HOU	N	Connie Grob Jim Bolger
Aug 8, 1963	SF	N	———	MIL	N	Cash

Dave LaRoche

Nov 30, 1971	MIN	A	———	CAL	A	Leo Cardenas
Nov 30, 1972	CHI	N	———	MIN	A	Bill Hands Joe Decker minor league P Bob Maneely
Feb 25, 1975	CLE	A	Brock Davis	CHI	N	Milt Wilcox
May 11, 1977	CAL	A	Dave Schuler	CLE	A	Bruce Bochte Sid Monge and $250,000.

Don Larsen

Nov 18, 1954	NY	A	Bob Turley Billy Hunter	BAL	A	Harry Byrd Jim McDonald Hal Smith Gus Triandos Gene Woodling Willie Miranda

(First part of 18-player trade completed on December 1, 1954; see Dick Kryhoski.)

Dec 11, 1959	KC	A	Hank Bauer Norm Siebern Marv Throneberry	NY	A	Roger Maris Joe DeMaestri Kent Hadley
June 10, 1961	CHI	A	Ray Herbert Andy Carey Al Pilarcik	KC	A	Wes Covington Bob Shaw Gerry Staley Stan Johnson
Nov 30, 1961	SF	N	Billy Pierce	CHI	A	Eddie Fisher Dom Zanni Verle Tiefenthaler Bob Farley
May 20, 1964	HOU	N	———	SF	N	Cash
April 24, 1965	BAL	A	———	HOU	N	Bob Saverine and cash

Dan Larson

Aug 15, 1974	HOU	N	Minor league P Ron Selak	STL	N	Claude Osteen
Dec 8, 1981	CHI	N	Keith Moreland Dickie Noles	PHI	N	Mike Krukow and cash

Date	Traded To		Traded With	Traded By		In Exchange For

Tony LaRussa

Date	Traded To		Traded With	Traded By		In Exchange For
Aug 14, 1971	ATL	N	———	OAK	A	Cash
Oct 20, 1972	CHI	N	———	ATL	N	Tom Phoebus

Frank Lary

Date	Traded To		Traded With	Traded By		In Exchange For
May 30, 1964	NY	N	———	DET	A	Cash
Aug 8, 1964	MIL	N	———	NY	N	Dennis Ribant and cash
March 20, 1965	NY	N	———	MIL	N	Cash
July 8, 1965	CHI	A	———	NY	N	Jimmie Schaffer

Lyn Lary

Date	Traded To		Traded With	Traded By		In Exchange For
May 15, 1934	BOS	A	———	NY	A	Freddie Muller and $20,000.
Oct 26, 1934	WAS	A	$225,000.	BOS	A	Joe Cronin
June 29, 1935	STL	A	———	WAS	A	Alan Strange
Jan 17, 1937	CLE	A	Ivy Andrews Moose Solters	STL	A	Bill Knickerbocker Joe Vosmik Oral Hildebrand
May 3, 1939	BKN	N	———	CLE	A	Cash
Aug 14, 1939	STL	N	———	BKN	N	Waiver price

Fred Lasher

Date	Traded To		Traded With	Traded By		In Exchange For
May 22, 1970	CLE	A	———	DET	A	Russ Nagelson Billy Rohr

Bill Laskey

Date	Traded To		Traded With	Traded By		In Exchange For
Dec 11, 1981	SF	N	Rich Gale	KC	A	Jerry Martin
Oct 24, 1985	SF	N	———	MON	N	Alonzo Powell George Riley

Bill Latham

Date	Traded To		Traded With	Traded By		In Exchange For
Jan 16, 1986	MIN	A	Billy Beane Joe Klink	NY	N	Tim Teufel Minor league OF Pat Crosby

Tacks Latimer

Date	Traded To		Traded With	Traded By		In Exchange For
Jan 1900	PIT	N	*See Honus Wagner*	LOU	N	———

Barry Latman

Date	Traded To		Traded With	Traded By		In Exchange For
April 18, 1960	CLE	A	———	CHI	A	Herb Score
Dec 2, 1963	LA	A	Joe Adcock	CLE	A	Leon Wagner
Dec 15, 1965	HOU	N	———	CAL	A	Minor league C Ed Pacheco and cash

Charlie Lau

Date	Traded To		Traded With	Traded By		In Exchange For
Oct 15, 1959	MIL	N	Don Lee	DET	A	Don Kaiser Mike Roarke Casey Wise
July 1, 1963	KC	A	———	BAL	A	Cash
June 15, 1964	BAL	A	———	KC	A	Wes Stock
May 31, 1967	ATL	N	———	BAL	A	Cash

George Lauzerique

Date	Traded To		Traded With	Traded By		In Exchange For
Dec 7, 1969	SEA	A	Ted Kubiak	OAK	A	Diego Segui Ray Oyler
Oct 20, 1970	STL	N	Jerry McNertney minor league P Jesse Higgins	MIL	A	Carl Taylor Jim Ellis

Cookie Lavagetto

Date	Traded To		Traded With	Traded By		In Exchange For
Dec 4, 1936	BKN	N	Ralph Birkofer	PIT	N	Ed Brandt

Mike LaValliere

Date	Traded To		Traded With	Traded By		In Exchange For
April 1, 1987	PIT	N	———	STL	N	*See Tony Pena*

Doc Lavan

Date	Traded To		Traded With	Traded By		In Exchange For
Aug 24, 1913	PHI	A	———	STL	A	Cash
Feb 5, 1914	STL	A	———	PHI	A	Cash
Dec 15, 1917	WAS	A	Burt Shotton	STL	A	Bert Gallia and $15,000.
Jan 1919	STL	N	———	WAS	A	Cash

Gary Lavelle

Date	Traded To		Traded With	Traded By		In Exchange For
Jan 26, 1985	TOR	A	———	SF	N	Jim Gott Minor league IF Augie Schmidt Minor league Jack McKnight

Jimmy Lavender

Date	Traded To		Traded With	Traded By		In Exchange For
Jan 16, 1917	PHI	N	$5,000.	CHI	N	Al Demaree

Ron Law

Date	Traded To		Traded With	Traded By		In Exchange For
Dec 5, 1969	WAS	A	Dave Nelson Horacio Pina	CLE	A	Dennis Higgins Barry Moore

Vance Law

Date	Traded To		Traded With	Traded By		In Exchange For
March 21, 1982	CHI	A	Ernie Camacho	PIT	N	Ross Baumgarten Butch Edge
Dec 7, 1984	MON	N	Bert Roberge	CHI	A	Bob James Bryan Little
Dec 19, 1987	CHI	N	———	MON	N	No compensation (free agent signing)

Tom Lawless

Date	Traded To		Traded With	Traded By		In Exchange For
Aug 16, 1984	MON	N	———	CIN	N	Pete Rose
			(Rose was named Cincinnati manager.)			
Feb 6, 1985	STL	N	———	MON	N	Mickey Mahler
			(St. Louis received Lawless on March 25, 1985.)			

Brooks Lawrence

Date	Traded To		Traded With	Traded By		In Exchange For
Jan 31, 1956	CIN	N	Sonny Senerchia	STL	N	Jackie Collum

Roxie Lawson

Date	Traded To		Traded With	Traded By		In Exchange For
May 13, 1939	STL	A	———	DET	A	*See Beau Bell*

Steve Lawson

Date	Traded To		Traded With	Traded By		In Exchange For
July 20, 1972	TEX	A	Marty Martinez Vic Harris	OAK	A	Don Mincher Ted Kubiak

Marcus Lawton

Date	Traded To		Traded With	Traded By		In Exchange For
July 10, 1989	NY	A	———	NY	N	Scott Nielsen

Bill Laxton

Date	Traded To		Traded With	Traded By		In Exchange For
Dec 15, 1967	PHI	N	Don Money Woodie Fryman minor league P Hal Clem	PIT	N	Jim Bunning
Dec 12, 1975	DET	A	Rusty Staub	NY	N	Mickey Lolich Billy Baldwin
Sept 9, 1977	CLE	A	Cash	SEA	A	Ray Fosse
June 22, 1978	SD	N	———	CLE	A	Dave Freisleben

Pete Layden

Date	Traded To		Traded With	Traded By		In Exchange For
Nov 17, 1947	STL	A	———	BOS	A	*See Vern Stephens*

Date	Traded To	Traded With	Traded By	In Exchange For

Charlie Lea
| Feb 4, 1988 | MIN A ——— | | MON N | No compensation (free agent signing) |

Freddy Leach
| Oct 29, 1928 | NY N ——— | | PHI N | Lefty O'Doul and cash |
| March 19, 1932 | BOS N ——— | | NY N | $10,000. |

Rick Leach
| Jan 23, 1989 | TEX A ——— | | TOR A | No compensation (free agent signing) |

Terry Leach
Sept 26, 1983	CHI N	Minor league 1B Mike Anicich	NY N	Minor league P Mitch Cook Minor league P Jim Adamczak
April 9, 1984	ATL N ———		CHI N	Ron Meridith
June 9, 1989	KC A ———		NY N	Player to be named later

(New York received P Aguedo Vasquez on Sept. 29, 1989.)

Tommy Leach
| Jan 1900 | PIT N | See Honus Wagner | LOU N ——— | |
| June 22, 1912 | CHI N | Lefty Leifield | PIT N | King Cole Solly Hofman |

Tom Leahy
| June 1901 | PHI A ——— | | MIL A | Phil Geier |

Luis Leal
| Feb 2, 1987 | ATL N | See Damaso Garcia | TOR A ——— | |

Fred Lear
| Feb 1920 | NY N ——— | | CHI N | Cash |

Tim Leary
| Jan 18, 1985 | MIL A ——— | | NY N | Frank Wills |

(Part of a four-team trade involving Texas, Milwaukee, Kansas City, and New York Mets.)

Dec 10, 1986	LA N	Tim Crews	MIL A	Greg Brock
July 18, 1989	CIN N	Lenny Harris	LA N	Kal Daniels Mariano Duncan
Dec 12, 1989	NY A	Van Snider	CIN N	Hal Morris Minor league P Rodney Imes

Bevo LeBourveau
| Feb 8, 1923 | PHI A ——— | | PHI N | Cash |

Bill Lee
| Aug 5, 1943 | PHI N ——— | | CHI N | Mickey Livingston |
| July 14, 1945 | BOS N ——— | | PHI N | Cash |

Bill Lee
| Dec 7, 1978 | MON N ——— | | BOS A | Stan Papi |

Bob Lee
| Dec 15, 1966 | LA N ——— | | CAL A | Nick Willhite |
| May 31, 1967 | CIN N ——— | | LA N | Cash |

Cliff Lee
| May 1921 | PHI N ——— | | PIT N | Waiver price |
| June 20, 1924 | CIN N ——— | | PHI N | Cash |

Don Lee
Oct 15, 1959	MIL N	Charlie Lau	DET A	Don Kaiser Mike Roarke Casey Wise
May 29, 1962	LA A ———		MIN A	Jim Donohue
June 1, 1965	HOU N ———		CAL A	Al Spangler

Hal Lee
Oct 14, 1930	PHI N	Clise Dudley Jumbo Elliott and cash	BKN N	Lefty O'Doul Fresco Thompson
June 17, 1933	BOS N	Pinky Whitney	PHI N	Fritz Knothe Wes Schulmerich and cash
Jan 27, 1937	NY N	Ben Cantwell	BOS N	Cash

Leron Lee
| June 11, 1971 | SD N | Fred Norman | STL N | Al Santorini |
| March 28, 1974 | CLE A ——— | | SD N | Cash |

Manny Lee
| Aug 28, 1984 | HOU N ——— | | NY N | See Ray Knight |

Mark Lee
| Aug 5, 1980 | PIT N | Kurt Bevacqua | SD N | Rick Lancellotti Luis Salazar |

Mark Lee
| Aug 31, 1988 | KC A ——— | | DET A | See Ted Power |

Mike Lee
| May 10, 1961 | STL N | Joe Morgan and cash | CLE A | Bob Nieman |

(St. Louis received Lee on September 25.)

Thornton Lee
| Dec 10, 1936 | CHI A ——— | | CLE A | Jack Salveson |

(Part of three-team trade involving Chicago, Cleveland, and Washington.)

Joe Lefebvre
| April 1, 1981 | SD N | Ruppert Jones Tim Lollar Chris Welsh | NY A | Jerry Mumphrey John Pacella |
| May 22, 1983 | PHI N ——— | | SD N | Sid Monge |

Craig Lefferts
| Dec 7, 1983 | SD N | Carmelo Martinez Fritz Connally | CHI N | Scott Sanderson |

(Part of three-team trade involving Chicago Cubs, San Diego, and Montreal.)

| July 4, 1987 | SF N | Kevin Mitchell Dave Dravecky | SD N | Chris Brown Mark Davis Keith Comstock Mark Grant |
| Dec 7, 1989 | SD N ——— | | SF N | No compensation (free agent signing) |

Ron LeFlore
| Dec 7, 1979 | MON N ——— | | DET A | Dan Schatzeder |
| Dec 6, 1980 | CHI A ——— | | MON N | No compensation (free agent signing) |

Date	Traded To		Traded With	Traded By		In Exchange For

Lou Legett

Date	Traded To		Traded With	Traded By		In Exchange For
Nov 7, 1928	BOS	N	Socks Seibold Percy Jones Freddie Maguire Bruce Cunningham and $200,000.	CHI	N	Rogers Hornsby

Ken Lehman

Date	Traded To		Traded With	Traded By		In Exchange For
June 4, 1957	BAL	A	———	BKN	N	$30,000.
Oct 2, 1958	PHI	N	———	BAL	A	Waiver price
March 20, 1962	CLE	A	Tony Curry	PHI	N	Mel Roach

Paul Lehner

Date	Traded To		Traded With	Traded By		In Exchange For
Dec 13, 1949	PHI	A	Bob Dillinger	STL	A	Ray Coleman Frankie Gustine Billy DeMars minor league OF Ray Ippolito and $100,000.
April 30, 1951	CHI	A	Minnie Minoso	PHI	A	Gus Zernial Dave Philley

(Part of three-team trade involving Chicago White Sox, Philadelphia A's, and Cleveland.)

Date	Traded To		Traded With	Traded By		In Exchange For
June 4, 1951	STL	A	Kermit Wahl and cash	CHI	A	Don Lenhardt
July 19, 1951	CLE	A	———	STL	A	Waiver price
June 25, 1952	BOS	A	———	CLE	A	Waiver price

Hank Leiber

Date	Traded To		Traded With	Traded By		In Exchange For
Dec 6, 1938	CHI	N	Dick Bartell Gus Mancuso	NY	N	Frank Demaree Bill Jurges Ken O'Dea
Dec 4, 1941	NY	N	———	CHI	N	Bob Bowman

Nemo Leibold

Date	Traded To		Traded With	Traded By		In Exchange For
July 7, 1915	CHI	A	———	CLE	A	Waiver price
March 4, 1921	BOS	A	Shano Collins	CHI	A	Harry Hooper
May 26, 1923	WAS	A	———	BOS	A	Waiver price

Charlie Leibrandt

Date	Traded To		Traded With	Traded By		In Exchange For
June 7, 1983	KC	A	———	CIN	N	Bob Tufts
Dec 15, 1989	ATL	N	Rick Luecken	KC	A	Gerald Perry Minor league P Jim Lemasters

Lefty Leifield

Date	Traded To		Traded With	Traded By		In Exchange For
May 1911	CHI	N	———	PIT	N	Cash
June 22, 1912	CHI	N	Tommy Leach	PIT	N	King Cole Solly Hofman

Ed Leip

Date	Traded To		Traded With	Traded By		In Exchange For
April 1940	PIT	N	———	WAS	A	Cash

Dave Leiper

Date	Traded To		Traded With	Traded By		In Exchange For
Aug 30, 1987	SD	N	———	OAK	A	Storm Davis

Al Leiter

Date	Traded To		Traded With	Traded By		In Exchange For
April 30, 1989	TOR	A	———	NY	A	Jesse Barfield

Dummy Leitner

Date	Traded To		Traded With	Traded By		In Exchange For
May 1902	CHI	A	———	CLE	A	Cash

Frank Leja

Date	Traded To		Traded With	Traded By		In Exchange For
March 30, 1962	LA	A	———	STL	N	Cash

Jack Lelivelt

Date	Traded To		Traded With	Traded By		In Exchange For
Dec 1911	NY	A	Gabby Street	WAS	A	John Knight Roxy Roach
May 20, 1913	CLE	A	Bill Stumpf	NY	A	Roger Peckinpaugh

Dave Lemanczyk

Date	Traded To		Traded With	Traded By		In Exchange For
June 3, 1980	CAL	A	———	TOR	A	Ken Schrom

Denny Lemaster

Date	Traded To		Traded With	Traded By		In Exchange For
Oct 8, 1967	HOU	N	Denis Menke	ATL	N	Sonny Jackson Chuck Harrison
Oct 14, 1971	MON	N	———	HOU	N	Cash

Johnnie LeMaster

Date	Traded To		Traded With	Traded By		In Exchange For
May 7, 1985	CLE	A	———	SF	N	Mike Jeffcoat Luis Quinones
May 30, 1985	PIT	N	———	CLE	A	Scott Bailes

(Cleveland received Bailes on July 3, 1985.)

Dick LeMay

Date	Traded To		Traded With	Traded By		In Exchange For
Nov 30, 1962	HOU	N	Manny Mota	SF	N	Joey Amalfitano
March 28, 1963	CHI	N	Merritt Ranew Hal Haydel	HOU	N	Dave Gerard Danny Murphy

Chet Lemon

Date	Traded To		Traded With	Traded By		In Exchange For
June 15, 1975	CHI	A	Dave Hamilton	OAK	A	Stan Bahnsen Skip Pitlock
Nov 27, 1981	DET	A	———	CHI	A	Steve Kemp

Jim Lemon

Date	Traded To		Traded With	Traded By		In Exchange For
May 12, 1954	WAS	A	———	CLE	A	Cash
May 4, 1963	PHI	N	———	MIN	A	Cash
June 28, 1963	CHI	A	———	PHI	N	Cash

Dave Lemonds

Date	Traded To		Traded With	Traded By		In Exchange For
Nov 30, 1970	CHI	A	Pat Jacquez Roe Skidmore	CHI	N	Jose Ortiz Ossie Blanco

Mark Lemongello

Date	Traded To		Traded With	Traded By		In Exchange For
Dec 6, 1975	HOU	N	———	DET	A	*See Milt May*
Nov 27, 1978	TOR	A	Joe Cannon Pedro Hernandez	HOU	N	Alan Ashby
April 7, 1980	CHI	N	———	TOR	A	Cash

Don Lenhardt

Date	Traded To		Traded With	Traded By		In Exchange For
June 4, 1951	CHI	A	———	STL	A	Paul Lehner Kermit Wahl and cash
Nov 13, 1951	BOS	A	Randy Gumpert	CHI	A	Mel Hoderlein Chuck Stobbs
June 3, 1952	DET	A	———	BOS	A	*See George Kell*
Aug 14, 1952	STL	A	*See Vic Wertz*	DET	A	———
Feb 12, 1954	BOS	A	———	BAL	A	Cash

Bob Lennon

Date	Traded To		Traded With	Traded By		In Exchange For
April 16, 1957	CHI	N	Dick Littlefield	NY	N	Ray Jablonski Ray Katt

Jim Lentine

Date	Traded To		Traded With	Traded By		In Exchange For
June 2, 1980	DET	A	———	STL	N	John Martin Al Greene
April 3, 1981	HOU	N	Cash	CLE	A	Mike Fischlin

Date	Traded To	Traded With	Traded By	In Exchange For

Eddie Leon

Date	Traded To		Traded With	Traded By		In Exchange For
Oct 19, 1972	CHI	A	———	CLE	A	Walt Williams
Dec 5, 1974	NY	A	———	CHI	A	Cecil Upshaw

Dutch Leonard

Dec 3, 1936	STL	N	Frenchy Bordagaray Jimmy Jordan	BKN	N	Tom Winsett
Dec 9, 1946	PHI	N	———	WAS	A	Cash
Dec 14, 1948	CHI	N	Monk Dubiel	PHI	N	Hank Borowy Eddie Waitkus

Dutch Leonard

Dec 18, 1918	NY	A	Ernie Shore Duffy Lewis	BOS	A	Frank Gilhooley Slim Love Ray Caldwell Roxy Walters and $15,000.
May 18, 1919	DET	A	———	NY	A	Cash

Jeffrey Leonard

July 1, 1978	HOU	N	Rafael Landestoy	LA	N	Joe Ferguson and cash
April 20, 1981	SF	N	Dave Bergman	HOU	N	Mike Ivie
June 8, 1988	MIL	A	———	SF	N	Ernest Riles
Dec 7, 1988	SEA	A	———	MIL	A	No compensation (free agent signing)

Joe Leonard

Aug 18, 1916	WAS	A	Elmer Smith	CLE	A	Joe Boehling Danny Moeller

Ted Lepcio

May 2, 1959	DET	A	Dave Sisler	BOS	A	Billy Hoeft
Dec 5, 1959	PHI	N	Ken Walters minor league P Alex Cosmidis	DET	A	Chico Fernandez Ray Semproch
April 3, 1961	CHI	A	———	PHI	N	Cash

Don Leppert

Dec 1, 1954	BAL	A	———	NY	A	*See Dick Kryhoski*

Don Leppert

Dec 15, 1962	WAS	A	———	PIT	N	Minor league P Ron Honeycutt and cash

Randy Lerch

March 1, 1981	MIL	A	———	PHI	N	Dick Davis
Aug 14, 1982	MON	N	———	MIL	A	Cash

Barry Lersch

Dec 3, 1973	ATL	N	Craig Robinson	PHI	N	Ron Schueler
Sept 14, 1974	STL	N	———	ATL	N	Cash

Don Leshnock

Oct 25, 1972	PHI	N	Tom Haller	DET	A	Cash

Brad Lesley

Nov 13, 1984	MIL	A	———	CIN	N	Cash

Sam Leslie

June 16, 1933	BKN	N	———	NY	N	Lefty O'Doul Watty Clark
Feb 20, 1936	NY	N	———	BKN	N	Cash

Ed Levy

Jan 22, 1943	PHI	N	Tom Padden Al Gerheauser Al Gettel and $10,000.	NY	A	Nick Etten

Dennis Lewallyn

Nov 23, 1977	MIN	A	———	LA	N	Cash
			(Lewallyn was returned to the Dodgers on March 15, 1978.)			
Sept 13, 1980	TEX	A	———	LA	N	Pepe Frias
Aug 25, 1981	CLE	A	———	TEX	A	Cash

Duffy Lewis

Dec 18, 1918	NY	A	Ernie Shore Dutch Leonard	BOS	A	Frank Gilhooley Slim Love Ray Caldwell Roxy Walters and $15,000.
Jan 20, 1921	WAS	A	George Mogridge	NY	A	Braggo Roth

Jim Lewis

Nov 1, 1979	NY	A	———	SEA	A	*See Jim Beattie*

Johnny Lewis

Dec 7, 1964	NY	N	Gordie Richardson	STL	N	Tracy Stallard Elio Chacon

Terry Ley

Dec 2, 1971	TEX	A	Gary Jones	NY	A	Bernie Allen

Sixto Lezcano

Dec 12, 1980	STL	N	David Green Lary Sorensen Dave LaPoint	MIL	A	Pete Vuckovich Rollie Fingers Ted Simmons
Dec 10, 1981	SD	N	Garry Templeton Luis DeLeon	STL	N	Ozzie Smith Steve Mura Al Olmsted
			(Templeton and Smith were exchanged on February 11, 1982; Olmsted and DeLeon were exchanged on February 19.)			
Aug 31, 1983	PHI	N	Steve Fireovid	SD	N	Lance McCullers Ed Wojna Marty Decker Minor league P Darren Burroughs
Jan 22, 1985	PIT	N	———	PHI	N	No compensation (free agent signing)

Francisco Libran

April 25, 1969	SD	N	Joe Niekro Gary Ross	CHI	N	Dick Selma

Don Liddle

Feb 1, 1954	NY	N	*See Johnny Antonelli*	MIL	N	———
June 14, 1956	STL	N	———	NY	N	*See Red Schoendienst*

Fred Liese

Feb 1910	BOS	N	———	CHI	N	Ginger Beaumont

Gene Lillard

Dec 27, 1939	STL	N	Steve Mesner and cash	CHI	N	Ken Raffensberger

Bob Lillis

May 30, 1961	STL	N	Carl Warwick	LA	N	Daryl Spencer

Date	Traded To	Traded With	Traded By	In Exchange For		Date	Traded To	Traded With	Traded By	In Exchange For

Vive Lindaman

Date	Traded To		Traded With	Traded By		In Exchange For
Dec 15, 1905	BOS	N	Dave Brain Del Howard	PIT	N	Vic Willis

Paul Lindblad

Date	Traded To		Traded With	Traded By		In Exchange For
May 8, 1971	WAS	A	Frank Fernandez Don Mincher and cash	OAK	A	Mike Epstein Darold Knowles
Oct 30, 1972	OAK	A	——	TEX	A	Bill McNulty Brant Alyea
Feb 19, 1977	TEX	A	——	OAK	A	$400,000.
Aug 2, 1978	NY	A	——	TEX	A	Cash
Nov 30, 1978	SEA	A	——	NY	A	Cash

Johnny Lindell

Date	Traded To		Traded With	Traded By		In Exchange For
May 15, 1950	STL	N	——	NY	A	Cash
Aug 31, 1953	PHI	N	——	PIT	N	Cash

Jim Lindeman

Date	Traded To		Traded With	Traded By		In Exchange For
Dec 6, 1989	DET	A	Matt Kinzer	STL	N	Minor league 2B Pat Austin Minor league C Bill Henderson Minor league P Marcos Betances

Bill Lindsey

Date	Traded To		Traded With	Traded By		In Exchange For
July 30, 1986	CHI	A	——	NY	A	*See Ron Kittle*

Jim Lindsey

Date	Traded To		Traded With	Traded By		In Exchange For
May 30, 1934	STL	N	——	CIN	N	Cash

Freddie Lindstrom

Date	Traded To		Traded With	Traded By		In Exchange For
Dec 12, 1932	PIT	N	——	NY	N	Glenn Spencer Gus Dugas

(Part of three-team trade involving New York, Philadelphia, and Pittsburgh.)

Date	Traded To		Traded With	Traded By		In Exchange For
Nov 22, 1934	CHI	N	Larry French	PIT	N	Guy Bush Jim Weaver Babe Herman

Fred Link

Date	Traded To		Traded With	Traded By		In Exchange For
Sept 1910	STL	A	——	CLE	A	Cash

Ed Linke

Date	Traded To		Traded With	Traded By		In Exchange For
Dec 1, 1937	STL	A	——	WAS	A	Chief Hogsett

Larry Lintz

Date	Traded To		Traded With	Traded By		In Exchange For
July 25, 1975	STL	N	——	MON	N	Jim Dwyer
Oct 28, 1975	OAK	A	——	STL	N	Charlie Chant

Phil Linz

Date	Traded To		Traded With	Traded By		In Exchange For
Nov 29, 1965	PHI	N	——	NY	A	Ruben Amaro
July 11, 1967	NY	N	——	PHI	N	Chuck Hiller

Frank Linzy

Date	Traded To		Traded With	Traded By		In Exchange For
May 19, 1970	STL	N	——	SF	N	Jerry Johnson
March 26, 1972	MIL	A	——	STL	N	Minor league P Rich Stonum
Nov 7, 1973	PHI	N	——	MIL	A	Billy Wilson

Johnny Lipon

Date	Traded To		Traded With	Traded By		In Exchange For
June 3, 1952	BOS	A	*See George Kell*	DET	A	——
Sept 8, 1953	STL	A	——	BOS	A	Cash

Johnny Lipon *continued*

Date	Traded To		Traded With	Traded By		In Exchange For
Feb 5, 1954	CHI	A	Johnny Groth	BAL	A	Neil Berry Sam Mele
April 18, 1954	CIN	N	——	CHI	A	Grady Hatton

Joe Lis

Date	Traded To		Traded With	Traded By		In Exchange For
Nov 30, 1972	MIN	A	Ken Sanders Ken Reynolds	PHI	N	Cesar Tovar
June 5, 1974	CLE	A	——	MIN	A	Cash

Hod Lisenbee

Date	Traded To		Traded With	Traded By		In Exchange For
Dec 15, 1928	BOS	A	Milt Gaston Bobby Reeves Grant Gillis Elliott Bigelow	WAS	A	Buddy Myer

Rick Lisi

Date	Traded To		Traded With	Traded By		In Exchange For
Feb 19, 1982	BAL	A	——	TEX	A	Steve Luebber

Mark Littell

Date	Traded To		Traded With	Traded By		In Exchange For
Dec 8, 1977	STL	N	Buck Martinez	KC	A	Al Hrabosky

Bryan Little

Date	Traded To		Traded With	Traded By		In Exchange For
Dec 7, 1984	CHI	A	Bob James	MON	N	Vance Law Bert Roberge
July 2, 1986	NY	A	——	CHI	A	Cash

Scott Little

Date	Traded To		Traded With	Traded By		In Exchange For
May 29, 1987	PIT	N	Al Pedrique	NY	N	Bill Almon

Dick Littlefield

Date	Traded To		Traded With	Traded By		In Exchange For
Dec 10, 1950	CHI	A	Joe Dobson Al Zarilla	BOS	A	Ray Scarborough Bill Wight
Nov 27, 1951	STL	A	Joe DeMaestri Gus Niarhos Gordon Goldsberry Jim Rivera	CHI	A	Al Widmar Sherm Lollar Tom Upton
Feb 14, 1952	DET	A	Ben Taylor Cliff Mapes	STL	A	Gene Bearden Bob Cain Dick Kryhoski
Aug 14, 1952	STL	A	Marlin Stuart Don Lenhardt Vic Wertz	DET	A	Jim Delsing Ned Garver Dave Madison Bill Black
May 25, 1954	PIT	N	——	BAL	A	Cal Abrams
May 17, 1956	STL	N	Bobby Del Greco	PIT	N	Bill Virdon
June 14, 1956	NY	N	*See Red Schoendienst*	STL	N	——
Dec 13, 1956	BKN	N	$30,000.	NY	N	Jackie Robinson

(Trade was cancelled when Robinson retired.)

Date	Traded To		Traded With	Traded By		In Exchange For
April 16, 1957	CHI	N	Bob Lennon	NY	N	Ray Jablonski Ray Katt
March 30, 1958	MIL	N	——	CHI	N	Cash

John Littlefield

Date	Traded To		Traded With	Traded By		In Exchange For
Dec 8, 1980	SD	N	——	STL	N	*See Rollie Fingers*

Larry Littleton

Date	Traded To		Traded With	Traded By		In Exchange For
Dec 21, 1979	CLE	A	minor league P John Burden	PIT	N	Larry Andersen
July 3, 1982	MIN	A	——	CLE	A	Larry Milbourne

Danny Litwhiler

Date	Traded To		Traded With	Traded By		In Exchange For
June 1, 1943	STL	N	Earl Naylor	PHI	N	Buster Adams Coaker Triplett Dain Clay
June 9, 1946	BOS	N	——	STL	N	Cash
May 11, 1948	CIN	N	——	BOS	N	Marv Rickert

Date	Traded To		Traded With	Traded By		In Exchange For

Mickey Livingston

Date	Traded To		Traded With	Traded By		In Exchange For
Nov 11, 1940	PHI	N	Vito Tamulis Bill Crouch and $100,000.	BKN	N	Kirby Higbe
Aug 5, 1943	CHI	N	——	PHI	N	Bill Lee
July 7, 1947	NY	N	——	CHI	N	Waiver price

Paddy Livingston

Date	Traded To		Traded With	Traded By		In Exchange For
Dec 6, 1911	CLE	A	——	PHI	A	Cash

Hans Lobert

Date	Traded To		Traded With	Traded By		In Exchange For
March 1906	CIN	N	Jake Weimer	CHI	N	Harry Steinfeldt
Feb 1911	PHI	N	Fred Beebe Jack Rowan Dode Paskert	CIN	N	Johnny Bates Eddie Grant George McQuillan Lew Moren
Jan 1915	NY	N	——	PHI	N	Al Demaree Milt Stock Bert Adams

Harry Lochhead

Date	Traded To		Traded With	Traded By		In Exchange For
April 1901	PHI	A	——	DET	A	Cash

Don Lock

Date	Traded To		Traded With	Traded By		In Exchange For
July 11, 1962	WAS	A	——	NY	A	Dale Long
Nov 30, 1966	PHI	N	——	WAS	A	Darold Knowles and cash
May 5, 1969	BOS	A	——	PHI	N	Rudy Schlesinger

Larry Locke

Date	Traded To		Traded With	Traded By		In Exchange For
Nov 27, 1961	CHI	N	——	CLE	A	Jerry Kindall
April 7, 1962	STL	N	——	CLE	A	Minor league OF Al Herring
April 28, 1962	PHI	N	Cash	STL	N	Don Ferrarese
Oct 15, 1964	LA	A	——	PHI	N	Cash
July 28, 1965	CIN	N	——	CAL	A	Cash
June 3, 1966	CAL	A	——	CIN	N	Cash

Bob Locker

Date	Traded To		Traded With	Traded By		In Exchange For
June 8, 1969	SEA	A	——	CHI	A	Gary Bell
June 15, 1970	OAK	A	——	MIL	A	Cash
Nov 21, 1972	CHI	N	——	OAK	A	Billy North
Dec 3, 1973	OAK	A	——	CHI	N	Horacio Pina
Oct 23, 1974	CHI	N	Darold Knowles Manny Trillo	OAK	A	Billy Williams

Gene Locklear

Date	Traded To		Traded With	Traded By		In Exchange For
June 12, 1973	SD	N	Mike Johnson and cash	CIN	N	Fred Norman
July 10, 1976	NY	A	——	SD	N	Rick Sawyer

Whitey Lockman

Date	Traded To		Traded With	Traded By		In Exchange For
June 14, 1956	STL	N	Alvin Dark Ray Katt Don Liddle	NY	N	Jackie Brandt Red Schoendienst Bobby Stephenson Dick Littlefield Bill Sarni
Feb 26, 1957	NY	N	——	STL	N	Hoyt Wilhelm
Feb 14, 1959	BAL	A	——	SF	N	Cash
June 23, 1959	CIN	N	——	BAL	A	Walt Dropo

Skip Lockwood

Date	Traded To		Traded With	Traded By		In Exchange For
Oct 22, 1973	CAL	A	Ellie Rodriguez Gary Ryerson Ollie Brown Joe Lahoud	MIL	A	Clyde Wright Steve Barber Ken Berry Art Kusnyer and cash
Dec 3, 1974	NY	A	——	CAL	A	Bill Sudakis

Skip Lockwood continued

Date	Traded To		Traded With	Traded By		In Exchange For
July 28, 1975	NY	N	——	OAK	A	Cash
Nov 27, 1979	BOS	A	——	NY	N	No compensation (free agent signing)

Dario Lodigiani

Date	Traded To		Traded With	Traded By		In Exchange For
Dec 16, 1940	CHI	A	——	PHI	A	Jack Knott

Billy Loes

Date	Traded To		Traded With	Traded By		In Exchange For
May 14, 1956	BAL	A	——	BKN	N	$20,000.
April 1, 1959	WAS	A	——	BAL	A	Vito Valentinetti
(Trade was cancelled on April 8, 1959, by Commissioner Frick due to Loes's sore arm.)						
Nov 30, 1959	SF	N	Billy O'Dell	BAL	A	Jackie Brandt Gordon Jones Roger McCardell
Oct 16, 1961	NY	N	——	SF	N	Cash

Johnny Logan

Date	Traded To		Traded With	Traded By		In Exchange For
June 15, 1961	PIT	N	——	MIL	N	Gino Cimoli

Lucky Lohrke

Date	Traded To		Traded With	Traded By		In Exchange For
Dec 13, 1951	PHI	N	——	NY	N	Minor league C Jake Schmitt
Jan 13, 1954	PIT	N	Andy Hansen and $70,000.	PHI	N	Murry Dickson

Bill Lohrman

Date	Traded To		Traded With	Traded By		In Exchange For
Dec 11, 1941	STL	N	Ken O'Dea Johnny McCarthy and $50,000.	NY	N	Johnny Mize
May 5, 1942	NY	N	——	STL	N	Cash
July 31, 1943	BKN	N	Bill Sayles Joe Orengo	NY	N	Dolf Camilli Johnny Allen
(Camilli refused to report to New York and retired.)						

Mickey Lolich

Date	Traded To		Traded With	Traded By		In Exchange For
Dec 12, 1975	NY	N	Billy Baldwin	DET	A	Rusty Staub Bill Laxton

Sherm Lollar

Date	Traded To		Traded With	Traded By		In Exchange For
Dec 20, 1946	NY	A	Ray Mack	CLE	A	Hal Peck Al Gettel Gene Bearden
Dec 13, 1948	STL	A	Red Embree Dick Starr and $100,000.	NY	A	Fred Sanford Roy Partee
Nov 27, 1951	CHI	A	Al Widmar Tom Upton	STL	A	Joe DeMaestri Dick Littlefield Gus Niarhos Gordon Goldsberry Jim Rivera

Tim Lollar

Date	Traded To		Traded With	Traded By		In Exchange For
April 1, 1981	SD	N	Ruppert Jones Joe Lefebvre Chris Welsh	NY	A	Jerry Mumphrey John Pacella
Dec 6, 1984	CHI	A	——	SD	N	See LaMarr Hoyt
July 11, 1985	BOS	A	——	CHI	A	Reid Nichols

Ernie Lombardi

Date	Traded To		Traded With	Traded By		In Exchange For
March 14, 1932	CIN	N	Babe Herman Wally Gilbert	BKN	N	Tony Cuccinello Joe Stripp Clyde Sukeforth
Feb 7, 1942	BOS	N	——	CIN	N	Cash
April 27, 1943	NY	N	——	BOS	N	Hugh Poland Connie Ryan

Date	Traded To	Traded With	Traded By	In Exchange For

Phil Lombardi

Date				
Dec 11, 1987	NY N	Steve Frey Minor league OF Darren Reed	NY A	Rafael Santana Minor league P Victor Garcia

Vic Lombardi

Dec 8, 1947	PIT N	Dixie Walker Hal Gregg	BKN N	Preacher Roe Billy Cox Gene Mauch

Steve Lombardozzi

March 21, 1989	HOU N	——	MIN A	Two players to be named

(Minnesota received P Gordon Farmer and OF Ramon Cedeno on Sept. 15, 1989.)

Jim Lonborg

Oct 11, 1971	MIL A	George Scott Billy Conigliaro Joe Lahoud Ken Brett Don Pavletich	BOS A	Marty Pattin Lew Krausse Tommy Harper Minor leaguer Pat Skrable
Oct 31, 1972	PHI N	Ken Sanders Ken Brett Earl Stephenson	MIL A	Don Money John Vukovich Billy Champion

Bill Long

Dec 6, 1984	CHI A	——	SD N	See LaMarr Hoyt

Dale Long

June 1, 1951	STL A	——	PIT N	Waiver price
May 1, 1957	CHI N	Lee Walls	PIT N	Gene Baker Dee Fondy
April 5, 1960	SF N	——	CHI N	Cash
Aug 22, 1960	NY A	——	SF N	Cash
July 11, 1962	NY A	——	WAS A	Don Lock

Herman Long

June 10, 1903	DET A	Ernie Courtney	NY A	Kid Elberfeld

Jeoff Long

July 7, 1964	CHI A	——	STL N	Cash
Dec 1, 1964	PHI N	Ray Herbert	CHI A	Danny Cater Lee Elia

Joe Lonnett

June 13, 1958	MIL N	——	PHI N	Carl Sawatski

Ed Lopat

Feb 24, 1948	NY A	——	CHI A	Aaron Robinson Fred Bradley Bill Wight
July 30, 1955	BAL A	——	NY A	Jim McDonald

Stan Lopata

March 31, 1959	MIL N	Ted Kazanski Johnny O'Brien	PHI N	Gene Conley Joe Koppe Harry Hanebrink

Davey Lopes

Feb 8, 1982	OAK A	——	LA N	Minor league 2B Lance Hudson
July 15, 1984	CHI N	——	OAK A	Chuck Rainey

(The Cubs received Lopes on August 31.)

July 21, 1986	HOU N	——	CHI N	Frank DiPino

Al Lopez

Dec 12, 1935	BOS N	Tony Cuccinello Ray Benge Bobby Reis	BKN N	Ed Brandt Randy Moore
June 14, 1940	PIT N	——	BOS N	Ray Berres and $40,000.
Dec 7, 1946	CLE A	——	PIT N	Gene Woodling

Aurelio Lopez

Dec 4, 1978	DET A	Jerry Morales	STL N	Bob Sykes and minor league P Jack Murphy
June 3, 1986	HOU N	——	DET A	No compensation (free agent signing)

Carlos Lopez

Dec 7, 1977	BAL A	Tommy Moore	SEA A	Mike Parrott

Hector Lopez

May 26, 1959	NY A	Ralph Terry	KC A	Johnny Kucks Tom Sturdivant Jerry Lumpe

Marcelino Lopez

Sept 9, 1964	LA A	Cash	PHI N	Vic Power
June 15, 1967	BAL A	minor league P Tom Arruda	CAL A	Woodie Held
April 5, 1971	MIL A	——	BAL A	Roric Harrison and minor leaguer Marion Jackson
March 29, 1972	CLE A	——	MIL A	Cash

Bris Lord

July 25, 1910	PHI A	——	CLE A	Joe Jackson
Dec 1912	BOS N	——	PHI A	Cash

Harry Lord

Aug 9, 1910	CHI A	Amby McConnell	BOS A	Frank Smith Billy Purtell

Baldy Louden

Dec 23, 1915	CIN N	——	BUF F	Cash

Slim Love

Dec 18, 1918	BOS A	——	NY A	See Duffy Lewis
Jan 17, 1919	DET A	Eddie Ainsmith Chick Shorten	BOS A	Ossie Vitt

Vance Lovelace

Jan 20, 1983	LA N	Minor League OF Dan Cataline	CHI N	Ron Cey

Jay Loviglio

April 1, 1981	CHI A	——	PHI N	Mike Proly
Nov 29, 1982	CHI N	——	CHI A	Cash

Joe Lovitto

Dec 12, 1975	NY N	——	TEX A	Gene Clines

Date	Traded To		Traded With	Traded By		In Exchange For

Grover Lowdermilk

Date	Traded To		Traded With	Traded By		In Exchange For
Dec 15, 1912	CIN	N	Joe Tinker Harry Chapman	CHI	N	Bert Humphries Red Corriden Pete Knisely Art Phelan Mike Mitchell
Aug 18, 1915	DET	A	Bill James	STL	A	Baby Doll Jacobson
Aug 1916	CLE	A	———	DET	A	Cash
Oct 1917	STL	A	———	CLE	A	Waiver price
May 1919	CHI	A	———	STL	A	Cash

Bobby Lowe

Date	Traded To		Traded With	Traded By		In Exchange For
July 1902	CHI	N	———	BOS	N	Charlie Dexter
April 20, 1904	PIT	N	———	CHI	N	Cash
April 30, 1904	DET	A	———	PIT	N	Cash

John Lowenstein

Date	Traded To		Traded With	Traded By		In Exchange For
Dec 6, 1976	TOR	A	Rick Cerone	CLE	A	Rico Carty
March 29, 1977	CLE	A	———	TOR	A	Hector Torres
Feb 28, 1978	TEX	A	Tom Buskey	CLE	A	Willie Horton David Clyde
Nov 27, 1978	BAL	A	———	TEX	A	Cash

Turk Lown

Date	Traded To		Traded With	Traded By		In Exchange For
May 8, 1958	CIN	N	———	CHI	N	Hersh Freeman
June 23, 1958	CHI	N	———	CIN	N	Waiver price

Peanuts Lowrey

Date	Traded To		Traded With	Traded By		In Exchange For
June 15, 1949	CIN	N	Harry Walker	CHI	N	Frankie Baumholtz Hank Sauer
Sept 7, 1950	STL	N	———	CIN	N	Cash

Mike Loynd

Date	Traded To		Traded With	Traded By		In Exchange For
March 25, 1988	HOU	N	———	TEX	A	Robbie Wine

Johnny Lucadello

Date	Traded To		Traded With	Traded By		In Exchange For
March 1, 1947	NY	A	———	STL	A	Waiver price

Gary Lucas

Date	Traded To		Traded With	Traded By		In Exchange For
Dec 7, 1983	MON	N	———	SD	N	Scott Sanderson
Dec 27, 1985	MON	N	———	CAL	A	Luis Sanchez Minor league P Tim Arnold

Red Lucas

Date	Traded To		Traded With	Traded By		In Exchange For
Nov 17, 1933	PIT	N	Wally Roettger	CIN	N	Adam Comorosky Tony Piet

Fred Luderus

Date	Traded To		Traded With	Traded By		In Exchange For
July 1910	PHI	N	———	CHI	N	Bill Foxen

Steve Luebber

Date	Traded To		Traded With	Traded By		In Exchange For
Feb 19, 1982	TEX	A	———	BAL	A	Rick Lisi

Dick Luebke

Date	Traded To		Traded With	Traded By		In Exchange For
Dec 15, 1962	CIN	N	minor league IF Willard Oplinger	BAL	A	Joe Gaines

Rick Luecken

Date	Traded To		Traded With	Traded By		In Exchange For
Dec 10, 1986	KC	A	Danny Tartabull	SEA	A	Scott Bankhead Mike Kingery Steve Shields
Aug 24, 1989	ATL	N	Minor league P Pat Gomez	CHI	N	Paul Assenmacher

Rick Luecken continued

Date	Traded To		Traded With	Traded By		In Exchange For
Dec 15, 1989	ATL	N	Charlie Leibrandt	KC	A	Gerald Perry Minor league P Jim Lemasters

Mike Lum

Date	Traded To		Traded With	Traded By		In Exchange For
Dec 12, 1975	CIN	N	———	ATL	N	Darrel Chaney
Feb 15, 1979	ATL	N	———	CIN	N	No compensation (free agent signing)

Jerry Lumpe

Date	Traded To		Traded With	Traded By		In Exchange For
May 26, 1959	KC	A	Johnny Kucks Tom Sturdivant	NY	A	Hector Lopez Ralph Terry
Nov 18, 1963	DET	A	Ed Rakow Dave Wickersham	KC	A	Rocky Colavito Bob Anderson and $50,000.

Don Lund

Date	Traded To		Traded With	Traded By		In Exchange For
June 28, 1948	STL	A	———	BKN	N	Waiver price
Jan 20, 1949	DET	A	———	STL	A	$15,000.

Gordon Lund

Date	Traded To		Traded With	Traded By		In Exchange For
Nov 28, 1967	BAL	A	John O'Donoghue	CLE	A	Eddie Fisher minor leaguers P Bob Scott and IF John Scruggs
March 31, 1969	SEA	A	Gene Brabender	BAL	A	Chico Salmon

Tony Lupien

Date	Traded To		Traded With	Traded By		In Exchange For
April 13, 1944	PHI	N	———	BOS	A	Waiver price
Jan 26, 1949	DET	A	———	CHI	A	Waiver price

Al Luplow

Date	Traded To		Traded With	Traded By		In Exchange For
Nov 29, 1965	NY	N	———	CLE	A	Cash
June 21, 1967	PIT	N	———	NY	N	Cash

Dolf Luque

Date	Traded To		Traded With	Traded By		In Exchange For
Feb 1930	BKN	N	———	CIN	N	Doug McWeeny

Billy Lush

Date	Traded To		Traded With	Traded By		In Exchange For
Jan 1904	CLE	A	———	DET	A	Jesse Stovall Ed Killian

Johnny Lush

Date	Traded To		Traded With	Traded By		In Exchange For
June 10, 1907	STL	N	———	PHI	N	Charlie Brown

Greg Luzinski

Date	Traded To		Traded With	Traded By		In Exchange For
March 30, 1981	CHI	A	———	PHI	N	Cash

Sparky Lyle

Date	Traded To		Traded With	Traded By		In Exchange For
March 22, 1972	NY	A	———	BOS	A	Danny Cater
Nov 10, 1978	TEX	A	Domingo Ramos Mike Heath Larry McCall Dave Rajsich and cash	NY	A	Dave Righetti Juan Beniquez Mike Griffin Paul Mirabella minor league P Greg Jemison
Sept 13, 1980	PHI	N	———	TEX	A	Kevin Saucier
Aug 21, 1982	CHI	A	———	PHI	N	Cash

Ed Lynch

Date	Traded To		Traded With	Traded By		In Exchange For
Aug 12, 1979	NY	N	Mike Jorgensen	TEX	A	Willie Montanez

Date	Traded To		Traded With	Traded By		In Exchange For

Ed Lynch *continued*

Date	Traded To		Traded With	Traded By		In Exchange For
June 30, 1986	CHI	N	——	NY	N	Minor league P Dave Lenderman Minor league C David Liddell

Jerry Lynch

May 23, 1963	PIT	N	——	CIN	N	Bob Skinner

Fred Lynn

Jan 23, 1981	CAL	A	Steve Renko	BOS	A	Frank Tanana Jim Dorsey Joe Rudi
Dec 11, 1984	BAL	A	——	CAL	A	Free agent signing

(California selected Donnie Moore from Atlanta as compensation.)

Aug 31, 1988	DET	A	——	BAL	A	Chris Hoiles Minor league P Robinson Garces Minor league P Cesar Mejia
Dec 6, 1989	SD	N	——	DET	A	No compensation (free agent signing)

Red Lynn

May 9, 1939	NY	N	——	DET	A	Cash

Al Lyons

Aug 4, 1947	PIT	N	——	NY	A	Cash
Nov 18, 1947	BOS	N	Jim Russell Bill Salkeld	PIT	N	Johnny Hopp Danny Murtaugh

Steve Lyons

June 29, 1986	CHI	A	——	BOS	A	Tom Seaver

Rick Lysander

Feb 10, 1981	HOU	N	——	OAK	A	Jimmy Sexton
Jan 12, 1983	MIN	A	——	HOU	N	Bob Veselic

Jim Lyttle

Oct 13, 1971	CHI	A	——	NY	A	Rich Hinton
Feb 1, 1973	KC	A	——	CHI	A	Joe Keough
July 10, 1973	MON	N	——	KC	A	Cash
July 18, 1975	MON	N	——	CHI	A	Cash

Duke Maas

Nov 20, 1957	KC	A	——	DET	A	*See Billy Martin*
June 15, 1958	NY	A	Virgil Trucks	KC	A	Bob Grim Harry Simpson
April 4, 1961	NY	A	——	LA	A	Fritzie Brickell

Bob Mabe

Oct 3, 1958	CIN	N	——	STL	N	*See George Crowe*

Danny MacFayden

June 5, 1932	NY	A	——	BOS	A	Ivy Andrews Hank Johnson and $50,000.
Nov 13, 1934	CIN	N	——	NY	A	Cash
June 15, 1935	BOS	N	——	CIN	N	Waiver price
Dec 8, 1939	PIT	N	——	BOS	N	Bill Swift and cash

Ken Macha

Jan 15, 1981	TOR	A	——	MON	N	Cash

Dave Machemer

March 3, 1976	BOS	A	John Balaz Dick Sharon	CAL	A	Dick Drago

Ray Mack

Dec 20, 1946	NY	A	Sherm Lollar	CLE	A	Hal Peck Al Gettel Gene Bearden

Pete Mackanin

Dec 5, 1974	MON	N	Don Stanhouse	TEX	A	Willie Davis
Sept 5, 1978	PHI	N	——	MON	N	Cash
Dec 7, 1979	MIN	A	——	PHI	N	Paul Thormodsgard
Feb 11, 1982	CHI	A	——	MIN	A	No compensation (free agent signing)

Ken MacKenzie

Oct 11, 1961	NY	N	Johnny Antonelli	MIL	N	Cash
Aug 5, 1963	STL	N	——	NY	N	Ed Bauta
Oct 1, 1963	SF	N	——	STL	N	Jimmie Coker

Max Macon

Sept 1939	BKN	N	——	STL	N	Cash

Mike Madden

Aug 30, 1982	HOU	N	Kevin Bass Frank DiPino and cash	MIL	A	Don Sutton

Morris Madden

Aug 9, 1987	PIT	N	——	DET	A	*See Jim Morrison*

Tom Madden

May 1911	PHI	N	——	BOS	A	Waiver price

Elliott Maddox

Oct 9, 1970	WAS	A	*See Denny McLain*	DET	A	——
March 23, 1974	NY	A	——	TEX	A	Cash
Jan 20, 1977	BAL	A	Rick Bladt	NY	A	Paul Blair
Nov 30, 1977	NY	A	——	BAL	A	No compensation (free agent signing)

Garry Maddox

May 4, 1975	PHI	N	——	SF	N	Willie Montanez

Art Madison

Jan 1900	LOU	N	——	PIT	N	*See Honus Wagner*

Dave Madison

April 7, 1952	STL	A	——	NY	A	Cash
Aug 14, 1952	DET	A	——	STL	A	*See Vic Wertz*

Scotti Madison

Jan 6, 1982	LA	N	——	MIN	A	*See Bobby Castillo*

Ed Madjeski

May 15, 1934	CHI	A	——	PHI	A	Cash

Bill Madlock

Oct 25, 1973	CHI	N	Vic Harris	TEX	A	Ferguson Jenkins

Date	Traded To		Traded With	Traded By		In Exchange For

Bill Madlock *continued*

Date	Traded To		Traded With	Traded By		In Exchange For
Feb 11, 1977	SF	N	Rob Sperring	CHI	N	Bobby Murcer Steve Ontiveros minor league P Andy Muhlstock
June 28, 1979	PIT	N	Lenny Randle Dave Roberts	SF	N	Ed Whitson Fred Breining Al Holland
Aug 31, 1985	LA	N	———	PIT	N	R. J. Reynolds Sid Bream Cecil Espy

(Pittsburgh received Reynolds on Sept. 3 and Bream and Espy on September 9, 1985.)

Alex Madrid

Date	Traded To		Traded With	Traded By		In Exchange For
Aug 24, 1988	PHI	N	———	MIL	A	Mike Young

Bill Magee

Date	Traded To		Traded With	Traded By		In Exchange For
May 1901	NY	N	———	STL	N	Chauncey Fisher
May 1902	PHI	N	———	NY	N	Cash

Lee Magee

Date	Traded To		Traded With	Traded By		In Exchange For
Feb 10, 1916	NY	A	———	BKN	F	Cash
July 15, 1917	STL	A	———	NY	A	Armando Marsans
April 28, 1918	NY	A	———	STL	A	Tim Hendryx
April 28, 1918	CIN	N	———	NY	A	Tommy Clarke
April 18, 1919	BKN	N	———	CIN	N	Cash
June 2, 1919	CHI	N	———	BKN	N	Pete Kilduff

Sherry Magee

Date	Traded To		Traded With	Traded By		In Exchange For
Dec 24, 1914	BOS	N	———	PHI	N	Cash
Aug 1, 1917	CIN	N	———	BOS	N	Waiver price

Sal Maglie

Date	Traded To		Traded With	Traded By		In Exchange For
July 31, 1955	CLE	A	———	NY	N	Waiver price
May 15, 1956	BKN	N	———	CLE	A	Cash
Sept 1, 1957	NY	A	———	BKN	N	Waiver price
June 14, 1958	STL	N	———	NY	A	Joe McClain and $25,000.

George Magoon

Date	Traded To		Traded With	Traded By		In Exchange For
June 9, 1903	CHI	A	———	CIN	N	Cozy Dolan Tom Daly

Tom Magrann

Date	Traded To		Traded With	Traded By		In Exchange For
Nov 15, 1988	CLE	A	Minor league OF Gary Holtz	BAL	A	Minor league 1B Don Lovell Minor league P John Githens

Pete Magrini

Date	Traded To		Traded With	Traded By		In Exchange For
Aug 3, 1967	NY	A	Ron Klimkowski	BOS	A	Elston Howard

Freddie Maguire

Date	Traded To		Traded With	Traded By		In Exchange For
Nov 7, 1928	BOS	N	Socks Seibold Percy Jones Lou Legett Bruce Cunningham and $200,000.	CHI	N	Rogers Hornsby

Jack Maguire

Date	Traded To		Traded With	Traded By		In Exchange For
June 5, 1951	PIT	N	———	NY	N	Waiver price
July 16, 1951	STL	A	———	PIT	N	Waiver price

Art Mahaffey

Date	Traded To		Traded With	Traded By		In Exchange For
Oct 27, 1965	STL	N	Pat Corrales Alex Johnson	PHI	N	Bill White Dick Groat Bob Uecker
April 1, 1967	NY	N	Jerry Buchek Tony Martinez	STL	N	Ed Bressoud Danny Napoleon and cash

Roy Mahaffey

Date	Traded To		Traded With	Traded By		In Exchange For
Jan 29, 1936	STL	A	———	PHI	A	Waiver price

Greg Mahlberg

Date	Traded To		Traded With	Traded By		In Exchange For
Dec 15, 1980	CIN	N	*See Danny Walton*	TEX	A	———

Mickey Mahler

Date	Traded To		Traded With	Traded By		In Exchange For
April 1, 1981	CAL	A	Ed Ott	PIT	N	Jason Thompson
Feb 6, 1985	MON	N	———	STL	N	Tom Lawless

(St. Louis received Lawless on March 25, 1985.)

Rick Mahler

Date	Traded To		Traded With	Traded By		In Exchange For
Dec 4, 1988	CIN	N	———	ATL	N	No compensation (free agent signing)

Bob Mahoney

Date	Traded To		Traded With	Traded By		In Exchange For
May 29, 1951	STL	A	———	CHI	A	Waiver price
Oct 14, 1952	BKN	N	Stan Rojek Ray Coleman and $90,000.	STL	A	Billy Hunter

Jim Mahoney

Date	Traded To		Traded With	Traded By		In Exchange For
Oct 5, 1961	CLE	A	Dick Donovan Gene Green	WAS	A	Jimmy Piersall
July 20, 1966	CHI	A	Cash	HOU	N	Gene Freese

Duster Mails

Date	Traded To		Traded With	Traded By		In Exchange For
May 10, 1917	PIT	N	———	BKN	N	Waiver price

Fritz Maisel

Date	Traded To		Traded With	Traded By		In Exchange For
Jan 22, 1918	STL	A	———	NY	A	*See Eddie Plank*

Hank Majeski

Date	Traded To		Traded With	Traded By		In Exchange For
Sept 25, 1942	NY	A	———	BOS	N	Cash
June 14, 1946	PHI	A	———	NY	A	Cash
Dec 14, 1949	CHI	A	———	PHI	A	Eddie Klieman
June 4, 1951	PHI	A	———	CHI	A	Kermit Wahl
June 10, 1952	CLE	A	———	PHI	A	Cash
June 27, 1955	BAL	A	———	CLE	A	Bobby Young

Candy Maldonado

Date	Traded To		Traded With	Traded By		In Exchange For
Dec 11, 1985	SF	N	———	LA	N	Alex Trevino
Nov 28, 1989	CLE	A	———	SF	N	No compensation (free agent signing)

Jim Maler

Date	Traded To		Traded With	Traded By		In Exchange For
Jan 15, 1984	NY	N	———	SEA	A	Minor league P John Semprini

Sheldon Mallory

Date	Traded To		Traded With	Traded By		In Exchange For
Dec 8, 1976	CHI	N	———	KC	A	Pete LaCock

(Part of three-team trade involving Kansas City, Chicago Cubs, and New York Mets.)

Date	Traded To		Traded With	Traded By		In Exchange For
Dec 8, 1976	NY	N	———	CHI	N	Jim Dwyer

(Part of three-team trade involving Chicago Cubs, New York Mets, and Kansas City.)

Date	Traded To		Traded With	Traded By		In Exchange For
April 4, 1977	OAK	A	———	NY	N	Cash

Date	Traded To	Traded With	Traded By	In Exchange For

Sheldon Mallory *continued*

Date	Traded To		Traded With	Traded By		In Exchange For
March 25, 1978	TOR	A	———	OAK	A	Steve Staggs
Nov 3, 1978	CLE	A	———	TOR	A	Dave Freisleben

Bob Malloy

April 28, 1947	PIT	N	———	CIN	N	Waiver price

Harry Malmberg

April 7, 1955	DET	A	———	CLE	A	Waiver price

Pat Malone

Oct 26, 1934	STL	N	———	CHI	N	Ken O'Dea
March 26, 1935	NY	A	———	STL	N	$15,000.

Billy Maloney

Dec 30, 1905	BKN	N	Jack McCarthy Doc Casey Buttons Briggs and $2,000.	CHI	N	Jimmy Sheckard

Jim Maloney

Dec 15, 1970	CAL	A	———	CIN	N	Greg Garrett

Al Mamaux

Jan 9, 1918	BKN	N	Chuck Ward Burleigh Grimes	PIT	N	Casey Stengel George Cutshaw

Frank Mancuso

Dec 16, 1946	STL	A	———	WAS	A	Jake Early

Gus Mancuso

Oct 10, 1932	NY	N	Ray Starr	STL	N	Ethan Allen Bob O'Farrell Bill Walker Jim Mooney
Dec 6, 1938	CHI	N	Dick Bartell Hank Leiber	NY	N	Frank Demaree Bill Jurges Ken O'Dea
Dec 8, 1939	BKN	N	Newt Kimball	CHI	N	Al Todd
Dec 4, 1940	STL	N	Minor league P John Pintar and $65,000.	BKN	N	Mickey Owen
May 5, 1942	NY	N	———	STL	N	Cash

Jim Mangan

March 5, 1956	NY	N	———	PIT	N	Cash

Angel Mangual

Sept 14, 1970	OAK	A	———	PIT	N	Mudcat Grant

(Oakland received Mangual on October 20.)

Pepe Mangual

July 21, 1976	NY	N	Jim Dwyer	MON	N	Del Unser Wayne Garrett

Leo Mangum

Jan 15, 1927	WAS	A	Sloppy Thurston	CHI	A	Roger Peckinpaugh

Phil Mankowski

Oct 31, 1979	NY	N	Jerry Morales	DET	A	Richie Hebner

Les Mann

Feb 10, 1916	CHI	N	*See Three Finger Brown*	CHI	F	———
Aug 1919	BOS	N	Charlie Pick	CHI	N	Buck Herzog
Nov 9, 1920	STL	N	———	BOS	N	Cash
July 18, 1927	NY	N	———	BOS	N	Waiver price

Rick Manning

June 6, 1983	MIL	A	Rick Waits	CLE	A	Gorman Thomas Jamie Easterly Ernie Camacho

Fred Manrique

April 7, 1985	MON	N	———	TOR	A	Cash
March 31, 1986	STL	N	———	MON	N	Tom Nieto
Dec 22, 1986	CHI	A	———	STL	N	Bill Dawley
July 29, 1989	TEX	A	Harold Baines	CHI	A	Scott Fletcher Sammy Sosa Wilson Alvarez

Felix Mantilla

Dec 11, 1962	BOS	A	———	NY	N	Tracy Stallard Pumpsie Green Al Moran
April 3, 1966	HOU	N	———	BOS	A	Eddie Kasko

Jerry Manuel

March 15, 1980	MON	N	———	DET	A	Duffy Dyer
May 22, 1982	SD	N	———	MON	N	Kim Seaman
June 8, 1982	MON	N	———	SD	N	Mike Griffin
April 10, 1984	CHI	A	———	CHI	N	Minor league IF Tim Gourley

Heinie Manush

Dec 2, 1927	STL	A	Lu Blue	DET	A	Chick Galloway Elam Vangilder Harry Rice
June 13, 1930	WAS	A	General Crowder	STL	A	Goose Goslin
Dec 17, 1935	BOS	A	———	WAS	A	Carl Reynolds Roy Johnson
May 1938	PIT	N	———	BKN	N	Waiver price

Dick Manville

Dec 3, 1952	PIT	N	$25,000.	CHI	N	Clyde McCullough

Cliff Mapes

July 31, 1951	STL	A	———	NY	A	Bobby Hogue Kermit Wahl Tom Upton Lou Sleater
Feb 14, 1952	DET	A	———	STL	A	*See Gene Bearden*
Oct 27, 1952	STL	A	Neil Berry and $25,000.	DET	A	Rufus Crawford

Georges Maranda

Aug 20, 1962	CLE	A	Jackie Collum and cash	MIN	A	Ruben Gomez

Rabbit Maranville

Feb 23, 1921	PIT	N	———	BOS	N	Billy Southworth Fred Nicholson Walter Barbare and $15,000.
Oct 27, 1924	CHI	N	Charlie Grimm Wilbur Cooper	PIT	N	Vic Aldridge George Grantham Al Niehaus
Nov 9, 1925	BKN	N	———	CHI	N	Waiver price
Dec 8, 1928	BOS	N	———	STL	N	Cash

Date	Traded To		Traded With	Traded By		In Exchange For

Firpo Marberry

| Dec 14, 1932 | DET | A | Carl Fischer | WAS | A | Earl Whitehill |

Johnny Marcum

Dec 10, 1935	BOS	A	Jimmie Foxx	PHI	A	Gordon Rhodes minor league C George Savino and $150,000.
Dec 6, 1938	STL	A	———	BOS	A	Tom Carey
June 2, 1939	CHI	A	———	STL	A	John Whitehead

Leo Marentette

| April 3, 1969 | MON | N | Howie Reed | HOU | N | Cash |

Juan Marichal

| Dec 7, 1973 | BOS | A | ——— | SF | N | Cash |

Roger Maris

June 15, 1958	KC	A	Dick Tomanek Preston Ward	CLE	A	Woodie Held Vic Power
Dec 11, 1959	NY	A	Joe DeMaestri Kent Hadley	KC	A	Hank Bauer Don Larsen Norm Siebern Marv Throneberry
Dec 8, 1966	STL	N	———	NY	A	Charley Smith

Dick Marlowe

| Sept 17, 1956 | CHI | A | ——— | DET | A | Waiver price |

Rube Marquard

Aug 31, 1915	BKN	N	———	NY	N	Waiver price
Dec 15, 1920	CIN	N	———	BKN	N	Dutch Ruether
Feb 18, 1922	BOS	N	———	CIN	N	Larry Kopf Jack Scott

Gonzalo Marquez

| Aug 29, 1973 | CHI | N | ——— | OAK | A | Pat Bourque |

Luis Marquez

| June 14, 1954 | PIT | N | ——— | CHI | N | Hal Rice |

Bob Marquis

| Aug 28, 1952 | CIN | N | ——— | NY | A | See Ewell Blackwell |

Bill Marriott

| April 1926 | BKN | N | ——— | BOS | N | Cash |

Armando Marsans

| Feb 10, 1916 | STL | A | See Eddie Plank | STL | F | ——— |
| July 15, 1917 | NY | A | ——— | STL | A | Lee Magee |

Freddie Marsh

April 1, 1951	STL	A	$35,000.	CLE	A	Snuffy Stirnweiss Merrill Combs
May 12, 1952	WAS	A	Lou Sleater	STL	A	Cass Michaels
June 10, 1952	STL	A	———	WAS	A	Earl Rapp
Jan 20, 1953	CHI	A	———	STL	A	Dixie Upright and $25,000.
Dec 6, 1954	BAL	A	———	CHI	A	See Clint Courtney

Cuddles Marshall

| May 15, 1950 | STL | A | ——— | NY | A | Cash |

Dave Marshall

| Dec 12, 1969 | NY | N | Ray Sadecki | SF | N | Bob Heise Jim Gosger |
| Nov 30, 1972 | SD | N | ——— | NY | N | Al Severinsen |

Doc Marshall

May 1904	NY	N	———	PHI	N	Cash
Aug 7, 1904	BOS	N	———	NY	N	Cash
July 13, 1906	STL	N	Sam Mertes	NY	N	Spike Shannon
June 1908	CHI	N	———	STL	N	Cash
Nov 1908	BKN	N	———	CHI	N	Waiver price

Jim Marshall

Dec 3, 1957	BAL	A	Jack Harshman Russ Heman Larry Doby	CHI	A	Tito Francona Ray Moore Billy Goodman
Aug 23, 1958	CHI	A	———	BAL	A	Waiver price
Nov 21, 1959	BOS	A	Dave Hillman	CHI	A	Dick Gernert
March 16, 1960	CLE	A	Sammy White	BOS	A	Russ Nixon
			(Trade was cancelled when White decided to retire.)			
March 29, 1960	SF	N	———	BOS	A	Al Worthington
Oct 13, 1961	NY	N	———	SF	N	Cash
May 7, 1962	PIT	N	———	NY	N	Vinegar Bend Mizell

Mike Marshall

| Dec 20, 1989 | NY | N | Alejandro Pena | LA | N | Juan Samuel |

Mike Marshall

Dec 5, 1973	LA	N	———	MON	N	Willie Davis
June 23, 1976	ATL	N	———	LA	N	Elias Sosa Lee Lacy
April 30, 1977	TEX	A	———	ATL	N	Cash

Willard Marshall

Dec 14, 1949	BOS	N	Sid Gordon Buddy Kerr Red Webb	NY	N	Eddie Stanky Alvin Dark
June 4, 1952	CIN	N	———	BOS	N	Cash
Dec 10, 1953	CHI	A	———	CIN	N	Saul Rogovin Connie Ryan Rocky Krsnich

Billy Martin

June 15, 1957	KC	A	Woodie Held Ralph Terry Bob Martyn	NY	A	Ryne Duren Jim Pisoni Milt Graff Harry Simpson
Nov 20, 1957	DET	A	Gus Zernial Tom Morgan Lou Skizas Mickey McDermott Tim Thompson	KC	A	Bill Tuttle Jim Small Duke Maas John Tsitouris Frank House Kent Hadley Jim McManus
Nov 20, 1958	CLE	A	Al Cicotte	DET	A	Don Mossi Ray Narleski Ossie Alvarez
Dec 15, 1959	CIN	N	Cal McLish Gordy Coleman	CLE	A	Johnny Temple
Dec 3, 1960	MIL	N	———	CIN	N	Cash
June 1, 1961	MIN	A	———	MIL	N	Billy Consolo

Gene Martin

| Nov 3, 1970 | PHI | N | Greg Goossen Jeff Terpko | WAS | A | Curt Flood |

J. C. Martin

| July 22, 1967 | NY | N | Bill Southworth | CHI | A | Ken Boyer |
| March 29, 1970 | CHI | N | ——— | NY | N | Randy Bobb |

Date	Traded To	Traded With	Traded By	In Exchange For

Jack Martin
July 3, 1914   PHI   N   ——   BOS   N   Josh Devore

Jerry Martin
Feb 23, 1979   CHI   N   Barry Foote   PHI   N   Manny Trillo
    Ted Sizemore   Dave Rader
    Derek Botelho   Greg Gross
    minor league
    P Henry Mack

Dec 12, 1980   SF   N   Jesus Figueroa   CHI   N   Joe Strain
    minor league   Phil Nastu
    IF Mike Turgeon

Dec 11, 1981   KC   A   ——   SF   N   Rich Gale
    Bill Laskey

March 17, 1984   NY   N   ——   KC   A   No compensation
    (free agent signing)

Joe Martin
July 1903   STL   A   ——   WAS   A   Barry McCormick

John Martin
June 2, 1980   STL   N   Al Greene   DET   A   Jim Lentine
Aug 4, 1983   DET   A   ——   STL   N   Cash

Morrie Martin
June 11, 1954   CHI   A   Ed McGhee   PHI   A   Sonny Dixon
    Al Sima
    Bill Wilson
    and $20,000.

July 13, 1956   BAL   A   ——   CHI   A   Waiver price
July 2, 1958   CLE   A   ——   STL   N   Waiver price

Renie Martin
March 30, 1982   SF   N   Craig Chamberlain   KC   A   Vida Blue
    Atlee Hammaker   Bob Tufts
    Brad Wellman

Aug 20, 1984   PHI   N   Al Oliver   SF   N   Kelly Downs
    George Riley

Speed Martin
July 14, 1917   STL   A   ——   CHI   A   Cash

Stu Martin
Dec 2, 1940   PIT   N   ——   STL   N   Cash

Buck Martinez
Dec 16, 1968   KC   A   Tommy Smith   HOU   N   Minor league
    and minor league   C John Jones
    IF Mickey Sinnerud

Dec 8, 1977   STL   N   Mark Littell   KC   A   Al Hrabosky
Dec 8, 1977   MIL   A   ——   STL   N   George Frazier
May 10, 1981   TOR   A   ——   MIL   A   Gil Kubski

Carlos Martinez
July 30, 1986   CHI   A   ——   NY   A   *See Ron Kittle*

Carmelo Martinez
Dec 7, 1983   SD   N   Craig Lefferts   CHI   N   Scott Sanderson
    Fritz Connally
    (Part of three-team trade involving Chicago Cubs, San Diego, and Montreal.)

Dec 1, 1989   PHI   N   ——   SD   N   No compensation
    (free agent signing)

Dave Martinez
July 14, 1988   MON   N   ——   CHI   N   Mitch Webster

Dennis Martinez
June 16, 1986   MON   N   ——   BAL   A   Rene Gonzales
    (Baltimore received Gonzales on Dec. 16, 1986.)

Marty Martinez
Dec 4, 1968   HOU   N   ——   ATL   N   Bob Aspromonte
Nov 3, 1971   STL   N   ——   HOU   N   Bob Stinson
May 18, 1972   OAK   A   ——   STL   N   Brant Alyea
    (Alyea was returned to Oakland on July 23.)

July 20, 1972   TEX   A   Vic Harris   OAK   A   Don Mincher
    Steve Lawson   Ted Kubiak

Silvio Martinez
Dec 10, 1976   CHI   A   Richie Zisk   PIT   N   Terry Forster
    Goose Gossage

Aug 31, 1977   STL   N   Nyls Nyman   CHI   A   Clay Carroll
    Dave Hamilton

Nov 20, 1981   CLE   A   Lary Sorensen   STL   N   Lonnie Smith
    (Part of three-team trade involving Cleveland, Philadelphia, and St. Louis.)

Teddy Martinez
Dec 11, 1974   STL   N   ——   NY   N   Jack Heidemann
    Mike Vail

May 18, 1975   OAK   A   ——   STL   N   Minor league
    P Steve Staniland
    Mike Barlow

Tippy Martinez
June 15, 1976   BAL   A   Rudy May   NY   A   Ken Holtzman
    Dave Pagan   Doyle Alexander
    Scott McGregor   Grant Jackson
    Rick Dempsey   Ellie Hendricks
    Jimmy Freeman

Tony Martinez
April 1, 1967   NY   N   Jerry Buchek   STL   N   Ed Bressoud
    Art Mahaffey   Danny Napoleon
    and cash

Joe Marty
May 29, 1939   PHI   N   Ray Harrell   CHI   N   Claude Passeau
    Kirby Higbe

Bob Martyn
June 15, 1957   KC   A   *See Ralph Terry*   NY   A   ——
April 12, 1959   NY   A   Mike Baxes   KC   A   Russ Snyder
    Tommy Carroll

Randy Martz
Jan 25, 1983   CHI   A   Scott Fletcher   CHI   N   Steve Trout
    Pat Tabler   Warren Brusstar
    Dick Tidrow

Clyde Mashore
June 15, 1970   MON   N   ——   CIN   N   Ty Cline

Phil Masi
June 15, 1949   PIT   N   ——   BOS   N   Ed Sauer
Feb 2, 1950   CHI   A   ——   PIT   N   Cash

Don Mason
Dec 4, 1970   SD   N   minor league   SF   N   Steve Huntz
    P Bill Frost

Date	Traded To		Traded With	Traded By		In Exchange For

Jim Mason

Date	Traded To		Traded With	Traded By		In Exchange For
Dec 6, 1973	NY	A	———	TEX	A	Cash
May 9, 1977	TEX	A	Steve Hargan and $200,000.	TOR	A	Roy Howell
Dec 8, 1978	MON	N	———	TEX	A	Mike Hart

Mike Mason

Date	Traded To		Traded With	Traded By		In Exchange For
May 16, 1987	CHI	N	———	TEX	A	Minor league P Dave Pavlas

Roger Mason

Date	Traded To		Traded With	Traded By		In Exchange For
April 5, 1985	SF	N	———	DET	A	Alejandro Sanchez

Walt Masterson

Date	Traded To		Traded With	Traded By		In Exchange For
June 13, 1949	BOS	A	———	WAS	A	Sam Mele Mickey Harris
June 10, 1952	WAS	A	Randy Gumpert	BOS	A	Sid Hudson

Tom Matchick

Date	Traded To		Traded With	Traded By		In Exchange For
Dec 13, 1969	BOS	A	———	DET	A	Dalton Jones
May 28, 1970	KC	A	———	BOS	A	Mike Fiore
May 11, 1971	MIL	A	———	KC	A	Ted Savage
April 5, 1973	NY	A	———	BAL	A	Frank Baker

Eddie Mathews

Date	Traded To		Traded With	Traded By		In Exchange For
Dec 31, 1966	HOU	N	Sandy Alomar Arnie Umbach	ATL	N	Dave Nicholson Bob Bruce
Aug 17, 1967	DET	A	———	HOU	N	Fred Gladding and cash

Nelson Mathews

Date	Traded To		Traded With	Traded By		In Exchange For
Dec 15, 1963	KC	A	———	CHI	N	Fred Norman

Christy Mathewson

Date	Traded To		Traded With	Traded By		In Exchange For
Dec 15, 1900	NY	N	———	CIN	N	Amos Rusie
July 20, 1916	CIN	N	Edd Roush Bill McKechnie	NY	N	Buck Herzog Red Killefer

John Matias

Date	Traded To		Traded With	Traded By		In Exchange For
Nov 29, 1967	CHI	A	*See Luis Aparicio*	BAL	A	———
Oct 13, 1970	KC	A	Gail Hopkins	CHI	A	Pat Kelly Don O'Riley

Jon Matlack

Date	Traded To		Traded With	Traded By		In Exchange For
Dec 8, 1977	TEX	A	John Milner	NY	N	Willie Montanez Ken Henderson Tom Grieve

(Part of four-team trade involving Texas, New York Mets, Pittsburgh, and Atlanta.)

Gary Matthews

Date	Traded To		Traded With	Traded By		In Exchange For
Nov 17, 1976	ATL	N	———	SF	N	No compensation (free agent signing)
March 25, 1981	PHI	N	———	ATL	N	Bob Walk
March 26, 1984	CHI	N	Bob Dernier Porfi Altamirano	PHI	N	Bill Campbell Mike Diaz
July 12, 1987	SEA	A	———	CHI	N	Minor league P David Hartnett

Wid Matthews

Date	Traded To		Traded With	Traded By		In Exchange For
Jan 1924	WAS	A	———	PHI	A	Cash

Bobby Mattick

Date	Traded To		Traded With	Traded By		In Exchange For
Dec 4, 1940	CIN	N	Jim Gleeson	CHI	N	Billy Myers

Len Matuszek

Date	Traded To		Traded With	Traded By		In Exchange For
April 1, 1985	TOR	A	———	PHI	N	Dave Shipanoff Minor league OF Ken Kinnard

Gene Mauch

Date	Traded To		Traded With	Traded By		In Exchange For
May 3, 1947	PIT	N	Kirby Higbe Hank Behrman Cal McLish Dixie Howell	BKN	N	Al Gionfriddo and $100,000.
Dec 8, 1947	BKN	N	Preacher Roe Billy Cox	PIT	N	Dixie Walker Hal Gregg Vic Lombardi
June 17, 1948	CHI	N	———	BKN	N	Waiver price
Dec 14, 1949	BOS	N	Cash	CHI	N	Bill Voiselle
March 26, 1952	STL	N	———	NY	A	Waiver price

Al Maul

Date	Traded To		Traded With	Traded By		In Exchange For
Feb 1900	PHI	N	———	BKN	N	Cash

Carmen Mauro

Date	Traded To		Traded With	Traded By		In Exchange For
May 26, 1953	WAS	A	———	BKN	N	Waiver price
June 30, 1953	PHI	A	———	WAS	A	Waiver price
Dec 16, 1953	NY	A	*See Harry Byrd*	PHI	A	———

Dal Maxvill

Date	Traded To		Traded With	Traded By		In Exchange For
Aug 30, 1972	OAK	A	———	STL	N	Minor leaguers IF Joe Lindsey and C Gene Dusan
July 7, 1973	PIT	N	———	OAK	A	Cash

Charlie Maxwell

Date	Traded To		Traded With	Traded By		In Exchange For
Nov 24, 1954	BAL	A	———	BOS	A	Cash
May 11, 1955	DET	A	———	BAL	A	Cash
June 25, 1962	CHI	A	———	DET	A	Bob Farley

Carlos May

Date	Traded To		Traded With	Traded By		In Exchange For
May 18, 1976	NY	A	———	CHI	A	Ken Brett Rich Coggins
Sept 16, 1977	CAL	A	———	NY	A	Cash

Dave May

Date	Traded To		Traded With	Traded By		In Exchange For
June 15, 1970	MIL	A	———	BAL	A	Dick Baney Buzz Stephen
Nov 2, 1974	ATL	N	minor league P Roger Alexander	MIL	A	Hank Aaron
Dec 9, 1976	TEX	A	Ken Henderson Carl Morton Roger Moret Adrian Devine and $250,000.	ATL	N	Jeff Burroughs
May 17, 1978	MIL	A	———	TEX	A	Cash
Sept 13, 1978	PIT	N	———	MIL	A	Cash

Jakie May

Date	Traded To		Traded With	Traded By		In Exchange For
Oct 14, 1930	CHI	N	———	CIN	N	Cash

Jerry May

Date	Traded To		Traded With	Traded By		In Exchange For
Dec 2, 1970	KC	A	*See Freddie Patek*	PIT	N	———
May 14, 1973	NY	N	———	KC	A	Cash

Lee May

Date	Traded To		Traded With	Traded By		In Exchange For
Nov 29, 1971	HOU	N	Tommy Helms Jimmy Stewart	CIN	N	Joe Morgan Denis Menke Jack Billingham Ed Armbrister Cesar Geronimo

Date	Traded To	Traded With	Traded By	In Exchange For

Lee May continued

Date	Traded To	Traded With	Traded By	In Exchange For
Dec 3, 1974	BAL A	Jay Schlueter	HOU N	Enos Cabell Rob Andrews
Dec 9, 1980	KC A	——	BAL A	No compensation (free agent signing)

Milt May

Date	Traded To	Traded With	Traded By	In Exchange For
Oct 31, 1973	HOU N	——	PIT N	Jerry Reuss
Dec 6, 1975	DET A	Dave Roberts Jim Crawford	HOU N	Leon Roberts Terry Humphrey Gene Pentz Mark Lemongello
May 27, 1979	CHI A	——	DET A	Cash
Nov 1, 1979	SF N	——	CHI A	No compensation (free agent signing)
Aug 19, 1983	PIT N	Cash	SF N	Steve Nicosia

Rudy May

Date	Traded To	Traded With	Traded By	In Exchange For
Oct 15, 1964	PHI N	——	CHI A	Bill Heath minor league P Joel Gibson
Dec 3, 1964	LA A	Costen Shockley	PHI N	Bo Belinsky
June 15, 1974	NY A	——	CAL A	Cash
June 15, 1976	BAL A	Tippy Martinez Dave Pagan Scott McGregor Rick Dempsey	NY A	Ken Holtzman Doyle Alexander Grant Jackson Ellie Hendricks Jimmy Freeman
Dec 7, 1977	MON N	Randy Miller Bryn Smith	BAL A	Don Stanhouse Joe Kerrigan Gary Roenicke
Nov 8, 1979	NY A	——	MON N	No compensation (free agent signing)

Scott May

Date	Traded To	Traded With	Traded By	In Exchange For
June 29, 1989	MIL A	Minor league OF Mike Wilson	TEX A	LaVel Freeman Minor league P Todd Simmons

John Mayberry

Date	Traded To	Traded With	Traded By	In Exchange For
Dec 2, 1971	KC A	minor league IF Dave Grangaard	HOU N	Jim York Lance Clemons
April 4, 1978	TOR A	——	KC A	Cash
May 5, 1982	NY A	——	TOR A	Dave Revering minor league 3B Jeff Reynolds

Lee Maye

Date	Traded To	Traded With	Traded By	In Exchange For
May 13, 1965	HOU N	——	MIL N	Ken Johnson Jim Beauchamp
Jan 4, 1967	CLE A	Ken Retzer	HOU N	Jim Landis Jim Weaver Doc Edwards
June 20, 1969	WAS A	——	CLE A	Bill Denehy and cash
Sept 10, 1970	CHI A	——	WAS A	Cash

Ed Mayer

Date	Traded To	Traded With	Traded By	In Exchange For
April 20, 1957	CHI N	Bobby Del Greco	STL N	Jim King

Erskine Mayer

Date	Traded To	Traded With	Traded By	In Exchange For
July 1, 1918	PIT N	——	PHI N	Elmer Jacobs
Aug 1919	CHI A	——	PIT N	Waiver price

Wally Mayer

Date	Traded To	Traded With	Traded By	In Exchange For
Feb 28, 1919	STL A	——	BOS A	$5000

Eddie Mayo

Date	Traded To	Traded With	Traded By	In Exchange For
Dec 4, 1936	BOS N	——	NY N	Mickey Haslin

Carl Mays

Date	Traded To	Traded With	Traded By	In Exchange For
July 29, 1919	NY A	——	BOS A	Allen Russell Bob McGraw and $40,000.
Dec 11, 1923	CIN N	——	NY A	Cash

Willie Mays

Date	Traded To	Traded With	Traded By	In Exchange For
May 11, 1972	NY N	——	SF N	Charlie Williams and $50,000.

Lee Mazzilli

Date	Traded To	Traded With	Traded By	In Exchange For
April 1, 1982	TEX A	——	NY N	Ron Darling Walt Terrell
Aug 8, 1982	NY A	——	TEX A	Bucky Dent
Dec 22, 1982	PIT N	——	NY A	Tim Burke Minor league P John Holland Minor league 1B Jose Rivera Minor league OF Don Aubin
Aug 2, 1989	TOR A	——	NY N	Waiver price

Bill McAfee

Date	Traded To	Traded With	Traded By	In Exchange For
Oct 14, 1930	BOS N	Wes Schulmerich	CHI N	Bob Smith Jimmy Welsh
Dec 1933	STL A	——	WAS A	Cash

Sport McAllister

Date	Traded To	Traded With	Traded By	In Exchange For
Sept 1902	BAL A	——	DET A	Cash
(Baltimore returned McAllister to Detroit later in September.)				

Jim McAnany

Date	Traded To	Traded With	Traded By	In Exchange For
April 1, 1961	CHI N	——	LA A	Lou Johnson

Jim McAndrew

Date	Traded To	Traded With	Traded By	In Exchange For
Dec 20, 1973	SD N	——	NY N	Steve Simpson

Ike McAuley

Date	Traded To	Traded With	Traded By	In Exchange For
May 24, 1917	STL N	——	PIT N	Waiver price

Dick McAuliffe

Date	Traded To	Traded With	Traded By	In Exchange For
Oct 23, 1973	BOS A	——	DET A	Ben Oglivie

Al McBean

Date	Traded To	Traded With	Traded By	In Exchange For
April 17, 1969	LA N	——	SD N	Tommy Dean Leon Everitt

Algie McBride

Date	Traded To	Traded With	Traded By	In Exchange For
May 30, 1901	NY N	——	CIN N	Cash

Bake McBride

Date	Traded To	Traded With	Traded By	In Exchange For
June 15, 1977	PHI N	Steve Waterbury	STL N	Tom Underwood Dane Iorg Rick Bosetti
Feb 16, 1982	CLE A	——	PHI N	Sid Monge

George McBride

Date	Traded To	Traded With	Traded By	In Exchange For
July 4, 1905	STL N	——	PIT N	Dave Brain

Date	Traded To	Traded With	Traded By	In Exchange For

Tom McBride
| May 14, 1947 | WAS A | ——— | BOS A | Cash |

Bill McCabe
| May 1920 | BKN N | ——— | CHI N | Cash |

Joe McCabe
| Oct 15, 1964 | WAS A | ——— | MIN A | Ken Retzer |

Larry McCall
Sept 16, 1974	CAL A	———	BAL A	Cash
Nov 10, 1978	TEX A	———	NY A	*See Dave Righetti*
Jan 4, 1980	CLE A	Gary Gray minor league 3B-OF Mike Bucci	TEX A	David Clyde Jim Norris

Roger McCardell
| Nov 30, 1959 | BAL A | Jackie Brandt Gordon Jones | SF N | Billy O'Dell Billy Loes |

Alex McCarthy
| Sept 5, 1915 | CHI N | ——— | PIT N | Cash |
| July 1916 | PIT N | ——— | CHI N | Cash |

Jack McCarthy
| Feb 10, 1900 | CHI N | ——— | PIT N | $2,000. |
| Dec 30, 1905 | BKN N | Billy Maloney Doc Casey Buttons Briggs and $2,000. | CHI N | Jimmy Sheckard |

Johnny McCarthy
| Jan 1936 | NY N | ——— | BKN N | $40,000. |
| Dec 11, 1941 | STL N | Ken O'Dea Bill Lohrman and $50,000. | NY N | Johnny Mize |

Tom McCarthy
| Nov 13, 1985 | NY N | *See Bob Ojeda* | BOS A | ——— |
| Aug 4, 1988 | CHI A | Minor league IF Steve Springer | NY N | Minor league OF Vince Harris Minor league 1B Mike Maksodian |

Tom McCarthy
| Jan 1908 | PIT N | ——— | CIN N | Cash |
| June 18, 1908 | BOS N | Harley Young | PIT N | Irv Young |

Lew McCarty
| Aug 20, 1916 | NY N | ——— | BKN N | Fred Merkle |
| July 4, 1920 | STL N | ——— | NY N | Cash |

Tim McCarver
| Oct 7, 1969 | PHI N | Curt Flood Joe Hoerner Byron Browne | STL N | Dick Allen Cookie Rojas Jerry Johnson |

(Flood refused to report to the Philadelphia Phillies, and the Cardinals sent Willie Montanez and Bob Browning on April 8, 1970 to complete the trade.)

June 14, 1972	MON N	———	PHI N	John Bateman
Nov 6, 1972	STL N	———	MON N	Jorge Roque
Sept 1, 1974	BOS A	———	STL N	Cash

Joe McClain
| June 14, 1958 | NY A | $25,000. | STL N | Sal Maglie |

Lloyd McClendon
| Dec 16, 1982 | CIN N | Charlie Puleo Minor league OF Jason Felice | NY N | Tom Seaver |
| Dec 9, 1988 | CHI N | ——— | CIN N | Rolando Roomes |

Bob McClure
| Dec 6, 1976 | MIL A | Jim Wohlford Jamie Quirk | KC A | Jim Colborn Darrell Porter |
| June 8, 1986 | MON N | ——— | MIL A | Cash |

Amby McConnell
| Aug 9, 1910 | CHI A | Harry Lord | BOS A | Frank Smith Billy Purtell |

George McConnell
| Sept 23, 1913 | CHI N | ——— | NY A | Cash |
| Feb 10, 1916 | CHI N | *See Three Finger Brown* | CHI F | ——— |

Billy McCool
| April 2, 1970 | STL N | ——— | SD N | Steve Huntz |

Barry McCormick
| July 1903 | WAS A | ——— | STL A | Joe Martin |

Frank McCormick
| Dec 10, 1945 | PHI N | ——— | CIN N | $30,000. |

Mike McCormick
Dec 15, 1962	BAL A	Stu Miller John Orsino	SF N	Jack Fisher Jimmie Coker Billy Hoeft
April 4, 1965	WAS A	———	BAL A	Minor league P Steve Herman and $20,000.
Dec 13, 1966	SF N	———	WAS A	Cap Peterson Bob Priddy
July 20, 1970	NY A	———	SF N	John Cumberland

Mike McCormick
June 3, 1946	BOS N	———	CIN N	Cash
Dec 15, 1948	BKN N	———	BOS N	Pete Reiser
Dec 11, 1950	WAS A	———	CHI A	Bud Stewart

Moose McCormick
July 1903	NY N	———	PHI N	Cash
July 3, 1904	CIN N	———	NY N	Mike Donlin
Aug 9, 1904	PIT N	———	NY N	Cash
Aug 11, 1904	PIT N	———	CIN N	Jimmy Sebring
Dec 20, 1904	PHI N	Kitty Bransfield Otto Krueger	PIT N	Del Howard
May 1908	NY N	———	PHI N	Cash

Barney McCosky
May 18, 1946	PHI A	———	DET A	George Kell
May 4, 1951	CIN N	———	PHI A	Cash
July 21, 1951	CLE A	———	CIN N	Waiver price

Willie McCovey
Oct 25, 1973	SD N	Bernie Williams	SF N	Mike Caldwell
Aug 30, 1976	OAK A	———	SD N	Cash
Jan 6, 1977	SF N	———	OAK A	No compensation (free agent signing)

Benny McCoy

Date	Traded To		Traded With	Traded By		In Exchange For
Dec 9, 1939	PHI	A	—	DET	A	Wally Moses

(Commissioner Landis ruled that Detroit had kept McCoy covered up in the minors and declared him a free agent, cancelling the deal. McCoy then signed with Philadelphia for a $10,000 bonus.)

Tom McCraw

Date	Traded To		Traded With	Traded By		In Exchange For
March 29, 1971	WAS	A	—	CHI	A	Ed Stroud
April 3, 1972	CLE	A	Roy Foster	TEX	A	Ted Ford
April 2, 1973	CAL	A	minor league 2B Bob Marcano	CLE	A	Leo Cardenas
July 17, 1974	CLE	A	—	CAL	A	Cash

Tom McCreery

Date	Traded To		Traded With	Traded By		In Exchange For
May 1901	BKN	N	—	PIT	N	Lefty Davis
June 1903	BOS	N	—	BKN	N	Cash

Lance McCullers

Date	Traded To		Traded With	Traded By		In Exchange For
Aug 31, 1983	SD	N	Ed Wojna, Marty Decker, Minor league P Darren Burroughs	PHI	N	Sixto Lezcano, Steve Fireovid
Oct 24, 1988	NY	A	Jimmy Jones, Stan Jefferson	SD	N	Jack Clark, Pat Clements

Clyde McCullough

Date	Traded To		Traded With	Traded By		In Exchange For
Dec 8, 1948	PIT	N	Cliff Chambers	CHI	N	Cal McLish, Frankie Gustine
Dec 3, 1952	CHI	N	—	PIT	N	Dick Manville and $25,000.

Harry McCurdy

Date	Traded To		Traded With	Traded By		In Exchange For
Dec 11, 1929	PHI	N	Grover Alexander	STL	N	Homer Peel, Bob McGraw
Nov 1933	CIN	N	—	PHI	N	Cash

Lindy McDaniel

Date	Traded To		Traded With	Traded By		In Exchange For
Oct 17, 1962	CHI	N	Larry Jackson, Jimmie Schaffer	STL	N	George Altman, Don Cardwell, Moe Thacker
Dec 2, 1965	SF	N	Don Landrum, Jim Rittwage	CHI	N	Randy Hundley, Bill Hands
July 12, 1968	NY	A	—	SF	N	Bill Monbouquette
Dec 7, 1973	KC	A	—	NY	A	Lou Piniella, Ken Wright

Mickey McDermott

Date	Traded To		Traded With	Traded By		In Exchange For
Dec 9, 1953	WAS	A	Tommy Umphlett	BOS	A	Jackie Jensen
Feb 8, 1956	NY	A	Bobby Kline	WAS	A	Lou Berberet, Bob Wiesler, Herb Plews, Whitey Herzog, Dick Tettelbach
Feb 19, 1957	KC	A	See Billy Hunter	NY	A	—
Nov 20, 1957	DET	A	See Billy Martin	KC	A	—
July 21, 1961	KC	A	—	STL	N	Cash

Danny McDevitt

Date	Traded To		Traded With	Traded By		In Exchange For
Dec 16, 1960	NY	A	—	LA	N	Cash
June 14, 1961	MIN	A	—	NY	A	Billy Gardner
April 10, 1962	KC	A	—	MIN	A	Cash

Dave McDonald

Date	Traded To		Traded With	Traded By		In Exchange For
May 15, 1970	MON	N	—	NY	A	Gary Waslewski
Dec 30, 1970	SF	N	—	MON	N	Ron Hunt

Hank McDonald

Date	Traded To		Traded With	Traded By		In Exchange For
May 28, 1933	STL	A	—	PHI	A	Cash

Jim McDonald

Date	Traded To		Traded With	Traded By		In Exchange For
May 17, 1951	STL	A	Matt Batts, Jim Suchecki and $100,000.	BOS	A	Les Moss
Nov 23, 1951	NY	A	—	STL	A	Clint Courtney
Nov 18, 1954	BAL	A	—	NY	A	See Bob Turley
July 30, 1955	NY	A	—	BAL	A	Ed Lopat

Tex McDonald

Date	Traded To		Traded With	Traded By		In Exchange For
June 1913	BOS	N	—	CIN	N	Cash
Aug 1914	BUF	F	—	PIT	F	Frank Delahanty

Oddibe McDowell

Date	Traded To		Traded With	Traded By		In Exchange For
Dec 6, 1988	CLE	A	Pete O'Brien, Jerry Browne	TEX	A	Julio Franco
July 2, 1989	ATL	N	—	CLE	A	Dion James

Roger McDowell

Date	Traded To		Traded With	Traded By		In Exchange For
June 18, 1989	PHI	N	Len Dykstra, Tom Edens	NY	N	Juan Samuel

(Philadelphia received Edens on July 26, 1989.)

Sam McDowell

Date	Traded To		Traded With	Traded By		In Exchange For
Nov 29, 1971	SF	N	—	CLE	A	Gaylord Perry, Frank Duffy
June 7, 1973	NY	A	—	SF	N	Cash

Will McEnaney

Date	Traded To		Traded With	Traded By		In Exchange For
Dec 16, 1976	MON	N	Tony Perez	CIN	N	Woodie Fryman, Dale Murray
March 29, 1978	PIT	N	—	MON	N	Tim Jones

Leon McFadden

Date	Traded To		Traded With	Traded By		In Exchange For
June 13, 1970	STL	N	Jim Beauchamp	HOU	N	George Culver

Chappie McFarland

Date	Traded To		Traded With	Traded By		In Exchange For
June 3, 1906	PIT	N	—	STL	N	Cash
Aug 1, 1906	BKN	N	—	PIT	N	Waiver price

Herm McFarland

Date	Traded To		Traded With	Traded By		In Exchange For
May 5, 1902	BAL	A	John Katoll	CHI	A	Cash

Orlando McFarlane

Date	Traded To		Traded With	Traded By		In Exchange For
April 10, 1967	CAL	A	—	DET	A	Cash

Andy McGaffigan

Date	Traded To		Traded With	Traded By		In Exchange For
March 30, 1982	SF	N	Ted Wilborn	NY	A	Doyle Alexander
Feb 27, 1984	MON	N	Fred Breining, Max Venable	SF	N	Al Oliver

(San Francisco sent McGaffigan to Montreal on April 1, 1984, after Breining reported to the Expos with a sore arm.)

Date	Traded To		Traded With	Traded By		In Exchange For
July 26, 1984	CIN	N	minor league P Jim Jefferson	MON	N	Dan Driessen
Dec 19, 1985	MON	N	—	CIN	N	See Bill Gullickson

Dan McGann

Date	Traded To		Traded With	Traded By		In Exchange For
Jan 17, 1900	STL	N	Gus Weyhing	WAS	N	Cash

Date	Traded To		Traded With	Traded By		In Exchange For

Dan McGann *continued*

Date	Traded To		Traded With	Traded By		In Exchange For
Dec 3, 1907	BOS	N	Frank Bowerman Bill Dahlen George Browne George Ferguson	NY	N	Fred Tenney Al Bridwell Tom Needham

Bill McGee

Date	Traded To		Traded With	Traded By		In Exchange For
May 14, 1941	NY	N	——	STL	N	Harry Gumbert Paul Dean and cash

Willie McGee

Date	Traded To		Traded With	Traded By		In Exchange For
Oct 21, 1981	STL	N	——	NY	A	Bob Sykes

Ed McGhee

Date	Traded To		Traded With	Traded By		In Exchange For
Jan 27, 1953	PHI	A	Joe DeMaestri Eddie Robinson	CHI	A	Ferris Fain minor league 2B Bob Wilson
June 11, 1954	CHI	A	Morrie Martin	PHI	A	Sonny Dixon Al Sima Bill Wilson and $20,000.

Randy McGilberry

Date	Traded To		Traded With	Traded By		In Exchange For
June 17, 1980	NY	N	——	KC	A	Kevin Kobel

Dan McGinn

Date	Traded To		Traded With	Traded By		In Exchange For
April 7, 1972	CHI	N	——	MON	N	Hector Torres Hal Breeden

Joe McGinnity

Date	Traded To		Traded With	Traded By		In Exchange For
Jan 1900	BKN	N	Jimmy Sheckard Jerry Nops Broadway Aleck Smith Frank Kitson Harry Howell	BAL	N	Cash

Lynn McGlothen

Date	Traded To		Traded With	Traded By		In Exchange For
Dec 7, 1973	STL	N	John Curtis Mike Garman	BOS	A	Reggie Cleveland Diego Segui Terry Hughes
Dec 10, 1976	SF	N	——	STL	N	Ken Reitz
June 15, 1978	CHI	N	——	SF	N	Hector Cruz
Aug 15, 1981	CHI	A	——	CHI	N	Bob Molinaro

(Cubs received Molinaro on March 29, 1982.)

Jim McGlothlin

Date	Traded To		Traded With	Traded By		In Exchange For
Nov 25, 1969	CIN	N	Pedro Borbon Vern Geishert	CAL	A	Alex Johnson Chico Ruiz
Aug 29, 1973	CHI	A	——	CIN	N	Steve Kealey

Bob McGraw

Date	Traded To		Traded With	Traded By		In Exchange For
July 29, 1919	BOS	A	Allen Russell and $40,000.	NY	A	Carl Mays
May 1927	STL	N	——	BKN	N	Jake Flowers
Dec 1927	PHI	N	——	STL	N	Cash
Dec 11, 1929	STL	N	Homer Peel	PHI	N	Grover Alexander Harry McCurdy

John McGraw

Date	Traded To		Traded With	Traded By		In Exchange For
Feb 11, 1900	STL	N	Bill Keister Wilbert Robinson	BAL	N	Cash

Tug McGraw

Date	Traded To		Traded With	Traded By		In Exchange For
Dec 3, 1974	PHI	N	Don Hahn Dave Schneck	NY	N	Del Unser John Stearns Mac Scarce

Scott McGregor

Date	Traded To		Traded With	Traded By		In Exchange For
June 15, 1976	BAL	A	Rudy May Tippy Martinez Dave Pagan Rick Dempsey	NY	A	Ken Holtzman Doyle Alexander Grant Jackson Ellie Hendricks Jimmy Freeman

Fred McGriff

Date	Traded To		Traded With	Traded By		In Exchange For
Dec 9, 1982	TOR	A	Dave Collins Mike Morgan and $400,000	NY	A	Dale Murray Minor league OF Tom Dodd

Deacon McGuire

Date	Traded To		Traded With	Traded By		In Exchange For
Jan 1904	NY	A	——	DET	A	Cash
June 29, 1907	BOS	A	——	NY	A	Waiver price

(McGuire was named Boston manager.)

Date	Traded To		Traded With	Traded By		In Exchange For
Aug 1908	CLE	A	——	BOS	A	Cash

Marty McHale

Date	Traded To		Traded With	Traded By		In Exchange For
May 1916	CLE	A	——	BOS	A	Cash

Vance McHenry

Date	Traded To		Traded With	Traded By		In Exchange For
Jan 27, 1983	TEX	A	——	SEA	A	Bob Babcock

Stuffy McInnis

Date	Traded To		Traded With	Traded By		In Exchange For
Jan 10, 1918	BOS	A	——	PHI	A	Larry Gardner Tilly Walker Hick Cady
Dec 24, 1921	CLE	A	——	BOS	A	George Burns Joe Harris Elmer Smith
Jan 1923	BOS	N	——	CLE	A	Waiver price

Joe McIntosh

Date	Traded To		Traded With	Traded By		In Exchange For
Dec 11, 1975	HOU	N	Larry Hardy	SD	N	Doug Rader

Matty McIntyre

Date	Traded To		Traded With	Traded By		In Exchange For
Jan 1911	CHI	A	——	DET	A	Cash

Archie McKain

Date	Traded To		Traded With	Traded By		In Exchange For
Dec 15, 1938	DET	A	Pinky Higgins	BOS	A	Eldon Auker Jake Wade Chet Morgan
Aug 4, 1941	STL	A	——	DET	A	Cash
July 15, 1943	BKN	N	Fritz Ostermueller	STL	A	Bobo Newsom

Bill McKechnie

Date	Traded To		Traded With	Traded By		In Exchange For
Dec 1912	BOS	N	——	PIT	N	Cash
April 15, 1913	NY	A	——	BOS	N	Waiver price
Dec 23, 1915	NY	N	Bill Rariden	NWK	F	Cash
July 20, 1916	CIN	N	Christy Mathewson Edd Roush	NY	N	Buck Herzog Red Killefer
March 1918	PIT	N	——	CIN	N	$20,000.

Rich McKinney

Date	Traded To		Traded With	Traded By		In Exchange For
Dec 2, 1971	NY	A	——	CHI	A	Stan Bahnsen
Nov 24, 1972	OAK	A	Rob Gardner	NY	A	Matty Alou

Date	Traded To	Traded With		Traded By		In Exchange For

Jim McKnight

| June 15, 1960 | CHI | N | ——— | STL | N | Walt Moryn |
| Dec 3, 1962 | MIL | N | ——— | CHI | N | Ken Aspromonte |

Denny McLain

Oct 9, 1970	WAS	A	Don Wert	DET	A	Joe Coleman
			Norm McRae			Ed Brinkman
			Elliott Maddox			Aurelio Rodriguez
						Jim Hannan
March 4, 1972	OAK	A	———	TEX	A	Don Stanhouse
						Jim Panther
June 29, 1972	ATL	N	———	OAK	A	Orlando Cepeda

Bo McLaughlin

| May 25, 1979 | ATL | N | ——— | HOU | N | Frank LaCorte |

Byron McLaughlin

| Dec 12, 1980 | MIN | A | ——— | SEA | A | Willie Norwood |

Joey McLaughlin

| Dec 5, 1979 | TOR | A | Barry Bonnell | ATL | N | Chris Chambliss |
| | | | Pat Rockett | | | Luis Gomez |

Warren McLaughlin

| March 1903 | PHI | N | ——— | PIT | N | Waiver price |

Larry McLean

Dec 12, 1903	STL	N	Jack Taylor	CHI	N	Three Finger Brown
						Jack O'Neill
Aug 6, 1913	NY	N	———	STL	N	Doc Crandall

Cal McLish

May 3, 1947	PIT	N	Kirby Higbe	BKN	N	Al Gionfriddo
			Hank Behrman			and $100,000.
			Gene Mauch			
			Dixie Howell			
Dec 8, 1948	CHI	N	Frankie Gustine	PIT	N	Clyde McCullough
						Cliff Chambers
Dec 15, 1959	CIN	N	Billy Martin	CLE	A	Johnny Temple
			Gordy Coleman			
Dec 15, 1960	CHI	A	Juan Pizarro	CIN	N	Gene Freese
Dec 15, 1961	PHI	N	Frank Barnes	CHI	A	Bob Sadowski
			Andy Carey			Taylor Phillips
						minor league
						IF Lou Vassie

(Carey refused to report, and the Phillies received McLish in exchange for Vassie to complete the trade on March 24, 1962.)

Jack McMahan

| June 23, 1956 | KC | A | ——— | PIT | N | Spook Jacobs |
| Feb 19, 1957 | NY | A | ——— | KC | A | *See Billy Hunter* |

Don McMahon

May 9, 1962	HOU	N	———	MIL	N	Cash
Sept 30, 1963	CLE	A	———	HOU	N	Cash
June 2, 1966	BOS	A	Lee Stange	CLE	A	Dick Radatz
June 3, 1967	CHI	A	minor league	BOS	A	Jerry Adair
			P Bob Snow			
July 21, 1968	DET	A	———	CHI	A	Dennis Ribant
Aug 9, 1969	SF	N	———	DET	A	Cash

Frank McManus

| July 25, 1904 | NY | A | ——— | DET | A | Monte Beville |

Jim McManus

| Nov 20, 1957 | KC | A | ——— | DET | A | *See Billy Martin* |

Marty McManus

Jan 15, 1927	DET	A	Bobby LaMotte	STL	A	Lefty Stewart
			Pinky Hargrave			Frank O'Rourke
						Billy Mullen
						Otto Miller
Aug 31, 1931	BOS	A	———	DET	A	Muddy Ruel

Norm McMillan

Jan 30, 1923	BOS	A	Camp Skinner	NY	A	Herb Pennock
			George Murray			
			and $50,000.			
Dec 1923	STL	A	———	BOS	A	Homer Ezzell

Roy McMillan

Dec 15, 1960	MIL	N	———	CIN	N	Joey Jay
						Juan Pizarro
May 8, 1964	NY	N	———	MIL	N	Jay Hook
						Adrian Garrett

Tommy McMillan

| Dec 5, 1978 | PIT | N | ——— | SEA | A | *See Mario Mendoza* |

Tommy McMillan

| May 1910 | CIN | N | ——— | BKN | N | Cash |

Ken McMullen

Dec 4, 1964	WAS	A	Frank Howard	LA	N	Claude Osteen
			Phil Ortega			John Kennedy
			Pete Richert			and $100,000.
			Dick Nen			
April 27, 1970	CAL	A	———	WAS	A	Aurelio Rodriguez
						Rick Reichardt
Nov 28, 1972	LA	N	Andy Messersmith	CAL	A	Frank Robinson
						Bill Singer
						Mike Strahler
						Billy Grabarkewitz
						Bobby Valentine
Feb 25, 1977	MIL	A	———	OAK	A	Cash

Craig McMurtry

| Feb 2, 1987 | TOR | A | ——— | ATL | N | Damaso Garcia |
| | | | | | | Luis Leal |

Eric McNair

Jan 4, 1936	BOS	A	Doc Cramer	PHI	A	Hank Johnson
						Al Niemiec
						and $75,000.
Dec 21, 1938	CHI	A	———	BOS	A	Boze Berger
Dec 18, 1940	DET	A	———	CHI	A	Waiver price
July 17, 1942	WAS	A	———	DET	A	Jack Wilson
			(McNair refused to report.)			
July 25, 1942	PHI	A	———	DET	A	Cash

Dave McNally

Dec 4, 1974	MON	N	Rich Coggins	BAL	A	Ken Singleton
			minor league			Mike Torrez
			P Bill Kirkpatrick			

Mike McNally

Dec 15, 1920	NY	A	*See Waite Hoyt*	BOS	A	———
Dec 10, 1924	BOS	A	———	NY	A	Howard Shanks
Dec 11, 1924	WAS	A	———	BOS	A	Doc Prothro
Feb 1925	WAS	A	———	NY	A	Cash

2453

Date	Traded To	Traded With	Traded By	In Exchange For

Tim McNamara

Date				
April 17, 1925	NY N	——	BOS N	Rosy Ryan

Rusty McNealy

Dec 9, 1981	OAK A	minor league P Tim Hallgren	SEA A	Roy Thomas
Dec 7, 1983	MON N	Cash	OAK A	Ray Burris

Earl McNeely

Oct 19, 1927	STL A	Dick Coffman	WAS A	Milt Gaston

Jerry McNertney

Oct 20, 1970	STL N	George Lauzerique minor league P Jesse Higgins	MIL A	Carl Taylor Jim Ellis
May 4, 1973	PIT N	——	OAK A	Cash

Bill McNulty

Aug 31, 1971	CHI N	Frank Fernandez	OAK A	Adrian Garrett
Oct 30, 1972	TEX A	Brant Alyea	OAK A	Paul Lindblad
March 28, 1973	NY N	——	TEX A	Bill Sudakis

George McQuillan

Feb 1911	CIN N	Johnny Bates Eddie Grant Lew Moren	PHI N	Fred Beebe Jack Rowan Dode Paskert Hans Lobert
Feb 14, 1915	PHI N	——	PIT N	Waiver price

Hugh McQuillan

July 30, 1922	NY N	——	BOS N	Fred Toney Larry Benton and $100,000.

(Toney refused to report and remained Giants' property.)

June 12, 1927	BOS N	Kent Greenfield Doc Farrell	NY N	Zack Taylor Larry Benton Herb Thomas

George McQuinn

Oct 16, 1945	PHI A	——	STL A	Dick Siebert

Hal McRae

Nov 30, 1972	KC A	Wayne Simpson	CIN N	Roger Nelson Richie Scheinblum

Norm McRae

Oct 9, 1970	WAS A	See Denny McLain	DET A	——
May 30, 1972	DET A		TEX A	Dalton Jones
Nov 30, 1972	PIT N	Jim Foor	DET A	Dick Sharon

Kevin McReynolds

Dec 11, 1986	NY N	Gene Walter Minor league IF Adam Ging	SD N	Kevin Mitchell Stan Jefferson Shawn Abner Minor league Ps Kevin Armstrong and Kevin Brown.

Doug McWeeny

Feb 1930	CIN N	——	BKN N	Dolf Luque

Larry McWilliams

June 30, 1982	PIT N	——	ATL N	Pascual Perez minor league SS Carlos Rios
Sept 2, 1989	KC A	——	PHI N	Player to be named later

(Philadelphia received C Jeff Hulse on Oct. 20, 1989.)

Bobby Meacham

Dec 5, 1988	TEX A	——	NY A	Bob Brower

Lee Meadows

July 14, 1919	PHI N	Gene Paulette	STL N	Elmer Jacobs Frank Woodward Doug Baird
May 22, 1923	PIT N	Johnny Rawlings	PHI N	Whitey Glazner Cotton Tierney and $50,000.

Doc Medich

Dec 11, 1975	PIT N	——	NY A	Willie Randolph Ken Brett Dock Ellis
March 15, 1977	OAK A	Dave Giusti Doug Bair Rick Langford Tony Armas Mitchell Page	PIT N	Phil Garner Tommy Helms Chris Batton
Sept 13, 1977	SEA A	——	OAK A	Cash
Sept 26, 1977	NY N	——	SEA A	Cash
Nov 11, 1977	TEX A	——	NY N	No compensation (free agent signing)
Aug 11, 1982	MIL A	——	TEX A	Cash

Scott Medvin

Oct 7, 1985	SF N	——	DET A	See Dave LaPoint
Aug 12, 1987	PIT N	Jeff Robinson	SF N	Rick Reuschel

Joe Medwick

June 12, 1940	BKN N	Curt Davis	STL N	Ernie Koy Carl Doyle Sam Nahem Bert Haas and $125,000.
July 6, 1943	NY N	——	BKN N	Cash
June 16, 1945	BOS N	Ewald Pyle	NY N	Clyde Kluttz

Jouett Meekin

Jan 1900	PIT N	——	BOS N	Cash

Dave Meier

March 17, 1988	CHI N	Greg Tabor	TEX A	Ray Hayward

Roman Mejias

Nov 26, 1962	BOS A	——	HOU N	Pete Runnels

Sam Mejias

June 7, 1976	STL N	——	MIL A	Danny Frisella
Nov 6, 1976	MON N	Bill Greif Angel Torres	STL N	Steve Dunning Pat Scanlon Tony Scott
Dec 14, 1978	CHI N	——	MON N	Rodney Scott Jerry White
July 4, 1979	CIN N	——	CHI N	Cash

Sam Mele

June 13, 1949	WAS A	Mickey Harris	BOS A	Walt Masterson

Date	Traded To	Traded With	Traded By	In Exchange For
Sam Mele _continued_				
May 3, 1952	CHI A	———	WAS A	Jim Busby Mel Hoderlein
Feb 5, 1954	BAL A	Neil Berry	CHI A	Johnny Groth Johnny Lipon
July 29, 1954	BOS A	———	BAL A	Waiver price
June 23, 1955	CIN N	———	BOS A	Cash
Francisco Melendez				
March 24, 1989	BAL A	———	SF N	Ken Gerhart
Luis Melendez				
May 19, 1976	SD N	———	STL N	Bill Greif
Oscar Melillo				
May 21, 1935	BOS A	———	STL A	Moose Solters and cash
Paul Meloan				
April 1911	STL A	———	CHI A	Cash
Bill Melton				
Dec 11, 1975	CAL A	Steve Dunning	CHI A	Jim Spencer Morris Nettles
Dec 3, 1976	CLE A	———	CAL A	Stan Perzanowski and cash
Rube Melton				
Dec 12, 1942	BKN N	———	PHI N	Johnny Allen and $30,000.
Bob Melvin				
Oct 7, 1985	SF N	Juan Berenguer Scott Medvin	DET A	Dave LaPoint Matt Nokes Eric King
(San Francisco received Medvin on Dec. 11, 1985.)				
Jan 24, 1989	BAL A	———	SF N	Terry Kennedy
Mario Mendoza				
Dec 5, 1978	SEA A	Odell Jones Rafael Vasquez	PIT N	Enrique Romo Rick Jones Tommy McMillan
Dec 12, 1980	TEX A	_See Rick Honeycutt_	SEA A	———
Denis Menke				
Oct 8, 1967	HOU N	Denny Lemaster	ATL N	Sonny Jackson Chuck Harrison
Nov 29, 1971	CIN N	_See Joe Morgan_	HOU N	
Feb 18, 1974	HOU N	———	CIN N	Pat Darcy and cash
Mike Menosky				
Feb 10, 1916	WAS A	———	PIT F	Cash
Jan 20, 1920	BOS A	Harry Harper Eddie Foster	WAS A	Braggo Roth Red Shannon
Mike Meola				
July 1936	BOS A	———	STL A	Cash
Rudi Meoli				
Sept 17, 1975	SD N	Bobby Valentine	CAL A	Gary Ross
April 5, 1976	CIN N	Cash	SD N	Merv Rettenmund

Date	Traded To	Traded With	Traded By	In Exchange For
Orlando Mercado				
April 4, 1985	TEX A	———	SEA A	Donnie Scott
March 24, 1987	DET A	———	TEX A	Player to be named
(Texas received OF Ruben Guzman on May 8, 1987.)				
Win Mercer				
Feb 9, 1900	NY N	———	WAS N	Cash
Spike Merena				
Sept 24, 1934	DET A	———	BOS A	Cash
Ron Meridith				
Feb 14, 1984	ATL N	———	HOU N	Jose Alvarez
April 9, 1984	CHI N	———	ATL N	Terry Leach
July 26, 1986	TEX A	———	CHI N	Rick Surhoff Minor league P Bryan Dial
Fred Merkle				
Aug 20, 1916	BKN N	———	NY N	Lew McCarty
Aug 16, 1917	CHI N	———	BKN N	$3,500.
Lloyd Merriman				
Feb 10, 1955	CHI A	———	CIN N	Cash
April 16, 1955	CHI N	———	CHI A	Cash
Jim Merritt				
Nov 21, 1968	CIN N	———	MIN A	Leo Cardenas
Dec 1, 1972	TEX A	———	CIN N	Hal King Minor leaguer Jim Driscoll
Lloyd Merritt				
June 15, 1959	LA N	Chuck Essegian	STL N	Dick Gray
Sam Mertes				
July 13, 1906	STL N	Doc Marshall	NY N	Spike Shannon
Steve Mesner				
Dec 27, 1939	STL N	Gene Lillard and cash	CHI N	Ken Raffensberger
Feb 1, 1943	BKN N	———	CIN N	Waiver price
(Landis voided the sale because Mesner had already been drafted at the time of the deal.)				
Andy Messersmith				
Nov 28, 1972	LA N	Ken McMullen	CAL A	Frank Robinson Bill Singer Mike Strahler Billy Grabarkewitz Bobby Valentine
April 10, 1976	ATL N	———	LA N	No compensation (free agent signing)
Dec 7, 1977	NY A	———	ATL N	Cash
Catfish Metkovich				
April 2, 1947	CLE A	———	BOS A	Cash
Dec 9, 1947	STL A	$50,000.	CLE A	Johnny Berardino
(Metkovich was returned to Cleveland because of a broken finger and the St. Louis Browns received another $15,000 to complete the trade.)				

Date	Traded To		Traded With	Traded By		In Exchange For

Catfish Metkovich *continued*

Date	Traded To		Traded With	Traded By		In Exchange For
June 4, 1953	CHI	N	Ralph Kiner / Joe Garagiola / Howie Pollet	PIT	N	Toby Atwell / Bob Schultz / Preston Ward / George Freese / Bob Addis / Gene Hermanski / $150,000.
Dec 7, 1953	MIL	N	———	CHI	N	Cash

Charlie Metro

Date	Traded To		Traded With	Traded By		In Exchange For
Aug 13, 1944	PHI	A	———	DET	A	Cash

Butch Metzger

Date	Traded To		Traded With	Traded By		In Exchange For
Dec 6, 1974	SD	N	Tito Fuentes	SF	N	Derrel Thomas
May 17, 1977	STL	N	———	SD	N	John D'Acquisto / Pat Scanlon
April 5, 1978	NY	N	———	STL	N	Cash
July 4, 1978	PHI	N	———	NY	N	Cash

Roger Metzger

Date	Traded To		Traded With	Traded By		In Exchange For
Oct 12, 1970	HOU	N	———	CHI	N	Hector Torres
June 15, 1978	SF	N	———	HOU	N	Cash

Alex Metzler

Date	Traded To		Traded With	Traded By		In Exchange For
July 21, 1930	STL	A	———	CHI	A	Cash

Bob Meusel

Date	Traded To		Traded With	Traded By		In Exchange For
Oct 16, 1929	CIN	N	———	NY	A	Waiver price

Irish Meusel

Date	Traded To		Traded With	Traded By		In Exchange For
July 25, 1921	NY	N	———	PHI	N	Curt Walker / Butch Henline / Jesse Winters / and $30,000.

Benny Meyer

Date	Traded To		Traded With	Traded By		In Exchange For
May 1914	BUF	F	———	PIT	F	Cash

Bob Meyer

Date	Traded To		Traded With	Traded By		In Exchange For
June 12, 1964	LA	A	———	NY	A	Cash
July 29, 1964	KC	A	———	LA	A	Cash
Aug 29, 1969	SEA	A	Pete Koegel	OAK	A	Fred Talbot

Dan Meyer

Date	Traded To		Traded With	Traded By		In Exchange For
Dec 9, 1981	OAK	A	———	SEA	A	Rich Bordi

Dutch Meyer

Date	Traded To		Traded With	Traded By		In Exchange For
April 27, 1945	CLE	A	Don Ross	DET	A	Roy Cullenbine

Russ Meyer

Date	Traded To		Traded With	Traded By		In Exchange For
Oct 11, 1948	PHI	N	———	CHI	N	Cash
Feb 16, 1953	MIL	N	Cash	PHI	N	Earl Torgeson

(Part of four-team trade involving Milwaukee Braves, Philadelphia Phillies, Brooklyn, and Cincinnati.)

Date	Traded To		Traded With	Traded By		In Exchange For
Feb 16, 1953	BKN	N	———	MIL	N	Rocky Bridges / Jim Pendleton

(Part of four-team trade involving Milwaukee, Philadelphia Phillies, Brooklyn, and Cincinnati.)

Date	Traded To		Traded With	Traded By		In Exchange For
Dec 9, 1955	CHI	N	Don Hoak / Walt Moryn	BKN	N	Randy Jackson / Don Elston
Sept 1, 1956	CIN	N	———	CHI	N	Waiver price
April 13, 1957	BOS	A	———	CIN	N	Waiver price

Scott Meyer

Date	Traded To		Traded With	Traded By		In Exchange For
March 1, 1982	DET	A	Jeff Cox	OAK	A	Darrell Brown / minor league Ps Mark Fellows / and Jack Smith

Chief Meyers

Date	Traded To		Traded With	Traded By		In Exchange For
Feb 10, 1916	BKN	N	———	NY	N	Waiver price
Aug 16, 1917	BOS	N	———	BKN	N	Waiver price

Gene Michael

Date	Traded To		Traded With	Traded By		In Exchange For
Dec 1, 1966	LA	N	Bob Bailey	PIT	N	Maury Wills
Nov 30, 1967	NY	A	———	LA	N	Cash

Cass Michaels

Date	Traded To		Traded With	Traded By		In Exchange For
May 31, 1950	WAS	A	Bob Kuzava / John Ostrowski	CHI	A	Al Kozar / Ray Scarborough / Eddie Robinson
May 12, 1952	STL	A	———	WAS	A	Lou Sleater / Freddie Marsh
Aug 5, 1952	PHI	A	———	STL	A	Waiver price
Dec 8, 1953	CHI	A	———	PHI	A	Cash

Ed Mickelson

Date	Traded To		Traded With	Traded By		In Exchange For
Oct 1, 1952	STL	A	———	STL	N	Waiver price

Pete Mikkelsen

Date	Traded To		Traded With	Traded By		In Exchange For
Dec 10, 1965	PIT	N	Cash	NY	A	Bob Friend
Aug 4, 1967	CHI	N	———	PIT	N	Waiver price
April 22, 1968	STL	N	Dave Dowling	CHI	N	Jack Lamabe / Ron Piche
Oct 21, 1968	LA	N	———	STL	N	Cash

Eddie Miksis

Date	Traded To		Traded With	Traded By		In Exchange For
June 15, 1951	CHI	N	Bruce Edwards / Joe Hatten / Gene Hermanski	BKN	N	Johnny Schmitz / Rube Walker / Andy Pafko / Wayne Terwilliger
Dec 11, 1956	STL	N	Hobie Landrith / Jim Davis / Sam Jones	CHI	N	Tom Poholsky / Jackie Collum / Ray Katt / minor league P Wally Lammers
Sept 19, 1957	BAL	A	———	STL	N	Waiver price

Larry Milbourne

Date	Traded To		Traded With	Traded By		In Exchange For
March 30, 1977	SEA	A	———	HOU	N	Roy Thomas
Nov 18, 1980	NY	A	———	SEA	A	Brad Gulden / and $150,000.
May 12, 1982	MIN	A	John Pacella / Pete Filson / and cash	NY	A	Butch Wynegar / Roger Erickson
July 3, 1982	CLE	A	———	MIN	A	Larry Littleton
Dec 9, 1982	PHI	N	———	CLE	A	Cash
July 16, 1983	NY	A	———	PHI	N	Cash
Feb 14, 1984	SEA	A	———	NY	A	Scott Nielsen / Minor league P Eric Parent

Johnny Miljus

Date	Traded To		Traded With	Traded By		In Exchange For
July 10, 1928	CLE	A	———	PIT	N	Waiver price

Felix Millan

Date	Traded To		Traded With	Traded By		In Exchange For
Nov 2, 1972	NY	N	George Stone	ATL	N	Gary Gentry / Danny Frisella

Date	Traded To		Traded With	Traded By		In Exchange For

Bill Miller

Date	Traded To		Traded With	Traded By		In Exchange For
Dec 1, 1954	BAL	A	———	NY	A	*See Dick Kryhoski*

Bing Miller

Date	Traded To		Traded With	Traded By		In Exchange For
Jan 10, 1922	PHI	A	Jose Acosta	WAS	A	Joe Dugan
	(Part of three-team trade involving Boston, Philadelphia, and Washington.)					
June 15, 1926	STL	A	———	PHI	A	Baby Doll Jacobson
Dec 13, 1927	PHI	A	———	STL	A	Sam Gray
Jan 14, 1935	BOS	A	———	PHI	A	Cash

Bob Miller

Date	Traded To		Traded With	Traded By		In Exchange For
May 7, 1962	NY	N	Cliff Cook	CIN	N	Don Zimmer

Bob Miller

Date	Traded To		Traded With	Traded By		In Exchange For
Nov 30, 1962	LA	N	———	NY	N	Tim Harkness Larry Burright
Nov 28, 1967	MIN	A	Johnny Roseboro Ron Perranoski	LA	N	Mudcat Grant Zoilo Versalles
Dec 10, 1969	CLE	A	Dean Chance Graig Nettles Ted Uhlaender	MIN	A	Luis Tiant Stan Williams
June 15, 1970	CHI	A	Barry Moore	CLE	A	Buddy Bradford
Sept 1, 1970	CHI	N	———	CHI	A	Cash
Aug 10, 1971	PIT	N	———	SD	N	John Jeter Ed Acosta
June 22, 1973	SD	N	———	DET	A	Cash
Sept 23, 1973	NY	N	———	SD	N	Cash

Bruce Miller

Date	Traded To		Traded With	Traded By		In Exchange For
Aug 17, 1972	CAL	A	Bruce Kimm	CHI	A	Eddie Fisher
April 14, 1973	SF	N	———	CAL	A	Al Gallagher

Doc Miller

Date	Traded To		Traded With	Traded By		In Exchange For
April 1910	BOS	N	———	CHI	N	Lew Richie
July 1, 1912	PHI	N	———	BOS	N	John Titus
Dec 1913	CIN	N	———	PHI	N	Cash

Dots Miller

Date	Traded To		Traded With	Traded By		In Exchange For
Dec 12, 1913	STL	N	Art Butler Cozy Dolan Owen Wilson Hank Robinson	PIT	N	Ed Konetchy Mike Mowrey Bob Harmon
Jan 1920	PHI	N	———	STL	N	Cash

Dusty Miller

Date	Traded To		Traded With	Traded By		In Exchange For
Unknown	STL	N	———	CIN	N	Cash

Dyar Miller

Date	Traded To		Traded With	Traded By		In Exchange For
June 13, 1977	CAL	A	———	BAL	A	Dick Drago
June 6, 1979	TOR	A	———	CAL	A	Cash
July 30, 1979	MON	N	———	TOR	A	Tony Solaita

Eddie Miller

Date	Traded To		Traded With	Traded By		In Exchange For
Dec 8, 1977	ATL	N	Adrian Devine Tommy Boggs	TEX	A	Willie Montanez
	(Part of four-team trade involving Texas, Atlanta, Pittsburgh, and New York Mets.)					
March 23, 1982	DET	A	———	ATL	N	Roger Weaver

Eddie Miller

Date	Traded To		Traded With	Traded By		In Exchange For
Aug 10, 1938	BOS	N	———	CIN	N	Tommy Reis Johnny Babich Gil English Johnny Riddle Vince DiMaggio and Cash

Eddie Miller *continued*

Date	Traded To		Traded With	Traded By		In Exchange For
Dec 4, 1942	CIN	N	———	BOS	N	Eddie Joost Nate Andrews and $25,000.
Feb 7, 1948	PHI	N	———	CIN	N	Johnny Wyrostek and cash
April 3, 1950	STL	N	———	PHI	N	Waiver price

Elmer Miller

Date	Traded To		Traded With	Traded By		In Exchange For
July 23, 1915	NY	A	———	STL	N	Cash
July 23, 1922	BOS	A	Chick Fewster Johnny Mitchell Lefty O'Doul and $50,000.	NY	A	Joe Dugan Elmer Smith

Frank Miller

Date	Traded To		Traded With	Traded By		In Exchange For
Oct 1919	WAS	A	———	PIT	N	Cash

John Miller

Date	Traded To		Traded With	Traded By		In Exchange For
April 3, 1967	LA	N	Jack Cullen and $25,000.	NY	A	John Kennedy

John Miller

Date	Traded To		Traded With	Traded By		In Exchange For
May 10, 1967	NY	N	———	BAL	A	Cash

Larry Miller

Date	Traded To		Traded With	Traded By		In Exchange For
Oct 15, 1964	NY	N	———	LA	N	Dick Smith

Norm Miller

Date	Traded To		Traded With	Traded By		In Exchange For
April 22, 1973	ATL	N	———	HOU	N	Cecil Upshaw

Otto Miller

Date	Traded To		Traded With	Traded By		In Exchange For
Jan 15, 1927	STL	A	———	DET	A	*See Marty McManus*

Ox Miller

Date	Traded To		Traded With	Traded By		In Exchange For
Aug 18, 1943	STL	A	Ellis Clary and cash	WAS	A	Harlond Clift Johnny Niggeling

Randy Miller

Date	Traded To		Traded With	Traded By		In Exchange For
Dec 7, 1977	MON	N	Rudy May Bryn Smith	BAL	A	Don Stanhouse Joe Kerrigan Gary Roenicke

Rick Miller

Date	Traded To		Traded With	Traded By		In Exchange For
Dec 21, 1977	CAL	A	———	BOS	A	No compensation (free agent signing)
Dec 10, 1980	BOS	A	Carney Lansford Mark Clear	CAL	A	Rick Burleson Butch Hobson

Roscoe Miller

Date	Traded To		Traded With	Traded By		In Exchange For
Feb 1904	PIT	N	———	NY	N	Cash

Stu Miller

Date	Traded To		Traded With	Traded By		In Exchange For
May 11, 1956	PHI	N	Harvey Haddix Ben Flowers	STL	N	Murry Dickson Herm Wehmeier
Oct 11, 1956	NY	N	———	PHI	N	Jim Hearn
Dec 15, 1962	BAL	A	Mike McCormick John Orsino	SF	N	Jack Fisher Jimmie Coker Billy Hoeft
April 1, 1968	ATL	N	———	BAL	A	Cash

Ward Miller

Date	Traded To		Traded With	Traded By		In Exchange For
May 28, 1909	CIN	N	Cash	PIT	N	Kid Durbin

Ward Miller *continued*

Date	Traded To		Traded With	Traded By		In Exchange For
Feb 10, 1916	STL	A	*See Eddie Plank*	STL	F	————

Randy Milligan

Date	Traded To		Traded With	Traded By		In Exchange For
March 26, 1988	PIT	N	Minor league P Scott Henion	NY	N	Mackey Sasser Tim Drummond
Nov 9, 1988	BAL	A	————	PIT	N	player to be named

(Pittsburgh received P Pete Blohm on December 7, 1988.)

Buster Mills

Date	Traded To		Traded With	Traded By		In Exchange For
Dec 2, 1937	STL	A	Bobo Newsom Red Kress	BOS	A	Joe Vosmik
Oct 26, 1938	NY	A	Oral Hildebrand	STL	A	Joe Glenn Myril Hoag

Lefty Mills

Date	Traded To		Traded With	Traded By		In Exchange For
Feb 5, 1941	BKN	N	————	STL	A	Cash

Al Milnar

Date	Traded To		Traded With	Traded By		In Exchange For
Aug 27, 1943	STL	A	————	CLE	A	Cash

Eddie Milner

Date	Traded To		Traded With	Traded By		In Exchange For
Jan 8, 1987	SF	N	————	CIN	N	Frank Williams Minor league P Timber Mead Minor league P Mike Villa
Feb 10, 1988	CIN	N	————	SF	N	No compensation (free agent signing)

John Milner

Date	Traded To		Traded With	Traded By		In Exchange For
Dec 8, 1977	TEX	A	Jon Matlack	NY	N	Willie Montanez Ken Henderson Tom Grieve

(Part of four-team trade involving Texas, New York Mets, Pittsburgh, and Atlanta.)

Date	Traded To		Traded With	Traded By		In Exchange For
Dec 8, 1977	PIT	N	Bert Blyleven	TEX	A	Al Oliver Nelson Norman

(Part of four-team trade involving Texas, New York Mets, Pittsburgh, and Atlanta.)

Date	Traded To		Traded With	Traded By		In Exchange For
Aug 20, 1981	MON	N	————	PIT	N	Willie Montanez

Don Mincher

Date	Traded To		Traded With	Traded By		In Exchange For
April 4, 1960	WAS	A	Earl Battey and $150,000.	CHI	A	Roy Sievers
Dec 2, 1966	CAL	A	Jimmie Hall Pete Cimino	MIN	A	Dean Chance Jackie Hernandez
Jan 15, 1970	OAK	A	Ron Clark	MIL	A	Mike Hershberger Lew Krausse Phil Roof Ken Sanders
May 8, 1971	WAS	A	Frank Fernandez Paul Lindblad and cash	OAK	A	Mike Epstein Darold Knowles
July 20, 1972	OAK	A	Ted Kubiak	TEX	A	Marty Martinez Vic Harris Steve Lawson

Craig Minetto

Date	Traded To		Traded With	Traded By		In Exchange For
Feb 24, 1982	BAL	A	————	OAK	A	Minor league P Allen Edwards
Dec 21, 1983	HOU	N	————	BAL	A	Bobby Sprowl

Paul Minner

Date	Traded To		Traded With	Traded By		In Exchange For
Oct 14, 1949	CHI	N	Preston Ward	BKN	N	$100,000.

Minnie Minoso

Date	Traded To		Traded With	Traded By		In Exchange For
April 30, 1951	CHI	A	Paul Lehner	PHI	A	Gus Zernial Dave Philley

(Part of three-team trade involving Chicago White Sox, Philadelphia A's, and Cleveland.)

Date	Traded To		Traded With	Traded By		In Exchange For
April 30, 1951	PHI	A	Sam Zoldak Ray Murray	CLE	A	Lou Brissie

(Part of three-team trade involving Cleveland, Philadelphia A's, and Chicago White Sox.)

Date	Traded To		Traded With	Traded By		In Exchange For
Dec 4, 1957	CLE	A	Fred Hatfield	CHI	A	Early Wynn Al Smith
Dec 6, 1959	CHI	A	Dick Brown Don Ferrarese Jake Striker	CLE	A	Johnny Romano Bubba Phillips Norm Cash
Nov 27, 1961	STL	N	————	CHI	A	Joe Cunningham
April 2, 1963	WAS	A	————	STL	N	Cash and minor league player to be named later

Jim Minshall

Date	Traded To		Traded With	Traded By		In Exchange For
Oct 15, 1976	SEA	A	————	PIT	N	Cash

Greg Minton

Date	Traded To		Traded With	Traded By		In Exchange For
April 2, 1973	SF	N	————	KC	A	Fran Healy

Paul Mirabella

Date	Traded To		Traded With	Traded By		In Exchange For
Nov 10, 1978	NY	A	*See Dave Righetti*	TEX	A	
Nov 1, 1979	TOR	A	*See Chris Chambliss*	NY	A	
Dec 28, 1981	CHI	A	————	TOR	A	Dave Geisel
March 26, 1982	TEX	A	minor league P Paul Semall and cash	CHI	N	Bump Wills

Willie Miranda

Date	Traded To		Traded With	Traded By		In Exchange For
Oct 24, 1951	CHI	A	————	WAS	A	Floyd Baker
June 15, 1952	STL	A	Al Zarilla	CHI	A	Tom Wright Leo Thomas
June 28, 1952	CHI	A	————	STL	A	Waiver price
Oct 16, 1952	STL	A	Hank Edwards	CHI	A	Joe DeMaestri Tommy Byrne
June 12, 1953	NY	A	————	STL	A	Cash
Nov 18, 1954	BAL	A	————	NY	A	*See Bob Turley*

Bobby Mitchell

Date	Traded To		Traded With	Traded By		In Exchange For
Jan 6, 1982	MIN	A	*See Bobby Castillo*	LA	N	————

Bobby Mitchell

Date	Traded To		Traded With	Traded By		In Exchange For
June 7, 1971	MIL	A	Frank Tepedino	NY	A	Danny Walton

Charlie Mitchell

Date	Traded To		Traded With	Traded By		In Exchange For
Dec 12, 1985	MIN	A	————	BOS	A	Mike Stenhouse

Clarence Mitchell

Date	Traded To		Traded With	Traded By		In Exchange For
Oct 16, 1917	BKN	N	————	CIN	N	Waiver price
Feb 11, 1923	PHI	N	————	BKN	N	George Smith
May 15, 1930	NY	N	————	STL	N	Ralph Judd

Dale Mitchell

Date	Traded To		Traded With	Traded By		In Exchange For
July 29, 1956	BKN	N	————	CLE	A	Cash

Fred Mitchell

Date	Traded To		Traded With	Traded By		In Exchange For
April 1902	PHI	A	————	BOS	A	Cash
Aug 18, 1904	BKN	N	————	PHI	N	Cash
Dec 14, 1916	CHI	N	————	BOS	N	Joe Kelly

Date	Traded To		Traded With	Traded By		In Exchange For

John Mitchell

Date	Traded To		Traded With	Traded By		In Exchange For
Nov 13, 1985	NY	N	Bob Ojeda Tom McCarthy Minor league P Chris Bayer	BOS	A	Calvin Schiraldi Wes Gardner John Christensen LaSchelle Tarver
Dec 5, 1989	BAL	A	Minor league OF Joaquin Contreras	NY	N	Keith Hughes Minor league P Cesar Mejia

Johnny Mitchell

Date	Traded To		Traded With	Traded By		In Exchange For
July 23, 1922	BOS	A	Chick Fewster Elmer Miller Lefty O'Doul and $50,000.	NY	A	Joe Dugan Elmer Smith
Nov 1923	BKN	N	—	BOS	A	Cash

Kevin Mitchell

Date	Traded To		Traded With	Traded By		In Exchange For
Dec 11, 1986	SD	N	Stan Jefferson Shawn Abner Minor league Ps Kevin Armstrong and Kevin Brown.	NY	N	Kevin McReynolds Gene Walter Minor league IF Adam Ging
July 4, 1987	SF	N	Craig Lefferts Dave Dravecky	SD	N	Chris Brown Mark Davis Keith Comstock Mark Grant

Mike Mitchell

Date	Traded To		Traded With	Traded By		In Exchange For
Dec 15, 1912	CHI	N	Bert Humphries Red Corriden Pete Knisely Art Phelan	CIN	N	Joe Tinker Grover Lowdermilk Harry Chapman
July 29, 1913	PIT	N	—	CHI	N	Waiver price
July 20, 1914	WAS	A	—	PIT	N	Waiver price

Paul Mitchell

Date	Traded To		Traded With	Traded By		In Exchange For
April 2, 1976	OAK	A	—	BAL	A	*See Reggie Jackson*
Aug 4, 1977	SEA	A	—	OAK	A	Cash
June 7, 1979	MIL	A	—	SEA	A	Randy Stein

Roy Mitchell

Date	Traded To		Traded With	Traded By		In Exchange For
April 1918	CIN	N	—	CHI	A	Cash

Willie Mitchell

Date	Traded To		Traded With	Traded By		In Exchange For
June 20, 1916	DET	A	—	CLE	A	Waiver price

George Mitterwald

Date	Traded To		Traded With	Traded By		In Exchange For
Dec 6, 1973	CHI	N	—	MIN	A	Randy Hundley

Johnny Mize

Date	Traded To		Traded With	Traded By		In Exchange For
Dec 13, 1934	CIN	N	—	STL	N	Cash

(Mize was returned to St. Louis because of a bad knee.)

Date	Traded To		Traded With	Traded By		In Exchange For
Dec 11, 1941	NY	N	—	STL	N	Ken O'Dea Bill Lohrman Johnny McCarthy and $50,000.
Aug 22, 1949	NY	A	—	NY	N	$40,000.

Vinegar Bend Mizell

Date	Traded To		Traded With	Traded By		In Exchange For
May 28, 1960	PIT	N	Dick Gray	STL	N	Julian Javier Ed Bauta
May 7, 1962	NY	N	—	PIT	N	Jim Marshall

Dave Moates

Date	Traded To		Traded With	Traded By		In Exchange For
May 23, 1977	NY	A	—	TEX	A	Cash

Danny Moeller

Date	Traded To		Traded With	Traded By		In Exchange For
Aug 18, 1916	CLE	A	Joe Boehling	WAS	A	Elmer Smith Joe Leonard

Randy Moffitt

Date	Traded To		Traded With	Traded By		In Exchange For
Feb 15, 1983	TOR	A	—	HOU	N	No compensation (free agent signing)

Herb Moford

Date	Traded To		Traded With	Traded By		In Exchange For
Dec 2, 1958	BOS	A	—	DET	A	Lou Berberet

George Mogridge

Date	Traded To		Traded With	Traded By		In Exchange For
Feb 1915	NY	A	—	CHI	A	Cash
Jan 20, 1921	WAS	A	Duffy Lewis	NY	A	Braggo Roth
June 8, 1925	STL	A	Pinky Hargrave	WAS	A	Hank Severeid
March 1926	NY	A	Cash	STL	A	Wally Schang
June 1926	BOS	N	—	NY	A	Waiver price

Dale Mohorcic

Date	Traded To		Traded With	Traded By		In Exchange For
Aug 30, 1988	NY	A	—	TEX	A	Cecilio Guante

Johnny Mokan

Date	Traded To		Traded With	Traded By		In Exchange For
July 14, 1922	PHI	N	—	PIT	N	Cash
Dec 13, 1927	STL	N	Jimmy Cooney Bubber Jonnard	PHI	N	Johnny Schulte Jimmy Ring

Bob Molinaro

Date	Traded To		Traded With	Traded By		In Exchange For
Sept 22, 1977	CHI	A	—	DET	A	Cash
Aug 30, 1979	BAL	A	—	CHI	A	Cash
Oct 3, 1979	CHI	A	—	BAL	A	Cash
Aug 15, 1981	CHI	N	—	CHI	A	Lynn McGlothen

(Cubs received Molinaro on March 29, 1982.)

Date	Traded To		Traded With	Traded By		In Exchange For
Sept 1, 1982	PHI	N	—	CHI	N	Cash

Fritz Mollwitz

Date	Traded To		Traded With	Traded By		In Exchange For
July 20, 1914	CIN	N	—	CHI	N	Claud Derrick
July 22, 1916	CHI	N	—	CIN	N	Cash
Feb 4, 1917	PIT	N	—	CHI	N	Cash
Aug 1919	STL	N	—	PIT	N	Cash

Bill Monbouquette

Date	Traded To		Traded With	Traded By		In Exchange For
Oct 4, 1965	DET	A	—	BOS	A	George Smith George Thomas
July 12, 1968	SF	N	—	NY	A	Lindy McDaniel
Dec 21, 1968	HOU	N	—	SF	N	Cash

(Monbouquette was returned to San Francisco on April 5, 1969.)

Rick Monday

Date	Traded To		Traded With	Traded By		In Exchange For
Nov 29, 1971	CHI	N	—	OAK	A	Ken Holtzman
Jan 11, 1977	LA	N	Mike Garman	CHI	N	Bill Buckner Ivan DeJesus minor league P Jeff Albert

Don Money

Date	Traded To		Traded With	Traded By		In Exchange For
Dec 15, 1967	PHI	N	Woodie Fryman Bill Laxton minor league P Hal Clem	PIT	N	Jim Bunning
Oct 31, 1972	MIL	A	John Vukovich Billy Champion	PHI	N	Jim Lonborg Ken Sanders Ken Brett Earl Stephenson

Date	Traded To	Traded With	Traded By	In Exchange For

Sid Monge

Date	Traded To		Traded With	Traded By		In Exchange For
May 11, 1977	CLE	A	Bruce Bochte and $250,000.	CAL	A	Dave LaRoche Dave Schuler
Feb 16, 1982	PHI	N	——	CLE	A	Bake McBride
May 22, 1983	SD	N	——	PHI	N	Joe Lefebvre
June 10, 1984	DET	A	——	SD	N	Cash

John Monroe

Date	Traded To		Traded With	Traded By		In Exchange For
June 1921	PHI	N		NY	N	Cash

John Montague

Date	Traded To		Traded With	Traded By		In Exchange For
Sept 2, 1975	PHI	N		MON	N	Cash
Nov 6, 1976	SEA	A		PHI	N	Cash
Aug 29, 1979	CAL	A	——	SEA	A	Jim Anderson

Rafael Montalvo

Date	Traded To		Traded With	Traded By		In Exchange For
July 10, 1985	HOU	N	German Rivera	LA	N	Enos Cabell

Willie Montanez

Date	Traded To		Traded With	Traded By		In Exchange For
April 8, 1970	PHI	N	minor league P Bob Browning	STL	N	Completion of Curt Flood trade of October 7, 1969
May 4, 1975	SF	N	——	PHI	N	Garry Maddox
June 13, 1976	ATL	N	Craig Robinson Mike Eden Jake Brown	SF	N	Darrell Evans Marty Perez
Dec 8, 1977	TEX	A	——	ATL	N	Adrian Devine Tommy Boggs Eddie Miller

(Part of four-team trade involving Texas, Atlanta, Pittsburgh, and New York Mets.)

Date	Traded To		Traded With	Traded By		In Exchange For
Dec 8, 1977	NY	N	Ken Henderson Tom Grieve	TEX	A	Jon Matlack John Milner

(Part of four-team trade involving Texas, New York Mets, Pittsburgh, and Atlanta.)

Date	Traded To		Traded With	Traded By		In Exchange For
Aug 12, 1979	TEX	A	——	NY	N	Ed Lynch Mike Jorgensen
Feb 15, 1980	SD	N	——	TEX	A	Gaylord Perry Tucker Ashford minor league P Joe Carroll
Aug 31, 1980	MON	N	——	SD	N	Tony Phillips
Aug 20, 1981	PIT	N	——	MON	N	John Milner

Aurelio Monteagudo

Date	Traded To		Traded With	Traded By		In Exchange For
May 17, 1966	HOU	N	——	KC	A	Cash
Sept 27, 1966	CIN	N	——	HOU	N	Cash
Aug 14, 1973	PHI	N	Chris Coletta Billy Grabarkewitz	CAL	A	Denny Doyle

John Montefusco

Date	Traded To		Traded With	Traded By		In Exchange For
Dec 12, 1980	ATL	N	minor league OF Craig Landis	SF	N	Doyle Alexander
March 6, 1982	SD	N	——	ATL	N	No compensation (free agent signing)
Aug 26, 1983	NY	A	——	SD	N	Dennis Rasmussen Edwin Rodriguez and $200,000.

Manny Montejo

Date	Traded To		Traded With	Traded By		In Exchange For
Dec 1, 1961	HOU	N	Bob Bruce	DET	A	Sam Jones

Rich Monteleone

Date	Traded To		Traded With	Traded By		In Exchange For
Dec 12, 1985	SEA	A	——	DET	A	Darnell Coles

Jeff Montgomery

Date	Traded To		Traded With	Traded By		In Exchange For
Feb 15, 1988	KC	A	——	CIN	N	Van Snider

Wally Moon

Date	Traded To		Traded With	Traded By		In Exchange For
Dec 4, 1958	LA	N	Phil Paine	STL	N	Gino Cimoli

Jim Mooney

Date	Traded To		Traded With	Traded By		In Exchange For
Oct 10, 1932	STL	N	Ethan Allen Bob O'Farrell Bill Walker	NY	N	Gus Mancuso Ray Starr

Balor Moore

Date	Traded To		Traded With	Traded By		In Exchange For
April 13, 1978	TOR	A	——	CAL	A	Cash

Barry Moore

Date	Traded To		Traded With	Traded By		In Exchange For
Dec 5, 1969	CLE	A	Dennis Higgins	WAS	A	Dave Nelson Horacio Pina Ron Law
June 15, 1970	CHI	A	Bob Miller	CLE	A	Buddy Bradford
Dec 3, 1970	NY	A	——	CHI	A	Bill Robinson

Cy Moore

Date	Traded To		Traded With	Traded By		In Exchange For
Dec 15, 1932	PHI	N	Mickey Finn Jack Warner	BKN	N	Ray Benge and $15,000.

Donnie Moore

Date	Traded To		Traded With	Traded By		In Exchange For
Oct 17, 1979	STL	N	——	CHI	N	Mike Tyson
Sept 3, 1981	MIL	A	——	STL	N	Cash

(Moore was returned on November 5.)

Date	Traded To		Traded With	Traded By		In Exchange For
Feb 1, 1982	ATL	N	——	STL	N	Dan Morogiello
Jan 24, 1985	CAL	A	——	ATL	N	

(Claimed in compensation draft after California lost free agent Fred Lynn to Baltimore.)

Earl Moore

Date	Traded To		Traded With	Traded By		In Exchange For
May 16, 1907	NY	A	——	CLE	A	Walter Clarkson
Oct 1907	PHI	N	——	NY	A	Waiver price
July 1913	CHI	N	——	PHI	N	Cash

Eddie Moore

Date	Traded To		Traded With	Traded By		In Exchange For
July 20, 1926	BOS	N	——	PIT	N	Cash

Euel Moore

Date	Traded To		Traded With	Traded By		In Exchange For
Aug 2, 1935	NY	N	——	PHI	N	Cash

Gene Moore

Date	Traded To		Traded With	Traded By		In Exchange For
Feb 6, 1936	BOS	N	Johnny Babich	BKN	N	Fred Frankhouse
Dec 13, 1938	BKN	N	Ira Hutchinson	BOS	N	Jimmy Outlaw Buddy Hassett
May 29, 1940	BOS	N	——	BKN	N	Cash
Feb 5, 1942	NY	A	Buddy Hassett	BOS	N	Tommy Holmes
March 1, 1944	STL	N	Tony Giuliani and cash	WAS	A	Rick Ferrell

(Giuliani announced his retirement, and St. Louis received Moore to complete the trade.)

Jim Moore

Date	Traded To		Traded With	Traded By		In Exchange For
April 24, 1932	CLE	A	Bill Cissell	CHI	A	Johnny Hodapp Bob Seeds

Johnny Moore

Date	Traded To		Traded With	Traded By		In Exchange For
Nov 30, 1932	CIN	N	Bob Smith Rollie Hemsley Lance Richbourg	CHI	N	Babe Herman
May 16, 1934	PHI	N	Syl Johnson	CIN	N	Ted Kleinhans Wes Schulmerich Art Ruble

Date	Traded To	Traded With	Traded By	In Exchange For

Kelvin Moore

Date	Traded To	Traded With	Traded By	In Exchange For
Feb 19, 1984	MIL A ———	.	NY N	Minor league IF Billy Max

Mike Moore

Nov 28, 1988	OAK A ———		SEA A	No compensation (free agent signing)

Randy Moore

Dec 12, 1935	BKN N	Ed Brandt	BOS N	Tony Cuccinello Al Lopez Ray Benge Bobby Reis
July 1937	STL N ———		BKN N	Cash

Ray Moore

Dec 3, 1957	CHI A ———		BAL A	See Larry Doby
June 13, 1960	WAS A ———		CHI A	Cash

Roy Moore

July 13, 1922	DET A ———		PHI A	Cash

Tommy Moore

Oct 13, 1974	STL N	Ray Sadecki	NY N	Joe Torre
June 4, 1975	TEX A	Ed Brinkman	STL N	Willie Davis
Oct 24, 1976	SEA A ———		TEX A	Cash
Dec 7, 1977	BAL N	Carlos Lopez	SEA A	Mike Parrott

Wilcy Moore

May 1, 1932	NY A ———		BOS A	Gordon Rhodes

Jerry Morales

Nov 7, 1973	CHI N ———		SD N	Glenn Beckert Bobby Fenwick
Dec 8, 1977	STL N	Steve Swisher and cash	CHI N	Dave Rader Hector Cruz
Dec 4, 1978	DET A	Aurelio Lopez	STL N	Bob Sykes and minor league P Jack Murphy
Oct 31, 1979	NY N	Phil Mankowski	DET A	Richie Hebner

Jose Morales

Sept 18, 1973	MON N ———		OAK A	Cash
March 29, 1978	MIN A ———		MON N	Cash
Dec 23, 1980	BAL A ———		MIN A	No compensation (free agent signing)
April 28, 1982	LA N ———		BAL A	Leo Hernandez

Rich Morales

May 26, 1973	SD N ———		CHI A	Cash

Al Moran

Dec 11, 1962	NY N	Tracy Stallard Pumpsie Green	BOS A	Felix Mantilla

Billy Moran

June 11, 1964	CLE A ———		LA A	Jerry Kindall
(Part of three-team trade involving Los Angeles Angels, Cleveland, and Minnesota.)				

Charlie Moran

July 14, 1904	STL A ———		WAS A	Hunter Hill Frank Huelsman
(Huelsmann went to Washington on loan.)				

Herbie Moran

Date	Traded To	Traded With	Traded By	In Exchange For
Aug 1908	BOS N ———		PHI A	Cash
Jan 1914	BOS N ———		CIN N	Cash
April 1914	CIN N	Earl Yingling	BKN N	Dick Egan

Pat Moran

Feb 1906	CHI N ———		BOS N	Cash

Ray Morehart

Jan 13, 1927	NY A	Johnny Grabowski	CHI A	Aaron Ward

Seth Morehead

May 12, 1959	CHI N ———		PHI N	Taylor Phillips
March 31, 1961	MIL N	Moe Drabowsky	CHI N	Andre Rodgers Daryl Robertson

Keith Moreland

Dec 8, 1981	CHI N	Dan Larson Dickie Noles	PHI N	Mike Krukow and cash
Feb 12, 1988	SD N	Mike Brumley	CHI N	Goose Gossage Ray Hayward
Oct 28, 1988	DET A	Chris Brown	SD N	Walt Terrell
July 28, 1989	BAL A ———		DET A	Brian Dubois

Lew Moren

Feb 1911	CIN N ———		PHI N	See Dode Paskert

Jose Moreno

March 27, 1979	NY N	Richie Hebner	PHI N	Nino Espinosa
Dec 15, 1980	SD N	John Pacella	NY N	Randy Jones

Omar Moreno

Dec 10, 1982	HOU N ———		PIT N	No compensation (free agent signing)
Aug 10, 1983	NY A ———		HOU N	Jerry Mumphrey

Roger Moret

Dec 12, 1975	ATL N ———		BOS A	Tom House
Dec 9, 1976	TEX A	Ken Henderson Dave May Carl Morton Adrian Devine and $250,000.	ATL N	Jeff Burroughs

Bobby Morgan

March 28, 1954	PHI N ———		BKN N	Dick Young and $50,000.
May 14, 1956	STL N ———		PHI N	Solly Hemus
Nov 19, 1956	PHI N	Rip Repulski	STL N	Del Ennis
May 13, 1957	CHI N ———		PHI N	Cash

Chet Morgan

Dec 15, 1938	BOS A	Eldon Auker Jake Wade	DET A	Pinky Higgins Archie McKain

Cy Morgan

Aug 1, 1907	BOS A ———		STL A	Cash

Eddie Morgan

March 6, 1938	PHI N	$45,000.	BKN N	Dolf Camilli

2461

Date	Traded To		Traded With		Traded By		In Exchange For

Joe Morgan

Date	Traded To		Traded With		Traded By		In Exchange For
Nov 29, 1971	CIN	N	Denis Menke Jack Billingham Ed Armbrister Cesar Geronimo		HOU	N	Lee May Tommy Helms Jimmy Stewart
Jan 31, 1980	HOU	N	——		CIN	N	No compensation (free agent signing)
Dec 14, 1982	PHI	N	Al Holland		SF	N	Mike Krukow Mark Davis minor league OF Charles Penigar
Dec 13, 1983	OAK	A	——		PHI	N	No compensation (free agent signing)

Joe Morgan

Date	Traded To		Traded With		Traded By		In Exchange For
June 23, 1960	PHI	N	——		MIL	N	Alvin Dark
Aug 9, 1960	CLE	A	——		PHI	N	Cash
May 10, 1961	STL	N	Mike Lee and cash		CLE	A	Bob Nieman

(St. Louis received Lee on September 25.)

Mike Morgan

Date	Traded To		Traded With		Traded By		In Exchange For
Nov 3, 1980	NY	A	——		OAK	A	Fred Stanley Brian Doyle
Dec 9, 1982	TOR	A	——		OAK	A	Fred Stanley Brian Doyle
Dec 9, 1982	TOR	A	*See Dave Collins*		NY	A	——
Dec 9, 1987	BAL	A	——		SEA	A	Ken Dixon
March 11, 1989	LA	N	——		BAL	A	Mike Devereaux

Tom Morgan

Date	Traded To		Traded With		Traded By		In Exchange For
Feb 19, 1957	KC	A	*See Billy Hunter*		NY	A	——
Nov 20, 1957	DET	A	*See Billy Martin*		KC	A	——
July 22, 1960	WAS	A	——		DET	A	Bill Fischer
Jan 31, 1961	LA	A	——		WAS	A	Cash

George Moriarty

Date	Traded To		Traded With		Traded By		In Exchange For
Jan 1909	DET	A	——		NY	A	Cash

Dan Morogiello

Date	Traded To		Traded With		Traded By		In Exchange For
Feb 1, 1982	STL	N	——		ATL	N	Donnie Moore

Jeff Moronko

Date	Traded To		Traded With		Traded By		In Exchange For
April 4, 1985	TEX	A	——		CLE	A	Kevin Buckley

(Texas received Moronko on April 29, 1985.)

Hal Morris

Date	Traded To		Traded With		Traded By		In Exchange For
Dec 12, 1989	CIN	N	Minor league P Rodney Imes		NY	A	Tim Leary Van Snider

John Morris

Date	Traded To		Traded With		Traded By		In Exchange For
May 17, 1985	STL	N	——		KC	A	Lonnie Smith

John Morris

Date	Traded To		Traded With		Traded By		In Exchange For
Dec 15, 1966	BAL	A	——		PHI	N	Dick Hall

Jim Morrison

Date	Traded To		Traded With		Traded By		In Exchange For
April 13, 1979	CHI	A	——		PHI	N	Jack Kucek
June 14, 1982	PIT	N	——		CHI	A	Eddie Solomon
Aug 9, 1987	DET	A	——		PIT	N	Darnell Coles Morris Madden

Bubba Morton

Date	Traded To		Traded With		Traded By		In Exchange For
May 4, 1963	MIL	N	——		DET	A	Cash

Bubba Morton *continued*

Date	Traded To		Traded With		Traded By		In Exchange For
June 15, 1965	CAL	A	Cash		CLE	A	Phil Roof

(California received Morton on September 15, 1965.)

Carl Morton

Date	Traded To		Traded With		Traded By		In Exchange For
Feb 28, 1973	ATL	N	——		MON	N	Pat Jarvis
Dec 9, 1976	TEX	A	Ken Henderson Dave May Roger Moret Adrian Devine and $250,000.		ATL	N	Jeff Burroughs

Walt Moryn

Date	Traded To		Traded With		Traded By		In Exchange For
Dec 9, 1955	CHI	N	Don Hoak Russ Meyer		BKN	N	Randy Jackson Don Elston
June 15, 1960	STL	N	——		CHI	N	Jim McKnight
June 15, 1961	PIT	N	——		STL	N	Cash

Lloyd Moseby

Date	Traded To		Traded With		Traded By		In Exchange For
Dec 7, 1989	DET	A	——		TOR	A	No compensation (free agent signing)

Earl Moseley

Date	Traded To		Traded With		Traded By		In Exchange For
Dec 23, 1915	CIN	N	——		NWK	F	$5,000.

Walter Moser

Date	Traded To		Traded With		Traded By		In Exchange For
June 1911	STL	A	——		BOS	A	Cash

Gerry Moses

Date	Traded To		Traded With		Traded By		In Exchange For
Oct 11, 1970	CAL	A	*See Tony Conigliaro*		BOS	A	——
Oct 5, 1971	CLE	A	*See Alex Johnson*		CAL	A	——
Nov 27, 1972	NY	A	*See Graig Nettles*		CLE	A	——
March 19, 1974	DET	A	——		NY	A	Rick Sawyer Walt Williams Ed Farmer

(Part of three-team trade involving Detroit, New York Yankees, and Cleveland.)

Date	Traded To		Traded With		Traded By		In Exchange For
Jan 30, 1975	NY	N	——		DET	A	Cash
April 28, 1975	SD	N	——		CHI	A	Cash
July 18, 1975	CHI	A	——		SD	N	Cash

Wally Moses

Date	Traded To		Traded With		Traded By		In Exchange For
Dec 9, 1939	DET	A	——		PHI	A	Benny McCoy

(Commissioner Landis ruled that Detroit had kept McCoy covered up in the minors and declared him a free agent, cancelling the deal. McCoy then signed with Philadelphia for a $10,000 bonus.)

Date	Traded To		Traded With		Traded By		In Exchange For
Dec 9, 1941	CHI	A	——		PHI	A	Mike Kreevich Jack Hallett
July 23, 1946	BOS	A	——		CHI	A	Cash

Paul Moskau

Date	Traded To		Traded With		Traded By		In Exchange For
Feb 9, 1982	BAL	A	——		CIN	N	Wayne Krenchicki
April 3, 1982	PIT	N	——		BAL	A	Cash

Les Moss

Date	Traded To		Traded With		Traded By		In Exchange For
May 17, 1951	BOS	A	——		STL	A	Matt Batts Jim Suchecki Jim McDonald and $100,000.
Nov 28, 1951	STL	A	Tom Wright		BOS	A	Ken Wood Gus Niarhos
June 6, 1955	CHI	A	——		BAL	A	Harry Dorish

Ray Moss

Date	Traded To		Traded With		Traded By		In Exchange For
May 28, 1931	BOS	N	——		BKN	N	Cash

Date		Traded To	Traded With		Traded By		In Exchange For

Don Mossi

Date		Traded To	Traded With		Traded By		In Exchange For
Nov 20, 1958	DET	A	Ray Narleski Ossie Alvarez		CLE	A	Billy Martin Al Cicotte
March 18, 1964	CHI	A	———		DET	A	Cash

Manny Mota

Nov 30, 1962	HOU	N	Dick LeMay		SF	N	Joey Amalfitano
April 4, 1963	PIT	N	———		HOU	N	Howie Goss and cash
June 11, 1969	LA	N	Maury Wills		MON	N	Ron Fairly Paul Popovich

Darryl Motley

| Sept 23, 1986 | ATL | N | ——— | | KC | A | Steve Shields |

Curt Motton

| Dec 9, 1971 | MIL | A | ——— | | BAL | A | Bob Reynolds
and cash |

Glen Moulder

| April 6, 1948 | CHI | A | ——— | | STL | A | Cash |

Mike Mowrey

Oct 1908	CIN	N	———		PHI	N	Cash
Aug 22, 1909	STL	N	———		CIN	N	Chappy Charles
Dec 12, 1913	PIT	N	Ed Konetchy Bob Harmon		STL	N	Art Butler Dots Miller Cozy Dolan Owen Wilson Hank Robinson
Feb 10, 1916	BKN	N	———		PIT	F	Cash

Jamie Moyer

| Dec 5, 1988 | TEX | A | Rafael Palmeiro
Drew Hall | | CHI | N | Mitch Williams
Paul Kilgus
Steve Wilson
Curtis Wilkerson
Minor league
IF Luis Benitez
Minor league
OF Pablo Delgado |

Don Mueller

| March 21, 1958 | CHI | A | ——— | | SF | N | Cash |

Heinie Mueller

| June 14, 1926 | NY | N | ——— | | STL | N | Billy Southworth |

Ray Mueller

Dec 16, 1938	PIT	N	———		BOS	N	Al Todd Johnny Dickshot and cash
June 13, 1949	NY	N	———		CIN	N	Walker Cooper
May 17, 1950	PIT	N	———		NY	N	Cash

Billy Muffett

| Oct 8, 1958 | SF | N | Hobie Landrith
Benny Valenzuela | | STL | N | Ernie Broglio
Marv Grissom |

Hugh Mulcahy

| Jan 1947 | PIT | N | ——— | | PHI | N | Cash |

Terry Mulholland

Date		Traded To	Traded With		Traded By		In Exchange For
June 18, 1989	PHI	N	Dennis Cook Charlie Hayes		SF	N	Steve Bedrosian Minor league IF Rick Parker

Greg Mulleavy

| Dec 15, 1932 | BOS | A | Johnny Hodapp
Bob Fothergill
Bob Seeds | | CHI | A | Ed Durham
Hal Rhyne |

Billy Mullen

| Jan 15, 1927 | STL | A | ——— | | DET | A | *See Marty McManus* |

Freddie Muller

| May 15, 1934 | NY | A | $20,000. | | BOS | A | Lyn Lary |

George Mullin

| May 17, 1913 | WAS | A | ——— | | DET | A | Waiver price |

Jim Mullin

| Aug 31, 1904 | WAS | A | ——— | | PHI | A | Cash |

Rance Mulliniks

| Dec 6, 1979 | KC | A | Willie Aikens | | CAL | A | Al Cowens
Todd Cruz
Craig Eaton |
| March 25, 1982 | TOR | A | ——— | | KC | A | Phil Huffman |

Fran Mullins

| Nov 21, 1983 | CIN | N | ——— | | CHI | A | Steve Christmas |
| Jan 23, 1986 | CLE | A | ——— | | SF | N | Cash |

Jerry Mumphrey

Dec 7, 1979	CLE	A	John Denny		STL	N	Bobby Bonds
Feb 15, 1980	SD	N	———		CLE	A	Bob Owchinko Jim Wilhelm
April 1, 1981	NY	A	John Pacella		SD	N	Ruppert Jones Joe Lefebvre Tim Lollar Chris Welsh
Aug 10, 1983	HOU	N	———		NY	A	Omar Moreno
Dec 16, 1985	CHI	N	———		HOU	N	Billy Hatcher Steve Engel

Bob Muncrief

Nov 20, 1947	CLE	A	Walt Judnich		STL	A	Dick Kokos Bryan Stephens Joe Frazier and $25,000.
Nov 20, 1948	PIT	N	———		CLE	A	$20,000.
June 6, 1949	CHI	N	———		PIT	N	Waiver price

George Munger

| May 3, 1952 | PIT | N | ——— | | STL | N | Bill Werle |

Scott Munninghoff

| Nov 20, 1981 | CLE | A | Lonnie Smith | | PHI | N | Bo Diaz |
| | | | (Part of three-team trade involving Cleveland, Philadelphia, and St. Louis.) | | | | |

Date	Traded To	Traded With	Traded By	In Exchange For

Steve Mura

Date	Traded To		Traded With	Traded By		In Exchange For
Dec 10, 1981	STL	N	Ozzie Smith Al Olmsted	SD	N	Sixto Lezcano Garry Templeton Luis DeLeon

(Templeton and Smith were exchanged on February 11, 1982; Olmsted and DeLeon were exchanged on February 19.)

Jan 26, 1983	CHI	N	——	STL	N	

(Claimed in compensation draft after Chicago lost free agent OF Steve Kemp to Yankees.)

Bobby Murcer

Date	Traded To		Traded With	Traded By		In Exchange For
Oct 22, 1974	SF	N	——	NY	A	Bobby Bonds
Feb 11, 1977	CHI	N	Steve Ontiveros minor league P Andy Muhlstock	SF	N	Bill Madlock Rob Sperring
June 26, 1979	NY	A	——	CHI	N	Minor league P Pete Semall

Danny Murphy

Date	Traded To		Traded With	Traded By		In Exchange For
March 28, 1963	HOU	N	Dave Gerard	CHI	N	Merritt Ranew Hal Haydel Dick LeMay
Dec 10, 1963	CHI	A	Jim Golden and cash	HOU	N	Nellie Fox
March 31, 1971	BOS	A	Duane Josephson	CHI	A	Vicente Romo Tony Muser

Eddie Murphy

Date	Traded To		Traded With	Traded By		In Exchange For
July 15, 1915	CHI	A	——	PHI	A	$13,500.

Frank Murphy

Date	Traded To		Traded With	Traded By		In Exchange For
July 1901	NY	N	——	BOS	N	Cash

Rob Murphy

Date	Traded To		Traded With	Traded By		In Exchange For
Dec 13, 1988	BOS	A	Nick Esasky	CIN	N	Todd Benzinger Jeff Sellers player to be named

(Cincinnati received P Luis Vasquez on January 12, 1989.)

Tom Murphy

Date	Traded To		Traded With	Traded By		In Exchange For
May 5, 1972	KC	A	——	CAL	A	Bob Oliver
May 8, 1973	STL	N	——	KC	A	Al Santorini
Dec 8, 1973	MIL	A	——	STL	N	Bob Heise
June 3, 1976	BOS	A	Bobby Darwin	MIL	A	Bernie Carbo
July 27, 1977	TOR	A	——	BOS	A	Cash

Dale Murray

Date	Traded To		Traded With	Traded By		In Exchange For
Dec 16, 1976	CIN	N	Woodie Fryman	MON	N	Tony Perez Will McEnaney
May 19, 1978	NY	N	——	CIN	N	Ken Henderson
Aug 30, 1979	MON	N	——	NY	N	Cash
Dec 9, 1982	NY	A	minor league OF Tom Dodd	TOR	A	Dave Collins Mike Morgan Fred McGriff and $400,000.

Eddie Murray

Date	Traded To		Traded With	Traded By		In Exchange For
Dec 4, 1988	LA	N	——	BAL	A	Brian Holton Ken Howell Juan Bell

George Murray

Date	Traded To		Traded With	Traded By		In Exchange For
Jan 30, 1923	BOS	A	Camp Skinner Norm McMillan and $50,000.	NY	A	Herb Pennock

Larry Murray

Date	Traded To		Traded With	Traded By		In Exchange For
April 27, 1977	OAK	A	Dock Ellis Marty Perez	NY	A	Mike Torrez

Ray Murray

Date	Traded To		Traded With	Traded By		In Exchange For
April 30, 1951	PHI	A	Sam Zoldak Minnie Minoso	CLE	A	Lou Brissie

(Part of three-team trade involving Cleveland, Philadelphia A's, and Chicago White Sox.)

March 28, 1954	BAL	A	——	PHI	A	$25,000.

Red Murray

Date	Traded To		Traded With	Traded By		In Exchange For
Dec 12, 1908	NY	N	Admiral Schlei Bugs Raymond	STL	N	Roger Bresnahan

Ivan Murrell

Date	Traded To		Traded With	Traded By		In Exchange For
April 1, 1974	ATL	N	——	SD	N	Cash

Danny Murtaugh

Date	Traded To		Traded With	Traded By		In Exchange For
Nov 18, 1947	PIT	N	Johnny Hopp	BOS	N	Jim Russell Bill Salkeld Al Lyons

Tony Muser

Date	Traded To		Traded With	Traded By		In Exchange For
March 31, 1971	CHI	A	Vicente Romo	BOS	A	Duane Josephson Danny Murphy
June 15, 1975	BAL	A	——	CHI	A	Jesse Jefferson

Jeff Musselman

Date	Traded To		Traded With	Traded By		In Exchange For
July 31, 1989	NY	N	Minor league P Mike Brady	TOR	A	Mookie Wilson

Ron Musselman

Date	Traded To		Traded With	Traded By		In Exchange For
Dec 21, 1982	TEX	A	——	SEA	A	Pat Putnam

Buddy Myer

Date	Traded To		Traded With	Traded By		In Exchange For
May 2, 1927	BOS	A	——	WAS	A	Topper Rigney
Dec 15, 1928	WAS	A	——	BOS	A	Milt Gaston Hod Lisenbee Bobby Reeves Grant Gillis Elliott Bigelow

Billy Myers

Date	Traded To		Traded With	Traded By		In Exchange For
Dec 14, 1934	CIN	N	Cash	NY	N	Mark Koenig Allyn Stout
Dec 4, 1940	CHI	N	——	CIN	N	Jim Gleeson Bobby Mattick

Elmer Myers

Date	Traded To		Traded With	Traded By		In Exchange For
March 1, 1919	CLE	A	Larry Gardner Charlie Jamieson	PHI	A	Braggo Roth
June 1920	BOS	A	——	CLE	A	Waiver price

Hap Myers

Date	Traded To		Traded With	Traded By		In Exchange For
May 1911	BOS	A	——	STL	A	Cash

Date	Traded To		Traded With	Traded By		In Exchange For

Hy Myers

Date	Traded To		Traded With	Traded By		In Exchange For
Feb 15, 1923	STL	N	Ray Schmandt	BKN	N	Jack Fournier
April 22, 1925	CIN	N		STL	N	Cash
May 4, 1925	STL	N		CIN	N	Cash

Randy Myers

Date	Traded To		Traded With	Traded By		In Exchange For
Dec 6, 1989	CIN	N	Minor league P Kip Gross	NY	N	John Franco Minor league OF Don Brown

Bob Myrick

Date	Traded To		Traded With	Traded By		In Exchange For
June 15, 1979	TEX	A	Mike Bruhert	NY	N	Dock Ellis

Bill Nagel

Date	Traded To		Traded With	Traded By		In Exchange For
March 21, 1941	PHI	N		PHI	A	Cash

Russ Nagelson

Date	Traded To		Traded With	Traded By		In Exchange For
May 22, 1970	DET	A	Billy Rohr	CLE	A	Fred Lasher

Judge Nagle

Date	Traded To		Traded With	Traded By		In Exchange For
June 21, 1911	BOS	A		PIT	N	Cash

Mike Nagy

Date	Traded To		Traded With	Traded By		In Exchange For
Jan 24, 1973	STL	N		BOS	A	Lance Clemons
Feb 1, 1973	TEX	A	Charles Hudson	STL	N	Mike Thompson
(Thompson and Nagy were exchanged on March 31.)						
June 6, 1973	STL	N	John Wockenfuss	TEX	A	Jim Bibby

Sam Nahem

Date	Traded To		Traded With	Traded By		In Exchange For
June 12, 1940	STL	N	Ernie Koy Carl Doyle Bert Haas and $125,000.	BKN	N	Joe Medwick Curt Davis

Bill Nahorodny

Date	Traded To		Traded With	Traded By		In Exchange For
Sept 8, 1977	CHI	A		PHI	N	Cash
Dec 3, 1979	ATL	N		CHI	A	Minor league P Rick Wieters

Danny Napoleon

Date	Traded To		Traded With	Traded By		In Exchange For
April 1, 1967	STL	N	Ed Bressoud and cash	NY	N	Jerry Buchek Art Mahaffey Tony Martinez

Hal Naragon

Date	Traded To		Traded With	Traded By		In Exchange For
May 25, 1959	WAS	A	Hal Woodeshick	CLE	A	Ed Fitz Gerald

Ray Narleski

Date	Traded To		Traded With	Traded By		In Exchange For
Nov 20, 1958	DET	A	Don Mossi Ossie Alvarez	CLE	A	Billy Martin Al Cicotte

Jerry Narron

Date	Traded To		Traded With	Traded By		In Exchange For
Nov 1, 1979	SEA	A	*See Jim Beattie*	NY	A	

Buster Narum

Date	Traded To		Traded With	Traded By		In Exchange For
March 31, 1964	WAS	A		BAL	A	Lou Piniella
Feb 13, 1968	CHI	A		WAS	A	*See Ron Hansen*

Cotton Nash

Date	Traded To		Traded With	Traded By		In Exchange For
May 6, 1967	CHI	A	Cash	CAL	A	Bill Skowron

Jim Nash

Date	Traded To		Traded With	Traded By		In Exchange For
Dec 3, 1969	ATL	N		OAK	A	Felipe Alou
June 15, 1972	PHI	N	Gary Neibauer	ATL	N	Joe Hoerner Andre Thornton

Phil Nastu

Date	Traded To		Traded With	Traded By		In Exchange For
Dec 12, 1980	CHI	N	Joe Strain	SF	N	Jerry Martin Jesus Figueroa minor league IF Mike Turgeon

Julio Navarro

Date	Traded To		Traded With	Traded By		In Exchange For
April 28, 1964	DET	A		LA	A	Willie Smith
June 14, 1966	BOS	A	Don Demeter	DET	A	Earl Wilson Joe Christopher

Earl Naylor

Date	Traded To		Traded With	Traded By		In Exchange For
June 1, 1943	STL	N	Danny Litwhiler	PHI	N	Buster Adams Coaker Triplett Dain Clay

Charlie Neal

Date	Traded To		Traded With	Traded By		In Exchange For
Dec 15, 1961	NY	N		LA	N	Lee Walls and $100,000.
July 1, 1963	CIN	N	Sammy Taylor	NY	N	Jesse Gonder

Greasy Neale

Date	Traded To		Traded With	Traded By		In Exchange For
Feb 22, 1921	PHI	N	Jimmy Ring	CIN	N	Eppa Rixey
June 2, 1921	CIN	N		PHI	N	Waiver price

Tom Needham

Date	Traded To		Traded With	Traded By		In Exchange For
Dec 3, 1907	NY	N	*See Fred Tenney*	BOS	N	
Dec 1908	CHI	N		NY	N	Cash

Cal Neeman

Date	Traded To		Traded With	Traded By		In Exchange For
May 13, 1960	PHI	N	Tony Taylor	CHI	N	Ed Bouchee Don Cardwell

Ron Negray

Date	Traded To		Traded With	Traded By		In Exchange For
April 5, 1957	BKN	N		PHI	N	*See Chico Fernandez*

Art Nehf

Date	Traded To		Traded With	Traded By		In Exchange For
Aug 15, 1919	NY	N		BOS	N	Joe Oeschger Red Causey Johnny Jones Mickey O'Neil and $55,000.
May 11, 1926	CIN	N		NY	N	Cash
Sept 4, 1927	CHI	N		CIN	N	Cash

Gary Neibauer

Date	Traded To		Traded With	Traded By		In Exchange For
June 15, 1972	PHI	N	Jim Nash	ATL	N	Joe Hoerner Andre Thornton

Bernie Neis

Date	Traded To		Traded With	Traded By		In Exchange For
Feb 4, 1925	BOS	N		BKN	N	Cotton Tierney
June 15, 1927	CHI	A		CLE	A	Cash

Dave Nelson

Date	Traded To		Traded With	Traded By		In Exchange For
Dec 5, 1969	WAS	A	Horacio Pina Ron Law	CLE	A	Dennis Higgins Barry Moore
Nov 12, 1975	KC	A		TEX	A	Nellie Briles

Date	Traded To	Traded With	Traded By	In Exchange For

Gene Nelson

Date				
Aug 1, 1979	NY A	Oscar Gamble Ray Fontenot minor league 3B Amos Lewis	TEX A	Mickey Rivers minor league Ps Bob Polinsky Neil Mersch and Mark Softy
April 1, 1982	SEA A	Bill Caudill Bobby Brown	NY A	Shane Rawley
June 29, 1984	CHI A	Jerry Don Gleaton	SEA A	Salome Barojas
Dec 11, 1986	OAK A	Bruce Tanner	CHI A	Donnie Hill
		(Oakland received Tanner on Dec. 18, 1986.)		

Jamie Nelson

Dec 7, 1984	CHI N	——	MIL A	Cash

Lynn Nelson

Feb 23, 1940	DET A	——	PHI A	Waiver price

Red Nelson

Aug 1912	PHI N	——	STL A	Cash
June 5, 1913	CIN N	John Dodge	PHI N	Josh Devore Beals Becker

Ricky Nelson

Dec 17, 1986	NY N	——	SEA A	Doug Gwosdz
May 11, 1987	CLE A	——	NY N	Don Schulze

Rocky Nelson

May 17, 1951	PIT N	Erv Dusak	STL N	Stan Rojek
Sept 20, 1951	CHI A	——	PIT N	Waiver price
July 30, 1956	STL N	——	BKN N	Waiver price

Roger Nelson

Nov 29, 1967	BAL A	——	CHI A	See Luis Aparicio
Nov 30, 1972	CIN N	Richie Scheinblum	KC A	Hal McRae Wayne Simpson
Oct 25, 1974	CHI A	——	CIN N	Cash

Dick Nen

Dec 4, 1964	WAS A	See Frank Howard	LA N	——
April 3, 1968	CHI N	——	WAS A	Cash
Oct 1, 1968	WAS A	——	CHI N	Cash

Graig Nettles

Dec 10, 1969	CLE A	Dean Chance Bob Miller Ted Uhlaender	MIN A	Luis Tiant Stan Williams
Nov 27, 1972	NY A	Gerry Moses	CLE A	John Ellis Jerry Kenney Charlie Spikes Rusty Torres
March 30, 1984	SD N	——	NY A	Dennis Rasmussen minor league P Darin Cloninger

Morris Nettles

Dec 11, 1975	CHI A	Jim Spencer	CAL A	Bill Melton Steve Dunning

Dan Neumeier

Oct 23, 1973	HOU N	——	CHI A	Hector Torres

Ernie Nevel

Aug 28, 1952	CIN N	——	NY A	See Ewell Blackwell

Ernie Nevel *continued*

June 9, 1954	BKN N	Charlie Kress Johnny Bucha and cash	DET A	Wayne Belardi

Don Newcombe

June 15, 1958	CIN N	——	LA N	Steve Bilko Johnny Klippstein
July 29, 1960	CLE A	——	CIN N	Cash

Al Newman

Feb 23, 1987	MIN A	——	MON N	Minor league P Mike Shade

Jeff Newman

Dec 6, 1982	BOS A	Tony Armas	OAK A	Carney Lansford Garry Hancock minor league P Jerry King

Ray Newman

Dec 6, 1973	DET A	——	MIL A	Mike Strahler

Bobo Newsom

May 21, 1935	WAS A	——	STL A	$40,000.
June 11, 1937	BOS A	Ben Chapman	WAS A	Wes Ferrell Rick Ferrell Mel Almada
Dec 2, 1937	STL A	Red Kress Buster Mills	BOS A	Joe Vosmik
May 13, 1939	DET A	Beau Bell Red Kress Jim Walkup	STL A	Vern Kennedy Bob Harris George Gill Roxie Lawson Chet Laabs Mark Christman
March 31, 1942	WAS A	——	DET A	$40,000.
Aug 30, 1942	BKN N	——	WAS A	$25,000.
July 15, 1943	STL A	——	BKN N	Fritz Ostermueller Archie McKain
Aug 31, 1943	WAS A	——	STL A	Cash
Dec 13, 1943	PHI A	——	WAS A	Roger Wolff
July 11, 1947	NY A	——	WAS A	Waiver price

Skeeter Newsome

Dec 12, 1945	PHI N	——	BOS A	Cash

Doc Newton

July 1901	BKN N	——	CIN N	Cash

Gus Niarhos

June 27, 1950	CHI A	——	NY A	$10,000.
Nov 27, 1951	STL A	——	CHI A	See Sherm Lollar
Nov 28, 1951	BOS A	Ken Wood	STL A	Les Moss Tom Wright

Carl Nichols

March 31, 1989	HOU N	——	BAL A	Dave Johnson Minor league OF Victor Hithe

Kid Nichols

July 16, 1905	PHI N	——	STL N	Waiver price

Date	Traded To		Traded With	Traded By		In Exchange For

Reid Nichols
| July 11, 1985 | CHI | A | —— | BOS | A | Tim Lollar |

Bill Nicholson
| Oct 4, 1948 | PHI | N | | CHI | N | Harry Walker |

Dave Nicholson
Jan 14, 1963	CHI	A	Hoyt Wilhelm Pete Ward Ron Hansen	BAL	A	Luis Aparicio Al Smith
Dec 1, 1965	HOU	N	Bill Heath	CHI	A	Jack Lamabe minor league P Ray Cordeiro and cash
Dec 31, 1966	ATL	N	Bob Bruce	HOU	N	Sandy Alomar Eddie Mathews Arnie Umbach

Fred Nicholson
| June 30, 1919 | PIT | N | —— | DET | A | Waiver price |
| Feb 23, 1921 | BOS | N | Billy Southworth
Walter Barbare
and $15,000. | PIT | N | Rabbit Maranville |

Steve Nicosia
| Aug 19, 1983 | SF | N | —— | PIT | N | Milt May
and cash |
| Feb 15, 1985 | MON | N | —— | SF | N | No compensation
(free agent signing) |

Tom Niedenfuer
| May 22, 1987 | BAL | A | —— | LA | N | John Shelby
Brad Havens |
| Dec 7, 1988 | SEA | A | —— | BAL | A | No compensation
(free agent signing) |

Al Niehaus
| Oct 27, 1924 | PIT | N | Vic Aldridge
George Grantham | CHI | N | Charlie Grimm
Rabbit Maranville
Wilbur Cooper |
| May 20, 1925 | CIN | N | —— | PIT | N | Tom Sheehan |

Bert Niehoff
Nov 1914	PHI	N	——	CIN	N	Red Dooin
April 4, 1918	STL	N	$500.	PHI	N	Milt Watson
May 18, 1918	NY	N	——	STL	N	Waiver price

Joe Niekro
April 25, 1969	SD	N	Gary Ross Francisco Libran	CHI	N	Dick Selma
Dec 4, 1969	DET	N	——	SD	N	Pat Dobson Dave Campbell
Aug 7, 1973	ATL	N	——	DET	N	Cash
April 6, 1975	HOU	N	——	ATL	N	$35,000.
Sept 15, 1985	NY	A	——	HOU	N	Jim Deshaies Two players to be named

(Houston received IF Neder Horta and P Dody Rather on Jan. 11, 1986.)

| June 6, 1987 | MIN | A | —— | NY | A | Mark Salas |

Phil Niekro
| Jan 6, 1984 | NY | A | —— | ATL | N | No compensation
(free agent signing) |
| Aug 9, 1987 | TOR | A | —— | CLE | A | Minor league
OF Darryl Landrum |

Scott Nielsen
Feb 14, 1984	NY	A	Minor league P Eric Parent	SEA	A	Larry Milbourne
Jan 5, 1987	CHI	A	Minor league IF Mike Soper	NY	A	Pete Filson Randy Velarde
Nov 13, 1987	NY	A	See Richard Dotson	CHI	A	
July 10, 1989	NY	A	——	NY	A	Marcus Lawton

Bob Nieman
Dec 4, 1952	DET	A	Owen Friend J. W. Porter	STL	A	Virgil Trucks Hal White Johnny Groth
Dec 6, 1954	CHI	A	Walt Dropo Ted Gray	DET	A	Chris Cristante Ferris Fain Jack Phillips
May 21, 1956	BAL	A	Mike Fornieles Connie Johnson George Kell	CHI	A	Jim Wilson Dave Philley
Dec 2, 1959	STL	N	——	BAL	A	Gene Green minor league C Charles Staniland
May 10, 1961	CLE	A	——	STL	N	Joe Morgan Mike Lee and cash

(St. Louis received Lee on September 25.)

| April 29, 1962 | SF | N | —— | CLE | A | Cash |

Randy Niemann
| June 15, 1977 | HOU | N | Mike Fischlin
Dave Bergman | NY | A | Cliff Johnson |

(Houston received Bergman on November 23.)

| Aug 31, 1981 | PIT | N | Johnny Ray
minor league
OF Kevin Houston | HOU | N | Phil Garner |
| Sept 7, 1983 | CHI | A | —— | PIT | N | Miguel Dilone
minor league
P Mike Maitland |

Al Niemiec
| Jan 4, 1936 | PHI | A | Hank Johnson
and $75,000. | BOS | A | Doc Cramer
Eric McNair |

Tom Nieto
March 31, 1986	MON	N	——	STL	N	Fred Manrique
Feb 3, 1987	MIN	A	See Jeff Reardon	MON	N	
Oct 24, 1988	PHI	N	Tommy Herr Eric Bullock	MIN	A	Shane Rawley and cash

Johnny Niggeling
| Jan 4, 1940 | STL | A | —— | CIN | N | Waiver price |
| Aug 18, 1943 | WAS | A | Harlond Clift | STL | A | Ellis Clary
Ox Miller
and cash |

Harry Niles
Nov 1907	NY	A	——	STL	A	Cash
Aug 17, 1908	BOS	A	——	NY	A	Frank LaPorte
May 1910	CLE	A	——	BOS	A	Cash

Rabbit Nill
| Aug 11, 1907 | CLE | A | —— | WAS | A | Pete O'Brien
Howard Wakefield |

Al Nipper
| Dec 8, 1987 | CHI | N | —— | BOS | A | See Lee Smith |

Ron Nischwitz
| Nov 27, 1962 | CLE | A | Gordon Seyfried | DET | A | Bubba Phillips |

Date	Traded To		Traded With	Traded By		In Exchange For

Donell Nixon

Date	Traded To		Traded With	Traded By		In Exchange For
March 19, 1988	SF	N	——	SEA	A	Rod Scurry

(San Francisco received Nixon on June 23, 1988.)

Otis Nixon

Date	Traded To		Traded With	Traded By		In Exchange For
Feb 5, 1984	CLE	A	——	NY	A	*See Toby Harrah*

Russ Nixon

Date	Traded To		Traded With	Traded By		In Exchange For
March 16, 1960	BOS	A	——	CLE	A	Sammy White / Jim Marshall

(Trade was cancelled when White decided to retire.)

| June 13, 1960 | BOS | A | Carroll Hardy | CLE | A | Marty Keough / Ted Bowsfield |
| April 6, 1966 | MIN | A | Chuck Schilling | BOS | A | Dick Stigman and minor league 1B Jose Calero |

Junior Noboa

Date	Traded To		Traded With	Traded By		In Exchange For
March 30, 1988	CAL	A	——	CLE	A	Minor league OF Ted Milner

Paul Noce

Date	Traded To		Traded With	Traded By		In Exchange For
April 2, 1989	SEA	A	Minor League IF Chuck Baldwin	CLE	A	Dave Hengel

Matt Nokes

Date	Traded To		Traded With	Traded By		In Exchange For
Oct 7, 1985	DET	A	Dave LaPoint / Eric King	SF	N	Juan Berenguer / Bob Melvin / Scott Medvin

(San Francisco received Medvin on Dec. 11, 1985.)

Gary Nolan

Date	Traded To		Traded With	Traded By		In Exchange For
June 15, 1977	CAL	A	——	CIN	N	Minor league IF Craig Henderson

Joe Nolan

Date	Traded To		Traded With	Traded By		In Exchange For
March 26, 1982	BAL	A	——	CIN	N	Dallas Williams minor league P Brooks Carey

Dickie Noles

Date	Traded To		Traded With	Traded By		In Exchange For
Dec 8, 1981	CHI	N	Keith Moreland / Dan Larson	PHI	N	Mike Krukow and cash
July 1, 1984	TEX	A	——	CHI	N	Dwayne Henry minor league IF Jorge Gomez

(The Cubs received Henry and Gomez on December 22.)

| Sept 22, 1987 | DET | A | —— | CHI | N | Player to be named |

(Noles was returned to Chicago on Oct. 23, 1987.)

Pete Noonan

Date	Traded To		Traded With	Traded By		In Exchange For
July 1, 1906	STL	N	Fred Beebe and cash	CHI	N	Jack Taylor

Jerry Nops

Date	Traded To		Traded With	Traded By		In Exchange For
Jan 1900	BKN	N	Jimmy Sheckard / Broadway Aleck Smith / Frank Kitson / Harry Howell / Joe McGinnity	BAL	N	Cash

Tim Nordbrook

Date	Traded To		Traded With	Traded By		In Exchange For
Sept 9, 1976	CAL	A	——	BAL	A	Cash
Aug 30, 1977	TOR	A	——	CHI	A	Cash
April 29, 1978	MIL	A	——	TOR	A	Tim Johnson

Wayne Nordhagen

Date	Traded To		Traded With	Traded By		In Exchange For
June 7, 1973	ATL	N	Frank Tepedino / Al Closter / Dave Cheadle	NY	A	Pat Dobson
May 28, 1975	STL	N	Ron Reed	ATL	N	Elias Sosa / Ray Sadecki
July 14, 1976	CHI	A	——	PHI	N	Rich Coggins
April 2, 1982	TOR	A	——	CHI	A	Aurelio Rodriguez
June 15, 1982	PHI	N	——	TOR	A	Dick Davis
June 15, 1982	PIT	N	——	PHI	N	Bill Robinson
June 22, 1982	TOR	A	——	PIT	N	Dick Davis
Dec 10, 1982	CHI	N	——	TOR	A	No compensation (free agent signing)

Irv Noren

Date	Traded To		Traded With	Traded By		In Exchange For
May 3, 1952	NY	A	Tom Upton	WAS	A	Jackie Jensen / Spec Shea / Jerry Snyder / Archie Wilson
Feb 19, 1957	KC	A	*See Billy Hunter*	NY	A	
Aug 31, 1957	STL	N	——	KC	A	Waiver price
May 19, 1959	CHI	N	——	STL	N	Charlie King

Dan Norman

Date	Traded To		Traded With	Traded By		In Exchange For
June 15, 1977	NY	N	Pat Zachry / Doug Flynn / Steve Henderson	CIN	N	Tom Seaver
May 29, 1981	MON	N	Jeff Reardon	NY	N	Ellis Valentine

Fred Norman

Date	Traded To		Traded With	Traded By		In Exchange For
Dec 15, 1963	CHI	N	——	KC	A	Nelson Mathews
Sept 28, 1970	STL	N	——	LA	N	Cash
June 11, 1971	SD	N	Leron Lee	STL	N	Al Santorini
June 12, 1973	CIN	N	——	SD	N	Gene Locklear / Mike Johnson and cash

Nelson Norman

Date	Traded To		Traded With	Traded By		In Exchange For
Dec 8, 1977	TEX	A	Al Oliver	PIT	N	Bert Blyleven / John Milner

(Part of four-team trade involving Texas, New York Mets, Pittsburgh, and Atlanta.)

Jim Norris

Date	Traded To		Traded With	Traded By		In Exchange For
Jan 4, 1980	TEX	A	David Clyde	CLE	A	Larry McCall / Gary Gray / minor league 3B-OF Mike Bucci

Billy North

Date	Traded To		Traded With	Traded By		In Exchange For
Nov 21, 1972	OAK	A	——	CHI	N	Bob Locker
May 17, 1978	LA	N	——	OAK	A	Glenn Burke

Lou North

Date	Traded To		Traded With	Traded By		In Exchange For
June 17, 1924	BOS	N	——	STL	N	Cash

Hub Northen

Date	Traded To		Traded With	Traded By		In Exchange For
April 1911	BKN	N	——	CIN	N	Cash

Ron Northey

Date	Traded To		Traded With	Traded By		In Exchange For
May 3, 1947	STL	N	——	PHI	N	Harry Walker / Freddy Schmidt
Dec 14, 1949	CIN	N	Lou Klein	STL	N	Harry Walker
June 7, 1950	CHI	N	——	CIN	N	Bob Scheffing

Jim Northrup

Date	Traded To		Traded With	Traded By		In Exchange For
Aug 7, 1974	MON	N	——	DET	A	Cash

Date	Traded To	Traded With	Traded By	In Exchange For

Jim Northrup *continued*

Date	Traded To	Traded With	Traded By	In Exchange For
Sept 16, 1974	BAL A ———		MON N	Cash

Willie Norwood

| Dec 12, 1980 | SEA A ——— | | MIN A | Byron McLaughlin |

Joe Nossek

| May 11, 1966 | KC A ——— | | MIN A | Cash |
| July 12, 1969 | STL N ——— | | OAK A | Bob Johnson |

Don Nottebart

| Nov 30, 1962 | HOU N ——— | | MIL N | Cash |
| April 27, 1969 | CHI N ——— | | CIN N | Minor league IF Jim Armstrong and cash |

Wynn Noyes

| Aug 1919 | CHI A ——— | | PHI A | Cash |

Les Nunamaker

May 13, 1914	NY A ———		BOS A	Cash
Jan 22, 1918	STL A ———		NY A	*See Eddie Plank*
March 1919	CLE A ———		STL A	Josh Billings

Edwin Nunez

| July 11, 1988 | NY N ——— | | SEA A | Gene Walter |

Jose Nunez

| Dec 7, 1989 | CHI N ——— | | TOR A | Paul Kilgus |

Howie Nunn

| Dec 21, 1961 | NY N ——— | | CIN N | Cash |

(Nunn was returned to Cincinnati on April 2, 1962.)

Joe Nuxhall

| Jan 25, 1961 | KC A ——— | | CIN N | John Tsitouris Johnny Briggs |

Rich Nye

| Dec 4, 1969 | STL N ——— | | CHI N | Boots Day |
| May 15, 1970 | MON N ——— | | STL N | Cash |

Jerry Nyman

| March 30, 1970 | SD N ——— | | CHI A | Tommie Sisk |

Nyls Nyman

| Aug 31, 1977 | STL N | Dave Hamilton Silvio Martinez | CHI A | Clay Carroll |

Rebel Oakes

| Feb 1910 | STL N | Miller Huggins Frank Corridon | CIN N | Fred Beebe Alan Storke |

Johnny Oates

Nov 30, 1972	ATL N ———		BAL A	*See Earl Williams*
May 7, 1975	PHI N	Dick Allen	ATL N	Jim Essian Barry Bonnell and cash
Dec 20, 1976	LA N	minor league P Quincy Hill	PHI N	Ted Sizemore

Ken Oberkfell

Date	Traded To	Traded With	Traded By	In Exchange For
June 15, 1984	ATL N ———		STL N	Mike Jorgensen Ken Dayley
Aug 28, 1988	PIT N ———		ATL N	Tommy Gregg

(Atlanta received Gregg on September 1, 1988.)

| May 10, 1989 | SF N ——— | | PIT N | Roger Samuels |
| Dec 6, 1989 | HOU N ——— | | SF N | No compensation (free agent signing) |

Frank Oberlin

| Aug 11, 1907 | WAS A ——— | | BOS A | Cash |

Mike O'Berry

Aug 17, 1979	CHI N Cash		BOS A	Ted Sizemore
Oct 17, 1980	CIN N ———		CHI N	Jay Howell
Jan 10, 1983	CAL A ———		CIN N	John Harris
Dec 8, 1983	NY A ———		CAL A	No compensation (free agent signing)

Bob O'Brien

| Dec 2, 1971 | BAL A ——— | | LA N | *See Frank Robinson* |

Buck O'Brien

| July 1913 | CHI A ——— | | BOS A | Cash |

Charlie O'Brien

| March 30, 1986 | MIL A ——— | | OAK A | *See Moose Haas* |

Dan O'Brien

| Nov 9, 1979 | SEA A ——— | | STL N | Cash |

Jack O'Brien

| May 1901 | CLE A ——— | | WAS A | Cash |

John O'Brien

| Jan 1900 | LOU N ——— | | PIT N | *See Honus Wagner* |

Johnny O'Brien

| June 15, 1958 | STL N | Gene Freese | PIT N | Dick Schofield and cash |
| March 31, 1959 | MIL N | Stan Lopata Ted Kazanski | PHI N | Gene Conley Joe Koppe Harry Hanebrink |

Pete O'Brien

| Dec 1906 | CLE A ——— | | STL A | Fritz Buelow |
| Aug 11, 1907 | WAS A | Howard Wakefield | CLE A | Rabbit Nill |

Pete O'Brien

| Dec 6, 1988 | CLE A | Oddibe McDowell Jerry Browne | TEX A | Julio Franco |
| Dec 7, 1989 | SEA A ——— | | CLE A | No compensation (free agent signing) |

Syd O'Brien

| Dec 13, 1969 | CHI A | minor league P Billy Farmer Gerry Janeski | BOS A | Don Pavletich Gary Peters |

(Janeski replaced Farmer, who retired.)

| Nov 30, 1970 | CAL A | *See Ken Berry* | CHI A ——— | |
| July 28, 1972 | MIL A | Joe Azcue | CAL A | Paul Ratliff Ron Clark |

Date	Traded To	Traded With	Traded By	In Exchange For

Tom O'Brien

Date	Traded To	Traded With	Traded By	In Exchange For
Feb 1900	PIT N	——	NY N	Cash

Tommy O'Brien

Date	Traded To	Traded With	Traded By	In Exchange For
May 8, 1950	WAS A	Merrill Combs	BOS A	Clyde Vollmer

Danny O'Connell

Date	Traded To	Traded With	Traded By	In Exchange For
Dec 26, 1953	MIL N	——	PIT N	Sid Gordon / Max Surkont / Sam Jethroe / Curt Raydon / Fred Walters / minor league / P Larry Lasalle
June 15, 1957	NY N	Ray Crone / Bobby Thomson	MIL N	Red Schoendienst

Jack O'Connor

Date	Traded To	Traded With	Traded By	In Exchange For
Jan 9, 1985	MON N	——	MIN A	Mike Stenhouse

Jack O'Connor

Date	Traded To	Traded With	Traded By	In Exchange For
May 10, 1900	PIT N	——	STL N	Cash
Oct 26, 1903	STL A	——	NY A	John Anderson
Jan 1904	STL A	Harry Howell	NY A	Jack Powell

Ken O'Dea

Date	Traded To	Traded With	Traded By	In Exchange For
Oct 26, 1934	CHI N	——	STL N	Pat Malone
Dec 6, 1938	NY N	Frank Demaree / Bill Jurges	CHI N	Dick Bartell / Hank Leiber / Gus Mancuso
Dec 11, 1941	STL N	Bill Lohrman / Johnny McCarthy / and $50,000.	NY N	Johnny Mize
July 8, 1946	BOS N	——	STL N	Cash

Billy O'Dell

Date	Traded To	Traded With	Traded By	In Exchange For
Nov 30, 1959	SF N	Billy Loes	BAL A	Jackie Brandt / Gordon Jones / Roger McCardell
Feb 1, 1965	MIL N	——	SF N	Ed Bailey
June 15, 1966	PIT N	——	ATL N	Don Schwall

Blue Moon Odom

Date	Traded To	Traded With	Traded By	In Exchange For
May 20, 1975	CLE A	Cash	OAK A	Dick Bosman / Jim Perry
June 7, 1975	ATL N	Bob Belloir	CLE A	Roric Harrison
June 15, 1976	CHI A	——	ATL N	Pete Varney

John O'Donoghue

Date	Traded To	Traded With	Traded By	In Exchange For
April 6, 1966	CLE A	——	KC A	Ralph Terry / and cash
Nov 28, 1967	BAL A	Gordon Lund	CLE A	Eddie Fisher / minor leaguers / P Bob Scott and / IF John Scruggs
April 30, 1969	SEA A	Tom Fisher / and minor league / P Lloyd Fourroux	BAL A	Gerry Schoen / Mike Ferraro
June 15, 1970	MON N	——	MIL A	Cash

Lefty O'Doul

Date	Traded To	Traded With	Traded By	In Exchange For
July 23, 1922	BOS A	Chick Fewster / Elmer Miller / Johnny Mitchell / and $50,000.	NY A	Joe Dugan / Elmer Smith
Oct 29, 1928	PHI N	Cash	NY N	Freddy Leach

Lefty O'Doul *continued*

Date	Traded To	Traded With	Traded By	In Exchange For
Oct 14, 1930	BKN N	Fresco Thompson	PHI N	Clise Dudley / Jumbo Elliott / Hal Lee / and cash
June 16, 1933	NY N	Watty Clark	BKN N	Sam Leslie

Bryan Oelkers

Date	Traded To	Traded With	Traded By	In Exchange For
Jan 7, 1986	MIN A	——	CLE A	Ken Schrom

Joe Oeschger

Date	Traded To	Traded With	Traded By	In Exchange For
May 27, 1919	NY N	——	PHI N	George Smith
Aug 15, 1919	BOS N	Red Causey / Johnny Jones / Mickey O'Neil / and $55,000.	NY N	Art Nehf
Nov 12, 1923	NY N	Billy Southworth	BOS N	Casey Stengel / Dave Bancroft / Bill Cunningham
(Bancroft was named Boston manager.)				
July 1, 1924	PHI N	——	NY N	Waiver price
April 20, 1925	BKN N	——	PHI N	Waiver price

Bob O'Farrell

Date	Traded To	Traded With	Traded By	In Exchange For
May 23, 1925	STL N	——	CHI N	Mike Gonzalez / Howard Freigau
May 1, 1928	NY N	——	STL N	George Harper
Oct 10, 1932	STL N	Ethan Allen / Bill Walker / Jim Mooney	NY N	Gus Mancuso / Ray Starr
Jan 11, 1934	CIN N	Syl Johnson	STL N	Glenn Spencer
(O'Farrell was named Cincinnati manager.)				

Rowland Office

Date	Traded To	Traded With	Traded By	In Exchange For
Dec 4, 1979	MON N	——	ATL N	No compensation (free agent signing)

Curly Ogden

Date	Traded To	Traded With	Traded By	In Exchange For
June 19, 1924	WAS A	——	PHI A	Cash

Jack Ogden

Date	Traded To	Traded With	Traded By	In Exchange For
May 7, 1933	STL N	*See Leo Durocher*	CIN N	——

Ben Oglivie

Date	Traded To	Traded With	Traded By	In Exchange For
Oct 23, 1973	DET A	——	BOS A	Dick McAuliffe
Dec 9, 1977	MIL A	——	DET A	Jim Slaton / Rich Folkers

Hal O'Hagen

Date	Traded To	Traded With	Traded By	In Exchange For
July 1902	NY N	——	CHI N	Jack Hendricks

Bob Ojeda

Date	Traded To	Traded With	Traded By	In Exchange For
Nov 13, 1985	NY N	John Mitchell / Tom McCarthy / Minor league / P Chris Bayer	BOS A	Calvin Schiraldi / Wes Gardner / John Christensen / LaSchelle Tarver

Bob Oldis

Date	Traded To	Traded With	Traded By	In Exchange For
Oct 13, 1961	PHI N	——	PIT N	Cash

Rube Oldring

Date	Traded To	Traded With	Traded By	In Exchange For
Oct 2, 1905	PHI A	——	NY A	Cash

Date	Traded To		Traded With	Traded By		In Exchange For

Al Oliver

Date	Traded To		Traded With	Traded By		In Exchange For
Dec 8, 1977	TEX	A	Nelson Norman	PIT	N	Bert Blyleven
						John Milner

(Part of four-team trade involving Texas, New York Mets, Pittsburgh, and Atlanta.)

Date	Traded To		Traded With	Traded By		In Exchange For
March 31, 1982	MON	N	——	TEX	A	Larry Parrish
						Dave Hostetler
Feb 27, 1984	SF	N	——	MON	N	Fred Breining
						Max Venable
						Andy McGaffigan

(San Francisco sent McGaffigan to Montreal on April 1, 1984, after Breining reported to the Expos with a sore arm.)

Date	Traded To		Traded With	Traded By		In Exchange For
Aug 20, 1984	PHI	N	Renie Martin	SF	N	Kelly Downs
						George Riley
Feb 4, 1985	LA	N	——	PHI	N	Pat Zachry
July 9, 1985	TOR	A	——	LA	N	Len Matuszek

Bob Oliver

Date	Traded To		Traded With	Traded By		In Exchange For
Dec 2, 1967	MIN	A	——	PIT	N	Ron Kline
May 5, 1972	CAL	A	——	KC	A	Tom Murphy
Sept 11, 1974	BAL	A	——	CAL	A	Mickey Scott
						Cash
Dec 1, 1974	NY	A	——	BAL	A	Cash

Dave Oliver

Date	Traded To		Traded With	Traded By		In Exchange For
July 11, 1980	MON	N	——	CLE	A	Ross Grimsley

Gene Oliver

Date	Traded To		Traded With	Traded By		In Exchange For
June 15, 1963	MIL	N	Bob Sadowski	STL	N	Lew Burdette
June 6, 1967	PHI	N		ATL	N	Bob Uecker
Dec 15, 1967	BOS	A	Dick Ellsworth	PHI	N	Mike Ryan
						and cash
June 27, 1968	CHI	N	——	BOS	A	Cash

Nate Oliver

Date	Traded To		Traded With	Traded By		In Exchange For
Feb 13, 1968	SF	N	Ron Hunt	LA	N	Tom Haller
						minor league
						P Frank Kasmeta
Dec 6, 1968	NY	A	——	SF	N	Charley Smith
April 19, 1969	CHI	N	——	NY	A	Lee Elia

Tom Oliver

Date	Traded To		Traded With	Traded By		In Exchange For
Jan 29, 1930	BOS	A	——	PHI	A	Cash

Chi Chi Olivo

Date	Traded To		Traded With	Traded By		In Exchange For
Nov 29, 1966	NY	A	Bill Robinson	ATL	N	Clete Boyer

Diomedes Olivo

Date	Traded To		Traded With	Traded By		In Exchange For
Nov 19, 1962	STL	N	Dick Groat	PIT	N	Julio Gotay
						Don Cardwell

Luis Olmo

Date	Traded To		Traded With	Traded By		In Exchange For
Dec 24, 1949	BOS	N	——	BKN	N	Jim Russell
						Ed Sauer
						and cash

Al Olmsted

Date	Traded To		Traded With	Traded By		In Exchange For
Dec 8, 1980	SD	N	——	STL	N	*See Rollie Fingers*
Dec 10, 1981	STL	N	Ozzie Smith	SD	N	Sixto Lezcano
			Steve Mura			Garry Templeton
						Luis DeLeon

(Templeton and Smith were exchanged on February 11, 1982; Olmsted and DeLeon were exchanged on February 19.)

Ivy Olson

Date	Traded To		Traded With	Traded By		In Exchange For
Dec 14, 1914	CIN	N	——	CLE	A	Cash
July 17, 1915	BKN	N	——	CIN	N	Waiver price

Karl Olson

Date	Traded To		Traded With	Traded By		In Exchange For
Nov 8, 1955	WAS	A	——	BOS	A	*See Mickey Vernon*
April 30, 1957	BOS	A	——	WAS	A	Cash
April 30, 1957	DET	A	——	BOS	A	Jack Phillips

Ed Olwine

Date	Traded To		Traded With	Traded By		In Exchange For
April 2, 1986	ATL	N	——	NY	N	Minor league
						P Mike Santiago

Tom O'Malley

Date	Traded To		Traded With	Traded By		In Exchange For
Aug 31, 1984	CHI	A	——	SF	N	Minor leaguers
						1B Pat Adams and
						P Mike Treiyillo
Sept 1, 1988	MON	N	——	TEX	A	Jack Daugherty

(Texas received Daugherty on Sept. 13, 1988.)

Date	Traded To		Traded With	Traded By		In Exchange For
March 28, 1989	NY	N	Mark Bailey	MON	N	Steve Frey

Randy O'Neal

Date	Traded To		Traded With	Traded By		In Exchange For
Jan 27, 1987	ATL	N	Chuck Cary	DET	A	Terry Harper
						Minor league
						OF Freedie Tiburco
July 23, 1987	STL	N	——	ATL	N	Joe Boever

Mickey O'Neil

Date	Traded To		Traded With	Traded By		In Exchange For
Aug 15, 1919	BOS	N	Joe Oeschger	NY	N	Art Nehf
			Red Causey			
			Johnny Jones			
			and $55,000.			
Oct 7, 1925	BKN	N	Jesse Barnes	BOS	N	Zack Taylor
			Gus Felix			Jimmy Johnston
						Eddie Brown
Dec 1926	WAS	A	——	BKN	N	Cash
May 25, 1927	NY	N	——	WAS	A	Cash

Bill O'Neill

Date	Traded To		Traded With	Traded By		In Exchange For
July 4, 1904	WAS	A	——	BOS	A	Kip Selbach

Jack O'Neill

Date	Traded To		Traded With	Traded By		In Exchange For
Dec 12, 1903	CHI	N	Three Finger Brown	STL	N	Jack Taylor
						Larry McLean
Jan 1906	BOS	N	——	CHI	N	Waiver price

Steve O'Neill

Date	Traded To		Traded With	Traded By		In Exchange For
Aug 20, 1911	CLE	A	——	PHI	A	Cash
Jan 7, 1924	BOS	A	Danny Boone	CLE	A	George Burns
			Joe Connolly			Roxy Walters
			Bill Wambsganss			Chick Fewster
Dec 12, 1924	NY	A	——	BOS	A	Waiver price

Steve Ontiveros

Date	Traded To		Traded With	Traded By		In Exchange For
Feb 11, 1977	CHI	N	Bobby Murcer	SF	N	Bill Madlock
			minor league			Rob Sperring
			P Andy Muhlstock			

Jose Oquendo

Date	Traded To		Traded With	Traded By		In Exchange For
April 2, 1985	STL	N	Minor league	NY	N	Angel Salazar
			P Mark J. Davis			Minor league
						P John Young

Joe Orengo

Date	Traded To		Traded With	Traded By		In Exchange For
Nov 25, 1940	NY	N	——	STL	N	Cash
July 31, 1943	BKN	N	Bill Lohrman	NY	N	Dolf Camilli
			Bill Sayles			Johnny Allen

(Camilli refused to report to New York and retired.)

Date	Traded To		Traded With	Traded By		In Exchange For
Dec 12, 1944	CHI	A	——	DET	A	Skeeter Webb

Don O'Riley

Date	Traded To		Traded With	Traded By		In Exchange For
Oct 13, 1970	CHI	A	Pat Kelly	KC	A	Gail Hopkins / John Matias

Jesse Orosco

Date	Traded To		Traded With	Traded By		In Exchange For
Dec 8, 1978	NY	N	minor league P Greg Field	MIN	A	Jerry Koosman
Dec 11, 1987	LA	N	———	NY	N	Jack Savage / Wally Whitehurst / Kevin Tapani

(Part of a three-team trade involving Los Angeles, Oakland, and New York Mets.)

Date	Traded To		Traded With	Traded By		In Exchange For
Dec 3, 1988	CLE	A	———	LA	N	No compensation (free agent signing)

Frank O'Rourke

Date	Traded To		Traded With	Traded By		In Exchange For
Jan 1920	WAS	A	———	BKN	N	Cash
Jan 10, 1922	BOS	A	Joe Dugan	WAS	A	Roger Peckinpaugh

(Part of three-team trade involving Boston, Philadelphia, and Washington.)

Date	Traded To		Traded With	Traded By		In Exchange For
Oct 24, 1922	DET	A	———	BOS	A	Waiver price
Jan 15, 1927	STL	A	Lefty Stewart / Billy Mullen / Otto Miller	DET	A	Marty McManus / Bobby LaMotte / Pinky Hargrave

John Orsino

Date	Traded To		Traded With	Traded By		In Exchange For
Dec 15, 1962	BAL	A	Mike McCormick / Stu Miller	SF	N	Jack Fisher / Jimmie Coker / Billy Hoeft
Oct 12, 1965	WAS	A	———	BAL	A	Woodie Held

Joe Orsulak

Date	Traded To		Traded With	Traded By		In Exchange For
Nov 6, 1987	BAL	A	———	PIT	N	Minor league IF Terry Crowley, Jr. / Minor league 3B Rico Rossy

Jorge Orta

Date	Traded To		Traded With	Traded By		In Exchange For
Dec 19, 1979	CLE	A	———	CHI	A	No compensation (free agent signing)
Dec 9, 1981	LA	N	Larry White / Jack Fimple	CLE	A	Rick Sutcliffe / Jack Perconte
Dec 28, 1982	NY	N	———	LA	N	Pat Zachry
Feb 4, 1983	TOR	A	———	NY	N	Steve Senteney
Dec 20, 1983	KC	A	———	TOR	A	Willie Aikens

Phil Ortega

Date	Traded To		Traded With	Traded By		In Exchange For
Dec 4, 1964	WAS	A	Frank Howard / Pete Richert / Dick Nen / Ken McMullen	LA	N	Claude Osteen / John Kennedy / and $100,000.
April 4, 1969	CAL	A	———	WAS	A	Cash

Frank Ortenzio

Date	Traded To		Traded With	Traded By		In Exchange For
Feb 15, 1978	CHI	A	———	MON	N	Cash

(Ortenzio was returned to Montreal on April 4, 1978.)

Al Orth

Date	Traded To		Traded With	Traded By		In Exchange For
July 13, 1904	NY	A	———	WAS	A	Long Tom Hughes / Bill Wolfe

Jose Ortiz

Date	Traded To		Traded With	Traded By		In Exchange For
Nov 30, 1970	CHI	N	Ossie Blanco	CHI	A	Pat Jacquez / Dave Lemonds / Roe Skidmore

Junior Ortiz

Date	Traded To		Traded With	Traded By		In Exchange For
June 14, 1983	NY	N	Minor league P Arthur Ray	PIT	N	Marvell Wynne / Steve Senteney

Roberto Ortiz

Date	Traded To		Traded With	Traded By		In Exchange For
March 8, 1943	BKN	N	———	PHI	N	Cash

Bob Osborn

Date	Traded To		Traded With	Traded By		In Exchange For
Jan 1931	PIT	N	———	CHI	N	Cash

Danny Osborn

Date	Traded To		Traded With	Traded By		In Exchange For
Dec 12, 1975	ATL	N	Ken Henderson / Dick Ruthven	CHI	A	Ralph Garr / Larvell Blanks

Bobo Osborne

Date	Traded To		Traded With	Traded By		In Exchange For
March 23, 1963	WAS	A	———	DET	A	Wayne Comer

Tiny Osborne

Date	Traded To		Traded With	Traded By		In Exchange For
May 16, 1924	BKN	N	———	CHI	N	Cash

Pat Osburn

Date	Traded To		Traded With	Traded By		In Exchange For
Oct 22, 1974	MIL	A	———	CIN	N	John Vukovich

Dan Osinski

Date	Traded To		Traded With	Traded By		In Exchange For
July 23, 1962	LA	A	———	KC	A	Gordie Windhorn / Ted Bowsfield

(Kansas City received Bowsfield on November 30.)

Date	Traded To		Traded With	Traded By		In Exchange For
Oct 14, 1964	MIL	N	———	LA	A	Phil Roof / Ron Piche
Dec 15, 1965	BOS	A	Bob Sadowski	MIL	N	Lee Thomas / Arnie Earley / Jay Ritchie

Champ Osteen

Date	Traded To		Traded With	Traded By		In Exchange For
Jan 1904	NY	A	———	WAS	A	Cash

Claude Osteen

Date	Traded To		Traded With	Traded By		In Exchange For
Sept 16, 1961	WAS	A	———	CIN	N	Dave Sisler and cash
Dec 4, 1964	LA	N	John Kennedy and $100,000.	WAS	A	Frank Howard / Phil Ortega / Pete Richert / Dick Nen / Ken McMullen
Dec 6, 1973	HOU	N	minor league P Dave Culpepper	LA	N	Jimmy Wynn
Aug 15, 1974	STL	N	———	HOU	N	Minor league P Ron Selak / Dan Larson

Darrell Osteen

Date	Traded To		Traded With	Traded By		In Exchange For
Oct 20, 1967	KC	A	Floyd Robinson	CIN	N	Ron Tompkins

Fritz Ostermueller

Date	Traded To		Traded With	Traded By		In Exchange For
Dec 3, 1940	STL	A	———	BOS	A	Cash
July 15, 1943	BKN	N	Archie McKain	STL	A	Bobo Newsom

Joe Ostrowski

Date	Traded To		Traded With	Traded By		In Exchange For
Nov 17, 1947	STL	A	———	BOS	A	*See Vern Stephens*
June 15, 1950	NY	A	———	STL	A	*See Snuffy Stirnweiss*

John Ostrowski

Date	Traded To		Traded With	Traded By		In Exchange For
May 31, 1950	WAS	A	———	CHI	A	*See Eddie Robinson*

Amos Otis

Date	Traded To		Traded With	Traded By		In Exchange For
Dec 3, 1969	KC	A	Bob Johnson	NY	N	Joe Foy

Date	Traded To	Traded With	Traded By	In Exchange For
Amos Otis *continued*				
Dec 19, 1983	PIT N	——	KC A	No compensation (free agent signing)
Denny O'Toole				
Oct 26, 1973	STL N	——	CHI A	Jim Kremmel
Jim O'Toole				
Dec 15, 1966	CHI A	——	CIN N	Floyd Robinson
Marty O'Toole				
Aug 14, 1914	NY N	——	PIT N	Cash
Ed Ott				
April 1, 1981	CAL A	Mickey Mahler	PIT N	Jason Thompson
Jimmy Outlaw				
Dec 13, 1938	BKN N	——	CIN N	Lew Krausse and cash
Dec 13, 1938	BOS N	Buddy Hassett	BKN N	Gene Moore Ira Hutchinson
Orval Overall				
June 2, 1906	CHI N	——	CIN N	Bob Wicker and $2,000.
Stubby Overmire				
Dec 1, 1949	STL A	——	DET A	Waiver price
June 15, 1951	NY A	——	STL A	Tommy Byrne and $25,000.
May 13, 1952	STL A	——	NY A	Waiver price
Bob Owchinko				
Feb 15, 1980	CLE A	Jim Wilhelm	SD N	Jerry Mumphrey
Dec 9, 1980	PIT N	——	CLE A	*See Bert Blyleven*
April 6, 1981	OAK A	——	PIT N	Ernie Camacho and cash
Nov 12, 1983	CIN N	——	PIT N	Cash
Dave Owen				
Dec 11, 1985	SF N	——	CHI N	Manny Trillo
Marv Owen				
Dec 2, 1937	CHI A	Mike Tresh Gee Walker	DET A	Vern Kennedy Tony Piet Dixie Walker
Dec 8, 1939	BOS A	——	CHI A	Cash
Mickey Owen				
Dec 4, 1940	BKN N	——	STL N	Gus Mancuso Minor league P John Pintar and $65,000.
Spike Owen				
Aug 19, 1986	BOS A	Dave Henderson	SEA A	Rey Quinones Mike Trujillo John Christensen Mike Brown
Dec 8, 1988	MON N	Minor league P Dan Gakeler	BOS A	John Dopson Luis Rivera
Jim Owens				
Nov 27, 1962	CIN N	——	PHI N	Cookie Rojas
Rick Ownbey				
June 15, 1983	STL N	Neil Allen	NY N	Keith Hernandez
Ray Oyler				
Dec 7, 1969	OAK A	Diego Segui	SEA A	Ted Kubiak George Lauzerique
April 17, 1970	CAL A	——	OAK A	Cash
John Pacella				
Dec 15, 1980	SD N	Jose Moreno	NY N	Randy Jones
April 1, 1981	NY A	Jerry Mumphrey	SD N	Ruppert Jones Joe Lefebvre Tim Lollar Chris Welsh
May 12, 1982	MIN A	Larry Milbourne Pete Filson and cash	NY A	Butch Wynegar Roger Erickson
Nov 1, 1982	TEX A	——	MIN A	Len Whitehouse
Pat Pacillo				
July 13, 1988	MON N	*See Tracy Jones*	CIN N	——
Tom Paciorek				
Nov 17, 1975	ATL N	Jimmy Wynn Lee Lacy Jerry Royster	LA N	Dusty Baker Ed Goodson
Dec 11, 1981	CHI A	——	SEA A	Todd Cruz Jim Essian Rod Allen
July 12, 1985	NY N	——	CHI A	Dave Cochrane
Gene Packard				
Feb 10, 1916	CHI N	Charlie Pechous	KC F	Cash
April 1917	STL N	——	CHI N	Cash
Jan 21, 1919	PHI N	Doug Baird Stuffy Stewart	STL N	Milt Stock Pickles Dillhoefer Dixie Davis
Tom Padden				
Oct 1937	STL N	minor leaguer Bernie Cobb	PIT N	Johnny Rizzo
Jan 22, 1943	PHI N	Al Gerheauser Ed Levy Al Gettel and $10,000.	NY A	Nick Etten
Del Paddock				
Jan 1912	NY A	——	CHI A	Cash
Don Padgett				
Dec 10, 1941	BKN N	——	STL N	$30,000.
June 12, 1946	BOS N	——	BKN N	Cash
March 27, 1947	PHI N	——	BOS N	Andy Karl
Ernie Padgett				
Feb 1926	CLE A	——	BOS N	Cash
Dennis Paepke				
Dec 12, 1968	KC A	Ed Kirkpatrick	CAL A	Hoyt Wilhelm

Date	Traded To		Traded With		Traded By		In Exchange For

Andy Pafko

| June 15, 1951 | BKN | N | Johnny Schmitz
Rube Walker
Wayne Terwilliger | CHI | N | Bruce Edwards
Joe Hatten
Eddie Miksis
Gene Hermanski |
| Jan 17, 1953 | MIL | N | ——— | BKN | N | Roy Hartsfield
and $50,000. |

Dave Pagan

| June 15, 1976 | BAL | A | *See Tippy Martinez* | NY | A | ——— |
| July 27, 1977 | PIT | N | ——— | SEA | A | Rick Honeycutt |

Jose Pagan

| May 22, 1965 | PIT | N | ——— | SF | N | Dick Schofield |

Mitchell Page

| March 15, 1977 | OAK | A | ——— | PIT | N | *See Phil Garner* |

Karl Pagel

| June 23, 1980 | CLE | A | Cash | CHI | N | Cliff Johnson |

Jim Pagliaroni

Nov 20, 1962	PIT	N	Don Schwall	BOS	A	Jack Lamabe Dick Stuart
Dec 3, 1967	OAK	A	———	PIT	N	Cash
May 27, 1969	SEA	A	———	OAK	A	Cash

Mike Pagliarulo

| July 22, 1989 | SD | N | Don Schulze | NY | A | Walt Terrell
Fred Toliver |

(New York received Toliver on Sept. 27, 1989.)

Phil Paine

| April 19, 1958 | STL | N | ——— | MIL | N | Waiver price |
| Dec 4, 1958 | LA | N | Wally Moon | STL | N | Gino Cimoli |

Rey Palacios

| Aug 31, 1988 | KC | A | Mark Lee | DET | A | Ted Power |

Erv Palica

| March 17, 1955 | BAL | A | ——— | BKN | N | Frank Kellert
and cash |

Rafael Palmeiro

| Dec 5, 1988 | TEX | A | Jamie Moyer
Drew Hall | CHI | N | Mitch Williams
Paul Kilgus
Steve Wilson
Curtis Wilkerson
Minor league
IF Luis Benitez
Minor league
OF Pablo Delgado |

Lowell Palmer

Sept 18, 1972	CLE	A	———	STL	N	Cash
June 12, 1973	NY	A	———	CLE	A	Mike Kekich
May 31, 1974	SD	N	———	NY	A	Cash

Stan Palys

| April 30, 1955 | CIN | N | ——— | PHI | N | *See Andy Seminick* |
| April 3, 1958 | DET | A | ——— | CIN | N | Waiver price |

Jim Panther

| March 4, 1972 | TEX | A | Don Stanhouse | OAK | A | Denny McLain |
| Oct 27, 1972 | ATL | N | ——— | TEX | A | Rico Carty |

Al Papai

| May 4, 1949 | STL | A | ——— | STL | N | Waiver price |
| Dec 1, 1949 | BOS | A | ——— | STL | A | Waiver price |

Stan Papi

June 8, 1973	STL	N	———	HOU	N	Ray Busse
Dec 7, 1978	BOS	A	———	MON	N	Bill Lee
March 30, 1980	PHI	N	Cash	BOS	A	Dave Rader
May 29, 1980	DET	A	———	PHI	N	Cash

Frank Papish

| Dec 2, 1948 | CLE | A | ——— | CHI | A | Bob Kuzava
Ernie Groth |
| Dec 14, 1949 | PIT | N | ——— | CLE | A | Cash |

Milt Pappas

Dec 9, 1965	CIN	N	Jack Baldschun Dick Simpson	BAL	A	Frank Robinson
June 11, 1968	ATL	N	Ted Davidson Bob Johnson	CIN	N	Woody Woodward Clay Carroll Tony Cloninger
June 23, 1970	CHI	N	———	ATL	N	Cash

Freddy Parent

| April 1908 | CHI | A | ——— | BOS | A | Cash |

Kelly Paris

| March 31, 1983 | CIN | N | ——— | STL | N | Minor league
P Jim Strichek |
| Nov 28, 1983 | CHI | A | ——— | CIN | N | Cash |

Clay Parker

| Dec 22, 1987 | NY | A | ——— | SEA | A | *See Steve Trout* |

Dave Parker

Dec 7, 1983	CIN	N	———	PIT	N	No compensation (free agent signing)
Dec 8, 1987	OAK	A	———	CIN	N	Jose Rijo Tim Birtsas
Dec 3, 1989	MIL	A	———	OAK	A	No compensation (free agent signing)

Harry Parker

Oct 18, 1971	NY	N	———	STL	N	*See Jim Bibby*
Aug 4, 1975	STL	N	———	NY	N	Cash
April 7, 1976	CLE	A	———	STL	N	Roric Harrison

Roy Parmelee

| Dec 9, 1935 | STL | N | Phil Weintraub
and cash | NY | N | Burgess Whitehead |
| Oct 8, 1936 | CHI | N | Ripper Collins | STL | N | Lon Warneke |

Jeff Parrett

| Dec 6, 1988 | PHI | N | Floyd Youmans | MON | N | Kevin Gross |

Sam Parrilla

| Dec 16, 1970 | BAL | A | Grant Jackson
Jim Hutto | PHI | N | Roger Freed |

Date	Traded To		Traded With	Traded By		In Exchange For

Lance Parrish

Date	Traded To		Traded With	Traded By		In Exchange For
March 12, 1987	PHI	N	———	DET	A	No compensation (free agent signing)
Oct 3, 1988	CAL	A	———	PHI	N	Minor league P David Holdridge

Larry Parrish

Date	Traded To		Traded With	Traded By		In Exchange For
March 31, 1982	TEX	A	Dave Hostetler	MON	N	Al Oliver

Mike Parrott

Date	Traded To		Traded With	Traded By		In Exchange For
Dec 7, 1977	SEA	A	———	BAL	A	Carlos Lopez Tommy Moore
March 5, 1982	MIL	A	———	SEA	A	Thad Bosley

Bill Parsons

Date	Traded To		Traded With	Traded By		In Exchange For
June 24, 1974	OAK	A	Cash	MIL	A	Deron Johnson
Dec 2, 1974	STL	N	———	OAK	A	Cash
June 30, 1975	CHI	A	Cash	STL	N	Buddy Bradford

Tom Parsons

Date	Traded To		Traded With	Traded By		In Exchange For
Oct 19, 1965	HOU	N	Cash	NY	N	Jerry Grote

Roy Partee

Date	Traded To		Traded With	Traded By		In Exchange For
Nov 17, 1947	STL	A	———	BOS	A	*See Vern Stephens*
Dec 13, 1948	NY	A	Fred Sanford	STL	A	Sherm Lollar Red Embree Dick Starr and $100,000.

Camilo Pascual

Date	Traded To		Traded With	Traded By		In Exchange For
Dec 3, 1966	WAS	A	Bernie Allen	MIN	A	Ron Kline
July 7, 1969	CIN	N	———	WAS	A	Cash
May 22, 1971	SD	N	———	CLE	A	Cash

(Pascual was returned to Cleveland on May 26, 1971.)

Johnny Pasek

Date	Traded To		Traded With	Traded By		In Exchange For
Dec 12, 1933	PHI	A	$100,000.	DET	A	Mickey Cochrane
Dec 12, 1933	CHI	A	George Earnshaw	PHI	A	Charlie Berry and $20,000.

Larry Pashnick

Date	Traded To		Traded With	Traded By		In Exchange For
Dec 8, 1983	MIN	A	———	DET	A	Rusty Kuntz

Dode Paskert

Date	Traded To		Traded With	Traded By		In Exchange For
Feb 1911	PHI	N	Fred Beebe Jack Rowan Hans Lobert	CIN	N	Johnny Bates Eddie Grant George McQuillan Lew Moren
Dec 26, 1917	CHI	N	———	PHI	N	Cy Williams
Dec 1920	CIN	N	———	CHI	N	Waiver price

Kevin Pasley

Date	Traded To		Traded With	Traded By		In Exchange For
Sept 8, 1977	SEA	A	———	LA	N	Cash

Dan Pasqua

Date	Traded To		Traded With	Traded By		In Exchange For
Nov 13, 1987	CHI	A	Mark Salas Steve Rosenberg	NY	A	Richard Dotson Scott Nielsen

Claude Passeau

Date	Traded To		Traded With	Traded By		In Exchange For
Nov 21, 1935	PHI	N	Earl Grace	PIT	N	Al Todd
May 29, 1939	CHI	N	———	PHI	N	Joe Marty Ray Harrell Kirby Higbe

Freddie Patek

Date	Traded To		Traded With	Traded By		In Exchange For
Dec 2, 1970	KC	A	Bruce Dal Canton Jerry May	PIT	N	Bob Johnson Jackie Hernandez Jim Campanis
Dec 5, 1979	CAL	A	———	KC	A	No compensation (free agent signing)

Casey Patten

Date	Traded To		Traded With	Traded By		In Exchange For
July 1908	BOS	A	———	WAS	A	Jesse Tannehill Bob Unglaub

Bob Patterson

Date	Traded To		Traded With	Traded By		In Exchange For
April 3, 1986	PIT	N	———	SD	N	Marvell Wynne

Daryl Patterson

Date	Traded To		Traded With	Traded By		In Exchange For
May 22, 1971	OAK	A	———	DET	A	John Donaldson
June 25, 1971	STL	N	———	OAK	A	Cash

(Patterson was returned to Oakland on October 21, 1971.)

Mike Patterson

Date	Traded To		Traded With	Traded By		In Exchange For
May 20, 1981	NY	A	Dave Revering minor league P Chuck Dougherty	OAK	A	Jim Spencer Tom Underwood

Reggie Patterson

Date	Traded To		Traded With	Traded By		In Exchange For
Dec 10, 1982	CHI	N	———	CHI	A	Tye Waller

Marty Pattin

Date	Traded To		Traded With	Traded By		In Exchange For
Oct 11, 1971	BOS	A	Lew Krausse Tommy Harper Minor leaguer Pat Skrable	MIL	A	George Scott Billy Conigliaro Joe Lahoud Jim Lonborg Ken Brett Don Pavletich
Oct 24, 1973	KC	A	———	BOS	A	Dick Drago

Mike Paul

Date	Traded To		Traded With	Traded By		In Exchange For
Dec 2, 1971	TEX	A	———	CLE	A	*See Del Unser*
Aug 31, 1973	CHI	N	———	TEX	A	Larry Gura

Gene Paulette

Date	Traded To		Traded With	Traded By		In Exchange For
May 1917	STL	N	———	STL	A	Waiver price
July 14, 1919	PHI	N	Lee Meadows	STL	N	Elmer Jacobs Frank Woodward Doug Baird

Don Pavletich

Date	Traded To		Traded With	Traded By		In Exchange For
Dec 5, 1968	CHI	A	Don Secrist	CIN	N	Jack Fisher
Dec 13, 1969	BOS	A	Gary Peters	CHI	A	Syd O'Brien minor league P Billy Farmer Gerry Janeski

(Janeski replaced Farmer, who retired.)

Date	Traded To		Traded With	Traded By		In Exchange For
Oct 11, 1971	MIL	A	*See George Scott*	BOS	A	———

Mike Paxton

Date	Traded To		Traded With	Traded By		In Exchange For
March 30, 1978	CLE	A	———	BOS	A	*See Dennis Eckersley*

Mike Pazik

Date	Traded To		Traded With	Traded By		In Exchange For
May 4, 1974	MIN	A	———	NY	A	Dick Woodson

Johnny Peacock

Date	Traded To		Traded With	Traded By		In Exchange For
June 11, 1944	PHI	N	———	BOS	A	Cash
June 15, 1945	BKN	N	———	PHI	N	Ben Chapman

Albie Pearson

Date	Traded To	Traded With	Traded By	In Exchange For
Jan 23, 1958	WAS A	Norm Zauchin	BOS A	Pete Runnels
May 26, 1959	BAL A	———	WAS A	Lenny Green

Monte Pearson

Date	Traded To	Traded With	Traded By	In Exchange For
Dec 11, 1935	NY A	Steve Sundra	CLE A	Johnny Allen
Dec 30, 1940	CIN N	———	NY A	Don Lang and $20,000.

Charlie Pechous

Date	Traded To	Traded With	Traded By	In Exchange For
Feb 10, 1916	CHI N	Gene Packard	KC F	Cash

Hal Peck

Date	Traded To	Traded With	Traded By	In Exchange For
May 15, 1943	CHI N	———	BKN N	Cash
June 20, 1946	NY A	———	PHI A	Cash
Dec 20, 1946	CLE A	Al Gettel Gene Bearden	NY A	Sherm Lollar Ray Mack

Roger Peckinpaugh

Date	Traded To	Traded With	Traded By	In Exchange For
May 20, 1913	NY A	———	CLE A	Bill Stumpf Jack Lelivelt
Dec 20, 1921	BOS A	Jack Quinn Rip Collins Bill Piercy	NY A	Everett Scott Joe Bush Sad Sam Jones
Jan 10, 1922	WAS A	———	BOS A	Joe Dugan Frank O'Rourke

(Part of three-team trade involving Boston, Philadelphia, and Washington.)

Date	Traded To	Traded With	Traded By	In Exchange For
Jan 15, 1927	CHI A	———	WAS A	Sloppy Thurston Leo Mangum

Al Pedrique

Date	Traded To	Traded With	Traded By	In Exchange For
May 29, 1987	PIT N	Scott Little	NY N	Bill Almon

Homer Peel

Date	Traded To	Traded With	Traded By	In Exchange For
May 11, 1928	PHI N	Spud Davis	STL N	Jimmie Wilson
Dec 11, 1929	STL N	Bob McGraw	PHI N	Grover Alexander Harry McCurdy

Heinie Peitz

Date	Traded To	Traded With	Traded By	In Exchange For
Dec 1905	PIT N	———	CIN N	Ed Phelps

Eddie Pellagrini

Date	Traded To	Traded With	Traded By	In Exchange For
Nov 17, 1947	STL A	———	BOS A	*See Vern Stephens*
Dec 10, 1951	CIN N	———	PHI N	*See Smoky Burgess*
April 17, 1953	PIT N	———	CIN N	Waiver price

Barney Pelty

Date	Traded To	Traded With	Traded By	In Exchange For
June 1912	WAS A	———	STL A	Cash

Brock Pemberton

Date	Traded To	Traded With	Traded By	In Exchange For
Dec 9, 1976	STL N	Leon Brown	NY N	Minor league 1B Ed Kurpiel

Alejandro Pena

Date	Traded To	Traded With	Traded By	In Exchange For
Dec 20, 1989	NY N	Mike Marshall	LA N	Juan Samuel

Hipolito Pena

Date	Traded To	Traded With	Traded By	In Exchange For
March 30, 1988	NY A	———	PIT N	Orestes Destrade

Orlando Pena

Date	Traded To	Traded With	Traded By	In Exchange For
June 23, 1965	DET A	———	KC A	Cash
May 6, 1967	CLE A	———	DET A	Cash

Orlando Pena *continued*

Date	Traded To	Traded With	Traded By	In Exchange For
June 15, 1973	STL N	———	BAL A	Cash
Sept 5, 1974	CAL A	———	STL N	Rich Hand

(St. Louis received Hand on October 15, 1974.)

Roberto Pena

Date	Traded To	Traded With	Traded By	In Exchange For
Dec 9, 1964	CHI N	Cash	PIT N	Andre Rodgers
March 24, 1970	OAK A	———	SD N	Ramon Webster
May 18, 1970	MIL A	———	OAK A	John Donaldson

Tony Pena

Date	Traded To	Traded With	Traded By	In Exchange For
April 1, 1987	STL N	———	PIT N	Andy Van Slyke Mike LaValliere Mike Dunne
Nov 27, 1989	BOS A	———	STL N	No compensation (free agent signing)

Jim Pendleton

Date	Traded To	Traded With	Traded By	In Exchange For
Feb 16, 1953	MIL N	Rocky Bridges	BKN N	Russ Meyer

(Part of four-team trade involving Milwaukee, Philadelphia Phillies, Brooklyn, and Cincinnati.)

Date	Traded To	Traded With	Traded By	In Exchange For
April 3, 1957	PIT N	———	MIL N	Dick Cole
Jan 30, 1959	CIN N	———	PIT N	*See Harvey Haddix*

Herb Pennock

Date	Traded To	Traded With	Traded By	In Exchange For
June 13, 1915	BOS A	———	PHI A	Waiver price
Jan 30, 1923	NY A	———	BOS A	Camp Skinner Norm McMillan George Murray and $50,000.

Gene Pentz

Date	Traded To	Traded With	Traded By	In Exchange For
Dec 6, 1975	HOU N	———	DET A	*See Milt May*

Joe Pepitone

Date	Traded To	Traded With	Traded By	In Exchange For
Dec 4, 1969	HOU N	———	NY A	Curt Blefary
July 29, 1970	CHI N	———	HOU N	Cash
May 19, 1973	ATL N	———	CHI N	Andre Thornton

Don Pepper

Date	Traded To	Traded With	Traded By	In Exchange For
March 25, 1969	MON N	———	DET A	Cash

Oswaldo Peraza

Date	Traded To	Traded With	Traded By	In Exchange For
Aug 31, 1987	BAL A	———	TOR A	Mike Flanagan

Jack Perconte

Date	Traded To	Traded With	Traded By	In Exchange For
Dec 9, 1981	CLE A	Rick Sutcliffe	LA N	Jorge Orta Larry White Jack Fimple
Dec 7, 1983	SEA A	Gorman Thomas	CLE A	Tony Bernazard

Hub Perdue

Date	Traded To	Traded With	Traded By	In Exchange For
June 1914	STL N	———	BOS N	Possum Whitted Ted Cather

Marty Perez

Date	Traded To	Traded With	Traded By	In Exchange For
Oct 21, 1970	ATL N	———	CAL A	Minor league C John Burns
June 13, 1976	SF N	*See Darrell Evans*	ATL N	
March 14, 1977	NY A	———	SF N	Terry Whitfield
April 27, 1977	OAK A	Dock Ellis Larry Murray	NY A	Mike Torrez

Date		Traded To	Traded With		Traded By	In Exchange For

Melido Perez

Date		Traded To	Traded With		Traded By	In Exchange For
Dec 10, 1987	CHI	A	John Davis Greg Hibbard Minor league P Chuck Mount	KC	A	Floyd Bannister Dave Cochrane

Pascual Perez

Date		Traded To	Traded With		Traded By	In Exchange For
June 30, 1982	ATL	N	minor league SS Carlos Rios	PIT	N	Larry McWilliams
Nov 21, 1989	NY	A	——	MON	N	No compensation (free agent signing)

Tony Perez

Date		Traded To	Traded With		Traded By	In Exchange For
Dec 16, 1976	MON	N	Will McEnaney	CIN	N	Woodie Fryman Dale Murray
Nov 20, 1979	BOS	A	——	MON	N	No compensation (free agent signing)
Dec 6, 1983	CIN	N		PHI	N	Cash

Broderick Perkins

Date		Traded To	Traded With		Traded By	In Exchange For
Nov 18, 1982	CLE	A	Juan Eichelberger	SD	N	Ed Whitson

Cy Perkins

Date		Traded To	Traded With		Traded By	In Exchange For
Dec 10, 1930	NY	A	——	PHI	A	Cash

Harry Perkowski

Date		Traded To	Traded With		Traded By	In Exchange For
Oct 1, 1954	CHI	N	Ted Tappe Jim Bolger	CIN	N	Johnny Klippstein Jim Willis

Ron Perranoski

Date		Traded To	Traded With		Traded By	In Exchange For
April 8, 1960	LA	N	John Goryl minor league OF Lee Handley and $25,000.	CHI	N	Don Zimmer
Nov 28, 1967	MIN	A	Johnny Roseboro Bob Miller	LA	N	Mudcat Grant Zoilo Versalles
July 30, 1971	DET	A	——	MIN	A	Cash

Pol Perritt

Date		Traded To	Traded With		Traded By	In Exchange For
Feb 18, 1915	NY	N	——	STL	N	Cash
June 1921	DET	A	——	NY	N	Cash

Gaylord Perry

Date		Traded To	Traded With		Traded By	In Exchange For
Nov 29, 1971	CLE	A	Frank Duffy	SF	N	Sam McDowell
June 13, 1975	TEX	A	——	CLE	A	Jim Bibby Jackie Brown Rick Waits and $100,000.
Jan 25, 1978	SD	N	——	TEX	A	Dave Tomlin and $125,000.
Feb 15, 1980	TEX	A	Tucker Ashford minor league P Joe Carroll	SD	N	Willie Montanez
Aug 14, 1980	NY	A	——	TEX	A	Ken Clay minor league OF Marvin Thompson
Jan 12, 1981	ATL	N	——	NY	A	No compensation (free agent signing)

Gerald Perry

Date		Traded To	Traded With		Traded By	In Exchange For
Dec 15, 1989	KC	A	Minor league P Jim Lemasters	ATL	N	Charlie Leibrandt Rick Luecken

Jim Perry

Date		Traded To	Traded With		Traded By	In Exchange For
May 2, 1963	MIN	A	——	CLE	A	Jack Kralick
March 27, 1973	DET	A	——	MIN	A	Dan Fife and cash

Jim Perry *continued*

Date		Traded To	Traded With		Traded By	In Exchange For
March 19, 1974	CLE	A	——	DET	A	Rick Sawyer Walt Williams
			(Part of three-team trade involving Detroit, Cleveland, and New York Yankees.)			
May 20, 1975	OAK	A	Dick Bosman	CLE	A	Blue Moon Odom and cash

Pat Perry

Date		Traded To	Traded With		Traded By	In Exchange For
Aug 30, 1987	CIN	N	——	STL	N	Scott Terry
May 19, 1988	CHI	N	Cash	CIN	N	Leon Durham

Scott Perry

Date		Traded To	Traded With		Traded By	In Exchange For
April 26, 1917	CIN	N	——	CHI	N	Waiver price
May 28, 1917	BOS	N	——	CIN	N	Waiver price
April 1918	PHI	A	——	BOS	N	Cash

Stan Perzanowski

Date		Traded To	Traded With		Traded By	In Exchange For
Feb 25, 1975	TEX	A	——	CHI	A	Steve Dunning
May 28, 1976	CLE	A	Cash	TEX	A	Fritz Peterson
Dec 3, 1976	CAL	A	Cash	CLE	A	Bill Melton

Johnny Pesky

Date		Traded To	Traded With		Traded By	In Exchange For
June 3, 1952	DET	A	Walt Dropo Bill Wight Fred Hatfield Don Lenhardt	BOS	A	Dizzy Trout George Kell Johnny Lipon Hoot Evers
June 14, 1954	WAS	A	——	DET	A	Mel Hoderlein

Gary Peters

Date		Traded To	Traded With		Traded By	In Exchange For
Dec 13, 1969	BOS	A	Don Pavletich	CHI	A	Syd O'Brien minor league P Billy Farmer Gerry Janeski
			(Janeski replaced Farmer, who retired.)			

Ray Peters

Date		Traded To	Traded With		Traded By	In Exchange For
April 22, 1971	PHI	N	Pete Koegel	MIL	A	John Briggs

Rusty Peters

Date		Traded To	Traded With		Traded By	In Exchange For
Dec 7, 1946	STL	A	——	CLE	A	Cash

Cap Peterson

Date		Traded To	Traded With		Traded By	In Exchange For
Dec 13, 1966	WAS	A	Bob Priddy	SF	N	Mike McCormick
March 31, 1969	CLE	A	——	WAS	A	Minor league P George Woodson

Fritz Peterson

Date		Traded To	Traded With		Traded By	In Exchange For
April 27, 1974	CLE	A	Steve Kline Fred Beene Tom Buskey	NY	A	Chris Chambliss Dick Tidrow Cecil Upshaw
May 28, 1976	TEX	A	——	CLE	A	Stan Perzanowski and cash

Kent Peterson

Date		Traded To	Traded With		Traded By	In Exchange For
May 23, 1952	PHI	N	Johnny Wyrostek	CIN	N	Bubba Church

Geno Petralli

Date		Traded To	Traded With		Traded By	In Exchange For
May 8, 1984	CLE	A	——	TOR	A	Cash

Dan Petry

Date		Traded To	Traded With		Traded By	In Exchange For
Nov 13, 1987	CAL	A	——	DET	A	Gary Pettis

Date	Traded To		Traded With	Traded By		In Exchange For

Joe Pettini

Date	Traded To		Traded With	Traded By		In Exchange For
June 13, 1979	SF	N	Cash	MON	N	John Tamargo

Gary Pettis

| Nov 13, 1987 | DET | A | —— | CAL | A | Dan Petry |
| Nov 24, 1989 | TEX | A | —— | DET | A | No compensation (free agent signing) |

Jesse Petty

| Dec 11, 1928 | PIT | N | Harry Riconda | BKN | N | Glenn Wright |
| Aug 24, 1930 | CHI | N | —— | PIT | N | Cash |

Pretzels Pezzullo

| Nov 1, 1934 | PHI | N | Blondy Ryan Johnny Vergez George Watkins and cash | NY | N | Dick Bartell |

Big Jeff Pfeffer

| Jan 1906 | BOS | N | —— | CHI | N | Cash |
| Jan 1911 | BOS | N | Scotty Ingerton | CHI | N | Dave Shean |

Jeff Pfeffer

| June 18, 1921 | STL | N | —— | BKN | N | Ferdie Schupp Hal Janvrin |
| May 1924 | PIT | N | —— | STL | N | Waiver price |

Bobby Pfeil

April 10, 1965	STL	N	minor league P Hal Gibson	CHI	N	Bob Humphreys
Feb 8, 1972	MIL	A	——	PHI	N	Minor league 3B Chico Vaughns
March 20, 1972	BOS	A	——	MIL	A	Cash

Art Phelan

| Dec 15, 1912 | CHI | N | —— | CIN | N | See Joe Tinker |

Babe Phelps

Dec 31, 1934	BKN	N	——	CHI	N	Waiver price
Dec 12, 1941	PIT	N	Pete Coscarart Luke Hamlin Jimmy Wasdell	BKN	N	Arky Vaughan
Dec 30, 1943	PHI	N	Cash	PIT	N	Babe Dahlgren

Ed Phelps

| Dec 1905 | CIN | N | —— | PIT | N | Heinie Peitz |
| May 20, 1906 | PIT | N | —— | CIN | N | Cash |

Ken Phelps

Jan 19, 1982	MON	N	——	KC	A	Grant Jackson
March 31, 1983	SEA	A	——	MON	N	Cash
July 21, 1988	NY	A	——	SEA	A	Jay Buhner Minor league P Rich Balabon player to be named

(Seattle received P Troy Evers on October 12, 1988.)

| Aug 30, 1989 | OAK | A | —— | NY | A | Minor league P Scott Holcomb |

Dave Philley

| April 30, 1951 | PHI | A | Gus Zernial | CHI | A | Paul Lehner Minnie Minoso |

(Part of three-team trade involving Chicago White Sox, Philadelphia A's, and Cleveland.)

Dave Philley continued

Date	Traded To		Traded With	Traded By		In Exchange For
Feb 19, 1954	CLE	A	——	PHI	A	Bill Upton Lee Wheat
July 2, 1955	BAL	A	——	CLE	A	Waiver price
May 21, 1956	CHI	A	Jim Wilson	BAL	A	Bob Nieman Mike Fornieles Connie Johnson George Kell
June 14, 1957	DET	A	——	CHI	A	Earl Torgeson
Dec 11, 1957	PHI	N	——	DET	A	Cash
May 12, 1960	SF	N	——	PHI	N	Cash
Sept 1, 1960	BAL	A	——	SF	N	Cash
March 24, 1962	BOS	A	——	HOU	N	Tom Borland

Deacon Phillippe

| Jan 1900 | PIT | N | See Honus Wagner | LOU | N | —— |

Adolfo Phillips

| April 21, 1966 | CHI | N | John Herrnstein Ferguson Jenkins | PHI | N | Larry Jackson Bob Buhl |
| June 11, 1969 | MON | N | Jack Lamabe | CHI | N | Paul Popovich |

Bubba Phillips

Nov 30, 1955	CHI	A	——	DET	A	Virgil Trucks
Dec 6, 1959	CLE	A	See Norm Cash	CHI	A	——
Nov 27, 1962	DET	A	——	CLE	A	Gordon Seyfried Ron Nischwitz

Eddie Phillips

| Jan 1931 | PIT | N | —— | PHI | N | Cash |
| Dec 1934 | CLE | A | —— | WAS | A | Cash |

Jack Phillips

Aug 6, 1949	PIT	N	——	NY	A	Cash
Dec 6, 1954	DET	A	See Ferris Fain	CHI	A	——
April 30, 1957	BOS	A	——	DET	A	Karl Olson

Mike Phillips

May 3, 1975	NY	N	——	SF	N	Cash
June 15, 1977	STL	N	——	NY	N	Joel Youngblood
Dec 8, 1980	SD	N	——	STL	N	See Rollie Fingers
May 10, 1981	MON	N	——	SD	N	Cash

Taylor Phillips

Dec 5, 1957	CHI	N	Sammy Taylor	MIL	N	Eddie Haas Don Kaiser Bob Rush
May 12, 1959	PHI	N	——	CHI	N	Seth Morehead
Dec 15, 1961	CHI	A	Bob Sadowski minor league IF Lou Vassie	PHI	N	Frank Barnes Andy Carey Cal McLish

(Carey refused to report, and the Phillies received McLish in exchange for Vassie to complete the trade on March 24, 1962.)

Tony Phillips

Aug 31, 1980	SD	N	——	MON	N	Willie Montanez
March 27, 1981	OAK	A	Kevin Bell minor league P Eric Mustard	SD	N	Bob Lacey minor league P Ray Moretti
Dec 5, 1989	DET	A	——	OAK	A	No compensation (free agent signing)

Tom Phoebus

Dec 1, 1970	SD	N	Al Severinsen Fred Beene Enzo Hernandez	BAL	A	Pat Dobson Tom Dukes
April 20, 1972	CHI	N	——	SD	N	Cash
Oct 20, 1972	ATL	N	——	CHI	N	Tony LaRussa

Date	Traded To		Traded With	Traded By		In Exchange For

Wiley Piatt

Date	Traded To		Traded With	Traded By		In Exchange For
July 1901	CHI	A	——	PHI	A	Cash

Rob Picciolo

Date	Traded To		Traded With	Traded By		In Exchange For
May 14, 1982	MIL	A	——	OAK	A	Mike Warren minor league 1B John Evans
Feb 6, 1984	CAL	A	——	MIL	A	No compensation (free agent signing)

Ron Piche

Date	Traded To		Traded With	Traded By		In Exchange For
Oct 14, 1964	LA	A	Phil Roof	MIL	N	Dan Osinski
April 22, 1968	CHI	N	Jack Lamabe	STL	N	Pete Mikkelsen Dave Dowling

Val Picinich

Date	Traded To		Traded With	Traded By		In Exchange For
Feb 10, 1923	BOS	A	Howard Shanks Ed Goebel	WAS	A	Muddy Ruel Allen Russell
Feb 10, 1926	CIN	N	——	BOS	A	$7,500.
April 18, 1929	BKN	N	——	CIN	N	Johnny Gooch Rube Ehrhardt
June 23, 1933	PIT	N	——	BKN	N	Cash

Charlie Pick

Date	Traded To		Traded With	Traded By		In Exchange For
Aug 1919	BOS	N	Les Mann	CHI	N	Buck Herzog

Ollie Pickering

Date	Traded To		Traded With	Traded By		In Exchange For
Feb 1903	PHI	A	——	CLE	A	Cash
Oct 5, 1907	WAS	A	——	STL	A	Charlie Jones

Billy Pierce

Date	Traded To		Traded With	Traded By		In Exchange For
Nov 10, 1948	CHI	A	$10,000.	DET	A	Aaron Robinson
Nov 30, 1961	SF	N	Don Larsen	CHI	A	Eddie Fisher Dom Zanni Verle Tiefenthaler Bob Farley

Jack Pierce

Date	Traded To		Traded With	Traded By		In Exchange For
March 29, 1975	DET	A	——	ATL	N	Reggie Sanders

Bill Piercy

Date	Traded To		Traded With	Traded By		In Exchange For
Dec 20, 1921	BOS	A	——	NY	A	See Joe Bush

Marino Pieretti

Date	Traded To		Traded With	Traded By		In Exchange For
June 9, 1948	CHI	A	——	WAS	A	Earl Harrist
April 16, 1950	CLE	A	——	CHI	A	Waiver price

Jimmy Piersall

Date	Traded To		Traded With	Traded By		In Exchange For
Dec 2, 1958	CLE	A	——	BOS	A	Vic Wertz Gary Geiger
Oct 5, 1961	WAS	A	——	CLE	A	Dick Donovan Gene Green Jim Mahoney
May 23, 1963	NY	N	——	WAS	A	Gil Hodges

(Hodges was named Washington manager.)

Tony Piet

Date	Traded To		Traded With	Traded By		In Exchange For
Nov 17, 1933	CIN	N	Adam Comorosky	PIT	N	Red Lucas Wally Roettger
June 4, 1935	CHI	A	——	CIN	N	Cash
Dec 2, 1937	DET	A	Vern Kennedy Dixie Walker	CHI	A	Marv Owen Mike Tresh Gee Walker

Joe Pignatano

Date	Traded To		Traded With	Traded By		In Exchange For
Jan 31, 1961	KC	A	——	LA	N	Cash
Dec 15, 1961	SF	N	——	KC	A	Jose Tartabull
July 13, 1962	NY	N	——	SF	N	Cash

Al Pilarcik

Date	Traded To		Traded With	Traded By		In Exchange For
Oct 11, 1956	BAL	A	Art Ceccarelli	KC	A	Ryne Duren Jim Pisoni
Jan 24, 1961	KC	A	——	BAL	A	See Russ Snyder
June 10, 1961	CHI	A	——	KC	A	See Wes Covington

Duane Pillette

Date	Traded To		Traded With	Traded By		In Exchange For
June 15, 1950	STL	A	Jim Delsing Don Johnson Snuffy Stirnweiss and $50,000.	NY	A	Tom Ferrick Joe Ostrowski Leo Thomas Sid Schacht

Horacio Pina

Date	Traded To		Traded With	Traded By		In Exchange For
Dec 5, 1969	WAS	A	Dave Nelson Ron Law	CLE	A	Dennis Higgins Barry Moore
Nov 30, 1972	OAK	A	——	TEX	A	Mike Epstein
Dec 3, 1973	CHI	N	——	OAK	A	Bob Locker
July 28, 1974	CAL	A	——	CHI	N	Rick Stelmaszek

Babe Pinelli

Date	Traded To		Traded With	Traded By		In Exchange For
Dec 1919	DET	A	——	CHI	A	Cash

Lou Piniella

Date	Traded To		Traded With	Traded By		In Exchange For
March 31, 1964	BAL	A	——	WAS	A	Buster Narum
April 1, 1969	KC	A	——	SEA	A	Steve Whitaker John Gelnar
Dec 7, 1973	NY	A	Ken Wright	KC	A	Lindy McDaniel

Vada Pinson

Date	Traded To		Traded With	Traded By		In Exchange For
Oct 11, 1968	STL	N	——	CIN	N	Wayne Granger Bobby Tolan
Nov 21, 1969	CLE	A	——	STL	N	Jose Cardenal
Oct 5, 1971	CAL	A	Frank Baker Alan Foster	CLE	A	Alex Johnson Gerry Moses
Feb 23, 1974	KC	A	——	CAL	A	Barry Raziano and cash

George Pipgras

Date	Traded To		Traded With	Traded By		In Exchange For
Jan 3, 1923	NY	A	Harvey Hendrick	BOS	A	Al DeVormer and cash
May 12, 1933	BOS	A	Bill Werber	NY	A	$100,000.

Wally Pipp

Date	Traded To		Traded With	Traded By		In Exchange For
Jan 7, 1915	NY	A	——	DET	A	Waiver price
Feb 1, 1926	CIN	N	——	NY	A	$7,500.

Cotton Pippen

Date	Traded To		Traded With	Traded By		In Exchange For
Sept 12, 1939	DET	A	——	PHI	A	Waiver price

Jim Pisoni

Date	Traded To		Traded With	Traded By		In Exchange For
Oct 11, 1956	KC	A	Ryne Duren	BAL	A	Art Ceccarelli Al Pilarcik
June 15, 1957	NY	A	——	KC	A	See Ralph Terry

Skip Pitlock

Date	Traded To		Traded With	Traded By		In Exchange For
June 15, 1975	OAK	A	Stan Bahnsen	CHI	A	Dave Hamilton Chet Lemon

Date	Traded To		Traded With	Traded By		In Exchange For

Chris Pittaro

| Jan 18, 1986 | MIN | A | Alejandro Sanchez | DET | A | Dave Engle |

Togie Pittinger

| Dec 20, 1904 | PHI | N | —— | BOS | N | Chick Fraser |
| | | | | | | Harry Wolverton |

Joe Pittman

June 8, 1982	SD	N	——	HOU	N	Danny Boone
Dec 6, 1983	SF	N	minor league	SD	N	Champ Summers
			OF Tommy Francis			

Juan Pizarro

Dec 15, 1960	CIN	N	Joey Jay	MIL	N	Roy McMillan
Dec 15, 1960	CHI	A	Cal McLish	CIN	N	Gene Freese
Oct 12, 1966	PIT	N	——	CHI	A	Wilbur Wood
June 27, 1968	BOS	A	——	PIT	N	Cash
April 19, 1969	CLE	A	See Ken Harrelson	BOS	A	——
Sept 21, 1969	OAK	A	——	CLE	A	Cash
July 9, 1970	CHI	N	——	CAL	A	Archie Reynolds

Eddie Plank

Feb 10, 1916	STL	A	Babe Borton	STL	F	Cash
			Harry Chapman			
			Doc Crandall			
			Charlie Deal			
			Bob Groom			
			Grover Hartley			
			Armando Marsans			
			Ward Miller			
			Johnny Tobin			
			Ernie Johnson			
Jan 22, 1918	NY	A	Del Pratt	STL	A	Les Nunamaker
			and $15,000.			Fritz Maisel
						Nick Cullop
						Urban Shocker
						Joe Gedeon

Whitey Platt

| April 20, 1946 | CHI | A | —— | CHI | N | Waiver price |

Herb Plews

Feb 8, 1956	WAS	A	See Whitey Herzog	NY	A	——
June 11, 1959	BOS	A	Dick Hyde	WAS	A	Billy Consolo
						Murray Wall

(Hyde was returned to Washington and Wall was returned to Boston.)

Bill Plummer

Jan 9, 1969	CIN	N	Clarence Jones	CHI	N	Ted Abernathy
			minor league			
			P Ken Myette			

Eric Plunk

Dec 8, 1984	OAK	A	——	NY	A	See Rickey Henderson
June 21, 1989	NY	A	Greg Cadaret	OAK	A	Rickey Henderson
			Luis Polonia			

Ray Poat

| June 6, 1949 | PIT | N | Bobby Rhawn | NY | N | Kirby Higbe |

Bud Podbielan

| June 15, 1952 | CIN | N | —— | BKN | N | Bud Byerly |
| | | | | | | and cash |

Johnny Podgajny

| June 15, 1943 | PIT | N | —— | PHI | N | Dutch Dietz |

Johnny Podres

| May 10, 1966 | DET | A | —— | LA | N | Cash |

John Poff

| Sept 1, 1980 | MIL | A | —— | PHI | N | Cash |
| April 1, 1981 | CHI | A | —— | MIL | A | Thad Bosley |

Boots Poffenberger

| Jan 1939 | BKN | N | —— | DET | A | Waiver price |

Tom Poholsky

Dec 11, 1956	CHI	N	Jackie Collum	STL	N	Hobie Landrith
			Ray Katt			Jim Davis
			minor league			Sam Jones
			P Wally Lammers			Eddie Miksis
Dec 10, 1957	NY	N	——	CHI	N	Freddy Rodriguez

Aaron Pointer

| May 4, 1968 | CHI | N | —— | HOU | N | Byron Browne |

Hugh Poland

| April 27, 1943 | BOS | N | Connie Ryan | NY | N | Ernie Lombardi |
| June 14, 1947 | CIN | N | Ken Raffensberger | PHI | N | Al Lakeman |

Gus Polidor

| Dec 7, 1988 | MIL | A | —— | CAL | A | Bill Schroeder |

Howie Pollet

June 15, 1951	PIT	N	Bill Howerton	STL	N	Cliff Chambers
			Ted Wilks			Wally Westlake
			Joe Garagiola			
			Dick Cole			
June 4, 1953	CHI	N	Ralph Kiner	PIT	N	Toby Atwell
			Joe Garagiola			Bob Schultz
			Catfish Metkovich			Preston Ward
						George Freese
						Bob Addis
						Gene Hermanski
						$150,000.
April 16, 1956	PIT	N	——	CHI	A	Cash

John Poloni

| Dec 14, 1977 | BOS | A | Cash | TEX | A | Ferguson Jenkins |

Luis Polonia

| June 21, 1989 | NY | A | Eric Plunk | OAK | A | Rickey Henderson |
| | | | Greg Cadaret | | | |

Elmer Ponder

| July 1, 1921 | CHI | N | —— | PIT | N | Dave Robertson |

Ed Poole

| April 1902 | CIN | N | —— | PIT | N | Cash |
| Feb 1904 | BKN | N | —— | CIN | N | Cash |

Dave Pope

| June 15, 1955 | BAL | A | Wally Westlake | CLE | A | Gene Woodling |
| | | | | | | Billy Cox |

(Cox refused to report and announced retirement. Cleveland received $15,000 to

Date	Traded To	Traded With	Traded By	In Exchange For

Dave Pope *continued*

		complete trade.)		
May 13, 1956	CLE A	——	BAL A	Hoot Evers

Paul Popovich

Nov 30, 1967	LA N	Jim Williams	CHI N	Lou Johnson
June 11, 1969	MON N	Ron Fairly	LA N	Maury Wills Manny Mota
June 11, 1969	CHI N	——	MON N	Adolfo Phillips Jack Lamabe
April 1, 1974	PIT N	——	CHI N	Tom Dettore and cash

Tom Poquette

June 13, 1979	BOS A	——	KC A	George Scott
Aug 12, 1981	TEX A	——	BOS A	Cash
Jan 15, 1982	KC A	——	TEX A	No compensation (free agent signing)

Darrell Porter

Dec 6, 1976	KC A	Jim Colborn	MIL A	Jim Wohlford Jamie Quirk Bob McClure
Dec 13, 1980	STL N	——	KC A	No compensation (free agent signing)
Jan 28, 1986	TEX A	——	STL N	No compensation (free agent signing)

Dick Porter

May 25, 1934	BOS A	Wes Ferrell	CLE A	Bob Weiland Bob Seeds and $25,000.

J. W. Porter

July 28, 1952	STL A	Ray Coleman	CHI A	Jim Rivera Darrell Johnson
Dec 4, 1952	DET A	——	STL A	*See Virgil Trucks*
Feb 18, 1958	CLE A	Hal Woodeshick	DET A	Jim Hegan Hank Aguirre
Oct 27, 1958	WAS A	——	CLE A	Ossie Alvarez
July 25, 1959	STL N	——	WAS A	Waiver price

Bob Porterfield

June 15, 1951	WAS A	Fred Sanford Tom Ferrick	NY A	Bob Kuzava
Nov 8, 1955	BOS A	Johnny Schmitz Mickey Vernon Tommy Umphlett	WAS A	Karl Olson Dick Brodowski Tex Clevenger Neil Chrisley and minor league P Al Curtis
May 7, 1958	PIT N	——	BOS A	Cash
June 13, 1959	CHI N	——	BOS A	Cash
June 13, 1959	PIT N	Waiver price	CHI N	Cash

Arnie Portocarrero

April 17, 1958	BAL A	——	KC A	Bud Daley

Mark Portugal

Dec 4, 1988	HOU N	——	MIN A	Minor league P Todd McClure

Bill Posedel

March 31, 1939	BOS N	——	BKN N	Al Todd

Wally Post

Dec 16, 1957	PHI N	——	CIN N	Harvey Haddix

Wally Post *continued*

June 15, 1960	CIN N	Harry Anderson minor league 1B Fred Hopke	PHI N	Tony Gonzalez Lee Walls
May 16, 1963	MIN A	——	CIN N	Cash

Dykes Potter

Feb 10, 1916	CHI N	*See Three Finger Brown*	CHI F	——

Mike Potter

June 26, 1978	SEA A	——	STL N	Jose Baez

Nels Potter

June 30, 1941	BOS A	——	PHI A	Cash
May 15, 1948	PHI A	——	STL A	$17,500.

Alonzo Powell

Oct 24, 1985	MON N	George Riley	SF N	Bill Laskey
Aug 28, 1989	MIN A	——	MON N	Jim Dwyer
	(Minnesota received Powell on Sept. 15, 1989.)			

Boog Powell

Feb 25, 1975	CLE A	Don Hood	BAL A	Dave Duncan and minor league OF Al McGrew

Dennis Powell

Dec 10, 1986	SEA A	Minor league IF Mike Watters	LA N	Matt Young

Hosken Powell

Dec 28, 1981	TOR A	——	MIN A	Boomer Wells

Jack Powell

Jan 1904	NY A	——	STL A	Harry Howell Jack O'Connor
Feb 1904	NY A	——	STL A	Cash
Sept 1, 1905	STL A	——	NY A	Cash

Jake Powell

June 14, 1936	NY A	——	WAS A	Ben Chapman

Paul Ray Powell

Oct 22, 1971	LA N	——	MIN A	Bobby Darwin

Ray Powell

Dec 15, 1923	PHI N	Hod Ford	BOS N	Cotton Tierney
	(Powell announced his intention to retire after the 1924 season. He remained with Boston, and Philadelphia received cash instead.)			

Ted Power

Oct 15, 1982	CIN N	——	LA N	Minor league IF Mike Ramsey
Nov 6, 1987	KC A	Kurt Stillwell	CIN N	Danny Jackson Angel Salazar
Aug 31, 1988	DET A	——	KC A	Rey Palacios Mark Lee
Nov 20, 1989	PIT N	——	STL N	No compensation (free agent signing)

Date	Traded To		Traded With	Traded By		In Exchange For

Vic Power

Date	Traded To		Traded With	Traded By		In Exchange For
Dec 16, 1953	PHI	A	Don Bollweg John Gray Jim Robertson Jim Finigan Bill Renna	NY	A	Harry Byrd Eddie Robinson Tom Hamilton Carmen Mauro Loren Babe
June 15, 1958	CLE	A	Woodie Held	KC	A	Roger Maris Dick Tomanek Preston Ward
April 2, 1962	MIN	A	Dick Stigman	CLE	A	Pedro Ramos
June 11, 1964	LA	A	Lenny Green	MIN	A	Jerry Kindall Frank Kostro

(Part of three-team trade involving Los Angeles Angels, Minnesota, and Cleveland.)

Date	Traded To		Traded With	Traded By		In Exchange For
Sept 9, 1964	PHI	N	——	LA	A	Marcelino Lopez and cash
Nov 30, 1964	LA	A	——	PHI	N	Cash

Johnny Powers

Date	Traded To		Traded With	Traded By		In Exchange For
Jan 30, 1959	CIN	N	——	PIT	N	See Harvey Haddix
Dec 15, 1959	BAL	A	——	CIN	N	Cash
May 12, 1960	CLE	A	——	BAL	A	Waiver price
June 2, 1960	PIT	N	——	CLE	A	Hank Foiles

Les Powers

Date	Traded To		Traded With	Traded By		In Exchange For
Dec 7, 1938	PHI	N	——	NY	N	Cash

Mike Powers

Date	Traded To		Traded With	Traded By		In Exchange For
July 13, 1905	NY	A	——	PHI	A	Cash
Aug 7, 1905	PHI	A	——	NY	A	Cash

Willie Prall

Date	Traded To		Traded With	Traded By		In Exchange For
March 19, 1974	CHI	N	——	SF	N	Ken Rudolph

Johnny Pramesa

Date	Traded To		Traded With	Traded By		In Exchange For
Oct 4, 1951	CHI	N	Bob Usher	CIN	N	Bob Borkowski Smoky Burgess

Del Pratt

Date	Traded To		Traded With	Traded By		In Exchange For
Jan 22, 1918	NY	A	Eddie Plank and $15,000.	STL	A	Les Nunamaker Fritz Maisel Nick Cullop Urban Shocker Joe Gedeon
Dec 15, 1920	BOS	A	Muddy Ruel Sammy Vick Hank Thormahlen	NY	A	Waite Hoyt Harry Harper Wally Schang Mike McNally
Oct 30, 1922	DET	A	Rip Collins	BOS	A	Carl Holling Howard Ehmke Danny Clark Babe Herman and $25,000.

Larry Pratt

Date	Traded To		Traded With	Traded By		In Exchange For
Feb 1915	NWK	F	Hugh Bradley Tom Seaton	BKN	F	Cy Falkenberg

Mike Prendergast

Date	Traded To		Traded With	Traded By		In Exchange For
Dec 11, 1917	PHI	N	Pickles Dillhoefer and $55,000.	CHI	N	Grover Alexander Bill Killefer

George Prentiss

Date	Traded To		Traded With	Traded By		In Exchange For
June 1902	BAL	A	——	BOS	A	Cash

Tot Pressnell

Date	Traded To		Traded With	Traded By		In Exchange For
Nov 19, 1940	STL	N	——	BKN	N	Cash
Dec 16, 1940	CIN	N	——	STL	N	Cash

Tot Pressnell *continued*

Date	Traded To		Traded With	Traded By		In Exchange For
Feb 4, 1941	CHI	N	——	CIN	N	Cash

Jim Price

Date	Traded To		Traded With	Traded By		In Exchange For
April 7, 1967	DET	A	——	PIT	N	Cash

Joe Price

Date	Traded To		Traded With	Traded By		In Exchange For
Feb 5, 1987	SF	N	——	CIN	N	No compensation (free agent signing)

Bob Priddy

Date	Traded To		Traded With	Traded By		In Exchange For
Feb 11, 1965	SF	N	Bob Burda	PIT	N	Del Crandall
Dec 13, 1966	WAS	A	Cap Peterson	SF	N	Mike McCormick
Feb 13, 1968	CHI	A	——	WAS	A	See Ron Hansen
May 14, 1969	CAL	A	Sandy Alomar	CHI	A	Bobby Knoop
Sept 9, 1969	ATL	N	——	CAL	A	Cash

Gerry Priddy

Date	Traded To		Traded With	Traded By		In Exchange For
Jan 29, 1943	WAS	A	Milo Candini	NY	A	Bill Zuber and cash
Nov 22, 1947	STL	A	——	WAS	A	Johnny Berardino

(Berardino announced his retirement to go into movies. Commissioner Chandler cancelled the trade. Berardino then unretired.)

Date	Traded To		Traded With	Traded By		In Exchange For
Dec 8, 1947	STL	A	——	WAS	A	$25,000.
Dec 14, 1949	DET	A	——	STL	A	Lou Kretlow and $100,000.

Mike Proly

Date	Traded To		Traded With	Traded By		In Exchange For
April 1, 1981	PHI	N	——	CHI	A	Jay Loviglio

Doc Prothro

Date	Traded To		Traded With	Traded By		In Exchange For
Dec 11, 1924	BOS	A	——	WAS	A	Mike McNally

Ron Pruitt

Date	Traded To		Traded With	Traded By		In Exchange For
Dec 9, 1975	CLE	A	Stan Thomas	TEX	A	John Ellis
June 13, 1980	CHI	A	——	CLE	A	Alan Bannister

Greg Pryor

Date	Traded To		Traded With	Traded By		In Exchange For
Feb 17, 1977	NY	A	Brian Doyle and cash	TEX	A	Sandy Alomar
Nov 28, 1977	CHI	A	——	NY	A	No compensation (free agent signing)
March 24, 1982	KC	A	——	CHI	A	Jeff Schattinger

Charlie Puleo

Date	Traded To		Traded With	Traded By		In Exchange For
April 6, 1981	NY	N	Cash	TOR	A	Mark Bomback
Dec 16, 1982	CIN	N	Lloyd McClendon Minor league OF Jason Felice	NY	N	Tom Seaver
June 5, 1985	ATL	N	——	CIN	N	Cash

Alfonso Pulido

Date	Traded To		Traded With	Traded By		In Exchange For
Dec 20, 1984	NY	A	——	PIT	N	$400,000.

Bob Purkey

Date	Traded To		Traded With	Traded By		In Exchange For
Dec 9, 1957	CIN	N	——	PIT	N	Don Gross
Dec 14, 1964	STL	N	——	CIN	N	Charlie James Roger Craig
April 7, 1966	PIT	N	——	STL	N	Cash

Billy Purtell

Date	Traded To		Traded With	Traded By		In Exchange For
Aug 9, 1910	BOS	A	Frank Smith	CHI	A	Harry Lord Amby McConnell

Ed Putman

Date	Traded To		Traded With	Traded By		In Exchange For
March 20, 1979	DET	A	——	CHI	N	Steve Dillard

Pat Putnam

Date	Traded To		Traded With	Traded By		In Exchange For
Dec 21, 1982	SEA	A	——	TEX	A	Ron Musselman
Aug 29, 1984	MIN	A	——	SEA	A	Cash
Feb 7, 1985	KC	A	——	MIN	A	No compensation (free agent signing)

Ewald Pyle

Date	Traded To		Traded With	Traded By		In Exchange For
June 16, 1945	BOS	N	Joe Medwick	NY	N	Clyde Kluttz

Frankie Pytlak

Date	Traded To		Traded With	Traded By		In Exchange For
Dec 12, 1940	BOS	A	Odell Hale Joe Dobson	CLE	A	Gene Desautels Jim Bagby Gee Walker

Tim Pyznarski

Date	Traded To		Traded With	Traded By		In Exchange For
June 12, 1986	MIL	A	——	SD	N	Randy Ready

(Milwaukee received Pyznarski on Oct. 29, 1986.)

Jimmy Qualls

Date	Traded To		Traded With	Traded By		In Exchange For
April 22, 1970	MON	N	——	CHI	N	Cash

Tom Qualters

Date	Traded To		Traded With	Traded By		In Exchange For
April 30, 1958	CHI	A	——	PHI	N	Cash

Mel Queen

Date	Traded To		Traded With	Traded By		In Exchange For
Oct 24, 1969	CAL	A	——	CIN	N	Cash

Mel Queen

Date	Traded To		Traded With	Traded By		In Exchange For
July 11, 1947	PIT	N	——	NY	A	Cash

Jack Quinn

Date	Traded To		Traded With	Traded By		In Exchange For
Dec 20, 1921	BOS	A	Roger Peckinpaugh Rip Collins Bill Piercy	NY	A	Everett Scott Joe Bush Sad Sam Jones
July 10, 1925	PHI	A	——	BOS	A	Waiver price

Joe Quinn

Date	Traded To		Traded With	Traded By		In Exchange For
Jan 1900	STL	N	Jack Harper Otto Krueger Jim Hughey	CLE	N	Cash
May 1900	CIN	N	——	STL	N	Cash

Luis Quinones

Date	Traded To		Traded With	Traded By		In Exchange For
Dec 6, 1983	CLE	A	——	OAK	A	Jim Essian
May 7, 1985	SF	N	Mike Jeffcoat	CLE	A	Johnnie LeMaster
Jan 30, 1987	CHI	N	——	OAK	A	Ron Cey

Rey Quinones

Date	Traded To		Traded With	Traded By		In Exchange For
Aug 19, 1986	SEA	A	Mike Trujillo John Christensen Mike Brown	BOS	A	Dave Henderson Spike Owen
April 21, 1989	PIT	N	Bill Wilkinson	SEA	A	Mike Dunne Minor league OF Mark Merchant Minor league P Mike Walker

Luis Quintana

Date	Traded To		Traded With	Traded By		In Exchange For
April 1, 1988	CHI	N	——	CIN	N	Bill Landrum

Jamie Quirk

Date	Traded To		Traded With	Traded By		In Exchange For
Dec 6, 1976	MIL	A	Jim Wohlford Bob McClure	KC	A	Jim Colborn Darrell Porter
Aug 3, 1978	KC	A	——	MIL	A	Minor league P Gerry Ako and cash
Feb 16, 1983	STL	N	——	KC	A	No compensation (free agent signing)
Sept 23, 1984	CLE	A	——	CHI	A	Cash
Dec 19, 1988	NY	A	——	KC	A	No compensation (free agent signing)
Dec 13, 1989	OAK	A	——	BAL	A	No compensation (free agent signing)

Johnny Rabb

Date	Traded To		Traded With	Traded By		In Exchange For
April 17, 1985	ATL	N	——	SF	N	Alex Trevino

Marv Rackley

Date	Traded To		Traded With	Traded By		In Exchange For
May 18, 1949	PIT	N	——	BKN	N	Johnny Hopp and $25,000.

(Trade was cancelled on June 7, 1949.)

Date	Traded To		Traded With	Traded By		In Exchange For
Oct 14, 1949	CIN	N	——	BKN	N	$60,000.

Dick Radatz

Date	Traded To		Traded With	Traded By		In Exchange For
June 2, 1966	CLE	A	——	BOS	A	Don McMahon Lee Stange
April 25, 1967	CHI	N	——	CLE	A	Bob Raudman and cash
June 15, 1969	MON	N	——	DET	A	Cash

Rip Radcliff

Date	Traded To		Traded With	Traded By		In Exchange For
Dec 8, 1939	STL	A	——	CHI	A	Moose Solters
May 5, 1941	DET	A	——	STL	A	$25,000.
Oct 11, 1943	PHI	A	——	DET	A	Don Heffner Bob Swift

Dave Rader

Date	Traded To		Traded With	Traded By		In Exchange For
Oct 20, 1976	STL	N	*See Mike Caldwell*	SF	N	——
Dec 8, 1977	CHI	N	Hector Cruz	STL	N	Jerry Morales Steve Swisher and cash
Feb 23, 1979	PHI	N	*See Manny Trillo*	CHI	N	——
March 30, 1980	BOS	A	——	PHI	N	Stan Papi and cash
Feb 2, 1981	CAL	A	——	BOS	A	No compensation (free agent signing)

Doug Rader

Date	Traded To		Traded With	Traded By		In Exchange For
Dec 11, 1975	SD	N	——	HOU	N	Joe McIntosh Larry Hardy
June 8, 1977	TOR	A	——	SD	N	Cash

Ken Raffensberger

Date	Traded To		Traded With	Traded By		In Exchange For
Dec 27, 1939	CHI	N	——	STL	N	Steve Mesner Gene Lillard and cash
June 14, 1947	CIN	N	Hugh Poland	PHI	N	Al Lakeman

Pat Ragan

Date	Traded To		Traded With	Traded By		In Exchange For
May 20, 1909	CHI	N	——	CIN	N	Cash
April 28, 1915	BOS	N	——	BKN	N	Cash
May 21, 1919	NY	N	——	BOS	N	Jim Thorpe
Sept 1919	CHI	A	——	NY	N	Waiver price

Tom Ragland

Date	Traded To		Traded With	Traded By		In Exchange For
Nov 30, 1972	CLE	A	——	TEX	A	Vince Colbert

Date	Traded To		Traded With	Traded By		In Exchange For

Chuck Rainey

Date	Traded To		Traded With	Traded By		In Exchange For
Dec 10, 1982	CHI	N	———	BOS	A	Doug Bird
July 15, 1984	OAK	A	———	CHI	N	Davey Lopes

(The Cubs received Lopes on August 31.)

Dave Rajsich

Date	Traded To		Traded With	Traded By		In Exchange For
Nov 10, 1978	TEX	A	———	NY	A	*See Dave Righetti*
Oct 20, 1981	PHI	N	———	TEX	A	Ramon Aviles

Gary Rajsich

Date	Traded To		Traded With	Traded By		In Exchange For
April 3, 1981	NY	N	———	HOU	N	Minor league OF John Csefalvay
April 4, 1984	STL	N	———	NY	N	Cash
Feb 1, 1985	SF	N	David Green Jose Uribe Dave LaPoint	STL	N	Jack Clark

Ed Rakow

Date	Traded To		Traded With	Traded By		In Exchange For
March 30, 1961	KC	A	———	LA	N	Howie Reed and cash
Nov 18, 1963	DET	A	———	KC	A	*See Rocky Colavito*

Bob Ramazzotti

Date	Traded To		Traded With	Traded By		In Exchange For
May 16, 1949	CHI	N	———	BKN	N	Hank Schenz

Milt Ramirez

Date	Traded To		Traded With	Traded By		In Exchange For
Nov 28, 1972	HOU	N	Skip Jutze	STL	N	Ray Busse Bobby Fenwick

Rafael Ramirez

Date	Traded To		Traded With	Traded By		In Exchange For
Dec 8, 1987	HOU	N	———	ATL	N	Ed Whited Minor league P Mike Stoker

Bobby Ramos

Date	Traded To		Traded With	Traded By		In Exchange For
April 5, 1982	NY	A	———	MON	N	Brad Gulden
Nov 3, 1982	MON	N	———	NY	A	Cash

Domingo Ramos

Date	Traded To		Traded With	Traded By		In Exchange For
Nov 10, 1978	TEX	A	———	NY	A	*See Dave Righetti*
Nov 5, 1979	TOR	A	———	TEX	A	Cash

Pedro Ramos

Date	Traded To		Traded With	Traded By		In Exchange For
April 2, 1962	CLE	A	———	MIN	A	Dick Stigman Vic Power
Sept 5, 1964	NY	A	———	CLE	A	Ralph Terry Bud Daley and $75,000.
Dec 14, 1966	PHI	N	———	NY	A	Joe Verbanic and cash

Willie Ramsdell

Date	Traded To		Traded With	Traded By		In Exchange For
May 10, 1950	CIN	N	———	BKN	N	Cash
Jan 3, 1952	CHI	N	———	CIN	N	Frank Hiller

Mike Ramsey

Date	Traded To		Traded With	Traded By		In Exchange For
July 1, 1984	MON	N	———	STL	N	Chris Speier

Newt Randall

Date	Traded To		Traded With	Traded By		In Exchange For
June 24, 1907	BOS	N	Bill Sweeney	CHI	N	Del Howard

Lenny Randle

Date	Traded To		Traded With	Traded By		In Exchange For
April 26, 1977	NY	N	———	TEX	A	Rick Auerbach and cash
June 28, 1979	PIT	N	*See Bill Madlock*	SF	N	
Aug 2, 1979	NY	N	———	PIT	N	Cash
March 8, 1980	SEA	A	———	NY	N	No compensation (free agent signing)
April 2, 1980	CHI	N	———	SEA	A	Cash
April 6, 1981	SEA	A	———	CHI	N	No compensation (free agent signing)

Willie Randolph

Date	Traded To		Traded With	Traded By		In Exchange For
Dec 11, 1975	NY	A	Ken Brett Dock Ellis	PIT	N	Doc Medich
Dec 10, 1988	LA	N	———	NY	A	No compensation (free agent signing)

Merritt Ranew

Date	Traded To		Traded With	Traded By		In Exchange For
March 28, 1963	CHI	N	Hal Haydel Dick LeMay	HOU	N	Dave Gerard Danny Murphy
June 3, 1964	MIL	N	$40,000.	CHI	N	Len Gabrielson

Earl Rapp

Date	Traded To		Traded With	Traded By		In Exchange For
Sept 1, 1951	STL	A	———	NY	N	Waiver price
June 10, 1952	WAS	A	———	STL	A	Freddie Marsh

Goldie Rapp

Date	Traded To		Traded With	Traded By		In Exchange For
July 1, 1921	PHI	N	Lee King Lance Richbourg	NY	N	Casey Stengel Johnny Rawlings Red Causey

Vern Rapp

Date	Traded To		Traded With	Traded By		In Exchange For
May 7, 1949	CHI	A	———	DET	A	Don Kolloway

Bill Rariden

Date	Traded To		Traded With	Traded By		In Exchange For
Dec 23, 1915	NY	N	Bill McKechnie	NWK	F	Cash
Feb 2, 1919	CIN	N	———	NY	N	Hal Chase

Vic Raschi

Date	Traded To		Traded With	Traded By		In Exchange For
Feb 23, 1954	STL	N	———	NY	A	$85,000.

Dennis Rasmussen

Date	Traded To		Traded With	Traded By		In Exchange For
Aug 31, 1982	NY	A	———	CAL	A	Tommy John
Aug 26, 1983	SD	N	Edwin Rodriguez and $200,000.	NY	A	John Montefusco
March 30, 1984	NY	A	minor league P Darin Cloninger	SD	N	Graig Nettles
Aug 26, 1987	CIN	N	———	NY	A	Bill Gullickson
June 8, 1988	SD	N	———	CIN	N	Candy Sierra

Eric Rasmussen

Date	Traded To		Traded With	Traded By		In Exchange For
May 26, 1978	SD	N	———	STL	N	George Hendrick
Aug 2, 1983	KC	A	———	STL	N	Cash

Morrie Rath

Date	Traded To		Traded With	Traded By		In Exchange For
May 1910	CLE	A	———	PHI	A	Cash

Gene Ratliff

Date	Traded To		Traded With	Traded By		In Exchange For
Oct 13, 1966	ATL	N	———	HOU	N	*See Tom Dukes*

Paul Ratliff

Date	Traded To		Traded With	Traded By		In Exchange For
July 8, 1971	MIL	A	———	MIN	A	Phil Roof
July 28, 1972	CAL	A	Ron Clark	MIL	A	Syd O'Brien Joe Azcue

Date	Traded To		Traded With	Traded By		In Exchange For

Steve Ratzer
Date	Traded To		Traded With	Traded By		In Exchange For
Dec 11, 1981	NY	N	Cash	MON	N	Frank Taveras

Bob Rauch
Nov 27, 1972	CLE	A	Brent Strom	NY	N	Phil Hennigan

Bob Raudman
April 25, 1967	CLE	A	Cash	CHI	N	Dick Radatz
Nov 21, 1967	CIN	N	George Culver Fred Whitfield	CLE	A	Tommy Harper

Lance Rautzhan
May 11, 1979	MIL	A	——	LA	N	Cash
Oct 24, 1979	KC	A	——	MIL	A	Minor league OF Kevin Gillen

Shane Rawley
May 21, 1977	CIN	N	Angel Torres	MON	N	Santo Alcala
Dec 9, 1977	SEA	A	——	CIN	N	Dave Collins
April 1, 1982	NY	A	——	SEA	A	Bill Caudill Gene Nelson Bobby Brown
June 30, 1984	PHI	N	——	NY	A	Marty Bystrom Keith Hughes
Oct 24, 1988	MIN	A	Cash	PHI	N	Tommy Herr Tom Nieto Eric Bullock

Johnny Rawlings
June 1920	PHI	N	——	BOS	N	Cash
July 1, 1921	NY	N	Casey Stengel Red Causey	PHI	N	Goldie Rapp Lee King Lance Richbourg
May 11, 1923	PHI	N	——	NY	N	Waiver price
May 22, 1923	PIT	N	Lee Meadows	PHI	N	Whitey Glazner Cotton Tierney and $50,000.

Jim Ray
Feb 24, 1967	NY	N	——	HOU	N	Cash

(Ray was returned to Houston on March 24.)

Dec 3, 1973	DET	A	Gary Sutherland	HOU	N	Fred Scherman and cash
Dec 6, 1974	PIT	N	——	DET	A	Cash

Johnny Ray
Aug 31, 1981	PIT	N	minor league OF Kevin Houston Randy Niemann	HOU	N	Phil Garner
Aug 29, 1987	CAL	A	——	PIT	N	Miguel Garcia Minor league IF Bill Merrifield

Curt Raydon
Dec 26, 1953	PIT	N	——	MIL	N	*See Danny O'Connell*

Floyd Rayford
June 5, 1979	BAL	A	Cash	CAL	A	Larry Harlow
June 15, 1983	STL	N	——	BAL	A	Tito Landrum
March 30, 1984	BAL	A	——	STL	N	Cash

Bugs Raymond
Dec 12, 1908	NY	N	Admiral Schlei Red Murray	STL	N	Roger Bresnahan

Claude Raymond
Oct 10, 1963	HOU	N	——	MIL	N	$30,000.
June 15, 1967	ATL	N	——	HOU	N	Wade Blasingame
Aug 19, 1969	MON	N	——	ATL	N	Cash

Barry Raziano
Feb 23, 1974	CAL	A	Cash	KC	A	Vada Pinson

Randy Ready
June 12, 1986	SD	N	——	MIL	A	Tim Pyznarski

(Milwaukee received Pyznarski on Oct. 29, 1986.)

June 2, 1989	PHI	N	John Kruk	SD	N	Chris James

Jeff Reardon
May 29, 1981	MON	N	Dan Norman	NY	N	Ellis Valentine
Feb 3, 1987	MIN	A	Tom Nieto	MON	N	Neal Heaton Jeff Reed Minor league P Yorkis Perez Minor league P Al Cardwood
Dec 6, 1989	BOS	A	——	MIN	A	No compensation (free agent sighning)

Frank Reberger
Dec 5, 1969	SF	N	——	SD	N	Bob Barton Ron Herbel Bobby Etheridge

Gary Redus
Dec 11, 1985	PHI	N	Tom Hume	CIN	N	John Denny Jeff Gray
March 27, 1987	CHI	A	——	PHI	N	Joe Cowley
Aug 19, 1988	PIT	N	——	CHI	A	Barry Jones

Howie Reed
March 30, 1961	LA	N	Cash	KC	A	Ed Rakow
May 27, 1966	CAL	A	——	LA	N	Dick Egan and minor league IF John Butler
April 3, 1969	MON	N	Leo Marentette	HOU	N	Cash

Jeff Reed
Feb 3, 1987	MON	N	——	MIN	A	*See Jeff Reardon*
July 13, 1988	CIN	N	Herm Winningham Randy St. Claire	MON	N	Tracy Jones Pat Pacillo

Jerry Reed
Sept 12, 1982	CLE	A	Wil Culmer Roy Smith	PHI	N	John Denny

Ron Reed
May 28, 1975	STL	N	Wayne Nordhagen	ATL	N	Elias Sosa Ray Sadecki
Dec 9, 1975	PHI	N	——	STL	N	Mike Anderson
Dec 5, 1983	CHI	A	——	PHI	N	Jerry Koosman

Jimmy Reese
Jan 1932	STL	N	——	NY	A	Waiver price

Rich Reese
Nov 30, 1972	DET	A	——	MIN	A	Cash

Date	Traded To	Traded With	Traded By	In Exchange For

Bobby Reeves

Date	Traded To	Traded With	Traded By	In Exchange For
Dec 15, 1928	BOS A	Milt Gaston Hod Lisenbee Grant Gillis Elliott Bigelow	WAS A	Buddy Myer

Bill Regan

Date	Traded To	Traded With	Traded By	In Exchange For
Jan 1931	PIT N	——	BOS A	Waiver price

Phil Regan

Date	Traded To	Traded With	Traded By	In Exchange For
Dec 15, 1965	LA N	——	DET A	Dick Tracewski
April 23, 1968	CHI N	Jim Hickman	LA N	Ted Savage Jim Ellis
June 2, 1972	CHI A		CHI N	Cash

Wally Rehg

Date	Traded To	Traded With	Traded By	In Exchange For
Jan 1913	BOS A	——	PIT N	Waiver price
Feb 1919	CIN N	——	BOS N	Lena Blackburne

Herm Reich

Date	Traded To	Traded With	Traded By	In Exchange For
April 30, 1949	WAS A	——	CLE A	Waiver price
(Reich was returned to Cleveland on May 10.)				
May 18, 1949	CHI N	——	CLE A	Waiver price
Feb 2, 1950	CHI A	——	CHI N	Cash

Rick Reichardt

Date	Traded To	Traded With	Traded By	In Exchange For
April 27, 1970	WAS A	Aurelio Rodriguez	CAL A	Ken McMullen
Feb 9, 1971	CHI A	——	WAS A	Gerry Janeski

Bill Reidy

Date	Traded To	Traded With	Traded By	In Exchange For
July 1903	BKN N	——	STL A	Clarence Wright

Bobby Reis

Date	Traded To	Traded With	Traded By	In Exchange For
Dec 12, 1935	BOS N	Tony Cuccinello Al Lopez Ray Benge	BKN N	Ed Brandt Randy Moore

Tommy Reis

Date	Traded To	Traded With	Traded By	In Exchange For
May 23, 1938	BOS N	——	PHI N	Cash
Aug 10, 1938	CIN N	Johnny Babich Gil English Johnny Riddle Vince DiMaggio and Cash	BOS N	Eddie Miller

Pete Reiser

Date	Traded To	Traded With	Traded By	In Exchange For
Dec 15, 1948	BOS N	——	BKN N	Mike McCormick

Heinie Reitz

Date	Traded To	Traded With	Traded By	In Exchange For
Feb 1900	PHI N	Tully Sparks	PIT N	Duff Cooley

Ken Reitz

Date	Traded To	Traded With	Traded By	In Exchange For
Dec 8, 1975	SF N	——	STL N	Pete Falcone
Dec 10, 1976	STL N	——	SF N	Lynn McGlothen
Dec 9, 1980	CHI N	Leon Durham Tye Waller	STL N	Bruce Sutter

Jerry Remy

Date	Traded To	Traded With	Traded By	In Exchange For
Dec 8, 1977	BOS A	——	CAL A	Don Aase and cash

Hal Reniff

Date	Traded To	Traded With	Traded By	In Exchange For
June 29, 1967	NY N		NY A	Cash

Steve Renko

Date	Traded To	Traded With	Traded By	In Exchange For
June 15, 1969	MON N	Kevin Collins minor league Ps Bill Carden and Dave Colon	NY N	Donn Clendenon
May 17, 1976	CHI N	Larry Biittner	MON N	Andre Thornton
Aug 18, 1977	CHI A	——	CHI N	Larry Anderson and cash
March 30, 1978	OAK A	Jim Essian	CHI A	Pablo Torrealba
Jan 20, 1979	BOS A	——	OAK A	No compensation (free agent signing)
Jan 23, 1981	CAL A	Fred Lynn	BOS A	Frank Tanana Jim Dorsey Joe Rudi
Feb 9, 1983	KC A	——	CAL A	No compensation (free agent signing)

Bill Renna

Date	Traded To	Traded With	Traded By	In Exchange For
Dec 16, 1953	PHI A	——	NY A	*See Harry Byrd*
June 14, 1956	NY A	Moe Burtschy and cash	KC A	Lou Skizas Eddie Robinson

Tony Rensa

Date	Traded To	Traded With	Traded By	In Exchange For
June 1930	PHI N	——	DET A	Waiver price

Rich Renteria

Date	Traded To	Traded With	Traded By	In Exchange For
Dec 5, 1986	SEA A	——	PIT N	player to be named
(Pittsburgh received P Bob Siegel on Dec. 10, 1986.)				

Andy Replogle

Date	Traded To	Traded With	Traded By	In Exchange For
April 4, 1978	MIL A	——	BAL A	Cash

Roger Repoz

Date	Traded To	Traded With	Traded By	In Exchange For
June 10, 1966	KC A	Gil Blanco Bill Stafford	NY A	Fred Talbot Billy Bryan
June 15, 1967	CAL A	——	KC A	Jack Sanford Jackie Warner
June 10, 1972	BAL A	——	CAL A	Jerry DaVanon

Rip Repulski

Date	Traded To	Traded With	Traded By	In Exchange For
Nov 19, 1956	PHI N	Bobby Morgan	STL N	Del Ennis
Dec 23, 1958	LA N	Jim Golden Gene Snyder	PHI N	Sparky Anderson
May 6, 1960	BOS A	——	LA N	Nels Chittum

Dino Restelli

Date	Traded To	Traded With	Traded By	In Exchange For
Sept 19, 1951	WAS A	——	PIT N	Waiver price
Dec 17, 1951	CLE A	——	WAS A	Cash

Merv Rettenmund

Date	Traded To	Traded With	Traded By	In Exchange For
Dec 4, 1973	CIN N	Junior Kennedy and minor league C Bill Wood	BAL A	Ross Grimsley and minor league C Wally Williams
April 5, 1976	SD N	——	CIN N	Rudi Meoli and cash

Ken Retzer

Date	Traded To	Traded With	Traded By	In Exchange For
Oct 15, 1964	MIN A	——	WAS A	Joe McCabe
Jan 4, 1967	CLE A	Lee Maye	HOU N	Jim Landis Jim Weaver Doc Edwards

Date	Traded To		Traded With	Traded By		In Exchange For

Ed Reulbach

Date	Traded To		Traded With	Traded By		In Exchange For
July 1913	BKN	N	———	CHI	N	Eddie Stack and cash
April 12, 1916	BOS	N	———	PIT	N	Cash

Paul Reuschel

Date	Traded To		Traded With	Traded By		In Exchange For
June 26, 1978	CLE	A	———	CHI	N	Denny DeBarr

Rick Reuschel

Date	Traded To		Traded With	Traded By		In Exchange For
June 12, 1981	NY	A	———	CHI	N	Doug Bird Mike Griffin and $400,000.
Feb 28, 1985	PIT	N	———	CHI	N	No compensation (free agent signing)
Aug 12, 1987	SF	N	———	PIT	N	Jeff Robinson Scott Medvin

Jerry Reuss

Date	Traded To		Traded With	Traded By		In Exchange For
April 15, 1972	HOU	N	———	STL	N	Scipio Spinks Lance Clemons
Oct 31, 1973	PIT	N	———	HOU	N	Milt May
April 7, 1979	LA	N	———	PIT	N	Rick Rhoden
July 31, 1989	MIL	A	———	CHI	A	Minor league P Brian Drahman

Dave Revering

Date	Traded To		Traded With	Traded By		In Exchange For
Feb 25, 1978	OAK	A	Cash	CIN	N	Doug Bair
May 20, 1981	NY	A	Mike Patterson minor league P Chuck Dougherty	OAK	A	Jim Spencer Tom Underwood
May 5, 1982	TOR	A	minor league 3B Jeff Reynolds	NY	A	John Mayberry
Aug 6, 1982	SEA	A	———	TOR	A	No compensation (free agent signing)

Gilberto Reyes

Date	Traded To		Traded With	Traded By		In Exchange For
March 27, 1989	MON	N	———	LA	N	Jeff Fischer

Allie Reynolds

Date	Traded To		Traded With	Traded By		In Exchange For
Oct 19, 1946	NY	A	———	CLE	A	Joe Gordon Eddie Bockman

Archie Reynolds

Date	Traded To		Traded With	Traded By		In Exchange For
July 9, 1970	CAL	A	———	CHI	N	Juan Pizarro

Bob Reynolds

Date	Traded To		Traded With	Traded By		In Exchange For
June 15, 1971	STL	N	———	MON	N	Mike Torrez
July 29, 1971	MIL	A	Jose Cardenal Dick Schofield	STL	N	Ted Kubiak minor league P Charlie Loseth
Dec 9, 1971	BAL	A	Cash	MIL	A	Curt Motton
May 29, 1975	DET	A	———	BAL	A	Fred Holdsworth
Aug 26, 1975	CLE	A	———	DET	A	Cash

Carl Reynolds

Date	Traded To		Traded With	Traded By		In Exchange For
Dec 4, 1931	WAS	A	John Kerr	CHI	A	Jackie Hayes Bump Hadley Sad Sam Jones
Dec 14, 1932	STL	A	Sammy West Lloyd Brown and $20,000.	WAS	A	Goose Goslin Fred Schulte Lefty Stewart
Dec 14, 1933	BOS	A	———	STL	A	Ivy Andrews Smead Jolley and cash
Dec 17, 1935	WAS	A	Roy Johnson	BOS	A	Heinie Manush

Craig Reynolds

Date	Traded To		Traded With	Traded By		In Exchange For
Dec 7, 1976	SEA	A	Jimmy Sexton	PIT	N	Grant Jackson
Dec 8, 1978	HOU	N	———	SEA	A	Floyd Bannister

Ken Reynolds

Date	Traded To		Traded With	Traded By		In Exchange For
Nov 30, 1972	MIN	A	Ken Sanders Joe Lis	PHI	N	Cesar Tovar
March 27, 1973	MIL	A	———	MIN	A	Mike Ferraro
April 8, 1976	SD	N	minor leaguer Bob Stewart	STL	N	Danny Frisella
March 21, 1977	TOR	A	———	SD	N	Cash

R. J. Reynolds

Date	Traded To		Traded With	Traded By		In Exchange For
Aug 31, 1985	PIT	N	Sid Bream Cecil Espy	LA	N	Bill Madlock

(Pittsburgh received Reynolds on Sept. 3 and Bream and Espy on September 9, 1985.)

Ronn Reynolds

Date	Traded To		Traded With	Traded By		In Exchange For
Jan 16, 1986	PHI	N	Jeff Bittiger	NY	N	Minor league P Rodger Cole Minor league 1B Ronnie Gideon
April 2, 1987	HOU	N	———	PHI	N	Jeff Calhoun

Tommie Reynolds

Date	Traded To		Traded With	Traded By		In Exchange For
May 16, 1970	CAL	A	———	OAK	A	Cash
Jan 26, 1972	MIL	A	———	CAL	A	Andy Kosco

Bobby Rhawn

Date	Traded To		Traded With	Traded By		In Exchange For
June 6, 1949	PIT	N	Ray Poat	NY	N	Kirby Higbe

Flint Rhem

Date	Traded To		Traded With	Traded By		In Exchange For
May 30, 1932	PHI	N	Eddie Delker	STL	N	Cash
Feb 11, 1934	STL	N	———	PHI	N	Cash
June 23, 1934	BOS	N	———	STL	N	Cash

Bob Rhoads

Date	Traded To		Traded With	Traded By		In Exchange For
April 1903	STL	N	———	CHI	N	Bob Wicker

Rick Rhoden

Date	Traded To		Traded With	Traded By		In Exchange For
April 7, 1979	PIT	N	———	LA	N	Jerry Reuss
Nov 26, 1986	NY	A	Cecilio Guante Pat Clements	PIT	N	Doug Drabek Logan Easley Brian Fisher
Jan 10, 1989	HOU	N	———	NY	A	John Fishel Minor league P Mike Hook Minor league P Pedro DeLeon

Charlie Rhodes

Date	Traded To		Traded With	Traded By		In Exchange For
May 1908	STL	N	———	CIN	N	Waiver price

Gordon Rhodes

Date	Traded To		Traded With	Traded By		In Exchange For
May 1, 1932	BOS	A	———	NY	A	Wilcy Moore
Dec 10, 1935	PHI	A	minor league C George Savino and $150,000.	BOS	A	Jimmie Foxx Johnny Marcum

Hal Rhyne

Date	Traded To		Traded With	Traded By		In Exchange For
Dec 15, 1932	CHI	A	Ed Durham	BOS	A	Johnny Hodapp Greg Mulleavy Bob Fothergill Bob Seeds

Date	Traded To		Traded With	Traded By		In Exchange For

Dennis Ribant

Date	Traded To		Traded With	Traded By		In Exchange For
Aug 8, 1964	NY	N	Cash	MIL	N	Frank Lary
Dec 6, 1966	PIT	N	Gary Kolb	NY	N	Don Bosch
						Don Cardwell
Nov 28, 1967	DET	A	——	PIT	N	Dave Wickersham
July 21, 1968	CHI	A	——	DET	A	Don McMahon
Dec 15, 1968	KC	A	——	DET	A	Cash

Frank Riccelli

Date	Traded To		Traded With	Traded By		In Exchange For
Oct 25, 1977	STL	N	——	SF	N	Jim Dwyer
			(San Francisco received Dwyer on June 15, 1978.)			
June 8, 1978	HOU	N	——	STL	N	Bob Coluccio

Del Rice

Date	Traded To		Traded With	Traded By		In Exchange For
June 3, 1955	MIL	N	——	STL	N	Pete Whisenant

Hal Rice

Date	Traded To		Traded With	Traded By		In Exchange For
June 14, 1953	PIT	N	Cash	STL	N	Pete Castiglione
June 14, 1954	CHI	N	——	PIT	N	Luis Marquez

Harry Rice

Date	Traded To		Traded With	Traded By		In Exchange For
Dec 2, 1927	DET	A	Chick Galloway	STL	A	Heinie Manush
			Elam Vangilder			Lu Blue
May 30, 1930	NY	A	Ownie Carroll	DET	A	Waite Hoyt
			Yats Wuestling			Mark Koenig
Jan 13, 1931	WAS	A	——	NY	A	Waiver price

Lee Richard

Date	Traded To		Traded With	Traded By		In Exchange For
Dec 12, 1975	STL	N	——	CHI	A	Buddy Bradford
						Greg Terlecky

Gene Richards

Date	Traded To		Traded With	Traded By		In Exchange For
March 31, 1984	SF	N	——	SD	N	No compensation
						(free agent signing)

Paul Richards

Date	Traded To		Traded With	Traded By		In Exchange For
Dec 1932	NY	N	——	BKN	N	Waiver price
May 25, 1935	PHI	A	——	NY	N	Cash

Gordie Richardson

Date	Traded To		Traded With	Traded By		In Exchange For
Dec 7, 1964	NY	N	Johnny Lewis	STL	N	Tracy Stallard
						Elio Chacon

Mike Richardt

Date	Traded To		Traded With	Traded By		In Exchange For
May 25, 1984	HOU	N	——	TEX	A	Alan Bannister

Lance Richbourg

Date	Traded To		Traded With	Traded By		In Exchange For
July 1, 1921	PHI	N	Goldie Rapp	NY	N	Casey Stengel
			Lee King			Johnny Rawlings
						Red Causey
Dec 17, 1931	CHI	N	——	BOS	N	Waiver price
Nov 30, 1932	CIN	N	Bob Smith	CHI	N	Babe Herman
			Rollie Hemsley			
			Johnny Moore			

Pete Richert

Date	Traded To		Traded With	Traded By		In Exchange For
Dec 4, 1964	WAS	A	Frank Howard	LA	N	Claude Osteen
			Phil Ortega			John Kennedy
			Dick Nen			and $100,000.
			Ken McMullen			
May 29, 1967	BAL	A	——	WAS	A	Mike Epstein
						Frank Bertaina

Pete Richert *continued*

Date	Traded To		Traded With	Traded By		In Exchange For
Dec 2, 1971	LA	N	Frank Robinson	BAL	A	Doyle Alexander
						Bob O'Brien
						Sergio Robles
						Royle Stillman
Dec 5, 1973	STL	N	——	LA	N	Tommie Agee
June 21, 1974	PHI	N	——	STL	N	Cash

Lew Richie

Date	Traded To		Traded With	Traded By		In Exchange For
July 16, 1909	BOS	N	Buster Brown	PHI	N	Johnny Bates
			Dave Shean			Charlie Starr
April 1910	CHI	N	——	BOS	N	Doc Miller

Marv Rickert

Date	Traded To		Traded With	Traded By		In Exchange For
Oct 8, 1947	CIN	N	——	CHI	N	Cash
May 11, 1948	BOS	N	——	CIN	N	Danny Litwhiler
Dec 14, 1949	PIT	N	——	BOS	N	Cash
May 29, 1950	CHI	A	——	PIT	N	Cash

Dave Ricketts

Date	Traded To		Traded With	Traded By		In Exchange For
Oct 21, 1969	PIT	N	Dave Giusti	STL	N	Carl Taylor
						minor league
						OF Frank Vanzin

Branch Rickey

Date	Traded To		Traded With	Traded By		In Exchange For
Feb 1905	STL	A	——	CHI	A	Frank Roth
Dec 1906	NY	A	——	STL	A	Cash

Fred Rico

Date	Traded To		Traded With	Traded By		In Exchange For
June 13, 1970	STL	N	——	KC	A	Cookie Rojas
Sept 1, 1971	MIN	A	minor league	STL	N	Stan Williams
			P Dan Ford			

Harry Riconda

Date	Traded To		Traded With	Traded By		In Exchange For
Dec 11, 1928	PIT	N	Jesse Petty	BKN	N	Glenn Wright

Elmer Riddle

Date	Traded To		Traded With	Traded By		In Exchange For
Dec 10, 1947	PIT	N	——	CIN	N	Cash

Johnny Riddle

Date	Traded To		Traded With	Traded By		In Exchange For
Aug 10, 1938	CIN	N	Tommy Reis	BOS	N	Eddie Miller
			Johnny Babich			
			Gil English			
			Vince DiMaggio			
			and Cash			

Denny Riddleberger

Date	Traded To		Traded With	Traded By		In Exchange For
Aug 31, 1970	WAS	A	Cash	PIT	N	George Brunet
Dec 2, 1971	CLE	A	*See Del Unser*	TEX	A	——

Steve Ridzik

Date	Traded To		Traded With	Traded By		In Exchange For
April 30, 1955	CIN	N	——	PHI	N	*See Andy Seminick*
April 13, 1966	PHI	N	——	WAS	A	Cash

Joe Riggert

Date	Traded To		Traded With	Traded By		In Exchange For
June 1914	STL	N	——	BKN	N	Casey Hageman

Lew Riggs

Date	Traded To		Traded With	Traded By		In Exchange For
Nov 3, 1934	CIN	N	——	STL	N	$30,000.
Dec 9, 1940	BKN	N	——	CIN	N	Pep Young

Date	Traded To	Traded With	Traded By	In Exchange For

Dave Righetti

Date	Traded To	Traded With	Traded By	In Exchange For
Nov 10, 1978	NY A	Juan Beniquez Mike Griffin Paul Mirabella minor league P Greg Jemison	TEX A	Domingo Ramos Mike Heath Sparky Lyle Larry McCall Dave Rajsich and cash

Topper Rigney

Date	Traded To	Traded With	Traded By	In Exchange For
April 7, 1926	BOS A	——	DET A	Cash
May 2, 1927	WAS A	——	BOS A	Buddy Myer

Jose Rijo

Date	Traded To	Traded With	Traded By	In Exchange For
Dec 8, 1984	OAK A	Jay Howell Stan Javier Tim Birtsas Eric Plunk	NY A	Rickey Henderson Bert Bradley and cash
Dec 8, 1987	CIN N	Tim Birtsas	OAK A	Dave Parker

Ernest Riles

Date	Traded To	Traded With	Traded By	In Exchange For
June 8, 1988	SF N	——	MIL A	Jeffrey Leonard

George Riley

Date	Traded To	Traded With	Traded By	In Exchange For
Aug 20, 1984	SF N	Kelly Downs	PHI N	Al Oliver Renie Martin
Oct 24, 1985	MON N	——	SF N	See Bill Laskey

Jimmy Ring

Date	Traded To	Traded With	Traded By	In Exchange For
Feb 22, 1921	PHI N	Greasy Neale	CIN N	Eppa Rixey
Dec 30, 1925	NY N	——	PHI N	Jack Bentley Wayland Dean
Dec 20, 1926	STL N	Frankie Frisch	NY N	Rogers Hornsby
Dec 13, 1927	PHI N	Johnny Schulte	STL N	Johnny Mokan Jimmy Cooney Bubber Jonnard

Juan Rios

Date	Traded To	Traded With	Traded By	In Exchange For
March 25, 1969	KC A	——	MON N	Cash
Sept 15, 1970	MIL A	——	KC A	Cash

Allen Ripley

Date	Traded To	Traded With	Traded By	In Exchange For
April 6, 1980	SF N	——	BOS A	Cash
Dec 7, 1981	CHI N	——	SF N	Doug Capilla

Jimmy Ripple

Date	Traded To	Traded With	Traded By	In Exchange For
Aug 23, 1939	BKN N	——	NY N	Ray Hayworth
Aug 23, 1940	CIN N	——	BKN N	Waiver price

Claude Ritchey

Date	Traded To	Traded With	Traded By	In Exchange For
Jan 1900	PIT N	See Honus Wagner	LOU N	——
Dec 1906	BOS N	Ginger Beaumont Patsy Flaherty	PIT N	Ed Abbaticchio

Jay Ritchie

Date	Traded To	Traded With	Traded By	In Exchange For
Dec 15, 1965	MIL N	Lee Thomas Arnie Earley	BOS A	Bob Sadowski Dan Osinski
Oct 10, 1967	CIN N	Jim Beauchamp Mack Jones	ATL N	Deron Johnson

Jim Rittwage

Date	Traded To	Traded With	Traded By	In Exchange For
Dec 1, 1965	CLE A	Jim Landis	KC A	Phil Roof Joe Rudi
Dec 2, 1965	SF N	——	CHI N	See Randy Hundley

German Rivera

Date	Traded To	Traded With	Traded By	In Exchange For
July 10, 1985	HOU N	——	LA N	See Enos Cabell

Jim Rivera

Date	Traded To	Traded With	Traded By	In Exchange For
Nov 27, 1951	STL A	Joe DeMaestri Dick Littlefield Gus Niarhos Gordon Goldsberry	CHI A	Al Widmar Sherm Lollar Tom Upton
July 28, 1952	CHI A	Darrell Johnson	STL A	J. W. Porter Ray Coleman

Luis Rivera

Date	Traded To	Traded With	Traded By	In Exchange For
Dec 8, 1988	BOS A	——	MON N	See Spike Owen

Mickey Rivers

Date	Traded To	Traded With	Traded By	In Exchange For
Dec 11, 1975	NY A	Ed Figueroa	CAL A	Bobby Bonds
Aug 1, 1979	TEX A	minor league Ps Bob Polinsky Neil Mersch and Mark Softy	NY A	Oscar Gamble Ray Fontenot Gene Nelson minor league 3B Amos Lewis

Eppa Rixey

Date	Traded To	Traded With	Traded By	In Exchange For
Feb 22, 1921	CIN N	——	PHI N	Jimmy Ring Greasy Neale

Johnny Rizzo

Date	Traded To	Traded With	Traded By	In Exchange For
Oct 1937	PIT N	——	STL N	Tom Padden minor leaguer Bernie Cobb
May 8, 1940	CIN N	——	PIT N	Vince DiMaggio
June 15, 1940	PHI N	——	CIN N	Morrie Arnovich
Dec 10, 1941	BKN N	——	PHI N	Cash

Mel Roach

Date	Traded To	Traded With	Traded By	In Exchange For
May 9, 1961	CHI N	——	MIL N	Frank Thomas
March 20, 1962	PHI N	——	CLE A	Ken Lehman Tony Curry

Roxy Roach

Date	Traded To	Traded With	Traded By	In Exchange For
Dec 1911	WAS A	John Knight	NY A	Gabby Street Jack Lelivelt

Mike Roarke

Date	Traded To	Traded With	Traded By	In Exchange For
Oct 15, 1959	DET A	Don Kaiser Casey Wise	MIL N	Charlie Lau Don Lee

Bert Roberge

Date	Traded To	Traded With	Traded By	In Exchange For
Dec 7, 1984	MON N	Vance Law	CHI A	Bob James Bryan Little

Curt Roberts

Date	Traded To	Traded With	Traded By	In Exchange For
Feb 19, 1957	NY A	——	KC A	See Billy Hunter

Dale Roberts

Date	Traded To	Traded With	Traded By	In Exchange For
Dec 7, 1967	ATL N	Bob Tillman	NY A	Bobby Cox

Dave Roberts

Date	Traded To	Traded With	Traded By	In Exchange For
Dec 3, 1971	HOU N	——	SD N	Derrel Thomas Bill Greif Mark Schaeffer

Dave Roberts *continued*

Date	Traded To		Traded With	Traded By		In Exchange For
Dec 6, 1975	DET	A	Milt May Jim Crawford	HOU	N	Leon Roberts Terry Humphrey Gene Pentz Mark Lemongello
July 30, 1977	CHI	N	——	DET	A	Cash
June 28, 1979	PIT	N	*See Bill Madlock*	SF	N	
April 24, 1980	SEA	N	——	PIT	N	Cash
Dec 23, 1980	NY	N	——	SEA	A	No compensation (free agent signing)

Dave Roberts

Date	Traded To		Traded With	Traded By		In Exchange For
Sept 12, 1966	BAL	A	——	PIT	N	Cash

Dave Roberts

Date	Traded To		Traded With	Traded By		In Exchange For
Nov 22, 1976	TOR	A	John Scott Dave Hilton	SD	N	Cash
Feb 16, 1977	SD	N	——	TOR	A	Jerry Johnson
Oct 25, 1978	TEX	A	Oscar Gamble and $300,000.	SD	N	Mike Hargrove Kurt Bevacqua Bill Fahey
Dec 10, 1980	HOU	N	——	TEX	A	No compensation (free agent signing)
March 28, 1982	PHI	N	——	HOU	N	Minor league P Steve Dunnegan

Leon Roberts

Date	Traded To		Traded With	Traded By		In Exchange For
Dec 6, 1975	HOU	N	Terry Humphrey Gene Pentz Mark Lemongello	DET	A	Milt May Dave Roberts Jim Crawford
Dec 5, 1977	SEA	A	——	HOU	N	Jimmy Sexton
Dec 12, 1980	TEX	A	*See Rick Honeycutt*	SEA	A	
July 15, 1982	TOR	A	——	TEX	A	Cash
Feb 5, 1983	KC	A	——	TOR	A	Cecil Fielder

Robin Roberts

Date	Traded To		Traded With	Traded By		In Exchange For
Oct 16, 1961	BAL	A	——	PHI	N	Cash

Andre Robertson

Date	Traded To		Traded With	Traded By		In Exchange For
June 29, 1986	ATL	N	——	NY	A	*See Claudell Washington*

Charlie Robertson

Date	Traded To		Traded With	Traded By		In Exchange For
Dec 31, 1925	STL	A	——	CHI	A	Waiver price

Daryl Robertson

Date	Traded To		Traded With	Traded By		In Exchange For
March 31, 1961	CHI	N	Andre Rodgers	MIL	N	Moe Drabowsky Seth Morehead
June 5, 1962	STL	N	Bobby Gene Smith	CHI	N	Don Landrum Alex Grammas

Dave Robertson

Date	Traded To		Traded With	Traded By		In Exchange For
July 25, 1919	CHI	N	——	NY	N	Phil Douglas
July 1, 1921	PIT	N	——	CHI	N	Elmer Ponder
April 20, 1922	NY	N	——	PIT	N	Cash

Gene Robertson

Date	Traded To		Traded With	Traded By		In Exchange For
Sept 17, 1929	BOS	N	——	NY	A	Cash

Jerry Robertson

Date	Traded To		Traded With	Traded By		In Exchange For
Dec 3, 1969	DET	A	——	MON	N	Joe Sparma
March 30, 1971	NY	N	——	DET	A	Dean Chance Bill Denehy

Jim Robertson

Date	Traded To		Traded With	Traded By		In Exchange For
Dec 16, 1953	PHI	A	——	NY	A	*See Harry Byrd*

Rich Robertson

Date	Traded To		Traded With	Traded By		In Exchange For
Feb 7, 1972	CHI	A	——	SF	N	Cash

(Robertson was returned to San Francisco on March 19.)

Sherry Robertson

Date	Traded To		Traded With	Traded By		In Exchange For
May 19, 1952	PHI	A	——	WAS	A	Waiver price

Aaron Robinson

Date	Traded To		Traded With	Traded By		In Exchange For
Feb 24, 1948	CHI	A	Fred Bradley Bill Wight	NY	A	Ed Lopat
Nov 10, 1948	DET	A	——	CHI	A	Billy Pierce and $10,000.
Aug 6, 1951	BOS	A	——	DET	A	Waiver price

Bill Robinson

Date	Traded To		Traded With	Traded By		In Exchange For
Nov 29, 1966	NY	A	Chi Chi Olivo	ATL	N	Clete Boyer
Dec 3, 1970	CHI	A	——	NY	A	Barry Moore
Dec 3, 1971	PHI	N	——	CHI	A	Minor league C Jerry Rodriguez
April 5, 1975	PIT	N	——	PHI	N	Wayne Simpson
June 15, 1982	PHI	N	——	PIT	N	Wayne Nordhagen

Bruce Robinson

Date	Traded To		Traded With	Traded By		In Exchange For
Feb 3, 1979	NY	A	——	OAK	A	$400,000.

Craig Robinson

Date	Traded To		Traded With	Traded By		In Exchange For
Dec 3, 1973	ATL	N	Barry Lersch	PHI	N	Ron Schueler
June 11, 1975	SF	N	——	ATL	N	Ed Goodson
June 13, 1976	ATL	N	——	SF	N	*See Darrell Evans*

Dewey Robinson

Date	Traded To		Traded With	Traded By		In Exchange For
Oct 30, 1981	PHI	N	Gary Holle	CHI	A	Minor league IF Jose Castro

Don Robinson

Date	Traded To		Traded With	Traded By		In Exchange For
July 31, 1987	SF	N	——	PIT	N	Mackey Sasser Cash

Earl Robinson

Date	Traded To		Traded With	Traded By		In Exchange For
Dec 15, 1960	BAL	A	——	LA	N	Cash

Eddie Robinson

Date	Traded To		Traded With	Traded By		In Exchange For
Dec 14, 1948	WAS	A	Joe Haynes Eddie Klieman	CLE	A	Mickey Vernon Early Wynn
May 31, 1950	CHI	A	Al Kozar Ray Scarborough	WAS	A	Bob Kuzava Cass Michaels John Ostrowski
Jan 27, 1953	PHI	A	Joe DeMaestri Ed McGhee	CHI	A	Ferris Fain minor league 2B Bob Wilson
Dec 16, 1953	NY	A	Harry Byrd Tom Hamilton Carmen Mauro Loren Babe	PHI	A	Don Bollweg John Gray Jim Robertson Jim Finigan Vic Power Bill Renna
June 14, 1956	KC	A	Lou Skizas	NY	A	Moe Burtschy Bill Renna and cash
Dec 5, 1956	DET	A	Jim Finigan Jack Crimian Bill Harrington	KC	A	Ned Garver Gene Host Virgil Trucks Wayne Belardi and $20,000.

Floyd Robinson

Date	Traded To		Traded With	Traded By		In Exchange For
Dec 15, 1966	CIN	N	——	CHI	A	Jim O'Toole

Date	Traded To		Traded With	Traded By		In Exchange For

Floyd Robinson *continued*

Date	Traded To		Traded With	Traded By		In Exchange For
Oct 20, 1967	KC	A	Darrell Osteen	CIN	N	Ron Tompkins
July 31, 1968	BOS	A	——	OAK	A	Cash

Frank Robinson

Dec 9, 1965	BAL	A	——	CIN	N	Milt Pappas
						Jack Baldschun
						Dick Simpson
Dec 2, 1971	LA	N	Pete Richert	BAL	A	Doyle Alexander
						Bob O'Brien
						Sergio Robles
						Royle Stillman
Nov 28, 1972	CAL	A	Bill Singer	LA	N	Andy Messersmith
			Mike Strahler			Ken McMullen
			Billy Grabarkewitz			
			Bobby Valentine			
Sept 12, 1974	CLE	A	——	CAL	A	Ken Suarez
						Rusty Torres
						and cash

Hank Robinson

Dec 12, 1913	STL	N	——	PIT	N	*See Ed Konetchy*
June 20, 1918	NY	A	——	STL	N	Cash

Humberto Robinson

April 11, 1959	CLE	A	——	MIL	N	Mickey Vernon
May 16, 1959	PHI	N	——	CLE	A	Granny Hamner

Jackie Robinson

Dec 13, 1956	NY	N	——	BKN	N	Dick Littlefield
						and $30,000.

(Trade was cancelled when Robinson retired.)

Jeff Robinson

Aug 12, 1987	PIT	N	Scott Medvin	SF	N	Rick Reuschel
Dec 4, 1989	NY	A	Minor league	PIT	N	Don Slaught
			P Willie Smith			

Wilbert Robinson

Feb 11, 1900	STL	N	John McGraw	BAL	N	Cash
			Bill Keister			

Rafael Robles

June 20, 1972	STL	N	——	SD	N	Mike Fiore
						Bob Chlupsa

(Fiore was returned to St. Louis on July 3.)

Sergio Robles

Dec 2, 1971	BAL	A	——	LA	N	*See Frank Robinson*

Mickey Rocco

May 1946	CHI	N	——	CLE	A	Heinz Becker

Pat Rockett

Dec 5, 1979	TOR	A	Barry Bonnell	ATL	N	Chris Chambliss
			Joey McLaughlin			Luis Gomez

Andre Rodgers

Oct 31, 1960	MIL	N	——	SF	N	Alvin Dark
March 31, 1961	CHI	N	Daryl Robertson	MIL	N	Moe Drabowsky
						Seth Morehead
Dec 9, 1964	PIT	N	——	CHI	N	Roberto Pena
						and cash

Bill Rodgers

May 1915	BOS	A	——	CLE	A	Cash
June 1915	CIN	N	——	BOS	A	Cash

Aurelio Rodriguez

April 27, 1970	WAS	A	Rick Reichardt	CAL	A	Ken McMullen
Oct 9, 1970	DET	A	Joe Coleman	WAS	A	Denny McLain
			Ed Brinkman			Don Wert
			Jim Hannan			Norm McRae
						Elliott Maddox
Dec 7, 1979	SD	N	——	DET	A	$200,000.
Aug 4, 1980	NY	A	——	SD	N	Cash
Nov 17, 1981	TOR	A	——	NY	A	Minor league
						C Mike Lebo
April 2, 1982	CHI	A	——	TOR	A	Wayne Nordhagen
Feb 7, 1983	BAL	A	——	CHI	A	No compensation
						(free agent signing)

Ed Rodriguez

Feb 26, 1979	KC	A	——	MIL	A	Cash

Edwin Rodriguez

Aug 26, 1983	SD	N	Dennis Rasmussen	NY	A	John Montefusco
			and $200,000.			

Ellie Rodriguez

Feb 2, 1971	MIL	A	——	KC	A	Carl Taylor
Oct 22, 1973	CAL	A	——	MIL	A	*See Clyde Wright*
March 21, 1976	LA	N	——	CAL	A	Orlando Alvarez
						and cash

Freddy Rodriguez

Dec 10, 1957	CHI	N	——	NY	N	Tom Poholsky

Roberto Rodriguez

May 26, 1970	SD	N	——	OAK	A	Cash
June 23, 1970	CHI	N	——	SD	N	Cash

Ruben Rodriguez

March 17, 1989	MIL	A	——	PIT	N	Lou Thornton

Vic Rodriguez

Feb 7, 1985	SD	N	——	BAL	A	Fritz Connally

Preacher Roe

Dec 8, 1947	BKN	N	Billy Cox	PIT	N	Dixie Walker
			Gene Mauch			Hal Gregg
						Vic Lombardi
Dec 13, 1954	BAL	A	Billy Cox	BKN	N	Minor leaguers
						John Jancse and
						Harry Schwegeman
						and $50,000.

(Roe retired; Erv Palica trade of March 17, 1955 was additional compensation.)

Ed Roebuck

July 20, 1963	WAS	A	——	LA	N	Marv Breeding
April 21, 1964	PHI	N	——	WAS	A	Cash

Gary Roenicke

Dec 7, 1977	BAL	A	Don Stanhouse	MON	N	Rudy May
			Joe Kerrigan			Randy Miller
						Bryn Smith
Dec 12, 1985	NY	A	Leo Hernandez	BAL	A	Rich Bordi
						Rex Hudler

Date	Traded To		Traded With	Traded By		In Exchange For

Gary Roenicke *continued*

Date	Traded To		Traded With	Traded By		In Exchange For
Jan 21, 1987	ATL	N	———	NY	A	No compensation (free agent signing)

Wally Roettger

April 10, 1930	NY	N	———	STL	N	Showboat Fisher Doc Farrell
Oct 29, 1930	CIN	N	———	NY	N	Cash
June 15, 1931	STL	N	———	CIN	N	Taylor Douthit
Dec 1931	CIN	N	———	STL	N	Cash
Nov 17, 1933	PIT	N	Red Lucas	CIN	N	Adam Comorosky Tony Piet

Billy Rogell

| Dec 6, 1939 | CHI | N | ——— | DET | A | Dick Bartell |

Tom Rogers

| April 1919 | PHI | A | ——— | STL | A | Cash |

Garry Roggenburk

| Sept 7, 1966 | BOS | A | ——— | MIN | A | Cash |
| June 23, 1969 | SEA | A | ——— | BOS | A | Cash |

Saul Rogovin

| May 15, 1951 | CHI | A | ——— | DET | A | Bob Cain |
| Dec 10, 1953 | CIN | N | Connie Ryan Rocky Krsnich | CHI | A | Willard Marshall |

Dan Rohn

| April 1, 1985 | CLE | A | ——— | CHI | N | Jay Baller |
| April 3, 1987 | OAK | A | *See Dennis Eckersley* | CHI | N | ——— |

Billy Rohr

| May 22, 1970 | DET | A | Russ Nagelson | CLE | A | Fred Lasher |

Cookie Rojas

Nov 27, 1962	PHI	N	———	CIN	N	Jim Owens
Oct 7, 1969	STL	N	———	PHI	N	*See Curt Flood*
June 13, 1970	KC	A	———	STL	N	Fred Rico

Stan Rojek

Nov 14, 1947	PIT	N	———	BKN	N	Cash
May 17, 1951	STL	N	———	PIT	N	Erv Dusak Rocky Nelson
Jan 24, 1952	STL	A	———	STL	N	Waiver price
Oct 14, 1952	BKN	N	Bob Mahoney Ray Coleman and $90,000.	STL	A	Billy Hunter

Jim Roland

Feb 24, 1969	OAK	A	———	MIN	A	Cash
April 28, 1972	NY	A	———	OAK	A	Cash
Aug 30, 1972	TEX	A	———	NY	A	Casey Cox

Ron Romanick

| Dec 19, 1986 | NY | A | ——— | CAL | A | Butch Wynegar |

Johnny Romano

| Dec 6, 1959 | CLE | A | Bubba Phillips Norm Cash | CHI | A | Dick Brown Don Ferrarese Jake Striker Minnie Minoso |

Johnny Romano *continued*

Date	Traded To		Traded With	Traded By		In Exchange For
Jan 20, 1965	CHI	A	Tommy John Tommie Agee	CLE	A	Rocky Colavito Camilo Carreon

(Part of three-team trade involving Kansas City, Cleveland, and Chicago White Sox.)

| Dec 14, 1966 | STL | N | minor league P Lee White | CHI | A | Walt Williams Don Dennis |

Ed Romero

| Dec 11, 1985 | BOS | A | ——— | MIL | A | Mark Clear |
| Aug 23, 1989 | MIL | A | ——— | ATL | N | Jay Aldrich |

Enrique Romo

| Dec 5, 1978 | PIT | N | Rick Jones Tommy McMillan | SEA | A | Odell Jones Rafael Vasquez Mario Mendoza |

Vicente Romo

April 19, 1969	BOS	A	———	CLE	A	*See Ken Harrelson*
March 31, 1971	CHI	A	Tony Muser	BOS	A	Duane Josephson Danny Murphy
Oct 28, 1972	SD	N	———	CHI	A	John Jeter

Gene Roof

| Sept 16, 1983 | MON | N | ——— | STL | N | Cash |

Phil Roof

| Oct 14, 1964 | LA | A | Ron Piche | MIL | N | Dan Osinski |
| June 15, 1965 | CLE | A | ——— | CAL | A | Bubba Morton and cash |

(California received Morton on September 15, 1965.)

Dec 1, 1965	KC	A	Joe Rudi	CLE	A	Jim Landis Jim Rittwage
Jan 15, 1970	MIL	A	Mike Hershberger Lew Krausse Ken Sanders	OAK	A	Don Mincher Ron Clark
July 8, 1971	MIN	A	———	MIL	A	Paul Ratliff
Oct 21, 1976	TOR	A	———	CHI	A	

Jim Rooker

| Sept 30, 1968 | NY | A | ——— | DET | A | Cash |
| Oct 25, 1972 | PIT | N | ——— | KC | A | Gene Garber |

Rolando Roomes

| Dec 9, 1988 | CIN | N | ——— | CHI | N | Lloyd McClendon |

Pat Rooney

| Dec 20, 1983 | NY | A | ——— | MON | N | Tim Burke |

Jorge Roque

| Nov 6, 1972 | MON | N | ——— | STL | N | Tim McCarver |

Buddy Rosar

Dec 17, 1942	CLE	A	Roy Cullenbine	NY	A	Roy Weatherly Oscar Grimes
May 29, 1945	PHI	A	———	CLE	A	Frankie Hayes
Oct 8, 1949	BOS	A	———	PHI	A	Billy Hitchcock

Don Rose

| Dec 10, 1971 | CAL | A | Nolan Ryan Leroy Stanton Francisco Estrada | NY | N | Jim Fregosi |

Date	Traded To	Traded With	Traded By	In Exchange For

Pete Rose

Date	Traded To	Traded With	Traded By	In Exchange For
Dec 5, 1978	PHI N	——	CIN N	No compensation (free agent signing)
Jan 20, 1984	MON N	——	PHI N	No compensation (free agent signing)
Aug 16, 1984	CIN N	——	MON N	Tom Lawless

(Rose was named Cincinnati manager.)

Johnny Roseboro

Date	Traded To	Traded With	Traded By	In Exchange For
Nov 28, 1967	MIN A	Ron Perranoski Bob Miller	LA N	Mudcat Grant Zoilo Versalles

Dave Rosello

Date	Traded To	Traded With	Traded By	In Exchange For
Dec 5, 1977	CLE A	——	CHI N	Minor leaguers P Norm Churchill and OF Bruce Compton

Goody Rosen

Date	Traded To	Traded With	Traded By	In Exchange For
April 27, 1946	NY N	——	BKN N	Cash

Steve Rosenberg

Date	Traded To	Traded With	Traded By	In Exchange For
Nov 13, 1987	CHI A	——	NY A	*See Richard Dotson*

Larry Rosenthal

Date	Traded To	Traded With	Traded By	In Exchange For
May 29, 1941	CLE A	——	CHI A	Cash
July 6, 1944	PHI A	——	NY A	Cash

Buck Ross

Date	Traded To	Traded With	Traded By	In Exchange For
April 30, 1941	CHI A	——	PHI A	Cash

Don Ross

Date	Traded To	Traded With	Traded By	In Exchange For
Sept 14, 1938	BKN N	——	DET A	Cash
April 27, 1945	CLE A	Dutch Meyer	DET A	Roy Cullenbine

Gary Ross

Date	Traded To	Traded With	Traded By	In Exchange For
April 25, 1969	SD N	Joe Niekro Francisco Libran	CHI N	Dick Selma
Sept 17, 1975	CAL A	——	SD N	Bobby Valentine Rudi Meoli

Mark Ross

Date	Traded To	Traded With	Traded By	In Exchange For
Dec 9, 1985	STL N	——	HOU N	Player to be named

(Ross was returned to Houston on March 31, 1986.)

Joe Rossi

Date	Traded To	Traded With	Traded By	In Exchange For
Oct 14, 1952	PIT N	Cal Abrams Gail Henley	CIN N	Gus Bell

Claude Rossman

Date	Traded To	Traded With	Traded By	In Exchange For
Dec 1906	DET A	——	CLE A	Cash
Aug 20, 1909	STL A	——	DET A	Tom Jones

Braggo Roth

Date	Traded To	Traded With	Traded By	In Exchange For
Aug 21, 1915	CLE A	Larry Chappell Ed Klepfer and $31,500.	CHI A	Joe Jackson
March 1, 1919	PHI A	——	CLE A	Larry Gardner Elmer Myers Charlie Jamieson
June 27, 1919	BOS A	Red Shannon	PHI A	Amos Strunk Jack Barry

(Barry refused to report, and retired.)

Braggo Roth *continued*

Date	Traded To	Traded With	Traded By	In Exchange For
Jan 20, 1920	WAS A	Red Shannon	BOS A	Mike Menosky Harry Harper Eddie Foster
Jan 20, 1921	NY A	——	WAS A	Duffy Lewis George Mogridge

Frank Roth

Date	Traded To	Traded With	Traded By	In Exchange For
Feb 1905	CHI A	——	STL A	Branch Rickey

Jack Rothrock

Date	Traded To	Traded With	Traded By	In Exchange For
April 30, 1932	CHI A	——	BOS A	Cash

Edd Roush

Date	Traded To	Traded With	Traded By	In Exchange For
Dec 23, 1915	NY N	——	NWK F	$7,500.
July 20, 1916	CIN N	Christy Mathewson Bill McKechnie	NY N	Buck Herzog Red Killefer
Feb 9, 1927	NY N	——	CIN N	George Kelly and cash

Jack Rowan

Date	Traded To	Traded With	Traded By	In Exchange For
Feb 1911	PHI N	*See Dode Paskert*	CIN N	——
Aug 1911	CHI N	——	PHI N	Cliff Curtis

Wade Rowdon

Date	Traded To	Traded With	Traded By	In Exchange For
Aug 23, 1982	CIN N	Leo Garcia	CHI A	Jim Kern
Feb 17, 1987	CHI N	——	CIN N	Guy Hoffman
	(Chicago received Rowdon on Feb. 23, 1987.)			
March 29, 1988	BAL A	——	CHI N	Minor league SS Nick Ramirez Minor league P Tom Michno

Ken Rowe

Date	Traded To	Traded With	Traded By	In Exchange For
Sept 10, 1964	BAL A	——	LA N	Cash

Schoolboy Rowe

Date	Traded To	Traded With	Traded By	In Exchange For
April 30, 1942	BKN N	——	DET A	Cash
March 24, 1943	PHI N	——	BKN N	Cash

Bama Rowell

Date	Traded To	Traded With	Traded By	In Exchange For
March 6, 1948	BKN N	Ray Sanders and $40,000.	BOS N	Eddie Stanky
April 15, 1948	PHI N	——	BKN N	Waiver price

Luther Roy

Date	Traded To	Traded With	Traded By	In Exchange For
July 24, 1929	BKN N	——	PHI N	Lou Koupal

Jerry Royster

Date	Traded To	Traded With	Traded By	In Exchange For
Nov 17, 1975	ATL N	Jimmy Wynn Tom Paciorek Lee Lacy	LA N	Dusty Baker Ed Goodson
Jan 3, 1985	SD N	——	ATL N	No compenstion (free agent signing)
Jan 21, 1987	CHI A	——	SD N	No compensation (free agent signing)
Aug 26, 1987	NY A	Minor league IF Mike Soper	CHI A	Minor league P Ken Patterson player to be named

(Chicago received P Jeff Pries on Sept. 19, 1987.)

Dick Rozek

Date	Traded To	Traded With	Traded By	In Exchange For
Dec 19, 1952	PHI A	minor league 2B Bob Wilson	CLE A	Bob Hooper

Date	Traded To	Traded With	Traded By	In Exchange For

Dave Rozema

| Dec 27, 1984 | TEX A ——— | | DET A | No compensation (free agent signing) |

Vic Roznovsky

| March 30, 1966 | BAL A ——— | | CHI N | Carl Warwick |

Sonny Ruberto

| May 22, 1969 | SD N | John Sipin | STL N | Bill Davis Jerry DaVanon |

Jorge Rubio

| Nov 29, 1967 | CIN N | Bill Kelso | CAL A | Sammy Ellis |

Art Ruble

| May 16, 1934 | CIN N | Ted Kleinhans Wes Schulmerich | PHI N | Syl Johnson Johnny Moore |

Dave Rucker

| June 22, 1983 | STL N ——— | | DET A | Doug Bair |
| April 6, 1985 | PHI N ——— | | STL N | Ivan DeJesus Bill Campbell |

Joe Rudi

Dec 1, 1965	KC A	Phil Roof	CLE A	Jim Landis Jim Rittwage
Nov 17, 1976	CAL A ———		OAK A	No compensation (free agent signing)
Jan 23, 1981	BOS A	Frank Tanana Jim Dorsey	CAL A	Fred Lynn Steve Renko
Dec 4, 1981	OAK A ———		BOS A	No compensation (free agent signing)

Don Rudolph

| May 1, 1959 | CIN N | Lou Skizas | CHI A | Del Ennis |
| May 3, 1962 | WAS A | Steve Hamilton | CLE A | Willie Tasby |

Ken Rudolph

March 19, 1974	SF N ———		CHI N	Willie Prall
Oct 14, 1974	STL N	Elias Sosa	SF N	Marc Hill
March 31, 1977	SF N ———		STL N	Cash
July 27, 1977	BAL A ———		SF N	Cash

Muddy Ruel

Aug 21, 1917	NY A ———		STL A	Cash
Dec 15, 1920	BOS A	Del Pratt Sammy Vick Hank Thormahlen	NY A	Waite Hoyt Harry Harper Wally Schang Mike McNally
Feb 10, 1923	WAS A	Allen Russell	BOS A	Val Picinich Howard Shanks Ed Goebel
Dec 15, 1930	BOS A ———		WAS A	Cash
Aug 31, 1931	DET A ———		BOS A	Marty McManus
Dec 1932	STL A ———		DET A	Waiver price

Dutch Ruether

July 17, 1917	CIN N ———		CHI N	Waiver price
Dec 15, 1920	BKN N ———		CIN N	Rube Marquard
Dec 17, 1924	WAS A ———		BKN N	Cash
Aug 27, 1926	NY A ———		WAS A	Garland Braxton Nick Cullop

(New York sent Braxton and Cullop to Washington on October 19, 1926.)

Rudy Rufer

| June 9, 1952 | BKN N | Cash | CIN N | Cal Abrams |

Red Ruffing

| May 6, 1930 | NY A ——— | | BOS A | Cedric Durst and $50,000. |

Vern Ruhle

| Dec 20, 1984 | CLE A ——— | | HOU N | No compensation (free agent signing) |

Chico Ruiz

| Nov 25, 1969 | CAL A | Alex Johnson | CIN N | Pedro Borbon Jim McGlothlin Vern Geishert |

Pete Runnels

| Jan 23, 1958 | BOS A ——— | | WAS A | Albie Pearson Norm Zauchin |
| Nov 26, 1962 | HOU N ——— | | BOS A | Roman Mejias |

Bob Rush

| Dec 5, 1957 | MIL N | Eddie Haas Don Kaiser | CHI N | Taylor Phillips Sammy Taylor |
| June 11, 1960 | CHI A ——— | | MIL N | Cash |

Amos Rusie

| Dec 15, 1900 | CIN N ——— | | NY N | Christy Mathewson |

Allen Russell

| July 29, 1919 | BOS A | Bob McGraw and $40,000. | NY A | Carl Mays |
| Feb 10, 1923 | WAS A | Muddy Ruel | BOS A | Val Picinich Howard Shanks Ed Goebel |

Jack Russell

June 10, 1932	CLE A ———		BOS A	Pete Appleton
Dec 15, 1932	WAS A	Bruce Connatser	CLE A	Harley Boss
June 13, 1936	BOS A ———		WAS A	Joe Cascarella

Jeff Russell

| July 19, 1985 | TEX A | Duane Walker | CIN N | Buddy Bell |

Jim Russell

| Nov 18, 1947 | BOS N | Bill Salkeld Al Lyons | PIT N | Johnny Hopp Danny Murtaugh |
| Dec 24, 1949 | BKN N | Ed Sauer and cash | BOS N | Luis Olmo |

John Russell

| March 25, 1989 | ATL N ——— | | PHI N | Cash |

Babe Ruth

| Jan 3, 1920 | NY A ——— | | BOS A | $125,000 and a $300,000 loan to Boston owner Harry Frazee |

Dick Ruthven

| Dec 10, 1975 | CHI A | Roy Thomas Alan Bannister | PHI N | Jim Kaat Mike Buskey |

Date			Traded To	Traded With	Traded By		In Exchange For

Dick Ruthven *continued*

Date			Traded To	Traded With	Traded By		In Exchange For
Dec 12, 1975	ATL	N		Ken Henderson Danny Osborn	CHI	A	Ralph Garr Larvell Blanks
June 15, 1978	PHI	N		——	ATL	N	Gene Garber
May 22, 1983	CHI	N		Bill Johnson	PHI	N	Guillermo Hernandez

Blondy Ryan

| Nov 1, 1934 | PHI | N | | Pretzels Pezzullo
Johnny Vergez
George Watkins
and cash | NY | N | Dick Bartell |
| Aug 6, 1935 | NY | A | | —— | PHI | N | Cash |

Connie Ryan

April 27, 1943	BOS	N		Hugh Poland	NY	N	Ernie Lombardi
May 10, 1950	CIN	N		——	BOS	N	Walker Cooper
Dec 10, 1951	PHI	N		Smoky Burgess Howie Fox	CIN	N	Andy Seminick Eddie Pellagrini Dick Sisler Niles Jordan
Aug 25, 1953	CHI	A		——	PHI	N	Waiver price
Dec 10, 1953	CIN	N		Saul Rogovin Rocky Krsnich	CHI	A	Willard Marshall

Jack Ryan

| Feb 18, 1909 | BOS | A | | Charlie Chech
and $12,500. | CLE | A | Cy Young |

Mike Ryan

| Dec 15, 1967 | PHI | N | | Cash | BOS | A | Dick Ellsworth
Gene Oliver |
| Jan 31, 1974 | PIT | N | | —— | PHI | N | Jackie Hernandez |

Nolan Ryan

Dec 10, 1971	CAL	A		Don Rose Leroy Stanton Francisco Estrada	NY	N	Jim Fregosi
Nov 19, 1979	HOU	N		——	CAL	A	No compensation (free agent signing)
Dec 7, 1988	TEX	A		——	HOU	N	No compensation (free agent signing)

Rosy Ryan

| April 17, 1925 | BOS | N | | —— | NY | N | Tim McNamara |

Gary Ryerson

| Oct 22, 1973 | CAL | A | | —— | MIL | A | *See Clyde Wright* |

Ray Sadecki

May 8, 1966	SF	N		——	STL	N	Orlando Cepeda
Dec 12, 1969	NY	N		Dave Marshall	SF	N	Bob Heise Jim Gosger
Oct 13, 1974	STL	N		Tommy Moore	NY	N	Joe Torre
May 28, 1975	ATL	N		Elias Sosa	STL	N	Ron Reed Wayne Nordhagen
June 30, 1975	KC	A		Cash	ATL	N	Bruce Dal Canton Norm Angelini Al Autry

(Atlanta received Angelini and Autry on September 4.)

Bob Sadowski

| June 15, 1963 | MIL | N | | Gene Oliver | STL | N | Lew Burdette |
| Dec 15, 1965 | BOS | A | | Dan Osinski | MIL | N | Lee Thomas
Arnie Earley
Jay Ritchie |

Bob Sadowski

| Dec 15, 1961 | CHI | A | | Taylor Phillips
minor league
IF Lou Vassie | PHI | N | Frank Barnes
Andy Carey
Cal McLish |

(Carey refused to report, and the Phillies received McLish in exchange for Vassie to complete the trade on March 24, 1962.)

Jim Sadowski

| Nov 6, 1976 | CIN | N | | —— | PIT | N | Tom Carroll |

Tom Saffell

| Sept 14, 1955 | KC | A | | —— | PIT | N | Waiver price |
| April 16, 1956 | BKN | N | | Lee Wheat
and cash | KC | A | Tim Thompson |

Johnny Sain

| Aug 30, 1951 | NY | A | | —— | BOS | N | Lew Burdette
and $50,000. |
| May 11, 1955 | KC | A | | Enos Slaughter | NY | A | Sonny Dixon
and cash |

Ebba St. Claire

| Feb 1, 1954 | NY | N | | *See Johnny Antonelli* | MIL | N | —— |

Randy St. Claire

| July 13, 1988 | CIN | N | | —— | MON | N | *See Tracy Jones* |

Lenn Sakata

| Dec 6, 1979 | BAL | A | | —— | MIL | A | John Flinn |
| Dec 16, 1986 | NY | A | | —— | OAK | A | No compensation
(free agent signing) |

Mark Salas

| June 6, 1987 | NY | A | | —— | MIN | A | Joe Niekro |
| Nov 13, 1987 | CHI | A | | Dan Pasqua
Steve Rosenberg | NY | A | Richard Dotson
Scott Nielsen |

Angel Salazar

| Jan 24, 1985 | STL | N | | —— | MON | N | |

(Claimed in compensation draft after St. Louis lost free agent P Bruce Sutter to Atlanta.)

April 2, 1985	NY	N		Minor league P John Young	STL	N	Jose Oquendo Minor league P Mark J. Davis
April 1, 1986	KC	A		——	NY	N	Tony Ferreira
Nov 6, 1987	CIN	N		Danny Jackson	KC	A	Ted Power Kurt Stillwell

Luis Salazar

Aug 5, 1980	SD	N		Rick Lancellotti	PIT	N	Kurt Bevacqua Mark Lee
Dec 6, 1984	CHI	A		——	SD	N	*See LaMarr Hoyt*
March 23, 1989	SD	N		——	DET	A	Mike Brumley
Aug 30, 1989	CHI	N		Marvell Wynne	SD	N	Calvin Schiraldi Darrin Jackson Phil Stephenson

(San Diego Received Stephenson on Sept. 5, 1989).

Bill Salkeld

| Nov 18, 1947 | BOS | N | | Jim Russell
Al Lyons | PIT | N | Johnny Hopp
Danny Murtaugh |
| Sept 26, 1949 | CHI | A | | —— | BOS | N | Cash |

Slim Sallee

| July 23, 1916 | NY | N | | —— | STL | N | $10,000. |

Date	Traded To	Traded With	Traded By	In Exchange For

Slim Sallee continued

Date	Traded To		Traded By		In Exchange For
March 8, 1919	CIN N	———	NY	N	Waiver price
Sept 5, 1920	NY N	———	CIN	N	Waiver price

Chico Salmon

April 1, 1964	CLE A	———	MIL	N	Mike de la Hoz
March 31, 1969	BAL A	———	SEA	A	Gene Brabender
					Gordon Lund

Jack Salveson

Dec 11, 1934	PIT N	———	NY	N	Waiver price
June 16, 1935	CHI A	———	PIT	N	Cash
Dec 10, 1936	CLE A	———	CHI	A	Thornton Lee

(Part of three-team trade involving Chicago, Cleveland, and Washington.)

| Dec 10, 1936 | WAS A | ——— | CLE | A | Earl Whitehill |

(Part of three-team trade involving Chicago, Cleveland, and Washington.)

Manny Salvo

| June 15, 1940 | BOS N | Al Glossop | NY | N | Tony Cuccinello |
| May 12, 1943 | PHI N | ——— | BOS | N | Cash |

Ron Samford

April 8, 1955	DET A	———	NY	N	Waiver price
Dec 6, 1958	WAS A	———	DET	A	See Eddie Yost
April 3, 1960	BAL A	Clint Courtney	WAS	A	Billy Gardner

Billy Sample

| Feb 27, 1985 | NY A | player to be named | TEX | A | Toby Harrah |

(New York received P Eric Dersin on July 14, 1985.)

| Dec 6, 1985 | MIL A | ——— | NY | A | Minor league |
| | | | | | IF Miguel Sosa |

Amado Samuel

| Oct 15, 1963 | NY N | ——— | MIL | N | Cash |

Juan Samuel

June 18, 1989	NY N	———	PHI	N	Len Dykstra
					Roger McDowell
					Tom Edens

(Philadelphia received Edens on July 26, 1989.)

| Dec 20, 1989 | LA N | ——— | NY | N | Alejandro Pena |
| | | | | | Mike Marshall |

Roger Samuels

| May 10, 1989 | PIT N | ——— | SF | N | Ken Oberkfell |

Alejandro Sanchez

March 24, 1984	SF N	———	PHI	N	Dave Bergman
April 5, 1985	DET A	———	SF	N	Roger Mason
Jan 18, 1986	MIN A	———	DET	A	See Dave Engle

Luis Sanchez

Oct 24, 1975	CIN N	minor league	HOU	N	Joaquin Andujar
		P Carlos Alfonso			
Dec 27, 1985	CAL A	Minor league	MON	N	Gary Lucas
		P Tim Arnold			

Orlando Sanchez

| May 17, 1984 | BAL A | ——— | KC | A | Cash |

Heinie Sand

| Dec 13, 1928 | STL N | $10,000. | PHI | N | Tommy Thevenow |

Ryne Sandberg

| Jan 27, 1982 | CHI N | Larry Bowa | PHI | N | Ivan DeJesus |

Ken Sanders

June 13, 1966	KC A	Jim Gosger	BOS	A	John Wyatt
		Guido Grilli			Rollie Sheldon
					Jose Tartabull
Jan 15, 1970	MIL A	———	OAK	A	See Don Mincher
Oct 31, 1972	PHI N	———	MIL	A	See Don Money
Nov 30, 1972	MIN A	Ken Reynolds	PHI	N	Cesar Tovar
		Joe Lis			
Aug 3, 1973	CLE A	———	MIN	A	Cash
March 22, 1975	NY N	———	CAL	A	Ike Hampton
Sept 17, 1976	KC A	———	NY	N	Cash

Ray Sanders

April 15, 1946	BOS N	———	STL	N	$25,000.
March 6, 1948	BKN N	Bama Rowell	BOS	N	Eddie Stanky
		and $40,000.			
April 19, 1948	BOS N	———	BKN	N	$60,000.

Reggie Sanders

| May 9, 1972 | DET A | ——— | OAK | A | Mike Kilkenny |
| March 29, 1975 | ATL N | ——— | DET | A | Jack Pierce |

Scott Sanderson

Dec 7, 1983	SD N	———	MON	N	Gary Lucas
Dec 7, 1983	CHI N	———	SD	N	Carmelo Martinez
					Craig Lefferts
					Fritz Connally

(Part of three-team trade involving Chicago Cubs, San Diego, and Montreal.)

| Dec 13, 1989 | OAK A | ——— | CHI | N | No compensation |
| | | | | | (free agent signing) |

Mike Sandlock

| Dec 19, 1953 | PHI N | ——— | PIT | N | Cash |

Charlie Sands

| April 2, 1973 | DET A | ——— | PIT | N | Chris Zachary |

Tom Sandt

| March 25, 1977 | STL N | ——— | OAK | A | Cash |

Fred Sanford

Dec 13, 1948	NY A	Roy Partee	STL	A	Sherm Lollar
					Red Embree
					Dick Starr
					and $100,000.
June 15, 1951	WAS A	Tom Ferrick	NY	A	Bob Kuzava
		Bob Porterfield			
July 30, 1951	STL A	———	WAS	A	Dick Starr

Jack Sanford

Dec 3, 1958	SF N	———	PHI	N	Valmy Thomas
					Ruben Gomez
Aug 18, 1965	CAL A	———	SF	N	Cash
June 15, 1967	KC A	Jackie Warner	CAL	A	Roger Repoz

Manny Sanguillen

Nov 5, 1976	OAK A	$100,000.	PIT	N	Chuck Tanner
April 4, 1978	PIT N	———	OAK	A	Miguel Dilone
					Elias Sosa
					Mike Edwards
Dec 9, 1980	CLE A	Bert Blyleven	PIT	N	Gary Alexander
					Victor Cruz
					Rafael Vasquez
					Bob Owchinko

Date	Traded To	Traded With	Traded By	In Exchange For

Rafael Santana

Date	Traded To		Traded With	Traded By		In Exchange For
Feb 16, 1981	STL	N	——	NY	A	Cash
Dec 11, 1987	NY	A	Minor league P Victor Garcia	NY	N	Phil Lombardi Steve Frey Minor league OF Darren Reed

Jose Santiago

Date	Traded To		Traded With	Traded By		In Exchange For
May 16, 1956	KC	A	——	CLE	A	Cash

Ron Santo

Date	Traded To		Traded With	Traded By		In Exchange For
Dec 11, 1973	CHI	A	——	CHI	N	Steve Stone Ken Frailing Steve Swisher Jim Kremmel

Al Santorini

Date	Traded To		Traded With	Traded By		In Exchange For
June 11, 1971	STL	N	——	SD	N	Leron Lee Fred Norman
May 8, 1973	KC	A	——	STL	N	Tom Murphy

Manny Sarmiento

Date	Traded To		Traded With	Traded By		In Exchange For
April 8, 1981	BOS	A	——	SEA	A	Dick Drago
Oct 23, 1981	PIT	N	——	BOS	A	Cash

Bill Sarni

Date	Traded To		Traded With	Traded By		In Exchange For
June 14, 1956	NY	N	See Red Schoendienst	STL	N	——

Mackey Sasser

Date	Traded To		Traded With	Traded By		In Exchange For
July 31, 1987	PIT	N	Cash	SF	N	Don Robinson
March 26, 1988	NY	N	Tim Drummond	PIT	N	Randy Milligan Minor league P Scott Henion

Tom Satriano

Date	Traded To		Traded With	Traded By		In Exchange For
June 15, 1969	BOS	A	——	CAL	A	Joe Azcue

Kevin Saucier

Date	Traded To		Traded With	Traded By		In Exchange For
Sept 13, 1980	TEX	A	——	PHI	N	Sparky Lyle
Dec 10, 1980	DET	A	——	TEX	A	Mark Wagner

Ed Sauer

Date	Traded To		Traded With	Traded By		In Exchange For
June 15, 1949	PIT	N	——	STL	N	Cash
June 15, 1949	BOS	N	——	PIT	N	Phil Masi
Dec 24, 1949	BKN	N	Jim Russell and cash	BOS	N	Luis Olmo

Hank Sauer

Date	Traded To		Traded With	Traded By		In Exchange For
June 15, 1949	CHI	N	Frankie Baumholtz	CIN	N	Harry Walker Peanuts Lowrey
March 30, 1956	STL	N	——	CHI	N	Pete Whisenant

Bob Savage

Date	Traded To		Traded With	Traded By		In Exchange For
Dec 16, 1948	STL	A	——	PHI	A	Waiver price

Jack Savage

Date	Traded To		Traded With	Traded By		In Exchange For
Dec 11, 1987	NY	N	——	LA	N	See Jesse Orosco
July 31, 1989	MIN	A	——	NY	N	See Frank Viola

Ted Savage

Date	Traded To		Traded With	Traded By		In Exchange For
Nov 28, 1962	PIT	N	Pancho Herrera	PHI	N	Don Hoak
May 14, 1967	CHI	N	——	STL	N	Cash

Ted Savage continued

Date	Traded To		Traded With	Traded By		In Exchange For
April 23, 1968	LA	N	Jim Ellis	CHI	N	Jim Hickman Phil Regan
March 30, 1969	CIN	N	——	LA	N	Jimmie Schaffer
April 5, 1970	MIL	A	——	CIN	N	Cash
May 11, 1971	KC	A	——	MIL	A	Tom Matchick

Bob Saverine

Date	Traded To		Traded With	Traded By		In Exchange For
April 24, 1965	HOU	N	Cash	BAL	A	Don Larsen

Carl Sawatski

Date	Traded To		Traded With	Traded By		In Exchange For
Nov 30, 1953	CHI	A	——	CHI	N	Waiver price
June 13, 1958	PHI	N	——	MIL	N	Joe Lonnett
Dec 4, 1959	STL	N	——	PHI	N	Bobby Gene Smith Bill Smith

Rick Sawyer

Date	Traded To		Traded With	Traded By		In Exchange For
March 19, 1974	DET	A	Walt Williams	CLE	A	Jim Perry
			(Part of three-team trade involving Detroit, Cleveland, and New York Yankees.)			
March 19, 1974	NY	A	Walt Williams Ed Farmer	DET	A	Gerry Moses
			(Part of three-team trade involving Detroit, New York Yankees, and Cleveland.)			
July 10, 1976	SD	N	——	NY	A	Gene Locklear
Sept 29, 1977	MON	N	——	SD	N	Cash

Steve Sax

Date	Traded To		Traded With	Traded By		In Exchange For
Nov 23, 1988	NY	A	——	LA	N	No compensation (free agent signing)

Bill Sayles

Date	Traded To		Traded With	Traded By		In Exchange For
July 31, 1943	BKN	N	Bill Lohrman Joe Orengo	NY	N	Dolf Camilli Johnny Allen
			(Camilli refused to report to New York and retired.)			

Doc Scanlan

Date	Traded To		Traded With	Traded By		In Exchange For
Aug 1, 1904	BKN	N	——	PIT	N	Cash

Pat Scanlon

Date	Traded To		Traded With	Traded By		In Exchange For
Nov 6, 1976	STL	N	Steve Dunning Tony Scott	MON	N	Bill Greif Angel Torres Sam Mejias
May 17, 1977	SD	N	John D'Acquisto	STL	N	Butch Metzger

Randy Scarbery

Date	Traded To		Traded With	Traded By		In Exchange For
Aug 12, 1977	STL	N	——	OAK	A	Steve Dunning
June 12, 1980	CAL	A	——	CHI	A	Todd Cruz

Ray Scarborough

Date	Traded To		Traded With	Traded By		In Exchange For
May 31, 1950	CHI	A	Al Kozar Eddie Robinson	WAS	A	Bob Kuzava Cass Michaels John Ostrowski
Dec 10, 1950	BOS	A	Bill Wight	CHI	A	Joe Dobson Dick Littlefield Al Zarilla
Aug 22, 1952	NY	A	——	BOS	A	Cash

Mac Scarce

Date	Traded To		Traded With	Traded By		In Exchange For
Dec 3, 1974	NY	N	Del Unser John Stearns	PHI	N	Tug McGraw Don Hahn Dave Schneck
April 15, 1975	CIN	N	——	NY	N	Tom Hall
Dec 13, 1978	TEX	A	——	MIN	A	Mike Bacsik

Les Scarsella

Date	Traded To		Traded With	Traded By		In Exchange For
Dec 6, 1939	BOS	N	Cash	CIN	N	Jim Turner

Date	Traded To		Traded With	Traded By		In Exchange For

Paul Schaal

Date	Traded To		Traded With	Traded By		In Exchange For
April 30, 1974	CAL	A	——	KC	A	Richie Scheinblum

Sid Schacht

Date	Traded To		Traded With	Traded By		In Exchange For
June 15, 1950	NY	A		STL	A	*See Snuffy Stirnweiss*
May 13, 1951	BOS	N	——	STL	A	Waiver price

Germany Schaefer

Date	Traded To		Traded With	Traded By		In Exchange For
Aug 13, 1909	WAS	A	Red Killefer	DET	A	Jim Delahanty
Feb 10, 1916	NY	A	——	NWK	F	Cash

Mark Schaeffer

Date	Traded To		Traded With	Traded By		In Exchange For
Dec 3, 1971	SD	N	Derrel Thomas Bill Greif	HOU	N	Dave Roberts

Jimmie Schaffer

Date	Traded To		Traded With	Traded By		In Exchange For
Oct 17, 1962	CHI	N	*See Larry Jackson*	STL	N	——
Dec 1, 1964	CHI	A		CHI	N	Frank Baumann
July 8, 1965	NY	N	——	CHI	A	Frank Lary
Feb 22, 1966	PHI	N	Bobby Klaus Wayne Graham	NY	N	Dick Stuart
March 30, 1969	LA	N		CIN	N	Ted Savage

Joe Schaffernoth

Date	Traded To		Traded With	Traded By		In Exchange For
July 7, 1961	CLE	A	——	CHI	N	Cash
Oct 14, 1961	WAS	A	——	CLE	A	Cash

Art Schallock

Date	Traded To		Traded With	Traded By		In Exchange For
May 11, 1955	BAL	A	——	NY	A	Waiver price

Bobby Schang

Date	Traded To		Traded With	Traded By		In Exchange For
June 1915	NY	N	——	PIT	N	Cash

Wally Schang

Date	Traded To		Traded With	Traded By		In Exchange For
Dec 14, 1917	BOS	A	Amos Strunk Joe Bush	PHI	A	Vean Gregg Merlin Kopp Pinch Thomas and $60,000.
Dec 15, 1920	NY	A	Waite Hoyt Harry Harper Mike McNally	BOS	A	Muddy Ruel Del Pratt Sammy Vick Hank Thormahlen
March 1926	STL	A	——	NY	A	George Mogridge and cash
Dec 11, 1929	PHI	A	——	STL	A	Sammy Hale

George Scharein

Date	Traded To		Traded With	Traded By		In Exchange For
Dec 8, 1936	PHI	N	Cash	NY	N	Lou Chiozza

Jeff Schattinger

Date	Traded To		Traded With	Traded By		In Exchange For
March 24, 1982	CHI	A	——	KC	A	Greg Pryor

Dan Schatzeder

Date	Traded To		Traded With	Traded By		In Exchange For
Dec 7, 1979	DET	A	——	MON	N	Ron LeFlore
Dec 9, 1981	SF	N	Mike Chris	DET	A	Larry Herndon
June 15, 1982	MON	N		SF	N	Cash
July 24, 1986	PHI	N	Skeeter Barnes	MON	N	Tom Foley Larry Sorensen
June 23, 1987	MIN	A	Cash	PHI	N	Minor league P Danny Clay Minor league 3B Tom Schwarz

Rube Schauer

Date	Traded To		Traded With	Traded By		In Exchange For
Jan 1917	PHI	A	——	NY	N	Waiver price

Bob Scheffing

Date	Traded To		Traded With	Traded By		In Exchange For
June 7, 1950	CIN	N	——	CHI	N	Ron Northey
Aug 1, 1951	STL	N	——	CIN	N	Waiver price

Carl Scheib

Date	Traded To		Traded With	Traded By		In Exchange For
May 7, 1954	STL	N	——	PHI	A	Cash

(Scheib was returned to Philadelphia on June 1.)

Richie Scheinblum

Date	Traded To		Traded With	Traded By		In Exchange For
Oct 23, 1970	WAS	A	——	CLE	A	Cash
Oct 21, 1971	KC	A	——	WAS	A	Cash
Nov 30, 1972	CIN	N	Roger Nelson	KC	A	Hal McRae Wayne Simpson
June 15, 1973	CAL	A	——	CIN	N	Terry Wilshusen minor league P Thor Skogan
April 30, 1974	KC	A	——	CAL	A	Paul Schaal
Aug 5, 1974	STL	N	——	KC	A	Cash

Hank Schenz

Date	Traded To		Traded With	Traded By		In Exchange For
May 16, 1949	BKN	N	——	CHI	N	Bob Ramazzotti
Nov 4, 1949	PIT	N	——	BKN	N	Cash
July 10, 1951	NY	N	——	PIT	N	Waiver price

Fred Scherman

Date	Traded To		Traded With	Traded By		In Exchange For
Dec 3, 1973	HOU	N	Cash	DET	A	Jim Ray Gary Sutherland
June 8, 1975	MON	N	——	HOU	N	Cash

Bill Scherrer

Date	Traded To		Traded With	Traded By		In Exchange For
Aug 27, 1984	DET	A	——	CIN	N	Carl Willis and cash

Chuck Schilling

Date	Traded To		Traded With	Traded By		In Exchange For
April 6, 1966	MIN	A	Russ Nixon	BOS	A	Dick Stigman and minor league 1B Jose Calero

Curt Schilling

Date	Traded To		Traded With	Traded By		In Exchange For
July 29, 1988	BAL	A	——	BOS	A	*See Mike Boddicker*

Calvin Schiraldi

Date	Traded To		Traded With	Traded By		In Exchange For
Nov 13, 1985	BOS	A	Wes Gardner John Christensen LaSchelle Tarver	NY	N	Bob Ojeda John Mitchell Tom McCarthy Minor league P Chris Bayer
Dec 8, 1987	CHI	N	Al Nipper	BOS	A	Lee Smith
Aug 30, 1989	SD	N	Darrin Jackson Phil Stephenson	CHI	N	Marvell Wynne Luis Salazar

(San Diego Received Stephenson on Sept. 5, 1989).

Admiral Schlei

Date	Traded To		Traded With	Traded By		In Exchange For
Dec 12, 1908	STL	N	——	CIN	N	Ed Karger Art Fromme
Dec 12, 1908	NY	N	Bugs Raymond Red Murray	STL	N	Roger Bresnahan

Rudy Schlesinger

Date	Traded To		Traded With	Traded By		In Exchange For
Nov 30, 1967	CHI	N	Cash	BOS	A	Ray Culp
May 5, 1969	PHI	N		BOS	A	Don Lock

Date	Traded To	Traded With	Traded By	In Exchange For

Dutch Schliebner
| May 1923 | STL A | —— | BKN N | Cash |

Jay Schlueter
| Dec 3, 1974 | BAL A | Lee May | HOU N | Enos Cabell / Rob Andrews |

Norm Schlueter
| Dec 29, 1939 | STL A | —— | CHI A | Cash |

Ray Schmandt
| Feb 15, 1923 | STL N | Hy Myers | BKN N | Jack Fournier |

George Schmees
| June 30, 1952 | BOS A | —— | STL A | Waiver price |

Bob Schmidt
| April 27, 1961 | CIN N | Don Blasingame / Sherman Jones | SF N | Ed Bailey |
| Dec 15, 1961 | WAS A | Dave Stenhouse | CIN N | Johnny Klippstein / Marty Keough |

Dave Schmidt
| Nov 25, 1985 | CHI A | Wayne Tolleson | TEX A | Ed Correa / Scott Fletcher / player to be named |

(Texas received IF Jose Mota on Dec. 12, 1985.)

| Jan 15, 1987 | BAL A | —— | CHI A | No compensation (free agent signing) |
| Dec 13, 1989 | MON N | —— | BAL A | No compensation (free agent signing) |

Freddy Schmidt
| May 3, 1947 | PHI N | Harry Walker | STL N | Ron Northey |

Willard Schmidt
| Dec 5, 1957 | CIN N | Marty Kutyna / Ted Wieand | STL N | Curt Flood / Joe Taylor |

Johnny Schmitz
June 15, 1951	BKN N	Rube Walker / Andy Pafko / Wayne Terwilliger	CHI N	Bruce Edwards / Joe Hatten / Eddie Miksis / Gene Hermanski
Aug 1, 1952	NY A	——	BKN N	Waiver price
Aug 28, 1952	CIN N	Jim Greengrass / Ernie Nevel / Bob Marquis / and $35,000.	NY A	Ewell Blackwell
Feb 17, 1953	NY A	——	CIN N	Cash
May 13, 1953	WAS A	——	NY A	Waiver price
Nov 8, 1955	BOS A	Bob Porterfield / Mickey Vernon / Tommy Umphlett	WAS A	Karl Olson / Dick Brodowski / Tex Clevenger / Neil Chrisley / and minor league P Al Curtis
May 14, 1956	BAL A	——	BOS A	Cash

Dave Schneck
| Dec 3, 1974 | PHI N | *See Tug McGraw* | NY N | —— |
| Feb 16, 1977 | CHI N | —— | CIN N | Champ Summers |

Dan Schneider
| Oct 13, 1966 | HOU N | *See Tom Dukes* | ATL N | —— |

Jeff Schneider
| Jan 28, 1982 | CAL A | Doug DeCinces | BAL A | Dan Ford |

Pete Schneider
| Dec 9, 1918 | NY A | —— | CIN N | Cash |

Gerry Schoen
| April 30, 1969 | BAL A | Mike Ferraro | SEA A | John O'Donoghue / Tom Fisher / and minor league P Lloyd Fourroux |

Red Schoendienst
| June 14, 1956 | NY N | Jackie Brandt / Bobby Stephenson / Dick Littlefield / Bill Sarni | STL N | Alvin Dark / Ray Katt / Don Liddle / Whitey Lockman |
| June 15, 1957 | MIL N | —— | NY N | Danny O'Connell / Ray Crone / Bobby Thomson |

Dick Schofield
June 15, 1958	PIT N	Cash	STL N	Gene Freese / Johnny O'Brien
May 22, 1965	SF N	——	PIT N	Jose Pagan
May 11, 1966	NY A	——	SF N	Cash
Sept 10, 1966	LA N	——	NY A	Thad Tillotson / and cash
Dec 2, 1968	BOS A	——	STL N	Gary Waslewski
Oct 21, 1970	STL N	——	BOS A	Jim Campbell
July 29, 1971	MIL A	Jose Cardenal / Bob Reynolds	STL N	Ted Kubiak / minor league P Charlie Loseth

Gene Schott
| May 5, 1939 | BKN N | —— | CIN N | Cash |

Ossee Schreckengost
Oct 1901	CLE A	——	BOS A	Cash
June 1902	PHI A	Frank Bonner	CLE A	Bill Bernhard
May 1908	CHI A	——	PHI A	Cash

Pop Schriver
| Unknown | STL N | —— | PIT N | Cash |

Bob Schroder
| Dec 1, 1969 | WAS A | —— | SF N | Cash |

Bill Schroeder
| Dec 7, 1988 | CAL A | —— | MIL A | Gus Polidor |

Al Schroll
| Dec 1, 1959 | CHI N | —— | BOS A | Bobby Thomson |

Ken Schrom
| June 3, 1980 | TOR A | —— | CAL A | Dave Lemanczyk |
| Jan 7, 1986 | CLE A | —— | MIN A | Bryan Oelkers |

Rick Schu
| March 21, 1988 | BAL A | Jeff Stone / Keith Hughes | PHI N | Mike Young / player to be named |

(Philadelphia received OF Frank Bellino on June 14, 1988.)

| May 19, 1989 | DET A | —— | BAL A | Cash |

Date	Traded To	Traded With		Traded By		In Exchange For

Ron Schueler

Dec 3, 1973	PHI	N	——	ATL	N	Barry Lersch
						Craig Robinson
March 31, 1977	MIN	A	——	PHI	N	Cash

Dave Schuler

May 11, 1977	CAL	A	Dave LaRoche	CLE	A	Bruce Bochte
						Sid Monge
						and $250,000.

Wes Schulmerich

Oct 14, 1930	BOS	N	Bill McAfee	CHI	N	Bob Smith
						Jimmy Welsh
June 17, 1933	PHI	N	Fritz Knothe	BOS	N	Hal Lee
			and cash			Pinky Whitney
May 16, 1934	CIN	N	Ted Kleinhans	PHI	N	Syl Johnson
			Art Ruble			Johnny Moore

Art Schult

| June 12, 1957 | WAS | A | —— | CIN | N | Cash |

Fred Schulte

Dec 14, 1932	WAS	A	Goose Goslin	STL	A	Sammy West
			Lefty Stewart			Carl Reynolds
						Lloyd Brown
						and $20,000.
Jan 30, 1936	PIT	N	——	WAS	A	Waiver price

Johnny Schulte

Dec 13, 1927	PHI	N	Jimmy Ring	STL	N	Johnny Mokan
						Jimmy Cooney
						Bubber Jonnard
April 1929	CHI	N	——	PHI	N	Cash

Wildfire Schulte

July 29, 1916	PIT	N	Bill Fischer	CHI	N	Art Wilson
						Otto Knabe
June 14, 1917	PHI	N	——	PIT	N	Waiver price
Dec 1917	WAS	A	——	PHI	N	Cash

Barney Schultz

| June 24, 1963 | STL | N | —— | CHI | N | Leo Burke |

Bob Schultz

| June 4, 1953 | PIT | N | —— | CHI | N | See Ralph Kiner |
| Dec 29, 1954 | DET | A | —— | PIT | N | Cash |

Buddy Schultz

| Feb 28, 1977 | STL | N | —— | CHI | N | Minor league |
| | | | | | | P Mark Covert |

Howie Schultz

| May 10, 1947 | PHI | N | —— | BKN | N | Cash |

Joe Schultz

Aug 1915	CHI	N	$3,000.	BKN	N	Larry Cheney
Jan 1916	PIT	N	——	CHI	N	Cash
June 6, 1924	PHI	N	——	STL	N	Cash
June 23, 1925	CIN	N	——	PHI	N	Cash

Al Schulz

| Feb 10, 1916 | CIN | N | —— | BUF | F | Cash |

Don Schulze

June 13, 1984	CLE	A	——	CHI	N	See Rick Sutcliffe
May 11, 1987	NY	N	——	CLE	A	Ricky Nelson
March 28, 1988	DET	A	——	MIN	A	Karl Best
July 22, 1989	SD	N	Mike Pagliarulo	NY	A	Walt Terrell
						Fred Toliver

(New York received Toliver on Sept. 27, 1989.)

Ferdie Schupp

July 1919	STL	N	——	NY	N	Frank Snyder
June 18, 1921	BKN	N	Hal Janvrin	STL	N	Jeff Pfeffer
Dec 1921	CHI	A	——	BKN	N	Cash

Bill Schuster

| June 15, 1939 | BOS | N | Cash | PIT | N | Elbie Fletcher |

Don Schwall

Nov 20, 1962	PIT	N	Jim Pagliaroni	BOS	A	Jack Lamabe
						Dick Stuart
June 15, 1966	ATL	N	——	PIT	N	Billy O'Dell

Herb Score

| April 18, 1960 | CHI | A | —— | CLE | A | Barry Latman |

Dick Scott

| Dec 13, 1963 | CHI | N | —— | LA | N | Jim Brewer |
| | | | | | | Cuno Barragan |

Donnie Scott

| April 4, 1985 | SEA | A | —— | TEX | A | Orlando Mercado |

Everett Scott

Dec 20, 1921	NY	A	Joe Bush	BOS	A	Roger Peckinpaugh
			Sad Sam Jones			Jack Quinn
						Rip Collins
						Bill Piercy
June 17, 1925	WAS	A	——	NY	A	Cash
March 1926	CHI	A	——	WAS	A	Waiver price
July 6, 1926	CIN	N	——	CHI	A	Waiver price

George Scott

Oct 11, 1971	MIL	A	Billy Conigliaro	BOS	A	Marty Pattin
			Joe Lahoud			Lew Krausse
			Jim Lonborg			Tommy Harper
			Ken Brett			Minor leaguer
			Don Pavletich			Pat Skrable
Dec 6, 1976	BOS	A	Bernie Carbo	MIL	A	Cecil Cooper
June 13, 1979	KC	A	——	BOS	A	Tom Poquette

Jack Scott

Feb 18, 1922	CIN	N	Larry Kopf	BOS	N	Rube Marquard
Jan 9, 1927	PHI	N	Fresco Thompson	NY	N	George Harper
						Butch Henline

(Part of three-team trade involving Philadelphia, New York, and Brooklyn.)

John Scott

Nov 22, 1976	TOR	A	Dave Roberts	SD	N	Cash
			Dave Hilton			
Dec 6, 1977	STL	N	Pete Vuckovich	TOR	A	Tom Underwood
						Victor Cruz
Oct 23, 1978	CHI	A	——	STL	N	Jim Willoughby

Mickey Scott

| Dec 18, 1969 | CHI | A | Cash | NY | A | Pete Ward |
| May 22, 1973 | MON | N | —— | BAL | A | Cash |

Date	Traded To	Traded With	Traded By	In Exchange For

Mickey Scott continued

Date	Traded To		Traded With	Traded By		In Exchange For
Sept 11, 1974	CAL	A	Cash	BAL	A	Bob Oliver

Mike Scott

Dec 10, 1982	HOU	N	———	NY	N	Danny Heep

Pete Scott

Nov 28, 1927	PIT	N	Sparky Adams	CHI	N	Kiki Cuyler

Rodney Scott

Dec 12, 1975	MON	N	———	KC	A	Cash
March 15, 1977	TEX	A	———	MON	N	Jeff Terpko
March 26, 1977	OAK	A	Jim Umbarger and cash	TEX	A	Claudell Washington
March 29, 1978	CHI	N	Cash	OAK	A	Pete Broberg
Dec 14, 1978	MON	N	Jerry White	CHI	N	Sam Mejias

Tony Scott

Nov 6, 1976	STL	N	Steve Dunning Pat Scanlon	MON	N	Bill Greif Angel Torres Sam Mejias
June 7, 1981	HOU	N	———	STL	N	Joaquin Andujar

Rod Scurry

Aug 14, 1985	NY	A	———	PIT	N	Cash
March 19, 1988	SEA	A	———	SF	N	Donell Nixon

(San Francisco received Nixon on June 23, 1988.)

Kim Seaman

Dec 5, 1978	STL	N	Tom Grieve	NY	N	Pete Falcone
Dec 8, 1980	SD	N	———	STL	N	*See Rollie Fingers*
May 22, 1982	MON	N	———	SD	N	Jerry Manuel

Ray Searage

Jan 8, 1982	CLE	A	———	NY	N	Tom Veryzer
Dec 15, 1982	SD	N	———	CLE	A	Cash

(Searage was returned to San Diego on March 28, 1983.)

July 23, 1986	CHI	A	———	MIL	A	Al Jones Minor league OF Tom Hartley

Tom Seaton

Feb 1915	NWK	F	Hugh Bradley Larry Pratt	BKN	F	Cy Falkenberg
Feb 10, 1916	CHI	N	———	NWK	F	Cash

Tom Seaver

June 15, 1977	CIN	N	———	NY	N	Pat Zachry Doug Flynn Steve Henderson Dan Norman
Dec 16, 1982	NY	N	———	CIN	N	Charlie Puleo Lloyd McClendon Minor league OF Jason Felice
Jan 20, 1984	CHI	A	———	NY	N	

(Claimed in compensation draft after Chicago lost free agent P Dennis Lamp to Toronto.)

June 29, 1986	BOS	A	———	CHI	A	Steve Lyons

Bob Sebra

Nov 2, 1985	MON	N	Jim Anderson	TEX	A	Pete Incaviglia
Sept 1, 1988	PHI	N	———	MON	N	Minor league P Travis Chambers
July 13, 1989	CIN	N	———	PHI	N	Jeff Gray

(Philadelphia received Gray on Sept. 6, 1989.)

Jimmy Sebring

Aug 11, 1904	CIN	N	———	PIT	N	Moose McCormick
Sept 1909	WAS	A	———	BKN	N	Cash

Don Secrist

Dec 5, 1968	CHI	A	Don Pavletich	CIN	N	Jack Fisher

Bob Seeds

April 24, 1932	CHI	A	Johnny Hodapp	CLE	A	Bill Cissell Jim Moore
Dec 15, 1932	BOS	A	Johnny Hodapp Greg Mulleavy Bob Fothergill	CHI	A	Ed Durham Hal Rhyne
May 25, 1934	CLE	A	Bob Weiland and $25,000.	BOS	A	Wes Ferrell Dick Porter
Jan 11, 1935	DET	A	———	CLE	A	Cash

Pat Seerey

June 2, 1948	CHI	A	Al Gettel	CLE	A	Bob Kennedy

Herman Segelke

Oct 15, 1982	SF	N	———	CHI	N	Alan Hargesheimer

Kal Segrist

Dec 1, 1954	BAL	A	———	NY	A	*See Dick Kryhoski*

Diego Segui

April 13, 1966	WAS	A	———	KC	A	Cash
July 30, 1966	KC	A	———	WAS	A	Jim Duckworth
Dec 7, 1969	OAK	A	Ray Oyler	SEA	A	Ted Kubiak George Lauzerique
June 7, 1972	STL	N	———	OAK	A	Cash
Dec 7, 1973	BOS	A	Reggie Cleveland Terry Hughes	STL	N	Lynn McGlothen John Curtis Mike Garman
Oct 22, 1976	SEA	A	———	SD	N	Cash

Socks Seibold

Nov 7, 1928	BOS	N	Percy Jones Lou Legett Freddie Maguire Bruce Cunningham and $200,000.	CHI	N	Rogers Hornsby

Kip Selbach

Feb 29, 1900	NY	N	———	CIN	N	Cash
July 4, 1904	BOS	A	———	WAS	A	Bill O'Neill

Jeff Sellers

Dec 13, 1988	CIN	N	———	BOS	A	*See Nick Esasky*

Dick Selma

April 25, 1969	CHI	N	———	SD	N	Joe Niekro Gary Ross Francisco Libran
Nov 17, 1969	PHI	N	Oscar Gamble	CHI	N	Johnny Callison
July 29, 1974	MIL	A	———	CAL	A	Cash

(Selma was returned to California on August 12, 1974.)

Andy Seminick

Dec 10, 1951	CIN	N	Eddie Pellagrini Dick Sisler Niles Jordan	PHI	N	Smoky Burgess Howie Fox Connie Ryan

Date	Traded To	Traded With	Traded By	In Exchange For

Andy Seminick *continued*

Date	Traded To	Traded With	Traded By	In Exchange For
April 30, 1955	PHI N	Glen Gorbous, Jim Greengrass	CIN N	Smoky Burgess, Steve Ridzik, Stan Palys

Ray Semproch

Date	Traded To	Traded With	Traded By	In Exchange For
Dec 5, 1959	DET A	Chico Fernandez	PHI N	Ken Walters, Ted Lepcio, minor league P Alex Cosmidis
June 15, 1960	LA N	Cash	DET A	Clem Labine
April 7, 1961	LA A	——	WAS A	Cash

Sonny Senerchia

Date	Traded To	Traded With	Traded By	In Exchange For
Jan 31, 1956	CIN N	Brooks Lawrence	STL N	Jackie Collum

Steve Senteney

Date	Traded To	Traded With	Traded By	In Exchange For
Feb 4, 1983	NY N	——	TOR A	Jorge Orta
June 14, 1983	PIT N	Marvell Wynne	NY N	Junior Ortiz, Minor league P Arthur Ray

Bill Serena

Date	Traded To	Traded With	Traded By	In Exchange For
Sept 30, 1954	CHI A	——	CHI N	Waiver price

Walter Sessi

Date	Traded To	Traded With	Traded By	In Exchange For
Jan 30, 1947	BKN N	——	STL N	Cash

Hank Severeid

Date	Traded To	Traded With	Traded By	In Exchange For
June 8, 1925	WAS A	——	STL A	George Mogridge, Pinky Hargrave
July 22, 1926	NY A	——	WAS A	Waiver price

Al Severinsen

Date	Traded To	Traded With	Traded By	In Exchange For
Dec 1, 1970	SD N	——	BAL A	*See Pat Dobson*
Nov 30, 1972	NY N	——	SD N	Dave Marshall

Luke Sewell

Date	Traded To	Traded With	Traded By	In Exchange For
Jan 7, 1933	WAS A	——	CLE A	Roy Spencer
Jan 22, 1935	STL A	——	WAS A	Bump Hadley
Jan 22, 1935	CHI A	——	STL A	Cash
Dec 19, 1938	BKN N	——	CHI A	Cash

Jimmy Sexton

Date	Traded To	Traded With	Traded By	In Exchange For
Dec 7, 1976	SEA A	Craig Reynolds	PIT N	Grant Jackson
Dec 5, 1977	HOU N	——	SEA A	Leon Roberts
Feb 10, 1981	OAK A	——	HOU N	Rick Lysander

Gordon Seyfried

Date	Traded To	Traded With	Traded By	In Exchange For
Nov 27, 1962	CLE A	Ron Nischwitz	DET A	Bubba Phillips

Cy Seymour

Date	Traded To	Traded With	Traded By	In Exchange For
July 14, 1906	NY N	——	CIN N	$12,000.

Art Shamsky

Date	Traded To	Traded With	Traded By	In Exchange For
Nov 8, 1967	NY N	——	CIN N	Bob Johnson
Oct 18, 1971	STL N	Jim Bibby, Rich Folkers, Charles Hudson	NY N	Jim Beauchamp, Chuck Taylor, Harry Parker, Tom Coulter
June 28, 1972	OAK A	——	CHI N	Cash

Howard Shanks

Date	Traded To	Traded With	Traded By	In Exchange For
Feb 10, 1923	BOS A	Val Picinich, Ed Goebel	WAS A	Muddy Ruel, Allen Russell
Dec 10, 1924	NY A	——	BOS A	Mike McNally

Red Shannon

Date	Traded To	Traded With	Traded By	In Exchange For
June 27, 1919	BOS A	Braggo Roth	PHI A	Amos Strunk, Jack Barry

(Barry refused to report, and retired.)

Date	Traded To	Traded With	Traded By	In Exchange For
Jan 20, 1920	WAS A	Braggo Roth	BOS A	Mike Menosky, Harry Harper, Eddie Foster
July 1920	PHI A	——	WAS A	Fred Thomas

Spike Shannon

Date	Traded To	Traded With	Traded By	In Exchange For
July 13, 1906	NY N	——	STL N	Sam Mertes, Doc Marshall
July 1908	PIT N	——	NY N	Cash

Bobby Shantz

Date	Traded To	Traded With	Traded By	In Exchange For
Feb 19, 1957	NY A	Art Ditmar, Jack McMahan, Wayne Belardi, Curt Roberts, Clete Boyer	KC A	Billy Hunter, Rip Coleman, Tom Morgan, Mickey McDermott, Milt Graff, Irv Noren

(New York received Roberts on April 4, and Boyer on June 4, 1957.)

Date	Traded To	Traded With	Traded By	In Exchange For
Dec 16, 1960	PIT N	——	WAS A	Bennie Daniels, Harry Bright, R C Stevens
May 7, 1962	STL N	——	HOU N	Carl Warwick, John Anderson
June 15, 1964	CHI N	Ernie Broglio, Doug Clemens	STL N	Lou Brock, Jack Spring, Paul Toth
Aug 15, 1964	PHI N	——	CHI N	Cash

Dick Sharon

Date	Traded To	Traded With	Traded By	In Exchange For
Nov 30, 1972	DET A	——	PIT N	Jim Foor, Norm McRae
Nov 18, 1974	SD N	Ed Brinkman, Bob Strampe	DET A	Nate Colbert

(Part of three-team trade involving San Diego, Detroit, and St. Louis Cardinals.)

Date	Traded To	Traded With	Traded By	In Exchange For
Oct 20, 1975	STL N	——	SD N	Willie Davis
Jan 12, 1976	CAL A	——	STL N	Minor league P Bill Rothan
March 3, 1976	BOS A	John Balaz, Dave Machemer	CAL A	Dick Drago

Bill Sharp

Date	Traded To	Traded With	Traded By	In Exchange For
May 8, 1975	MIL A	——	CHI A	Bob Coluccio

Bud Sharpe

Date	Traded To	Traded With	Traded By	In Exchange For
Sept 1910	PIT N	——	BOS N	Cash

Mike Sharperson

Date	Traded To	Traded With	Traded By	In Exchange For
Sept 21, 1987	LA N	——	TOR A	Minor league P Juan Guzman

Joe Shaute

Date	Traded To	Traded With	Traded By	In Exchange For
Dec 1933	CIN N	——	BKN N	Cash

Al Shaw

Date	Traded To	Traded With	Traded By	In Exchange For
Jan 1908	CHI A	——	BOS A	Cash

Date	Traded To		Traded With	Traded By		In Exchange For

Bob Shaw

Date	Traded To		Traded With	Traded By		In Exchange For
June 15, 1958	CHI	A	Ray Boone	DET	A	Bill Fischer Tito Francona
June 10, 1961	KC	A	Wes Covington Gerry Staley Stan Johnson	CHI	A	Ray Herbert Don Larsen Andy Carey Al Pilarcik
Dec 15, 1961	MIL	N	Lou Klimchock	KC	A	Joe Azcue Ed Charles Manny Jimenez
Dec 3, 1963	SF	N	——	MIL	N	See Felipe Alou
June 10, 1966	NY	N	——	SF	N	Cash
July 24, 1967	CHI	N	——	NY	N	Cash

Don Shaw

Date	Traded To		Traded With	Traded By		In Exchange For
May 15, 1972	OAK	A	——	STL	N	Dwain Anderson

Bob Shawkey

Date	Traded To		Traded With	Traded By		In Exchange For
July 7, 1915	NY	A	——	PHI	A	$18,000.

Merv Shea

Date	Traded To		Traded With	Traded By		In Exchange For
May 9, 1933	STL	A	Cash	BOS	A	Rick Ferrell Lloyd Brown
Dec 11, 1933	CHI	A	——	STL	A	Cash

Spec Shea

Date	Traded To		Traded With	Traded By		In Exchange For
May 3, 1952	WAS	A	Jackie Jensen Jerry Snyder Archie Wilson	NY	A	Irv Noren Tom Upton

Steve Shea

Date	Traded To		Traded With	Traded By		In Exchange For
April 3, 1969	MON	N	——	HOU	N	Cash

Dave Shean

Date	Traded To		Traded With	Traded By		In Exchange For
July 16, 1909	BOS	N	Buster Brown Lew Richie	PHI	N	Johnny Bates Charlie Starr
Jan 1911	CHI	N	——	BOS	N	Scotty Ingerton Big Jeff Pfeffer
Oct 1911	BOS	N	——	CHI	N	Cash
April 1918	BOS	A	——	CIN	N	Rube Foster

(Foster refused to report to Cincinnati; Cincinnati received cash instead.)

Jimmy Sheckard

Date	Traded To		Traded With	Traded By		In Exchange For
Jan 1900	BKN	N	Jerry Nops Broadway Aleck Smith Frank Kitson Harry Howell Joe McGinnity	BAL	N	Cash
Dec 30, 1905	CHI	N	——	BKN	N	Billy Maloney Jack McCarthy Doc Casey Buttons Briggs and $2,000.
April 1913	STL	N	——	CHI	N	Cash
July 1913	CIN	N	——	STL	N	Waiver price

Tom Sheehan

Date	Traded To		Traded With	Traded By		In Exchange For
May 20, 1925	PIT	N	——	CIN	N	Al Niehaus

Tommy Sheehan

Date	Traded To		Traded With	Traded By		In Exchange For
Jan 1908	BKN	N	——	PIT	N	Cash

John Shelby

Date	Traded To		Traded With	Traded By		In Exchange For
May 22, 1987	LA	N	Brad Havens	BAL	A	Tom Niedenfuer

Rollie Sheldon

Date	Traded To		Traded With	Traded By		In Exchange For
May 3, 1965	KC	A	Johnny Blanchard	NY	A	Doc Edwards
June 13, 1966	BOS	A	See John Wyatt	KC	A	——
Aug 15, 1966	CIN	N	Dick Stigman	BOS	A	Hank Fischer

(Cincinnati received Stigman and Sheldon on December 15, 1966.)

Jim Shellenback

Date	Traded To		Traded With	Traded By		In Exchange For
May 17, 1969	WAS	A	——	PIT	N	Frank Kreutzer

Bill Sherdel

Date	Traded To		Traded With	Traded By		In Exchange For
June 16, 1930	BOS	N	Fred Frankhouse	STL	N	Burleigh Grimes
May 18, 1932	STL	N	——	BOS	N	Waiver price

Pat Sheridan

Date	Traded To		Traded With	Traded By		In Exchange For
June 16, 1989	SF	N	——	DET	A	Tracy Jones

Larry Sherry

Date	Traded To		Traded With	Traded By		In Exchange For
April 9, 1964	DET	A	——	LA	N	Lou Johnson and $10,000.
June 29, 1967	HOU	N	——	DET	A	Jim Landis

Norm Sherry

Date	Traded To		Traded With	Traded By		In Exchange For
Oct 11, 1962	NY	N	——	LA	N	Cash

Barry Shetrone

Date	Traded To		Traded With	Traded By		In Exchange For
Dec 5, 1962	WAS	A	——	CHI	A	See Eddie Robinson

Charlie Shields

Date	Traded To		Traded With	Traded By		In Exchange For
Sept 1902	STL	A	——	BAL	A	Cash

Steve Shields

Date	Traded To		Traded With	Traded By		In Exchange For
Sept 23, 1986	KC	A	——	ATL	N	Darryl Motley
Dec 10, 1986	SEA	A	Scott Bankhead Mike Kingery	KC	A	Danny Tartabull Rick Luecken
March 20, 1989	MIN	A	——	NY	A	Balvino Galvez

Dave Shipanoff

Date	Traded To		Traded With	Traded By		In Exchange For
April 1, 1985	PHI	N	Minor league OF Ken Kinnard	TOR	A	Len Matuszek

Craig Shipley

Date	Traded To		Traded With	Traded By		In Exchange For
April 1, 1988	NY	N	——	LA	N	John Gibbons

Art Shires

Date	Traded To		Traded With	Traded By		In Exchange For
June 16, 1930	WAS	A	——	CHI	A	Garland Braxton Bennie Tate

Bob Shirley

Date	Traded To		Traded With	Traded By		In Exchange For
Dec 8, 1980	STL	N	See Rollie Fingers	SD	N	——
April 1, 1982	CIN	N	——	STL	N	Jeff Lahti minor league P Jose Brito
Dec 15, 1982	NY	A	——	CIN	N	No compensation (free agent signing)

Urban Shocker

Date	Traded To		Traded With	Traded By		In Exchange For
Jan 22, 1918	STL	A	Les Nunamaker Fritz Maisel Nick Cullop Joe Gedeon	NY	A	Eddie Plank Del Pratt and $15,000.

Date	Traded To	Traded With	Traded By	In Exchange For

Urban Shocker *continued*

Date	Traded To	Traded With	Traded By	In Exchange For
Dec 17, 1924	NY A	——	STL A	Joe Bush
				Milt Gaston
				Joe Giard

Costen Shockley

Date	Traded To	Traded With	Traded By	In Exchange For
Dec 3, 1964	LA A	Rudy May	PHI N	Bo Belinsky

Milt Shoffner

Date	Traded To	Traded With	Traded By	In Exchange For
Aug 19, 1939	CIN N	——	BOS N	Waiver price

Ernie Shore

Date	Traded To	Traded With	Traded By	In Exchange For
Dec 18, 1918	NY A	Duffy Lewis	BOS A	Frank Gilhooley
		Dutch Leonard		Slim Love
				Ray Caldwell
				Roxy Walters
				and $15,000.

Bill Short

Date	Traded To	Traded With	Traded By	In Exchange For
Aug 15, 1966	BOS A	——	BAL A	Cash
Oct 17, 1966	PIT N	——	BOS A	Cash
Nov 29, 1967	NY N	——	PIT N	Cash

Chick Shorten

Date	Traded To	Traded With	Traded By	In Exchange For
Jan 17, 1919	DET A	Eddie Ainsmith	BOS A	Ossie Vitt
		Slim Love		
Dec 14, 1921	STL A	——	DET A	Waiver price

Burt Shotton

Date	Traded To	Traded With	Traded By	In Exchange For
Dec 15, 1917	WAS A	Doc Lavan	STL A	Bert Gallia
				and $15,000.
Feb 1, 1919	STL N	——	WAS A	Waiver price

Clyde Shoun

Date	Traded To	Traded With	Traded By	In Exchange For
April 16, 1938	STL N	Curt Davis	CHI N	Dizzy Dean
		Tuck Stainback		
		and $185,000.		
May 6, 1942	CIN N	——	STL N	Cash
June 7, 1947	BOS N	——	CIN N	Cash
May 11, 1949	CHI A	——	BOS N	Cash

Harry Shuman

Date	Traded To	Traded With	Traded By	In Exchange For
July 27, 1944	PHI N	——	PIT N	Waiver price

Eddie Sicking

Date	Traded To	Traded With	Traded By	In Exchange For
May 14, 1919	PHI N	——	NY N	Cash
July 2, 1920	CIN N	——	NY N	Cash

Norm Siebern

Date	Traded To	Traded With	Traded By	In Exchange For
Dec 11, 1959	KC A	Hank Bauer	NY A	Roger Maris
		Don Larsen		Joe DeMaestri
		Marv Throneberry		Kent Hadley
Nov 27, 1963	BAL A	——	KC A	Jim Gentile
				and cash
Dec 2, 1965	CAL A	——	BAL A	Dick Simpson
Dec 14, 1966	SF N	——	CAL A	Len Gabrielson
July 16, 1967	BOS A	——	SF N	Cash

Dick Siebert

Date	Traded To	Traded With	Traded By	In Exchange For
Oct 16, 1945	STL A	——	PHI A	George McQuinn

Paul Siebert

Date	Traded To	Traded With	Traded By	In Exchange For
June 15, 1977	NY N	Bobby Valentine	SD N	Dave Kingman
Oct 2, 1978	STL N	——	NY N	Bob Coluccio

Sonny Siebert

Date	Traded To	Traded With	Traded By	In Exchange For
April 19, 1969	BOS A	Joe Azcue	CLE A	Ken Harrelson
		Vicente Romo		Juan Pizarro
				Dick Ellsworth
May 4, 1973	TEX A	——	BOS A	Cash
Oct 26, 1973	STL N	——	TEX A	Tommy Cruz
				and cash
Nov 18, 1974	SD N	Alan Foster	STL N	Ed Brinkman
		Rich Folkers		Danny Breeden
(Part of three-team trade involving San Diego, Detroit, and St. Louis Cardinals.)				
May 16, 1975	OAK A	——	SD N	Ted Kubiak

Candy Sierra

Date	Traded To	Traded With	Traded By	In Exchange For
June 8, 1988	CIN N	——	SD N	Dennis Rasmussen

Ed Siever

Date	Traded To	Traded With	Traded By	In Exchange For
Dec 1902	STL A	——	DET A	Cash

Roy Sievers

Date	Traded To	Traded With	Traded By	In Exchange For
Feb 18, 1954	WAS A	——	BAL A	Gil Coan
April 4, 1960	CHI A	——	WAS A	Earl Battey
				Don Mincher
				and $150,000.
Nov 28, 1961	PHI N	——	CHI A	John Buzhardt
				Charley Smith
July 16, 1964	WAS A	——	PHI N	Cash

Frank Sigafoos

Date	Traded To	Traded With	Traded By	In Exchange For
June 22, 1929	CHI A	——	DET A	Cash

Charlie Silvera

Date	Traded To	Traded With	Traded By	In Exchange For
Dec 11, 1956	CHI N	——	NY A	Cash

Ken Silvestri

Date	Traded To	Traded With	Traded By	In Exchange For
Dec 31, 1940	NY A	——	CHI A	Bill Knickerbocker

Al Sima

Date	Traded To	Traded With	Traded By	In Exchange For
June 11, 1954	PHI A	Sonny Dixon	CHI A	Ed McGhee
		Bill Wilson		Morrie Martin
		and $20,000.		

Al Simmons

Date	Traded To	Traded With	Traded By	In Exchange For
Sept 28, 1932	CHI A	Jimmy Dykes	PHI A	$100,000.
		Mule Haas		
Dec 10, 1935	DET A	——	CHI A	$75,000.
April 4, 1937	WAS A	——	DET A	$15,000.
Dec 29, 1938	BOS N	——	WAS A	$3,000.
Aug 31, 1939	CIN N	——	BOS N	Cash

Curt Simmons

Date	Traded To	Traded With	Traded By	In Exchange For
June 22, 1966	CHI N	——	STL N	Cash
Aug 2, 1967	CAL A	——	CHI N	Cash

Ted Simmons

Date	Traded To	Traded With	Traded By	In Exchange For
Dec 12, 1980	MIL A	Pete Vuckovich	STL N	Sixto Lezcano
		Rollie Fingers		David Green
				Lary Sorensen
				Dave LaPoint
March 5, 1986	ATL N	——	MIL A	Rick Cerone
				Minor league
				SS Flavio Alfaro

Dick Simpson

Date	Traded To	Traded With	Traded By	In Exchange For
Dec 2, 1965	BAL A	——	CAL A	Norm Siebern

Date	Traded To		Traded With	Traded By		In Exchange For

Dick Simpson *continued*

Date	Traded To		Traded With	Traded By		In Exchange For
Dec 9, 1965	CIN	N	Milt Pappas Jack Baldschun	BAL	A	Frank Robinson
Jan 11, 1968	STL	N	——	CIN	N	Alex Johnson
June 15, 1968	HOU	N	Hal Gilson	STL	N	Ron Davis
Dec 4, 1968	NY	A	——	HOU	N	Dooley Womack
May 19, 1969	SEA	A	——	NY	A	Jose Vidal
Dec 12, 1969	SF	N	Steve Whitaker	SEA	A	Bobby Bolin

Harry Simpson

Date	Traded To		Traded With	Traded By		In Exchange For
May 11, 1955	KC	A	——	CLE	A	Cash
June 15, 1957	NY	A	Ryne Duren Jim Pisoni Milt Graff	KC	A	Billy Martin Woodie Held Ralph Terry Bob Martyn
June 15, 1958	KC	A	Bob Grim	NY	A	Duke Maas Virgil Trucks
May 2, 1959	CHI	A	——	KC	A	Ray Boone
Aug 25, 1959	PIT	N	minor league IF Bob Sagers	CHI	A	Ted Kluszewski
Oct 13, 1959	CHI	A	——	PIT	N	Cash

Steve Simpson

Date	Traded To		Traded With	Traded By		In Exchange For
Dec 20, 1973	NY	N	——	SD	N	Jim McAndrew

Wayne Simpson

Date	Traded To		Traded With	Traded By		In Exchange For
Nov 30, 1972	KC	A	Hal McRae	CIN	N	Roger Nelson Richie Scheinblum
March 28, 1974	PIT	N	——	KC	A	Jim Foor
April 5, 1975	PHI	N	——	PIT	N	Bill Robinson
April 8, 1976	CAL	A	——	PHI	N	Cash

Duke Sims

Date	Traded To		Traded With	Traded By		In Exchange For
Dec 11, 1970	LA	N	——	CLE	A	Alan Foster Ray Lamb
Aug 4, 1972	DET	A	——	LA	N	Cash
Sept 24, 1973	NY	A	——	DET	A	Cash
May 8, 1974	TEX	A	——	NY	A	Larry Gura and cash

Matt Sinatro

Date	Traded To		Traded With	Traded By		In Exchange For
April 6, 1989	HOU	N	——	OAK	A	Troy Afenir

Bill Singer

Date	Traded To		Traded With	Traded By		In Exchange For
Nov 28, 1972	CAL	A	Frank Robinson Mike Strahler Billy Grabarkewitz Bobby Valentine	LA	N	Andy Messersmith Ken McMullen
Dec 10, 1975	TEX	A	——	CAL	A	Jim Spencer and $100,000.
June 1, 1976	MIN	A	Roy Smalley Mike Cubbage Jim Gideon and $250,000.	TEX	A	Bert Blyleven Danny Thompson

Elmer Singleton

Date	Traded To		Traded With	Traded By		In Exchange For
Sept 30, 1946	PIT	N	Billy Herman Stan Wentzel Whitey Wietelmann	BOS	N	Bob Elliott Hank Camelli
Nov 13, 1956	CHI	N	Ray Jablonski	CIN	N	Don Hoak Warren Hacker Pete Whisenant

Ken Singleton

Date	Traded To		Traded With	Traded By		In Exchange For
April 5, 1972	MON	N	Tim Foli Mike Jorgensen	NY	N	Rusty Staub
Dec 4, 1974	BAL	A	Mike Torrez	MON	N	Dave McNally Rich Coggins minor league P Bill Kirkpatrick

John Sipin

Date	Traded To		Traded With	Traded By		In Exchange For
May 22, 1969	SD	N	Sonny Ruberto	STL	N	Bill Davis Jerry DaVanon

Doug Sisk

Date	Traded To		Traded With	Traded By		In Exchange For
Dec 8, 1987	BAL	A	——	NY	N	Blaine Beatty Minor league P Greg Talamantez

Tommie Sisk

Date	Traded To		Traded With	Traded By		In Exchange For
March 28, 1969	SD	N	Chris Cannizzaro	PIT	N	Ron Davis Bobby Klaus
March 30, 1970	CHI	A	——	SD	N	Jerry Nyman

Dave Sisler

Date	Traded To		Traded With	Traded By		In Exchange For
May 2, 1959	DET	A	Ted Lepcio	BOS	A	Billy Hoeft
Sept 16, 1961	CIN	N	Cash	WAS	A	Claude Osteen

Dick Sisler

Date	Traded To		Traded With	Traded By		In Exchange For
April 7, 1948	PHI	N	——	STL	N	Ralph LaPointe and $30,000.
Dec 10, 1951	CIN	N	Andy Seminick Eddie Pellagrini Niles Jordan	PHI	N	Smoky Burgess Howie Fox Connie Ryan
May 13, 1952	STL	N	Virgil Stallcup	CIN	N	Eddie Kazak Wally Westlake

George Sisler

Date	Traded To		Traded With	Traded By		In Exchange For
Dec 14, 1927	WAS	A	——	STL	A	$25,000.
May 27, 1928	BOS	N	——	WAS	A	$7,500.

Jim Siwy

Date	Traded To		Traded With	Traded By		In Exchange For
June 21, 1984	CLE	A	——	CHI	A	Dan Spillner

Ted Sizemore

Date	Traded To		Traded With	Traded By		In Exchange For
Oct 5, 1970	STL	N	Bob Stinson	LA	N	Dick Allen
March 2, 1976	LA	N	——	STL	N	Willie Crawford
Dec 20, 1976	PHI	N	——	LA	N	Johnny Oates minor league P Quincy Hill
Feb 23, 1979	CHI	N	——	PHI	N	*See Manny Trillo*
Aug 17, 1979	BOS	A	——	CHI	N	Mike O'Berry and cash

Dave Skaggs

Date	Traded To		Traded With	Traded By		In Exchange For
May 13, 1980	CAL	A	——	BAL	A	Cash

Roe Skidmore

Date	Traded To		Traded With	Traded By		In Exchange For
Nov 30, 1970	CHI	A	Pat Jacquez Dave Lemonds	CHI	N	Jose Ortiz Ossie Blanco
July 27, 1973	STL	N	Ed Sprague	CIN	N	Ed Crosby minor league C Gene Dusan

Bob Skinner

Date	Traded To		Traded With	Traded By		In Exchange For
May 23, 1963	CIN	N	——	PIT	N	Jerry Lynch
June 13, 1964	STL	N	——	CIN	N	Minor league C Jim Saul and cash

Camp Skinner

Date	Traded To		Traded With	Traded By		In Exchange For
Jan 30, 1923	BOS	A	Norm McMillan George Murray and $50,000.	NY	A	Herb Pennock

Date	Traded To	Traded With	Traded By	In Exchange For

Joel Skinner

Date	Traded To	Traded With		Traded By		In Exchange For
Feb 2, 1982	CHI	A ———		PIT	N	

(Claimed in compensation draft after Chicago lost free agent P Ed Farmer to Philadelphia.)

July 30, 1986	NY	A	Ron Kittle	CHI	A	Ron Hassey
			Wayne Tolleson			Carlos Martinez
						Bill Lindsey

(Chicago received Lindsey on Dec. 24, 1986.)

March 19, 1989	CLE	A	Minor league	NY	A	Mel Hall
			OF Turner Ward			

Lou Skizas

June 14, 1956	KC	A	Eddie Robinson	NY	A	Moe Burtschy
						Bill Renna
						and cash
Nov 20, 1957	DET	A	*See Billy Martin*	KC	A	
May 1, 1959	CIN	N	Don Rudolph	CHI	A	Del Ennis

Craig Skok

Nov 17, 1975	TEX	A	Juan Beniquez	BOS	A	Ferguson Jenkins
			Steve Barr			

Bill Skowron

Nov 26, 1962	LA	N ———	NY	A	Stan Williams
Dec 6, 1963	WAS	A ———	LA	N	Cash
July 13, 1964	CHI	A Carl Bouldin	WAS	A	Joe Cunningham
					Frank Kreutzer
May 6, 1967	CAL	A ———	CHI	A	Cotton Nash
					and cash

Gordon Slade

Feb 1933	STL	N	Dazzy Vance	BKN	N	Jake Flowers
						Ownie Carroll
Dec 1933	CIN	N ———		STL	N	Waiver price

Jimmy Slagle

Jan 1900	PHI	N ———	WAS	N	Cash
June 1901	BOS	N ———	PHI	N	Shad Barry

Jim Slaton

Dec 9, 1977	DET	A	Rich Folkers	MIL	A	Ben Oglivie
Nov 29, 1978	MIL	A ———		DET	A	No compensation
						(free agent signing)
Dec 20, 1983	CAL	A ———		MIL	A	Bobby Clark

Jack Slattery

April 1903	CHI	A ———	CLE	A	Cash

Don Slaught

Jan 18, 1985	TEX	A ———	MIL	A	Danny Darwin
					Minor league
					C Bill Hance

(Part of a four-team trade involving Texas, Milwaukee, Kansas City, and New York Mets.)

Jan 18, 1985	MIL	A	Frank Wills	KC	A	Jim Sundberg

(Part of a four-team deal involving Texas, Milwaukee, Kansas City, and New York Mets.)

Nov 2, 1987	NY	A ———	TEX	A	Brad Arnsberg
Dec 4, 1989	PIT	N ———	NY	A	Jeff Robinson
					Minor league
					P Willie Smith

Enos Slaughter

April 11, 1954	NY	A ———	STL	N	Bill Virdon
					Mel Wright
					minor league
					OF Emil Tellinger

Enos Slaughter *continued*

May 11, 1955	KC	A	Johnny Sain	NY	A	Sonny Dixon
						and cash
Aug 25, 1956	NY	A ———		KC	A	Waiver price
Sept 12, 1959	MIL	N ———		NY	A	Waiver price

Lou Sleater

July 31, 1951	NY	A	Bobby Hogue	STL	A	Cliff Mapes
			Kermit Wahl			
			Tom Upton			
May 12, 1952	WAS	A	Freddie Marsh	STL	A	Cass Michaels
April 28, 1955	KC	A ———		NY	A	Cash
June 2, 1958	BAL	A ———		DET	A	Waiver price

Jim Small

Nov 20, 1957	KC	A ———	DET	A	*See Billy Martin*

Roy Smalley

June 1, 1976	MIN	A	Bill Singer	TEX	A	Bert Blyleven
			Mike Cubbage			Danny Thompson
			Jim Gideon			
			and $250,000.			
April 10, 1982	NY	A ———		MIN	A	Ron Davis
						Paul Boris
						Greg Gagne
July 17, 1984	CHI	A ———		NY	A	Doug Drabek
						Kevin Hickey
Feb 19, 1985	MIN	A ———		CHI	A	Randy Johnson
						Minor league
						OF Ron Scheer
Feb 8, 1988	CHI	A ———		MIN	A	Cash

Roy Smalley

March 20, 1954	MIL	N ———	CHI	N	Dave Cole
					and cash
April 30, 1955	PHI	N ———	MIL	N	Cash

Al Smith

Dec 20, 1937	STL	N ———	NY	N	Cash
Dec 29, 1937	PHI	N ———	STL	N	Waiver price

Al Smith

Dec 4, 1957	CHI	A	Early Wynn	CLE	A	Fred Hatfield
						Minnie Minoso
Jan 14, 1963	BAL	A	Luis Aparicio	CHI	A	Hoyt Wilhelm
						Pete Ward
						Ron Hansen
						Dave Nicholson
Dec 4, 1963	CLE	A	$25,000.	BAL	A	Willie Kirkland

Bill Smith

Dec 4, 1959	PHI	N	Bobby Gene Smith	STL	N	Carl Sawatski

Bob Smith

Oct 14, 1930	CHI	N	Jimmy Welsh	BOS	N	Bill McAfee
						Wes Schulmerich
Nov 30, 1932	CIN	N	Rollie Hemsley	CHI	N	Babe Herman
			Johnny Moore			
			Lance Richbourg			
Aug 2, 1933	BOS	N ———		CIN	N	Waiver price

Bob Smith

May 14, 1957	PIT	N ———	STL	N	Cash
June 13, 1959	DET	A ———	PIT	N	Waiver price

Bobby Gene Smith

Dec 4, 1959	PHI	N	Bill Smith	STL	N	Carl Sawatski

Date	Traded To		Traded With	Traded By		In Exchange For

Bobby Gene Smith continued

Date	Traded To		Traded With	Traded By		In Exchange For
April 26, 1962	CHI	N	——	NY	N	Sammy Taylor
June 5, 1962	STL	N	Daryl Robertson	CHI	N	Don Landrum Alex Grammas

Broadway Aleck Smith

Date	Traded To		Traded With	Traded By		In Exchange For
Jan 1900	BKN	N	Jimmy Sheckard Jerry Nops Frank Kitson Harry Howell Joe McGinnity	BAL	N	Cash

Bryn Smith

Date	Traded To		Traded With	Traded By		In Exchange For
Dec 7, 1977	MON	N	Rudy May Randy Miller	BAL	A	Don Stanhouse Joe Kerrigan Gary Roenicke
Nov 28, 1989	STL	N	——	MON	N	No compensation (free agent signing)

Carr Smith

Date	Traded To		Traded With	Traded By		In Exchange For
Dec 12, 1924	CLE	A	Byron Speece	WAS	A	Stan Coveleski

Charley Smith

Date	Traded To		Traded With	Traded By		In Exchange For
May 4, 1961	PHI	N	Don Demeter	LA	N	Dick Farrell Joe Koppe
Nov 28, 1961	CHI	A	John Buzhardt	PHI	N	Roy Sievers
April 23, 1964	NY	N	——	CHI	A	Chico Fernandez minor league C Bobby Catton and cash
Oct 20, 1965	STL	N	Al Jackson	NY	N	Ken Boyer
Dec 8, 1966	NY	A	——	STL	N	Roger Maris
Dec 6, 1968	SF	N	——	NY	A	Nate Oliver
March 28, 1969	CHI	N	——	SF	N	Cash

Charlie Smith

Date	Traded To		Traded With	Traded By		In Exchange For
Sept 1909	BOS	A	——	WAS	A	Doc Gessler
April 1911	CHI	N	——	BOS	A	Cash

Chris Smith

Date	Traded To		Traded With	Traded By		In Exchange For
March 31, 1980	MON	N	LaRue Washington	TEX	A	Rusty Staub
Feb 2, 1983	SF	N	——	MON	N	Jim Wohlford

Dick Smith

Date	Traded To		Traded With	Traded By		In Exchange For
Oct 11, 1962	NY	N	——	LA	N	Cash
Oct 15, 1964	LA	N	——	NY	N	Larry Miller

Earl Smith

Date	Traded To		Traded With	Traded By		In Exchange For
May 31, 1921	WAS	A	——	STL	A	Frank Ellerbe

Earl Smith

Date	Traded To		Traded With	Traded By		In Exchange For
June 7, 1923	BOS	N	Jesse Barnes	NY	N	Hank Gowdy Mule Watson
July 6, 1924	PIT	N	——	BOS	N	Cash
July 10, 1928	STL	N	——	PIT	N	Cash

Eddie Smith

Date	Traded To		Traded With	Traded By		In Exchange For
April 27, 1939	CHI	A	——	PHI	A	Waiver price

Elmer Smith

Date	Traded To		Traded With	Traded By		In Exchange For
Aug 8, 1900	NY	N	——	CIN	N	Cash
Jan 1901	PIT	N	——	NY	N	Cash
May 1901	BOS	N	——	PIT	N	Cash

Elmer Smith

Date	Traded To		Traded With	Traded By		In Exchange For
Aug 18, 1916	WAS	A	Joe Leonard	CLE	A	Joe Boehling Danny Moeller
June 13, 1917	CLE	A	——	WAS	A	$4,000.
Dec 24, 1921	BOS	A	George Burns Joe Harris	CLE	A	Stuffy McInnis
July 23, 1922	NY	A	Joe Dugan	BOS	A	Chick Fewster Elmer Miller Johnny Mitchell Lefty O'Doul and $50,000.

Frank Smith

Date	Traded To		Traded With	Traded By		In Exchange For
Aug 9, 1910	BOS	A	Billy Purtell	CHI	A	Harry Lord Amby McConnell
May 11, 1911	CIN	N	——	BOS	A	$5,000.
June 1915	BKN	F	——	BAL	F	Steve Evans

Frank Smith

Date	Traded To		Traded With	Traded By		In Exchange For
Dec 8, 1954	STL	N	——	CIN	N	Ray Jablonski Gerry Staley
April 10, 1956	CIN	N	——	STL	N	Waiver price

Fred Smith

Date	Traded To		Traded With	Traded By		In Exchange For
July 1915	BKN	F	——	BUF	F	Ed Gagnier Ed Lafitte

George Smith

Date	Traded To		Traded With	Traded By		In Exchange For
June 20, 1918	NY	N	——	CIN	N	Cash
July 15, 1918	BKN	N	——	NY	N	Cash
Oct 1918	NY	N	——	BKN	N	Cash
May 27, 1919	PHI	N	——	NY	N	Joe Oeschger
Feb 11, 1923	BKN	N	——	PHI	N	Clarence Mitchell

George Smith

Date	Traded To		Traded With	Traded By		In Exchange For
Oct 4, 1965	BOS	A	George Thomas	DET	A	Bill Monbouquette

Hal Smith

Date	Traded To		Traded With	Traded By		In Exchange For
Nov 18, 1954	BAL	A	——	NY	A	See Bob Turley
Aug 17, 1956	KC	A	——	BAL	A	Joe Ginsberg
Dec 15, 1959	PIT	N	——	KC	A	Ken Hamlin Dick Hall

Harry Smith

Date	Traded To		Traded With	Traded By		In Exchange For
Jan 1908	BOS	N	——	PIT	N	Cash

Heinie Smith

Date	Traded To		Traded With	Traded By		In Exchange For
June 1901	NY	N	——	PIT	N	Ed Doheny

Jack Smith

Date	Traded To		Traded With	Traded By		In Exchange For
April 19, 1926	BOS	N	——	STL	N	Cash

Jimmy Smith

Date	Traded To		Traded With	Traded By		In Exchange For
Sept 1915	BAL	F	Adam Johnson	CHI	F	Bill Bailey
Feb 10, 1916	PIT	N	Otto Knabe	BAL	F	Cash
Jan 1917	NY	N	——	PIT	N	Waiver price
Oct 1918	BOS	N	——	NY	N	Cash
Feb 1919	NY	N	——	BOS	N	Walter Holke
Feb 1919	CIN	N	——	NY	N	Cash
June 28, 1921	PHI	N	——	CIN	N	Cash

Lee Smith

Date	Traded To		Traded With	Traded By		In Exchange For
Dec 8, 1987	BOS	A	——	CHI	N	Calvin Schiraldi Al Nipper

Date	Traded To	Traded With	Traded By	In Exchange For

Lonnie Smith

Date	Traded To	Traded With	Traded By	In Exchange For
Nov 20, 1981	CLE A	Scott Munninghoff	PHI N	Bo Diaz
(Part of three-team trade involving Cleveland, Philadelphia, and St. Louis.)				
Nov 20, 1981	STL N	——	CLE A	Lary Sorensen
				Silvio Martinez
(Part of three-team trade involving Cleveland, Philadelphia, and St. Louis.)				
May 17, 1985	KC A	——	STL N	John Morris

Mike Smith

Date	Traded To	Traded With	Traded By	In Exchange For
Nov 14, 1988	BAL A	——	MON N	player to be named
(Montreal received P Doug Cline on December 7, 1988.)				

Milt Smith

Date	Traded To	Traded With	Traded By	In Exchange For
May 1, 1956	STL N		CIN N	Paul LaPalme

Nate Smith

Date	Traded To	Traded With	Traded By	In Exchange For
Sept 10, 1962	BAL A	——	LA A	Cash

Ozzie Smith

Date	Traded To	Traded With	Traded By	In Exchange For
Dec 10, 1981	STL N	Steve Mura	SD N	Sixto Lezcano
		Al Olmsted		Garry Templeton
				Luis DeLeon
(Templeton and Smith were exchanged on February 11, 1982; Olmsted and DeLeon were exchanged on February 19.)				

Paul Smith

Date	Traded To	Traded With	Traded By	In Exchange For
May 6, 1958	CHI N	——	PIT N	Cash

Pete Smith

Date	Traded To	Traded With	Traded By	In Exchange For
Dec 10, 1985	ATL N	——	PHI N	*See Steve Bedrosian*

Ray Smith

Date	Traded To	Traded With	Traded By	In Exchange For
Dec 7, 1984	SD N	——	MIN A	Floyd Chiffer

Red Smith

Date	Traded To	Traded With	Traded By	In Exchange For
Aug 10, 1914	BOS N	——	BKN N	Cash

Reggie Smith

Date	Traded To	Traded With	Traded By	In Exchange For
Oct 26, 1973	STL N	Ken Tatum	BOS A	Rick Wise
				Bernie Carbo
June 15, 1976	LA N	——	STL N	Joe Ferguson
				Bob Detherage
				minor league
				IF Fred Tisdale
Feb 27, 1982	SF N	——	LA N	No compensation
				(free agent signing)

Riverboat Smith

Date	Traded To	Traded With	Traded By	In Exchange For
March 9, 1959	CHI N	——	BOS A	Chuck Tanner
May 4, 1959	CLE A	——	CHI N	Randy Jackson

Roy Smith

Date	Traded To	Traded With	Traded By	In Exchange For
Sept 12, 1982	CLE A	Wil Culmer	PHI N	John Denny
		Jerry Reed		

Sherry Smith

Date	Traded To	Traded With	Traded By	In Exchange For
Sept 18, 1922	CLE A	——	BKN N	Waiver price

Syd Smith

Date	Traded To	Traded With	Traded By	In Exchange For
July 1908	STL A		PHI A	Bert Blue

Tommy Smith

Date	Traded To	Traded With	Traded By	In Exchange For
Dec 16, 1968	KC A	Buck Martinez	HOU N	Minor league
		and minor league		C John Jones
		IF Mickey Sinnerud		

Willie Smith

Date	Traded To	Traded With	Traded By	In Exchange For
April 28, 1964	LA A	——	DET A	Julio Navarro
Oct 13, 1966	CLE A	——	CAL A	Cash
June 28, 1968	CHI N	——	CLE A	Lou Johnson
Nov 30, 1970	CIN N	——	CHI N	Danny Breeden

Zane Smith

Date	Traded To	Traded With	Traded By	In Exchange For
July 2, 1989	MON N	——	ATL N	Sergio Valdez
				Minor league
				P Nate Minchey
				Minor league
				OF Kevin Dean

Mike Smithson

Date	Traded To	Traded With	Traded By	In Exchange For
April 9, 1982	TEX A	——	BOS A	John Henry Johnson
Dec 7, 1983	MIN A	John Butcher	TEX A	Gary Ward
		minor league		
		C Sam Sorce		
Dec 21, 1989	CAL A	——	BOS A	No compensation
				(free agent signing)

John Smoltz

Date	Traded To	Traded With	Traded By	In Exchange For
Aug 12, 1987	ATL N	——	DET A	Doyle Alexander

Homer Smoot

Date	Traded To	Traded With	Traded By	In Exchange For
July 25, 1906	CIN N	——	STL N	Carl Druhot
				Shad Barry

Harry Smythe

Date	Traded To	Traded With	Traded By	In Exchange For
May 28, 1934	BKN N	——	NY A	Waiver price

Duke Snider

Date	Traded To	Traded With	Traded By	In Exchange For
April 1, 1963	NY N	——	LA N	Cash
April 14, 1964	SF N	——	NY N	Cash

Van Snider

Date	Traded To	Traded With	Traded By	In Exchange For
Feb 15, 1988	CIN N	——	KC A	Jeff Montgomery
Dec 12, 1989	NY A	Tim Leary	CIN N	Hal Morris
				Minor league
				P Rodney Imes

Fred Snodgrass

Date	Traded To	Traded With	Traded By	In Exchange For
Aug 1915	BOS N	——	NY N	Cash

Frank Snyder

Date	Traded To	Traded With	Traded By	In Exchange For
July 1919	NY N	——	STL N	Ferdie Schupp

Gene Snyder

Date	Traded To	Traded With	Traded By	In Exchange For
Dec 23, 1958	LA N	Rip Repulski	PHI N	Sparky Anderson
		Jim Golden		

Jerry Snyder

Date	Traded To	Traded With	Traded By	In Exchange For
May 3, 1952	WAS A	*See Jackie Jensen*	NY A	——

Russ Snyder

Date	Traded To	Traded With	Traded By	In Exchange For
April 12, 1959	KC A	Tommy Carroll	NY A	Mike Baxes
				Bob Martyn

Date	Traded To	Traded With	Traded By		In Exchange For

Russ Snyder *continued*

Date	Traded To	Traded With	Traded By		In Exchange For
Jan 24, 1961	BAL A	Whitey Herzog	KC	A	Wayne Causey Jim Archer Bob Boyd Al Pilarcik
Nov 29, 1967	CHI A	Luis Aparicio John Matias	BAL	A	Don Buford Bruce Howard Roger Nelson
June 13, 1968	CLE A	——	CHI	A	Leon Wagner
April 4, 1970	MIL A	Max Alvis	CLE	A	Roy Foster Frank Coggins and cash

Eric Soderholm

Date	Traded To	Traded With	Traded By		In Exchange For
Nov 26, 1976	CHI A	——	MIN	A	No compensation (free agent signing)
June 15, 1979	TEX A	——	CHI	A	Ed Farmer Gary Holle
Nov 14, 1979	NY A	——	TEX	A	Minor league 3B Amos Lewis minor league P Ricky Burdette and cash

Tony Solaita

Date	Traded To	Traded With	Traded By		In Exchange For
July 14, 1976	CAL A	——	KC	A	Cash
Dec 5, 1978	MON N	——	CAL	A	Cash
July 30, 1979	TOR A	——	MON	N	Dyar Miller

Julio Solano

Date	Traded To	Traded With	Traded By		In Exchange For
Sept 30, 1987	SEA A	——	HOU	A	Minor league P Doug Givler

Eddie Solomon

Date	Traded To	Traded With	Traded By		In Exchange For
May 2, 1975	CHI N	Geoff Zahn	LA	N	Burt Hooton
March 28, 1980	PIT N	——	ATL	N	Minor league P Greg Field
June 14, 1982	CHI A	——	PIT	N	Jim Morrison

Moose Solters

Date	Traded To	Traded With	Traded By		In Exchange For
May 21, 1935	STL A	Cash	BOS	A	Oscar Melillo
Jan 17, 1937	CLE A	Ivy Andrews Lyn Lary	STL	A	Bill Knickerbocker Joe Vosmik Oral Hildebrand
Aug 2, 1939	STL A	——	CLE	A	Waiver price
Dec 8, 1939	CHI A	——	STL	A	Rip Radcliff

Bill Sommers

Date	Traded To	Traded With	Traded By		In Exchange For
Nov 18, 1947	STL A	——	BOS	A	See Ellis Kinder

Don Songer

Date	Traded To	Traded With	Traded By		In Exchange For
May 9, 1927	NY N	——	PIT	N	Cash

Lary Sorensen

Date	Traded To	Traded With	Traded By		In Exchange For
Dec 12, 1980	STL N	——	MIL	A	See Rollie Fingers
Nov 20, 1981	CLE A	Silvio Martinez	STL	N	Lonnie Smith
					(Part of three-team trade involving Cleveland, Philadelphia, and St. Louis.)
Jan 23, 1984	OAK A	——	CLE	A	No compensation (free agent signing)
Dec 18, 1984	CHI N	——	OAK	A	No compensation (free agent signing)
July 24, 1986	MON N	Tom Foley	PHI	N	Dan Schatzeder Skeeter Barnes

Paul Sorrento

Date	Traded To	Traded With	Traded By		In Exchange For
Nov 3, 1988	MIN A	Mike Cook Minor league P Rob Wassenaar	CAL	A	Bert Blyleven Minor league P Kevin Trudeau

Elias Sosa

Date	Traded To	Traded With	Traded By		In Exchange For
Oct 14, 1974	STL N	Ken Rudolph	SF	N	Marc Hill
May 28, 1975	ATL N	Ray Sadecki	STL	N	Ron Reed Wayne Nordhagen
June 23, 1976	LA N	Lee Lacy	ATL	N	Mike Marshall
Jan 31, 1978	PIT N	——	LA	N	Cash
April 4, 1978	OAK A	Miguel Dilone Mike Edwards	PIT	N	Manny Sanguillen
Jan 9, 1979	MON N	——	OAK	A	No compensation (free agent signing)
March 30, 1982	DET A	——	MON	N	Cash
Oct 7, 1982	SD N	——	DET	A	Cash

Sammy Sosa

Date	Traded To	Traded With	Traded By		In Exchange For
July 29, 1989	CHI A	Scott Fletcher Wilson Alvarez	TEX	A	Harold Baines Fred Manrique

Denny Sothern

Date	Traded To	Traded With	Traded By		In Exchange For
Aug 7, 1930	PIT N	——	PHI	N	Fred Brickell

Allen Sothoron

Date	Traded To	Traded With	Traded By		In Exchange For
Jan 1921	BOS A	——	STL	A	Waiver price
April 1921	CLE A	——	BOS	A	Waiver price

Steve Souchock

Date	Traded To	Traded With	Traded By		In Exchange For
Dec 14, 1948	CHI A	——	NY	A	Jim Delsing

Bill Southworth

Date	Traded To	Traded With	Traded By		In Exchange For
July 22, 1967	NY N	J. C. Martin	CHI	A	Ken Boyer

Billy Southworth

Date	Traded To	Traded With	Traded By		In Exchange For
Feb 23, 1921	BOS N	Fred Nicholson Walter Barbare and $15,000.	PIT	N	Rabbit Maranville
Nov 12, 1923	NY N	Joe Oeschger	BOS	N	Casey Stengel Dave Bancroft Bill Cunningham
		(Bancroft was named Boston manager.)			
June 14, 1926	STL N	——	NY	N	Heinie Mueller

Bob Spade

Date	Traded To	Traded With	Traded By		In Exchange For
April 1910	STL A	——	CIN	N	Cash

Warren Spahn

Date	Traded To	Traded With	Traded By		In Exchange For
Nov 23, 1964	NY N	——	MIL	N	Cash

Al Spangler

Date	Traded To	Traded With	Traded By		In Exchange For
June 1, 1965	CAL A	——	HOU	N	Don Lee

Tully Sparks

Date	Traded To	Traded With	Traded By		In Exchange For
Feb 1900	PHI N	Heinie Reitz	PIT	N	Duff Cooley

Joe Sparma

Date	Traded To	Traded With	Traded By		In Exchange For
Dec 3, 1969	MON N	——	DET	A	Jerry Robertson

Bob Speake

Date	Traded To	Traded With	Traded By		In Exchange For
April 3, 1958	SF N	Cash	CHI	N	Bobby Thomson

Tris Speaker

Date	Traded To	Traded With	Traded By		In Exchange For
April 12, 1916	CLE A	——	BOS	A	Sad Sam Jones Fred Thomas and $55,000.

Date	Traded To		Traded With	Traded By		In Exchange For

Byron Speece

| Dec 12, 1924 | CLE | A | Carr Smith | WAS | A | Stan Coveleski |

Chris Speier

April 27, 1977	MON	N	——	SF	N	Tim Foli
July 1, 1984	STL	N	——	MON	N	Mike Ramsey
Aug 19, 1984	MIN	A	——	STL	N	Cash and player to be named

(St. Louis received P Jay Pettibone on Oct. 2, 1984.)

| April 8, 1985 | CHI | N | —— | MIN | A | No compensation (free agent signing) |
| Dec 10, 1986 | SF | N | —— | CHI | N | No compensation (free agent signing) |

Stan Spence

Dec 13, 1941	WAS	A	Jack Wilson Johnny Welaj	BOS	A	Ken Chase
Dec 10, 1947	BOS	A	——	WAS	A	Leon Culberson Al Kozar
May 8, 1949	STL	A	Cash	BOS	A	Al Zarilla

Daryl Spencer

| Dec 15, 1959 | STL | N | Leon Wagner | SF | N | Don Blasingame |
| May 30, 1961 | LA | N | —— | STL | N | Bob Lillis Carl Warwick |

Glenn Spencer

| Dec 12, 1932 | NY | N | Gus Dugas | PIT | N | Freddie Lindstrom |

(Part of three-team trade involving New York, Philadelphia, and Pittsburgh.)

| Nov 15, 1933 | CIN | N | —— | NY | N | George Grantham |
| Jan 11, 1934 | STL | N | —— | CIN | N | Bob O'Farrell Syl Johnson |

(O'Farrell was named Cincinnati manager.)

Jim Spencer

May 20, 1973	TEX	A	Lloyd Allen	CAL	A	Mike Epstein Rich Hand Rick Stelmaszek
Dec 10, 1975	CAL	A	$100,000.	TEX	A	Bill Singer
Dec 11, 1975	CHI	A	Morris Nettles	CAL	A	Bill Melton Steve Dunning
Dec 12, 1977	NY	A	Tommy Cruz minor league P Bob Polinsky	CHI	A	Stan Thomas minor league P Ed Ricks
May 20, 1981	OAK	A	Tom Underwood	NY	A	Dave Revering Mike Patterson minor league P Chuck Dougherty

Roy Spencer

| Jan 7, 1933 | CLE | A | —— | WAS | A | Luke Sewell |

Tom Spencer

| Nov 6, 1976 | CHI | A | —— | CIN | N | Hugh Yancy |

Tubby Spencer

| Dec 12, 1908 | BOS | A | —— | STL | A | Lou Criger |

Rob Sperring

| Feb 11, 1977 | SF | N | Bill Madlock | CHI | N | Bobby Murcer Steve Ontiveros minor league P Andy Muhlstock |
| March 26, 1977 | HOU | N | Willie Crawford | SF | N | Rob Andrews and cash |

Ed Spiezio

| Dec 3, 1968 | SD | N | Danny Breeden Ron Davis minor league P Phil Knuckles | STL | N | Dave Giusti |
| July 9, 1972 | CHI | A | —— | SD | N | Don Eddy and cash |

Charlie Spikes

| Nov 27, 1972 | CLE | A | —— | NY | A | See Graig Nettles |
| Dec 9, 1977 | DET | A | —— | CLE | A | Tom Veryzer |

Dan Spillner

| June 14, 1978 | CLE | A | —— | SD | N | Dennis Kinney |
| June 21, 1984 | CHI | A | —— | CLE | A | Jim Siwy |

Harry Spilman

| June 8, 1981 | HOU | N | —— | CIN | N | Rafael Landestoy |

Scipio Spinks

| April 15, 1972 | STL | N | Lance Clemons | HOU | N | Jerry Reuss |
| March 23, 1974 | CHI | N | —— | STL | N | Jim Hickman |

Al Spohrer

| June 15, 1928 | BOS | N | Ben Cantwell Bill Clarkson Virgil Barnes | NY | N | Joe Genewich |

Ed Sprague

Oct 20, 1970	CIN	N	——	OAK	A	Cash
July 27, 1973	STL	N	Roe Skidmore	CIN	N	Ed Crosby minor league C Gene Dusan
Sept 4, 1973	MIL	A	——	STL	N	Cash

George Spriggs

| March 15, 1971 | NY | N | —— | KC | A | Cash |

Jack Spring

June 24, 1958	WAS	A	——	BOS	A	Bud Byerly
May 15, 1964	CHI	N	——	LA	A	Cash
June 15, 1964	STL	N	See Lou Brock	CHI	N	

Bobby Sprowl

| June 13, 1979 | HOU | N | Pete Ladd and cash | BOS | A | Bob Watson |
| Dec 21, 1983 | BAL | A | —— | HOU | N | Craig Minetto |

Eddie Stack

| Dec 1911 | BKN | N | —— | PHI | N | Cash |
| July 1913 | CHI | N | Cash | BKN | N | Ed Reulbach |

Marv Staehle

| July 29, 1967 | CLE | A | Jim King | CHI | A | Rocky Colavito |
| Sept 13, 1969 | MON | N | —— | SEA | A | Cash |

Bill Stafford

| June 10, 1966 | KC | A | Gil Blanco Roger Repoz | NY | A | Fred Talbot Billy Bryan |

Steve Staggs

| March 25, 1978 | OAK | A | —— | TOR | A | Sheldon Mallory |

Jake Stahl

Date	Traded To	Traded With	Traded By	In Exchange For
Jan 16, 1904	WAS A	—	BOS A	Cash
March 1907	CHI A	—	WAS A	Cash
(Stahl refused to report and was sold by Chicago to the New York Yankees.)				
Oct 1907	NY A	—	CHI A	Cash
July 10, 1908	BOS A	—	NY A	Cash

Larry Stahl

Date	Traded To	Traded With	Traded By	In Exchange For
Oct 14, 1966	NY N	—	KC A	Waiver price
Nov 30, 1972	CIN N	—	SD N	Cash

Roy Staiger

Date	Traded To	Traded With	Traded By	In Exchange For
Dec 9, 1977	NY A	—	NY N	Sergio Ferrer

Tuck Stainback

Date	Traded To	Traded With	Traded By	In Exchange For
April 16, 1938	STL N	Curt Davis Clyde Shoun and $185,000.	CHI N	Dizzy Dean
June 1938	PHI N	—	STL N	Waiver price
July 11, 1938	BKN N	—	PHI N	Gib Brack

Gerry Staley

Date	Traded To	Traded With	Traded By	In Exchange For
Dec 8, 1954	CIN N	Ray Jablonski	STL N	Frank Smith
Sept 11, 1955	NY A	—	CIN N	Waiver price
May 28, 1956	CHI A	—	NY A	Waiver price
June 10, 1961	KC A	Wes Covington Bob Shaw Stan Johnson	CHI A	Ray Herbert Don Larsen Andy Carey Al Pilarcik
Aug 2, 1961	DET A	Reno Bertoia	KC A	Ozzie Virgil Bill Fischer

Tracy Stallard

Date	Traded To	Traded With	Traded By	In Exchange For
Dec 11, 1962	NY N	Pumpsie Green Al Moran	BOS A	Felix Mantilla
Dec 7, 1964	STL N	Elio Chacon	NY N	Johnny Lewis Gordie Richardson

Virgil Stallcup

Date	Traded To	Traded With	Traded By	In Exchange For
May 13, 1952	STL N	Dick Sisler	CIN N	Eddie Kazak Wally Westlake

Oscar Stanage

Date	Traded To	Traded With	Traded By	In Exchange For
May 17, 1906	CIN N	—	STL N	Cash

Charley Stanceu

Date	Traded To	Traded With	Traded By	In Exchange For
May 1946	PHI N	—	NY A	Waiver price

Lee Stange

Date	Traded To	Traded With	Traded By	In Exchange For
June 15, 1964	CLE A	George Banks	MIN A	Mudcat Grant
June 2, 1966	BOS A	Don McMahon	CLE A	Dick Radatz
June 29, 1970	CHI A	—	BOS A	Cash

Don Stanhouse

Date	Traded To	Traded With	Traded By	In Exchange For
March 4, 1972	TEX A	Jim Panther	OAK A	Denny McLain
Dec 5, 1974	MON N	Pete Mackanin	TEX A	Willie Davis
Dec 7, 1977	BAL A	Joe Kerrigan Gary Roenicke	MON N	Rudy May Randy Miller Bryn Smith
Nov 17, 1979	LA N	—	BAL A	No compensation (free agent signing)

Eddie Stanky

Date	Traded To	Traded With	Traded By	In Exchange For
June 6, 1944	BKN N	—	CHI N	Bob Chipman

Eddie Stanky *continued*

Date	Traded To	Traded With	Traded By	In Exchange For
March 6, 1948	BOS N	—	BKN N	Bama Rowell Ray Sanders and $40,000.
Dec 14, 1949	NY N	Alvin Dark	BOS N	Sid Gordon Buddy Kerr Willard Marshall Red Webb
Dec 11, 1951	STL N	—	NY N	Chuck Diering Max Lanier
(Stanky was named St. Louis manager.)				

Fred Stanley

Date	Traded To	Traded With	Traded By	In Exchange For
June 11, 1972	SD N	—	CLE A	Mike Kilkenny
Nov 3, 1980	OAK A	Brian Doyle	NY A	Mike Morgan

Leroy Stanton

Date	Traded To	Traded With	Traded By	In Exchange For
Dec 10, 1971	CAL A	Nolan Ryan Don Rose Francisco Estrada	NY N	Jim Fregosi

Mike Stanton

Date	Traded To	Traded With	Traded By	In Exchange For
March 29, 1978	TOR A	—	HOU N	Cash
Dec 7, 1981	STL N	—	CLE A	Cash
Feb 8, 1982	CLE A	—	STL N	Cash

Dave Stapleton

Date	Traded To	Traded With	Traded By	In Exchange For
Dec 23, 1986	SEA A	—	BOS A	No compensation (free agent signing)

Charlie Starr

Date	Traded To	Traded With	Traded By	In Exchange For
July 16, 1909	PHI N	Johnny Bates	BOS N	Buster Brown Lew Richie Dave Shean
Sept 1909	BOS N	—	PIT N	Cash

Dick Starr

Date	Traded To	Traded With	Traded By	In Exchange For
Dec 13, 1948	STL A	Sherm Lollar Red Embree and $100,000.	NY A	Fred Sanford Roy Partee
July 30, 1951	WAS A	—	STL A	Fred Sanford

Ray Starr

Date	Traded To	Traded With	Traded By	In Exchange For
Oct 10, 1932	NY N	Gus Mancuso	STL N	Ethan Allen Bob O'Farrell Bill Walker Jim Mooney
June 12, 1933	BOS N	—	NY N	Cash
May 27, 1944	PIT N	—	CIN N	Cash
June 23, 1945	CHI N	—	PIT N	Waiver price

Jigger Statz

Date	Traded To	Traded With	Traded By	In Exchange For
July 1920	BOS A	—	NY N	Cash

Rusty Staub

Date	Traded To	Traded With	Traded By	In Exchange For
Jan 22, 1969	MON N	—	HOU N	Jesus Alou Donn Clendenon Jack Billingham Skip Guinn and $100,000.
(Clendenon refused to report, and Houston sent Billingham, Guinn, and Cash on April 8, 1969.)				
April 5, 1972	NY N	—	MON N	Tim Foli Ken Singleton Mike Jorgensen
Dec 12, 1975	DET A	Bill Laxton	NY N	Mickey Lolich Billy Baldwin

Date	Traded To		Traded With	Traded By		In Exchange For

Rusty Staub *continued*

Date	Traded To		Traded With	Traded By		In Exchange For
July 20, 1979	MON	N	———	DET	A	Minor league C Randy Schafer and cash
March 31, 1980	TEX	A	———	MON	N	LaRue Washington Chris Smith
Dec 16, 1980	NY	N	———	TEX	A	No compensation (free agent signing)

John Stearns

Dec 3, 1974	NY	N	Del Unser Mac Scarce	PHI	N	Tug McGraw Don Hahn Dave Schneck

Bill Steele

July 1914	BKN	N	———	STL	N	Cash

Bob Steele

June 14, 1917	PIT	N	———	STL	N	Doug Baird
June 1918	NY	N	———	PIT	N	Cash

Elmer Steele

Feb 1910	PIT	N	———	BOS	A	Waiver price
Sept 16, 1911	BKN	N	———	PIT	N	Cash

Farmer Steelman

Jan 1900	BKN	N	———	LOU	N	Cash
April 1901	PHI	A	———	BKN	N	Cash

James Steels

Aug 30, 1989	MON	N	———	SF	N	Player to be named

Bill Steen

June 1915	DET	A	———	CLE	A	Cash

John Stefero

Dec 8, 1986	MON	N	———	BAL	A	Rene Gonzales

(Baltimore received Gonzales on Dec. 16, 1986, also completing Dennis Martinez deal.)

Dave Stegman

Dec 12, 1980	SD	N	———	DET	A	Dennis Kinney

Bill Stein

Dec 19, 1980	TEX	A	———	SEA	A	No compensation (free agent signing)

Justin Stein

June 10, 1938	CIN	N	———	PHI	N	Buck Jordan

Randy Stein

June 7, 1979	SEA	A	———	MIL	A	Paul Mitchell

Ray Steineder

May 25, 1924	PHI	N	———	PIT	N	Cash

Harry Steinfeldt

March 1906	CHI	N	———	CIN	N	Hans Lobert Jake Weimer
March 1911	BOS	N	———	CHI	N	Cash

Rick Stelmaszek

May 20, 1973	CAL	A	*See Mike Epstein*	TEX	A	———
July 28, 1974	CHI	N	———	CAL	A	Horacio Pina

Casey Stengel

Jan 9, 1918	PIT	N	George Cutshaw	BKN	N	Chuck Ward Burleigh Grimes Al Mamaux
Aug 1919	PHI	N	———	PIT	N	Possum Whitted
July 1, 1921	NY	N	Johnny Rawlings Red Causey	PHI	N	Goldie Rapp Lee King Lance Richbourg
Nov 12, 1923	BOS	N	Dave Bancroft Bill Cunningham	NY	N	Billy Southworth Joe Oeschger

(Bancroft was named Boston manager.)

Dave Stenhouse

Dec 15, 1961	WAS	A	Bob Schmidt	CIN	N	Johnny Klippstein Marty Keough

Mike Stenhouse

Jan 9, 1985	MIN	A	———	MON	N	Jack O'Connor
Dec 12, 1985	BOS	A	———	MIN	A	Charlie Mitchell

Rennie Stennett

Nov 29, 1979	SF	N	———	PIT	N	No compensation (free agent signing)

Buzz Stephen

June 15, 1970	BAL	A	Dick Baney	MIL	A	Dave May

Bryan Stephens

Nov 20, 1947	STL	A	Dick Kokos Joe Frazier and $25,000.	CLE	A	Bob Muncrief Walt Judnich

Gene Stephens

June 9, 1960	BAL	A	———	BOS	A	Willie Tasby
June 8, 1961	KC	A	———	BAL	A	Marv Throneberry

Vern Stephens

Nov 17, 1947	BOS	A	Jack Kramer	STL	A	Roy Partee Jim Wilson Al Widmar Eddie Pellagrini Pete Layden Joe Ostrowski and $310,000.
Feb 9, 1953	CHI	A	———	BOS	A	Hal Brown Marv Grissom Bill Kennedy
July 20, 1953	STL	A	———	CHI	A	Waiver price

Bobby Stephenson

June 14, 1956	NY	N	*See Red Schoendienst*	STL	N	———

Earl Stephenson

Dec 3, 1971	MIL	A	Brock Davis Jim Colborn	CHI	N	Jose Cardenal
Oct 31, 1972	PHI	N	———	MIL	A	*See Don Money*

Johnny Stephenson

June 12, 1967	CHI	N	Rob Gardner	NY	N	Bob Hendley

Date	Traded To	Traded With	Traded By	In Exchange For

Phil Stephenson

Date	Traded To	Traded With	Traded By	In Exchange For
Aug 30, 1989	SD N	Calvin Schiraldi Darrin Jackson	CHI N	Marvell Wynne Luis Salazar

(San Diego Received Stephenson on Sept. 5, 1989).

Ed Stevens

Date	Traded To	Traded With	Traded By	In Exchange For
Nov 14, 1947	PIT N	——	BKN N	Cash

R C Stevens

Date	Traded To	Traded With	Traded By	In Exchange For
Dec 16, 1960	WAS A	Bennie Daniels Harry Bright	PIT N	Bobby Shantz

Bud Stewart

Date	Traded To	Traded With	Traded By	In Exchange For
May 13, 1948	WAS A	——	NY A	Leon Culberson and $15,000.
Dec 11, 1950	CHI A	——	WAS A	Mike McCormick

Dave Stewart

Date	Traded To	Traded With	Traded By	In Exchange For
Aug 19, 1983	TEX A	Ricky Wright and $200,000.	LA N	Rick Honeycutt
Sept 13, 1985	PHI N	——	TEX A	Rick Surhoff

Jimmy Stewart

Date	Traded To	Traded With	Traded By	In Exchange For
May 22, 1967	CHI A	——	CHI N	Cash
Nov 29, 1971	HOU N	——	CIN N	*See Joe Morgan*

Lefty Stewart

Date	Traded To	Traded With	Traded By	In Exchange For
Jan 15, 1927	STL A	Frank O'Rourke Billy Mullen Otto Miller	DET A	Marty McManus Bobby LaMotte Pinky Hargrave
Dec 14, 1932	WAS A	Goose Goslin Fred Schulte	STL A	Sammy West Carl Reynolds Lloyd Brown and $20,000.
May 14, 1935	CLE A	——	WAS A	Belve Bean

Sammy Stewart

Date	Traded To	Traded With	Traded By	In Exchange For
Dec 17, 1985	BOS A	——	BAL A	Jackie Gutierrez

Stuffy Stewart

Date	Traded To	Traded With	Traded By	In Exchange For
Jan 21, 1919	PHI N	Doug Baird Gene Packard	STL N	Milt Stock Pickles Dillhoefer Dixie Davis

Dick Stigman

Date	Traded To	Traded With	Traded By	In Exchange For
April 2, 1962	MIN A	Vic Power	CLE A	Pedro Ramos
April 6, 1966	BOS A	minor league 1B Jose Calero	MIN A	Russ Nixon Chuck Schilling
Aug 15, 1966	CIN N	Rollie Sheldon	BOS A	Hank Fischer

(Cincinnati received Stigman and Sheldon on December 15, 1966.)

Royle Stillman

Date	Traded To	Traded With	Traded By	In Exchange For
Dec 2, 1971	BAL A	——	LA N	*See Frank Robinson*

Kurt Stillwell

Date	Traded To	Traded With	Traded By	In Exchange For
Nov 6, 1987	KC A	Ted Power	CIN N	Danny Jackson Angel Salazar

Craig Stimac

Date	Traded To	Traded With	Traded By	In Exchange For
Jan 27, 1982	CLE A	——	SD N	Cash

Bob Stinson

Date	Traded To	Traded With	Traded By	In Exchange For
Oct 5, 1970	STL N	Ted Sizemore	LA N	Dick Allen
Nov 3, 1971	HOU N	——	STL N	Marty Martinez
March 28, 1973	MON N	——	HOU N	Cash
March 31, 1975	KC A	——	MON N	Cash

Snuffy Stirnweiss

Date	Traded To	Traded With	Traded By	In Exchange For
June 15, 1950	STL A	Jim Delsing Don Johnson Duane Pillette and $50,000.	NY A	Tom Ferrick Joe Ostrowski Leo Thomas Sid Schacht
April 1, 1951	CLE A	Merrill Combs	STL A	Freddie Marsh and $35,000.

Chuck Stobbs

Date	Traded To	Traded With	Traded By	In Exchange For
Nov 13, 1951	CHI A	Mel Hoderlein	BOS A	Randy Gumpert Don Lenhardt
Dec 10, 1952	WAS A	——	CHI A	Mike Fornieles
July 9, 1958	STL N	——	WAS A	Waiver price

Milt Stock

Date	Traded To	Traded With	Traded By	In Exchange For
Jan 1915	PHI N	Al Demaree Bert Adams	NY N	Hans Lobert
Jan 21, 1919	STL N	Pickles Dillhoefer Dixie Davis	PHI N	Doug Baird Stuffy Stewart Gene Packard
April 27, 1924	BKN N	——	STL N	Mike Gonzalez

Wes Stock

Date	Traded To	Traded With	Traded By	In Exchange For
June 15, 1964	KC A	——	BAL A	Charlie Lau

Bob Stoddard

Date	Traded To	Traded With	Traded By	In Exchange For
April 18, 1986	SD N	Minor league OF Kevin Russ	OAK A	Rusty Tillman

Tim Stoddard

Date	Traded To	Traded With	Traded By	In Exchange For
Dec 8, 1983	OAK A	——	BAL A	Wayne Gross
March 26, 1984	CHI N	——	OAK A	Minor leaguers P Stan Kyles and OF Stan Boderick
Jan 8, 1985	SD N	——	CHI N	No compensation (free agent signing)
July 9, 1986	NY A	——	SD N	Ed Whitson

Dean Stone

Date	Traded To	Traded With	Traded By	In Exchange For
April 29, 1957	BOS A	Bob Chakales	WAS A	Milt Bolling Russ Kemmerer Faye Throneberry
March 15, 1959	STL N	——	BOS A	Nels Chittum
June 22, 1962	CHI A	——	HOU N	Russ Kemmerer

George Stone

Date	Traded To	Traded With	Traded By	In Exchange For
Nov 2, 1972	NY N	Felix Millan	ATL N	Gary Gentry Danny Frisella
Feb 24, 1976	TEX A	——	NY N	Bill Hands

George Stone

Date	Traded To	Traded With	Traded By	In Exchange For
Jan 16, 1904	WAS A	——	BOS A	Cash
Jan 16, 1905	BOS A	——	WAS A	Cash
Jan 16, 1905	STL A	——	BOS A	Jesse Burkett

Jeff Stone

Date	Traded To	Traded With	Traded By	In Exchange For
March 21, 1988	BAL A	Rick Schu Keith Hughes	PHI N	Mike Young player to be named

(Philadelphia received OF Frank Bellino on June 14, 1988.)

Date	Traded To	Traded With	Traded By	In Exchange For

John Stone

| Dec 20, 1933 | WAS A | —— | DET A | Goose Goslin |

Ron Stone

| Jan 20, 1969 | PHI N | —— | BAL A | Clay Dalrymple |

Steve Stone

Nov 28, 1972	CHI A	Ken Henderson	SF N	Tom Bradley
Dec 11, 1973	CHI N	Ken Frailing Steve Swisher Jim Kremmel	CHI A	Ron Santo
Nov 24, 1976	CHI A	——	CHI N	No compensation (free agent signing)
Nov 29, 1978	BAL A	——	CHI A	No compensation (free agent signing)

Bill Stoneman

| April 4, 1974 | CAL A | —— | MON N | Cash |

Alan Storke

| Aug 19, 1909 | STL N | Jap Barbeau | PIT N | Bobby Byrne |
| Feb 1910 | CIN N | Fred Beebe | STL N | Miller Huggins Rebel Oakes Frank Corridon |

Allyn Stout

| May 7, 1933 | CIN N | —— | STL N | See Leo Durocher |
| Dec 14, 1934 | NY N | Mark Koenig | CIN N | Billy Myers and cash |

George Stovall

| Jan 1912 | STL A | —— | CLE A | Lefty George |

Jesse Stovall

| Jan 1904 | DET A | Ed Killian | CLE A | Billy Lush |

Mike Strahler

| Nov 28, 1972 | CAL A | —— | LA N | See Andy Messersmith |
| Dec 6, 1973 | MIL A | —— | DET A | Ray Newman |

Joe Strain

| Dec 12, 1980 | CHI N | Phil Nastu | SF N | Jerry Martin Jesus Figueroa minor league IF Mike Turgeon |

Bob Strampe

| Nov 18, 1974 | SD N | Ed Brinkman Dick Sharon | DET A | Nate Colbert |

(Part of three-team trade involving San Diego, Detroit, and St. Louis Cardinals.)

Sammy Strang

Feb 1901	NY N	——	CHI N	Jack Doyle
March 1903	BKN N	——	CHI N	Cash
Feb 1905	NY N	——	BKN N	Cash

Alan Strange

| June 29, 1935 | WAS A | —— | STL A | Lyn Lary |

Gabby Street

| June 6, 1905 | BOS N | —— | CIN N | Cash |
| July 30, 1905 | CIN N | —— | BOS N | Cash |

Gabby Street *continued*

| Dec 1911 | NY A | Jack Lelivelt | WAS A | John Knight Roxy Roach |

George Strickland

| Aug 18, 1952 | CLE A | Ted Wilks | PIT N | Johnny Berardino minor league P Charlie Sipple and $50,000. |

Jake Striker

| Dec 6, 1959 | CHI A | —— | CLE A | See Norm Cash |

Nick Strincevich

| May 7, 1941 | PIT N | —— | BOS N | Lloyd Waner |
| May 15, 1948 | PHI N | —— | PIT N | Cash |

Joe Stripp

March 14, 1932	BKN N	Tony Cuccinello Clyde Sukeforth	CIN N	Babe Herman Wally Gilbert Ernie Lombardi
Oct 4, 1937	STL N	Johnny Cooney Jim Bucher Roy Henshaw	BKN N	Leo Durocher
Aug 1, 1938	BOS N	——	STL N	Cash
Dec 13, 1938	BKN N	——	BOS N	Fred Frankhouse

John Strohmayer

| July 16, 1973 | NY N | —— | MON N | Cash |

Brent Strom

| Nov 27, 1972 | CLE A | Bob Rauch | NY N | Phil Hennigan |
| June 15, 1974 | SD N | minor league P Jerry Lee | CLE A | Steve Arlin |

Ed Stroud

| June 15, 1967 | WAS A | —— | CHI A | Jim King |
| March 29, 1971 | CHI A | —— | WAS A | Tom McCraw |

Steve Stroughter

| Dec 19, 1980 | MIN A | —— | SEA A | Mike Bacsik |

Amos Strunk

| Dec 14, 1917 | BOS A | Joe Bush Wally Schang | PHI A | Vean Gregg Merlin Kopp Pinch Thomas and $60,000. |
| June 27, 1919 | PHI A | Jack Barry | BOS A | Braggo Roth Red Shannon |

(Barry refused to report, and retired.)

| July 23, 1920 | CHI A | —— | PHI A | Waiver price |
| Aug 1924 | PHI A | —— | CHI A | Waiver price |

Dick Stuart

Nov 20, 1962	BOS A	Jack Lamabe	PIT N	Jim Pagliaroni Don Schwall
Nov 29, 1964	PHI N	——	BOS A	Dennis Bennett
Feb 22, 1966	NY N	——	PHI N	Jimmie Schaffer Bobby Klaus Wayne Graham

Marlin Stuart

| Aug 14, 1952 | STL A | See Vic Wertz | DET A | —— |
| July 4, 1954 | NY A | —— | BAL A | Waiver price |

Date	Traded To	Traded With	Traded By	In Exchange For

Bill Stumpf

Date	Traded To	Traded With	Traded By	In Exchange For
May 20, 1913	CLE A	Jack Lelivelt	NY A	Roger Peckinpaugh

John Stuper

Date	Traded To	Traded With	Traded By	In Exchange For
Sept 10, 1984	CIN N	——	STL N	Paul Householder
Dec 19, 1985	MON N	——	CIN N	*See Bill Gullickson*

Tom Sturdivant

Date	Traded To	Traded With	Traded By	In Exchange For
May 26, 1959	KC A	Johnny Kucks Jerry Lumpe	NY A	Hector Lopez Ralph Terry
Dec 3, 1959	BOS A	——	KC A	Pete Daley
June 29, 1961	PIT N	——	WAS A	Tom Cheney
May 4, 1963	DET A	——	PIT N	Cash
July 23, 1963	KC A	——	DET A	Cash

Bobby Sturgeon

Date	Traded To	Traded With	Traded By	In Exchange For
March 1, 1948	BOS N	——	CHI N	Dick Culler

Ken Suarez

Date	Traded To	Traded With	Traded By	In Exchange For
Dec 2, 1971	TEX A	——	CLE A	*See Del Unser*
Feb 12, 1974	CLE A	——	TEX A	Leo Cardenas
Sept 12, 1974	CAL A	Rusty Torres and cash	CLE A	Frank Robinson

Jim Suchecki

Date	Traded To	Traded With	Traded By	In Exchange For
May 17, 1951	STL A	Matt Batts Jim McDonald and $100,000.	BOS A	Les Moss
March 4, 1952	PIT N	——	STL A	Cash
May 5, 1952	CHI A	——	PIT N	Waiver price

Bill Sudakis

Date	Traded To	Traded With	Traded By	In Exchange For
March 27, 1972	NY N	——	LA N	Cash
March 28, 1973	TEX A	——	NY N	Bill McNulty
Dec 7, 1973	NY A	——	TEX A	Cash
Dec 3, 1974	CAL A	——	NY A	Skip Lockwood

Willie Sudhoff

Date	Traded To	Traded With	Traded By	In Exchange For
Dec 1905	WAS A	——	STL A	Beany Jacobson

Joe Sugden

Date	Traded To	Traded With	Traded By	In Exchange For
Feb 1902	STL A	——	CHI A	Cash

Gus Suhr

Date	Traded To	Traded With	Traded By	In Exchange For
July 28, 1939	PHI N	——	PIT N	Max Butcher

Clyde Sukeforth

Date	Traded To	Traded With	Traded By	In Exchange For
March 14, 1932	BKN N	Tony Cuccinello Joe Stripp	CIN N	Babe Herman Wally Gilbert Ernie Lombardi

Billy Sullivan

Date	Traded To	Traded With	Traded By	In Exchange For
Jan 29, 1936	CLE A	——	CIN N	Cash
Feb 10, 1938	STL A	Ed Cole Roy Hughes	CLE A	Rollie Hemsley
Jan 30, 1940	DET A	——	STL A	
March 13, 1942	BKN N	——	DET A	Cash

Denny Sullivan

Date	Traded To	Traded With	Traded By	In Exchange For
Sept 1908	CLE A	——	BOS A	Cash

Frank Sullivan

Date	Traded To	Traded With	Traded By	In Exchange For
Dec 15, 1960	PHI N	——	BOS A	Gene Conley

Haywood Sullivan

Date	Traded To	Traded With	Traded By	In Exchange For
Dec 29, 1960	KC A	——	WAS A	Marty Kutyna and cash

Joe Sullivan

Date	Traded To	Traded With	Traded By	In Exchange For
June 20, 1941	PIT N	——	BOS N	Cash

John Sullivan

Date	Traded To	Traded With	Traded By	In Exchange For
May 11, 1921	CHI N	——	BOS N	Cash

John Sullivan

Date	Traded To	Traded With	Traded By	In Exchange For
Oct 4, 1948	STL A	Tom Ferrick and $25,000.	WAS A	Sam Dente

Marc Sullivan

Date	Traded To	Traded With	Traded By	In Exchange For
Dec 14, 1987	HOU N	——	BOS A	player to be named

(Boston received SS Randy Randle on October 4, 1988.)

Homer Summa

Date	Traded To	Traded With	Traded By	In Exchange For
Jan 5, 1929	PHI A	——	CLE A	Cash

Champ Summers

Date	Traded To	Traded With	Traded By	In Exchange For
April 6, 1975	CHI N	Cash	OAK A	Jim Todd
Feb 16, 1977	CIN N	——	CHI N	Dave Schneck
May 25, 1979	DET A	——	CIN N	Sheldon Burnside
March 4, 1982	SF N	——	DET A	Enos Cabell and cash
Dec 6, 1983	SD N	——	SF N	Joe Pittman minor league OF Tommy Francis

Jim Sundberg

Date	Traded To	Traded With	Traded By	In Exchange For
Dec 8, 1983	MIL A	——	TEX A	Ned Yost minor league P Dan Scarpetta
Jan 18, 1985	KC A	——	MIL A	Frank Wills Don Slaught

(Part of a four-team deal involving Texas, Milwaukee, Kansas City, and New York Mets.)

Date	Traded To	Traded With	Traded By	In Exchange For
March 26, 1987	CHI N	——	KC A	Thad Bosley Dave Gumpert

Steve Sundra

Date	Traded To	Traded With	Traded By	In Exchange For
Dec 11, 1935	NY A	Monte Pearson	CLE A	Johnny Allen
March 27, 1941	WAS A	——	NY A	Cash
June 7, 1942	STL A	Mike Chartak	WAS A	Roy Cullenbine Bill Trotter

Rick Surhoff

Date	Traded To	Traded With	Traded By	In Exchange For
Sept 13, 1985	TEX A	——	PHI N	Dave Stewart
July 26, 1986	CHI N	Minor league P Bryan Dial	TEX A	Ron Meridith

Max Surkont

Date	Traded To	Traded With	Traded By	In Exchange For
Dec 26, 1953	PIT N	Sid Gordon Sam Jethroe Curt Raydon Fred Walters minor league P Larry Lasalle	MIL N	Danny O'Connell
May 5, 1956	STL N	——	PIT N	Luis Arroyo

Date	Traded To		Traded With	Traded By		In Exchange For

George Susce

| May 12, 1958 | DET | A | —— | BOS | A | Waiver price |

Rick Sutcliffe

Dec 9, 1981	CLE	A	Jack Perconte	LA	N	Jorge Orta
						Larry White
						Jack Fimple
June 13, 1984	CHI	N	George Frazier	CLE	A	Mel Hall
			Ron Hassey			Joe Carter
						Don Schulze
						Minor league
						P Darryl Banks

Gary Sutherland

Dec 3, 1973	DET	A	Jim Ray	HOU	N	Fred Scherman
						and cash
June 10, 1976	MIL	A	——	DET	A	Pedro Garcia

Bruce Sutter

Dec 9, 1980	STL	N	——	CHI	N	Leon Durham
						Ken Reitz
						Tye Waller
Dec 7, 1984	ATL	N	——	STL	N	

(Free agent signing) (St. Louis claimed SS Argenis Salazar from Montreal in the compensation draft.)

Jack Sutthoff

| July 20, 1904 | PHI | N | Frank Corridon | CHI | N | Shad Barry |

Don Sutton

Dec 4, 1980	HOU	N	——	LA	N	No compensation
						(free agent signing)
Aug 30, 1982	MIL	A	——	HOU	N	Kevin Bass
						Frank DiPino
						Mike Madden
						and cash
Dec 7, 1984	OAK	A	——	MIL	A	Ray Burris
						minor league
						P Eric Barry
						and a player
						to be named later
Sept 10, 1985	CAL	A	——	OAK	A	Two players to be named

(Oakland received P Robert Sharpnack and OF Jerome Nelson on Sept. 25, 1985.)

Johnny Sutton

| Oct 22, 1976 | STL | N | —— | TEX | A | Mike Wallace |

Bill Sweeney

| June 24, 1907 | BOS | N | Newt Randall | CHI | N | Del Howard |
| Feb 1914 | CHI | N | Cash | BOS | N | Johnny Evers |

Rick Sweet

| May 21, 1982 | SEA | A | —— | NY | N | Cash |

Leo Sweetland

| Oct 13, 1930 | CHI | N | —— | PHI | N | Cash |

Steve Swetonic

| Feb 23, 1934 | BOS | N | —— | PIT | N | Cash |

Bill Swift

| Dec 8, 1939 | BOS | N | Cash | PIT | N | Danny MacFayden |

Bob Swift

| June 1, 1942 | PHI | A | Bob Harris | STL | A | Frankie Hayes |
| Oct 11, 1943 | DET | A | Don Heffner | PHI | A | Rip Radcliff |

Steve Swisher

Dec 11, 1973	CHI	N	Steve Stone	CHI	A	Ron Santo
			Ken Frailing			
			Jim Kremmel			
Dec 8, 1977	STL	N	Jerry Morales	CHI	N	Dave Rader
			and cash			Hector Cruz
Dec 8, 1980	SD	N	——	STL	N	See Rollie Fingers

Ron Swoboda

| March 31, 1971 | MON | N | Rich Hacker | NY | N | Don Hahn |
| June 25, 1971 | NY | A | —— | MON | N | Ron Woods |

Bob Sykes

Dec 4, 1978	STL	N	minor league	DET	A	Jerry Morales
			P Jack Murphy			Aurelio Lopez
Oct 21, 1981	NY	A	——	STL	N	Willie McGee

Jerry Tabb

| March 15, 1977 | OAK | A | —— | CHI | N | Cash |

Pat Tabler

| Aug 19, 1981 | CHI | N | —— | NY | A | Bill Caudill |
| | | | | | | Jay Howell |

(New York received Caudill on April 1, 1982, and Howell on August 2, 1982.)

Jan 25, 1983	CHI	A	Scott Fletcher	CHI	N	Steve Trout
			Randy Martz			Warren Brusstar
			Dick Tidrow			
April 1, 1983	CLE	A	——	CHI	A	Jerry Dybzinski
June 3, 1988	KC	A	——	CLE	A	Bud Black

Greg Tabor

| March 17, 1988 | CHI | N | Dave Meier | TEX | A | Ray Hayward |

Jim Tabor

| Jan 22, 1946 | PHI | N | —— | BOS | A | Cash |

Doug Taitt

| May 23, 1929 | CHI | A | —— | BOS | A | Bill Barrett |

Fred Talbot

| Jan 20, 1965 | KC | A | Jim Landis | CHI | A | Rocky Colavito |
| | | | Mike Hershberger | | | |

(Part of three-team trade involving Kansas City, Cleveland, and the Chicago White Sox.)

June 10, 1966	NY	A	Billy Bryan	KC	A	Gil Blanco
						Roger Repoz
						Bill Stafford
May 20, 1969	SEA	A	——	NY	A	Jack Aker
Aug 29, 1969	OAK	A	——	SEA	A	Bob Meyer
						Pete Koegel

John Tamargo

July 18, 1978	SF	N	——	STL	N	Rob Dressler
June 13, 1979	MON	N	——	SF	N	Joe Pettini
						and cash

Vito Tamulis

May 20, 1938	BKN	N	——	STL	A	Waiver price
Nov 11, 1940	PHI	N	Bill Crouch	BKN	N	Kirby Higbe
			Mickey Livingston			
			and $100,000.			

Date	Traded To	Traded With	Traded By	In Exchange For
Vito Tamulis *continued*				
May 6, 1941	BKN N ——		PHI N	Lee Grissom

Frank Tanana

Date	Traded To	Traded With	Traded By	In Exchange For
Jan 23, 1981	BOS A	Jim Dorsey Joe Rudi	CAL A	Fred Lynn Steve Renko
Jan 6, 1982	TEX A ——		BOS A	No compensation (free agent signing)
June 20, 1985	DET A ——		TEX A	Minor league P Duane James

Jesse Tannehill

Date	Traded To	Traded With	Traded By	In Exchange For
Dec 1903	BOS A ——		NY A	Long Tom Hughes
July 1908	WAS A	Bob Unglaub	BOS A	Casey Patten

Bruce Tanner

Date	Traded To	Traded With	Traded By	In Exchange For
Dec 11, 1986	OAK A	Gene Nelson	CHI A	Donnie Hill
(Oakland received Tanner on Dec. 18, 1986.)				

Chuck Tanner

Date	Traded To	Traded With	Traded By	In Exchange For
June 8, 1957	CHI N ——		MIL N	Waiver price
March 9, 1959	BOS A ——		CHI N	Riverboat Smith
Nov 5, 1976	PIT N ——		OAK A	Manny Sanguillen and $100,000.

Kevin Tapani

Date	Traded To	Traded With	Traded By	In Exchange For
Dec 11, 1987	NY N	Jack Savage Wally Whitehurst	LA N	Jesse Orosco
(Part of a three-team trade involving Los Angeles, Oakland, and New York Mets.)				
July 31, 1989	MIN A ——		NY N	*See Frank Viola*

Ted Tappe

Date	Traded To	Traded With	Traded By	In Exchange For
Oct 1, 1954	CHI N	Harry Perkowski Jim Bolger	CIN N	Johnny Klippstein Jim Willis

Danny Tartabull

Date	Traded To	Traded With	Traded By	In Exchange For
Dec 10, 1986	KC A	Rick Luecken	SEA A	Scott Bankhead Mike Kingery Steve Shields

Jose Tartabull

Date	Traded To	Traded With	Traded By	In Exchange For
Dec 15, 1961	KC A ——		SF N	Joe Pignatano
June 13, 1966	BOS A	John Wyatt Rollie Sheldon	KC A	Jim Gosger Ken Sanders Guido Grilli
May 7, 1969	OAK A ——		BOS A	Cash

LaSchelle Tarver

Date	Traded To	Traded With	Traded By	In Exchange For
Nov 13, 1985	BOS A ——		NY N	*See Bob Ojeda*

Willie Tasby

Date	Traded To	Traded With	Traded By	In Exchange For
June 9, 1960	BOS A ——		BAL A	Gene Stephens
May 3, 1962	CLE A ——		WAS A	Steve Hamilton Don Rudolph

Bennie Tate

Date	Traded To	Traded With	Traded By	In Exchange For
June 16, 1930	CHI A	Garland Braxton	WAS A	Art Shires
April 29, 1932	BOS A	Smead Jolley Cliff Watwood	CHI A	Charlie Berry

Jarvis Tatum

Date	Traded To	Traded With	Traded By	In Exchange For
Oct 11, 1970	BOS A ——		CAL A	*See Tony Conigliaro*

Ken Tatum

Date	Traded To	Traded With	Traded By	In Exchange For
Oct 11, 1970	BOS A ——		CAL A	*See Tony Conigliaro*
Oct 26, 1973	STL N	Reggie Smith	BOS A	Rick Wise Bernie Carbo
April 27, 1974	CHI A ——		STL N	Luis Alvarado

Tommy Tatum

Date	Traded To	Traded With	Traded By	In Exchange For
May 13, 1947	CIN N ——		BKN N	Cash

Jackie Tavener

Date	Traded To	Traded With	Traded By	In Exchange For
Dec 11, 1928	CLE A	Ken Holloway	DET A	George Uhle

Frank Taveras

Date	Traded To	Traded With	Traded By	In Exchange For
April 19, 1979	NY N ——		PIT N	Tim Foli minor league P Greg Field
Dec 11, 1981	MON N ——		NY N	Steve Ratzer and cash

Ben Taylor

Date	Traded To	Traded With	Traded By	In Exchange For
Feb 14, 1952	DET A ——		STL A	*See Gene Bearden*

Carl Taylor

Date	Traded To	Traded With	Traded By	In Exchange For
Oct 21, 1969	STL N	minor league OF Frank Vanzin	PIT N	Dave Giusti Dave Ricketts
Oct 20, 1970	MIL A	Jim Ellis	STL N	Jerry McNertney George Lauzerique minor league P Jesse Higgins
Feb 2, 1971	KC A ——		MIL A	Ellie Rodriguez
Sept 3, 1971	PIT N ——		KC A	Cash

Chuck Taylor

Date	Traded To	Traded With	Traded By	In Exchange For
Feb 17, 1964	HOU N	Jim Beauchamp	STL N	Carl Warwick
June 15, 1965	STL N	Hal Woodeshick	HOU N	Mike Cuellar Ron Taylor
Oct 18, 1971	NY N ——		STL N	*See Jim Bibby*
Sept 13, 1972	MIL A ——		NY N	Cash

Danny Taylor

Date	Traded To	Traded With	Traded By	In Exchange For
May 7, 1932	BKN N ——		CHI N	Cash

Hawk Taylor

Date	Traded To	Traded With	Traded By	In Exchange For
Dec 2, 1963	NY N ——		MIL N	Cash
July 24, 1967	CAL A ——		NY N	Don Wallace and cash

Jack Taylor

Date	Traded To	Traded With	Traded By	In Exchange For
Dec 12, 1903	STL N	Larry McLean	CHI N	Three Finger Brown Jack O'Neill
July 1, 1906	CHI N ——		STL N	Fred Beebe Pete Noonan and cash

Joe Taylor

Date	Traded To	Traded With	Traded By	In Exchange For
Dec 5, 1957	STL N	Curt Flood	CIN N	Marty Kutyna Ted Wieand Willard Schmidt
July 25, 1958	BAL A ——		STL N	Waiver price

Ron Taylor

Date	Traded To	Traded With	Traded By	In Exchange For
Dec 15, 1962	STL N	Jack Kubiszyn	CLE A	Fred Whitfield
June 15, 1965	HOU N	Mike Cuellar	STL N	Hal Woodeshick Chuck Taylor
Feb 10, 1967	NY N ——		HOU N	Cash

Date	Traded To	Traded With	Traded By	In Exchange For
Ron Taylor *continued*				
Oct 20, 1971	MON N	——	NY N	Cash
Sammy Taylor				
Dec 5, 1957	CHI N	Taylor Phillips	MIL N	Eddie Haas
				Don Kaiser
				Bob Rush
April 26, 1962	NY N	——	CHI N	Bobby Gene Smith
July 1, 1963	CIN N	Charlie Neal	NY N	Jesse Gonder
Aug 1, 1963	CLE A	——	CIN N	Gene Green
Tony Taylor				
May 13, 1960	PHI N	Cal Neeman	CHI N	Ed Bouchee
				Don Cardwell
June 12, 1971	DET A	——	PHI N	Minor league
				Ps Mike Fremuth and
				Carl Cavanaugh
Zack Taylor				
Oct 7, 1925	BOS N	Jimmy Johnston	BKN N	Jesse Barnes
		Eddie Brown		Mickey O'Neil
				Gus Felix
June 12, 1927	NY N	Larry Benton	BOS N	Hugh McQuillan
		Herb Thomas		Kent Greenfield
				Doc Farrell
Feb 1928	BOS N	——	NY N	Cash
July 6, 1929	CHI N	——	BOS N	Waiver price
Bud Teachout				
Dec 1931	STL N	Hack Wilson	CHI N	Burleigh Grimes
Birdie Tebbetts				
May 20, 1947	BOS A	——	DET A	Hal Wagner
Dec 13, 1950	CLE A	——	BOS A	Cash
Wil Tejada				
Nov 20, 1988	SF N	——	MON N	Angel Escobar
Kent Tekulve				
April 20, 1985	PHI N	——	PIT N	Al Holland
				Minor league
				P Frankie Griffin
Tom Tellmann				
Oct 15, 1982	MIL A	——	SD N	Minor league
				Ps Weldon Swift
				and Tim Cook
Johnny Temple				
Dec 15, 1959	CLE A	——	CIN N	Cal McLish
				Billy Martin
				Gordy Coleman
Nov 16, 1961	BAL A	——	CLE A	Ray Barker
				Harry Chiti
				and minor leaguer
				Art Kay
Aug 11, 1962	HOU N	——	BAL A	Cash
Garry Templeton				
Dec 10, 1981	SD N	Sixto Lezcano	STL N	Ozzie Smith
		Luis DeLeon		Steve Mura
				Al Olmsted

(Templeton and Smith were exchanged on February 11, 1982; Olmsted and DeLeon were exchanged on February 19.)

Date	Traded To	Traded With	Traded By	In Exchange For
Gene Tenace				
Dec 14, 1976	SD N	——	OAK A	No compensation
				(free agent signing)
Dec 8, 1980	STL N	Rollie Fingers	SD N	Terry Kennedy
		Bob Shirley		Steve Swisher
		minor league		Mike Phillips
		C Bob Geren		John Littlefield
				John Urrea
				Kim Seaman
				Al Olmsted
Dec 1, 1982	PIT N	——	STL N	No compensation
				(free agent signing)
Fred Tenney				
Dec 3, 1907	NY N	Al Bridwell	BOS N	Dan McGann
		Tom Needham		Frank Bowerman
				Bill Dahlen
				George Browne
				George Ferguson
Frank Tepedino				
June 7, 1971	MIL A	Bobby Mitchell	NY A	Danny Walton
June 7, 1973	ATL N	Wayne Nordhagen	NY A	Pat Dobson
		Al Closter		
		Dave Cheadle		
Greg Terlecky				
Dec 12, 1975	CHI A	Buddy Bradford	STL N	Lee Richard
Jeff Terpko				
Nov 3, 1970	PHI N	Greg Goossen	WAS A	Curt Flood
		Gene Martin		
March 15, 1977	MON N	——	TEX A	Rodney Scott
Walt Terrell				
April 1, 1982	NY N	Ron Darling	TEX A	Lee Mazzilli
Dec 7, 1984	DET A	——	NY N	Howard Johnson
Oct 28, 1988	SD N	——	DET A	Keith Moreland
				Chris Brown
July 22, 1989	NY A	Fred Toliver	SD N	Mike Pagliarulo
				Don Schulze

(New York received Toliver on Sept. 27, 1989.)

Date	Traded To	Traded With	Traded By	In Exchange For
Nov 29, 1989	PIT N	——	NY A	No compensation
				(free agent signing)
Ralph Terry				
June 15, 1957	KC A	Billy Martin	NY A	Ryne Duren
		Woodie Held		Jim Pisoni
		Bob Martyn		Milt Graff
				Harry Simpson
May 26, 1959	NY A	Hector Lopez	KC A	Johnny Kucks
				Tom Sturdivant
				Jerry Lumpe
Sept 5, 1964	CLE A	Bud Daley	NY A	Pedro Ramos
		and $75,000.		
April 6, 1966	KC A	Cash	CLE A	John O'Donoghue
Aug 6, 1966	NY A	——	KC A	Cash
Scott Terry				
Aug 30, 1987	STL N	——	CIN N	Pat Perry
Zeb Terry				
Jan 1920	CHI N	——	PIT N	Cash
Wayne Terwilliger				
June 15, 1951	BKN N	*See Andy Pafko*	CHI N	
Sept 23, 1952	WAS A	——	BKN N	Waiver price

Date	Traded To	Traded With	Traded By	In Exchange For

Dick Tettelbach

| Feb 8, 1956 | WAS A | *See Whitey Herzog* | NY A | —— |

Tim Teufel

| Jan 16, 1986 | NY N | Minor league OF Pat Crosby | MIN A | Billy Beane Bill Latham Joe Klink |

Bob Tewksbury

| July 12, 1987 | CHI N | Dean Wilkins Minor League P Rich Scheid | NY A | Steve Trout Cash |

Moe Thacker

| Oct 17, 1962 | STL N | —— | CHI N | *See Larry Jackson* |

Ron Theobald

| May 11, 1970 | MIL A | Hank Allen | WAS A | Wayne Comer |

Tommy Thevenow

Dec 13, 1928	PHI N		STL N	Heinie Sand and $10,000.
Nov 6, 1930	PIT N	Claude Willoughby	PHI N	Dick Bartell
Dec 12, 1935	CIN N	——	PIT N	Cash
Jan 6, 1937	BOS N	——	CIN N	Cash

Henry Thielman

| Jan 1903 | BKN N | | CIN N | Cash |

Jake Thielman

| Aug 1908 | BOS A | —— | NY A | Cash |

Bud Thomas

| May 1, 1939 | WAS A | —— | PHI A | Waiver price |
| May 18, 1939 | DET A | —— | WAS A | Waiver price |

Derrel Thomas

Dec 3, 1971	SD N	Bill Greif Mark Schaeffer	HOU N	Dave Roberts
Dec 6, 1974	SF N	——	SD N	Tito Fuentes Butch Metzger
Feb 28, 1978	SD N	——	SF N	Mike Ivie
Nov 14, 1978	LA N	——	SD N	No compensation (free agent signing)
Feb 7, 1984	MON N	——	LA N	No compensation (free agent signing)
Sept 6, 1984	CAL A	——	MON N	Cash

Frank Thomas

Jan 30, 1959	CIN N	Whammy Douglas Jim Pendleton Johnny Powers	PIT N	Smoky Burgess Harvey Haddix Don Hoak
Dec 6, 1959	CHI N	——	CIN N	Bill Henry Lou Jackson Lee Walls
May 9, 1961	MIL N	——	CHI N	Mel Roach
Nov 28, 1961	NY N	——	MIL N	Gus Bell and cash

(Milwaukee received Bell on May 21, 1962.)

Aug 7, 1964	PHI N	——	NY N	Gary Kroll Wayne Graham and cash
July 10, 1965	HOU N	——	PHI N	Cash
Sept 1, 1965	MIL N	——	HOU N	Minor league IF Mickey Sinnerud

Fred Thomas

April 12, 1916	BOS A	Sad Sam Jones and $55,000.	CLE A	Tris Speaker
Jan 1919	PHI A	——	BOS A	Cash
July 1920	WAS A	——	PHI A	Red Shannon

George Thomas

June 26, 1961	LA A	——	DET A	Cash
June 15, 1963	DET A	Cash	LA A	Frank Kostro Paul Foytack
Oct 4, 1965	BOS A	George Smith	DET A	Bill Monbouquette

Gorman Thomas

Aug 20, 1977	TEX A	——	MIL A	Ed Kirkpatrick
Feb 8, 1978	MIL A	——	TEX A	Cash
June 6, 1983	CLE A	Jamie Easterly Ernie Camacho	MIL A	Rick Manning Rick Waits
Dec 7, 1983	SEA A	Jack Perconte	CLE A	Tony Bernazard

Herb Thomas

| June 12, 1927 | NY N | Zack Taylor Larry Benton | BOS N | Hugh McQuillan Kent Greenfield Doc Farrell |

Ira Thomas

| Dec 12, 1907 | DET A | —— | NY A | Cash |
| Dec 8, 1908 | PHI A | —— | DET A | Cash |

Kite Thomas

| June 30, 1953 | WAS A | —— | PHI A | Waiver price |
| March 27, 1954 | CHI A | —— | WAS A | Tom Wright |

Lee Thomas

May 8, 1961	LA A	Ryne Duren Johnny James	NY A	Tex Clevenger Bob Cerv
June 4, 1964	BOS A	——	LA A	Lu Clinton
Dec 15, 1965	MIL N	Arnie Earley Jay Ritchie	BOS A	Bob Sadowski Dan Osinski
May 28, 1966	CHI N	——	ATL N	Ted Abernathy
Feb 9, 1968	HOU N	——	CHI N	Minor league OFs Tom Murray and Levi Brown

Leo Thomas

| June 15, 1950 | NY A | —— | STL A | *See Snuffy Stirnweiss* |
| June 15, 1952 | CHI A | Tom Wright | STL A | Willie Miranda Al Zarilla |

Myles Thomas

| June 18, 1929 | WAS A | —— | NY A | Cash |

Pinch Thomas

| Dec 14, 1917 | PHI A | Vean Gregg Merlin Kopp and $60,000. | BOS A | Amos Strunk Joe Bush Wally Schang |
| June 1, 1918 | CLE A | —— | BOS A | Cash |

Roy Thomas

| April 1908 | PIT N | —— | PHI N | Cash |
| Feb 1909 | BOS N | —— | PIT N | Cash |

Roy Thomas

| Dec 10, 1975 | CHI A | Dick Ruthven Alan Bannister | PHI N | Jim Kaat Mike Buskey |
| March 30, 1977 | HOU N | —— | SEA A | Larry Milbourne |

Roy Thomas *continued*

Date	Traded To		Traded With	Traded By		In Exchange For
June 23, 1978	STL	N	———	HOU	N	Cash
Dec 9, 1981	SEA	A	———	OAK	A	Rusty McNealy / minor league / P Tim Hallgren

Stan Thomas

Date	Traded To		Traded With	Traded By		In Exchange For
Dec 9, 1975	CLE	A	Ron Pruitt	TEX	A	John Ellis
Aug 2, 1977	NY	A	———	SEA	A	Cash
Dec 12, 1977	CHI	A	minor league / P Ed Ricks	NY	A	Jim Spencer / Tommy Cruz / minor league / P Bob Polinsky

Tommy Thomas

Date	Traded To		Traded With	Traded By		In Exchange For
June 11, 1932	WAS	A	———	CHI	A	Cash
May 20, 1935	PHI	N	———	WAS	A	Waiver price
Jan 1936	STL	A	———	PHI	N	Cash

Valmy Thomas

Date	Traded To		Traded With	Traded By		In Exchange For
Dec 3, 1958	PHI	N	Ruben Gomez	SF	N	Jack Sanford

Gary Thomasson

Date	Traded To		Traded With	Traded By		In Exchange For
March 15, 1978	OAK	A	———	SF	N	*See Vida Blue*
June 15, 1978	NY	A	———	OAK	A	Dell Alston / Mickey Klutts / and $50,000.
Feb 15, 1979	LA	N	———	NY	A	Brad Gulden

Bobby Thompson

Date	Traded To		Traded With	Traded By		In Exchange For
Dec 6, 1978	SEA	A	———	TEX	A	Cash

Danny Thompson

Date	Traded To		Traded With	Traded By		In Exchange For
June 1, 1976	TEX	A	———	MIN	A	*See Roy Smalley*

Fresco Thompson

Date	Traded To		Traded With	Traded By		In Exchange For
Jan 9, 1927	PHI	N	Jack Scott	NY	N	George Harper / Butch Henline

(Part of three-team trade involving Philadelphia, New York, and Brooklyn.)

Date	Traded To		Traded With	Traded By		In Exchange For
Oct 14, 1930	BKN	N	Lefty O'Doul	PHI	N	Clise Dudley / Jumbo Elliott / Hal Lee / and cash

Jason Thompson

Date	Traded To		Traded With	Traded By		In Exchange For
May 27, 1980	CAL	A	———	DET	A	Al Cowens
April 1, 1981	PIT	N	———	CAL	A	Ed Ott / Mickey Mahler
April 4, 1986	MON	N	———	PIT	N	two players to be named

(Pittsburgh received OF Ben Abner and IF Ronnie Giddens on April 7, 1985.)

Mike Thompson

Date	Traded To		Traded With	Traded By		In Exchange For
Feb 1, 1973	STL	N	———	TEX	A	Charles Hudson / Mike Nagy

(Thompson and Nagy were exchanged on March 31.)

Date	Traded To		Traded With	Traded By		In Exchange For
Sept 10, 1974	ATL	N	———	STL	N	Cash
April 7, 1976	CIN	N	———	ATL	N	Terry Crowley
Nov 8, 1976	TEX	A	———	CIN	N	Minor league / P Art DeFilippis

Milt Thompson

Date	Traded To		Traded With	Traded By		In Exchange For
Dec 10, 1985	PHI	N	Steve Bedrosian	ATL	N	Ozzie Virgil / Pete Smith
Dec 16, 1988	STL	N	———	PHI	N	Curt Ford / Steve Lake

Rich Thompson

Date	Traded To		Traded With	Traded By		In Exchange For
Dec 16, 1985	MIL	A	———	CLE	A	Minor league / P Scott Roberts

Scot Thompson

Date	Traded To		Traded With	Traded By		In Exchange For
Aug 1, 1985	MON	N	player to be named	SF	N	Dan Driessen

(Montreal returned Bill Laskey on Oct. 24 to complete deal.)

Tim Thompson

Date	Traded To		Traded With	Traded By		In Exchange For
April 16, 1956	KC	A	———	BKN	N	Lee Wheat / Tom Saffell / and cash
Nov 20, 1957	DET	A	*See Billy Martin*	KC	A	———

Tommy Thompson

Date	Traded To		Traded With	Traded By		In Exchange For
April 27, 1939	STL	A	———	CHI	A	Cash

Bobby Thomson

Date	Traded To		Traded With	Traded By		In Exchange For
Feb 1, 1954	MIL	N	Sammy Calderone	NY	N	Johnny Antonelli / Don Liddle / Ebba St. Claire / Billy Klaus / and $50,000.
June 15, 1957	NY	N	Danny O'Connell / Ray Crone	MIL	N	Red Schoendienst
April 3, 1958	CHI	N	———	SF	N	Bob Speake / and cash
Dec 1, 1959	BOS	A	———	CHI	N	Al Schroll

Dickie Thon

Date	Traded To		Traded With	Traded By		In Exchange For
April 1, 1981	HOU	N	———	CAL	A	Ken Forsch
Feb 18, 1988	SD	N	———	HOU	N	No compensation (free agent signing)
Jan 27, 1989	PHI	N	———	SD	N	Cash

Jack Thoney

Date	Traded To		Traded With	Traded By		In Exchange For
Sept 1902	BAL	A	———	CLE	A	
May 8, 1904	NY	A	———	WAS	A	Cash

Hank Thormahlen

Date	Traded To		Traded With	Traded By		In Exchange For
Dec 15, 1920	BOS	A	———	NY	A	*See Waite Hoyt*

Paul Thormodsgard

Date	Traded To		Traded With	Traded By		In Exchange For
Dec 7, 1979	PHI	N	———	MIN	A	Pete Mackanin

Andre Thornton

Date	Traded To		Traded With	Traded By		In Exchange For
June 15, 1972	ATL	N	Joe Hoerner	PHI	N	Jim Nash / Gary Neibauer
May 19, 1973	CHI	N	———	ATL	N	Joe Pepitone
May 17, 1976	MON	N	———	CHI	N	Steve Renko / Larry Biittner
Dec 10, 1976	CLE	A	———	MON	N	Jackie Brown

Lou Thornton

Date	Traded To		Traded With	Traded By		In Exchange For
March 17, 1989	PIT	N	———	MIL	A	Ruben Rodriguez

Jim Thorpe

Date	Traded To		Traded With	Traded By		In Exchange For
April 24, 1917	CIN	N	———	NY	N	Cash

(Thorpe was returned to the Giants on August 1, 1917.)

Date	Traded To		Traded With	Traded By		In Exchange For
May 21, 1919	BOS	N	———	NY	N	Pat Ragan

Faye Throneberry

Date	Traded To		Traded With	Traded By		In Exchange For
April 29, 1957	WAS	A	Milt Bolling / Russ Kemmerer	BOS	A	Dean Stone / Bob Chakales

Date	Traded To	Traded With	Traded By	In Exchange For

Marv Throneberry

Date	Traded To	Traded With	Traded By	In Exchange For
Dec 11, 1959	KC A	Hank Bauer, Don Larsen, Norm Siebern	NY A	Roger Maris, Joe DeMaestri, Kent Hadley
June 8, 1961	BAL A	—	KC A	Gene Stephens
May 9, 1962	NY N	—	BAL A	Hobie Landrith and cash

George Throop

April 27, 1979	HOU N	—	KC A	Keith Drumright

Mark Thurmond

July 9, 1986	DET A	—	SD N	Dave LaPoint
Feb 27, 1988	BAL A	—	DET A	Ray Knight

Sloppy Thurston

May 12, 1923	CHI A	—	STL A	Cash
Jan 15, 1927	WAS A	Leo Mangum	CHI A	Roger Peckinpaugh

Luis Tiant

Dec 10, 1969	MIN A	Stan Williams	CLE A	Dean Chance, Bob Miller, Graig Nettles, Ted Uhlaender
Nov 13, 1978	NY A	—	BOS A	No compensation (free agent signing)

Jay Tibbs

June 15, 1984	CIN N	Eddie Williams, Minor league P Matt Bullinger	NY N	Bruce Berenyi
Dec 19, 1985	MON N	Andy McGaffigan, Dann Bilardello, John Stuper	CIN N	Bill Gullickson, Sal Butera
Feb 16, 1988	BAL A	Minor league P Al Cardwood	MON N	Minor league Ps John Hoover, Doug Cinnella, Rick Carriger

Dick Tidrow

April 27, 1974	NY A	Chris Chambliss, Cecil Upshaw	CLE A	Fritz Peterson, Steve Kline, Fred Beene, Tom Buskey
May 23, 1979	CHI N	—	NY A	Ray Burris
Jan 25, 1983	CHI A	Scott Fletcher, Pat Tabler, Randy Martz	CHI N	Steve Trout, Warren Brusstar
Jan 27, 1984	NY N	—	CHI A	No compensation (free agent signing)

Bobby Tiefenauer

Sept 8, 1955	DET A	—	STL N	Ben Flowers
March 30, 1968	CHI N	—	CLE A	Rob Gardner

Verle Tiefenthaler

Nov 30, 1961	CHI A	—	SF N	See Billy Pierce

Cotton Tierney

May 22, 1923	PHI N	Whitey Glazner and $50,000.	PIT N	Lee Meadows, Johnny Rawlings
Dec 15, 1923	BOS N	—	PHI N	Hod Ford, Ray Powell

(Powell announced his intention to retire after the 1924 season. He remained with Boston, and Philadelphia received cash instead.)

Feb 4, 1925	BKN N	—	BOS N	Bernie Neis

Les Tietje

Date	Traded To	Traded With	Traded By	In Exchange For
May 5, 1936	STL A	—	CHI A	Sugar Cain

Bob Tillman

Aug 8, 1967	NY A	—	BOS A	Cash
Dec 7, 1967	ATL N	Dale Roberts	NY A	Bobby Cox
Dec 2, 1970	MIL A	—	ATL N	Hank Allen, minor leaguers P Paul Click and IF John Ryan

Rusty Tillman

March 31, 1985	SD N	—	NY N	Rick Lancellotti
April 18, 1986	OAK A	—	SD N	Bob Stoddard, Minor league OF Kevin Russ

Thad Tillotson

Sept 10, 1966	NY A	Cash	LA N	Dick Schofield

Tom Timmerman

June 15, 1973	CLE A	Kevin Collins	DET A	Ed Farmer

Ron Tingley

Sept 6, 1989	CAL A	—	CLE A	Player to be named

Joe Tinker

Dec 15, 1912	CIN N	Grover Lowdermilk, Harry Chapman	CHI N	Bert Humphries, Red Corriden, Pete Knisely, Art Phelan, Mike Mitchell
Dec 1913	BKN N	—	CIN N	Dick Egan and $6,500.

(Tinker demanded $2,000 of the purchase price; when this was refused, he jumped to the Federal League and the deal was cancelled.)

Feb 10, 1916	CHI N	See Three Finger Brown	CHI F	—

Bud Tinning

Nov 21, 1934	STL N	Dick Ward and cash	CHI N	Tex Carleton

Joe Tipton

Nov 22, 1948	CHI A	—	CLE A	Joe Haynes
Oct 19, 1949	PHI A	—	CHI A	Nellie Fox
June 23, 1952	CLE A	—	PHI A	Waiver price
Jan 20, 1954	WAS A	—	CLE A	Mickey Grasso

John Titus

July 1, 1912	BOS N	—	PHI N	Doc Miller

Dave Tobik

March 24, 1983	TEX A	—	DET A	Johnny Grubb

Jack Tobin

Feb 1926	WAS A	Joe Bush	STL A	Tom Zachary, Win Ballou
July 31, 1926	BOS A	—	WAS A	Cash

Jim Tobin

Dec 6, 1939	BOS N	Cash	PIT N	Johnny Lanning
Aug 1945	DET A	—	BOS N	Cash

Date	Traded To	Traded With	Traded By	In Exchange For

Johnny Tobin

Date	Traded To	Traded With	Traded By	In Exchange For
Feb 10, 1916	STL A	*See Eddie Plank*	STL F	——

Al Todd

Date	Traded To	Traded With	Traded By	In Exchange For
Nov 21, 1935	PIT N	——	PHI N	Claude Passeau Earl Grace
Dec 16, 1938	BOS N	Johnny Dickshot and cash	PIT N	Ray Mueller
March 31, 1939	BKN N	——	BOS N	Bill Posedel
Dec 8, 1939	CHI N	——	BKN N	Gus Mancuso Newt Kimball

Jackson Todd

Date	Traded To	Traded With	Traded By	In Exchange For
March 27, 1978	PHI N	——	NY N	Minor league C Ed Cuervo

Jim Todd

Date	Traded To	Traded With	Traded By	In Exchange For
April 6, 1975	OAK A	——	CHI N	Champ Summers and cash
March 15, 1977	CHI N	——	OAK A	Joe Coleman
April 20, 1977	SEA A	——	CHI N	Pete Broberg

Phil Todt

Date	Traded To	Traded With	Traded By	In Exchange For
Feb 3, 1931	PHI A	——	BOS A	Cash

Bobby Tolan

Date	Traded To	Traded With	Traded By	In Exchange For
Oct 11, 1968	CIN N	Wayne Granger	STL N	Vada Pinson
Nov 9, 1973	SD N	Dave Tomlin	CIN N	Clay Kirby

Fred Toliver

Date	Traded To	Traded With	Traded By	In Exchange For
Nov 4, 1981	CIN N	minor league P Bryan Ryder	NY A	Ken Griffey
Aug 8, 1985	PHI N	——	CIN N	*See Bo Diaz*
Feb 5, 1988	MIN A	——	PHI N	Minor league C Chris Calvert
June 29, 1989	SD N	——	MIN A	Greg Booker
July 22, 1989	NY A	Walt Terrell	SD N	Mike Pagliarulo Don Schulze

(New York received Toliver on Sept. 27, 1989.)

Wayne Tolleson

Date	Traded To	Traded With	Traded By	In Exchange For
Nov 25, 1985	CHI A	Dave Schmidt	TEX A	Ed Correa Scott Fletcher player to be named

(Texas received IF Jose Mota on Dec. 12, 1985.)

Date	Traded To	Traded With	Traded By	In Exchange For
July 30, 1986	NY A	Ron Kittle Joel Skinner	CHI A	Ron Hassey Carlos Martinez Bill Lindsey

(Chicago received Lindsey on Dec. 24, 1986.)

Dick Tomanek

Date	Traded To	Traded With	Traded By	In Exchange For
June 15, 1958	KC A	Roger Maris Preston Ward	CLE A	Woodie Held Vic Power

Dave Tomlin

Date	Traded To	Traded With	Traded By	In Exchange For
Nov 9, 1973	SD N	Bobby Tolan	CIN N	Clay Kirby
Jan 25, 1978	TEX A	$125,000.	SD N	Gaylord Perry
March 28, 1978	CIN N	——	TEX A	Cash
Sept 8, 1982	MON N	——	CIN N	Cash
Aug 2, 1983	PIT N	——	MON N	Cash

Ron Tompkins

Date	Traded To	Traded With	Traded By	In Exchange For
Oct 20, 1967	CIN N	——	KC A	Floyd Robinson Darrell Osteen
Oct 21, 1969	KC A	——	ATL N	Dave Wickersham

Fred Toney

Date	Traded To	Traded With	Traded By	In Exchange For
Feb 22, 1915	CIN N	——	BKN N	Waiver price
July 25, 1918	NY N	——	CIN N	Cash
July 30, 1922	BOS N	Larry Benton and $100,000.	NY N	Hugh McQuillan

(Toney refused to report and remained Giants' property.)

Date	Traded To	Traded With	Traded By	In Exchange For
Oct 1922	STL N	——	NY N	Waiver price

Jeff Torborg

Date	Traded To	Traded With	Traded By	In Exchange For
March 13, 1971	CAL A	——	LA N	Cash
Dec 6, 1973	STL N	——	CAL A	John Andrews

Earl Torgeson

Date	Traded To	Traded With	Traded By	In Exchange For
Feb 16, 1953	PHI N	——	MIL N	Russ Meyer and cash

(Part of four-team trade involving Milwaukee Braves, Philadelphia Phillies, Brooklyn, and Cincinnati.)

Date	Traded To	Traded With	Traded By	In Exchange For
June 15, 1955	DET A	——	PHI N	Cash
June 14, 1957	CHI A	——	DET A	Dave Philley

Joe Torre

Date	Traded To	Traded With	Traded By	In Exchange For
March 17, 1969	STL N	——	ATL N	Orlando Cepeda
Oct 13, 1974	NY N	——	STL N	Ray Sadecki Tommy Moore

Pablo Torrealba

Date	Traded To	Traded With	Traded By	In Exchange For
March 29, 1977	OAK A	——	ATL N	Cash
March 30, 1978	CHI A	——	OAK A	Steve Renko Jim Essian

Angel Torres

Date	Traded To	Traded With	Traded By	In Exchange For
Nov 6, 1976	MON N	Bill Greif Sam Mejias	STL N	Steve Dunning Pat Scanlon Tony Scott
May 21, 1977	CIN N	Shane Rawley	MON N	Santo Alcala

Hector Torres

Date	Traded To	Traded With	Traded By	In Exchange For
Aug 7, 1967	HOU N	——	CAL A	Jim Weaver
Oct 12, 1970	CHI N	——	HOU N	Roger Metzger
April 7, 1972	MON N	Hal Breeden	CHI N	Dan McGinn
April 4, 1973	HOU N	——	MON N	Cash
Oct 23, 1973	CHI A	——	HOU N	Dan Neumeier
Dec 8, 1976	CLE A	Johnny Grubb Fred Kendall	SD N	George Hendrick
March 29, 1977	TOR A	——	CLE A	John Lowenstein

Rusty Torres

Date	Traded To	Traded With	Traded By	In Exchange For
Nov 27, 1972	CLE A	——	NY A	*See Graig Nettles*
Sept 12, 1974	CAL A	Ken Suarez and cash	CLE A	Frank Robinson
May 16, 1978	CHI A	Claudell Washington	TEX A	Bobby Bonds

Mike Torrez

Date	Traded To	Traded With	Traded By	In Exchange For
June 15, 1971	MON N	——	STL N	Bob Reynolds
Dec 4, 1974	BAL A	Ken Singleton	MON N	Dave McNally Rich Coggins minor league P Bill Kirkpatrick
April 2, 1976	OAK A	Don Baylor Paul Mitchell	BAL A	Reggie Jackson Ken Holtzman minor leaguer Bill Van Bommell
April 27, 1977	NY A	——	OAK A	Dock Ellis Marty Perez Larry Murray
Nov 23, 1977	BOS A	——	NY A	No compensation (free agent signing)
Jan 14, 1983	NY N	——	BOS A	Minor league 3B Mike Davis

Date	Traded To	Traded With	Traded By	In Exchange For

Lou Tost
March 25, 1947 — PIT N ——— — BOS N — Cash

Paul Toth
Sept 1, 1962 — CHI N — — STL N — Harvey Branch
June 15, 1964 — STL N — *See Lou Brock* — CHI N ———

Cesar Tovar
Dec 4, 1964 — MIN A ——— — CIN N — Jerry Arrigo
Nov 30, 1972 — PHI N — — MIN A — Ken Sanders
Ken Reynolds
Joe Lis
Dec 7, 1973 — TEX A ——— — PHI N — Cash
Aug 31, 1975 — OAK A ——— — TEX A — Cash

Jack Townsend
Jan 1906 — CLE A ——— — WAS A — Cash

Dick Tracewski
Dec 15, 1965 — DET A ——— — LA N — Phil Regan

Jim Tracy
Dec 9, 1981 — HOU N — — CHI N — Gary Woods

Walt Tragesser
July 15, 1919 — PHI N ——— — BOS N — Cash

Bill Travers
Jan 26, 1981 — CAL A ——— — MIL A — No compensation (free agent signing)

Jeff Treadway
March 25, 1989 — ATL N ——— — CIN N — Cash

Mike Tresh
Dec 2, 1937 — CHI A — Marv Owen
Gee Walker — DET A — Vern Kennedy
Tony Piet
Dixie Walker
Jan 12, 1949 — CLE A ——— — CHI A — Cash

Tom Tresh
June 14, 1969 — DET A ——— — NY A — Ron Woods

Alex Trevino
Feb 10, 1982 — CIN N — Jim Kern
Greg Harris — NY N — George Foster
April 24, 1984 — ATL N — — CIN N — Cash
April 17, 1985 — SF N ——— — ATL N — Johnny Rabb
Dec 11, 1985 — LA N ——— — SF N — Candy Maldonado

Gus Triandos
Nov 18, 1954 — BAL A ——— — NY A — *See Bob Turley*
Nov 26, 1962 — DET A — Whitey Herzog — BAL A — Dick Brown
Dec 4, 1963 — PHI N — Jim Bunning — DET A — Don Demeter
Jack Hamilton
June 14, 1965 — HOU N ——— — PHI N — Cash

Manny Trillo
Oct 23, 1974 — CHI N — Darold Knowles
Bob Locker — OAK A — Billy Williams

Manny Trillo *continued*
Feb 23, 1979 — PHI N — Dave Rader
Greg Gross — CHI N — Barry Foote
Ted Sizemore
Jerry Martin
Derek Botelho
minor league
P Henry Mack
Dec 9, 1982 — CLE A — George Vukovich
Jay Baller
Julio Franco
Jerry Willard — PHI N — Von Hayes
Aug 17, 1983 — MON N ——— — CLE A — Minor league
OF Don Carter
and $300,000.
Dec 21, 1983 — SF N — — MON N — No compensation (free agent signing)
Dec 11, 1985 — CHI N ——— — SF N — Dave Owen
Dec 21, 1988 — CIN N ——— — CHI N — No compensation (free agent signing)

Ken Trinkle
Dec 14, 1948 — PHI N ——— — NY N — Cash

Coaker Triplett
June 1, 1943 — PHI N — Buster Adams
Dain Clay — STL N — Danny Litwhiler
Earl Naylor

Hal Trosky
Nov 6, 1943 — CHI A ——— — CLE A — Cash

Bill Trotter
June 7, 1942 — WAS A — Roy Cullenbine — STL A — Mike Chartak
Steve Sundra

Dizzy Trout
June 3, 1952 — BOS A — George Kell
Johnny Lipon
Hoot Evers — DET A — Walt Dropo
Bill Wight
Fred Hatfield
Johnny Pesky
Don Lenhardt

Steve Trout
Jan 25, 1983 — CHI N — Warren Brusstar — CHI A — Scott Fletcher
Pat Tabler
Randy Martz
Dick Tidrow
July 12, 1987 — NY A — Cash — CHI N — Bob Tewksbury
Dean Wilkins
Minor League
P Rich Scheid
Dec 22, 1987 — SEA A — Henry Cotto — NY A — Lee Guetterman
Clay Parker
Minor league
P Wade Taylor

Bob Trowbridge
Oct 12, 1959 — KC A ——— — MIL N — Cash

Virgil Trucks
Dec 4, 1952 — STL A — Hal White
Johnny Groth — DET A — Owen Friend
Bob Nieman
J. W. Porter
June 13, 1953 — CHI A — Bob Elliott — STL A — Darrell Johnson
Lou Kretlow
and $75,000.
Nov 30, 1955 — DET A ——— — CHI A — Bubba Phillips
Dec 5, 1956 — KC A — Ned Garver
Gene Host
Wayne Belardi
and $20,000. — DET A — Jim Finigan
Jack Crimian
Bill Harrington
Eddie Robinson

Date	Traded To		Traded With	Traded By		In Exchange For

Virgil Trucks *continued*

Date	Traded To		Traded With	Traded By		In Exchange For
June 15, 1958	NY	A	Duke Maas	KC	A	Bob Grim Harry Simpson

Mike Trujillo

Aug 19, 1986	SEA	A	———	BOS	A	*See Dave Henderson*

John Tsitouris

Nov 20, 1957	KC	A	———	DET	A	*See Billy Martin*
Jan 25, 1961	CIN	N	Johnny Briggs	KC	A	Joe Nuxhall

Thurman Tucker

Jan 27, 1948	CLE	A	———	CHI	A	Ralph Weigel

John Tudor

Dec 6, 1983	PIT	N	———	BOS	A	Mike Easler
Dec 12, 1984	STL	N	Brian Harper	PIT	N	George Hendrick minor league C Steve Barnard
Aug 16, 1988	LA	N	———	STL	N	Pedro Guerrero
Dec 14, 1989	STL	N	———	LA	N	No compensation (free agent signing)

Bob Tufts

March 30, 1982	KC	A	*See Vida Blue*	SF	N	———
June 7, 1983	CIN	N	———	KC	A	Charlie Leibrandt

Bob Turley

Nov 18, 1954	NY	A	Don Larsen Billy Hunter	BAL	A	Harry Byrd Jim McDonald Hal Smith Gus Triandos Gene Woodling Willie Miranda

(First part of 18-player trade completed on December 1, 1954; see Dick Kryhoski.)

Oct 29, 1962	LA	A	———	NY	A	Cash

Jerry Turner

Sept 9, 1981	CHI	A	———	SD	N	Cash
Feb 12, 1982	DET	A	———	CHI	A	No compensation (free agent signing)

Jim Turner

Dec 6, 1939	CIN	N	———	BOS	N	Les Scarsella and Cash
July 16, 1942	NY	A	———	CIN	N	Frankie Kelleher

Shane Turner

June 10, 1987	PHI	N	Keith Hughes	NY	A	Mike Easler

Terry Turner

Jan 1919	PHI	A	———	CLE	A	Waiver price

Tom Turner

July 31, 1944	STL	A	———	CHI	A	Cash

Bill Tuttle

Nov 20, 1957	KC	A	———	DET	A	*See Billy Martin*
June 1, 1961	MIN	A	———	KC	A	Paul Giel Reno Bertoia

(Giel was returned to Minnesota for a cash payment.)

Wayne Twitchell

Date	Traded To		Traded With	Traded By		In Exchange For
Nov 21, 1969	SEA	A	———	HOU	N	Cash
June 15, 1977	MON	N	Tim Blackwell	PHI	N	Barry Foote Dan Warthen
Aug 19, 1979	SEA	A	———	NY	N	Cash

Lefty Tyler

Jan 4, 1918	CHI	N	———	BOS	N	Larry Doyle Art Wilson and $15,000.

Dave Tyriver

Oct 14, 1961	WAS	A	———	CLE	A	Cash

Mike Tyson

Oct 17, 1979	CHI	N	———	STL	N	Donnie Moore

Bob Uecker

April 9, 1964	STL	N	———	MIL	N	Jimmie Coker Gary Kolb
Oct 27, 1965	PHI	N	Bill White Dick Groat	STL	N	Pat Corrales Art Mahaffey Alex Johnson
June 6, 1967	ATL	N	———	PHI	N	Gene Oliver

Ted Uhlaender

Dec 10, 1969	CLE	A	*See Graig Nettles*	MIN	A	———
Dec 6, 1971	CIN	N	———	CLE	A	Milt Wilcox

George Uhle

Dec 11, 1928	DET	A	———	CLE	A	Jackie Tavener Ken Holloway
April 21, 1933	NY	N	———	DET	A	$20,000.

Arnie Umbach

Dec 31, 1966	HOU	N	Sandy Alomar Eddie Mathews	ATL	N	Dave Nicholson Bob Bruce

Jim Umbarger

March 26, 1977	OAK	A	Rodney Scott and cash	TEX	A	Claudell Washington
Aug 25, 1977	TEX	A	———	OAK	A	Cash

Tommy Umphlett

Dec 9, 1953	WAS	A	Mickey McDermott	BOS	A	Jackie Jensen
Nov 8, 1955	BOS	A	*See Mickey Vernon*	WAS	A	———
June 12, 1962	NY	A	Cash	BOS	A	Billy Gardner

Pat Underwood

June 30, 1983	CIN	N	———	DET	A	Wayne Krenchicki

Tom Underwood

June 15, 1977	STL	N	Dane Iorg Rick Bosetti	PHI	N	Bake McBride Steve Waterbury
Dec 6, 1977	TOR	A	Victor Cruz	STL	N	Pete Vuckovich John Scott
Nov 1, 1979	NY	A	Rick Cerone Ted Wilborn	TOR	A	Chris Chambliss Damaso Garcia Paul Mirabella
May 20, 1981	OAK	A	Jim Spencer	NY	A	Dave Revering Mike Patterson minor league P Chuck Dougherty

Date	Traded To	Traded With	Traded By	In Exchange For

Tom Underwood *continued*

| Feb 6, 1984 | BAL | A | ——— | | OAK | A | Free agent signing |

(Oakland selected P Tim Belcher of New York Yankees from the compensation pool.)

Bob Unglaub

| June 18, 1904 | BOS | A | ——— | NY | A | Patsy Dougherty |
| July 1908 | WAS | A | Jesse Tannehill | BOS | A | Casey Patten |

Del Unser

Dec 2, 1971	CLE	A	Denny Riddleberger Gary Jones minor league P Terry Ley	TEX	A	Roy Foster Ken Suarez Mike Paul Rich Hand
Nov 30, 1972	PHI	N	minor league IF Terry Wedgewood	CLE	A	Oscar Gamble Roger Freed
Dec 3, 1974	NY	N	John Stearns Mac Scarce	PHI	N	Tug McGraw Don Hahn Dave Schneck
July 21, 1976	MON	N	Wayne Garrett	NY	N	Jim Dwyer Pepe Mangual

Dixie Upright

| Jan 20, 1953 | STL | A | $25,000. | CHI | A | Freddie Marsh |

Cecil Upshaw

April 22, 1973	HOU	N	———	ATL	N	Norm Miller
Dec 3, 1973	CLE	A	———	HOU	N	Jerry Johnson
April 27, 1974	NY	A	*See Chris Chambliss*	CLE	A	
Dec 5, 1974	CHI	A	———	NY	A	Eddie Leon

Willie Upshaw

| March 25, 1988 | CLE | A | ——— | TOR | A | Cash |

Bill Upton

| Feb 19, 1954 | PHI | A | Lee Wheat | CLE | A | Dave Philley |

Tom Upton

July 31, 1951	NY	A	Bobby Hogue Kermit Wahl Lou Sleater	STL	A	Cliff Mapes
Nov 27, 1951	CHI	A	*See Sherm Lollar*	STL	A	
Nov 27, 1951	WAS	A	———	CHI	A	Sam Dente
May 3, 1952	NY	A	———	WAS	A	*See Jackie Jensen*

Jack Urban

| April 5, 1957 | KC | A | ——— | NY | A | Continuation of Billy Hunter February 19, 1957. |
| April 8, 1959 | NY | A | ——— | KC | A | Mark Freeman |

(Freeman was returned to the Yankees on May 8, 1959.)

Jose Uribe

| Feb 1, 1985 | SF | N | David Green
Dave LaPoint
Gary Rajsich | STL | N | Jack Clark |

John Urrea

| Dec 8, 1980 | SD | N | ——— | STL | N | *See Rollie Fingers* |

Bob Usher

| Oct 4, 1951 | CHI | N | Johnny Pramesa | CIN | N | Bob Borkowski
Smoky Burgess |
| May 15, 1957 | WAS | A | ——— | CLE | A | Cash |

Tex Vache

| Dec 9, 1925 | DET | A | Homer Ezzell | BOS | A | Fred Haney |

Mike Vail

Dec 11, 1974	NY	N	Jack Heidemann	STL	N	Teddy Martinez
March 26, 1978	CLE	A	———	NY	N	Cash
June 15, 1978	CHI	N	———	CLE	A	Joe Wallis
Dec 12, 1980	CIN	N	———	CHI	N	Hector Cruz
Jan 5, 1983	SF	N	———	CIN	N	Rich Gale
May 25, 1983	MON	N	———	SF	N	Wallace Johnson

Sandy Valdespino

| Aug 30, 1969 | SEA | A | Danny Walton | HOU | N | Tommy Davis |

Sergio Valdez

| July 2, 1989 | ATL | N | Minor league
P Nate Minchey
Minor league
OF Kevin Dean | MON | N | Zane Smith |

Bobby Valentine

Nov 28, 1972	CAL	A	———	LA	N	*See Andy Messersmith*
Sept 17, 1975	SD	N	Rudi Meoli	CAL	A	Gary Ross
June 15, 1977	NY	N	Paul Siebert	SD	N	Dave Kingman

Corky Valentine

| April 9, 1956 | MIL | N | Bob Hazle | CIN | N | George Crowe |

Ellis Valentine

| May 29, 1981 | NY | N | ——— | MON | N | Jeff Reardon
Dan Norman |
| Jan 24, 1983 | CAL | A | ——— | NY | N | No compensation (free agent signing) |

Fred Valentine

| Oct 11, 1963 | WAS | A | ——— | BAL | A | Cash |
| June 15, 1968 | BAL | A | ——— | WAS | A | Bruce Howard |

Vito Valentinetti

May 23, 1957	CHI	N	Jackie Collum	BKN	N	Don Elston
Aug 24, 1957	CLE	A	———	CHI	N	Cash
March 27, 1958	DET	A	Milt Bolling	CLE	A	Pete Wojey and $20,000.
June 23, 1958	WAS	A	———	DET	A	Al Cicotte
April 1, 1959	BAL	A	———	WAS	A	Billy Loes

(Trade was cancelled on April 8, 1959, by Commissioner Frick due to Loes's sore arm.)

Benny Valenzuela

| Oct 8, 1958 | SF | N | Hobie Landrith
Billy Muffett | STL | N | Ernie Broglio
Marv Grissom |

Elmer Valo

| April 5, 1957 | BKN | N | Ron Negray
Tim Harkness
Ben Flowers
minor league
SS Mel Geho | PHI | N | Chico Fernandez |

Russ Van Atta

| May 15, 1935 | STL | A | ——— | NY | A | Cash |

Deacon Van Buren

| April 30, 1904 | PHI | N | Jack Doyle | BKN | N | Cash |

Date	Traded To		Traded With	Traded By		In Exchange For

Dazzy Vance

Date	Traded To		Traded With	Traded By		In Exchange For
March 1915	NY	A	———	PIT	N	Cash
Feb 1933	STL	N	Gordon Slade	BKN	N	Jake Flowers
						Ownie Carroll
June 25, 1934	CIN	N	———	STL	N	Waiver price

Ed Vande Berg

Date	Traded To		Traded With	Traded By		In Exchange For
Dec 11, 1985	LA	N	———	SEA	A	Steve Yeager
Feb 2, 1988	TEX	A	———	CLE	A	No compensation (free agent signing)

Hy Vandenburg

Date	Traded To		Traded With	Traded By		In Exchange For
Jan 1941	STL	N		NY	N	Cash

Johnny Vander Meer

Date	Traded To		Traded With	Traded By		In Exchange For
Feb 10, 1950	CHI	N	———	CIN	N	Cash

Elam Vangilder

Date	Traded To		Traded With	Traded By		In Exchange For
Dec 2, 1927	DET	A	Chick Galloway	STL	A	Heinie Manush
			Harry Rice			Lu Blue

Andy Van Slyke

Date	Traded To		Traded With	Traded By		In Exchange For
April 1, 1987	PIT	N	Mike LaValliere	STL	N	Tony Pena
			Mike Dunne			

Pete Varney

Date	Traded To		Traded With	Traded By		In Exchange For
June 15, 1976	ATL	N	———	CHI	A	Blue Moon Odom

Rafael Vasquez

Date	Traded To		Traded With	Traded By		In Exchange For
Dec 5, 1978	SEA	A	*See Mario Mendoza*	PIT	N	———
Dec 6, 1979	CLE	A	Bud Anderson and minor league P Bob Pietroburgo	SEA	A	Ted Cox
Dec 9, 1980	PIT	N	———	CLE	A	*See Bert Blyleven*

Arky Vaughan

Date	Traded To		Traded With	Traded By		In Exchange For
Dec 12, 1941	BKN	N	———	PIT	N	Pete Coscarart
						Luke Hamlin
						Babe Phelps
						Jimmy Wasdell

Fred Vaughn

Date	Traded To		Traded With	Traded By		In Exchange For
Jan 2, 1946	CHI	A	Alex Carrasquel	WAS	A	Cash

Hippo Vaughn

Date	Traded To		Traded With	Traded By		In Exchange For
June 26, 1912	WAS	A	———	NY	A	Waiver price

Bobby Veach

Date	Traded To		Traded With	Traded By		In Exchange For
March 12, 1924	BOS	A	———	DET	A	Cash
May 5, 1925	NY	A	Alex Ferguson	BOS	A	Ray Francis and $9,000.
Aug 17, 1925	WAS	A	———	NY	A	Waiver price

Coot Veal

Date	Traded To		Traded With	Traded By		In Exchange For
Nov 21, 1961	PIT	N	———	WAS	A	Cash

Bob Veale

Date	Traded To		Traded With	Traded By		In Exchange For
Sept 2, 1972	BOS	A	———	PIT	N	Cash

Randy Velarde

Date	Traded To		Traded With	Traded By		In Exchange For
Jan 5, 1987	NY	A	Pete Filson	CHI	A	Scott Nielsen
						Minor league
						IF Mike Soper

Freddie Velazquez

Date	Traded To		Traded With	Traded By		In Exchange For
June 3, 1969	OAK	A	———	SEA	A	Cash

Max Venable

Date	Traded To		Traded With	Traded By		In Exchange For
Feb 27, 1984	MON	N	Fred Breining Andy McGaffigan	SF	N	Al Oliver
(San Francisco sent McGaffigan to Montreal on April 1, 1984, after Breining reported to the Expos with a sore arm.)						
April 26, 1985	CIN	N	———	MON	N	Skeeter Barnes

Emil Verban

Date	Traded To		Traded With	Traded By		In Exchange For
May 2, 1946	PHI	N	———	STL	N	Clyde Kluttz
Aug 3, 1948	CHI	N	———	PHI	N	Waiver price

Joe Verbanic

Date	Traded To		Traded With	Traded By		In Exchange For
Dec 14, 1966	NY	A	Cash	PHI	N	Pedro Ramos

Johnny Vergez

Date	Traded To		Traded With	Traded By		In Exchange For
Nov 1, 1934	PHI	N	Pretzels Pezzullo Blondy Ryan George Watkins and cash	NY	N	Dick Bartell
July 1936	STL	N	———	PHI	N	Cash

John Verhoeven

Date	Traded To		Traded With	Traded By		In Exchange For
June 15, 1977	CHI	A	Don Kirkwood John Flannery	CAL	A	Ken Brett
Jan 26, 1982	BOS	A	———	MIN	A	Cash

Mickey Vernon

Date	Traded To		Traded With	Traded By		In Exchange For
Dec 14, 1948	CLE	A	Early Wynn	WAS	A	Joe Haynes
						Eddie Klieman
						Eddie Robinson
June 14, 1950	WAS	A	———	CLE	A	Dick Weik
Nov 8, 1955	BOS	A	Bob Porterfield Johnny Schmitz Tommy Umphlett	WAS	A	Karl Olson
						Dick Brodowski
						Tex Clevenger
						Neil Chrisley
						and minor league
						P Al Curtis
Jan 29, 1958	CLE	A	———	BOS	A	Waiver price
April 11, 1959	MIL	N	———	CLE	A	Humberto Robinson

Zoilo Versalles

Date	Traded To		Traded With	Traded By		In Exchange For
Nov 28, 1967	LA	N	Mudcat Grant	MIN	A	Johnny Roseboro
						Ron Perranoski
						Bob Miller
Oct 21, 1968	CLE	A	———	SD	N	Bill Davis
July 26, 1969	WAS	A	———	CLE	A	Cash

Tom Veryzer

Date	Traded To		Traded With	Traded By		In Exchange For
Dec 9, 1977	CLE	A	———	DET	A	Charlie Spikes
Jan 8, 1982	NY	N	———	CLE	A	Ray Searage
April 2, 1983	CHI	N	———	NY	N	Minor league
						Ps Craig Weissman
						and Bob Schilling

Bob Veselic

Date	Traded To		Traded With	Traded By		In Exchange For
Jan 12, 1983	HOU	N	———	MIN	A	Rick Lysander

Date	Traded To		Traded With	Traded By		In Exchange For

Sammy Vick
Dec 15, 1920 | BOS | A | —— | NY | A | *See Waite Hoyt*

Jose Vidal
May 19, 1969 | NY | A | —— | SEA | A | Dick Simpson

Rube Vinson
Feb 1906 | CHI | A | —— | CLE | A | Cash

Frank Viola
July 31, 1989 | NY | N | —— | MIN | A | Rick Aguilera
David West
Tim Drummond
Kevin Tapani
Jack Savage

(Minnesota received Savage on Oct. 16, 1989.)

Bill Virdon
April 11, 1954 | STL | N | Mel Wright minor league OF Emil Tellinger | NY | A | Enos Slaughter
May 17, 1956 | PIT | N | —— | STL | N | Dick Littlefield Bobby Del Greco

Ozzie Virgil
Jan 28, 1958 | DET | A | Gail Harris | SF | N | Jim Finigan and $25,000.
Aug 2, 1961 | KC | A | Bill Fischer | DET | A | Gerry Staley Reno Bertoia
Oct 1, 1965 | SF | N | Joe Gibbon | PIT | N | Matty Alou

Ozzie Virgil
Dec 10, 1985 | ATL | N | Pete Smith | PHI | N | Steve Bedrosian Milt Thompson

Ossie Vitt
Jan 17, 1919 | BOS | A | —— | DET | A | Eddie Ainsmith Chick Shorten Slim Love

Bill Voiselle
June 13, 1947 | BOS | N | Cash | NY | N | Mort Cooper
Dec 14, 1949 | CHI | N | —— | BOS | N | Gene Mauch and cash

Clyde Vollmer
May 8, 1950 | BOS | A | —— | WAS | A | Tommy O'Brien Merrill Combs
April 22, 1953 | WAS | A | —— | BOS | A | Cash

Joe Vosmik
Jan 17, 1937 | STL | A | Bill Knickerbocker Oral Hildebrand | CLE | A | Ivy Andrews Lyn Lary Moose Solters
Dec 2, 1937 | BOS | A | —— | STL | A | Bobo Newsom Red Kress Buster Mills
Feb 12, 1940 | BKN | N | —— | BOS | A | $25,000.

Bill Voss
Jan 20, 1969 | CAL | A | minor league P Andy Rubicotta | CHI | A | Sammy Ellis
Jan 28, 1971 | MIL | A | —— | CAL | A | Gene Brabender
June 20, 1972 | OAK | A | —— | MIL | A | Ron Clark

Bill Voss *continued*
Aug 27, 1972 | STL | N | minor league P Steve Easton | OAK | A | Matty Alou
Nov 28, 1972 | CIN | N | —— | STL | N | Pat Jacquez

Pete Vuckovich
Dec 6, 1977 | STL | N | John Scott | TOR | A | Tom Underwood Victor Cruz
Dec 12, 1980 | MIL | A | Rollie Fingers Ted Simmons | STL | N | Sixto Lezcano David Green Lary Sorensen Dave LaPoint

George Vukovich
Dec 9, 1982 | CLE | A | Manny Trillo Jay Baller Julio Franco Jerry Willard | PHI | N | Von Hayes

John Vukovich
Oct 31, 1972 | MIL | A | *See Don Money* | PHI | N | ——
Oct 22, 1974 | CIN | N | —— | MIL | A | Pat Osburn

Rube Waddell
Jan 1900 | PIT | N | *See Honus Wagner* | LOU | N | ——
May 1901 | CHI | N | —— | PIT | N | Cash
Feb 7, 1908 | STL | A | —— | PHI | A | Cash

Ben Wade
Aug 8, 1954 | STL | N | —— | BKN | N | Waiver price
Jan 11, 1955 | PIT | N | Cash | STL | N | Paul LaPalme

Gale Wade
Nov 16, 1954 | CHI | N | Sam Jones and $60,000. | CLE | A | Ralph Kiner

Jake Wade
Dec 15, 1938 | BOS | A | Eldon Auker Chet Morgan | DET | A | Pinky Higgins Archie McKain
Sept 1939 | STL | A | —— | BOS | A | Cash
Dec 15, 1944 | NY | A | —— | CHI | A | Johnny Johnson

Bill Wagner
Oct 1917 | BOS | N | —— | PIT | N | Cash

Gary Wagner
Sept 6, 1969 | BOS | A | —— | PHI | N | Mike Jackson

Hal Wagner
May 7, 1944 | BOS | A | —— | PHI | A | Ford Garrison
May 20, 1947 | DET | A | —— | BOS | A | Birdie Tebbetts
Sept 13, 1948 | PHI | N | —— | DET | A | Waiver price

Date	Traded To		Traded With	Traded By		In Exchange For

Honus Wagner

Jan 1900	PIT	N	Patsy Flaherty	LOU	N	Jack Chesbro
			Deacon Phillippe			Paddy Fox
			Walt Woods			John O'Brien
			Rube Waddell			Art Madison
			Icebox Chamberlain			and $25,000.
			Chief Zimmer			
			Tacks Latimer			
			Claude Ritchey			
			Fred Clarke			
			Tommy Leach			
			Mike Kelly			
			Conny Doyle			
			OF Tom Massitt			

(Sale of the chief assets of the Louisville franchise to Pittsburgh after Louisville was dropped by the National League.)

Leon Wagner

Dec 15, 1959	STL	N	Daryl Spencer	SF	N	Don Blasingame
Jan 26, 1961	LA	A	Cal Browning	STL	N	Al Cicotte
			Ellis Burton			
			and cash			
Dec 2, 1963	CLE	A	———	LA	A	Joe Adcock
						Barry Latman
June 13, 1968	CHI	A	———	CLE	A	Russ Snyder
Dec 5, 1968	CIN	N	———	CHI	A	Cash

(Wagner was returned to Chicago on April 5, 1969.)

Mark Wagner

Dec 10, 1980	TEX	A	———	DET	A	Kevin Saucier

Kermit Wahl

June 4, 1951	CHI	A	———	PHI	A	Hank Majeski
June 4, 1951	STL	A	Paul Lehner	CHI	A	Don Lenhardt
			and cash			
July 31, 1951	NY	A	Bobby Hogue	STL	A	Cliff Mapes
			Tom Upton			
			Lou Sleater			

Eddie Waitkus

Dec 14, 1948	PHI	N	Hank Borowy	CHI	N	Monk Dubiel
						Dutch Leonard
March 16, 1954	BAL	A	———	PHI	N	$40,000.

Rick Waits

June 13, 1975	CLE	A	Jim Bibby	TEX	A	Gaylord Perry
			Jackie Brown			
			and $100,000.			
June 6, 1983	MIL	A	Rick Manning	CLE	A	Gorman Thomas
						Jamie Easterly
						Ernie Camacho

Bill Wakefield

Nov 4, 1963	NY	N	George Altman	STL	N	Roger Craig

Dick Wakefield

Dec 17, 1949	NY	A	———	DET	A	Dick Kryhoski

Howard Wakefield

Feb 1906	WAS	A	———	CLE	A	Cash
Feb 1907	CLE	A	———	WAS	A	Cash
Aug 11, 1907	WAS	A	Pete O'Brien	CLE	A	Rabbit Nill

Rube Walberg

April 1923	PHI	A	———	NY	N	Waiver price
Dec 12, 1933	BOS	A	Lefty Grove	PHI	A	Bob Kline
			Max Bishop			Rabbit Warstler
						and $125,000.

Bob Walk

March 25, 1981	ATL	N	———	PHI	N	Gary Matthews

Bill Walker

Oct 10, 1932	STL	N	Ethan Allen	NY	N	Gus Mancuso
			Bob O'Farrell			Ray Starr
			Jim Mooney			
Aug 6, 1936	CIN	N	———	STL	N	Si Johnson

Chico Walker

Sept 22, 1987	CAL	A	———	CHI	N	Minor league
						P Todd Fischer

Curt Walker

July 25, 1921	PHI	N	Butch Henline	NY	N	Irish Meusel
			Jesse Winters			
			and $30,000.			
May 30, 1924	CIN	N	———	PHI	N	George Harper

Dixie Walker

May 4, 1936	CHI	A	———	NY	A	Waiver price
Dec 2, 1937	DET	A	Vern Kennedy	CHI	A	Marv Owen
			Tony Piet			Mike Tresh
						Gee Walker
July 24, 1939	BKN	N	———	DET	A	Waiver price
Dec 8, 1947	PIT	N	Hal Gregg	BKN	N	Preacher Roe
			Vic Lombardi			Billy Cox
						Gene Mauch

Duane Walker

July 19, 1985	TEX	A	Jeff Russell	CIN	N	Buddy Bell

Gee Walker

Dec 2, 1937	CHI	A	Marv Owen	DET	A	Vern Kennedy
			Mike Tresh			Tony Piet
						Dixie Walker
Dec 8, 1939	WAS	A	———	CHI	A	Taffy Wright
						Pete Appleton
Dec 12, 1940	BOS	A	———	WAS	A	Doc Cramer
Dec 12, 1940	CLE	A	Gene Desautels	BOS	A	Frankie Pytlak
			Jim Bagby			Odell Hale
						Joe Dobson
March 26, 1942	CIN	N	———	CLE	A	Cash

Harry Walker

May 3, 1947	PHI	N	Freddy Schmidt	STL	N	Ron Northey
Oct 4, 1948	CHI	N	———	PHI	N	Bill Nicholson
June 15, 1949	CIN	N	Peanuts Lowrey	CHI	N	Frankie Baumholtz
						Hank Sauer
Dec 14, 1949	STL	N	———	CIN	N	Lou Klein
						Ron Northey

Jerry Walker

April 12, 1961	KC	A	Chuck Essegian	BAL	A	Dick Hall
						Dick Williams
Feb 27, 1963	CLE	A	———	KC	A	Chuck Essegian

Luke Walker

Dec 5, 1973	DET	A	———	PIT	N	Cash

Rube Walker

June 15, 1951	BKN	N	*See Andy Pafko*	CHI	N	———

Tilly Walker

Oct 1912	STL	A	———	WAS	A	Cash

Date	Traded To	Traded With	Traded By	In Exchange For

Tilly Walker *continued*

Date	Traded To	Traded With	Traded By	In Exchange For
April 8, 1916	BOS A	——	STL A	Cash
Jan 10, 1918	PHI A	Larry Gardner Hick Cady	BOS A	Stuffy McInnis

Tom Walker

Date	Traded To	Traded With	Traded By	In Exchange For
Dec 4, 1974	DET A	Terry Humphrey	MON N	Woodie Fryman
Feb 3, 1976	STL N	——	DET A	Cash
July 13, 1977	CAL A	——	MON N	Cash

Tony Walker

Date	Traded To	Traded With	Traded By	In Exchange For
March 31, 1983	HOU N	*See Bill Dawley*	CIN N	——

Jim Walkup

Date	Traded To	Traded With	Traded By	In Exchange For
May 13, 1939	DET A	*See Beau Bell*	STL A	——

Joe Wall

Date	Traded To	Traded With	Traded By	In Exchange For
July 1902	BKN N	Roy Evans	NY N	Cash

Murray Wall

Date	Traded To	Traded With	Traded By	In Exchange For
June 11, 1959	WAS A	Billy Consolo	BOS A	Dick Hyde Herb Plews

(Hyde was returned to Washington and Wall was returned to Boston.)

Don Wallace

Date	Traded To	Traded With	Traded By	In Exchange For
July 24, 1967	NY N	Cash	CAL A	Hawk Taylor

Mike Wallace

Date	Traded To	Traded With	Traded By	In Exchange For
May 3, 1974	NY A	——	PHI N	Ken Wright
June 13, 1975	STL N	——	NY A	Cash
Oct 22, 1976	TEX N	——	STL N	Johnny Sutton

Jack Wallaesa

Date	Traded To	Traded With	Traded By	In Exchange For
Dec 13, 1946	CHI A	——	PHI A	Cash

Tye Waller

Date	Traded To	Traded With	Traded By	In Exchange For
Dec 9, 1980	CHI N	Leon Durham Ken Reitz	STL N	Bruce Sutter
Dec 10, 1982	CHI A	——	CHI N	Reggie Patterson

Denny Walling

Date	Traded To	Traded With	Traded By	In Exchange For
June 15, 1977	HOU N	Cash	OAK A	Willie Crawford
Aug 31, 1988	STL N	——	HOU N	Bob Forsch

Joe Wallis

Date	Traded To	Traded With	Traded By	In Exchange For
June 15, 1978	CLE A	——	CHI N	Mike Vail
June 15, 1978	OAK A	——	CLE A	Gary Alexander

Lee Walls

Date	Traded To	Traded With	Traded By	In Exchange For
May 1, 1957	CHI N	Dale Long	PIT N	Gene Baker Dee Fondy
Dec 6, 1959	CIN N	Bill Henry Lou Jackson	CHI N	Frank Thomas
June 15, 1960	PHI N	Tony Gonzalez	CIN N	Harry Anderson Wally Post minor league 1B Fred Hopke
Dec 15, 1961	LA N	$100,000.	NY N	Charlie Neal

Jimmy Walsh

Date	Traded To	Traded With	Traded By	In Exchange For
June 10, 1914	PHI A	——	NY A	Tom Daley
Sept 2, 1916	BOS A	——	PHI A	Ray Haley

Jimmy Walsh

Date	Traded To	Traded With	Traded By	In Exchange For
Sept 1915	STL F	——	BAL F	Cash

Gene Walter

Date	Traded To	Traded With	Traded By	In Exchange For
Dec 11, 1986	NY N	*See Kevin McReynolds*	SD N	——
July 11, 1988	SEA A	——	NY N	Edwin Nunez

Bucky Walters

Date	Traded To	Traded With	Traded By	In Exchange For
June 14, 1934	PHI N	——	BOS A	Cash
June 13, 1938	CIN N	——	PHI N	Spud Davis Al Hollingsworth and $50,000.

Charley Walters

Date	Traded To	Traded With	Traded By	In Exchange For
March 21, 1970	WAS A	Joe Grzenda	MIN A	Brant Alyea

Fred Walters

Date	Traded To	Traded With	Traded By	In Exchange For
Dec 26, 1953	PIT N	——	MIL N	*See Danny O'Connell*

Ken Walters

Date	Traded To	Traded With	Traded By	In Exchange For
Dec 5, 1959	PHI N	Ted Lepcio minor league P Alex Cosmidis	DET A	Chico Fernandez Ray Semproch

Mike Walters

Date	Traded To	Traded With	Traded By	In Exchange For
May 12, 1982	MIN A	Tom Brunansky and $400,000.	CAL A	Doug Corbett Rob Wilfong

Roxy Walters

Date	Traded To	Traded With	Traded By	In Exchange For
Dec 18, 1918	BOS A	——	NY A	*See Duffy Lewis*
Jan 7, 1924	CLE A	——	BOS A	*See Bill Wambsganss*

Danny Walton

Date	Traded To	Traded With	Traded By	In Exchange For
Aug 30, 1969	SEA A	Sandy Valdespino	HOU N	Tommy Davis
June 7, 1971	NY A	——	MIL A	Frank Tepedino Bobby Mitchell
Oct 27, 1972	MIN A	——	NY A	Rick Dempsey
Dec 15, 1980	CIN N	Greg Mahlberg	TEX A	Don Werner Minor leaguer Greg Hughes

Reggie Walton

Date	Traded To	Traded With	Traded By	In Exchange For
April 9, 1982	PIT N	——	SEA A	Cash

Bill Wambsganss

Date	Traded To	Traded With	Traded By	In Exchange For
Jan 7, 1924	BOS A	Danny Boone Steve O'Neill Joe Connolly	CLE A	George Burns Roxy Walters Chick Fewster
Dec 12, 1925	PHI A	——	BOS A	$4,000.

Lloyd Waner

Date	Traded To	Traded With	Traded By	In Exchange For
May 7, 1941	BOS N	——	PIT N	Nick Strincevich
June 12, 1941	CIN N	——	BOS N	Johnny Hutchings
March 9, 1943	BKN N	Al Glossop	PHI N	Babe Dahlgren

Aaron Ward

Date	Traded To	Traded With	Traded By	In Exchange For
Jan 13, 1927	CHI A	——	NY A	Johnny Grabowski Ray Morehart
March 4, 1928	CLE A	——	CHI A	Waiver price

Date	Traded To		Traded With	Traded By		In Exchange For

Chuck Ward

Date	Traded To		Traded With	Traded By		In Exchange For
Jan 9, 1918	BKN	N	Burleigh Grimes, Al Mamaux	PIT	N	Casey Stengel, George Cutshaw

Colin Ward

Date	Traded To		Traded With	Traded By		In Exchange For
Nov 11, 1985	SF	N	——	CIN	N	Bob Buchanan

Dick Ward

Date	Traded To		Traded With	Traded By		In Exchange For
Nov 21, 1934	STL	N	Bud Tinning and cash	CHI	N	Tex Carleton

Duane Ward

Date	Traded To		Traded With	Traded By		In Exchange For
July 6, 1986	TOR	A	——	ATL	N	Doyle Alexander

Gary Ward

Date	Traded To		Traded With	Traded By		In Exchange For
Dec 7, 1983	TEX	A	——	MIN	A	Mike Smithson, John Butcher, minor league C Sam Sorce
Dec 24, 1986	NY	A	——	TEX	A	No compensation (free agent signing)

Joe Ward

Date	Traded To		Traded With	Traded By		In Exchange For
March 1909	NY	A	——	PHI	N	Cash

(Ward was returned to Philadelphia on May 20.)

Pete Ward

Date	Traded To		Traded With	Traded By		In Exchange For
Jan 14, 1963	CHI	A	Hoyt Wilhelm, Ron Hansen, Dave Nicholson	BAL	A	Luis Aparicio, Al Smith
Dec 18, 1969	NY	A	——	CHI	A	Mickey Scott and cash

Preston Ward

Date	Traded To		Traded With	Traded By		In Exchange For
Oct 14, 1949	CHI	N	Paul Minner	BKN	N	$100,000.
June 4, 1953	PIT	N	——	CHI	N	See Ralph Kiner
May 15, 1956	CLE	A	——	PIT	N	Hank Foiles
June 15, 1958	KC	A	Roger Maris, Dick Tomanek	CLE	A	Woodie Held, Vic Power

Curt Wardle

Date	Traded To		Traded With	Traded By		In Exchange For
Aug 1, 1985	CLE	A	——	MIN	A	See Bert Blyleven
Feb 23, 1987	OAK	A	——	CLE	A	Jeff Kaiser

Lon Warneke

Date	Traded To		Traded With	Traded By		In Exchange For
Oct 8, 1936	STL	N	——	CHI	N	Ripper Collins, Roy Parmelee
July 8, 1942	CHI	N	——	STL	N	$75,000.

Jack Warner

Date	Traded To		Traded With	Traded By		In Exchange For
Jan 1905	STL	N	——	NY	N	Cash
Aug 10, 1905	DET	A	——	STL	N	Cash
Aug 13, 1906	WAS	A	——	DET	A	Cash

Jack Warner

Date	Traded To		Traded With	Traded By		In Exchange For
Dec 19, 1928	WAS	A	——	DET	A	Bucky Harris

(Harris was named Detroit manager.)

Date	Traded To		Traded With	Traded By		In Exchange For
Dec 15, 1932	PHI	N	Cy Moore, Mickey Finn	BKN	N	Ray Benge and $15,000.

Jackie Warner

Date	Traded To		Traded With	Traded By		In Exchange For
June 15, 1967	KC	A	Jack Sanford	CAL	A	Roger Repoz

Bennie Warren

Date	Traded To		Traded With	Traded By		In Exchange For
Sept 9, 1942	PIT	N	——	PHI	N	Waiver price

(Deal was cancelled by Commissioner Landis.)

Date	Traded To		Traded With	Traded By		In Exchange For
Nov 17, 1942	CHI	N	——	PIT	N	Cash
April 4, 1946	NY	N	——	CHI	N	Waiver price

Mike Warren

Date	Traded To		Traded With	Traded By		In Exchange For
May 14, 1982	OAK	A	minor league 1B John Evans	MIL	A	Rob Picciolo

Rabbit Warstler

Date	Traded To		Traded With	Traded By		In Exchange For
Dec 12, 1933	PHI	A	Bob Kline and $125,000.	BOS	A	Lefty Grove, Rube Walberg, Max Bishop
July 6, 1936	BOS	N	——	PHI	A	Waiver price
July 24, 1940	CHI	N	——	BOS	N	Waiver price

Dan Warthen

Date	Traded To		Traded With	Traded By		In Exchange For
June 15, 1977	PHI	N	Barry Foote	MON	N	Wayne Twitchell, Tim Blackwell

Carl Warwick

Date	Traded To		Traded With	Traded By		In Exchange For
May 30, 1961	STL	N	Bob Lillis	LA	N	Daryl Spencer
May 7, 1962	HOU	N	John Anderson	STL	N	Bobby Shantz
Feb 17, 1964	STL	N	——	HOU	N	Jim Beauchamp, Chuck Taylor
July 24, 1965	BAL	A	——	STL	N	Cash
March 30, 1966	CHI	N	——	BAL	A	Vic Roznovsky

Jimmy Wasdell

Date	Traded To		Traded With	Traded By		In Exchange For
May 25, 1940	BKN	N	——	WAS	A	Cash
Dec 12, 1941	PIT	N	Pete Coscarart, Luke Hamlin, Babe Phelps	BKN	N	Arky Vaughan
April 30, 1943	PHI	N	——	PIT	N	Cash

George Washburn

Date	Traded To		Traded With	Traded By		In Exchange For
April 16, 1943	PHI	N	——	CHI	N	Cash
April 22, 1943	BKN	N	Johnny Allen	PHI	N	Cash

Ray Washburn

Date	Traded To		Traded With	Traded By		In Exchange For
Nov 5, 1969	CIN	N	——	STL	N	George Culver

Claudell Washington

Date	Traded To		Traded With	Traded By		In Exchange For
March 26, 1977	TEX	A	——	OAK	A	Jim Umbarger, Rodney Scott and cash
May 16, 1978	CHI	A	Rusty Torres	TEX	A	Bobby Bonds
June 7, 1980	NY	N	——	CHI	A	Minor league P jesse Anderson
Nov 17, 1980	ATL	N	——	NY	N	No compensation (free agent signing)
June 29, 1986	NY	A	Paul Zuvella	ATL	N	Ken Griffey, Andre Robertson

(Atlanta received Robertson on July 3, 1986.)

Date	Traded To		Traded With	Traded By		In Exchange For
Jan 17, 1989	CAL	A	——	NY	A	No compensation (free agent signing)

LaRue Washington

Date	Traded To		Traded With	Traded By		In Exchange For
March 31, 1980	MON	N	Chris Smith	TEX	A	Rusty Staub

U. L. Washington

Date	Traded To		Traded With	Traded By		In Exchange For
April 24, 1986	PIT	N	——	MON	N	No compensation (free agent signing)

Date	Traded To		Traded With	Traded By		In Exchange For

Mark Wasinger
| April 17, 1987 | SF | N | Minor league P Tom Meagher | SD | N | Minor league P Colin Ward Minor league IF Steve Miller |

Gary Waslewski
Dec 2, 1968	STL	N	——	BOS	A	Dick Schofield
June 3, 1969	MON	N	——	STL	N	Mudcat Grant
May 15, 1970	NY	A	——	MON	N	Dave McDonald

Steve Waterbury
| June 15, 1977 | PHI | N | Bake McBride | STL | N | Tom Underwood Dane Iorg Rick Bosetti |

George Watkins
Feb 1934	NY	N	——	STL	N	Kiddo Davis
Nov 1, 1934	PHI	N	Pretzels Pezzullo Blondy Ryan Johnny Vergez and cash	NY	N	Dick Bartell
May 1936	BKN	N	——	PHI	N	Cash

Bob Watson
June 13, 1979	BOS	A	——	HOU	N	Pete Ladd Bobby Sprowl and cash
Nov 8, 1979	NY	A	——	BOS	A	No compensation (free agent signing)
April 23, 1982	ATL	N	——	NY	A	Minor league P Scott Patterson

Milt Watson
| April 4, 1918 | PHI | N | —— | STL | N | Bert Niehoff and $500. |

Mule Watson
May 28, 1920	PIT	N	——	BOS	N	Waiver price
June 30, 1920	BOS	N	——	PIT	N	Waiver price
June 7, 1923	NY	N	Hank Gowdy	BOS	N	Jesse Barnes Earl Smith

Eddie Watt
| Dec 7, 1973 | PHI | N | —— | BAL | A | Cash |

Cliff Watwood
| April 29, 1932 | BOS | A | Bennie Tate Smead Jolley | CHI | A | Charlie Berry |

Roy Weatherly
| Dec 17, 1942 | NY | A | Oscar Grimes | CLE | A | Roy Cullenbine Buddy Rosar |

Art Weaver
| June 1903 | PIT | N | —— | STL | N | Cash |

Floyd Weaver
| June 30, 1971 | MIL | A | —— | CHI | A | Cash |

Jim Weaver
| Jan 4, 1967 | HOU | N | Jim Landis Doc Edwards | CLE | A | Lee Maye Ken Retzer |
| Aug 7, 1967 | CAL | N | —— | HOU | N | Hector Torres |

Jim Weaver
May 15, 1934	CHI	N	——	STL	A	Waiver price
Nov 22, 1934	PIT	N	Guy Bush Babe Herman	CHI	N	Larry French Freddie Lindstrom
Jan 1938	STL	A	——	PIT	N	Cash
April 25, 1938	CIN	N	——	STL	A	Cash

Jim Weaver
| Aug 1, 1985 | CLE | A | Curt Wardle | MIN | A | Bert Blyleven |

Monte Weaver
| Feb 1939 | BOS | A | —— | WAS | A | Cash |

Orlie Weaver
| June 10, 1911 | BOS | N | See Johnny Kling | CHI | N | —— |

Roger Weaver
| March 23, 1982 | ATL | N | —— | DET | A | Eddie Miller |

Earl Webb
April 4, 1930	WAS	A	——	CIN	N	Waiver price
April 30, 1930	BOS	A	——	WAS	A	Bill Barrett
June 12, 1932	DET	A	——	BOS	A	Dale Alexander Roy Johnson
May 14, 1933	CHI	A	——	DET	A	Waiver price

Hank Webb
| Feb 7, 1977 | LA | N | minor league P Dick Sander | NY | N | Rick Auerbach |

Red Webb
| Dec 14, 1949 | BOS | N | Sid Gordon Buddy Kerr Willard Marshall | NY | N | Eddie Stanky Alvin Dark |

Skeeter Webb
| Dec 12, 1944 | DET | A | —— | CHI | A | Joe Orengo |

Mitch Webster
June 22, 1985	MON	N	——	TOR	A	Cash
July 14, 1988	CHI	N	——	MON	N	Dave Martinez
Nov 20, 1989	CLE	A	——	CHI	N	Dave Clark

Ramon Webster
March 24, 1970	SD	N	——	OAK	A	Roberto Pena
Oct 19, 1970	OAK	A	——	SD	N	Cash
June 17, 1971	CHI	N	——	OAK	A	Cash

Ray Webster
| Jan 8, 1960 | BOS | A | —— | CLE | A | Leo Kiely |

Johnny Weekly
| June 15, 1964 | BAL | A | Cash | HOU | N | Joe Gaines |
| Jan 6, 1966 | NY | N | Cash | HOU | N | Gary Kroll |

Herm Wehmeier
June 12, 1954	PHI	N	——	CIN	N	Cash
May 11, 1956	STL	N	Murry Dickson	PHI	N	Harvey Haddix Ben Flowers Stu Miller
May 13, 1958	DET	A	——	STL	N	Cash

Date	Traded To	Traded With	Traded By	In Exchange For

Dave Wehrmeister
| June 15, 1979 | NY | A | —— | SD | N | Jay Johnstone |

Ralph Weigel
| Jan 27, 1948 | CHI | A | —— | CLE | A | Thurman Tucker |
| April 15, 1949 | WAS | A | —— | CHI | A | Cash |

Dick Weik
| June 14, 1950 | CLE | A | —— | WAS | A | Mickey Vernon |
| June 15, 1953 | DET | A | *See Ray Boone* | CLE | A | —— |

Bob Weiland
Dec 2, 1931	BOS	A	——	CHI	A	Milt Gaston
May 25, 1934	CLE	A	Bob Seeds and $25,000.	BOS	A	Wes Ferrell Dick Porter
Nov 20, 1934	STL	A	Johnny Burnett and cash	CLE	A	Bruce Campbell

Jake Weimer
| March 1906 | CIN | N | Hans Lobert | CHI | N | Harry Steinfeldt |

Phil Weintraub
| Dec 9, 1935 | STL | N | Roy Parmelee and cash | NY | N | Burgess Whitehead |

Al Weis
| Dec 15, 1967 | NY | N | Tommie Agee | CHI | A | Tommy Davis Jack Fisher Billy Wynne Buddy Booker |

Johnny Welaj
| Dec 13, 1941 | BOS | A | Ken Chase | WAS | A | Stan Spence Jack Wilson |

Bob Welch
| Dec 11, 1987 | OAK | A | Matt Young | LA | N | Alfredo Griffin Jay Howell |

(Part of three-team trade involving Oakland, Los Angeles and New York Mets.)

Frank Welch
| Nov 1926 | BOS | A | —— | PHI | A | Cash |

Johnny Welch
| July 1936 | PIT | N | —— | BOS | A | Waiver price |

Brad Wellman
| March 30, 1982 | SF | N | —— | KC | A | *See Vida Blue* |

Boomer Wells
| Dec 28, 1981 | MIN | A | —— | TOR | A | Hosken Powell |

Ed Wells
| Dec 1932 | STL | A | —— | NY | A | Cash |

Chris Welsh
April 1, 1981	SD	N	Ruppert Jones Joe Lefebvre Tim Lollar	NY	A	Jerry Mumphrey John Pacella
May 4, 1983	MON	N	——	SD	N	Cash
Nov 8, 1984	TEX	A	——	MON	N	Dave Hostetler

Jimmy Welsh
Jan 10, 1928	NY	N	Shanty Hogan	BOS	N	Rogers Hornsby
June 14, 1929	BOS	N	——	NY	N	Doc Farrell
Oct 14, 1930	CHI	N	Bob Smith	BOS	N	Bill McAfee Wes Schulmerich

Butch Wensloff
| April 12, 1948 | CLE | A | —— | NY | A | Cash |

Stan Wentzel
| Sept 30, 1946 | PIT | N | Billy Herman Elmer Singleton Whitey Wietelmann | BOS | N | Bob Elliott Hank Camelli |

Fred Wenz
| Nov 25, 1969 | PHI | N | —— | BOS | A | Cash |

Bill Werber
May 12, 1933	BOS	A	George Pipgras	NY	A	$100,000.
Dec 9, 1936	PHI	A	——	BOS	A	Pinky Higgins
March 16, 1939	CIN	N	——	PHI	A	Cash
Dec 9, 1941	NY	N	——	CIN	N	Cash

Johnny Werhas
| May 10, 1967 | CAL | A | —— | LA | N | Len Gabrielson |

Bill Werle
| May 3, 1952 | STL | N | —— | PIT | N | George Munger |
| Oct 2, 1952 | BOS | A | —— | STL | N | Waiver price |

Don Werner
| Dec 15, 1980 | TEX | A | Minor leaguer Greg Hughes | CIN | N | Danny Walton Greg Mahlberg |

Don Wert
| Oct 9, 1970 | WAS | A | *See Denny McLain* | DET | A | —— |

Dennis Werth
| March 24, 1982 | KC | A | —— | NY | A | Minor league P Scott Behan |

Vic Wertz
Aug 14, 1952	STL	A	Dick Littlefield Marlin Stuart Don Lenhardt	DET	A	Jim Delsing Ned Garver Dave Madison Bill Black
June 1, 1954	CLE	A	——	BAL	A	Bob Chakales
Dec 2, 1958	BOS	A	Gary Geiger	CLE	A	Jimmy Piersall
Sept 8, 1961	DET	A	——	BOS	A	Waiver price

David West
| July 31, 1989 | MIN | A | Rick Aguilera Tim Drummond Kevin Tapani Jack Savage | NY | N | Frank Viola |

(Minnesota received Savage on Oct. 16, 1989.)

Max West
| April 18, 1946 | CIN | N | —— | BOS | N | Jim Konstanty and cash |

Date	Traded To	Traded With	Traded By	In Exchange For

Sammy West

Date		Traded With		In Exchange For
Dec 14, 1932	STL A	Carl Reynolds Lloyd Brown and $20,000.	WAS A	Goose Goslin Fred Schulte Lefty Stewart
June 15, 1938	WAS A	——	STL A	Mel Almada

Wally Westlake

June 15, 1951	STL N	Cliff Chambers	PIT N	Bill Howerton Howie Pollet Ted Wilks Joe Garagiola Dick Cole
May 13, 1952	CIN N	Eddie Kazak	STL N	Dick Sisler Virgil Stallcup
Aug 7, 1952	CLE A	——	CIN N	Cash
June 15, 1955	BAL A	Dave Pope	CLE A	Gene Woodling Billy Cox

(Cox refused to report and announced retirement. Cleveland received $15,000 to complete trade.)

Gus Weyhing

Jan 17, 1900	STL N	Dan McGann	WAS N	Cash
July 1900	BKN N	——	STL N	Cash

Lee Wheat

Feb 19, 1954	PHI A	Bill Upton	CLE A	Dave Philley
April 16, 1956	BKN N	Tom Saffell and cash	KC A	Tim Thompson

Mack Wheat

Jan 12, 1920	PHI N	——	BKN N	Cash

Pete Whisenant

June 3, 1955	STL N	——	MIL N	Del Rice
March 30, 1956	CHI N	——	STL N	Hank Sauer
Nov 13, 1956	CIN N	Don Hoak Warren Hacker	CHI N	Elmer Singleton Ray Jablonski
April 29, 1960	CLE A	——	CIN N	Cash
May 15, 1960	WAS A	——	CLE A	Ken Aspromonte

Steve Whitaker

April 1, 1969	SEA A	John Gelnar	KC A	Lou Piniella
Dec 12, 1969	SF N	Dick Simpson	SEA A	Bobby Bolin

Bill White

March 25, 1959	STL N	Ray Jablonski	SF N	Sam Jones Don Choate
Oct 27, 1965	PHI N	Dick Groat Bob Uecker	STL N	Pat Corrales Art Mahaffey Alex Johnson
April 3, 1969	STL N	——	PHI N	Jim Hutto Jerry Buchek

Charlie White

Feb 10, 1954	MIL N	$10,000.	BAL A	Vern Bickford

Ernie White

May 14, 1946	BOS N	——	STL N	Cash

Hal White

Dec 4, 1952	STL A	Virgil Trucks Johnny Groth	DET A	Owen Friend Bob Nieman J. W. Porter
June 2, 1953	STL N	——	STL A	Waiver price

Jerry White

June 9, 1978	CHI N	——	MON N	Woodie Fryman
Dec 14, 1978	MON N	Rodney Scott	CHI N	Sam Mejias

Jo-Jo White

Aug 19, 1944	CIN N	——	PHI A	Cash

Kirby White

June 1, 1910	PIT N	——	BOS N	Sam Frock

Larry White

Dec 9, 1981	LA N	Jorge Orta Jack Fimple	CLE A	Rick Sutcliffe Jack Perconte

Sammy White

March 16, 1960	CLE A	Jim Marshall	BOS A	Russ Nixon

(Trade was cancelled when White decided to retire.)

June 15, 1961	MIL N	——	BOS A	Cash

Ed Whited

Dec 8, 1987	ATL N	Minor league P Mike Stoker	HOU N	Rafael Ramirez

Burgess Whitehead

Dec 9, 1935	NY N	——	STL N	Roy Parmelee Phil Weintraub and cash

John Whitehead

June 2, 1939	STL A	——	CHI A	Johnny Marcum

Earl Whitehill

Dec 14, 1932	WAS A	——	DET A	Firpo Marberry Carl Fischer
Dec 10, 1936	CLE A	——	WAS A	Jack Salveson

(Part of three-team trade involving Chicago, Cleveland, and Washington.)

Len Whitehouse

Nov 1, 1982	MIN A	——	TEX A	John Pacella

Wally Whitehurst

Dec 11, 1987	NY N	Jack Savage Kevin Tapani	LA N	Jesse Orosco

(Part of a three-team trade involving Los Angeles, Oakland, and New York Mets.)

Fred Whitfield

Dec 15, 1962	CLE A	——	STL N	Ron Taylor Jack Kubiszyn
Nov 21, 1967	CIN N	George Culver Bob Raudman	CLE A	Tommy Harper

Terry Whitfield

March 14, 1977	SF N	——	NY A	Marty Perez

Dick Whitman

Nov 14, 1949	PHI N	——	BKN N	Cash
June 8, 1951	BKN N	Cash	PHI N	Tommy Brown

Date	Traded To		Traded With	Traded By		In Exchange For

Pinky Whitney

Date	Traded To		Traded With	Traded By		In Exchange For
June 17, 1933	BOS	N	Hal Lee	PHI	N	Fritz Knothe Wes Schulmerich and cash
April 30, 1936	PHI	N	——	BOS	N	Mickey Haslin

Ed Whitson

Date	Traded To		Traded With	Traded By		In Exchange For
June 28, 1979	SF	N	Fred Breining Al Holland	PIT	N	Bill Madlock Lenny Randle Dave Roberts
Nov 14, 1981	CLE	A	——	SF	N	Duane Kuiper
Nov 18, 1982	SD	N	——	CLE	A	Juan Eichelberger Broderick Perkins
Dec 27, 1984	NY	A	——	SD	N	No compensation (free agent signing)
July 9, 1986	SD	N	——	NY	A	Tim Stoddard

Ernie Whitt

Date	Traded To		Traded With	Traded By		In Exchange For
Dec 17, 1989	ATL	N	Kevin Batiste	TOR	A	Minor league P Rick Trlicek

Possum Whitted

Date	Traded To		Traded With	Traded By		In Exchange For
June 1914	BOS	N	Ted Cather	STL	N	Hub Perdue
Feb 10, 1915	PHI	N	Oscar Dugey	BOS	N	Cash
Aug 1919	PIT	N	——	PHI	N	Casey Stengel
March 14, 1922	BKN	N	——	PIT	N	Cash

Bob Wicker

Date	Traded To		Traded With	Traded By		In Exchange For
April 1903	CHI	N	——	STL	N	Bob Rhoads
June 2, 1906	CIN	N	$2,000.	CHI	N	Orval Overall

Floyd Wicker

Date	Traded To		Traded With	Traded By		In Exchange For
June 1, 1971	SF	N	——	MIL	A	Bob Heise

Dave Wickersham

Date	Traded To		Traded With	Traded By		In Exchange For
Nov 18, 1963	DET	A	——	KC	A	See Rocky Colavito
Nov 28, 1967	PIT	N	——	DET	A	Dennis Ribant
Oct 21, 1968	KC	A	——	PIT	N	Cash
Oct 21, 1969	ATL	N	——	KC	A	Ron Tompkins

Al Wickland

Date	Traded To		Traded With	Traded By		In Exchange For
June 1, 1915	PIT	F	——	CHI	F	Cash
Jan 1919	NY	A	——	BOS	N	Cash

Al Widmar

Date	Traded To		Traded With	Traded By		In Exchange For
Nov 17, 1947	STL	A	——	BOS	A	See Vern Stephens
Nov 27, 1951	CHI	A	See Sherm Lollar	STL	A	

Ted Wieand

Date	Traded To		Traded With	Traded By		In Exchange For
Dec 5, 1957	CIN	N	Marty Kutyna Willard Schmidt	STL	N	Curt Flood Joe Taylor

Tom Wieghaus

Date	Traded To		Traded With	Traded By		In Exchange For
Feb 24, 1984	HOU	N	——	MON	N	George Bjorkman

(Montreal received Bjorkman on March 26, 1984.)

Bob Wiesler

Date	Traded To		Traded With	Traded By		In Exchange For
Feb 8, 1956	WAS	A	See Whitey Herzog	NY	A	——

Whitey Wietelmann

Date	Traded To		Traded With	Traded By		In Exchange For
Sept 30, 1946	PIT	N	Billy Herman Elmer Singleton Stan Wentzel	BOS	N	Bob Elliott Hank Camelli

Alan Wiggins

Date	Traded To		Traded With	Traded By		In Exchange For
June 27, 1985	BAL	A	——	SD	N	Roy Lee Jackson player to be named

(San Diego received P Rich Caldwell on Sept. 16, 1985.)

Bill Wight

Date	Traded To		Traded With	Traded By		In Exchange For
Feb 24, 1948	CHI	A	Aaron Robinson Fred Bradley	NY	A	Ed Lopat
Dec 10, 1950	BOS	A	Ray Scarborough	CHI	A	Joe Dobson Dick Littlefield Al Zarilla
June 3, 1952	DET	A	——	BOS	A	See George Kell
June 15, 1953	CLE	A	Art Houtteman Owen Friend Joe Ginsberg	DET	A	Ray Boone Al Aber Steve Gromek Dick Weik
July 13, 1955	BAL	A	——	CLE	A	Hoot Evers
Dec 4, 1957	CIN	N	——	BAL	A	Waiver price

Del Wilber

Date	Traded To		Traded With	Traded By		In Exchange For
May 12, 1952	BOS	A	——	PHI	N	Cash
Dec 14, 1954	NY	N	——	BOS	A	Billy Klaus

Ted Wilborn

Date	Traded To		Traded With	Traded By		In Exchange For
Nov 1, 1979	NY	A	——	TOR	A	See Chris Chambliss
March 30, 1982	SF	N	Andy McGaffigan	NY	A	Doyle Alexander

Milt Wilcox

Date	Traded To		Traded With	Traded By		In Exchange For
Dec 6, 1971	CLE	A	——	CIN	N	Ted Uhlaender
Feb 25, 1975	CHI	N	——	CLE	A	Dave LaRoche Brock Davis

Randy Wiles

Date	Traded To		Traded With	Traded By		In Exchange For
Aug 23, 1977	STL	N	——	CHI	A	Cash
Dec 9, 1977	HOU	N	——	STL	N	Minor league P Ron Selak

Mark Wiley

Date	Traded To		Traded With	Traded By		In Exchange For
Sept 12, 1978	TOR	A	——	SD	N	Minor league OF Andy Dyes

Rob Wilfong

Date	Traded To		Traded With	Traded By		In Exchange For
May 12, 1982	CAL	A	Doug Corbett	MIN	A	Tom Brunansky Mike Walters and $400,000.

Hoyt Wilhelm

Date	Traded To		Traded With	Traded By		In Exchange For
Feb 26, 1957	STL	N	——	NY	N	Whitey Lockman
Sept 21, 1957	CLE	A	——	STL	N	Cash
Aug 23, 1958	BAL	A	——	CLE	A	Waiver price
Jan 14, 1963	CHI	A	Pete Ward Ron Hansen Dave Nicholson	BAL	A	Luis Aparicio Al Smith
Dec 12, 1968	CAL	A	——	KC	A	Ed Kirkpatrick Dennis Paepke
Sept 8, 1969	ATL	N	——	CAL	A	Cash
Sept 21, 1970	CHI	N	——	ATL	N	Cash
Nov 30, 1970	ATL	N	——	CHI	N	Hal Breeden

Jim Wilhelm

Date	Traded To		Traded With	Traded By		In Exchange For
Feb 15, 1980	CLE	A	Bob Owchinko	SD	N	Jerry Mumphrey

Kaiser Wilhelm

Date	Traded To		Traded With	Traded By		In Exchange For
Jan 1904	BOS	N	——	PIT	N	Cash

Date	Traded To	Traded With	Traded By	In Exchange For

Joe Wilhoit

| July 29, 1917 | PIT | N —— | BOS | N | Waiver price |
| Aug 5, 1917 | NY | N —— | PIT | N | Waiver price |

Curtis Wilkerson

| Dec 5, 1988 | CHI | N —— | TEX | A | *See Rafael Palmeiro* |

Dean Wilkins

| July 12, 1987 | CHI | N | Bob Tewksbury Minor League P Rich Scheid | NY | A | Steve Trout Cash |

Bill Wilkinson

| April 21, 1989 | PIT | N | *See Rey Quinones* | SEA | A | —— |

Ted Wilks

| June 15, 1951 | PIT | N | Bill Howerton Howie Pollet Joe Garagiola Dick Cole | STL | N | Cliff Chambers Wally Westlake |
| Aug 18, 1952 | CLE | A | George Strickland | PIT | N | Johnny Berardino minor league P Charlie Sipple and $50,000. |

Jerry Willard

| Dec 9, 1982 | CLE | A | Manny Trillo George Vukovich Jay Baller Julio Franco | PHI | N | Von Hayes |

Carl Willey

| March 23, 1963 | NY | N —— | MIL | N | Cash |

Nick Willhite

Oct 15, 1964	WAS	A ——	LA	N	Cash
May 11, 1965	LA	N ——	WAS	A	Cash
Dec 15, 1966	CAL	A ——	LA	N	Bob Lee
June 10, 1967	NY	N ——	CAL	A	Jack Hamilton

Bernie Williams

| Oct 25, 1973 | SD | N | Willie McCovey | SF | N | Mike Caldwell |

Billy Williams

| Oct 23, 1974 | OAK | A —— | CHI | N | Darold Knowles Bob Locker Manny Trillo |

Buff Williams

| Jan 1912 | WAS | A —— | BOS | A | Waiver price |

Charlie Williams

| May 11, 1972 | SF | N | $50,000. | NY | N | Willie Mays |

Cy Williams

| Dec 26, 1917 | PHI | N —— | CHI | N | Dode Paskert |

Dallas Williams

| March 26, 1982 | CIN | N | minor league P Brooks Carey | BAL | A | Joe Nolan |
| March 30, 1984 | DET | A —— | CIN | N | Minor league P Charlie Nail |

Dana Williams

| Aug 2, 1989 | CHI | A —— | BOS | A | Ray Chadwick |

Dib Williams

| May 1, 1935 | BOS | A —— | PHI | A | Cash |

Dick Williams

June 25, 1956	BAL	A ——	BKN	N	Waiver price
June 13, 1957	CLE	A ——	BAL	A	Jim Busby
April 1, 1958	BAL	A	Bud Daley Gene Woodling	CLE	A	Larry Doby Don Ferrarese
Oct 2, 1958	KC	A ——	BAL	A	Chico Carrasquel
April 12, 1961	BAL	A	Dick Hall	KC	A	Jerry Walker Chuck Essegian
Oct 12, 1962	HOU	N ——	BAL	A	Cash
Dec 10, 1962	BOS	A ——	HOU	N	Carroll Hardy

Earl Williams

Nov 30, 1972	BAL	A	Taylor Duncan	ATL	N	Pat Dobson Roric Harrison Davey Johnson Johnny Oates
April 17, 1975	ATL	N ——	BAL	A	Jimmy Freeman and $75,000.
July 24, 1976	MON	N ——	ATL	N	Cash

Eddie Williams

| June 15, 1984 | CIN | N —— | NY | N | *See Bruce Berenyi* |
| Jan 23, 1989 | CHI | A —— | CLE | A | Ed Wojna Joel Davis |

Frank Williams

| Jan 8, 1987 | CIN | N | Minor league P Timber Mead Minor league P Mike Villa | SF | N | Eddie Milner |
| Jan 16, 1989 | DET | A —— | CIN | N | No compensation (free agent signing) |

Jim Williams

| Nov 30, 1967 | LA | N | Paul Popovich | CHI | N | Lou Johnson |

Jimmy Williams

| Feb 1908 | STL | A | Hobe Ferris Danny Hoffman | NY | A | Fred Glade Charlie Hemphill |

Jimy Williams

| Feb 8, 1968 | CIN | N | Pat Corrales | STL | N | Johnny Edwards |

Ken Williams

| Dec 15, 1927 | BOS | A —— | STL | A | $10,000. |
| Jan 29, 1930 | NY | A —— | BOS | A | Waiver price |

Ken Williams

| March 23, 1989 | DET | A —— | CHI | A | Eric King |

Mitch Williams

| April 6, 1985 | TEX | A —— | SD | N | Randy Asadoor |
| Dec 5, 1988 | CHI | N | Paul Kilgus Steve Wilson Curtis Wilkerson Minor league IF Luis Benitez Minor league OF Pablo Delgado | TEX | A | Rafael Palmeiro Jamie Moyer Drew Hall |

Date	Traded To		Traded With	Traded By		In Exchange For

Otto Williams

| July 1903 | CHI | N | ——— | STL | N | Cash |

Pop Williams

| April 1903 | PHI | N | ——— | CHI | N | Cash |
| June 1903 | BOS | N | ——— | PHI | N | Cash |

Reggie Williams

| April 5, 1988 | CLE | A | ——— | LA | N | Minor league P Greg LaFever |

Stan Williams

Nov 26, 1962	NY	A	———	LA	N	Bill Skowron
March 30, 1965	CLE	A	———	NY	A	Cash
Dec 10, 1969	MIN	A	———	CLE	A	*See Graig Nettles*
Sept 1, 1971	STL	N	———	MIN	A	Fred Rico and minor league P Dan Ford

Walt Williams

Dec 14, 1966	CHI	A	Don Dennis	STL	N	Johnny Romano and minor league P Lee White
Oct 19, 1972	CLE	A	———	CHI	A	Eddie Leon
March 19, 1974	DET	A	Rick Sawyer	CLE	A	Jim Perry

(Part of three-team trade involving Detroit, Cleveland, and New York Yankees.)

| March 19, 1974 | NY | A | Rick Sawyer Ed Farmer | DET | A | Gerry Moses |

(Part of three-team trade involving Detroit, New York Yankees, and Cleveland.)

Woody Williams

| Sept 10, 1940 | CIN | N | ——— | BKN | N | Waiver price |

Mark Williamson

| Oct 30, 1986 | BAL | A | Terry Kennedy | SD | N | Storm Davis |

Carl Willis

| Aug 27, 1984 | CIN | N | Cash | DET | A | Bill Scherrer |
| Jan 19, 1988 | CHI | A | ——— | CIN | N | Minor league OF Darrell Pruitt |

Jim Willis

| Oct 1, 1954 | CIN | N | Johnny Klippstein | CHI | N | Ted Tappe Harry Perkowski Jim Bolger |

Joe Willis

| April 1911 | STL | N | ——— | STL | A | Cash |

Ron Willis

| Aug 8, 1969 | HOU | N | ——— | STL | N | Cash |

(Willis was returned to St. Louis on October 15.)

Vic Willis

| Dec 15, 1905 | PIT | N | ——— | BOS | N | Dave Brain Del Howard Vive Lindaman |
| Jan 1910 | STL | N | ——— | PIT | N | Cash |

Claude Willoughby

| Nov 6, 1930 | PIT | N | Tommy Thevenow | PHI | N | Dick Bartell |

Jim Willoughby

Oct 14, 1974	STL	N	———	SF	N	Tom Heintzelman
April 4, 1975	BOS	A	———	STL	N	Mario Guerrero
April 5, 1978	CHI	A	———	BOS	A	Cash
Oct 23, 1978	STL	N	———	CHI	A	John Scott

Bump Wills

| March 26, 1982 | CHI | N | ——— | TEX | A | Paul Mirabella minor league P Paul Semall and cash |

Frank Wills

| Jan 18, 1985 | MIL | A | Don Slaught | KC | A | Jim Sundberg |

(Part of a four-team deal involving Texas, Milwaukee, Kansas City, and New York Mets.)

| Jan 18, 1985 | NY | N | ——— | MIL | A | Tim Leary |

(Part of a four-team trade involving Texas, Milwaukee, Kansas City, and New York Mets.)

| March 29, 1985 | SEA | A | ——— | NY | N | Minor league P Wray Bergendahl |

Maury Wills

| Dec 1, 1966 | PIT | N | ——— | LA | N | Bob Bailey Gene Michael |
| June 11, 1969 | LA | N | Manny Mota | MON | N | Ron Fairly Paul Popovich |

Ted Wills

| May 8, 1962 | CIN | N | ——— | BOS | A | Cash |

Terry Wilshusen

| June 15, 1973 | CIN | N | minor league P Thor Skogan | CAL | A | Richie Scheinblum |

Archie Wilson

| May 3, 1952 | WAS | A | *See Jackie Jensen* | NY | A | ——— |
| June 9, 1952 | BOS | A | ——— | WAS | A | Ken Wood |

Art Wilson

Feb 10, 1916	PIT	N	———	CHI	F	Cash
July 29, 1916	CHI	N	Otto Knabe	PIT	N	Wildfire Schulte Bill Fischer
Jan 4, 1918	BOS	N	Larry Doyle and $15,000.	CHI	N	Lefty Tyler

Bill Wilson

| June 11, 1954 | PHI | A | Sonny Dixon Al Sima and $20,000. | CHI | A | Ed McGhee Morrie Martin |

Billy Wilson

| Nov 7, 1973 | MIL | A | ——— | PHI | N | Frank Linzy |

Earl Wilson

| June 14, 1966 | DET | A | Joe Christopher | BOS | A | Julio Navarro Don Demeter |
| July 15, 1970 | SD | N | ——— | DET | A | Cash |

Frank Wilson

| May 10, 1928 | STL | A | ——— | CLE | A | Cash |

Date	Traded To	Traded With	Traded By	In Exchange For

Glenn Wilson

Date				
March 24, 1984	PHI N	John Wockenfuss	DET A	Guillermo Hernandez Dave Bergman
Dec 9, 1987	SEA A	Mike Jackson Minor league OF Dave Grundage	PHI N	Phil Bradley Minor league P John Fortugno
July 22, 1988	PIT N	——	SEA A	Darnell Coles
Aug 18, 1989	HOU N	——	PIT N	Billy Hatcher

Grady Wilson

April 5, 1948	PIT N	——	PHI N	Cash

Hack Wilson

Dec 1931	STL N	Bud Teachout	CHI N	Burleigh Grimes
Jan 23, 1932	BKN N	——	STL N	Minor league P Bob Parham and $45,000.

Jack Wilson

Dec 13, 1941	WAS A	Stan Spence	BOS A	Ken Chase Johnny Welaj
July 17, 1942	DET A	——	WAS A	Eric McNair

(McNair refused to report.)

Jim Wilson

Nov 17, 1947	STL A	——	BOS A	*See Vern Stephens*
April 13, 1955	BAL A	——	MIL N	Cash
May 21, 1956	CHI A	Dave Philley	BAL A	Bob Nieman Mike Fornieles Connie Johnson George Kell

Jimmie Wilson

May 11, 1928	STL N	——	PHI N	Spud Davis Homer Peel
Nov 15, 1933	PHI N	——	STL N	Spud Davis Eddie Delker

(Wilson was named manager of the Phillies.)

Mookie Wilson

July 31, 1989	TOR A	——	NY N	Jeff Musselman Minor league P Mike Brady

Owen Wilson

Dec 12, 1913	STL N	Art Butler Dots Miller Cozy Dolan Hank Robinson	PIT N	Ed Konetchy Mike Mowrey Bob Harmon

Red Wilson

May 29, 1954	DET A	——	CHI A	Matt Batts
July 26, 1960	CLE A	Rocky Bridges	DET A	Hank Foiles

Steve Wilson

Dec 5, 1988	CHI N	——	TEX A	*See Rafael Palmeiro*

Tack Wilson

March 28, 1983	MIN A	——	LA N	Minor league SS Ivan Mesa

Ted Wilson

May 8, 1952	NY N	——	CHI A	$25,000.
Aug 22, 1956	NY A	——	NY N	Waiver price

Hal Wiltse

April 25, 1928	STL A	——	BOS A	Wally Gerber

Snake Wiltse

July 1901	PHI A	——	PIT N	Cash
July 1902	BAL A	——	PHI A	Cash

Gordie Windhorn

April 5, 1960	LA N	minor league 1B Dick Sanders	NY A	Fred Kipp
May 12, 1962	LA A	——	KC A	Marlan Coughtry
July 23, 1962	KC A	Ted Bowsfield	LA A	Dan Osinski

(Kansas City received Bowsfield on November 30.)

Robbie Wine

March 25, 1988	TEX A	——	HOU N	Mike Loynd
May 17, 1988	NY A	——	TEX A	Cash

Dave Winfield

Dec 15, 1980	NY A	——	SD N	No compensation (free agent signing)

Jim Winford

March 1939	BKN N	——	STL N	Waiver price

Ted Wingfield

Sept 10, 1924	BOS A	——	WAS A	Cash

Ivy Wingo

April 8, 1915	CIN N	——	STL N	Mike Gonzalez

Lave Winham

Feb 1903	PIT N	——	BKN N	Waiver price

Herm Winningham

Dec 10, 1984	MON N	——	NY N	*See Gary Carter*
July 13, 1988	CIN N	Jeff Reed Randy St. Claire	MON N	Tracy Jones Pat Pacillo

Tom Winsett

Dec 3, 1936	BKN N	——	STL N	Frenchy Bordagaray Dutch Leonard Jimmy Jordan

George Winter

Jan 1908	DET A	——	BOS A	Cash

Jesse Winters

July 25, 1921	PHI N	Curt Walker Butch Henline and $30,000.	NY N	Irish Meusel

Alan Wirth

March 15, 1978	OAK A	——	SF N	*See Vida Blue*

Casey Wise

Nov 10, 1957	MIL N	——	CHI N	Ben Johnson Charlie King minor league OF Len Williams

Date	Traded To	Traded With	Traded By	In Exchange For

Casey Wise continued

Date	Traded To		Traded With	Traded By		In Exchange For
Oct 15, 1959	DET	A	Don Kaiser Mike Roarke	MIL	N	Charlie Lau Don Lee

Rick Wise

Feb 25, 1972	STL	N	——	PHI	N	Steve Carlton
Oct 26, 1973	BOS	A	Bernie Carbo	STL	N	Reggie Smith Ken Tatum
March 30, 1978	CLE	A	Bo Diaz Mike Paxton Ted Cox	BOS	A	Dennis Eckersley Fred Kendall
Nov 19, 1979	SD	N	——	CLE	A	No compensation (free agent signing)

George Witt

Oct 10, 1961	LA	A	——	PIT	N	Cash

Whitey Witt

April 17, 1922	NY	A	——	PHI	A	Cash

John Wockenfuss

June 6, 1973	STL	N	Mike Nagy	TEX	A	Jim Bibby
March 24, 1984	PHI	N	Glenn Wilson	DET	A	Guillermo Hernandez Dave Bergman

Jim Wohlford

Dec 6, 1976	MIL	A	Jamie Quirk Bob McClure	KC	A	Jim Colborn Darrell Porter
Nov 29, 1979	SF	N	——	MIL	A	No compensation (free agent signing)
Feb 2, 1983	MON	N	——	SF	N	Chris Smith

Pete Wojey

March 27, 1958	CLE	A	$20,000.	DET	A	Milt Bolling Vito Valentinetti

Ed Wojna

Aug 31, 1983	SD	N	——	PHI	N	See Sixto Lezcano
Jan 23, 1989	CLE	A	Joel Davis	CHI	A	Eddie Williams

Wally Wolf

Jan 20, 1964	CIN	N	Jim Dickson and cash	HOU	N	Eddie Kasko

Bill Wolfe

July 13, 1904	WAS	A	Long Tom Hughes	NY	A	Al Orth

Harry Wolfe

Aug 1917	PIT	N	——	CHI	N	Cash

Larry Wolfe

Feb 3, 1979	BOS	A	——	MIN	A	Dave Coleman

Roger Wolff

Dec 13, 1943	WAS	A	——	PHI	A	Bobo Newsom
March 4, 1947	CLE	A	——	WAS	A	George Case
June 14, 1947	PIT	N	——	CLE	A	Cash

Harry Wolter

June 17, 1907	PIT	N	——	CIN	N	Cash
July 4, 1907	STL	N	——	PIT	N	Cash
May 10, 1910	NY	A	——	BOS	A	Clyde Engle

Harry Wolverton

April 28, 1900	PHI	N	——	CHI	N	Cash
Dec 20, 1904	BOS	N	Chick Fraser	PHI	N	Togie Pittinger

Dooley Womack

Dec 4, 1968	HOU	N	——	NY	A	Dick Simpson
Aug 24, 1969	SEA	A	Roric Harrison	HOU	N	Jim Bouton

Jake Wood

June 23, 1967	CIN	N	——	DET	A	Cash

Ken Wood

Nov 28, 1951	BOS	A	Gus Niarhos	STL	A	Les Moss Tom Wright
June 9, 1952	WAS	A	——	BOS	A	Archie Wilson

Roy Wood

Jan 1914	CLE	A	——	PIT	N	Cash

Smoky Joe Wood

Feb 24, 1917	CLE	A	——	BOS	A	$15,000.

Wilbur Wood

Oct 12, 1966	CHI	A	——	PIT	N	Juan Pizarro

Hal Woodeshick

Feb 18, 1958	CLE	A	J. W. Porter	DET	A	Jim Hegan Hank Aguirre
May 25, 1959	WAS	A	Hal Naragon	CLE	A	Ed Fitz Gerald
June 5, 1961	DET	A	——	WAS	A	Chuck Cottier
June 15, 1965	STL	N	Chuck Taylor	HOU	N	Mike Cuellar Ron Taylor

Gene Woodling

Dec 7, 1946	PIT	N	——	CLE	A	Al Lopez
Nov 18, 1954	BAL	A	——	NY	A	See Bob Turley
June 15, 1955	CLE	A	Billy Cox	BAL	A	Dave Pope Wally Westlake

(Cox refused to report and announced retirement. Cleveland received $15,000 to complete trade.)

April 1, 1958	BAL	A	Bud Daley Dick Williams	CLE	A	Larry Doby Don Ferrarese
June 15, 1962	NY	N	——	WAS	A	Cash

Al Woods

Nov 5, 1982	OAK	A	——	TOR	A	Cliff Johnson

Gary Woods

Dec 4, 1978	HOU	N	——	TOR	A	Minor league OF Don Pisker
Dec 9, 1981	CHI	N	——	HOU	N	Jim Tracy

Jim Woods

Jan 11, 1960	PHI	N	——	CHI	N	See Richie Ashburn

Ron Woods

June 14, 1969	NY	A	——	DET	A	Tom Tresh
June 25, 1971	MON	N	——	NY	A	Ron Swoboda

Walt Woods

Jan 1900	PIT	N	See Honus Wagner	LOU	N	——

Date	Traded To	Traded With	Traded By	In Exchange For		Date	Traded To	Traded With	Traded By	In Exchange For

Dick Woodson

Date					
May 4, 1974	NY	A	——	MIN	A	Mike Pazik

Tracy Woodson

| Nov 9, 1989 | CHI | A | —— | LA | N | Jeff Bittiger |

Frank Woodward

| July 14, 1919 | STL | N | Elmer Jacobs | PHI | N | Lee Meadows |
| | | | Doug Baird | | | Gene Paulette |

Woody Woodward

June 11, 1968	CIN	N	Clay Carroll	ATL	N	Milt Pappas
			Tony Cloninger			Ted Davidson
						Bob Johnson

Chuck Workman

| June 12, 1946 | PIT | N | —— | BOS | N | Johnny Barrett |

Ralph Works

| Aug 1912 | CIN | N | —— | DET | A | Cash |

Rich Wortham

| Dec 12, 1980 | MON | N | —— | CHI | A | Tony Bernazard |

Al Worthington

| March 29, 1960 | BOS | A | —— | SF | N | Jim Marshall |

Red Worthington

| Sept 11, 1934 | STL | N | —— | BOS | N | Waiver price |

Clarence Wright

| July 1903 | STL | A | —— | BKN | N | Bill Reidy |

Clyde Wright

Oct 22, 1973	MIL	A	Steve Barber	CAL	A	Ellie Rodriguez
			Ken Berry			Skip Lockwood
			Art Kusnyer			Gary Ryerson
			and cash			Ollie Brown
						Joe Lahoud
Dec 5, 1974	TEX	A	——	MIL	A	Pete Broberg

George Wright

| June 18, 1986 | MON | N | —— | TEX | A | Cash |

Glenn Wright

| Dec 11, 1928 | BKN | N | —— | PIT | N | Jesse Petty |
| | | | | | | Harry Riconda |

Ken Wright

| Dec 7, 1973 | NY | A | Lou Piniella | KC | A | Lindy McDaniel |
| May 3, 1974 | PHI | N | —— | NY | A | Mike Wallace |

Mel Wright

April 11, 1954	STL	N	Bill Virdon	NY	A	Enos Slaughter
			minor league			
			OF Emil Tellinger			

Ricky Wright

| Aug 19, 1983 | TEX | A | Dave Stewart | LA | N | Rick Honeycutt |
| | | | and $200,000. | | | |

Taffy Wright

| Dec 8, 1939 | CHI | A | Pete Appleton | WAS | A | Gee Walker |
| Nov 15, 1948 | PHI | A | —— | CHI | A | Cash |

Tom Wright

Nov 28, 1951	STL	A	Les Moss	BOS	A	Ken Wood
						Gus Niarhos
June 15, 1952	CHI	A	Leo Thomas	STL	A	Willie Miranda
						Al Zarilla
March 27, 1954	WAS	A	——	CHI	A	Kite Thomas
						Waiver price

Russ Wrightstone

| May 29, 1928 | NY | N | —— | PHI | N | Art Jahn |

Yats Wuestling

| May 30, 1930 | NY | A | Ownie Carroll | DET | A | Waite Hoyt |
| | | | Harry Rice | | | Mark Koenig |

John Wyatt

June 13, 1966	BOS	A	Rollie Sheldon	KC	A	Jim Gosger
			Jose Tartabull			Ken Sanders
						Guido Grilli
May 18, 1968	NY	A	——	BOS	A	Cash
June 15, 1968	DET	A	——	NY	A	Cash

Whit Wyatt

| June 2, 1933 | CHI | A | —— | DET | A | Vic Frasier |
| March 28, 1945 | PHI | N | —— | BKN | N | $20,000. |

Butch Wynegar

May 12, 1982	NY	A	Roger Erickson	MIN	A	John Pacella
						Larry Milbourne
						Pete Filson
						and cash
Dec 19, 1986	CAL	A	——	NY	A	Ron Romanick

Early Wynn

Dec 14, 1948	CLE	A	Mickey Vernon	WAS	A	Joe Haynes
						Eddie Klieman
						Eddie Robinson
Dec 4, 1957	CHI	A	Al Smith	CLE	A	Fred Hatfield
						Minnie Minoso

Jimmy Wynn

Dec 6, 1973	LA	N	——	HOU	N	Claude Osteen
						minor league
						P Dave Culpepper
Nov 17, 1975	ATL	N	Tom Paciorek	LA	N	Dusty Baker
			Lee Lacy			Ed Goodson
			Jerry Royster			
Nov 29, 1976	NY	A	——	ATL	N	Cash

Billy Wynne

| Dec 15, 1967 | CHI | A | —— | NY | N | *See Tommie Agee* |
| Nov 30, 1970 | CAL | A | *See Ken Berry* | CHI | A | —— |

Marvell Wynne

March 31, 1981	NY	N	minor league	KC	A	Juan Berenguer
			P John Skinner			
June 14, 1983	PIT	N	Steve Senteney	NY	N	Junior Ortiz
						Minor league
						P Arthur Ray
April 3, 1986	SD	N	——	PIT	N	Bob Patterson

Date	Traded To	Traded With	Traded By	In Exchange For

Marvell Wynne *continued*

Date	Traded To	Traded With	Traded By	In Exchange For
Aug 30, 1989	CHI N	Luis Salazar	SD N	Calvin Schiraldi
				Darrin Jackson
				Phil Stephenson

(San Diego Received Stephenson on Sept. 5, 1989).

Johnny Wyrostek

Date	Traded To	Traded With	Traded By	In Exchange For
Feb 5, 1946	PHI N		STL N	Cash
Feb 7, 1948	CIN N	Cash	PHI N	Eddie Miller
May 23, 1952	PHI N	Kent Peterson	CIN N	Bubba Church

Hugh Yancy

Date	Traded To	Traded With	Traded By	In Exchange For
Nov 6, 1976	CIN N		CHI A	Tom Spencer

Al Yates

Date	Traded To	Traded With	Traded By	In Exchange For
June 24, 1967	BOS A	Cash	NY N	Dennis Bennett

Steve Yeager

Date	Traded To	Traded With	Traded By	In Exchange For
Dec 11, 1985	SEA A		LA N	Ed Vande Berg

Steve Yerkes

Date	Traded To	Traded With	Traded By	In Exchange For
Feb 10, 1916	CHI N		PIT F	Cash

Rich Yett

Date	Traded To	Traded With	Traded By	In Exchange For
Dec 29, 1989	MIN A		CLE A	No compensation (free agent signing)

Earl Yingling

Date	Traded To	Traded With	Traded By	In Exchange For
April 1914	CIN N	Herbie Moran	BKN N	Dick Egan

Jim York

Date	Traded To	Traded With	Traded By	In Exchange For
Dec 2, 1971	HOU N	Lance Clemons	KC A	John Mayberry
				minor league
				IF Dave Grangaard
Jan 8, 1976	NY A		HOU N	Cash

Rudy York

Date	Traded To	Traded With	Traded By	In Exchange For
Jan 3, 1946	BOS A		DET A	Eddie Lake
June 14, 1947	CHI A		BOS A	Jake Jones

Eddie Yost

Date	Traded To	Traded With	Traded By	In Exchange For
Dec 6, 1958	DET A	Rocky Bridges	WAS A	Reno Bertoia
		Neil Chrisley		Ron Samford
				Jim Delsing

Ned Yost

Date	Traded To	Traded With	Traded By	In Exchange For
Dec 8, 1983	TEX A	minor league	MIL A	Jim Sundberg
		P Dan Scarpetta		

Floyd Youmans

Date	Traded To	Traded With	Traded By	In Exchange For
Dec 10, 1984	MON N	Hubie Brooks	NY N	Gary Carter
		Mike Fitzgerald		
		Herm Winningham		
Dec 6, 1988	PHI N	Jeff Parrett	MON N	Kevin Gross

Babe Young

Date	Traded To	Traded With	Traded By	In Exchange For
June 7, 1947	CIN N		NY N	Joe Beggs

Bobby Young

Date	Traded To	Traded With	Traded By	In Exchange For
June 27, 1955	CLE A		BAL A	Hank Majeski

Cy Young

Date	Traded To	Traded With	Traded By	In Exchange For
Feb 18, 1909	CLE A		BOS A	Charlie Chech
				Jack Ryan
				and $12,500.
July 1911	BOS N		CLE A	Waiver price

Dick Young

Date	Traded To	Traded With	Traded By	In Exchange For
March 28, 1954	BKN N	$50,000.	PHI N	Bobby Morgan

Don Young

Date	Traded To	Traded With	Traded By	In Exchange For
May 14, 1967	STL N		CHI N	Cash
Aug 1, 1967	CHI N		STL N	Cash

Gerald Young

Date	Traded To	Traded With	Traded By	In Exchange For
Aug 28, 1984	HOU N	Manny Lee	NY N	Ray Knight
		Minor league		
		P Mitch Cook		

Harley Young

Date	Traded To	Traded With	Traded By	In Exchange For
June 18, 1908	BOS N	Tom McCarthy	PIT N	Irv Young

Irv Young

Date	Traded To	Traded With	Traded By	In Exchange For
June 18, 1908	PIT N		BOS N	Tom McCarthy
				Harley Young

Matt Young

Date	Traded To	Traded With	Traded By	In Exchange For
Dec 10, 1986	LA N		SEA A	Dennis Powell
				Minor league
				IF Mike Watters
Dec 11, 1987	OAK A	*See Bob Welch*	LA N	
Dec 15, 1989	SEA A		OAK A	No compensation (free agent signing)

Mike Young

Date	Traded To	Traded With	Traded By	In Exchange For
Jan 7, 1985	MON N		KC A	Mike Kinnunen
				Minor League
				OF Ken Baker
March 21, 1988	PHI N	player to be named	BAL A	Rick Schu
				Jeff Stone
				Keith Hughes

(Philadelphia received OF Frank Bellino on June 14, 1988.)

Date	Traded To	Traded With	Traded By	In Exchange For
Aug 24, 1988	MIL A		PHI N	Alex Madrid

Pep Young

Date	Traded To	Traded With	Traded By	In Exchange For
Dec 9, 1940	CIN N		BKN N	Lew Riggs

Ralph Young

Date	Traded To	Traded With	Traded By	In Exchange For
April 3, 1922	PHI A		DET A	Waiver price

Joel Youngblood

Date	Traded To	Traded With	Traded By	In Exchange For
March 28, 1977	STL N		CIN N	Bill Caudill
June 15, 1977	NY N		STL N	Mike Phillips
Aug 4, 1982	MON N		NY N	Tom Gorman
Feb 7, 1983	SF N		MON N	No compensation (free agent signing)
Dec 21, 1988	CIN N		SF N	No compensation (free agent signing)

Sal Yvars

Date	Traded To	Traded With	Traded By	In Exchange For
June 15, 1953	STL N		NY N	$12,500.

Chris Zachary

Date	Traded To	Traded With	Traded By	In Exchange For
July 1, 1970	STL N		KC A	Ted Abernathy
April 2, 1973	PIT N		DET A	Charlie Sands

Date	Traded To		Traded With	Traded By		In Exchange For

Tom Zachary

Date	Traded To		Traded With	Traded By		In Exchange For
Feb 1926	STL	A	Win Ballou	WAS	A	Joe Bush
						Jack Tobin
July 7, 1927	WAS	A	——	STL	A	General Crowder
Aug 23, 1928	NY	A	——	WAS	A	Waiver price
May 12, 1930	BOS	N	——	NY	A	Waiver price

Elmer Zacher

Date	Traded To		Traded With	Traded By		In Exchange For
May 8, 1910	STL	N		NY	N	Cash

Pat Zachry

Date	Traded To		Traded With	Traded By		In Exchange For
June 15, 1977	NY	N	Doug Flynn	CIN	N	Tom Seaver
			Steve Henderson			
			Dan Norman			
Dec 28, 1982	LA	N	——	NY	N	Jorge Orta
Feb 4, 1985	PHI	N	——	LA	N	Al Oliver

Geoff Zahn

Date	Traded To		Traded With	Traded By		In Exchange For
May 2, 1975	CHI	N	Eddie Solomon	LA	N	Burt Hooton
Dec 2, 1980	CAL	A	——	MIN	A	No compensation (free agent signing)

Paul Zahniser

Date	Traded To		Traded With	Traded By		In Exchange For
April 26, 1925	BOS	A	Roy Carlyle	WAS	A	Joe Harris

Dom Zanni

Date	Traded To		Traded With	Traded By		In Exchange For
Nov 30, 1961	CHI	A	——	SF	N	See Billy Pierce
May 5, 1963	CIN	N	——	CHI	A	Jim Brosnan

Al Zarilla

Date	Traded To		Traded With	Traded By		In Exchange For
May 8, 1949	BOS	A	——	STL	A	Stan Spence and cash
Dec 10, 1950	CHI	A	Joe Dobson	BOS	A	Ray Scarborough
			Dick Littlefield			Bill Wight
June 15, 1952	STL	A	Willie Miranda	CHI	A	Tom Wright
						Leo Thomas
Aug 31, 1952	BOS	A	——	STL	A	Cash

Norm Zauchin

Date	Traded To		Traded With	Traded By		In Exchange For
Jan 23, 1958	WAS	A	Albie Pearson	BOS	A	Pete Runnels

Joe Zdeb

Date	Traded To		Traded With	Traded By		In Exchange For
Jan 15, 1980	CHI	A	——	KC	A	Eddie Bane

Rollie Zeider

Date	Traded To		Traded With	Traded By		In Exchange For
June 1, 1913	NY	A	Babe Borton	CHI	A	Hal Chase
Feb 10, 1916	CHI	N	See Three Finger Brown	CHI	F	

Bill Zepp

Date	Traded To		Traded With	Traded By		In Exchange For
March 29, 1971	DET	A	——	MIN	A	Bob Adams and minor league P Art Clifford

Gus Zernial

Date	Traded To		Traded With	Traded By		In Exchange For
April 30, 1951	PHI	A	Dave Philley	CHI	A	Paul Lehner
						Minnie Minoso

(Part of three-team trade involving Chicago White Sox, Philadelphia A's, and Cleveland.)

Date	Traded To		Traded With	Traded By		In Exchange For
Nov 20, 1957	DET	A	Billy Martin	KC	A	Bill Tuttle
			Tom Morgan			Jim Small
			Lou Skizas			Duke Maas
			Mickey McDermott			John Tsitouris
			Tim Thompson			Frank House
						Kent Hadley
						Jim McManus

Chief Zimmer

Date	Traded To		Traded With	Traded By		In Exchange For
Jan 1900	PIT	N	See Honus Wagner	LOU	N	——
Jan 1903	PHI	N	——	PIT	N	Waiver price

Don Zimmer

Date	Traded To		Traded With	Traded By		In Exchange For
April 8, 1960	CHI	N	——	LA	N	Ron Perranoski
						John Goryl
						minor league OF Lee Handley and $25,000.
May 7, 1962	CIN	N	——	NY	N	Bob Miller
						Cliff Cook
Jan 24, 1963	LA	N	——	CIN	N	Minor league P Scott Breeden
June 24, 1963	WAS	A	——	LA	N	Cash

Heinie Zimmerman

Date	Traded To		Traded With	Traded By		In Exchange For
Aug 28, 1916	NY	N	Mickey Doolan	CHI	N	Larry Doyle
						Herb Hunter
						Merwin Jacobson

Jerry Zimmerman

Date	Traded To		Traded With	Traded By		In Exchange For
Jan 30, 1962	MIN	A	——	CIN	N	Dan Dobbek

Guy Zinn

Date	Traded To		Traded With	Traded By		In Exchange For
Dec 1912	BOS	N	George Davis	NY	A	Cash

Richie Zisk

Date	Traded To		Traded With	Traded By		In Exchange For
Dec 10, 1976	CHI	A	Silvio Martinez	PIT	N	Terry Forster
						Goose Gossage
Nov 9, 1977	TEX	A	——	CHI	A	No compensation (free agent signing)
Dec 12, 1980	SEA	A	Rick Auerbach	TEX	A	Rick Honeycutt
			Ken Clay			Mario Mendoza
			Jerry Don Gleaton			Larry Cox
			Brian Allard			Leon Roberts
			Minor league			Willie Horton
			P Steve Finch			

Billy Zitzmann

Date	Traded To		Traded With	Traded By		In Exchange For
June 1919	CIN	N	——	PIT	N	Cash

Sam Zoldak

Date	Traded To		Traded With	Traded By		In Exchange For
Feb 17, 1944	STL	A	minor league OF Barney Lutz	PHI	A	Frankie Hayes
June 15, 1948	CLE	A	——	STL	A	Bill Kennedy and $100,000.
April 30, 1951	PHI	A	Ray Murray	CLE	A	Lou Brissie
			Minnie Minoso			

(Part of three-team trade involving Cleveland, Philadelphia A's, and Chicago White Sox.)

Bill Zuber

Date	Traded To		Traded With	Traded By		In Exchange For
April 21, 1941	WAS	A	——	CLE	A	Cash
Jan 29, 1943	NY	A	Cash	WAS	A	Gerry Priddy
						Milo Candini
June 18, 1946	BOS	A	——	NY	A	Cash

Paul Zuvella

Date	Traded To		Traded With	Traded By		In Exchange For
June 29, 1986	NY	A	Claudell Washington	ATL	N	Ken Griffey
						Andre Robertson

(Atlanta received Robertson on July 3, 1986.)

George Zuverink

Date	Traded To		Traded With	Traded By		In Exchange For
April 26, 1954	DET	A	——	CIN	N	Cash
July 8, 1955	BAL	A	——	DET	A	Waiver price

PART TEN

National Association Register

Alphabetical List of Every Man Who Ever
Played in the National Association
and His Record in that League

National Association Register

This section contains an alphabetical listing of every man who played in the National Association, baseball's first professional league, which lasted from 1871 through 1875. In addition to the facts about the players and their year-by-year batting and pitching records, there are team and managerial records for each year. Information about the National Association is not as complete as the other data that appears in this book. This is because many statistical items are not available as a result of poor newspaper coverage.

The records of men who played in the National Association and in the major leagues are not combined because the National Association is not considered a major league. The reasons for this, as defined by the Special Baseball Records Committee, were the erratic schedule and procedures of the National Association. For men who played in the National Association and went on to play or manage in the major leagues, their major league records can be found in the appropriate sections of this book. Appearing last, after the alphabetical player listing, are the yearly league standings and team data. All information and abbreviations that may appear unfamiliar are explained in the sample format presented below.

		Manager	W	L	Manager	W	L
1871	Philadelphia Athletics	Dick McBride	21	7			
	Chicago White Stockings	Jimmy Wood	19	9			
	Boston Red Stockings	Harry Wright	20	10			
	Washington Olympics	Nick Young	15	15			
	New York Mutuals	Bob Ferguson	16	17			
	Troy Haymakers	Lip Pike	1	3	Bill Craver	12	12
	Ft. Wayne Kekiongas	Bill Lennon	5	9	Harry Deane	2	3
	Cleveland Forest Citys	Charlie Pabor	10	19			
	Rockford Forest Citys	Scott Hastings	4	21			

Team Column Headings and Statistical Information

	Manager	W	L	Manager	W	L

W   Wins

L   Losses

PCT   Winning Percentage

GB   Games Behind the League Leader

R   Runs Scored

AB   At Bats

H   Hits

BA   Batting Average

Manager   The name and record of the man who managed the team. Teams with more than one manager have the managers listed in the order of when they managed.

The following is the record of John Doe, a fictitious player used as an example to illustrate the information about the players:

	G	AB	H	R	BA	W	L	PCT	G by POS

John Doe

DOE, JOHN LEE (Slim)
Played as John Cherry part of 1871.
Born John Lee Doughnut   Brother of Bill Doe.
B. Jan. 1, 1850, New York, N. Y.   D. July 1, 1955, New York, N. Y.
Hall of Fame 1946.
Manager 1872.

BR   TR   6'2"   165 lbs.

	G	AB	H	R	BA	W	L	PCT	G by POS
1871 Philadelphia Athletics	26	132	65	45	.492	2	2	.500	3B-22, P-4
1872 Boston Red Stockings	35	169	43	25	.254	6	4	.600	3B-20, P-15
1873	51	238	59	36	.248	7	3	.700	3B-36, P-15
1874 2 teams New York Mutuals (25G. .314 W-2 L-2) Lord Baltimores (25G. .296 W-3 L-0)									
" total	50	196	60	36	.305	5	2	.714	3B-40, P-10
1875 Brooklyn Atlantics	1	0	0	0	—	0	0	—	P-1
5 yrs.	163	735	227	142	.309	20	11	.645	3B-118, P-45

Player Information

John Doe

This shortened version of the player's full name is the name most familiar to the fans. All players in this section are alphabetically arranged by the last name part of this name.

Doe, John Lee

Player's full name. The arrangement is last name first, then first and middle name(s).

(Slim)

Player's nickname. Any name appearing in parentheses is a nickname.

BR TR

The player's batting and throwing style. Doe, for instance, batted and threw right-handed. A "BB" would mean Doe was a switch hitter, a "BL" would mean that he batted left-handed, and a "TL" would mean that he threw left-handed.

6'2"

Player's height.

165 lbs.

Player's average playing weight.

Played as John Cherry part of 1871

The player at one time in his career played under another name and can be found in box scores or newspaper stories under that name. In the case of Doe, he was still an amateur athlete when he entered baseball in 1871, and in order to protect his amateur standing he adopted an alias.

Born John Lee Doughnut

The name the player was given at birth. (For the most part, the player never used this name while playing in the National Association, but if he did, it would be listed as "played as," which is explained above under the heading "Played as John Cherry part of 1871.")

Brother of Bill Doe

The player's brother. (Relatives indicated here are fathers, sons, and brothers who played or managed in the National Association and the major leagues.)

B. Jan. 1, 1850, New York, N.Y.

Date and place of birth.

D. July 1, 1955, New York, N.Y.

Date and place of death. (Since all men who played in the National Association are dead, the word "deceased" is shown if no information is now available.)

Hall of Fame 1946

Doe was elected to the Baseball Hall of Fame in 1946.

Manager 1872

Doe also served as a manager. All men who were managers, along with their managerial records, can also be found with the team information.

Player Column Headings Information

G	Games Played
AB	At Bats
H	Hits
R	Runs Scored
BA	Batting Average
W	Wins as a Pitcher
L	Losses as a Pitcher
PCT	Pitcher's Winning Percentage
G by POS	Games by Position (All fielding positions that a man played within the given year are shown. The position where the most games were played is listed first.)

Team Information

```
1871  Philadelphia Athletics
1872  Boston Red Stockings
1873
1874  2 teams  New York Mutuals (25G.  .314  W-2  L-2)  Lord Baltimores (25G.  .296  W-3  L-0)
  "     total                  50     196    60    36    .305     5       2    .714   3B-40, P-10
1875  Brooklyn Atlantics
        5 yrs.
```

Blank space appearing beneath a team indicates that the team is the same. Doe, for example, played for the Boston Red Stockings from 1872 through 1873.

2 Teams Total. Indicates a player played for more than one team in the same year. Doe played for two teams in 1874. The number of games he played, his batting average, and pitching decisions for each team are also shown. Directly beneath this line, following the word "total," is Doe's combined record for both teams in 1874.

Player Statistical Information

	G	AB	H	R	BA	W	L	PCT	G by POS

John Doe

DOE, JOHN LEE (Slim)   BR TR 6'2" 165 lbs.
Played as John Cherry part of 1871.
Born John Lee Doughnut   Brother of Bill Doe.
B. Jan. 1, 1850, New York, N. Y.   D. July 1, 1955, New York, N. Y.
Hall of Fame 1946.
Manager 1872.

Year	Team	G	AB	H	R	BA	W	L	PCT	G by POS
1871	Philadelphia Athletics	26	132	65	45	**.492**	2	2	.500	3B-22, P-4
1872	Boston Red Stockings	35	169	43	25	.254	6	4	.600	3B-20, P-15
1873		51	238	59	36	.248	7	3	.700	3B-36, P-15
1874	2 teams New York Mutuals (25G. .314 W-2 L-2) Lord Baltimores (25G. .296 W-3 L-0)									
"	total	50	196	60	36	.305	5	2	.714	3B-40, P-10
1875	Brooklyn Atlantics	1	0	0	0	—	0	0	—	P-1
	5 yrs.	163	735	227	142	.309	20	11	.645	3B-118, P-45

Meaningless Averages. Indicated by the use of a dash (—). In the case of Doe, a dash is shown for his 1875 batting average. This means that although he played one game he had no official at bats. A batting average of .000 would mean he had at least one at bat with no hits. If a dash is shown in place of a pitcher's winning percentage, as it is in the case of Doe in 1875, it means that although he pitched in one game he never had a decision. A percentage of .000 would mean he had at least one loss.

League Leaders. Statistics that appear in boldfaced print indicate the player led the league that year in a particular statistical category. Doe, for example, led the National Association in batting in 1871. When there is a tie for league lead, the figures for all the men who tied are shown in boldface.

		G	AB	H	R	BA	W	L	PCT	G BY POS

John Abadie

ABADIE, JOHN
B. Nov. 4, 1854, Philadelphia, Pa.   D. May 17, 1905, Pemberton, N. J.

BR TR 6'   192 lbs.

1875 2 teams   Brooklyn Atlantics (1G .250)   Philadelphia Centennials (11G .217)

		G	AB	H	R	BA				G BY POS
"	total	12	50	11	4	.220				1B-12

Dave Abercrombie

ABERCROMBIE, DAVID
B. May, 1840, Falkirk, Scotland   D. Sept. 2, 1916, Baltimore Md.

1871 Troy Haymakers	1	4	0	0	.000				SS-1

Bob Addy

ADDY, ROBERT EDWARD (The Magnet)
B. Feb., 1845, Rochester, N. Y.   D. Apr. 9, 1910, Pocatello, Ida.
Manager 1875, 1877.

BL TL 5'8"   160 lbs.

1871 Rockford Forest Cities	25	122	31	29	.254				SS-3

1873 2 teams   Boston Red Stockings (31G .340)   Philadelphias (10G .286)

"	total	41	218	71	49	.326				OF-31, 2B-10
1874 Hartfords		50	208	55	26	.264				2B-45, 3B-4, SS-1
1875 Philadelphias		69	308	81	60	.263				OF-66, 2B-3
	4 yrs.	185	856	238	164	.278				OF-97, 2B-58, 3B-4, SS-4

Ham Allen

ALLEN, HOMER S.
B. Aug., 1854, Hamden, Conn.   D. Jan. 7, 1892, Hamden, Conn.

1872 Middletown Mansfields	16	71	12	8	.169				OF-10, SS-6

Andy Allison

ALLISON, ANDREW K.
B. 1848, New York, N. Y.   Deceased.

5'10"   150 lbs.

1872 Brooklyn Eckfords	25	107	15	11	.140				1B-23, OF-2

Art Allison

ALLISON, ARTHUR ALGERNON
Brother of Doug Allison.
B. Jan. 29, 1849, Philadelphia, Pa.   D. Feb. 25, 1916, Washington, D. C.

5'8"   150 lbs.

1871 Cleveland Forest Cities	29	140	36	27	.257				OF-29
1872	18	88	23	13	.261				OF-18
1873 Elizabeth Resolutes	23	102	31	12	.304				OF-20, 1B-2, C-1

1875 2 teams   Hartfords (35G .242)   Washington Nationals (27G .169)

"	total	62	279	59	42	.211				OF-36, 1B-24, C-1, 2B-1
	4 yrs.	132	609	149	94	.245				OF-103, 1B-26, C-2, 2B-1

Bill Allison

ALLISON, WILLIAM ANDREW
B. Sept. 18, 1848, Philadelphia, Pa.   D. June 12, 1923

1872 Brooklyn Eckfords	3	11	2	3	.182				OF-2, 2B-1

Doug Allison

ALLISON, DOUGLAS L.
Brother of Art Allison.
B. 1846, Philadelphia, Pa.   D. Dec. 19, 1916, Washington, D. C.

BR TR 5'10½" 160 lbs.

1871 Washington Olympics	27	132	44	28	.333				C-27

1872 2 teams   Brooklyn Eckfords (18G .299)   Troy Haymakers (23G .319)

"	total	41	206	64	41	.311				C-40, SS-1

1873 2 teams   New York Mutuals (11G .245)   Elizabeth Resolutes (18G .275)

"	total	29	144	38	17	.264				C-26, OF-3
1874 New York Mutuals		65	326	88	65	.270				OF-41, C-24
1875 Hartfords		61	293	68	38	.232				C-59, 1B-3
	5 yrs.	223	1101	302	189	.274				C-176, OF-44, 1B-3, SS-1

Cap Anson

ANSON, ADRIAN CONSTANTINE (Old Anse)
B. Apr. 11, 1852, Marshalltown, Iowa   D. Apr. 14, 1922, Chicago, Ill.
Manager 1875, 1879-98.
Hall of Fame 1939.

BR TR 6'   227 lbs.

1871 Rockford Forest Cities	25	122	43	30	.352				3B-20, C-3, 2B-2, OF-1
1872 Philadelphia Athletics	45	231	88	60	.381				3B-45
1873	51	272	96	52	.353				1B-36, 3B-10, 2B-4, OF-1 C-1
1874	55	267	98	51	.367				1B-22, 3B-20, OF-8, SS-5
1875	69	330	105	84	.318				1B-32, OF-22, C-11, 3B-4
5 yrs.	245	1222	430	277	.352				3B-99, 1B-90, OF-32, C-15 2B-6, SS-5

Sam Armstrong

ARMSTRONG, SAMUEL
B. 1850, Baltimore, Md.   Deceased.

6'2"   160 lbs.

1871 Fort Wayne Kekiongas	12	48	11	9	.229				OF-12

Billy Arnold

ARNOLD, WILLIS S.
B. Mar. 2, 1851, Middletown, Conn.   D. Jan. 18, 1899, Albany, N. Y.

1872 Middletown Mansfields	2	8	1	2	.125				OF-2

Harry Arundel

ARUNDEL, HARRY
B. 1854, Philadelphia, Pa.   D. Mar. 25, 1904, Cleveland, Ohio

1875 Brooklyn Atlantics	1	4	0	0	.000				OF-1

Ed Atkinson

ATKINSON, EDWARD
B. Baltimore, Md.   Deceased.

1873 Washington Nationals	2	9	0	2	.000				OF-2

Henry Austin

AUSTIN, HENRY C.
B. 1844, Brooklyn, N. Y.   D. Amityville, N. Y.

1873 Elizabeth Resolutes	23	106	24	11	.226				OF-23

Stud Bancker

BANCKER, JOHN
B. Philadelphia, Pa.   Deceased.

1875 New Havens	19	77	11	3	.143				C-12, 3B-3, 2B-3, SS-1

Al Barker

BARKER, ALFRED L
B. Jan. 18, 1839, Rockford, Ill.   D. Sept. 15, 1912, Rockford, Ill.

1871 Rockford Forest Citys	1	5	1	0	.200				OF-1

	G	AB	H	R	BA	W	L	PCT	G BY POS
Tom Barlow									
BARLOW, THOMAS H.									
Deceased.									
1872 Brooklyn Atlantics	35	174	48	31	.276				C-34, SS-2
1873	55	283	71	48	.251				C-55
1874 Hartfords	32	157	49	37	.312				SS-32
1875 2 teams Brooklyn Atlantics (1G .000) New Havens (1G .200)									
" total	2	9	1	1	.111				SS-1, 2B-1
4 yrs.	124	623	169	117	.271				C-89, SS-35, 2B-1
Ross Barnes									
BARNES, ROSCOE CHARLES									BR TR 5'8½" 145 lbs.
B. May 8, 1850, Mount Morris, N. Y. D. Feb. 5, 1915, Chicago, Ill.									
1871 Boston Red Stockings	31	172	65	66	.378				2B-16, SS-15, 3B-1
1872	45	240	97	81	.404				2B-45
1873	60	338	136	126	.402				2B-47, 3B-13
1874	52	277	94	73	.339				2B-52
1875	78	398	148	116	.372				2B-78
5 yrs.	266	1425	540	462	.379				2B-238, SS-15, 3B-14
Billy Barnie									
BARNIE, WILLIAM HARRISON (Bald Billy)									5'7" 157 lbs.
B. Jan. 26, 1853, New York, N. Y. D. July 15, 1900, Hartford, Conn.									
Manager 1883-94, 1897-98.									
1874 Hartfords	45	184	36	19	.196				C-23, OF-21, SS-1
1875 2 teams New York Mutuals (10G .150) Keokuk Westerns (10G .108)									
" total	20	77	10	4	.130				OF-10, C-10
2 yrs.	65	261	46	23	.176				C-33, OF-31, SS-1
Bill Barrett									
BARRETT, WILLIAM									
B. Washington, D. C. Deceased.									
1871 Fort Wayne Kekiongas	1	5	1	1	.200				C-1, 3B-1
1872 2 teams Brooklyn Atlantics (7G .267) Washington Olympics (1G .000)									
" total	8	35	8	4	.229				OF-7, C-1
1873 Lord Baltimores	1	4	1	0	.250				OF-1, SS-1
3 yrs.	10	44	10	5	.227				OF-8, C-2, 3B-1, SS-1
Jim Barron									
BARRON, JAMES									
B. St. Louis, Mo. Deceased.									
1874 Lord Baltimores	16	76	22	6	.289				OF-16
Frank Barrows									
BARROWS, FRANK LEWIS									
B. Boston, Mass. D. Sept. 24, 1901, Boston, Mass.									
1871 Boston Red Stockings	18	87	14	13	.161				OF-17, 2B-1
John Bass									
BASS, JOHN E.									5'6" 150 lbs.
B. 1850, Baltimore, Md. Deceased.									
1871 Cleveland Forest Citys	22	91	25	18	.275				SS-22
1872 Brooklyn Atlantics	1	4	1	0	.250				OF-1
2 yrs.	23	95	26	18	.274				SS-22, OF-1
Joe Battin									
BATTIN, JOSEPH V.									BR TR
B. Nov. 11, 1851, Philadelphia, Pa. D. Dec. 10, 1937, Akron, Ohio									
Manager 1883-84.									
1871 Cleveland Forest Citys	1	4	0	0	.000				OF-1
1873 Philadelphia Athletics	1	6	3	4	.500				OF-1
1874	51	228	62	41	.272				2B-40, OF-7, SS-4
1875 St. Louis	66	278	73	32	.263				2B-60, 3B-6
4 yrs.	119	516	138	77	.267				2B-100, OF-9, 3B-6, SS-4
Tommy Beals									
BEALS, THOMAS L.									BR 5'5" 144 lbs.
B. Hartford, Conn. D. Oct. 2, 1915, San Francisco, Calif.									
1871 Washington Olympics	10	38	7	7	.184				OF-8, 2B-2
1872	9	39	11	8	.282				2B-5, OF-2, SS-2
1873 Washington Nationals	37	170	46	35	.271				2B-26, C-11, OF-1
1874 Boston Red Stockings	18	98	20	20	.204				2B-10, OF-8
1875	35	157	46	38	.293				OF-31, 2B-6
5 yrs.	109	502	130	108	.259				OF-50, 2B-49, C-11, SS-2
Charlie Bearman									
BEARMAN, CHARLES S.									6' 180 lbs.
B. 1848, Hoboken, N. J. D. Feb. 4, 1879, Hoboken, N. J.									
1871 Fort Wayne Kekiongas	1	3	0	0	.000				1B-1
George Bechtel									
BECHTEL, GEORGE A.									5'11" 165 lbs.
B. Sept. 2, 1848, Philadelphia, Pa. Deceased.									
1871 Philadelphia Athletics	20	94	30	23	.319	1	2	.333	OF-15, P-3, 3B-2
1872 New York Mutuals	52	262	79	64	.302				OF-51, 1B-1
1873 Philadelphias	53	266	62	54	.233	0	3	.000	OF-50, P-3
1874	31	153	43	29	.281	1	3	.250	OF-27, P-4
1875 2 teams Philadelphia Athletics (34G .292 W-3 L-1) Philadelphia Centennials (14G .266 W-2 L-12)									
" total	48	218	62	44	.284	5	13	.143	OF-30, P-18
5 yrs.	204	993	276	214	.278	7	21	.250	OF-173, P-28, 2B-2, 1B-1
Steve Bellan									
BELLAN, ESTEBAN ENRIQUE									5'6" 154 lbs.
B. 1850, Havana, Cuba D. Aug. 8, 1932, Havana, Cuba									
1871 Troy Haymakers	29	136	29	25	.213				3B-28, SS-1
1872	23	115	32	22	.278				SS-9, 3B-8, OF-6
1873 New York Mutuals	7	37	7	4	.189				3B-7
3 yrs.	59	288	68	51	.236				3B-43, SS-10, OF-6
Cy Bentley									
BENTLEY, CLYTUS G.									
B. Nov. 23, 1850, East Haven, Conn. D. Feb. 26, 1873, Middletown, Conn.									
1872 Middletown Mansfields	23	113	27	26	.239	2	14	.125	P-16, OF-8

	G	AB	H	R	BA	W	L	PCT	G BY POS

Nate Berkenstock

BERKENSTOCK, NATHAN
B. 1831, Pa.   D. Feb. 23, 1900, Philadelphia, Pa.

	G	AB	H	R	BA				G BY POS
1871 Philadelphia Athletics	1	4	0	0	.000				OF-1

Tom Berry

BERRY, THOMAS HANEY   5'6"   140 lbs.
B. Dec. 31, 1842, Chester, Pa.   D. June 6, 1915, Chester, Pa.

	G	AB	H	R	BA				G BY POS
1871 Philadelphia Athletics	1	4	1	0	.250				OF-1

Harry Berthrong

BERTHRONG, HARRY W.   5'6½"   140 lbs.
B. Dec. 31, 1843, Munford, N. Y.   D. Apr. 24, 1928, Chelsea, Mass.

	G	AB	H	R	BA				G BY POS
1871 Washington Olympics	17	78	17	17	.218				OF-12, 2B-4, 3B-1

Bestick

BESTICK,
Deceased.

	G	AB	H	R	BA				G BY POS
1872 Brooklyn Eckfords	4	14	3	0	.214				C-4

E. P. Bevans

BEVANS, E. P.   5'8"   138 lbs.
B. 1848, N. Y.   Deceased.

	G	AB	H	R	BA				G BY POS
1871 Troy Haymakers	3	15	5	7	.333				2B-3
1872 Brooklyn Atlantics	10	44	9	7	.205				2B-8, OF-1, SS-1
2 yrs.	13	59	14	14	.237				2B-11, OF-1, SS-1

Oscar Bielaski

BIELASKI, OSCAR   BR TR
B. Mar. 21, 1847, Washington, D. C.   D. Nov. 8, 1911, Washington, D. C.

	G	AB	H	R	BA				G BY POS
1872 Washington Nationals	10	47	8	12	.170				OF-10
1873	38	187	49	35	.262				OF-38
1874 Lord Baltimores	28	126	26	18	.206				OF-26, 2B-1, 1B-1
1875 Chicago White Stockings	52	211	49	21	.232				OF-52
4 yrs.	128	571	132	86	.231				OF-126, 2B-1, 1B-1

George Bird

BIRD, GEORGE RAYMOND   BR TR 5'9"   150 lbs.
B. June 23, 1850, Stillman Valley, Ill.   D. Nov. 9, 1940, Rockford, Ill.

	G	AB	H	R	BA				G BY POS
1871 Rockford Forest Citys	25	112	24	18	.214				OF-25

Dave Birdsall

BIRDSALL, DAVID SOLOMON   5'9"   126 lbs.
B. July 16, 1838, New York, N. Y.   D. Dec. 30, 1896, Boston, Mass.

	G	AB	H	R	BA				G BY POS
1871 Boston Red Stockings	29	155	43	51	.277				OF-26, C-3
1872	14	78	14	10	.179				C-11, OF-5
1873	3	12	1	4	.083				OF-3
3 yrs.	46	245	58	65	.237				OF-34, C-14

Joe Blong

BLONG, JOSEPH MYLES   BR TR
B. Sept. 17, 1853, St. Louis, Mo.   D. Sept. 22, 1892, St. Louis, Mo.

	G	AB	H	R	BA	W	L	PCT	G BY POS
1875 St. Louis Reds	16	70	10	3	.143	3	11	.214	P-14, OF-3

Fred Boardman

BOARDMAN, FREDERICK
B. Chicago, Ill.

	G	AB	H	R	BA				G BY POS
1874 Lord Baltimores	1	3	1	0	.333				OF-1

Boland

BOLAND,
Deceased.

	G	AB	H	R	BA				G BY POS
1875 Brooklyn Atlantics	1	4	0	0	.000				OF-1

Tommy Bond

BOND, THOMAS HENRY   BR TR 5'7½"   160 lbs.
B. Apr. 2, 1856, Granard, Ireland   D. Jan. 24, 1941, Boston, Mass.
Manager 1882.

	G	AB	H	R	BA	W	L	PCT	G BY POS
1874 Brooklyn Atlantics	55	249	54	25	.217	22	32	.407	P-55
1875 Hartfords	71	297	78	30	.263	19	16	.543	P-39, OF-29, 2B-2, 1B-2
2 yrs.	126	546	132	55	.242	41	48	.461	P-94, OF-29, 2B-2, 1B-2

Eddie Booth

BOOTH, EDWARD H.
B. Brooklyn, N. Y.

	G	AB	H	R	BA				G BY POS
1872 2 teams Brooklyn Atlantics (14G .250) Middletown Mansfields (24G .336)									
" total	38	180	55	36	.306				2B-21, OF-17
1873 2 teams Brooklyn Atlantics (15G .171) Elizabeth Resolutes (18G .299)									
" total	33	147	35	17	.238				OF-31, 2B-2
1874 Brooklyn Atlantics	44	194	46	24	.237				OF-44
1875 New York Mutuals	68	286	57	33	.199				OF-62, 2B-6
4 yrs.	183	807	193	110	.239				OF-154, 2B-29

Joe Borden

BORDEN, JOSEPH EMLEY   BR TR 5'9"   140 lbs.
Also appeared in box score as Josephs
B. May 9, 1854, Jacobstown, N. J.   D. Oct. 14, 1929, Yeadon, Pa.

	G	AB	H	R	BA	W	L	PCT	G BY POS
1875 Philadelphias	7	29	3	3	.103	2	4	.333	P-7

Bill Boyd

BOYD, WILLIAM J.   250 lbs.
B. Dec. 22, 1852, New York   D. Oct. 1, 1912, Queens, N. Y.

	G	AB	H	R	BA				G BY POS
1872 New York Mutuals	35	169	43	25	.254				3B-33, OF-1, SS-1
1873 Brooklyn Atlantics	48	233	63	31	.270				OF-43, 3B-5
1874 Hartfords	26	123	47	22	.382				3B-25, OF-21
1875 Brooklyn Atlantics	36	154	45	14	.292				2B-15, OF-11, 3B-9, 1B-1
4 yrs.	145	679	198	92	.292				OF-76, 3B-72, 2B-15, SS-1, 1B-1

George Bradley

BRADLEY, GEORGE WASHINGTON (Grin)   BR TR 5'10½"   175 lbs.
B. July 13, 1852, Reading, Pa.   D. Oct. 2, 1931, Philadelphia, Pa.

	G	AB	H	R	BA	W	L	PCT	G BY POS
1875 St. Louis	61	250	67	28	.268	33	26	.559	P-60, OF-1, 3B-1

Brady

BRADY,
Deceased.

	G	AB	H	R	BA				G BY POS
1875 Chicago White Stockings	1	4	1	1	.250				OF-1

		G	AB	H	R	BA	W	L	PCT	G BY POS

Steve Brady — BRADY, STEPHEN A.
Brother of Tom Brady.
B. July 14, 1851, Worcester, Mass.   D. Nov. 1, 1917, Hartford, Conn.

5'9½"   165 lbs.

		G	AB	H	R	BA	W	L	PCT	G BY POS
1874	Hartfords	25	110	37	18	.336				3B-17, OF-8
1875	Washington Nationals	19	83	11	4	.133				2B-16, OF-2, 1B-1
	2 yrs.	44	193	48	22	.249				3B-17, 2B-16, OF-10, 1B-1

Tom Brady — BRADY, THOMAS A.
Brother of Steve Brady.
B. Hartford, Conn.   D. Aug. 27, 1923, Hartford, Conn.

		G	AB	H	R	BA				G BY POS
1875	Hartfords	1	4	0	0	.000				OF-1

Asa Brainard — BRAINARD, ASA (Count)
B. 1841, Albany, N. Y.   D. Dec. 29, 1888, Denver, Colo.

TR 5'8½" 150 lbs.

		G	AB	H	R	BA	W	L	PCT	G BY POS
1871	Washington Olympics	30	140	28	24	.200	13	15	.464	P-30
1872	2 teams Middletown Mansfields (7G		.161	W-0 L-3)		Washington Olympics	(9G	.405	W-2 L-7)	
"	total	16	73	22	10	.301	2	10	.222	P-12, 2B-4
1873	Lord Baltimores	15	64	16	16	.250	4	7	.364	P-13, OF-2
1874		47	209	50	19	.239	5	24	.172	P-29, 2B-17, OF-2
	4 yrs.	108	486	116	69	.239	24	56	.300	P-84, 2B-21, OF-4

Mike Brannock — BRANNOCK, MICHAEL J
B. 1853, Guelph Ont., Canada   Deceased.

5'8"   162 lbs.

		G	AB	H	R	BA				G BY POS
1871	Chicago White Stockings	3	13	1	1	.077				3B-3
1875		2	9	1	2	.111				3B-2
	2 yrs.	5	22	2	4	.091				3B-5

Jim Britt — BRITT, JAMES EDWARD
B. Feb. 25, 1856   D. Dec. 23, 1925, San Francisco, Calif.

		G	AB	H	R	BA	W	L	PCT	G BY POS
1872	Brooklyn Atlantics	35	155	34	24	.219	8	27	.229	P-35
1873		54	246	47	29	.191	17	36	.321	P-54
	2 yrs.	89	401	81	53	.202	25	63	.284	P-89

Brown — BROWN,
Deceased.

		G	AB	H	R	BA				G BY POS
1874	Lord Baltimores	1	5	0	0	.000				SS-1

Oliver Brown — BROWN, OLIVER E.
B. Brooklyn, N. Y.   D. Sept. 23, 1932, Brooklyn, N. Y.

		G	AB	H	R	BA				G BY POS
1872	Brooklyn Atlantics	4	17	1	0	.059				OF-4
1875		3	14	1	0	.071				1B-4
	2 yrs.	7	31	2	0	.065				OF-4, 1B-4

Jack Burdock — BURDOCK, JOHN JOSEPH (Black Jack)
B. 1851, Brooklyn, N. Y.   D. Nov. 28, 1931, Brooklyn, N. Y.
Manager 1883.

BR TR 5'9½" 158 lbs.

		G	AB	H	R	BA				G BY POS
1872	Brooklyn Atlantics	35	176	44	27	.250				SS-33, C-2, 2B-1
1873		55	261	62	56	.238				2B-55
1874	New York Mutuals	61	284	78	46	.275				3B-61
1875	Hartfords	73	360	102	72	.283				2B-72, 3B-1
	4 yrs.	224	1081	286	201	.265				2B-128, 3B-62, SS-33, C-2

Henry Burroughs — BURROUGHS, HENRY F.
B. 1845, Detroit, Mich.   Deceased.

5'8"   147 lbs.

		G	AB	H	R	BA				G BY POS
1871	Washington Olympics	12	63	14	11	.222				OF-8, 3B-5
1872		2	8	1	1	.125				OF-2
	2 yrs.	14	71	15	12	.211				OF-10, 3B-5

Doc Bushong — BUSHONG, ALBERT JOHN
B. Sept. 15, 1856, Philadelphia, Pa.   D. Aug. 19, 1908, Brooklyn, N. Y.

BR TR 5'11" 165 lbs.

		G	AB	H	R	BA				G BY POS
1875	Brooklyn Atlantics	1	5	3	0	.600				C-1

Frank Buttery — BUTTERY, FRANK
B. May 13, 1851, Silver Mine, Conn.   D. Dec. 16, 1902, Silver Mine, Conn.

		G	AB	H	R	BA	W	L	PCT	G BY POS
1872	Middletown Mansfields	17	88	26	18	.295	3	2	.600	OF-6, P-6, 3B-6

Hugh Campbell — CAMPBELL, HUGH F.
D. 1881, Elizabeth, N. J.

		G	AB	H	R	BA	W	L	PCT	G BY POS
1873	Elizabeth Resolutes	20	93	12	9	.129	2	16	.111	P-18, OF-1, 2B-1

Mike Campbell — CAMPBELL, MICHAEL
B. N. J.   Deceased.

		G	AB	H	R	BA				G BY POS
1873	Elizabeth Resolutes	21	89	13	9	.146				1B-17, SS-3, OF-1

John Carbine — CARBINE, JOHN C.
B. Oct. 12, 1855, Syracuse, N. Y.   D. Sept. 11, 1915, Forest Park, Ill.

6'   187 lbs.

		G	AB	H	R	BA				G BY POS
1875	Keokuk Westerns	10	39	2	1	.051				1B-10

Tom Carey — CAREY, THOMAS JOHN
Born J. J. Norton.
B. 1849, Brooklyn, N. Y.   D. Feb. 13, 1899, Los Angeles Calif.,
Manager 1873-74.

BR TR 5'8"   145 lbs.

		G	AB	H	R	BA				G BY POS
1871	Fort Wayne Kekiongas	19	85	20	15	.235				2B-18, SS-1
1872	Lord Baltimores	41	196	58	39	.296				2B-26, SS-8, OF-3, 3B-3, 1B-1
1873		55	292	95	72	.325				2B-51, 3B-3, SS-3
1874	New York Mutuals	64	292	83	55	.284				SS-51, 2B-13
1875	Hartfords	85	390	99	63	.254				SS-85
	5 yrs.	264	1255	355	244	.283				SS-148, 2B-108, 3B-6, OF-3, 1B-1

		G	AB	H	R	BA	W	L	PCT	G BY POS
Lew Carl	**CARL, LEWIS** B. Baltimore, Md. Deceased.									
	1874 Lord Baltimores	1	4	0	0	.000				C-1
Jim Carlton	**CARLTON, JAMES** B. 1849, N. Y. Deceased.									5'8" 155 lbs.
	1871 Cleveland Forest Citys	29	136	32	31	.235				1B-29
	1872	7	38	12	8	.316				1B-7
	2 yrs.	36	174	44	39	.253				1B-36
John Cassidy	**CASSIDY, JOHN P.** B. 1855, Brooklyn, N. Y. D. July 2, 1891, Brooklyn, N. Y.									BR TL 5'8" 168 lbs.
	1875 2 teams Brooklyn Atlantics (40G .168 W-1 L-25) New Havens (6G .125)									
	" total	46	191	31	16	.162	1	25	.038	P-27, 1B-13, OF-10
Jack Chapman	**CHAPMAN, JOHN CURTIS** B. May 8, 1843, Brooklyn, N. Y. D. June 10, 1916, Brooklyn, N. Y. Manager 1876-78, 1882-85, 1889-92.									TR 5'11" 170 lbs.
	1874 Brooklyn Atlantics	53	248	64	32	.258				OF-52, 1B-1
	1875 St. Louis	43	187	46	27	.246				OF-43
	2 yrs.	96	435	110	59	.253				OF-95, 1B-1
Bobby Clack	**CLACK, ROBERT S. (Gentlemanly Bobby)** Born Robert S. Clark. B. 1851, Brooklyn, N. Y. D. Oct. 22, 1933, Danvers, Mass.									BR TR 5'9" 153 lbs.
	1874 Brooklyn Atlantics	32	134	21	22	.157				OF-30, 1B-2
	1875	17	60	6	1	.100				OF-17
	2 yrs.	49	194	27	23	.139				OF-47, 1B-2
John Clapp	**CLAPP, JOHN EDGAR** Brother of Aaron Clapp. B. July 17, 1851, Ithaca, N. Y. D. Dec. 18, 1904, Ithaca, N. Y. Manager 1878, 1872, 1879-80, 1883.									BR TR 5'7" 194 lbs.
	1872 Middletown Mansfields	19	98	30	30	.306				C-19
	1873 Philadelphia Athletics	45	219	63	35	.288				C-42, SS-2, 2B-1
	1874	39	169	56	46	.331				C-26, OF-13, SS-1
	1875	60	298	74	65	.248				C-60
	4 yrs.	163	784	223	176	.284				C-147, OF-13, SS-3, 2B-1
Denny Clare	**CLARE, DENNIS J.** B. 1852, Brooklyn, N. Y. D. Nov. 26, 1928, Brooklyn, N. Y.									
	1872 Brooklyn Atlantics	2	7	1	1	.143				2B-2
Jim Clinton	**CLINTON, JAMES LAWRENCE (Big Jim)** B. Aug. 10, 1850, New York, N. Y. D. Sept. 3, 1921, Brooklyn, N. Y. Manager 1872.									BR TR 5'8½" 174 lbs.
	1872 Brooklyn Eckfords	24	101	19	11	.188				3B-9, OF-8, SS-4, 2B-3
	1873 Elizabeth Resolutes	9	40	9	5	.225				3B-8, OF-1
	1874 Brooklyn Atlantics	2	11	2	3	.182				OF-1, 2B-1
	1875	22	83	10	3	.120	1	12	.077	P-14, OF-5, 1B-4, 2B-1
	4 yrs.	57	235	40	22	.170	1	12	.077	3B-17, OF-15, P-14, 2B-5 SS-4, 1B-4
Dan Collins	**COLLINS, DANIEL THOMAS** B. July 12, 1854, St. Louis, Mo. D. Sept. 21, 1883, New Orleans La.,									
	1874 Chicago White Stockings	3	12	1	1	.083	1	1	.500	OF-2, P-2, SS-1
Fred Cone	**CONE, JOSEPH FREDERICK** B. May, 1848, Rockford, Ill. D. Apr. 13, 1909, Chicago, Ill.									5'9½" 171 lbs.
	1871 Boston Red Stockings	18	85	20	17	.235				OF-18
Terry Connell	**CONNELL, TERENCE G.** B. June 17, 1855, Philadelphia, Pa. D. Mar. 25, 1924, Philadelphia, Pa.									
	1874 Chicago White Stockings	1	4	0	0	.000	0	0	.000	C-1
Ned Connors	**CONNORS, JOSEPH P.** B. 1850, N. Y. Deceased.									5'9" 156 lbs.
	1871 Troy Haymakers	7	33	6	7	.182				1B-4, OF-2, 2B-1
William Coon	**COON, WILLIAM K.** B. Mar. 21, 1855, Philadelphia, Pa. D. Aug. 30, 1915, Burlington, N. J.									
	1875 Philadelphia Athletics	4	14	2	1	.143				C-4
Dennis Coughlin	**COUGHLIN, DENNIS F.** Deceased.									
	1872 Washington Nationals	8	37	12	5	.324				OF-5, SS-2, 2B-1
Fred Crane	**CRANE, FREDERICK WILLIAM HOTCHKISS** B. Nov. 4, 1840, Saybrook, Conn. D. Apr. 27, 1925, Brooklyn, N. Y.									
	1873 Elizabeth Resolutes	1	4	1	0	.250				2B-1
	1875 Brooklyn Atlantics	21	81	17	7	.210				1B-20, OF-1
	2 yrs.	22	85	18	7	.212				1B-20, OF-1, 2B-1
Bill Craver	**CRAVER, WILLIAM H.** B. 1844, Troy, N. Y. D. June 17, 1901, Troy, N. Y. Manager 1871-72, 1874.									BR TR 5'9" 160 lbs.
	1871 Troy Haymakers	27	122	37	26	.303				2B-18, SS-4, C-3, 1B-2
	1872 Lord Baltimores	33	180	50	52	.278				C-25, OF-5, 3B-2, 2B-2
	1873	36	185	52	38	.281				C-20, SS-12, OF-3, 1B-1
	1874 Philadelphias	55	275	95	71	.345				2B-53, C-3

	G	AB	H	R	BA	W	L	PCT	G BY POS

Bill Craver *continued*

1875 2 teams Philadelphia Athletics (54G .314) Philadelphia Centennials (14G .265)

" total	68	332	101	79	.304				2B-53, SS-9, 3B-4, C-1 1B-1
5 yrs.	219	1094	335	266	.306				2B-126, C-52, SS-25, OF-8 3B-6, 1B-4

Art Croft

CROFT, ARTHUR F.
B. Jan. 23, 1855, St. Louis, Mo.   D. Mar. 16, 1884, St. Louis, Mo.

1875 St. Louis Reds	18	72	11	4	.153				OF-18

Bill Crowley

CROWLEY, WILLIAM MICHAEL   BR TR 5'7½" 159 lbs.
B. Apr. 8, 1857, Philadelphia, Pa.   D. July 14, 1891, Gloucester, N. J.

1875 Philadelphias	9	37	4	4	.108				OF-4, 3B-3, 2B-1, 1B-1

Candy Cummings

CUMMINGS, WILLIAM ARTHUR   BR TR 5'9" 120 lbs.
B. Oct. 18, 1848, Ware, Mass.   D. May 16, 1924, Toledo, Ohio
Hall of Fame 1939.

1872 New York Mutuals	55	260	51	36	.196	33	20	.623	P-55, OF-1
1873 Lord Baltimores	42	200	50	31	.250	28	14	.667	P-42
1874 Philadelphias	54	240	50	30	.208	28	26	.519	P-54
1875 Hartfords	52	235	43	32	.183	35	12	.745	P-47, OF-6
4 yrs.	203	935	194	129	.207	124	72	.633	P-198, OF-7

Ned Cuthbert

CUTHBERT, EDGAR EDWARD   BR TR 5'6" 140 lbs.
B. June 20, 1845, Philadelphia, Pa.   D. Feb. 6, 1905, St. Louis, Mo.
Manager 1882.

1871 Philadelphia Athletics	28	162	39	47	.241				OF-27, C-1
1872	46	265	87	80	.328				OF-46
1873 Philadelphias	51	284	75	79	.264				OF-51
1874 Chicago White Stockings	58	306	79	64	.258				OF-55, C-3
1875 St. Louis	68	308	82	69	.266				OF-67, C-2
5 yrs.	251	1325	362	339	.273				OF-246, C-6

John Dailey

DAILEY, JOHN J.
B. Brooklyn, N. Y.   D. Jan. 8, 1898, Brooklyn, N. Y.

1875 2 teams Brooklyn Atlantics (2G .125) Washington Nationals (26G .208)

" total	28	114	23	18	.202				SS-17, 3B-7, 2B-2, OF-1 1B-1

Harry Deane

DEANE, JOHN HENRY   5'7" 150 lbs.
B. May 6, 1846, Trenton, N. J.   D. May 31, 1925, Indianapolis, Ind.
Manager 1871.

1871 Fort Wayne Kekiongas	5	24	4	3	.167				OF-5
1874 Lord Baltimores	47	212	49	29	.231				OF-45, 2B-2
2 yrs.	52	236	53	32	.225				OF-50, 2B-2

Dutch Dehlman

DEHLMAN, HERMAN J.
B. 1850, Catasauqua, Pa.   D. Mar. 13, 1885, Wilkes-Barre, Pa.
Manager 1876.

1872 Brooklyn Atlantics	35	164	33	26	.201				1B-35
1873	54	236	50	50	.212				1B-54
1874	53	232	51	40	.220				1B-53
1875 St. Louis	67	284	61	43	.215				1B-67
4 yrs.	209	916	195	159	.213				1B-209

Jim Devlin

DEVLIN, JAMES ALEXANDER   BR TR 5'11" 175 lbs.
B. 1849, Philadelphia, Pa.   D. Oct. 10, 1883, Philadelphia, Pa.

1873 Philadelphias	22	104	26	18	.250				1B-12, 3B-5, SS-3, OF-2
1874 Chicago White Stockings	44	215	59	28	.274				1B-22, OF-16, 3B-6
1875	70	336	95	60	.283	6	16	.273	1B-43, P-26, OF-3
3 yrs.	136	655	180	106	.275	6	16	.273	1B-77, P-26, OF-21, 3B-11 SS-3

J. Dillon

DILLON, J.
Brother of Packy Dillon.
B. St. Louis, Mo.

1875 St. Louis Reds	1	1	0	0	.000				SS-1

Packy Dillon

DILLON, PACKARD ANDREW
Brother of J. Dillon.
B. St. Louis, Mo.   D. Jan. 9, 1890, Guelph, Ont., Canada

1875 St. Louis Reds	3	15	3	1	.200				C-3

Lester Dole

DOLE, LESTER CARRINGTON   5'11"
B. July 8, 1855, Meriden, Conn.   D. Dec. 10, 1918, Concord, N. H.

1875 New Havens	1	4	2	1	.500				OF-1

T. J. Donnelly

DONNELLY, T. J.
Deceased.

1871 Fort Wayne Kekiongas	9	35	7	8	.200				OF-9, 3B-1
1873 Washington Nationals	30	141	35	15	.248				SS-13, 2B-11, OF-6
1874 Philadelphias	5	21	5	2	.238				OF-2, SS-2, 2B-1
3 yrs.	44	197	47	25	.239				OF-17, SS-15, 2B-12, 3B-1

Herm Doscher

DOSCHER, JOHN HENRY, SR.   BR TR 5'10" 182 lbs.
Father of Jack Doscher.
B. Dec. 20, 1852, New York, N. Y.   D. Mar. 20, 1934, Buffalo, N. Y.

1872 Brooklyn Atlantics	6	26	9	4	.346				OF-6
1873	1	6	1	1	.167				OF-1
1875 Washington Nationals	21	75	12	3	.160				3B-19, SS-2
3 yrs.	28	107	22	8	.206				3B-19, OF-7, SS-2

	G	AB	H	R	BA	W	L	PCT	G BY POS

Joe Doyle

DOYLE, JOSEPH K.
B. Cincinnati, Ohio   Deceased.

	G	AB	H	R	BA				G BY POS
1872 Washington Nationals	8	36	8	4	.222				SS-6, 3B-1, 2B-1

Ed Duffy

DUFFY, EDWARD CHARLES — TR 5'7½" 152 lbs.
B. 1844, Ireland   D. June, 1889, Brooklyn, N. Y.

1871 Chicago White Stockings	25	121	28	31	.231				SS-24, 3B-1

Edwards

EDWARDS,
Deceased.

1875 Brooklyn Atlantics	1	5	1	1	.200	0	0	.000	OF-1, P-1

Dave Eggler

EGGLER, DAVID DANIEL — BR TR 5'9" 165 lbs.
B. Apr. 30, 1851, Brooklyn, N. Y.   D. Apr. 5, 1902, Buffalo, N. Y.

1871 New York Mutuals	33	150	47	37	.313				OF-33
1872	56	295	102	95	.346				OF-56
1873	53	281	92	83	.327				OF-53
1874 Philadelphias	58	306	96	70	.314				OF-56, 2B-2
1875 Philadelphia Athletics	66	302	87	65	.288				OF-66
5 yrs.	266	1334	424	350	.318				OF-264, 2B-2

Eland

ELAND,
Deceased.

1873 Marylands	1	4	0	0	.000				OF-1

Joe Ellick

ELLICK, JOSEPH J. — 5'10" 162 lbs.
B. Apr. 3, 1854, Cincinnati, Ohio   D. Apr. 21, 1923, Kansas City, Mo.
Manager 1884.

1875 St. Louis Reds	6	24	5	1	.208				3B-3, OF-2, SS-1

Evans

EVANS,

1875 New Havens	1	4	2	1	.500				OF-1

G. Ewell

EWELL, G.
Deceased.

1871 Cleveland Forest Citys	1	4	0	0	.000				OF-1

Jack Farrell

FARRELL, JOHN (Hartford Jack)
B. Jan. 2, 1856, Hartford, Conn.   D. Nov. 15, 1916, Hartford, Conn.

1874 Hartfords	3	15	5	3	.333				OF-3

John Farrow

FARROW, JOHN JACOB — BL TR
B. 1852, Verplanck's Point, N. Y.   D. Dec. 31, 1914, Perth Amboy, N. J.

1873 Elizabeth Resolutes	12	51	8	2	.157				C-7, OF-2, SS-2, 1B-1
1874 Brooklyn Atlantics	27	125	26	16	.208				C-15, 2B-12
2 yrs.	39	176	34	18	.193				C-22, 2B-12, OF-2, SS-2 1B-1

Bob Ferguson

FERGUSON, ROBERT V. (Death to Flying Things) — BB TR 5'9½" 149 lbs.
B. Jan. 31, 1845, Brooklyn, N. Y.   D. May 3, 1894, Brooklyn, N. Y.
Manager 1871-84, 1886-87.

1871 New York Mutuals	33	156	34	30	.218				3B-19, 2B-10, C-4
1872 Brooklyn Atlantics	35	164	43	34	.262				3B-35
1873	51	238	59	36	.248	0	1	.000	3B-50, P-1
1874	56	249	64	34	.257	0	1	.000	3B-55, C-2, P-1
1875 Hartfords	84	373	87	65	.233				3B-84
5 yrs.	259	1180	287	199	.243	0	2	.000	3B-243, 2B-10, C-6, P-2

Sam Field

FIELD, SAMUEL JAY — BR TR 5'9½" 182 lbs.
B. Oct. 12, 1848, Philadelphia, Pa.   D. Oct. 28, 1904, Sinking Spring, Pa.

1875 2 teams Philadelphia Centennials (3G .091) Washington Nationals (5G .235)									
" total	8	28	5	2	.179				C-6, OF-2

George Fields

FIELDS, GEORGE W.
B. 1851, Waterbury, Conn.   D. Sept. 22, 1933, Waterbury, Conn.

1872 Middletown Mansfields	17	71	20	18	.282				3B-10, OF-6, SS-1

Cherokee Fisher

FISHER, WILLIAM CHARLES — BR TR 5'9" 164 lbs.
B. Dec., 1845, Philadelphia, Pa.   D. Sept. 26, 1912, New York, N. Y.

1871 Rockford Forest Citys	25	124	28	24	.226	4	20	.167	P-24, SS-1
1872 Lord Baltimores	44	234	48	39	.205	9	3	.750	3B-17, OF-16, P-13
1873 Philadelphia Athletics	51	259	66	51	.255	2	2	.500	OF-45, P-7, 1B-1
1874 Hartfords	52	231	53	29	.229	14	21	.400	P-35, OF-10, 3B-6, SS-1
1875 Philadelphias	41	169	39	26	.231	22	18	.550	P-40, OF-1
5 yrs.	213	1017	234	169	.230	51	64	.443	P-119, OF-72, 3B-23, SS-2 1B-1

Wes Fisler

FISLER, WESTON DICKSON — 5'6" 137 lbs.
B. July 5, 1841, Camden, N. J.   D. Dec. 25, 1922, Philadelphia, Pa.

1871 Philadelphia Athletics	28	150	44	43	.293				1B-26, 2B-2
1872	46	248	81	50	.327				2B-46
1873	43	227	71	42	.313				2B-35, 1B-8
1874	37	175	67	27	.383				1B-28, 2B-9
1875	57	272	75	54	.276				1B-44, OF-9, 2B-4
5 yrs.	211	1072	338	216	.315				1B-106, 2B-96, OF-9

Frank Fleet

FLEET, FRANK H.
B. 1848, New York, N. Y.   D. June 13, 1900, New York, N. Y.

1871 New York Mutuals	1	5	2	1	.400	0	1	.000	P-1
1872 Brooklyn Eckfords	13	58	11	10	.190				3B-10, 2B-2, OF-1
1873 Elizabeth Resolutes	22	96	22	11	.229	0	3	.000	2B-8, SS-7, P-3, 3B-3 1B-1

		G	AB	H	R	BA	W	L	PCT	G BY POS

Frank Fleet *continued*

		G	AB	H	R	BA	W	L	PCT	G BY POS
1874	Brooklyn Atlantics	20	94	22	18	.234				C-12, 2B-7, OF-1
1875	2 teams Brooklyn Atlantics (26G .216 W-0 L-1) St. Louis (3G .083 W-2 L-1)									
"	total	29	128	26	14	.203	2	2	.667	2B-11, C-10, SS-6, P-4
	5 yrs.	85	381	83	54	.218	2	6	.250	2B-28, C-22, 3B-13, SS-13 P-8, OF-2, 1B-1

Fletcher

FLETCHER, G. H. E.
B. Brooklyn, N. Y. Deceased.

		G	AB	H	R	BA	W	L	PCT	G BY POS
1872	Brooklyn Eckfords	2	8	2	1	.250				OF-2

Silver Flint

FLINT, FRANK SYLVESTER
B. Aug. 3, 1855, Philadelphia, Pa. D. Jan. 14, 1892, Chicago, Ill.
Manager 1879.

BR TR 6' 180 lbs.

		G	AB	H	R	BA	W	L	PCT	G BY POS
1875	St. Louis Reds	16	58	5	3	.086				C-15, 3B-1

Dickie Flowers

FLOWERS, CHARLES RICHARD
B. 1850, Philadelphia, Pa. D. Oct. 5, 1892, Philadelphia, Pa.

		G	AB	H	R	BA	W	L	PCT	G BY POS
1871	Troy Haymakers	21	109	33	40	.303				SS-20, 2B-1
1872	Philadelphia Athletics	3	17	4	1	.235				SS-3
	2 yrs.	24	126	37	41	.294				SS-23, 2B-1

Clipper Flynn

FLYNN, WILLIAM
B. Apr. 29, 1849, Lansingburg, N. Y. D. Nov. 2, 1881, Troy, N. Y.

TR 5'7" 140 lbs.

		G	AB	H	R	BA	W	L	PCT	G BY POS
1871	Troy Haymakers	29	148	46	44	.311				1B-19, OF-9, 3B-1
1872	Washington Olympics	9	41	9	4	.220				1B-9
	2 yrs.	38	189	55	48	.291				1B-28, OF-9, 3B-1

Tom Foley

FOLEY, THOMAS J.
B. Aug. 16, 1842, Cashel, Ireland D. Nov. 3, 1926, Chicago, Ill.
Manager 1871.

5'9½" 157 lbs.

		G	AB	H	R	BA	W	L	PCT	G BY POS
1871	Chicago White Stockings	18	84	21	18	.250				OF-14, C-3, 3B-1

Will Foley

FOLEY, WILLIAM BROWN
B. Nov. 15, 1855, Chicago, Ill. D. Nov. 12, 1916, Chicago, Ill.

BR TR 5'9½" 150 lbs.

		G	AB	H	R	BA	W	L	PCT	G BY POS
1875	Chicago White Stockings	3	14	3	0	.214				3B-3

Jim Foran

FORAN, JAMES H.
B. 1848, N. Y. Deceased.

5'6½" 159 lbs.

		G	AB	H	R	BA	W	L	PCT	G BY POS
1871	Fort Wayne Kekiongas	19	90	31	20	.344				1B-15, OF-4

Davy Force

FORCE, DAVID W. (Tom Thumb)
B. July 27, 1849, New York, N. Y. D. June 21, 1918, Englewood, N. J.

BR TR 5'4" 130 lbs.

		G	AB	H	R	BA	W	L	PCT	G BY POS
1871	Washington Olympics	32	166	44	45	.265				SS-31, 3B-1
1872	2 teams Lord Baltimores (18G .409) Troy Haymakers (25G .414)									
"	total	43	226	93	69	.412				3B-34, SS-9
1873	Lord Baltimores	48	250	85	75	.340	1	1	.500	3B-32, SS-15, P-2
1874	Chicago White Stockings	59	305	92	61	.302				3B-38, SS-20, OF-1, P-1
1875	Philadelphia Athletics	77	391	122	77	.312				SS-77
	5 yrs.	259	1338	436	327	.326	1	1	.500	SS-152, 3B-105, P-3, OF-1

Bill French

FRENCH, WILLIAM
B. Baltimore, Md. Deceased.

		G	AB	H	R	BA	W	L	PCT	G BY POS
1873	Marylands	5	19	4	3	.211	0	1	.000	OF-2, 1B-2, P-1

Chick Fulmer

FULMER, CHARLES JOHN
Brother of Washington Fulmer.
B. Feb. 12, 1851, Philadelphia, Pa. D. Feb. 15, 1940, Philadelphia, Pa.
Manager 1876.

BR TR 6' 158 lbs.

		G	AB	H	R	BA	W	L	PCT	G BY POS
1871	Rockford Forest Citys	16	70	17	12	.243				SS-15, 1B-1
1872	New York Mutuals	36	169	51	29	.302				3B-23, SS-13
1873	Philadelphias	49	244	64	41	.262				SS-48, C-1
1874		57	265	70	49	.264				SS-31, 3B-26
1875		68	288	64	49	.222				SS-54, 3B-14
	5 yrs.	226	1036	266	180	.257				SS-161, 3B-63, C-1, 1B-1

Washington Fulmer

FULMER, WASHINGTON LAFAYETTE
Brother of Chick Fulmer.
B. June 15, 1840, Philadelphia, Pa. D. Dec. 8, 1907, Philadelphia, Pa.

		G	AB	H	R	BA	W	L	PCT	G BY POS
1875	Brooklyn Atlantics	1	4	2	1	.500				3B-1

John Galvin

GALVIN, JOHN S.
B. 1851 D. Apr. 20, 1904, Brooklyn, N. Y.

		G	AB	H	R	BA	W	L	PCT	G BY POS
1872	Brooklyn Atlantics	1	4	0	0	.000				2B-1
1874		1	4	0	1	.000				2B-1
	2 yrs.	2	8	0	1	.000				2B-2

Pud Galvin

GALVIN, JAMES FRANCIS (Gentle Jeems, The Little Steam Engine)
B. Dec. 25, 1856, St. Louis, Mo. D. Mar. 7, 1902, Pittsburgh, Pa.
Manager 1885.
Hall of Fame 1965.

BR TR 5'8" 190 lbs.

		G	AB	H	R	BA	W	L	PCT	G BY POS
1875	St. Louis	12	37	8	8	.216	4	2	.667	P-8, OF-5

Count Gedney

GEDNEY, ALFRED W.
B. May 10, 1849, Brooklyn, N. Y. D. Mar. 26, 1922, Hackensack, N. J.

5'9" 140 lbs.

		G	AB	H	R	BA	W	L	PCT	G BY POS
1872	2 teams Brooklyn Eckfords (18G .158) Troy Haymakers (9G .413)									
"	total	27	122	31	23	.254				OF-27
1873	New York Mutuals	53	236	60	41	.254				OF-53
1874	Philadelphia Athletics	54	235	76	48	.323				OF-50, 1B-4
1875	New York Mutuals	67	263	52	29	.198	1	0	1.000	OF-66, P-1
	4 yrs.	201	856	219	141	.256	1	0	1.000	OF-196, 1B-4, P-1

		G	AB	H	R	BA	W	L	PCT	G BY POS		

Billy Geer

GEER, WILLIAM HENRY HARRISON
Born George Harrison Geer.
B. Aug. 13, 1849, Syracuse, N. Y.   D. Jan. 5, 1922, Syracuse, N. Y.

TR 5'8"   160 lbs.

		G	AB	H	R	BA				G BY POS
1874	New York Mutuals	2	8	2	0	.250				OF-2
1875	New Havens	37	173	39	20	.225				OF-17, 2B-13, SS-5, 3B-1, 1B-1
	2 yrs.	39	181	41	20	.227				OF-19, 2B-13, SS-5, 3B-1, 1B-1

Joe Gerhardt

GERHARDT, JOHN JOSEPH (Move Up Joe)
B. Feb. 14, 1855, Washington, D. C.   D. Mar. 11, 1922, Middletown, N. Y.
Manager 1883-84.

BR TR 6'   160 lbs.

1873	Washington Nationals	13	56	11	6	.196				SS-13
1874	Lord Baltimores	14	65	20	10	.308				SS-14
1875	New York Mutuals	57	254	54	29	.213				3B-44, 2B-12, SS-1
	3 yrs.	84	375	85	45	.227				3B-44, SS-28, 2B-12

Barney Gilligan

GILLIGAN, ANDREW BERNARD
B. Jan. 3, 1856, Cambridge, Mass.   D. Apr. 1, 1934, Lynn, Mass.

BR TR 5'6½" 130 lbs.

1875	Brooklyn Atlantics	2	8	2	2	.250				OF-1, C-1

Jim Gilmore

GILMORE, JAMES
B. May, 1853, Baltimore, Md.   D. Nov. 18, 1928, Baltimore, Md.

1875	Washington Nationals	4	15	5	4	.333				C-2, 3B-1, 2B-1

Gilroy

GILROY,
Deceased.

1874	Chicago White Stockings	8	39	8	4	.205				C-8
1875	Philadelphia Athletics	2	8	2	0	.250				OF-1, C-1
	2 yrs.	10	47	10	4	.213				C-9, OF-1

John Glenn

GLENN, JOHN W.
B. 1849, Rochester, N. Y.   D. Nov. 10, 1888, Sandy Hill, N. Y.

BR TR 5'8½" 169 lbs.

1871	Washington Olympics	26	123	37	24	.301				OF-26
1872	2 teams Washington Nationals (1G .500) Washington Olympics (9G .150)									
"	total	10	44	8	5	.182				OF-10
1873	Washington Nationals	39	194	49	39	.253				1B-39
1874	Chicago White Stockings	55	245	64	34	.261				1B-38, OF-17
1875		70	325	76	48	.234				OF-44, 1B-26
	5 yrs.	200	931	234	150	.251				1B-103, OF-97

Mike Golden

GOLDEN, MICHAEL HENRY
B. Sept. 11, 1851, Shirley, Mass.   D. Jan. 11, 1929, Rockford, Ill.

BR TR 5'7"   166 lbs.

1875	2 teams Chicago White Stockings (39G .242 W-7 L-7) Keokuk Westerns (13G .140 W-1 L-12)									
"	total	52	211	46	21	.218	8	19	.077	P-28, OF-24, 1B-1

Fred Goldsmith

GOLDSMITH, FRED ERNEST
B. May 15, 1852, New Haven, Conn.   D. Mar. 28, 1939, Berkley, Mich.

BR TR 6'1"   195 lbs.

1875	New Havens	1	4	2	0	.500				2B-1

Wally Goldsmith

GOLDSMITH, WALLACE
B. 1849, Baltimore, Md.   Deceased.

5'7"   146 lbs.

1871	Fort Wayne Kekiongas	19	91	19	9	.209				SS-12, 3B-5, C-1, 2B-1
1872	Washington Olympics	9	40	9	4	.225				SS-5, 2B-4
1873	Marylands	1	4	0	0	.000				2B-1
1875	Keokuk Westerns	13	53	6	3	.113				3B-13
	4 yrs.	42	188	34	16	.181				3B-18, SS-17, 2B-6, C-1

Charlie Gould

GOULD, CHARLES HARVEY
B. Aug. 21, 1847, Cincinnati, Ohio   D. Apr. 10, 1917, Flushing, N. Y.
Manager 1875-76.

BR TR 6'   172 lbs.

1871	Boston Red Stockings	31	156	42	38	.269				1B-30, OF-1
1872		45	223	57	41	.256				1B-44, OF-2
1874	Lord Baltimores	33	151	34	20	.225				1B-32, C-1
1875	New Havens	27	115	29	9	.252				1B-26, OF-1
	4 yrs.	136	645	162	108	.251				1B-132, OF-4, C-1

Greyson

GREYSON,
Deceased.

TL

1873	Washington Nationals	8	35	5	4	.143	1	7	.125	P-8

Bill Hague

HAGUE, WILLIAM L.
Born William L. Haug.
B. 1852, Philadelphia, Pa.   Deceased.

BR TR 5'9"   164 lbs.

1875	St. Louis	62	261	59	24	.226				3B-61, 1B-1

George Hall

HALL, GEORGE WILLIAM
B. Mar. 29, 1849, Stepney, England   D. June 11, 1923, Ridgewood N. Y.,

BL 5'7"   142 lbs.

1871	Washington Olympics	32	146	38	31	.260				OF-32
1872	Lord Baltimores	54	263	79	69	.300				OF-53, 1B-1
1873		34	169	54	43	.320				OF-34
1874	Boston Red Stockings	47	209	67	58	.321				OF-47
1875	Philadelphia Athletics	77	362	108	70	.298				OF-77
	5 yrs.	244	1149	346	271	.301				OF-243, 1B-1

Jim Hall

HALL, JAMES
D. Jan. 30, 1886, Brooklyn, N. Y.

1872	Brooklyn Atlantics	13	57	14	8	.246				2B-12, OF-1
1874		2	8	1	0	.125				2B-2
1875	Keokuk Westerns	1	4	1	0	.250				OF-1
	3 yrs.	16	69	16	8	.232				2B-14, OF-2

		G	AB	H	R	BA	W	L	PCT	G BY POS

Jimmy Hallinan

HALLINAN, JAMES H.
B. May 27, 1849, Ireland   D. Oct. 28, 1879, Chicago, Ill.

BL TL 5'9"   172 lbs.

1871 Fort Wayne Kekiongas	5	25	5	7	.200				SS-5
1875 2 teams New York Mutuals (44G .299) Keokuk Westerns (13G .241)									
" total	57	262	75	42	.286				SS-56, 3B-1
2 yrs.	62	287	80	49	.279				SS-61, 3B-1

Ralph Ham

HAM, RALPH A.
B. 1850, Troy, N. Y.   D. Feb. 13, 1905, Troy, N. Y.

5'8"   158 lbs.

1871 Rockford Forest Citys	25	118	26	25	.220				OF-18, 3B-7, SS-2
1872 Middletown Mansfields	1	6	2	0	.333				SS-1
2 yrs.	26	124	28	25	.226				OF-18, 3B-7, SS-3

Bill Harbidge

HARBIDGE, WILLIAM ARTHUR
B. Mar. 29, 1855, Philadelphia, Pa.   D. Mar. 17, 1924, Philadelphia, Pa.

BL TL   162 lbs.

1875 Hartfords	51	227	49	32	.216				C-25, OF-13, 2B-10, 1B-3

Rit Harrison

HARRISON, WASHINGTON RITTER
B. Sept. 16, 1849, Haverstraw, N. Y.   D. Nov. 7, 1888, Bridgeport, Conn.

1875 New Havens	1	4	2	0	.500				C-1

Scott Hastings

HASTINGS, WINFIELD SCOTT
B. Aug. 10, 1846, Hillsboro, Ohio   D. Aug. 14, 1907, Sawtelle, Calif.
Manager 1871-72.

BR TR 5'8"   161 lbs.

1871 Rockford Forest Citys	25	120	28	27	.233				C-23, 2B-2, OF-1
1872 2 teams Lord Baltimores (11G .196) Cleveland Forest Citys (21G .422)									
" total	32	172	60	52	.349				C-20, OF-7, 2B-6
1873 Lord Baltimores	30	160	41	42	.256				C-19, OF-10, 2B-1
1874 Hartfords	52	237	88	60	.371				C-31, OF-20, 2B-1
1875 Chicago White Stockings	66	298	74	43	.248				C-39, OF-25, 2B-2
5 yrs.	205	987	291	224	.295				C-132, OF-63, 2B-12

John Hatfield

HATFIELD, JOHN VAN BUSKIRK
Brother of Gil Hatfield.
B. July 20, 1847, N. J.   D. Feb. 20, 1909, Long Island City, N. Y.
Manager 1873.

5'10"   165 lbs.

1871 New York Mutuals	33	168	44	41	.262				OF-24, 2B-7, 3B-2
1872	56	297	90	75	.303				2B-56
1873	52	260	76	54	.292				3B-42, 2B-10
1874	63	299	67	47	.224	0	0	.000	OF-59, 3B-4, P-1, 1B-1
1875	2	9	4	2	.444				OF-2
5 yrs.	206	1033	281	219	.272	0	0	.000	OF-85, 2B-73, 3B-48, P-1
									1B-1

Charlie Hautz

HAUTZ, CHARLES A.
B. Feb. 5, 1852, St. Louis, Mo.   D. Jan. 24, 1929, St. Louis, Mo.

5'7"   150 lbs.

1875 St. Louis Reds	18	75	23	5	.307				1B-18

Hearn

HEARN,
Deceased.

1872 Washington Olympics	1	3	1	0	.333				SS-1

Frank Heifer

HEIFER, FRANKLIN (Heck)
B. Jan. 18, 1854, Reading, Pa.   D. Aug. 29, 1893, Reading, Pa.

5'10½"   175 lbs.

1875 Boston Red Stockings	11	48	16	11	.333	0	0	.000	1B-7, OF-5, P-1

Hellings

HELLINGS,
B. Philadelphia, Pa.   Deceased.

1875 Brooklyn Atlantics	1	4	1	0	.250				2B-1

George Heubel

HEUBEL, GEORGE A.
B. 1849, Paterson, N. J.   D. Jan. 22, 1896, Philadelphia, Pa.

5'11½"   178 lbs.

1871 Philadelphia Athletics	17	78	25	10	.321				OF-16, 1B-1
1872 Washington Olympics	5	24	3	2	.125				OF-5
2 yrs.	22	102	28	12	.275				OF-21, 1B-1

Nat Hicks

HICKS, NATHANIEL WOODHULL
B. Apr. 19, 1845, Hempstead, N. Y.   D. Apr. 21, 1907, Hoboken, N. J.
Manager 1875.

BR TR 6'1"   186 lbs.

1872 New York Mutuals	56	276	85	54	.308				C-55, OF-2
1873	28	132	28	12	.212				C-28
1874 Philadelphias	58	284	73	51	.257				C-56, OF-2
1875 New York Mutuals	62	270	63	32	.233				C-59, OF-3
4 yrs.	204	962	249	149	.259				C-198, OF-7

Higby

HIGBY,
Deceased.

1872 Brooklyn Atlantics	1	4	0	0	.000				OF-1

Dick Higham

HIGHAM, RICHARD
B. July, 1851, England   D. Mar. 18, 1905, Chicago, Ill.
Manager 1874.

BL TR

1871 New York Mutuals	21	97	32	21	.330				2B-11, OF-8, C-1, 3B-1
1872 Lord Baltimores	46	242	82	67	.339				C-21, OF-18, 2B-6, 1B-1
1873 New York Mutuals	49	247	75	57	.304				OF-18, 2B-16, C-14, 3B-1
1874	65	342	87	58	.254				C-41, OF-23, 2B-1
1875 2 teams Chicago White Stockings (43G .234) New York Mutuals (15G .333)									
" total	58	280	72	55	.257				C-30, 2B-19, OF-7, 1B-2
5 yrs.	239	1208	348	258	.288				C-107, OF-74, 2B-53, 1B-3
									3B-2

		G	AB	H	R	BA	W	L	PCT	G BY POS
Paul Hines	**HINES, PAUL A.** B. Mar. 1, 1852, Washington, D. C. D. July 10, 1935, Hyattsville, Md.									BR TR 5'9½" 173 lbs.
	1872 Washington Nationals	11	49	14	10	.286				1B-10, 3B-1
	1873	39	186	61	33	.328				OF-36, 2B-2, C-1
	1874 Chicago White Stockings	59	283	78	47	.276				OF-46, 2B-12, SS-2
	1875	69	322	101	42	.314				OF-41, 2B-28
	4 yrs.	178	840	254	132	.302				OF-123, 2B-42, 1B-10, SS-2 C-1, 3B-1
Charlie Hodes	**HODES, CHARLES** B. 1848, New York, N. Y. D. Feb. 14, 1875, Brooklyn, N. Y.									TR 5'11½" 175 lbs.
	1871 Chicago White Stockings	28	138	34	32	.246				C-18, 3B-7, OF-2, SS-1
	1872 Troy Haymakers	13	65	15	17	.231				SS-5, OF-4, C-3, 3B-1
	1874 Brooklyn Atlantics	21	84	12	8	.143				OF-19, 2B-2
	3 yrs.	62	287	61	57	.213				OF-25, C-21, 3B-8, SS-6 2B-2
Jim Holdsworth	**HOLDSWORTH, JAMES (Long Jim)** B. July 14, 1850, New York, N. Y. D. Mar. 22, 1918, New York, N. Y.									BR TR
	1872 2 teams Cleveland Forest Citys (21G .321) Brooklyn Eckfords (2G .250)									
	" total	23	117	37	19	.316				SS-23
	1873 New York Mutuals	53	232	71	45	.306				SS-53
	1874 Philadelphias	58	302	99	59	.328				3B-31, SS-23, OF-4
	1875 New York Mutuals	71	339	92	47	.271				OF-45, SS-26
	4 yrs.	205	990	299	170	.302				SS-125, OF-49, 3B-31
Holly Hollingshead	**HOLLINGSHEAD, JOHN SAMUEL** Also appeared in box score as Holly B. Jan. 17, 1853, Washington, D. C. D. Oct. 6, 1926, Washington, D. C. Manager 1875, 1884.									
	1872 Washington Nationals	9	45	14	12	.311				2B-9
	1873	30	137	35	25	.255				OF-30, 2B-1
	1875	19	88	20•	8	.227				OF-19
	3 yrs.	58	270	69	45	.256				OF-49, 2B-10
Mike Hooper	**HOOPER, MICHAEL H.** B. Feb. 20, 1850, Baltimore, Md. D. Dec. 1, 1927, Baltimore, Md.									5'6" 165 lbs.
	1873 Marylands	2	9	0	0	.000				OF-1, C-1
Dick Hunt	**HUNT, RICHARD M.** B. 1847, N. Y. D. Nov. 20, 1895, New York, N. Y.									5'9" 145 lbs.
	1872 Brooklyn Eckfords	11	52	15	11	.288				OF-8, 2B-3
Dick Hurley	**HURLEY, WILLIAM F.** B. 1847, Honesdale, Pa. Deceased.									BL 5'7" 160 lbs.
	1872 Washington Olympics	2	8	0	0	.000				OF-2
Sam Jackson	**JACKSON, SAMUEL** B. Mar. 24, 1849, Ripon, England D. Aug. 4, 1893, Clifton Springs, N. Y.									BR TR 5'5½" 160 lbs.
	1871 Boston Red Stockings	15	77	15	15	.195				2B-14, OF-1
	1872 Brooklyn Atlantics	3	13	2	0	.154				OF-3
	2 yrs.	18	90	17	15	.189				2B-14, OF-4
Nat Jewett	**JEWETT, NATHAN W.** B. Dec. 25, 1842, New York, D. Feb. 23, 1914, Bronx, N. Y.									5'6" 137 lbs.
	1872 Brooklyn Eckfords	2	8	1	1	.125				C-2
Tom Johns	**JOHNS, THOMAS PEARCE** B. Sept. 7, 1851, Baltimore, Md. D. Apr. 13, 1927, Baltimore, Md.									5'11" 170 lbs.
	1873 Marylands	1	5	0	0	.000				OF-1
Caleb Johnson	**JOHNSON, CALEB CLARK** B. May 23, 1844, Fulton, Ill. D. Mar. 7, 1925, Sterling, Ill.									
	1871 Cleveland Forest Citys	16	65	16	10	.246				2B-8, OF-7, SS-1
Charley Jones	**JONES, CHARLES WESLEY (Long Charley)** Born Benjamin Wesley Rippay. B. Apr. 3, 1850, County, N. C. Deceased.									BR TR 5'11½" 202 lbs.
	1875 Keokuk Westerns	12	52	13	4	.250				OF-12
Kavanaugh	**KAVANAUGH,** Deceased.									
	1872 Brooklyn Eckfords	5	22	4	5	.182				1B-4, OF-1
Jim Keenan	**KEENAN, JAMES WILLIAM** B. Feb. 10, 1858, New Haven, Conn. D. Sept. 21, 1926, Cincinnati, Ohio									BR TR 5'10" 186 lbs.
	1875 New Havens	3	12	1	1	.083				3B-2, C-1
George Keerl	**KEERL, GEORGE HENRY (Cap)** B. Apr. 10, 1847, Baltimore, Md. D. Sept. 13, 1923, Menominee, Mich.									BR TR 5'7" 145 lbs.
	1875 Chicago White Stockings	6	26	3	2	.115				2B-6
Bill Kelley	**KELLEY, WILLIAM J.** B. New York, N. Y. Deceased.									
	1871 Fort Wayne Kekiongas	18	71	15	17	.211				OF-17, 1B-1
John Kenney	**KENNEY, JOHN** Deceased.									
	1872 Brooklyn Atlantics	5	21	0	0	.000				2B-3, OF-2
Joe Kernan	**KERNAN, JOSEPH** B. Baltimore, Md. Deceased.									
	1873 Marylands	2	8	3	1	.375				OF-1, 2B-1

		G	AB	H	R	BA	W	L	PCT	G BY POS
Henry Kessler	**KESSLER, HENRY (Lucky)** B. 1847, Brooklyn, N. Y. D. Jan. 9, 1900, Franklin, Pa.									BR TR 5'10" 144 lbs.
	1873 Brooklyn Atlantics	1	6	1	0	.167				1B-1
	1874	14	57	16	8	.281				C-8, 2B-4, OF-2, 3B-1
	1875	25	108	26	17	.241				SS-18, OF-6, C-1, 2B-1
	3 yrs.	40	171	43	25	.251				SS-18, C-9, OF-8, 2B-5 3B-1, 1B-1
Gene Kimball	**KIMBALL, EUGENE BOYNTON** B. Aug. 31, 1850, Rochester, N. Y. D. Aug. 2, 1882, Rochester, N. Y.									5'10" 160 lbs.
	1871 Cleveland Forest Citys	29	136	25	18	.184				2B-17, OF-6, SS-6
Mart King	**KING, MARSHALL NEY** B. Dec., 1848, Troy, N. Y. D. Oct. 19, 1911, Troy, N. Y.									TR 5'9½" 176 lbs.
	1871 Chicago White Stockings	20	109	16	23	.147				OF-10, C-7, SS-3
	1872 Troy Haymakers	3	12	0	0	.000				OF-3
	2 yrs.	23	121	16	23	.132				OF-13, C-7, SS-3
Steve King	**KING, STEPHEN F.** B. 1845, Troy, N. Y. D. July 8, 1895, Troy, N. Y.									5'9" 175 lbs.
	1871 Troy Haymakers	29	144	57	45	.396				OF-29
	1872	25	128	38	31	.297				OF-25
	2 yrs.	54	272	95	76	.349				OF-54
George Knight	**KNIGHT, GEORGE HENRY** B. Nov. 24, 1855, Lakeville, Conn. D. Oct. 4, 1912, Lakeville, Conn.									
	1875 New Havens	1	4	0	0	.000	1	0	1.000	P-1
Lon Knight	**KNIGHT, ALONZO P.** B. June 16, 1853, Philadelphia, Pa. D. Apr. 23, 1932, Philadelphia, Pa. Manager 1885.									BR TR 5'11½" 165 lbs.
	1875 Philadelphia Athletics	13	51	6	5	.118	6	5	.545	P-13
Jake Knowdell	**KNOWDELL, JACOB AUGUSTUS** B. July 27, 1840, Brooklyn, N. Y. Deceased.									5'7½" 148 lbs.
	1874 Brooklyn Atlantics	23	90	12	8	.133				C-20, OF-3
	1875	43	165	32	17	.194				C-33, SS-8, OF-3
	2 yrs.	66	255	44	25	.173				C-53, SS-8, OF-6
Henry Kohler	**KOHLER, HENRY C.** B. May 5, 1852, Baltimore, Md. D. Aug. 27, 1934, Baltimore, Md.									
	1871 Fort Wayne Kekiongas	3	12	2	0	.167				1B-2, 3B-1
	1873 Marylands	5	22	3	2	.136				3B-5, C-1
	1874 Lord Baltimores	1	4	0	0	.000				1B-1
	3 yrs.	9	38	5	2	.132				3B-6, 1B-3, C-1
Frank Latham	**LATHAM, GEORGE WALTER** B. Oct. 16, 1854, N. Y. D. June 17, 1907, New York, N. Y.									
	1872 Middletown Mansfields	19	85	23	17	.271				OF-19
Juice Latham	**LATHAM, GEORGE WARREN (Jumbo)** B. Sept. 6, 1852, Utica, N. Y. D. May 26, 1914, Utica, N. Y. Manager 1875, 1882.									BR TR 240 lbs.
	1875 2 teams Boston Red Stockings (16G .321) New Havens (20G .183) " total	36	160	40	28	.250				1B-29, SS-4, 3B-3
Ben Laughlin	**LAUGHLIN, BENJAMIN** Deceased.									
	1873 Elizabeth Resolutes	12	54	12	3	.222				2B-10, 3B-1, 1B-1
Mike Ledwith	**LEDWITH, MICHAEL** B. Brooklyn, N. Y. D. Jan. 2, 1929, Bronx, N. Y.									
	1874 Brooklyn Atlantics	1	4	1	0	.250				C-1
Billy Lennon	**LENNON, WILLIAM F.** B. 1848, Brooklyn, N. Y. Deceased. Manager 1871.									5'7" 145 lbs.
	1871 Fort Wayne Kekiongas	12	48	11	4	.229				C-12
	1872 Washington Nationals	11	52	12	11	.231				C-11
	1873 Marylands	4	15	3	1	.200				1B-3, C-1, 3B-1
	3 yrs.	27	115	26	16	.226				C-24, 1B-3, 3B-1
Andy Leonard	**LEONARD, ANDREW JACKSON** B. June 1, 1846, County Cavan, Ireland D. Aug. 22, 1903, Roxbury, Mass.									BR TR 5'7" 168 lbs.
	1871 Washington Olympics	31	151	43	34	.285				2B-20, OF-10, SS-1
	1872 Boston Red Stockings	46	252	86	60	.341				OF-37, 3B-6, 2B-3
	1873	58	319	95	83	.298				OF-45, 2B-12, SS-1
	1874	71	350	119	71	.340				OF-51, SS-11, 2B-9
	1875	80	396	128	87	.323				OF-73, 3B-3, SS-3, 2B-1
	5 yrs.	286	1468	471	335	.321				OF-216, 2B-45, SS-16, 3B-9
Leutz	**LEUTZ,** Deceased.									
	1872 Brooklyn Eckfords	4	15	2	3	.133				C-4
Marshall Locke	**LOCKE, MARSHALL** B. Indianapolis, Ind. Deceased.									
	1874 Lord Baltimores	1	5	0	0	.000				SS-1
Len Lovett	**LOVETT, LEONARD WALKER** B. July 17, 1852, County, Pa. D. Nov. 18, 1922, Newark, Del.									BR TR
	1873 Elizabeth Resolutes	1	5	2	1	.400	0	1	.000	P-1

		G	AB	H	R	BA	W	L	PCT	G BY POS

Len Lovett *continued*

	G	AB	H	R	BA	W	L	PCT	G BY POS
1875 Philadelphia Centennials	5	22	4	2	.182				OF-5
2 yrs.	6	27	6	3	.222	0	1	.000	OF-5, P-1

Charlie Lowe

LOWE, CHARLES
B. Baltimore, Md.   Deceased.

	G	AB	H	R	BA	W	L	PCT	G BY POS
1872 Brooklyn Atlantics	6	27	4	1	.148				2B-6

John Lowry

LOWRY, JOHN D.
B. Baltimore, Md.   Deceased.

	G	AB	H	R	BA	W	L	PCT	G BY POS
1875 Washington Nationals	5	17	3	1	.176				OF-5

Henry Luff

LUFF, HENRY T.   5'11"   175 lbs.
B. Sept. 14, 1856, Philadelphia, Pa.   D. Oct. 11, 1916, Philadelphia, Pa.

	G	AB	H	R	BA	W	L	PCT	G BY POS
1875 New Havens	38	172	45	15	.262	1	7	.125	3B-26, P-8, OF-4

Denny Mack

MACK, DENNIS JOSEPH   BR TR 5'7"   164 lbs.
Born Dennis Joseph McGee.
B. 1851, Easton, Pa.   D. Apr. 10, 1888, Wilkes-Barre, Pa.
Manager 1882.

	G	AB	H	R	BA	W	L	PCT	G BY POS
1871 Rockford Forest Cities	25	130	31	34	.238	0	1	.000	1B-24, P-1, SS-1
1872 Philadelphia Athletics	46	227	56	66	.247				1B-24, SS-22
1873 Philadelphias	46	218	61	54	.280				1B-40, OF-4, SS-1, 2B-1
1874	56	261	53	47	.203				1B-56
4 yrs.	173	836	201	201	.240	0	1	.000	1B-144, SS-24, OF-4, P-1, 2B-1

Malone

MALONE,
Deceased.

	G	AB	H	R	BA	W	L	PCT	G BY POS
1872 Brooklyn Eckfords	4	16	4	1	.250	0	3	.000	P-3, OF-1

Fergy Malone

MALONE, FERGUSON G.   BR TL 5'8"   156 lbs.
B. 1842, Ireland   D. Jan. 1, 1905, Seattle, Wash.
Manager 1873-74, 1884.

	G	AB	H	R	BA	W	L	PCT	G BY POS
1871 Philadelphia Athletics	27	145	46	33	.317				C-27
1872	39	216	58	46	.269				C-21, 1B-18
1873 Philadelphias	53	284	76	59	.268				C-52, SS-1
1874 Chicago White Stockings	47	238	53	33	.223				C-47
1875 Philadelphias	27	114	26	15	.228				1B-21, C-4, OF-2
5 yrs.	193	997	259	186	.260				C-151, 1B-39, OF-2, SS-1

Jack Manning

MANNING, JOHN E.   BR TR 5'8½"   158 lbs.
B. Dec. 20, 1853, Braintree, Mass.   D. Aug. 15, 1929, Boston, Mass.

	G	AB	H	R	BA	W	L	PCT	G BY POS
1873 Boston Red Stockings	33	169	44	30	.260				1B-28, OF-5
1874 2 teams Lord Baltimores (42G .299 W-4 L-14) Hartfords (1G .250)									
" total	43	188	56	36	.298	4	14	.222	2B-20, P-19, SS-5, 3B-1
1875 Boston Red Stockings	77	351	100	71	.285	13	3	.813	OF-58, P-17, 3B-2, 1B-2
3 yrs.	153	708	200	137	.282	17	17	.500	OF-63, P-36, 1B-30, 2B-20, SS-5, 3B-3

Al Martin

MARTIN, ALBERT
Deceased.

	G	AB	H	R	BA	W	L	PCT	G BY POS
1872 Brooklyn Eckfords	4	19	5	2	.263				2B-4
1874 Brooklyn Atlantics	7	35	4	1	.114				2B-6, OF-1
1875	6	26	3	1	.115				OF-6
3 yrs.	17	80	12	4	.150				2B-10, OF-7

Phoney Martin

MARTIN, ALPHONSE CASE   5'7"   148 lbs.
B. Aug. 4, 1845, New York, N. Y.   D. May 24, 1933, Hollis, N. Y.

	G	AB	H	R	BA	W	L	PCT	G BY POS
1872 2 teams Brooklyn Eckfords (18G .183 W-2 L-8) Troy Haymakers (25G .287 W-1 L-2)									
" total	43	204	50	37	.245	3	10	.333	OF-31, P-13
1873 New York Mutuals	29	139	29	12	.209	0	2	.000	OF-27, P-2
2 yrs.	72	343	79	49	.230	3	12	.200	OF-58, P-15

Charlie Mason

MASON, CHARLES E.   TR
B. June 25, 1853, New Orleans, La.   D. Oct. 21, 1936, Philadelphia, Pa.
Manager 1882, 1884-85, 1887.

	G	AB	H	R	BA	W	L	PCT	G BY POS
1875 2 teams Philadelphia Centennials (12G .229) Washington Nationals (7G .100)									
" total	19	78	14	6	.179				OF-17, 1B-2

Bobby Mathews

MATHEWS, ROBERT T.   BR TR 5'5½"   140 lbs.
B. Nov. 21, 1851, Baltimore, Md.   D. Apr. 17, 1898, Baltimore, Md.

	G	AB	H	R	BA	W	L	PCT	G BY POS
1871 Fort Wayne Kekiongas	19	89	25	17	.281	7	12	.368	P-19
1872 Lord Baltimores	47	218	50	30	.229	25	16	.610	P-45, OF-3, 3B-2
1873 New York Mutuals	52	235	43	39	.183	29	22	.569	P-51, OF-1
1874	65	303	71	46	.234	42	23	.646	P-65
1875	70	278	49	23	.176	29	38	.433	P-70
5 yrs.	253	1123	238	155	.212	132	111	.543	P-250, OF-4, 3B-2

Bub McAtee

McATEE, MICHAEL JAMES (Butch, Butcher)   TR 6'1"   160 lbs.
B. Mar., 1845, Troy, N. Y.   D. Oct. 18, 1876, Troy, N. Y.

	G	AB	H	R	BA	W	L	PCT	G BY POS
1871 Chicago White Stockings	26	141	39	34	.277				1B-26
1872 Troy Haymakers	25	129	27	31	.209				1B-25
2 yrs.	51	270	66	65	.244				1B-51

Dick McBride

McBRIDE, JAMES DICKSON   TR 5'9"   150 lbs.
B. 1845, Philadelphia, Pa.   D. Oct. 10, 1916, Philadelphia, Pa.
Manager 1871-75.

	G	AB	H	R	BA	W	L	PCT	G BY POS
1871 Philadelphia Athletics	25	141	30	36	.213	20	5	.800	P-25
1872	46	262	72	58	.275	30	14	.682	P-46
1873	49	267	68	42	.255	25	21	.543	P-46, OF-5

		G	AB	H	R	BA	W	L	PCT	G BY POS
Dick McBride *continued*										
	1874	55	268	72	31	.269	33	22	.600	P-55
	1875	60	275	73	43	.265	44	14	.759	P-60
	5 yrs.	235	1213	315	210	.260	152	76	.667	P-232, OF-5

McCloskey
McCLOSKEY,
B. Brooklyn, N. Y.   Deceased.

	1875 Washington Nationals	10	38	5	1	.132				C-10

Joe McDermott
McDERMOTT, JOSEPH
Deceased.

	1871 Fort Wayne Kekiongas	2	9	1	3	.111				OF-2
	1872 Brooklyn Eckfords	7	33	9	3	.273	0	7	.000	P-7
	2 yrs.	9	42	10	6	.238	0	7	.000	P-7, OF-2

Jack McDonald
McDONALD, DANIEL
B. 1847, Brooklyn, N. Y.   D. Nov. 23, 1880, Brooklyn, N. Y.

	1872 2 teams Brooklyn Atlantics (14G .214) Brooklyn Eckfords (1G .000)									
	" total	15	61	12	8	.197				OF-14, SS-1

McDoolan
McDOOLAN,
Deceased.

	1873 Marylands	1	4	0	1	.000	0	1	.000	P-1

Mike McGeary
McGEARY, MICHAEL HENRY   BR TR 5'7"   138 lbs.
B. 1851, Philadelphia, Pa.   Deceased.
Manager 1875, 1880-81.

	1871 Troy Haymakers	29	156	38	42	.244				C-26, SS-3
	1872 Philadelphia Athletics	46	227	78	67	.344				C-25, SS-20, OF-1
	1873	52	286	81	63	.283				SS-43, C-10
	1874	54	276	100	61	.362				SS-26, C-24, OF-4
	1875 Philadelphias	69	313	92	71	.294				3B-24, 2B-23, SS-18, OF-3 C-1
	5 yrs.	250	1258	389	304	.309				SS-110, C-86, 3B-24, 2B-23 OF-8

Pat McGee
McGEE, PATRICK
B. Philadelphia, Pa.   D. June 21, 1889, New York, N. Y.

	1874 Brooklyn Atlantics	16	66	10	4	.152				OF-15, SS-2, 2B-1
	1875 2 teams Brooklyn Atlantics (18G .134) New York Mutuals (25G .158)									
	" total	43	168	25	7	.149				OF-38, 2B-5
	2 yrs.	59	234	35	11	.150				OF-53, 2B-6, SS-2

Tim McGinley
McGINLEY, TIMOTHY S.   5'9½"   155 lbs.
B. Philadelphia, Pa.   D. Nov. 2, 1899, Oakland, Calif.

	1875 2 teams Philadelphia Centennials (13G .226) New Havens (33G .255)									
	" total	46	194	48	19	.247				C-45, OF-1

John McKelvey
McKELVEY, JOHN WELLINGTON   BR TR 5'7½"   175 lbs.
B. Aug. 27, 1847, Rochester, N. Y.   D. May 31, 1944, Rochester, N. Y.

	1875 New Havens	43	202	42	26	.208				OF-39, 3B-4

Ed McKenna
McKENNA, EDWARD J.
B. St. Louis, Mo.   Deceased.

	1874 Philadelphias	1	4	0	0	.000				1B-1

John McMullin
McMULLIN, JOHN F. (Lefty)   BR TL 5'9"   160 lbs.
B. 1849, Philadelphia, Pa.   D. Apr. 11, 1881, Philadelphia, Pa.

	1871 Troy Haymakers	29	145	38	38	.262	13	15	.464	P-29
	1872 New York Mutuals	54	256	60	49	.234	1	0	1.000	OF-53, P-2
	1873 Philadelphia Athletics	52	240	61	54	.254	1	0	1.000	OF-51, P-1
	1874	55	271	105	61	.387				OF-54, C-1
	1875 Philadelphias	54	225	56	34	.249	0	1	.000	OF-53, P-1
	5 yrs.	244	1137	320	236	.281	15	16	.484	OF-211, P-33, C-1

Trick McSorley
McSORLEY, JOHN BERNARD   TR 5'4"   142 lbs.
B. Dec. 16, 1858, St. Louis, Mo.   D. Feb. 9, 1936, St. Louis, Mo.

	1875 St. Louis Reds	14	51	9	4	.176				3B-8, OF-6

Cal McVey
McVEY, CALVIN ALEXANDER   BR TR 5'9"   170 lbs.
B. Aug. 30, 1850, Montrose, Iowa   D. Aug. 20, 1926, San Francisco, Calif.
Manager 1873, 1878-79.

	1871 Boston Red Stockings	29	155	65	43	.419				C-28, OF-1
	1872	46	242	74	56	.306				C-40, OF-9
	1873 Lord Baltimores	35	187	69	47	.369				C-17, OF-6, SS-5, 2B-3 1B-3, 3B-1
	1874 Boston Red Stockings	70	343	131	90	.382				OF-55, C-15
	1875	82	392	138	90	.352	1	0	1.000	1B-54, OF-17, C-11, P-2
	5 yrs.	262	1319	477	326	.362	1	0	1.000	C-111, OF-88, 1B-57, SS-5 2B-3, P-2, 3B-1

Bob Metcalf
METCALF, ROBERT
B. Brooklyn, N. Y.   Deceased.

	1875 New York Mutuals	7	31	6	1	.194				3B-4, OF-2, SS-1

Levi Meyerle
MEYERLE, LEVI SAMUEL (Long Levi)   BR TR 6'1"   177 lbs.
B. July, 1845, Philadelphia, Pa.   D. Nov. 4, 1921, Philadelphia, Pa.

	1871 Philadelphia Athletics	26	132	65	45	.492				3B-26
	1872	27	154	49	30	.318				OF-25, 3B-1, SS-1
	1873 Philadelphias	48	248	82	52	.331				3B-48
	1874 Chicago White Stockings	52	263	97	63	.369				2B-26, 3B-14, OF-7, SS-5

		G	AB	H	R	BA	W	L	PCT	G BY POS

Levi Meyerle *continued*

		G	AB	H	R	BA	W	L	PCT	G BY POS
1875 Philadelphias		68	296	93	55	.314				2B-32, 3B-21, 1B-15
5 yrs.		221	1093	386	245	.353				3B-110, 2B-58, OF-32, 1B-15 SS-6

Joe Miller

MILLER, JOSEPH WICK   5'10½" 169 lbs.
B. July 24, 1850, Germany   D. Aug. 30, 1891, White Bear Lake, Minn.

		G	AB	H	R	BA	W	L	PCT	G BY POS
1872 Washington Nationals		1	4	1	0	.250				1B-1
1875 2 teams Chicago White Stockings (16G .138) Keokuk Westerns (13G .111)										
" total		29	119	15	6	.126				2B-27, OF-2
2 yrs.		30	123	16	6	.130				2B-27, OF-2, 1B-1

Reddy Miller

MILLER, THOMAS P.   5'10½" 160 lbs.
B. Philadelphia, Pa.   D. May 29, 1876, Philadelphia, Pa.

		G	AB	H	R	BA	W	L	PCT	G BY POS
1874 Philadelphia Athletics		4	16	8	1	.500				C-4
1875 St. Louis		54	211	35	17	.166				C-52, 3B-3
2 yrs.		58	227	43	18	.189				C-56, 3B-3

Charlie Mills

MILLS, CHARLES   6'
B. Brooklyn, N. Y.   D. Apr. 10, 1874, Brooklyn, N. Y.

		G	AB	H	R	BA	W	L	PCT	G BY POS
1871 New York Mutuals		32	149	37	27	.248				C-28, OF-3, 2B-1
1872		6	30	4	6	.133				OF-5, C-2
2 yrs.		38	179	41	33	.229				C-30, OF-8, 2B-1

Everett Mills

MILLS, EVERETT   6'1" 174 lbs.
B. 1845, Newark, N. J.   D. June 22, 1908, Newark, N. J.
Manager 1872.

		G	AB	H	R	BA	W	L	PCT	G BY POS
1871 Washington Olympics		32	161	44	38	.273				1B-32
1872 Lord Baltimores		53	259	71	52	.274				1B-53
1873		53	262	83	62	.317				1B-52, OF-1
1874 Hartfords		53	242	69	40	.285				1B-53
1875		78	353	92	58	.261				1B-78
5 yrs.		269	1277	359	250	.281				1B-268, OF-1

Ed Mincher

MINCHER, EDWARD JOHN
B. Baltimore, Md.   Deceased.

		G	AB	H	R	BA	W	L	PCT	G BY POS
1871 Fort Wayne Kekiongas		9	36	8	4	.222				OF-9
1872 Washington Nationals		11	51	6	5	.118				OF-11
2 yrs.		20	87	14	9	.161				OF-20

Maury Moore

MOORE, MAURICE
D. Feb. 24, 1881, New York, N. Y.

		G	AB	H	R	BA	W	L	PCT	G BY POS
1875 Brooklyn Atlantics		23	90	20	6	.222				SS-14, 1B-6, 3B-3

Bill Morgan

MORGAN, HENRY WILLIAM
B. Brooklyn, N. Y.   Deceased.

		G	AB	H	R	BA	W	L	PCT	G BY POS
1875 St. Louis Reds		18	73	15	11	.205	1	3	.250	OF-8, 3B-6, P-5

Mullen

MULLEN,
Deceased.

		G	AB	H	R	BA	W	L	PCT	G BY POS
1872 Cleveland Forest Citys		1	6	4	1	.667				OF-1

Munn

MUNN,
Deceased.

		G	AB	H	R	BA	W	L	PCT	G BY POS
1875 Brooklyn Atlantics		1	4	0	0	.000				2B-1

Tim Murnane

MURNANE, TIMOTHY HAYES   BL TR 5'9½" 172 lbs.
B. June 4, 1852, Naugatuck, Conn.   D. Feb. 7, 1917, Boston, Mass.
Manager 1884.

		G	AB	H	R	BA	W	L	PCT	G BY POS
1872 Middletown Mansfields		24	115	34	29	.296				1B-24
1873 Philadelphia Athletics		42	201	43	54	.214				OF-29, 1B-8, 2B-6
1874		19	84	21	9	.250				OF-12, 2B-6, 1B-1
1875 Philadelphias		69	316	90	71	.285				1B-31, OF-26, 2B-12
4 yrs.		154	716	188	163	.263				OF-67, 1B-64, 2B-24

Candy Nelson

NELSON, JOHN W.   BL TR 5'6" 145 lbs.
B. Mar. 12, 1854, Portland, Me.   D. Sept. 4, 1910, Brooklyn, N. Y.

		G	AB	H	R	BA	W	L	PCT	G BY POS
1872 2 teams Brooklyn Eckfords (18G .235) Troy Haymakers (4G .368)										
" total		22	100	26	14	.260				OF-11, 2B-8, 3B-2, SS-1
1873 New York Mutuals		36	177	54	27	.305				2B-27, OF-6, 3B-3
1874		65	.313	69	57	.220				2B-51, SS-14
1875		70	300	56	28	.187				2B-47, 3B-22, OF-1
4 yrs.		193	890	205	126	.230				2B-133, 3B-27, OF-18, SS-15

Nevins

NEVINS,
Deceased.

		G	AB	H	R	BA	W	L	PCT	G BY POS
1873 Elizabeth Resolutes		13	56	11	7	.196				3B-11, OF-1, 2B-1

Al Nichols

NICHOLS, ALFRED H.   5'11" 180 lbs.
B. Brooklyn, N. Y.   Deceased.

		G	AB	H	R	BA	W	L	PCT	G BY POS
1875 Brooklyn Atlantics		32	132	21	4	.159				3B-32

Tricky Nichols

NICHOLS, FREDERICK C.   BR TR 5'7½" 150 lbs.
B. July 26, 1850, Bridgeport, Conn.   D. Aug. 22, 1897, Bridgeport Conn.,

		G	AB	H	R	BA	W	L	PCT	G BY POS
1875 New Havens		33	126	22	12	.175	4	28	.125	P-32, OF-1

Pete Norton

NORTON, PETER J.
B. June 19, 1850, Watertown, Wis.   D. Feb. 8, 1923, Oak Park, Ill.

		G	AB	H	R	BA	W	L	PCT	G BY POS
1871 Washington Olympics		1		0	0	.000				OF-1

		G	AB	H	R	BA	W	L	PCT	G BY POS

Fancy O'Neal

O'NEAL,
B. Hartford, Conn.   Deceased.

		G	AB	H	R	BA	W	L	PCT	G BY POS
1874	Hartfords	1	3	0	0	.000				OF-1

O'Neill

O'NEILL,
B. Bedford, Pa.   Deceased.

| 1875 | Brooklyn Atlantics | 7 | 26 | 3 | 3 | .115 | 0 | 4 | .000 | P-4, OF-3 |

Tom Oran

ORAN, THOMAS
D. Sept. 22, 1886, St. Louis, Mo.

| 1875 | St. Louis Reds | 18 | 79 | 14 | 8 | .177 | | | | OF-18 |

O'Rourke

O'ROURKE,
Deceased.

| 1872 | Brooklyn Eckfords | 1 | 4 | 2 | 0 | .500 | 0 | 1 | .000 | P-1 |

Jim O'Rourke

O'ROURKE, JAMES HENRY (Orator Jim)   BR TR 5'8"   185 lbs.
Brother of John O'Rourke.
B. Sept. 1, 1850, Bridgeport, Conn.   D. Jan. 8, 1919, Bridgeport, Conn.
Manager 1881-84, 1893.
Hall of Fame 1945.

1872	Middletown Mansfields	23	101	29	23	.287				SS-16, C-5, 3B-2
1873	Boston Red Stockings	57	300	99	79	.330				1B-32, OF-20, C-5
1874		70	334	115	80	.344				1B-70
1875		75	374	108	96	.289				OF-45, 3B-27, 1B-3
	4 yrs.	225	1109	351	278	.317				1B-105, OF-65, 3B-29, SS-16 C-10

Charlie Pabor

PABOR, CHARLES HENRY (The Old Woman In The Red Cap)   BL TL 5'8"   155 lbs.
B. Sept. 24, 1846, Brooklyn, N. Y.   D. Apr. 22, 1913, New Haven, Conn.
Manager 1871, 1875.

1871	Cleveland Forest Citys	29	142	44	24	.310	0	1	.000	OF-28, P-1
1872		20	93	25	12	.269	1	0	1.000	OF-19, P-1
1873	Brooklyn Atlantics	55	237	82	36	.346				OF-55
1874	Philadelphias	17	83	18	11	.217				OF-17
1875	2 teams Brooklyn Atlantics (42G .229 W-0 L-0) New Havens (6G .320)									
"	total	48	182	44	19	.242	0	0	.000	OF-47, P-2
	5 yrs.	169	737	213	102	.289	1	1	.500	OF-166, P-4

Bill Parks

PARKS, WILLIAM ROBERT   BR TR 5'8"   150 lbs.
B. June 4, 1849, Easton, Pa.   D. Oct. 10, 1911, Easton, Pa.
Manager 1875.

| 1875 | 2 teams   Washington Nationals (26G .183 W-3 L-9) Philadelphias (2G .125) | | | | | | | | | |
| " | total | 28 | 123 | 22 | 12 | .179 | 3 | 9 | .250 | OF-17, P-12 |

Dan Patterson

PATTERSON, DANIEL THOMAS   TL 5'9"   143 lbs.
B. 1846, New York, N. Y.   Deceased.

1871	New York Mutuals	32	151	31	31	.205				OF-31, 2B-1
1872	Brooklyn Eckfords	12	50	8	5	.160				OF-11, 1B-1
1874	New York Mutuals	1	5	2	1	.400				OF-1, 1B-1
1875	Brooklyn Atlantics	10	38	8	3	.211				OF-5, 2B-5
	4 yrs.	55	244	49	40	.201				OF-48, 2B-6, 1B-2

Dickey Pearce

PEARCE, RICHARD J.   BR TR 5'3½" 161 lbs.
B. Feb. 29, 1836, Brooklyn, N. Y.   D. Oct. 12, 1908, Onset, Mass.
Manager 1872, 1875.

1871	New York Mutuals	33	165	44	31	.267				SS-33
1872		43	208	39	28	.188				SS-42, OF-1
1873	Brooklyn Atlantics	55	279	72	42	.258				SS-55
1874		56	262	76	49	.290				SS-56, 3B-2
1875	St. Louis	70	293	75	49	.256				SS-70
	5 yrs.	257	1207	306	199	.254				SS-256, 3B-2, OF-1

Johnny Peters

PETERS, JOHN PAUL   BR TR   180 lbs.
B. Apr. 8, 1850, Louisiana, Mo.   D. Jan. 4, 1924, St. Louis, Mo.

1874	Chicago White Stockings	54	248	69	39	.278				SS-32, 2B-21, 3B-1
1875		70	314	87	40	.277				SS-66, 2B-4
	2 yrs.	124	562	156	79	.278				SS-98, 2B-25, 3B-1

Neal Phelps

PHELPS, CORNELIUS CARMAN
B. Nov. 19, 1840, New York, N. Y.   D. Feb. 12, 1885, New York, N. Y.

1871	Fort Wayne Kekiongas	1	4	0	0	.000				1B-1
1873	New York Mutuals	1	6	0	0	.000				OF-1
1874		6	23	3	5	.130				OF-6
1875		2	6	2	1	.333				OF-2
	4 yrs.	10	39	5	6	.128				OF-9, 1B-1

Lip Pike

PIKE, LIPMAN EMANUEL (The Iron Batter)   BL TL 5'8"   158 lbs.
Brother of Jay Pike.
B. May 25, 1845, New York, N. Y.   D. Oct. 10, 1893, Brooklyn, N. Y.
Manager 1871, 1874, 1877.

1871	Troy Haymakers	28	134	47	42	.351				OF-18, 2B-6, 1B-4
1872	Lord Baltimores	54	278	80	69	.288				OF-24, 2B-21, 3B-9
1873		56	301	89	73	.296				OF-56, 2B-1
1874	Hartfords	52	228	79	58	.346				OF-27, SS-18, 2B-7
1875	St. Louis	70	313	107	61	.342				OF-62, 2B-8
	5 yrs.	260	1254	402	303	.321				OF-187, 2B-43, SS-18, 3B-9 1B-4

Ed Pinkham

PINKHAM, EDWARD   TL 5'7"   142 lbs.
B. 1849, Brooklyn, N. Y.   Deceased.

| 1871 | Chicago White Stockings | 24 | 110 | 25 | 27 | .227 | 1 | 0 | 1.000 | 3B-16, OF-7, P-1 |

		G	AB	H	R	BA	W	L	PCT	G BY POS

Al Pratt

PRATT, ALBERT G. (Uncle Al)
B. Nov. 19, 1847, Pittsburgh, Pa.   D. Nov. 21, 1937, Pittsburgh, Pa.
Manager 1882-83.

										TR 5'7" 140 lbs.
1871 Cleveland Forest Citys		29	130	33	32	.254	10	18	.357	P-28, OF-1
1872		15	69	18	10	.261	3	9	.250	P-13, OF-3
2 yrs.		44	199	51	42	.256	13	27	.325	P-41, OF-4

Tom Pratt

PRATT, THOMAS J.
B. 1840, Chelsea, Mass.   D. Sept. 28, 1908, Philadelphia, Pa.
Manager 1884.

										5'7½" 150 lbs.
1871 Philadelphia Athletics		1	6	2	2	.333				1B-1

Joe Quest

QUEST, JOSEPH L.
B. Nov., 1851, New Castle, Pa.   Deceased.

										BR TR 5'6" 150 lbs.
1871 Cleveland Forest Citys		3	16	3	1	.188				2B-2, SS-1

Quinlan

QUINLAN,
Deceased.

1874 Philadelphias		1	3	0	0	.000				SS-1

Joe Quinn

QUINN, JOSEPH C.
B. 1851, Chicago, Ill.   D. Jan. 2, 1909, Chicago, Ill.

										5'8½" 148 lbs.
1871 Fort Wayne Kekiongas		5	21	4	8	.190				C-5
1875 2 teams Chicago White Stockings (17G .194) Keokuk Westerns (11G .298)										
" total		31	124	28	16	.226				C-19, OF-13
2 yrs.		36	145	32	24	.221				C-24, OF-13

Paddy Quinn

QUINN, PATRICK
B. Boston, Mass.   D. Mar., 1893

1875 Brooklyn Atlantics		2	8	1	2	.125				OF-2

John Radcliffe

RADCLIFFE, JOHN Y.
B. 1846, Camden, N. J.   D. July 26, 1911, Ocean City, N. J.

										5'6" 140 lbs.
1871 Philadelphia Athletics		28	153	40	47	.261				SS-28
1872 Lord Baltimores		54	293	83	71	.283				SS-48, 3B-5, 2B-1
1873		44	246	69	57	.280				3B-22, SS-22
1874 Philadelphias		23	102	21	19	.206				OF-16, 2B-3, SS-2, 3B-1
										1B-1
1875 Philadelphia Centennials		5	25	4	2	.160				SS-5
5 yrs.		154	819	217	196	.265				SS-105, 3B-28, OF-16, 2B-4
										1B-1

Al Reach

REACH, ALFRED JAMES
Brother of Bob Reach.
B. May 25, 1840, London, England   D. Jan. 14, 1928, Atlantic City, N. J.
Manager 1874-75, 1890.

										BL TL 5'6" 155 lbs.
1871 Philadelphia Athletics		26	135	47	43	.348				2B-26
1872		23	115	22	21	.191				OF-19, 1B-4
1873		13	64	15	13	.234				OF-8, 2B-5
1874		14	53	9	8	.170				OF-14
1875		5	22	5	4	.227				OF-3, 2B-2
5 yrs.		81	389	98	89	.252				OF-44, 2B-33, 1B-4

Bob Reach

REACH, ROBERT
Brother of Al Reach.
B. Aug. 28, 1843, Brooklyn, N. Y.   D. May 19, 1922, Springfield, Mass.

										5'5" 155 lbs.
1872 Washington Olympics		1	5	1	1	.200				SS-1
1873 Washington Nationals		1	5	1	1	.200				SS-1
2 yrs.		2	10	2	2	.200				SS-2

Billy Redmond

REDMOND, WILLIAM T.
B. Brooklyn, N. Y.   Deceased.

										BL TL
1875 St. Louis Reds		18	80	14	10	.175				SS-17, C-1, 3B-1

Hugh Reed

REED, HUGH
B. 1837, Chicago, Ill.   D. Nov. 3, 1883, Chicago, Ill.

1874 Lord Baltimores		1	4	0	0	.000				OF-1

Jack Remsen

REMSEN, JOHN J.
B. Apr., 1851, Brooklyn, N. Y.   Deceased.

										BR TR 5'11" 170 lbs.
1872 Brooklyn Atlantics		35	166	34	22	.205				OF-35
1873		51	215	63	29	.293				OF-51
1874 New York Mutuals		64	286	64	51	.224				OF-63, 1B-1
1875 Hartfords		85	371	95	71	.256				OF-85
4 yrs.		235	1038	256	173	.247				OF-234, 1B-1

Larry Ressler

RESSLER, LAWRENCE P.
B. Aug. 10, 1848, France   D. June 12, 1918, Reading, Pa.

1875 Washington Nationals		26	106	20	15	.189				OF-19, 2B-7

Revels

REVELS,
Deceased.

1874 Lord Baltimores		1	4	0	0	.000				OF-1

Rexter

REXTER,
Deceased.

1875 Brooklyn Atlantics		1	5	0	0	.000				OF-1

John Richmond

RICHMOND, JOHN H.
B. 1854, Pennsylvania   Deceased.

										TR
1875 Philadelphia Athletics		29	122	26	30	.213				2B-16, OF-11, C-2

		G	AB	H	R	BA	W	L	PCT	G BY POS
Billy Riley	**RILEY, WILLIAM JAMES (Pigtail Billy)**									BR TR 5'10" 160 lbs.
	B. 1857, Cincinnati, Ohio D. Nov. 9, 1887, Cincinnati, Ohio									
	1875 Keokuk Westerns	8	34	5	4	.147				OF-8
Tom Roberts	**ROBERTS, THOMAS**									
	B. Baltimore, Md. Deceased.									
	1874 Brooklyn Atlantics	1	4	0	0	.000				OF-1
Al Robinson	**ROBINSON, ALFRED N.**									
	Deceased.									
	1872 Washington Olympics	7	32	6	6	.188				OF-7
Adam Rocap	**ROCAP, ADAM**									5'9" 170 lbs.
	B. 1854, Philadelphia, Pa. D. Mar. 29, 1892, Philadelphia, Pa.									
	1875 Philadelphia Athletics	14	70	12	13	.171				OF-11, 2B-3
Fraley Rogers	**ROGERS, FRALEY W.**									5'8" 184 lbs.
	B. 1850, Brooklyn, N. Y. D. May 10, 1881, New York, N. Y.									
	1872 Boston Red Stockings	46	201	59	40	.294				OF-42, 1B-6
Johnny Ryan	**RYAN, JOHN JOSEPH**									5'7½" 150 lbs.
	B. Oct., 1853, Philadelphia, Pa. D. Mar. 22, 1902, Philadelphia, Pa.									
	1873 Philadelphias	2	9	2	1	.222				OF-1, 1B-1
	1874 Lord Baltimores	47	196	35	28	.179				OF-47
	1875 New Havens	37	153	23	17	.150	1	5	.167	OF-29, P-6, 3B-1, SS-1
	3 yrs.	86	358	60	46	.168	1	5	.167	OF-77, P-6, 3B-1, SS-1 1B-1
Pony Sager	**SAGER, SAMUEL B.**									140 lbs.
	B. 1847, Marshalltown, Iowa Deceased.									
	1871 Rockford Forest Citys	8	40	12	9	.300				OF-4, SS-4
Lew Say	**SAY, LOUIS I.**									BR TR 5'7" 145 lbs.
	Brother of Jimmy Say.									
	B. Feb. 4, 1854, Baltimore, Md. D. June 5, 1930, Fallston, Md.									
	1873 Marylands	3	12	2	1	.167				SS-2, OF-1
	1874 Lord Baltimores	18	71	12	3	.169				SS-18
	1875 Washington Nationals	10	38	9	4	.237				SS-8, OF-1, 2B-1
	3 yrs.	31	121	23	8	.190				SS-28, OF-2, 2B-1
Harry Schafer	**SCHAFER, HARRY C. (Silk Stocking)**									BR TR 5'9½" 143 lbs.
	B. Aug. 14, 1846, Philadelphia, Pa. D. Feb. 28, 1935, Philadelphia, Pa.									
	1871 Boston Red Stockings	31	151	41	38	.272				3B-31, 2B-1
	1872	48	225	59	50	.262				3B-43, OF-5
	1873	60	301	79	64	.262				3B-47, OF-13
	1874	71	324	86	71	.265				3B-71
	1875	51	224	66	50	.295				3B-50, OF-1
	5 yrs.	261	1225	331	273	.270				3B-242, OF-19, 2B-1
Frank Selman	**SELMAN, FRANK C.**									
	Played as Frank Williams From 1871-73.									
	B. Baltimore, Md. Deceased.									
	1871 Fort Wayne Kekiongas	14	69	15	12	.217				3B-13, C-2, SS-1
	1872 Washington Olympics	8	40	11	3	.275				C-6, 3B-2
	1873 Marylands	1	5	1	1	.200	0	1	.000	P-1
	1874 Lord Baltimores	12	58	16	9	.276				SS-7, C-6, OF-1
	4 yrs.	35	172	43	25	.250	0	1	.000	3B-15, C-14, SS-8, OF-1 P-1
Count Sensenderfer	**SENSENDERFER, JOHN PHILLIPS JENKINS (Sen-Sen)**									5'9" 170 lbs.
	B. Dec. 28, 1847, Philadelphia, Pa. D. May 3, 1903, Philadelphia, Pa.									
	1871 Philadelphia Athletics	25	127	43	38	.339				OF-25
	1872	1	5	2	2	.400				OF-1
	1873	19	88	22	12	.250				OF-19
	1874	4	16	4	3	.250				OF-4
	4 yrs.	49	236	71	55	.301				OF-49
George Seward	**SEWARD, GEORGE E.**									5'7½" 145 lbs.
	B. St. Louis, Mo. Deceased.									
	1875 St. Louis	24	95	20	12	.211				C-17, OF-5, 2B-2
Shaffer	**SHAFFER,**									
	Deceased.									
	1875 Brooklyn Atlantics	1	4	0	0	.000				OF-1
Orator Shaffer	**SHAFFER, GEORGE**									BL TR 5'9" 165 lbs.
	Brother of Taylor Shaffer.									
	B. 1852, Philadelphia, Pa. Deceased.									
	1874 2 teams Hartfords (9G .200) New York Mutuals (1G .167)									
	" total	10	41	8	7	.195				OF-10
	1875 Philadelphias	18	79	19	11	.241				OF-10, 3B-6, 1B-2
	2 yrs.	28	120	27	18	.225				OF-20, 3B-6, 1B-2
John Sheppard	**SHEPPARD, JOHN**									
	B. Baltimore, Md. Deceased.									
	1873 Marylands	2	7	0	0	.000				OF-1, C-1
Sheridan	**SHERIDAN,**									
	Deceased.									
	1875 Brooklyn Atlantics	1	4	0	0	.000				OF-1

		G	AB	H	R	BA	W	L	PCT	G BY POS

Joe Simmons

SIMMONS, JOSEPH S.
B. June 13, 1845, New York, N. Y.   D. Dec. 10, 1888, Brooklyn, N. Y.
Manager 1875, 1884.   5'9½"   166 lbs.

		G	AB	H	R	BA	W	L	PCT	G BY POS
1871	Chicago White Stockings	27	134	27	29	.201				OF-25, 1B-2
1872	Cleveland Forest Citys	17	87	20	11	.230				1B-14, OF-3
1875	Keokuk Westerns	13	56	9	5	.161				OF-10, 1B-3
3 yrs.		57	277	56	45	.202				OF-38, 1B-19

Marty Simpson

SIMPSON, MARTIN
B. Baltimore, Md.   Deceased.

		G	AB	H	R	BA				G BY POS
1873	Marylands	3	11	0	2	.000				2B-2, C-1

Bill Smiley

SMILEY, WILLIAM B.
B. 1856, Baltimore, Md.   D. July 11, 1884, Baltimore, Md.

		G	AB	H	R	BA				G BY POS
1874	Lord Baltimores	2	7	0	0	.000				3B-2

Bill Smith

SMITH, WILLIAM J.
B. Baltimore, Md.   D. Aug. 9, 1886, Baltimore, Md.
Manager 1873.

		G	AB	H	R	BA				G BY POS
1873	Marylands	4	16	1	1	.063				OF-3, C-1

Charlie Smith

SMITH, CHARLES J.
B. Dec. 11, 1840, Brooklyn, N. Y.   D. Nov. 15, 1897, Great Neck, N. Y.   5'10½"   150 lbs.

		G	AB	H	R	BA				G BY POS
1871	New York Mutuals	14	72	17	15	.236				3B-11, 2B-3

John Smith

SMITH, JOHN
B. Baltimore, Md.   Deceased.

		G	AB	H	R	BA				G BY POS
1873	Marylands	5	21	4	1	.190				OF-2, SS-2, 2B-1
1874	Lord Baltimores	5	19	3	1	.158				SS-5, OF-1
1875	New Havens	1	4	0	0	.000				SS-1
3 yrs.		11	44	7	2	.159				SS-8, OF-3, 2B-1

Tom Smith

SMITH, THOMAS N.
B. 1851, Guelph, Ontario, Canada   D. Mar. 28, 1889, Detroit, Mich.

		G	AB	H	R	BA				G BY POS
1875	Brooklyn Atlantics	3	14	1	0	.071				2B-3

Charlie Snow

SNOW, CHARLES M.
B. Aug. 3, 1849, Lowell, Mass.   Deceased.

		G	AB	H	R	BA				G BY POS
1874	Brooklyn Atlantics	1	1	0	0	.000				OF-1

Jim Snyder

SNYDER, JAMES
B. Sept. 15, 1847, Brooklyn, N. Y.   D. Dec. 1, 1922, Rockaway Beach, N. Y.   5'7"   130 lbs.

		G	AB	H	R	BA				G BY POS
1872	Brooklyn Eckfords	26	109	30	15	.275				SS-22, OF-3, C-1

Josh Snyder

SNYDER, JOSHUA M.
B. Mar., 1844, Brooklyn, N. Y.   D. Apr. 21, 1881, Brooklyn, N. Y.

		G	AB	H	R	BA				G BY POS
1872	Brooklyn Eckfords	9	41	7	3	.171				OF-9

Pop Snyder

SNYDER, CHARLES N.
B. Oct. 6, 1854, Washington, D. C.   D. Oct. 29, 1924, Washington, D. C.   BR TR 5'11½" 184 lbs.
Manager 1882-84, 1891.

		G	AB	H	R	BA				G BY POS
1873	Washington Nationals	28	118	18	16	.153				C-28, OF-1
1874	Lord Baltimores	39	168	32	23	.190				C-39
1875	Philadelphias	66	206	62	39	.301				C-65, OF-1
3 yrs.		133	492	112	78	.228				C-132, OF-2

Ed Somerville

SOMERVILLE, EDWARD
B. Philadelphia, Pa.   D. Sept. 30, 1877, Hamilton, Ont., Canada   BR TR

		G	AB	H	R	BA				G BY POS
1875	2 teams Philadelphia Centennials (14G .220) New Havens (33G .207)									
"	total	47	204	43	21	.211				2B-44, 3B-1, SS-1, 1B-1

Al Spalding

SPALDING, ALBERT GOODWILL
B. Sept. 2, 1850, Byron, Ill.   D. Sept. 9, 1915, San Diego, Calif.   BR TR 6'1"   170 lbs.
Manager 1876-77.
Hall of Fame 1939.

		G	AB	H	R	BA	W	L	PCT	G BY POS
1871	Boston Red Stockings	31	151	40	43	.265	20	10	.667	P-31, OF-2
1872		48	248	84	59	.339	37	8	.822	P-48, OF-2
1873		60	331	105	85	.317	41	15	.732	P-57, OF-3
1874		71	363	121	80	.333	52	18	.743	P-71
1875		74	352	112	67	.318	57	5	.919	P-66, OF-10, 1B-2
5 yrs.		284	1445	462	334	.320	207	56	.787	P-273, OF-17, 1B-2

Spencer

SPENCER,
Deceased.

		G	AB	H	R	BA				G BY POS
1872	Washington Nationals	2	10	2	3	.200				SS-2

Joe Start

START, JOSEPH (Old Reliable)
B. Oct. 14, 1842, New York, N. Y.   D. Mar. 27, 1927, Providence, R. I.   BL TL 5'9"   165 lbs.
Manager 1873.

		G	AB	H	R	BA				G BY POS
1871	New York Mutuals	33	165	56	35	.339				1B-33
1872		55	281	77	62	.274				1B-55
1873		53	262	66	44	.252				1B-53
1874		63	321	93	68	.290				1B-63
1875		69	324	90	57	.278				1B-69
5 yrs.		273	1353	382	266	.282				1B-273

Bill Stearns

STEARNS, WILLIAM E.
B. Washington, D. C.   D. Dec. 30, 1898, Washington, D. C.   TR

		G	AB	H	R	BA	W	L	PCT	G BY POS
1871	Washington Olympics	2	11	0	1	.000	2	0	1.000	P-2
1872	Washington Nationals	11	47	12	7	.255	0	11	.000	P-11
1873		31	140	24	22	.171	7	24	.226	P-31
1874	Hartfords	32	130	25	16	.192	2	16	.111	P-18, OF-14

		G	AB	H	R	BA	W	L	PCT	G BY POS

Bill Stearns *continued*

	G	AB	H	R	BA	W	L	PCT	G BY POS
1875 Washington Nationals	21	78	20	9	.256	1	14	.067	P-16, OF-6
5 yrs.	97	406	81	55	.200	12	65	.156	P-78, OF-20

Gat Stires

STIRES, GARRETT
B. Oct. 13, 1849, Hunterdon County, N. J.   D. June 13, 1933, Byron, Ill.   BL TR 5'8"   180 lbs.

	G	AB	H	R	BA				G BY POS
1871 Rockford Forest Citys	25	118	32	23	.271				OF-25

Stoddard

STODDARD,
Deceased.

	G	AB	H	R	BA				G BY POS
1875 Brooklyn Atlantics	2	9	1	1	.111				OF-2

Ed Stratton

STRATTON, WILLIAM EDWARD
B. Baltimore, Md.   Deceased.

	G	AB	H	R	BA	W	L	PCT	G BY POS
1873 Marylands	3	12	2	1	.167	0	2	.000	P-2, OF-1

Sy Studley

STUDLEY, SEYMOUR L. (Warhorse)
B. Washington, D. C.   D. 1874, Washington, D. C.

	G	AB	H	R	BA				G BY POS
1872 Washington Nationals	5	22	3	3	.136				OF-5

Sullivan

SULLIVAN,
B. Bistol, R. I.   Deceased.

	G	AB	H	R	BA				G BY POS
1875 New Havens	2	10	3	3	.300				OF-2

Ezra Sutton

SUTTON, EZRA BALLOU
B. Sept. 17, 1850, Palmyra, N. Y.   D. June 20, 1907, Braintree, Mass.   BR TR 5'8½"   153 lbs.

	G	AB	H	R	BA				G BY POS
1871 Cleveland Forest Citys	29	130	45	35	.346				3B-29
1872	21	110	31	30	.282				3B-21
1873 Philadelphia Athletics	51	258	82	52	.318				3B-44, SS-7, 2B-1
1874	55	246	85	54	.346				3B-36, SS-20
1875	75	357	117	85	.328				3B-73, OF-1, 1B-1
5 yrs.	231	1101	360	256	.327				3B-203, SS-27, OF-1, 2B-1 1B-1

Marty Swandell

SWANDELL, JOHN MARTIN
B. 1845, Brooklyn, N. Y.   Deceased.   TL 5'10½" 146 lbs.

	G	AB	H	R	BA				G BY POS
1872 Brooklyn Eckfords	14	58	12	6	.207				3B-8, OF-4, 2B-1, 1B-1
1873 Elizabeth Resolutes	2	10	1	1	.100				OF-1, 1B-1
2 yrs.	16	68	13	7	.191				3B-8, OF-5, 1B-2, 2B-1

Charlie Sweasy

SWEASY, CHARLES JAMES
Also known as Charles James Swasey.
B. Nov. 2, 1847, Newark, N. J.   D. Mar. 30, 1908, Newark, N. J.   BR TR 5'9"   172 lbs.
Manager 1875.

	G	AB	H	R	BA				G BY POS
1871 Washington Olympics	5	20	4	4	.200				2B-5
1872 Cleveland Forest Citys	11	54	12	8	.222				2B-10, OF-1
1873 Boston Red Stockings	1	5	1	0	.200				2B-1
1874 2 teams Brooklyn Atlantics (10G .128) Lord Baltimores (8G .235)									
" total	18	73	13	6	.178				2B-17, OF-1
1875 St. Louis Reds	18	72	12	5	.167				2B-18
5 yrs.	53	224	42	23	.188				2B-51, OF-2

Taylor

TAYLOR,
Deceased.

	G	AB	H	R	BA				G BY POS
1874 Lord Baltimores	13	51	10	3	.196				1B-13

Terry

TERRY,
Deceased.

	G	AB	H	R	BA				G BY POS
1875 Washington Nationals	6	24	2	0	.083				OF-4, 1B-2

Al Thake

THAKE, ALBERT
B. Sept. 21, 1849, Wymondham, England   D. Sept. 1, 1872, Ft. Hamilton, N. Y.   6'

	G	AB	H	R	BA				G BY POS
1872 Brooklyn Atlantics	17	73	20	12	.274				OF-16, 2B-1

Thompson

THOMPSON,

	G	AB	H	R	BA				G BY POS
1875 Brooklyn Atlantics	1	5	2	1	.400				OF-1

Andrew Thompson

THOMPSON, ANDREW M.
B. 1846, Ill.
Manager 1884.

	G	AB	H	R	BA				G BY POS
1875 Washington Nationals	11	42	4	3	.095				C-10, OF-1

Jim Tipper

TIPPER, JAMES
B. June 18, 1849, Middletown, Conn.   D. Apr. 19, 1895, New Haven, Conn.   5'5½"   148 lbs.

	G	AB	H	R	BA				G BY POS
1872 Middletown Mansfields	24	110	29	23	.264				OF-18, 3B-6
1874 Hartfords	45	196	60	36	.306				OF-45
1875 New Havens	41	170	25	9	.147				OF-41
3 yrs.	110	476	114	68	.239				OF-104, 3B-6

Fred Treacey

TREACEY, FREDERICK S.
Brother of Pete Treacey.
B. 1847, Brooklyn, N. Y.   Deceased.   TR 5'9½"   145 lbs.

	G	AB	H	R	BA				G BY POS
1871 Chicago White Stockings	25	125	43	39	.344				OF-25
1872 Philadelphia Athletics	46	242	62	53	.256				OF-46
1873 Philadelphias	51	246	62	49	.252				OF-51
1874 Chicago White Stockings	35	160	28	18	.175				OF-35
1875 2 teams Philadelphia Centennials (11G .271) Philadelphias (42G .207)									
" total	53	227	50	28	.220				OF-53
5 yrs.	210	1000	245	187	.245				OF-210

		G	AB	H	R	BA	W	L	PCT	G BY POS

George Trenwith

TRENWITH, GEORGE
B. Philadelphia, Pa.   D. Feb. 1, 1890, Philadelphia, Pa.
1875 2 teams   Philadelphia Centennials (10G .174)   New Havens (6G .200)

		G	AB	H	R	BA				G BY POS
"	total	16	71	13	6	.183				3B-16

Charlie Waitt

WAITT, CHARLES C.   5'11"   165 lbs.
B. Oct. 14, 1853, Hallowell, Me.   D. Oct. 21, 1912, San Francisco Calif.,

1875 St. Louis	31	122	26	14	.213	OF-29, 1B-2

Oscar Walker

WALKER, OSCAR   BL TL 5'10"   166 lbs.
B. Mar. 18, 1854, Brooklyn, N. Y.   D. May 20, 1889, Brooklyn, N. Y.

1875 Brooklyn Atlantics	1	3	0	0	.000	OF-1

Wall

WALL,
Deceased.

1873 Washington Nationals	1	4	1	1	.250	SS-1

Fred Warner

WARNER, FREDERICK JOHN RODNEY   5'7"   155 lbs.
B. 1855, Philadelphia, Pa.   D. Feb. 13, 1886, Philadelphia, Pa.

1875 Philadelphia Centennials	14	59	14	11	.237	OF-14

Fred Waterman

WATERMAN, FREDERICK A.   5'7½"   148 lbs.
B. 1845, New York, N. Y.   D. Dec. 16, 1899, Cincinnati, Ohio

	G	AB	H	R	BA	G BY POS
1871 Washington Olympics	32	167	51	46	.305	3B-27, C-6
1872	9	45	18	13	.400	3B-7, C-2
1873 Washington Nationals	15	81	27	20	.333	SS-9, OF-4, 3B-2
1875 Chicago White Stockings	5	23	6	2	.261	3B-4, 2B-1
4 yrs.	61	316	102	81	.323	3B-40, SS-9, C-8, OF-4 2B-1

Sam Weaver

WEAVER, SAMUEL H.   BR TR   185 lbs.
B. July 10, 1855, Philadelphia, Pa.   D. Feb. 1, 1914, Philadelphia, Pa.

	G	AB	H	R	BA	W	L	PCT	G BY POS
1875 Philadelphias	1	4	1	1	.250	1	0	1.000	P-1

Billy West

WEST, WILLIAM NELSON
B. Aug. 21, 1840, Philadelphia, Pa.   D. Aug. 18, 1891, Radnor, Pa.

1874 Brooklyn Atlantics	10	43	8	4	.186	2B-10

Deacon White

WHITE, JAMES LAURIE   BL TR 5'11"   175 lbs.
Brother of Will White.
B. Dec. 7, 1847, Caton, N. Y.   D. July 7, 1939, Aurora, Ill.
Manager 1872, 1879.

	G	AB	H	R	BA	G BY POS
1871 Cleveland Forest Citys	29	149	47	40	.315	C-27, 2B-2
1872	21	110	37	21	.336	C-13, 2B-6, OF-3
1873 Boston Red Stockings	60	325	124	76	.382	C-55, OF-5
1874	69	349	112	73	.321	C-55, OF-12, 2B-1, 1B-1
1875	80	383	136	77	.355	C-72, OF-7, 1B-1
5 yrs.	259	1316	456	287	.347	C-222, OF-27, 2B-9, 1B-2

Elmer White

WHITE, ELMER
B. Dec. 7, 1850, Caton, N. Y.   D. Mar. 17, 1872, Caton, N. Y.

1871 Cleveland Forest Citys	15	71	20	13	.282	OF-13, C-2

Warren White

WHITE, WILLIAM WARREN
D. Mar. 3, 1898
Manager 1872, 1874.

	G	AB	H	R	BA	G BY POS
1871 Washington Olympics	1	4	0	0	.000	2B-1
1872 Washington Nationals	10	44	14	8	.318	3B-9, SS-1
1873	39	166	44	29	.265	3B-37, SS-2
1874 Lord Baltimores	45	224	57	21	.254	3B-45
1875 Chicago White Stockings	70	304	72	37	.237	3B-61, SS-4, OF-3, 2B-2
5 yrs.	165	742	187	95	.252	3B-152, SS-7, OF-3, 2B-3

Rynie Wolters

WOLTERS, REINDERS ALBERTIS   TR 6'   165 lbs.
B. Dec. 18, 1842, U. S. A.   D. Jan. 3, 1917, Newark, N. J.

	G	AB	H	R	BA	W	L	PCT	G BY POS
1871 New York Mutuals	32	150	48	33	.320	16	16	.500	P-32
1872 Cleveland Forest Citys	15	77	17	7	.221	2	6	.250	OF-8, P-8
1873 Elizabeth Resolutes	1	4	0	1	.000	0	1	.000	P-1
3 yrs.	48	231	65	41	.281	18	23	.439	P-41, OF-8

Wood

WOOD,
Deceased.

1874 Lord Baltimores	1	6	0	0	.000	2B-1

Jimmy Wood

WOOD, JAMES LEON   TR 5'8½"   150 lbs.
B. Dec. 1, 1844, Brooklyn, N. Y.   D. Nov. 30, 1886, New York, N. Y.
Manager 1871-75.

		G	AB	H	R	BA	G BY POS
1871 Chicago White Stockings		28	145	51	44	.352	2B-28
1872 2 teams	Brooklyn Eckfords (7G .176) Troy Haymakers (25G .322)						
"	total	32	152	44	49	.289	2B-32
1873 Philadelphias		42	224	66	67	.295	2B-42
3 yrs.		102	521	161	160	.309	2B-102

Red Woodhead

WOODHEAD, JAMES   5'6"   160 lbs.
B. July, 1851, Chelsea, Mass.   D. Sept. 7, 1881, Boston, Mass.

1873 Marylands	1	5	0	1	.000	SS-1

Favel Wordsworth

WORDSWORTH, FAVEL PERRY (Red)
B. Jan., 1851, New York, N. Y.   D. Aug. 12, 1888, New York, N. Y.

1873 Elizabeth Resolutes	11	45	10	6	.222	SS-11

		G	AB	H	R	BA	W	L	PCT	G BY POS
Herb Worth	**WORTH, HERBERT** B. May 2, 1847 D. Apr. 27, 1914, Brooklyn, N. Y.									
	1872 Brooklyn Atlantics	1	6	1	1	.167				OF-1
George Wright	**WRIGHT, GEORGE** Brother of Harry Wright. Brother of Sam Wright. B. Jan. 28, 1847, Yonkers, N. Y. D. Aug. 21, 1937, Boston, Mass. Manager 1879. Hall of Fame 1937.									BR TR 5'9½" 150 lbs.
	1871 Boston Red Stockings	16	88	36	35	.409				SS-15, 1B-1
	1872	48	253	85	86	.336				SS-48
	1873	59	333	126	98	.378				SS-59
	1874	60	319	110	75	.345				SS-60
	1875	79	407	137	105	.337				SS-79
	5 yrs.	262	1400	494	399	.353				SS-261, 1B-1
Harry Wright	**WRIGHT, WILLIAM HENRY** Brother of Sam Wright. Brother of George Wright. B. Jan. 10, 1835, Sheffield, England D. Oct. 3, 1895, Atlantic City, N. J. Manager 1871-93. Hall of Fame 1953.									BR TR 5'9½" 157 lbs.
	1871 Boston Red Stockings	31	161	43	42	.267	0	0	.000	OF-30, P-2, SS-1
	1872	48	214	56	38	.262	2	0	1.000	OF-48, P-2
	1873	58	283	66	57	.233	2	1	.667	OF-55, P-3
	1874	41	189	58	44	.307				OF-40, C-1
	1875	1	4	1	1	.250				OF-1
	5 yrs.	179	851	224	182	.263	4	1	.800	OF-174, P-7, C-1, SS-1
Sam Wright	**WRIGHT, SAMUEL** Brother of Harry Wright. Brother of George Wright. B. Nov. 25, 1848, New York, N. Y. D. May 6, 1928, Boston, Mass.									BR TR 5'7½" 146 lbs.
	1875 New Havens	33	137	24	11	.175				SS-33
Bill Yeatman	**YEATMAN, WILLIAM S.** B. 1849 D. Apr. 20, 1901, York, Pa.									
	1872 Washington Nationals	1	3	0	0	.000				OF-2
Tom York	**YORK, THOMAS J.** B. July 13, 1851, Brooklyn, N. Y. D. Feb. 17, 1936, New York, N. Y. Manager 1878, 1881.									BL 5'9" 165 lbs.
	1871 Troy Haymakers	29	156	34	37	.218				OF-29
	1872 Lord Baltimores	49	249	67	60	.269				OF-49
	1873	56	279	79	68	.283				OF-56
	1874 Philadelphias	50	241	60	37	.249				OF-50
	1875 Hartfords	85	387	110	66	.284				OF-85
	5 yrs.	269	1312	350	268	.267				OF-269
George Zettlein	**ZETTLEIN, GEORGE (The Charmer)** B. July 18, 1844, Brooklyn, N. Y. D. May 23, 1905, Patchogue, N. Y.									BR TR 5'9" 162 lbs.
	1871 Chicago White Stockings	28	130	31	23	.238	18	9	.667	P-27, OF-1
	1872 2 teams Brooklyn Eckfords (9G .059 W-1 L-7) Troy Haymakers (25G .248 W-14 L-8)									
	" total	34	151	31	26	.205	15	15	.636	P-31, OF-4
	1873 Philadelphias	50	235	49	40	.209	36	14	.720	P-50
	1874 Chicago White Stockings	57	247	46	26	.186	27	30	.474	P-57
	1875 2 teams Chicago White Stockings (32G .216 W-17 L-14) Philadelphias (21G .203 W-12 L-8)									
	" total	53	213	45	19	.211	29	22	.600	P-52, 1B-2
	5 yrs.	222	976	202	134	.207	125	90	.581	P-217, OF-5, 1B-2

FINAL NATIONAL ASSOCIATION STANDINGS

Year	Team	W	L	PCT	GB	R	AB	H	BA	Manager	W	L	Manager	W	L
1871	Philadelphia Athletics	21	7	.750		367	1331	412	.310	Dick McBride	21	7			
	Chicago White Stockings	19	9	.679	2	302	1250	316	.253	Jimmy Wood	19	9			
	Boston Red Stockings	20	10	.667	2	401	1438	424	.295	Harry Wright	20	10			
	Washington Olympics	15	15	.500	7	310	1400	371	.265	Nick Young	15	15			
	New York Mutuals	16	17	.485	7.5	302	1428	392	.275	Bob Ferguson	16	17			
	Troy Haymakers	13	15	.464	8	353	1302	370	.284	Lip Pike	1	3	Bill Craver	12	12
	Fort Wayne Kekiongas	7	12	.368	9.5	137	765	179	.234	Bill Lennon	5	9	Harry Deane	2	3
	Cleveland Forest Cities	10	19	.345	12.5	249	1214	326	.269	Charlie Pabor	10	19			
	Rockford Forest Cities	4	21	.160	15.5	231	1081	273	.253	Scott Hastings	4	21			
1872	Boston Red Stockings	39	8	.830		521	2176	671	.308	Harry Wright	39	8			
	Philadelphia Athletics	30	14	.682	7.5	534	2209	659	.298	Dick McBride	30	14			
	Lord Baltimores	34	19	.642	8	597	2561	717	.280	Bill Craver	27	13	Everett Mills	7	6
	New York Mutuals	34	20	.630	8.5	523	2503	681	.272	Dickey Pearce	34	20			
	Troy Haymakers	15	10	.600	13	272	1123	333	.297	Jimmy Wood	15	10			
	Cleveland Forest Cities	6	15	.286	20	171	957	283	.296	Scott Hastings	6	13	Deacon White	0	2
	Brooklyn Atlantics	8	27	.229	25	220	1452	334	.230	Bob Ferguson	8	27			
	Washington Olympics	2	7	.222	18	54	372	93	.250	Nick Young	2	7			
	Middletown Mansfields	5	19	.208	22.5	223	1013	277	.273	John Clapp	5	19			
	Brooklyn Eckfords	3	26	.103	27	151	1133	233	.206	Jim Clinton	0	11	Jimmy Wood	3	15
	Washington Nationals	0	11	.000	21	80	449	107	.238	Joe Miller	0	11			
1873	Boston Red Stockings	43	16	.729		739	2878	931	.323	Harry Wright	43	16			
	Philadelphias (White Stockings)	36	17	.679	4	526	2418	641	.265	Fergy Malone	8	2	Jimmy Wood	28	15
	Lord Baltimores	33	22	.600	8	624	2599	783	.301	Cal McVey	19	13	Tom Carey	14	9
	Philadelphia Athletics	28	23	.549	11	474	2387	671	.281	Dick McBride	28	23			
	New York Mutuals	29	24	.547	11	424	2297	614	.267	John Hatfield	11	17	Joe Start	18	7
	Brooklyn Atlantics	17	37	.315	23.5	366	2310	583	.252	Bob Ferguson	17	37			
	Washington Nationals	8	31	.205	25	283	1629	406	.249	Nick Young	8	31			
	Elizabeth Resolutes	2	21	.087	23	98	923	204	.221	John Benjamin	2	21			
	Marylands	0	5	.000	27	15	169	23	.136	John Smith	0	5			
1874	Boston Red Stockings	52	18	.743		735	3155	1033	.327	Harry Wright	52	18			
	New York Mutuals	42	23	.646	7.5	500	2808	708	.252	Tom Carey	13	12	Dick Higham	29	11
	Philadelphia Athletics	33	23	.589	12	441	2304	763	.331	Dick McBride	33	23			
	Philadelphias (White Stockings)	29	29	.500	17	475	2540	683	.269	Bill Craver	29	29			
	Chicago White Stockings	28	31	.475	18.5	418	2565	674	.263	Fergy Malone	18	18	Jimmy Wood	10	13
	Brooklyn Atlantics	22	33	.400	22.5	301	2233	495	.222	Bob Ferguson	22	33			
	Hartfords (Dark Blues)	17	37	.315	27	371	2103	611	.291	Lip Pike	17	37			
	Lord Baltimores	9	38	.191	31.5	227	1893	431	.228	Warren White	9	38			
1875	Boston Red Stockings	71	8	.899		832	3564	1161	.326	Harry Wright	71	8			
	Philadelphia Athletics	53	20	.726	15	699	3292	942	.286	Dick McBride	49	18	Cap Anson	4	2
	Hartfords (Dark Blues)	54	28	.659	18.5	554	3466	863	.249	Bob Ferguson	54	28			
	St. Louis (Brown Stockings)	39	29	.574	26.5	385	2651	660	.249	Dickey Pearce	39	29			
	Philadelphias (White Stockings)	37	31	.544	28.5	469	2645	683	.258	Mike McGeary	34	27	Bob Addy	3	4
	Chicago White Stockings	30	37	.448	35	380	2832	709	.250	Jimmy Wood	30	37			
	New York Mutuals	30	38	.441	35.5	328	2771	630	.227	Nat Hicks	30	38			
	St. Louis Reds	4	14	.222	36.5	55	670	121	.181	Charlie Sweasy	4	14			
	New Havens (Elm Citys)	7	40	.149	48	171	1818	370	.204	Charlie Gould	2	21	Juice Latham	4	14
										Charlie Pabor	1	5			
	Washington Nationals	4	23	.148	41	96	990	181	.183	Holly Hollingshead	4	16	Bill Parks	0	7
	Philadelphia Centennials	2	12	.143	36.5	70	549	125	.228	Bill Craver	2	12			
	Keokuk Westerns	1	12	.077	37	45	484	81	.167	Joe Simmons	1	12			
	Brooklyn Atlantics	2	42	.045	51.5	132	1590	306	.192	Charlie Pabor	2	40	Bill Boyd	0	2

PART ELEVEN

Negro Leagues Register

Player Register
Pitcher Register

The Negro Leagues

In this, the eighth edition of *The Baseball Encyclopedia*, the editors are proud to include vital pitching and playing statistics comprising the career accomplishments of some of the biggest stars from the old Negro leagues.

As most baseball fans know, long before the major leagues became integrated in 1947, hundreds of the most talented ballplayers in this nation were denied an opportunity to play in the majors because of the color of their skin. That injustice, of course, can never be corrected, but it is the collective editorial opinion of the *Baseball Encyclopedia* staff that we should at least recognize the accomplishments of those talented men. To that end, we have tapped the resources of the best-known Negro league historians as well as some of the players themselves to help us compile this new and exciting section of the book.

However, as you'll notice in scanning these pages, some of the data here is still incomplete, despite the very diligent efforts of a most capable research staff headed by John Holway, Dick Clark, and Jim Riley, all baseball historians and members of the Society for American Baseball Research (SABR). Their research here represents literally years of painstakingly detailed effort, but even they are the first to admit that we're eager to fill in the gaps in the research.

Therefore, we are putting forth an open invitation to those baseball fans worldwide who can help us in our continuing research. We fully expect that by the time the next edition of *The Baseball Encyclopedia* is published, this section will be even more complete, with more names and statistics. Again, this section is not meant to be a full compilation of every man who played in the Negro leagues, but rather a listing of over 130 of the best, selected by our research staff. In fairness to our staff, gathering this kind of data was a most difficult process. And as mentioned, some of the statistics usually used do not exist, at least not where our historians could locate them. For example, pitchers' earned run averages do not exist nor were runs batted in kept. Sadly, these statistics are not reflected in our research, but we certainly hope to fill in the missing data in the years to come. The Negro leagues statistics were edited by Dick Clark, Jim Riley, and John Holway. The following persons contributed to the research: Russ Adams, Joe Adler, Shaikh Aizaz, Chris Allen, Terry Baxter, Gary Brinkmeyer, Daniel Coffeen, Craig Cohen, Karen Constantino, Harry Conwell, Dick Cramer, Debbie Crawford, Tracy Curtis, Michael Deault, Rod Drew, Greg Ficery, Garret Finney, Dan Friedman, Jared Gardner, Bob Gill, Troy Greene, Richard Hall, Pete Hegarty, David Heller, Jim Holway, John Holway, Jr., Joel Hurwitz, Carolyn Jones, Tim Joyce, Merl Kleinknecht, Jeff Krosse, Paul Kubicek, Catherine Kuchar, Neil Lanctot, Rob Langenderfer, Jeff Lapin, Kevin Lemmer, Larry Lester, Adam Levine, Peter Levitt, Raymond Marks, Willa Martin, Michael Mazur, Joe McGillen, Jeremy Myers, Steve Neumann, Erick Norlin, Jim O'Connor, Denise Oliver, Josh Orenstein, Joe Overfield, Mona Peach, Frank Perretti, Edward Pettit, Walt Peycha, Jonathan Pine, Katrina Powers, Mark Presswood, Jeff Rhodes, Cynthia Rigg, Greg Rosenstein, Paul Rubin, Rob Ruck, Warren Rush, Robin Rutledge, Mike Sampson, Susan Scheller, Bill Schopmeyer, Arthur Schott, Norm Schrager, Dawn Schurek, Jonathan Seamon, Andrew Shields, Jonathan Shiffman, Mathew Shine, Prashant Shukla, Andy Siegel, Amanda Siegfried, Tania Sims, Justin Sloss, David Stark, Roger Still, A. D. Suehsdorf, Diane Walker, Lance Wallace, Dan Wilkison, Edie Williams, Bill Wold, Wendell Wolff, and Charles Zarelli.

About the Negro Leagues

As you might imagine, not all black games were reported in the press. Some cities covered their home teams very well, in both the black and white press, while other localities ignored the black games. Games in neutral third cities were often unreported. The black press had good coverage of games in the 1920s, but the hard times of the Depression caused cutbacks in coverage. Black papers relied on teams sending in their own box scores, which not every team did. And deadlines meant that the last two days before weekly publication went uncovered.

Occasionally two or more papers covered the same game—with slightly different box scores. At other times box score figures did not add up correctly, or the game account and the box score differed.

Some black papers did not have an at-bats column. This forced us to estimate at-bats, based on the score, total hits, walks, and sacrifices (if known), errors, position in the batting order, and so forth.

Some box scores did not carry extra-base hits, stolen bases, or the pitching breakdown of strikeouts, walks, innings pitched, and the like. Sometimes some or all of this could be found in the game accounts. However, this information is certainly underrepresented in the statistical profiles. Thus home runs do not relate to at-bats, nor strikeouts to innings pitched.

Sometimes all we had was a brief game account without a box score, giving only the winning pitcher and any home runs hit. So, just as we sometimes had at-bats without knowing the home runs, occasionally we had information on a home run without knowing the at-bats. Stolen bases were especially neglected in the box scores. Most probably, the box score compilers simply forgot to report steals.

Some pitching data had to be derived from line scores only, which gave the hits and runs for complete-game pitchers, but did not break them down if two or more pitchers were involved. In almost no cases did the box score give offensive strikeouts or walks, or runs batted in. When this project was first undertaken, about twenty years ago, we arbitrarily (and mistakenly) decided not to count runs either.

The seasons usually ran from early May to early September. In the 1920s, especially in the West, teams played six games a week, or about one hundred games a season. In the 1930s, the hard-pressed teams in both sections cut way back on league games, doing more barnstorming against white semipro clubs. Thus players whose careers were primarily in the '20s will have larger totals than those such as Josh Gibson, who played mostly in the '30s and '40s.

Games were arbitrarily designated "league" games or "exhibition" games. The former counted towards the pennant race. However, the distinction was often blurry, even though the competition was equally fierce in boths types of contest. We have decided to count all games between major black teams, including interleague games between clubs of the Eastern and Western leagues.

Rosters varied from fourteen to eighteen players. Pitching staffs were small. Rarely did a starter see a reliever in the bullpen behind him. Thus saves were rare. And starters paced themselves. Back then pitchers threw only as hard as necessary to win. (Christy Mathewson, Walter Johnson, et al., said they did the same thing in the white leagues.) A pitcher might win 12–9 or 2–1, depending on how much run support he received.

Negro league scores tended to be higher than major league scores of that era. Shutouts and no-hitters were rare. Balls favored the pitchers. They were cheaper than those used by the white majors, and black veterans say they didn't have the bounce that the Reach and Spalding balls had. There were also tobacco juice and manifold trick pitches to contend with.

Parks varied widely. The Chicago American Giants played in huge Southside Park, home of the famous "Hitless Wonders" White Sox of the 1906 era. The St. Louis Stars played in a bandbox with a left-field foul line estimated at between 250 and 260 feet. The teams also used white big-league stadia, which also varied widely, from the cozy Polo Grounds to wide-open Griffith Stadium and Forbes Field. This wide difference affected both the pitching and batting stats. A good example is home run king Mule Suttles, who went from spacious Rickwood Park in Birmingham to the little St. Louis field, to the open spaces of Chicago, and finally to friendly Ruppert Stadium, Newark. His home run totals reflected his travels. Josh Gibson was generally handicapped by his home fields in Pittsburgh and Washington.

There were many variables within the black leagues and between the black leagues and the white. But in the many postseason exhibitions against white big leaguers, Negro league pitchers and hitters performed generally as they had against black competition. A .350 hitter in the black leagues hit about as well against white league hurlers as against black.

> The first black league, the Negro National League, was founded in 1920 and included six Midwestern cities. It lasted through 1930. In 1923 six Eastern clubs formed the Eastern Colored League and raided the West for its stars. It survived, with a change of name, through 1929. For four years, 1924–1927, the two winners met in a World Series.
>
> The stock market crash wiped out the leagues and many teams. From 1931 to 1932 teams were born and folded in rapid succession. In 1933 one league of six to eight teams was formed, the Negro National League. It split into two half-seasons, and the two winners met in a championship series. The league endured for four years.
>
> In 1937 the two regional leagues reappeared—the Negro National League, now in the East, and the Negro American League in the West. Each had six teams. Again the champions faced each other in a black world series each September or October. Raids by the Dominican Republic and Mexico, however, took much of the black talent away from these leagues.
>
> Jackie Robinson's signing a contract with the Brooklyn Dodgers organization in 1945 was the death knell for the Negro leagues. As they lost more of their stars to the white raiders, the black teams began to die off. By 1949 the league remained in name only.
>
> John B. Holway

The Negro Leagues Player and Pitcher registers are alphabetical listings of more than 130 of the best Negro league players. The registers follow the format of the registers of major league players and pitchers in Parts Eight and Nine, but because of the difficulty of compiling statistics, the register formats have been modified.

Player Information

		G	AB	H	2B	3B	HR	SB	BA	POS			
John Doe	**DOE, JOHN LEE** (Slim)										BR	TR 6'2" 165 lb.	
	Brother of Bill Doe.												
	B. Jan. 1, 1910, Bronx, N. Y. D. July 1, 1985, Bronx, N. Y.												
	Manager 1945.												
	Major leagues 1947–49.												
	Hall of Fame 1976.												
	1941 PHI Stars	73	274	61	1	1	1	4	.223	3B			
	1942	**68**	284	66	4	1	1	1	.232	3B			
	1943	**39**	**154**	**45**	2	0	3	0	.292	3B			
	1944	17	58	13	0	0		0	.224	3B			
	1945	9	27	1	0	0	0	0	.037	3B			
	5 years	208	797	186	7	2	(5)	5	.233				

John Doe
This shortened version of the player's full name is the name most familiar to the fans.

DOE, JOHN LEE
Player's full name. The arrangement is last name first, then first and middle name(s).

(Slim)
Player's nickname. Any name appearing in parentheses is a nickname.

BR TR
The player's main batting and throwing style. Doe, for instance, batted and threw right-handed.

6'2"
Player's height.

165 lbs.
Player's average playing weight.

Brother of Bill Doe
The player's brother.

B. Jan. 1, 1910, Bronx, N.Y.
Date and place of birth.

D. July 1, 1985, Bronx, N.Y.
Date and place of death. (Players are listed simply as "deceased" if no certification of death or other information is available, but it is reasonably certain they are dead.)

Manager 1945
Doe also served as a Negro league manager.

Major leagues 1947–49
Doe played in the major leagues from 1947 to 1949. See the major league registers.

Hall of Fame 1976
Doe was elected to the Baseball Hall of Fame in 1976.

Column Headings Information

G	AB	H	2B	3B	HR	SB	BA	POS

G	Games
AB	At Bats
H	Hits
2B	Doubles
3B	Triples
HR	Home Runs
SB	Stolen Bases
BA	Batting Average
POS	Position

Negro Leagues Ballclubs

ATL	Black Crackers	Atlanta Black Crackers
AC	Bacharach Giants	Atlantic City Bacharach Giants
BAL	Black Sox	Baltimore Black Sox
BAL	Elite Giants	Baltimore Elite Giants
BIR	Black Barons	Birmingham Black Barons
BKN	Eagles	Brooklyn Eagles
BKN	Royal Giants	Brooklyn Royal Giants
CHI	Am. Giants	Chicago American Giants
CHI	Giants	Chicago Giants
CHI	Union Giants	Chicago Union Giants
CIN	Buckeyes	Cincinnati Buckeyes
CIN	Clowns	Cincinnati Clowns
CIN	Tigers	Cincinnati Tigers
CLA	Tigers	Claybrook (Ark.) Tigers
CLE	Bears	Cleveland Bears
CLE	Browns	Cleveland Browns
CLE	Buckeyes	Cleveland Buckeyes
CLE	Cubs	Cleveland Cubs
CLE	Hornets	Cleveland Hornets
CLE	Red Sox	Cleveland Red Sox
CLE	Tate Stars	Cleveland Tate Stars
COL	Blue Birds	Columbus Blue Birds

COL	Buckeyes	Columbus Buckeyes
COL	Elite Giants	Columbus Elite Giants
	Cuban Stars	Cuban Stars
DAY	Marcos	Dayton Marcos
DET	Stars	Detroit Stars
DET	Wolves	Detroit Wolves
HBG	Giants	Harrisburg Giants
	Homestead Grays	Homestead Grays
HOU	Eagles	Houston Eagles
IND	ABCs	Indianapolis ABCs
IND	Clowns	Indianapolis Clowns
JAC	Red Caps	Jacksonville Red Caps
KC	Monarchs	Kansas City Monarchs
LOU	Black Caps	Louisville Black Caps
MAD	Stars	Madison Stars (farm team)
MEM	Red Sox	Memphis Red Sox
MIL	Bears	Milwaukee Bears
MRO	Monarchs	Monroe Monarchs
NAS	Elite Giants	Nashville Elite Giants
NOR		New Orleans
NWK	Browns	Newark Browns
NWK	Dodgers	Newark Dodgers
NWK	Eagles	Newark Eagles
NY	Black Yankees	New York Black Yankees
NY	Cubans	New York Cubans
NY	Harlem Stars	New York Harlem Stars
NY	Lincoln Giants	New York Lincoln Giants
PHI	Hilldales	Philadelphia Hilldales
PHI	Stars	Philadelphia Stars
PIT	Crawfords	Pittsburgh Crawfords
STL	Giants	St. Louis Giants
STL	Stars	St. Louis Stars
TOL	Crawfords	Toledo Crawfords
TOL	Tigers	Toledo Tigers
WAS	Black Senators	Washington Black Senators
WAS	Elite Giants	Washington Elite Giants
WAS	Homestead Grays	Washington Homestead Grays
WAS	Pilots	Washington Pilots
WAS	Potomacs	Washington Potomacs
WB	Sprudels	West Baden (Ind.) Sprudels
WIL	Hornets	Wilmington Hornets

The following teams were not in the Negro leagues, but played against league teams:

	Cuban HoD	Cuban House of David
	Ethiopian Clowns	Ethiopian Clowns
MAD	Stars	Madison Stars

Statistical Information

League Leaders. Statistics that appear in boldfaced print indicate the player led his league that year in a particular statistical category. Doe, for example, led the Negro leagues in doubles in 1943. When there is a tie for league lead, the figures for all the men who tied are shown in boldface.

Unavailable Information. Any time a blank space is shown in a particular statistical column, such as in Doe's 1944 home run total, it indicates the information was unavailable or incomplete.

Partial Career Totals. Indicated by parentheses. Doe's career home run total of (5) is based on incomplete information. Whenever a player's statistics in a particular category are incomplete, his lifetime total appears in parentheses.

Pitcher Register Column Headings Information

W	L	PCT	G	GS	CG	IP	H	BB	SO	ShO	SV

Total Pitching (including all starting and relief appearances)

W	Wins
L	Losses
PCT	Winning Percentage
G	Games Pitched In
GS	Games Started
CG	Complete Games
IP	Innings Pitched
H	Hits Allowed
BB	Bases on Balls Allowed
SO	Strikeouts
ShO	Shutouts

Relief Pitching

SV	Saves

Negro Leagues Player Register

	G	AB	H	2B	3B	HR	SB	BA	POS

Newt Allen

ALLEN, NEWTON HENRY (Colt)   BB   TR   5'8"   158 lbs.
B. May 19, 1901, Austin, Tex.   D. June 11, 1988, Cincinnati, Ohio
Manager 1941

Year/Team	G	AB	H	2B	3B	HR	SB	BA	POS
1922 KC Monarchs	1	4	3	0	0	0	0	.750	2B
1923	14	53	13	0	1	0	0	.245	3B, SS
1924	**88**	**364**	101	11	3	2	0	.277	2B
1925	82	334	103	6	9	4	15	.308	2B
1926	71	278	72	14	3	1	10	.259	2B
1927	77	293	98	16	3	2	7	.334	SS
1928	70	282	79	13	4	2	12	.280	SS, 2B
1929	77	303	100	24	6	3	23	.330	2B
1930	57	235	81	12	4	2	9	.345	2B
1931 2 teams KC Monarchs STL Stars									
" total	41	117	32	9	2	2	0	.274	SS, 2B
1932 2 teams DET Wolves KC Monarchs									
" total	25	95	31	2	0	0	4	.326	2B
1935 KC Monarchs	2	8	4	1	0	0	0	.500	2B
1936	7	26	10	3	1	0	1	.385	2B
1937	**33**	146	**53**	4	2	0	**6**	.363	2B
1938	22	77	21	2	0	0	2	.273	2B
1939	31	102	26	2	1	0	0	.255	2B
1940	22	96	31	4	1	1	1	.323	OF, 2B, SS
1941	22	82	25	2	1	0	1	.305	SS, 3B
1942		103	28	2	0	1	0	.272	3B
1943		75	14	1	0	0	0	.178	3B
1944	50	177	36	7	1	0	4	.203	3B
21 years	(792)	3250	961	135	42	20	95	.296	

Sam Bankhead

BANKHEAD, SAM   BR   TR   5'8"   175 lbs.
B. Sept. 18, 1905, Empire, Ala.   D. 1976, Pittsburgh, Pa.

Year/Team	G	AB	H	2B	3B	HR	SB	BA	POS
1931 BIR Black Barons	1	4	2	1	1	0	0	.500	2B
1932 3 teams Lou Black Caps BIR Black Barons NAS Elite Giants									
" total	5	10	4	1	0	0	0	.400	P
1933 NAS Elite Giants	22	86	27	3	1	1	3	.314	C, OF
1934	19	80	27	0	1	0	4	.338	SS
1935 PIT Crawfords	59	235	79	14	6	1	4	.336	OF
1936	29	125	27	5	0	0	1	.216	2B, OF
1937 Dominican Republic									
1938 PIT Crawfords	14	50	10	3	0	1	3	.200	OF
1939 Homestead Grays	25	78	26	3	0	5	1	.333	2B
1940 Mexico									
1941 Mexico									
1942 Homestead Grays	37	126	33	3	3	2	0	.241	SS
1943		162	39	1	1	1	8	.356	SS
1944	40	150	43	8	4	0	4	.287	SS
1945	35	124	35	5	2	1	3	.282	SS
1946		120	43	2	3	4	0	.358	SS
1947		244	60	12		3	8	.246	SS
14 years	(286)	1594	455	61	(22)	19	39	.285	

Ernie Banks

BANKS, ERNEST   BR   TR   6'1"   180 lbs.
B. Jan. 31, 1931, Dallas, Tex.
Major Leagues 1953–71.
Hall of Fame 1977.

Year/Team	G	AB	H	2B	3B	HR	SB	BA	POS
1950 KC Monarchs	53	196	50	11	1	1	3	.255	SS

Bernardo Baro

BARO, BERNARDO
B. Cuba

Year/Team	G	AB	H	2B	3B	HR	SB	BA	POS
1917 Cuban Stars	1	4	1	0	0	0	0	.250	OF
1918 No data available									
1919 No data available									
1920 Cuban Stars	20	83	28	6	3	1	2	.337	OF
1921	32	212	42	6	4	3	13	.198	OF
1923	16	63	24	0	0	0	6	.381	OF
1924	10	33	12	3	3	2	4	.364	1B
1925	39	159	46	1	2	0	4	.289	1B, P
1926	19	79	15	2	0	1	1	.190	OF, P
1927	39	150	45	4	2	0	2	.300	OF, P
1928	17	72	21	4	0	0	4	.292	OF
1929	36	131	36	5	0	0	0	.275	OF
(10 years)	(229)	(986)	(270)	(31)	(14)	(7)	(36)	(.274)	

		G	AB	H	2B	3B	HR	SB	BA	POS

John Beckwith

BECKWITH, JOHN BR TR 6'3" 230 lbs.
B. 1902, Louisville, Ky. D. 1956, New York, N. Y.

		G	AB	H	2B	3B	HR	SB	BA	POS
1920	CHI Giants	15	46	10	1	1	0	1	.217	SS, C, P
1921		34	113	45	5	4	4	0	.398	SS
1922	CHI Am. Giants	48	159	48	11	2	3	3	.302	UT
1923		60	232	75	**19**	9	13	5	.323	3B, 1B
1924	2 teams Homestead Grays BAL Black Sox									
"	total	33	119	48	8	1	7	7	.403	SS
1925	BAL Black Sox	47	174	70	14	1	14	2	.402	SS
1926	2 teams BAL Black Sox HBG Giants									
"	total	34	119	43	7	1	9	1	.361	SS, UT
1927	HBG Giants	46	188	63	13	2	7	1	.335	3B, UT
1929	2 teams Homestead Grays NY Lincoln Giants									
"	total	40	163	62	10	2	11	6	.380	3B, 1B, SS, OF
1930	2 teams NY Lincoln Giants BAL Black Sox									
"	total	**50**	**200**	**96**	10	3	**19**	0	**.480**	3B
1931	2 teams BAL Black Sox NWK Browns									
"	total	51	190	66	3	0	**16**	0	.316	3B
1932	NWK Browns	3	12	4	1	0	1	0	.333	3B
1933	NY Black Yankees	2	9	4	0	0	0	0	.444	3B
1934	2 teams NY Black Yankees NWK Browns									
"	total	12	11	3	1	0	0	0	.273	PH
1935	Homestead Grays	1	4	0	0	0	0	0	.000	C
	15 years	476	1739	637	103	26	104	26	.366	

Cool Papa Bell

BELL, JAMES THOMAS BB TL 6' 165 lbs.
B. May 17, 1903, Starkville, Miss.
Hall of Fame 1974.

		G	AB	H	2B	3B	HR	SB	BA	POS
1922	STL Stars	22	60	25	3	1	3	0	.417	P, OF
1923		34	74	22	5	1	1	0	.297	P, OF, 1B
1924		59	216	67	15	1	0	9	.310	OF, P
1925		89	**362**	**128**	29	7	11	24	.354	OF
1926		85	370	134	24	7	15	23	.362	OF
1927		93	**401**	128	18	3	5	13	.319	OF
1928		72	310	103	16	6	4	7	.332	OF
1929		**89**	**359**	112	25	6	4	**28**	.312	OF
1930		62	264	93	17	6	7	15	.332	OF
1931		17	59	19	0	1	0	0	.322	OF
1932	2 teams DET Wolves KC Monarchs									
"	total	37	138	53	7	3	2	3	.384	OF
1933	PIT Crawfords	37	**137**	41	6	6	1	**6**	.299	OF
1934		50	199	63	4	1	1	**8**	.317	OF
1935		53	214	73	7	8	1	4	.341	OF
1936		21	82	22	1	1	0	1	.268	OF
1937	Dominican Republic									
1938	Mexico									
1939	Mexico									
1940	Mexico									
1941	Mexico									
1942	CHI Am. Giants		73	27	3	0	0	0	.370	OF
1943	Homestead Grays		163	58	4	4	0	**10**	.356	OF
1944		51	206	78	10	2	1	10	.379	OF
1945		48	188	56	8	3	0	10	.298	OF
1946			77	33	1	1	0	2	.429	OF
	25 years	(919)	3952	1335	203	68	56	**173**	.338	

Gene Benson

BENSON, GENE BL TL 5'8" 190 lbs.
B. Oct. 4, 1913, Pittsburgh, Pa.

		G	AB	H	2B	3B	HR	SB	BA	POS
1934	AC Bacharach Giants	7	27	11	0	0	0	0	.407	OF
1936		2	8	2	0	0	0	0	.250	OF
1937	PHI Stars	**35**	**143**	**40**	4	0	3	2	.280	OF
1938	2 teams PHI Stars PIT Crawfords									
"	total	24	96	23	0	0	0	0	.240	OF
1939	PHI Stars	51	169	62	**7**	0	1	1	.367	OF
1940		60	233	65	5	5	2	1	.279	OF
1941		37	140	38	**9**	1	1	3	.271	OF
1942		44	158	37	3	0	0	0	.234	OF
1943			178	61	7	6	0	2	.343	OF
1944		48	186	59	7	7	1	4	.317	OF
1945		40	162	60	8	3	2	2	.370	OF
1946			155	51	4	2	0	0	.329	OF
1947		87	217	62	12		1	4	.286	OF
	13 years	(435)	1872	571	66	(24)	11	19	.305	

	G	AB	H	2B	3B	HR	SB	BA	POS

Charles Blackwell

BLACKWELL, CHARLES   BL
    D. May 12, 1935

	G	AB	H	2B	3B	HR	SB	BA	POS
1915 WB Sprudels	2	4	1	1	0	1	0	.250	OF
1920 STL Giants	52	183	59	7	4	4	9	.322	OF
1921	62	221	99	16	8	10	27	.448	OF
1922	73	275	105	21	10	7	17	.382	OF
1923	52	180	56	10	6	3	8	.311	OF
1924 STL Stars	57	194	50	5	3	6	1	.258	OF
1925 BIR Black Barons	75	296	91	11	4	15	9	.307	OF
1926 DET Stars	73	246	68	11	5	4	11	.276	OF
1928 STL Giants	5	19	9	0	0	1	0	.474	OF
1929 NAS Elite Giants	20	70	18	3	1	2	0	.257	OF
10 years	471	1688	556	85	41	53	82	.329	

Bob Boyd

BOYD, ROBERT RICHARD (The Rope)   BL   TL   5'10"   170 lbs.
    B. Oct. 1, 1926, Potts Camp, Miss.
    Major leagues 1951–61.

	G	AB	H	2B	3B	HR	SB	BA	POS
1947 MEM Red Sox	**73**	283	96	0	0	4	0	.339	1B
1948	**77**	303	114		9			.376	1B
1949	76	293	110					.375	1B
1950	63	250	89	**27**	8	7	9	.356	1B
4 years	289	1129	409	(27)	(17)	(11)	(9)	.362	

Larry Brown

BROWN, LARRY   BR   TR   5'7"   160 lbs.
    B. Sept. 5, 1905, Pratt City, Ala.   D. Apr. 7, 1972, Memphis, Tenn.
    Manager 1935, 1939–48.

	G	AB	H	2B	3B	HR	SB	BA	POS
1923 2 teams IND ABCs MEM Red Sox									
" total	10	28	4	0	0	0	1	.143	C
1924 MEM Red Sox	57	172	35	5	6	1	3	.203	C
1925	50	151	30	6	3	1	0	.199	C
1926 DET Stars	47	135	33	3	4	2	1	.244	C
1927 2 teams MEM Red Sox CHI Am. Giants									
" total	79	198	50	10	3	0	4	.253	C
1928 MEM Red Sox	76	257	75	15	2	1	1	.292	C
1929 2 teams MEM Red Sox CHI Am. Giants									
" total	71	235	68	9	2	5	0	.289	C
1930 NY Lincoln Giants	39	133	34	2	1	0		.256	C
1931 2 teams NY Lincoln Giants MEM Red Sox									
" total	7	12	5	0	0	1	0	.417	C
1932 CHI Am. Giants	22	72	31	4	0	0	0	.431	C
1933	26	84	22	1	2	0	1	.262	C
1934	22	72	31	4	0	0	0	.431	C
1935	25	85	21	1	3	0	0	.247	C
1936 PHI Stars	26	82	16	1	1	0	0	.195	C
1937	19	65	7	0	0	0	0	.108	C
1938 MEM Red Sox	12	34	5	0	0	0	0	.147	C
1939	18	61	16	1	0	0	1	.262	C
1940 2 teams MEM Red Sox CHI Am. Giants									
" total	20	70	18	2	1	0	1	.257	C
1941 MEM Red Sox	10	30	6	1	0	0	0	.200	C
1942	14	43	10	3	0	0	0	.233	C
1943		38	8	1	1	1	0	.211	C
1944	36	82	16	2	1	0	2	.195	C
1945	16	28	8	2	0	0	0	.286	C
1946	1	1	0	0	0	0	0	.000	
1947	50	211	71	4	2	1	1	.336	C
1948	14	18	0	0	0	0	0	.000	C
26 years	(767)	2397	620	77	32	13	16	.259	

Willard Brown

BROWN, WILLARD JESSIE (Home Run)   BR   TR   6'1"   190 lbs.
    B. June 26, 1911, Shreveport, La.
    Major leagues 1947.

	G	AB	H	2B	3B	HR	SB	BA	POS
1935 KC Monarchs	2	7	2	0	0	1	1	.286	SS
1936	6	30	11	0	0	1	2	.367	SS
1937	32	**143**	**53**	10	3	**8**	4	**.371**	SS
1938	**29**	**104**	37	3	3	6	10	**.356**	OF
1939	31	119	40	9	1	1	4	.336	OF
1940	2	7	0	0	0	0	0	.000	OF
1941	23	89	30	5	4	2	2	.337	OF
1942		181	**66**	7	2	6	4	.365	OF

		G	AB	H	2B	3B	HR	SB	BA	POS

Willard Brown *continued*

1943			113	**39**	5	0	**6**	0	.345	OF
1944	US Army									
1945	US Army									
1946	KC Monarchs	58	230	80	**8**	4	**13**	3	.348	OF
1947		50	211	71					.336	OF
1948		66	262	98	20	5	**18**	13	.374	OF
1949		83	291	108					.371	OF
	13 years	(382)	1787	635	(67)	(22)	(62)	(43)	.355	

Pee Wee Butts

BUTTS, TOM BR TR 5'9" 145 lbs.
B. 1919, Atlanta, Ga.   D. Jan. 1973, Atlanta, Ga.

1938	ATL Black Crackers	6	21	8	0	1	0	0	.381	SS
1939	2 teams IND ABCs BAL Elite Giants									
"	total	20	66	32	2	0	0	1	.485	SS
1940	BAL Elite Giants	44	176	52	10	1	1	2	.295	SS
1941		45	167	30	4	0	0	0	.180	SS
1942		40	151	34	3	2	0	4	.225	SS
1943	No data available									
1944	BAL Elite Giants	41	143	44	4	4	0	1	.308	SS
1945		35	123	37	7	1	0	2	.301	SS
1946		22	77	24	3	1	1	0	.312	SS
1947		74	296	97	7	0	1	6	.328	SS
1948									.281	SS
1949		86	333	87					.261	SS
1950	2 teams BAL Elite Giants IND ABCs									
"	total	65	208	45	5	1	0	4	.216	SS, P
	(12 years)	(478)	(1761)	(490)	(45)	(11)	(3)	(20)	(.278)	

Roy Campanella

CAMPANELLA, ROY BR TR 5'9½" 190 lbs.
B. Nov. 19, 1921, Philadelphia, Pa.
Major leagues 1948–56.
Hall of Fame 1969.

1938	BAL Elites	2	3	0	0	0	0	0	.000	C
1939		16	46	13	1	0	1	0	.283	C
1940		26	82	25	2	1	5	1	.305	C
1941		23	68	25	7	2	3	1	.368	C
1942		30	111	33	4	3	1	1	.297	C
1943	Mexico									
1944	BAL Elites	48	175	64	19	4	3	6	.366	C
1945		43	146	51	8	2	5	1	.349	C
	7 years	188	631	211	41	12	18	10	.334	

Rev Cannady

CANNADY, WALTER TR

1922	CLE Tate Stars	14	38	12	3	2	0	3	.316	P, OF, SS
1923	Homestead Grays	Team not in the league								
1924		Team not in the league								
1925	HBG Giants	69	262	104	14	1	12	10	.397	SS
1926		26	101	24	3	0	0	2	.238	SS
1927		50	189	61	12	7	2	7	.323	SS, 3B
1928	NY Lincoln Giants	52	205	61	4	3	2	5	.298	SS
1929	Homestead Grays	30	107	36	5	2	2	3	.336	SS, 2B, 1B
1930	NY Lincoln Giants	55	216	63	10	2	10	0	.292	2B
1932	2 teams Homestead Grays PIT Crawfords									
"	total	26	88	20	3	1	1	0	.227	
1933	NY Black Yankees	2	8	1	0	0	0	0	.125	2B
1934		13	45	7	0	0	0	0	.156	2B
1936		16	66	18	2	0	0	3	.273	
1937		13	45	14	2	0	0	0	.311	3B
1938		13	45	5	0	1	0	1	.111	3B
1939		14	55	17	0	0	2	0	.309	SS, 3B
	14 years	393	1470	443	58	19	31	34	.301	

Tank Carr

CARR, GEORGE BB TR 6'2" 230 lbs.
B. 1895, Calif. (?)

1920	KC Monarchs	28	115	34	4	2	2	8	.296	1B
1921		55	196	61	9	8	5	5	.311	UT
1922		69	252	69	6	2	8	6	.274	UT
1923	PHI Hilldales	18	69	14	1	1	1	3	.203	1B
1924		52	161	49	12	4	1	9	.304	1B

		G	AB	H	2B	3B	HR	SB	BA	POS

Tank Carr *continued*

		G	AB	H	2B	3B	HR	SB	BA	POS
1925		67	259	94	19	**9**	10	**24**	.363	1B
1926		80	282	89	21	4	2	19	.316	1B
1927		58	198	67	1	1	1	6	.338	1B
1928	3 teams PHI Hilldales NY Lincoln Giants AC Bacharach Giants									
"	total	74	**270**	83	10	2	7	7	.307	1B
1929	AC Bacharach Giants	5	34	14	1	0	0	3	.412	1B
1933		2	8	1	0	0	0	0	.125	1B
1934	PHI Stars	4	14	6	1	0	0	0	.429	1B
	12 years	512	1858	581	85	33	37	90	.313	

Oscar Charleston

CHARLESTON, OSCAR MCKINLEY BL TL 6'1" 185 lbs.
B. Oct. 14, 1896, Indianapolis, Ind. D. Oct. 6, 1954, Philadelphia, Pa.
Manager 1932–38, 1940–41.
Hall of Fame 1976.

		G	AB	H	2B	3B	HR	SB	BA	POS
1915	IND ABCs	10	23	6	1	1	1	5	.261	OF
1916	No data available									
1917	No data available									
1918	No data available									
1919	2 teams DET Stars CHI Am. Giants									
"	total	4	16	5	1	0	0	0	.313	OF
1920	IND ABCs	40	154	54	8	**4**	6	6	.351	OF
1921	STL Giants	60	212	92	14	**11**	15	34	.434	OF
1922	IND ABCs	66	281	104	23	8	**16**	23	.370	OF
1923		66	238	74	15	8	9	18	.311	OF
1924	HBG Giants	56	175	72	13	1	**14**	3	.411	OF
1925		68	238	**106**	**21**	4	**20**	15	**.445**	OF
1926		27	93	32	7	0	7	11	.344	OF, P
1927		49	185	71	14	1	**11**	7	.384	OF
1928	PHI Hilldales	52	204	74	8	2	8	9	.363	OF
1929		58	204	76	5	4	6	10	.373	OF
1930	Homestead Grays	17	69	23	2	6	6	0	.333	1B
1931		34	137	52	12	4	4	0	.380	1B
1932	PIT Crawfords	43	**171**	**49**	7	2	5	2	.287	1B
1933		40	129	48	9	4	10	3	**.372**	1B, PH, P
1934	2 teams PIT Crawfords CHI Am. Giants									
"	total	52	192	54	7	2	7	2	.281	1B
1935	PIT Crawfords	52	191	58	10	1	5	5	.304	1B
1936		15	46	12	**5**	0	1	0	.261	1B
1937		8	26	5	2	0	0	0	.192	1B
1938		1	1	0	0	0	0	0	.000	PH
1939	No data available									
1940	TOL Crawfords	2	4	2	0	0	0	0	.500	1B
1941		1	3	0	0	0	0	0	.000	1B
	23 years	(821)	(2992)	(1069)	(184)	(63)	(151)	(153)	.357	

Francisco Coimbre

COIMBRE, FRANCISCO (Pancho) BR TR
B. Jan. 29, 1909, Coamo, Puerto Rico D. Nov. 8, 1989, Ponce, Puerto Rico

		G	AB	H	2B	3B	HR	SB	BA	POS
1940	NY Cubans		157	50	3	1	2	0	.318	OF
1941		30	126	41	4	1	3	0	.325	OF
1943			117	51	9	0	1	0	.436	OF
1944		32	118	46	7	1	2	3	.390	OF
	4 years	(62)	518	188	23	3	8	3	.363	

Dewey Creacy

CREACY, DEWEY BR TR 5'9" 160 lbs.

		G	AB	H	2B	3B	HR	SB	BA	POS
1924	STL Stars	56	182	56	7	9	0	3	.308	3B
1925		78	313	102	19	4	12	16	.326	3B
1926		89	369	126	24	7	23	2	.341	3B
1927		90	324	103	12	9	10	1	.318	3B
1928		72	272	89	17	4	7	2	.327	3B
1929		86	320	82	5	2	6	1	.256	3B
1930		73	270	77	4	5	7	7	.285	3B
1931	2 teams STL Stars WAS Pilots									
"	total	20	63	13	0	0	0	0	.206	3B
1932	2 teams DET Wolves WAS Pilots									
"	total	25	90	23	4	2	1	0	.256	3B
1933	COL Blue Birds	21	69	22	6	2	0	1	.319	3B
1934	PHI Stars	73	274	61	1	1	1	4	.223	3B
1935		**68**	284	66	1	1	4	1	.232	3B

		G	AB	H	2B	3B	HR	SB	BA	POS

Dewey Creacy *continued*

		G	AB	H	2B	3B	HR	SB	BA	POS
1936		**39**	**154**	**45**	3	0	2	0	.292	3B
1937		17	58	13	0	0	0	0	.224	3B
1938		9	27	1	0	0	0	0	.037	3B
	15 years	816	3069	879	103	46	73	38	.286	

Ray Dandridge

DANDRIDGE, RAYMOND EMMETT　　　　　BR TR 5'7" 175 lbs.
B. Aug. 31, 1913, Richmond, Va.
Hall of Fame 1987.

		G	AB	H	2B	3B	HR	SB	BA	POS
1933	2 teams DET Stars NAS Elite Giants									
"	total	11	38	8	1	2	0	0	.211	SS
1934	NWK Dodgers	29	110	48	5	2	0	0	.436	3B
1935		44	137	45	11	3	0	0	.328	3B
1936	NWK Eagles	31	103	31	4	0	1	1	.301	3B
1937		25	96	34	3	1	1	0	.354	3B
1938		14	52	21	0	0	0	0	**.404**	3B
1939	Mexico									
1940	Mexico									
1941	Mexico									
1942	NWK Eagles	25	85	14	1	0	0	0	.165	3B, 2B
1943	Mexico									
1944	NWK Eagles	50	**203**	**75**	15	5	2	0	.369	2B
	8 years	229	824	276	40	13	4	1	.335	

Cherokee Davis

DAVIS, JOHN　　　　　BR TR 6'3" 215 lbs.
B. Feb. 6, 1918, Newark, N.J.　D. Nov. 17, 1982, Ft. Lauderdale, Fla.

		G	AB	H	2B	3B	HR	SB	BA	POS
1941	NWK Eagles	13	48	9	0	0	1	1	.188	OF
1942		15	42	17	1	2	2	1	.405	OF
1943			118	36	4	0	3	0	.305	OF
1944		51	154	53	10	1	4	1	.344	OF
1945		38	138	44	14	3	6	1	.319	OF
1946			142	38	7	0	5	0	.268	
1947		80	262	69	13	0	13	3	.263	OF
1948		82	299	113					.378	OF
1949		66	262	60					.229	OF
	9 years	(345)	1465	439	(49)	(6)	(34)	(7)	.300	

Piper Davis

DAVIS, LORENZO　　　　　BR TR 6'3" 187 lbs.
B. July 3, 1917, Piper, Ala.
Manager 1948–50.

		G	AB	H	2B	3B	HR	SB	BA	POS
1942	BIR Black Barons	2	4	0	0	0	0	0	.000	IF
1943			57	22	9	1	1	1	.386	IF
1944		64	253	38	3	3	2	7	.150	IF
1945		58	211	66	10	7	3	7	.313	IF
1946		4	11	3	0	1	0	0	.273	2B
1947		56	228	62	1	0	2	0	.272	IF
1948		76	295	104	19	8	7	6	.353	IF
1949		82	299	113					.378	IF
1950		42	149	57	10	2	3	4	.383	2B, SS
	9 years	(384)	1507	465	(52)	(22)	(18)	(25)	.309	

Leon Day

DAY, LEON　　　　　BR TR 5'8" 175 lbs.
B. Oct. 30, 1916, Alexandria, Va.

		G	AB	H	2B	3B	HR	SB	BA	POS
1934	No data available									
1935	BKN Eagles	11	29	7	3	0	0	0	.241	P
1936	NWK Eagles	6	11	3	0	0	0	0	.273	P
1937	No data available									
1938	No data available									
1939	NWK Eagles	10	28	8	0	2	0	0	.286	P
1940	No data available									
1941	NWK Eagles	30	122	41	10	5	1	1	.336	P, OF
1942			100	31	4	1	0	1	.310	P, OF
1943			54	11	2	1	1	0	.204	P
1944	US Army									
1945	US Army									
1946	NWK Eagles		51	18	0	0	1	0	.353	P
1947	Mexico									
1948	Mexico									
1949	NWK Eagles	57	181	49					.271	P
	(8 years)	(114)	(576)	(168)	(19)	(9)	(3)	(2)	(.292)	

	G	AB	H	2B	3B	HR	SB	BA	POS

Bingo DeMoss

DEMOSS, ELWOOD   BR TR 6'2" 175 lbs.
B. Sept. 5, 1889, Topeka, Kans. D. Jan. 26, 1965, Chicago, Ill.
Manager 1926–29.

	G	AB	H	2B	3B	HR	SB	BA	POS
1915 IND ABCs	14	31	8	3	0	0	8	.258	2B
1916 No data available									
1917 CHI Am. Giants	1	4	1	0	0	0	0	.250	2B
1918 No data available									
1919 CHI Am. Giants	2	7	0	0	0	0	0	.000	2B
1920	35	133	38	6	1	0	9	.286	2B
1921	60	222	58	9	2	1	14	.261	2B
1923	65	236	60	6	1	2	10	.254	2B
1924	62	210	47	4	1	0	6	.224	2B
1925	58	185	42	6	0	0	4	.227	2B
1926 IND ABCs	67	306	80	9	3	0	**26**	.261	2B
1927 DET Stars	38	133	28	3	2	1	0	.211	2B, 1B
1928	43	129	20	5	1	0	0	.155	2B
1929	13	51	16	1	0	0	4	.314	2B
(12 years)	(458)	(1647)	(398)	(52)	(11)	(4)	(81)	(.242)	

Martin Dihigo

DIHIGO, MARTIN   BR TR 6'1" 190 lbs.
B. May 25, 1905, Matanzas, Cuba D. May 22, 1971, Cienfuegos, Cuba
Hall of Fame 1977.

	G	AB	H	2B	3B	HR	SB	BA	POS
1923 Cuban Stars	17	63	17	1	1	0	1	.270	1B, P
1924	52	190	47	8	3	3	4	.247	2B, OF, P
1925	41	149	45	7	1	2	3	.302	UT
1926	21	76	32	5	0	8	3	.421	UT, P
1927	40	154	57	3	2	10	9	.370	SS, UT, P
1928 Grays	No data available								
1929 PHI Hilldales	68	207	77	8	1	13	7	.372	3B, SS, 2B, 1B, P
1930 Cuban Stars	22	89	35	5	2	6	1	.393	3B, P
1931 2 teams BAL Black Sox PHI Hilldales									
" total	50	193	51	1	3	2	0	.264	3B, OF, P
1932 Did not play									
1933 Venezuela									
1934 Did not play									
1935 NY Cubans	51	160	47	9	4	7	2	.294	1B, P
1936	33	93	31	6	1	10	2	.333	OF, 2B, SS, 3B, P
1937 Latin America									
1938 Latin America									
1939 Latin America									
1940 Latin America									
1944 Latin America									
1945 NY Cubans	20	61	14	0	0	3	0	.230	P
12 years	(415)	(1435)	(453)	(53)	(18)	(64)	(32)	(.316)	

Rap Dixon

DIXON, HERBERT ALBERT   BR TR 6'2" 185 lbs.
B. Sept. 2, 1902, Kingston, Ga. D. July 20, 1945, Detroit, Mich. (?)

	G	AB	H	2B	3B	HR	SB	BA	POS
1924 HBG Giants	40	132	29	0	0	3	1	.220	OF
1925	70	266	95	10	5	7	15	.357	OF
1926	26	109	39	6	3	3	4	.358	OF
1927	14	48	11	0	1	0	2	.229	OF
1928 2 teams HBG Giants BAL Black Sox									
" total	35	131	46	10	3	8	7	.351	OF
1929 BAL Black Sox	52	217	83	12	7	9	18	.382	OF
1930	25	165	33	1	0	0	0	.200	OF
1931 2 teams BAL Black Sox PHI Hilldales									
" total	52	201	46	5	3	0	2	.229	OF
1932 2 teams WAS Pilots PIT Crawfords									
" total	33	126	39	6	2	2	0	.310	OF
1933 PHI Stars	11	38	14	2	1	0	0	.368	OF
1934 2 teams BAL Black Sox PIT Crawfords									
" total	2	10	4	0	0	0	0	.400	OF
1935 2 teams BKN Eagles NY Cubans									
" total	35	113	34	7	0	4	1	.301	OF
12 teams	395	1556	473	59	25	36	50	.304	

Larry Doby

DOBY, LAWRENCE EUGENE
B. Dec. 13, 1924, Camden, S. C.
Also played as Larry Walker.
Major leagues 1947–59.

	G	AB	H	2B	3B	HR	SB	BA	POS
1942 NWK Eagles	26	92	36	4	1	1	2	.391	
1943	23	85	24	1	1	2	1	.282	
1944 U.S. Navy									

	G	AB	H	2B	3B	HR	SB	BA	POS

Larry Doby *continued*

1945 U.S. Navy									
1946 NWK Eagles		145	56	6	**6**	3	0	.386	2B
1947	41	162	67	16		**14**		.414	2B
4 years	(90)	484	183	27	(8)	20	(3)	.378	

Valentin Dreke

DREKE, VALENTIN   BR TR 5'8" 160 lbs.
  B. June 21, 1898, Union de Reyes, Cuba   D. Sept. 25, 1929

1919 Cuban Stars	5	20	5	0	0	0	0	.250	OF
1920	20	85	30	2	1	0	2	.353	OF
1921	33	134	38	4	3	0	3	.284	OF
1922	65	254	74	13	4	2	13	.291	OF
1923	46	188	71	7	4	2	1	.378	OF
1924	51	212	91	15	1	2	6	.429	OF
1925	48	207	66	11	4	2	6	.319	OF
1926	45	177	56	6	1	1	0	.316	OF
1927	56	208	68	7	4	1	6	.327	OF
9 years	369	1485	499	65	22	10	37	.336	

Frank Duncan

DUNCAN, FRANK   BR TR 6' 170 lbs.
  B. Feb. 14, 1901, Kansas City, Mo.   D. Dec. 4, 1973, Kansas City, Mo.
  Manager 1942–45.

1921 2 teams CHI Am. Giants KC Monarchs									
" total	39	115	26	1	0	0	4	.226	C
1922 KC Monarchs	77	281	62	11	3	3	5	.221	C
1923	40	165	35	6	0	0	5	.212	C
1924	80	283	70	12	2	0	0	.247	C
1925	49	141	33	4	0	1	2	.234	C
1926	53	155	44	9	1	4	2	.284	C
1927	15	43	17	2	3	0	1	.395	C
1928	44	140	40	7	1	2	2	.286	C
1929	44	136	47	4	4	1	7	.346	C, 1B
1930	50	148	55	9	5	1	4	.372	C
1931 2 teams KC Monarchs NY Harlem Stars									
" total	14	46	9	2	0	0	0	.196	C
1932 2 teams Homestead Grays PIT Crawfords									
" total	16	50	11	0	1	0	0	.220	C
1935 NY Cubans	40	128	22	4	0	0	0	.172	C
1936	28	94	22	1	0	1	0	.234	C
1937 KC Monarchs	23	78	16	3	0	0	1	.205	C
1938 2 teams KC Monarchs CHI Am. Giants									
" total	27	77	20	2	2	0	2	.260	C
1939 No data available									
1940 No data available									
1941 KC Monarchs	7	20	3	1	0	0	0	.150	C
1942	12	23	3	1	1	0	0	.130	C
1943		23	0	0	0	0	0	.000	C
1944	23	44	6	2	0	0	0	.136	C
1945	12	29	5	3	0	0	0	.172	C
(22 years)	(693)	(2219)	(546)	(84)	(23)	(13)	(35)	(.246)	

Luke Easter

EASTER, LUSCIOUS LUKE   BL TR 6'4½" 240 lbs.
  B. Aug. 4, 1914, St. Louis, Mo.   D. Mar. 29, 1979, Euclid, Ohio
  Major leagues 1949–54.

1947 WAS Homestead Grays		219	68	11	0	10	1	.311	OF
1948	58	215	78	22	8	13		.363	OF
2 years	(58)	434	146	33	8	23	(1)	.336	

Howard Easterling

EASTERLING, HOWARD   BR TR 6' 180 lbs.
  B. Nov. 26, 1911, Mount Olive, Miss.

1937 CIN Tigers	18	70	27	4	2	0	0	.386	SS
1938 No data available									
1939 No data available									
1940 WAS Homestead Grays	46	165	59	7	7	3	4	.358	3B
1941	31	114	35	5	2	2	3	.307	3B
1942	39	137	31	5	1	1	2	.226	3B
1943		164	74	8	5	1	1	.451	3B
1944 US Army									

		G	AB	H	2B	3B	HR	SB	BA	POS

Howard Easterling *continued*

		G	AB	H	2B	3B	HR	SB	BA	POS
1945	US Army									
1946	WAS Homestead Grays		80	24	4	3	1	0	.300	3B
1947	No data available									
1948	No data available									
1949	NY Cubans	45	189	57					.302	
	(7 years)	(179)	(919)	(307)	(33)	(20)	(8)	(10)	(.334)	

Red Farrell

FARRELL, LUTHER   TL   6'1"   190 lbs.

		G	AB	H	2B	3B	HR	SB	BA	POS
1928	AC Bacharach Giants	43	106	39	2	0	13	0	.368	P, OF
1930	NY Lincoln Giants	16	46	25	3	2	4	0	.543	OF, P
	2 years	59	152	64	5	2	17	0	.421	

Jelly Gardner

GARDNER, FLOYD   BL TR   5'7"   160 lbs.
B. Sept. 26, 189?, Russellville, Ark.   D. 1976, Chicago, Ill.

		G	AB	H	2B	3B	HR	SB	BA	POS
1920	CHI Am. Giants	14	55	10	3	1	0	3	.182	OF
1921		53	169	37	3	0	0	11	.219	OF
1922		57	178	42	1	1	0	6	.236	OF
1923		69	258	78	9	0	0	15	.302	OF
1924		74	269	96	11	1	0	6	.357	OF
1925		92	348	100	12	3	1	5	.287	OF
1926		59	216	72	11	4	0	5	.333	OF
1927	No data available									
1928	2 teams CHI Am. Giants Homestead Grays									
"	total	49	173	50	7	2	0	8	.289	OF
1929	CHI Am. Giants	68	241	73	8	4	0	6	.303	OF
1930		30	86	20	3	0	0	1	.233	OF
1931	DET Wolves	27	88	17	2	0	0	6	.193	OF
	(11 years)	(592)	(2081)	(595)	(70)	(16)	(1)	(72)	(.286)	

Josh Gibson

GIBSON, JOSHUA   BR TR   6'2"   217 lbs.
B. Dec. 21, 1911, Buena Vista, Ga.   D. Jan. 20, 1947, Pittsburgh, Pa.
Hall of Fame 1972.

		G	AB	H	2B	3B	HR	SB	BA	POS
1930	Homestead Grays	10	33	8	1	0	1	1	.242	C
1931		32	128	47	8	4	6	0	.367	C
1932		46	147	42	3	5	7	1	.286	C, OF
1933		34	116	42	8	1	6	1	.362	C, 3B, P, PH
1934	PIT Crawfords	50	190	56	13	4	12	0	.295	C
1935		49	191	58	11	2	13	8	.304	C
1936		23	75	27	3	0	11	0	.360	C
1937	Homestead Grays	12	42	21	0	4	7	0	.500	C
1938		18	60	21	2	0	4	1	.350	C
1939		27	72	24	2	2	16	0	.333	C
1940		1	6	1	0	0	0	0	.167	C
1941	Mexico									
1942	Homestead Grays	40	125	43	6	1	9	3	.344	C
1943			190	90	32	8	14	0	.474	C
1944		48	165	57	8	5	8	2	.345	C
1945		49	161	64	6	4	9	0	.398	C
1946			119	43	7	5	18	0	.361	C
	16 years	(439)	1820	644	110	45	141	17	.354	

George Giles

GILES, GEORGE FRANKLIN   BL TR   6'1"   175 lbs.
B. May 2, 1909. Junction City, Kans.

		G	AB	H	2B	3B	HR	SB	BA	POS
1927	KC Monarchs	51	171	50	8	5	0	1	.292	1B
1928		67	252	76	11	7	1	4	.302	1B
1929	Semipro									
1930	STL Stars	66	272	87	15	4	3	7	.320	1B
1931		19	67	16	0	0	0	0	.239	1B
1932	3 teams KC Monarchs DET Wolves Homestead Grays									
"	total	29	117	36	3	0	0	6	.308	1B
1933	BAL Black Sox	2	6	2	1	0	0	0	.333	1B
1935	BKN Eagles	47	189	69	9	3	4	3	.365	1B
1936	NY Black Yankees	17	65	18	2	1	0	2	.277	1B
1937		12	43	16	1	0	0	0	.372	1B
1938	2 teams PIT Crawfords PHI Stars									
"	total	29	116	31	0	1	0	1	.267	1B
	10 years	339	1298	401	50	21	8	24	.309	

		G	AB	H	2B	3B	HR	SB	BA	POS

Jim Gilliam

GILLIAM, JAMES WILLIAM (Junior)   BB   TR   5′10½″   175 lbs.
B. Oct. 17, 1928, Nashville, Tenn.   D. Oct. 8, 1978, Inglewood, Calif.
Major leagues 1953–66.

		G	AB	H	2B	3B	HR	SB	BA	POS
1946	BAL Elite Giants		9	1	0	0	0	0	.111	2B
1947		71	257	65	1		0	9	.253	2B
1948	No data available									
1949	No data available									
1950	BAL Elite Giants	42	162	43	10	5	2	13	.265	2B
	(3 years)	(113)	(428)	(109)	(11)	(5)	(2)	(22)	.255	

Vic Harris

HARRIS, ELANDER VICTOR   BL   TR   5′10″   164 lbs.
B. June 10, 1905, Pensacola, Fla.   D. Feb. 23, 1978, San Fernando, Calif.
Manager 1935–43, 1945.

		G	AB	H	2B	3B	HR	SB	BA	POS
1923	2 teams TOL Tigers CLE Tate Stars									
"	total	20	69	21	1	0	0	0	.304	3B, IN
1924	2 teams CLE Browns CHI Am. Giants									
"	total	39	137	38	5	2	2	1	.277	OF
1925	Homestead Grays	Team not in the league								
1926		Team not in the league								
1927		Team not in the league								
1928	Homestead Grays	8	30	7	1	0	0	0	.233	OF
1929		41	159	59	12	5	5	2	.371	OF
1930		17	74	24	2	3	0	0	.324	OF
1931		22	76	18	2	1	0	0	.237	OF
1932	2 teams DET Wolves Homestead Grays									
"	total	37	132	46	9	2	3	3	**.348**	OF
1933	Homestead Grays	16	74	26	3	0	2	1	.351	OF
1934	PIT Crawfords	47	178	64	7	2	3	2	.360	OF
1935	Homestead Grays	46	181	67	10	0	7	4	.370	OF
1936		5	19	2	2	0	0	0	.105	OF
1937	WAS Homestead Grays	18	79	18	1	0	1	0	.228	OF
1938		14	55	14	1	0	0	0	.255	OF
1939		26	74	16	3	0	0	0	.216	OF
1940		47	181	49	4	7	1	1	.271	OF, C
1941		29	102	24	5	2	0	1	.235	OF
1942		32	102	22	4	2	0	0	.216	OF
1943			68	21	3	1	0	0	.309	OF
1944	Defense work									
1945	WAS Homestead Grays	13	19	5	0	1	0	0	.263	OF, PH
	19 years	(477)	1809	541	75	28	24	15	.299	

Pete Hill

HILL, PRESTON (Pete)   BL   TR
B. 1880   D. 1951, Buffalo, NY
Manager 1920, 1921, 1924, 1925.

		G	AB	H	2B	3B	HR	SB	BA	POS
1914	CHI Am. Giants	3	13	4	0	1	0	0	.308	OF
1915			27	4	1	0	0	0	.148	OF
1916		4	16	2	1	0	0	0	.125	OF
1917		1	4	2	0	1	0	0	.500	OF
1920	DET Stars	33	98	28	4	1	2	4	.286	OF
1921		41	138	54	5	5	3	3	.391	OF, 1B
1923	MIL Bears	13	46	15	2	0	0	1	.326	OF
1924	BAL Black Sox	16	52	14	2	0	0	1	.269	OF, PH
1925		6	13	4	0	0	1	0	.308	1B, OF, PH
	9 years	(117)	407	127	15	8	6	9	.312	

Elston Howard

HOWARD, ELSTON GENE (Ellie)   BR   TR   6′2″   196 lbs.
B. Feb. 23, 1929, St. Louis, Mo.   D. Dec. 14, 1980, New York, N. Y.
Major leagues 1955–67.

		G	AB	H	2B	3B	HR	SB	BA	POS
1949	KC Monarchs	85	307	83					.270	
1950		49	188	60	13	5	3	0	.319	OF
	2 years	134	495	143	(13)	(5)	(3)	(0)	.289	

Robert Hudspeth

HUDSPETH, ROBERT (High Pockets)

		G	AB	H	2B	3B	HR	SB	BA	POS
1920	IND ABCs	5	11	2	0	0	0	0	.182	1B
1921	COL Buckeyes	56	224	62	13	2	4	2	.277	1B
1922	AC Bacharach Giants	24	86	26	6	3	3	1	.302	1B
1923	NY Lincoln Giants	23	87	32	1	4	2	1	.336	1B
1924		62	221	80	17	2	7	2	.362	1B
1925		49	183	49	8	0	7	1	.268	1B
1926		40	156	57	7	3	7	0	**.365**	1B

		G	AB	H	2B	3B	HR	SB	BA	POS

Robert Hudspeth *continued*

		G	AB	H	2B	3B	HR	SB	BA	POS
1927	BKN Royal Giants	21	87	23	0	0	3	0	.264	1B
1928		10	36	7	0	0	0	0	.194	1B
1929	2 teams BKN Royal Giants PHI Hilldales									
"	total	44	158	43	9	1	0	2	.272	1B
1930	BKN Royal Giants	6	25	5	0	0	1	0	.200	1B
1932	NY Black Yankees	6	24	6	0	0	0	0	.250	1B
	12 years	346	1298	392	61	15	34	9	.302	

Sammy T. Hughes

HUGHES, SAMUEL THOMAS   BR TR 6'3" 190 lbs.
B. Oct. 20, 1910, Louisville, Ky. D. 1973, Los Angeles, Calif.

		G	AB	H	2B	3B	HR	SB	BA	POS
1930	Lou Black Caps	16	54	14	0	2	1	1	.259	2B
1931	2 teams LOU Black Caps PIT Crawfords									
"	total	8	27	5	0	0	0	0	.185	2B, SS, P
1932	WAS Pilots	11	36	12	0	0	1	0	.333	2B
1933	NAS Elite Giants	13	51	18	3	2	0	0	.353	2B
1934	2 teams CLE Red Sox NAS Elite Giants									
"	total	24	96	22	3	0	1	2	.229	2B
1935	COL Elite Giants	24	107	38	4	1	0	1	.355	2B
1936	WAS Elite Giants	31	102	36	0	1	3	0	.353	2B
1937		24	91	29	5	0	2	0	.319	2B
1938	BAL Elite Giants	17	63	19	4	1	1	3	.302	2B
1939		23	87	30	5	2	0	1	.345	2B
1940		48	185	47	10	1	5	2	.254	2B
1941	Mexico									
1942	BAL Elite Giants	38	146	44	9	1	1	0	.301	2B
1943	US Army									
1944	US Army									
1945	US Army									
1946	BAL Elite Giants	10	35	6	0	0	0	0	.171	3B
	13 years	287	1080	320	43	11	15	10	.296	

Monte Irvin

IRVIN, MERRILL MONFORD   BR TR 6'2" 195 lbs.
B. Feb. 25, 1919, Columbia, Ala.
Major leagues 1949–56.
Hall of Fame 1973.

		G	AB	H	2B	3B	HR	SB	BA	POS
1939	NWK Eagles	22	72	29	4	0	3	1	.403	3B, OF
1940		36	133	48	8	5	2	3	.361	SS
1941		30	108	41	9	1	5	2	.380	OF
1942		8	32	17	6	4	2	1	.531	OF
1943	Mexico									
1944	US Army									
1945	NWK Eagles	5	18	4	1	0	1	0	.222	OF
1946			123	41	8	0	7	0	.333	SS
1947		81	287	91	18	0	14	19	.317	OF
1948		42	135	43					.319	OF
	8 years	(224)	908	314	(54)	(10)	(34)	(26)	.346	

Fats Jenkins

JENKINS, CLARENCE R.   BL TL 5'7"
B. Jan. 19, 1898, New York, N.Y. D. Dec. 6, 1968, Philadelphia Pa.

		G	AB	H	2B	3B	HR	SB	BA	POS
1920	NY Lincoln Giants	1	4	2	0	0	0	0	.500	OF
1921	No data available									
1922	AC Bacharach Giants	2	6	3	0	0	0	0	.500	OF
1923	HBG Giants	Team not in the league								
1924		56	183	58	4	0	0	4	.317	OF
1925		69	289	91	9	2	2	15	.315	OF
1926		27	106	30	1	1	0	5	.283	OF
1927		50	216	86	8	4	4	10	.398	OF
1928	2 teams NY Lincoln Giants AC Bacharach Giants									
"	total	63	248	94	4	3	0	2	.379	OF
1929	AC Bacharach Giants	44	179	68	5	0	2	4	.380	OF
1930	NY Lincoln Giants	21	79	26	1	2	0	1	.329	OF
1931		17	66	17	2	0	1	0	.258	OF
1932	2 teams PIT Crawfords NY Black Yankees									
"	total	15	66	19	2	0	0	1	.288	OF
1934	NY Lincoln Giants	15	49	16	1	0	0	1	.327	OF
1935	BKN Eagles	49	196	63	7	1	2	0	.321	OF
1936	NY Black Yankees	15	62	12	3	0	0	2	.194	OF
1937		14	40	12	2	0	2	0	.300	OF
1938	2 teams PIT Crawfords NY Black Yankees									
"	total	10	37	13	0	0	0	2	.351	OF
	(17 years)	(468)	(1826)	(610)	(49)	(13)	(13)	(47)	(.334)	

		G	AB	H	2B	3B	HR	SB	BA	POS

Sam Jethroe

JETHROE, SAMUEL (Jet)   BB   TR   6'1"   178 lbs.
B. Jan. 20, 1922, East St. Louis, Ill.
Major Leagues 1950–54.

Year	Team	G	AB	H	2B	3B	HR	SB	BA	POS
1942	CLE Buckeyes		39	19	5	1	0	1	.487	OF
1943			98	28	**8**	**4**	2	0	.286	OF
1944		68	**275**	97	14	2	2	**18**	**.353**	OF
1945		56	214	84	10	10	3	**21**	**.393**	OF
1946		**62**	226	70			6	20	.310	OF
1947		70	**288**	98	**5**	0	2	3	.340	OF
	6 years	(256)	1140	396	(42)	(17)	15	63	.347	

Heavy Johnson

JOHNSON, OSCAR   250 lbs.
B. 1896, Atchison, Kans.   D. 1966, Cleveland, Ohio

Year	Team	G	AB	H	2B	3B	HR	SB	BA	POS
1922	KC Monarchs	55	208	81	17	10	7	6	**.389**	OF
1923		46	179	68	**19**	9	**18**	6	.380	OF
1924		81	299	123	18	11	7	1	.411	OF
1925	BAL Black Sox	55	200	69	13	3	7	4	.345	OF
1926		28	95	32	3	2	6	12	.337	OF
1927	HBG Giants	40	152	48	8	3	3	0	.316	OF
1928	2 teams CLE Hornets MEM Red Sox									
"	total	56	197	62	13	3	1	1	.315	OF
1929	No data available									
1930	MEM Red Sox	7	17	6	0	1	0	1	.353	OF, PH
	(8 years)	(368)	(1347)	(489)	(91)	(42)	(49)	(31)	(.363)	

Judy Johnson

JOHNSON, WILLIAM JULIUS   BR   TR   5'11"   150 lbs.
B. Oct. 20, 1900, Snow Hill, Md.   D. June 15, 1989, Wilmington, Del.
Hall of Fame 1975.

Year	Team	G	AB	H	2B	3B	HR	SB	BA	POS
1919	MAD Stars	1	4	0	0	0	0	0	.000	3B
1920	No data available									
1921	PHI Hilldales	22	88	20	3	2	2	1	.227	SS, 3B
1922		7	25	2	0	0	0	0	.080	SS
1923		27	86	31	**12**	1	1	2	.360	3B
1924		71	245	84	**19**	**6**	2	4	.343	3B
1925		66	249	97	12	8	4	7	.390	3B
1926		87	339	111	21	6	2	14	.327	3B
1927		51	183	49	5	2	1	2	.268	3B
1928		52	205	46	3	3	1	0	.224	3B
1929		74	256	104	13	1	3	12	.406	3B, SS
1930	Homestead Grays	16	69	19	0	1	0		.275	3B
1931	PHI Hilldales	56	205	56	3	3	0	2	.273	3B
1932	2 teams PHI Hilldales PIT Crawfords									
"	total	32	115	31	2	4	1	2	.270	3B
1933	PIT Crawfords	36	121	27	8	0	0	0	.223	3B
1934		50	192	49	9	3	1	2	.255	3B
1935		55	222	68	12	3	1	2	.306	3B
1936		25	88	22	3	1	0	1	.250	3B
	(18 years)	(728)	(2692)	(816)	(125)	(44)	(19)	(51)	(.303)	

Newt Joseph

JOSEPH, NEWTON   BL   TR
B. Oct. 27, 1899, Montgomery, Ala.   D. Jan. 18, 1953, Kansas City, Mo.

Year	Team	G	AB	H	2B	3B	HR	SB	BA	POS
1922	KC Monarchs	70	261	61	10	1	2	8	.234	3B
1923		32	121	22	6	2	8	1	.182	3B
1924		84	338	113	24	7	8	2	.334	3B
1925		50	193	63	12	0	1	9	.326	3B
1926		59	203	60	10	4	4	3	.296	3B
1927		69	238	69	15	5	5	7	.290	3B
1928		72	261	69	12	2	1	16	.264	3B
1929		72	233	66	7	3	5	6	.283	3B
1930		52	175	47	10	3	3	14	.269	3B
1931		8	27	10	3	0	0	0	.370	3B
1932		3	8	0	0	0	0	1	.000	3B
1933	Team not in the league									
1934	Team not in the league									
1935	KC Monarchs	2	6	1	0	0	0	0	.167	3B
	12 years	573	2064	581	109	27	37	67	.281	

		G	AB	H	2B	3B	HR	SB	BA	POS

Jumbo Kimbro

KIMBRO, HENRY ALLEN   BL   TL   5'8"   175 lbs.
B. Feb. 10, 1912, Nashville, Tenn.

Year	Team	G	AB	H	2B	3B	HR	SB	BA	POS
1937	WAS Elite Giants	25	98	27	3	1	5	0	.276	OF
1938		21	85	27	1	1	0	0	.318	OF
1939	BAL Elite Giants	30	116	36	3	0	1	0	.310	OF
1940			282	68	5	0	1	3	.241	OF
1941			60	22	1	0	0	1	.367	OF
1942		32	131	37	5	3	2	3	.282	OF
1943			121	32	3	0	0	0	.264	OF
1944		43	158	52	10	4	5	10	.329	OF
1945		41	172	50	10	6	2	5	.291	OF
1946		22	85	27	2	1	5	0	.318	OF
1947		77	284	103					.363	OF
1948		71	239	75					.314	OF
1949		83	307	108					.352	OF
1950		45	165	61	11	4	2	9	.370	OF
14 years		(490)	2303	725	(54)	(20)	(23)	(31)	.315	

Buck Leonard

LEONARD, WALTER FENNER   BL   TL   5'10"   185 lbs.
B. Sept. 8, 1907, Rocky Mount, N.C.
Hall of Fame 1972.

Year	Team	G	AB	H	2B	3B	HR	SB	BA	POS
1934	WAS Homestead Grays	9	35	14	1	0	2	0	.400	1B
1935		39	151	51	**14**	2	2	0	.338	1B
1936		5	21	5	1	0	3	0	.238	1B
1937		14	54	18	1	0	2	0	.333	1B
1938		18	58	20	0	0	4	0	.345	1B
1939		25	69	22	2	0	4	0	.319	1B
1940		52	175	67	15	3	8	2	**.383**	1B
1941		34	107	25	4	4	6	2	.234	1B
1942		20	79	14	4	0	0	3	.177	1B
1943			187	56	11	**11**	3	0	.299	1B
1944		48	161	51	11	6	7	1	.317	1B
1945		40	144	54	9	4	6	1	.375	1B
1946			84	12	1	3	4	0	.143	1B
1947		31	105	43	11	0	7	1	.410	1B
1948		47	157	62				13	**.395**	1B
15 years		(382)	1587	514	(85)	(33)	71	(10)	.324	

Pop Lloyd

LLOYD, JOHN HENRY   BL   TR   6'   178 lbs.
B. Apr. 25, 1884, Palatka, Fla.   D. Mar. 19, 1964, Atlantic City, N.J.
Manager 1921–31.
Hall of Fame 1977.

Year	Team	G	AB	H	2B	3B	HR	SB	BA	POS
1914	2 teams CHI Am. Giants NY Lincoln Giants									
"	total	5	21	9	1	1	1	2	.429	SS
1915	No data available									
1916	NY Lincoln Giants	4	19	5	0	0	0	0	.263	SS
1917	CHI Am. Giants	1	4	0	0	0	0	0	.000	SS
1918	BKN Royal Giants	3	12	2	0	0	0	0	.167	SS
1919		2	8	3	0	0	0	0	.375	SS
1920		11	45	14	0	0	0	1	.311	SS
1921	COL Buckeyes	63	247	83	17	3	1	17	.336	SS
1922	AC Bacharach Giants	24	75	29	6	0	1	3	.387	SS, 2B
1923	PHI Hilldales	19	70	27	10	1	2	4	.386	SS
1924	AC Bacharach Giants	59	194	84	10	2	1	3	**.433**	2B
1925		61	221	73	5	5	2	9	.330	2B
1926	NY Lincoln Giants	40	146	51	6	3	1	4	.349	2B
1927		20	80	30	9	0	2	1	.375	2B
1928		37	149	84	4	1	**11**	10	**.564**	1B
1929		55	206	80	15	3	2	1	.388	1B
1930		52	199	62	6	0	2	0	.312	1B
1931	2 teams NY Harlem Stars AC Bacharach Giants									
"	total	18	62	12	1	0	0	1	.194	1B
1932	AC Bacharach Giants	3	11	3	0	0	0	0	.273	1B
(18 years)		(477)	(1769)	(651)	(90)	(18)	(26)	(56)	(.368)	

Lester Lockett

LOCKETT, LESTER   BR   TR   6'0"   195 lbs.

Year	Team	G	AB	H	2B	3B	HR	SB	BA	POS
1938	BIR Black Barons	2	5	0	0	0	0	0	.000	SS
1939	No data available									
1940	No data available									

		G	AB	H	2B	3B	HR	SB	BA	POS

Lester Lockett *continued*

Year	Team	G	AB	H	2B	3B	HR	SB	BA	POS
1941	BIR Black Barons	20	67	22	1	0	1	0	.328	
1942		15	54	17	0	2	0	0	.315	
1943			76	31	5	4	2	0	**.408**	
1944		57	191	49	8	4	0	3	.257	
1945		61	229	70	11	2	3	8	.306	
1946	CIN Clowns	3	14	2	1	1	0	0	.143	3B, OF
1947	BAL Elite Giants	76	278	87	11	0	1	4	.313	
1948		**71**	**277**	**107**					.386	
1949	No data available									
1950	CHI Am. Giants	31	103	31	7	0	2	9	.301	OF
	(9 years)	(336)	(1294)	(416)	(44)	(13)	(9)	(24)	(.321)	

Dick Lundy

LUNDY, RICHARD (King Richard) BB TR
B. July 10, 1898, Jacksonville, Fla.   D. 1965, Jacksonville, Fla.
Manager 1926–34, 1937.

Year	Team	G	AB	H	2B	3B	HR	SB	BA	POS
1918	AC Bacharach Giants	2	8	1	0	0	0	0	.125	SS
1919	2 teams AC Bacharach Giants PHI Hilldales									
"	total	11	41	15	0	0	1	0	.366	SS
1920	AC Bacharach Giants	9	32	11	3	0	2	1	**.344**	SS
1921		25	91	33	5	4	3	5	.363	SS
1922		8	30	10	1	0	1	0	.333	SS
1923		19	71	22	6	3	4	2	.310	SS
1924		60	228	84	9	3	14	11	.368	SS
1925		62	236	64	10	1	5	5	.271	SS
1926		33	121	42	5	1	1	1	.347	SS
1927		55	202	62	5	0	2	1	.307	SS
1928		57	208	85	11	3	7	6	.409	SS
1929	BAL Black Sox	57	213	67	11	0	4	8	.315	SS
1930		32	134	43	6	1	2	1	.321	SS
1931		63	232	61	2	2	4	1	.263	SS
1932		25	85	29	0	0	0	1	.341	SS, PH
1933	PHI Stars	12	39	6	0	0	0	0	.154	
1934	BKN Eagles	17	55	13	0	0	0	0	.236	SS
1935	2 teams NY Cubans NWK Dodgers									
"	total	25	90	29	3	0	1	0	.322	2B, SS
1936	No data available									
1937	NWK Eagles	12	43	8	1	2	0	0	.186	SS
	(19 years)	(584)	(2159)	(685)	(78)	(20)	(51)	(43)	(.317)	

Jimmy Lyons

LYONS, JIMMY BL TR 5'8" 175 lbs.
B. Chicago, Ill.

Year	Team	G	AB	H	2B	3B	HR	SB	BA	POS
1914	BKN Royal Giants	4	16	6	0	0	1	5	.375	OF
1920	CHI Am. Giants	44	166	64	11	4	8	22	.386	OF, P
1921		58	194	56	2	3	4	28	.289	OF
1922		53	201	50	4	3	2	8	.249	OF
1923		56	183	46	12	1	0	13	.251	OF
1924		2	0	0	0	0	0	0	.000	
	6 years	217	760	222	29	11	15	76	.292	

Biz Mackey

MACKEY, RALEIGH BB TR 6'2" 210 lbs.
B. July 27, 1897, Eagle Pass, Tex.   D. 1959, Los Angeles, Calif.
Manager 1940–41, 1945–46.

Year	Team	G	AB	H	2B	3B	HR	SB	BA	POS
1920	IND ABCs	17	49	15	3	1	1	0	.306	UT
1921		66	226	67	8	9	11	4	.296	C, SS
1922		62	219	79	15	13	6	5	.361	OF, C
1923	PHI Hilldales	24	90	39	4	2	4	1	.433	C, SS
1924		**71**	**255**	**86**	16	3	4	6	.337	C, SS
1925		60	206	72	14	3	6	12	.350	C, SS
1926		85	315	103	19	3	10	14	.327	C
1927		16	56	21	1	1	0	1	.375	C
1928		53	205	67	3	2	2	3	.337	C
1929		29	135	45	2	0	1	2	.333	C, SS
1930		29	105	42	6	4	4	2	.400	3B, C, SS
1931		51	173	65	2	1	2	0	.376	C
1932	No data available									
1933	PHI Stars	13	47	14	2	0	0	0	.298	C

	G	AB	H	2B	3B	HR	SB	BA	POS
Biz Mackey *continued*									
1934	29	98	26	3	0	2	0	.265	C
1935	57	186	52	2	0	4	1	.280	C
1936 BAL Elite Giants	23	87	21	3	1	0	0	.241	C
1937	16	50	16	2	0	0	0	.320	C
1938	20	70	18	0	0	0	0	.257	C
1939 2 teams BAL Elite Giants NWK Eagles									
" total	21	78	20	1	0	4	0	.256	C
1940 NWK Eagles	35	122	33	3	1	1	0	.270	C
1941	16	36	14	1	0	2	0	.389	C
1942 No data available									
1943 No data available									
1944 No data available									
1945 NWK Eagles	36	114	35	2	2	1	0	.307	C
1946	4	4	0	0	0	0	0	.000	
1947		92	21	4	0	1	0	.228	C
(24 years)	(833)	(3018)	(971)	(116)	(46)	(66)	(51)	(.322)	

Dave Malarcher

MALARCHER, DAVID JULIUS (Gentleman Dave)   BB TR 5'7" 147 lbs.
B. Oct. 18, 1894, Whitehall, La.   D. May 11, 1982, Chicago, Ill.
Manager 1925–28, 1931, 1933–34.

	G	AB	H	2B	3B	HR	SB	BA	POS
1920 CHI Am. Giants	29	114	31	3	1	0	4	.272	3B
1921	58	208	46	5	1	0	11	.221	3B
1922	25	81	13	0	0	0	2	.160	3B
1923	65	234	69	15	3	1	12	.295	3B
1924	72	287	84	9	1	0	14	.293	3B
1925	84	321	106	9	0	2	12	.330	3B, 2B
1926	70	250	64	8	0	1	8	.256	3B, 2B
1927	77	276	69	7	3	1	16	.250	3B
1928	17	57	14	0	0	0	2	.246	3B
1929 No data available									
1930 No data available									
1931 CHI Am. Giants	13	39	11	0	0	0	0	.282	3B
1932 No data available									
1933 CHI Am. Giants	2	7	0	0	0	0	0	.000	3B
1934	1	1	0	0	0	0	0	.000	PH
(12 years)	(513)	(1875)	(507)	(56)	(9)	(5)	(81)	(.270)	

Oliver Marcelle

MARCELLE, OLIVER (Ghost)   BR TR 5'9" 160 lbs.
B. June 24, 1897, Thibedeaux, La.   D. June 12, 1949, Denver, Colo.

	G	AB	H	2B	3B	HR	SB	BA	POS
1918 BKN Royal Giants	3	11	1	0	0	0	0	.091	3B
1919	7	30	14	0	1	0	0	.467	3B
1920 AC Bacharach Giants	9	29	6	0	2	0	1	.207	3B
1921	**43**	**164**	**50**	7	3	1	7	.305	3B
1922	**27**	**99**	**36**	5	1	0	2	.364	3B
1923	15	61	18	0	0	2	**6**	.295	3B
1924 NY Lincoln Giants	45	175	60	13	3	1	12	.343	3B
1925 2 teams NY Lincoln Giants AC Bacharach Giants									
" total	58	195	60	5	3	2	3	.308	3B
1926 AC Bacharach Giants	31	106	27	1	1	1	1	.255	3B
1927	48	180	55	4	3	2	2	.306	3B
1928		169	50	2	3	3	0	.296	3B
1929 BAL Black Sox	58	207	57	4	2	0	7	.275	3B
1930 BKN Royal Giants	5	25	8	1	0	0	0	.320	3B
13 years	349	1451	442	42	22	12	41	.305	

Willie Mays

MAYS, WILLIE HOWARD (Say Hey)   BR TR 5'10½" 170 lbs.
B. May 6, 1931, Westfield, Ala.
Major leagues 1951–73.
Hall of Fame 1979.

	G	AB	H	2B	3B	HR	SB	BA	POS
1948 BIR Black Barons	28	84	22	3	0	1	1	.262	OF
1949	75	270	64					.237	OF
1950	27	106	35	7	2	4	2	.330	OF
3 years	130	460	121	(10)	(2)	(5)	(3)	.263	

Terris McDuffie

MCDUFFIE, TERRIS (The Great)   BR TR 6'2" 200 lbs.
B. July 22, 1910, Mobile, Ala.   D. New York, N.Y.

	G	AB	H	2B	3B	HR	SB	BA	POS
1930 BIR Black Barons	61	186	54	10	2	3	**16**	.290	OF
1932 BAL Black Sox	11	33	11	0	0	0	0	.333	OF
2 years	72	219	65	10	2	3	16	.297	

		G	AB	H	2B	3B	HR	SB	BA	POS

Hurley McNair

MCNAIR, HURLEY ALLEN   BB TR 5′6″ 155 lbs.
B. Oct. 28, 1888, Marshall, Tex.   D. Dec. 2, 1948, Kansas City, Mo.

Year	Team	G	AB	H	2B	3B	HR	SB	BA	POS
1914	CHI Union Giants	3	13	4	0	1	0	0	.308	OF
1915	CHI Am. Giants	7	22	7	3	0	0	0	.318	OF, P
1920	KC Monarchs	28	125	39	9	2	2	3	.312	OF
1921		53	196	60	9	8	5	5	.306	OF, P
1922		86	**331**	**124**	19	4	11	10	.375	OF, P
1923		43	181	64	6	3	11	5	.354	OF
1924		80	331	103	18	7	5	4	.311	OF
1925		74	289	104	11	9	3	10	.360	OF
1926		59	211	59	11	2	0	10	.280	OF
1927		77	277	77	15	5	6	7	.278	OF
1928	DET Stars	68	241	66	8	6	3	6	.274	OF
	11 years	578	2217	707	109	47	46	60	.319	

Pablo Mesa

MESA, PABLO
B. Cuba

Year	Team	G	AB	H	2B	3B	HR	SB	BA	POS
1922	Cuban Stars	2	9	2	1	0	0	0	.222	OF
1923		17	66	17	3	2	1	1	.258	OF
1924		47	196	58	13	2	1	14	.296	OF
1925		41	161	50	4	1	2	2	.311	OF
1926		17	65	18	3	0	0	0	.277	OF
1927		19	69	15	0	0	0	1	.217	OF
	6 years	143	566	160	24	5	4	18	.283	

Minnie Minoso

MINOSO, SATURNINO ORESTES ARMAS ARRIETA   BR TR 5′10″ 175 lbs.
B. Nov. 29, 1922, Havana, Cuba
Major leagues 1949–80.

Year	Team	G	AB	H	2B	3B	HR	SB	BA	POS
1946	NY Cubans		55	17	1	2	0	0	.309	3B
1947		55	228	67	14	0	3	7	.294	3B
	2 years	(55)	283	84	15	2	3	7	.297	

Dobie Moore

MOORE, DOBIE   BR TR 5′11″ 230 lbs.
B. 1893, Ga.   D. Detroit, Mich. (?)

Year	Team	G	AB	H	2B	3B	HR	SB	BA	POS
1920	KC Monarchs	21	84	23	3	0	2	2	.274	SS
1921		36	125	33	7	4	6	4	.264	SS
1922		77	312	120	22	3	8	11	.385	SS
1923		43	170	62	7	8	8	2	.365	SS
1924		79	307	**139**	**26**	9	10	1	**.453**	SS
1925		83	332	108	20	**12**	7	9	.325	SS
1926		18	63	24	3	3	0	2	.381	SS
	7 years	357	1393	509	88	39	41	31	.365	

Alejandro Oms

OMS, ALEJANDRO   BL TL 5′8″ 190 lbs.
B. Mar. 13, 1895, Santa Clara, Cuba   D. Nov. 9, 1946

Year	Team	G	AB	H	2B	3B	HR	SB	BA	POS
1921	Cuban Stars	1					3			OF
1922		2	9	3	1	0	0	0	.333	OF
1923		16	65	26	2	2	1	2	.400	OF
1924		39	129	42	9	4	4	3	.326	OF
1925		43	157	50	13	1	6	4	.318	OF
1926		20	73	25	5	2	2	1	.342	OF
1927		39	132	46	10	2	3	5	.348	OF
1928		29	117	36	11	0	6	1	.308	OF
1929	No data available									
1930	NY Cubans	18	72	24	7	2	1	1	.333	OF, P
1931		8	33	2	0	0	1	0	.061	OF
1933	No data available									
1934	Team not in the league									
1935	NY Cubans	44	147	56	8	0	2	1	.381	OF
	(11 years)	(259)	(934)	(310)	(66)	(13)	(29)	(18)	(.332)	

Buck O'Neil

O'NEIL, JOHN JORDAN   BR TR 6′2″ 190 lbs.
B. Nov. 13, 1911, Carrabelle, Fla.
Manager 1948–50.

Year	Team	G	AB	H	2B	3B	HR	SB	BA	POS
1937	MEM Red Sox	3	11	1	0	0	0	0	.091	2B, OF
1938	KC Monarchs	27	89	23	5	2	1	7	.258	1B
1939		30	101	26	7	2	2	3	.257	1B

		G	AB	H	2B	3B	HR	SB	BA	POS

Buck O'Neil *continued*

		G	AB	H	2B	3B	HR	SB	BA	POS
1940		30	113	39	**5**	**3**	1	6	.345	1B
1941		23	88	21	3	2	0	3	.239	1B
1942			**182**	45	6	1	1	0	.247	1B
1943			99	22	1	1	2	1	.222	1B
1944	US Navy									
1945	US Navy									
1946	KC Monarchs	58	197	69	1	1	2	1	.350	1B
1947		46	162	58					.358	1B
1948		42	162	41	6	1	1	3	.253	1B
1949		45	109	36					.330	1B
1950		31	83	21	5	2	1	5	.253	1B
	12 years	(335)	1396	402	(39)	(15)	(11)	(29)	.288	

Red Parnell

PARNELL, ROY

		G	AB	H	2B	3B	HR	SB	BA	POS
1927	BIR Black Barons	78	305	130	19	6	10	**18**	**.426**	OF
1928		64	224	73	18	7	7	3	.326	OF
1929	No data available									
1930	No data available									
1934	WAS Elite Giants	2	9	2	1	0	0	0	.222	OF
1935		26	109	28	4	0	0	2	.257	OF
1936	PHI Stars	34	145	45	3	0	0	1	.310	OF
1937	NY Black Yankees	6	23	11	0	0	0	2	.478	OF
1938	PHI Stars	29	148	30	2	0	5	0	.203	OF
1939		39	134	36	2	1	1	0	.269	OF
1940		55	200	67	9	4	3	0	.335	OF
1941		62	264	67	9	6	1	2	.254	OF
1942		43	166	49	8	0	1	0	.295	OF
1943			146	50	2	3	0	0	.342	OF
	(12 years)	(438)	(1873)	(588)	(77)	(27)	(28)	(28)	(.314)	

Lenny Pearson

PEARSON, LEONARD CURTIS (Horse)   · BR TR 6'2" 200 lbs.
B. May 23, 1918, Akron, Ohio   D. 1984, Newark, N.J.

		G	AB	H	2B	3B	HR	SB	BA	POS
1938	NWK Eagles	8	16	10	0	0	1	1	.625	OF
1939		17	64	16	0	0	0	0	.250	OF, 3B, 1B
1940			199	63	6	2	6	2	.317	3B
1941		20	65	21	1	0	2	0	.323	
1942		31	112	33	7	0	5	0	.295	
1943		26	95	30	5	3	5	2	.316	
1944			172	56	11	2	2	3	.326	
1945		33	123	38	8	5	2	6	.309	
1946			134	37	7	0	5	0	.276	1B
1947	NWK Eagles	80	**313**	91	**19**		10	10	.291	OF
1948			6	4	3	0	1	0	.667	OF
1949	BAL Elite Giants	90	331	110					.332	
	(12 years)	(305)	1630	509	(67)	(12)	(39)	(24)	.312	

Cy Perkins

PERKINS, WILLIAM GEORGE (Bill)   BR TR 6'
B. Ga.

		G	AB	H	2B	3B	HR	SB	BA	POS
1928	BIR Black Barons	53	201	49	7	4	5	2	.244	C
1929	No data available									
1930	BIR Black Barons	59	201	64	7	3	5	7	.318	C
1931	2 teams CLE Cubs PIT Crawfords									
"	total	10	40	8	0	0	1	0	.200	OF, C
1932	PIT Crawfords	22	81	33	3	3	4	0	.407	C
1933		28	82	23	1	2	0	0	.280	C, OF, PH, 3B
1934		6	23	4	1	1	0	0	.174	C, UT
1935		50	184	62	17	4	3	0	.337	C, OF
1936		21	65	16	1	0	0	0	.246	C
1937	Dominican Republic									
1938	PHI Stars	21	115	36	0	0	4	0	.313	C
1939		26	67	20	1	1	2	0	.299	C
1940	BAL Elite Giants	42	147	41	7	3	1	0	.279	C, OF
1941	No data available									
1942	No data available									
1943	No data available									
1944	No data available									
1945	BAL Elite Giants	22	72	16	2	1	0	1	.222	C, OF

	G	AB	H	2B	3B	HR	SB	BA	POS

Cy Perkins *continued*

1946 2 teams NY Black Yankees PHI Stars									
" total	4	14	6	0	0	0	0	.429	C
1947 PHI Stars		36	5	0	0	0	0	.139	C, OF
(13 years)	(364)	(1328)	(383)	(47)	(22)	(25)	(10)	(.288)	

Bruce Petway

PETWAY, BRUCE (Buddy)   BL TR 170 lbs.
B. 1883 (?), Nashville, Tenn. D. July 4, 1941, Chicago, Ill.
Manager 1922–25.

1917 CHI Am. Giants	1	3	0	0	0	0	0	.000	C
1918 No data available									
1919 DET Stars	3	8	0	0	0	0	0	.000	OF
1920	30	97	18	1	0	0	4	.186	C
1921	43	143	44	6	2	2	9	.308	C
1922	30	82	22	2	0	2	3	.268	C
1923	49	89	30	2	1	0	0	.337	C
1924	32	86	29	3	3	1	1	.337	C, OF, 1B
1925	18	36	7	1	0	0	1	.194	C, PH
(8 years)	(206)	(544)	(150)	(15)	(6)	(5)	(18)	(.276)	

Alec Radcliff

RADCLIFF, ALEXANDER   BR TR 6' 190 lbs.
Brother of Ted Radcliffe.
B. July 26, 1905, Mobile, Ala. D. July 18, 1983, Chicago, Ill.

1926 DAY Marcos	1	3	0	0	0	0	0	.000	SS
1932 CHI Am. Giants	42	142	39	9	0	5	2	.275	3B
1933	25	101	33	10	3	0	3	.327	3B
1934	25	94	29	5	0	1	1	.309	3B
1935	42	181	64	10	2	1	0	.354	3B
1936 2 teams NY Cubans CHI Am. Giants									
" total	17	68	24	6	0	1	0	.353	3B
1937 CHI Am. Giants	29	104	24	1	5	1	1	.231	3B, SS
1938	24	64	14	5	3	0	5	.219	SS, 3B
1939	18	65	19	3	3	1	0	.292	3B
1940 No data available									
1941 CHI Am. Giants	3	9	3	1	0	0	0	.333	3B
1942		74	15	1	1	0	0	.203	3B
1943		96	34	1	0	2	1	.354	3B, P
1944	48	174	50	11	0	5	3	.287	3B
1945	50	175	58	7	1	7	3	.331	3B
1946 MEM Red Sox	2	7	1	0	0	0	0	.143	3B, SS
1947 No data available									
1948 No data available									
1949 CHI Am. Giants	57	180	43					.239	3B
(16 years)	(383)	(1537)	(450)	(70)	(18)	(24)	(19)	(.293)	

Double Duty Radcliffe

RADCLIFFE, TED   BR TR 5'10" 212 lbs.
Brother of Alec Radcliff.
B. July 7, 1902, Mobile, Ala.
Manager 1937–38, 1943.

1928 DET Stars	67	256	68	13	4	8	1	.266	C
1929	32	126	39	7	2	3	4	.310	C
1930 STL Stars	56	180	51	11	2	6	4	.283	P, C
1931 2 teams DET Wolves Homestead Grays									
" total	17	47	14	3	1	1	0	.298	C, P
1932 PIT Crawfords	15	47	11	3	0	2	0	.234	C, P
1933 3 teams Homestead Grays CLE Giants COL Blue Birds									
" total	12	47	15	1	1	0	1	.319	P, C
1934 CHI Am. Giants	1	2	2	0	0	0	0	1.000	P, C
1935 BKN Eagles	16	42	11	2	0	0	0	.262	C, P
1936 Semi-pro									
1937 CLA Tigers	24	87	31	3	2	0	0	.356	C
1938 MEM Red Sox	11	31	7	0	0	0	2	.226	C, P, PH
1939	13	26	8	0	0	0	0	.308	P, C, PH
1940 Mexico									
1941 CLE Red Sox	6	6	2	1	0	0	0	.333	P
1942 2 teams BIR Black Barons CHI Am. Giants									
" total		33	11	0	0	0	0	.333	C
1943 CHI Am. Giants		52	13	1	0	0	0	.250	C, P
1944 BIR Black Barons	26	93	20	4	0	0	1	.215	P, C
1945 No data available									
(15 years)	(296)	(1075)	(303)	(49)	(12)	(20)	(13)	(.282)	

	G	AB	H	2B	3B	HR	SB	BA	POS

Frog Redus

REDUS, WILSON   BR   TR   5'5"   155 lbs.
B. Jan. 29, 1905, Muskogee, Okla.   D. 1986 (?), Okla.

	G	AB	H	2B	3B	HR	SB	BA	POS
1924 3 teams IND ABCs CLE Browns STL Stars									
" total	19	70	25	2	2	2	0	.357	OF
1925 STL Stars	70	244	96	15	7	11	0	.393	OF
1926	61	215	71	9	6	6	4	.330	OF
1927	97	367	131	18	7	15	1	.357	OF
1928	73	278	96	12	6	21	1	.345	OF
1929	85	324	104	24	2	11	6	.321	OF
1930		60	21	5	3	3	0	.350	OF
1931	6	16	5	0	0	0	0	.313	OF
1932 No data available									
1933 2 teams COL Blue Birds CLE Red Sox									
" total	21	81	26	6	1	9	1	.321	OF
1934 CLE Red Sox	8	30	11	0	0	0	0	.367	OF
1935 CHI Am. Giants	42	150	26	1	1	1	0	.173	OF
1936	11	50	7	0	0	0	0	.140	OF
1937	27	93	22	2	0	0	2	.237	OF
1938	29	77	22	6	0	1	4	.286	OF
1939 No data available									
1940 CHI Am. Giants	5	8	3	0	0	0	0	.375	OF
(16 years)	(554)	(2063)	(666)	(100)	(35)	(80)	(19)	(.323)	

Orville Riggins

RIGGINS, ORVILLE   TR

	G	AB	H	2B	3B	HR	SB	BA	POS
1920 2 teams CHI Am. Giants DET Stars									
" total	45	160	46	11	2	1	1	.288	SS
1921 DET Stars	52	206	67	17	2	1	4	.325	SS
1922	61	218	75	10	5	12	6	.344	SS
1923	60	223	64	9	3	5	1	.287	SS
1924	60	255	76	7	6	1	5	.298	SS
1925	86	332	92	16	9	8	18	.277	SS
1926	80	295	89	16	7	7	16	.302	SS
1927 CLE Hornets	34	125	42	5	3	3	2	.336	SS
1928 No data available									
1929 NY Lincoln Giants	60	228	70	13	3	4	6	.307	3B, 2B
1930	29	114	39	2	0	5	0	.342	SS
1931 NY Harlem Stars	21	75	18	14	2	0	2	.240	SS
(11 years)	(588)	(2231)	(678)	(120)	(42)	(47)	(61)	(.304)	

Ed Rile

RILE, ED (Huck)   BB   TR(?)   6'4"   230 lbs.

	G	AB	H	2B	3B	HR	SB	BA	POS
1920 2 teams IND ABCs NY Lincoln Giants									
" total	2	8	3	1	0	0	0	.375	P
1921 2 teams NY Lincoln Giants COL Buckeyes									
" total	2	8	4	0	1	0	0	.500	1B, P
1922 CHI Am. Giants	No data available								
1923 No data available									
1924 No data available									
1925 IND ABCs	No data available								
1926	59	215	70	16	5	2	2	.326	1B, P
1927 DET Stars	70	242	96	23	6	10	3	.397	1B, P
1928	84	302	111	27	2	8	7	.368	1B, P
1929	68	251	75	12	2	10	2	.299	1B, P
1930	61	226	73	17	9	8	7	.323	1B, P
1931 BKN Royal Giants	2	5	0	0	0	0	0	.000	1B
(8 years)	(348)	(1257)	(432)	(96)	(25)	(38)	(21)	(.344)	

Jackie Robinson

ROBINSON, JACK ROOSEVELT   BR   TR   5'11½"   195 lbs.
B. Jan. 31, 1919, Cairo, Ga.   D. Oct. 24, 1972, Stamford, Conn.
Hall of Fame 1962.
Major leagues 1947–56.

	G	AB	H	2B	3B	HR	SB	BA	POS
1945 KC Monarchs	47	163	63	14	4	5	13	.387	SS

Neil Robinson

ROBINSON, NEIL   BR   TR   5'11"   182 lbs.
B. July 7, 1908, Grand Rapids, Mich.   D.

	G	AB	H	2B	3B	HR	SB	BA	POS
1936 CIN Tigers	3	13	5	1	1	0	0	.385	OF
1937	25	84	33	4	3	2	0	.393	OF
1938 MEM Red Sox	17	58	19	4	1	4	0	.328	SS
1939	30	70	19	5	1	1	2	.271	OF
1940		49	10	2	0	1	0	.204	OF

		G	AB	H	2B	3B	HR	SB	BA	POS

Neil Robinson *continued*

		G	AB	H	2B	3B	HR	SB	BA	POS
1941		9	29	10	1	1	1	0	.345	OF
1942		19	70	22	6	1	3	0	.314	OF
1943			49	11	1	2	3	0	.224	OF
1944		64	232	74	12	5	4	17	.319	OF
1945		60	198	60	7	1	3	3	.303	OF
1946		1	3	0	0	0	0	0	.000	OF
1947								2		
1948		74	258	86	**23**	4	7	4	.333	OF
1949		71	232	63					.272	OF
1950		66	251	71	14	3	10	7	.283	OF
15 years		(439)	(1596)	(483)	(80)	(23)	(41)	(33)	(.303)	

Bullet Joe Rogan

ROGAN, WILBER (Bullet Joe)   BR TR 5'7"
B. 1898, Oklahoma City, Okla. D. 1964

		G	AB	H	2B	3B	HR	SB	BA	POS
1920	KC Monarchs	19	76	21	4	3	0	6	.276	P, UT
1921		45	137	36	7	2	3	13	.263	P, OF, 2B
1922		74	251	88	9	8	**16**	17	.351	P, OF
1923		27	89	37	3	1	7	6	.416	P, OF
1924		52	153	63	11	7	5	0	.412	P, OF
1925		58	161	59	12	8	3	6	.366	P, OF
1926		46	118	37	6	3	2	3	.314	P, OF
1927		50	103	34	3	2	2	1	.330	P, OF
1928		62	201	71	15	4	6	5	.353	2B, OF, P
1929		76	270	92	18	8	7	23	.341	OF, P
1930		28	103	32	5	0	1	6	.311	OF, P
1931		7	24	7	1	0	0	2	.292	OF
1932	Team not in the league									
1933	Team not in the league									
1934	Team not in the league									
1935	Team not in the league									
1936	KC Monarchs	3	5	3	0	0	0	0	.600	1B, P
1937		13	22	11	1	1	0	1	.500	OF, P, 1B, PH
1938		10	33	8	0	0	0	1	.242	OF, PH
15 years		570	1746	599	95	47	52	90	.343	

Nat Rogers

ROGERS, NAT   BL TR 5'11" 160 lbs.
B. June 7, 1893, Spartanburg, S.C. D.

		G	AB	H	2B	3B	HR	SB	BA	POS
1927	2 teams MEM Red Sox CHI Am. Giants									
"	total	66	243	72	12	7	3	5	.296	OF
1928	2 teams CHI Am. Giants MEM Red Sox									
"	total	36	132	44	6	4	2	2	.333	OF
1929	MEM Red Sox	52	197	56	7	1	3	0	.284	OF
1930	2 teams MEM Red Sox BIR Black Barons									
"	total	69	251	85	21	7	5	5	.339	OF
1931	CHI Am. Giants	18	66	28	6	1	0	1	.424	OF
1932		39	134	42	8	1	0	4	.313	OF
1937	MEM Red Sox	6	24	9	0	0	0	0	.375	OF
1938		16	51	16	2	1	1	1	.314	OF
1939		11	25	2	0	0	0	0	.080	OF, PH
1940			28	6	0	0	0	0	.214	
1941		2	6	3	2	0	0	0	.500	
1942	No data available									
1943	MEM Red Sox		32	4	0	0	0	0	.125	OF
1944	2 teams MEM Red Sox CHI Am. Giants									
"	total	26	46	8	2	1	0	0	.174	OF
1945	MEM Red Sox	22	35	8	1	0	0	0	.229	OF, PH
(14 years)		(363)	(1270)	(383)	(67)	(23)	(14)	(18)	(.302)	

Johnny Russell

RUSSELL, JOHN HENRY (Pistol)   BR TR

		G	AB	H	2B	3B	HR	SB	BA	POS
1922	STL Giants	64	252	77	8	5	3	10	.306	2B
1923	MEM Red Sox	18	66	22	2	3	0	2	.333	2B
1924		53	203	58	8	4	0	6	.286	2B
1925		72	277	78	10	4	0	2	.282	2B
1926	STL Stars	82	313	97	14	6	5	15	.310	2B
1927		83	273	78	10	5	10	2	.286	2B
1928		73	269	68	6	2	2	0	.253	2B

		G	AB	H	2B	3B	HR	SB	BA	POS

Johnny Russell *continued*

		G	AB	H	2B	3B	HR	SB	BA	POS
1929		59	199	53	1	2	1	0	.266	2B
1930		72	260	79	11	6	5	2	.304	2B
1931	2 teams IND ABCs PIT Crawfords									
"	total	8	21	6	0	0	0	0	.286	2B
1932	2 teams DET Wolves PIT Crawfords									
"	total	41	149	41	4	1	0	0	.275	2B
1933	PIT Crawfords	30	109	23	8	0	0	0	.211	2B
	12 years	655	2391	680	82	38	26	39	.284	

Lazaro Salazar

SALAZAR, LAZARO BL TL 5'9" 177 lbs.
B. Feb. 4, 1912, Havana, Cuba   D. Apr. 25, 1957

		G	AB	H	2B	3B	HR	SB	BA	POS
1930	NY Cubans	39	138	31	3	2	1	1	.225	OF, P
1932		14	45	16	0	0	0	3	.356	P, OF
1933		3	11	7	0	0	0	0	.636	OF
1934	Team not in the league									
1935	NY Cubans	46	146	52	12	2	3	4	.356	1B, P, OF
1936		28	98	36	6	0	4	**4**	**.367**	OF, PH
1937	Team not in the league									
1938	Team not in the league									
1939	No data available									
	(5 years)	(130)	(438)	(142)	(21)	(4)	(8)	(12)	(.324)	

Louis Santop

SANTOP, LOUIS LOFTIN (Top) BL TR 6'4" 242 lbs.
B. Jan. 17, 1890, Tyler, Tex.   D. Jan. 6, 1942, Philadelphia, Pa.

		G	AB	H	2B	3B	HR	SB	BA	POS
1916	NY Lincoln Giants	4	16	4	0	1	0	0	.250	C
1917		1						1		C
1918	PHI Hilldales	4	12	5	0	2	1	0	.417	C
1919		4	16	4	0	0	0	1	.250	C
1920		16	59	16	1	0	0	0	.271	C
1921		30	107	33	6	1	**6**	6	.308	C, OF
1922		7	22	12	2	0	0	0	.545	C, 1B
1923		15	55	14	3	2	1	4	.255	C
1924		48	167	65	7	1	4	2	.389	C
1925		21	30	5	1	0	0	1	.167	C, PH
1926		12	26	10	0	0	0	1	.385	C
	11 years	162	(510)	(168)	(20)	(7)	13	(15)	(.329)	

George Scales

SCALES, GEORGE (Tubby) BR TR 5'11" 195 lbs.
B. Aug. 16, 1900, Talladega, Ala.   D. Apr. 1976, Los Angeles, Calif.

		G	AB	H	2B	3B	HR	SB	BA	POS
1921	STL Giants	10	35	7	2	0	0	1	.200	
1922		24	72	15	7	0	1	1	.208	3B
1923	2 teams STL Stars NY Lincoln Giants									
"	total	50	154	66	10	7	11	6	.429	3B, 2B
1924	NY Lincoln Giants	54	180	66	14	1	5	4	.367	2B
1925	2 teams NY Lincoln Giants Homestead Grays									
"	total	31	108	39	8	0	5	2	.361	SS, 3B
1926	2 teams NY Lincoln Giants Homestead Grays									
"	total	13	45	10	1	1	0	0	.222	SS
1927	NY Lincoln Giants	19	65	29	8	1	3	1	.446	3B
1928		36	130	44	**17**	2	8	**10**	.338	IF
1929		48	181	73	12	0	9	6	.403	2B
1930	Homestead Grays	18	66	20	0	2	2	2	.303	2B, 3B
1931	2 teams Homestead Grays NY Black Yankees									
"	total	31	112	44	9	5	2	0	**.393**	2B, 3B
1932	NY Black Yankees	13	46	10	3	0	1	0	.217	2B
1933		2	8	2	0	0	0	0	.250	OF
1934		14	48	7	2	0	0	2	.146	2B
1935	Homestead Grays	41	152	40	7	0	4	0	.263	1B, 2B, 3B, PH
1936	NY Black Yankees	15	58	13	0	1	4	1	.224	3B
1937	Dominican Republic									
1938	BAL Elite Giants	9	16	3	0	0	0	0	.188	3B
1939	NY Black Yankees	14	47	10	0	1	2	0	.213	3B
1940	BAL Elite Giants	41	115	35	10	1	5	1	.304	
1941		25	59	14	1	0	2	0	.237	IF
1942		39	127	31	8	0	2	0	.244	
1943			99	25	6	1	0	0	.253	1B, 3B
1944		26	80	24	7	1	0	0	.300	IF

		G	AB	H	2B	3B	HR	SB	BA	POS

George Scales *continued*

		G	AB	H	2B	3B	HR	SB	BA	POS
1945		19	55	17	0	2	0	0	.309	IF
1946		5	10	4	0	0	0	0	.400	1B
	25 years	(597)	2068	648	132	26	66	37	.313	

Dick Seay

SEAY, RICHARD WILLIAM   BR TR 5'8" 160 lbs.
   B. Nov. 30, 1904, West New York, N.J.   D. Apr. 6, 1981, Jersey City, N.J.

		G	AB	H	2B	3B	HR	SB	BA	POS
1926	BAL Black Sox	11	33	4	0	0	0	0	.121	SS
1927	BKN Royal Giants	13	49	9	1	0	0	0	.184	SS
1928	Team not in the league									
1929	Team not in the league									
1930	BKN Royal Giants	6	20	4	0	0	0	0	.200	2B
1931		4	14	0	0	0	0	0	.000	2B
1932	BAL Black Sox	29	104	32	0	0	0	0	.308	2B
1933		20	73	22	0	0	0	3	.301	2B
1934	PHI Stars	65	249	34	0	0	0	3	.137	2B
1935		71	274	59	2	3	3	2	.215	2B
1936	NY Black Yankees	1	6	3	0	0	0	0	.500	2B
1937	NWK Eagles	19	78	9	1	0	1	2	.115	2B
1938		15	57	16	0	0	0	0	.281	2B
1939		29	112	20	0	0	2	0	.179	2B
1940		27	107	33	4	1	3	2	.308	2B
1941	NY Black Yankees		41	10	0	0	1	0	.244	
1942			69	15	3	0	1	2	.217	2B
1943	US Army									
1944	US Army									
1945	US Army									
1946	NY Black Yankees		28	5	0	0	0			2B
1947			78	15	1	0	0	1	.192	2B
	16 years	(310)	(1364)	313	17	4	11	15	(.229)	

Harry Simpson

SIMPSON, HARRY LEON (Suitcase)   BL TR 6'1" 180 lbs.
   B. Dec. 3, 1925, Atlanta, Ga.   D. Apr. 3, 1979, Akron, Ohio
   Major leagues 1951–59.

		G	AB	H	2B	3B	HR	SB	BA	POS
1946	PHIL Stars		51	17	0	1	3	1	.333	OF
1947			135	33	5		1	0	.244	OF
	2 years		186	50	5	(1)	4	(1)	.269	

Chino Smith

SMITH, CHARLIE   BL TR

		G	AB	H	2B	3B	HR	SB	BA	POS
1925	BKN Royal Giants	35	131	43	7	0	5	2	.328	2B, OF
1927		24	85	41	8	2	5	2	.482	OF, UT
1928		9	37	10	2	1	0	0	.270	OF
1929	NY Lincoln Giants	60	229	104	22	1	**20**	4	**.454**	OF
1930		34	126	59	17	5	7	3	.468	OF
	5 years	162	608	257	56	9	37	11	**.423**	

Turkey Stearnes

STEARNES, NORMAN THOMAS   BL TL 6' 170 lbs.
   Name also spelled Turkey Stearns.
   B. May 8, 1901, Nashville, Tenn.   D. Sept. 4, 1979, Detroit, Mich.

		G	AB	H	2B	3B	HR	SB	BA	POS
1923	DET Stars	60	244	89	16	**15**	**17**	1	.365	OF
1924		60	240	86	7	**12**	10	3	.358	OF
1925		88	336	124	22	11	**18**	11	.369	OF
1926		82	301	113	24	10	20	13	.375	OF
1927		85	312	108	**24**	**12**	20	13	.346	OF
1928		82	313	102	18	7	**24**	5	.326	OF
1929		69	259	98	15	5	19	12	.378	OF
1930	2 teams NY Lincoln Giants DET Stars									
"	total	56	215	73	15	12	7	7	.340	OF
1931	2 teams DET Stars KC Monarchs									
"	total	40	137	48	9	3	8	5	.350	OF
1932	CHI Am. Giants	**43**	141	**42**	**10**	**4**	**5**	13	.298	OF
1933		30	120	41	11	1	7	2	.342	OF
1934		27	107	40	2	4	6	1	.374	OF
1935		43	149	64	8	4	6	0	**.430**	OF
1936	PHI Stars	40	178	53	1	0	7	1	.298	OF
1937	2 teams DET Stars CHI Am. Giants									
"	total	18	47	18	2	2	2	0	.383	OF

		G	AB	H	2B	3B	HR	SB	BA	POS

Turkey Stearnes *continued*

		G	AB	H	2B	3B	HR	SB	BA	POS
1938	2 teams CHI Am. Giants KC Monarchs									
"	total	17	48	14	4	2	2	1	.292	OF
1939	KC Monarchs	**35**	120	**42**	8	0	**2**	4	.350	OF
1940		30	105	31	3	2	5	1	.295	
	18 years	905	3372	1186	199	106	**185**	93	.359	

Jake Stephens

STEPHENS, PAUL EUGENE BR TR 5'6" 158 lbs.
Name also spelled Jake Stevens.
B. Feb. 10, 1900, Pleasureville, Pa.   D. Feb. 5, 1981, York, Pa.

		G	AB	H	2B	3B	HR	SB	BA	POS
1921	PHI Hilldales	7	26	4	2	0	0	0	.154	SS
1922		1	4	1	0	0	0	0	.250	SS
1923		6	11	0	0	0	0	0	.000	SS
1924		28	105	22	4	1	0	3	.210	SS
1925		51	172	37	9	2	0	9	.215	SS
1926		65	205	51	5	1	0	13	.249	SS
1927		60	212	45	2	2	0	8	.212	SS
1928		47	194	31	2	0	0	0	.160	SS
1929		5	20	9	1	0	0	1	.450	SS
1930	Homestead Grays	17	74	24	1	2	1	1	.324	SS
1931		10	40	8	4	0	0	0	.200	SS
1932	2 teams Homestead Grays PIT Crawfords									
"	total	29	114	23	2	0	0	2	.202	SS
1933	PHI Stars	12	47	15	0	0	1	0	.319	SS
1934		64	130	30	2	0	0	3	.231	SS
1935		61	220	51	0	0	0	0	.232	SS
1936	NY Black Yankees	14	54	9	0	0	0	0	.167	SS
1937		9	26	7	0	0	0	0	.269	SS, 2B
	17 years	486	1654	367	34	8	2	40	.222	

Ed Stone

STONE, ED BL TR 6'2" 190 lbs.
B. 1909 or 1910, Black Cat, Del.   D. Mar. 20, 1983, New York, N.Y.

		G	AB	H	2B	3B	HR	SB	BA	POS
1931	AC Bacharach Giants	4	16	5	0	0	0	0	.313	OF
1932	WIL Hornets	1	3	0	0	0	0	0	.000	OF
1933	AC Bacharach Giants	2	8	2	0	0	0	0	.250	OF
1935	BKN Eagles	45	167	54	4	2	3	2	.323	OF
1936	NWK Eagles	13	41	13	2	2	1	0	.317	OF
1937		22	82	15	1	3	4	0	.183	OF
1938		10	45	10	0	0	3	0	.222	OF
1939		29	107	**47**	2	1	4	1	.439	OF
1940			141	35	3	5	2	1	.248	OF
1941		2	8	1	0	0	0	0	.125	OF
1942		31	118	27	4	1	3	0	.229	OF
1943		12	36	9	1	1	1	2	.250	
1944	PHI Stars	37	140	42	6	7	1	4	.300	OF
1945		35	131	39	9	0	1	3	.298	OF
	14 years	(243)	1043	299	32	22	23	13	.287	

Mule Suttles

SUTTLES, GEORGE BR TR 6'1" 212 lbs.
B. Mar. 2, 1901, Brockton, Ala.   D. 1968, Newark, N.J.

		G	AB	H	2B	3B	HR	SB	BA	POS
1923	BIR Black Barons	35	132	34	4	3	1	3	.258	OF
1924		85	296	93	23	3	2	1	.314	OF
1925		74	266	88	5	5	13	6	.331	OF
1926	STL Stars	87	342	**143**	25	19	27	11	**.418**	1B, OF
1927		30	79	36	8	3	8	1	.456	1B
1928		72	274	102	12	**9**	19	1	**.372**	1B
1929		82	304	108	**29**	7	20	3	.355	1B
1930	2 teams STL Stars BAL Black Sox									
"	total	50	192	74	14	8	17	0	.385	1B, OF
1931	2 teams STL Stars WAS Black Senators									
"	total	20	59	18	6	1	2	1	.305	1B
1932	2 teams DET Wolves WAS Pilots									
"	total	28	96	33	11	0	5	1	.344	1B
1933	CHI Am. Giants	30	94	25	4	1	7	4	.266	1B
1934		26	104	29	2	1	6	1	.279	1B
1935		38	111	34	6	0	7	1	.306	1B, OF, PH
1936	NWK Eagles	30	118	41	3	1	10	0	.347	1B
1937		27	91	29	2	0	**12**	0	.319	1B, OF

		G	AB	H	2B	3B	HR	SB	BA	POS

Mule Suttles *continued*

		G	AB	H	2B	3B	HR	SB	BA	POS
1938		21	55	15	0	0	9	1	.273	1B
1939	2 teams NWK Eagles IND ABCs									
"	total	30	123	35	3	2	10	0	.285	1B
1940	NWK Eagles	37	125	36	7	0	5	2	.288	OF
1941	NY Black Yankees		46	12	1	0	0	0	.261	1B
1942		7	12	5	1	0	0	1	.417	
1943	No data available									
1944	NWK Eagles	21	43	11	1	0	3	0	.256	1B
	(21 years)	(830)	(2962)	(1001)	(167)	(63)	(183)	(38)	.338	

Ben Taylor

TAYLOR, BEN BL TL 6' 190 lbs.
Brother of C.L. Taylor and Candy Jim Taylor.
B. 1888, Anderson, S.C. D. Jan. 23, 1953, Baltimore, Md.
Manager 1924, 1926–29.

		G	AB	H	2B	3B	HR	SB	BA	POS
1919	AC Bacharach Giants	5	21	3	0	0	0	0	.143	1B
1920	IND ABCs	40	133	43	9	1	3	8	.323	1B, P
1921		77	268	109	21	6	4	14	.407	1B
1922		64	257	92	24	4	2	1	.358	1B
1923	WAS Potomacs	Team not in the league								
1924		59	207	65	4	1	2	4	.314	1B
1925	HBG Giants	67	251	82	12	5	3	0	.327	1B
1926	BAL Black Sox	30	99	24	2	1	0	2	.242	1B
1927		52	189	58	12	6	1	0	.307	1B
1928		31	119	40	5	1	2	0	.336	1B
1929		18	59	19	1	0	1	1	.322	1B
	10 years	443	1603	535	90	25	18	30	.334	

Clint Thomas

THOMAS, CLINTON C. (Buckeye) BR TR 5'8" 185 lbs.
B. Nov. 25, 1896, Greenup, Ky.

		G	AB	H	2B	3B	HR	SB	BA	POS
1921	COL Buckeyes	56	221	62	7	9	5	7	.281	2B
1922	DET Stars	60	231	79	15	7	7	7	.342	2B, OF
1923	PHI Hilldales	25	105	23	2	1	1	5	.219	OF
1924		70	233	83	7	6	5	11	.356	OF
1925		67	241	86	21	3	6	16	.357	OF
1926		88	326	102	16	9	8	23	.313	OF
1927		57	202	53	9	3	1	5	.262	OF
1928	3 teams PHI Hilldales AC Bacharach Giants NY Lincoln Giants									
"	total	47	186	44	6	5	2	2	.237	OF
1929	AC Bacharach Giants	31	119	41	6	0	7	5	.345	OF
1930	NY Lincoln Giants	34	134	47	18	2	2	0	.351	OF
1931	NY Harlem Stars	22	78	13	1	1	0	1	.167	OF
1932	2 teams IND ABCs NY Black Yankees									
"	total	46	164	48	12	0	2	8	.293	OF
1933	NY Black Yankees	2	9	2	0	0	0	0	.222	OF
1934		16	48	11	0	0	2	0	.229	OF
1936	2 teams NY Cubans NWK Eagles									
"	total	17	41	9	0	0	0	8	.220	OF
1937	NY Black Yankees	14	43	12	1	1	3	0	.279	OF
1938		3	10	2	1	0	0	0	.200	OF
	17 years	655	2391	717	122	47	51	98	.300	

Showboat Thomas

THOMAS, DAVID BL TL 6'0" 180 lbs.
B. 1904

		G	AB	H	2B	3B	HR	SB	BA	POS
1930	BAL Black Sox	8	26	8	1	0	0	0	.308	1B
1931		61	219	39	7	1	3	0	.178	1B
1932	2 teams BAL Black Sox NY Black Yankees									
"	total	24	90	21	1	0	1	0	.233	1B
1933	NY Black Yankees	3	9	3	0	0	1	0	.333	1B
1934		15	52	10	0	0	0	0	.192	1B
1935	NY Cubans	17	66	20	3	1	1	0	.303	1B
1936		31	129	32	6	0	0	0	.248	1B
1937	No data available									
1938	WAS Black Senators	9	38	13	2	1	1	0	.342	1B
1940	NY Cubans	2	7	0	0	0	0	0	.000	1B
1941		2	6	2	0	1	0	0	.333	1B
1942		17	65	15	3	3	0	0	.231	1B
1943			123	41	8	0	2	0	.333	1B

	G	AB	H	2B	3B	HR	SB	BA	POS

Showboat Thomas *continued*

		G	AB	H	2B	3B	HR	SB	BA	POS
1944	No data available									
1945	NY Cubans	20	71	18	5	3	1	1	.254	1B
1946			84	33	3	0	1	0	.393	1B
	(14 years)	(209)	(985)	(255)	(39)	(10)	(11)	(1)	(.259)	

Hank Thompson

THOMPSON, HENRY CURTIS   BL   TR   5'9"   174 lbs.
    B. Dec. 8, 1925, Oklahoma City, Okla.   D. Sept. 30, 1969, Fresno, Calif.
    Major leagues 1947–1956.

		G	AB	H	2B	3B	HR	SB	BA	POS
1943	KC Monarchs		70	22	6	1	2	1	.314	2B
1944	Military service									
1945	KC Monarchs	5	6	1	0	0	0	0	.167	2B
1946		8	27	6	0	0	4	2	.222	2B
1947		48	189	65	3	2	2	0	.344	IF
1948		70	267	100	20	8	11	**20**	.375	IF
	5 years	(131)	559	194	29	11	19	23	.347	

Cristobal Torriente

TORRIENTE, CRISTOBAL   BL   TL   5'10"   190 lbs.
    B. 1895, Cuba   D. 1938 (?), New York, N.Y.

		G	AB	H	2B	3B	HR	SB	BA	POS
1914	CHI Am. Giants	3	11	2	2	2	0	0	.182	OF, P
1915	NY Cubans	9	28	13	1	5	0	2	.464	OF
1920	CHI Am. Giants	35	129	53	11	4	2	5	.411	OF, P
1921		64	201	68	5	**10**	7	18	.338	OF, P
1922		36	117	40	1	2	3	3	.342	OF, P
1923		63	233	**96**	18	3	7	1	**.412**	OF, P
1924		72	253	85	22	4	9	11	.336	OF
1925		86	292	70	8	6	6	2	.240	OF
1926	KC Monarchs	70	254	86	17	5	4	5	.339	OF
1927	DET Stars	83	297	95	17	2	4	6	.320	OF, P
1928		40	119	39	5	3	2	3	.328	OF, P
1932	CLE Cubs	1	4	1	0	0	0	0	.250	1B
	12 years	562	1938	648	107	46	44	56	.334	

Tetelo Vargas

VARGAS, JUAN ESTEBAN VARGAS MARCANO   BR   TR
    B. Apr. 11, 1906, Santo Domingo de Guzman, Dominican Republic   D. 1971, Guayama, Puerto Rico

		G	AB	H	2B	3B	HR	SB	BA	POS
1931	NY Cubans	5	20	6	1	0	0	0	.300	OF
1938		1	4	2	0	0	0	0	.500	OF
1939		15	55	17	1	0	1	0	.309	OF
1940	No data available									
1941	NY Cubans	14	49	11	0	0	0	0	.224	
1942		15	52	15	3	1	0	1	.288	
1943			122	61	8	3	0	1	.500	
1944		31	108	29	8	3	0	2	.269	
	(7 years)	(81)	(410)	(141)	(21)	(7)	(1)	(4)	(.344)	

Frank Warfield

WARFIELD, FRANCIS XAVIER   BR   TR   5'7"   170 lbs.
    B. 1895, Indianapolis, Ind.   D. July 24, 1932, Pittsburgh, Pa.
    Manager 1925–28, 1932.

		G	AB	H	2B	3B	HR	SB	BA	POS
1920	DET Stars	48	199	54	11	4	1	5	.271	2B, 3B
1921		54	197	53	8	5	2	9	.269	2B
1922		58	228	78	10	3	0	10	.342	2B, 3B
1923	PHI Hilldales	26	100	30	9	2	0	5	.300	2B
1924		71	240	82	16	1	2	**20**	.342	2B
1925		66	230	71	11	5	3	14	.309	2B
1926		88	331	83	10	3	3	12	.251	2B
1927		64	225	49	7	5	0	**10**	.218	2B
1928		53	210	41	1	1	2	0	.195	2B
1929	BAL Black Sox	59	232	61	4	1	0	8	.263	2B
1930		28	112	24	2	0	0	0	.214	2B
1931	2 teams BAL Black Sox WAS Pilots									
"	total	58	201	31	2	0	0	1	.154	2B, 3B
1932	WAS Pilots	12	43	10	0	0	0	1	.233	2B
	13 years	685	2548	667	91	30	13	95	.262	

		G	AB	H	2B	3B	HR	SB	BA	POS

Willie Wells

WELLS, WILLIE JAMES (Devil)   BR TR 5'9" 166 lbs.
Father of Willie Wells, Jr.
B. Aug. 10, 1908, Austin, Tex.   D. Jan. 22, 1989, Austin, Tex.

Year	Team	G	AB	H	2B	3B	HR	SB	BA	POS
1924	STL Stars	54	208	55	16	3	1	2	.264	SS
1925		89	325	96	13	6	6	15	.295	SS
1926		78	254	96	13	3	12	8	.378	SS
1927		96	351	**134**	18	5	23	5	.382	SS
1928		72	289	102	22	4	17	2	.353	SS
1929		88	334	**123**	21	6	**27**	21	.368	SS
1930		72	273	110	31	3	14	16	**.403**	SS
1931		19	68	19	1	0	1	0	.279	SS
1932	3 teams KC Monarchs DET Wolves Homestead Grays									
"	total	36	130	34	14	3	1	6	.262	SS
1933	CHI Am. Giants	26	109	31	3	3	0	**6**	.284	SS
1934		26	104	25	7	5	0	2	.240	SS
1935		42	163	55	**14**	3	2	1	.337	SS
1936	NWK Eagles	27	101	27	5	0	3	0	.267	SS
1937		21	85	25	4	0	1	1	.294	SS
1938		15	53	21	1	0	3	1	.396	SS
1939		28	104	36	2	1	4	1	.346	SS
1940	Mexico									
1941	Mexico									
1942	NWK Eagles	34	131	45	6	0	5	**4**	**.344**	SS
1943	No data available									
1944	Mexico									
1945	2 teams NY Black Yankees NWK Eagles									
"	total	37	129	36	9	1	0	0	.279	SS
1946	2 teams NY Black Yankees BAL Elite Giants									
"	total		94	24	3	2	1	0	.255	2B, 3B
1947	No data available									
1948	MEM Red Sox	49	137	45	9	1	2	0	.328	SS
	(20 years)	(909)	(3442)	(1139)	(212)	(49)	(123)	(91)	.331	

Edgar Wesley

WESLEY, EDGAR   BL

Year	Team	G	AB	H	2B	3B	HR	SB	BA	POS
1920	DET Stars	50	188	52	**13**	1	**11**	3	.277	1B
1921	2 teams DET Stars COL Buckeyes									
"	total	40	145	42	8	0	7	3	.290	1B
1922	DET Stars	61	218	75	10	5	12	6	.344	1B
1923		61	225	76	13	0	**17**	0	.338	1B
1924	HBG Giants	55	177	47	7	5	2	2	.266	1B
1925	DET Stars	57	214	89	13	6	**18**	9	**.416**	1B
1926		74	257	77	6	1	15	5	.300	1B
1927	2 teams DET Stars CLE Hornets									
"	total	37	140	59	8	2	0	2	.421	1B
1931	AC Bacharach Giants	4	13	1	0	0	0	0	.077	1B
	9 years	439	1577	518	78	20	82	30	.328	

Jim West

WEST, JIM (Shifty)   BB TR 6'2" 216 lbs.
B. 1912, Mobile, Ala.   D. 1970 (?), Philadelphia, Pa.

Year	Team	G	AB	H	2B	3B	HR	SB	BA	POS
1930	2 teams BIR Black Barons MEM Red Sox									
"	total	44	149	39	8	2	1	3	.262	1B
1931	CLE Cubs	16	57	12	2	1	1	0	.211	1B
1932	2 teams BIR Black Barons MEM Red Sox									
"	total	9	30	10	0	1	0	2	.333	1B
1933	NAS Elite Giants	22	79	17	1	0	0	0	.215	1B
1934	BAL Elite Giants	20	83	35	4	1	0	1	.422	C, OF
1935	COL Elite Giants	22	72	20	1	5	4	0	.278	1B
1936	WAS Elite Giants	19	62	25	3	1	0	0	.403	1B
1937		29	107	40	1	0	6	0	.374	1B
1938	BAL Elite Giants	21	77	31	**5**	0	2	0	.403	1B
1939	2 teams BAL Elite Giants PHI Stars									
"	total	42	149	38	5	2	2	0	.255	1B
1940	PHI Stars	62	223	70	12	5	1	1	.314	1B
1941		70	246	55	2	1	3	0	.224	1B
1942		**47**	**168**	47	6	**5**	3	1	.280	1B
1943			164	52	5	3	0	2	.317	1B
1944		47	176	60	11	**7**	1	1	.341	1B
1945		41	166	44	2	5	3	0	.265	1B
1946	No data available									
1947	PHI Stars		33	8	1	0	1	0	.242	1B
	(17 years)	(511)	(2041)	(603)	(69)	(39)	(28)	(11)	(.295)	

		G	AB	H	2B	3B	HR	SB	BA	POS

Chaney White

WHITE, CHANEY   BR   TL   5'10"   195 lbs.
B. Dallas, Tex.   D. 1966 (?)

		G	AB	H	2B	3B	HR	SB	BA	POS
1919	PHI Hilldales	8	34	6	0	0	0	0	.176	OF
1920		10	40	6	0	0	0	0	.150	OF
1921		37	144	40	10	2	1	11	.278	OF
1922		7	32	10	2	0	0	3	.313	OF
1923	AC Bacharach Giants	14	52	20	3	1	0	1	.385	OF
1924	2 teams AC Bacharach Giants WAS Potomacs									
"	total	43	165	58	4	2	2	4	.352	OF
1925	2 teams WIL Hornets AC Bacharach Giants									
"	total	54	207	74	10	3	6	9	.357	OF
1926	AC Bacharach Giants	35	122	36	6	2	1	2	.295	OF
1927		56	208	57	7	0	2	4	.274	OF
1928			237	80	1	4	5	2	.338	OF
1929		47	183	66	7	3	4	1	.361	OF
1930	Homestead Grays	15	63	21	2	0	1	0	.333	OF
1931	PHI Hilldales	54	214	59	4	2	1	1	.276	OF
1932	No data available									
1933	PHI Stars	11	44	12	1	0	0	0	.273	OF
1934		27	108	29	1	0	0	0	.269	OF
1935		68	270	68	1	0	1	1	.252	OF
	(16 years)	(486)	(2123)	(642)	(59)	(19)	(24)	(39)	(.302)	

Artie Wilson

WILSON, ARTHUR LEE   BL   TR   5'11"   162 lbs.
B. Oct. 28, 1920, Springfield, Ala.
Major leagues 1951.

		G	AB	H	2B	3B	HR	SB	BA	POS
1940	BIR Black Barons	2	7	2					.286	
1942	No data available									
1943	No data available									
1944	BIR Black Barons	65	266	92	9	6	0	17	.346	2B
1945		63	249	90	8	2	3	17	.361	2B
1946		2	4	0	0	0	0	1	.000	2B
1947		53	212	79	1	0	0	0	.373	2B
1948		76	333	134	19	8	2	10	.402	2B
	(6 years)	(261)	(1071)	(397)	(37)	(16)	(5)	(45)	(.371)	

Jud Wilson

WILSON, JUDSON ERNEST (Boojum)   BL   TR   5'8"   195 lbs.
B. Feb. 28, 1899, Remington, Va.   D. June 26, 1963, Washington, D.C.

		G	AB	H	2B	3B	HR	SB	BA	POS
1922	BAL Black Sox	7	22	10	0	0	0	0	.455	UT
1923		44	158	59	8	3	3	4	.373	1B
1924		49	167	63	8	0	2	6	.377	1B
1925		54	200	79	14	3	6	9	.395	1B, 3B
1926		32	104	36	7	1	3	19	.346	UT
1927		53	196	92	22	4	7	10	.469	3B, UT
1928		27	109	41	14	0	2	5	.376	IF
1929		52	217	76	10	1	10	20	.350	1B, OF
1930		38	148	55	12	2	2	2	.372	3B
1931	Homestead Grays	32	127	41	10	3	3	0	.323	3B
1932	2 teams Homestead Grays PIT Crawfords									
"	total	18	72	20	1	0	1	0	.278	3B
1933	PHI Stars	13	48	17	2	0	1	0	.354	3B
1934		63	243	83	6	1	7	2	.342	
1935		65	250	81	5	1	7	3	.324	1B, OF
1936		41	168	53	2	1	6	0	.315	1B
1937		23	88	34	5	0	1	0	.386	1B, 3B
1938		27	89	19	1	1	0	0	.213	3B, 1B
1939		42	135	33	5	1	3	0	.244	3B
1940	WAS Homestead Grays	36	97	27	4	0	0	0	.278	3B, PH
1941		19	48	20	2	1	0	1	.417	3B
1942		32	67	15	3	1	1	0	.224	
1943			119	41	4	9	0	0	.345	
1944		5	12	5	0	1	0	0	.417	PH, IF
1945	No data available									
1946	Homestead Grays		123	36	3	6	0	2	.293	3B
	(24 years)	(772)	(3007)	(1036)	(148)	(40)	(65)	(83)	(.345)	

Parnell Woods

WOODS, PARNELL   TR
B. 1912   D. July 22, 1977, Cleveland, Ohio

		G	AB	H	2B	3B	HR	SB	BA	POS
1936	BIR Black Barons	2	6	1	0	0	0	0	.167	
1937		23	93	25	1	3	5	0	.269	3B, 2B
1938		14	43	11	1	1	1	1	.256	3B, 2B

		G	AB	H	2B	3B	HR	SB	BA	POS
Parnell Woods *continued*										
1939	CLE Bears	21	67	23	1	3	0	1	.343	3B
1940	BIR Black Barons	16	66	21	2	0	0	0	.318	
1941	JAC Red Caps	4	11	1	0	0	0	2	.091	
1942	2 teams JAC Red Caps CIN Buckeyes									
"	total		35	12	0	1	1	0	.343	3B
1943	CLE Buckeyes		59	17	2	1	0	1	.288	3B
1944		62	217	70	10	6	1	11	.323	3B
1945	2 teams CLE Buckeyes PHI Stars									
"	total	74	290	80	14	4	0	16	.276	3B
1950	MEM Red Sox	24	46	8	3	0	1	0	.174	
	11 years	(240)	933	269	34	19	9	32	.288	

		G	AB	H	2B	3B	HR	SB	BA	POS
WRIGHT, BURNIS (Wild Bill)								BB TR 6'4" 225 lbs.		
1932	NAS Elite Giants	12	40	12	1	1	0	2	.300	
1933		21	78	19	2	2	0	0	.244	OF
1934		12	50	6	0	1	3	2	.300	OF
1935	COL Elite Giants	21	82	20	1	0	2	4	.244	OF
1936	WAS Elite Giants	21	74	25	2	5	1	2	.338	OF
1937		31	100	41	4	2	7	0	**.410**	OF
1938	BAL Elite Giants	22	81	19	2	0	0	3	.235	OF
1939		27	99	40	1	3	3	2	.404	OF
1940	Mexico									
1941	Mexico									
1942	BAL Elite Giants	40	146	43	8	2	1	2	.295	OF
1943	Mexico									
1944	Mexico									
1945	BAL Elite Giants	44	165	62	12	5	3	5	.376	OF
	10 years	251	915	287	33	21	20	22	.314	

Bill Wright

Negro Leagues Pitcher Register

	W	L	PCT	G	GS	CG	IP	H	BB	SO	ShO	SV

Dan Bankhead

BANKHEAD, DANIEL ROBERT   BR TR 6'1" 184 lbs.
B. May 3, 1920, Empire, Ala.   D. May 2, 1976, Houston, Tex.
Brother of Sam Bankhead.
Major leagues 1947–51.

		W	L	PCT	G	GS	CG	IP	H	BB	SO	ShO	SV
1942	CLE Buckeyes	0	0	.000	1								
1943	No record												
1944	No record												
1945	No record												
1946	MEM Red Sox	5	2	.714	8	7	6	63	24	8	36	1	
1947		4	4	.500	9	9	6	54	41	7	24	0	
	(3 years)	(9)	(6)	(.600)	(18)	(16)	(12)	(117)	(65)	(15)	(60)	(1)	

Sam Bankhead

BANKHEAD, SAM   BR TR 5'8" 175 lbs.
B. Sept. 18, 1905, Empire Ala.   D. 1976, Pittsburgh, Pa.
Brother of Dan Bankhead.

		W	L	PCT									
1932	3 teams LOU Black Caps BIR Black Barons NAS Elite Giants												
"	total	2	6	.250				No further data available					

Dave Barnhill

BARNHILL, DAVID (Impo, Skinny)   BB TL 5'7" 155 lbs.
B. Oct. 30, 1914, Greenville, N.C.   D. Jan. 8, 1983, Miami, Fla.

		W	L	PCT	G	GS	CG	IP	H	BB	SO	ShO	SV
1938	2 teams JAC Red Caps IND Clowns												
"	total	1	0	1.000	2		0	9	8			0	0
1939	No data available												
1940	Ethio. Clowns	2	0	1.000	3	3	1	13	5	0	20	0	0
1941	NY Cubans	9	6	.600	16	15	13	124	92	25	71	0	0
1942		4	7	.364	11	10	10	89	77	16	43	1	0
1943		11	3	.786	17	15	12	129	88	25	55	4	0
1944		4	1	.800	6		2	46	33	13	12		
1945		1	3	.250	5		2	23	29	9	21	0	
1946		8	3	.727	10	8	7	72	47	13	19	0	0
1947		4	0	1.000	7			47	39		35	2	
1948		2	0	1.000	2	2	2	18	9		9		0
	(10 years)	(46)	(23)	(.666)	(79)	(53)	(49)	(570)	(427)	(101)	(285)	(7)	(0)

Bernardo Baro

BARO, BERNARDO
B. Cuba

		W	L	PCT									
1925	Cuban Stars	0	2	.000				No further data available					
1926		1	1	.500				No further data available					
1927		0	1	.000				No further data available					
	3 years	1	4	.200									

Cool Papa Bell

BELL, JAMES THOMAS   BB TL 6' 165 lbs.
B. May 17, 1903, Starkville, Miss.
Hall of Fame 1974.

		W	L	PCT									
1922	STL Stars	7	6	.538				No further data available					
1923	No data available												
1924		3	1	.750				No further data available					
	(2 years)	(10)	(7)	(.588)									

William Bell

BELL, WILLIAM   BR TR 5'10" 180 lbs.
B. Lazaca County, Tex.   D. 1979, El Campo, Tex.

		W	L	PCT	G	GS	CG	IP	H	BB	SO	ShO	SV
1923	KC Monarchs	0	1	.000	3	2	1	19	12	2	3	0	0
1924		10	2	.833	16	13	8	114	110	26	36	0	0
1925		9	3	.750	17	12	7	95	45	26	40	1	1
1926		16	3	.842	23	18	15	156	100	22	49	1	2
1927		13	6	.684	26	19	14	166	142	31	47	2	0
1928		10	7	.588	25	16	13	164	153	22	71	1	0
1929		17	4	.810	29	19	13	166	146	29	91	0	3
1930		9	3	.750	13	11	11	100	90	13	65	2	1
1931	No data available												
1932	2 teams DET Wolves Homestead Grays												
"	total	5	1	.833	7	6	4	42	31	4	9	0	0
	(9 years)	(89)	(30)	(.748)	(159)	(116)	(86)	(1022)	(829)	(175)	(411)	(7)	(7)

		W	L	PCT	G	GS	CG	IP	H	BB	SO	ShO	SV

Joe Black

BLACK, JOE
B. Feb. 8, 1924, Plainfield, N.J.
Major leagues 1952–57.

BR TR 6'2" 220 lbs.

Year	Team	W	L	PCT	G	GS	CG	IP	H	BB	SO	ShO	SV
1944	BAL Elite Giants	3	3	.500	9	4		59	58	19	27		
1945		0	1	.000	1	1	1	7	6	2	3	0	0
1946		3	9	.250	15	9	9	96	44	9	18	0	1
1947		9	9	.500	26		12	148	**174**		78	0	
1948		10	5	.667	**21**				117	36	**90**		
1949		11	7	.611	23		13	153	164	44	64	1	
1950		8	3	.727	13		8	94	87		1		
	7 Years	44	37	.543	108	(14)	(43)	(557)	650	(110)	(280)	(2)	(1)

Eugene Bremer

BREMER, EUGENE
B. June 16, 1915, New Orleans, La.   Deceased

BR TR 5'8" 160 lbs.

Year	Team	W	L	PCT	G	GS	CG	IP	H	BB	SO	ShO	SV
1937	CIN Tigers	4	0	1.000	4			36	25		13	0	0
1938	MEM Red Sox	1	1	.500	4	3	2	21	19	0	4	0	0
1939		0	5	.000	6	6	3	42	37	17	9	0	0
1940		5	2	.714	7	6	6	53	20	16	10	2	0
1941	No data available												
1942	CIN Buckeyes	5	1	.833	6	6	6	36	27	0	5	1	0
1943	CLE Buckeyes	8	2	.800	11	11	**10**	84	55	6	11	3	0
1944		10	6	.625	20			113	109	34	44	2	
1945		8	4	.667	15		10	96	78	17	30		
1946		1	0	1.000	2	2	0	8	7	1	2	0	0
1947		1	0	1.000								0	
1948		0	1	.000							0		
	(11 years)	(43)	(22)	(.662)	(75)	(34)	(37)	(489)	(377)	(91)	(128)	(8)	(0)

Chet Brewer

BREWER, CHESTER ARTHUR
B. Jan. 14, 1907, Leavenworth, Kans.

BL TR 6'4" 176 lbs.

Year	Team	W	L	PCT	G	GS	CG	IP	H	BB	SO	ShO	SV
1925	KC Monarchs	1	0	1.000	9	5	0	20	21	16	11	0	0
1926		12	1	**.923**	16	12	8	110	72	**40**	63	2	0
1927		8	7	.533	20	14	7	103	98	38	46	1	0
1928		7	9	.438	19	15	10	135	130	27	51	0	1
1929		**17**	3	**.850**	24	17	16	167	124	35	83	2	1
1930		8	8	.500	17	15	15	145	150	35	85	1	1
1931		2	2	.500	4	4	3	31	14	3	4	2	0
1932	2 teams KC Monarchs WAS Pilots												
"	total	5	1	.833	7	5	5	45	32	7	13	3	0
1933	Semi-pro												
1934	No data available												
1935	KC Monarchs	0	1	.000	1	1	0	25	16			0	0
1936	NY Cubans	4	6	.400	12	10	8	86	64	25	40	0	0
1937	KC Monarchs	1	1	.500	1	1	1	9	1			0	0
1938	Latin America												
1939	Latin America												
1940	Latin America												
1941	2 teams PHI Stars KC Monarchs												
"	total	3	7	.300	13	8	8	87	67	9	16	0	0
1942	Latin America												
1943	Latin America												
1944	Latin America												
1945	Latin America												
1946	2 teams CHI Am. Giants CLE Buckeyes												
"	total	4	6	.400	8	**8**	6	51	31	0	4	1	0
1947	CLE Buckeyes	12	6	.667					137	29	81	**2**	0
1948		5	5	.500	15		10	96	118	19	55		
	(15 years)	(89)	(63)	.586	(166)	(115)	(97)	(1110)	(1075)	(283)	(552)	(14)	(3)

Dave Brown

BROWN, DAVE
B. 1896 or 1897, Tex.

TL 5'10" 170 lbs.

Year	Team	W	L	PCT	G	GS	CG	IP	H	BB	SO	ShO	SV
1920	CHI Am. Giants	10	2	**.833**	14	13	10	107	51	33	62	1	0
1921		11	3	**.786**	22	16	13	148	98	26	88	5	2
1922		8	3	.727	18	9	5	75	57	30	61	2	0
1923	NY Lincoln Giants	4	7	.364	12	**12**	6	62	65	6	**25**	1	0
1924		12	7	.632	**27**	18	17	175	155	28	**88**	1	**2**
1925		1	0	1.000	1	1	1	9	7	6	8	0	0
	6 years	46	22	.676	94	69	52	576	433	129	332	10	4

			W	L	PCT	G	GS	CG	IP	H	BB	SO	ShO	SV

Ray Brown

BROWN, RAYMOND   BB TR 6'1" 195 lbs.
B. Feb. 23, 1908, Ashland Grove, Ohio D. Dayton, Ohio.

Year	Team	W	L	PCT	G	GS	CG	IP	H	BB	SO	ShO	SV
1932	2 teams DET Wolves Homestead Grays												
"	total	7	5	.583	15	11	10	91	63	7	7	1	0
1933	Homestead Grays	6	1	.857	8	6	6	47	41	5	18	0	0
1934		2	1	.667	3	3	3	26	13	1	6	0	0
1935		12	3	.800	**18**	13	12	120	**82**	34	**45**	2	0
1936		0	1	.000	2	1	1	9	9	0	4	0	0
1937	WAS Homestead Grays	3	2	.600	6	4	4	41	31	2	13	0	0
1938		7	0	**1.000**	9	7	6	36	28			3	0
1939		4	1	.800	6	5	5	48	34	4	3	0	0
1940		**24**	4	**.857**	32	25	25	240	178	36	63	4	0
1941		13	6	.684	**22**	15	15	147	**128**	37	42	1	2
1942		12	4	.750	**17**	12	10	114	**78**	30	**39**	2	0
1943		4	1	.800	8	6	4	47	41	13	17	1	0
1944		11	3	.786	20		11	125	116	21	38	3	
1945		4	2	.667	7		6	46	55	9	17	1	
	14 years	109	34	.762	173	(108)	(118)	1137	897	(199)	(312)	18	(2)

Pee Wee Butts

BUTTS, TOM   BR TR 5'9" 145 lbs.
B. 1919, Atlanta, Ga. D. Jan. 1973, Atlanta, Ga.

Year	Team	W	L	PCT									
1950	2 teams BAL Elite Giants IND ABCs												
	total	8	8	.500			No further data available						

Bill Byrd

BYRD, BILL   BB TR 6'1" 200 lbs.
B. Jul. 15, 1907, Canton, Ohio

Year	Team	W	L	PCT	G	GS	CG	IP	H	BB	SO	ShO	SV
1933	NAS Elite Giants	3	6	.333	13	9	7	70	60	4	13	0	3
1934	CLE Red Sox	1	6	.143	7	6	3	40	43	4	9	0	0
1935	COL Elite Giants	2	3	.400	8	4	2	25	14	3	11	0	0
1936	WAS Elite Giants	8	4	.667	11	8	6	79	54	4	14	2	0
1937		5	3	.625	12	9	6	65	48	4	8	0	0
1938	BAL Elite Giants	6	3	.667	7	6	3	46	45	1	7	0	0
1939		9	4	.692	14	13	13	98	103	11	25	0	0
1940	No data available												
1941	BAL Elite Giants	7	4	.636	3	10	8	87	70	8	19	2	1
1942		9	2	**.818**	14	11	8	91	66	16	36	1	1
1943		9	4	.692	15	11	10	114	**102**	**29**	**57**	1	0
1944		10	7	.588	19		13	124	103	20	75	2	
1945		11	6	.647	17		12	123	117	20	79	0	
1946		3	5	.375	12	6	6	73	67	4	19	0	2
1947		9	6	.600	18		13	134	124		68	0	
1948		**11**	6	.647	20				**124**	23	82		
1949		12	3	**.800**	25		11	144	145	30	57	0	
1950		0	0	–	1		0	2				0	0
	(17 years)	(115)	(72)	(.615)	(216)	(93)	(121)	(1315)	(1285)	(181)	(579)	(8)	(7)

Rev Cannady

CANNADY, WALTER   TR
1922 CLE Tate Stars

		W	L	PCT									
		3	3	.500			No further data available						

Oscar Charleston

CHARLESTON, OSCAR McKINLEY   BL TL 6'1" 185 lbs.
B. Oct. 14, 1896, Indianapolis, Ind. D. Oct. 6, 1954, Philadelphia, Pa.
Hall of Fame 1976.

Year	Team	W	L	PCT									
1926	HBG Giants	0	1	.000			No further data available						
1933	PIT Crawfords	0	0										0
	2 years	0	1	.000									0

Phil Cockrell

COCKRELL, PHIL   BR TR
B. 1898, Augusta, Ga. D. Apr. 7, 1951, Philadelphia, Pa.

Year	Team	W	L	PCT	G	GS	CG	IP	H	BB	SO	ShO	SV
1918	PHI Hilldales	4	1	.800	5	4	2	29				0	0
1919		5	2	.714	7	7	7	46	20			0	0
1920		2	2	.500	6	5	5	47	39			0	0
1921		9	6	.600	17	12	10	87	63	12	34	1	0
1922		3	0	1.000	4	4	3					2	0
1923		2	4	.333	6	4	4	39	51	0	2	0	0
1924		10	1	**.909**	16	15	8	104	76	23	33	0	0
1925		13	3	.813	20	15	13	141	116	36	47	1	0

	W	L	PCT	G	GS	CG	IP	H	BB	SO	ShO	SV

Phil Cockrell *continued*

	W	L	PCT	G	GS	CG	IP	H	BB	SO	ShO	SV
1926	10	3	**.769**	16	16	12	119	102	35	52	1	0
1927	11	13	.458	26	24	15	61	71	15	31	1	0
1928	8	12	.400	24	17	4	138	117	16	18	0	0
1929	2	3	.400	8	5	3	31	18	8	9	0	0
1930	1	5	.167	9	6	6	54	71	20	21	0	0
1931	5	0	1.000	6	2	2	48	17	2	2	1	0
1932 2 teams PHI Hilldales AC Bacharach Giants												
" total	2	7	.222	10	7	5	62	50			0	0
1933 AC Bacharach Giants	0	0		1	0	0	9	11			0	0
1934 PHI Stars	1	4	.200	8	5	2	34	35			0	0
17 years	88	66	.571	189	148	101	(1049)	(857)	(167)	(249)	7	0

Andy Cooper

COOPER, ANDY (Lefty)   TL 6'1" 210 lbs.
B. Mar. 4, 1896, Waco, Tex. D. June 10, 1941, Waco, Tex.
Manager, Kansas City 1934–41.

	W	L	PCT	G	GS	CG	IP	H	BB	SO	ShO	SV
1920 DET Stars	0	2	.000	8	3	1	37	31	19	10	0	1
1921	5	9	.357	24	17	9	117	125	13	29	1	0
1922	14	5	**.737**	25	22	16	153	132	21	43	4	0
1923	15	8	.652	37	20	14	173	147	43	60	1	5
1924	12	5	.706	31	13	7	128	124	33	76	1	6
1925	12	1	**.923**	31	12	6	137	51	25	47	1	6
1926	12	8	.600	36	22	12	178	178	21	48	1	4
1927	7	3	.700	13	11	6	80	89	3	34	0	1
1928 KC Monarchs	13	7	.650	27	19	11	144	146	53	18	2	1
1929	13	3	.813	24	15	11	147	146	22	61	2	4
1930 DET Stars	15	6	.714	27	20	16	161	161	10	50	2	0
11 years	118	57	.674	283	174	109	1455	1330	263	476	15	30

Rube Currie

CURRIE, REUBEN   BR TR 6'4" 195 lbs.
B. 1898 (?), Kansas City, Mo. D. 1969, Chicago, Ill.

	W	L	PCT	G	GS	CG	IP	H	BB	SO	ShO	SV
1920 KC Monarchs	10	12	.455	27	19	13	**188**	166	31	**89**	1	2
1921	12	10	.545	24	16	14	140	118	24	57	0	0
1922	12	7	.632	22	20	16	179	**190**	40	92	1	0
1923	14	7	.667	26	18	16	187	160	30	66	1	0
1924 PHI Hilldales	1	5	.167	10	6	2	34	28	7	9	0	0
1925	13	1	**.929**	22	17	11	139	128	14	44	0	2
1926 CHI Am. Giants	8	3	.727	17	13	7	108	114	22	42	2	1
1927	4	5	.444	13	13	8	96	94	13	22	2	0
1928 KC Monarchs	6	6	.500	20	13	7	95	99	17	21	1	0
9 years	80	56	.588	181	135	94	1166	1097	198	442	8	5

Cherokee Davis

DAVIS, JOHN   BR TR
B. Feb. 6, 1918, Newark, N.J. D. Ft. Lauderdale, Fla. Nov. 7, 1982

	W	L	PCT	G	GS	CG	IP	H	BB	SO	ShO	SV
1944 NWK Eagles	3	0	1.000									2
1946	1	1	.500				No further data available					
1947	1	0	1.000				No further data available					
1950 HOU Eagles	1	0	1.000				No further data available					
4 years	6	1	.857									2

Leon Day

DAY, LEON   BR TR 5'8" 175 lbs.
B. Oct. 30, 1916, Alexandria, Va.

	W	L	PCT	G	GS	CG	IP	H	BB	SO	ShO	SV
1934 BAL Black Sox	0	1	.000	2					1	1	0	0
1935 BKN Eagles	9	2	.818	12	10	8	79	60	7	38	0	1
1936 NWK Eagles	3	4	.429	7	4	4	34	28	4	24	0	0
1937	6	0	1.000	8	6	6	55	36	0	16	0	0
1938	1	1	.500	3	3	1					1	0
1939	12	4	.750	17	15	11	113	98	11	16	3	0
1940 No data available												
1941 NWK Eagles	1	1	.500	2	2	1	15	14	6	4		
1942	7	1	**.875**	9	8	8	74	39	18	65	2	0
1943	4	3	.571	10	8	3	46	45	10	27	0	0
1944 US Army												
1945 US Army												
1946 NWK Eagles	13	4	.765	19	18	16	141	97	34	65	3	0
1947 Mexico												

Leon Day *continued*

	W	L	PCT	G	GS	CG	IP	H	BB	SO	ShO	SV
1948 Mexico												
1949 NWK Eagles	7	5	.583	14	9	5	110	25	51	0	0	
(11 years)	(63)	(26)	(.708)	(103)	(83)	(63)	(667)	(442)	(142)	(256)	(9)	(1)

Martin Dihigo

DIHIGO, MARTIN   BR TR 6'1" 190 lbs.
B. May 25, 1905, Matanzas, Cuba   D. May 22, 1971, Cienfuegos, Cuba
Hall of Fame 1977.

	W	L	PCT	G	GS	CG	IP	H	BB	SO	ShO	SV
1923 Cuban Stars	1	0	1.000				No further data available					
1924	2	2	.500	5	3	3	28	9	0	8	0	0
1925	3	3	.500	8	6	6	53	52	16	12	0	1
1926	2	0	1.000	2	1	1	9	3	1	6	0	0
1927	1	0	1.000				No further data available					
1928 Homestead Grays	1	1	.500	2	1	1	9	9	0	10	0	0
1929 PHI Hilldales	4	2	.667	2	2	2	16	11	2	5	0	0
1930 NY Cubans	0	3	.000	3							0	0
1931 PHI Hilldales	1	2	.333	4	3	3	27	19	2	6	0	0
1935 NY Cubans	7	3	.700	14	9	9	94	72	25	33	0	0
1936	5	4	.556	9	8	7	67	54	12	39	0	0
1945 Cuban Stars	0	1	.000	1		0	6	6	3	7	0	0
12 years	27	21	.563	(50)	(33)	(32)	(309)	(235)	(61)	(126)	(0)	(1)

Bill Drake

DRAKE, WILLIAM P. (Plunk)   BR TR 6'0" 209 lbs.
B. June 8, 1895, Sedalia, Mo.   D. Oct. 30, 1977, St. Louis, Mo.

	W	L	PCT	G	GS	CG	IP	H	BB	SO	ShO	SV
1920 STL Giants	9	12	.429	24	22	**18**	181	**196**	50	72	1	1
1921	**20**	10	.667	**33**	26	22	231	204	66	123	3	**4**
1922 KC Monarchs	8	8	.500	20	14	5	96	108	32	46	0	0
1923	9	7	.563	19	16	11	128	92	31	24	0	0
1924	10	**8**	.556	25	19	11	140	135	**57**	60	0	1
1925	9	5	.643	22	13	8	113	96	33	62	3	0
1926 DAY Marcos	6	6	.500	17	9	9	86	55	20	20	0	0
1927 DET Stars	8	6	.571	16	14	8	115	110	44	35	0	0
1928 No data available												
1929 No data available												
1930 STL Stars	1	0	1.000	1	0	0	8	12	3	2	0	0
(9 years)	(80)	(62)	(.563)	(177)	(133)	(92)	(1098)	(1008)	(336)	(444)	(7)	(6)

Red Farrell

FARRELL, LUTHER   TL 6'1" 190 lbs.

	W	L	PCT	G	GS	CG	IP	H	BB	SO	ShO	SV
1920 3 teams NY Lincoln Giants STL Giants CHI Giants												
" total	3	8	.273	12	10	7	68	45	16	26	0	
1921 CHI Giants	3	6	.333	14	10	6	73	86	22	18	0	
1923 CHI Am. Giants	1	0	1.000	2	1	1	9	11	2	2	0	
1924 Semi-pro												
1925 2 teams NY Lincoln Giants AC Bacharach Giants												
" total	3	7	.300	13	9	7	74	72	12	34	0	
1926 AC Bacharach Giants	1	2	.333	4	3	2	18	17				
1927	17	13	.567	33	22	14				2		
1928	9	10	.474	**26**	**20**	16	155	**140**	15	37		**2**
1929	0	2	.000	3	3	2	16	24	2	7	0	
1930 NY Lincoln Giants	8	1	.889	12	10	8	75	97	24	34	0	1
1931 No data available												
1932 NY Black Yankees	0	3	.000	5	1						0	
1933 No data available												
1934 AC Bacharach Giants	1	3	.250	6	2	1	14	12	3	2	0	
(11 years)	(46)	(55)	(.455)	(130)	(91)	(64)	(502)	(504)	(96)	(160)	(2)	(3)

Bill Foster

FOSTER, WILLIAM HENDRICK   BB TL 6'1" 196 lbs.
Brother of Rube Foster.
B. June 12, 1904, Calvert, Tex.   D. Sept. 16, 1978, Lorman, Miss.

	W	L	PCT	G	GS	CG	IP	H	BB	SO	ShO	SV
1923 2 teams MEM Red Sox CHI Am. Giants												
" total	5	2	.714	11	8	6	64	34	14	38	1	0
1924 2 teams MEM Red Sox CHI Am. Giants												
" total	6	1	.857	11	8	5	59	34	19	38	3	0
1925 2 teams CHI Am. Giants BIR Black Barons												
" total	7	1	.875	14	10	7	87	24	20	40	2	0
1926 CHI Am. Giants	11	4	.733	20	14	10	137	86	37	**72**	4	1

	W	L	PCT	G	GS	CG	IP	H	BB	SO	ShO	SV

Bill Foster *continued*

	W	L	PCT	G	GS	CG	IP	H	BB	SO	ShO	SV
1927	21	3	.875	29	21	18	199	164	21	50	5	0
1928	14	10	.583	30	21	20	208	85	55	118	2	0
1929	11	7	.611	26	18	15	152	60	39	75	3	3
1930	16	10	.615	34	20	18	199	173	51	134	3	3
1931 2 teams Homestead Grays KC Monarchs												
" total	9	2	.818	14	11	11	103	35	10	40	3	0
1932 CHI Am. Giants	15	8	.652	28	23	23	198	100	61	49	4	0
1933	8	4	.667	17	12	10	96	55	8	52	1	2
1934	3	2	.600	7	4	4	36	29	10	6	1	0
1935	4	2	.667	7	4	3	36	28	11	10	1	0
1936 PIT Crawfords	2	2	.500	4	4	3	24	18	9	4	0	0
1937 CHI Am. Giants	5	4	.555	13	14	8	61	47	5	8	1	0
15 years	137	62	.688	265	192	161	1659	972	370	734	34	12

Josh Gibson

GIBSON, JOSHUA   BR TR 6'2" 217 lbs.
B. Dec. 21, 1911, Buena Vista, Ga. D. Jan. 20, 1947, Pittsburgh, Pa.
Hall of Fame 1972.

	W	L	PCT	G	GS	CG	IP	H	BB	SO	ShO	SV
1933 Homestead Grays	0	0										1

Rats Henderson

HENDERSON, ARTHUR CHAUNCEY   BR TR 5'7" 180 lbs.
B. Aug. 29, 1897, Richmond, Va. D. Wilmington, Del.

	W	L	PCT	G	GS	CG	IP	H	BB	SO	ShO	SV
1923 AC Bacharach Giants	8	6	.571	16	12	10	96	75	2	7	0	2
1924	8	1	.889	11	10	8	78	55	5	23	1	0
1925	14	10	.583	29	23	20	206	104	38	80	2	1
1926	7	3	.700	11	10	9	88	70	9	10	1	0
1927	19	7	.731	30	20	13	18	12	0	6	2	1
1928	8	4	.667	15	11	7	82	59	6	16	0	0
1929	5	6	.455	16	9	8	70	84	19	19	1	0
7 years	69	37	.651	128	95	75	638	459	79	161	7	4

Bill Holland

HOLLAND, ELVIS WILLIAM   BB TR 5'8½" 175 lbs.
B. Feb. 2, 1901, Indianapolis, Ind. D. New York, N.Y.

	W	L	PCT	G	GS	CG	IP	H	BB	SO	ShO	SV
1920 DET Stars	12	7	.632	27	20	14	175	146	43	84	1	2
1921 2 teams DET Stars CHI Am. Giants												
" total	13	12	.520	32	22	20	190	169	38	104	1	0
1922 DET Stars	16	13	.552	35	23	18	204	182	25	95	2	1
1923 NY Lincoln Giants	2	5	.286	10	6	3	31	35	3	13	0	1
1924	8	5	.615	16	12	10	109	100	14	26	0	0
1925 BKN Royal Giants	3	5	.375	10	7	5	51	74	14	33	0	0
1926	0	3	.000	3	3	2	16	12	3	8	0	0
1927	3	4	.429	7	5	4	35	44	1	5	0	0
1928	1	1	.500	2	1	1	17	22	1	12	0	0
1929 NY Lincoln Giants	13	7	.650	18	16	15	124	122	19	53	1	0
1930 NY Black Yankees	12	1	.923	14	10	10	86	91	31	59	0	0
1931	2	4	.333	7	6	6	47	7	2	6	0	0
1932	6	1	.857	9	9	9	83	39	10	19	0	0
1933 No data available												
1934 NY Black Yankees	0	3	.000	3	3	2	16	9	1	7	0	0
1936	4	2	.667	5	5	5	45	43	10	22	0	0
1937	1	1	.500	3	3	2	23	23	3	2	0	0
1938	2	3	.400	10	6	5	59	52	2	15	0	1
1939 No data available												
1940 NY Black Yankees	1	3	.250	4	4	2	25	33	9	12	0	0
1941	0	1	.000									
(19 years)	(99)	(81)	(.550)	(215)	(161)	(133)	(1336)	(1203)	(229)	(575)	(7)	(5)

Sammy T. Hughes

HUGHES, SAMUEL THOMAS   BR TR 6'3" 190 lbs.
B. Oct. 20, 1910, Louisville, Ky. D. 1973, Los Angeles, Calif.

	W	L	PCT	G	GS	CG	IP	H	BB	SO	ShO	SV
1931 LOU Black Caps	0	1	.000	No further data available

Connie Johnson

JOHNSON, CLIFFORD (Connie)   BR TR 6'4" 200 lbs.
B. Dec. 27, 1922, Stone Mountain, Ga.
Major leagues 1953–1958.

	W	L	PCT	G	GS	CG	IP	H	BB	SO	ShO	SV
1941 KC Monarchs	2	2	.500	2	0	0	8	3	0	4	0	
1942	3	0	1.000									
1943 Military service												

	W	L	PCT	G	GS	CG	IP	H	BB	SO	ShO	SV

Connie Johnson *continued*

	W	L	PCT	G	GS	CG	IP	H	BB	SO	ShO	SV
1944 Military service												
1945 Military service												
1946 KC Monarchs	**9**	3	.750	**13**	7	**6**	**85**	**33**	**9**	18	1	
1947	1	1	.500	3	1	1	10	5			0	
4 years	15	6	.714	(18)	(8)	(7)	(103)	(41)	(9)	(22)	(1)	

Stuart Jones

JONES, STUART (Slim) BL TL 6'6" 185 lbs.
B. May 6, 1913, Baltimore, Md.   D. Dec. 1938, Baltimore, Md.

	W	L	PCT	G	GS	CG	IP	H	BB	SO	ShO	SV
1933 BAL Black Sox	4	2	.667	8	4	2	31	16	10	31	0	0
1934 PHI Stars	22	3	**.880**	29	20	19	180	109	14	83	4	0
1935	4	10	.286	19	10	7	86	34	13	13	0	0
1936	3	3	.500	11	5	2	18	11	11	11	0	0
1937	1	0	1.000	1	1	0	5				0	0
1938	2	1	.667	4	1	1				0	0	0
	36	19	.655	72	41	31	(320)	(170)	(48)	(138)	(4)	(0)

Jimmy Lyons

LYONS, JIMMY BL TR 5'8" 175 lbs.
B. Chicago, Ill.

	W	L	PCT	G	GS	CG	IP	H	BB	SO	ShO	SV
1920 CHI Am. Giants	1	1	.500	No further data available								

Max Manning

MANNING, MAX BL TR 6'4" 180 lbs.
B. Nov. 18, 1919, Rome, Ga.

	W	L	PCT	G	GS	CG	IP	H	BB	SO	ShO	SV
1939 NWK Eagles	1	2	.333	5	3	2	21	11	0	3	0	0
1940	11	6	.647	25	14	7	105	95	24	33	0	0
1941	5	5	.500	20	11	7	92	92	10	24	0	0
1942	6	6	.500	15	11	5	82	58	14	21	1	0
1943 Military service												
1944 Military service												
1945 Military service												
1946 NWK Eagles	10	0	**1.000**	13	9	9	86	39	0	10	0	0
1947	15	6	.714	23		18	**169**	153		104	0	
1948	10	4	.714	16				95	35	73		
1949	8	4	.667	16		8	94	87	16	28	1	
8 years	66	33	.667	133	(48)	(56)	(649)	630	(99)	296	(2)	(0)

Verdell Mathis

MATHIS, VERDELL (Lefty) BL TL 5'11" 150 lb.
B. Nov. 18, 1921, Crawfordville, Ark.

	W	L	PCT	G	GS	CG	IP	H	BB	SO	ShO	SV
1940 MEM Red Sox	2	2	.500	4	3	2	24	15	2	16	0	0
1941	1	2	.333	5	3	2	19	22	4	12	0	0
1942	6	5	.545	13	7	5	**65**	35	8	20	**2**	0
1943	6	5	.545	17	14	9	83	41	9	14	1	0
1944	9	9	.500	21			130	130	35	86	1	
1945	10	11	.476	25		18	168	162	32	85		
1946	2	6	.250				35	22	2	6	1	1
1947	5	5	.500	15			75	77		38	1	1
1948	9	12	.429	31		10	153	196	48	82		
1949	9	11	.450	23		12	155	166		70	0	
10 years	59	68	.465	(154)	(27)	(58)	907	866	(140)	(429)	(6)	(2)

Leroy Matlock

MATLOCK, LEROY BL TL 5'10" 180 lbs.
B. Mar. 12, 1907, Moberly, Mo.   D. Feb. 6, 1968, St. Paul, Minn.

	W	L	PCT	G	GS	CG	IP	H	BB	SO	ShO	SV
1929 STL Stars	5	2	.714	13	8	4	65	75	42	73	1	0
1930	11	3	**.786**	17	14	8	89	92	24	24	1	0
1931	0	1	.000	No further data available								
1932 2 teams WAS Pilots Homestead Grays												
" total	2	4	.333	10	6	2	46	19	14	23	0	0
1933 PIT Crawfords	7	3	.700	12	8	6	85	75	14	38	1	0
1934	5	3	.625	14	7	7	66	31	3	17	1	0
1935	18	0	1.000	18	16	16	159	77	7	29	**2**	0
1936	3	2	.600	5	4	2	20	19	2	3	0	0
1937 Dominican Republic												
1938 PIT Crawfords	2	4	.333	6	4	4	34	28			0	0
9 years	53	22	.707	95	67	49	564	416	(106)	(207)	6	0

			W	L	PCT	G	GS	CG	IP	H	BB	SO	ShO	SV

Webster McDonald

MCDONALD, WEBSTER
B. Jan. 1, 1900, Wilmington, Del.   D. June 12, 1982, Philadelphia, Pa.
Manager 1934–40.

BL TR 6′ 180 lbs.

Year	Team		W	L	PCT	G	GS	CG	IP	H	BB	SO	ShO	SV
1925	CHI Am. Giants		6	2	.750	11	8	6	76	22	19	47	2	0
1926			14	9	.609	20	14	9	112	100	27	70	0	1
1927			10	5	.667	18	14	11	136	111	26	64	1	0
1928	Homestead Grays		2	0	1.000	2	2	2	14	8	1	7	2	0
1929	CHI Am. Giants		2	2	.500	4	4	3	33	34	5	10	0	0
1930	3 teams CHI Am. Giants BAL Black Sox PHI Hilldales													
″	total		12	13	.480	35	25	13	172	186	28	42	2	1
1931	2 teams PHI Hilldales CHI Am. Giants													
″	total		8	2	.800	11	10	10	93	58	9	21	5	0
1932	Semi-pro													
1933	PHI Stars		3	2	.600	6	6	5	46	57			0	0
1934			8	2	.800	17	13	8	103	66	3	17	0	0
1935			10	6	.625	25	14	8	129	98	14	9	0	0
1936			7	2	**.778**	17	2	0	28		5		0	0
1937			4	**4**	.500	**13**	9	5	60	23		9	0	0
1938			4	5	.444	13	3	7	38	29	5	0	1	0
1939			2	5	.286	14	4	4	47	40	0	3	0	0
1940			0	1	.000									
	15 years		92	60	.605	(206)	(128)	(91)	(1087)	(832)	(142)	(299)	(13)	(2)

Terris McDuffie

MCDUFFIE, TERRIS (The Great)
B. July 22, 1910, Mobile, Ala.   D. New York, N.Y.

BR TR 6′2″ 200 lbs.

Year	Team		W	L	PCT	G	GS	CG	IP	H	BB	SO	ShO	SV
1932	BAL Black Sox		4	0	1.000	5	2	2	37	31	5	5	0	0
1933	No data available													
1934	No data available													
1935	NWK Eagles		0	0	.000	1	1	0	5	10	1	3	0	0
1936			2	2	.500	5	2	2	16	10	6	6	0	0
1937			7	3	.700	11	**10**	10	79	54	5	9	1	0
1938	2 teams NWK Eagles NY Black Yankees													
″	total		**11**	3	.786	**17**	13	10	108	**86**	5	**19**	0	0
1939	NY Black Yankees		5	3	.625	9	7	0	54	44	6	9	1	0
1940	PHI Stars		5	3	.625	9	7	5	47	34	5	7	1	0
1941	WAS Homestead Grays		1	2	.333	3	1	0	9	4	2	1	0	0
1942	PHI Stars		5	3	.625				No further data available					
1943	No data available													
1944	NWK Eagles		5	6	.455	**25**	7		90	98	21	33	0	
1945			2	1	.667	4		2	25	29	5	12	1	
	(11 years)		(47)	(26)	(.644)	(89)	(50)	(31)	(470)	(400)	(61)	(109)	(4)	(0)

Hurley McNair

MCNAIR, HURLEY ALLEN
B. Oct. 28, 1888, Marshall, Tex.   D. Dec. 2, 1948, Kansas City, Mo.

BB TR 5′6″ 155 lbs.

Year	Team		W	L	PCT	G	GS	CG	IP	H	BB	SO	ShO	SV
1915	CHI Am. Giants		0	1	.000			No further data available						
1921	KC Monarchs		1	1	.500			No further data available						
1922			2	0	1.000			No further data available						
	(3 years)		(3)	(2)	(.600)									

Don Newcombe

NEWCOMBE, DONALD (Newk)
B. June 14, 1926, Madison, N. J.
Major leagues 1949–1960.

BR TR 6′4″ 220 lbs.

Year	Team		W	L	PCT	G	GS	CG	IP	H	BB	SO	ShO	SV
1944	NWK Eagles		1	3	.250	14		2	48	53	24	27		
1945			8	4	.667	15		12	115	102	55	78		
	2 years		9	7	.563	29		14	163	155	79	105		

Alejandro Oms

OMS, ALEJANDRO
B. Mar. 13, 1895, Santa Clara, Cuba   D. Nov. 9, 1946

BL TL 5′8″ 190 lbs.

Year	Team		W	L	PCT	G	GS	CG	IP	H	BB	SO	ShO	SV
1930	Cuban Stars		2	0	1.000			No further data available						

Satchel Paige

PAIGE, LEROY ROBERT
B. July 7, 1906, Mobile, Ala.   D. June 8, 1982, Kansas City, Mo.
Major leagues, 1948–49, 1951–53, 1965.
Hall of Fame 1971.

BR TR 6′3½″ 180 lbs.

Year	Team		W	L	PCT	G	GS	CG	IP	H	BB	SO	ShO	SV
1927	BIR Black Barons		8	3	.727	20	9	6	93	63	19	80	3	1
1928			12	4	.750	26	16	10	120	107	19	112	3	0
1929			11	11	.500	31	20	15	**196**	191	39	**184**	0	3

	W	L	PCT	G	GS	CG	IP	H	BB	SO	ShO	SV

Satchel Paige *continued*

	W	L	PCT	G	GS	CG	IP	H	BB	SO	ShO	SV
1930 2 teams BIR Black Barons BAL												
" total	11	4	.733	18	13	12	120	92	15	86	3	1
1931 2 teams CLE Cubs PIT Crawfords												
" total	5	5	.500	12	6	5	60	36	4	23	1	0
1932 PIT Crawfords	14	8	.636	29	23	19	181	92	13	109	3	2
1933	5	7	.417	13	12	10	95	39	10	57	0	0
1934	13	3	.813	20	17	15	154	85	21	97	6	0
1935 KC Monarchs	0	0		2	2	0	7	0	0	10	0	0
1936 PIT Crawfords	7	2	.778	9	9	9	70	54	11	59	3	0
1937 STL Stars	1	2	.333	3	3	2	26	22	6	11	0	0
1938 Mexico												
1939 Monarchs' B team												
1940 KC Monarchs	1	1	.500	2	2	2	12	10	0	15	1	0
1941	7	1	.875	13	11	3	67	38	6	61	0	0
1942	8	5	.615	20	18	6	100	68	12	78	1	0
1943	5	9	.357	24	20	4	88	80	16	54	0	1
1944	5	5	.500	13			78	47	8	70	2	0
1945	3	5	.375	13	7	1	68	65	12	48	0	0
1946	5	1	.833	9	9	1	38	22	2	23	0	0
1947	1	1	.500	2	2	2	11	5			0	0
1948 Cleveland Indians												
1949 Cleveland Indians												
1950 2 teams KC Monarchs PHI Stars												
" total	1	2	.333		8		0	26	28			0
20 years	123	79	.609	279	(207)	(122)	1584	1142	(241)	(1177)	26	(8)

Willie Powell

POWELL, ERNEST (Piggie)   BL   TR   5'9"   154 lbs.
B. Oct. 30, 1903, Eutah, Ala.   D. May 16, 1987, Three Rivers, Mich.

	W	L	PCT	G	GS	CG	IP	H	BB	SO	ShO	SV
1925 CHI Am. Giants	3	2	.600	5	4	4	33	15	7	20	0	0
1926	2	2	.500	5	4	0	18	17	11	13	0	0
1927	9	4	.692	15	14	7	114	119	31	57	2	0
1928	9	9	.500	22	21	15	156	135	20	82	4	1
1929	3	1	.750	9	4	3	53	60	26	20	0	0
1930 DET Stars	9	10	.474	25	19	12	143	145	27	60	2	2
1931 DET Wolves	4	7	.364	14	11	9	80	71	20	30	2	0
1932 CHI Am. Giants	13	7	.650	22	18	13	147	87	20	20	5	0
1933	6	3	.667	10	6	3	31	14	0	3	1	0
9 years	58	45	.563	127	101	66	775	663	162	305	16	3

Double Duty Radcliffe

RADCLIFFE, TED   BR   TR   5'10"   212 lbs.
Brother of Alec Radcliff.
B. July 7, 1902, Mobile, Ala.
Manager 1937–38, 1943.

	W	L	PCT	G	GS	CG	IP	H	BB	SO	ShO	SV
1930 STL Stars	9	3	.750	20	11	9	94	89	24	40	1	3
1931 2 teams DET Wolves Homestead Grays												
" total	9	5	.643	17	13	12	106	22	15	39	0	0
1932 PIT Crawfords	13	5	.722	24	21	14	156	60	14	17	0	1
1933 3 teams Homestead Grays NY Black Yankees COL Blue Birds												
" total	0	1	.000	1		0					0	0
1934 CHI Am. Giants	0	1	.000	2		0	6	3			0	0
1935 BKN Eagles	4	6	.400	13	8	6	58	59	9	19	0	0
1936 Semi-pro												
1937 CLA Tigers	0	1	.000	1	0	0				4	0	0
1938 CLE Red Sox	3	2	.600	8	4	4	38	20	0	3	0	0
1939	4	3	.571	10	6	5	49	45	26	9	0	0
1940 Mexico												
1941 MEM Red Sox	1	2	.333	7	2	1	35	38	1	7	0	1
1942 No data available												
1943 No data available												
1944 No data available												
1945 KC Monarchs	3	0	1.000			No other data available						
1946 2 teams BIR Black Barons WAS Homestead Grays												
" total	7	4	.636	21							0	4
(12 years)	(53)	(33)	(.616)	(124)	(65)	(51)	(542)	(336)	(89)	(138)	(1)	(9)

Connie Rector

RECTOR, CONNIE (Broadway)   BR   TR   5'8"   170 lbs.

	W	L	PCT	G	GS	CG	IP	H	BB	SO	ShO	SV
1920 PHI Hilldales	1	1	.500	3	3	3	20	12	4	12	0	0
1921	5	1	.833	10	6	5	69	38	24	19	0	0
1922 No data available												

	W	L	PCT	G	GS	CG	IP	H	BB	SO	ShO	SV

Connie Rector *continued*

		W	L	PCT	G	GS	CG	IP	H	BB	SO	ShO	SV
1923	PHI Hilldales	3	1	.750	5	4	3	27	32	2	5	0	0
1924	BKN Royal Giants	1	1	.500	4	3	2	25	17	2	6	0	0
1925		3	2	.600	9	7	4	47	48	8	10	0	0
1926		1	2	.333	4	4	3	35	44	10	6	0	0
1927	NY Lincoln Giants	6	6	.500	12	9	8	78	65	24	14	0	1
1928		6	9	.400	20	14	14	132	151	12	16	0	2
1929		20	2	.909	25	15	13	161	122	24	25	1	0
1930	NY Black Yankees	3	1	.750	6	5	3	41	25	14	7	1	0
1931		2	6	.250	8	8	6	50	14	0	3	0	0
1932		4	1	.800	5	4	1	18	9			0	0
1933	Team not in the league												
1934	Team not in the league												
1935	Team not in the league												
1936	No data available												
1937	No data available												
1938	NY Black Yankees	0	0		1	0	0					0	0
1939	NY Cubans	0	1	.000	6	0	0					0	0
1940	No data available												
1941	NY Black Yankees	3	5	.375	10	3	3	28	24	6	4	0	0
	(15 years)	(58)	(39)	(.598)	(128)	(85)	(68)	(731)	(601)	(130)	(127)	(2)	(3)

Dick Redding

REDDING, DICK (Cannonball)   BR TR 6'4" 210 lbs.
B. 1891, Atlanta, Ga. D. 1940 (?), Islip, N.Y.
Manager 1923–31.

		W	L	PCT	G	GS	CG	IP	H	BB	SO	ShO	SV
1916	NY Lincoln Giants	1	0	1.000									
1917	No data available												
1918	No data available												
1919	BKN Royal Giants	3	3	.500	6	6	6	45	9			0	0
1920		6	3	.667	10	9	8	78	42	8	17	3	1
1921	AC Bacharach Giants	17	12	.586	30	23	21	213	189	38	81	3	1
1922		8	8	.500	14	13	12	113	59	10	14	2	0
1923	BKN Royal Giants	3	1	.750	5	4	2	21	17	2	2	0	0
1924		1	4	.200	6	6	5	42	56	2	13	0	0
1925		3	3	.500	6	6	4	55	24	4	12	0	0
1926		0	1	.000	2							0	0
1927		3	6	.333	11	9	5					0	0
1928		1	0	1.000	1	1	1	9	10			0	0
1929	Team not in the league												
1930	BKN Royal Giants	0	2	.000	2	1	1	18	24	1	3	0	0
1931		0	1	.000	1	1	0	4	7	1	0	0	0
	(14 years)	(45)	(44)	.506	(94)	(79)	(65)	(598)	(437)	(66)	(142)	(8)	(2)

Ed Rile

RILE, ED (Huck)   BB TR(?) 6'4" 230 lbs.

		W	L	PCT	G	GS	CG	IP	H	BB	SO	ShO	SV
1920	IND ABCs	2	1	.667	7	6	3	27	14	24	17	1	0
1921	2 teams COL Buckeyes NY Lincoln Giants												
"	total	4	1	.800	3	3	3	29	15	7	11	2	0
1922	CHI Am. Giants	4	5	.444	16	10	6	77	45	18	22	0	0
1923		14	8	.636	26	15	13	159	120	34	64	2	0
1924		5	1	.833	12	7	2	59	70	32	18	0	0
1925	IND ABCs	2	8	.200	13	10	9	83	107	19	46	0	0
1926		4	1	.800	10	6	4	40	35	7	13	2	1
1927	DET Stars	14	6	.700	21	19	12	163	139	19	47	2	0
1928		2	2	.500	4	4	3	106	63	2	3	1	0
1929		0	2	.000	3	2	0	7	19	1	1	0	0
1930		2	0	1.000	3	2	1	7	8			0	0
	11 years	53	35	.602	118	84	56	757	635	(163)	(242)	10	1

Bullet Joe Rogan

ROGAN, WILBER JOE   BR TR 5'9" 175 lbs.
B. July 28, 1889, Oklahoma City, Okla. D. March 4, 1967, Kansas City, Mo.

		W	L	PCT	G	GS	CG	IP	H	BB	SO	ShO	SV
1920	KC Monarchs	7	5	.583	14	12	12	114	97	44	77	0	1
1921		14	7	.667	21	20	20	172	123	46	68	3	2
1922		13	6	.684	23	18	18	172	146	36	96	2	1
1923		11	7	.611	20	18	15	178	124	38	71	4	1
1924		16	5	.762	23	22	17	176	154	50	101	1	0
1925		15	2	.882	22	16	15	154	122	28	69	4	2
1926		12	4	.750	19	11	9	105	87	21	46	0	1
1927		15	6	.714	30	16	15	152	121	30	89	4	6

	W	L	PCT	G	GS	CG	IP	H	BB	SO	ShO	SV

Bullet Joe Rogan *continued*

	W	L	PCT	G	GS	CG	IP	H	BB	SO	ShO	SV
1928	9	3	.750	16	11	9	102	117	14	52	0	0
1929	0	0		2	0	0	6	7	1	5	0	1
1930 No data available												
1931 No data available												
1932 Team not in the league												
1933 Team not in the league												
1934 Team not in the league												
1935 Team not in the league												
1936 KC Monarchs	1	0	1.000	1	1	1	6	3	0	3	0	0
1937	0	0		1		0				0		
1938 No data available												
(12 years)	(113)	(45)	(.715)	(192)	(145)	(131)	(1337)	(1101)	(308)	(677)	(18)	(15)

Lazaro Salazar

SALAZAR, LAZARO BL TL 5'9" 177 lbs.
B. Feb. 4, 1912, Havana, Cuba   D. Apr. 25, 1957

	W	L	PCT									
1930 NY Cubans	1	2	.333	No further data available								
1932	2	1	.667	No further data available								
2 years	3	3	.500									

Harry Salmon

SALMON, HARRY BR TR 5'10" 180 lbs.
B. Birmingham, Ala.   D. Pittsburgh, Pa.

	W	L	PCT	G	GS	CG	IP	H	BB	SO	ShO	SV
1923 BIR Black Barons	7	3	.700	14	10	9	92	82	11	45	3	0
1924 2 teams MEM Red Sox BIR Black Barons												
" total	8	3	.727	13	10	8	88	88	20	42	1	0
1925 BIR Black Barons	7	6	.538	20	13	11	127	139	28	56	0	0
1926 Team not in the league												
1927 BIR Black Barons	14	6	.700	27	18	13	199	164	27	74	1	0
1928	11	10	.524	24	20	11	164	170	16	84	3	0
1929	10	15	.400	34	22	18	177	144	19	92	3	3
1930 2 teams BIR Black Barons MEM Red Sox												
" total	11	11	.500	28	18	15	176	200	34	101	0	2
1931 BIR Black Barons	1	0	1.000	1	1	1	9	6			0	0
1932	1	0	1.000	1	1	1	9				0	0
9 years	70	54	.565	162	113	87	1041	(993)	(155)	(494)	11	5

Hilton Smith

SMITH, HILTON BR TR
B. Feb. 27, 1912, Giddings, Tex.   D. Nov. 18, 1983, Kansas City, Mo.

	W	L	PCT	G	GS	CG	IP	H	BB	SO	ShO	SV
1933 NOR	1	0	1.000	2	0	0	3	6			0	0
1934 Team not in the league												
1935 Team not in the league												
1937 Team not in the league												
1937 KC Monarchs	6	4	.600	11	9	6	54	28	7	28	1	0
1938	8	1	.889	14	9	4	84	28	6	54	1	0
1939	8	2	.800	7	3	3	70	49	12	60	1	6
1940	5	3	.625	10	5	4	37	20	36	11	0	1
1941	10	0	1.000	19	7	4	89	34	5	31	2	3
1942	8	3	.727	13	6	4	68	76	16	28	0	3
1943	4	4	.500	11	8	7	76	42	2	17	0	0
1944	2	5	.286	11	0	0	53	55	12	10	0	0
1945	5	3	.625	13		6	76	67	11	43		
1946	8	2	.800	13	10	5	46	26	7	15	1	3
1947	7	3	.700	11			88	90		30		
1948	1	2	.333	11	0	2	46	68	23	27		
13 years	72	32	.692	146	(57)	(45)	787	583	(137)	(354)	(6)	(16)

Sam Streeter

STREETER, SAMUEL BR TL 5'7" 170 lbs.
B. Sept. 17, 1900, New Market, Ala.   D. Aug. 9, 1985, Pittsburgh, Pa.

	W	L	PCT	G	GS	CG	IP	H	BB	SO	ShO	SV
1921 CHI Am. Giants	0	1	.000	4	2	1	16	13	4	6	0	0
1922 AC Bacharach Giants	1	0	1.000	4	4	3					0	0
1923 NY Lincoln Giants	2	2	.500	11	10	0	61	38	0	0	1	0
1924 BIR Black Barons	14	7	.667	27	24	21	208	201	20	127	2	1
1925	0	1	.000	3	0	0	8	18	1	4	0	0
1926 Team not in the league												
1927 BIR Black Barons	14	12	.538	29	21	18	204	160	28	89	2	0
1928 2 teams BIR Black Barons Homestead Grays												
" total	4	3	.571	9	7	7	73	69	14	30	1	0
1929 Homestead Grays	9	5	.643	18	10	4	69	71	16	22	0	1
1930 2 teams BIR Black Barons BAL Black Sox												
" total	14	12	.538	33	27	22	210	220	35	61	2	1

			W	L	PCT	G	GS	CG	IP	H	BB	SO	ShO	SV

Sam Streeter *continued*

		W	L	PCT	G	GS	CG	IP	H	BB	SO	ShO	SV
1931	2 teams CLE Cubs PIT Crawfords												
"	total	3	2	.600	5	3	3	26	11	0	7	0	0
1932	PIT Crawfords	4	5	.444	12	7	6	66	47	10	23	0	0
1933		2	3	.400	5	5	5	44	35	0	3	0	0
1934		3	0	1.000	10	5	1	36	24	8	5	2	0
1935		2	0	1.000	5	2	2	18	21	3	2	0	0
1936		3	1	.750	5	5	3	32	26	3	5	0	0
	15 years	75	54	.581	180	132	96	(1071)	(954)	(142)	(384)	10	3

Ben Taylor

TAYLOR, BEN   BL TL 6′ 190 lbs.
    Brother of C.L. Taylor and Candy Jim Taylor.
    B. 1888, Anderson, S.C.   D. Jan. 23, 1953, Baltimore, Md.

		W	L	PCT									
1920	IND ABCs	1	1	.500	No further data available								

Luis Tiant

TIANT, LUIS, SR.   TL 5′10″ 165 lbs.
    Father of Luis Tiant.
    B. Aug. 27, 1906, Havana, Cuba   D. Dec. 12, 1971

		W	L	PCT	G	GS	CG	IP	H	BB	SO	ShO	SV
1930	NY Cubans	4	13	.235	23	18	11	121	128	33	67	1	0
1931	Cuban HoD	1	3	.250	4	3	2	16	31	2	2	0	0
1932	NY Cubans	4	1	.800	7	4	2	50	16	6	12	1	0
1933	Team not in the league												
1934	Team not in the league												
1935	NY Cubans	7	4	.636	15	8	5	70	31	26	51	3	0
1936		1	0	1.000	4	1	1	14		3	4	0	0
1937	Team not in the league												
1938	Team not in the league												
1939	NY Cubans	1	3	.250	6	4	3	37	41	3	4	0	0
1940	No data available												
1941	No data available												
1942	No data available												
1943	NY Cubans	0	0		2	0	0					0	0
1944		0	0		1	1	0	3		1	0	0	
1945		2	1	.667	6	6	1	26	31	10	20	1	
1946		1	1	.500	5	2	2	72	47	6	13	0	0
1947		10	0	1.000	17		8	90	80		46	3	0
	(11 years)	(31)	(26)	(.544)	(90)	(47)	(35)	(499)	(405)	(90)	(219)	(9)	(0)

Cristobal Torriente

TORRIENTE, CRISTOBAL   BL TL 5′10″ 190 lbs.
    B. 1895, Cuba   D. 1938 (?), New York, N.Y.

		W	L	PCT									SV
1914	CHI Am. Giants	0	1	.000									0
1920		0	1	.000									0
1921		4	1	.800									0
1922		1	0	1.000									0
1923		1	0	1.000									0
1927	DET Stars	2	1	.667									0
1928		7	3	.700									2
	7 years	15	7	.682									2

Ted Trent

TRENT, THEODORE (Ted, Big Florida)   BR TR 6′3″ 185 lbs.
    B. Dec. 17, 1903, Jacksonville, Fla.   D. Jan. 10, 1944, Chicago, Ill.

		W	L	PCT	G	GS	CG	IP	H	BB	SO	ShO	SV
1927	STL Stars	15	11	.577	**35**	**25**	16	**204**	155	**71**	**127**	2	0
1928		21	2	**.913**	28	**22**	16	185	162	36	86	2	0
1929		12	8	.600	29	**22**	14	174	167	**42**	73	3	1
1930		12	2	.857	20	11	7	103	103	34	56	1	1
1931		3	1	.750	5	3	2	21	11	3	8	1	0
1932	2 teams DET Wolves WAS Pilots												
"	total	5	4	.556	14	10	5	77	77	17	20	1	0
1933	NY Black Yankees	0	0		1	0	0					0	0
1934	2 teams NY Black Yankees CHI Am. Giants												
"	total	4	4	.500	9	7	7	73	61	8	22	0	0
1935	CHI Am. Giants	4	7	.364	13	8	7	78	62	19	32	0	0
1936		2	1	.667	5	1	0	24	24	2	5	0	0
1937		8	2	.800	14	9	9	91	41	13	37	5	1
1938		6	4	.600	18	11	7	83	57	3	26	1	0
1939		2	3	.400	12	2	1	26	21	4	13	0	0
	13 years	94	49	.657	203	131	91	(1139)	(941)	(252)	(505)	16	3

Joe Williams

	W	L	PCT	G	GS	CG	IP	H	BB	SO	ShO	SV
WILLIAMS, JOE (Smokey, Cyclone)									BR	TR	6'4"	200 lbs.
B. Apr. 6, 1885 (?), Seguin, Tex. D. Mar. 12, 1946, New York, N.Y.												
1918 NY Lincoln Giants	7	1	.875	8	7	7	67	73	3	21	1	0
1919	8	2	.800	11	10	10	101	53	29	53	2	0
1920	0	2	.000	2	2	2	18		0	11	0	0
1921 2 teams NY Lincoln Giants AC Bacharach Giants												
" total	5	1	.833	8	6	6	52	19	1	8	0	0
1922 No data available												
1923 NY Lincoln Giants	3	6	.333	10	9	4	44	57	1	16	0	0
1924 BKN Royal Giants	3	6	.333	13	10	7	89	90	10	28	1	0
1925 Team not in the league												
1926 Team not in the league												
1927 Homestead Grays	1	0	1.000	1	1	1	9	9	0	8	1	0
1928	2	1	.667	4	2	2	21	3	8	6	0	0
1929	12	7	.632	23	12	7	77	24	8	10	0	1
1930	7	1	.875	10	7	7	72	40	8	46	0	0
1931	5	6	.455	13	13	9	85	28	3	3	0	0
1932 2 teams DET Wolves Homestead Grays												
" total	6	3	.667	12	10	6	80	50	8	5	0	0
(12 years)	(59)	(36)	(.621)	(115)	(89)	(68)	(715)	(446)	(79)	(215)	(5)	(1)

Nip Winters

	W	L	PCT	G	GS	CG	IP	H	BB	SO	ShO	SV
WINTERS, JESSE (Nip)									BL	TL	6'5"	235 lbs.
B. 1899, Washington, D.C. D. Dec. 1971, Hokessin, Del.												
1921 AC Bacharach Giants	3	2	.600	6	6	5	40	22	16	10	3	0
1922	4	3	.571	7	6	5	38	22	22	32	0	0
1923	6	3	.667	11	10	9	81	51	6	16	0	0
1924 PHI Hilldales	**19**	**5**	.792	**27**	**22**	**20**	**190**	131	24	72	2	2
1925	**21**	**10**	.677	**32**	**27**	**22**	**254**	**213**	**39**	**86**	1	0
1926	**15**	5	.750	23	17	14	149	116	46	62	2	1
1927	14	8	.636	22	22	12	81	72	34	32	1	0
1928 NY Lincoln Giants	8	7	.533	16	15	10	120	122	19	28	0	0
1929	3	5	.375	12	8	6	52	44	10	7	0	0
1930 No data available												
1931 3 teams PHI Hilldales NWK Browns AC Bacharach Giants												
" total	1	5	.167	9	6	5	2	39	10			0
1932 AC Bacharach Giants	1	1	.500	1	1	1	9	5			0	0
(11 years)	(95)	(54)	(.638)	(166)	(140)	(109)	(1016)	(837)	(226)	(345)	(9)	(3)

PART TWELVE

The World Series and Championship Playoffs

Results and Highlights of Each Playoff
And Series and Composite Box Scores

The World Series

Before the World Series started in 1903 there were other post-season championships which took place as early as 1884. Although they are not officially recognized as part of World Series history, they provided a basis for the establishment of the World Series. The first of these was between the 1884 pennant winners. The National League's Providence team swept the three-game series from the American Association's New York Metropolitans. Post-season series between the two league champions continued until 1891 when renewed fighting between the leagues prevented the games.

The twelve-team National League played a split season in 1892 to create a post-season playoff. Cleveland, first-half winners, met Boston, the second-half champions. Boston's momentum continued as they won five of the six games, Cleveland managing only one tie. In 1893 the split season was dropped and no playoffs were held. Then, in 1894, William C. Temple, a Pittsburgh sportsman, donated an expensive trophy in his name to be awarded to the winner of a playoff series between the teams that finished first and second in the pennant race. These best four-out-of-seven-game series lasted for four years, but the games were often ragged and one-sided and public interest was never very great.

Then, in 1903, with the National League sharing the spotlight with its junior competitor, the American League, the first World Series was held. The American League won the Series and caused an embarrassment that prevented the games from being held in 1904. Both leagues made peace in 1905 and signed an agreement governing the rules of post-season championship play, and the World Series was resumed, becoming an annual feature and attracting millions of people.

This section provides information on all World Series through today. Included are facts about the individual games and series and lifetime leaders. Most of the information is self-explanatory. That which may appear unfamiliar is listed below. Appearing first, before the individual series information, is a table showing the number of World Series games each franchise has played along with their wins, losses, and winning percentage.

When teams in this section are listed by an abbreviation of the city in which the team played, they appear as follows:

BAL	Baltimore	CLE	Cleveland
BKN	Brooklyn	DET	Detroit
BOS	Boston	KC	Kansas City
CHI	Chicago	LA	Los Angeles
CIN	Cincinnati	MIL	Milwaukee
MIN	Minnesota	SD	San Diego
NY	New York	SF	San Francisco
OAK	Oakland	STL	St. Louis
PHI	Philadelphia	WAS	Washington
PIT	Pittsburgh		

Franchise Summary

TEAM	LEAGUE	SERIES			GAMES		
		WON	LOST	PCT.	WON	LOST	PCT.
Oakland	AL	4	1	.800	17	11	.607
Pittsburgh	NL	5	2	.714	23	24	.489
New York	AL	22	11	.667	109	77	.586
New York Mets	NL	2	1	.667	11	8	.579
Cleveland	AL	2	1	.667	9	8	.529
Philadelphia	AL	5	3	.625	24	19	.558
St. Louis	NL	9	6	.600	48	48	.500
Boston	AL	5	4	.556	33	26	.559
Los Angeles	NL	5	4	.556	25	24	.510
Cincinnati	NL	4	4	.500	22	25	.468
Baltimore	AL	3	3	.500	19	14	.576
Chicago	AL	2	2	.500	13	13	.500
Boston	NL	1	1	.500	6	4	.600
Kansas City Royals	AL	1	1	.500	6	7	.462
Milwaukee	NL	1	1	.500	7	7	.500
Minnesota	AL	1	1	.500	7	7	.500
Detroit	AL	4	5	.444	26	29	.473
New York Giants	NL	5	9	.357	39	41	.488
Washington	AL	1	2	.333	8	11	.421
Philadelphia	NL	1	3	.250	6	14	.300
Chicago	NL	2	8	.200	19	33	.365
Brooklyn	NL	1	8	.111	20	36	.357
Milwaukee	AL	0	1	.000	3	4	.429
St. Louis	AL	0	1	.000	2	4	.333
San Diego	NL	0	1	.000	1	4	.200
San Francisco	NL	0	2	.000	3	8	.273

Individual Game Information

Innings Pitched. Pitchers are listed in the order of appearance. In parentheses, following each pitcher's name, are the number of innings he pitched in the game. For example: Doe (2.1) would mean that he pitched $2\frac{1}{3}$ innings.

Winning and Losing Pitchers. Indicated by boldfaced print.

Save. The pitcher who is credited with a Save is indicated by the abbreviation SV, which appears in boldfaced print after his innings pitched.

Home Runs. Players are listed in the order their home runs were hit.

Composite Box Score Information

The following is an explanation of the column headings:

Batting and Fielding
(Pitchers who would appear with all zeros in their information are not included.)

AB	At Bats
H	Hits
2B	Doubles
3B	Triples
HR	Home Runs
R	Runs Scored
RBI	Runs Batted In
BA	Batting Average

(Errors and Stolen Bases appear beneath this information.)

Pitching

W	Wins
L	Losses
ERA	Earned Run Average
IP	Innings Pitched
H	Hits allowed
BB	Bases on Balls Allowed
SO	Strike-outs
SV	Saves

1903 WORLD SERIES

LINE SCORES	PITCHERS (innings pitched)	HOME RUNS (men on)	HIGHLIGHTS

Boston (A.L.) defeats Pittsburgh (N.L.) 5 games to 3

GAME 1 - OCTOBER 1

PIT	N	401 100 100	7 12 2	Phillippe (9)	Sebring	
BOS	A	000 000 201	3 6 4	Young (9)		

Four runs in the first, three of them unearned, were enough to stake Phillippe to a win over the Red Sox. Phillippe struck out ten, Sebring had four RBIs, and Leach contributed four hits.

GAME 2 - OCTOBER 2

PIT	N	000 000 000	0 3 2	Leever (1), Veil (7)	
BOS	A	200 001 00x	3 9 0	Dinneen (9)	Dougherty, Dougherty

The Red Sox evened the Series behind Dinneen's 11-strikeout pitching performance and Dougherty's two home runs.

GAME 3 - OCTOBER 3

PIT	N	012 000 010	4 7 0	Phillippe (9)	
BOS	A	000 100 010	2 4 2	Hughes (2), Young (7)	

The Pirates built an early 3-0 lead and scored an insurance run on Young's error in the eighth to give Phillippe his second victory.

GAME 4 - OCTOBER 6

BOS	A	000 010 003	4 9 1	Dinneen (8)	
PIT	N	100 010 30x	5 12 1	Phillippe (9)	

After a one-day rain delay, Phillippe returned with his third complete-game win of the Series. Boston had the tying run on second with one out in the ninth but could not bring it across.

GAME 5 - OCTOBER 7

BOS	A	000 006 410	11 14 2	Young (9)	
PIT	N	000 000 020	2 6 4	Kennedy (7), Thompson (2)	

The Red Sox sent ten men to the plate in the sixth, breaking open a scoreless game. Dougherty had three hits, including two of Boston's five triples.

GAME 6 - OCTOBER 8

BOS	A	003 020 100	6 10 1	Dinneen (9)	
PIT	N	000 000 300	3 10 3	Leever (9)	

Three singles, a walk, a steal, and an error added up to three runs in the Boston third. Beaumont had four hits and two stolen bases in a losing effort.

GAME 7 - OCTOBER 10

BOS	A	200 202 010	7 11 4	Young (9)	
PIT	N	000 101 001	3 10 3	Phillippe (9)	

The Pirates put men on base in every inning but stranded nine as Young scattered ten hits to pin the first loss on Deacon Phillippe.

GAME 8 - OCTOBER 13

PIT	N	000 000 000	0 4 3	Phillippe (8)	
BOS	A	000 201 00x	3 8 0	Dinneen (9)	

Phillippe threw his fifth complete game of the Series, but was outdone by Dinneen's four-hitter. Boston bunched six of their eight hits into their two scoring frames to take the Series.

Team totals

		W	AB	H	2B	3B	HR	R	RBI	BA	BB	SO	ERA
BOS	A	5	282	71	4	16	2	39	35	.252	13	27	2.03
PIT	N	3	271	64	7	9	1	24	23	.236	14	45	3.73

Individual Batting

BOSTON (A.L.)

	AB	H	2B	3B	HR	R	RBI	BA
J. Collins, 3b	36	9	1	2	0	5	1	.250
P. Dougherty, of	34	8	0	2	2	3	5	.235
C. Stahl, of	33	10	1	3	0	6	3	.303
F. Parent, ss	32	9	0	3	0	8	3	.281
B. Freeman, of	32	9	0	3	0	6	4	.281
H. Ferris, 2b	31	9	0	1	0	3	7	.290
C. LaChance, 1b	27	6	2	1	0	5	4	.222
L. Criger, c	26	6	0	0	0	1	4	.231
C. Young, p	15	2	0	1	0	1	3	.133
B. Dinneen, p	12	3	0	0	0	1	0	.250
D. Farrell	2	0	0	0	0	0	1	.000
J. O'Brien	2	0	0	0	0	0	0	.000

Errors: L. Criger (3), C. LaChance (3), F. Parent (2), H. Ferris (2), J. Collins (2), P. Dougherty, C. Young
Stolen Bases: J. Collins (3), C. Stahl (2)

PITTSBURGH (N.L.)

	AB	H	2B	3B	HR	R	RBI	BA
G. Beaumont, of	34	9	0	1	0	6	0	.265
F. Clarke, of	34	9	2	1	0	3	2	.265
T. Leach, 3b	33	9	0	4	0	3	7	.273
J. Sebring, of	30	11	0	1	1	3	5	.367
Bransfield, 1b	30	6	0	2	0	3	1	.200
C. Ritchey, 2b	27	3	1	0	0	2	2	.111
H. Wagner, ss	27	6	1	0	0	2	3	.222
E. Phelps, c	26	6	2	0	0	1	2	.231
D. Phillippe, p	18	4	0	0	0	1	1	.222
S. Leever, p	4	0	0	0	0	0	0	.000
H. Smith, c	3	0	0	0	0	0	0	.000
B. Veil, p	2	0	0	0	0	0	0	.000
B. Kennedy, p	2	1	1	0	0	0	0	.500
G. Thompson, p	1	0	0	0	0	0	0	.000

Errors: H. Wagner (6), T. Leach (4), Bransfield (2), E. Phelps (2), D. Phillippe, H. Smith, B. Veil, F. Clarke
Stolen Bases: H. Wagner (3), T. Leach (2), G. Beaumont (2), Bransfield, F. Clarke, C. Ritchey

Individual Pitching

BOSTON (A.L.)

	W	L	ERA	IP	H	BB	SO	SV
B. Dinneen	3	1	2.06	35	29	8	28	0
C. Young	2	1	1.59	34	31	4	17	0
L. Hughes	0	1	9.00	2	4	2	0	0

PITTSBURGH (N.L.)

	W	L	ERA	IP	H	BB	SO	SV
D. Phillippe	3	2	3.27	44	38	3	20	0
S. Leever	0	2	6.30	10	13	3	2	0
B. Kennedy	0	1	5.14	7	11	3	3	0
B. Veil	0	0	1.29	7	6	4	1	0
G. Thompson	0	0	4.50	2	3	0	1	0

1905 WORLD SERIES

LINE SCORES	PITCHERS (innings pitched)	HOME RUNS (men on)	HIGHLIGHTS

New York (N.L.) defeats Philadelphia (A.L.) 4 games to 1

GAME 1 - OCTOBER 9

NY	N	000 020 001	3 10 1	Mathewson (9)	
PHI	A	000 000 000	0 4 0	Plank (9)	

The Giants refused to play the Series in 1904, but acceded to public demand a year later. Mathewson opened the Series masterfully, allowing just four hits and walking none.

GAME 2 - OCTOBER 10

PHI	A	001 000 020	3 6 2	Bender (9)	
NY	N	000 000 000	0 4 2	McGinnity (8), Ames (1)	

Bender, Philadelphia's tall Indian, evened the Series with his shutout, aided by Bris Lord's two RBIs.

GAME 3 - OCTOBER 12

NY	N	200 050 002	9 9 1	Mathewson (9)	
PHI	A	000 000 000	0 4 5	Coakley (9)	

A day of rain allowed Mathewson to return to post his second shutout, once again holding the Athletics to four hits. McGann drove in four runs on three hits.

GAME 4 - OCTOBER 13

PHI	A	000 000 000	0 5 2	Plank (8)	
NY	N	000 100 00x	1 4 1	McGinnity (9)	

Plank allowed just four hits, but was beaten by McGinnity's shutout. An unearned run in the fourth accounted for all the scoring.

GAME 5 - OCTOBER 14

PHI	A	000 000 000	0 6 0	Bender (8)	
NY	N	000 010 01x	2 5 1	Mathewson (9)	

Mathewson gained his third shutout to clinch a Series in which every game was a shutout. In his three victories, Matty allowed just fourteen hits, struck out eighteen, and walked but one.

Team totals

		W	AB	H	2B	3B	HR	R	RBI	BA	BB	SO	ERA
NY	N	4	153	32	7	0	0	15	13	.209	15	26	0.00
PHI	A	1	155	25	5	0	0	3	2	.161	5	25	1.47

Individual Batting

NEW YORK (N.L.)

	AB	H	2B	3B	HR	R	RBI	BA
G. Browne, of	22	4	0	0	0	2	1	.182
M. Donlin, of	19	6	1	0	0	4	1	.316
B. Gilbert, 2b	17	4	0	0	0	1	1	.235
D. McGann, 1b	17	4	2	0	0	1	4	.235
S. Mertes, of	17	3	1	0	0	2	3	.176
A. Devlin, 3b	16	4	1	0	0	1	0	.250
R. Bresnahan, c	16	5	2	0	0	3	1	.313
B. Dahlen, ss	15	0	0	0	0	1	1	.000
C. Mathewson, p	8	2	0	0	0	1	0	.250
McGinnity, p	5	0	0	0	0	0	0	.000
S. Strang	1	0	0	0	0	0	0	.000

Errors: A. Devlin (2), M. Donlin (2), C. Mathewson, D. McGann
Stolen Bases: A. Devlin (3), M. Donlin (2), G. Browne (2), B. Dahlen (2), R. Bresnahan, B. Gilbert

PHILADELPHIA (A.L.)

	AB	H	2B	3B	HR	R	RBI	BA
H. Davis, 1b	20	4	1	0	0	0	0	.200
B. Lord, of	20	2	0	0	0	0	2	.100
L. Cross, 3b	19	2	0	0	0	0	0	.105
M. Cross, ss	17	3	0	0	0	0	0	.176
T. Hartsel, of	17	5	1	0	0	1	0	.294
D. Murphy, 2b	16	3	1	0	0	0	0	.188
S. Seybold, of	16	2	0	0	0	0	0	.125
Schreckengost, c	9	2	1	0	0	2	0	.222
M. Powers, c	7	1	1	0	0	0	0	.143
E. Plank, p	6	1	0	0	0	0	0	.167
C. Bender, p	5	0	0	0	0	0	0	.000
A. Coakley, p	2	0	0	0	0	0	0	.000
D. Hoffman	1	0	0	0	0	0	0	.000

Errors: D. Murphy (4), L. Cross (2), M. Cross (2), T. Hartsel
Stolen Bases: T. Hartsel (2)

Individual Pitching

NEW YORK (N.L.)

	W	L	ERA	IP	H	BB	SO	SV
C. Mathewson	3	0	0.00	27	14	1	18	0
McGinnity	1	1	0.00	17	10	3	6	0
R. Ames	0	0	0.00	1	1	1	1	0

PHILADELPHIA (A.L.)

	W	L	ERA	IP	H	BB	SO	SV
C. Bender	1	1	1.06	17	9	6	13	0
E. Plank	0	2	1.59	17	14	4	11	0
A. Coakley	0	1	2.00	9	9	5	2	0

1906 WORLD SERIES

LINE SCORES	PITCHERS (innings pitched)	HOME RUNS (men on)	HIGHLIGHTS

Chicago (A.L.) defeats Chicago (N.L.) 4 games to 2

GAME 1 - OCTOBER 9

CHI	A	000 011 000	2 4 1	Altrock (9)		
CHI	N	000 001 000	1 4 2	Brown (9)		

Isbell scored Jones with the tie-breaking run on a single in the sixth in a game played in bitterly cold weather and snow flurries.

GAME 2 - OCTOBER 10

CHI	N	031 001 020	7 10 2	Reulbach (9)	
CHI	A	000 010 000	1 1 2	White (3), Owen (6)	

Reulbach pitched six no-hit innings before yielding a single to Donahue. He finished with a one-hitter, but walked six and hit one batter.

GAME 3 - OCTOBER 11

CHI	A	000 003 000	3 4 1	Walsh (9)	
CHI	N	000 000 000	0 2 2	Pfiester (9)	

Rohe's three-run triple in the sixth broke open the game and aided Walsh's record 12-strikeout pitching performance.

GAME 4 - OCTOBER 12

CHI	N	000 000 100	1 7 1	Brown (9)	
CHI	A	000 000 000	0 2 1	Altrock (9)	

Evers singled in Chance in the seventh to back up Brown's two-hitter.

GAME 5 - OCTOBER 13

CHI	A	102 401 000	8 12 6	Walsh (6.1), White (2.2) SV	
CHI	N	300 102 000	6 6 0	Reulbach (2), Pfiester (1.1), Overall (5.2)	

Isbell hit four doubles, scored three runs and drove in two to pace the White Sox' twelve-hit attack.

GAME 6 - OCTOBER 14

CHI	N	100 010 001	3 7 0	Brown (1.2), Overall (6.1)	
CHI	A	340 000 01x	8 14 3	White (9)	

The White Sox jumped to a 7-1 lead after two innings and won the Series as Hahn contributed four hits and Donahue and Davis each drove in three runs.

Team totals

		W	AB	H	2B	3B	HR	R	RBI	BA	BB	SO	ERA
CHI	A	4	187	37	10	3	0	22	19	.198	18	35	1.67
CHI	N	2	184	36	9	0	0	18	11	.196	18	28	3.40

Individual Batting

CHICAGO (A.L.)

	AB	H	2B	3B	HR	R	RBI	BA
F. Isbell, 2b	26	8	4	0	0	4	4	.308
E. Hahn, of	22	6	0	0	0	4	0	.273
F. Jones, of	21	2	0	0	0	4	0	.095
G. Rohe, 3b	21	7	1	2	0	2	4	.333
B. Sullivan, c	21	0	0	0	0	0	0	.000
P. Dougherty, of	20	2	0	0	0	1	1	.100
J. Donahue, 1b	18	6	2	1	0	0	4	.333
G. Davis, ss	13	4	3	0	0	4	6	.308
L. Tannehill, ss	9	1	0	0	0	1	0	.111
E. Walsh, p	4	0	0	0	0	1	0	.000
N. Altrock, p	4	1	0	0	0	0	0	.250
D. White, p	3	0	0	0	0	0	0	.000
F. Owen, p	2	0	0	0	0	0	0	.000
McFarland	1	0	0	0	0	0	0	.000
B. O'Neill, of	1	0	0	0	0	1	0	.000
B. Towne	1	0	0	0	0	0	0	.000

Errors: F. Isbell (5), G. Rohe (3), G. Davis (2), J. Donahue, P. Dougherty, B. Sullivan, E. Walsh
Stolen Bases: G. Rohe (2), P. Dougherty (2), F. Isbell, G. Davis

CHICAGO (N.L.)

	AB	H	2B	3B	HR	R	RBI	BA
W. Schulte, of	26	7	3	0	0	1	3	.269
S. Hofman, of	23	7	1	0	0	3	2	.304
F. Chance, 1b	21	5	1	0	0	3	0	.238
J. Sheckard, of	21	0	0	0	0	0	1	.000
Steinfeldt, 3b	20	5	1	0	0	2	2	.250
J. Evers, 2b	20	3	1	0	0	2	1	.150
J. Tinker, ss	18	3	0	0	0	4	1	.167
J. Kling, c	17	3	1	0	0	2	0	.176
T. Brown, p	6	2	0	0	0	0	0	.333
O. Overall, p	4	1	1	0	0	1	0	.250
E. Reulbach, p	3	0	0	0	0	0	1	.000
P. Moran	2	0	0	0	0	0	0	.000
J. Pfiester, p	2	0	0	0	0	0	0	.000
D. Gessler	1	0	0	0	0	0	0	.000

Errors: J. Tinker (2), T. Brown, J. Evers, J. Kling, J. Pfiester, Steinfeldt
Stolen Bases: J. Tinker (2), F. Chance (2), J. Evers (2), S. Hofman, J. Sheckard

Individual Pitching

CHICAGO (A.L.)

	W	L	ERA	IP	H	BB	SO	SV
N. Altrock	1	1	1.00	18	11	2	5	0
E. Walsh	2	0	1.80	15	7	6	17	0
D. White	1	1	1.80	15	12	7	4	1
F. Owen	0	0	3.00	6	6	3	2	0

CHICAGO (N.L.)

	W	L	ERA	IP	H	BB	SO	SV
T. Brown	1	2	3.66	19.2	14	4	12	0
O. Overall	0	0	1.50	12	10	3	8	0
E. Reulbach	1	0	2.45	11	6	8	4	0
J. Pfiester	0	2	6.10	10.1	7	3	11	0

1907 WORLD SERIES

LINE SCORES	PITCHERS (innings pitched)	HOME RUNS (men on)	HIGHLIGHTS

Chicago (N.L.) defeats Detroit (A.L.) 4 games to 0

GAME 1 - OCTOBER 8

DET	A	000 000 030 000	3	9	3	Donovan (12)
CHI	N	000 100 002 000	3	10	5	Overall (9), Reulbach (3)

Schmidt's third-strike passed ball with two out in the ninth allowed the Cubs to even the game, which ended after 12 in a 3-3 tie. Donovan struck out 12 and the Cubs stole seven bases.

GAME 2 - OCTOBER 9

DET	A	010 000 000	1	9	1	Mullin (8)
CHI	N	010 200 00x	3	9	1	Pfiester (9)

Slagle drove in the go-ahead run with a single in the fourth, then scored an insurance run on Sheckard's double.

GAME 3 - OCTOBER 10

DET	A	000 001 000	1	6	1	Siever (4), Killian (4)
CHI	N	010 310 00x	5	10	1	Reulbach (9)

Evers's three hits led the Cubs' attack as Reulbach subdued the Tigers on six scattered hits.

GAME 4 - OCTOBER 11

CHI	N	000 020 301	6	7	2	Overall (9)
DET	A	000 100 000	1	5	2	Donovan (9)

Overall aided his own cause with a go-ahead two-run single in the fifth as he held the Tigers to five hits.

GAME 5 - OCTOBER 12

CHI	N	110 000 000	2	7	1	Brown (9)
DET	A	000 000 000	0	7	2	Mullin (9)

The Cubs swept the Series behind Brown's shutout. The Cubs swiped 18 bases in the five games, and held batting champ Ty Cobb to a .200 average.

Team totals

		W	AB	H	2B	3B	HR	R	RBI	BA	BB	SO	ERA
CHI	N	4	167	43	6	1	0	19	16	.257	12	25	0.75
DET	A	0	172	36	1	2	0	6	6	.209	9	22	1.96

Individual Batting

CHICAGO (N.L.)

	AB	H	2B	3B	HR	R	RBI	BA
J. Slagle, of	22	6	0	0	0	3	4	.273
J. Sheckard, of	21	5	2	0	0	0	2	.238
W. Schulte, of	20	5	0	0	0	3	2	.250
J. Evers, 2b, ss	20	7	2	0	0	2	1	.350
J. Kling, c	19	4	0	0	0	2	1	.211
Steinfeldt, 3b	17	8	1	1	0	2	2	.471
F. Chance, 1b	14	3	1	0	0	3	0	.214
J. Tinker, ss	13	2	0	0	0	4	1	.154
D. Howard, 1b	5	1	0	0	0	0	0	.200
O. Overall, p	5	1	0	0	0	0	2	.200
E. Reulbach, p	5	1	0	0	0	0	1	.200
T. Brown, p	3	0	0	0	0	0	0	.000
J. Pfiester, p	2	0	0	0	0	0	0	.000
H. Zimmerman, 2b	1	0	0	0	0	0	0	.000
P. Moran	0	0	0	0	0	0	0	–

Errors: J. Tinker (3), W. Schulte (2), J. Evers (2), J. Slagle, J. Kling.
Stolen Bases: J. Slagle (6), J. Evers (3), F. Chance (3), J. Tinker (2), Steinfeldt, D. Howard, W. Schulte, J. Sheckard

DETROIT (A.L.)

	AB	H	2B	3B	HR	R	RBI	BA
S. Crawford, of	21	5	1	0	0	1	2	.238
G. Schaefer, 2b	21	3	0	0	0	1	0	.143
C. Rossman, 1b	20	8	0	1	0	1	2	.400
T. Cobb, of	20	4	0	1	0	1	1	.200
B. Coughlin, 3b	20	5	0	0	0	0	0	.250
C. O'Leary, ss	17	1	0	0	0	0	0	.059
D. Jones, of	17	6	0	0	0	1	0	.353
B. Schmidt, c	12	2	0	0	0	0	0	.167
W. Donovan, p	8	0	0	0	0	0	0	.000
G. Mullin, p	6	0	0	0	0	0	0	.000
F. Payne, c	4	1	0	0	0	0	1	.250
J. Archer, c	3	0	0	0	0	0	0	.000
E. Killian, p	2	1	0	0	0	1	0	.500
E. Siever, p	1	0	0	0	0	0	0	.000

Errors: B. Schmidt (2), B. Coughlin (2), C. O'Leary (2), F. Payne, D. Jones, C. Rossman
Stolen Bases: D. Jones (3), C. Rossman (2), G. Schaefer, B. Coughlin

Individual Pitching

CHICAGO (N.L.)

	W	L	ERA	IP	H	BB	SO	SV
O. Overall	1	0	1.00	18	14	4	11	0
E. Reulbach	1	0	0.75	12	6	3	4	0
J. Pfiester	1	0	1.00	9	9	1	3	0
T. Brown	1	0	0.00	9	7	1	4	0

DETROIT (A.L.)

	W	L	ERA	IP	H	BB	SO	SV
W. Donovan	0	1	1.29	21	17	5	16	0
G. Mullin	0	2	2.12	17	16	6	7	0
E. Siever	0	1	4.50	4	7	0	1	0
E. Killian	0	0	2.25	4	3	1	1	0

1908 WORLD SERIES

LINE SCORES	PITCHERS (innings pitched)	HOME RUNS (men on)	HIGHLIGHTS

Chicago (N.L.) defeats Detroit (A.L.) 4 games to 1

GAME 1 - OCTOBER 10

CHI	N	004 000 105	10 14 2	Reulbach (6.2), Overall (0.1), **Brown** (2)	
DET	A	100 000 320	6 10 4	Killian (2.1), **Summers** (6.2)	

Five Cub runs in the ninth, four scoring on two-run singles by Hofman and Kling, broke open a game played in heavy rain.

GAME 2 - OCTOBER 11

DET	A	000 000 001	1 4 1	Donovan (8)	
CHI	N	000 000 06x	6 7 1	**Overall** (9)	Tinker (1 on)

Donovan held the Cubs to one hit in seven innings, but Tinker's homer sparked a six-run rally that broke up a scoreless deadlock.

GAME 3 - OCTOBER 12

DET	A	100 005 020	8 11 4	**Mullin** (9)	
CHI	N	000 300 000	3 7 2	Pfiester (8), Reulbach (1)	

Cobb's four hits led the Detroit attack to a come-from-behind victory.

GAME 4 - OCTOBER 13

CHI	A	002 000 001	3 10 0	**Brown** (9)	
DET	N	000 000 000	0 4 1	Summers (8), Winter (1)	

Back-to-back scoring singles by Steinfeldt and Hofman in the third gave Brown all the runs he needed to subdue the Tigers.

GAME 5 - OCTOBER 14

CHI	N	100 010 000	2 10 0	**Overall** (9)	
DET	A	000 000 000	0 3 0	Donovan (9)	

Three hits and one RBI each by Evers and Chance aided Overall's 10-strikeout pitching in the Series clincher.

Team totals

		W	AB	H	2B	3B	HR	R	RBI	BA	BB	SO	ERA
CHI	N	4	164	48	4	2	1	24	20	.293	13	26	2.60
DET	A	1	158	32	5	0	0	15	14	.203	12	26	3.48

Individual Batting

CHICAGO (N.L.)

	AB	H	2B	3B	HR	R	RBI	BA
J. Sheckard, of	21	5	2	0	0	2	1	.238
J. Evers, 2b	20	7	1	0	0	5	2	.350
S. Hofman, of	19	6	0	1	0	2	4	.316
F. Chance, 1b	19	8	0	0	0	4	2	.421
J. Tinker, ss	19	5	0	0	1	2	5	.263
W. Schulte, of	18	7	0	1	0	4	2	.389
Steinfeldt, 3b	16	4	0	0	0	3	3	.250
J. Kling, c	16	4	1	0	0	2	1	.250
O. Overall, p	6	2	0	0	0	0	0	.333
T. Brown, p	4	0	0	0	0	0	0	.000
E. Reulbach, p	3	0	0	0	0	0	0	.000
J. Pfiester, p	2	0	0	0	0	0	0	.000
D. Howard	1	0	0	0	0	0	0	.000

Errors: F. Chance (3), J. Evers, Steinfeldt
Stolen Bases: F. Chance (5), J. Evers (2), S. Hofman (2), W. Schulte (2), J. Sheckard, Steinfeldt, J. Tinker

DETROIT (A.L.)

	AB	H	2B	3B	HR	R	RBI	BA
S. Crawford, of	21	5	1	0	0	2	1	.238
C. O'Leary, ss	19	3	0	0	0	2	0	.158
C. Rossman, 1b	19	4	0	0	0	3	3	.211
T. Cobb, of	19	7	1	0	0	3	4	.368
M. McIntyre, of	18	4	1	0	0	2	0	.222
G. Schaefer, 3b, 2b	16	2	0	0	0	0	0	.125
B. Schmidt, c	14	1	0	0	0	0	1	.071
B. Coughlin, 3b	8	1	0	0	0	0	1	.125
R. Downs, 2b	6	1	1	0	0	1	1	.167
E. Summers, p	5	1	0	0	0	0	1	.200
I. Thomas, c	4	2	1	0	0	0	1	.500
W. Donovan, p	4	0	0	0	0	0	0	.000
G. Mullin, p	3	1	0	0	0	1	1	.333
D. Jones	2	0	0	0	0	0	0	.000

Errors: C. Rossman (2), T. Cobb (2), B. Coughlin, W. Donovan, R. Downs, M. McIntyre, C. O'Leary, G. Schaefer
Stolen Bases: T. Cobb (2), W. Donovan, M. McIntyre

Individual Pitching

CHICAGO (N.L.)

	W	L	ERA	IP	H	BB	SO	SV
O. Overall	2	0	0.98	18.1	7	7	15	0
T. Brown	2	0	0.00	11	6	1	5	0
J. Pfiester	0	1	7.88	8	10	3	1	0
E. Reulbach	0	0	4.70	7.2	9	1	5	0

DETROIT (A.L.)

	W	L	ERA	IP	H	BB	SO	SV
W. Donovan	0	2	4.24	17	17	4	10	0
E. Summers	0	2	4.30	14.2	18	4	7	0
G. Mullin	1	0	1.00	9	7	1	8	0
E. Killian	0	0	7.71	2.1	5	3	1	0
G. Winter	0	0	0.00	1	1	1	0	0

1909 WORLD SERIES

LINE SCORES	PITCHERS (innings pitched)	HOME RUNS (men on)	HIGHLIGHTS

Pittsburgh (N.L.) defeats Detroit (A.L.) 4 games to 3

GAME 1 - OCTOBER 8

DET	A	100 000 000	1 6 4	Mullin (8)	
PIT	N	000 121 00x	4 5 0	Adams (9)	Clarke

Leach made a running catch of Cobb's fly in the seventh with two on and two out to preserve the 4-1 lead.

GAME 2 - OCTOBER 9

DET	A	023 020 000	7 9 3	Donovan (9)	
PIT	N	200 000 000	2 5 1	Camnitz (2.2), Willis (6.1)	

Three in the third, capped by Cobb's steal of home, broke open the game. Every Tiger hitter except Donovan had at least one hit.

GAME 3 - OCTOBER 11

PIT	N	510 000 002	8 10 3	Maddox (9)	
DET	A	000 000 402	6 10 5	Summers (0.1), Willett (6.2), Works (2)	

The Pirates held off a late Tiger rally for the win. Wagner was the hitting star, with three singles, three RBIs, three stolen bases.

GAME 4 - OCTOBER 12

PIT	N	000 000 000	0 5 6	Leifield (4), Phillippe (4)	
DET	A	020 300 00x	5 8 0	Mullin (9)	

Cobb and Stanage contributed two RBIs each as the Tigers evened the Series, Mullin striking out ten Pirates.

GAME 5 - OCTOBER 13

DET	A	100 002 010	4 6 1	Summers (7), Willett (1)	D. Jones, Crawford
PIT	N	111 000 41x	8 10 2	Adams (9)	Clarke (2 on)

Clarke's two-run homer in the seventh broke open the 3-3 deadlock, off-setting Crawford's 3-for-4 performance that included a double and homer of his own.

GAME 6 - OCTOBER 14

PIT	N	300 000 001	4 7 3	Willis (5), Camnitz (1), Phillippe (2)	
DET	A	100 211 00x	5 10 3	Mullin (9)	

The Tigers suffered four injuries in the ninth but hung on to win. Tom Jones ran over Wilson to let in one run, but Schmidt and Moriarty ended the game by recording putouts while being spiked on close plays at the plate and at third.

GAME 7 - OCTOBER 16

PIT	N	020 203 010	8 7 0	Adams (9)	
DET	A	000 000 000	0 6 3	Donovan (3), Mullin (6)	

Clarke is walked four times and Wagner and Miller each had two RBIs to pace the Pirates' Series victory. Eighteen Buc stolen bases tied the Series record set by the Cubs in 1906.

Team totals

		W	AB	H	2B	3B	HR	R	RBI	BA	BB	SO	ERA
PIT	N	4	223	49	13	1	2	34	25	.220	20	34	3.10
DET	A	3	233	55	16	0	2	28	26	.236	20	22	3.10

Individual Batting

PITTSBURGH (N.L.)

	AB	H	2B	3B	HR	R	RBI	BA
D. Miller, 2b	28	7	1	0	0	2	4	.250
B. Abstein, 1b	26	6	2	0	0	3	2	.231
O. Wilson, of	26	4	1	0	0	2	1	.154
G. Gibson, c	25	6	2	0	0	2	2	.240
T. Leach, of, 3b	25	8	4	0	0	8	2	.320
B. Byrne, 3b	24	6	1	0	0	5	0	.250
H. Wagner, ss	24	8	2	1	0	4	6	.333
F. Clarke, of	19	4	0	0	2	7	7	.211
B. Adams, p	9	0	0	0	0	0	0	.000
H. Hyatt, of	4	0	0	0	0	1	1	.000
N. Maddox, p	4	0	0	0	0	0	0	.000
V. Willis, p	4	0	0	0	0	0	0	.000
P. O'Connor	1	0	0	0	0	0	0	.000
D. Phillippe, p	1	0	0	0	0	0	0	.000
L. Leifield, p	1	0	0	0	0	0	0	.000
H. Camnitz, p	1	0	0	0	0	0	0	.000
Abbaticchio	1	0	0	0	0	0	0	.000

Errors: B. Abstein (5), D. Miller (3), D. Phillippe (2), H. Wagner (2), F. Clarke, B. Byrne, O. Wilson

Stolen Bases: H. Wagner (6), D. Miller (3), F. Clarke (3), G. Gibson (2), T. Leach, O. Wilson, B. Abstein, B. Byrne

DETROIT (A.L.)

	AB	H	2B	3B	HR	R	RBI	BA
D. Jones, of	30	7	0	0	1	6	2	.233
S. Crawford, of, 1b	28	7	3	0	1	4	3	.250
T. Cobb, of	26	6	3	0	0	3	6	.231
J. Delahanty, 2b	26	9	4	0	0	2	4	.346
T. Jones, 1b	24	6	1	0	0	3	2	.250
D. Bush, ss	23	6	1	0	0	5	2	.261
G. Moriarty, 3b	22	6	1	0	0	4	1	.273
B. Schmidt, c	18	4	2	0	0	0	4	.222
G. Mullin, p	16	3	1	0	0	1	0	.188
O. Stanage, c	5	1	0	0	0	0	2	.200
W. Donovan, p	4	0	0	0	0	0	0	.000
C. O'Leary, 3b	3	0	0	0	0	0	0	.000
M. McIntyre, of	3	0	0	0	0	0	0	.000
E. Summers, p	3	0	0	0	0	0	0	.000
E. Willett, p	2	0	0	0	0	0	0	.000

Errors: D. Bush (5), B. Schmidt (5), S. Crawford (2), J. Delahanty (2), W. Donovan, D. Jones, T. Jones, T. Cobb, E. Willett

Stolen Bases: T. Cobb (2), S. Crawford, D. Bush, D. Jones, T. Jones

Individual Pitching

PITTSBURGH (N.L.)

	W	L	ERA	IP	H	BB	SO	SV
B. Adams	3	0	1.33	27	18	6	11	0
V. Willis	0	1	4.76	11.1	10	8	3	0
N. Maddox	1	0	1.00	9	10	2	4	0
D. Phillippe	0	0	0.00	6	2	1	2	0
L. Leifield	0	1	11.25	4	7	1	0	0
H. Camnitz	0	1	12.27	3.2	8	2	2	0

DETROIT (A.L.)

	W	L	ERA	IP	H	BB	SO	SV
G. Mullin	2	1	2.25	32	22	8	20	0
W. Donovan	1	1	3.00	12	7	8	7	0
E. Summers	0	2	8.59	7.1	13	4	4	0
E. Willett	0	0	0.00	7.2	3	0	1	0
R. Works	0	0	9.00	2	4	0	2	0

1910 WORLD SERIES

LINE SCORES	PITCHERS (innings pitched)	HOME RUNS (men on)	HIGHLIGHTS

Philadelphia (A.L.) defeats Chicago (N.L.) 4 games to 1

GAME 1 - OCTOBER 17

CHI	N	000 000 001	1	3	1	Overall (3), McIntire (5)		Baker's single, two doubles, and two RBIs paced the Athletics' attack. Bender lost his shutout in the ninth thanks to errors by Thomas and Strunk.
PHI	A	021 000 01x	4	7	2	Bender (9)		

GAME 2 - OCTOBER 18

CHI	N	100 000 101	3	8	3	Brown (7), Richie (1)		The Athletics broke open the game with a six-run seventh featuring four Athletics doubles. Everyone in the Philadelphia lineup contributed at least one hit.
PHI	A	002 010 06x	9	14	4	Coombs (9)		

GAME 3 - OCTOBER 20

PHI	A	125 000 400	12	15	1	Coombs (9)	Murphy (2 on)	Murphy's three-run homer sparked a five-run third inning to put the game out of reach of the Cubs. Coombs aided his own cause with three hits and three RBIs.
CHI	N	120 000 020	5	6	5	Reulbach (2), McIntire (0.1) Pfiester (6.2)		

GAME 4 - OCTOBER 22

PHI	A	001 200 000 0	3	11	3	Bender (9.2)		Chance's triple with one out in the ninth tied the game and Sheckard's game-winning single in the bottom of the tenth prevented a Series sweep.
CHI	N	100 100 001 1	4	9	1	Cole (8), Brown (2)		

GAME 5 - OCTOBER 23

PHI	A	100 010 050	7	9	1	Coombs (9)		Athletics scored five times in the eighth to break open a tight game and wrap up the series in five games. Coombs posted his third victory and Collins led the offense with three hits and two RBIs.
CHI	N	010 000 010	2	9	2	Brown (9)		

Team totals

		W	AB	H	2B	3B	HR	R	RBI	BA	BB	SO	ERA
PHI	A	4	177	56	19	1	1	35	29	.316	17	24	2.76
CHI	N	1	158	35	11	1	0	15	13	.222	18	31	4.70

Individual Batting

PHILADELPHIA (A.L.)

	AB	H	2B	3B	HR	R	RBI	BA
F. Baker, 3b	22	9	3	0	0	6	4	.409
B. Lord, of	22	4	2	0	0	3	1	.182
E. Collins, 2b	21	9	4	0	0	5	3	.429
D. Murphy, of	20	7	3	0	1	6	8	.350
A. Strunk, of	18	5	1	1	0	2	2	.278
H. Davis, 1b	17	6	3	0	0	5	2	.353
J. Barry, ss	17	4	2	0	0	3	3	.235
J. Coombs, p	13	5	1	0	0	0	3	.385
I. Thomas, c	12	3	0	0	0	2	1	.250
C. Bender, p	6	2	0	0	0	1	1	.333
T. Hartsel, of	5	1	0	0	0	2	0	.200
J. Lapp, c	4	1	0	0	0	0	1	.250

Errors: H. Davis (3), F. Baker (3), J. Coombs (2), E. Collins, A. Strunk, I. Thomas
Stolen Bases: E. Collins (4), T. Hartsel (2), D. Murphy

CHICAGO (N.L.)

	AB	H	2B	3B	HR	R	RBI	BA
Steinfeldt, 3b	20	2	1	0	0	0	1	.100
J. Tinker, ss	18	6	2	0	0	2	0	.333
W. Schulte, of	17	6	3	0	0	3	2	.353
F. Chance, 1b	17	6	1	1	0	1	4	.353
H. Zimmerman, 2b	17	4	1	0	0	0	2	.235
S. Hofman, of	15	4	0	0	0	2	2	.267
J. Sheckard, of	14	4	2	0	0	5	1	.286
J. Kling, c	13	1	0	0	0	0	1	.077
J. Archer, c, 1b	11	2	1	0	0	1	0	.182
T. Brown, p	7	0	0	0	0	0	0	.000
K. Cole, p	2	0	0	0	0	0	0	.000
J. Pfiester, p	2	0	0	0	0	0	0	.000
G. Beaumont	2	0	0	0	0	1	0	.000
O. Overall, p	1	0	0	0	0	0	0	.000
H. McIntire, p	1	0	0	0	0	0	0	.000
T. Needham	1	0	0	0	0	0	0	.000
J. Kane	0	0	0	0	0	0	0	–

Errors: Steinfeldt (4), J. Tinker (2), H. Zimmerman, T. Brown, S. Hofman, H. McIntire, W. Schulte, J. Sheckard
Stolen Bases: J. Sheckard, J. Tinker, H. Zimmerman

Individual Pitching

PHILADELPHIA (A.L.)

	W	L	ERA	IP	H	BB	SO	SV
J. Coombs	3	0	3.33	27	23	14	17	0
C. Bender	1	1	1.93	18.2	12	4	14	0

CHICAGO (N.L.)

	W	L	ERA	IP	H	BB	SO	SV
T. Brown	1	2	5.00	18	23	7	14	0
K. Cole	0	0	3.38	8	10	3	5	0
J. Pfiester	0	0	0.00	6.2	9	1	1	0
H. McIntire	0	1	6.75	5.1	4	3	3	0
O. Overall	0	1	9.00	3	6	1	1	0
E. Reulbach	0	0	13.50	2	3	2	0	0
L. Richie	0	0	0.00	1	1	0	0	0

1911 WORLD SERIES

LINE SCORES	PITCHERS (innings pitched)	HOME RUNS (men on)	HIGHLIGHTS

Philadelphia (A.L.) defeats New York (N.L.) 4 games to 2

GAME 1 - OCTOBER 14

PHI	A	010 000 000	1 6 2	Bender (8)	
NY	N	000 100 10x	2 5 0	Mathewson (9)	

Devore's go-ahead single in the seventh gave Mathewson and the Giants a 2-1 victory over Bender, who struck out 11 in a losing cause.

GAME 2 - OCTOBER 16

NY	N	010 000 000	1 5 3	Marquard (7), Crandall (1)	
PHI	A	100 002 00x	3 4 0	Plank (9)	Baker (1 on)

Baker's two-run homer in the sixth broke a 1-1 deadlock and evened the Series.

GAME 3 - OCTOBER 17

PHI	A	000 000 001 02	3 9 2	Coombs (11)	Baker
NY	N	001 000 000 01	2 3 5	Mathewson (11)	

Baker's homer in the top of the ninth sent the game into extra innings. The Athletics scored twice in the 11th; Davis's RBI single proved the deciding run as the Giants countered with a run in their half of the inning.

GAME 4 - OCTOBER 24

NY	N	200 000 000	2 7 3	Mathewson (7), Wiltse (1)	
PHI	A	000 310 00x	4 11 1	Bender (9)	

The Giants' two-run lead was overcome in the fourth as the Athletics scored three times. Baker, Murphy, and Barry led the attack with two doubles each.

GAME 5 - OCTOBER 25

PHI	A	003 000 000 0	3 7 1	Coombs (9), Plank (0.2)	Oldring (2 on)
NY	N	000 000 102 1	4 9 2	Marquard (3), Ames (4), Crandall (3)	

The Giants scored two runs in the ninth, tying the game and offsetting Oldring's third inning three-run shot. Merkle's sacrifice fly in the bottom of the tenth drove in the winning run.

GAME 6 - OCTOBER 26

NY	N	100 000 001	2 4 3	Ames (4), Wiltse (2.1), Marquard (1.2)	
PHI	A	001 401 70x	13 13 5	Bender (9)	

Six singles, a double, an error, and a wild pitch led to seven Philadelphia runs and a World Series crown.

Team totals

		W	AB	H	2B	3B	HR	R	RBI	BA	BB	SO	ERA
PHI	A	4	205	50	15	0	3	27	20	.244	4	31	1.29
NY	N	2	189	33	11	1	0	13	10	.175	14	44	2.83

Individual Batting

PHILADELPHIA (A.L.)

	AB	H	2B	3B	HR	R	RBI	BA
B. Lord, of	27	5	2	0	0	2	1	.185
R. Oldring, of	25	5	2	0	1	2	3	.200
H. Davis, 1b	24	5	1	0	0	3	5	.208
F. Baker, 3b	24	9	2	0	2	7	5	.375
D. Murphy, of	23	7	3	0	0	4	2	.304
E. Collins, 2b	21	6	1	0	0	4	1	.286
J. Barry, ss	19	7	4	0	0	2	2	.368
I. Thomas, c	12	1	0	0	0	1	0	.083
C. Bender, p	11	1	0	0	0	0	0	.091
J. Lapp, c	8	2	0	0	0	1	0	.250
J. Coombs, p	8	2	0	0	0	1	0	.250
E. Plank, p	3	0	0	0	0	0	0	.000
S. McInnis, 1b	0	0	0	0	0	0	0	–
A. Strunk	0	0	0	0	0	0	0	–

Errors: E. Collins (4), J. Barry (3), F. Baker (2), D. Murphy, R. Oldring
Stolen Bases: E. Collins (2), J. Barry (2)

NEW YORK (N.L.)

	AB	H	2B	3B	HR	R	RBI	BA
J. Devore, of	24	4	1	0	0	1	3	.167
L. Doyle, 2b	23	7	3	1	0	3	1	.304
A. Fletcher, ss	23	3	1	0	0	1	1	.130
R. Murray, of	21	0	0	0	0	0	0	.000
B. Herzog, 3b	21	4	2	0	0	3	0	.190
F. Merkle, 1b	20	3	1	0	0	1	1	.150
C. Meyers, c	20	6	2	0	0	2	2	.300
F. Snodgrass, of	19	2	0	0	0	1	1	.105
C. Mathewson, p	7	2	0	0	0	0	0	.286
B. Becker	3	0	0	0	0	0	0	.000
R. Ames, p	2	1	0	0	0	0	0	.500
D. Crandall, p	2	1	1	0	0	1	1	.500
R. Marquard, p	2	0	0	0	0	0	0	.000
A. Wilson, c	1	0	0	0	0	0	0	.000
H. Wiltse, p	1	0	0	0	0	0	0	.000

Errors: A. Fletcher (4), R. Murray (3), B. Herzog (3), F. Merkle (2), C. Mathewson, L. Doyle, R. Ames, J. Devore
Stolen Bases: L. Doyle (2), B. Herzog (2)

Individual Pitching

PHILADELPHIA (A.L.)

	W	L	ERA	IP	H	BB	SO	SV
C. Bender	2	1	1.04	26	16	8	20	0
J. Coombs	1	0	1.35	20	11	6	16	0
E. Plank	1	1	1.86	9.2	6	0	8	0

NEW YORK (N.L.)

	W	L	ERA	IP	H	BB	SO	SV
C. Mathewson	1	2	2.00	27	25	2	13	0
R. Marquard	0	1	1.54	11.2	9	1	8	0
R. Ames	0	1	2.25	8	6	1	6	0
D. Crandall	1	0	0.00	4	2	0	2	0
H. Wiltse	0	0	18.90	3.1	8	0	2	0

1912 WORLD SERIES

LINE SCORES	PITCHERS (innings pitched)	HOME RUNS (men on)	HIGHLIGHTS

Boston (A.L.) defeats New York (N.L.) 4 games to 3

GAME 1 - OCTOBER 8

BOS	A	000 001 300	4 6 1	Wood (9)
NY	N	002 000 001	3 8 1	Tesreau (7), Crandall (2)

Yerkes's single in the seventh drove in the go-ahead and deciding runs and Wood held off the Giants' ninth-inning rally. Wood had 11 strikeouts in the game.

GAME 2 - OCTOBER 9

NY	N	010 100 030 10	6 11 5	Mathewson (11)
BOS	A	300 010 010 10	6 10 1	Collins (7.1), Hall (2.2), Bedient (1)

Five Giant errors, three by Fletcher, led to four unearned Boston runs in a game called on account of darkness after eleven innings.

GAME 3 - OCTOBER 10

NY	N	010 010 000	2 7 1	Marquard (9)
BOS	A	000 000 001	1 7 0	O'Brien (8), Bedient (1)

Devore's running catch in the bottom of the ninth with two on and two out saved the game for the Giants.

GAME 4 - OCTOBER 11

BOS	A	010 100 001	3 8 1	Wood (9)
NY	N	000 000 100	1 9 1	Tesreau (7), Ames (2)

Wood scattered nine hits, struck out eight, and drove in one man with a single to aid his own cause.

GAME 5 - OCTOBER 12

NY	N	000 000 100	1 3 1	Mathewson (8)
BOS	A	002 000 00x	2 5 1	Bedient (9)

Back-to-back triples by Hooper and Yerkes and Doyle's error in the third gave the Red Sox their two runs. Mathewson settled down to retire the last 17 batters in a row, but the Giants managed just three hits against Bedient.

GAME 6 - OCTOBER 14

BOS	A	020 000 000	2 7 2	O'Brien (1), Collins (7)
NY	N	500 000 00x	5 11 2	Marquard (9)

The Giants took charge with five runs in the first, including back-to-back RBI doubles by Merkle and Herzog.

GAME 7 - OCTOBER 15

NY	N	610 002 101	11 16 4	Tesreau (9)
BOS	A	010 000 210	4 9 3	Wood (1), Hall (8)

HOME RUNS: Doyle (1 on); Gardner

The Giants again jumped to an early lead and held to to even the Series.

GAME 8 - OCTOBER 16

NY	N	001 000 000 1	2 9 2	Mathewson (9.2)
BOS	A	000 000 100 2	3 8 5	Bedient (7), Wood (3)

New York scored in the top of the tenth, but Snodgrass dropped a fly ball and Merkle let Speaker's foul pop get away, allowing the Red Sox to tie the game before winning on a sacrifice fly by Gardner.

Team totals

		W	AB	H	2B	3B	HR	R	RBI	BA	BB	SO	ERA
BOS	A	4	273	60	14	6	1	25	21	.220	19	36	2.92
NY	N	3	274	74	14	4	1	31	25	.270	22	39	1.83

Individual Batting

BOSTON (A.L.)

	AB	H	2B	3B	HR	R	RBI	BA
D. Lewis, of	32	5	3	0	0	4	2	.156
J. Stahl, 1b	32	9	2	0	0	3	2	.281
S. Yerkes, 2b	32	8	2	0	3	4		.250
H. Hooper, of	31	9	2	1	0	3	2	.290
T. Speaker, of	30	9	1	2	0	4	2	.300
H. Wagner, ss	30	5	1	0	0	1	0	.167
L. Gardner, 3b	28	5	2	1	1	4	4	.179
H. Cady, c	22	3	0	0	0	1	1	.136
B. Carrigan, c	7	0	0	0	0	0	0	.000
S. Wood, p	7	2	0	0	0	1	1	.286
H. Bedient, p	6	0	0	0	0	0	0	.000
R. Collins, p	5	0	0	0	0	0	0	.000
C. Hall, p	4	3	1	0	0	0	0	.750
C. Engle	3	1	1	0	0	1	2	.333
B. O'Brien, p	2	0	0	0	0	0	0	.000
O. Henriksen	1	1	1	0	0	0	1	1.000
N. Ball	1	0	0	0	0	0	0	.000

Errors: L. Gardner (4), H. Wagner (3), T. Speaker (2), J. Stahl, S. Yerkes, H. Cady, C. Hall, D. Lewis
Stolen Bases: J. Stahl (2), H. Hooper (2), T. Speaker, H. Wagner

NEW YORK (N.L.)

	AB	H	2B	3B	HR	R	RBI	BA
L. Doyle, 2b	33	8	1	0	1	5	2	.242
F. Merkle, 1b	33	9	2	1	0	5	3	.273
F. Snodgrass, of	33	7	2	0	0	2	2	.212
R. Murray, of	31	10	4	1	0	5	5	.323
B. Herzog, 3b	30	12	4	1	0	6	4	.400
A. Fletcher, ss	28	5	1	0	0	1	3	.179
C. Meyers, c	28	10	1	0	0	2	3	.357
J. Devore, of	24	6	0	0	0	4	0	.250
C. Mathewson, p	12	2	0	0	0	0	0	.167
J. Tesreau, p	8	3	0	0	0	0	2	.375
McCormick	4	1	0	0	0	0	1	.250
R. Marquard, p	4	0	0	0	0	0	0	.000
B. Becker, of	4	0	0	0	0	1	0	.000
D. Crandall, p	1	0	0	0	0	0	0	.000
A. Wilson, c	1	1	0	0	0	0	0	1.000
T. Shafer, ss	0	0	0	0	0	0	0	–

Errors: L. Doyle (4), A. Fletcher (4), F. Merkle (3), J. Devore (2), R. Marquard, C. Meyers, F. Snodgrass, A. Wilson
Stolen Bases: J. Devore (4), L. Doyle (2), B. Herzog (2), F. Merkle, C. Meyers, F. Snodgrass, A. Fletcher

Individual Pitching

BOSTON (A.L.)

	W	L	ERA	IP	H	BB	SO	SV
S. Wood	3	1	3.68	22	27	3	21	0
H. Bedient	1	0	0.50	18	10	7	7	0
R. Collins	0	0	1.88	14.1	14	0	6	0
C. Hall	0	0	3.38	10.2	11	9	1	0
B. O'Brien	0	2	7.00	9	12	3	4	0

NEW YORK (N.L.)

	W	L	ERA	IP	H	BB	SO	SV
C. Mathewson	0	2	1.57	28.2	23	5	10	0
J. Tesreau	1	2	3.13	23	19	11	15	0
R. Marquard	2	0	0.50	18	14	2	9	0
R. Ames	0	0	4.50	2	3	1	0	0
D. Crandall	0	0	0.00	2	1	0	2	0

1913 WORLD SERIES

LINE SCORES	PITCHERS (innings pitched)	HOME RUNS (men on)	HIGHLIGHTS

Philadelphia (A.L.) defeats New York (N.L.) 4 games to 1

GAME 1 - OCTOBER 7

PHI	A	000 320 010	6 11 1	Bender (9)	Baker (1 on)	Baker had three RBIs and three hits including a home run in the fifth for the A's.
NY	N	001 030 000	4 11 0	Marquard (5), Crandall (2), Tesreau (2)		

GAME 2 - OCTOBER 8

NY	N	000 000 000 3	3 7 2	Mathewson (10)	The Giants scored three times in the tenth as Mathewson drove in the game-winning run with a single.
PHI	A	000 000 000 0	0 8 2	Plank (10)	

GAME 3 - OCTOBER 9

PHI	A	320 000 210	8 12 1	Bush (9)	Schang	The Athletics jumped to an early 5-0 lead and coasted on to the victory, paced by Collins's second three-hit game of the Series.
NY	N	000 010 100	2 5 1	Tesreau (6.1), Crandall (2.2)		

GAME 4 - OCTOBER 10

NY	N	000 000 320	5 8 2	Demaree (4), Marquard (4)	Merkle (2 on)	Bender posted his second victory, aided by Schang's three RBIs. He wavered in the late innings, giving up Merkle's three-run homer in the seventh and three more hits in the eighth, but held on for the win.
PHI	A	010 320 00x	6 9 0	Bender (9)		

GAME 5 - OCTOBER 11

PHI	A	102 000 000	3 6 1	Plank (9)	Plank allowed just two hits, singles by Mathewson and McLean, and faced only 29 men in leading the Athletics to their third Series triumph in four years.
NY	N	000 010 000	1 2 2	Mathewson (9)	

Team totals

		W	AB	H	2B	3B	HR	R	RBI	BA	BB	SO	ERA
PHI	A	4	174	46	4	4	2	23	21	.264	7	16	2.15
NY	N	1	164	33	3	1	1	15	15	.201	8	19	3.60

Individual Batting

PHILADELPHIA (A.L.)

	AB	H	2B	3B	HR	R	RBI	BA
E. Murphy, of	22	5	0	0	0	2	0	.227
R. Oldring, of	22	6	0	1	0	5	0	.273
F. Baker, 3b	20	9	0	0	1	2	7	.450
J. Barry, ss	20	6	3	0	0	3	2	.300
E. Collins, 2b	19	8	0	2	0	5	3	.421
S. McInnis, 1b	17	2	1	0	0	1	2	.118
A. Strunk, of	17	2	0	0	0	3	0	.118
W. Schang, c	14	5	0	1	1	2	6	.357
C. Bender, p	8	0	0	0	0	0	1	.000
E. Plank, p	7	1	0	0	0	0	0	.143
J. Bush, p	4	1	0	0	0	0	0	.250
J. Lapp, c	4	1	0	0	0	0	0	.250

Errors: F. Baker, J. Barry, E. Collins, E. Plank, W. Schang
Stolen Bases: E. Collins (3), F. Baker, R. Oldring

NEW YORK (N.L.)

	AB	H	2B	3B	HR	R	RBI	BA
L. Doyle, 2b	20	3	0	0	0	1	2	.150
B. Herzog, 3b	19	1	0	0	0	1	0	.053
G. Burns, of	19	3	2	0	0	2	1	.158
T. Shafer, 3b, of	19	3	1	1	0	2	1	.158
A. Fletcher, ss	18	5	0	0	0	1	4	.278
R. Murray, of	16	4	0	0	0	2	1	.250
F. Merkle, 1b	13	3	0	0	1	3	3	.231
L. McLean, c	12	6	0	0	0	0	2	.500
C. Mathewson, p	5	3	0	0	0	1	1	.600
D. Crandall, p	4	0	0	0	0	0	0	.000
C. Meyers, c	4	0	0	0	0	0	0	.000
F. Snodgrass, 1b, of	3	1	0	0	0	0	0	.333
A. Wilson, c	3	0	0	0	0	0	0	.000
H. Wiltse, 1b	2	0	0	0	0	0	0	.000
J. Tesreau, p	2	0	0 –	0	0	0	0	.000
McCormick	2	1	0	0	0	0	1	.500
A. Demaree, p	1	0	0	0	0	0	0	.000
E. Grant	1	0	0	0	0	1	0	.000
R. Marquard, p	1	0	0	0	0	0	0	.000
C. Cooper	0	0	0	0	0	0	0	–

Errors: L. Doyle (3), F. Merkle (2), A. Fletcher, G. Burns
Stolen Bases: R. Murray (2), G. Burns, C. Cooper, A. Fletcher

Individual Pitching

PHILADELPHIA (A.L.)

	W	L	ERA	IP	H	BB	SO	SV
E. Plank	1	1	0.95	19	9	3	7	0
C. Bender	2	0	4.00	18	19	1	9	0
J. Bush	1	0	1.00	9	5	4	3	0

NEW YORK (N.L.)

	W	L	ERA	IP	H	BB	SO	SV
C. Mathewson	1	1	0.95	19	14	2	7	0
R. Marquard	0	1	7.00	9	10	3	3	0
J. Tesreau	0	1	5.40	8.1	11	1	4	0
D. Crandall	0	0	3.86	4.2	4	0	2	0
A. Demaree	0	1	4.50	4	7	1	0	0

1914 WORLD SERIES

LINE SCORES	PITCHERS (innings pitched)	HOME RUNS (men on)	HIGHLIGHTS

Boston (N.L.) defeats Philadelphia (A.L.) 4 games to 0

GAME 1 - OCTOBER 9

BOS N 020 013 010   7 11 2   Rudolph (9)

PHI A 010 000 000   1 5 0   Bender (5.1), Wyckoff (3.2)

Gowdy's single, double, and triple paced the attack as the Braves knocked Bender out of the box for the first time in his ten World Series starts.

GAME 2 - OCTOBER 10

BOS N 000 000 001   1 7 1   James (9)

PHI A 000 000 000   0 2 1   Plank (9)

Deal reached second with one out in the top of the ninth when Strunk misplayed his fly ball, and scored on Mann's two-out single for the game's only run.

GAME 3 - OCTOBER 12

PHI A 100 100 000 200   4 8 2   Bush (11)

BOS N 010 100 000 201   5 9 1   Tyler (10), James (2)   Gowdy

Bush's wild throw in the bottom of the 12th allowed the winning run to score. The Braves nearly gave the Athletics the game in the tenth when Evers muffed a grounder with the bases loaded to allow a run, and then continued to hold the ball, letting Murphy score. But Gowdy's homer and Connolly's sac fly to score Moran evened the game in the Braves' half of the 10th.

GAME 4 - OCTOBER 13

PHI A 000 010 000   1 7 0   Shawkey (5), Pennock (3)

BOS N 000 120 00x   3 6 0   Rudolph (9)

The Braves swept the Series on Evers's go-ahead two-run single in the fifth. The hitting star of the Series for the Braves was Gowdy, who batted .545 with five extra-base hits in eleven at bats.

Team totals

		W	AB	H	2B	3B	HR	R	RBI	BA	BB	SO	ERA
BOS	N	4	135	33	6	2	1	16	14	.244	15	18	1.15
PHI	A	0	128	22	9	0	0	6	5	.172	13	28	3.65

Individual Batting

BOSTON (N.L.)

	AB	H	2B	3B	HR	R	RBI	BA
B. Schmidt, 1b	17	5	0	0	0	2	2	.294
C. Deal, 3b	16	2	2	0	0	1	0	.125
J. Evers, 2b	16	7	0	0	0	2	2	.438
P. Whitted, of	14	3	0	1	0	2	2	.214
Maranville, ss	13	4	0	0	0	1	3	.308
H. Moran, of	13	1	1	0	0	2	0	.077
H. Gowdy, c	11	6	3	1	1	3	3	.545
J. Connolly, of	9	1	0	0	0	1	1	.111
L. Mann, of	7	2	0	0	0	1	1	.286
D. Rudolph, p	6	2	0	0	0	1	0	.333
T. Cather, of	5	0	0	0	0	0	0	.000
B. James, p	4	0	0	0	0	0	0	.000
L. Tyler, p	3	0	0	0	0	0	0	.000
J. Devore	1	0	0	0	0	0	0	.000
L. Gilbert	0	0	0	0	0	0	0	–

Errors: J. Connolly, J. Evers, Maranville, H. Moran

Stolen Bases: Maranville (2), C. Deal (2), J. Evers, H. Gowdy, H. Moran, B. Schmidt, P. Whitted

PHILADELPHIA (A.L.)

	AB	H	2B	3B	HR	R	RBI	BA
F. Baker, 3b	16	4	2	0	0	0	2	.250
E. Murphy, of	16	3	2	0	0	2	0	.188
R. Oldring, of	15	1	0	0	0	0	0	.067
S. McInnis, 1b	14	2	1	0	0	2	0	.143
E. Collins, 2b	14	3	0	0	0	0	1	.214
J. Barry, ss	14	1	0	0	0	1	0	.071
W. Schang, c	12	2	1	0	0	1	0	.167
A. Strunk, of	7	2	0	0	0	0	0	.286
J. Walsh, of	6	2	1	0	0	0	1	.333
J. Bush, p	5	0	0	0	0	0	0	.000
C. Bender, p	2	0	0	0	0	0	0	.000
B. Shawkey, p	2	1	1	0	0	0	1	.500
E. Plank, p	2	0	0	0	0	0	0	.000
H. Pennock, p	1	0	0	0	0	0	0	.000
J. Lapp, c	1	0	0	0	0	0	0	.000
J. Wyckoff, p	1	1	1	0	0	0	0	1.000

Errors: J. Bush, S. McInnis, W. Schang

Stolen Bases: J. Barry, E. Collins

Individual Pitching

BOSTON (N.L.)

	W	L	ERA	IP	H	BB	SO	SV
D. Rudolph	2	0	0.50	18	12	4	15	0
B. James	2	0	0.00	11	2	6	9	0
L. Tyler	0	0	3.60	10	8	3	4	0

PHILADELPHIA (A.L.)

	W	L	ERA	IP	H	BB	SO	SV
J. Bush	0	1	3.27	11	9	4	4	0
E. Plank	0	1	1.00	9	7	4	6	0
B. Shawkey	0	1	5.40	5	4	2	0	0
C. Bender	0	1	10.13	5.1	8	2	3	0
J. Wyckoff	0	0	2.45	3.2	3	1	2	0
H. Pennock	0	0	0.00	3	2	2	3	0

1915 WORLD SERIES

LINE SCORES	PITCHERS (innings pitched)	HOME RUNS (men on)	HIGHLIGHTS

Boston (A.L.) defeats Philadelphia (N.L.) 4 games to 1

GAME 1 - OCTOBER 8

BOS A 000 000 010   1 8 1   Shore (8)
PHI N 000 100 02x   3 5 1   Alexander (9)

Cravath drove in the deciding run in the eighth on a groundout as Alexander scattered eight singles.

GAME 2 - OCTOBER 9

BOS A 100 000 001   2 10 0   Foster (9)
PHI N 000 010 000   1 3 1   Mayer (9)

Foster faced only 30 men and drove in the game-winning run with his single in the top of the ninth.

GAME 3 - OCTOBER 11

PHI N 001 000 000   1 3 0   Alexander (8.2)
BOS A 000 100 001   2 6 1   Leonard (9)

Lewis singled home Hooper in the bottom of the ninth to support Leonard's three-hitter. Leonard retired the last twenty batters to face him.

GAME 4 - OCTOBER 12

PHI N 000 000 010   1 7 0   Chalmers (8)
BOS A 001 001 00x   2 8 1   Shore (9)

Lewis doubled in Hoblitzell with what proved to be the deciding run in the sixth. Shore lost his shutout when Cravath's hit bounced over Speaker's head for a triple and Luderus singled him home.

GAME 5 - OCTOBER 13

BOS A 011 000 021   5 10 1   Foster (9)   Hooper, Lewis (1 on), Hooper
PHI N 200 200 000   4 9 1   Mayer (2.1), Rixey (6.2)   Luderus

Hooper hit his second home run of the game in the top of the ninth to give Boston the Series. Lewis's two-run homer in the eighth tied the score and cancelled out Luderus's three RBIs.

Team totals

		W	AB	H	2B	3B	HR	R	RBI	BA	BB	SO	ERA
BOS	A	4	159	42	2	2	3	12	11	.264	11	25	1.84
PHI	N	1	148	27	4	1	1	10	9	.182	10	25	2.27

Individual Batting

BOSTON (A.L.)

	AB	H	2B	3B	HR	R	RBI	BA
H. Hooper, of	20	7	0	0	2	4	3	.350
D. Lewis, of	18	8	1	0	1	1	5	.444
E. Scott, ss	18	1	0	0	0	0	0	.056
T. Speaker, of	17	5	0	1	0	2	0	.294
L. Gardner, 3b	17	4	0	1	0	2	0	.235
J. Barry, 2b	17	3	0	0	0	1	1	.176
Hoblitzell, 1b	16	5	0	0	0	1	1	.313
R. Foster, p	8	4	1	0	0	0	1	.500
H. Cady, c	6	2	0	0	0	0	0	.333
E. Shore, p	5	1	0	0	0	0	0	.200
P. Thomas, c	5	1	0	0	0	0	0	.200
D. Gainer, 1b	3	1	0	0	0	1	0	.333
D. Leonard, p	3	0	0	0	0	0	0	.000
O. Henriksen	2	0	0	0	0	0	0	.000
B. Carrigan, c	2	0	0	0	0	0	0	.000
H. Janvrin, ss	1	0	0	0	0	0	0	.000
B. Ruth	1	0	0	0	0	0	0	.000

Errors: J. Barry, Hoblitzell, H. Hooper, E. Shore
Stolen Bases: Hoblitzell

PHILADELPHIA (N.L.)

	AB	H	2B	3B	HR	R	RBI	BA
D. Paskert, of	19	3	0	0	0	2	0	.158
M. Stock, 3b	17	2	1	0	0	1	0	.118
D. Bancroft, ss	17	5	0	0	0	2	1	.294
B. Niehoff, 2b	16	1	0	0	0	1	0	.063
F. Luderus, 1b	16	7	2	0	1	1	6	.438
G. Cravath, of	16	2	1	1	0	2	1	.125
E. Burns, c	16	3	0	0	0	1	0	.188
P. Whitted, of, 1b	15	1	0	0	0	0	1	.067
G. Alexander, p	5	1	0	0	0	0	0	.200
E. Mayer, p	4	0	0	0	0	0	0	.000
G. Chalmers, p	3	1	0	0	0	0	0	.333
E. Rixey, p	2	1	0	0	0	0	0	.500
B. Byrne	1	0	0	0	0	0	0	.000
B. Killefer	1	0	0	0	0	0	0	.000
O. Dugey	0	0	0	0	0	0	0	—
B. Becker, of	0	0	0	0	0	0	0	—

Errors: D. Bancroft, E. Burns, F. Luderus
Stolen Bases: O. Dugey, P. Whitted

Individual Pitching

BOSTON (A.L.)

	W	L	ERA	IP	H	BB	SO	SV
R. Foster	2	0	2.00	18	12	2	13	0
E. Shore	1	1	2.12	17	12	8	6	0
D. Leonard	1	0	1.00	9	3	0	6	0

PHILADELPHIA (N.L.)

	W	L	ERA	IP	H	BB	SO	SV
G. Alexander	1	1	1.53	17.2	14	4	10	0
E. Mayer	0	1	2.38	11.1	16	2	7	0
G. Chalmers	0	1	2.25	8	8	3	6	0
E. Rixey	0	1	4.05	6.2	4	2	2	0

1916 WORLD SERIES

LINE SCORES	PITCHERS (innings pitched)	HOME RUNS (men on)	HIGHLIGHTS

Boston (A.L.) defeats Brooklyn (N.L.) 4 games to 1

GAME 1 - OCTOBER 7

BKN N	000 100 004	5 10 4	Marquard (7), Pfeffer (1)	
BOS A	001 010 31x	6 8 1	Shore (8.2), Mays (0.1) SV	

The Dodgers' ninth-inning rally fell short when Scott made a great stop of Daubert's hard grounder with two out and the bases filled.

GAME 2 - OCTOBER 9

BKN N	100 000 000 000 00	1 6 2	Smith (13.1)	Myers
BOS A	001 000 000 000 01	2 7 1	Ruth (14)	

Gainor's pinch single in the 14th scored pinch-runner McNally to break the 1-1 deadlock. The only Dodger run off Ruth came on Myers's inside-the-park homer in the first.

GAME 3 - OCTOBER 10

BOS A	000 002 100	3 7 1	Mays (5), Foster (3)	Gardner
BKN N	001 120 00x	4 10 0	Coombs (6.1), Pfeffer (2.2) SV	

Pfeffer retired all eight men he faced after relieving Coombs in the seventh to preserve Brooklyn's one-run lead.

GAME 4 - OCTOBER 11

BOS A	030 110 100	6 10 1	Leonard (9)	Gardner (2 on)
BKN N	200 000 000	2 5 4	Marquard (4), Cheney (3), Rucker (2)	

Gardner's three-run homer in the second paced Boston's attack. Leonard held the Dodgers to three hits and no runs after their two-run first.

GAME 5 - OCTOBER 12

BKN N	010 000 000	1 3 3	Pfeffer (7), Dell (1)	
BOS A	012 010 00x	4 7 2	Shore (9)	

Shore held Brooklyn hitless for four and a third innings and then scattered three singles in locking up the Series for Boston.

Team totals

		W	AB	H	2B	3B	HR	R	RBI	BA	BB	SO	ERA
BOS	A	4	164	39	7	6	2	21	18	.238	18	25	1.47
BKN	N	1	170	34	2	5	1	13	11	.200	14	19	2.85

Individual Batting

BOSTON (A.L.)

	AB	H	2B	3B	HR	R	RBI	BA
H. Janvrin, 2b	23	5	3	0	0	2	1	.217
H. Hooper, of	21	7	1	1	0	6	1	.333
Hoblitzell, 1b	17	4	1	1	0	3	2	.235
L. Gardner, 3b	17	3	0	2	2	2	6	.176
D. Lewis, of	17	6	2	1	0	3	1	.353
E. Scott, ss	16	2	0	1	0	1	1	.125
T. Walker, of	11	3	1	0	1	1	1	.273
C. Shorten, of	7	4	0	0	0	0	2	.571
P. Thomas, c	7	1	0	1	0	0	0	.143
E. Shore, p	7	0	0	0	0	0	0	.000
B. Ruth, p	5	0	0	0	0	0	1	.000
H. Cady, c	4	1	0	0	0	1	0	.250
B. Carrigan, c	3	2	0	0	0	0	1	.667
D. Leonard, p	3	0	0	0	0	0	0	.000
J. Walsh, of	3	0	0	0	0	0	0	.000
C. Mays, p	1	0	0	0	0	0	0	.000
R. Foster, p	1	0	0	0	0	0	0	.000
D. Gainer	1	1	0	0	0	0	1	1.000
O. Henriksen	0	0	0	0	0	1	0	—
M. McNally	0	0	0	0	0	1	0	—

Errors: L. Gardner (2), H. Janvrin (2), E. Scott (2)
Stolen Bases: H. Hooper

BROOKLYN (N.L.)

	AB	H	2B	3B	HR	R	RBI	BA
H. Myers, of	22	4	0	1	1	2	3	.182
Z. Wheat, of	19	4	0	1	0	2	1	.211
G. Cutshaw, 2b	19	2	1	0	0	2	2	.105
J. Daubert, 1b	17	3	0	1	0	1	0	.176
M. Mowrey, 3b	17	3	0	0	0	2	1	.176
I. Olson, ss	16	4	0	1	0	1	2	.250
C. Stengel, of	11	4	0	0	0	2	0	.364
C. Meyers, c	10	2	0	1	0	0	1	.200
J. Johnston, of	10	3	0	1	0	1	0	.300
O. Miller, c	8	1	0	0	0	0	0	.125
S. Smith, p	5	1	1	0	0	0	0	.200
J. Pfeffer, p	4	1	0	0	0	0	0	.250
F. Merkle, 1b	4	1	0	0	0	0	0	.250
R. Marquard, p	3	0	0	0	0	0	0	.000
J. Coombs, p	3	1	0	0	0	0	1	.333
G. Getz	1	0	0	0	0	0	0	.000
O. O'Mara	1	0	0	0	0	0	0	.000

Errors: I. Olson (4), M. Mowrey (2), G. Cutshaw (2), L. Cheney, J. Johnston, F. Merkle, C. Stengel, Z. Wheat
Stolen Bases: Z. Wheat

Individual Pitching

BOSTON (A.L.)

	W	L	ERA	IP	H	BB	SO	SV
E. Shore	2	0	1.53	17.2	12	4	9	0
B. Ruth	1	0	0.64	14	6	3	4	0
D. Leonard	1	0	1.00	9	5	4	3	0
C. Mays	0	1	5.06	5.1	8	3	2	1
R. Foster	0	0	0.00	3	3	0	1	0

BROOKLYN (N.L.)

	W	L	ERA	IP	H	BB	SO	SV
S. Smith	0	1	1.35	13.1	7	6	2	0
R. Marquard	0	2	4.91	11	12	6	9	0
J. Pfeffer	0	1	2.53	10.2	7	4	5	1
J. Coombs	1	0	4.26	6.1	7	1	1	0
L. Cheney	0	0	3.00	3	4	1	5	0
N. Rucker	0	0	0.00	2	1	0	3	0
W. Dell	0	0	0.00	1	1	0	0	0

1917 WORLD SERIES

LINE SCORES			PITCHERS (innings pitched)	HOME RUNS (men on)	HIGHLIGHTS

Chicago (A.L.) defeats New York (N.L.) 4 games to 2

GAME 1 - OCTOBER 6

NY	N	000 010 000	1 7 1	Sallee (8)	
CHI	A	001 100 00x	2 7 1	Cicotte (9)	Felsch

Felsch's homer in the fourth and Shano Collins's three hits backed up Cicotte's seven-hit pitching.

GAME 2 - OCTOBER 7

NY	N	020 000 000	2 8 1	Schupp (1.1), Anderson (2), Perritt (3.2), Tesreau (1)	
CHI	A	020 500 00x	7 14 1	Faber (9)	

Six singles led to five fourth-inning runs for Chicago, allowing Faber to coast on in for the victory.

GAME 3 - OCTOBER 10

CHI	A	000 000 000	0 5 3	Cicotte (8)	
NY	N	000 200 00x	2 8 2	Benton (9)	

Robertson's triple and Holke's double in the fourth gave the Giants the lead and the game. Benton walked none in his five-hit shutout.

GAME 4 - OCTOBER 11

CHI	A	000 000 000	0 7 0	Faber (7), Danforth (1)	
NY	N	000 110 12x	5 10 1	Schupp (9)	Kauff, Kauff (1 on)

Kauff's two homers paced the Giants attack as Schupp allowed seven hits in posting a 5-0 shutout.

GAME 5 - OCTOBER 13

NY	N	200 200 100	5 12 3	Sallee (7.1), Perritt (0.2)	
CHI	A	001 001 33x	8 14 6	Russell (0), Cicotte (6), Williams (1), Faber (2)	

Eddie Collins singled in the go-ahead run in a three-run eighth to break open a 5-5 deadlock as the teams combined for 26 hits.

GAME 6 - OCTOBER 15

CHI	A	000 300 001	4 7 1	Faber (9)	
NY	N	000 020 000	2 6 3	Benton (5), Perritt (4)	

The White Sox scored all of their runs on Giant miscues as Faber scattered six hits for his third win of the Series.

Team totals

		W	AB	H	2B	3B	HR	R	RBI	BA	BB	SO	ERA
CHI	A	4	197	54	6	0	1	21	18	.274	11	28	2.77
NY	N	2	199	51	5	4	2	17	16	.256	6	27	2.82

Individual Batting

CHICAGO (A.L.)

	AB	H	2B	3B	HR	R	RBI	BA
F. McMullin, 3b	24	3	1	0	0	1	2	.125
J. Jackson, of	23	7	0	0	0	4	2	.304
C. Gandil, 1b	23	6	1	0	0	1	5	.261
H. Felsch, of	22	6	1	0	1	4	3	.273
E. Collins, 2b	22	9	1	0	0	4	0	.409
S. Collins, of	21	6	1	0	0	2	0	.286
B. Weaver, ss	21	7	1	0	0	3	1	.333
R. Schalk, c	19	5	0	0	0	1	0	.263
R. Faber, p	7	1	0	0	0	0	0	.143
E. Cicotte, p	7	1	0	0	0	0	0	.143
N. Leibold, of	5	2	0	0	0	1	2	.400
S. Risberg	2	1	0	0	0	0	1	.500
B. Lynn	1	0	0	0	0	0	0	.000

Errors: B. Weaver (4), S. Collins (3), R. Schalk (2), E. Cicotte, C. Gandil, L. Williams
Stolen Bases: E. Collins (3), C. Gandil, J. Jackson, R. Schalk

NEW YORK (N.L.)

	AB	H	2B	3B	HR	R	RBI	BA
H. Zimmerman, 3b	25	3	0	1	0	1	0	.120
B. Kauff, of	25	4	1	0	2	2	5	.160
A. Fletcher, ss	25	5	1	0	0	2	0	.200
B. Herzog, 2b	24	6	0	1	0	1	2	.250
D. Robertson, of	22	11	1	1	0	3	1	.500
G. Burns, of	22	5	0	0	0	3	2	.227
W. Holke, 1b	21	6	2	0	0	2	1	.286
B. Rariden, c	13	5	0	0	0	2	2	.385
S. Sallee, p	6	1	0	0	0	0	1	.167
L. McCarty, c	5	2	0	1	0	1	1	.400
F. Schupp, p	4	1	0	0	0	0	1	.250
R. Benton, p	4	0	0	0	0	0	0	.000
P. Perritt, p	2	2	0	0	0	0	0	1.000
J. Wilhoit	1	0	0	0	0	0	0	.000
J. Thorpe, of	0	0	0	0	0	0	0	–

Errors: A. Fletcher (3), B. Herzog (2), H. Zimmerman (2), W. Holke, B. Kauff, L. McCarty, D. Robertson
Stolen Bases: D. Robertson (2), G. Burns, B. Kauff

Individual Pitching

CHICAGO (A.L.)

	W	L	ERA	IP	H	BB	SO	SV
R. Faber	3	1	2.33	27	21	3	9	0
E. Cicotte	1	1	1.96	23	23	2	13	0
D. Danforth	0	0	18.00	1	3	0	2	0
L. Williams	0	0	9.00	1	2	0	3	0
R. Russell	0	0	∞	0.0	2	1	0	0

NEW YORK (N.L.)

	W	L	ERA	IP	H	BB	SO	SV
S. Sallee	0	2	4.70	15.1	20	4	4	0
R. Benton	1	1	0.00	14	9	1	8	0
F. Schupp	1	0	1.74	10.1	11	2	9	0
P. Perritt	0	0	2.16	8.1	9	3	3	0
F. Anderson	0	1	18.00	2	5	0	3	0
J. Tesreau	0	0	0.00	1	0	1	1	0

1918 WORLD SERIES

LINE SCORES	PITCHERS (innings pitched)	HOME RUNS (men on)	HIGHLIGHTS

Boston (A.L.) defeats Chicago (N.L.) 4 games to 2

GAME 1 - SEPTEMBER 5

BOS	A	000 100 000	1 5 0	Ruth (9)	
CHI	N	000 000 000	0 6 0	Vaughn (9)	

Ruth and Vaughn allowed just eleven singles between them, but Boston packaged two of them with a walk in the fourth for the game's only run.

GAME 2 - SEPTEMBER 6

BOS	A	000 000 001	1 6 1	Bush (8)	
CHI	N	030 000 00x	3 7 1	Tyler (9)	

Tyler went the distance and singled in two runs in the second. The shutout was spoiled when Strunk and Whiteman tripled in the ninth.

GAME 3 - SEPTEMBER 7

BOS	A	000 200 000	2 7 0	Mays (9)	
CHI	N	000 010 000	1 7 1	Vaughn (9)	

Scott singled home McInnis with the deciding run in the fourth. Pick tried to score from second on a passed ball with two out in the bottom of the ninth, but got caught in a rundown and retired.

GAME 4 - SEPTEMBER 9

CHI	N	000 000 020	2 7 1	Tyler (7), Douglas (1)	
BOS	A	000 200 01x	3 4 0	Ruth (8), Bush (1) SV	

Schang scored the go-ahead run in the eighth on Killefer's passed ball and Douglas's wild throw. Ruth's record scoreless inning streak dating back to the 1916 Series was stopped in the eighth after 29.2 innings.

GAME 5 - SEPTEMBER 10

CHI	N	001 000 020	3 7 0	Vaughn (9)	
BOS	A	000 000 000	0 5 0	Jones (9)	

Vaughn stopped Boston on five hits after two hard-luck losses.

GAME 6 - SEPTEMBER 11

CHI	N	000 100 000	1 3 2	Tyler (7), Hendrix (1)	
BOS	A	002 000 00x	2 5 0	Mays (9)	

Flack's error in the third let in two runs as Mays subdued Chicago on three hits.

Team totals

		W	AB	H	2B	3B	HR	R	RBI	BA	BB	SO	ERA
BOS	A	4	172	32	2	3	0	9	6	.186	16	21	1.70
CHI	N	2	176	37	5	1	0	10	10	.210	18	14	1.04

Individual Batting

BOSTON (A.L.)

	AB	H	2B	3B	HR	R	RBI	BA
A. Strunk, of	23	4	1	1	0	1	0	.174
G. Whiteman, of	20	5	0	1	0	2	1	.250
E. Scott, ss	20	2	0	0	0	0	1	.100
H. Hooper, of	20	4	0	0	0	0	0	.200
S. McInnis, 1b	20	5	0	0	0	2	1	.250
D. Shean, 2b	19	4	1	0	0	2	0	.211
F. Thomas, 3b	17	2	0	0	0	0	1	.118
W. Schang, c	9	4	0	0	0	1	1	.444
S. Agnew, c	9	0	0	0	0	0	0	.000
C. Mays, p	5	1	0	0	0	1	0	.200
B. Ruth, of, p	5	1	0	1	0	0	2	.200
J. Bush, p	2	0	0	0	0	0	0	.000
J. Dubuc	1	0	0	0	0	0	0	.000
S. Jones, p	1	0	0	0	0	0	0	.000
H. Miller	1	0	0	0	0	0	0	.000

Errors: G. Whiteman
Stolen Bases: W. Schang, D. Shean, G. Whiteman

CHICAGO (N.L.)

	AB	H	2B	3B	HR	R	RBI	BA
L. Mann, of	22	5	2	0	0	0	2	.227
C. Hollocher, ss	21	4	0	1	0	2	0	.190
D. Paskert, of	21	4	1	0	0	2	0	.190
M. Flack, of	19	5	0	0	0	2	1	.263
C. Pick, 2b	18	7	1	0	0	2	0	.389
F. Merkle, 1b	18	5	0	0	0	1	1	.278
C. Deal, 3b	17	3	0	0	0	0	0	.176
B. Killefer, c	17	2	1	0	0	2	2	.118
H. Vaughn, p	10	0	0	0	0	0	0	.000
L. Tyler, p	5	1	0	0	0	0	2	.200
B. O'Farrell, c	3	0	0	0	0	0	0	.000
T. Barber	2	0	0	0	0	0	0	.000
B. McCabe	1	0	0	0	0	1	0	.000
C. Hendrix, p	1	1	0	0	0	0	0	1.000
C. Wortman, 2b	1	0	0	0	0	0	0	.000
R. Zeider, 3b	0	0	0	0	0	0	0	–

Errors: C. Deal, P. Douglas, M. Flack, C. Hollocher, L. Tyler
Stolen Bases: C. Hollocher (2), M. Flack

Individual Pitching

BOSTON (A.L.)

	W	L	ERA	IP	H	BB	SO	SV
C. Mays	2	0	1.00	18	10	3	5	0
B. Ruth	2	0	1.06	17	13	7	4	0
J. Bush	0	1	3.00	9	7	3	0	1
S. Jones	0	1	3.00	9	7	5	5	0

CHICAGO (N.L.)

	W	L	ERA	IP	H	BB	SO	SV
H. Vaughn	1	2	1.00	27	17	5	17	0
L. Tyler	1	1	1.17	23	14	11	4	0
P. Douglas	0	1	0.00	1	1	0	0	0
C. Hendrix	0	0	0.00	1	0	0	0	0

1919 WORLD SERIES

LINE SCORES	PITCHERS (innings pitched)	HOME RUNS (men on)	HIGHLIGHTS

Cincinnati (N.L.) defeats Chicago (A.L.) 5 games to 3

GAME 1 - OCTOBER 1

CHI A 010 000 000   1 6 1   Cicotte (3.2), Wilkinson (3.1), Lowdermilk(1)

CIN N 100 500 21x   9 14 1   Ruether (9)

The Reds' five runs off Cicotte in the fourth broke a 1-1 deadlock. Ruether held Chicago to six hits and had three of his own.

GAME 2 - OCTOBER 2

CHI A 000 000 200   2 10 1   Williams (8)

CIN N 000 301 00x   4 4 2   Sallee (9)

Kopf's two-run triple in the fourth capped a three-run inning after Williams walked three.

GAME 3 - OCTOBER 3

CIN N 000 000 000   0 3 1   Fisher (7), Luque (1)

CHI A 020 100 00x   3 7 0   Kerr (9)

Kerr allowed three hits in shutting out the Reds. Gandil's double drove in Jackson and Felsch in the second.

GAME 4 - OCTOBER 4

CIN N 000 020 000   2 5 2   Ring (9)

CHI A 000 000 000   0 3 2   Cicotte (9)

Ring allowed three hits and posted a shutout as the Reds scored twice in the fifth on Cicotte's two errors.

GAME 5 - OCTOBER 6

CIN N 000 004 001   5 4 0   Eller (9)

CHI A 000 000 000   0 3 3   Williams (8), Mayer (1)

Four runs in the sixth capped by Roush's triple broke open a tie game. Eller fanned nine, six in succession. (There is no taint on the streak; among those fanned were Schalk, Leibold, and Eddie Collins.)

GAME 6 - OCTOBER 7

CHI A 000 013 000 1   5 10 3   Kerr (10)

CIN N 002 200 000 0   4 11 0   Ruther (5), Ring (5)

Gandil singled home Weaver in the tenth with the deciding run.

GAME 7 - OCTOBER 8

CHI A 101 020 000   4 10 1   Cicotte (9)

CIN N 000 001 000   1 7 4   Sallee (4.1), Fisher (0.2), Luque (4)

Shano Collins scored the deciding run on Jackson's single as Cicotte scattered seven hits.

GAME 8 - OCTOBER 9

CIN N 410 013 010   10 16 2   Eller (9)

CHI A 001 000 040   5 10 1   Williams (0.1), James (4.2), Wilkinson (4)   Jackson

The Reds scored four times in the first to wrap up the series on Williams's third loss of the Series. (Williams, Cicotte, Gandil, Felsch, Jackson, McMullin, Risberg and Weaver were later barred for life for their part in fixing the Series.)

Team totals

		W	AB	H	2B	3B	HR	R	RBI	BA	BB	SO	ERA
CIN	N	5	251	64	10	7	0	35	33	.255	25	22	1.63
CHI	A	3	263	59	10	3	1	20	17	.224	15	30	3.68

Individual Batting

CINCINNATI (N.L.)

	AB	H	2B	3B	HR	R	RBI	BA
M. Rath, 2b	31	7	1	0	0	5	2	.226
H. Groh, 3b	29	5	2	0	0	6	1	.172
J. Daubert, 1b	29	7	0	1	0	4	1	.241
E. Roush, of	28	6	2	1	0	6	7	.214
G. Neale, of	28	10	1	1	0	3	4	.357
L. Kopf, ss	27	6	0	2	0	3	2	.222
P. Duncan, of	26	7	2	0	0	3	8	.269
B. Rariden, c	19	4	0	0	0	0	2	.211
I. Wingo, c	7	4	0	0	0	1	1	.571
H. Eller, p	7	2	1	0	0	2	0	.286
D. Ruether, p	6	4	1	2	0	2	4	.667
J. Ring, p	5	0	0	0	0	0	0	.000
S. Sallee, p	4	0	0	0	0	0	0	.000
S. Magee	2	1	0	0	0	0	0	.500
R. Fisher, p	2	1	0	0	0	0	0	.500
D. Luque, p	1	0	0	0	0	0	0	.000
J. Smith	0	0	0	0	0	0	0	–

Errors: M. Rath (2), E. Roush (2), J. Daubert (2), H. Groh (2), L. Kopf, R. Fisher, G. Neale, B. Rariden.

Stolen Bases: M. Rath (2), E. Roush (2), J. Daubert, G. Neale, B. Rariden.

CHICAGO (A.L.)

	AB	H	2B	3B	HR	R	RBI	BA
B. Weaver, 3b	34	11	4	1	0	4	0	.324
J. Jackson, of	32	12	3	0	1	5	6	.375
E. Collins, 2b	31	7	1	0	0	2	1	.226
C. Gandil, 1b	30	7	0	1	0	1	5	.233
H. Felsch, of	26	5	1	0	0	2	3	.192
S. Risberg, ss	25	2	0	1	0	3	0	.080
R. Schalk, c	23	7	0	0	0	1	2	.304
N. Leibold, of	18	1	0	0	0	0	0	.056
S. Collins, of	16	4	1	0	0	2	0	.250
E. Cicotte, p	8	0	0	0	0	0	0	.000
D. Kerr, p	6	1	0	0	0	0	0	.167
L. Williams, p	5	1	0	0	0	0	0	.200
R. Wilkinson, p	2	0	0	0	0	0	0	.000
E. Murphy	2	0	0	0	0	0	0	.000
B. James, p	2	0	0	0	0	0	0	.000
F. McMullin	2	1	0	0	0	0	0	.500
B. Lynn, c	1	0	0	0	0	0	0	.000

Errors: S. Risberg (4), E. Cicotte (2), E. Collins (2), H. Felsch (2), C. Gandil, R. Schalk.

Stolen Bases: E. Collins, C. Gandil, N. Leibold, S. Risberg, R. Schalk.

Individual Pitching

CINCINNATI (N.L.)

	W	L	ERA	IP	H	BB	SO	SV
H. Eller	2	0	2.00	18	13	2	15	0
J. Ring	1	1	0.64	14	7	6	4	0
D. Ruether	1	0	2.57	14	12	4	1	0
S. Sallee	1	1	1.35	13.1	19	1	2	0
R. Fisher	0	1	2.35	7.2	7	2	2	0
D. Luque	0	0	0.00	5	1	0	6	0

CHICAGO (A.L.)

	W	L	ERA	IP	H	BB	SO	SV
E. Cicotte	1	2	2.91	21.2	19	5	7	0
D. Kerr	2	0	1.42	19	14	3	6	0
L. Williams	0	3	6.61	16.1	12	8	4	0
R. Wilkinson	0	0	3.68	7.1	9	4	3	0
B. James	0	0	5.79	4.2	8	3	2	0
Lowdermilk	0	0	9.00	1	2	1	0	0
E. Mayer	0	0	0.00	1	0	1	0	0

1920 WORLD SERIES

LINE SCORES	PITCHERS (innings pitched)	HOME RUNS (men on)	HIGHLIGHTS

Cleveland (A.L.) defeats Brooklyn (N.L.) 5 games to 2

GAME 1 - OCTOBER 5

CLE	A	020 100 000	3 5 0	Coveleski (9)		O'Neill drove in two runs and Wood scored two to back up Coveleski's five-hitter.
BKN	N	000 000 100	1 5 1	Marquard (6), Mamaux (2), Cadore (1)		

GAME 2 - OCTOBER 6

CLE	A	000 000 000	0 7 1	Bagby (6), Uhle (2)		Brooklyn bounced back as Grimes, like Coveleski a spitballer, blanked the Tribe on seven hits.
BKN	N	101 010 00x	3 7 0	Grimes (9)		

GAME 3 - OCTOBER 7

CLE	A	000 100 000	1 3 1	Caldwell (0.1), Mails (6.2), Uhle (1)		The Dodgers made quick work of Caldwell, batting him out in the first, and Sherry Smith allowed just three hits while inducing twenty ground-ball outs.
BKN	N	200 000 00x	2 6 1	S. Smith (9)		

GAME 4 - OCTOBER 9

BKN	N	000 100 000	1 5 1	Cadore (1), Mamaux (1), Marquard (3), Pfeffer (3)		Coveleski again baffled Brooklyn as Wambsganss and Speaker each had two hits and scored two runs.
CLE	A	202 001 00x	5 12 2	Coveleski (9)		

GAME 5 - OCTOBER 10

BKN	N	000 000 001	1 13 1	Grimes (3.1), Mitchell (4.2)	E. Smith (3 on)	In a strange and memorable game, Elmer Smith hit the first World Series grand slam and Bagby hit the first home run by a pitcher. But they were overshadowed by Wambsganss's unassisted triple play in the fifth, as he caught Mitchell's line drive, stepped on second before Kildruff could duck back, and tagged Miller, running from first on the pitch.
CLE	A	400 310 00x	8 12 2	Bagby (9)	Bagby (2 on)	

GAME 6 - OCTOBER 11

BKN	N	000 000 000	0 3 0	S. Smith (8)		The Indians scored the only run in the sixth when Speaker singled with two out and tallied on a double by Burns to the centerfield fence.
CLE	A	000 001 00x	1 7 3	Mails (9)		

GAME 7 - OCTOBER 12

BKN	N	000 000 000	0 5 2	Grimes (7), Mamaux (1)		Coveleski won for the third time with a superb shutout, yielding five harmless singles: three starts, three wins, three five-hitters.
CLE	A	000 110 10x	3 7 3	Coveleski (9)		

Team totals

		W	AB	H	2B	3B	HR	R	RBI	BA	BB	SO	ERA
CLE	A	5	217	53	9	2	2	21	18	.244	21	21	0.89
BKN	N	2	215	44	5	1	0	8	8	.205	10	20	2.59

Individual Batting

CLEVELAND (A.L.)

	AB	H	2B	3B	HR	R	RBI	BA
Wambsganss, 2b	26	4	0	0	0	3	1	.154
T. Speaker, of	25	8	2	1	0	6	1	.320
L. Gardner, 3b	24	5	1	0	0	1	1	.208
J. Sewell, ss	23	4	0	0	0	0	0	.174
S. O'Neill, c	21	7	3	0	0	1	2	.333
C. Jamieson, of	15	5	1	0	0	2	1	.333
E. Smith, of	13	4	0	1	1	1	6	.308
J. Evans, of	13	4	0	0	0	0	0	.308
D. Johnston, 1b	11	3	0	0	0	1	0	.273
S. Wood, of	10	2	1	0	0	2	0	.200
S. Coveleski, p	10	1	0	0	0	2	0	.100
G. Burns, 1b	10	3	1	0	0	1	3	.300
J. Bagby, p	6	2	0	1	1	1	3	.333
D. Mails, p	5	0	0	0	0	0	0	.000
J. Graney, of	3	0	0	0	0	0	0	.000
L. Nunamaker, c	2	1	0	0	0	0	0	.500
H. Lunte, ss	0	0	0	0	0	0	0	–
P. Thomas, c	0	0	0	0	0	0	0	–

Errors: J. Sewell (6), L. Gardner (2), S. Coveleski, J. Bagby, G. Burns, S. O'Neill

Stolen Bases: C. Jamieson, D. Johnston

BROOKLYN (N.L.)

	AB	H	2B	3B	HR	R	RBI	BA
Z. Wheat, of	27	9	2	0	0	2	2	.333
H. Myers, of	26	6	0	0	0	0	1	.231
I. Olson, ss	25	8	1	0	0	2	0	.320
E. Konetchy, 1b	23	4	0	1	0	0	2	.174
P. Kilduff, 2b	21	2	0	0	0	0	0	.095
T. Griffith, of	21	4	2	0	0	1	3	.190
J. Johnston, 3b	14	3	0	0	0	2	0	.214
O. Miller, c	14	2	0	0	0	0	0	.143
J. Sheehan, 3b	11	2	0	0	0	0	0	.182
S. Smith, p	6	0	0	0	0	0	0	.000
B. Grimes, p	6	2	0	0	0	1	0	.333
E. Krueger, c	6	1	0	0	0	0	0	.167
B. Neis, of	5	0	0	0	0	0	0	.000
C. Mitchell, p	3	1	0	0	0	0	0	.333
B. Lamar	3	0	0	0	0	0	0	.000
A. Mamaux, p	1	0	0	0	0	0	0	.000
R. Marquard, p	1	0	0	0	0	0	0	.000
J. Pfeffer, p	1	0	0	0	0	0	0	.000
R. Schmandt	1	0	0	0	0	0	0	.000
B. McCabe	0	0	0	0	0	0	0	–

Errors: J. Sheehan (2), Z. Wheat (2), B. Grimes, E. Konetchy

Stolen Bases: J. Johnston

Individual Pitching

CLEVELAND (A.L.)

	W	L	ERA	IP	H	BB	SO	SV
S. Coveleski	3	0	0.67	27	15	2	8	0
J. Bagby	1	1	1.80	15	20	1	3	0
D. Mails	1	0	0.00	15.2	6	6	6	0
G. Uhle	0	0	0.00	3	1	0	3	0
R. Caldwell	0	1	27.00	0.1	2	1	0	0

BROOKLYN (N.L.)

	W	L	ERA	IP	H	BB	SO	SV
B. Grimes	1	2	4.19	19.1	23	9	4	0
S. Smith	1	1	0.53	17	10	3	3	0
R. Marquard	0	1	2.00	9	7	3	6	0
A. Mamaux	0	0	4.50	4	2	0	5	0
C. Mitchell	0	0	0.00	4.2	3	3	1	0
J. Pfeffer	0	0	3.00	3	4	2	1	0
L. Cadore	0	1	9.00	2	4	1	1	0

1921 WORLD SERIES

LINE SCORES	PITCHERS (innings pitched)	HOME RUNS (men on)	HIGHLIGHTS

New York (N.L.) defeats New York (A.L.) 5 games to 3

GAME 1 - OCTOBER 5

NY	A	100 011 000	3 7 0	Mays (9)			Mays's underhand delivery baffled all the Giants but Frisch, who collected four of their five hits in the losing cause.
NY	N	000 000 000	0 5 0	Douglas (8), Barnes (1)			

GAME 2 - OCTOBER 6

NY	N	000 000 000	0 2 3	Nehf (8)			The Giants are shut out for the second day in a row, Hoyt allowing only singles by Frisch and Rawlings.
NY	A	000 100 02x	3 3 0	Hoyt (9)			

GAME 3 - OCTOBER 7

NY	A	004 000 010	5 8 0	Shawkey (2.1), Quinn (3.2), Collins (1.2), Rogers (1.1)			An eight-run explosion in the seventh made a rout of the contest with the Giants pounding out 20 hits, including four each by Burns and Snyder.
NY	N	004 000 81x	13 20 0	Toney (2), Barnes (7)			

GAME 4 - OCTOBER 9

NY	N	000 000 031	4 9 1	Douglas (9)			Douglas squared the Series in his second meeting with Mays on a two-run double by Burns that provided the winning margin.
NY	A	000 010 001	2 7 1	Mays (9)	Ruth		

GAME 5 - OCTOBER 10

NY	A	001 200 000	3 6 1	Hoyt (9)			A surprise bunt single by Ruth started off the winning rally as Hoyt allowed only one run, that one unearned.
NY	N	100 000 000	1 10 1	Nehf (9)			

GAME 6 - OCTOBER 11

NY	N	030 401 000	8 13 0	Toney (0.2), Barnes (8.1)	Meusel (1 on), Snyder		Barnes picked up his second win in relief of Toney, striking out ten. Injuries kept Ruth out of the Yankee lineup.
NY	A	320 000 000	5 7 2	Harper (1.1), Shawkey (6.2), Piercy (1)	Fewster (1 on)		

GAME 7 - OCTOBER 12

NY	A	010 000 000	1 8 1	Mays (8)			A double by Snyder drove in the winning run as Douglas edged Mays for the second time in their three meetings.
NY	N	000 100 10x	2 6 0	Douglas (9)			

GAME 8 - OCTOBER 13

NY	N	100 000 000	1 6 0	Nehf (9)			The only run off Hoyt was unearned, scoring on a bobble by Peckinpaugh, but it was enough as Nehf held the Yankees scoreless to win the Series.
NY	A	000 000 000	0 4 1	Hoyt (9)			

Team totals

		W	AB	H	2B	3B	HR	R	RBI	BA	BB	SO	ERA
NY	N	5	264	71	13	4	2	29	26	.269	22	38	2.54
NY	A	3	241	50	7	1	2	22	20	.207	27	44	3.09

Individual Batting

NEW YORK (N.L.)

	AB	H	2B	3B	HR	R	RBI	BA
D. Bancroft, ss	33	5	1	0	0	3	3	.152
G. Burns, of	33	11	4	1	0	2	2	.333
F. Frisch, 3b	30	9	0	1	0	5	1	.300
G. Kelly, 1b	30	7	1	0	0	3	3	.233
J. Rawlings, 2b	30	10	3	0	0	2	4	.333
I. Meusel, of	29	10	2	1	1	4	7	.345
R. Youngs, of	25	7	1	1	0	3	3	.280
F. Snyder, c	22	8	1	0	1	4	3	.364
A. Nehf, p	9	0	0	0	0	0	0	.000
J. Barnes, p	9	4	0	0	0	3	0	.444
P. Douglas, p	7	0	0	0	0	0	0	.000
E. Smith, c	7	0	0	0	0	0	0	.000

Errors: F. Frisch (2), A. Nehf, D. Bancroft, E. Smith
Stolen Bases: F. Frisch (3), R. Youngs (2), I. Meusel, G. Burns

NEW YORK (A.L.)

	AB	H	2B	3B	HR	R	RBI	BA
E. Miller, of	31	5	1	0	0	3	2	.161
B. Meusel, of	30	6	2	0	0	3	3	.200
Peckinpaugh, ss	28	5	1	0	0	2	0	.179
W. Pipp, 1b	26	4	1	0	0	1	2	.154
A. Ward, 2b	26	6	0	0	0	1	4	.231
W. Schang, c	21	6	1	1	0	1	1	.286
M. McNally, 3b	20	4	1	0	0	3	1	.200
B. Ruth, of	16	5	0	0	1	3	4	.313
C. Fewster, of	10	2	0	0	1	3	2	.200
W. Hoyt, p	9	2	0	0	0	0	1	.222
C. Mays, p	9	1	0	0	0	0	0	.111
F. Baker, 3b	8	2	0	0	0	0	0	.250
B. Shawkey, p	4	2	0	0	0	2	0	.500
J. Quinn, p	2	0	0	0	0	0	0	.000
A. DeVormer, c	1	0	0	0	0	0	0	.000

Errors: M. McNally (3), A. Ward (2), Peckinpaugh
Stolen Bases: B. Ruth (2), M. McNally (2), B. Meusel, W. Pipp

Individual Pitching

NEW YORK (N.L.)

	W	L	ERA	IP	H	BB	SO	SV
P. Douglas	2	1	2.08	26	24	5	17	0
A. Nehf	1	2	1.38	26	13	13	8	0
J. Barnes	2	0	1.65	16.1	6	6	18	0
F. Toney	0	0	23.63	2.2	7	3	1	0

NEW YORK (A.L.)

	W	L	ERA	IP	H	BB	SO	SV
W. Hoyt	2	1	0.00	27	18	11	18	0
C. Mays	1	2	1.73	26	20	0	9	0
B. Shawkey	0	1	7.00	9	13	6	5	0
J. Quinn	0	1	9.82	3.2	8	2	2	0
T. Rogers	0	0	6.75	1.1	3	0	1	0
B. Piercy	0	0	0.00	1	2	0	2	0
H. Harper	0	0	20.25	1.1	3	2	1	0
R. Collins	0	0	54.00	0.2	4	1	0	0

1922 WORLD SERIES

LINE SCORES	PITCHERS (innings pitched)	HOME RUNS (men on)	HIGHLIGHTS

New York (N.L.) defeats New York (A.L.) 4 games to 0

GAME 1 - OCTOBER 4

NY	A	000 001 100	2 7 0	Bush (7), Hoyt (1)		
NY	N	000 000 03x	3 11 3	Nehf (7), Ryan (2)		

Irish Meusel's two-run single and sacrifice fly by Youngs gave the Giants three in the eighth for the win. Groh went three-for-three for the victors.

GAME 2 - OCTOBER 5

NY	N	300 000 000 0	3 8 1	Barnes (10)	Irish Meusel (2 on)	
NY	A	100 100 010 0	3 8 0	Shawkey (10)	Ward	

The sun was high in the sky when the game was called "on account of darkness." Judge Landis was so irate at the decision that he donated the receipts to charity.

GAME 3 - OCTOBER 6

NY	A	000 000 000	0 4 1	Hoyt (7), Jones (1)	
NY	N	002 000 10x	3 12 1	Scott (9)	

Jack Scott, rescued from the sore arm junkheap by McGraw, whitewashed the Yankees, holding the powerful Yankee lineup to a double and three singles.

GAME 4 - OCTOBER 7

NY	N	000 040 000	4 9 1	McQuillan (9)	
NY	A	200 000 100	3 8 0	Mays (8), Jones (1)	Ward

The Giants scored all their runs in the fifth, Bancroft's bad-hop single over Ward's head driving in the first two.

GAME 5 - OCTOBER 8

NY	A	100 010 100	3 5 0	Bush (8)	
NY	N	020 000 03x	5 10 0	Nehf (9)	

Kelly's clean single in the eighth gave the Giants the winning margin as Nehf won the decisive game for the second year in a row. Ruth ended a poor Series with his third consecutive hitless game.

Team totals

		W	AB	H	2B	3B	HR	R	RBI	BA	BB	SO	ERA
NY	N	4	162	50	2	1	1	18	18	.309	12	15	1.76
NY	A	0	158	32	6	1	2	11	11	.203	8	20	3.35

Individual Batting

NEW YORK (N.L.)

	AB	H	2B	3B	HR	R	RBI	BA
I. Meusel, of	20	5	0	0	1	3	7	.250
H. Groh, 3b	19	9	0	1	0	4	0	.474
D. Bancroft, ss	19	4	0	0	0	4	2	.211
G. Kelly, 1b	18	5	0	0	0	0	2	.278
F. Frisch, 2b	17	8	1	0	0	3	2	.471
R. Youngs, of	16	6	0	0	0	2	2	.375
F. Snyder, c	15	5	0	0	0	1	0	.333
Cunningham, of	10	2	0	0	0	0	2	.200
E. Smith, c	7	1	0	0	0	0	0	.143
C. Stengel, of	5	2	0	0	0	0	0	.400
J. Scott, p	4	1	0	0	0	0	0	.250
McQuillan, p	4	1	1	0	0	1	0	.250
J. Barnes, p	4	0	0	0	0	0	0	.000
A. Nehf, p	3	0	0	0	0	0	0	.000
L. King, of	1	1	0	0	0	0	1	1.000

Errors: R. Youngs (2), F. Snyder, F. Frisch, A. Nehf, D. Bancroft
Stolen Bases: F. Frisch

NEW YORK (A.L.)

	AB	H	2B	3B	HR	R	RBI	BA
W. Pipp, 1b	21	6	1	0	0	0	3	.286
B. Meusel, of	20	6	1	0	0	2	2	.300
J. Dugan, 3b	20	5	1	0	0	4	0	.250
W. Witt, of	18	4	1	1	0	1	0	.222
B. Ruth, of	17	2	1	0	0	1	1	.118
W. Schang, c	16	3	1	0	0	0	0	.188
E. Scott, ss	14	2	0	0	0	0	1	.143
A. Ward, 2b	13	2	0	0	2	3	3	.154
J. Bush, p	6	1	0	0	0	0	1	.167
B. Shawkey, p	4	0	0	0	0	0	0	.000
E. Smith	2	0	0	0	0	0	0	.000
W. Hoyt, p	2	1	0	0	0	0	0	.500
C. Mays, p	2	0	0	0	0	0	0	.000
N. McMillan, of	2	0	0	0	0	0	0	.000
F. Baker	1	0	0	0	0	0	0	.000
M. McNally, 2b	0	0	0	0	0	0	0	—

Errors: A. Ward
Stolen Bases: B. Meusel, W. Pipp

Individual Pitching

NEW YORK (N.L.)

	W	L	ERA	IP	H	BB	SO	SV
A. Nehf	1	0	2.25	16	11	3	6	0
J. Barnes	0	0	1.80	10	8	3	6	0
McQuillan	1	0	3.00	9	8	2	4	0
J. Scott	1	0	0.00	9	4	1	2	0
R. Ryan	1	0	0.00	2	1	0	2	0

NEW YORK (A.L.)

	W	L	ERA	IP	H	BB	SO	SV
J. Bush	0	2	4.80	15	21	5	6	0
B. Shawkey	0	0	2.70	10	8	2	4	0
C. Mays	0	1	4.50	8	9	2	1	0
W. Hoyt	0	1	1.13	8	11	2	4	0
S. Jones	0	0	0.00	2	1	1	0	0

1923 WORLD SERIES

LINE SCORES	PITCHERS (innings pitched)	HOME RUNS (men on)	HIGHLIGHTS

New York (A.L.) defeats New York (N.L.) 4 games to 2

GAME 1 - OCTOBER 10

NY	N	004 000 001	5 8 0	Watson (2), **Ryan** (7)	Stengel	Stengel's inside-the-park home run with two out in the ninth won the game for the Giants.
NY	A	120 000 100	4 12 1	Hoyt (2.1), **Bush** (6.2)		

GAME 2 - OCTOBER 11

NY	A	010 210 000	4 10 0	**Pennock** (9)	Ward, Ruth, Ruth	Two long home runs by Ruth enabled Pennock to win. Ruth's longest blow was a drive to deepest center field caught by Stengel in the ninth.
NY	N	010 001 000	2 9 2	McQuillan (3.2), Bentley (5.1)	I. Meusel	

GAME 3 - OCTOBER 12

NY	N	000 000 100	1 4 0	**Nehf** (9)	Stengel	Stengel again provided the winning margin with his seventh-inning drive into the bleachers in right field.
NY	A	000 000 000	0 6 1	Jones (8), Bush (1)		

GAME 4 - OCTOBER 13

NY	A	061 100 000	8 13 1	**Shawkey** (7.2), Pennock (1.1) SV	Youngs	The Yankees evened the Series thanks to a six-run outburst in the second. Shawkey allowed twelve hits and had to yield to Pennock in the eighth.
NY	N	000 000 031	4 13 1	J. Scott (1), Ryan (0.2) McQuillan (5.1), Jonnard (1), Barnes (1)		

GAME 5 - OCTOBER 14

NY	N	010 000 000	1 3 2	Bentley (1.1), J. Scott (2), Barnes (3.2), Jonnard (1)		Dugan's four hits paced the Yankees' 14-hit attack as Irish Meusel had all three of the Giants' hits.
NY	A	340 100 00x	8 14 0	**Bush** (9)	Dugan (2 on)	

GAME 6 - OCTOBER 15

NY	A	100 000 050	6 5 0	**Pennock** (7), Jones (2) SV	Ruth	Nehf allowed two hits in the first seven innings, but after allowing two more in the eighth walked the eventual tying and winning runs on eight straight balls.
NY	N	100 111 000	4 10 1	Nehf (7.1), Ryan (1.2)	Snyder	

Team totals

		W	AB	H	2B	3B	HR	R	RBI	BA	BB	SO	ERA
NY	A	4	205	60	8	4	5	30	29	.293	20	22	2.83
NY	N	2	201	47	2	3	5	17	17	.234	12	18	4.25

Individual Batting

NEW YORK (A.L.)

	AB	H	2B	3B	HR	R	RBI	BA
B. Meusel, of	26	7	1	2	0	1	8	.269
J. Dugan, 3b	25	7	2	1	1	5	5	.280
W. Witt, of	25	6	2	0	0	1	4	.240
A. Ward, 2b	24	10	0	0	1	4	2	.417
W. Schang, c	22	7	1	0	0	3	0	.318
E. Scott, ss	22	7	0	0	0	2	3	.318
W. Pipp, 1b	20	5	0	0	0	2	2	.250
B. Ruth, 1b, of	19	7	1	1	3	8	3	.368
J. Bush, p	7	3	1	0	0	2	1	.429
H. Pennock, p	6	0	0	0	0	0	0	.000
B. Shawkey, p	3	1	0	0	0	0	1	.333
S. Jones, p	2	0	0	0	0	0	0	.000
H. Hendrick	1	0	0	0	0	0	0	.000
F. Hofmann	1	0	0	0	0	0	0	.000
W. Hoyt, p	1	0	0	0	0	0	0	.000
H. Haines, of	1	0	0	0	0	1	0	.000
E. Johnson, ss	0	0	0	0	0	1	0	—

Errors: B. Ruth, W. Schang, E. Scott
Stolen Bases: A. Ward

NEW YORK (N.L.)

	AB	H	2B	3B	HR	R	RBI	BA
F. Frisch, 2b	25	10	0	1	0	2	1	.400
I. Meusel, of	25	7	1	1	1	3	2	.280
D. Bancroft, ss	24	2	0	0	0	1	1	.083
R. Youngs, of	23	8	0	0	1	2	3	.348
G. Kelly, 1b	22	4	0	0	0	1	1	.182
H. Groh, 3b	22	4	0	1	0	3	2	.182
F. Snyder, c	17	2	0	0	1	1	2	.118
C. Stengel, of	12	5	0	0	2	3	4	.417
Cunningham, of	7	1	0	0	0	0	1	.143
A. Nehf, p	6	1	0	0	0	0	0	.167
J. Bentley, p	5	3	1	0	0	0	0	.600
H. Gowdy, c	4	0	0	0	0	0	0	.000
McQuillan, p	3	0	0	0	0	0	0	.000
R. Ryan, p	2	0	0	0	0	0	0	.000
J. Scott, p	1	0	0	0	0	0	0	.000
J. O'Connell	1	0	0	0	0	0	0	.000
T. Jackson	1	0	0	0	0	0	0	.000
V. Barnes, p	1	0	0	0	0	0	0	.000
D. Gearin	0	0	0	0	0	0	0	—
F. Maguire	0	0	0	0	0	1	0	—

Errors: R. Youngs (2), Cunningham, F. Frisch, G. Kelly, M. Watson
Stolen Bases: D. Bancroft

Individual Pitching

NEW YORK (A.L.)

	W	L	ERA	IP	H	BB	SO	SV
H. Pennock	2	0	3.63	17.1	19	1	8	1
J. Bush	1	1	1.08	16.2	7	4	5	0
S. Jones	0	1	0.90	10	5	2	3	1
B. Shawkey	1	0	3.52	7.2	12	4	2	0
W. Hoyt	0	0	15.43	2.1	4	1	0	0

NEW YORK (N.L.)

	W	L	ERA	IP	H	BB	SO	SV
A. Nehf	1	1	2.76	16.1	10	6	7	0
R. Ryan	1	0	0.96	9.1	11	3	3	0
McQuillan	0	1	5.00	9	11	4	3	0
J. Bentley	0	1	9.45	6.2	10	4	1	0
V. Barnes	0	0	0.00	4.2	4	0	4	0
J. Scott	0	1	12.00	3	9	1	2	0
M. Watson	0	0	13.50	2	4	1	1	0
C. Jonnard	0	0	0.00	2	1	1	1	0

1924 WORLD SERIES

LINE SCORES	PITCHERS (innings pitched)	HOME RUNS (men on)	HIGHLIGHTS

Washington (A.L.) defeats New York (N.L.) 4 games to 3

GAME 1 - OCTOBER 4

NY	N	010 100 000 002	4 14 1	Nehf (12)	Kelly, Terry	Johnson, in his first World Series after 18 years in the majors, fanned 12 but lost on Youngs' bases-loaded single in the twelfth.
WAS	A	000 001 001 001	3 10 1	Johnson (12)		

GAME 2 - OCTOBER 5

NY	N	000 000 102	3 6 0	Bentley (8.1)		Peckinpaugh's double in the ninth drove in the winning run after the Senators blew an early lead built on homers by Goslin and Harris.
WAS	A	200 010 001	4 6 1	Zachary (8.2), Marberry (0.1) SV	Goslin (1 on), Harris	

GAME 3 - OCTOBER 6

WAS	A	000 200 011	4 9 2	Marberry (3), Russell (3), Martina (1), Speece (1)		Harris's error on an attempted double play in the second set up two runs for the Giants and gave them a lead they never relinquished.
NY	N	021 101 01x	6 12 0	McQuillan (3.2), Ryan (4.2), Jonnard (0), Watson (0.2) SV	Ryan	

GAME 4 - OCTOBER 7

WAS	A	003 020 020	7 13 3	Mogridge (7.1), Marberry (1.2) SV	Goslin (2 on)	Goslin's four hits, including a home run, sparked the Senators to an easy triumph.
NY	N	100 001 011	4 6 1	Barnes (5), Baldwin (2), Dean (2)		

GAME 5 - OCTOBER 8

WAS	A	000 100 010	2 9 1	Johnson (8)	Goslin	Johnson again lost as Lindstrom had four hits and Bentley added a two-run homer.
NY	N	001 020 03x	6 13 0	Bentley (7.1), McQuillan (1.2) SV	Bentley (1 on)	

GAME 6 - OCTOBER 9

NY	N	100 000 000	1 7 1	Nehf (7), Ryan (1)		The duel of southpaws went to Zachary when Harris's single scored two runs in the fifth.
WAS	A	000 020 00x	2 4 0	Zachary (9)		

GAME 7 - OCTOBER 10

NY	N	000 003 000 000	3 8 3	Barnes (7.2), Nehf (0.2), McQuillan (1.2), Bentley (1.1)		The Series closed as it opened: with a 12-inning encounter, but this time Johnson was the winner when McNeely's roller hopped over Lindstrom's head at third base.
WAS	A	000 100 020 001	4 10 4	Ogden (0.1), Mogridge (4.2), Marberry (3), Johnson (4)	Harris	

Team totals

		W	AB	H	2B	3B	HR	R	RBI	BA	BB	SO	ERA
WAS	A	4	248	61	9	0	5	26	25	.246	29	34	2.28
NY	N	3	253	66	9	2	4	27	21	.261	25	40	3.11

Individual Batting

WASHINGTON (A.L.)

	AB	H	2B	3B	HR	R	RBI	BA
B. Harris, 2b	33	11	0	0	2	5	7	.333
G. Goslin, of	32	11	1	0	3	4	7	.344
S. Rice, of	29	6	0	0	0	2	1	.207
E. McNeely, of	27	6	3	0	0	4	1	.222
J. Judge, 1b	26	10	1	0	0	4	0	.385
O. Bluege, ss, 3b	26	5	0	0	0	2	3	.192
M. Ruel, c	21	2	1	0	0	2	0	.095
Peckinpaugh, ss	12	5	2	0	0	1	2	.417
R. Miller, 3b	11	2	0	0	0	0	2	.182
W. Johnson, p	9	1	0	0	0	0	0	.111
N. Leibold, of	6	1	1	0	0	1	0	.167
G. Mogridge, p	5	0	0	0	0	0	0	.000
T. Zachary, p	5	0	0	0	0	0	0	.000
T. Taylor, 3b	2	0	0	0	0	0	0	.000
F. Marberry, p	2	0	0	0	0	0	0	.000
M. Shirley	2	1	0	0	0	1	1	.500
B. Tate	0	0	0	0	0	0	0	—

Errors: O. Bluege (3), B. Harris (2), R. Miller (2), S. Rice, J. Judge, E. McNeely, W. Johnson, T. Taylor
Stolen Bases: S. Rice (2), Peckinpaugh, O. Bluege, E. McNeely

NEW YORK (N.L.)

	AB	H	2B	3B	HR	R	RBI	BA
G. Kelly, 1b, 2b, of	31	9	1	0	1	7	4	.290
F. Frisch, 2b, 3b	30	10	4	1	0	1	0	.333
F. Lindstrom, 3b	30	10	2	0	0	1	4	.333
H. Wilson, of	30	7	1	0	0	1	3	.233
R. Youngs, of	27	5	1	0	0	3	1	.185
H. Gowdy, c	27	7	0	0	0	4	1	.259
T. Jackson, ss	27	2	0	0	0	3	1	.074
B. Terry, 1b	14	6	1	1	1	3	1	.429
I. Meusel, of	13	2	0	0	0	0	1	.154
A. Nehf, p	7	3	0	0	0	1	0	.429
J. Bentley, p	7	2	0	0	1	1	2	.286
V. Barnes, p	4	0	0	0	0	0	0	.000
R. Ryan, p	2	1	0	0	1	1	2	.500
F. Snyder	1	0	0	0	0	0	0	.000
Southworth, of	1	0	0	0	0	1	0	.000
McQuillan, p	1	1	0	0	0	0	1	1.000
H. Groh	1	1	0	0	0	0	0	1.000

Errors: T. Jackson (3), G. Kelly, H. Gowdy, I. Meusel
Stolen Bases: R. Youngs, F. Frisch, T. Jackson

Individual Pitching

WASHINGTON (A.L.)

	W	L	ERA	IP	H	BB	SO	SV
W. Johnson	1	2	2.63	24	30	11	20	0
T. Zachary	2	0	2.04	17.2	13	3	3	0
G. Mogridge	1	0	2.25	12	7	6	5	0
F. Marberry	0	1	1.13	8	9	4	10	2
A. Russell	0	0	3.00	3	4	0	0	0
B. Speece	0	0	9.00	1	3	0	0	0
J. Martina	0	0	0.00	1	0	0	1	0
C. Ogden	0	0	0.00	0.1	0	1	1	0

NEW YORK (N.L.)

	W	L	ERA	IP	H	BB	SO	SV
A. Nehf	1	1	1.83	19.2	15	9	7	0
J. Bentley	1	2	3.18	17	18	8	10	0
V. Barnes	0	1	5.68	12.2	15	1	9	0
McQuillan	0	0	2.57	7	2	6	2	1
R. Ryan	1	0	3.18	5.2	7	4	3	0
W. Dean	0	0	4.50	2	3	0	2	0
H. Baldwin	0	0	0.00	2	1	0	1	0
C. Jonnard	0	0	—	0.0	0	1	0	0
M. Watson	0	0	0.00	0.2	0	0	0	1

1925 WORLD SERIES

LINE SCORES	PITCHERS (innings pitched)	HOME RUNS (men on)	HIGHLIGHTS

Pittsburgh (N.L.) defeats Washington (A.L.) 4 games to 3

GAME 1 - OCTOBER 7

WAS	A	010 020 001	4	8	1	
PIT	N	000 010 000	1	5	0	

Johnson (9)
Meadows (8), Morrison (1)

J. Harris
Traynor

Johnson checked the Pirates and struck out ten as Rice delivered the key blow with a single in the fifth driving in two runs to decide the game.

GAME 2 - OCTOBER 8

WAS	A	010 000 001	2	8	2	
PIT	N	000 100 02x	3	7	0	

Coveleski (8)
Aldridge (9)

Judge
Wright, Cuyler (1 on)

Peckinpaugh's two errors in the eighth, one of which allowed the tying run to get on base before Cuyler's homer, helped the Pirates to their victory.

GAME 3 - OCTOBER 10

PIT	N	010 101 000	3	8	3	
WAS	A	001 001 02x	4	10	1	

Kremer (8)
Ferguson (7), Marberry (2) SV

Goslin

With the Senators leading 4-3 in the bottom of the eighth, Earl Smith hit a ball to the center field bleachers. Rice, attempting to catch it, fell over the bleacher railing and disappeared. He then reappeared with the ball for the most controversial "out" in Series play.

GAME 4 - OCTOBER 11

PIT	N	000 000 000	0	6	1	
WAS	A	004 000 00x	4	12	0	

Yde (2.1), Morrison (4.2), B. Adams (1)
Johnson (9)

Goslin (2 on), J. Harris

Back-to-back homers by Goslin and Joe Harris staked Johnson to a four-run third inning lead as he posted his only post-season shutout.

GAME 5 - OCTOBER 12

PIT	N	002 000 211	6	13	0	
WAS	A	100 100 100	3	8	1	

Aldridge (9)
Coveleski (6.1), Ballou (0.2),
Zachary (1.2), Marberry (0.1)

J. Harris

Back-to-back RBI singles by Cuyler and Barnhart broke a 2-2 tie as Pittsburgh staved off elimination.

GAME 6 - OCTOBER 13

WAS	A	110 000 000	2	6	2	
PIT	N	002 010 00x	3	7	1	

Ferguson (7), Ballou (1)
Kremer (9)

Goslin
Moore

Moore's solo homer in the fifth gave the Pirates a tie in the Series. The temporary screen in center field turned Joe Harris's bid for a game-tying homer in the ninth into a double.

GAME 7 - OCTOBER 15

WAS	A	400 200 010	7	7	2	
PIT	N	003 010 23x	9	15	2	

Johnson (8)
Aldridge (0.1), Morrison (3.2), Kremer (4), Oldham (1) SV

Peckinpaugh

The Pirates battered Johnson for 15 hits in their come-from-behind win. The Pirates were the first team to come back from 3-1 down in a seven-game Series.

Team totals

		W	AB	H	2B	3B	HR	R	RBI	BA	BB	SO	ERA
PIT	N	4	230	61	12	2	4	25	25	.265	17	32	3.54
WAS	A	3	225	59	8	0	8	26	24	.262	17	32	2.85

Individual Batting

PITTSBURGH (N.L.)

	AB	H	2B	3B	HR	R	RBI	BA
C. Barnhart, of	28	7	1	0	0	1	5	.250
G. Wright, ss	27	5	1	0	1	3	3	.185
P. Traynor, 3b	26	9	0	2	1	2	4	.346
K. Cuyler, of	26	7	3	0	1	3	6	.269
E. Moore, 2b	26	6	1	0	1	7	2	.231
M. Carey, of	24	11	4	0	0	6	2	.458
E. Smith, c	20	7	1	0	0	0	0	.350
G. Grantham, 1b	15	2	0	0	0	0	0	.133
S. McInnis, 1b	14	4	0	0	0	0	1	.286
R. Kremer, p	7	1	0	0	0	0	0	.143
V. Aldridge, p	7	0	0	0	0	0	0	.000
C. Bigbee, of	3	1	1	0	0	1	1	.333
J. Gooch, c	3	0	0	0	0	0	0	.000
J. Morrison, p	2	1	0	0	0	0	1	.500
L. Meadows, p	1	0	0	0	0	0	0	.000
E. Yde, p	1	0	0	0	0	1	0	.000

Errors: G. Wright (2), M. Carey, K. Cuyler, R. Kremer, E. Moore, E. Smith

Stolen Bases: M. Carey (3), C. Bigbee, G. Grantham, P. Traynor, C. Barnhart

WASHINGTON (A.L.)

	AB	H	2B	3B	HR	R	RBI	BA
S. Rice, of	33	12	0	0	0	5	3	.364
G. Goslin, of	26	8	1	0	3	6	5	.308
J. Harris, of	25	11	2	0	3	5	6	.440
Peckinpaugh, ss	24	6	1	0	1	1	2	.250
B. Harris, 2b	23	2	0	0	0	2	0	.087
J. Judge, 1b	23	4	1	0	1	2	4	.174
M. Ruel, c	19	6	1	0	0	0	1	.316
O. Bluege, 3b	18	5	1	0	0	2	2	.278
W. Johnson, p	11	1	0	0	0	0	0	.091
B. Myer, 3b	8	2	0	0	0	0	0	.250
A. Ferguson, p	4	0	0	0	0	0	0	.000
S. Coveleski, p	3	0	0	0	0	0	0	.000
H. Severeid, c	3	1	0	0	0	0	0	.333
N. Leibold	2	1	1	0	0	1	0	.500
S. Adams, 2b	1	0	0	0	0	0	0	.000
D. Ruether	1	0	0	0	0	0	0	.000
B. Veach	1	0	0	0	0	0	1	.000
E. McNeely, of	0	0	0	0	0	2	0	–

Errors: Peckinpaugh (8), H. Severeid

Stolen Bases: Peckinpaugh, G. Goslin, E. McNeely

Individual Pitching

PITTSBURGH (N.L.)

	W	L	ERA	IP	H	BB	SO	SV
R. Kremer	2	1	3.00	21	17	4	9	0
V. Aldridge	2	0	3.93	18.1	18	9	9	0
J. Morrison	0	0	2.89	9.1	11	1	7	0
L. Meadows	0	1	3.38	8	6	0	4	0
E. Yde	0	1	11.57	2.1	5	3	1	0
R. Oldham	0	0	0.00	1	0	0	2	1
B. Adams	0	0	0.00	1	2	0	0	0

WASHINGTON (A.L.)

	W	L	ERA	IP	H	BB	SO	SV
W. Johnson	2	1	2.08	26	26	4	15	0
S. Coveleski	0	2	3.77	14.1	16	5	3	0
A. Ferguson	1	1	3.21	14	13	6	11	0
F. Marberry	0	0	0.00	2.1	3	0	2	1
T. Zachary	0	0	10.80	1.2	3	1	0	0
W. Ballou	0	0	0.00	1.2	0	1	1	0

1926 WORLD SERIES

LINE SCORES	PITCHERS (innings pitched)	HOME RUNS (men on)	HIGHLIGHTS

St. Louis (N.L.) defeats New York (A.L.) 4 games to 3

GAME 1 - OCTOBER 2

STL	N	100 000 000	1 3 1	Sherdel (7), Haines (1)	
NY	A	100 001 00x	2 6 0	Pennock (9)	

Gehrig's single in the sixth sent Ruth home to break a 1-1 tie. Bottomley collected two of the Cardinals' three hits in the loss.

GAME 2 - OCTOBER 3

STL	N	002 000 301	6 12 1	Alexander (9)	Southworth (2 on), Thevenow
NY	A	020 000 000	2 4 0	Shocker (7), Shawkey (1), Jones (1)	

Alexander struck out ten Yankees and retired the last 21 men in succession as Southworth's three-run homer in the seventh won the game.

GAME 3 - OCTOBER 5

NY	A	000 000 000	0 5 1	Ruether (4.1), Shawkey (2.2), Thomas (1)	
STL	N	000 310 00x	4 8 0	Haines (9)	Haines (1 on)

The Cardinals put together three runs in the fourth to break open the game. Haines aided his own cause with two hits, one a two-run homer.

GAME 4 - OCTOBER 6

NY	A	101 142 100	10 14 1	Hoyt (9)	Ruth, Ruth, Ruth (1 on)
STL	N	100 300 001	5 14 0	Rhem (4), Reinhart (0), H. Bell (2), Hallahan (2), Keen (1)	

Ruth unloaded a record three home runs in leading the Yankee bombardment which knotted the Series.

GAME 5 - OCTOBER 7

NY	A	000 001 001 1	3 9 1	Pennock (10)	
STL	N	000 100 100 0	2 7 1	Sherdel (10)	

Lazzeri's sacrifice fly in the tenth scored Koenig with the winning tally of the game after Sherdel's wild pitch set up the run. O'Farrell had three hits in the losing cause.

GAME 6 - OCTOBER 9

STL	N	300 010 501	10 13 2	Alexander (9)	L. Bell (1 on)
NY	A	000 100 100	2 8 1	Shawkey (6.1), Shocker (0.2), Thomas (2)	

Les Bell had three hits and four RBIs that capped Cardinal rallies in the first and seventh. Alexander won his second complete game of the Series.

GAME 7 - OCTOBER 10

STL	N	000 300 000	3 8 0	Haines (6.2), Alexander (2.1) SV	
NY	A	001 001 000	2 8 3	Hoyt (6), Pennock (3)	Ruth

The Cardinals scored three unearned runs in the fourth and Alexander saved the victory in the seventh when, with two out and the bases loaded, he struck out Lazzeri.

Team totals

		W	AB	H	2B	3B	HR	R	RBI	BA	BB	SO	ERA
STL	N	4	239	65	12	1	4	31	30	.272	11	30	2.57
NY	A	3	223	54	10	1	4	21	19	.242	31	31	3.14

Individual Batting

ST. LOUIS (N.L.)

	AB	H	2B	3B	HR	R	RBI	BA
J. Bottomley, 1b	29	10	3	0	0	4	5	.345
Southworth, of	29	10	1	1	1	6	4	.345
R. Hornsby, 2b	28	7	1	0	0	2	4	.250
L. Bell, 3b	27	7	1	0	1	4	6	.259
C. Hafey, of	27	5	2	0	0	2	0	.185
T. Thevenow, ss	24	10	1	0	1	5	4	.417
B. O'Farrell, c	23	7	1	0	0	2	2	.304
W. Holm, of	16	2	0	0	0	1	1	.125
T. Douthit, of	15	4	2	0	0	3	1	.267
G. Alexander, p	7	0	0	0	0	1	0	.000
J. Haines, p	5	3	0	0	1	1	2	.600
B. Sherdel, p	5	0	0	0	0	0	0	.000
J. Flowers	3	0	0	0	0	0	0	.000
F. Rhem, p	1	0	0	0	0	0	0	.000
S. Toporcer	0	0	0	0	0	0	1	–

Errors: L. Bell (2), T. Thevenow (2), G. Alexander
Stolen Bases: R. Hornsby, Southworth

NEW YORK (A.L.)

	AB	H	2B	3B	HR	R	RBI	BA
M. Koenig, ss	32	4	1	0	0	2	2	.125
E. Combs, of	28	10	2	0	0	3	2	.357
T. Lazzeri, 2b	26	5	1	0	0	2	3	.192
J. Dugan, 3b	24	8	1	0	0	2	2	.333
L. Gehrig, 1b	23	8	2	0	0	1	3	.348
H. Severeid, c	22	6	1	0	0	1	1	.273
B. Meusel, of	21	5	1	1	0	3	0	.238
B. Ruth, of	20	6	0	0	4	6	5	.300
H. Pennock, p	7	1	1	0	0	1	0	.143
W. Hoyt, p	6	0	0	0	0	0	0	.000
D. Ruether, p	4	0	0	0	0	0	0	.000
B. Paschal	4	1	0	0	0	0	1	.250
P. Collins, c	2	0	0	0	0	0	0	.000
B. Shawkey, p	2	0	0	0	0	0	0	.000
U. Shocker, p	2	0	0	0	0	0	0	.000
S. Adams	0	0	0	0	0	0	0	–
M. Gazella, 3b	0	0	0	0	0	0	0	–

Errors: M. Koenig (4), T. Lazzeri, B. Meusel, J. Dugan
Stolen Bases: B. Ruth

Individual Pitching

ST. LOUIS (N.L.)

	W	L	ERA	IP	H	BB	SO	SV
G. Alexander	2	0	0.89	20.1	12	4	17	1
B. Sherdel	0	2	2.12	17	15	8	3	0
J. Haines	2	0	1.08	16.2	13	9	5	0
F. Rhem	0	0	6.75	4	7	2	4	0
B. Hallahan	0	0	4.50	2	2	3	1	0
H. Bell	0	0	9.00	2	4	1	1	0
V. Keen	0	0	0.00	1	0	0	0	0
A. Reinhart	0	1	∞	0.0	1	4	0	0

NEW YORK (A.L.)

	W	L	ERA	IP	H	BB	SO	SV
H. Pennock	2	0	1.23	22	13	4	8	0
W. Hoyt	1	1	1.20	15	19	1	10	0
B. Shawkey	0	1	5.40	10	8	2	7	0
U. Shocker	0	1	5.87	7.2	13	0	3	0
D. Ruether	0	1	8.31	4.1	7	2	1	0
M. Thomas	0	0	3.00	3	3	0	0	0
S. Jones	0	0	9.00	1	2	2	1	0

1927 WORLD SERIES

LINE SCORES	PITCHERS (innings pitched)	HOME RUNS (men on)	HIGHLIGHTS

New York (A.L.) defeats Pittsburgh (N.L.) 4 games to 0

GAME 1 - OCTOBER 5

NY	A	103 010 000	5 6 1	Hoyt (7.1), Moore (1.2) SV	
PIT	N	101 010 010	4 9 2	Kremer (5), Miljus (4)	

Three hits by Ruth and two RBIs by Gehrig gave the Yankees the win. Paul Waner had three hits of his own for the losers.

GAME 2 - OCTOBER 6

NY	A	003 000 030	6 11 0	Pipgras (9)	
PIT	N	100 000 010	2 7 2	Aldrich (7.1), Cvengros (0.2), Dawson (1)	

The Yankees again scored three in the third with Gehrig's double highlighting the frame, enabling Pipgras to breeze. Koenig had three hits for New York.

GAME 3 - OCTOBER 7

PIT	N	000 000 010	1 3 1	Meadows (6.1), Cvengros (1.2)	
NY	A	200 000 60x	8 9 0	Pennock (9)	Ruth (2 on)

Pennock retired the first 22 men in succession before Traynor broke the spell with a single in the eighth. Gehrig's two-run triple settled the issue in the first and Ruth's three-run homer added icing in the seventh.

GAME 4 - OCTOBER 8

PIT	N	100 000 200	3 10 1	Hill (6), Miljus (2.2)	
NY	A	100 020 001	4 12 2	Moore (9)	Ruth (1 on)

A walk, a bunt, a wild pitch, and an intentional walk loaded the bases for Yanks in the bottom of the ninth. Miljus then struck out Gehrig and Meusel, but then threw a wild pitch to bring home the Series-ending run.

Team totals

		W	AB	H	2B	3B	HR	R	RBI	BA	BB	SO	ERA
NY	A	4	136	38	6	2	2	23	20	.279	13	25	2.00
PIT	N	0	130	29	6	1	0	10	10	.223	4	7	5.19

Individual Batting

NEW YORK (A.L.)

	AB	H	2B	3B	HR	R	RBI	BA
M. Koenig, ss	18	9	2	0	0	5	2	.500
B. Meusel, of	17	2	0	0	0	1	1	.118
E. Combs, of	16	5	0	0	0	6	2	.313
J. Dugan, 3b	15	3	0	0	0	2	0	.200
T. Lazzeri, 2b	15	4	1	0	0	1	2	.267
B. Ruth, of	15	6	0	0	2	4	7	.400
L. Gehrig, 1b	13	4	2	2	0	2	5	.308
W. Moore, p	5	1	0	0	0	0	0	.200
P. Collins, c	5	3	1	0	0	0	0	.600
B. Bengough, c	4	0	0	0	0	1	0	.000
H. Pennock, p	4	0	0	0	0	1	1	.000
G. Pipgras, p	3	1	0	0	0	0	0	.333
W. Hoyt, p	3	0	0	0	0	0	0	.000
J. Grabowski, c	1	0	0	0	0	0	0	.000
C. Durst	1	0	0	0	0	0	0	.000

Errors: T. Lazzeri, B. Meusel, W. Moore
Stolen Bases: B. Meusel, B. Ruth

PITTSBURGH (N.L.)

	AB	H	2B	3B	HR	R	RBI	BA
C. Barnhart, of	16	5	1	0	0	0	4	.313
J. Harris, 1b	15	3	0	0	0	0	1	.200
P. Traynor, 3b	15	3	1	0	0	1	0	.200
L. Waner, of	15	6	1	1	0	5	0	.400
P. Waner, of	15	5	1	0	0	0	3	.333
G. Wright, ss	13	2	0	0	0	1	2	.154
G. Grantham, 2b	11	4	1	0	0	0	0	.364
E. Smith, c	8	0	0	0	0	0	0	.000
J. Gooch, c	5	0	0	0	0	0	0	.000
H. Rhyne, 2b	4	0	0	0	0	0	0	.000
L. Meadows, p	2	0	0	0	0	0	0	.000
J. Miljus, p	2	0	0	0	0	0	0	.000
R. Kremer, p	2	1	1	0	0	1	0	.500
F. Brickell	2	0	0	0	0	1	0	.000
V. Aldridge, p	2	0	0	0	0	0	0	.000
H. Groh	1	0	0	0	0	0	0	.000
C. Hill, p	1	0	0	0	0	0	0	.000
R. Spencer, c	1	0	0	0	0	0	0	.000
E. Yde	0	0	0	0	0	0	1	—

Errors: L. Waner (2), G. Wright, G. Grantham, E. Smith, P. Traynor

Individual Pitching

NEW YORK (A.L.)

	W	L	ERA	IP	H	BB	SO	SV
W. Moore	1	0	0.84	10.2	11	2	2	1
H. Pennock	1	0	1.00	9	3	0	1	0
G. Pipgras	1	0	2.00	9	7	1	2	0
W. Hoyt	1	0	4.91	7.1	8	1	2	0

PITTSBURGH (N.L.)

	W	L	ERA	IP	H	BB	SO	SV
V. Aldridge	0	1	7.36	7.1	10	4	4	0
C. Hill	0	0	4.50	6	9	1	6	0
L. Meadows	0	1	9.95	6.1	7	1	6	0
J. Miljus	0	1	1.35	6.2	4	4	6	0
R. Kremer	0	1	3.60	5	5	3	1	0
M. Cvengros	0	0	3.86	2.1	3	0	2	0
J. Dawson	0	0	0.00	1	0	0	0	0

1928 WORLD SERIES

LINE SCORES	PITCHERS (innings pitched)	HOME RUNS (men on)	HIGHLIGHTS

New York (A.L.) defeats St. Louis (N.L.) 4 games to 0

GAME 1 - OCTOBER 4

STL	N	000 000 100	1 3 1	Sherdel (7), Johnson (1)	Bottomley	
NY	A	100 200 01x	4 7 0	Hoyt (9)	Meusel (1 on)	

Hoyt opened with a win for the second year in a row, notching a three-hitter. Meusel's homer in the fourth scored two; Bottomley's blast spoiled the shutout.

GAME 2 - OCTOBER 5

STL	N	030 000 000	3 4 1	Alexander (2.1), Mitchell (5.2)	
NY	A	314 000 10x	9 8 2	Pipgras (9)	Gehrig (2 on)

Gehrig's homer in the first led the Yankees to a revenge win over Alexander, the hero of the 1926 classic. Pipgras, relying on curve balls, went the distance despite a shaky start.

GAME 3 - OCTOBER 7

NY	A	010 203 100	7 7 2	Zachary (9)	Gehrig, Gehrig (1 on)
STL	N	200 010 000	3 9 3	Haines (6), Johnson (1), Rhem (2)	

Zachary, a surprise southpaw starter, had an easy task when Gehrig connected twice for homers, batting in three as the Yankees dispose of Haines in six.

GAME 4 - OCTOBER 9

NY	A	000 100 420	7 15 2	Hoyt (9)	Ruth, Ruth, Gehrig, Durst, Ruth
STL	N	001 100 001	3 11 0	Sherdel (6.1), Alexander (2.2)	

Ruth rose to heights with three homers, aided by the umpire's ruling depriving Sherdel of a strikeout on a "quick-pitch."

Team totals

		W	AB	H	2B	3B	HR	R	RBI	BA	BB	SO	ERA
NY	A	4	134	37	7	0	9	27	25	.276	13	12	2.00
STL	N	0	131	27	5	1	1	10	8	.206	11	29	6.09

Individual Batting

NEW YORK (A.L.)

	AB	H	2B	3B	HR	R	RBI	BA
M. Koenig, ss	19	3	0	0	0	1	0	.158
B. Ruth, of	16	10	3	0	3	9	4	.625
B. Meusel, of	15	3	1	0	1	5	3	.200
B. Bengough, c	13	3	0	0	0	1	1	.231
T. Lazzeri, 2b	12	3	1	0	0	2	0	.250
L. Gehrig, 1b	11	6	1	0	4	5	9	.545
B. Paschal, of	10	2	0	0	0	0	1	.200
G. Robertson, 3b	8	1	0	0	0	1	2	.125
C. Durst, of	8	3	0	0	1	3	2	.375
W. Hoyt, p	7	1	0	0	0	0	0	.143
J. Dugan, 3b	6	1	0	0	0	0	1	.167
T. Zachary, p	4	0	0	0	0	0	0	.000
G. Pipgras, p	2	0	0	0	0	0	1	.000
L. Durocher, 2b	2	0	0	0	0	0	0	.000
P. Collins, c	1	1	1	0	0	0	0	1.000
E. Combs	0	0	0	0	0	0	1	—

Errors: M. Koenig (2), T. Lazzeri (2), W. Hoyt, G. Robertson
Stolen Bases: T. Lazzeri (2), B. Meusel (2)

ST. LOUIS (N.L.)

	AB	H	2B	3B	HR	R	RBI	BA
A. High, 3b	17	5	2	0	0	1	1	.294
C. Hafey, of	15	3	0	0	0	0	0	.200
J. Bottomley, 1b	14	3	0	1	1	1	3	.214
F. Frisch, 2b	13	3	0	0	0	1	1	.231
Maranville, ss	13	4	1	0	0	2	0	.308
T. Douthit, of	11	1	0	0	0	1	0	.091
J. Wilson, c	11	1	1	0	0	1	1	.091
G. Harper, of	9	1	0	0	0	1	0	.111
E. Orsatti, of	7	2	1	0	0	1	0	.286
W. Holm, of	6	1	0	0	0	0	1	.167
B. Sherdel, p	5	0	0	0	0	0	0	.000
E. Smith, c	4	3	0	0	0	0	0	.750
J. Haines, p	2	0	0	0	0	0	0	.000
C. Mitchell, p	2	0	0	0	0	0	0	.000
G. Alexander, p	1	0	0	0	0	0	1	.000
R. Blades	1	0	0	0	0	0	0	.000
P. Martin	0	0	0	0	0	1	0	—
T. Thevenow, ss	0	0	0	0	0	0	0	—

Errors: J. Wilson (2), C. Hafey, Maranville, C. Mitchell
Stolen Bases: F. Frisch (2), Maranville

Individual Pitching

NEW YORK (A.L.)

	W	L	ERA	IP	H	BB	SO	SV
W. Hoyt	2	0	1.50	18	14	6	14	0
G. Pipgras	1	0	2.00	9	4	4	8	0
T. Zachary	1	0	3.00	9	9	1	7	0

ST. LOUIS (N.L.)

	W	L	ERA	IP	H	BB	SO	SV
B. Sherdel	0	2	4.73	13.1	15	3	3	0
J. Haines	0	1	4.50	6	6	3	3	0
C. Mitchell	0	0	1.59	5.2	2	2	2	0
G. Alexander	0	1	19.80	5	10	4	2	0
F. Rhem	0	0	0.00	2	0	0	1	0
S. Johnson	0	0	4.50	2	4	1	1	0

1929 WORLD SERIES

LINE SCORES	PITCHERS (innings pitched)	HOME RUNS (men on)	HIGHLIGHTS

Philadelphia (A.L.) defeats Chicago (N.L.) 4 games to 1

GAME 1 - OCTOBER 8

PHI	A	000 000 102	3 6 1	Ehmke (9)
CHI	N	000 000 001	1 8 2	Root (7), Bush (2)

Home Runs: Foxx

Ehmke struck out 13, surpassing the Series record of 12 set by Walsh in 1906. Foxx's home run in the seventh broke a scoreless deadlock, and Miller's two-run single in the ninth applied the crusher.

GAME 2 - OCTOBER 9

PHI	A	003 300 120	9 12 0	Earnshaw (4.2), Grove (4.1) SV
CHI	N	000 030 000	3 10 1	Malone (3.2), Blake (1.1), Carlson (3), Nehf (1)

Home Runs: Foxx (2 on), Simmons (1 on)

Foxx again took charge, his three-run homer in the third launching the scoring. Earnshaw got credit for the win despite being relieved by Grove in the fifth.

GAME 3 - OCTOBER 11

CHI	N	000 003 000	3 6 1	Bush (9)
PHI	A	000 010 000	1 9 1	Earnshaw (9)

A two-run single in the sixth by Cuyler gives the National League its first Series victory after ten straight setbacks. Earnshaw, on one day's rest, struck out ten, but lost on two unearned runs.

GAME 4 - OCTOBER 12

CHI	N	000 205 1 00	8 10 2	Root (6.1), Nehf (0), Blake (0), Malone (0.2), Carlson (1)
PHI	A	000 000 (10)0x	10 15 2	Quinn (5), Walberg (1), Rommel (1), Grove (2) SV

Home Runs: Grimm (1 on); Simmons, Haas (2 on)

A fabulous ten-run seventh overcame an 8-0 deficit and lifted the A's to an incredible triumph. Wilson contributed to the scoring binge by losing two balls in the sun.

GAME 5 - OCTOBER 14

CHI	N	000 200 000	2 8 0	Malone (8.2)
PHI	A	000 000 003	3 6 0	Ehmke (3.2), Walberg (5.1)

Home Runs: Haas (1 on)

Three runs in the last of the ninth brought a dramatic end to the Series. A two-run homer by Haas tied the score before Simmons and Miller doubled to score the winning run.

Team totals

		W	AB	H	2B	3B	HR	R	RBI	BA	BB	SO	ERA
PHI	A	4	171	48	5	0	6	26	26	.281	13	27	2.40
CHI	N	1	173	43	6	2	1	17	15	.249	13	50	4.33

Individual Batting

PHILADELPHIA (A.L.)

	AB	H	2B	3B	HR	R	RBI	BA
M. Bishop, 2b	21	4	0	0	0	2	1	.190
M. Haas, of	21	5	0	0	2	3	6	.238
A. Simmons, of	20	6	1	0	2	6	5	.300
J. Foxx, 1b	20	7	1	0	2	5	5	.350
J. Dykes, 3b	19	8	1	0	0	2	4	.421
B. Miller, of	19	7	1	0	0	1	4	.368
J. Boley, ss	17	4	0	0	0	1	1	.235
M. Cochrane, c	15	6	1	0	0	5	0	.400
G. Earnshaw, p	5	0	0	0	0	1	0	.000
H. Ehmke, p	5	1	0	0	0	0	0	.200
G. Burns	2	0	0	0	0	0	0	.000
J. Quinn, p	2	0	0	0	0	0	0	.000
L. Grove, p	2	0	0	0	0	0	0	.000
H. Summa	1	0	0	0	0	0	0	.000
R. Walberg, p	1	0	0	0	0	0	0	.000
W. French	1	0	0	0	0	0	0	.000

Errors: J. Dykes (2), B. Miller, R. Walberg

CHICAGO (N.L.)

	AB	H	2B	3B	HR	R	RBI	BA
W. English, ss	21	4	2	0	0	1	0	.190
R. Hornsby, 2b	21	5	1	1	0	4	1	.238
N. McMillan, 3b	20	2	0	0	0	0	0	.100
K. Cuyler, of	20	6	1	0	0	4	4	.300
Stephenson, of	19	6	1	0	0	3	3	.316
C. Grimm, 1b	18	7	0	0	1	2	4	.389
Z. Taylor, c	17	3	0	0	0	0	3	.176
H. Wilson, of	17	8	0	1	0	2	0	.471
C. Root, p	5	0	0	0	0	0	0	.000
P. Malone, p	4	1	1	0	0	0	0	.250
G. Hartnett	3	0	0	0	0	0	0	.000
G. Bush, p	3	0	0	0	0	1	0	.000
F. Blair	1	0	0	0	0	0	0	.000
S. Blake, p	1	1	0	0	0	0	0	1.000
M. Gonzalez, c	1	0	0	0	0	0	0	.000
C. Heathcote	1	0	0	0	0	0	0	.000
C. Tolson	1	0	0	0	0	0	0	.000

Errors: W. English (4), R. Hornsby, H. Wilson, K. Cuyler
Stolen Bases: N. McMillan

Individual Pitching

PHILADELPHIA (A.L.)

	W	L	ERA	IP	H	BB	SO	SV
G. Earnshaw	1	1	2.63	13.2	14	6	17	0
H. Ehmke	1	0	1.42	12.2	14	3	13	0
L. Grove	0	0	0.00	6.1	3	1	10	2
R. Walberg	1	0	0.00	6.1	3	0	8	0
J. Quinn	0	0	9.00	5	7	2	2	0
E. Rommel	1	0	9.00	1	2	1	0	0

CHICAGO (N.L.)

	W	L	ERA	IP	H	BB	SO	SV
C. Root	0	1	4.73	13.1	12	2	8	0
P. Malone	0	2	4.15	13	12	7	11	0
G. Bush	1	0	0.82	11	12	2	4	0
H. Carlson	0	0	6.75	4	7	1	3	0
S. Blake	0	1	13.50	1.1	4	0	1	0
A. Nehf	0	0	18.00	1	1	1	0	0

1930 WORLD SERIES

LINE SCORES	PITCHERS (innings pitched)	HOME RUNS (men on)	HIGHLIGHTS

Philadelphia (A.L.) defeats St. Louis (N.L.) 4 games to 2

GAME 1 - OCTOBER 1

STL	N	002 000 000	2 9 0	Grimes (8)		The Athletics got only five hits in five different innings off Grimes but all were for extra bases and each produced a run.
PHI	A	010 101 11x	5 5 0	Grove (9)	Simmons, Cochrane	

GAME 2 - OCTOBER 2

STL	N	010 000 000	1 6 2	Rhem (3.1), Lindsey (2.2), Johnson (2)	Watkins	The Athletics scored six runs off Rhem in the first four innings to win easily. Earnshaw walked one and struck out eight.
PHI	A	202 200 00x	6 7 2	Earnshaw (9)	Cochrane	

GAME 3 - OCTOBER 4

PHI	A	000 000 000	0 7 0	Walberg (4.2), Shores (1.1), Quinn (2)		Hallahan had an easy shutout after escaping from a first inning jam.
STL	N	000 110 21x	5 10 0	Hallahan (9)	Douthit	

GAME 4 - OCTOBER 5

PHI	A	100 000 000	1 4 1	Grove (8)		Dykes's error allowed the Cardinals to score twice in the fourth. Haines did not allow a hit after the third inning.
STL	N	001 200 00x	3 5 1	Haines (9)		

GAME 5 - OCTOBER 6

PHI	A	000 000 002	2 5 0	Earnshaw (7), **Grove** (2)	Foxx (1 on)	Foxx's homer won for the Athletics in the ninth as Earnshaw and Grove kept the Cardinals from reaching third.
STL	N	000 000 000	0 3 1	Grimes (9)		

GAME 6 - OCTOBER 8

STL	N	000 000 001	1 5 1	Hallahan (2), Johnson (3), Lindsey (2), Bell (1)		Once again the Athletics got only extra base hits and turned each into a run as Earnshaw, with only one day's rest, pitched a strong five-hitter.
PHI	A	201 211 00x	7 7 0	Earnshaw (9)	Simmons, Dykes (1 on)	

Team totals

		W	AB	H	2B	3B	HR	R	RBI	BA	BB	SO	ERA
PHI	A	4	178	35	10	2	6	21	20	.197	24	32	1.73
STL	N	2	190	38	10	1	2	12	11	.200	11	33	3.35

Individual Batting

PHILADELPHIA (A.L.)

	AB	H	2B	3B	HR	R	RBI	BA
A. Simmons, of	22	8	2	0	2	4	4	.364
B. Miller, of	21	3	2	0	0	3	3	.143
J. Boley, ss	21	2	0	0	0	1	1	.095
J. Foxx, 1b	21	7	2	1	1	3	3	.333
M. Haas, of	18	2	0	1	0	1	1	.111
M. Cochrane, c	18	4	1	0	2	5	3	.222
J. Dykes, 3b	18	4	3	0	1	2	5	.222
M. Bishop, 2b	18	4	0	0	0	5	0	.222
G. Earnshaw, p	9	0	0	0	0	0	0	.000
L. Grove, p	6	0	0	0	0	0	0	.000
J. Moore, of	3	1	0	0	0	0	0	.333
R. Walberg, p	2	0	0	0	0	0	0	.000
E. McNair	1	0	0	0	0	0	0	.000

Errors: J. Boley, M. Cochrane, J. Dykes

ST. LOUIS (N.L.)

	AB	H	2B	3B	HR	R	RBI	BA
F. Frisch, 2b	24	5	2	0	0	0	0	.208
T. Douthit, of	24	2	0	0	1	1	2	.083
J. Bottomley, 1b	22	1	1	0	0	1	0	.045
C. Hafey, of	22	6	5	0	0	2	2	.273
S. Adams, 3b	21	3	0	0	0	0	1	.143
C. Gelbert, ss	17	6	0	1	0	2	2	.353
J. Wilson, c	15	4	1	0	0	0	2	.267
G. Watkins, of	12	2	0	0	1	2	1	.167
R. Blades, of	9	1	0	0	0	2	0	.111
G. Mancuso, c	7	2	0	0	0	1	0	.286
B. Grimes, p	5	2	0	0	0	0	0	.400
S. Fisher	2	1	1	0	0	0	0	.500
J. Haines, p	2	1	0	0	0	0	1	.500
B. Hallahan, p	2	0	0	0	0	0	0	.000
A. High, 3b	2	1	0	0	0	1	0	.500
J. Lindsey, p	1	1	0	0	0	0	0	1.000
E. Orsatti	1	0	0	0	0	0	0	.000
Puccinelli	1	0	0	0	0	0	0	.000
F. Rhem, p	1	0	0	0	0	0	0	.000

Errors: F. Frisch (3), F. Rhem, G. Watkins
Stolen Bases: F. Frisch

Individual Pitching

PHILADELPHIA (A.L.)

	W	L	ERA	IP	H	BB	SO	SV
G. Earnshaw	2	0	0.72	25	13	7	19	0
L. Grove	2	1	1.42	19	15	3	10	0
R. Walberg	0	1	3.86	4.2	4	1	3	0
J. Quinn	0	0	4.50	2	3	0	1	0
B. Shores	0	0	13.50	1.1	3	0	0	0

ST. LOUIS (N.L.)

	W	L	ERA	IP	H	BB	SO	SV
B. Grimes	0	2	3.71	17	10	6	13	0
B. Hallahan	1	1	1.64	11	9	8	8	0
J. Haines	1	0	1.00	9	4	4	2	0
S. Johnson	0	0	7.20	5	4	3	4	0
J. Lindsey	0	0	1.93	4.2	1	1	2	0
F. Rhem	0	1	10.80	3.1	7	2	3	0
H. Bell	0	0	0.00	1	0	0	0	0

1931 WORLD SERIES

LINE SCORES	PITCHERS (innings pitched)	HOME RUNS (men on)	HIGHLIGHTS

St. Louis (N.L.) defeats Philadelphia (A.L.) 4 games to 3

GAME 1 - OCTOBER 1

PHI	A	004 000 200	6 11 0	Grove (9)	Simmons (1 on)	The A's gave Grove four third-inning runs, and he coasted from there. He scattered twelve hits, three by Pepper Martin.
STL	N	200 000 000	2 12 0	Derringer (7), Johnson (2)

GAME 2 - OCTOBER 2

PHI	A	000 000 000	0 3 0	Earnshaw (8)		Pepper Martin, with two hits and two stolen bases, scored both Cardinal runs to support Hallahan's shutout pitching.
STL	N	010 000 01x	2 6 1	Hallahan (9)

GAME 3 - OCTOBER 5

STL	N	020 200 001	5 12 0	Grimes (9)		Grimes supported his two-hitter with a two-run single in the fourth.
PHI	A	000 000 002	2 2 0	Grove (8), Mahaffey (1)	Simmons (1 on)

GAME 4 - OCTOBER 6

STL	N	000 000 000	0 2 1	Johnson (5.2), Lindsey (1.1), Derringer (1)		Simmons doubled home Bishop in the first to give Earnshaw the only run he needed. Martin had both Cardinal hits.
PHI	A	100 002 00x	3 10 0	Earnshaw (9)	Foxx

GAME 5 - OCTOBER 7

STL	N	100 002 011	5 12 0	Hallahan (9)	Martin (1 on)	Martin, with three hits and a long fly, drove in four runs to lead the Cardinal attack.
PHI	A	000 000 100	1 9 0	Hoyt (6), Walberg (2), Rommel (1)

GAME 6 - OCTOBER 9

PHI	A	000 040 400	8 8 1	Grove (9)		The Athletics broke a scoreless tie with four runs in the fifth on two singles, four walks and an error.
STL	N	000 001 000	1 5 2	Derringer (4.2), Johnson (1.1), Lindsey (2), Rhem (1)

GAME 7 - OCTOBER 10

PHI	A	000 000 002	2 7 1	Earnshaw (7), Walberg (1)		Watkins's two-run homer in the third gave the Cardinals a 4-0 lead and enabled them to withstand a late Athletics rally, Hallahan nailing down the final out for a tiring Grimes.
STL	N	202 000 00x	4 5 0	Grimes (8.2), Hallahan (0.1) SV	Watkins (1 on)

Team totals

		W	AB	H	2B	3B	HR	R	RBI	BA	BB	SO	ERA
STL	N	4	229	54	11	0	2	19	17	.236	9	41	2.32
PHI	A	3	227	50	5	0	3	22	20	.220	28	46	2.66

Individual Batting

ST. LOUIS (N.L.)

	AB	H	2B	3B	HR	R	RBI	BA
F. Frisch, 2b	27	7	2	0	0	2	1	.259
J. Bottomley, 1b	25	4	1	0	0	2	2	.160
C. Hafey, of	24	4	0	0	0	1	0	.167
P. Martin, of	24	12	4	0	1	5	5	.500
J. Wilson, c	23	5	0	0	0	0	2	.217
C. Gelbert, ss	23	6	1	0	0	0	3	.261
A. High, 3b	15	4	0	0	0	3	0	.267
W. Roettger, of	14	4	1	0	0	1	0	.286
G. Watkins, of	14	4	1	0	1	4	2	.286
J. Flowers, 3b	11	1	1	0	0	1	0	.091
B. Grimes, p	7	2	0	0	0	0	2	.286
B. Hallahan, p	6	0	0	0	0	0	0	.000
S. Adams, 3b	4	1	0	0	0	0	0	.250
E. Orsatti, of	3	0	0	0	0	0	0	.000
S. Johnson, p	2	0	0	0	0	0	0	.000
R. Blades	2	0	0	0	0	0	0	.000
R. Collins	2	0	0	0	0	0	0	.000
P. Derringer, p	2	0	0	0	0	0	0	.000
G. Mancuso, c	1	0	0	0	0	0	0	.000

Errors: J. Wilson, J. Bottomley, J. Flowers, C. Hafey
Stolen Bases: P. Martin (5), F. Frisch, C. Hafey, G. Watkins

PHILADELPHIA (A.L.)

	AB	H	2B	3B	HR	R	RBI	BA
M. Bishop, 2b	27	4	0	0	0	4	0	.148
A. Simmons, of	27	9	2	0	2	4	8	.333
B. Miller, of	26	7	1	0	0	3	1	.269
D. Williams, ss	25	8	1	0	0	2	1	.320
M. Cochrane, c	25	4	0	0	0	2	1	.160
J. Foxx, 1b	23	8	0	0	1	3	3	.348
M. Haas, of	23	3	1	0	0	1	0	.130
J. Dykes, 3b	22	5	0	0	0	2	2	.227
L. Grove, p	10	0	0	0	0	0	0	.000
G. Earnshaw, p	8	0	0	0	0	0	0	.000
J. Moore, of	3	1	0	0	0	0	0	.333
E. McNair, 2b	2	0	0	0	0	1	0	.000
W. Hoyt, p	2	0	0	0	0	0	0	.000
D. Cramer	2	1	0	0	0	0	2	.500
J. Boley	1	0	0	0	0	0	0	.000
J. Heving	1	0	0	0	0	0	0	.000
P. Todt	0	0	0	0	0	0	0	—

Errors: M. Cochrane, J. Foxx

Individual Pitching

ST. LOUIS (N.L.)

	W	L	ERA	IP	H	BB	SO	SV
B. Hallahan	2	0	0.49	18.1	12	8	12	1
B. Grimes	2	0	2.04	17.2	9	9	11	0
P. Derringer	0	2	4.26	12.2	14	7	14	0
S. Johnson	0	1	3.00	9	10	1	6	0
J. Lindsey	0	0	5.40	3.1	4	3	2	0
F. Rhem	0	0	0.00	1	1	0	1	0

PHILADELPHIA (A.L.)

	W	L	ERA	IP	H	BB	SO	SV
L. Grove	2	1	2.42	26	28	2	16	0
G. Earnshaw	1	2	1.88	24	12	4	20	0
W. Hoyt	0	1	4.50	6	7	0	1	0
R. Walberg	0	0	3.00	3	3	2	4	0
R. Mahaffey	0	0	9.00	1	1	1	0	0
E. Rommel	0	0	9.00	1	3	0	0	0

1932 WORLD SERIES

LINE SCORES	PITCHERS (innings pitched)	HOME RUNS (men on)	HIGHLIGHTS

New York (A.L.) defeats Chicago (N.L.) 4 games to 0

GAME 1 - SEPTEMBER 28

CHI	N	200 000 220	6 10 1	Bush (5.1), Grimes (1.2), Smith (1)			Bush retired the first nine batters, but the Yanks exploded, thanks to Gehrig's two-run homer in the fourth, and two-run singles by Dickey and Combs. Ruffing struck out ten in going the distance.
NY	A	000 305 31x	12 8 2	Ruffing (9)	Gehrig (1 on)		

GAME 2 - SEPTEMBER 29

CHI	N	101 000 000	2 9 0	Warneke (8)		Chapman's single in the third gave the Yankees the lead, and Gomez shut the Cubs down. Gehrig had three hits and scored two runs.
NY	A	202 010 00x	5 10 1	Gomez (9)		

GAME 3 - OCTOBER 1

NY	A	301 020 001	7 8 1	Pipgras (8), Pennock (1) SV	Ruth (2 on), Gehrig, Ruth, Gehrig	In a home run carnival which featured two homers each by Ruth and Gehrig, the Yankees took a commanding three-game lead in the Series. Back-to-back home runs in the fifth by the two sluggers decided the game.
CHI	N	102 100 001	5 9 4	Root (4.1), Malone (2.2), May (1.1), Tinning (0.2)	Cuyler, Hartnett	

GAME 4 - OCTOBER 2

NY	A	102 002 404	13 19 4	W. Moore (5.1), Pennock (3) SV	Lazzeri (1 on), Combs, Lazzeri (1 on)	The Yankees came back from a 4-1 first inning deficit to sweep the Series. The Cubs held Ruth to just one single, but six other Yankees had two or more hits on the day.
CHI	N	400 001 001	6 9 1	Bush (0.1), Warneke (2.2), May (3.1), Tinning (1.2), Grimes (1)	Demaree (2 on)	

Team totals

		W	AB	H	2B	3B	HR	R	RBI	BA	BB	SO	ERA
NY	A	4	144	45	6	0	8	37	36	.313	23	26	3.25
CHI	N	0	146	37	8	2	3	19	16	.253	11	24	9.26

Individual Batting

NEW YORK (A.L.)

	AB	H	2B	3B	HR	R	RBI	BA
B. Chapman, of	17	5	1	0	0	1	6	.294
L. Gehrig, 1b	17	9	1	0	3	9	8	.529
T. Lazzeri, 2b	17	5	0	0	2	4	5	.294
B. Dickey, c	16	7	0	0	0	2	4	.438
E. Combs, 2b, of	16	6	2	0	1	8	4	.375
F. Crosetti, ss	15	2	1	0	0	2	0	.133
J. Sewell, 3b	15	5	1	0	0	4	3	.333
B. Ruth, of	15	5	0	0	2	6	6	.333
G. Pipgras, p	5	0	0	0	0	0	0	.000
R. Ruffing, p	4	0	0	0	0	0	0	.000
W. Moore, p	3	1	0	0	0	0	0	.333
L. Gomez, p	3	0	0	0	0	0	0	.000
H. Pennock, p	1	0	0	0	0	0	0	.000
M. Hoag	0	0	0	0	0	1	0	—
S. Byrd, of	0	0	0	0	0	0	0	—

Errors: F. Crosetti (4), L. Gehrig, T. Lazzeri, B. Ruth, J. Sewell

CHICAGO (N.L.)

	AB	H	2B	3B	HR	R	RBI	BA
K. Cuyler, of	18	5	1	1	1	2	2	.278
Stephenson, of	18	8	1	0	0	2	4	.444
B. Herman, 2b	18	4	1	0	0	5	1	.222
W. English, 3b	17	3	0	0	0	2	1	.176
G. Hartnett, c	16	5	2	0	1	2	1	.313
C. Grimm, 1b	15	5	2	0	0	2	1	.333
B. Jurges, ss	11	4	1	0	0	1	1	.364
J. Moore, of	7	0	0	0	0	1	0	.000
F. Demaree, of	7	2	0	0	1	1	4	.286
M. Koenig, ss	4	1	0	1	0	1	1	.250
L. Warneke, p	4	0	0	0	0	0	0	.000
R. Hemsley, c	3	0	0	0	0	0	0	.000
M. Gudat	2	0	0	0	0	0	0	.000
J. May, p	2	0	0	0	0	0	0	.000
C. Root, p	2	0	0	0	0	0	0	.000
B. Grimes, p	1	0	0	0	0	0	0	.000
G. Bush, p	1	0	0	0	0	0	0	.000
S. Hack	0	0	0	0	0	0	0	—

Errors: B. Jurges (2), F. Demaree, W. English, G. Hartnett, B. Herman

Stolen Bases: K. Cuyler, B. Jurges

Individual Pitching

NEW YORK (A.L.)

	W	L	ERA	IP	H	BB	SO	SV
R. Ruffing	1	0	4.00	9	10	6	10	0
L. Gomez	1	0	1.00	9	9	1	8	0
G. Pipgras	1	0	4.50	8	9	3	1	0
W. Moore	1	0	0.00	5.1	2	0	1	0
H. Pennock	0	0	2.25	4	2	1	4	2
J. Allen	0	0	40.50	0.2	5	0	0	0

CHICAGO (N.L.)

	W	L	ERA	IP	H	BB	SO	SV
L. Warneke	0	1	5.91	10.2	15	5	8	0
G. Bush	0	1	14.29	5.2	5	6	2	0
J. May	0	1	11.57	4.2	9	3	4	0
C. Root	0	1	10.38	4.1	6	3	4	0
B. Tinning	0	0	0.00	2.1	0	3	0	0
B. Grimes	0	0	23.63	2.2	7	2	0	0
P. Malone	0	0	0.00	2.2	1	4	4	0
B. Smith	0	0	9.00	1	2	0	1	0

1933 WORLD SERIES

LINE SCORES	PITCHERS (innings pitched)	HOME RUNS (men on)	HIGHLIGHTS

New York (N.L.) defeats Washington (A.L.) 4 games to 1

GAME 1 - OCTOBER 3

WAS	A	000 100 001	2 5 3	Stewart (2), Russell (5), Thomas (1)		Ott had four hits and three RBIs and Hubbell struck out ten and allowed two unearned runs.
NY	N	202 000 00x	4 10 2	Hubbell (9)	Ott (1 on)	

GAME 2 - OCTOBER 4

WAS	A	001 000 000	1 5 0	Crowder (5.2), Thomas (0.1), McCool (2)	Goslin	The Giants overcame a 1-0 deficit with six in the sixth. O'Doul drove in two with a pinch single and Mancuso drove in another with a bunt single.
NY	N	000 006 00x	6 10 0	Schumacher (9)		

GAME 3 - OCTOBER 5

NY	N	000 000 000	0 5 0	Fitzsimmons (7), Bell (1)		The Senators scored two in the first on Myer's single and doubles by Goslin and Schulte to support Whitehill's six-hit shutout.
WAS	A	210 000 10x	4 9 1	Whitehill (9)		

GAME 4 - OCTOBER 6

NY	N	000 100 000 01	2 11 1	Hubbell (11)	Terry	Jackson, although suffering from a severe leg injury, led off the eleventh by beating out a bunt, moved to second on a a sacrifice, and scored on Ryan's single. Hubbell secured the victory by getting pinch-hitter Bolton to ground into a double play with the bases loaded and one out in the bottom of the eleventh.
WAS	A	000 000 100 00	1 8 0	Weaver (10.1), Russell (0.2)		

GAME 5 - OCTOBER 7

NY	N	020 001 000 1	4 11 1	Schumacker (5.2), Luque (4.1)	Ott	Ott's homer in the tenth won the Series after Schulte tied the game with a two-out three-run homer in the sixth.
WAS	A	000 003 000 0	3 10 0	Crowder (5.1), Russell (4.2)	Schulte (2 on)	

Team totals

		W	AB	H	2B	3B	HR	R	RBI	BA	BB	SO	ERA
NY	N	4	176	47	5	0	3	16	16	.267	11	21	1.53
WAS	A	1	173	37	4	0	2	11	11	.214	13	25	2.74

Individual Batting

NEW YORK (N.L.)

	AB	H	2B	3B	HR	R	RBI	BA
H. Critz, 2b	22	3	0	0	0	2	0	.136
J. Moore, of	22	5	1	0	0	1	1	.227
B. Terry, 1b	22	6	1	0	1	3	1	.273
K. Davis, of	19	7	1	0	0	1	0	.368
M. Ott, of	18	7	0	0	2	3	4	.389
T. Jackson, 3b	18	4	1	0	0	3	2	.222
B. Ryan, ss	18	5	0	0	0	0	1	.278
G. Mancuso, c	17	2	1	0	0	2	2	.118
C. Hubbell, p	7	2	0	0	0	0	0	.286
Schumacher, p	7	2	0	0	0	0	3	.286
H. Peel, of	2	1	0	0	0	0	0	.500
Fitzsimmons, p	2	1	0	0	0	0	0	.500
L. O'Doul	1	1	0	0	0	1	2	1.000
D. Luque, p	1	1	0	0	0	0	0	1.000

Errors: T. Jackson, B. Ryan, H. Critz, C. Hubbell

WASHINGTON (A.L.)

	AB	H	2B	3B	HR	R	RBI	BA
J. Cronin, ss	22	7	0	0	0	1	2	.318
F. Schulte, of	21	7	1	0	1	1	4	.333
G. Goslin, of	20	5	1	0	1	2	1	.250
B. Myer, 2b	20	6	1	0	0	2	2	.300
J. Kuhel, 1b	20	3	0	0	0	1	1	.150
H. Manush, of	18	2	0	0	0	2	0	.111
L. Sewell, c	17	3	0	0	0	1	1	.176
O. Bluege, 3b	16	2	1	0	0	1	0	.125
G. Crowder, p	4	1	0	0	0	0	0	.250
M. Weaver, p	4	0	0	0	0	0	0	.000
E. Whitehill, p	3	0	0	0	0	0	0	.000
C. Bolton	2	0	0	0	0	0	0	.000
D. Harris, of	2	0	0	0	0	0	0	.000
J. Russell, p	2	0	0	0	0	0	0	.000
S. Rice	1	1	0	0	0	0	0	1.000
L. Stewart, p	1	0	0	0	0	0	0	.000
J. Kerr	0	0	0	0	0	0	0	—

Errors: B. Myer (3), J. Cronin
Stolen Bases: L. Sewell

Individual Pitching

NEW YORK (N.L.)

	W	L	ERA	IP	H	BB	SO	SV
C. Hubbell	2	0	0.00	20	13	6	15	0
Schumacher	1	0	2.45	14.2	13	5	3	0
Fitzsimmons	0	1	5.14	7	9	0	2	0
D. Luque	1	0	0.00	4.1	2	2	5	0
H. Bell	0	0	0.00	1	0	0	0	0

WASHINGTON (A.L.)

	W	L	ERA	IP	H	BB	SO	SV
G. Crowder	0	1	7.36	11	16	5	7	0
M. Weaver	0	1	1.74	10.1	11	4	3	0
J. Russell	0	1	0.87	10.1	8	0	7	0
E. Whitehill	1	0	0.00	9	5	2	2	0
L. Stewart	0	1	9.00	2	6	0	0	0
A. McColl	0	0	0.00	2	0	0	0	0
T. Thomas	0	0	0.00	1.1	1	0	2	0

1934 WORLD SERIES

LINE SCORES	PITCHERS (innings pitched)	HOME RUNS (men on)	HIGHLIGHTS

St. Louis (N.L.) defeats Detroit (A.L.) 4 games to 3

GAME 1 - OCTOBER 3

STL N	021 014 000	8 13 2	D. Dean (9)	Medwick
DET A	001 001 010	3 8 5	Crowder (5), Marberry (0.2), Hogsett (3.1)	Greenberg

The Cardinals capitalized on five errors by the Tiger infield. Medwick leads the attack with four hits.

GAME 2 - OCTOBER 4

STL N	011 000 000 000	2 7 3	Hallahan (8.1), B. Walker (3)	
DET A	000 100 001 001	3 7 0	Rowe (12)	

Gee Walker, given a chance when Collins and Delancey failed to catch his pop foul, singled in the tying run for the Tigers in the ninth. They went on to win in the twelfth when Goslin singled following walks to Gehringer and Greenberg.

GAME 3 - OCTOBER 5

DET A	000 000 001	1 8 2	Bridges (4), Hogsett (4)	
STL N	110 020 00x	4 9 1	P. Dean (9)	

The Tigers left 13 men on base as Martin's double, triple, and two runs scored led the Cardinals.

GAME 4 - OCTOBER 6

DET A	003 100 150	10 13 1	Auker (9)	
STL N	011 200 000	4 10 5	Carleton (2.2), Vance (1.1), B. Walker (3.1), Haines (0.2), Mooney (1)	

The Tigers evened the Series thanks to Greenberg's three hits and three RBIs and Rogell's four RBIs.

GAME 5 - OCTOBER 7

DET A	010 002 000	3 7 0	Bridges (9)	Gehringer
STL N	000 000 100	1 7 1	D. Dean (8), Carleton (1)	Delancey

Bridges returned after a day's rest to subdue the Cardinals. Gehringer's home run in the sixth was the game-winner.

GAME 6 - OCTOBER 8

STL N	100 020 100	4 10 2	P. Dean (9)	
DET A	001 002 000	3 7 1	Rowe (9)	

Paul Dean aided his own cause with a single in the seventh that sent in the deciding run.

GAME 7 - OCTOBER 9

STL N	007 002 200	11 17 1	D. Dean (9)	
DET A	000 000 000	0 6 3	Auker (2.1), Rowe (0.1), Hogsett (0), Bridges (4.1), Marberry (1), Crowder (1)	

The Cardinals easily romped to the Series crown. Medwick was replaced for his own protection in the sixth after the crowd pelted him with fruit and bottles.

Team totals

		W	AB	H	2B	3B	HR	R	RBI	BA	BB	SO	ERA
STL	N	4	262	73	14	5	2	34	32	.279	11	31	2.34
DET	A	3	250	56	12	1	2	23	20	.224	25	43	3.74

Individual Batting

ST. LOUIS (N.L.)

	AB	H	2B	3B	HR	R	RBI	BA
F. Frisch, 2b	31	6	1	0	0	2	4	.194
P. Martin, 3b	31	11	3	1	0	8	3	.355
J. Rothrock, of	30	7	3	1	0	3	6	.233
R. Collins, 1b	30	11	1	0	0	4	4	.367
J. Medwick, of	29	11	0	1	1	4	5	.379
B. DeLancey, c	29	5	3	0	1	3	4	.172
L. Durocher, ss	27	7	1	1	0	4	0	.259
E. Orsatti, of	22	7	0	1	0	3	2	.318
D. Dean, p	12	3	2	0	0	3	1	.250
P. Dean, p	6	1	0	0	0	0	2	.167
C. Fullis, of	5	2	0	0	0	0	0	.400
B. Hallahan, p	3	0	0	0	0	0	0	.000
B. Walker, p	2	0	0	0	0	0	0	.000
P. Crawford	2	0	0	0	0	0	0	.000
S. Davis	2	2	0	0	0	1	0	1.000
T. Carleton, p	2	0	0	0	0	0	0	.000
B. Whitehead, ss	0	0	0	0	0	0	0	—

Errors: P. Martin (4), E. Orsatti (2), F. Frisch (2), B. DeLancey, C. Fullis, B. Hallahan, R. Collins, P. Dean, J. Rothrock, B. Walker
Stolen Bases: P. Martin (2)

DETROIT (A.L.)

	AB	H	2B	3B	HR	R	RBI	BA
C. Gehringer, 2b	29	11	1	0	1	5	2	.379
G. Goslin, of	29	7	1	0	0	2	2	.241
M. Owen, 3b	29	2	0	0	0	0	1	.069
B. Rogell, ss	29	8	1	0	0	3	4	.276
H. Greenberg, 1b	28	9	2	1	1	4	7	.321
P. Fox, of	28	8	6	0	0	1	2	.286
M. Cochrane, c	28	6	1	0	0	2	1	.214
J. White, of	23	3	0	0	0	6	0	.130
S. Rowe, p	7	0	0	0	0	0	0	.000
T. Bridges, p	7	1	0	0	0	0	0	.143
E. Auker, p	4	0	0	0	0	0	0	.000
G. Walker	3	1	0	0	0	0	1	.333
C. Hogsett, p	3	0	0	0	0	0	0	.000
F. Doljack, of	2	0	0	0	0	0	0	.000
G. Crowder, p	1	0	0	0	0	0	0	.000
R. Hayworth, c	0	0	0	0	0	0	0	—

Errors: C. Gehringer (3), B. Rogell (3), M. Owen (2), G. Goslin (2), H. Greenberg, J. White
Stolen Bases: C. Gehringer, H. Greenberg, M. Owen, J. White

Individual Pitching

ST. LOUIS (N.L.)

	W	L	ERA	IP	H	BB	SO	SV
D. Dean	2	1	1.73	26	20	5	17	0
P. Dean	2	0	1.00	18	15	7	11	0
B. Hallahan	0	0	2.16	8.1	6	4	6	0
B. Walker	0	2	7.11	6.1	6	6	2	0
T. Carleton	0	0	7.36	3.2	5	2	2	0
J. Mooney	0	0	0.00	1	1	0	0	0
D. Vance	0	0	0.00	1.1	2	1	3	0
J. Haines	0	0	0.00	0.2	1	0	2	0

DETROIT (A.L.)

	W	L	ERA	IP	H	BB	SO	SV
S. Rowe	1	1	2.95	21.1	19	0	12	0
T. Bridges	1	1	3.63	17.1	21	1	12	0
E. Auker	1	1	5.56	11.1	16	5	2	0
C. Hogsett	0	0	1.23	7.1	6	3	3	0
G. Crowder	0	1	1.50	6	6	1	2	0
F. Marberry	0	0	21.60	1.2	5	1	0	0

1935 WORLD SERIES

LINE SCORES	PITCHERS (innings pitched)	HOME RUNS (men on)	HIGHLIGHTS

Detroit (A.L.) defeats Chicago (N.L.) 4 games to 2

GAME 1 - OCTOBER 2

CHI N	200 000 001	3 7 0	Warneke (9)	Demaree
DET A	000 000 000	0 4 3	Rowe (9)	

Chicago scored twice in the first on hits by Galan and Hartnett and Rowe's error as Warneke pitched a four-hit shutout.

GAME 2 - OCTOBER 3

CHI N	000 010 200	3 6 1	Root (0), Henshaw (3.2), Kowalik (4.1)	
DET A	400 300 10x	8 9 2	Bridges (9)	Greenberg (1 on)

Hits by the first four batters in the Tiger first, capped by Greenberg's homer, chased Root and ensured the victory.

GAME 3 - OCTOBER 4

DET A	000 001 040 01	6 12 2	Auker (6), Hogsett (1), Rowe (4)	
CHI N	020 010 002 00	5 10 3	Lee (7.1), Warneke (1.2), French (2)	Demaree

White's single scored Owen with the winning run in the eleventh after the Cubs tied the game in the ninth on singles by Hack, Klein, and O'Dea and a long fly by Galan.

GAME 4 - OCTOBER 5

DET A	001 001 000	2 7 0	Crowder (9)	
CHI N	010 000 000	1 5 2	Carleton (7), Root (2)	Hartnett

The Tigers scored the winning run in the sixth on errors by Galan and Jurges.

GAME 5 - OCTOBER 6

DET A	000 000 001	1 7 1	Rowe (8)	
CHI N	002 000 10x	3 8 0	Warneke (6), Lee (3) SV	Klein (1 on)

The Cubs scored twice in the third on Herman's triple and Klein's homer. Warneke left after six shutout innings because of a sore shoulder. Lee had to retire Clifton with two out and runners on second and third in the ninth to preserve the victory.

GAME 6 - OCTOBER 7

CHI N	001 020 000	3 12 0	French (8.2)	Herman (1 on)
DET A	100 101 001	4 12 1	Bridges (9)	

The Tigers won in the ninth inning when Cochrane singled, Gehringer's grounder moved him to second, and Goslin's single brought him in for the Series-ending run.

Team totals

		W	AB	H	2B	3B	HR	R	RBI	BA	BB	SO	ERA
DET	A	4	206	51	11	1	1	21	18	.248	25	27	2.29
CHI	N	2	202	48	6	2	5	18	17	.238	11	29	2.81

Individual Batting

DETROIT (A.L.)

	AB	H	2B	3B	HR	R	RBI	BA
P. Fox, of	26	10	3	1	0	4	4	.385
C. Gehringer, 2b	24	9	3	0	0	4	4	.375
B. Rogell, ss	24	7	2	0	0	1	1	.292
M. Cochrane, c	24	7	1	0	0	3	1	.292
G. Goslin, of	22	6	1	0	0	2	3	.273
M. Owen, 3b, 1b	20	1	0	0	0	2	1	.050
J. White, of	19	5	0	0	0	3	1	.263
F. Clifton, 3b	16	0	0	0	0	1	0	.000
T. Bridges, p	8	1	0	0	0	1	1	.125
S. Rowe, p	8	2	1	0	0	0	0	.250
H. Greenberg, 1b	6	1	0	0	1	1	2	.167
G. Walker, of	4	1	0	0	0	1	0	.250
G. Crowder, p	3	1	0	0	0	1	0	.333
E. Auker, p	2	0	0	0	0	0	0	.000

Errors: H. Greenberg (3), G. Goslin, M. Owen, S. Rowe, F. Clifton, M. Cochrane, P. Fox
Stolen Bases: C. Gehringer

CHICAGO (N.L.)

	AB	H	2B	3B	HR	R	RBI	BA
A. Galan, of	25	4	1	0	0	2	2	.160
Cavarretta, 1b	24	3	0	0	0	1	0	.125
F. Demaree, of	24	6	1	0	2	2	2	.250
G. Hartnett, c	24	7	0	0	1	1	2	.292
B. Herman, 2b	24	8	2	1	1	3	6	.333
S. Hack, ss, 3b	22	5	1	1	0	2	0	.227
B. Jurges, ss	16	4	0	0	0	3	1	.250
F. Lindstrom, 3b, of	15	3	1	0	0	0	0	.200
C. Klein, of	12	4	0	0	1	2	2	.333
L. Warneke, p	5	1	0	0	0	0	0	.200
L. French, p	4	1	0	0	0	1	0	.250
F. Kowalik, p	2	1	0	0	0	1	0	.500
B. Lee, p	1	0	0	0	0	0	0	.000
K. O'Dea	1	1	0	0	0	0	1	1.000
Stephenson	1	0	0	0	0	0	0	.000
T. Carleton, p	1	0	0	0	0	0	0	.000
R. Henshaw, p	1	0	0	0	0	0	0	.000

Errors: Cavarretta, A. Galan, B. Herman, B. Jurges, F. Kowalik, F. Lindstrom
Stolen Bases: S. Hack

Individual Pitching

DETROIT (A.L.)

	W	L	ERA	IP	H	BB	SO	SV
S. Rowe	1	2	2.57	21	19	1	14	0
T. Bridges	2	0	2.50	18	18	4	9	0
G. Crowder	1	0	1.00	9	5	3	5	0
E. Auker	0	0	3.00	6	6	2	1	0
C. Hogsett	0	0	0.00	1	0	1	0	0

CHICAGO (N.L.)

	W	L	ERA	IP	H	BB	SO	SV
L. Warneke	2	0	0.54	16.2	9	4	5	0
B. Lee	0	0	3.48	10.1	11	5	5	1
L. French	0	2	3.38	10.2	15	2	8	0
T. Carleton	0	1	1.29	7	6	7	4	0
F. Kowalik	0	0	2.08	4.1	3	1	1	0
R. Henshaw	0	0	7.36	3.2	2	5	2	0
C. Root	0	1	18.00	2	5	1	2	0

1936 WORLD SERIES

LINE SCORES	PITCHERS (innings pitched)	HOME RUNS (men on)	HIGHLIGHTS

New York (A.L.) defeats New York (N.L.) 4 games to 2

GAME 1 - SEPTEMBER 30

NY	A	001 000 000	1 7 2	Ruffing (8)	Selkirk	Hubbell's masterful pitching ended a Yankee streak of 12 consecutive
NY	N	000 011 04x	6 9 1	Hubbell (9)	Bartell	Series victories. Giant outfielders had no fielding chances.

GAME 2 - OCTOBER 2

NY	A	207 001 206	18 17 0	Gomez (9)	Lazzeri (3 on), Dickey (2 on)	The Yankees set a Series record by scoring 18 runs as every man in
NY	N	010 300 000	4 6 1	Schumacher (2), Smith (0.1), Coffman (1.2), Gabler (4), Gumbert (1)		their line-up had at least one hit and scored at least one run. Lazzeri and Dickey paced the onslaught with five RBIs each.

GAME 3 - OCTOBER 3

NY	N	000 010 000	1 11 0	Fitzsimmons (8)	Ripple	Crosetti's single scored Powell with the winning run in the eighth
NY	A	010 000 01x	2 4 0	Hadley (8), Malone (1) SV	Gehrig	after Ripple's homer tied the game for the Giants in the fifth.

GAME 4 - OCTOBER 4

NY	N	000 100 010	2 7 1	Hubbell (7), Gabler (1)		Three in the third on Crosetti'e double, Rolfe's single, and Gehrig's
NY	A	013 000 01x	5 10 1	Pearson (9)	Gehrig (1 on)	homer provided the cushion for Pearson.

GAME 5 - OCTOBER 5

NY	N	300 001 000 1	5 8 3	Schumacher (10)		Jackson's error enabled the Yankees to tie the game with two in the
NY	A	011 002 000 0	4 10 1	Ruffing (6), Malone (4)	Selkirk	sixth, but the Giants won in the tenth on Moore's double, Bartell's sacrifice, and Terry's long fly.

GAME 6 - OCTOBER 6

NY	A	021 200 017	13 17 2	Gomez (6.1), Murphy (2.2) SV	Powell (1 on)	The Yankees broke open a 6-5 game with seven runs in the ninth on
NY	N	200 010 110	5 9 1	Fitzsimmons (3.2), Castleman (4.1), Coffman (0), Gumbert (1)	Morre, Ott	five hits and four walks.

Team totals

		W	AB	H	2B	3B	HR	R	RBI	BA	BB	SO	ERA
NY	A	4	215	65	8	1	7	43	41	.302	26	35	3.33
NY	N	2	203	50	9	0	4	23	20	.246	21	33	6.79

Individual Batting

NEW YORK (A.L.)

	AB	H	2B	3B	HR	R	RBI	BA
J. DiMaggio, of	26	9	3	0	0	3	3	.346
F. Crosetti, ss	26	7	2	0	0	5	3	.269
B. Dickey, c	25	3	0	0	1	5	5	.120
R. Rolfe, 3b	25	10	0	0	0	5	4	.400
G. Selkirk, of	24	8	0	1	2	6	3	.333
L. Gehrig, 1b	24	7	1	0	2	5	7	.292
J. Powell, of	22	10	1	0	1	8	5	.455
T. Lazzeri, 2b	20	5	0	0	1	4	7	.250
L. Gomez, p	8	2	0	0	0	1	3	.250
R. Ruffing, p	5	0	0	0	0	0	0	.000
M. Pearson, p	4	2	1	0	0	0	0	.500
J. Murphy, p	2	1	0	0	0	1	1	.500
B. Hadley, p	2	0	0	0	0	0	0	.000
R. Johnson	1	0	0	0	0	0	0	.000
P. Malone, p	1	1	0	0	0	0	0	1.000
B. Seeds	0	0	0	0	0	0	0	–

Errors: F. Crosetti (2), B. Dickey, J. DiMaggio, R. Rolfe, G. Selkirk
Stolen Bases: J. Powell

NEW YORK (N.L.)

	AB	H	2B	3B	HR	R	RBI	BA
J. Moore, of	28	6	2	0	1	4	1	.214
B. Terry, 1b	25	6	0	0	0	1	5	.240
M. Ott, of	23	7	2	0	1	4	3	.304
B. Whitehead, 2b	21	1	0	0	0	1	2	.048
D. Bartell, ss	21	8	3	0	1	5	3	.381
T. Jackson, 3b	21	4	0	0	0	1	1	.190
G. Mancuso, c	19	5	2	0	0	3	1	.263
J. Ripple, of	12	4	0	0	1	2	3	.333
H. Leiber, of	6	0	0	0	0	0	0	.000
C. Hubbell, p	6	2	0	0	0	0	1	.333
Fitzsimmons, p	4	2	0	0	0	0	0	.500
Schumacher, p	4	0	0	0	0	0	0	.000
S. Leslie	3	2	0	0	0	0	0	.667
M. Koenig, 2b	3	1	0	0	0	0	0	.333
H. Danning, c	2	0	0	0	0	0	0	.000
K. Davis	2	1	0	0	0	0	2	.500
S. Castleman, p	2	1	0	0	0	0	0	.500
E. Mayo, 3b	1	0	0	0	0	0	0	.000

Errors: T. Jackson (3), M. Ott, D. Bartell, H. Danning, C. Hubbell

Individual Pitching

NEW YORK (A.L.)

	W	L	ERA	IP	H	BB	SO	SV
L. Gomez	2	0	4.70	15.1	14	11	9	0
R. Ruffing	0	1	4.50	14	16	5	12	0
M. Pearson	1	0	2.00	9	7	2	7	0
B. Hadley	1	0	1.13	8	10	1	2	0
P. Malone	0	1	1.80	5	2	1	2	1
J. Murphy	0	0	3.38	2.2	1	1	1	1

NEW YORK (N.L.)

	W	L	ERA	IP	H	BB	SO	SV
C. Hubbell	1	1	2.25	16	15	2	10	0
Schumacher	1	1	5.25	12	13	10	11	0
Fitzsimmons	0	2	5.40	11.2	13	2	6	0
F. Gabler	0	0	7.20	5	7	4	0	0
S. Castleman	0	0	2.08	4.1	3	2	5	0
H. Gumbert	0	0	36.00	2	7	4	2	0
D. Coffman	0	0	32.40	1.2	5	1	1	0
A. Smith	0	0	81.00	0.1	2	1	0	0

1937 WORLD SERIES

LINE SCORES	PITCHERS (innings pitched)	HOME RUNS (men on)	HIGHLIGHTS

New York (A.L.) defeats New York (N.L.) 4 games to 1

GAME 1 - OCTOBER 6

NY	N	000 010 000	1 6 2	Hubbell (5.1), Gumbert (0), Coffman (1.2), Smith (1)	
NY	A	000 007 01x	8 7 0	Gomez (9)	Lazzeri

The Yankees, losing 1-0, racked Hubbell, Gumbert, and Coffman for seven in the sixth. DiMaggio and Selkirk each drove in two runs with bases-loaded singles.

GAME 2 - OCTOBER 7

NY	N	100 000 000	1 7 0	Melton (4), Gumbert (1.1), Coffman (2.2)	
NY	A	000 024 20x	8 12 0	Ruffing (9)	

The Yankees again overcame a 1-0 Giant lead and romped to an easy win. Ruffing supported his pitching with two hits and three RBIs.

GAME 3 - OCTOBER 8

NY	A	012 110 000	5 9 0	Pearson (8.2), Murphy (0.1) **SV**	
NY	N	000 000 100	1 5 4	Schumacher (6), Melton (2), Brennan (1)	

The Yankees scored early and often, with Dickey's triple in the third the big hit. Pearson loaded the bases in the ninth, but Murphy retired Danning to preserve the victory.

GAME 4 - OCTOBER 9

NY	A	101 000 010	3 6 0	Hadley (1.1), Andrews (5.2), Wicker (1)	Gehrig
NY	N	060 000 10x	7 12 3	Hubbell (9)	

Leiber had two hits in the six-run second inning as Hubbell pitched the Giants to their only win of the Series.

GAME 5 - OCTOBER 10

NY	A	011 020 000	4 8 0	Gomez (9)	DiMaggio, Hoag
NY	N	002 000 000	2 10 0	Melton (5), Smith (2), Brennan (2)	Ott (1 on)

With the score tied 2-2, Lazzeri led off the Yankee fifth with a triple and Gomez, a career .147 hitter, drove in the winning run with a single off Whitehead's glove.

Team totals

		W	AB	H	2B	3B	HR	R	RBI	BA	BB	SO	ERA
NY	A	4	169	42	6	4	4	28	25	.249	21	21	2.45
NY	N	1	169	40	6	0	1	12	12	.237	11	21	4.81

Individual Batting

NEW YORK (A.L.)	AB	H	2B	3B	HR	R	RBI	BA
J. DiMaggio, of	22	6	0	0	1	2	4	.273
F. Crosetti, ss	21	1	0	0	0	2	0	.048
M. Hoag, of	20	6	1	0	1	4	2	.300
R. Rolfe, 3b	20	6	2	1	0	3	1	.300
G. Selkirk, of	19	5	1	0	0	5	6	.263
B. Dickey, c	19	4	0	1	0	3	3	.211
L. Gehrig, 1b	17	5	1	1	1	4	3	.294
T. Lazzeri, 2b	15	6	0	1	1	3	2	.400
L. Gomez, p	6	1	0	0	0	2	1	.167
R. Ruffing, p	4	2	1	0	0	0	3	.500
M. Pearson, p	3	0	0	0	0	0	0	.000
I. Andrews, p	2	0	0	0	0	0	0	.000
J. Powell	1	0	0	0	0	0	0	.000

NEW YORK (N.L.)	AB	H	2B	3B	HR	R	RBI	BA
J. Moore, of	23	9	1	0	0	1	1	.391
D. Bartell, ss	21	5	1	0	0	3	1	.238
M. Ott, 3b	20	4	0	0	1	1	3	.200
J. McCarthy, 1b	19	4	1	0	0	1	1	.211
J. Ripple, of	17	5	0	0	0	2	0	.294
B. Whitehead, 2b	16	4	2	0	1	0	0	.250
H. Danning, c	12	3	1	0	0	0	2	.250
H. Leiber, of	11	4	0	0	0	2	2	.364
G. Mancuso, c	8	0	0	0	0	0	1	.000
L. Chiozza, of	7	2	0	0	0	0	0	.286
C. Hubbell, p	6	0	0	0	0	1	1	.000
W. Berger	3	0	0	0	0	0	0	.000
C. Melton, p	2	0	0	0	0	0	0	.000
B. Ryan	1	0	0	0	0	0	0	.000
Schumacher, p	1	0	0	0	0	0	0	.000
D. Coffman, p	1	0	0	0	0	0	0	.000
S. Leslie	1	0	0	0	0	0	0	.000

Errors: D. Bartell (3), J. McCarthy (2), C. Melton, M. Ott, B. Whitehead, L. Chiozza
Stolen Bases: B. Whitehead

Individual Pitching

NEW YORK (A.L.)	W	L	ERA	IP	H	BB	SO	SV
L. Gomez	2	0	1.50	18	16	2	8	0
R. Ruffing	1	0	1.00	9	7	3	8	0
M. Pearson	1	0	1.04	8.2	5	2	4	0
I. Andrews	0	0	3.18	5.2	6	4	1	0
B. Hadley	0	1	33.75	1.1	6	0	0	0
K. Wicker	0	0	0.00	1	0	0	0	0
J. Murphy	0	0	0.00	0.1	0	0	0	1

NEW YORK (N.L.)	W	L	ERA	IP	H	BB	SO	SV
C. Hubbell	1	1	3.77	14.1	12	4	7	0
C. Melton	0	2	4.91	11	12	6	7	0
Schumacher	0	1	6.00	6	9	4	3	0
D. Coffman	0	0	4.15	4.1	2	5	1	0
D. Brennan	0	0	0.00	3	1	1	1	0
A. Smith	0	0	3.00	3	2	0	1	0
H. Gumbert	0	0	27.00	1.1	4	1	1	0

1938 WORLD SERIES

LINE SCORES	PITCHERS (innings pitched)	HOME RUNS (men on)	HIGHLIGHTS

New York (A.L.) defeats Chicago (N.L.) 4 games to 0

GAME 1 - OCTOBER 5

NY	A	020 000 100	3 12 1	Ruffing (9)	
CHI	N	001 000 000	1 9 1	Lee (8), Russell (1)	

Dickey's four singles led the New York attack in support of Ruffing's nine-hit effort.

GAME 2 - OCTOBER 6

NY	A	020 000 022	6 7 2	Gomez (7), Murphy (2) SV	Crosetti (1 on), DiMaggio (1 on)
CHI	N	102 000 000	3 11 0	Dean (8), French (1)	

Crosetti batted in the tying and winning runs with an eighth-inning homer after Dizzy Dean, with no fastball left due to a sore arm, had held the Yankees to five hits in the first seven innings.

GAME 3 - OCTOBER 8

CHI	N	000 010 010	2 5 1	Bryant (5.1), Russell (0.2), French (2)	Marty
NY	A	000 022 01x	5 7 2	Pearson (9)	Gordon, Dickey

Gordon's homer in the fifth was the first Yankee hit off Bryant, and his two-run single in the sixth gave the Yankees a three-run cushion.

GAME 4 - OCTOBER 9

CHI	N	000 100 020	3 8 1	Lee (3), Root (3), Page (1.1), French (0.1), Carleton (0), Dean (0.1)	O'Dea (1 on)
NY	A	030 001 04x	8 11 1	Ruffing (9)	Henrich

New York scored three runs in the second on a two-out error by Jurges, two singles, and Crosetti's triple. Four more in the eighth ensured the clincher after O'Dea's homer in the top of the eighth narrowed the lead to one run.

Team totals

		W	AB	H	2B	3B	HR	R	RBI	BA	BB	SO	ERA
NY	A	4	135	37	6	1	5	22	21	.274	11	16	1.75
CHI	N	0	136	33	4	1	2	9	8	.243	6	26	5.03

Individual Batting

NEW YORK (A.L.)

	AB	H	2B	3B	HR	R	RBI	BA
R. Rolfe, 3b	18	3	0	0	0	0	1	.167
F. Crosetti, ss	16	4	2	1	1	1	6	.250
T. Henrich, of	16	4	1	0	1	3	1	.250
J. Gordon, 2b	15	6	2	0	1	3	6	.400
B. Dickey, c	15	6	0	0	1	2	2	.400
J. DiMaggio, of	15	4	0	0	1	4	2	.267
L. Gehrig, 1b	14	4	0	0	0	4	0	.286
G. Selkirk, of	10	2	0	0	0	1	0	.200
R. Ruffing, p	6	1	0	0	0	1	1	.167
M. Hoag, of	5	2	1	0	0	3	1	.400
M. Pearson, p	3	1	0	0	0	1	0	.333
L. Gomez, p	2	0	0	0	0	0	0	.000
J. Powell, of	0	0	0	0	0	0	0	—

Errors: R. Rolfe (2), J. Gordon (2), T. Henrich, F. Crosetti
Stolen Bases: R. Rolfe, B. Dickey, J. Gordon

CHICAGO (N.L.)

	AB	H	2B	3B	HR	R	RBI	BA
S. Hack, 3b	17	8	1	0	0	3	1	.471
B. Herman, 2b	16	3	0	0	0	1	0	.188
R. Collins, 1b	15	2	0	0	0	1	0	.133
B. Jurges, ss	13	3	1	0	0	0	0	.231
Cavarretta, of	13	6	1	0	0	1	0	.462
J. Marty, of	12	6	1	0	1	1	5	.500
C. Reynolds, of	12	0	0	0	0	0	0	.000
G. Hartnett, c	11	1	0	1	0	0	0	.091
F. Demaree, of	10	1	0	0	0	1	0	.100
K. O'Dea, c	5	1	0	0	1	1	2	.200
B. Lee, p	3	0	0	0	0	0	0	.000
D. Dean, p	3	2	0	0	0	0	0	.667
A. Galan	2	0	0	0	0	0	0	.000
T. Lazzeri	2	0	0	0	0	0	0	.000
C. Bryant, p	2	0	0	0	0	0	0	.000

Errors: B. Herman (2), B. Jurges

Individual Pitching

NEW YORK (A.L.)

	W	L	ERA	IP	H	BB	SO	SV
R. Ruffing	2	0	1.50	18	17	2	11	0
M. Pearson	1	0	1.00	9	5	2	9	0
L. Gomez	1	0	3.86	7	9	1	5	0
J. Murphy	0	0	0.00	2	2	1	1	1

CHICAGO (N.L.)

	W	L	ERA	IP	H	BB	SO	SV
B. Lee	0	2	2.45	11	15	1	8	0
D. Dean	0	1	6.48	8.1	8	1	2	0
C. Bryant	0	1	6.75	5.1	6	5	3	0
L. French	0	0	2.70	3.1	1	1	2	0
C. Root	0	0	3.00	3	3	0	1	0
J. Russell	0	0	0.00	1.2	1	1	0	0
V. Page	0	0	13.50	1.1	2	0	0	0
T. Carleton	0	0	∞	0.0	1	2	0	0

1939 WORLD SERIES

LINE SCORES	PITCHERS (innings pitched)	HOME RUNS (men on)	HIGHLIGHTS

New York (A.L.) defeats Cincinnati (N.L.) 4 games to 0

GAME 1 - OCTOBER 4

CIN N 000 100 000   1 4 0   Derringer (8.1)
NY A 000 010 001   2 6 0   Ruffing (9)

Keller led off the Yankee ninth with a triple just past Goodman's lunge. After an intentional walk to DiMaggio, Dickey singled home the winning run.

GAME 2 - OCTOBER 5

CIN N 000 000 000   0 2 0   Walters (8)
NY A 003 100 00x   4 9 0   Pearson (9)   Dahlgren

Pearson had a no-hitter for seven and a third innings before Lombardi singled to break it up. Dahlgren's double and homer gave Pearson all the help he needed.

GAME 3 - OCTOBER 7

NY A 202 030 000   7 5 1   Gomez (1), Hadley (8)   Keller (1 on), DiMaggio (1 on),
CIN N 120 000 000   3 10 0   Thompson (4.2), Grissom (1.1), Moore (3)   Keller (1 on), Dickey

Keller spearheaded the Yankee attack with two homers, four RBIs, and three runs scored. Gomez and Hadley allowed ten Cincinnati hits, but all ten were singles and only three came after the second inning.

GAME 4 - OCTOBER 8

NY A 000 000 202 3   7 7 1   Hildebrand (4), Sundra (2.2), Murphy (3.1)   Keller, Dickey
CIN N 000 000 310 0   4 11 4   Derringer (7), Walters (3)

Myers's error on a potential double-play ball in the ninth allowed one run to score and set up the tying run. Three more Red errors in the tenth helped the Yankees score three runs and sweep the Series.

Team totals

		W	AB	H	2B	3B	HR	R	RBI	BA	BB	SO	ERA
NY	A	4	131	27	4	1	7	20	18	.206	9	20	1.22
CIN	N	0	133	27	3	1	0	8	8	.203	6	22	4.33

Individual Batting

NEW YORK (A.L.)

	AB	H	2B	3B	HR	R	RBI	BA
J. DiMaggio, of	16	5	0	0	1	3	3	.313
F. Crosetti, ss	16	1	0	0	0	2	1	.063
R. Rolfe, 3b	16	2	0	0	0	2	0	.125
C. Keller, of	16	7	1	1	3	8	6	.438
B. Dickey, c	15	4	0	0	2	2	5	.267
B. Dahlgren, 1b	14	3	2	0	1	2	2	.214
J. Gordon, 2b	14	2	0	0	0	1	1	.143
G. Selkirk, of	12	2	1	0	0	0	0	.167
R. Ruffing, p	3	1	0	0	0	0	0	.333
B. Hadley, p	3	0	0	0	0	0	0	.000
J. Murphy, p	2	0	0	0	0	0	0	.000
M. Pearson, p	2	0	0	0	0	0	0	.000
Hildebrand, p	1	0	0	0	0	0	0	.000
L. Gomez, p	1	0	0	0	0	0	0	.000

Errors: R. Rolfe, B. Hadley

CINCINNATI (N.L.)

	AB	H	2B	3B	HR	R	RBI	BA
L. Frey, 2b	17	0	0	0	0	0	0	.000
B. Werber, 3b	16	4	0	0	0	1	2	.250
I. Goodman, of	15	5	1	0	0	3	1	.333
McCormick, 1b	15	6	1	0	0	1	1	.400
W. Berger, of	15	0	0	0	0	0	1	.000
E. Lombardi, c	14	3	0	0	0	0	2	.214
B. Myers, ss	12	4	0	1	0	2	0	.333
H. Craft, of	11	1	0	0	0	0	0	.091
P. Derringer, p	5	1	0	0	0	0	0	.200
A. Simmons, of	4	1	1	0	0	1	0	.250
B. Walters, p	3	0	0	0	0	0	0	.000
Hershberger, c	2	1	0	0	0	0	1	.500
W. Moore, p	1	0	0	0	0	0	0	.000
L. Gamble	1	0	0	0	0	0	0	.000
J. Thompson, p	1	1	0	0	0	0	0	1.000
Bongiovanni	1	0	0	0	0	0	0	.000
Bordagaray	0	0	0	0	0	0	0	–

Errors: B. Myers (2), I. Goodman, E. Lombardi
Stolen Bases: I. Goodman

Individual Pitching

NEW YORK (A.L.)

	W	L	ERA	IP	H	BB	SO	SV
R. Ruffing	1	0	1.00	9	4	1	4	0
M. Pearson	1	0	0.00	9	2	1	8	0
B. Hadley	1	0	2.25	8	7	3	2	0
Hildebrand	0	0	0.00	4	2	0	3	0
J. Murphy	1	0	2.70	3.1	5	0	2	0
S. Sundra	0	0	0.00	2.2	4	1	2	0
L. Gomez	0	0	9.00	1	3	0	1	0

CINCINNATI (N.L.)

	W	L	ERA	IP	H	BB	SO	SV
P. Derringer	0	1	2.35	15.1	9	3	9	0
B. Walters	0	2	4.91	11	13	1	6	0
J. Thompson	0	1	13.50	4.2	5	4	3	0
W. Moore	0	0	0.00	3	0	0	2	0
L. Grissom	0	0	0.00	1.1	0	1	0	0

1940 WORLD SERIES

LINE SCORES	PITCHERS (innings pitched)	HOME RUNS (men on)	HIGHLIGHTS

Cincinnati (N.L.) defeats Detroit (A.L.) 4 games to 3

GAME 1 - OCTOBER 2

DET	A	050 020 000	7 10 1	Newsom (9)	Campbell (1 on)
CIN	N	000 100 010	2 8 3	Derringer (1.1), Moore (6.2), Riddle (1)	

Derringer was knocked out in the second as Newsom breezed to the American League's tenth successive World Series triumph.

GAME 2 - OCTOBER 3

DET	A	200 001 000	3 3 1	Rowe (3.1), Gorsica (4.2)	
CIN	N	022 100 00x	5 9 0	Walters (9)	Ripple (1 on)

Walters pitched a three-hitter with Ripple's third-inning home run providing the winning run.

GAME 3 - OCTOBER 4

CIN	N	100 000 012	4 10 1	Turner (6), Moore (1), Beggs (1)	
DET	A	000 100 42x	7 13 1	Bridges (9)	York (1 on), Higgins (1 on)

Two-run homers by York and Higgins in the seventh decided the outcome.

GAME 4 - OCTOBER 5

CIN	N	201 100 010	5 11 1	Derringer (9)
DET	A	001 001 000	2 5 1	Trout (2), Smith (4), McKain (3)

Derringer coasted to victory. Werber, Frank McCormick, Goodman, and Mike McCormick, the first four Cincinnati hitters, each had two hits.

GAME 5 - OCTOBER 6

CIN	N	000 000 000	0 3 0	Thompson (3.1), Moore (0.2) Vander Meer (3), Hutchings (1)	
DET	A	003 400 01x	8 13 0	Newsom (9)	Greenberg (2 on)

Newsom held the Reds to three singles for the shutout win, backed by 13 hits including Greenberg's three-run homer.

GAME 6 - OCTOBER 7

DET	A	000 000 000	0 5 0	Rowe (0.1), Gorsica (6.2), Hutchinson (1)	
CIN	N	200 001 01x	4 10 2	Walters (9)	Walters

Walters drew the Reds even with a shutout and contributed a homer to his cause. The Reds chased Rowe with four hits and two runs in a third of an inning.

GAME 7 - OCTOBER 8

DET	A	001 000 000	1 7 0	Newsom (8)
CIN	N	000 000 20x	2 7 1	Derringer (9)

Doubles by McCormick and Ripple and a long fly by Myers brought Cincinnati its first World Championship since the tainted Series of 1919.

Team totals

		W	AB	H	2B	3B	HR	R	RBI	BA	BB	SO	ERA
CIN	N	4	232	58	14	0	2	22	21	.250	15	30	3.69
DET	A	3	228	56	9	3	4	28	24	.246	30	30	3.00

Individual Batting

CINCINNATI (N.L.)

	AB	H	2B	3B	HR	R	RBI	BA
I. Goodman, of	29	8	2	0	0	5	5	.276
McCormick, of	29	9	3	0	0	1	2	.310
McCormick, 1b	28	6	1	0	0	2	0	.214
B. Werber, 3b	27	10	4	0	0	5	2	.370
E. Joost, 2b	25	5	0	0	0	0	2	.200
B. Myers, ss	23	3	0	0	0	0	2	.130
J. Ripple, of	21	7	2	0	1	3	6	.333
J. Wilson, c	17	6	0	0	0	2	0	.353
B. Walters, p	7	2	1	0	1	2	2	.286
P. Derringer, p	7	0	0	0	0	0	0	.000
B. Baker, c	4	1	0	0	0	1	0	.250
E. Lombardi, c	3	1	1	0	0	0	0	.333
L. Riggs	3	0	0	0	0	1	0	.000
J. Turner, p	2	0	0	0	0	0	0	.000
W. Moore, p	2	0	0	0	0	0	0	.000
L. Frey	2	0	0	0	0	0	0	.000
H. Craft	1	0	0	0	0	0	0	.000
J. Thompson, p	1	0	0	0	0	0	0	.000
M. Arnovich, of	1	0	0	0	0	0	0	.000

Errors: B. Myers (2), B. Werber (2), McCormick (2), McCormick, B. Baker.
Stolen Bases: J. Wilson

DETROIT (A.L.)

	AB	H	2B	3B	HR	R	RBI	BA
H. Greenberg, of	28	10	2	1	1	5	6	.357
C. Gehringer, 2b	28	6	0	0	0	3	1	.214
D. Bartell, ss	26	7	2	0	0	2	3	.269
R. York, 1b	26	6	0	1	1	3	2	.231
B. Campbell, of	25	9	1	0	1	4	5	.360
P. Higgins, 3b	24	8	3	1	1	2	6	.333
B. McCosky, of	23	7	1	0	0	5	1	.304
B. Sullivan, c	13	2	0	0	0	3	0	.154
B. Tebbetts, c	11	0	0	0	0	0	0	.000
B. Newsom, p	10	1	0	0	0	1	0	.100
J. Gorsica, p	4	0	0	0	0	0	0	.000
E. Averill	3	0	0	0	0	0	0	.000
T. Bridges, p	3	0	0	0	0	0	0	.000
P. Fox	1	0	0	0	0	0	0	.000
S. Rowe, p	1	0	0	0	0	0	0	.000
C. Smith, p	1	0	0	0	0	0	0	.000
D. Trout, p	1	0	0	0	0	0	0	.000
F. Croucher, ss	0	0	0	0	0	0	0	–

Errors: P. Higgins (2), D. Bartell, B. Tebbetts

Individual Pitching

CINCINNATI (N.L.)

	W	L	ERA	IP	H	BB	SO	SV
P. Derringer	2	1	2.79	19.1	17	10	6	0
B. Walters	2	0	1.50	18	8	6	6	0
W. Moore	0	0	3.24	8.1	8	6	7	0
J. Turner	0	1	7.50	6	8	0	4	0
Vander Meer	0	0	0.00	3	2	3	2	0
J. Thompson	0	1	16.20	3.1	8	4	2	0
E. Riddle	0	0	0.00	1	0	2	0	0
J. Hutchings	0	0	9.00	1	2	1	0	0
J. Beggs	0	0	9.00	1	3	0	1	0

DETROIT (A.L.)

	W	L	ERA	IP	H	BB	SO	SV
B. Newsom	2	1	1.38	26	18	4	17	0
J. Gorsica	0	0	0.79	11.1	6	4	4	0
T. Bridges	1	0	3.00	9	10	1	5	0
C. Smith	0	0	2.25	4	1	3	1	0
S. Rowe	0	2	17.18	3.2	12	1	1	0
A. McKain	0	0	3.00	3	4	0	0	0
D. Trout	0	1	9.00	2	6	1	1	0
Hutchinson	0	0	9.00	1	1	1	1	0

1941 WORLD SERIES

LINE SCORES		PITCHERS (innings pitched)	HOME RUNS (men on)	HIGHLIGHTS

New York (A.L.) defeats Brooklyn (N.L.) 4 games to 1

GAME 1 - OCTOBER 1

BKN	N	000 010 100	2 6 0	Davis (5.1), Casey (0.2), Allen (2)	
NY	A	010 101 00x	3 6 1	Ruffing (9)	Gordon

The Brooklyn rally in the seventh fell short when Reese was thrown out trying to go from second to third with one out on Wasdell's foul pop to Rolfe.

GAME 2 - OCTOBER 2

BKN	N	000 021 000	3 6 2	Wyatt (9)	
NY	A	011 000 000	2 9 1	Chandler (5), Murphy (4)	

Camilli's single in the sixth brought home Walker with the deciding run of the game, stopping the Yankees' Series winning streak at ten games.

GAME 3 - OCTOBER 4

NY	A	000 000 020	2 8 0	Russo (9)	
BKN	N	000 000 010	1 4 0	Fitzsimmons (7), Casey (0.1), French (0.2), Allen (1)	

The Dodgers' Series hopes were shaken when Russo's savage drive caromed off Fitzsimmons's leg in the seventh, forcing him out of the game. The Yankees, who had just four hits to that point, reached Casey for four more and two runs.

GAME 4 - OCTOBER 5

NY	A	100 200 004	7 12 0	Donald (4), Breuer (3), Murphy (2)	
BKN	N	000 220 000	4 9 1	Higbe (3.2), French (0.1), Allen (0.2), Casey (4.1)	Reiser (1 on)

The Dodgers led 4-3 in the top of the ninth with two outs. Casey threw strike three past Henrich, but it also got past catcher Owen, allowing Henrich to reach first. The Yankees then pounced for four runs to take a commanding 3-1 Series lead. Keller's double, scoring two runs, keyed the big inning.

GAME 5 - OCTOBER 6

NY	A	020 010 000	3 6 0	Bonham (9)	Henrich
BKN	N	001 000 000	1 4 1	Wyatt (9)	

Bonham allows only one hit after the third to check the Dodgers and bring the Yankees another Series victory. Gordon's single in the second sent home Keller with the deciding run.

Team totals

		W	AB	H	2B	3B	HR	R	RBI	BA	BB	SO	ERA
NY	A	4	166	41	5	1	2	17	16	.247	23	18	1.80
BKN	N	1	159	29	7	2	1	11	11	.182	14	21	2.66

Individual Batting

NEW YORK (A.L.)

	AB	H	2B	3B	HR	R	RBI	BA
J. Sturm, 1b	21	6	0	0	0	0	2	.286
R. Rolfe, 3b	20	6	0	0	0	2	0	.300
J. DiMaggio, of	19	5	0	0	0	1	1	.263
B. Dickey, c	18	3	1	0	0	3	1	.167
T. Henrich, of	18	3	1	0	1	4	1	.167
C. Keller, of	18	7	2	0	0	5	5	.389
P. Rizzuto, ss	18	2	0	0	0	0	0	.111
J. Gordon, 2b	14	7	1	1	1	2	5	.500
E. Bonham, p	4	0	0	0	0	0	0	.000
M. Russo, p	4	0	0	0	0	0	0	.000
R. Ruffing, p	3	0	0	0	0	0	0	.000
G. Selkirk	2	1	0	0	0	0	0	.500
J. Murphy, p	2	0	0	0	0	0	0	.000
A. Donald, p	2	0	0	0	0	0	0	.000
S. Chandler, p	2	1	0	0	0	0	1	.500
M. Breuer, p	1	0	0	0	0	0	0	.000
Bordagaray	0	0	0	0	0	0	0	–
B. Rosar, c	0	0	0	0	0	0	0	–

Errors: J. Gordon, P. Rizzuto
Stolen Bases: P. Rizzuto, J. Sturm

BROOKLYN (N.L.)

	AB	H	2B	3B	HR	R	RBI	BA
P. Reese, ss	20	4	0	0	0	1	2	.200
P. Reiser, of	20	4	1	1	1	1	3	.200
D. Camilli, 1b	18	3	1	0	0	1	1	.167
D. Walker, of	18	4	2	0	0	3	0	.222
J. Medwick, of	17	4	1	0	0	1	0	.235
M. Owen, c	12	2	0	1	0	1	2	.167
C. Lavagetto, 3b	10	1	0	0	0	1	0	.100
B. Herman, 2b	8	1	0	0	0	0	0	.125
L. Riggs, 3b	8	2	0	0	0	0	1	.250
P. Coscarart, 2b	7	0	0	0	0	1	0	.000
W. Wyatt, p	6	1	0	0	0	1	0	.167
J. Wasdell, of	5	1	1	0	0	0	2	.200
H. Casey, p	2	1	0	0	0	0	0	.500
C. Davis, p	2	0	0	0	0	0	0	.000
Fitzsimmons, p	2	0	0	0	0	0	0	.000
A. Galan	2	0	0	0	0	0	0	.000
K. Higbe	1	1	0	0	0	0	0	1.000
H. Franks, c	1	0	0	0	0	0	0	.000

Errors: P. Reese (3), M. Owen

Individual Pitching

NEW YORK (A.L.)

	W	L	ERA	IP	H	BB	SO	SV
M. Russo	1	0	1.00	9	4	2	5	0
E. Bonham	1	0	1.00	9	4	2	2	0
R. Ruffing	1	0	1.00	9	6	3	5	0
J. Murphy	1	0	0.00	6	2	1	3	0
S. Chandler	0	1	3.60	5	4	2	2	0
A. Donald	0	0	9.00	4	6	3	2	0
M. Breuer	0	0	0.00	3	3	1	2	0

BROOKLYN (N.L.)

	W	L	ERA	IP	H	BB	SO	SV
W. Wyatt	1	1	2.50	18	15	10	14	0
Fitzsimmons	0	0	0.00	7	4	3	1	0
H. Casey	0	2	3.38	5.1	9	2	1	0
C. Davis	0	1	5.06	5.1	6	3	1	0
J. Allen	0	0	0.00	3.2	1	3	0	0
K. Higbe	0	0	7.36	3.2	6	2	1	0
L. French	0	0	0.00	1	0	0	0	0

1942 WORLD SERIES

LINE SCORES	PITCHERS (innings pitched)	HOME RUNS (men on)	HIGHLIGHTS

St. Louis (N.L.) defeats New York (A.L.) 4 games to 1

GAME 1 - SEPTEMBER 30

NY	A	000 110 032	7 11 0	Ruffing (8.2), Chandler (0.1) SV		
STL	N	000 000 004	4 7 4	M. Cooper (7.2), Gumbert (0.1), Lanier (1)		

The Yankees made an early lead stand up, but four in the ninth by the Cardinals gave an omen of things to come. Ruffing did not allow a hit until there were two out in the eighth to become the first pitcher to win seven World Series games.

GAME 2 - OCTOBER 1

NY	A	000 000 030	3 10 2	Bonham (8)	Keller (1 on)
STL	N	200 000 11x	4 6 0	Beazley (9)	

A two-run homer by Keller tied the score in the eighth, but the Cardinals eked out a win in the home half when Slaughter doubled and Musial singled. Slaughter then saved the day by throwing out Stainback going from first to third on a single with none out in the ninth.

GAME 3 - OCTOBER 3

STL	N	001 000 001	2 5 1	White (9)	
NY	A	000 000 000	0 6 1	Chandler (8), Breuer (0), Turner (1)	

White's six-hit gem is the first Series whitewash of the Yankees since Haines did the trick in 1926. The Cardinals got their runs on Brown's infield out in the third and Slaughter's single in the ninth.

GAME 4 - OCTOBER 4

STL	N	000 600 201	9 12 1	M. Cooper (5.1), Gumbert (0.1), Pollet (0.1), Lanier (3)	
NY	A	100 005 000	6 10 1	Borowy (3), Donald (3), Bonham (3)	Keller (2 on)

The teams traded big innings before the Cardinals took charge in the seventh. Walker Cooper's single scored Slaughter, and Marion hit a long fly, scoring Musial for the decisive two runs.

GAME 5 - OCTOBER 5

STL	N	000 101 002	4 9 4	Beazley (9)	Kurowski (1 on)
NY	A	100 100 000	2 7 1	Ruffing (9)	Rizzuto

Kurowski's two-run homer in the ninth gave the Cardinals the Series. It was the Yankees' first Series defeat in their last nine appearances, dating back to St. Louis's victory over them in 1926.

Team totals

		W	AB	H	2B	3B	HR	R	RBI	BA	BB	SO	ERA
STL	N	4	163	39	4	2	2	23	23	.239	17	19	2.60
NY	A	1	178	44	6	0	3	18	14	.247	8	22	4.50

Individual Batting

ST. LOUIS (N.L.)

	AB	H	2B	3B	HR	R	RBI	BA
W. Cooper, c	21	6	1	0	0	3	4	.286
J. Brown, 2b	20	6	0	0	0	2	1	.300
E. Slaughter, of	19	5	1	0	1	3	2	.263
M. Marion, ss	18	2	1	0	2	3	.111
S. Musial, of	18	4	1	0	0	2	2	.222
T. Moore, of	17	5	1	0	0	2	2	.294
J. Hopp, 1b	17	3	0	0	0	3	0	.176
W. Kurowski, 3b	15	4	0	1	1	3	5	.267
J. Beazley, p	7	1	0	0	0	0	0	.143
M. Cooper, p	5	1	0	0	0	1	2	.200
E. White, p	2	0	0	0	0	0	0	.000
H. Walker	1	0	0	0	0	0	0	.000
M. Lanier, p	1	1	0	0	0	0	1	1.000
R. Sanders	1	0	0	0	0	1	0	.000
K. O'Dea	1	1	0	0	0	0	1	1.000
C. Crespi	0	0	0	0	0	1	0	–

Errors: J. Brown (3), M. Lanier (2), W. Kurowski, E. Slaughter, J. Beazley, W. Cooper, J. Hopp

NEW YORK (A.L.)

	AB	H	2B	3B	HR	R	RBI	BA
J. DiMaggio, of	21	7	0	0	0	3	3	.333
J. Gordon, 2b	21	2	1	0	0	1	.095
P. Rizzuto, ss	21	8	0	0	1	2	1	.381
C. Keller, of	20	4	0	0	2	2	5	.200
B. Dickey, c	19	5	0	0	0	1	0	.263
Cullenbine, of	19	5	1	0	0	3	2	.263
R. Rolfe, 3b	17	6	2	0	0	5	0	.353
G. Priddy, 1b, 3b	10	1	1	0	0	0	1	.100
B. Hassett, 1b	9	3	1	0	0	1	2	.333
R. Ruffing, p	9	2	0	0	0	0	0	.222
F. Crosetti, 3b	3	0	0	0	0	0	0	.000
S. Chandler, p	2	0	0	0	0	0	0	.000
E. Bonham, p	2	0	0	0	0	0	0	.000
A. Donald, p	2	0	0	0	0	0	0	.000
H. Borowy, p	1	0	0	0	0	0	0	.000
G. Selkirk	1	0	0	0	0	0	0	.000
B. Rosar	1	1	0	0	0	0	0	1.000
T. Stainback	0	0	0	0	0	0	0	–

Errors: M. Breuer, B. Dickey, B. Hassett, G. Priddy, P. Rizzuto
Stolen Bases: P. Rizzuto (2), Cullenbine

Individual Pitching

ST. LOUIS (N.L.)

	W	L	ERA	IP	H	BB	SO	SV
J. Beazley	2	0	2.50	18	17	3	6	0
M. Cooper	0	1	5.54	13	17	4	9	0
E. White	1	0	0.00	9	6	0	6	0
M. Lanier	1	0	0.00	4	3	1	1	0
H. Pollet	0	0	0.00	0.1	0	0	0	0
H. Gumbert	0	0	0.00	0.2	1	0	0	0

NEW YORK (A.L.)

	W	L	ERA	IP	H	BB	SO	SV
R. Ruffing	1	1	4.08	17.2	14	7	11	0
E. Bonham	0	1	4.09	11	9	3	3	0
S. Chandler	0	1	1.08	8.1	5	1	3	1
A. Donald	0	1	6.00	3	3	2	1	0
H. Borowy	0	0	18.00	3	6	3	1	0
J. Turner	0	0	0.00	1	0	1	0	0
M. Breuer	0	0	–	0.0	2	0	0	0

1943 WORLD SERIES

LINE SCORES	PITCHERS (innings pitched)	HOME RUNS (men on)	HIGHLIGHTS

New York (A.L.) defeats St. Louis (N.L.) 4 games to 1

GAME 1 - OCTOBER 5

STL N 010 010 000   2 7 2   Lanier (7), Brecheen (1)

NY A 000 202 00x   4 8 2   Chandler (9)   Gordon

The Yankees broke a 2-2 tie in the sixth with two runs on singles by Crosetti, Johnson and Dickey and a wild pitch by Lanier.

GAME 2 - OCTOBER 6

STL N 001 300 000   4 7 2   M. Cooper (9)   Marion, Sanders (1 on)

NY A 000 100 002   3 6 0   Bonham (8), Murphy (1)

Three in the fourth for the Cards on singles by Musial and Kurowski and a homer by Sanders stood up for the win, as New York's ninth inning rally fell short.

GAME 3 - OCTOBER 7

STL N 000 200 000   2 6 4   Brazle (7.1), Krist (0), Brecheen (0.2)

NY A 000 001 05x   6 8 0   Borowy (8), Murphy (1) SV

The Yankees erased a 2-1 deficit with five in the eighth as Johnson drove in three with a bases-loaded triple.

GAME 4 - OCTOBER 10

NY A 000 100 010   2 6 2   Russo (9)

STL N 000 000 100   1 7 1   Lanier (7), Brecheen (2)

Russo allowed one unearned run and scored the winning run in the eighth on his double and a long fly by Crosetti.

GAME 5 - OCTOBER 11

NY A 000 002 000   2 7 1   Chandler (9)   Dickey (1 on)

STL N 000 000 000   0 10 1   M. Cooper (7), Lanier (1.1), Dickson (0.2)

Dickey's homer followed Keller's single in the sixth for the only runs as the Cardinals stranded eleven runners.

Team totals

		W	AB	H	2B	3B	HR	R	RBI	BA	BB	SO	ERA
NY	A	4	159	35	5	2	2	17	14	.220	12	30	1.40
STL	N	1	165	37	5	0	2	9	8	.224	11	26	2.51

Individual Batting

NEW YORK (A.L.)

	AB	H	2B	3B	HR	R	RBI	BA
B. Johnson, 3b	20	6	1	1	0	3	3	.300
N. Etten, 1b	19	2	0	0	0	0	2	.105
F. Crosetti, ss	18	5	0	0	0	4	1	.278
B. Dickey, c	18	5	0	0	1	1	4	.278
C. Keller, of	18	4	0	1	0	3	2	.222
J. Gordon, 2b	17	4	1	0	1	2	2	.235
T. Stainback, of	17	3	0	0	0	0	0	.176
J. Lindell, of	9	1	0	0	0	1	0	.111
B. Metheny, of	8	1	0	0	0	0	0	.125
S. Chandler, p	6	1	0	0	0	0	0	.167
M. Russo, p	3	2	2	0	0	1	0	.667
E. Bonham, p	2	0	0	0	0	0	0	.000
H. Borowy, p	2	1	1	0	0	1	0	.500
Stirnweiss	1	0	0	0	0	1	0	.000
R. Weatherly	1	0	0	0	0	0	0	.000

Errors: F. Crosetti (3), N. Etten, B. Johnson
Stolen Bases: F. Crosetti, C. Keller

ST. LOUIS (N.L.)

	AB	H	2B	3B	HR	R	RBI	BA
L. Klein, 2b	22	3	0	0	0	0	0	.136
W. Kurowski, 3b	18	4	1	0	0	2	1	.222
H. Walker, of	18	3	1	0	0	0	0	.167
S. Musial, of	18	5	0	0	0	2	0	.278
R. Sanders, 1b	17	5	0	0	1	3	2	.294
W. Cooper, c	17	5	0	0	0	1	0	.294
D. Litwhiler, of	15	4	1	0	0	0	2	.267
M. Marion, ss	14	5	2	0	1	1	2	.357
D. Garms, of	5	0	0	0	0	0	0	.000
M. Cooper, p	5	0	0	0	0	0	0	.000
J. Hopp, of	4	0	0	0	0	0	0	.000
M. Lanier, p	4	1	0	0	0	0	1	.250
K. O'Dea, c	3	2	0	0	0	0	0	.667
A. Brazle, p	3	0	0	0	0	0	0	.000
S. Narron	1	0	0	0	0	0	0	.000
F. Demaree	1	0	0	0	0	0	0	.000
E. White	0	0	0	0	0	0	0	—

Errors: W. Cooper (2), L. Klein (2), W. Kurowski (2), H. Walker (2), M. Lanier, M. Marion
Stolen Bases: M. Marion

Individual Pitching

NEW YORK (A.L.)

	W	L	ERA	IP	H	BB	SO	SV
S. Chandler	2	0	0.50	18	17	3	10	0
M. Russo	1	0	0.00	9	7	1	2	0
E. Bonham	0	1	4.50	8	6	3	9	0
H. Borowy	1	0	2.25	8	6	3	4	0
J. Murphy	0	0	0.00	2	1	1	1	1

ST. LOUIS (N.L.)

	W	L	ERA	IP	H	BB	SO	SV
M. Cooper	1	1	2.81	16	11	3	10	0
M. Lanier	0	1	1.76	15.1	13	3	13	0
A. Brazle	0	1	3.68	7.1	5	2	4	0
H. Brecheen	0	1	2.45	3.2	5	3	3	0
M. Dickson	0	0	0.00	0.2	0	1	0	0
H. Krist	0	0	—	0.0	1	0	0	0

1944 WORLD SERIES

LINE SCORES	PITCHERS (innings pitched)	HOME RUNS (men on)	HIGHLIGHTS

St. Louis (N.L.) defeats St. Louis (A.L.) 4 games to 2

GAME 1 - OCTOBER 4

STL	A	000 200 000	2 2 0	Galehouse (9)	McQuinn (1 on)	Cooper allowed just two hits, but one was McQuinn's homer in the fourth, which gave Galehouse enough for the win.
STL	N	000 000 001	1 7 0	M. Cooper (7), Donnelly (2)		

GAME 2 - OCTOBER 5

STL	A	000 000 200 00	2 7 4	Potter (6), Muncrief (4.1)		Donnelly struck out seven and allowed only three balls to be hit out of the infield in four innings of relief. The Cardinals won in the eleventh on O'Dea's pinch-hit single with two on.
STL	N	001 100 000 01	3 7 0	Lanier (7), Donnelly (4)		

GAME 3 - OCTOBER 6

STL	N	100 000 100	2 7 0	Wilks (2.2), Schmidt (3.1), Jurisich (0.2), Byerly (1.1)		Five straight singles, a walk, and a wild pitch, all after two out, gave the Browns four runs and a 2-1 lead in the Series.
STL	A	004 000 20x	6 8 2	Kramer (9)		

GAME 4 - OCTOBER 7

STL	N	202 001 000	5 12 0	Brecheen (9)	Musial (1 on)	Musial's three hits paced the Cardinals to a 5-0 lead. The Browns' only threat was cutoff in the eighth by a spectacular double play started by Marion.
STL	A	000 000 010	1 9 1	Jakucki (3), Hollingsworth (4), Shirley (2)		

GAME 5 - OCTOBER 8

STL	N	000 001 010	2 6 1	M. Cooper (9)	Sanders, Litwhiler	Homers by Sanders and Litwhiler decided the duel as Cooper struck out 12 and Galehouse 10.
STL	A	000 000 000	0 7 1	Galehouse (9)		

GAME 6 - OCTOBER 9

STL	A	010 000 000	1 3 2	Potter (3.2), Muncrief (2.1), Kramer (2)		Wilks entered the game in the sixth with one out and men on second and third, and retired the last 11 batters in a row to preserve the 3-1 margin.
STL	N	000 300 00x	3 10 0	Lanier (5.1), Wilks (3.2) SV		

Team totals

		W	AB	H	2B	3B	HR	R	RBI	BA	BB	SO	ERA
STL	N	4	204	49	9	1	3	16	15	.240	19	43	1.96
STL	A	2	197	36	9	1	1	12	9	.183	23	49	1.49

Individual Batting

ST. LOUIS (N.L.)

	AB	H	2B	3B	HR	R	RBI	BA
J. Hopp, of	27	5	0	0	0	2	0	.185
W. Kurowski, 3b	23	5	1	0	0	2	1	.217
S. Musial, of	23	7	2	0	1	2	2	.304
M. Marion, ss	22	5	3	0	0	1	2	.227
W. Cooper, c	22	7	2	1	0	1	2	.318
R. Sanders, 1b	21	6	0	0	1	5	1	.286
D. Litwhiler, of	20	4	1	0	1	2	1	.200
E. Verban, 2b	17	7	0	0	0	1	2	.412
A. Bergamo, of	6	0	0	0	0	0	1	.000
M. Cooper, p	4	0	0	0	0	0	0	.000
H. Brecheen, p	4	0	0	0	0	0	0	.000
M. Lanier, p	4	2	0	0	0	0	1	.500
K. O'Dea	3	1	0	0	0	0	2	.333
T. Wilks, p	2	0	0	0	0	0	0	.000
G. Fallon, 2b	2	0	0	0	0	0	0	.000
D. Garms	2	0	0	0	0	0	0	.000
B. Donnelly, p	1	0	0	0	0	0	0	.000
F. Schmidt, p	1	0	0	0	0	0	0	.000

Errors: S. Musial

ST. LOUIS (A.L.)

	AB	H	2B	3B	HR	R	RBI	BA
M. Kreevich, of	26	6	3	0	0	0	0	.231
V. Stephens, ss	22	5	1	0	0	2	0	.227
G. Moore, of	22	4	0	0	0	4	0	.182
M. Christman, 3b	22	2	0	0	0	0	1	.091
Gutteridge, 2b	21	3	1	0	0	1	0	.143
R. Hayworth, c	17	2	1	0	0	1	1	.118
G. McQuinn, 1b	16	7	2	0	1	2	5	.438
C. Laabs, of	15	3	1	0	0	1	0	.200
A. Zarilla, of	10	1	0	0	0	1	1	.100
D. Galehouse, p	5	1	0	0	0	0	0	.200
J. Kramer, p	4	0	0	0	0	0	0	.000
N. Potter, p	4	0	0	0	0	0	0	.000
F. Mancuso, c	3	2	0	0	0	0	1	.667
M. Byrnes	2	0	0	0	0	0	0	.000
M. Chartak	2	0	0	0	0	0	0	.000
F. Baker, 2b	2	0	0	0	0	0	0	.000
E. Clary	1	0	0	0	0	0	0	.000
B. Muncrief, p	1	0	0	0	0	0	0	.000
T. Turner	1	0	0	0	0	0	0	.000
Hollingsworth, p	1	0	0	0	0	0	0	.000

Errors: Gutteridge (3), V. Stephens (3), N. Potter (2), R. Hayworth, M. Christman

Individual Pitching

ST. LOUIS (N.L.)

	W	L	ERA	IP	H	BB	SO	SV
M. Cooper	1	1	1.13	16	9	5	16	0
M. Lanier	1	0	2.19	12.1	8	8	11	0
H. Brecheen	1	0	1.00	9	9	4	4	0
B. Donnelly	1	0	0.00	6	2	1	9	0
T. Wilks	0	1	5.68	6.1	5	3	7	1
F. Schmidt	0	0	0.00	3.1	1	1	1	0
B. Byerly	0	0	0.00	1.1	0	0	1	0
A. Jurisich	0	0	27.00	0.2	2	1	0	0

ST. LOUIS (A.L.)

	W	L	ERA	IP	H	BB	SO	SV
D. Galehouse	1	1	1.50	18	13	5	15	0
J. Kramer	1	0	0.00	11	9	4	12	0
N. Potter	0	1	0.93	9.2	10	3	6	0
B. Muncrief	0	1	1.35	6.2	5	4	4	0
Hollingsworth	0	0	2.25	4	5	2	1	0
S. Jakucki	0	1	9.00	3	5	0	4	0
T. Shirley	0	0	0.00	2	1	2	1	0

1945 WORLD SERIES

LINE SCORES	PITCHERS (innings pitched)	HOME RUNS (men on)	HIGHLIGHTS

Detroit (A.L.) defeats Chicago (N.L.) 4 games to 3

GAME 1 - OCTOBER 3

CHI	N	403 000 200	9 13 0	Borowy (9)	Cavarretta
DET	A	000 000 000	0 6 0	Newhouser (2.2), Benton (1.1), Tobin (3), Mueller (2)	

Newhouser gave up seven hits and eight runs in the first three innings as Cavarretta and Pafko scored three runs each and Nicholson had three RBIs.

GAME 2 - OCTOBER 4

CHI	N	000 100 000	1 7 0	Wyse (6), Erickson (2)	
DET	A	000 040 00x	4 7 0	Trucks (9)	Greenberg (2 on)

Greenberg's homer with two on in the fifth broke open the game.

GAME 3 - OCTOBER 5

CHI	N	000 200 100	3 8 0	Passeau (9)
DET	A	000 000 000	0 1 2	Overmire (6), Benton (3)

Passeau allowed only a single to York in the third and a walk to Swift in the sixth.

GAME 4 - OCTOBER 6

DET	A	000 400 000	4 7 1	Trout (9)
CHI	N	000 001 000	1 5 1	Prim (3.1), Derringer (1.2), Vandenburg (2), Erickson (2)

Prim retired the first ten batters in the game, but the Tigers knocked him out with four in the fourth.

GAME 5 - OCTOBER 7

DET	A	001 004 102	8 11 0	Newhouser (9)
CHI	N	001 000 201	4 7 2	Borowy (5), Vandenburg (0.2), Chipman (0.1), Derringer (2), Erickson (1)

Newhouser benefitted from another four-run Tiger rally and struck nine Cubs in the victory. Greenberg's three doubles keyed the attack.

GAME 6 - OCTOBER 8

DET	A	010 000 240 000	7 13 1	Trucks (4.1), Caster (0.2), Bridges (1.2), Benton (0.1), Trout (4.2)	Greenberg
CHI	N	000 041 200 001	8 15 3	Passeau (6.2), Wyse (0.2), Prim (0.2), Borowy (4)	

Hack's drive bounced past Greenberg for a double and brought home the winning run in the twelfth after Greenberg tied the game with a homer in the eighth. Borowy held the Tigers hitless over the last four innings.

GAME 7 - OCTOBER 10

DET	A	510 000 120	9 9 1	Newhouser (9)
CHI	N	100 100 010	3 10 0	Borowy (0), Derringer (1.2), Vandenberg (3.1), Erickson (2), Passeau (1), Wyse (1)

The Cubs gambled and sent in Borowy with only a day's rest. The Tigers hit three successive singles to knock him out in the first, and went on to score five in the frame to sew up the Series.

Team totals

		W	AB	H	2B	3B	HR	R	RBI	BA	BB	SO	ERA
DET	A	4	242	54	10	0	2	32	32	.223	33	22	3.84
CHI	N	3	246	65	16	3	1	29	27	.264	19	48	4.15

Individual Batting

DETROIT (A.L.)

	AB	H	2B	3B	HR	R	RBI	BA
D. Cramer, of	29	11	0	0	0	7	4	.379
E. Mayo, 2b	28	7	1	0	0	4	2	.250
J. Outlaw, 3b	28	5	0	0	0	1	3	.179
R. York, 1b	28	5	1	0	0	1	3	.179
S. Webb, ss	27	5	0	0	0	4	1	.185
H. Greenberg, of	23	7	3	0	2	7	7	.304
Cullenbine, of	22	5	2	0	0	5	4	.227
P. Richards, c	19	4	2	0	0	0	6	.211
H. Newhouser, p	8	0	0	0	0	0	0	.000
D. Trout, p	6	1	0	0	0	0	0	.167
V. Trucks, p	4	0	0	0	0	0	0	.000
B. Swift, c	4	1	0	0	0	1	0	.250
J. McHale	3	0	0	0	0	0	0	.000
J. Hoover, ss	3	1	0	0	0	1	1	.333
C. Hostetler	3	0	0	0	0	0	0	.000
H. Walker	2	1	1	0	0	1	0	.500
J. Tobin, p	1	0	0	0	0	0	0	.000
B. Maier	1	1	0	0	0	0	0	1.000
Z. Eaton	1	0	0	0	0	0	0	.000
S. Overmire, p	1	0	0	0	0	0	0	.000
R. Borom	1	0	0	0	0	0	0	.000
Mierkowicz, of	0	0	0	0	0	0	0	–

Errors: P. Richards, S. Webb, R. York, E. Mayo, H. Newhouser
Stolen Bases: J. Outlaw, D. Cramer, Cullenbine

CHICAGO (N.L.)

	AB	H	2B	3B	HR	R	RBI	BA
S. Hack, 3b	30	11	3	0	0	1	4	.367
D. Johnson, 2b	29	5	2	1	0	4	0	.172
P. Lowrey, of	29	9	1	0	0	4	0	.310
B. Nicholson, of	28	6	1	1	0	1	8	.214
A. Pafko, of	28	6	2	1	0	5	2	.214
Cavarretta, 1b	26	11	2	0	1	7	5	.423
Livingston, c	22	8	3	0	0	3	4	.364
R. Hughes, ss	17	5	1	0	0	1	3	.294
C. Passeau, p	7	0	0	0	0	1	1	.000
P. Gillespie, c	6	0	0	0	0	0	0	.000
H. Borowy, p	5	1	0	0	0	1	0	.200
F. Secory	5	2	0	0	0	0	4	.400
H. Wyse, p	3	0	0	0	0	0	0	.000
D. Williams, c	2	0	0	0	0	0	0	.000
E. Sauer	2	0	0	0	0	0	0	.000
L. Merullo, ss	2	0	0	0	0	0	0	.000
H. Becker	2	1	0	0	0	0	0	.500
McCullough	1	0	0	0	0	0	0	.000
B. Schuster, ss	1	0	0	0	0	0	0	.000
Vandenburg, p	1	0	0	0	0	0	0	.000
C. Block	0	0	0	0	0	0	0	–

Errors: S. Hack (3), D. Johnson, B. Nicholson, A. Pafko
Stolen Bases: P. Lowrey

Individual Pitching

DETROIT (A.L.)

	W	L	ERA	IP	H	BB	SO	SV
H. Newhouser	2	1	6.10	20.2	25	4	22	0
D. Trout	1	1	0.66	13.2	9	3	9	0
V. Trucks	1	0	3.38	13.1	14	5	7	0
S. Overmire	0	1	3.00	6	4	2	2	0
A. Benton	0	0	1.93	4.2	6	0	5	0
J. Tobin	0	0	6.00	3	4	1	0	0
L. Mueller	0	0	0.00	2	0	1	1	0
T. Bridges	0	0	16.20	1.2	3	3	1	0
G. Caster	0	0	0.00	0.2	0	1	0	0

CHICAGO (N.L.)

	W	L	ERA	IP	H	BB	SO	SV
H. Borowy	2	2	4.00	18	21	6	8	0
C. Passeau	1	0	2.70	16.2	7	8	3	0
P. Erickson	0	0	3.86	7	8	3	5	0
H. Wyse	0	1	7.04	7.2	8	4	1	0
Vandenburg	0	0	0.00	6	1	3	3	0
P. Derringer	0	0	6.75	5.1	5	7	1	0
R. Prim	0	1	9.00	4	4	1	1	0
B. Chipman	0	0	0.00	0.1	0	1	0	0

1946 WORLD SERIES

LINE SCORES	PITCHERS (innings pitched)	HOME RUNS (men on)	HIGHLIGHTS

St. Louis (N.L.) defeats Boston (A.L.) 4 games to 3

GAME 1 - OCTOBER 6

BOS A 010 000 001 1   3 9 2   Hughson (8), **Johnson** (2)   York
STL N 000 001 010 0   2 7 0   Pollet (10)

The Red Sox tied the game in the ninth when a ground ball took a freak bounce through Marion's legs, setting the stage for York, who homered in the tenth.

GAME 2 - OCTOBER 7

BOS A 000 000 000   0 4 1   Harris (7), Dobson (1)
STL N 001 020 00x   3 6 0   **Brecheen** (9)

Brecheen drove in the first run of the game and allowed only four singles.

GAME 3 - OCTOBER 9

STL N 000 000 000   0 6 1   Dickson (7), Wilks (1)   York (2 on)
BOS A 300 000 01x   4 8 0   **Ferriss** (9)

The Red Sox broke the game open in the first on York's three-run homer. Ferriss's shutout is the 50th in Series history.

GAME 4 - OCTOBER 10

STL N 033 010 104   12 20 1   **Munger** (9)   Slaughter
BOS A 000 100 020   3 9 4   Hughson (2), Bagby (3), Zuber (2), Brown (1), Ryba (0.2), Dreiserwerd (0.1)   Doerr (1 on)

Slaughter, Kurowski, and Garagiola each had four hits as the Cardinals tied a Series record with their 20 hits.

GAME 5 - OCTOBER 11

STL N 010 000 020   3 4 1   Pollet (0.1), Brazle (6.2), Beazley (1)
BOS A 110 001 30x   6 11 3   **Dobson** (9)   Culberson

Higgins's double in the seventh scored DiMaggio for the deciding run of the game. All three St. Louis runs off Dobson were unearned.

GAME 6 - OCTOBER 13

BOS A 000 000 100   1 7 0   Harris (2.2), Hughson (4.1), Johnson (1)
STL N 003 000 01x   4 8 0   **Brecheen** (9)

Brecheen shut down the Red Sox on seven hits as the Cardinals evened the Series.

GAME 7 - OCTOBER 15

BOS A 100 000 020   3 8 0   Ferriss (4.1), Dobson (2.2), **Klinger** (0.2), Johnson (0.1)
STL N 010 020 01x   4 9 1   Dickson (7), **Brecheen** (2)

Pesky hesitated throwing the ball in after Walker's hit in the eighth and Slaughter raced home from first with the deciding run. Brecheen recorded his third victory of the Series.

Team totals

		W	AB	H	2B	3B	HR	R	RBI	BA	BB	SO	ERA
STL	N	4	232	60	19	2	1	28	27	.259	19	30	2.32
BOS	A	3	233	56	7	1	4	20	18	.240	22	28	2.95

Individual Batting

ST. LOUIS (N.L.)

	AB	H	2B	3B	HR	R	RBI	BA
Schoendienst, 2b	30	7	1	0	0	3	1	.233
S. Musial, 1b	27	6	4	1	0	3	4	.222
W. Kurowski, 3b	27	8	3	0	0	5	2	.296
T. Moore, of	27	4	0	0	0	1	2	.148
E. Slaughter, of	25	8	1	1	1	5	2	.320
M. Marion, ss	24	6	2	0	0	1	4	.250
J. Garagiola, c	19	6	2	0	0	2	4	.316
H. Walker, of	17	7	2	0	0	3	6	.412
H. Brecheen, p	8	1	0	0	0	2	1	.125
D. Rice, c	6	3	1	0	0	2	0	.500
M. Dickson, p	5	2	2	0	0	1	1	.400
E. Dusak, of	4	1	1	0	0	0	0	.250
H. Pollet, p	4	0	0	0	0	0	0	.000
G. Munger, p	4	1	0	0	0	0	0	.250
D. Sisler	2	0	0	0	0	0	0	.000
A. Brazle, p	2	0	0	0	0	0	0	.000
N. Jones	1	0	0	0	0	0	0	.000

Errors: M. Marion (2), W. Kurowski, Schoendienst
Stolen Bases: S. Musial, Schoendienst, E. Slaughter

BOSTON (A.L.)

	AB	H	2B	3B	HR	R	RBI	BA
J. Pesky, ss	30	7	0	0	0	2	0	.233
D. DiMaggio, of	27	7	3	0	0	2	3	.259
T. Williams, of	25	5	0	0	0	2	1	.200
P. Higgins, 3b	24	5	1	0	0	1	2	.208
R. York, 1b	23	6	1	1	2	6	5	.261
B. Doerr, 2b	22	9	1	0	1	1	3	.409
H. Wagner, c	13	0	0	0	0	0	0	.000
W. Moses, of	12	5	0	0	1	0	0	.417
T. McBride, of	12	2	0	0	0	0	1	.167
R. Partee, c	10	1	0	0	0	1	1	.100
L. Culberson, of	9	2	0	1	1	1	1	.222
B. Ferriss, p	6	0	0	0	0	0	0	.000
Gutteridge, 2b	5	2	0	0	0	1	1	.400
M. Harris, p	3	1	0	0	0	0	0	.333
J. Dobson, p	3	0	0	0	0	0	0	.000
T. Hughson, p	3	1	0	0	0	0	0	.333
C. Metkovich	2	1	1	0	0	1	0	.500
R. Russell, 3b	2	2	0	0	0	1	0	1.000
E. Johnson, p	1	0	0	0	0	0	0	.000
J. Bagby, p	1	0	0	0	0	0	0	.000
P. Campbell	0	0	0	0	0	0	0	—

Errors: J. Pesky (4), P. Higgins (2), M. Ryba, T. Hughson, T. McBride, R. York
Stolen Bases: L. Culberson, J. Pesky

Individual Pitching

ST. LOUIS (N.L.)

	W	L	ERA	IP	H	BB	SO	SV
H. Brecheen	3	0	0.45	20	14	5	11	0
M. Dickson	0	1	3.86	14	11	4	7	0
H. Pollet	0	1	3.48	10.1	12	4	3	0
G. Munger	1	0	1.00	9	9	3	2	0
A. Brazle	0	1	5.40	6.2	7	6	4	0
J. Beazley	0	0	0.00	1	1	0	1	0
T. Wilks	0	0	0.00	1	2	0	0	0

BOSTON (A.L.)

	W	L	ERA	IP	H	BB	SO	SV
T. Hughson	0	1	3.14	14.1	14	3	8	0
B. Ferriss	1	0	2.03	13.1	13	2	4	0
J. Dobson	1	0	0.00	12.2	4	3	10	0
M. Harris	0	2	3.72	9.2	11	4	5	0
J. Bagby	0	0	3.00	3	6	1	1	0
E. Johnson	1	0	2.70	3.1	1	2	1	0
B. Zuber	0	0	4.50	2	3	1	1	0
M. Brown	0	0	27.00	1	4	1	0	0
Dreiserwerd	0	0	0.00	0.1	0	0	0	0
B. Klinger	0	1	13.50	0.2	2	1	0	0
M. Ryba	0	0	13.50	0.2	2	1	0	0

1947 WORLD SERIES

LINE SCORES	PITCHERS (innings pitched)	HOME RUNS (men on)	HIGHLIGHTS

New York (A.L.) defeats Brooklyn (N.L.) 4 games to 3

GAME 1 - SEPTEMBER 30

BKN	N	100 001 100	3 6 0	Branca (4), Behrman (2), Casey (2)		Branca retired the first twelve batters but was knocked out as the Yankees got five in the fifth on three hits, three walks, and a hit batsman.
NY	A	000 050 00x	5 4 0	Shea (5), Page (4) **SV**		

GAME 2 - OCTOBER 1

BKN	N	001 100 001	3 9 2	Lombardi (4), Gregg (2), Behrman (0.1), Barney (1.2)	Walker	Reynolds spaced nine Dodger hits and fanned 12 as he breezed to an easy win.
NY	A	101 121 40x	10 15 1	Reynolds (9)	Henrich	

GAME 3 - OCTOBER 2

NY	A	002 221 100	8 13 0	Newsom (1.2), Raschi (0.1), Drew (1), Chandler (2), Page (3)	DiMaggio (1 on), Berra	The Dodgers jumped on Newsom and Raschi for six runs in the second to outlast the Yankees in the slugfest. Berra's pinch homer was the first in Series history.
BKN	N	061 200 00x	9 13 1	Hatten (4.1), Branca (2), **Casey** (2.2)		

GAME 4 - OCTOBER 3

NY	A	100 100 000	2 8 1	Bevens (8.2)		Bevens was one out from the first Series no-hitter when Lavagetto doubled home two men to win the game for the Dodgers.
BKN	N	000 010 002	3 1 3	Taylor (0), Gregg (7), Behrman (1.1), **Casey** (0.2)		

GAME 5 - OCTOBER 4

NY	A	000 110 000	2 5 0	Shea (9)	DiMaggio	A fifth-inning homer by DiMaggio proved the deciding run. Shea aided his own cause with two hits and an RBI.
BKN	N	000 001 000	1 4 1	Barney (4.2), Hatten (1.1), Behrman (1), Casey (2)		

GAME 6 - OCTOBER 5

BKN	N	202 004 000	8 12 1	Lombardi (2.2), **Branca** (2.1), Hatten (3), Casey (1) **SV**		A record 38 players were used as the Dodgers knotted the Series. Gionfriddo's great catch of DiMaggio's 415-foot drive in the sixth with two aboard helped to subdue the Yankees.
NY	A	004 100 001	6 15 2	Reynolds (2.1), Drews (2), **Page** (1), Newsom (0.2), Raschi (1), Wensloff (2)		

GAME 7 - OCTOBER 6

BKN	N	020 000 000	2 7 0	Gregg (3.2), Behrman (1.2), Hatten (0.1), Barney (0.1), Casey (2)		Page, the Yankees' relief ace, checked the Dodgers on one hit for the last five innings to give the Yankees the Series victory. Henrich's go-ahead RBI single in the fourth marked the third time in the Series that he delivered the clutch run.
NY	A	010 201 10x	5 7 0	Shea (1.1), Bevens (2.2), **Page** (5)		

Team totals

		W	AB	H	2B	3B	HR	R	RBI	BA	BB	SO	ERA
NY	A	4	238	67	11	5	4	38	36	.282	38	37	4.09
BKN	N	3	226	52	13	1	1	29	26	.230	30	32	5.55

Individual Batting

NEW YORK (A.L.)

	AB	H	2B	3B	HR	R	RBI	BA
T. Henrich, of	31	10	2	0	1	2	5	.323
Stirnweiss, 2b	27	7	0	1	0	3	3	.259
P. Rizzuto, ss	26	8	1	0	0	3	2	.308
J. DiMaggio, of	26	6	0	0	2	4	5	.231
B. Johnson, 3b	26	7	0	3	0	8	2	.269
G. McQuinn, 1b	23	3	0	0	0	3	1	.130
Y. Berra, c, of	19	3	0	0	1	2	2	.158
J. Lindell, of	18	9	3	1	0	3	7	.500
A. Robinson, c	10	2	0	0	0	2	1	.200
S. Shea, p	5	2	1	0	0	0	1	.400
A. Reynolds, p	4	2	0	0	0	2	1	.500
J. Page, p	4	0	0	0	0	0	0	.000
S. Lollar, c	4	3	2	0	0	3	1	.750
B. Bevens, p	4	0	0	0	0	0	0	.000
B. Brown	3	3	2	0	0	2	3	1.000
A. Clark, of	2	1	0	0	0	1	1	.500
K. Drews, p	2	0	0	0	0	0	0	.000
J. Phillips, 1b	2	0	0	0	0	0	0	.000
L. Frey	1	0	0	0	0	0	1	.000
R. Houk	1	1	0	0	0	0	0	1.000

Errors: Y. Berra (2), G. McQuinn, A. Robinson
Stolen Bases: P. Rizzuto (2)

BROOKLYN (N.L.)

	AB	H	2B	3B	HR	R	RBI	BA
J. Robinson, 1b	27	7	2	0	0	3	3	.259
B. Edwards, c	27	6	1	0	0	3	2	.222
D. Walker, of	27	6	1	0	1	1	4	.222
E. Stanky, 2b	25	6	1	0	0	4	2	.240
P. Reese, ss	23	7	1	0	0	5	4	.304
S. Jorgensen, 3b	20	4	2	0	0	1	3	.200
G. Hermanski, of	19	3	0	1	0	4	1	.158
C. Furillo, of	17	6	2	0	0	2	3	.353
P. Reiser, of	8	2	0	0	0	1	0	.250
C. Lavagetto, 3b	7	1	1	0	0	0	3	.143
E. Miksis, of, 2b	4	1	0	0	0	1	0	.250
R. Branca, p	4	0	0	0	0	0	0	.000
V. Lombardi, p	3	0	0	0	0	0	0	.000
Gionfriddo, of	3	0	0	0	0	2	0	.000
H. Gregg, p	3	0	0	0	0	0	0	.000
J. Hatten, p	3	1	0	0	0	1	0	.333
A. Vaughan	2	1	1	0	0	0	0	.500
G. Hodges	1	0	0	0	0	0	0	.000
H. Casey, p	1	0	0	0	0	0	0	.000
B. Bragan	1	1	0	0	0	0	1	1.000
R. Barney, p	1	0	0	0	0	0	0	.000
D. Bankhead	0	0	0	0	0	1	0	–

Errors: S. Jorgensen (2), E. Miksis, B. Edwards, C. Furillo, E. Stanky, P. Reese, P. Reiser
Stolen Bases: P. Reese (3), J. Robinson (2), Gionfriddo, D. Walker

Individual Pitching

NEW YORK (A.L.)

	W	L	ERA	IP	H	BB	SO	SV
S. Shea	2	0	2.35	15.1	10	8	10	0
J. Page	1	1	4.15	13	12	2	7	1
A. Reynolds	1	0	4.76	11.1	15	3	6	0
B. Bevens	0	1	2.38	11.1	3	11	7	0
K. Drews	0	0	3.00	3	2	1	0	0
B. Newsom	0	1	19.29	2.1	6	2	0	0
B. Wensloff	0	0	0.00	2	0	0	0	0
S. Chandler	0	0	9.00	2	2	3	1	0
V. Raschi	0	0	6.75	1.1	2	0	1	0

BROOKLYN (N.L.)

	W	L	ERA	IP	H	BB	SO	SV
H. Gregg	0	1	3.55	12.2	9	8	10	0
H. Casey	2	0	0.87	10.1	5	1	3	1
J. Hatten	0	0	7.00	9	12	7	5	0
R. Branca	1	1	8.64	8.1	12	5	8	0
R. Barney	0	1	2.70	6.2	4	10	3	0
H. Behrman	0	0	7.11	6.1	9	5	3	0
V. Lombardi	0	1	12.15	6.2	14	1	5	0
H. Taylor	0	0	–	0.0	2	1	0	0
D. Bankhead	0	0	–	0.0	0	0	0	0

1948 WORLD SERIES

LINE SCORES	PITCHERS (innings pitched)	HOME RUNS (men on)	HIGHLIGHTS

Cleveland (A.L.) defeats Boston (N.L.) 4 games to 2

GAME 1 - OCTOBER 6

CLE	A	000 000 000	0 4 0	Feller (8)	
BOS	N	000 000 01x	1 2 2	Sain (9)	

Holmes singled Masi home in the eighth after Masi was almost picked off second by Feller.

GAME 2 - OCTOBER 7

CLE	A	000 210 001	4 8 1	Lemon (9)	
BOS	N	100 000 000	1 8 3	Spahn (4.1), Barrett (2.2), Potter (2)	

The Indians went ahead with two runs in the fourth on hits by Boudreau, Gordon, and Doby.

GAME 3 - OCTOBER 8

BOS	N	000 000 000	0 5 1	Bickford (3.1), Voiselle (3.2), Barrett (1)	
CLE	A	001 100 00x	2 5 0	Bearden (9)	

Bearden faced only 30 batters and doubled in the third, scoring the go-ahead run on Dark's error. Hegan singled in an insurance run in the fourth.

GAME 4 - OCTOBER 9

BOS	N	000 000 100	1 7 0	Sain (8)	Rickert
CLE	A	101 000 00x	2 5 0	Gromek (9)	Doby

Doby's homer in the third became decisive when Rickert homered to spoil Gromek's shutout attempt in the seventh.

GAME 5 - OCTOBER 10

BOS	N	301 001 600	11 12 0	Potter (3.1), Spahn (5.2)	Elliott (2 on), Elliott, Salkeld
CLE	A	100 400 000	5 6 2	Feller (6.1), Klieman (0), Christopher (0), Paige (0.2), Muncrief (2)	Mitchell, Hegan (2 on)

Elliott's two home runs drove in four runs in the first and third. The Braves broke a 5-5 tie with six runs in the seventh on five singles off four Indian pitchers.

GAME 6 - OCTOBER 11

CLE	A	001 002 010	4 10 0	Lemon (7.1), Bearden (1.2) SV	Gordon
BOS	N	000 100 020	3 9 0	Voiselle (7), Spahn (2)	

Masi's pinch-hit double off Bearden in the eighth brought the Braves within one run of the Indians, but Bearden retired the next four men to nail down the win.

Team totals

		W	AB	H	2B	3B	HR	R	RBI	BA	BB	SO	ERA
CLE	A	4	191	38	7	0	4	17	16	.199	12	26	2.72
BOS	N	2	187	43	6	0	4	17	16	.230	16	19	2.60

Individual Batting

CLEVELAND (A.L.)

	AB	H	2B	3B	HR	R	RBI	BA
D. Mitchell, of	23	4	1	0	1	4	1	.174
L. Doby, of	22	7	1	0	1	1	2	.318
J. Gordon, 2b	22	4	0	0	1	3	2	.182
L. Boudreau, ss	22	6	4	0	0	1	3	.273
K. Keltner, 3b	21	2	0	0	0	3	0	.095
E. Robinson, 1b	20	6	0	0	0	0	1	.300
J. Hegan, c	19	4	0	0	1	2	5	.211
W. Judnich, of	13	1	0	0	0	1	1	.077
B. Lemon, p	7	0	0	0	0	0	0	.000
B. Feller, p	4	0	0	0	0	0	0	.000
G. Bearden, p	4	2	1	0	0	1	0	.500
A. Clark, of	3	0	0	0	0	0	0	.000
S. Gromek, p	3	0	0	0	0	0	0	.000
T. Tucker, of	3	1	0	0	0	1	0	.333
B. Kennedy, of	2	1	0	0	0	0	1	.500
R. Boone	1	0	0	0	0	0	0	.000
A. Rosen	1	0	0	0	0	0	0	.000
J. Tipton	1	0	0	0	0	0	0	.000
H. Peck, of	0	0	0	0	0	0	0	-

Errors: J. Gordon, K. Keltner, L. Doby
Stolen Bases: J. Gordon, J. Hegan

BOSTON (N.L.)

	AB	H	2B	3B	HR	R	RBI	BA
T. Holmes, of	26	5	0	0	0	3	1	.192
A. Dark, ss	24	4	1	0	0	2	0	.167
McCormick, of	23	6	0	0	0	1	2	.261
B. Elliott, 3b	21	7	0	0	2	4	5	.333
M. Rickert, of	19	4	0	0	1	2	2	.211
E. Torgeson, 1b	18	7	3	0	0	2	1	.389
E. Stanky, 2b	14	4	1	0	0	0	1	.286
B. Salkeld, c	9	2	0	0	1	2	1	.222
P. Masi, c	8	1	1	0	0	1	1	.125
McCormick, 1b	5	1	0	0	0	0	0	.200
J. Sain, p	5	1	0	0	0	0	0	.200
W. Spahn, p	4	0	0	0	0	0	1	.000
C. Conatser, of	4	0	0	0	0	0	1	.000
B. Voiselle, p	2	0	0	0	0	0	0	.000
N. Potter, p	2	1	0	0	0	0	0	.500
C. Ryan	1	0	0	0	0	0	0	.000
R. Sanders	1	0	0	0	0	0	0	.000
S. Sisti, 2b	1	0	0	0	0	0	0	.000

Errors: A. Dark (3), B. Elliott (3)
Stolen Bases: E. Torgeson

Individual Pitching

CLEVELAND (A.L.)

	W	L	ERA	IP	H	BB	SO	SV
B. Lemon	2	0	1.65	16.1	16	7	6	0
B. Feller	0	2	5.02	14.1	10	5	7	0
G. Bearden	1	0	0.00	10.2	6	1	4	1
S. Gromek	1	0	1.00	9	7	1	2	0
B. Muncrief	0	0	0.00	2	1	0	0	0
S. Paige	0	0	0.00	0.2	0	0	0	0
E. Klieman	0	0	∞	0.0	1	2	0	0
Christopher	0	0	∞	0.0	2	0	0	0

BOSTON (N.L.)

	W	L	ERA	IP	H	BB	SO	SV
J. Sain	1	1	1.06	17	9	0	9	0
W. Spahn	1	1	3.00	12	10	3	12	0
B. Voiselle	0	1	2.53	10.2	8	2	2	0
N. Potter	0	0	8.44	5.1	6	2	1	0
R. Barrett	0	0	0.00	3.2	1	0	1	0
V. Bickford	0	1	2.70	3.1	4	5	1	0

1949 WORLD SERIES

LINE SCORES	PITCHERS (innings pitched)	HOME RUNS (men on)	HIGHLIGHTS

New York (A.L.) defeats Brooklyn (N.L.) 4 games to 1

GAME 1 - OCTOBER 5

BKN	N	000 000 000	0 2 0	Newcombe (8)	
NY	A	000 000 001	1 5 1	Reynolds (9)	Henrich

A stirring pitching duel was resolved in the ninth when Henrich hit a leadoff homer for the game's only run.

GAME 2 - OCTOBER 6

BKN	N	010 000 000	1 7 2	Roe (9)	
NY	A	000 000 000	0 6 1	Raschi (8), Page (1)	

The Dodgers reversed the score and squared accounts when Roe blanked the Yankees on six hits. Robinson scored the only Dodger run on Hodges's single.

GAME 3 - OCTOBER 7

NY	A	001 000 003	4 5 0	Byrne (3.1), Page (5.2)	
BKN	N	000 100 002	3 5 0	Branca (8.2), Banta (0.1)	Reese, Olmo, Campanella

With the score tied 1-1 in the ninth, the Yankees scored three times, and the Dodgers came back with two. A two-run pinch single by Mize is the big blow for the Bombers, while homers by Olmo and Campanella left Brooklyn one run short.

GAME 4 - OCTOBER 8

NY	A	000 330 000	6 10 0	Lopat (5.2), Reynolds (3.1) SV	
BKN	N	000 004 000	4 9 1	Newcombe (3.2), Hatten (1.1), Erskine (1), Banta (3)	

Reynolds came into the game with runners on first and third and two out in the sixth. He retired all ten batters who faced him to save Lopat's win.

GAME 5 - OCTOBER 9

NY	A	203 113 000	10 11 1	Raschi (6.2), Page (2.1) SV	DiMaggio
BKN	N	001 001 400	6 11 2	Barney (2.2), Banta (2.1), Erskine (0.2), Hatten (0.1), Palica (2), Minner (1)	Hodges (2 on)

Barney's wildness enabled the Yankees to take an early lead and Page relieved Raschi to choke off the Dodger comeback effort.

Team totals

		W	AB	H	2B	3B	HR	R	RBI	BA	BB	SO	ERA
NY	A	4	164	37	10	2	2	21	20	.226	18	27	2.80
BKN	N	1	162	34	7	1	4	14	14	.210	15	38	4.30

Individual Batting

NEW YORK (A.L.)

	AB	H	2B	3B	HR	R	RBI	BA
J. Coleman, 2b	20	5	3	0	0	0	4	.250
T. Henrich, 1b	19	5	0	0	1	4	1	.263
J. DiMaggio, of	18	2	0	0	1	2	2	.111
P. Rizzuto, ss	18	3	0	0	0	2	1	.167
Y. Berra, c	16	1	0	0	0	2	1	.063
B. Brown, 3b	12	6	1	2	0	4	5	.500
C. Mapes, of	10	1	1	0	0	3	2	.100
G. Woodling, of	10	4	3	0	0	4	0	.400
J. Lindell, of	7	1	0	0	0	0	0	.143
B. Johnson, 3b	7	1	0	0	0	0	0	.143
H. Bauer, of	6	1	0	0	0	0	0	.167
V. Raschi, p	5	1	0	0	0	0	1	.200
A. Reynolds, p	4	2	1	0	0	0	0	.500
J. Page, p	4	0	0	0	0	0	0	.000
E. Lopat, p	3	1	1	0	0	0	1	.333
J. Mize	2	2	0	0	0	0	2	1.000
C. Silvera, c	2	0	0	0	0	0	0	.000
T. Byrne, p	1	1	0	0	0	0	0	1.000
G. Niarhos, c	0	0	0	0	0	0	0	–
Stirnweiss	0	0	0	0	0	0	0	–

Errors: J. Coleman, J. Lindell, C. Mapes
Stolen Bases: B. Johnson, P. Rizzuto

BROOKLYN (N.L.)

	AB	H	2B	3B	HR	R	RBI	BA
D. Snider, of	21	3	1	0	0	2	0	.143
P. Reese, ss	19	6	1	0	1	2	2	.316
G. Hodges, 1b	17	4	0	0	1	2	4	.235
J. Robinson, 2b	16	3	1	0	0	2	2	.188
Campanella, c	15	4	1	0	1	2	2	.267
G. Hermanski, of	13	4	0	1	0	1	2	.308
L. Olmo, of	11	3	0	0	1	2	2	.273
S. Jorgensen, 3b	11	2	2	0	0	1	0	.182
C. Furillo, of	8	1	0	0	0	0	0	.125
E. Miksis, 3b	7	2	1	0	0	0	0	.286
M. Rackley, of	5	0	0	0	0	0	0	.000
D. Newcombe, p	4	0	0	0	0	0	0	.000
P. Roe, p	3	0	0	0	0	0	0	.000
B. Cox, 3b	3	1	0	0	0	0	0	.333
R. Branca, p	3	0	0	0	0	0	0	.000
T. Brown	2	0	0	0	0	0	0	.000
B. Edwards	2	1	0	0	0	0	0	.500
J. Banta, p	1	0	0	0	0	0	0	.000
D. Whitman	1	0	0	0	0	0	0	.000
McCormick, of	0	0	0	0	0	0	0	–

Errors: R. Barney, E. Miksis, P. Reese, J. Robinson, P. Roe
Stolen Bases: P. Reese

Individual Pitching

NEW YORK (A.L.)

	W	L	ERA	IP	H	BB	SO	SV
V. Raschi	1	1	4.30	14.2	15	5	11	0
A. Reynolds	1	0	0.00	12.1	2	4	14	1
J. Page	1	0	2.00	9	6	3	8	1
E. Lopat	1	0	6.35	5.2	9	1	4	0
T. Byrne	0	0	2.70	3.1	2	2	1	0

BROOKLYN (N.L.)

	W	L	ERA	IP	H	BB	SO	SV
D. Newcombe	0	2	3.09	11.2	10	3	11	0
P. Roe	1	0	0.00	9	6	3	0	0
R. Branca	0	0	4.15	8.2	4	4	6	0
J. Banta	0	0	3.18	5.2	5	1	4	0
R. Barney	0	0	16.88	2.2	3	6	2	0
E. Palica	0	0	0.00	2	1	1	1	0
P. Minner	0	0	0.00	1	1	0	0	0
C. Erskine	0	0	16.20	1.2	3	1	0	0
J. Hatten	0	0	16.20	1.2	4	2	0	0

1950 WORLD SERIES

LINE SCORES	PITCHERS (innings pitched)	HOME RUNS (men on)	HIGHLIGHTS

New York (A.L.) defeats Philadelphia (N.L.) 4 games to 0

GAME 1 - OCTOBER 4

NY	A	000 100 000	1	5	0	Raschi (9)
PHI	N	000 000 000	0	2	1	Konstanty (8), Meyer (1)

Raschi allowed only two singles. The Yankees scored in the fourth on a double by Brown and long flies by Bauer and Coleman.

GAME 2 - OCTOBER 5

NY	A	010 000 000 1	2	10	0	Reynolds (10)	DiMaggio
PHI	N	000 010 000 0	1	7	0	Roberts (10)	

DiMaggio homered in the tenth to decide pitcher's duel between Reynolds and Roberts.

GAME 3 - OCTOBER 6

PHI	N	000 001 100	2	10	2	Heintzelman (7.2), Konstanty (0.1), Meyer (0.2)
NY	A	001 000 011	3	7	0	Lopat (8), Ferrick (1)

Coleman's single in the ninth drove in Woodling with the winning run after the Yankees tied the game in the eighth on Hamner's bases-loaded error.

GAME 4 - OCTOBER 7

PHI	N	000 000 002	2	7	1	Miller (0.1), Konstanty (6.2), Roberts (1)	
NY	A	200 003 00x	5	8	2	Ford (8.2), Reynolds (0.1) SV	Berra

Berra's homer and Brown's triple highlighted the Yankees' three-run fifth. Ford held the Phillies to seven hits, but needed ninth inning help from Reynolds, who struck out Lopata with two men on.

Team totals

		W	AB	H	2B	3B	HR	R	RBI	BA	BB	SO	ERA
NY	A	4	135	30	3	1	2	11	10	.222	13	12	0.73
PHI	N	0	128	26	6	1	0	5	3	.203	7	24	2.27

Individual Batting

NEW YORK (A.L.)

	AB	H	2B	3B	HR	R	RBI	BA
H. Bauer, of	15	2	0	0	0	0	1	.133
Y. Berra, c	15	3	0	0	1	2	2	.200
J. Mize, 1b	15	2	0	0	0	0	0	.133
P. Rizzuto, ss	14	2	0	0	0	1	0	.143
G. Woodling, of	14	6	0	0	0	2	1	.429
J. Coleman, 2b	14	4	1	0	0	2	3	.286
J. DiMaggio, of	13	4	1	0	1	2	2	.308
B. Brown, 3b	12	4	1	1	0	2	1	.333
B. Johnson, 3b	6	0	0	0	0	0	0	.000
C. Mapes, of	4	0	0	0	0	0	0	.000
V. Raschi, p	3	1	0	0	0	0	0	.333
A. Reynolds, p	3	1	0	0	0	0	0	.333
W. Ford, p	3	0	0	0	0	0	0	.000
E. Lopat, p	2	1	0	0	0	0	0	.500
J. Hopp, 1b	2	0	0	0	0	0	0	.000
J. Jensen	0	0	0	0	0	0	0	–
J. Collins, 1b	0	0	0	0	0	0	0	–

Errors: G. Woodling, B. Brown
Stolen Bases: P. Rizzuto

PHILADELPHIA (N.L.)

	AB	H	2B	3B	HR	R	RBI	BA
R. Ashburn, of	17	3	0	0	0	0	1	.176
D. Sisler, of	17	1	0	0	0	0	1	.059
E. Waitkus, 1b	15	4	1	0	0	0	0	.267
W. Jones, 3b	14	4	1	0	0	1	0	.286
D. Ennis, of	14	2	1	0	0	1	0	.143
M. Goliat, 2b	14	3	0	0	0	1	1	.214
G. Hamner, ss	14	6	2	1	0	1	0	.429
A. Seminick, c	11	2	0	0	0	0	0	.182
J. Konstanty, p	4	1	0	0	0	0	0	.250
Heintzelman, p	2	0	0	0	0	0	0	.000
R. Roberts, p	2	0	0	0	0	0	0	.000
D. Whitman	2	0	0	0	0	0	0	.000
S. Lopata, c	1	0	0	0	0	0	0	.000
P. Caballero	1	0	0	0	0	0	0	.000
K. Johnson	0	0	0	0	0	1	0	–
Bloodworth, 2b	0	0	0	0	0	0	0	–
J. Mayo, of	0	0	0	0	0	0	0	–
K. Silvestri, c	0	0	0	0	0	0	0	–

Errors: M. Goliat, G. Hamner, W. Jones, A. Seminick
Stolen Bases: G. Hamner

Individual Pitching

NEW YORK (A.L.)

	W	L	ERA	IP	H	BB	SO	SV
A. Reynolds	1	0	0.87	10.1	7	4	7	1
V. Raschi	1	0	0.00	9	2	1	5	0
W. Ford	1	0	0.00	8.2	7	1	7	0
E. Lopat	0	0	2.25	8	9	0	5	0
T. Ferrick	1	0	0.00	1	1	1	1	0

PHILADELPHIA (N.L.)

	W	L	ERA	IP	H	BB	SO	SV
J. Konstanty	0	1	2.40	15	9	4	3	0
R. Roberts	0	1	1.64	11	11	3	5	0
Heintzelman	0	0	1.17	7.2	4	6	3	0
R. Meyer	0	1	5.40	1.2	4	0	1	0
B. Miller	0	1	27.00	0.1	2	0	0	0

1951 WORLD SERIES

LINE SCORES	PITCHERS (innings pitched)	HOME RUNS (men on)	HIGHLIGHTS

New York (A.L.) defeats New York (N.L.) 4 games to 2

GAME 1 - OCTOBER 4

NY	N	200 003 000	5 10 1	Koslo (9)	Dark (2 on)	Irvin's four hits and steal of home paced the Giant attack as surprise starter Koslo went the distance.
NY	A	010 000 000	1 7 1	Reynolds (6), Hogue (1), Morgan (2)		

GAME 2 - OCTOBER 5

NY	N	000 000 100	1 5 1	Jansen (6), Spencer (2)		Irvin hit safely three times but the Giants had only two more hits off Lopat. Collins contributed a home run to the Yankee cause.
NY	A	110 000 01x	3 6 0	Lopat (9)	Collins	

GAME 3 - OCTOBER 6

NY	A	000 000 011	2 5 2	Raschi (4.1), Hogue (1.2), Ostrowski (2)	Woodling	Stanky kicked the ball out of Rizzuto's glove on a steal attempt, setting up the Giants' explosion in the fifth, capped by Lockman's three-run homer.
NY	N	010 050 00x	6 7 2	Hearn (7.2), Jones (1.1) **SV**	Lockman (2 on)	

GAME 4 - OCTOBER 8

NY	A	010 120 200	6 12 0	Reynolds (9)	DiMaggio (1 on)	DiMaggio, hitless in the first three games, paced the Yankee attack with a single and a two-run homer.
NY	N	100 000 001	2 8 2	Maglie (5), Jones (3), Kennedy (1)		

GAME 5 - OCTOBER 9

NY	A	005 202 400	13 12 1	Lopat (9)	McDougald (3 on), Rizzuto (1 on)	The Yankees took the lead in the Series for the first time as McDougald's grand slam in the third started a rout.
NY	N	100 000 000	1 5 3	Jansen (3), Kennedy (2), Spencer (1.1), Corwin (1.2), Konikowski (1)		

GAME 6 - OCTOBER 10

NY	N	000 010 002	3 11 1	Koslo (6), Hearn (1), Jansen (1)		Bauer's three-run triple in the sixth led the Yankees to victory.
NY	A	100 003 00x	4 7 0	Raschi (6), Sain (2), Kuzava (1) **SV**		

Team totals

		W	AB	H	2B	3B	HR	R	RBI	BA	BB	SO	ERA
NY	A	4	199	49	7	2	5	29	25	.246	26	23	1.87
NY	N	2	194	46	7	1	2	18	15	.237	25	22	4.67

Individual Batting

NEW YORK (A.L.)

	AB	H	2B	3B	HR	R	RBI	BA
P. Rizzuto, ss	25	8	0	0	1	5	3	.320
McDougald, 2b, 3b	23	6	1	0	1	2	7	.261
J. DiMaggio, of	23	6	2	0	1	3	5	.261
Y. Berra, c	23	6	1	0	0	4	0	.261
H. Bauer, of	18	3	0	1	0	0	3	.167
J. Collins, 1b, of	18	4	0	1	2	3	.222
G. Woodling, of	18	3	1	1	1	6	1	.167
B. Brown, 3b	14	5	1	0	0	1	0	.357
J. Coleman, 2b	8	2	0	0	2	0	.250
E. Lopat, p	8	1	0	0	0	0	1	.125
J. Mize, 1b	7	2	1	0	0	2	1	.286
A. Reynolds, p	6	2	0	0	0	0	1	.333
M. Mantle, of	5	1	0	0	0	1	0	.200
V. Raschi, p	2	0	0	0	0	0	0	.000
J. Sain, p	1	0	0	0	0	0	0	.000
B. Martin	0	0	0	0	0	1	0	—
J. Hopp	0	0	0	0	0	0	0	—

Errors: Y. Berra, McDougald, P. Rizzuto, G. Woodling

NEW YORK (N.L.)

	AB	H	2B	3B	HR	R	RBI	BA
W. Lockman, 1b	25	6	2	0	1	1	4	.240
A. Dark, ss	24	10	3	0	1	5	4	.417
M. Irvin, of	24	11	0	1	0	4	2	.458
W. Mays, of	22	4	0	0	1	1	1	.182
E. Stanky, 2b	22	3	0	0	0	3	1	.136
B. Thomson, 3b	21	5	1	0	0	1	2	.238
W. Westrum, c	17	4	1	0	0	1	0	.235
H. Thompson, of	14	2	0	0	0	2	0	.143
D. Koslo, p	5	0	0	0	0	0	0	.000
C. Hartung, of	4	0	0	0	0	0	0	.000
B. Rigney	4	1	0	0	0	0	1	.250
J. Hearn, p	3	0	0	0	0	0	0	.000
L. Jansen, p	2	0	0	0	0	0	0	.000
L. Lohrke	2	0	0	0	0	0	0	.000
R. Noble, c	2	0	0	0	0	0	0	.000
D. Williams	1	0	0	0	0	0	0	.000
S. Yvars	1	0	0	0	0	0	0	.000
S. Maglie, p	1	0	0	0	0	0	0	.000
H. Schenz	0	0	0	0	0	0	0	—

Errors: W. Lockman (2), H. Thompson (2), B. Thomson (2), E. Stanky, W. Westrum, C. Hartung, M. Irvin

Stolen Bases: M. Irvin (2)

Individual Pitching

NEW YORK (A.L.)

	W	L	ERA	IP	H	BB	SO	SV
E. Lopat	2	0	0.50	18	10	3	4	0
A. Reynolds	1	1	4.20	15	16	11	8	0
V. Raschi	1	1	0.87	10.1	12	8	4	0
T. Morgan	0	0	0.00	2	2	1	3	0
J. Ostrowski	0	0	0.00	2	1	0	1	0
B. Hogue	0	0	0.00	2.2	1	0	0	0
J. Sain	0	0	9.00	2	4	2	2	0
B. Kuzava	0	0	0.00	1	0	0	0	1

NEW YORK (N.L.)

	W	L	ERA	IP	H	BB	SO	SV
D. Koslo	1	1	3.00	15	12	7	6	0
L. Jansen	0	2	6.30	10	8	4	6	0
J. Hearn	1	0	1.04	8.2	5	8	1	0
S. Maglie	0	1	7.20	5	8	2	3	0
S. Jones	0	0	2.08	4.1	5	1	2	1
M. Kennedy	0	0	6.00	3	3	1	4	0
G. Spencer	0	0	18.90	3.1	6	3	0	0
Konikowski	0	0	0.00	1	1	0	0	0
A. Corwin	0	0	0.00	1.2	1	0	1	0

1952 WORLD SERIES

LINE SCORES		PITCHERS (innings pitched)	HOME RUNS (men on)	HIGHLIGHTS

New York (A.L.) defeats Brooklyn (N.L.) 4 games to 3

GAME 1 - OCTOBER 1

NY	A	001 000 010	2 6 2	Reynolds (7), Scarborough (1)	McDougald	Snider's two-run homer in the sixth gave the Dodgers a lead they never relinquished.
BKN	N	010 002 01x	4 6 0	Black (9)	Robinson, Snider (1 on), Reese	

GAME 2 - OCTOBER 2

NY	A	000 115 000	7 10 0	Raschi (9)	Martin (2 on)	Martin's double, homer, and four RBIs led the Yankee attack. Brooklyn got all three of their hits in the third.
BKN	N	001 000 000	1 3 1	Erskine (5), Loes (2), Lehman (2)		

GAME 3 - OCTOBER 3

BKN	N	001 010 012	5 11 0	Roe (9)		A passed ball by Berra let in two runs in the ninth. Mize's pinch-hit homer in the bottom of the frame went for naught.
NY	A	010 000 011	3 6 2	Lopat (8.1), Gorman (0.2)	Berra, Mize	

GAME 4 - OCTOBER 4

BKN	N	000 000 000	0 4 1	Black (7), Rutherford (1)		Reynolds allowed four singles and struck out ten as the Yankees scored on Mize's homer in the fourth, and Mantle's triple and Reese's error in the eighth.
NY	A	000 100 01x	2 4 1	Reynolds (9)	Mize	

GAME 5 - OCTOBER 5

BKN	N	010 030 100 01	6 10 0	Erskine (11)	Snider (1 on)	Erskine retired the last 19 batters after the Yankees scored five runs in the fifth. Snider's single drove in the winning run in the eleventh.
NY	A	000 050 000 00	5 5 1	Blackwell (5), Sain (6)	Mize (2 on)	

GAME 6 - OCTOBER 6

NY	A	000 000 210	3 9 0	Raschi (7.2), Reynolds (1.1) SV	Berra, Mantle	Berra's homer, Woodling's single, a balk by Loes, and Raschi's ground single off Loes's knee gave the Yanks the lead in the seventh, and Mantle's homer in the eighth insured the victory.
BKN	N	000 001 010	2 8 1	Loes (8.1), Roe (0.2)	Snider, Snider	

GAME 7 - OCTOBER 7

NY	A	000 111 100	4 10 4	Lopat (3), Reynolds (3), Raschi (0.1), Kuzava (2.2) SV	Woodling, Mantle	The Yankees went ahead on Mantle's homer in the sixth and Kuzava saved the victory by retiring the last eight batters.
BKN	N	000 110 000	2 8 1	Black (5.1), Roe (1.2), Erskine (2)		

Team totals

		W	AB	H	2B	3B	HR	R	RBI	BA	BB	SO	ERA
NY	A	4	232	50	5	2	10	26	24	.216	31	32	2.81
BKN	N	3	233	50	7	0	6	20	18	.215	24	49	3.52

Individual Batting

NEW YORK (A.L.)

	AB	H	2B	3B	HR	R	RBI	BA
M. Mantle, of	29	10	1	1	2	5	3	.345
Y. Berra, c	28	6	1	0	2	2	3	.214
P. Rizzuto, ss	27	4	1	0	0	2	0	.148
McDougald, 3b	25	5	0	0	1	5	3	.200
B. Martin, 2b	23	5	0	0	1	2	4	.217
G. Woodling, of	23	8	1	1	1	4	1	.348
H. Bauer, of	18	1	0	0	0	2	1	.056
J. Mize, 1b	15	6	1	0	3	3	6	.400
J. Collins, 1b	12	0	0	0	0	1	0	.000
I. Noren, of	10	3	0	0	0	0	1	.300
A. Reynolds, p	7	0	0	0	0	0	0	.000
V. Raschi, p	6	1	0	0	0	0	1	.167
E. Lopat, p	3	1	0	0	0	0	1	.333
J. Sain, p	3	0	0	0	0	0	0	.000
R. Houk	1	0	0	0	0	0	0	.000
B. Kuzava, p	1	0	0	0	0	0	0	.000
E. Blackwell, p	1	0	0	0	0	0	0	.000

Errors: McDougald (4), A. Reynolds (2), Y. Berra, B. Martin, P. Rizzuto, G. Woodling
Stolen Bases: McDougald

BROOKLYN (N.L.)

	AB	H	2B	3B	HR	R	RBI	BA
D. Snider, of	29	10	2	0	4	5	8	.345
P. Reese, ss	29	10	0	0	1	4	4	.345
Campanella, c	28	6	0	0	0	0	1	.214
B. Cox, 3b	27	8	2	0	0	4	0	.296
J. Robinson, 2b	23	4	0	0	1	4	2	.174
C. Furillo, of	23	4	2	0	0	1	0	.174
G. Hodges, 1b	21	0	0	0	0	1	1	.000
A. Pafko, of	21	4	0	0	0	2	2	.190
G. Shuba, of	10	3	1	0	0	0	0	.300
C. Erskine, p	6	0	0	0	0	1	0	.000
J. Black, p	6	0	0	0	0	0	0	.000
B. Loes, p	3	1	0	0	0	0	0	.333
R. Nelson	3	0	0	0	0	0	0	.000
P. Roe, p	2	0	0	0	0	0	0	.000
B. Morgan, 3b	1	0	0	0	0	0	0	.000
T. Holmes, of	1	0	0	0	0	0	0	.000
S. Amoros	0	0	0	0	0	0	0	–

Errors: P. Reese (2), B. Cox, G. Hodges
Stolen Bases: J. Robinson (2), D. Snider, B. Loes, P. Reese

Individual Pitching

NEW YORK (A.L.)

	W	L	ERA	IP	H	BB	SO	SV
A. Reynolds	2	1	1.77	20.1	12	6	18	1
V. Raschi	2	0	1.59	17	12	8	18	0
E. Lopat	0	1	4.76	11.1	14	4	3	0
J. Sain	0	1	3.00	6	6	3	3	0
E. Blackwell	0	0	7.20	5	4	3	4	0
B. Kuzava	0	0	0.00	2.2	0	0	2	1
Scarborough	0	0	9.00	1	1	0	1	0
T. Gorman	0	0	0.00	0.2	1	0	0	0

BROOKLYN (N.L.)

	W	L	ERA	IP	H	BB	SO	SV
J. Black	1	2	2.53	21.1	15	8	9	0
C. Erskine	1	1	4.50	18	12	10	10	0
P. Roe	1	0	3.18	11.1	9	6	7	0
B. Loes	0	1	4.35	10.1	11	5	5	0
K. Lehman	0	0	0.00	2	2	1	0	0
Rutherford	0	0	9.00	1	1	1	1	0

1953 WORLD SERIES

LINE SCORES	PITCHERS (innings pitched)	HOME RUNS (men on)	HIGHLIGHTS

New York (A.L.) defeats Brooklyn (N.L.) 4 games to 2

GAME 1 - SEPTEMBER 30

BKN	N	000 013 100	5 12 2	Erskine (1), Hughes (4), **Labine** (1.2), Wade (1.1)	Gilliam, Hodges, Shuba (1 on)	Martin's triple with the bases loaded in the first gave the Yankees the lead, and after the Dodgers tied the score in the sixth, Collins's homer in the seventh provided the go-ahead run.
NY	A	400 010 13x	9 12 0	Reynolds (5.1), **Sain** (3.2)	Berra, Collins	

GAME 2 - OCTOBER 1

BKN	N	000 200 000	2 9 1	**Roe** (8)		Mantle homered in the eighth to break the deadlock.
NY	A	100 000 12x	4 5 0	Lopat (9)	Martin, Mantle (1 on)	

GAME 3 - OCTOBER 2

NY	A	000 010 010	2 6 0	**Raschi** (8)		Erskine struck out 14, including Mantle four times in four appearances, to set a new Series record.
BKN	N	000 011 01x	3 9 0	Erskine (9)	Campanella	

GAME 4 - OCTOBER 3

NY	A	000 020 001	3 9 0	**Ford** (1), Gorman (3), Sain (2), Schallock (2)	McDougald (1 on)	Snider drove in four runs with two doubles and a homer.
BKN	N	300 102 10x	7 12 0	Loes (8), Labine (1) SV	Snider	

GAME 5 - OCTOBER 4

NY	A	105 000 311	11 11 1	**McDonald** (7.2), Kuzava (0.2), Reynolds (0.2) SV	Woodling, Mantle (3 on), Martin (1 on), McDougald	Mantle homered with the bases full after a two-out error by Hodges in the third. A Series record was set as both teams combined for 47 total bases.
BKN	N	010 010 041	7 14 1	**Podres** (2.2), Meyer (4.1), Wade (1), Black (1)	Cox (2 on), Gilliam	

GAME 6 - OCTOBER 5

BKN	N	000 001 002	3 8 3	Erskine (4), Milliken (2), **Labine** (2.1)	Furillo (1 on)	Martin's twelfth hit of the Series in the bottom of the ninth scored Bauer for the winning run. The win gave the Yankees their fifth consecutive World Series crown, an all-time record.
NY	A	210 000 001	4 13 0	Ford (7), **Reynolds** (2)		

Team totals

		W	AB	H	2B	3B	HR	R	RBI	BA	BB	SO	ERA
NY	A	4	201	56	6	4	9	33	32	.279	25	43	4.50
BKN	N	2	213	64	13	1	8	27	26	.300	15	30	4.91

Individual Batting

NEW YORK (A.L.)

	AB	H	2B	3B	HR	R	RBI	BA
M. Mantle, of	24	5	0	0	2	3	7	.208
J. Collins, 1b	24	4	1	0	1	4	2	.167
B. Martin, 2b	24	12	1	2	2	5	8	.500
McDougald, 3b	24	4	0	1	2	2	4	.167
H. Bauer, of	23	6	0	1	0	6	1	.261
Y. Berra, c	21	9	1	0	1	3	4	.429
G. Woodling, of	20	6	0	0	1	5	3	.300
P. Rizzuto, ss	19	6	1	0	0	4	0	.316
J. Mize	3	0	0	0	0	0	0	.000
W. Ford, p	3	1	0	0	0	0	0	.333
E. Lopat, p	3	0	0	0	0	0	0	.000
D. Bollweg, 1b	2	0	0	0	0	0	0	.000
J. McDonald, p	2	1	1	0	0	0	1	.500
V. Raschi, p	2	0	0	0	0	0	0	.000
A. Reynolds, p	2	1	0	0	0	0	0	.500
J. Sain, p	2	1	1	0	0	1	2	.500
I. Noren	1	0	0	0	0	0	0	.000
T. Gorman, p	1	0	0	0	0	0	0	.000
B. Kuzava, p	1	0	0	0	0	0	0	.000

Errors: P. Rizzuto
Stolen Bases: B. Martin, P. Rizzuto

BROOKLYN (N.L.)

	AB	H	2B	3B	HR	R	RBI	BA
J. Gilliam, 2b	27	8	3	0	2	4	4	.296
D. Snider, of	25	8	3	0	1	3	5	.320
J. Robinson, of	25	8	2	0	0	3	2	.320
P. Reese, ss	24	5	0	1	0	0	0	.208
C. Furillo, of	24	8	2	0	1	4	4	.333
B. Cox, 3b	23	7	3	0	1	3	6	.304
Campanella, c	22	6	0	0	1	6	2	.273
G. Hodges, 1b	22	8	0	0	1	3	1	.364
C. Erskine, p	4	1	0	0	0	0	0	.250
B. Loes, p	3	2	0	0	0	0	0	.667
P. Roe, p	3	0	0	0	0	0	0	.000
D. Williams	2	1	0	0	0	0	0	.500
C. Labine, p	2	0	0	0	0	0	0	.000
W. Belardi	2	0	0	0	0	0	0	.000
R. Meyer, p	1	0	0	0	0	0	0	.000
J. Hughes, p	1	0	0	0	0	0	0	.000
G. Shuba	1	1	0	0	0	1	1	1.000
B. Morgan	1	0	0	0	0	0	0	.000
J. Podres, p	1	1	0	0	0	0	0	1.000
D. Thompson, of	0	0	0	0	0	0	0	–

Errors: C. Furillo (2), B. Cox, C. Erskine, J. Hughes, J. Gilliam, G. Hodges
Stolen Bases: G. Hodges, J. Robinson

Individual Pitching

NEW YORK (A.L.)

	W	L	ERA	IP	H	BB	SO	SV
E. Lopat	1	0	2.00	9	9	4	3	0
V. Raschi	0	1	3.38	8	9	3	4	0
A. Reynolds	1	0	6.75	8	9	4	9	1
W. Ford	0	1	4.50	8	9	2	7	0
J. McDonald	1	0	5.87	7.2	12	0	3	0
J. Sain	1	0	4.76	5.2	8	1	1	0
T. Gorman	0	0	3.00	3	4	0	1	0
A. Schallock	0	0	4.50	2	2	1	1	0
B. Kuzava	0	0	13.50	0.2	2	0	1	0

BROOKLYN (N.L.)

	W	L	ERA	IP	H	BB	SO	SV
C. Erskine	1	0	5.79	14	14	9	16	0
B. Loes	1	0	3.38	8	8	2	8	0
P. Roe	0	1	4.50	8	5	4	4	0
C. Labine	0	2	3.60	5	10	1	3	1
J. Hughes	0	0	2.25	4	3	1	3	0
R. Meyer	0	0	6.23	4.1	8	4	5	0
B. Wade	0	0	15.43	2.1	4	1	2	0
B. Milliken	0	0	0.00	2	2	1	0	0
J. Podres	0	1	3.38	2.2	2	1	2	0
J. Black	0	0	9.00	1	1	0	2	0

1954 WORLD SERIES

LINE SCORES	PITCHERS (innings pitched)	HOME RUNS (men on)	HIGHLIGHTS

New York (N.L.) defeats Cleveland (A.L.) 4 games to 0

GAME 1 - SEPTEMBER 29

CLE	A	200 000 000 0	2 8 0	Lemon (9.1)		With the score tied 2-2, Mays made a back-to-the-plate catch of Wertz's 440-foot fly with two men on in the eighth to preserve the tie until the tenth, when Rhodes delivered a pinch homer with two on to win the game.
NY	N	002 000 000 3	5 9 3	Maglie (7), Liddle (0.1), **Grissom** (2.2)	Rhodes (2 on)	

GAME 2 - SEPTEMBER 30

CLE	A	100 000 000	1 8 0	Wynn (7), Mossi (1)	Smith	Rhodes again proved the big gun with a pinch-hit single in the fifth that tied the game and a home run in the seventh that provided an insurance run. The Indians' early lead came on Smith's home run off Antonelli's first pitch.
NY	N	000 020 10x	3 4 0	Antonelli (9)	Rhodes	

GAME 3 - OCTOBER 1

NY	N	103 011 000	6 10 1	Gomez (7.1), Wilhelm (1.2) **SV**		Rhodes pinch-hit for Irvin in the third with the bases loaded and singled to drive in two runs, giving the Giants a 3-0 lead. The Indians broke through in the seventh and knocked Gomez out in the eighth as he faltered behind uneven fielding. Wilhelm relieved and checked the Indians, retiring the last five batters in a row.
CLE	A	000 000 110	2 4 2	Garcia (3), Houtteman (2), Narleski (3), Mossi (1)	Wertz	

GAME 4 - OCTOBER 2

NY	N	021 040 000	7 10 3	Liddle (6.2), Wilhelm (0.2), Antonelli (1.2) **SV**		Rhodes rested as the Giants jumped out to a 7-0 lead to nail down the first National League Series victory since 1946. The Indian pitching staff was the disappointment of the Series as they allowed 21 runs in four games after going through the regular season with a 2.78 ERA.
CLE	A	000 030 100	4 6 2	Lemon (4), Newhouser (0), Narleski (1), Mossi (2), Garcia (2)		

Team totals

		W	AB	H	2B	3B	HR	R	RBI	BA	BB	SO	ERA
NY	N	4	130	33	3	0	2	21	20	.254	17	24	1.46
CLE	A	0	137	26	5	1	3	9	9	.190	16	23	4.84

Individual Batting

NEW YORK (N.L.)

	AB	H	2B	3B	HR	R	RBI	BA
W. Lockman, 1b	18	2	0	0	0	2	0	.111
D. Mueller, of	18	7	0	0	0	4	1	.389
A. Dark, ss	17	7	0	0	0	2	0	.412
W. Mays, of	14	4	1	0	0	4	3	.286
H. Thompson, 3b	11	4	1	0	0	6	2	.364
W. Westrum, c	11	3	0	0	0	0	3	.273
D. Williams, 2b	11	0	0	0	0	0	1	.000
M. Irvin, of	9	2	1	0	0	1	2	.222
D. Rhodes, of	6	4	0	0	2	2	7	.667
R. Gomez, p	4	0	0	0	0	0	0	.000
J. Antonelli, p	3	0	0	0	0	0	1	.000
D. Liddle, p	3	0	0	0	0	0	0	.000
S. Maglie, p	3	0	0	0	0	0	0	.000
M. Grissom, p	1	0	0	0	0	0	0	.000
H. Wilhelm, p	1	0	0	0	0	0	0	.000

Errors: D. Mueller (2), D. Liddle, H. Wilhelm, D. Williams, A. Dark, M. Irvin
Stolen Bases: W. Mays

CLEVELAND (A.L.)

	AB	H	2B	3B	HR	R	RBI	BA
V. Wertz, 1b	16	8	2	1	1	2	3	.500
L. Doby, of	16	2	0	0	0	0	0	.125
B. Avila, 2b	15	2	0	0	0	1	0	.133
A. Smith, of	14	3	0	0	1	2	2	.214
J. Hegan, c	13	2	1	0	0	1	0	.154
A. Rosen, 3b	12	3	0	0	0	0	0	.250
Strickland, ss	9	0	0	0	0	0	0	.000
D. Philley, of	8	1	0	0	0	0	0	.125
W. Westlake, of	7	1	0	0	0	0	0	.143
B. Lemon, p	6	0	0	0	0	0	0	.000
H. Majeski, 3b	6	1	0	0	1	1	3	.167
S. Dente, ss	3	0	0	0	0	1	0	.000
D. Pope, of	3	0	0	0	0	0	0	.000
R. Regalado, 3b	3	1	0	0	0	0	1	.333
E. Wynn, p	2	1	0	0	0	0	0	.500
B. Glynn, 1b	2	1	1	0	0	1	0	.500
D. Mitchell	2	0	0	0	0	0	0	.000
H. Naragon, c	0	0	0	0	0	0	0	—
M. Grasso, c	0	0	0	0	0	0	0	—

Errors: M. Garcia, Strickland, V. Wertz, W. Westlake

Individual Pitching

NEW YORK (N.L.)

	W	L	ERA	IP	H	BB	SO	SV
J. Antonelli	1	0	0.84	10.2	8	7	12	1
R. Gomez	1	0	2.45	7.1	4	3	2	0
D. Liddle	1	0	1.29	7	5	1	2	0
S. Maglie	0	0	2.57	7	7	2	2	0
H. Wilhelm	0	0	0.00	2.1	1	0	3	1
M. Grissom	1	0	0.00	2.2	1	3	2	0

CLEVELAND (A.L.)

	W	L	ERA	IP	H	BB	SO	SV
B. Lemon	0	2	6.75	13.1	16	8	11	0
E. Wynn	0	1	3.86	7	4	2	5	0
M. Garcia	0	1	5.40	5	6	4	4	0
D. Mossi	0	0	0.00	4	3	0	1	0
R. Narleski	0	0	2.25	4	1	1	2	0
A. Houtteman	0	0	4.50	2	2	1	1	0
H. Newhouser	0	0	∞	0.0	1	1	1	0

1955 WORLD SERIES

LINE SCORES	PITCHERS (innings pitched)	HOME RUNS (men on)	HIGHLIGHTS

Brooklyn (N.L.) defeats New York (A.L.) 4 games to 3

GAME 1 - SEPTEMBER 28

BKN	N	021 000 020	5 10 0	Newcombe (5.2), Bessent (1.1), Labine (1)	Furillo, Snider
NY	A	021 102 00x	6 9 1	Ford (8), Grim (1) **SV**	Howard (1 on), Collins, Collins (1 on)

Collins's two-run homer in the sixth put the Yankees ahead 6-3. Robinson stole home in the eighth to bring the Dodgers within one run of a tie.

GAME 2 - SEPTEMBER 29

BKN	N	000 110 000	2 5 2	Loes (3.2), Bessent (0.1), Spooner (3), Labine (1)	
NY	A	000 400 00x	4 8 0	Byrne (9)	

Byrne capped a four-run fourth-inning with a two-run single and became the first lefty to pitch a complete game victory over the Dodgers in 1955.

GAME 3 - SEPTEMBER 30

NY	A	020 000 100	3 7 0	Turley (1.1), Morgan (2.2), Kucks (2), Sturdivant (2)	Mantle
BKN	N	220 200 20x	8 11 1	Podres (9)	Campanella (1 on)

Campanella led the Dodger attack with three hits and three RBIs.

GAME 4 - OCTOBER 1

NY	A	110 102 000	5 9 0	Larsen (4), Kucks (1), Coleman (1), Morgan (1), Sturdivant (1)	McDougald
BKN	N	001 330 10x	8 14 1	Erskine (3), Bessent (1.2), Labine (4.1)	Campanella, Hodges (1 on), Snider (2 on)

Homers by Campanella and Hodges gave the Dodgers a 4-3 lead in the fourth and Snider's three-run homer in the fifth insured the victory.

GAME 5 - OCTOBER 2

NY	A	100 100 110	3 6 0	Grim (6), Turley (2)	Cerv, Berra
BKN	N	021 010 01x	5 9 2	Craig (6), Labine (3) **SV**	Amoros (1 on), Snider, Snider

Three homers off Grim in the first five innings (two by Snider) paced the Dodger victory.

GAME 6 - OCTOBER 3

BKN	N	000 100 000	1 4 1	Spooner (0.1), Meyer (5.2), Roebuck (2)	
NY	A	500 000 00x	5 8 0	Ford (9)	Skowron (2 on)

The Yankees knocked out Spooner with five runs in the first on two walks, singles by Berra and Bauer, and Skowron's homer.

GAME 7 - OCTOBER 4

BKN	N	000 101 000	2 5 0	Podres (9)	
NY	A	000 000 000	0 8 1	Byrne (5.1), Grim (1.2), Turley (2)	

The Dodgers won their first Series on Podres's shutout and two RBIs by Hodges. Amoros saved the game in the sixth with a spectacular running catch of Berra's fly down the left field line.

Team totals

		W	AB	H	2B	3B	HR	R	RBI	BA	BB	SO	ERA
BKN	N	4	223	58	8	1	9	31	30	.260	33	38	3.75
NY	A	3	222	55	4	2	8	26	25	.248	22	39	4.20

Individual Batting

BROOKLYN (N.L.)

	AB	H	2B	3B	HR	R	RBI	BA
Campanella, c	27	7	3	0	2	4	4	.259
C. Furillo, of	27	8	1	0	1	4	3	.296
P. Reese, ss	27	8	1	0	0	5	2	.296
D. Snider, of	25	8	1	0	4	5	7	.320
J. Gilliam, 2b, of	24	7	1	0	0	2	3	.292
G. Hodges, 1b	24	7	0	0	2	5	5	.292
J. Robinson, 3b	22	4	1	1	0	5	1	.182
S. Amoros, of	12	4	0	0	1	3	3	.333
D. Zimmer, 2b	9	2	0	0	0	0	2	.222
J. Podres, p	7	1	0	0	0	1	0	.143
C. Labine, p	4	0	0	0	0	0	0	.000
F. Kellert	3	1	0	0	0	0	0	.333
D. Hoak, 3b	3	1	0	0	0	0	0	.333
D. Newcombe, p	3	0	0	0	0	0	0	.000
R. Meyer, p	2	0	0	0	0	0	0	.000
G. Shuba	1	0	0	0	0	0	0	.000
C. Erskine, p	1	0	0	0	0	0	0	.000
B. Loes, p	1	0	0	0	0	0	0	.000
D. Bessent, p	1	0	0	0	0	0	0	.000

Errors: J. Robinson (2), D. Zimmer (2), Campanella, P. Reese
Stolen Bases: J. Gilliam, J. Robinson

NEW YORK (A.L.)

	AB	H	2B	3B	HR	R	RBI	BA
McDougald, 3b	27	7	0	0	1	2	1	.259
E. Howard, of	26	5	0	0	1	3	3	.192
B. Martin, 2b	25	8	1	1	0	2	4	.320
Y. Berra, c	24	10	1	0	1	5	2	.417
B. Cerv, of	16	2	0	0	1	1	1	.125
I. Noren, of	16	1	0	0	0	0	0	.063
P. Rizzuto, ss	15	4	0	0	0	2	1	.267
H. Bauer, of	14	6	0	0	0	1	1	.429
J. Collins, 1b, of	12	2	0	0	2	6	3	.167
B. Skowron, 1b	12	4	2	0	1	2	3	.333
M. Mantle, of	10	2	0	0	1	1	1	.200
W. Ford, p	6	0	0	0	0	1	0	.000
T. Byrne, p	6	1	0	0	0	0	2	.167
J. Coleman, ss	3	0	0	0	0	0	0	.000
E. Robinson, 1b	3	2	0	0	0	0	1	.667
B. Grim, p	2	0	0	0	0	0	0	.000
D. Larsen, p	2	0	0	0	0	0	0	.000
A. Carey	2	1	0	1	0	0	1	.500
B. Turley, p	1	0	0	0	0	0	0	.000
T. Carroll	0	0	0	0	0	0	0	—

Errors: McDougald, B. Skowron
Stolen Bases: P. Rizzuto (2), J. Collins

Individual Pitching

BROOKLYN (N.L.)

	W	L	ERA	IP	H	BB	SO	SV
J. Podres	2	0	1.00	18	15	4	10	0
C. Labine	1	0	2.89	9.1	6	2	2	1
R. Craig	1	0	3.00	6	4	5	4	0
R. Meyer	0	0	0.00	5.2	4	2	4	0
D. Newcombe	0	1	9.53	5.2	8	2	4	0
C. Erskine	0	0	9.00	3	3	2	3	0
B. Loes	0	1	9.82	3.2	7	1	5	0
K. Spooner	0	1	13.50	3.1	4	3	6	0
D. Bessent	0	0	0.00	3.1	3	1	1	0
E. Roebuck	0	0	0.00	2	1	0	0	0

NEW YORK (A.L.)

	W	L	ERA	IP	H	BB	SO	SV
W. Ford	2	0	2.12	17	13	8	10	0
T. Byrne	1	1	1.88	14.1	8	8	8	0
B. Grim	0	1	4.15	8.2	8	5	8	1
B. Turley	0	1	8.44	5.1	7	4	7	0
D. Larsen	0	1	11.25	4	5	2	2	0
T. Morgan	0	0	4.91	3.2	3	3	1	0
J. Kucks	0	0	6.00	3	4	1	1	0
Sturdivant	0	0	6.00	3	5	2	0	0
R. Coleman	0	0	9.00	1	5	0	1	0

1956 WORLD SERIES

LINE SCORES		PITCHERS (innings pitched)	HOME RUNS (men on)	HIGHLIGHTS

New York (A.L.) defeats Brooklyn (N.L.) 4 games to 3

GAME 1 - OCTOBER 3

NY A — 200 100 000 — 3 9 1 — Ford (3), Kucks (2), Morgan (2), Turley (1) — Mantle (1 on), Martin Robinson, Hodges (2 on)
BKN N — 023 100 00x — 6 9 0 — Maglie (9)

Hodges' three-run homer in the third broke a 2-2 deadlock.

GAME 2 - OCTOBER 5

NY A — 150 100 001 — 8 12 2 — Larsen (1.2), Kucks (0), Byrne (0.1), Sturdivant (0.2), Morgan (2), Turley (0.1), McDermott (3) — Berra (3 on)
BKN N — 061 220 02x — 13 12 0 — Newcombe (1.2), Roebuck (0.1), Bessent (7) — Snider (2 on)

The Yankees used seven pitchers to set a Series record as the Dodgers won the slugfest in the longest nine-inning game in Series history (3 hours, 26 minutes).

GAME 3 - OCTOBER 6

BKN N — 010 001 100 — 3 8 1 — Craig (6), Labine (2)
NY A — 010 003 01x — 5 8 1 — Ford (9) — Martin, Slaughter (2 on)

Slaughter's three-run homer in the sixth put the Yankees ahead to stay.

GAME 4 - OCTOBER 7

BKN N — 000 100 001 — 2 6 0 — Erskine (4), Roebuck (2), Drysdale (2)
NY A — 100 201 20x — 6 7 2 — Sturdivant (9) — Mantle, Bauer (1 on)

Martin's single in the fourth scored the go-ahead run, and homers by Mantle in the sixth and Bauer in the seventh iced the game.

GAME 5 - OCTOBER 8

BKN N — 000 000 000 — 0 0 0 — Maglie (8)
NY A — 000 101 00x — 2 5 0 — Larsen (9) — Mantle

Larsen threw 97 pitches in hurling a perfect game for the first World Series no-hitter.

GAME 6 - OCTOBER 9

NY A — 000 000 000 0 — 0 7 0 — Turley (9.2)
BKN N — 000 000 000 1 — 1 4 0 — Labine (10)

Robinson singled in the winning run in the tenth on a fly ball misjudged by Slaughter.

GAME 7 - OCTOBER 10

NY A — 202 100 400 — 9 10 0 — Kucks (9) — Berra (1 on), Berra (1 on), Howard, Skowron (3 on)
BKN N — 000 000 000 — 0 3 1 — Newcombe (3), Bessent (3), Craig (0), Roebuck (2), Erskine (1)

Kucks allowed three hits and Skowron hit a grand-slam homer to give the Yankees the Series victory.

Team totals

		W	AB	H	2B	3B	HR	R	RBI	BA	BB	SO	ERA
NY	A	4	229	58	6	0	12	33	33	.253	21	43	2.48
BKN	N	3	215	42	8	1	3	25	24	.195	32	47	4.72

Individual Batting

NEW YORK (A.L.)

	AB	H	2B	3B	HR	R	RBI	BA
H. Bauer, of	32	9	0	0	1	3	3	.281
B. Martin, 2b, 3b	27	8	0	0	2	5	3	.296
Y. Berra, c	25	9	2	0	3	5	10	.360
M. Mantle, of	24	6	1	0	3	6	4	.250
McDougald, ss	21	3	0	0	0	0	1	.143
J. Collins, 1b	21	5	2	0	0	2	2	.238
E. Slaughter, of	20	7	0	0	1	6	4	.350
A. Carey, 3b	19	3	0	0	0	2	0	.158
B. Skowron, 1b	10	1	0	0	1	1	4	.100
E. Howard, of	5	2	1	0	1	1	1	.400
W. Ford, p	4	0	0	0	0	0	0	.000
B. Turley, p	4	0	0	0	0	0	0	.000
Sturdivant, p	3	1	0	0	0	0	0	.333
J. Kucks, p	3	0	0	0	0	0	0	.000
D. Larsen, p	3	1	0	0	0	1	1	.333
J. Coleman, 2b	2	0	0	0	0	0	0	.000
T. Byrne, p	1	0	0	0	0	0	0	.000
B. Cerv	1	1	0	0	0	0	0	1.000
McDermott, p	1	1	0	0	0	0	0	1.000
T. Morgan, p	1	1	0	0	0	1	0	1.000
N. Siebern	1	0	0	0	0	0	0	.000
T. Wilson	1	0	0	0	0	0	0	.000

Errors: A. Carey (2), J. Collins (2), B. Skowron, H. Bauer
Stolen Bases: H. Bauer, M. Mantle

BROOKLYN (N.L.)

	AB	H	2B	3B	HR	R	RBI	BA
P. Reese, ss	27	6	0	1	0	3	2	.222
C. Furillo, of	25	6	2	0	0	2	1	.240
J. Gilliam, 2b, of	24	2	0	0	0	2	2	.083
J. Robinson, 3b	24	6	1	0	1	5	2	.250
D. Snider, of	23	7	1	0	1	5	4	.304
G. Hodges, 1b	23	7	2	0	1	5	8	.304
Campanella, c	22	4	1	0	0	2	3	.182
S. Amoros, of	19	1	0	0	0	1	1	.053
S. Maglie, p	5	0	0	0	0	0	0	.000
D. Mitchell	4	0	0	0	0	0	0	.000
C. Neal, 2b	4	0	0	0	0	0	0	.000
C. Labine, p	4	1	1	0	0	0	0	.250
R. Jackson	3	0	0	0	0	0	0	.000
R. Craig, p	2	1	0	0	0	0	0	.500
D. Bessent, p	2	1	0	0	0	0	1	.500
R. Walker	2	0	0	0	0	0	0	.000
D. Newcombe, p	1	0	0	0	0	0	0	.000
C. Erskine, p	1	0	0	0	0	0	0	.000
G. Cimoli, of	0	0	0	0	0	0	0	–

Errors: C. Neal, P. Reese
Stolen Bases: J. Gilliam

Individual Pitching

NEW YORK (A.L.)

	W	L	ERA	IP	H	BB	SO	SV
W. Ford	1	1	5.25	12	14	2	8	0
J. Kucks	1	0	0.82	11	6	3	2	0
B. Turley	0	1	0.82	11	4	8	14	0
D. Larsen	1	0	0.00	10.2	1	4	7	0
Sturdivant	1	0	2.79	9.2	8	8	9	0
T. Morgan	0	1	9.00	4	6	4	3	0
McDermott	0	0	3.00	3	2	3	3	0
T. Byrne	0	0	0.00	0.1	1	0	1	0

BROOKLYN (N.L.)

	W	L	ERA	IP	H	BB	SO	SV
S. Maglie	1	1	2.65	17	14	6	15	0
C. Labine	1	0	0.00	12	8	3	7	0
D. Bessent	1	0	1.80	10	8	3	5	0
R. Craig	0	1	12.00	6	10	3	4	0
C. Erskine	0	1	5.40	5	4	2	2	0
D. Newcombe	0	1	21.21	4.2	11	3	4	0
E. Roebuck	0	0	2.08	4.1	1	0	5	0
D. Drysdale	0	0	9.00	2	2	1	1	0

1957 WORLD SERIES

LINE SCORES	PITCHERS (innings pitched)	HOME RUNS (men on)	HIGHLIGHTS

Milwaukee (N.L.) defeats New York (A.L.) 4 games to 3

GAME 1 - OCTOBER 2

						Pitchers	Home Runs	Highlights
MIL	N	000 000 100	1	5	0	Spahn (5.1), Johnson (0.2), McMahon (2)		Carey knocked out Spahn with a run-scoring single in the sixth and Coleman then squeezed across an insurance run.
NY	A	000 012 00x	3	9	1	Ford (9)		

GAME 2 - OCTOBER 3

						Pitchers	Home Runs	Highlights
MIL	N	011 200 000	4	8	0	Burdette (9)	Logan	The Braves broke a 2-2 tie in the fourth on three singles and an error by Kubek. Covington's spectacular catch snuffed out a Yankee rally in the second.
NY	A	011 000 000	2	7	2	Shantz (3), Ditmar (4), Grim (2)	Bauer	

GAME 3 - OCTOBER 5

						Pitchers	Home Runs	Highlights
NY	A	302 200 500	12	9	0	Turley (1.2), Larsen (7.1)	Kubek, Mantle (1 on), Kubek (2 on)	The Yankees capitalized on 11 walks allowed by six Brave pitchers with Kubek leading the attack with two homers and four RBIs.
MIL	N	010 020 000	3	8	1	Buhl (0.2), Pizarro (1.2), Conley (1.2), Johnson (2), Trowbridge (1), McMahon (2)	Aaron (1 on)	

GAME 4 - OCTOBER 6

						Pitchers	Home Runs	Highlights
NY	A	100 000 003 1	5	11	0	Sturdivant (4), Shantz (3), Kucks (0.2), Byrne (1.1), Grim (0.1),	Howard (2 on)	The Yankees, down 4-1 with two out in the ninth, tied the game on Howard's homer and went ahead in the tenth on Kubek's single and Bauer's triple. In the bottom of the tenth, Jones was ruled hit by a pitch after a long argument, Logan doubled to tie, and Mathews homered to win.
MIL	N	000 400 000 3	7	7	0	Spahn (10)	Aaron (2 on), Torre, Mathews (1 on)	

GAME 5 - OCTOBER 7

						Pitchers	Home Runs	Highlights
NY	A	000 000 000	0	7	0	Ford (7), Turley (1)		Adcock's single in the sixth drove in the only run after Covington's catch robbed McDougald of a possible home run in the fourth.
MIL	N	000 001 00x	1	6	1	Burdette (9)		

GAME 6 - OCTOBER 9

						Pitchers	Home Runs	Highlights
MIL	N	000 010 100	2	4	0	Buhl (2.2), Johnson (4.1), McMahon (1)	Torre, Aaron	Aaron's homer in the top of the seventh tied the score at 2-2, but Bauer homered in the bottom of the inning for the decisive run.
NY	A	002 000 10x	3	7	0	Turley (9)	Berra (1 on), Bauer	

GAME 7 - OCTOBER 10

						Pitchers	Home Runs	Highlights
MIL	N	004 000 010	5	9	1	Burdette (9)	Crandall	Burdette won his third complete game of the Series and posted his second successive shutout as Kubek's error paved the way for four runs in the third.
NY	A	000 000 000	0	7	3	Larsen (2.1), Shantz (0.2), Ditmar (2), Sturdivant (2), Byrne (2)		

Team totals

		W	AB	H	2B	3B	HR	R	RBI	BA	BB	SO	ERA
MIL	N	4	225	47	6	1	8	23	22	.209	22	40	3.48
NY	A	3	230	57	7	1	7	25	25	.248	22	34	2.89

Individual Batting

MILWAUKEE (N.L.)

	AB	H	2B	3B	HR	R	RBI	BA
H. Aaron, of	28	11	0	1	3	5	7	.393
J. Logan, ss	27	5	1	0	1	5	2	.185
W. Covington, of	24	5	1	0	0	1	1	.208
E. Mathews, 3b	22	5	3	0	1	4	4	.227
D. Crandall, c	19	4	0	0	1	1	1	.211
Schoendienst, 2b	18	5	1	0	0	0	0	.278
J. Adcock, 1b	15	3	0	0	0	1	2	.200
A. Pafko, of	14	3	0	0	0	1	0	.214
B. Hazle, of	13	2	0	0	0	2	0	.154
F. Mantilla, 2b	10	0	0	0	0	1	0	.000
F. Torre, 1b	10	3	0	0	2	2	3	.300
L. Burdette, p	8	0	0	0	0	0	0	.000
D. Rice, c	6	1	0	0	0	0	0	.167
W. Spahn, p	4	0	0	0	0	0	0	.000
C. Sawatski	2	0	0	0	0	0	0	.000
N. Jones	2	0	0	0	0	0	0	.000
J. Pizarro, p	1	0	0	0	0	0	0	.000
B. Buhl, p	1	0	0	0	0	0	0	.000
E. Johnson, p	1	0	0	0	0	0	0	.000
J. DeMerit	0	0	0	0	0	0	0	–

Errors: E. Mathews, J. Adcock, B. Buhl
Stolen Bases: W. Covington

NEW YORK (A.L.)

	AB	H	2B	3B	HR	R	RBI	BA
H. Bauer, of	31	8	2	1	2	3	6	.258
T. Kubek, of, 3b	28	8	0	0	2	4	4	.286
Y. Berra, c	25	8	1	0	1	5	2	.320
McDougald, ss	24	6	0	0	0	3	2	.250
J. Coleman, 2b	22	8	2	0	0	2	2	.364
M. Mantle, of	19	5	0	0	1	3	2	.263
J. Lumpe, 3b	14	4	0	0	0	0	2	.286
H. Simpson, 1b	12	1	0	0	0	0	1	.083
E. Slaughter, of	12	3	1	0	0	2	0	.250
E. Howard, 1b	11	3	0	0	1	2	3	.273
A. Carey, 3b	7	2	1	0	0	0	1	.286
J. Collins, 1b	5	0	0	0	0	0	0	.000
W. Ford, p	5	0	0	0	0	0	0	.000
B. Turley, p	4	0	0	0	0	0	0	.000
B. Skowron, 1b	4	0	0	0	0	0	0	.000
D. Larsen, p	2	0	0	0	0	1	0	.000
T. Byrne, p	2	1	0	0	0	0	0	.500
A. Ditmar, p	1	0	0	0	0	0	0	.000
B. Shantz, p	1	0	0	0	0	0	0	.000
Sturdivant, p	1	0	0	0	0	0	0	.000
Richardson, 2b	0	0	0	0	0	0	0	–

Errors: T. Kubek (2), Y. Berra, E. Howard, M. Mantle, McDougald
Stolen Bases: McDougald

Individual Pitching

MILWAUKEE (N.L.)

	W	L	ERA	IP	H	BB	SO	SV
L. Burdette	3	0	0.67	27	21	4	13	0
W. Spahn	1	1	4.70	15.1	18	2	2	0
E. Johnson	0	1	1.29	7	2	1	8	0
D. McMahon	0	0	0.00	5	3	3	5	0
B. Buhl	0	1	10.80	3.1	6	6	4	0
G. Conley	0	0	10.80	1.2	2	1	0	0
J. Pizarro	0	0	10.80	1.2	3	2	1	0
Trowbridge	0	0	45.00	1	2	3	1	0

NEW YORK (A.L.)

	W	L	ERA	IP	H	BB	SO	SV
W. Ford	1	1	1.13	16	11	5	7	0
B. Turley	1	0	2.31	11.2	7	6	12	0
D. Larsen	1	1	3.72	9.2	8	5	6	0
B. Shantz	0	1	4.05	6.2	8	2	7	0
Sturdivant	0	0	6.00	6	6	1	2	0
A. Ditmar	0	0	0.00	6	2	0	2	0
T. Byrne	0	0	5.40	3.1	1	2	1	0
B. Grim	0	1	7.71	2.1	3	0	2	0
J. Kucks	0	0	0.00	0.2	1	1	1	0

1958 WORLD SERIES

LINE SCORES	PITCHERS (innings pitched)	HOME RUNS (men on)	HIGHLIGHTS

New York (A.L.) defeats Milwaukee (N.L.) 4 games to 3

GAME 1 - OCTOBER 1

NY	A	000 120 000 0	3 8 1	Ford (7), **Duren** (2.2)	Skowron, Bauer (1 on)	The Braves won in the tenth on singles by Adcock, Crandall, and Bruton.
MIL	N	000 200 010 1	4 10 0	Spahn (10)		

GAME 2 - OCTOBER 2

NY	A	100 100 003	5 7 0	Turley (0.1), Maas (0.1), Kucks (3.1), Dickson (3), Monroe (1)	Mantle, Bauer, Mantle (1 on)	The Braves battered Turley and Maas for seven runs in the first inning capped by Burdette's homer.
MIL	N	710 000 23x	13 15 1	Burdette (9)	Bruton, Burdette (2 on)	

GAME 3 - OCTOBER 4

MIL	N	000 000 000	0 6 0	Rush (6), McMahon (2)		Bauer drove in all the runs on a single following three walks in the fifth, and a two-run homer off McMahon in the seventh.
NY	A	000 020 20x	4 4 0	Larsen (7), Duren (2) SV	Bauer (1 on)	

GAME 4 - OCTOBER 5

MIL	N	000 001 110	3 9 0	Spahn (9)		Spahn pitched a two-hitter and stopped Bauer's 17-game Series hitting streak. Siebern lost two fly balls in the sun to set up runs for the Braves.
NY	A	000 000 000	0 2 1	Ford (7), Kucks (1), Dickson (1)		

GAME 5 - OCTOBER 6

MIL	N	000 000 000	0 5 0	Burdette (5.1), Pizarro (1.2), Willey (1)		The Yankees broke open the game with a six-run seventh after McDougald's homer gave them a 1-0 lead in the third inning.
NY	A	001 006 00x	7 10 0	Turley (9)	McDougald	

GAME 6 - OCTOBER 8

NY	A	100 001 000 2	4 10 1	Ford (1), Ditmar (3.2), **Duren** (4.2), Turley (0.1) SV	Bauer, McDougald	The Yankees scored twice in the tenth on a homer by McDougald and singles by Howard, Berra, and Skowron. Turley retired Torre with the tying run at third and two out to pick up the save.
MIL	N	110 000 000 1	3 10 4	Spahn (9.2), McMahon (0.1)		

GAME 7 - OCTOBER 9

NY	A	020 000 040	6 8 0	Larsen (2.1), **Turley** (6.2)	Skowron (2 on)	The Yankees became the first team since 1925 to win the Series after being down three games to one as they scored four runs in the eighth after two out on Howard's tie-breaking single and Skowron's homer.
MIL	N	100 001 000	2 5 2	Burdette (8), McMahon (1)	Crandall	

Team totals

		W	AB	H	2B	3B	HR	R	RBI	BA	BB	SO	ERA
NY	A	4	233	49	5	1	10	29	29	.210	21	42	3.39
MIL	N	3	240	60	10	1	3	25	24	.250	27	56	3.71

Individual Batting

NEW YORK (A.L.)

	AB	H	2B	3B	HR	R	RBI	BA
H. Bauer, of	31	10	0	0	4	6	8	.323
McDougald, 2b	28	9	2	0	2	5	4	.321
Y. Berra, c	27	6	3	0	0	3	2	.222
B. Skowron, 1b	27	7	0	0	2	3	7	.259
M. Mantle, of	24	6	0	1	2	4	3	.250
T. Kubek, ss	21	1	0	0	0	0	1	.048
E. Howard, of	18	4	0	0	0	4	2	.222
A. Carey, 3b	12	1	0	0	0	1	0	.083
J. Lumpe, 3b, ss	12	2	0	0	0	0	0	.167
N. Siebern, of	8	1	0	0	0	1	0	.125
Richardson, 3b	5	0	0	0	0	0	0	.000
B. Turley, p	5	1	0	0	0	0	2	.200
W. Ford, p	4	0	0	0	0	1	0	.000
R. Duren, p	3	0	0	0	0	0	0	.000
E. Slaughter	3	0	0	0	0	1	0	.000
D. Larsen, p	2	0	0	0	0	0	0	.000
A. Ditmar, p	1	0	0	0	0	0	0	.000
J. Kucks, p	1	1	0	0	0	0	0	1.000
Throneberry	1	0	0	0	0	0	0	.000

Errors: T. Kubek (2), A. Ditmar
Stolen Bases: E. Howard

MILWAUKEE (N.L.)

	AB	H	2B	3B	HR	R	RBI	BA
Schoendienst, 2b	30	9	3	1	0	5	0	.300
H. Aaron, of	27	9	2	0	0	3	2	.333
W. Covington, of	26	7	0	0	0	2	4	.269
D. Crandall, c	25	6	0	0	1	4	3	.240
J. Logan, ss	25	3	2	0	0	3	2	.120
E. Mathews, 3b	25	4	2	0	0	3	3	.160
F. Torre, 1b	17	3	0	0	0	0	1	.176
B. Bruton, of	17	7	0	0	1	2	2	.412
J. Adcock, 1b	13	4	0	0	1	1	0	.308
W. Spahn, p	12	4	0	0	0	0	3	.333
A. Pafko, of	9	3	1	0	0	0	1	.333
L. Burdette, p	9	1	0	0	1	1	3	.111
H. Hanebrink	2	0	0	0	0	0	0	.000
B. Rush, p	2	0	0	0	0	0	0	.000
C. Wise	1	0	0	0	0	0	0	.000
F. Mantilla, ss	0	0	0	0	0	0	1	0	–

Errors: J. Logan (2), F. Torre (2), Schoendienst, E. Mathews, B. Bruton
Stolen Bases: E. Mathews

Individual Pitching

NEW YORK (A.L.)

	W	L	ERA	IP	H	BB	SO	SV
B. Turley	2	1	2.76	16.1	10	7	13	1
W. Ford	0	1	4.11	15.1	19	5	16	0
R. Duren	1	1	1.93	9.1	7	6	14	1
D. Larsen	1	0	0.96	9.1	9	6	9	0
J. Kucks	0	0	2.08	4.1	4	1	0	0
M. Dickson	0	0	4.50	4	4	0	1	0
A. Ditmar	0	0	0.00	3.2	2	0	2	0
Z. Monroe	0	0	27.00	1	3	1	1	0
D. Maas	0	0	81.00	0.1	2	1	0	0

MILWAUKEE (N.L.)

	W	L	ERA	IP	H	BB	SO	SV
W. Spahn	2	1	2.20	28.2	19	8	18	0
L. Burdette	1	2	5.64	22.1	22	4	12	0
B. Rush	0	1	3.00	6	3	5	2	0
D. McMahon	0	0	5.40	3.1	3	3	5	0
J. Pizarro	0	0	5.40	1.2	2	1	3	0
C. Willey	0	0	0.00	1	0	0	2	0

1959 WORLD SERIES

LINE SCORES		PITCHERS (innings pitched)	HOME RUNS (men on)	HIGHLIGHTS

Los Angeles (N.L.) defeats Chicago (A.L.) 4 games to 2

GAME 1 - OCTOBER 1

LA	N	000 000 000	0 8 3	Craig (2.1), Churn (0.2), Labine (1), Koufax (2), Klippstein (2)		Wynn and Staley subdued the Dodgers as Kluszewski's five RBIs pace the 11-run attack.
CHI	A	207 200 00x	11 11 0	Wynn (7), Staley (2) SV	Kluszewski (1 on), Kluszewski (1 on)	

GAME 2 - OCTOBER 2

LA	N	000 010 300	4 9 1	Podres (6), Sherry (3) SV	Neal, Essegian, Neal (1 on)	Two home runs by Neal and Essegian's two-out pinch homer in the seventh gave the Dodgers the win.
CHI	A	200 000 010	3 8 0	Shaw (6.2), Lown (2.1)		

GAME 3 - OCTOBER 4

CHI	A	000 000 010	1 12 0	Donovan (6.2), Staley (1.1)		Furillo's pinch-hit single in the seventh with the bases full broke a scoreless tie and provided the winning margin.
LA	N	000 000 21x	3 5 0	Drysdale (7), Sherry (2) SV		

GAME 4 - OCTOBER 5

CHI	A	000 000 400	4 10 3	Wynn (2.2), Lown (0.1), Pierce (3), Staley (2)	Lollar (2 on)	Hodges's homer in the eighth broke the deadlock after Lollar's three-run shot in the seventh pulled the White Sox even.
LA	N	004 000 01x	5 9 0	Craig (7), Sherry (2)	Hodges	

GAME 5 - OCTOBER 6

CHI	A	000 100 000	1 5 0	Shaw (7.1), Pierce (0), Donovan (1.2) SV		Rivera's back-to-the-plate catch of Neal's fly with two men on and two out in the seventh choked off a Dodger rally. The White Sox set a Series record by using three pitchers in posting a 1-0 shutout. The game was witnessed by a record crowd of 92,706.
LA	N	000 000 000	0 9 0	Koufax (7), Williams (2)		

GAME 6 - OCTOBER 8

LA	N	002 600 001	9 13 0	Podres (3.1), Sherry (5.2)	Snider (1 on), Moon (1 on), Essegian	The Dodgers jumped to an early 8-0 lead. Kluszewski homered for three runs in the fourth before Sherry came on to check the White Sox. It was Sherry's second win to go along with his two saves.
CHI	A	000 300 000	3 6 1	Wynn (3.1), Donavan (0), Lown (0.2), Staley (3), Pierce (1), Moore (1)	Kluszewski (2 on)	

Team totals

		W	AB	H	2B	3B	HR	R	RBI	BA	BB	SO	ERA
LA	N	4	203	53	3	1	7	21	19	.261	12	27	3.23
CHI	A	2	199	52	10	0	4	23	19	.261	20	33	3.46

Individual Batting

LOS ANGELES (N.L.)

	AB	H	2B	3B	HR	R	RBI	BA
C. Neal, 2b	27	10	2	0	2	4	6	.370
J. Gilliam, 3b	25	6	0	0	0	2	0	.240
G. Hodges, 1b	23	9	0	1	1	2	2	.391
W. Moon, of	23	6	0	0	1	3	2	.261
J. Roseboro, c	21	2	0	0	0	0	1	.095
M. Wills, ss	20	5	0	0	0	2	1	.250
N. Larker, of	16	3	0	0	0	2	0	.188
D. Demeter, of	12	3	0	0	0	2	0	.250
D. Snider, of	10	2	0	0	1	1	2	.200
L. Sherry, p	4	2	0	0	0	0	0	.500
C. Furillo, of	4	1	0	0	0	0	2	.250
J. Podres, p	4	2	1	0	0	1	1	.500
C. Essegian	3	2	0	0	2	2	2	.667
R. Fairly, of	3	0	0	0	0	0	0	.000
R. Craig, p	3	0	0	0	0	0	0	.000
D. Drysdale, p	2	0	0	0	0	0	0	.000
S. Koufax, p	2	0	0	0	0	0	0	.000
D. Zimmer, ss	1	0	0	0	0	0	0	.000
R. Repulski, of	0	0	0	0	0	0	0	–
J. Pignatano, c	0	0	0	0	0	0	0	–

Errors: D. Snider (2), C. Neal, M. Wills
Stolen Bases: J. Gilliam (2), W. Moon, C. Neal, M. Wills

CHICAGO (A.L.)

	AB	H	2B	3B	HR	R	RBI	BA
L. Aparicio, ss	26	8	1	0	0	1	0	.308
J. Landis, of	24	7	0	0	0	6	1	.292
N. Fox, 2b	24	9	3	0	0	4	0	.375
Kluszewski, 1b	23	9	1	0	3	5	10	.391
S. Lollar, c	22	5	0	0	1	3	5	.227
A. Smith, of	20	5	3	0	0	1	1	.250
B. Goodman, 3b	13	3	0	0	0	1	1	.231
J. Rivera, of	11	0	0	0	0	1	0	.000
B. Phillips, 3b, of	10	3	1	0	0	0	0	.300
J. McAnany, of	5	0	0	0	0	0	0	.000
E. Wynn, p	5	1	1	0	0	0	1	.200
B. Shaw, p	4	1	0	0	0	0	0	.250
N. Cash	4	0	0	0	0	0	0	.000
D. Donovan, p	3	1	0	0	0	0	0	.333
S. Esposito, 3b	2	0	0	0	0	0	0	.000
G. Staley, p	1	0	0	0	0	0	0	.000
E. Torgeson, 1b	1	0	0	0	0	1	0	.000
J. Romano	1	0	0	0	0	0	0	.000

Errors: L. Aparicio (2), J. Landis, B. Pierce
Stolen Bases: L. Aparicio, J. Landis

Individual Pitching

LOS ANGELES (N.L.)

	W	L	ERA	IP	H	BB	SO	SV
L. Sherry	2	0	0.71	12.2	8	2	5	2
J. Podres	1	0	4.82	9.1	7	6	4	0
R. Craig	0	1	8.68	9.1	15	5	8	0
S. Koufax	0	1	1.00	9	5	1	7	0
D. Drysdale	1	0	1.29	7	11	4	5	0
Klippstein	0	0	0.00	2	1	0	2	0
S. Williams	0	0	0.00	2	0	2	1	0
C. Labine	0	0	0.00	1	0	0	1	0
C. Churn	0	0	27.00	0.2	5	0	0	0

CHICAGO (A.L.)

	W	L	ERA	IP	H	BB	SO	SV
B. Shaw	1	1	2.57	14	17	2	2	0
E. Wynn	1	1	5.54	13	19	4	10	0
G. Staley	0	1	2.16	8.1	8	0	3	1
D. Donovan	0	1	5.40	8.1	4	3	5	1
B. Pierce	0	0	0.00	4	2	2	3	0
T. Lown	0	0	0.00	3.1	2	1	3	0
R. Moore	0	0	9.00	1	1	0	1	0

1960 WORLD SERIES

LINE SCORES	PITCHERS (innings pitched)	HOME RUNS (men on)	HIGHLIGHTS

Pittsburgh (N.L.) defeats New York (A.L.) 4 games to 3

GAME 1 - OCTOBER 5

NY A 100 100 002   4 13 2   Ditmar (0.1), Coates (3.2), Maas (2), Duren (2)   Maris, Howard (1 on)   Mazeroski's two-run homer in the fourth gave the Pirates enough of a lead to withstand Howard's homer in the ninth.

PIT N 300 201 00x   6 8 0   Law (7), Face (2) SV   Mazeroski (1 on)

GAME 2 - OCTOBER 6

NY A 002 127 301   16 19 1   Turley (8.1), Shantz (0.2) SV   Mantle (1 on), Mantle (2 on)   The two teams combined for a Series record of 32 hits as Mantle led the assault with two homers and five RBIs. Kubek and Richardson scored three runs apiece.

PIT N 000 100 002   3 13 1   Friend (4), Green (1), Labine (0.2), Witt (0.1), Gibbon (2), Cheney (1)

GAME 3 - OCTOBER 8

PIT N 000 000 000   0 4 0   Mizell (0.1), Labine (0.1), Green (3), Witt (1.1), Cheney (2), Gibbon (1)   Richardson set a Series record with 6 RBIs as the Yankees romped behind Ford.

NY A 600 400 00x   10 16 1   Ford (9)   Richardson (3 on), Mantle (1 on)

GAME 4 - OCTOBER 9

PIT N 000 030 000   3 7 0   Law (6.1), Face (2.2) SV   Law's double and Virdon's single capped the Pirates' three-run fifth and gave them the lead. Face retired all eight men he faced in relief of Law.

NY A 000 100 100   2 8 0   Terry (6.1), Shantz (0.2), Coates (2)   Skowron

GAME 5 - OCTOBER 10

PIT N 031 000 001   5 10 2   Haddix (6.1), Face (2.2) SV   Face again pitched 2 2/3 innings of hitless relief to save a Pirate victory.

NY A 011 000 000   2 5 2   Ditmar (1.1), Arroyo (0.2), Stafford (5), Duren (2)   Maris

GAME 6 - OCTOBER 12

NY A 015 002 220   12 17 1   Ford (9)   Ford got his second shutout in another laugher. Richardson hit two triples and established a Series record with 12 RBIs.

PIT N 000 000 000   0 7 1   Friend (2), Cheney (1), Mizell (2), Green (0), Labine (3), Witt (1)

GAME 7 - OCTOBER 13

NY A 000 014 022   9 13 1   Turley (1), Stafford (1), Shantz (5), Coates (0.2), Terry (0.1)   Skowron, Berra (2 on)   Capitalizing on a break when a ground ball took a bad hop and struck Kubek in the neck, the Pirates scored five in the eighth, capped by Smith's three-run homer. New York tied the score but Mazeroski's homer in the bottom of the ninth won it.

PIT N 220 000 051   10 11 0   Law (5), Face (3), Friend (0), Haddix (1)   Nelson (1 on), Smith (2 on), Mazeroski

Team totals

		W	AB	H	2B	3B	HR	R	RBI	BA	BB	SO	ERA
PIT	N	4	234	60	11	0	4	27	26	.256	12	26	7.11
NY	A	3	269	91	13	4	10	55	54	.338	18	40	3.54

Individual Batting

PITTSBURGH (N.L.)

	AB	H	2B	3B	HR	R	RBI	BA
B. Virdon, of	29	7	3	0	0	2	5	.241
R. Clemente, of	29	9	0	0	0	1	3	.310
D. Groat, ss	28	6	2	0	0	3	2	.214
B. Mazeroski, 2b	25	8	2	0	2	4	5	.320
D. Hoak, 3b	23	5	2	0	0	3	3	.217
D. Stuart, 1b	20	3	0	0	0	0	0	.150
G. Cimoli, of	20	5	0	0	0	4	1	.250
S. Burgess, c	18	6	1	0	0	2	0	.333
R. Nelson, 1b	9	3	0	0	1	2	2	.333
H. Smith, c	8	3	0	0	1	1	3	.375
V. Law, p	6	2	1	0	0	1	1	.333
B. Skinner, of	5	1	0	0	0	2	1	.200
D. Schofield, ss	3	1	0	0	0	0	0	.333
H. Haddix, p	3	1	0	0	0	0	0	.333
G. Baker	3	0	0	0	0	0	0	.000
R. Face, p	3	0	0	0	0	0	0	.000
F. Green, p	1	0	0	0	0	0	0	.000
B. Friend, p	1	0	0	0	0	0	0	.000
Christopher	0	0	0	0	0	2	0	—
B. Oldis, c	0	0	0	0	0	0	0	—

Errors: D. Groat (2), D. Hoak, B. Virdon
Stolen Bases: B. Virdon, B. Skinner

NEW YORK (A.L.)

	AB	H	2B	3B	HR	R	RBI	BA
B. Skowron, 1b	32	12	2	0	2	7	6	.375
Richardson, 2b	30	11	2	2	1	8	12	.367
R. Maris, of	30	8	1	0	2	6	2	.267
T. Kubek, ss, of	30	10	1	0	0	6	3	.333
M. Mantle, of	25	10	1	0	3	8	11	.400
Y. Berra, of, c	22	7	0	0	1	6	8	.318
McDougald, 3b	18	5	1	0	0	4	2	.278
B. Cerv, of	14	5	0	0	1	0	1	.357
E. Howard, c	13	6	1	1	1	4	4	.462
C. Boyer, 3b, ss	12	3	2	1	0	1	1	.250
J. Blanchard, c	11	5	2	0	0	2	2	.455
W. Ford, p	8	2	0	0	0	1	2	.250
H. Lopez, of	7	3	0	0	0	0	0	.429
B. Turley, p	4	1	0	0	0	0	0	.250
B. Shantz, p	3	1	0	0	0	0	0	.333
D. Long	3	1	0	0	0	0	0	.333
DeMaestri, ss	2	1	0	0	0	1	0	.500
R. Terry, p	2	0	0	0	0	0	0	.000
B. Stafford, p	1	0	0	0	0	0	0	.000
J. Coates, p	1	0	0	0	0	0	0	.000
L. Arroyo, p	1	0	0	0	0	0	0	.000
E. Grba	0	0	0	0	0	0	0	

Errors: T. Kubek (3), Richardson (2), B. Cerv, R. Maris, McDougald

Individual Pitching

PITTSBURGH (N.L.)

	W	L	ERA	IP	H	BB	SO	SV
V. Law	2	0	3.44	18.1	22	3	8	0
R. Face	0	0	5.23	10.1	9	2	4	3
H. Haddix	2	0	2.45	7.1	6	2	6	0
B. Friend	0	2	13.50	6	13	3	7	0
F. Green	0	0	22.50	4	11	1	3	0
C. Labine	0	0	13.50	4	13	1	2	0
T. Cheney	0	0	4.50	4	4	1	6	0
J. Gibbon	0	0	9.00	3	4	1	2	0
V. Mizell	0	1	15.43	2.1	4	2	1	0
G. Witt	0	0	0.00	2.2	5	2	1	0

NEW YORK (A.L.)

	W	L	ERA	IP	H	BB	SO	SV
W. Ford	2	0	0.00	18	11	2	8	0
B. Turley	1	0	4.82	9.1	15	4	0	0
B. Stafford	0	0	1.50	6	5	1	2	0
R. Terry	0	2	5.40	6.2	7	1	5	0
B. Shantz	0	0	4.26	6.1	4	1	1	1
J. Coates	0	0	5.68	6.1	6	1	3	0
R. Duren	0	0	2.25	4	2	1	5	0
D. Maas	0	0	4.50	2	2	0	1	0
A. Ditmar	0	2	21.60	1.2	6	1	0	0
L. Arroyo	0	0	13.50	0.2	2	0	1	0

1961 WORLD SERIES

LINE SCORES	PITCHERS (innings pitched)	HOME RUNS (men on)	HIGHLIGHTS

New York (A.L.) defeats Cincinnati (N.L.) 4 games to 1

GAME 1 - OCTOBER 4

CIN	N	000 000 000	0 2 0	O'Toole (7), Brosnan (1)			
NY	A	000 101 00x	2 6 0	Ford (9)	Howard, Skowron		

Howard and Skowron powered Ford to his record eighth World Series victory. Richardson had three of the Yankees' six hits.

GAME 2 - OCTOBER 5

CIN	N	000 211 020	6 9 0	Jay (9)	Coleman (1 on)
NY	A	000 200 000	2 4 3	Terry (7), Arroyo (2)	Berra (1 on)

Chacon's alert base-running gave the Reds the go-ahead run. The game was then iced when the Yankees twice intentionally walked batters to face Edwards, and he upset their strategy by batting in runs each time.

GAME 3 - OCTOBER 7

NY	A	000 000 111	3 6 1	Stafford (6.2), Daley (0.1), Arroyo (2)	Blanchard, Maris
CIN	N	001 000 100	2 8 0	Purkey (9)	

Blanchard delivered a clutch pinch-hit homer in the top of the eighth to tie the score before Maris won the game with a homer in the ninth. The Yankees' first run came on a two-out blooper by Berra that scored Kubek when Chacon and Robinson collided on the play.

GAME 4 - OCTOBER 8

NY	A	000 112 300	7 11 0	Ford (5), Coates (4) SV	
CIN	N	000 000 000	0 5 1	O'Toole (5), Brosnan (3), Henry (1)	

An ankle injury forced Ford to retire in the sixth after he extended his Series scoreless inning streak to 32 and eclipsed Ruth's record of 29.2 innings.

GAME 5 - OCTOBER 9

NY	A	510 502 000	13 15 1	Terry (2.1), Daley (6.2)	Blanchard (1 on), Lopez (2 on)
CIN	N	003 020 000	5 11 3	Jay (0.2), Maloney (0.2), K. Johnson (0.2), Henry (1.1), Jones (0.2), Purkey (2), Brosnan (2), Hunt (1)	Robinson (2 on), Post (1 on)

With Mantle and Berra out of the lineup with injuries and with Maris finishing the Series with a .105 batting average, the Yankees resorted to their bench and erupted for five runs in the first and five more in the fourth. Lopez drove in five runs, and Blanchard added two more.

Team totals

		W	AB	H	2B	3B	HR	R	RBI	BA	BB	SO	ERA
NY	A	4	165	42	8	1	7	27	26	.255	24	25	1.60
CIN	N	1	170	35	8	0	3	13	11	.206	8	27	4.91

Individual Batting

NEW YORK (A.L.)

	AB	H	2B	3B	HR	R	RBI	BA
Richardson, 2b	23	9	1	0	0	2	0	.391
T. Kubek, ss	22	5	0	0	0	3	1	.227
E. Howard, c	20	5	3	0	1	5	1	.250
R. Maris, of	19	2	1	0	1	4	2	.105
B. Skowron, 1b	17	6	0	0	1	3	5	.353
C. Boyer, 3b	15	4	2	0	0	0	3	.267
Y. Berra, of	11	3	0	0	1	2	3	.273
J. Blanchard, of	10	4	1	0	2	4	3	.400
H. Lopez, of	9	3	0	1	1	3	7	.333
M. Mantle, of	6	1	0	0	0	0	0	.167
W. Ford, p	5	0	0	0	0	1	0	.000
R. Terry, p	3	0	0	0	0	0	0	.000
B. Stafford, p	2	0	0	0	0	0	0	.000
B. Gardner	1	0	0	0	0	0	0	.000
J. Coates, p	1	0	0	0	0	0	0	.000
B. Daley, p	1	0	0	0	0	0	1	.000
J. Reed, of	0	0	0	0	0	0	0	—

Errors: B. Daley, B. Stafford, L. Arroyo, Y. Berra, C. Boyer
Stolen Bases: Richardson

CINCINNATI (N.L.)

	AB	H	2B	3B	HR	R	RBI	BA
V. Pinson, of	22	2	1	0	0	0	0	.091
E. Kasko, ss	22	7	0	0	0	1	1	.318
G. Coleman, 1b	20	5	0	0	1	2	2	.250
W. Post, of	18	6	1	0	1	3	2	.333
G. Freese, 3b	16	1	1	0	0	0	0	.063
F. Robinson, of	15	3	2	0	1	3	4	.200
E. Chacon, 2b	12	3	0	0	0	2	0	.250
J. Edwards, c	11	4	2	0	0	1	2	.364
Blasingame, 2b	7	1	0	0	0	1	0	.143
D. Gernert	4	0	0	0	0	0	0	.000
J. Jay, p	4	0	0	0	0	0	0	.000
D. Johnson, c	4	2	0	0	0	0	0	.500
J. Lynch	3	0	0	0	0	0	0	.000
B. Purkey, p	3	0	0	0	0	0	0	.000
J. O'Toole, p	3	0	0	0	0	0	0	.000
L. Cardenas	3	1	1	0	0	0	0	.333
G. Bell	3	0	0	0	0	0	0	.000
J. Zimmerman, c	0	0	0	0	0	0	0	—

Errors: G. Coleman, E. Kasko, V. Pinson, B. Purkey

Individual Pitching

NEW YORK (A.L.)

	W	L	ERA	IP	H	BB	SO	SV
W. Ford	2	0	0.00	14	6	1	7	0
R. Terry	0	1	4.82	9.1	12	2	7	0
B. Daley	1	0	0.00	7	5	0	3	0
B. Stafford	0	0	2.70	6.2	7	2	5	0
L. Arroyo	1	0	2.25	4	4	2	3	0
J. Coates	0	0	0.00	4	1	1	2	1

CINCINNATI (N.L.)

	W	L	ERA	IP	H	BB	SO	SV
J. O'Toole	0	2	3.00	12	11	7	4	0
B. Purkey	0	1	1.64	11	6	3	5	0
J. Jay	1	1	5.59	9.2	8	6	6	0
J. Brosnan	0	0	7.50	6	9	4	5	0
B. Henry	0	0	19.29	2.1	4	2	3	0
K. Hunt	0	0	0.00	1	0	1	1	0
K. Johnson	0	0	0.00	0.2	0	0	0	0
S. Jones	0	0	0.00	0.2	0	0	0	0
J. Maloney	0	0	27.00	0.2	4	1	1	0

1962 WORLD SERIES

LINE SCORES	PITCHERS (innings pitched)	HOME RUNS (men on)	HIGHLIGHTS

New York (A.L.) defeats San Francisco (N.L.) 4 games to 3

GAME 1 - OCTOBER 4

NY	A	200 000 121	6 11 0	Ford (9)	Boyer
SF	N	011 000 000	2 10 0	O'Dell (7.1), Larsen (1), Miller (0.2)	

Ford's tenth Series triumph came when Clete Boyer broke a 2-2 tie with his seventh-inning homer.

GAME 2 - OCTOBER 5

NY	A	000 000 000	0 3 1	Terry (7), Daley (1)	
SF	N	100 000 10x	2 6 0	Sanford (9)	McCovey

Sanford held the Yankees to three hits; the lead run scored when Hiller doubled and scored on an infield out. The insurance tally came on McCovey's seventh-inning homer.

GAME 3 - OCTOBER 7

SF	N	000 000 002	2 4 3	Pierce (6), Larsen (1), Bolin (1)	Bailey (1 on)
NY	A	000 000 30x	3 5 1	Stafford (9)	

Maris singled off Pierce to drive in the first two Yankee runs. The Giants rallied on Bailey's homer but fell short.

GAME 4 - OCTOBER 8

SF	N	020 000 401	7 9 1	Marichal (4), Bolin (1.2), Larsen (0.1), O'Dell (3) SV	Haller (1 on), Hiller (3 on)
NY	A	000 002 001	3 9 1	Ford (6), Coates (0.1), Bridges (2.2)	

Hiller connected off Bridges for the first National League grand slam in Series competition, breaking a tie in the seventh.

GAME 5 - OCTOBER 10

SF	N	001 010 001	3 8 2	Sanford (7.1), Miller (0.2)	Pagan
NY	A	000 101 03x	5 6 0	Terry (9)	Tresh (2 on)

Sanford struck out ten, but a three-run homer by Tresh won the game for Terry.

GAME 6 - OCTOBER 15

NY	A	000 010 010	2 3 2	Ford (4.2), Coates (2.1), Bridges (1)	Maris
SF	N	000 320 00x	5 10 1	Pierce (9)	

After a three-day rain delay, Pierce was masterful as Cepeda ignited the Giant attack with three hits.

GAME 7 - OCTOBER 16

NY	A	000 010 000	1 7 0	Terry (9)	
SF	N	000 000 000	0 4 1	Sanford (7), O'Dell (2)	

McCovey's line drive with two out and two on in the ninth was caught by Richardson, providing a dramatic end to the Series.

Team totals

		W	AB	H	2B	3B	HR	R	RBI	BA	BB	SO	ERA
NY	A	4	221	44	6	1	3	20	17	.199	21	39	2.95
SF	N	3	226	51	10	2	5	21	19	.226	12	39	2.66

Individual Batting

NEW YORK (A.L.)

	AB	H	2B	3B	HR	R	RBI	BA
T. Kubek, ss	29	8	1	0	0	2	1	.276
T. Tresh, of	28	9	1	0	1	5	4	.321
Richardson, 2b	27	4	0	0	0	3	0	.148
M. Mantle, of	25	3	1	0	0	2	0	.120
R. Maris, of	23	4	1	0	1	4	5	.174
C. Boyer, 3b	22	7	1	0	1	2	4	.318
E. Howard, c	21	3	1	0	0	1	1	.143
B. Skowron, 1b	18	4	0	1	0	1	1	.222
R. Terry, p	8	1	0	0	0	0	0	.125
W. Ford, p	7	0	0	0	0	0	0	.000
D. Long, 1b	5	1	0	0	0	0	1	.200
B. Stafford, p	3	0	0	0	0	0	0	.000
H. Lopez	2	0	0	0	0	0	0	.000
Y. Berra, c	2	0	0	0	0	0	0	.000
J. Blanchard	1	0	0	0	0	0	0	.000

Errors: C. Boyer (2), W. Ford, T. Kubek, Richardson
Stolen Bases: M. Mantle (2), T. Tresh (2)

SAN FRANCISCO (N.L.)

	AB	H	2B	3B	HR	R	RBI	BA
W. Mays, of	28	7	2	0	0	3	1	.250
C. Hiller, 2b	26	7	3	0	1	4	5	.269
F. Alou, of	26	7	1	1	0	2	1	.269
J. Davenport, 3b	22	3	1	0	0	1	1	.136
O. Cepeda, 1b	19	3	1	0	0	1	2	.158
J. Pagan, ss	19	7	0	0	1	2	2	.368
W. McCovey, of, 1b	15	3	0	1	1	2	1	.200
T. Haller, c	14	4	1	0	1	1	3	.286
E. Bailey, c	14	1	0	0	1	1	2	.071
M. Alou, of	12	4	1	0	0	2	1	.333
H. Kuenn, of	12	1	0	0	0	1	0	.083
J. Sanford, p	7	3	0	0	0	0	0	.429
B. Pierce, p	5	0	0	0	0	0	0	.000
B. O'Dell, p	3	1	0	0	0	0	0	.333
J. Marichal, p	2	0	0	0	0	0	0	.000
J. Orsino, c	1	0	0	0	0	0	0	.000
E. Bowman, ss	1	0	0	0	0	1	0	.000
B. Nieman	0	0	0	0	0	0	0	—

Errors: J. Davenport (3), W. McCovey (2), J. Pagan, C. Hiller, F. Alou
Stolen Bases: W. Mays

Individual Pitching

NEW YORK (A.L.)

	W	L	ERA	IP	H	BB	SO	SV
R. Terry	2	1	1.80	25	17	2	16	0
W. Ford	1	1	4.12	19.2	24	4	12	0
B. Stafford	1	0	2.00	9	4	2	5	0
M. Bridges	0	0	4.91	3.2	4	2	3	0
J. Coates	0	1	6.75	2.2	1	1	3	0
B. Daley	0	0	0.00	1	1	1	1	0

SAN FRANCISCO (N.L.)

	W	L	ERA	IP	H	BB	SO	SV
J. Sanford	1	2	1.93	23.1	16	8	19	0
B. Pierce	1	1	2.40	15	8	2	5	0
B. O'Dell	0	1	4.38	12.1	12	3	9	1
J. Marichal	0	0	0.00	4	2	4	0	0
D. Larsen	1	0	3.86	2.1	1	2	0	0
B. Bolin	0	0	6.75	2.2	4	2	2	0
S. Miller	0	0	0.00	1.1	1	2	0	0

1963 WORLD SERIES

LINE SCORES	PITCHERS (innings pitched)	HOME RUNS (men on)	HIGHLIGHTS

Los Angeles (N.L.) defeats New York (A.L.) 4 games to 0

GAME 1 - OCTOBER 2

LA	N	041 000 000	5 9 0	Koufax (9)	Roseboro (2 on)
NY	A	000 000 020	2 6 0	Ford (5), Williams (3), Hamilton (1)	Tresh (1 on)

Koufax struck out 15 to set a new Series record and Roseboro hit a three-run homer in the second. Yankee pitchers struck out ten Dodgers, bringing the two-team total to 25 strikeouts, also a record.

GAME 2 - OCTOBER 3

LA	N	200 100 010	4 10 1	Podres (8.1), Perranoski (0.2) SV	Skowron
NY	A	000 000 001	1 7 0	Downing (5), Terry (3), Reniff (1)	

Willie Davis drove in two runs in the first on a ball that went for a double after Maris slipped chasing the hit.

GAME 3 - OCTOBER 5

NY	A	000 000 000	0 3 0	Bouton (7), Reniff (1)	
LA	N	100 000 00x	1 4 1	Drysdale (9)	

Drysdale allowed three hits in pitching a shutout, walking only one batter while striking out nine. The Dodgers' run came in the first when Gilliam scored on Tommy Davis's single.

GAME 4 - OCTOBER 6

NY	A	000 000 100	1 6 1	Ford (7), Reniff (1)	Mantle
LA	N	000 010 10x	2 2 1	Koufax (9)	F. Howard

Pepitone lost Boyer's throw in the shirts in the crowd, and Gilliam sped around to third to lead off the seventh. Willie Davis's sacrifice fly then scored him with the winning run.

Team totals

		W	AB	H	2B	3B	HR	R	RBI	BA	BB	SO	ERA
LA	N	4	117	25	3	2	3	12	12	.214	11	25	1.00
NY	A	0	129	22	3	0	2	4	4	.171	5	37	2.91

Individual Batting

LOS ANGELES (N.L.)

	AB	H	2B	3B	HR	R	RBI	BA
T. Davis, of	15	6	0	2	0	0	2	.400
M. Wills, ss	15	2	0	0	0	1	0	.133
J. Roseboro, c	14	2	0	0	1	1	3	.143
B. Skowron, 1b	13	5	0	0	1	2	3	.385
D. Tracewski, 2b	13	2	0	0	0	1	0	.154
J. Gilliam, 3b	13	2	0	0	0	3	0	.154
W. Davis, of	12	2	2	0	0	2	3	.167
F. Howard, of	10	3	1	0	1	2	1	.300
S. Koufax, p	6	0	0	0	0	0	0	.000
J. Podres, p	4	1	0	0	0	0	0	.250
D. Drysdale, p	1	0	0	0	0	0	0	.000
R. Fairly, of	1	0	0	0	0	0	0	.000

Errors: J. Podres, D. Tracewski, M. Wills
Stolen Bases: T. Davis, M. Wills

NEW YORK (A.L.)

	AB	H	2B	3B	HR	R	RBI	BA
T. Kubek, ss	16	3	0	0	0	1	0	.188
E. Howard, c	15	5	0	0	0	0	1	.333
T. Tresh, of	15	3	0	0	1	1	2	.200
M. Mantle, of	15	2	0	0	1	1	1	.133
Richardson, 2b	14	3	1	0	0	0	0	.214
J. Pepitone, 1b	13	2	0	0	0	0	0	.154
C. Boyer, 3b	13	1	0	0	0	0	0	.077
H. Lopez, of	8	2	2	0	0	1	0	.250
R. Maris, of	5	0	0	0	0	0	0	.000
W. Ford, p	3	0	0	0	0	0	0	.000
P. Linz	3	1	0	0	0	0	0	.333
J. Blanchard, of	3	0	0	0	0	0	0	.000
J. Bouton, p	2	0	0	0	0	0	0	.000
H. Bright	2	0	0	0	0	0	0	.000
A. Downing, p	1	0	0	0	0	0	0	.000
Y. Berra	1	0	0	0	0	0	0	.000

Errors: J. Pepitone

Individual Pitching

LOS ANGELES (N.L.)

	W	L	ERA	IP	H	BB	SO	SV
S. Koufax	2	0	1.50	18	12	3	23	0
D. Drysdale	1	0	0.00	9	3	1	9	0
J. Podres	1	0	1.08	8.1	6	1	4	0
Perranoski	0	0	0.00	0.2	1	0	1	1

NEW YORK (A.L.)

	W	L	ERA	IP	H	BB	SO	SV
W. Ford	0	2	4.50	12	10	3	8	0
J. Bouton	0	1	1.29	7	4	5	4	0
A. Downing	0	1	5.40	5	7	1	6	0
H. Reniff	0	0	0.00	3	0	1	1	0
R. Terry	0	0	3.00	3	3	1	0	0
S. Williams	0	0	0.00	3	1	0	5	0
S. Hamilton	0	0	0.00	1	0	0	1	0

1964 WORLD SERIES

LINE SCORES	PITCHERS (innings pitched)	HOME RUNS (men on)	HIGHLIGHTS

St. Louis (N.L.) defeats New York (A.L.) 4 games to 3

GAME 1 - OCTOBER 7

NY	A	030 010 010	5 12 2	Ford (5.1), Downing (1.2), Sheldon (0.2), Mikkelsen (0.1)	Tresh (1 on)	The Cardinals erased a 4-2 deficit with four runs in the sixth as Shannon's homer tied the game, and Warwick's pinch single and Flood's triple drove in the go-ahead runs.
STL	N	110 004 03x	9 12 0	Sadecki (6), Schultz (3) **SV**	Shannon (1 on)	

GAME 2 - OCTOBER 8

NY	A	000 101 204	8 12 0	Stottlemyre (9)	Linz	The Yankees broke the game open with four runs in the ninth after Gibson was removed for a pinch-hitter.
STL	N	001 000 011	3 7 0	Gibson (8), Schultz (0.1), G. Richardson (0.1), Craig (0.1)		

GAME 3 - OCTOBER 10

STL	N	000 010 000	1 6 0	Simmons (8), **Schultz** (0)		Mantle led off the bottom of the ninth with a home run off Schultz's first pitch after Simmons was removed for a pinch-hitter.
NY	A	010 000 001	2 5 2	**Bouton** (9)	Mantle	

GAME 4 - OCTOBER 11

STL	N	000 040 000	4 6 1	Sadecki (0.1) **Craig** (4.2) Taylor (4) **SV**	K. Boyer (3 on)	A grand-slam homer by Ken Boyer in the fifth wiped out a 3-0 Yankee lead. Craig and Taylor allowed only two hits in eight and two-thirds innings of relief pitching.
NY	A	300 000 000	3 6 1	**Downing** (6), Mikkelsen (1), Terry (2)		

GAME 5 - OCTOBER 12

STL	N	000 020 000 3	5 10 1	Gibson (10)	McCarver (2 on)	McCarver's three-run homer in the tenth won after Tresh's two-run homer tied the game with two out in the ninth. Gibson struck out 13.
NY	A	000 000 002 0	2 6 2	Stottlemyre (7), **Reniff** (0.1), Mikkelsen (2.2)	Tresh (1 on)	

GAME 6 - OCTOBER 14

NY	A	000 012 050	8 10 0	**Bouton** (8.1), Hamilton (0.2) **SV**	Maris, Mantle, Pepitone (3 on)	Consecutive homers by Maris and Mantle gave the Yankees a 3-1 lead in the sixth. Pepitone's grand slam in the eighth insured the victory.
STL	N	100 000 011	3 10 1	**Simmons** (6.1), Taylor (0.2), Schultz (0.2), G. Richardson (0.1), Humphreys (1)		

GAME 7 - OCTOBER 15

NY	A	000 003 002	5 9 2	**Stottlemyre** (4), Downing (0), Sheldon (2), Hamilton (1.1), Mikkelsen (0.2)	Mantle (2 on), C. Boyer, Linz	Gibson pitched his second complete game of the Series and struck out nine for a Series total of 31. Richardson set an all-time Series record with 13 hits.
STL	N	000 330 10x	7 10 1	**Gibson** (9)	Brock, K. Boyer	

Team totals

		W	AB	H	2B	3B	HR	R	RBI	BA	BB	SO	ERA
STL	N	4	240	61	8	3	5	32	29	.254	18	39	4.29
NY	A	3	239	60	11	0	10	33	33	.251	25	54	3.77

Individual Batting

ST. LOUIS (N.L.)

	AB	H	2B	3B	HR	R	RBI	BA
C. Flood, of	30	6	0	1	0	5	3	.200
L. Brock, of	30	9	2	0	1	2	5	.300
M. Shannon, of	28	6	0	0	1	6	2	.214
K. Boyer, 3b	27	6	1	0	2	5	6	.222
B. White, 1b	27	3	1	0	0	2	2	.111
D. Groat, ss	26	5	1	1	0	3	1	.192
T. McCarver, c	23	11	1	1	1	4	5	.478
D. Maxvill, 2b	20	4	1	0	0	0	1	.200
B. Gibson, p	9	2	0	0	0	1	0	.222
C. Warwick	4	3	0	0	0	2	1	.750
C. Simmons, p	4	2	0	0	0	0	1	.500
B. Skinner	3	2	1	0	0	0	1	.667
C. James	3	0	0	0	0	0	0	.000
R. Sadecki, p	2	1	0	0	0	0	1	.500
B. Schultz, p	1	0	0	0	0	0	0	.000
J. Buchek, 2b	1	1	0	0	0	1	0	1.000
R. Craig, p	1	0	0	0	0	0	0	.000
R. Taylor, p	1	0	0	0	0	0	0	.000
J. Javier, 2b	0	0	0	0	0	1	0	—

Errors: D. Groat (2), K. Boyer, L. Brock
Stolen Bases: T. McCarver, M. Shannon, B. White

NEW YORK (A.L.)

	AB	H	2B	3B	HR	R	RBI	BA
Richardson, 2b	32	13	2	0	0	3	3	.406
P. Linz, ss	31	7	1	0	2	5	2	.226
R. Maris, of	30	6	0	0	1	4	1	.200
J. Pepitone, 1b	26	4	1	0	1	1	5	.154
M. Mantle, of	24	8	2	0	3	8	8	.333
E. Howard, c	24	7	1	0	0	5	2	.292
C. Boyer, 3b	24	5	1	0	1	2	3	.208
T. Tresh, of	22	6	2	0	2	4	7	.273
Stottlemyre, p	8	1	0	0	0	0	0	.125
J. Bouton, p	7	1	0	0	0	0	1	.143
J. Blanchard	4	1	1	0	0	0	0	.250
A. Downing, p	2	0	0	0	0	0	0	.000
H. Lopez, of	2	0	0	0	0	0	0	.000
M. Hegan	1	0	0	0	0	1	0	.000
W. Ford, p	1	1	0	0	0	0	1	1.000
P. Gonzalez, 3b	1	0	0	0	0	0	0	.000

Errors: C. Boyer (2), P. Linz (2), M. Mantle (2), Richardson (2), E. Howard
Stolen Bases: C. Boyer, Richardson

Individual Pitching

ST. LOUIS (N.L.)

	W	L	ERA	IP	H	BB	SO	SV
B. Gibson	2	1	3.00	27	23	8	31	0
C. Simmons	0	1	2.51	14.1	11	3	8	0
R. Sadecki	1	0	8.53	6.1	12	5	2	0
R. Craig	1	0	0.00	5	2	3	9	0
B. Schultz	0	1	18.00	4	9	3	1	1
R. Taylor	0	0	0.00	4.2	0	1	2	1
B. Humphreys	0	0	0.00	1	0	0	1	0
Richardson	0	0	40.50	0.2	3	2	0	0

NEW YORK (A.L.)

	W	L	ERA	IP	H	BB	SO	SV
Stottlemyre	1	1	3.15	20	18	6	12	0
J. Bouton	2	0	1.56	17.1	15	5	7	0
A. Downing	0	1	8.22	7.2	9	2	5	0
W. Ford	0	1	8.44	5.1	8	1	4	0
P. Mikkelsen	0	1	5.79	4.2	4	2	4	0
S. Hamilton	0	0	4.50	2	3	0	2	1
R. Terry	0	0	0.00	2	2	0	3	0
R. Sheldon	0	0	0.00	2.2	0	2	2	0
H. Reniff	0	0	0.00	0.1	2	0	0	0

1965 WORLD SERIES

LINE SCORES	PITCHERS (innings pitched)	HOME RUNS (men on)	HIGHLIGHTS

Los Angeles (N.L.) defeats Minnesota (A.L.) 4 games to 3

GAME 1 - OCTOBER 6

LA N	010 000 001	2 10 1	Drysdale (2.2), Reed (1.1), Brewer (2), Perranoski (2)	Fairly
MIN A	016 001 00x	8 10 0	Grant (9)	Mincher, Versalles (2 on)

The Twins broke away on a six-run third- inning barrage featuring Versalles's three-run homer and Quilici's two singles.

GAME 2 - OCTOBER 7

LA N	000 000 100	1 7 3	Koufax (6), Perranoski (1.2), Miller (0.1)	
MIN A	000 002 12x	5 9 0	Kaat (9)	

The Twins rolled behind Kaat as Oliva and Killebrew supplied the hitting. Allison made a diving catch of Lefebvre's drive to spark the defense.

GAME 3 - OCTOBER 9

MIN A	000 000 000	0 5 0	Pascual (5), Merritt (2), Klippstein (1)	
LA N	000 211 00x	4 10 1	Osteen (9)	

Roseboro opened the scoring with a single driving in two runs as Osteen checked the Twins on five hits.

GAME 4 - OCTOBER 10

MIN A	000 101 000	2 5 2	Grant (5), Worthington (2), Pleis (1)	Killebrew, Oliva
LA N	110 103 01x	7 10 0	Drysdale (9)	Parker, Johnson

Drysdale returned with an 11-strikeout performance as Fairly drove in three runs.

GAME 5 - OCTOBER 11

MIN A	000 000 000	0 4 1	Kaat (2.1), Boswell (2.2), Perry (3)	
LA N	202 100 20x	7 14 0	Koufax (9)	

Koufax regained his form, striking out ten and scattering four singles. Wills had two singles and two doubles, while Willie Davis stole three bases.

GAME 6 - OCTOBER 13

LA N	000 000 100	1 6 1	Osteen (5), Reed (2), Miller (1)	Fairly
MIN A	000 203 00x	5 6 1	Grant (9)	Allison (1 on), Grant (2 on)

The Twins tied the Series behind Grant's six-hit pitching and his three-run homer.

GAME 7 - OCTOBER 14

LA N	000 200 000	2 7 0	Koufax (9)	Johnson
MIN A	000 000 000	0 3 1	Kaat (3), Worthington (2), Klippstein (1.2), Merritt (1.1) Perry (1)	

Koufax ended the Series with a flourish, earning his second shutout and again fanning ten. Lou Johnson's homer provided the winning margin.

Team totals

	W	AB	H	2B	3B	HR	R	RBI	BA	BB	SO	ERA
LA N	4	234	64	10	1	5	24	21	.274	13	31	2.10
MIN A	3	215	42	7	2	6	20	19	.195	19	54	3.15

Individual Batting

LOS ANGELES (N.L.)

	AB	H	2B	3B	HR	R	RBI	BA
M. Wills, ss	30	11	3	0	0	3	3	.367
R. Fairly, of	29	11	3	0	2	7	6	.379
J. Gilliam, 3b	28	6	1	0	0	2	2	.214
L. Johnson, of	27	8	2	0	2	3	4	.296
W. Davis, of	26	6	0	0	0	3	0	.231
W. Parker, 1b	23	7	0	1	1	3	2	.304
J. Roseboro, c	21	6	1	0	0	1	3	.286
D. Tracewski, 2b	17	2	0	0	0	0	0	.118
J. Lefebvre, 2b	10	4	0	0	0	2	0	.400
S. Koufax, p	9	1	0	0	0	0	1	.111
D. Drysdale, p	5	0	0	0	0	0	0	.000
C. Osteen, p	3	1	0	0	0	0	0	.333
W. Moon	2	0	0	0	0	0	0	.000
W. Crawford	2	1	0	0	0	0	0	.500
J. Kennedy, 3b	1	0	0	0	0	0	0	.000
D. LeJohn	1	0	0	0	0	0	0	.000

Errors: J. Gilliam (2), L. Johnson, J. Kennedy, J. Lefebvre, D. Tracewski
Stolen Bases: M. Wills (3), W. Davis (3), W. Parker (2), J. Roseboro

MINNESOTA (A.L.)

	AB	H	2B	3B	HR	R	RBI	BA
Z. Versalles, ss	28	8	1	1	1	3	4	.286
T. Oliva, of	26	5	1	0	1	2	2	.192
E. Battey, c	25	3	0	1	0	1	2	.120
D. Mincher, 1b	23	3	0	0	1	3	1	.130
H. Killebrew, 3b	21	6	0	0	1	2	2	.286
J. Nossek, of	20	4	0	0	0	0	0	.200
F. Quilici, 2b	20	4	2	0	0	2	1	.200
B. Allison, of	16	2	1	0	1	3	2	.125
Valdespino, of	11	3	1	0	0	1	0	.273
M. Grant, p	8	2	1	0	1	3	3	.250
J. Hall, of	7	1	0	0	0	0	0	.143
J. Kaat, p	6	1	0	0	0	0	2	.167
R. Rollins	2	0	0	0	0	0	0	.000
C. Pascual, p	1	0	0	0	0	0	0	.000
J. Zimmerman, c	1	0	0	0	0	0	0	.000

Errors: F. Quilici (2), Worthington, H. Killebrew, T. Oliva
Stolen Bases: B. Allison, Z. Versalles

Individual Pitching

LOS ANGELES (N.L.)

	W	L	ERA	IP	H	BB	SO	SV
S. Koufax	2	1	0.38	24	13	5	29	0
C. Osteen	1	1	0.64	14	9	5	4	0
D. Drysdale	1	1	3.86	11.2	12	3	15	0
Perranoski	0	0	7.36	3.2	3	4	1	0
H. Reed	0	0	8.10	3.1	2	2	4	0
J. Brewer	0	0	4.50	2	3	0	1	0
B. Miller	0	0	0.00	1.1	0	0	0	0

MINNESOTA (A.L.)

	W	L	ERA	IP	H	BB	SO	SV
M. Grant	2	1	2.74	23	22	2	12	0
J. Kaat	1	2	3.77	14.1	18	2	6	0
C. Pascual	0	1	5.40	5	8	1	0	0
J. Perry	0	0	4.50	4	5	2	4	0
Worthington	0	0	0.00	4	2	2	2	0
J. Merritt	0	0	2.70	3.1	2	0	1	0
Klippstein	0	0	0.00	2.2	2	1	3	0
D. Boswell	0	0	3.38	2.2	3	2	3	0
B. Pleis	0	0	9.00	1	2	0	0	0

1966 WORLD SERIES

LINE SCORES		PITCHERS (innings pitched)	HOME RUNS (men on)	HIGHLIGHTS

Baltimore (A.L.) defeats Los Angeles (N.L.) 4 games to 0

GAME 1 - OCTOBER 5

BAL	A	310 100 000	5 9 0	McNally (2.1), Drabowsky (6.2)	F. Robinson (1 on), B. Robinson
LA	N	011 000 000	2 3 0	Drysdale (2), Moeller (2), Miller (3), Perranoski (2)	Lefebvre

Superb relief work by Drabowsky, who fanned 11 (including six in a row) after rushing to the aid of McNally in the third, preserved the victory for the Orioles. Baltimore took the early lead on back-to-back homers in the first by Frank and Brooks Robinson.

GAME 2 - OCTOBER 6

BAL	A	000 031 020	6 8 0	Palmer (9)	
LA	N	000 000 000	0 4 6	Koufax (6), Perranoski (1.1), Regan (0.2), Brewer (1)	

Palmer blanked the Dodgers as Koufax was victimized by Willie Davis's three successive errors in the fifth.

GAME 3 - OCTOBER 8

LA	N	000 000 000	0 6 0	Osteen (7), Regan (1)	
BAL	A	000 010 00x	1 3 0	Bunker (9)	Blair

Blair's 430-foot homer in the fifth gave Bunker all the edge he needed. The Dodgers doubled the Orioles' hit total, but were unable to score as only one of their six hits went for extra bases.

GAME 4 - OCTOBER 9

LA	N	000 000 000	0 4 0	Drysdale (8)	
BAL	A	000 100 00x	1 4 0	McNally (9)	F. Robinson

The Orioles swept the Series on a fourth-inning homer by Frank Robinson as the Dodgers went scoreless again, completing a streak of 33 consecutive innings without a run.

Team totals

		W	AB	H	2B	3B	HR	R	RBI	BA	BB	SO	ERA
BAL	A	4	120	24	3	1	4	13	10	.200	11	17	0.50
LA	N	0	120	17	3	0	1	2	2	.142	13	28	2.65

Individual Batting

BALTIMORE (A.L.)

	AB	H	2B	3B	HR	R	RBI	BA
L. Aparicio, ss	16	4	1	0	0	0	2	.250
B. Powell, 1b	14	5	1	0	1	1	1	.357
B. Robinson, 3b	14	3	0	0	1	2	1	.214
F. Robinson, of	14	4	0	1	2	4	3	.286
D. Johnson, 2b	14	4	1	0	1	1	1	.286
C. Blefary, of	13	1	0	0	0	0	0	.077
Etchebarren, c	12	1	0	0	0	0	0	.083
P. Blair, of	6	1	0	0	1	2	1	.167
R. Snyder, of	6	1	0	0	0	1	1	.167
J. Palmer, p	4	0	0	0	0	0	0	.000
D. McNally, p	3	0	0	0	0	0	0	.000
W. Bunker, p	2	0	0	0	0	0	0	.000
M. Drabowsky, p	2	0	0	0	0	0	0	.000

LOS ANGELES (N.L.)

	AB	H	2B	3B	HR	R	RBI	BA
W. Davis, of	16	1	0	0	0	0	0	.063
L. Johnson, of	15	4	1	0	1	0	0	.267
J. Roseboro, c	14	1	0	0	0	0	0	.071
W. Parker, 1b	13	3	2	0	0	0	0	.231
M. Wills, ss	13	1	0	0	0	0	0	.077
J. Lefebvre, 2b	12	2	0	0	1	1	1	.167
T. Davis, of	8	2	0	0	0	0	0	.250
R. Fairly, of, 1b	7	1	0	0	0	0	0	.143
J. Gilliam, 3b	6	0	0	0	0	0	1	.000
J. Kennedy, 3b	5	1	0	0	0	0	0	.200
S. Koufax, p	2	0	0	0	0	0	0	.000
C. Osteen, p	2	0	0	0	0	0	0	.000
D. Stuart	2	0	0	0	0	0	0	.000
D. Drysdale, p	2	0	0	0	0	0	0	.000
W. Covington	1	0	0	0	0	0	0	.000
J. Barbieri	1	0	0	0	0	0	0	.000
A. Ferrara	1	1	0	0	0	0	0	1.000
N. Oliver	0	0	0	0	0	0	0	—

Errors: W. Davis (3), Perranoski, R. Fairly, J. Gilliam
Stolen Bases: M. Wills

Individual Pitching

BALTIMORE (A.L.)

	W	L	ERA	IP	H	BB	SO	SV
D. McNally	1	0	1.59	11.1	6	7	5	0
J. Palmer	1	0	0.00	9	4	3	6	0
W. Bunker	1	0	0.00	9	6	1	6	0
M. Drabowsky	1	0	0.00	6.2	1	2	11	0

LOS ANGELES (N.L.)

	W	L	ERA	IP	H	BB	SO	SV
D. Drysdale	0	2	4.50	10	8	3	6	0
C. Osteen	0	1	1.29	7	3	1	3	0
S. Koufax	0	1	1.50	6	6	2	2	0
B. Miller	0	0	0.00	3	2	2	1	0
Perranoski	0	0	5.40	3.1	4	1	2	0
J. Moeller	0	0	4.50	2	1	1	0	0
J. Brewer	0	0	0.00	1	0	0	1	0
P. Regan	0	0	0.00	1.2	0	1	2	0

1967 WORLD SERIES

LINE SCORES	PITCHERS (innings pitched)	HOME RUNS (men on)	HIGHLIGHTS

St. Louis (N.L.) defeats Boston (A.L.) 4 games to 3

GAME 1 - OCTOBER 4

STL	N	001 000 100	2 10 0	B. Gibson (9)
BOS	A	001 000 000	1 6 0	Santiago (7), Wyatt (2)

Home Runs: Santiago

Highlights: Gibson scattered six hits and struck out ten as Brock collected four singles and two stolen bases to pace the Cardinal attack.

GAME 2 - OCTOBER 5

STL	N	000 000 000	0 1 1	Hughes (5.1), Willis (0.2), Hoerner (0.2), Lamabe (1.1)
BOS	A	000 101 30x	5 9 0	Lonborg (9)

Home Runs: Yastrzemski, Yastrzemski (2 on)

Highlights: Lonborg retired the first 20 batters until Javier doubled for the only Cardinal hit of the game. Yastrzemski homered twice for Red Sox.

GAME 3 - OCTOBER 7

BOS	A	000 001 100	2 7 1	Bell (2), Waslewski (3), Stange (2), Osinski (1)
STL	N	120 001 01x	5 10 0	Briles (9)

Home Runs: Smith, Shannon (1 on)

Highlights: Shannon homered with Maxvill on base in the second for the deciding runs. Briles held Boston to seven hits.

GAME 4 - OCTOBER 8

BOS	A	000 000 000	0 5 0	Santiago (0.2), Bell (1.1), Stephenson (2), Morehead (3), Brett (1)
STL	N	402 000 00x	6 9 0	B. Gibson (9)

Highlights: Gibson allowed five hits and coasted to a 6-0 shutout win.

GAME 5 - OCTOBER 9

BOS	A	001 000 002	3 6 1	Lonborg (9)
STL	N	000 000 001	1 3 2	Carlton (6), Washburn (2), Willis (0), Lamabe (1)

Home Runs: Maris

Highlights: Howard's single in the ninth inning with the bases filled scored the deciding run. Maris homered in the bottom of the inning for the Cardinals' only run.

GAME 6 - OCTOBER 11

STL	N	002 000 200	4 8 0	Hughes (3.2), Willis (0.1), Briles (2), Lamabe (0.1), Hoerner (0), Jaster (0.1), Washburn (0.1), Woodshick (1)
BOS	A	010 300 40x	8 12 1	Waslewski (5.1), Wyatt (1.2), Bell (2) SV

Home Runs: Brock (1 on); Petrocelli, Yastrzemski, Smith, Petrocelli

Highlights: Fourth-inning home runs by Yastrzemski, Smith, and Petrocelli set a Series record, and St. Louis tied another record by using eight pitchers.

GAME 7 - OCTOBER 12

STL	N	002 023 000	7 10 1	B. Gibson (9)
BOS	A	000 010 010	2 3 1	Lonborg (6), Santiago (2), Morehead (0.1), Osinski (0.1), Brett (0.1)

Home Runs: B. Gibson, Javier (2 on)

Highlights: Gibson allowed three hits and struck out ten as St. Louis routed Lonborg for the Series victory.

Team totals

		W	AB	H	2B	3B	HR	R	RBI	BA	BB	SO	ERA
STL	N	4	229	51	11	2	5	25	24	.223	17	30	2.66
BOS	A	3	222	48	6	1	8	21	19	.216	17	49	3.39

Individual Batting

ST. LOUIS (N.L.)

	AB	H	2B	3B	HR	R	RBI	BA
L. Brock, of	29	12	2	1	1	8	3	.414
O. Cepeda, 1b	29	3	2	0	0	1	1	.103
C. Flood, of	28	5	1	0	0	2	3	.179
R. Maris, of	26	10	1	0	1	3	7	.385
J. Javier, 2b	25	9	3	0	1	2	4	.360
T. McCarver, c	24	3	1	0	0	3	2	.125
M. Shannon, 3b	24	5	1	0	1	3	2	.208
D. Maxvill, ss	19	3	0	1	0	1	1	.158
B. Gibson, p	11	1	0	0	1	1	1	.091
D. Hughes, p	3	0	0	0	0	0	0	.000
N. Briles, p	3	0	0	0	0	0	0	.000
D. Ricketts	3	0	0	0	0	0	0	.000
B. Tolan	2	0	0	0	0	0	0	.000
E. Spiezio	1	0	0	0	0	0	0	.000
P. Gagliano	1	0	0	0	0	0	0	.000
S. Carlton, p	1	0	0	0	0	0	0	.000
E. Bressoud, ss	0	0	0	0	0	0	0	–

Errors: M. Shannon (2), R. Maris, J. Javier
Stolen Bases: L. Brock (7)

BOSTON (A.L.)

	AB	H	2B	3B	HR	R	RBI	BA
G. Scott, 1b	26	6	1	1	0	3	0	.231
Yastrzemski, of	25	10	2	0	3	4	5	.400
R. Smith, of	24	6	1	0	2	3	3	.250
Petrocelli, ss	20	4	1	0	2	3	3	.200
E. Howard, c	18	2	0	0	0	0	1	.111
D. Jones, 3b	18	7	0	0	0	2	1	.389
J. Adair, 2b	16	2	0	0	0	0	1	.125
J. Foy, 3b	15	2	1	0	0	2	1	.133
K. Harrelson, of	13	1	0	0	0	0	0	.077
M. Andrews, 2b	13	4	0	0	0	2	1	.308
J. Tartabull, of	13	2	0	0	0	1	0	.154
J. Lonborg, p	9	0	0	0	0	0	0	.000
N. Siebern, of	3	1	0	0	0	0	1	.333
M. Ryan, c	2	0	0	0	0	0	0	.000
J. Santiago, p	2	1	0	1	1	1	1	.500
G. Thomas, of	2	0	0	0	0	0	0	.000
R. Gibson, c	2	0	0	0	0	0	0	.000
G. Waslewski, p	1	0	0	0	0	0	0	.000

Errors: Petrocelli (2), J. Foy, L. Stange
Stolen Bases: J. Adair

Individual Pitching

ST. LOUIS (N.L.)

	W	L	ERA	IP	H	BB	SO	SV
B. Gibson	3	0	1.00	27	14	5	26	0
N. Briles	1	0	1.64	11	7	1	4	0
D. Hughes	0	1	5.00	9	9	3	7	0
S. Carlton	0	1	0.00	6	3	2	5	0
J. Lamabe	0	1	6.75	2.2	5	0	4	0
R. Washburn	0	0	0.00	2.1	1	1	2	0
R. Willis	0	0	27.00	1	2	4	1	0
Woodeshick	0	0	0.00	1	1	0	0	0
L. Jaster	0	0	0.00	0.1	2	0	0	0
J. Hoerner	0	0	40.50	0.2	4	1	0	0

BOSTON (A.L.)

	W	L	ERA	IP	H	BB	SO	SV
J. Lonborg	2	1	2.63	24	14	2	11	0
J. Santiago	0	2	5.59	9.2	16	3	6	0
G. Waslewski	0	0	2.16	8.1	4	2	7	0
G. Bell	0	1	5.06	5.1	8	1	1	1
D. Morehead	0	0	0.00	3.1	0	4	3	0
J. Wyatt	1	0	4.91	3.2	1	3	1	0
L. Stange	0	0	0.00	2	3	0	0	0
Stephenson	0	0	9.00	2	3	1	0	0
K. Brett	0	0	0.00	1.1	0	1	1	0
D. Osinski	0	0	6.75	1.1	2	0	0	0

1968 WORLD SERIES

LINE SCORES	PITCHERS (innings pitched)	HOME RUNS (men on)	HIGHLIGHTS

Detroit (A.L.) defeats St. Louis (N.L.) 4 games to 3

GAME 1 - OCTOBER 2

DET A 000 000 000   0 5 3   McLain (5), Dobson (2), McMahon (1)

STL N 000 300 10x   4 6 0   Gibson (9)   Brock

Gibson subdued the Tigers on a Series record 17-strikeout performance as McLain, the first 30-game winner since 1931, lasted only until the sixth.

GAME 2 - OCTOBER 3

DET A 011 003 102   8 13 1   Lolich (9)   Horton, Lolich, Cash

STL N 000 001 000   1 6 1   Briles (5), Carlton (1), Willis (2), Hoerner (1)

Lolich hit his first homer in the majors, aiding his own cause as he allowed the Cardinals six singles.

GAME 3 - OCTOBER 5

STL N 000 040 300   7 13 0   Washburn (5.1), Hoerner (3.2) SV   McCarver (2 on), Cepeda (2 on)

DET A 002 010 000   3 4 0   Wilson (4.1), Dobson (0.2), McMahon (1), Patterson (1), Hiller (2)   Kaline (1 on), McAuliffe

McCarver's go-ahead three-run homer in the fifth and Cepeda's three-run homer in the seventh upended the Tigers.

GAME 4 - OCTOBER 6

STL N 202 200 040   10 13 0   Gibson (9)   Brock, Gibson

DET A 000 100 000   1 5 4   McLain (2.2), Sparma (0.1), Patterson (2), Lasher (2), Hiller (0), Dobson (2)   Northrup

Gibson coasted to his seventh straight victory, a Series record, striking out ten as Brock collected four RBIs.

GAME 5 - OCTOBER 7

STL N 300 000 000   3 9 0   Briles (6.1), Hoerner (0), Willis (1.2)   Cepeda (2 on)

DET A 000 200 30x   5 9 1   Lolich (9)

Brock failed to slide on a play at the plate in the fifth and was tagged out after colliding with Freehan. Detroit went on to win the game on Kaline's bases-loaded single in the seventh.

GAME 6 - OCTOBER 9

DET A 02(10) 010 000   13 12 1   McLain (9)   Northrup (3 on), Kaline

STL N 00 0 000 001   1 9 1   Washburn (2), Jaster (0), Willis (0.2), Hughes (0.1), Carlton (3), Granger (2), Nelson (1)

Northrup's grand slam highlighted the Tigers' ten-run third-inning barrage.

GAME 7 - OCTOBER 10

DET A 000 000 301   4 8 1   Lolich (9)

STL N 000 000 001   1 5 0   Gibson (9)   Shannon

The Tigers won the Series behind Northrup's go-ahead, two-run triple in the seventh. Gibson's eight strikeouts gave him a single-Series record of 35. Key plays came in the sixth when Lolich picked Brock and Flood off first.

Team totals

		W	AB	H	2B	3B	HR	R	RBI	BA	BB	SO	ERA
DET	A	4	231	56	4	3	8	34	33	.242	27	59	3.48
STL	N	3	239	61	7	3	7	27	27	.255	21	40	4.65

Individual Batting

DETROIT (A.L.)

	AB	H	2B	3B	HR	R	RBI	BA
A. Kaline, of	29	11	2	0	2	6	8	.379
M. Stanley, ss, of	28	6	0	1	0	4	0	.214
J. Northrup, of	28	7	0	1	2	4	8	.250
McAuliffe, 2b	27	6	0	0	1	5	3	.222
N. Cash, 1b	26	10	0	0	1	5	5	.385
B. Freehan, c	24	2	1	0	0	0	2	.083
W. Horton, of	23	7	1	1	1	6	3	.304
D. Wert, 3b	17	2	0	0	0	1	2	.118
M. Lolich, p	12	3	0	0	1	2	2	.250
D. McLain, p	6	0	0	0	0	0	0	.000
E. Mathews, 3b	3	1	0	0	0	0	0	.333
T. Matchick	3	0	0	0	0	0	0	.000
J. Price	2	0	0	0	0	0	0	.000
E. Wilson, p	1	0	0	0	0	0	0	.000
W. Comer	1	1	0	0	0	0	0	1.000
G. Brown	1	0	0	0	0	0	0	.000
D. Tracewski, 3b	0	0	0	0	0	1	0	–
R. Oyler, ss	0	0	0	0	0	0	0	–

Errors: J. Northrup (2), M. Stanley (2), N. Cash (2), B. Freehan (2), W. Horton, E. Mathews, D. McLain

ST. LOUIS (N.L.)

	AB	H	2B	3B	HR	R	RBI	BA
M. Shannon, 3b	29	8	1	0	1	3	4	.276
L. Brock, of	28	13	3	1	2	6	5	.464
O. Cepeda, 1b	28	7	0	0	2	2	6	.250
C. Flood, of	28	8	1	0	0	4	2	.286
T. McCarver, c	27	9	0	2	1	3	4	.333
J. Javier, 2b	27	9	1	0	0	1	3	.333
D. Maxvill, ss	22	0	0	0	0	1	0	.000
R. Maris, of	19	3	1	0	0	5	1	.158
B. Gibson, p	8	1	0	0	1	2	2	.125
R. Davis, of	7	0	0	0	0	0	0	.000
N. Briles, p	4	0	0	0	0	0	0	.000
P. Gagliano	3	0	0	0	0	0	0	.000
R. Washburn, p	3	0	0	0	0	0	0	.000
J. Hoerner, p	2	1	0	0	0	0	0	.500
J. Edwards	1	0	0	0	0	0	0	.000
E. Spiezio	1	1	0	0	0	0	0	1.000
B. Tolan	1	0	0	0	0	0	0	.000
D. Ricketts	1	1	0	0	0	0	0	1.000
D. Schofield	0	0	0	0	0	0	0	–

Errors: L. Brock, M. Shannon

Stolen Bases: L. Brock (7), C. Flood (3), J. Javier

Individual Pitching

DETROIT (A.L.)

	W	L	ERA	IP	H	BB	SO	SV
M. Lolich	3	0	1.67	27	20	6	21	0
D. McLain	1	2	3.24	16.2	18	4	13	0
E. Wilson	0	1	6.23	4.1	4	6	3	0
P. Dobson	0	0	3.86	4.2	5	1	0	0
D. Patterson	0	0	0.00	3	1	1	0	0
D. McMahon	0	0	13.50	2	4	0	1	0
J. Hiller	0	0	13.50	2	6	3	1	0
F. Lasher	0	0	0.00	2	1	0	1	0
J. Sparma	0	0	54.00	0.1	2	0	0	0

ST. LOUIS (N.L.)

	W	L	ERA	IP	H	BB	SO	SV
B. Gibson	2	1	1.67	27	18	4	35	0
N. Briles	0	1	5.56	11.1	13	4	7	0
R. Washburn	1	1	9.82	7.1	7	7	6	0
R. Willis	0	0	8.31	4.1	2	4	3	0
J. Hoerner	0	1	3.86	4.2	5	5	3	1
S. Carlton	0	0	6.75	4	7	1	3	0
W. Granger	0	0	0.00	2	0	1	1	0
M. Nelson	0	0	0.00	1	0	0	1	0
D. Hughes	0	0	0.00	0.1	2	0	0	0
L. Jaster	0	0	∞	0.0	2	1	0	0

1969 NATIONAL LEAGUE CHAMPIONSHIP SERIES

LINE SCORES	PITCHERS (innings pitched)	HOME RUNS (men on)	HIGHLIGHTS

New York (East) defeats Atlanta (West) 3 games to 0

GAME 1 - OCTOBER 4

NY	E	020 200 050	9 10 1	Seaver (7), Taylor (2) SV	
ATL	W	012 010 100	5 10 2	Niekro (8), Upshaw (1)	Gonzalez, H. Aaron

Aaron's home run off Seaver gave Atlanta a 5-4 lead in the seventh. But the Mets scored five in the eighth off Niekro as Garrett doubled past Boyer, Jones looped a single to left, Shamsky singled, Jones stole third when caught off second, Kranepool's grounder and Martin pinch hit a two-run single after an intentional pass to Harrelson. The fifth run scored as Gonzalez let Martin's hit bounce past in center.

GAME 2 - OCTOBER 5

NY	E	132 210 200	11 13 1	Koosman (4.2), Taylor (1.1), McGraw (3) SV	Agee (1 on), Boswell (1 on), Jones (1 on)
ATL	W	000 150 000	6 9 3	Reed (1.2), Doyle (1), Pappas (2.1), Britton (0.1), Upshaw (2.2), Neibauer (1)	H. Aaron (2 on)

The Mets piled up an 8-0 lead in four innings, scoring on a double steal and an infield hit in the first, on Agee's homer and a scoring single by Shamsky in the second, and on Boswell's homer in the fourth. Koosman was knocked out in the fifth by Aaron's homer, a walk, Cepeda's double and Boyer's two-run single, all with two out. But with the score 9-6, Taylor and McGraw stifled the Braves while Jones's homer gives New York an extra safety margin in the seventh.

GAME 3 - OCTOBER 6

ATL	W	200 020 000	4 8 1	Jarvis (4.1), Stone (1), Upshaw (2.2)	H. Aaron (1 on), Cepeda (1 on)
NY	E	001 231 00x	7 14 0	Gentry (2), Ryan (7)	Agee, Boswell (1 on), Garrett (1 on)

After Aaron's homer in the first, Ryan relieved Gentry with two on, none out in the third and a one-ball, two-strike count on Carty. He struck out Carty, and got out of the inning. Agee's homer in the third and Boswell's homer in the fourth put the Mets ahead, 3-2, but Cepeda's homer in the fifth made the score 4-3. But in the Met fifth, Garrett greeted reliever Stone with a homer and Jones followed with a double. Boswell's single off Upshaw made it 6-4 and Ryan coasted home.

Team totals

		W	AB	H	2B	3B	HR	R	RBI	BA	BB	SO	ERA
NY	E	3	113	37	8	1	6	27	24	.327	10	25	5.00
ATL	W	0	106	27	9	0	5	15	15	.255	11	20	6.92

Individual Batting

NEW YORK (EAST)

	AB	H	2B	3B	HR	R	RBI	BA
T. Agee, of	14	5	1	0	2	4	4	.357
C. Jones, of	14	6	2	0	1	4	4	.429
A. Shamsky, of	13	7	0	0	0	3	1	.538
W. Garrett, 3b	13	5	2	0	1	3	3	.385
K. Boswell, 2b	12	4	0	0	2	4	5	.333
E. Kranepool, 1b	12	3	1	0	0	2	1	.250
J. Grote, c	12	2	1	0	0	3	1	.167
B. Harrelson, ss	11	2	1	1	0	2	3	.182
N. Ryan, p	4	2	0	0	0	1	0	.500
T. Seaver, p	3	0	0	0	0	0	0	.000
J. Koosman, p	2	0	0	0	0	1	0	.000
J. Martin	2	1	0	0	0	0	2	.500
A. Weis, 2b	1	0	0	0	0	0	0	.000
R. Gaspar, of	0	0	0	0	0	0	0	–

Errors: B. Harrelson, K. Boswell
Stolen Bases: T. Agee (2), C. Jones (2), W. Garrett

ATLANTA (WEST)

	AB	H	2B	3B	HR	R	RBI	BA
H. Aaron, of	14	5	2	0	3	3	7	.357
T. Gonzalez, of	14	5	1	0	1	4	2	.357
F. Millan, 2b	12	4	1	0	0	2	0	.333
B. Didier, c	11	0	0	0	0	0	0	.000
O. Cepeda, 1b	11	5	2	0	1	2	3	.455
R. Carty, of	10	3	2	0	0	4	0	.300
G. Garrido, ss	10	2	0	0	0	0	0	.200
C. Boyer, 3b	9	1	0	0	0	0	3	.111
Aspromonte	3	0	0	0	0	0	0	.000
P. Niekro, p	3	0	0	0	0	0	0	.000
M. Lum, of	2	2	1	0	0	0	0	1.000
P. Jarvis, p	2	0	0	0	0	0	0	.000
F. Alou	1	0	0	0	0	0	0	.000
G. Stone, p	1	0	0	0	0	0	0	.000
C. Upshaw, p	1	0	0	0	0	0	0	.000
M. Pappas, p	1	0	0	0	0	0	0	.000
T. Aaron	1	0	0	0	0	0	0	.000
B. Tillman, c	0	0	0	0	0	0	0	–
S. Jackson, ss	0	0	0	0	0	0	0	–

Errors: O. Cepeda (2), T. Gonzalez, H. Aaron, C. Boyer, F. Millan
Stolen Bases: O. Cepeda

Individual Pitching

NEW YORK (EAST)

	W	L	ERA	IP	H	BB	SO	SV
T. Seaver	1	0	6.43	7	8	3	2	0
N. Ryan	1	0	2.57	7	3	2	7	0
J. Koosman	0	0	11.57	4.2	7	4	5	0
R. Taylor	1	0	0.00	3.1	3	0	4	1
T. McGraw	0	0	0.00	3	1	1	1	1
G. Gentry	0	0	9.00	2	5	1	1	0

ATLANTA (WEST)

	W	L	ERA	IP	H	BB	SO	SV
P. Niekro	0	1	4.50	8	9	4	4	0
C. Upshaw	0	0	2.84	6.1	5	1	4	0
P. Jarvis	0	1	12.46	4.1	10	0	6	0
M. Pappas	0	0	11.57	2.1	4	0	4	0
R. Reed	0	1	21.60	1.2	5	3	3	0
G. Stone	0	0	9.00	1	2	0	1	0
G. Neibauer	0	0	0.00	1	0	0	1	0
P. Doyle	0	0	0.00	1	2	1	3	0
J. Britton	0	0	0.00	0.1	0	1	0	0

1969 AMERICAN LEAGUE CHAMPIONSHIP SERIES

LINE SCORES	PITCHERS (innings pitched)	HOME RUNS (men on)	HIGHLIGHTS

Baltimore (East) defeats Minnesota (West) 3 games to 0

GAME 1 · OCTOBER 4

MIN W 000 010 200 000   3 4 2   Perry (8), **Perranoski** (3.2)   Oliva (1 on)

BAL E 000 110 001 001   4 10 1   **Cuellar** (8), Richert (1), Watt (2), Lopez (0.1), Hall (0.2)   F. Robinson, Belanger, Powell

Belanger raced home with the winning run in the 12th-inning on Blair's two-out suicide squeeze bunt to give Baltimore the edge over Minnesota in the opening of the first Championship Playoff Series since 1897. The American League's Eastern Division winners were boosted by three solo home runs: Frank Robinson's in fourth-inning, Belanger's in the fifth, Powell's in the ninth, which tied the game and erased Minnesota's 3-2 lead which came in the seventh on Oliva's home run with Carew aboard.

GAME 2 · OCTOBER 5

MIN W 000 000 000 00   0 3 1   **Boswell** (10.2), Perranoski (0)

BAL E 000 000 000 01   1 8 0   **McNally** (11)

McNally struck out ten batters in going the extra distance to shut out Minnesota. The duel ended in the 11th-inning when, with two outs, Motton pinch hit for Hendricks and drove in Powell with a liner over second baseman Carew's out-stretched glove. Baltimore again pitched around Killebrew, walking him for the fifth time in two games.

GAME 3 · OCTOBER 6

BAL E 030 201 023   11 18 0   **Palmer** (9)   Blair (1 on)

MIN W 100 010 000   2 10 2   **Miller** (1.2), Woodson (1.2), Hall (0.2), Worthington (1.1), Grzenda (0.2), Chance (2), Perranoski (1)

Baltimore wrapped up the American League pennant by routing Minnesota 11-2, as Blair led the attack with a home run and two doubles in a 5-for-6 day with five RBIs. Buford chipped in with four hits of his own, and Hendricks drove in 3 runs. Baltimore's three-game sweep was aided by their holding Carew, the AL batting champ, to one hit in 14 trips, as well as avoiding Killebrew's power.

Team totals

		W	AB	H	2B	3B	HR	R	RBI	BA	BB	SO	ERA
BAL	E	3	123	36	8	1	4	16	15	.293	13	14	1.13
MIN	W	0	110	17	3	1	1	5	5	.155	12	27	4.02

Individual Batting

BALTIMORE (EAST)

	AB	H	2B	3B	HR	R	RBI	BA
M. Belanger, ss	15	4	0	1	1	4	1	.267
P. Blair, of	15	6	2	0	1	1	6	.400
B. Robinson, 3b	14	7	1	0	0	1	0	.500
D. Buford, of	14	4	1	0	0	3	1	.286
D. Johnson, 2b	13	3	0	0	0	2	0	.231
B. Powell, 1b	13	5	0	0	1	2	1	.385
F. Robinson, of	12	4	2	0	1	1	2	.333
E. Hendricks, c	8	2	2	0	0	2	3	.250
J. Palmer, p	5	0	0	0	0	0	0	.000
D. McNally, p	4	0	0	0	0	0	0	.000
Etchebarren, c	4	0	0	0	0	0	0	.000
M. Cuellar, p	2	0	0	0	0	0	0	.000
C. Motton	2	1	0	0	0	0	1	.500
D. May	1	0	0	0	0	0	0	.000
C. Salmon	1	0	0	0	0	0	0	.000
Rettenmund	0	0	0	0	0	0	0	–

Errors: F. Robinson

MINNESOTA (WEST)

	AB	H	2B	3B	HR	R	RBI	BA
R. Carew, 2b	14	1	0	0	0	0	0	.071
L. Cardenas, ss	13	2	0	1	0	0	0	.154
C. Tovar, of	13	1	0	0	0	0	0	.077
T. Oliva, of	13	5	2	0	1	3	2	.385
R. Reese, 1b	12	2	0	0	0	0	2	.167
H. Killebrew, 3b	8	1	1	0	0	2	0	.125
B. Allison, of	8	0	0	0	0	0	1	.000
Mitterwald, c	7	1	0	0	0	0	0	.143
T. Uhlaender, of	6	1	0	0	0	0	0	.167
J. Roseboro, c	5	1	0	0	0	0	0	.200
D. Boswell, p	4	0	0	0	0	0	0	.000
J. Perry, p	3	0	0	0	0	0	0	.000
Perranoski, p	1	0	0	0	0	0	0	.000
G. Nettles	1	1	0	0	0	0	0	1.000
R. Renick	1	0	0	0	0	0	0	.000
D. Woodson, p	1	1	0	0	0	0	0	1.000
C. Manuel	0	0	0	0	0	0	0	–

Errors: T. Oliva (2), L. Cardenas, T. Uhlaender, R. Carew
Stolen Bases: T. Oliva

Individual Pitching

BALTIMORE (EAST)

	W	L	ERA	IP	H	BB	SO	SV
D. McNally	1	0	0.00	11	3	5	11	0
J. Palmer	1	0	2.00	9	10	2	4	0
M. Cuellar	0	0	2.25	8	3	1	7	0
E. Watt	0	0	0.00	2	0	0	2	0
P. Richert	0	0	0.00	1	0	2	2	0
D. Hall	1	0	0.00	0.2	0	0	1	0
M. Lopez	0	0	0.00	0.1	1	2	0	0

MINNESOTA (WEST)

	W	L	ERA	IP	H	BB	SO	SV
D. Boswell	0	1	0.84	10.2	7	7	4	0
J. Perry	0	0	3.38	8	6	3	3	0
Perranoski	0	1	5.79	4.2	8	0	2	0
D. Chance	0	0	13.50	2	4	0	2	0
B. Miller	0	1	5.40	1.2	5	0	0	0
Worthington	0	0	6.75	1.1	3	0	1	0
D. Woodson	0	0	10.80	1.2	3	3	2	0
T. Hall	0	0	0.00	0.2	0	0	0	0
J. Grzenda	0	0	0.00	0.2	0	0	0	0

1969 WORLD SERIES

LINE SCORES	PITCHERS (innings pitched)	HOME RUNS (men on)	HIGHLIGHTS

New York (N.L.) defeats Baltimore (A.L.) 4 games to 1

GAME 1 · OCTOBER 11

NY	N	000 000 100	1 6 1	Seaver (5), Cardwell (1), Taylor (2)		Buford greeted Seaver with a home run on his second pitch. The Orioles added three in the fourth, and Cuellar scattered six hits for the win.
BAL	A	100 300 00x	4 6 0	Cuellar (9)	Buford	

GAME 2 · OCTOBER 12

NY	N	000 100 001	2 6 0	Koosman (8.2), Taylor (0.1) SV	Clendenon	Koosman pitched six no-hit innings until singles by Blair and Brooks Robinson broke the spell and tied the score. The Mets won the game on two-out singles by Charles, Grote, and Weis in the ninth.
BAL	A	000 000 100	1 2 0	McNally (9)		

GAME 3 · OCTOBER 14

BAL	A	000 000 000	0 4 1	Palmer (6), Leonhard (2)		Agee homered in first and made two spectacular catches (one in left center and one in right center) that saved five runs for Gentry and Ryan.
NY	N	120 001 01x	5 6 0	Gentry (6.2), Ryan (2.1) SV	Agee, Kranepool	

GAME 4 · OCTOBER 15

BAL	A	000 000 001 0	1 6 1	Cuellar (7), Watt (2), Hall (0), Richert (0)		Seaver took a 1-0 lead into ninth, thanks to Clendenon's homer in second. But Frank Robinson and Powell singled with one out, and Swoboda's diving catch robbed Brooks Robinson of a triple but the tying run scored. Grote led off the 10th with a double, and scored when Richert's throw on Martin's bunt hit his wrist and went wide of first.
NY	N	010 000 000 1	2 10 1	Seaver (10)	Clendenon	

GAME 5 · OCTOBER 16

BAL	A	003 000 000	3 5 2	McNally (7), Watt (1)	McNally (1 on), F. Robinson	Third-inning homers by McNally and Frank Robinson gave Baltimore a 3-0 lead. But Clendenon's homer in sixth after a pitch nicked Jones's shoe, and Weis's homer in seventh tied it. Doubles by Jones and Swoboda off Watt scored the winning run in eighth.
NY	N	000 002 12x	5 7 0	Koosman (9)	Clendenon (1 on), Weis	

Team totals

		W	AB	H	2B	3B	HR	R	RBI	BA	BB	SO	ERA
NY	N	4	159	35	8	0	6	15	13	.220	15	35	1.80
BAL	A	1	157	23	1	0	3	9	9	.146	15	28	2.72

Individual Batting

NEW YORK (N.L.)

	AB	H	2B	3B	HR	R	RBI	BA
J. Grote, c	19	4	2	0	0	1	1	.211
C. Jones, of	19	3	1	0	0	2	0	.158
T. Agee, of	18	3	0	0	1	1	1	.167
B. Harrelson, ss	17	3	0	0	0	1	0	.176
R. Swoboda, of	15	6	1	0	0	1	1	.400
E. Charles, 3b	15	2	1	0	0	1	0	.133
D. Clendenon, 1b	14	5	1	0	3	4	4	.357
A. Weis, 2b	11	5	0	0	1	1	3	.455
J. Koosman, p	7	1	1	0	0	0	0	.143
A. Shamsky, of	6	0	0	0	0	0	0	.000
E. Kranepool, 1b	4	1	0	0	1	1	1	.250
T. Seaver, p	4	0	0	0	0	0	0	.000
G. Gentry, p	3	1	1	0	0	0	2	.333
K. Boswell, 2b	3	1	0	0	0	1	0	.333
R. Gaspar, of	2	0	0	0	0	1	0	.000
D. Dyer	1	0	0	0	0	0	0	.000
W. Garrett, 3b	1	0	0	0	0	0	0	.000
J. Martin	0	0	0	0	0	0	0	—

Errors: A. Weis, W. Garrett
Stolen Bases: T. Agee

BALTIMORE (A.L.)

	AB	H	2B	3B	HR	R	RBI	BA
P. Blair, of	20	2	0	0	0	1	0	.100
D. Buford, of	20	2	1	0	1	1	2	.100
B. Robinson, 3b	19	1	0	0	0	0	2	.053
B. Powell, 1b	19	5	0	0	0	0	0	.263
D. Johnson, 2b	16	1	0	0	0	1	0	.063
F. Robinson, of	16	3	0	0	1	2	1	.188
M. Belanger, ss	15	3	0	0	0	2	1	.200
E. Hendricks, c	10	1	0	0	0	1	0	.100
Etchebarren, c	6	0	0	0	0	0	0	.000
M. Cuellar, p	5	2	0	0	0	0	1	.400
D. McNally, p	5	1	0	0	1	1	2	.200
J. Palmer, p	2	0	0	0	0	0	0	.000
C. Dalrymple	2	2	0	0	0	0	0	1.000
D. May	1	0	0	0	0	0	0	.000
C. Motton	1	0	0	0	0	0	0	.000
Rettenmund	0	0	0	0	0	0	0	—
C. Salmon	0	0	0	0	0	0	0	—

Errors: J. Palmer, B. Powell, P. Richert, E. Watt
Stolen Bases: P. Blair

Individual Pitching

NEW YORK (N.L.)

	W	L	ERA	IP	H	BB	SO	SV
J. Koosman	2	0	2.04	17.2	7	4	9	0
T. Seaver	1	1	3.00	15	12	3	9	0
G. Gentry	1	0	0.00	6.2	3	5	4	0
N. Ryan	0	0	0.00	2.1	1	2	3	1
R. Taylor	0	0	0.00	2.1	0	1	3	1
D. Cardwell	0	0	0.00	1	0	0	0	0

BALTIMORE (A.L.)

	W	L	ERA	IP	H	BB	SO	SV
M. Cuellar	1	0	1.13	16	13	4	13	0
D. McNally	0	1	2.81	16	11	5	13	0
J. Palmer	0	1	6.00	6	5	4	5	0
E. Watt	0	1	3.00	3	4	0	3	0
D. Leonhard	0	0	4.50	2	1	1	1	0
P. Richert	0	0	—	0.0	0	0	0	0
D. Hall	0	1	—	0.1	1	1	0	0

1970 NATIONAL LEAGUE CHAMPIONSHIP SERIES

LINE SCORES	PITCHERS (innings pitched)	HOME RUNS (men on)	HIGHLIGHTS

Cincinnati (West) defeats Pittsburgh (East) 3 games to 0

GAME 1 - OCTOBER 3

CIN	W	000 000 000 3	3 9 0	Nolan (9), Carroll (1), SV		
PIT	E	000 000 000 0	0 8 0	Ellis (9.2), Gibbon (0.1)		

Pete Rose's run-scoring single in the 10th inning followed by Lee May's two-run double broke up a scoreless pitching duel between Gary Nolan and Dock Ellis.

GAME 2 - OCTOBER 4

CIN	W	001 010 010	3 8 1	Merritt (5.1), Carroll (0.1), Gullett (3.1), SV	Tolan	
PIT	E	000 001 000	1 5 2	Walker (7), Giusti (2)		

Tolan cracked three hits including a home run, and scored all three Cincinnati runs as starter Jim Merritt earned his seventh straight victory over the Pirates.

GAME 3 - OCTOBER 5

PIT	E	100 010 000	2 10 0	Moose (7.2), Gibbon (0), Giusti (0.1)		
CIN	W	200 000 01x	3 5 0	Cloninger (5), Wilcox (3), Granger (0.1), Gullett (0.1), SV	Perez, Bench	

Pinch hitter Ty Cline walked in the eighth and came home on successive singles by Rose and Tolan, enabling the Reds to snap a 2-2 tie for a sweep.

Team totals

		W	AB	H	2B	3B	HR	R	RBI	BA	BB	SO	ERA
CIN	W	3	100	22	3	1	3	9	8	.220	8	12	0.96
PIT	E	0	102	23	6	0	0	3	3	.225	12	19	2.67

Individual Batting

CINCINNATI (WEST)

	AB	H	2B	3B	HR	R	RBI	BA
P. Rose, of	13	3	0	0	0	1	1	.231
T. Perez, 3b, 1b	12	4	2	0	1	1	2	.333
B. Tolan, of	12	5	0	0	1	3	2	.417
L. May, 1b	12	2	1	0	0	0	2	.167
T. Helms, 2b	11	3	0	0	0	0	0	.273
W. Woodward, ss, 3b	10	1	0	0	0	0	0	.100
J. Bench, c	9	2	0	0	1	2	1	.222
B. Carbo, of	6	0	0	0	0	0	0	.000
H. McRae, of	4	0	0	0	0	0	0	.000
G. Nolan, p	3	1	0	0	0	0	0	.333
J. Merritt, p	2	0	0	0	0	0	0	.000
J. Stewart, of	2	0	0	0	0	0	0	.000
T. Cline, of	1	1	0	1	0	2	0	1.000
T. Cloninger, p	1	0	0	0	0	0	0	.000
A. Bravo	1	0	0	0	0	0	0	.000
D. Gullett, p	1	0	0	0	0	0	0	.000
Concepcion, ss	0	0	0	0	0	0	0	—

Stolen Bases: B. Tolan

PITTSBURGH (EAST)

	AB	H	2B	3B	HR	R	RBI	BA
R. Clemente, of	14	3	0	0	0	1	1	.214
W. Stargell, of	12	6	1	0	0	0	1	.500
M. Alou, of	12	3	1	0	0	1	0	.250
Sanguillen, c	12	2	0	0	0	0	0	.167
A. Oliver, 1b	8	2	0	0	0	0	1	.250
D. Cash, 2b	8	1	1	0	0	1	0	.125
G. Alley, ss	7	0	0	0	0	0	0	.000
R. Hebner, 3b	6	4	2	0	0	0	0	.667
B. Robertson, 1b	5	1	1	0	0	0	0	.200
B. Moose, p	4	0	0	0	0	0	0	.000
J. Pagan, 3b	3	1	0	0	0	0	0	.333
F. Patek, ss	3	0	0	0	0	0	0	.000
D. Ellis, p	2	0	0	0	0	0	0	.000
J. Jeter, of	2	0	0	0	0	0	0	.000
L. Walker, p	2	0	0	0	0	0	0	.000
B. Mazeroski, 2b	2	0	0	0	0	0	0	.000

Errors: L. Walker, Sanguillen

Individual Pitching

CINCINNATI (WEST)

	W	L	ERA	IP	H	BB	SO	SV
G. Nolan	1	0	0.00	9	8	4	6	0
T. Cloninger	0	0	3.60	5	7	4	1	0
J. Merritt	1	0	1.69	5.1	3	0	2	0
D. Gullett	0	0	0.00	3.2	1	2	3	2
M. Wilcox	1	0	0.00	3	1	2	5	0
C. Carroll	0	0	0.00	1.1	2	0	2	1
W. Granger	0	0	0.00	0.2	1	0	0	0

PITTSBURGH (EAST)

	W	L	ERA	IP	H	BB	SO	SV
D. Ellis	0	1	2.79	9.2	9	4	1	0
L. Walker	0	1	1.29	7	5	1	5	0
B. Moose	0	1	3.52	7.2	4	2	4	0
D. Giusti	0	0	3.86	2.1	3	1	1	0
J. Gibbon	0	0	0.00	0.1	1	0	1	0

1970 AMERICAN LEAGUE CHAMPIONSHIP SERIES

LINE SCORES	PITCHERS (innings pitched)	HOME RUNS (men on)	HIGHLIGHTS

Baltimore (East) defeats Minnesota (West) 3 games to 0

GAME 1 - OCTOBER 3

BAL E 020 701 000 — 10 13 0 — Cuellar (4.1), R. Hall (4.2) — Buford, Cuellar (3 on), Powell (1 on) — With the score tied at 2-2 in the fourth inning, the Orioles erupted for seven runs to hang the defeat on Twins starter Jim Perry. Pitcher Mike Cuellar's grand slam homer led the attack.

MIN W 110 130 000 — 6 11 2 — Perry (3.1), Zepp (0.2), Woodson (1), Williams (3), Perranoski (1) — Killebrew (1 on)

GAME 2 - OCTOBER 4

BAL E 102 100 007 — 11 13 0 — McNally (9) — F. Robinson (1 on), Johnson (2 on), Killebrew (1 on), Oliva — Dave McNally went the distance, permitting six hits, the Minnesota runs coming on home runs by Harmon Killebrew and Tony Oliva.

MIN W 000 300 000 — 3 6 2 — T. Hall (3.1), Zepp (2.3), Williams (3), Perranoski (1), Tiant (0.2)

GAME 3 - OCTOBER 5

MIN W 000 010 000 — 1 7 2 — Kaat (2), Blyleven (2), Hall (2), Perry (2) — Brooks Robinson enjoyed another 3-hit game and Davey Johnson hit another homer as the Orioles wrapped up the pennant early, scoring five runs in the first three innings.

BAL E 113 000 10x — 6 10 0 — Palmer (9) — Johnson

Team totals

		W	AB	H	2B	3B	HR	R	RBI	BA	BB	SO	ERA
BAL	E	3	109	36	7	0	6	27	24	.330	12	19	3.33
MIN	W	0	101	24	4	1	3	10	10	.238	9	22	7.62

Individual Batting

BALTIMORE (EAST)

	AB	H	2B	3B	HR	R	RBI	BA
B. Powell, 1b	14	6	2	0	1	2	6	.429
P. Blair, of	13	1	0	0	0	0	0	.077
M. Belanger, ss	12	4	0	0	0	5	1	.333
B. Robinson, 3b	12	7	2	0	0	4	1	.583
D. Johnson, 2b	11	4	0	0	2	4	4	.364
F. Robinson, of	10	2	0	0	1	3	2	.200
Etchebarren, c	9	1	0	0	1	0	1	.111
D. Buford, of	7	3	1	0	1	2	3	.429
D. McNally, p	5	2	1	0	0	1	1	.400
E. Hendricks, c	5	2	0	0	0	2	0	.400
J. Palmer, p	4	1	1	0	0	1	1	.250
Rettenmund, of	3	1	0	0	0	1	1	.333
D. Hall, p	2	1	0	0	0	0	0	.500
M. Cuellar, p	2	1	0	0	1	1	4	.500

Stolen Bases: Rettenmund, D. McNally

MINNESOTA (WEST)

	AB	H	2B	3B	HR	R	RBI	BA
C. Tovar, of, 2b	13	5	0	1	0	2	1	.385
T. Oliva, of	12	6	2	0	1	2	1	.500
L. Cardenas, ss	11	2	0	0	0	1	1	.182
H. Killebrew, 3b, 1b	11	3	0	0	2	2	4	.273
Mitterwald, c	8	4	1	0	0	2	2	.500
D. Thompson, 2b	8	1	1	0	0	0	0	.125
B. Alyea, of	7	0	0	0	0	1	0	.000
R. Reese, 1b	7	1	0	0	0	0	0	.143
R. Renick, 3b	5	1	0	0	0	0	0	.200
J. Holt, of	5	0	0	0	0	0	0	.000
P. Ratliff, c	4	1	0	0	0	0	0	.250
F. Quilici, 2b	2	0	0	0	0	0	0	.000
B. Allison	2	0	0	0	0	0	0	.000
R. Carew	2	0	0	0	0	0	0	.000
T. Hall, p	1	0	0	0	0	0	0	.000
C. Manuel	1	0	0	0	0	0	0	.000
J. Kaat, p	1	0	0	0	0	0	0	.000
J. Perry, p	1	0	0	0	0	0	0	.000

Errors: L. Cardenas (2), P. Ratliff, J. Holt, D. Thompson

Individual Pitching

BALTIMORE (EAST)

	W	L	ERA	IP	H	BB	SO	SV
D. McNally	1	0	3.00	9	6	5	5	0
J. Palmer	1	0	1.00	9	7	3	12	0
M. Cuellar	0	0	12.46	4.1	10	1	2	0
D. Hall	1	0	0.00	4.2	1	0	3	0

MINNESOTA (WEST)

	W	L	ERA	IP	H	BB	SO	SV
S. Williams	0	0	0.00	6	2	1	2	0
T. Hall	0	1	6.75	5.1	6	4	6	0
J. Perry	0	1	13.50	5.1	10	1	3	0
B. Blyleven	0	0	0.00	2	2	0	2	0
J. Kaat	0	1	9.00	2	6	2	1	0
Perranoski	0	0	19.29	2.1	5	1	3	0
D. Woodson	0	0	9.00	1	2	1	0	0
B. Zepp	0	0	6.75	1.1	2	2	2	0
L. Tiant	0	0	13.50	0.2	1	0	0	0

1970 WORLD SERIES

LINE SCORES	PITCHERS (innings pitched)	HOME RUNS (men on)	HIGHLIGHTS

Baltimore (A.L.) defeats Cincinnati (N.L.) 4 games to 1

GAME 1 - OCTOBER 10

BAL A 000 210 100   4 7 2   Palmer (8.2), Richert (0.1), **SV**   Powell (1 on), Hendricks, B. Robinson

CIN N 102 000 000   3 5 0   Nolan (6.2), Carroll (2.1)   May (1 on)

Powell hit a two-run homer, and Hendricks and B. Robinson added solo shots, enabling the Orioles to overcome a 3-0 deficit and spoil the Reds' first Series game in Riverfront Stadium.

GAME 2 - OCTOBER 11

BAL A 000 150 000   6 10 2   Cuellar (2.1), Phoebus (1.2), Drabowsky (2.1), Lopez (0.1), Hall (2.1), **SV**   Powell

CIN N 301 001 000   5 7 0   McGlothlin (4.1), Wilcox (0.1), Carroll (2.1), Gullett (2)   Bench, Tolan

Reds again took an early 3-0 lead, and again lost by one run, as Powell smashed his second homer of Series and Hendricks capped a five-run rally in the fifth with a two-run double.

GAME 3 - OCTOBER 13

CIN N 010 000 200   3 9 0   Cloninger (5.1), Granger (0.2), Gullett (2)

BAL A 201 014 10x   9 10 1   **McNally (9)**   F. Robinson, Buford, McNally (3 on)

McNally helped his own cause with a grand slam homer, while Frank Robinson and Buford also homered, and Brooks Robinson contributed a two-run double and two fielding gems.

GAME 4 - OCTOBER 14

CIN N 011 010 030   6 8 3   Nolan (2.2), Gullett (2.2), **Carroll (3.2)**   Rose, May (2 on)

BAL A 013 001 000   5 8 0   Palmer (7), **Watt (1)**, Drabowsky (1)   B. Robinson

May's clutch three-run homer in eighth gave the Reds their first victory and ended Baltimore's 17-game winning streak, including the last 11 games of the regular season and three in the A.L. playoffs.

GAME 5 - OCTOBER 15

CIN N 300 000 000   3 6 0   Merritt (1.2), Granger (0.2), Wilcox (1.2), Cloninger (2), Washburn (1.1), Carroll (0.2)

BAL A 222 010 02x   9 15 0   **Cuellar (9)**   F. Robinson (1 on), Rettenmund

The Orioles again overcame a three-run deficit, as Frank Robinson and Rettenmund each homered and drove in two runs. Cuellar allowed only two hits after first inning.

Team totals

		W	AB	H	2B	3B	HR	R	RBI	BA	BB	SO	ERA
BAL	A	4	171	50	7	0	10	33	32	.292	20	33	3.40
CIN	N	1	164	35	6	1	5	20	20	.213	15	23	6.70

Individual Batting

BALTIMORE (A.L.)

	AB	H	2B	3B	HR	R	RBI	BA
F. Robinson, of	22	6	0	0	2	5	4	.273
B. Robinson, 3b	21	9	2	0	2	5	6	.429
M. Belanger, ss	19	2	0	0	0	1	0	.105
P. Blair, of	19	9	1	0	0	5	3	.474
B. Powell, 1b	17	5	1	0	2	6	5	.294
D. Johnson, 2b	16	5	2	0	0	2	2	.313
D. Buford, of	15	4	0	0	1	3	1	.267
E. Hendricks, c	11	4	1	0	1	1	4	.364
Etchebarren, c	7	1	0	0	0	1	0	.143
J. Palmer, p	7	1	0	0	0	1	0	.143
Rettenmund, of	5	2	0	0	1	2	2	.400
D. McNally, p	4	1	0	0	1	1	4	.250
M. Cuellar, p	4	0	0	0	0	0	0	.000
M. Drabowsky, p	1	0	0	0	0	0	0	.000
D. Hall, p	1	0	0	0	0	0	0	.000
T. Crowley	1	0	0	0	0	0	0	.000
C. Salmon	1	1	0	0	0	1	0	1.000

Errors: B. Robinson, E. Hendricks, M. Belanger, P. Blair, Etchebarren

CINCINNATI (N.L.)

	AB	H	2B	3B	HR	R	RBI	BA
P. Rose, of	20	5	1	0	1	2	2	.250
B. Tolan, of	19	4	1	0	1	5	1	.211
J. Bench, c	19	4	0	0	1	3	3	.211
T. Perez, 3b	18	1	0	0	0	2	0	.056
T. Helms, 2b	18	4	0	0	0	1	0	.222
L. May, 1b	18	7	2	0	2	6	8	.389
H. McRae, of	11	5	2	0	0	1	3	.455
Concepcion, ss	9	3	0	1	0	0	3	.333
B. Carbo, of	8	0	0	0	0	0	0	.000
W. Woodward, ss	5	1	0	0	0	0	0	.200
G. Nolan, p	3	0	0	0	0	0	0	.000
T. Cline	3	1	0	0	0	0	0	.333
T. Cloninger, p	2	0	0	0	0	0	0	.000
McGlothlin, p	2	0	0	0	0	0	0	.000
J. Stewart	2	0	0	0	0	0	0	.000
A. Bravo	2	0	0	0	0	0	0	.000
D. Chaney, ss	1	0	0	0	0	0	0	.000
D. Gullett, p	1	0	0	0	0	0	0	.000
J. Merritt, p	1	0	0	0	0	0	0	.000
P. Corrales	1	0	0	0	0	0	0	.000
C. Carroll, p	1	0	0	0	0	0	0	.000

Errors: T. Perez, P. Rose, B. Tolan
Stolen Bases: B. Tolan

Individual Pitching

BALTIMORE (A.L.)

	W	L	ERA	IP	H	BB	SO	SV
J. Palmer	1	0	4.60	15.2	11	9	9	0
M. Cuellar	1	0	3.18	11.1	10	2	5	0
D. McNally	1	0	3.00	9	9	2	5	0
M. Drabowsky	0	0	2.70	3.1	2	1	1	0
D. Hall	0	0	0.00	2.1	0	0	0	1
T. Phoebus	1	0	0.00	1.2	0	1	0	0
E. Watt	0	1	9.00	1	2	1	3	0
P. Richert	0	0	0.00	0.1	0	0	0	1
M. Lopez	0	0	0.00	0.1	0	0	0	0

CINCINNATI (N.L.)

	W	L	ERA	IP	H	BB	SO	SV
C. Carroll	1	0	0.00	9	5	2	11	0
G. Nolan	0	1	7.71	9.1	9	3	9	0
T. Cloninger	0	1	7.36	7.1	10	5	4	0
D. Gullett	0	0	1.35	6.2	5	4	4	0
McGlothlin	0	0	8.31	4.1	6	2	2	0
M. Wilcox	0	1	9.00	2	3	0	0	0
W. Granger	0	0	33.75	1.1	7	1	1	0
J. Merritt	0	1	21.60	1.2	3	1	0	0
R. Washburn	0	0	13.50	1.1	2	2	0	0

1971 NATIONAL LEAGUE CHAMPIONSHIP SERIES

LINE SCORES	PITCHERS (innings pitched)	HOME RUNS (men on)	HIGHLIGHTS

Pittsburgh (East) defeats San Francisco (West) 3 games to 1

GAME 1 - OCTOBER 2

PIT	E	002 000 200	4 9 0	Blass (5), Moose (2), Giusti (1)	
SF	W	001 040 00x	5 7 2	Perry (9)	McCovey (1 on), Fuentes (1 on)

Tito Fuentes and Willie McCovey poled two-run home runs in the fifth inning as the Giants overcame a 2-1 deficit.

GAME 2 - OCTOBER 3

PIT	E	010 210 401	9 15 0	Ellis (5), Miller (3), Giusti (1), SV	Robertson (1 on), Robertson (2 on), Robertson, Clines
SF	W	110 000 002	4 9 0	Cumberland (3), Barr (1), McMahon (2), Carrithers (0), Bryant (2), Hamilton (1)	Mays

Bob Robertson, in a one-man display of power, hammered three home runs and a double to drive in five runs as the Pirates evened the series.

GAME 3 - OCTOBER 5

SF	W	000 001 000	1 5 2	Marichal (8)	
PIT	E	010 000 01x	2 4 1	Johnson (8), Giusti (1), SV	Robertson, Hebner

Richie Hebner's homer off Juan Marichal in the eighth inning snapped a 1-1 tie and gave Bob Johnson a 2-1 victory.

GAME 4 - OCTOBER 6

SF	W	140 000 000	5 10 0	Perry (5.2), Johnson (1.1), McMahon (1)	Speier, McCovey (2 on)
PIT	E	230 004 00x	9 11 2	Blass (2), Kison (4.2), Giusti (2.1) SV	Hebner (2 on), Oliver (2 on)

Richie Hebner drove in three runs with three hits including a home run, and rookie right-hander Bruce Kison pitched two-hit scoreless ball in 4.2 innings.

Team totals

		W	AB	H	2B	3B	HR	R	RBI	BA	BB	SO	ERA
PIT	E	3	144	39	4	0	8	24	23	.271	5	33	3.34
SF	W	1	132	31	5	0	5	15	14	.235	16	28	6.09

Individual Batting

PITTSBURGH (EAST)

	AB	H	2B	3B	HR	R	RBI	BA
D. Cash, 2b	19	8	2	0	0	5	1	.421
R. Clemente, of	18	6	0	0	0	2	4	.333
R. Hebner, 3b	17	5	1	0	2	3	4	.294
B. Robertson, 1b	16	7	1	0	4	5	6	.438
Sanguillen, c	15	4	0	0	0	1	1	.267
W. Stargell, of	14	0	0	0	0	1	0	.000
J. Hernandez, ss	13	3	0	0	0	2	1	.231
A. Oliver, of	12	3	0	0	1	2	5	.250
D. Ellis, p	3	0	0	0	0	0	0	.000
G. Clines, of	3	1	0	0	1	1	1	.333
B. Kison, p	2	0	0	0	0	0	0	.000
B. Johnson, p	2	0	0	0	0	0	0	.000
V. Davalillo	2	0	0	0	0	0	0	.000
G. Alley, ss	2	1	0	0	0	1	0	.500
S. Blass, p	1	0	0	0	0	0	0	.000
D. Giusti, p	1	0	0	0	0	0	0	.000
B. Mazeroski	1	1	0	0	0	1	0	1.000
B. Miller, p	1	0	0	0	0	0	0	.000
J. Pagan, 3b	1	0	0	0	0	0	0	.000
M. May	1	0	0	0	0	0	0	.000

Errors: J. Hernandez, R. Hebner, D. Cash
Stolen Bases: Sanguillen, D. Cash

SAN FRANCISCO (WEST)

	AB	H	2B	3B	HR	R	RBI	BA
T. Fuentes, 2b	16	5	1	0	1	4	2	.313
K. Henderson, of	16	5	1	0	0	3	2	.313
D. Dietz, c	15	1	0	0	0	0	0	.067
W. Mays, of	15	4	2	0	1	2	3	.267
W. McCovey, 1b	14	6	0	0	2	2	6	.429
C. Speier, ss	14	5	1	0	1	4	1	.357
A. Gallagher, 3b	10	1	0	0	0	0	0	.100
D. Kingman, of	9	1	0	0	0	0	0	.111
B. Bonds, of	8	2	0	0	0	0	0	.250
J. Hart, 3b	5	0	0	0	0	0	0	.000
G. Perry, p	4	1	0	0	0	0	0	.250
J. Marichal, p	3	0	0	0	0	0	0	.000
H. Lanier, 3b	1	0	0	0	0	0	0	.000
F. Duffy	1	0	0	0	0	0	0	.000
J. Barr, p	1	0	0	0	0	0	0	.000
J. Rosario	0	0	0	0	0	0	0	—

Errors: T. Fuentes, W. McCovey, B. Bonds, C. Speier
Stolen Bases: K. Henderson, W. Mays

Individual Pitching

PITTSBURGH (EAST)

	W	L	ERA	IP	H	BB	SO	SV
B. Johnson	1	0	0.00	8	5	3	7	0
S. Blass	0	1	11.57	7	14	2	11	0
D. Giusti	0	0	0.00	5.1	1	2	3	3
D. Ellis	1	0	3.60	5	6	4	1	0
B. Kison	1	0	0.00	4.2	2	2	3	0
B. Miller	0	0	6.00	3	3	3	3	0
B. Moose	0	0	0.00	2	0	0	0	0

SAN FRANCISCO (WEST)

	W	L	ERA	IP	H	BB	SO	SV
G. Perry	1	1	6.14	14.2	19	3	11	0
J. Marichal	0	1	2.25	8	4	0	6	0
D. McMahon	0	0	0.00	3	0	0	3	0
Cumberland	0	0	9.00	3	7	0	4	0
R. Bryant	0	0	4.50	2	1	1	2	0
S. Hamilton	0	0	9.00	1	1	0	3	0
J. Johnson	0	0	13.50	1.1	1	1	2	0
J. Barr	0	0	9.00	1	3	0	2	0
Carrithers	0	0	∞	0.0	3	0	0	0

1971 AMERICAN LEAGUE CHAMPIONSHIP SERIES

LINE SCORES	PITCHERS (innings pitched)	HOME RUNS (men on)	HIGHLIGHTS

Baltimore (East) defeats Oakland (West) 3 games to 0

GAME 1 - OCTOBER 3

OAK	W	020 100 000	3 9 0	Blue (7), Fingers (1)	
BAL	E	000 100 40x	5 7 1	McNally (7), Watt (2), SV	

Paul Blair's two-run double climaxed a four-run uprising against Vida Blue in the seventh to give the Orioles a 5-3 victory.

GAME 2 - OCTOBER 4

OAK	W	000 100 000	1 6 0	Hunter (8)	
BAL	E	011 000 12x	5 7 0	Cuellar (9)	Powell (1 on), Powell, Hendricks, B. Robinson

The Orioles managed only seven hits off Catfish Hunter but four of them were home runs. Boog Powell hit two and drove in three runs.

GAME 3 - OCTOBER 5

BAL	E	100 020 200	5 12 0	Palmer (9)	
OAK	W	001 001 010	3 7 0	Segui (4.2), Fingers (1.1), Knowles (0.1), Locker (0.2), Grant (0.2)	Jackson, Jackson, Bando

Brooks Robinson singled home two runs after A's manager Dick Williams had ordered an intentional pass to Ellie Hendricks, loading the bases. Jim Palmer yielded three home runs, two to Reggie Jackson, but all came with the bases empty.

Team totals

		W	AB	H	2B	3B	HR	R	RBI	BA	BB	SO	ERA
BAL	E	3	95	26	7	1	4	15	14	.274	13	22	2.33
OAK	W	0	96	22	8	1	3	7	7	.229	5	16	5.40

Individual Batting

BALTIMORE (EAST)

	AB	H	2B	3B	HR	R	RBI	BA
F. Robinson, of	12	1	1	0	0	2	1	.083
B. Robinson, 3b	11	4	1	0	1	2	3	.364
B. Powell, 1b	10	3	0	0	2	4	3	.300
D. Johnson, 2b	10	3	2	0	0	2	0	.300
P. Blair, of	9	3	1	0	0	1	2	.333
M. Belanger, ss	8	2	0	0	0	1	1	.250
Rettenmund, of	8	2	1	0	0	0	1	.250
D. Buford, of	7	3	0	1	0	1	0	.429
Etchebarren, c	5	0	0	0	0	0	0	.000
J. Palmer, p	5	1	0	0	0	1	0	.200
E. Hendricks, c	4	2	0	0	1	1	2	.500
M. Cuellar, p	3	1	0	0	0	0	0	.333
D. McNally, p	2	0	0	0	0	0	0	.000
C. Motton	1	1	1	0	0	0	1	1.000

Errors: D. Johnson

OAKLAND (WEST)

	AB	H	2B	3B	HR	R	RBI	BA
Campaneris, ss	12	2	1	0	0	0	0	.167
A. Mangual, of	12	2	1	1	0	1	2	.167
R. Jackson, of	12	4	1	0	2	2	2	.333
S. Bando, 3b	11	4	2	0	1	3	1	.364
T. Davis, 1b	8	3	1	0	0	1	0	.375
D. Green, 2b	7	2	0	0	0	0	0	.286
J. Rudi, of	7	1	1	0	0	0	0	.143
D. Duncan, c	6	3	1	0	0	0	2	.500
M. Epstein, 1b	5	1	0	0	0	0	0	.200
R. Monday, of	3	0	0	0	0	0	0	.000
C. Hunter, p	3	0	0	0	0	0	0	.000
V. Blue, p	3	0	0	0	0	0	0	.000
G. Tenace, c	3	0	0	0	0	0	0	.000
D. Segui, p	2	0	0	0	0	0	0	.000
M. Hegan	1	0	0	0	0	0	0	.000
C. Blefary	1	0	0	0	0	0	0	.000

Individual Pitching

BALTIMORE (EAST)

	W	L	ERA	IP	H	BB	SO	SV
M. Cuellar	1	0	1.00	9	6	1	2	0
J. Palmer	1	0	3.00	9	7	3	8	0
D. McNally	1	0	3.86	7	7	1	5	0
E. Watt	0	0	0.00	2	2	0	1	1

OAKLAND (WEST)

	W	L	ERA	IP	H	BB	SO	SV
C. Hunter	0	1	5.63	8	7	2	6	0
V. Blue	0	1	6.43	7	7	2	8	0
D. Segui	0	1	5.79	4.2	6	6	4	0
R. Fingers	0	0	7.71	2.1	2	1	2	0
M. Grant	0	0	0.00	2	3	0	2	0
D. Knowles	0	0	0.00	0.1	1	0	0	0
B. Locker	0	0	0.00	0.2	0	2	0	0

1971 WORLD SERIES

LINE SCORES	PITCHERS (innings pitched)	HOME RUNS (men on)	HIGHLIGHTS

Pittsburgh (N.L.) defeats Baltimore (A.L.) 4 games to 3

GAME 1 - OCTOBER 9

PIT	N	030 000 000	3 3 0	Ellis (2.1), Moose (3.2), Miller (2)
BAL	A	013 010 00x	5 10 3	McNally (9)

HOME RUNS: F. Robinson, Rettenmund (2 on), Buford

Rettenmund's three-run homer and solo blasts by Frank Robinson and Buford backed McNally, who allowed three hits, none after the third inning.

GAME 2 - OCTOBER 11

PIT	N	000 000 030	3 8 1	R. Johnson (3.1), Kison (0), Moose (1), Veale (0.2), Miller (2), Giusti (1)
BAL	A	010 361 00x	11 14 1	Palmer (8), Hall (1), SV

HOME RUNS: Hebner (2 on)

The Orioles rapped out 14 singles and Brooks Robinson tied a Series record by reaching base five straight times on three hits and two walks.

GAME 3 - OCTOBER 12

BAL	A	000 000 100	1 3 3	Cuellar (6), Dobson (1), Watt (1)
PIT	N	100 001 30x	5 7 0	Blass (9)

HOME RUNS: F. Robinson, Robertson (2 on)

Blass silenced the Orioles' bats on three hits and eight strikeouts before a record Pittsburgh crowd of 50,403.

GAME 4 - OCTOBER 13

BAL	A	300 000 000	3 4 1	Dobson (5.1), Jackson (0.2), Watt (1.1), Richert (0.2)
PIT	N	201 000 01x	4 14 0	Walker (0.2), Kison (6.1), Giusti (2) SV

Rookie Kison pitched one-hit relief for 6.1 innings and May delivered a tie-breaking, run-scoring pinch single as Pittsburgh rallied from a 3-0 deficit to win the first night game in World Series history.

GAME 5 - OCTOBER 14

BAL	A	000 000 000	0 2 1	McNally (4), Leonhard (1), Dukes (3)
PIT	N	021 010 00x	4 9 0	Briles (9)

HOME RUNS: Robertson

Briles, with only four complete games during regular season, permitted only two singles and helped himself with a run-scoring single, while Clemente hit safely in his 12th straight Series game.

GAME 6 - OCTOBER 16

PIT	N	011 000 000 0	2 9 1	Moose (5), R. Johnson (1.2), Giusti (2.1), Miller (0.2)
BAL	A	000 001 100 1	3 8 0	Palmer (9), Dobson (0.2), McNally (0.1)

HOME RUNS: Clemente; Buford

Brooks Robinson's sacrifice fly, following singles by Frank Robinson and Rettenmund in the 10th inning gave the Orioles a dramatic victory, after McNally escaped a bases-loaded jam in the top of inning.

GAME 7 - OCTOBER 17

PIT	N	000 100 010	2 6 1	Blass (9)
BAL	A	000 000 010	1 4 0	Cuellar (8), Dobson (0.2), McNally (0.1)

HOME RUNS: Clemente

The Pirates became only the sixth club in Series history to take the title after losing the first two games, thanks to Blass's sparkling four-hitter.

Team totals

		W	AB	H	2B	3B	HR	R	RBI	BA	BB	SO	ERA
PIT	N	4	238	56	9	2	5	23	21	.235	26	47	3.50
BAL	A	3	219	45	3	1	5	24	22	.205	20	35	2.66

Individual Batting

PITTSBURGH (N.L.)

	AB	H	2B	3B	HR	R	RBI	BA
D. Cash, 2b	30	4	1	0	0	2	1	.133
Sanguillen, c	29	11	1	0	0	3	0	.379
R. Clemente, of	29	12	2	1	2	3	4	.414
B. Robertson, 1b	25	6	0	0	2	4	5	.240
W. Stargell, of	24	5	1	0	0	3	1	.208
A. Oliver, of	19	4	2	0	0	1	2	.211
J. Hernandez, ss	18	4	0	0	0	2	1	.222
J. Pagan, 3b	15	4	2	0	0	0	2	.267
R. Hebner, 3b	12	2	0	0	1	2	3	.167
G. Clines, of	11	1	0	1	0	2	0	.091
S. Blass, p	7	0	0	0	0	0	0	.000
V. Davalillo, of	3	1	0	0	0	1	0	.333
B. Johnson, p	3	0	0	0	0	0	0	.000
B. Kison, p	2	0	0	0	0	0	0	.000
M. May	2	1	0	0	0	0	1	.500
B. Moose, p	2	0	0	0	0	0	0	.000
N. Briles, p	2	1	0	0	0	0	1	.500
G. Alley, ss	2	0	0	0	0	0	0	.000
B. Mazeroski	1	0	0	0	0	0	0	.000
C. Sands	1	0	0	0	0	0	0	.000
D. Ellis, p	1	0	0	0	0	0	0	.000

Errors: R. Hebner, A. Oliver, B. Robertson
Stolen Bases: Sanguillen (2), J. Hernandez, D. Cash, G. Clines

BALTIMORE (A.L.)

	AB	H	2B	3B	HR	R	RBI	BA
B. Powell, 1b	27	3	0	0	0	1	1	.111
D. Johnson, 2b	27	4	0	0	0	1	3	.148
Rettenmund, of	27	5	0	0	1	3	4	.185
F. Robinson, of	25	7	0	0	2	5	2	.280
D. Buford, of	23	6	1	0	2	3	4	.261
B. Robinson, 3b	22	7	0	0	0	2	5	.318
M. Belanger, ss	21	5	0	1	0	4	0	.238
E. Hendricks, c	19	5	1	0	0	3	1	.263
P. Blair, of	9	3	1	0	0	2	0	.333
T. Shopay	4	0	0	0	0	0	0	.000
D. McNally, p	4	0	0	0	0	0	0	.000
J. Palmer, p	4	0	0	0	0	0	2	.000
M. Cuellar, p	3	0	0	0	0	0	0	.000
Etchebarren, c	2	0	0	0	0	0	0	.000
P. Dobson, p	2	0	0	0	0	0	0	.000

Errors: M. Belanger (3), B. Robinson (2), E. Hendricks, P. Blair, M. Cuellar, B. Powell
Stolen Bases: M. Belanger

Individual Pitching

PITTSBURGH (N.L.)

	W	L	ERA	IP	H	BB	SO	SV
S. Blass	2	0	1.00	18	7	4	13	0
N. Briles	1	0	0.00	9	2	2	2	0
B. Moose	0	0	6.52	9.2	12	2	7	0
B. Kison	1	0	0.00	6.1	1	2	3	0
B. Johnson	0	1	9.00	5	5	3	3	0
D. Giusti	0	0	0.00	5.1	3	2	4	1
B. Miller	0	1	3.86	4.2	7	1	2	0
D. Ellis	0	1	15.43	2.1	4	1	1	0
B. Veale	0	0	13.50	0.2	1	2	0	0
L. Walker	0	0	40.50	0.2	3	1	0	0

BALTIMORE (A.L.)

	W	L	ERA	IP	H	BB	SO	SV
J. Palmer	1	0	2.65	17	15	9	15	0
M. Cuellar	0	2	3.86	14	11	6	10	0
D. McNally	2	1	1.98	13.2	10	5	12	0
P. Dobson	0	0	4.05	6.2	13	4	6	0
T. Dukes	0	0	0.00	4	2	0	1	0
E. Watt	0	1	3.86	2.1	4	0	2	0
D. Hall	0	0	0.00	1	1	0	1	1
D. Leonhard	0	0	0.00	1	0	1	0	0
G. Jackson	0	0	0.00	0.2	0	1	0	0
P. Richert	0	0	0.00	0.2	0	0	1	0

1972 NATIONAL LEAGUE CHAMPIONSHIP SERIES

LINE SCORES	PITCHERS (innings pitched)	HOME RUNS (men on)	HIGHLIGHTS

Cincinnati (West) defeats Pittsburgh (East) 3 games to 2

GAME 1 - OCTOBER 7

CIN W 100 000 000 — 1 8 0 Gullett (6), Borbon (2) — Morgan — Joe Morgan, second batter to face Steve Blass, hit a home run, but the Pirates came up with three runs in their half of the first inning, more than enough to win the opener, 5-1.
PIT E 300 020 00x — 5 6 0 **Blass** (8.1), Hernandez (0.2) **SV** — Oliver (1 on)

GAME 2 - OCTOBER 8

CIN W 400 000 010 — 5 8 1 Billingham (4.2), **Hall** (4.1) — Morgan — Pirate starter Bob Moose failed to retire a batter as the Reds raked him for five straight hits in the first inning.
PIT E 000 111 000 — 3 7 1 Moose (0), Johnson (5), Kison (1), Hernandez (2), Giusti (1)

GAME 3 - OCTOBER 9

PIT E 000 010 110 — 3 7 0 Briles (6), **Kison** (1.1), Giusti (1.2) **SV** — Sanguillen — Manny Sanguillen homered for the first Pittsburgh run and drove in the tie-breaking run in the eighth inning to give the Pirates a 3-2 victory.
CIN W 002 000 000 — 2 8 1 Nolan (6), Borbon (0.1), **Carroll** (1.2), McGlothlin (1)

GAME 4 - OCTOBER 10

PIT E 000 000 100 — 1 2 3 Ellis (5), Johnson (1), Walker (1), Miller (1) — Clemente — Ross Grimsley handcuffed the hard-hitting Pirates, limiting them to two hits, including Roberto Clemente's solo homer.
CIN W 100 202 20x — 7 11 1 **Grimsley** (9)

GAME 5 - OCTOBER 11

PIT E 020 100 000 — 3 8 0 Blass (7.1), Hernandez (0.2), **Giusti** (0), Moose (0.2) — Geronimo, Bench — Pittsburgh was leading 3-2 as the Reds came to bat in the ninth. Bench, the first batter to face Giusti, hit a home run to tie the game. When Perez and Menke followed with singles, manager Bill Virdon brought in Bob Moose. With pinch hitter Hal McRae at the plate, Moose uncorked a wild pitch and Foster raced home with the winning run.
CIN W 001 010 002 — 4 7 1 Gullett (3), Borbon (2), Hall (3), **Carroll** (1)

Team totals

		W	AB	H	2B	3B	HR	R	RBI	BA	BB	SO	ERA
CIN	W	3	166	42	9	2	4	19	16	.253	10	28	3.07
PIT	E	2	158	30	6	1	3	15	14	.190	9	27	3.30

Individual Batting

CINCINNATI (WEST)

	AB	H	2B	3B	HR	R	RBI	BA
B. Tolan, of	21	5	1	1	0	3	4	.238
T. Perez, 1b	20	4	1	0	0	0	2	.200
P. Rose, of	20	9	4	0	0	1	2	.450
C. Geronimo, of	20	2	0	0	1	2	1	.100
J. Morgan, 2b	19	5	0	0	2	5	3	.263
J. Bench, c	18	6	1	1	1	3	2	.333
D. Menke, 3b	16	4	1	0	0	1	0	.250
D. Chaney, ss	16	3	0	0	0	3	1	.188
R. Grimsley, p	4	2	1	0	0	0	1	.500
D. Gullett, p	2	1	0	0	0	0	0	.500
Concepcion, ss	2	0	0	0	0	0	0	.000
T. Uhlaender	2	1	0	0	0	0	0	.500
G. Nolan, p	2	0	0	0	0	0	0	.000
Billingham, p	2	0	0	0	0	0	0	.000
T. Hall, p	1	0	0	0	0	0	0	.000
J. Hague	1	0	0	0	0	0	0	.000
H. McRae	0	0	0	0	0	0	0	—
G. Foster	0	0	0	0	0	1	0	—

Errors: D. Chaney (3), J. Bench
Stolen Bases: J. Bench (2), D. Chaney, J. Morgan

PITTSBURGH (EAST)

	AB	H	2B	3B	HR	R	RBI	BA
R. Stennett, of, 2b	21	6	0	0	0	2	1	.286
A. Oliver, of	20	5	2	1	1	3	3	.250
D. Cash, 2b	19	4	0	0	0	3		.211
R. Clemente, of	17	4	1	0	1	1	2	.235
G. Alley, ss	16	0	0	0	0	1	0	.000
R. Hebner, 3b	16	3	1	0	0	2	1	.188
Sanguillen, c	16	5	1	0	1	4	2	.313
W. Stargell, 1b, of	16	1	1	0	0	1	1	.063
S. Blass, p	6	0	0	0	0	0	0	.000
N. Briles, p	2	0	0	0	0	0	0	.000
B. Mazeroski	2	1	0	0	0	0	0	.500
M. May, c	2	1	0	0	0	0	1	.500
G. Clines	2	0	0	0	0	1	0	.000
B. Johnson, p	1	0	0	0	0	0	0	.000
D. Ellis, p	1	0	0	0	0	0	0	.000
D. Giusti, p	1	0	0	0	0	0	0	.000
V. Davalillo	0	0	0	0	0	0	0	—
B. Robertson, 1b	0	0	0	0	0	0	0	—

Errors: G. Alley (2), Sanguillen, D. Cash

Individual Pitching

CINCINNATI (WEST)

	W	L	ERA	IP	H	BB	SO	SV
R. Grimsley	1	0	1.00	9	2	0	5	0
D. Gullett	0	1	8.00	9	12	6	6	0
T. Hall	1	0	1.23	7.1	3	3	8	0
G. Nolan	0	0	1.50	6	4	1	4	0
Billingham	0	0	3.86	4.2	5	2	4	0
P. Borbon	0	0	2.08	4.1	2	0	1	0
C. Carroll	1	1	3.38	2.2	2	3	0	0
McGlothlin	0	0	0.00	1	0	0	0	0

PITTSBURGH (EAST)

	W	L	ERA	IP	H	BB	SO	SV
S. Blass	1	0	1.72	15.2	12	6	5	0
N. Briles	0	0	3.00	6	6	1	3	0
B. Johnson	0	0	3.00	6	4	2	7	0
D. Ellis	0	1	0.00	5	5	1	3	0
R. Hernandez	0	0	2.70	3.1	1	0	3	1
B. Kison	1	0	0.00	2.1	1	0	3	0
D. Giusti	0	1	6.75	2.2	5	0	3	1
B. Miller	0	0	0.00	1	0	0	1	0
L. Walker	0	0	18.00	1	3	0	0	0
B. Moose	0	1	54.00	0.2	5	0	0	0

1972 AMERICAN LEAGUE CHAMPIONSHIP SERIES

LINE SCORES	PITCHERS (innings pitched)	HOME RUNS (men on)	HIGHLIGHTS

Oakland (West) defeats Detroit (East) 3 games to 2

GAME 1 - OCTOBER 7

DET	E	010 000 000 01	2 6 2	Lolich (10), Seelbach (0.1)	Cash, Kaline
OAK	W	001 000 000 02	3 10 1	Hunter (8), Blue (0), **Fingers** (3)	

Mickey Lolich carried a 2-1 lead into the last of the 11th, but the A's scored twice to beat the Tiger ace, 3-2. Gonzalo Marquez drove in the tying run, and the winning run scored on Kaline's throwing error.

GAME 2 - OCTOBER 8

DET	E	000 000 000	0 3 1	Fryman (4.1), Zachary (0), Scherman (2.2), LaGrow (1), Hiller (2)	
OAK	W	100 040 00x	5 8 0	**Odom** (9)	

Blue Moon Odom pitched a magnificent three-hitter and did not walk a batter as the A's made it two straight, 5-0.

GAME 3 - OCTOBER 10

OAK	W	000 000 000	0 7 0	Holtzman (4), Fingers (1.2), Blue (0.1), Locker (2)	
DET	E	000 200 01x	3 8 1	**Coleman** (6)	Freehan

Joe Coleman struck out 14, setting a playoff record, as the Tigers bounced back to win the third game, 3-0.

GAME 4 - OCTOBER 11

OAK	W	000 000 100 2	3 9 2	Hunter (7.1), Fingers (0.2), Blue (1), Locker (3), **Horlen** (0), Hamilton (0)	Epstein
DET	E	001 000 000 3	4 10 1	Lolich (9), Seelbach (0.2), **Hiller** (0.1)	McAuliffe

The Tigers appeared hopelessly lost coming to bat in the 10th after the A's scored twice in the top of the inning to take a 3-1 lead. Detroit's comeback began with singles by Dick McAuliffe and Al Kaline. A wild pitch, a walk, and an error produced one run before Hamilton walked home the tying run and Jim Northrup knocked in the game- winner.

GAME 5 - OCTOBER 12

OAK	W	010 100 000	2 4 0	Odom (5), Blue (4), SV	
DET	E	100 000 000	1 5 2	Fryman (8), Hiller (1)	

Gene Tenace's only hit of the series, a single with two out in the fourth, drove home George Hendrick from second with the winning run.

Team totals

		W	AB	H	2B	3B	HR	R	RBI	BA	BB	SO	ERA
OAK	W	3	170	38	8	0	1	13	10	.224	12	35	1.76
DET	E	2	162	32	6	1	4	10	10	.198	13	25	2.14

Individual Batting

OAKLAND (WEST)

	AB	H	2B	3B	HR	R	RBI	BA
M. Alou, of	21	8	4	0	0	2	2	.381
S. Bando, 3b	20	4	0	0	0	0	0	.200
J. Rudi, of	20	5	1	0	0	1	2	.250
R. Jackson, of	18	5	0	0	0	1	2	.278
G. Tenace, c, 1b	17	1	0	0	0	1	1	.059
M. Epstein, 1b	16	3	0	0	1	1	1	.188
D. Green, 2b	8	1	1	0	0	0	0	.125
D. Maxvill, ss, 2b	8	1	0	0	0	0	0	.125
Campaneris, ss	7	3	0	0	0	3	0	.429
G. Hendrick, of	7	1	0	0	0	2	0	.143
C. Hunter, p	6	1	0	0	0	0	0	.167
T. Kubiak, 2b, ss	4	2	0	0	0	0	1	.500
B. Odom, p	4	1	1	0	0	0	0	.250
A. Mangual	3	0	0	0	0	0	0	.000
G. Marquez	3	2	0	0	0	1	1	.667
D. Duncan, c	2	0	0	0	0	0	0	.000
T. Cullen, ss	1	0	0	0	0	0	0	.000
R. Fingers, p	1	0	0	0	0	0	0	.000
V. Blue, p	1	0	0	0	0	0	0	.000
D. Mincher	1	0	0	0	0	0	0	.000
M. Hegan, 1b	1	0	0	0	0	1	0	.000
K. Holtzman, p	1	0	0	0	0	0	0	.000

Errors: R. Jackson

Stolen Bases: R. Jackson (2), Campaneris (2), M. Alou, D. Maxvill

DETROIT (EAST)

	AB	H	2B	3B	HR	R	RBI	BA
McAuliffe, ss, 2b	20	4	0	0	1	3	1	.200
A. Kaline, of	19	5	0	0	1	3	1	.263
A. Rodriguez, 3b	16	0	0	0	0	0	0	.000
T. Taylor, 2b	15	2	2	0	0	0	0	.133
N. Cash, 1b	15	4	0	0	1	1	2	.267
J. Northrup, of	14	5	0	0	0	0	1	.357
D. Sims, c, of	14	3	2	1	0	0	0	.214
B. Freehan, c	12	3	1	0	1	2	3	.250
W. Horton, of	10	1	0	0	0	0	0	.100
M. Lolich, p	7	0	0	0	0	0	0	.000
M. Stanley, of	6	2	0	0	0	0	0	.333
E. Brinkman, ss	4	1	1	0	0	0	0	.250
W. Fryman, p	3	0	0	0	0	0	0	.000
G. Brown	2	0	0	0	0	1	0	.000
J. Coleman, p	2	1	0	0	0	0	0	.500
I. Brown, 1b	2	1	0	0	0	0	2	.500
T. Haller	1	0	0	0	0	0	0	.000
J. Niekro	0	0	0	0	0	0	0	–
J. Knox	0	0	0	0	0	0	0	–

Errors: A. Kaline, A. Rodriguez, McAuliffe, D. Sims

Individual Pitching

OAKLAND (WEST)

	W	L	ERA	IP	H	BB	SO	SV
C. Hunter	0	0	1.17	15.1	10	5	9	0
B. Odom	2	0	0.00	14	5	2	5	0
R. Fingers	1	0	1.69	5.1	4	1	3	0
V. Blue	0	0	0.00	5.1	4	1	5	1
K. Holtzman	0	1	4.50	4	4	2	2	0
B. Locker	0	0	13.50	2	4	0	1	0
J. Horlen	0	1	∞	0.0	0	1	0	0
D. Hamilton	0	0	–	0.0	1	1	0	0

DETROIT (EAST)

	W	L	ERA	IP	H	BB	SO	SV
M. Lolich	0	1	1.42	19	14	5	10	0
W. Fryman	0	2	3.65	12.1	11	2	8	0
J. Coleman	1	0	0.00	9	7	3	14	0
J. Hiller	1	0	0.00	3.1	1	1	1	0
L. LaGrow	0	0	0.00	1	0	0	1	0
C. Seelbach	0	0	18.00	1	4	0	0	0
C. Zachary	0	0	∞	0.0	1	0	1	0
F. Scherman	0	0	0.00	0.2	1	0	1	0

1972 WORLD SERIES

| LINE SCORES | | PITCHERS (innings pitched) | HOME RUNS (men on) | HIGHLIGHTS |

Oakland (A.L.) defeats Cincinnati (N.L.) 4 games to 3

GAME 1 - OCTOBER 14

| OAK | A | 020 010 000 | 3 4 0 | Holtzman (5), Fingers (1.2), Blue (2.1) **SV** | Tenace (1 on), Tenace | Tenace made Series history, becoming the first player to hit home runs in his first two Series at bats. He knocked in all three Oakland runs before a record Cincinnati crowd of 52,918. |
| CIN | N | 010 100 000 | 2 7 0 | Nolan (6), Borbon (1), Carroll (2) | | |

GAME 2 - OCTOBER 15

| OAK | A | 011 000 000 | 2 9 2 | Hunter (8.2), Fingers (0.1), **SV** | Rudi | Rudi excelled at bat and in the field, with a home run and game-saving catch in the ninth before another Cincinnati record crowd—53,224. |
| CIN | N | 000 000 001 | 1 6 0 | Grimsley (5), Borbon (2), Hall (2) | | |

GAME 3 - OCTOBER 18

| CIN | N | 000 000 100 | 1 4 2 | Billingham (8), Carroll (1), **SV** | | The Reds got the game's only run in the seventh on Perez's single, Menke's bunt and Geronimo's single. Odom struck out eleven and allowed just three hits in a losing cause. |
| OAK | A | 000 000 000 | 0 3 2 | Odom (7), Blue (0.1), Fingers (1.2) | | |

GAME 4 - OCTOBER 19

| CIN | N | 000 000 020 | 2 7 1 | Gullett (7), Borbon (1.1), **Carroll** (0) | | The A's scored two in the ninth on four straight singles—three by pinch-hitters —in posting their third one-run victory of the Series. Hits by Marquez, Tenace, Mincher and Mangual won it. |
| OAK | A | 000 010 002 | 3 10 1 | Holtzman (7.2), Blue (0.1), **Fingers** (1) | Tenace | |

GAME 5 - OCTOBER 20

| CIN | N | 100 110 011 | 5 8 0 | McGlothlin (3), Borbon (1), Hall (2), Carroll (1.2), **Grimsley** (0.2), Billingham (0.2), **SV** | Rose, Menke | Rose began the scoring with a first-pitch homer and ended it with a run-scoring single in ninth. The Reds threw out the tying run at home in the bottom of ninth. |
| OAK | A | 030 100 000 | 4 7 2 | Hunter (4.2), **Fingers** (3.2), Hamilton (0.2) | Tenace (2 on) | |

GAME 6 - OCTOBER 21

| OAK | A | 000 010 000 | 1 7 1 | Blue (5.2), Locker (0.1), Hamilton (0.2), Horlen (1.1) | | The Reds ended their seven-game Series home losing streak, with Tolan and Geronimo each knocking in two runs. |
| CIN | N | 000 111 50x | 8 10 0 | Nolan (4.2), **Grimsley** (1) Borbon (1), Hall (2.1), **SV** | Bench | |

GAME 7 - OCTOBER 22

| OAK | A | 100 002 000 | 3 6 1 | Odom (4.1), **Hunter** (2.2), Holtzman (0), Fingers (2), **SV** | | The A's won their first World Series title since 1930, with Tenace the unlikely hero on two hits and two RBIs. |
| CIN | N | 000 010 010 | 2 4 2 | Billingham (5), **Borbon** (0.2), Carroll (1), Granger (0.1), Hall (2) | | |

Team totals

		W	AB	H	2B	3B	HR	R	RBI	BA	BB	SO	ERA
OAK	A	4	220	46	4	0	5	16	16	.209	21	37	3.05
CIN	N	3	220	46	8	1	3	21	21	.209	27	46	2.17

Individual Batting

OAKLAND (A.L.)

	AB	H	2B	3B	HR	R	RBI	BA
Campaneris, ss	28	5	0	0	0	1	0	.179
S. Bando, 3b	26	7	1	0	0	2	1	.269
J. Rudi, of	25	6	0	0	1	1	1	.240
M. Alou, of	24	1	0	0	0	0	0	.042
G. Tenace, c, 1b	23	8	1	0	4	5	9	.348
D. Green, 2b	18	6	2	0	0	0	1	.333
M. Epstein, 1b	16	0	0	0	0	1	0	.000
G. Hendrick, of	15	2	0	0	0	3	0	.133
A. Mangual, of	10	3	0	0	0	1	1	.300
M. Hegan, 1b	5	1	0	0	0	0	0	.200
K. Holtzman, p	5	0	0	0	0	0	0	.000
C. Hunter, p	5	1	0	0	0	0	1	.200
G. Marquez	5	3	0	0	0	0	1	.600
D. Duncan, c	5	1	0	0	0	0	0	.200
B. Odom, p	4	0	0	0	0	0	0	.000
T. Kubiak, 2b	3	1	0	0	0	0	0	.333
R. Fingers, p	1	0	0	0	0	0	0	.000
V. Blue, p	1	0	0	0	0	0	0	.000
D. Mincher	1	1	0	0	0	0	1	1.000
A. Lewis	0	0	0	0	0	2	0	—

Errors: M. Epstein (2), K. Holtzman, S. Bando, Campaneris, M. Alou, C. Hunter, G. Tenace, A. Mangual

Stolen Bases: M. Alou

CINCINNATI (N.L.)

	AB	H	2B	3B	HR	R	RBI	BA
P. Rose, of	28	6	0	0	1	3	2	.214
B. Tolan, of	26	7	1	0	0	2	6	.269
D. Menke, 3b	24	2	0	0	1	1	2	.083
J. Morgan, 2b	24	3	2	0	0	4	1	.125
T. Perez, 1b	23	10	2	0	0	3	2	.435
J. Bench, c	23	6	1	0	1	4	1	.261
C. Geronimo, of	19	3	0	0	0	1	3	.158
Concepcion, ss	13	4	0	1	0	2	2	.308
H. McRae, of	9	4	1	0	0	1	2	.444
D. Chaney, ss	7	0	0	0	0	0	0	.000
Billingham, p	5	0	0	0	0	0	0	.000
T. Uhlaender	4	1	1	0	0	0	0	.250
G. Nolan, p	3	0	0	0	0	0	0	.000
J. Hague, of	3	0	0	0	0	0	0	.000
R. Grimsley, p	2	0	0	0	0	0	0	.000
D. Gullett, p	2	0	0	0	0	0	0	.000
T. Hall, p	2	0	0	0	0	0	0	.000
J. Javier	2	0	0	0	0	0	0	.000
McGlothlin, p	1	0	0	0	0	0	0	.000
G. Foster, of	0	0	0	0	0	0	0	—

Errors: J. Morgan, T. Perez, B. Tolan, J. Bench, Concepcion

Stolen Bases: B. Tolan (5), J. Morgan (2), J. Bench (2), C. Geronimo, Concepcion, P. Rose

Individual Pitching

OAKLAND (A.L.)

	W	L	ERA	IP	H	BB	SO	SV
C. Hunter	2	0	2.81	16	12	6	11	0
K. Holtzman	1	0	2.13	12.2	11	3	4	0
B. Odom	0	1	1.59	11.1	5	6	13	0
R. Fingers	1	1	1.74	10.1	4	4	11	2
V. Blue	0	1	4.15	8.2	8	5	5	1
D. Hamilton	0	0	27.00	1.1	3	1	1	0
J. Horlen	0	0	6.75	1.1	2	2	1	0
B. Locker	0	0	0.00	0.1	1	0	0	0

CINCINNATI (N.L.)

	W	L	ERA	IP	H	BB	SO	SV
Billingham	1	0	0.00	13.2	6	4	11	1
G. Nolan	0	1	3.38	10.2	7	2	3	0
T. Hall	0	0	0.00	8.1	6	2	7	1
P. Borbon	0	1	3.86	7	7	2	4	0
R. Grimsley	2	1	2.57	7	7	3	2	0
D. Gullett	0	0	1.29	7	5	2	4	0
C. Carroll	0	1	1.59	5.2	6	4	3	1
McGlothlin	0	0	12.00	3	2	2	3	0

1973 NATIONAL LEAGUE CHAMPIONSHIP SERIES

LINE SCORES	PITCHERS (innings pitched)	HOME RUNS (men on)	HIGHLIGHTS

New York (East) defeats Cincinnati (West) 3 games to 2

GAME 1 - OCTOBER 6

NY	E	010 000 000	1 3 0	Seaver (9)		
CIN	W	000 000 011	2 6 0	Billingham (8), Hall (0), **Borbon** (1)	Rose, Bench	

Tom Seaver set a league playoff record by striking out 13 Reds, but after seven superb scoreless innings, Pete Rose homered in the eighth and Johnny Bench in the ninth as the Reds won.

GAME 2 - OCTOBER 7

NY	E	000 100 004	5 7 0	**Matlack** (9)	Staub	
CIN	W	000 000 000	0 2 0	Gullett (5), Carroll (3), Hall (0.1), Borbon (0.2)		

Jon Matlack pitched a two-hitter and struck out nine pitching the Mets to a 5-0 triumph that evened the Series.

GAME 3 - OCTOBER 8

CIN	W	002 000 000	2 8 1	Grimsley (1.2), Hall (0.1), Tomlin (1.2), Nelson (2.1), Borbon (2)	Menke	
NY	E	151 200 00x	9 11 1	**Koosman** (9)	Staub, Staub (2 on)	

Rusty Staub homered in his first two times at bat to lead Jerry Koosman to an easy win in a game marred by a brawl triggered by Rose's hard slide into Bud Harrelson in the fifth.

GAME 4 - OCTOBER 9

CIN	W	000 000 100 001	2 8 0	Norman (5), Gullett (4), **Carroll** (2), Borbon (1) SV	Perez, Rose	
NY	E	001 000 000 000	1 3 2	Stone (6.2), McGraw (4.1), **Parker** (1)		

Pete Rose hit a home run off Harry Parker in the 12th inning to give the Reds a 2-1 victory that evened the series at two games apiece.

GAME 5 - OCTOBER 10

CIN	W	001 010 000	2 7 1	Billingham (4), Gullett (0), Carroll (2), Grimsley (2)		
NY	E	200 041 00x	7 13 1	**Seaver** (8.1), McGraw (0.2) SV		

Tom Seaver, a victim of non-support most of the regular season, was backed by a 13-hit attack and easily outpitched Cincinnati ace Jack Billingham to give the Mets a 7-2 victory and the pennant.

Team totals

		W	AB	H	2B	3B	HR	R	RBI	BA	BB	SO	ERA
NY	E	3	168	37	5	0	3	23	22	.220	19	28	1.33
CIN	W	2	167	31	6	0	5	8	8	.186	13	42	4.50

Individual Batting

NEW YORK (EAST)

	AB	H	2B	3B	HR	R	RBI	BA
W. Garrett, 3b	23	2	1	0	0	1	1	.087
C. Jones, of	20	6	2	0	0	3	3	.300
J. Grote, c	19	4	0	0	0	2	2	.211
F. Millan, 2b	19	6	0	0	0	5	2	.316
B. Harrelson, ss	18	3	0	0	0	1	2	.167
D. Hahn, of	17	4	0	0	0	2	1	.235
J. Milner, 1b	17	3	0	0	0	2	1	.176
R. Staub, of	15	3	0	0	3	4	5	.200
T. Seaver, p	6	2	2	0	0	1	1	.333
J. Koosman, p	4	2	0	0	1	1	1	.500
W. Mays, of	3	1	0	0	0	1	1	.333
E. Kranepool, of	2	1	0	0	0	0	2	.500
J. Matlack, p	2	0	0	0	0	0	0	.000
K. Boswell	1	0	0	0	0	0	0	.000
G. Stone, p	1	0	0	0	0	0	0	.000
T. McGraw, p	1	0	0	0	0	0	0	.000

Errors: J. Grote, C. Jones, T. McGraw, W. Garrett

CINCINNATI (WEST)

	AB	H	2B	3B	HR	R	RBI	BA
T. Perez, 1b	22	2	0	0	1	1	2	.091
P. Rose, of	21	8	1	0	2	3	2	.381
J. Morgan, 2b	20	2	1	0	0	1	1	.100
J. Bench, c	19	5	2	0	1	1	1	.263
C. Geronimo, of	15	1	0	0	0	0	0	.067
D. Driessen, 3b	12	2	1	0	0	0	1	.167
A. Kosco, of	10	3	0	0	0	0	0	.300
D. Menke, 3b, ss	9	2	0	0	1	1	1	.222
D. Chaney, ss	9	0	0	0	0	0	0	.000
K. Griffey, of	7	1	1	0	0	0	0	.143
Armbrister, of	6	1	0	0	0	0	0	.167
L. Stahl	4	2	0	0	0	1	0	.500
Billingham, p	3	0	0	0	0	0	0	.000
P. Gagliano	3	0	0	0	0	0	0	.000
H. King	2	1	0	0	0	0	0	.500
E. Crosby, ss	2	1	0	0	0	0	0	.500
D. Gullett, p	1	0	0	0	0	0	0	.000
R. Nelson, p	1	0	0	0	0	0	0	.000
F. Norman, p	1	0	0	0	0	0	0	.000

Errors: A. Kosco, D. Driessen

Individual Pitching

NEW YORK (EAST)

	W	L	ERA	IP	H	BB	SO	SV
T. Seaver	1	1	1.62	16.2	13	5	17	0
J. Koosman	1	0	2.00	9	8	0	9	0
J. Matlack	1	0	0.00	9	2	3	9	0
G. Stone	0	0	1.35	6.2	3	2	4	0
T. McGraw	0	0	0.00	5	4	3	3	1
H. Parker	0	1	9.00	1	1	0	0	0

CINCINNATI (WEST)

	W	L	ERA	IP	H	BB	SO	SV
Billingham	0	1	4.50	12	9	4	9	0
D. Gullett	0	1	2.00	9	4	3	6	0
C. Carroll	1	0	1.29	7	5	1	2	0
F. Norman	0	0	1.80	5	1	3	3	0
P. Borbon	1	0	0.00	4.2	3	0	3	1
R. Grimsley	0	1	12.27	3.2	7	2	3	0
R. Nelson	0	0	0.00	2.1	1	1	0	0
D. Tomlin	0	0	16.20	1.2	5	1	1	0
T. Hall	0	0	67.50	0.2	3	4	1	0

1973 AMERICAN LEAGUE CHAMPIONSHIP SERIES

| LINE SCORES | PITCHERS (innings pitched) | HOME RUNS (men on) | HIGHLIGHTS |

Oakland (West) defeats Baltimore (East) 3 games to 2

GAME 1 - OCTOBER 6

OAK W 000 000 000   0 5 1   Blue (0.2), Pina (2), Odom (5), Fingers (0.1)

BAL E 400 000 11x   6 12 0   Palmer (9)

Baltimore pounced upon Vida Blue, knocking him out of the box in the first with a four-run barrage.

GAME 2 - OCTOBER 7

OAK W 100 002 021   6 9 0   Hunter (7.1), Fingers (1.2), SV

BAL E 100 001 010   3 8 0   McNally (7.2), Reynolds (1), Jackson (0.1)

Bando (1 on), Bando, Rudi, Campaneris

Sal Bando, robbed of a home run when Al Bumbry made a spectacular leaping catch of his drive in the third inning, followed with two four-baggers, one with a runner aboard, to lead the A's to a 6-3 triumph.

GAME 3 - OCTOBER 9

BAL E 010 000 000 00   1 3 0   Cuellar (10)

OAK W 000 000 010 01   2 4 3   Holtzman (11)

Williams Campaneris

Bert Campaneris, not known for his batting power, hammered a home run off Mike Cuellar leading off the bottom of the 11th inning to give the A's a thrilling 2-1 triumph over the Orioles.

GAME 4 - OCTOBER 10

BAL E 000 000 410   5 8 0   Palmer (1.1), Reynolds (4.2), Watt (0.1), Jackson (2.2)

OAK W 030 001 000   4 7 0   Blue (6.1), Fingers (2.2)

Etchebarren (2 on), Grich

Bobby Grich hit a home run in the eighth inning to break a 4-4 tie and give the Orioles a 5-4 comeback victory.

GAME 5 - OCTOBER 11

BAL E 000 000 000   0 5 2   Alexander (3.2), Palmer (4.1)

OAK W 001 200 00x   3 7 0   Hunter (9)

Catfish Hunter overpowered the Orioles in the final game, shutting them out 3-0 on a five-hitter. Not a single Oriole reached third base and no more than one runner was on base in any one inning.

Team totals

		W	AB	H	2B	3B	HR	R	RBI	BA	BB	SO	ERA
OAK	W	3	160	32	5	1	5	15	15	.200	17	39	2.74
BAL	E	2	171	36	7	0	3	15	15	.211	16	25	2.80

Individual Batting

OAKLAND (WEST)

	AB	H	2B	3B	HR	R	RBI	BA
R. Jackson, of	21	3	0	0	0	0	0	.143
Campaneris, ss	21	7	1	0	2	3	3	.333
S. Bando, 3b	18	3	0	0	2	2	3	.167
J. Rudi, of	18	4	0	0	1	1	3	.222
G. Tenace, 1b, c	17	4	1	0	0	3	0	.235
D. Green, 2b	13	1	1	0	0	0	1	.077
R. Fosse, c	11	1	1	0	0	2	3	.091
D. Johnson, dh	10	1	0	0	0	0	0	.100
A. Mangual, of	9	1	0	0	0	1	0	.111
V. Davalillo, of, 1b	8	5	1	1	0	2	1	.625
J. Alou, dh	6	2	0	0	0	0	1	.333
Conigliaro, of	4	0	0	0	0	0	0	.000
T. Kubiak, 2b	2	0	0	0	0	0	0	.000
P. Bourque, dh	1	0	0	0	0	0	0	.000
M. Andrews, 1b, dh	1	0	0	0	0	0	0	.000
A. Lewis	0	0	0	0	0	1	0	—

Errors: D. Green (2), Campaneris, V. Davalillo
Stolen Bases: Campaneris (3), G. Tenace

BALTIMORE (EAST)

	AB	H	2B	3B	HR	R	RBI	BA
T. Davis, dh	21	6	1	0	0	1	2	.286
B. Robinson, 3b	20	5	2	0	0	1	2	.250
B. Grich, 2b	20	2	0	0	1	1	1	.100
E. Williams, 1b, c	18	5	2	0	1	2	4	.278
P. Blair, of	18	3	0	0	0	2	0	.167
M. Belanger, ss	16	2	0	0	0	0	1	.125
Etchebarren, c	14	5	1	0	1	1	4	.357
Rettenmund, of	11	1	0	0	0	1	0	.091
D. Baylor, of	11	3	0	0	0	3	1	.273
R. Coggins, of	9	4	1	0	0	1	0	.444
A. Bumbry, of	7	0	0	0	0	0	0	.000
B. Powell, 1b	4	0	0	0	0	1	0	.000
T. Crowley, of	2	0	0	0	0	0	0	.000
F. Baker, ss	0	0	0	0	0	0	0	—
D. Hood	0	0	0	0	0	0	0	—
L. Brown, 3b	0	0	0	0	0	0	0	—

Errors: B. Robinson, A. Bumbry

Individual Pitching

OAKLAND (WEST)

	W	L	ERA	IP	H	BB	SO	SV
C. Hunter	2	0	1.65	16.1	12	5	6	0
K. Holtzman	1	0	0.82	11	3	1	7	0
V. Blue	0	1	10.29	7	8	5	3	0
B. Odom	0	0	1.80	5	6	2	4	0
R. Fingers	0	1	1.93	4.2	4	2	4	1
H. Pina	0	0	0.00	2	3	1	1	0

BALTIMORE (EAST)

	W	L	ERA	IP	H	BB	SO	SV
J. Palmer	1	0	1.84	14.2	11	8	15	0
M. Cuellar	0	1	1.80	10	4	3	11	0
D. McNally	0	1	5.87	7.2	7	2	7	0
B. Reynolds	0	0	3.18	5.2	5	3	5	0
D. Alexander	0	1	4.91	3.2	5	0	1	0
G. Jackson	1	0	0.00	3	0	1	0	0
E. Watt	0	0	0.00	0.1	0	0	0	0

1973 WORLD SERIES

LINE SCORES	PITCHERS (innings pitched)	HOME RUNS (men on)	HIGHLIGHTS

Oakland (A.L.) defeats New York (N.L.) 4 games to 3

GAME 1 - OCTOBER 13

NY	N	000 100 000	1 7 2	Matlack (6), McGraw (2)	
OAK	A	002 000 00x	2 4 0	Holtzman (5), Fingers (3.1), Knowles (0.2) SV	

Oakland scored two unearned runs in the third, with help from errors by Millan and Mays, and hung on for the victory.

GAME 2 - OCTOBER 14

NY	N	011 004 000 004	10 15 1	Koosman (2.1), Sadecki (1.2), Parker (1), McGraw (6), Stone (1), SV	Jones, Garrett
OAK	A	210 000 102 001	7 13 5	Blue (5.1), Pina (0), Knowles (1.2), Odom (2), Fingers (2.2), Lindblad (0.1)	

In the longest (4:13) and perhaps the loosest Series game in history, the Mets prevailed by virtue of two costly errors by Andrews in the 12th, when New York pushed across four runs. The two teams tied a record by using 11 pitchers.

GAME 3 - OCTOBER 16

OAK	A	000 001 010 01	3 10 1	Hunter (6), Knowles (2), Lindblad (2), Fingers (1), SV	
NY	N	200 000 000 00	2 10 2	Seaver (8), Sadecki (0), McGraw (2), Parker (1)	Garrett

Campaneris got the decisive hit, rapping a single following a walk and passed ball on a third strike in the 11th. Seaver fanned 12 in eight innings.

GAME 4 - OCTOBER 17

OAK	A	000 100 000	1 5 1	Holtzman (0.1), Odom (2.2), Knowles (1), Pina (3), Lindblad (1)	
NY	N	300 300 00x	6 13 1	Matlack (8), Sadecki (1), SV	Staub (2 on)

Staub had a perfect night with three singles and a three-run homer for five RBIs, while Matlack throttled the A's on three hits in eight innings.

GAME 5 - OCTOBER 18

OAK	A	000 000 000	0 3 1	Blue (5.2), Knowles (0.1), Fingers (2)	
NY	N	010 001 00x	2 7 1	Koosman (6.1), McGraw (2.2), SV	

Jones doubled in a run in the second and Hahn tripled home the other in the sixth. Koosman and McGraw allowed just two singles and a double.

GAME 6 - OCTOBER 20

NY	N	000 000 010	1 6 2	Seaver (7), McGraw (1)	
OAK	A	101 000 01x	3 7 0	Hunter (7.1), Knowles (0.1), Fingers (1.1) SV	

Jackson ripped two RBI doubles, then singled and scored the A's other run.

GAME 7 - OCTOBER 21

NY	N	000 001 001	2 8 1	Matlack (2.2), Parker (1.1), Sadecki (2), Stone (2)	
OAK	A	004 010 00x	5 9 1	Holtzman (5.1), Fingers (3.1), Knowles (0.1), SV	Campaneris (1 on), Jackson (1 on)

Campaneris and Jackson bashed two-run homers in third inning for the A's first two homers of Series as Oakland captured their second World Series title in a row. After the game, A's manager Dick Williams quit.

Team totals

		W	AB	H	2B	3B	HR	R	RBI	BA	BB	SO	ERA
OAK	A	4	241	51	12	3	2	21	20	.212	28	62	2.32
NY	N	3	261	66	7	2	4	24	16	.253	26	36	2.22

Individual Batting

OAKLAND (A.L.)

	AB	H	2B	3B	HR	R	RBI	BA
Campaneris, ss	31	9	0	1	1	6	3	.290
R. Jackson, of	29	9	3	1	1	3	6	.310
J. Rudi, of	27	9	2	0	0	3	4	.333
S. Bando, 3b	26	6	1	1	0	5	1	.231
J. Alou, of	19	3	1	0	0	0	3	.158
R. Fosse, c	19	3	1	0	0	0	0	.158
G. Tenace, c, 1b	19	3	1	0	0	0	3	.158
D. Green, 2b	16	1	0	0	0	0	0	.063
V. Davalillo, 1b, of	11	1	0	0	0	0	0	.091
D. Johnson, 1b	10	3	1	0	0	0	0	.300
A. Mangual, of	6	0	0	0	0	0	0	.000
C. Hunter, p	5	0	0	0	0	0	0	.000
V. Blue, p	4	0	0	0	0	0	0	.000
R. Fingers, p	3	1	0	0	0	0	0	.333
Conigliaro	3	0	0	0	0	0	0	.000
T. Kubiak, 2b	3	0	0	0	0	1	0	.000
K. Holtzman, p	3	2	2	0	0	2	0	.667
M. Andrews, 2b	3	0	0	0	0	0	0	.000
P. Bourque, 1b	2	1	0	0	0	0	0	.500
P. Lindblad, p	1	0	0	0	0	0	0	.000
B. Odom, p	1	0	0	0	0	0	0	.000
A. Lewis	0	0	0	0	0	1	0	–

Errors: M. Andrews (2), G. Tenace (2), S. Bando, Campaneris, D. Green, C. Hunter, D. Knowles
Stolen Bases: Campaneris (3)

NEW YORK (N.L.)

	AB	H	2B	3B	HR	R	RBI	BA
F. Millan, 2b	32	6	1	1	0	3	1	.188
W. Garrett, 3b	30	5	0	0	2	4	2	.167
J. Grote, c	30	8	0	0	0	0	2	.267
D. Hahn, of	29	7	1	1	0	2	2	.241
C. Jones, of	28	8	2	0	1	5	1	.286
J. Milner, 1b	27	8	0	0	1	2	2	.296
R. Staub, of	26	11	2	0	1	1	6	.423
B. Harrelson, ss	24	6	1	0	0	2	1	.250
W. Mays, of	7	2	0	0	0	1	1	.286
T. Seaver, p	5	0	0	0	0	0	0	.000
J. Koosman, p	4	0	0	0	0	0	0	.000
J. Matlack, p	4	1	0	0	0	0	0	.250
J. Beauchamp	4	0	0	0	0	0	0	.000
E. Kranepool	3	0	0	0	0	0	0	.000
K. Boswell	3	3	0	0	0	1	0	1.000
T. McGraw, p	3	1	0	0	0	1	0	.333
G. Theodore, of	2	0	0	0	0	0	0	.000
R. Hodges	0	0	0	0	0	0	0	–
T. Martinez	0	0	0	0	0	0	0	–

Errors: F. Millan (3), W. Garrett (3), J. Koosman, D. Hahn, C. Jones, W. Mays

Individual Pitching

OAKLAND (A.L.)

	W	L	ERA	IP	H	BB	SO	SV
C. Hunter	1	0	2.03	13.1	11	4	6	0
R. Fingers	0	1	0.66	13.2	13	4	8	2
V. Blue	0	1	4.91	11	10	3	8	0
K. Holtzman	2	1	4.22	10.2	13	5	6	0
D. Knowles	0	0	0.00	6.1	4	5	5	2
B. Odom	0	0	3.86	4.2	5	2	2	0
P. Lindblad	1	0	0.00	3.1	4	1	1	0
H. Pina	0	0	0.00	3	6	2	0	0

NEW YORK (N.L.)

	W	L	ERA	IP	H	BB	SO	SV
J. Matlack	1	2	2.16	16.2	10	5	11	0
T. Seaver	0	1	2.40	15	13	3	18	0
T. McGraw	1	0	2.63	13.2	8	9	14	1
J. Koosman	1	0	3.12	8.2	9	7	8	0
R. Sadecki	0	0	1.93	4.2	5	1	6	1
G. Stone	0	0	0.00	3	4	1	3	1
H. Parker	0	1	0.00	3.1	2	2	2	0

1974 NATIONAL LEAGUE CHAMPIONSHIP SERIES

LINE SCORES		PITCHERS (innings pitched)	HOME RUNS (men on)	HIGHLIGHTS

Los Angeles (West) defeats Pittsburgh (East) 3 games to 1

GAME 1 - OCTOBER 5

LA	W	010 000 002	3 9 2	Sutton (9)	
PIT	E	000 000 000	0 4 0	Reuss (7), Giusti (2)	

Don Sutton pitched a 4-hitter for his 10th straight victory while Jimmy Wynn, Joe Ferguson and Dave Lopes drove in a run each off loser Jerry Reuss in the Dodgers' opening win.

GAME 2 - OCTOBER 6

LA	W	100 100 030	5 12 0	Messersmith (7), Marshall (2)	Cey
PIT	E	000 000 200	2 8 3	Rooker (7), Giusti (0), Demery (0), Hernandez (2)	

Ron Cey slammed a homer, two doubles and a single as the Dodgers racked four Pittsburgh pitchers for 12 hits and gained a 2-0 lead in the series. Andy Messersmith was the winner.

GAME 3 - OCTOBER 8

PIT	E	502 000 000	7 10 0	Kison (6.2), Hernandez (2.1)	Hebner (1 on), Stargell (2 on)
LA	W	000 000 000	0 4 5	Rau (0.2), Hough (2.1), Downing (4), Solomon (2)	

Willie Stargell and Richie Hebner each hammered two hits, including home runs, and drove in six runs between them as the Pirates broke through for their only victory. Bruce Kison and Ramon Hernandez combined on the shutout.

GAME 4 - OCTOBER 9

PIT	E	000 000 100	1 3 1	Reuss (2.2), Brett (2.1), Demery (1), Giusti (1.1), Pizarro (0.2)	Stargell
LA	W	102 022 23x	12 12 0	Sutton (8), Marshall (1)	Garvey (1 on), Garvey

Steve Garvey slammed two home runs and two singles, driving in four runs as the Dodgers clobbered 5 Pittsburgh pitchers for 12 hits to clinch the series. Don Sutton hurled his 2nd series win and 11th consecutive victory of the year.

Team totals

		W	AB	H	2B	3B	HR	R	RBI	BA	BB	SO	ERA
LA	W	3	138	37	8	1	3	20	19	.268	30	16	2.00
PIT	E	1	129	25	1	1	3	10	10	.194	8	17	4.89

Individual Batting

LOS ANGELES (WEST)

	AB	H	2B	3B	HR	R	RBI	BA
B. Russell, ss	18	7	0	0	0	1	3	.389
S. Garvey, 1b	18	7	1	0	2	4	5	.389
B. Buckner, of	18	3	1	0	0	0	0	.167
R. Cey, 3b	16	5	3	0	1	2	1	.313
D. Lopes, 2b	15	4	0	1	0	4	3	.267
J. Ferguson, of, c	13	3	0	0	0	3	2	.231
J. Wynn, of	10	2	2	0	0	4	2	.200
S. Yeager, c	9	0	0	0	0	1	0	.000
D. Sutton, p	7	2	0	0	0	0	1	.286
W. Crawford, of	4	1	0	0	0	1	1	.250
M. Mota, of	3	1	0	0	0	0	1	.333
Messersmith, p	3	0	0	0	0	0	0	.000
R. Auerbach	1	1	1	0	0	0	0	1.000
A. Downing, p	1	0	0	0	0	0	0	.000
K. McMullen	1	0	0	0	0	0	0	.000
T. Paciorek, of	1	1	0	0	0	0	0	1.000
L. Lacy	0	0	0	0	0	0	0	–
V. Joshua	0	0	0	0	0	0	0	–

Errors: R. Cey (2), J. Ferguson, C. Hough, D. Lopes, A. Downing, S. Garvey
Stolen Bases: D. Lopes (3), J. Wynn, S. Yeager

PITTSBURGH (EAST)

	AB	H	2B	3B	HR	R	RBI	BA
Sanguillen, c	16	4	1	0	0	0	0	.250
R. Stennett, 2b	16	1	0	0	0	1	0	.063
W. Stargell, of	15	6	0	0	2	3	4	.400
A. Oliver, of	14	2	0	0	0	1	1	.143
R. Hebner, 3b	13	3	0	0	1	1	4	.231
R. Zisk, of	10	3	0	0	0	0	1	.300
Kirkpatrick, 1b	9	0	0	0	0	0	0	.000
D. Parker, of	8	1	0	0	0	0	0	.125
M. Mendoza, ss	5	1	0	0	0	0	1	.200
P. Popovich, ss	5	3	0	0	0	0	0	.600
B. Robertson, 1b	5	0	0	0	0	1	0	.000
B. Kison, p	3	0	0	0	0	0	0	.000
J. Reuss, p	2	0	0	0	0	0	0	.000
F. Taveras, ss	2	0	0	0	0	0	0	.000
J. Rooker, p	2	1	0	0	0	0	0	.500
R. Hernandez, p	1	0	0	0	0	0	0	.000
K. Brett, p	1	0	0	0	0	0	0	.000
A. Howe	1	0	0	0	0	0	0	.000
G. Clines, of	1	0	0	0	0	1	0	.000

Errors: Sanguillen (2), J. Rooker, R. Stennett
Stolen Bases: F. Taveras

Individual Pitching

LOS ANGELES (WEST)

	W	L	ERA	IP	H	BB	SO	SV
D. Sutton	2	0	0.53	17	7	2	13	0
Messersmith	1	0	2.57	7	8	3	0	0
A. Downing	0	0	0.00	4	1	1	0	0
M. Marshall	0	0	0.00	3	0	0	1	0
C. Hough	0	0	7.71	2.1	4	0	2	0
E. Solomon	0	0	0.00	2	2	1	1	0
D. Rau	0	1	40.50	0.2	3	1	0	0

PITTSBURGH (EAST)

	W	L	ERA	IP	H	BB	SO	SV
J. Reuss	0	2	3.72	9.2	7	8	3	0
J. Rooker	0	0	2.57	7	6	5	4	0
B. Kison	1	0	0.00	6.2	2	6	5	0
R. Hernandez	0	0	0.00	4.1	3	1	2	0
D. Giusti	0	1	21.60	3.1	13	5	1	0
K. Brett	0	0	7.71	2.1	3	2	1	0
L. Demery	0	0	27.00	1	3	2	0	0
J. Pizarro	0	0	0.00	0.2	0	1	0	0

1974 AMERICAN LEAGUE CHAMPIONSHIP SERIES

LINE SCORES	PITCHERS (innings pitched)	HOME RUNS (men on)	HIGHLIGHTS

Oakland (West) defeats Baltimore (East) 3 games to 1

GAME 1 - OCTOBER 5

BAL E 100 140 000 6 10 0   Cuellar (8), Grimsley (1)   Blair, Robinson (1 on), Grich (1 on)

OAK W 001 010 001 3 9 0   Hunter (4.2), Odom (3.1), Fingers (1)

A 2-run homer by Bobby Grich and solo homers by Paul Blair and Brooks Robinson supported Mike Cuellar's 9-hit pitching as Baltimore drew first blood at the expense of Catfish Hunter.

GAME 2 - OCTOBER 6

BAL E 000 000 000 0 5 2   McNally (5.2), Garland (0.2), Reynolds (1.1), Jackson (0.1)   Fosse (2 on), Bando

OAK W 000 101 03x 5 8 0   Holtzman (9)

Ray Fosse hit a 3-run homer, Sal Bando hit his first homer of the year off Baltimore pitching, and Ken Holtzman hurled a 5-hit shutout as the A's evened the series.

GAME 3 - OCTOBER 8

OAK W 000 100 000 1 4 2   Blue (9)   Bando

BAL E 000 000 000 0 2 1   Palmer (9)

Vida Blue pitched a masterful two-hitter, striking out seven and walking none, and Bando added another homer to provide the game's only run.

GAME 4 - OCTOBER 9

OAK W 000 010 100 2 1 0   Hunter (7), Fingers (2), SV

BAL E 000 000 001 1 5 1   Cuellar (4.2), Grimsley (4.1)

One hit was all the A's needed to win the final game. They drew 11 walks, nine off loser Cuellar, who walked Gene Tenace in the 5th to force in a run. Reggie Jackson doubled in Bando with what proved to be the winning run in the seventh.

Team totals

		W	AB	H	2B	3B	HR	R	RBI	BA	BB	SO	ERA
OAK	W	3	120	22	4	1	3	11	11	.183	22	16	1.75
BAL	E	1	124	22	1	0	3	7	7	.177	5	20	1.80

Individual Batting

OAKLAND (WEST)

	AB	H	2B	3B	HR	R	RBI	BA
Campaneris, ss	17	3	0	0	0	0	3	.176
B. North, of	16	1	1	0	0	3	0	.063
S. Bando, 3b	13	3	0	0	2	4	2	.231
J. Rudi, of	13	2	0	1	0	0	1	.154
R. Jackson, of, dh	12	2	1	0	0	0	1	.167
R. Fosse, c	12	4	1	0	1	1	3	.333
G. Tenace, 1b	11	0	0	0	0	1	1	.000
Washington, of	11	3	1	0	0	1	0	.273
D. Green, 2b	9	2	0	0	0	0	0	.222
A. Mangual, dh	4	1	0	0	0	0	0	.250
D. Maxvill, 2b	1	0	0	0	0	0	0	.000
J. Alou	1	1	0	0	0	0	0	1.000
J. Holt, 1b	0	0	0	0	0	0	0	—
Washington	0	0	0	0	0	0	0	—
M. Trillo	0	0	0	0	0	1	0	—

Errors: D. Green (2)
Stolen Bases: G. Tenace, B. North, Campaneris

BALTIMORE (EAST)

	AB	H	2B	3B	HR	R	RBI	BA
B. Grich, 2b	16	4	1	0	1	2	2	.250
D. Baylor, of	15	4	0	0	0	0	0	.267
T. Davis, dh	15	4	0	0	0	0	1	.267
P. Blair, of	14	4	0	1	1	3	2	.286
B. Robinson, 3b	12	1	0	1	1	1	1	.083
R. Coggins, of	11	0	0	0	0	0	0	.000
M. Belanger, ss	9	0	0	0	0	0	0	.000
B. Powell, 1b	8	1	0	0	0	0	1	.125
E. Hendricks, c	6	1	0	0	0	1	0	.167
E. Williams, 1b	6	0	0	0	0	0	0	.000
Etchebarren, c	6	2	0	0	0	0	0	.333
E. Cabell, of	4	1	0	0	0	0	0	.250
A. Bumbry	1	0	0	0	0	0	0	.000
C. Motton	1	0	0	0	0	0	0	.000
F. Baker, ss	0	0	0	0	0	0	0	—

Errors: M. Belanger, E. Williams, F. Baker, B. Grich

Individual Pitching

OAKLAND (WEST)

	W	L	ERA	IP	H	BB	SO	SV
C. Hunter	1	1	4.63	11.2	11	2	6	0
V. Blue	1	0	0.00	9	2	0	7	0
K. Holtzman	1	0	0.00	9	5	2	3	0
B. Odom	0	0	0.00	3.1	1	0	1	0
R. Fingers	0	0	3.00	3	3	1	3	1

BALTIMORE (EAST)

	W	L	ERA	IP	H	BB	SO	SV
M. Cuellar	1	1	2.84	12.2	9	13	6	0
J. Palmer	0	1	1.00	9	4	1	4	0
D. McNally	0	1	1.59	5.2	6	2	2	0
R. Grimsley	0	0	1.69	5.1	1	2	2	0
B. Reynolds	0	0	0.00	1.1	0	3	1	0
W. Garland	0	0	0.00	0.2	1	1	0	0
G. Jackson	0	0	0.00	0.1	1	0	1	0

1974 WORLD SERIES

LINE SCORES	PITCHERS (innings pitched)	HOME RUNS (men on)	HIGHLIGHTS

Oakland (A.L.) defeats Los Angeles (N.L.) 4 games to 1

GAME 1 - OCTOBER 12

OAK	A	010 010 010	3 6 2	Holtzman (4.1), **Fingers** (4.1), Hunter (0.1), SV	Jackson
LA	N	000 010 001	2 11 1	Messersmith (8), Marshall (1)	Wynn

A second-inning home run by Jackson proved to be the difference. Starting pitcher Holtzman doubled in the fifth and scored on a squeeze bunt by Campaneris. Fingers, in relief, was credited with the victory.

GAME 2 - OCTOBER 13

OAK	A	000 000 002	2 6 0	Blue (7), Odom (1)	
LA	N	010 002 00x	3 6 1	**Sutton** (8), Marshall (1), SV	Ferguson (1 on)

Ferguson's home run with a runner on base in the sixth off Blue gave Sutton the victory with help from Marshall, who picked off designated pinch runner Herb Washington in the ninth.

GAME 3 - OCTOBER 15

LA	N	000 000 011	2 7 2	Downing (3.2), Brewer (0.1), Hough (2), Marshall (2)	Buckner, Crawford
OAK	A	002 100 00x	3 5 2	**Hunter** (7.1), Fingers (1.2), SV	

Two unearned runs in the third brought about the downfall of Al Downing and gave the A's their second victory in three 3-2 decisions. Fingers saved win for Hunter.

GAME 4 - OCTOBER 16

LA	N	000 200 000	2 7 1	Messersmith (8), Marshall	
OAK	A	001 004 00x	5 7 0	**Holtzman** (7.2), Fingers (1.1), SV	Holtzman

Holtzman helped his cause with a home run after the Dodgers had taken a 2-1 lead on Russell's two-run triple. The A's erupted for 4 runs in the sixth. Pinch hitter Holt drove in two runs with a single.

GAME 5 - OCTOBER 17

LA	N	000 002 000	2 5 1	Sutton (5), Marshall (3)	
OAK	A	110 000 10x	3 6 1	Blue (6.2), **Odom** (0.1), Fingers (2), SV	Fosse, Rudi

Rudi's home run off ace reliever Marshall broke a 2-2 tie in the 7th, giving the A's their third 3-2 victory and their third straight Series title. Fingers matched Larry Sherry's feat from 1959 by figuring in all four Oakland wins with three saves and a win.

Team totals

		W	AB	H	2B	3B	HR	R	RBI	BA	BB	SO	ERA
OAK	A	4	142	30	4	0	4	16	14	.211	16	42	2.05
LA	N	1	158	36	4	1	4	11	10	.228	16	32	2.79

Individual Batting

OAKLAND (A.L.)

	AB	H	2B	3B	HR	R	RBI	BA
J. Rudi, 1b, of	18	6	0	0	1	1	4	.333
B. North, of	17	1	0	0	0	3	0	.059
Campaneris, ss	17	6	2	0	1	1	2	.353
S. Bando, 3b	16	1	0	0	0	3	2	.063
R. Fosse, c	14	2	0	0	1	1	1	.143
R. Jackson, of	14	4	1	0	1	3	1	.286
D. Green, 2b	13	0	0	0	0	1	1	.000
G. Tenace, 1b	9	2	0	0	0	0	0	.222
Washington, of	7	4	0	0	0	1	0	.571
V. Blue, p	4	0	0	0	0	0	0	.000
K. Holtzman, p	4	2	1	0	1	2	1	.500
J. Holt, 1b	3	2	0	0	0	0	2	.667
R. Fingers, p	2	0	0	0	0	0	0	.000
C. Hunter, p	2	0	0	0	0	0	0	.000
J. Alou	1	0	0	0	0	0	0	.000
A. Mangual	1	0	0	0	0	0	0	.000
Washington	0	0	0	0	0	0	0	—
D. Maxvill, 2b	0	0	0	0	0	0	0	—
L. Haney, c	0	0	0	0	0	0	0	—

Errors: Campaneris (2), D. Green, R. Jackson, B. North
Stolen Bases: Campaneris, R. Jackson, B. North

LOS ANGELES (N.L.)

	AB	H	2B	3B	HR	R	RBI	BA
S. Garvey, 1b	21	8	0	0	0	2	1	.381
B. Buckner, of	20	5	1	0	1	1	1	.250
D. Lopes, 2b	18	2	0	0	0	2	0	.111
B. Russell, ss	18	4	0	1	0	0	2	.222
R. Cey, 3b	17	3	0	0	0	1	0	.176
J. Ferguson, c, of	16	2	0	0	1	2	2	.125
J. Wynn, of	16	3	1	0	1	1	2	.188
S. Yeager, c	11	4	1	0	0	0	1	.364
W. Crawford, of	6	2	0	0	1	1	0	.333
V. Joshua	4	0	0	0	0	0	0	.000
Messersmith, p	4	2	0	0	0	0	0	.500
D. Sutton, p	3	0	0	0	0	0	0	.000
T. Paciorek	2	1	1	0	0	1	0	.500
L. Lacy	1	0	0	0	0	0	0	.000
A. Downing, p	1	0	0	0	0	0	0	.000
M. Marshall, p	0	0	0	0	0	0	1	—
R. Auerbach	0	0	0	0	0	0	0	—

Errors: J. Ferguson (2), S. Yeager, B. Russell, Messersmith, R. Cey
Stolen Bases: D. Lopes (2), J. Ferguson

Individual Pitching

OAKLAND (A.L.)

	W	L	ERA	IP	H	BB	SO	SV
V. Blue	0	1	3.29	13.2	10	7	9	0
K. Holtzman	1	0	1.50	12	13	4	10	0
R. Fingers	1	0	1.93	9.1	8	2	6	2
C. Hunter	1	0	1.17	7.2	5	2	5	1
B. Odom	1	0	0.00	1.1	0	1	2	0

LOS ANGELES (N.L.)

	W	L	ERA	IP	H	BB	SO	SV
Messersmith	0	2	4.50	14	11	7	12	0
D. Sutton	1	0	2.77	13	9	3	12	0
M. Marshall	0	1	1.00	9	6	1	10	1
A. Downing	0	1	2.45	3.2	4	4	3	0
C. Hough	0	0	0.00	2	0	1	4	0
J. Brewer	0	0	0.00	0.1	0	0	1	0

1975 NATIONAL LEAGUE CHAMPIONSHIP SERIES

LINE SCORES	PITCHERS (innings pitched)	HOME RUNS (men on)	HIGHLIGHTS

Cincinnati (West) defeats Pittsburgh (East) 3 games to 0

GAME 1 - OCTOBER 4

PIT E 020 000 001   3 8 0   Reuss (2.2), Brett (1.2), Demery (2), Ellis (2)

CIN W 013 040 00x   8 11 0 Gullett (9)   Gullett

Gullett pitched an 8-hitter and had 3 RBIs with a homer and single.

GAME 2 - OCTOBER 5

PIT E 000 100 000   1 5 0   Rooker (4), Tekulve (1), Brett (1), Kison (2)

CIN W 200 201 10x   6 12 1 Norman (6), Eastwick (3) SV   Perez (1 on)

Perez drove in 3 runs with a home run and single, and Eastwick saved Norman's victory.

GAME 3 - OCTOBER 7

CIN W 010 000 020 2 5 6 0 Nolan (6), C. Carroll (1), McEnaney (1.1), Eastwick (0.2), Borbon (1) SV   Rose (1 on), Concepcion

PIT E 000 002 001 0 3 7 2 Candelaria (7.2), Giusti (1.2), Hernandez (0.2), Tekulve (0.1)   Oliver (1 on)

Rose's 2-run home run and Armbrister's tie-breaking sacrifice fly ruined rookie Candelaria's 14-strikeout performance.

Team totals

		W	AB	H	2B	3B	HR	R	RBI	BA	BB	SO	ERA
CIN	W	3	102	29	4	0	4	19	18	.284	9	28	2.25
PIT	E	0	101	20	3	0	1	7	7	.198	10	18	6.58

Individual Batting

CINCINNATI (WEST)

	AB	H	2B	3B	HR	R	RBI	BA
P. Rose, 3b	14	5	0	0	1	3	2	.357
J. Bench, c	13	1	0	0	0	1	0	.077
T. Perez, 1b	12	5	0	0	1	3	4	.417
K. Griffey, of	12	4	1	0	0	4	4	.333
Concepcion, ss	11	5	0	0	1	2	1	.455
J. Morgan, 2b	11	3	3	0	0	2	1	.273
G. Foster, of	11	4	0	0	0	3	0	.364
C. Geronimo, of	10	0	0	0	0	0	1	.000
D. Gullett, p	4	2	0	0	1	1	3	.500
G. Nolan, p	2	0	0	0	0	0	0	.000
Rettenmund	1	0	0	0	0	0	0	.000
F. Norman, p	1	0	0	0	0	0	1	.000
T. Crowley	0	0	0	0	0	0	0	–
Armbrister	0	0	0	0	0	0	1	–

Errors: Concepcion

Stolen Bases: J. Morgan (4), K. Griffey (3), Concepcion (2), J. Bench, G. Foster

PITTSBURGH (EAST)

	AB	H	2B	3B	HR	R	RBI	BA
R. Stennett, 2b, ss	14	3	0	0	0	0	0	.214
R. Hebner, 3b	12	4	1	0	0	2	2	.333
Sanguillen, c	12	2	0	0	0	0	0	.167
W. Stargell, 1b	11	2	1	0	0	1	0	.182
A. Oliver, of	11	2	0	0	1	1	2	.182
R. Zisk, of	10	5	1	0	0	0	0	.500
D. Parker, of	10	0	0	0	0	2	0	.000
F. Taveras, ss	7	1	0	0	0	0	1	.143
Candelaria, p	3	0	0	0	0	0	0	.000
W. Randolph, 2b	2	0	0	0	0	1	0	.000
B. Robertson, 1b	2	1	0	0	0	0	1	.500
Kirkpatrick	2	0	0	0	0	0	0	.000
B. Robinson	2	0	0	0	0	0	0	.000
J. Rooker, p	1	0	0	0	0	0	0	.000
C. Reynolds, ss	1	0	0	0	0	0	0	.000
J. Reuss, p	1	0	0	0	0	0	0	.000
D. Dyer	0	0	0	0	0	0	1	–

Errors: Sanguillen, C. Reynolds

Individual Pitching

CINCINNATI (WEST)

	W	L	ERA	IP	H	BB	SO	SV
D. Gullett	1	0	3.00	9	8	2	5	0
F. Norman	1	0	1.50	6	4	5	4	0
G. Nolan	0	0	3.00	6	5	0	5	0
R. Eastwick	0	0	0.00	3.2	2	1	1	1
W. McEnaney	0	0	6.75	1.1	1	0	1	0
P. Borbon	0	0	0.00	1	0	0	1	0
C. Carroll	0	0	0.00	1	0	1	1	0

PITTSBURGH (EAST)

	W	L	ERA	IP	H	BB	SO	SV
Candelaria	0	0	3.52	7.2	3	2	14	0
J. Rooker	0	1	9.00	4	7	0	5	0
D. Ellis	0	0	0.00	2	2	0	2	0
J. Reuss	0	1	13.50	2.2	4	1	1	0
L. Demery	0	0	18.00	2	4	1	1	0
K. Brett	0	0	0.00	2.1	1	0	1	0
B. Kison	0	0	4.50	2	2	1	1	0
K. Tekulve	0	0	6.75	1.1	3	1	2	0
D. Giusti	0	0	0.00	1.1	0	0	1	0
R. Hernandez	0	1	27.00	0.2	3	0	0	0

1975 AMERICAN LEAGUE CHAMPIONSHIP SERIES

LINE SCORES	PITCHERS (innings pitched)	HOME RUNS (men on)	HIGHLIGHTS

Boston (East) defeats Oakland (West) 3 games to 0

GAME 1 - OCTOBER 4

OAK	W	000 000 010	1 3 4	Holtzman (6.1), Todd (0), Lindblad (0.1) Bosman (0.1), Abbott (1)	
BOS	E	200 000 50x	7 8 3	Tiant (9)	

Tiant pitched a three-hitter and Lynn doubled home two runs in Boston's five-run seventh to put the game away.

GAME 2 - OCTOBER 5

OAK	W	200 100 000	3 10 0	Blue (3), Todd (1), Fingers (4)	Jackson (1 on)
BOS	E	000 301 11x	6 12 0	Cleveland (5), Moret (1), Drago (3) SV	Petrocelli, Yastrzemski (1 on)

Boston's win featured Yastrzemski's homer and Drago's scoreless relief pitching.

GAME 3 - OCTOBER 7

BOS	E	000 130 010	5 11 1	Wise (7.1), Drago (2.1) SV	
OAK	W	000 001 020	3 6 2	Holtzman (4.2), Todd (0), Lindblad (4.1)	

Yastrzemski cracked two hits and made two defensive gems to spark the Red Sox to a three-game sweep.

Team totals

		W	AB	H	2B	3B	HR	R	RBI	BA	BB	SO	ERA
BOS	E	3	98	31	8	0	2	18	14	.316	3	12	1.67
OAK	W	0	98	19	6	0	1	7	7	.194	9	14	4.32

Individual Batting

BOSTON (EAST)

	AB	H	2B	3B	HR	R	RBI	BA
Petrocelli, 3b	12	2	0	0	1	1	2	.167
J. Beniquez, dh	12	3	0	0	0	2	1	.250
C. Fisk, c	12	5	1	0	0	4	2	.417
F. Lynn, of	11	4	1	0	0	1	3	.364
D. Doyle, 2b	11	3	0	0	0	3	1	.273
Yastrzemski, of	11	5	1	0	1	4	2	.455
C. Cooper, 1b	10	4	2	0	0	0	1	.400
D. Evans, of	10	1	1	0	0	1	1	.100
R. Burleson, ss	9	4	2	0	0	2	1	.444

Errors: R. Burleson, F. Lynn, C. Cooper, D. Doyle
Stolen Bases: J. Beniquez (2), C. Fisk

OAKLAND (WEST)

	AB	H	2B	3B	HR	R	RBI	BA
S. Bando, 3b	12	6	2	0	0	1	2	.500
Washington, of, dh	12	3	1	0	0	1	1	.250
R. Jackson, of	12	5	0	0	1	1	3	.417
J. Rudi, 1b, of	12	3	2	0	0	1	0	.250
Campaneris, ss	11	0	0	0	0	1	0	.000
B. North, of	10	0	0	0	0	0	1	.000
G. Tenace, 1b, c	9	0	0	0	0	0	0	.000
B. Williams, dh	8	0	0	0	0	0	0	.000
P. Garner, 2b	5	0	0	0	0	0	0	.000
J. Holt, 1b	3	1	1	0	0	0	0	.333
R. Fosse, c	2	0	0	0	0	0	0	.000
C. Tovar, 2b	2	1	0	0	0	2	0	.500
T. Harper	0	0	0	0	0	0	0	–
D. Hopkins, dh	0	0	0	0	0	0	0	–
T. Martinez, 2b	0	0	0	0	0	0	0	–

Errors: Washington (2), B. North, P. Garner, S. Bando, C. Tovar

Individual Pitching

BOSTON (EAST)

	W	L	ERA	IP	H	BB	SO	SV
L. Tiant	1	0	0.00	9	3	3	8	0
R. Wise	1	0	2.45	7.1	6	3	2	0
R. Cleveland	0	0	5.40	5	7	1	2	0
D. Drago	0	0	0.00	4.2	2	1	2	2
R. Moret	1	0	0.00	1	1	1	0	0

OAKLAND (WEST)

	W	L	ERA	IP	H	BB	SO	SV
K. Holtzman	0	2	4.09	11	12	1	7	0
P. Lindblad	0	0	0.00	4.2	5	1	0	0
R. Fingers	0	1	6.75	4	5	1	3	0
V. Blue	0	0	9.00	3	6	0	2	0
J. Todd	0	0	9.00	1	3	0	0	0
G. Abbott	0	0	4.04	1	0	0	0	0
D. Bosman	0	0	0.00	0.1	0	0	0	0

1975 WORLD SERIES

LINE SCORES	PITCHERS (innings pitched)	HOME RUNS (men on)	HIGHLIGHTS

Cincinnati (N.L.) defeats Boston (A.L.) 4 games to 3

GAME 1 - OCTOBER 11

CIN	N	000 000 000	0 5 0	Gullett (6), Carroll (0), McEnaney (1)
BOS	A	000 000 60x	6 12 0	Tiant (9)

Tiant pitched a five-hitter, singled and scored the first run to lead Boston to a 6-0 victory over Cincinnati.

GAME 2 - OCTOBER 12

CIN	N	000 100 002	3 7 1	Billingham (5.2), Borbon (0.1), McEnaney (1), Eastwick (2)
BOS	A	100 001 000	2 7 0	Lee (8), Drago (1)

Trailing 2-1 in the ninth, Bench doubled against Boston starter Lee. Drago retired two batters, but Concepcion singled home Bench, stole second, and scored on Griffey's double.

GAME 3 - OCTOBER 14

BOS	A	010 001 102 0	5 10 2	Wise (4.1), Burton (0.1), Cleveland (1.1), Willoughby (3), Moret (0.1)	Fisk, Carbo, Evans (1 on)
CIN	N	000 230 000 1	6 7 0	Nolan (4), Darcy (2), Carroll (0.2), McEnaney (1.2), Eastwick (1.2)	Bench, Concepcion, Geronimo

A record six home runs were hit but a 10th inning bunt was decisive as the Reds scored in the extra inning for a 6-5 victory. Trailing 5-1, the Red Sox had rallied to score the tying run on Evans's ninth-inning homer.

GAME 4 - OCTOBER 15

BOS	A	000 500 000	5 11 1	Tiant (9)
CIN	N	200 200 000	4 9 1	Norman (3.1), Borbon (0.2), Carroll (2), Eastwick (3)

Although he needed 163 pitches to do it, Tiant went the distance defeating the Reds 5-4 to even the series at two apiece.

GAME 5 - OCTOBER 16

BOS	A	100 000 001	2 5 0	Cleveland (5), Willoughby (2), Pole (0), Segui (1)	
CIN	N	000 113 01x	6 8 0	Gullett (8.2), Eastwick (0.1) SV	Perez (2 on), Perez

After going 0-for-15, Perez broke loose, driving in four runs with two home runs to lead the Reds to a 6-2 victory and a 3 games to 2 edge.

GAME 6 - OCTOBER 21

CIN	N	000 030 210 000	6 14 0	Nolan (2), Norman (0.2), Billingham (1.1), Carroll (1), Eastwick (1), McEnaney (1) Borbon (2), Darcy (2)	Geronimo
BOS	A	300 000 030 001	7 10 1	Tiant (7), Moret (1), Drago (3), Wise (1)	Lynn (2 on), Carbo (2 on), Fisk

After tying the score in the 8th on pinch hitter Carbo's 3-run homer, the Red Sox filled the bases with nobody out in the 9th but failed to score. Fisk's home run off the foul pole in the 12th ended one of the most thrilling games in Series history.

GAME 7 - OCTOBER 22

CIN	N	000 002 101	4 9 0	Gullett (4), Billingham (2), Carroll (2), McEnaney (1), SV	Perez (1 on)
BOS	A	003 000 000	3 5 2	Lee (6.1), Moret (0.1), Willoughby (1.1), Burton (0.2), Cleveland (0.1)	

The Reds overcame a 3-0 deficit, defeating the Red Sox 4-3 on Morgan's single with two out in the 9th. It was the Reds' first world championship since 1940.

Team totals

		W	AB	H	2B	3B	HR	R	RBI	BA	BB	SO	ERA
CIN	N	4	244	59	9	3	7	29	29	.242	25	30	3.88
BOS	A	3	239	60	7	2	6	30	30	.251	30	40	3.88

Individual Batting

CINCINNATI (N.L.)

	AB	H	2B	3B	HR	R	RBI	BA
G. Foster, lf	29	8	1	0	0	1	2	.276
J. Bench, c	29	6	2	0	1	5	4	.207
T. Perez, 1b	28	5	0	0	3	4	7	.179
Concepcion, ss	28	5	1	0	1	3	4	.179
P. Rose, 3b	27	10	1	1	0	3	2	.370
J. Morgan, 2b	27	7	1	0	0	4	3	.259
K. Griffey, rf	26	7	3	1	0	4	4	.269
C. Geronimo, cf	25	7	0	1	2	3	3	.280
D. Gullett, p	7	2	0	0	0	1	0	.286
Rettenmund	3	0	0	0	0	0	0	.000
Billingham, p	2	0	0	0	0	0	0	.000
D. Driessen	2	0	0	0	0	0	0	.000
T. Crowley	2	1	0	0	0	0	0	.500
D. Chaney	2	0	0	0	0	0	0	.000
P. Borbon, p	1	0	0	0	0	0	0	.000
P. Darcy, p	1	0	0	0	0	0	0	.000
R. Eastwick, p	1	0	0	0	0	0	0	.000
W. McEnaney, p	1	1	0	0	0	0	0	1.000
Armbrister	1	0	0	0	0	1	0	.000
G. Nolan, p	1	0	0	0	0	0	0	.000
F. Norman, p	1	0	0	0	0	0	0	.000

Errors: T. Perez, Concepcion
Stolen Bases: Concepcion (3), K. Griffey (2), J. Morgan (2), T. Perez, G. Foster

BOSTON (A.L.)

	AB	H	2B	3B	HR	R	RBI	BA
D. Doyle, 2b	30	8	1	1	0	3	0	.267
Yastrzemski, 1b, of	29	9	0	0	0	7	4	.310
Petrocelli, 3b	26	8	1	0	0	3	4	.308
C. Fisk, c	25	6	0	0	2	5	4	.240
F. Lynn, cf	25	7	1	0	1	3	5	.280
R. Burleson, ss	24	7	1	0	0	1	2	.292
D. Evans, rf	24	7	1	1	1	3	5	.292
C. Cooper, 1b	19	1	1	0	0	0	1	.053
J. Beniquez, of	8	1	0	0	0	0	1	.125
L. Tiant, p	8	2	0	0	0	2	0	.250
B. Carbo, lf	7	3	1	0	2	3	4	.429
B. Lee, p	6	1	0	0	0	0	0	.167
R. Wise, p	2	0	0	0	0	0	0	.000
R. Cleveland, p	2	0	0	0	0	0	0	.000
R. Miller, of	2	0	0	0	0	0	0	.000
Montgomery	1	0	0	0	0	0	0	.000
D. Griffin	1	0	0	0	0	0	0	.000

Errors: D. Doyle (3), C. Fisk (2), R. Burleson

Individual Pitching

CINCINNATI (N.L.)

	W	L	ERA	IP	H	BB	SO	SV
D. Gullett	1	1	4.34	18.2	19	10	15	0
Billingham	0	0	1.00	9	8	5	7	0
R. Eastwick	2	0	2.25	8	6	3	4	1
W. McEnaney	0	0	2.70	6.2	3	2	5	1
G. Nolan	0	0	6.00	6	6	1	2	0
C. Carroll	1	0	3.18	5.2	4	2	3	0
F. Norman	0	1	9.00	4	8	3	2	0
P. Darcy	0	1	4.50	4	3	2	1	0
P. Borbon	0	0	6.00	3	3	2	1	0

BOSTON (A.L.)

	W	L	ERA	IP	H	BB	SO	SV
L. Tiant	2	0	3.60	25	25	8	12	0
B. Lee	0	0	3.14	14.1	12	3	7	0
Willoughby	0	1	0.00	6.1	3	0	2	0
R. Cleveland	0	1	6.75	6.2	7	3	5	0
R. Wise	1	0	8.44	5.1	6	2	2	0
D. Drago	0	1	2.25	4	3	1	1	0
J. Burton	0	1	9.00	1	1	3	1	0
R. Moret	0	0	0.00	1.2	2	3	1	0
D. Segui	0	0	0.00	1	0	0	0	0
D. Pole	0	0	∞	0.0	0	2	0	0

1976 NATIONAL LEAGUE CHAMPIONSHIP SERIES

LINE SCORES		PITCHERS (innings pitched)	HOME RUNS (men on)	HIGHLIGHTS

Cincinnati (West) defeats Philadelphia (East) 3 games to 0

GAME 1 - OCTOBER 9

CIN	W	001 002 030	6 10 0	Gullett (8), Eastwick (1)	Foster
PHI	E	100 000 002	3 6 1	Carlton (7), McGraw (2)	

George Foster homered, Pete Rose got 3 hits and Don Gullett allowed 2 hits in 8 innings.

GAME 2 - OCTOBER 10

CIN	W	000 004 200	6 6 0	Zachry (5.1), Borbon (4), SV	
PHI	E	010 010 000	2 10 1	Lonborg (5.1), Garber (0.2), McGraw (0.1), Reed (2.2)	Luzinski

Pete Rose and Ken Griffey had 2 hits each, and Pedro Borbon saved Pat Zachry's victory with 4 scoreless innings in relief.

GAME 3 - OCTOBER 12

PHI	E	000 100 221	6 11 0	Kaat (6), Reed (2), Garber (0), Underwood (0.1)	
CIN	W	000 000 403	7 9 2	Nolan (5.2), Sarmiento (1), Borbon, Eastwick (2)	Foster, Bench

Trailing 6-4, the Reds rallied for 3 runs in the 9th. Foster and Bench hit successive homers to ignite the pennant-clinching rally.

Team totals

		W	AB	H	2B	3B	HR	R	RBI	BA	BB	SO	ERA
CIN	W	3	99	25	5	3	3	19	17	.253	15	16	3.33
PHI	E	0	100	27	8	1	1	11	11	.270	12	9	5.13

Individual Batting

CINCINNATI (WEST)

	AB	H	2B	3B	HR	R	RBI	BA
P. Rose, 3b	14	6	2	1	0	3	2	.429
K. Griffey, of	13	5	0	1	0	2	2	.385
J. Bench, c	12	4	1	0	1	3	1	.333
G. Foster, of	12	2	0	0	2	2	4	.167
C. Geronimo, of	11	2	0	1	0	0	2	.182
Concepcion, ss	10	2	1	0	0	4	0	.200
T. Perez, 1b	10	2	0	0	0	1	3	.200
J. Morgan, 2b	7	0	0	0	0	2	0	.000
D. Gullett, p	4	2	1	0	0	1	3	.500
P. Borbon, p	2	0	0	0	0	1	0	.000
M. Sarmiento, p	1	0	0	0	0	0	0	.000
M. Lum	1	0	0	0	0	0	0	.000
D. Driessen	1	0	0	0	0	0	0	.000
P. Zachry, p	1	0	0	0	0	0	0	.000
Armbrister	0	0	0	0	0	0	0	–
D. Flynn, 2b	0	0	0	0	0	0	0	–

Errors: T. Perez, P. Rose
Stolen Bases: K. Griffey (2), J. Morgan (2), J. Bench

PHILADELPHIA (EAST)

	AB	H	2B	3B	HR	R	RBI	BA
G. Maddox, of	13	3	1	0	0	2	1	.231
M. Schmidt, 3b	13	4	2	0	0	1	2	.308
D. Cash, 2b	13	4	1	0	0	1	1	.308
G. Luzinski, of	11	3	2	0	1	2	3	.273
D. Allen, 1b	9	2	0	0	0	1	0	.222
J. Johnstone, of	9	7	1	1	0	1	2	.778
L. Bowa, ss	8	1	1	0	0	1	1	.125
B. Boone, c	7	2	0	0	0	0	1	.286
T. McCarver, c	4	0	0	0	0	0	0	.000
J. Kaat, p	2	1	0	0	0	0	0	.500
B. Tolan, of, 1b	2	0	0	0	0	0	0	.000
O. Brown, of	2	0	0	0	0	0	0	.000
S. Carlton, p	2	0	0	0	0	0	0	.000
T. Hutton	1	0	0	0	0	0	0	.000
R. Reed, p	1	0	0	0	0	0	0	.000
J. Lonborg, p	1	0	0	0	0	0	0	.000
J. Oates, c	1	0	0	0	0	0	0	.000
J. Martin, of	1	0	0	0	0	1	0	.000
T. Harmon	0	0	0	0	0	1	0	–

Errors: D. Allen, M. Schmidt

Individual Pitching

CINCINNATI (WEST)

	W	L	ERA	IP	H	BB	SO	SV
D. Gullett	1	0	1.13	8	2	3	4	0
P. Zachry	1	0	3.60	5	6	3	3	0
G. Nolan	0	0	1.59	5.2	6	2	1	0
P. Borbon	0	0	0.00	4.1	4	1	0	1
R. Eastwick	1	0	12.00	3	7	2	1	0
M. Sarmiento	0	0	18.00	1	2	1	0	0

PHILADELPHIA (EAST)

	W	L	ERA	IP	H	BB	SO	SV
S. Carlton	0	1	5.14	7	8	5	6	0
J. Kaat	0	0	3.00	6	2	2	1	0
J. Lonborg	0	1	1.69	5.1	2	2	2	0
R. Reed	0	0	7.71	4.2	6	2	2	0
T. McGraw	0	0	11.57	2.1	4	1	5	0
G. Garber	0	1	13.50	0.2	2	1	0	0
T. Underwood	0	0	0.00	0.1	1	2	0	0

1976 AMERICAN LEAGUE CHAMPIONSHIP SERIES

LINE SCORES	PITCHERS (innings pitched)	HOME RUNS (men on)	HIGHLIGHTS

New York (East) defeats Kansas City (West) 3 games to 2

GAME 1 - OCTOBER 9

NY	E	200 000 002	4 12 0	Hunter (9)	
KC	W	000 000 010	1 5 2	Gura (8.2), Littell (0.1)	

A pair of misplays by George Brett gave the Yankees two unearned runs in the first inning, and Hunter made them stand up as he held Royals to 5 hits.

GAME 2 - OCTOBER 10

NY	E	012 000 000	3 12 5	Figueroa (5.1), Tidrow (2.2)	
KC	W	200 002 03x	7 9 0	Leonard (2.1), Splittorff (5.2), Mingori (1)	

Paul Splittorff pitched 5.2 innings of scoreless relief, and Tom Poquette and Buck Martinez each had two RBIs.

GAME 3 - OCTOBER 12

KC	W	300 000 000	3 6 0	Hassler (5), Pattin (0), Hall (0.1), Mingori (0), Littell (2.2)	
NY	E	000 203 00x	5 9 0	Ellis (8), Lyle (1) SV	Chambliss (1 on)

Chambliss got two hits, one a homer, and drove in three runs as Yanks overcame early 3-0 deficit.

GAME 4 - OCTOBER 13

KC	W	030 201 010	7 9 1	Gura (2), Bird (4.2), Mingori (2.1) SV	
NY	E	020 000 101	4 11 0	Hunter (3), Tidrow (3.2), Jackson (2.1)	Nettles (1 on), Nettles

Freddie Patek drove in three runs with three hits, and Doug Bird pitched strong relief to even the series.

GAME 5 - OCTOBER 14

KC	W	210 000 030	6 11 1	Leonard (0), Splittorff (3.2), Pattin (0.1), Hassler (2.1), Littell (1.2)	Mayberry (1 on), Brett (2 on)
NY	E	202 002 001	7 11 1	Figueroa (7), Jackson (1), Tidrow (1)	Chambliss

Chambliss's homer off Mark Littell in the bottom of the 9th snapped a 6-6 tie, giving Yanks their first A.L. pennant in 12 years. Royals had tied game on Brett's three run homer in the eighth.

Team totals

		W	AB	H	2B	3B	HR	R	RBI	BA	BB	SO	ERA
NY	E	3	174	55	13	2	4	23	21	.316	16	15	4.70
KC	W	2	162	40	6	4	2	24	24	.247	11	18	4.40

Individual Batting

NEW YORK (EAST)

	AB	H	2B	3B	HR	R	RBI	BA
M. Rivers, of	23	8	0	1	0	5	0	.348
T. Munson, c	23	10	2	0	0	3	3	.435
C. Chambliss, 1b	21	11	1	1	2	5	8	.524
W. Randolph, 2b	17	2	0	0	0	0	1	.118
R. White, of	17	5	3	0	0	4	3	.294
G. Nettles, 3b	17	4	1	0	2	2	4	.235
F. Stanley, ss	15	5	2	0	0	1	0	.333
L. Piniella, dh	11	3	1	0	0	1	0	.273
C. May, dh	10	2	1	0	0	1	0	.200
E. Maddox, of	9	2	1	0	0	0	1	.222
O. Gamble, of	8	2	1	0	0	1	1	.250
S. Alomar, dh	1	0	0	0	0	0	0	.000
E. Hendricks	1	1	0	0	0	0	0	1.000
O. Velez	1	0	0	0	0	0	0	.000
J. Mason, ss	0	0	0	0	0	0	0	—

Errors: T. Munson (2), O. Gamble (2), F. Stanley, C. Chambliss
Stolen Bases: C. Chambliss (2), R. White, W. Randolph

KANSAS CITY (WEST)

	AB	H	2B	3B	HR	R	RBI	BA
A. Cowens, of	21	4	0	1	0	3	0	.190
J. Mayberry, 1b	18	4	0	0	1	4	3	.222
F. Patek, ss	18	7	2	0	0	2	4	.389
G. Brett, 3b	18	8	1	1	1	4	5	.444
H. McRae, of, dh	17	2	1	1	0	2	1	.118
T. Poquette, of	16	3	2	0	0	1	4	.188
B. Martinez, c	15	5	0	0	0	0	4	.333
J. Wohlford, of	11	2	0	0	0	3	0	.182
C. Rojas, 2b	9	3	0	0	0	2	1	.333
F. White, 2b	8	1	0	0	0	2	0	.125
J. Quirk, dh	7	1	0	1	0	1	2	.143
D. Nelson	2	0	0	0	0	0	0	.000
B. Stinson, c	1	0	0	0	0	0	0	.000
A. Otis, of	1	0	0	0	0	0	0	.000
J. Wathan, c	0	0	0	0	0	0	0	—

Errors: G. Brett (3), D. Bird
Stolen Bases: A. Cowens (2), J. Wohlford (2), C. Rojas

Individual Pitching

NEW YORK (EAST)

	W	L	ERA	IP	H	BB	SO	SV
C. Hunter	1	1	4.50	12	10	1	5	0
E. Figueroa	0	1	5.84	12.1	14	2	5	0
D. Ellis	1	0	3.38	8	6	2	5	0
D. Tidrow	1	0	3.68	7.1	6	4	0	0
G. Jackson	0	0	8.10	3.1	4	1	3	0
S. Lyle	0	0	0.00	1	0	1	0	1

KANSAS CITY (WEST)

	W	L	ERA	IP	H	BB	SO	SV
L. Gura	0	1	4.22	10.2	18	1	4	0
Splittorff	1	0	1.93	9.1	7	5	2	0
A. Hassler	0	1	6.14	7.1	8	6	4	0
D. Bird	1	0	1.93	4.2	4	0	1	0
M. Littell	0	1	1.93	4.2	4	1	3	0
S. Mingori	0	0	2.70	3.1	4	0	1	1
D. Leonard	0	0	19.29	2.1	9	2	0	0
T. Hall	0	0	0.00	0.1	1	0	0	0
M. Pattin	0	0	27.00	0.1	0	1	0	0

1976 WORLD SERIES

LINE SCORES	PITCHERS (innings pitched)	HOME RUNS (men on)	HIGHLIGHTS

Cincinnati (N.L.) defeats New York (A.L.) 4 games to 0

GAME 1 - OCTOBER 16

NY	A	010 000 000	1 5 1	Alexander (6), Lyle (2)	
CIN	N	101 001 20x	5 10 1	Gullett (7.1), Borbon (1.2)	Morgan

The Yankees returned to World Series play after a 12-year absence, but ran into an inspired Reds club. Three hits by Perez and Gullett's five-hit pitching gave Cincinnati the opener.

GAME 2 - OCTOBER 17

NY	A	000 100 200	3 9 1	Hunter (8.2)
CIN	N	030 000 001	4 10 0	Norman (6.1), Billingham (2.2)

The Reds broke a 3-3 tie with two out in the 9th when Stanley threw Griffey's grounder into the dugout for two bases. Griffey then scored on Perez's single.

GAME 3 - OCTOBER 19

CIN	N	030 100 020	6 13 2	Zachry (6.2), McEnaney (2.1), SV	Driessen
NY	A	000 100 100	2 8 0	Ellis (3.1), Jackson (3.2), Tidrow (2)	Mason

Driessen cracked three hits, including a home run, and Zachry and McEnaney scattered eight hits for the win.

GAME 4 - OCTOBER 21

CIN	N	000 300 004	7 9 2	Nolan (6.2), McEnaney (2.1), SV	Bench (1 on), Bench (2 on)
NY	A	100 010 000	2 8 0	Figueroa (8), Tidrow (0.1), Lyle (0.2)	

Bench drove in five runs with a pair of homers as the Reds won in four straight. Bench ended the Series with a .533 average, overshadowing Munson's fine .529 performance.

Team totals

		W	AB	H	2B	3B	HR	R	RBI	BA	BB	SO	ERA
CIN	N	4	134	42	10	3	4	22	21	.313	12	16	2.00
NY	A	0	135	30	3	1	1	8	8	.222	12	16	5.45

Individual Batting

CINCINNATI (N.L.)

	AB	H	2B	3B	HR	R	RBI	BA
K. Griffey, of	17	1	0	0	0	2	1	.059
T. Perez, 1b	16	5	1	0	0	1	2	.313
P. Rose, 3b	16	3	1	0	0	1	1	.188
J. Morgan, 2b	15	5	1	1	1	3	2	.333
J. Bench, c	15	8	1	1	2	4	6	.533
G. Foster, of	14	6	1	0	0	3	4	.429
Concepcion, ss	14	5	1	1	0	1	3	.357
D. Driessen, dh	14	5	2	0	1	4	1	.357
C. Geronimo, of	13	4	2	0	0	3	1	.308

Errors: J. Morgan (2), C. Geronimo, Concepcion, P. Zachry
Stolen Bases: J. Morgan (2), C. Geronimo (2), Concepcion, D. Driessen, K. Griffey

NEW YORK (A.L.)

	AB	H	2B	3B	HR	R	RBI	BA
M. Rivers, of	18	3	0	0	0	1	0	.167
T. Munson, c	17	9	0	0	0	2	2	.529
C. Chambliss, 1b	16	5	1	0	0	1	1	.313
R. White, of	15	2	0	0	0	0	0	.133
W. Randolph, 2b	14	1	0	0	0	1	0	.071
G. Nettles, 3b	12	3	0	0	0	0	2	.250
L. Piniella, dh, of	9	3	1	0	0	1	0	.333
C. May, dh	9	0	0	0	0	0	0	.000
O. Gamble, of	8	1	0	0	0	0	1	.125
F. Stanley, ss	6	1	1	0	0	1	1	.167
E. Maddox, of, dh	5	1	0	1	0	0	0	.200
O. Velez	3	0	0	0	0	0	0	.000
E. Hendricks	2	0	0	0	0	0	0	.000
J. Mason, ss	1	1	0	0	1	1	1	1.000

Errors: F. Stanley, C. Chambliss
Stolen Bases: M. Rivers

Individual Pitching

CINCINNATI (N.L.)

	W	L	ERA	IP	H	BB	SO	SV
D. Gullett	1	0	1.23	7.1	5	3	4	0
P. Zachry	1	0	2.70	6.2	6	5	6	0
F. Norman	0	0	4.26	6.1	9	2	2	0
G. Nolan	1	0	2.70	6.2	8	1	1	0
W. McEnaney	0	0	0.00	4.2	2	1	2	2
Billingham	1	0	0.00	2.2	0	0	1	0
P. Borbon	0	0	0.00	1.2	0	0	0	0

NEW YORK (A.L.)

	W	L	ERA	IP	H	BB	SO	SV
C. Hunter	0	1	3.12	8.2	10	4	5	0
E. Figueroa	0	1	5.63	8	6	5	2	0
D. Alexander	0	1	7.50	6	9	2	1	0
D. Ellis	0	1	10.80	3.1	7	0	1	0
G. Jackson	0	0	4.91	3.2	4	0	3	0
S. Lyle	0	0	0.00	2.2	1	0	3	0
D. Tidrow	0	0	7.71	2.1	5	1	1	0

1977 NATIONAL LEAGUE CHAMPIONSHIP SERIES

LINE SCORES	PITCHERS (innings pitched)	HOME RUNS (men on)	HIGHLIGHTS

Los Angeles (West) defeats Philadelphia (East) 3 games to 1

GAME 1 - OCTOBER 4

PHI E	200 021 002	7 9 0	Carlton (6.2), Garber (1.1), McGraw (1) SV	Luzinski (1 on)	The Phillies broke a 5-5 tie in the ninth on singles by Bake McBride, Larry Bowa and Mike Schmidt, good for two runs.
LA W	000 010 400	5 9 2	John (4.2), Garman (0.1), Hough (2), Sosa (2)	Cey (3 on)	

GAME 2 - OCTOBER 5

PHI E	001 000 000	1 9 1	Lonborg (4), Reed (2), Brusstar (2)	McBride	Dusty Baker's grand slam snapped a 1-1 tie, and Don Sutton spaced 9 hits.
LA W	001 401 10x	7 9 1	Sutton (9)	Baker (3 on)	

GAME 3 - OCTOBER 7

LA W	020 100 003	6 12 2	Hooton (1.2), Rhoden (4.1), Rau (1), Sosa (0.2), Rautzhan (0.1), Garman (1) SV	The Dodgers rallied for three runs with two outs in the 9th. Pinch hitter Manny Mota doubled after Vic Davalillo singled. Davey Lopes singled in the tying run and scored the winning run on a single by Bill Russell.
PHI E	030 000 020	5 6 2	Christenson (3.1), Brusstar (0.2), Reed (2), Garber (3)	

GAME 4 - OCTOBER 8

LA W	020 020 000	4 5 0	John (9)	Baker (1 on)	Dusty Baker drove in 2 runs with his second homer, scored twice, and Tommy John permitted only 7 hits as the Dodgers clinched the series.
PHI E	000 100 000	1 7 0	Carlton (5), Reed (1), McGraw (2), Garber (1)		

Team totals

		W	AB	H	2B	3B	HR	R	RBI	BA	BB	SO	ERA
LA	W	3	133	35	6	1	3	22	20	.263	14	22	2.25
PHI	E	1	138	31	3	0	2	14	12	.225	11	21	5.40

Individual Batting

LOS ANGELES (WEST)

	AB	H	2B	3B	HR	R	RBI	BA
B. Russell, ss	18	5	1	0	0	3	2	.278
D. Lopes, 2b	17	4	0	0	0	2	3	.235
R. Smith, of	16	3	0	1	0	2	1	.188
D. Baker, of	14	5	1	0	2	4	8	.357
S. Yeager, c	13	3	0	0	0	1	2	.231
R. Cey, 3b	13	4	1	0	1	4	4	.308
S. Garvey, 1b	13	4	0	0	0	2	0	.308
G. Burke, of	7	0	0	0	0	0	0	.000
R. Monday, of	7	2	1	0	0	1	0	.286
T. John, p	5	1	0	0	0	0	0	.200
D. Sutton, p	3	0	0	0	0	0	0	.000
M. Mota	1	1	1	0	0	1	0	1.000
V. Davalillo	1	1	0	0	0	1	0	1.000
E. Goodson	1	0	0	0	0	0	0	.000
B. Hooton, p	1	1	1	0	0	0	0	1.000
R. Rhoden, p	1	0	0	0	0	0	0	.000
L. Lacy	1	1	0	0	0	1	0	1.000
E. Sosa, p	1	0	0	0	0	0	0	.000
J. Grote, c	0	0	0	0	0	0	0	–

Errors: B. Russell (2), R. Smith, R. Cey, D. Lopes
Stolen Bases: R. Smith, S. Garvey, R. Cey

PHILADELPHIA (EAST)

	AB	H	2B	3B	HR	R	RBI	BA
B. McBride, of	18	4	0	0	1	2	2	.222
L. Bowa, ss	17	2	0	0	0	2	1	.118
M. Schmidt, 3b	16	1	0	0	0	2	1	.063
G. Luzinski, of	14	4	1	0	1	2	2	.286
R. Hebner, 1b	14	5	2	0	0	2	0	.357
T. Sizemore, 2b	13	3	0	0	0	1	0	.231
B. Boone, c	10	4	0	0	0	1	0	.400
G. Maddox, of	7	3	0	0	0	1	2	.429
T. McCarver, c	6	1	0	0	0	1	0	.167
J. Johnstone, of	5	1	0	0	0	0	0	.200
D. Johnson, 1b	4	1	0	0	0	0	2	.250
J. Martin, of	4	0	0	0	0	0	0	.000
S. Carlton, p	4	2	0	0	0	0	1	.500
T. Hutton, 1b, ph	3	0	0	0	0	0	0	.000
O. Brown	2	0	0	0	0	0	0	.000
J. Lonborg, p	1	0	0	0	0	0	0	.000
Christenson, p	0	0	0	0	0	0	1	–

Errors: T. Sizemore (2), G. Garber
Stolen Bases: G. Luzinski

Individual Pitching

LOS ANGELES (WEST)

	W	L	ERA	IP	H	BB	SO	SV
T. John	1	0	0.66	13.2	11	5	11	0
D. Sutton	1	0	1.00	9	9	0	4	0
R. Rhoden	0	0	0.00	4.1	2	2	0	0
C. Hough	0	0	4.50	2	2	0	3	0
E. Sosa	0	1	10.13	2.2	5	0	0	0
D. Rau	0	0	0.00	1	0	0	1	0
B. Hooton	0	0	16.20	1.2	2	4	1	0
M. Garman	0	0	0.00	1.1	0	0	1	1
L. Rautzhan	1	0	0.00	0.1	0	0	0	0

PHILADELPHIA (EAST)

	W	L	ERA	IP	H	BB	SO	SV
S. Carlton	0	1	6.94	11.2	13	8	6	0
R. Reed	0	0	1.80	5	3	2	5	0
G. Garber	1	1	3.38	5.1	4	0	3	0
J. Lonborg	0	1	11.25	4	5	1	1	0
T. McGraw	0	0	0.00	3	1	2	3	1
Christenson	0	0	8.10	3.1	7	0	2	0
W. Brusstar	0	0	3.38	2.2	2	1	2	0

1977 AMERICAN LEAGUE CHAMPIONSHIP SERIES

LINE SCORES		PITCHERS (innings pitched)	HOME RUNS (men on)	HIGHLIGHTS

New York (East) defeats Kansas City (West) 3 games to 2

GAME 1 - OCTOBER 5

KC	W	222 000 010	7 9 0	Splittorff (8), Bird (1)	McRae (1 on), Mayberry (1 on), Cowens
NY	E	002 000 000	2 9 0	Gullett (2), Tidrow (6.2), Lyle (0.1)	Munson (1 on)

Hal McRae, John Mayberry and Al Cowens homered to account for five Royals' runs.

GAME 2 - OCTOBER 6

KC	W	001 001 000	2 3 1	Hassler (5.2), Littell (2), Mingori (0.1)	
NY	E	000 023 01x	6 10 1	Guidry (9)	Johnson

Ron Guidry pitched a 3-hitter, and Cliff Johnson homered as Yanks tied series.

GAME 3 - OCTOBER 7

NY	E	000 010 001	2 4 1	Torrez (5.2), Lyle (2.1)	
KC	W	011 012 10x	6 12 1	Leonard (9)	

Hal McRae doubled twice and scored twice, and Amos Otis hit a pinch double in support of Dennis Leonard's 4-hitter.

GAME 4 - OCTOBER 8

NY	E	121 100 001	6 13 0	Figueroa (3.1), Tidrow (0.1), Lyle (5.1)	
KC	W	002 200 000	4 8 2	Gura (2), Pattin (6), Mingori (0.1), Bird (0.1)	

Mickey Rivers banged four hits and Sparky Lyle hurled scoreless ball through 5.2 relief innings as the Yankees evened the series.

GAME 5 - OCTOBER 9

NY	E	001 000 013	5 10 0	Guidry (2.1), Torrez (5.1), Lyle (1.1)	
KC	W	201 000 000	3 10 1	Splittorff (7), Bird (0.1), Mingori (0.2), Gura (0), Leonard (0), Littell (1)	

Trailing 3-1, the Yanks scored one run in the 8th and three in the 9th to win the pennant. Rivers delivered the game-winning hit, and Lyle gained his second straight victory in relief.

Team totals

		W	AB	H	2B	3B	HR	R	RBI	BA	BB	SO	ERA
NY	E	3	175	46	12	0	2	21	17	.263	9	16	4.50
KC	W	2	163	42	9	3	3	22	21	.258	15	22	3.27

Individual Batting

NEW YORK (EAST)

	AB	H	2B	3B	HR	R	RBI	BA
M. Rivers, of	23	9	2	0	0	5	2	.391
T. Munson, c	21	6	1	0	1	3	5	.286
L. Piniella, of, dh	21	7	3	0	0	1	2	.333
G. Nettles, 3b	20	3	0	0	0	1	1	.150
W. Randolph, 2b	18	5	1	0	0	4	2	.278
C. Chambliss, 1b	17	1	0	0	0	0	0	.059
R. Jackson, of, dh	16	2	0	0	0	1	1	.125
C. Johnson, dh	15	6	2	0	1	2	2	.400
B. Dent, ss	14	3	1	0	0	1	2	.214
P. Blair, of	5	2	0	0	0	1	0	.400
R. White, of, dh	5	2	2	0	0	2	0	.400
F. Stanley, ss	0	0	0	0	0	0	0	—

Errors: B. Dent, R. White
Stolen Bases: R. Jackson, M. Rivers

KANSAS CITY (WEST)

	AB	H	2B	3B	HR	R	RBI	BA
G. Brett, 3b	20	6	0	2	0	2	2	.300
A. Cowens, of	19	5	0	0	1	2	5	.263
F. Patek, ss	18	7	3	1	0	4	5	.389
H. McRae, of, dh	18	8	3	0	1	6	2	.444
F. White, 2b	18	5	1	0	0	1	2	.278
A. Otis, of	16	2	1	0	0	1	2	.125
D. Porter, c	15	5	0	0	0	3	0	.333
J. Mayberry, 1b	12	2	1	0	1	1	3	.167
J. Zdeb, of	9	0	0	0	0	0	0	.000
J. Wathan, 1b, c, dh	6	0	0	0	0	0	0	.000
T. Poquette, of	6	1	0	0	0	0	0	.167
C. Rojas, dh	4	1	0	0	0	0	0	.250
P. LaCock, 1b	1	0	0	0	0	0	0	.000
J. Lahoud, dh	1	0	0	0	0	2	0	.000

Errors: J. Mayberry (2), G. Brett (2), F. Patek
Stolen Bases: A. Otis (2), J. Zdeb, F. White, C. Rojas

Individual Pitching

NEW YORK (EAST)

	W	L	ERA	IP	H	BB	SO	SV
M. Torrez	0	1	4.09	11	11	5	5	0
R. Guidry	1	0	3.97	11.1	9	3	8	0
S. Lyle	2	0	0.96	9.1	7	0	3	0
D. Tidrow	0	0	3.86	7	6	3	3	0
E. Figueroa	0	0	10.80	3.1	5	2	3	0
D. Gullett	0	1	18.00	2	4	2	0	0

KANSAS CITY (WEST)

	W	L	ERA	IP	H	BB	SO	SV
Splittorff	1	0	2.40	15	14	3	4	0
D. Leonard	1	1	3.00	9	5	2	4	0
M. Pattin	0	0	1.50	6	6	0	0	0
A. Hassler	0	1	4.76	5.2	5	0	3	0
M. Littell	0	0	3.00	3	5	3	1	0
L. Gura	0	1	18.00	2	7	1	2	0
D. Bird	0	0	0.00	2	4	0	1	0
S. Mingori	0	0	0.00	1.1	0	0	1	0

1977 WORLD SERIES

LINE SCORES	PITCHERS (innings pitched)	HOME RUNS (men on)	HIGHLIGHTS

New York (A.L.) defeats Los Angeles (N.L.) 4 games to 2

GAME 1 - OCTOBER 11

LA	N	200 000 001 000	3 6 0	Sutton (7), Rautzhan (0.1), Sosa (0.2), Garman (3), Rhoden (0)	
NY	A	100 001 010 001	4 11 0	Gullett (8.1), Lyle (3.2)	Randolph

Randolph doubled in the twelfth and scored on a single by Blair against loser Rhoden.

GAME 2 - OCTOBER 12

LA	N	212 000 001	6 9 0	Hooton (9)	Cey (1 on), Yeager, Smith (1 on), Garvey
NY	A	000 100 000	1 5 0	Hunter (2.1), Tidrow (2.2), Clay (3), Lyle (1)	

The Dodgers exploded for four homers to rout Hunter. Hooton allowed just five singles.

GAME 3 - OCTOBER 14

NY	A	300 110 000	5 10 0	Torrez (9)	
LA	N	003 000 000	3 7 1	John (6), Hough (3)	Baker (2 on)

Rivers cracked three hits, including two doubles, to lead the Yankees' attack against loser John.

GAME 4 - OCTOBER 15

NY	A	030 001 000	4 7 0	Guidry (9)	Jackson
LA	N	002 000 000	2 4 0	Rau (1), Rhoden (7), Garman (1)	Lopes (1 on)

Jackson homered and doubled in support of Ron Guidry's four-hitter. Guidry fanned seven.

GAME 5 - OCTOBER 16

NY	A	000 000 220	4 9 2	Gullett (4.1), Clay (0.2), Tidrow (1), Hunter (2)	Munson, Jackson
LA	N	100 432 00x	10 13 0	Sutton (9)	Yeager (2 on), Smith (1 on)

Yeager homered and drove in four runs, Baker had three hits, and Sutton breezed to an easy victory.

GAME 6 - OCTOBER 18

LA	N	201 000 001	4 9 0	Hooton (3), Sosa (1.2), Rau (1.1), Hough (2)	Smith
NY	A	020 320 01x	8 8 1	Torrez (9)	Chambliss (1 on), Jackson (1 on), Jackson (1 on), Jackson

Jackson hit three successive homers, each on the first pitch, each off a different pitcher, amounting to five RBIs to give the Yankees their first World Series title since 1962.

Team totals

		W	AB	H	2B	3B	HR	R	RBI	BA	BB	SO	ERA
NY	A	4	205	50	10	0	8	26	25	.244	11	37	4.02
LA	N	2	208	48	5	3	9	28	28	.231	16	36	4.09

Individual Batting

NEW YORK (A.L.)

	AB	H	2B	3B	HR	R	RBI	BA
M. Rivers, of	27	6	2	0	0	1	1	.222
W. Randolph, 2b	25	4	2	0	1	5	1	.160
T. Munson, c	25	8	2	0	1	4	3	.320
C. Chambliss, 1b	24	7	2	0	1	4	4	.292
L. Piniella, of	22	6	0	0	0	1	3	.273
G. Nettles, 3b	21	4	1	0	0	1	2	.190
R. Jackson, of	20	9	1	0	5	10	8	.450
B. Dent, ss	19	5	0	0	0	0	2	.263
M. Torrez, p	6	0	0	0	0	0	0	.000
P. Blair, of	4	1	0	0	0	0	1	.250
R. White, ph	2	0	0	0	0	0	0	.000
S. Lyle, p	2	0	0	0	0	0	0	.000
R. Guidry, p	2	0	0	0	0	0	0	.000
D. Gullett, p	2	0	0	0	0	0	0	.000
G. Zeber, ph	2	0	0	0	0	0	0	.000
C. Johnson, c	1	0	0	0	0	0	0	.000
D. Tidrow, p	1	0	0	0	0	0	0	.000
F. Stanley, ss	0	0	0	0	0	0	0	—

Errors: L. Piniella, G. Nettles, B. Dent
Stolen Bases: M. Rivers

LOS ANGELES (N.L.)

	AB	H	2B	3B	HR	R	RBI	BA
B. Russell, ss	26	4	0	1	0	3	2	.154
D. Baker, of	24	7	0	0	1	4	5	.292
S. Garvey, 1b	24	9	1	1	1	5	3	.375
D. Lopes, 2b	24	4	0	1	1	3	2	.167
R. Smith, of	22	6	1	0	3	7	5	.273
R. Cey, 3b	21	4	1	0	1	2	3	.190
S. Yeager, c	19	6	1	0	2	2	5	.316
R. Monday, of	12	2	0	0	0	0	0	.167
L. Lacy, of	7	3	0	0	0	1	2	.429
D. Sutton, p	6	0	0	0	0	0	0	.000
G. Burke, of	5	1	0	0	0	0	0	.200
B. Hooton, p	5	0	0	0	0	0	0	.000
M. Mota	3	0	0	0	0	0	0	.000
V. Davalillo	3	1	0	0	0	0	1	.333
T. John, p	2	0	0	0	0	0	0	.000
R. Rhoden, p	2	1	1	0	0	1	0	.500
E. Goodson	1	0	0	0	0	0	0	.000
J. Oates, c	1	0	0	0	0	0	0	.000
J. Grote, c	1	0	0	0	0	0	0	.000
R. Landestoy	0	0	0	0	0	0	0	—

Errors: D. Baker
Stolen Bases: D. Lopes (2)

Individual Pitching

NEW YORK (A.L.)

	W	L	ERA	IP	H	BB	SO	SV
M. Torrez	2	0	2.50	18	16	5	15	0
D. Gullett	0	1	6.39	12.2	13	7	10	0
R. Guidry	1	0	2.00	9	4	3	7	0
C. Hunter	0	1	10.38	4.1	6	0	1	0
S. Lyle	1	0	1.93	4.2	2	0	2	0
K. Clay	0	0	2.45	3.2	2	1	0	0
D. Tidrow	0	0	4.91	3.2	5	0	1	0

LOS ANGELES (N.L.)

	W	L	ERA	IP	H	BB	SO	SV
D. Sutton	1	0	3.94	16	17	1	6	0
B. Hooton	1	1	3.75	12	8	2	9	0
R. Rhoden	0	1	2.57	7	4	1	5	0
T. John	0	1	6.00	6	9	3	7	0
C. Hough	0	0	1.80	5	3	0	5	0
M. Garman	0	0	0.00	4	2	1	3	0
D. Rau	0	1	11.57	2.1	4	0	1	0
E. Sosa	0	0	11.57	2.1	3	1	1	0
L. Rautzhan	0	0	0.00	0.1	0	2	0	0

1978 NATIONAL LEAGUE CHAMPIONSHIP SERIES

LINE SCORES	PITCHERS (innings pitched)	HOME RUNS (men on)	HIGHLIGHTS

Los Angeles (West) defeats Philadelphia (East) 3 games to 1

GAME 1 - OCTOBER 4

LA W 004 211 001 9 13 1 Hooton (4.2), **Welch** (4.1) Lopes, Yeager, Garvey, Garvey (1 on) Garvey drove in four runs with 2 home runs and a triple, and Welch pitched two-hit ball for 4.1 innings in relief.

PHI E 010 030 001 5 12 1 **Christensen** (4.1), Brusstar (0.2), Eastwick (1), McGraw (3) Martin

GAME 2 - OCTOBER 5

LA W 000 120 100 4 8 0 John (9) Lopes (1 on) Tommy John pitched a 4-hit shutout, and Davey Lopes drove in 3 runs with a homer, triple and single.

PHI E 000 000 000 0 4 0 **Ruthven** (4.2), Brusstar (1.1), Reed (2), McGraw (1)

GAME 3 - OCTOBER 6

PHI E 040 003 101 9 11 1 Carlton (9) Carlton (2 on), Luzinski Carlton helped his cause at bat, driving in 4 runs with a home run and sacrifice fly as he went the route on an 8-hitter.

LA W 012 000 010 4 8 2 **Sutton** (5.2), Rautzhan (1.1), Hough (2) Garvey

GAME 4 - OCTOBER 7

PHI E 002 000 100 0 3 8 2 Lerch (5.1), Brusstar (0.2), Reed (2), McGraw (1.2) Luzinski (1 on), McBride Bill Russell's 10th inning single, after a muff of a fly ball by Garry Maddox, scored Ron Cey with the winning run giving the Dodgers the NL championship.

LA W 010 101 000 1 4 13 0 Rau (5), Rhoden (4), **Forster** (1) Cey, Garvey

Team totals

		W	AB	H	2B	3B	HR	R	RBI	BA	BB	SO	ERA
LA	W	3	147	42	8	3	8	21	21	.286	9	22	3.41
PHI	E	1	140	35	3	2	5	17	16	.250	9	21	4.62

Individual Batting

LOS ANGELES (WEST)

	AB	H	2B	3B	HR	R	RBI	BA
D. Lopes, 2b	18	7	1	1	2	3	5	.389
S. Garvey, 1b	18	7	1	1	4	6	7	.389
B. Russell, ss	17	7	1	0	1	2	2	.412
R. Smith, of	16	3	1	0	0	2	1	.188
R. Cey, 3b	16	5	1	0	1	4	3	.313
D. Baker, of	15	7	2	0	0	1	1	.467
S. Yeager, c	13	3	0	0	1	2	2	.231
R. Monday, of	10	2	0	1	0	2	0	.200
B. North, of	8	0	0	0	0	0	0	.000
T. John, p	3	0	0	0	0	0	0	.000
D. Sutton, p	2	0	0	0	0	0	0	.000
J. Ferguson	2	0	0	0	0	0	0	.000
L. Lacy	2	0	0	0	0	0	0	.000
B. Welch, p	2	0	0	0	0	0	0	.000
B. Hooton, p	2	0	0	0	0	0	0	.000
D. Rau, p	1	0	0	0	0	0	0	.000
R. Rhoden, p	1	0	0	0	0	0	0	.000
M. Mota	1	1	1	0	0	0	0	1.000
J. Grote, c	0	0	0	0	0	0	0	–

Errors: D. Lopes (2), R. Smith
Stolen Bases: D. Lopes, S. Yeager

PHILADELPHIA (EAST)

	AB	H	2B	3B	HR	R	RBI	BA
G. Maddox, of	19	5	0	0	0	1	2	.263
L. Bowa, ss	18	6	0	0	0	3	0	.333
G. Luzinski, of	16	6	0	1	2	3	3	.375
M. Schmidt, 3b	15	3	2	0	0	1	1	.200
T. Sizemore, 2b	13	5	0	1	0	3	1	.385
B. Boone, c	11	2	0	0	0	0	0	.182
B. McBride, of	9	2	0	1	2	1	.222	
J. Martin, of	9	2	1	0	1	1	2	.222
R. Hebner, 1b	9	1	0	0	0	0	1	.111
J. Cardenal, 1b	6	1	0	0	0	0	0	.167
S. Carlton, p	4	2	0	1	2	4	.500	
T. McCarver, c	4	0	0	0	2	1	.000	
R. Lerch, p	2	0	0	0	0	0	0	.000
O. Gonzalez	1	0	0	0	0	0	0	.000
J. Morrison	1	0	0	0	0	0	0	.000
D. Ruthven, p	1	0	0	0	0	0	0	.000
Christenson, p	1	0	0	0	0	0	0	.000
B. Foote	1	0	0	0	0	0	0	.000

Errors: M. Schmidt (2), B. Boone, G. Maddox

Individual Pitching

LOS ANGELES (WEST)

	W	L	ERA	IP	H	BB	SO	SV
T. John	1	0	0.00	9	4	2	4	0
D. Sutton	0	1	6.35	5.2	7	2	0	0
D. Rau	0	0	3.60	5	5	2	1	0
B. Welch	1	0	2.08	4.1	2	0	5	0
B. Hooton	0	0	7.71	4.2	10	0	5	0
R. Rhoden	0	0	2.25	4	2	1	3	0
C. Hough	0	0	4.50	2	1	0	1	0
L. Rautzhan	0	0	6.75	1.1	3	2	0	0
T. Forster	1	0	0.00	1	1	0	2	0

PHILADELPHIA (EAST)

	W	L	ERA	IP	H	BB	SO	SV
S. Carlton	1	0	4.00	9	8	2	8	0
T. McGraw	0	1	1.59	5.2	3	5	5	0
R. Lerch	0	0	5.06	5.1	7	0	0	0
Christenson	0	1	12.46	4.1	7	1	3	0
D. Ruthven	0	1	5.79	4.2	6	0	3	0
R. Reed	0	0	2.25	4	6	0	2	0
W. Brusstar	0	0	0.00	2.2	2	1	0	0
R. Eastwick	0	0	9.00	1	3	0	1	0

1978 AMERICAN LEAGUE CHAMPIONSHIP SERIES

LINE SCORES	PITCHERS (innings pitched)	HOME RUNS (men on)	HIGHLIGHTS

New York (East) defeats Kansas City (West) 3 games to 1

GAME 1 - OCTOBER 3

NY E 011 020 030   7 16 0   **Beattie** (5.1), Clay (3.2), SV   Jackson (2 on)   Jackson accounted for 5 runs, scoring two and driving in three with 3 hits, including a double and a homer.

KC W 000 001 000   1 2 2   **Leonard** (4), Mingori (3.2), Hrabosky (0.1), Bird (1)

GAME 2 - OCTOBER 4

NY E 000 000 220   4 12 1   Figueroa (1), Tidrow (5.2), Lyle (1.1)   Kansas City raked three Yankee pitchers for sixteen hits and an easy win.

KC W 140 000 32x   10 16 1   **Gura** (6.1), Pattin (0.2), Hrabosky (2)   Patek (1 on)

GAME 3 - OCTOBER 6

KC W 101 010 020   5 10 1   Splittorff (7.1), **Bird** (0), Hrabosky (0.2)   Brett, Brett, Brett   Munson's 8th inning homer with White on base gave the Yankees an uphill victory and a 2-1 lead in games, offsetting Brett's 3 home runs.

NY E 010 201 02x   6 10 0   **Hunter** (6), Gossage (3)   Jackson (1 on), Munson (1 on)

GAME 4 - OCTOBER 7

KC W 100 000 000   1 7 0   **Leonard** (8)   White broke a 1-1 tie with a homer in the 6th, giving the Yankees their third straight championship series win over the Royals.

NY E 010 001 00x   2 4 0   **Guidry** (8), Gossage (1), SV   Nettles, White

Team totals

		W	AB	H	2B	3B	HR	R	RBI	BA	BB	SO	ERA
NY	E	3	140	42	3	1	5	19	18	.300	7	18	3.86
KC	W	1	133	35	6	3	4	17	16	.263	14	21	4.76

Individual Batting

NEW YORK (EAST)

	AB	H	2B	3B	HR	R	RBI	BA
T. Munson, c	18	5	1	0	1	2	2	.278
L. Piniella, of	17	4	0	0	0	2	0	.235
R. White, of, dh	16	5	1	0	1	5	1	.313
G. Nettles, 3b	15	5	0	1	1	3	2	.333
C. Chambliss, 1b	15	6	0	0	0	1	2	.400
B. Dent, ss	15	3	0	0	0	0	4	.200
R. Jackson, of, dh	13	6	1	0	2	5	6	.462
M. Rivers, of	11	5	0	0	0	0	0	.455
B. Doyle, 2b	7	2	0	0	0	0	1	.286
P. Blair, of, 2b	6	0	0	0	0	1	0	.000
F. Stanley, 2b	5	1	0	0	0	0	0	.200
C. Johnson	1	0	0	0	0	0	0	.000
G. Thomasson, of	1	0	0	0	0	0	0	.000

Errors: B. Dent

KANSAS CITY (WEST)

	AB	H	2B	3B	HR	R	RBI	BA
G. Brett, 3b	18	7	1	1	3	7	3	.389
A. Cowens, of	15	2	0	0	0	2	1	.133
H. McRae, dh	14	3	0	0	0	0	2	.214
A. Otis, of	14	6	2	0	0	2	1	.429
D. Porter, c	14	5	1	0	0	1	3	.357
F. Patek, ss	13	1	0	0	1	2	2	.077
F. White, 2b	13	3	0	0	0	1	2	.231
P. LaCock, 1b	11	4	2	1	0	1	1	.364
C. Hurdle, of	8	3	1	0	0	1	1	.375
S. Braun, of	5	0	0	0	0	0	0	.000
W. Wilson, of	4	1	0	0	0	0	0	.250
J. Wathan, 1b	3	0	0	0	0	0	0	.000
T. Poquette	1	0	0	0	0	0	0	.000

Errors: F. Patek (2), G. Brett, A. Otis
Stolen Bases: A. Otis (4), H. McRae, P. LaCock

Individual Pitching

NEW YORK (EAST)

	W	L	ERA	IP	H	BB	SO	SV
R. Guidry	1	0	1.13	8	7	1	7	0
C. Hunter	0	0	4.50	6	7	3	5	0
J. Beattie	1	0	1.69	5.1	2	5	3	0
D. Tidrow	0	0	4.76	5.2	8	2	1	0
G. Gossage	1	0	4.50	4	3	0	3	1
K. Clay	0	0	0.00	3.2	0	3	2	1
S. Lyle	0	0	13.50	1.1	3	0	0	0
E. Figueroa	0	1	27.00	1	5	0	0	0

KANSAS CITY (WEST)

	W	L	ERA	IP	H	BB	SO	SV
D. Leonard	0	2	3.75	12	13	2	11	0
Splittorff	0	0	4.91	7.1	9	0	2	0
L. Gura	1	0	2.84	6.1	8	2	2	0
A. Hrabosky	0	0	3.00	3	3	0	2	0
S. Mingori	0	0	7.36	3.2	5	3	0	0
D. Bird	0	1	9.00	1	2	0	1	0
M. Pattin	0	0	27.00	0.2	2	0	0	0

1978 WORLD SERIES

LINE SCORES	PITCHERS (innings pitched)	HOME RUNS (men on)	HIGHLIGHTS

New York (A.L.) defeats Los Angeles (N.L.) 4 games to 2

GAME 1 - OCTOBER 10

NY A 000 000 320   5 9 1   Figueroa (1.2), Clay (2.1), Lindblad (2.1), Tidrow (1.2)   Jackson

LA N 030 310 31x   11 15 2   John (7.2), Foster (1.1)   Lopes (1 on), Lopes (2 on), Baker

Lopes hammered two homers for five RBIs while Russell and Baker had three hits each as the Dodgers rapped four Yankee pitchers for 15 hits.

GAME 2 - OCTOBER 11

NY A 002 000 100   3 11 0   Hunter (6), Gossage (2)

LA N 000 103 00x   4 7 0   Hooton (6), Forster (2.1), Welch (0.2), **SV**   Cey (2 on)

Cey drove in all four runs with a single and three-run homer off Hunter. Welch saved Hooton's victory by striking out Jackson in the ninth.

GAME 3 - OCTOBER 13

LA N 001 000 000   1 8 0   Sutton (6.1), Rautzhan (0.2), Hough (1)

NY A 110 000 30x   5 10 1   Guidry (9)   White

Aided by the spectacular fielding of third baseman Nettles, who made four dazzling stops, Guidry went the distance despite allowing 8 hits and 7 walks.

GAME 4 - OCTOBER 14

LA N 000 030 000 0   3 6 1   John (7), Forster (0.1), Welch (2.1)   Smith (2 on)

NY A 000 002 010 1   4 9 0   Figueroa (5), Tidrow (3), **Gossage** (2)

Piniella's single off Welch with two out in the tenth enabled the Yankees to square the Series. The hit scored White, who had walked and was singled to second by Reggie Jackson.

GAME 5 - OCTOBER 15

LA N 101 000 000   2 9 3   Hooton (2.1), Rautzahn (1.1), Hough (4.1)

NY A 004 300 41x   12 18 0   Beattie (9)

The Yankees routed three Dodger pitchers with an 18-hit attack that included 3 each by Rivers, Doyle and Dent. Jim Beattie went the route for the first time in his major league career.

GAME 6 - OCTOBER 17

NY A 030 002 200   7 11 0   Hunter (7), Gossage (2)   Jackson

LA N 101 000 000   2 7 1   Sutton (5.2), Welch (1.1), Rau (2)   Lopes

Hunter scattered 6 hits in 7 innings, and Doyle and Dent had 3 hits apiece as the Yankees wrapped up their 22nd world championship. Dent was named the Series MVP.

Team totals

		W	AB	H	2B	3B	HR	R	RBI	BA	BB	SO	ERA
NY	A	4	222	68	8	0	3	36	34	.306	16	40	3.74
LA	N	2	199	52	8	0	6	23	22	.261	20	31	5.46

Individual Batting

NEW YORK (A.L.)

	AB	H	2B	3B	HR	R	RBI	BA
L. Piniella, of	25	7	0	0	0	3	4	.280
G. Nettles, 3b	25	4	0	0	0	2	1	.160
T. Munson, c	25	8	3	0	0	5	7	.320
R. White, of	24	8	0	0	1	9	4	.333
B. Dent, ss	24	10	1	0	0	3	7	.417
R. Jackson, dh	23	9	1	0	2	2	8	.391
M. Rivers, of	18	6	0	0	0	2	1	.333
B. Doyle, 2b	16	7	1	0	0	4	2	.438
J. Spencer, 1b	12	2	0	0	0	3	0	.167
C. Chambliss, 1b	11	2	0	0	0	1	0	.182
P. Blair, of, 2b	8	3	1	0	0	2	0	.375
F. Stanley, 2b	5	1	1	0	0	0	0	.200
G. Thomasson, of	4	1	0	0	0	0	0	.250
C. Johnson	2	0	0	0	0	0	0	.000
M. Heath, c	0	0	0	0	0	0	0	—
J. Johnstone, of	0	0	0	0	0	0	0	—

Errors: B. Dent (2)

Stolen Bases: R. White (2), T. Munson, L. Piniella, M. Rivers

LOS ANGELES (N.L.)

	AB	H	2B	3B	HR	R	RBI	BA
D. Lopes, 2b	26	8	0	0	3	7	7	.308
B. Russell, ss	26	11	2	0	0	1	2	.423
R. Smith, of	25	5	0	0	1	3	5	.200
S. Garvey, 1b	24	5	1	0	0	1	0	.208
R. Cey, 3b	21	6	0	0	1	2	4	.286
D. Baker, of	21	5	0	0	1	2	1	.238
L. Lacy, dh	14	2	0	0	0	0	1	.143
S. Yeager, c	13	3	1	0	0	2	0	.231
R. Monday, of, dh	13	2	1	0	0	2	0	.154
B. North, of	8	1	1	0	0	2	2	.125
J. Ferguson, c	4	2	2	0	0	1	0	.500
V. Davalillo, dh	3	1	0	0	0	0	0	.333
J. Oates, c	1	1	0	0	0	0	0	1.000
M. Mota	0	0	0	0	0	0	0	—
J. Grote	0	0	0	0	0	0	0	—

Errors: B. Russell (3), R. Smith, D. Lopes, S. Garvey, J. Ferguson

Stolen Bases: D. Lopes (2), B. Russell, S. Garvey, B. North

Individual Pitching

NEW YORK (A.L.)

	W	L	ERA	IP	H	BB	SO	SV
C. Hunter	1	1	4.15	13	13	1	5	0
R. Guidry	1	0	1.00	9	8	7	4	0
J. Beattie	1	0	2.00	9	9	4	8	0
E. Figueroa	0	1	8.10	6.2	9	5	2	0
G. Gossage	1	0	0.00	6	1	1	4	0
D. Tidrow	0	0	1.93	4.2	4	0	5	0
K. Clay	0	0	11.57	2.1	4	2	2	0
P. Lindblad	0	0	11.57	2.1	4	0	1	0

LOS ANGELES (N.L.)

	W	L	ERA	IP	H	BB	SO	SV
T. John	1	0	3.07	14.2	14	4	6	0
D. Sutton	0	2	7.50	12	17	4	8	0
B. Hooton	1	1	6.48	8.1	13	3	6	0
C. Hough	0	0	8.44	5.1	10	2	5	0
B. Welch	0	1	6.23	4.1	4	2	6	1
T. Forster	0	0	0.00	4	5	1	6	0
L. Rautzhan	0	0	13.50	2	4	0	0	0
D. Rau	0	0	0.00	2	1	0	3	0

1979 NATIONAL LEAGUE CHAMPIONSHIP SERIES

LINE SCORES	PITCHERS (innings pitched)	HOME RUNS (men on)	HIGHLIGHTS

Pittsburgh (East) defeats Cincinnati (West) 3 games to 0

GAME 1 - OCTOBER 2

PIT	E	002 000 000 03	5 10 0	Candelaria (7), Romo (0.1), Tekulve (1.2), Jackson (0.1), Robinson (1.2) SV	Garner, Stargell (2 on)	Stargell's 3-run homer in the 11th broke a 2-2 tie.
CIN	W	000 200 000 00	2 7 0	Seaver (8), Hume (2.1), Tomlin (0.2)	Foster (1 on)	

GAME 2 - OCTOBER 3

PIT	E	000 110 000 1	3 11 0	Bibby (7), Jackson (0.1), Romo (0), Tekulve (1), Roberts (0), Robinson (1.2)		Singles by Moreno and Parker sandwiched around Foli's sacrifice broke a 2-2 tie in the 10th inning.
CIN	W	010 000 001 0	2 8 0	Pastore (7), Tomlin (0.2), Hume (1.1),		

GAME 3 - OCTOBER 5

CIN	W	000 001 000	1 8 1	LaCoss (1.2), Norman (2), Leibrandt (0.1), Soto (2), Tomlin (1.2), Hume (0.1)	Bench	Blyleven went the route, scattering 8 hits and fanning 9, while Stargell socked his second homer as Bucs completed series sweep.
PIT	E	112 200 01x	7 7 0	Blyleven (9)	Madlock, Stargell	

Team totals

		W	AB	H	2B	3B	HR	R	RBI	BA	BB	SO	ERA
PIT	E	3	105	28	3	2	4	15	14	.267	13	13	1.50
CIN	W	0	107	23	4	1	2	5	5	.215	11	26	4.34

Individual Batting

PITTSBURGH (EAST)

	AB	H	2B	3B	HR	R	RBI	BA
E. Ott, c	13	3	0	0	0	0	0	.231
O. Moreno, of	12	3	0	1	0	3	0	.404
T. Foli, ss	12	4	1	0	0	1	3	.333
P. Garner, 2b, ss	12	5	0	1	1	4	1	.417
B. Madlock, 3b	12	3	0	0	1	1	2	.250
D. Parker, of	12	4	0	0	0	2	2	.333
W. Stargell, 1b	11	5	2	0	2	2	6	.455
J. Milner, of	9	0	0	0	0	0	0	.000
B. Robinson, of	3	0	0	0	0	0	0	.000
B. Blyleven, p	3	1	0	0	0	1	0	.333
Candelaria, p	3	0	0	0	0	0	0	.000
K. Tekulve, p	1	0	0	0	0	0	0	.000
G. Jackson, p	1	0	0	0	0	0	0	.000
M. Easler	1	0	0	0	0	0	0	.000
R. Stennett, 2b	0	0	0	0	0	0	0	–
M. Alexander	0	0	0	0	0	1	0	–

Stolen Bases: B. Madlock (2), D. Parker, O. Moreno

CINCINNATI (WEST)

	AB	H	2B	3B	HR	R	RBI	BA
D. Collins, of	14	5	1	0	0	0	1	.357
Concepcion, ss	14	6	1	0	0	1	0	.429
R. Knight, 3b	14	4	1	0	0	0	0	.286
J. Bench, c	12	3	0	1	1	1	1	.250
D. Driessen, 1b	12	1	0	0	0	1	0	.083
J. Morgan, 2b	11	0	0	0	0	0	0	.000
G. Foster, of	10	2	0	0	1	1	2	.200
C. Geronimo, of	7	1	0	0	0	0	0	.143
H. Cruz, of	5	1	1	0	0	1	0	.200
H. Spilman	2	0	0	0	0	0	0	.000
R. Auerbach	2	0	0	0	0	0	0	.000
T. Seaver, p	2	0	0	0	0	0	0	.000
F. Norman, p	1	0	0	0	0	0	0	.000
T. Hume, p	1	0	0	0	0	0	0	.000
F. Pastore, p	0	0	0	0	0	0	1	–

Errors: C. Geronimo
Stolen Bases: D. Collins (2), J. Morgan, R. Knight

Individual Pitching

PITTSBURGH (EAST)

	W	L	ERA	IP	H	BB	SO	SV
B. Blyleven	1	0	1.00	9	8	0	9	0
J. Bibby	0	0	1.29	7	4	4	5	0
Candelaria	0	0	2.57	7	5	1	4	0
K. Tekulve	0	0	3.00	3	2	2	2	0
G. Jackson	1	0	0.00	2	1	1	2	0
D. Robinson	1	0	0.00	2	0	1	3	1
E. Romo	0	0	0.00	0.1	3	1	1	0
D. Roberts	0	0	–	0.0	0	1	0	0

CINCINNATI (WEST)

	W	L	ERA	IP	H	BB	SO	SV
T. Seaver	0	0	2.25	8	5	2	5	0
F. Pastore	0	0	2.57	7	7	3	1	0
T. Hume	0	1	6.75	4	6	0	2	0
D. Tomlin	0	0	0.00	3	3	2	3	0
F. Norman	0	0	18.00	2	4	1	1	0
M. Soto	0	0	0.00	2	0	0	1	0
M. LaCoss	0	1	10.80	1.2	1	4	0	0
D. Bair	0	1	9.00	1	2	1	0	0
C. Leibrandt	0	0	0.00	0.1	0	0	0	0

1979 AMERICAN LEAGUE CHAMPIONSHIP SERIES

LINE SCORES	PITCHERS (innings pitched)	HOME RUNS (men on)	HIGHLIGHTS

Baltimore (East) defeats California (West) 3 games to 1

GAME 1 - OCTOBER 3

CAL	W	101 001 000 0	3 7 1	Ryan (7), Montague (2.2)	Ford
BAL	E	002 100 000 3	6 6 0	Palmer (9), Stanhouse (1)	Lowenstein (2 on)

John Lowenstein, a pinch hitter, stroked a 10th-inning homer with two on to snap a 3-3 tie.

GAME 2 - OCTOBER 4

CAL	W	100 001 132	8 10 1	Frost (1.1), Clear (5.2), Aase (1)	Ford
BAL	E	441 000 00x	9 11 1	Flanagan (7), Stanhouse (2)	Murray (2 on)

Eddie Murray drove in 4 runs with a single and a homer to give the Orioles an early 9-1 lead. California scored 7 runs in the last 4 innings to fall short by one run.

GAME 3 - OCTOBER 5

BAL	E	000 101 100	3 8 3	D. Martinez (8.2), Stanhouse (0.1)	
CAL	W	100 100 002	4 9 0	Tanana (5), Aase (4)	Baylor

California rallied for 2 runs in the 9th to pull the game out the fire. Larry Harlow's looping double off relief ace Stanhouse drove in the winning run.

GAME 4 - OCTOBER 6

BAL	E	002 100 500	8 12 1	McGregor (9)	Kelly (2 on)
CAL	W	000 000 000	0 6 0	Knapp (2.1), LaRoche (1.1), Frost (3), Montague (1.1), Barlow (1)	

McGregor hurled a 6-hitter and Pat Kelly knocked in 3 runs with a homer and single to help the Orioles win the championship in four games.

Team totals

		W	AB	H	2B	3B	HR	R	RBI	BA	BB	SO	ERA
BAL	E	3	133	37	5	1	3	26	25	.278	18	24	2.97
CAL	W	1	137	32	7	0	3	15	14	.234	7	13	5.80

Individual Batting

BALTIMORE (EAST)

	AB	H	2B	3B	HR	R	RBI	BA
K. Singleton, of	16	6	2	0	0	4	2	.375
A. Bumbry, of	16	4	0	1	0	5	0	.250
D. DeCinces, 3b	13	4	1	0	0	4	3	.308
E. Murray, 1b	12	5	0	0	1	3	5	.417
R. Dauer, 2b	11	2	0	0	0	0	0	.182
K. Garcia, ss	11	3	0	0	1	2	2	.273
P. Kelly, of, dh	11	4	0	0	1	3	4	.364
R. Dempsey, c	10	4	2	0	0	3	2	.400
L. May, dh	7	1	0	0	0	0	1	.143
Lowenstein, of	6	1	0	0	1	2	3	.167
M. Belanger, ss	5	1	0	0	0	0	1	.200
G. Roenicke, of	5	1	0	0	0	1	1	.200
B. Smith, 2b	4	0	0	0	0	0	0	.000
D. Skaggs, c	4	0	0	0	0	0	0	.000
T. Crowley	2	1	0	0	0	0	1	.500

Errors: K. Garcia (2), E. Murray (2), A. Bumbry
Stolen Bases: P. Kelly (2), A. Bumbry (2), R. Dempsey

CALIFORNIA (WEST)

	AB	H	2B	3B	HR	R	RBI	BA
D. Ford, of	17	5	1	0	2	2	4	.294
R. Carew, 1b	17	7	3	0	0	4	1	.412
C. Lansford, 3b	17	5	0	0	0	2	3	.294
R. Miller, of	16	4	0	0	0	2	0	.250
D. Baylor, of, dh	16	3	0	0	1	2	2	.188
B. Downing, c	15	3	0	0	0	1	1	.200
B. Grich, 2b	13	2	1	0	0	0	2	.154
J. Anderson, ss	11	1	0	0	0	0	0	.091
L. Harlow, of	8	1	1	0	0	0	1	.125
B. Clark, of	3	0	0	0	0	0	0	.000
Rettenmund, dh	2	0	0	0	0	0	0	.000
W. Davis	2	1	1	0	0	1	0	.500
Campaneris, ss	0	0	0	0	0	0	0	—
D. Thon, ss	0	0	0	0	0	1	0	—

Errors: D. Ford, B. Grich
Stolen Bases: R. Carew, C. Lansford

Individual Pitching

BALTIMORE (EAST)

	W	L	ERA	IP	H	BB	SO	SV
J. Palmer	0	0	3.00	9	7	2	3	0
S. McGregor	1	0	0.00	9	6	1	4	0
D. Martinez	0	0	3.24	8.1	8	0	4	0
M. Flanagan	1	0	5.14	7	6	1	2	0
D. Stanhouse	1	1	6.00	3	5	3	0	0

CALIFORNIA (WEST)

	W	L	ERA	IP	H	BB	SO	SV
N. Ryan	0	0	1.29	7	4	3	8	0
M. Clear	0	0	4.76	5.2	4	2	3	0
F. Tanana	0	0	3.60	5	6	2	3	0
D. Aase	1	0	1.80	5	4	2	6	0
D. Frost	0	1	18.69	4.1	8	5	1	0
J. Montague	0	1	9.00	4	4	2	2	0
C. Knapp	0	1	7.71	2.1	5	1	0	0
M. Barlow	0	0	0.00	1	0	0	0	0
D. LaRoche	0	0	6.75	1.1	2	1	1	0

1979 WORLD SERIES

LINE SCORES	PITCHERS (innings pitched)	HOME RUNS (men on)	HIGHLIGHTS

Pittsburgh (N.L.) defeats Baltimore (A.L.) 4 games to 3

GAME 1 - OCTOBER 10

PIT	N	000 102 010	4 11 3	Kison (0.1), Rooker (3.2), Romo (1), D. Robinson (2), Jackson (1)
BAL	A	500 000 00x	5 6 3	Flanagan (9)

Home Runs: Stargell / DeCinces (1 on)

Baltimore erupted for 5 runs in the first inning and Flanagan withstood a late Pittsburgh rally, going the route despite giving up 11 hits.

GAME 2 - OCTOBER 11

PIT	N	020 000 001	3 11 2	Blyleven (6), B. Robinson (2), Tekulve (1) SV
BAL	A	010 001 000	2 6 1	Palmer (7), T. Martinez (1), Stanhouse (1)

Home Runs: Murray

Sanguillen, a pinch hitter, singled with two out in the 9th to score Ed Ott with the tie-breaking run off Oriole relief ace Stanhouse.

GAME 3 - OCTOBER 12

BAL	A	002 500 100	8 13 0	McGregor (9)
PIT	N	120 001 000	4 9 2	Candelaria (3), Romo (3.2), Jackson (0.1), Tekulve (2)

Home Runs: Ayala (1 on)

Kiko Garcia enjoyed a 4-for-4 day, including a double and a triple, and drove in 4 runs as McGregor went the distance spacing 9 hits.

GAME 4 - OCTOBER 13

BAL	A	003 000 060	9 12 0	D. Martinez (1.1), Stewart (2.2), Stone (2), Stoddard (3)
PIT	N	040 011 000	6 17 1	Bibby (6.1), Jackson (0.2), D. Robinson (0.1), Tekulve (1.2)

Home Runs: Stargell

Baltimore exploded for 6 runs in the 8th to overcome a 6-3 deficit. Doubles by pinch hitters Lowenstein and Crowley accounted for 4 of the runs.

GAME 5 - OCTOBER 14

BAL	A	000 010 000	1 6 2	Flanagan (6), Stoddard (0.2), T. Martinez (0.1), Stanhouse (1)
PIT	N	000 002 23x	7 13 1	Rooker (5), Blyleven (4)

Bill Madlock had 4 hits and Tim Foli drove in 3 runs as Pittsburgh staved off elimination. Blyleven pitched four shutout innings in relief to gain the victory.

GAME 6 - OCTOBER 16

PIT	N	000 000 220	4 10 0	Candelaria (6), Tekulve (3) SV
BAL	A	000 000 000	0 7 1	Palmer (8), Stoddard (1)

Candelaria and Tekulve combined to blank the Orioles on 7 hits to square the Series. Moreno led the 10-hit attack on Palmer with 3 singles.

GAME 7 - OCTOBER 17

PIT	N	000 002 002	4 10 0	Bibby (4), D. Robinson (0.2) Jackson (2.2), Tekulve (1.2) SV
BAL	A	001 000 000	1 4 2	McGregor (8), Stoddard (0.1), Flanagan (0), Stanhouse (0), T. Martinez (0), D. Martinez (0.2)

Home Runs: Stargell (1 on)

Stargell homered with one on in the 6th as Pittsburgh overcame a 1-0 deficit and went on to defeat McGregor and the Orioles to win the World Series, after trailing three games to one.

Team totals

		W	AB	H	2B	3B	HR	R	RBI	BA	BB	SO	ERA
PIT	N	4	251	81	18	1	3	32	32	.323	16	35	3.19
BAL	A	3	233	54	10	1	4	26	23	.232	26	41	4.35

Individual Batting

PITTSBURGH (N.L.)

	AB	H	2B	3B	HR	R	RBI	BA
O. Moreno, of	33	11	2	0	0	4	3	.333
T. Foli, ss	30	10	1	1	0	6	3	.333
W. Stargell, 1b	30	12	4	0	3	7	7	.400
D. Parker, of	29	10	3	0	0	2	4	.345
P. Garner, 2b	24	12	4	0	0	4	5	.500
B. Madlock, 3b	24	9	1	0	0	2	3	.375
B. Robinson, of	19	5	1	0	0	2	2	.263
S. Nicosia, c	16	1	0	0	0	1	0	.063
E. Ott, c	12	4	1	0	0	2	3	.333
J. Milner, of	9	3	1	0	0	2	1	.333
J. Bibby, p	4	0	0	0	0	0	0	.000
L. Lacy	4	1	0	0	0	0	0	.250
B. Blyleven, p	3	0	0	0	0	0	0	.000
Sanguillen	3	1	0	0	0	0	1	.333
Candelaria, p	3	1	0	0	0	0	0	.333
K. Tekulve, p	2	0	0	0	0	0	0	.000
J. Rooker, p	2	0	0	0	0	0	0	.000
G. Jackson, p	1	0	0	0	0	0	0	.000
R. Stennett	1	1	0	0	0	0	0	1.000
E. Romo, p	1	0	0	0	0	0	0	.000
M. Easler	1	0	0	0	0	0	0	.000
M. Alexander, of	0	0	0	0	0	0	0	–

Errors: T. Foli (3), P. Garner (2), W. Stargell (2), B. Madlock, D. Parker

BALTIMORE (A.L.)

	AB	H	2B	3B	HR	R	RBI	BA
K. Singleton, of	28	10	1	0	0	1	2	.357
E. Murray, 1b	26	4	1	0	1	3	2	.154
D. DeCinces, 3b	25	5	0	0	1	2	3	.200
A. Bumbry, of	21	3	0	0	0	3	1	.143
R. Dempsey, c	21	6	2	0	0	3	0	.286
K. Garcia, ss	20	8	2	1	0	4	6	.400
R. Dauer, 2b	17	5	1	0	1	2	1	.294
G. Roenicke, of	16	2	1	0	0	1	0	.125
Lowenstein, of	13	3	1	0	0	2	3	.231
B. Smith, 2b	7	2	0	0	0	1	0	.286
B. Ayala, of	6	2	0	0	1	1	2	.333
M. Belanger, ss	6	0	0	0	0	1	0	.000
M. Flanagan, p	5	0	0	0	0	0	0	.000
P. Kelly	4	1	0	0	0	0	0	.250
T. Crowley	4	1	1	0	0	0	2	.250
S. McGregor, p	4	0	0	0	0	0	1	.000
J. Palmer, p	4	0	0	0	0	0	0	.000
D. Skaggs, c	3	1	0	0	0	0	1	.333
T. Stoddard, p	1	1	0	0	0	0	1	1.000
L. May	1	0	0	0	0	0	0	.000
S. Stewart, p	1	0	0	0	0	0	0	.000

Errors: D. DeCinces (3), M. Belanger, T. Stoddard, K. Garcia, Lowenstein, A. Bumbry, D. Stanhouse
Stolen Bases: D. DeCinces, E. Murray

Individual Pitching

PITTSBURGH (N.L.)

	W	L	ERA	IP	H	BB	SO	SV
J. Bibby	0	0	2.61	10.1	10	2	10	0
B. Blyleven	1	0	1.80	10	8	3	4	0
K. Tekulve	0	1	2.89	9.1	4	3	10	3
Candelaria	1	1	5.00	9	14	2	4	0
J. Rooker	0	0	1.04	8.2	5	3	4	0
D. Robinson	1	0	5.40	5	4	6	3	0
G. Jackson	1	0	0.00	4.2	1	2	2	0
E. Romo	0	0	3.86	4.2	5	3	4	0
B. Kison	0	1	∞	0.1	3	2	0	0

BALTIMORE (A.L.)

	W	L	ERA	IP	H	BB	SO	SV
S. McGregor	1	1	3.18	17	16	2	8	0
M. Flanagan	1	1	3.00	15	18	2	13	0
J. Palmer	0	1	3.60	15	18	5	8	0
T. Stoddard	1	0	5.40	5	6	1	3	0
D. Martinez	0	0	18.00	2	6	0	0	0
D. Stanhouse	0	1	13.50	2	6	3	0	0
S. Stewart	0	0	0.00	2.2	4	1	0	0
S. Stone	0	0	9.00	2	4	2	2	0
T. Martinez	0	0	6.75	1.1	3	0	1	0

1980 NATIONAL LEAGUE CHAMPIONSHIP SERIES

LINE SCORES	PITCHERS (innings pitched)	HOME RUNS (men on)	HIGHLIGHTS

Philadelphia (East) defeats Houston (West) 3 games to 2

GAME 1 - OCTOBER 7

HOU	W	001 000 000	1 7 0	K. Forsch (8)		
PHI	E	000 002 10x	3 8 1	Carlton (7), McGraw (2) SV	Luzinski (1 on)	

A two-run homer by Luzinski lifted the Phillies to a 3-1 victory. Carlton got the victory and McGraw the save.

GAME 2 - OCTOBER 8

HOU	W	001 000 110 4	7 8 1	Ryan (6.2), Sambito (0.1), D. Smith (1.2), LaCorte (1), Andujar (1) SV
PHI	E	000 200 010 1	4 14 2	Ruthven (7), McGraw (1), Reed (1.1), Saucier (0.2)

Jose Cruz singled in one run and Bergman tripled in two to highlight a 4-run outburst in the 10th, snapping a 3-3 deadlock and evening the series.

GAME 3 - OCTOBER 10

PHI	E	000 000 000 00	0 7 1	Christenson (6), Noles (1.1), McGraw (3)
HOU	W	000 000 000 01	1 6 1	J. Niekro (10), D. Smith (1)

Joe Morgan's leadoff triple in the 11th and Walling's sacrifice fly off loser Tug McGraw accounted for the game's only run. Joe Niekro pitched 10 scoreless innings for the Astros, but Smith got the win.

GAME 4 - OCTOBER 11

PHI	E	000 000 030 2	5 13 0	Carlton (5.1), Noles (1.1), Saucier (0), Reed (0.1), Brusstar (2), McGraw (1) SV
HOU	W	000 110 001 0	3 5 1	Ruhle (7), D. Smith (0), Sambito (3)

Luzinski and Trillo followed Rose's single with doubles for a 2-run rally in the 10th to give the Phillies the winning runs in a controversial see-saw game.

GAME 5 - OCTOBER 12

PHI	E	020 000 050 1	8 13 2	Bystrom (5.1), Brusstar (0.2), Christenson (0.2), Reed (0.1), McGraw (1), Ruthven (2)
HOU	W	100 001 320 0	7 14 0	Ryan (7), Sambito (0.1), K. Forsch (0.2), LaCorte (2)

A double by Maddox in the 10th inning drove Unser home with the decisive run as the Phillies outlasted the Astros to win the 5th game and capture their first pennant since 1950. The Phillies rallied for 5 runs in the 8th to take a 7-5 lead but the Astros tallied twice in their half to force the fourth straight overtime game.

Team totals

		W	AB	H	2B	3B	HR	R	RBI	BA	BB	SO	ERA
PHI	E	3	190	55	8	1	1	20	19	.289	13	37	0.33
HOU	W	2	172	40	7	5	0	19	18	.233	31	19	3.49

Individual Batting

PHILADELPHIA (EAST)

	AB	H	2B	3B	HR	R	RBI	BA
M. Schmidt, 3b	24	5	1	0	0	1	1	.208
B. McBride, of	21	5	0	0	0	0	0	.238
M. Trillo, 2b	21	8	2	1	0	1	4	.381
G. Maddox, of	20	6	2	0	0	2	3	.300
P. Rose, 1b	20	8	0	0	0	3	2	.400
L. Bowa, ss	19	6	0	0	0	2	0	.316
B. Boone, c	18	4	0	0	0	1	2	.222
G. Luzinski, of	17	5	2	0	1	3	4	.294
L. Smith, of	5	3	0	0	0	2	0	.600
D. Unser, of	5	2	1	0	0	2	1	.400
S. Carlton, p	4	0	0	0	0	0	0	.000
G. Gross, of	4	3	0	0	0	2	1	.750
G. Vukovich, of	3	0	0	0	0	0	0	.000
M. Bystrom, p	2	0	0	0	0	0	0	.000
Christenson, p	2	0	0	0	0	0	0	.000
D. Ruthven, p	2	0	0	0	0	0	0	.000
T. McGraw, p	1	0	0	0	0	0	0	.000
W. Brusstar, p	1	0	0	0	0	0	0	.000
K. Moreland, c	1	0	0	0	0	0	1	.000
R. Aviles	0	0	0	0	0	1	0	—

Errors: G. Luzinski, M. Schmidt, Christenson, B. McBride, M. Trillo, L. Bowa.

Stolen Bases: G. Maddox (2), B. McBride (2), L. Smith, M. Schmidt, L. Bowa

HOUSTON (WEST)

	AB	H	2B	3B	HR	R	RBI	BA
E. Cabell, 3b	21	5	1	0	0	1	0	.238
T. Puhl, of	19	10	2	0	0	4	3	.526
J. Cruz, of	15	6	1	1	0	3	4	.400
A. Howe, 1b	15	3	1	1	0	0	2	.200
J. Morgan, 2b	13	2	1	1	0	1	0	.154
C. Reynolds, ss	13	2	1	0	0	2	0	.154
C. Cedeno, of	11	2	0	0	0	1	1	.182
L. Pujols, c	10	1	0	1	0	1	0	.100
R. Landestoy, 2b, ss	9	2	0	0	0	3	2	.222
D. Walling, of, 1b	9	1	0	0	0	2	2	.111
G. Woods, of	8	2	0	0	0	0	1	.250
A. Ashby, c	8	1	0	0	0	1	0	.125
N. Ryan, p	4	0	0	0	0	1	0	.000
J. Niekro, p	3	0	0	0	0	0	0	.000
D. Bergman, 1b	3	1	0	1	0	0	2	.333
V. Ruhle, p	3	0	0	0	0	0	0	.000
J. Leonard, of	3	0	0	0	0	0	0	.000
K. Forsch, p	2	2	0	0	0	0	0	1.000
F. LaCorte, p	1	0	0	0	0	0	0	.000
B. Bochy, c	1	0	0	0	0	0	0	.000
D. Heep	1	0	0	0	0	0	0	.000

Errors: D. Bergman, C. Reynolds.

Stolen Bases: T. Puhl (2), G. Woods, R. Landestoy

Individual Pitching

PHILADELPHIA (EAST)

	W	L	ERA	IP	H	BB	SO	SV
S. Carlton	1	0	2.19	12.1	11	8	6	0
D. Ruthven	1	0	2.00	9	3	5	4	0
T. McGraw	0	1	4.50	8	8	4	5	2
Christenson	0	0	4.05	6.2	5	5	2	0
M. Bystrom	0	0	1.69	5.1	7	2	1	0
D. Noles	0	0	0.00	2.2	1	3	0	0
R. Reed	0	1	18.00	2	3	1	1	0
W. Brusstar	1	0	3.38	2.2	1	1	0	0
K. Saucier	0	0	0.00	0.2	1	2	0	0

HOUSTON (WEST)

	W	L	ERA	IP	H	BB	SO	SV
N. Ryan	0	0	5.40	13.1	16	3	14	0
J. Niekro	0	0	0.00	10	6	1	2	0
K. Forsch	0	1	4.15	8.2	10	1	6	0
V. Ruhle	0	0	3.86	7	8	1	3	0
F. LaCorte	1	1	3.00	3	7	2	2	0
J. Sambito	0	1	4.91	3.2	4	2	6	0
D. Smith	1	0	3.86	2.1	4	2	4	0
J. Andujar	0	0	0.00	1	0	1	0	1

1980 AMERICAN LEAGUE CHAMPIONSHIP SERIES

LINE SCORES	PITCHERS (innings pitched)	HOME RUNS (men on)	HIGHLIGHTS

Kansas City (West) defeats New York (East) 3 games to 0

GAME 1 - OCTOBER 8

NY	E	020 000 000	2 10 1	Guidry (3), Davis (4), Underwood (1)	Cerone, Piniella	
KC	W	022 000 12x	7 10 0	Gura (9)	G. Brett	

Gura spaced ten hits and White drove in two runs with three hits.

GAME 2 - OCTOBER 9

NY	E	000 020 000	2 8 0	May (8)	Nettles
KC	W	003 000 00x	3 6 0	Leonard (8), Quisenberry (1) SV	

Four straight hits accounted for all of KC's runs in the 3rd inning. Wilson drove in two with a triple and Washington doubled in the other run. Game ended with Randolph tagged out at plate trying to score tying run.

GAME 3 - OCTOBER 10

KC	W	000 010 300	4 12 1	Splittorff (5.1), Quisenberry (3.2)	G. Brett (2 on), White
NY	E	000 002 000	2 8 0	John (6.2), Gossage (0.1), Underwood (2)	

Powered by George Brett's three-run blast in the 7th off Goose Gossage, the Royals swept the Yanks for their first American League pennant.

Team totals

		W	AB	H	2B	3B	HR	R	RBI	BA	BB	SO	ERA
KC	W	3	97	28	6	1	3	14	14	.289	9	15	1.67
NY	E	0	102	26	7	1	3	6	5	.255	6	16	4.32

Individual Batting

KANSAS CITY (WEST)

	AB	H	2B	3B	HR	R	RBI	BA
W. Wilson, of	13	4	2	1	0	2	4	.308
A. Otis, of	12	4	1	0	0	2	0	.333
W. Aikens, 1b	11	4	0	0	0	0	2	.364
Washington, ss	11	4	1	0	0	1	1	.364
G. Brett, 3b	11	3	1	0	2	3	4	.273
F. White, 2b	11	6	1	0	1	3	3	.545
D. Porter, c	10	1	0	0	0	2	0	.100
H. McRae, dh	10	2	0	0	0	0	0	.200
J. Wathan, of	6	0	0	0	0	1	0	.000
C. Hurdle, of	2	0	0	0	0	0	0	.000
P. LaCock, 1b	0	0	0	0	0	0	0	–

Errors: F. White

Stolen Bases: A. Otis (2), F. White

NEW YORK (EAST)

	AB	H	2B	3B	HR	R	RBI	BA
W. Randolph, 2b	13	5	2	0	0	0	1	.385
R. Cerone, c	12	4	0	0	1	1	2	.333
B. Watson, 1b	12	6	3	1	0	0	0	.500
R. Jackson, of	11	3	1	0	0	1	0	.273
B. Dent, ss	11	2	0	0	0	0	0	.182
B. Brown, of	10	0	0	0	0	1	0	.000
E. Soderholm, dh	6	1	0	0	0	0	0	.167
G. Nettles, 3b	6	1	0	0	1	1	1	.167
A. Rodriguez, 3b	6	2	1	0	0	0	0	.333
L. Piniella, of	5	1	0	0	1	1	1	.200
O. Gamble, of, dh	5	1	0	0	0	1	0	.200
B. Murcer, dh	4	0	0	0	0	0	0	.000
J. Spencer	1	0	0	0	0	0	0	.000
J. Lefebvre, of	0	0	0	0	0	0	0	–

Errors: B. Watson

Individual Pitching

KANSAS CITY (WEST)

	W	L	ERA	IP	H	BB	SO	SV
L. Gura	1	0	2.00	9	10	1	4	0
D. Leonard	1	0	2.25	8	7	1	8	0
Splittorff	0	0	1.69	5.1	5	2	3	0
Quisenberry	1	0	0.00	4.2	4	2	1	1

NEW YORK (EAST)

	W	L	ERA	IP	H	BB	SO	SV
R. May	0	1	3.38	8	6	3	4	0
T. John	0	0	2.70	6.2	8	1	3	0
R. Davis	0	0	2.25	4	3	1	3	0
T. Underwood	0	0	0.00	3	3	0	3	0
R. Guidry	0	1	12.00	3	5	4	2	0
G. Gossage	0	1	54.00	0.1	3	0	0	0

1980 WORLD SERIES

LINE SCORES	PITCHERS (innings pitched)	HOME RUNS (men on)	HIGHLIGHTS

Philadelphia (N.L.) defeats Kansas City (A.L.) 4 games to 2

GAME 1 - OCTOBER 14

KC	A	022 000 020	6 9 1	
PHI	N	005 110 00x	7 11 0	

Pitchers: Leonard (3.2), Martin (4), Quisenberry (0.1) / Walk (7), McGraw (2) SV

Home Runs: Aikens (1 on), Aikens (1 on), Otis (1 on) / McBride (2 on)

Highlights: The Phillies erupted for 5 runs in the 3rd inning to offset an early 4-0 Kansas City lead. McBride's 3-run homer was the big blow. Aikens slammed a pair of 2-run homers for the Royals.

GAME 2 - OCTOBER 15

KC	A	000 001 300	4 11 0	
PHI	N	000 020 04x	6 8 1	

Pitchers: Gura (6), Quisenberry (2) / Carlton (8), Reed (1) SV

Highlights: Philadelphia came from behind, pummeling relief ace Quisenberry for 4 runs in the 8th to overcome a 4-2 deficit. Doubles by pinch hitter Unser and Mike Schmidt were the key blows.

GAME 3 - OCTOBER 17

PHI	N	010 010 010 0	3 14 0	
KC	A	100 100 100 1	4 11 0	

Pitchers: Ruthven (9), McGraw (0.2) / Gale (4.1), Martin (3.1) Quisenberry (2.1)

Home Runs: Schmidt / Brett, Otis

Highlights: Aikens's first major league triple scored Willie Wilson with the winning run in the 10th inning. Quisenberry, in relief, was the winner, McGraw the loser.

GAME 4 - OCTOBER 18

PHI	N	010 000 110	3 10 1	
KC	A	410 000 00x	5 10 2	

Pitchers: Christenson (0.1), Noles (4.2), Saucier (0.2), Brusstar (2.1) / Leonard (7), Quisenberry (2) SV

Home Runs: Aikens, Aikens (1 on)

Highlights: Aikens drove in 3 runs with 2 home runs, becoming the first player to have two multiple-homer games in the same Series.

GAME 5 - OCTOBER 19

PHI	N	000 200 002	4 7 0	
KC	A	000 012 000	3 12 2	

Pitchers: Bystrom (5), Reed (1), McGraw (3) / Gura (6.1), Quisenberry (2.2)

Home Runs: Schmidt (1 on) / Otis

Highlights: Pinch-hitter Unser doubled home Schmidt with the tying run in the 9th and Trillo followed with a game-winning single as the Phillies defeated Quisenberry for the second time. McGraw fanned Cardenal with the bases full in the bottom of the 9th inning.

GAME 6 - OCTOBER 21

KC	A	000 000 010	1 7 2	
PHI	N	002 011 00x	4 9 0	

Pitchers: Gale (2), Martin (2.1), Splittorff (1.2), Pattin (1), Quisenberry (1) / Carlton (7), McGraw (2) SV

Highlights: Schmidt knocked in 2 runs and relief ace McGraw twice stopped the Royals with the bases full as the Phillies won the first World Series in their history.

Team totals

		W	AB	H	2B	3B	HR	R	RBI	BA	BB	SO	ERA
PHI	N	4	201	59	13	0	3	27	26	.294	15	17	3.67
KC	A	2	207	60	9	2	8	23	22	.290	26	49	4.15

Individual Batting

PHILADELPHIA (N.L.)

	AB	H	2B	3B	HR	R	RBI	BA
L. Bowa, ss	24	9	1	0	0	3	2	.375
P. Rose, 1b	23	6	1	0	0	2	1	.261
B. McBride, of	23	7	1	0	1	3	5	.304
M. Trillo, 2b	23	5	2	0	0	4	2	.217
G. Maddox, of	22	5	2	0	0	1	1	.227
M. Schmidt, 3b	21	8	1	0	2	6	7	.381
L. Smith, of, dh	19	5	1	0	0	2	1	.263
B. Boone, c	17	7	2	0	0	3	4	.412
K. Moreland, dh	12	4	0	0	0	1	1	.333
G. Luzinski, of, dh	9	0	0	0	0	0	0	.000
D. Unser, of	6	3	2	0	0	2	2	.500
G. Gross, of	2	0	0	0	0	0	0	.000

Errors: Christenson, M. Trillo
Stolen Bases: L. Bowa (3)

KANSAS CITY (A.L.)

	AB	H	2B	3B	HR	R	RBI	BA
W. Wilson, of	26	4	1	0	0	3	0	.154
F. White, 2b	25	2	0	0	0	0	0	.080
G. Brett, 3b	24	9	2	1	1	3	3	.375
H. McRae, dh	24	9	3	0	0	3	1	.375
A. Otis, of	23	11	2	0	3	4	7	.478
Washington, ss	22	6	0	0	0	1	2	.273
W. Aikens, 1b	20	8	0	1	4	5	8	.400
D. Porter, c	14	2	0	0	0	1	0	.143
C. Hurdle, of	12	5	1	0	0	1	0	.417
J. Cardenal, of	10	2	0	0	0	0	0	.200
J. Wathan, c, of	7	2	0	0	0	1	1	.286
P. LaCock, 1b	0	0	0	0	0	0	0	—
Concepcion	0	0	0	0	0	0	0	—
D. Chalk, 3b	0	0	0	0	0	1	0	—

Errors: W. Aikens (2), F. White (2), Washington, G. Brett, D. Leonard
Stolen Bases: W. Wilson (2), C. Hurdle, G. Brett, D. Chalk, F. White

Individual Pitching

PHILADELPHIA (N.L.)

	W	L	ERA	IP	H	BB	SO	SV
S. Carlton	2	0	2.40	15	14	9	17	0
D. Ruthven	0	0	3.00	9	9	0	7	0
B. Walk	1	0	7.71	7	8	3	3	0
T. McGraw	1	1	1.17	7.2	7	8	10	2
M. Bystrom	0	0	5.40	5	10	1	4	0
D. Noles	0	0	1.93	4.2	5	2	6	0
R. Reed	0	0	0.00	2	2	0	2	1
W. Brusstar	0	0	0.00	2.1	0	1	0	0
K. Saucier	0	0	0.00	0.2	0	2	0	0
Christenson	0	1	∞	0.1	5	0	0	0

KANSAS CITY (A.L.)

	W	L	ERA	IP	H	BB	SO	SV
L. Gura	0	0	2.19	12.1	8	3	4	0
D. Leonard	1	1	6.75	10.2	15	2	5	0
Quisenberry	1	2	5.23	10.1	10	3	0	1
R. Martin	0	0	2.79	9.2	11	3	2	0
R. Gale	0	1	4.26	6.1	11	4	4	0
Splittorff	0	0	5.40	1.2	4	0	0	0
M. Pattin	0	0	0.00	1	0	0	2	0

1981 NATIONAL LEAGUE EASTERN DIVISION PLAYOFF

LINE SCORES	PITCHERS (innings pitched)	HOME RUNS (men on)	HIGHLIGHTS

Montreal defeats Philadelphia 3 games to 2

GAME 1 - OCTOBER 7

PHI E 010 000 000   1 10 1   Carlton (6), R. Reed (2)   Moreland   Speier drove in a run and scored another to lead the Expos to a 3-1 win over the Phillies.
MON E 110 100 00x   3 8 0   Rogers (8.1), Reardon (0.2) SV

GAME 2 - OCTOBER 8

PHI E 000 000 010   1 6 2   Ruthven (4), Brusstar (2), Lyle (1), McGraw (1)   Speier's run-scoring single and Carter's two-run homer carried the Expos to a second 3-1 triumph over the Phillies.
MON E 012 000 00x   3 7 0   Gullickson (7.2), Reardon (1.1) SV   Carter (1 on)

GAME 3 - OCTOBER 9

MON E 010 000 010   2 8 2   Burris (5.1), Lee (0.2), Sosa (2)   The Phillies pounded four pitchers for 13 hits, including 3 by Matthews, to stave off elimination. Christenson allowed 4 hits in 6 innings.
PHI E 020 002 20x   6 13 0   Christenson (6), Lyle (1), R. Reed (2)

GAME 4 - OCTOBER 10

MON E 000 112 100 0   5 10 1   Sanderson (2.2), Bahnsen (1.1), Sosa (1), Fryman (1.1), Reardon (2.2)   Carter   A pinch homer by Vukovich in the bottom of the 10th enabled the Phillies to edge out the Expos, 6-5. McGraw pitched 1-hit relief for 3 innings to gain credit for the win.
PHI E 202 001 000 1   6 9 0   Noles (4), Brusstar (1.2), Lyle (0.1), R. Reed (1), McGraw (3)   Schmidt (1 on), Matthews, Vukovich

GAME 5 - OCTOBER 11

MON E 000 021 000   3 8 1   Rogers (9)   Rogers pitched a 6-hit shutout and knocked in 2 runs with a pair of hits as the Expos defeated Carlton for the second time, 3-0, to capture the NL East Division Series.
PHI E 000 000 000   0 6 0   Carlton (8), R. Reed (1)

Team totals

		W	AB	H	2B	3B	HR	R	RBI	BA	BB	SO	ERA
MON	E	3	161	41	10	1	2	16	16	.255	18	36	2.05
PHI	E	2	166	44	6	1	4	14	12	.265	13	19	3.07

Individual Batting

MONTREAL

	AB	H	2B	3B	HR	R	RBI	BA
W. Cromartie, 1b	22	5	2	0	0	1	1	.227
L. Parrish, 3b	20	3	1	0	0	3	1	.150
A. Dawson, of	20	6	0	1	0	1	0	.300
G. Carter, c	19	8	3	0	2	3	6	.421
J. White, of	18	3	1	0	0	3	1	.167
C. Speier, ss	15	6	2	0	0	4	3	.400
J. Manuel, 2b	14	1	0	0	0	0	0	.071
T. Francona, of	12	4	0	0	0	0	0	.333
S. Rogers, p	5	2	0	0	0	0	2	.400
T. Wallach, of	4	1	1	0	0	1	0	.250
Gullickson, p	3	0	0	0	0	0	0	.000
J. Milner	2	1	0	0	0	0	0	.500
W. Johnson	2	1	0	0	0	0	1	.500
R. Burris, p	2	0	0	0	0	0	0	.000
M. Phillips, 2b	1	0	0	0	0	0	0	.000
S. Sanderson, p	1	0	0	0	0	0	0	.000
J. Reardon, p	1	0	0	0	0	0	0	.000
B. Mills	0	0	0	0	0	0	0	–

Errors: J. Manuel (3), A. Dawson, W. Cromartie, E. Sosa
Stolen Bases: J. White (3), A. Dawson (2), T. Francona (2)

PHILADELPHIA

	AB	H	2B	3B	HR	R	RBI	BA
G. Matthews, of	20	8	1	1	3	1	.400	
P. Rose, 1b	20	6	1	0	0	1	2	.300
L. Smith, of	19	5	1	0	0	1	0	.263
L. Bowa, ss	17	3	1	0	0	0	1	.176
M. Trillo, 2b	16	3	0	0	0	1	1	.188
M. Schmidt, 3b	16	4	1	0	1	3	2	.250
B. McBride, of	15	3	1	0	0	1	0	.200
K. Moreland, c	13	6	0	0	1	2	3	.462
G. Vukovich, of	9	4	0	0	1	1	2	.444
B. Boone, c	5	0	0	0	0	0	0	.000
G. Gross, of	4	0	0	0	0	0	0	.000
S. Carlton, p	4	1	0	0	0	0	0	.250
G. Maddox, of	3	1	1	0	0	0	0	.333
D. Davis, of	2	0	0	0	0	0	0	.000
Christenson, p	2	0	0	0	0	0	0	.000
D. Ruthven, p	1	0	0	0	0	0	0	.000
R. Aviles	0	0	0	0	0	0	0	–
L. Aguayo	0	0	0	0	0	1	0	–

Errors: M. Schmidt, K. Moreland, L. Bowa

Individual Pitching

MONTREAL

	W	L	ERA	IP	H	BB	SO	SV
S. Rogers	2	0	0.51	17.2	16	3	5	0
Gullickson	1	0	1.17	7.2	6	1	3	0
R. Burris	0	1	5.06	5.1	7	4	4	0
J. Reardon	0	1	2.08	4.1	1	1	2	2
E. Sosa	0	0	3.00	3	4	0	1	0
S. Sanderson	0	0	6.75	2.2	4	2	2	0
S. Bahnsen	0	0	0.00	1.1	1	1	1	0
W. Fryman	0	0	6.75	1.1	3	1	0	0
B. Lee	0	0	0.00	0.2	2	0	1	0

PHILADELPHIA

	W	L	ERA	IP	H	BB	SO	SV
S. Carlton	0	2	3.86	14	14	8	13	0
R. Reed	0	0	3.00	6	5	3	4	0
Christenson	1	0	1.50	6	4	1	8	0
D. Ruthven	0	1	4.50	4	3	1	0	0
T. McGraw	1	0	0.00	4	2	0	2	0
D. Noles	0	0	4.50	4	4	2	5	0
W. Brusstar	0	0	4.91	3.2	5	1	3	0
S. Lyle	0	0	0.00	2.1	4	2	1	0

1981 NATIONAL LEAGUE WESTERN DIVISION PLAYOFF

LINE SCORES	PITCHERS (innings pitched)	HOME RUNS (men on)	HIGHLIGHTS

Los Angeles defeats Houston 3 games to 2

GAME 1 - OCTOBER 6

LA	W	000 000 100	1 2 0	Valenzuela (8), **Stewart** (0.2)	Garvey
HOU	W	000 001 002	3 8 0	Ryan (9)	Ashby (1 on)

Ashby's 2-run homer in the 9th lifted Ryan and the Astros to a 3-1 win.

GAME 2 - OCTOBER 7

LA	W	000 000 000 00	0 9 1	Reuss (9), S. Howe (1), Stewart (0), Forster (0.1), Niedenfuer (0.1)	
HOU	W	000 000 000 01	1 9 0	J. Niekro (8), D. Smith (2) **Sambito** (1)	

Pinch hitter Dennis Walling singled with 2 out and the bases full in the 11th inning to drive in the run that gave the Astros a 1-0 victory and a 2-0 lead in the series.

GAME 3 - OCTOBER 9

HOU	W	001 000 000	1 3 2	Knepper (5), LaCorte (2), Sambito (0.2), B. Smith (0.1)	A. Howe
LA	W	300 000 03x	6 10 0	Hooton (7), S. Howe (1), Welch (1)	Garvey (1 on)

A 2-run homer by Garvey capped a 3-run first inning that sent the Dodgers to a 6-1 win. Hooton allowed 3 hits in 7 innings for the victory.

GAME 4 - OCTOBER 10

HOU	W	000 000 001	1 4 0	Ruhle (8)	
LA	W	000 010 10x	2 4 0	Valenzuela (9)	Guerrero

A home run by Guerrero and a run-producing single by Russell gave the Dodgers a 2-1 win and tied the series.

GAME 5 - OCTOBER 11

HOU	W	000 000 000	0 5 3	Ryan (6), D. Smith (0.1), LaCorte (1.2)	
LA	W	000 003 10x	4 7 2	Reuss (9)	

A 3-run outburst in the 6th broke up a scoreless duel between Reuss and Ryan and enabled the Dodgers to win three straight after losing the first two games. Garvey led the attack with a single and triple as the Dodgers won the NL West Division Series.

Team totals

		W	AB	H	2B	3B	HR	R	RBI	BA	BB	SO	ERA
LA	W	3	162	32	6	1	3	13	12	.198	13	34	1.17
HOU	E	2	162	29	3	0	2	6	6	.179	13	24	2.45

Individual Batting

LOS ANGELES

	AB	H	2B	3B	HR	R	RBI	BA
D. Lopes, 2b	20	4	1	0	1	0	0	.200
K. Landreaux, of	20	4	1	0	0	1	1	.200
S. Garvey, 1b	19	7	0	1	2	4	4	.368
D. Baker, of	18	3	1	0	0	2	1	.167
P. Guerrero, 3b	17	3	1	0	1	1	1	.176
B. Russell, ss	16	4	1	0	0	1	2	.250
R. Monday, of	14	3	0	0	0	1	1	.214
M. Scioscia, c	13	2	0	0	0	0	1	.154
J. Reuss, p	8	0	0	0	0	0	0	.000
S. Yeager, c	5	2	1	0	0	1	0	.400
Valenzuela, p	4	0	0	0	0	0	0	.000
B. Hooton, p	3	0	0	0	0	0	0	.000
D. Thomas, of	2	0	0	0	0	1	0	.000
M. Marshall	1	0	0	0	0	0	0	.000
J. Johnstone	1	0	0	0	0	0	0	.000
R. Smith	1	0	0	0	0	0	1	.000
S. Sax, 2b	0	0	0	0	0	0	0	–

Errors: B. Russell (2), P. Guerrero
Stolen Bases: D. Lopes, P. Guerrero

HOUSTON

	AB	H	2B	3B	HR	R	RBI	BA
T. Puhl, of	21	4	1	0	0	2	0	.190
J. Cruz, of	20	6	1	0	0	0	0	.300
T. Scott, of	20	3	0	0	0	0	2	.150
P. Garner, 2b	18	2	0	0	0	1	0	.111
A. Howe, 3b	17	4	0	0	1	1	1	.235
C. Cedeno, 1b	13	3	1	0	0	0	0	.231
D. Thon, ss	11	2	0	0	0	0	0	.182
A. Ashby, c	9	1	0	0	1	1	2	.111
D. Walling, 1b, of	6	2	0	0	0	0	1	.333
L. Pujols, c	6	0	0	0	0	0	0	.000
K. Garcia, ss	4	0	0	0	0	0	0	.000
N. Ryan, p	4	1	0	0	0	0	0	.250
C. Reynolds, ss	3	1	0	0	0	1	0	.333
G. Woods	2	0	0	0	0	0	0	.000
J. Niekro, p	2	0	0	0	0	0	0	.000
J. Pittman	2	0	0	0	0	0	0	.000
D. Roberts	1	0	0	0	0	0	0	.000
B. Knepper, p	1	0	0	0	0	0	0	.000
V. Ruhle, p	1	0	0	0	0	0	0	.000
H. Spilman	1	0	0	0	0	0	0	.000

Errors: J. Cruz, D. Walling, C. Cedeno, D. Thon, P. Garner
Stolen Bases: C. Cedeno (2), T. Puhl, J. Cruz

Individual Pitching

LOS ANGELES

	W	L	ERA	IP	H	BB	SO	SV
J. Reuss	1	0	0.00	18	10	5	7	0
Valenzuela	1	0	1.06	17	10	3	10	0
B. Hooton	1	0	1.29	7	3	3	2	0
S. Howe	0	0	0.00	2	1	0	2	0
B. Welch	0	0	0.00	1	0	1	1	0
Niedenfuer	0	0	0.00	0.1	1	1	1	0
T. Forster	0	0	4.04	0.1	0	0	0	0
D. Stewart	0	2	40.50	0.2	4	0	1	0

HOUSTON

	W	L	ERA	IP	H	BB	SO	SV
N. Ryan	1	1	1.80	15	6	3	14	0
J. Niekro	0	0	0.00	8	7	3	4	0
V. Ruhle	0	1	2.25	8	4	2	1	0
B. Knepper	0	1	5.40	5	6	2	4	0
F. LaCorte	0	0	0.00	3.2	1	2	5	0
D. Smith	0	0	3.86	2.1	2	0	4	0
J. Sambito	1	0	16.20	1.2	5	2	2	0
B. Smith	0	0	0.00	0.1	0	0	0	0

1981 NATIONAL LEAGUE CHAMPIONSHIP SERIES

LINE SCORES	PITCHERS (innings pitched)	HOME RUNS (men on)	HIGHLIGHTS

Los Angeles (West) defeats Montreal (East) 3 games to 2

GAME 1 - OCTOBER 13

MON E 000 000 001   1 9 0   Gullickson (7), Reardon (1)
LA   W 020 000 03x   5 8 0   Hooton (7.1), Welch (0.2), Howe (1)   Guerrero (2 on), Scioscia

Cey, activated prior to the start of the series, doubled home the first run and scored another to lead the Dodgers to an opening win over the Expos. Homers by Guerrero and Scioscia ensured victory.

GAME 2 - OCTOBER 14

MON E 020 001 000   3 10 1   Burris (9)
LA   W 000 000 000   0 5 1   Valenzuela (6), Niedenfuer (0.1), Forster (0.1), Pena (1.1), Castillo (1)

Burris pitched a 5-hitter and Raines rapped 3 hits to enable the Expos to deadlock the series with a 3-0 victory.

GAME 3 - OCTOBER 16

LA   W 000 100 000   1 7 0   Reuss (7), Pena (1)
MON E 000 004 00x   4 7 1   Rogers (9)   White (2 on)

A 3-run homer by White highlighted a 4-run outburst in the 6th that carried the Expos to a 4-1 triumph behind Rogers's seven-hit pitching.

GAME 4 - OCTOBER 17

LA   W 001 000 024   7 12 1   Hooton (7.1), Welch (0.2), Howe (1)   Garvey (1 on)
MON E 000 100 000   1 5 1   Gullickson (7.1), Fryman (1), Sosa (0.1), Lee (0.1)

Garvey's 2-run homer in the 8th broke a 1-1 tie and led the Dodgers to a 7-1 win that evened the series at 2 games apiece.

GAME 5 - OCTOBER 19

LA   W 000 010 001   2 6 0   Valenzuela (8.2), Welch (0.1) **SV**   Monday
MON E 100 000 000   1 3 1   Burris (8), Rogers (1)

Monday walloped a 2-out homer in the 9th inning, giving the Dodgers a 2-1 victory over the Expos and the NL pennant. Valenzuela allowed 3 hits but needed help from Welch to get the last out.

Team totals

		W	AB	H	2B	3B	HR	R	RBI	BA	BB	SO	ERA
LA	W	3	163	38	3	1	4	15	15	.233	12	23	1.84
MON	E	2	158	34	7	0	1	10	8	.215	12	25	2.86

Individual Batting

LOS ANGELES (WEST)

	AB	H	2B	3B	HR	R	RBI	BA
S. Garvey, 1b	21	6	0	0	1	2	2	.286
D. Baker, of	19	6	1	0	0	3	3	.316
P. Guerrero, of	19	2	0	0	1	1	2	.105
D. Lopes, 2b	18	5	0	0	0	0	0	.278
R. Cey, 3b	18	5	1	0	0	1	3	.278
B. Russell, ss	16	5	0	1	0	2	1	.313
M. Scioscia, c	15	2	0	0	1	1	1	.133
K. Landreaux, of	10	1	1	0	0	0	0	.100
R. Monday, of	9	3	0	0	1	2	1	.333
B. Hooton, p	5	0	0	0	0	0	0	.000
Valenzuela, p	5	0	0	0	0	0	0	.000
S. Yeager, c	2	1	0	0	0	1	0	.500
J. Johnstone	2	0	0	0	0	0	0	.000
J. Reuss, p	2	0	0	0	0	0	0	.000
R. Smith	1	1	0	0	0	0	1	1.000
D. Thomas, 3b, of	1	1	0	0	0	2	0	1.000
S. Sax, 2b	0	0	0	0	0	0	0	–

Errors: R. Cey, D. Baker
Stolen Bases: D. Lopes (5)

MONTREAL (EAST)

	AB	H	2B	3B	HR	R	RBI	BA
T. Raines, of	21	5	2	0	0	1	1	.238
A. Dawson, of	20	3	0	0	0	2	0	.150
L. Parrish, 3b	19	5	2	0	0	2	2	.263
W. Cromartie, 1b	18	3	1	0	0	0	2	.167
R. Scott, 2b	18	3	0	0	0	0	0	.167
G. Carter, c	16	7	1	0	0	3	0	.438
J. White, of	16	5	1	0	1	2	3	.313
C. Speier, ss	16	3	0	0	0	0	0	.188
R. Burris, p	6	0	0	0	0	0	0	.000
Gullickson, p	3	0	0	0	0	0	0	.000
S. Rogers, p	2	0	0	0	0	0	0	.000
T. Wallach	1	0	0	0	0	0	0	.000
T. Francona, of	1	0	0	0	0	0	0	.000
J. Milner	1	0	0	0	0	0	0	.000
J. Manuel	0	0	0	0	0	0	0	–

Errors: C. Speier (2), L. Parrish, R. Scott
Stolen Bases: J. White, R. Scott

Individual Pitching

LOS ANGELES (WEST)

	W	L	ERA	IP	H	BB	SO	SV
B. Hooton	2	0	0.00	14.2	11	6	7	0
Valenzuela	1	1	2.45	14.2	10	5	10	0
J. Reuss	0	1	5.14	7	7	1	2	0
S. Howe	0	0	0.00	2	1	0	2	0
A. Pena	0	0	0.00	2.1	1	0	0	0
B. Welch	0	0	5.40	1.2	2	0	2	1
B. Castillo	0	0	0.00	1	0	0	1	0
T. Forster	0	0	0.00	0.1	0	0	1	0
Niedenfuer	0	0	0.00	0.1	2	0	0	0

MONTREAL (EAST)

	W	L	ERA	IP	H	BB	SO	SV
R. Burris	1	0	0.53	17	10	3	4	0
Gullickson	0	2	2.51	14.1	12	6	12	0
S. Rogers	1	1	1.80	10	8	1	6	0
J. Reardon	0	0	27.00	1	3	0	0	0
W. Fryman	0	0	36.00	1	3	1	1	0
B. Lee	0	0	0.00	0.1	1	0	0	0
E. Sosa	0	0	0.00	0.1	1	1	1	0

1981 AMERICAN LEAGUE EASTERN DIVISION PLAYOFF

LINE SCORES	PITCHERS (innings pitched)	HOME RUNS (men on)	HIGHLIGHTS

New York defeats Milwaukee 3 games to 2

GAME 1 - OCTOBER 7

NY	E	000 400 001	5 13 1	Guidry (4.1), **Davis** (2.2), Gossage (2) **SV**	Gamble (1 on)
MIL	E	011 010 000	3 8 3	Haas (3.1), Bernard (0.2), McClure (1.1), Slaton (2.1), Fingers (1.1)	

Gamble's 2-run homer highlighted a 4-run 4th inning, giving the Yankees a 5-3 win. Davis and Gossage were superb in relief.

GAME 2 - OCTOBER 8

NY	E	000 100 002	3 7 0	**Righetti** (6), Davis (0.1), Gossage (2.2) **SV**	Piniella, Jackson (1 on)
MIL	E	000 000 000	0 7 0	Caldwell (8.1), Slaton (0.2)	

Homers by Piniella and Jackson accounted for all Yankee runs. Righetti, Davis, and Gossage fanned 14 Brewers.

GAME 3 - OCTOBER 9

MIL	E	000 000 320	5 9 0	Lerch (6), **Fingers** (3)	Simmons (1 on), Molitor
NY	E	000 100 200	3 8 2	John (7), May (2)	

Molitor's homer in the 8th inning broke a 3-3 tie enabling the Brewers to stave off elimination. Simmons hit a 2-run homer for the Brewers in the 7th.

GAME 4 - OCTOBER 10

MIL	E	000 200 000	2 4 2	**Vuckovich** (5), Easterly (1), Slaton (1.2), McClure (1), Fingers (0.1) **SV**	
NY	E	000 001 000	1 5 0	Reuschel (6), Davis (3)	

Oglivie's 2-out double drove in what proved to be the winning run as the Brewers evened the series at two wins apiece. Vuckovich, despite a heavy cold, pitched 5 innings for the victory with Fingers getting the save.

GAME 5 - OCTOBER 11

MIL	E	011 000 100	3 8 0	Haas (3.1), Caldwell (0), Bernard (1.2), McClure (1), Slaton (1.1), Easterly (0.1), Vuckovich (0.1)	Thomas
NY	E	000 400 12x	7 13 0	**Guidry** (4), Righetti (3), Gossage (2) **SV**	Jackson (1 on), Gamble, Cerone

Pounding Milwaukee pitching for 13 hits, including 3 homers, the Yankees downed the Brewers 7-3 to capture the AL Divisional crown in the East. Gossage earned his third save.

Team totals

		W	AB	H	2B	3B	HR	R	RBI	BA	BB	SO	ERA
NY	E	3	171	46	8	0	6	19	18	.269	9	22	2.60
MIL	E	2	162	36	6	1	3	13	13	.222	13	39	3.48

Individual Batting

NEW YORK

	AB	H	2B	3B	HR	R	RBI	BA
J. Mumphrey, of	21	2	0	0	0	2	0	.095
D. Winfield, of	20	7	3	0	0	2	0	.350
R. Jackson, of	20	6	0	0	2	4	4	.300
W. Randolph, 2b	20	4	0	0	0	0	1	.200
L. Milbourne, ss	19	6	1	0	0	4	0	.316
R. Cerone, c	18	6	2	0	1	1	5	.333
G. Nettles, 3b	17	1	0	0	0	1	1	.059
B. Watson, 1b	16	7	0	0	0	2	1	.438
L. Piniella, dh	10	2	1	0	1	1	3	.200
O. Gamble, dh	9	5	1	0	2	2	3	.556
B. Murcer	1	0	0	0	0	0	0	.000
B. Foote	0	0	0	0	0	0	0	—
B. Brown	0	0	0	0	0	0	0	—
D. Revering, 1b	0	0	0	0	0	0	0	—

Errors: R. Cerone, R. May, B. Watson
Stolen Bases: J. Mumphrey

MILWAUKEE

	AB	H	2B	3B	HR	R	RBI	BA
P. Molitor, of	20	5	0	0	1	2	1	.250
T. Simmons, c	19	4	1	0	1	1	4	.211
R. Yount, ss	19	6	0	1	0	4	1	.316
C. Cooper, 1b	18	4	0	0	0	1	3	.222
B. Oglivie, of	18	3	1	0	0	0	1	.167
S. Bando, 3b	17	5	3	0	0	1	1	.294
G. Thomas, of, dh	17	2	0	0	1	2	1	.118
J. Gantner, 2b	14	2	1	0	0	1	0	.143
C. Moore, of, dh	9	2	0	0	0	0	1	.222
R. Howell, dh	5	2	0	0	0	0	0	.400
D. Money, 2b, dh	3	0	0	0	0	0	0	.000
E. Romero, 2b	2	1	0	0	0	0	1	.500
M. Edwards, of	1	0	0	0	0	0	0	.000
T. Bosley, dh	0	0	0	0	0	0	0	—

Errors: J. Gantner (2), C. Cooper, R. Yount, T. Simmons
Stolen Bases: R. Yount

Individual Pitching

NEW YORK

	W	L	ERA	IP	H	BB	SO	SV
D. Righetti	2	0	1.00	9	8	3	13	0
R. Guidry	0	0	5.40	8.1	11	3	8	0
T. John	0	1	6.43	7	8	2	0	0
R. Davis	1	0	0.00	6	1	2	6	0
R. Reuschel	0	1	3.00	6	4	1	3	0
G. Gossage	0	0	0.00	6.2	3	2	8	3
R. May	0	0	0.00	2	1	0	1	0

MILWAUKEE

	W	L	ERA	IP	H	BB	SO	SV
M. Caldwell	0	1	4.32	8.1	9	0	4	0
M. Haas	0	2	9.45	6.2	13	1	1	0
R. Lerch	0	0	1.50	6	3	4	3	0
J. Slaton	0	0	3.00	6	6	0	2	0
P. Vuckovich	1	0	0.00	5.1	2	3	4	0
R. Fingers	1	0	3.66	4.2	7	1	5	1
B. McClure	0	0	0.00	3.1	4	0	2	0
D. Bernard	0	0	0.00	2.1	0	0	0	0
J. Easterly	0	0	6.75	1.1	2	0	1	0

1981 AMERICAN LEAGUE WESTERN DIVISION PLAYOFF

LINE SCORES	PITCHERS (innings pitched)	HOME RUNS (men on)	HIGHLIGHTS

Oakland defeats Kansas City 3 games to 0

GAME 1 - OCTOBER 6

OAK	W	000 300 010		4	8	2	Norris (9)	Gross (2 on), Murphy
KC	W	000 000 000		0	4	1	Leonard (8), Martin (1)	

Homers by Gross and Murphy, backed by the 4-hit pitching of Norris, propelled the A's to a 4-0 win in AL West playoffs opener.

GAME 2 - OCTOBER 7

OAK	W	100 000 010	2	10	1	McCatty (9)	
KC	W	000 010 000	1	6	0	Jones (8), Quisenberry (1)	

Armas drilled a double through Brett's legs to score Murphy in the 8th with the tie-breaking run. McCatty scattered 10 hits.

GAME 3 - OCTOBER 9

KC	W	000 100 000	1	10	3	Gura (3.2), Martin (4.1)	
OAK	W	101 200 00x	4	7	0	Langford (7.1), Underwood (0.1), Beard (1.1) SV	McKay

Henderson reached base all 4 times and scored three times as the A's swept the series, winning 4-1 behind Langford.

Team totals

		W	AB	H	2B	3B	HR	R	RBI	BA	BB	SO	ERA
OAK	W	3	99	25	5	0	3	10	9	.253	6	10	0.67
KC	E	0	98	20	1	0	0	2	2	.204	7	11	2.08

Individual Batting

OAKLAND

	AB	H	2B	3B	HR	R	RBI	BA
T. Armas, of	11	6	2	0	0	1	3	.545
R. Henderson, of	11	2	0	0	0	3	0	.182
D. Murphy, of	11	6	1	0	1	4	2	.545
D. McKay, 2b	11	3	0	0	1	1	1	.273
K. Moore, 1b	8	0	0	0	0	0	0	.000
M. Heath, c	8	0	0	0	0	0	0	.000
M. Klutts, 3b	7	1	0	0	0	0	0	.143
C. Johnson, dh	7	2	1	0	0	0	0	.286
F. Stanley, ss	6	0	0	0	0	0	0	.000
W. Gross, 3b	5	2	0	0	1	1	3	.400
K. Drumright, dh	4	1	0	0	0	0	0	.250
J. Spencer, 1b	4	1	1	0	0	0	0	.250
R. Picciolo, ss	3	1	0	0	0	0	0	.333
J. Newman, c	3	0	0	0	0	0	0	.000
R. Bosetti, of	0	0	0	0	0	0	0	–

Errors: T. Armas, D. McKay, M. Norris
Stolen Bases: R. Henderson (2)

KANSAS CITY

	AB	H	2B	3B	HR	R	RBI	BA
W. Wilson, of	13	4	0	0	0	0	1	.308
A. Otis, of	12	0	0	0	0	0	1	.000
G. Brett, 3b	12	2	0	0	0	0	0	.167
F. White, 2b	11	2	0	0	0	1	0	.182
C. Hurdle, of	11	3	0	0	0	0	0	.273
H. McRae, dh	11	1	1	0	0	0	0	.091
J. Wathan, c	10	3	0	0	0	1	0	.300
W. Aikens, 1b	9	3	0	0	0	0	0	.333
Washington, ss	9	2	0	0	0	0	0	.222
L. May, 1b	0	0	0	0	0	0	0	–
C. Geronimo	0	0	0	0	0	0	0	–

Errors: F. White, G. Brett, Washington, J. Wathan

Individual Pitching

OAKLAND

	W	L	ERA	IP	H	BB	SO	SV
M. Norris	1	0	0.00	9	4	3	2	0
S. McCatty	1	0	1.00	9	6	4	3	0
R. Langford	1	0	1.23	7.1	10	0	3	0
D. Beard	0	0	0.00	1.1	0	0	2	1
T. Underwood	0	0	0.00	0.1	0	0	1	0

KANSAS CITY

	W	L	ERA	IP	H	BB	SO	SV
M. Jones	0	1	2.25	8	9	0	2	0
D. Leonard	0	1	1.13	8	7	1	3	0
R. Martin	0	0	0.00	5.1	1	2	2	0
L. Gura	0	1	7.36	3.2	7	3	2	0
Quisenberry	0	0	0.00	1	1	0	0	0

1981 AMERICAN LEAGUE CHAMPIONSHIP SERIES

LINE SCORES	PITCHERS (innings pitched)	HOME RUNS (men on)	HIGHLIGHTS

New York (East) defeats Oakland (West) 3 games to 0

GAME 1 - OCTOBER 13

OAK	W	000 010 000	1 8 1	Norris (7.1), Underwood (0.2)	
NY	E	300 000 00x	3 7 1	John (6), Davis (1.1), Gossage (1.2) SV	

A 3-run double by Nettles in the first inning triggered the Yankees' 3-1 win over the A's. Gossage preserved John's victory.

GAME 2 - OCTOBER 14

OAK	W	001 200 000	3 11 1	McCatty (3.1), Beard (0.2), Jones (2), Kingman (0.1), Owchinko (1.2)	
NY	E	100 701 40x	13 19 0	May (3.1), Frazier (5.2)	Nettles (2 on), Piniella (2 on)

Three-run homers by Nettles and Piniella were the most telling blows in the Yankees' 13-3 rout of the A's. Frazier pitched 5.2 innings of shutout relief to gain the victory.

GAME 3 - OCTOBER 15

NY	E	000 001 003	4 10 0	Righetti (6), Davis (2), Gossage (1)	Randolph
OAK	W	000 000 000	0 5 2	Keough (8.1), Underwood (0.2)	

Randolph broke up a scoreless duel with a 2-out homer in the 6th inning to back five-hit pitching by Righetti, Davis and Gossage, as the Yankees swept the AL championship.

Team totals

		W	AB	H	2B	3B	HR	R	RBI	BA	BB	SO	ERA
NY	E	3	107	36	4	0	3	20	20	.336	13	10	1.33
OAK	W	0	99	22	4	1	0	4	4	.222	6	23	6.84

Individual Batting

NEW YORK (EAST)

	AB	H	2B	3B	HR	R	RBI	BA
D. Winfield, of	13	2	1	0	0	2	2	.154
L. Milbourne, ss	13	6	0	0	0	4	1	.462
J. Mumphrey, of	12	6	1	0	0	2	0	.500
W. Randolph, 2b	12	4	0	0	1	2	2	.333
G. Nettles, 3b	12	6	2	0	1	2	9	.500
B. Watson, 1b	12	3	0	0	0	1	0	.250
R. Cerone, c	10	1	0	0	0	1	0	.100
O. Gamble, dh	6	1	0	0	0	2	1	.167
L. Piniella, of, dh	5	3	0	0	1	2	3	.600
R. Jackson, of	4	0	0	0	0	1	1	.000
B. Murcer, dh	3	1	0	0	0	0	0	.333
D. Revering, 1b	2	1	0	0	0	0	0	.500
B. Brown, of	1	1	0	0	0	2	0	1.000
A. Robertson, ss	1	0	0	0	0	0	0	.000
B. Foote, c	1	1	0	0	0	0	0	1.000
A. Rodriguez, 3b	0	0	0	0	0	0	0	–

Errors: G. Nettles
Stolen Bases: D. Winfield, R. Jackson

OAKLAND (WEST)

	AB	H	2B	3B	HR	R	RBI	BA
T. Armas, of	12	2	0	0	0	0	0	.167
D. McKay, 2b	11	3	0	0	0	0	1	.273
R. Henderson, of	11	4	2	1	0	0	1	.364
K. Moore, 1b	9	2	0	0	0	0	0	.222
D. Murphy, of	8	2	1	0	0	0	1	.250
M. Klutts, 3b	7	3	0	0	1	0	0	.429
M. Heath, c, of	6	2	0	0	0	1	0	.333
C. Johnson, dh	6	0	0	0	0	0	0	.000
R. Picciolo, ss	5	1	0	0	1	0	0	.200
W. Gross, 3b	5	0	0	0	0	0	0	.000
J. Newman, c	5	0	0	0	0	0	0	.000
R. Bosetti, of, dh	4	1	1	0	0	1	0	.250
K. Drumright, dh	4	0	0	0	0	0	0	.000
F. Stanley, ss	3	1	0	0	0	0	1	.333
J. Spencer, 1b	2	0	0	0	0	0	0	.000
M. Davis	1	1	0	0	0	0	0	1.000

Errors: D. McKay, R. Henderson, M. Klutts, R. Picciolo
Stolen Bases: R. Henderson (2)

Individual Pitching

NEW YORK (EAST)

	W	L	ERA	IP	H	BB	SO	SV
D. Righetti	1	0	0.00	6	4	2	4	0
T. John	1	0	1.50	6	6	1	3	0
G. Frazier	1	0	0.00	5.2	5	1	5	0
R. May	0	0	8.10	3.1	6	0	5	0
R. Davis	0	0	0.00	3.1	0	2	4	0
G. Gossage	0	0	0.00	2.2	1	0	2	1

OAKLAND (WEST)

	W	L	ERA	IP	H	BB	SO	SV
M. Keough	0	1	1.08	8.1	7	6	2	0
M. Norris	0	1	3.68	7.1	6	2	4	0
S. McCatty	0	1	13.50	3.1	6	2	2	0
J. Jones	0	0	4.50	2	2	1	0	0
B. Owchinko	0	0	5.40	1.2	3	0	0	0
T. Underwood	0	0	13.50	1.1	4	2	2	0
D. Beard	0	0	40.50	0.2	5	0	0	0
B. Kingman	0	0	81.00	0.1	3	0	0	0

1981 WORLD SERIES

LINE SCORES		PITCHERS (innings pitched)	HOME RUNS (men on)	HIGHLIGHTS

Los Angeles (N.L.) defeats New York (A.L.) 4 games to 2

GAME 1 - OCTOBER 20

LA	N	000 010 020	3 5 0	Reuss (2.2), Castillo (1), Goltz (0.1), Niedenfuer (3), Stewart (1)	Yeager
NY	A	301 100 00x	5 6 0	Guidry (7), Davis (0), Gossage (2) SV	Watson (2 on)

Watson homered with two on in the first inning to propel the Yankees to a 5-3 win. Gossage quelled a Dodger rally in the 8th to preserve Guidry's triumph.

GAME 2 - OCTOBER 21

LA	N	000 000 000	0 4 2	Hooton (6), Forster (1.0), Howe (0.1), Stewart (0.2)	
NY	A	000 010 02x	3 6 1	John (7), Gossage (2) SV	

John and Gossage combined to shut out the Dodgers on 4 hits. Watson continued his hot streak with 2 hits and an RBI.

GAME 3 - OCTOBER 23

NY	A	022 000 000	4 9 0	Righetti (2), **Frazier (2)**, May (3), Davis (1)	Watson, Cerone (1 on)
LA	N	300 020 00x	5 11 1	Valenzuela (9)	Cey (2 on)

Cey hit a 3-run homer but the winning run crossed the plate on a double play as the Dodgers came from behind to win 5-4. Valenzuela staggered to victory despite giving up 9 hits and 7 walks.

GAME 4 - OCTOBER 24

NY	A	211 002 010	7 13 1	Reuschel (3), May (1.1), Davis (1), **Frazier (0.2)**, John (2)	Randolph, Jackson
LA	N	002 013 20x	8 14 2	Welch (0), Goltz (3), Forster (1), Niedenfuer (2), **Howe (3)**	Johnstone (1 on)

A pinch 2-run homer by Johnstone and some shoddy fielding by Yankee outfielders helped the Dodgers score 5 runs in the 7th and 8th innings and overcome a 6-3 deficit. The 8-7 victory tied the Series at 2 games each.

GAME 5 - OCTOBER 25

NY	A	010 000 000	1 5 0	Guidry (7), Gossage (1)	
LA	N	000 000 20x	2 4 3	Reuss (9)	Guerrero, Yeager

Seventh inning back-to-back homers by Guerrero and Yeager off Guidry provided the Dodgers with their third straight win over the Yankees. Reuss allowed only 5 hits.

GAME 6 - OCTOBER 28

LA	N	000 134 010	9 13 1	Hooton (5.1), Howe (3.1)	Guerrero
NY	A	001 001 000	2 7 2	John (4), **Frazier (1)**, Davis (0.2), Reuschel (0.2), May (2), LaRoche (1)	Randolph

Guerrero drove in 5 runs as the Dodgers pounded 6 pitchers for 13 hits to win their 4th straight and capture the World Series, 4 games to 2. Frazier, in relief, was charged with his 3rd loss.

Team totals

		W	AB	H	2B	3B	HR	R	RBI	BA	BB	SO	ERA
LA	N	4	198	51	6	1	6	27	26	.258	20	44	3.29
NY	A	2	193	46	8	1	6	22	22	.238	33	24	4.24

Individual Batting

LOS ANGELES (N.L.)

	AB	H	2B	3B	HR	R	RBI	BA
B. Russell, ss	25	6	0	0	0	1	2	.240
D. Baker, of	24	4	0	0	0	3	1	.167
S. Garvey, 1b	24	10	1	0	0	3	0	.417
D. Lopes, 2b	22	5	1	0	0	6	2	.227
P. Guerrero, of	21	7	1	1	2	2	7	.333
R. Cey, 3b	20	7	0	0	1	3	6	.350
S. Yeager, c	14	4	1	0	2	2	4	.286
R. Monday, of	13	3	1	0	0	1	0	.231
D. Thomas, 3b, ss, of	7	0	0	0	0	2	1	.000
K. Landreaux, of	6	1	0	0	0	1	0	.167
B. Hooton, p	4	0	0	0	0	0	0	.000
M. Scioscia, c	4	1	0	0	0	0	0	.250
Valenzuela, p	3	0	0	0	0	0	0	.000
J. Johnstone	3	2	0	0	1	1	3	.667
J. Reuss, p	3	0	0	0	0	0	0	.000
R. Smith	2	1	0	0	0	0	0	.500
S. Howe, p	2	0	0	0	0	0	0	.000
S. Sax, 2b	1	0	0	0	0	0	0	.000

Errors: D. Lopes (6), S. Howe, B. Russell, D. Stewart
Stolen Bases: D. Lopes (4), K. Landreaux, B. Russell

NEW YORK (A.L.)

	AB	H	2B	3B	HR	R	RBI	BA
B. Watson, 1b	22	7	1	0	2	2	7	.318
D. Winfield, of	22	1	0	0	0	0	1	.045
R. Cerone, c	21	4	1	0	1	2	3	.190
L. Milbourne, ss	20	5	2	0	0	2	3	.250
W. Randolph, 2b	18	4	1	1	2	5	3	.222
L. Piniella, of	16	7	1	0	0	2	3	.438
J. Mumphrey, of	15	3	0	0	0	2	0	.200
A. Rodriguez, 3b	12	5	0	0	0	1	0	.417
R. Jackson, of, dh	12	4	1	0	1	3	1	.333
G. Nettles, 3b	10	4	1	0	0	1	0	.400
O. Gamble, of	6	2	0	0	1	1	1	.333
R. Guidry, p	5	0	0	0	0	0	0	.000
B. Murcer	3	0	0	0	0	0	0	.000
T. John, p	2	0	0	0	0	0	0	.000
R. Reuschel, p	2	0	0	0	0	0	0	.000
G. Frazier, p	2	0	0	0	0	0	0	.000
B. Brown, of	1	0	0	0	0	1	0	.000
D. Righetti, p	1	0	0	0	0	0	0	.000
B. Foote	1	0	0	0	0	0	0	.000
G. Gossage, p	1	0	0	0	0	0	0	.000
R. May, p	1	0	0	0	0	0	0	.000
A. Robertson	0	0	0	0	0	0	0	–

Errors: L. Milbourne (2), R. Jackson, G. Nettles
Stolen Bases: W. Randolph, D. Winfield, L. Piniella, J. Mumphrey

Individual Pitching

LOS ANGELES (N.L.)

	W	L	ERA	IP	H	BB	SO	SV
J. Reuss	1	1	3.86	11.2	10	3	8	0
B. Hooton	1	1	1.59	11.1	8	9	3	0
Valenzuela	1	0	4.00	9	9	7	6	0
S. Howe	1	0	3.86	7	7	1	4	1
Niedenfuer	0	0	0.00	5	3	1	0	0
D. Goltz	0	0	5.40	3.1	4	1	2	0
T. Forster	0	0	0.00	2	1	3	0	0
B. Castillo	0	0	9.00	1	0	5	0	0
D. Stewart	0	0	0.00	1.2	1	2	1	0
B. Welch	0	0	∞	0.0	3	1	0	0

NEW YORK (A.L.)

	W	L	ERA	IP	H	BB	SO	SV
R. Guidry	1	1	1.93	14	8	4	15	0
T. John	1	0	0.69	13	11	0	8	0
R. May	0	0	2.84	6.1	5	1	5	0
G. Gossage	0	0	0.00	5	2	2	5	2
R. Reuschel	0	0	4.91	3.2	7	3	2	0
G. Frazier	0	3	17.18	3.2	9	3	2	0
R. Davis	0	0	23.14	2.1	4	5	4	0
D. Righetti	0	0	13.50	2	5	2	1	0
D. LaRoche	0	0	0.00	1	0	0	2	0

1982 NATIONAL LEAGUE CHAMPIONSHIP SERIES

LINE SCORES	PITCHERS (innings pitched)	HOME RUNS (men on)	HIGHLIGHTS

St. Louis (East) defeats Atlanta (West) 3 games to 0

GAME 1 - OCTOBER 7

ATL	W	000 000 000	0	3	0
STL	E	001 005 01x	7	13	1

Perez (5), Bedrosian (0.2), Moore (1.1), Walk (1)
B. Forsch (9)

Game 1 came a day late after rain washed away the previous day's effort with Atlanta leading 1-0 in the fifth. In the game that counted, the Cardinals scored five in the sixth to break open a 1-0 game. Bob Forsch scattered three hits and walked none for the win.

GAME 2 - OCTOBER 9

ATL	W	002 010 000	3	6	0
STL	E	100 001 011	4	9	1

Niekro (6), Garber (2.1)
Stuper (6), Bair (1), Sutter (2)

Another day of rain allowed Phil Niekro, who pitched in the Game 1 washout, to come back on two days' rest. Niekro left the game with a 3-2 lead, but Garber could not hold it. Ken Oberkfell, 6-for-10 against Garber in the season, singled home the winning run with first base open in the bottom of the ninth.

GAME 3 - OCTOBER 10

STL	E	040 010 001	6	12	0
ATL	W	000 000 200	2	6	1

Andujar (6.2), Sutter (2.1) SV
Camp (1), Perez (3.2), Moore (1.1), Mahler (1.2), Bedrosian (0.1), Garber (1)

McGee

Five Cardinal hits, topped by rookie Willie McGee's triple, led to four runs in the second inning to chase Rick Camp. McGee added a homer in the ninth and Bruce Sutter set down seven straight hitters to nail down the Cardinals' first pennant in fourteen years.

Team totals

		W	AB	H	2B	3B	HR	R	RBI	BA	BB	SO	ERA
STL	E	3	103	34	4	2	1	17	16	.330	12	16	1.33
ATL	W	0	89	15	1	0	0	5	3	.169	6	15	0.60

Individual Batting

ST. LOUIS (EAST)

	AB	H	2B	3B	HR	R	RBI	BA
K. Oberkfell, 3b	15	3	0	0	0	1	2	.200
G. Hendrick, of	13	4	0	0	0	2	2	.308
T. Herr, 2b	13	3	1	0	0	1	0	.231
W. McGee, of	13	4	0	2	1	4	5	.308
K. Hernandez, 1b	12	4	0	0	0	3	1	.333
L. Smith, of	11	3	0	0	0	1	1	.273
D. Porter, c	9	5	3	0	0	3	1	.556
O. Smith, ss	9	5	0	0	0	0	3	.556
B. Forsch, p	3	2	0	0	0	1	1	.667
B. Sutter, p	1	0	0	0	0	0	0	.000
S. Braun	1	0	0	0	0	0	0	.000
J. Andujar, p	1	0	0	0	0	0	0	.000
D. Green, of	1	1	0	0	0	1	0	1.000
J. Stuper, p	1	0	0	0	0	0	0	.000

Errors: K. Oberkfell, W. McGee
Stolen Bases: O. Smith

ATLANTA (WEST)

	AB	H	2B	3B	HR	R	RBI	BA
D. Murphy, of	11	3	0	0	0	1	0	.273
J. Royster, of, 3b	11	2	0	0	0	0	0	.182
R. Ramirez, ss	11	2	0	0	0	1	1	.182
B. Horner, 3b	11	1	0	0	0	0	0	.091
C. Chambliss, 1b	10	0	0	0	0	0	0	.000
Washington, of	9	3	0	0	0	0	0	.333
G. Hubbard, 2b	9	2	0	0	0	1	1	.222
B. Benedict, c	8	2	1	0	0	1	0	.250
P. Perez, p	3	0	0	0	0	0	0	.000
L. Whisenton	2	0	0	0	0	0	0	.000
B. Pocoroba	1	0	0	0	0	0	0	.000
G. Garber, p	1	0	0	0	0	0	0	.000
T. Harper, of	1	0	0	0	0	1	0	.000
B. Butler, of	1	0	0	0	0	0	0	.000
P. Niekro, p	0	0	0	0	0	0	1	—

Errors: R. Ramirez
Stolen Bases: D. Murphy

Individual Pitching

ST. LOUIS (EAST)

	W	L	ERA	IP	H	BB	SO	SV
B. Forsch	1	0	0.00	9	3	0	6	0
J. Andujar	1	0	2.70	6.2	6	2	4	0
J. Stuper	0	0	3.00	6	4	1	4	0
B. Sutter	1	0	0.00	4.1	0	0	1	1
D. Bair	0	0	0.00	1	2	3	0	0

ATLANTA (WEST)

	W	L	ERA	IP	H	BB	SO	SV
P. Perez	0	1	5.19	8.2	10	2	4	0
P. Niekro	0	0	3.00	6	6	4	5	0
G. Garber	0	1	8.10	3.1	4	1	3	0
D. Moore	0	0	0.00	2.2	2	0	1	0
R. Camp	0	1	36.00	1	4	1	0	0
R. Mahler	0	0	0.00	1.2	3	2	0	0
B. Walk	0	0	9.00	1	2	1	1	0
S. Bedrosian	0	0	18.00	1	3	1	2	0

1982 AMERICAN LEAGUE CHAMPIONSHIP SERIES

LINE SCORES	PITCHERS (innings pitched)	HOME RUNS (men on)	HIGHLIGHTS

Milwaukee (East) defeats California (West) 3 games to 2

GAME 1 - OCTOBER 5

MIL	E	021 000 000	3 7 2	Caldwell (3), Slaton (3), Ladd (1), Bernard (1)	Thomas (1 on)		Don Baylor tied a Championship Series record with five RBIs as Tommy John hurled a seven-hitter, shutting out the Brewers over the final six innings.
CAL	W	104 210 00x	8 10 0	John (9)	Lynn		

GAME 2 - OCTOBER 6

MIL	E	000 020 000	2 5 0	Vuckovich (8)	Molitor (1 on)	Bruce Kison's five-hitter put the Angels up two games to none. Reggie Jackson's solo homer in the fourth gave California a 4-0 lead before Molitor's homer cut it to 4-2.
CAL	W	021 100 00x	4 6 0	Kison (9)	Re. Jackson	

GAME 3 - OCTOBER 8

CAL	W	000 000 030	3 8 0	Zahn (3.2), Witt (3), Hassler (1.1)	Boone	Don Sutton and the Brewers staved off elimination with a 5-3 victory at home. Paul Molitor's two-run home run provided the margin.
MIL	E	000 300 20x	5 6 0	Sutton (7.2), Ladd (1.1) SV	Molitor (1 on)	

GAME 4 - OCTOBER 9

CAL	W	000 001 040	5 5 3	John (3.1), Goltz (3.2), Sanchez (1)	Baylor (3 on)	Mark Brouhard, a reserve outfielder, had three hits, three RBIs, and four runs scored as the Brewers evened the series.
MIL	E	030 301 02x	9 9 2	Haas (7.1), Slaton (1.2) SV	Brouhard (1 on)	

GAME 5 - OCTOBER 10

CAL	W	101 100 000	3 11 1	Kison (5), Sanchez (1.2), Hassler (1.1)		Cecil Cooper singled in the tying and winning runs in the seventh to give the Brewers their first AL title. They also became the first team to win a Championship Series after trailing two games to none.
MIL	E	100 100 20x	4 6 4	Vuckovich (6.1), McClure (1.2), Ladd (1) SV	Oglivie	

Team totals

		W	AB	H	2B	3B	HR	R	RBI	BA	BB	SO	ERA
MIL	E	3	151	33	4	0	5	23	20	.219	15	28	4.19
CAL	W	2	157	40	8	1	4	23	23	.255	16	34	4.29

Individual Batting

MILWAUKEE (EAST)

	AB	H	2B	3B	HR	R	RBI	BA
C. Cooper, 1b	20	3	2	0	0	1	4	.150
P. Molitor, 3b	19	6	1	0	2	4	5	.316
T. Simmons, c	18	3	0	0	0	3	1	.167
R. Yount, ss	16	4	0	0	0	1	0	.250
J. Gantner, 2b	16	3	0	0	0	1	2	.188
B. Oglivie, of	15	2	0	0	1	1	1	.133
G. Thomas, of	15	1	0	0	1	1	3	.067
C. Moore, of	13	6	0	0	0	3	0	.462
D. Money, dh	11	2	0	0	0	2	1	.182
M. Brouhard, of	4	3	1	0	1	4	3	.750
R. Howell, dh	3	0	0	0	0	0	0	.000
M. Edwards, of, dh	1	0	0	0	0	2	0	.000

Errors: C. Cooper (2), P. Molitor (2), B. Oglivie (2), R. Yount, M. Caldwell

Stolen Bases: P. Molitor, M. Edwards

CALIFORNIA (WEST)

	AB	H	2B	3B	HR	R	RBI	BA
D. DeCinces, 3b	19	6	2	0	0	5	0	.316
B. Downing, of	19	3	1	0	0	4	0	.158
R. Jackson, of	18	2	0	0	1	2	2	.111
F. Lynn, of	18	11	2	0	1	4	5	.611
D. Baylor, dh	17	5	1	1	1	2	10	.294
R. Carew, 1b	17	3	1	0	0	2	0	.176
T. Foli, ss	16	2	0	0	0	0	1	.125
B. Boone, c	16	4	0	0	1	3	4	.250
B. Grich, 2b	15	3	1	0	0	1	1	.200
R. Wilfong	1	0	0	0	0	0	0	.000
R. Jackson	1	1	0	0	0	0	0	1.000
J. Beniquez, of	0	0	0	0	0	0	0	—
B. Clark, of	0	0	0	0	0	0	0	—

Errors: D. DeCinces (3), F. Lynn

Stolen Bases: R. Carew

Individual Pitching

MILWAUKEE (EAST)

	W	L	ERA	IP	H	BB	SO	SV
P. Vuckovich	0	1	4.40	14.1	15	7	8	0
M. Haas	1	0	4.91	7.1	5	5	7	0
D. Sutton	1	0	3.52	7.2	8	2	9	0
J. Slaton	0	0	1.93	4.2	3	1	3	1
M. Caldwell	0	1	15.00	3	7	1	2	0
P. Ladd	0	0	0.00	3.1	0	0	5	2
D. Bernard	0	0	0.00	1	0	0	0	0
B. McClure	1	0	0.00	1.2	2	0	0	0

CALIFORNIA (WEST)

	W	L	ERA	IP	H	BB	SO	SV
B. Kison	1	0	1.93	14	8	3	12	0
T. John	1	1	5.11	12.1	11	6	6	0
M. Witt	0	0	6.00	3	2	2	3	0
D. Goltz	0	0	7.36	3.2	4	2	2	0
G. Zahn	0	1	7.36	3.2	4	1	2	0
L. Sanchez	0	1	6.75	2.2	4	1	1	0
A. Hassler	0	0	0.00	2.2	0	0	2	0

1982 WORLD SERIES

LINE SCORES	PITCHERS (innings pitched)	HOME RUNS (men on)	HIGHLIGHTS

St. Louis (N.L.) defeats Milwaukee (A.L.) 4 games to 3

GAME 1 - OCTOBER 12

MIL A 200 112 004 10 17 0 — Caldwell (9) — Simmons — Caldwell allowed three hits as Milwaukee hammered four Cardinal pitchers. Molitor had the first five-hit game in World Series history, and Yount added four of his own.
STL N 000 000 000 0 3 1 — Forsch (5.2), Kaat (1.1), LaPoint (1.2), Lahti (0.1)

GAME 2 - OCTOBER 13

MIL A 012 010 000 4 10 1 — Sutton (6), **McClure** (1.1), Ladd (0.2) — Simmons — Porter doubled in two runs in the sixth and had a key single in the Cards' game-winning rally in the eighth.
STL N 002 002 01x 5 8 0 — Stuper (4), Kaat (0.2), Bair (2), **Sutter** (2.1)

GAME 3 - OCTOBER 15

STL N 000 030 201 6 6 1 — Andujar (6.1), Kaat (0.1), Bair (0), Sutter (2.1) SV — McGee (2 on), McGee — Rookie McGee sparkled with two home runs and a great catch at the wall, driving in four runs and saving another. Andujar was hit on the leg with a line drive, and had to leave the game, leading to an early appearance by relief ace Sutter.
MIL A 000 000 020 2 5 3 — Vuckovich (8.2), McClure (0.1) — Cooper (1 on)

GAME 4 - OCTOBER 16

STL N 130 001 000 5 8 1 — LaPoint (6.2), **Bair** (0), Kaat (0), Lahti (1.1) — With Sutter unavailable, four Cardinal pitchers could not stop the Brewers from rallying for a 7-5 win after LaPoint's error opened the door in the seventh.
MIL A 000 010 60x 7 10 2 — Haas (5.1), **Slaton** (2), McClure (1.2) SV

GAME 5 - OCTOBER 17

STL N 001 000 102 4 15 2 — Forsch (7), Sutter (1) — Yount became the first in Series history to have two four-hit games. Caldwell got his second win, McClure his second save.
MIL A 101 010 12x 6 11 1 — Caldwell (8.1), McClure (0.2) SV — Yount

GAME 6 - OCTOBER 19

MIL A 000 000 001 1 4 4 — **Sutton** (4.1), Slaton (0.2), Medich (2), Bernard (1) — Rookie Stuper earned a complete-game win despite two rain delays totalling more than two and a half hours. Dane Iorg led the way with two doubles and a triple.
STL N 020 326 00x 13 12 1 — Stuper (9) — Hernandez (1 on), Porter (1 on)

GAME 7 - OCTOBER 20

MIL A 000 012 000 3 7 0 — Vuckovich (5.1), **McClure** (0.1), Haas (2), Caldwell (0.1) — Oglivie — A three-run rally in the sixth, capped by Hendrick's go-ahead single, overcame a 3-1 deficit to give St. Louis the championship.
STL N 000 103 02x 6 15 1 — **Andujar** (7), Sutter (2) SV

Team totals

		W	AB	H	2B	3B	HR	R	RBI	BA	BB	SO	ERA
STL	N	4	245	67	16	3	4	39	34	.273	20	26	3.84
MIL	A	3	238	64	12	2	5	33	28	.269	19	28	4.80

Individual Batting

ST. LOUIS (N.L.)

	AB	H	2B	3B	HR	R	RBI	BA
G. Hendrick, of	28	9	0	0	0	5	5	.321
L. Smith, of, dh	28	9	4	1	0	6	1	.321
D. Porter, c	28	8	2	0	1	1	5	.286
K. Hernandez, 1b	27	7	2	0	1	4	8	.259
T. Herr, 2b	25	4	2	0	0	2	5	.160
W. McGee, of	25	6	0	0	2	6	5	.240
O. Smith, ss	24	5	0	0	0	3	1	.208
K. Oberkfell, 3b	24	7	1	0	0	4	1	.292
D. Iorg, dh	17	9	4	1	0	4	1	.529
D. Green, of, dh	10	2	1	1	0	3	0	.200
G. Tenace, dh	6	0	0	0	0	0	0	.000
S. Braun, dh	2	1	0	0	0	0	2	.500
M. Ramsey, 3b	1	0	0	0	0	1	0	.000
G. Brummer, c	0	0	0	0	0	0	0	—

Errors: K. Hernandez (2), J. Andujar, B. Forsch, K. Oberkfell, T. Herr, D. LaPoint
Stolen Bases: K. Oberkfell (2), L. Smith (2), W. McGee (2), O. Smith

MILWAUKEE (A.L.)

	AB	H	2B	3B	HR	R	RBI	BA
P. Molitor, 3b	31	11	0	0	0	5	2	.355
R. Yount, ss	29	12	3	0	1	6	6	.414
C. Cooper, 1b	28	8	1	0	1	3	6	.286
B. Oglivie, of	27	6	0	1	1	4	1	.222
C. Moore, of	26	9	3	0	0	3	2	.346
G. Thomas, of	26	3	0	0	0	3	0	.115
J. Gantner, 2b	24	8	4	1	0	5	4	.333
T. Simmons, c	23	4	0	0	2	2	3	.174
D. Money, dh	13	3	1	0	0	4	1	.231
R. Howell, dh	11	0	0	0	0	1	0	.000
N. Yost, c	0	0	0	0	0	0	0	—
M. Edwards, of	0	0	0	0	0	0	0	—

Errors: J. Gantner (5), R. Yount (3), C. Cooper, B. Oglivie, T. Simmons
Stolen Bases: P. Molitor

Individual Pitching

ST. LOUIS (N.L.)

	W	L	ERA	IP	H	BB	SO	SV
J. Andujar	2	0	1.35	13.1	10	1	4	0
J. Stuper	1	0	3.46	13	10	5	5	0
B. Forsch	0	2	4.97	12.2	18	3	4	0
D. LaPoint	0	0	3.24	8.1	10	2	3	0
B. Sutter	1	0	4.70	7.2	6	3	6	2
D. Bair	0	1	9.00	2	2	2	3	0
J. Kaat	0	0	3.86	2.1	4	2	2	0
J. Lahti	0	0	10.80	1.2	4	1	1	0

MILWAUKEE (A.L.)

	W	L	ERA	IP	H	BB	SO	SV
M. Caldwell	2	0	2.04	17.2	19	3	6	0
P. Vuckovich	0	1	4.50	14	16	5	4	0
D. Sutton	0	1	7.84	10.1	12	1	5	0
M. Haas	0	0	7.36	7.1	8	3	4	0
B. McClure	0	2	4.15	4.1	5	3	5	2
J. Slaton	1	0	0.00	2.2	1	2	1	0
D. Medich	0	0	18.00	2	5	1	0	0
D. Bernard	0	0	0.00	1	0	0	1	0
P. Ladd	0	0	0.00	0.2	1	2	0	0

1983 NATIONAL LEAGUE CHAMPIONSHIP SERIES

LINE SCORES	PITCHERS (innings pitched)	HOME RUNS (men on)	HIGHLIGHTS

Philadelphia (East) defeats Los Angeles (West) 3 games to 1

GAME 1 - OCTOBER 4

PHI E 100 000 000   1 5 1   Carlton (7.2), Holland (1.1) SV   Schmidt
LA W 000 000 000   0 7 0   Reuss (8), Niedenfuer (1)

Mike Schmidt's first-inning homer accounted for all the scoring, and Al Holland shut down a bases-loaded threat in the eighth to preserve the 1-0 win.

GAME 2 - OCTOBER 5

PHI E 010 000 000   1 7 2   Denny (6), Reed (2)   Matthews
LA W 100 020 01x   4 6 1   Valenzuela (8), Niedenfuer (1) SV

Two Philadelphia errors and a two-run triple by Pedro Guerrero gave the Dodgers the win behind Valenzuela's and Niedenfuer's seven-hitter.

GAME 3 - OCTOBER 7

LA W 000 200 000   2 4 0   Welch (1.1), Pena (2.2), Honeycutt (0.1), Beckwith (1.2), Zachry (2)   Marshall (1 on)
PHI E 021 120 10x   7 9 1   Hudson (9)   Matthews

Gary Matthews went three-for-three and drove in four runs as rookie Charlie Hudson went the distance for the Phillies.

GAME 4 - OCTOBER 8

LA W 000 100 010   2 10 0   Reuss (4), Beckwith (0.2), Honeycutt (1.1), Zachry (2)   Baker
PHI E 300 022 00x   7 13 1   Carlton (6), Reed (1.1), Holland (1.2)   Matthews (2 on), Lezcano (1 on)

Gary Matthews's three-run homer in the first and Sixto Lezcano's three hits led the 13-hit attack that gave Steve Carlton his second victory and Philadelphia the National League pennant.

Team totals

		W	AB	H	2B	3B	HR	R	RBI	BA	BB	SO	ERA
PHI	E	3	130	34	4	0	5	16	15	.262	15	22	1.03
LA	W	1	129	27	5	1	2	8	7	.209	11	31	3.97

Individual Batting

PHILADELPHIA (EAST)

	AB	H	2B	3B	HR	R	RBI	BA
P. Rose, 1b	16	6	0	0	0	3	0	.375
J. Morgan, 2b	15	1	0	0	0	1	0	.067
M. Schmidt, 3b	15	7	2	0	1	5	2	.467
G. Matthews, of	14	6	0	0	3	4	8	.429
B. Diaz, c	13	2	1	0	0	0	0	.154
S. Lezcano, of	13	4	0	0	1	2	2	.308
I. DeJesus, ss	12	3	0	0	0	0	1	.250
G. Maddox, of	11	3	1	0	0	0	1	.273
G. Gross, of	5	0	0	0	0	1	0	.000
S. Carlton, p	5	1	0	0	0	0	0	.200
C. Hudson, p	4	0	0	0	0	0	0	.000
V. Hayes, of	2	0	0	0	0	0	0	.000
J. Lefebvre, of	2	0	0	0	0	0	1	.000
O. Virgil	1	0	0	0	0	0	0	.000
T. Perez	1	1	0	0	0	0	0	1.000
J. Denny, p	1	0	0	0	0	0	0	.000
B. Dernier, of	0	0	0	0	0	0	0	—
J. Samuel	0	0	0	0	0	0	0	—

Errors: I. DeJesus (2), S. Lezcano, G. Maddox, M. Schmidt
Stolen Bases: G. Matthews, P. Rose

LOS ANGELES (WEST)

	AB	H	2B	3B	HR	R	RBI	BA
S. Sax, 2b	16	4	0	0	0	0	0	.250
M. Marshall, 1b, of	15	2	1	0	1	1	2	.133
K. Landreaux, of	14	2	0	0	0	0	1	.143
B. Russell, ss	14	4	0	0	0	1	0	.286
D. Baker, of	14	5	1	0	1	4	1	.357
P. Guerrero, 3b	12	3	1	1	0	1	2	.250
D. Thomas, of	9	4	1	0	0	0	0	.444
G. Brock, 1b	9	0	0	0	0	1	0	.000
J. Fimple, c	7	1	0	0	0	0	1	.143
S. Yeager, c	6	1	1	0	0	0	0	.167
Valenzuela, p	3	0	0	0	0	0	0	.000
J. Reuss, p	3	0	0	0	0	0	0	.000
R. Landestoy	2	0	0	0	0	0	0	.000
J. Morales	2	0	0	0	0	0	0	.000
C. Maldonado	2	0	0	0	0	0	0	.000
A. Pena, p	1	1	0	0	0	0	0	1.000
R. Monday	0	0	0	0	0	0	0	—

Errors: B. Russell
Stolen Bases: B. Russell, D. Thomas, S. Sax

Individual Pitching

PHILADELPHIA (EAST)

	W	L	ERA	IP	H	BB	SO	SV
S. Carlton	2	0	0.66	13.2	13	5	13	0
C. Hudson	1	0	2.00	9	4	2	9	0
J. Denny	0	1	0.00	6	5	3	3	0
A. Holland	0	0	0.00	3	1	0	3	1
R. Reed	0	0	2.70	3.1	4	1	3	0

LOS ANGELES (WEST)

	W	L	ERA	IP	H	BB	SO	SV
J. Reuss	0	2	4.50	12	14	3	4	0
Valenzuela	1	0	1.13	8	7	4	5	0
P. Zachry	0	0	2.25	4	4	2	2	0
J. Beckwith	0	0	0.00	2.1	1	2	3	0
Niedenfuer	0	0	0.00	2	0	1	3	1
A. Pena	0	0	6.75	2.2	4	1	3	0
R. Honeycutt	0	0	21.60	1.2	4	0	2	0
B. Welch	0	1	6.75	1.1	0	2	0	0

1983 AMERICAN LEAGUE CHAMPIONSHIP SERIES

LINE SCORES		PITCHERS (innings pitched)	HOME RUNS (men on)	HIGHLIGHTS

Baltimore (East) defeats Chicago (West) 3 games to 1

GAME 1 - OCTOBER 5

CHI	W	001 001 000	2 7 0	Hoyt (9)	
BAL	E	000 000 001	1 5 0	McGregor (6.2), Stewart (0.1), T. Martinez (2)	

Five-hit pitching by LaMarr Hoyt carried the White Sox to victory in Game 1. Rudy Law had three hits and scored a run to pace the Chicago attack.

GAME 2 - OCTOBER 6

CHI	W	000 000 000	0 5 2	Bannister (6), Barojas (1), Lamp (1)	
BAL	E	010 102 00x	4 6 0	Boddicker (9)	Roenicke (1 on)

Mike Boddicker struck out 14 batters in his five-hit shutout effort. Gary Roenicke slammed a two-run homer and scored three runs for the Orioles.

GAME 3 - OCTOBER 7

BAL	E	310 020 014	11 8 1	Flanagan (5), Stewart (4) SV	Murray (2 on)
CHI	W	010 000 000	1 6 1	Dotson (5), Tidrow (2), Koosman (0.1), Lamp (0.2)	

Eddie Murray drove in three runs and scored four as Mike Flanagan and Sammy Stewart combined on a six-hitter. Cal Ripken chipped in with two hits and scored three times.

GAME 4 - OCTOBER 8

BAL	E	000 000 000 3	3 9 0	Davis (6), T. Martinez (4)	Landrum
CHI	W	000 000 000 0	0 10 0	Burns (9.1), Barojas (0), Agosto (0.1), Lamp (0.1)	

Tito Landrum's tenth-inning homer snapped a scoreless tie and ignited a three-run outburst that gave Baltimore the American League pennant.

Team totals

		W	AB	H	2B	3B	HR	R	RBI	BA	BB	SO	ERA
BAL	E	3	129	28	9	0	3	19	17	.217	16	24	0.49
CHI	W	1	133	28	4	0	0	3	2	.211	12	26	4.00

Individual Batting

BALTIMORE (EAST)

	AB	H	2B	3B	HR	R	RBI	BA
E. Murray, 1b	15	4	0	0	1	5	3	.267
T. Cruz, 3b	15	2	0	0	0	0	1	.133
C. Ripken, ss	15	6	2	0	0	5	1	.400
R. Dauer, 2b	14	0	0	0	0	0	1	.000
K. Singleton, dh	12	3	2	0	0	0	1	.250
R. Dempsey, c	12	2	0	0	0	1	0	.167
T. Landrum, of	10	2	0	0	1	2	1	.200
J. Shelby, of	9	2	0	0	0	1	0	.222
A. Bumbry, of	8	1	1	0	0	0	1	.125
Lowenstein, of, dh	6	1	1	0	0	0	2	.167
D. Ford, of, dh	5	1	1	0	0	0	0	.200
G. Roenicke, of	4	3	1	0	1	4	4	.750
J. Dwyer, of	4	1	1	0	0	1	0	.250
J. Nolan	0	0	0	0	0	0	1	—
J. Palmer, dh	0	0	0	0	0	0	0	—
B. Ayala, dh	0	0	0	0	0	0	1	—

Errors: R. Dempsey, E. Murray
Stolen Bases: E. Murray, J. Shelby

CHICAGO (WEST)

	AB	H	2B	3B	HR	R	RBI	BA
R. Law, of	18	7	1	0	0	1	0	.389
C. Fisk, c	17	3	1	0	0	0	0	.176
T. Paciorek, 1b, of	16	4	0	0	0	1	1	.250
H. Baines, of	16	2	0	0	0	0	0	.125
G. Luzinski, dh	15	2	1	0	0	0	0	.133
J. Cruz, 2b	12	4	0	0	0	0	0	.333
V. Law, 3b	11	2	0	0	0	0	1	.182
S. Fletcher, ss	7	0	0	0	0	0	0	.000
R. Kittle, of	7	2	1	0	0	1	0	.286
M. Squires, 1b	4	0	0	0	0	0	0	.000
J. Dybzinski, ss	4	1	0	0	0	0	0	.250
G. Walker, 1b	3	1	0	0	0	0	0	.333
J. Hairston, of	3	0	0	0	0	0	0	.000
A. Rodriguez, 3b	0	0	0	0	0	0	0	—

Errors: A. Rodriguez, V. Law, J. Hairston
Stolen Bases: J. Cruz (2), R. Law (2)

Individual Pitching

BALTIMORE (EAST)

	W	L	ERA	IP	H	BB	SO	SV
M. Boddicker	1	0	0.00	9	5	3	14	0
S. Davis	0	0	0.00	6	5	2	2	0
T. Martinez	1	0	0.00	6	5	3	5	0
S. McGregor	0	1	1.35	6.2	6	3	2	0
M. Flanagan	1	0	1.80	5	5	0	1	0
S. Stewart	0	0	0.00	4.1	2	1	2	1

CHICAGO (WEST)

	W	L	ERA	IP	H	BB	SO	SV
B. Burns	0	1	0.96	9.1	6	5	8	0
L. Hoyt	1	0	1.00	9	5	0	4	0
F. Bannister	0	1	4.50	6	5	1	5	0
R. Dotson	0	1	10.80	5	6	3	3	0
D. Tidrow	0	0	3.00	3	1	3	3	0
D. Lamp	0	0	0.00	2	0	2	1	0
S. Barojas	0	0	18.00	1	4	0	0	0
J. Agosto	0	0	0.00	0.1	0	0	0	0
J. Koosman	0	0	54.00	0.1	1	2	0	0

1983 WORLD SERIES

LINE SCORES	PITCHERS (innings pitched)	HOME RUNS (men on)	HIGHLIGHTS

Baltimore (A.L.) defeats Philadelphia (N.L.) 4 games to 1

GAME 1 - OCTOBER 11

PHI N 000 001 010 2 5 0   Denny (7.2), Holland (1.2) **SV**   Morgan, Maddox   Homers by Morgan and Maddox offset Dwyer's first-inning shot to give the Phillies a 1-0 lead in the Series.
BAL A 100 000 000 1 5 1   McGregor (8), Stewart (0.2), T. Martinez (0.1)   Dwyer

GAME 2 - OCTOBER 12

PHI N 000 100 000 1 3 0   Hudson (4.1), Hernandez (0.2), Andersen (2), Reed (1)   Boddicker pitched a masterful three-hitter to even the Series. Lowenstein rapped out three hits to lead the Baltimore attack.
BAL A 000 030 10x 4 9 1   Boddicker (9)   Lowenstein

GAME 3 - OCTOBER 14

BAL A 000 001 200 3 6 1   Flanagan (4), Palmer (2), Stewart (2), T. Martinez (1) **SV**   Ford   DeJesus's error in the seventh let in the game-winning run as the Orioles came back from a 2-0 deficit. Dempsey hit two doubles and shut down the Phils' running game in this pivotal contest.
PHI N 011 000 000 2 8 2   Carlton (6.2), Holland (2.1)   Matthews, Morgan

GAME 4 - OCTOBER 15

BAL A 000 202 100 5 10 1   Davis (5), Stewart (2.1) T. Martinez (1.2) **SV**   Dauer broke a 1-for-25 slump with three hits and three RBIs and manager Altobelli used four consecutive pinch-hitters to forge the go-ahead rally in the sixth as Baltimore took a commanding three games to one edge.
PHI N 000 120 001 4 10 0   Denny (5.1), Hernandez (0.1), Reed (1.1), Andersen (2)

GAME 5 - OCTOBER 16

BAL A 011 210 000 5 5 0   McGregor (9)   Murray, Dempsey, Murray (1 on)   McGregor scattered five hits and Murray blasted two homers as the Orioles won their third straight on the road to clinch the Series. Dempsey homered and doubled, and was named the series MVP.
PHI N 000 000 000 0 5 1   Hudson (4.0), Bystrom (1), Hernandez (3)

Team totals

		W	AB	H	2B	3B	HR	R	RBI	BA	BB	SO	ERA
BAL	A	4	164	35	8	0	6	18	17	.213	10	37	1.60
PHI	N	1	159	31	4	1	4	9	9	.195	7	29	3.48

Individual Batting

BALTIMORE (A.L.)

	AB	H	2B	3B	HR	R	RBI	BA
E. Murray, 1b	20	5	0	0	2	2	3	.250
R. Dauer, 2b, 3b	19	4	1	0	0	2	3	.211
C. Ripken, ss	18	3	0	0	0	2	1	.167
T. Cruz, 3b	16	2	0	0	0	1	0	.125
Lowenstein, of	13	5	1	0	1	2	1	.385
R. Dempsey, c	13	5	4	0	1	3	2	.385
D. Ford, of	12	2	0	0	1	1	1	.167
A. Bumbry, of	11	1	1	0	0	0	1	.091
J. Shelby, of	9	4	0	0	0	1	1	.444
J. Dwyer, of	8	3	1	0	1	3	1	.375
G. Roenicke, of	7	0	0	0	0	0	0	.000
S. McGregor, p	5	0	0	0	0	0	0	.000
M. Boddicker, p	3	0	0	0	0	0	1	.000
S. Davis, p	2	0	0	0	0	0	0	.000
J. Nolan, c	2	0	0	0	0	0	0	.000
S. Stewart, p	2	0	0	0	0	0	0	.000
K. Singleton	1	0	0	0	0	0	1	.000
L. Sakata, 2b	1	0	0	0	0	0	0	.000
M. Flanagan, p	1	0	0	0	0	0	0	.000
B. Ayala	1	1	0	0	0	1	1	1.000
T. Landrum, of	0	0	0	0	0	0	0	–

Errors: T. Cruz (2), Lowenstein, E. Murray
Stolen Bases: T. Landrum

PHILADELPHIA (N.L.)

	AB	H	2B	3B	HR	R	RBI	BA
M. Schmidt, 3b	20	1	0	0	0	0	0	.050
J. Morgan, 2b	19	5	0	1	2	3	2	.263
P. Rose, 1b, of	16	5	1	0	0	1	1	.313
I. DeJesus, ss	16	2	0	0	0	0	0	.125
G. Matthews, of	16	4	0	0	1	1	1	.250
B. Diaz, c	15	5	1	0	0	1	0	.333
G. Maddox, of	12	3	1	0	1	1	1	.250
T. Perez, 1b	10	2	0	0	0	0	0	.200
S. Lezcano, of	8	1	0	0	0	0	0	.125
G. Gross, of	6	0	0	0	0	0	0	.000
J. Denny, p	5	1	0	0	0	0	1	.200
J. Lefebvre, of	5	1	1	0	0	0	2	.200
S. Carlton, p	3	0	0	0	0	0	0	.000
V. Hayes, of	3	0	0	0	0	0	0	.000
C. Hudson, p	2	0	0	0	0	0	0	.000
O. Virgil, c	2	1	0	0	0	0	1	.500
J. Samuel	1	0	0	0	0	0	0	.000
B. Dernier	0	0	0	0	0	1	0	–

Errors: I. DeJesus, B. Diaz, M. Schmidt
Stolen Bases: J. Morgan

Individual Pitching

BALTIMORE (A.L.)

	W	L	ERA	IP	H	BB	SO	SV
S. McGregor	1	1	1.06	17	9	2	12	0
M. Boddicker	1	0	0.00	9	3	0	6	0
S. Davis	1	0	5.40	5	6	1	3	0
S. Stewart	0	0	0.00	5	2	2	6	0
M. Flanagan	0	0	4.50	4	6	1	1	0
T. Martinez	0	0	3.00	3	3	0	0	2
J. Palmer	1	0	0.00	2	2	1	1	0

PHILADELPHIA (N.L.)

	W	L	ERA	IP	H	BB	SO	SV
J. Denny	1	1	3.46	13	12	3	9	0
C. Hudson	0	2	8.64	8.1	9	1	6	0
S. Carlton	0	1	2.70	6.2	5	3	7	0
L. Andersen	0	0	2.25	4	4	0	1	0
G. Hernandez	0	0	0.00	4	0	1	4	0
A. Holland	0	0	0.00	3.2	1	0	5	1
R. Reed	0	0	2.70	3.1	4	2	4	0
M. Bystrom	0	0	0.00	1	0	0	1	0

1984 NATIONAL LEAGUE CHAMPIONSHIP SERIES

LINE SCORES	PITCHERS (innings pitched)	HOME RUNS (men on)	HIGHLIGHTS

San Diego (West) defeats Chicago (East) 3 games to 2

GAME 1 - OCTOBER 2

SD W 000 000 000   0 6 1   Show (4), Harris (2), Booker (2)
CHI E 203 062 00x   13 16 0   Sutcliffe (7), Brusstar (2)

Dernier, Matthews, Sutcliffe, Matthews (2 on), Cey

In the first playoff appearance for both clubs, the Cubs set NL LCS records for runs, hits, home runs, and total bases in battering the Padres. A strike by major league umpires caused the league to call in college and former pro umps to work the games.

GAME 2 - OCTOBER 3

SD W 000 101 000   2 5 0   Thurmond (3.2), Hawkins (1.1), Dravecky (2), Lefferts (1)
CHI E 102 100 00x   4 8 1   Trout (8.1), Smith (0.2) SV

Trout scattered five hits before yielding to Lee Smith, who nailed down the win. Sandberg and Moreland each had two hits for the Cubs.

GAME 3 - OCTOBER 4

CHI E 010 000 000   1 5 0   Eckersley (5.1), Frazier (1.2), Stoddard (1)
SD W 000 034 00x   7 11 0   Whitson (8), Gossage (1)

McReynolds (2 on)

Templeton's two-run double in the fifth gave the Padres their first lead of the series, and McReynolds's homer in the sixth put the game away. Whitson allowed five hits over eight innings to keep San Diego's hopes alive.

GAME 4 - OCTOBER 6

CHI E 000 300 020   5 8 1   Sanderson (4.2), Brusstar (1.1), Stoddard (1), Smith (1.1)
SD W 002 010 202   7 11 0   Lollar (4.1), Hawkins (0.2), Dravecky (2), Gossage (1), Lefferts (1)

Davis (1 on), Durham

Garvey (1 on)

Garvey capped a four-for-five, five RBI game with his two run homer in the bottom of the ninth to win one of the most dramatic LCS games ever played.

GAME 5 - OCTOBER 7

CHI E 210 000 000   3 5 1   Sutcliffe (6.1), Trout (0.2), Brusstar (1)
SD W 000 002 40x   6 8 0   Show (1.1), Hawkins (1.2), Dravecky (2), Lefferts (2), Gossage (2) SV

Durham (1 on), Davis

The Padres became the first National League team to come back from two games down to win the series. Durham's error allowed Martinez to score the tying run and then three straight singles capped the four run 7th inning rally that won San Diego's first pennant.

Team totals

		W	AB	H	2B	3B	HR	R	RBI	BA	BB	SO	ERA
SD	W	3	155	41	5	1	2	22	20	.265	14	22	5.23
CHI	E	2	162	42	11	0	9	26	25	.259	20	28	4.25

Individual Batting

SAN DIEGO (WEST)

	AB	H	2B	3B	HR	R	RBI	BA
S. Garvey, 1b	20	8	1	0	1	1	7	.400
T. Gwynn, of	19	7	3	0	0	6	3	.368
A. Wiggins, 2b	19	6	0	0	0	4	1	.316
T. Kennedy, c	18	4	0	0	0	2	1	.222
C. Martinez, of	17	3	0	0	0	1	0	.176
G. Templeton, ss	15	5	1	0	0	2	2	.333
G. Nettles, 3b	14	2	0	0	0	1	2	.143
McReynolds, of	10	3	0	0	1	2	4	.300
L. Salazar, 3b, of	5	1	0	1	0	0	0	.200
B. Brown, of	4	0	0	0	0	1	0	.000
E. Whitson, p	3	0	0	0	0	0	0	.000
K. Bevacqua	2	0	0	0	0	0	0	.000
C. Summers	2	0	0	0	0	0	0	.000
M. Ramirez	2	0	0	0	0	0	0	.000
T. Flannery	2	1	0	0	0	2	0	.500
T. Lollar, p	1	0	0	0	0	0	0	.000
E. Show, p	1	0	0	0	0	0	0	.000
M. Thurmond, p	1	1	0	0	0	0	0	1.000

Errors: G. Templeton
Stolen Bases: B. Brown, G. Templeton

CHICAGO (EAST)

	AB	H	2B	3B	HR	R	RBI	BA
L. Durham, 1b	20	3	0	0	2	2	4	.150
R. Sandberg, 2b	19	7	2	0	0	3	2	.368
R. Cey, 3b	19	3	1	0	1	3	3	.158
J. Davis, c	18	7	2	0	2	3	6	.389
K. Moreland, of	18	6	2	0	0	3	2	.333
B. Dernier, of	17	4	2	0	1	5	1	.235
G. Matthews, of	15	3	0	0	2	4	5	.200
L. Bowa, ss	15	3	1	0	0	1	1	.200
R. Sutcliffe, p	6	3	0	0	1	1	1	.500
T. Bosley	2	0	0	0	0	0	0	.000
D. Eckersley, p	2	0	0	0	0	0	0	.000
S. Trout, p	2	1	0	0	0	0	0	.500
S. Sanderson, p	2	0	0	0	0	0	0	.000
W. Brusstar, p	1	0	0	0	0	0	0	.000
D. Lopes, of	1	0	0	0	0	0	0	.000
S. Lake, c	1	1	1	0	0	0	0	1.000
H. Cotto, of	1	1	0	0	0	1	0	1.000
T. Veryzer, 3b, ss	1	0	0	0	0	0	0	.000
R. Hebner	1	0	0	0	0	0	0	.000
G. Woods, of	1	0	0	0	0	0	0	.000

Errors: S. Trout, L. Durham, R. Sandberg
Stolen Bases: R. Sandberg (3), B. Dernier (2), G. Matthews

Individual Pitching

SAN DIEGO (WEST)

	W	L	ERA	IP	H	BB	SO	SV
E. Whitson	1	0	1.13	8	5	2	6	0
D. Dravecky	0	0	0.00	6	2	0	5	0
E. Show	0	1	13.50	5.1	8	4	2	0
G. Gossage	0	0	4.50	4	5	1	5	1
C. Lefferts	2	0	0.00	4	1	1	1	0
T. Lollar	0	0	6.23	4.1	3	4	3	0
M. Thurmond	0	1	9.82	3.2	7	2	1	0
A. Hawkins	0	0	0.00	3.2	0	2	1	0
G. Booker	0	0	0.00	2	2	1	2	0
G. Harris	0	0	31.50	2	9	3	2	0

CHICAGO (EAST)

	W	L	ERA	IP	H	BB	SO	SV
R. Sutcliffe	1	1	3.38	13.1	9	8	10	0
S. Trout	1	0	2.00	9	5	3	3	0
D. Eckersley	0	1	8.44	5.1	9	0	0	0
W. Brusstar	0	0	0.00	4.2	6	0	1	0
S. Sanderson	0	0	5.79	4.2	6	1	2	0
L. Smith	0	1	9.00	2	3	0	3	1
T. Stoddard	0	0	4.50	2	1	2	2	0
G. Frazier	0	0	10.80	1.2	2	0	1	0

1984 AMERICAN LEAGUE CHAMPIONSHIP SERIES

LINE SCORES	PITCHERS (innings pitched)	HOME RUNS (men on)	HIGHLIGHTS

Detroit (East) defeats Kansas City (West) 3 games to 0

GAME 1 · OCTOBER 2

DET	E	200 110 121	8 14 0	**Morris** (7), Hernandez (2)	Herndon, Trammell, Parrish
KC	W	000 000 100	1 5 1	**Black** (5), Huismann (2.2), M. Jones (1.1)	

Trammell led the Detroit attack with three hits, including a triple and a solo homer, and three RBIs to support Morris's five-hitter.

GAME 2 · OCTOBER 3

DET	E	201 000 000 02	5 8 1	Petry (7), Hernandez (1), **Lopez** (3)	Gibson
KC	W	000 100 110 00	3 10 3	Saberhagen (8), **Quisenberry** (3)	

The Royals rallied from three runs down on RBI pinch hits by Iorg and McRae in the seventh and eighth, but Grubb's two-run double in the eleventh gave the Tigers the victory.

GAME 3 · OCTOBER 5

KC	W	000 000 000	0 3 3	**Leibrandt** (8)	
DET	E	010 000 00x	1 3 0	**Wilcox** (8), Hernandez (1) SV	

Leibrandt allowed just three hits in eight innings, but Wilcox was even better, giving up two before yielding to Hernandez, who locked up Detroit's first pennant in sixteen years.

Team totals

		W	AB	H	2B	3B	HR	R	RBI	BA	BB	SO	ERA
DET	E	3	107	25	4	1	4	14	14	.234	8	17	1.24
KC	W	0	106	18	1	1	0	4	4	.170	6	21	3.86

Individual Batting

DETROIT (EAST)

	AB	H	2B	3B	HR	R	RBI	BA
L. Whitaker, 2b	14	2	0	0	0	3	0	.143
C. Lemon, of	13	0	0	0	0	1	0	.000
L. Parrish, c	12	3	1	0	1	1	3	.250
K. Gibson, of	12	5	1	0	1	2	2	.417
A. Trammell, ss	11	4	0	1	1	2	3	.364
D. Evans, 1b, 3b	10	3	1	0	0	1	1	.300
B. Garbey, dh	9	3	0	0	0	1	0	.333
M. Castillo, 3b	8	2	0	0	0	0	2	.250
L. Herndon, of	5	1	0	0	1	1	1	.200
R. Jones, of	5	0	0	0	0	1	0	.000
J. Grubb	4	1	1	0	0	0	2	.250
T. Brookens, 3b, 2b	2	0	0	0	0	0	0	.000
R. Kuntz, of	1	0	0	0	0	0	0	.000
D. Bergman, 1b	1	1	0	0	0	1	0	1.000
D. Baker, ss	0	0	0	0	0	0	0	—

Errors: T. Brookens

Stolen Bases: K. Gibson, M. Castillo, D. Evans, D. Bergman

KANSAS CITY (WEST)

	AB	H	2B	3B	HR	R	RBI	BA
W. Wilson, of	13	2	0	0	0	0	0	.154
G. Brett, 3b	13	3	0	0	0	0	0	.231
D. Motley, of	12	2	0	0	0	0	1	.167
F. White, 2b	12	1	0	0	0	1	0	.083
D. Slaught, c	11	4	0	0	0	0	0	.364
J. Orta, dh	10	1	0	1	0	1	1	.100
S. Balboni, 1b	10	1	0	0	0	0	0	.100
Concepcion, ss	7	0	0	0	0	0	0	.000
P. Sheridan, of	6	0	0	0	0	1	0	.000
L. Jones, of	5	1	0	0	0	1	0	.200
D. Iorg	2	1	0	0	0	0	1	.500
H. McRae	2	2	1	0	0	0	1	1.000
J. Wathan	1	0	0	0	0	0	0	.000
Washington	1	0	0	0	0	0	0	.000
Biancalana, ss	1	0	0	0	0	0	0	.000
G. Pryor, 3b	0	0	0	0	0	0	0	—

Errors: D. Slaught (3), Saberhagen, Concepcion, P. Sheridan, S. Balboni

Individual Pitching

DETROIT (EAST)

	W	L	ERA	IP	H	BB	SO	SV
M. Wilcox	1	0	0.00	8	2	2	8	0
D. Petry	0	0	2.57	7	4	1	4	0
J. Morris	1	0	1.29	7	5	1	4	0
G. Hernandez	0	0	2.25	4	3	1	3	1
A. Lopez	1	0	0.00	3	4	1	2	0

KANSAS CITY (WEST)

	W	L	ERA	IP	H	BB	SO	SV
Saberhagen	0	0	2.25	8	6	1	5	0
C. Leibrandt	0	1	1.13	8	3	4	6	0
B. Black	0	1	7.20	5	7	1	3	0
Quisenberry	0	1	3.00	3	2	1	1	0
M. Huismann	0	0	10.13	2.2	6	1	2	0
M. Jones	0	0	6.75	1.1	1	0	0	0

1984 WORLD SERIES

LINE SCORES	PITCHERS (innings pitched)	HOME RUNS (men on)	HIGHLIGHTS

Detroit (A.L.) defeats San Diego (N.L.) 4 games to 1

GAME 1 - OCTOBER 9

DET A 100 020 000   3 8 0   Morris (9)   Herndon (1 on)

SD N 200 000 000   2 8 0   Thurmond (5), Hawkins (2.2), Dravecky (1.1)

Herndon's two-run homer in the fifth powered the Tigers to the win. San Diego's best hope to even the score was cut off when Gibson threw Bevacqua out as he tried to stretch a leadoff double into a triple in the seventh.

GAME 2 - OCTOBER 10

DET A 300 000 000   3 7 2   Petry (4.1), Lopez (0.2), Scherrer (1.1) Bair (0.2), Hernandez (1)

SD N 100 130 00x   5 11 0   Whitson (0.2), Hawkins (5.1), Lefferts (3) SV   Bevacqua (2 on)

Bevacqua's three-run homer in the fifth brought the Padres back from an early deficit to even the Series. Hawkins allowed one hit in five and a third innings of relief to earn the victory.

GAME 3 - OCTOBER 12

SD N 001 000 100   2 10 0   Lollar (1.2), Booker (1), Harris (5.1)

DET A 041 000 00x   5 7 0   Wilcox (6), Scherrer (0.2), Hernandez (2.1) SV   Castillo (1 on)

San Diego pitchers walked eleven Tigers to tie a Series record in a slow-moving, sloppily played contest. Castillo was the surprise hero for Detroit with his two-run homer. Detroit left 14 runners on base, and the Padres stranded 10.

GAME 4 - OCTOBER 13

SD N 010 000 001   2 5 2   Show (2.2), Dravecky (3.1), Lefferts (1) Gossage (1)   Kennedy

DET A 202 000 00x   4 7 0   Morris (9)   Trammell (1 on), Trammell (1 on)

A pair of two-run homers by Trammell provided Morris with all the scoring he needed to back up his five-hitter.

GAME 5 - OCTOBER 14

SD N 001 200 010   4 10 1   Thurmond (0.1), Hawkins (4), Lefferts (2), Gossage (1.2)   Bevacqua

DET A 300 010 13x   8 11 1   Petry (3.2), Scherrer (1), Lopez (2.1) Hernandez (2) SV   Gibson (1 on), Parrish, Gibson (2 on)

Gibson cracked two homers and drove in five as the Tigers won the Series. He also scored the run that put Detroit ahead to stay in the fifth on a popup fielded by Wiggins in short right field. Detroit battered Padre starters for a 13.94 ERA in the Series as Sparky Anderson became the first to manage a World Series winner in both leagues.

Team totals

		W	AB	H	2B	3B	HR	R	RBI	BA	BB	SO	ERA
DET	A	4	158	40	4	0	7	23	23	.253	24	27	3.07
SD	N	1	166	44	7	0	3	15	14	.265	11	26	4.71

Individual Batting

DETROIT (A.L.)

	AB	H	2B	3B	HR	R	RBI	BA
A. Trammell, ss	20	9	1	0	2	5	6	.450
L. Whitaker, 2b	18	5	2	0	0	6	0	.278
L. Parrish, c	18	5	1	0	1	3	2	.278
K. Gibson, of	18	6	0	0	2	4	7	.333
C. Lemon, of	17	5	0	0	0	1	1	.294
L. Herndon, of	15	5	0	0	1	1	3	.333
D. Evans, 1b	15	1	0	0	0	1	1	.067
B. Garbey, dh	12	0	0	0	0	0	0	.000
M. Castillo, 3b	9	3	0	0	1	2	2	.333
D. Bergman, 1b	5	0	0	0	0	0	0	.000
R. Jones, of	3	0	0	0	0	0	0	.000
T. Brookens, 3b	3	0	0	0	0	0	0	.000
J. Grubb, dh	3	1	0	0	0	0	0	.333
H. Johnson	1	0	0	0	0	0	0	.000
R. Kuntz	1	0	0	0	0	0	1	.000

Errors: K. Gibson (2), A. Trammell, L. Parrish
Stolen Bases: K. Gibson (3), C. Lemon (2), A. Trammell, L. Parrish

SAN DIEGO (N.L.)

	AB	H	2B	3B	HR	R	RBI	BA
A. Wiggins, 2b	22	8	1	0	0	2	1	.364
S. Garvey, 1b	20	4	2	0	0	2	2	.200
T. Gwynn, of	19	5	0	0	0	1	0	.263
T. Kennedy, c	19	4	1	0	1	2	3	.211
G. Templeton, ss	19	6	1	0	0	1	0	.316
C. Martinez, of	17	3	0	0	0	0	0	.176
K. Bevacqua, dh	17	7	2	0	2	4	4	.412
B. Brown, of	15	1	0	0	0	1	2	.067
G. Nettles, 3b	12	3	0	0	0	2	2	.250
L. Salazar, 3b, of	3	1	0	0	0	0	0	.333
T. Flannery, 2b	1	1	0	0	0	0	0	1.000
C. Summers	1	0	0	0	0	0	0	.000
B. Bochy	1	1	0	0	0	0	0	1.000
R. Roenicke, of	0	0	0	0	0	0	0	—

Errors: A. Wiggins (2), T. Gwynn, C. Martinez
Stolen Bases: T. Gwynn, A. Wiggins

Individual Pitching

DETROIT (A.L.)

	W	L	ERA	IP	H	BB	SO	SV
J. Morris	2	0	2.00	18	13	3	13	0
D. Petry	0	1	9.00	8	14	5	4	0
M. Wilcox	1	0	1.50	6	7	2	4	0
G. Hernandez	0	0	1.69	5.1	4	2	0	2
A. Lopez	1	0	0.00	3	1	1	4	0
B. Scherrer	0	0	3.00	3	5	0	0	0
D. Bair	0	0	0.00	0.2	0	0	1	0

SAN DIEGO (N.L.)

	W	L	ERA	IP	H	BB	SO	SV
A. Hawkins	1	1	0.75	12	4	6	4	0
C. Lefferts	0	0	0.00	6	2	1	7	1
M. Thurmond	0	1	10.13	5.1	12	3	2	0
G. Harris	0	0	0.00	5.1	3	3	5	0
D. Dravecky	0	0	0.00	4.2	3	1	5	0
E. Show	0	1	10.13	2.2	4	1	2	0
G. Gossage	0	0	13.50	2.2	3	1	2	0
T. Lollar	0	1	21.60	1.2	4	4	0	0
G. Booker	0	0	9.00	1	0	4	0	0
E. Whitson	0	0	40.50	0.2	5	0	0	0

1985 NATIONAL LEAGUE CHAMPIONSHIP SERIES

LINE SCORES	PITCHERS (innings pitched)	HOME RUNS (men on)	HIGHLIGHTS

St. Louis (East) defeats Los Angeles (West) 4 games to 2

GAME 1 - OCTOBER 9

STL	E	000 000 100	1 8 1		Tudor (5.2), Dayley (0.1), Campbell (1.0), Worrell (1)
LA	W	000 103 00x	4 8 0		Valenzuela (6.1), Niedenfuer (2.2) SV

Uncharactistic Cardinal fielding lapses led to all four Dodger runs as Los Angeles chased St. Louis's ace Tudor, winner of twenty of his last twenty-one decisions.

GAME 2 - OCTOBER 10

STL	E	001 000 001	2 8 1		Andujar (4.1), Horton (1.1), Campbell (0.1), Dayley (1), Lahti (1)
LA	W	003 212 00x	8 13 1	Brock (1 on)	Hershiser (9)

Every Dodger starter had at least one hit, battering five Cardinal pitchers to take a 2-0 lead in the series.

GAME 3 - OCTOBER 12

LA	W	000 100 100	2 7 2		Welch (2.2), Honeycutt (1.1), Diaz (2), Howell (2)
STL	E	220 000 00x	4 8 0	Herr	Cox (6.0), Horton (0.2), Worrell (1.1), Dayley (1) SV

The St. Louis running game revived with the move to Busch Stadium's artificial surface; their first three runs were aided by three stolen bases and two errors on pickoff attempts.

GAME 4 - OCTOBER 13

LA	W	000 000 110	2 5 2	Madlock	Reuss (1.2), Honeycutt (0), Castillo (5.1), Diaz (1)
STL	E	090 110 01x	12 15 0		Tudor (7), Horton (1), Campbell (1)

The Cardinals sent fourteen men to the plate in the home second, scoring an LCS-record nine runs on eight singles, two walks, and an error.

GAME 5 - OCTOBER 14

LA	W	000 200 000	2 5 1	Madlock (1 on)	Valenzuela (8), Niedenfuer (0.1)
STL	E	200 000 001	3 5 1	Smith	Forsch (3.1), Dayley (2.2), Worrell (2), Lahti (1)

Ozzie Smith's one-out homer in the ninth (his first ever from the left side of the plate) was the game-winning blow.

GAME 6 - OCTOBER 16

STL	E	001 000 303	7 12 1	Clark (2 on)	Andujar (6), Worrell (2), Dayley (1) SV
LA	W	110 020 010	5 8 0	Madlock, Marshall	Hershiser (6.1), Niedenfuer (2.2)

Marshall's eighth-inning home run gave the Dodgers a 5-4 lead. But with two out in the ninth and runners on second and third, the Dodgers chose to pitch to Jack Clark. Clark's towering homer gave the Cardinals the pennant.

Team totals

		W	AB	H	2B	3B	HR	R	RBI	BA	BB	SO	ERA
STL	E	4	201	56	10	1	3	29	26	.279	30	34	3.46
LA	W	2	197	46	12	1	5	23	23	.234	19	31	3.51

Individual Batting

ST. LOUIS (EAST)

	AB	H	2B	3B	HR	R	RBI	BA
W. McGee, of	26	7	1	0	0	6	3	.269
T. Pendleton, 3b	24	5	1	0	0	2	4	.208
O. Smith, ss	23	10	1	1	1	4	3	.435
J. Clark, 1b	21	8	0	0	1	4	4	.381
T. Herr, 2b	21	7	4	0	1	2	6	.333
D. Porter, c	15	4	1	0	0	1	0	.267
T. Landrum, of	14	6	0	0	0	2	4	.429
V. Coleman, of	14	4	0	0	0	2	1	.286
C. Cedeno, of	12	2	1	0	0	2	0	.167
A. Van Slyke, of	11	1	0	0	0	1	1	.091
J. Tudor, p	4	0	0	0	0	1	0	.000
J. Andujar, p	4	1	1	0	0	1	0	.250
T. Nieto, c	3	0	0	0	0	1	0	.000
D. Cox, p	2	0	0	0	0	0	0	.000
K. Dayley, p	2	1	0	0	0	0	0	.500
S. Braun	2	0	0	0	0	0	0	.000
M. Jorgensen	2	0	0	0	0	0	0	.000
B. Harper	1	0	0	0	0	0	0	.000

Errors: J. Andujar (2), D. Porter, T. Pendleton
Stolen Bases: W. McGee (2), V. Coleman, T. Herr, T. Landrum, O. Smith

LOS ANGELES (WEST)

	AB	H	2B	3B	HR	R	RBI	BA
B. Madlock, 3b	24	8	1	0	3	5	7	.333
M. Marshall, of	23	5	2	0	1	1	3	.217
S. Sax, 2b	20	6	3	0	0	1	1	.300
P. Guerrero, of	20	5	1	0	0	2	4	.250
K. Landreaux, of	18	7	3	0	0	4	2	.389
M. Duncan, ss	18	4	2	1	0	2	1	.222
M. Scioscia, c	16	4	0	0	0	2	1	.250
E. Cabell, 1b	13	1	0	0	0	1	0	.077
G. Brock, 1b	12	1	0	0	1	2	2	.083
O. Hershiser, p	7	2	0	0	0	1	1	.286
C. Maldonado, of	7	1	0	0	0	0	1	.143
Valenzuela, p	5	1	0	0	0	0	0	.200
D. Anderson, ss, 3b	5	0	0	0	0	1	0	.000
S. Yeager, c	2	0	0	0	0	0	0	.000
B. Castillo, p	2	0	0	0	0	0	0	.000
B. Welch, p	1	0	0	0	0	0	0	.000
B. Bailor, 3b	1	0	0	0	0	0	0	.000
J. Johnstone	1	0	0	0	0	0	0	.000
Niedenfuer, p	1	0	0	0	0	0	0	.000
L. Matuszek, of, 1b	1	1	0	0	0	1	1	1.000
T. Whitfield	0	0	0	0	0	0	0	–

Errors: J. Reuss, B. Welch, M. Scioscia, Valenzuela, C. Maldonado, M. Duncan
Stolen Bases: P. Guerrero (2), M. Duncan, B. Madlock

Individual Pitching

ST. LOUIS (EAST)

	W	L	ERA	IP	H	BB	SO	SV
J. Tudor	1	1	2.84	12.2	10	3	8	0
J. Andujar	0	1	6.97	10.1	14	4	9	0
K. Dayley	0	0	0.00	6	2	1	3	2
D. Cox	1	0	3.00	6	4	5	4	0
T. Worrell	1	0	1.42	6.1	4	2	3	0
R. Horton	0	0	9.00	3	4	2	1	0
B. Forsch	0	0	5.40	3.1	3	2	0	0
J. Lahti	1	0	0.00	2	2	0	1	0
B. Campbell	0	0	0.00	2.1	3	0	2	0

LOS ANGELES (WEST)

	W	L	ERA	IP	H	BB	SO	SV
O. Hershiser	1	0	3.52	15.1	17	6	5	0
Valenzuela	1	0	1.88	14.1	11	10	13	0
Niedenfuer	0	2	6.35	5.2	5	2	5	1
B. Castillo	0	0	3.38	5.1	4	2	4	0
C. Diaz	0	0	3.00	3	5	1	2	0
K. Howell	0	0	0.00	2	1	0	2	0
B. Welch	0	1	6.75	2.2	5	6	2	0
J. Reuss	0	1	10.80	1.2	5	1	0	0
R. Honeycutt	0	0	13.50	1.1	4	2	1	0

1985 AMERICAN LEAGUE CHAMPIONSHIP SERIES

LINE SCORES		PITCHERS (innings pitched)	HOME RUNS (men on)	HIGHLIGHTS

Kansas City (West) defeats Toronto (East) 4 games to 3

GAME 1 - OCTOBER 8

KC	W	000 000 001	1 5 1	Leibrandt (2.0), Farr (2), Gubicza (3), Jackson (1)	
TOR	E	023 100 00x	6 11 0	**Stieb (8)**, Henke (1)	

Stieb scattered three hits over eight innings, striking out eight, as the Blue Jays took the first ALCS game ever played in Canada.

GAME 2 - OCTOBER 9

KC	W	002 100 001 1	5 10 3	Black (7), **Quisenberry (2.2)**	Wilson (1 on), Sheridan
TOR	E	000 102 010 2	6 10 0	Key (3.1), Lamp (3.2), Lavelle (0), **Henke (3)**	

The Royals fought back on Sheridan's pinch homer in the ninth and White's disputed single in the tenth. But singles by Fernandez, Moseby and Oliver provided the winning runs.

GAME 3 - OCTOBER 11

TOR	E	000 050 000	5 13 1	Alexander (5.0), Lamp (2), **Clancy (1)**	Barfield (1 on), Mulliniks (1 on)
KC	W	100 112 01x	6 10 1	Saberhagen (4.1), Black (0.1), **Farr (4.1)**	Brett, Brett (1 on), Sundberg

George Brett's extraordinary display (four-for-four, four runs, three RBI, eleven total bases) drove the Royals past the Blue Jays despite a shaky performance by their 20-game winner Saberhagen.

GAME 4 - OCTOBER 12

TOR	E	000 000 003	3 7 0	**Stieb (6.2)**, Henke (2.1)	
KC	W	000 001 000	1 2 0	Leibrandt (8.0), Quisenberry (1)	

Oliver's ninth-inning double drove in the winning runs, as Quisenberry failed to hold the Blue Jays in check for the second time in the series.

GAME 5 - OCTOBER 13

TOR	E	000 000 000	0 8 0	Key (5.1), Acker (2.2)	
KC	W	110 000 00x	2 8 0	**Jackson (9)**	

Danny Jackson's eight-hit shutout helped the Royals stave off elimination. Lonnie Smith snapped a 2-for-14 slump with three hits, scoring his first run.

GAME 6 - OCTOBER 15

KC	W	101 012 000	5 8 1	**Gubicza (5.1)**, Black (3.1), Quisenberry (0.1) SV	Brett
TOR	E	101 001 000	3 8 2	**Alexander (5.1)**, Lamp (3.2)	

Brett's third home run of the series, all of them off Alexander, put the Royals ahead to stay in the fifth to force a seventh game.

GAME 7 - OCTOBER 16

KC	W	010 104 000	6 8 0	**Saberhagen (3)**, Leibrandt (5.1) Quisenberry (0.2)	Sheridan
TOR	E	000 010 001	2 8 1	**Stieb (5.2)**, Acker (3.1)	

Sundberg's bases-loaded triple broke open a 2-1 game and gave the Royals their third straight win and the AL pennant.

Team totals

		W	AB	H	2B	3B	HR	R	RBI	BA	BB	SO	ERA
KC	W	4	227	51	9	1	7	26	26	.225	22	51	3.16
TOR	E	3	242	65	19	0	2	25	23	.269	16	37	3.77

Individual Batting

KANSAS CITY (WEST)

	AB	H	2B	3B	HR	R	RBI	BA
W. Wilson, of	29	9	0	0	1	5	2	.310
L. Smith, of	28	7	2	0	0	2	1	.250
S. Balboni, 1b	25	3	0	0	0	1	1	.120
F. White, 2b	25	5	0	0	0	1	3	.200
J. Sundberg, c	24	4	1	1	1	3	6	.167
H. McRae, dh	23	6	2	0	0	1	3	.261
G. Brett, 3b	23	8	2	0	3	6	5	.348
P. Sheridan, of	20	3	0	0	2	4	3	.150
Biancalana, ss	18	4	1	0	0	2	1	.222
J. Orta, dh	5	0	0	0	0	0	0	.000
D. Motley, of	3	1	0	0	0	1	0	.333
D. Iorg	2	1	1	0	0	0	0	.500
Concepcion, ss	1	0	0	0	0	0	0	.000
J. Quirk	1	0	0	0	0	0	0	.000
L. Jones, of	0	0	0	0	0	0	0	–

Errors: G. Brett (2), S. Balboni (2), J. Sundberg, L. Smith
Stolen Bases: W. Wilson, L. Smith

TORONTO (EAST)

	AB	H	2B	3B	HR	R	RBI	BA
L. Moseby, of	31	7	1	0	0	5	4	.226
D. Garcia, 2b	30	7	4	0	0	4	1	.233
G. Bell, of	28	9	3	0	0	4	1	.321
W. Upshaw, 1b	26	6	2	0	0	2	1	.231
J. Barfield, of	25	7	1	0	1	3	4	.280
T. Fernandez, ss	24	8	2	0	0	2	2	.333
E. Whitt, c	21	4	1	0	0	1	2	.190
C. Johnson, dh	19	7	2	0	0	1	2	.368
G. Iorg, 3b	15	2	0	0	0	1	0	.133
R. Mulliniks, 3b	11	4	1	0	1	1	3	.364
A. Oliver, dh	8	3	1	0	0	0	3	.375
C. Fielder	3	1	1	0	0	0	0	.333
J. Burroughs	1	0	0	0	0	0	0	.000
J. Hearron, c	0	0	0	0	0	0	0	–
M. Lee, 2b	0	0	0	0	0	0	0	–
L. Thornton	0	0	0	0	0	1	0	–

Errors: T. Fernandez (2), W. Upshaw, J. Barfield
Stolen Bases: L. Moseby, J. Barfield

Individual Pitching

KANSAS CITY (WEST)

	W	L	ERA	IP	H	BB	SO	SV
C. Leibrandt	1	2	5.28	15.1	17	4	6	0
B. Black	0	0	1.69	10.2	11	4	8	0
D. Jackson	1	0	0.00	10	10	1	7	0
M. Gubicza	1	0	3.24	8.1	4	4	4	0
Saberhagen	0	0	6.14	7.1	12	2	6	0
S. Farr	1	0	1.42	6.1	4	1	3	0
Quisenberry	0	1	3.86	4.2	7	0	3	1

TORONTO (EAST)

	W	L	ERA	IP	H	BB	SO	SV
D. Stieb	1	1	3.10	20.1	11	10	18	0
D. Alexander	0	1	8.71	10.1	14	3	9	0
D. Lamp	0	0	0.00	9.1	2	1	10	0
J. Key	0	1	5.19	8.2	15	2	5	0
T. Henke	2	0	4.26	6.1	5	4	4	0
J. Acker	0	0	0.00	6	2	0	5	0
J. Clancy	0	1	9.00	1	2	1	0	0
G. Lavelle	0	0	–	0.0	0	1	0	0

1985 WORLD SERIES

LINE SCORES	PITCHERS (innings pitched)	HOME RUNS (men on)	HIGHLIGHTS

Kansas City (A.L.) defeats St. Louis (N.L.) 4 games to 3

GAME 1 - OCTOBER 19

STL	N	001 100 001	3 7 1		
KC	A	010 000 000	1 8 0		

Tudor (6.2), Worrell (2.1) SV
Jackson (7), Quisenberry (1.2), Black (0.1)

St. Louis bunched their seven hits to produce three runs and take game one of the so-called I-70 Series, named for the highway linking the two cities.

GAME 2 - OCTOBER 20

STL	N	000 000 004	4 6 0		
KC	A	000 200 000	2 9 0		

Cox (7), Dayley (1), Lahti (1) SV
Leibrandt (8.2), Quisenberry (0.1)

Charlie Leibrandt had allowed just two hits in the first eight innings. But two-out hits by Clark, Landrum, and Pendleton, the last a bases-loaded double, gave the Cards four runs and a come-from-behind win.

GAME 3 - OCTOBER 22

KC	A	000 220 200	6 11 0		
STL	N	000 010 000	1 6 0		

Saberhagen (9)
Andujar (4.0), Campbell (1), Horton (2), Dayley (2)

White (1 on)

White, batting cleanup in the absence of McRae (no DH this year), drove in three runs with a double and the first home run of the Series.

GAME 4 - OCTOBER 23

KC	A	000 000 000	0 5 1		
STL	N	011 010 00x	3 6 0		

Black (5), Beckwith (2), Quisenberry (1)
Tudor (9)

Landrum, McGee

Tudor shut out the Royals on five hits, striking out eight while walking one. Cardinal runs scored on solo homers by Landrum and McGee, and a surprise two-strike squeeze bunt by Tom Nieto.

GAME 5 - OCTOBER 24

KC	A	130 000 011	6 11 2		
STL	N	100 000 000	1 5 1		

Jackson (9)
Forsch (1.2), Horton (2), Campbell (1.1), Worrell (2), Lahti (2)

As he had in game five of the LCS, Jackson gave the Royals a complete-game win to keep them alive. Cardinals rookie Todd Worrell tied a Series record by striking out six straight batters in his perfect two-inning stint for the Cards.

GAME 6 - OCTOBER 26

STL	N	000 000 010	1 5 0		
KC	A	000 000 002	2 10 0		

Cox (7), Dayley (1), **Worrell** (0.1)
Leibrandt (7.2), **Quisenberry** (1.1)

A disputed play at first, a single, a passed ball, and an intentional pass set up Dane Iorg's two-run pinch single in the ninth that evened the Series.

GAME 7 - OCTOBER 27

STL	N	000 000 000	0 5 0		
KC	A	023 060 00x	11 14 0		

Tudor (2.1), Campbell (1.2), Lahti (0.2), Horton (0), Andujar (0), Forsch (1.1), Dayley (2)
Saberhagen (9)

Motley (1 on)

The Royals romped to their first World Series title in a laugher. They became the sixth team to win after trailing 3-1 in games, and the first to win after losing the first two games at home.

Team totals

		W	AB	H	2B	3B	HR	R	RBI	BA	BB	SO	ERA
KC	A	4	236	68	12	2	2	28	26	.288	28	56	1.89
STL	N	3	216	40	10	1	2	13	13	.185	18	42	3.96

Individual Batting

KANSAS CITY (A.L.)

	AB	H	2B	3B	HR	R	RBI	BA
W. Wilson, of	30	11	0	1	0	2	3	.367
F. White, 2b	28	7	3	0	1	4	6	.250
G. Brett, 3b	27	10	1	0	0	5	1	.370
L. Smith, of	27	9	0	0	0	4	4	.333
S. Balboni, 1b	25	8	0	0	0	2	3	.320
J. Sundberg, c	24	6	2	0	0	6	1	.250
P. Sheridan, of	18	4	2	0	0	0	1	.222
Biancalana, ss	18	5	0	0	0	2	2	.278
D. Motley, of	11	4	0	0	1	1	3	.364
Saberhagen, p	7	0	0	0	0	1	0	.000
D. Jackson, p	6	0	0	0	0	0	0	.000
C. Leibrandt, p	4	0	0	0	0	0	0	.000
L. Jones, of	3	2	1	1	0	0	0	.667
J. Orta	3	1	0	0	0	0	0	.333
D. Iorg	2	1	0	0	0	0	2	.500
H. McRae	1	0	0	0	0	0	0	.000
J. Wathan	1	0	0	0	0	0	0	.000
B. Black, p	1	0	0	0	0	0	0	.000
Concepcion, ss	0	0	0	0	0	1	0	—
G. Pryor, 3b	0	0	0	0	0	0	0	—

Errors: B. Black, D. Jackson, G. Brett
Stolen Bases: W. Wilson (3), L. Smith (2), G. Brett, F. White

ST. LOUIS (N.L.)

	AB	H	2B	3B	HR	R	RBI	BA
W. McGee, of	27	7	2	0	1	2	2	.259
T. Herr, 2b	26	4	2	0	0	2	0	.154
T. Landrum, of	25	9	2	0	1	3	1	.360
J. Clark, 1b	25	6	2	0	0	1	4	.240
O. Smith, ss	23	2	0	0	0	1	0	.087
T. Pendleton, 3b	23	6	1	1	0	3	3	.261
D. Porter, c	15	2	0	0	0	0	0	.133
C. Cedeno, of	15	2	1	0	0	1	1	.133
A. Van Slyke, of	11	1	0	0	0	0	0	.091
T. Nieto, c	5	0	0	0	0	0	1	.000
J. Tudor, p	5	0	0	0	0	0	0	.000
B. Harper	4	1	0	0	0	0	1	.250
D. Cox, p	4	0	0	0	0	0	0	.000
M. Jorgensen, of	3	0	0	0	0	0	0	.000
I. DeJesus	1	0	0	0	0	0	0	.000
S. Braun	1	0	0	0	0	0	0	.000
R. Horton, p	1	0	0	0	0	0	0	.000
T. Worrell, p	1	0	0	0	0	0	0	.000
J. Andujar, p	1	0	0	0	0	0	0	.000
T. Lawless	0	0	0	0	0	0	0	—

Errors: O. Smith, T. Pendleton
Stolen Bases: O. Smith, W. McGee

Individual Pitching

KANSAS CITY (A.L.)

	W	L	ERA	IP	H	BB	SO	SV
Saberhagen	2	0	0.50	18	11	1	10	0
D. Jackson	1	1	1.69	16	9	5	12	0
C. Leibrandt	0	1	2.76	16.1	10	4	10	0
B. Black	0	1	5.06	5.1	4	5	4	0
Quisenberry	1	0	2.08	4.1	5	3	3	0
J. Beckwith	0	0	0.00	2	1	0	3	0

ST. LOUIS (N.L.)

	W	L	ERA	IP	H	BB	SO	SV
J. Tudor	2	1	3.00	18	15	7	14	0
D. Cox	0	0	1.29	14	14	4	13	0
K. Dayley	1	0	0.00	6	1	3	5	0
R. Horton	0	0	6.75	4	4	5	5	0
B. Campbell	0	0	2.25	4	2	5	5	0
T. Worrell	0	1	3.86	4.2	4	2	6	1
J. Andujar	0	1	9.00	4	10	4	3	0
B. Forsch	0	1	12.00	3	6	1	3	0
J. Lahti	0	0	12.27	3.2	10	0	2	1

1986 NATIONAL LEAGUE CHAMPIONSHIP SERIES

LINE SCORES		PITCHERS (innings pitched)	HOME RUNS (men on)	HIGHLIGHTS

New York (East) defeats Houston (West) 4 games to 2

GAME 1 - OCTOBER 8

NY	E	000 000 000	0 5 0	Gooden (7), Orosco (1)	
HOU	W	010 000 00x	1 7 1	Scott (9)	Davis

Scott struck out 14 to tie an NLCS mark as he shut down the Mets on five hits.

GAME 2 - OCTOBER 9

NY	E	000 230 000	5 10 0	Ojeda (9)	
HOU	W	000 000 100	1 10 2	Ryan (5), Andersen (2), Lopez (1.1), Kerfeld (0.2)	

New York evened the LCS at one game apiece on Ojeda's ten-hitter, backed by RBIs from Carter and Strawberry in the fourth and Hernandez's two-run triple in the fifth.

GAME 3 - OCTOBER 11

HOU	W	220 000 100	5 8 1	Knepper (7), Kerfeld (1), Smith (0.1)	Doran (1 on)
NY	E	000 004 002	6 10 1	Darling (5), Aguilera (2), Orosco (2)	Strawberry (2 on), Dykstra (1 on)

Trailing 4-0, the Mets rallied for four in the sixth, the big blow coming on Strawberry's homer. Houston took the lead aided by Knight's error in the seventh, but Dykstra's homer won the game in the bottom of the ninth.

GAME 4 - OCTOBER 12

HOU	W	020 010 000	3 4 1	Scott (9)	Ashby (1 on), Thon
NY	E	000 000 010	1 3 0	Fernandez (6), McDowell (2), Sisk (1)	

Scott stymied the Mets again, this time on three hits, with Houston's runs coming on homers by Ashby and Thon.

GAME 5 - OCTOBER 14

HOU	W	000 010 000 000	1 9 1	Ryan (9), Kerfeld (2.1)	
NY	E	000 010 000 001	2 4 0	Gooden (10), Orosco (2)	Strawberry

Carter's single broke a 1-for-21 slump to drive in the winning run in the 12th inning, overshadowing Ryan's nine innings of two-hit, 12-strikeout pitching for the Astros.

GAME 6 - OCTOBER 15

NY	E	000 000 003 000 010 3	7 11 0	Ojeda (5), Aguilera (3), McDowell (5), Orosco (3)	
HOU	W	300 000 000 000 010 2	6 11 1	Knepper (8.1), Smith (1.2), Andersen (3), Lopez (2.0), Calhoun (1)	Hatcher

New York rallied from three down in the top of the ninth on RBIs by Wilson, Hernandez, and Knight. Backman's single in the 14th put the Mets up a run, but Hatcher's towering homer tied the score. Three in the top of the 16th put the Mets ahead, but the outcome was in doubt until Orosco struck out Bass with two on to clinch the pennant.

Team totals

		W	AB	H	2B	3B	HR	R	RBI	BA	BB	SO	ERA
NY	E	4	227	43	4	2	3	21	19	.189	14	57	2.29
HOU	W	2	225	49	6	0	5	17	17	.218	17	40	2.87

Individual Batting

NEW YORK (EAST)

	AB	H	2B	3B	HR	R	RBI	BA
G. Carter, c	27	4	1	0	0	1	2	.148
K. Hernandez, 1b	26	7	1	1	0	3	3	.269
M. Wilson, of	26	3	0	0	0	2	1	.115
R. Knight, 3b	24	4	0	0	0	1	2	.167
L. Dykstra, of	23	7	1	1	1	3	3	.304
Strawberry, of	22	5	1	0	2	4	5	.227
W. Backman, 2b	21	5	0	0	0	5	2	.238
R. Santana, ss	17	3	0	0	0	0	0	.176
K. Mitchell, of	8	2	0	0	0	1	0	.250
T. Teufel, 2b	6	1	0	0	0	0	0	.167
D. Gooden, p	5	0	0	0	0	0	0	.000
B. Ojeda, p	5	0	0	0	0	1	0	.000
L. Mazzilli	5	1	0	0	0	0	0	.200
D. Heep, of	4	1	0	0	0	0	1	.250
K. Elster, ss	3	0	0	0	0	0	0	.000
H. Johnson	2	0	0	0	0	0	0	.000
R. McDowell, p	1	0	0	0	0	0	0	.000
R. Darling, p	1	0	0	0	0	0	0	.000
S. Fernandez, p	1	0	0	0	0	0	0	.000

Errors: R. Knight

Stolen Bases: L. Dykstra, W. Backman, M. Wilson, Strawberry

HOUSTON (WEST)

	AB	H	2B	3B	HR	R	RBI	BA
B. Doran, 2b	27	6	0	0	1	3	3	.222
G. Davis, 1b	26	7	1	0	1	3	3	.269
J. Cruz, of	26	5	0	0	0	0	2	.192
B. Hatcher, of	25	7	0	0	1	4	2	.280
K. Bass, of	24	7	2	0	0	0	0	.292
A. Ashby, c	23	3	1	0	1	2	2	.130
D. Walling, 3b	19	3	1	0	0	1	2	.158
C. Reynolds, ss	12	4	0	0	0	1	0	.333
D. Thon, ss	12	3	0	0	1	1	1	.250
P. Garner, 3b	9	2	1	0	0	1	2	.222
M. Scott, p	6	0	0	0	0	0	0	.000
B. Knepper, p	5	0	0	0	0	0	0	.000
N. Ryan, p	4	0	0	0	0	0	0	.000
T. Puhl	3	2	0	0	0	0	0	.667
J. Pankovits	2	0	0	0	0	0	0	.000
D. Lopes	2	0	0	0	0	1	0	.000

Errors: C. Reynolds (2), M. Scott, K. Bass, G. Davis, B. Hatcher, C. Kerfeld

Stolen Bases: B. Hatcher (3), K. Bass (2), B. Doran (2), T. Puhl

Individual Pitching

NEW YORK (EAST)

	W	L	ERA	IP	H	BB	SO	SV
D. Gooden	0	1	1.06	17	16	5	9	0
B. Ojeda	1	0	2.57	14	15	4	6	0
J. Orosco	3	0	3.38	8	5	2	10	0
R. McDowell	0	0	4.04	7	1	0	3	0
S. Fernandez	0	1	4.50	6	3	1	5	0
R. Darling	0	0	7.20	5	6	2	5	0
R. Aguilera	0	0	0.00	5	2	2	2	0
D. Sisk	0	0	0.00	1	1	1	0	0

HOUSTON (WEST)

	W	L	ERA	IP	H	BB	SO	SV
M. Scott	2	0	0.50	18	8	1	19	0
B. Knepper	0	0	3.52	15.1	13	1	9	0
N. Ryan	0	1	3.86	14	9	1	17	0
L. Andersen	0	0	0.00	5	1	2	3	0
C. Kerfeld	0	1	2.25	4	2	1	4	0
A. Lopez	0	1	8.10	3.1	7	4	3	0
D. Smith	0	1	9.00	2	2	3	2	0
J. Calhoun	0	0	9.00	1	1	1	0	0

1986 AMERICAN LEAGUE CHAMPIONSHIP SERIES

LINE SCORES	PITCHERS (innings pitched)	HOME RUNS (men on)	HIGHLIGHTS

Boston (East) defeats California (West) 4 games to 3

GAME 1 - OCTOBER 7

CAL W 041 000 030   8 11 0   Witt (9)

BOS E 000 001 000   1 5 1   Clemens (7.1), Sambito (0.1), Stanley (1.1)

Witt shut down the Red Sox on five hits as the Angels reached 24-game winner Clemens for four in the second after two were out.

GAME 2 - OCTOBER 8

CAL W 000 110 000   2 11 3   McCaskill (7), Lucas (0.2), Corbett (0.1)   Joyner

BOS E 110 010 33x   9 13 2   Hurst (9)   Rice (1 on)

In a sloppy game played in late afternoon sun, Boston evened the LCS as Grich lost Evans's pop double in the fifth, and three Angel errors led to three Boston runs in the 7th.

GAME 3 - OCTOBER 10

BOS E 010 000 020   3 9 1   Boyd (6.2), Sambito (0.1), Schiraldi (1)

CAL W 000 001 31x   5 8 0   Candelaria (7), Moore (2) SV   Schofield, Pettis (1 on)

Seventh-inning homers by Schofield and Pettis off Boston starter Boyd lifted the Angels to the win.

GAME 4 - OCTOBER 11

BOS E 000 001 020 00   3 6 1   Clemens (8.1), Schiraldi (2)

CAL W 000 000 003 01   4 11 2   Sutton (6.1), Lucas (0.1), Ruhle (0.2), Finley (0), Corbett (3.2)   DeCinces

Schiraldi hit Downing with two out and the bases loaded to force in the tying run in the ninth, and Grich's single in the 11th drove in Narron with the game-winner.

GAME 5 - OCTOBER 12

BOS E 020 000 004 01   7 12 0   Hurst (6), Stanley (2.1), Sambito (0) Crawford (1.2), Schiraldi (1) SV   Henderson (1 on)

CAL W 001 002 201 00   6 13 0   Witt (8.2), Lucas (0), Moore (2), Finley (0.1)   Boone, Grich (1 on)

Henderson's dramatic two-out two-run homer with the Red Sox one strike away from elimination gave Boston a 6-5 lead. Wilfong's single tied the game in the bottom of the ninth, but a Henderson sacrifice fly in the 11th proved the winner and sent the LCS back to Boston.

GAME 6 - OCTOBER 14

CAL W 200 000 110   4 11 1   McCaskill (2.1), Lucas (1.1), Corbett (2.2), Finley (1.2)   Downing

BOS E 205 010 20x   10 16 1   Boyd (7), Stanley (2)

Boston batted around in the third, battering McCaskill for the second time in the LCS. Owen had four hits for Boston, and Barrett had three.

GAME 7 - OCTOBER 15

CAL W 000 000 010   1 6 2   Candelaria (3.2), Sutton (3.1), Moore (1)

BOS E 030 400 10x   8 8 1   Clemens (7.0), Schiraldi (2)   Rice (2 on), Evans

Errors by Schofield and Pettis led to seven unearned runs off Candelaria and sealed the victory for Boston, extending Gene Mauch's streak to 25 years of managing without a pennant.

Team totals

		W	AB	H	2B	3B	HR	R	RBI	BA	BB	SO	ERA
BOS	E	4	254	69	11	2	6	41	35	.272	19	31	3.58
CAL	W	3	256	71	11	0	7	30	29	.277	20	44	3.94

Individual Batting

BOSTON (EAST)

	AB	H	2B	3B	HR	R	RBI	BA
J. Rice, of	31	5	1	0	2	8	6	.161
M. Barrett, 2b	30	11	2	0	0	4	5	.367
W. Boggs, 3b	30	7	1	1	0	3	2	.233
B. Buckner, 1b	28	6	1	0	0	3	3	.214
R. Gedman, c	28	10	1	0	1	4	6	.357
D. Evans, of	28	6	1	0	1	2	4	.214
D. Baylor, dh	26	9	3	0	1	6	2	.346
S. Owen, ss	21	9	0	1	0	5	3	.429
T. Armas, of	16	2	1	0	0	1	0	.125
D. Henderson, of	9	1	0	0	1	3	4	.111
D. Stapleton, 1b	3	2	0	0	0	2	0	.667
E. Romero, ss	2	0	0	0	0	0	0	.000
M. Greenwell	2	1	0	0	0	0	0	.500

Errors: S. Owen (5), W. Boggs (2)

Stolen Bases: S. Owen

CALIFORNIA (WEST)

	AB	H	2B	3B	HR	R	RBI	BA
D. DeCinces, 3b	32	9	3	0	1	2	3	.281
D. Schofield, ss	30	9	1	0	1	4	2	.300
B. Downing, of	27	6	0	0	1	2	7	.222
G. Pettis, of	26	9	1	0	1	4	4	.346
R. Jackson, dh	26	5	2	0	0	2	2	.192
B. Grich, 2b, 1b	24	5	0	0	1	1	3	.208
B. Boone, c	22	10	0	0	1	4	2	.455
R. Jones, of	17	3	1	0	0	4	2	.176
R. Wilfong, 2b	13	4	1	0	0	1	2	.308
G. Hendrick, 1b, of	12	1	0	0	0	0	0	.083
R. Burleson, 2b, dh	11	3	0	0	0	0	0	.273
W. Joyner, 1b	11	5	2	0	1	3	2	.455
D. White, of	2	1	0	0	0	2	0	.500
J. Narron, c	2	1	0	0	0	1	0	.500
J. Howell	1	0	0	0	0	0	0	.000

Errors: B. Grich (3), D. Schofield (2), D. DeCinces (2), G. Pettis

Stolen Bases: D. Schofield

Individual Pitching

BOSTON (EAST)

	W	L	ERA	IP	H	BB	SO	SV
R. Clemens	1	1	4.37	22.2	22	7	17	0
B. Hurst	1	0	2.40	15	18	1	8	0
O. Boyd	1	1	4.61	13.2	17	3	8	0
C. Schiraldi	0	1	1.50	6	5	3	9	1
B. Stanley	0	0	4.76	5.2	7	3	1	0
S. Crawford	1	0	0.00	1.2	1	2	1	0
J. Sambito	0	0	0.00	0.2	1	1	0	0

CALIFORNIA (WEST)

	W	L	ERA	IP	H	BB	SO	SV
M. Witt	1	0	2.55	17.2	13	2	8	0
Candelaria	1	1	0.84	10.2	11	6	7	0
D. Sutton	0	0	1.86	9.2	6	1	4	0
McCaskill	0	2	7.71	9.1	16	5	7	0
D. Corbett	1	0	5.40	6.2	9	2	2	0
D. Moore	0	1	7.20	5	8	2	0	1
G. Lucas	0	0	11.57	2.1	3	1	2	0
C. Finley	0	0	0.00	2	1	0	1	0
V. Ruhle	0	0	13.50	0.2	2	0	0	0

1986 WORLD SERIES

LINE SCORES	PITCHERS (innings pitched)	HOME RUNS (men on)	HIGHLIGHTS

New York (N.L.) defeats Boston (A.L.) 4 games to 3

GAME 1 - OCTOBER 18

BOS A 000 000 100   1 5 0   Hurst (8), Schiraldi (1) SV

NY N 000 000 000   0 4 1   Darling (7), McDowell (2)

A walk to Rice, a wild pitch, and Teufel's error led to the only run of the game as Hurst allowed the Mets just four singles.

GAME 2 - OCTOBER 19

BOS A 003 120 201   9 18 0   Clemens (4.1), Crawford (1.2), Stanley (3) SV   Henderson, Evans (1 on)

NY N 002 010 000   3 8 1   Gooden (5), Aguilera (1.0), Orosco (2), Fernandez (0.1), Sisk (0.2)

Boston exploded for eighteen hits to take a 2-0 lead in the Series, as the much ballyhooed Clemens-Gooden matchup failed to last through the fifth.

GAME 3 - OCTOBER 21

NY N 400 000 210   7 13 0   Ojeda (7), McDowell (2)   Dykstra

BOS A 001 000 000   1 5 0   Boyd (7), Sambito (0), Stanley (2)

Dykstra's leadoff homer triggered a four-run outburst in the first. Ojeda earned the win against the team that sent him to the Mets the previous winter.

GAME 4 - OCTOBER 22

NY N 000 300 210   6 12 0   Darling (7), McDowell (0.2), Orosco (1.1) SV   Carter (1 on), Dykstra (1 on), Carter

BOS A 000 000 020   2 7 1   Nipper (6), Crawford (2), Stanley (1)

Carter's two homers, combined with Darling's seven innings of four-hit pitching, helped even the Series at two games apiece.

GAME 5 - OCTOBER 23

NY N 000 000 011   2 10 1   Gooden (4.0), Fernandez (4)   Teufel

BOS A 011 020 00x   4 12 0   Hurst (9)

Hurst scattered 10 hits for his second victory, as the Red Sox became the first home team to lead in any game.

GAME 6 - OCTOBER 25

BOS A 110 000 100 2   5 13 3   Clemens (7), Schiraldi (2.2), Stanley (0)   Henderson

NY N 000 020 010 3   6 8 2   Ojeda (6), McDowell (1.2), Orosco (0.1), Aguilera (2)

With two out and nobody on in the bottom of the tenth, the Mets staged one of the most dramatic comebacks in World Series history. Twice a strike away from elimination, they bunched three singles, a Stanley wild pitch, and a grounder through Buckner's legs for a miraculous come-from-behind victory.

GAME 7 - OCTOBER 27

BOS A 030 000 020   5 9 0   Hurst (6), Schiraldi (0.1), Sambito (0.1), Stanley (0.1), Nipper (0.1), Crawford (0.2)   Evans, Gedman

NY N 000 003 32x   8 10 0   Darling (3.2), Fernandez (2.1), McDowell (1.0), Orosco (2) SV   Knight, Strawberry

Knight's leadoff homer in the seventh proved the game-winning blow as the Mets overcame a 3-0 deficit to win the Series. For Boston, it was the fourth Series appearance since their last win in '18, all seven-game defeats.

Team totals

		W	AB	H	2B	3B	HR	R	RBI	BA	BB	SO	ERA
NY	N	4	240	65	6	0	7	32	29	.271	21	43	3.29
BOS	A	3	248	69	11	2	5	27	26	.278	28	53	4.31

Individual Batting

NEW YORK (N.L.)

	AB	H	2B	3B	HR	R	RBI	BA
G. Carter, c	29	8	2	0	2	4	9	.276
L. Dykstra, of	27	8	0	0	2	4	3	.296
K. Hernandez, 1b	26	6	0	0	0	1	4	.231
M. Wilson, of	26	7	1	0	0	3	0	.269
Strawberry, of	24	5	1	0	1	4	1	.208
R. Knight, 3b	23	9	1	0	1	4	5	.391
R. Santana, ss	20	5	0	0	0	3	2	.250
W. Backman, 2b	18	6	0	0	0	4	1	.333
D. Heep, dh, of	11	1	0	0	0	0	2	.091
T. Teufel, 2b	9	4	1	0	1	1	1	.444
K. Mitchell, of, dh	8	2	0	0	0	1	0	.250
L. Mazzilli, of, dh	5	2	0	0	0	2	0	.400
H. Johnson, 3b, ss	5	0	0	0	0	0	0	.000
R. Darling, p	3	0	0	0	0	0	0	.000
D. Gooden, p	2	1	0	0	0	1	0	.500
B. Ojeda, p	2	0	0	0	0	0	0	.000
J. Orosco, p	1	1	0	0	0	0	1	1.000
K. Elster, ss	1	0	0	0	0	0	0	.000

Errors: K. Hernandez, R. Knight, R. Santana, T. Teufel, K. Elster
Stolen Bases: M. Wilson (3), Strawberry (3), W. Backman

BOSTON (A.L.)

	AB	H	2B	3B	HR	R	RBI	BA
B. Buckner, 1b	32	6	0	0	0	2	1	.188
W. Boggs, 3b	31	9	3	0	0	3	3	.290
M. Barrett, 2b	30	13	2	0	0	1	4	.433
R. Gedman, c	30	6	1	0	1	1	1	.200
J. Rice, of	27	9	1	1	0	6	0	.333
D. Evans, of	26	8	2	0	2	4	9	.308
D. Henderson, of	25	10	1	1	2	6	5	.400
S. Owen, ss	20	6	0	0	0	2	2	.300
D. Baylor, dh	11	2	1	0	0	1	1	.182
R. Clemens, p	4	0	0	0	0	1	0	.000
M. Greenwell	3	0	0	0	0	0	0	.000
B. Hurst, p	3	0	0	0	0	0	0	.000
E. Romero, ss	1	0	0	0	0	0	0	.000
B. Stanley, p	1	0	0	0	0	0	0	.000
D. Stapleton, 1b	1	0	0	0	0	0	0	.000
S. Crawford, p	1	0	0	0	0	0	0	.000
T. Armas	1	0	0	0	0	0	0	.000
C. Schiraldi, p	1	0	0	0	0	0	0	.000

Errors: R. Gedman (2), D. Evans, B. Buckner

Individual Pitching

NEW YORK (N.L.)

	W	L	ERA	IP	H	BB	SO	SV
R. Darling	1	1	1.53	17.2	13	10	12	0
B. Ojeda	1	0	2.08	13	13	5	9	0
D. Gooden	0	2	8.00	9	17	4	9	0
R. McDowell	1	0	4.91	7.1	10	6	2	0
S. Fernandez	0	0	1.35	6.2	6	1	10	0
J. Orosco	0	0	0.00	5.2	2	0	6	2
R. Aguilera	1	0	12.00	3	8	1	4	0
D. Sisk	0	0	0.00	0.2	0	1	1	0

BOSTON (A.L.)

	W	L	ERA	IP	H	BB	SO	SV
B. Hurst	2	0	1.96	23	18	6	17	0
R. Clemens	0	0	3.18	11.1	9	6	11	0
O. Boyd	0	1	7.71	7	9	1	3	0
A. Nipper	0	1	7.11	6.1	10	2	2	0
B. Stanley	0	0	0.00	6.1	5	1	4	1
S. Crawford	1	0	6.23	4.1	5	4	4	0
C. Schiraldi	0	2	13.50	4	7	3	2	1
J. Sambito	0	0	27.00	0.1	2	2	0	0

1987 NATIONAL LEAGUE CHAMPIONSHIP SERIES

LINE SCORES	PITCHERS (innings pitched)	HOME RUNS (men on)	HIGHLIGHTS

St. Louis (East) defeats San Francisco (West) 4 games to 3

GAME 1 - OCTOBER 6

SF W 100 100 010   3 7 1   Reuschel (6), Lefferts (1), Garrelts (1)   Leonard   Mathews allowed four hits over seven innings and singled in two runs in a three run sixth that gave the Cards a win in the series opener.
STL E 001 103 00x   5 10 1   **Mathews** (7.1), Worrell (0.1), Dayley (1.1) **SV**

GAME 2 - OCTOBER 7

SF W 020 100 020   5 10 0   **Dravecky** (9)   W. Clark (1 on), Leonard   Dravecky hurled a two hitter and Will Clark and Jeff Leonard supplied the firepower as the Giants evened the series.
STL E 000 000 000   0 2 1   Tudor (8), Forsch (1)

GAME 3 - OCTOBER 9

STL E 000 002 400   6 11 1   Magrane (4), **Forsch** (2), Worrell (3) **SV**   Lindeman (1 on)   Lindeman drove in three runs with a home run and a sacrifice fly to give the Cards a 2-1 lead in the series. The Cards trailed 4-0 after five innings.
SF W 031 000 001   5 7 1   Hammaker (6.0), **Robinson** (0), Lefferts (1), LaCoss (2)   Leonard, Spilman

GAME 4 - OCTOBER 10

STL E 020 000 000   2 9 0   **Cox** (8)   Leonard homered in his fourth consecutive game, his homer coming with one on in the fifth to give the Giants the lead in a 4-2 victory as Mike Krukow went the distance giving up nine hits.
SF W 000 120 01x   4 9 4   Krukow (9)   Leonard (1 on), Thompson, Brenly

GAME 5 - OCTOBER 11

STL E 101 100 000   3 7 0   Mathews (3), **Forsch** (0), Horton (3), Dayley (2)   Uribe delivered a two run single to highlight a four run fourth inning and Joe Price pitched five innings of one hit shutout relief to earn the victory, giving the Giants a 3-2 lead.
SF W 101 400 00x   6 7 1   Reuschel (4), **Price** (5)   Mitchell

GAME 6 - OCTOBER 13

SF W 000 000 000   0 6 0   **Dravecky** (6), Robinson (2)   Pena tripled in the second inning and scored on Oquendo's short sacrfice fly to account for the only run as three Cardinal pitchers combined on a six hitter.
STL E 010 000 00x   1 5 0   Tudor (7.2), Worrell (1), Dayley (.2) **SV**

GAME 7 - OCTOBER 14

SF W 000 000 000   0 8 1   Hammaker (2), Price (0.2), Downs (1.1), Garrelts (1.2), Lefferts (0), LaCoss (1.1), Robinson (1)   Cox scattered eight hits and Oquendo belted a three run homer as the Cards captured the NL Pennant in seven games. The Giants were held scoreless over the last 22 innings.
STL E 040 002 00x   6 12 0   **Cox** (9)   Oquendo (2 on)

Team totals

		W	AB	H	2B	3B	HR	R	RBI	BA	BB	SO	ERA
STL	E	4	215	56	4	4	2	23	22	.260	16	42	2.95
SF	W	3	226	54	7	1	9	23	20	.239	17	51	3.30

Individual Batting

ST. LOUIS (EAST)

	AB	H	2B	3B	HR	R	RBI	BA
T. Herr, 2b	27	6	0	0	0	0	3	.222
V. Coleman, of	26	7	1	0	0	3	4	.269
W. McGee, of	26	8	1	1	0	2	2	.308
O. Smith, ss	25	5	0	1	0	2	1	.200
T. Pena, c	21	8	0	1	0	5	0	.381
T. Pendleton, 3b	19	4	0	1	0	3	1	.211
J. Lindeman, 1b	13	4	0	0	1	1	3	.308
D. Driessen, 1b	12	3	2	0	0	1	1	.250
J. Oquendo, 3b, of	12	2	0	0	1	3	4	.167
C. Ford, of	9	3	0	0	0	2	0	.333
D. Cox, p	6	2	0	0	0	0	1	.333
T. Lawless, 3b, of	6	2	0	0	0	0	0	.333
J. Tudor, p	4	0	0	0	0	0	0	.000
J. Morris, of	3	0	0	0	0	0	0	.000
G. Mathews, p	2	2	0	0	0	0	2	1.000
T. Worrell, of, p	1	0	0	0	0	0	0	.000
J. Magrane, p	1	0	0	0	0	0	0	.000
T. Pagnozzi, c	1	0	0	0	0	0	0	.000
J. Clark, 1b	1	0	0	0	0	0	0	.000
L. Johnson, of	0	0	0	0	0	1	0	—

Errors: O. Smith, T. Herr, D. Driessen
Stolen Bases: T. Herr, T. Pena, V. Coleman, L. Johnson

SAN FRANCISCO (WEST)

	AB	H	2B	3B	HR	R	RBI	BA
K. Mitchell, 3b	30	8	1	0	1	2	2	.267
J. Uribe, ss	26	7	1	0	0	1	2	.269
W. Clark, 1b	25	9	2	0	1	3	3	.360
J. Leonard, of	24	10	0	0	4	5	5	.417
C. Davis, of	20	3	1	0	0	2	0	.150
R. Thompson, 2b	20	2	0	1	1	4	2	.100
C. Maldonado, of	19	4	1	0	0	2	2	.211
B. Brenly, c	17	4	1	0	1	3	2	.235
M. Aldrete, of	10	1	0	0	0	0	1	.100
B. Melvin, c	7	3	0	0	0	0	0	.429
E. Milner, of	7	1	0	0	0	0	0	.143
D. Dravecky, p	6	1	0	0	0	0	0	.167
C. Speier, 2b	5	0	0	0	0	0	0	.000
A. Hammaker, p	3	0	0	0	0	0	0	.000
R. Reuschel, p	2	0	0	0	0	0	0	.000
H. Spilman, 1b	2	1	0	0	1	1	1	.500
M. Krukow, p	2	0	0	0	0	0	0	.000
J. Price, p	1	0	0	0	0	0	0	.000

Errors: C. Davis, R. Reuschel, J. Uribe, K. Mitchell, W. Clark, R. Thompson
Stolen Bases: R. Thompson (2), J. Uribe, K. Mitchell, W. Clark

Individual Pitching

ST. LOUIS (EAST)

	W	L	ERA	IP	H	BB	SO	SV
D. Cox	1	1	2.12	17	17	3	11	0
J. Tudor	1	1	1.76	15.1	16	5	12	0
G. Mathews	1	0	3.48	10.1	6	3	10	0
J. Magrane	0	0	9.00	4	4	2	3	0
K. Dayley	0	0	0.00	4	1	2	4	2
T. Worrell	0	2	2.08	4.1	4	1	6	1
R. Horton	0	0	0.00	3	2	0	2	0
B. Forsch	1	1	12.00	3	4	1	3	0

SAN FRANCISCO (WEST)

	W	L	ERA	IP	H	BB	SO	SV
D. Dravecky	1	1	0.60	15	7	4	14	0
R. Reuschel	0	1	6.30	10	15	2	2	0
M. Krukow	1	0	2.00	9	9	1	3	0
A. Hammaker	0	1	7.88	8	12	0	7	0
J. Price	1	0	0.00	5.2	3	1	7	0
M. LaCoss	0	0	0.00	3.1	1	3	2	0
D. Robinson	0	1	9.00	3	3	0	3	0
S. Garrelts	0	0	6.75	2.2	2	4	4	0
C. Lefferts	0	0	0.00	2	3	1	0	0
K. Downs	0	0	0.00	1.1	1	0	0	0

1987 AMERICAN LEAGUE CHAMPIONSHIP SERIES

LINE SCORES	PITCHERS (innings pitched)	HOME RUNS (men on)	HIGHLIGHTS

Minnesota (West) defeats Detroit (East) 4 games to 1

GAME 1 - OCTOBER 7

DET E 001 001 120 5 10 0 — Alexander, (7.1), Henneman (0), Hernandez (0.1), King (0.1) — Gibson, Heath (1 on)

MIN W 010 030 04x 8 10 0 — Viola (7), **Reardon** (2) — Gaetti, Gaetti

An RBI double by Puckett, a pinch single by Baylor, and a two run double by Brunansky in the eighth inning rallied the Twins to victory. Gaetti homered twice for the winners.

GAME 2 - OCTOBER 8

DET E 020 000 010 3 7 1 — **Morris** (8) — Lemon (1 on), Whitaker

MIN W 030 210 00x 6 6 0 — Blyleven (7.1), Berenguer (1.2) **SV** — Hrbek

Laudner and Gladden drove in two runs apiece and Hrbek added a solo home run to give the Twins a 2-0 edge in the series.

GAME 3 - OCTOBER 10

MIN W 000 202 200 6 8 1 — Straker (2.2), Schatzeder (3.1), Berenguer (1), **Reardon** (1) — Gagne, Brunansky (1 on)

DET E 005 000 02x 7 7 0 — Terrell (6.0), **Henneman** (3) — Sheridan (1 on)

The Tigers squandered a 5-0 lead, but won in the eighth on Pat Sheridan's two run homer. It was Detroit's finest hour.

GAME 4 - OCTOBER 11

MIN W 001 111 010 5 7 1 — Viola (5), Atherton (0.1), Berenguer (2.2), **Reardon** (1) **SV** — Puckett, Gagne

DET E 100 011 000 3 7 3 — **Tanana** (5.1), Petry (3.1), Thurmond (0.1)

Solo homers by Puckett and Gagne powered the Twins to their first victory on the road and a 3-1 series advantage.

GAME 5 - OCTOBER 12

MIN W 040 000 113 9 15 1 — Blyleven (6), Schatzeder (1), Berenguer (0.2), Reardon (1.1) **SV** — Brunansky

DET E 000 300 011 5 9 1 — **Alexander** (1.2), King (5), Henneman (2), Robinson (0.1) — Lemon, Nokes (1 on)

Brunansky's two run double and RBI singles by Gladden and Puckett produced four second inning runs that propelled the Twins to their first AL Pennant since 1965.

Team totals

		W	AB	H	2B	3B	HR	R	RBI	BA	BB	SO	ERA
MIN	W	4	171	46	13	1	8	34	33	.269	20	25	4.50
DET	E	1	167	40	4	0	7	23	21	.240	18	35	6.70

Individual Batting

MINNESOTA (WEST)

	AB	H	2B	3B	HR	R	RBI	BA
K. Puckett, of	24	5	1	0	1	3	3	.208
D. Gladden, of	20	7	2	0	0	5	5	.350
G. Gaetti, 3b	20	6	1	0	2	5	5	.300
K. Hrbek, 1b	20	3	0	0	1	4	1	.150
G. Gagne, ss	18	5	3	0	2	5	3	.278
T. Brunansky, of	17	7	4	0	2	5	9	.412
Lombardozzi, 2b	15	4	0	0	0	2	1	.267
T. Laudner, c	14	1	1	0	0	1	2	.071
R. Bush, dh	12	3	0	1	0	4	2	.250
D. Baylor, dh	5	2	0	0	0	0	1	.400
S. Butera, c	3	2	0	0	0	0	0	.667
A. Newman, 2b	2	0	0	0	0	0	0	.000
G. Larkin, of	1	1	1	0	0	0	1	1.000
M. Davidson, of	0	0	0	0	0	0	0	—

Errors: G. Gagne (2), Lombardozzi
Stolen Bases: R. Bush (3), K. Puckett

DETROIT (EAST)

	AB	H	2B	3B	HR	R	RBI	BA
K. Gibson, of	21	6	1	0	1	4	4	.286
A. Trammell, ss	20	4	1	0	0	3	2	.200
C. Lemon, of	18	5	0	0	2	4	4	.278
L. Whitaker, 2b	17	3	0	0	1	4	1	.176
D. Evans, 1b, 3b	17	5	0	0	0	0	0	.294
M. Nokes, c, dh	14	2	0	0	1	2	2	.143
T. Brookens, 3b	13	0	0	0	0	0	0	.000
P. Sheridan, of	10	3	1	0	1	2	2	.300
L. Herndon, of, dh	9	3	1	0	0	1	2	.333
J. Grubb, dh	7	4	0	0	0	0	0	.571
M. Heath, c	7	2	0	0	1	1	2	.286
J. Morrison, 3b, dh	5	2	0	0	0	1	0	.400
B. Madlock, dh	5	0	0	0	0	0	0	.000
D. Bergman, 1b, dh	4	1	0	0	0	0	2	.250
J. Morris, p	0	0	0	0	0	1	0	—

Errors: D. Evans (3), L. Herndon, A. Trammell
Stolen Bases: K. Gibson (3), P. Sheridan, L. Whitaker

Individual Pitching

MINNESOTA (WEST)

	W	L	ERA	IP	H	BB	SO	SV
B. Blyleven	2	0	4.05	13.1	12	3	9	0
F. Viola	1	0	5.25	12	14	5	9	0
J. Berenguer	0	0	1.50	6	1	3	6	1
J. Reardon	1	1	5.06	5.1	7	3	5	2
Schatzeder	0	0	0.00	4.1	2	0	5	0
L. Straker	0	0	16.88	2.2	3	4	1	0
K. Atherton	0	0	0.00	0.1	1	0	0	0

DETROIT (EAST)

	W	L	ERA	IP	H	BB	SO	SV
D. Alexander	0	2	10.00	9	14	1	5	0
J. Morris	0	1	6.75	8	6	3	7	0
W. Terrell	0	0	9.00	6	7	4	4	0
E. King	0	0	1.69	5.1	3	2	4	0
F. Tanana	0	1	5.06	5.1	6	4	1	0
M. Henneman	1	0	10.80	5	6	6	3	0
D. Petry	0	0	0.00	3.1	1	0	1	0
M. Thurmond	0	0	0.00	0.1	0	0	0	0
G. Hernandez	0	0	0.00	0.1	2	0	0	0
J. Robinson	0	0	0.00	0.1	1	0	0	0

1987 WORLD SERIES

LINE SCORES	PITCHERS (innings pitched)	HOME RUNS (men on)	HIGHLIGHTS

Minnesota (A.L.) defeats St. Louis (N.L.) 4 games to 3

GAME 1 · OCTOBER 17

STL	N	010 000 000	1 5 1	Magrane (3.0), Forsch (3), Horton (2)
MIN	A	000 720 10x	10 11 0	Viola (8), Atherton (1)

Gladden (3 on), Lombardozzi (1 on)

Gladden highlighted the seven run fourth inning with a grand slam and Viola allowed five hits in eight innings as the Twins won the opener.

GAME 2 · OCTOBER 18

STL	N	000 010 120	4 9 0	Cox (3.2), Tunnell (2.1), Dayley (1.1), Worrell (0.2)
MIN	A	010 601 00x	8 10 0	Blyleven (7), Berenguer (1), Reardon (1)

Gaetti, Laudner

Bush's bases loaded double highlighted a six run fourth inning as the Twins romped to their second straight win.

GAME 3 · OCTOBER 20

MIN	A	000 001 000	1 5 1	Straker (6), Berenguer (0.1), Schatzeder (1.2)
STL	N	000 000 30x	3 9 1	Tudor (7), Worrell (2) SV

Coleman doubled home two runs as the Cardinals rallied against reliever Berenguer for three runs in the seventh to overcome a 1-0 Twins lead.

GAME 4 · OCTOBER 21

MIN	A	001 010 000	2 7 1	Viola (3.1), Schatzeder (0.2), Niekro (2), Frazier (2)
STL	N	001 600 00x	7 10 1	Mathews (3.2), Forsch (2.2), Dayley (2.2) SV

Gagne

Lawless (2 on)

Three run homer by Lawless sparked a six run fourth inning as the Cards evened the Series at 2-2.

GAME 5 · OCTOBER 22

MIN	A	000 000 020	2 6 1	Blyleven (6), Atherton (0.1), Reardon (1.2)
STL	N	000 003 10x	4 10 0	Cox (7.1), Dayley (0.1), Worrell (1.1) SV

Ford's bases loaded single with two out in the sixth inning broke up a scoreless pitching duel between Cox and Blyleven, giving the Cards a 3-2 Series lead.

GAME 6 · OCTOBER 24

STL	N	110 210 000	5 11 2	Tudor (4.0), Horton (1.0), Forsch (0.2), Dayley (0.1), Tunnell (2)
MIN	A	200 044 01x	11 15 0	Straker (3.0), Schatzeder (2), Berenguer (3), Reardon (1)

Herr

Baylor (1 on), Hrbek (3 on)

Baylor hit a game-tying two run homer in the fifth inning and Hrbek hit a grand slam in the sixth as the Twins tied the Series 3-3.

GAME 7 · OCTOBER 25

STL	N	020 000 000	2 6 1	Magrane (4.1), Cox (0.2), Worrell (3)
MIN	A	010 011 01x	4 10 0	Viola (8), Reardon (1) SV

Viola pitched a six-hitter for eight innings to post his second Series win and bring the Minnesota Twins their first World Championship.

Team totals

		W	AB	H	2B	3B	HR	R	RBI	BA	BB	SO	ERA
MIN	A	4	238	64	10	3	7	38	38	.269	29	36	3.75
STL	N	3	232	60	8	0	2	26	25	.259	13	44	5.64

Individual Batting

MINNESOTA (A.L.)

	AB	H	2B	3B	HR	R	RBI	BA
D. Gladden, of	31	9	2	1	1	3	7	.290
G. Gagne, ss	30	6	1	0	1	5	3	.200
K. Puckett, of	28	10	1	1	0	5	3	.357
G. Gaetti, 3b	27	7	2	1	1	4	4	.259
T. Brunansky, of	25	5	0	0	0	5	2	.200
K. Hrbek, 1b	24	5	0	0	1	4	6	.208
T. Laudner, c	22	7	1	0	1	4	4	.318
Lombardozzi, 2b	17	7	1	0	1	3	4	.412
D. Baylor, dh	13	5	0	0	1	3	3	.385
R. Bush, dh	6	1	1	0	0	1	2	.167
A. Newman, 2b	5	1	0	0	0	0	0	.200
G. Larkin, 1b, dh	3	0	0	0	0	1	0	.000
L. Straker, p	2	0	0	0	0	0	0	.000
R. Smalley, ss	2	1	1	0	0	0	0	.500
B. Blyleven, p	1	0	0	0	0	0	0	.000
F. Viola, p	1	0	0	0	0	0	0	.000
M. Davidson, of	1	0	0	0	0	0	0	.000
S. Butera, c	0	0	0	0	0	0	0	–

Errors: G. Gagne (2), K. Puckett
Stolen Bases: G. Gaetti (2), D. Gladden (2), T. Brunansky, K. Puckett

ST. LOUIS (N.L.)

	AB	H	2B	3B	HR	R	RBI	BA
V. Coleman, of	28	4	2	0	0	5	2	.143
O. Smith, ss	28	6	0	0	0	3	2	.214
T. Herr, 2b	28	7	0	0	1	2	1	.250
W. McGee, of	27	10	2	0	0	2	4	.370
J. Oquendo, 3b, of	24	6	0	0	0	2	2	.250
T. Pena, c, dh	22	9	1	0	0	2	4	.409
J. Lindeman, 1b, of	15	5	1	0	0	3	2	.333
C. Ford, of	13	4	0	0	0	1	2	.308
D. Driessen, 1b	13	3	2	0	0	3	1	.231
T. Lawless, 3b	10	1	0	0	1	1	3	.100
T. Pendleton, dh	7	3	0	0	0	2	1	.429
T. Pagnozzi, dh	4	1	0	0	0	0	0	.250
S. Lake, c	3	1	0	0	0	0	1	.333
J. Morris, of	2	0	0	0	0	0	0	.000
D. Cox, p	2	0	0	0	0	0	0	.000
J. Tudor, p	2	0	0	0	0	0	0	.000
B. Forsch, p	2	0	0	0	0	0	0	.000
K. Dayley, p	1	0	0	0	0	0	0	.000
G. Mathews, p	1	0	0	0	0	0	0	.000
L. Johnson, of	0	0	0	0	0	0	0	–

Errors: J. Lindeman (3), W. McGee, T. Pena, T. Lawless
Stolen Bases: V. Coleman (6), O. Smith (2), T. Pendleton (2), T. Pena, L. Johnson

Individual Pitching

MINNESOTA (A.L.)

	W	L	ERA	IP	H	BB	SO	SV
F. Viola	2	1	3.72	19.1	17	3	16	0
B. Blyleven	1	1	2.77	13	13	2	12	0
L. Straker	0	0	4.00	9	9	3	6	0
J. Reardon	0	0	0.00	4.2	5	0	3	1
Schatzeder	1	0	6.23	4.1	4	3	3	0
J. Berenguer	0	1	10.38	4.1	10	0	1	0
G. Frazier	0	0	0.00	2	1	0	2	0
J. Niekro	0	0	0.00	2	1	1	1	0
K. Atherton	0	0	6.75	1.1	0	1	0	0

ST. LOUIS (N.L.)

	W	L	ERA	IP	H	BB	SO	SV
D. Cox	1	2	7.71	11.2	13	8	9	0
J. Tudor	1	1	5.73	11	15	3	8	0
T. Worrell	0	0	1.29	7	6	4	3	2
J. Magrane	0	1	8.59	7.1	5	5	5	0
B. Forsch	1	0	9.95	6.1	8	5	3	0
K. Dayley	0	0	1.93	4.2	2	0	3	1
L. Tunnell	0	0	2.08	4.1	4	2	1	0
G. Mathews	0	0	2.45	3.2	2	2	3	0
R. Horton	0	0	6.00	3	5	0	1	0

1988 NATIONAL LEAGUE CHAMPIONSHIP SERIES

LINE SCORES	PITCHERS (innings pitched)	HOME RUNS (men on)	HIGHLIGHTS

Los Angeles (West) defeats New York (East) 4 games to 3

GAME 1 - OCTOBER 4

NY	E	000 000 003	3 8 1	Gooden (7), Myers (2)
LA	W	100 000 100	2 4 0	Hershiser (8.1), Howell (0.2)

New York rallied for three runs in the ninth inning to overcome a 2-0 deficit. Strawberry doubled home the first run against Hershiser, and Carter's 2-out bloop double off Howell plated the tying and winning runs.

GAME 2 - OCTOBER 5

NY	E	000 200 001	3 6 0	Cone (2), Aguilera (3), Leach (2), McDowell (1)
LA	W	140 010 00x	6 7 0	Belcher (8.1), Orosco (0), Pena (0.2) SV

Home Runs: Hernandez (1 on)

Los Angeles jumped to an early 5-0 lead behind the rookie Belcher, who struck out 10. Hernandez homered and drove in all three New York runs.

GAME 3 - OCTOBER 8

LA	W	021 000 010	4 7 2	Hershiser (7), Howell (0), Pena (0.2), Orosco (0), Horton (0.1)
NY	E	001 002 05x	8 9 2	Darling (6), McDowell (1.2), Myers (0.1), Cone (1)

New York sent 10 men to the plate during a 5 run eighth inning rally in which Dodger reliever Howell was ejected and subsequently suspended for having pine tar in his glove.

GAME 4 - OCTOBER 9

LA	W	200 000 002 001	5 7 1	Tudor (5), Holton (1), Horton (2), Pena (3), Leary (0.1), Orosco (0.1), Hershiser (0.1) SV
NY	E	000 301 000 000	4 10 2	Gooden (8.1), Myers (2.1), McDowell

Home Runs: Scioscia (1 on), Gibson; Strawberry (1 on), McReynolds

Scioscia belted a 2 run homer in the ninth inning off Gooden to tie the game, then Gibson connected off McDowell in the 12th as Los Angeles evened the series 2-2.

GAME 5 - OCTOBER 10

LA	W	000 330 001	7 12 0	Belcher (7), Horton (0.1), Holton (1.2) SV
NY	E	000 030 010	4 9 1	Fernandez (4.0), Leach (1), Aguilera (2), McDowell (2)

Home Runs: Gibson (2 on); Dykstra (2 on)

Dodgers scored three times in both the fourth and fifth innings and held off Mets to take series lead for the first time. Big blow was Gibson's three run homer which gave Los Angeles a 6-0 lead.

GAME 6 - OCTOBER 11

NY	E	101 021 000	5 11 0	Cone (9)
LA	W	000 010 000	1 5 2	Leary (4.0), Holton (1.1), Horton (1.2), Orosco (2)

Home Runs: McReynolds (1 on)

Cone went the distance on a five hitter, while McReynolds went 4 for 4 with a home run and 3 RBI as Mets forced a seventh game.

GAME 7 - OCTOBER 12

NY	E	000 000 000	0 5 2	Darling (1.0), Gooden (3), Leach (2), Aguilera (2)
LA	W	150 000 00x	6 10 0	Hershiser (9)

Los Angeles completed upset of heavily favored Mets, who had beaten them 10 times in 11 meetings during the regular season. Series MVP Hershiser pitched a 5 hit shutout to wrap up Dodgers' first flag in seven years.

Team totals

		W	AB	H	2B	3B	HR	R	RBI	BA	BB	SO	ERA
LA	W	4	243	52	7	1	3	31	30	.214	25	54	3.32
NY	E	3	240	58	12	1	5	27	27	.242	28	42	3.94

Individual Batting

LOS ANGELES (WEST)

	AB	H	2B	3B	HR	R	RBI	BA
M. Marshall, of	30	7	1	1	0	3	5	.233
S. Sax, 2b	30	8	0	0	0	7	3	.267
K. Gibson, of	26	4	0	0	2	2	6	.154
A. Griffin, ss	25	4	1	0	0	1	3	.160
J. Shelby, of	24	4	0	0	0	3	3	.167
J. Hamilton, 3b	23	5	0	0	0	2	1	.217
M. Scioscia, c	22	8	1	0	1	3	2	.364
M. Hatcher, 1b, of	21	5	2	0	0	4	3	.238
O. Hershiser, p	9	0	0	0	0	1	1	.000
F. Stubbs, 1b	8	2	0	0	0	0	0	.250
T. Belcher, p	8	1	0	0	0	1	0	.125
R. Dempsey, c	5	2	2	0	0	1	2	.400
T. Woodson, 1b	4	1	0	0	0	0	0	.250
J. Tudor, p	2	0	0	0	0	0	0	.000
M. Davis	2	0	0	0	0	0	0	.000
T. Leary, p	1	0	0	0	0	0	0	.000
D. Heep	1	0	0	0	0	0	0	.000
Sharperson, 3b, ss	1	0	0	0	0	0	1	.000
B. Holton, p	1	1	0	0	0	1	0	1.000
J. Gonzalez, of	0	0	0	0	0	2	0	–

Errors: M. Hatcher (2), J. Hamilton (2)
Stolen Bases: S. Sax (5), J. Shelby (2), K. Gibson (2)

NEW YORK (EAST)

	AB	H	2B	3B	HR	R	RBI	BA
Strawberry, of	30	9	2	0	1	5	6	.300
McReynolds, of	28	7	2	0	2	4	4	.250
G. Jefferies, 3b	27	9	2	0	0	2	1	.333
G. Carter, c	27	6	1	1	0	0	4	.222
K. Hernandez, 1b	26	7	0	0	1	2	5	.269
W. Backman, 2b	22	6	1	0	0	2	2	.273
H. Johnson, ss, 3b	18	1	0	0	0	3	0	.056
L. Dykstra, of	14	6	3	0	1	6	3	.429
M. Wilson, of	13	2	0	0	0	2	1	.154
K. Elster, ss	8	2	1	0	0	1	1	.250
M. Sasser, c	5	1	0	0	0	0	0	.200
D. Gooden, p	5	1	0	0	0	0	0	.200
D. Cone, p	4	0	0	0	0	0	0	.000
D. Magadan	3	0	0	0	0	0	0	.000
R. Darling, p	3	0	0	0	0	0	0	.000
T. Teufel, 2b	3	0	0	0	0	0	0	.000
L. Mazzilli	2	1	0	0	0	0	0	.500
S. Fernandez, p	1	0	0	0	0	0	0	.000
R. Aguilera, p	0	0	0	0	0	0	0	.000

Errors: K. Elster (2), W. Backman (2), H. Johnson, R. McDowell, K. Hernandez, G. Jefferies
Stolen Bases: McReynolds (2), K. Hernandez, L. Mazzilli, W. Backman, H. Johnson

Individual Pitching

LOS ANGELES (WEST)

	W	L	ERA	IP	H	BB	SO	SV
O. Hershiser	1	0	1.09	24.2	18	7	15	1
T. Belcher	2	0	4.11	15.1	12	4	16	0
J. Tudor	0	0	7.20	5	8	1	1	0
T. Leary	0	1	6.23	4.1	8	3	3	0
A. Pena	1	1	4.15	4.1	1	5	1	1
R. Horton	0	0	0.00	4.1	4	2	3	0
B. Holton	0	0	2.25	4	2	1	2	1
J. Orosco	0	0	7.71	2.1	4	3	0	0
J. Howell	0	1	27.00	0.2	1	2	1	0

NEW YORK (EAST)

	W	L	ERA	IP	H	BB	SO	SV
D. Gooden	0	0	2.95	18.1	10	8	20	0
D. Cone	1	1	4.50	12	10	5	9	0
R. Darling	0	1	7.71	7	11	4	7	0
R. Aguilera	0	0	1.29	7	3	2	4	0
R. McDowell	0	1	4.50	6	6	2	5	0
T. Leach	0	0	0.00	5	4	1	4	0
S. Fernandez	0	1	13.50	4	7	1	5	0
R. Myers	2	0	0.00	4.2	1	2	0	0

1988 AMERICAN LEAGUE CHAMPIONSHIP SERIES

LINE SCORES	PITCHERS (innings pitched)	HOME RUNS (men on)	HIGHLIGHTS

Oakland (West) defeats Boston (East) 4 games to 0

GAME 1 - OCTOBER 5

OAK W 000 100 010   2 6 0   Stewart (6.1), Honeycutt (0.2), Eckersley (2) **SV**   Canseco

BOS E 000 000 100   1 6 0   Hurst (9)

Henderson's eighth inning RBI single gave Oakland the series opener. A's scored on Canseco's fourth inning homer, before Boston drew even on sacrifice fly by Boggs in seventh. Hurst pitched a complete game in losing effort for Red Sox.

GAME 2 - OCTOBER 6

OAK W 000 000 301   4 10 1   Davis (6.1), Caderet (0.1), **Nelson** (1.1), Eckersley (1) **SV**   Canseco (1 on)

BOS E 000 002 100   3 4 1   Clemens (7), Stanley (0.1), **Smith** (1.2)   Gedman

Oakland posted their second consecutive late inning victory as Weiss singled home winning run in ninth inning. Boston scored twice in sixth to lead 2-0, but Oakland responded an inning later with Canseco's two run homer and McGwire's RBI single off Clemens. Boston tied it in bottom of the seventh on Gedman's homer.

GAME 3 - OCTOBER 8

BOS E 320 000 100   6 12 0   Boddicker (2.2), Gardner (4.2), Stanley (0.2)   McGwire,

OAK W 042 010 12x   10 15 1   Welch (1.2), **Nelson** (3.1), Young (1.1), Plunk (0.1), Honeycutt (0.1), Eckersley (2) **SV**   Lansford (1 on), Hassey (1 on), Henderson (1 on)

Oakland slammed four homers to charge back from early 5-0 deficit. McGwire's solo shot got Athletics on the board, then Lansford's 2 run homer brought them within a run in the second. Hassey gave them the lead for good an inning later with his two run homer. Henderson added another two run blast in the eighth to close out the scoring.

GAME 4 - OCTOBER 9

BOS E 000 001 000   1 4 0   Hurst (4), Smithson (2.1), Smith (1.2)

OAK W 101 000 02x   4 10 0   Stewart (7.0), Honeycutt (1), Eckersley (1) **SV**   Canseco

In winning their first pennant since 1974, Oakland became the first team to sweep a best-of-seven League Championship Series. Eckersley saved all 4 games to set a playoff record and win the series MVP award. Canseco hit his third homer of the series to open the scoring.

Team totals

		W	AB	H	2B	3B	HR	R	RBI	BA	BB	SO	ERA
OAK	W	4	137	41	8	0	7	20	20	.299	10	35	2.00
BOS	E	0	126	26	4	0	2	11	10	.206	18	23	5.29

Individual Batting

OAKLAND (WEST)

	AB	H	2B	3B	HR	R	RBI	BA
C. Lansford, 3b	17	5	1	0	1	4	2	.294
D. Henderson, of	16	6	1	0	1	2	4	.375
J. Canseco, of	16	5	1	0	3	4	4	.313
M. McGwire, 1b	15	5	0	0	1	4	3	.333
W. Weiss, ss	15	5	2	0	0	2	2	.333
D. Parker, of, dh	12	3	1	0	0	1	0	.250
M. Gallego, 2b	12	1	0	0	0	1	0	.083
R. Hassey, c	8	4	1	0	1	2	3	.500
T. Phillips, 2b, of	7	2	1	0	0	0	0	.286
D. Baylor, dh	6	0	0	0	0	0	1	.000
L. Polonia, of	5	2	0	0	0	0	0	.400
S. Javier, of	4	2	0	0	0	0	1	.500
T. Steinbach, c	4	1	0	0	0	0	0	.250

Errors: D. Henderson (2), D. Parker
Stolen Bases: J. Canseco

BOSTON (EAST)

	AB	H	2B	3B	HR	R	RBI	BA
E. Burks, of	17	4	1	0	0	2	1	.235
M. Barrett, 2b	15	1	0	0	0	2	0	.067
R. Gedman, c	14	5	0	0	1	1	1	.357
M. Greenwell, of	14	3	1	0	1	2	3	.214
W. Boggs, 3b	13	5	0	0	0	2	3	.385
J. Rice, dh	13	2	0	0	0	0	1	.154
D. Evans, of	12	2	1	0	0	1	1	.167
T. Benzinger, 1b	11	1	0	0	0	0	0	.091
J. Reed, ss	11	3	1	0	0	0	0	.273
L. Parrish, 1b, dh	6	0	0	0	0	0	0	.000
E. Romero	0	0	0	0	0	0	0	—
S. Owen	0	0	0	0	0	0	0	—
K. Romine	0	0	0	0	0	1	0	—

Errors: R. Clemens

Individual Pitching

OAKLAND (WEST)

	W	L	ERA	IP	H	BB	SO	SV
D. Stewart	1	0	1.35	13.1	9	6	11	0
D. Eckersley	0	0	0.00	6	1	2	5	4
S. Davis	0	0	0.00	6.1	2	5	4	0
G. Nelson	2	0	0.00	4.2	5	1	0	0
R. Honeycutt	1	0	0.00	2	0	2	0	0
B. Welch	0	0	27.00	1.2	6	2	0	0
C. Young	0	0	0.00	1.1	1	0	2	0
E. Plunk	0	0	0.00	0.1	1	1	0	0
G. Cadaret	0	0	27.00	0.1	1	0	0	0

BOSTON (EAST)

	W	L	ERA	IP	H	BB	SO	SV
B. Hurst	0	2	2.77	13	10	5	12	0
R. Clemens	0	0	3.86	7	6	0	8	0
W. Gardner	0	0	5.79	4.2	6	2	8	0
L. Smith	0	1	8.10	3.1	6	1	4	0
M. Smithson	0	0	0.00	2.1	3	0	1	0
M. Boddicker	0	1	20.25	2.2	8	1	2	0
B. Stanley	0	0	9.00	1	2	1	0	0

1988 WORLD SERIES

LINE SCORES	PITCHERS (innings pitched)	HOME RUNS (men on)	HIGHLIGHTS

Los Angeles (N.L.) defeats Oakland (A.L.) 4 games to 1

GAME 1 - OCTOBER 15

OAK A	040 000 000	4 7 0	Stewart (8), Eckersley (0.2)
LA N	200 001 002	5 7 0	Belcher (2), Leary (3), Holton (2), **Pena** (2)

Home Runs: Canseco (3 on); Hatcher (1 on), Gibson (1 on)

Highlights: Two out, two run pinch homer by Gibson in ninth off relief ace Eckersley gave Dodgers a dramatic Series opening victory. Grand slam by Canseco gave Oakland the lead until Gibson's blast. It was to be injured Gibson's only appearance in the Series.

GAME 2 - OCTOBER 16

OAK A	000 000 000	0 3 0	Davis (3.1), Nelson (1.2), Young (1), Plunk (1), Honeycutt (1)
LA N	005 100 00x	6 10 1	**Hershiser** (9)

Home Runs: Marshall (2 on)

Highlights: Hershiser limited Oakland to three hits while collecting three himself, as Los Angeles took a 2-0 series lead. Dodgers tallied five times in the third inning, capped by Marshall's 3 run homer. Parker had all three Oakland hits off Hershiser.

GAME 3 - OCTOBER 18

LA N	000 010 000	1 8 1	Tudor (1.1), Leary (3.2), Pena (3), **Howell** (0.1)
OAK A	001 000 001	2 5 0	Welch (5.0), Cadaret (0.1), Nelson (1.2), **Honeycutt** (2)

Home Runs: McGwire

Highlights: Ninth inning homer by McGwire powered Athletics to their only victory of the Series. Los Angeles left 10 runners on base and failed to capitalize on a bases loaded, nobody out opportunity in the sixth inning.

GAME 4 - OCTOBER 19

LA N	201 000 100	4 8 1	**Belcher** (6.2), Howell (2.1) SV
OAK A	100 001 100	3 9 2	Stewart (6.1), Cadaret (1.2), Eckersley (1)

Highlights: Los Angeles took advantage of sloppy fielding by Oakland to take a 3-1 lead in the Series. Errors by infielders Hubbard and Weiss, along with Steinbach's passed ball led to Dodgers' first three runs. Strong relief work by Howell saved win for Belcher.

GAME 5 - OCTOBER 20

LA N	200 201 000	5 8 0	**Hershiser** (9)
OAK A	001 000 010	2 4 0	Davis (4.2), Cadaret (0), Nelson (3) Honeycutt (0.1), Plunk (0.2), Burns (0.1)

Home Runs: Hatcher (1 on); Davis (1 on)

Highlights: Injury-riddled Dodgers climaxed a miraculous postseason by defeating Athletics 4 games to 1 to win their second World Championship of the 1980's. Series MVP Hershiser wrapped up the title with a 4 hitter, receiving support from Hatcher and Davis, who each smacked a two run homer.

Team totals

		W	AB	H	2B	3B	HR	R	RBI	BA	BB	SO	ERA
LA	N	4	167	41	8	1	5	21	19	.246	13	36	2.05
OAK	A	1	158	28	3	0	2	11	11	.177	17	41	3.89

Individual Batting

LOS ANGELES (N.L.)

	AB	H	2B	3B	HR	R	RBI	BA
S. Sax, 2b	20	6	0	0	0	3	0	.300
J. Hamilton, 3b	19	2	0	0	1	0	0	.105
M. Hatcher, of	19	7	1	0	2	5	5	.368
J. Shelby, of	18	4	1	0	0	0	1	.222
F. Stubbs, 1b	17	5	2	0	0	3	2	.294
A. Griffin, ss	16	3	0	0	0	2	0	.188
M. Scioscia, c	14	3	0	0	0	0	1	.214
M. Marshall, of	13	3	0	1	1	2	3	.231
D. Heep, of, dh	8	2	1	0	0	0	0	.250
M. Davis, dh, of	7	1	0	0	1	3	2	.143
R. Dempsey, c	5	1	1	0	0	0	1	.200
T. Woodson, 1b	4	0	0	0	0	0	1	.000
O. Hershiser, p	3	3	2	0	0	1	1	1.000
J. Gonzalez, of	2	0	0	0	0	0	0	.000
D. Anderson, dh	1	0	0	0	0	0	0	.000
K. Gibson	1	1	0	0	1	1	2	1.000

Errors: A. Griffin, M. Scioscia, J. Hamilton
Stolen Bases: M. Davis (2), S. Sax, J. Shelby

OAKLAND (A.L.)

	AB	H	2B	3B	HR	R	RBI	BA
D. Henderson, of	20	6	2	0	0	1	1	.300
J. Canseco, of	19	1	0	0	1	1	5	.053
C. Lansford, 3b	18	3	0	0	0	2	1	.167
M. McGwire, 1b	17	1	0	0	1	1	1	.059
W. Weiss, ss	16	1	0	0	0	1	0	.063
D. Parker, of, dh	15	3	0	0	0	0	0	.200
G. Hubbard, 2b	12	3	0	0	0	2	0	.250
T. Steinbach, c, dh	11	4	1	0	0	0	0	.364
L. Polonia, of	9	1	0	0	0	1	0	.111
R. Hassey, c	8	2	0	0	0	0	1	.250
T. Phillips, 2b, of	4	1	0	0	0	1	0	.250
S. Javier, of	4	2	0	0	0	0	2	.500
D. Stewart, p	3	0	0	0	0	1	0	.000
S. Davis, p	1	0	0	0	0	0	0	.000
D. Baylor	1	0	0	0	0	0	0	.000
M. Gallego, 2b	0	0	0	0	0	0	0	—

Errors: G. Hubbard, W. Weiss
Stolen Bases: G. Hubbard, J. Canseco, W. Weiss

Individual Pitching

LOS ANGELES (N.L.)

	W	L	ERA	IP	H	BB	SO	SV
O. Hershiser	2	0	1.00	18	7	6	17	0
T. Belcher	1	0	6.23	8.2	10	6	10	0
T. Leary	0	0	1.35	6.2	6	2	4	0
A. Pena	1	0	0.00	5	2	1	7	0
B. Holton	0	0	0.00	2	0	1	0	0
J. Howell	0	1	3.38	2.2	3	1	2	1
J. Tudor	0	0	0.00	1.1	0	0	1	0

OAKLAND (A.L.)

	W	L	ERA	IP	H	BB	SO	SV
D. Stewart	0	1	3.14	14.1	12	5	5	0
S. Davis	0	2	11.25	8	14	1	7	0
G. Nelson	0	0	1.42	6.1	4	3	3	0
B. Welch	0	0	1.80	5	6	3	8	0
R. Honeycutt	1	0	0.00	3.1	0	0	5	0
G. Cadaret	0	0	0.00	2	2	0	3	0
C. Young	0	0	0.00	1	1	0	0	0
E. Plunk	0	0	0.00	1.2	0	0	3	0
D. Eckersley	0	1	10.80	1.2	2	1	2	0
T. Burns	0	0	0.00	0.1	0	0	0	0

1989 NATIONAL LEAGUE CHAMPIONSHIP SERIES

LINE SCORES		PITCHERS (innings pitched)	HOME RUNS (men on)	HIGHLIGHTS

San Francisco (West) defeats Chicago (East) 4 games to 1

GAME 1 - OCTOBER 4

SF W 301 400 030   11 13 0   Garrelts (7), Brantley (1), Hammaker (1)

CHI E 201 000 000   3 10 0   Maddux (4), Kilgus (3), Wilson (2)

HOME RUNS: Clark, Clark (3 on), Mitchell (2 on), Grace (1 on), Sandberg

HIGHLIGHTS: Clark went 4-for-4, homered twice and drove in a playoff-record 6 runs to lead Giants. Clark's fourth inning grand slam off Maddux gave Giants an 8-3 lead, breaking open a tight game.

GAME 2 - OCTOBER 5

SF W 000 200 021   5 10 0   Reuschel (0.2), Downs (4.2), Lefferts (0.2), Brantley (1), Bedrosian (1)

CHI E 600 003 00x   9 11 0   Bielecki (4.2), Assenmacher (0.1), Lancaster (4)

HOME RUNS: Mitchell (1 on), Williams (1 on), Thompson

HIGHLIGHTS: Chicago evened the series by scoring a playoff-record six runs in the opening inning. Walton singled twice in the frame, scored the first run and drove in the sixth.

GAME 3 - OCTOBER 7

CHI E 200 100 100   4 10 0   Sutcliffe (6), Assenmacher (0.1), Lancaster (1.2)

SF W 300 000 20x   5 8 3   LaCoss (3.0), Brantley (3), Robinson (1.2), Lefferts (0.1), Bedrosian (1) SV

HOME RUNS: Thompson

HIGHLIGHTS: Robby Thompson's two-run homer in seventh inning gave San Francisco a 5-4 victory and the lead in the series. Chicago had taken a 4-3 lead in the top of the seventh on Sandberg's sacrifice fly.

GAME 4 - OCTOBER 8

CHI E 110 020 000   4 12 1   Maddux (3.1), Wilson (1.2), Sanderson (2.0), Williams (1)

SF W 102 120 00x   5 9 1   Garrelts (4.2), Downs (4), Bedrosian (0.1) SV

HOME RUNS: Salazar / Williams

HIGHLIGHTS: Two-run homer by Matt Williams in the fifth inning snapped a 4-4 tie, and strong relief work by Downs and Bedrosian made the lead stand up. Chicago loaded the bases in the ninth inning with two out, but Dawson struck out on three pitches to end the game.

GAME 5 - OCTOBER 9

CHI E 001 000 001   2 10 1   Bielecki (7.2), Williams (0), Lancaster (0.1)

SF W 000 000 12x   3 4 1   Reuschel (8), Bedrosian (1) SV

HIGHLIGHTS: Clark's bases-loaded single in the eighth inning carried Giants to their first pennant since 1962. Bielecki retired the first two Giants in the eighth, but walked the next three. Williams relieved, and Clark singled to center for a 3-1 lead. Chicago's ninth-inning rally fell a run short. Clark, who hit .650 in the five games, was named MVP of the series.

Team totals

		W	AB	H	2B	3B	HR	R	RBI	BA	BB	SO	ERA
SF	W	4	165	44	6	2	8	30	29	.267	17	29	4.09
CHI	E	1	175	53	9	3	3	22	21	.303	16	27	5.57

Individual Batting

SAN FRANCISCO (WEST)

	AB	H	2B	3B	HR	R	RBI	BA
M. Williams, 3b, ss	20	6	1	0	2	2	9	.300
W. Clark, 1b	20	13	3	1	2	8	8	.650
B. Butler, of	19	4	0	0	0	6	0	.211
R. Thompson, 2b	18	5	0	0	2	5	3	.278
K. Mitchell, of	17	6	0	0	2	5	7	.353
J. Uribe, ss	17	4	1	0	0	2	1	.235
T. Kennedy, c	16	3	1	0	0	0	0	.188
P. Sheridan, of	13	2	0	1	0	1	0	.154
S. Garrelts, p	4	0	0	0	0	0	0	.000
K. Oberkfell, 3b	4	0	0	0	0	0	0	.000
C. Maldonado, of	3	0	0	0	0	1	1	.000
K. Downs, p	3	0	0	0	0	0	0	.000
D. Nixon, of	3	0	0	0	0	0	0	.000
K. Manwaring, c	2	0	0	0	0	0	0	.000
R. Reuschel, p	2	0	0	0	0	0	0	.000
E. Riles	1	0	0	0	0	0	0	.000
B. Bathe	1	0	0	0	0	0	0	.000
M. LaCoss, p	1	0	0	0	0	0	0	.000
G. Litton	1	1	0	0	0	0	0	1.000

Errors: J. Uribe (2), M. LaCoss, K. Mitchell, D. Nixon

Stolen Bases: J. Uribe, D. Nixon

CHICAGO (EAST)

	AB	H	2B	3B	HR	R	RBI	BA
J. Walton, of	22	8	0	0	0	4	2	.364
R. Sandberg, 2b	20	8	3	1	1	6	4	.400
L. Salazar, 3b	19	7	0	1	1	2	2	.368
S. Dunston, ss	19	6	0	0	0	2	0	.316
A. Dawson, of	19	2	1	0	0	0	3	.105
M. Grace, 1b	17	11	3	1	1	3	8	.647
D. Smith, of	15	3	1	0	0	2	0	.200
J. Girardi, c	10	1	0	0	0	0	1	.100
M. Wynne, of	6	1	0	0	0	0	0	.167
M. Bielecki, p	5	1	0	0	0	0	2	.200
R. Wrona, c	5	0	0	0	0	0	0	.000
McClendon, c, of	3	2	0	0	0	0	0	.667
G. Maddux, p	3	0	0	0	0	0	1	.000
M. Webster, of	3	1	0	0	0	0	0	.333
V. Law, 3b	3	0	0	0	0	0	0	.000
R. Sutcliffe, p	2	1	1	0	0	0	0	.500
C. Wilkerson, 3b	2	1	0	0	0	1	0	.500
L. Lancaster, p	1	0	0	0	0	0	0	.000
D. Ramos	1	0	0	0	0	0	0	.000

Errors: G. Maddux, L. Salazar, S. Dunston

Stolen Bases: S. Dunston, M. Grace, D. Smith

Individual Pitching

SAN FRANCISCO (WEST)

	W	L	ERA	IP	H	BB	SO	SV
S. Garrelts	1	0	5.40	11.2	16	2	8	0
R. Reuschel	1	1	5.19	8.2	12	2	5	0
K. Downs	1	0	3.12	8.2	8	6	6	0
J. Brantley	0	0	0.00	5	1	2	3	0
S. Bedrosian	0	0	2.70	3.1	4	2	2	3
M. LaCoss	0	0	9.00	3	7	0	2	0
D. Robinson	1	0	0.00	1.2	3	0	0	0
A. Hammaker	0	0	0.00	1	1	0	0	0
C. Lefferts	0	0	9.00	1	1	2	1	0

CHICAGO (EAST)

	W	L	ERA	IP	H	BB	SO	SV
M. Bielecki	0	1	3.65	12.1	7	6	11	0
G. Maddux	0	1	13.50	7.1	13	4	5	0
L. Lancaster	1	1	6.00	6	6	1	3	0
R. Sutcliffe	0	0	4.50	6	5	4	2	0
S. Wilson	0	1	4.91	3.2	3	1	4	0
P. Kilgus	0	0	0.00	3	4	1	1	0
S. Sanderson	0	0	0.00	2	2	0	1	0
M. Williams	0	0	0.00	1	1	0	2	0
Assenmacher	0	0	13.50	0.2	3	0	0	0

1989 AMERICAN LEAGUE CHAMPIONSHIP SERIES

LINE SCORES	PITCHERS (innings pitched)	HOME RUNS (men on)	HIGHLIGHTS

Oakland (West) defeats Toronto (East) 4 games to 1

GAME 1 - OCTOBER 3

TOR E 020 100 000 — 3 5 1 — Stieb (5.1), Acker (1.2), Ward (1) — Whitt

OAK W 010 013 02x — 7 11 0 — Stewart (8), Eckersley (1) — D. Henderson, McGwire

Athletics rallied for three sixth-inning runs to take series opener as Stewart and Eckersley combined on a five-hitter. Liriano's wild throw on attempted double play allowed Oakland to score twice after McGwire's homer tied the game.

GAME 2 - OCTOBER 4

TOR E 001 000 020 — 3 5 1 — Stottlemyre (5.0), Acker (0.1), Wells (1), Henke (0.2), Cerutti (1)

OAK A 000 203 10x — 6 9 1 — Moore (7), Honeycutt (0), Eckersley (2) SV — Parker

Rickey Henderson's postseason-record four stolen bases helped Oakland take a 2-0 lead in the series. Trailing 1-0, Athletics scored twice in the fourth inning. Henderson walked, stole second and third, and scored on single by Lansford. McGwire's double drove in the go-ahead run.

GAME 3 - OCTOBER 6

OAK W 101 100 000 — 3 8 1 — Davis (6.1), Honeycutt (0), Nelson (1.1), M. Young (0.1) — Parker

TOR E 000 400 30x — 7 8 0 — Key (6), Acker (2), Henke (1)

Toronto tallied four times in the fourth inning to erase 3-0 deficit. Two-run double by Fernandez tied the score, and go-ahead run scored on Whitt's RBI single. Parker homered for Oakland.

GAME 4 - OCTOBER 7

OAK A 003 020 100 — 6 11 1 — Welch (5.2), Honeycutt (1.2), Eckersley (1.2) SV — R. Henderson (1 on), Canseco, R. Henderson (1 on)

TOR E 000 101 120 — 5 13 0 — Flanagan (4.1), Ward (2.2), Cerutti (1.2), Acker (0.1)

Rickey Henderson hit two, two-run homers and Canseco belted a massive shot into the Skydome's upper deck to help Oakland build a 5-1 lead. Jays cut the lead to 6-5 in the eighth inning before Eckersley shut the door.

GAME 5 - OCTOBER 8

OAK A 101 000 200 — 4 4 0 — Stewart (8.0), Eckersley (1) SV

TOR E 000 000 012 — 3 9 0 — Stieb (6.0), Acker (2), Henke (1) — Moseby, Bell

Stewart bested Stieb for the second time in the series as Athletics became first team to win back-to-back pennants since 1978 Yankees and Dodgers. Rickey Henderson set a postseason series record with eight stolen bases, and was named series MVP.

Team totals

	W	AB	H	2B	3B	HR	R	RBI	BA	BB	SO	ERA
OAK W	4	158	43	9	1	7	26	23	.272	20	32	3.89
TOR E	1	165	40	5	0	3	21	19	.242	15	24	5.02

Individual Batting

OAKLAND (WEST)

	AB	H	2B	3B	HR	R	RBI	BA
D. Henderson, of	19	5	3	0	1	4	1	.263
T. Phillips, 2b, 3b	18	3	1	0	0	1	1	.167
M. McGwire, 1b	18	7	1	0	1	3	3	.389
J. Canseco, of	17	5	0	0	1	3	3	.294
D. Parker, dh	16	3	0	0	2	2	3	.188
T. Steinbach, c, dh	15	3	0	0	0	0	1	.200
R. Henderson, of	15	6	1	1	2	8	5	.400
C. Lansford, 3b	11	5	0	0	0	2	4	.455
M. Gallego, 2b, ss	11	3	1	0	0	3	1	.273
W. Weiss, ss	9	1	1	0	0	2	0	.111
R. Hassey, c	6	1	0	0	0	0	1	.167
S. Javier, of	2	0	0	0	0	0	0	.000
K. Phelps	1	1	0	0	0	0	0	1.000
Blankenship, 2b	0	0	0	0	0	0	0	—

Errors: R. Henderson, J. Canseco, M. McGwire
Stolen Bases: R. Henderson (8), T. Phillips (2), C. Lansford (2), W. Weiss

TORONTO (EAST)

	AB	H	2B	3B	HR	R	RBI	BA
F. McGriff, 1b	21	3	0	0	0	1	3	.143
T. Fernandez, ss	20	7	3	0	0	6	1	.350
G. Bell, dh, of	20	4	0	0	1	2	2	.200
M. Wilson, of	19	5	0	0	0	2	2	.263
K. Gruber, 3b	17	5	1	0	0	2	1	.294
L. Moseby, of	16	5	0	0	1	4	2	.313
E. Whitt, c	16	2	0	0	1	1	3	.125
J. Felix, of	11	3	1	0	0	0	3	.273
M. Lee, 2b	8	2	0	0	0	2	0	.250
L. Mazzilli, dh	8	0	0	0	0	0	0	.000
N. Liriano, 2b	7	3	0	0	0	1	1	.429
R. Mulliniks	1	0	0	0	0	0	0	.000
P. Borders, c	1	1	0	0	0	0	1	1.000

Errors: F. McGriff, N. Liriano
Stolen Bases: T. Fernandez (5), N. Liriano (3), K. Gruber, L. Moseby, M. Wilson

Individual Pitching

OAKLAND (WEST)

	W	L	ERA	IP	H	BB	SO	SV
D. Stewart	2	0	2.81	16	13	3	9	0
M. Moore	1	0	0.00	7	3	2	3	0
S. Davis	0	1	7.11	6.1	5	2	3	0
B. Welch	1	0	3.18	5.2	8	1	4	0
D. Eckersley	0	0	1.59	5.2	4	0	2	3
R. Honeycutt	0	0	32.40	1.2	6	5	1	0
G. Nelson	0	0	0.00	1.1	1	0	2	0
M. Young	0	0	0.00	0.1	0	2	0	0

TORONTO (EAST)

	W	L	ERA	IP	H	BB	SO	SV
D. Stieb	0	2	6.35	11.1	12	6	10	0
J. Acker	0	0	1.42	6.1	4	1	4	0
J. Key	1	0	4.50	6	7	2	2	0
Stottlemyre	0	1	7.20	5	7	2	3	0
M. Flanagan	0	1	10.38	4.1	7	1	3	0
D. Ward	0	0	7.36	3.2	6	3	5	0
J. Cerutti	0	0	0.00	2.2	0	3	1	0
T. Henke	0	0	0.00	2.2	0	0	3	0
D. Wells	0	0	0.00	1	0	2	1	0

1989 WORLD SERIES

LINE SCORES	PITCHERS (innings pitched)	HOME RUNS (men on)	HIGHLIGHTS

Oakland (A.L.) defeats San Francisco (N.L.) 4 games to 0

GAME 1 - OCTOBER 14

SF	N	000 000 000	0 5 1	Garrelts (4), Hammaker (1.2), Brantley (1.1), LaCoss (1)	
OAK	A	031 100 00x	5 11 1	Stewart (9)	Parker, Weiss

Athletics took opener behind Stewart's five-hitter. Oakland jumped out to 3-0 lead in the second inning, and solo homers by Parker and Weiss added to the lead.

GAME 2 - OCTOBER 15

SF	N	001 000 000	1 4 0	Reuschel (4.0), Downs (2), Lefferts (1), Bedrosian (1)	
OAK	A	100 400 00x	5 7 0	Moore (7.0), Honeycutt (1.1), Eckersley (1)	Steinbach (2 on)

A's broke open a 1-1 game by scoring four times in the fourth inning. Parker's RBI double snapped the tie, then Steinbach followed with a three run homer. Moore pitched seven strong innings as the Giants were held to four hits.

GAME 3 - OCTOBER 27

OAK	A	200 241 040	13 14 0	Stewart (7), Honeycutt (1), Nelson (0.2), Burns (0.1)	D. Henderson, Phillips, Canseco (2 on), D. Henderson, Lansford
SF	N	010 200 004	7 10 3	Garrelts (3.1), Downs (1), Brantley (2.2), Hammaker (0.2), Lefferts (1.1)	Williams, Bathe (2 on)

A devastating earthquake hit the Bay Area minutes before the scheduled start of Game 3 on October 17. The Series was then postponed for ten days. When play resumed on October 27, the Athletics hit a record-tying five home runs (2 by Dave Henderson) to take a 3-0 Series lead. The teams combined for seven round-trippers, setting a series record for one game. Stewart became the first pitcher to ever win two games in both the LCS and World Series, and was later named MVP of the Series.

GAME 4 - OCTOBER 28

OAK	A	130 031 010	9 12 0	Moore (6), Nelson (0.1), Honeycutt (0.1), Burns (1.1), Eckersley (1) SV	R. Henderson
SF	N	000 002 400	6 9 0	Robinson (1.2), LaCoss (3.1), Brantley (1), Downs (1.2), Lefferts (0.1), Bedrosian (1.2)	Mitchell (1 on), Litton (1 on)

Athletics raced out to an 8-0 lead and held off the Giants to sweep the Series and win their first World Championship in fifteen years. Rickey Henderson led off the game with a home run, and winning pitcher Moore doubled home two runs an inning later. Mitchell and Litton homered for San Francisco.

Team totals

		W	AB	H	2B	3B	HR	R	RBI	BA	BB	SO	ERA
OAK	A	4	146	44	8	3	9	32	30	.301	18	22	3.50
SF	N	0	134	28	4	1	4	14	14	.209	8	27	8.21

Individual Batting

OAKLAND (A.L.)

	AB	H	2B	3B	HR	R	RBI	BA
R. Henderson, of	19	9	1	2	1	4	3	.474
T. Phillips, 2b, 3b, of	17	4	1	0	1	2	3	.235
M. McGwire, 1b	17	5	1	0	0	0	1	.294
C. Lansford, 3b	16	7	1	0	1	5	4	.438
T. Steinbach, c	16	4	0	1	1	3	7	.250
W. Weiss, ss	15	2	0	0	1	3	1	.133
J. Canseco, of	14	5	0	0	1	5	3	.357
D. Henderson, of	13	4	2	0	2	6	4	.308
D. Parker, dh	9	2	1	0	1	2	2	.222
M. Moore, p	3	1	1	0	0	1	2	.333
D. Stewart, p	3	0	0	0	0	0	0	.000
Blankenship, 2b	2	1	0	0	0	1	0	.500
K. Phelps	1	0	0	0	0	0	0	.000
M. Gallego, 2b, 3b	1	0	0	0	0	0	0	.000
S. Javier, of	0	0	0	0	0	0	0	–

Errors: D. Stewart
Stolen Bases: R. Henderson (3), J. Canseco

SAN FRANCISCO (N.L.)

	AB	H	2B	3B	HR	R	RBI	BA
K. Mitchell, of	17	5	0	0	1	2	2	.294
W. Clark, 1b	16	4	1	0	0	2	0	.250
M. Williams, ss, 3b	16	2	0	0	1	1	1	.125
B. Butler, of	14	4	1	0	0	1	1	.286
T. Kennedy, c	12	2	0	0	0	1	2	.167
C. Maldonado, of	11	1	0	1	0	1	0	.091
R. Thompson, 2b	11	1	0	0	0	0	2	.091
E. Riles, dh	8	0	0	0	0	0	0	.000
G. Litton, 2b, 3b	6	3	1	0	1	1	3	.500
K. Oberkfell, 3b	6	2	0	0	0	1	0	.333
D. Nixon, of	5	1	0	0	0	1	0	.200
J. Uribe, ss	5	1	0	0	0	1	0	.200
B. Bathe	2	1	0	0	1	1	3	.500
P. Sheridan, of	2	0	0	0	0	0	0	.000
S. Garrelts, p	1	0	0	0	0	0	0	.000
M. LaCoss, p	1	0	0	0	0	0	0	.000
K. Manwaring, c	1	1	1	0	0	1	0	1.000

Errors: C. Lefferts, K. Mitchell, K. Oberkfell, T. Kennedy
Stolen Bases: B. Butler (2)

Individual Pitching

OAKLAND (A.L.)

	W	L	ERA	IP	H	BB	SO	SV
D. Stewart	2	0	1.69	16	10	2	14	0
M. Moore	2	0	2.08	13	9	3	10	0
R. Honeycutt	0	0	6.75	2.2	4	0	2	0
G. Nelson	0	0	54.00	1	4	2	1	0
D. Eckersley	0	0	0.00	1.2	0	0	0	1
T. Burns	0	0	0.00	1.2	1	1	0	0

SAN FRANCISCO (N.L.)

	W	L	ERA	IP	H	BB	SO	SV
S. Garrelts	0	2	9.82	7.1	13	1	8	0
R. Reuschel	0	1	11.25	4	5	4	2	0
M. LaCoss	0	0	6.23	4.1	4	3	2	0
K. Downs	0	0	7.71	4.2	3	2	4	0
J. Brantley	0	0	4.15	4.1	5	3	1	0
S. Bedrosian	0	0	0.00	2.2	0	2	2	0
C. Lefferts	0	0	3.38	2.2	2	2	1	0
A. Hammaker	0	0	15.43	2.1	8	0	2	0
D. Robinson	0	1	21.60	1.2	4	1	0	0

PART THIRTEEN

All-Star Games

Scores and Highlights of
Every All-Star Game

All-Star Games

Baseball's midsummer classic, the All-Star Game, began in 1933. With the exception of 1959–62, when two games were held yearly, and 1945, when no game was played due to wartime restrictions, the game has been an annual event which features the best talent of the American and National leagues. This section provides information about these games through today. Included are facts about the individual games, the pitchers, home run hitters, and highlights which feature key plays, all-time records, and special achievements. Most of the information is self-explanatory. That which may appear unfamiliar is listed below:

Innings Pitched. Pitchers are listed in the order of appearance. In parentheses, following each pitcher's name, are the number of innings he pitched in the game. For example, J. Doe (2.1) would mean that he pitched 2⅓ innings.

Winning and Losing Pitchers. Indicated by boldfaced print.

Save. The relief pitcher who is credited with a save is indicated by the abbreviation SV, which appears in boldfaced print after his innings pitched.

Home Runs. Players are listed in the order their home runs were hit.

LINE SCORES	PITCHERS (innings pitched)	HOME RUNS (men on)	HIGHLIGHTS
1933 - JULY 6 AT CHICAGO N 000 002 000 2 8 0 A 012 001 00x 4 9 1	Hallahan (2), Warneke (4), D. Dean (2) **Gomez** (3), Crowder (3), Grove (3) **SV**	Frisch Ruth (1 on)	Ruth's third-inning homer with one on gave the American League a 3-0 lead and proved enough of a margin to win the first All-Star Game.
1934 - JULY 10 AT NEW YORK A 000 261 000 9 14 1 N 103 030 000 7 8 1	Gomez (3), Ruffing (1), **Harder** (5) Hubbell (3), Warneke (1), **Mungo** (1), D. Dean (3), Frankhouse (1)	Frisch, Medwick (2 on)	Hubbell struck out Ruth, Gehrig, Foxx, Simmons, and Cronin consecutively as the National League jumped to a 4-0 lead before the American League exploded for six runs in the fifth. Harder kept the senior circuit in check with one hit through the final five innings and Averill captured the hitting honors with a double, triple, and three RBIs.
1935 - JULY 8 AT CLEVELAND N 000 100 000 1 4 1 A 210 010 00x 4 8 0	Walker (2), Schumacher (4), Derringer (1), J. Dean (1) **Gomez** (6), Harder (3) **SV**	Foxx (1 on)	Foxx drove in three runs with a two-run homer and an RBI single to lead the American League to victory behind Gomez's three-hit six-inning pitching performance.
1936 - JULY 7 AT BOSTON A 000 000 300 3 7 1 N 020 020 00x 4 9 0	Grove (3), Rowe (3), Harder (2) D. Dean (3), **Hubbell** (3), Davis (0.2), Warneke (2.1) **SV**	Gehrig Galan	The National League won for the first time as they jumped out to a 4-0 lead before the American League scored three times in the seventh. Shutout pitching by Hubbell and Dean aided in the victory as Medwick's RBI single in the fifth proved the deciding run.
1937 - JULY 7 AT WASHINGTON N 000 111 000 3 13 0 A 002 312 00x 8 13 2	D. Dean (3), Hubbell (0.2), Blanton (0.1), Grissom (1.1), Mungo (2), Walters (1) **Gomez** (3), Bridges (3), Harder (3) **SV**	Gehrig (1 on)	Led by Gehrig's four RBIs and homer in the third with DiMaggio aboard, the American League easily coasted to a victory. Medwick stroked four hits in the losing cause and Dizzy Dean broke his toe on an Averill line drive which would prove his undoing. He returned too soon after the injury, and by favoring his bad foot, developed a sore arm.
1938 - JULY 6 AT CINCINNATI A 000 000 001 1 7 4 N 100 100 20x 4 8 0	Gomez (3), Allen (3), Grove (2) **Vander Meer** (3), Lee (3), Brown (3) **SV**		The National League scored four times before the American League got on the board in the ninth inning to break the shutout. The victory was sparked by the pitching of Vander Meer and Lee. Medwick and Goodman excelled in the field.
1939 - JULY 11 AT NEW YORK N 001 000 000 1 7 1 A 000 210 00x 3 6 1	Derringer (3), **Lee** (3), Fette (2) Ruffing (3), **Bridges** (2.1), Feller (3.2) **SV**	J. DiMaggio	Feller saved the American League's 3-1 lead when he entered the game in the sixth with one out and the bases loaded and forced Vaughn to hit into a double play. Joe DiMaggio's homer in the fifth with the score 2-1 provided an insurance run.
1940 - JULY 10 AT ST. LOUIS A 000 000 000 0 3 1 N 300 000 01x 4 7 0	**Ruffing** (3), Newsom (3), Feller (2) **Derringer** (2), Walters (2), Wyatt (2), French (2), Hubbell (1) **SV**	West (2 on)	Before Ruffing could retire a single man, the National League jumped off to a 3-0 lead in the first on West's homer and coasted to the first shutout in All-Star Game history. Manager McKechnie led the Nationals to their mid-summer victory, led the Cincinnati Reds to a World Series championship, and also piloted a National League club to a 2-1 win over the junior circuit in an impromptu All-Star Game held in Tampa, Florida on St. Patrick's Day for the benefit of the Finnish Relief fund.
1941 - JULY 8 AT DETROIT N 000 001 220 5 10 2 A 000 101 014 7 11 3	Wyatt (2), Derringer (2), Walters (2), **Passeau** (2.2) Feller (3), Lee (3), Hudson (1), **E. Smith** (2)	Vaughan (1 on), Vaughan (1 on) Williams (2 on)	The American League was losing 5-4 in the bottom of the ninth and only one out away from defeat when Williams delivered a clutch home run with two men aboard to end the game. Vaughan's two home runs set an All-Star record.
1942 - JULY 6 AT NEW YORK A 300 000 000 3 7 0 N 000 000 010 1 6 1	**Chandler** (4), Benton (5) **SV** **M. Cooper** (3), Vander Meer (3), Passeau (2), Walters (1)	Boudreau, York (1 on) Owen	Boudreau's homer, followed by Henrich's double and York's homer in the first, carried the American League to an easy victory. Owen's pinch-hit homer in the eighth spoiled the shutout. The next night at Cleveland, in an All-Star Game which took place for the Ball and Bat and Army-Navy relief, the American League handed Mickey Cochrane's Service All-Stars, made up largely of major leaguers in the armed forces, a 5-0 defeat.
1943 - JULY 13 AT PHILADELPHIA N 100 000 101 3 10 3 A 031 010 00x 5 8 1	M. Cooper (2.1), Vander Meer (2.2), Sewell (1), Javery (2) **Leonard** (3), Newhouser (3), Hughson (3) **SV**	V. DiMaggio Doerr (2 on)	Doerr's three-run homer in the second paced the junior circuit in the first night All-Star Game. In the course of losing, Vander Meer tied a record with six strikeouts and Vince DiMaggio had a single, triple, and homer. American fighting men throughout the world heard the game via shortwave radio.
1944 - JULY 11 AT PITTSBURGH A 010 000 000 1 6 3 N 000 040 21x 7 12 1	Borowy (3), **Hughson** (1.2), Muncrief (1.1), Newhouser (1.2), Newsom (0.1) Walters (3), **Raffensberger** (2), Sewell (3), Tobin (1) **SV**		The National League scored four times in the fifth to put the game out of reach. Cavaretta set an All-Star Game record as he reached base five times with a triple, a single, and three walks.
1945 - NO GAME PLAYED			
1946 - JULY 9 AT BOSTON N 000 000 000 0 3 0 A 200 130 24x 12 14 1	Passeau (3), Higbe (1.1), Blackwell (2.2), Sewell (1) **Feller** (3), Newhouser (3), Kramer (3) **SV**	Keller (1 on), Williams, Williams (2 on)	The All-Star Game resumed after a one-year wartime interruption as Williams led a one-man assault with four hits and five RBIs in the most one-sided midsummer-classic in history. His two home runs tied Vaughan's 1941 record-setting feat, and his five RBIs set a record. In the last three innings, Kramer held the Nationals hitless.
1947 - JULY 8 AT CHICAGO A 000 001 100 2 8 0 N 000 100 000 1 5 1	Newhouser (3), **Shea** (3), Masterson (1.2), Page (1.1) **SV** Blackwell (3), **Brecheen** (3), Sain (1), Spahn (2)	Mize	The National League held a 1-0 lead on Mize's home run until the sixth when the American League tied the score on a double-play ball hit by Joe DiMaggio which brought Appling home. Spence singled home Doerr with the deciding run in the next inning after Doerr reached third as the result of a pick-off attempt by Sain that wound up in center field.
1948 - JULY 13 AT ST. LOUIS N 200 000 000 2 8 0 A 011 300 00x 5 6 0	Branca (3), **Schmitz** (0.1), Sain (1.2), Blackwell (3) Masterson (3), **Raschi** (3), Coleman (3) **SV**	Musial (1 on) Evers	The American League defeated the National League 5-2 despite the absence of DiMaggio, Williams, Kell, and Newhouser. Raschi aided his own cause with a single in the fourth producing two RBIs.

LINE SCORES | PITCHERS (innings pitched) | HOME RUNS (men on) | HIGHLIGHTS

1949 - JULY 12 AT BROOKLYN

A 400 202 300   11 13 1
N 212 002 000   7 12 5

Pitchers:
Parnell (1), **Trucks** (2), Brissie (3), Raschi (3) SV
Spahn (1.1), **Newcombe** (2.2), Munger (1), Bickford (1), Pollett (1), Blackwell (1), Roe (1)

Home Runs: Musial (1 on), Kiner (1 on)

Highlights: In a see-saw slugfest, the Americans proved the victor in a game that marked the appearance of Robinson, Newcombe, Campanella, and Doby, the first Negroes in All-Star play. The key play of the game came in the second with the bases filled when Williams made a spectacular catch of Newcombe's slicing liner in the left field corner. Raschi's one-hit pitching over the last three innings also aided in checking the Nationals.

1950 - JULY 11 AT CHICAGO

N 020 000 001 000 01   4 10 0
A 001 020 000 000 00   3 8 1

Pitchers:
Roberts (3), Newcombe (2), Konstanty (1), Jansen (5), **Blackwell** (3)
Raschi (3), Lemon (3), Houtteman (3), Reynolds (3), **Gray** (1.1), Feller (0.2)

Home Runs: Kiner, Schoendienst

Highlights: Kiner's homer in the top of the ninth sent the game into extra innings before Schoendienst settled the contest in the 14th with a home run. Jansen allowed one hit and struck out six in checking the American League for five innings. The contest was marred as Williams broke his elbow while making a catch against the left field wall in the first, and was lost to the Red Sox until the end of the season.

1951 - JULY 10 AT DETROIT

N 100 302 110   8 12 1
A 010 110 000   3 10 2

Pitchers:
Roberts (2), **Maglie** (3), Newcombe (3), Blackwell (1) SV
Garver (3), **Lopat** (1), Hutchinson (3), Parnell (1), Lemon (1)

Home Runs: Musial, Elliott (1 on), Kiner, Hodges (1 on), Wertz, Kell

Highlights: Home run records fell as both leagues combined to hit six round trippers. The National League, with four of the home runs, used them to send six runs across and topple the American League in what marked the first back-to-back victories in All-Star play for the senior circuit.

1952 - JULY 8 AT PHILADELPHIA

A 000 20   2 5 0
N 100 20   3 3 0

Pitchers:
Raschi (2), **Lemon** (2), Shantz (1)
Simmons (3), Rush (2)

Home Runs: Robinson, Sauer (1 on)

Highlights: Sauer's homer with Musial aboard in the fourth proved the deciding run in a five-inning game shortened by rain.

1953 - JULY 14 AT CINCINNATI

A 000 000 001   1 5 0
N 000 020 12x   5 10 0

Pitchers:
Pierce (3), **Reynolds** (2), Garcia (2), Paige (1)
Roberts (3), **Spahn** (2), Simmons (2), Dickson (2) SV

Highlights: Slaughter's two hits, RBI, two runs, and diving catch of Kuenn's line drive sparked the National League. The American League broke the shutout with two outs in the ninth as Minoso singled home Fain.

1954 - JULY 13 AT CLEVELAND

N 000 520 020   9 14 0
A 004 121 03x   11 17 1

Pitchers:
Roberts (3), Antonelli (2), Spahn (0.2), Grissom (1.1), Conley (0.1), Erskine (0.2)
Ford (3), Consuegra (0.1), Lemon (0.2), Porterfield (3), Keegan (0.2), Stone (0.1), Trucks (1) SV

Home Runs: Kluszewski (1 on), Bell (1 on); Rosen (2 on), Boone, Rosen (1 on), Doby

Highlights: Doby's pinch-hit homer in the eighth, followed by Fox's single which sent two runs home, ended the highest scoring All-Star Game in history. The victory broke a five-year losing streak for the American League and produced two hit records: 17 for the junior circuit and a combined total of 31 for the game. Rosen's five RBIs and two home runs also tied the All-Star Game record.

1955 - JULY 12 AT MILWAUKEE

A 400 001 000 000   5 10 2
N 000 000 230 001   6 13 1

Pitchers:
Pierce (3), Wynn (3), Ford (1.2), Sullivan (3.1)
Roberts (3), Haddix (3), Newcombe (1), Jones (0.2), Nuxhall (3.1), **Conley** (1)

Home Runs: Mantle (2 on); Musial

Highlights: Conley struck out the side in the 12th and Musial hit a homer to give the National League a victory after being down 5-0. The American League's first inning barrage of four runs featured Mantle's homer with two on.

1956 - JULY 10 AT WASHINGTON

N 001 211 200   7 11 0
A 000 003 000   3 11 0

Pitchers:
Friend (3), Spahn (2), Antonelli (4) SV
Pierce (3), Ford (1), Wilson (1), Brewer (2), Score (1), Wynn (1)

Home Runs: Mays (1 on), Musial; Williams (1 on), Mantle

Highlights: Three sparkling fielding plays by Ken Boyer, along with his three hits, paced the National League as they score five times before the American League got on the board with back-to-back homers in the sixth by Williams and Mantle.

1957 - JULY 9 AT ST. LOUIS

A 020 001 003   6 10 0
N 000 000 203   5 9 1

Pitchers:
Bunning (3), Loes (3), Wynn (0.1), Pierce (1.2), Mossi (0.2), Grim (0.1) SV
Simmons (1), Burdette (4), Sanford (1), Jackson (2), Labine (1)

Highlights: Minoso's running catch of Hodges' line drive with one on and two out in the ninth ended a three-run National League rally and preserved the victory for the American League, who also scored their final three runs in the ninth.

1958 - JULY 8 AT BALTIMORE

N 210 000 000   3 4 2
A 110 011 00x   4 9 2

Pitchers:
Spahn (3), **Friend** (2.1), L. Jackson (0.2), Farrell (2)
Turley (1.2), Narleski (3.1), **Wynn** (1), O'Dell (1) SV

Highlights: McDougald's pinch-hit single in the sixth scored Malzone for the deciding run in the first All-Star Game played without an extra base hit. O'Dell pitched perfect ball to check the National League.

1959 - JULY 7 AT PITTSBURGH

A 000 100 030   4 8 0
N 100 000 22x   5 9 1

Pitchers:
Wynn (3), Duren (3), Bunning (1), **Ford** (0.1), Daley (0.2)
Drysdale (3), Burdette (3), Face (1.2), **Antonelli** (0.1), Elston (1) SV

Home Runs: Kaline; Mathews

Highlights: Aaron knocked in the tying run with a single and scored the deciding run as Mays tripled him home in the eighth. Drysdale got the National League off to a good start by pitching perfect ball for three innings.

1959 - AUGUST 3 AT LOS ANGELES

A 012 000 110   5 6 0
N 100 010 100   3 6 3

Pitchers:
Walker (3), Wynn (2), Wilhelm (1), McLish (2), O'Dell (1) SV
Drysdale (3), Conley (2), Jones (2), Face (2)

Home Runs: Malzone, Berra (1 on), Colavito; Robinson, Gilliam

Highlights: Five homers were hit, but Fox decided the game on his go-ahead RBI single in the fourth to cap the American League victory.

1960 - JULY 11 AT KANSAS CITY

N 311 000 000   5 12 4
A 000 001 020   3 6 1

Pitchers:
Friend (3), McCormick (2.1), Jackson (1), Henry (1), McDaniel (1)
Monbouquette (2), Estrada (1), Coates (2), Bell (2), Lary (1), Daley (1)

Home Runs: Banks (1 on), Crandall, Musial, K. Boyer (1 on); Kaline (1 on)

Highlights: The National League jumped to a 5-0 lead and held on to win as Mays paced the attack with a single, double, and triple. Face relieved with the bases full in the sixth and retired the side as he forced Aparicio to hit into a double play.

1960 - JULY 13 AT NEW YORK

N 021 000 102   6 10 0
A 000 000 000   0 8 0

Pitchers:
Law (2), Podres (2), S. Williams (2), Jackson (1), Henry (1), McDaniel (1) SV
Ford (3), Wynn (2), Staley (2), Lary (1), Bell (1)

Home Runs: Mathews (1 on), Mays, Musial, K. Boyer (1 on)

Highlights: The game was sparked by Mays's three hits, Musial's pinch-hit homer in the seventh, and the shutout pitching of the National League.

1961 - JULY 11 AT SAN FRANCISCO

A 000 001 002 1   4 4 2
N 010 100 010 2   5 11 5

Pitchers:
Ford (3), Lary (0), Donovan (2), Bunning (2), Fornieles (0.1), **Wilhelm** (1.2)
Spahn (3), Purkey (2), McCormick (3), **Face** (0.1), Koufax (0), Miller (1.2)

Home Runs: Killebrew; Altman

Highlights: Clemente hit a game-winning single in the bottom of the tenth after Mays tied the game with a double that drove in Aaron. Seven errors by both sides set an All-Star Game record.

LINE SCORES	PITCHERS (innings pitched)	HOME RUNS (men on)	HIGHLIGHTS

1961 - JULY 31 AT BOSTON

N   000 001 000   1 5 1
A   100 000 000   1 4 0

Purkey (2), Mahaffey (2), Koufax (2), Miller (3)
Bunning (3), Schwall (3), Pasqual (3)

Colavito

The first tie game in All-Star history occured as rain fell after the ninth inning to end the contest and cancel excellent pitching performances. Colavito's homer in the first was the only run scored until White drove in Mathews on a single in the sixth.

1962 - JULY 10 AT WASHINGTON

N   000 002 010   3 8 0
A   000 001 000   1 4 0

Drysdale (3), Marichal (2), Purkey (2), Shaw (2) SV
Bunning (3), Pascual (3), Donovan (2), Pappas (1)

Entering the game in the sixth inning, Wills sparked the National League and scored the first run of the game. In the eighth inning he scored the insurance run. Clemente led the attack with three hits.

1962 - JULY 30 AT CHICAGO

A   001 201 302   9 10 0
N   010 000 111   4 10 4

Stenhouse (2), Herbert (3), Aguirre (3), Pappas (1) SV
Podres (2), Mahaffey (2), Gibson (2), Farrell (1), Marichal (2)

Runnels, Wagner (1 on), Colavito (2 on)
Roseboro

With one man on and one out in the seventh, Moran hit a line drive which umpire Burkhart ruled trapped by Aaron. After Maris tapped a roller to force Moran, Colavito hit a home run to make the score 7-1 and ice the game. Two double plays in the middle of the game also helped to subdue the Nationals.

1963 - JULY 9 AT CLEVELAND

N   012 010 010   5 6 0
A   012 000 000   3 11 1

O'Toole (2), Jackson (2), Culp (1), Woodeshick (2), Drysdale (2) SV
McBride (3), Bunning (2), Bouton (1), Pizarro (1), Radatz (2)

The National League used only six singles to win as Mays led the attack with two RBIs, two runs, two stolen bases, and a catch against the center field fence to rob Pepitone of an extra base hit. Musial's 24th All-Star appearance set a record. A tribute was paid to Mantle as the players named him starting centerfielder even though he was unable to play because of a broken foot.

1964 - JULY 7 AT NEW YORK

A   100 002 100   4 9 1
N   000 210 004   7 8 0

Chance (3), Wyatt (1), Pascual (2), Radatz (2.2)
Drysdale (3), Bunning (2), Short (1), Farrell (2), Marichal (1)

Williams, Boyer, Callison (2 on)

Mays walked, stole second, and scored in the last of the ninth to tie the game on Cepeda's bloop single before Callison's homer with two on gave the National League a dramatic come-from-behind victory.

1965 - JULY 13 AT MINNESOTA

N   320 000 100   6 11 0
A   000 140 000   5 8 0

Marichal (3), Maloney (1.2), Drysdale (0.1), Koufax (1), Farrell (1), Gibson (2) SV
Pappas (1), Grant (2), Richert (2), McDowell (2), Fisher (2)

Mays, Torre (1 on), Stargell (1 on)
McAuliffe (1 on), Killebrew (1 on)

The National League jumped to a 5-0 lead on three homers before McAuliffe and Killebrew hit two-run homers in the fifth to tie the game. Santo's single in the seventh drove in the deciding run. An American League rally was cut off in the eighth as Mays recovered after slipping to make a leaping, backhanded catch of Hall's fly with two men and two out.

1966 - JULY 12 AT ST. LOUIS

A   010 000 000 0   1 6 0
N   000 100 000 1   2 6 0

McLain (3), Kaat (2), Stottlemyre (2), Siebert (2), Richert (0.1)
Koufax (3), Bunning (2), Marichal (3), Perry (2)

A single in the bottom of the tenth by Wills sent McCarver home with the winning run in a game that took place in 105-degree temperature. The victory came in spite of Brooks Robinson's three hits and McLain's three perfect innings. After Aaron lost Robinson's fly in the background of white shirts for a triple in the second, Koufax uncorked a wild pitch to lose the shutout.

1967 - JULY 11 AT CALIFORNIA

N   010 000 000 000 001   2 9 0
A   000 001 000 000 000   1 8 0

Marichal (3), Jenkins (3), Gibson (2), Short (2), Cuellar (2), Drysdale (2), Seaver (1) SV
Chance (3), McGlothin (2), Peters (3), Downing (2), Hunter (5)

Allen, Perez
B. Robinson

After Allen's homer in the second and Brooks Robinson's equalizer in the sixth, Perez homered in the 15th inning to end the longest All-Star Game in history. The pitching proved superior as 30 batters go down via the strikeout route. The American League's five pitchers allowed no walks. Jenkins proved the most spectacular of the seven National League pitchers as he equalled the record of Hubbell and Vander Meer by striking out six.

1968 - JULY 9 AT HOUSTON

A   000 000 000   0 3 1
N   100 000 000   1 5 0

Tiant (2), Odom (2), McLain (2), McDowell (1), Stottlemyre (0.1), John (0.2)
Drysdale (3), Marichal (2), Carlton (1), Seaver (2), Reed (0.2), Koosman (0.1) SV

Mays scored on a double-play ball in the first to give the National League mound staff all the support they needed in winning the first 1-0 game in All-Star history. Seaver sparkled with five strikeouts in a game that typified the pitchers' stranglehold on the batters.

1969 - JULY 23 AT WASHINGTON

N   125 100 000   9 11 0
A   011 100 000   3 6 2

Carlton (3), Gibson (1), Singer (2), Koosman (1.2), Dierker (0.1), Niekro (1) SV
Stottlemyre (2), Odom (0.1), Knowles (0.2), McLain (1), McNally (2), McDowell (2), Culp (1)

Bench (1 on), McCovey, McCovey (1 on)
Freehan, Howard

San Francisco's Willie McCovey became the fourth player in All-Star history to hit two home runs in a game and drove in three runs to lead the National League to its seventh straight victory. Bench of the Reds also homered and knocked in a pair of runs as the winners battered seven American League pitchers for 11 hits in a game played in the nation's capital to help celebrate baseball's 100th anniversary.

1970 - JULY 14 AT CINCINNATI

A   000 001 120 000   4 12 0
N   000 000 103 001   5 10 0

Palmer (3), McDowell (3), J. Perry (2), Hunter (0.1), Peterson (0), Stottlemyre (1.2), Wright (1.2)
Seaver (3), Merritt (2), G. Perry (2), Gibson (2), Osteen (3)

Dietz

The National League, after trailing 4-1 in the ninth, won in the 12th on singles by Rose, Grabarkewitz and Hickman for their eighth straight triumph. The game marked the first time since 1957 that the starters were elected by the fans.

1971 - JULY 13 AT DETROIT

N   021 000 010   4 5 0
A   004 002 00x   6 7 0

Ellis (3), Marichal (2), Jenkins (1), Wilson (2)
Blue (3), Palmer (2), Cuellar (2), Lolich (2) SV

Bench (1 on), Aaron, Clemente
Jackson (1 on), F. Robinson (1 on), Killebrew (1 on)

The American League finally snaps the NL's dominance, winning for the first time since 1962 with a power display by Jackson, Frank Robinson and Killebrew. Jackson's homer was an epic shot off the light towers, and Robinson's made him the first to homer for each league. Aaron's homer was his first in All-Star competition.

1972 - JULY 25 AT ATLANTA

A   001 000 020 0   3 6 0
N   000 002 001 1   4 8 0

Palmer (3), Lolich (2), Perry (2), Wood (2), McNally (0.1)
Gibson (2), Blass (1), Sutton (1), Carlton (1), Stoneman (2), McGraw (2)

Rojas (1 on)
Aaron (1 on)

The seventh extra-inning All-Star game ended in the 10th inning when Colbert walked, was sacrificed to second, and raced home on Morgan's hit to make the National League 7-for-7 in extra-inning games. The most popular hit was Aaron's homer before his home fans.

LINE SCORES	PITCHERS (innings pitched)	HOME RUNS (men on)	HIGHLIGHTS
1973 - JULY 24 AT KANSAS CITY N 002 122 000 7 10 0 A 010 000 000 1 5 0	**Wise** (2), Osteen (2), Sutton (1), Twitchell (1), Giusti (1), Seaver (1), Brewer (1) **SV** Hunter (1.1), Holtzman (0.2), **Blyleven** (1), Singer (2), Ryan (1), Lyle (1), Fingers (1)	Bonds, Davis (1 on), Bench	A record 54 players (28 by the National League and 26 by the American) are used as the NL continued to assert its power. Aaron broke a 1-1 tie with his RBI single in third before Bench, Bonds and Davis rap insurance homers.
1974 - JULY 23 AT PITTSBURGH A 002 000 000 2 4 1 N 010 210 12x 7 10 1	Perry (3), Tiant (2), Hunter (2), Fingers (1) Messersmith (3), **Brett** (2), Matlack (1), McGlothen (1), Marshall (2)	Smith	Steve Garvey, who was not even listed on the All-Star ballot, was the hero of the National League's victory, hitting a double and single, driving in one run and scoring another. In addition, he made several sparkling defensive plays at first base to give the National League their 11th victory in the last 12 games.
1975 - JULY 15 AT MILWAUKEE N 021 000 003 6 13 1 A 000 003 000 3 10 1	Reuss (3), Sutton (2), Seaver (1), **Matlack** (2), Jones (1) Blue (2), Busby (2), Kaat (2), **Hunter** (2), Gossage (1)	Garvey, Wynn Yastrzemski (2 on)	A three-run outburst in the ninth inning against Hunter and Gossage snapped a 3-3 tie and gave the NL their 12th victory in 13 games. A single by Madlock with the bases full was the key blow. Yastrzemski accounted for all the AL's runs with a three-run pinch homer.
1976 - JULY 13 AT PHILADELPHIA A 000 100 000 1 5 0 N 202 000 03x 7 10 0	Fidrych (2), Hunter (2), Tiant (2), Tanana (2) **Jones** (3), Seaver (2), Montefusco (2), Rhoden (1), K. Forsch (1)	Lynn Foster (1 on), Cedeno (1 on)	Scoring early and often, the NL tagged Fidrych and his 3 successors for 10 hits, including home runs by Foster and Cedeno. The rout was the National League's fifth straight victory, giving them 13 of the last 14.
1977 - JULY 19 AT NEW YORK N 401 000 020 7 9 1 A 000 002 102 5 8 0	**Sutton** (3), Lavelle (2), Seaver (2), R. Reuschel (1), Gossage (1) Palmer (2), Kern (1), Eckersley (2), LaRoche (1), Campbell (1), Lyle (2)	Morgan, Garvey, Luzinski (1 on) Scott (1 on)	The NL rocked Palmer for four runs in the first inning, sparked by homers from Morgan and Luzinski, and went on to defeat the AL 7-5 for its sixth straight.
1978 - JULY 11 AT SAN DIEGO A 201 000 000 3 8 1 N 003 000 04x 7 10 0	Palmer (2.2), Keough (0.1), Sorensen (3), Kern (0.2), Guidry (0.1), **Gossage** (1) Blue (3), Rogers (2), Fingers (1), **Sutter** (1.2), P. Niekro (0.1)		The NL spotted the AL three runs then came roaring from behind to win on a four-run assault against Gossage in the eighth. Garvey, whose single tied the score in the third, tripled in the tie-breaking run.
1979 - JULY 17 AT SEATTLE N 211 001 011 7 10 0 A 302 001 000 6 10 0	Carlton (1), Andujar (2), Rogers (2), Perry (0), Sambito (0.2), LaCoss (1.1), **Sutter** (2) Ryan (2), Stanley (2), Clear (1), **Kern** (2.2), Guidry (0.1)	Mazzilli Lynn (1 on)	Mazzilli of the Mets hit a game-winning pinch home run in the eighth on his first All-Star at bat, and walked with the bases full in the ninth to give the National League its eighth straight win.
1980 - JULY 8 AT LOS ANGELES A 000 020 000 2 7 1 N 000 012 10x 4 7 0	Stone (2), **John** (2.1), Farmer (0.2), Stieb (1), Gossage (1) Richard (2), Welch (3), Reuss (1), Bibby (1), Sutter (2) **SV**	Lynn (1 on) Griffey	Griffey led the National League to its ninth straight victory, 4-2, with a single and a home run as five pitchers held the American League to seven hits. Lynn accounted for the AL's runs with a two-run homer in the fifth that gave the losers a temporary 2-0 lead. It was the NL's 17th win in 18 games.
1981 - AUGUST 9 AT CLEVELAND N 000 011 120 5 9 1 A 010 003 000 4 11 1	Valenzuela (1), Seaver (1), Knepper (2), Hooton (1.2), Ruthven (0.1) Blue (1), Ryan (1), Sutter (1) **SV** Morris (2), Barker (2), K. Forsch (1), Norris (1), Davis (1), **Fingers** (0.1), Stieb (1.2)	Carter, Carter, Parker, Schmidt (1 on) Singleton	Schmidt hit a 2-run homer off Fingers in the eighth inning to to lift the National League to a 5-4 victory over the American League before 72,086, the largest crowd ever to see an All-Star Game. It was the NL's tenth straight win and the 18th in the last 19 meetings with the AL. The game, held on August 9, was the latest All-Star Game ever held, owing to the ten-week player strike.
1982 - JULY 13 AT MONTREAL A 100 000 000 1 8 2 N 021 001 00x 4 8 1	**Eckersley** (3), Clancy (1), Bannister (1), Quisenberry (2), Fingers (1) **Rogers** (3), Carlton (2), Soto (2), Valenzuela (0.2), Minton (0.2), Howe (0.1), Hume (0.1) **SV**	Concepcion (1 on)	Led by Concepcion's two-run homer, the National League maintained its mastery over the American, winning its 11th straight. The game was the first All-Star Game played outside the United States.
1983 - JULY 6 AT CHICAGO N 100 110 000 3 8 3 A 117 000 22x 13 15 2	Soto (2), Hammaker (0.2), Dawley (1.1), Dravecky (2), Perez (0.2), Orosco (0.1), L. Smith (1) **Stieb** (3), Honeycutt (2), Stanley (2), Young (1), Quisenberry (1)	Rice, Lynn (3 on)	Paced by Fred Lynn's grand slam, the American League tallied seven runs in the third to break the Nationals' winning streak in taking the 50th anniversary game. The game was played at Comiskey Park, site of the first mid-summer classic.
1984 - JULY 10 AT SAN FRANCISCO A 010 000 000 1 7 2 N 110 000 01x 3 8 0	Stieb (2), Morris (2), Dotson (2), Caudill (1), W. Hernandez (1) **Lea** (2), Valenzuela (2), Gooden (2), Soto (2), Gossage (1) **SV**	Brett Carter, Murphy	Pitchers prevailed in the San Francisco twilight, as a nine-inning-record twenty-one strikeouts were recorded. Nineteen-year-old Dwight Gooden, the youngest All-Star ever, combined with Fernando Valenzuela to strike out six consecutive hitters, breaking Carl Hubbell's fifty-year-old mark.
1985 - JULY 16 AT MINNESOTA N 011 020 002 6 9 1 A 100 000 000 1 5 0	**Hoyt** (3), Ryan (3), Valenzuela (1), Reardon (1), Gossage (1) **Morris** (2.2), Key (0.1), Blyleven (1), Stieb (1), Moore (2), Petry (0.1), Hernandez (0.2)		Steve Garvey's two-out single in the third inning, which scored Tommy Herr from second base was enough to put the National League ahead to stay. Rickey Henderson scored the lone American League run on George Brett's sacrifice fly in the first inning. The American League managed only five singles. This win made it 21 of the last 23 for the Nationals.
1986 - JULY 15 AT HOUSTON A 020 000 010 0 3 5 0 N 000 000 002 0 2 5 1	**Clemens** (3), Higuera (3), Hough (1.2), Righetti (0.2), Aase (0.2) **SV** **Gooden** (3), Valenzuela (3), Scott (1), Fernandez (1), Krukow (1)	Whitaker (1 on), White	Lou Whitaker's two run homer in the second inning off Dwight Gooden was the key blow for the American League. Frank White added a solo shot for a needed insurance run as the Nationals rallied in the eighth with two runs and left the tying and winning runs on base in the ninth.

LINE SCORES	PITCHERS (innings pitched)	HOME RUNS (men on)	HIGHLIGHTS
1987 - JULY 14 AT OAKLAND N 000 000 000 000 2 2 8 2 A 000 000 000 000 0 0 6 1	Scott (2), Sutcliffe (2), Hershiser (2), Reuschel (1.1), Franco (0.2), Bedrosian (1), **L. Smith** (3), Fernandez (1) **SV** Saberhagen (3), Morris (2), Langston (2), Plesac (1), Righetti (0.1), Henke (2.2), **Howell** (2)		Tim Raines, hitless in six previous All-Star contests, hit a two-out triple in the top of the 13th inning to drive home the only runs scored in the game. The National League has won all eight extra inning All-Star games.
1988 - JULY 12 AT CINCINNATI A 001 100 000 0 2 6 2 N 000 100 000 0 1 5 0	**Viola** (2), Clemens (1), Gubicza (2), Stieb (1), Russell (1), Jones (0.2), Plesac (0.1), Eckersley (1) **SV** **Gooden** (3), Knepper (1), Cone (1), Gross (1), Davis (0.2), Walk (0.1), Hershiser (1), Worrell (1)	Steinbach	Steinbach's third inning homer and fourth inning sacrifice fly was all the American League needed to turn back the Nationals. It was the A.L.'s second victory in the last three meetings.
1989 - JULY 11 AT ANAHEIM N 200 000 010 3 9 1 A 212 000 00x 5 12 0	Reuschel (1), **Smoltz** (1), Sutcliffe (1), Burke (2), M. Davis (1), Howell (1), Williams (1) Stewart (1), **Ryan** (2), Gubicza (1), Moore (1), Swindell (1.2), Russell (1), Plesac (0), Jones (1.1) **SV**	Jackson, Boggs	All nine A.L. starters hit safely as they won consecutive games for the first time in 31 years. Bo Jackson and Wade Boggs hit back-to-back first inning homers to wipe out a 2-0 deficit. 42 year old Nolan Ryan became the oldest All-Star winner in the first game played with the designated hitter.

Appendices

A. Sources

B. Decisions of the Special Baseball
Records Committee

C. Major Changes in Playing Rules
and Scoring Rules

Appendix A

Sources

The following is the list of official documents, private collections, and newspapers that were used during the research of this volume:

Official Records

American League, 1905–present
National League, 1903–present

Collections

Lee Allen   John Tattersall   Files of the National Baseball Hall of Fame and Museum, Cooperstown, N.Y.

Trade Papers

The Sporting Life (1885–1916)   *The Sporting News* (1916—)
The Sporting Times (1890)

Newspapers

Albany, N.Y.	*Argus*
Altoona, Pa.	*Morning Tribune, Times*
Baltimore, Md.	*American, Herald, Sun*
Boston, Mass.	*Globe, Herald, Morning Journal, Post, Daily Advertiser, Evening Transcript*
Brooklyn, N.Y.	*Daily Eagle*
Buffalo, N.Y.	*Courier-Express, Evening News, Times*
Chicago, Ill.	*Daily News, Evening Journal, Evening Mail, Herald Interocean, Record, Record Herald, Times, Tribune*
Cincinnati, Ohio	*Commercial Gazette, Commercial Tribune, Enquirer, Evening Telegram, News Journal, Post, Times-Star*
Cleveland, Ohio	*Evening Herald, Leader, Plain Dealer, World*
Columbus, Ohio	*Dispatch, Evening Post, Evening Press, Ohio State Journal*
Detroit, Mich.	*Evening News, Free Press, Journal, Post and Tribune, Times, Tribune*
Hartford, Conn.	*Courant, Times*
Indianapolis, Ind.	*Journal, News Sentinel, Star*
Kansas City, Mo.	*Journal, Star, Star-Times, Times*
Louisville, Ky.	*Commercial, Courier-Journal*
Milwaukee, Wis.	*Daily News, Evening Wisconsin, Journal, Sentinel*
Newark, N.J.	*Eagle, News, Star-Ledger*
New York, N.Y.	*American, Clipper, Herald, Journal, Mail, News, Post, Press, Sun, Telegram, Times, Tribune, World*
Philadelphia, Pa.	*Evening Bulletin, Inquirer, Item, Ledger, North American, Press, Record, Times*
Pittsburgh, Pa.	*Chronicle-Telegraph, Dispatch, Gazette, Leader, Post, Press, Times*
Providence, R.I.	*Evening Bulletin, Journal, Press, Telegram*
Richmond, Va.	*Dispatch, State, Whig*
Rochester, N.Y.	*Democrat and Chronicle, Herald, Post and Express, Union and Advertiser*
St. Louis, Mo.	*Globe-Democrat, Missouri Republican, Post-Dispatch, Star-Times*
Syracuse, N.Y.	*Courier, Daily Standard, Herald, Journal*
Toledo, Ohio	*Bee, Blade*
Troy, N.Y.	*Press, Telegram, Times*
Washington, D.C.	*Evening Star, Herald, Post, Sunday Chronicle, Sunday Sentinel, Times*
Wilmington, Del.	*Journal Every Evening, Morning News, Star*
Worcester, Mass.	*Evening Gazette, Spy*

The following is the Editorial Staff listing which appeared in the landmark first edition of *The Baseball Encyclopedia,* published in 1969. While considerable work has been done on the *Encyclopedia* since then, the work of these people formed the foundation on which all subsequent efforts have been based.

Editorial Staff

DAVID S. NEFT

Director of Research,
Information Concepts
Incorporated

LEE ALLEN

Historian,
National Baseball
Hall of Fame
and Museum

ROBERT MARKEL

Executive Editor,
The Macmillan
Company

John C. Tattersall
Consulting Editor

Neil R. Armann
Systems Manager

Jordan A. Deutsch
Associate Editor

Research Supervisors
Richard M. Cohen, Donald C. Henry, Roland T. Johnson

Researchers
Gary R. Abram, N. Richard Anderson, Eugene B. Galusha, Irving Moss, Alan Stolowitz

Associate Researchers
William R. Bevilacqua, Stephen Hirdt, John G. Hogrogian, John Liscio, Dennis J. Murphy, William J. Murphy, George A. Shanahan, James M. Taylor, Raymond J. Walsh, Richard Wangeman

Assistant Researchers
Thomas E. Alberto, Charles D. Blatz, John Boyle, Robert F. Brennan, Calvin Clark, Alphonso Cook, Jr., Michael J. Kitson, Mati Kuuskmae, Edward Madera, James C. Madera, Thomas J. Malvey, Philip A. Marino, Robert Re, Richard J. Riccardi

Programmers
Joanne Cotterill, Senior Programmer
Harriet Cinque, Anselmo O. Clarke, Robert A. Hyslop, R. William Ihrie, Basil M. Jarrett, Lawrence A. Lenczewski

Design and Production
Abe Lerner, Faulkner Lewis

Additional research for the eighth edition has been provided by members of the Society for American Baseball Research, including Robert Anderson, Richard Bozzone, William Carle, L. Robert Davids, Harold Dellinger, Jack Dougherty, Genevieve Duffin, Michael Dugan, William Haber, Ralph Horton, Thomas Hufford, Louis Jacobson, Dr. José J. Jiménez, Francis Kinlaw, Gary Koca, Martin LaCoste, Erwin Lynn, Robert McConnell, Steve Nadel, Gary Nuthals, Joseph Overfield, Frank Phelps, Robert Richardson, Emil Rothe, Richard Schrader, John Schwartz, Thomas Shea, Joseph Simenic, Jack Smalling, Lyle Spatz, A. D. Suehsdorf, Richard Thompson, David Vincent, William Weiss, Walter Wilson, and Ralph Winnie.

Appendix B

Decisions of the Special Baseball Records

Committee

In 1887 eleven men had batting averages higher than .400. It is an astonishing feat, until one learns that bases on balls were counted as hits in the official averages that year. There are other such records based on definitions which were either incomplete or inconsistent with the rest of baseball history. It was because of these factors that it became necessary to draw up a code of rules governing record-keeping procedures. A group was formed for this purpose and was called the Special Baseball Records Committee.

It should be noted that the Committee's concern was not with laying future ground rules, which is the duty of the Baseball Rules Committee, but rather to establish the rules governing record-keeping procedures that mostly concern past play.

David Grote, director of public relations for the National League, and Robert Holbrook, executive assistant to the president of the American League, served as co-chairmen of the Special Baseball Records Committee.

Other members included Jack Lang, secretary-treasurer of the Baseball Writers Association of America, Joseph Reichler, director of public relations of the office of the Commissioner of Baseball, and Lee Allen, historian of the Baseball Hall of Fame.

The Committee met twice in 1968. At the first meeting, which took place in St. Petersburg, Florida, on March 5, they voted on the issues in question. The Committee met again in New York City on November 14, and reviewed their decisions after they were given an opportunity to see what changes had resulted in the records after much of the research was completed. In addition to these meetings, the Committee is continually informed of all errors found in the official records.

Most of the important issues concerned the period before 1920, a time that was somewhat chaotic in baseball record-keeping procedures. The following is a list of the decisions on seventeen issues as voted by the Committee:

1. The following leagues are defined as "major":

National League, 1876 to the present	Federal League, 1914–15
American League, 1901 to the present	Players' League, 1890
American Association, 1882–91	Union Association, 1884

The National Association, 1871–1875, shall not be considered as a "major league" due to its erratic schedule and procedures, but it will continue to be recognized as the first professional baseball league.

2. Major league baseball shall have one set of records, starting in 1876, without any arbitrary division into nineteenth- and twentieth-century data.

3. There shall be no change in rules used in past years governing the minimum appearances necessary for recognition as a league leader for averages (batting average, slugging average, fielding average, earned run average, and pitchers' winning percentage).

4. For all-time single season records, no asterisk or official sign shall be used to indicate the number of games scheduled.

5. Performances in all tie games of five or more innings shall be included in the official averages. (Before 1885 this was not done.)

6. Several games in the National League in 1877, 1879, and 1899 that were subsequently declared "unofficial" for varying reasons, shall now be counted as "official."

7. All appearances by a player in an official game shall be counted as a game played. (Before 1912 many pinch hitters, pinch runners, and substitutes who did not bat were not credited with a game played.)

8. Bases on balls shall always be treated as neither a time at bat nor a hit for the batter. (In 1887 bases on balls were scored as hits and in 1876 bases on balls were scored as outs.)

9. A distinction shall be made in the definition of stolen bases. Before 1898 stolen bases were credited any time a runner advanced an extra base on a hit or out. Since these bases advanced cannot be separated from bases stolen, according to the modern definition, there shall be two sets of records, one starting with 1898 and the other before 1898.

10. Bases on balls, wild pitches, passed balls, balks, and hit batsmen shall not be counted as errors. (These items were frequently scored as errors before 1889.)

11. A pitcher shall not be credited with an assist on a strikeout. (Before 1889 pitchers were usually awarded an assist on a strikeout.)

12. Scoring rules governing won and lost decisions by a pitcher did not become official until 1950. It was decided that all pitching decisions during the period 1901–49 shall stand as they are in the official records, but that for the period 1876–1900 the 1950 ruling shall be in effect. The reason for this was that since 1920 the official scorer did exist, and he had the explicit authority to award the victory based on common practice, which was very close to the rule adopted in 1950. In the pre-1901 period, however, there was no official scoring rule or common practice for wins by a pitcher and for many years no official scorer.

13. The present definition on earned runs, as was established in 1969 by the Baseball Scoring Rules Committee, shall be effective from that date on in defining earned runs. Prior to that date, the

1917–73 definition of earned runs shall be applied to the years 1876–1911, and to the American League in 1912. (Before 1912 there was a period when there was no official compilation of earned runs, and a time where bases on balls, hit batsmen, and wild pitches were considered errors in the computation of earned runs.)

14. Fractional innings pitched shall be used in the calculation of earned run averages.

15. The earned run average of a pitcher who allowed one or more earned runs during a season without retiring a batter shall be "infinity."

16. 1894 shall be considered the starting date for exempting a man from a time at bat for a sacrifice bunt hit. Before 1894 a batter was credited with a sacrifice hit and charged with a time at bat every time he advanced a runner on any type of out.

17. Sudden Death Home Runs. Before 1920, when the team batting last won the game in the ninth or in an extra inning, the ruling was that the team could not win by more than one run. If a man hit an outside-the-park home run, which, under present rules, would have resulted in a victory by more than one run, he was given credit for a lesser hit and only the winning run counted. The committee originally voted that before 1920 any ball hit outside the park in a sudden death situation should be counted as a home run. However, after the committee had a further opportunity to review their ruling and polled their colleagues on the issue, they reversed their decision on May 5, 1969. The following 37 players lost home runs because of the rulings:

DATE	BATTER	TEAM	LEAGUE	OPP.	HIT
June 17, 1884	Roger Connor	N.Y.	N.L.	Bos.	Single
Sept. 6, 1884	Hardy Richardson	Buf.	N.L.	Bos.	Triple
April 21, 1885	Fred Mann	Pit.	A.A.	Lou.	Double
July 30, 1885	Tommy McCarthy	Bos.	N.L.	Det.	Double
Aug. 20, 1885	Paul Hines	Pro.	N.L.	Bos.	Single
June 5, 1890	Sam Thompson	Phi.	N.L.	Bkn.	Single
July 30, 1890	Al McCauley	Phi.	N.L.	Chi.	Triple
June 17, 1890	Mike Griffin	N.Y.	P.L.	Phi.	Double
May 7, 1891	King Kelly	Cin.	A.A.	Bos.	Single
Sept. 13, 1891 (first game)	George Wood	Phi.	A.A.	Mil.	Double
July 7, 1892	Buck Ewing	N.Y.	N.L.	St. L.	Single
May 13, 1893	Lou Bierbauer	Pit.	N.L.	Lou.	Single
Aug. 9, 1893	George Van Haltren	Pit.	N.L.	Chi.	Double
Aug. 27, 1895	Bill Lange	Chi.	N.L.	Was.	Single
Sept. 2, 1895	Mike Tiernan	N.Y.	N.L.	Cle.	Triple
Sept. 27, 1895	Duke Farrell	N.Y.	N.L.	Bal.	Triple

DATE	BATTER	TEAM	LEAGUE	OPP.	HIT
July 27, 1896	Charlie Irwin	Cin.	N.L.	Cle.	Triple
June 4, 1897	Parke Wilson	N.Y.	N.L.	Lou.	Double
July 15, 1899	Jimmy Collins	Bos.	N.L.	Pit.	Single
July 24, 1899	Ginger Beaumont	Pit.	N.L.	Phi.	Triple
July 24, 1900	Jimmy Collins	Bos.	N.L.	St. L.	Single
July 27, 1900	Chick Stahl	Bos.	N.L.	Pit.	Single
May 17, 1901	Bill Coughlin	Was.	A.L.	Phi.	Single
Sept. 1, 1902	Ed Gremminger	Bos.	N.L.	Cin.	Double
June 26, 1903	Pat Moran	Bos.	N.L.	Chi.	Triple
Sept. 10, 1904	Roger Bresnahan	N.Y.	N.L.	Phi.	Double
May 5, 1906	Sherry Magee	Phi.	N.L.	Bkn.	Triple
June 2, 1906	Tim Jordan	Bkn.	N.L.	Bos.	Double
May 25, 1908	Joe Tinker	Chi.	N.L.	N.Y.	Double
Sept. 28, 1908	Cy Seymour	N.Y.	N.L.	Phi.	Single
April 23, 1910	Doc Crandall	N.Y.	N.L.	Bkn.	Single
Aug. 24, 1911	Tex Erwin	Bkn.	N.L.	Chi.	Triple
June 17, 1914	Sherry Magee	Phi.	N.L.	St. L.	Double
April 19, 1917	Ping Bodie	Phi.	A.L.	Bos.	Triple
July 8, 1918	Babe Ruth	Bos.	A.L.	Cle.	Triple
July 18, 1918 (second game)	Frank Baker	N.Y.	A.L.	Det.	Single
April 19, 1918	Irish Meusel	Phi.	N.L.	Bos.	Triple

The Commissioner's Committee on Baseball History

From time to time, certain questions are raised regarding the accuracy of the material and data found in the *Encyclopedia*. To that end, the late Commissioner A. Bartlett Giamatti put together a blue-ribbon panel of baseball historians to hear all questions and challenges put forth regarding the historical record of baseball (e.g., *The Baseball Encyclopedia*).

The Committee would be glad to hear and respond to any questions or challenges of merit as long as the challenges are submitted in writing along with any and all pieces of evidence or documentation. Please feel free to submit any questions to the editorial director of the *Encyclopedia*, c/o Macmillan Publishing Inc., 866 Third Avenue, New York, NY 10022. Please note that all challenges must be in writing, along with complete and full documentation, in order for the Committee to consider such questions of historical accuracy.

The Committee currently consists of professor David Voigt, Professor George Kirsch, and Joseph Durso of the *New York Times*.

Appendix C

Major Changes in Playing Rules

and Scoring Rules

Part of the history of major league baseball is the history of playing and scoring rules. This is a continual process of trying to maintain the delicate balance between offense and defense, trying to insure the fairest possible scoring decisions, and closing obscure loopholes discovered by alert observers. Listed here are the major changes in the rules since 1876 as they have been adopted. Included are scoring practices which were not officially adopted as rules but which were used in the compilation of the official averages. An asterisk (*) before a rule indicates that this scoring rule was affected by a decision of the Special Baseball Records Committee (see Appendix B).

1877   *Time at bat not charged to the batter on a base on balls.

1880   Base on balls on eight balls instead of nine.
        Runner out if hit by a batted ball.
        Catcher must catch ball on a fly to retire the batter on a strikeout.

1881   Pitcher's box located 50 feet from home plate instead of 45 feet.

1882   Base on balls on seven balls.

1883   *Error charged to the pitcher for a base on balls, wild pitch, hit batter, and balk.
        *Error charged to the catcher for a passed ball.
        Foul ball caught on the first bounce is no longer an out.

1884   Pitcher's motion limited to a shoulder-high delivery, instead of a delivery where his hand must pass below his hip.
        Base on balls on six balls.

1885   *Official averages to include performances in all tie games of five or more innings.
        A portion of one side of the bat may be flat instead of round.
        Pitcher credited with an assist on batter's strikeout.

1886   Pitcher's box changed to 4 × 7 feet, instead of 6 × 6 feet.
        Base on balls on seven balls.
        *Stolen base credited to the runner for each base advanced by his own volition (i.e., if the runner advances from first to third on a single, he is credited with a stolen base).

1887   Batter no longer allowed to call for a high or low pitch.
        Strike zone defined as the area between the top of the shoulder and the bottom of the knee.
        Pitcher's box changed to 4 × 5½ feet.

Batter hit by pitched ball entitled to first base and not charged with the time at bat.
Base on balls on five balls.
*Batter's base on balls credited as a hit, and charged as a time at bat.
No error charged to the catcher on a passed ball.
No error charged to the pitcher for a base on balls, wild pitch, hit batter, and balk.
Strikeout on four strikes instead of three strikes, where the first called third strike did not count.

1888   Batter's base on balls not a hit or a time at bat.
        *Error charged to the pitcher for a base on balls, wild pitch, hit batter, and balk.
        Batter credited with a hit if the base runner is struck by a batted ball.
        Strikeout on three strikes.
        Ground rule double instead of a home run if the ball is batted over the fence in fair territory where the fence is less than 210 feet from home plate.
        *Error charged to the catcher on a passed ball.

1889   No error charged to the catcher on a passed ball.
        No error charged to the pitcher for a base on balls, wild pitch, hit batter, and balk.
        Sacrifice bunt recognized, but the batter charged with a time at bat.
        Bases on balls on four balls.
        Pitcher not credited with an assist for batter's strikeout.

1891   Any player may be substituted during a game, but the player substituted for may not re-enter the game. (Before this, substitutions could be made only in case of an injury or with the permission of the opposing team.)

1892   Ground rule double if the ball is hit over the fence in fair territory where the fence is less than 235 feet from home plate.

1893   Pitching distance lengthened to 60 feet 6 inches, and marked by a rubber slab 12 inches long and 4 inches wide.
        The bat must be completely round.

1894   *When a bunt results in advancing a base runner and the batter is put out, or could have been put out, the batter is credited with a sacrifice hit and not charged with a time at bat. (This rule was actually adopted in 1893, but was not used at all until 1894 and not uniformly recognized until 1897.)

Batter charged with a strike for hitting a foul bunt.

1895   Pitcher's rubber enlarged to 24 × 6 inches.

Maximum diameter of the bat increased to 2¾ inches from 2½ inches.

Batter automatically out on an infield fly when there is one out and first and second or first, second, and third bases are occupied.

Strike charged to a batter on a foul tip.

1897   *Earned run is a run scored by the aid of hits only.

1898   *Stolen base credited to the base runner whenever he reaches a base he attempted to steal without the aid of battery or fielding errors or a hit by the batter.

Error not charged to the infielder attempting to complete a double play unless the throw is so wild it gives the runner an additional base.

Error not charged against the catcher attempting to prevent a stolen base unless the throw is so wild it gives the runner an additional base.

1900   A pitcher must win at least 15 games to qualify as the league leader in Winning Percentage, instead of appearing in at least 25 games.

Home plate changed from a 12-inch square to a 5-sided figure 17 inches wide.

1901   Infield fly rule changed to be in effect when there are no outs, as well as when there is one out.

Any foul ball not caught on a fly is a strike unless the batter has two strikes on him (National League).

1903   Pitcher's mound must not be higher than 15 inches above the base lines and home plate.

Any foul ball not caught on a fly is a strike unless the batter has two strikes on him (American League).

1907   *All appearances by a player in an official game count as a game played (American League). Before this, pinch hitters, pinch runners, and defensive substitutes often were not credited with a game played.

1908   Batter credited with a sacrifice fly and not charged with a time at bat if he hits a fly ball which is caught, but a runner scores on the catch.

1909   Pitcher or catcher charged with an error if a wild pitch or passed ball on the third strike allows the batter to reach first base.

Stolen base not credited to any runner on an attempted double steal if either runner is thrown out.

Bunt on third strike is a strikeout and the catcher is credited with the put out.

1912   Earned run charged to the pitcher every time a player scores by the aid of safe hits, sacrifice hits, base on balls, hit batters, wild pitches, and balks before fielding chances have been offered to retire the side.

*All appearances by a player in an official game count as a game played (National League). Before this, pinch hitters, pinch runners, and defensive substitutes often were not credited with a game played.

1917   Earned runs also include runs scored by the aid of stolen bases.

1920   The spitball and other unorthodox deliveries abolished. Special provision made to allow each team to name two pitchers as spitball pitchers for the 1920 season and thereafter no spitballers will be allowed.

If the batter hits a home run in the bottom of the ninth or subsequent innings with the winning run on base, all runners, including the batter, shall score, instead of just the winning run, and the batter shall be credited with a home run instead of the number of bases necessary to score the winning run.

A ball hit over the fence will be judged fair or foul in respect to where the ball was when it passed over the fence, instead of where it landed.

If the winning run is on base in the bottom half of the final inning and the batter drives the run home, credit the batter with as many bases as the runner had to take in order to score, instead of the number of bases the batter made before the runner scored.

Stolen base not credited to the runner if no effort is made to put the runner out.

A player must appear in at least 100 games to qualify as the league leader in Batting Average and Slugging Average. (Before 1920 there was no rule, but it was the practice that a man had to play in at least 60% of the scheduled number of games to qualify.) Note: The one exception to this rule was in 1938 when the American League awarded the batting championship to Jimmie Foxx instead of Taffy Wright, who had a higher percentage and appeared in 100 games, but only had 263 at bats.

An infielder or outfielder must play in at least 100 games at a fielding position to qualify as the league leader in Fielding Average at that position. (Before 1920 there was no rule, but it was the practice that a man had to play in at least 60% of the scheduled number of games to qualify.)

A catcher must catch in at least 90 games to qualify as the league leader in Fielding Average. (Before 1920 there was no rule, but it was the practice that a man had to catch in at least one-half of the scheduled number of games to qualify.)

Official scorer to determine the winning pitcher if more than one pitcher is used by the winning team.

1921   Eight National League and nine American League pitchers named as spitball pitchers, and allowed to use the spitball for the rest of their careers.

1926   Ground rule double if the ball is batted over the fence in fair territory where the fence is less than 250 feet from home plate.

Batter credited with a sacrifice fly and not charged with a time at bat if he hits a fly ball which is caught, but any runner advances on the catch.

Pitcher not credited with a strikeout if the batter reaches first base due to a wild pitch on the third strike.

1931   A fair hit ball which bounces through or over a fence, or into the stands, is considered a ground rule double instead of a home run.

When the batter drives in the winning run in the bottom half of the final inning, he should be credited with the number of bases that the scorer believes he would have made.

When a runner is hit by a batted ball, the putout is credited to the fielder nearest the runner.

Pitchers not credited with an assist on runners put out while trying to steal home on the pitch.

Batter no longer credited with a sacrifice fly.

1939   Batter credited with a sacrifice fly and not charged with a time at bat if he hits a fly ball which is caught, but a runner scores on the catch.

Batter not credited for a Run Batted In if he grounds into a double play and a runner scores.

1940   Batter no longer credited with a sacrifice fly.

1945   A player must have at least 400 at bats to qualify as the league leader in Batting Average or Slugging Average.

1950   Strike zone to include only the area from the batter's armpits to the top of his knee.

A player must play in at least two-thirds of his team's scheduled games in order to qualify as the league leader in Batting Average or Slugging Average.

Formal Rules Governing Designations of a Winning Pitcher When More Than One Man Pitches for the Winning Team:

A starting pitcher receives the win if he pitches at least 5 innings and his team is in the lead when the relief pitcher enters the game and never relinquishes the lead. (If the game lasts only 5 innings the starter must pitch at least 4 innings to get credit for the win.)

If the starting pitcher does not pitch the required number of innings but relief pitchers keep the lead, the official scorer credits the victory to the relief pitcher he believed to be the most effective.

If the starting pitcher does not get the win because his team loses the lead after he is replaced, then the relief pitcher who was in the game when his team scored and went ahead to stay is given credit for the win. (Note: If a pitcher is removed for a pinch hitter, he receives "credit" for the runs scored by his team during that inning.) A win will not be credited to any relief pitcher who pitches briefly and ineffectively. In such a case the official scorer shall credit the victory to another relief pitcher.

1951   A pitcher must pitch a total of at least one inning for every scheduled game to qualify as the league leader in Earned Run Average or Fielding Average. (Before 1951 the rule was that the man had to pitch at least ten complete games and at least 100 innings to qualify, but men who met the 1951 standard were usually recognized as leaders even if they did not pitch ten complete games.)

A player must have at least 400 times at bat to qualify as the league leader in Batting Average or Slugging Average. However, if there is any player with fewer than the required number of times at bat whose average *would* be the highest if he were charged with this required at bat total, then the player shall be recognized as the league leader in Batting Average or Slugging Average.

1954   Batter credited with a sacrifice fly and not charged with a time at bat if he hits a fly ball, but the runner scores on the catch.

1955   Batter no longer eligible to be the league leader in Batting Average or Slugging Average if he does not have 400 times

at bat, instead of the 1951 rule, which makes an exception to the required number of at bats.

1957   A player must have a total of at least 3.1 plate appearances for every scheduled game to qualify as the league leader in Batting Average or Slugging Average.

An infielder or outfielder must play in at least two-thirds of the scheduled number of games at a fielding position to qualify as the league leader in Fielding Average at that position.

A catcher must catch in at least one-half of the scheduled number of games to qualify as the league leader in Fielding Average.

1959   Professional fields constructed after June 1, 1958, must have a minimum distance of 325 feet on both the first and third base foul lines to the outfield fence, and a minimum of 400 feet to the center field fence.

1963   Strike zone to include the area from the top of the shoulder to the bottom of the knee.

1967   A player must have a total of at least 3.1 plate appearances for every scheduled game to qualify as the league leader in Batting Average or Slugging Average. However, if there is any player with fewer than the required number of plate appearances whose average *would* be the highest if he were charged with this required number of plate appearances, then the player shall be recognized as the league leader in Batting Average or Slugging Average.

1969   Strike zone to include only the area from the armpit to the top of the knee.

Earned runs for a relief pitcher entering a game in the middle of an inning are determined by treating the pitcher as if he entered the game at the beginning of an inning.

Pitcher's mound lowered to 10 inches above the base lines and home plate.

1971   The Official Major League Scoring Committee, at the behest of the Baseball Writers' Association of America, changed the qualifications for a rookie. In order to qualify for a rookie, a player must have not more than 130 at bats or 50 innings pitched in the major leagues during a previous season or seasons, nor more than 45 days on a major league roster during the 25-player limit from the start of the season to August 31 (excluding time in a military service).

1973   Formal Rules Governing Designations of Relief Pitchers' Saves:

A pitcher shall be credited with a save when, in entering the game as a relief pitcher, he finds the potential tying or winning run either on base or at the plate or pitches at least three or more effective innings and, in either case, preserves the lead.

When more than one relief pitcher qualifies for a save under the provisions of this rule, credit the save to the relief pitcher judged by the scorer to have been the most effective. It is not mandatory to credit a save. Only one save can be credited in any game.

(In the preparation of this book, however, for the period 1876 through 1968, a save was awarded only to the relief pitcher who finished a game since that exception occurs very infrequently, and takes a deliberate judgmental decision on the part of the official scorer to award a save to a relief pitcher who doesn't finish a game.)

The American League voted unanimously for a designated hitter rule on a three-year experimental basis.

DESIGNATED HITTER (DH) RULE

A hitter may be designated to bat for the starting pitcher and all subsequent pitchers in any game without otherwise affecting the status of the pitcher(s) in the game. A DH for the pitcher must be selected prior to the game and must be included in the lineup cards presented to the umpire-in-chief.

It is not mandatory that a club designate a hitter for the pitcher, but failure to do so prior to the game precludes the use of a DH for that game.

Pinch-hitters for a DH may be used. Any substitute for a DH himself becomes a DH. A replaced DH shall not re-enter the game in any capacity.

The DH may be used defensively, continuing to bat in the same position in the batting order, but the pitcher then must bat in the place of the substituted defensive player, unless more than one substitution is made, and the manager then must designate their spots in the batting order.

A runner may be substituted for the DH and the runner assumes the role of the DH.

A DH is "locked" into the batting order. No multiple substitutions may be made that will alter the batting rotation of the DH.

Once the game pitcher is switched from the mound to a defensive position this move shall terminate the DH role for the remainder of the game. Once a pinch-hitter bats for any player in the batting order and then enters the game to pitch, this move shall terminate the DH role for the remainder of the game.

Once the game pitcher bats for the DH this move shall terminate the DH role for the remainder of the game. (The game pitcher may only pinch hit for the DH.)

Once a DH assumes a defensive position this move shall terminate the DH role for the remainder of the game.

A DH is eligible for all American League batting titles.

1975   In their December 1975 meeting, the American League adopted the designated hitter as a permanent official rule. The National League decided against adopting the designated hitter rule for its use.

The relief pitcher's save rule was amended again. A pitcher shall be credited with a save when he is the finishing but not the winning pitcher and when he qualifies under one of the following conditions: (1) he enters the game with a lead of no more than three runs and pitches for at least one inning; (2) he enters the game with the potential tying run either on base, at bat, or on deck; or (3) he pitches effectively for at least three innings regardless of his team's lead.

1978   On December 5, 1978, at a meeting of the Baseball Playing Rules Committee, several rules changes were adopted. The changes were to be effective with the start of the 1979 season.

The first change alters Playing Rules 4.11 and 4.12 creating, under certain circumstances, suspended games instead of reverting to a prior inning when rain forces the calling of games. In fairness to the visiting team which does not control game conditions, revised section 4.11(d) is amended to read:

(d) A called game ends at the moment the umpire terminates play.

EXCEPTION: If the game is called while an inning is in progress and before it is completed, the game becomes a SUSPENDED GAME in each of the following situations:

(1) The visiting team has scored one or more runs to tie the score and the home team has not scored.

(2) The visiting team has scored one or more runs to take the lead and the home team has not tied the score or retaken the lead.

The change on protested games reads as follows: "Even if it is held that the protested decision violated the rules, no replay of the game will be ordered unless in the opinion of the League President the violation adversely affected the protesting team's chances of winning the game" (4.19). This rule revision will protect a team that won a game convincingly on its merits from being penalized on a technicality.

A victory will not be credited to a relief pitcher who is ineffective in a brief appearance when a succeeding relief pitcher pitches effectively in helping his team maintain the lead. In such cases, the succeeding relief pitcher will be credited with the victory.

A new official statistic has been added: The RBI that gives a club the lead which it never relinquishes.

A pitcher who pitches only one-third of an inning in an entire season will not have his total ERA "rounded off" as is the normal procedure. In such cases, his total for innings pitched will be carried as one-third. Any games played to break a divisional tie shall be included in the statistics for that championship season.

Official Scoring Rules will now include the examples that currently appear on the Official Score Sheet.

1987   In early December, Commissioner Peter Ueberroth announced a further clarification of the strike zone. Specifically, that the strike zone is that area over home plate, the upper limit of which is a horizontal line at the midpoint between the top of the shoulders and the top of the uniform pants, and the lower level is a line at the top of the knees. The strike zone shall be determined from the batter's stance as the batter is prepared to swing at a pitched ball.

1989   The game-winning RBI has been eliminated as an official statistic.

Note:
The following were the qualifications used in this volume to determine league leaders in categories where no formal rule has ever been adopted:
A relief pitcher must win at least 8 games in relief to qualify as the league leader in Winning Percentage.
A relief pitcher must pitch at least one-third of an inning in relief for every scheduled game to qualify as the league leader in Earned Run Average and all relief pitching averages other than Winning Percentage.

Pinch Hit Batting Average—A pinch hitter must have at least 30 at bats to qualify as the league leader.

For All Other Batting Averages and Percentages—It is the rule that was used for Batting Average in effect at the time.

For All Other Fielding Averages and Percentages—It is the rule that was used for Fielding Averages at the particular position in effect at the time.

For All Other Pitching Averages and Percentages—It is the rule that was used for Earned Run Averages in effect at the time.